Lexicomp®

Drug Information Handbook *for Dentistry*

Including Oral Medicine for Medically Compromised Patients & Specific Oral Conditions

23rd Edition

DRUG INFORMATION HANDBOOK for DENTISTRY

Including Oral Medicine for Medically-Compromised Patients & Specific Oral Conditions

Richard L. Wynn, BSPharm, PhD
Professor of Pharmacology
Baltimore College of Dental Surgery
Dental School
University of Maryland Baltimore
Baltimore, Maryland

Timothy F. Meiller, DDS, PhD
Professor
Oncology and Diagnostic Sciences
Baltimore College of Dental Surgery
Professor of Oncology
Marlene and Stewart Greenebaum Cancer Center
University of Maryland Medical System
Baltimore, Maryland

Harold L. Crossley, DDS, MS, PhD
Professor Emeritus
Baltimore College of Dental Surgery
Dental School
University of Maryland Baltimore
Baltimore, Maryland

Lexicomp®

NOTICE

This data is intended to serve the user as a handy reference and not as a complete drug information resource. It does not include information on every therapeutic agent available. The publication covers over 1,700 commonly used drugs. In addition, it does not include all potentially relevant information about any particular drug. Instead, it is intended to present important aspects of drug data in a more concise and accessible format than is typically found in medical literature or product material supplied by manufacturers.

The nature of drug information is that it is constantly evolving because of ongoing research and clinical experience and is often subject to interpretation. While Wolters Kluwer Clinical Drug Information makes reasonable efforts to publish accurate information, users are advised that the authors, editors, reviewers, contributors, and publishers cannot be responsible for the continued currency of the information or for any errors, omissions, or the application of this information, or for any consequences arising therefrom. Therefore, the authors, editors, reviewers, contributors, and publishers shall have no liability to any person or entity with regard to claims, loss, or damage caused, or alleged to be caused, directly or indirectly, by the use of information contained herein. Because of the dynamic nature of drug information and the characteristics and needs unique to individual patients, readers are advised that decisions regarding drug therapy must be based on the independent judgment of the clinician. Users must regularly consult multiple sources (eg, medical literature and a manufacturer's most current product information) to remain aware of changing information about a drug and medical practices regarding its use. Therefore, this data is intended to be used in conjunction with other necessary information and is not intended to be solely relied upon by any user. The user of this data hereby and forever releases the authors, editors, reviewers, contributors, and publishers of this data from any and all liability of any kind that might arise out of the use of this data. The authors, editors, reviewers, contributors, and publishers are not responsible for any inaccurate source materials developed by third-parties or for any user misunderstandings that may arise from the data.

Certain of the authors, editors, reviewers, and contributors have written portions of this book in their individual capacities. The inclusion of content is not intended to indicate that it has been reviewed or endorsed by any federal or state agency, pharmaceutical company, or regulatory body.

The publishers have made reasonable efforts to avoid reproducing without permission, any content that may be subject to third-party copyright claims. Any questions regarding content that may be subject to such claims will be addressed at the first opportunity.

If you have any suggestions or questions regarding any information presented in this data, please contact our drug information pharmacists at (855) 633-0577. Book revisions are available at our website at http://www.wolterskluwercdi.com/clinical-notices/revisions/.

Natural product content is adapted from *The Review of Natural Products*. Facts & Comparisons [database online]. Clinical Drug Information, LLC; 2017

This manual was produced using LIMS — a complete publishing service of Wolters Kluwer Clinical Drug Information, Inc.

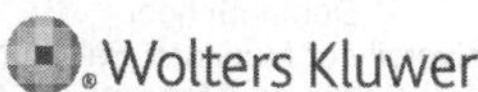

ISBN 978-1-59195-363-0

Wolters Kluwer

TABLE OF CONTENTS

ABOUT THE EDITORS

Richard L. Wynn, BSPharm, PhD

Richard L. Wynn, PhD, is Professor of Pharmacology at the Baltimore College of Dental Surgery, Dental School, University of Maryland Baltimore. Dr Wynn has served as a dental educator, researcher, and teacher of dental pharmacology and dental hygiene pharmacology for his entire professional career. He holds a BS in Pharmacy, an MS (physiology), and a PhD (pharmacology) from the University of Maryland. He was a practicing pharmacist for 10 years in the Baltimore area. Dr Wynn chaired the Department of Pharmacology at the University of Maryland Dental School from 1980 to 1995. Previously, he chaired the Department of Oral Biology at the University of Kentucky College of Dentistry, for six years.

Dr Wynn has to his credit over 400 publications, including original research articles in scientific journals, textbooks, textbook chapters, monographs, and articles in continuing education journals. He has given over 600 continuing education seminars to dental professionals in the US, Canada, and Europe. Dr Wynn has been a consultant to the drug industry for over 30 years and his research laboratories have contributed to the development of new analgesics and anesthetics. He is a former consultant to the Academy of General Dentistry, the American Dental Association, and a former consultant to the Council on Dental Education, Commission on Accreditation. One of his primary interests continues to be keeping dental professionals informed on all aspects of drug use in dental practice.

Timothy F. Meiller, DDS, PhD

Dr Meiller is Professor of Oncology and Diagnostic Sciences at the University of Maryland Dental School and Professor of Oncology at the Marlene and Stewart Greenebaum Comprehensive Cancer Center, University of Maryland Medical System in Baltimore. He is Director of the Oral Medicine Program in the dental school and the cancer center. He has held his position at the Dental School for 40 years.

Dr Meiller is a Diplomate of the American Board of Oral Medicine and a graduate of Johns Hopkins University and the University of Maryland Dental and Graduate Schools, holding a DDS and a PhD in Immunology/Virology. He has over 200 publications to his credit, maintains an active general dental practice, and is a consultant to the National Institutes of Health and the Veterans Administration. He is currently engaged in ongoing investigations into cellular immune dysfunction in premalignant oral lesions, oral diseases associated with AIDS, in patients receiving therapies for cancer, and in other medically-compromised patients.

Harold L. Crossley, DDS, MS, PhD

Dr Crossley is Professor Emeritus at the University of Maryland Dental School. A native of Rhode Island, Dr Crossley received a Bachelor of Science degree in Pharmacy from the University of Rhode Island in 1964. He later was awarded the Master of Science (1970) and Doctorate degrees (1972) in Pharmacology. The University of Maryland Dental School in Baltimore awarded Dr Crossley the DDS degree in 1980. The liaison between the classroom and his dental practice, which he maintained on a part-time basis in the Dental School Intramural Faculty Practice, produced a practical approach to understanding the pharmacology of drugs used in the dental office.

Dr Crossley has coauthored a number of articles and four books dealing with a variety of topics within the field of pharmacology. Other areas of expertise include the pharmacology of street drugs and chemical dependency. He serves on the Maryland State Dental Association's Well-Being Committee. He is an active member of Phi Kappa Phi, Omicron Kappa Upsilon Honorary Dental Society, the American College of Dentists, International College of Dentists, and an honorary member of the Thomas B. Hinman Dental Society. He was the recipient of the 2008 Gordon Christensen Lecturer Recognition award presented by the Chicago Dental Society, and the recipient of the 2012 Award of Distinction presented by the Academy of Dentistry International for his efforts in continuing dental education. He has been a consultant for the United States Drug Enforcement Administration and other law enforcement agencies since 1974. Drawing on this unique background, Dr Crossley has become nationally and internationally recognized as an expert on street drugs and chemical dependency as well as the clinical pharmacology of dental drugs.

DRUG INTERACTIONS EDITORIAL ADVISORY PANEL

Kay Burke, PharmD
Senior Clinical Editor
Wolters Kluwer

Jamie Hoffman, PharmD, BCPS
Senior Clinical Editor
Wolters Kluwer

Jooran Kim, PharmD
Pharmacotherapy Contributor
Vancouver, Canada

Carrie Nemerovski, PharmD, BCPS
Senior Clinical Content Specialist
Wolters Kluwer

Sacha R. Pollard, PharmD, BCPS
Pharmacotherapy Contributor
Fort Mill, South Carolina

Steve Sklar, PharmD
Senior Clinical Manager
Wolters Kluwer

Stephen Marc Stout, PharmD, MS, BCPS
Director, Clinical Content
Wolters Kluwer

Dan Streetman, PharmD, RPh
Clinical Manager, Metabolism, Interactions, & *Genomics Group*
Wolters Kluwer

David M. Weinstein, PhD, RPh
Senior Director, Clinical Content
Wolters Kluwer

EDITORIAL ADVISORY PANEL

J. Emanuel Finet, MD
Attending Physician, Advanced Heart Care and Cardio-Oncology Programs
IU Health Methodist Hospital

Christine Fitzgerald, PharmD, BCPS
Pharmacotherapy Contributor
Valleio, California

Margaret A. Fitzgerald, MS, APRN, BC, NP-C, FAANP
President
Fitzgerald Health Education Associates, Inc.
Family Nurse Practitioner
Greater Lawrence Family Health Center

Carole W. Fuseck, MSN, RN, ACCNS-AG, VA-BC
Clinical Nurse Specialist, Critical Care
Louis Stokes Cleveland Department of Veteran Affairs Medical Center

Joyce Generali, RPh, MS, FASHP
Senior Clinical Manager, In-depth Content
Wolters Kluwer

Ann Gentry, PharmD
Medical Writer
Gentry Medical Communications

Riane Ghamrawi, PharmD, BCPS
Clinical Pharmacist Specialist, Adult Antimicrobial Stewardship
University Hospitals Case Medical Center

Heather L. Girand, PharmD
Professor of Pharmacy, Pediatrics
Pharmacy Practice, Ferris State University College of Pharmacy

Meredith D. Girard, MD, FACP
Medical Staff
Department of Internal Medicine, Summa Health Systems
Assistant Professor Internal Medicine
Northeast Ohio Medical University (NEOMED)

Morton P. Goldman, RPh, PharmD, BCPS, FCCP
Health Care Consultant
American Pharmacotherapy, Inc

Julie A. Golembiewski, PharmD
Clinical Associate Professor and *Clinical Pharmacist, Anesthesia/Pain*
Colleges of Pharmacy and Medicine, University of Illinois

Jeffrey P. Gonzales, PharmD, BCPS
Critical Care Clinical Pharmacy Specialist
University of Maryland Medical Center

John Grabenstein, RPh, PhD, FAPhA
Pharmacotherapy Contributor
West Point, Pennsylvania

Tracy Hagemann, PharmD
Associate Dean and *Professor of Clinical Pharmacy*
University of Tennessee College of Pharmacy

Martin D. Higbee, PharmD
Retired Associate Professor
Department of Pharmacy Practice and Science, The University of Arizona

Mark T. Holdsworth, PharmD
Associate Professor of Pharmacy & Pediatrics and *Pharmacy Practice Area Head*
College of Pharmacy, The University of New Mexico

Edward Horn, PharmD, BCPS
Clinical Specialist, Transplant/Cardiothoracic Surgery
Allegheny General Hospital

Collin A. Hovinga, PharmD
Director of Research and *Associate Professor*
Dell Children's Medical Center, UT Austin School of Pharmacy

Jane Hurlburt Hodding, PharmD
Executive Director, Inpatient Pharmacy Services and Clinical Nutrition Services
Long Beach Memorial Medical Center and Miller Children's Hospital

Makiko Iwasawa, PharmD, BCPS
Chief Pharmacist, Drug Information Center
National Cerebral and Cardiovascular Center

Adam B. Jackson, PharmD, BCPS
Clinical Pharmacy Specialist in Infectious Diseases
Kaiser Permanente

Anna M. Wodlinger Jackson, PharmD, BCPS AQ Cardiology
Pharmacotherapy Contributor
Fort Lauderdale, Florida

Douglas L. Jennings, PharmD, AACC, BCPS-AQ Cardiology, FCCP
Clinical Pharmacy Manager, Heart Transplant and Mechanical Circulatory Support
New York Presbyterian Columbia Medical Center

Sallie Johnson, PharmD, BCPS, AQ Cardiology
Clinical Pharmacy Specialist, Cardiology
Penn State Milton S. Hershey Medical Center

Michael A. Kahn, DDS
Professor and Chairman
Department of Oral and Maxillofacial Pathology, Tufts University School of Dental Medicine

Julie J. Kelsey, PharmD
Clinical Specialist
Women's Health and Family Medicine, Department of Pharmacy Services, University of Virginia Health System

Patrick J. Kiel, PharmD, BCPS, BCOP
Clinical Pharmacy Specialist
Hematology and Stem Cell Transplant, Indiana University Simon Cancer Center

Jooran Kim, PharmD
Pharmacotherapy Contributor
Vancouver, Canada

Polly E. Kintzel, PharmD, BCPS, BCOP
Clinical Pharmacy Specialist – Oncology
Spectrum Health

Michael Klepser, PharmD, FCCP
Professor of Pharmacy
Department of Pharmacy Practice, Ferris State University

Sandra Knowles, RPh, BScPhm
Drug Information Pharmacist
Sunnybrook Health Sciences Centre

Julie Miller, PharmD
Pharmacy Clinical Specialist, Cardiology
Nationwide Children's Hospital

Stacy E. Miller, PharmD, BCPS, BCPP
Senior Clinical Content Specialist
Wolters Kluwer

Katherine Mills, PharmD
Pharmacotherapy Contributor
Bristow, Virginia

Stephanie S. Minich, PharmD, BCOP
Senior Clinical Content Specialist
Wolters Kluwer

Brady Moffett, PharmD, MPH
Clinical Pharmacist
Texas Children's Hospital

Lauri Moore, RPh, MBA
Vice President, Content Development
Wolters Kluwer

John M. Moorman, PharmD, BCPS
Pharmacotherapy Specialist, Endocrinology
Cleveland Clinic Akron General

Erika Mora, PharmD, BCOP
Clinical Pharmacist Specialist – Pediatric Hematology/Oncology
Beaumount Hospital, Royal Oak

Kara M. Morris, DDS, MS
Pediatric Dentist
Olentangy Pediatric Dentistry

Naoto Nakagawa, PharmD, PhD
Chief Pharmacist
Drug Information Center, Japan

Lynne Nakashima, PharmD
Professional Practice Leader, Clinical Professor
B.C. Cancer Agency, Vancouver Centre, University of BC

Carrie Nemerovski, PharmD, BCPS
Senior Clinical Content Specialist
Wolters Kluwer

Elizabeth A. Neuner, PharmD, BCPS
Infectious Diseases Clinical Specialist
Cleveland Clinic

Kimberly Novack, PharmD, BCPS
Clinical Pharmacy Specialist, Cystic Fibrosis and Pharmacy Clinical Coordinator
Nationwide Children's Hospital

Charla E. Miller Nowak, RPh, PharmD
Neonatal Clinical Pharmacy Specialist
Wolfson Children's Hospital

Carlene N. Oliverio, PharmD, BCPS
Clinical Content Specialist
Wolters Kluwer

Neeta O'Mara, PharmD, BCPS
Clinical Pharmacist
Dialysis Clinic

Tom Palma, MS, RPh, BCPS
Clinical Content Specialist
Wolters Kluwer

Ji Hyun Park, PharmD, RPh
Clinical Pharmacist
KEPCO Medical Center, Hanjeon Hospital, KMC

Susie H. Park, PharmD, BCPP
Assistant Professor of Clinical Pharmacy
University of Southern California

Nicole Passerrello, PharmD, BCPPS, BCPS
Senior Clinical Content Specialist
Wolters Kluwer

Rebecca Pettit, PharmD, MBA, BCPS
Pediatric Pulmonary Clinical Pharmacy Specialist
Riley Hospital for Children, Indiana University Health, Department of Pharmacy

Cameron Phillips, BPharm, MClin Pharm
Clinical Pharmacist
Flinders Medical Center

Jennifer L. Placencia, PharmD
Neonatal Clinical Pharmacy Specialist
Texas Children's Hospital

Sacha R. Pollard, PharmD, BCPS
Pharmacotherapy Contributor
Fort Mill, South Carolina

Amy L. Potts, PharmD, BCPS
Assistant Director
Department of Pharmacy
PGY1 & PGY2 Residency Program Director
Monroe Carell Jr. Children's Hospital at Vanderbilt

Saira Rab, PharmD, BCPS (AQ-ID), AAHIVP
Infectious Diseases/HIV Clinical Pharmacist Specialist
Grady Health System

Sally Rafie, PharmD, BCPS
Medical Safety Pharmacist
UC San Diego Health System

Esta Razavi, PharmD
Clinical Content Specialist
Wolters Kluwer

James Reissig, PharmD, BCPS
Assistant Director, Clinical Services
Cleveland Clinic Akron General

A.J. (Fred) Remillard, PharmD
Assistant Dean, Research and Graduate Affairs
College of Pharmacy and Nutrition, University of Saskatchewan

Neil Reynolds, BPharm, MSc
Senior Pharmacist
Fiona Stanley Hospital

Elizabeth Rich, RN, BSN, BA
Registered Nurse – Medical Intensive Care Unit
Cleveland Clinic

Amy Rybarczyk, PharmD, BCPS
Pharmacotherapy Specialist, Internal Medicine
Cleveland Clinic Akron General

Rikki L. Rychel, PharmD, BCPS, CDE
Clinical Pharmacy Specialist, Ambulatory Care
Louis Stokes Cleveland Department of Veterans Affairs Medical Center

JoEllen L. Weilnau, PharmD
Clinical Coordinator
Department of Hematology/Oncology/Bone Marrow Transplant, Children's Hospital of Akron

David M. Weinstein, PhD, RPh
Senior Director, Clinical Content
Wolters Kluwer

Regine L. White, PharmD, RPh
Clinical Pharmacist
University of Michigan Health System

Greg Wiggers, PharmD, PhD
Clinical Content Specialist
Wolters Kluwer

Sherri J. Willard Argyres, MA, PharmD
Senior Clinical Content Specialist
Wolters Kluwer

Andrea Williams, RPh
Clinical Content Specialist
Wolters Kluwer

Nathan Wirick, PharmD, BCPS
Clinical Specialist in Infectious Diseases and Antibiotic Management
Hillcrest Hospital

Adrian Wong, PharmD, BCPS, BCCCP
Senior Pharmacist, Fellow, Outcomes Research and Pharmacy Informatics
Brigham and Women's Hospital

Wende Wood, RPh, BSPharm, BCPP
Pharmacotherapy Contributor
Toronto, Ontario, Canada

Richard L. Wynn, BSPharm, PhD
Professor of Pharmacology
Baltimore College of Dental Surgery, University of Maryland

Sevasti Yeropoli, MD
OB/GYN
Paragon Obstetrics and Gynecology

Jessica Zatroch, DDS
Private Practice Dentist
Willoughby Hills, OH

PREFACE TO THE TWENTY-THIRD EDITION

The editors of the 23rd edition of the *Drug Information Handbook for Dentistry* are extremely proud that the book remains as popular and as successful as its readers have affirmed. We thank each practitioner and student who has made the previous editions so widely accepted in the field of dentistry. In this new 23rd edition, we have responded to all of the comments and creative suggestions that come from our readership each year. We know that our text remains the premier companion to the daily practice of dentistry and that it complements Oral Medicine and medical reference libraries that every clinician has available in their office.

As in each previous edition, the Oral Medicine chapters have been updated offering a now clearly highlighted selection of common dental office prescription choices and Rx examples for management of common oral conditions often encountered during patient care. These example prescriptions have been updated and are presented in a stand-alone section for quicker reference.

The latest Guidelines for Antimicrobial Stewardship endorsed by the ADA have been added, including the guideline effects on the management of patients at risk of endocarditis or those with joint prostheses. The chapter related to the dentist's involvement with the cancer patient now has an expanded section for salivary testing for HPV and HPV vaccines as well as addresses diagnostic testing in the dental office. Stand-alone sections have been updated for the crucial topics of Antiplatelet and Anticoagulation Considerations in Dentistry, adding information on the newly approved reversal agent for one of the novel anticoagulation drugs. Medication related osteonecrosis of the jaw (MRONJ) information has been updated. Recommended readings have been edited for chapter subsections. Sections have been expanded and added related to prescribing medications with NSAIDs including their risk association with MI and stroke, acetaminophen, and sarcoidosis. Prescribing information options are outlined and are available for easy cross-referencing for the busy dental practitioner.

In addition to the extensive information presented, we are confident that the dental practitioners and dental hygienists who utilize the text will find the size format to be easy to navigate. The complete cross-referencing of generic and brand names along with the foreign brands, makes the text the truly complete drug reference guide for dental practice.

The monographs now include over 1,700 drugs and these have been updated in the 23rd edition with the fields expanded in common monographs to make them easier to read and identify for all of the drugs. The fields most important to practicing dentists have been enhanced. The drugs most commonly used in dentistry have the added fields regarding specific use considerations in dentistry. Medical drugs also include dosing and dose formulation information. In addition, the adverse reaction section and the important uses and effects on dental treatment for all drugs have been updated throughout the text.

The alphabetical index at the back of the text continues to guide the reader through the text. The natural products section; drug synonyms; and US, Canadian, and Mexican brand names have all been updated. We hope that the active general dentist, the specialist, the dental hygienist, and the advanced student of dentistry remain better prepared for patient care while using this new 23rd edition of the DIHD.

Richard L. Wynn

Timothy F. Meiller

Harold L. Crossley

DESCRIPTION OF SECTIONS AND FIELDS USED IN THIS HANDBOOK

The *Drug Information Handbook for Dentistry, 23rd Edition* is organized into six sections: Introductory text; sample prescriptions, alphabetical listing of drug monographs; natural products; oral medicine topics; appendix; and indexes which include pharmacologic categories and alphabetical listings containing generic product names and index terms, as well as US, Canadian, and Mexican brand names.

INTRODUCTORY TEXT

Helpful guides to understanding the organization and format of the information in this handbook.

SAMPLE PRESCRIPTIONS

Examples provided for prototype drugs and popular prescriptions. Prescriptions included for the following uses: Prevention of endocarditis and to reduce the risk of late infections of joint prostheses, oral pain, bacterial infections and periodontal diseases, sinus infection treatment, antimicrobial oral rinse, fungal infections, viral infections, ulcerative and erosive disorders, sedation (prior to dental treatment).

DRUG MONOGRAPHS

This alphabetical listing of drugs contains comprehensive monographs for medications commonly prescribed in dentistry and concise monographs for other popular drugs which dental patients may be taking. Monographs may contain the following fields:

Generic Name	US adopted name
Pronunciation	Phonetic pronunciation guide
Related Information	Cross-reference(s) to pertinent information in other sections of this handbook
Related Sample Prescriptions	Cross-reference(s) to sample prescriptions.
Brand Names: US	Trade names found in the United States (manufacturer-specific). The symbol [DSC] appears after trade names that have been recently discontinued.
Brand Names: Canada	Trade names found in Canada.
Generic Availability (US)	Indicates availability of generic products in the United States
Pharmacologic Category	Indicates one or more systematic classifications of the drug
Dental Use	Information in the **Dental Use** field indicates when a drug has an established use specific to dentistry and/or oral medicine. In some cases, these uses are considered to be unlabeled, as they are not included in the FDA-approved product labeling (see Description of Dental Use).
Use	Statements under the **Use** field reflect the approved labeling by the FDA based on accepted clinical evaluation on safety and efficacy of the drug as submitted in the New Drug Application (NDA). The "gold standard" of clinical testing of a new drug requires a randomly selected cohort of subjects, using a double-blind and placebo controlled protocol and an acceptable method of assessment to test differences between test compound and placebo. It is assumed that by their approval of the labeling, the FDA considers the new drug "safe and effective" for treating a particular condition in a given patient population.
Local Anesthetic/Vasoconstrictor Precautions	Specific information for the dental health professional to prevent potential drug interactions related to anesthesia
Effects on Dental Treatment	Includes significant side effects of drug therapy which may directly or indirectly affect dental treatment or diagnosis; may also contain suggested management approaches and patient handling or care.
Effects on Bleeding	How the product affects bleeding during dental procedures
Adverse Reactions	Side effects are grouped by percentage of incidence (if known) and/or body system; in the interest of saving space, <1% effects are grouped only by percentage.
General Dosage Range	Amount of drug used during therapy; reported as a general range. Not indication or country specific. Prior to use, individual product labeling should be consulted.
Dental Usual Dosage	The amount of the drug to be typically given or taken during dental treatment for children and adults

Dosing	The amount of drug to be typically given or taken during therapy; may include the following:
Adult	The recommended amount of drug to be given to adult patients
Adult & Geriatric	This combined field is only used to indicate that no specific adjustments for elderly patients were identified. However, other issues should be considered (eg, renal or hepatic impairment). Also refer to Geriatric Considerations for additional information related to elderly patients.
Geriatric	A suggested amount of drug to be given to elderly patients; may include adjustments from adult dosing (lack of information in the monograph may imply that the drug is not used in the elderly patient or no specific adjustments could be identified)
Pediatric	Suggested amount of drug to be given to neonates, infants, and children. The following age group definitions are utilized to characterize age-related dosing unless otherwise specified in the monograph: Neonate (0 to 28 days of age), infant (>28 days to 1 year of age), children (1 to 12 years of age), and adolescent (13 to 18 years of age).
Renal Impairment	Suggested dosage adjustments based on compromised renal function; may include dosing instructions for patients on dialysis
Hepatic Impairment	Suggested dosage adjustments based on compromised liver function
Obesity	Dosing adjustment or dosing considerations for the obese adult patient. Obesity is defined as a BMI ≥30 kg/m^2 (based on the World Health Organization [WHO]).
Adjustment for Toxicity	Suggested dosage adjustments in the event specific toxicities related to therapy are noted, such as hematologic toxicities related to cancer chemotherapy
Mechanism of Action	How the drug works in the body to elicit a response
Contraindications	Information pertaining to inappropriate use of the drug as dictated by approved labeling
Warnings/Precautions	Precautionary considerations, hazardous conditions related to use of the drug, and disease states or patient populations in which the drug should be cautiously used. Boxed warnings, when present, are clearly identified and are adapted from the FDA approved labeling. Consult the product labeling for the exact black box warning through the manufacturer's or the FDA website.
Drug Interactions	
Metabolism/Transport Effects	If a drug has demonstrated involvement with cytochrome P450 enzymes, or other metabolism or transport proteins, this field will identify the drug as an inhibitor, inducer, or substrate of the specific enzyme(s) (eg, CYP1A2 or UGT1A1). CYP450 isoenzymes are identified as substrates (minor or major), inhibitors (weak, moderate, or strong), and inducers (weak or strong).
Avoid Concomitant Use	Designates drug combinations which should not be used concomitantly, due to an unacceptable risk:benefit assessment. Frequently, the concurrent use of the agents is explicitly prohibited or contraindicated by the product labeling.
Increased Effect/Toxicity	Drug combinations that result in an increased or toxic therapeutic effect between the drug listed in the monograph and other drugs or drug classes.
Decreased Effect	Drug combinations that result in a decreased therapeutic effect between the drug listed in the monograph and other drugs or drug classes.
Food Interactions	Possible important interactions between the drug listed in the monograph and food, alcohol, or other beverages.
Dietary Considerations	Specific dietary modifications and/or restrictions (eg, information about sodium content)
Pharmacodynamics/Kinetics	
Onset of Action	The time after drug administration when therapeutic effect is observed; may also include time for peak therapeutic effect.
Duration of Action	Length of therapeutic effect.
Half-life Elimination	The reported half-life of elimination for the parent or metabolites of the drug

Time to Peak	Describes the relative time after ingestion when concentration achieves the highest serum concentration
Pregnancy Risk Factor	Five categories established by the FDA to indicate the potential of a systemically absorbed drug for causing risk to fetus.
Pregnancy Considerations	A summary of human and/or animal information pertinent to or associated with the use of the drug as it relates to clinical effects on the fetus, newborn, or pregnant women.
Breastfeeding Considerations	Information pertinent to or associated with the human use of the drug as it relates to clinical effects on the breastfeeding infant or postpartum woman.
Product Availability	Provides availability information on products that have been approved by the FDA but are not yet available for use. Estimates for when a product may be available are included, when this information is known. May also provide any unique or critical drug availability issues.
Controlled Substance	Contains controlled substance schedule information as assigned by the United States Drug Enforcement Administration (DEA) or Canada's Controlled Drugs and Substance Act (CDSA). CDSA information is only provided for drugs available in Canada and not available in the US.
Prescribing and Access Restrictions	Provides information on any special requirements regarding the prescribing, obtaining, or dispensing of drugs, including access restrictions pertaining to drugs with REMS elements and those drugs whose access restrictions are not REMS-related.
Dosage Forms Considerations	More specific information regarding product concentrations, ingredients, package sizes, amount of doses per container, and other important details pertaining to various formulations of medications
Dosage Forms	Information with regard to form, strength, and availability of the drug in the United States. **Note:** Additional formulation information (eg, excipients, preservatives) is included when available. Please consult product labeling for further information.
Dosage Forms: Canada	Information with regard to form, strength, and availability of products that are uniquely available in Canada, but currently not available in the United States.
Dental Comment	Pharmacology-related comments and considerations relevant to the dental professional

NATURAL PRODUCTS: HERBAL AND DIETARY SUPPLEMENTS

The natural product content is adapted from *The Review of Natural Products* a Facts & Comparisons online database. This section consists of a clinical overview that summarizes the uses, dosing, contraindications, pregnancy/lactation, interactions, adverse reactions, and toxicology information for each natural product. The dental-specific information is also included to further assist the dental professional in patient care.

ORAL MEDICINE TOPICS

This section is divided into two major parts and contains text on Oral Medicine topics. In each subsection, the systemic condition or the oral disease state is described briefly, followed by the pharmacologic considerations with which the dentist must be familiar.

I. **Dental Management and Therapeutic Considerations in Medically Compromised Patients:** Focuses on common medical conditions and their associated drug therapies with which the dentist must be familiar. Patient profiles with commonly associated drug regimens are described.

II. **Dental Management and Therapeutic Considerations in Patients With Specific Oral Conditions:** Focuses on therapies the dentist may choose to prescribe for patients suffering from oral disease or who are in need of special care. Some overlap between these sections has resulted from systemic conditions that have oral manifestations and vice-versa. Cross-references to the descriptions and the monographs for individual drugs described elsewhere in this handbook allow for easy retrieval of information. Example prescriptions for drugs commonly used in the treatment of each condition are presented so that the clinician can evaluate alternate approaches to treatment. Seldom is there a single drug of choice.
Note: Prescriptions listed represent prototype drugs and popular prescriptions and are examples only. The pharmacologic category index is available for cross-referencing if alternatives or additional drugs are sought.

APPENDIX

The appendix is broken down into various sections for easy use and offers a compilation of tables and guidelines which can often be helpful when considering patient care.

INDEXES

This section includes a pharmacologic category index with an easy-to-use classification system in alphabetical order and an alphabetical index which provides a quick reference for generic names, index terms, US, Canadian, and Mexican brand names. From this index, the reader can cross-reference to the monographs.

DESCRIPTION OF DENTAL USE

Unlabeled Use and Routes of Administration in Dentistry and Oral Medicine

The off-label use of a medication may involve differences in either the intended purpose or the route of administration of a particular medication. In dentistry, there are some situations which are common (clindamycin for endocarditis prophylaxis), and uncommon (application of Oralone paste to the oral mucosa) which may be termed "unlabeled use". Depending on the degree of familiarity, the prescription of a drug for an off-label purpose may create concern on the part of healthcare professionals who are less familiar with the dental use of these medications. For example, a pharmacist may note the statement "for external use only" on the label of a tube of topical cream and question whether the drug should be applied to the oral mucosa. Usually, reinforcement of the use of a drug as well as an analysis of the likely systemic exposure/toxicity, can address these concerns.

The dentist who prescribes a drug bears the responsibility for deciding on the purpose of the prescription and the detail of the dosing regimen. These professional decisions are based on information from a variety of sources, including (but not limited to) the official labeling, sound scientific evidence, expert medical judgment, or published literature. In selected situations, these sources may justify the use of a drug in an off-label manner. Accepted professional standards indicate off-label use of a drug must be initiated in good faith, serve the best interest of the patient, and must be undertaken without fraudulent intent. Healthcare providers should recognize that the approved labeling is not intended to limit the practitioners in the exercise of his or her best professional judgment in serving the interest of patients. However, it should be noted that a practitioner may be accountable for the negligent use in a civil action regardless of whether the FDA has approved the use of the drug in question. Based on these assertions, at least one medical organization (the American Academy of Pediatrics) has published in an official policy statement that the practice of medicine may actually require a practitioner to use drugs in an off-label manner in order to provide the most appropriate treatment for a given patient. Off-label use in dentistry and oral medicine is a frequently encountered issue. A discussion of the off-label use of drugs in dentistry appears in the *ADA/PDR Guide to Dental Therapeutics*, 5th Edition, edited by Sebastian G. Ciancio, DDS in cooperation with the ADA Division of Legal Affairs.

CONTROLLED SUBSTANCES

Schedule I = C-I

The drugs and other substances in this schedule have no legal medical uses except research. They have a **high** potential for abuse. They include selected opiates such as heroin, opium derivatives, and hallucinogens.

Schedule II = C-II

The drugs and other substances in this schedule have legal medical uses and a **high** abuse potential which may lead to severe dependence. They include former "Class A" opioids, amphetamines, barbiturates, and other drugs.

Schedule III = C-III

The drugs and other substances in this schedule have legal medical uses and a **lesser** degree of abuse potential which may lead to **moderate** dependence. They include former "Class B" opioids and other drugs.

Schedule IV = C-IV

The drugs and other substances in this schedule have legal medial uses and **low** abuse potential which may lead to **moderate** dependence. They include barbiturates, benzodiazepines, propoxyphenes, and other drugs.

Schedule V = C-V

The drugs and other substances in this schedule have legal medical uses and **low** abuse potential which may lead to **moderate** dependence. They include opioids cough preparations, diarrhea preparations, and other drugs.

Note: These are federal classifications. Your individual state may place a substance into a more restricted category. When this occurs, the more restricted category applies. Consult your state law.

PREGNANCY CATEGORIES

Pregnancy Categories (sometimes referred to as pregnancy risk factors) are a letter system presented under the *Teratogenic Effects* subsection of the product labeling. The system was initiated in 1979. The categories were required to be part of the package insert for prescription drugs that are systemically absorbed. The Food and Drug Administration (FDA) has updated prescribing labeling requirements and as of June 2015, the pregnancy categories will no longer be part of new product labeling. Prescription products which currently have a pregnancy category letter will be phasing this out of their product information.

The categories are defined as follows:

A — Adequate and well-controlled studies in pregnant women have not shown that the drug increases the risk of fetal abnormalities.

B — Animal reproduction studies show no evidence of impaired fertility or harm to the fetus; however, no adequate and well-controlled studies have been conducted in pregnant women.
or
Animal reproduction studies have shown adverse events; however, studies in pregnant women have not shown that the drug increases the risk of abnormalities.

C — Animal reproduction studies have shown an adverse effect on the fetus. There are no adequate and well-controlled studies in humans and the benefits from the use of the drug in pregnant women may be acceptable, despite its potential risks.
or
Animal reproduction studies have not been conducted.

D — Based on human data, the drug can cause fetal harm when administered to pregnant women, but the potential benefits from the use of the drug may be acceptable, despite its potential risks.

X — Studies in animals or humans have demonstrated fetal abnormalities (or there is positive evidence of fetal risk based on reports and/or marketing experience) and the risk of using the drug in pregnant women clearly outweighs any possible benefit (for example, safer drugs or other forms of therapy are available).

In 2008, the Food and Drug Administration (FDA) proposed new labeling requirements which would eliminate the use of the pregnancy category system and replace it with scientific data and other information specific to the use of the drug in pregnant women. These proposed changes were suggested because the current category system may be misleading. For instance, some practitioners may believe that risk increases from category A to B to C to D to X, which is not the intent. In addition, practitioners may not be aware that some medications are categorized based on animal data, while others are based on human data. The new labeling requirements will contain pregnancy and lactation subsections, each describing a risk summary, clinical considerations, and section for specific data.

For full descriptions of the final rule, refer to the following website: http://www.fda.gov/Drugs/DevelopmentApprovalProcess/DevelopmentResources/Labeling/ucm093307.htm

FDA NAME DIFFERENTIATION PROJECT: THE USE OF TALL-MAN LETTERS

Confusion between similar drug names is an important cause of medication errors. For years, The Institute For Safe Medication Practices (ISMP), has urged generic manufacturers to use a combination of large and small letters as well as bolding (ie, chlorpro**MAZINE** and chlorpro**PAMIDE**) to help distinguish drugs with look-alike names, especially when they share similar strengths. Recently the FDA's Division of Generic Drugs began to issue recommendation letters to manufacturers suggesting this novel way to label their products to help reduce this drug name confusion. Although this project has had marginal success, the method has successfully eliminated problems with products such as diphenhydr**AMINE** and dimenhy**DRINATE**. Hospitals should also follow suit by making similar changes in their own labels, preprinted order forms, computer screens and printouts, and drug storage location labels.

Lexi-Comp, Inc. Medical Publishing will use "Tall-Man" letters for the drugs suggested by the FDA or recommended by ISMP.

The following is a list of generic and brand name product names and recommended revisions.

Drug Product	**Recommended Revision**
acetazolamide	aceta**ZOLAMIDE**
alprazolam	**ALPRAZ**olam
amiloride	a**MIL**oride
amlodipine	am**LODIP**ine
aripiprazole	**ARIP**iprazole
atomoxetine	ato**MOX**etine
atorvastatin	atorva**STAT**in
Avinza	**AVIN**za
azacitidine	aza**CITID**ine
azathioprine	aza**THIO**prine
bupropion	bu**PROP**ion
buspirone	bus**PIR**one
carbamazepine	car**BAM**azepine
carboplatin	**CARBO**platin
cefazolin	ce**FAZ**olin
cefotetan	cefo**TE**tan
cefoxitin	cef**OX**itin
ceftazidime	cef**TAZ**idime
ceftriaxone	cef**TRIAX**one
Celebrex	Cele**BREX**
Celexa	Cele**XA**
chlordiazepoxide	chlordiaze**POXIDE**
chlorpromazine	chlorpro**MAZINE**
chlorpropamide	chlorpro**PAMIDE**
cisplatin	**CIS**platin
clobazam	clo**BAZ**am
clomiphene	clomi**PHENE**
clomipramine	clomi**PRAMINE**
clonazepam	clonaze**PAM**
clonidine	clo**NID**ine
clozapine	clo**ZAP**ine
cycloserine	cyclo**SERINE**
cyclosporine	cyclo**SPORINE**
dactinomycin	**DACTIN**omycin
daptomycin	**DAPTO**mycin
daunorubicin	**DAUNO**rubicin

(continued)

Drug Product	Recommended Revision
Depo-Medrol	**DEPO**-Medrol
diazepam	diaze**PAM**
diltiazem	dil**tiaz**em
dimenhydrinate	dimenhy**DRINATE**
diphenhydramine	diphenhydr**AMINE**
dobutamine	**DOBUT**amine
docetaxel	**DOCE**taxel
dopamine	**DOP**amine
doxorubicin	**DOXO**rubicin
duloxetine	**DUL**oxetine
ephedrine	e**PHED**rine
epinephrine	**EPINEPH**rine
epirubicin	epi**RUB**icin
eribulin	eri**BUL**in
fentanyl	fenta**NYL**
flavoxate	flavox**ATE**
fluoxetine	**FLU**oxetine
fluphenazine	flu**PHENAZ**ine
fluvoxamine	fluvoxa**MINE**
glipizide	glipi**ZIDE**
glyburide	gly**BURIDE**
guaifenesin	guai**FEN**esin
guanfacine	guan**FACINE**
Humalog	Huma**LOG**
Humulin	Humu**LIN**
hydralazine	hydr**ALAZINE**
hydrochlorothiazide	hydro**CHLORO**thiazide
hydrocodone	**HYDRO**codone
hydromorphone	**HYDRO**morphone
hydroxyprogesterone	**HYDROXY**progesterone
hydroxyzine	hydr**OXY**zine
idarubicin	**IDA**rubicin
idarucizumab	idaru**CIZU**mab
infliximab	in**FLIX**imab
Invanz	**INV**anz
isotretinoin	**ISO**tretinoin
Klonopin	Klono**PIN**
Lamictal	La**MIC**tal
Lamisil	Lam**ISIL**
lamivudine	lami**VUD**ine
lamotrigine	lamo**TRI**gine
levetiracetam	Lev**ETIRA**cetam
levocarnitine	lev**OCARN**itine
levofloxacin	levo**FLOX**acin
levoleucovorin	**LEVO**leucovorin
lorazepam	**LOR**azepam
medroxyprogesterone	medroxy**PROGESTER**one
metformin	met**FORMIN**
methazolamide	methazol**AMIDE**

(continued)

Drug Product	Recommended Revision
methimazole	meth**IMA**zole
methylprednisolone	methyl**PREDNIS**olone
methyltestosterone	methyl**TESTOSTER**one
metolazone	met**OL**azone
metronidazole	metro**NIDAZOLE**
metyrapone	metyra**PONE**
metyrosine	metyro**SINE**
mifepristone	mi**FEPRIS**tone
misoprostol	mi**SOPROS**tol
mitomycin	mito**MY**cin
mitoxantrone	Mito**XANTRONE**
Nexavar	Nex**AVAR**
Nexium	Nex**IUM**
nicardipine	ni**CAR**dipine
nifedipine	**NIFE**dipine
nimodipine	ni**MOD**ipine
Novolin	Novo**LIN**
Novolog	Novo**LOG**
olanzapine	**OLANZ**apine
oxcarbazepine	**OX**carbazepine
oxycodone	oxy**CODONE**
Oxycontin	Oxy**CONTIN**
oxymorphone	oxy**MOR**phone
paclitaxel	**PACL**itaxel
paroxetine	**PAR**oxetine
pazopanib	**PAZOP**anib
pemetrexed	**PEME**trexed
penicillamine	penicill**AMINE**
pentobarbital	**PENT**obarbital
phenobarbital	**PHEN**obarbital
ponatinib	**PONAT**inib
pralatrexate	**PRALA**trexate
prednisolone	predniso**LONE**
prednisone	predni**SONE**
Prilosec	Pri**LOSEC**
Prozac	**PRO**zac
quetiapine	**QUE**tiapine
quinidine	qui**NID**ine
quinine	qui**NINE**
rabeprazole	**RABE**prazole
ranitidine	ra**NITI**dine
rifampin	rif**AMP**in
rifaximin	rif**AXIM**in
rimantadine	ri**MANTA**dine
Risperdal	Risper**DAL**
risperidone	risperi**DONE**
rituximab	ri**TUX**imab
romidepsin	romi**DEP**sin
romiplostim	romi**PLOS**tim

(continued)

Drug Product	Recommended Revision
ropinirole	r**OPINIR**ole
Sandimmune	sand**IMMUNE**
Sandostatin	Sando**STATIN**
saxagliptin	**SAX**agliptin
Seroquel	**SERO**quel
Sinequan	**SINE**quan
sitagliptin	**SIT**agliptin
Solu-Cortef	Solu-**CORTEF**
Solu-Medrol	**SOLU**-Medrol
sorafenib	**SORA**fenib
sufentanil	**SUF**entanil
sulfadiazine	sulf**ADIAZINE**
sulfasalazine	sulfa**SALA**zine
sumatriptan	**SUMA**triptan
sunitinib	**SUNI**tinib
Tegretol	**TEG**retol
tiagabine	tia**GAB**ine
tizanidine	ti**ZAN**idine
tolazamide	**TOLAZ**amide
tolbutamide	**TOLBUT**amide
tramadol	tra**MAD**ol
trazodone	tra**ZOD**one
Trental	**TREN**tal
valacyclovir	val**ACY**clovir
valganciclovir	val**GAN**ciclovir
vinblastine	vin**BLAS**tine
vincristine	vin**CRIS**tine
zolmitriptan	**ZOLM**itriptan
Zyprexa	Zy**PREXA**
Zyrtec	Zyr**TEC**

FDA and ISMP lists of look-alike drug names with recommended tall man letter. http://www.ismp.org/tools/tallmanletters.pdf. Accessed January 6, 2011.

Name differentiation project. http://www.fda.gov/Drugs/DrugSafety/MedicationErrors/ucm164587.htm. Accessed January 6, 2011.

U.S. Pharmacopeia. USP quality review: use caution – avoid confusion. March 2001, No. 76. http://www.usp.org

PRESCRIPTION WRITING

Doctor's Name
Address
Phone Number

Patient's Name/Date

Patient's Address/Age

Rx

Drug Name/Dosage Size
Disp: Number of tablets, capsules, ounces to be dispensed (roman numerals added as precaution for abused drugs)
Sig: Direction on how drug is to be taken

Doctor's signature
State license number
DEA number (if required)

PRESCRIPTION REQUIREMENTS

1. Date
2. Full name and address of patient
3. Name and address of prescriber
4. Signature of prescriber

If Class II drug, Drug Enforcement Agency (DEA) number necessary.

If Class II and Class III opioid, a triplicate prescription form (in the state of California) is necessary and it must be handwritten by the prescriber.

Please turn to appropriate oral medicine chapters for examples of prescriptions.

PREVENTING PRESCRIBING ERRORS

Prescribing errors account for the majority of reported medication errors and have prompted health care professionals to focus on the development of steps to make the prescribing process safer. Prescription legibility has been attributed to a portion of these errors and legislation has been enacted in several states to address prescription legibility. However, eliminating handwritten prescriptions and ordering medications through the use of technology [eg, computerized prescriber order entry (CPOE)] has been the primary recommendation. Whether a prescription is electronic, typed, or hand-printed, additional safe practices should be considered for implementation to maximize the safety of the prescribing process. Listed below are suggestions for safer prescribing:

- Ensure correct patient by using at least 2 patient identifiers on the prescription (eg, full name, birth date, or address). Review prescription with the patient or patient's caregiver.
- If pediatric patient, document patient's birth date or age and most recent weight. If geriatric patient, document patient's birth date or age.
- Prevent drug name confusion: For more information, see http://www.ismp.org/tools/confuseddrugnames.pdf.
  - Use TALLman lettering (eg, buPROPion, busPIRone, predniSONE, prednisoLONE). For more information, see http://www.fda.gov/drugs/drugsafety/medicationerrors/default.htm.
  - Avoid abbreviated drug names (eg, MSO_4, $MgSO_4$, MS, HCT, 6MP, MTX), as they may be misinterpreted and cause error.
  - Avoid investigational names for drugs with FDA approval (eg, FK-506, CBDCA).
  - Avoid chemical names such as 6-mercaptopurine or 6-thioguanine, as sixfold overdoses have been given when these were not recognized as chemical names. The proper names of these drugs are mercaptopurine or thioguanine.
  - Use care when prescribing drugs that look or sound similar (eg, look- alike, sound-alike drugs). Common examples include: CeleBREX vs CeleXA, hydrOXYzine vs hydrALAZINE, ZyPREXA vs ZyrTEC.
- Avoid dangerous, error-prone abbreviations (eg, regardless of letter-case: U, IU, QD, QOD, µg, cc, @). Do not use apothecary system or symbols. Additionally, text messaging abbreviations (eg, "2Day") should never be used.
  - For more information, see http://www.ismp.org/tools/errorproneabbreviations.pdf.
- Always use a leading zero for numbers <1 (0.5 mg is correct and .5 mg is **incorrect**) and never use a trailing zero for whole numbers (2 mg is correct and 2.0 mg is **incorrect**).
- Always use a space between a number and its units as it is easier to read. There should be no periods after the abbreviations mg or mL (10 mg is correct and 10mg is **incorrect**).
- For doses that are ≥1,000 dosing units, use properly placed commas to prevent 10-fold errors (100,000 units is correct and 100000 units is **incorrect**).
- Do not prescribe drug dosage by the type of container in which the drug is available (eg, do not prescribe "1 amp", "2 vials", etc).
- Do not write vague or ambiguous orders which have the potential for misinterpretation by other health care providers. Examples of vague orders to avoid: "Resume pre-op medications," "give drug per protocol," or "continue home medications."
- Review each prescription with patient (or patient's caregiver) including the medication name, indication, and directions for use.
- Take extra precautions when prescribing *high alert drugs* (drugs that can cause significant patient harm when prescribed in error). Common examples of these drugs include: Anticoagulants, chemotherapy, insulins, opioids, and sedatives.
  - For more information, see http://www.ismp.org/tools/institutionalhighalert.asp or http://www.ismp.org/communityRx/tools/ambulatoryhighalert.asp.

To Err Is Human: Building a Safer Health System, Kohn LT, Corrigan JM, Donaldson MS, eds. Washington, D.C.: National Academy Press. 2000.

A Complete Outpatient Prescription[1]

A complete outpatient prescription can prevent the prescriber, the pharmacist, and/or the patient from making a mistake and can eliminate the need for further clarification. The complete outpatient prescription should contain:

- Patient's full name
- Medication indication
- Allergies
- Prescriber name and telephone or pager number
- For pediatric patients: Their birth date or age and current weight
- For geriatric patients: Their birth date or age

- Drug name, dosage form and strength
- For pediatric patients: Intended daily weight-based dose so that calculations can be checked by the pharmacist (ie, mg/kg/day or units/kg/day)
- Number or amount to be dispensed
- Complete instructions for the patient or caregiver, including the purpose of the medication, directions for use (including dose), dosing frequency, route of administration, duration of therapy, and number of refills.
- Dose should be expressed in convenient units of measure.
- When there are recognized contraindications for a prescribed drug, the prescriber should indicate knowledge of this fact to the pharmacist (ie, when prescribing a potassium salt for a patient receiving an ACE inhibitor, the prescriber should write "K serum leveling being monitored").

Upon dispensing of the final product, the pharmacist should ensure that the patient or caregiver can effectively demonstrate the appropriate administration technique. An appropriate measuring device should be provided or recommended. Household teaspoons and tablespoons should not be used to measure liquid medications due to their variability and inaccuracies in measurement; oral medication syringes are recommended.

For additional information, see http://www.ismp.org/Newsletters/acutecare/articles/20020601.asp

[1]Levine SR, Cohen MR, Blanchard NR, et al. Guidelines for preventing medication errors in pediatrics. *J Pediatr Pharmacol Ther.* 2001;6:426-442.

SAMPLE PRESCRIPTIONS

Drug prescriptions shown in this section represent prototype drugs and popular prescriptions and are examples only. The pharmacologic category index is available for cross-referencing if alternatives and additional drugs are sought. See the Oral Medicine Chapters for a complete description of Diagnosis and Management considerations.

TABLE OF CONTENTS

ORAL PAIN - SAMPLE PRESCRIPTIONS

MILD/MODERATE ORAL PAIN

General Prescription Comments

Recently, the FDA has formally requested manufacturers to limit the amount of acetaminophen in prescription combination products (eg, Vicodin, Lortab) to no more than 325 mg per dosage unit. The FDA is also requiring manufacturers to update labeling of all prescription combination acetaminophen products to warn of the potential risk for severe liver injury (see Oral Pain on page 1830 for more information). Some manufacturers have already reduced acetaminophen amounts to 300 to 325 mg per tablet in combination prescription products.

Note: Numerous brand name products for infants and children that contain ibuprofen or acetaminophen have been voluntarily recalled by manufacturers due to investigation by the FDA.

Closely monitor and reevaluate response at least every 2 weeks. If response is inadequate, reevaluate diagnosis, medication choice, and dosage.
Note: The following sample prescriptions are for **adults.**

Sample Prescriptions

For additional information, see Acetaminophen on page 56, Diflunisal on page 506, Ibuprofen on page 851, Naproxen on page 1169

Rx:

Acetaminophen 325 mg tablets
Disp: To be determined by practitioner
Sig: Take 2 tablets every 4 hours

Note: Products include Tylenol and others.
Note: Acetaminophen can be given if patient has allergies, bleeding problems, or stomach upset secondary to aspirin or NSAIDs.

Rx:

Ibuprofen 200 mg tablets
Disp: To be determined by practitioner
Sig: Take 1 to 2 tablets every 4 hours

Note: Ibuprofen is an available OTC as Advil, Motrin IB, and many store brand generic names. NSAIDs should not be combined with aspirin. NSAIDs may increase post-treatment bleeding. Use with caution in patients receiving anticoagulants or antiplatelet drugs.

Rx:

Naproxen sodium 220 mg tablets
Disp: To be determined by practitioner
Sig: Take 1 to 2 tablets every 8 hours

Note: Naproxen sodium is an available OTC as Aleve and many store brand generic names.

Rx:

Ibuprofen 400 mg tablets
Disp: 20 tablets
Sig: Take 1 tablet every 4 to 6 hours as needed for pain

Note: Prescription strength ibuprofen is available as the brand name Motrin.

Rx:

Dolobid 500 mg tablets
Disp: 16 tablets
Sig: Take 2 tablets initially, then 1 tablet every 12 hours as needed for pain

Ingredient: Diflunisal

MODERATE/MODERATELY SEVERE ORAL PAIN

General Prescription Comments

Closely monitor and reevaluate response at least every 2 weeks. If response is inadequate, reevaluate diagnosis, medication choice, and dosage.
Note: The following sample prescriptions are for **adults.**

Sample Prescriptions

For additional information, see Acetaminophen and Codeine on page 61, Acetaminophen and Tramadol on page 65, Hydrocodone and Acetaminophen on page 825, Hydrocodone and Ibuprofen on page 828, Ibuprofen on page 851, Naproxen on page 1169, TraMADol on page 1586

Rx:

Ibuprofen 800 mg tablets
Disp: 16 tablets
Sig: Take 1 tablet 3 times/day as needed for pain

Note: For severe pain can be given up to 4 times/day. Also available as 600 mg tablets.

Rx:

TraMADol 50 mg tablets
Disp: 36 tablets
Sig: Take 1 to 2 tablets every 4 to 6 hours as needed for pain (maximum: 400 mg/day)

Note: Also available as the brand name Ultram.

Important notification regarding TraMADol: Effective August 18, 2014, Tramadol will be classified as a Schedule IV controlled dangerous substance (CDS) under federal regulation. If you dispense Tramadol to your patients, you are required to report this to the Prescription Drug Monitoring Program (PDMP). If you write a prescription for Tramadol, but do **not** dispense this medication, you are not required to report to the PDMP. The Division of Drug Control (DDC) has posted the following information on its website: USDOJ/DEA, 21 CFR (Federal Register) Part 1308: Schedules of Controlled Dangerous Substances: Placement of Tramadol Into Schedule IV (Final Rule). DEA (CFR Final Rule) Tramadol Schedule IV Placement (Effective: 8/18/14).

Rx:

Ultracet tablets
Disp: 36 tablets
Sig: Take 2 tablets every 4 to 6 hours as needed for pain, not to exceed 8 tablets in 24 hours

Ingredients: Acetaminophen 325 mg and Tramadol 37.5 mg

Rx:

Vicoprofen tablets
Disp: 16 tablets
Sig: Take 1 to 2 tablets every 4 to 6 hours as needed for pain (maximum: 5 tablets/day)

Note: Restrictions: C-II; no refills
Ingredients: Hydrocodone 7.5 mg and ibuprofen 200 mg; available as generic equivalent

Rx:

Vicodin ES tablets 7.5 mg hydrocodone/300 mg acetaminophen (per tablet)
Disp: 16 tablets
Sig: Take 1 tablet every 4 to 6 hours as needed for pain (maximum: 5 tablets/day)

Note: Restrictions: C-II; no refills
Ingredients: Hydrocodone bitartrate 7.5 mg and acetaminophen 300 mg; available as generic equivalent.

Rx:

Norco 10 mg
Disp: 16 tablets
Sig: Take 1 or 2 tablets every 4 hours as needed for pain; not to exceed 8 tablets in 24 hours

Note: Restrictions: C-II; no refills
Ingredients: Hydrocodone 10 mg and acetaminophen 325 mg; available as generic equivalent

Rx:

Tylenol #3
Disp: 16 tablets
Sig: Take 1 tablet every 4 hours as needed for pain

Note: Restrictions: C-III; no refills
Ingredients: Codeine 30 mg and acetaminophen 300 mg; available as generic equivalent

Rx:

Naproxen 275 mg tablets
Disp: 16 tablets
Sig: Take 2 tablets initially, then one tablet 3 times/day as needed for pain

SEVERE ORAL PAIN

General Prescription Comments

Closely monitor and reevaluate response at least every 2 weeks. If response is inadequate, reevaluate diagnosis, medication choice, and dosage.

Liquid volumes are suggested for a typical 2-week course. Check with pharmacist for available sizes.

Cream and ointment tube sizes may vary based on availability. Refer to individual monograph or check with pharmacist for available sizes.

Note: The following sample prescriptions are for **adults**.

Sample Prescriptions

For additional information, see Oxycodone and Acetaminophen on page 1261.

Rx:

Percocet tablets
Disp: 16 tablets
Sig: Take 1 tablet every 6 hours as needed for pain

Note: Restrictions: C-II; no refills
Ingredients: Oxycodone 5 mg and acetaminophen 325 mg; available as generic equivalent; triplicate prescription required in some states

Rx:

Oxycodone and Ibuprofen tablets
Disp: 16 tablets
Sig: Take 1 tablet every 6 hours as needed for pain

Note: Restrictions: C-II; no refills
Ingredients: Oxycodone 5 mg and ibuprofen 400 mg; triplicate prescription required in some states

ANTIMICROBIAL ORAL RINSE - SAMPLE PRESCRIPTIONS

General Prescription Comments

Closely monitor and reevaluate response at least every 2 weeks. If response is inadequate, reevaluate diagnosis, medication choice, and dosage.

Liquid volumes for antimicrobial rinses are suggested for a typical 1 month course. Check with pharmacist for available sizes.

Sample Prescriptions

For additional information, see Chlorhexidine Gluconate on page 344, Mouthwash (Antiseptic) on page 1150.

Rx:

Chlorhexidine gluconate 0.12% oral rinse
Disp: 32 oz bottle
Sig: Rinse vigorously twice daily with 15 to 20 mL for 30 seconds and expectorate

Note: Chlorhexidine gluconate available as the following brands: Peridex, PerioGard; it is also available in an alcohol-free formulation in some pharmaceutical locations. Advise patient of risk of reversible tooth staining.

Rx:

Listerine antiseptic mouthwash [OTC]
Disp: Bottle
Sig: Rinse vigorously twice daily with 15 to 20 mL for 30 seconds and expectorate

Note: Various formulations, such as Cool Mint, are also available in an alcohol-free formulation.

BACTERIAL INFECTIONS AND PERIODONTAL DISEASES - SAMPLE PRESCRIPTIONS

General Prescription Comments

For the use of all antibiotic medications, prescribers should review the guidelines related to antimicrobial stewardship endorsed by the ADA that is cited in Bacterial Infections on page 1835. Sample prescription dosing is for adults. Closely monitor and reevaluate response at least every 2 weeks. If response is inadequate, reevaluate diagnosis, medication choice, and dosage.

Sample Prescriptions

For additional information, see Bacterial Infections on page 1835, Amoxicillin on page 121, Amoxicillin and Clavulanate on page 126, Azithromycin (Systemic) on page 194, Cephalexin on page 333, Clindamycin (Systemic) on page 382, Doxycycline on page 540, Erythromycin (Systemic) on page 596, LevoFLOXacin (Systemic) on page 979, MetroNIDAZOLE (Systemic) on page 1110, Minocycline on page 1127, Penicillin V Potassium on page 1311

Rx:
Penicillin V potassium 500 mg
Disp: 40 tablets
Sig: Take 1 tablet 4 times/day for 7 to 10 days (consider a loading dose of 1 g for acute infection)

Rx:
Clindamycin (Systemic) 150 mg
Disp: 40 capsules
Sig: Take 1 capsule 4 times/day for 7 to 10 days

Note: Prescription usually selected for patients allergic to penicillin; may be prescribed for 3 or 4 times/day. Recommend to be taken after food to reduce GI concerns.

Rx:
Clindamycin (Systemic) 300 mg
Disp: 40 capsules
Sig: Take 1 capsule 4 times/day for 7 to 10 days

Note: Prescription usually selected for patients allergic to penicillin; may be prescribed for 3 or 4 times/day. Recommend to be taken after food to reduce GI concerns.

Rx:
Azithromycin (Systemic) 250 mg
Disp: 1 Z-Pak
Sig: 2 tablets day 1, then 1 tablet/day until gone

OTHER ANTIBIOTICS:

Rx:
Amoxicillin 250 mg
Disp: 30 capsules
Sig: Take 1 capsule 3 times/day for 7 to 10 days

Rx:
Amoxicillin 500 mg
Disp: 30 capsules or tablets
Sig: Take 1 capsule or tablet 3 times/day for 7 to 10 days

Rx:
Amoxicillin 875 mg
Disp: 20 tablets
Sig: Take 1 tablet twice daily

Rx:
Augmentin 250 mg
Disp: 30 tablets
Sig: Take 1 tablet 3 times/day for 7 to 10 days

Rx:
Augmentin 500 mg
Disp: 30 tablets
Sig: Take 1 tablet 3 times/day for 7 to 10 days

Rx:

Augmentin 875 mg
Disp: 20 tablets
Sig: Take 1 tablet twice daily for 7 to 10 days

Rx:

Augmentin XR 1,000 mg
Disp: 20 tablets
Sig: Take 1 tablet twice daily for 7 to 10 days; not the same as taking two 500 mg tablets

Rx:

Cephalexin 250 mg
Disp: 40 capsules
Sig: Take 1 capsule 4 times/day for 7 to 10 days

Rx:

MetroNIDAZOLE (Systemic) 500 mg
Disp: 40 tablets
Sig: Take 1 tablet 3 or 4 times/day for 7 to 10 days

Note: For acute periodontal infections or as therapy in osteonecrosis of the jaw, usually used in combination with amoxicillin or amoxicillin plus clavulanic acid; may be prescribed for 3 or 4 times/day. When prescribed at 500 mg tid the patient can take both medications together enhancing compliance.

Rx:

Erythromycin (Systemic) 250 mg
Disp: 40 tablets
Sig: Take 1 tablet 4 times/day for 7 to 10 days

Note: Prescription for patients allergic to penicillin, however, is seldom prescribed due to concern over general efficacy and considerable GI effects.

Rx:

Zithromax TRI-PAK 500 mg
Disp: 1 PAK
Sig: Follow package insert directions until gone

Ingredient: Azithromycin (Systemic)

Rx:

Levaquin 500 mg
Disp: 10 tablets
Sig: Take 1 tablet/day until gone

Ingredient: LevoFLOXacin, available as 250, 500, and 750 mg tablets

Note: Not the ideal drug for general dental and/or periodontal infections; however, levofloxacin is approved for treatment of acute bacterial rhinosinusitis.

PERIODONTAL DISEASE

Note: Sample prescriptions based on dosing suggestions from the American Academy of Periodontology

Rx:

Azithromycin (Systemic) 500 mg tablets
Disp: Dispense a dose pack
Sig: Take 1 tablet daily for 4 to 7 days as directed

Rx:

Clindamycin (Systemic) 300 mg tablets
Disp: 24 tablets
Sig: Take 1 tablet 3 times/day for 8 days

Rx:

Doxycycline or Minocycline 100 to 200 mg tablets
Disp: 21 tablets of selected dose
Sig: Take 1 tablet daily for 21 days

Rx:

Doxycycline 100 mg tablets
Disp: 42 tablets
Sig: Take 1 tablet twice daily for 21 days

Note: Prescription used for Lyme disease: Early stage (erythema migrans)

Rx:
MetroNIDAZOLE (Systemic) 500 mg
Disp: 24 tablets
Sig: Take 1 tablet 3 times/day for 8 days

Note: Metronidazole is often used in acute periodontal infections and in the early management of infected osteonecrosis of the jaw in combination with amoxicillin, or amoxicillin plus clavulanic acid.

Rx:
MetroNIDAZOLE (Systemic) and Amoxicillin 250 mg or 500 mg tablets
Disp: 24 tablets of each drug
Sig: Take 1 tablet of each drug 3 times/day for 8 days

FUNGAL INFECTIONS - SAMPLE PRESCRIPTIONS

FUNGAL INFECTIONS REQUIRING TOPICAL THERAPY

General Prescription Comments

Closely monitor and reevaluate response at least every 2 weeks. If response is inadequate, reevaluate diagnosis, medication choice, and dosage.

Liquid volumes are suggested for a typical 2-week course. Check with pharmacist for available sizes.

Cream and ointment tube may vary from 5 g, 15 g, 30 g, 45 g, or 60 g sizes, based on availability. Refer to individual monograph or check with pharmacist for available sizes.

Sample Prescriptions

For additional information, see Fungal Infections on page 1847, Clotrimazole (Oral) on page 404, Nystatin (Oral) on page 1214, Nystatin (Topical) on page 1215

Rx:

Nystatin (Oral) 100,000 units/mL oral suspension
Disp: 300 mL
Sig: Rinse with 1 teaspoon (5 mL) for 2 minutes 4 to 5 times/day and expectorate

Rx:

Nystatin (Topical) ointment
Disp: 15 g tube
Sig: Apply locally as directed with a thin coat to inner surface of denture and the affected area 4 to 5 times/day

Rx:

Mycelex 10 mg troches
Disp: 70 troches
Sig: Dissolve 1 troche in mouth 4 to 5 times/day until gone; leave any prosthesis out during treatment and soak prosthesis in nystatin liquid suspension overnight

Ingredient: Clotrimazole (Oral)

FUNGAL INFECTIONS REQUIRING SYSTEMIC THERAPY

General Prescription Comments

Note: Decision to use systemic antifungals should be based on diagnostic culture results or positive smear.

Closely monitor and reevaluate response at least every 2 weeks. If response is inadequate, reevaluate diagnosis, medication choice, and dosage.

Sample Prescriptions

For additional information, see Fluconazole on page 721, Ketoconazole (Systemic) on page 940, Posaconazole on page 1358

Rx:

Diflucan 100 mg tablets
Disp: 14 tablets
Sig: Take 1 tablet/day until gone

Note: Sometimes a shorter course is adequate. However, oral infections are more commonly difficult to eradicate and often a 21-day course, or even a second course, may be necessary.

Ingredient: Fluconazole

Rx:

Nizoral 200 mg tablets
Disp: 14 tablets
Sig: Take 1 tablet/day with a meal for 2 weeks

Note: May cause irreversible liver damage; liver function should be monitored with long-term use (ie, >3 weeks)

Ingredient: Ketoconazole (Systemic)

Rx:

Posaconazole 100 mg tablets
Disp: 14 tablets
Sig: Take 2 tablets the first day, followed by 1 tablet each day for 13 days

Note: Posaconazole has been recently approved for use in patients refractory to itraconazole or fluconazole

ANGULAR CHEILITIS

General Prescription Comments

Closely monitor and reevaluate response at least every 2 weeks. If response is inadequate, reevaluate diagnosis, medication choice, and dosage. Other associated etiologies for angular cheilitis must also be considered, such as loss of vertical dimension, trauma, and vitamin deficiencies.

Cream and ointment tube may vary from 15 g, 30 g, or 45 g sizes, based on availability. Refer to individual monograph or check with pharmacist for available sizes.

Sample Prescriptions

For additional information, see Iodoquinol and Hydrocortisone on page 914.

Rx:

Nystatin and Triamcinolone acetonide ointment
Disp: 30 g tube
Sig: Apply locally as directed to affected area 4 times/day for 10 to 14 days and then reevaluate

Rx:

Iodoquinol and Hydrocortisone cream
Disp: 45 g tube
Sig: Apply locally as directed 3 to 4 times/day for 10 days to 2 weeks and then reevaluate

PREVENTION OF ENDOCARDITIS AND TO REDUCE THE RISK OF LATE INFECTIONS OF JOINT PROSTHESES - SAMPLE PRESCRIPTIONS

General Prescription Comments

For any patients requiring preprocedural antibiotics for prevention of infective endocarditis or to reduce the risk of late infections in joint prostheses, the dental team must be aware of significant changes in the practice guidelines endorsed by the American Dental Association, the American Heart Association, and the American Association of Orthopedic Surgeons. The American Association of Orthopedic Surgeons (AAOS) has developed Appropriate Use Criteria (AUC) for thirteen selected situations encountered by orthopedists, including, "Management of patients with orthopedic implants undergoing dental procedures". This was added as of November 2016.

Regarding antibiotic selection, when after consultation preprocedural antibiotics are deemed necessary, one important change occurred. In the latest release from the AAOS, clindamycin is no longer recommended as the suggested alternative in patients allergic to penicillins. The AAOS now recommends, in allergic patients still able to take oral medication, 2 g cephalexin, or 500 mg of azithromycin or clarithromycin, in that order of selection. Since this release the ADA and the AHA have not taken any steps to alter their endocarditis recommendations. Terico AT, Gallagher JC. Beta-lactam hypersensitivity and cross-reactivity. *J Pharm Pract*. 2014;27(6):530-544 is cited as the reference for considerations of cross-allergenicity of cephalosporins and penicillins.

Preprocedural antibiotics are only recommended in very specific medical circumstances relative to endocarditis and they are generally not recommended for patients with joint prostheses. The dentist is encouraged as always to record a thorough medical history to determine risks and to consult with the appropriate physician in order to make the final decision to prescribe antibiotic prophylaxis or not. See Antibiotic Prophylaxis on page 1812 for additional information regarding high-risk patients and the goals of consultation.

Prescriptions dispense amounts are for three visits. These numbers can be adjusted for each patient treatment plan.

Sample Prescriptions

For additional information, see Amoxicillin on page 121, Azithromycin (Systemic) on page 194, Cephalexin on page 333, Clarithromycin on page 377, Clindamycin (Systemic) on page 382

Rx:
Amoxicillin 500 mg
Disp: 12 tablets
Sig: 4 tablets (2 g) 30 to 60 minutes prior to dental visit and repeat at each appointment

Rx:
Clindamycin (Systemic) 150 mg
Disp: 12 capsules
Sig: 4 capsules (600 mg) 30 to 60 minutes prior to dental visit and repeat at each appointment

Rx:
Cephalexin 500 mg
Disp: 12 tablets
Sig: 4 tablets (2 g) 30 to 60 minutes prior to dental visit and repeat at each appointment
Note: Clindamycin is no longer recommended in the AAOS guidelines but is still an alternative in the AHA and ADA guidelines.

Rx:
Azithromycin (Systemic) 500 mg
Disp: 3 tablets
Sig: 1 tablet 30 to 60 minutes prior to dental visit and repeat at each appointment

Rx:
Clarithromycin 500 mg
Disp: 3 tablets
Sig: 1 tablet 30 to 60 minutes prior to dental visit and repeat at each appointment

SINUS INFECTION TREATMENT - SAMPLE PRESCRIPTIONS

General Prescription Comments

Please review the guidelines related to antimicrobial stewardship endorsed by the ADA that is cited in Bacterial Infections on page 1835. Closely monitor and reevaluate response at least every 2 weeks. If response is inadequate, reevaluate diagnosis, medication choice, and dosage.

Sinus infections represent a common condition which may present with confounding dental complaints. Treatment is sometimes instituted by the dentist, but due to the often chronic and recurrent nature of sinus infections, early involvement of an otolaryngologist is advised. These infections may require antibiotics of varying spectrum, as well as requiring the management of sinus congestion. Although amoxicillin is usually adequate, many otolaryngologists initially prescribe Augmentin. Second generation cephalosporins, azithromycin, and clarithromycin are sometimes used depending on the chronicity of the problem. Although not the ideal drug for general dental and/or periodontal infections, levofloxacin (Levoquin) is approved for treatment of acute bacterial rhinosinusitis.

Sample Prescriptions

For additional information, see Amoxicillin on page 121, Amoxicillin and Clavulanate on page 126, Azithromycin (Systemic) on page 194, Chlorpheniramine on page 349, LevoFLOXacin (Systemic) on page 979, Oxymetazoline (Nasal) on page 1273, Pseudoephedrine on page 1404

Rx:
Afrin nasal spray [OTC]
Disp: 15 mg
Sig: Spray once in each nostril every 6 to 8 hours for no more than 3 days

Ingredient: Oxymetazoline (Nasal)

Rx:
Sudafed 60 mg tablets [OTC]
Disp: 30 tablets
Sig: Take 1 tablet every 4 to 6 hours as needed for congestion

Note: Some reports have suggested alterations in blood pressure with pseudoephedrine which can range from minor to significant. This should be considered prior to prescribing.
Ingredient: Pseudoephedrine

Rx:
Chlor-Trimeton 4 mg [OTC]
Disp: 14 tablets
Sig: Take 1 tablet twice daily

Ingredient: Chlorpheniramine

ANTIBIOTICS:

Note: Antibiotics are not always required but may be useful in acute management of infection.

Rx:
Azithromycin (Systemic) 250 mg
Disp: 1 Z-Pak
Sig: 2 tablets day 1, then 1 tablet/day until gone

Rx:
Amoxicillin 250 mg
Disp: 30 capsules
Sig: Take 1 capsule 3 times/day for 7 to 10 days

Rx:
Amoxicillin 500 mg
Disp: 30 capsules or tablets
Sig: Take 1 capsule or tablet 3 times/day for 7 to 10 days

Rx:
Amoxicillin 875 mg
Disp: 20 tablets
Sig: Take 1 tablet twice daily

Rx:
Augmentin 250 mg
Disp: 30 tablets
Sig: Take 1 tablet 3 times/day for 7 to 10 days

Rx:
Augmentin 500 mg
Disp: 30 tablets
Sig: Take 1 tablet 3 times/day for 7 to 10 days

Rx:
Augmentin 875 mg
Disp: 20 tablets
Sig: Take 1 tablet twice daily for 7 to 10 days

Rx:
Augmentin XR 1,000 mg
Disp: 20 tablets
Sig: Take 2 tablets twice daily for 7 to 10 days

Rx:
LevoFLOXacin
Disp: Either five 750 mg tablets or seven or fourteen 500 mg tablets
Sig: Depending on the reference therapy you are following, select 1 tablet/day from the dosage and durations above

Note: For Acute Bacterial Rhinosinusitis, available as 500 mg or 750 mg tablets. Not generally recommended for dental or periodontal infections.

VIRAL INFECTIONS - SAMPLE PRESCRIPTIONS

HERPES SIMPLEX (PRIMARY)

General Prescription Comments

Closely monitor and reevaluate response at least every 2 weeks. If response is inadequate, reevaluate diagnosis, medication choice, and dosage.

Sample Prescriptions

For additional information, see Acyclovir (Systemic) on page 73, Acyclovir (Topical) on page 77

Rx:

Zovirax 200 mg capsules
Disp: 50 or 60 capsules
Sig: Take 1 capsule 5 times/day for 10 days or 2 capsules 3 times/day for 10 days

Ingredient: Acyclovir (Systemic)

Rx:

Zovirax ointment 5%
Disp: 15 g tube
Sig: Apply thin layer to lesions 6 times/day for 7 days.

Ingredient: Acyclovir (Topical)

HERPES SIMPLEX (RECURRENT)

General Prescription Comments

Closely monitor and reevaluate response at least every 2 weeks. If response is inadequate, reevaluate diagnosis, medication choice, and dosage.

Cream and ointment tube sizes may vary based on availability. Refer to individual monograph or check with pharmacist for available sizes.

Sample Prescriptions

For additional information, see Acyclovir (Topical) on page 77, Docosanol on page 524, Famciclovir on page 686, Penciclovir on page 1307, ValACYclovir on page 1622

Rx:

Denavir topical cream 1%
Disp: 1.5 g tube
Sig: Apply locally as directed to lesion every 2 hours during waking hours (begin when prodromal symptoms first occur)

Ingredient: Penciclovir

Rx:

Famciclovir 500 mg tablets
Disp: 3 tablets
Sig: Take 3 tablets (1,500 mg) as a single dose; therapy should be initiated at the first sign of any prodrome such as tingling, burning, or itching

Note: Dispense in multiples of 3 so that patient has drug on hand for any recurrences; available as generic equivalent

Rx:

ValACYclovir 500 mg
Disp: 8 caplets
Sig: 4 caplets twice daily for 1 day (separate doses by 12 hours); therapy should be initiated at the first sign of any prodrome such as tingling, burning, or itching

Rx:

Abreva cream [OTC]
Disp: 2 g tube
Sig: Apply to lesion 5 times/day during waking hours for 4 days (begin when symptoms first occur)

Ingredient: Docosanol

Rx:

Zovirax cream 5%
Disp: 2 g tube; 5 g tube
Sig: Apply 5 times/day for 4 days

Ingredient: Acyclovir (Topical)

SHINGLES (VARICELLA-ZOSTER VIRUS)

General Prescription Comments

Closely monitor and reevaluate response at least every 2 weeks. If response is inadequate, reevaluate diagnosis, medication choice, and dosage.

Sample Prescriptions

For additional information, see Acyclovir (Systemic) on page 73, Famciclovir on page 686, ValACYclovir on page 1622

Rx:

Zovirax 200 mg capsules
Disp: 200 capsules
Sig: Take 4 capsules 5 times/day for 10 days

Ingredient: Acyclovir (Systemic)

Rx:

ValACYclovir 500 mg
Disp: 42 caplets
Sig: Take 2 caplets 3 times/day for 7 days

Rx:

Famciclovir 500 mg
Disp: 21 tablets
Sig: 1 tablet 3 times/day for 7 days

SEDATION (PRIOR TO DENTAL TREATMENT) - SAMPLE PRESCRIPTIONS

General Prescription Comments

Sample prescription doses are for healthy adults. Use of these drugs and/or dosage may not be appropriate for children, elderly, and/or debilitated patients. Dental sedation should be used cautiously in these patients. Patients receiving sedative agents must be advised that they will need to have someone drive them to and from their appointment.

Sample Prescriptions for Adults

For additional information, see ALPRAZolam on page 101, DiazePAM on page 491, HydrOXYzine on page 844, LORazepam on page 1020, Triazolam on page 1606

Rx:

Valium 5 mg
Disp: 1 tablet
Sig: Take 1 tablet 1 hour before appointment

Note: Also available as 2 mg and 10 mg
Ingredient: DiazePAM

Rx:

Ativan 1 mg
Disp: 2 tablets
Sig: Take 2 tablets 1 hour before appointment

Note: Also available as 0.5 mg and 2 mg
Ingredient: LORazepam

Rx:

Xanax 0.5 mg
Disp: 1 tablet
Sig: Take 1 tablet 1 hour before appointment

Ingredient: ALPRAZolam

Rx:

Vistaril 25 mg
Disp: 2 capsules
Sig: Take 2 capsules 1 hour before appointment

Ingredient: HydrOXYzine

Rx:

Halcion 0.25 mg
Disp: 1 tablet
Sig: Take 1 tablet 1 hour before appointment

Ingredient: Triazolam

ULCERATIVE AND EROSIVE DISORDERS - SAMPLE PRESCRIPTIONS

RECURRENT APHTHOUS STOMATITIS

General Prescription Comments

Some intraoral uses are off-label. Write directions as "use locally as directed" and closely monitor and reevaluate response at least every 2 weeks. If response is inadequate, reevaluate diagnosis, medication choice, and dosage.

Liquid volumes are suggested for a typical 2-week course. Check with pharmacist for available sizes.

Cream, gel, and ointment tube sizes may vary based on availability. Refer to individual monograph or check with pharmacist for available sizes.

Sample Prescriptions

For additional information, see Betamethasone (Topical) on page 221, Clobetasol on page 390, Dexamethasone (Systemic) on page 474, DiphenhydrAMINE (Systemic) on page 517, Fluocinonide on page 734, Triamcinolone (Topical) on page 1604

Palliative

Rx:

Orabase Protective Barrier [OTC]
Disp: 1 package
Sig: Apply locally as directed, every 6 hours as needed

Rx:

Benadryl liquid 12.5 mg per 5 mL (mix 50/50) with Kaopectate
Disp: 8 oz total
Sig: Rinse with 1 to 2 teaspoonfuls every 2 hours and expectorate

Note: Maalox can be used in place of Kaopectate if constipation is a problem. Benadryl is available as a generic DiphenhydrAMINE liquid.

Rx:

Benadryl liquid 12.5 mg per 5 mL / Kaopectate / Lidocaine viscous (mix 1/3, 1/3, 1/3)
Disp: 8 oz total
Sig: Rinse with 1 to 2 teaspoonfuls every 2 hours and expectorate

Note: Maalox can be used in place of Kaopectate if constipation is a problem. Benadryl is available as a generic DiphenhydrAMINE liquid. Lidocaine viscous is available as a prescription only.

Rx:

Benadryl liquid 12.5 mg per 5 mL
Disp: 4 oz bottle
Sig: Rinse with 1 to 2 teaspoonfuls every 2 hours and expectorate

Note: Benadryl is available as a generic DiphenhydrAMINE liquid.

Therapy-Based (Contain Steroids)

Rx:

Oralone 0.1%
Disp: 5 g tube
Sig: Apply locally as directed to the lesion after each meal and at bedtime

Ingredient: Triamcinolone (Topical)

Rx:

Fluocinonide 0.05% gel
Disp: 45 g tube
Sig: Apply locally as directed to lesion 4 times/day

Rx:

Temovate 0.05%
Disp: 45 g tube
Sig: Apply locally as directed a small quantity with a Q-tip to affected area 3 to 4 times/day

Ingredient: Clobetasol propionate

Note: Pharmacies can be asked to compound drugs with higher potency, such as clobetasol with Orabase to achieve bioadhesive properties to help deliver the steroid effects.

Rx:
Betamethasone 0.1% ointment
Disp: 45 g tube
Sig: Apply a small quantity with a Q-tip locally as directed to affected area 3 to 4 times/day

Rx:
Decadron elixir 0.5 mg per 5 mL
Disp: 300 mL
Sig: Rinse with 1 teaspoon for 2 minutes 4 times/day and expectorate

Ingredient: Dexamethasone (Systemic)

Note: Depending on severity of ulceration, instructions can be tailored to include swallowing initial doses and then tapering to every other dose eventually over 4 to 7 days to no swallowing. See Erosive Lichen Planus, Other Biopsy-Proven Desquamative Oral Diseases, and Major Aphthae for more examples.

MILD LICHEN PLANUS

General Prescription Comments

Some intraoral uses are off-label. Write directions as "use locally as directed" and closely monitor and reevaluate response at least every 2 weeks. If response is inadequate, reevaluate diagnosis, medication choice, and dosage.

Cream and ointment tube sizes may vary based on availability. Refer to individual monograph or check with pharmacist for available sizes.

Sample Prescriptions

For additional information, see Betamethasone (Topical) on page 221, Clobetasol on page 390, Dexamethasone (Systemic) on page 474, Fluocinonide on page 734, Triamcinolone (Topical) on page 1604

Rx:
Oralone 0.1%
Disp: 5 g tube
Sig: Apply locally as directed by coating the lesion with a thin film after each meal and at bedtime

Ingredient: Triamcinolone (Topical) 0.1%

Rx:
Fluocinonide 0.05% gel
Disp: 45 g tube
Sig: Apply locally as directed to lesion 4 times/day

Rx:
Temovate 0.05%
Disp: 45 g tube
Sig: Apply a small quantity with a Q-tip locally as directed to affected area 3 to 4 times/day

Ingredient: Clobetasol

Note: The pharmacist can compound potent steroids, such as clobetasol with Orabase, to enhance adherence to oral tissues.

Rx:
Betamethasone 0.1% ointment
Disp: 45 g tube
Sig: Apply a small quantity with a Q-tip locally as directed to affected area 3 to 4 times/day

Rx:
Decadron elixir 0.5 mg per 5 mL
Disp: 300 mL
Sig: Rinse with 1 teaspoon for 2 minutes 4 times/day and expectorate

Ingredient: Dexamethasone (Systemic)

Note: Depending on severity of ulceration, instructions can be tailored to include swallowing initial doses and then tapering to every other dose eventually over 4 to 7 days to no swallowing. See Erosive Lichen Planus, Other Biopsy-Proven Desquamative Oral Diseases, and Major Aphthae for more examples.

EROSIVE LICHEN PLANUS, OTHER BIOPSY-PROVEN DESQUAMATIVE ORAL DISEASES, AND MAJOR APHTHAE

General Prescription Comments

Some intraoral uses are off-label. Write directions as "use locally as directed" and closely monitor and reevaluate response at least every 2 weeks. If response is inadequate, reevaluate diagnosis, medication choice, and dosage.

Liquid volumes are suggested for a typical 2-week course. Check with pharmacist for available sizes.

Cream, gel, and ointment formulations should only be selected if the sites of the oral lesions are localized and are accessible for applications.

Cream, gel, and ointment tube sizes may vary based on availability. Refer to individual monograph or check with pharmacist for available sizes.

Note: Soft, thin, vacuum-formed trays can be made (similar to bleaching trays but extending slightly onto the gingiva) to deliver steroid ointments or creams to gingival lesions. Also, the pharmacist can compound potent steroids, such as clobetasol with Orabase, to enhance adherence to oral tissues. For chronically recurring lesions, prednisone can be prescribed at 40 mg/day for week 1, 30 mg/day for week 2, continue tapering dose each week to 0. Occasionally, the clinician needs to tailor the regimen by using alternating doses every other day, such as 20 mg day 1, 10 mg day 2, then back to 20 mg. It is important to assess patient compliance when such a regimen is considered.

Sample Prescriptions

For additional information, see Clobetasol on page 390, Dexamethasone (Systemic) on page 474, MethylPREDNISolone on page 1097, PredniSONE on page 1377

Rx:

Decadron 0.5 mg per 5 mL elixir
Disp: 400 mL bottle
Sig: For 3 days, rinse with 1 tablespoonful (15 mL) 4 times/day and swallow; then for 3 days, rinse with 1 teaspoonful (5 mL) 4 times/day and swallow; then for 3 days, rinse with 1 teaspoonful (5 mL) 4 times/day and swallow every other time. Then for 3 days rinse with 1 teaspoonful (5 mL) 4 times/day and expectorate. Continue the rinse and expectorate mode for 2 minutes but discontinue medication when mouth becomes completely comfortable.

Ingredient: Dexamethasone (Systemic); the practitioner can tailor this rinse, hold expectorate and/or swallow prescription to the severity and lesion location for each individual patient.

Rx:

Temovate 0.05% cream
Disp: 15 g tube
Sig: Apply locally as directed 4 to 5 times/day

Ingredient: Clobetasol; high potency topical steroid

Rx:

PredniSONE 5 mg tablets
Disp: 40 tablets
Sig: Take 5 tablets in the morning for 5 days, then 5 tablets in the morning every other day until gone

Rx:

PredniSONE 10 mg tablets
Disp: 50 tablets
Sig: Take 4 tablets in the morning for 5 days, then decrease by 1 tablet on each successive series of 5 days.
Note: Longer durations of a regimen (eg, 7 to 10 days) can be tailored to the severity of the oral condition.

Rx:

Medrol Dose Pak
Disp: 1 Pack
Sig: Follow package insert directions until gone

Ingredient: MethylPREDNISolone

Rx:

Protopic ointment (available in 0.03% and 0.1% strengths)
Disp: Available in 30 g, 60 g, and 100 g tubes
Sig: Apply locally as directed 2 times/day

Ingredient: Tacrolimus (Calcineurin Inhibitor; Immunosuppressant Agent)

ALPHABETICAL LISTING OF DRUGS

Abacavir (a BAK a veer)

Related Information

HIV Infection and AIDS *on page 1785*

Brand Names: US Ziagen

Brand Names: Canada Ziagen

Pharmacologic Category Antiretroviral, Reverse Transcriptase Inhibitor, Nucleoside (Anti-HIV)

Use HIV-1 infection: Treatment of HIV-1 infection in combination with other antiretroviral agents

Local Anesthetic/Vasoconstrictor Precautions No information available to require special precautions

Effects on Dental Treatment No significant effects or complications reported

Effects on Bleeding No information available to require special precautions relative to altered hemostasis

Adverse Reactions Rates of adverse reactions were defined during combination therapy with other antiretrovirals. Frequency not always defined. *Incidence not specifically defined but reported in the range of >10%. **Incidence not specifically defined but reported in the range of 1% to 10%.

Central nervous system: Fatigue*, headache (adults: >10%; children: 1% to 10%), malaise*, abnormal dreams**, anxiety**, chills**, depression**, dizziness**, migraine**, sleep disorder**

Dermatologic: Skin rash**

Endocrine & metabolic: Hypertriglyceridemia**, increased gamma-glutamyl transferase

Gastrointestinal: Nausea*, abdominal pain**, diarrhea (increased incidence with once daily dosing)**, gastritis**, gastrointestinal disease**, increased serum amylase**, nausea and vomiting**, vomiting**, pancreatitis

Hematologic & oncologic: Neutropenia**, thrombocytopenia**

Hepatic: Increased serum ALT**, increased serum AST**

Hypersensitivity: Hypersensitivity reaction (including anaphylaxis and multiorgan failure; 8%; excluding subjects carrying the HLA-B*5701 allele: 1%)

Neuromuscular & skeletal: Increased creatinine phosphokinase**, musculoskeletal pain**

Respiratory: Bronchitis**, ENT infection**, pneumonia (children)**, viral respiratory tract infection**

Miscellaneous: Fever**

<1%, postmarketing, and/or case reports: Anemia, erythema multiforme, hepatomegaly, hepatotoxicity, hyperglycemia, immune reconstitution syndrome, lactic acidosis, leukopenia, liver steatosis, myocardial infarction, pain, redistribution of body fat, renal disease, Stevens-Johnson syndrome, toxic epidermal necrolysis

General Dosage Range Dosage adjustment recommended in patients with hepatic impairment

Oral:

Infants ≥3 months, Children, and Adolescents:

Oral solution: 16 mg/kg/day in 1 to 2 divided doses (maximum: 600 mg/day)

Tablet: 14 to <20 kg: 300 mg once daily or 150 mg twice daily; ≥20 to <25 kg: 450 mg once daily or 150 mg in the morning and 300 mg in the evening; ≥25 kg: 600 mg once daily or 300 mg twice daily

Adults: 600 mg/day in 1 to 2 divided doses (maximum: 600 mg/day)

Mechanism of Action Nucleoside reverse transcriptase inhibitor. Abacavir is a guanosine analogue which is phosphorylated to carbovir triphosphate which interferes with HIV viral RNA-dependent DNA polymerase resulting in inhibition of viral replication.

Pharmacodynamics/Kinetics

Half-life Elimination

Serum:

Pediatric patients ≥3 months to ≤13 years: 1 to 1.5 hours (Hughes 1999; Kline 1999)

Adults: 1.54 ± 0.63 hours

Hepatic impairment (mild): Increases half-life by 58%

Intracellular: 12 to 26 hours

Time to Peak Pediatric patients ≥3 months to ≤13 years: Within 1.5 hours (Hughes 1999); Adults: 0.7 to 1.7 hours

Pregnancy Considerations Abacavir has a high level of transfer across the human placenta. No increased risk of overall birth defects has been observed following first trimester exposure according to data collected by the antiretroviral pregnancy registry. Maternal antiretroviral therapy may increase the risk of preterm delivery, although available information is conflicting possibly due to variability of maternal factors (disease severity; initiation of therapy); however, maternal antiretroviral medication should not be withheld due to concerns of preterm birth. Information related to stillbirth, low birth weight, and small for gestational age infants is limited. Long-term follow-up is recommended for all infants exposed to antiretroviral medications; children who develop significant organ system abnormalities of unknown etiology (particularly of the CNS or heart) should be evaluated for potential mitochondrial dysfunction. Cases of lactic acidosis and hepatic steatosis related to mitochondrial toxicity have been reported with use of nucleoside reverse transcriptase inhibitors (NRTIs). These adverse events are similar to other rare but life-threatening syndromes which occur during pregnancy (eg, HELLP syndrome). In general nucleoside reverse transcriptase inhibitors are well tolerated and the benefits of use generally outweigh potential risk.

Combination antiretroviral therapy (cART) therapy is recommended for all HIV-infected pregnant women to keep the viral load below the limit of detection and reduce the risk of perinatal transmission. When HIV is diagnosed during pregnancy in a woman who has never received antiretroviral therapy, cART should begin as soon as possible after diagnosis. The Health and Human Services (HHS) Perinatal HIV Guidelines consider abacavir in combination with lamivudine to be a preferred NRTI backbone for initial therapy in antiretroviral-naive pregnant women (do not use in women who are positive for the HLA-B*5701 allele). This backbone is not recommended with atazanavir/ritonavir or efavirenz if pretreatment HIV RNA is >100,000 copies/mL. The pharmacokinetics of abacavir are not significantly changed by pregnancy and dose adjustment is not needed for pregnant women. In general, women who become pregnant on a stable cART regimen may continue that regimen if viral suppression is effective, appropriate drug exposure can be achieved, contraindications for use in pregnancy are not present, and the regimen is well tolerated. Monitoring during pregnancy is more frequent than in non-pregnant adults; cART should be continued postpartum.

For HIV-infected couples planning a pregnancy, maximum viral suppression with combination antiretroviral therapy (cART) is recommended prior to conception for the HIV-infected partner(s) and expert consultation is recommended; modification of therapy (if needed) and optimization of the woman's health should be done prior to conception. HIV-infected women not planning a pregnancy may use any available type of contraception, considering possible drug interactions and contraindications of the specific method. In addition, consistent use of condoms is also recommended (even during pregnancy) to prevent transmission of HIV or other sexually transmitted diseases.

Health care providers are encouraged to enroll pregnant women exposed to antiretroviral medications as early in pregnancy as possible in the Antiretroviral Pregnancy Registry (1-800-258-4263 or www.APRegistry.com). Health care providers caring for HIV-infected women and their infants may contact the National Perinatal HIV Hotline (888-448-8765) for clinical consultation (HHS [perinatal] 2016).

Abacavir and Lamivudine

(a BAK a veer & la MI vyoo deen)

Related Information

Abacavir *on page 48*

LamiVUDine *on page 956*

Brand Names: US Epzicom

Brand Names: Canada Apo-Abacavir-Lamivudine; Kivexa; Mylan-Abacavir/Lamivudine; Teva-Abacavir/Lamivudine

Pharmacologic Category Antiretroviral, Reverse Transcriptase Inhibitor, Nucleoside (Anti-HIV)

Use HIV-1 infection: Treatment of HIV infection in combination with other antiretroviral agents

Local Anesthetic/Vasoconstrictor Precautions No information available to require special precautions

Effects on Dental Treatment No significant effects or complications reported

Effects on Bleeding No information available to require special precautions relative to altered hemostasis

Adverse Reactions See individual agents as well as other combination products for additional information. Rates of adverse reactions were defined during combination therapy with other antiretrovirals.

1% to 10%:

Central nervous system: Abnormal dreams, anxiety, depression, dizziness, fatigue, headache, insomnia, malaise, migraine, vertigo

Dermatologic: Skin rash

Gastrointestinal: Abdominal pain, diarrhea, gastritis

Hypersensitivity: Hypersensitivity (including multiorgan failure and anaphylaxis; ≤9%; higher incidence in subjects carrying the HLA-B*5701 allele)

Miscellaneous: Fever

<1%, postmarketing, and/or case reports: Abnormal breath sounds, alopecia, anemia (including pure red cell aplasia and severe anemias progressing on therapy), aplastic anemia, erythema multiforme, exacerbation of hepatitis B, hepatitis, hyperglycemia, immune reconstitution syndrome, increased creatine phosphokinase, lactic acidosis, liver steatosis, lymphadenopathy, myasthenia, paresthesia, peripheral neuropathy, redistribution of body fat, rhabdomyolysis, seizure, splenomegaly, Stevens-Johnson syndrome, stomatitis, weakness, wheezing

General Dosage Range Oral: *Children and Adolescents ≥25 kg and Adults:* One tablet (abacavir 600 mg and lamivudine 300 mg) once daily

Mechanism of Action Nucleoside reverse transcriptase inhibitor combination.

Abacavir is a guanosine analogue which is phosphorylated to carbovir triphosphate which interferes with HIV viral RNA-dependent DNA polymerase resulting in inhibition of viral replication.

Lamivudine is a cytosine analog. After lamivudine is triphosphorylated, the principle mode of action is inhibition of HIV reverse transcription via viral DNA chain termination; inhibits RNA-dependent DNA polymerase activities of reverse transcriptase.

Pregnancy Considerations

The Health and Human Services (HHS) Perinatal HIV Guidelines consider abacavir in combination with lamivudine to be a preferred nucleoside reverse transcriptase inhibitor (NRTI) backbone for initial use in antiretroviral-naive pregnant women (do not use in women who are positive for the HLA-B*5701 allele). This backbone is not recommended with atazanavir/ritonavir or efavirenz if pretreatment HIV RNA is >100,000 copies/mL.

In general, women who become pregnant on a stable combination antiretroviral therapy (cART) regimen may continue that regimen if viral suppression is effective, appropriate drug exposure can be achieved, contraindications for use in pregnancy are not present, and the regimen is well tolerated (HHS [perinatal] 2016). See individual agents.

Abacavir, Dolutegravir, and Lamivudine

(a BAK a veer, doe loo TEG ra vir, & la MI vyoo deen)

Brand Names: US Triumeq

Brand Names: Canada Triumeq

Pharmacologic Category Antiretroviral, Integrase Inhibitor (Anti-HIV); Antiretroviral, Reverse Transcriptase Inhibitor, Nucleoside (Anti-HIV)

Use

HIV infection: Treatment of human immunodeficiency virus type 1 (HIV-1) infection

Limitations of use: Not recommended for use in patients with current or past history of resistance to abacavir, dolutegravir, or lamivudine; not recommended in patients with resistance-associated integrase substitutions or clinically suspected integrase strand transfer inhibitor resistance because the dose of dolutegravir is insufficient in these subpopulations.

Local Anesthetic/Vasoconstrictor Precautions No information available to require special precautions

Effects on Dental Treatment No significant effects or complications reported

Effects on Bleeding No information available to require special precautions

Adverse Reactions See individual agents as well as other combination products for additional information.

>10%:

Endocrine & metabolic: Hyperglycemia (≥126 mg/dL)

Gastrointestinal: Increased serum lipase (>1.5 x ULN)

Neuromuscular & skeletal: Increased creatine phosphokinase (≥6.0 x ULN)

1% to 10%:

Central nervous system: Drowsiness (<2%), lethargy (<2%), nightmares (<2%), sleep disorder (<2%), suicidal ideation (<2%), depression, fatigue, headache, insomnia

Dermatologic: Pruritus (<2%)

Endocrine & metabolic: Hypertriglyceridemia (<2%)

Gastrointestinal: Abdominal distention (<2%), abdominal distress (<2%), abdominal pain (<2%), anorexia (<2%), dyspepsia (<2%), flatulence (<2%),

gastroesophageal reflux disease (<2%), upper abdominal pain (<2%), vomiting (<2%)
Hematologic & oncologic: Decreased neutrophils
Hepatic: Hepatitis (<2%), increased serum ALT (>2.5 x ULN), increased serum AST (>2.5 x ULN)
Neuromuscular & skeletal: Arthralgia (<2%), myositis (<2%)
Renal: Renal insufficiency (<2%)
Miscellaneous: Fever (<2%)
<1%, postmarketing, and/or case reports: Abnormal dreams, diarrhea, dizziness, hypersensitivity reaction, immune reconstitution syndrome, nausea, skin rash

General Dosage Range Dosage adjustment recommended in patients on concomitant therapy.

Oral: *Adults*: One tablet daily

Mechanism of Action Dolutegravir inhibits HIV integrase by binding to the integrase active site and blocking the strand transfer step of retroviral DNA integration. Abacavir is converted by cellular enzymes to the active metabolite, carbovir triphosphate (CBV-TP), an analogue of deoxyguanosine-5'-triphosphate (dGTP). CBV-TP inhibits the activity of HIV-1 reverse transcriptase (RT) both by competing with the natural substrate dGTP and by its incorporation into viral DNA. Intracellularly, lamivudine is phosphorylated to its active 5'-triphosphate metabolite, lamivudine triphosphate (3TC-TP). The principal mode of action of 3TC-TP is inhibition of reverse transcriptase via DNA chain termination after incorporation of the nucleotide analogue.

Pregnancy Risk Factor C

Pregnancy Considerations Animal reproduction studies have not been conducted with this combination. In general, women who become pregnant on a stable combination antiretroviral therapy (cART) regimen may continue that regimen if viral suppression is effective, appropriate drug exposure can be achieved, contraindications for use in pregnancy are not present, and the regimen is well tolerated (HHS [perinatal] 2016). Evaluate individual components when choosing initial therapy for antiretroviral-naive pregnant women.

Abacavir, Lamivudine, and Zidovudine

(a BAK a veer, la MI vyoo deen, & zye DOE vyoo deen)

Related Information

Abacavir *on page 48*
HIV Infection and AIDS *on page 1785*
LamiVUDine *on page 956*
Zidovudine *on page 1672*

Brand Names: US Trizivir

Brand Names: Canada Trizivir

Pharmacologic Category Antiretroviral, Reverse Transcriptase Inhibitor, Nucleoside (Anti-HIV)

Use

HIV infection: Treatment of HIV-1 infection alone or in combination with other antiretroviral agents.

Limitations of use: Limited data exist on use alone in patients with higher baseline viral load levels (>100,000 copies/mL).

Local Anesthetic/Vasoconstrictor Precautions No information available to require special precautions

Effects on Dental Treatment No significant effects or complications reported

Effects on Bleeding No information available to require special precautions relative to altered hemostasis

Adverse Reactions See individual agents as well as other combination products for additional information. Frequency not always defined.

Central nervous system: Headache (13%), fatigue (12%), malaise (12%), depression (6%), anxiety (5%)
Dermatologic: Skin rash (5%)
Endocrine & metabolic: Increased amylase (2%), increased serum triglycerides (grade 3-4: 2%), increased gamma-glutamyl transferase, redistribution of body fat
Gastrointestinal: Nausea (19%), nausea and vomiting (10%), diarrhea (7%), pancreatitis
Hematologic & oncologic: Neutropenia (5%)
Hepatic: Increased serum ALT (6%)
Hypersensitivity: Hypersensitivity (1% to 9%; based on abacavir component; higher risk in carriers of the HLA-B*5701 allele)
Immunologic: Immune reconstitution syndrome
Infection: Viral infection (5%)
Miscellaneous: Fever and chills (6%)
Neuromuscular & skeletal: Increased creatine phosphokinase (7%)
Respiratory: ENT infection (5%)
<1%, postmarketing, and/or case reports: Abdominal pain, abnormal breath sounds, allergic sensitization (including anaphylaxis), alopecia, anemia, anorexia, aplastic anemia, arthralgia, cardiomyopathy, decreased appetite, dizziness, dyspepsia, erythema multiforme, exacerbation of hepatitis B (posttreatment), gynecomastia, increased serum bilirubin, increased serum transaminases, insomnia, lactic acidosis, liver steatosis, lymphadenopathy, myalgia, myasthenia, oral mucosa hyperpigmentation, paresthesia, peripheral neuropathy, rhabdomyolysis, seizure, sleep disorder, splenomegaly, Stevens-Johnson syndrome, stomatitis, thrombocytopenia, urticaria, vasculitis, weakness, wheezing

General Dosage Range Oral: *Children and Adolescents ≥40 kg and Adults:* One tablet twice daily

Mechanism of Action The combination of abacavir, lamivudine, and zidovudine is believed to act synergistically to inhibit reverse transcriptase via DNA chain termination after incorporation of the nucleoside analogue as well as to delay the emergence of mutations conferring resistance.

Pregnancy Considerations In general, women who become pregnant on a stable combination antiretroviral therapy (cART) regimen may continue that regimen if viral suppression is effective, appropriate drug exposure can be achieved, contraindications for use in pregnancy are not present, and the regimen is well tolerated. The Health and Human Services (HHS) Perinatal HIV Guidelines generally do not recommend this combination as initial therapy in antiretroviral-naive pregnant women due to inferior virologic activity (HHS [perinatal] 2016). See individual agents.

Abatacept (ab a TA sept)

Related Information

Rheumatoid Arthritis, Osteoarthritis, and Osteoporosis *on page 1792*

Brand Names: US Orencia; Orencia ClickJect

Brand Names: Canada Orencia

Pharmacologic Category Antirheumatic, Disease Modifying; Selective T-Cell Costimulation Blocker

Use

Rheumatoid arthritis: Treatment of moderately to severely active adult rheumatoid arthritis (RA); may be used as monotherapy or in combination with other DMARDs

Juvenile idiopathic arthritis: Treatment of moderately to severely active polyarticular juvenile idiopathic arthritis (JIA); may be used as monotherapy or in combination with methotrexate

Note: Abatacept should **not** be used in combination with anakinra or TNF-blocking agents

Local Anesthetic/Vasoconstrictor Precautions No information available to require special precautions

Effects on Dental Treatment No significant effects or complications reported

Effects on Bleeding No information available to require special precautions

Adverse Reactions Note: Percentages not always reported; COPD patients experienced a higher frequency of COPD-related adverse reactions (COPD exacerbation, cough, dyspnea, pneumonia, rhonchi)

>10%:

Central nervous system: Headache (≤18%)
Gastrointestinal: Nausea
Respiratory: Nasopharyngitis (12%), upper respiratory tract infection
Miscellaneous: Infection (adults 54%; children 36%), antibody development (2% to 41%)

1% to 10%:

Cardiovascular: Hypertension (7%)
Central nervous system: Dizziness (9%)
Dermatologic: Skin rash (4%)
Gastrointestinal: Dyspepsia (6%), abdominal pain, diarrhea
Genitourinary: Urinary tract infection (6%)
Immunologic: Immunogenicity (1% to 2%)
Infection: Herpes simplex infection, influenza
Local: Injection site reaction (3%)
Neuromuscular & skeletal: Back pain (7%), limb pain (3%)
Respiratory: Cough (8%), bronchitis, pneumonia, rhinitis, sinusitis
Miscellaneous: Infusion-related reaction (≤9%), fever

<1%, postmarketing, and/or case reports: Acute lymphocytic leukemia, anaphylactoid reaction, anaphylaxis, cellulitis, diverticulitis, dyspnea, exacerbation of arthritis, exacerbation of chronic obstructive pulmonary disease, flushing, hypersensitivity, hypotension, joint wear, malignant lymphoma, malignant neoplasm (including malignant melanoma, malignant neoplasm of the bile duct, malignant neoplasm of bladder, malignant neoplasm of breast, malignant neoplasm of cervix, malignant neoplasm of kidney, malignant neoplasm of prostate, malignant neoplasm of skin, malignant neoplasm of thyroid, myelodysplastic syndrome, and uterine neoplasm), malignant neoplasm of lung, ovarian cyst, pruritus, pyelonephritis, rhonchi, urticaria, varicella, vasculitis (including hypersensitivity angiitis [cutaneous vasculitis and leukocytoclastic vasculitis]), wheezing

General Dosage Range

IV: Repeat dose at 2 weeks and 4 weeks, then every 4 weeks thereafter

Children ≥6 years and <75 kg: 10 mg/kg/dose
Children ≥6 years and 75-100 kg: 750 mg/dose
Children ≥6 years and >100 kg: 1000 mg/dose
Adults <60 kg: 500 mg/dose
Adults 60-100 kg: 750 mg/dose
Adults >100 kg: 1000 mg/dose

SubQ: *Adults:* 125 mg/dose once weekly

Mechanism of Action Selective costimulation modulator; inhibits T-cell (T-lymphocyte) activation by binding to CD80 and CD86 on antigen presenting cells (APC), thus blocking the required CD28 interaction between APCs and T cells. Activated T lymphocytes are found in the synovium of rheumatoid arthritis patients.

Pharmacodynamics/Kinetics

Half-life Elimination

RA: 13.1 days (range: 8 to 25 days)

Clearance: 0.22 to 0.23 mL/hour/kg; Children 6 to 17 years: JIA: 0.4 mL/hour/kg (increases with baseline body weight)

Pregnancy Considerations Adverse effects were not observed in animal studies. Information related to the use of abatacept in pregnancy is limited (Kumar 2015). Until additional data are available, it is recommended to discontinue use and switch to a safer medication prior to conception unless no other pregnancy compatible medication is able to control maternal disease (Götestam Skorpen 2016)

A pregnancy registry has been established to monitor outcomes of women exposed to abatacept during pregnancy (1-877-311-8972).

Product Availability Orencia 50 mg/0.4 mL and 87.5 mg/0.7 mL prefilled syringes: FDA approved March 2017; anticipated availability is currently unknown. Consult the prescribing information for additional information.

Abciximab (ab SIK si mab)

Related Information

Cardiovascular Diseases *on page 1752*

Brand Names: US ReoPro

Brand Names: Canada ReoPro

Pharmacologic Category Antiplatelet Agent, Glycoprotein IIb/IIIa Inhibitor

Use Prevention of cardiac ischemic complications in patients undergoing percutaneous coronary intervention (PCI); prevention of cardiac ischemic complications in patients with unstable angina (UA)/non-ST-elevation myocardial infarction (NSTEMI) unresponsive to conventional therapy when PCI is scheduled within 24 hours

Note: Intended for use with aspirin and heparin, at a minimum.

Local Anesthetic/Vasoconstrictor Precautions No information available to require special precautions

Effects on Dental Treatment Key adverse event(s) related to dental treatment: Bleeding is a potential adverse effect of abciximab during dental surgery. See Effects on Bleeding.

Effects on Bleeding As with all antiplatelet drugs, bleeding is a potential adverse effect of abciximab during dental surgery; risk is dependent on multiple variables, including the intensity of anticoagulation and patient susceptibility. Medical consult is suggested. It is unlikely that ambulatory patients presenting for dental treatment will be taking intravenous antiplatelet therapy such as abciximab.

Adverse Reactions As with all drugs which may affect hemostasis, bleeding is associated with abciximab. Hemorrhage may occur at virtually any site. Risk is dependent on multiple variables, including the concurrent use of multiple agents which alter hemostasis and patient susceptibility.

>10%:

Cardiovascular: Hypotension (14%), chest pain (11%)
Gastrointestinal: Nausea (14%)
Hematologic & oncologic: Minor hemorrhage (4% to 17%), major hemorrhage (1% to 14%)
Neuromuscular & skeletal: Back pain (18%)

Miscellaneous: Antibody development (HACA, first exposure: 6%; readministration: 27%; four or more exposures: 44%)

1% to 10%:

Cardiovascular: Bradycardia (5%), peripheral edema (2%)

Gastrointestinal: Abdominal pain (3%)

Hematologic & oncologic: Thrombocytopenia: <100,000 cells/mm^3 (3% to 6%); <50,000 cells/mm^3 (0.4% to 2%)

Local: Pain at injection site (4%)

<1%: Abdominal distension, abnormality in thinking, abscess, agitation, allergic reaction (possible), anaphylaxis (possible), anemia, anxiety, arteriovenous fistula, bladder pain, bronchitis, bronchospasm, bullous skin disease, cellulitis, cerebrovascular accident, cold extremities, coma, complete atrioventricular block, confusion, diabetes mellitus, diaphoresis, diarrhea, diplopia, dizziness, dyspepsia, dysuria, edema, embolism, gastroesophageal reflux disease, hyperkalemia, hypertonia, hypoesthesia, incisional pain, incomplete atrioventricular block, inflammation, intestinal obstruction, intracranial hemorrhage, leukocytosis, muscle spasm, myalgia, nodal arrhythmia, pain, pallor, palpitations, petechiae, pleural effusion, pleurisy, pneumonia, prostatitis, pruritus, pseudoaneurysm, pulmonary alveolar hemorrhage, pulmonary embolism, rales, renal insufficiency, rhonchi, thrombophlebitis, urinary frequency, urinary incontinence, urinary retention, ventricular tachycardia, visual disturbance, weakness, wound, xerostomia

General Dosage Range IV: *Adults:* Bolus: 0.25 mg/kg; Infusion: 0.125 mcg/kg/minute (maximum: 10 mcg/minute)

Mechanism of Action Fab antibody fragment of the chimeric human-murine monoclonal antibody 7E3; this agent binds to platelet IIb/IIIa receptors, resulting in steric hindrance, thus inhibiting platelet aggregation

Pharmacodynamics/Kinetics

Onset of Action Rapid; platelet aggregation reduced to <20% of baseline at 10 minutes

Duration of Action Up to 72 hours for restoration of normal hemostasis (Schror, 2003)

Half-life Elimination Plasma: ~30 minutes; dissociation half-life from GP IIb/IIIa receptors: up to 4 hours (Schror, 2003). Note: 29% and 13% of abciximab estimated to remain on GP IIb/IIIa receptors at 8 and 15 days, respectively (Mascelli, 1998). Platelet function may remain abnormal for up to 7 days post infusion (Osende, 2001).

Time to Peak Platelet inhibition: ~30 minutes (Mascelli, 1998)

Pregnancy Risk Factor C

Pregnancy Considerations Animal reproduction studies have not been conducted. *In vitro* studies have shown only small amounts of abciximab to cross the placenta. It is not known whether abciximab can cause fetal harm when administered to a pregnant woman or can affect reproduction capacity.

Abiraterone Acetate (a bir A ter one AS e tate)

Brand Names: US Zytiga

Brand Names: Canada Zytiga

Pharmacologic Category Antiandrogen; Antineoplastic Agent, Antiandrogen

Use Prostate cancer: Treatment of metastatic, castration-resistant prostate cancer (in combination with prednisone)

Local Anesthetic/Vasoconstrictor Precautions No information available to require special precautions

Effects on Dental Treatment No significant effects or complications reported

Effects on Bleeding No information available to require special precautions

Adverse Reactions Adverse reactions reported for use in combination with prednisone.

>10%:

Cardiovascular: Edema (25% to 27%; includes anasarca, peripheral edema, pitting edema), hypertension (9% to 22%)

Central nervous system: Fatigue (39%), insomnia (14%)

Dermatologic: Bruise (13%)

Endocrine & metabolic: Hypertriglyceridemia (63%), hyperglycemia (57%), hypernatremia (33%), hypokalemia (17% to 28%), hypophosphatemia (24%; grades 3/4: 7%), hot flash (19% to 22%)

Gastrointestinal: Constipation (23%), diarrhea (18% to 22%), dyspepsia (6% to 11%)

Genitourinary: Urinary tract infection (12%)

Hematologic & oncologic: Lymphocytopenia (38%; grades 3/4: 9%)

Hepatic: Increased serum ALT (11% to 42%; grades 3/4: 1% to 6%), increased serum AST (37%; grades 3/4: 3%)

Neuromuscular & skeletal: Joint swelling (30%, includes arthralgia, arthritis, joint discomfort, joint stiffness), myalgia (26%; includes muscle rigidity, muscle spasm, musculoskeletal discomfort, musculoskeletal pain)

Respiratory: Cough (11% to 17%), upper respiratory infection (5% to 13%), dyspnea (12%), nasopharyngitis (11%)

1% to 10%:

Cardiovascular: Cardiac arrhythmia (7%; includes atrial fibrillation, atrial tachycardia, bradycardia, cardiac conduction disturbance, complete atrioventricular block, supraventricular tachycardia, tachycardia), chest pain (4%, includes angina pectoris, chest discomfort, unstable angina pectoris), cardiac failure (2%; includes cardiogenic shock, cardiomegaly, cardiomyopathy, congestive heart failure, left ventricular dysfunction, reduced ejection fraction)

Central nervous system: Falling (6%)

Dermatologic: Skin rash (8%)

Genitourinary: Hematuria (10%), groin pain (7%), urinary frequency (7%), nocturia (6%)

Hepatic: Increased serum bilirubin (7%; grades 3/4: <1%)

Neuromuscular & skeletal: Bone fracture (6%)

Miscellaneous: Fever (9%)

<1%, postmarketing, and/or case reports: Acute hepatic failure, adrenocortical insufficiency, fulminant hepatitis, myopathy (includes rhabdomyolysis), pneumonia

General Dosage Range Dosage adjustment recommended in patients with hepatic impairment, on concomitant therapy, or who develop toxicity.

Oral: *Adults:* 1000 mg once daily

Mechanism of Action Selectively and irreversibly inhibits CYP17 (17 alpha-hydroxylase/C17,20-lyase), an enzyme required for androgen biosynthesis which is expressed in testicular, adrenal, and prostatic tumor tissues. Inhibits the formation of the testosterone precursors dehydroepiandrosterone (DHEA) and androstenedione.

Pharmacodynamics/Kinetics

Half-life Elimination 14.4 to 16.5 hours (Acharya 2012)

Time to Peak 2 hours (Acharya 2012)

Pregnancy Risk Factor X

Pregnancy Considerations Adverse effects were observed in animal reproduction studies at doses resulting in less systemic exposure than in humans. Adverse effects were also observed in the reproductive system of animals during toxicology and pharmacology studies. Based on the mechanism of action, abiraterone may cause fetal harm or fetal loss if administered during pregnancy. Abiraterone is not indicated for use in women and is specifically contraindicated in women who are or may become pregnant. It is not known if abiraterone is excreted in semen, therefore, men should use a condom and another method of birth control during treatment and for 1 week following therapy if having intercourse with a woman of reproductive age. Women who are or may become pregnant should wear gloves if contact with tablets may occur.

AbobotulinumtoxinA

(aye bo BOT yoo lin num TOKS in aye)

Brand Names: US Dysport; Dysport (Glabellar Lines) [DSC]

Pharmacologic Category Neuromuscular Blocker Agent, Toxin

Use

Cervical dystonia: Treatment of adults with cervical dystonia.

Glabellar lines: Temporary improvement in the appearance of moderate to severe glabellar lines associated with corrugator and procerus muscle activity in adults <65 years.

Lower limb spasticity: Treatment of lower limb spasticity in pediatric patients ≥2 years.

Upper limb spasticity: Treatment of upper limb spasticity in adults, to decrease the severity of increased muscle tone in elbow flexors, wrist flexors, and finger flexors.

Local Anesthetic/Vasoconstrictor Precautions No information available to require special precautions

Effects on Dental Treatment Key adverse event(s) related to dental treatment: Xerostomia (normal salivary flow resumes upon discontinuation) and facial paresis.

Effects on Bleeding No information available to require special precautions

Adverse Reactions

Cervical dystonia: Frequency not always defined.

Cardiovascular: Decreased heart rate

Central nervous system: Voice disorder (≤28%), fatigue (12%), headache (11%), facial paresis (≤11%), dizziness (4%)

Endocrine & metabolic: Increased serum glucose

Gastrointestinal: Dysphagia (15% to 39%), xerostomia (13% to 39%)

Immunologic: Antibody development (binding or neutralizing; 3%)

Infection: Infection (13%)

Local: Discomfort at injection site (13% to 22%), pain at injection site (5%)

Neuromuscular & skeletal: Myasthenia (11% to 56%), musculoskeletal pain (7%), amyotrophy (1%)

Ophthalmic: Eye disease (≤17%; includes accommodation disorder, blurred vision, decreased visual acuity, diplopia, dryness, pain, pruritus)

Respiratory: Dyspnea (3%; onset: ~1 week; duration: ~3 weeks)

Glabellar lines: 1% to 10%:

Central nervous system: Headache (9%)

Dermatologic: Contact dermatitis (2% to 3%)

Gastrointestinal: Nausea (2%)

Genitourinary: Hematuria (2%)

Immunologic: Antibody development (<1%)

Infection: Influenza (2% to 3%)

Local: Pain at injection site (3%), discomfort at injection site (2% to 3%), injection site reaction (2% to 3%), swelling at injection site (2% to 3%)

Ophthalmic: Blepharoptosis (2%), eyelid edema (2%)

Respiratory: Nasopharyngitis (10%), upper respiratory tract infection (3%), bronchitis (2% to 3%), cough (2% to 3%), pharyngolaryngeal pain (2% to 3%), sinusitis (2%)

Upper limb spasticity: Frequency not always defined; as reported with doses of 500 units to 1,000 units.

Cardiovascular: Hypertension (1% to 2%), syncope (1% to 2%)

Central nervous system: Myasthenia (2% to 4%), dizziness (3%), falling (3%), depression (2% to 3%), convulsions (2%), fatigue (2%), headache (2%), hypoesthesia (2%), seizure (partial; ≤2%), abnormal gait (<1%), feeling of heaviness (<1%), hypertonia (<1%)

Endocrine & metabolic: Increased serum triglycerides (1% to 2%)

Gastrointestinal: Constipation (2%), nausea (2%), diarrhea (1% to 2%), dysphagia (<1%)

Genitourinary: Urinary tract infection (3%)

Hematologic & oncologic: Bruise (1% to 2%)

Immunologic Antibody development (7%; neutralizing: ≤4%)

Infection: Infection (2%), influenza (2%)

Local: Injection site reaction

Neuromuscular & skeletal: Musculoskeletal pain (3%), back pain (2%), limb pain (2%), weakness (1% to 2%)

Respiratory: Nasopharyngitis (4%), cough (2%)

Miscellaneous: Accidental injury (2%)

Lower limb spasticity: As reported in children and adolescents.

>10%:

Infection: Influenza (10% to 14%)

Respiratory: Upper respiratory tract infection (20%), nasopharyngitis (9% to 16%), cough (7% to 14%), pharyngitis (11%)

Miscellaneous: Fever (7% to 12%)

1% to 10%:

Central nervous system: Epilepsy (≤7%), seizure (≤7%), myasthenia (5%)

Gastrointestinal: Vomiting (6% to 8%), nausea (2% to 5%), viral gastroenteritis (2% to 4%)

Immunologic: Antibody development (4%; neutralizing: 2%)

Infection: Varicella (5%)

Neuromuscular & skeletal: Limb pain (7%)

Otic: Otic infection (4%)

Respiratory: Bronchitis (7% to 8%), rhinitis (5%), viral respiratory tract infection (2% to 5%), oropharyngeal pain (2% to 4%)

Any indication: Postmarketing and/or case reports: Burning sensation, connective tissue disease (excessive granulation tissue), dysarthria, erythema, photophobia, urinary incontinence, vertigo

General Dosage Range IM:

Children ≥2 years and Adolescents: Lower limb spasticity: 10 to 15 units/kg total dose per limb per treatment session; maximum total dose per treatment session: 15 units/kg (unilateral injections), 30 units/kg (bilateral injections), or 1,000 units, whichever is less.

Adults:

Cervical dystonia: Initial: 500 units/treatment; usual dosage: 250 to 1,000 units

Upper limb spasticity: Usual dosage: 100 to 400 units

Adults <65 years: Reduction of glabellar lines: 10 units into each site (total dose: 50 units)

Mechanism of Action AbobotulinumtoxinA (previously known as botulinum toxin type A) is a neurotoxin produced by *Clostridium botulinum*, spore-forming anaerobic bacillus, which appears to affect only the presynaptic membrane of the neuromuscular junction in humans, where it prevents calcium-dependent release of acetylcholine and produces a state of denervation. Muscle inactivation persists until new fibrils grow from the nerve and form junction plates on new areas of the muscle-cell walls.

Pharmacodynamics/Kinetics

Onset of Action Peak effect: Cervical dystonia: 2 to 4 weeks; Upper limb spasticity: 1 week

Duration of Action Cervical dystonia, glabellar lines: ≥4 months; Lower limb spasticity: ≥5 ½ months; Upper limb spasticity: ≥5 months

Pregnancy Considerations Adverse events have been observed in animal reproduction studies.

Acamprosate (a kam PROE sate)

Brand Names: US Campral [DSC]

Brand Names: Canada Campral®

Pharmacologic Category GABA Agonist/Glutamate Antagonist

Use

Alcohol abstinence: Maintenance of abstinence from alcohol in patients with alcohol dependence who are abstinent at treatment initiation, as part of a comprehensive management program

Limitations of use: Efficacy has not been demonstrated in subjects who have not undergone detoxification and not achieved alcohol abstinence prior to beginning treatment. Efficacy in promoting abstinence from alcohol in polysubstance abusers has not been adequately assessed.

Local Anesthetic/Vasoconstrictor Precautions No information available to require special precautions

Effects on Dental Treatment Key adverse event(s) related to dental treatment: Xerostomia and changes in salivation (normal salivary flow resumes upon discontinuation) and taste perversion.

Effects on Bleeding No information available to require special precautions

Adverse Reactions Many adverse effects associated with treatment may be related to alcohol abstinence; reported frequency range may overlap with placebo.

>10%: Gastrointestinal: Diarrhea (10% to 17%)

1% to 10%:

Cardiovascular: Chest pain, hypertension, palpitations, peripheral edema, syncope, vasodilatation

Central nervous system: Insomnia (6% to 9%), anxiety (5% to 8%), depression (4% to 8%), dizziness (3% to 4%), pain (2% to 4%), paresthesia (2% to 3%), abnormality in thinking, amnesia, attempted suicide, chills, drowsiness, headache

Dermatologic: Pruritus (3% to 4%), diaphoresis (2% to 3%), skin rash

Endocrine & metabolic: Decreased libido, weight gain

Gastrointestinal: Anorexia (2% to 5%), nausea (3% to 4%), flatulence (1% to 4%), xerostomia (1% to 3%), abdominal pain, constipation, dysgeusia, dyspepsia, increased appetite, vomiting

Genitourinary: Impotence

Infection: Infection

Neuromuscular & skeletal: Weakness (5% to 7%), arthralgia, back pain, myalgia, tremor

Ophthalmic: Visual disturbance

Respiratory: Bronchitis, dyspnea, flu-like symptoms, increased cough, pharyngitis, rhinitis

<1%, postmarketing, and/or case reports: Abnormal hepatic function tests, agitation, alopecia, anemia, angina pectoris, asthma, brain disease, colitis, confusion, deafness, diabetes mellitus, duodenal ulcer, eosinophilia, epistaxis, exfoliative dermatitis, fever, gastrointestinal hemorrhage, gout, hallucination, hemorrhage, hepatic cirrhosis, hepatitis, hostility, hyperbilirubinemia, hyperesthesia, hyperglycemia, hypersensitivity reaction, hyperuricemia, hyponatremia, hypotension, hypothyroidism, increased serum creatinine, increased serum transaminases, leukopenia, lymphadenopathy, lymphocytosis, myocardial infarction, nephrolithiasis, neuralgia, ophthalmic inflammation, orthostatic hypotension, pancreatitis, pneumonia, psychoneurosis, psychosis, pulmonary embolism, rectal hemorrhage, renal failure, seizure, skin photosensitivity, suicidal ideation, tachycardia, thrombocytopenia, urticaria, withdrawal syndrome

General Dosage Range Dosage adjustment recommended in patients with renal impairment.

Oral: *Adults:* 666 mg 3 times daily (maximum: 1,998 mg daily)

Mechanism of Action Mechanism not fully defined. Structurally similar to gamma-amino butyric acid (GABA), acamprosate appears to increase the activity of the GABA-ergic system, and decreases activity of glutamate within the CNS, including a decrease in activity at N-methyl D-aspartate (NMDA) receptors; may also affect CNS calcium channels. Restores balance to GABA and glutamate activities which appear to be disrupted in alcohol dependence. During therapeutic use, reduces alcohol intake, but does not cause a disulfiram-like reaction following alcohol ingestion. Insignificant CNS activity, outside its effect on alcohol dependence, was observed including no anxiolytic, anticonvulsant, or antidepressant activity.

Pharmacodynamics/Kinetics

Half-life Elimination 20 to 33 hours

Time to Peak Plasma: 3 to 8 hours

Pregnancy Risk Factor C

Pregnancy Considerations Adverse events were observed in animal reproduction studies.

Acarbose (AY car bose)

Related Information

Endocrine Disorders and Pregnancy *on page 1781*

Brand Names: US Precose

Brand Names: Canada Glucobay

Pharmacologic Category Antidiabetic Agent, Alpha-Glucosidase Inhibitor

Use Diabetes mellitus, type 2: Adjunct to diet and exercise to improve glycemic control in adults with type 2 diabetes mellitus (noninsulin dependent, NIDDM)

Local Anesthetic/Vasoconstrictor Precautions No information available to require special precautions

Effects on Dental Treatment No significant effects or complications reported

Effects on Bleeding No information available to require special precautions

Adverse Reactions

>10%: Gastrointestinal: Frequency and intensity of flatulence (74%) tend to abate with time; diarrhea (31%) and abdominal pain (19%) tend to return to pretreatment levels over time

1% to 10%: Hepatic: Increased serum transaminases (≤4%)

<1%, postmarketing, and/or case reports: Edema, erythema, hepatic injury, hepatitis, intestinal obstruction, jaundice, pneumatosis cystoides intestinalis, skin rash, thrombocytopenia, urticaria

General Dosage Range Oral: *Adults:* Initial: 25 mg 1 to 3 times daily; Maintenance: 75 to 300 mg/day in 3 divided doses (maximum: ≤60 kg: 150 mg/day; >60 kg: 300 mg/day).

Mechanism of Action Competitive inhibitor of pancreatic α-amylase and intestinal brush border α-glucosidases, resulting in delayed hydrolysis of ingested complex carbohydrates and disaccharides and absorption of glucose; dose-dependent reduction in postprandial serum insulin and glucose peaks; inhibits the metabolism of sucrose to glucose and fructose

Pharmacodynamics/Kinetics

Half-life Elimination ~2 hours

Time to Peak Active drug: ~1 hour

Pregnancy Risk Factor B

Pregnancy Considerations Adverse events have not been observed in animal reproduction studies. Less than 2% of an oral dose of acarbose is absorbed systemically, which should limit fetal exposure.

In women with diabetes, maternal hyperglycemia can be associated with congenital malformations as well as adverse effects in the fetus, neonate, and the mother (ACOG 2005; ADA 2016c; Kitzmiller 2008; Metzger 2007). To prevent adverse outcomes, prior to conception and throughout pregnancy, maternal blood glucose and HbA_{1c} should be kept as close to target goals as possible but without causing significant hypoglycemia (ACOG 2013; ADA 2016c; Blumer 2013; Kitzmiller 2008). Agents other than acarbose are currently recommended to treat diabetes in pregnant women (ACOG 2013; Blumer 2013).

Acebutolol (a se DYOO toe lole)

Related Information

Cardiovascular Diseases *on page* 1752

Brand Names: US Sectral [DSC]

Brand Names: Canada Apo-Acebutolol®; Ava-Acebutolol; Mylan-Acebutolol; Mylan-Acebutolol (Type S); Nu-Acebutolol; Rhotral; Sandoz-Acebutolol; Sectral®; Teva-Acebutolol

Pharmacologic Category Antiarrhythmic Agent, Class II; Antihypertensive; Beta-Blocker With Intrinsic Sympathomimetic Activity

Use Treatment of hypertension; management of ventricular arrhythmias

The 2014 guideline for the management of high blood pressure in adults (Eighth Joint National Committee [JNC 8; James, 2013]) recommends initiation of pharmacologic treatment to lower blood pressure for the following patients:

- Patients ≥60 years of age with systolic blood pressure (SBP) ≥150 mm Hg or diastolic blood pressure (DBP) ≥90 mm Hg. Goal of therapy is SBP <150 mm Hg and DBP <90 mm Hg.
- Patients <60 years of age with SBP ≥140 mm Hg or DBP ≥90 mm Hg. Goal of therapy is SBP <140 mm Hg and DBP <90 mm Hg.
- Patients ≥18 years of age with diabetes and SBP ≥140 mm Hg or DBP ≥90 mm Hg. Goal of therapy is SBP <140 mm Hg and DBP <90 mm Hg.
- Patients ≥18 years of age with chronic kidney disease (CKD) and SBP ≥140 mm Hg or DBP ≥90 mm Hg. Goal of therapy is SBP <140 mm Hg and DBP <90 mm Hg.

In patients with CKD, regardless of race or diabetes status, the use of an ACE inhibitor (ACEI) or angiotensin receptor blocker (ARB) as initial therapy is recommended to improve kidney outcomes. In the general nonblack population (without CKD), including those with diabetes, initial antihypertensive treatment should consist of a thiazide-type diuretic, calcium channel blocker, ACEI, or ARB. In the general black population (without CKD), including those with diabetes, initial antihypertensive treatment should consist of a thiazide-type diuretic or a calcium channel blocker instead of an ACEI or ARB.

Local Anesthetic/Vasoconstrictor Precautions No information available to require special precautions. Local anesthetic with vasoconstrictor can be safely used in patients medicated with acebutolol.

Effects on Dental Treatment Acebutolol is a cardioselective beta-blocker. Local anesthetic with vasoconstrictor can be safely used in patients medicated with acebutolol. Nonselective beta-blockers (ie, propranolol, nadolol) enhance the pressor response to epinephrine, or levonordefrin resulting in hypertension and bradycardia; this has not been reported for acebutolol. Many nonsteroidal anti-inflammatory drugs, such as ibuprofen and indomethacin, can reduce the hypotensive effect of beta-blockers after 3 or more weeks of therapy with the NSAID. Short-term NSAID use (ie, 3 days) requires no special precautions in patients taking beta-blockers.

Effects on Bleeding No information available to require special precautions

Adverse Reactions

>10%: Central nervous system: Fatigue (11%)

1% to 10%:

Cardiovascular: Chest pain (2%), edema (2%), bradycardia, congestive heart failure, hypotension

Central nervous system: Dizziness (6%), headache (6%), insomnia (3%), abnormal dreams (2%), depression (2%), anxiety, hyperesthesia, hypoesthesia

Dermatologic: Skin rash (2%), pruritus

Gastrointestinal: Constipation (4%), diarrhea (4%), dyspepsia (4%), nausea (4%), flatulence (3%), abdominal pain, vomiting

Genitourinary: Urinary frequency (3%), dysuria, impotence, nocturia

Neuromuscular & skeletal: Myalgia (2%), arthralgia, back pain

Ophthalmic: Visual disturbance (2%), conjunctivitis, dry eye syndrome, eye pain

Respiratory: Dyspnea (4%), rhinitis (2%), cough (1%), pharyngitis, wheezing

<1%, postmarketing, and/or case reports: Anorexia, atrioventricular block, cold extremities, facial edema, hepatotoxicity, increased serum alkaline phosphatase, increased serum bilirubin, increased serum transaminases, lichen planus, lupus-like syndrome, palpitations, pleurisy, pneumonitis, pulmonary granuloma, renal insufficiency, systemic lupus erythematosus, urinary retention, ventricular arrhythmia, xerostomia

General Dosage Range Dosage adjustment recommended in patients with renal impairment

Oral:

Adults: 200 to 1200 mg/day in 2 divided doses (maximum: 1200 mg/day)

Elderly: 200 to 800 mg/day in 2 divided doses (maximum: 800 mg/day)

Mechanism of Action Competitively blocks $beta_1$-adrenergic receptors with little or no effect on $beta_2$-receptors except at high doses; exhibits membrane stabilizing and intrinsic sympathomimetic activity

Pharmacodynamics/Kinetics

Onset of Action 1 to 2 hours

Duration of Action 12 to 24 hours

Half-life Elimination Parent drug: 3 to 4 hours; Metabolite: 8 to 13 hours

Time to Peak 2 to 4 hours

Pregnancy Risk Factor B

Pregnancy Considerations Adverse effects were observed in some animal reproduction studies. Acebutolol and diacetolol (active metabolite) cross the placenta. Decreases in birth weight, blood pressure, and heart rate have been observed in neonates following maternal use of acebutolol during pregnancy. Hypoglycemia has also been found following in utero exposure to beta-blockers as a class. The half-life of acebutolol is 6 to 14 hours in the newborn. The half-life of diacetolol is 24 to 30 hours for the first 24 hours of life, then 12 to 16 hours. Adequate facilities for monitoring infants at birth should be available. The plasma elimination half-life of acebutolol is longer in pregnant women at term (Bianchetti 1981a; Boutroy 1982).

Untreated chronic maternal hypertension and preeclampsia are also associated with adverse events in the fetus, infant, and mother (ACOG 2015; Magee 2014). When treatment of hypertension in pregnancy is indicated, beta-blockers may be used. Specific recommendations vary by guideline. Although other agents are preferred (ACOG 2013), use of acebutolol may be considered (Magee 2014).

Acetaminophen (a seet a MIN oh fen)

Related Information

Oral Pain *on page 1830*

Related Sample Prescriptions

Oral Pain - Sample Prescriptions *on page 28*

Brand Names: US Acephen [OTC]; Aspirin Free Anacin Extra Strength [OTC]; Cetafen Extra [OTC]; Cetafen [OTC]; FeverAll Adult [OTC]; FeverAll Children's [OTC]; FeverAll Infants' [OTC]; FeverAll Junior Strength [OTC]; Little Fevers [OTC]; Mapap Arthritis Pain [OTC]; Mapap Children's [OTC]; Mapap Extra Strength [OTC]; Mapap Infants' [OTC] [DSC]; Mapap [OTC]; Non-Aspirin Pain Reliever [OTC]; Nortemp Children's [OTC]; Ofirmev; Pain & Fever Children's [OTC]; Pain Eze [OTC]; Pharbetol Extra Strength [OTC]; Pharbetol [OTC]; Q-Pap Children's [OTC]; Q-Pap Extra Strength [OTC]; Q-Pap Infants' [OTC] [DSC]; Q-Pap [OTC]; Silapap Children's [OTC]; Silapap Infants' [OTC] [DSC]; Triaminic Children's Fever Reducer Pain Reliever [OTC]; Tylenol 8 HR Arthritis Pain [OTC]; Tylenol 8 HR [OTC] [DSC]; Tylenol Children's Meltaways [OTC] [DSC]; Tylenol Children's [OTC]; Tylenol Extra Strength [OTC]; Tylenol Infants' [OTC]; Tylenol Jr. Meltaways [OTC] [DSC]; Tylenol [OTC]; Valorin Extra [OTC]; Valorin [OTC]

Brand Names: Canada Abenol; Apo-Acetaminophen; Atasol; Novo-Gesic; Pediatrix; Tempra; Tylenol

Generic Availability (US) Yes: Excludes extended release products; injectable formulation

Pharmacologic Category Analgesic, Nonopioid

Dental Use Treatment of postoperative pain

Use

Pain:

Injection: Management of mild to moderate pain in patients ≥2 years of age; management of moderate to severe pain when combined with opioid analgesia in patients ≥2 years

Oral, Rectal: Temporary relief of minor aches, pains, and headache

Fever: Temporary reduction of fever

Local Anesthetic/Vasoconstrictor Precautions No information available to require special precautions

Effects on Dental Treatment No significant effects or complications reported (see Dental Comment)

Effects on Bleeding As a single agent, acetaminophen does not appear to affect bleeding or platelet aggregation. Acetaminophen may prolong the INR and increase bleeding in patients taking warfarin (Coumadin). For patients taking warfarin, single acetaminophen doses or acetaminophen therapy of short duration should be safe, but if large (>1.3 g/day) doses are administered for longer than 10-14 days, then the INR should be monitored (see Dental Comment).

Adverse Reactions

Oral, Rectal: Frequency not defined:

Dermatologic: Skin rash

Endocrine & metabolic: Decreased serum bicarbonate, decreased serum calcium, decreased serum sodium, hyperchloremia, hyperuricemia, increased serum glucose

Genitourinary: Nephrotoxicity (with chronic overdose)

Hematologic & oncologic: Anemia, leukopenia, neutropenia, pancytopenia

Hepatic: Increased serum alkaline phosphatase, increased serum bilirubin

Hypersensitivity: Hypersensitivity reaction (rare)

Renal: Hyperammonemia, renal disease (analgesic)

IV:

>10%: Gastrointestinal: Nausea (adults 34%; children ≥5%), vomiting (adults 15%; children ≥5%)

1% to 10%:

Cardiovascular: Hypertension, hypotension, peripheral edema, tachycardia

Central nervous system: Headache (adults 10%; children ≥1%), insomnia (adults 7%; children ≥1%), agitation (children ≥5%), anxiety, fatigue, trismus

Dermatologic: Pruritus (children ≥5%), skin rash

Endocrine & metabolic: Hypervolemia, hypoalbuminemia, hypokalemia, hypomagnesemia, hypophosphatemia

Gastrointestinal: Constipation (children ≥5%), abdominal pain, diarrhea

Genitourinary: Oliguria (children ≥1%)

Hematologic & oncologic: Anemia

Hepatic: Increased serum transaminases

Local: Infusion site reaction (pain)

Neuromuscular & skeletal: Limb pain, muscle spasm

Ophthalmic: Periorbital edema

Respiratory: Atelectasis (children ≥5%), abnormal breath sounds, dyspnea, hypoxia, pleural effusion, pulmonary edema, stridor, wheezing

Miscellaneous: Fever (children ≥1%)

All formulations: <1%, postmarketing, and/or case reports: Anaphylaxis, hepatic injury (dose-related), hypersensitivity reaction, severe dermatological reaction (acute generalized exanthematous pustulosis, Stevens-Johnson syndrome, toxic epidermal necrolysis)

Dental Usual Dosage Postoperative pain: Oral, rectal:

Children <12 years: 10 to 15 mg/kg/dose every 4 to 6 hours as needed; do **not** exceed 5 doses (2.6 g) in 24 hours

Adults: 325 to 650 mg every 4 to 6 hours or 1000 mg 3 to 4 times/day; do **not** exceed 4 g/day

Dosing

Adult & Geriatric Note: In 2011, McNeil Consumer Healthcare reduced the maximum doses and increased the dosing interval on the labeling of some of their acetaminophen OTC products used in older pediatric patients (usually children ≥ 12 years and adolescents) and adults in an attempt to protect consumers from inadvertent overdoses. For example, the maximum daily dose of Tylenol Extra Strength and Tylenol Regular Strength was decreased and the dosing interval for Tylenol Extra Strength was increased. Health care professionals may still prescribe or recommend the 4 g daily maximum to patients (but are advised to use their own discretion and clinical judgment) (McNeil Consumer Healthcare, 2014).

Pain or fever:

Oral: **Note:** OTC dosing recommendations may vary by product and/or manufacturer. When calculating the maximum daily dose, consider all sources of acetaminophen (prescription and OTC) and all routes of administration. Do not exceed the maximum recommended daily dose. No dose adjustment required when converting between different acetaminophen formulations.

Immediate-release:

Regular strength: 650 mg every 4 to 6 hours; maximum daily dose: 3250 mg **daily** unless directed by health care provider; under health care provider supervision, daily doses ≤4 g may be used

Extra strength: 1000 mg every 6 hours; maximum daily dose: 3000 mg **daily** unless directed by a health care provider; under health care provider supervision, daily doses ≤4 g may be used

Extended-release: 1300 mg every 8 hours; maximum daily dose: 3900 mg **daily**

Rectal: 650 mg every 4 to 6 hours; maximum daily dose: 3900 mg **daily**

IV:

<50 kg: 12.5 mg/kg every 4 hours or 15 mg/kg every 6 hours; maximum single dose: 15 mg/kg/dose (≤750 mg/dose); maximum daily dose: 75 mg/kg/day (≤3.75 g/day)

≥50 kg: 650 mg every 4 hours or 1,000 mg every 6 hours; maximum single dose: 1,000 mg/dose; maximum daily dose: 4 g/day

Pediatric Note: In 2011, McNeil Consumer Healthcare reduced the maximum doses and increased the dosing interval on the labeling of some of their acetaminophen OTC products used in older pediatric patients (usually children ≥12 years and adolescents) in an attempt to protect consumers from inadvertent overdoses. For example, the maximum daily dose of Tylenol Extra Strength OTC and Tylenol Regular Strength OTC was decreased and the dosing interval for Tylenol Extra Strength OTC was increased. Health care professionals may still prescribe or recommend the 4 g daily maximum to patients (but are advised to use their own discretion and clinical judgment) (McNeil Consumer Healthcare, 2014).

Pain or fever:

Oral: **Note:** When calculating the maximum daily dose, consider all sources of acetaminophen (prescription and OTC) and all routes of administration. Do not exceed the maximum recommended daily dose (see dosing information for further detail).

Weight-based dosing: Infants, Children, and Adolescents: 10 to 15 mg/kg/dose every 4 to 6 hours as needed (APS, 2008; Sullivan, 2011); do **not** exceed 5 doses in 24 hours; maximum daily dose: 75 mg/kg/day not to exceed 4 g daily.

Fixed dosing: Oral suspension, chewable tablets: Infants and Children <12 years: Consult specific product formulations for appropriate age groups. See table; use of weight to select dose is preferred; if weight is not available, then use age; doses may be repeated every 4 hours; maximum: 5 doses daily.

Acetaminophen Pediatric Dosing (Oral)[1]

Weight (kg)	Weight (lbs)	Age	Dosage (mg)
2.7-5.3	6-11	0-3 mo	40
5.4-8.1	12-17	4-11 mo	80
8.2-10.8	18-23	1-2 y	120
10.9-16.3	24-35	2-3 y	160
16.4-21.7	36-47	4-5 y	240
21.8-27.2	48-59	6-8 y	320
27.3-32.6	60-71	9-10 y	400
32.7-43.2	72-95	11 y	480

[1]Manufacturer's recommendations are based on weight in pounds (OTC labeling); weight in kg listed here is derived from pounds and rounded; kg weight listed also is adjusted to allow for continuous weight ranges in kg. OTC labeling instructs consumer to consult with health care provider for dosing instructions in infants and children under 2 years of age.

Immediate release solid dosage formulations: **Note:** Actual OTC dosing recommendations may vary by product and/or manufacturer:

Children 6 to 11 years: 325 mg every 4 to 6 hours; maximum daily dose: 1625 mg **daily**; **Note:** Do not use for more than 5 days unless directed by a health care provider

Children ≥12 years and Adolescents: Refer to adult dosing.

Extended release: Children ≥12 years and Adolescents: Refer to adult dosing.

Rectal:

Infants 6 to 11 months: 80 mg every 6 hours; maximum daily dose: 320 mg **daily**

Infants and Children 12 to 36 months: 80 mg every 4 to 6 hours; maximum daily dose: 400 mg **daily**

Children >3 to 6 years: 120 mg every 4 to 6 hours; maximum daily dose: 600 mg **daily**

Children >6 up to 12 years: 325 mg every 4 to 6 hours; maximum daily dose: 1625 mg **daily**

Children ≥12 years and Adolescents: Refer to adult dosing.

IV:

Neonates (including premature neonates born ≥32 weeks gestational age) up to 28 days (fever only): 12.5 mg/kg every 6 hours; maximum daily dose: 50 mg/kg/day.

Infants 29 days to 2 years of age (fever only): 15 mg/kg every 6 hours; maximum daily dose: 60 mg/kg/day.

Children 2 to 12 years: 12.5 mg/kg every 4 hours or 15 mg/kg every 6 hours; maximum single dose: 15 mg/kg/dose (≤750 mg/dose); maximum daily dose: 75 mg/kg/day (≤3.75 g/day)

Adolescents: Refer to adult dosing.

Renal Impairment

Oral (Aronoff 2007):

Adults:

GFR ≥50 mL/minute: No dosage adjustment necessary.

GFR 10 to 50 mL/minute: Administer every 6 hours.

GFR <10 mL/minute: Administer every 8 hours.

CRRT: Administer every 6 hours.

Infants, Children, and Adolescents:

GFR ≥10 mL/minute/1.73 m^2: No dosage adjustment necessary.

GFR <10 mL/minute/1.73 m^2: Administer every 8 hours.

Intermittent hemodialysis or peritoneal dialysis: Administer every 8 hours.

CRRT: No dosage adjustment necessary.

IV: Children, Adolescents, and Adults:

CrCl >30 mL/minute: There are no dosage adjustments provided in the manufacturer's labeling.

CrCl ≤30 mL/minute: There are no dosage adjustments provided in the manufacturer's labeling. Use with caution; consider decreasing daily dose and extending dosing interval.

Hepatic Impairment

Oral: Use with caution. Limited, low-dose therapy is usually well tolerated in hepatic disease/cirrhosis. However, cases of hepatotoxicity at daily acetaminophen dosages <4 g daily have been reported.

IV:

Mild to moderate impairment: There are no dosage adjustments provided in the manufacturer's labeling. Use with caution; a reduced total daily dosage may be warranted.

Severe impairment: Use is contraindicated.

Mechanism of Action Although not fully elucidated, believed to inhibit the synthesis of prostaglandins in the central nervous system and work peripherally to block pain impulse generation; produces antipyresis from inhibition of hypothalamic heat-regulating center

Contraindications

Injection: Hypersensitivity to acetaminophen or any component of the formulation; severe hepatic impairment or severe active liver disease

OTC labeling: When used for self-medication, do not use with other drug products containing acetaminophen or if allergic to acetaminophen or any of the inactive ingredients

Warnings/Precautions **[Injection: US Boxed Warning]: Acetaminophen has been associated with acute liver failure, at times resulting in liver transplant and death. Hepatotoxicity is usually associated with excessive acetaminophen intake and often involves more than one product that contains acetaminophen.** Do not exceed the maximum recommended daily dose (>4 g daily in adults). In addition, chronic daily dosing may also result in liver damage in some patients. Limit acetaminophen dose from all sources (prescription, OTC, combination products) and all routes of administration (IV, oral, rectal) to ≤4 g/day (adults). Use with caution in patients with alcoholic liver disease; consuming ≥3 alcoholic drinks/day may increase the risk of liver damage. Use caution in patients with hepatic impairment or active liver disease; use of IV formulation is contraindicated in patients with severe hepatic impairment or severe active liver disease.

[Injection: US Boxed Warning]: Take care to avoid dosing errors with acetaminophen injection, which could result in accidental overdose and death; ensure that the dose in mg is not confused with mL, dosing in patients <50 kg is based on body weight, infusion pumps are properly programmed, and total daily dose of acetaminophen from all sources does not exceed the maximum daily limits.

Hypersensitivity and anaphylactic reactions have been reported including life-threatening anaphylaxis; discontinue immediately if symptoms occur. Serious and potentially fatal skin reactions, including acute generalized exanthematous pustulosis (AGEP), Stevens-Johnson syndrome (SJS), and toxic epidermal necrolysis (TEN), have occurred rarely with acetaminophen use. Discontinue therapy at the first appearance of skin rash.

Benzyl alcohol and derivatives: Some dosage forms may contain benzyl alcohol and/or sodium benzoate/benzoic acid; benzoic acid (benzoate) is a metabolite of benzyl alcohol; large amounts of benzyl alcohol (≥99 mg/kg/day) have been associated with a potentially fatal toxicity ("gasping syndrome") in neonates; the "gasping syndrome" consists of metabolic acidosis, respiratory distress, gasping respirations, CNS dysfunction (including convulsions, intracranial hemorrhage), hypotension and cardiovascular collapse (AAP ["Inactive" 1997]; CDC, 1982); some data suggests that benzoate displaces bilirubin from protein binding sites (Ahlfors, 2001); avoid or use dosage forms containing benzyl alcohol and/or benzyl alcohol derivative with caution in neonates. See manufacturer's labeling.

Polysorbate 80: Some dosage forms may contain polysorbate 80 (also known as Tweens). Hypersensitivity reactions, usually a delayed reaction, have been reported following exposure to pharmaceutical products containing polysorbate 80 in certain individuals (Isaksson, 2002; Lucente 2000; Shelley, 1995). Thrombocytopenia, ascites, pulmonary deterioration, and renal and hepatic failure have been reported in premature neonates after receiving parenteral products containing polysorbate 80 (Alade, 1986; CDC, 1984). See manufacturer's labeling. Some products may contain aspartame which is metabolized to phenylalanine and must be avoided (or used with caution) in patients with phenylketonuria.

Propylene glycol: Some dosage forms may contain propylene glycol; large amounts are potentially toxic and have been associated hyperosmolality, lactic acidosis, seizures, and respiratory depression; use caution (AAP ["Inactive" 1997]; Zar, 2007).

When used for self-medication (OTC), patients should be instructed to contact healthcare provider if symptoms get worse or new symptoms appear, redness or swelling is present in the painful area, fever lasts >3 days (all ages), or pain (excluding sore throat) lasts longer than: Adults: 10 days, Children and Adolescents: 5 days, Infants: 3 days. When treating children with sore throat, if sore throat is severe, persists for >2 days, or is followed by fever, rash, headache, nausea, or vomiting, consult health care provider immediately.

Use with caution in patients with chronic malnutrition or severe renal impairment; use intravenous formulation with caution in patients with severe hypovolemia. Use with caution in patients with known G6PD deficiency.

Drug Interactions

Metabolism/Transport Effects Substrate of CYP1A2 (minor), CYP2A6 (minor), CYP2C9 (minor), CYP2D6 (minor), CYP2E1 (minor), CYP3A4 (minor); **Note:** Assignment of Major/Minor substrate status based on clinically relevant drug interaction potential

Avoid Concomitant Use There are no known interactions where it is recommended to avoid concomitant use.

Increased Effect/Toxicity

Acetaminophen may increase the levels/effects of: Busulfan; Dasatinib; Imatinib; Mipomersen; Phenylephrine (Systemic); Prilocaine; Sodium Nitrite; SORAfenib; Vitamin K Antagonists

The levels/effects of Acetaminophen may be increased by: Alcohol (Ethyl); Dapsone (Topical); Dasatinib; Isoniazid; MetyraPONE; Nitric Oxide; Probenecid; SORAfenib; Tetracaine (Topical)

Decreased Effect

Acetaminophen may decrease the levels/effects of: LamoTRIgine

The levels/effects of Acetaminophen may be decreased by: Barbiturates; CarBAMazepine; Cholestyramine Resin; Fosphenytoin-Phenytoin

Food Interactions Rate of absorption may be decreased when given with food. Management: Administer without regard to food.

Dietary Considerations Some products may contain phenylalanine and/or sodium.

Pharmacodynamics/Kinetics

Onset of Action

Oral: <1 hour

IV: Analgesia: 5 to 10 minutes; Antipyretic: Within 30 minutes

Peak effect: IV: Analgesic: 1 hour

Duration of Action

IV, Oral: Analgesia: 4 to 6 hours

IV: Antipyretic: ≥6 hours

Half-life Elimination Prolonged following toxic doses

Neonates: 7 hours (range: 4 to 10 hours)

Infants: ~4 hours (range: 1 to 7 hours)

Children: 3 hours (range: 2 to 5 hours)

Adolescents: ~3 hours (range: 2 to 4 hours)

Adults: ~2 hours (range: 2 to 3 hours); may be slightly prolonged in severe renal insufficiency (CrCl <30 mL/minute): 2 to 5.3 hours

Time to Peak Serum: Oral: Immediate release: 10 to 60 minutes (may be delayed in acute overdoses); IV: 15 minutes

Pregnancy Considerations Acetaminophen crosses the placenta and can be detected in cord blood, newborn serum, and urine immediately after delivery (Levy 1975; Naga Rani 1989; Wang 1997). An increased risk of teratogenic effects has not been observed following maternal use of acetaminophen during pregnancy. Prenatal constriction of the ductus arteriosus has been noted in case reports following maternal use during the third trimester (Suhag 2008; Wood 2005). The use of acetaminophen in normal doses during pregnancy is not associated with an increased risk of miscarriage or still birth; however, an increase in fetal death or spontaneous abortion may be seen following maternal overdose if treatment is delayed (Li 2003; Rebordosa 2009; Riggs 1989). Frequent maternal use of acetaminophen during pregnancy may be associated with wheezing and asthma in early childhood (Perzanowki 2010).

Breastfeeding Considerations Acetaminophen is excreted in breast milk (Notarianni 1987).

The relative infant dose (RID) of acetaminophen is 3.98% when calculated using the highest breast milk concentration located and compared to an infant therapeutic dose of 60 mg/kg/day. In general, breastfeeding is considered acceptable when the RID is <10%; when an RID is >25% breastfeeding should generally be avoided (Anderson 2016; Ito 2000). Using the highest milk concentration (15.9 mcg/mL), the estimated daily infant dose via breast milk is 2.385 mg/kg/day. This milk concentration was obtained following a single maternal dose of oral acetaminophen 1,000 mg (Hurden 1980).

Following a single oral maternal dose of acetaminophen 650 mg, the half-life of acetaminophen is 1.35 to 3.5 hours in breast milk (Berlin 1980). Acetaminophen can be detected in the urine of nursing infants (Notarianni 1987). Except for a single case report of a rash (Matheson 1985), adverse reactions have generally not been observed in nursing infants (Ito 1993).

Current guidelines note that nonopioid analgesics are preferred for the treatment of pain in breastfeeding women and acetaminophen is one of the preferred non-narcotic agents (Montgomery 2012; Sachs 2013). Acetaminophen is considered compatible with breastfeeding when used in usual recommended doses (WHO 2002).

Product Availability Ofirmev 100 mL IV bag formulation: FDA approved November 2016; availability anticipated in the second quarter of 2017.

Dosage Forms

Caplet, oral: 500 mg

Cetafen Extra [OTC]: 500 mg

Mapap Extra Strength [OTC]: 500 mg

Pain Eze [OTC]: 650 mg

Tylenol [OTC]: 325 mg

Tylenol Extra Strength [OTC]: 500 mg

Caplet, extended release, oral:

Mapap Arthritis Pain [OTC]: 650 mg

Tylenol 8 HR Arthritis Pain [OTC]: 650 mg

Capsule, oral:

Mapap Extra Strength [OTC]: 500 mg

Injection, solution [preservative free]:

Ofirmev: 10 mg/mL (100 mL)

Liquid, oral: 160 mg/5 mL (120 mL, 473 mL); 500 mg/5 mL (240 mL)

Mapap Extra Strength [OTC]: 500 mg/5 mL (237 mL)

Q-Pap Children's [OTC]: 160 mg/5 mL (118 mL, 473 mL)

Silapap Children's [OTC]: 160 mg/5 mL (118 mL, 237 mL, 473 mL)

Solution, oral: 160 mg/5 mL (5 mL, 10 mL, 20 mL, 118 mL, 473 mL)

Pain & Fever Children's [OTC]: 160 mg/5 mL (118 mL, 473 mL)

Suppository, rectal: 120 mg (12s, 50s, 100s); 325 mg (12s); 650 mg (12s, 50s, 100s)

Acephen [OTC]: 120 mg (12s, 50s, 100s); 325 mg (6s, 12s, 50s, 100s); 650 mg (12s, 50s, 100s)

Feverall [OTC]: 80 mg (6s, 50s); 120 mg (6s, 50s); 325 mg (6s, 50s); 650 mg (50s)

Suspension, oral: 160 mg/5 mL (5 mL, 10 mL, 10.15 mL, 20 mL, 20.3 mL)

Mapap Children's [OTC]: 160 mg/5 mL (118 mL)

Nortemp Children's [OTC]: 160 mg/5 mL (118 mL)

Pain & Fever Children's [OTC]: 160 mg/5 mL (60 mL)

Q-Pap Children's [OTC]: 160 mg/5 mL (118 mL)

Tylenol Children's [OTC]: 160 mg/5 mL (60 mL, 120 mL)

Tylenol Infants' [OTC]: 160 mg/5 mL (60 mL)

Syrup, oral:
Triaminic Children's Fever Reducer Pain Reliever [OTC]: 160 mg/5 mL (118 mL)

Tablet, oral: 325 mg, 500 mg
Aspirin Free Anacin Extra Strength [OTC]: 500 mg
Cetafen [OTC]: 325 mg
Mapap [OTC]: 325 mg
Mapap Extra Strength [OTC]: 500 mg
Non-Aspirin Pain Reliever [OTC]: 325 mg
Pharbetol [OTC]: 325 mg
Pharbetol Extra Strength [OTC]: 500 mg
Q-Pap [OTC]: 325 mg
Q-Pap Extra Strength [OTC]: 500 mg
Tylenol [OTC]: 325 mg
Tylenol Extra Strength [OTC]: 500 mg
Valorin [OTC]: 325 mg
Valorin Extra [OTC]: 500 mg

Tablet, chewable, oral: 80 mg
Mapap Children's [OTC]: 80 mg

Tablet, dispersible, oral: 80 mg, 160 mg
Mapap Children's [OTC]: 80 mg
Tylenol Jr. Meltaways [OTC]: 160 mg

Dental Comment Although the ***OTC product labeling*** for acetaminophen products state to limit the maximum dose to 3,000 mg daily (for extra strength) or 3,250 mg (for regular strength) (see this site for details: http://www.tylenolprofessional.com/extra-strength-tylenol-dosage-faq.html), it is still appropriate for patients to take up to 4,000 mg daily "under the direction of a health care provider" (http://www.tylenolprofessional.com/assets/v4/faqs-new-dosing.pdf).

The acetaminophen component requires use with caution in patients who use alcohol, with preexisting liver disease, and those receiving more than one source of acetaminophen-containing medication.

Hepatotoxicity caused by acetaminophen is potentiated by chronic alcohol consumption. People who are taking acetaminophen, even at therapeutic doses, and consume alcohol are at risk of developing hepatotoxicity.

Acetaminophen may increase the levels and enhance the anticoagulant effects of vitamin K antagonists acenocoumarol and warfarin (Coumadin). Studies have reported that acetaminophen has increased the INR in warfarin-treated patients with daily acetaminophen doses as low as 2 g, particularly when taking acetaminophen for >1 week (Gebauer 2003; Hylek 1998). In addition, case reports of bleeding as a result of increased INR have been published (Bagheri 1999). There is no known mechanism of the interaction; furthermore, some studies have failed to demonstrate this interaction (Gadisseur 2003; Kwan 1995; van den Bemt 2002). In terms of risk, the data suggest that acetaminophen and warfarin could interact in some clinically significant manner but that the benefits of concomitant use of acetaminophen for pain control in dental patients taking warfarin usually outweigh the risks. An appropriate monitoring plan should be in place to identify potential negative effects and dosage adjustments may be necessary in a minority of patients. The interaction may be more likely to occur with daily acetaminophen doses of >1.3 g for >1 week. In a review of seven random controlled trials comparing acetaminophen versus placebo in warfarin-treated patients (Caldeira 2015), acetaminophen was associated with a mean 0.62 INR increase compared to placebo. Specifically, there was 0.17 mean increase of the INR per each daily gram of acetaminophen. Statistically, this was significant; however, the clinical relevance was questionable since the reviewed studies did not report any major bleeding event.

There are no reports of acetaminophen interacting with antiplatelet drugs such as aspirin, clopidogrel (Plavix), ticagrelor (Brilinta), or prasugrel (Effient). Also, there are no reports of acetaminophen in combination with hydrocodone, codeine, or oxycodone interacting with warfarin (Coumadin).

Acetaminophen and Caffeine

(a seet a MIN oh fen & KAF een)

Brand Names: US Excedrin Tension Headache [OTC]

Pharmacologic Category Analgesic, Nonopioid

Use Pain: For the temporary relief of pain caused by headache or muscle aches

Local Anesthetic/Vasoconstrictor Precautions
No information available to require special precautions

Effects on Dental Treatment No significant effects or complications reported

Effects on Bleeding As a single agent, acetaminophen does not appear to affect bleeding or platelet aggregation. Acetaminophen may prolong the INR and increase bleeding in patients taking warfarin (Coumadin). For patients taking warfarin, single acetaminophen doses or acetaminophen therapy of short duration should be safe, but if large (>1.3 g/day) doses are administered for longer than 10 to 14 days, then the INR should be monitored (see Dental Comment).

Adverse Reactions See individual agents.

Mechanism of Action
Acetaminophen is believed to inhibit the synthesis of prostaglandins in the central nervous system (Graham 2005); produces antipyretic and analgesic activity.

Caffeine blocks adenosine receptors (mainly A1 and A2A subtypes), induces calcium mobilization from the sarcoplasmic reticulum and inhibits calcium reuptake, increases levels of cyclic AMP by inhibiting phosphodiesterase (Cappelletti 2015).

Pregnancy Considerations See individual agents.

Dental Comment
Although the OTC product labeling for acetaminophen products state to limit the maximum dose to 3,000 mg daily (for extra strength) or 3,250 mg (for regular strength) (see this site for details: http://www.-tylenolprofessional.com/extra-strength-tylenol-dosage-faq.html), it is still appropriate for patients to take up to 4,000 mg daily "under the direction of a health care provider" (http://www.tylenolprofessional.com/assets/v4/faqs-new-dosing.pdf).

The acetaminophen component requires use with caution in patients who use alcohol, with preexisting liver disease, and those receiving more than one source of acetaminophen-containing medication.

Hepatotoxicity caused by acetaminophen is potentiated by chronic alcohol consumption. People who are taking acetaminophen, even at therapeutic doses, and consume alcohol are at risk of developing hepatotoxicity.

Acetaminophen may increase the levels and enhance the anticoagulant effects of vitamin K antagonists acenocoumarol and warfarin (Coumadin). Studies have reported that acetaminophen has increased the INR in warfarin-treated patients with daily acetaminophen doses as low as 2 g, particularly when taking acetaminophen for >1 week (Gebauer 2003; Hylek 1998). In addition, case reports of bleeding as a result of increased INR have been published (Bagheri 1999).

There is no known mechanism of the interaction; furthermore, some studies have failed to demonstrate this interaction (Gadisseur 2003; Kwan 1995; van den Bemt 2002). In terms of risk, the data suggest that acetaminophen and warfarin could interact in some clinically significant manner but that the benefits of concomitant use of acetaminophen for pain control in dental patients taking warfarin usually outweigh the risks. An appropriate monitoring plan should be in place to identify potential negative effects and dosage adjustments may be necessary in a minority of patients. The interaction may be more likely to occur with daily acetaminophen doses of >1.3 g for >1 week. In a review of seven random controlled trials comparing acetaminophen versus placebo in warfarin-treated patients (Caldeira 2015), acetaminophen was associated with a mean 0.62 INR increase compared to placebo. Specifically, there was 0.17 mean increase of the INR per each daily gram of acetaminophen. Statistically, this was significant; however, the clinical relevance was questionable since the reviewed studies did not report any major bleeding event.

There are no reports of acetaminophen interacting with antiplatelet drugs such as aspirin, clopidogrel (Plavix), ticagrelor (Brilinta), or prasugrel (Effient). Also, there are no reports of acetaminophen in combination with hydrocodone, codeine, or oxycodone interacting with warfarin (Coumadin).

Acetaminophen and Codeine

(a seet a MIN oh fen & KOE deen)

Related Information

Acetaminophen *on page 56*

Codeine *on page 410*

Related Sample Prescriptions

Oral Pain - Sample Prescriptions *on page 28*

Brand Names: US Capital/Codeine [DSC]; Tylenol with Codeine #3; Tylenol with Codeine #4

Brand Names: Canada Acet-Codeine; PHL-Acet-Codeine; PMS-Acetaminophen with Codeine Elixir; Procet-30; ratio-Emtec-30; ratio-Lenoltec No. 4

Generic Availability (US) May be product dependent

Pharmacologic Category Analgesic Combination (Opioid); Analgesic, Opioid

Dental Use Treatment of postoperative pain

Use

Pain management: Management of mild to moderate pain where treatment with an opioid is appropriate and for which alternative treatments are inadequate.

Limitations of use: Reserve for use in patients for whom alternative treatment options (eg, nonopioid analgesics) are ineffective, not tolerated, or would be otherwise inadequate.

Local Anesthetic/Vasoconstrictor Precautions No information available to require special precautions

Effects on Dental Treatment No significant effects or complications reported (see Dental Comment)

Effects on Bleeding As a single agent, acetaminophen does not appear to affect bleeding or platelet aggregation. Acetaminophen may prolong the INR and increase bleeding in patients taking warfarin (Coumadin). For patients taking warfarin, single acetaminophen doses or acetaminophen therapy of short duration should be safe, but if large (>1.3 g/day) doses are administered for longer than 10-14 days, then the INR should be monitored (see Dental Comment).

Adverse Reactions Also see individual agents.

Frequency not defined:

Central nervous system: Dizziness, drowsiness, dysphoria, euphoria, sedation, serotonin syndrome

Dermatologic: Pruritus, skin rash

Endocrine & metabolic: Adrenocortical insufficiency

Gastrointestinal: Abdominal pain, constipation, nausea, vomiting

Hematologic & oncologic: Agranulocytosis, thrombocytopenia

Hypersensitivity: Hypersensitivity reaction

Respiratory: Dyspnea

<1%, postmarketing, and/or case reports: Hypogonadism (Brennan 2013; Debono 2011), respiratory depression

Dental Usual Dosage Postoperative pain: Adults: Analgesic: Based on codeine (30-60 mg/dose) every 4-6 hours (maximum: 4000 mg/24 hours based on acetaminophen component)

Dosing

Adult Note: Adult doses ≥60 mg codeine fail to give commensurate relief of pain but merely prolong analgesia and are associated with an appreciably increased incidence of side effects.

US labeling:

Pain management: Oral:

Solution or suspension: Acetaminophen 120 mg/codeine 12 mg per 5 mL: 15 mL every 4 hours as needed; adjust dose according to severity of pain and response of patient (maximum: acetaminophen 4,000 mg per 24 hours).

Tablets: Acetaminophen (300 to 1,000 mg/dose)/codeine (15 to 60 mg/dose) every 4 hours as needed; adjust dose according to severity of pain and response of patient (maximum: acetaminophen 4,000 mg/codeine 360 mg per 24 hours).

Discontinuation of therapy: For patients on long term opioid therapy, decrease dose by 25% to 50% every 2 to 4 days; monitor carefully for signs/symptoms of withdrawal. If patient displays withdrawal symptoms, increase dose to the previous level and then reduce dose more slowly by increasing interval between dose reductions, decreasing amount of daily dose reduction, or both.

Canadian labeling:

Mild to moderate pain: Oral: Solution: Acetaminophen 160 mg and codeine 8 mg per 5 mL: 10 to 20 mL every 4 hours as needed (maximum: 100 mL [acetaminophen 3,200 mg and codeine 160 mg] per 24 hours)

Mild to severe pain: Oral: Tablets: Acetaminophen (300 to 600 mg/dose) and codeine (30 to 60 mg/dose) every 4 to 6 hours as needed (maximum: Acetaminophen 3,600 mg and codeine 360 mg per 24 hours)

Geriatric Refer to adult dosing. Use with caution and consider initiation at the low end of the dosing range; titrate slowly.

Pediatric

US labeling: **Pain management:** Oral: Solution or suspension: Acetaminophen 120 mg/codeine 12 mg per 5 mL:

Children 3 to 6 years: 5 mL 3 to 4 times daily as needed

Children 7 to 12 years: 10 mL 3 to 4 times daily as needed

Adolescents: Refer to adult dosing

Canadian labeling: Children ≥12 years and Adolescents: Refer to adult dosing.

Renal Impairment There are no dosage adjustments provided in the manufacturer's labeling; use with caution.

Hepatic Impairment There are no dosage adjustments provided in the manufacturer's labeling; use with caution.

Mechanism of Action

Acetaminophen: Although not fully elucidated, believed to inhibit the synthesis of prostaglandins in the central nervous system and peripherally block pain impulse generation; produces antipyresis from inhibition of hypothalamic heat-regulating center.

Codeine: Binds to opiate receptors in the CNS, causing inhibition of ascending pain pathways, altering the perception of and response to pain; causes cough suppression by direct central action in the medulla; produces generalized CNS depression.

Contraindications

Hypersensitivity (eg, anaphylaxis) to acetaminophen, codeine, or any component of the formulation; acute or severe bronchial asthma in an unmonitored setting or in the absence of resuscitative equipment; postoperative pain management in children who have undergone tonsillectomy and/or adenoidectomy; significant respiratory depression; GI obstruction, including paralytic ileus (known or suspected); concurrent use with monoamine oxidase inhibitors (MAOIs) or use of MAOIs within the last 14 days.

Canadian labeling: Additional contraindications (not in US labeling): Use in pediatric patients <12 years. Some products may contraindicate use in patients <18 years (refer to specific product labeling).

Documentation of allergenic cross-reactivity for opioids is limited. However, because of similarities in chemical structure and/or pharmacologic actions, the possibility of cross-sensitivity cannot be ruled out with certainty.

Warnings/Precautions [US Boxed Warning]: Respiratory depression and death have occurred in children who received codeine following tonsillectomy and/or adenoidectomy and were found to have evidence of being ultrarapid metabolizers of codeine due to a CYP2D6 polymorphism; children with obstructive sleep apnea may be at increased risk. Deaths have also occurred in breastfeeding infants after being exposed to high concentrations of morphine because the mothers were ultrarapid metabolizers. Use is contraindicated in the postoperative pain management of children who have undergone tonsillectomy and/or adenoidectomy. **[US Boxed Warning]: Prolonged use during pregnancy can cause neonatal opioid withdrawal syndrome, which may be life-threatening if not recognized and treated according to protocols developed by neonatology experts. If opioid use is required for a prolonged period in a pregnant woman, advise the patient of the risk of neonatal opioid withdrawal syndrome and ensure that appropriate treatment will be available**. Signs and symptoms include irritability, hyperactivity and abnormal sleep pattern, high pitched cry, tremor, vomiting, diarrhea and failure to gain weight. Onset, duration, and severity depend on the drug used, duration of use, maternal dose, and rate of drug elimination by the newborn.

Avoid use of codeine in patients with impaired consciousness or coma as these patients are susceptible to intracranial effects of CO_2 retention. Some products may contain metabisulfite which may cause allergic reactions. Use caution in patients with two or more copies of the variant CYP2D6*2 allele; may have extensive conversion to morphine and thus increased opioid-mediated effects. Avoid the use of codeine in these patients; consider alternative analgesics such as morphine or a nonopioid agent (Crews 2012). The occurrence of this phenotype is seen in 0.5% to 1% of Chinese and Japanese, 0.5% to 1% of Hispanics, 1% to 10% of Caucasians, 3% of African-Americans, and 16% to 28% of North Africans, Ethiopians, and Arabs.

Serious and potentially fatal skin reactions, including acute generalized exanthematous pustulosis (AGEP), Stevens-Johnson syndrome (SJS), and toxic epidermal necrolysis (TEN) have occurred rarely with acetaminophen use. Discontinue therapy at the first appearance of skin rash or any other sign of hypersensitivity. Limit acetaminophen dose from all sources (prescription, OTC, combination products) to <4 g/day in adults. Do not use acetaminophen/codeine concomitantly with other acetaminophen-containing products.

[US Boxed Warning]: Acetaminophen has been associated with cases of acute liver failure, at times resulting in liver transplant and death. Most of the cases of liver injury are associated with the use of acetaminophen at dosages that exceed 4 g/day, and often involve more than one acetaminophen-containing product. Risk is increased with alcohol use, preexisting liver disease, and intake of more than one source of acetaminophen-containing medications. Chronic daily dosing in adults has also resulted in liver damage in some patients. Hypersensitivity and anaphylactic reactions have been reported with acetaminophen use; discontinue immediately if symptoms of allergic or hypersensitivity reactions occur. Use with caution in patients with hypersensitivity reactions to other phenanthrene-derivative opioid agonists (hydrocodone, hydromorphone, levorphanol, oxycodone, oxymorphone). Use acetaminophen with caution in patients with known G6PD deficiency. Use with caution in patients with alcoholic liver disease; consuming ≥3 alcoholic drinks/day may increase the risk of liver damage.

May cause CNS depression, which may impair physical or mental abilities; patients must be cautioned about performing tasks which require mental alertness (eg, operating machinery or driving). **[US Boxed Warning]: Use exposes patients and other users to the risks of opioid addiction, abuse, and misuse, which can lead to overdose and death. Assess each patient's risk prior to prescribing oxycodone/acetaminophen, and monitor all patients regularly for the development of these behaviors or conditions.** Use with caution in patients with a history of drug abuse or acute alcoholism; potential for drug dependency exists. Other factors associated with increased risk for misuse include younger age, concomitant depression (major), and psychotropic medication use. Consider offering naloxone prescriptions in patients with factors associated with an increased risk for overdose, such as history of overdose or substance use disorder, higher opioid dosages (≥50 morphine milligram equivalents/day orally), and concomitant benzodiazepine use (Dowell [CDC 2016]). Abuse or misuse of ER tablets by crushing, chewing, snorting, or injecting the dissolved product will result in the uncontrolled delivery of the oxycodone and can result in overdose and death.

Chronic pain (outside of end-of-life or palliative care, active cancer treatment, sickle cell disease, or medication-assisted treatment for opioid use disorder) in outpatient setting in adults: Opioids should **not** be used as first-line therapy for chronic pain management (pain >3-month duration or beyond time of normal tissue healing) due to limited short-term benefits, undetermined long-term benefits, and association with serious risks (eg, overdose, MI, auto accidents, risk of developing opioid use disorder). Preferred management includes nonpharmacologic therapy and nonopioid therapy (eg, NSAIDs, acetaminophen, certain anticonvulsants and antidepressants). If opioid therapy is initiated, it should be combined with nonpharmacologic and nonopioid therapy, as appropriate. Prior to initiation, known risks of opioid therapy should be discussed and realistic treatment goals for pain/function should be established, including consideration for discontinuation if benefits do not outweigh risks. Therapy should be continued only if clinically meaningful improvement in pain/function outweighs risks. Therapy should be initiated at the lowest effective dosage using immediate-release opioids (instead of extended-release/long-acting opioids). Risk associated with use increases with higher opioid dosages. Risks and benefits should be re-evaluated when increasing dosage to ≥50 morphine milligram equivalents (MME)/day orally; dosages ≥90 MME/day orally should be avoided unless carefully justified (Dowell [CDC 2016]).

Concurrent use of mixed agonist/antagonist (eg, pentazocine, nalbuphine, butorphanol) or partial agonist (eg, buprenorphine) analgesics may precipitate withdrawal symptoms and/or reduced analgesic efficacy in patients following prolonged therapy with mu opioid agonists. Abrupt discontinuation following prolonged use may also lead to withdrawal symptoms. Taper dose gradually when discontinuing. Potentially significant drug-drug interactions may exist, requiring dose or frequency adjustment, additional monitoring, and/or selection of alternative therapy. **[US Boxed Warning]: Concomitant use of opioids with benzodiazepines or other CNS depressants, including alcohol, may result in profound sedation, respiratory depression, coma, and death. Reserve concomitant prescribing of acetaminophen/codeine and benzodiazepines or other CNS depressants for use in patients for whom alternative treatment options are inadequate. Limit dosages and durations to the minimum required. Follow patients for signs and symptoms of respiratory depression and sedation. [US Boxed Warning]: The concomitant use of codeine with all CYP450 3 A4 inducers or discontinuation of a CYP450 3A4 inhibitor may result in lower codeine levels, greater norcodeine levels, and less metabolism via 2D6 with resultant lower morphine levels. The concomitant use of codeine with all CYP450 2D6 inhibitors may result in an increase in codeine plasma concentrations and a decrease in the plasma concentration of the active metabolite, morphine. The discontinuation of a CYP450 2D6 inhibitor may result in a decrease in codeine plasma concentrations and an increase in the plasma concentration of the active metabolite, morphine. Follow patients receiving acetaminophen/codeine and any CYP2D6 inhibitor or CYP3A4 inhibitor or inducer for signs and symptoms that may reflect opioid toxicity and opioid withdrawal when acetaminophen/codeine are used in conjunction with inhibitors of CYP2D6 or inhibitors and inducers of CYP3A4. The concomitant use of codeine with all cytochrome P450 3A4 inhibitors or discontinuation of a CYP450 3A4 inducer may result in an increase in codeine plasma concentrations with subsequently greater metabolism by CYP450 2D6, resulting in greater morphine levels, which could increase or prolong adverse reactions and may cause potentially fatal respiratory depression.**

Use with caution in cachectic or debilitated patients, or in morbidly obese patients; adrenal insufficiency (including Addison disease); biliary tract impairment (including acute pancreatitis); renal or severe hepatic impairment; toxic psychosis; delirium tremens; thyroid disorders; prostatic hyperplasia and/or urethral stricture; seizure disorder; head injury, intracranial lesions or increased intracranial pressure. May cause or aggravate constipation; chronic use may result in obstructive bowel disease, particularly in those with underlying intestinal motility disorders. May also be problematic in patients with unstable angina and patients post-myocardial infarction. Consider preventive measures (eg, stool softener, increased fiber) to reduce the potential for constipation. **[US Boxed Warning]: Serious, life-threatening, or fatal respiratory depression may occur with use. Monitor for respiratory depression, especially during initiation of therapy or following a dose increase.** Carbon dioxide retention from opioid-induced respiratory depression can exacerbate the sedating effects of opioids. Use with caution and monitor for respiratory depression in patients with significant chronic obstructive pulmonary disease or cor pulmonale, and those with a substantially decreased respiratory reserve, hypoxia, hypercapnia, or preexisting respiratory depression, particularly when initiating and titrating therapy; critical respiratory depression may occur, even at therapeutic dosages. Consider the use of alternative nonopioid analgesics in these patients. May obscure diagnosis or clinical course of patients with acute abdominal conditions. Use with caution in the elderly; may be more sensitive to adverse effects, such as respiratory depression. Use opioids for chronic pain with caution in this age group; monitor closely due to an increased potential for risks, including certain risks such as falls/fracture, cognitive impairment, and constipation. Clearance may also be reduced in older adults (with or without renal impairment) resulting in a narrow therapeutic window and increasing the risk for respiratory depression or overdose (Dowell [CDC 2016]).

[US Boxed Warning]: Accidental ingestion of even one dose of acetaminophen/codeine, especially by children, can result in a fatal overdose of codeine. [US Boxed Warning]: Dosing errors due to confusion between mg and mL, and other acetaminophen/codeine oral suspensions of different concentrations can result in accidental overdose and death. Ensure accuracy when prescribing, dispensing, and administering oral suspension. May cause severe hypotension (including orthostatic hypotension and syncope); use with caution in patients with hypovolemia, cardiovascular disease (including acute MI), or drugs which may exaggerate hypotensive effects (including phenothiazines or general anesthetics). Monitor for symptoms of hypotension following initiation or dose titration. Avoid use in patients with circulatory shock. Use opioids with caution for chronic pain in patients with mental health conditions (eg, depression, anxiety disorders, post-traumatic stress disorder) due to increased risk for opioid use disorder and overdose; more frequent monitoring is recommended (Dowell [CDC 2016]). Use opioids with caution for chronic pain and titrate dosage cautiously in patients with risk factors for sleep-disordered breathing, including HF and obesity. Avoid opioids in patients with moderate to severe sleep-disordered breathing (Dowell [CDC 2016]). An opioid-containing analgesic regimen should be tailored to each patient's needs and based upon the type of pain being treated (acute versus chronic), the route of administration, degree of tolerance for opioids (naive versus chronic user), age, weight, and medical condition. The optimal analgesic dose varies widely among patients; doses should be titrated to pain relief/prevention. Opioids decrease bowel motility; monitor for decreased bowel motility in postop patients receiving opioids. Use with caution in the perioperative setting; individualize treatment when transitioning from parenteral to oral analgesics.

Some dosage forms may contain propylene glycol; large amounts are potentially toxic and have been associated hyperosmolality, lactic acidosis, seizures and respiratory depression; use caution (AAP ["Inactive" 1997]; Zar 2007).

Some dosage forms may contain sodium benzoate/benzoic acid; benzoic acid (benzoate) is a metabolite of benzyl alcohol; large amounts of benzyl alcohol (≥99 mg/kg/day) have been associated with a potentially fatal toxicity ("gasping syndrome") in neonates; the "gasping syndrome" consists of metabolic acidosis, respiratory distress, gasping respirations, CNS dysfunction (including convulsions, intracranial hemorrhage), hypotension, and cardiovascular collapse (AAP ["Inactive" 1997]; CDC 1982); some data suggests that benzoate displaces bilirubin from protein binding sites (Ahlfors 2001); avoid or use dosage forms containing benzyl alcohol derivative with caution in neonates. See manufacturer's labeling.

Drug Interactions

Metabolism/Transport Effects Refer to individual components.

Avoid Concomitant Use

Avoid concomitant use of Acetaminophen and Codeine with any of the following: Azelastine (Nasal); Eluxadoline; Mixed Agonist / Antagonist Opioids; Orphenadrine; Oxomemazine; Paraldehyde; Thalidomide

Increased Effect/Toxicity

Acetaminophen and Codeine may increase the levels/effects of: Alvimopan; Analgesics (Opioid); Azelastine (Nasal); Blonanserin; Busulfan; Dasatinib; Desmopressin; Diuretics; Eluxadoline; Flunitrazepam; HYDROcodone; Imatinib; Methotrimeprazine; MetyroSINE; Mipomersen; Orphenadrine; OxyCODONE; Paraldehyde; Phenylephrine (Systemic); Piribedil; Pramipexole; Prilocaine; Ramosetron; ROPINIRole; Rotigotine; Selective Serotonin Reuptake Inhibitors; Serotonin Modulators; Sodium Nitrite; SORAfenib; Suvorexant; Thalidomide; Vitamin K Antagonists; Zolpidem

The levels/effects of Acetaminophen and Codeine may be increased by: Amphetamines; Anticholinergic Agents; Brimonidine (Topical); Cannabis; Chlormethiazole; Chlorphenesin Carbamate; CNS Depressants; Dapsone (Topical); Dasatinib; Dimethindene (Topical); Dronabinol; Droperidol; Isoniazid; Kava Kava; Lofexidine; Magnesium Sulfate; MAO Inhibitors; Methotrimeprazine; MetyraPONE; Minocycline; Nabilone; Nitric Oxide; Oxomemazine; Perampanel; Probenecid; Rufinamide; Sodium Oxybate; Somatostatin Analogs; SORAfenib; Succinylcholine; Tapentadol; Tetracaine (Topical); Tetrahydrocannabinol

Decreased Effect

Acetaminophen and Codeine may decrease the levels/effects of: Diuretics; Gastrointestinal Agents (Prokinetic); Pegvisomant

The levels/effects of Acetaminophen and Codeine may be decreased by: Cholestyramine Resin; CYP2D6 Inhibitors (Moderate); CYP2D6 Inhibitors (Strong); Mixed Agonist / Antagonist Opioids; Nalmefene; Naltrexone

Pregnancy Risk Factor C

Pregnancy Considerations Animal reproduction studies have not been conducted with this combination. **[US Boxed Warning]: Prolonged use of opioids during pregnancy can cause neonatal opioid withdrawal syndrome, which may be life-threatening if not recognized and treated according to protocols developed by neonatology experts. If opioid use is required for a prolonged period in a pregnant woman, advise the patient of the risk of neonatal opioid withdrawal syndrome and ensure that appropriate treatment will be available.** Refer to individual agents.

Breastfeeding Considerations Acetaminophen and codeine are excreted in breast milk. According to the manufacturer, the decision to continue or discontinue breastfeeding during therapy should take into account the risk of infant exposure, the benefits of breastfeeding to the infant, and benefits of treatment to the mother. Refer to individual agents.

Controlled Substance Liquid products: C-V; Tablet: C-III

Dosage Forms

Solution, Oral:

Generic: Acetaminophen 120 mg and codeine phosphate 12 mg per 5 mL (5 mL, 12.5 mL, 118 mL, 120 mL, 473 mL)

Tablet, Oral:

Tylenol with Codeine #3: Acetaminophen 300 mg and codeine phosphate 30 mg

Tylenol with Codeine #4: Acetaminophen 300 mg and codeine phosphate 60 mg

Generic: Acetaminophen 300 mg and codeine phosphate 15 mg, Acetaminophen 300 mg and codeine phosphate 30 mg, Acetaminophen 300 mg and codeine phosphate 60 mg

Dosage Forms: Canada

Solution, Oral:

pms-Acetaminophen with Codeine Elixir: Acetaminophen 160 mg and codeine phosphate 8 mg per 5 mL

Tablet:

Acet-Codeine, Procet-30, ratio-Emtec-30, Triatec-30: Acetaminophen 300 mg and codeine phosphate 30 mg

Acet-Codeine, ratio-Lenoltec No. 4: Acetaminophen 300 mg and codeine phosphate 60 mg

Dental Comment Although the ***OTC product labeling*** for acetaminophen products state to limit the maximum dose to 3,000 mg daily (for extra strength) or 3,250 mg (for regular strength) (see this site for details: http://www.tylenolprofessional.com/extra-strength-tylenol-dosage-faq.html), it is still appropriate for patients to take up to 4,000 mg daily "under the direction of a healthcare provider" (http://www.tylenolprofessional.com/assets/v4/faqs-new-dosing.pdf).

The acetaminophen component requires use with caution in patients who use alcohol, with preexisting liver disease, and those receiving more than one source of acetaminophen-containing medication.

Hepatotoxicity caused by acetaminophen is potentiated by chronic alcohol consumption. People who are taking acetaminophen, even at therapeutic doses, and consume alcohol are at risk of developing hepatotoxicity.

Acetaminophen may increase the levels and enhance the anticoagulant effects of vitamin K antagonists acenocoumarol and warfarin (Coumadin). Studies have reported that acetaminophen has increased the INR in warfarin treated patients with daily acetaminophen doses as low as 2 g, particularly when taking acetaminophen for >1 week (Antlitz, 1968; Boeijinga, 1982; Gebauer, 2003; Hylek, 1998; Rubin, 1984). In addition, case reports of bleeding as a result of increased INR have been published (Bagheri, 1999; Bartle, 1991). There is no known mechanism of the interaction; furthermore, some studies have failed to demonstrate this interaction (Gadisseur, 2003; Kwan, 1995; van den Bemt, 2002). In terms of risk, the data suggest that acetaminophen and warfarin could interact in some clinically significant manner but that the benefits of concomitant use of acetaminophen for pain control in dental patients taking warfarin usually outweigh the risks. An appropriate monitoring plan should be in place to identify potential negative effects and dosage adjustments may be necessary in a minority of patients. The interaction may be more likely to occur with daily acetaminophen doses of >1.3 g for >1 week.

There are no reports of acetaminophen interacting with antiplatelet drugs such as aspirin, clopidogrel (Plavix), ticagrelor (Brilinta), or prasugrel (Effient). Also, there are no reports of acetaminophen in combination with hydrocodone, codeine, or oxycodone interacting with warfarin (Coumadin).

Acetaminophen and Diphenhydramine

(a seet a MIN oh fen & dye fen HYE dra moon)

Related Information

Acetaminophen *on page 56*

DiphenhydrAMINE (Systemic) *on page 517*

Brand Names: US Aceta-Gesic [OTC]; Acetadryl [OTC]; Excedrin PM [OTC]; Goody's PM [OTC] [DSC]; Legatrin PM [OTC]; Mapap PM [OTC]; Percogesic Extra Strength [OTC]; Tylenol PM Extra Strength [OTC]; Tylenol Severe Allergy [OTC] [DSC]

Pharmacologic Category Analgesic, Nonopioid

Use Aid in the relief of insomnia accompanied by minor pain

Local Anesthetic/Vasoconstrictor Precautions No information available to require special precautions

Effects on Dental Treatment Key adverse event(s) related to dental treatment: Xerostomia (normal salivary flow resumes upon discontinuation) (see Dental Comment).

Effects on Bleeding As a single agent, acetaminophen does not appear to affect bleeding or platelet aggregation. Acetaminophen may prolong the INR and increase bleeding in patients taking warfarin (Coumadin). For patients taking warfarin, single acetaminophen doses or acetaminophen therapy of short duration should be safe, but if large (>1.3 g/day) doses are administered for longer than 10-14 days, then the INR should be monitored (see Dental Comment).

Adverse Reactions See individual agents.

General Dosage Range Oral: *Children ≥12 years and Adults:* 50 mg of diphenhydramine HCl (76 mg diphenhydramine citrate) at bedtime

Dental Comment Although the ***OTC product labeling*** for acetaminophen products state to limit the maximum dose to 3,000 mg daily (for extra strength) or 3,250 mg (for regular strength) (see this site for details: http://www.tylenolprofessional.com/extra-strength-tylenol-dosage-faq.html), it is still appropriate for patients to take up to 4,000 mg daily "under the direction of a health care provider" (http://www.tylenolprofessional.com/assets/v4/faqs-new-dosing.pdf).

The acetaminophen component requires use with caution in patients who use alcohol, with preexisting liver disease, and those receiving more than one source of acetaminophen-containing medication.

Hepatotoxicity caused by acetaminophen is potentiated by chronic alcohol consumption. People who are taking acetaminophen, even at therapeutic doses, and consume alcohol are at risk of developing hepatotoxicity.

Acetaminophen may increase the levels and enhance the anticoagulant effects of vitamin K antagonists acenocoumarol and warfarin (Coumadin). Studies have reported that acetaminophen has increased the INR in warfarin-treated patients with daily acetaminophen doses as low as 2 g, particularly when taking acetaminophen for >1 week (Gebauer 2003; Hylek 1998). In addition, case reports of bleeding as a result of increased INR have been published (Bagheri 1999). There is no known mechanism of the interaction; furthermore, some studies have failed to demonstrate this interaction (Gadisseur 2003; Kwan 1995; van den Bemt 2002). In terms of risk, the data suggest that acetaminophen and warfarin could interact in some clinically significant manner but that the benefits of concomitant use of acetaminophen for pain control in dental patients taking warfarin usually outweigh the risks. An appropriate monitoring plan should be in place to identify potential negative effects and dosage adjustments may be necessary in a minority of patients. The interaction may be more likely to occur with daily acetaminophen doses of >1.3 g for >1 week. In a review of seven random controlled trials comparing acetaminophen versus placebo in warfarin-treated patients (Caldeira 2015), acetaminophen was associated with a mean 0.62 INR increase compared to placebo. Specifically, there was 0.17 mean increase of the INR per each daily gram of acetaminophen. Statistically, this was significant; however, the clinical relevance was questionable since the reviewed studies did not report any major bleeding event.

There are no reports of acetaminophen interacting with antiplatelet drugs such as aspirin, clopidogrel (Plavix), ticagrelor (Brilinta), or prasugrel (Effient). Also, there are no reports of acetaminophen in combination with hydrocodone, codeine, or oxycodone interacting with warfarin (Coumadin).

Acetaminophen and Tramadol

(a seet a MIN oh fen & TRA ma dole)

Related Information

Acetaminophen *on page 56*

Oral Pain *on page 1830*

TraMADol *on page 1586*

Related Sample Prescriptions

Oral Pain - Sample Prescriptions *on page 28*

Brand Names: US Ultracet

Brand Names: Canada ACT Tramadol/Acet; Apo-Tramadol/Acet; JAMP-ACET-Tramadol; Mar-Tramadol/Acet; Mint-Tramadol/Acet; PMS-Tramadol/Acet; Priva-Tramadol/Acet; RAN-Tramadol/Acet; TEVA-Tramadol/Acetaminophen; Tramacet

Generic Availability (US) Yes

Pharmacologic Category Analgesic Combination (Opioid); Analgesic, Opioid

Dental Use Treatment of postoperative pain (≤5 days)

Use

Pain management: Short-term (≤5 days) management of acute pain severe enough to require an opioid analgesic and for which alternative treatments are inadequate.

Limitations of use: Reserve tramadol/acetaminophen for use in patients for whom alternative treatment options (eg, nonopioid analgesics) are ineffective, not tolerated, or would be otherwise inadequate to provide sufficient management of pain.

Local Anesthetic/Vasoconstrictor Precautions No information available to require special precautions

Effects on Dental Treatment Key adverse event(s) related to dental treatment: Xerostomia and changes in salivation (normal salivary flow resumes upon discontinuation) (see Dental Comment).

Effects on Bleeding As a single agent, acetaminophen does not appear to affect bleeding or platelet aggregation. Acetaminophen may prolong the INR and increase bleeding in patients taking warfarin (Coumadin). For patients taking warfarin, single acetaminophen doses or acetaminophen therapy of short duration should be safe, but if large (>1.3 g/day) doses are administered for longer than 10-14 days, then the INR should be monitored (see Dental Comment).

Adverse Reactions Also see individual agents.

1% to 10%:

Central nervous system: Drowsiness (6%), dizziness (3%), insomnia (2%), anxiety, confusion, euphoria, fatigue, headache, nervousness

Dermatologic: Diaphoresis (4%), pruritus (2%), skin rash

Endocrine & metabolic: Hot flash

Gastrointestinal: Constipation (6%), anorexia (3%), diarrhea (3%), nausea (3%), xerostomia (2%), abdominal pain, dyspepsia, flatulence, vomiting

Genitourinary: Prostatic disease (2%)

Neuromuscular & skeletal: Tremor, weakness

<1%, postmarketing, and/or case reports: Abnormality in thinking, albuminuria, amnesia, anemia, ataxia, cardiac arrhythmia, changes in liver function, chest pain, convulsions, depersonalization, depression, drug abuse, dysphagia, dyspnea, emotional lability, exacerbation of migraine headache, exacerbation of hypertension, hallucination, hypertension, hypertonia, hypotension, impotence, melena, migraine, muscle spasm, nightmares, oliguria, palpitations, paresthesia, rigors, stupor, syncope, tachycardia, tinnitus, tongue edema, urinary retention, urination disorder, vertigo, visual disturbance, weight loss, withdrawal syndrome (with abrupt discontinuation; includes anxiety, diarrhea, hallucinations [rare], nausea, pain, piloerection, rigors, sweating, and tremor; uncommon discontinuation symptoms may include severe anxiety, panic attacks, or paresthesia)

Dental Usual Dosage Acute postoperative pain (≤5 days): Adults: Oral: Two tablets every 4-6 hours as needed for pain relief (maximum: 8 tablets/day); treatment should not exceed 5 days

Dosing

Adult Pain management: Oral: Acetaminophen 325 mg/tramadol 37.5 mg: Two tablets every 4 to 6 hours as needed for pain relief (maximum: 8 tablets/day [acetaminophen 2,600 mg/tramadol 300 mg per day]); do not exceed 5 days of therapy

Geriatric Refer to adult dosing. Use with caution.

Renal Impairment

CrCl ≥30 mL/minute: No dosage adjustment necessary.

CrCl <30 mL/minute: Maximum: Two tablets every 12 hours

Hepatic Impairment Use is not recommended (acetaminophen and tramadol undergo extensive hepatic metabolism).

Mechanism of Action

Acetaminophen: Inhibits the synthesis of prostaglandins in the central nervous system and peripherally blocks pain impulse generation; produces antipyresis from inhibition of hypothalamic heat-regulating center

Tramadol: Binds to μ-opiate receptors in the CNS causing inhibition of ascending pain pathways, altering the perception of and response to pain; also inhibits the reuptake of norepinephrine and serotonin, which also modifies the ascending pain pathway

Contraindications

Hypersensitivity to acetaminophen, tramadol, or any component of the formulation; significant respiratory depression; acute or severe bronchial asthma in an unmonitored setting or in the absence of resuscitative equipment; GI obstruction, including paralytic ileus (known or suspected); concomitant use with or within 14 days following MAO inhibitor therapy

Documentation of allergenic cross-reactivity for opioids is limited. However, because of similarities in chemical structure and/or pharmacologic actions, the possibility of cross-sensitivity cannot be ruled out with certainty.

Canadian labeling: Additional contraindications (not in US labeling): Known or suspected mechanical GI obstruction or any disease/condition that affects bowel transit; severe hepatic or renal dysfunction; acute asthma, other obstructive airway, and status asthmaticus; acute respiratory depression, hypercapnia, or cor pulmonale; acute alcoholism, delirium tremens, or seizure disorder; severe CNS depression, increased cerebrospinal or intracranial pressure, or head injury; during or within 14 days following MAO inhibitor therapy; breastfeeding; pregnancy; use during labor and delivery

Warnings/Precautions See individual agents.

Drug Interactions

Metabolism/Transport Effects Refer to individual components.

Avoid Concomitant Use

Avoid concomitant use of Acetaminophen and Tramadol with any of the following: Azelastine (Nasal); CarBAMazepine; Dapoxetine; Eluxadoline; Methylene Blue; Mixed Agonist / Antagonist Opioids; Moclobemide; Orphenadrine; Oxomemazine; Paraldehyde; Thalidomide

Increased Effect/Toxicity

Acetaminophen and Tramadol may increase the levels/effects of: Alvimopan; Azelastine (Nasal); Blonanserin; Busulfan; CarBAMazepine; Dasatinib; Desmopressin; Diuretics; Eluxadoline; Flunitrazepam; HYDROcodone; Imatinib; Iohexol; Iomeprol; Iopamidol; Methotrimeprazine; Metoclopramide; MetyroSINE; Mipomersen; Moclobemide; Orphenadrine; OxyCODONE; Paraldehyde; Phenylephrine (Systemic); Piribedil; Pramipexole; Prilocaine;

Ramosetron; ROPINIRole; Rotigotine; Serotonin Modulators; Sodium Nitrite; SORAfenib; Suvorexant; Thalidomide; Vitamin K Antagonists; Zolpidem

The levels/effects of Acetaminophen and Tramadol may be increased by: Amphetamines; Anticholinergic Agents; Anti-Parkinson Agents (Monoamine Oxidase Inhibitor); Brimonidine (Topical); Cannabis; Chlormethiazole; Chlorphenesin Carbamate; CNS Depressants; CYP2D6 Inhibitors (Strong); CYP3A4 Inhibitors (Strong); Dapoxetine; Dapsone (Topical); Dasatinib; Dimethindene (Topical); Dronabinol; Droperidol; Isoniazid; Kava Kava; Linezolid; Lofexidine; Magnesium Sulfate; Methotrimeprazine; Methylene Blue; Methylphenidate; MetyraPONE; Minocycline; Nabilone; Nitric Oxide; Oxomemazine; Perampanel; Probenecid; Ritonavir; Rufinamide; Serotonin Modulators; Sodium Oxybate; SORAfenib; Succinylcholine; Tapentadol; Tedizolid; Tetracaine (Topical); Tetrahydrocannabinol

Decreased Effect

Acetaminophen and Tramadol may decrease the levels/effects of: CarBAMazepine; Diuretics; Gastrointestinal Agents (Prokinetic); Pegvisomant

The levels/effects of Acetaminophen and Tramadol may be decreased by: Antiemetics (5HT3 Antagonists); Bosentan; CarBAMazepine; Cholestyramine Resin; CYP2D6 Inhibitors (Moderate); CYP2D6 Inhibitors (Strong); CYP3A4 Inducers (Moderate); CYP3A4 Inducers (Strong); Dabrafenib; Deferasirox; Enzalutamide; Mitotane; Mixed Agonist / Antagonist Opioids; Nalmefene; Naltrexone; Ritonavir; Siltuximab; St John's Wort; Tocilizumab

Food Interactions Food may delay time to peak plasma levels, however, the extent of absorption is not affected. Management: Administer without regard to meals.

Pregnancy Considerations Adverse events have been observed in some animal reproduction studies using this combination. Acetaminophen and tramadol cross the placenta. Use is not recommended for use prior to or during labor and delivery. **[US Boxed Warning]: Prolonged use of opioids during pregnancy can cause neonatal withdrawal syndrome, which may be life-threatening if not recognized and treated according to protocols developed by neonatology experts. If opioid use is required for a prolonged period in a pregnant woman, advise the patient of the risk of neonatal opioid withdrawal syndrome and ensure that appropriate treatment will be available.** Refer to individual monographs.

Breastfeeding Considerations Acetaminophen and tramadol can be detected in breast milk. The manufacturer does not recommend this combination for use as a preoperative medication or for postdelivery analgesia in nursing mothers. Refer to individual monographs.

Controlled Substance

C-IV

Dosage Forms

Tablet, Oral:

Ultracet: Acetaminophen 325 mg and tramadol 37.5 mg

Generic: Acetaminophen 325 mg and tramadol 37.5 mg

Dosage Forms: Canada

Tablet, Oral: Acetaminophen 325 mg and tramadol hydrochloride 37.5 mg

Tramacet: Acetaminophen 325 mg and tramadol hydrochloride 37.5 mg

Dental Comment Although the ***OTC product labeling*** for acetaminophen products state to limit the maximum dose to 3,000 mg daily (for extra strength) or 3,250 mg (for regular strength) (see this site for details: http://www.tylenolprofessional.com/extra-strength-tylenol-dosage-faq.html), it is still appropriate for patients to take up to 4,000 mg daily "under the direction of a healthcare provider" (http://www.tylenolprofessional.com/assets/v4/faqs-new-dosing.pdf).

The acetaminophen component requires use with caution in patients who use alcohol, with preexisting liver disease, and those receiving more than one source of acetaminophen-containing medication.

Hepatotoxicity caused by acetaminophen is potentiated by chronic alcohol consumption. People who are taking acetaminophen, even at therapeutic doses, and consume alcohol are at risk of developing hepatotoxicity.

Acetaminophen may increase the levels and enhance the anticoagulant effects of vitamin K antagonists acenocoumarol and warfarin (Coumadin®). Studies have reported that acetaminophen has increased the INR in warfarin treated patients with daily acetaminophen doses as low as 2 g, particularly when taking acetaminophen for >1 week (Antlitz, 1968; Boeijinga, 1982; Gebauer, 2003; Hylek, 1998; Rubin, 1984). In addition, case reports of bleeding as a result of increased INR have been published (Bagheri, 1999; Bartle, 1991). There is no known mechanism of the interaction; furthermore, some studies have failed to demonstrate this interaction (Gadisseur, 2003; Kwan, 1995; van den Bemt, 2002). In terms of risk, the data suggest that acetaminophen and warfarin could interact in some clinically significant manner but that the benefits of concomitant use of acetaminophen for pain control in dental patients taking warfarin usually outweigh the risks. An appropriate monitoring plan should be in place to identify potential negative effects and dosage adjustments may be necessary in a minority of patients. The interaction may be more likely to occur with daily acetaminophen doses of >1.3 g for >1 week.

There are no reports of acetaminophen interacting with antiplatelet drugs such as aspirin, clopidogrel (Plavix®), or prasugrel (Effient™). Also, there are no reports of acetaminophen in combination with hydrocodone, codeine, or oxycodone interacting with warfarin (Coumadin®).

Acetaminophen, Aspirin, and Caffeine

(a seet a MIN oh fen, AS pir in, & KAF een)

Related Information

Acetaminophen *on page 56*

Aspirin *on page 168*

Caffeine *on page 276*

Brand Names: US Anacin Advanced Headache Formula [OTC]; Excedrin Extra Strength [OTC]; Excedrin Migraine [OTC]; Fem-Prin [OTC]; Goody's Extra Strength Headache Powder [OTC]; Goody's Extra Strength Pain Relief [OTC] [DSC]; Pain-Off [OTC]; Vanquish Extra Strength Pain Reliever [OTC]

Pharmacologic Category Analgesic, Nonopioid

Use

Migraine: Relief of migraine headache

Pain: Relief of minor aches and pain

Local Anesthetic/Vasoconstrictor Precautions No information available to require special precautions

Effects on Dental Treatment Key adverse event(s) related to dental treatment: As with all drugs which may affect hemostasis, bleeding is associated with aspirin. Hemorrhage may occur at virtually any site; risk is dependent on multiple variables including dosage, concurrent use of multiple agents which alter hemostasis, and patient susceptibility. Many adverse effects of aspirin are dose related, and are rare at low dosages. Other serious reactions are idiosyncratic, related to allergy or individual sensitivity (see Dental Comment).

Aspirin as sole antiplatelet agent: Patients taking aspirin for ischemic stroke prevention are safe to continue it during dental procedures (Armstrong, 2013).

Concurrent aspirin use with other antiplatelet agents: Aspirin in combination with clopidogrel (Plavix®), prasugrel (Effient®), or ticagrelor (Brilinta™) is the primary prevention strategy against stent thrombosis after placement of drug-eluting metal stents in coronary patients. Premature discontinuation of combination antiplatelet therapy (ie, dual antiplatelet therapy) strongly increases the risk of a catastrophic event of stent thrombosis leading to myocardial infarction and/or death, so says a science advisory issued in January 2007 from the American Heart Association in collaboration with the American Dental Association and other professional healthcare organizations. The advisory stresses a 12-month therapy of dual antiplatelet therapy after placement of a drug-eluting stent in order to prevent thrombosis at the stent site. Any elective surgery should be postponed for 1 year after stent implantation, and if surgery must be performed, consideration should be given to continuing the antiplatelet therapy during the perioperative period in high-risk patients with drug-eluting stents.

This advisory was issued from a science panel made up of representatives from the American Heart Association (AHA), the American College of Cardiology, the Society for Cardiovascular Angiography and Interventions, the American College of Surgeons, the American Dental Association (ADA), and the American College of Physicians (Grines, 2007).

Effects on Bleeding As a single agent, acetaminophen does not appear to affect bleeding or platelet aggregation. Acetaminophen may prolong the INR and increase bleeding in patients taking warfarin (Coumadin). For patients taking warfarin, single acetaminophen doses or acetaminophen therapy of short duration should be safe, but if large (>1.3 g/day) doses are administered for longer than 10-14 days, then the INR should be monitored (see Dental Comment).

Aspirin irreversibly inhibits platelet aggregation which can prolong bleeding. Upon discontinuation, normal platelet function returns only when new platelets are released (~7-10 days). However, in the case of dental surgery, there is no scientific evidence to support discontinuation of aspirin. This was recently supported by the American Academy of Neurology in patients with ischemic cerebrovascular disease (Armstrong, 2013). A recent study compared blood loss after a single tooth extraction in coronary artery disease patients who were either on aspirin (100 mg daily) or off aspirin for the extraction. The mean volume of bleeding was not statistically different between the groups. Local hemostatic measures were sufficient to control bleeding and there were no reported episodes of hemorrhaging intra- or postoperatively (Medeiros, 2011).

Adverse Reactions See individual agents.

General Dosage Range

Oral:

Children >12 years, Adolescents, and Adults: Minor aches and pains: 1 to 2 tablets every 6 hours as needed (maximum: 8 tablets per 24 hours) or contents of 1 powder packet every 6 hours as needed (maximum: 4 powder packets per 24 hours)

Adults: Migraine headache: Two tablets once every 24 hours (maximum: 2 tablets per 24 hours)

Pregnancy Considerations See individual agents.

Dental Comment Although the ***OTC product labeling*** for acetaminophen products state to limit the maximum dose to 3,000 mg daily (for extra strength) or 3,250 mg (for regular strength) (see this site for details: http://www.tylenolprofessional.com/extra-strength-tylenol-dosage-faq.html), it is still appropriate for patients to take up to 4,000 mg daily "under the direction of a health care provider" (http://www.tylenolprofessional.com/assets/v4/faqs-new-dosing.pdf).

The acetaminophen component requires use with caution in patients who use alcohol, with preexisting liver disease, and those receiving more than one source of acetaminophen-containing medication.

Hepatotoxicity caused by acetaminophen is potentiated by chronic alcohol consumption. People who are taking acetaminophen, even at therapeutic doses, and consume alcohol are at risk of developing hepatotoxicity.

Acetaminophen may increase the levels and enhance the anticoagulant effects of vitamin K antagonists acenocoumarol and warfarin (Coumadin). Studies have reported that acetaminophen has increased the INR in warfarin-treated patients with daily acetaminophen doses as low as 2 g, particularly when taking acetaminophen for >1 week (Gebauer 2003; Hylek 1998). In addition, case reports of bleeding as a result of increased INR have been published (Bagheri 1999). There is no known mechanism of the interaction; furthermore, some studies have failed to demonstrate this interaction (Gadisseur 2003; Kwan 1995; van den Bemt 2002). In terms of risk, the data suggest that acetaminophen and warfarin could interact in some clinically significant manner but that the benefits of concomitant use of acetaminophen for pain control in dental patients taking warfarin usually outweigh the risks. An appropriate monitoring plan should be in place to identify potential negative effects and dosage adjustments may be necessary in a minority of patients. The interaction may be more likely to occur with daily acetaminophen doses of >1.3 g for >1 week. In a review of seven random controlled trials comparing acetaminophen versus placebo in warfarin-treated patients (Caldeira 2015), acetaminophen was associated with a mean 0.62 INR increase compared to placebo. Specifically, there was 0.17 mean increase of the INR per each daily gram of acetaminophen. Statistically, this was significant; however, the clinical relevance was questionable since the reviewed studies did not report any major bleeding event.

There are no reports of acetaminophen interacting with antiplatelet drugs such as aspirin, clopidogrel (Plavix), ticagrelor (Brilinta), or prasugrel (Effient). Also, there are no reports of acetaminophen in combination with hydrocodone, codeine, or oxycodone interacting with warfarin (Coumadin).

Acetaminophen, Caffeine, and Isometheptene Mucate

(a seet a MIN oh fen, KAF een, & eye soe meth EP teen MUE kate)

Related Information

Acetaminophen *on page 56*

Caffeine *on page 276*

Brand Names: US Prodrin

Pharmacologic Category Antimigraine Agent

Use Headache: Relief of tension headache and vascular headache (possibly effective for relief of migraine headache)

Local Anesthetic/Vasoconstrictor Precautions No information available to require special precautions

Effects on Dental Treatment No significant effects or complications reported (see Dental Comment)

Effects on Bleeding As a single agent, acetaminophen does not appear to affect bleeding or platelet aggregation. Acetaminophen may prolong the INR and increase bleeding in patients taking warfarin (Coumadin). For patients taking warfarin, single acetaminophen doses or acetaminophen therapy of short duration should be safe, but if large (>1.3 g/day) doses are administered for longer than 10-14 days, then the INR should be monitored (see Dental Comment).

Adverse Reactions See individual agents.

General Dosage Range Oral: *Adults:* Initial: 1 or 2 caplets followed by 1 caplet every hour until relief is obtained; maximum 5 caplets in 12 hours **or** 1or 2 caplets every 4 hours; maximum 8 caplets in 24 hours

Mechanism of Action

Acetaminophen: Nonopioid analgesic which reduces the perception of pain impulses originating from dilated cerebral vessels.

Caffeine: A cranial vasoconstrictor to enhance the vasoconstrictor effect. It is also used as a central stimulant for relief of headache.

Isometheptene mucate: Sympathomimetic amine which acts by constricting dilated cranial and cerebral arterioles, thus reducing the stimuli that lead to vascular headaches.

Pregnancy Considerations Refer to the Acetaminophen and Caffeine monographs for information.

Dental Comment Although the ***OTC product labeling*** for acetaminophen products state to limit the maximum dose to 3,000 mg daily (for extra strength) or 3,250 mg (for regular strength) (see this site for details: http://www.tylenolprofessional.com/extra-strength-tylenol-dosage-faq.html), it is still appropriate for patients to take up to 4,000 mg daily "under the direction of a health care provider" (http://www.tylenolprofessional.com/assets/v4/faqs-new-dosing.pdf).

The acetaminophen component requires use with caution in patients who use alcohol, with preexisting liver disease, and those receiving more than one source of acetaminophen-containing medication.

Hepatotoxicity caused by acetaminophen is potentiated by chronic alcohol consumption. People who are taking acetaminophen, even at therapeutic doses, and consume alcohol are at risk of developing hepatotoxicity.

Acetaminophen may increase the levels and enhance the anticoagulant effects of vitamin K antagonists acenocoumarol and warfarin (Coumadin). Studies have reported that acetaminophen has increased the INR in warfarin-treated patients with daily acetaminophen doses as low as 2 g, particularly when taking acetaminophen for >1 week (Gebauer 2003; Hylek 1998). In addition, case reports of bleeding as a result of increased INR have been published (Bagheri 1999). There is no known mechanism of the interaction; furthermore, some studies have failed to demonstrate this interaction (Gadisseur 2003; Kwan 1995; van den Bemt 2002). In terms of risk, the data suggest that acetaminophen and warfarin could interact in some clinically significant manner but that the benefits of concomitant use of acetaminophen for pain control in dental patients taking warfarin usually outweigh the risks. An appropriate monitoring plan should be in place to identify potential negative effects and dosage adjustments may be necessary in a minority of patients. The interaction may be more likely to occur with daily acetaminophen doses of >1.3 g for >1 week. In a review of seven random controlled trials comparing acetaminophen versus placebo in warfarin-treated patients (Caldeira 2015), acetaminophen was associated with a mean 0.62 INR increase compared to placebo. Specifically, there was 0.17 mean increase of the INR per each daily gram of acetaminophen. Statistically, this was significant; however, the clinical relevance was questionable since the reviewed studies did not report any major bleeding event.

There are no reports of acetaminophen interacting with antiplatelet drugs such as aspirin, clopidogrel (Plavix), ticagrelor (Brilinta), or prasugrel (Effient). Also, there are no reports of acetaminophen in combination with hydrocodone, codeine, or oxycodone interacting with warfarin (Coumadin).

Acetaminophen, Isometheptene, and Dichloralphenazone

(a seet a MIN oh fen, eye soe me THEP teen, & dye KLOR al FEN a zone)

Related Information

Acetaminophen *on page 56*

Brand Names: US Migragesic IDA [DSC]; Nodolor

Pharmacologic Category Analgesic, Nonopioid; Sedative; Sympathomimetic

Use Headache: Relief of tension headache and vascular headache (potentially effective for relief of migraine headache).

Local Anesthetic/Vasoconstrictor Precautions No information available to require special precautions

Effects on Dental Treatment No significant effects or complications reported (see Dental Comment)

Effects on Bleeding As a single agent, acetaminophen does not appear to affect bleeding or platelet aggregation. Acetaminophen may prolong the INR and increase bleeding in patients taking warfarin (Coumadin). For patients taking warfarin, single acetaminophen doses or acetaminophen therapy of short duration should be safe, but if large (>1.3 g/day) doses are administered for longer than 10-14 days, then the INR should be monitored (see Dental Comment).

Adverse Reactions Frequency not defined.

Central nervous system: Dizziness (transient)

Dermatologic: Skin rash

General Dosage Range Oral: *Adults:* 2 capsules initially, then 1 capsule every hour until relief; alternatively, 1-2 capsules every 4 hours (maximum: 5 capsules/12 hours or 8 capsules/day)

Mechanism of Action

Acetaminophen: Although not fully elucidated, believed to inhibit the synthesis of prostaglandins in the central nervous system and work peripherally to block pain impulse generation; produces antipyresis from inhibition of hypothalamic health-regulating center

Dichloralphenazone: Prodrug, converted to chloral hydrate (sedative) and antipyrine (analgesic/antipyretic) that reduces patient's emotional response to painful stimuli

Isometheptene: A sympathomimetic that reduces stimuli leading to vascular headaches via constriction of dilated cranial and cerebral arterioles

Controlled Substance C-IV

Dental Comment Although the ***OTC product labeling*** for acetaminophen products state to limit the maximum dose to 3,000 mg daily (for extra strength) or 3,250 mg (for regular strength) (see this site for details: http://www.tylenolprofessional.com/extra-strength-tylenol-dosage-faq.html), it is still appropriate for patients to take up to 4,000 mg daily "under the direction of a health care provider" (http://www.tylenolprofessional.com/assets/v4/faqs-new-dosing.pdf).

The acetaminophen component requires use with caution in patients who use alcohol, with preexisting liver disease, and those receiving more than one source of acetaminophen-containing medication.

Hepatotoxicity caused by acetaminophen is potentiated by chronic alcohol consumption. People who are taking acetaminophen, even at therapeutic doses, and consume alcohol are at risk of developing hepatotoxicity.

Acetaminophen may increase the levels and enhance the anticoagulant effects of vitamin K antagonists acenocoumarol and warfarin (Coumadin). Studies have reported that acetaminophen has increased the INR in warfarin-treated patients with daily acetaminophen doses as low as 2 g, particularly when taking acetaminophen for >1 week (Gebauer 2003; Hylek 1998). In addition, case reports of bleeding as a result of increased INR have been published (Bagheri 1999). There is no known mechanism of the interaction; furthermore, some studies have failed to demonstrate this interaction (Gadisseur 2003; Kwan 1995; van den Bemt 2002). In terms of risk, the data suggest that acetaminophen and warfarin could interact in some clinically significant manner but that the benefits of concomitant use of acetaminophen for pain control in dental patients taking warfarin usually outweigh the risks. An appropriate monitoring plan should be in place to identify potential negative effects and dosage adjustments may be necessary in a minority of patients. The interaction may be more likely to occur with daily acetaminophen doses of >1.3 g for >1 week. In a review of seven random controlled trials comparing acetaminophen versus placebo in warfarin-treated patients (Caldeira 2015), acetaminophen was associated with a mean 0.62 INR increase compared to placebo. Specifically, there was 0.17 mean increase of the INR per each daily gram of acetaminophen. Statistically, this was significant; however, the clinical relevance was questionable since the reviewed studies did not report any major bleeding event.

There are no reports of acetaminophen interacting with antiplatelet drugs such as aspirin, clopidogrel (Plavix), ticagrelor (Brilinta), or prasugrel (Effient). Also, there are no reports of acetaminophen in combination with hydrocodone, codeine, or oxycodone interacting with warfarin (Coumadin).

AcetaZOLAMIDE (a set a ZOLE a mide)

Brand Names: US Diamox Sequels

Brand Names: Canada Acetazolam; Diamox

Pharmacologic Category Anticonvulsant, Miscellaneous; Carbonic Anhydrase Inhibitor; Diuretic, Carbonic Anhydrase Inhibitor; Ophthalmic Agent, Antiglaucoma

Use Treatment of glaucoma (chronic simple open-angle, secondary glaucoma, preoperatively in acute angle-closure); drug-induced edema or edema due to congestive heart failure (adjunctive therapy; IV and immediate release dosage forms); centrencephalic epilepsies (IV and immediate release dosage forms); prevention or amelioration of symptoms associated with acute mountain sickness (immediate and extended release dosage forms)

Local Anesthetic/Vasoconstrictor Precautions No information available to require special precautions

Effects on Dental Treatment Key adverse event(s) related to dental treatment: Metallic taste (resolves upon discontinuation)

Effects on Bleeding No information available to require special precautions

Adverse Reactions Frequency not defined.

Cardiovascular: Flushing

Central nervous system: Ataxia, confusion, convulsions, depression, dizziness, drowsiness, excitement, fatigue, flaccid paralysis, headache, malaise, paresthesia

Dermatologic: Allergic skin reaction, skin photosensitivity, Stevens-Johnson syndrome, toxic epidermal necrolysis, urticaria

Endocrine & metabolic: Electrolyte imbalance, growth retardation (children), hyperglycemia, hypoglycemia, hypokalemia, hyponatremia, metabolic acidosis

Gastrointestinal: Decreased appetite, diarrhea, dysgeusia, glycosuria, melena, nausea, vomiting

Genitourinary: Crystalluria, hematuria

Hematologic and oncologic: Agranulocytosis, aplastic anemia, leukopenia, thrombocytopenia, thrombocytopenic purpura

Hepatic: Abnormal hepatic function tests, cholestatic jaundice, fulminant hepatic necrosis, hepatic insufficiency

Hypersensitivity: Anaphylaxis

Local: Pain at injection site

Ophthalmic: Myopia

Otic: Auditory disturbance, tinnitus

Renal: Polyuria, renal failure

Miscellaneous: Fever

General Dosage Range Dosage adjustment recommended in patients with renal impairment

IV: *Adults:* 250-1000 mg/day

Oral:

Immediate release:

Children: 8-30 mg/kg/day divided in 1-4 doses (maximum: 30 mg/kg/day or 1 g/day)

Adults: 250-1000 mg/day **or** 8-30 mg/kg/day in 1-4 divided doses (maximum: 30 mg/kg/day or 1 g/day) **or** 125-250 mg every 4 hours

Elderly: Initial: 250-500 mg/day

Extended release:

Adults: 500-1000 mg/day

Mechanism of Action Reversible inhibition of the enzyme carbonic anhydrase resulting in reduction of hydrogen ion secretion at renal tubule and an increased renal excretion of sodium, potassium, bicarbonate, and water. Decreases production of aqueous humor and inhibits carbonic anhydrase in central nervous system to retard abnormal and excessive discharge from CNS neurons.

Pharmacodynamics/Kinetics

Onset of Action

Capsule (extended release): 2 hours; Tablet (immediate release): 1 to 1.5 hours; IV: 2 to 10 minutes

Peak effect: Capsule (extended release): 8 to 18 hours; IV: 15 minutes; Tablet: 2 to 4 hours

Duration of Action Inhibition of aqueous humor secretion: Capsule (extended release): 18 to 24 hours; IV: 4 to 5 hours; Tablet: 8 to 12 hours

Half-life Elimination 2.4 to 5.8 hours

Time to Peak Plasma: Capsule (extended release): 3 to 6 hours; Tablet: 1 to 4 hours; IV: 15 minutes

Pregnancy Risk Factor C

Pregnancy Considerations Adverse events have been observed in animal reproduction studies. Limited data is available following the use of acetazolamide in pregnant women for the treatment of idiopathic intracranial hypertension (Falardeau, 2013; Kesler, 2013).

Pregnant women exposed to acetazolamide during pregnancy for the treatment of seizure disorders are encouraged to enroll themselves into the AED Pregnancy Registry by calling 1-888-233-2334. Additional information is available at aedpregnancyregistry.org

Acetohydroxamic Acid
(a SEE toe hye droks am ik AS id)

Brand Names: US Lithostat

Brand Names: Canada Lithostat

Pharmacologic Category Urinary Tract Product

Use Chronic urea-splitting urinary infection: Adjunctive therapy in chronic urea-splitting urinary infection

Local Anesthetic/Vasoconstrictor Precautions No information available to require special precautions

Effects on Dental Treatment No significant effects or complications reported

Effects on Bleeding Has been associated with bone marrow suppression and hemolytic anemia. No information to require specific precautions related to dental procedures.

Adverse Reactions

Frequency not always defined.

>10%:

Central nervous system: Headache (30%), malaise (20% to 25%), anxiety (20%), depression (20%), nervousness (20%)

Gastrointestinal: Anorexia (20% to 25%), nausea (20% to 25%), vomiting (20% to 25%)

Hematologic & oncologic: Hemolytic anemia (3% to 15%)

Neuromuscular & skeletal: Tremor (20%)

1% to 10%:

Cardiovascular: Deep vein thrombosis (rare), embolism, flushing, palpitations, phlebitis

Dermatologic: Alopecia, macular eruption

Hematologic & oncologic: Reticulocytosis (5% to 6%)

General Dosage Range Dosage adjustment recommended in patients with renal impairment.

Oral:

Children and Adolescents: Initial: 10 mg/kg/day in 2 or 3 divided doses

Adults: 250 mg 3 to 4 times daily maximum: 1500 mg daily)

Mechanism of Action Acetohydroxamic acid inhibits bacterial urease enzymes, decreasing the formation of ammonia in the urine by urea-splitting organisms. A reduction in urinary ammonia and decreased pH may increase the activity of some antimicrobial agents.

Pharmacodynamics/Kinetics

Half-life Elimination 5-10 hours (increased in patients with reduced renal function)

Time to Peak 0.25-1 hour

Pregnancy Risk Factor X

Pregnancy Considerations Adverse effects were observed in animal reproduction studies. Use is contraindicated in pregnant women or women of childbearing potential who are not using a reliable form of contraception.

Acetylcholine (a se teel KOE leen)

Brand Names: US Miochol-E

Brand Names: Canada Miochol®-E

Pharmacologic Category Cholinergic Agonist; Ophthalmic Agent, Miotic

Use Produces complete miosis in cataract surgery, keratoplasty, iridectomy, and other anterior segment surgery where rapid miosis is required

Local Anesthetic/Vasoconstrictor Precautions No information available to require special precautions

Effects on Dental Treatment No significant effects or complications reported

Effects on Bleeding No information available to require special precautions

Adverse Reactions Frequency not defined.

Cardiovascular: Bradycardia, flushing, hypotension

Dermatologic: Diaphoresis

Ophthalmic: Cloudy vision, corneal decompensation, corneal edema

Respiratory: Dyspnea

General Dosage Range Intraocular: *Adults:* Instill 0.5-2 mL of 1% injection (5-20 mg)

Mechanism of Action Causes contraction of the sphincter muscles of the iris, resulting in miosis and contraction of the ciliary muscle, leading to accommodation spasm

Pharmacodynamics/Kinetics

Onset of Action Rapid

Duration of Action ~20 minutes (Kanski 1968); duration as long as 6 hours has been reported (Roszkowska 1998)

Acetylcysteine (a se teel SIS teen)

Brand Names: US Acetadote; Cetylev

Brand Names: Canada Acetylcysteine Injection; Acetylcysteine Solution; Mucomyst; Parvolex

Pharmacologic Category Antidote; Mucolytic Agent

Use

Acetaminophen overdose: To prevent or lessen hepatic injury after ingestion of a potentially hepatotoxic quantity of acetaminophen in patients with acute ingestion or from repeated supratherapeutic ingestion (RSTI).

Mucolytic: Adjunct therapy in patients with abnormal, viscid, or inspissated mucous secretions in conditions such as: chronic bronchopulmonary disease (chronic emphysema, emphysema with bronchitis, chronic asthmatic bronchitis, tuberculosis, bronchiectasis, primary amyloidosis of the lung); acute bronchopulmonary disease (pneumonia, bronchitis, tracheobronchitis); pulmonary complications of cystic fibrosis; tracheostomy care; pulmonary complications associated with surgery; use during anesthesia; post-traumatic chest conditions; atelectasis due to mucous obstruction; diagnostic bronchial studies (bronchograms, bronchospirometry, bronchial wedge catheterization).

Local Anesthetic/Vasoconstrictor Precautions No information available to require special precautions

Effects on Dental Treatment Key adverse event(s) related to dental treatment: Stomatitis, bronchospasm, rhinorrhea

Effects on Bleeding No information available to require special precautions

Adverse Reactions

Intravenous:

>10%:

Immunologic: Autoimmune disease (14% to 18%)

Miscellaneous: Anaphylactoid reaction (1% to 18%)

1% to 10%:

Cardiovascular: Flushing (1% to 3%), tachycardia (1% to 4%), edema (1% to 2%)

Dermatologic: Urticaria (≤21%), rash (2% to ≤21%), pruritus (1% to ≤21%)

Gastrointestinal: Vomiting (2% to 10%), nausea (1% to 6%)

Respiratory: Pharyngitis (≤1%), rhinorrhea (≤1%), rhonchi (≤1%), throat tightness (≤1%)

<1%, postmarketing, and/or case reports (limited to important or life-threatening): Anaphylaxis, angioedema, bronchospasm, chest tightness, cough, dizziness (Sandilands 2008), dyspnea (Sandilands 2008), hypotension, respiratory distress, stridor, wheezing

Oral: Frequency not defined.

Cardiovascular: Chest tightness, hypotension (Bebarta 2010; Sandilands 2008)

Dermatologic: Rash (with or without fever), urticaria

Gastrointestinal: Gastrointestinal symptoms, nausea, vomiting

Hypersensitivity: Hypersensitivity reaction

Respiratory: Bronchospasm, bronchitis

<1%, postmarketing, and/or case reports (limited to important or life-threatening): Angioedema (Bebarta 2010), pruritus (Bebarta 2010), tachycardia (Bebarta 2010)

General Dosage Range

Inhalation:

Nebulization:

Infants: 1 to 2 mL of 20% solution or 2 to 4 mL 10% solution 3 to 4 times/day

Children and Adults: 1 to 10 mL of 20% solution or 2 to 20 mL of 10% solution every 2 to 6 hours

Direct instillation: *Adults:* 1 to 4 mL of 10% or 1 to 2 mL of 20% solution every 1 to 4 hours

IV: Acetadote:

Infants, Children, Adolescents, and Adults: 21-hour regimen: Consists of 3 doses; total dose delivered: 300 mg/kg

Loading dose: 150 mg/kg (maximum: 15 g) infused over 1 hour

Second dose: 50 mg/kg (maximum: 5 g) infused over 4 hours

Third dose: 100 mg/kg (maximum: 10 g) infused over 16 hours

Oral:

Children and Adults: Acetaminophen overdose: 72-hour regimen: Consists of 18 doses; total dose delivered: 1,330 mg/kg

Loading dose: 140 mg/kg

Maintenance dose: 70 mg/kg every 4 hours

Mechanism of Action

Acetaminophen overdose: Acetylcysteine acts as a hepatoprotective agent by restoring hepatic glutathione, serving as a glutathione substitute, and enhancing the nontoxic sulfate conjugation of acetaminophen.

Mucolytic: Exerts mucolytic action through its free sulfhydryl group which opens up the disulfide bonds in the mucoproteins thus lowering mucous viscosity.

Prevention of contrast-induced nephropathy (off-label use): The presumed mechanism in preventing contrast-induced nephropathy is its ability to scavenge oxygen-derived free radicals and improve endothelium-dependent vasodilation.

Pharmacodynamics/Kinetics

Onset of Action Inhalation: 5 to 10 minutes

Duration of Action Inhalation: >1 hour

Half-life Elimination

Reduced acetylcysteine: 2 hours; Total acetylcysteine: Adults: 5.6 hours, Newborns: 11 hours

Effervescent tablets: Terminal half-life: 18.1 hours

Time to Peak Plasma: Oral solution: 1 to 2 hours; Effervescent tablets: 1 to 3.5 hours (median: 2 hours)

Pregnancy Considerations

Adverse events have not been observed in animal reproduction studies. Based on limited reports using acetylcysteine to treat acetaminophen overdose in pregnant women, acetylcysteine has been shown to cross the placenta and may provide protective concentrations in the fetus.

Acetylcysteine may be used to treat acetaminophen overdose in during pregnancy (Wilkes 2005). In general, medications used as antidotes should take into consideration the health and prognosis of the mother; antidotes should be administered to pregnant women if there is a clear indication for use and should not be withheld because of fears of teratogenicity (Bailey 2003).

Aclidinium (a kli DIN ee um)

Related Information

Respiratory Diseases *on page 1777*

Brand Names: US Tudorza Pressair

Brand Names: Canada Tudorza Genuair

Pharmacologic Category Anticholinergic Agent; Anticholinergic Agent, Long-Acting

Use Chronic obstructive pulmonary disease: Long-term maintenance treatment of bronchospasm associated with chronic obstructive pulmonary disease (COPD) including bronchitis and emphysema

Local Anesthetic/Vasoconstrictor Precautions No information available to require special precautions

Effects on Dental Treatment Key adverse event(s) related to dental treatment: Cough, nasopharyngitis, rhinitis, sinusitis, and toothache have been reported.

Effects on Bleeding No information available to require special precautions

Adverse Reactions

1% to 10%:

Central nervous system: Headache (7%), falling (1%)

Gastrointestinal: Diarrhea (3%), toothache (1%), vomiting (1%)

Respiratory: Nasopharyngitis (6%), cough (3%), rhinitis (2%), sinusitis (2%)

<1%, postmarketing, and/or case reports: Anaphylaxis, angioedema (including swelling of the lips, tongue, or throat), bronchospasm, cardiac failure, cardiopulmonary arrest, diabetes mellitus, dizziness, dyspnea, dysuria, first degree atrioventricular block, hypersensitivity reaction (immediate), nausea, osteoarthritis, palpitations, pruritus, skin rash, tachycardia, urinary retention, urticaria, xerostomia

General Dosage Range Inhalation, oral: *Adults:* 400 mcg twice daily

Mechanism of Action Competitively and reversibly inhibits the action of acetylcholine at type 3 muscarinic (M_3) receptors in bronchial smooth muscle causing bronchodilation

Pharmacodynamics/Kinetics

Half-life Elimination 5-8 hours (following inhalation)

Time to Peak Plasma: Within 10 minutes (steady state, following inhalation)

Pregnancy Risk Factor C

Pregnancy Considerations Adverse events have been observed in animal reproduction studies.

Acyclovir (Systemic) (ay SYE kloe veer)

Related Information

Systemic Viral Diseases *on page 1806*

ValACYclovir *on page 1622*

Viral Infections *on page 1849*

Related Sample Prescriptions

Viral Infections - Sample Prescriptions *on page 40*

Brand Names: US Zovirax

Brand Names: Canada Acyclovir Sodium Injection; Apo-Acyclovir; Mylan-Acyclovir; ratio-Acyclovir; Teva-Acyclovir; Zovirax

Generic Availability (US) Yes

Pharmacologic Category Antiviral Agent

Dental Use Treatment of initial and prophylaxis of recurrent mucosal and cutaneous herpes simplex (HSV-1 and HSV-2) infections in immunocompromised patients

Use

Oral:

Herpes zoster (shingles): Acute treatment of herpes zoster (shingles).

Herpes simplex virus (HSV), genital: Treatment of initial episodes and the management of recurrent episodes of genital herpes.

Varicella (chickenpox): Treatment of varicella (chickenpox).

Injection:

Herpes simplex virus (HSV), mucocutaneous infection in immunocompromised patients: Treatment of initial and recurrent mucosal and cutaneous herpes simplex (HSV-1 and HSV-2) in immunocompromised patients.

Herpes simplex virus (HSV), genital infection (severe): Treatment of severe initial clinical episodes of genital herpes in immunocompetent patients.

Herpes simplex encephalitis: Treatment of herpes simplex encephalitis.

Herpes simplex virus (HSV), neonatal: Treatment of neonatal herpes infections.

Herpes zoster (shingles) in immunocompromised patients: Treatment of herpes zoster (shingles) in immunocompromised patients.

Local Anesthetic/Vasoconstrictor Precautions No information available to require special precautions

Effects on Dental Treatment No significant effects or complications reported (see Dental Comment)

Effects on Bleeding No information available to require special precautions

Adverse Reactions

Oral:

>10%: Central nervous system: Malaise (≤12%)

1% to 10%:

Central nervous system: Headache (≤2%)

Gastrointestinal: Nausea (2% to 5%), vomiting (≤3%), diarrhea (2% to 3%)

Parenteral:

1% to 10%:

Dermatologic: Hives (2%), itching (2%), rash (2%)

Gastrointestinal: Nausea/vomiting (7%)

Hepatic: Liver function tests increased (1% to 2%)

Local: Inflammation at injection site or phlebitis (9%)

Renal: BUN increased (5% to 10%), creatinine increased (5% to 10%), acute renal failure

All forms: <1%, postmarketing, and/or case reports: Abdominal pain, aggression, agitation, anemia, anorexia, ataxia, coma, confusion, consciousness decreased, delirium, desquamation, disseminated intravascular coagulopathy (DIC), dizziness, dysarthria, encephalopathy, fatigue, fever, gastrointestinal distress, hallucinations, hematuria, hemolysis, hepatitis, hyperbilirubinemia, hypotension, insomnia, jaundice, leukocytoclastic vasculitis, leukocytosis, leukopenia, lymphadenopathy, mental depression, myalgia, neutrophilia, pain, psychosis, renal failure, renal pain, seizure, somnolence, sore throat, thrombocytopenia, thrombocytopenic purpura/hemolytic uremic syndrome (TTP/HUS), thrombocytosis, visual disturbances

Dental Usual Dosage

Mucocutaneous HSV: Adults:

Immunocompromised (off-label use): Oral: 400 mg 5 times a day for 7-14 days

Chronic suppression of recurrent herpes labialis (cold sores) (off-label use): Immunocompetent adults: oral: 400 mg twice daily (Rooney 1993)

Dosing

Adult & Geriatric

Bell's palsy (off-label use; alternate therapy): Oral: 2,000 mg/day in divided doses for 10 days in combination with corticosteroids (Gronseth 2012)

Herpes simplex virus (HSV), genital infection:

Immunocompetent:

IV: Initial episode, severe:

Manufacturer's labeling: 5 mg/kg/dose every 8 hours for 5 to 7 days

Alternate recommendation: 5 to 10 mg/kg/dose every 8 hours for 2 to 7 days, follow with oral therapy to complete at least 10 days of therapy (CDC [Workowski 2015])

Oral:

Initial episode:

Manufacturer's labeling: 200 mg 5 times daily while awake for 10 days

Alternate recommendation: 200 mg 5 times daily for 7 to 10 days **or** 400 mg 3 times daily for 7 to 10 days (CDC [Workowski 2015])

Recurrence: **Note:** Begin at earliest signs of disease

Manufacturer's labeling: 200 mg 5 times daily while awake for 5 days

Alternate recommendation: 400 mg 3 times daily for 5 days **or** 800 mg twice daily for 5 days **or** 800 mg 3 times daily for 2 days (CDC [Workowski 2015])

Chronic suppression: 400 mg twice daily for up to 12 months (followed by re-evaluation); **Note:** Safety and efficacy have been documented in patients receiving daily therapy with acyclovir for up to 6 years (CDC [Workowski 2015])

HIV-infected patients (off-label use):

Initial or recurrent episodes: 400 mg 3 times daily for 5 to 14 days (HHS [OI adult 2015]) **or** 400 mg

3 times daily for 5 to 10 days (CDC [Workowski 2015])

Chronic suppressive therapy: 400 mg twice daily; continue indefinitely regardless of CD4 count in patients with severe recurrences of genital herpes or in patients who want to minimize frequency of recurrences (HHS [OI adult 2015]) **or** 400 to 800 mg 2 to 3 times daily (CDC [Workowski 2015])

HSV encephalitis: IV: Independent of HIV status:

Manufacturer's labeling: 10 mg/kg/dose every 8 hours for 10 days

Alternate recommendation: 10 mg/kg/dose every 8 hours for 14 to 21 days (*Red Book* [AAP 2012])

HSV, mucocutaneous treatment:

Immunocompromised:

IV:

Manufacturer's labeling: 5 mg/kg/dose every 8 hours for 7 days

Alternate recommendations: 5 to 10 mg/kg/dose every 8 hours for 7 days (Leflore 2000)

Oral (off-label use): 400 mg 5 times daily for 7 days (Leflore 2000)

HIV-infected patients: (off-label use)

IV: 5 mg/kg/dose every 8 hours; may switch to oral after lesions begin to heal (HHS [OI adult 2015])

Oral: After initial IV therapy, may switch to 400 mg 3 times daily; continue until lesions are completely healed (HHS [OI adult 2015])

HSV, orolabial (cold sores) (off-label use): Oral:

Immunocompetent:

Treatment: (episodic/recurrent): 200 to 400 mg 5 times daily for 5 days (Cernik 2008; Leflore 2000; Spruance 1990).

Chronic suppression: 400 mg 2 times daily (has been clinically evaluated for up to 1 year) (Cernik 2008; Rooney 1993)

HIV-infected patients: Treatment: 400 mg 3 times daily for 5 to 10 days (HHS [OI adult 2015])

Herpes zoster (shingles), treatment:

Manufacturer's labeling:

IV: Immunocompromised: 10 mg/kg/dose every 8 hours for 7 days

Oral: Immunocompetent: 800 mg 5 times daily for 7 to 10 day

Alternate recommendations: HIV-infected patients (HHS [OI adult 2015]):

IV: *Extensive cutaneous lesions or visceral involvement:* 10 to 15 mg/kg/dose every 8 hours until clinical improvement; switch to oral famciclovir or valacyclovir (preferred) or acyclovir (alternative) to complete a 10 to 14 day course when formation of new lesions has ceased and signs/symptoms of visceral infection are improving

Oral (off-label use): *Acute localized infection (as an alternative to valacyclovir or famciclovir):* 800 mg 5 times daily for 7 to 10 days; consider longer duration if lesions resolve slowly

Prevention of early HSV reactivation in seropositive hematopoietic stem cell transplant (HSCT) recipients (off-label use): Note: Start at the beginning of conditioning therapy and continue until engraftment or until mucositis resolves (~30 days) (Tomblyn 2009)

Adults ≥40 kg:

Oral: 400 to 800 mg twice daily

IV: 250 mg/m² every 12 hours

Prevention of late HSV reactivation in seropositive HSCT recipients (off-label use): Adults ≥40 kg: Oral: 800 mg twice daily; continue therapy for 1 year after HSCT (Tomblyn 2009).

Prevention of HSV reactivation in seropositive patients undergoing acute myeloid leukemia induction or reinduction (off-label use): Adults ≥40 kg: Oral: 400 mg twice daily; continue during active therapy and throughout periods of neutropenia (Bergmann 1995; Freifeld 2011)

Prevention of VZV reactivation in HSCT recipients (off-label use): Oral: 800 mg twice daily; continue therapy for 1 year after HSCT (Tomblyn 2009).

Prophylaxis of CMV in low-risk allogeneic HSCT (off-label use; alternate therapy): Note: Begin at engraftment and continue to day 100; requires close monitoring for CMV reactivation (due to weak activity); not for use in patients at high risk for CMV disease (Tomblyn 2009)

Oral: 800 mg 4 times daily

IV: 500 mg/m² every 8 hours

Varicella (chickenpox), treatment: Begin treatment within the first 24 hours of rash onset:

Oral:

Immunocompetent (>40 kg): 800 mg 4 times daily for 5 days

HIV-infected patients (off-label use): *Uncomplicated cases (as an alternative to valacyclovir or famciclovir):* 800 mg 5 times daily for 5 to 7 days (HHS [OI adult 2015])

IV: HIV- infected patients (off-label use): Severe or complicated cases: 10 to 15 mg/kg/dose every 8 hours for 7 to 10 days; may switch to oral famciclovir or valacyclovir (preferred) or acyclovir (alternative) after defervescence if no evidence of visceral involvement (HHS [OI adult 2015])

Varicella-zoster virus acute retinal necrosis (ARN) in HIV-infected patients (off-label use): IV: 10 to 15 mg/kg/dose every 8 hours for 10 to 14 days, followed by valacyclovir for 6 weeks plus intravitreal ganciclovir twice weekly for 1 to 2 doses (HHS [OI adult 2015])

Pediatric

Herpes simplex virus (HSV), genital infection:

IV: Children ≥12 years and Adolescents: Immunocompetent: Initial episode, severe: *Manufacturer's labeling:* 5 mg/kg/dose every 8 hours for 5 to 7 days

Oral:

Infants and Children <12 years: Immunocompetent (off-label use):

Initial episode: 40 to 80 mg/kg/day divided into 3 to 4 doses for 5-10 days (maximum: 1,000 mg daily) (*Red Book* [AAP 2012])

Chronic suppression: 40 to 80 mg/kg/day in 3 divided doses for ≤12 months; (maximum: 1,000 mg daily) (*Red Book* [AAP 2009])

Children ≥12 years and Adolescents: Immunocompetent (off-label use):

Initial episode: 200 mg every 4 hours while awake (5 times daily) **or** 400 mg 3 times daily for 7 to 10 days; treatment can be extended beyond 10 days if healing is not complete (*Red Book* [AAP 2012])

Chronic suppression: 800 mg daily in 2 divided doses for ≤12 continuous months (*Red Book* [AAP 2012])

Children: HIV-exposed/-positive (off-label use):
Children <45 kg:
Initial episode: 60 mg/kg/day divided into 3 doses daily for 5 to 14 days (maximum: 1,200 mg daily) (CDC 2009)
Chronic suppression: 20 mg/kg/dose twice daily (maximum dose: 400 mg) (CDC 2009)
Children ≥45 kg:
Initial episode: 400 mg twice daily for 5 to 14 days (CDC 2009)
Chronic suppression: 20 mg/kg/dose twice daily (maximum dose: 400 mg) (CDC 2009)
Children <12 years: Recurrence: Immunocompetent: Oral: 20 to 25 mg/kg/dose twice daily; maximum dose: 400 mg (Bradley 2011)
Children ≥12 years: Recurrence: Immunocompetent:
Manufacturer's labeling: 200 mg every 4 hours while awake (5 times daily) for 5 days
Alternate recommendation: 400 mg 3 times daily for 5 days **or** 800 mg twice daily for 5 days **or** 800 mg 3 times daily for 2 days (CDC [Workowski 2015]; *Red Book* [AAP 2015])
Adolescents: HIV-positive patients: (off-label use): Refer to adult dosing.

HSV encephalitis: IV:
Infants and Children 3 months to <12 years:
Immunocompetent:
Manufacturer's labeling: 20 mg/kg/dose every 8 hours for 10 days. **Note:** Doses ≥20 mg/kg may be associated with a higher incidence of nephrotoxicity (*Red Book* [AAP 2012])
Alternate recommendation: 10 to 15 mg/kg/dose every 8 hours for 14 to 21 days (*Red Book* [AAP 2012])
HIV-exposed/-positive: 10 mg/kg/dose every 8 hours for 21 days; do not discontinue therapy until a repeat HSV DNA PCR assay of the cerebrospinal fluid is negative (CDC 2009)
Children ≥12 years and Adolescents: Independent of HIV status:
Manufacturer's labeling: 10 mg/kg/dose every 8 hours for 10 days
Alternate recommendation: 10 mg/kg/dose every 8 hours for 14 to 21 days (*Red Book* [AAP 2012])

HSV gingivostomatitis (off-label use): HIV-exposed/-positive:
Mild, symptomatic: Oral: Infants and Children: 20 mg/kg/dose 3 times daily for 5 to 10 days (maximum dose: 400 mg) (CDC 2009)
Moderate to severe, symptomatic: IV: Infants and Children: 5 to 10 mg/kg/dose every 8 hours; **Note:** switch to oral therapy once lesions begin to regress (CDC 2009)

HSV, mucocutaneous treatment:
Immunocompromised:
IV:
Infants, Children, and Adolescents: 10 mg/kg/dose every 8 hours for 7 to 14 days (*Red Book* [AAP 2012])
Oral (off-label use):
Children ≥2 years and Adolescents: 1,000 mg daily in 3 to 5 divided doses for 7 to 14 days; some suggest the maximum daily dose should not exceed 80 mg/kg/day (*Red Book* [AAP 2009]; Red Book [AAP 2012])
HIV-infected patients (off-label use): Adolescents: IV, Oral: Refer to adult dosing.

Suppression, chronic (cutaneous, ocular) episodes:
Immunocompromised: Oral:
Infants and Children (HIV-exposed/-positive): 20 mg/kg/dose twice daily for 5 to 14 days; maximum dose: 400 mg (CDC 2009)
Children and Adolescents ≥12 years (independent of HIV status): 400 mg twice daily for up to 12 months (*Red Book* [AAP 2012])

HSV, neonatal: IV: Infants: Birth to 3 months: Treatment:
Manufacturer's labeling: 10 mg/kg/dose every 8 hours for 10 days
Alternate recommendations: 20 mg/kg/dose every 8 hours for 14 days (skin and mucous membrane disease) to 21 days (disseminated disease and CNS disease) (CDC [Workowski 2015]; Kimberlin 2013; *Red Book* [AAP 2012])

HSV, orolabial (cold sores) (off-label use): Oral:
Immunocompetent: Chronic suppression: Children: 30 mg/kg/day in 3 divided doses for up to 12 months (maximum: 1,000 mg/day). **Note:** Re-evaluate after 12 months (*Red Book* [AAP 2012])
HIV-infected patients: Treatment: Adolescents: Refer to adult dosing.

Herpes zoster (shingles), treatment:
IV:
Immunocompetent (off-label use):
Infants: 10 mg/kg/dose every 8 hours for 7 to 10 days (*Red Book* [AAP 2012])
Children ≥1 year and Adolescents: 500 mg/m²/dose every 8 hours for 7 to 10 days; some experts recommend 10 mg/kg/dose every 8 hours (*Red Book* [AAP 2012])
Immunocompromised:
Children <12 years: (off-label dose): 10 mg/kg/dose every 8 hours for 7 to 10 days (*Red Book* [AAP 2012])
Children ≥12 years and Adolescents: Manufacturer's labeling: Refer to adult dosing.
HIV-infected patients: Adolescents (off-label dose): *Extensive cutaneous lesions or visceral involvement:* Refer to adult dosing.
Oral:
Immunocompetent:
Children ≥12 years and Adolescents (off-label dose): 800 mg 5 times daily for 5 to 7 days (*Red Book* [AAP 2012])
Immunocompromised: HIV-infected patients (off-label use): *Acute localized infection (as an alternative to valacyclovir or famciclovir):* Adolescents: Refer to adult dosing.

Prevention of HSV reactivation in HIV-exposed/-positive patients (off-label use): Oral: Children: 20 mg/kg/dose twice daily (maximum: 400 mg per dose) (CDC 2009)

Prevention of early HSV reactivation in seropositive hematopoietic stem cell transplant (HSCT) recipients (off-label use): Note: Start at the beginning of conditioning therapy and continue until engraftment or until mucositis resolves (~30 days) (Tomblyn 2009):
Oral:
Children and Adolescents <40 kg (alternate therapy): 60 to 90 mg/kg/day in 2 to 3 divided doses
Children and Adolescents ≥40 kg: Refer to adult dosing.

IV:

Children and Adolescents <40 kg: 250 mg/m^2 every 8 hours or 125 mg/m^2 every 6 hours (maximum daily dose: 80 mg/kg/day)

Children and Adolescents ≥40 kg: Refer to adult dosing.

Prevention of late HSV reactivation in seropositive HSCT recipients (off-label use): Note: Continue therapy for 1 year after HSCT (Tomblyn 2009).

Children and Adolescents <40 kg: Oral: 60 to 90 mg/kg/day in 2 to 3 divided doses (maximum dose: 800 mg twice daily)

Children and Adolescents ≥40 kg: Refer to adult dosing.

Prevention of VZV reactivation in HSCT recipients (off-label use): Note: Continue therapy for 1 year after HSCT (Tomblyn 2009)

Children and Adolescents <40 kg: Oral: 60 to 80 mg/kg/day in 2 to 3 divided doses

Children and Adolescents ≥40 kg: Refer to adult dosing.

Prophylaxis of CMV in low-risk allogeneic HSCT (off-label use; alternate therapy): Note: Begin at engraftment and continue to day 100; requires close monitoring for CMV reactivation (due to weak activity); not for use in patients at high risk for CMV disease (Tomblyn 2009)

Oral:

Infants, Children, and Adolescents <40 kg: 600 mg/m^2 4 times daily

Children and Adolescents ≥40 kg: 800 mg 4 times daily

IV: Infants, Children, and Adolescents: 500 mg/m^2 every 8 hours

Varicella (chickenpox), treatment: Begin treatment within the first 24 hours of rash onset:

Oral:

Immunocompetent:

Children ≥2 years and ≤40 kg: 20 mg/kg/dose (maximum: 800 mg per dose) 4 times daily for 5 days

Children >40 kg: Refer to adult dosing.

HIV-infected patients (off-label use):

Infants and Children: Mild, uncomplicated disease and no or moderate immune suppression: 20 mg/kg/dose (maximum dose: 800 mg) 4 times daily for 7 to 10 days or until no new lesions for 48 hours (CDC 2009)

Adolescents: Uncomplicated cases (as an alternative to valacyclovir or famciclovir): Refer to adult dosing.

IV:

Immunocompetent (off-label use): Children ≥2 years: 10 mg/kg/dose or 500 mg/m^2/dose every 8 hours for 7 to 10 days (CDC 2009; *Red Book* [AAP 2012])

Immunocompromised (off-label use):

Infants (off-label dose): 10 mg/kg/dose every 8 hours for 7 to 10 days (*Red Book* [AAP 2012])

Children and Adolescents (off-label dose): 500 mg/m^2/dose every 8 hours for 7 to 10 days; some experts recommend 10 mg/kg/dose every 8 hours (*Red Book* [AAP 2012])

HIV-exposed/-positive (off-label use):

Infants: 10 mg/kg/dose every 8 hours for 7 to 10 days or until no new lesions for 48 hours (CDC 2009)

Children ≥1 year: 10 mg/kg/dose or 500 mg/m^2/dose every 8 hours for 7 to 10 days or until no new lesions for 48 hours (CDC 2009)

Adolescents: Refer to adult dosing.

Varicella-zoster virus acute retinal necrosis in HIV-exposed/-positive patients (off-label use): IV:

Infants and Children: 10 to 15 mg/kg/dose every 8 hours for 10 to 14 days, followed by oral acyclovir or valacyclovir for 4 to 6 weeks (CDC 2009)

Adolescents: Refer to adult dosing.

Renal Impairment

Oral:

CrCl 10-25 mL/minute/1.73 m^2: Normal dosing regimen 800 mg 5 times daily: Administer 800 mg every 8 hours

CrCl <10 mL/minute/1.73 m^2:

Normal dosing regimen 200 mg 5 times daily or 400 mg every 12 hours: Administer 200 mg every 12 hours

Normal dosing regimen 800 mg 5 times daily: Administer 800 mg every 12 hours

Intermittent hemodialysis (IHD): Dialyzable (60% reduction following a 6-hour session):

Normal dosing regimen 200 mg 5 times daily or 400 mg every 12 hours: Administer 200 mg every 12 hours; administer after hemodialysis on dialysis days

Normal dosing regimen 800 mg 5 times daily: Administer 800 mg every 12 hours; administer after hemodialysis on dialysis days

IV:

CrCl 25-50 mL/minute/1.73 m^2: Administer recommended dose every 12 hours

CrCl 10-25 mL/minute/1.73 m^2: Administer recommended dose every 24 hours

CrCl <10 mL/minute/1.73 m^2: Administer 50% of recommended dose every 24 hours

Intermittent hemodialysis (IHD) (administer after hemodialysis on dialysis days): Dialyzable (60% reduction following a 6-hour session): 2.5-5 mg/kg every 24 hours (Heintz 2009). **Note:** Dosing dependent on the assumption of 3 times weekly, complete IHD sessions.

Peritoneal dialysis (PD): Administer 50% of normal dose once daily; no supplemental dose needed (Aronoff 2007)

Continuous renal replacement therapy (CRRT) (Heintz 2009; Trotman 2005): Drug clearance is highly dependent on the method of renal replacement, filter type, and flow rate. Appropriate dosing requires close monitoring of pharmacologic response, signs of adverse reactions due to drug accumulation, as well as drug concentrations in relation to target trough (if appropriate). The following are general recommendations only (based on dialysate flow/ultrafiltration rates of 1-2 L/hour and minimal residual renal function) and should not supersede clinical judgment:

CVVH: 5-10 mg/kg every 24 hours

CVVHD/CVVHDF: 5-10 mg/kg every 12-24 hours

Note: The higher end of dosage range (eg, 10 mg/kg every 12 hours for CVVHDF) is recommended for viral meningoencephalitis and varicella-zoster virus infections.

Hepatic Impairment Oral, IV: There are no dosage adjustments provided in the manufacturer's labeling; use caution in patients with severe impairment.

Obesity Obese patients should be dosed using ideal body weight.

Mechanism of Action Acyclovir is converted to acyclovir monophosphate by virus-specific thymidine kinase then further converted to acyclovir triphosphate by other cellular enzymes. Acyclovir triphosphate inhibits DNA synthesis and viral replication by competing with deoxyguanosine triphosphate for viral DNA polymerase and being incorporated into viral DNA.

Contraindications Hypersensitivity to acyclovir, valacyclovir, or any component of the formulation

Warnings/Precautions Use with caution in immunocompromised patients; thrombocytopenic purpura/hemolytic uremic syndrome (TTP/HUS) has been reported. Use caution in the elderly, preexisting renal disease (may require dosage modification), or in those receiving other nephrotoxic drugs. Renal failure (sometimes fatal) has been reported. Maintain adequate hydration during oral or intravenous therapy. Use IV preparation with caution in patients with underlying neurologic abnormalities, serious hepatic or electrolyte abnormalities, or substantial hypoxia.

Varicella-zoster: Treatment should begin within 24 hours of appearance of rash; oral route not recommended for routine use in otherwise healthy children with varicella, but may be effective in patients at increased risk of moderate-to-severe infection (>12 years of age, chronic cutaneous or pulmonary disorders, long-term salicylate therapy, corticosteroid therapy).

Drug Interactions

Metabolism/Transport Effects Inhibits CYP1A2 (weak)

Avoid Concomitant Use

Avoid concomitant use of Acyclovir (Systemic) with any of the following: Foscarnet; Varicella Virus Vaccine; Zoster Vaccine

Increased Effect/Toxicity

Acyclovir (Systemic) may increase the levels/effects of: CloZAPine; Mycophenolate; Tenofovir Products; TiZANidine; Zidovudine

The levels/effects of Acyclovir (Systemic) may be increased by: Foscarnet; Mycophenolate; Tenofovir Products

Decreased Effect

Acyclovir (Systemic) may decrease the levels/effects of: Talimogene Laherparepvec; Varicella Virus Vaccine; Zoster Vaccine

Food Interactions Food does not affect absorption of oral acyclovir.

Dietary Considerations May be taken with or without food. Some products may contain sodium.

Pharmacodynamics/Kinetics

Half-life Elimination Terminal: Neonates: 4 hours; Children 1 to 12 years: 2 to 3 hours; Adults: 2 to 3.5 hours (with normal renal function); hemodialysis: ~5 hours

Time to Peak Serum: Oral: Within 1.5 to 2 hours

Pregnancy Risk Factor B

Pregnancy Considerations Teratogenic effects were not observed in animal reproduction studies. Acyclovir has been shown to cross the human placenta (Henderson 1992). Results from a pregnancy registry, established in 1984 and closed in 1999, did not find an increase in the number of birth defects with exposure to acyclovir when compared to those expected in the general population. However, due to the small size of the registry and lack of long-term data, the manufacturer recommends using during pregnancy with caution and only when clearly needed. Acyclovir is recommended for the treatment of genital herpes in pregnant women (CDC [Workowski 2015]).

Breastfeeding Considerations Acyclovir is excreted in breast milk. The manufacturer recommends that caution be exercised when administering acyclovir to nursing women. Limited data suggest exposure to the nursing infant of ~0.3 mg/kg/day following oral administration of acyclovir to the mother. Acyclovir may be used for the treatment of genital herpes in breastfeeding women (CDC [Workowski 2015]). breastfeeding mothers with herpetic lesions near or on the breast should avoid breastfeeding (Gartner 2005).

Dosage Forms

Capsule, Oral:
- Zovirax: 200 mg
- Generic: 200 mg

Solution, Intravenous:
- Generic: 50 mg/mL (10 mL, 20 mL)

Solution Reconstituted, Intravenous:
- Generic: 500 mg (1 ea)

Suspension, Oral:
- Zovirax: 200 mg/5 mL (473 mL)
- Generic: 200 mg/5 mL (473 mL)

Tablet, Oral:
- Zovirax: 400 mg, 800 mg
- Generic: 400 mg, 800 mg

Dental Comment Although some conflicting data, dental treatment may be a risk factor for asymptomatic viral shedding of herpes simplex virus type-1 (HSV-1) into human saliva in patients with previous exposure to the virus (Hyland 2007).

It is recommended to reappoint the patient if an active lesion is present. If the lesion is already "crusted" over, treatment will not induce spread of the virus but treatment is aimed at patient comfort during the procedure relating to the wound healing on their lip.

Acyclovir (Topical) (ay SYE kloe veer)

Related Information

Systemic Viral Diseases *on page 1806*
Viral Infections *on page 1849*

Related Sample Prescriptions

Viral Infections - Sample Prescriptions *on page 40*

Brand Names: US Sitavig; Zovirax

Brand Names: Canada Zovirax

Generic Availability (US) May be product dependent

Pharmacologic Category Antiviral Agent, Topical

Dental Use Treatment of initial and prophylaxis of recurrent mucosal and cutaneous herpes simplex (HSV-1 and HSV-2) infections in immunocompromised patients

Use Herpes virus:

Buccal tablet: Treatment of recurrent herpes labialis (cold sores) in immunocompetent adults.

Cream: Treatment of recurrent herpes labialis (cold sores) in immunocompetent children ≥12 years of age, adolescents, and adults.

Ointment: Management of initial genital herpes and in limited non-life-threatening mucocutaneous herpes simplex virus infections in immunocompromised patients.

Local Anesthetic/Vasoconstrictor Precautions No information available to require special precautions

Effects on Dental Treatment Key adverse event(s) related to dental treatment: Topical (Zovirax cream): Dry/cracked lips and dry/flaky skin were reported in fewer than 1 in 100 patients in clinical studies.

Effects on Bleeding No information available to require special precautions

Adverse Reactions

>10%: Dermatologic: Local pain (ointment 30%; mild; includes transient burning and stinging)

1% to 10%:

Central nervous system: Lethargy (buccal tablet 1%)

Dermatologic: Erythema (buccal tablet 1%), skin rash (buccal tablet 1%)

Gastrointestinal: Aphthous stomatitis (buccal tablet 1%), gingival pain (buccal tablet 1%)

Local: Application site reaction (cream 5%; including dry lips, desquamation, dryness of skin, cracked lips, burning skin, pruritus, flakiness of skin, and stinging on skin); application site irritation (buccal tablet 1%)

<1%, postmarketing, and/or case reports: Anaphylaxis, angioedema, contact dermatitis, eczema, localized edema, local pruritus, pruritus

Dental Usual Dosage

Herpes labialis (cold sores): Children ≥12 years and Adults: Topical: Cream: Apply 5 times/day for 4 days

Mucocutaneous HSV: Adults: Nonlife-threatening, immunocompromised: Topical: Ointment: 1/2" ribbon of ointment for a 4" square surface area every 3 hours (6 times/day) for 7 days

Dosing

Adult & Geriatric

Genital HSV: Topical ointment: Initial episode: 1/2" ribbon of ointment for a 4" square surface area every 3 hours (6 times daily) for 7 days

Herpes labialis (cold sores):

Topical cream: Apply 5 times daily for 4 days

Buccal tablet: Apply one 50 mg tablet as a single dose to the upper gum region (canine fossa).

Mucocutaneous HSV (non-life-threatening, immunocompromised): Topical ointment: 1/2" ribbon of ointment for a 4" square surface area every 3 hours (6 times daily) for 7 days

Pediatric Herpes labialis (cold sores): Children ≥12 years and Adolescents: Topical cream: Refer to adult dosing.

Renal Impairment There are no dosage adjustments provided in the manufacturer's labeling. However, dosage adjustment is unlikely due to low systemic absorption.

Hepatic Impairment There are no dosage adjustments provided in the manufacturer's labeling. However, dosage adjustment is unlikely due to low systemic absorption.

Mechanism of Action Acyclovir is converted to acyclovir monophosphate by virus-specific thymidine kinase then further converted to acyclovir triphosphate by other cellular enzymes. Acyclovir triphosphate inhibits DNA synthesis and viral replication by competing with deoxyguanosine triphosphate for viral DNA polymerase and being incorporated into viral DNA.

Contraindications

Buccal tablet: Hypersensitivity to acyclovir, valacyclovir, milk protein concentrate or any component of the formulation

Cream, ointment: Hypersensitivity to acyclovir, valacyclovir, or any component of the formulation

Warnings/Precautions

Genital herpes: Physical contact should be avoided when lesions are present; transmission may also occur in the absence of symptoms. Treatment should begin with the first signs or symptoms. There are no data to support the use of acyclovir ointment to prevent transmission of infection to other persons or prevent recurrent infections if no signs or symptoms are present.

Herpes labialis: Treatment should begin with the first signs or symptoms. Cream is for external use only to the lips and face; do not apply to eye or inside the mouth or nose, or any mucous membranes. Ointment should also not be used in the eye and be used with caution in immunocompromised patients. Cream may be irritating and cause contact sensitization. Buccal tablets are applied to the area of the upper gum above the incisor tooth on the same side as the symptoms; do not apply to the inside of the lip or cheek. Some products may contain milk protein concentrate.

Drug Interactions

Metabolism/Transport Effects None known.

Avoid Concomitant Use There are no known interactions where it is recommended to avoid concomitant use.

Increased Effect/Toxicity There are no known significant interactions involving an increase in effect.

Decreased Effect

Acyclovir (Topical) may decrease the levels/effects of: Talimogene Laherparepvec

Pregnancy Risk Factor B

Pregnancy Considerations Teratogenic effects were not observed in animal studies. When administered orally, acyclovir crosses the placenta. Refer to the Acyclovir (Systemic) monograph for details. The amount of acyclovir available systemically following topical application of the cream or ointment is significantly less in comparison to oral doses.

Breastfeeding Considerations When administered orally, acyclovir enters breast milk. Refer to the Acyclovir (Systemic) monograph for details. The amount of acyclovir available systemically following topical application of the cream or ointment is significantly less in comparison to oral doses. Nursing mothers with herpetic lesions near or on the breast should avoid breast-feeding.

Dosage Forms

Cream, External:

Zovirax: 5% (5 g)

Ointment, External:

Zovirax: 5% (30 g)

Generic: 5% (5 g, 15 g, 30 g)

Tablet, Buccal:

Sitavig: 50 mg

Dental Comment Although some conflicting data, dental treatment may be a risk factor for asymptomatic viral shedding of herpes simplex virus type-1 (HSV-1) into human saliva in patients with previous exposure to the virus (Hyland 2007).

It is recommended to reappoint the patient if an active lesion is present. If the lesion is already "crusted" over, treatment will not induce spread of the virus but treatment is aimed at patient comfort during the procedure relating to the wound healing on their lip.

Acyclovir and Hydrocortisone

(ay SYE kloe veer & hye droe KOR ti sone)

Related Information

Acyclovir (Topical) *on page 77*

Hydrocortisone (Topical) *on page 836*

Brand Names: US Xerese

Generic Availability (US) No

Pharmacologic Category Antiviral Agent, Topical; Corticosteroid, Topical

Use Herpes labialis: Treatment of recurrent herpes labialis (cold sores) in children ≥6 years and adults.

Local Anesthetic/Vasoconstrictor Precautions No information available to require special precautions

Effects on Dental Treatment No significant effects or complications reported (see Dental Comment)

Effects on Bleeding No information available to require special precautions

Adverse Reactions <1%, postmarketing, and/or case reports: Allergic contact sensitivity, application site reaction, burning sensation of skin, contact dermatitis (when applied under occlusion), dyschromia, erythema, exfoliation of skin, tingling of skin, xeroderma

Dosing

Adult & Geriatric Herpes labialis (cold sores): Topical: Apply 5 times/day for 5 days

Pediatric Herpes labialis (cold sores): Topical: Children ≥6 years and Adolescents: Refer to adult dosing.

Renal Impairment There are no dosage adjustments provided in the manufacturer's labeling.

Hepatic Impairment There are no dosage adjustments provided in the manufacturer's labeling.

Mechanism of Action

Acyclovir: Acyclovir is converted to acyclovir monophosphate by virus-specific thymidine kinase then further converted to acyclovir triphosphate by other cellular enzymes. Acyclovir triphosphate inhibits DNA synthesis and viral replication by competing with deoxyguanosine triphosphate for viral DNA polymerase and being incorporated into viral DNA.

Hydrocortisone: Topical corticosteroids have anti-inflammatory, antipruritic, and vasoconstrictive properties.

Contraindications There are no contraindications listed in the manufacturer's labeling.

Warnings/Precautions Treatment should begin with the first signs or symptoms. For external use only to the lips and around the mouth; do not apply to eye, inside the mouth or nose, or on the genitals. Contact healthcare provider if cold sore does not heal in 2 weeks. Use with caution in immunocompromised patients. Use has been associated with local sensitization (irritation). Potentially significant interactions may exist, requiring dose or frequency adjustment, additional monitoring, and/or selection of alternative therapy.

Drug Interactions

Metabolism/Transport Effects Refer to individual components.

Avoid Concomitant Use

Avoid concomitant use of Acyclovir and Hydrocortisone with any of the following: Aldesleukin

Increased Effect/Toxicity

Acyclovir and Hydrocortisone may increase the levels/effects of: Ceritinib; Deferasirox

Decreased Effect

Acyclovir and Hydrocortisone may decrease the levels/effects of: Aldesleukin; Corticorelin; Hyaluronidase; Talimogene Laherparepvec

Pregnancy Risk Factor B

Pregnancy Considerations Animal reproduction studies and studies in pregnant women have not been conducted with Xerese. Systemic exposure of acyclovir and hydrocortisone after topical administration is minimal. See individual agents.

Breastfeeding Considerations Systemic exposure of acyclovir and hydrocortisone after topical administration is minimal. See individual agents.

Dosage Forms

Cream, topical:

Xerese: Acyclovir 5% and hydrocortisone 1% (5 g)

Dental Comment Although some conflicting data, dental treatment may be a risk factor for asymptomatic viral shedding of herpes simplex virus type-1 (HSV-1) into human saliva in patients with previous exposure to the virus (Hyland 2007).

It is recommended to reappoint the patient if an active lesion is present. If the lesion is already "crusted" over, treatment will not induce spread of the virus but treatment is aimed at patient comfort during the procedure relating to the wound healing on their lip.

Adalimumab (a da LIM yoo mab)

Related Information

Rheumatoid Arthritis, Osteoarthritis, and Osteoporosis *on page 1792*

Brand Names: US Humira; Humira Pediatric Crohns Start; Humira Pen; Humira Pen-Crohns Starter; Humira Pen-Psoriasis Starter

Brand Names: Canada Humira

Pharmacologic Category Antirheumatic, Disease Modifying; Gastrointestinal Agent, Miscellaneous; Monoclonal Antibody; Tumor Necrosis Factor (TNF) Blocking Agent

Use

Ankylosing spondylitis: Treatment (to reduce signs/symptoms) of active ankylosing spondylitis in adults

Crohn disease: Treatment (to reduce signs/symptoms and to induce and maintain clinical remission) of active Crohn disease (moderate to severe) in adults and pediatric patients ≥6 years (Humira only) with an inadequate response to conventional therapy or who have lost response to or are intolerant to infliximab.

Hidradenitis suppurativa (Humira only): Treatment of moderate to severe hidradenitis suppurativa

Juvenile idiopathic arthritis: Treatment (to reduce signs/symptoms) of active polyarticular juvenile idiopathic arthritis (moderate to severe) in pediatric patients ≥2 years (Humira) or ≥4 years (Amjevita); may be used alone or in combination with methotrexate

Plaque psoriasis: Treatment of chronic plaque psoriasis (moderate to severe) in adults who are candidates for systemic therapy or phototherapy, and when other systemic therapies are less appropriate (with close monitoring and regular follow-up)

Psoriatic arthritis: Treatment (to reduce signs/symptoms, inhibit progression of structural damage, and improve physical function) of active psoriatic arthritis in adults; may be used alone or in combination with nonbiologic disease-modifying antirheumatic drugs (DMARDs)

Rheumatoid arthritis: Treatment (to reduce signs/symptoms, induce major clinical response, inhibit progression of structural damage, and improve physical function) of active rheumatoid arthritis (moderate to severe) in adults; may be used alone or in combination with methotrexate or other nonbiologic DMARDs

Ulcerative colitis: Treatment (to induce and sustain clinical remission) of active ulcerative colitis (moderate to severe) in adults who have had an inadequate response to immunosuppressants such as corticosteroids, azathioprine, or 6-mercaptopurine. (**Note:** Efficacy in patients that are intolerant to or no longer responsive to other TNF blockers has not been established.)

Uveitis (Humira only): Treatment of non-infectious intermediate, posterior, and panuveitis in adults

Local Anesthetic/Vasoconstrictor Precautions No information available to require special precautions

Effects on Dental Treatment No significant effects or complications reported

Effects on Bleeding Rare reports of pancytopenia (including aplastic anemia), as well as medically significant thrombocytopenia, have been reported with tumor necrosis factor-alpha therapy; in patients undergoing active treatment, a medical consult is recommended

Adverse Reactions

>10%:

Central nervous system: Headache (12%)

Dermatologic: Skin rash (6% to 12%)

Hematologic & oncologic: Positive ANA titer (12%)

Immunologic: Antibody development (3% to 26%; significance unknown)

Local: Injection site reaction (12% to 20%; includes erythema, itching, hemorrhage, pain, swelling)

Neuromuscular & skeletal: Increased creatine phosphokinase (15%)

Respiratory: Upper respiratory tract infection (17%), sinusitis (11%)

1% to 10%:

Cardiovascular: Hypertension (5%), atrial fibrillation (<5%), cardiac arrest (<5%), cardiac arrhythmia (<5%), chest pain (<5%), coronary artery disease (<5%), deep vein thrombosis (<5%), hypertensive encephalopathy (<5%), myocardial infarction (<5%), palpitations (<5%), pericardial effusion (<5%), pericarditis (<5%), peripheral edema (<5%), subdural hematoma (<5%), syncope (<5%), tachycardia (<5%)

Central nervous system: Confusion (<5%), myasthenia (<5%), paresthesia (<5%), torso pain (<5%)

Dermatologic: Cellulitis, erysipelas

Endocrine & metabolic: Hyperlipidemia (7%), hypercholesterolemia (6%), dehydration (<5%), ketosis (<5%), menstrual disease (<5%), parathyroid disease (<5%)

Gastrointestinal: Nausea (9%), abdominal pain (7%), cholecystitis (<5%), cholelithiasis (<5%), esophagitis (<5%), gastrointestinal hemorrhage (<5%), vomiting (<5%), diverticulitis

Genitourinary: Urinary tract infection (≤8%), hematuria (5%), cystitis (<5%), pelvic pain (<5%)

Hematologic & oncologic: Adenoma (<5%), agranulocytosis (<5%), paraproteinemia (<5%), polycythemia (<5%), carcinoma (including breast, gastrointestinal, skin, urogenital), malignant lymphoma, malignant melanoma

Hepatic: Increased serum alkaline phosphatase (5%), hepatic necrosis (<5%)

Hypersensitivity: Hypersensitivity reaction (children 6%; adults 1%)

Infection: Serious infection (9%; including dental caries, gastroenteritis, rotavirus, varicella), herpes simplex infection (≤4%), herpes zoster (≤4%), sepsis

Local: Injection site reaction (8%; other than erythema, itching, hemorrhage, pain, swelling)

Neuromuscular & skeletal: Back pain (6%), arthritis (<5%), arthropathy (<5%), bone disease (<5%), bone fracture (<5%), limb pain (<5%), muscle cramps (<5%), myasthenia (<5%), osteonecrosis (<5%), septic arthritis (<5%), synovitis (<5%), tendon disease (<5%), tremor (<5%), arthralgia (3%; plaque psoriasis)

Ophthalmic: Cataract (<5%)

Renal: Nephrolithiasis (<5%), pyelonephritis

Respiratory: Flu-like symptoms (7%), asthma (<5%), bronchospasm (<5%), dyspnea (<5%), pleural effusion (<5%), respiratory depression (<5%), pharyngitis (juvenile idiopathic arthritis: ≤4%), pneumonia (≤4%), tuberculosis (including reactivation of latent infection; disseminated, miliary, lymphatic, peritoneal, and pulmonary)

Miscellaneous: Accidental injury (10%), abnormal healing (<5%), postoperative complication (infection)

<1%, postmarketing, and/or case reports: Abscess (limb, perianal), alopecia, anal fissure, anaphylactoid reaction, anaphylaxis, anemia, angioedema, aplastic anemia, appendicitis, bacterial infection, basal cell carcinoma, blepharitis, bronchitis, cardiac failure, cerebrovascular accident, cervical dysplasia, circulatory shock, clonus, cytopenia, dermal ulcer, diarrhea, diplopia, endometrial hyperplasia, eosinophilia, erythema multiforme, fever, fixed drug eruption, fulminant necrotizing fasciitis, fungal infection, Guillain-Barré syndrome, hepatic failure, hepatitis B (reactivation), hepatosplenic T-cell lymphomas (children, adolescents, and young adults), hepatotoxicity (idiosyncratic) (Chalasani 2014), histoplasmosis, hyperreflexia, hypersensitivity angiitis, increased serum transaminases, interstitial pulmonary disease (eg, pulmonary fibrosis), intestinal obstruction, intestinal perforation, leukemia, leukopenia, liver metastases, lupus-like syndrome, lymphadenopathy, lymphocytosis, malignant neoplasm of ovary, meningitis (viral), Merkel cell carcinoma, multiple sclerosis, musculoskeletal chest pain, mycobacterium avium complex, myositis (children and adolescents), neutropenia, nocturia, optic neuritis, pancreatitis, pancytopenia, protozoal infection, psoriasis (including new onset, palmoplantar, pustular, or exacerbation), pulmonary embolism, respiratory failure, sarcoidosis, septic shock, skin granuloma (annulare; children and adolescents), Stevens-Johnson syndrome, streptococcal pharyngitis (children and adolescents), supraventricular cardiac arrhythmia, swelling of eye, systemic lupus erythematosus, testicular neoplasm, thrombocytopenia, urticaria, vascular disease, vasculitis (systemic), viral infection, weakness

General Dosage Range SubQ:

Children ≥2 years and Adolescents: Dosage varies greatly depending on indication.

Adults: Initial: 40 to 160 mg; Maintenance: 40 mg every other week

Mechanism of Action Adalimumab is a recombinant monoclonal antibody that binds to human tumor necrosis factor alpha (TNF-alpha), thereby interfering with binding to TNFα receptor sites and subsequent cytokine-driven inflammatory processes. Elevated TNF levels in the synovial fluid are involved in the pathologic pain and joint destruction in immune-mediated arthritis. Adalimumab decreases signs and symptoms of psoriatic arthritis, rheumatoid arthritis, and ankylosing spondylitis. It inhibits progression of structural damage of rheumatoid and psoriatic arthritis. Reduces signs and symptoms and maintains clinical remission in Crohn disease and ulcerative colitis; reduces epidermal thickness and inflammatory cell infiltration in plaque psoriasis.

Pharmacodynamics/Kinetics

Half-life Elimination Terminal: ~2 weeks (range: 10 to 20 days)

Time to Peak Serum: SubQ: 131 ± 56 hours

Pregnancy Considerations Adalimumab crosses the placenta and can be detected in cord blood at birth at concentrations higher than those in the maternal serum. In one study of pregnant women with inflammatory bowel disease, adalimumab was found to be measurable in a newborn for up to 11 weeks following delivery. Maternal doses of adalimumab were 40 mg every other week (n=9) or 40 mg weekly (n=1) and the last dose was administered 0.14 to 8 weeks prior to delivery (median 5.5 weeks) (Mahadevan 2013). If therapy for inflammatory bowel disease is needed during pregnancy, adalimumab should be discontinued before 30 weeks gestation in order to decrease exposure to the newborn. In addition, the administration of live vaccines should be postponed until anti-TNF concentrations in the infant are negative (Habal 2012; Mahadeven 2013; Zelinkova 2013).

Women exposed to adalimumab during pregnancy for the treatment of an autoimmune disease (eg, inflammatory bowel disease) may contact the OTIS Autoimmune Diseases Study at 877-311-8972.

Product Availability Amjevita (adalimumab-atto): FDA approved September 2016; anticipated availability is currently unknown. Amjevita is approved as biosimilar to Humira. Consult the prescribing information for additional information.

Adapalene (a DAP a leen)

Brand Names: US Differin; Differin [OTC]

Brand Names: Canada Differin; Differin XP

Pharmacologic Category Acne Products; Topical Skin Product, Acne

Use Acne vulgaris: Treatment of acne vulgaris.

Local Anesthetic/Vasoconstrictor Precautions No information available to require special precautions

Effects on Dental Treatment No significant effects or complications reported

Effects on Bleeding No information available to require special precautions

Adverse Reactions

>10%: Dermatologic: Xeroderma (≤45%), exfoliation of skin (≤44%), erythema (≤38%), burning sensation of skin (≤29%), stinging of the skin (≤29%)

1% to 10%: Dermatologic: Skin abnormalities (1% to 6%; discomfort), desquamation (2%), pruritus (≤2%), skin irritation (1% to 2%), sunburn (1% to 2%)

≤1%, postmarketing, and/or case reports: Acne flare, angioedema (gel), application site pain (gel), conjunctivitis, contact dermatitis, dermatitis, eczema, eyelid edema, facial edema (gel), skin discoloration, skin rash (cream/gel), swelling of lips (gel)

General Dosage Range Topical: *Children ≥12 years, Adolescents, and Adults:* Apply once daily; use cream and gel in the evening before bedtime

Mechanism of Action Retinoid-like compound which is a modulator of cellular differentiation, keratinization, and inflammatory processes, all of which represent important features in the pathology of acne vulgaris

Pharmacodynamics/Kinetics

Onset of Action 8 to 12 weeks

Half-life Elimination Terminal: 7 to 51 hours (gel)

Pregnancy Risk Factor C

Pregnancy Considerations Adverse effects were observed in animal reproduction studies. Retinoids may cause harm when administered during pregnancy. A case report described maternal use of adapalene 1 month prior to pregnancy and through 13 weeks gestation; cerebral and ocular malformations were reported in the exposed fetus which resulted in termination of pregnancy (Autret, 1997). In clinical trials, women of childbearing potential were required to have a negative pregnancy test prior to therapy.

Adefovir (a DEF o veer)

Related Information

HIV Infection and AIDS *on page 1785*

Systemic Viral Diseases *on page 1806*

Brand Names: US Hepsera

Brand Names: Canada Hepsera

Pharmacologic Category Antihepadnaviral, Reverse Transcriptase Inhibitor, Nucleotide (Anti-HBV)

Use Treatment of chronic hepatitis B with evidence of active viral replication (based on persistent elevation of ALT/AST or histologic evidence), including patients with lamivudine-resistant hepatitis B

Local Anesthetic/Vasoconstrictor Precautions No information available to require special precautions

Effects on Dental Treatment No significant effects or complications reported

Effects on Bleeding No information available to require special precautions

Adverse Reactions In liver transplant patients with baseline renal dysfunction, frequency of increased serum creatinine has been observed to be as high as 32% to 51% at 48 and 96 weeks post-transplantation, respectively; considering the concomitant use of other potentially nephrotoxic medications, baseline renal insufficiency, and predisposing comorbidities, the role of adefovir in these changes could not be established.

>10%:

Central nervous system: Headache (24% to 25%)

Gastrointestinal: Abdominal pain (15%), diarrhea (≤13%)

Genitourinary: Hematuria (grade ≥3: 11%)

Hepatic: Hepatitis (exacerbation; ≤25% within 12 weeks of adefovir discontinuation)

Neuromuscular & skeletal: Weakness (≤25%)

1% to 10%:

Dermatologic: Pruritus, skin rash

Endocrine & metabolic: Hypophosphatemia (<2 mg/dL: 1% and 3% in pre-/post-liver transplant patients, respectively)

Gastrointestinal: Flatulence (≤8%), dyspepsia (5% to 9%), nausea, vomiting

Neuromuscular & skeletal: Back pain (≤10%)

Renal: Increased serum creatinine (≥0.5 mg/dL: 2% to 3% in compensated liver disease; incidence may be higher in patients with decompensated cirrhosis or in liver transplant recipients), renal failure

Respiratory: Cough (6% to 8%), rhinitis (≤5%)

<1%, postmarketing, and/or case reports: Fanconi's syndrome, hepatitis, myopathy, nephrotoxicity, osteomalacia, pancreatitis, proximal tubular nephropathy

General Dosage Range Dosage adjustment recommended in patients with renal impairment

Oral: *Children ≥12 years and Adults:* 10 mg once daily

Mechanism of Action Acyclic nucleotide reverse transcriptase inhibitor (adenosine analog) which interferes with HBV viral RNA-dependent DNA polymerase resulting in inhibition of viral replication.

Pharmacodynamics/Kinetics

Half-life Elimination 7.5 hours; prolonged in renal impairment

Time to Peak Median: 1.75 hours (range: 0.58 to 4 hours)

Pregnancy Risk Factor C

Pregnancy Considerations Adverse events have been observed in animal reproduction studies.

Health care providers are encouraged to enroll women exposed to adefovir during pregnancy in the Hepsera pregnancy registry (800-258-4263).

Adenosine (a DEN oh seen)

Brand Names: US Adenocard; Adenoscan

Brand Names: Canada Adenocard; Adenosine Injection, USP; PMS-Adenosine

Pharmacologic Category Antiarrhythmic Agent, Miscellaneous; Diagnostic Agent

Use

Paroxysmal supraventricular tachycardia: Adenocard: Treatment of paroxysmal supraventricular tachycardia (PSVT) including that associated with accessory bypass tracts (Wolff-Parkinson-White syndrome); when clinically advisable, appropriate vagal maneuvers should be attempted prior to adenosine administration; **not effective for conversion of atrial fibrillation, atrial flutter, or ventricular tachycardia**

Note: While adenosine will not convert atrial fibrillation or atrial flutter, the transient AV-nodal block may aid in the identification of the arrhythmia by exposing the underlying atrial fibrillation or flutter electrocardiographic morphology.

Guideline recommendations: The American College of Cardiology/American Heart Association/Heart Rhythm Society supraventricular tachycardia (SVT) guidelines recommends adenosine in the acute management of a variety of SVTs (eg, AV nodal reentrant tachycardia [AVNRT], AV reentrant tachycardia [AVRT]) (ACC/AHA/HRS [Page 2015]).

Diagnostic aid: Adenoscan: Pharmacologic stress agent used in myocardial perfusion thallium-201 scintigraphy

Local Anesthetic/Vasoconstrictor Precautions No information available to require special precautions

Effects on Dental Treatment No significant effects or complications reported

Effects on Bleeding No information available to require special precautions

Adverse Reactions Note: Frequency varies based on use and is not always defined; higher frequency of infusion-related effects, such as flushing and lightheadedness/dizziness, were reported with continuous infusion (Adenoscan).

>10%:

Cardiovascular: Cardiac arrhythmia (transient and new arrhythmia after cardioversion; eg, atrial premature contractions, atrial fibrillation, premature ventricular contractions; 55%), chest pressure (and discomfort; 7% to 40%)

Central nervous system: Headache (2% to 18%), dizziness (≤12%)

Dermatologic: Facial flushing (18% to 44%)

Gastrointestinal: Gastrointestinal distress (13%)

Neuromuscular & skeletal: Neck discomfort (includes throat, jaw; <1% to 15%)

Respiratory: Dyspnea (12% to 28%)

1% to 10%:

Cardiovascular: Atrioventricular block (infusion 6%; third-degree <1%), depression of ST segment on ECG (3%), hypotension (<1% to 2%), chest pain, palpitations

Central nervous system: Nervousness (2%), paresthesia (≤2%), numbness (1%), apprehension

Dermatologic: Diaphoresis

Gastrointestinal: Nausea (3%)

Neuromuscular & skeletal: Upper extremity discomfort (≤4%)

Respiratory: Hyperventilation

<1%, postmarketing, and/or case reports: Asystole (prolonged), atrial fibrillation, blurred vision, bradycardia, bronchospasm, burning sensation, cardiac arrest (fatal and nonfatal), increased intracranial pressure, injection site reaction, loss of consciousness, metallic taste, myocardial infarction, respiratory arrest, seizure, torsades de pointes, transient hypertension, ventricular arrhythmia, ventricular fibrillation, ventricular tachycardia

General Dosage Range IV:

Children <50 kg: Initial: 0.05 to 0.1 mg/kg/dose (maximum initial dose: 6 mg); repeat: 0.05 to 0.3 mg/kg/dose (maximum: 0.3 mg/kg/dose or 12 mg/dose)

Children ≥50 kg and Adults: Initial: 6 mg; if not effective, 12 mg may be given; may repeat 12 mg if needed (maximum: 12 mg/dose)

Mechanism of Action

Antiarrhythmic actions: Slows conduction time through the AV node, interrupting the re-entry pathways through the AV node, restoring normal sinus rhythm

Myocardial perfusion scintigraphy: Adenosine also causes coronary vasodilation and increases blood flow in normal coronary arteries with little to no increase in stenotic coronary arteries; thallium-201 uptake into the stenotic coronary arteries will be less than that of normal coronary arteries revealing areas of insufficient blood flow.

Pharmacodynamics/Kinetics

Onset of Action Rapid

Duration of Action Very brief

Half-life Elimination <10 seconds

Pregnancy Risk Factor C

Pregnancy Considerations Animal reproduction studies have not been conducted. Adenosine is an endogenous substance and adverse fetal effects would not be anticipated. Adenosine is recommended for the acute treatment of SVT in pregnant women. The usual recommended doses may be used, although higher doses may be needed in some cases (Page [ACC/AHA/HRS 2015]). ACLS guidelines suggest use is safe and effective in pregnancy (ACLS [Neumar 2010]).

Ado-Trastuzumab Emtansine
(a do tras TU zoo mab em TAN seen)

Brand Names: US Kadcyla

Brand Names: Canada Kadcyla

Pharmacologic Category Antineoplastic Agent, Anti-HER2; Antineoplastic Agent, Antibody Drug Conjugate; Antineoplastic Agent, Antimicrotubular; Antineoplastic Agent, Monoclonal Antibody

Use Breast cancer, metastatic: Treatment (single-agent) of HER2-positive, metastatic breast cancer in patients who previously received trastuzumab and a taxane, separately or in combination, and have either received prior therapy for metastatic disease or developed disease recurrence during or within 6 months of completing adjuvant therapy.

Local Anesthetic/Vasoconstrictor Precautions No information available to require special precautions

Effects on Dental Treatment Key adverse event(s) related to dental treatment: Abnormal taste, oral discomfort, xerostomia and changes in salivation (normal salivary flow resumes upon discontinuation)

Effects on Bleeding Chemotherapy may result in significant myelosuppression, thrombocytopenia (31%; grades 3/4: 15%; Asians grades 3/4: 45%), anemia (14%; grades 3/4: 4%), neutropenia (7%; grades 3/4: 2%). In patients who are under active treatment with these agents, medical consult is suggested.

Adverse Reactions

>10%:

Central nervous system: Fatigue (36%), headache (28%), peripheral neuropathy (21%; grades 3/4: 2%), insomnia (12%)

Dermatologic: Skin rash (12%)

Endocrine & metabolic: Decreased serum potassium (33%; grade 3: 3%)

Gastrointestinal: Nausea (40%), constipation (27%), diarrhea (24%), abdominal pain (19%), vomiting (19%), xerostomia (17%), stomatitis (14%)

Hematologic & oncologic: Decreased platelet count (83% [nadir by day 8]; grade 3: 14%; grade 4: 3%), decreased hemoglobin (60%; grade 3: 4%; grade 4: 1%), decreased neutrophils (39%; grade 3: 3%; grade 4: <1%), hemorrhage (32%; grades 3/4: 2%), thrombocytopenia (31%; grades 3/4: 15%; Asians grades 3/4: 45%), anemia (14%; grades 3/4: 4%)

Hepatic: Increased serum AST (98%; grades 3/4: <8%), increased serum ALT (82%; grades 3/4: <6%), increased serum transaminases (29%), increased serum bilirubin (17%)

Neuromuscular & skeletal: Musculoskeletal pain (36%), arthralgia (19%), weakness (18%), myalgia (14%)

Respiratory: Epistaxis (23%), cough (18%), dyspnea (12%)

Miscellaneous: Fever (19%)

1% to 10%:

Cardiovascular: Peripheral edema (7%), hypertension (5%; grades 3/4: 1%), left ventricular dysfunction (2%; grades 3/4: <1%)

Central nervous system: Dizziness (10%), chills (8%)

Dermatologic: Pruritus (6%)

Endocrine & metabolic: Hypokalemia (10%; grades 3/4: 3%)

Gastrointestinal: Dyspepsia (9%), dysgeusia (8%)

Genitourinary: Urinary tract infection (9%)

Hematologic & oncologic: Neutropenia (7%; grades 3/4: 2%)

Hepatic: Increased serum alkaline phosphatase (5%)

Hypersensitivity: Hypersensitivity (2%)

Immunologic: Antibody development (5%)

Ophthalmic: Blurred vision (5%), conjunctivitis (4%), dry eye syndrome (4%), increased lacrimation (3%)

Respiratory: Pneumonitis (≤1%)

Miscellaneous: Infusion related reaction (1%)

<1%: Anaphylactoid reaction, hepatic encephalopathy, hepatotoxicity, nodular regenerative hyperplasia, portal hypertension

General Dosage Range Dosage reduction recommended in patients who develop toxicities.

IV: *Adults:* 3.6 mg/kg every 3 weeks; maximum dose: 3.6 mg/kg

Mechanism of Action Ado-trastuzumab emtansine is a HER2 antibody drug conjugate which incorporates the HER2 targeted actions of trastuzumab with the microtubule inhibitor DM1 (a maytansine derivative). The conjugate, which is linked via a stable thioether linker, allows for selective delivery into HER2 overexpressing cells, resulting in cell cycle arrest and apoptosis.

Pharmacodynamics/Kinetics

Half-life Elimination ~4 days

Time to Peak Near the end of the infusion

Pregnancy Considerations Animal reproduction studies have not been conducted. **[US Boxed Warning]: Exposure to ado-trastuzumab emtansine during pregnancy may cause embryo-fetal harm. Effective contraception must be used in women of reproductive potential.** Oligohydramnios and oligohydramnios sequence (manifested as pulmonary hypoplasia, skeletal malformations and neonatal death) were observed following trastuzumab exposure during pregnancy (trastuzumab is the antibody component of ado-trastuzumab emtansine). Monitor for oligohydramnios if trastuzumab exposure occurs during pregnancy or within 7 months prior to conception; conduct appropriate fetal testing if oligohydramnios occurs. Based on the mechanism of action, the DM1 component of the ado-trastuzumab emtansine formulation may also cause fetal harm if administered during pregnancy. Verify pregnancy status (in females of reproductive potential) prior to therapy. Effective contraception is recommended during therapy and for 7 months after the last dose for women of childbearing potential. Males with female partners of reproductive potential should use effective contraception during therapy and for 4 months after the last dose. Ado-trastuzumab emtansine may impair fertility in females and males.

If ado-trastuzumab emtansine exposure occurs during pregnancy or within 7 months prior to conception, healthcare providers should report the exposure to the Genentech Adverse Event Line (888-835-2555). Women exposed to ado-trastuzumab emtansine during pregnancy or within 7 months prior to conception are encouraged to enroll in MotHER Pregnancy Registry (1-800-690-6720).

European Society for Medical Oncology (ESMO) guidelines for cancer during pregnancy recommend delaying treatment with HER-2 targeted agents until after delivery in pregnant patients with HER-2 positive disease (Peccatori 2013).

Agalsidase Beta (aye GAL si days BAY ta)

Brand Names: US Fabrazyme

Brand Names: Canada Fabrazyme

Pharmacologic Category Enzyme

Use Fabry disease: For use in patients with Fabry disease. Agalsidase beta reduces globotriaosylceramide (GL-3) deposition in capillary endothelium of the kidney and certain other cell types.

Local Anesthetic/Vasoconstrictor Precautions No information available to require special precautions

Effects on Dental Treatment No significant effects or complications reported

Effects on Bleeding No information available to require special precautions

Adverse Reactions

>10%:

Cardiovascular: Peripheral edema (21%), hypertension (14%)

Central nervous system: Chills (43%), headache (39%), paresthesia (31%), procedural pain (25%), fatigue (24%), dizziness (21%), pain (16%), sensation of cold (11%)

Dermatologic: Skin rash (20%)

Immunologic: Development of IgG Antibodies (69% to 79%)

Local: Infusion site reaction (50% to 55%, severe ≥5%)

Neuromuscular & skeletal: Limb pain (19%), back pain (16%), myalgia (14%)
Respiratory: Upper respiratory tract infection (44%), cough (33%), nasal congestion (19%), lower respiratory tract infection (18%)
Miscellaneous: Fever (39%)
1% to 10%:
Cardiovascular: Tachycardia (9%), bradycardia (≥5%), chest discomfort (≥5%), chest pain (≥5%), facial edema (≥5%), flushing (≥5%), hypotension (≥5%), ventricular hypertrophy (5%)
Central nervous system: Hypoesthesia (9%), anxiety (6%), burning sensation (6%), depression (6%), falling (6%)
Dermatologic: Pruritus (10%), excoriation (9%), pallor (≥5%), urticaria (≥5%), thermal injury (4%)
Gastrointestinal: Toothache (6%), abdominal pain (≥5%), diarrhea (≥5%), nausea (≥5%), vomiting (≥5%), xerostomia (4%)
Hematologic & oncologic: Bruise (4%)
Hypersensitivity: Anaphylaxis, hypersensitivity reaction
Infection: Fungal infection (5%), viral infection (5%), localized infection (4%)
Neuromuscular & skeletal: Muscle spasm (5%)
Otic: Tinnitus (8%), hypoacusis (5%)
Renal: Increased serum creatinine (9%)
Respiratory: Sinusitis (9%), dyspnea (8%), respiratory congestion (8%), pharyngitis (6%), wheezing (6%), pharyngeal edema (≥5%)
Miscellaneous: Procedural complications (postprocedure, 10%)
Frequency not defined:
Cardiovascular: Cardiac arrhythmia, cerebrovascular accident, low cardiac output
Central nervous system: Ataxia, vertigo
Genitourinary: Nephrotic syndrome
<1%, postmarketing, and/or case reports: Anaphylactic shock, angioedema (including auricular edema, dysphagia, lip edema, ocular edema, pharyngeal edema, tongue edema), arthralgia, bronchospasm, cardiac failure, decreased oxygen saturation, erythema, hyperhidrosis, hypersensitivity angiitis, hypoxia, increased lacrimation, lymphadenopathy, myocardial infarction, palpitations, pneumonia, renal failure, respiratory failure, rhinorrhea, sepsis, weakness

General Dosage Range IV: *Children ≥8 years, Adolescents, and Adults:* 1 mg/kg every 2 weeks

Mechanism of Action Agalsidase beta is a recombinant form of the enzyme alpha-galactosidase-A, which is required for the hydrolysis of GL-3 and other glycosphingolipids. The compounds may accumulate (over many years) within the tissues of patients with Fabry disease, leading to renal and cardiovascular complications. In clinical trials of limited duration, agalsidase been noted to reduce tissue inclusions of a key sphingolipid (GL-3). It is believed that long-term enzyme replacement may reduce clinical manifestations of renal failure, cardiomyopathy, and stroke. However, the relationship to a reduction in clinical manifestations has not been established.

Pharmacodynamics/Kinetics

Half-life Elimination
Dose dependent: Children: 86 to 151 minutes; Adults: 45 to 119 minutes

Pregnancy Risk Factor B

Pregnancy Considerations Adverse events have not been observed in animal reproduction studies. Women of childbearing potential are encouraged to enroll in the Fabry registry (www.registrynxt.com or 1-800-745-4447).

Albendazole (al BEN da zole)

Brand Names: US Albenza

Pharmacologic Category Anthelmintic

Use

Hydatid disease: Treatment of cystic hydatid disease of the liver, lung, and peritoneum caused by the larval form of the dog tapeworm, *Echinococcus granulosus*.

Neurocysticercosis: Treatment of parenchymal neurocysticercosis due to active lesions caused by larval forms of the pork tapeworm, *Taenia solium*.

Local Anesthetic/Vasoconstrictor Precautions
No information available to require special precautions

Effects on Dental Treatment No significant effects or complications reported

Effects on Bleeding No information available to require special precautions

Adverse Reactions
>10%:
Central nervous system: Headache (neurocysticercosis: 11%; hydatid: 1%)
Hepatic: Increased liver enzymes (hydatid: 16%; neurocysticercosis: <1%)
1% to 10%:
Central nervous system: Increased intracranial pressure (≤2%), dizziness (≤1%), vertigo (≤1%), meningism (1%)
Dermatologic: Alopecia (<1% to 2%)
Gastrointestinal: Abdominal pain (≤6%), nausea and vomiting (4% to 6%)
Miscellaneous: Fever (≤1%)
<1%, postmarketing, and/or case reports: Acute hepatic failure, acute renal failure, agranulocytosis, aplastic anemia, erythema multiforme, granulocytopenia, hepatitis, hypersensitivity reaction, leukopenia, neutropenia, pancytopenia, skin rash, Stevens-Johnson syndrome, thrombocytopenia, urticaria

General Dosage Range Oral:
Children, Adolescents, and Adults <60 kg: 15 mg/kg/day in 2 divided doses (maximum: 800 mg/day)
Children, Adolescents, and Adults ≥60 kg: 800 mg/day in 2 divided doses (maximum: 800 mg/day)

Mechanism of Action Active metabolite, albendazole sulfoxide, causes selective degeneration of cytoplasmic microtubules in intestinal and tegmental cells of intestinal helminths and larvae; glycogen is depleted, glucose uptake and cholinesterase secretion are impaired, and desecratory substances accumulate intracellulary. ATP production decreases causing energy depletion, immobilization, and worm death.

Pharmacodynamics/Kinetics

Half-life Elimination 8 to 12 hours (albendazole sulfoxide)

Time to Peak Serum: 2 to 5 hours for the metabolite

Pregnancy Risk Factor C

Pregnancy Considerations Adverse events were observed in animal reproduction studies. Albendazole should not be used during pregnancy, if at all possible. The manufacturer recommends a pregnancy test prior to therapy in women of reproductive potential. Women should be advised to avoid pregnancy during and for at least 1 month following therapy. Discontinue if pregnancy occurs during treatment.

Albiglutide (al bi GLOO tide)

Brand Names: US Tanzeum

Pharmacologic Category Antidiabetic Agent, Glucagon-Like Peptide-1 (GLP-1) Receptor Agonist

Use Diabetes mellitus, type 2: Adjunct to diet and exercise to improve glycemic control in the treatment of type 2 diabetes mellitus (noninsulin dependent, NIDDM)

Local Anesthetic/Vasoconstrictor Precautions No information available to require special precautions

Effects on Dental Treatment Key adverse event(s) related to dental treatment: Schedule type 1 and type 2 diabetic patients for dental treatment in the morning in order to minimize chance of stress-induced hypoglycemia.

Effects on Bleeding No information available to require special precautions

Adverse Reactions Reactions reported from monotherapy and combination therapy.

>10%:

Endocrine & metabolic: Hypoglycemia (combination therapy; 3% to 17%)

Gastrointestinal: Diarrhea (13%), nausea (11%)

Local: Injection site reaction (11% to 18%, including erythema at injection site [2%], hypersensitivity reaction at injection site [1%], rash at injection site [1%], itching at injection site)

Respiratory: Upper respiratory tract infection (14%)

1% to 10%:

Cardiovascular: Atrial fibrillation (1%)

Endocrine & metabolic: Increased gamma-glutamyl transferase (2%)

Gastrointestinal: Gastroesophageal reflux disease (4%), vomiting (4%)

Immunologic: Antibody development (non-neutralizing; 6%)

Infection: Influenza (5%)

Neuromuscular & skeletal: Arthralgia (7%), back pain (7%)

Respiratory: Cough (7%), pneumonia (2%)

<1%: Appendicitis, atrial flutter, constipation, hypersensitivity, increased heart rate (1-2 bpm), increased serum ALT, increased serum bilirubin, pancreatitis

General Dosage Range

SubQ: *Adults:* 30 to 50 mg once weekly

Mechanism of Action Albiglutide is an agonist of human glucagon-like peptide-1 (GLP-1) receptor and augments glucose-dependent insulin secretion and slows gastric emptying.

Pharmacodynamics/Kinetics

Half-life Elimination ~5 days

Time to Peak 3 to 5 days

Pregnancy Risk Factor C

Pregnancy Considerations Adverse events have been observed in some animal reproduction studies. Because of the long washout period, consider stopping albiglutide at least 1 month before a planned pregnancy.

In women with diabetes, maternal hyperglycemia can be associated with congenital malformations as well as adverse effects in the fetus, neonate, and the mother (ACOG 2005; ADA 2016c; Kitzmiller 2008; Metzger 2007). To prevent adverse outcomes, prior to conception and throughout pregnancy maternal blood glucose and HbA_{1c} should be kept as close to target goals as possible but without causing significant hypoglycemia (ACOG 2013; ADA 2016c; Blumer 2013; Kitzmiller 2008). Agents other than albiglutide are currently recommended to treat diabetes in pregnant women (ACOG 2013; Blumer 2013).

Albuterol (al BYOO ter ole)

Related Information

Respiratory Diseases *on page 1777*

Brand Names: US AccuNeb [DSC]; ProAir HFA; ProAir RespiClick; Proventil HFA; Ventolin HFA; VoSpire ER

Brand Names: Canada Airomir; Apo-Salvent; Apo-Salvent AEM; Apo-Salvent CFC Free; Apo-Salvent Sterules; Dom-Salbutamol; Novo-Salbutamol HFA; PHL-Salbutamol; PMS-Salbutamol; ratio-Ipra-Sal; ratio-Salbutamol; Salbutamol HFA; Sandoz-Salbutamol; Teva-Salbutamol Sterinebs P.F.; Ventolin Diskus; Ventolin HFA; Ventolin I.V. Infusion; Ventolin Nebules P.F.; Ventolin Respirator

Pharmacologic Category $Beta_2$ Agonist

Use Treatment or prevention of bronchospasm in patients with reversible obstructive airway disease; prevention of exercise-induced bronchospasm

Local Anesthetic/Vasoconstrictor Precautions No information available to require special precautions

Effects on Dental Treatment Key adverse event(s) related to dental treatment: Xerostomia (normal salivary flow resumes upon discontinuation)

Effects on Bleeding No information available to require special precautions

Adverse Reactions Incidence of adverse effects is dependent upon age of patient, dose, and route of administration. Frequency not always defined.

>10%:

Central nervous system: Excitement (children and adolescents 2 to 14 years: 20%), nervousness (4% to 15%)

Neuromuscular & skeletal: Tremor (≥5% to 38%; frequency increases with age)

Respiratory: Upper respiratory tract infection (≥5% to 21%), rhinitis (5% to 16%), bronchospasm (8% to 15%; exacerbation of underlying pulmonary disease), pharyngitis (14%), exacerbation of asthma (11% to 13%)

1% to 10%:

Cardiovascular: Tachycardia (≤7%), hypertension (1% to 3%), chest pain (<3%), edema (<3%), extrasystoles (<3%), chest discomfort, flushing, palpitations

Central nervous system: Shakiness (children and adolescents 6 to 14 years: 9%), headache (3% to 7%), dizziness (<7%), insomnia (1% to 3%), anxiety (<3%), ataxia (<3%), depression (<3%), drowsiness (<3%), rigors (<3%), voice disorder (<3%), hyperactivity (children and adolescents 6 to 14 years: 2%), malaise (2%), pain (2%), migraine (≤2%), emotional lability (1%), fatigue (1%), restlessness, vertigo

Dermatologic: Diaphoresis (<3%), skin rash (<3%), urticaria (≤2%), pallor (children 2 to 6 years: 1%)

Endocrine & metabolic: Increased serum glucose (10%), diabetes mellitus (<3%)

Gastrointestinal: Nausea (2% to 10%), vomiting (3% to 7%), unpleasant taste (inhalation site, 4%), gastroenteritis (3%), increased appetite (children and adolescents 6 to 14 years: 3%), viral gastroenteritis (1% to 3%), diarrhea (<3%), eructation (<3%), flatulence (<3%), glossitis (<3%), xerostomia (<3%), gastrointestinal symptoms (children 2 to 6 years: 2%), dyspepsia (1% to 2%), anorexia (children 2 to 6 years: 1%)

Genitourinary: Urinary tract infection (≤3%), difficulty in micturition
Hematologic & oncologic: Decreased hematocrit (7%), decreased hemoglobin (7%), decreased white blood cell count (4%), lymphadenopathy (3%)
Hepatic: Increased serum ALT (5%), increased serum AST (4%)
Hypersensitivity: Hypersensitivity reaction (3% to 6%)
Infection: Cold symptoms (3%), infection (<3%; skin/appendage: ≤2%)
Local: Application site reaction (HFA inhaler: 6%)
Neuromuscular & skeletal: Muscle cramps (1% to 7%; frequency increases with age), musculoskeletal pain (3% to 5%), back pain (2% to 4%), hyperkinesia (≤4%), leg cramps (<3%)
Ophthalmic: Conjunctivitis (children 2 to 6 years: 1%)
Otic: Otitis media (≤4%), ear disease (<3%), otalgia (<3%), tinnitus (<3%)
Respiratory: Throat irritation (10%), viral upper respiratory tract infection (7%), respiratory tract disease (6%), nasopharyngitis (≥5%; children: 2%), oropharyngeal pain (≥5%; children: 2%), sinusitis (≥5%), upper respiratory tract inflammation (5%), cough (≥3%), flu-like symptoms (3%), dyspnea (<3%), laryngitis (<3%), oropharyngeal edema (<3%), pulmonary disease (<3%), bronchitis (≥2%), increased bronchial secretions (2%), wheezing (1% to 2%), epistaxis (children and adolescents 6 to 14 years: 1%), nasal congestion (1%), sinus headache (1%)
Miscellaneous: Fever (≥5% to 6%), accidental injury (<3%)

<1%, postmarketing, and/or case reports: Anaphylaxis, angina pectoris, angioedema, atrial fibrillation, dysgeusia, exacerbation of diabetes mellitus, gag reflex, hoarseness, hyperglycemia, hypokalemia, hypotension, irritability, ketoacidosis, lactic acidosis, metabolic acidosis, muscle spasm (children and adolescents 6 to 14 years), mydriasis (children and adolescents 6 to 14 years), oropharyngeal irritation, paradoxical bronchospasm, peripheral vasodilation, stomach pain (children and adolescents 6 to 14 years), supraventricular tachycardia, tongue ulcer, weakness

General Dosage Range

Inhalation via metered-dose inhaler (90 mcg/actuation): *Children, Adolescents, and Adults:* 2 inhalations every 4 to 6 hours **or** 4 to 8 inhalations every 1 to 4 hours [acute symptoms] **or** 1 to 2 inhalations prior to exercise

Nebulization:

Children <12 years: 0.15 to 0.3 mg/kg (maximum: 10 mg) every 1 to 4 hours **or** 0.63 to 1.25 mg 3 to 4 times daily **or** 0.5 mg/kg/hour by continuous nebulization

Children ≥12 years and Adolescents: 2.5 to 10 mg every 1 to 4 hours **or** 10 to 15 mg/hour by continuous nebulization

Adults: 2.5 to 10 mg every 1 to 4 hours **or** 10 to 15 mg/hour by continuous nebulization

Oral:

Regular release:

Children 2 to 6 years: 0.1 to 0.2 mg/kg/dose 3 times daily (maximum: 12 mg daily)

Children 6 to 12 years: 2 mg/dose 3 to 4 times daily (maximum: 24 mg daily)

Children >12 years, Adolescents, and Adults: 2 to 4 mg/dose 3 to 4 times daily (maximum: 32 mg daily)

Extended release:

Children 6 to 12 years: 4 mg every 12 hours (maximum: 24 mg daily)

Children >12 years, Adolescents, and Adults: 8 mg every 12 hours (maximum: 32 mg daily)

Mechanism of Action Relaxes bronchial smooth muscle by action on beta$_2$-receptors with little effect on heart rate

Pharmacodynamics/Kinetics

Onset of Action Peak effect:

Nebulization/oral inhalation: 0.5 to 2 hours
CFC-propelled albuterol: 10 minutes
Inhalation powder: 30 minutes
Ventolin HFA: 25 minutes
Oral: Immediate release: 2 to 3 hours

Duration of Action Nebulization/oral inhalation: 2 to 5 hours; Oral: Immediate release: 4 to 6 hours; Extended release tablets: Up to 12 hours

Half-life Elimination Inhalation: 3.8 to ~5 hours; Oral: 3.7 to 5 hours

Pregnancy Risk Factor C

Pregnancy Considerations Adverse events have been observed in some animal reproduction studies. Albuterol crosses the placenta (Boulton, 1997). Congenital anomalies (cleft palate, limb defects) have rarely been reported following maternal use during pregnancy. Multiple medications were used in most cases, no specific pattern of defects has been reported, and no relationship to albuterol has been established. The amount of albuterol available systemically following inhalation is significantly less in comparison to oral doses.

Uncontrolled asthma is associated with adverse events on pregnancy (increased risk of perinatal mortality, preeclampsia, preterm birth, low birth weight infants). Albuterol is the preferred short acting beta agonist when treatment for asthma is needed during pregnancy (NAEPP, 2005; NAEPP, 2007).

Albuterol may affect uterine contractility. Maternal pulmonary edema and other adverse events have been reported when albuterol was used for tocolysis. Albuterol is not approved for use as a tocolytic; use caution when needed to treat bronchospasm in pregnant women. Use of the injection (Canadian product; not available in the U.S.) is specifically contraindicated in women during the first or second trimester who may be at risk of threatened abortion.

Alcaftadine (al KAF ta deen)

Brand Names: US Lastacaft

Pharmacologic Category Histamine H$_1$ Antagonist; Histamine H$_1$ Antagonist, Second Generation; Mast Cell Stabilizer

Use Allergic conjunctivitis: Prevention of itching associated with allergic conjunctivitis

Local Anesthetic/Vasoconstrictor Precautions No information available to require special precautions

Effects on Dental Treatment No significant effects or complications reported

Effects on Bleeding No information available to require special precautions

Adverse Reactions 1% to 10%:

Central nervous system: Headache (<3%)
Ophthalmic: Burning sensation of eyes (<4%), eye irritation (<4%), eye pruritus (<4%), eye redness (<4%), stinging of eyes (<4%)
Respiratory: Nasopharyngitis (<3%)

<1%, postmarketing, and/or case reports: Allergic dermatitis, blurred vision, drowsiness, erythema of eyelid,

eye discharge, eyelid edema, facial edema, hypersensitivity, increased lacrimation, swelling of eye

General Dosage Range Ophthalmic: *Children ≥2 years, Adolescents, and Adults:* Instill 1 drop into each eye once daily

Mechanism of Action Direct H_1-receptor antagonist and inhibitor of histamine release from mast cells

Pharmacodynamics/Kinetics

Half-life Elimination Carboxylic acid: ~2 hours

Pregnancy Risk Factor B

Pregnancy Considerations Adverse events were not observed in animal reproduction studies. The amount of alcaftadine absorbed systemically following ophthalmic administration is minimal.

Alclometasone (al kloe MET a sone)

Brand Names: US Aclovate

Pharmacologic Category Corticosteroid, Topical

Use Treatment of inflammation of corticosteroid-responsive dermatosis (low to medium potency topical corticosteroid)

Local Anesthetic/Vasoconstrictor Precautions No information available to require special precautions

Effects on Dental Treatment No significant effects or complications reported

Effects on Bleeding No information available to require special precautions

Adverse Reactions Frequency not always defined.

Central nervous system: Localized burning (1% to 2%)

Dermatologic: Local dryness (2%), papular rash (2%), erythema (1% to 2%), pruritus (1% to 2%), acne vulgaris, allergic dermatitis, atrophic striae, folliculitis, hypopigmentation, miliaria, perioral dermatitis, skin atrophy

Endocrine & metabolic: Cushing's syndrome, growth suppression, HPA-axis suppression

Infection: Secondary infection

Local: Local irritation (2%)

General Dosage Range Topical: *Children ≥1 year and Adults:* Apply a thin film to the affected area 2-3 times/day

Mechanism of Action Topical corticosteroids have anti-inflammatory, antipruritic, and vasoconstrictive properties. May depress the formation, release, and activity of endogenous chemical mediators of inflammation (kinins, histamine, liposomal enzymes, prostaglandins) through the induction of phospholipase A_2 inhibitory proteins (lipocortins) and sequential inhibition of the release of arachidonic acid. Alclometasone has low range potency.

Pharmacodynamics/Kinetics

Onset of Action Initial response (Ruthven 1988): Eczema: 5.3 days; Psoriasis: 6.7 days

Time to Peak Peak response (Ruthven 1988): Eczema: 13.9 days; Psoriasis: 14.8 days

Pregnancy Risk Factor C

Pregnancy Considerations Some corticosteroids were found to be teratogenic following topical application in animal reproduction studies. Topical products are not recommended for extensive use, in large quantities, or for long periods of time in pregnant women.

Aldesleukin (al des LOO kin)

Brand Names: US Proleukin

Brand Names: Canada Proleukin

Pharmacologic Category Antineoplastic Agent, Biological Response Modulator; Antineoplastic Agent, Miscellaneous

Use

Melanoma, metastatic: Treatment of metastatic melanoma

Renal cell cancer, metastatic: Treatment of metastatic renal cell cancer

Limitations of use: Careful patient selection is necessary. Assess performance status (PS); patients with a more favorable PS (Eastern Cooperative Oncology Group [ECOG] PS 0) at treatment initiation respond better to aldesleukin (higher response rate and lower toxicity). Experience in patients with ECOG PS >1 is limited.

Local Anesthetic/Vasoconstrictor Precautions No information available to require special precautions

Effects on Dental Treatment Key adverse event(s) related to dental treatment: Stomatitis

Effects on Bleeding Chemotherapy may result in significant myelosuppression, including thrombocytopenia. In patients who are under active treatment, a medical consult is suggested.

Adverse Reactions

>10%:

Cardiovascular: Hypotension (71%, grade 4: 3%), peripheral edema (28%), tachycardia (23%), edema (15%), vasodilatation (13%), supraventricular tachycardia (12%, grade 4: 1%), cardiac disease (11%; includes blood pressure changes, HF and ECG changes)

Central nervous system: Chills (52%), confusion (34%, grade 4: 1%), malaise (27%), drowsiness (22%), anxiety (12%), pain (12%), dizziness (11%)

Dermatologic: Skin rash (42%), pruritus (24%), exfoliative dermatitis (18%)

Endocrine & metabolic: Weight gain (16%), acidosis (12%, grade 4: 1%), hypomagnesemia (12%), hypocalcemia (11%)

Gastrointestinal: Diarrhea (67%, grade 4: 2%), vomiting (19% to 50%, grade 4: 1%), nausea (19% to 35%), stomatitis (22%), anorexia (20%), abdominal pain (11%)

Genitourinary: Oliguria (63%, grade 4: 6%)

Hematologic & oncologic: Thrombocytopenia (37%, grade 4: 1%), anemia (29%), leukopenia (16%)

Hepatic: Hyperbilirubinemia (40%, grade 4: 2%), increased serum AST (23%, grade 4: 1%)

Immunologic: Antibody development (66% to 74%)

Infection: Infection (13%, grade 4: 1%)

Miscellaneous: Fever (29%, grade 4: 1%)

Neuromuscular & skeletal: Weakness (23%)

Renal: Increased serum creatinine (33%, grade 4: 1%)

Respiratory: Dyspnea (43%, grade 4: 1%), pulmonary disease (24%; includes pulmonary congestion, rales, rhonchi), cough (11%), respiratory tract disease (11%; includes acute respiratory distress syndrome, pulmonary infiltrates, and pulmonary changes)

1% to 10%:

Cardiovascular: Cardiac arrhythmia (10%), cardiac arrest (grade 4: 1%), myocardial infarction (grade 4: 1%), ventricular tachycardia (grade 4: 1%)

Central nervous system: Coma (grade 4: 2%), psychosis (grade 4: 1%), stupor (grade 4: 1%)

Gastrointestinal: Enlargement of abdomen (10%)

Genitourinary: Anuria (grade 4: 5%)

Hematologic & oncologic: Blood coagulation disorder (grade 4: 1%; includes intravascular coagulopathy)

Hepatic: Increased serum alkaline phosphatase (10%)

Infection: Sepsis (grade 4: 1%)

Renal: Acute renal failure (grade 4: 1%)
Respiratory: Rhinitis (10%), apnea (grade 4: 1%)

<1%, postmarketing, and/or case reports: Agitation, allergic interstitial nephritis, anaphylaxis, angioedema, asthma, atrial arrhythmia, atrioventricular block, blindness (transient or permanent), bowel infarction, bradycardia, brain disease, bullous pemphigoid, capillary leak syndrome, cardiomyopathy, cellulitis, cerebral edema, cerebral lesion, cerebral vasculitis, cerebrovascular accident, cholecystitis, colitis, delirium, depression (severe; leading to suicide), diabetes mellitus, duodenal ulcer, endocarditis, eosinophilia, exacerbation of Crohn's disease, extrapyramidal reaction, gastritis, hematemesis, hemoptysis, hemorrhage (including cerebral, gastrointestinal, retroperitoneal, subarachnoid, subdural), hepatic failure, hepatitis, hepatosplenomegaly, hypertension, hyperthyroidism, hyperuricemia, hyperventilation, hypothermia, hypoventilation, hypoxia, IgA glomerulonephritis (crescentic), increased blood urea nitrogen, increased nonprotein nitrogen, inflammatory arthritis, insomnia, intestinal necrosis, intestinal obstruction, intestinal perforation, ischemic heart disease, leukocytosis, lymphocytopenia, malignant hyperthermia, meningitis, myasthenia gravis (oculo-bulbar), mydriasis, myocarditis, myopathy, myositis, neuralgia, neuritis, neuropathy, neutropenia, optic neuritis, pancreatitis, paranoia, pericardial effusion, pericarditis, peripheral gangrene, phlebitis, pneumonia, pneumothorax, pulmonary edema, pulmonary embolism, renal tubular necrosis, respiratory acidosis, respiratory arrest, respiratory failure, restricted systemic blood flow, rhabdomyolysis, scleroderma, seizure, shock, Stevens-Johnson syndrome, syncope, thrombosis, thyroiditis, tissue necrosis at injection site, tracheoesophageal fistula, transient ischemic attacks, urticaria, ventricular premature contractions

General Dosage Range Dosage adjustment recommended in patients who develop toxicities

IV: *Adults:* 600,000 units/kg every 8 hours (maximum: 14 doses); may repeat after 9 days for a total of 28 doses/course

Mechanism of Action Aldesleukin is a human recombinant interleukin-2 product which promotes proliferation, differentiation, and recruitment of T and B cells, natural killer (NK) cells, and thymocytes; causes cytolytic activity in a subset of lymphocytes and subsequent interactions between the immune system and malignant cells; can stimulate lymphokine-activated killer (LAK) cells and tumor-infiltrating lymphocytes (TIL) cells.

Pharmacodynamics/Kinetics

Half-life Elimination

IV:

Children: Distribution: 14 ± 6 minutes; Elimination: 51 ± 11 minutes

Adults: Distribution: 13 minutes; Terminal: 85 minutes

Pregnancy Risk Factor C

Pregnancy Considerations Adverse events were observed in animal reproduction studies. Use during pregnancy only if benefits to the mother outweigh potential risk to the fetus. Effective contraception is recommended for fertile males and/or females using this medication.

Alectinib (al EK ti nib)

Brand Names: US Alecensa

Brand Names: Canada Alecensaro

Pharmacologic Category Antineoplastic Agent, Anaplastic Lymphoma Kinase Inhibitor; Antineoplastic Agent, Tyrosine Kinase Inhibitor

Use Non-small cell lung cancer, metastatic: Treatment of patients with anaplastic lymphoma kinase (ALK)-positive, metastatic non-small cell lung cancer (NSCLC) who have progressed on or are intolerant to crizotinib.

Local Anesthetic/Vasoconstrictor Precautions No information available to require special precautions

Effects on Dental Treatment No significant effects or complications reported

Effects on Bleeding No reports of bleeding or thrombocytopenia.

Adverse Reactions

>10%:

Cardiovascular: Edema (30%), bradycardia (8% to 20%)

Central nervous system: Fatigue (≤41%), headache (17%)

Dermatologic: Skin rash (18%)

Endocrine & metabolic: Hyperglycemia (36%), hypocalcemia (32%), hypokalemia (29%), hypophosphatemia (21%), hyponatremia (20%), weight gain (11%)

Gastrointestinal: Constipation (34%), nausea (18%), diarrhea (16%), vomiting (12%)

Hematologic & oncologic: Anemia (56%, grades 3/4: 2%), lymphocytopenia (22%, grades 3/4: 5%)

Hepatic: Increased serum AST (51%, grades 3/4: 4%), increased serum alkaline phosphatase (47%), hyperbilirubinemia (39%, grades 3/4: 2% to 3%), increased serum ALT (34%, grades 3/4: 5%)

Neuromuscular & skeletal: Increased creatinine phosphokinase (43%, grades 3/4: 5%), weakness (≤41%), musculoskeletal pain (≤29%), myalgia (≤29%), back pain (12%)

Renal: Increased serum creatinine (28%)

Respiratory: Cough (19%), dyspnea (16%)

1% to 10%:

Cardiovascular: Pulmonary embolism (1%)

Dermatologic: Photosensitivity dermatitis (10%)

Ophthalmic: Visual disturbances (10%)

<1%, postmarketing, and/or case reports: Interstitial pulmonary disease, pneumonitis

General Dosage Range Dosage adjustment recommended in patients who develop toxicities.

Oral: *Adults:* 600 mg twice daily

Mechanism of Action Alectinib is a tyrosine kinase receptor inhibitor which inhibits anaplastic lymphoma kinase (ALK) and RET (with similar potency to ALK; Ou 2016). ALK gene abnormalities due to mutations or translocations may result in expression of oncogenic fusion proteins (eg, ALK fusion protein) which alter signaling and expression and result in increased cellular proliferation and survival in tumors which express these fusion proteins. Inhibition of ALK phosphorylation and ALK-mediated activation of downstream signaling results in decreased tumor cell viability. Alectinib is more potent than crizotinib against ALK, and can inhibit most of the clinically observed acquired ALK resistance mutations to crizotinib (Ou 2016).

Pharmacodynamics/Kinetics

Half-life Elimination Parent drug: 33 hours; M4: 31 hours

Time to Peak 4 hours

Pregnancy Considerations Based on data from animal reproduction studies and its mechanism of action, alectinib may be expected to cause fetal harm if administered during pregnancy. Women of reproductive potential should use effective contraception during therapy and for 1 week after the final dose. Males with female partners of reproductive potential should use effective contraception during therapy and for 3 months after the last dose.

Prescribing and Access Restrictions Available through specialty pharmacies and distributors. Further information may be obtained from the manufacturer, Genentech, at 1-888-249-4918 or at https://www.alecensa.com/.

Alemtuzumab (ay lem TU zoo mab)

Brand Names: US Campath; Lemtrada

Brand Names: Canada Lemtrada; MabCampath

Pharmacologic Category Antineoplastic Agent, Anti-CD52; Antineoplastic Agent, Monoclonal Antibody; Monoclonal Antibody

Use

B-cell chronic lymphocytic leukemia: Campath or MabCampath [Canadian product]: Treatment (as a single agent) of B-cell chronic lymphocytic leukemia (B-CLL)

Multiple sclerosis, relapsing: Lemtrada: Treatment of patients with relapsing forms of multiple sclerosis (MS), generally who have had an inadequate response to 2 or more medications indicated for the treatment of MS.

Local Anesthetic/Vasoconstrictor Precautions No information available to require special precautions

Effects on Dental Treatment Key adverse event(s) related to dental treatment: Stomatitis and mucositis.

Effects on Bleeding Chemotherapy may result in significant myelosuppression, including thrombocytopenia. In patients who are under active treatment, a medical consult is suggested.

Adverse Reactions

>10%:

Central nervous system: Headache (44% to 52%), fatigue (8% to 21%), insomnia (11% to 17%), paresthesia (10% to 12%)

Dermatologic: Skin rash (43% to 53%), urticaria (15% to 17%), pruritus (13% to 17%)

Endocrine & metabolic: Thyroid disease (13% to 34%)

Gastrointestinal: Nausea (16% to 22%), diarrhea (12%), oral candidiasis (3% to 12%)

Genitourinary: Urinary tract infection (18% to 19%), vulvovaginal candidiasis (3% to 12%)

Hematologic & oncologic: Lymphocytopenia (6% to 100%)

Immunologic: Antibody development (8% to 85%; no effect on drug efficacy; anti-alemtuzumab: 2%)

Infection: Infection (71%), herpes virus infection (16%), fungal infection (12% to 13%)

Local: Infusion related reaction (92%)

Neuromuscular & skeletal: Arthralgia (12% to 13%), limb pain (13%), back pain (12%)

Respiratory: Nasopharyngitis (24% to 25%), upper respiratory tract infection (15% to 16%), oropharyngeal pain (11%), sinusitis (11%)

Miscellaneous: Fever (26% to 30%)

1% to 10%:

Cardiovascular: Flushing (10%), chest discomfort (7% to 8%), tachycardia (6% to 8%), peripheral edema (5%), palpitations (4%), bradycardia (3%), hypotension (3%), chest pain (2%), cold extremities (1%)

Central nervous system: Chills (9% to 10%), dizziness (10%), anxiety (7%), pain (5% to 7%), vertigo (4%), equilibrium disturbance (3%), hyperthermia (3%), increased body temperature (3%), drowsiness (2%), facial hypoesthesia (2%), hypertonia (2%)

Dermatologic: Skin rash (generalized; 7% to 8%), erythema (6%), acne vulgaris (3%), allergic dermatitis (3%), alopecia (3%), erythematous rash (3%), hyperhidrosis (3%), pruritic rash (3%), papular rash (2%), pruritus (generalized; 2%), skin blister (1%), xeroderma (1%)

Endocrine & metabolic: Hypothyroidism (5%), hypermenorrhea (4%), hyperthyroidism (4%), chronic lymphocytic thyroiditis (2%), Graves' disease (2%), thyroid stimulating hormone suppression (2%), goiter (1%)

Gastrointestinal: Vomiting (10%), abdominal pain (5% to 10%), oral herpes (9%), dyspepsia (6% to 9%), dysgeusia (8%), gastroenteritis (4%), upper abdominal pain (4%), abdominal distention (2%), oral mucosa ulcer (1%)

Genitourinary: Occult blood in urine (4% to 8%), uterine hemorrhage (5%), hematuria (3%), cystitis (2%), fungal vaginosis (2%), increase in urinary protein (2%), irregular menses (2%), proteinuria (2%), abnormal urinalysis (1%), herpes genitalis (1%), vaginal hemorrhage (1%)

Hematologic & oncologic: Bruise (10%), decreased CD-4 cell count (5% to 6%), decreased CD-8 cell counts (5% to 6%), decreased absolute lymphocyte count (4% to 5%), decreased T cell lymphocytes (4%), reduction of B-cells (4%), abnormal white blood cell differential (lymphocyte percentage decreased: 3%; lymphocyte percentage increased: 2%), immune thrombocytopenia (2%), nonthrombocytopenic purpura (2%), hematoma (1%), petechia (1%)

Hypersensitivity: Cytokine release syndrome (2%)

Infection: Influenza (8%), herpes zoster (4%), bacterial infection (3%), herpes simplex infection (2%), human papilloma virus infection (2%)

Local: Catheter pain (1%)

Neuromuscular & skeletal: Myalgia (6% to 7%), myasthenia (7%), muscle spasm (6%), weakness (5% to 6%), neck pain (5%), joint sprain (2%), joint swelling (2%), musculoskeletal chest pain (2%)

Ophthalmic: Blurred vision (5%), conjunctivitis (2%), Graves' ophthalmopathy (1%)

Otic: Otalgia (3%), otic infection (3%)

Respiratory: Cough (9%), dyspnea (8% to 9%), bronchitis (7%), epistaxis (5%), pharyngitis (4%), rhinitis (4%), sinus congestion (3%), nasal congestion (2%), wheezing (2%), bronchospasm (1%)

<1%, postmarketing, and/or case reports: Abnormal gait, abnormal hepatic function tests, acquired blood coagulation disorder, agitation, allodynia, altered blood pressure, amenorrhea, anaphylactic shock, anaphylaxis, anemia, angina pectoris, angioedema, anti-GBM disease, antithyroid antibody positive, aphthous stomatitis, aplastic anemia, asthma, ataxia, atrial fibrillation, autoimmune hemolytic anemia, autoimmune thrombocytopenia, bacterial vaginosis, bacteriuria, bacteriuria (asymptomatic), burning sensation, candidiasis, cardiac failure, cardiomyopathy, casts in urine, catheter-site erythema, catheter-site reaction (rash), cellulitis, cervical dysplasia, cervicitis, choking sensation, chronic inflammatory demyelinating polyradiculoneuropathy, connective tissue disease (undifferentiated), constipation, constriction of the pharynx, crystalluria, cutaneous papilloma, decreased appetite, decreased free T4, decreased hematocrit, decreased hemoglobin, decreased monocytes, decreased neutrophils, decreased T3 level,

dehydration, depression, desquamation, diaphoresis, disturbance in attention, dry eye syndrome, dysesthesia, dysmenorrhea, dysphagia, dyssomnia, dysuria, ecchymoses, eczema, edema, eosinopenia, eosinophilia, Epstein-Barr-associated lymphoproliferative disorder, Epstein-Barr infection, esophageal candidiasis, esophagitis, eye pain, eyelid edema, facial edema, facial pain, facial swelling, feeling of heaviness, flatulence, fungal skin infection, furuncle, gastritis, gastroesophageal reflux disease, gastrointestinal disease, gingival hemorrhage, gingival pain, gingivitis, glossalgia, glycosuria, graft versus host disease (transfusion associated), Guillain-Barre syndrome, hematochezia, hemiparesis, hemolytic anemia, hemophilia A (acquired [anti-Factor VIII antibodies]), hemoptysis, hiccups, hyperemia, hyperesthesia, hypersensitivity reaction, hypopigmentation, increased blood pressure, increased free T4, increased heart rate, increased monocytes, increased serum alkaline phosphatase, increased serum ALT, increased serum AST, increased serum bilirubin, increased T3 level, infusion site reaction, iron deficiency anemia, irritability, joint stiffness, labyrinthitis, laryngitis, leukocytosis, leukocyturia, limb pain, local alterations in temperature sensations, lower respiratory tract infection, lymphoproliferative disorder, macular eruption, maculopapular rash, major hemorrhage, malignant lymphoma, malignant melanoma, malignant neoplasm of thyroid, membranous glomerulonephritis, memory impairment, meningitis due to listeria monocytogenes, meningitis (herpes), menstrual disease, microcytic anemia, migraine, mucosal inflammation, multiple sclerosis, muscle spasticity, musculoskeletal pain, natural killer cell count increased, neutropenia, night sweats, noncardiac chest pain, onychomycosis, optic neuropathy, oropharyngeal blistering, ostealgia, ovarian cyst, pain at injection site, painful respiration, pallor, pancytopenia, papule, periorbital edema, peripheral neuropathy, pharyngeal erythema, photophobia, pityriasis rosea, pleurisy, pneumonia, pneumonitis, pollakiuria, positive direct Coombs test, postherpetic neuralgia, presyncope, progressive multifocal leukoencephalopathy, protozoal infection, prurigo, pruritus of ear, psychomotor agitation, pyelonephritis, reactivation of disease, reduced ejection fraction, respiratory congestion (upper), respiratory tract infection, restless leg syndrome, restlessness, retinal pigment changes (epitheliopathy), rheumatoid arthritis, rhinorrhea, seasonal allergy, sensation of cold, sensory disturbance, serum sickness, skin hyperpigmentation, skin infection, skin irritation, skin lesion, stiffness, streptococcal pharyngitis, subacute thyroiditis, suicidal ideation, suicidal tendencies, syncope, tachypnea, throat irritation, thrombocytopenia, thyroiditis, tinea, tinea pedis, tinea versicolor, tinnitus, tongue discoloration, tonsillitis, tooth abscess, tooth infection, toothache, tracheobronchitis, tuberculosis, tumor lysis syndrome, type 1 diabetes mellitus, upper airway symptoms (cough syndrome), urethritis, urinary incontinence, urinary urgency, urine abnormality, vaginal infection, varicella, viral infection, viral respiratory tract infection, visual disturbance, vitiligo, voice disorder, weight gain, weight loss, xerostomia

General Dosage Range Dosage adjustment recommended in patients who develop toxicities

IV (infusion): *Adults:* Initial: 3 mg/day, then 10 mg/day; Maintenance: 30 mg/day 3 times/week on alternate days; Maximum dose: 30 mg/day; 90 mg/week (cumulative) **or** 12 mg daily for 5 days, followed 1 year later by 12 mg daily for 3 days.

Mechanism of Action Binds to CD52, a nonmodulating antigen present on the surface of B and T lymphocytes, a majority of monocytes, macrophages, NK cells, and a subpopulation of granulocytes. After binding to $CD52^+$ cells, an antibody-dependent lysis of malignant cells occurs. In multiple sclerosis, alemtuzumab immunomodulatory effects may include alteration in the number, proportions, and properties of some lymphocyte subsets following treatment.

Pharmacodynamics/Kinetics

Half-life Elimination IV: Campath: 11 hours (following first 30 mg dose; range: 2 to 32 hours); 6 days (following the last 30 mg dose; range: 1 to 14 days); Lemtrada: ~2 weeks

Pregnancy Risk Factor C

Pregnancy Considerations Adverse events were observed in animal reproduction studies. Human IgG is known to cross the placental barrier; therefore, alemtuzumab may also cross the barrier and cause fetal B- and T-lymphocyte depletion. Use during pregnancy only if the benefit to the mother outweighs the potential risk to the fetus. Effective contraception is recommended during and for at least 6 months (Campath) or 4 months (Lemtrada) after treatment for women of childbearing potential and men of reproductive potential.

Prescribing and Access Restrictions As of September 4, 2012, alemtuzumab (Campath) is no longer commercially available in the United States (or Europe); a restricted distribution program will allow access (free of charge) for appropriate patients. Information on necessary documentation and requirements is available at Campath Distribution Program (1-877-422-6728) or Genzyme Medical Information (1-800-745-4447, option 2).

Alendronate (a LEN droe nate)

Related Information

Osteonecrosis of the Jaw *on page 1796*

Rheumatoid Arthritis, Osteoarthritis, and Osteoporosis *on page 1792*

Brand Names: US Binosto; Fosamax

Brand Names: Canada ACH-Alendronate; Alendronate-70; Alendronate-FC; Apo-Alendronate; Auro-Alendronate; CO Alendronate; Dom-Alendronate; Fosamax; JAMP-Alendronate; Mint-Alendronate; Mylan-Alendronate; PHL-Alendronate; PMS-Alendronate; PMS-Alendronate-FC; Q-Alendronate; Ran-Alendronate; ratio-Alendronate; Riva-Alendronate; Sandoz-Alendronate; Teva-Alendronate

Generic Availability (US) May be product dependent

Pharmacologic Category Bisphosphonate Derivative

Use

Osteoporosis: Treatment of osteoporosis in postmenopausal females (Fosamax, Binosto); prevention of osteoporosis in postmenopausal females (Fosamax); treatment of osteoporosis in males (Fosamax, Binosto); treatment of Paget disease of the bone in patients who are symptomatic, at risk for future complications, or with alkaline phosphatase ≥2 times the upper limit of normal (Fosamax); treatment of glucocorticoid-induced osteoporosis in males and females with low bone mineral density who are receiving a daily dosage ≥7.5 mg of prednisone (or equivalent) (Fosamax)

Canadian labeling: Additional use (not in US labeling): Prevention of glucocorticoid-induced osteoporosis in males and females

Local Anesthetic/Vasoconstrictor Precautions No information available to require special precautions

Effects on Dental Treatment Osteonecrosis of the jaw (ONJ), generally associated with local infection and/or tooth extraction and often with delayed healing, has been reported in patients taking bisphosphonates. Symptoms included nonhealing extraction socket or an exposed jawbone. Most reported cases of bisphosphonate-associated osteonecrosis have been in cancer patients treated with intravenous bisphosphonates. However, some have occurred in patients with postmenopausal osteoporosis taking oral bisphosphonates. The risk of developing ONJ in patients taking oral bisphosphonates remains low with an estimated prevalence of 0.1% (one out of every 1000 cases of patients exposed to oral bisphosphonates). The benefits of using the oral bisphosphonates to prevent osteoporosis significantly outweighs the small risk of developing bisphosphonate-associated ONJ. Also, at the present time, there are no validated diagnostic techniques to determine which patients are at increased risk of developing ONJ. ONJ in patients taking these drugs can occur spontaneously. In addition, the risk of ONJ increases with specific procedures that increase bone trauma, particularly tooth extractions. Other factors that increase risk of ONJ in patients taking these drugs are age (>65 years of age), periodontitis, use of bisphosphonates for >2 years, smoking, wearing dentures, and diabetes. Patients who develop ONJ while on bisphosphonate therapy should receive care by an oral surgeon. See Dental Comment.

Effects on Bleeding No information available to require special precautions

Adverse Reactions Note: Incidence of adverse effects (mostly GI) increases significantly in patients treated for Paget's disease at 40 mg/day.

>10%: Endocrine & metabolic: Decreased serum calcium (18%; transient, mild)

1% to 10%:

Central nervous system: Headache (3%)

Endocrine & metabolic: Decreased serum phosphate (10%; transient, mild)

Gastrointestinal: Abdominal pain (2% to 7%), acid regurgitation (1% to 5%), flatulence (≤4%), gastroesophageal reflux disease (3%), constipation (≤3%), diarrhea (≤3%), dyspepsia (1% to 3%), nausea (1% to 3%), esophageal ulcer (2%), dysphagia (1%), melena (1%), abdominal distension (≤1%), gastric ulcer (≤1%; may be severe with complications), gastritis (≤1%)

Neuromuscular & skeletal: Musculoskeletal pain (≤6%; includes bone pain, joint pain, and muscle pain), muscle cramps (≤1%)

<1%, postmarketing, and/or case reports: Alopecia, cholesteatoma, conjunctivitis, dizziness, duodenal ulcer (may be severe with complications), dysgeusia, episcleritis, erythema, erosive esophagitis, esophageal perforation, esophageal stenosis, esophageal ulcer, esophagitis, exacerbation of asthma, femur fracture (low-energy fractures, including subtrochanteric and diaphyseal), fever, hypersensitivity reaction (includes angioedema and urticaria), hypocalcemia (symptomatic), joint swelling, malaise, oropharyngeal ulcer; osteonecrosis of the jaw (generally associated with tooth extraction and/or local infection with delayed healing), peripheral edema, pruritus, scleritis, skin rash (occasionally with photosensitivity), Stevens-Johnson syndrome, toxic epidermal necrolysis, uveitis, vertigo, weakness

Dosing

Adult & Geriatric Note: Consider discontinuing after 3 to 5 years of use for osteoporosis in patients at low-risk for fracture. Patients should receive supplemental calcium and vitamin D if dietary intake is inadequate.

Osteoporosis in postmenopausal females: Oral:

Prophylaxis: 5 mg once daily **or** 35 mg once weekly

Treatment: 10 mg once daily **or** 70 mg once weekly

Osteoporosis in males: Oral: Treatment: 10 mg once daily **or** 70 mg once weekly

Osteoporosis secondary to glucocorticoids in males and females: Oral: Treatment (US labeling) or Treatment and prevention (Canadian labeling): 5 mg once daily; a dose of 10 mg once daily should be used in postmenopausal females who are not receiving estrogen

Paget disease of bone in males and females: Oral: 40 mg once daily for 6 months

Re-treatment: Following a 6-month post-treatment evaluation period, treatment with alendronate may be considered in patients who have relapsed based on increases in serum alkaline phosphatase, which should be measured periodically. Re-treatment may also be considered in those who failed to normalize their serum alkaline phosphatase. The Endocrine Society guidelines suggest re-treatment may be required between 2 and 6 years (Singer 2014).

Missed doses (once weekly): If a once-weekly dose is missed, it should be given the next morning after remembered; may then return to the original once-weekly schedule (original scheduled day of the week), however, do not give 2 doses on the same day.

Osteogenesis imperfecta (off-label use): Oral: 10 mg once daily (Chevrel 2006) **or** 70 mg once weekly (Shapiro 2010).

Renal Impairment

CrCl ≥35 mL/minute: No dosage adjustment necessary.

CrCl <35 mL/minute: Use not recommended.

Hepatic Impairment No dosage adjustment necessary.

Mechanism of Action A bisphosphonate which inhibits bone resorption via actions on osteoclasts or on osteoclast precursors; decreases the rate of bone resorption, leading to an indirect increase in bone mineral density. In Paget's disease, characterized by disordered resorption and formation of bone, inhibition of resorption leads to an indirect decrease in bone formation; but the newly-formed bone has a more normal architecture.

Contraindications

Hypersensitivity to alendronate, other bisphosphonates, or any component of the formulation; hypocalcemia; abnormalities of the esophagus (eg, stricture, achalasia) which delay esophageal emptying; inability to stand or sit upright for at least 30 minutes; increased risk of aspiration (effervescent tablets; oral solution)

Canadian labeling: Additional contraindications (not in US labeling): Renal insufficiency with creatinine clearance <35 mL/minute

Warnings/Precautions Use caution in patients with renal impairment (not recommended for use in patients with CrCl <35 mL/minute); hypocalcemia must be corrected before therapy initiation; ensure adequate calcium and vitamin D intake. May cause irritation to upper gastrointestinal mucosa. Esophagitis, dysphagia, esophageal ulcers, esophageal erosions, and esophageal stricture (rare) have been reported; risk increases in patients unable to comply with dosing instructions. Use with caution in patients with dysphagia, esophageal disease, gastritis, duodenitis, or ulcers (may worsen underlying condition). Discontinue use if new or worsening symptoms develop.

Osteonecrosis of the jaw (ONJ), also referred to as medication-related osteonecrosis of the jaw (MRONJ), has been reported in patients receiving bisphosphonates. Known risk factors for MRONJ include invasive dental procedures (eg, tooth extraction, dental implants, boney surgery), cancer diagnosis, concomitant therapy (eg, chemotherapy, corticosteroids, angiogenesis inhibitors), poor oral hygiene, ill-fitting dentures, and comorbid disorders (anemia, coagulopathy, infection, preexisting dental or periodontal disease). Risk may increase with increased duration of bisphosphonate use. According to a position paper by the American Association of Maxillofacial Surgeons (AAOMS), MRONJ has been associated with bisphosphonate and other antiresorptive agents (denosumab), and antiangiogenic agents (eg, bevacizumab, sunitinib) used for the treatment of osteoporosis or malignancy; risk of MRONJ is significantly higher in cancer patients receiving antiresorptive therapy compared to patients receiving osteoporosis treatment (regardless of medication used or dosing schedule). MRONJ risk is also increased with intravenous antiresorptive use compared to the minimal risk associated with oral bisphosphonate use, although risk appears to increase with oral bisphosphonates when duration of therapy exceeds 4 years (AAOMS [Ruggiero 2014]). The manufacturer's labeling states that in patients requiring invasive dental procedures, discontinuing bisphosphonates may reduce the risk of ONJ and clinical judgment should guide the decision. However, the AAOMS suggests there is currently no evidence that interrupting oral bisphosphonate therapy alters the risk of ONJ following tooth extraction, and that in patients receiving oral bisphosphonates for <4 years who have no clinical risk factors, no alternations or delay in any procedure common to oral/maxillofacial surgeons, periodontists, and other dental providers is necessary (special considerations apply to patients receiving dental implants). Conversely, in patients receiving oral bisphosphonates for >4 years **or** in patients receiving oral bisphosphonates for <4 years who have also taken corticosteroids or antiangiogenic medications concomitantly, the AAOMS recommends considering a 2-month, drug-free period prior to invasive dental procedures (recommendation based on a theoretical benefit). Patients developing ONJ during therapy should receive care by an oral surgeon (AAOMS [Ruggiero 2014]). According to the manufacturer, discontinuation of the bisphosphonate therapy should be considered (based on risk/benefit evaluation) in patients who develop ONJ.

Atypical femur fractures have been reported in patients receiving bisphosphonates for treatment/prevention of osteoporosis. The fractures include subtrochanteric femur (bone just below the hip joint) and diaphyseal femur (long segment of the thigh bone). Some patients experience prodromal pain weeks or months before the fracture occurs. It is unclear if bisphosphonate therapy is the cause for these fractures, although the majority of cases have been reported in patients taking bisphosphonates. Patients receiving long-term (>3 to 5 years) therapy may be at an increased risk. Discontinue bisphosphonate therapy in patients who develop a femoral shaft fracture.

Severe (and occasionally debilitating) bone, joint, and/or muscle pain have been reported during bisphosphonate treatment. The onset of pain ranged from a single day to several months. Consider discontinuing therapy in patients who experience severe symptoms; symptoms usually resolve upon discontinuation. Some patients experienced recurrence when rechallenged with same drug or another bisphosphonate; avoid use in patients with a history of these symptoms in association with bisphosphonate therapy. In the management of osteoporosis, re-evaluate the need for continued therapy periodically; the optimal duration of treatment has not yet been determined. Consider discontinuing after 3 to 5 years of use in patients at low-risk for fracture; following discontinuation, re-evaluate fracture risk periodically.

Conjunctivitis, uveitis, episcleritis, and scleritis have been reported with alendronate; patients presenting with signs of ocular inflammation may require further ophthalmologic evaluation. Potentially significant drug-drug interactions may exist, requiring dose or frequency adjustment, additional monitoring, and/or selection of alternative therapy. Consult drug interactions database for more detailed information. Each effervescent tablet contains 650 mg of sodium (NaCl 1650 mg); use with caution in patients following a sodium-restricted diet.

Drug Interactions

Metabolism/Transport Effects None known.

Avoid Concomitant Use

Avoid concomitant use of Alendronate with any of the following: Parathyroid Hormone

Increased Effect/Toxicity

Alendronate may increase the levels/effects of: Deferasirox

The levels/effects of Alendronate may be increased by: Aminoglycosides; Aspirin; Nonsteroidal Anti-Inflammatory Agents; Systemic Angiogenesis Inhibitors

Decreased Effect

Alendronate may decrease the levels/effects of: Parathyroid Hormone

The levels/effects of Alendronate may be decreased by: Antacids; Calcium Salts; Iron Salts; Magnesium Salts; Multivitamins/Minerals (with ADEK, Folate, Iron); Multivitamins/Minerals (with AE, No Iron); Proton Pump Inhibitors

Food Interactions All food and beverages interfere with absorption. Coadministration with dairy products may decrease alendronate absorption. Beverages (especially orange juice, coffee, and mineral water) and food may reduce the absorption of alendronate as much as 60%. Management: Alendronate must be taken first thing in the morning and ≥30 minutes before the first food, beverage (except plain water), or other medication of the day.

Dietary Considerations Ensure adequate calcium and vitamin D intake; if dietary intake is inadequate, dietary supplementation is recommended. Women and men should consume:

Calcium: 1,000 mg/day (men: 50 to 70 years) **or** 1,200 mg/day (women ≥51 years and men ≥71 years) (IOM 2011; NOF [Cosman 2014])

Vitamin D: 800 to 1,000 int. units/day (men and women ≥50 years) (NOF [Cosman 2014]). Recommended Dietary Allowance (RDA): 600 int. units daily (men and women ≤70 years) **or** 800 int. units/day (men and women ≥71 years) (IOM 2011).

Pharmacodynamics/Kinetics

Half-life Elimination Exceeds 10 years

Pregnancy Risk Factor C

Pregnancy Considerations Adverse events were observed in animal reproduction studies. It is not known if bisphosphonates cross the placenta, but fetal exposure is expected (Djokanovic 2008; Stathopoulos 2011). Bisphosphonates are incorporated into the bone matrix and gradually released over time. The amount available in the systemic circulation varies by dose and duration of therapy. Theoretically, there may be a risk of fetal harm when pregnancy follows the completion of therapy; however, available data have not shown that exposure to bisphosphonates during pregnancy significantly increases the risk of adverse fetal events (Djokanovic 2008; Levy 2009; Stathopoulos 2011). Until additional data is available, most sources recommend discontinuing bisphosphonate therapy in women of reproductive potential as early as possible prior to a planned pregnancy; use in premenopausal women should be reserved for special circumstances when rapid bone loss is occurring (Bhalla 2010; Pereira 2012; Stathopoulos 2011). Because hypocalcemia has been described following *in utero* bisphosphonate exposure, exposed infants should be monitored for hypocalcemia after birth (Djokanovic 2008; Stathopoulos 2011).

Breastfeeding Considerations It is not known if alendronate is excreted into breast milk. The manufacturer recommends that caution be exercised when administering alendronate to nursing women.

Dosage Forms

Solution, Oral:

Generic: 70 mg/75 mL (75 mL)

Tablet, Oral:

Fosamax: 70 mg

Generic: 5 mg, 10 mg, 35 mg, 40 mg, 70 mg

Tablet Effervescent, Oral:

Binosto: 70 mg

Dosage Forms: Canada Refer to Dosage Forms. **Note:** Effervescent tablet and oral solution are not available in Canada.

Dental Comment A review of 2,408 published cases of bisphosphonate-associated osteonecrosis of the jaw bone (BP-associated ONJ) was done by Filleul 2010. BP therapy was associated with 89% of the cases to treat malignancies and 11% of the cases to treat nonmalignant conditions. Information on the specific bisphosphonate used was available for 1,694 of the patients. Intravenous therapy (primarily zoledronic acid) was received by 88% of the patients and 12% received oral treatment (primarily alendronate). Of all the cases of BP-associated ONJ, 67% were preceded by tooth extraction and for 26% of patients, there was no predisposing factor identified.

A 2010 retrospective case review reported the prevalence of BP-associated ONJ in patients using alendronate-type drugs was one out of 952 patients or ~0.1% (Lo 2010). Of the 8,572 respondents, nine cases of ONJ were identified; five had developed ONJ spontaneously and four developed ONJ after tooth extraction. When extrapolated to patient-years of bisphosphonate exposure, this prevalence rate of 0.1% equates to a frequency of 28 cases per 100,000 person-years of oral bisphosphonate treatment. An Australian group (Mavrokokki 2007), identified the frequency of BP-associated ONJ in osteoporotic patients, mainly taking weekly oral alendronate, was 1 in 8,470 to 1 in 2,260 (0.01% to 0.04%) patients. If extractions were carried out, the calculated frequency was 1 in 1,130 to 1 in 296 (0.09% to 0.34%) patients. The median time to onset of ONJ in alendronate patients was 24 months.

According to the 2011 report by the American Dental Association (ADA), the incidence of BP-associated ONJ remains low and the benefits of using oral bisphosphonates significantly outweighs the risk of developing BP-associated ONJ for treatment and prevention of osteoporosis and cancer treatment (Hellstein 2011). The full 47-page report can be accessed at http://www.ada.org/~/media/ADA/Member%20Center/FIles/topics_ARONJ_report.ashx.

The ADA review of 2011 stated the incidence of oral BP-associated ONJ was one case for every 1,000 individuals exposed to oral bisphosphonates (0.1%) (Hellstein 2011).

The most comprehensive review to date on osteonecrosis of the jaw bone (ONJ) has been published in the *Journal of Bone and Mineral Research* (Khan 2015), and written by an International Task Force of authors, totaling 34, from academe; industry; clinical medical and dental practice; oral and maxillofacial surgery; bone and mineral research; epidemiology; medical and dental oncology; orthopedic surgery; osteoporosis research; muscle and bone research; endocrinology and diagnostic sciences. The work provides a systematic review of the literature and international consensus on the classification, incidence, pathophysiology, diagnosis, and management of ONJ in both oncology and osteoporosis patient populations. This review of the literature from January 2003 to April 2014, with 299 references, offers recommendations for management of ONJ based on multidisciplinary international consensus.

Prevalence and incidence of ONJ in osteoporosis patients from the Task Force report:

Prevalence – the percent of osteoporotic population affected with ONJ

After reviewing all literature reports on this subject, the Task Force concluded that the prevalence of ONJ in patients prescribed oral BPs for the treatment of osteoporosis ranges from 0% to 0.04% with the majority being below 0.001%. However, the Task Force does cite the study of (Lo et al) that evaluated the Kaiser Permanente database and found the prevalence of ONJ in those receiving BPs for more than 2 years to range from 0.05% to 0.21% and appeared to be related to duration of exposure. As mentioned above, the American Dental Association has previously reported that the prevalence of ONJ in osteoporosis patients using oral BPs to be 1 out of 1,000 or 0.1% (Hellstein 2011).

Incidence - the rate at which ONJ occurs or the number of times it happens

From currently available data, the incidence of ONJ in the osteoporosis patient population appears to be low ranging from 0.15% to less than 0.001% person-years drug exposure. In terms of the osteoporosis patient population taking oral BPs, the incidence ranges from 1.04 to 69 per 100,000 patient years of drug exposure.

Alendronate and Cholecalciferol

(a LEN droe nate & kole e kal SI fer ole)

Related Information

Alendronate *on page 90*
Cholecalciferol *on page 354*

Brand Names: US Fosamax Plus D

Brand Names: Canada Fosavance; Teva-Alendronate/Cholecalciferol

Pharmacologic Category Bisphosphonate Derivative; Vitamin D Analog

Use

Osteoporosis: Treatment of osteoporosis in postmenopausal females; increase bone mass in males with osteoporosis

Limitations of use: Not for use in the treatment of vitamin D deficiency.

Local Anesthetic/Vasoconstrictor Precautions No information available to require special precautions

Effects on Dental Treatment Osteonecrosis of the jaw (ONJ), generally associated with local infection and/or tooth extraction and often with delayed healing, has been reported in patients taking bisphosphonates. Symptoms included nonhealing extraction socket or an exposed jawbone. Most reported cases of bisphosphonate-associated osteonecrosis have been in cancer patients treated with intravenous bisphosphonates. However, some have occurred in patients with postmenopausal osteoporosis taking oral bisphosphonates. The risk of developing ONJ in patients taking oral bisphosphonates remains low with an estimated prevalence of 0.1% (one out of every 1000 cases of patients exposed to oral bisphosphonates). The benefits of using the oral bisphosphonates to prevent osteoporosis significantly outweighs the small risk of developing bisphosphonate-associated ONJ. Also, at the present time, there are no validated diagnostic techniques to determine which patients are at increased risk of developing ONJ. ONJ in patients taking these drugs can occur spontaneously. In addition, the risk of ONJ increases with specific procedures that increase bone trauma, particularly tooth extractions. Other factors that increase risk of ONJ in patients taking these drugs are age (>65 years of age), periodontitis, use of bisphosphonates for >2 years, smoking, wearing dentures, and diabetes. Patients who develop ONJ while on bisphosphonate therapy should receive care by an oral surgeon. See Dental Comment.

Effects on Bleeding No information available to require special precautions

Adverse Reactions See individual agents.

General Dosage Range Oral: *Adults:* One tablet (alendronate 70 mg/cholecalciferol 2,800 to 5,600 units) once weekly

Mechanism of Action See individual agents.

Pregnancy Risk Factor C

Pregnancy Considerations Animal reproduction studies have not been conducted with this combination. The Canadian labeling recommends avoiding use in pregnant women. See individual agents.

Dental Comment See Alendronate monograph.

Alfacalcidol

(Al fa CAL ce dol)

Brand Names: Canada One-Alpha

Pharmacologic Category Vitamin D Analog

Use Note: Not approved in the US

Chronic kidney disease-mineral and bone disorder: Management of hypocalcemia, secondary hyperparathyroidism, and osteodystrophy in patients with chronic renal failure

Local Anesthetic/Vasoconstrictor Precautions No information available to require special precautions

Effects on Dental Treatment Key adverse event(s) related to dental treatment: Xerostomia (normal salivary flow resumes upon discontinuation) or abnormal taste.

Effects on Bleeding No information available to require special precautions

Adverse Reactions Frequency not defined; as associated with Hypervitaminosis D.

Cardiovascular: Cardiac arrhythmia, hypertension

Central nervous system: Headache, hyperthermia, psychosis (rare), drowsiness

Dermatologic: Pruritus

Gastrointestinal: Anorexia, constipation, dysgeusia, nausea, pancreatitis, vomiting, xerostomia

Genitourinary: Nocturia

Endocrine & metabolic: Decreased libido, hypercalcemia, hypercholesterolemia, hyperphosphatemia, polydipsia, weight loss

Hepatic: Increased serum ALT, increased serum AST

Neuromuscular & skeletal: Myalgia, ostealgia, weakness

Ophthalmic: Conjunctivitis, corneal deposits (calcification), photophobia

Renal: Increased blood urea nitrogen, polyuria

Respiratory: Rhinorrhea

General Dosage Range Individualize dosage:

Oral: *Adults:* 0.25-3 mcg/day

IV: *Adults:* 1-12 mcg/week (with dialysis)

Mechanism of Action Alfacalcidol is rapidly converted to the active metabolite of vitamin D (1,25-dihydroxyvitamin D_3) in the liver, effectively bypassing renal metabolic conversion; promotes intestinal absorption of calcium and phosphorous, resorption of calcium from the bone, and possibly renal reabsorption of calcium

Pharmacodynamics/Kinetics

Onset of Action 6 hours

Duration of Action Effect on intestinal calcium absorption levels: 1,25-$(OH)_2$ D_3: 48 hours

Half-life Elimination Renal insufficiency: ~3 hours

Time to Peak Active vitamin D levels: Oral: 12 hours; IV: 4 hours

Pregnancy Considerations Adverse events have been observed in animal reproduction studies.

Product Availability Not available in the US

Alfentanil

(al FEN ta nil)

Brand Names: Canada Alfenta; Alfentanil Injection, USP

Pharmacologic Category Analgesic, Opioid; Anilidopiperidine Opioid

Use

Analgesia: Analgesic adjunct for the maintenance of anesthesia with barbiturate/nitrous oxide/oxygen; analgesic with nitrous oxide/oxygen in the maintenance of general anesthesia; analgesic component for monitored anesthesia care.

Anesthetic: Primary anesthetic for induction of anesthesia in general surgery when endotracheal intubation and mechanical ventilation are required.

Local Anesthetic/Vasoconstrictor Precautions No information available to require special precautions

Effects on Dental Treatment Key adverse event(s) related to dental treatment: Patients may experience

orthostatic hypotension as they stand up after treatment; especially if lying in dental chair for extended periods of time. Use caution with sudden changes in position during and after dental treatment.

Erythromycin inhibits the liver metabolism of alfentanil resulting in increased sedation and prolonged respiratory depression. Clarithromycin may act similarly.

Effects on Bleeding No information available to require special precautions

Adverse Reactions

>10%:

Cardiovascular: Hypertension (18%), chest wall rigidity (17%), bradycardia (14%), tachycardia (12%)

Gastrointestinal: Nausea (28%), vomiting (18%)

1% to 10%:

Cardiovascular: Hypotension (10%), cardiac arrhythmia (1% to 3%)

Central nervous system: Dizziness (3% to 9%), drowsiness (≤3%), sedation (≤3%; postoperative)

Neuromuscular & skeletal: Muscle movements (3% to 9%; skeletal)

Ophthalmic: Blurred vision (1% to 3%)

Respiratory: Apnea (3% to 9%), respiratory depression (1% to 3%; postoperative)

Frequency not defined:

Cardiovascular: Peripheral vasodilation

Gastrointestinal: Constipation

Ophthalmic: Miosis

<1%, postmarketing, and/or case reports: Anaphylaxis, bronchospasm, confusion (postoperative), drug dependence, euphoria (postoperative), headache, hypercapnia, laryngospasm, muscle rigidity (neck and extremities), myoclonus, pruritus, shivering, urticaria

General Dosage Range IV:

Anesthetic induction: *Children ≥12 years, Adolescents, and Adults:* Initial: 130 to 245 mcg/kg; Maintenance: 0.5 to 1.5 mcg/kg/minute

Continuous infusion: *Children ≥12 years, Adolescents, and Adults:* Initial: 50 to 75 mcg/kg; Maintenance: 0.5 to 3 mcg/kg/minute

Incremental injection: *Children ≥12 years, Adolescents, and Adults:*

≤30 minutes anesthesia: Initial: 8 to 20 mcg/kg; Maintenance: 3 to 5 mcg/kg every 5 to 20 minutes or 0.5 to 1 mcg/kg/minute (may give up to 8 to 40 mcg/kg total dose)

≥30 minutes anesthesia: Initial: 20 to 50 mcg/kg; Maintenance: 5 to 15 mcg/kg every 5 to 20 minutes (may give up to 75 mcg/kg total dose)

Monitored anesthesia care (MAC): *Children ≥12 years, Adolescents, and Adults:* Initial: 3 to 8 mcg/kg; Maintenance: 3 to 5 mcg/kg every 5 to 20 minutes or 0.25 to 1 mcg/kg/minute (may give up to 3 to 40 mcg/kg total dose)

Mechanism of Action Binds with stereospecific receptors at many sites within the CNS, increases pain threshold, alters pain perception, inhibits ascending pain pathways; is an ultra short-acting opioid

Pharmacodynamics/Kinetics

Onset of Action Rapid, within 5 minutes

Duration of Action Dose dependent: 30 to 60 minutes

Half-life Elimination

Newborns (premature): 5.33 to 9 hours (Davis 1988; Marlow 1990)

Children: 40 to 63 minutes (Davis 1988; Meistelman 1987; Roure 1987)

Adults: 90 to 111 minutes

Pregnancy Considerations Adverse events have been observed in some animal reproduction studies. Alfentanil is known to cross the placenta, which may result in severe respiratory depression in the newborn (Mattingly 2003). When used for pain relief during labor, opioids may temporarily affect the heart rate of the fetus (ACOG 2002). Use during labor and immediately prior to labor is not recommended by the manufacturer.

Controlled Substance C-II

Alfuzosin (al FYOO zoe sin)

Related Information

Clinical Risk Related to Drugs Prolonging QT Interval *on page 1772*

Brand Names: US Uroxatral

Brand Names: Canada Apo-Alfuzosin®; Sandoz-Alfuzosin; Teva-Alfuzosin PR; Xatral

Pharmacologic Category Alpha$_1$ Blocker

Use Benign prostatic hyperplasia: Treatment of signs and symptoms of benign prostatic hyperplasia (BPH)

Local Anesthetic/Vasoconstrictor Precautions Alfuzosin is one of the drugs confirmed to prolong the QT interval and is accepted as having a risk of causing torsade de pointes. The risk of drug-induced torsade de pointes is extremely low when a single QT interval prolonging drug is prescribed. In terms of epinephrine, it is not known what effect vasoconstrictors in the local anesthetic regimen will have in patients with a known history of congenital prolonged QT interval or in patients taking any medication that prolongs the QT interval. Until more information is obtained, it is suggested that the clinician consult with the physician prior to the use of a vasoconstrictor in suspected patients, and that the vasoconstrictor (epinephrine, mepivacaine and levonordefrin [Carbocaine® 2% with Neo-Cobefrin®]) be used with caution.

Effects on Dental Treatment No significant effects or complications reported

Effects on Bleeding No information available to require special precautions

Adverse Reactions

1% to 10%:

Central nervous system: Dizziness (6%), fatigue (3%), headache (3%), pain (1% to 2%)

Gastrointestinal: Abdominal pain (1% to 2%), constipation (1% to 2%), dyspepsia (1% to 2%), nausea (1% to 2%)

Genitourinary: Impotence (1% to 2%)

Respiratory: Upper respiratory tract infection (3%), bronchitis (1% to 2%), pharyngitis (1% to 2%), sinusitis (1% to 2%)

<1%, postmarketing, and/or case reports: Angina pectoris (pre-existing CAD), angioedema, atrial fibrillation, chest pain, diarrhea, edema, flushing, hepatic injury (including cholestatic), hypotension, intraoperative floppy iris syndrome (with cataract surgery), jaundice, orthostatic hypotension, priapism, pruritus, rhinitis, skin rash, syncope, tachycardia, thrombocytopenia, toxic epidermal necrolysis, urticaria

General Dosage Range Oral: *Adults:* 10 mg once daily

Mechanism of Action An antagonist of alpha$_1$-adrenoreceptors in the lower urinary tract. Smooth muscle tone is mediated by the sympathetic nervous stimulation of alpha$_1$-adrenoreceptors, which are abundant in the prostate, prostatic capsule, prostatic urethra, and bladder neck. Blockade of these adrenoreceptors can cause smooth muscles in the bladder neck and prostate ▶

to relax, resulting in an improvement in urine flow rate and a reduction in BPH symptoms.

Pharmacodynamics/Kinetics

Half-life Elimination 10 hours

Time to Peak Plasma: 8 hours following a meal

Pregnancy Risk Factor B

Pregnancy Considerations Adverse events have not been observed in animal reproduction studies.

Dental Comment See Local Anesthetic/Vasoconstrictor Precautions

Alirocumab (al i ROK ue mab)

Brand Names: US Praluent

Brand Names: Canada Praluent

Pharmacologic Category Antilipemic Agent, PCSK9 Inhibitor; Monoclonal Antibody

Use

Hyperlipidemia, primary: Adjunct to diet and maximally tolerated statin therapy for the treatment of adults with heterozygous familial hypercholesterolemia or clinical atherosclerotic cardiovascular disease, who require additional lowering of LDL-cholesterol (LDL-C).

Limitation of use: The effect of alirocumab on cardiovascular morbidity and mortality has not been determined.

Local Anesthetic/Vasoconstrictor Precautions No information available to require special precautions

Effects on Dental Treatment No significant effects or complications reported

Effects on Bleeding No information available to require special precautions

Adverse Reactions

1% to 10%:

Gastrointestinal: Diarrhea (5%)

Hepatic: Liver enzyme disorder (3%), increased serum transaminases (>3 X ULN; 2%)

Immunologic: Immunogenicity (5%; neutralizing: 1%; efficacy effected: <1%)

Infection: Influenza (6%)

Local: Injection site reaction (7%)

Neuromuscular & skeletal: Myalgia (4%), muscle spasm (3%)

Respiratory: Cough (3%)

Frequency not defined:

Hypersensitivity: Hypersensitivity reaction

<1%, postmarketing, and/or case reports: Confusion, decreased LDL cholesterol (≤25 mg/dL), memory impairment

General Dosage Range SubQ: *Adults:* Initial: 75 mg once every two weeks; Maximum dose: 150 mg once every 2 weeks.

Mechanism of Action Alirocumab is a human monoclonal antibody (IgG1isotype) that binds to proprotein convertase subtilisin kexin type 9 (PCSK9). PCSK9 binds to the low-density lipoprotein receptors (LDLR) on hepatocyte surfaces to promote LDLR degradation within the liver. LDLR is the primary receptor that clears circulating LDL; therefore, the decrease in LDLR levels by PCSK9 results in higher blood levels of LDL-cholesterol (LDL-C). By inhibiting the binding of PCSK9 to LDLR, alirocumab increases the number of LDLRs available to clear LDL, thereby lowering LDL-C levels.

Pharmacodynamics/Kinetics

Onset of Action Peak effect: Proprotein convertase subtilisin kexin type 9 (PCSK9) suppression: 4 to 8 hours

Half-life Elimination SubQ: Steady-state: 17 to 20 days; reduced to 12 days when administered with a statin

Time to Peak SubQ: 3 to 7 days

Pregnancy Considerations Adverse events were not observed in animal reproduction studies. Information specific to alirocumab in pregnancy is not available. However, IgG molecules are known to cross the placenta, with increasing amounts during the second and third trimesters of pregnancy.

Prescribing and Access Restrictions Only available via specialty pharmacies. Call 844-772-5836 or visit https://www.praluenthcp.com/support for additional information..

Aliskiren (a lis KYE ren)

Related Information

Cardiovascular Diseases *on page 1752*

Brand Names: US Tekturna

Brand Names: Canada Rasilez

Pharmacologic Category Renin Inhibitor

Use

Hypertension: Management of hypertension

Note: According to the Eighth Joint National Committee (JNC 8) guidelines, aliskiren is **not** recommended for the initial treatment of hypertension (James 2013).

Local Anesthetic/Vasoconstrictor Precautions No information available to require special precautions

Effects on Dental Treatment No significant effects or complications required

Effects on Bleeding No information available to require special precautions

Adverse Reactions

1% to 10%:

Dermatologic: Skin rash (1%)

Gastrointestinal: Diarrhea (2%)

Neuromuscular & skeletal: Increased creatine phosphokinase (>300% increase: 1%)

Renal: Increased blood urea nitrogen (≤7%), increased serum creatinine (≤7%)

Respiratory: Cough (1%)

<1%, postmarketing, and/or case reports: Abdominal pain, anaphylaxis, anemia, angioedema, decreased hematocrit, decreased hemoglobin, dyspepsia, erythema, gastroesophageal reflux disease, gout, hepatic insufficiency, hyperkalemia, hyponatremia, increased liver enzymes, increased uric acid, myositis, nausea, nephrolithiasis, periorbital edema, peripheral edema, pruritus, rhabdomyolysis, seizure, severe hypotension, Stevens-Johnson syndrome, tonic-clonic seizures, toxic epidermal necrolysis, urticaria, vomiting

General Dosage Range Oral: *Adults:* 150 to 300 mg once daily (maximum: 300 mg/day)

Mechanism of Action Decreases plasma renin activity and inhibits conversion of angiotensinogen to angiotensin I.

Pharmacodynamics/Kinetics

Onset of Action Maximum antihypertensive effect: Within 2 weeks

Half-life Elimination ~24 hours (range: 16 to 32 hours)

Time to Peak 1 to 3 hours

Pregnancy Considerations [US Boxed Warning]: Drugs that act on the renin-angiotensin system can cause injury and death to the developing fetus. Discontinue as soon as possible once pregnancy is detected. The use of drugs which act on the renin-angiotensin system are associated with oligohydramnios. Oligohydramnios, due to decreased fetal renal function, may lead to fetal lung hypoplasia and skeletal malformations. Use is also associated with anuria, hypotension, renal failure, skull hypoplasia, and death in the fetus/neonate. The exposed fetus should be monitored for fetal growth, amniotic fluid volume, and organ formation. Infants exposed *in utero* should be monitored for hyperkalemia, hypotension, and oliguria.

Aliskiren and Amlodipine

(a lis KYE ren & am LOE di peen)

Related Information

Aliskiren *on page 96*
AmLODIPine *on page 117*

Brand Names: US Tekamlo [DSC]

Pharmacologic Category Antianginal Agent; Antihypertensive; Calcium Channel Blocker; Calcium Channel Blocker, Dihydropyridine; Renin Inhibitor

Use Hypertension: Management of hypertension (monotherapy or in combination with other antihypertensives).

Local Anesthetic/Vasoconstrictor Precautions No information available to require special precautions

Effects on Dental Treatment Fewer reports of gingival hyperplasia with amlodipine than with other calcium channel blockers (usually resolves upon discontinuation); consultation with physician is suggested.

Effects on Bleeding No information available to require special precautions

Adverse Reactions Frequencies reported with combination product. See individual monographs for additional adverse effects reported with each agent.

1% to 10%: Cardiovascular: Peripheral edema (6% to 9%)

<1%, postmarketing, and/or case reports: Angioedema, hyperkalemia, hypotension, increased blood urea nitrogen, increased serum creatinine

General Dosage Range Oral: *Adults:* Initial: Aliskiren 150 mg/amlodipine 5 mg once daily; maximum: aliskiren 300 mg/amlodipine 10 mg per day.

Mechanism of Action

Aliskiren: Decreases plasma renin activity and inhibits conversion of angiotensinogen to angiotensin I.

Amlodipine: Inhibits calcium ion from entering the "slow channels" or select voltage-sensitive areas of vascular smooth muscle and myocardium during depolarization, producing a relaxation of coronary vascular smooth muscle and coronary vasodilation; increases myocardial oxygen delivery in patients with vasospastic angina. Amlodipine directly acts on vascular smooth muscle to produce peripheral arterial vasodilation reducing peripheral vascular resistance and blood pressure.

Pregnancy Considerations [US Boxed Warning]: Drugs that act on the renin-angiotensin system can cause injury and death to the developing fetus. Discontinue as soon as possible once pregnancy is detected. Animal reproduction studies have not been conducted with this combination. See individual agents.

Alitretinoin (Systemic)

(a li TRET i noyn)

Brand Names: Canada Toctino

Pharmacologic Category Anti-inflammatory Agent; Immunomodulator, Systemic; Retinoic Acid Derivative

Use Note: Not approved in the US.

Eczema of the hand: Treatment of severe chronic hand eczema refractory to high-potency topical corticosteroids

Local Anesthetic/Vasoconstrictor Precautions No information available to require special precautions

Effects on Dental Treatment No significant effects or complications reported

Effects on Bleeding No information available to require special precautions

Adverse Reactions

>10%:

Central nervous system: Headache (11% to 22%)

Endocrine & metabolic: Increased serum triglycerides (30 mg: 35%; 10 mg: 17%), increased LDL cholesterol (>10%)

1% to 10%:

Cardiovascular: Flushing (2% to 6%), hypertension (1% to 2%)

Central nervous system: Depression (3%), dizziness (2%)

Dermatologic: Erythema (2% to 7%), cheilosis (4% to 6%), xeroderma (3%), cheilitis (2%), alopecia (≤2%)

Endocrine & metabolic: Decreased HDL cholesterol (5% to 10%), decreased thyroid hormones (TSH and T4, reversible: 3% to 10%), hypercholesterolemia (1% to 10%), decreased serum iron (1% to 5%), high total iron binding capacity (1% to 5%), weight gain (1%), hot flash (<1%)

Gastrointestinal: Nausea (3%), xerostomia (3%), dyspepsia (1%), upper abdominal pain (1%), vomiting (1%)

Hematologic & oncologic: Reticulocytopenia (1% to 5%)

Infection: Influenza (2%)

Neuromuscular & skeletal: Increased creatine phosphokinase (2% to 3%), arthralgia (2%), back pain (2%)

Ophthalmic: Dry eye syndrome (2% to 3%), conjunctivitis (2%), abnormal sensation in eyes (≤1%)

Respiratory: Nasopharyngitis (6%), pharyngitis (1%)

<1%, postmarketing, and/or case reports: Acute pancreatitis, aggressive behavior, anaphylaxis, ankylosing spondylitis, anxiety, blurred vision, cataract, decreased hematocrit, decreased hemoglobin, decreased red blood cells, epistaxis, exfoliation of skin, exostosis, eye irritation, hypersensitivity reaction, increased serum transaminases, inflammatory bowel disease, mood changes, nocturnal amblyopia, peripheral edema, pruritus, psychotic symptoms, skin rash, suicidal ideation, suicidal tendencies, thrombocythemia, tinnitus, vasculitis

General Dosage Range Oral: *Adults:* 10 to 30 mg once daily

Mechanism of Action Binds to both retinoid acid receptor (RAR) and retinoid X receptor (RXR); anti-inflammatory and immunomodulating effects occur through down-regulation of CXCR3 ligands and CCL20 chemokine expression in cytokine-induced dermal cells and suppressed expansion of cytokine-induced leukocytes and antigen presenting cells.

Pharmacodynamics/Kinetics

Duration of Action Serum concentrations of endogenous alitretinoin return to normal range within 48 to 72 hours after discontinuation

Half-life Elimination Alitretinoin: 9 hours; 4-oxo-alitretinoin: 10 hours

Time to Peak 3 to 4 hours (Weber 1997)

Pregnancy Considerations [Canadian Boxed Warning]: Alitretinoin is a known teratogen and is contraindicated in pregnancy. Females must avoid

becoming pregnant while receiving alitretinoin and for at least 1 month after discontinuation of therapy. Discontinue immediately if pregnancy is discovered during treatment or within 1 month after discontinuation. Fetal abnormalities and spontaneous abortion may occur. The risk for severe birth defects is high, with any dose or even with short treatment duration. If treatment with alitretinoin is required in women of childbearing potential, two effective and reliable forms of birth control should be used simultaneously for at least 1 month prior to starting therapy, during therapy, and for at least 1 month after treatment. Two negative pregnancy tests (sensitivity at least 25 milliunits/mL) and onset of next menses for 2 or 3 days are required prior to initiating therapy. Patients should be advised of the potential harm to the fetus and the physician and patient should discuss the desire to maintain the pregnancy.

Only physicians familiar with systemic retinoid therapy should prescribe alitretinoin. Females of childbearing potential must be able to fulfill all conditions for use prior to initiating therapy (consult manufacturer labeling for further detail). Physicians are required to use the Toctino Pregnancy Prevention Program, which includes comprehensive information regarding conditions that must be met prior to initiating therapy, birth control options, potential risks of therapy, informed consent, and monthly pregnancy reminders. Even women with amenorrhea, a history of infertility, or those who claim an absence of sexual activity must comply with these conditions.

Small amounts of alitretinoin have been detected in the semen of some healthy male volunteers, although accumulation in the semen is not anticipated. Systemic exposure of female partners or fetus is expected to be negligible. The manufacturer labeling suggests that there is no apparent fetal risk in pregnant females whose male partners are receiving alitretinoin.

Product Availability Not available in the US

Prescribing and Access Restrictions Prescriptions must be limited to a 30-day supply for women of childbearing potential; further treatment requires a new prescription. The evaluation of pregnancy test results and the issuance and dispensing of a prescription should preferably occur on the same day. Alitretinoin should be dispensed within 7 days of a medically supervised pregnancy test.

Alitretinoin (Topical) (a li TRET i noyn)

Brand Names: US Panretin

Pharmacologic Category Antineoplastic Agent, Retinoic Acid Derivative

Use Topical treatment of cutaneous lesions in AIDS-related Kaposi's sarcoma. Not indicated when systemic therapy is necessary (eg, >10 new lesions in previous month, symptomatic visceral involvement, symptomatic pulmonary Kaposi's sarcoma, symptomatic lymphedema)

Local Anesthetic/Vasoconstrictor Precautions No information available to require special precautions

Effects on Dental Treatment No significant effects or complications reported

Effects on Bleeding No information available to require special precautions

Adverse Reactions

>10%:

Central nervous system: Pain (≤34%), paresthesia (3% to 22%)

Dermatologic: Skin rash (25% to 77%), pruritus (8% to 11%)

1% to 10%:

Cardiovascular: Edema (3% to 8%)

Dermatologic: Exfoliative dermatitis (3% to 9%), dermatological disease (≤8%)

General Dosage Range Dosage adjustment may be necessary for application site toxicity.

Topical: *Adults:* Initial: Apply twice daily; Range: Apply 2-4 times daily

Mechanism of Action Naturally occurring endogenous retinoid that binds to and activates intracellular retinoid receptors (RAR and RXR); this results in altered expression of the genes controlling cellular differentiation and proliferation in normal and neoplastic cells, inhibiting the growth of Kaposi's sarcoma

Pregnancy Risk Factor D

Pregnancy Considerations Adverse events were observed in animal reproduction studies using an oral preparation; studies have not been conducted using the topical product. Alitretinoin may cause fetal harm if significant absorption occurs in a woman who is pregnant. Women of childbearing potential should avoid becoming pregnant.

Allopurinol (al oh PURE i nole)

Brand Names: US Aloprim; Zyloprim

Brand Names: Canada Allopurin; Apo-Allopurinol; JAMP-Allopurinol; Mar-Allopurinol; Novo-Purol; Zyloprim

Pharmacologic Category Antigout Agent; Xanthine Oxidase Inhibitor

Use

Oral:

Calcium oxalate calculi (recurrent): Management of recurrent calcium oxalate calculi (with uric acid excretion >800 mg/day in men and >750 mg/day in women)

Cancer therapy-induced hyperuricemia: Management of hyperuricemia associated with cancer treatment for leukemia, lymphoma, and other malignancies

Gout: Management of primary or secondary gout (acute attack, tophi, joint destruction, uric acid lithiasis, and/or nephropathy)

Limitations of use: Allopurinol is not recommended for the treatment of asymptomatic hyperuricemia. Allopurinol reduces serum and urinary uric acid concentrations; its use should be individualized for each patient and requires an understanding of its mode of action and pharmacokinetics.

IV: **Cancer therapy-induced hyperuricemia:** Management of hyperuricemia associated with cancer treatment for leukemia, lymphoma, or solid tumor malignancies in patients who cannot tolerate oral therapy.

Local Anesthetic/Vasoconstrictor Precautions No information available to require special precautions

Effects on Dental Treatment No significant effects or complications reported

Effects on Bleeding No information available to require special precautions

Adverse Reactions

Most commonly reported:

Dermatologic: Skin rash

Endocrine & metabolic: Gout (acute)

Gastrointestinal: Diarrhea, nausea

Hepatic: Increased liver enzymes, increased serum alkaline phosphatase

<1%, postmarketing, and/or case reports: Abdominal pain, ageusia, agranulocytosis, alopecia, angioedema, aplastic anemia, arthralgia, bronchospasm, cataract, cholestatic jaundice, drowsiness, dysgeusia, dyspepsia, ecchymoses, eczematoid dermatitis, eosinophilia, epistaxis, exfoliative dermatitis, fever, gastritis, gynecomastia, headache, hepatic necrosis, hepatitis, hepatomegaly, hepatotoxicity (idiosyncratic) (Chalasani, 2014), hyperbilirubinemia, hypersensitivity reaction, leukocytosis, leukopenia, lichen planus, macular retinitis, myopathy, necrotizing angiitis, nephritis, neuritis, neuropathy, onycholysis, pancreatitis, paresthesia, pruritus, purpura, renal failure, skin granuloma (annulare), Stevens-Johnson syndrome, thrombocytopenia, toxic epidermal necrolysis, toxic pustuloderma, uremia, vasculitis, vesicobullous dermatitis, vomiting

General Dosage Range Dosage adjustment recommended in patients with renal impairment

IV:

Children: Initial: 200 mg/m^2 daily as a single infusion or in equally divided doses at 6, 8, or 12 hour intervals

Adults: 200 to 400 mg/m^2 daily as a single infusion or in equally divided doses at 6, 8, or 12 hour intervals (maximum dose: 600 mg daily)

Oral:

Children <6 years: 150 mg daily

Children 6 to 10 years: 300 mg daily

Children >10 years: 600 to 800 mg daily in divided doses

Adults: 100 to 800 mg daily in single or divided doses

Mechanism of Action Allopurinol inhibits xanthine oxidase, the enzyme responsible for the conversion of hypoxanthine to xanthine to uric acid. Allopurinol is metabolized to oxypurinol which is also an inhibitor of xanthine oxidase; allopurinol acts on purine catabolism, reducing the production of uric acid without disrupting the biosynthesis of vital purines.

Pharmacodynamics/Kinetics

Onset of Action

Gout: Decrease in serum and urine uric acid: 2 to 3 days; peak effect: 1 week or longer; normal serum urate levels achieved typically within 1 to 3 weeks

Cancer therapy-induced hyperuricemia: Median time to plasma uric acid control: 27 hours (Cortes 2010)

Half-life Elimination

Parent drug: ~1 to 2 hours; Oxypurinol: ~15 hours

Time to Peak Plasma: Oral: Allopurinol: 1.5 hours; Oxypurinol: 4.5 hours

Pregnancy Risk Factor C

Pregnancy Considerations Adverse events were observed in some animal reproduction studies. Allopurinol crosses the placenta (Torrance 2009). An increased risk of adverse fetal events has not been observed (limited data) (Hoeltzenbein 2013).

Almotriptan (al moh TRIP tan)

Related Information

Temporomandibular Dysfunction (TMD), Chronic Pain, and Fibromyalgia *on page 1868*

Brand Names: US Axert

Brand Names: Canada Axert; Mylan-Almotriptan; Sandoz-Almotriptan

Pharmacologic Category Antimigraine Agent; Serotonin 5-HT$_{1B,\ 1D}$ Receptor Agonist

Use Acute treatment of migraine with or without aura in adults (with a history of migraine) and adolescents (with a history of migraine lasting ≥4 hours when left untreated)

Local Anesthetic/Vasoconstrictor Precautions No information available to require special precautions

Effects on Dental Treatment Key adverse effect(s) related to dental treatment: Xerostomia (normal salivary flow resumes upon discontinuation)

Effects on Bleeding No information available to require special precautions

Adverse Reactions

1% to 10%:

Central nervous system: Drowsiness (≤5%), dizziness (≤4%), headache (≤2%)

Gastrointestinal: Nausea (1% to 3%), vomiting (≤2%), xerostomia (1%)

Neuromuscular & skeletal: Paresthesia (≤1%)

<1%, postmarketing, and/or case reports: Abdominal cramps, abdominal discomfort, abdominal pain, abnormal dreams, altered sense of smell, anaphylactic shock, anaphylaxis, angina pectoris, angioedema, anxiety, arthralgia, arthritis, ataxia, back pain, blepharospasm, blurred vision, bronchitis, central nervous system stimulation, chest pain, chills, cold extremities, colitis, confusion, conjunctivitis, coronary artery vasospasm, decreased visual acuity, depression, dermatitis, diaphoresis, diarrhea, diplopia, dry eye syndrome, dysgeusia, dysmenorrhea, dyspepsia, dyspnea, epistaxis, erythema, euphoria, eye irritation, eye pain, fatigue, fever, gastritis, gastroenteritis, gastroesophageal reflux disease, hemiplegia, hyperacusis, hypercholesterolemia, hyperglycemia, hyperhidrosis, hyperreflexia, hypersensitivity reaction, hypertension, hypertonia, hyperventilation, hypoesthesia, increased creatine phosphokinase, increased gamma-glutamyl transferase, increased thirst, insomnia, ischemic heart disease, lack of concentration, laryngismus, laryngitis, limb pain, malaise, mastalgia, myalgia, myasthenia, myocardial infarction, myopathy, neck pain, neck stiffness, nervousness, neuropathy, nightmares, nystagmus, otalgia, otitis media, palpitations, pharyngitis, pruritus, restlessness, rhinitis, scotoma, seizure, shakiness, sialorrhea, sinusitis, skin photosensitivity, skin rash, sneezing, syncope, tachycardia, tinnitus, tremor, vasodilation, ventricular fibrillation, ventricular tachycardia, vertigo, weakness

General Dosage Range Dosage adjustment recommended in patients with hepatic or renal impairment and/or on concomitant therapy

Oral: *Children ≥12 years and Adults:* 6.25-12.5 mg in a single dose; may repeat after 2 hours (maximum daily dose: 25 mg)

Mechanism of Action Selective agonist for serotonin (5-HT$_{1B}$ and 5-HT$_{1D}$ receptors) in cranial arteries; causes vasoconstriction and reduces sterile inflammation associated with antidromic neuronal transmission correlating with relief of migraine

Pharmacodynamics/Kinetics

Half-life Elimination Mean: 3 to 5 hours (Baldwin 2004; McEnroe 2005)

Time to Peak Plasma: 1 to 3 hours

Pregnancy Risk Factor C

Pregnancy Considerations Adverse events were observed in animal reproduction studies. Information related to almotriptan use in pregnancy is limited (Källén, 2011; Nezvalová-Henriksen, 2010; Nezvalová-Henriksen, 2012). Until additional information is available, other agents are preferred for the initial treatment of migraine in pregnancy (Da Silva, 2012; MacGregor, 2012; Williams, 2012).

Alogliptin (al oh GLIP tin)

Brand Names: US Nesina

Brand Names: Canada Nesina

Pharmacologic Category Antidiabetic Agent, Dipeptidyl Peptidase 4 (DPP-4) Inhibitor

Use Diabetes mellitus, type 2: Management of adults with type 2 diabetes mellitus (noninsulin dependent, NIDDM) as an adjunct to diet and exercise as monotherapy or in combination therapy

Local Anesthetic/Vasoconstrictor Precautions No information available to require special precautions

Effects on Dental Treatment Alogliptin-dependent patients with diabetes (noninsulin dependent, type 2) should be appointed for dental treatment in morning in order to minimize chance of stress-induced hypoglycemia.

Effects on Bleeding No information available to require special precautions

Adverse Reactions

1% to 10%:

Cardiovascular: Cardiac failure (4%)

Central nervous system: Headache (4%)

Genitourinary: Decreased estimated GFR (5%)

Hepatic: Increased serum ALT (>3 times ULN: 1%)

Renal: Renal function abnormality (3%; patients with high cardiovascular risk: 23%), renal disease (patients with high cardiovascular risk: 17%), renal insufficiency (patients with high cardiovascular risk: 8%)

Respiratory: Nasopharyngitis (5%), upper respiratory tract infection (5%)

<1%, postmarketing, and/or case reports: Anaphylaxis, angioedema, constipation, decreased creatinine clearance, diarrhea, hepatic failure, hypersensitivity reaction, increased liver enzymes, intestinal obstruction, nausea, pancreatitis, serum sickness, severe arthralgia (FDA Safety Alert, Aug 28, 2015), skin rash, Stevens-Johnson syndrome, urticaria

General Dosage Range Dosage adjustment recommended in patients with renal impairment.

Oral: *Adults:* 25 mg once daily

Mechanism of Action Alogliptin inhibits dipeptidyl peptidase 4 (DPP-4) enzyme resulting in prolonged active incretin levels. Incretin hormones (eg, glucagon-like peptide-1 [GLP-1] and glucose-dependent insulinotropic polypeptide [GIP]) regulate glucose homeostasis by increasing insulin synthesis and release from pancreatic beta cells and decreasing glucagon secretion from pancreatic alpha cells. Decreased glucagon secretion results in decreased hepatic glucose production. Under normal physiologic circumstances, incretin hormones are released by the intestine throughout the day and levels are increased in response to a meal; incretin hormones are rapidly inactivated by the DPP-4 enzyme.

Pharmacodynamics/Kinetics

Half-life Elimination ~21 hours

Time to Peak ~1 to 2 hours

Pregnancy Considerations Adverse events were not observed in animal reproduction studies.

In women with diabetes, maternal hyperglycemia can be associated with congenital malformations as well as adverse effects in the fetus, neonate, and the mother (ACOG 2005; ADA 2016c; Kitzmiller 2008; Metzger 2007). To prevent adverse outcomes, prior to conception and throughout pregnancy, maternal blood glucose and HbA_{1c} should be kept as close to target goals as possible but without causing significant hypoglycemia (ACOG 2013; ADA 2016c; Blumer 2013; Kitzmiller 2008). Agents other than alogliptin are currently recommended to treat diabetes in pregnant women (ACOG 2013; Blumer 2013).

Alosetron (a LOE se tron)

Brand Names: US Lotronex

Pharmacologic Category Selective 5-HT_3 Receptor Antagonist

Use Irritable bowel syndrome: Treatment of women with severe diarrhea-predominant irritable bowel syndrome (IBS) who have chronic IBS symptoms (generally lasting 6 months or longer), have had anatomic or biochemical abnormalities of the GI tract excluded, and who have not responded adequately to conventional therapy.

Local Anesthetic/Vasoconstrictor Precautions No information available to require special precautions

Effects on Dental Treatment No significant effects or complications reported

Effects on Bleeding No information available to require special precautions

Adverse Reactions

>10%: Gastrointestinal: Constipation (9% to 29%; dose related)

1% to 10%:

Central nervous system: Fatigue (≥3%), headache (≥3%)

Gastrointestinal: Abdominal distress (≤1% to 7%), abdominal pain (≤1% to 7%), nausea (6%), gastrointestinal distress (≤5%), gastrointestinal pain (≤5%), gastroenteritis (≥3%), vomiting (≥3%), diarrhea (2% to 3%), flatulence (1% to 3%), hemorrhoids (1% to 3%), abdominal distention (2%), acid regurgitation (≤2%), gastroesophageal reflux disease (≤2%)

Genitourinary: Urinary tract infection (≥3%)

Neuromuscular & skeletal: Muscle spasm (≥3%)

Respiratory: Cough (≥3%), nasopharyngitis (≥3%), upper respiratory tract infection (≥3%)

<1%, postmarketing, and/or case reports: Abnormal bilirubin levels, abnormal erythrocytes, active gastrointestinal lesion, allergic skin reaction, alopecia, anxiety, cardiac arrhythmia, cholecystitis, cognitive dysfunction, colitis, confusion, cystitis, decreased gastrointestinal motility, depression, dermatitis, diaphoresis, disruption of body temperature regulation, disturbance in fluid balance, diverticulitis, drowsiness, dyspepsia, extrasystoles, fecal impaction, gastrointestinal obstruction, gastrointestinal perforation, gastrointestinal spasm, gastrointestinal ulcer, hematoma, hemoglobinopathy, hemorrhage, hepatitis, hyperacidity, hyperglycemia, hypertension, hypoesthesia, hypoglycemia, hypothalamic disease, intestinal

obstruction, intussusception, ischemic colitis, memory impairment, mesenteric ischemia (small bowel), muscle cramps, muscle rigidity, myalgia, occult blood in stools, ostealgia, pain, pituitary insufficiency, proctitis, respiratory tract disease, sedation, sexual disorder, skeletal pain, skin rash, tachyarrhythmia, tremor, ulcerative colitis, urinary frequency, urticaria

General Dosage Range Oral: *Adults:* Initial: 0.5 mg twice daily; may increase to 1 mg twice daily if needed (maximum dose: 2 mg/day)

Mechanism of Action Alosetron is a potent and selective antagonist of a subtype of the serotonin 5-HT_3 receptor. 5-HT_3 receptors are ligand-gated ion channels extensively distributed on enteric neurons in the human gastrointestinal tract, as well as other peripheral and central locations. Activation of these channels affect the regulation of visceral pain, colonic transit, and gastrointestinal secretions. In patients with irritable bowel syndrome, blockade of these channels may reduce pain, abdominal discomfort, urgency, and diarrhea.

Pharmacodynamics/Kinetics

Half-life Elimination 1.5 hours

Time to Peak 1 hour

Pregnancy Risk Factor B

Pregnancy Considerations Adverse events have not been observed in animal reproduction studies. Alosetron should be used in pregnant women only if clearly needed.

ALPRAZolam (al PRAY zoe lam)

Related Information

Dentin Hypersensitivity, Acid Erosion, High Caries Index, Management of Alveolar Osteitis, and Xerostomia *on page 1857*

Management of the Patient With Anxiety or Depression *on page 1873*

Temporomandibular Dysfunction (TMD), Chronic Pain, and Fibromyalgia *on page 1868*

Related Sample Prescriptions

Sedation (Prior to Dental Treatment) - Sample Prescriptions *on page 42*

Brand Names: US ALPRAZolam Intensol; ALPRAZolam XR; Niravam [DSC]; Xanax; Xanax XR

Brand Names: Canada Apo-Alpraz; Apo-Alpraz TS; Jamp-Alprazolam; Mylan-Alprazolam; Nat-Alprazolam; Riva-Alpraz; Teva-Alprazolam; Xanax; Xanax TS

Generic Availability (US) May be product dependent

Pharmacologic Category Benzodiazepine

Dental Use Preoperative anxiety

Use

Anxiety disorders (immediate release tablet, oral concentrate, orally-disintegrating tablets): Treatment of generalized anxiety disorder (GAD), short-term anxiety and anxiety association with depression

Panic disorder (extended-release tablets, oral solution, orally-disintegrating tablets, immediate-release tablets): Treatment of panic disorder, with or without agoraphobia

Local Anesthetic/Vasoconstrictor Precautions No information available to require special precautions

Effects on Dental Treatment Key adverse event(s) related to dental treatment: Significant xerostomia and changes in salivation (normal salivary flow resumes upon discontinuation)

Effects on Bleeding No information available to require special precautions

Adverse Reactions

>10%:

Central nervous system: Drowsiness (immediate-release: 41% to 77%; extended-release: 23%), fatigue (immediate-release: 49%; extended-release: 14%), sedation (extended-release: 45%), ataxia (immediate-release: 40%; extended-release: 7% to 9%), memory impairment (immediate-release: 33%; extended-release: 15%), irritability (immediate-release: 33%; extended-release: ≥1%), cognitive dysfunction (immediate-release: 29%), dysarthria (immediate-release: 23%; extended-release: 11%), dizziness (immediate-release: 2% to 21%; extended-release: ≥1%), depression (extended-release: 1% to 12%)

Dermatologic: Skin rash (immediate-release: 11%; extended-release: <1%)

Endocrine & metabolic: Weight gain (immediate-release: 27%; extended-release: 5%), weight loss (immediate-release: 23%), decreased libido (6% to 14%)

Gastrointestinal: Increased appetite (immediate-release: 33%; extended-release: 7%), decreased appetite (immediate-release: 28%), constipation (immediate-release: 26%; extended-release: 8%), xerostomia (immediate-release: 15%)

Genitourinary: Difficulty in micturition (immediate-release: 12%; extended-release: ≥1%)

1% to 10%:

Cardiovascular: Hypotension (immediate-release: 5%; extended-release: <1%), chest pain (extended-release: ≥1%), palpitations (extended-release: ≥1%)

Central nervous system: Confusion (immediate-release: 10%; extended-release: 2%), altered mental status (extended-release: 7%), disinhibition (immediate-release: 3%), disturbance in attention (extended-release: 3%), equilibrium disturbance (extended-release: 3%), akathisia (immediate-release: 2%), disorientation (extended-release: 2%), lethargy (extended-release: 2%), talkativeness (immediate-release: 2%), derealization (≥1% to 2%), agitation (extended-release: ≥1%), depersonalization (extended-release: ≥1%), headache (extended-release: ≥1%), insomnia (extended-release: ≥1%), malaise (extended-release: ≥1%), nervousness (extended-release: ≥1%), nightmares (extended-release: ≥1%), restlessness (≥1%), vertigo (extended-release: ≥1%), anxiety (extended-release: 1%), feeling hot (immediate-release: 1%; extended-release: <1%), hypersomnia (extended-release: 1%), hypoesthesia (extended-release: 1%), dystonia

Dermatologic: Allergic skin reaction (≤4%), dermatitis (immediate-release: ≤4%), diaphoresis (extended-release: ≥1%), pruritus (extended-release: 1%)

Endocrine & metabolic: Menstrual disease (immediate-release: 10%; extended-release: 2%), increased libido (immediate-release: 8%; extended-release: ≥1%), change in libido (immediate-release: 7%), hot flash (extended-release: 2%)

Gastrointestinal: Nausea (extended-release: 6%), sialorrhea (immediate-release: 4% to 6%; extended-release: ≥1%), anorexia (extended-release: 2%), abdominal pain (extended-release: ≥1%), diarrhea (extended-release: ≥1%), dyspepsia (extended-release: ≥1%), vomiting (extended-release: ≥1%)

Genitourinary: Sexual disorder (immediate-release: 7%; extended-release: 2%), dysmenorrhea (extended-release: 4%), urinary incontinence (immediate-release: 2%; extended-release: <1%)

Neuromuscular & skeletal: Arthralgia (extended-release: 2%), dyskinesia (extended-release: 2%), myalgia (extended-release: 2%), back pain (extended-release: ≥1%), muscle cramps (extended-release: ≥1%), muscle twitching (extended-release: ≥1%), tremor (extended-release: ≥1%), weakness (extended-release: ≥1%), limb pain (extended-release: 1%)

Ophthalmic: Blurred vision (extended-release: ≥1%)

Respiratory: Dyspnea (extended-release: 2%), hyperventilation (extended-release: ≥1%), nasal congestion (extended-release: ≥1%), allergic rhinitis (extended-release: 1%)

Frequency not defined:

Central nervous system: Drug dependence, drug withdrawal

<1%, postmarketing, and/or case reports: Abnormal dreams, aggressive behavior, amnesia, angioedema, apathy, bradyphrenia, chest tightness, choking sensation, clammy skin, clumsiness, diplopia, dysgeusia, dysphagia, edema, emotional lability, epistaxis, euphoria, falling, feeling drunk, fever, galactorrhea, gastrointestinal disease, gynecomastia, hallucination, hangover effect, hepatic failure, hepatitis, homicidal ideation, hyperprolactinemia, hypomania, hypotonia, impaired consciousness, impulse control disorder, increased energy, increased liver enzymes, increased serum bilirubin, increased thirst, jaundice, jitteriness, loss of control of legs, mania, mydriasis, otalgia, outbursts of anger, peripheral edema, photophobia, psychomotor retardation, relaxation, rhinorrhea, rigors, seizure, sensation of cold, sinus tachycardia, skin photosensitivity, sleep apnea, sleep talking, Stevens-Johnson syndrome, stupor, suicidal ideation, syncope, tinnitus, urinary frequency, urticaria, voice disorder

Dental Usual Dosage Preoperative anxiety (off-label use) Adults: Oral: 0.5 mg 60-90 minutes before procedure (De Witte, 2002)

Dosing

Adult Note: Titrate dose gradually as needed and tolerated. Periodic reassessment and consideration of dosage reduction is recommended.

Anxiety disorders: Oral: *Immediate release tablet, oral concentrate, orally-disintegrating tablet:* Initial: 0.25 to 0.5 mg 3 times daily; titrate dose every 3 to 4 days; usual maximum: 4 mg/day. Patients requiring doses >4 mg/day should be increased cautiously.

Panic disorder: Oral:

Immediate release tablet, oral concentrate, orally-disintegrating tablet: Initial: 0.5 mg 3 times daily; titrate dose every 3 to 4 days in increments ≤1 mg/day. Mean effective dosage: 5 to 6 mg/day, in 3 or 4 divided doses; some patients may require as much as 10 mg/day.

Extended release: 0.5 to 1 mg once daily; titrate dose every 3 to 4 days in increments ≤1 mg/day (range: 3 to 6 mg/day).

Switching from immediate release to extended release: Patients may be switched to extended release tablets by taking the total daily dose of the immediate release tablets and giving it once daily using the extended release preparation.

Preoperative anxiety (off-label use): Oral: 0.5 mg 60-90 minutes before procedure (De Witte, 2002)

Dose reduction: Abrupt discontinuation should be avoided. Daily dose may be decreased by 0.5 mg every 3 days; however, some patients may require a slower reduction. If withdrawal symptoms occur, resume previous dose and discontinue on a less rapid schedule.

Geriatric Note: Titrate gradually, if needed and tolerated. Periodic reassessment and consideration of dosage reduction is recommended.

Immediate release: Initial 0.25 mg 2 to 3 times/day

Extended release: Initial: 0.5 mg once daily

Dose reduction: Refer to adult dosing.

Pediatric

Anxiety (off-label use): Oral: Immediate release: Initial: 0.005 mg/kg/dose or 0.125 mg/dose 3 times/day; increase in increments of 0.125 to 0.25 mg, up to a maximum of 0.02 mg/kg/dose or 0.06 mg/kg/day (range of doses reported in one study: 0.375 to 3 mg/day) (Pfefferbaum, 1987). See "Dose Reduction" comment in adult dosing.

Renal Impairment There are no dosage adjustments provided in the manufacturer's labeling; use caution.

Hepatic Impairment Advanced liver disease:

Immediate release tablet, oral concentrate, orally-disintegrating tablet: 0.25 mg 2 to 3 times daily.

Extended release: 0.5 mg once daily

Mechanism of Action Binds to stereospecific benzodiazepine receptors on the postsynaptic GABA neuron at several sites within the central nervous system, including the limbic system, reticular formation. Enhancement of the inhibitory effect of GABA on neuronal excitability results by increased neuronal membrane permeability to chloride ions. This shift in chloride ions results in hyperpolarization (a less excitable state) and stabilization. Benzodiazepine receptors and effects appear to be linked to the GABA-A receptors. Benzodiazepines do not bind to GABA-B receptors.

Contraindications Hypersensitivity to alprazolam or any component of the formulation (cross-sensitivity with other benzodiazepines may exist); acute narrow-angle glaucoma; concurrent use with ketoconazole, itraconazole, or other potent CYP3A4 inhibitors.

Warnings/Precautions [U.S. Boxed warning]: Concomitant use of benzodiazepines and opioids may result in profound sedation, respiratory depression, coma, and death. Reserve concomitant prescribing of these drugs for use in patients for whom alternative treatment options are inadequate. Limit dosages and durations to the minimum required. Follow patients for signs and symptoms of respiratory depression and sedation.

Rebound or withdrawal symptoms, including seizures, may occur following abrupt discontinuation or large decreases in dose (more common in adult patients receiving >4 mg/day or prolonged treatment); the risk of seizures appears to be greatest 24 to 72 hours following discontinuation of therapy. Breakthrough anxiety may occur at the end of dosing interval. Potentially significant interactions may exist, requiring dose or frequency adjustment, additional monitoring, and/or selection of alternative therapy. Use with caution in patients receiving concurrent CYP3A4 inhibitors, moderate or strong CYP3A4 inducers, and major CYP3A4 substrates; consider alternative agents that avoid or lessen the potential for CYP-mediated interactions. Use with caution in renal impairment or predisposition to urate nephropathy; has weak uricosuric properties. Use with caution in or debilitated patients (use lower starting dose), patients with hepatic disease (including alcoholics) or respiratory disease, or obese patients. Cigarette smoking may decrease alprazolam concentrations up to 50%.

Causes CNS depression (dose related) which may impair physical and mental capabilities. Patients must be cautioned about performing tasks that require mental alertness (eg, operating machinery or driving). Effects with other sedative drugs or ethanol may be potentiated. Benzodiazepines have been associated with falls and traumatic injury and should be used with extreme caution in patients who are at risk of these events.

Use caution in patients with depression, particularly if suicidal risk may be present. Episodes of mania or hypomania have occurred in depressed patients treated with alprazolam. May cause physical or psychological dependence. Acute withdrawal may be precipitated in patients after administration of flumazenil. Tolerance does not develop to the anxiolytic effects (Vinkers, 2012). Chronic use of this agent may increase the perioperative benzodiazepine dose needed to achieve desired effect.

Benzodiazepines have been associated with anterograde amnesia. Paradoxical reactions have been reported with benzodiazepines, particularly in adolescent/pediatric or psychiatric patients. Does not have analgesic, antidepressant, or antipsychotic properties.

Drug Interactions

Metabolism/Transport Effects Substrate of CYP3A4 (major); **Note:** Assignment of Major/Minor substrate status based on clinically relevant drug interaction potential; **Inhibits** CYP3A4 (weak)

Avoid Concomitant Use

Avoid concomitant use of ALPRAZolam with any of the following: Azelastine (Nasal); Conivaptan; Fusidic Acid (Systemic); Idelalisib; Indinavir; Itraconazole; Ketoconazole (Systemic); Methadone; OLANZapine; Orphenadrine; Oxomemazine; Paraldehyde; Pimozide; Sodium Oxybate; Thalidomide

Increased Effect/Toxicity

ALPRAZolam may increase the levels/effects of: Alcohol (Ethyl); Analgesics (Opioid); ARIPiprazole; Azelastine (Nasal); Blonanserin; Buprenorphine; CloZAPine; CNS Depressants; Dofetilide; Flibanserin; Flunitrazepam; HYDROcodone; Lomitapide; Methadone; Methotrimeprazine; MetyroSINE; Mirtazapine; NiMODipine; Orphenadrine; OxyCODONE; Paraldehyde; Pimozide; Piribedil; Pramipexole; ROPINIRole; Rotigotine; Selective Serotonin Reuptake Inhibitors; Sodium Oxybate; Suvorexant; Thalidomide, Zolpidem

The levels/effects of ALPRAZolam may be increased by: Aprepitant; Boceprevir; Brimonidine (Topical); Cannabis; Chlormethiazole; Chlorphenesin Carbamate; Conivaptan; CYP3A4 Inhibitors (Moderate); CYP3A4 Inhibitors (Strong); Dasatinib; Dimethindene (Topical); Doxylamine; Dronabinol; Droperidol; FluvoxaMINE; Fosaprepitant; Fusidic Acid (Systemic); HydrOXYzine; Idelalisib; Indinavir; Itraconazole; Ivacaftor; Kava Kava; Ketoconazole (Systemic); Lofexidine; Macrolide Antibiotics; Magnesium Sulfate; Methotrimeprazine; MiFEPRIStone; Minocycline; Nabilone; Netupitant; OLANZapine; Ombitasvir, Paritaprevir, and Ritonavir; Ombitasvir, Paritaprevir, Ritonavir, and Dasabuvir; Oxomemazine; Palbociclib; Perampanel; Protease Inhibitors; Rufinamide; Simeprevir; Stiripentol; Tapentadol; Teduglutide; Telaprevir; Tetrahydrocannabinol; Trimeprazine

Decreased Effect

The levels/effects of ALPRAZolam may be decreased by: Bosentan; CYP3A4 Inducers (Moderate); CYP3A4 Inducers (Strong); Dabrafenib; Deferasirox; Enzalutamide; Mitotane; Siltuximab; St John's Wort; Theophylline Derivatives; Tocilizumab; Yohimbine

Food Interactions Alprazolam serum concentration is unlikely to be increased by grapefruit juice because of alprazolam's high oral bioavailability. The C_{max} of the extended release formulation is increased by 25% when a high-fat meal is given 2 hours before dosing. T_{max} is decreased 33% when food is given immediately prior to dose and increased by 33% when food is given ≥1 hour after dose. Management: Administer without regard to food.

Dietary Considerations Extended release tablet should be taken once daily in the morning. Orally-disintegrating tablets may contain phenylalanine.

Pharmacodynamics/Kinetics

Half-life Elimination

Adults: Mean: 11.2 hours (Immediate release range: 6.3 to 26.9 hours; Extended release range: 10.7 to 15.8 hours); Orally-disintegrating tablet: Mean: 12.5 hours (range: 7.9 to 19.2 hours)

Alcoholic liver disease: 19.7 hours (range: 5.8 to 65.3 hours)

Obesity: 21.8 hours (range: 9.9 to 40.4 hours)

Elderly: 16.3 hours (range: 9 to 26.9 hours)

Time to Peak

Immediate release: 1 to 2 hours

Extended release: Adolescents and Adults: ~9 hours, relatively steady from 4 to 12 hours (Glue 2006); decreased by 1 hour when administered at bedtime (as compared to morning administration); decreased by 33% when administered with a high-fat meal; increased by 33% when administered ≥1 hour after a high-fat meal

Orally-disintegrating tablet: 1.5 to 2 hours; occurs ~15 minutes earlier when administered with water; increased to ~4 hours when administered with a high-fat meal

Pregnancy Risk Factor D

Pregnancy Considerations Benzodiazepines have the potential to cause harm to the fetus. Alprazolam and its metabolites cross the human placenta. Teratogenic effects have been observed with some benzodiazepines; however, additional studies are needed. The incidence of premature birth and low birth weights may be increased following maternal use of benzodiazepines; hypoglycemia and respiratory problems in the neonate may occur following exposure late in pregnancy. Neonatal withdrawal symptoms may occur within days to weeks after birth and "floppy infant syndrome" (which also includes withdrawal symptoms) has been reported with some benzodiazepines (Bergman, 1992; Iqbal, 2002; Wikner, 2007).

Breastfeeding Considerations Benzodiazepines are excreted into breast milk. In a study of eight postpartum women, peak concentrations of alprazolam were found in breast milk ~1 hour after the maternal dose and the half-life was ~14 hours. Samples were obtained over 36 hours following a single oral dose of alprazolam 0.5 mg. Metabolites were not detected in breast milk. In this study, the estimated exposure to the breastfeeding infant was ~3% of the weight-adjusted maternal dose (Oo, 1995). Drowsiness, lethargy, or weight loss in nursing infants have been observed in case reports following maternal use of some benzodiazepines (Iqbal, 2002). breastfeeding is not recommended by the manufacturer.

Controlled Substance C-IV

Dosage Forms

Concentrate, Oral:

ALPRAZolam Intensol: 1 mg/mL (30 mL)

Tablet, Oral:

Xanax: 0.25 mg, 0.5 mg, 1 mg, 2 mg

Generic: 0.25 mg, 0.5 mg, 1 mg, 2 mg

Tablet Dispersible, Oral:

Generic: 0.25 mg, 0.5 mg, 1 mg, 2 mg

Tablet Extended Release 24 Hour, Oral:

ALPRAZolam XR: 0.5 mg, 1 mg, 2 mg, 3 mg

Xanax XR: 0.5 mg, 1 mg, 2 mg, 3 mg

Generic: 0.5 mg, 1 mg, 2 mg, 3 mg

Dental Comment Patient should not drive themselves to and from the dental office. It is recommended an adult companion accompany the patient to their appointment.

Alprostadil (al PROS ta dill)

Brand Names: US Caverject; Caverject Impulse; Edex; Muse; Prostin VR

Brand Names: Canada Alprostadil Injection USP; Caverject; Muse Pellet; Prostin VR

Pharmacologic Category Prostaglandin; Vasodilator

Use

Patent ductus arteriosus (Prostin VR Pediatric): Temporary maintenance of patency of ductus arteriosus in neonates with ductal-dependent congenital heart disease until surgery can be performed. These defects include cyanotic (eg, pulmonary atresia, pulmonary stenosis, tricuspid atresia, Fallot's tetralogy, transposition of the great vessels) and acyanotic (eg, interruption of aortic arch, coarctation of aorta, hypoplastic left ventricle) heart disease.

Erectile dysfunction:

Caverject, Edex, Caverject Impulse: Treatment of erectile dysfunction due to vasculogenic, psychogenic, neurogenic, or mixed etiology; Caverject may be a useful adjunct to other diagnostic tests in the diagnosis of erectile dysfunction

Muse: Treatment of erectile dysfunction

Local Anesthetic/Vasoconstrictor Precautions No information available to require special precautions

Effects on Dental Treatment No significant effects or complications reported

Effects on Bleeding No information available to require special precautions

Adverse Reactions

Intraurethral:

>10%: Genitourinary: Penile pain, urethral burning

2% to 10%:

Central nervous system: Dizziness, headache, pain

Genitourinary: Testicular pain, urethral bleeding (minor), vulvovaginal pruritus (female partner)

<2%: Leg pain, perineal pain, tachycardia

Intracavernosal injection:

>10%: Genitourinary: Penile pain

1% to 10%:

Cardiovascular: Hypertension

Central nervous system: Dizziness, headache

Genitourinary: Prolonged erection (>4 hours, 4%), penile disease, penile rash, penile swelling, Peyronie's disease

Local: Bruising at injection site, hematoma at injection site

<1%: Balanitis, injection site hemorrhage, priapism (0.4%)

Intravenous:

>10%:

Cardiovascular: Flushing

Respiratory: Apnea

Miscellaneous: Fever

1% to 10%:

Cardiovascular: Bradycardia, cardiac arrest, edema, hypertension, hypotension, tachycardia

Central nervous system: Dizziness, headache, seizure

Endocrine & metabolic: Hypokalemia

Gastrointestinal: Diarrhea

Hematologic & oncologic: Disseminated intravascular coagulation

Infection: Sepsis

Local: Local pain (in structures other than the injection site)

Neuromuscular & skeletal: Back pain

Respiratory: Cough, flu-like symptoms, nasal congestion, sinusitis, upper respiratory tract infection

<1%: Anemia, anuria, bradypnea, cardiac failure, cerebral hemorrhage, gastroesophageal reflux disease, hematuria, hemorrhage, hyperbilirubinemia, hyperemia, hyperirritability, hyperkalemia, hypoglycemia, hypothermia, jitteriness, lethargy, neck hyperextension, peritonitis, second degree atrioventricular block, shock, stiffness, supraventricular tachycardia, thrombocytopenia, ventricular fibrillation, wheezing (bronchial)

General Dosage Range

IV: *Neonates:* Initial: 0.05-0.1 mcg/kg/minute; Maintenance: 0.01-0.4 mcg/kg/minute

Intracavernous: *Adults:* Initial: 1.25-2.5 mcg; Maintenance: Increase to effective dose no more than 3 times/week with at least 24 hours between doses (maximum: 40 mcg/dose [Edex]; 60 mcg/dose [Caverject])

Intraurethral: *Adults:* Initial: 125-250 mcg; Maintenance: As needed (maximum: 2 doses/day)

Mechanism of Action Causes vasodilation by means of direct effect on vascular and ductus arteriosus smooth muscle; relaxes trabecular smooth muscle by dilation of cavernosal arteries when injected along the penile shaft, allowing blood flow to and entrapment in the lacunar spaces of the penis (ie, corporeal veno-occlusive mechanism)

Pharmacodynamics/Kinetics

Onset of Action Erectile dysfunction: 5 to 20 minutes

Duration of Action Ductus arteriosus will begin to close within 1 to 2 hours after drug is stopped; Erectile dysfunction: Intended duration <1 hour

Half-life Elimination 30 seconds to 10 minutes

Time to Peak Acyanotic congenital heart disease: Usual: 1.5 to 3 hours; Range: 15 minutes to 11 hoursCyanotic congenital heart disease: Usual: ~30 minutesErectile dysfunction: Intracavernosal: 30 to 60 minutes; Transurethral: ~16 minutes

Pregnancy Risk Factor C (Muse)

Pregnancy Considerations Adverse events have been observed in animal reproduction studies. Alprostadil is not indicated for use in women. The manufacturer of Muse recommends a condom barrier when being used during sexual intercourse with a pregnant woman.

Alteplase (AL te plase)

Related Information

Cardiovascular Diseases *on page 1752*

Brand Names: US Activase; Cathflo Activase

Brand Names: Canada Activase rt-PA; Cathflo Activase

Pharmacologic Category Thrombolytic Agent

Use Activase:

Acute ischemic stroke: Treatment of acute ischemic stroke (AIS) within 3 hours of symptom onset.

Pulmonary embolism: Management of acute massive pulmonary embolism (PE)

ST-elevation myocardial infarction: Management of ST-elevation myocardial infarction (STEMI) for the lysis of thrombi in coronary arteries.

Limitations of use: The risk of stroke may outweigh the benefit produced by thrombolytic therapy in patients whose acute myocardial infarction (MI) puts them at low risk for death or heart failure.

Recommended criteria for treatment:

STEMI (ACCF/AHA [O'Gara 2013]): Ischemic symptoms within 12 hours of treatment or evidence of ongoing ischemia 12 to 24 hours after symptom onset with a large area of myocardium at risk or hemodynamic instability.

STEMI ECG definition: New ST-segment elevation at the J point in at least 2 contiguous leads of ≥2 mm (0.2 mV) in men or ≥1.5 mm (0.15 mV) in women in leads V_2-V_3 and/or of ≥1 mm (0.1 mV) in other contiguous precordial leads or limb leads. New or presumably new left bundle branch block (LBBB) may interfere with ST-elevation analysis and should not be considered diagnostic in isolation.

At non-PCI-capable hospitals, the ACCF/AHA recommends thrombolytic therapy administration when the anticipated first medical contact (FMC)-to-device time at a PCI-capable hospital is >120 minutes due to unavoidable delays.

AIS: Onset of stroke symptoms within 3 hours of treatment

Acute PE: Age ≤75 years: Documented massive PE (defined as acute PE with sustained hypotension [SBP <90 mm Hg for ≤15 minutes or requiring inotropic support], persistent profound bradycardia [HR <40 bpm with signs or symptoms of shock], or pulselessness); alteplase may be considered for submassive PE with clinical evidence of adverse prognosis (eg, new hemodynamic instability, worsening respiratory insufficiency, severe right ventricular (RV) dysfunction, or major myocardial necrosis) and low risk of bleeding complications. **Note:** Not recommended for patients with low-risk PE (eg, normotensive, no RV dysfunction, normal biomarkers) or submassive acute PE with minor RV dysfunction, minor myocardial necrosis, and no clinical worsening (AHA [Jaff 2011]).

Cathflo Activase: Restoration of function to central venous access device

Local Anesthetic/Vasoconstrictor Precautions No information available to require special precautions

Effects on Dental Treatment Key adverse event(s) related to dental treatment: As with all drugs which may affect hemostasis, bleeding is the major adverse effect associated with alteplase. Hemorrhage may occur at virtually any site; risk is dependent on multiple variables, including the dosage administered, concurrent use of multiple agents which alter hemostasis, and patient predisposition. Rapid lysis of coronary artery thrombi by thrombolytic agents may be associated with reperfusion-related atrial and/or ventricular arrhythmias. See Effects on Bleeding.

Effects on Bleeding Bleeding is the major adverse effect associated with thrombolytic agents, such as alteplase. It is unlikely that ambulatory patients presenting for dental treatment will be taking parenteral thrombolytic therapy.

Adverse Reactions As with all drugs which may affect hemostasis, bleeding is the major adverse effect associated with alteplase. Hemorrhage may occur at virtually any site. Risk is dependent on multiple variables, including the dosage administered, concurrent use of multiple agents which alter hemostasis, and patient predisposition. Rapid lysis of coronary artery thrombi by thrombolytic agents may be associated with reperfusion-related atrial and/or ventricular arrhythmia. **Note:** Lowest rate of bleeding complications expected with dose used to restore catheter function.

1% to 10%:

Cardiovascular: Hypotension

Central nervous system: Fever

Dermatologic: Bruising (1%)

Gastrointestinal: GI hemorrhage (5%), nausea, vomiting

Genitourinary: GU hemorrhage (4%)

Hematologic: Bleeding (0.5% major, 7% minor: GUSTO trial)

Local: Bleeding at catheter puncture site (15.3%, accelerated administration)

<1% (Limited to important or life-threatening): Angioedema (orolingual), intracranial hemorrhage (0.4% to 0.87% when adult dose is ≤100 mg), retroperitoneal hemorrhage, pericardial hemorrhage, gingival hemorrhage, epistaxis, allergic reaction (anaphylaxis, anaphylactoid reactions, laryngeal edema, rash, and urticaria [<0.02%])

Additional cardiovascular events associated **with use in STEMI:** AV block, cardiogenic shock, heart failure, cardiac arrest, recurrent ischemia/infarction, myocardial rupture, electromechanical dissociation, pericardial effusion, pericarditis, mitral regurgitation, cardiac tamponade, thromboembolism, pulmonary edema, asystole, ventricular tachycardia, bradycardia, ruptured intracranial AV malformation, seizure, hemorrhagic bursitis, cholesterol crystal embolization

Additional events associated **with use in pulmonary embolism:** Pulmonary re-embolization, pulmonary edema, pleural effusion, thromboembolism

Additional events associated **with use in stroke:** Cerebral edema, cerebral herniation, seizure, new ischemic stroke

General Dosage Range

Intracatheter:

Children <30 kg: 110% of the internal lumen volume of the catheter; retain in catheter for 0.5 to 2 hours; may repeat once (maximum: 2 mg/2 mL per dose)

Children ≥30 kg, Adolescents, and Adults: 2 mg/2 mL retain in catheter for 0.5 to 2 hours; may repeat once

IV infusion: *Adults:* Dosage varies greatly depending on indication

Mechanism of Action Initiates local fibrinolysis by binding to fibrin in a thrombus (clot) and converts entrapped plasminogen to plasmin

Pharmacodynamics/Kinetics

Duration of Action >50% present in plasma cleared ~5 minutes after infusion terminated, ~80% cleared within 10 minutes; fibrinolytic activity persists for up to 1 hour after infusion terminated (Semba 2000)

Half-life Elimination Initial: 5 minutes

Pregnancy Risk Factor C

Pregnancy Considerations Adverse events have been observed in animal reproduction studies. The risk of bleeding may be increased in pregnant women. Outcome information is available following alteplase use in pregnancy (Hirano 2013; Leonhardt 2006; Li 2012; Özkan 2013). Currently, most guidelines consider pregnancy to be a relative contraindication for its use (Jaff 2011; Jauch 2013; O'Gara 2013; O'Connor 2010). Alteplase should not be withheld from pregnant women in life-threatening situations but should be avoided when safer alternatives are available (Bates 2012; Leonhardt 2006; Li 2012).

Altretamine (al TRET a meen)

Brand Names: US Hexalen

Brand Names: Canada Hexalen

Pharmacologic Category Antineoplastic Agent, Alkylating Agent

Use Ovarian cancer (persistent or recurrent): Palliative treatment (single agent) of persistent or recurrent ovarian cancer after first-line treatment with a cisplatin and/or alkylating agent-based combination.

Local Anesthetic/Vasoconstrictor Precautions No information available to require special precautions

Effects on Dental Treatment No significant effects or complications reported

Effects on Bleeding Chemotherapy may result in significant myelosuppression, including thrombocytopenia. In patients who are under active treatment, a medical consult is suggested.

Adverse Reactions

>10%:

- Central nervous system: Peripheral sensory neuropathy (31%; mild: 9%; moderate-to-severe: 9%)
- Gastrointestinal: Nausea and vomiting (33%; severe 1%)
- Hematologic & oncologic: Anemia (33%), leukopenia (5% to 15%, grade 4: <1%)

1% to 10%:

- Central nervous system: Fatigue, seizure
- Gastrointestinal: Anorexia
- Hematologic & oncologic: Thrombocytopenia
- Hepatic: Increased serum alkaline phosphatase
- Renal: Increased blood urea nitrogen, increased serum creatinine

<1%, postmarketing, and/or case reports: Alopecia, ataxia, depression, dizziness, hepatotoxicity, mood disorder, neurotoxicity, pruritus, skin rash, vertigo

General Dosage Range Dosage adjustment recommended in patients who develop toxicities

Oral: *Adults:* 260 mg/m^2/day in 4 divided doses for 14 or 21 days of a 28-day cycle

Mechanism of Action Altretamine structurally resembles alkylating agents, although has demonstrated activity in tumors resistant to classic alkylating agents. Cytotoxic effect not fully characterized, however it is likely that after activation, metabolites form crosslinks with DNA and RNA and inhibit DNA and RNA synthesis (Perry 2012). Altretamine has demonstrated more activity in platinum-sensitive ovarian cancers than platinum-resistant disease (Alberts 2004).

Pharmacodynamics/Kinetics

Half-life Elimination 4.7 to 10.2 hours

Time to Peak Plasma: 0.5 to 3 hours

Pregnancy Risk Factor D

Pregnancy Considerations Adverse effects were observed in animal reproduction studies. Altretamine may cause fetal harm if administered during pregnancy. Women of childbearing potential should avoid becoming pregnant while on therapy.

Aluminum Acetate (a LOO mi num AS e tate)

Brand Names: US Boro-Packs [OTC]; Pedi-Boro Soak [OTC]

Pharmacologic Category Topical Skin Product

Use Skin irritation: Temporary relief of minor skin irritations due to poison ivy, oak, or sumac; itching; insect bites; athlete's foot; and rashes caused by soaps, detergents, cosmetics, or jewelry.

Local Anesthetic/Vasoconstrictor Precautions No information available to require special precautions

Effects on Dental Treatment No significant effects or complications reported

Effects on Bleeding No information available to require special precautions

Adverse Reactions Frequency not defined.

1% to 10%: Local: Local irritation

General Dosage Range Topical: *Children, Adolescents, and Adults:* Soak affected area in solution or apply wet dressing/compress to affected area for 15 to 30 minutes; repeat as needed.

Pregnancy Considerations Animal reproduction studies have not been conducted. The amount of aluminum acetate available systemically following topical application is unknown.

Aluminum Chloride (a LOO mi num KLOR ide)

Related Information

Antiplatelet and Anticoagulation Considerations in Dentistry *on page* 1764

Brand Names: US Hemoban; Hemodent; ViscoStat Clear

Pharmacologic Category Astringent; Hemostatic Agent

Use Hemostatic

Local Anesthetic/Vasoconstrictor Precautions No information available to require special precautions

Effects on Dental Treatment Aids in local tissue hemostasis when applied to intraoral tissue.

Effects on Bleeding When applied to tissue intraorally, it slows bleeding at the site of application.

Adverse Reactions No data reported.

General Dosage Range Topical: *Adults:* Apply retraction cord as directed

Mechanism of Action Precipitates tissue and blood proteins causing a mechanical obstruction to hemorrhage from injured blood vessels

Aluminum Hydroxide
(a LOO mi num hye DROKS ide)

Brand Names: US DermaMed [OTC]

Brand Names: Canada Amphojel; Basaljel

Pharmacologic Category Antacid; Antidote; Protectant, Topical

Use

Oral: Antacid: For the temporary relief of heartburn, acid indigestion, and sour stomach

Topical: Temporary protection and relief of chafed and abraded skin, minor burns and wounds, and skin irritations resulting from friction and rubbing.

Local Anesthetic/Vasoconstrictor Precautions No information available to require special precautions

Effects on Dental Treatment Key adverse event(s) related to dental treatment: Chalky taste. Aluminum and magnesium ions prevent GI absorption of tetracycline by forming a large ionized chelated molecule with the aluminum ion and tetracyclines in the stomach. Aluminum hydroxide prevents GI absorption of ketoconazole and itraconazole by increasing the pH in the GI tract. Any of these drugs should be administered at least 1 hour before $Al(OH)_3$.

Effects on Bleeding No information available to require special precautions

Adverse Reactions Frequency not defined.

Gastrointestinal: Constipation, fecal discoloration (white speckles), fecal impaction, nausea, stomach cramps, vomiting

Endocrine & metabolic: Hypomagnesemia, hypophosphatemia

General Dosage Range

Oral: *Adults:* 640 mg 5 to 6 times daily (maximum: 3,840 mg in 24 hours)

Topical: *Adults:* Apply to affected area as needed or as directed.

Mechanism of Action As an antacid, aluminum hydroxide neutralizes hydrochloride in the stomach to form Al $(Cl)_3$ salt + H_2O, resulting in increased gastric pH and inhibition of pepsin activity (Weberg, 1998). As an agent for the short term treatment of hyperphosphatemia (off-label use), aluminum hydroxide binds phosphate in the gastrointestinal tract preventing absorption of phosphate (Schucker, 2005).

Pharmacodynamics/Kinetics

Duration of Action Dependent on gastric emptying time: Fasting state: 20-60 minutes; One hour after meals: Up to 3 hours

Pregnancy Considerations Most aluminum-containing antacids are considered low risk during pregnancy (Mahadevan, 2006).

Aluminum Hydroxide and Magnesium Carbonate

(a LOO mi num hye DROKS ide & mag NEE zhum KAR bun nate)

Related Information

Aluminum Hydroxide *on page 106*

Brand Names: US Acid Gone Extra Strength [OTC]; Acid Gone [OTC]; Gaviscon Extra Strength [OTC]; Gaviscon Liquid [OTC]

Pharmacologic Category Antacid

Use Antacid: Relief of heartburn, acid indigestion, sour stomach and GI upset associated with these symptoms

Local Anesthetic/Vasoconstrictor Precautions No information available to require special precautions

Effects on Dental Treatment Key adverse event(s) related to dental treatment: Chalky taste. Aluminum and magnesium ions prevent GI absorption of tetracycline by forming a large ionized chelated molecule with the tetracyclines in the stomach. Aluminum hydroxide prevents GI absorption of ketoconazole and itraconazole by increasing the pH in the GI tract. Any of these drugs should be administered at least 1 hour before aluminum hydroxide.

Effects on Bleeding No information available to require special precautions

Adverse Reactions 1% to 10%:

Endocrine & metabolic: Hypermagnesemia, hypophosphatemia

Gastrointestinal: Constipation, diarrhea

Neuromuscular & skeletal: Osteomalacia

Miscellaneous: Aluminum toxicity (prolonged use and concomitant renal failure)

General Dosage Range Oral: *Children ≥12 years, Adolescents, and Adults:* 10 to 30 mL **or** 2 to 4 tablets 4 times daily (maximum: 120 mL or 16 tablets per 24 hours)

Mechanism of Action Aluminum hydroxide neutralizes hydrochloride in the stomach to form Al (Cl)3 salt + H2O, resulting in increased gastric pH and inhibition of pepsin activity (Weberg, 1998). Magnesium salts have a similar mechanism. Alginic acid is a natural polysaccharide polymer that precipitates into a low-density viscous gel of near-neutral pH within minutes of contacting gastric acid. The change in pH triggers the sodium bicarbonate in the formulation to release carbon dioxide, which becomes trapped in the alginate gel, causing it to float to the top of the gastric contents. (Rohof 2013).

Pregnancy Considerations Most aluminum- and magnesium-containing antacids are considered low risk during pregnancy (Mahadevan, 2006).

Aluminum Hydroxide and Magnesium Hydroxide

(a LOO mi num hye DROKS ide & mag NEE zhum hye DROK side)

Related Information

Aluminum Hydroxide *on page 106*

Magnesium Hydroxide *on page 1035*

Brand Names: US Mag-Al [OTC]

Brand Names: Canada Diovol; Diovol Ex; Gelusil Extra Strength; Mylanta

Pharmacologic Category Antacid

Use Antacid: Relief of heartburn, acid indigestion, sour stomach and GI upset associated with these symptoms

Local Anesthetic/Vasoconstrictor Precautions No information available to require special precautions

Effects on Dental Treatment Key adverse event(s) related to dental treatment: Chalky taste. Aluminum and magnesium ions prevent GI absorption of tetracycline by forming a large ionized chelated molecule with the tetracyclines in the stomach. Aluminum hydroxide prevents GI absorption of ketoconazole and itraconazole by increasing the pH in the GI tract. Any of these drugs should be administered at least 1 hour before aluminum hydroxide.

Effects on Bleeding No information available to require special precautions

Adverse Reactions Frequency not defined.

Central nervous system: Calcium or chalky taste

Endocrine & metabolic: Hypermagnesemia (rare), hypophosphatemia (rare)

Gastrointestinal: Abdominal cramps, constipation, fecal discoloration (white speckles), fecal impaction, nausea, vomiting

General Dosage Range Oral: *Children ≥12 years, Adolescents, and Adults:* 10 to 20 mL 4 times daily (maximum: 80 mL per 24 hours)

Pharmacodynamics/Kinetics

Duration of Action Dependent on gastric emptying time: Fasting state: 20-60 minutes; 1 hour after meals: May be up to 3 hours

Pregnancy Considerations Most aluminum- and magnesium-containing antacids are considered low risk during pregnancy (Mahadevan 2006).

Aluminum Hydroxide and Magnesium Trisilicate

(a LOO mi num hye DROKS ide & mag NEE zhum trye SIL i kate)

Related Information

Aluminum Hydroxide *on page 106*

Brand Names: US Gaviscon Tablet [OTC]

Pharmacologic Category Antacid

Use Antacid: Temporary relief of heartburn and acid indigestion due to acid reflux

Local Anesthetic/Vasoconstrictor Precautions No information available to require special precautions

Effects on Dental Treatment Key adverse event(s) related to dental treatment: Chalky taste. Aluminum and magnesium ions prevent GI absorption of tetracycline by forming a large ionized chelated molecule with the tetracyclines in the stomach. Aluminum hydroxide prevents GI absorption of ketoconazole and itraconazole by increasing the pH in the GI tract. Any of these drugs should be administered at least 1 hour before aluminum hydroxide.

Effects on Bleeding No information available to require special precautions

General Dosage Range Oral: *Adults:* Chew 2 to 4 tablets 4 times daily (maximum: 16 tablets per 24 hours)

Mechanism of Action Aluminum hydroxide neutralizes hydrochloride in the stomach to form Al (Cl)3 salt + H2O, resulting in increased gastric pH and inhibition of pepsin activity (Weberg, 1998). Magnesium salts have a similar mechanism. Alginic acid is a natural polysaccharide polymer that precipitates into a low-density viscous gel of near-neutral pH within minutes of contacting gastric acid. The change in pH triggers the sodium bicarbonate in the formulation to release carbon dioxide, which becomes trapped in the alginate gel, causing it to float to the top of the gastric contents. (Rohof 2013).

Pregnancy Considerations Most aluminum-containing antacids are considered low risk during pregnancy; however, use of antacids containing magnesium trisilicate should be avoided (Mahadevan 2006).

Aluminum Hydroxide, Magnesium Hydroxide, and Simethicone

(a LOO mi num hye DROKS ide, mag NEE zhum hye DROKS ide, & sye METH i kone)

Related Information

Aluminum Hydroxide *on page 106*

Magnesium Hydroxide *on page 1035*

Simethicone *on page 1479*

Brand Names: US Alamag Plus [OTC] [DSC]; Aldroxicon I [OTC]; Aldroxicon II [OTC]; Almacone Double Strength [OTC]; Almacone [OTC]; Gelusil [OTC]; Geri-Mox [OTC]; HyVee Advanced Antacid [OTC]; Maalox Advanced Maximum Strength [OTC]; Maalox Advanced Regular Strength [OTC] [DSC]; Mi-Acid Maximum Strength [OTC] [DSC]; Mi-Acid [OTC]; Mintox Plus [OTC]; Mylanta Classic Maximum Strength Liquid [OTC]; Mylanta Classic Regular Strength Liquid [OTC]; Rulox [OTC]

Brand Names: Canada Diovol Plus; Gelusil; Mylanta Double Strength; Mylanta Extra Strength; Mylanta Regular Strength

Pharmacologic Category Antacid; Antiflatulent

Use Antacid/antigas: Relief of acid indigestion, heartburn, sour stomach, or upset stomach and gas associated with these symptoms

Local Anesthetic/Vasoconstrictor Precautions No information available to require special precautions

Effects on Dental Treatment Key adverse event(s) related to dental treatment: Chalky taste. Aluminum and magnesium ions prevent GI absorption of tetracycline by forming a large ionized chelated molecule with the tetracyclines in the stomach. Aluminum hydroxide prevents GI absorption of ketoconazole and itraconazole by increasing the pH in the GI tract. Any of these drugs should be administered at least 1 hour before aluminum hydroxide.

Effects on Bleeding No information available to require special precautions

Adverse Reactions

>10%: Gastrointestinal: Constipation, decreased gastrointestinal motility, fecal impaction, hemorrhoids, stomach cramps, unpleasant taste (chalky)

1% to 10%: Gastrointestinal: Fecal discoloration (white speckles), nausea, vomiting

<1%, postmarketing, and/or case reports: Dehydration, fluid retention, hypomagnesemia, hypophosphatemia

General Dosage Range Oral: *Children ≥12 years, Adolescents and Adults:* 10 to 20 mL or 1 to 4 tablets 4 times daily

Mechanism of Action Aluminum hydroxide and magnesium hydroxide are antacids; simethicone is used to relieve symptoms of gas

Alvimopan (al VI moe pan)

Brand Names: US Entereg

Pharmacologic Category Gastrointestinal Agent, Miscellaneous; Opioid Antagonist, Peripherally-Acting

Use Postoperative ileus: To accelerate the time to upper and lower GI recovery following surgeries including partial bowel resection with primary anastomosis

Local Anesthetic/Vasoconstrictor Precautions No information available to require special precautions

Effects on Dental Treatment No significant effects or complications reported

Effects on Bleeding No information available to require special precautions

Adverse Reactions Note: Incidence reported limited to bowel resection patients only.

1% to 10%:

- Endocrine & metabolic: Hypokalemia (10%)
- Gastrointestinal: Dyspepsia (2% to 7%)
- Genitourinary: Urinary retention (3%)
- Hematologic and oncologic: Anemia (5%)
- Neuromuscular & skeletal: Back pain (3%)

Frequency not defined:

- Cardiovascular: Myocardial infarction

General Dosage Range Oral: *Adults:* Initial: 12 mg prior to surgery; Maintenance: 12 mg twice daily (maximum: 15 doses)

Mechanism of Action An opioid receptor antagonist which blocks opioid binding at the mu receptor; alvimopan has restricted ability to cross the blood-brain barrier at therapeutic doses. It selectively and competitively binds to the GI tract mu opioid receptors and antagonizes the peripheral effects of opioids on gastrointestinal motility and secretion. Does not affect opioid analgesic effects or induce opioid withdrawal symptoms.

Pharmacodynamics/Kinetics

Half-life Elimination 10-17 hours

Time to Peak Plasma: Parent drug: ~2 hours; Metabolite: 36 hours

Pregnancy Risk Factor B

Pregnancy Considerations Adverse events have not been observed in animal reproduction studies.

Prescribing and Access Restrictions As a requirement of the REMS program, access to this medication is restricted. Only hospitals enrolled in the ENTEREG Access Support and Education (E.A.S.E.™) Program may administer this medication. Hospital staff must be educated on the need to limit to short-term (no more than 15 doses) and inpatient use. Hospitals may contact the E.A.S.E.™ program at 1-800-278-0340.

Amantadine (a MAN ta deen)

Related Information

Systemic Viral Diseases *on page 1806*

Brand Names: Canada Dom-Amantadine; Mylan-Amantadine; PHL-Amantadine; PMS-Amantadine

Pharmacologic Category Anti-Parkinson Agent, Dopamine Agonist; Antiviral Agent; Antiviral Agent, Adamantane

Use

Drug-induced extrapyramidal reactions: Treatment of drug-induced extrapyramidal reactions.

Influenza A prophylaxis: Chemoprophylaxis against signs and symptoms of influenza A virus infection; also refer to current Advisory Committee on Immunization Practices (ACIP) guidelines for recommendations during current influenza season.

Influenza A treatment: Treatment of uncomplicated respiratory tract illness caused by influenza A virus strains; also refer to current ACIP guidelines for recommendations during current influenza season.

Parkinson disease: Treatment of idiopathic Parkinson disease (paralysis agitans), postencephalitic parkinsonism, parkinsonism in association with cerebral arteriosclerosis, and symptomatic parkinsonism, which may follow injury to the nervous system by carbon monoxide intoxication.

Local Anesthetic/Vasoconstrictor Precautions No information available to require special precautions

Effects on Dental Treatment Key adverse event(s) related to dental treatment: Xerostomia (prolonged use may cause significant xerostomia; normal salivary flow resumes upon discontinuation); Patients may experience orthostatic hypotension as they stand up after treatment; especially if lying in dental chair for extended periods of time. Use caution with sudden changes in position during and after dental treatment.

Effects on Bleeding No information available to require special precautions

Adverse Reactions

1% to 10%:

Cardiovascular: Livedo reticularis (1% to 5%), orthostatic hypotension (1% to 5%), peripheral edema (1% to 5%)

Central nervous system: Dizziness (5% to 10%), insomnia (5% to 10%), abnormal dreams (1% to 5%), agitation (1% to 5%), anxiety (1% to 5%), ataxia (1% to 5%), confusion (1% to 5%), depression (1% to 5%), drowsiness (1% to 5%), fatigue (1% to 5%), hallucination (1% to 5%), headache (1% to 5%), irritability (1% to 5%), nervousness (1% to 5%)

Gastrointestinal: Nausea (5% to 10%), anorexia (1% to 5%), constipation (1% to 5%), diarrhea (1% to 5%), xerostomia (1% to 5%)

Respiratory: Dry nose (1% to 5%)

<1%, postmarketing, and/or case reports: Abnormal gait, abnormality in thinking, acute respiratory tract failure, aggressive behavior, agranulocytosis, amnesia, anaphylaxis, cardiac arrhythmia (including malignant arrhythmias), coma, congestive heart failure, corneal edema, decreased libido, decreased visual acuity, delirium, delusions, diaphoresis, dysphagia, dyspnea, eczema, edema, EEG pattern changes, euphoria, fever, hyperkinesia, hypersensitivity reaction, hypertension, hypertonia, hypokinesia, hypotension, impulse control disorder (including urges to spend money uncontrollably), increased blood urea nitrogen, increased creatine phosphokinase, increased gamma-glutamyl transferase, increased lactate dehydrogenase, increased libido, increased serum alkaline phosphatase, increased serum ALT, increased serum AST, increased serum bilirubin, increased serum creatinine, keratitis, leukocytosis, leukopenia, mania, muscle spasm, mydriasis, neuroleptic malignant syndrome (associated with dosage reduction or abrupt withdrawal of amantadine), neutropenia, oculogyric crisis, optic nerve palsy, paranoia, paresthesia, pathological gambling, pruritus, psychosis, pulmonary edema, seizure, skin photosensitivity, skin rash, slurred speech, stupor, suicidal ideation, tachycardia, tachypnea, tremor, urinary retention, visual disturbance (including punctate subepithelial or other corneal opacity), vomiting, weakness

General Dosage Range Dosage adjustment recommended in patients with renal impairment

Oral:

Children 1 to 9 years: 4.4 to 8.8 mg/kg/day in 2 divided doses (maximum: 150 mg/day)

Children ≥10 years and <40 kg: 5 mg/kg/day in 2 divided doses

Children ≥10 years and ≥40 kg: 100 mg twice daily

Adults: 200 to 400 mg/day in 2 divided doses (maximum: 400 mg/day)

Elderly: 100 to 400 mg/day in 2 divided doses (maximum: 400 mg/day)

Mechanism of Action

Antiviral:

The mechanism of amantadine's antiviral activity has not been fully elucidated. It appears to primarily prevent the release of infectious viral nucleic acid into the host cell by interfering with the transmembrane domain of the viral M2 protein. Amantadine is also known to prevent viral assembly during replication. Amantadine inhibits the replication of influenza A virus isolates from each of the subtypes (ie, H1N1, H2N2 and H3N2), but has very little or no activity against influenza B virus isolates.

Parkinson disease:

The exact mechanism of amantadine in the treatment of Parkinson disease and drug-induced extrapyramidal reactions is not known. Data from early animal studies suggest that amantadine may have direct and indirect effects on dopamine neurons; however, recent studies have demonstrated that amantadine is a weak, noncompetitive NMDA receptor antagonist. Although amantadine has not been shown to possess direct anticholinergic activity, clinically, it exhibits anticholinergic-like side effects (dry mouth, urinary retention, and constipation).

Pharmacodynamics/Kinetics

Onset of Action Antidyskinetic: Within 48 hours

Half-life Elimination Normal renal function: 16 ± 6 hours (9 to 31 hours); Healthy, older (≥60 years) males: 29 hours (range: 20 to 41 hours) (Aoki 1988); End-stage renal disease: 8 days

Time to Peak Plasma: 2-4 hours

Pregnancy Risk Factor C

Pregnancy Considerations Adverse events have been observed in animal reproduction studies and teratogenic events have been observed in humans (case reports).

Untreated influenza infection is associated with an increased risk of adverse events to the fetus and an increased risk of complications or death to the mother. Other agents are currently recommended for the treatment or prophylaxis influenza in pregnant women and women up to 2 weeks postpartum. Appropriate antiviral agents are currently recommended as an adjunct to vaccination and should not be used as a substitute for vaccination in pregnant women (CDC 2011; CDC 2014).

Health care providers are encouraged to refer women exposed to influenza vaccine, or who have taken an antiviral medication during pregnancy to the Vaccines and Medications in Pregnancy Surveillance System (VAMPSS) by contacting The Organization of Teratology Information Specialists (OTIS) at (877) 311-8972.

Ambrisentan (am bri SEN tan)

Brand Names: US Letairis

Brand Names: Canada Volibris

Pharmacologic Category Endothelin Receptor Antagonist; Vasodilator

Use Pulmonary arterial hypertension: Treatment of pulmonary artery hypertension (PAH) (World Health Organization [WHO] Group I) to improve exercise ability and delay clinical worsening; in combination with tadalafil to reduce the risks of disease progression and hospitalization for worsening PAH, and to improve exercise ability. Studies establishing effectiveness included predominantly patients with WHO Functional Class II to III symptoms and etiologies of idiopathic or heritable PAH (60%) or PAH associated with connective tissue diseases (34%).

Note: According to treatment guidelines from the Fifth World Symposium on Pulmonary Hypertension (WSPH), only a small number of PAH patients with WHO-FC IV symptoms (ie, severely ill patients) were included in clinical trials, therefore, most experts consider ambrisentan second-line therapy in these patients (WSPH [Gailè 2013]).

Local Anesthetic/Vasoconstrictor Precautions No information available to require special precautions

Effects on Dental Treatment Key adverse event(s) related to dental treatment: Endothelin antagonists have caused bleeding gums; there have been no specific reports for ambrisentan

Effects on Bleeding No information available to require special precautions

Adverse Reactions Frequency not always defined.

Cardiovascular: Peripheral edema (14% to 38%), flushing (4%)

Central nervous system: Headache (34%)

Gastrointestinal: Dyspepsia (3%)

Genitourinary: Oligospermia

Hematologic & oncologic: Decreased hemoglobin (7% to 10%; dose-dependent), anemia (7%), decreased hematocrit

Respiratory: Nasal congestion (6% to 16%), cough (13%), bronchitis (4%), sinusitis (3%)

<1%, postmarketing, and/or case reports: Cardiac failure, dizziness, fatigue, fluid retention, hypersensitivity, hypotension, increased liver enzymes, nausea, vomiting, weakness

General Dosage Range Dosage adjustment recommended in patients on concomitant therapy.

Oral: *Adults:* Initial: 5 mg once daily (maximum: 10 mg/day)

Mechanism of Action Blocks endothelin receptor subtypes ET_A and ET_B on vascular endothelium and smooth muscle. Stimulation of ET_A receptors, located primarily in pulmonary vascular smooth muscle cells is associated with vasoconstriction and cellular proliferation. Stimulation of ET_B receptors, located in both pulmonary vascular endothelial cells and smooth muscle cells is associated with vasodilation, antiproliferative effects, and endothelin clearance. Although ambrisentan blocks both ET_A and ET_B receptors, the affinity is greater for the ET_A receptor (>4,000-fold higher affinity).

Pharmacodynamics/Kinetics

Half-life Elimination ~9 hours

Time to Peak ~2 hours

Pregnancy Risk Factor X

Pregnancy Considerations [US Boxed Warning]: May cause birth defects; use in pregnancy is contraindicated. Exclude pregnancy prior to initiation of therapy and obtain pregnancy tests monthly during treatment and for 1 month after therapy is complete. Reliable contraception must be used during therapy and for 1 month after stopping treatment. Based on animal studies, ambrisentan is likely to produce major birth defects if used by pregnant women. Two reliable methods of contraception (eg, hormone method with a barrier method or 2 barrier methods) must be used throughout treatment and for 1 month after stopping treatment. Patients who have undergone a tubal ligation or the insertion of a contraceptive implant or intrauterine device (Copper T 380A or LNg 20) do not require additional contraceptive measures. A missed menses or suspected pregnancy should be reported to a healthcare provider and prompt immediate pregnancy testing. Sperm counts may be reduced in men during treatment (as observed with bosentan). Women with pulmonary arterial hypertension are encouraged to avoid pregnancy (McLaughlin 2009; Taichman 2014).

Prescribing and Access Restrictions As a requirement of the REMS program, access to this medication is restricted. Only prescribers and pharmacies registered with this program may prescribe and dispense ambrisentan. Further information may be obtained from the manufacturer, Gilead Sciences, Inc at www.-letairisrems.com or 1-866-664-5327.

Amifostine (am i FOS teen)+

Brand Names: US Ethyol

Brand Names: Canada Ethyol

Pharmacologic Category Antidote; Chemoprotective Agent

Use

Renal toxicity (cisplatin-induced): Reduce the cumulative renal toxicity associated with repeated administration of cisplatin in patients with advanced ovarian cancer.

Xerostomia due to radiation therapy for head and neck cancer: Reduce the incidence of moderate-to-severe xerostomia in patients undergoing postoperative radiation treatment for head and neck cancer, where the radiation port includes a substantial portion of the parotid glands.

Limitations of use: The clinical data do not suggest the efficacy of cisplatin-based chemotherapy or radiation therapy for the approved indications is altered by amifostine. Data on the effects of amifostine on the efficacy of chemotherapy or radiotherapy in other settings is limited. Do not administer amifostine in other settings where chemotherapy can produce a significant survival benefit or cure, or in patients receiving definitive radiotherapy, unless within the context of a clinical study.

Local Anesthetic/Vasoconstrictor Precautions No information available to require special precautions

Effects on Dental Treatment No significant effects or complications reported

Effects on Bleeding No information available to require special precautions

Adverse Reactions

>10%:

Cardiovascular: Hypotension (15% to 61%; grades 3/4: 3% to 8%; dose dependent)

Gastrointestinal: Nausea and vomiting (53% to 96%; grades 3/4: 8% to 30%; dose dependent)

1% to 10%: Endocrine & metabolic: Hypocalcemia (clinically significant: 1%)

<1%, postmarketing, and/or case reports: Anaphylactoid reaction, anaphylaxis, apnea, atrial fibrillation, atrial flutter, back pain, bradycardia, cardiac arrest, cardiac arrhythmia, chest pain, chest tightness, chills, dizziness, drowsiness, erythema multiforme, exfoliative dermatitis, extrasystoles, fever, flushing, hiccups, hypersensitivity reaction (fever, skin rash, hypoxia, dyspnea, laryngeal edema), hypoxia, ischemic heart disease, malaise, myocardial infarction, pruritus, renal failure, respiratory arrest, rigors, seizure, skin rash (including mild), sneezing, Stevens-Johnson syndrome, supraventricular tachycardia, syncope, tachycardia, toxic epidermal necrolysis, toxoderma, transient hypertension, urticaria

General Dosage Range IV: *Adults:* 910 mg/m^2 once daily 30 minutes prior to cytotoxic therapy **or** 200 mg/m^2/day 15 to 30 minutes prior to radiation therapy

Mechanism of Action Amifostine is a prodrug that is dephosphorylated by alkaline phosphatase in tissues to a pharmacologically-active free thiol metabolite. The free thiol is available to bind to, and detoxify, reactive metabolites of cisplatin; and can also act as a scavenger of free radicals that may be generated (by cisplatin or radiation therapy) in tissues.

Pharmacodynamics/Kinetics

Half-life Elimination Children: 9.3 minutes (Fouladi 2001); Adults: ~8 minutes

Pregnancy Considerations Adverse events have been observed in animal reproduction studies.

Amikacin (am i KAY sin)

Brand Names: Canada Amikacin Sulfate Injection, USP, Amikin

Pharmacologic Category Antibiotic, Aminoglycoside

Use Serious infections: Treatment of serious infections (eg, bone infections, respiratory tract infections, endocarditis, septicemia) due to gram-negative organisms, including *Pseudomonas*, *Escherichia coli*, *Proteus*, *Providencia*, *Klebsiella*, *Enterobacter*, *Serratia*, and *Acinetobacter*

Local Anesthetic/Vasoconstrictor Precautions No information available to require special precautions

Effects on Dental Treatment No significant effects or complications reported

Effects on Bleeding No information available to require special precautions

Adverse Reactions

1% to 10%:

Central nervous system: Neurotoxicity

Genitourinary: Nephrotoxicity

Otic: Auditory ototoxicity, vestibular ototoxicity

<1%, postmarketing, and/or case reports: Arthralgia, drowsiness, drug fever, dyspnea, eosinophilia, headache, hypersensitivity reaction, hypotension, nausea, paresthesia, skin rash, tremor, vomiting, weakness

General Dosage Range Dosage adjustment recommended in patients with renal impairment

IM, IV: *Infants, Children, Adolescents, and Adults:* 5 to 7.5 mg/kg/dose every 8 to 12 hours (maximum: 15 mg/kg/day)

Mechanism of Action Inhibits protein synthesis in susceptible bacteria by binding to 30S ribosomal subunits

Pharmacodynamics/Kinetics

Half-life Elimination Renal function and age dependent:

Infants: Low birth weight (1 to 3 days): 7 to 9 hours; Full-term >7 days: 4 to 5 hours (Howard 1975)

Children: 1.6 to 2.5 hours

Adolescents: 1.5 ± 1 hour

Adults: Normal renal function: ~2 hours; Anuria/end-stage renal disease: 17 to 150 hours (Aronoff 2007)

Time to Peak Serum: IM: 60 minutes; IV: Within 30 minutes following a 30-minute infusion

Pregnancy Risk Factor D

Pregnancy Considerations Adverse events were not observed in the initial animal reproduction studies. Amikacin crosses the placenta and produces detectable concentrations in the fetus. Aminoglycosides may cause fetal harm if administered to a pregnant woman. There are several reports of total irreversible bilateral congenital deafness in children whose mothers received another aminoglycoside (streptomycin) during pregnancy. Although serious side effects to the fetus/infant have not been reported following maternal use of all aminoglycosides, a potential for harm exists.

Due to pregnancy-induced physiologic changes, some pharmacokinetic parameters of amikacin may be altered (Bernard 1977).

AMILoride (a MIL oh ride)

Related Information

Cardiovascular Diseases *on page 1752*

Brand Names: Canada Midamor

Pharmacologic Category Antihypertensive; Diuretic, Potassium-Sparing

Use

Heart failure or hypertension: Counteracts potassium loss induced by other diuretics in the treatment of hypertension or heart failure; usually used in conjunction with more potent diuretics such as thiazides or loop diuretics

According to the Eighth Joint National Committee (JNC 8) guidelines, potassium-sparing diuretics are not recommended for the initial treatment of hypertension (James, 2013). The American Society of Hypertension/International Society of Hypertension (ASH/ISH) suggests that amiloride in combination with other diuretics (eg, hydrochlorothiazide) may be used to prevent hypokalemia associated with diuretics used to manage hypertension (Weber, 2014).

Local Anesthetic/Vasoconstrictor Precautions No information available to require special precautions

Effects on Dental Treatment No significant effects or complications reported

Effects on Bleeding No information available to require special precautions

Adverse Reactions

1% to 10%:

Central nervous system: Dizziness, fatigue, headache

Endocrine & metabolic: Hyperkalemia (up to 10%; risk reduced in patients receiving kaliuretic diuretics), dehydration, gynecomastia, hyperchloremic metabolic acidosis, hyponatremia

Gastrointestinal: Abdominal pain, change in appetite, constipation, diarrhea, gas pain, nausea, vomiting

Genitourinary: Impotence

Neuromuscular & skeletal: Muscle cramps, weakness

Respiratory: Cough, dyspnea

<1%, postmarketing, and/or case reports: Alopecia, bladder spasm, cardiac arrhythmia, chest pain, dysuria, gastrointestinal hemorrhage, increased intraocular pressure, jaundice, orthostatic hypotension, palpitations, polyuria

General Dosage Range Dosage adjustment recommended in patients with renal impairment

Oral: *Adults:* 5 to 10 mg daily in 1 to 2 divided doses (maximum: 20 mg daily)

Mechanism of Action Blocks epithelial sodium channels in the late distal convoluted tubule (DCT), and collecting duct which inhibits sodium reabsorption from the lumen. This effectively reduces intracellular sodium, decreasing the function of Na+/K+ATPase, leading to potassium retention and decreased calcium, magnesium, and hydrogen excretion. As sodium uptake capacity in the DCT/collecting duct is limited, the natriuretic, diuretic, and antihypertensive effects are generally considered weak.

Pharmacodynamics/Kinetics

Onset of Action Within 2 hours; Peak effect: 6 to 10 hours

Duration of Action ~24 hours

Half-life Elimination Normal renal function: 6 to 9 hours; renal impairment (CrCl <50 mL/minute): 21 to 144 hours (George 1980)

Time to Peak Serum:3 to 4 hours

Pregnancy Risk Factor B

Pregnancy Considerations Adverse events were not observed in animal reproduction studies.

Amiloride and Hydrochlorothiazide

(a MIL oh ride & hye droe klor oh THYE a zide)

Related Information

AMILoride *on page 111*

HydroCHLOROthiazide *on page 820*

Brand Names: Canada Ami-Hydro; Apo-Amilzide®; Gen-Amilazide; Moduret; Novamilor; Nu-Amilzide

Pharmacologic Category Antihypertensive; Diuretic, Combination

Use Heart failure, Hypertension: For the treatment of patients with congestive heart failure (CHF) or hypertension who develop hypokalemia when thiazides or other kaliuretic diuretics are used alone, or in whom maintenance of normal potassium levels is considered to be clinically important (eg, digitalized patients or patients with significant cardiac arrhythmias).

Local Anesthetic/Vasoconstrictor Precautions No information available to require special precautions

Effects on Dental Treatment No significant effects or complications reported

Effects on Bleeding No information available to require special precautions

Adverse Reactions Also see individual agents.

1% to 10%:

Cardiovascular: Cardiac arrhythmia (>1%)

Central nervous system: Dizziness (3% to 8%), headache (3% to 8%), fatigue (>1%)

Dermatologic: Skin rash (3% to 8%), pruritus (>1%)

Endocrine & metabolic: Hyperkalemia (1% to 2%), increased serum potassium (>1%; >5.5 mEq/L)

Gastrointestinal: Nausea (3% to 8%), abdominal pain (>1%), diarrhea (>1%), gastrointestinal pain (>1%)

Neuromuscular & skeletal: Leg pain (>1%), weakness (3% to 8%)

Respiratory: Dyspnea (>1%)

<1%, postmarketing, and/or case reports: Alopecia, angina pectoris, anorexia, arthralgia, back pain, change in appetite, chest pain, confusion, constipation, dehydration, depression, diaphoresis, digitalis intoxication, drowsiness, dysuria, erythema multiforme, exfoliative dermatitis, flatulence, flushing, gastrointestinal distress, gastrointestinal fullness, gastrointestinal hemorrhage, gout, gynecomastia, hiccups, hyponatremia (symptomatic), impotence, increased thirst, insomnia, malaise, muscle cramps, muscle spasm, nasal congestion, nervousness, nocturia, numbness, orthostatic hypertension, paresthesia, renal failure, renal insufficiency, Stevens-Johnson syndrome, stupor, syncope, tachycardia, toxic epidermal necrolysis, unpleasant taste, urinary incontinence, vertigo, visual disturbance, vomiting

General Dosage Range Dosage adjustment recommended in patients with renal impairment

Oral: *Adults:* 1 to 2 tablets daily (maximum: 2 tablets/day)

Pregnancy Risk Factor B

Pregnancy Considerations Adverse events have not been observed in animal reproduction studies. See individual agents.

Aminocaproic Acid (a mee noe ka PROE ik AS id)

Related Information

Antiplatelet and Anticoagulation Considerations in Dentistry *on page 1764*

Brand Names: US Amicar

Pharmacologic Category Antifibrinolytic Agent; Antihemophilic Agent; Hemostatic Agent; Lysine Analog

Use To enhance hemostasis when fibrinolysis contributes to bleeding (causes may include cardiac surgery, hematologic disorders, neoplastic disorders, abruptio placentae, hepatic cirrhosis, and urinary fibrinolysis)

Local Anesthetic/Vasoconstrictor Precautions No information available to require special precautions

Effects on Dental Treatment No significant effects or complications reported (see Effects on Bleeding)

Effects on Bleeding Used as an off-label indication to prevent or treat dental bleeding in patients with Hemophilia A; may cause thrombocytopenia

Adverse Reactions Frequency not defined.

Cardiovascular: Arrhythmia, bradycardia, edema, hypotension, intracranial hypertension, peripheral ischemia, syncope, thrombosis

Central nervous system: Confusion, delirium, dizziness, fatigue, hallucinations, headache, malaise, seizure, stroke
Dermatologic: Rash, pruritus
Gastrointestinal: Abdominal pain, anorexia, cramps, diarrhea, GI irritation, nausea, vomiting
Genitourinary: Dry ejaculation
Hematologic: Agranulocytosis, bleeding time increased, leukopenia, thrombocytopenia
Local: Injection site necrosis, injection site pain, injection site reactions
Neuromuscular & skeletal: CPK increased, myalgia, myositis, myopathy, rhabdomyolysis (rare), weakness
Ophthalmic: Vision decreased, watery eyes
Otic: Tinnitus
Renal: BUN increased, intrarenal obstruction (glomerular capillary thrombosis), myoglobinuria (rare), renal failure (rare)
Respiratory: Dyspnea, nasal congestion, pulmonary embolism
Miscellaneous: Allergic reaction, anaphylactoid reaction, anaphylaxis
Postmarketing and/or case reports: Hepatic lesion, hyperkalemia, myocardial lesion

General Dosage Range

IV: *Adults:* Dosage varies greatly depending on indication

Oral: *Adults:* Initial: Loading dose: 4-5 g for first hour; Maintenance: 1 g/hour (or 1.25 g/hour using oral solution) for 8 hours or until bleeding controlled (maximum: 30 g/day)

Mechanism of Action Binds competitively to plasminogen; blocking the binding of plasminogen to fibrin and the subsequent conversion to plasmin, resulting in inhibition of fibrin degradation (fibrinolysis).

Pharmacodynamics/Kinetics

Onset of Action ~1 to 72 hours

Half-life Elimination 1 to 2 hours

Time to Peak Oral: 1.2 ± 0.45 hours

Pregnancy Risk Factor C

Pregnancy Considerations Animal reproduction studies have not been conducted.

Aminolevulinic Acid (a MEE noh lev yoo lin ik AS id)

Brand Names: US Ameluz; Levulan Kerastick

Brand Names: Canada Levulan Kerastick

Pharmacologic Category Photosensitizing Agent, Topical; Topical Skin Product

Use

Actinic keratoses:

Gel (Ameluz): Lesion-directed and field-directed treatment of mild to moderate actinic keratosis of the face and scalp; to be used in conjunction with photodynamic therapy with narrowband red light illumination (using BF-RhodoLED lamp).

Solution (Levulan Kerastick): Treatment of minimally to moderately thick actinic keratoses of the face or scalp; to be used in conjunction with photodynamic therapy with blue light illumination (using BLU-U blue light).

Local Anesthetic/Vasoconstrictor Precautions No information available to require special precautions

Effects on Dental Treatment Key adverse event(s) related to dental treatment: Bleeding/hemorrhage (limited to application/treatment site).

Effects on Bleeding Bleeding/hemorrhage at application or treatment site.

Adverse Reactions

>10%:

Central nervous system: Severe burning skin (≤50%; occurred during or shortly after illumination; most cases resolved in 1 to 4 days)
Dermatologic: Burning sensation of skin (≤92%), crusted skin (≤64% to 71%), desquamation (≤64% to 71%), stinging of the skin (severe: ≤50%), hyperpigmentation (≤22% to 36%), hypopigmentation (≤22% to 36%), exfoliation of skin (19%), scabbing (≤2% to 19%), skin erosion (2% to 14%), dermatological disease (5% to 12%), localized vesiculation (4% to 12%)
Endocrine & metabolic: Edematous lesion (35%)
Local: Application site erythema (92% to 99%), local pain (≤1% to 92%; severe: ≤30%), application site irritation (72%), application site pruritus (14% to 34%), application site induration (12%)

1% to 10%:

Cardiovascular: Edema (≤1% to 35%)
Central nervous system: Paresthesia (9%), hyperalgesia (≤5%), local discomfort (3%), dysesthesia (≤2%), chills, headache
Dermatologic: Local flare (≤2% to 7%), urticaria (<2% to 7%), dermal ulcer (2% to 4%), pustules (1% to ≤4%), excoriation (≤1%), oozing (≤1%)
Hematologic & oncologic: Hemorrhage (1% to 4%)
Local: Application site reaction (4%), application site discharge (2%), localized tenderness (1% to 2%)

<1%, postmarketing, and/or case reports: Blurred vision, diplopia, eye irritation, eyelid edema, feeling hot, fever, local inflammation, local swelling, nervousness, ocular hyperemia, pain, petechia, photophobia, pruritus, pustular rash, skin blister, skin discoloration, ulcer

General Dosage Range Topical: *Adults:*

Gel: Apply ~1 mm thick to actinic keratosis and to ~5 mm of surrounding skin; application area should not exceed 20 cm^2 and a maximum of 2 g at one time. May repeat after 3 months.

Solution: Apply to actinic keratoses once; may repeat (once) after 8 weeks

Mechanism of Action Aminolevulinic acid is a metabolic precursor of the photosensitizer protoporphyrin IX (PpIX). Photosensitization following local/topical application of aminolevulinic acid occurs through the metabolic conversion to PpIX. When exposed to light of appropriate wavelength and energy, accumulated PpIX produces a photodynamic reaction resulting in local cytotoxicity. Precancerous and cancerous cells exhibit a higher rate of porphyrin induction compared to normal cells.

Pharmacodynamics/Kinetics

Onset of Action Peak fluorescence intensity of protoporphyrin IX (PpIX): Actinic keratosis: Solution: 11 hours ± 1 hour; Perilesional skin: 12 hours ± 1 hour

Half-life Elimination Mean fluorescence clearance half-life of PpIX for lesions: Solution: 30 ± 10 hours

Time to Peak Gel: 3 hours

Pregnancy Risk Factor C

Pregnancy Considerations Animal reproduction studies have not been conducted. Systemic absorption following topical application of the gel is negligible.

Aminophylline (am in OFF i lin)

Related Information

Respiratory Diseases *on page 1777*

Theophylline *on page 1557*

Brand Names: Canada Aminophylline Injection; JAA-Aminophylline

Pharmacologic Category Phosphodiesterase Enzyme Inhibitor, Nonselective

Use

Treatment of symptoms and reversible airway obstruction due to asthma or other chronic lung diseases (eg, emphysema, chronic bronchitis)

Note: The 2007 National Heart, Lung, and Blood Institute Asthma Guidelines and the 2015 Global Initiative for Asthma Guidelines (GINA) recommend against aminophylline IV for the treatment of asthma exacerbations because of poor efficacy and safety concerns (GINA, 2015; NAEPP, 2007).

Local Anesthetic/Vasoconstrictor Precautions No information available to require special precautions

Effects on Dental Treatment Prescribe erythromycin products with caution to patients taking theophylline products. Erythromycin will delay the normal metabolic inactivation of theophyllines leading to increased blood levels; this has resulted in nausea, vomiting, and CNS restlessness.

Effects on Bleeding No information available to require special precautions

Adverse Reactions Frequency not defined. Adverse events observed at therapeutic serum levels:

Central nervous system: Headache, insomnia, irritability, restlessness, seizure

Dermatologic: Allergic skin reaction, exfoliative dermatitis

Gastrointestinal: Diarrhea, nausea, vomiting

Genitourinary: Diuresis (transient)

Neuromuscular & skeletal: Tremor

General Dosage Range

IV:

Infants to Adults: Loading dose: 5.7 mg/kg

Children 6 weeks to 1 year: Maintenance: Dose (mg/kg/hour) = [(0.008 x age in weeks) + 0.21] divided by 0.79

Children 1-9 years: Maintenance: 1.01 mg/kg/hour

Children 9-12 years: Maintenance: 0.89 mg/kg/hour

Adolescents 12-16 years (smokers): Maintenance: 0.89 mg/kg/hour

Adolescents 12-16 years (nonsmokers): Maintenance: 0.63 mg/kg/hour

Adolescents >16 years and Adults ≤60 years (nonsmokers): Maintenance: 0.51 mg/kg/hour (maximum: 900 mg/day)

Adults >60 years (nonsmokers): Maintenance: 0.38 mg/kg/hour (maximum: 400 mg/day)

Oral:

Children 1-15 years and <45 kg (without risk factors for impaired clearance): Initial: 15.2-17.7 mg/kg/day divided every 4-6 hours for 3 days (maximum: 380 mg), then increase to 20.3 mg/kg/day divided every 4-6 hours for 3 days (maximum: 400 mg/day); Maintenance: 25.3 mg/kg/day divided every 4-6 hours (maximum: 760 mg/day)

Children ≥45 kg and Adults: Initial: 380 mg/day divided every 6-8 hours for 3 days, then 507 mg/day divided every 6-8 hours for 3 days; Maintenance: 760 mg/day divided every 6-8 hours

Mechanism of Action Causes bronchodilatation, diuresis, CNS and cardiac stimulation, and gastric acid secretion by blocking phosphodiesterase which increases tissue concentrations of cyclic adenine monophosphate (cAMP) which in turn promote catecholamine stimulation of lipolysis, glycogenolysis, and gluconeogenesis and induce release of epinephrine from adrenal medulla cells

Pharmacodynamics/Kinetics

Half-life Elimination Theophylline: Highly variable and dependent upon age, liver function, cardiac function, lung disease, and smoking history

Premature infants, postnatal age 3-15 days: 30 hours (range: 17-43 hours)

Premature infants, postnatal age 25-57 days: 20 hours (range: 9.4-30.6 hours)

Children 1-4 yrs: 3.4 hours (range: 1.2-5.6 hours); 6-17 years: 3.7 hours (range: 1.5-5.9 hours)

Adults 16-60 years with asthma, nonsmoking, otherwise healthy: 8.7 hours (range: 6.1-12.8 hours)

Time to Peak Oral: 1-2 hours; IV: Within 30 minutes

Pregnancy Risk Factor C

Pregnancy Considerations Refer to Theophylline monograph.

Aminosalicylic Acid (a mee noe sal i SIL ik AS id)

Brand Names: US Paser

Pharmacologic Category Antitubercular Agent

Use Adjunctive treatment of tuberculosis used in combination with other antitubercular agents

Local Anesthetic/Vasoconstrictor Precautions No information available to require special precautions

Effects on Dental Treatment NSAID formulations are known to reversibly decrease platelet aggregation via mechanisms different than observed with aspirin. The dentist should be aware of the potential of abnormal coagulation. Caution should also be exercised in the use of NSAIDs in patients already on anticoagulant therapy with drugs such as warfarin (Coumadin®).

Effects on Bleeding No information available to require special precautions

Adverse Reactions Frequency not defined.

Cardiovascular: Pericarditis, vasculitis

Central nervous system: Brain disease

Dermatologic: Skin rash (including exfoliative dermatitis)

Endocrine & metabolic: Goiter (with or without myxedema), hypoglycemia, hypothyroidism

Gastrointestinal: Abdominal pain, diarrhea, nausea, vomiting

Hematologic & oncologic: Agranulocytosis, hemolytic anemia, leukopenia, thrombocytopenia

Hepatic: Hepatitis, jaundice

Miscellaneous: Fever

Ophthalmic: Optic neuritis

Respiratory: Eosinophilic pneumonitis

General Dosage Range Dosage adjustment recommended in patients with renal impairment

Oral:

Children: 200-300 mg/kg/day in 2-4 divided doses

Adults: 8-12 g/day in 2-3 divided doses

Mechanism of Action Aminosalicylic acid (PAS) is a highly-specific bacteriostatic agent active against *M. tuberculosis*. Structurally related to para-aminobenzoic acid (PABA) and its mechanism of action is thought to be similar to the sulfonamides, a competitive antagonism with PABA; disrupts plate biosynthesis in sensitive organisms.

Pharmacodynamics/Kinetics

Half-life Elimination Reduced with renal impairment

Time to Peak Serum: 6 hours

Pregnancy Risk Factor C

Pregnancy Considerations Teratogenic effects have been reported in animal reproduction studies. Salicylates have been noted to cross the placenta and enter fetal circulation. Aminosalicylic acid has been used safely during pregnancy; however, it should only be used if there are no alternatives for the treatment of multidrug-resistant tuberculosis (*MMWR*, 2003).

Amiodarone (a MEE oh da rone)

Related Information

Cardiovascular Diseases *on page 1752*

Clinical Risk Related to Drugs Prolonging QT Interval *on page 1772*

Brand Names: US Cordarone [DSC]; Nexterone; Pacerone

Brand Names: Canada Amiodarone Hydrochloride For Injection; Apo-Amiodarone; Cordarone; Dom-Amiodarone; Mylan-Amiodarone; PHL-Amiodarone; PMS-Amiodarone; PRO-Amiodarone; Riva-Amiodarone; Sandoz-Amiodarone; Teva-Amiodarone

Pharmacologic Category Antiarrhythmic Agent, Class III

Use Ventricular arrhythmias: Management of life-threatening recurrent ventricular fibrillation (VF) or recurrent hemodynamically-unstable ventricular tachycardia (VT) refractory to other antiarrhythmic agents or in patients intolerant of other agents used for these conditions

Local Anesthetic/Vasoconstrictor Precautions Amiodarone is one of the drugs confirmed to prolong the QT interval and is accepted as having a risk of causing torsade de pointes. The risk of drug-induced torsade de pointes is extremely low when a single QT interval prolonging drug is prescribed. In terms of epinephrine, it is not known what effect vasoconstrictors in the local anesthetic regimen will have in patients with a known history of congenital prolonged QT interval or in patients taking any medication that prolongs the QT interval. Until more information is obtained, it is suggested that the clinician consult with the physician prior to the use of a vasoconstrictor in suspected patients, and that the vasoconstrictor (epinephrine, mepivacaine and levonordefrin [Carbocaine® 2% with Neo-Cobefrin®]) be used with caution.

Effects on Dental Treatment Key adverse event(s) related to dental treatment: Oral: Abnormal salivation and taste

Effects on Bleeding No information available to require special precautions

Adverse Reactions

Frequency not always defined.

Cardiovascular: Hypotension (IV: 16%, refractory in rare cases), bradycardia (2% to 5%), atrioventricular block (<2% to 5%), cardiac arrest (3%), cardiac arrhythmia (1% to 3%), cardiac failure (1% to 3%), ventricular tachycardia (2%), asystole (≤2%; IV), atrial fibrillation (<2%), cardiogenic shock (<2%), torsades de pointes (<2%, rare), ventricular fibrillation (<2%), atrioventricular dissociation, cardiac conduction disturbance, edema, flushing, peripheral thrombophlebitis (IV, with concentrations >3 mg/mL), pulseless electrical activity (PEA)

Central nervous system: Abnormal gait (4% to 40%), ataxia (4% to 40%), dizziness (4% to 40%), fatigue (4% to 40%), involuntary body movements (4% to 40%), malaise (4% to 40%), peripheral neuropathy (4% to 40%), memory impairment (3% to 40%), paresthesia (4% to 9%), altered sense of smell (1% to 3%), headache (1% to 3%), insomnia (1% to 3%), sleep disorder (1% to 3%)

Dermatologic: Blue-gray skin pigmentation (oral: ≤15% with prolonged exposure to amiodarone), skin photosensitivity (4% to 10%)

Endocrine & metabolic: Hypothyroidism (1% to 10%), decreased libido (1% to 3%), hyperthyroidism (1% to 3%)

Gastrointestinal: Nausea (oral: 10% to 33%; IV: 4%), vomiting (10% to 33%), anorexia (≤25%), constipation (≤25%), altered salivation (1% to 3%), dysgeusia (1% to 3%), abdominal pain (1% to 3%), diarrhea (<2%)

Hematologic & oncologic: Blood coagulation disorder (1% to 3%)

Hepatic: Increased serum transaminases (IV: <2% to 54%; oral: 3% to 9%), abnormal hepatic function tests (4% to 9%), hepatic disease (1% to 3%)

Neuromuscular & skeletal: Tremor (≤40%)

Ophthalmic: Corneal deposits (>90%; causes visual disturbance in <10%), visual halos (≤10%), visual disturbance (2% to 9%), optic neuritis (1%), photophobia

Respiratory: Pulmonary toxicity (2% to 17%), pulmonary edema (IV: <2%), hypersensitivity pneumonitis, interstitial pneumonitis, pulmonary fibrosis

Miscellaneous: Fever

<1%, postmarketing, and/or case reports: Acute pancreatitis, acute renal failure, adult respiratory distress syndrome, agranulocytosis, alopecia, altered thyroid hormone levels (increased T_4, decreased T_3, increased inactive reverse T_3), anaphylactic shock, anaphylactoid reaction, anaphylaxis, angioedema, aplastic anemia, back pain, bronchiolitis obliterans organizing pneumonia, bronchospasm, bullous dermatitis, cholestasis, cholestatic hepatitis, confusion, cough, decreased T_3 level, delirium, demyelinating polyneuropathy, disorientation, DRESS syndrome, drug-induced Parkinson disease, dyspnea, eczema, eosinophilic pneumonia, epididymitis, erythema multiforme, exfoliation of skin, exfoliative dermatitis, fever, hallucination, hemolytic anemia, hemoptysis, hepatic cirrhosis, hepatic failure, hepatitis, hepatotoxicity (idiosyncratic) (Chalasani 2014), hypoesthesia, hypotension, hypoxia, impotence, increased intracranial pressure, increased lactate dehydrogenase, increased serum alkaline phosphatase, increased serum ALT, increased serum AST, increased serum creatinine, injection site reaction, jaundice, leukocytoclastic vasculitis, malignant neoplasm of skin, mass (pulmonary), myasthenia, myopathy, neutropenia, optic neuropathy, pancytopenia, pleural effusion, pleurisy, prolonged Q-T interval on ECG (associated with worsening arrhythmia), pruritus, pseudotumor cerebri, pulmonary alveolar hemorrhage, pulmonary infiltrates, pulmonary phospholipidosis, renal insufficiency, respiratory arrest, respiratory distress syndrome, respiratory failure, rhabdomyolysis, SIADH, sinoatrial arrest, sinus node dysfunction, skin carcinoma, skin granuloma, skin rash, skin sclerosis, spontaneous ecchymoses, Stevens-Johnson syndrome, superior vena cava syndrome, thrombocytopenia, thyroid cancer, thyroid nodule, thyrotoxicosis, tissue necrosis at injection site, toxic epidermal necrolysis, urticaria, vasculitis, vortex keratopathy (Chan 2015), wheezing, xerostomia

General Dosage Range

I.O.: *Children (PALS dosing):* 5 mg/kg (maximum: 300 mg per dose); may repeat twice up to maximum dose of 15 mg/kg/day

IV:

Children (PALS dosing): 5 mg/kg (maximum: 300 mg per dose); may repeat twice up to maximum dose of 15 mg/kg/day

Adults: Initial: 150 to 300 mg bolus; Maintenance: 1200 to 1800 mg daily continuous infusion until 10 g total **or** 1 mg/minute infusion for 6 hours, then 0.5 mg/minute infusion for 18 hours (maximum: 2.1 g daily)

Oral: *Adults:* Initial: 600 to 1600 mg daily until 10 g total; Maintenance: 100 to 400 mg daily

Mechanism of Action Class III antiarrhythmic agent which inhibits adrenergic stimulation (alpha- and beta-blocking properties), affects sodium, potassium, and calcium channels, prolongs the action potential and refractory period in myocardial tissue; decreases AV conduction and sinus node function

Pharmacodynamics/Kinetics

Onset of Action Oral: 2 days to 3 weeks; IV: (electrophysiologic effects) within hours; antiarrhythmic effects: 2 to 3 days to 1 to 3 weeks; mean onset of effect may be shorter in children vs adults and in patients receiving IV loading doses; Peak effect: 1 week to 5 months

Duration of Action

After discontinuing therapy: Variable, 2 weeks to months: Children: Less than a few weeks; Adults: Several months

Note: Duration after discontinuation may be shorter in children than adults

Half-life Elimination

Note: Half-life is shortened in children vs adults

Amiodarone:

Single dose: 58 days (range: 15 to 142 days)

Oral chronic therapy: Mean range: 40 to 55 days (range: 26 to 107 days)

IV single dose: Mean range: 9 to 36 days

N-desethylamiodarone (active metabolite): Prolonged in severe left ventricular dysfunction

Single dose: 36 days (range: 14 to 75 days)

Oral chronic therapy: 61 days

IV single dose: Mean range: 9 to 30 days

Time to Peak Oral: Serum: 3 to 7 hours

Pregnancy Considerations Adverse events have been observed in some animal reproduction studies. Amiodarone crosses the placenta (~10% to 50%) and may cause fetal harm when administered to a pregnant woman. Reported risks include neonatal bradycardia, QT prolongation, and periodic ventricular extrasystoles; neonatal hypothyroidism (with or without goiter); neonatal hyperthyroxinemia; neurodevelopmental abnormalities independent of thyroid function; jerk nystagmus with synchronous head titubation; fetal growth retardation; and/or premature birth. Oral or IV amiodarone should be used in pregnant women only to treat arrhythmias refractory to other treatments or when other treatments are contraindicated (Page [ACC/AHA/HRS 2015]; Regitz-Zagrosek [ESG/AEPC/DGesGM/ESC] 2011).

Dental Comment See Local Anesthetic/Vasoconstrictor Precautions

Amitriptyline (a mee TRIP ti leen)

Related Information

Dentin Hypersensitivity, Acid Erosion, High Caries Index, Management of Alveolar Osteitis, and Xerostomia *on page 1857*

Temporomandibular Dysfunction (TMD), Chronic Pain, and Fibromyalgia *on page 1868*

Vasoconstrictor Interactions With Antidepressants *on page 1913*

Brand Names: US Elavil

Brand Names: Canada Apo-Amitriptyline; Bio-Amitriptyline; Elavil; Levate; Novo-Triptyn; PMS-Amitriptyline

Pharmacologic Category Antidepressant, Tricyclic (Tertiary Amine)

Use Depression: Treatment of depression

Local Anesthetic/Vasoconstrictor Precautions

Amitriptyline is one of the drugs confirmed to prolong the QT interval and is accepted as having a risk of causing torsade de pointes. In terms of epinephrine, it is not known what effect vasoconstrictors in the local anesthetic regimen will have in patients with a known history of congenital prolonged QT interval or in patients taking any medication that prolongs the QT interval. Until more information is obtained, it is suggested that the clinician consult with the physician prior to the use of a vasoconstrictor in suspected patients, and that the vasoconstrictor (epinephrine, mepivacaine and levonordefrin [Carbocaine® 2% with Neo-Cobefrin®]) be used with caution. See Dental Comment.

Effects on Dental Treatment Key adverse event(s) related to dental treatment: Xerostomia and changes in salivation (normal salivary flow resumes upon discontinuation), stomatitis, peculiar taste, and black tongue. Patients may experience orthostatic hypotension as they stand up after treatment; especially if lying in dental chair for extended periods of time. Use caution with sudden changes in position during and after dental treatment. Amitriptyline is the most anticholinergic and sedating of the antidepressants; has pronounced effects on the cardiovascular system. Long-term treatment with TCAs such as amitriptyline increases the risk of caries by reducing salivation and salivary buffer capacity. In a study by Rundergren, et al, pathological alterations were observed in the oral mucosa of 72% of 58 patients; 55% had new carious lesions after taking TCAs for a median of 5½ years. Current research is investigating the use of the salivary stimulant pilocarpine (Salagen®) to overcome the xerostomia from amitriptyline.

Effects on Bleeding May cause thrombocytopenia

Adverse Reactions Anticholinergic effects may be pronounced; moderate to marked sedation can occur (tolerance to these effects usually occurs).

Frequency not defined.

Cardiovascular: Atrioventricular conduction disturbance, cardiac arrhythmia, cardiomyopathy (rare), cerebrovascular accident, ECG changes (nonspecific), edema, facial edema, heart block, hypertension, myocardial infarction, orthostatic hypotension, palpitations, syncope, tachycardia

Central nervous system: Anxiety, ataxia, cognitive dysfunction, coma, confusion, delusions, disorientation, dizziness, drowsiness, drug withdrawal (nausea, headache, malaise, irritability, restlessness, dream and sleep disturbance, mania [rare], and hypomania [rare]), dysarthria, EEG pattern changes, excitement, extrapyramidal reaction (including abnormal involuntary movements and tardive dyskinesia), fatigue, hallucination, headache, hyperpyrexia, insomnia, lack of concentration, nightmares, numbness, paresthesia, peripheral neuropathy, restlessness, sedation, seizure, tingling of extremities

Dermatologic: Allergic skin rash, alopecia, diaphoresis, skin photosensitivity, urticaria

Endocrine & metabolic: Altered serum glucose, decreased libido, galactorrhea, gynecomastia, increased libido, SIADH, weight gain, weight loss

Gastrointestinal: Ageusia, anorexia, constipation, diarrhea, melanoglossia, nausea, paralytic ileus, parotid gland enlargement, stomatitis, unpleasant taste, vomiting, xerostomia

Genitourinary: Breast hypertrophy, impotence, testicular swelling, urinary frequency, urinary retention, urinary tract dilation

Hematologic & oncologic: Bone marrow depression (including agranulocytosis, leukopenia, and thrombocytopenia), eosinophilia, purpura

Hepatic: Hepatic failure, hepatitis (rare; including altered liver function and jaundice)

Hypersensitivity: Tongue edema

Neuromuscular & skeletal: Lupus-like syndrome, tremor, weakness

Ophthalmic: Accommodation disturbance, blurred vision, increased intraocular pressure, mydriasis

Otic: Tinnitus

Postmarketing and/or case reports: Angle-closure glaucoma, neuroleptic malignant syndrome (rare; Stevens, 2008), serotonin syndrome (rare)

General Dosage Range Oral:

Adolescents: 10 mg 3 times daily and 20 mg at bedtime (recommended by the manufacturer).

Adults: 25-300 mg daily as a single dose at bedtime or in divided doses

Elderly: 10 mg 3 times daily and 20 mg at bedtime (recommended by the manufacturer).

Mechanism of Action Increases the synaptic concentration of serotonin and/or norepinephrine in the central nervous system by inhibition of their reuptake by the presynaptic neuronal membrane pump.

Pharmacodynamics/Kinetics

Onset of Action Individual responses may vary, however 4 to 8 weeks of treatment are needed before determining if a patient with depression is partially or non-responsive; similarly 8 to 12 weeks are required for an adequate migraine prophylaxis trial (APA, 2010; Prinsheim, 2012); desired therapeutic effect (for analgesia) may take as long as 1 to 3 weeks.

Half-life Elimination ~13 to 36 hours (Schulz, 1985)

Time to Peak Serum: ~2 to 5 hours (Schulz, 1985)

Pregnancy Risk Factor C

Pregnancy Considerations Adverse events have been observed in some animal reproduction studies. Amitriptyline crosses the human placenta; CNS effects, limb deformities, and developmental delay have been noted in case reports (causal relationship not established). Tricyclic antidepressants may be associated with irritability, jitteriness, and convulsions (rare) in the neonate (Yonkers, 2009).

The ACOG recommends that therapy for depression during pregnancy be individualized; treatment should incorporate the clinical expertise of the mental health clinician, obstetrician, primary healthcare provider, and pediatrician (ACOG, 2008). According to the American Psychiatric Association (APA), the risks of medication treatment should be weighed against other treatment options and untreated depression. For women who discontinue antidepressant medications during pregnancy and who may be at high risk for postpartum depression, the medications can be restarted following delivery (APA, 2010). Treatment algorithms have been developed by the ACOG and the APA for the management of depression in women prior to conception and during pregnancy (Yonkers, 2009). Although not a first-line agent, amitriptyline may be used for the treatment of post-traumatic stress disorder in pregnant women (Bandelow, 2008). Migraine prophylaxis should be avoided during pregnancy; if needed, amitriptyline may be used if other agents are ineffective or contraindicated (Pringsheim, 2012).

Pregnant women exposed to antidepressants during pregnancy are encouraged to enroll in the National Pregnancy Registry for Antidepressants (NPRAD). Women 18 to 45 years of age or their health care providers may contact the registry by calling 844-405-6185. Enrollment should be done as early in pregnancy as possible.

Dental Comment See Local Anesthetic/Vasoconstrictor Precautions

AmLODIPine (am LOE di peen)

Related Information

Calcium Channel Blockers and Gingival Hyperplasia *on page 1908*

Cardiovascular Diseases *on page 1752*

Brand Names: US Norvasc

Brand Names: Canada Accel-Amlodipine; ACT-Amlodipine; Amlodipine-Odan; Apo-Amlodipine; Auro-Amlodipine; Bio-Amlodipine; Dom-Amlodipine; GD-Amlodipine; JAMP-Amlodipine; Mar-Amlodipine; Mint-Amlodipine; Mylan-Amlodipine; Norvasc; PHL Amlodipine; PMS-Amlodipine; Q-Amlodipine; RAN-Amlodipine; ratio-Amlodipine; Riva-Amlodipine; Sandoz Amlodipine; Septa-Amlodipine; Teva-Amlodipine

Generic Availability (US) Yes

Pharmacologic Category Antianginal Agent; Antihypertensive; Calcium Channel Blocker; Calcium Channel Blocker, Dihydropyridine

Use

Coronary artery disease (CAD):

Chronic stable angina: Treatment of symptomatic chronic stable angina. May be used alone or in combination with other antianginal agents.

Vasospastic angina (Prinzmetal or variant angina): Treatment of confirmed or suspected vasospastic angina. May be used alone or in combination with other antianginal agents.

Angiographically documented CAD: Reduce the risk of hospitalization secondary to angina and to reduce the risk of a coronary revascularization procedure in patients with recently documented CAD by angiography (without heart failure or an ejection fraction of <40%).

The ACCF/AHA 2013 guidelines for management of heart failure state that, with the exception of amlodipine, calcium channel blockers should be avoided and withdrawn whenever possible in patients with heart failure with reduced ejection fraction (HFrEF). While amlodipine, like other calcium channel blockers, has no benefit on functioning or survival, it may be used for the treatment of hypertension or ischemic heart disease in patients with HFrEF (ACCF/AHA [Yancy 2013]).

Hypertension: Treatment of hypertension. May be used alone or in combination with other antihypertensive agents

The 2014 guideline for the management of high blood pressure in adults (JNC 8) recommends initiation of pharmacologic treatment to lower blood pressure for the following patients (JNC8 [James 2013]):

- Patients ≥60 years of age, with systolic blood pressure (SBP) ≥150 mm Hg or diastolic blood pressure (DBP) ≥90 mm Hg. Goal of therapy is SBP <150 mm Hg and DBP <90 mm Hg.
- Patients <60 years of age, with SBP ≥140 mm Hg or DBP ≥90 mm Hg. Goal of therapy is SBP <140 mm Hg and DBP <90 mm Hg.
- Patients ≥18 years of age with diabetes, with SBP ≥140 mm Hg or DBP ≥90 mm Hg. Goal of therapy is SBP <140 mm Hg and DBP <90 mm Hg.
- Patients ≥18 years of age with chronic kidney disease (CKD), with SBP ≥140 mm Hg or DBP ≥90 mm Hg. Goal of therapy is SBP <140 mm Hg and DBP <90 mm Hg.

In patients with chronic kidney disease (CKD), regardless of race or diabetes status, the use of an ACE inhibitor (ACEI) or angiotensin receptor blocker (ARB) as initial therapy is recommended to improve kidney outcomes. In the general nonblack population (without CKD) including those with diabetes, initial antihypertensive treatment should consist of a thiazide-type diuretic, calcium channel blocker, ACEI, or ARB. In the general black population (without CKD) including those with diabetes, initial antihypertensive treatment should consist of a thiazide-type diuretic or a calcium channel blocker **instead of** an ACEI or ARB.

Local Anesthetic/Vasoconstrictor Precautions No information available to require special precautions

Effects on Dental Treatment Fewer reports of gingival hyperplasia with amlodipine than with other calcium channel blockers (usually resolves upon discontinuation); consultation with physician is suggested if gingival hyperplasia is observed.

Effects on Bleeding No information available to require special precautions

Adverse Reactions

>10%:

Cardiovascular: Peripheral edema (2% to 11% dose related; female 15%; male 6%; HF patients 27% to 28% [Packer 1996; Packer 2013])

Respiratory: Pulmonary edema (HF patients 7% to 15% [Packer 1996; Packer 2013])

1% to 10%:

Cardiovascular: Palpitations (≤5%, dose related), flushing (≤3%, dose related, more frequent in females)

Central nervous system: Fatigue (5%), dizziness (1% to 3%, dose related), male sexual disorder (≤2%), drowsiness (1%)

Dermatologic: Pruritus (≤2%), skin rash (≤2%)

Gastrointestinal: Nausea (3%), abdominal pain (2%)

Neuromuscular & skeletal: Muscle cramps (≤2%), weakness (≤2%)

Respiratory: Dyspnea (≤2%)

<1%, postmarketing, and/or case reports: Abnormal dreams, acute interstitial nephritis (Ejaz 2000), angioedema, anorexia, anxiety, arthralgia, atrial fibrillation, back pain, bradycardia, cardiac arrhythmia, chest pain, cholestasis, conjunctivitis, constipation, depersonalization, depression, diaphoresis, diarrhea, difficulty in micturition, diplopia, dysphagia, epistaxis, erythema multiforme, erythematous rash, exfoliative dermatitis, extrapyramidal reaction, eye pain, female sexual disorder, flatulence, gingival hyperplasia, gynecomastia, hepatitis, hot flash, hyperglycemia, hypersensitivity angiitis, hypersensitivity reaction, hypoesthesia, increased serum transaminases, increased thirst, insomnia, jaundice, leukopenia, maculopapular rash, malaise, myalgia, nervousness, nocturia, nonthrombocytopenic purpura, orthostatic hypotension, osteoarthritis, pain, pancreatitis, paresthesia, peripheral ischemia, peripheral neuropathy, phototoxicity, purpura, rigors, syncope, tachycardia, thrombocytopenia, tinnitus, tremor, urinary frequency, vasculitis, ventricular tachycardia, vertigo, visual disturbance, vomiting, weight gain, weight loss, xerostomia

Dosing

Adult

Coronary artery disease (CAD) (chronic stable angina, vasospastic angina, angiographically documented CAD [without heart failure or ejection fraction <40%]): Oral: 5 to 10 mg once daily

Hypertension: Oral: Initial: 5 mg once daily **or** 2.5 mg once daily in small or frail patients, or when adding amlodipine to other antihypertensive therapy; maximum dose: 10 mg once daily. In general, titrate every 7 to 14 days. Titrate more rapidly, however, if clinically warranted, provided the patient is assessed frequently. Usual dosage range (ASH/ISH [Weber 2014]): 5 to 10 mg once daily. Target dose (JNC8 [James 2013]): 10 mg once daily.

Geriatric Dosing should start at the lower end of dosing range and titrated to response due to possible increased incidence of hepatic, renal, or cardiac impairment. Elderly patients also show decreased clearance of amlodipine.

Coronary artery disease (CAD) (chronic stable angina, vasospastic angina, angiographically documented CAD without heart failure or ejection fraction <40%): Oral: Initial: 5 mg once daily

Hypertension: Oral: Initial: 2.5 mg once daily; maximum dose: 10 mg once daily. In general, titrate every 7 to 14 days. Titrate more rapidly, however, if clinically warranted, provided the patient is assessed frequently. Usual dosage range (ASH/ISH [Weber 2014]): 5 to 10 mg once daily. Target dose (JNC8 [James 2013]): 10 mg once daily.

Pediatric Hypertension: Children ≥6 years and Adolescents: Oral: 2.5 to 5 mg once daily

Renal Impairment

No dosage adjustment necessary (Doyle 1989; Kungys 2003).

End-stage renal disease (ESRD) on dialysis: Hemodialysis and peritoneal dialysis do not enhance elimination; supplemental dose is not necessary (Kungys 2003).

Hepatic Impairment

Coronary artery disease (CAD) (chronic stable angina, vasospastic angina, angiographically documented CAD without heart failure or ejection fraction <40%): Initial: 5 mg once daily; titrate slowly in patients with severe hepatic impairment.

Hypertension: Initial: 2.5 mg once daily; titrate slowly in patients with severe hepatic impairment.

Mechanism of Action Inhibits calcium ion from entering the "slow channels" or select voltage-sensitive areas of vascular smooth muscle and myocardium during depolarization, producing a relaxation of coronary vascular smooth muscle and coronary vasodilation; increases myocardial oxygen delivery in patients with vasospastic angina. Amlodipine directly acts on vascular smooth muscle to produce peripheral arterial vasodilation reducing peripheral vascular resistance and blood pressure.

Contraindications Hypersensitivity to amlodipine or any component of the formulation

Canadian labeling: Additional contraindications (not in US labeling): Hypersensitivity to other dihydropyridines; severe hypotension (SBP less than 90 mmHg)

Warnings/Precautions Increased angina and/or MI has occurred with initiation or dosage titration of calcium channel blockers. Symptomatic hypotension can occur; acute hypotension upon initiation is unlikely due to the gradual onset of action. Blood pressure must be lowered at a rate appropriate for the patient's clinical condition. Use caution in severe aortic stenosis and/or hypertrophic cardiomyopathy with outflow tract obstruction. Use caution in patients with hepatic impairment; may require lower starting dose; titrate slowly with severe hepatic impairment. The most common side effect is peripheral edema; occurs within 2 to 3 weeks of starting therapy. Reflex tachycardia may occur with use. Peak antihypertensive effect is delayed; dosage titration should occur after 7 to 14 days on a given dose. Initiate at a lower dose in the elderly.

Drug Interactions

Metabolism/Transport Effects Substrate of CYP3A4 (major); **Note:** Assignment of Major/Minor substrate status based on clinically relevant drug interaction potential; **Inhibits** BCRP, CYP1A2 (weak), CYP2A6 (weak), CYP2C8 (weak), CYP2C9 (weak), CYP3A4 (weak)

Avoid Concomitant Use

Avoid concomitant use of AmLODIPine with any of the following: Amodiaquine; Conivaptan; Fusidic Acid (Systemic); Idelalisib; Pimozide

Increased Effect/Toxicity

AmLODIPine may increase the levels/effects of: Amifostine; Amodiaquine; Antipsychotic Agents (Second Generation [Atypical]); ARIPiprazole; Atosiban; Calcium Channel Blockers (Nondihydropyridine); CloZAPine; CycloSPORINE (Systemic); Dofetilide; DULoxetine; Flibanserin; Fosphenytoin; HYDROcodone; Hypotension-Associated Agents; Levodopa; Lomitapide; Magnesium Salts; Neuromuscular-Blocking Agents (Nondepolarizing); NiMODipine; Nitroprusside; Phenytoin; Pimozide; QuiNIDine; Simvastatin; Tacrolimus (Systemic); TiZANidine

The levels/effects of AmLODIPine may be increased by: Alfuzosin; Alpha1-Blockers; Antifungal Agents (Azole Derivatives, Systemic); Antihepaciviral Combination Products; Aprepitant; Barbiturates; Benperidol; Brimonidine (Topical); Calcium Channel Blockers (Nondihydropyridine); Ceritinib; Conivaptan; CycloSPORINE (Systemic); CYP3A4 Inhibitors (Moderate); CYP3A4 Inhibitors (Strong); Dapoxetine; Dasatinib; Diazoxide; Fluconazole; Fosaprepitant; Fusidic Acid (Systemic); Grapefruit Juice; Herbs (Hypotensive Properties); Idelalisib; Ivacaftor; Lormetazepam; Macrolide Antibiotics; Magnesium Salts; MiFEPRIStone; Molsidomine; Naftopidil; Netupitant; Nicergoline; Nicorandil; Obinutuzumab; Palbociclib; Pentoxifylline; Phosphodiesterase 5 Inhibitors; Prostacyclin Analogues; Quinagolide; QuiNIDine; Simeprevir; Stiripentol

Decreased Effect

AmLODIPine may decrease the levels/effects of: Clopidogrel; QuiNIDine

The levels/effects of AmLODIPine may be decreased by: Amphetamines; Barbiturates; Bosentan; Calcium Salts; CarBAMazepine; CYP3A4 Inducers (Moderate); CYP3A4 Inducers (Strong); Dabrafenib; Deferasirox; Efavirenz; Enzalutamide; Herbs (Hypertensive Properties); Melatonin; Methylphenidate; Mitotane; Phenytoin; Rifamycin Derivatives; Siltuximab; St John's Wort; Tocilizumab; Yohimbine

Food Interactions Grapefruit juice may modestly increase amlodipine levels. Management: Monitor closely with concurrent use.

Pharmacodynamics/Kinetics

Onset of Action Antihypertensive effect: Significant reductions in blood pressure at 24 to 48 hours after first dose; slight increase in heart rate within 10 hours of administration may reflect some vasodilating activity (Donnelly 1993)

Duration of Action Antihypertensive effect: At least 24 hours (Donnelly 1993); has been shown to extend to at least 72 hours when discontinued after 6 to 7 weeks of therapy (Biston 1999)

Half-life Elimination Terminal (biphasic): 30 to 50 hours; increased with hepatic dysfunction

Time to Peak Plasma: 6 to 12 hours

Pregnancy Risk Factor C

Pregnancy Considerations Adverse events have been observed in some animal reproduction studies. Untreated chronic maternal hypertension is associated with adverse events in the fetus, infant, and mother. If treatment for hypertension during pregnancy is needed, other agents are preferred (ACOG 2013).

Breastfeeding Considerations Amlodipine is excreted in breast milk. A study was conducted in 31 lactating women ~3 weeks postpartum. All women were administered amlodipine for pregnancy-induced hypertension (median daily dose 6.01 ± 2.31 mg). Sampling occurred ~10 days after dosing was initiated. The median predose amlodipine concentrations were 15.5 ng/mL (maternal serum) and 11.5 ng/mL (breast milk). The median estimated amlodipine exposure to the breastfeeding infant (relative infant dose) was 4.17 mcg/kg/day (median relative infant dose 4.18% based on the weight adjusted maternal dose). Variability was observed; the maximum relative infant dose calculated was 15.2% (Naito 2015). breastfeeding is not recommended by the manufacturer.

Dosage Forms

Tablet, Oral:

Norvasc: 2.5 mg, 5 mg, 10 mg
Generic: 2.5 mg, 5 mg, 10 mg

Amlodipine and Olmesartan

(am LOE di peen & olme SAR tan)

Related Information

AmLODIPine *on page 117*
Olmesartan *on page 1226*

Brand Names: US Azor

Pharmacologic Category Angiotensin II Receptor Blocker; Antianginal Agent; Antihypertensive; Calcium Channel Blocker; Calcium Channel Blocker, Dihydropyridine

Use Hypertension: Management of hypertension (monotherapy or with other antihypertensive agents).

Local Anesthetic/Vasoconstrictor Precautions No information available to require special precautions

Effects on Dental Treatment Key adverse event(s) related to dental treatment: Patients may experience orthostatic hypotension as they stand up after treatment; especially if lying in dental chair for extended periods of time. Use caution with sudden changes in position during and after dental treatment.

Fewer reports of gingival hyperplasia with amlodipine than with other CCBs (usually resolves upon discontinuation); consultation with physician is suggested.

Effects on Bleeding No information available to require special precautions

Adverse Reactions Reactions/percentages reported with combination product; also see individual agents

>10%: Cardiovascular: Peripheral edema (dose related: 18% to 26%)

Frequency not defined (limited to important or life-threatening): Anaphylaxis, hypotension, nocturia, orthostatic hypotension, palpitations, pruritus, skin rash, urinary frequency

General Dosage Range Oral: *Adults:* Initial: Amlodipine 5 mg/olmesartan 20 mg once daily. Maximum dose: Amlodipine 10 mg/olmesartan 40 mg per day.

Mechanism of Action

Amlodipine: Directly acts on vascular smooth muscle to produce peripheral arterial vasodilation reducing peripheral vascular resistance and blood pressure.

Olmesartan: Blocks the vasoconstrictor and aldosterone-secreting effects of angiotensin II.

Pregnancy Risk Factor D

Pregnancy Considerations [US Boxed Warning]: Drugs that act on the renin-angiotensin system can cause injury and death to the developing fetus. Discontinue as soon as possible once pregnancy is detected. See individual agents.

Ammonium Chloride (a MOE nee um KLOR ide)

Pharmacologic Category Electrolyte Supplement, Parenteral

Use Treatment of hypochloremic states or metabolic alkalosis

Local Anesthetic/Vasoconstrictor Precautions No information available to require special precautions

Effects on Dental Treatment No significant effects or complications reported

Effects on Bleeding No information available to require special precautions

Adverse Reactions Frequency not defined.

Central nervous system: Coma (with rapid infusion [Devlin 2014]), confusion (with rapid infusion [Devlin 2014]), seizure (with rapid infusion [Devlin 2014])

Endocrine & metabolic: Hypervolemia (from large volume diluent)

Local: Extravasation, injection site infection, injection site phlebitis, pain at injection site, venous thrombosis at injection site

Miscellaneous: Fever

Mechanism of Action Increases acidity by increasing free hydrogen ion concentration

Pregnancy Risk Factor C

Pregnancy Considerations Animal reproduction studies have not been conducted.

Amobarbital (am oh BAR bi tal)

Brand Names: US Amytal Sodium

Pharmacologic Category Barbiturate

Use Sedative/hypnotic: Use as a sedative, hypnotic, or preanesthetic

Local Anesthetic/Vasoconstrictor Precautions No information available to require special precautions

Effects on Dental Treatment No significant effects or complications reported

Effects on Bleeding No information available to require special precautions

Adverse Reactions Frequency not defined and is reported as barbiturate use (not specifically amobarbital).

Cardiovascular: Bradycardia, hypotension, syncope

Central nervous system: Abnormality in thinking, agitation, anxiety, ataxia, central nervous system depression, confusion, dizziness, drowsiness, hallucination, headache, insomnia, nervousness, nightmares, psychiatric disturbance

Gastrointestinal: Constipation, nausea, vomiting

Hematologic & oncologic: Megaloblastic anemia (following chronic phenobarbital use)

Hepatic: Hepatic injury

Hypersensitivity: Hypersensitivity reaction (including angioedema, skin rash, and exfoliative dermatitis)

Local: Injection site reaction

Neuromuscular & skeletal: Hyperkinesia

Respiratory: Apnea, atelectasis (postoperative), hypoventilation

Miscellaneous: Fever

General Dosage Range Dosage adjustment recommended in patients with hepatic or renal impairment

IM, IV:

Children >6 years and Adolescents: Sedative/hypnotic: 65 to 500 mg/dose

Adults:

Hypnotic: 65 to 200 mg at bedtime (maximum single dose: 1,000 mg)

Sedative: 30 to 50 mg 2 to 3 times/day (maximum single dose: 1,000 mg)

Mechanism of Action An intermediate-acting barbiturate; barbiturates depress the sensory cortex, decrease motor activity, and alter cerebellar function producing drowsiness, sedation, and hypnosis.

Pharmacodynamics/Kinetics

Onset of Action Rapid, within minutes

Duration of Action Variable

Half-life Elimination 16 to 40 hours (mean: 25 hours)

Time to Peak Maximum effect: Hours

Pregnancy Risk Factor D

Pregnancy Considerations Barbiturates cross the placenta and distribute in fetal tissue. Teratogenic effects have been reported with 1st trimester exposure. Exposure during the 3rd trimester may lead to symptoms of acute withdrawal following delivery; symptoms may be delayed up to 14 days.

Controlled Substance C-II

Amoxapine (a MOKS a peen)

Related Information

Dentin Hypersensitivity, Acid Erosion, High Caries Index, Management of Alveolar Osteitis, and Xerostomia *on page 1857*

Vasoconstrictor Interactions With Antidepressants *on page 1913*

Pharmacologic Category Antidepressant, Tricyclic (Secondary Amine)

Use Depression: For the relief of symptoms of depression in patients with neurotic or reactive depressive disorders as well as endogenous and psychotic depressions; for depression accompanied by anxiety or agitation.

Local Anesthetic/Vasoconstrictor Precautions Use with caution; epinephrine and levonordefrin have been shown to have an increased pressor response in combination with TCAs. Amoxapine is one of the drugs confirmed to prolong the QT interval and is accepted as having a risk of causing torsade de pointes. The risk of drug-induced torsade de pointes is extremely low when a single QT interval prolonging drug is prescribed. In terms of epinephrine, it is not known what effect vasoconstrictors in the local anesthetic regimen will have in patients with a known history of congenital prolonged QT interval or in patients taking any medication that prolongs the QT interval. Until more information is obtained, it is suggested that the clinician consult with the physician prior to the use of a vasoconstrictor in suspected patients, and that the vasoconstrictor (epinephrine, mepivacaine and levonordefrin [Carbocaine® 2% with Neo-Cobefrin®]) be used with caution.

Effects on Dental Treatment Key adverse event(s) related to dental treatment: Xerostomia and changes in salivation (normal salivary flow resumes upon discontinuation). Long-term treatment with TCAs, such as amoxapine, increases the risk of caries by reducing salivation and salivary buffer capacity.

Effects on Bleeding May cause thrombocytopenia

Adverse Reactions

>10%:

Central nervous system: Drowsiness (14%)

Gastrointestinal: Xerostomia (14%), constipation (12%)

1% to 10%:

Cardiovascular: Edema, palpitations

Central nervous system: Anxiety, ataxia, confusion, dizziness, EEG pattern changes, excitement, fatigue, headache, insomnia, nervousness, nightmares, restlessness

Dermatologic: Diaphoresis, skin rash

Endocrine & metabolic: Increased serum prolactin

Gastrointestinal: Increased appetite, nausea

Neuromuscular & skeletal: Tremor, weakness

Ophthalmic: Blurred vision (7%)

<1% (Limited to important or life-threatening): Abdominal pain, accommodation disturbance, agranulocytosis, alopecia, altered serum glucose, angle-closure glaucoma, anorexia, atrial arrhythmia, atrial fibrillation, breast hypertrophy, decreased libido, delayed micturition, diarrhea, disorientation, eosinophilia, epigastric distress, extrapyramidal reaction, fever, flatulence, galactorrhea, hallucination, heart block, hepatic insufficiency, hepatitis, hypersensitivity reaction, hypertension, hyperthermia, hypomania, hypotension, impotence, increased intraocular pressure, increased libido, jaundice, lack of concentration, lacrimation, leukopenia, menstrual disease, mydriasis, myocardial infarction, nasal congestion, neuroleptic malignant syndrome, numbness, painful ejaculation, pancreatitis, paralytic ileus, paresthesia, parotid swelling, petechia, pruritus, purpura, seizure, SIADH, skin photosensitivity, syncope, tachycardia, tardive dyskinesia, testicular swelling, thrombocytopenia, tingling sensation, tinnitus, unusual taste, urinary frequency, urinary retention, urticaria, vasculitis, vomiting, weight gain, weight loss

General Dosage Range Oral:

Adults: Initial: 50 mg once to 3 times daily; usual dosage: 100 to 400 mg daily; maximum: 600 mg daily (inpatient); 400 mg daily (outpatient)

Elderly: 25 mg 2 to 3 times daily; usual dosage: 100 to 150 mg daily; maximum: 300 mg daily

Mechanism of Action Reduces the reuptake of serotonin and norepinephrine. The metabolite, 7-OH-amoxapine has significant dopamine receptor blocking activity similar to antipsychotic agents.

Pharmacodynamics/Kinetics

Onset of Action Antidepressant effect: Usually occurs after 1 to 2 weeks, but may require 4 to 6 weeks

Half-life Elimination 8 hours; 8-hydroxyamoxapine metabolite: 30 hours

Time to Peak Serum: ~90 minutes

Pregnancy Risk Factor C

Pregnancy Considerations Adverse events were observed in some animal reproduction studies. Tricyclic antidepressants may be associated with irritability, jitteriness, and convulsions (rare) in the neonate (Yonkers, 2009).

The ACOG recommends that therapy for depression during pregnancy be individualized; treatment should incorporate the clinical expertise of the mental health clinician, obstetrician, primary healthcare provider, and pediatrician (ACOG, 2008). According to the American Psychiatric Association (APA), the risks of medication treatment should be weighed against other treatment options and untreated depression. For women who discontinue antidepressant medications during pregnancy and who may be at high risk for postpartum depression, the medications can be restarted following delivery (APA, 2010). Treatment algorithms have been developed by the ACOG and the APA for the management of depression in women prior to conception and during pregnancy (Yonkers, 2009).

Pregnant women exposed to antidepressants during pregnancy are encouraged to enroll in the National Pregnancy Registry for Antidepressants (NPRAD). Women 18 to 45 years of age or their health care providers may contact the registry by calling 844-405-6185. Enrollment should be done as early in pregnancy as possible.

Dental Comment See Local Anesthetic/Vasoconstrictor Precautions

Amoxicillin (a moks i SIL in)

Related Information

Antibiotic Prophylaxis *on page 1812*

Bacterial Infections *on page 1835*

Gastrointestinal Disorders *on page 1775*

Osteonecrosis of the Jaw *on page 1796*

Periodontal Diseases *on page 1844*

Related Sample Prescriptions

Bacterial Infections and Periodontal Diseases - Sample Prescriptions *on page 32*

Prevention of Endocarditis and to Reduce the Risk of Late Infections of Joint Prostheses - Sample Prescriptions *on page 37*

Sinus Infection Treatment - Sample Prescriptions *on page 38*

Brand Names: US Moxatag

Brand Names: Canada Apo-Amoxi; Mylan-Amoxicillin; Novamoxin; NTP-Amoxicillin; Nu-Amoxi; PHL-Amoxicillin; PMS-Amoxicillin; Pro-Amox-250; Pro-Amox-500

Generic Availability (US) Yes

Pharmacologic Category Antibiotic, Penicillin

Dental Use Antibiotic for standard prophylactic regimen for dental patients who are at risk for infective endocarditis; prophylaxis in total joint replacement patients undergoing dental procedures; antibiotic used to treat orofacial infections. Useful (as amoxicillin or amoxicillin/clavulanic acid) in combination with metronidazole in addition to scaling and root planing in the treatment of periodontitis associated with the presence of *Actinobacillus actinomycetemcomitans* (AA).

Use

Ear, nose, and throat infections (pharyngitis/tonsillitis, otitis media, rhinosinusitis): Immediate-release: Treatment of infections due to beta-lactamase-negative *Streptococcus* spp (alpha- and beta-hemolytic isolates only), *Streptococcus pneumoniae*, *Staphylococcus* spp., or *Haemophilus influenzae*.

Genitourinary tract infections: Immediate-release: Treatment of infections of the genitourinary tract due to beta-lactamase-negative *Escherichia coli*, *Proteus mirabilis*, or *Enterococcus faecalis*.

***Helicobacter pylori* eradication:** Immediate-release: Eradication of *H. pylori* to reduce the risk of duodenal ulcer recurrence as a component of combination therapy (triple or dual therapy as clinically indicated) in patients with active or 1 year history of duodenal ulcer disease.

Lower respiratory tract infections (including pneumonia): Immediate-release: Treatment of infections of the lower respiratory tract due to beta-lactamase-negative *Streptococcus* spp. (alpha- and beta-hemolytic strains only), *Streptococcus pneumoniae*, *Staphylococcus* spp., or *H. influenzae*.

Pharyngitis and tonsillitis: Extended-release: Treatment of tonsillitis and/or pharyngitis due to *Streptococcus pyogenes* in adults and pediatric patients ≥12 years.

Skin and skin structure infections: Immediate-release: Treatment of infections of the skin and skin structure due to beta-lactamase-negative *Streptococcus* spp. (alpha- and beta-hemolytic strains only), *Staphylococcus* spp., or *E. coli*.

Local Anesthetic/Vasoconstrictor Precautions No information available to require special precautions

Effects on Dental Treatment Prolonged use of penicillins may lead to development of oral candidiasis

Effects on Bleeding No information available to require special precautions

Adverse Reactions Frequency not defined.

Cardiovascular: Hypersensitivity angiitis

Central nervous system: Agitation, anxiety, behavioral changes, confusion, dizziness, headache, hyperactivity (reversible), insomnia, seizure

Dermatologic: Acute generalized exanthematous pustulosis, erythematous maculopapular rash, erythema multiforme, exfoliative dermatitis, Stevens-Johnson syndrome, toxic epidermal necrolysis, urticaria

Gastrointestinal: Dental discoloration (brown, yellow, or gray; rare), diarrhea, hemorrhagic colitis, melanoglossia, mucocutaneous candidiasis, nausea, pseudomembranous colitis, vomiting

Genitourinary: Crystalluria

Hematologic & oncologic: Agranulocytosis, anemia, eosinophilia, hemolytic anemia, leukopenia,thrombocytopenia, thrombocytopenia purpura

Hepatic: Cholestatic hepatitis, cholestatic jaundice, hepatitis (acute cytolytic), increased serum ALT, increased serum AST

Hypersensitivity: Anaphylaxis

Immunologic: Serum sickness-like reaction

Dental Usual Dosage Oral:

Children >3 months and <40 kg: Prophylaxis against infective endocarditis: 50 mg/kg 30-60 minutes before procedure. **Note:** American Heart Association (AHA) guidelines now recommend prophylaxis only in patients undergoing invasive procedures and in whom underlying cardiac conditions may predispose to a higher risk of adverse outcomes should infection occur.

Adults:

Periodontitis (aggressive) (in combination with metronidazole) associated with presence of *Actinobacillus actinomycetemcomitans* (AA): 500 mg every 8 hours for 10 days used in addition to scaling and root planing (Varela 2011). In aggressive periodontitis, greatest benefit is seen after 3 months of therapy. No benefit was seen after 6 months of therapy (Varela 2011).

Prophylaxis against infective endocarditis: 2 g 30-60 minutes before procedure. **Note:** American Heart Association (AHA) guidelines now recommend prophylaxis only in patients undergoing invasive procedures and in whom underlying cardiac conditions may predispose to a higher risk of adverse outcomes should infection occur.

Orofacial infection: 250-500 mg every 8 hours or 500-875 mg twice daily

Prophylaxis in total joint replacement patients undergoing dental procedures which produce bacteremia: 2 g 1 hour prior to procedure

Note: In general, patients with prosthetic joint implants do not require prophylactic antibiotics prior to dental procedures. In planning an invasive oral procedure, dental consultation with the patient's orthopedic surgeon may be advised to review the risks of infection.

Dosing

Adult & Geriatric Note: Unless otherwise specified, all dosing recommendations based on immediate release product formulations.

Usual dosage range: Oral:

Mild or moderate infection: 250 every 8 hours or 500 mg every 12 hours

Mild or moderate infection (lower respiratory tract): 500 mg every 8 hours or 875 mg every 12 hours

Severe infection (as step-down therapy): 500 mg every 8 hours or 875 mg every 12 hours

Extended-release: 775 mg once daily

Indication-specific dosing:

Anthrax, inhalational postexposure prophylaxis (CDC recommendations) (off-label use): Oral: 1,000 mg every 8 hours (Hendricks [CDC 2014]). **Note:** Use **only** if isolates of the specific *B. anthracis* are sensitive to amoxicillin (MIC ≤0.125 mcg/mL); may be administered to pregnant and breastfeeding women. Duration of antibiotic postexposure prophylaxis (PEP) is 60 days whether a patient is vaccinated, partially vaccinated, or unvaccinated (Hendricks [CDC 2014]).

Ear, nose, throat, genitourinary tract, or skin/skin structure infections: Note: IDSA guidelines recommend amoxicillin-clavulanate as preferred first-line treatment of acute bacterial rhinosinusitis (ABRS) (IDSA [Chow 2012]); AAO-HNS guidelines for adult sinusitis recommend either amoxicillin or amoxicillin-clavulanate as initial first-line therapy of ABRS, with consideration given for amoxicillin-clavulanate instead of amoxicillin in certain patients (eg, moderate to severe ABRS symptoms, antibiotic use in past month, high prevalence of resistant bacteria in community, history of recurrent ABRS, presence of comorbidities) (AAO-HNS [Rosenfeld 2015]).

Mild-to-moderate: Oral: 500 mg every 12 hours **or** 250 mg every 8 hours

Severe: Oral: 875 mg every 12 hours **or** 500 mg every 8 hours

Tonsillitis and/or pharyngitis: Oral: Extended release: 775 mg once daily for 10 days

Endocarditis, prophylaxis (off-label use): Oral: 2 g 30 to 60 minutes before procedure. **Note:** American Heart Association (AHA) guidelines now recommend prophylaxis only in patients undergoing invasive procedures and in whom underlying cardiac conditions may predispose to a higher risk of adverse outcomes should infection occur. As of April 2007, routine prophylaxis for GI/GU procedures is no longer recommended by the AHA.

Erysipeloid (off-label use): Oral: 500 mg 3 times daily for 7 to 10 days (IDSA [Stevens 2014])

***Helicobacter pylori* eradication:** Oral:

Manufacturer's labeling: 1,000 mg twice daily in combination therapy with clarithromycin and lansoprazole for 14 days

Alternate dosing: 1,000 mg twice daily, in combination with a proton pump inhibitor (PPI) and clarithromycin or metronidazole (triple therapy) **or** a PPI, clarithromycin, and metronidazole (quadruple therapy) for 14 days; use of triple therapy should be reserved for areas where clarithromycin resistance is low (<15%) or eradication rates are high (>85%) (Fallone 2016)

Lower respiratory tract infections: Oral:

Manufacturer's labeling: 875 mg every 12 hours **or** 500 mg every 8 hours

Alternate dosing: Pneumonia, community-acquired: Outpatient empiric therapy: 1,000 mg 3 times daily for a minimum of 5 days (patients should be afebrile for ≥48 hours and clinically stable before discontinuation of therapy); use in combination with a macrolide (preferred) or doxycycline (Mandell 2007)

Lyme disease (excluding neurologic disease) (off-label use) (IDSA [Wormser 2006]): Oral:

Acrodermatitis chronica atrophicans: 500 mg 3 times daily for 21 days

Erythema migrans: 500 mg 3 times daily for 14 to 21 days

Lyme arthritis: 500 mg 3 times daily for 28 days

Lyme carditis (mild): 500 mg 3 times daily for 14 to 21 days

Lyme neuroborreliosis (off-label use) (when doxycycline is contraindicated): Oral: 500 mg 3 times daily for 14 to 21 days. **Note:** Oral regimens should be reserved for patients with cranial nerve palsy without evidence of meningitis (IDSA [Wormser 2006]).

Periodontitis (aggressive) (in combination with metronidazole) associated with presence of *Actinobacillus actinomycetemcomitans* (AA) (off-label use): Oral: 500 mg every 8 hours for 10 days used in addition to scaling and root planing (Varela 2011)

Pharyngitis, group A streptococci: Oral: 1,000 mg once daily or 500 mg twice daily (maximum: 1,000 mg/day) for 10 days (IDSA [Shulman 2012])

Prophylaxis in total joint replacement patients undergoing dental procedures which produce bacteremia (off-label use): Oral: 2 g 1 hour prior to procedure (ADA/AAOS 2003). **Note:** In general, patients with prosthetic joint implants do not require prophylactic antibiotics prior to dental procedures. In planning an invasive oral procedure, dental consultation with the patient's orthopedic surgeon may be advised to review the risks of infection (Sollecito 2015).

Prosthetic joint infection, chronic antimicrobial suppression of prosthetic joint infection associated with beta-hemolytic streptococci, penicillin-susceptible *Enterococcus* spp, or *Propionibacterium* spp (off-label use): Oral: 500 mg 3 times daily (Osmon 2013)

Pediatric Note: Unless otherwise specified, all pediatric dosing recommendations based on immediate release product formulations (oral suspension, chewable tablet, tablet, and capsule).

Usual dosage range:

Mild to moderate infection:

Infants ≤3 months: Oral: 25 to 50 mg/kg/day in divided doses every 8 hours (*Red Book* [AAP 2015]). **Note:** Manufacturer's labeling recommends a maximum daily dose of 30 mg/kg/**day** divided into 2 doses per day for this age group.

Infants >3 months, Children, and Adolescents (<40 kg):

AAP recommendations (*Red Book* [AAP 2015]): Oral: 25 to 50 mg/kg/day in divided doses every 8 hours; maximum dose: 500 mg/dose

Manufacturer's labeling: Oral: 20 to 40 mg/kg/day in divided doses every 8 hours (maximum dose: 500 mg/dose) **or** 25 to 45 mg/kg/day in divided doses every 12 hours (maximum dose: 875 mg/dose)

Children, and Adolescents (≥40 kg): Refer to adult dosing.

Severe infection (as step-down therapy): Infants, Children, and Adolescents: Oral: 80 to 100 mg/kg/day in divided doses every 8 hours; maximum dose: 500 mg/dose for most indications (*Red Book* [AAP 2015])

Indication-specific dosing:

Anthrax (off-label use):

Cutaneous, without systemic involvement: Children and Adolescents: Oral: 75 mg/kg/day in 3 divided doses. Maximum dose: 1,000 mg/dose. Duration of therapy: 7 to 10 days for naturally acquired infection, up to 60 days for biological weapon-related exposure (AAP [Bradley 2014]).

Inhalational, postexposure prophylaxis: Children and Adolescents: Oral: 75 mg/kg/day in divided doses every 8 hours for 60 days after exposure; maximum dose: 1,000 mg/dose (AAP [Bradley 2014]).

Catheter (peritoneal dialysis), exit-site or tunnel infection (off-label use): Infants, Children, and Adolescents: Oral: 10 to 20 mg/kg once daily; maximum dose: 1,000 mg/dose (Warady [ISPD 2012])

Endocarditis, prophylaxis (off-label use): Infants, Children, and Adolescents: Oral: 50 mg/kg 1 hour before procedure (maximum dose: 2,000 mg/dose) (Wilson 2007)

***Helicobacter pylori* eradication:** Children and Adolescents: Oral: 50 mg/kg/day in 2 divided doses for 10 to 14 days; maximum daily dose: 2,000 mg/**day**. Administer in combination with a proton pump inhibitor or bismuth subsalicylate and at least one other antibiotic (clarithromycin and/or metronidazole) (NASPGHAN/ESPGHAN [Koletzko 2011]).

Lyme disease (off-label use): Infants, Children, and Adolescents: Oral: 50 mg/kg/day divided every 8 hours (maximum dose: 500 mg/dose) (Halperin 2007; Wormser 2006)

Otitis media, acute: Infants ≥2 months and Children: Oral: 80 to 90 mg/kg/day divided every 12 hours; variable duration of therapy, if <2 years of age or severe symptoms (any age): 10-day course; if 2 to 5 years of age with mild to moderate symptoms: 7-day course; ≥6 years of age with mild to moderate symptoms: 5- to 7-day course; some experts recommend initiating with 90 mg/kg/day (AAP [Lieberthal 2013]; *Red Book* [AAP 2015]); a maximum dose is not provided in the Guidelines for The Diagnosis and Management of Acute Otitis Media (AAP [Lieberthal 2013]); however, some experts suggest a maximum daily dose of 4,000 mg/day for high-dose amoxicillin therapy (Bradley 2015).

Peritonitis, prophylaxis (for patients receiving peritoneal dialysis who require dental procedures) (off-label use): Infants, Children, and Adolescents: Oral: 50 mg/kg administered 30 to 60 minutes before dental procedure (maximum dose: 2000 mg/dose) (Warady [ISPD 2012])

Pneumococcal infection prophylaxis for anatomic or functional asplenia (eg, sickle cell disease ([SCD]) (off-label use) (Price 2007; *Red Book* [AAP 2015]):

Infants (<2 months to 1 year, or as soon as SCD is diagnosed or asplenia occurs) and Children ≤5 years: Oral: 20 mg/kg/day in divided doses every 12 hours (maximum dose: 250 mg/dose)

Children ≥6 years and Adolescents: Oral: 250 mg every 12 hours. **Note:** The decision to discontinue penicillin prophylaxis after 5 years of age in children who have not experienced invasive pneumococcal infection and have received recommended pneumococcal immunizations is patient and clinician dependent.

Pneumonia, community-acquired (CAP) (Bradley [IDSA 2011]): Infants ≥3 months, Children, and Adolescents: **Note:** In pediatric patients 5 to 15 years of age, a macrolide antibiotic may be a more reasonable first choice as *M. pneumoniae* is the chief cause of pneumonia in this age group.

Empiric treatment: Oral: 90 mg/kg/day in divided doses every 12 hours (maximum daily dose: 4,000 mg/**day**)

Group A *Streptococcus*: Oral: 50 to 75 mg/kg/day in divided doses every 12 hours (maximum daily dose: 4,000 mg/**day**)

H. influenzae: Oral: 75 to 100 mg/kg/day in divided doses every 8 hours (maximum daily dose: 4,000 mg/**day**)

S. pneumoniae (MICs to penicillin ≤2 mcg/mL), mild infection or step-down therapy: Oral: 90 mg/kg/day in divided doses every 12 hours **or** 45 mg/kg/day in divided doses every 8 hours (maximum daily dose: 4,000 mg/**day**)

Rhinosinusitis, acute bacterial; uncomplicated: **Note:** AAP guidelines recommend amoxicillin as first-line empiric therapy for pediatric patients 1 to 18 years with uncomplicated cases and where resistance is not suspected; however, the IDSA guidelines consider amoxicillin/clavulanate as the preferred therapy (Chow 2012, Wald 2013):

Children and Adolescents:

Low dose: Oral: 45 mg/kg/day in divided doses every 12 hours

High dose (use reserved for select patients; see **Note**): Oral: 80 to 90 mg/kg/day in divided doses every 12 hours (maximum dose: 1,000 mg/dose). **Note:** Should only be used in the following: Mild to moderate infections in communities with a high prevalence of nonsusceptible *S. pneumoniae* resistance.

Tonsillopharyngitis; Group A streptococcal infection, treatment and primary prevention of rheumatic fever:

Immediate release: Children ≥3 years and Adolescents: Oral: 50 mg/kg once daily **or** 25 mg/kg twice daily for 10 days; maximum daily dose: 1,000 mg/**day** (Gerber 2009; Shulman 2012)

Extended release: Children ≥12 years and Adolescents: Oral: 775 mg once daily for 10 days. **Note:** Patient must be able to swallow tablet whole.

Urinary tract infection, prophylaxis (hydronephrosis, vesicoureteral reflux): Infants ≤2 months: Oral: 10 to 15 mg/kg once daily; some suggest administration in the evening (drug resides in bladder longer); **Note:** Due to resistance, amoxicillin should not be used for prophylaxis after 2 months of age (Belarmino 2006; Greenbaum 2006; Mattoo 2007).

Renal Impairment

Adults: Oral:

Immediate-release: **Note:** Avoid immediate-release 875 mg tablet in patients with GFR <30 mL/minute.

- GFR ≥30 mL/minute: No dosage adjustment necessary.
- GFR 10 to 30 mL/minute: 250 to 500 mg every 12 hours
- GFR <10 mL/minute: 250 to 500 mg every 24 hours
- Hemodialysis: Moderately dialyzable (20% to 50%); ~30% removed by 3-hour hemodialysis: 250 to 500 mg every 24 hours; administer after dialysis on dialysis days (Aronoff 2007)

Extended-release:

- CrCl ≥30 mL/minute: There are no dosage adjustments provided in the manufacturer's labeling (has not been studied).
- CrCl <30 mL/minute: Not recommended
- Hemodialysis: Not recommended.

Infants, Children, and Adolescents: Oral:

Immediate-release:

There are no dosage adjustments provided in the manufacturer's labeling; however, the following recommendations have been used by some clinicians (Aronoff 2007):

Mild to moderate infection: Dosing based on 25 to 50 mg/kg/day divided every 8 hours:

- GFR ≥30 mL/minute/1.73 m^2: No dosage adjustment necessary.
- GFR 10 to 29 mL/minute/1.73 m^2: 8 to 20 mg/kg/dose every 12 hours
- GFR <10 mL/minute/1.73 m^2: 8 to 20 mg/kg/dose every 24 hours
- Hemodialysis: Moderately dialyzable (20% to 50%); ~30% removed by 3-hour hemodialysis: 8 to 20 mg/kg/dose every 24 hours; give after dialysis.
- Peritoneal dialysis: 8 to 20 mg/kg/dose every 24 hours.

Severe infection (high dose): Dosing based on 80 to 90 mg/kg/day divided every 12 hours:

- GFR ≥30 mL/minute/1.73 m^2: No dosage adjustment necessary.

GFR 10 to 29 mL/minute/1.73 m^2: 20 mg/kg/dose every 12 hours; do not use the 875 mg tablet.

GFR <10 mL/minute/1.73 m^2: 20 mg/kg/dose every 24 hours; do not use the 875 mg tablet.

Hemodialysis: Moderately dialyzable (20% to 50%); ~30% removed by 3-hour hemodialysis: 20 mg/kg/dose every 24 hours; give after dialysis.

Peritoneal dialysis: 20 mg/kg/dose every 24 hours

Extended-release: Children ≥12 years and Adolescents:

CrCl ≥30 mL/minute: There are no dosage adjustments provided in the manufacturer's labeling (has not been studied).

CrCl <30 mL/minute: Not recommended.

Hemodialysis: Not recommended.

Hepatic Impairment There are no dosage adjustments provided in the manufacturer's labeling.

Mechanism of Action Inhibits bacterial cell wall synthesis by binding to one or more of the penicillin-binding proteins (PBPs) which in turn inhibits the final transpeptidation step of peptidoglycan synthesis in bacterial cell walls, thus inhibiting cell wall biosynthesis. Bacteria eventually lyse due to ongoing activity of cell wall autolytic enzymes (autolysins and murein hydrolases) while cell wall assembly is arrested.

Contraindications Serious hypersensitivity to amoxicillin (eg, anaphylaxis, Stevens-Johnson syndrome) or to other beta-lactams, or any component of the formulation

Warnings/Precautions In patients with renal impairment, doses and/or frequency of administration should be modified in response to the degree of renal impairment; dosage adjustment recommended in patients with GFR <30 mL/minute. Avoid extended release 775 mg tablet and immediate release 875 mg tablet in patients with GFR <30 mL/minute or patients requiring hemodialysis. A high percentage of patients with infectious mononucleosis develop an erythematous rash during amoxicillin therapy; avoid use in these patients. Serious and occasionally severe or fatal hypersensitivity (anaphylactic) reactions have been reported in patients on penicillin therapy, including amoxicillin, especially with a history of beta-lactam hypersensitivity (including severe reactions with cephalosporins) and/or a history of sensitivity to multiple allergens. Prolonged use may result in fungal or bacterial superinfection, including *C. difficile* associated diarrhea (CDAD) and pseudomembranous colitis; CDAD has been observed >2 months postantibiotic treatment. Potentially significant interactions may exist, requiring dose or frequency adjustment, additional monitoring, and/or selection of alternative therapy.

Chewable tablets may contain phenylalanine; see manufacturer's labeling.

Benzyl alcohol and derivatives: Some dosage forms may contain sodium benzoate/benzoic acid; benzoic acid (benzoate) is a metabolite of benzyl alcohol; large amounts of benzyl alcohol (≥99 mg/kg/day) have been associated with a potentially fatal toxicity ("gasping syndrome") in neonates; the "gasping syndrome" consists of metabolic acidosis, respiratory distress, gasping respirations, CNS dysfunction (including convulsions, intracranial hemorrhage), hypotension, and cardiovascular collapse (AAP ["Inactive" 1997]; CDC 1982); some data suggests that benzoate displaces bilirubin from protein binding sites (Ahlfors 2001); avoid or use dosage forms containing benzyl alcohol derivative with caution in neonates. See manufacturer's labeling.

Drug Interactions

Metabolism/Transport Effects None known.

Avoid Concomitant Use

Avoid concomitant use of Amoxicillin with any of the following: BCG (Intravesical); Cholera Vaccine

Increased Effect/Toxicity

Amoxicillin may increase the levels/effects of: Methotrexate; Vitamin K Antagonists

The levels/effects of Amoxicillin may be increased by: Allopurinol; Probenecid

Decreased Effect

Amoxicillin may decrease the levels/effects of: BCG (Intravesical); BCG Vaccine (Immunization); Cholera Vaccine; Lactobacillus and Estriol; Mycophenolate; Sodium Picosulfate; Typhoid Vaccine

The levels/effects of Amoxicillin may be decreased by: Tetracycline Derivatives

Dietary Considerations Some products may contain phenylalanine.

Pharmacodynamics/Kinetics

Half-life Elimination

Adults: Immediate release: 61.3 minutes; Extended-release: 90 minutes

Time to Peak Capsule; oral suspension: 1 to 2 hours; Chewable tablet: 1 hour; Extended-release tablet: 3.1 hours

Pregnancy Risk Factor B

Pregnancy Considerations Adverse events have not been observed in animal reproduction studies. Amoxicillin crosses the placenta (Muller 2009). Maternal use of amoxicillin has generally not resulted in an increased risk of adverse fetal effects; however, a possible association with cleft lip with cleft palate has been observed in some studies (more data is needed) (Lin 2012; Puhó 2007). Amoxicillin may be used for the management of *Bacillus anthracis* in pregnant women when penicillin susceptibility is documented (Meaney-Delman 2014). Amoxicillin is an alternative antibiotic for the treatment of chlamydial infections in pregnancy (CDC [Workowski 2015]). Amoxicillin can also be used in the management of preterm premature rupture of membranes and in certain situations prior to vaginal delivery in women at high risk for endocarditis (ACOG 120 2011; ACOG 139 2013).

Due to pregnancy-induced physiologic changes, some pharmacokinetic parameters of amoxicillin may be altered (Andrew 2007). Oral ampicillin-class antibiotics are poorly absorbed during labor.

Breastfeeding Considerations Amoxicillin is excreted in breast milk (Kafetzis 1981).

The relative infant dose (RID) of amoxicillin is 0.15% to 0.54% when calculated using the highest average breast milk concentration located and compared to an infant therapeutic dose of 25 to 90 mg/kg/day. In general, breastfeeding is considered acceptable when the RID is <10%; when an RID is >25% breastfeeding should generally be avoided (Anderson 2016; Ito 2000). Using the highest average milk concentration (0.9 mcg/mL), the estimated daily infant dose via breast milk is 0.135 mg/kg/day. This milk concentration was obtained following maternal administration of a single oral dose of amoxicillin 1,000 mg (Kafetzis 1981).

Self-limiting diarrhea, rash, and somnolence have been reported in nursing infants exposed to amoxicillin (Benyamini 2005; Goldstein 2009; Ito 1993); the manufacturer warns of the potential for allergic sensitization in the infant. In general, antibiotics that are present in breast milk may cause nondose-related modification of bowel flora. Monitor infants for GI disturbances, such as thrush or diarrhea (WHO 2002).

Although the manufacturer recommends that caution be exercised when administering amoxicillin to breastfeeding women, amoxicillin is considered compatible with breastfeeding when used in usual recommended doses (WHO 2002). Amoxicillin has been recommended to treat mastitis in breastfeeding women when penicillin susceptibility is documented (WHO 2000) and also for the management of *Bacillus anthracis* (Meaney-Delman 2014).

Dosage Forms

Capsule, Oral:
Generic: 250 mg, 500 mg

Suspension Reconstituted, Oral:
Generic: 125 mg/5 mL (80 mL, 100 mL, 150 mL); 200 mg/5 mL (50 mL, 75 mL, 100 mL); 250 mg/5 mL (80 mL, 100 mL, 150 mL); 400 mg/5 mL (50 mL, 75 mL, 100 mL)

Tablet, Oral:
Generic: 500 mg, 875 mg

Tablet Chewable, Oral:
Generic: 125 mg, 250 mg

Tablet Extended Release 24 Hour, Oral:
Moxatag: 775 mg

Amoxicillin and Clavulanate

(a moks i SIL in & klav yoo LAN ate)

Related Information

Amoxicillin *on page 121*
Bacterial Infections *on page 1835*

Related Sample Prescriptions

Bacterial Infections and Periodontal Diseases - Sample Prescriptions *on page 32*
Sinus Infection Treatment - Sample Prescriptions *on page 38*

Brand Names: US Augmentin; Augmentin ES-600; Augmentin XR

Brand Names: Canada Amoxi-Clav; Apo-Amoxi-Clav; Clavulin; Novo-Clavamoxin; ratio-Aclavulanate

Generic Availability (US) Yes

Pharmacologic Category Antibiotic, Penicillin

Dental Use Treatment of orofacial infections when beta-lactamase-producing staphylococci and beta-lactamase-producing *Bacteroides* are present

Use

Pneumonia, community-acquired: Extended-release tablets only: Treatment of patients with community-acquired pneumonia (CAP) caused by confirmed or suspected beta-lactamase-producing pathogens (ie, *Haemophilus influenzae, Moraxella catarrhalis, Haemophilus parainfluenzae, Klebsiella pneumoniae*, methicillin-susceptible *Staphylococcus aureus*) and *Streptococcus pneumoniae* with reduced susceptibility to penicillin (penicillin minimum inhibitory concentration [MIC] = 2 mcg/mL).

Limitations of use: Augmentin XR is not indicated for the treatment of infections caused by *S. pneumoniae* with penicillin MIC of 4 mcg/mL or greater (limited data).

Otitis media, acute:

Immediate-release tablets, chewable tablets, oral suspension (400/57 mg per 5 mL, 250/62.5 mg per 5 mL, 200/28.5 mg per 5 mL, and 125/31.25 mg per 5 mL only): Treatment of otitis media caused by beta-lactamase-producing strains of *H. influenzae* and *M. catarrhalis*.

Oral suspension (600/42.9 mg per 5 mL concentration): Treatment of acute otitis media, recurrent or persistent, caused by *S. pneumoniae* (penicillin MIC = 2 mcg/mL or less), *H. influenzae* (including beta-lactamase-producing strains), and *M. catarrhalis* (including beta-lactamase-producing strains) in pediatric patients with a history of antibiotic exposure for acute otitis media in the preceding 3 months and who are either 2 years or younger or attend day care; treatment of otitis media caused by beta-lactamase-producing strains of *H. influenzae* and *M. catarrhalis*.

Respiratory tract infections, lower: Immediate-release tablets, chewable tablets, oral suspension (400/57 mg per 5 mL, 250/62.5 mg per 5 mL, 200/28.5 mg per 5 mL, and 125/31.25 mg per 5 mL only): Treatment of lower respiratory tract infection caused by beta-lactamase-producing strains of *H. influenzae* and *M. catarrhalis*.

Sinusitis, acute bacterial:

Extended-release tablets: Treatment of patients with acute bacterial sinusitis caused by confirmed or suspected beta-lactamase-producing pathogens (ie, *H. influenzae, M. catarrhalis, H. parainfluenzae, K. pneumoniae*, methicillin-susceptible *S. aureus*) and *S. pneumoniae* with reduced susceptibility to penicillin (penicillin MIC = 2 mcg/mL).

Limitations of use: Augmentin XR is not indicated for the treatment of infections caused by *S. pneumoniae* with penicillin MIC of 4 mcg/mL or greater (limited data).

Immediate-release tablets, chewable tablets, oral suspension (400/57 mg per 5 mL, 250/62.5 mg per 5 mL, 200/28.5 mg per 5 mL, and 125/31.25 mg per 5 mL only): Treatment of sinusitis caused by beta-lactamase-producing strains of *H. influenzae* and *M. catarrhalis*.

Skin and skin structure infections: Immediate-release tablets, chewable tablets, oral suspension (400/57 mg per 5 mL, 250/62.5 mg per 5 mL, 200/28.5 mg per 5 mL, and 125/31.25 mg per 5 mL only): Treatment of skin and skin structure infections caused by beta-lactamase-producing strains of *S. aureus, Escherichia coli*, and *Klebsiella* spp.

Urinary tract infections: Immediate-release tablets, chewable tablets, oral suspension (400/57 mg per 5 mL, 250/62.5 mg per 5 mL, 200/28.5 mg per 5 mL, and 125/31.25 mg per 5 mL only): Treatment of urinary tract infections caused by beta-lactamase-producing strains of *E. coli, Klebsiella* spp, and *Enterobacter* spp.

Local Anesthetic/Vasoconstrictor Precautions No information available to require special precautions

Effects on Dental Treatment Prolonged use of penicillins may lead to development of oral candidiasis (see Dental Comment)

Effects on Bleeding No information available to require special precautions

Adverse Reactions

>10%: Gastrointestinal: Diarrhea (3% to 34%; incidence varies upon dose and regimen used)

1% to 10%:

Dermatologic: Diaper rash, skin rash, urticaria

Gastrointestinal: Abdominal distress, loose stools, nausea, vomiting

Genitourinary: Vaginitis

Infection: Candidiasis, vaginal mycosis

<1%, postmarketing, and/or case reports: Cholestatic jaundice, flatulence, headache, hepatic insufficiency,

hepatitis, hepatotoxicity (idiosyncratic) (Chalasani 2014), increased liver enzymes, increased serum alkaline phosphatase, prolonged prothrombin time, thrombocythemia, vasculitis (hypersensitivity)

Additional adverse reactions seen with **ampicillin-class antibiotics:** Acute generalized exanthematous pustulosis, agitation, agranulocytosis, anaphylaxis, anemia, angioedema, anxiety, behavioral changes, confusion, convulsions, crystalluria, dental discoloration, dizziness, dyspepsia, enterocolitis, eosinophilia, erythema multiforme, exfoliative dermatitis, gastritis, glossitis, hematuria, hemolytic anemia, hemorrhagic colitis, hyperactivity, immune thrombocytopenia, increased serum bilirubin, increased serum transaminases, insomnia, interstitial nephritis, leukopenia, melanoglossia, mucocutaneous candidiasis, pruritus, pseudomembranous colitis, serum sickness-like reaction, Stevens-Johnson syndrome, stomatitis, thrombocytopenia, toxic epidermal necrolysis

Dental Usual Dosage Orofacial infections: Children >40 kg and Adults: Oral: 250-500 mg every 8 hours or 875 mg every 12 hours

Dosing

Adult & Geriatric Note: Dose is based on the amoxicillin component. Dose and frequency are product specific; not all products are interchangeable. Using a product with the incorrect amoxicillin:clavulanate ratio could result in subtherapeutic clavulanic acid concentrations or severe diarrhea. For adults who have difficulty swallowing the tablets, the 125 mg/5 mL or 250 mg/5 mL suspension may be given in place of the 500 mg/125 mg tablet; the 200 mg/5 mL or 400 mg/5 mL suspension may be given in place of the 875 mg/125 mg tablet.

Susceptible infections: Oral: 250 mg every 8 hours or 500 mg every 8 to 12 hours **or** 875 mg every 12 hours **or** 2,000 mg every 12 hours

Bite wounds (animal/human) (off-label use): Oral: Immediate release: 875 mg every 12 hours (IDSA [Stevens 2014])

Chronic obstructive pulmonary disease (COPD) (off-label use): Oral: Immediate release: 500 mg every 8 hours (Llor 2012)

Cystitis, acute uncomplicated: Oral: Immediate release:

Manufacturer's labeling: 500 mg every 12 hours or 250 mg every 8 hours

Alternate dosing: 500 mg every 12 hours for 7 days (Colgan 2011; IDSA [Gupta 2011])

Impetigo (off-label use): Oral: Immediate release: 875 mg every 12 hours for 7 days, depending on response (IDSA [Stevens 2014])

Febrile neutropenia, empiric therapy in low-risk cancer patients (off-label use): Oral: Immediate release: 500 mg every 8 hours until resolution of neutropenia; use in combination with oral ciprofloxacin (Freifeld 1999; Pherwani 2015)

Group A streptococci chronic carrier, treatment (off-label use): Oral: Immediate release: Amoxicillin 40 mg/kg/day divided every 8 hours (maximum: Amoxicillin 2,000 mg/day) for 10 days (IDSA [Shulman 2012])

Pneumonia, community-acquired (CAP): Oral:

Manufacturer's labeling:

Immediate release: 875 mg every 12 hours **or** 500 mg every 8 hours

Extended release: 2,000 mg every 12 hours for 7 to 10 days

Alternate dosing:

Outpatient empiric therapy: Extended release: 2,000 mg every 12 hours for a minimum of 5 days (patients should be afebrile for ≥48 hours and clinically stable before discontinuation of therapy); use in combination with a macrolide (preferred) or doxycycline (Mandell 2007)

Meliodosis, treatment (eradication phase) and postexposure prophylaxis (off-label use) (HHS [Lipsitz 2012]): Oral: Immediate release: **Note:** Duration for eradication phase treatment is ≥12 weeks; duration for postexposure prophylaxis is 21 days.

>60 kg: 1,500 mg (three 500 mg tablets) every 8 hours

<60 kg: 1,000 mg (two 500 mg tablets) every 8 hours

Prosthetic joint infection, chronic antimicrobial suppression, oxacillin-susceptible *Staphylococci* (alternative to cephalexin or cefadroxil) (off-label use): Oral: Immediate release: 500 mg 3 times daily (IDSA [Osmon 2013])

Respiratory tract infections, lower: Oral Immediate release: 875 mg every 12 hours **or** 500 mg every 8 hours

Sinusitis, acute bacterial: Oral:

Manufacturer's labeling:

Immediate release: 500 mg every 8 hours or amoxicillin 875 mg every 12 hours

Extended release: Amoxicillin 2,000 mg every 12 hours for 10 days

Alternate dosing: IDSA recommendations:

Standard dose: Immediate release: 500 mg every 8 hours or 875 mg every 12 hours for 5 to 7 days

High dose: Extended release: 2,000 mg every 12 hours for 10 days. **Note:** Recommended for patients with any of the following: If initial therapy fails (as second-line therapy), in areas with high endemic rates of penicillin-nonsusceptible *S. pneumoniae*, those with severe infections, age >65 years, recent hospitalization, antibiotic use within the past month, or who are immunocompromised (AAO-HNS [Rosenfeld 2015]; IDSA [Chow 2012]).

Pediatric Note: Dose is based on the amoxicillin component. Dose and frequency are product specific; not all products are interchangeable. Using a product with the incorrect amoxicillin:clavulanate ratio could result in subtherapeutic clavulanic acid concentrations or severe diarrhea.

Usual dosage range:

Infants <3 months: Oral: Amoxicillin 30 mg/kg/day divided every 12 hours using the 125 mg per 5 mL suspension **only**

Infants ≥3 months, Children, and Adolescents <40 kg: Oral: Immediate release:

Mild to moderate infections: Amoxicillin 25 mg/kg/day in divided doses twice daily (using the 200 mg per 5 mL or 400 mg per 5 mL suspension or 200 mg or 400 mg chewable tablets) **or** amoxicillin 20 mg/kg/day in divided doses 3 times daily (using the 125 mg per 5 mL or 250 mg per 5 mL suspension) (maximum single dose: 500 mg amoxicillin)

Severe infections: Amoxicillin 45 mg/kg/day in divided doses twice daily (using the 200 mg per 5 mL or 400 mg per 5 mL suspension or 200 mg or 400 mg **chewable** tablets) (maximum single dose: Amoxicillin 875 mg) **or** amoxicillin 40 mg/kg/day in divided doses 3 times daily (using the 125 mg per 5 mL or 250 mg per 5 mL suspension) (maximum single dose: Amoxicillin 500 mg)

Children and Adolescents ≥40 kg: Oral:

Mild to moderate infections: Immediate release: Amoxicillin 500 mg every 12 hours (using the 500 mg tablet; if difficulty swallowing the 125 mg per 5 mL or 250 mg per 5 mL suspension may be used) **or** 250 mg amoxicillin every 8 hours (using the 250 mg tablet)

Severe infections:

Immediate release: Amoxicillin 875 mg every 12 hours (using the 875 mg tablet; if difficulty swallowing, the 200 mg per 5 mL or 400 mg per 5 mL suspension may be used) **or** amoxicillin 500 mg every 8 hours (using the 500 mg tablet; if difficulty swallowing, the 125 mg per 5 mL or 250 mg per 5 mL suspension may be used).

Extended release: Amoxicillin 2,000 mg every 12 hours

Indication-specific dosing:

Group A streptococci chronic carrier, treatment (off-label use): Infants ≥3 months, Children, and Adolescents: Oral: Immediate release: Amoxicillin 40 mg/kg/day divided every 8 hours for 10 days (using the 125 mg per 5 mL or 250 mg per 5 mL suspension) (IDSA [Shulman 2012])

Impetigo (off-label use): Infants ≥3 months, Children, and Adolescents: Oral: Immediate release: Amoxicillin 25 mg/kg/day in divided doses twice daily (using the 200 mg per 5 mL or 400 mg per 5 mL oral suspension or the 200 mg or 400 mg **chewable** tablets) (maximum single dose: 875 mg amoxicillin) (IDSA [Stevens 2014])

Otitis media, acute: Infants ≥6 months and Children: Oral: Immediate release: Amoxicillin 90 mg/kg/day divided every 12 hours (using the 600 mg per 5 mL suspension **only**). **Note:** Use for severe illness, those who have received amoxicillin in the past 30 days, who have treatment failure at 48 to 72 hours on first-line therapy, and when coverage for beta-lactamase positive *H. influenzae* and *M. catarrhalis* is needed. Variable duration of therapy; the manufacturer's labeling suggests 10-day course in all patients; however, new data suggest a shorter-course in some cases: If <2 years of age or severe symptoms (any age): 10-day course; if 2 to 5 years of age with mild to moderate symptoms: 7-day course; if ≥6 years of age with mild to moderate symptoms: 5- to 7-day course (AAP [Lieberthal 2013]). **Note:** Per the manufacturer, the 600 mg/5 mL formulation should only be used for patients weighing <40 kg.

Pneumonia, community-acquired (CAP) and respiratory tract infections, lower: Infants ≥3 months, Children, and Adolescents: Oral:

Manufacturer's labeling:

Patients weighing <40 kg: Immediate release: Amoxicillin 45 mg/kg/day in divided doses twice daily (using the 200 mg per 5 mL or 400 mg per 5 mL suspension or the 200 mg or 400 mg chewable tablets) (maximum single dose: Amoxicillin 875 mg) **or** amoxicillin 40 mg/kg/day in divided doses 3 times daily (using the 125 mg per 5 mL or 250 mg per 5 mL suspension) (maximum single dose: Amoxicillin 500 mg)

Patients weighing ≥40 kg:

Immediate release: Amoxicillin 875 mg every 12 hours using the 875 mg tablet or if difficulty swallowing, the 200 mg/5 mL or the 400 mg/5 mL oral suspension may be used or 500 mg amoxicillin every 8 hours using the 500 mg tablet or if difficulty swallowing, the 125 mg/5 mL or 250 mg/5 mL oral suspension may be used

Extended release: 2,000 mg amoxicillin every 12 hours

Alternate dosing (off-label dosing): Beta-lactamase positive *H. influenzae* strains (IDSA/PIDS [Bradley 2011]): Immediate release:

Standard dose: Amoxicillin 45 mg/kg/day in divided doses 3 times daily (using the 125 mg per 5 mL or 250 mg per 5 mL suspension) (maximum single dose: Amoxicillin 500 mg)

High dose: Amoxicillin 90 mg/kg/day in divided doses 2 times daily (using the 600 mg per 5 mL suspension). **Note:** A wider dosing range of 80 to 100 mg/kg/day divided every 8 hours has also been used (Bradley 2002).

Sinusitis, acute bacterial: Oral:

IDSA recommendations:

Infants ≥3 months, Children, and Adolescents <40 kg: Immediate release:

Standard dose: Amoxicillin 45 mg/kg/day divided every 12 hours for 10 to 14 days (using the 200 mg per 5 mL or 400 mg per 5 mL suspension or 200 mg or 400 mg chewable tablets **only**) (IDSA [Chow 2012])

High dose (off-label dose): Amoxicillin 90 mg/kg/day divided every 12 hours for 10 to 14 days (using the 600 mg per 5 mL suspension **only**). **Note:** Use recommended in the following: If initial therapy fails (as second-line therapy), in areas with high endemic rates of penicillin-nonsusceptible *S. pneumoniae*, those with severe infections, daycare attendance, age <2 years, recent hospitalization, antibiotic use within the past month, or who are immunocompromised (IDSA [Chow 2012]).

Children and Adolescents ≥40 kg: Refer to adult dosing.

AAP recommendations: Children and Adolescents: Immediate release:

High dose (off-label dose): Amoxicillin 80 to 90 mg/kg/day divided every 12 hours (using the 600 mg per 5 mL oral suspension **only**); treatment duration variable: 10 to 28 days, some have suggested discontinuation of therapy 7 days after resolution of signs and symptoms of infection. **Note:** Recommended for patients with any of the following: moderate to severe infection, age <2 years, childcare attendance, or recent antibiotic treatment. (Wald 2013)

Urinary tract infections: Infants and Children 2 to 24 months: Oral: Immediate release: Amoxicillin 20 to 40 mg/kg/day in divided doses 3 times daily (using the 125 mg per 5 mL or 250 mg per 5 mL suspension); (maximum single dose: Amoxicillin 500 mg) (AAP 2011)

Renal Impairment

Adults: **Note:** Renally adjusted dose recommendations are based on the amoxicillin 250 mg/clavulanate 125 mg and amoxicillin 500 mg/clavulanate 125 mg tablets.

CrCl ≥30 mL/minute: No dosage adjustment necessary.

CrCl 10 to 30 mL/minute: 250 to 500 mg every 12 hours; do not use 875 mg tablet or extended-release tablets

CrCl <10 mL/minute: 250 to 500 mg every 24 hours; do not use 875 mg tablet or extended-release tablets

End-stage renal disease (ESRD) on hemodialysis: 250 to 500 mg amoxicillin every 24 hours; administer dose both during and after dialysis. Do not use 875 mg tablet or extended-release tablets.

Infants, Children, and Adolescents: There are no dosage adjustments provided in the manufacturer's labeling; however, the following adjustments have been recommended (Aronoff 2007):

Mild to moderate infection: Dosing based on amoxicillin 25 to 50 mg/kg/day divided every 8 hours:

GFR ≥30 mL/minute/1.73 m^2: No dosage adjustment necessary

GFR 10 to 29 mL/minute/1.73 m^2: Amoxicillin 8 to 20 mg/kg/dose every 12 hours

GFR <10 mL/minute/1.73 m^2: Amoxicillin 8 to 20 mg/kg/dose every 24 hours

End-stage renal disease (ESRD):

Hemodialysis: Amoxicillin 8 to 20 mg/kg/dose every 24 hours; give after dialysis

Peritoneal dialysis: Amoxicillin 8 to 20 mg/kg/dose every 24 hours

Severe infection (high dose): Dosing based on amoxicillin 80 to 90 mg/kg/day divided every 12 hours:

CrCl ≥30 mL/minute/1.73 m^2: No dosage adjustment necessary

CrCl 10 to 29 mL/minute/1.73 m^2: Amoxicillin 20 mg/kg/dose every 12 hours; do not use the 875 mg tablet

CrCl <10 mL/minute/1.73 m^2: Amoxicillin 20 mg/kg/dose every 24 hours; do not use the 875 mg tablet

End-stage renal disease (ESRD):

Hemodialysis: Amoxicillin 20 mg/kg/dose every 24 hours; give after dialysis; do not use the 875 mg tablet

Peritoneal dialysis: Amoxicillin 20 mg/kg/dose every 24 hours; do not use the 875 mg tablet

Hepatic Impairment There are no dosage adjustments provided in the manufacturer's labeling; use with caution. Use contraindicated in patients with a history of amoxicillin and clavulanate-associated hepatic dysfunction.

Mechanism of Action Clavulanic acid binds and inhibits beta-lactamases that inactivate amoxicillin resulting in amoxicillin having an expanded spectrum of activity. Amoxicillin inhibits bacterial cell wall synthesis by binding to one or more of the penicillin-binding proteins (PBPs) which in turn inhibits the final transpeptidation step of peptidoglycan synthesis in bacterial cell walls, thus inhibiting cell wall biosynthesis. Bacteria eventually lyse due to ongoing activity of cell wall autolytic enzymes (autolysins and murein hydrolases) while cell wall assembly is arrested.

Contraindications

Hypersensitivity to amoxicillin, clavulanic acid, other beta-lactam antibacterial drugs (eg, penicillins, cephalosporins), or any component of the formulation; history of cholestatic jaundice or hepatic dysfunction with amoxicillin/clavulanate potassium therapy

Augmentin XR: Additional contraindications: Severe renal impairment (creatinine clearance <30 mL/minute) and hemodialysis patients

Canadian labeling: Additional contraindications (not in US labeling): Suspected or confirmed mononucleosis

Warnings/Precautions Hypersensitivity reactions, including anaphylaxis (some fatal), have been reported. Prolonged use may result in fungal or bacterial superinfection, including *C. difficile*-associated diarrhea (CDAD) and pseudomembranous colitis; CDAD has been observed >2 months postantibiotic treatment. Although rarely fatal, hepatic dysfunction (eg, cholestatic jaundice, hepatitis) has been reported. Patients at highest risk include those with serious underlying disease or concomitant medications. Hepatic toxicity is usually reversible. Monitor liver function tests at regular intervals in patients with hepatic impairment. High percentage of patients with infectious mononucleosis have developed rash during therapy; ampicillin class antibiotics not recommended in these patients. Incidence of diarrhea is higher than with amoxicillin alone. Due to differing content of clavulanic acid, not all formulations are interchangeable; use of an inappropriate product for a specific dosage could result in either diarrhea (which may be severe) or subtherapeutic clavulanic acid concentrations leading to decreased clinical efficacy. Low incidence of cross-allergy with cephalosporins exists. Monitor renal, hepatic, and hematopoietic function if therapy extends beyond approved duration times. Some products contain phenylalanine. Potentially significant drug-drug interactions may exist, requiring dose or frequency adjustment, additional monitoring, and/or selection of alternative therapy.

Drug Interactions

Metabolism/Transport Effects None known.

Avoid Concomitant Use

Avoid concomitant use of Amoxicillin and Clavulanate with any of the following: BCG (Intravesical); Cholera Vaccine

Increased Effect/Toxicity

Amoxicillin and Clavulanate may increase the levels/effects of: Methotrexate; Vitamin K Antagonists

The levels/effects of Amoxicillin and Clavulanate may be increased by: Allopurinol; Probenecid

Decreased Effect

Amoxicillin and Clavulanate may decrease the levels/effects of: BCG (Intravesical); BCG Vaccine (Immunization); Cholera Vaccine; Lactobacillus and Estriol; Mycophenolate; Sodium Picosulfate; Typhoid Vaccine

The levels/effects of Amoxicillin and Clavulanate may be decreased by: Tetracycline Derivatives

Dietary Considerations May be taken with meals or on an empty stomach; take with meals to increase absorption and decrease GI upset; may mix with milk, formula, or juice. Extended release tablets should be taken with food. Some products may contain sodium. Some products contain phenylalanine; if you have phenylketonuria or PKU, avoid use. All dosage forms contain potassium.

Pharmacodynamics/Kinetics

Half-life Elimination Clavulanic acid: 1 hour

Time to Peak Clavulanic acid: Serum: 1.5 hours

Pregnancy Risk Factor B

Pregnancy Considerations Adverse events have not been observed in animal reproduction studies. Both amoxicillin and clavulanic acid cross the placenta. Maternal use of amoxicillin/clavulanate has generally not resulted in an increased risk of birth defects. A possible increased risk of necrotizing enterocolitis in neonates or bowel disorders in children exposed to amoxicillin/clavulanate in utero has been observed. In women with acute infections during pregnancy, amoxicillin/clavulanate may be given if an antibiotic is required and appropriate based on bacterial sensitivity; however, use is not recommended in the management of preterm premature rupture of membranes. Oral ampicillin-class antibiotics are poorly absorbed during labor.

Breastfeeding Considerations Amoxicillin is excreted in breast milk following administration amoxicillin/clavulanate (Weber 1984).

The relative infant dose (RID) of amoxicillin following administration of amoxicillin/clavulanate is 0.02% to 0.07% when calculated using the highest average breast milk concentration located and compared to an infant therapeutic dose of 25 to 90 mg/kg/day. In general, breastfeeding is considered acceptable when the RID is <10%; when an RID is >25% breastfeeding should generally be avoided (Anderson 2016; Ito 2000). Using the highest average milk concentration (0.12 mcg/mL), the estimated daily infant dose via breast milk is 0.018 mg/kg/day. This milk concentration was obtained 4 to 6 hours following maternal administration of oral amoxicillin/clavulanate 250 mg/125 mg (Takase 1982).

Constipation, diarrhea, restlessness, and rash have been reported in breastfeeding infants exposed to amoxicillin and clavulanate; reversible elevations in AST and ALT have been noted in one infant (Benyami 2005). The manufacturer warns of the potential for allergic sensitization in the infant. In general, antibiotics that are present in breast milk may cause nondose-related modification of bowel flora. Monitor infants for GI disturbances, such as thrush and diarrhea (WHO 2002).

Although the manufacturer recommends that caution be exercised when administering amoxicillin and clavulanate to breastfeeding women, amoxicillin/clavulanate is considered compatible with breastfeeding when used in usual recommended doses (WHO 2002).

Dosage Forms

Powder for suspension, oral:

Augmentin:

125: Amoxicillin 125 mg and clavulanate potassium 31.25 mg per 5 mL

250: Amoxicillin 250 mg and clavulanate potassium 62.5 mg per 5 mL

Augmentin ES-600:

600: Amoxicillin 600 mg and clavulanate potassium 42.9 mg per 5 mL (75 mL, 125 mL, 200 mL) [contains phenylalanine 7 mg/5 mL, potassium 0.23 mEq/5 mL; strawberry cream flavor]

Generic: 200: Amoxicillin 200 mg and clavulanate potassium 28.5 mg per 5 mL; 250: Amoxicillin 250 mg and clavulanate potassium 62.5 mg per 5 mL; 400: Amoxicillin 400 mg and clavulanate potassium 57 mg per 5 mL; 600: Amoxicillin 600 mg and clavulanate potassium 42.9 mg per 5 mL

Tablet, oral:

Augmentin:

500: Amoxicillin 500 mg and clavulanate potassium 125 mg

875: Amoxicillin 875 mg and clavulanate potassium 125 mg

Generic: 250: Amoxicillin 250 mg and clavulanate potassium 125 mg; 500: Amoxicillin 500 mg and clavulanate potassium 125 mg; 875: Amoxicillin 875 mg and clavulanate potassium 125 mg

Tablet, chewable, oral:

Generic: 200: Amoxicillin 200 mg and clavulanate potassium 28.5 mg; 400: Amoxicillin 400 mg and clavulanate potassium 57 mg

Tablet, extended release, oral:

Augmentin XR: 1000: Amoxicillin 1000 mg and clavulanate acid 62.5 mg

Generic: 1000: Amoxicillin 1000 mg and clavulanate acid 62.5 mg

Dosage Forms: Canada Note: Also refer to Dosage Forms.

Powder for suspension, oral:

Clavulin:

125: Amoxicillin 125 mg and clavulanate potassium 31.25 mg per 5 mL

200: Amoxicillin 200 mg and clavulanate potassium 28.5 mg per 5 mL

250: Amoxicillin 250 mg and clavulanate potassium 62.5 mg per 5 mL

400: Amoxicillin 400 mg and clavulanate potassium 57 mg per 5 mL

Tablet, oral:

Clavulin:

500: Amoxicillin 500 mg and clavulanate potassium 125 mg

875: Amoxicillin 875 mg and clavulanate potassium 125 mg

Dental Comment In maxillary sinus, anterior nasal cavity, and deep neck infections, beta-lactamase-producing staphylococci and beta-lactamase-producing *Bacteroides* usually are present. In these situations, antibiotics that resist the beta-lactamase enzyme are indicated. Amoxicillin and clavulanic acid is administered orally for moderate infections. Ampicillin sodium and sulbactam sodium (Unasyn®) is administered parenterally for more severe infections.

Amphetamine (am FET a meen)

Related Information

Dentin Hypersensitivity, Acid Erosion, High Caries Index, Management of Alveolar Osteitis, and Xerostomia *on page 1857*

Management of the Chemically Dependent Patient *on page 1821*

Brand Names: US Adzenys XR-ODT; Dyanavel XR; Evekeo

Generic Availability (US) No

Pharmacologic Category Central Nervous System Stimulant

Use

Attention-deficit/hyperactivity disorder: Treatment of attention deficit hyperactivity disorder (ADHD)

Exogenous obesity (immediate-release tablet only): Short-term treatment of exogenous obesity as an adjunct to caloric restriction for patients refractory to alternative therapy (eg, repeated diets, group programs, other drugs)

Narcolepsy (immediate-release tablet only): Treatment of narcolepsy

Local Anesthetic/Vasoconstrictor Precautions Use vasoconstrictor with caution in patients taking amphetamine. Amphetamines enhance the sympathomimetic response of epinephrine and norepinephrine leading to potential hypertension and cardiotoxicity.

Effects on Dental Treatment Key adverse event(s) related to dental treatment: Amphetamines cause tachycardia, increases in blood pressure, and palpitations. Consider monitoring blood pressure prior to using local anesthetic with a vasoconstrictor. Symptoms associated with bruxism have been observed in some patients.

Effects on Bleeding No information available to require special precautions

Adverse Reactions As reported in children and adults unless otherwise noted.

1% to 10%:
Gastrointestinal: Upper abdominal pain (children: 4%)
Respiratory: Allergic rhinitis (children: 4%), epistaxis (children: 4%)
Frequency not defined:
Cardiovascular: Increased blood pressure, palpitations, Raynaud's phenomenon, tachycardia
Central nervous system: Dizziness, dysphoria, euphoria, exacerbation of Gilles de la Tourette's syndrome, headache, insomnia, overstimulation, psychosis, restlessness, tics (including exacerbation), vocal tics (exacerbation)
Dermatologic: Urticaria
Endocrine & metabolic: Change in libido, growth suppression (children), weight loss (children)
Gastrointestinal: Anorexia, constipation, diarrhea, dysgeusia, gastrointestinal disease, vomiting, xerostomia
Genitourinary: Erectile dysfunction (frequent or prolonged erections), impotence
Neuromuscular & skeletal: Dyskinesia, rhabdomyolysis, tremor
<1%, postmarketing, and/or case reports: Mania, peripheral vascular disease

Dosing

Adult & Geriatric Note: Administer at the lowest effective dose.

Attention-deficit/hyperactivity disorder:
Extended-release orally disintegrating tablet: Oral: 12.5 mg once daily.
Conversion: Do not substitute extended-release formulation for other amphetamine formulations on a mg-per-mg basis.
Converting from Adderall XR to Adzenys XR-ODT: Initial dose of Adzenys XR-ODT should be determined by the current dose of Adderall XR as follows:
Current Adderall XR dose of 5 mg once daily: Initial Adzenys XR-ODT dose of 3.1 mg once daily
Current Adderall XR dose of 10 mg once daily: Initial Adzenys XR-ODT dose of 6.3 mg once daily
Current Adderall XR dose of 15 mg once daily: Initial Adzenys XR-ODT dose of 9.4 mg once daily
Current Adderall XR dose of 20 mg once daily: Initial Adzenys XR-ODT dose of 12.5 mg once daily
Current Adderall XR dose of 25 mg once daily: Initial Adzenys XR-ODT dose of 15.7 mg once daily
Current Adderall XR dose of 30 mg once daily: Initial Adzenys XR-ODT dose of 18.8 mg once daily
Converting from all other amphetamine formulations to Adzenys XR-ODT: Discontinue that treatment and titrate Adzenys XR-ODT as per the recommended dosing schedule.
Extended-release suspension: Oral: Initial: 2.5 or 5 mg once daily; may increase in 2.5 to 10 mg/day increments every 4 to 7 days until optimal response is obtained (maximum: 20 mg/day).
Note: Do not substitute extended-release formulation for other amphetamine products on a mg-per-mg basis since base composition and pharmacokinetic profiles are not similar. If switching from other amphetamine products, discontinue that treatment, and titrate as per the recommended dosing schedule.

Exogenous obesity: Immediate-release tablet: Oral: Up to 30 mg daily in divided doses (5 to 10 mg per dose)
Narcolepsy: Immediate-release tablet: Oral: Initial: 10 mg once daily; increase daily dose in 10 mg increments at weekly intervals until optimal response is obtained; usual dosage range: 5 to 60 mg daily in divided doses

Pediatric Note: Administer at the lowest effective dose.

Attention-deficit/hyperactivity disorder:
Extended-release orally disintegrating tablet:
Children ≥6 years: Oral: Initial: 6.3 mg once daily; may increase in 3.1 mg or 6.3 mg increments every week until optimal response is obtained (maximum: 6 to 12 years: 18.8 mg/day).
Adolescents: Oral: Initial: 6.3 mg once daily; may increase in 3.1 mg or 6.3 mg increments every week until optimal response is obtained (maximum: 12.5 mg/day).
Conversion: Note: Do not substitute extended-release formulation for other amphetamine formulations on a mg-per-mg basis.
Converting from Adderall XR to Adzenys XR-ODT: Initial dose of Adzenys XR-ODT should be determined by the current dose of Adderall XR as follows:
Current Adderall XR dose of 5 mg once daily: Initial Adzenys XR-ODT dose of 3.1 mg once daily
Current Adderall XR dose of 10 mg once daily: Initial Adzenys XR-ODT dose of 6.3 mg once daily
Current Adderall XR dose of 15 mg once daily: Initial Adzenys XR-ODT dose of 9.4 mg once daily
Current Adderall XR dose of 20 mg once daily: Initial Adzenys XR-ODT dose of 12.5 mg once daily
Current Adderall XR dose of 25 mg once daily: Initial Adzenys XR-ODT dose of 15.7 mg once daily
Current Adderall XR dose of 30 mg once daily: Initial Adzenys XR-ODT dose of 18.8 mg once daily
Converting from all other amphetamine formulations to Adzenys XR-ODT: Discontinue that treatment and titrate Adzenys XR-ODT as per the recommended dosing schedule.
Extended-release suspension: Children ≥6 years and Adolescents: Oral: Refer to adult dosing.
Immediate-release tablet:
Children 3 to 5 years: Oral: Initial: 2.5 mg once daily; increase daily dose in 2.5 mg increments at weekly intervals until optimal response is obtained. Only in rare cases will it be necessary to exceed 40 mg daily.
Children ≥6 years and Adolescents: Oral: Initial: 5 mg once or twice daily; increase daily dose in 5 mg increments at weekly intervals until optimal response is obtained. Only in rare cases will it be necessary to exceed 40 mg daily.

Exogenous obesity: Immediate-release tablet: Children ≥12 years and Adolescents: Oral: Up to 30 mg daily in divided doses (5 to 10 mg per dose)
Narcolepsy: Immediate-release tablet:
Children 6 to 12 years: Oral: Initial: 5 mg once daily; increase daily dose in 5 mg increments at weekly intervals until optimal response is obtained; usual dosage range: 5 to 60 mg daily in divided doses

Children ≥12 years and Adolescents: Oral: Initial: 10 mg once daily; increase daily dose in 10 mg increments at weekly intervals until optimal response is obtained; usual dosage range: 5 to 60 mg daily in divided doses

Renal Impairment There are no dosage adjustments provided in the manufacturer's labeling.

Hepatic Impairment There are no dosage adjustments provided in the manufacturer's labeling.

Mechanism of Action Amphetamines are noncatecholamine sympathomimetic amines that promote release of catecholamines (primarily dopamine and norepinephrine) from their storage sites in the presynaptic nerve terminals. A less significant mechanism may include their ability to block the reuptake of catecholamines by competitive inhibition. The anorexigenic effect is probably secondary to the CNS-stimulating effect; the site of action is probably the hypothalamic feeding center.

Contraindications

Immediate release: Hypersensitivity or idiosyncrasy to amphetamine, other sympathomimetic amines, or any component of the formulation; advanced arteriosclerosis; symptomatic cardiovascular disease; moderate to severe hypertension; hyperthyroidism; agitated states; history of drug abuse; use during or within 14 days following MAO inhibitor.

Extended release: Hypersensitivity to amphetamine or any component of the formulation, anaphylactic reactions and angioedema have been reported; use during or within 14 days following MAO inhibitor.

Documentation of allergenic cross-reactivity for amphetamines is limited. However, because of similarities in chemical structure and/or pharmacologic actions, the possibility of cross-sensitivity cannot be ruled out with certainty.

Warnings/Precautions **[US Boxed Warning]: Potential for drug abuse and dependency exists; prolonged use may lead to drug dependency and must be avoided. Assess the risk for abuse prior to prescribing, and monitor for signs of abuse and dependence while on therapy. Consider the possibility of patients obtaining amphetamines for non-therapeutic use or distribution to others; prescribe sparingly.** Use of immediate-release formulation is contraindicated in patients with history of drug abuse. Write prescriptions for the smallest quantity consistent with good patient care to minimize possibility of overdose.

[US Boxed Warning]: Misuse may cause serious cardiovascular events including sudden death. Adverse effects have been reported at usual doses in patients with preexisting structural cardiac abnormalities or other serious heart problems (sudden death in children and adolescents; sudden death, stroke, and MI in adults). These products should be avoided in the patients with known serious structural cardiac abnormalities, cardiomyopathy, serious heart rhythm abnormalities, coronary artery disease, or other serious cardiac problems that could increase the risk of sudden death that these conditions alone carry. Patients should be carefully evaluated for cardiac disease prior to initiation of therapy. Patients who develop symptoms such as exertional chest pain, unexplained syncope, or other symptoms suggestive of cardiac disease during treatment should undergo a prompt cardiac evaluation. Hypertension and tachycardia may occur; monitor blood pressure and heart rate in all patients. May impair the ability to engage in potentially hazardous activities; patients must be cautioned about performing tasks that require mental alertness (eg, operating machinery or driving).

Stimulants are associated with peripheral vasculopathy, including Raynaud's phenomenon; signs/symptoms are usually mild and intermittent, and generally improve with dose reduction or discontinuation. Digital ulceration and/or soft tissue breakdown have been observed rarely; monitor for digital changes during therapy and seek further evaluation (eg, rheumatology) if necessary (Syed 2008). Difficulty in accommodation and blurred vision has been reported with the use of stimulants. Use with caution in patients with hypertension and other cardiovascular conditions that might be exacerbated by increases in blood pressure or heart rate (eg, preexisting hypertension, heart failure, recent myocardial infarction, ventricular arrhythmia). Use of immediate-release formulation is contraindicated in patients with advanced arteriosclerosis, moderate to severe hypertension, or symptomatic cardiovascular disease. Use with caution in patients with preexisting psychosis or bipolar disorder; may exacerbate symptoms of behavior and thought disorder or induce mixed/manic episode, respectively. Screen patients with comorbid depressive symptoms prior to initiating treatment to determine if they are at risk for bipolar disorder, including a family history of suicide, bipolar disorder, and depression. May be associated with aggressive behavior or hostility (causal relationship not established); monitor for development or worsening of these behaviors. New-onset psychosis or mania may also occur with stimulant use; consider discontinuing therapy if hallucinations, delusional thinking or mania occurs. Limited information exists regarding amphetamine use in seizure disorder (Cortese 2013). Use with caution in patients with a history of seizure disorder; may lower seizure threshold leading to new onset or breakthrough seizure activity. Use with caution in patients with Tourette syndrome or other tic disorders. Stimulants may exacerbate tics (motor and phonic) and Tourette syndrome; however, evidence demonstrating increased tics is limited. Evaluate for tics and Tourette syndrome prior to therapy initiation (AACAP [Murphy 2013]; Pliszka 2007). Potentially significant drug-drug interactions may exist, requiring dose or frequency adjustment, additional monitoring, and/or selection of alternative therapy. Potentially life-threatening serotonin syndrome (SS) may occur when amphetamine is used in combination with other serotonergic agents (eg, selective serotonin reuptake inhibitors, serotonin norepinephrine reuptake inhibitors, triptans, tricyclic antidepressants, fentanyl, lithium, tramadol, buspirone, St. John's wort, tryptophan), agents that impair metabolism of serotonin (eg, monoamine oxidase inhibitors) or CYP2D6 inhibitors that impair metabolism of amphetamine. Concomitant use with monoamine oxidase inhibitors is contraindicated. If concomitant use of amphetamine with serotonergic drugs or CYP2D6 inhibitors is indicated, initiate amphetamine at a low dose and monitor patient closely for signs and symptoms of SS. Discontinue treatment (and any concomitant serotonergic agent) immediately if signs/symptoms arise. Angioedema and anaphylactic reactions have been reported in patients with hypersensitivity reactions.

Appetite suppression may occur in children; monitor weight during therapy. Use of stimulants has been associated with weight loss and slowing of growth rate; monitor growth rate and weight during treatment.

Treatment interruption may be necessary in patients who are not increasing in height or gaining weight as expected.

Abrupt discontinuation following high doses or for prolonged periods may result in symptoms for withdrawal.

Drug Interactions

Metabolism/Transport Effects **Substrate** of CYP2D6 (minor); **Note:** Assignment of Major/Minor substrate status based on clinically relevant drug interaction potential

Avoid Concomitant Use

Avoid concomitant use of Amphetamine with any of the following: Acebrophylline; Iobenguane I 123; MAO Inhibitors

Increased Effect/Toxicity

Amphetamine may increase the levels/effects of: Analgesics (Opioid); Doxofylline; Iohexol; Iomeprol; Iopamidol; Sympathomimetics

The levels/effects of Amphetamine may be increased by: Acebrophylline; Alkalinizing Agents; Antacids; AtoMOXetine; Cannabinoid-Containing Products; Carbonic Anhydrase Inhibitors; Cocaine; Linezolid; MAO Inhibitors; Proton Pump Inhibitors; Tedizolid; Tricyclic Antidepressants

Decreased Effect

Amphetamine may decrease the levels/effects of: Antihistamines; Antihypertensive Agents; Ethosuximide; Iobenguane I 123; Ioflupane I 123; PHENobarbital; Phenytoin

The levels/effects of Amphetamine may be decreased by: Ammonium Chloride; Antipsychotic Agents; Ascorbic Acid; Gastrointestinal Acidifying Agents; Lithium; Methenamine; Multivitamins/Fluoride (with ADE); Multivitamins/Minerals (with ADEK, Folate, Iron); Multivitamins/Minerals (with AE, No Iron); Urinary Acidifying Agents

Food Interactions Amphetamine serum levels may be reduced if taken with acidic food, juices, or vitamin C. Management: Monitor response when taken concurrently.

Pharmacodynamics/Kinetics

Half-life Elimination Oral:

Adzenys XR-ODT:

Children 6 to 12 years: d-amphetamine 9 to 10 hours (mean) and l-amphetamine 10 to 11 hours (mean)

Adults: d-amphetamine 11 hours (mean) and l-amphetamine 14 hours (mean)

Dyanavel XR:

Children: d-amphetamine 10.43 ± 2.01 hours and l-amphetamine 12.14 ± 3.15 hours

Adults: d-amphetamine 12.36 ± 2.95 hours and l-amphetamine 15.12 ± 4.4 hours

Evekeo: 12 hours (de la Torre 2004)

Time to Peak Oral:

Adzenys XR-ODT: Median time d-amphetamine 5 hours (7 hours with food) and l-amphetamine 5.25 hours (7.75 hours with food)

Dyanavel XR:

Children: Median time d-amphetamine 3.9 hours and l-amphetamine 4.5 hours

Adults: 4 (2 to 7) hours

Evekeo: Serum: Within 4 hours (de la Torre 2004)

Pregnancy Risk Factor C

Pregnancy Considerations Adverse effects have been observed in animal reproduction studies. The majority of human data are based on illicit amphetamine/methamphetamine exposure and not from therapeutic maternal use (Golub, 2005). Use of amphetamines during pregnancy may lead to an increased risk of premature birth and low birth weight; newborns may experience symptoms of withdrawal. Behavioral problems may also occur later in childhood (LaGasse, 2012).

Breastfeeding Considerations Amphetamine is excreted in breast milk. The majority of human data are based on illicit amphetamine/methamphetamine exposure and not from therapeutic maternal use (Golub, 2005). Increased irritability, agitation, and crying have been reported in nursing infants (ACOG, 2011). breastfeeding is not recommended by the manufacturer.

Controlled Substance C-II

Dosage Forms

Suspension Extended Release, Oral:

Dyanavel XR: 2.5 mg/mL (464 mL)

Tablet, Oral:

Evekeo: 5 mg, 10 mg

Tablet Extended Release Dispersible, Oral:

Adzenys XR-ODT: 3.1 mg, 6.3 mg, 9.4 mg, 12.5 mg, 15.7 mg, 18.8 mg

Amphotericin B Cholesteryl Sulfate Complex

(am foe TER i sin bee kole LES te ril SUL fate KOM plecks)

Brand Names: US Amphotec [DSC]

Brand Names: Canada Amphotec

Pharmacologic Category Antifungal Agent, Parenteral

Use Treatment of invasive aspergillosis in patients who have failed amphotericin B deoxycholate treatment, or who have renal impairment or experience unacceptable toxicity which precludes treatment with amphotericin B deoxycholate in effective doses.

Local Anesthetic/Vasoconstrictor Precautions No information available to require special precautions

Effects on Dental Treatment No significant effects or complications reported

Effects on Bleeding No information available to require special precautions

Adverse Reactions Amphotericin B colloidal dispersion has an improved therapeutic index compared to conventional amphotericin B, and has been used safely in patients with amphotericin B-related nephrotoxicity; however, continued decline of renal function has occurred in some patients.

>10%:

Cardiovascular: Hypotension, tachycardia

Central nervous system: Chills

Endocrine & metabolic: Hypokalemia

Gastrointestinal: Vomiting

Hepatic: Hyperbilirubinemia

Renal: Increased serum creatinine

Miscellaneous: Fever

5% to 10%:

Cardiovascular: Chest pain, facial edema, hypertension

Central nervous system: Abnormality in thinking, drowsiness, headache, insomnia

Dermatologic: Diaphoresis, pruritus, skin rash

Endocrine & metabolic: Hyperglycemia, hypocalcemia, hypomagnesemia, hypophosphatemia

Gastrointestinal: Abdominal pain, diarrhea, enlargement of abdomen, hematemesis, nausea, stomatitis, xerostomia

Hematologic & oncologic: Anemia, hemorrhage, thrombocytopenia

Hepatic: Abnormal hepatic function tests, increased serum alkaline phosphatase, jaundice
Neuromuscular & skeletal: Back pain, muscle rigidity, tremor
Respiratory: Dyspnea, epistaxis, hypoxia, increased cough, rhinitis

<5%, postmarketing, and/or case reports: Acidosis, atrial arrhythmia, cardiac arrest, cardiac failure, gastrointestinal hemorrhage, hepatic failure, injection site reaction, oliguria, pain at injection site, pleural effusion, renal failure, seizure, syncope, ventricular arrhythmia

General Dosage Range IV: *Children and Adults:* 3-4 mg/kg/day

Mechanism of Action Binds to ergosterol altering cell membrane permeability in susceptible fungi and causing leakage of cell components with subsequent cell death. Proposed mechanism suggests that amphotericin causes an oxidation-dependent stimulation of macrophages (Lyman, 1992).

Pharmacodynamics/Kinetics

Half-life Elimination ~28 hours; prolonged with higher doses

Pregnancy Risk Factor B

Pregnancy Considerations Adverse events were not observed in animal reproduction studies. Amphotericin crosses the placenta and enters the fetal circulation. Amphotericin B is recommended for the treatment of serious systemic fungal diseases in pregnant women; refer to current guidelines (IDSA [Pappas 2016]; King 1998; Pilmis 2015).

Amphotericin B (Conventional)

(am foe TER i sin bee con VEN sha nal)

Related Information

Fungal Infections *on page 1847*

Brand Names: Canada Fungizone

Pharmacologic Category Antifungal Agent, Parenteral

Use

Life-threatening fungal infections: Treatment of patients with progressive, potentially life-threatening fungal infections: Aspergillosis, cryptococcosis (torulosis), North American blastomycosis, systemic candidiasis, coccidioidomycosis, histoplasmosis, zygomycosis (including mucormycosis due to susceptible species of the genera *Absidia, Mucor,* and *Rhizopus*), and infections due to related susceptible species of *Conidiobolus, Basidiobolus,* and sporotrichosis.

Leishmaniasis: May be useful in the treatment of American mucocutaneous leishmaniasis, but it is not the drug of choice as primary therapy.

Local Anesthetic/Vasoconstrictor Precautions No information available to require special precautions

Effects on Dental Treatment No significant effects or complications reported

Effects on Bleeding No information available to require special precautions

Adverse Reactions

Systemic:

>10%:

Cardiovascular: Hypotension
Central nervous system: Chills, headache (less frequent with I.T.), malaise, pain (less frequent with I.T.)
Endocrine & metabolic: Hypokalemia, hypomagnesemia
Gastrointestinal: Anorexia, diarrhea, epigastric pain, heartburn, nausea (less frequent with I.T.), stomach cramps, vomiting (less frequent with I.T.)
Hematologic & oncologic: Anemia (normochromic-normocytic)
Local: Pain at injection site (with or without phlebitis or thrombophlebitis [incidence may increase with peripheral infusion of admixtures])
Renal: Renal function abnormality (including azotemia, renal tubular acidosis, nephrocalcinosis [>0.1 mg/mL]), renal insufficiency
Respiratory: Tachypnea
Miscellaneous: Fever

1% to 10%:

Cardiovascular: Flushing, hypertension
Central nervous system: Arachnoiditis, delirium, neuralgia (lumbar; especially with intrathecal therapy), paresthesia (especially with intrathecal therapy)
Genitourinary: Urinary retention
Hematologic & oncologic: Leukocytosis

<1% (Limited to important or life-threatening): Acute hepatic failure, agranulocytosis, anuria, blood coagulation disorder, bone marrow depression, bronchospasm, cardiac arrest, cardiac arrhythmia, cardiac failure, convulsions, diplopia, dyspnea, eosinophilia, exfoliation of skin, hearing loss, hemorrhagic gastroenteritis, hepatitis, hypersensitivity pneumonitis, increased liver enzymes, jaundice, leukoencephalopathy, leukopenia, maculopapular rash, melena, nephrogenic diabetes insipidus, oliguria, peripheral neuropathy, pruritus, pulmonary edema, renal failure, renal tubular acidosis, shock, Stevens-Johnson syndrome, thrombocytopenia, tinnitus, toxic epidermal necrolysis, ventricular fibrillation, vertigo (transient), visual disturbance, wheezing

General Dosage Range Dosage adjustment recommended in patients who develop toxicities

IV:

Infants and Children: Test dose: 0.1 mg/kg/dose (maximum: 1 mg); Maintenance: 0.25 to 1 mg/kg/day given once daily; 1 to 1.5 mg/kg every other day may be given once therapy is established (maximum: 1.5 to 4 g cumulative dose)

Adults: Test dose: 1 mg infused; Maintenance: 0.3 to 1.5 mg/kg/day given once daily; 1 to 1.5 mg/kg every other day may be given once therapy is established (maximum: 1.5 mg/kg/day)

Mechanism of Action Binds to ergosterol altering cell membrane permeability in susceptible fungi and causing leakage of cell components with subsequent cell death. Proposed mechanism suggests that amphotericin causes an oxidation-dependent stimulation of macrophages (Lyman 1992).

Pharmacodynamics/Kinetics

Half-life Elimination

Premature neonates (GA: 27.4 ± 5 weeks): 14.8 hours (range: 5 to 82 hours) (Baley 1990)
Infants and Children (4 months to 14 years): 18.1 ± 6.6 hours (range: 11.9 to 40.3 hours) (Benson 1989)
Adults: Biphasic: Initial: 15 to 48 hours; Terminal: 15 days

Time to Peak Within 1 hour following a 4- to 6-hour dose

Pregnancy Risk Factor B

Pregnancy Considerations Adverse events were not observed in animal reproduction studies. Amphotericin crosses the placenta and enters the fetal circulation. Amphotericin B is recommended for the treatment of serious systemic fungal diseases in pregnant women.

Refer to current guidelines (IDSA [Pappas 2016]; King 1998; Pilmis 2015).

Amphotericin B (Lipid Complex)

(am foe TER i sin bee LIP id KOM pleks)

Brand Names: US Abelcet

Brand Names: Canada Abelcet

Pharmacologic Category Antifungal Agent, Parenteral

Use Treatment of invasive fungal infection in patients who are refractory to or intolerant of conventional amphotericin B (amphotericin B deoxycholate) therapy

Local Anesthetic/Vasoconstrictor Precautions No information available to require special precautions

Effects on Dental Treatment No significant effects or complications reported

Effects on Bleeding No information available to require special precautions

Adverse Reactions Nephrotoxicity and infusion-related hyperpyrexia, rigor, and chilling are reduced relative to amphotericin deoxycholate.

>10%:

Central nervous system: Chills (18%)

Renal: Increased serum creatinine (11%)

Miscellaneous: Fever (14%), multi-organ failure (11%)

1% to 10%:

Cardiovascular: Hypotension (8%), cardiac arrest (6%), hypertension (5%), chest pain (3%)

Central nervous system: Headache (6%), pain (5%)

Dermatologic: Skin rash (4%)

Endocrine & metabolic: Hypokalemia (5%)

Gastrointestinal: Nausea (9%), vomiting (8%), diarrhea (6%), abdominal pain (4%), gastrointestinal hemorrhage (4%)

Hematologic & oncologic: Thrombocytopenia (5%), anemia (4%), leukopenia (4%)

Hepatic: Hyperbilirubinemia (4%)

Infection: Sepsis (7%), infection (5%)

Renal: Renal failure (5%)

Respiratory: Respiratory failure (8%), dyspnea (6%), respiratory tract disease (4%)

<1%, postmarketing, and/or case reports: Acute hepatic failure, anaphylactoid reaction, anuria, asthma, blood coagulation disorder, brain disease, bronchospasm, cardiac arrhythmia, cardiomyopathy, cerebrovascular accident, cholangitis, cholecystitis, deafness, dysuria, eosinophilia, erythema multiforme, exfoliative dermatitis, extrapyramidal reaction, hearing loss, hematologic disease, hemoptysis, hepatic veno-occlusive disease, hepatitis, hepatomegaly, hepatotoxicity, hypercalcemia, hyperkalemia, hypersensitivity reaction, hypocalcemia, hypomagnesemia, increased blood urea nitrogen, increased serum transaminases, injection site reaction, jaundice, leukocytosis, myasthenia, myocardial infarction, oliguria, peripheral neuropathy, pleural effusion, pulmonary edema, pulmonary embolism, renal insufficiency, renal tubular acidosis, seizure, shock, tachycardia, thrombophlebitis, ventricular fibrillation, vertigo (transient), visual impairment

General Dosage Range IV: *Children and Adults:* 5 mg/kg once daily

Mechanism of Action Binds to ergosterol altering cell membrane permeability in susceptible fungi and causing leakage of cell components with subsequent cell death. Proposed mechanism suggests that amphotericin causes an oxidation-dependent stimulation of macrophages.

Pharmacodynamics/Kinetics

Half-life Elimination 173 hours following multiple doses

Pregnancy Risk Factor B

Pregnancy Considerations Adverse events were not observed in animal reproduction studies. Amphotericin crosses the placenta and enters the fetal circulation. Amphotericin B is recommended for the treatment of serious, systemic fungal diseases in pregnant women, refer to current guidelines (IDSA [Pappas 2016]; King 1998; Pilmus 2015).

Amphotericin B (Liposomal)

(am foe TER i sin bee lye po SO mal)

Brand Names: US AmBisome

Brand Names: Canada AmBisome

Pharmacologic Category Antifungal Agent, Parenteral

Use

Cryptococcal meningitis in HIV-infected patients: Treatment of cryptococcal meningitis in HIV-infected patients.

Fungal infections, empiric therapy: Empiric treatment in febrile neutropenic patients with presumed fungal infection.

Fungal infections, systemic therapy: Treatment of systemic infections caused by *Aspergillus* sp, *Candida* sp, and/or *Cryptococcus* sp in patients refractory to conventional amphotericin B deoxycholate therapy or when renal impairment or unacceptable toxicity precludes the use of the deoxycholate formulation.

Leishmaniasis (visceral): Treatment of visceral leishmaniasis.

Local Anesthetic/Vasoconstrictor Precautions No information available to require special precautions

Effects on Dental Treatment Key adverse event(s) related to dental treatment: Facial swelling, mucositis, stomatitis, and ulcerative stomatitis; Patients may experience orthostatic hypotension as they stand up after treatment; especially if lying in dental chair for extended periods of time. Use caution with sudden changes in position during and after dental treatment (see Dental Comment).

Effects on Bleeding No information available to require special precautions

Adverse Reactions Percentage of adverse reactions is dependent upon population studied and may vary with respect to premedications and underlying illness. Incidence of decreased renal function and infusion-related events are lower than rates observed with amphotericin B deoxycholate.

>10%:

Cardiovascular: Hypertension (8% to 20%), tachycardia (9% to 19%), peripheral edema (15%), edema (12% to 14%), hypotension (7% to 14%), chest pain (8% to 12%), localized phlebitis (9% to 11%)

Central nervous system: Chills (29% to 48%), insomnia (17% to 22%), headache (9% to 20%), pain (14%), anxiety (7% to 14%), confusion (9% to 13%)

Dermatologic: Skin rash (5% to 25%), pruritus (11%)

Endocrine & metabolic: Hypokalemia (31% to 51%), hypomagnesemia (15% to 50%), hyperglycemia (8% to 23%), hypocalcemia (5% to 18%), hyponatremia (9% to 12%), hypervolemia (8% to 12%)

Gastrointestinal: Nausea (16% to 40%), vomiting (11% to 32%), diarrhea (11% to 30%), abdominal pain (7% to 20%), constipation (15%), anorexia (10% to 14%)

Genitourinary: Nephrotoxicity (14% to 47%), hematuria (14%)

Hematologic & oncologic: Anemia (27% to 48%), leukopenia (15% to 17%), thrombocytopenia (6% to 13%)
Hepatic: Increased serum alkaline phosphatase (7% to 22%), hyperbilirubinemia (≤18%), increased serum ALT (15%), increased serum AST (13%), abnormal hepatic function tests (not specified) (4% to 13%)
Hypersensitivity: Transfusion reaction (9% to 18%)
Infection: Sepsis (7% to 14%), infection (11% to 13%)
Neuromuscular & skeletal: Weakness (6% to 13%), back pain (12%)
Renal: Increased serum creatinine (18% to 40%), increased blood urea nitrogen (7% to 21%)
Respiratory: Dyspnea (18% to 23%), pulmonary disease (14% to 18%), cough (2% to 18%), epistaxis (9% to 15%), pleural effusion (13%), rhinitis (11%)
Miscellaneous: Infusion related reactions (4% to 21%; fever [7% to 24%], chills [6% to 24%], vomiting [4% to 16%], nausea [8% to 14%], dyspnea [5% to 10%], tachycardia [2% to 10%], hypertension [2% to 9%], vasodilation [5%], hypotension [4%], hyperventilation [1%], hypoxia [≤1%])

2% to 10%:
Cardiovascular: Atrial fibrillation, bradycardia, cardiac arrest, cardiac arrhythmia, cardiomegaly, facial edema, flushing, heart valve disease, orthostatic hypotension, vascular disorder, vasodilatation
Central nervous system: Dizziness (7% to 9%), abnormality in thinking, agitation, coma, depression, drowsiness, dysesthesia, dystonia, hallucination, malaise, nervousness, paresthesia, rigors, seizure
Dermatologic: Diaphoresis (7%), alopecia, cellulitis, dermal ulcer, dermatological reaction, maculopapular rash, skin discoloration, urticaria, vesiculobullous dermatitis, xeroderma
Endocrine & metabolic: Hypernatremia (4%), acidosis, hyperchloremia, hyperkalemia, hypermagnesemia, hyperphosphatemia, hypophosphatemia, increased lactate dehydrogenase, increased nonprotein nitrogen
Gastrointestinal: Gastrointestinal hemorrhage (10%), aphthous stomatitis, dyspepsia, dysphagia, enlargement of abdomen, eructation, fecal incontinence, flatulence, gingival hemorrhage, hematemesis, hemorrhoids, hiccups, increased serum amylase, intestinal obstruction, mucositis, rectal disease, stomatitis, xerostomia
Genitourinary: Dysuria, toxic nephrosis, urinary incontence, vaginal hemorrhage
Hematologic & oncologic: Blood coagulation disorder, bruise, decreased prothrombin time, hemophthalmos, hemorrhage, hypoproteinemia, increased prothrombin time, oral hemorrhage, petechia, purpura
Hepatic: Hepatic injury, hepatic veno-occlusive disease, hepatomegaly
Hypersensitivity: Delayed hypersensitivity, hypersensitivity reaction
Immunologic: Graft versus host disease
Infection: Herpes simplex infection
Local: Inflammation at injection site
Neuromuscular & skeletal: Arthralgia, myalgia, neck pain, ostealgia, tremor
Ophthalmic: Conjunctivitis, dry eyes
Renal: Acute renal failure, renal failure, renal function abnormality
Respiratory: Hypoxia (6% to 8%), asthma, atelectasis, dry nose, flu-like symptoms, hemoptysis, hyperventilation, pharyngitis, pneumonia, pulmonary edema, respiratory alkalosis, respiratory failure, respiratory insufficiency, sinusitis
Miscellaneous: Procedural complication (8% to 10%)

Postmarketing and/or case reports: Agranulocytosis, angioedema, bronchospasm, cyanosis, erythema, hemorrhagic cystitis, hypoventilation, rhabdomyolysis

General Dosage Range IV: *Infants, Children, Adolescents, and Adults:* 3 to 6 mg/kg/day as a single daily dose (maximum: 6 mg/kg/day)

Mechanism of Action Binds to ergosterol altering cell membrane permeability in susceptible fungi and causing leakage of cell components with subsequent cell death. Proposed mechanism suggests that amphotericin causes an oxidation-dependent stimulation of macrophages (Lyman 1992).

Pharmacodynamics/Kinetics

Half-life Elimination 7 to 10 hours (following a single 24-hour dosing interval); Terminal half-life: 100 to 153 hours (following multiple dosing up to 49 days)

Pregnancy Risk Factor B

Pregnancy Considerations Adverse events were not observed in animal reproduction studies. Amphotericin crosses the placenta and enters the fetal circulation. Amphotericin B is recommended for the treatment of serious systemic fungal diseases in pregnant women; refer to current guidelines (IDSA [Pappas 2016]; King 1998; Pilmus 2015).

Dental Comment Amphotericin B, liposomal is a true single bilayer liposomal drug delivery system. Liposomes are closed, spherical vesicles created by mixing specific proportions of amphophilic substances such as phospholipids and cholesterol so that they arrange themselves into multiple concentric bilayer membranes when hydrated in aqueous solutions. Single bilayer liposomes are then formed by microemulsification of multilamellar vesicles using a homogenizer. Amphotericin B, liposomal consists of these unilamellar bilayer liposomes with amphotericin B intercalated within the membrane. Due to the nature and quantity of amphophilic substances used, and the lipophilic moiety in the amphotericin B molecule, the drug is an integral part of the overall structure of the amphotericin B liposomes. Amphotericin B, liposomal contains true liposomes that are <100 nm in diameter.

Ampicillin (am pi SIL in)

Related Information

Antibiotic Prophylaxis *on page 1812*

Brand Names: Canada Ampicillin for Injection; Apo-Ampi; Novo-Ampicillin; Nu-Ampi

Generic Availability (US) Yes

Pharmacologic Category Antibiotic, Penicillin

Dental Use IV or IM administration for the prevention of infective endocarditis in patients not allergic to penicillin and unable to take oral amoxicillin; IV or IM administration for prophylaxis in total joint replacement patients not allergic to penicillin and unable to take oral medications undergoing dental procedures

Use

Oral:

Genitourinary tract infections: Treatment of genitourinary tract infections caused by *Escherichia coli*, *Proteus mirabilis*, enterococci, *Shigella*, *Salmonella typhosa* and other *Salmonella*, and nonpenicillinase-producing *N. gonorrhoeae*. **Note:** Ampicillin is **not** recommended by the CDC as a first-line agent in the treatment of gonorrhea (CDC, 2010).

GI tract infections: Treatment of GI tract infections caused by *Shigella*, *S. typhosa* and other *Salmonella*, *E. coli*, *P. mirabilis*, and enterococci. **Note:** Ampicillin is not recommended as a first-line agent for Shigellosis, Salmonellosis (nontyphoid), or *Salmonella enterica* species (typhoid fever) due to development of resistance (CDC, 2014).

Respiratory tract infections: Treatment of respiratory tract infections caused by nonpenicillinase-producing *H. influenzae* and staphylococci, and streptococci, including *Streptococcus pneumoniae*.

Injection:

Bacterial meningitis: Treatment of bacterial meningitis caused by *E. coli*, group B streptococci, and other gram-negative bacteria (*N. meningitidis*).

Gastrointestinal infections: Treatment of GI infections caused by *S. typhi* (typhoid fever), other *Salmonella* species and *Shigella* species (dysentery). **Note:** Ampicillin is **not** recommended as a first-line agent for Shigellosis, Salmonellosis (nontyphoid), or *S. enterica* species (typhoid fever) due to development of resistance (CDC, 2014).

Respiratory tract infections: Treatment of respiratory tract infections caused by *S. pneumoniae*, *Staphylococcus aureus* (penicillinase and nonpenicillinase producing), *H. influenzae*, and group A beta-hemolytic streptococci.

Septicemia and endocarditis: Treatment of septicemia and endocarditis caused by susceptible gram-positive organisms, including Streptococcus species, penicillin G-susceptible staphylococci, and enterococci; gram-negative sepsis caused by *E. coli*, *P. mirabilis*, and *Salmonella* species.

Urinary tract infections: Treatment of urinary tract infections caused by *E. coli* and *P. mirabilis*.

Local Anesthetic/Vasoconstrictor Precautions No information available to require special precautions

Effects on Dental Treatment Key adverse event(s) related to dental treatment: Oral candidiasis, black hairy tongue, glossitis, sore mouth or tongue, and stomatitis.

Effects on Bleeding No information available to require special precautions

Adverse Reactions Frequency not defined.

Central nervous system: Brain disease (penicillin-induced), glossalgia, seizure, sore mouth

Dermatologic: Erythema multiforme, exfoliative dermatitis, skin rash, urticaria

Note: Appearance of a rash should be carefully evaluated to differentiate (if possible) nonallergic ampicillin rash from hypersensitivity reaction. Incidence is higher in patients with viral infection, *Salmonella* infection, lymphocytic leukemia, or patients that have hyperuricemia.

Gastrointestinal: Diarrhea, enterocolitis, glossitis, melanoglossia, nausea, oral candidiasis, pseudomembranous colitis, stomatitis, vomiting

Hematologic & oncologic: Agranulocytosis, anemia, eosinophilia, hemolytic anemia, immune thrombocytopenia, leukopenia

Hepatic: Increased serum AST

Hypersensitivity: Anaphylaxis

Immunologic: Serum sickness-like reaction

Renal: Interstitial nephritis (rare)

Respiratory: Stridor

Miscellaneous: Fever

Dental Usual Dosage

Infective endocarditis prophylaxis: IM, IV: Dental, oral, or respiratory tract procedures:

Infants and Children: 50 mg/kg within 30 to 60 minutes prior to procedure in patients not allergic to penicillin and unable to take oral amoxicillin.

Adults: 2 g within 30 to 60 minutes prior to procedure in patients not allergic to penicillin and unable to take oral amoxicillin.

Note: Intramuscular injections should be avoided in patients who are receiving anticoagulant therapy. In these circumstances, orally administered regimens should be given whenever possible. Intravenously administered antibiotics should be used for patients who are unable to tolerate or absorb oral medications.

Note: American Heart Association (AHA) guidelines now recommend prophylaxis only in patients undergoing invasive procedures and in whom underlying cardiac conditions may predispose to a higher risk of adverse outcomes should infection occur.

Prophylaxis in total joint replacement patient: Adults: IM, IV: 2 g 1 hour prior to the procedure

Note: In general, patients with prosthetic joint implants do not require prophylactic antibiotics prior to dental procedures. In planning an invasive oral procedure, dental consultation with the patient's orthopedic surgeon may be advised to review the risks of infection.

Dosing

Adult & Geriatric

Usual dosage range:

Oral: 250 to 500 mg every 6 hours

IM, IV: 1 to 2 g every 4 to 6 hours or 50 to 250 mg/kg/day in divided doses (maximum: 12 g/day)

Endocarditis, treatment (off-label dose; AHA [Baddour 2015]): IV:

Enterococcus, native or prosthetic valve (penicillin/gentamicin-susceptible strains): 2 g every 4 hours with concomitant ceftriaxone for 6 weeks **or** 2 g every 4 hours with concomitant gentamicin for 4 to 6 weeks (4 weeks for native valve **and** symptoms present <3 months; 6 weeks for native valve **and** symptoms present ≥3 months **or** for prosthetic valve)

Enterococcus, native or prosthetic valve (penicillin-susceptible/aminoglycoside-resistant strains): 2 g every 4 hours with concomitant ceftriaxone for 6 weeks

Enterococcus, native or prosthetic valve (penicillin-susceptible/gentamicin-resistant/streptomycin-susceptible strains): 2 g every 4 hours with concomitant streptomycin for 4 to 6 weeks (4 weeks for native valve **and** symptoms present <3 months; ≥6 weeks for native valve **and** symptoms present ≥3 months or prosthetic valve).

HACEK organisms, native or prosthetic valve (off-label use): 2 g every 4 hours for 4 weeks (native valve) or 6 weeks (prosthetic valve).

Viridans group streptococcus (VGS) and S. bovis:

Native valve: Highly penicillin-susceptible (MIC ≤0.12 mcg/mL): 2 g every 4 hours for 4 weeks (monotherapy) or for 2 weeks with concomitant gentamicin

Native valve: Relatively penicillin-resistant (MIC >0.12 to ≤0.5 mcg/mL): 2 g every 4 hours for 4 weeks with concomitant gentamicin for the first 2 weeks

Prosthetic valve: Highly penicillin-susceptible (MIC ≤0.12 mcg/mL): 2 g every 4 hours for 6 weeks

(with or without concomitant gentamicin for the first 2 weeks)

Prosthetic valve: Relatively or fully penicillin-resistant (MIC >0.12 mcg/mL): 2 g every 4 hours with concomitant gentamicin for 6 weeks

Endocarditis, prophylaxis (off-label use):

Dental, oral, or respiratory tract procedures: IM, IV: 2 g within 30 to 60 minutes prior to procedure in patients not allergic to penicillin and unable to take oral amoxicillin. IM injections should be avoided in patients who are receiving anticoagulant therapy. In these circumstances, orally administered regimens should be given whenever possible. Intravenously administered antibiotics should be used for patients who are unable to tolerate or absorb oral medications. **Note:** American Heart Association (AHA) guidelines now recommend prophylaxis only in patients undergoing invasive procedures and in whom underlying cardiac conditions may predispose to a higher risk of adverse outcomes should infection occur (Wilson 2007).

Genitourinary and gastrointestinal tract procedures: IM, IV: **Note:** Routine prophylaxis for GI/GU procedures is no longer recommended by the AHA. Consider only in patients with the highest risk of adverse outcome from endocarditis (eg, prosthetic heart valve, previous endocarditis, some categories of congenital heart disease, cardiac valvulopathy in cardiac transplant patients) who have an established GI or GU enterococcal infection or for those already receiving antibiotic therapy to prevent a wound infection or sepsis associated with a GI or GU procedure in which enterococcal coverage is desired (Wilson 2007).

High-risk patients: 2 g within 30 minutes prior to procedure, followed by ampicillin 1 g (or amoxicillin 1 g orally) 6 hours later; must be used in combination with gentamicin (Dajani 1997).

Moderate-risk patients: 2 g within 30 minutes prior to procedure (Dajani 1997).

Genitourinary or gastrointestinal infections: Oral, IM, IV: 500 mg every 6 hours

Group B streptococcus (maternal dose for neonatal prophylaxis) (off-label use): IV: 2 g initial dose, then 1 g every 4 hours until delivery (CDC 2010)

***Listeria* infections (off-label dosing; Lorber, 1997):** IV:

Bacteremia: 200 mg/kg/day divided every 6 hours for ≥2 weeks

Brain abscess or rhombencephalitis: 200 mg/kg/day divided every 4 hours with concomitant aminoglycoside for ≥6 weeks

Endocarditis: 200 mg/kg/day divided every 6 hours with concomitant aminoglycoside for ≥4 to 6 weeks

Meningitis: 200 mg/kg/day divided every 4 hours with concomitant aminoglycoside for ≥3 weeks

Mild to moderate infections: Oral: 250 to 500 mg every 6 hours

Osteomyelitis, native vertebral (off-label use): *Enterococcus* spp (penicillin-susceptible): IV: 12 g continuous infusion every 24 hours **or** 2 g every 4 hours for 6 weeks; the addition of an aminoglycoside for 4 to 6 weeks is recommended in patients with infective endocarditis (IDSA [Berbari 2015])

Prosthetic joint infection, *Enterococcus* spp (penicillin-susceptible) (off-label use): IV: 12 g continuous infusion every 24 hours **or** 2 g every 4 hours for 4 to 6 weeks; consider addition of aminoglycoside (Osmon, 2013).

Prophylaxis in total joint replacement patients undergoing dental procedures which produce bacteremia (off-label use): Note: In general, patients with prosthetic joint implants do not require prophylactic antibiotics prior to dental procedures. In planning an invasive oral procedure, dental consultation with the patient's orthopedic surgeon may be advised to review the risks of infection (Sollecito 2015).

IM, IV: 2 g 1 hour prior to procedure (ADA/AAOS 2003).

Respiratory tract infections:

Oral: 250 mg 4 times daily

IM, IV: 250 to 500 mg every 6 hours

Sepsis/meningitis: IM, IV: **Note:** administer doses IV initially; IM may be used later in therapy course: 150 to 200 mg/kg/day divided every 3 to 4 hours (range: 6 to 12 g/day)

Surgical (perioperative) prophylaxis in liver transplantation (off-label use): IV: 2 g within 60 minutes prior to surgery in combination with cefotaxime. Doses may be repeated in 2 hours if procedure is lengthy or if there is excessive blood loss (Bratzler, 2013).

Urinary tract infections (ampicillin-susceptible *Enterococcus*; off-label use): IV: 1 to 2 g every 4 to 6 hours with or without an aminoglycoside (Heintz 2010)

Pediatric

Usual dosage range: Infants, Children, and Adolescents:

Oral: 50 to 100 mg/kg/day divided every 6 hours (maximum: 2 to 4 g/day)

IM, IV: 25 to 200 mg/kg/day divided every 3 to 4 hours (maximum: 12 g/day)

Community-acquired pneumonia (CAP) (IDSA/PIDS 2011): Infants >3 months, Children, and Adolescents: IV: **Note:** May consider addition of vancomycin or clindamycin to empiric therapy if community-acquired MRSA suspected. In children ≥5 years, a macrolide antibiotic should be added if atypical pneumonia cannot be ruled out. Maximum daily dose of ampicillin: 12 g/day (*Red Book* [AAP 2012]).

Empiric treatment or *S. pneumoniae* (moderate to severe; MICs to penicillin ≤2.0 mcg/mL) or *H. influenzae* (beta-lactamase negative) (preferred): 150 to 200 mg/kg/day divided every 6 hours

Group A *Streptococcus* (moderate to severe) (preferred): 200 mg/kg/day divided every 6 hours

S. pneumoniae (moderate to severe; MICs to penicillin ≥4.0 mcg/mL) (alternative to ceftriaxone): 300 to 400 mg/kg/day divided every 6 hours

Endocarditis prophylaxis (off-label use): Infants, Children, and Adolescents: IM, IV:

Dental, oral, or respiratory tract procedures: 50 mg/kg within 30 to 60 minutes prior to procedure in patients not allergic to penicillin and unable to take oral amoxicillin. Maximum single dose of ampicillin: 2 g. IM injections should be avoided in patients who are receiving anticoagulant therapy. In these circumstances, orally administered regimens should be given whenever possible. Intravenously administered antibiotics should be used for patients who are unable to tolerate or absorb oral medications (Wilson, 2007).

Note: American Heart Association (AHA) guidelines now recommend prophylaxis only in patients undergoing invasive procedures and in whom underlying cardiac conditions may predispose to a higher risk of adverse outcomes should infection occur.

Genitourinary and gastrointestinal tract procedures: **Note:** Routine prophylaxis for GI/GU procedures is no longer recommended by the AHA. Consider only in patients with the highest risk of adverse outcome from endocarditis (eg, prosthetic heart valve, previous endocarditis, some categories of congenital heart disease, valvulopathy in cardiac transplant patients) who have an established GI or GU enterococcal infection or for those already receiving antibiotic therapy to prevent a wound infection or sepsis associated with a GI or GU procedure in which enterococcal coverage is desired (Wilson 2007).

High-risk patients: 50 mg/kg (maximum: 2 g) within 30 minutes prior to procedure, followed by ampicillin 25 mg/kg (or amoxicillin 25 mg/kg orally) 6 hours later; must be used in combination with gentamicin. Maximum single dose of ampicillin: 2 g (Dajani 1997). **Note:** Routine prophylaxis for GI/GU procedures is no longer recommended by the AHA (Wilson 2007).

Moderate-risk patients: 50 mg/kg within 30 minutes prior to procedure Maximum single dose of ampicillin: 2 g (Dajani 1997).

Endocarditis treatment (off-label dose): Infants, Children, and Adolescents: IV: 300 mg/kg/day in divided doses every 4 to 6 hours in combination with other antibiotics (maximum: 12 g/day) (Baddour 2005)

Genitourinary or gastrointestinal infections:

Oral:

Infants and Children ≤20 kg: 100 mg/kg/day in divided doses 4 times daily

Children and Adolescents >20 kg: 500 mg 4 times daily

IM, IV:

Infants and Children <40 kg: 50 mg/kg/day in divided doses every 6 to 8 hours

Children and Adolescents ≥40 kg: 500 mg every 6 hours

Mild to moderate infections: Infants, Children, and Adolescents:

Oral: 50 to 100 mg/kg/day divided every 6 hours (maximum: 2 to 4 g/day) (*Red Book* [AAP 2012])

IM, IV: 100 to 150 mg/kg/day divided every 6 hours (maximum: 2 to 4 g/day) (*Red Book* [AAP 2012])

Respiratory tract infections:

Oral:

Infants and Children ≤20 kg: 50 mg/kg/day in divided doses 3 to 4 times daily

Children and Adolescents >20 kg: 250 mg 4 times daily

IM, IV:

Infants and Children <40 kg: 25 to 50 mg/kg/day in divided doses every 6 to 8 hours

Children and Adolescents ≥40 kg: 250 to 500 mg every 6 hours

Severe infections, meningitis, septicemia: Infants, Children, and Adolescents: IM, IV: **Note:** Treatment should be initiated with IV infusion therapy and may be continued with IM injections if preferred.

Manufacturer's labeling: 150 to 200 mg/kg/day in divided doses every 3 to 4 hours

Alternative recommendation: 200 to 400 mg/kg/day in divided doses every 6 hours (maximum: 6 to 12 g/day) (*Red Book* [AAP 2012])

Surgical (perioperative) prophylaxis in liver transplantation (off-label use): Children ≥1 year: IV: 50 mg/kg within 60 minutes prior to surgery (maximum: 2,000 mg/dose) in combination with cefotaxime. Doses may be repeated in 2 hours if procedure is lengthy or if there is excessive blood loss (Bratzler 2013).

Renal Impairment There are no dosage adjustments provided in the manufacturer's labeling; however, the following adjustments have been recommended (Aronoff 2007):

CrCl >50 mL/minute: Administer every 6 hours

CrCl 10 to 50 mL/minute: Administer every 6 to 12 hours

CrCl <10 mL/minute: Administer every 12 to 24 hours

End-stage renal disease (ESRD) on intermittent hemodialysis (IHD) (administer after hemodialysis on dialysis days): Dialyzable (20% to 50%): IV: 1 to 2 g every 12 to 24 hours (administer after hemodialysis on dialysis days) (Heintz 2009). **Note:** Dosing dependent on the assumption of 3 times/week, complete IHD sessions.

Peritoneal dialysis (PD): IV: 250 mg every 12 hours (Aronoff, 2007)

Continuous renal replacement therapy (CRRT) (Heintz, 2009): Drug clearance is highly dependent on the method of renal replacement, filter type, and flow rate. Appropriate dosing requires close monitoring of pharmacologic response, signs of adverse reactions due to drug accumulation, as well as drug concentrations in relation to target trough (if appropriate). The following are general recommendations only (based on dialysate flow/ultrafiltration rates of 1 to 2 L/hour and minimal residual renal function) and should not supersede clinical judgment: IV:

CVVH: Loading dose of 2 g followed by 1 to 2 g every 8 to 12 hours

CVVHD: Loading dose of 2 g followed by 1 to 2 g every 8 hours

CVVHDF: Loading dose of 2 g followed by 1 to 2 g every 6 to 8 hours

Hepatic Impairment There are no dosage adjustments provided in the manufacturer's labeling.

Mechanism of Action Inhibits bacterial cell wall synthesis by binding to one or more of the penicillin-binding proteins (PBPs) which in turn inhibits the final transpeptidation step of peptidoglycan synthesis in bacterial cell walls, thus inhibiting cell wall biosynthesis. Bacteria eventually lyse due to ongoing activity of cell wall autolytic enzymes (autolysins and murein hydrolases) while cell wall assembly is arrested.

Contraindications Hypersensitivity (eg, anaphylaxis) to ampicillin, any component of the formulation, or other penicillins; infections caused by penicillinase-producing organisms

Warnings/Precautions Dosage adjustment may be necessary in patients with renal impairment. Serious and occasionally severe or fatal hypersensitivity (anaphylactoid) reactions have been reported in patients on penicillin therapy, especially with a history of beta-lactam hypersensitivity, history of sensitivity to multiple allergens, or previous IgE-mediated reactions (eg, anaphylaxis, angioedema, urticaria). Serious anaphylactoid reactions require emergency treatment and airway management. Appropriate treatments must be readily available. Use with caution in asthmatic patients. Appearance of any rash should be carefully evaluated to differentiate a nonallergic ampicillin rash from a hypersensitivity reaction. High percentage of patients with infectious mononucleosis have developed rash during therapy with ampicillin; ampicillin-class antibiotics not recommended in these patients This rash (generalized maculopapular and pruritic) usually appears 7 to 10 days after initiation and usually resolves within a week of discontinuation. It is not known whether these patients are truly allergic to ampicillin. Ampicillin rash occurs in 5% to 10% of children receiving ampicillin and is a generalized dull red, maculopapular rash, generally appearing 3 to 14 days after the start of therapy. It normally begins on the trunk and spreads over most of the body. It may be most intense at pressure areas, elbows, and knees. Prolonged use may result in fungal or bacterial superinfection, including *Clostridium difficile*-associated diarrhea (CDAD) and pseudomembranous colitis; CDAD has been observed >2 months postantibiotic treatment.

Drug Interactions

Metabolism/Transport Effects None known.

Avoid Concomitant Use

Avoid concomitant use of Ampicillin with any of the following: BCG (Intravesical); Cholera Vaccine

Increased Effect/Toxicity

Ampicillin may increase the levels/effects of: Methotrexate; Vitamin K Antagonists

The levels/effects of Ampicillin may be increased by: Allopurinol; Probenecid

Decreased Effect

Ampicillin may decrease the levels/effects of: Atenolol; BCG (Intravesical); BCG Vaccine (Immunization); Cholera Vaccine; Lactobacillus and Estriol; Mycophenolate; Sodium Picosulfate; Typhoid Vaccine

The levels/effects of Ampicillin may be decreased by: Chloroquine; Lanthanum; Tetracycline Derivatives

Food Interactions Food decreases ampicillin absorption rate; may decrease ampicillin serum concentration. Management: Take at equal intervals around-the-clock, preferably on an empty stomach (30 minutes before or 2 hours after meals). Maintain adequate hydration, unless instructed to restrict fluid intake.

Dietary Considerations Take on an empty stomach 30 minutes before or 2 hours after meals. Some products may contain sodium.

Pharmacodynamics/Kinetics

Half-life Elimination

Neonates:

PNA 2 to 7 days: 4 hours

PNA 8 to 14 days: 2.8 hours

PNA 15 to 30 days: 1.7 hours

Children and Adults: 1 to 1.8 hours (Bergan 1979)

Anuric patients: 8 to 20 hours

Time to Peak Serum concentration: Oral: Within 1 to 2 hours

Pregnancy Risk Factor B

Pregnancy Considerations Adverse events have not been observed in animal reproduction studies. Ampicillin crosses the placenta, providing detectable concentrations in the cord serum and amniotic fluid (Bolognese 1968; Fisher 1967; MacAulay 1966). Maternal use of ampicillin has generally not resulted in an increased risk of birth defects (Aselton 1985; Czeizel 2001b; Heinonen 1977; Jick 1981; Puhó 2007). Ampicillin is recommended for use in pregnant women for the management of preterm premature rupture of membranes (PPROM) and for the prevention of early-onset group B streptococcal (GBS) disease in newborns. Ampicillin may also be used in certain situations prior to vaginal delivery in women at high risk for endocarditis (ACOG 172, 2016; ACOG No. 120, 2011; ACOG No. 485, 2011; CDC [RR-10] 2010).

The volume of distribution of ampicillin is increased during pregnancy and the half-life is decreased. As a result, serum concentrations in pregnant patients are approximately 50% of those in nonpregnant patients receiving the same dose. Higher doses may be needed during pregnancy. Although oral absorption is not altered during pregnancy, oral ampicillin is poorly absorbed during labor (Philipson 1977; Philipson 1978; Wasz-Höckert 1970).

Breastfeeding Considerations Ampicillin is excreted in breast milk. The manufacturer recommends that caution be exercised when administering ampicillin to nursing women. Due to the low concentrations in human milk, minimal toxicity would be expected in the nursing infant. Nondose-related effects could include modification of bowel flora and allergic sensitization.

Dosage Forms

Capsule, Oral:

Generic: 250 mg, 500 mg

Solution Reconstituted, Injection:

Generic: 125 mg (1 ea); 250 mg (1 ea); 500 mg (1 ea); 1 g (1 ea); 2 g (1 ea); 10 g (1 ea)

Solution Reconstituted, Injection [preservative free]:

Generic: 250 mg (1 ea); 500 mg (1 ea)

Solution Reconstituted, Intravenous:

Generic: 1 g (1 ea); 2 g (1 ea); 10 g (1 ea)

Suspension Reconstituted, Oral:

Generic: 125 mg/5 mL (100 mL, 200 mL); 250 mg/5 mL (100 mL, 200 mL)

Ampicillin and Sulbactam

(am pi SIL in & SUL bak tam)

Related Information

Ampicillin *on page 136*

Brand Names: US Unasyn

Generic Availability (US) Yes

Pharmacologic Category Antibiotic, Penicillin

Dental Use Parenteral beta-lactamase-resistant antibiotic combination to treat more severe orofacial infections where beta-lactamase-producing staphylococci and beta-lactamase-producing *Bacteroides* are present

Use Bacterial infections: Treatment of susceptible bacterial infections involved with skin and skin structure, intra-abdominal infections, gynecological infections; spectrum is that of ampicillin plus organisms producing beta-lactamases such as *S. aureus*, *H. influenzae*, *E. coli*, *Klebsiella*, *Acinetobacter*, *Enterobacter*, and anaerobes

Local Anesthetic/Vasoconstrictor Precautions No information available to require special precautions

Effects on Dental Treatment Prolonged use of penicillins may lead to development of oral candidiasis (see Dental Comment)

Effects on Bleeding No information available to require special precautions

Adverse Reactions Also see Ampicillin.

>10%: Local: Pain at injection site (IM; 16%)

1% to 10%:

Cardiovascular: Thrombophlebitis (3%), phlebitis (1%)

Dermatologic: Skin rash (<2%)

Gastrointestinal: Diarrhea (3%)

Local: Pain at injection site (IV; 3%)

<1%: Abdominal distention, acute generalized exanthematous pustulosis, agranulocytosis, anemia, basophilia, candidiasis, casts in urine (hyaline), chest pain, chills, cholestasis, cholestatic hepatitis, cholestatic jaundice, *clostridium difficile* associated diarrhea, constriction of the pharynx, convulsions, decreased

hematocrit, decreased hemoglobin, decreased neutrophils, decreased red blood cells, decreased serum albumin, decreased serum total protein, dysuria, edema, eosinophilia, epistaxis, erythema, erythema multiforme, erythrocyturia, exfoliative dermatitis, facial swelling, fatigue, flatulence, gastritis, glossitis, hairy tongue, headache, hemolytic anemia, hepatic insufficiency, hepatitis, hyperbilirubinemia, hypersensitivity reaction, immune thrombocytopenia, increased blood urea nitrogen, increased lactate dehydrogenase, increased liver enzymes, increased monocytes, increased serum alkaline phosphatase, increased serum ALT, increased serum AST, increased serum creatinine, injection site reaction, interstitial nephritis, jaundice, leukopenia, lymphocytopenia, lymphocytosis (abnormal), malaise, mucous membrane bleeding, nausea, positive direct Coombs test, pruritus, pseudomembranous colitis, Stevens-Johnson syndrome, stomatitis, substernal pain, thrombocythemia, thrombocytopenia, toxic epidermal necrolysis, urinary retention, urticaria, vomiting

Dental Usual Dosage Severe orofacial infections: Adults: IM, IV: 1000 to 2000 mg ampicillin (1500 to 3000 mg Unasyn) every 6 hours (maximum: 8 g ampicillin/day, 12 g Unasyn)

Dosing

Adult & Geriatric Unasyn (ampicillin/sulbactam) is a combination product. **Note:** Dosage recommendations are expressed as grams of **ampicillin/sulbactam** combination.

Susceptible infections: IM, IV: 1.5 to 3 g every 6 hours (maximum: 12 g ampicillin/sulbactam daily)

Acute bacterial rhinosinusitis, severe infection requiring hospitalization (off-label use): IV: 1.5 to 3 g every 6 hours for 5 to 7 days (Chow 2012)

Amnionitis, cholangitis, diverticulitis, endomyometritis (with doxycycline), endophthalmitis, epididymitis/orchitis, liver abscess (with metronidazole), or peritonitis: IV: 3 g every 6 hours

Bite wounds (animal/human) (off-label use): IV: 1.5 to 3 g every 6 hours (human bites) or every 6 to 8 hours (animal bites) (IDSA [Stevens 2014])

Infective endocarditis, treatment (off-label use): *Enterococcus* (native or prosthetic valve; beta-lactamase producing strains resistant to penicillin/susceptible to aminoglycoside and vancomycin): IV: 3 g every 6 hours with a concomitant aminoglycoside for 6 weeks (AHA [Baddour 2015])

Intravascular catheter-associated bloodstream infection, *Acinetobacter* spp (off-label use) (IDSA 2009): IV: 3 g every 6 hours

Orbital cellulitis: IV: 3 g every 6 hours

Osteomyelitis (diabetic foot) (Lipsky 2004): IV: 3 g every 6 hours

Pelvic inflammatory disease (alternative to preferred therapy): IV: 3 g every 6 hours with doxycycline oral or IV; transition from parenteral to oral therapy can usually be initiated within 24 to 48 hours of clinical improvement for a total treatment duration of 14 days; if tubo-ovarian abscess is present, at least 24 hours of inpatient observation is recommended (CDC [Workowski 2015).

Peritonitis associated with CAPD: Intraperitoneal:

Intermittent: 3 g added to one exchange every 12 hours; allow to dwell for at least 6 hours (Blackwell 1990; Li 2010)

Continuous: Loading dose: 1.5 g per liter of dialysate; maintenance dose: 150 mg per liter of dialysate (Li 2010)

Pneumonia, community-acquired (off-label use): IV: 1.5 to 3 g every 6 hours for ≥5 days (Geckler 1994; Majcher-Peszynska 2014; Mandell 2007; Rossoff 1995). **Note:** In ICU patients, use in combination with azithromycin or a fluoroquinolone (Mandell 2007).

Pneumonia, hospital-acquired or ventilator-associated due to *Acinetobacter* (off-label use): IV: 3 g every 6 hours (Zalts 2016); duration of therapy is 7 days (may consider shorter or longer duration depending on rate of clinical improvement) (Kalil 2016)

Surgical (perioperative) prophylaxis (off-label use): IV: 3 g within 60 minutes prior to surgical incision. Doses may be repeated in 2 hours if procedure is lengthy or if there is excessive blood loss (Bratzler 2013).

Surgical site infections (intestinal or GI tract) (off-label use): IV: 3 g every 6 hours; in combination with gentamicin or tobramycin (IDSA [Stevens 2014])

Urinary tract infections, pyelonephritis: IV: 3 g every 6 hours for 14 days

Pediatric Unasyn (ampicillin/sulbactam) is a combination product. **Note:** Dosage recommendations are expressed as mg of the **ampicillin** component.

Susceptible infections: Children and Adolescents: IV: 100 to 200 mg **ampicillin**/kg/day divided every 6 hours (maximum: 8 g ampicillin daily or 12 g ampicillin/sulbactam daily).

Epiglottitis: Children and Adolescents: IV: 100 to 200 mg ampicillin/kg/day divided in 4 doses

Intra-abdominal infection, complicated (off-label): Infants, Children, and Adolescents: IV: 200 mg ampicillin/kg/day divided every 6 hours; **Note:** Due to high rates of *E. coli* resistance, not recommended for the treatment of community-acquired intra-abdominal infections (IDSA [Solomkin 2010]).

Infective endocarditis, treatment (off-label use) (AHA/IDSA [Baddour 2005]): Infants, Children, and Adolescents:

Bartonella spp. (Native valve): IV: 200 mg ampicillin/kg/day in 4 or 6 divided doses with concomitant gentamicin for 4 to 6 weeks.

Enterococcus organism (resistant to penicillin/susceptible to aminoglycoside and vancomycin): IV: 200 mg ampicillin/kg/day in 4 divided doses with concomitant gentamicin for 6 weeks. **Note:** If enterococcus is gentamicin resistant, then >6 weeks of ampicillin-sulbactam therapy needed.

HACEK organism: 200 mg ampicillin/kg/day in 4 or 6 divided doses for 4 weeks.

Intravascular catheter-associated bloodstream infection (off-label use) (IDSA 2009): Infants, Children, and Adolescents:

Infants: IV: 100 to 150 mg ampicillin/kg/day in 4 divided doses

Children and Adolescents: IV: 100 to 200 mg ampicillin/kg/day in 4 divided doses

Mild to moderate infections: Children and Adolescents: IV: 100 to 200 mg ampicillin/kg/day divided every 6 hours (maximum: 8 g ampicillin daily or 12 g ampicillin/sulbactam daily)

Peritonsillar and retropharyngeal abscess: Children and Adolescents: IV: 200 mg ampicillin/kg/day in 4 divided doses

Severe infections: Children and Adolescents: IV: 200 mg ampicillin/kg/day divided every 6 hours (maximum: 8 g ampicillin daily or 12 g ampicillin/sulbactam daily)

Surgical (perioperative) prophylaxis (off-label use): Children ≥1 year: IV: 50 mg ampicillin/kg within 60 minutes prior to surgical incision (maximum dose: 2000 mg ampicillin or 3 g ampicillin/sulbactam daily). Doses may be repeated in 2 hours if procedure is lengthy or if there is excessive blood loss (Bratzler 2013).

Renal Impairment Note: Estimation of renal function for the purpose of drug dosing should be done using the Cockcroft-Gault formula. Dosage recommendations are expressed as grams of **ampicillin/sulbactam** combination:

CrCl ≥30 mL/minute/1.73 m^2: No dosage adjustment necessary.

CrCl 15 to 29 mL/minute/1.73 m^2: 1.5 to 3 g every 12 hours

CrCl 5 to 14 mL/minute/1.73 m^2: 1.5 to 3 g every 24 hours

End stage renal disease (ESRD) on intermittent hemodialysis (IHD) (administer after hemodialysis on dialysis days): 1.5 to 3 g every 12 to 24 hours (Heintz 2009). **Note:** Dosing dependent on the assumption of 3 times weekly, complete IHD sessions.

Continuous renal replacement therapy (CRRT): Drug clearance is highly dependent on the method of renal replacement, filter type, and flow rate. Appropriate dosing requires close monitoring of pharmacologic response, signs of adverse reactions due to drug accumulation, as well as drug levels in relation to target trough (if appropriate). The following are general recommendations only (based on dialysate flow/ultrafiltration rates of 1 to 2 L/hour and minimal residual renal function) and should not supersede clinical judgment (Heintz 2009; Trotman 2005):

CVVH: Initial: 3 g; maintenance: 1.5 to 3 g every 8 to 12 hours

CVVHD: Initial: 3 g; maintenance: 1.5 to 3 g every 8 hours

CVVHDF: Initial: 3 g; maintenance: 1.5 to 3 g every 6 to 8 hours

Hepatic Impairment There is no dosage adjustment provided in the manufacturer's labeling.

Mechanism of Action Inhibits bacterial cell wall synthesis by binding to one or more of the penicillin-binding proteins (PBPs) which in turn inhibits the final transpeptidation step of peptidoglycan synthesis in bacterial cell walls, thus inhibiting cell wall biosynthesis. Bacteria eventually lyse due to ongoing activity of cell wall autolytic enzymes (autolysins and murein hydrolases) while cell wall assembly is arrested. The addition of sulbactam, a beta-lactamase inhibitor, to ampicillin extends the spectrum of ampicillin to include some beta-lactamase-producing organisms.

Contraindications Hypersensitivity (eg, anaphylaxis or Stevens-Johnson syndrome) to ampicillin, sulbactam, or to other beta-lactam antibacterial drugs (eg, penicillins, cephalosporins), or any component of the formulations; history of cholestatic jaundice or hepatic dysfunction associated with ampicillin/sulbactam

Warnings/Precautions Dosage adjustment may be necessary in patients with renal impairment. Serious and occasionally severe or fatal hypersensitivity (anaphylactic) reactions have been reported in patients on penicillin therapy, especially with a history of beta-lactam hypersensitivity, history of sensitivity to multiple allergens. Patients with a history of penicillin hypersensitivity have experienced severe reactions when treated with cephalosporins. Before initiating therapy, carefully investigate previous penicillin, cephalosporin, or other allergen hypersensitivity. If an allergic reaction occurs, discontinue and institute appropriate therapy. Hepatitis and cholestatic jaundice have been reported (including fatalities). Toxicity is usually reversible. Monitor hepatic function at regular intervals in patients with hepatic impairment. High percentage of patients with infectious mononucleosis have developed rash during therapy with ampicillin; ampicillin-class antibacterials are not recommended in these patients. Appearance of a rash should be carefully evaluated to differentiate a nonallergic ampicillin rash from a hypersensitivity reaction. Prolonged use may result in fungal or bacterial superinfection, including *C. difficile*-associated diarrhea (CDAD) and pseudomembranous colitis; CDAD has been observed >2 months postantibiotic treatment.

Drug Interactions

Metabolism/Transport Effects None known.

Avoid Concomitant Use

Avoid concomitant use of Ampicillin and Sulbactam with any of the following: BCG (Intravesical); Cholera Vaccine

Increased Effect/Toxicity

Ampicillin and Sulbactam may increase the levels/effects of: Methotrexate; Vitamin K Antagonists

The levels/effects of Ampicillin and Sulbactam may be increased by: Allopurinol; Probenecid

Decreased Effect

Ampicillin and Sulbactam may decrease the levels/effects of: Atenolol; BCG (Intravesical); BCG Vaccine (Immunization); Cholera Vaccine; Lactobacillus and Estriol; Mycophenolate; Sodium Picosulfate; Typhoid Vaccine

The levels/effects of Ampicillin and Sulbactam may be decreased by: Chloroquine; Lanthanum; Tetracycline Derivatives

Dietary Considerations Some products may contain sodium.

Pharmacodynamics/Kinetics

Half-life Elimination Sulbactam: Children 1 to 12 years (normal renal function): Mean range: ~0.7 to 0.9 hours (Nahata 1999); Adults (normal renal function): 1 to 1.3 hours; **Note:** Elimination kinetics of both ampicillin and sulbactam are similarly affected in patients with renal impairment, therefore, the blood concentration ratio is expected to remain constant regardless of renal function.

Pregnancy Risk Factor B

Pregnancy Considerations Adverse events have not been observed in animal reproduction studies. Both ampicillin and sulbactam cross the placenta. Maternal use of penicillins has generally not resulted in an increased risk of birth defects. When used during pregnancy, pharmacokinetic changes have been observed with ampicillin alone (refer to the Ampicillin monograph for details). Ampicillin/sulbactam may be considered for prophylactic use prior to cesarean delivery (consult current guidelines).

Breastfeeding Considerations Ampicillin and sulbactam are both excreted into breast milk in low concentrations. The manufacturer recommends that caution be used if administering to lactating women. Nondose-related effects could include modification of bowel flora and allergic sensitization of the infant. The maternal dose of sulbactam does not need altered in the postpartum period. Also refer to the Ampicillin monograph.

Dosage Forms

Injection, powder for reconstitution: 1.5 g [ampicillin 1 g and sulbactam 0.5 g]; 3 g [ampicillin 2 g and sulbactam 1 g]; 15 g [ampicillin 10 g and sulbactam 5 g]

Unasyn: 1.5 g [ampicillin 1 g and sulbactam 0.5 g]; 3 g [ampicillin 2 g and sulbactam 1 g]; 15 g [ampicillin 10 g and sulbactam 5 g]; 15 g [ampicillin 10 g and sulbactam 5 g

Dental Comment In maxillary sinus, anterior nasal cavity, and deep neck infections, beta-lactamase-producing staphylococci and beta-lactamase-producing *Bacteroides* usually are present. In these situations, antibiotics that resist the beta-lactamase enzyme should be administered. Amoxicillin and clavulanic acid is administered orally for moderate infections. Ampicillin sodium and sulbactam sodium (Unasyn) is administered parenterally for more severe infections.

Amsacrine (AM sah kreen)

Brand Names: Canada AMSA PD

Pharmacologic Category Antineoplastic Agent, Miscellaneous

Use Note: Not approved in the US.

Acute leukemia: Remission induction in refractory acute leukemia in adults

Local Anesthetic/Vasoconstrictor Precautions No information available to require special precautions

Effects on Dental Treatment Key adverse event(s) related to dental treatment: Oral ulcerations and stomatitis

Effects on Bleeding Chemotherapy may result in significant myelosuppression, potentially including significant reduction in platelet counts and altered hemostasis. In patients who are under active treatment with these agents, medical consult is suggested.

Adverse Reactions Frequency not always defined.

Cardiovascular: Atrial fibrillation, atrial tachycardia, bradycardia, cardiomyopathy (rare), cardiorespiratory arrest, congestive heart failure (rare), ECG changes (prolonged QT interval on ECG, nonspecific ST or T wave changes on ECG), hypotension, phlebitis, reduced ejection fraction, sinus tachycardia, tachycardia, ventricular arrhythmia, ventricular fibrillation, ventricular premature contractions, ventricular tachyarrhythmia

Central nervous system: Confusion, dizziness, emotional lability, headache, hypoesthesia, lethargy, paresthesia, seizure

Dermatologic: Allergic dermatitis, alopecia, dermatological reaction, maculopapular rash, urticaria

Endocrine & metabolic: Weight changes

Gastrointestinal: Abdominal pain (>10%), diarrhea (>10%), nausea (>10%), stomatitis (>10%), vomiting (>10%), anorexia, dysphagia, gingival hemorrhage, gingivitis, hematemesis

Genitourinary: Perirectal abscess (>10%), hematuria, proteinuria, urine abnormality (orange-red discoloration)

Hematologic & oncologic: Bone marrow depression (>10%), leukopenia (>10%; nadir: 11-13 days; recovery: days 17-25), anemia, granulocytopenia, hemorrhage, pancytopenia, purpura, purpuric rash, thrombocytopenia

Hepatic: Hepatic failure (progressive), hepatic insufficiency, hepatitis, hepatotoxicity, increased serum alkaline phosphatase, increased serum AST, increased serum bilirubin, jaundice

Hypersensitivity: Hypersensitivity reaction

Infection: Infection

Local: Inflammation at injection site

Neuromuscular & skeletal: Musculoskeletal pain, weakness

Renal: Increased blood urea nitrogen, increased serum creatinine, renal failure

Respiratory: Dyspnea

Miscellaneous: Fever

General Dosage Range Dosage adjustment recommended in patients with hepatic or renal impairment or patients who develop toxicities

IV: *Adults:* Induction: 75 to 125 mg/m^2/day for 5 days every 3 to 4 weeks; Maintenance: ~50% of induction dose every 4 to 8 weeks

Mechanism of Action Amsacrine has been shown to inhibit DNA synthesis by binding to, and intercalating with, DNA; inhibits topoisomerase II activity.

Pharmacodynamics/Kinetics

Half-life Elimination Terminal: Mean 7.4 hours; range: 6 to 10 hours (Hall, 1983)

Pregnancy Considerations Animal reproduction studies have not been conducted. Women of childbearing potential should avoid becoming pregnant while receiving treatment.

Product Availability Not available in the US

Amyl Nitrite (AM il NYE trite)

Pharmacologic Category Antianginal Agent; Antidote; Vasodilator

Local Anesthetic/Vasoconstrictor Precautions No information available to require special precautions

Effects on Dental Treatment Key adverse event(s) related to dental treatment: Patients may experience orthostatic hypotension as they stand up after treatment; especially if lying in dental chair for extended periods of time. Use caution with sudden changes in position during and after dental treatment.

Effects on Bleeding No information available to require special precautions

Adverse Reactions Frequency not defined.

Cardiovascular: Cerebral ischemia, facial flushing, hypotension, orthostatic hypotension, shock, syncope, tachycardia, vasodilatation

Central nervous system: Dizziness, headache, increased intracranial pressure, restlessness

Dermatologic: Dermatitis, diaphoresis, pallor, skin irritation

Gastrointestinal: Fecal incontinence, nausea, vomiting

Genitourinary: Urinary incontinence

Hematologic & oncologic: Hemolytic anemia, methemoglobinemia

Neuromuscular & skeletal: Weakness

Ophthalmic: Eye irritation, increased intraocular pressure

General Dosage Range Inhalation: *Adults:* 2 to 6 nasal inhalations from 1 crushed ampul; may repeat in 3 to 5 minutes

Mechanism of Action Relaxes vascular smooth muscle; decreases venous ratios and arterial blood pressure; reduces left ventricular work; decreases myocardial O_2 consumption. When used for cyanide poisoning, amyl nitrite promotes the formation of methemoglobin which competes with cytochrome oxidase for the cyanide ion. Cyanide combines with methemoglobin to form cyanomethemoglobin, thereby freeing the cytochrome oxidase and allowing aerobic metabolism to continue.

Pharmacodynamics/Kinetics

Onset of Action Angina: Within 30 seconds

Duration of Action Angina: 3-15 minutes; Pharmacologic provocation of latent left ventricular outflow tract (LVOT) gradient in hypertrophic cardiomyopathy (HCM): ~30 seconds (Reagan, 2005)

Half-life Elimination Amyl nitrite: <1 hour; Methemoglobin: 1 hour

Pregnancy Risk Factor C

Pregnancy Considerations Animal reproduction studies have not been conducted. Because amyl nitrite significantly decreases systemic blood pressure and therefore blood flow to the fetus, use is contraindicated in pregnancy (per manufacturer). In addition, fetal hemoglobin may be more susceptible methemoglobin conversion (Valenzuela, 1986).

Anagrelide (an AG gre lide)

Brand Names: US Agrylin

Brand Names: Canada Agrylin; Dom-Anagrelide; Mylan-Anagrelide; PMS-Anagrelide; Sandoz-Anagrelide

Pharmacologic Category Antiplatelet Agent; Phosphodiesterase-3 Enzyme Inhibitor

Use Thrombocythemia: Treatment of thrombocythemia associated with myeloproliferative disorders to reduce the risk of thrombosis and reduce associated symptoms (including thrombohemorrhagic events)

Local Anesthetic/Vasoconstrictor Precautions No information available to require special precautions

Effects on Dental Treatment Key adverse event(s) related to dental treatment: Patients may experience orthostatic hypotension as they stand up after treatment; especially if lying in dental chair for extended periods of time. Use caution with sudden changes in position during and after dental treatment.

Effects on Bleeding Anagrelide causes dose-related reduction in platelet production and could affect normal clotting; hemorrhage has been reported. Medical consult is suggested for patients under active treatment with anagrelide.

Adverse Reactions

Frequency not always defined; reactions similar in adult and pediatric patients unless otherwise noted.

Cardiovascular: Palpitations (26%), edema (21%), peripheral edema (9%), chest pain (8%), tachycardia (8%), angina pectoris (1% to <5%), cardiac arrhythmia (1% to <5%), cardiac failure (1% to <5%), hypertension (1% to <5%), orthostatic hypotension (1% to <5%), syncope (1% to <5%), vasodilatation (1% to <5%), atrial fibrillation, cardiomegaly, cardiomyopathy, cerebrovascular accident, complete atrioventricular block, decreased diastolic pressure (pediatric patients), increased heart rate (pediatric patients), myocardial infarction, pericardial effusion, systolic hypotension (pediatric patients)

Central nervous system: Headache (44%), dizziness (15%), pain (15%), malaise (6%), paresthesia (6%), amnesia (1% to <5%), chills (1% to <5%), confusion (1% to <5%), depression (1% to <5%), drowsiness (1% to <5%), insomnia (1% to <5%), migraine (1% to <5%), nervousness (1% to <5%), fatigue (pediatric patients)

Dermatologic: Skin rash (8%), pruritus (6%), alopecia (1% to <5%)

Gastrointestinal: Diarrhea (26%), nausea (17%), abdominal pain (16%), flatulence (10%), vomiting (10%), anorexia (8%), dyspepsia (5%), constipation (1% to <5%), gastritis (1% to <5%), gastrointestinal hemorrhage (1% to <5%), pancreatitis

Hematologic & oncologic: Anemia (1% to <5%), bruise (1% to <5%), hemorrhage (1% to <5%), thrombocytopenia (1% to <5%)

Hepatic: Increased liver enzymes (1% to <5%)

Neuromuscular & skeletal: Weakness (23%), back pain (6%), arthralgia (1% to <5%), myalgia (1% to <5%), muscle cramps (pediatric patients)

Ophthalmic: Diplopia (1% to <5%), visual field defect (1% to <5%)

Otic: Tinnitus (1% to <5%)

Renal: Hematuria (1% to <5%), renal failure (1%)

Respiratory: Dyspnea (12%), cough (6%), epistaxis (1% to <5%), flu-like symptoms (1% to <5%), pneumonia (1% to <5%), pleural effusion, pulmonary hypertension, pulmonary fibrosis, pulmonary infiltrates

Miscellaneous: Fever (9%)

<1%, postmarketing, and/or case reports: Eosinophilic pneumonitis, hepatotoxicity, hypersensitivity pneumonitis, increased serum ALT (>3 x ULN), increased serum AST (>3 x ULN), interstitial nephritis, interstitial pneumonitis, leukocytosis, prolonged Q-T interval on ECG, skin photosensitivity (pediatric patients), torsades de pointes, ventricular tachycardia

General Dosage Range Dosage adjustment recommended in patients with hepatic impairment

Oral:

Children: Initial: 0.5 mg once daily; Maintenance: 0.5 mg 1 to 4 times daily (maximum single dose: 2.5 mg; maximum daily dose: 10 mg)

Adults: Initial: 0.5 mg 4 times daily **or** 1 mg twice daily (maximum single dose: 2.5 mg; maximum daily dose: 10 mg)

Mechanism of Action Anagrelide appears to inhibit cyclic nucleotide phosphodiesterase and the release of arachidonic acid from phospholipase, possibly by inhibiting phospholipase A_2. It also causes a dose-related reduction in platelet production, which results from decreased megakaryocyte hypermaturation (disrupts the postmitotic phase of maturation).

Pharmacodynamics/Kinetics

Onset of Action Initial: Within 7 to 14 days; complete response (platelets ≤600,000/mm^3): 4 to 12 weeks

Duration of Action 6 to 24 hours; upon discontinuation, platelet count begins to rise within 4 days

Half-life Elimination Anagrelide: 1.5 hours, similar data reported in pediatric patients 7-14 years; 3-hydroxy anagrelide: 2.5 hours

Time to Peak Serum: 1 hour, similar data reported in pediatric patients 7-14 years

Pregnancy Risk Factor C

Pregnancy Considerations Adverse events were observed in some animal reproduction studies. Data regarding use of anagrelide during pregnancy is limited. The manufacturer recommends effective contraception in women of childbearing potential.

Anakinra (an a KIN ra)

Related Information

Rheumatoid Arthritis, Osteoarthritis, and Osteoporosis *on page 1792*

Brand Names: US Kineret

Brand Names: Canada Kineret

Pharmacologic Category Antirheumatic, Disease Modifying; Interleukin-1 Receptor Antagonist

Use

Neonatal-onset multisystem inflammatory disease: Treatment of neonatal-onset multisystem inflammatory disease (NOMID).

Rheumatoid arthritis: Reduction in signs and symptoms and slowing the progression of structural damage of moderately to severely active rheumatoid arthritis (RA) in patients 18 years and older who have failed 1 or more disease-modifying antirheumatic drugs (DMARDs).

Local Anesthetic/Vasoconstrictor Precautions No information available to require special precautions

Effects on Dental Treatment No significant effects or complications reported

Effects on Bleeding No information available to require special precautions

Adverse Reactions

>10%:

Central nervous system: Headache (12% to 14%)

Gastrointestinal: Vomiting (NOMID: 14%)

Immunologic: Antibody development (RA: 49%; neutralizing: 2%; no correlation of antibody development and adverse effects)

Infection: Infection (RA: 39%; serious infection: 2% to 3%; including cellulitis, pneumonia, and bone and joint infections)

Local: Injection site reaction (RA: 71%; mild: 73%; moderate: 24%; severe: 2% to 3%; NOMID: 16%; mild: 76%; moderate: 24%)

Neuromuscular & skeletal: Arthralgia (NOMID: 12%)

Respiratory: Nasopharyngitis (NOMID: 12%)

Miscellaneous: Fever (NOMID: 12%)

1% to 10%:

Gastrointestinal: Nausea (RA: 8%), diarrhea (RA: 7%)

Hematologic & oncologic: Eosinophilia (RA: 9%), decreased white blood cell count (RA: 8%), change in platelet count (RA; decreased: 2%

Frequency not defined:

Dermatologic: Skin rash (NOMID)

Endocrine & metabolic: Hypercholesterolemia (RA)

Respiratory: Upper respiratory tract infection (NOMID)

<1%, postmarketing, and/or case reports: Hepatitis (noninfectious), hypersensitivity reaction (including anaphylaxis, angioedema, pruritus, skin rash, urticaria), increased serum transaminases, metastases (malignant lymphoma, malignant melanoma), opportunistic infection, thrombocytopenia (including severe)

General Dosage Range Dosage adjustment recommended in patients with renal impairment

SubQ:

Infants, Children, and Adolescents: Initial: 1 to 2 mg/kg daily in 1 to 2 divided doses (maximum: 8 mg/kg/day)

Adults: 100 mg once daily **or** initial: 1 to 2 mg/kg daily in 1 to 2 divided doses (maximum: 8 mg/kg/day)

Mechanism of Action Antagonist of the interleukin-1 (IL-1) receptor. Endogenous IL-1 is induced by inflammatory stimuli and mediates a variety of immunological responses, including degradation of cartilage (loss of proteoglycans) and stimulation of bone resorption.

Pharmacodynamics/Kinetics

Half-life Elimination Terminal: 4 to 6 hours; Severe renal impairment (CrCl <30 mL/minute): ~7 hours; ESRD: 9.7 hours (Yang 2003)

Time to Peak SubQ: 3 to 7 hours

Pregnancy Risk Factor B

Pregnancy Considerations Adverse events have not been observed in animal reproduction studies. Information related to the use of anakinra during pregnancy is limited (Makol 2011; Ostensen 2011). Specific guidelines for use in pregnancy are not available (Saag [ACR] 2008); use should not be continued during pregnancy until more data is available (Makol 2011; Ostensen 2011).

Women exposed to anakinra during pregnancy may contact the Organization of Teratology Information Services (OTIS), Rheumatoid Arthritis and Pregnancy Study at 1-877-311-8972.

Anastrozole (an AS troe zole)

Brand Names: US Arimidex

Brand Names: Canada ACH-Anastrozole; ACT-Anastrozole; Apo-Anastrozole; Arimidex; Auro-Anastrozole; Bio-Anastrozole; JAMP-Anastrozole; Mar-Anastrozole; Med-Anastrozole; Mint-Anastrozole; Mylan-Anastrozole; Nat-Anastrozole; PMS-Anastrozole; RAN-Anastrozole; Riva-Anastrozole; Sandoz-Anastrozole; Taro-Anastrozole; Teva-Anastrozole; Zinda-Anastrozole

Pharmacologic Category Antineoplastic Agent, Aromatase Inhibitor

Use Breast cancer:

First-line treatment of locally-advanced or metastatic breast cancer (hormone receptor-positive or unknown) in postmenopausal women

Adjuvant treatment of early hormone receptor-positive breast cancer in postmenopausal women

Treatment of advanced breast cancer in postmenopausal women with disease progression following tamoxifen therapy

Local Anesthetic/Vasoconstrictor Precautions No information available to require special precautions

Effects on Dental Treatment Key adverse event(s) related to dental treatment: Xerostomia (normal salivary flow resumes upon discontinuation).

Effects on Bleeding No information available to require special precautions

Adverse Reactions

>10%:

Cardiovascular: Vasodilatation (25% to 36%), ischemic heart disease (4%; 17% in patients with preexisting ischemic heart disease), hypertension (2% to 13%), angina pectoris (2%; 12% in patients with pre-existing ischemic heart disease), edema (7% to 11%)

Central nervous system: Fatigue (19%), mood disorder (19%), headache (9% to 18%), pain (11% to 17%), depression (2% to 13%)

Dermatologic: Skin rash (6% to 11%)

Endocrine & metabolic: Hot flash (12% to 36%)

Gastrointestinal: Gastrointestinal distress (29% to 34%), nausea (11% to 20%), vomiting (8% to 13%)

Neuromuscular & skeletal: Weakness (13% to 19%), arthritis (17%), arthralgia (2% to 15%), back pain (10% to 12%), ostealgia (6% to 12%), osteoporosis (11%)

Respiratory: Pharyngitis (6% to 14%), dyspnea (8% to 11%), increased cough (7% to 11%)

1% to 10%:

Cardiovascular: Peripheral edema (5% to 10%), chest pain (5% to 7%), venous thrombosis (2% to 4%; including pulmonary embolism, thrombophlebitis, retinal vein thrombosis), myocardial infarction (1%)

Central nervous system: Insomnia (2% to 10%), dizziness (5% to 8%), paresthesia (5% to 7%), anxiety (2% to 6%), confusion (2% to 5%), drowsiness (2% to 5%), malaise (2% to 5%), nervousness (2% to

5%), carpal tunnel syndrome (3%), hypertonia (3%), cerebrovascular insufficiency (2%), lethargy (1%)

Dermatologic: Alopecia (2% to 5%), pruritus (2% to 5%), diaphoresis (1% to 5%)

Endocrine & metabolic: Hypercholesterolemia (9%), increased serum cholesterol (9%), weight gain (2% to 9%), increased gamma-glutamyl transferase (2% to 5%), weight loss (2% to 5%)

Gastrointestinal: Constipation (7% to 9%), diarrhea (7% to 9%), abdominal pain (6% to 9%), anorexia (5% to 8%), dyspepsia (7%), gastrointestinal disease (7%), xerostomia (4% to 6%)

Genitourinary: Mastalgia (2% to 8%), urinary tract infection (2% to 8%), pelvic pain (5% to 7%), vulvovaginitis (6%), vaginal dryness (1% to 5%), vaginal hemorrhage (1% to 5%), vaginal discharge (4%), vaginitis (4%), leukorrhea (2% to 3%)

Hematologic & oncologic: Lymphedema (10%), breast neoplasm (5%), neoplasm (5%), anemia (2% to 5%), leukopenia (2% to 5%), tumor flare (3%)

Hepatic: Increased serum alkaline phosphatase (2% to 5%), increased serum ALT (2% to 5%), increased serum AST (2% to 5%)

Infection: Infection (2% to 9%)

Neuromuscular & skeletal: Bone fracture (1% to 10%), arthrosis (7%), myalgia (2% to 6%), neck pain (2% to 5%), pathological fracture (2% to 5%)

Ophthalmic: Cataract (6%)

Respiratory: Flu-like symptoms (2% to 7%), sinusitis (2% to 6%), bronchitis (2% to 5%), rhinitis (2% to 5%)

Miscellaneous: Accidental injury (2% to 10%), cyst (5%), fever (2% to 5%)

<1%, postmarketing, and/or case reports: Anaphylaxis, angioedema, cerebral infarction, cerebral ischemia, decreased bone mineral density, dermal ulcer, endometrial carcinoma, erythema multiforme, hepatitis, hepatomegaly, hypercalcemia, hypersensitivity angiitis (including anaphylactoid purpura [IgA vasculitis]), increased serum bilirubin, jaundice, joint stiffness, pulmonary embolism, retinal thrombosis, skin blister, skin lesion, Stevens-Johnson syndrome, tenosynovitis (stenosing), urticaria

General Dosage Range Oral: *Adults:* 1 mg once daily

Mechanism of Action Potent and selective nonsteroidal aromatase inhibitor. By inhibiting aromatase, the conversion of androstenedione to estrone, and testosterone to estradiol, is prevented, thereby decreasing tumor mass or delaying progression in patients with tumors responsive to hormones. Anastrozole causes an 85% decrease in estrone sulfate levels.

Pharmacodynamics/Kinetics

Onset of Action Onset of estradiol reduction: 70% reduction after 24 hours; 80% after 2 weeks of therapy

Duration of Action Duration of estradiol reduction: 6 days

Half-life Elimination ~50 hours

Time to Peak Plasma: ~2 hours without food; 5 hours with food

Pregnancy Risk Factor X

Pregnancy Considerations Adverse events were observed in animal reproduction studies. Anastrozole is contraindicated in women who are or may become pregnant (may cause fetal harm if administered during pregnancy). Use in premenopausal women with breast cancer does not provide any clinical benefit.

Anidulafungin (ay nid yoo la FUN jin)

Related Information

Fungal Infections *on page 1847*

Brand Names: US Eraxis

Brand Names: Canada Eraxis

Pharmacologic Category Antifungal Agent, Parenteral; Echinocandin

Use Treatment of candidemia and other forms of *Candida* infections (including those of intra-abdominal, peritoneal, and esophageal locus)

Local Anesthetic/Vasoconstrictor Precautions No information available to require special precautions

Effects on Dental Treatment No significant effects or complications reported

Effects on Bleeding No information available to require special precautions

Adverse Reactions

>10%:

Cardiovascular: Hypotension (15%), hypertension (12%), peripheral edema (11%)

Central nervous system: Insomnia (15%)

Endocrine & metabolic: Hypokalemia (≤25%), hypomagnesemia (12%)

Gastrointestinal: Nausea (7% to 24%), diarrhea (9% to 18%), vomiting (7% to 18%)

Genitourinary: Urinary tract infection (15%)

Hepatic: Increased serum alkaline phosphatase (12%)

Infection: Bacteremia (18%)

Respiratory: Dyspnea (12%)

Miscellaneous: Fever (9% to 18%)

2% to 10%:

Cardiovascular: Deep vein thrombosis (10%), chest pain (5%)

Central nervous system: Confusion (8%), headache (8%), depression (6%)

Dermatologic: Decubitus ulcer (5%)

Endocrine & metabolic: Hypoglycemia (7%), dehydration (6%), hyperglycemia (6%), hyperkalemia (6%)

Gastrointestinal: Constipation (8%), dyspepsia (7%), abdominal pain (6%), oral candidiasis (5%)

Hematologic & oncologic: Anemia (8% to 9%), leukocytosis (5% to 8%), thrombocythemia (6%)

Hepatic: Increased serum transaminases (≤5%)

Infection: Sepsis (7%)

Neuromuscular & skeletal: Back pain (5%)

Renal: Increased serum creatinine (5%)

Respiratory: Pleural effusion (10%), cough (7%), pneumonia (6%), respiratory distress (6%)

<2%, postmarketing, and/or case reports: Anaphylactic shock, anaphylaxis, angioedema, atrial fibrillation, blood coagulation disorder, blurred vision, bronchospasm, cholestasis, clostridium infection, diaphoresis, dizziness, ECG abnormality (including ECG changes – prolonged Q-T interval), erythema, eye pain, flushing, hepatic insufficiency, hepatic necrosis, hepatitis, hot flash, increased amylase, increased blood urea nitrogen, increased creatine phosphokinase, increased gamma-glutamyl transferase, increased serum bilirubin, increased serum lipase, infusion related reaction, prolonged prothrombin time, pruritus, right bundle branch block, rigors, seizure, sinus arrhythmia, skin rash, thrombocytopenia, thrombophlebitis, urticaria, ventricular premature contractions, visual disturbance

General Dosage Range IV: *Adults:* Initial dose: 100-200 mg as a single dose; Subsequent dosing: 50-100 mg daily

Mechanism of Action Noncompetitive inhibitor of 1,3-beta-D-glucan synthase resulting in reduced formation of 1,3-beta-D-glucan, an essential polysaccharide comprising 30% to 60% of *Candida* cell walls (absent in mammalian cells); decreased glucan content leads to osmotic instability and cellular lysis

Pharmacodynamics/Kinetics

Half-life Elimination Terminal: 40-50 hours

Pregnancy Risk Factor B

Pregnancy Considerations Adverse effects were observed in animal reproduction studies. Other agents are currently preferred for the treatment of *Candida* infections in pregnant women (IDSA [Pappas 2016]).

Anthralin (AN thra lin)

Brand Names: US Dritho-Creme HP; Zithranol; Zithranol-RR

Brand Names: Canada Anthraforte; Anthranol; Anthrascalp; Micanol

Pharmacologic Category Antipsoriatic Agent; Keratolytic Agent

Use Plaque psoriasis: Treatment of stable plaque psoriasis

Local Anesthetic/Vasoconstrictor Precautions No information available to require special precautions

Effects on Dental Treatment No significant effects or complications reported

Effects on Bleeding No information available to require special precautions

Adverse Reactions Frequency not defined.

Dermatologic: Allergic contact sensitivity, erythema, hair discoloration (temporary), nail discoloration (temporary), skin discoloration (temporary)

Miscellaneous: Transient irritation (uninvolved skin)

General Dosage Range Topical:

Children ≥12 years, Adolescents, and Adults: Shampoo: Apply 3 to 4 times weekly

Adults: Cream: Generally, apply once daily or as directed, Shampoo: Apply 3 to 4 times weekly

Mechanism of Action Reduction of the mitotic rate and proliferation of epidermal cells in psoriasis by inhibiting synthesis of nucleic protein from inhibition of DNA synthesis to affected areas

Pregnancy Risk Factor C

Pregnancy Considerations Animal reproduction studies have not been conducted.

Anthrax Immune Globulin (Human)

(AN thraks i MYUN GLOB yoo lin YU man)

Pharmacologic Category Antidote; Blood Product Derivative; Immune Globulin

Use

Anthrax (inhalational exposure): Treatment of inhalational anthrax in adult and pediatric patients in combination with appropriate antibacterial drugs.

Limitations of use: Effectiveness is based solely on efficacy studies conducted in animal models of inhalational anthrax. Anthrax immune globulin (human) (AIGIV) does not have direct antibacterial activity, does not cross the blood-brain barrier, and does not prevent or treat meningitis. There have been no studies in the pediatric, geriatric, or obese populations.

Local Anesthetic/Vasoconstrictor Precautions No information available to require special precautions

Effects on Dental Treatment No significant effects or complications reported

Effects on Bleeding Intravenous immune globulin products have been associated with antiglobulin hemolysis (acute or delayed) resulting in hemolytic anemia; thrombosis may occur with immune globulin products even in the absence of risk factors for thrombosis.

Adverse Reactions Frequency not always defined.

Cardiovascular: Cardiac arrest, edema, hypotension, peripheral edema

Central nervous system: Headache (20%; dose dependent)

Endocrine & metabolic: Glycosuria (dose related), hyperkalemia, metabolic acidosis

Gastrointestinal: Nausea (9%)

Hematologic & oncologic: Blood coagulation disorder

Hepatic: Ascites

Local: Pain at injection site (9%), swelling at injection site (7%)

Renal: Renal insufficiency

Respiratory: Acute respiratory distress, pleural effusion, pulmonary edema

Mechanism of Action Antibodies obtained from pooled human plasma of individuals immunized with the anthrax vaccine provide passive immunity and neutralizes the anthrax toxin by binding to protective antigen (PA) to prevent PA-mediated cellular entry of anthrax edema factor and lethal factor.

Pharmacodynamics/Kinetics

Half-life Elimination 24 to 28 days

Time to Peak ~2.5 to 4 hours

Pregnancy Considerations Human data are not available related to the use of anthrax immune globulin in pregnancy. However, anthrax immune globulin is expected to cross the placenta. Anthrax infection is associated with maternal and fetal death. Criteria for treating pregnant and postpartum women should be the same as nonpregnant women unless other contraindications exist. Dosing of anthrax immune globulin in pregnancy should also follow the same weight-based dosing schedule (Meaney-Delman, 2014).

Product Availability Anthrasil: FDA approved March 2015; availability is limited to the US Strategic National Stockpile

Antihemophilic Factor (Human)

(an tee hee moe FIL ik FAK tor HYU man)

Brand Names: US Hemofil M; Koate; Koate-DVI; Monoclate-P

Brand Names: Canada Hemofil M

Pharmacologic Category Antihemophilic Agent; Blood Product Derivative

Use Hemophilia A: Control and prevention of bleeding episodes in patients with hemophilia A (classic hemophilia); perioperative management of hemophilia A.

Limitations of use: Not indicated for the treatment of von Willebrand disease.

Local Anesthetic/Vasoconstrictor Precautions No information available to require special precautions

Effects on Dental Treatment No significant effects or complications reported

Effects on Bleeding Following large doses, an increased bleeding tendency has rarely been reported. Mild thrombocytopenia has been reported. Due to underlying hemophilia and complications of thrombotic events, a medical consultation is warranted.

Adverse Reactions <1%, postmarketing, and/or case reports: Acute hemolytic anemia, anaphylaxis (rare), blurred vision, chest tightness, chills, drowsiness, fever, headache, hemorrhagic diathesis, hypersensitivity reaction (rare), increased factor VIII inhibitors, increased serum fibrinogen, jitteriness, lethargy, nausea, pain at injection site, stomach discomfort, tingling sensation, urticaria, vasomotor symptoms (with rapid infusion), vomiting

General Dosage Range IV: *Children, Adolescents, and Adults:* Dosage varies greatly depending on indication

Mechanism of Action Protein (factor VIII) in normal plasma which is necessary for clot formation and maintenance of hemostasis; activates factor X in conjunction with activated factor IX; activated factor X converts prothrombin to thrombin, which converts fibrinogen to fibrin, and with factor XIII forms a stable clot

Pharmacodynamics/Kinetics

Half-life Elimination Mean: 14.8 to 17.5 hours

Pregnancy Risk Factor C

Pregnancy Considerations Animal reproduction studies have not been conducted. Parvovirus B19 or hepatitis A, which may be present in plasma-derived products, may affect a pregnant woman more seriously than nonpregnant women.

Antihemophilic Factor (Recombinant)

(an tee hee moe FIL ik FAK tor ree KOM be nant)

Brand Names: US Advate; Afstyla; Helixate FS; Kogenate FS; Kogenate FS Bio-Set; Kovaltry; Novoeight; Nuwiq; Recombinate; Xyntha; Xyntha Solofuse

Brand Names: Canada Advate; Helixate FS; Kogenate FS; Kovaltry; Nuwiq; Xyntha; Xyntha Solofuse

Pharmacologic Category Antihemophilic Agent

Use

Hemophilia A:

Control and prevention of bleeding episodes: For the prevention and control of bleeding episodes in adults and children with hemophilia A.

Perioperative management: For surgical prophylaxis in adults and children with hemophilia A.

Routine prophylaxis to prevent or reduce the frequency of bleeding: For routine prophylactic treatment to prevent or reduce the frequency of bleeding episodes in adults and children with hemophilia A.

Routine prophylaxis to prevent bleeding episodes and joint damage (Helixate FS, Kogenate FS): For routine prophylactic treatment to reduce the frequency of bleeding episodes and the risk of joint damage in children without preexisting joint damage.

Limitations of use: Not indicated for the treatment of von Willebrand disease.

Local Anesthetic/Vasoconstrictor Precautions No information available to require special precautions

Effects on Dental Treatment Key adverse event(s) related to dental treatment: Taste perversion.

Effects on Bleeding Following large doses, an increased bleeding tendency has rarely been reported. Mild thrombocytopenia has been reported. Due to underlying hemophilia and complications of thrombotic events, a medical consultation is warranted.

Adverse Reactions Actual frequency may vary by product.

>10%:

Central nervous system: Headache (7% to 26%)

Dermatologic: Pruritus (≤16%), skin rash (≤16%), urticaria (≤16%)

Gastrointestinal: Nausea (6% to 13%), vomiting (7% to 12%)

Hematologic & oncologic: Increased factor VIII inhibitors (≤20%)

Local: Catheter infection (18% to 19%)

Neuromuscular & skeletal: Arthralgia (8% to 25%)

Respiratory: Cough (11% to 19%), nasopharyngitis (17%)

Miscellaneous: Fever (≤43%; in patients previously exposed to factor VIII products: <1%)

1% to 10%:

Cardiovascular: Chest discomfort (1%), palpitations (1%), sinus tachycardia (1%)

Central nervous system: Pain (8%), procedural pain (5%), insomnia (3%), chills (≤1%), dizziness (≤1%)

Dermatologic: Allergic dermatitis (1%)

Gastrointestinal: Diarrhea (5% to 8%), abdominal distress (2%), abdominal pain (2%), dyspepsia (2%)

Hematologic & oncologic: Lymphadenopathy (1%)

Hepatic: Increased liver enzymes (in patients previously exposed to factor VIII products: 1%)

Hypersensitivity: Hypersensitivity reaction (2%)

Local: injection site reaction (3% to 7%)

Neuromuscular & skeletal: Weakness (5% to 7%), back pain (≤3%; more common in children)

Otic: Otic infection (≤5%)

Respiratory: Pharyngolaryngeal pain (9%), upper respiratory tract infection (9%), nasal congestion (8%), rhinorrhea (5%)

Miscellaneous: Limb injury (10%)

<1%, postmarketing, and/or case reports: Anaphylaxis, angioedema, anorexia, catheter complication (venous catheter access), chest discomfort, cold extremities, cyanosis, drowsiness, dysgeusia, edema, epistaxis, erythema, facial edema, facial flushing, fatigue, feeling hot, flushing, hematoma, hot flash, hyperhidrosis, hypotension, inflammation at injection site, joint swelling, laryngeal edema, limb pain, loss of consciousness, maculopapular rash, malaise, myalgia, pain at injection site, pallor, paresthesia, restlessness, tachycardia, tremor, vasodilatation, vertigo, xerostomia

General Dosage Range IV: *Children, Adolescents, and Adults:* Dosage varies greatly depending on indication

Mechanism of Action Factor VIII replacement, necessary for clot formation and maintenance of hemostasis. It activates factor X in conjunction with activated factor IX; activated factor X converts prothrombin to thrombin, which converts fibrinogen to fibrin, and with factor XIII forms a stable clot.

Pharmacodynamics/Kinetics

Half-life Elimination

Advate: Children <12 years: 8.7 to 11.2 hours; Adolescents and Adults: 12 hours

Afstyla: Children <12 years: 10.2 to 10.4 hours; Children ≥12 years and Adolescents: 14.3 hours; Adults: 14.2 hours

Helixate FS, Kogenate FS: Children: 10.7 hours; Adults: 13.7 to 14.6 hours

Kovaltry: Children <12 years: ~12 hours; Children ≥12 years, Adolescents, and Adults: ~14 hours

Novoeight: Children <12 years: 7.7 to 10 hours; Adolescents and Adults: 11 to 12 hours

Nuwiq: Children ≤12 years: 11.9 to 13.1 hours; Adolescents and Adults: 17.1 hours

Recombinate: Adults: 14.6 hours

Xyntha, Xyntha Solofuse: Children and Adolescents: 6.9 to 8.3 hours; Adults: 11 to 17 hours

Pregnancy Risk Factor C

Pregnancy Considerations Animal reproduction studies have not been conducted. Factor VIII concentrations may increase in pregnant women with coagulation disorders. Pregnant women should have clotting factors monitored, particularly at 28 and 34 weeks gestation and prior to invasive procedures. Prophylaxis may be needed if concentrations are <50 units/mL at term and treatment should continue for 3 to 5 days postpartum depending on route of delivery. Because parvovirus infection may cause hydrops fetalis or fetal death, a recombinant product is preferred if prophylaxis or treatment is needed. The neonate may also be at an increased risk of bleeding following delivery and should be tested for the coagulation disorder (Kadir 2009; Lee 2006).

Product Availability Afstyla: FDA approved May 2016; availability anticipated in summer of 2016. Afstyla is indicated in adults and children with hemophilia A for the on-demand treatment and control of bleeding episodes, routine prophylaxis to reduce the frequency of bleeding episodes, and perioperative management of bleeding. Refer to the prescribing information for additional information.

Antihemophilic Factor (Recombinant [Fc Fusion Protein])

(an tee hee moe FIL ik FAK tor ree KOM be nant eff see FYOO zhun PRO teen)

Brand Names: US Eloctate

Brand Names: Canada Eloctate

Pharmacologic Category Antihemophilic Agent

Use Hemophilia A:

Control and prevention of bleeding episodes: For the prevention and control of bleeding episodes in adults and children with hemophilia A.

Perioperative management: For surgical prophylaxis in adults and children with hemophilia A.

Routine prophylaxis to prevent or reduce the frequency of bleeding: For routine prophylactic treatment to prevent or reduce the frequency of bleeding episodes in adults and children with hemophilia A.

Limitation of use: Not indicated for the treatment of von Willebrand disease.

Local Anesthetic/Vasoconstrictor Precautions No information available to require special precautions

Effects on Dental Treatment No significant effects or complications reported

Effects on Bleeding Following large doses, an increased bleeding tendency has rarely been reported. Mild thrombocytopenia has been reported. Due to underlying hemophilia and complications of thrombotic events, a medical consultation is warranted.

Adverse Reactions <1%, postmarketing, and/or case reports: Antibody development (Factor VIII inhibitor development), arthralgia, back pain, bradycardia, chest pain, cough, dizziness, dysgeusia, feeling hot, headache, hot flash, hypertension, joint swelling, lower abdominal pain, malaise, myalgia, procedural hypotension, sensation of cold, skin rash, venous pain (post-injection)

General Dosage Range IV: *Children, Adolescents, and Adults:* Dosage varies greatly depending on indication

Mechanism of Action Factor VIII replacement, necessary for clot formation and maintenance of hemostasis. It activates factor X in conjunction with activated factor IX; activated factor X converts prothrombin to thrombin, which converts fibrinogen to fibrin, and with factor XIII forms a stable clot.

Pharmacodynamics/Kinetics

Half-life Elimination Children <12 years: 12.7 to 14.9 hours; Children ≥12 years, Adolescents, and Adults: 16.4 to 19.7 hours

Pregnancy Considerations Animal reproduction studies have not been conducted. Factor VIII concentrations may increase in pregnant women with coagulation disorders. Pregnant women should have clotting factors monitored, particularly at 28 and 34 weeks gestation and prior to invasive procedures. Prophylaxis may be needed if concentrations are <50 units/mL at term and treatment should continue for 3 to 5 days postpartum depending on route of delivery. Because parvovirus infection may cause hydrops fetalis or fetal death, a recombinant product is preferred if prophylaxis or treatment is needed. The neonate may also be at an increased risk of bleeding following delivery and should be tested for the coagulation disorder (Kadir 2009; Lee 2006).

Antihemophilic Factor/von Willebrand Factor Complex (Human)

(an tee hee moe FIL ik FAK tor von WILL le brand FAK tor KOM plex HYU man)

Brand Names: US Alphanate; Humate-P; Wilate

Brand Names: Canada Humate-P

Pharmacologic Category Antihemophilic Agent; Blood Product Derivative

Use

Hemophilia A:

Alphanate: Treatment and prevention of bleeding in adult and pediatric patients with factor VIII deficiency due to hemophilia A (classical hemophilia).

Humate-P: Treatment and prevention of bleeding in adults with hemophilia A (classical hemophilia).

von Willebrand disease:

Alphanate: Surgical and/or invasive procedures in adult and pediatric patients with von Willebrand disease when desmopressin is either ineffective or contraindicated

Limitations of use: Not indicated for patients with severe von Willebrand disease (type 3) undergoing major surgery.

Humate-P: Treatment of spontaneous or trauma-induced bleeding, as well as prevention of excessive bleeding during and after surgery in adult and pediatric patients with severe von Willebrand disease, including mild or moderate von Willebrand disease where use of desmopressin is known or suspected to be inadequate.

Limitations of use: Safety and efficacy of prophylactic dosing to prevent spontaneous bleeding have not been conducted in patients with von Willebrand disease.

Wilate: On demand treatment and control of bleeding episodes, and perioperative management of bleeding in adult and pediatric patients with von Willebrand disease.

Local Anesthetic/Vasoconstrictor Precautions No information available to require special precautions

Effects on Dental Treatment No significant effects or complications reported

Effects on Bleeding Following large doses, an increased bleeding tendency has rarely been reported. Mild thrombocytopenia has been reported. Due to underlying hemophilia and complications of thrombotic events, a medical consultation is warranted.

Adverse Reactions Frequency not always defined.

Cardiovascular: Facial edema (>5%), peripheral edema (1%), vasodilatation (1%), chest pain, orthostatic hypotension, phlebitis, pulmonary embolism (large doses), subdural hematoma, thrombophlebitis

Central nervous system: Chills (>5%), fatigue (>5%), pain (>5%), paresthesia (3% to >5%), dizziness (1%), cerebral hemorrhage, drowsiness, headache, insomnia

Dermatologic: Skin rash (>5%), pruritus (1% to >5%), urticaria (1% to >5%), diaphoresis

Endocrine & metabolic: Hypermenorrhea

Gastrointestinal: Nausea (24%; postoperative), constipation, gastrointestinal hemorrhage, sore throat, vomiting

Genitourinary: Urinary retention, urinary tract infection

Hematologic & oncologic: Hemorrhage (30%; postoperative), anemia, decreased hematocrit (moderate), increased factor VIII inhibitors

Hepatic: Increased serum ALT

Hypersensitivity: Anaphylaxis, hypersensitivity reaction (2%)

Infection: Parvovirus B19 seroconversion (3%; not accompanied by clinical signs of disease), infection, sepsis

Local: Pain at injection site

Neuromuscular & skeletal: Arthralgia (>5%), limb pain (1%), back pain

Renal: Pyelonephritis

Respiratory: Respiratory distress (>5%), cough, pharyngitis

Miscellaneous: Postoperative pain (17%), fever (>5%)

Postmarketing and/or case reports: Abdominal pain, antibody development (neutralizing), cardiorespiratory arrest, chest discomfort, chest tightness, dyspnea, edema, flushing, hemolysis, hypervolemia, lethargy, parotid gland enlargement, seizure, shock, tachycardia, thromboembolic complications, venous thrombosis (femoral)

General Dosage Range IV: *Infants, Children, Adolescents, and Adults:* Dosage varies greatly depending on indication and product

Mechanism of Action Factor VIII and von Willebrand factor (VWF), obtained from pooled human plasma, are used to replace endogenous factor VIII and VWF in patients with hemophilia or von Willebrand disease. Factor VIII in conjunction with activated factor IX, activates factor X which converts prothrombin to thrombin and fibrinogen to fibrin. VWF promotes platelet aggregation and adhesion to damaged vascular endothelium and acts as a stabilizing carrier protein for factor VIII. (Circulating levels of functional VWF are measured as ristocetin cofactor activity [VWF:RCo]).

Pharmacodynamics/Kinetics

Onset of Action Shortening of bleeding time: Immediate; maximum effect: 1 to 2 hours

Duration of Action von Willebrand disease: Shortening of bleeding time: <6 hours postinfusion; presence of VWF multimers detected in the plasma: ≥24 hours (Alphanate)

Half-life Elimination

Factor VIII coagulant activity (FVIII:C): Range: 8 to 28 hours in patients with hemophilia A

VWF:RCo: Range (in patients with von Willebrand disease): Alphanate: 4 to 16 hours; Humate: 3 to 34 hours; Wilate: 6 to 49 hours

Pregnancy Risk Factor C

Pregnancy Considerations Animal reproduction studies have not been conducted. Parvovirus B19 or hepatitis A, which may be present in plasma-derived products, may affect a pregnant woman more seriously than nonpregnant women.

Women with von Willebrand disease have an increased risk of bleeding associated with invasive gynecologic procedures and delivery. The risk of miscarriage is also increased (NHLBI 2007; Pacheco 2010). Pregnant women with von Willebrand disease or hemophilia may have a transient increase in factor VIII during the second and third trimesters. Close monitoring is needed and therapy is recommended if levels are <50 units/dL prior to delivery (Pacheco 2010; Srivastava 2013). If otherwise indicated, therapy with von Willebrand factor concentrates should be used. Bleeding associated with postpartum hemorrhage is increased and may be delayed; women should be monitored after delivery for at least 2 weeks (Pacheco 2010).

Anti-inhibitor Coagulant Complex (Human)

(an TEE in HI bi tor coe AG yoo lant KOM pleks HYU man)

Brand Names: US FEIBA

Brand Names: Canada FEIBA NF

Pharmacologic Category Activated Prothrombin Complex Concentrate (aPCC); Antihemophilic Agent; Blood Product Derivative

Use

Hemorrhage in patients with hemophilia: For use in patients with hemophilia A and B with inhibitors for control and prevention of bleeding episodes.

Perioperative bleeding management in patients with hemophilia: For use in patients with hemophilia A and B with inhibitors for perioperative management.

Routine prophylaxis of bleeding events in patients with hemophilia: For use in patients with hemophilia A and B for routine prophylaxis to prevent or reduce the frequency of bleeding episodes.

Local Anesthetic/Vasoconstrictor Precautions No information available to require special precautions

Effects on Dental Treatment No significant effects or complications reported

Effects on Bleeding Due to underlying hemophilia and complications of thrombotic events, a medical consultation is warranted.

Adverse Reactions Frequency not defined.

Cardiovascular: Cerebrovascular accident (embolic/thrombotic stroke), chest discomfort, chest pain, decreased blood pressure, flushing, hypertension, hypotension, myocardial infarction, pulmonary embolism, tachycardia, thromboembolism, thrombosis (arterial thrombosis, venous thrombosis)

Central nervous system: Chills, dizziness, drowsiness, headache, hypoesthesia (including facial), malaise, paresthesia

Dermatologic: Pruritus, skin rash, urticaria

Gastrointestinal: Abdominal distress, diarrhea, dysgeusia, nausea, vomiting

Hematologic & oncologic: Disseminated intravascular coagulation

Hypersensitivity: Angioedema, hypersensitivity reaction (including anaphylaxis)

Immunologic: Antibody development (anamnestic response)

Local: Pain at injection site

Miscellaneous: Fever

Respiratory: Bronchospasm, cough, dyspnea, wheezing

General Dosage Range IV: *Children, Adolescents, and Adults:* 50-100 units/kg every 6-12 hours (maximum: 100 units/kg [single dose]; 200 units/kg/day [total daily dose])

Mechanism of Action Multiple interactions of the components in anti-inhibitor coagulant complex restore the impaired thrombin generation of hemophilia patients with inhibitors. *In vitro*, anti-inhibitor coagulant complex shortens the activated partial thromboplastin time of plasma containing factor VIII inhibitor.

Pharmacodynamics/Kinetics

Onset of Action Peak thrombin generation: Within 15-30 minutes (Varadi, 2003)

Duration of Action 8-12 hours (based on thrombin generation) (Varadi, 2003)

Half-life Elimination 4-7 hours (based on thrombin generation) (Varadi, 2003)

Pregnancy Risk Factor C

Pregnancy Considerations Animal reproduction studies have not been conducted.

Antipyrine and Benzocaine

(an tee PYE reen & BEN zoe kane)

Related Information

Benzocaine *on page 213*

Brand Names: US Aurodex [DSC]

Brand Names: Canada Auralgan®

Pharmacologic Category Otic Agent, Analgesic; Otic Agent, Cerumenolytic

Use Temporary relief of pain and reduction of swelling associated with acute congestive and serous otitis media; facilitates ear wax removal

Local Anesthetic/Vasoconstrictor Precautions No information available to require special precautions

Effects on Dental Treatment No significant effects or complications reported

Effects on Bleeding No information available to require special precautions

Adverse Reactions No adverse reactions are reported in the manufacturer's labeling. Refer to Benzocaine monograph.

General Dosage Range Otic: *Children and Adults:* Instill drops 3 times/day (ear wax removal) or fill ear canal every 1-2 hours (otitis media)

Mechanism of Action Antipyrine has analgesic properties; benzocaine is a local anesthetic; the glycerin base provides decreased middle ear pressure by osmosis.

Pharmacodynamics/Kinetics

Onset of Action Pain relief: ~30 minutes (Hoberman 1997)

Pregnancy Risk Factor C

Pregnancy Considerations Animal reproduction studies have not been conducted with this combination.

Antithrombin

(an tee THROM bin)

Brand Names: US ATryn; Thrombate III

Brand Names: Canada Antithrombin III NF; Thrombate III®

Pharmacologic Category Anticoagulant; Blood Product Derivative

Use

Treatment and prevention of antithrombin deficiency: Thrombate III: Treatment and prevention of thromboembolism and prevention of peri-operative and peri-partum thromboembolism in patients with hereditary antithrombin (AT) deficiency.

Prevention of thromboembolic events: ATryn: Prevention of perioperative and peripartum thromboembolic events in patients with hereditary antithrombin deficiency.

Limitations of use: Not indicated for treatment of thromboembolic events in patients with hereditary antithrombin deficiency.

Local Anesthetic/Vasoconstrictor Precautions No information available to require special precautions

Effects on Dental Treatment No significant effects or complications reported

Effects on Bleeding As with all anticoagulant drugs, bleeding is a potential adverse effect of antithrombin during dental surgery; risk is dependent on multiple variables, including the intensity of anticoagulation and patient susceptibility. Medical consult is suggested. It is unlikely that ambulatory patients presenting for dental treatment will be taking intravenous anticoagulant therapy such as antithrombin.

Adverse Reactions

1% to 10%:

- Cardiovascular: Chest pain (≤2%)
- Central nervous system: Dizziness (2%)
- Gastrointestinal: Liver enzyme abnormalities (≤2%)
- Genitourinary: Hematuria (≤2%)
- Hematologic & oncologic: Hemorrhage (≥5%), hematoma (≤2%)
- Local: Infusion site reaction (≥5%)
- Neuromuscular & skeletal: Hemarthrosis (≤2%)

<1%, postmarketing, and/or case reports: Blurred vision, chest tightness, chills, dizziness, dyspnea, fever, gastrointestinal fullness, muscle cramps, nausea, unpleasant taste, urticaria

General Dosage Range IV: *Adults:* Dosage varies greatly depending on indication

Mechanism of Action Antithrombin is the primary physiologic inhibitor of *in vivo* coagulation. It is an alpha$_2$-globulin. Its principal actions are the inactivation of thrombin, plasmin, and other active serine proteases of coagulation, including factors IXa, Xa, XIa, and XIIa. The inactivation of proteases is a major step in the normal clotting process. The strong activation of clotting enzymes at the site of every bleeding injury facilitates fibrin formation and maintains normal hemostasis. Thrombosis in the circulation would be caused by active serine proteases if they were not inhibited by antithrombin after the localized clotting process (Schwartz, 1989).

In patients with hereditary antithrombin (AT) deficiency, spontaneous thrombosis may occur due to decreased AT concentrations; therapy with human or recombinant AT restores functional AT activity.

Pharmacodynamics/Kinetics

Half-life Elimination

Plasma derived (Thrombate III): Biologic: 2.5 days (immunologic assay); 3.8 days (functional AT assay). Half-life may be decreased following surgery, with hemorrhage, acute thrombosis, and/or during heparin administration.

Recombinant derived (ATryn): 12-18 hours; surgery, childbirth hemorrhage, and/or concomitant heparin may shorten half-life

Pregnancy Risk Factor B (Thrombate III); C (ATryn)

Pregnancy Considerations

ATryn: Adverse events were observed in some animal reproduction studies. An increased risk of adverse fetal or neonatal effects has not been observed in studies involving a limited number of pregnant women in their 3rd trimester. Pharmacokinetic studies in pregnant women using the recombinant product showed an increase in clearance and volume of distribution compared to nonpregnant patients. Therefore, distinct initial dosing recommendations are provided for pregnant women compared to nonpregnant patients.

Thrombate III: Adverse events were not observed in animal reproduction studies. Dosing recommendations do not differ for obstetric patients compared to nonpregnant patients.

In patients with hereditary antithrombin (AT) deficiency, the risk of thromboembolic events such as VTE is increased; pregnancy and delivery further increase this risk. These products are specifically indicated for use in pregnant women with hereditary AT deficiency to decrease this risk, although use of other agents may be preferred (Bates, 2012).

Thromboembolism has been reported in children of women with hereditary AT deficiency; AT concentrations in neonates of parents with hereditary AT deficiency should be measured immediately after birth. Plasma AT levels are typically lower in neonates and infants than in adults. Low plasma AT concentrations in neonates may not be indicative of deficiency; consultation with a coagulation expert is recommended.

Antithymocyte Globulin (Equine)

(an te THY moe site GLOB yu lin, E kwine)

Brand Names: US Atgam

Brand Names: Canada Atgam

Pharmacologic Category Immune Globulin; Immunosuppressant Agent; Polyclonal Antibody

Use

Aplastic anemia: Treatment of moderate-to-severe aplastic anemia in patients not considered suitable candidates for bone marrow transplantation

Limitations of use: The usefulness of antithymocyte globulin (equine) has not been demonstrated in patients with aplastic anemia who are suitable candidates for transplantation, or in aplastic anemia secondary to neoplastic disease, storage disease, myelofibrosis, Fanconi syndrome, or in patients with known prior treatment with myelotoxic agents or radiation therapy

Local Anesthetic/Vasoconstrictor Precautions No information available to require special precautions

Effects on Dental Treatment Key adverse event(s) related to dental treatment: Stomatitis

Effects on Bleeding No information available to require special precautions

Adverse Reactions

>10%:

Central nervous system: Chills, headache

Dermatologic: Dermatological reaction (wheal/flare), pruritus, skin rash, urticaria

Hematologic & oncologic: Leukopenia, thrombocytopenia

Neuromuscular & skeletal: Arthralgia

Miscellaneous: Fever

1% to 10%:

Cardiovascular: Bradycardia, cardiac disease, cardiac failure, chest pain, edema, hypertension, hypotension, myocarditis, phlebitis, thrombophlebitis

Central nervous system: Agitation, brain disease (viral), burning sensation (burning of soles and burning of palms), dizziness, encephalitis, generalized ache, lethargy, seizure

Dermatologic: Diaphoresis, night sweats

Gastrointestinal: Diarrhea, nausea, stomatitis, vomiting

Genitourinary: Proteinuria

Hematologic & oncologic: Lymphadenopathy

Hepatic: Abnormal hepatic function tests, hepatosplenomegaly

Hypersensitivity: Anaphylaxis, serum sickness

Infection: Viral infection

Local: Injection site reaction (pain, redness, swelling)

Neuromuscular & skeletal: Back pain, joint stiffness, myalgia

Ophthalmic: Periorbital edema

Renal: Renal function test abnormality

Respiratory: Dyspnea, pleural effusion, respiratory distress

<1%, postmarketing, and/or case reports: Abdominal pain, acute renal failure, anaphylactoid reaction, anemia, apnea, confusion, cough, deep vein thrombosis, disorientation, dizziness, eosinophilia, epigastric pain, epistaxis, erythema, flank pain, gastrointestinal hemorrhage, gastrointestinal perforation, granulocytopenia, hemolysis, hemolytic anemia, herpes simplex infection (reactivation), hiccups, hyperglycemia, infection, involuntary body movements, laryngospasm, malaise, muscle rigidity, neutropenia, pancytopenia, paresthesia, pulmonary edema, pure red cell aplasia, renal artery thrombosis, sore mouth, sore throat, tachycardia, thrombosis of vein (iliac), toxic epidermal necrolysis, tremor, vasculitis, viral hepatitis, weakness, wound dehiscence

General Dosage Range IV: *Children, Adolescents, and Adults:* 10 to 20 mg/kg/day administered daily for 8 to 14 days; may be followed by administration every other day (maximum: 21 doses in 28 days)

Mechanism of Action Immunosuppressant involved in the elimination of antigen-reactive T lymphocytes (killer cells) in peripheral blood or alteration in the function of T-lymphocytes, which are involved in humoral immunity and partly in cell-mediated immunity; induces complete or partial hematologic response in aplastic anemia

Pharmacodynamics/Kinetics

Half-life Elimination 5.7 ± 3 days

Pregnancy Considerations

Adverse events were observed in some animal reproduction studies.

The National Transplantation Pregnancy Registry (NTPR) is a registry which follows pregnancies which occur in maternal transplant recipients or those fathered by male transplant recipients. The NTPR encourages reporting of pregnancies following solid organ transplant by contacting them at 877-955-6877 or NTPR@giftoflifeinstitute.org.

Apixaban (a PIX a ban)

Related Information

Antiplatelet and Anticoagulation Considerations in Dentistry *on page 1764*

Brand Names: US Eliquis

Brand Names: Canada Eliquis

Pharmacologic Category Anticoagulant; Anticoagulant, Factor Xa Inhibitor; Direct Oral Anticoagulant (DOAC)

Use

Deep vein thrombosis: Treatment of deep vein thrombosis; to reduce the risk of recurrent deep vein thrombosis following initial therapy

Nonvalvular atrial fibrillation: To reduce the risk of stroke and systemic embolism in patients with nonvalvular atrial fibrillation (AF)

Note: The 2014 American Heart Association/American College of Cardiology/Heart Rhythm Society guidelines for the management of AF recommend oral anticoagulation for patients with nonvalvular AF or atrial flutter with prior stroke, TIA, or a CHA_2DS_2-VASc score ≥2. As an alternative to warfarin, apixaban may also be used for 3 weeks prior and 4 weeks after cardioversion in patients with AF or atrial flutter of ≥48 hours duration or when the duration is unknown (January 2014)

Postoperative venous thromboprophylaxis following hip or knee replacement surgery: Prophylaxis of deep vein thrombosis, which may lead to pulmonary embolism, in patients who have undergone hip or knee replacement surgery

Pulmonary embolism: Treatment of pulmonary embolism; to reduce the risk of recurrent pulmonary embolism following initial therapy

Local Anesthetic/Vasoconstrictor Precautions No information available to require special precautions

Effects on Dental Treatment Key adverse event(s) related to dental treatment: Surgical site bleeding may occur. See Effects on Bleeding.

Effects on Bleeding Apixaban inhibits platelet activation and fibrin clot formation via direct, selective, and reversible inhibition of factor Xa. As with all anticoagulants, bleeding is the major adverse effect of apixaban. Hemorrhage may occur at virtually any site; risk is dependent on multiple variables including the intensity of anticoagulation and patient susceptibility. Medical consult is suggested.

Adverse Reactions

>10%: Hematologic & oncologic: Hemorrhage (1% to 12%; major: ≤3%; clinically relevant nonmajor bleeding: 2% to 4%)

1% to 10%:

Endocrine & metabolic: Increased gamma-glutamyl transferase (≤1%)

Gastrointestinal: Nausea (3%), gingival hemorrhage (≤1%)

Genitourinary: Hematuria (≤2%), hypermenorrhea (1%)

Hematologic & oncologic: Anemia (3%), bruise (1% to 2%), hematoma (1% to 2%), postprocedural hemorrhage (≤1%), rectal hemorrhage (≤1%)

Hepatic: Increased serum transaminases (≤1%)

Respiratory: Epistaxis (≤4%), hemoptysis (≤1%)

<1%, postmarketing, and/or case reports: Abnormal hepatic function tests, abnormal uterine bleeding, acute posthemorrhagic anemia, allergic edema, anal hemorrhage, anaphylaxis, conjunctival hemorrhage, gastrointestinal hemorrhage, genital bleeding, hematemesis, hematochezia, hematoma, hematoma at injection site, hemophthalmos, hemorrhoidal bleeding, hypersensitivity, hypotension, incision site hemorrhage, increased serum alkaline phosphatase, increased serum AST, increased serum bilirubin, intracranial hemorrhage, melena, muscle hemorrhage, occult blood in urine, perioperative blood loss, periorbital hematoma, petechia, postoperative hematoma (incision site), postprocedural hemorrhage, puncture site bleeding, retinal hemorrhage, skin rash, syncope, thrombocytopenia, vaginal hemorrhage, wound hemorrhage, wound secretion

General Dosage Range Dosage adjustment recommended in patients with multiple risk factors for bleeding including renal impairment or patients on concomitant therapy, and patients with body weight ≤60 kg

Oral: *Adults:* 2.5 to 5 mg twice daily

Mechanism of Action Inhibits platelet activation and fibrin clot formation via direct, selective and reversible inhibition of free and clot-bound factor Xa (FXa). FXa, as part of the prothrombinase complex consisting also of factor Va, calcium ions, and phospholipid, catalyzes the conversion of prothrombin to thrombin. Thrombin both activates platelets and catalyzes the conversion of fibrinogen to fibrin.

Pharmacodynamics/Kinetics

Onset of Action 3 to 4 hours

Half-life Elimination ~12 hours

Time to Peak 3 to 4 hours

Pregnancy Risk Factor B

Pregnancy Considerations Adverse events were not observed in animal reproduction studies. Data are insufficient to evaluate the safety of oral factor Xa inhibitors during pregnancy; use during pregnancy should be avoided (Bates 2012).

Dental Comment At this time there are no coagulation parameters for apixaban to predict the extent of bleeding. Increased bleeding may occur during invasive dental procedures in patients taking a total daily dose of 10 mg. Medical consult is suggested prior to dental invasive procedures.

Apomorphine (a poe MOR feen)

Brand Names: US Apokyn

Brand Names: Canada Movapo

Pharmacologic Category Anti-Parkinson Agent, Dopamine Agonist

Use Parkinson disease: Treatment of hypomobility "off" episodes with advanced Parkinson disease

Local Anesthetic/Vasoconstrictor Precautions Apomorphine is one of the drugs confirmed to prolong the QT interval and is accepted as having a risk of causing torsade de pointes. The risk of drug-induced torsade de pointes is extremely low when a single QT interval prolonging drug is prescribed. In terms of epinephrine, it is not known what effect vasoconstrictors in the local anesthetic regimen will have in patients with a known history of congenital prolonged QT interval or in patients taking any medication that prolongs the QT interval. Until more information is obtained, it is suggested that the clinician consult with the physician prior to the use of a vasoconstrictor in suspected patients, and that the vasoconstrictor (epinephrine, mepivacaine and levonordefrin [Carbocaine® 2% with Neo-Cobefrin®]) be used with caution.

Effects on Dental Treatment Key adverse event(s) related to dental treatment: Patients may experience orthostatic hypotension as they stand up after treatment; especially if lying in dental chair for extended periods of time. Use caution with sudden changes in position during and after dental treatment.

Effects on Bleeding No information available to require special precautions

Adverse Reactions Note: Frequency not always defined.

>10%:

Cardiovascular: Angina pectoris (15%), chest pain (15%), chest pressure (15%)

Central nervous system: Drowsiness (35%), dizziness (20%), orthostatic hypotension (20%)

Gastrointestinal: Nausea (30%), vomiting (30%)

Neuromuscular & skeletal: Dyskinesia (24% to 35%), falling (30%)

Respiratory: Yawning (40%), rhinorrhea (20%)

1% to 10%:

Cardiovascular: Edema (10%), vasodilatation (3%), hypotension (2%), syncope (2%), congestive heart failure

Central nervous system: Confusion (10%), hallucinations (10%), anxiety, depression, fatigue, headache, insomnia, pain
Dermatologic: Bruise
Endocrine & metabolic: Dehydration
Gastrointestinal: Constipation, diarrhea
Local: Injection site reaction
Neuromuscular & skeletal: Arthralgia, weakness
Miscellaneous: Diaphoresis

<1%, postmarketing, and/or case reports: Aggressive behavior, agitation, cardiac arrest, confusion, hemolytic anemia (combination therapy, Colosimo 1994; Frankel 1990), impulse control disorder, impulsivity, increased libido, myocardial infarction, panniculitis (focal), paranoia, priapism, psychosis (acute)

General Dosage Range Dosage adjustment recommended in patients with renal impairment

SubQ: *Adults:* Initial test dose: 2 mg; Starting dose: 2 to 3 mg/dose at time of "off" episode; Maintenance dose: 2 to 6 mg/dose at time of "off" episode (maximum: 6 mg/dose)

Mechanism of Action Stimulates postsynaptic D2-type receptors within the caudate putamen in the brain.

Pharmacodynamics/Kinetics

Onset of Action SubQ: Rapid

Half-life Elimination Terminal: ~40 minutes

Time to Peak Plasma: 10 to 60 minutes

Pregnancy Considerations Adverse events have been observed in animal reproduction studies.

Prescribing and Access Restrictions Apokyn is only available through specialty pharmacies and cannot be obtained through a retail pharmacy. For more information, contact 1-877-7APOKYN (1-877-727-6596).

Dental Comment See Local Anesthetic/Vasoconstrictor Precautions

Apraclonidine (a pra KLOE ni deen)

Brand Names: US Iopidine

Brand Names: Canada Iopidine

Pharmacologic Category $Alpha_2$ Agonist, Ophthalmic

Use

0.5% solution: Short-term, adjunctive therapy in patients who require additional reduction of IOP

1% solution: Prevention and treatment of postsurgical intraocular pressure (IOP) elevation following argon laser trabeculoplasty, argon laser iridotomy or Nd:YAG posterior capsulotomy

Local Anesthetic/Vasoconstrictor Precautions No information available to require special precautions

Effects on Dental Treatment Key adverse event(s) related to dental treatment: Xerostomia (normal salivary flow resumes upon discontinuation)

Effects on Bleeding No information available to require special precautions

Adverse Reactions

Frequency not always defined.

5% to 15%:

Gastrointestinal: Xerostomia (10%)
Ophthalmic: Eye discomfort, eye pruritus, ocular hyperemia

1% to 5%:

Cardiovascular: Cardiac arrhythmia (<3%), chest pain (<3%), facial edema (<3%), peripheral edema (<3%), localized blanching
Central nervous system: Altered sense of smell (<3%), ataxia (<3%), depression (<3%), dizziness (<3%), drowsiness (<3%), headache (<3%), insomnia (<3%), malaise (<3%), nervousness (<3%), paresthesia (<3%)
Dermatologic: Contact dermatitis (<3%), dermatitis (<3%)
Gastrointestinal: Constipation (<3%), dysgeusia (<3%), nausea (<3%)
Neuromuscular & skeletal: Myalgia (<3%), weakness (<3%)
Ophthalmic: Blurred vision, conjunctivitis, dry eye syndrome, eyelid edema, eye discharge, foreign body sensation of eye, lacrimation
Respiratory: Asthma (<3%), dry nose (<3%), dyspnea (<3%), pharyngitis (<3%), rhinitis (<3%)

<1%, postmarketing, and/or case reports: Blepharitis, blepharoconjunctivitis, bradycardia, conjunctival edema, corneal erosion, corneal infiltrates, corneal staining, crusting of eyelid, epithelial keratopathy, erythema of eyelid, eyelid disease, eyelid retraction, eye irritation, eye pain, follicular conjunctivitis, hypersensitivity reaction, keratitis, ocular edema, photophobia, scaling of eyelid, visual disturbance

General Dosage Range Ophthalmic: *Adults:* 0.5%: Instill 1 to 2 drops in the affected eye(s) 3 times daily; 1%: Instill 1 drop in operative eye 1 hour prior to and upon completion of surgery

Mechanism of Action Apraclonidine is a potent alpha-adrenergic agent similar to clonidine; relatively selective for $alpha_2$-receptors but does retain some binding to $alpha_1$-receptors; appears to result in reduction of aqueous humor formation; its penetration through the blood-brain barrier is more polar than clonidine which reduces its penetration through the blood-brain barrier and suggests that its pharmacological profile is characterized by peripheral rather than central effects.

Pharmacodynamics/Kinetics

Onset of Action 1 hour; Peak effect: Decreased intraocular pressure: 3 to 5 hours

Half-life Elimination Systemic: 0.5% solution: 8 hours

Pregnancy Risk Factor C

Pregnancy Considerations Adverse events have been observed in animal reproduction studies. If ophthalmic agents are needed during pregnancy, the minimum effective dose should be used in combination with punctual occlusion to decrease potential exposure to the fetus (Samples 1988).

Apremilast (a PRE mi last)

Brand Names: US Otezla

Brand Names: Canada Otezla

Pharmacologic Category Phosphodiesterase-4 Enzyme Inhibitor

Use

Psoriasis: Treatment of patients with moderate to severe plaque psoriasis who are candidates for phototherapy or systemic therapy

Psoriatic arthritis: Treatment of adult patients with active psoriatic arthritis (PsA)

Local Anesthetic/Vasoconstrictor Precautions No information available to require special precautions

Effects on Dental Treatment No significant effects or complications reported

Effects on Bleeding No information available to require special precautions

Adverse Reactions

Frequency not always defined.

Central nervous system: Tension headache (7%), headache (6%), fatigue (3%), depression (2%), insomnia (2%), migraine (2%), paresthesia (<2%)
Dermatologic: Skin rash (<2%), folliculitis (1%)
Endocrine & metabolic: Weight loss (≥5% of body weight: 19%; ≥10% of body weight: 6%)
Gastrointestinal: Diarrhea (18%), nausea (17%), vomiting (4%), decreased appetite (3%), dyspepsia (3%), abdominal distress (2%), abdominal pain (2%), frequent bowel movements (2%), upper abdominal pain (2%), abdominal distention (<2%), gastroesophageal reflux disease (<2%)
Hypersensitivity: Hypersensitivity (<2%)
Infection: Influenza (<2%), tooth abscess (1%)
Neuromuscular & skeletal: Back pain (2%), arthralgia (<2%), muscle spasm (<2%), myalgia (<2%)
Respiratory: Upper respiratory tract infection (8%), nasopharyngitis (7%), sinusitis (2%), bronchitis (<2%), cough (<2%), pharyngitis (<2%), rhinitis (<2%), sinus headache (<2%)
<1%: Atrial fibrillation, exacerbation of psoriasis (rebound following discontinuation), suicidal ideation, tachyarrhythmia

General Dosage Range

Oral: *Adults:* Initial: 10 mg in the morning. Titrate upward by additional 10 mg per day on days 2 to 5 as follows: Day 2: 10 mg twice daily; Day 3: 10 mg in the morning and 20 mg in the evening; Day 4: 20 mg twice daily; Day 5: 20 mg in the morning and 30 mg in the evening. Maintenance dose: 30 mg twice daily starting on day 6

Mechanism of Action Apremilast inhibits phosphodiesterase 4 (PDE4) specific for cyclic adenosine monophosphate (cAMP) which results in increased intracellular cAMP levels and regulation of numerous inflammatory mediators (eg, decreased expression of nitric oxide synthase, TNF-α, and interleukin [IL]-23, as well as increased IL-10) (Schafer, 2012).

Pharmacodynamics/Kinetics

Half-life Elimination ~6 to 9 hours

Time to Peak ~2.5 hours

Pregnancy Risk Factor C

Pregnancy Considerations Adverse events were observed in some animal reproduction studies. A registry is available for women exposed to apremilast during pregnancy (877-311-8972).

Aprepitant (ap RE pi tant)

Brand Names: US Emend

Brand Names: Canada Emend

Pharmacologic Category Antiemetic; Substance P/ Neurokinin 1 Receptor Antagonist

Use

Prevention of chemotherapy-induced nausea and vomiting:

Prevention of acute and delayed nausea and vomiting associated with **highly** emetogenic chemotherapy (initial and repeat courses; in combination with other antiemetics) in patients ≥12 years (capsules) and in patients ≥6 months (oral suspension).

Prevention of nausea and vomiting associated with **moderately** emetogenic chemotherapy (initial and repeat courses; in combination with other antiemetics) in patients ≥12 years (capsules) and in patients ≥6 months (oral suspension).

Postoperative nausea and vomiting: Prevention of postoperative nausea and vomiting (PONV) in adults.

Limitations of use: Aprepitant has not been studied for the management of existing nausea and vomiting. Chronic, continuous administration is not recommended (has not been studied and chronic use may alter aprepitant's drug interaction profile).

Local Anesthetic/Vasoconstrictor Precautions No information available to require special precautions

Effects on Dental Treatment Key adverse event(s) related to dental treatment: Hiccups, stomatitis, and mucous membrane disorder.

Effects on Bleeding No information available to require special precautions

Adverse Reactions Adverse reactions may be reported in combination with other antiemetic agents. As reported for highly emetogenic cancer chemotherapy or moderately emetogenic cancer chemotherapy, unless otherwise noted as reported for postoperative nausea and vomiting (PONV).

>10%:
Central nervous system: Fatigue (adults: 13%; children & adolescents: 5%)
Hematologic & oncologic: Neutropenia (children & adolescents: 13%; adults: <3%)

0.5% to 10%:
Cardiovascular: Hypotension (PONV: 6%), bradycardia (PONV: <3%), flushing (<3%), palpitations (<3%), peripheral edema (<3%), syncope (PONV: <3%)
Central nervous system: Headache (children & adolescents: 9%), dizziness (<3% to 5%), anxiety (<3%), hypoesthesia (PONV: <3%), hypothermia (PONV: <3%), malaise (<3%), peripheral neuropathy (<3%), abnormal behavior (children & adolescents: 2%), agitation (children & adolescents: 2%)
Dermatologic: Alopecia (<3%), hyperhidrosis (<3%), skin rash (<3%), urticaria (<3%)
Endocrine & metabolic: Dehydration (≤3%), decreased serum albumin (PONV: <3%), decreased serum potassium (PONV: <3%), decreased serum sodium (<3%), hot flash (<3), hypokalemia (<3%), hypovolemia (PONV: <3%), increased serum glucose (PONV: <3%), weight loss (<3%)
Gastrointestinal: Constipation (PONV: 9%), diarrhea (6% to 9%), dyspepsia (≤7%), abdominal pain (≤6%), hiccups (4% to 5%), decreased appetite (<3% to 5%), dysgeusia (<3%), eructation (<3%), flatulence (<3%), gastritis (<3%), gastroesophageal reflux disease (<3%), nausea (<3%), vomiting (<3%), xerostomia (<3%)
Genitourinary: Proteinuria (<3%)
Hematologic & oncologic: Decreased hemoglobin (children & adolescents: 5%), decreased white blood cell count (≤4%), anemia (<3%), febrile neutropenia (<3%), hematoma (PONV: <3%), thrombocytopenia (<3%)
Hepatic: Increased serum ALT (3%), increased serum alkaline phosphatase (<3%), increased serum AST (<3%), increased serum bilirubin (PONV: <3%)
Infection: Candidiasis (<3%), postoperative infection (PONV: <3%)
Neuromuscular & skeletal: Weakness (≤7%), musculoskeletal pain (<3%)
Renal: Increased blood urea nitrogen (<3%)
Respiratory: Cough (<3% to 5%), dyspnea (<3%), hypoxia (PONV: <3%), oropharyngeal pain (<3%), pharyngitis (<3%), respiratory depression (PONV: <3%)
Miscellaneous: Wound dehiscence (PONV: <3%)

<0.5%, postmarketing, and/or case reports: Anaphylaxis, angioedema, hypersensitivity reaction, pruritus,

Stevens-Johnson syndrome, toxic epidermal necrolysis

General Dosage Range Oral:

Infants ≥6 months (and ≥6 kg), Children <12 years (and ≥6 kg) and patients (any age and ≥6 kg) unable to swallow capsules: 3 mg/kg (maximum: 125 mg/dose) on day 1, followed by 2 mg/kg (maximum: 80 mg/dose) on days 2 and 3

Children ≥12 years and Adolescents: 125 mg on day 1, followed by 80 mg on days 2 and 3

Adults: 125 mg on day 1, followed by 80 mg on days 2 and 3 **or** 40 mg within 3 hours prior to anesthesia induction.

Mechanism of Action Prevents acute and delayed vomiting by inhibiting the substance P/neurokinin 1 (NK_1) receptor; augments the antiemetic activity of $5\text{-}HT_3$ receptor antagonists and corticosteroids to inhibit acute and delayed phases of chemotherapy-induced emesis.

Pharmacodynamics/Kinetics

Half-life Elimination Terminal: ~9 to 13 hours

Time to Peak Plasma: Pediatric: Capsule: ~4 hours; Suspension ~6 hours; Adults: 40 mg: ~3 hours; 125 mg followed by 80 mg for 2 days: ~4 hours

Pregnancy Considerations Adverse events were not observed in animal reproduction studies. Efficacy of hormonal contraceptive may be reduced during and for 28 days following the last aprepitant dose; alternative or additional effective methods of contraception should be used both during treatment with fosaprepitant or aprepitant and for at least 1 month following the last fosaprepitant/aprepitant dose.

Arformoterol (ar for MOE ter ol)

Related Information

Respiratory Diseases *on page 1777*

Brand Names: US Brovana

Pharmacologic Category $Beta_2$-Adrenergic Agonist; $Beta_2$-Adrenergic Agonist, Long-Acting

Use Chronic obstructive pulmonary disease: Long-term maintenance treatment of bronchoconstriction in patients with chronic obstructive pulmonary disease (COPD), including chronic bronchitis and emphysema

Local Anesthetic/Vasoconstrictor Precautions No information available to require special precautions

Effects on Dental Treatment No significant effects or complications reported

Effects on Bleeding No information available to require special precautions

Adverse Reactions

2% to 10%:

Cardiovascular: Chest pain (7%), peripheral edema (3%)

Central nervous system: Pain (8%)

Dermatologic: Skin rash (4%)

Gastrointestinal: Diarrhea (6%)

Neuromuscular & skeletal: Back pain (6%), leg cramps (4%)

Respiratory: Dyspnea (4%), sinusitis (5%), flu-like symptoms (3%), respiratory congestion (2%)

<2%: Abscess, agitation, arteriosclerosis, arthralgia, arthritis, atrial flutter, atrioventricular block, bone disease, calcium crystalluria, cardiac failure, cerebral infarction, constipation, cystitis, decreased glucose tolerance, dehydration, digitalis intoxication, drowsiness, ECG changes, edema, fever, gastritis, glaucoma, glycosuria, gout, heart block, hematuria, hernia, hyperglycemia, hyperlipidemia, hypersensitivity reaction, hypoglycemia, hypokalemia, hypokinesia, inversion T wave on ECG, lung carcinoma, melena, myocardial infarction, neck stiffness, neoplasm, nephrolithiasis, nocturia, oral candidiasis, paradoxical bronchospasm, paralysis, paresthesia (circumoral), pelvic pain, periodontal abscess, prolonged Q-T interval on ECG, prostate specific antigen increase, pyuria, rectal hemorrhage, retroperitoneal hemorrhage, rheumatoid arthritis, skin discoloration, skin hypertrophy, supraventricular tachycardia, tendinous contracture, tremor, urinary tract abnormality, urine abnormality, viral infection, visual disturbance, voice disorder, xeroderma

General Dosage Range Nebulization: *Adults:* 15 mcg twice daily (maximum: 30 mcg daily)

Mechanism of Action Arformoterol, the (R,R)-enantiomer of the racemic formoterol, is a long-acting $beta_2$-agonist that relaxes bronchial smooth muscle by selective action on $beta_2$-receptors with little effect on cardiovascular system.

Pharmacodynamics/Kinetics

Onset of Action 7-20 minutes; Peak effect: 1-3 hours

Half-life Elimination 26 hours

Time to Peak 0.5-3 hours

Pregnancy Risk Factor C

Pregnancy Considerations Adverse events were observed in some animal reproduction studies. Beta-agonists may interfere with uterine contractility if administered during labor.

Argatroban (ar GA troh ban)

Related Information

Cardiovascular Diseases *on page 1752*

Pharmacologic Category Anticoagulant; Anticoagulant, Direct Thrombin Inhibitor

Use

Heparin-induced thrombocytopenia: Prophylaxis or treatment of thrombosis in adult patients with heparin-induced thrombocytopenia (HIT).

Percutaneous coronary intervention: As an anticoagulant for percutaneous coronary intervention (PCI) in adult patients who have or are at risk of developing HIT.

Local Anesthetic/Vasoconstrictor Precautions No information available to require special precautions

Effects on Dental Treatment Key adverse event(s) related to dental treatment: Bleeding is a potential adverse effect of argatroban during dental surgery; it is unlikely that ambulatory patients presenting for dental treatment will be taking intravenous anticoagulant therapy. See Effects on Bleeding.

Effects on Bleeding As with all anticoagulants, bleeding is a potential adverse effect of argatroban during dental surgery; risk is dependent on multiple variables, including the intensity of anticoagulation and patient susceptibility. Medical consult is suggested. It is unlikely that ambulatory patients presenting for dental treatment will be taking intravenous anticoagulant therapy such as argatroban.

Adverse Reactions As with all anticoagulants, bleeding is the major adverse effect of argatroban. Hemorrhage may occur at virtually any site. Risk is dependent on multiple variables, including the intensity of anticoagulation and patient susceptibility.

>10%:

Cardiovascular: Chest pain (PCI related: <1% to 15%), hypotension (7% to 11%)

Genitourinary: Genitourinary tract hemorrhage (including hematuria; major: <1%; minor: 2% to 12%)

1% to 10%:

Cardiovascular: Vasodilation (1% to 10%), cardiac arrest (6%), bradycardia (5%), ventricular tachycardia (5%), myocardial infarction (PCI: 4%), angina pectoris (2%), coronary occlusion (2%), ischemic heart disease (2%), thrombosis (<1% to 2%)

Central nervous system: Headache (5%), pain (5%), intracranial hemorrhage (1% to 4%)

Dermatologic: Dermatological reaction (bullous eruption, rash; 1% to <10%)

Gastrointestinal: Nausea (5% to 7%), diarrhea (6%), vomiting (4% to 6%), abdominal pain (3% to 4%), gastrointestinal hemorrhage (major: <1% to 3%; minor: 3%)

Hematologic & oncologic: Decreased hematocrit (minor: ≤10%; major: <1%), decreased hemoglobin (minor: ≤10%; major: <1%; ≥2g/dL), groin bleeding (5%), brachial bleeding (2%), minor hemorrhage (CABG related: 2%)

Neuromuscular & skeletal: Back pain (PCI related: 8%)

Respiratory: Dyspnea (10%), cough (3% to 10%), hemoptysis (minor: ≤1% to 3%)

Miscellaneous: Fever (<1% to 7%)

<1% (Limited to important or life-threatening): Aortic valve stenosis, bleeding at injection site (or access site; minor),cerebrovascular disease, gastroesophageal reflux disease, hypersensitivity reaction, local hemorrhage (limb and below-the-knee stump), pulmonary edema, retroperitoneal bleeding

General Dosage Range Dosage adjustment and careful titration are recommended in patients with hepatic impairment

IV:

Infants, Children, and Adolescents ≤16 years: Continuous IV infusion: Initial dose: 0.75 mcg/kg/minute; dosage may be adjusted in increments of 0.1 to 0.25 mcg/kg/minute

Adults: Bolus IV dose: 150 to 350 mcg/kg during PCI procedure; Continuous IV Infusion: Initial: 2 mcg/kg/minute for HIT **or** 25 mcg/kg/minute during PCI procedure; Maintenance: 0.5 to 10 mcg/kg/minute (maximum: 10 mcg/kg/minute) for HIT **or** 25 to 40 mcg/kg/minute during PCI procedure

Mechanism of Action A direct, highly-selective thrombin inhibitor. Reversibly binds to the active thrombin site of free and clot-associated thrombin. Inhibits fibrin formation; activation of coagulation factors V, VIII, and XIII; activation of protein C; and platelet aggregation.

Pharmacodynamics/Kinetics

Onset of Action Immediate

Half-life Elimination 39 to 51 minutes; Hepatic impairment: 181 minutes

Time to Peak Steady-state: 1 to 3 hours

Pregnancy Risk Factor B

Pregnancy Considerations Adverse events have not been observed in animal reproduction studies. Information related to argatroban in pregnancy is limited. Use of parenteral direct thrombin inhibitors in pregnancy should be limited to those women who have severe allergic reactions to heparin, including heparin-induced thrombocytopenia, and who cannot receive danaparoid (Guyatt, 2012).

ARIPiprazole (ay ri PIP ray zole)

Brand Names: US Abilify; Abilify Discmelt [DSC]; Abilify Maintena

Brand Names: Canada Abilify; Abilify Maintena

Pharmacologic Category Second Generation (Atypical) Antipsychotic

Use

Oral:

Bipolar I disorder: Acute treatment of manic and mixed episodes associated with bipolar I disorder.

Irritability associated with autistic disorder: Treatment of irritability associated with autistic disorder.

Major depressive disorder: Adjunctive treatment of major depressive disorder.

Schizophrenia: Treatment of schizophrenia.

Tourette disorder: Treatment of Tourette disorder.

Injection:

Agitation associated with schizophrenia or bipolar mania (immediate-release injection only): Treatment of agitation associated with schizophrenia or bipolar mania.

Schizophrenia (extended-release injection only): Treatment of schizophrenia.

Local Anesthetic/Vasoconstrictor Precautions No information available to require special precautions

Effects on Dental Treatment Key adverse event(s) related to dental treatment: Extrapyramidal symptoms (similar to placebo) (see Dental Comment); xerostomia and changes in salivation (normal salivary flow resumes upon discontinuation).

Effects on Bleeding No information available to require special precautions

Adverse Reactions Unless otherwise noted, frequency of adverse reactions is shown as reported for adult patients receiving aripiprazole monotherapy with oral administration. Spectrum and incidence of adverse effects similar in children; exceptions noted when incidence much higher in children.

>10%:

Central nervous system: Headache (adults 27%; children and adolescents 10% to 12%; injection 12%), extrapyramidal reaction (dose-related; children and adolescents 6% to 27%; adults 5% to 13%), drowsiness (children and adolescents 10% to 26%; adults 8% to 13%), akathisia (dose-related; adults 2% to 25%; children and adolescents 6% to 11%), fatigue (dose-related; children and adolescents 4% to 22%; adults 6%; injection 1% to 2%), sedation (dose-related, children and adolescents 9% to 21%; adults 3% to 8%), agitation (oral 19%; injection <1%), insomnia (18%; injection ≥1%), anxiety (oral 17%; injection ≥1%)

Endocrine & metabolic: Weight gain (children and adolescents 3% to 26%; injection 17% to 22%; adults 2% to 8%), increased serum cholesterol (injection 4% to 22%; oral 1%), increased serum triglycerides (adults 7% to 10%; children and adolescents 5%; injection 7% to 20%; oral 5% to 10%), increased serum glucose (adults 8% to 18%; children and adolescents 3% to 5%), decreased HDL cholesterol (injection 14%; children and adolescents 4%), increased LDL cholesterol (injection 10% to 14%)

Gastrointestinal: Nausea (8% to 15%), vomiting (oral 8% to 14%; injection: 3%), constipation (10% to 11%; children and adolescents 2% to 3%)

Neuromuscular & skeletal: Tremor (dose-related; oral 5% to 12%; injection 3%)

1% to 10%:

Cardiovascular: Tachycardia (injection ≤2%), hypertension (≥1%), peripheral edema (≥1%), orthostatic hypotension (including injection; ≤1%)

Central nervous system: Dizziness (3% to 10%), drooling (children and adolescents 3% to 9%), restlessness (oral 5% to 6%; injection ≥1%), lethargy (older adults 5%; children 3% to 5%; injection <1%), pain (3%), dystonia (2%), irritability (children and adolescents 2%; injection <1%), ataxia (≥1%), hypersomnia (≤1%)

Dermatologic: Skin rash (≤2%)

Endocrine & metabolic: Weight loss (injection 4%; oral ≥1%)

Gastrointestinal: Dyspepsia (oral 9%; injection <1%), sialorrhea (dose-related; 3% to 8%), decreased appetite (children and adolescents 5% to 7%; injection <1%), increased appetite (children and adolescents 7%), xerostomia (5%; injection: 4%; children and adolescents 1%), toothache (4%), diarrhea (3% to 4%), gastric distress (3%), stomach discomfort (3%), upper abdominal pain (children and adolescents 3%; injection <1%), abdominal distress (2% to 3%), anorexia (≥1%)

Genitourinary: Urinary incontinence (older adults ≤5%; injection <1%), dysmenorrhea (children and adolescents 2%)

Hematologic & oncologic: Neutropenia (injection 6%)

Local: Pain at injection site (5%), injection site reaction (injection ≥1%; including erythema, induration, inflammation, hemorrhage, pruritus, swelling, rash)

Neuromuscular & skeletal: Arthralgia (injection 4%; children and adolescents 1%), back pain (injection 4%), limb pain (4%), myalgia (2% to 4%), stiffness (2% to 4%), musculoskeletal pain (injection 3%), muscle cramps (2%), muscle rigidity (children and adolescents 2%), muscle spasm (2%), weakness (1% to 2%), dyskinesia (children and adolescents 1%)

Ophthalmic: Blurred vision (oral 3% to 8%; injection <1%)

Respiratory: Nasopharyngitis (children and adolescents 6% to 9%; injection <1%), upper respiratory tract infection (4%), cough (3%), pharyngolaryngeal pain (3%), epistaxis (children and adolescents 2%), nasal congestion (injection: 2%; oral <1%), aspiration pneumonia (≥1%), dyspnea (≥1%)

Miscellaneous: Fever (children and adolescents 4% to 9%; injection <1%)

<1%, postmarketing, and/or case reports: Abnormal bilirubin levels, abnormal gait, abnormal hepatic function tests, aggressive behavior, agranulocytosis, akinesia, alopecia, altered serum glucose, amenorrhea, anaphylaxis, angina pectoris, angioedema, anorgasmia, atrial fibrillation, atrial flutter, atrioventricular block, bradycardia, bradykinesia, bruxism, cardiac arrhythmia, catatonia, cerebrovascular accident, change in libido, chest discomfort, chest pain, choreoathetosis, cogwheel rigidity, convulsions, decreased serum cholesterol, decreased serum triglycerides, delirium, depression, diabetes mellitus, diabetic ketoacidosis, diplopia, disruption of body temperature regulation, drug-induced Parkinson disease, dry tongue, dysgeusia, dysphagia, dystonia (oromandibular), edema, elevated glycosylated hemoglobin, erectile dysfunction, esophagitis, extrasystoles, eyelid edema, facial edema, falling, gastroesophageal reflux disease, glycosuria, gynecomastia, heatstroke, hepatic failure, hepatitis, hepatotoxicity, hirsutism, homicidal ideation, hostility, hyperglycemia, hyperhidrosis, hyperinsulinism, hyperlipidemia, hypersensitivity, hypersexuality, hypertonia, hypoglycemia, hypokalemia, hypokinesia, hyponatremia, hypothermia, hypotonia, impulse control disorder (including pathologic gambling and hypersexuality), increased blood urea nitrogen, increased creatinine clearance, increased creatine phosphokinase, increased gamma-glutamyl transferase, increased lactate dehydrogenase, increased liver enzymes, increased serum bilirubin, increased serum prolactin, inhibition of prolactin secretion, intentional injury, ischemic heart disease, jaundice, joint stiffness, laryngospasm, leukopenia, mastalgia, memory impairment, menstrual disease, mobility disorder, muscle twitching, myasthenia, myocardial infarction, myoclonus, neuroleptic malignant syndrome, nocturia, obesity, oculogyric crisis, oropharyngeal spasm, palpitations, pancreatitis, panic attack, photophobia, photopsia, pollakiuria, polydipsia, polyuria, presyncope, priapism, prolonged Q-T interval on ECG, pruritus, psychosis, rhabdomyolysis, seizure (including injection), skin photosensitivity, sleep apnea syndrome (obstructive) (Health Canada, August 16, 2016; Shirani 2011), sleep talking, somnambulism, speech disturbance, suicidal ideation, suicidal tendencies, supraventricular tachycardia, swollen tongue, syncope, tardive dyskinesia, thrombocytopenia, tics, tongue spasm, tonic-clonic seizures, torsades de pointes, transient ischemic attacks, uncontrolled diabetes mellitus, urinary retention, urticaria, venous thromboembolism, ventricular tachycardia

General Dosage Range Dosage adjustment recommended in patients on concomitant therapy or with CYP2D6 poor metabolizer status

IM (extended release): *Adults:* 400 mg once monthly.

IM (immediate release): *Adults:* 5.25 to 15 mg as a single dose (maximum: 30 mg daily)

Oral:

Children ≥6 years and Adolescents: Dosage varies greatly by indication

Adults: 2 to 15 mg once daily (maximum: 30 mg daily)

Mechanism of Action Aripiprazole is a quinolinone antipsychotic which exhibits high affinity for D_2, D_3, 5-HT_{1A}, and 5-HT_{2A} receptors; moderate affinity for D_4, 5-HT_{2C}, 5-HT_7, $alpha_1$ adrenergic, and H_1 receptors. It also possesses moderate affinity for the serotonin reuptake transporter; has no affinity for muscarinic (cholinergic) receptors. Aripiprazole functions as a partial agonist at the D_2 and 5-HT_{1A} receptors, and as an antagonist at the 5-HT_{2A} receptor (de Bartolomeis 2015).

Pharmacodynamics/Kinetics

Onset of Action Initial: 1 to 3 weeks

Half-life Elimination

Aripiprazole: 75 hours; dehydro-aripiprazole: 94 hours; IM, extended release (terminal): ~30 to 47 days (dose-dependent)

CYP2D6 poor metabolizers: Aripiprazole: 146 hours

Time to Peak Plasma:

IM:

Immediate release: 1 to 3 hours

Extended release (after multiple doses): 4 days (deltoid administration); 5 to 7 days (gluteal administration)

Tablet: 3 to 5 hours

With high-fat meal: Aripiprazole: Delayed by 3 hours; dehydro-aripiprazole: Delayed by 12 hours

Pregnancy Risk Factor C

Pregnancy Considerations Adverse events have been observed in animal reproduction studies. Aripiprazole crosses the placenta; aripiprazole and dehydro-aripiprazole can be detected in the cord blood at delivery (Nguyen 2011; Watanabe 2011). Antipsychotic use during the third trimester of pregnancy has a risk for abnormal muscle movements (extrapyramidal symptoms [EPS]) and/or withdrawal symptoms in newborns following delivery. Symptoms in the newborn may include agitation, feeding disorder, hypertonia, hypotonia, respiratory distress, somnolence, and tremor; these effects may be self-limiting or require hospitalization.

Treatment algorithms have been developed by the ACOG and the APA for the management of depression in women prior to conception and during pregnancy (Yonkers 2009). The ACOG recommends that therapy during pregnancy be individualized; treatment with psychiatric medications during pregnancy should incorporate the clinical expertise of the mental health clinician, obstetrician, primary health care provider, and pediatrician. Safety data related to atypical antipsychotics during pregnancy is limited and routine use is not recommended. However, if a woman is inadvertently exposed to an atypical antipsychotic while pregnant, continuing therapy may be preferable to switching to a typical antipsychotic that the fetus has not yet been exposed to; consider risk:benefit (ACOG 2008).

Health care providers are encouraged to enroll women exposed to aripiprazole during pregnancy in the National Pregnancy Registry for Atypical Antipsychotics (866-961-2388 or http://www.womensmentalhealth.org/clinical-and-research-programs/pregnancyregistry/).

Product Availability Abilify immediate-release injection (9.75 mg/1.3 mL) has been discontinued in the US for more than 1 year.

Dental Comment Aripiprazole works differently from the classic antipsychotics, such as chlorpromazine, in that it does not appear to block central dopaminergic receptors, but rather seems to be a stabilizer of dopamine-serotonin central systems. The risk of extrapyramidal reactions such as pseudoparkinsonism, acute dystonic reactions, akathisia, and tardive dyskinesia are low and the frequencies reported are similar to placebo. Aripiprazole may be associated with neuroleptic malignant syndrome (NMS).

ARIPiprazole Lauroxil (ay ri PIP ray zole lawr OX il)

Brand Names: US Aristada

Pharmacologic Category Second Generation (Atypical) Antipsychotic

Use Schizophrenia: Treatment of schizophrenia.

Local Anesthetic/Vasoconstrictor Precautions Adverse effects of palpitations, tachycardia have been observed; monitor, and if present, use caution with the use of vasoconstrictor

Effects on Dental Treatment Key adverse event(s) related to dental treatment: Xerostomia; Parkinson-like syndrome and restlessness in 3% to 4% of patients has been reported.

Effects on Bleeding No information available to require special precautions

Adverse Reactions

>10%: Central nervous system: Akathisia (11%)

1% to 10%:

Central nervous system: Headache (5%), parkinsonian-like syndrome (4%), insomnia (3% to 4%), restlessness (3%), dystonia (2%)

Endocrine & metabolic: Weight gain (2%; ≥7% increase: 9% to 10%)

Local: Pain at injection site (3% to 4%)

Neuromuscular & skeletal: Increased creatine phosphokinase (1% to 2%)

Frequency not defined:

Cardiovascular: Angina pectoris, palpitations, tachycardia

Central nervous system: Anxiety, dizziness, myasthenia

Gastrointestinal: Constipation, xerostomia

Neuromuscular & skeletal: Weakness

<1%, postmarketing, and/or case reports: Erythema at injection site, impulse control disorder (including pathologic gambling, binge eating, and hypersexuality) (FDA Safety Alert May 3, 2016), induration at injection site, orthostatic hypotension (patient taking 882 mg aripiprazole lauroxil), swelling at injection site

General Dosage Range

Dosage adjustment recommended in patients on concomitant therapy.

IM: *Adults:* 441 to 882 mg every 4 weeks or 882 mg every 6 weeks

Mechanism of Action Aripiprazole lauroxil is a prodrug of aripiprazole. Following intramuscular injection, aripiprazole lauroxil is likely converted by enzyme-mediated hydrolysis to N-hydroxymethyl aripiprazole, which is then hydrolyzed to aripiprazole. Aripiprazole is a quinolinone antipsychotic that exhibits high affinity for D_2, D_3, 5-HT_{1A}, and 5-HT_{2A} receptors; moderate affinity for D_4, 5-HT_{2C}, 5-HT_7, $alpha_1$ adrenergic, and H_1 receptors (de Bartolomeis 2015). It also possesses moderate affinity for the serotonin reuptake transporter; has no affinity for muscarinic (cholinergic) receptors. Aripiprazole functions as a partial agonist at the D_2 and 5-HT_{1A} receptors, and as an antagonist at the 5-HT_{2A} receptor.

Pharmacodynamics/Kinetics

Onset of Action 5 to 6 days following injection; 4 days following injection when administered concomitantly with oral aripiprazole.

Duration of Action 36 days following appearance in the systemic circulation.

Half-life Elimination 29 to 35 days.

Pregnancy Considerations

Aripiprazole crosses the placenta; aripiprazole and dehydro-aripiprazole can be detected in the cord blood at delivery (Nguyen 2011; Watanabe 2011).

Antipsychotic use during the third trimester of pregnancy has a risk for abnormal muscle movements (extrapyramidal symptoms [EPS]) and/or withdrawal symptoms in newborns following delivery. Symptoms in the newborn may include agitation, feeding disorder, hypertonia, hypotonia, respiratory distress, somnolence, and tremor; these effects may be self-limiting or require hospitalization.

Health care providers are encouraged to enroll women exposed to aripiprazole lauroxil during pregnancy in the National Pregnancy Registry for Atypical Antipsychotics at 1-866-961-2388 or visit http://womensmentalhealth.org/clinical-and-research-programs/pregnancyregistry.

Armodafinil (ar moe DAF i nil)

Brand Names: US Nuvigil

Pharmacologic Category Central Nervous System Stimulant

Use

Narcolepsy: To improve wakefulness in patients with excessive sleepiness associated with narcolepsy.

Obstructive sleep apnea: To improve wakefulness in patients with excessive sleepiness associated with obstructive sleep apnea (OSA).

Limitations of use: In OSA, armodafinil is indicated to treat excessive sleepiness and not as treatment for the underlying obstruction. If continuous positive airway pressure (CPAP) is the treatment of choice for a patient, a maximal effort to treat with CPAP for an adequate period of time should be made prior to initiating armodafinil for excessive sleepiness.

Shift-work disorder: To improve wakefulness in patients with excessive sleepiness associated with shift-work disorder.

Local Anesthetic/Vasoconstrictor Precautions Use vasoconstrictor with caution. Patients may experience heart palpitations and increased heart rate when taking armodafinil.

Effects on Dental Treatment Key adverse event(s) related to dental treatment: Armodafinil causes tachycardia, increases in blood pressure, and palpitations. Consider monitoring blood pressure prior to using local anesthetic with a vasoconstrictor. Symptoms associated with bruxism have been observed in some patients.

Effects on Bleeding No information available to require special precautions

Adverse Reactions

>10%: Central nervous system: Headache (14% to 23%; dose related)

1% to 10%:

Cardiovascular: Palpitations (2%), increased heart rate (1%)

Central nervous system: Insomnia (4% to 6%; dose related), dizziness (5%), anxiety (4%), depression (1% to 3%; dose related), fatigue (2%), agitation (1%), depressed mood (1%), lack of concentration (1%), migraine (1%), nervousness (1%), pain (1%), paresthesia (1%)

Dermatologic: Skin rash (1% to 4%; dose related), contact dermatitis (1%), diaphoresis (1%)

Endocrine & metabolic: Increased gamma-glutamyl transferase (1%), increased thirst (1%)

Gastrointestinal: Nausea (6% to 9%; dose related), xerostomia (2% to 7%; dose related), diarrhea (4%), dyspepsia (2%), upper abdominal pain (2%), anorexia (1%), constipation (1%), decreased appetite (1%), loose stools (1%), vomiting (1%)

Hypersensitivity: Seasonal allergy (1%)

Neuromuscular & skeletal: Tremor (1%)

Renal: Polyuria (1%)

Respiratory: Dyspnea (1%), flu-like symptoms (1%)

Miscellaneous: Fever (1%)

<1%, postmarketing, and/or case reports: Anaphylaxis, angioedema, DRESS syndrome, hypersensitivity, hypouricemia, increased liver enzymes, increased serum alkaline phosphatase, irritability, pancytopenia, Stevens-Johnson syndrome, suicidal ideation, systolic hypertension, toxic epidermal necrolysis

General Dosage Range

Oral: *Adults:* 150 to 250 mg once daily

Mechanism of Action The exact mechanism of action of armodafinil is unknown. It is the R-enantiomer of modafinil. Armodafinil binds to the dopamine transporter and inhibits dopamine reuptake, which may result in increased extracellular dopamine levels in the brain. However, it does not appear to be a dopamine receptor agonist and also does not appear to bind to or inhibit the most common receptors or enzymes that are relevant for sleep/wake regulation.

Pharmacodynamics/Kinetics

Half-life Elimination ~15 hours

Time to Peak 2 hours (fasted)

Pregnancy Considerations

Intrauterine growth restriction and spontaneous abortion have been reported in association with armodafinil. Efficacy of steroidal contraceptives may be decreased; alternate means of contraception should be considered during therapy and for 1 month after armodafinil is discontinued.

A pregnancy registry has been established for patients exposed to armodafinil; healthcare providers are encouraged to register pregnant patients or pregnant women may register themselves by calling 1-866-404-4106.

Controlled Substance C-IV

Artemether and Lumefantrine

(ar TEM e ther & loo me FAN treen)

Related Information

Clinical Risk Related to Drugs Prolonging QT Interval *on page 1772*

Brand Names: US Coartem

Pharmacologic Category Antimalarial Agent

Use Treatment of acute, uncomplicated malaria infections due to *Plasmodium falciparum*, including geographical regions where chloroquine resistance has been reported

Local Anesthetic/Vasoconstrictor Precautions Artemether and lumefantrine is one of the drugs confirmed to prolong the QT interval and is accepted as having a risk of causing torsade de pointes. The risk of drug-induced torsade de pointes is extremely low when a single QT interval prolonging drug is prescribed. In terms of epinephrine, it is not known what effect vasoconstrictors in the local anesthetic regimen will have in patients with a known history of congenital prolonged QT interval or in patients taking any medication that prolongs the QT interval. Until more information is obtained, it is suggested that the clinician consult with the physician prior to the use of a vasoconstrictor in suspected patients, and that the vasoconstrictor (epinephrine, mepivacaine and levonordefrin [Carbocaine® 2% with Neo-Cobefrin®]) be used with caution.

Effects on Dental Treatment No significant effects or complications reported

Effects on Bleeding No information available to require special precautions

Adverse Reactions

>10%:

Cardiovascular: Palpitation (adults: 18%)

Central nervous system: Headache (adults 56%; children 13%), dizziness (adults 39%; children 4%), fever (25% to 29%), chills (adults 23%; children 5%), sleep disorder (adults: 22%), fatigue (adults 17%; children 3%)

Gastrointestinal: Anorexia (adults 40%; children 13%), nausea (adults 26%; children 5%), vomiting (17% to 18%), abdominal pain (8% to 17%)

Infection: Plasmodium falciparum (exacerbation: children: 17%)

Neuromuscular & skeletal: Weakness (adults 38%; children 5%), arthralgia (adults 34%; children 3%), myalgia (adults 32%; children 3%)

Respiratory: Cough (adults 6%; children 23%)

Miscellaneous: Fever (25% to 29%)

3% to 10%:

Central nervous system: Insomnia (adults: 5%), malaise (adults: 3%), vertigo (adults: 3%)

Dermatologic: Pruritus (adults: 4%), skin rash (3%)

Gastrointestinal: Diarrhea (7% to 8%), increased serum aspartate aminotransferase (<3% to 4%)

Hematologic & oncologic: Anemia (4% to 9%)

Hepatic: Hepatomegaly (6% to 9%)

Infection: Malaria (≤3%)

Respiratory: Rhinitis (4%), nasopharyngitis (≤3%)

<3%, postmarketing, and/or case reports: Abnormal gait, abnormal lymphocytes, abscess, agitation, anapylaxis, angioedema, asthma, ataxia, back pain, bronchitis, bullous dermatitis, change in platelet count (increased), clonus, conjunctivitis, constipation, decreased hematocirt, decreased platelet count, decreased white blood cell count, dermatitis (hands and feet), dyspepsia, dysphagia, emotional lability, eosinophilia, fine motor control disorder, gastroenteritis, helminthiasis, hematuria, hookworm infection, hyper-reflexia, hypoesthesia, hypokalemia, impetigo, increased serum alanine aminotransferase, influenza, leukocytosis, leukopenia, lower respiratory tract infection, nystagmus, oral herpes, otic infection, peptic ulcer, pharyngolaryngeal pain, pneumonia, proteinuria, respiratory tract infection, subcutaneous abscess, tinnitus, tremor, upper respiratory tract infection, urinary tract infection, urticaria

General Dosage Range Oral:

Children 2 months to ≤16 years:

5 to <15 kg: Artemether 20 mg/lumefantrine 120 mg twice daily (maximum: 6 tablets per treatment course)

15 to <25 kg: Artemether 40 mg/lumefantrine 240 mg twice daily (maximum: 12 tablets per treatment course)

25 to <35 kg: Artemether 60 mg/lumefantrine 360 mg twice daily (maximum: 18 tablets per treatment course)

≥35 kg: Artemether 80 mg/lumefantrine 480 mg twice daily (maximum: 24 tablets per treatment course)

Children >16 years and Adults:

25 to <35 kg: Artemether 60 mg/lumefantrine 360 mg twice daily (maximum: 18 tablets per treatment course)

≥35 kg: Artemether 80 mg/lumefantrine 480 mg twice daily (maximum: 24 tablets per treatment course)

Mechanism of Action A coformulation of artemether and lumefantrine with activity against *Plasmodium falciparum*. Artemether and major metabolite dihydroartemisinin (DHA) are rapid schizontocides with activity attributed to the endoperoxide moiety common to each substance. Artemether inhibits an essential calcium adenosine triphosphatase. The exact mechanism of lumefantrine is unknown, but it may inhibit the formation of β-hematin by complexing with hemin. Both artemether and lumefantrine inhibit nucleic acid and protein synthesis. Artemether rapidly reduces parasite biomass and lumefantrine eliminates residual parasites.

Pharmacodynamics/Kinetics

Half-life Elimination Artemether: 1-2 hours; DHA: 2 hours; Lumefantrine: 72-144 hours

Time to Peak Plasma: Artemether: ~2 hours; Lumefantrine: ~6-8 hours

Pregnancy Risk Factor C

Pregnancy Considerations Adverse events were observed in some animal reproduction studies. Safety data from an observational pregnancy study included 500 pregnant women exposed to artemether/lumefantrine and did not show an increased in adverse outcomes or teratogenic effects over background rate. Approximately one-third of these patients were in the third trimester. Efficacy has not been established in pregnant patients. Treatment failures with standard doses have been reported in pregnant women in areas where drug resistant parasites are prevalent. This may be attributed to lower serum concentration of both artemether and lumefantrine in this population (McGready 2008). Malaria infection in pregnant women may be more severe than in nonpregnant women. Because *P. falciparum* malaria can cause maternal death and fetal loss, pregnant women traveling to malaria-endemic areas must use personal protection against mosquito bites. Artemether and lumefantrine may be used as an alternative treatment of malaria in pregnant women but use in the first trimester is generally avoided; consult current CDC guidelines.

Dental Comment See Local Anesthetic/Vasoconstrictor Precautions

Artesunate (ar TES oo nate)

Pharmacologic Category Antimalarial Agent; Artemisinin Derivative

Local Anesthetic/Vasoconstrictor Precautions No information available to require special precautions

Effects on Dental Treatment Key adverse event(s) related to dental treatment: Metallic taste has been reported

Effects on Bleeding No information available to require special precautions

Adverse Reactions Frequency not defined.

Cardiovascular: Hypotension

Central nervous system: Anxiety, ataxia, dizziness, headache, hyperreflexia, metallic taste, restlessness, slurred speech

Dermatologic: Erythema, pruritus, skin rash, urticaria

Endocrine & metabolic: Hypoglycemia

Gastrointestinal: Anorexia, diarrhea, nausea, vomiting

Hematologic & oncologic: Anemia, hemolysis, neutropenia, reticulocytopenia

Hepatic: Increased serum ALT

Hypersensitivity: Angioedema, hypersensitivity reaction

Neuromuscular & skeletal: Tremor

Renal: Increased blood urea nitrogen

Respiratory: Dyspnea

General Dosage Range IM, IV:

Infants and Children <20 kg: 3 mg/kg/dose initially, followed by 3 mg/kg/dose at 12 hours, 24 hours, and 48 hours after the initial dose for a total of 4 doses over a period of 3 days

Children and Adolescents ≥20 kg and Adults: 2.4 mg/kg/dose initially, followed by 2.4 mg/kg/dose at 12 hours, 24 hours, and 48 hours after the initial dose for a total of 4 doses

Mechanism of Action Artesunate, a semisynthetic derivative of artemisinin, is a prodrug which is converted to dihydroartemisinin (DHA). DHA is an antimalarial agent active against all of the erythrocytic stages of the parasite including gametocytes; inhibits parasite metabolism and enhances the clearance of infected erythrocytes.

Antiparasitic activity is hypothesized to involve cleavage of the Fe^{2+} of endoperoxide bridge, thereby producing free radicals and damaging parasite proteins. DHA may also inhibit calcium adenosine triphosphatase (cATP) of the sarcoplasmic endoplasmic reticulum and impair parasite protein folding.

Pharmacodynamics/Kinetics

Half-life Elimination Artesunate: Adults infected with severe malaria: 0.22 hours (range: 0.08 to 0.61 hours); Dihydroartemisinin (DHA): 0.34 hours (range: 0.14 to 0.87 hours) (Newton 2006)

Time to Peak Dihydroartemisinin (DHA): Adults infected with severe malaria: Within 15 minutes (Newton 2006)

Pregnancy Considerations Adverse events have been observed in some animal reproduction studies. Studies in pregnant women have not revealed an increased risk of congenital abnormalities in newborns (Kovacs 2015, McGready 1998, McGready 2008). Malaria infection in pregnant women may be more severe than in nonpregnant women. Because *P. falciparum* malaria can cause maternal death, congenital malaria, and fetal loss, pregnant women traveling to malaria-endemic areas must use personal protection against mosquito bites. Artesunate is recommended for the treatment of severe malaria in pregnant women (Kovacs 2015).

Prescribing and Access Restrictions Investigational agent – not approved for use in the U.S.

Artesunate is available in the U.S. for IV use in patients with malaria through an Investigational New Drug (IND) protocol. To obtain artesunate via the IND protocol, clinicians must contact the Centers for Disease Control (CDC) Malaria Hotline at 770-488-7788 (business hours) or 770-488-7100 (nonbusiness hours) and request to speak with a CDC Malaria Branch clinician.

Eligibility criteria under the IND protocol include (Callender 2011; Hess 2010):

- **Patients must have malaria:** Confirmation by microscopy or undetermined but strong clinical suspicion of *Plasmodium falciparum* or other *Plasmodium* spp. infection
- **Patients must require parenteral therapy:** Unable to take oral medications, high-density parasitemia (eg, >5%), or diagnosis of severe malaria (eg, seizures, shock, hemoglobin <7 g/dL, disseminated intravascular coagulation, or acute respiratory distress syndrome [ARDS]).
- **IV artesunate must be the preferred treatment:** IV artesunate is at least as readily available as IV quinidine or the patient has experienced quinidine failure (eg, parasitemia >10% baseline after 48 hours of quinidine therapy), quinidine intolerance (eg, persistent hypotension, QRS prolongation >50% of baseline or QTc interval prolongation >25% of baseline), or contraindications to quinidine (eg, allergy, left bundle branch block, myasthenia gravis, digoxin toxicity).

For medical access to IV artesunate in Canada, please refer to special access information on the Public Health Agency of Canada website, http://www.phac-aspc.gc.ca/tmp-pmv/quinine/.

Articaine and Epinephrine

(AR ti kane & ep i NEF rin)

Related Information

EPINEPHrine (Systemic) *on page 580*

Oral Pain *on page 1830*

Brand Names: US Articadent; Orabloc; Septocaine with Epinephrine 1:100,000; Septocaine with Epinephrine 1:200,000; Zorcaine

Brand Names: Canada Astracaine with Epinephrine 1:200,000; Astracaine with Epinephrine forte 1:100,000; Karticaine; Karticaine Forte; Orabloc 1:100,000; Orabloc 1:200,000; Posicaine N; Posicaine SP; Septanest N; Septanest SP; Ultracaine DS; Ultracaine DS Forte; Zorcaine

Generic Availability (US) No

Pharmacologic Category Local Anesthetic

Dental Use Local, infiltrative, or conductive anesthesia in both simple and complex dental and periodontal procedures

Use Dental anesthesia: Local, infiltrative, or conductive anesthesia in both simple and complex dental procedures

Local Anesthetic/Vasoconstrictor Precautions No information available to require special precautions (see Dental Comment)

Effects on Dental Treatment No significant effects or complications reported

Effects on Bleeding No information available to require special precautions

Adverse Reactions Frequency not always defined.

Adverse reactions are characteristic of those associated with other amide-type local anesthetics; adverse reactions to this group of drugs may also result from excessive plasma levels which may be due to overdosage, unintentional intravascular injection, or slow metabolic degradation.

Cardiovascular: Facial edema (1%), cardiac arrhythmia, cardiac insufficiency

Central nervous system: Pain (13%), headache (4%), paresthesia (1%), seizure

Gastrointestinal: Gingivitis (1%)

Hypersensitivity: Hypersensitivity reaction

Local: Injection site reaction

Respiratory: Asthma

Miscellaneous: Tissue necrosis

<1%, postmarketing, and/or case reports: Abdominal pain, accidental injury, arthralgia, back pain, constipation, dermatological disease, diarrhea, dizziness, drowsiness, dysgeusia, dysmenorrhea, dyspepsia, ecchymoses, edema, facial paralysis, gingival hemorrhage, glossitis, hemorrhage, hyperesthesia, increased thirst, lymphadenopathy, malaise, methemoglobinemia, migraine, myalgia, nausea, neck pain, nervousness, neuropathy, oral mucosa ulcer, osteomyelitis, otalgia, pharyngitis, pruritus, rhinitis, sialorrhea, stomatitis, syncope, tachycardia, tongue edema, vomiting, weakness, xerostomia

Dental Usual Dosage Adults:

Infiltration: Injection volume of 4% solution: 0.5-2.5 mL; total dose: 20-100 mg

Nerve block: Injection volume of 4% solution: 0.5-3.4 mL; total dose: 20-136 mg

Oral surgery: Injection volume of 4% solution: 1-5.1 mL; total dose: 40-204 mg

Note: These dosages are guides only; other dosages may be used; however, do not exceed maximum recommended dose

Special populations: The clinician is reminded that these doses serve only as a guide to the amount of anesthetic required for most routine procedures. The actual volumes to be used depend upon a number of factors, such as type and extent of surgical procedure, depth of anesthesia, degree of muscular relaxation, and condition of the patient. In all cases, the smallest dose that will produce the desired result should be given. Dosages should be reduced for pediatric patients, elderly patients, and patients with cardiac and/or liver disease.

Dosing

Adult

Dental anesthesia: Submucosal infiltration and/or nerve block: Articaine 4%/epinephrine: **Note:** These dosages are guides only; other dosages may be used; however, do not exceed maximum recommended dose. The actual volumes to be used depend upon a number of factors, such as type and extent of surgical procedure, depth of anesthesia, degree of muscular relaxation, and condition of the patient. In all cases, the smallest dose that will produce the desired result should be given. For most routine dental procedures, epinephrine 1:200,000 is preferred; when more pronounced hemostasis or improved visualization of the surgical field are required, epinephrine 1:100,000 may be used. Dosages should be reduced for patients with cardiac disease and acutely ill and/or debilitated patients:

Infiltration: 0.5 to 2.5 mL; total dose of articaine: 20 to 100 mg; maximum dose of articaine: 7 mg/kg (0.175 mL/kg).

Nerve block: 0.5 to 3.4 mL; total dose of articaine: 20 to 136 mg; maximum dose of articaine: 7 mg/kg (0.175 mL/kg).

Oral surgery: 1 to 5.1 mL; total dose of articaine: 40 to 204 mg; maximum dose of articaine: 7 mg/kg (0.175 mL/kg).

Geriatric

Dental anesthesia: Submucosal infiltration and/or nerve block: Articaine 4%/epinephrine: **Note:** These dosages are guides only; other dosages may be used; however, do not exceed maximum recommended dose. The actual volumes to be used depend upon a number of factors, such as type and extent of surgical procedure, depth of anesthesia, degree of muscular relaxation, and condition of the patient. In all cases, the smallest dose that will produce the desired result should be given. For most routine dental procedures, epinephrine 1:200,000 is preferred; when more pronounced hemostasis or improved visualization of the surgical field are required, epinephrine 1:100,000 may be used. Dosages should be reduced for patients with cardiac disease and acutely ill and/or debilitated patients:

65 to 75 years:

Simple procedures: 0.43 to 4.76 mg/kg of articaine.

Complex procedures: 1.05 to 4.27 mg/kg of articaine.

≥75 years:

Simple procedures: 0.78 to 4.76 mg/kg of articaine.

Complex procedures: 1.12 to 2.17 mg/kg of articaine.

Pediatric

Dental anesthesia: Submucosal infiltration and/or nerve block: Articaine 4%/epinephrine: Children and Adolescents 4 to 16 years: **Note:** These dosages are guides only; other dosages may be used; however, do not exceed maximum recommended dose. The actual volumes to be used depend upon a number of factors, such as type and extent of surgical procedure, depth of anesthesia, degree of muscular relaxation, and condition of the patient. In all cases, the smallest dose that will produce the desired result should be given. For most routine dental procedures, epinephrine 1:200,000 is preferred; when more pronounced hemostasis or improved visualization of the surgical field are required, epinephrine 1:100,000 may be used. Dosages should be reduced for patients with cardiac disease and acutely ill and/or debilitated patients:

Simple procedures: 0.76 to 5.65 mg/kg of articaine; maximum dose of articaine: 7 mg/kg (0.175 mL/kg).

Complex procedures: 0.37 to 7 mg/kg of articaine; maximum dose of articaine: 7 mg/kg (0.175 mL/kg).

Renal Impairment There are no dosage adjustments provided in the manufacturer's labeling (has not been studied).

Hepatic Impairment There are no dosage adjustments provided in the manufacturer's labeling (has not been studied). Use with caution in patients with severe hepatic disease.

Mechanism of Action

Articaine: Blocks both the initiation and conduction of nerve impulses by increasing the threshold for electrical excitation in the nerve, slowing the propagation of the nerve impulse, and reducing the rate of rise of the action potential.

Epinephrine: Increases the duration of action of articaine by causing vasoconstriction (via alpha effects) which slows the vascular absorption of articaine.

Contraindications

Sulfite hypersensitivity.

Documentation of allergenic cross-reactivity for local anesthetics is limited. However, because of similarities in chemical structure and/or pharmacologic actions, the possibility of cross-sensitivity cannot be ruled out with certainty.

Warnings/Precautions Systemic toxicity may occur. Systemic absorption of local anesthetics may produce cardiovascular and/or CNS effects. Toxic blood concentrations of local anesthetics depress cardiac conduction and excitability, which may lead to AV block, ventricular arrhythmias, and cardiac arrest (sometimes resulting in death). In addition, myocardial contractility is depressed and peripheral vasodilation occurs, leading to decreased cardiac output and arterial blood pressure. Restlessness, anxiety, tinnitus, dizziness, blurred vision, tremors, depression, or drowsiness may be early warning signs of CNS toxicity. Small doses of local anesthetics injected into dental blocks may produce adverse reactions similar to systemic toxicity, including confusion, convulsions, respiratory depression and/or respiratory arrest, and cardiovascular stimulation or depression; these reactions may be due to intra-arterial injection of the local anesthetic with retrograde flow to the cerebral circulation. Constantly monitor cardiovascular and respiratory vital signs and patient's state of consciousness carefully following each injection. Epinephrine may cause local toxicity, including ischemic injury or necrosis. Local anesthetics containing a vasoconstrictor may cause methemoglobinemia, especially in combination with methemoglobin-inducing agents.

Do not use in patients with congenital or idiopathic methemoglobinemia, or in patients who are receiving treatment with methemoglobin-inducing agents. Use with caution in patients with impaired cardiovascular function, including patients with heart block. Use local anesthetics containing a vasoconstrictor with caution in patients with vascular disease; patients with peripheral vascular disease or hypertensive vascular disease may exhibit exaggerated vasoconstrictor response, possibly resulting in ischemic injury or necrosis. Dosages should be reduced for patients with cardiac disease. Use with caution in patients with severe hepatic disease (has not been studied).

Administer reduced dosages, commensurate with age and physical condition to pediatric, elderly, debilitated and/or acutely-ill patients. Avoid intravascular injection; accidental intravascular injection may be associated with convulsions, followed by CNS or cardiorespiratory depression and coma, progressing ultimately to respiratory arrest. Aspiration should be performed prior to administration; the needle must be repositioned until no return of blood can be elicited by aspiration; however, absence of blood in the syringe does not guarantee that intravascular injection has been avoided. To avoid serious adverse effects and high plasma levels, use the lowest dosage resulting in effective anesthesia. Repeated doses may cause significant increases in blood levels due to the possibility of accumulation of the drug or its metabolites. Dosage recommendations should not be exceeded. Health care providers should be well trained in diagnosis and management of emergencies that may arise from the use of these agents. Resuscitative equipment, oxygen, and other resuscitative drugs should be available for immediate use. May contain sodium metabisulfite, which may cause allergic-type reactions (including anaphylactic symptoms, and life-threatening or less severe asthmatic episodes) in certain susceptible patients. The overall prevalence of the sulfite sensitivity in the general population is unknown, and is seen more frequently in asthmatic than in nonasthmatic persons. Potentially significant interactions may exist, requiring dose or frequency adjustment, additional monitoring, and/or selection of alternative therapy.

Drug Interactions

Metabolism/Transport Effects Refer to individual components.

Avoid Concomitant Use

Avoid concomitant use of Articaine and Epinephrine with any of the following: Blonanserin; Bupivacaine (Liposomal); Ergot Derivatives; Iobenguane I 123; Lurasidone

Increased Effect/Toxicity

Articaine and Epinephrine may increase the levels/effects of: Bupivacaine (Liposomal); Doxofylline; Lurasidone; Neuromuscular-Blocking Agents; Sympathomimetics

The levels/effects of Articaine and Epinephrine may be increased by: AtoMOXetine; Beta-Blockers; Cannabinoid-Containing Products; Cocaine; COMT Inhibitors; Ergot Derivatives; Hyaluronidase; Inhalational Anesthetics; Linezolid; MAO Inhibitors; Serotonin/Norepinephrine Reuptake Inhibitors; Tedizolid; Tricyclic Antidepressants

Decreased Effect

Articaine and Epinephrine may decrease the levels/effects of: Antidiabetic Agents; Benzylpenicilloyl Polylysine; Iobenguane I 123; Technetium Tc 99m Tilmanocept

The levels/effects of Articaine and Epinephrine may be decreased by: Alpha1-Blockers; Benperidol; Blonanserin; CloZAPine; Promethazine; Spironolactone

Pharmacodynamics/Kinetics

Onset of Action 1 to 9 minutes

Duration of Action Complete anesthesia: ~1 hour (infiltration); ~2 hours (nerve block)

Half-life Elimination Articaine/epinephrine: 43.8 to 44.4 minutes

Time to Peak Articaine: ~25 minutes (single dose); 48 minutes (3 doses)

Pregnancy Risk Factor C

Pregnancy Considerations Adverse events have been observed in some animal reproduction studies using this combination. Articaine crosses the placenta (Strasser 1977).

Breastfeeding Considerations It is not known if articaine or epinephrine are excreted in breast milk. The manufacturer recommends that caution be exercised when administering articaine/epinephrine to breastfeeding women; consideration may be given to pumping and discarding milk for 4 hours after the last dose. In general, women administered single dose local anesthesia for dental procedures may resume breastfeeding once they are awake and stable (Montgomery 2012).

Dosage Forms

Injection, solution [for dental use]:

Articadent: Articaine hydrochloride 4% [40 mg/mL] and epinephrine 1:100,000 (1.7 mL)

Articadent: Articaine hydrochloride 4% [40 mg/mL] and epinephrine 1:200,000 (1.7 mL)

Orabloc: Articaine hydrochloride 4% [40 mg/mL] and epinephrine 1:100,000 (1.8 mL)

Orabloc: Articaine hydrochloride 4% [40 mg/mL] and epinephrine 1:200,000 (1.8 mL)

Septocaine with epinephrine 1:100,000: Articaine 4% [40 mg/mL] and epinephrine 1:100,000 (1.7 mL)

Septocaine with epinephrine 1:200,000: Articaine 4% [40 mg/mL] and epinephrine 1:200,000 (1.7 mL)

Zorcaine: Articaine 4% [40 mg/mL] and epinephrine 1:100,000 (1.7 mL)

Dosage Forms: Canada

Injection, solution [for dental use]:

Astracaine with epinephrine 1:200,000: Articaine 4% and epinephrine 1:200,000 (1.8 mL)

Astracaine Forte with epinephrine forte 1:100,000: Articaine 4% and epinephrine 1:100,000 (1.8 mL)

Septanest N: Articaine 4% and epinephrine 1:200,000 (1.7 mL)

Septanest SP: Articaine 4% and epinephrine 1:100,000 (1.7 mL)

Ultracaine DS: Articaine 4% and epinephrine 1:200,000 (1.7 mL)

Ultracaine DS Forte: Articaine 4% and epinephrine 1:100,000 (1.7 mL)

Dental Comment Septocaine (articaine hydrochloride 4% and epinephrine 1:100,000) is the first FDA approval in 30 years of a new local dental anesthetic providing complete pulpal anesthesia for approximately 1 hour. Chemically, articaine contains both an amide linkage and an ester linkage, making it chemically unique in the class of local anesthetics. Since it contains the ester linkage, articaine HCl is rapidly metabolized by plasma carboxyesterase to its primary metabolite, articainic acid, which is an inactive product of this metabolism. According to the manufacturer, *in vitro* studies show that the human liver microsomal P450 isoenzyme system metabolizes approximately 5% to 10% of available articaine with nearly quantitative conversion to articainic acid. The elimination half-life of articaine is about 1.8 hours, and that of articainic acid is about 1.5 hours. Articaine is excreted primarily through urine with 53% to 57% of the administered dose eliminated in the first 24 hours following submucosal administration. Articainic acid is the primary metabolite in urine. A minor metabolite, articainic acid glucuronide, is also excreted in the urine. Articaine constitutes only 2% of the total dose excreted in urine.

The anesthetic efficacy of the articaine 4% with 1:200,000 epinephrine (A/200) was compared to that of articaine 4% with 1:100,000 (A/100) using electric pulp tester to assess anesthesia using 63 subjects after either maxillary infiltration (Moore, 2006) or inferior alveolar block (Hersh, 2006).

After maxillary infiltration of 1 mL of each formula, the onset times to anesthesia were 3.1 ± 2.3 minutes for articaine 4% and 1:200,000 epinephrine (A/200), 3 ± 2.1 minutes for articaine 4% and 1:100,000 epinephrine (A/100), 3 ± 2 minutes for articaine 4% with no epinephrine (A/no). These three mean times of onset were not statistically different. Durations of anesthesia were 41.6 ± 21.1 minutes A/200, 45 ± 23.6 minutes A/100, 13.3 ± 6.8 minutes for A/no. There was no statistically significant difference between the durations elicited by the A/200 and A/100 formulations (Moore, 2006). In the second trial of the study, also using 63 subjects, the investigators administered an inferior alveolar nerve block injection of one cartridge (1.7 mL) using a standard intra-oral injection technique for inferior alveolar block anesthesia. Pulpal anesthesia was measured again using the pulp tester.

The onset times to anesthesia were 4.7 ± 2.6 minutes A/200, 4.2 ± 2.8 minutes A/100, and 4.3 ± 2.5 minutes for A/no. There were no statistically significant differences in these times to onset. Durations of anesthesia were 51.2 ± 55.9 minutes A/200, 61.8 ± 59 minutes A/100, and 49.7 ± 44.6 minutes for A/no. There were no statistically significant differences in the duration between A/200, A/100, and A/no formulations (Hersh, 2006).

Oral paresthesia: The occurrence of oral paresthesia associated with 4% solutions of prilocaine or articaine, although rare, continue to be slightly more frequent than other local anesthetics. From 1999-2008, there were 182 cases of nonsurgical paresthesia (Gaffen, 2009). Of the cases, 172 involved mandibular block injection only. Another eight cases involved mandibular block combined with at least one other type of anesthetic injection. A single case involved infiltration around tooth number 35 (European numbering system; tooth number 20 for Universal numbering system) and the final case involved infiltration and intraligamentary injection in the maxillary anterior region.

A 2010 report, reviewed adverse events submitted voluntarily over a 10-year period involving the dental local anesthetics articaine, bupivacaine, lidocaine, mepivacaine, and prilocaine in the United States. Articaine reported incidence: One case per 4,159,848 cartridges sold. The reported incidence of paresthesia was one case for 13,800,970 cartridges of all local anesthetics sold in the U.S. (Garisto, 2010).

Ascorbic Acid (a SKOR bik AS id)

Related Information

Viral Infections *on page 1849*

Brand Names: US Acerola C 500 [OTC]; Asco-Tabs-1000 [OTC]; Ascocid [OTC]; Ascocid-ISO-pH [OTC]; BProtected Vitamin C [OTC]; C-500 [OTC]; C-Time [OTC]; Cemill SR [OTC]; Cemill [OTC]; Chew-C [OTC]; Fruit C 500 [OTC]; Fruit C [OTC]; Fruity C [OTC]; Mega-C/A Plus; Ortho-CS 250; Vita-C [OTC]; VitaChew Vit C Citrus Burst [OTC]

Brand Names: Canada Ascor L 500; Vitamin C

Pharmacologic Category Vitamin, Water Soluble

Use

Ascorbic acid deficiency: Treatment of symptoms of mild deficiency; use in conditions requiring an increased intake (eg, burns, wound healing)

Dietary supplement: As a dietary vitamin C supplement

Scurvy: Prevention and treatment of scurvy

Local Anesthetic/Vasoconstrictor Precautions No information available to require special precautions

Effects on Dental Treatment No significant effects or complications reported

Effects on Bleeding No information available to require special precautions

Adverse Reactions

1% to 10%: Endocrine & metabolic: Hyperoxaluria (with large doses)

<1%: Diarrhea, dizziness, fatigue, flank pain, flushing, headache, heartburn, nausea, vomiting

General Dosage Range Dosage varies greatly depending on indication.

Mechanism of Action Ascorbic acid is an essential water soluble vitamin that acts as a cofactor and antioxidant. Ascorbic acid is an electron donor used for collagen hydroxylation, carnitine biosynthesis, and hormone/amino acid biosynthesis. It is required for connective tissue synthesis as well as iron absorption and storage (IOM, 2000).

Pharmacodynamics/Kinetics

Onset of Action Reversal of scurvy symptoms: 2 days to 3 weeks

Half-life Elimination 10 hours (Schwedhelm 2003). Biological half-life: 8 to 40 days (IOM, 2000)

Pregnancy Risk Factor C

Pregnancy Considerations Animal reproduction studies have not been conducted. Maternal plasma concentrations of ascorbic acid decrease as pregnancy progresses due to hemodilution and increased transfer to the fetus. Some pregnant women (eg, smokers) may require supplementation greater than the RDA (IOM, 2000).

Asenapine (a SEN a peen)

Related Information

Clinical Risk Related to Drugs Prolonging QT Interval *on page 1772*

Brand Names: US Saphris

Brand Names: Canada Saphris

Pharmacologic Category Antimanic Agent; Second Generation (Atypical) Antipsychotic

Use

Bipolar disorder: Treatment of acute manic or mixed episodes associated with bipolar I disorder (as monotherapy in adult and pediatric patients 10 years and older or adjunctive treatment with lithium or valproate in adults) and maintenance treatment in adults (as monotherapy)

Schizophrenia: Treatment of adults with schizophrenia

Local Anesthetic/Vasoconstrictor Precautions Asenapine is one of the drugs confirmed to prolong the QT interval and is accepted as having a risk of causing torsade de pointes. The risk of drug-induced torsade de pointes is extremely low when a single QT interval prolonging drug is prescribed. In terms of epinephrine, it is not known what effect vasoconstrictors in the local anesthetic regimen will have in patients with a known history of congenital prolonged QT interval or in patients taking any medication that prolongs the QT interval. Until more information is obtained, it is suggested that the clinician consult with the physician prior to the use of a vasoconstrictor in suspected patients, and that the vasoconstrictor (epinephrine, mepivacaine and levonordefrin [Carbocaine® 2% with Neo-Cobefrin®]) be used with caution.

Effects on Dental Treatment Key adverse event(s) related to dental treatment: Xerostomia and increase in salivation (normal salivary flow resumes upon discontinuation). Abnormal taste, toothache, and edema of the tongue have been reported. Patients may experience orthostatic hypotension as they stand up after treatment; especially if lying in dental chair for extended periods of time. Use caution with sudden changes in position during and after dental treatment. Asenapine may cause extrapyramidal symptoms including tardive dyskinesia; risk may be greater with increased doses.

Effects on Bleeding No information available to require special precautions

Adverse Reactions Actual frequency may be dependent upon dose and/or indication.

>10%:

Central nervous system: Drowsiness (13% to 24%), insomnia (6% to 16%), extrapyramidal reaction (6% to 12%), headache (12%), akathisia (4% to 11%; dose related), dizziness (3% to 11%)

Endocrine & metabolic: Hypertriglyceridemia (13% to 15%), weight gain (2% to 15%)

Neuromuscular and skeletal: Increased creatine phosphokinase (6% to 11%)

1% to 10%:

Cardiovascular: Peripheral edema (3%), hypertension (2% to 3%)

Central nervous system: Hypoesthesia (4% to 7%), anxiety (4%), fatigue (3% to 4%), taste disorder (3%), depression (2%), irritability (1% to 2%)

Endocrine & metabolic: Increased serum cholesterol (8% to 9%), increased serum glucose (5% to 7%), hyperprolactinemia (2% to 3%)

Gastrointestinal: Constipation (4% to 7%), vomiting (4% to 7%), increased appetite (≤4%), sialorrhea (≤4%), dyspepsia (3% to 4%), dysgeusia (3%), toothache (3%), abdominal distress (≤3%), xerostomia (1% to 3%)

Hepatic: Increased serum transaminases (<1% to 3%)

Neuromuscular & skeletal: Arthralgia (3%), limb pain (2%)

<1%, postmarketing, and/or case reports: Accommodation disturbance, anaphylaxis, anemia, angioedema, application site reaction, bradycardia, bundle branch block (temporary), diabetes mellitus, dysarthria, dyskinesia, dysphagia, dyspnea, dystonia, fever, glossalgia, hyperglycemia, hypersensitivity, hyponatremia, hypotension, leukopenia, localized warm feeling, mucous membrane lesion, neuroleptic malignant syndrome, neutropenia, oral paresthesia, prolonged Q-T interval on ECG, seizure, skin rash, syncope, tachycardia, thrombocytopenia, tongue edema, wheezing

General Dosage Range Oral:

Children ≥10 years and Adolescents ≤17 years: 2.5 to 10 mg twice daily; maximum: 10 mg twice daily.

Adults: 5 to 10 mg twice daily; maximum: 10 mg twice daily.

Mechanism of Action Asenapine is a dibenzo-oxepino pyrrole atypical antipsychotic with mixed serotonin-dopamine antagonist activity. It exhibits high affinity for 5-HT_{1A}, 5-HT_{1B}, 5-HT_{2A}, 5-HT_{2B}, 5-HT_{2C}, 5-HT_{5-7}, D_{1-4}, H_1 and, alpha$_1$- and alpha$_2$-adrenergic receptors; moderate affinity for H_2 receptors. Asenapine has no significant affinity for muscarinic receptors. The binding affinity to the D_2 receptor is 19 times lower than the 5-HT_{2A} affinity (Weber 2009). The addition of serotonin antagonism to dopamine antagonism (classic neuroleptic mechanism) is thought to improve negative symptoms of psychoses and reduce the incidence of extrapyramidal side effects as compared to typical antipsychotics (Huttunen 1995).

Pharmacodynamics/Kinetics

Half-life Elimination Terminal: ~24 hours

Time to Peak 0.5 to 1.5 hours

Pregnancy Considerations Antipsychotic use during the third trimester of pregnancy has a risk for abnormal muscle movements (extrapyramidal symptoms [EPS]) and/or withdrawal symptoms in newborns following delivery. Symptoms in the newborn may include agitation, feeding disorder, hypertonia, hypotonia, respiratory distress, somnolence, and tremor; these effects may be self-limiting or require hospitalization; monitoring of the neonate is recommended. Asenapine may cause hyperprolactinemia, which may decrease reproductive function in both males and females.

The ACOG recommends that therapy during pregnancy be individualized; treatment with psychiatric medications during pregnancy should incorporate the clinical expertise of the mental health clinician, obstetrician, primary healthcare provider, and pediatrician. Safety data related to atypical antipsychotics during pregnancy is limited and routine use is not recommended. However, if a woman is inadvertently exposed to an atypical antipsychotic while pregnant, continuing therapy may be preferable to switching to a typical antipsychotic that the fetus has not yet been exposed to; consider risk: benefit (ACOG 2008).

Healthcare providers are encouraged to enroll women 18-45 years of age exposed to asenapine during pregnancy in the Atypical Antipsychotics Pregnancy Registry (866-961-2388 or http://www.womensmentalhealth.org/pregnancyregistry).

Dental Comment

See Local Anesthetic/Vasoconstrictor Precautions

Asparaginase (*E. coli*) (a SPEAR a ji nase e ko lye)

Brand Names: US Elspar [DSC]

Brand Names: Canada Kidrolase

Pharmacologic Category Antineoplastic Agent, Enzyme; Antineoplastic Agent, Miscellaneous

Use Acute lymphoblastic leukemia: Treatment of acute lymphoblastic leukemia (ALL) (in combination with other chemotherapy)

Local Anesthetic/Vasoconstrictor Precautions No information available to require special precautions

Effects on Dental Treatment Key adverse event(s) related to dental treatment: Stomatitis

Effects on Bleeding Thrombotic and hemorrhagic events have been reported with asparaginase *(E. coli)*. A medical consult is recommended.

Adverse Reactions Frequency not defined.

Cardiovascular: Cerebrovascular accident (hemorrhagic stroke and thrombotic stroke [Morgan 2011]), thrombosis (including cerebral thrombosis)

Central nervous system: Central nervous system disease (adults; includes delusion, disorientation, mild depression, Parkinsonian-like syndrome, personality disorder, seizure), cerebral hemorrhage, cerebrovascular hemorrhage (Morgan 2011)

Endocrine & metabolic: Amenorrhea, decreased glucose tolerance, hyperammonemia (with clinical signs of metabolic encephalopathy [eg, impaired consciousness with coma, confusion, and stupor]), hypercholesterolemia, hyperglycemia, hypertriglyceridemia, hypoalbuminemia, hypocholesterolemia, increased uric acid, weight loss

Gastrointestinal: Abdominal pain (infrequent), acute pancreatitis (may be fatal), cholestatic injury, diarrhea (infrequent), intestinal perforation (rare), nausea (frequent, but rarely severe; may be secondary to increased blood urea nitrogen and increased uric acid), vomiting (frequent, but rarely severe; may be secondary to increased blood urea nitrogen and increased uric acid)

Genitourinary: Azoospermia

Hematologic: Antithrombin III deficiency, blood coagulation disorder (change in hemostatic function), bone marrow depression, decreased clotting factors (factors VII, VIII, IX, and X), decreased plasminogen, hypofibrinogenemia, prolonged partial thromboplastin time, prolonged prothrombin time

Hepatic: Hepatic injury, hepatotoxicity (usually mild and regressive, but may be fatal rarely), hyperbilirubinemia, increased serum alkaline phosphatase, increased serum ALT, increased serum AST (mild), jaundice, liver steatosis

Hypersensitivity: Allergic reactions (includes anaphylactic shock, anaphylaxis, bronchospasm, edema, hypotension, laryngeal edema, skin rash, urticaria; onset usually within 1 hour of administration and risk increasing with increasing number of exposures)

Immunologic: Increased serum globulins (beta and gamma)

Infection: Septicemia (during bone marrow depression)

Renal: Increased blood urea nitrogen, renal failure

Respiratory: Respiratory distress (with retrosternal pressure)

Miscellaneous: Fever

General Dosage Range IM, IV: *Children, Adolescents, and Adults:* 200 to 1,000 units/kg/day or 400 units/kg on Monday and Wednesday and 600 units/kg on Friday

Mechanism of Action In leukemic cells, asparaginase hydrolyzes L-asparagine to ammonia and L-aspartic acid, leading to depletion of asparagine. Leukemia cells, especially lymphoblasts, require exogenous asparagine; normal cells can synthesize asparagine. Asparagine depletion in leukemic cells leads to inhibition of protein synthesis and apoptosis. Asparaginase is cycle-specific for the G_1 phase.

Pharmacodynamics/Kinetics

Half-life Elimination IM: 34 to 49 hours; IV: 8 to 30 hours

Time to Peak IM: 14 to 24 hours

Pregnancy Considerations Use is contraindicated.

Product Availability US product, Elspar, was discontinued more than 1 year ago.

Asparaginase (*Erwinia*)

(a SPEAR a ji nase er WIN i ah)

Brand Names: US Erwinaze

Brand Names: Canada Erwinase

Pharmacologic Category Antineoplastic Agent, Enzyme; Antineoplastic Agent, Miscellaneous

Use Acute lymphoblastic leukemia: Treatment (in combination with other chemotherapy) of acute lymphoblastic leukemia (ALL) in patients with hypersensitivity to *E. coli*-derived asparaginase

Local Anesthetic/Vasoconstrictor Precautions No information available to require special precautions

Effects on Dental Treatment No significant effects or complications reported

Effects on Bleeding Thrombotic and hemorrhagic events have been reported with asparaginase *(Erwinia)*. A medical consult is recommended.

Adverse Reactions

Frequency of adverse reactions is for both IM and IV routes unless specified.

>10%: Hypersensitivity: Hypersensitivity reaction (14% [IV: ≤37%]; grades 3/4: 4%; includes anaphylaxis, urticaria)

1% to 10%:

Cardiovascular: Thrombosis (2% [IV: ≤7%]; grades 3/4: ≤1%; includes pulmonary embolism and cerebrovascular accident)

Endocrine & metabolic: Hyperglycemia (4% [IV: ≤17%]; grades 3/4: 4%), abnormal transaminase (4%), decreased glucose tolerance (4%)

Gastrointestinal: Nausea (3% [IV: ≤20%]), vomiting (3% [IV: ≤17%]), pancreatitis (4%; grades 3/4: <1%), abdominal pain (1%), diarrhea (1%), mucositis (1%)

Local: Injection site reaction (3%)

Miscellaneous: Fever (4%)

<1%, postmarketing, and/or case reports: Acute renal failure, anorexia, azotemia, bone marrow depression (rare), changes in serum lipids, chills, decreased serum albumin, decreased serum cholesterol, disseminated intravascular coagulation, headache, hemorrhage, hepatomegaly, hyperammonemia, hyperbilirubinemia, irritability, malabsorption syndrome, proteinuria, seizure, transient ischemic attacks, weight loss

General Dosage Range IM, IV: *Children and Adults:* 25,000 units/m^2 3 times weekly (Mon, Wed, Fri) for 6 doses for each planned pegaspargase dose **or** 25,000 units/m^2 for each planned asparaginase (*E. coli*) dose

Mechanism of Action Asparaginase catalyzes the deamidation of asparagine to aspartic acid and ammonia, reducing circulating levels of asparagine. Leukemia cells lack asparagine synthetase and are unable to synthesize asparagine. Asparaginase reduces the exogenous asparagine source for the leukemic cells, resulting in cytotoxicity specific to leukemic cells.

Pharmacodynamics/Kinetics

Half-life Elimination IM: ~16 hours (Asselin, 1993; Avramis, 2005); IV: ~7.5 hours

Pregnancy Risk Factor C

Pregnancy Considerations Adverse events were observed in animal reproduction studies.

Prescribing and Access Restrictions Erwinaze is distributed through Accredo Health Group, Inc. (1-877-900-9223).

Aspirin (AS pir in)

Related Information

Antiplatelet and Anticoagulation Considerations in Dentistry *on page 1764*
Cardiovascular Diseases *on page 1752*
Oral Pain *on page 1830*
Rheumatoid Arthritis, Osteoarthritis, and Osteoporosis *on page 1792*

Brand Names: US Ascriptin Maximum Strength [OTC]; Ascriptin Regular Strength [OTC]; Aspercin [OTC]; Aspir-low [OTC]; Aspirtab [OTC]; Bayer Aspirin Extra Strength [OTC]; Bayer Aspirin Regimen Adult Low Strength [OTC]; Bayer Aspirin Regimen Children's [OTC]; Bayer Aspirin Regimen Regular Strength [OTC]; Bayer Genuine Aspirin [OTC]; Bayer Plus Extra Strength [OTC]; Bayer Women's Low Dose Aspirin [OTC]; Buffasal [OTC]; Bufferin Extra Strength [OTC]; Bufferin [OTC]; Buffinol [OTC]; Durlaza; Ecotrin Arthritis Strength [OTC]; Ecotrin Low Strength [OTC]; Ecotrin [OTC]; Halfprin [OTC] [DSC]; St Joseph Adult Aspirin [OTC]; Tri-Buffered Aspirin [OTC]

Brand Names: Canada Asaphen; Asaphen E.C.; Entrophen; Novasen; Praxis ASA EC 81 Mg Daily Dose; Pro-AAS EC-80

Generic Availability (US) May be product dependent

Pharmacologic Category Analgesic, Nonopioid; Antiplatelet Agent; Nonsteroidal Anti-inflammatory Drug (NSAID), Oral; Salicylate

Dental Use Treatment of postoperative pain

Use

Immediate release:

Analgesic/Antipyretic: For the temporary relief of headache, pain, and fever caused by colds, muscle aches and pains, menstrual pain, toothache pain, and minor aches and pains of arthritis.

Revascularization procedures: In patients who have undergone revascularization procedures (ie, coronary artery bypass graft [CABG], percutaneous transluminal coronary angioplasty, or carotid endarterectomy).

Rheumatoid disease: For the relief of the signs and symptoms of rheumatoid arthritis (RA), juvenile idiopathic arthritis (formerly called juvenile RA), osteoarthritis, spondyloarthropathies, and arthritis and pleurisy associated with systemic lupus erythematosus.

Vascular indications (ischemic stroke, transient ischemic attack, acute myocardial infarction, prevention of recurrent myocardial infarction, unstable angina, and chronic stable angina): To reduce the combined risk of death and nonfatal stroke in patients who have had ischemic stroke or transient ischemia of the brain due to fibrin platelet emboli; to reduce the risk of vascular mortality in patients with a suspected acute myocardial infarction (MI); to reduce the combined risk of death and nonfatal MI in patients with a previous MI or unstable angina; to reduce the combined risk of MI and sudden death in patients with chronic stable angina.

Extended-release capsules:

Chronic coronary artery disease: To reduce the risk of death and MI in patients with chronic coronary artery disease (eg, history of MI, unstable angina, or chronic stable angina).

History of ischemic stroke or transient ischemic attack: To reduce the risk of death and recurrent stroke in patients who have had an ischemic stroke or transient ischemic attack (TIA).

Limitations of use: Do not use extended-release capsules in situations for which a rapid onset of action is required (such as acute treatment of MI or before percutaneous coronary intervention); use immediate-release formulations instead.

Local Anesthetic/Vasoconstrictor Precautions No information available to require special precautions

Effects on Dental Treatment Key adverse event(s) related to dental treatment: As with all drugs which may affect hemostasis, bleeding is associated with aspirin. Hemorrhage may occur at virtually any site; risk is dependent on multiple variables including dosage, concurrent use of multiple agents which alter hemostasis, and patient susceptibility. Many adverse effects of aspirin are dose related, and are rare at low dosages. Other serious reactions are idiosyncratic, related to allergy or individual sensitivity (see Dental Comment).

Aspirin as sole antiplatelet agent: Patients taking aspirin for ischemic stroke prevention are safe to continue it during dental procedures (Armstrong, 2013).

Concurrent aspirin use with other antiplatelet agents: Aspirin in combination with clopidogrel (Plavix), prasugrel (Effient), or ticagrelor (Brilinta) is the primary prevention strategy against stent thrombosis after placement of drug-eluting metal stents in coronary patients. Premature discontinuation of combination antiplatelet therapy (ie, dual antiplatelet therapy) strongly increases the risk of a catastrophic event of stent thrombosis leading to myocardial infarction and/or death, so says a science advisory issued in January 2007 from the American Heart Association in collaboration with the American Dental Association and other professional healthcare organizations. The advisory stresses a 12-month therapy of dual antiplatelet therapy after placement of a drug-eluting stent in order to prevent thrombosis at the stent site. Any elective surgery should be postponed for 1 year after stent implantation, and if surgery must be performed, consideration should be given to continuing the antiplatelet therapy during the perioperative period in high-risk patients with drug-eluting stents.

This advisory was issued from a science panel made up of representatives from the American Heart Association (AHA), the American College of Cardiology, the Society for Cardiovascular Angiography and Interventions, the American College of Surgeons, the American Dental Association (ADA), and the American College of Physicians (Grines, 2007).

Effects on Bleeding Aspirin irreversibly inhibits platelet aggregation which can prolong bleeding. Upon discontinuation, normal platelet function returns only when new platelets are released (~7 to 10 days). However, in the case of dental surgery, there is no scientific evidence to support discontinuation of aspirin. This was recently supported by the American Academy of Neurology in patients with ischemic cerebrovascular disease (Armstrong, 2013). A recent study compared blood loss after a single tooth extraction in coronary artery disease patients who were either on aspirin (100 mg daily) or off aspirin for the extraction. The mean volume of bleeding was not statistically different between the groups. Local hemostatic measures were sufficient to control bleeding and there were no reported episodes of hemorrhaging intra- or postoperatively (Medeiros, 2011).

Adverse Reactions As with all drugs which may affect hemostasis, bleeding is associated with aspirin. Hemorrhage may occur at virtually any site. Risk is dependent on multiple variables including dosage, concurrent use of multiple agents which alter hemostasis, and patient susceptibility. Many adverse effects of aspirin are dose related, and are rare at low dosages. Other serious reactions are idiosyncratic, related to allergy or individual sensitivity. Accurate estimation of frequencies is not possible. The reactions listed below have been reported for aspirin.

Cardiovascular: Cardiac arrhythmia, edema, hypotension, tachycardia

Central nervous system: Agitation, cerebral edema, coma, confusion, dizziness, fatigue, headache, hyperthermia, insomnia, lethargy, nervousness, Reye's syndrome

Dermatologic: Skin rash, urticaria

Endocrine & metabolic: Acidosis, dehydration, hyperglycemia, hyperkalemia, hypernatremia (buffered forms), hypoglycemia (children)

Gastrointestinal: Gastrointestinal ulcer (6% to 31%), duodenal ulcer, dyspepsia, epigastric distress, gastritis, gastrointestinal erosion, heartburn, nausea, stomach pain, vomiting

Genitourinary: Postpartum hemorrhage, prolonged gestation, prolonged labor, proteinuria, stillborn infant

Hematologic & oncologic: Anemia, blood coagulation disorder, disseminated intravascular coagulation, hemolytic anemia, hemorrhage, iron deficiency anemia, prolonged prothrombin time, thrombocytopenia

Hepatic: Hepatitis (reversible), hepatotoxicity, increased serum transaminases

Hypersensitivity: Anaphylaxis, angioedema

Neuromuscular & skeletal: Acetabular bone destruction, rhabdomyolysis, weakness

Otic: Hearing loss, tinnitus

Renal: Increased blood urea nitrogen, increased serum creatinine, interstitial nephritis, renal failure (including cases caused by rhabdomyolysis), renal insufficiency, renal papillary necrosis

Respiratory: Asthma, bronchospasm, dyspnea, hyperventilation, laryngeal edema, noncardiogenic pulmonary edema, respiratory alkalosis, tachypnea

Miscellaneous: Low birth weight

Postmarketing and/or case reports: Anorectal stenosis (suppository), atrial fibrillation (toxicity), cardiac conduction disturbance (toxicity), cerebral infarction (ischemic), cholestatic jaundice, colitis, colonic ulceration, coronary artery vasospasm, delirium, esophageal obstruction, esophagitis (with esophageal ulcer), hematoma (esophageal), macular degeneration (age-related) (Li 2014), periorbital edema, rhinosinusitis

Dental Usual Dosage Postoperative pain:

Analgesic and antipyretic: Oral, rectal:

Children: 10 to 15 mg/kg/dose every 4 to 6 hours, up to a total of 4 g/day

Adults: 325 to 650 mg every 4 to 6 hours up to 4 g/day

Anti-inflammatory: Oral: Initial:

Children: 60 to 90 mg/kg/day in divided doses; usual maintenance: 80 to 100 mg/kg/day divided every 6 to 8 hours; monitor serum concentrations

Adults: 2.4 to 3.6 g/day in divided doses; usual maintenance: 3.6 to 5.4 g/day; monitor serum concentrations

Dosing

Adult & Geriatric Note: For most cardiovascular uses, typical maintenance dosing of aspirin is 81 mg once daily. Manufacturer recommended dosing for some indications have been superseded by more recent guideline recommended doses and therefore manufacturer recommended dosing may not be represented; terminologies may also differ from manufacturer's prescribing information.

Acute coronary syndrome (ST- elevation myocardial infarction [STEMI], non-ST-elevation acute coronary syndromes [NSTE-ACS]): Oral:

Initial: 162 to 325 mg given on presentation (patient should chew nonenteric-coated aspirin especially if not taking before presentation) (ACC/AHA [Amsterdam 2014]; ACCF/AHA [O'Gara 2013]); for patients unable to take oral, may use a rectal suppository dose of 600 mg (Maalouf 2009).

Maintenance (secondary prevention): 81 to 325 mg once daily continued indefinitely; when aspirin is used with ticagrelor, the recommended maintenance dose of aspirin is 81 mg/day (ACC/AHA [Amsterdam 2014]; ACCF/AHA [O'Gara 2013]) According to the STEMI guidelines, 81 mg once daily is preferred (ACCF/AHA [O'Gara 2013]).

Concomitant antiplatelet therapy:

STEMI: Aspirin is recommended in combination with either clopidogrel, prasugrel, or ticagrelor given as early as possible or at time of PCI. In addition to dual antiplatelet therapy, parenteral anticoagulant therapy is indicated. Post-PCI stenting, consult clinical practice guidelines for recommended duration of maintenance antiplatelet therapy depending on type of stenting (ACCF/AHA [O'Gara 2013]).

NSTE-ACS:

If early-invasive strategy chosen: Aspirin is recommended in combination with either clopidogrel or ticagrelor. In addition to dual antiplatelet therapy, parenteral anticoagulant therapy is indicated. In select high-risk patients (ie, troponin positive), an IV GP IIb/IIIa inhibitor may be considered as part of initial antiplatelet therapy (if given before PCI, eptifibatide and tirofiban are preferred agents). In patients post-PCI with stenting (bare metal or drug-eluting stent), aspirin should be given with either clopidogrel, ticagrelor, or prasugrel for at least 12 months (ACC/AHA [Amsterdam 2014])

If ischemia-guided strategy (ie, noninvasive strategy) chosen: Aspirin is recommended in combination with clopidogrel or ticagrelor for up to 12 months In addition to dual antiplatelet therapy, parenteral anticoagulant therapy is indicated. (ACC/AHA [Amsterdam 2014]).

Analgesic and antipyretic:

Oral: Immediate release: 325 to 650 mg as needed every 4 hours **or** 975 mg as needed every 6 hours **or** 500 to 1,000 mg as needed every 4 to 6 hours for no more than 10 days or as directed by health care provider; maximum daily dose: 4 g/day.

Rectal: 300 to 600 mg every 4 hours for no more than 10 days or as directed by health care provider

Anti-inflammatory (off-label dosing): Note: The use of non-aspirin NSAIDs has largely supplanted the use of aspirin for osteoarthritis, rheumatoid arthritis, and other inflammatory arthritides.

Immediate release: Oral: Usual maintenance dose: 2.1 to 7.3 g/day in divided doses (individualize dose); monitor serum salicylate concentrations especially when symptoms of salicylism (eg, tinnitus) appear; adjust dose accordingly (Csuka, 1989).

Aortic valve repair (off-label use): Immediate release: Oral: 50 to 100 mg once daily (ACCP [Guyatt 2012])

Atrial fibrillation (to prevent thromboembolism in patients not candidates for oral anticoagulation

or at low risk of ischemic stroke [CHA_2DS_2-VASc score of 1]) (off-label use): Immediate release: Oral: 75 to 325 mg once daily (AHA/ACC/HRS [January 2014]; AHA/ASA [Furie 2011]). **Note:** Combination therapy with clopidogrel has been suggested over aspirin alone for those patients who are unsuitable for or choose not to take oral anticoagulant for reasons other than concerns for bleeding (ACCP [Guyatt 2012]).

As an alternative to adjusted-dose warfarin in patients with atrial fibrillation and mitral stenosis: 75 to 325 mg once daily with (preferred) or without clopidogrel (ACCP [Guyatt 2012])

Carotid artery stenosis (asymptomatic) (off-label use): Immediate release: Oral: 75 to 100 mg once daily (ACCP [Alonso-Coello, 2012]). **Note:** The addition of statin therapy has also been recommended for asymptomatic carotid stenosis (AHA/ASA [Meschia, 2014]). When symptomatic, the use of clopidogrel or aspirin/extended-release dipyridamole has been suggested over aspirin alone (ACCP [Alonso-Coello 2012]).

Carotid endarterectomy (off-label dosing): Immediate release: Oral: 75 to 100 mg once daily (ACCP [Alonso-Coello 2012]; AHA [Biller 1998]). The use of clopidogrel or aspirin/extended-release dipyridamole has been suggested over aspirin alone (ACCP [Alonso-Coello 2012]).

Colorectal cancer risk reduction (off-label use): Note: The optimal dose and duration of therapy for colorectal cancer risk reduction are unknown. Consider risk versus benefit ratio when initiating aspirin for this indication.

Primary/Secondary prevention: Immediate release: Oral: 75 to 325 mg once daily (Rothwell, 2010; Sandler, 2003; Ye, 2013)

Hereditary nonpolyposis colon cancer (HNPCC; Lynch Syndrome) carriers: Immediate release: Oral: 600 mg once daily for at least 2 years (ASCO [Stoffel 2014]; Burn, 2011)

Coronary artery disease (CAD), established or chronic:

Immediate release (off-label dosing): Oral: 75 to 100 mg once daily (ACCP [Guyatt 2012])

Extended release capsule: Oral: 162.5 mg once daily

Percutaneous coronary intervention (PCI) (off-label dosing): Immediate release: Oral:

Non-emergent PCI: Preprocedure: 81 to 325 mg (325 mg [nonenteric coated] in aspirin-naive patients) starting at least 2 hours (preferably 24 hours) before procedure. Postprocedure: 81 mg once daily continued indefinitely (in combination with a $P2Y_{12}$ inhibitor [eg, clopidogrel, prasugrel, ticagrelor] up to 12 months) (ACCF/AHA/SCAI [Levine 2011])

Primary PCI: Preprocedure: 162 to 325 mg as early as possible prior to procedure; 325 mg preferred. Postprocedure: 81 mg once daily continued indefinitely (in combination with a P2Y12 inhibitor [eg, clopidogrel] for at least 14 days and up to 12 months) (ACCF/AHA [O'Gara 2013]).

Alternatively, in patients who have undergone elective PCI with either bare metal or drug-eluting stent placement: The American College of Chest Physicians recommends the use of 75 to 325 mg once daily (in combination with clopidogrel) for 1 month in patients receiving a bare metal stent or 3 to 6 months (dependent upon drug eluting stent type) followed by 75 to 100 mg once daily (in combination with clopidogrel) for up to 12 months. For patients who underwent PCI but did not have stent placement, 75 to 325 mg once daily (in combination with clopidogrel) for 1 month is recommended. In either case, single antiplatelet therapy (either aspirin or clopidogrel) is recommended indefinitely (ACCP [Guyatt 2012]).

Pericarditis (off-label use): Immediate release: Oral: Initial: 2.4 to 3.6 g daily in 3 to 4 divided doses; usual maintenance: 3.6 to 5.4 g daily in divided doses; gradually taper over 2- to 3-week period as appropriate (Imazio, 2004; Imazio, 2009).

Pericarditis in association with myocardial infarction (off-label use): Immediate release: Oral: Initial: 650 mg 4 times daily; may increase after 24 hours to 975 mg 4 times daily if necessary (ACCF/AHA [O'Gara 2013]; Berman, 1981).

Peripheral arterial disease (off-label use): Immediate release: Oral: 75 to 100 mg once daily (ACCP [Guyatt 2012]) **or** 75 to 325 mg once daily; may use in conjunction with clopidogrel in those who are not at an increased risk of bleeding but are of high cardiovascular risk. **Note:** These recommendations also pertain to those with intermittent claudication or critical limb ischemia, prior lower extremity revascularization, or prior amputation for lower extremity ischemia (Rooke, 2011).

Peripheral artery percutaneous transluminal angioplasty (with or without stenting) or peripheral artery bypass graft surgery, postprocedure (off-label use): Immediate release: Oral: 75 to 100 mg once daily (ACCP [Guyatt 2012]). **Note:** For below-knee bypass graft surgery with prosthetic grafts, combine with clopidogrel (ACCP [Guyatt 2012]).

Polycythemia vera (off-label use): Immediate release: Oral: 75 or 100 mg once daily. In pregnant women, administer 75 mg once daily throughout pregnancy and for 6 weeks after delivery (Barbui, 2006; McMullin, 2005).

Preeclampsia prevention (women at risk) (off-label use): Immediate release: Oral: 75 to 100 mg once daily starting in the second trimester (ACCP [Guyatt 2012]; USPSTF [LeFevre 2014]) **or** 60 to 80 mg once daily beginning late in the first trimester (ACOG, 2013).

Prevention (primary) of cardiovascular disease (off-label use): Immediate release: Oral:

American College of Chest Physicians: Select individuals ≥50 years of age (without symptomatic cardiovascular disease): 75 to 100 mg once daily (ACCP [Vandvik 2012])

American Diabetes Association: Individuals ≥50 years of age with diabetes type 1 or 2 who are increased cardiovascular risk (10-year risk >10%): 75 to 162 mg once daily (ADA 2016)

Prevention (secondary) after coronary artery bypass graft (CABG) surgery (off-label dosing): Immediate release: Oral: 81 to 325 mg once daily administered preoperatively and within 6 hours postoperatively; continue indefinitely. Following off-pump CABG, administer aspirin 81 to 162 mg in combination with clopidogrel for 12 months (AHA [Kulik 2015]).

Prosthetic heart valve (thromboprophylaxis) (off-label use): Immediate release: Oral:

Bioprosthetic aortic valve (patient in normal sinus rhythm): 50 to 100 mg once daily (ACCP [Guyatt 2012]).

Bioprosthetic mitral valve: 50 to 100 mg once daily after 3 months of anticoagulation with warfarin (ACCP [Guyatt 2012]).

Mechanical aortic or mitral valve:

Low risk of bleeding: 50 to 100 mg once daily (in combination with warfarin) (ACCP [Guyatt 2012])

History of thromboembolism while receiving oral anticoagulants: 75 to 100 mg once daily (in combination with warfarin) (Furie, 2011)

Transcatheter aortic bioprosthetic valve: 50 to 100 mg once daily (in combination with clopidogrel) (ACCP [Guyatt 2012])

Pregnant women, mechanical or bioprosthetic: 75 to 100 mg once daily during the second and third trimesters (when used for mechanical prosthetic valve, combine with warfarin) (AHA/ACC [Nishimura 2014]).

Stroke/TIA: Oral:

Acute ischemic stroke/TIA:

Immediate release (off-label dosing): Initial: 160 to 325 mg within 48 hours of stroke/TIA onset, followed by 75 to 100 mg once daily (ACCP [Guyatt 2012]). The AHA/ASA recommends an initial dose of 325 mg within 24 to 48 hours after stroke; do not administer aspirin within 24 hours after administration of alteplase (Jauch, 2013).

Extended-release capsule: Maintenance (secondary prevention): 162.5 mg once daily. **Note:** Not for initial dosing during acute ischemic stroke or TIA (use immediate release)

Cardioembolic, secondary prevention (oral anticoagulation unsuitable) (off-label dosing: Immediate release: 75 to 100 mg once daily (in combination with clopidogrel) (ACCP [Guyatt 2012]; The ACTIVE Investigators [Connolly 2009])

Cryptogenic with patent foramen ovale (PFO) or atrial septal aneurysm (off-label use): Immediate release: 50 to 100 mg once daily (ACCP [Guyatt 2012])

Noncardioembolic, secondary prevention (off-label use): Immediate release: 75 to 325 mg once daily (Smith, 2011) **or** 75 to 100 mg once daily (ACCP [Guyatt 2012]). **Note:** Combination aspirin/extended release dipyridamole or clopidogrel is preferred over aspirin alone (ACCP [Guyatt 2012]).

Women at high risk for first stroke, primary prevention: Immediate release: 81 mg once daily **or** 100 mg every other day (AHA/ASA [Meschia 2014]).

Pediatric Note: Do not use aspirin in children <12 years (APS, 2008) and adolescents (per manufacturer) who have or who are recovering from chickenpox or flu symptoms due to the association with Reye's syndrome (APS, 2008).

Analgesic: Immediate release:

Infants, Children, and Adolescents weighing <50 kg (off-label use): Oral, rectal: 10 to 15 mg/kg/dose every 4 to 6 hours; maximum daily dose: The lesser value of either 90 mg/kg/day or 4 g/day (APS, 2008)

Children ≥12 years and Adolescents weighing ≥50 kg:

Oral: 325 to 650 mg as needed every 4 hours **or** 975 mg as needed every 6 hours **or** 500 to 1,000 mg as needed every 4 to 6 hours for no more than 10 days or as directed by health care provider; maximum daily dose: 4 g/day

Rectal: 300 to 600 mg every 4 hours for no more than 10 days or as directed by health care provider

Anti-inflammatory (off-label use): Immediate release: Oral: Initial: 60 to 90 mg/kg/day in divided doses; usual maintenance: 80 to 100 mg/kg/day divided every 6 to 8 hours; monitor serum concentrations

Antiplatelet effects (off-label use): Adequate pediatric studies have not been performed; pediatric dosage is derived from adult studies and clinical experience and is not well established. Doses are typically rounded to a convenient amount (eg, 1/2 of 81 mg tablet).

Acute ischemic stroke (AIS) (off-label use): Immediate release: Oral:

Noncardioembolic: 1 to 5 mg/kg/dose once daily for ≥2 years; patients with recurrent AIS or TIAs should be transitioned to clopidogrel, LMWH, or warfarin (ACCP [Monagle 2012])

Secondary to Moyamoya and non-Moyamoya vasculopathy: 1 to 5 mg/kg/dose once daily. **Note:** In non-Moyamoya vasculopathy, continue aspirin for 3 months, with subsequent use guided by repeat cerebrovascular imaging (ACCP [Monagle 2012]).

Norwood, Fontan surgery (postoperative) (primary prophylaxis) (off-label use): Immediate release: Oral: 1 to 5 mg/kg/dose once daily (ACCP [Monagle 2011]; AHA [Giglia 2013])

Prosthetic heart valve (off-label use): Immediate release: Oral:

Bioprosthetic aortic valve (in normal sinus rhythm): 1 to 5 mg/kg/dose once daily (ACCP [Guyatt 2012]; ACCP [Monagle 2012])

Mechanical aortic and/or mitral valve: Low-dose aspirin (eg, 1 to 5 mg/kg/day) combined with vitamin K antagonist (eg, warfarin) is recommended as first-line antithrombotic therapy (ACCP [Guyatt 2012]). Alternative regimens: 6 to 20 mg/kg/dose once daily in combination with dipyridamole (Bradley 1985; El Makhlouf 1987; LeBlanc 1993; Serra 1987; Solymar 1991)

Shunts: Blalock-Taussig or Glenn (primary prophylaxis) (off-label use): Immediate release: Oral: 1 to 5 mg/kg/dose once daily (AHA [Giglia 2013]; ACCP [Monagle 2012])

Transcatheter Atrial Septal Defect (ASD) or Ventricular Septal Defect (VSD) devices (postprocedure prophylaxis) (off-label use): Immediate release: Oral: 1 to 5 mg/kg/dose once daily starting one to several days prior to implantation and continued for at least 6 months. For older children and adolescents, after device closure of ASD, an additional anticoagulant may be given with aspirin for 3 to 6 months, but the aspirin should continue for at least 6 months (AHA [Giglia 2013]).

Ventricular assist device (VAD) placement (off-label use): Immediate release: Oral: 1 to 5 mg/kg/dose once daily initiated within 72 hours of VAD placement; should be used with heparin (initiated between 8 to 48 hours following implantation) (ACCP [Monagle 2012]).

Kawasaki disease (off-label use): Immediate release: Oral: 80 to 100 mg/kg/day divided every 6 hours for up to 14 days (until fever resolves for at least 48 hours); then decrease dose to 1 to 5 mg/kg/day once daily (AHA and AAP suggest 3 to 5 mg/kg/day). Combine initial high-dose treatment with IV immune globulin within first 10 days of symptom onset. In patients without coronary artery abnormalities, give lower dose for at least 6 to 8 weeks. In patients with coronary artery abnormalities, low-dose aspirin should be continued indefinitely (in combination with warfarin) (ACCP [Monagle 2012]; AHA [Giglia 2013]; Newburger, 2004; *Red Book* [AAP 2015]).

Rheumatic fever (off-label use): Limited data available: Infants, Children, and Adolescents: Oral: Initial: 100 mg/kg/day divided into 4 to 5 doses; if response inadequate, may increase dose to 125 mg/kg/day; continue for 2 weeks; then decrease dose to 60 to 70 mg/kg/day in divided doses for an additional 3 to 6 weeks (WHO Guidelines 2004)

Migratory polyarthritis, with carditis without cardiomegaly or congestive heart failure: Initial: 100 mg/kg/day in 4 divided doses for 3 to 5 days, followed by 75 mg/kg/day in 4 divided doses for 4 weeks (Kliegman 2011)

Carditis and cardiomegaly or congestive heart failure: At the beginning of the tapering of the prednisone dose, aspirin should be started at 75 mg/kg/day in 4 divided doses for 6 weeks (Kliegman 2011)

Renal Impairment

Analgesia or anti-inflammatory uses: The manufacturer recommends avoiding in patients with CrCl <10 mL/minute. However, may use with caution and monitor renal function or consider the use of an alternative analgesic/anti-inflammatory agent (NKF [Henrich 1996], Whelton 2000).

Antiplatelet uses: The manufacturer recommends avoiding in patients with CrCl <10 mL/minute. However, in general, the benefit of low-dose aspirin outweighs any risk associated with nephropathy or other adverse effects even in the setting of severe renal impairment; the recommended aspirin dose should not be reduced in any patient with suspected or documented ACS, other cardiovascular disease, or other antithrombotic indication (Fernandez 2001, Harter 1979, Summaria 2015). In patients with diabetes and chronic kidney disease or in dialysis patients, the National Kidney Foundation recommends the use of antithrombotic doses of aspirin (ie, 75 to 162 mg daily) for prevention and management of ischemic heart disease or primary prevention of atherosclerotic disease (KDOQI 2005, KDOQI 2007).

Hemodialysis: Dialyzable (concentration dependent; higher salicylate concentrations are more readily dialyzable: 50% to 60%) (Juurlink 2015; Rosenberg 1981); consider administration after hemodialysis on dialysis days (Aronoff 2007).

Hepatic Impairment Avoid use in severe liver disease.

Mechanism of Action Irreversibly inhibits cyclooxygenase-1 and 2 (COX-1 and 2) enzymes, via acetylation, which results in decreased formation of prostaglandin precursors; irreversibly inhibits formation of prostaglandin derivative, thromboxane A_2, via acetylation of platelet cyclooxygenase, thus inhibiting platelet aggregation; has antipyretic, analgesic, and anti-inflammatory properties

Contraindications

Hypersensitivity to NSAIDs; patients with asthma, rhinitis, and nasal polyps; use in children or teenagers for viral infections, with or without fever.

Documentation of allergenic cross-reactivity for salicylates is limited. However, because of similarities in chemical structure and/or pharmacologic actions, the possibility of cross-sensitivity cannot be ruled out with certainty.

Warnings/Precautions Use with caution in patients with platelet and bleeding disorders, renal dysfunction, dehydration, or erosive gastritis. Avoid use in patients with active peptic ulcer disease. Heavy ethanol use (>3 drinks/day) can increase bleeding risks. When using high dosages (eg, analgesic or anti-inflammatory uses), use with caution and monitor renal function or consider the use of an alternative analgesic/anti-inflammatory agent (NKF [Henrich 1996], Whelton 2000). Low-dose aspirin (eg, 75 to 162 mg daily) may be safely used in patients with any degree of renal impairment (KDOQI 2005, KDOQI 2007). Avoid use in severe hepatic failure. Low-dose aspirin for cardioprotective effects is associated with a two- to fourfold increase in UGI events (eg, symptomatic or complicated ulcers); risks of these events increase with increasing aspirin dose; during the chronic phase of aspirin dosing, doses >81 mg are not recommended unless indicated (Bhatt, 2008). Use of safer agents for routine management of pain or headache throughout pregnancy should be considered. If possible, avoid use during the third trimester of pregnancy.

Discontinue use if tinnitus or impaired hearing occurs. Caution in mild-to-moderate renal failure (only at high dosages). Patients with sensitivity to tartrazine dyes, nasal polyps, and asthma may have an increased risk of salicylate sensitivity. In the treatment of acute ischemic stroke, avoid aspirin for 24 hours following administration of alteplase; administration within 24 hours increases the risk of hemorrhagic transformation (Jauch, 2013). Concurrent use of aspirin and clopidogrel is not recommended for secondary prevention of ischemic stroke or TIA in patients unable to take oral anticoagulants due to hemorrhagic risk (Furie, 2011). Surgical patients should avoid ASA if possible, for 1 to 2 weeks prior to surgery, to reduce the risk of excessive bleeding (except in patients with cardiac stents that have not completed their full course of dual antiplatelet therapy [aspirin, clopidogrel]; patient-specific situations need to be discussed with cardiologist; AHA/ACC/SCAI/ACS/ADA Science Advisory provides recommendations). When used concomitantly with ≤325 mg of aspirin, NSAIDs (including selective COX-2 inhibitors) substantially increase the risk of gastrointestinal complications (eg, ulcer); concomitant gastroprotective therapy (eg, proton pump inhibitors) is recommended (Bhatt, 2008). Potentially significant drug-drug interactions may exist, requiring dose or frequency adjustment, additional monitoring, and/or selection of alternative therapy.

When used for self-medication (OTC labeling): Children and teenagers who have or are recovering from chickenpox or flu-like symptoms should not use this product. Changes in behavior (along with nausea and vomiting) may be an early sign of Reye's syndrome; patients should be instructed to contact their healthcare provider if these occur.

Some dosage forms may contain polysorbate 80 (also known as Tweens). Hypersensitivity reactions, usually a delayed reaction, have been reported following exposure to pharmaceutical products containing polysorbate 80 in certain individuals (Isaksson, 2002; Lucente 2000; Shelley, 1995). Thrombocytopenia, ascites, pulmonary deterioration, and renal and hepatic failure have been reported in premature neonates after receiving parenteral products containing polysorbate 80 (Alade, 1986; CDC, 1984). See manufacturer's labeling.

Aspirin resistance is defined as measurable, persistent platelet activation that occurs in patients prescribed a therapeutic dose of aspirin. Clinical aspirin resistance, the recurrence of some vascular event despite a regular therapeutic dose of aspirin, is considered aspirin treatment failure. Estimates of biochemical aspirin resistance range from 5.5% to 60% depending on the population studied and the assays used (Gasparyan, 2008). Patients with aspirin resistance may have a higher risk of cardiovascular events compared to those who are aspirin sensitive (Gum, 2003).

Drug Interactions

Metabolism/Transport Effects **Substrate** of CYP2C9 (minor); **Note:** Assignment of Major/Minor substrate status based on clinically relevant drug interaction potential

Avoid Concomitant Use

Avoid concomitant use of Aspirin with any of the following: Dexketoprofen; Floctafenine; Influenza Virus Vaccine (Live/Attenuated); Ketorolac (Nasal); Ketorolac (Systemic); Omacetaxine; Sulfinpyrazone; Urokinase

Increased Effect/Toxicity

Aspirin may increase the levels/effects of: ACE Inhibitors; Agents with Antiplatelet Properties; Ajmaline; Alendronate; Anticoagulants; Apixaban; Blood Glucose Lowering Agents; Carbonic Anhydrase Inhibitors; Carisoprodol; Cephalothin; Collagenase (Systemic); Corticosteroids (Systemic); Dabigatran Etexilate; Deoxycholic Acid; Dexketoprofen; Edoxaban; Heparin; Ibritumomab; Methotrexate; Nicorandil; NSAID (COX-2 Inhibitor); Obinutuzumab; Omacetaxine; PRALAtrexate; Rivaroxaban; Salicylates; Talniflumate; Thrombolytic Agents; Ticagrelor; Tositumomab and Iodine I 131 Tositumomab; Urokinase; Valproate Products; Varicella Virus-Containing Vaccines; Vitamin K Antagonists

The levels/effects of Aspirin may be increased by: Agents with Antiplatelet Properties; Alcohol (Ethyl); Ammonium Chloride; Antidepressants (Tricyclic, Tertiary Amine); Calcium Channel Blockers (Nondihydropyridine); Dasatinib; Felbinac; Floctafenine; Ginkgo Biloba; Glucosamine; Herbs (Anticoagulant/Antiplatelet Properties); Ibrutinib; Influenza Virus Vaccine (Live/Attenuated); Ketorolac (Nasal); Ketorolac (Systemic); Limaprost; Loop Diuretics; Multivitamins/Fluoride (with ADE); Multivitamins/Minerals (with ADEK, Folate, Iron); Multivitamins/Minerals (with AE, No Iron); NSAID (Nonselective); Omega-3 Fatty Acids; Pentosan Polysulfate Sodium; Pentoxifylline; Potassium Acid Phosphate; Prostacyclin Analogues; Selective Serotonin Reuptake Inhibitors; Serotonin/Norepinephrine Reuptake Inhibitors; Tipranavir; Vitamin E (Systemic)

Decreased Effect

Aspirin may decrease the levels/effects of: ACE Inhibitors; Benzbromarone; Carisoprodol; Dexketoprofen; Hyaluronidase; Lesinurad; Loop Diuretics; Multivitamins/Fluoride (with ADE); Multivitamins/Minerals (with ADEK, Folate, Iron); Multivitamins/Minerals (with AE, No Iron); NSAID (Nonselective); Probenecid; Sulfinpyrazone; Ticagrelor; Tiludronate

The levels/effects of Aspirin may be decreased by: Alcohol (Ethyl); Corticosteroids (Systemic); Dexketoprofen; Floctafenine; Ketorolac (Nasal); Ketorolac (Systemic); NSAID (Nonselective)

Food Interactions Food may decrease the rate but not the extent of oral absorption. Benedictine liqueur, prunes, raisins, tea, and gherkins have a potential to cause salicylate accumulation. Fresh fruits containing vitamin C may displace drug from binding sites, resulting in increased urinary excretion of aspirin. Curry powder, paprika, licorice; may cause salicylate accumulation. These foods contain 6 mg salicylate/100 g. An ordinary American diet contains 10-200 mg/day of salicylate. Management: Administer with food or large volume of water or milk to minimize GI upset. Limit curry powder, paprika, licorice.

Pharmacodynamics/Kinetics

Onset of Action Immediate release: Platelet inhibition: Within 1 hour (nonenteric-coated). Onset of enteric-coated aspirin expected to be delayed (Eikelboom, 2012). **Note:** Chewing nonenteric-coated or enteric-coated tablets results in inhibition of platelet aggregation within 20 minutes; therefore, nonenteric-coated tablets should be chewed in settings where a more rapid onset is required (eg, acute MI) and enteric-coated tablets may be chewed when a rapid effect is required and immediate release nonenteric-coated tablets are not available (Eikelboom, 2012; Feldman, 1999; Sai, 2011).

Duration of Action Immediate release: 4 to 6 hours; however, platelet inhibitory effects last the lifetime of the platelet (~10 days) due to its irreversible inhibition of platelet COX-1 (Eikelboom, 2012).

Half-life Elimination Parent drug: Plasma concentration: 15 to 20 minutes; Salicylates (dose dependent): 3 hours at lower doses (300 to 600 mg), 5 to 6 hours (after 1 g), 10 hours with higher doses

Time to Peak Serum: Immediate release: ~1 to 2 hours (nonenteric-coated), 3 to 4 hours (enteric-coated) (Eikelboom, 2012); Extended-release capsule: ~2 hours. **Note:** Chewing nonenteric-coated tablets results in a time to peak concentration of 20 minutes (Feldman, 1999). Chewing enteric-coated tablets results in a time to peak concentration of 2 hours (Sai, 2011).

Pregnancy Considerations Salicylates have been noted to cross the placenta and enter fetal circulation. Adverse effects reported in the fetus include mortality, intrauterine growth retardation, salicylate intoxication, bleeding abnormalities, and neonatal acidosis. Use of aspirin close to delivery may cause premature closure of the ductus arteriosus. Adverse effects reported in the mother include anemia, hemorrhage, prolonged gestation, and prolonged labor (Østensen, 1998). Low-dose aspirin may be used to prevent preeclampsia in women with a history of early-onset preeclampsia and preterm delivery (<34 0/7 weeks), or preeclampsia in ≥1 prior pregnancy (ACOG, 2013). Low-dose aspirin is used to treat complications resulting from antiphospholipid syndrome in pregnancy (either primary or secondary to SLE) (ACCP [Guyatt, 2012]; Carp, 2004; Tincani, 2003). Low-dose aspirin to prevent thrombosis may also be used during the second and third trimesters in women with prosthetic valves (mechanical or bioprosthetic). The use of warfarin is recommended, along with low dose aspirin, in those with mechanical prosthetic valves (Nishimura, 2014). In general, low doses during pregnancy needed for the treatment of certain medical conditions have not been shown to cause fetal harm; however, discontinuing therapy prior to delivery is recommended (Østensen, 2006). Use of safer agents for routine management of pain or headache should be considered.

Breastfeeding Considerations Low amounts of aspirin can be found in breast milk. Milk/plasma ratios ranging from 0.03 to 0.3 have been reported. Peak levels in breast milk are reported to be at ~9 hours after a dose. Metabolic acidosis was reported in one infant following an aspirin dose of 3.9 g/day in the mother. The WHO considers occasional doses of aspirin to be compatible with breastfeeding, but to avoid long-term therapy and consider monitoring the infant for adverse effects (WHO, 2002). Other sources suggest avoiding aspirin while breastfeeding due to the theoretical risk of Reye's syndrome (Bar-Oz, 2003; Spigset, 2000). When used for vascular indications, breastfeeding may be continued during low-dose aspirin therapy (ACCP [Guyatt, 2012]).

Dosage Forms

Caplet, oral: 500 mg
- Ascriptin Maximum Strength [OTC]: 500 mg
- Bayer Aspirin Extra Strength [OTC]: 500 mg
- Bayer Genuine Aspirin [OTC]: 325 mg
- Bayer Plus Extra Strength [OTC]: 500 mg
- Bayer Women's Low Dose Aspirin [OTC]: 81 mg

Caplet, enteric coated, oral:
- Bayer Aspirin Regimen Regular Strength [OTC]: 325 mg

Capsule Extended Release, oral:
- Durlaza: 162.5 mg

Suppository, rectal: 300 mg (12s); 600 mg (12s)

Tablet, oral: 325 mg
- Ascriptin Regular Strength [OTC]: 325 mg
- Aspercin [OTC]: 325 mg
- Aspirtab [OTC]: 325 mg
- Bayer Genuine Aspirin [OTC]: 325 mg
- Buffasal [OTC]: 325 mg
- Bufferin [OTC]: 325 mg
- Bufferin Extra Strength [OTC]: 500 mg
- Buffinol [OTC]: 324 mg
- Tri-Buffered Aspirin [OTC]: 325 mg

Tablet, chewable, oral: 81 mg
- Bayer Aspirin Regimen Children's [OTC]: 81 mg
- St Joseph Adult Aspirin [OTC]: 81 mg

Tablet, enteric coated, oral: 81 mg, 325 mg, 650 mg
- Aspir-low [OTC]: 81 mg
- Bayer Aspirin Regimen Adult Low Strength [OTC]: 81 mg
- Ecotrin [OTC]: 325 mg
- Ecotrin Arthritis Strength [OTC]: 500 mg
- Ecotrin Low Strength [OTC]: 81 mg
- St Joseph Adult Aspirin [OTC]: 81 mg

Dental Comment The Food and Drug Administration (FDA), has issued a letter updating information and considerations regarding the use of ibuprofen (400 mg doses) in patients who are taking low dose aspirin (81 mg, immediate release; not enteric coated) for cardioprotection and stroke prevention. Ibuprofen, at these doses, may interfere with aspirin's antiplatelet effect depending upon when it is administered. Patients initiated on aspirin first (for ~1 week) then ibuprofen (400 mg 3 times/day for 10 days) seem to maintain aspirin's platelet effect (Cryer, 2005). Ibuprofen has the greatest impact on aspirin if administered less than 8 hours before aspirin (Catella-Lawson, 2001).

Patients may require counseling about the appropriate timing of ibuprofen dosing in relationship to aspirin therapy. With occasional use of ibuprofen, a clinically-significant interaction with aspirin in unlikely. To avoid interference during chronic dosing, a single dose of ibuprofen should be taken 30 to 120 minutes after aspirin ingestion or at least 8 hours should elapse after ibuprofen dosing before giving aspirin (Catella-Lawson, 2001; FDA, 2006).

The clinical implications of the interaction are unclear. There have not been any clinical endpoint studies conducted at this time. Avoidance of this interaction is potentially important because aspirin's vascular protection could be decreased or negated.

Other nonselective NSAIDs may have potential for a similar interaction with aspirin. Such has been described with naproxen (Capone, 2005). Acetaminophen does not appear to interfere with the antiplatelet effect of aspirin. Other clinical scenarios (use of smaller ibuprofen doses, other aspirin products, other doses of aspirin) have not been evaluated.

Additional information is available at: http://www.fda.gov/Drugs/DrugSafety/PostmarketDrugSafetyInformationforPatientsandProviders/ucm125222.htm

Aspirin and Dipyridamole

(AS pir in & dye peer ID a mole)

Related Information

Aspirin *on page 168*
Dipyridamole *on page 521*

Brand Names: US Aggrenox

Brand Names: Canada Aggrenox

Pharmacologic Category Antiplatelet Agent

Use Stroke prevention: Reduction in the risk of stroke in patients who have had transient ischemia of the brain or complete ischemic stroke due to thrombosis.

Local Anesthetic/Vasoconstrictor Precautions No information available to require special precautions

Effects on Dental Treatment Key adverse event(s) related to dental treatment: As with all drugs which may affect hemostasis, bleeding is associated with aspirin. Hemorrhage may occur at virtually any site; risk is dependent on multiple variables including dosage, concurrent use of multiple agents which alter hemostasis, and patient susceptibility. Many adverse effects of aspirin are dose related, and are rare at low dosages. Other serious reactions are idiosyncratic, related to allergy or individual sensitivity (see Dental Comment).

Aspirin as sole antiplatelet agent: Patients taking aspirin for ischemic stroke prevention are safe to continue it during dental procedures (Armstrong 2013).

Concurrent aspirin use with other antiplatelet agents: Aspirin in combination with clopidogrel (Plavix), prasugrel (Effient), or ticagrelor (Brilinta™) is the primary prevention strategy against stent thrombosis after placement of drug-eluting metal stents in coronary patients. Premature discontinuation of combination antiplatelet therapy (ie, dual antiplatelet therapy) strongly increases the risk of a catastrophic event of stent thrombosis leading to myocardial infarction and/or death, so says a science advisory issued in January 2007 from the American Heart Association in collaboration with the American Dental Association and other professional healthcare organizations. The advisory stresses a 12-month therapy of dual antiplatelet therapy after placement of a drug-eluting stent in order to prevent thrombosis at the stent site. Any elective surgery should be postponed for 1 year after stent implantation, and if surgery must be performed, consideration should be given to continuing the antiplatelet therapy during the perioperative period in high-risk patients with drug-eluting stents.

This advisory was issued from a science panel made up of representatives from the American Heart Association (AHA), the American College of Cardiology, the Society for Cardiovascular Angiography and Interventions, the American College of Surgeons, the American Dental Association (ADA), and the American College of Physicians (Grines 2007).

Effects on Bleeding Aspirin irreversibly inhibits platelet aggregation which can prolong bleeding. Upon discontinuation, normal platelet function returns only when new platelets are released (~7-10 days). However, in the case of dental surgery, there is no scientific evidence to support discontinuation of aspirin. This was recently supported by the American Academy of Neurology in patients with ischemic cerebrovascular disease (Armstrong 2013). A recent study compared blood loss after a single tooth extraction in coronary artery disease patients who were either on aspirin (100 mg daily) or off aspirin for the extraction. The mean volume of bleeding was not statistically different between the groups. Local hemostatic measures were sufficient to control bleeding and there were no reported episodes of hemorrhaging intra- or postoperatively (Medeiros 2011).

Adverse Reactions

>10%:

Central nervous system: Headache (39%; tolerance usually develops)

Gastrointestinal: Abdominal pain (18%), dyspepsia (18%), nausea (16%), diarrhea (13%)

1% to 10%:

Cardiovascular: Cardiac failure (2%), syncope (1%)

Central nervous system: Fatigue (6%), pain (6%), amnesia (2%), malaise (2%), seizure (2%), confusion (1%), drowsiness (1%)

Gastrointestinal: Vomiting (8%), gastrointestinal hemorrhage (1% to 4%), melena (2%), anorexia (1%), hemorrhoids (1%)

Hematologic & oncologic: Hemorrhage (3%), anemia (2%), rectal hemorrhage (2%), purpura (1%)

Neuromuscular & skeletal: Arthralgia (6%), back pain (5%), arthritis (2%), weakness (2%), arthropathy (1%), myalgia (1%)

Respiratory: Cough (2%), epistaxis (2%), upper respiratory tract infection (1%)

<1% (Limited to important or life-threatening): Ageusia, agitation, alopecia, anaphylaxis, angina pectoris, angioedema, antepartum hemorrhage, aplastic anemia, asthma, auditory impairment, blood coagulation disorder, bronchospasm, bruise, cardiac arrhythmia, cerebral edema, cerebral hemorrhage, changes in liver function, chest pain, cholelithiasis, coma, deafness, dehydration, disseminated intravascular coagulation, dizziness, dyspnea, ecchymoses, fever, flushing, gastritis, gastrointestinal perforation, gastrointestinal ulcer, gingival hemorrhage, hematemesis, hematoma, hematuria, hemoptysis, hepatic failure, hepatitis, hyperglycemia, hyperkalemia, hypersensitivity angiitis, hypersensitivity reaction, hyperventilation, hypoglycemia, hypokalemia, hypotension, hypothermia, increased thirst, interstitial nephritis, intracranial hemorrhage, jaundice, laryngeal edema, metabolic acidosis, migraine, palpitations, pancreatitis, pancytopenia, paresthesia, postpartum hemorrhage, prolonged prothrombin time, proteinuria, pruritus, pulmonary edema, renal failure, renal insufficiency, renal papillary necrosis, respiratory alkalosis, Reye's syndrome, rhabdomyolysis, skin rash, Stevens-Johnson syndrome, subarachnoid hemorrhage, supraventricular tachycardia, tachycardia, tachypnea, thrombocythemia, thrombocytopenia, tinnitus, urticaria, uterine hemorrhage

General Dosage Range Oral: *Adults:* 1 capsule (dipyridamole extended release 200 mg/aspirin 25 mg) twice daily

Mechanism of Action The antithrombotic action results from additive antiplatelet effects. Dipyridamole inhibits the uptake of adenosine into platelets, endothelial cells, and erythrocytes. Aspirin inhibits platelet aggregation by irreversible inhibition of platelet cyclooxygenase and thus inhibits the generation of thromboxane A_2.

Pregnancy Risk Factor D

Pregnancy Considerations

Adverse events have been observed in animal reproduction studies with this combination.

Low birth weight, increased risk of intracranial hemorrhage in premature infants, still birth, and neonatal death have been reported following maternal use of aspirin in the later stages of pregnancy. Use of aspirin close to delivery may cause premature closure of the ductus arteriosus in the neonate, prolonged gestation, prolonged labor and/or excessive blood loss in the mother at delivery. Avoid aspirin/dipyridamole during the third trimester of pregnancy.

Dental Comment The Food and Drug Administration (FDA), has issued a letter updating information and considerations regarding the use of ibuprofen (400 mg doses) in patients who are taking low dose aspirin (81 mg, immediate release; not enteric coated) for cardioprotection and stroke prevention. Ibuprofen, at these doses, may interfere with aspirin's antiplatelet effect depending upon when it is administered. Patients initiated on aspirin first (for ~1 week) then ibuprofen (400 mg 3 times/day for 10 days) seem to maintain aspirin's platelet effect (Cryer 2005). Ibuprofen has the greatest impact on aspirin if administered less than 8 hours before aspirin (Catella-Lawson 2001).

Patients may require counseling about the appropriate timing of ibuprofen dosing in relationship to aspirin therapy. With occasional use of ibuprofen, a clinically-significant interaction with aspirin in unlikely. To avoid interference during chronic dosing, a single dose of ibuprofen should be taken 30-120 minutes after aspirin ingestion or at least 8 hours should elapse after ibuprofen dosing before giving aspirin (Catella-Lawson 2001; FDA 2006).

The clinical implications of the interaction are unclear. There have not been any clinical endpoint studies conducted at this time. Avoidance of this interaction is potentially important because aspirin's vascular protection could be decreased or negated.

Other nonselective NSAIDs may have potential for a similar interaction with aspirin. Such has been described with naproxen (Capone 2005). Acetaminophen does not appear to interfere with the antiplatelet effect of aspirin. Other clinical scenarios (use of smaller ibuprofen doses, other aspirin products, other doses of aspirin) have not been evaluated.

Additional information is available at: http://www.fda.gov/Drugs/DrugSafety/PostmarketDrugSafetyInformationforPatientsandProviders/ucm125222.htm

Aspirin and Omeprazole

(AS pir in & oh MEP ra zole)

Brand Names: US Yosprala

Pharmacologic Category Analgesic, Nonopioid; Antiplatelet Agent; Nonsteroidal Anti-inflammatory Drug (NSAID), Oral; Proton Pump Inhibitor; Salicylate; Substituted Benzimidazole

Use

Secondary prevention of cardiovascular and cerebrovascular events: Reduction of the risk of aspirin-associated gastric ulcers in patients at risk of developing gastric ulcers due to age (≥55 years) or documented history of gastric ulcers who require aspirin for the secondary prevention of cardiovascular and cerebrovascular events.

Limitations of use: Not for use as the initial dose of aspirin therapy during onset of acute coronary syndrome, acute myocardial infarction or before percutaneous coronary intervention; has not been shown to reduce the risk of gastrointestinal bleeding due to aspirin.

Local Anesthetic/Vasoconstrictor Precautions No information available to require special precautions

Effects on Dental Treatment Key adverse event(s) related to dental treatment: As with all drugs which may affect hemostasis, bleeding is associated with aspirin. Hemorrhage may occur at virtually any site; risk is dependent on multiple variables including dosage, concurrent use of multiple agents which alter hemostasis, and patient susceptibility. Many adverse effects of aspirin are dose related, and are rare at low dosages. Other serious reactions are idiosyncratic, related to allergy or individual sensitivity (see Dental Comment).

Aspirin as sole antiplatelet agent: Patients taking aspirin for ischemic stroke prevention are safe to continue it during dental procedures (Armstrong 2013).

Concurrent aspirin use with other antiplatelet agents: Aspirin in combination with clopidogrel (Plavix), prasugrel (Effient), or ticagrelor (Brilinta) is the primary prevention strategy against stent thrombosis after placement of drug-eluting metal stents in coronary patients. Premature discontinuation of combination antiplatelet therapy (ie, dual antiplatelet therapy) strongly increases the risk of a catastrophic event of stent thrombosis leading to myocardial infarction and/or death, so says a science advisory issued in January 2007 from the American Heart Association in collaboration with the American Dental Association and other professional healthcare organizations. The advisory stresses a 12-month therapy of dual antiplatelet therapy after placement of a drug-eluting stent in order to prevent thrombosis at the stent site. Any elective surgery should be postponed for 1 year after stent implantation, and if surgery must be performed, consideration should be given to continuing the antiplatelet therapy during the perioperative period in high-risk patients with drug-eluting stents.

This advisory was issued from a science panel made up of representatives from the American Heart Association (AHA), the American College of Cardiology, the Society for Cardiovascular Angiography and Interventions, the American College of Surgeons, the American Dental Association (ADA), and the American College of Physicians (Grines 2007).

Effects on Bleeding Aspirin irreversibly inhibits platelet aggregation which can prolong bleeding. Upon discontinuation, normal platelet function returns only when new platelets are released (~7 to 10 days). However, in the case of dental surgery, there is no scientific evidence to support discontinuation of aspirin. This was recently supported by the American Academy of Neurology in patients with ischemic cerebrovascular disease (Armstrong 2013). A recent study compared blood loss after a single tooth extraction in coronary artery disease patients who were either on aspirin (100 mg daily) or off aspirin for the extraction. The mean volume of bleeding was not statistically different between the groups. Local hemostatic measures were sufficient to control bleeding and there were no reported episodes of hemorrhaging intra- or postoperatively (Medeiros 2011).

Adverse Reactions Also see individual agents.

>10%: Gastrointestinal: Gastritis (18%)

1% to 10%:

Central nervous system: Noncardiac chest pain (2%)

Gastrointestinal: Diarrhea (3%), nausea (3%), gastric polyp (2%)

<1%, postmarketing, and/or case reports: Gastrointestinal hemorrhage (including hematochezia and large intestinal hemorrhage), intestinal obstruction (small bowel), upper gastrointestinal hemorrhage (gastric or duodenal)

General Dosage Range Oral: *Adults:* One tablet (aspirin 81 mg/omeprazole 40 mg or aspirin 325 mg/omeprazole 40 mg) once daily.

Mechanism of Action

Aspirin: Irreversibly inhibits cyclooxygenase-1 and 2 (COX-1 and 2) enzymes, via acetylation, which results in decreased formation of prostaglandin precursors; irreversibly inhibits formation of prostaglandin derivative, thromboxane A2, via acetylation of platelet cyclooxygenase, thus inhibiting platelet aggregation; has antipyretic, analgesic, and anti-inflammatory properties.

Omeprazole: Suppresses gastric basal and stimulated acid secretion by inhibiting the parietal cell H+/K+ ATP pump

Pregnancy Considerations Use of aspirin in women ≥30 weeks gestation is associated with an increased risk for premature closure of the fetal ductus arteriosus; third trimester use may be also associated with an increased risk of neonatal complications. In addition, use of aspirin during labor may increase the risk for excessive blood loss at delivery. Use of this combination should be avoided in women ≥30 weeks gestation. Refer to individual monographs for additional information.

Dental Comment The Food and Drug Administration (FDA), has issued a letter updating information and considerations regarding the use of ibuprofen (400 mg doses) in patients who are taking low-dose aspirin (81 mg, immediate release; not enteric coated) for cardioprotection and stroke prevention. Ibuprofen, at these doses, may interfere with aspirin's antiplatelet effect depending upon when it is administered. Patients initiated on aspirin first (for ~1 week) then ibuprofen (400 mg 3 times/day for 10 days) seem to maintain aspirin's platelet effect (Cryer 2005). Ibuprofen has the greatest impact on aspirin if administered less than 8 hours before aspirin (Catella-Lawson 2001).

Patients may require counseling about the appropriate timing of ibuprofen dosing in relationship to aspirin therapy. With occasional use of ibuprofen, a clinically-significant interaction with aspirin in unlikely. To avoid interference during chronic dosing, a single dose of ibuprofen should be taken 30 to 120 minutes after aspirin ingestion or at least 8 hours should elapse after ibuprofen dosing before giving aspirin (Catella-Lawson 2001; FDA 2006).

The clinical implications of the interaction are unclear. There have not been any clinical endpoint studies conducted at this time. Avoidance of this interaction is potentially important because aspirin's vascular protection could be decreased or negated.

Other nonselective NSAIDs may have potential for a similar interaction with aspirin. Such has been described with naproxen (Capone 2005). Acetaminophen does not appear to interfere with the antiplatelet effect of aspirin. Other clinical scenarios (use of smaller ibuprofen doses, other aspirin products, other doses of aspirin) have not been evaluated.

Additional information is available at: http://www.fda.gov/Drugs/DrugSafety/PostmarketDrugSafetyInformationforPatientsandProviders/ucm125222.htm

Atazanavir (at a za NA veer)

Related Information

HIV Infection and AIDS *on page 1785*

Brand Names: US Reyataz

Brand Names: Canada Reyataz

Pharmacologic Category Antiretroviral, Protease Inhibitor (Anti-HIV)

Use HIV-1 Infection:

Treatment of HIV-1 infection in combination with other antiretroviral agents in patients ≥3 months weighing ≥5 kg

Limitations of use:

Not recommended for use in pediatric patients younger than 3 months due to the risk of kernicterus

Use in treatment-experienced patients should be guided by the number of baseline primary protease inhibitor resistance substitutions

Local Anesthetic/Vasoconstrictor Precautions No information available to require special precautions

Effects on Dental Treatment No significant effects or complications reported

Effects on Bleeding Increased bleeding has been noted with protease inhibitors, such as atazanavir, in patients with hemophilia A or B. Thrombocytopenia has been reported. No other information is available to require special precautions in other patients.

Adverse Reactions Includes data from both treatment-naive and treatment-experienced patients. Unless otherwise noted, frequency of adverse events is as reported in adults receiving combination antiretroviral therapy.

>10%:

Dermatologic: Skin rash (adults 3% to 21%; median onset: 7 weeks; children 14%)

Endocrine & metabolic: Increased serum cholesterol (≥240 mg/dL: 6% to 25%), increased amylase (adults: >2 x ULN: ≤14%)

Gastrointestinal: Nausea (3% to 14%)

Hepatic: Increased serum bilirubin (≥2.6 x ULN: adults 35% to 49%; children 16%), jaundice (children 13% to 15%; adults 5% to 9%)

Neuromuscular & skeletal: Increased creatine phosphokinase (>5 times ULN: 6% to 11%)

Respiratory: Cough (children 21%)

Miscellaneous: Fever (children 18% to 19%; adults 2%)

1% to 10%:

Cardiovascular: Peripheral edema (children 7%), first degree atrioventricular block (6%), second degree atrioventricular block (children ≤2%; adults [rare])

Central nervous system: Headache (adults 1% to 6%; children 7% to 8%), peripheral neuropathy (<1% to 4%), insomnia (<1% to 3%), depression (2%), dizziness (<1% to 2%)

Endocrine & metabolic: Increased serum triglycerides (≥751 mg/dL: <1% to 8%), hyperglycemia (≥251 mg/dL: 5%), hypoglycemia (children: grades 3/4: 4%)

Gastrointestinal: Vomiting (children 8% to 12%; adults 3% to 4%), diarrhea (children 8% to 9%; adults 1% to 3%), increased serum lipase (adults: >2 x ULN: ≤5%), abdominal pain (4%)

Hematologic & oncologic: Decreased neutrophils (<750 cells/mm^3: 3% to 7%), decreased hemoglobin (<8.0 g/dL: <1% to 5%), decreased platelet count (<50,000 cells/mm^3: 2%)

Hepatic: Increased serum ALT (adults and children: >5 x ULN: 3% to 9%; 10% to 25% in adult patients co-infected with hepatitis B and/or C), increased serum AST (>5 times ULN: 2% to 7%; 9% to 10% in patients co-infected with hepatitis B and/or C)

Neuromuscular & skeletal: Myalgia (4%), limb pain (children 6%)

Respiratory: Nasal congestion (children 6%), oropharyngeal pain (children 6%), rhinorrhea (children 6%), wheezing (children 6%)

Postmarketing and/or case reports: Alopecia, angioedema, arthralgia, cholecystitis, cholelithiasis, cholestasis, complete atrioventricular block (rare), diabetes mellitus, DRESS syndrome, edema, erythema multiforme, hepatic abnormality, immune reconstitution syndrome, interstitial nephritis, left bundle branch block, maculopapular rash, nephrolithiasis, pancreatitis, prolongation P-R interval on ECG, prolonged Q-T interval on ECG, pruritus, Stevens-Johnson syndrome, torsades de pointes

General Dosage Range Dosage adjustment recommended in patients with hepatic or renal impairment or on concomitant therapy

Oral:

Infants ≥3 months and Children weighing 5 to <25 kg:

5 to <15 kg: 200 mg once daily

15 to <25 kg: 250 mg once daily

Children ≥6 years and Adolescents <18 years:

15 to <20 kg: 150 mg once daily

20 to <40 kg: 200 mg once daily

≥40 kg: 300 mg once daily

Adolescents (≥40 kg) and Adults: 400 mg once daily (antiretroviral-naive) **or** 300 mg once daily

Mechanism of Action Binds to the site of HIV-1 protease activity and inhibits cleavage of viral Gag-Pol polyprotein precursors into individual functional proteins required for infectious HIV. This results in the formation of immature, noninfectious viral particles.

Pharmacodynamics/Kinetics

Half-life Elimination Unboosted therapy: 7 to 8 hours; Boosted therapy (with ritonavir): 9 to 18 hours; 12 hours in patients with hepatic impairment

Time to Peak Plasma: 2 to 3 hours

Pregnancy Considerations Atazanavir has a low level of transfer across the human placenta with cord blood concentrations reported as 13% to 21% of maternal serum concentrations at delivery. An increased risk of teratogenic effects has not been observed based on information collected by the antiretroviral pregnancy registry. A small increased risk of preterm birth has been associated with maternal use of protease inhibitor-based combination antiretroviral therapy during pregnancy; however, the benefits of use generally outweigh this risk and protease inhibitors (PIs) should not be withheld if otherwise recommended. Information related to stillbirth, low birth weight, and small for gestational age infants is limited. Long-term follow-up is recommended for all infants exposed to antiretroviral medications; children who develop significant organ system abnormalities (particularly of the CNS or heart) should be evaluated for potential mitochondrial dysfunction. Hyperglycemia, new onset of diabetes mellitus, or diabetic ketoacidosis have been reported with PIs; it is not clear if pregnancy increases this risk. Hyperbilirubinemia or hypoglycemia may occur in neonates following in utero exposure to atazanavir, although data are conflicting (monitor).

Combination antiretroviral therapy (cART) therapy is recommended for all HIV-infected pregnant women to keep the viral load below the limit of detection and reduce the risk of perinatal transmission. When HIV is diagnosed during pregnancy in a woman who has never received antiretroviral therapy, cART should begin as soon as possible after diagnosis. The Health and Human Services (HHS) Perinatal HIV Guidelines recommend atazanavir as a preferred PI as initial therapy in antiretroviral-naive pregnant women when combined with low-dose ritonavir boosting. Pharmacokinetic studies suggest that standard dosing during pregnancy may provide decreased plasma concentrations and some experts recommend increased doses during the second and third trimesters. However, the manufacturer notes that dose adjustment is not required unless using concomitant H_2-receptor blockers or tenofovir or for ARV-naive pregnant women taking efavirenz. In general, women who become pregnant on a stable cART regimen may continue that regimen if viral suppression is effective, appropriate drug exposure can be achieved, contraindications for use in pregnancy are not present, and the regimen is well tolerated. The HHS perinatal guidelines recommend avoiding atazanavir in treatment-experienced pregnant women taking and H_2-receptor blockers and tenofovir. May give as once-daily dosing

For HIV-infected couples planning a pregnancy, maximum viral suppression with combination antiretroviral therapy (cART) is recommended prior to conception for the HIV-infected partner(s) and expert consultation is recommended; modification of therapy (if needed) and optimization of the woman's health should be done prior to conception. HIV-infected women not planning a pregnancy may use any available type of contraception, considering possible drug interactions and contraindications of the specific method. In addition, consistent use of condoms is also recommended (even during pregnancy) to prevent transmission of HIV or other sexually transmitted diseases.

Health care providers are encouraged to enroll pregnant women exposed to antiretroviral medications as early in pregnancy as possible in the Antiretroviral Pregnancy Registry (1-800-258-4263 or www.APRegistry.com). Health care providers caring for HIV-infected women and their infants may contact the National Perinatal HIV Hotline (888-448-8765) for clinical consultation (HHS [perinatal] 2016).

Atazanavir and Cobicistat

(at a za NA veer & koe BIK i stat)

Brand Names: US Evotaz

Brand Names: Canada Evotaz

Pharmacologic Category Antiretroviral, Protease Inhibitor (Anti-HIV); Cytochrome P-450 Inhibitor

Use

HIV-1 infection: Treatment of human immunodeficiency virus (HIV-1) infection in adults in combination with other antiretroviral agents.

Limitations of use: Use in treatment-experienced patients should be guided by the number of baseline primary protease inhibitor resistance substitutions

Local Anesthetic/Vasoconstrictor Precautions No information available to require special precautions

Effects on Dental Treatment No significant effects or complications reported

Effects on Bleeding Increased bleeding has been noted with protease inhibitors, such as atazanavir, in patients with hemophilia A or B. Thrombocytopenia has been reported. No other information is available to require special precautions in other patients.

Adverse Reactions Frequency not always defined.

>10%:

Hepatic: Abnormal bilirubin levels (65%; >2.5 × ULN), jaundice (13%; grades 2 to 4: 5%)

Ophthalmic: Scleral icterus (15%; grades 2 to 4: 3%)

1% to 10%:

Cardiovascular: First-degree atrioventricular block (6%; asymptomatic), cardiac conduction disturbance (including but not limited to P-R interval prolongation and second degree atrioventricular block)

Central nervous system: Abnormal dreams (grades ≥2: <2%), depression (grades ≥2: <2%), fatigue (grades ≥2: <2%), headache (grades ≥2: <2%), insomnia (grades ≥2: <2%)

Dermatologic: Skin rash (5%; erythema multiforme, maculopapular rash, eosinophilia, and DRESS syndrome), Stevens-Johnson syndrome

Endocrine & metabolic: Glycosuria (3%; ≥1,000 mg/dL), increased gamma-glutamyl transferase (2%; >5.0 × ULN), Fanconi's syndrome (grades ≥2: <2%), buffalo hump, cushingoid appearance, increased HDL cholesterol, increased LDL cholesterol, increased serum cholesterol, increased serum triglycerides, truncal obesity

Gastrointestinal: Nausea (12%; grades 3/4: 2%), diarrhea (11%; grades ≥2: <2%), increased serum lipase (grades 3/4: 9%), increased serum amylase (4%; >2.0 × ULN), upper abdominal pain (grades ≥2: <2%), vomiting (grades ≥2: <2%)

Genitourinary: Hematuria (3%; >75 RBC/HPF), breast hypertrophy

Hematologic & oncologic: Hemorrhage (increased spontaneous bleeding in patients with hemophilia)

Hepatic: Increased serum ALT (3%; >5.0 × ULN), increased serum AST (3%; >5.0 × ULN), hepatotoxicity (in patients with hepatitis)

Immunologic: Immune reconstitution syndrome

Neuromuscular & skeletal: Increased creatine phosphokinase (5%; ≥10.0 × ULN), rhabdomyolysis (<2%), amyotrophy, lipoatrophy

Renal: Nephrolithiasis (2%), renal disease (grades ≥2: <2%), acute renal failure, decreased creatinine clearance, increased serum creatinine, renal insufficiency

<1%, postmarketing, and/or case reports: Cholelithiasis, diabetes mellitus (new-onset and exacerbation), hyperglycemia

General Dosage Range Oral: *Adults:* One tablet once daily.

Mechanism of Action

Atazanavir binds to the site of HIV-1 protease activity and inhibits cleavage of viral Gag-Pol polyprotein precursors into individual functional proteins required for infectious HIV. This results in the formation of immature, noninfectious viral particles.

Cobicistat is a mechanism-based inhibitor of cytochrome P450 3A (CYP3A). Inhibition of CYP3A-mediated metabolism by cobicistat and increases the systemic exposure of CYP3A substrates (eg, atazanavir).

Pregnancy Considerations In general, women who become pregnant on a stable combination antiretroviral therapy (cART) regimen may continue that regimen if viral suppression is effective, appropriate drug exposure can be achieved, contraindications for use in pregnancy are not present, and the regimen is well tolerated. The Health and Human Services (HHS) Perinatal HIV Guidelines note there are insufficient data to recommend this combination for routine use as initial therapy in antiretroviral-naive pregnant women (HHS [perinatal] 2016). See individual agents.

Atenolol (a TEN oh lole)

Related Information

Cardiovascular Diseases *on page 1752*

Brand Names: US Tenormin

Brand Names: Canada Apo-Atenol; Ava-Atenolol; CO Atenolol; Dom-Atenolol; JAMP-Atenolol; Mint-Atenolol; Mylan-Atenolol; Nu-Atenol; PMS-Atenolol; RAN-Atenolol; ratio-Atenolol; Riva-Atenolol; Sandoz-Atenolol; Septa-Atenolol; Tenormin; Teva-Atenolol

Generic Availability (US) Yes

Pharmacologic Category Antianginal Agent; Antihypertensive; Beta-Blocker, Beta-1 Selective

Use

Acute myocardial infarction: For the management of hemodynamically stable patients with definite or suspected acute MI to reduce cardiovascular mortality.

Angina pectoris caused by coronary atherosclerosis: For the long-term management of patients with angina pectoris.

Hypertension: Treatment of hypertension, alone or in combination with other agents

Guideline recommendations:

Hypertension: The 2014 guideline for the management of high blood pressure in adults (Eighth Joint National Committee [JNC 8]) recommends initiation of pharmacologic treatment to lower blood pressure for the following patients (JNC8 [James, 2013]):

- Patients ≥60 years of age with systolic blood pressure (SBP) ≥150 mm Hg or diastolic blood pressure (DBP) ≥90 mm Hg. Goal of therapy is SBP <150 mm Hg and DBP <90 mm Hg.
- Patients <60 years of age with SBP ≥140 mm Hg or DBP is ≥90 mm Hg. Goal of therapy is SBP <140 mm Hg and DBP <90 mm Hg.
- Patients ≥18 years of age with diabetes and SBP ≥140 mm Hg or DBP ≥90 mm Hg. Goal of therapy is SBP <140 mm Hg and DBP <90 mm Hg.
- Patients ≥18 years of age with chronic kidney disease (CKD) and SBP ≥140 mm Hg or DBP ≥90 mm Hg. Goal of therapy is SBP <140 mm Hg and DBP <90 mm Hg.

Chronic kidney disease (CKD) and hypertension: Regardless of race or diabetes status, the use of an ACE inhibitor (ACEI) or angiotensin receptor blocker (ARB) as initial therapy is recommended to improve kidney outcomes. In the general nonblack population (without CKD) including those with diabetes, initial antihypertensive treatment should consist of a thiazide-type diuretic, calcium channel blocker, ACEI, or ARB. In the general black population (without CKD) including those with diabetes, initial antihypertensive treatment should consist of a thiazide-type diuretic or a calcium channel blocker **instead of** an ACEI or ARB.

Coronary artery disease (CAD) and hypertension: The American Heart Association, American College of Cardiology and American Society of Hypertension (AHA/ACC/ASH) 2015 scientific statement for the treatment of hypertension in patients with coronary artery disease (CAD) recommends the use of a beta blocker as part of a regimen in patients with hypertension and chronic stable angina with a history of prior MI. A BP target of <140/90 mm Hg is reasonable for the secondary prevention of cardiovascular events. A lower target BP (<130/80 mm Hg) may be appropriate in some individuals with CAD, previous MI, stroke or transient ischemic attack, or CAD risk equivalents (AHA/ACC/ASH [Rosendorff 2015]).

Local Anesthetic/Vasoconstrictor Precautions No information available to require special precautions

Effects on Dental Treatment Atenolol is a cardioselective beta-blocker. Local anesthetic with vasoconstrictor can be safely used in patients medicated with atenolol. Nonselective beta-blockers (ie, propranolol, nadolol) enhance the pressor response to epinephrine, resulting in hypertension and bradycardia; this has not been reported for atenolol. Many nonsteroidal anti-inflammatory drugs, such as ibuprofen and indomethacin, can reduce the hypotensive effect of beta-blockers after 3 or more weeks of therapy with the NSAID. Short-term NSAID use (ie, 3 days) requires no special precautions in patients taking beta-blockers.

Effects on Bleeding No information available to require special precautions

Adverse Reactions

1% to 10%:

Cardiovascular: Bradycardia (persistent), cardiac failure, chest pain, cold extremities, complete atrioventricular block, edema, hypotension, Raynaud's phenomenon, second degree atrioventricular block

Central nervous system: Confusion, decreased mental acuity, depression, dizziness, fatigue, headache, insomnia, lethargy, nightmares

Gastrointestinal: Constipation, diarrhea, nausea

Genitourinary: Impotence

<1% (Limited to important or life-threatening): Alopecia, dyspnea (especially with large doses), hallucination, increased liver enzymes, lupus-like syndrome, Peyronie's disease, positive ANA titer, psoriasiform eruption, psychosis, thrombocytopenia, wheezing

Dosing

Adult

Hypertension: Oral: Initial: 25 to 50 mg once daily, after 1 to 2 weeks, may increase to 100 mg once daily; usual dose (ASH/ISH [Weber 2014]): 100 mg once daily; target dose (JNC 8 [James 2013]): 100 mg once daily. Doses >100 mg are unlikely to produce any further benefit.

Angina pectoris: Oral: 50 mg once daily; may increase to 100 mg daily. Some patients may require 200 mg daily.

Postmyocardial Infarction: Oral: 100 mg/day or 50 mg twice daily for 6 to 9 days postmyocardial infarction

Atrial fibrillation (rate control) (off-label use): Usual maintenance dose: 25 to 100 mg once daily (AHA/ACC/HRS [January 2014])

Supraventricular tachycardia (off-label use): Oral: Initial: 25 to 50 mg daily, maximum maintenance dose: 100 mg/day (ACC/AHA/HRS [Page 2015])

Thyrotoxicosis (off-label use): Oral: 25 to 100 mg once or twice daily (Bahn 2011)

Geriatric Refer to adult dosing. In the management of hypertension, consider lower initial doses and titrate to response (Aronow, 2011).

Pediatric Hypertension: Oral: Children: 0.5 to 1 mg/kg/dose given daily; range of 0.5 to 1.5 mg/kg/day; maximum dose: 2 mg/kg/day up to 100 mg/day

Renal Impairment

CrCl >35 mL/minute/1.73 m^2: No dosage adjustment necessary.

CrCl 15 to 35 mL/minute/1.73 m^2: Maximum dose: 50 mg daily

CrCl <15 mL/minute/1.73 m^2: Maximum dose: 25 mg daily

Hemodialysis: Moderately dialyzable (20% to 50%) via hemodialysis; administer dose postdialysis or administer 25 to 50 mg supplemental dose.

Peritoneal dialysis: Elimination is not enhanced; supplemental dose is not necessary.

Hepatic Impairment There are no dosage adjustments provided in the manufacturer's labeling; however, atenolol undergoes minimal hepatic metabolism.

Mechanism of Action Competitively blocks response to beta-adrenergic stimulation, selectively blocks beta$_1$-receptors with little or no effect on beta$_2$-receptors except at high doses

Contraindications

Hypersensitivity to atenolol or any component of the formulation; sinus bradycardia; sinus node dysfunction; heart block greater than first-degree (except in patients with a functioning artificial pacemaker); cardiogenic shock; uncompensated cardiac failure

Canadian labeling: Additional contraindications (not in US labeling): Bradycardia (regardless of origin); cor pulmonale; hypotension; severe peripheral arterial disorders; anesthesia with agents that produce myocardial depression; Pheochromocytoma (in the absence of alpha-blockade); metabolic acidosis

Warnings/Precautions Consider preexisting conditions such as sick sinus syndrome before initiating. Administer cautiously in compensated heart failure and monitor for a worsening of the condition (efficacy of atenolol in heart failure has not been established). **[US Boxed Warning]: Beta-blocker therapy should not be withdrawn abruptly (particularly in patients with CAD), but gradually tapered to avoid acute tachycardia, hypertension, and/or ischemia.** Beta-blockers without alpha1-adrenergic receptor blocking activity should be avoided in patients with Prinzmetal variant angina (Mayer, 1998). Chronic beta-blocker therapy should not be routinely withdrawn prior to major surgery. Beta-blockers should be avoided in patients with bronchospastic disease (asthma). Atenolol, with B$_1$ selectivity, has been used cautiously in bronchospastic disease with close monitoring. May precipitate or aggravate symptoms of arterial insufficiency in patients with PVD and Raynaud's disease; use with caution and monitor for progression of arterial obstruction. Use cautiously in patients with diabetes - may mask hypoglycemic symptoms. May mask signs of hyperthyroidism (eg, tachycardia); use caution if hyperthyroidism is suspected, abrupt withdrawal may precipitate thyroid storm. Alterations in thyroid function tests may be observed. Use cautiously in the renally impaired (dosage adjustment required). Caution in myasthenia gravis or psychiatric disease (may cause CNS depression). Bradycardia may be observed more frequently in elderly patients (>65 years of age); dosage reductions may be necessary. Adequate alpha-blockade is required prior to use of any beta-blocker for patients with untreated pheochromocytoma. May induce or exacerbate psoriasis. Use caution with history of severe anaphylaxis to allergens; patients taking beta-blockers may become more sensitive to repeated challenges. Treatment of anaphylaxis (eg, epinephrine) in patients taking beta-blockers may be ineffective or promote undesirable effects. Use with caution in patients on concurrent digoxin, verapamil, or diltiazem; bradycardia or heart block can occur. Use with caution in patients receiving inhaled anesthetic agents known to depress myocardial contractility.

Drug Interactions

Metabolism/Transport Effects None known.

Avoid Concomitant Use

Avoid concomitant use of Atenolol with any of the following: Ceritinib; Floctafenine; Methacholine; Rivastigmine

Increased Effect/Toxicity

Atenolol may increase the levels/effects of: Alpha-/Beta-Agonists (Direct-Acting); Alpha1-Blockers; Alpha2-Agonists; Amifostine; Antipsychotic Agents (Second Generation [Atypical]); Bradycardia-Causing Agents; Bupivacaine; Cardiac Glycosides; Ceritinib; Cholinergic Agonists; Disopyramide; DULoxetine; Ergot Derivatives; Fingolimod; Grass Pollen Allergen Extract (5 Grass Extract); Hypotension-Associated Agents; Insulin; Ivabradine; Lacosamide; Levodopa; Lidocaine (Systemic); Lidocaine (Topical); Mepivacaine; Methacholine; Midodrine; Nitroprusside; Sulfonylureas

The levels/effects of Atenolol may be increased by: Acetylcholinesterase Inhibitors; Alfuzosin; Alpha2-Agonists; Amiodarone; Anilidopiperidine Opioids; Barbiturates; Benperidol; Bretylium; Brimonidine (Topical); Calcium Channel Blockers (Nondihydropyridine); Diazoxide; Dipyridamole; Disopyramide; Dronedarone; Floctafenine; Glycopyrrolate (Systemic); Herbs (Hypotensive Properties); Lormetazepam; Methoxyflurane; Molsidomine; Naftopidil; Nicergoline; Nicorandil; NIFEdipine; Obinutuzumab; Pentoxifylline; Phosphodiesterase 5 Inhibitors; Prostacyclin Analogues; Quinagolide; Regorafenib; Reserpine; Rivastigmine; Ruxolitinib; Tofacitinib

Decreased Effect

Atenolol may decrease the levels/effects of: Beta2-Agonists; Theophylline Derivatives

The levels/effects of Atenolol may be decreased by: Amphetamines; Ampicillin; Herbs (Hypertensive Properties); Methylphenidate; Nonsteroidal Anti-Inflammatory Agents; Yohimbine

Food Interactions Atenolol serum concentrations may be decreased if taken with food. Management: Administer without regard to meals.

Dietary Considerations May be taken without regard to meals.

Pharmacodynamics/Kinetics

Onset of Action Oral: ≤1 hour; Peak effect: Oral: 2 to 4 hours

Duration of Action Normal renal function: Beta-blocking effect: 12 to 24 hours; Antihypertensive effect: Oral: 24 hours

Half-life Elimination Beta:

Newborns (<24 hours of age) born to mothers receiving atenolol: Mean: 16 hours; up to 35 hours (Rubin 1983)

Children and Adolescents 5 to 16 years of age: Mean: 4.6 hours; range: 3.5 to 7 hours; Patients >10 years of age may have longer half-life (>5 hours) compared to children 5 to 10 years of age (<5 hours) (Buck 1989)

Adults: Normal renal function: 6 to 7 hours, prolonged with renal impairment; End-stage renal disease (ESRD): 15 to 35 hours

Time to Peak Plasma: Oral: 2 to 4 hours

Pregnancy Risk Factor D

Pregnancy Considerations Atenolol crosses the placenta and is found in cord blood. Maternal use of atenolol may cause harm to the fetus. Adverse events, such as bradycardia, hypoglycemia and reduced birth weight, have been observed following in utero exposure to atenolol. Adequate facilities for monitoring infants at birth is generally recommended. The maternal pharmacokinetic parameters of atenolol during the second and third trimesters are within the ranges reported in nonpregnant patients (Hebert 2005).

Untreated chronic maternal hypertension and preeclampsia are associated with adverse events in the fetus, infant, and mother (ACOG 2015; Magee 2014). Although beta-blockers may be used when treatment of hypertension in pregnancy is indicated, agents other than atenolol are preferred (ACOG 2013; Magee 2014; Regitz-Zagrosek 2011).

Breastfeeding Considerations Atenolol is excreted in breast milk. Bradycardia has been observed in some nursing infants and neonates may also be at risk for hypoglycemia. Adverse events may be more likely in premature infants or infants with impaired renal function. The manufacturer recommends that caution be used if administered to a nursing woman.

Dosage Forms

Tablet, Oral:

Tenormin: 25 mg, 50 mg, 100 mg

Generic: 25 mg, 50 mg, 100 mg

Atenolol and Chlorthalidone

(a TEN oh lole & klor THAL i done)

Related Information

Atenolol *on page 179*

Chlorthalidone *on page 353*

Brand Names: US Tenoretic

Brand Names: Canada Apo-Atenidone; Novo-Atenolthalidone; Tenoretic; Teva-Atenolol Chlorthalidone

Pharmacologic Category Antihypertensive; Beta-Blocker, Beta-1 Selective; Diuretic, Thiazide

Use Treatment of hypertension with a cardioselective beta-blocker and a diuretic

Local Anesthetic/Vasoconstrictor Precautions No information available to require special precautions

Effects on Dental Treatment Atenolol is a cardioselective beta-blocker. Local anesthetic with vasoconstrictor can be safely used in patients medicated with atenolol. Nonselective beta-blockers (ie, propranolol, nadolol) enhance the pressor response to epinephrine, resulting in hypertension and bradycardia; this has not been reported for atenolol. Many nonsteroidal anti-inflammatory drugs, such as ibuprofen and indomethacin, can reduce the hypotensive effect of beta-blockers after 3 or more weeks of therapy with the NSAID. Short-term NSAID use (ie, 3 days) requires no special precautions in patients taking beta-blockers.

Effects on Bleeding No information available to require special precautions

Adverse Reactions See individual agents.

General Dosage Range Dosage adjustment recommended in patients with renal impairment.

Oral: *Adults:* Initial: Atenolol 50 mg and chlorthalidone 25 mg once daily; Maintenance: Atenolol 50-100 mg and chlorthalidone 25 mg once daily (maximum dose: Atenolol 100 mg/day; chlorthalidone 25 mg/day)

Pregnancy Risk Factor D

Pregnancy Considerations Atenolol and chlorthalidone cross the placenta. See individual agents.

AtoMOXetine (AT oh mox e teen)

Related Information

Dentin Hypersensitivity, Acid Erosion, High Caries Index, Management of Alveolar Osteitis, and Xerostomia *on page 1857*

Brand Names: US Strattera

Brand Names: Canada Apo-Atomoxetine; DOM-Atomoxetine; Mylan-Atomoxetine; PMS-Atomoxetine; RIVA-Atomoxetine; Sandoz-Atomoxetine; Strattera; Teva-Atomoxetine

Pharmacologic Category Norepinephrine Reuptake Inhibitor, Selective

Use Attention-deficit/hyperactivity disorder: Treatment of attention-deficit/hyperactivity disorder (ADHD)

Local Anesthetic/Vasoconstrictor Precautions Use vasoconstrictor with caution. Atomoxetine may increase heart rate or blood pressure in the presence of pressor agents. Pressor agents include the vasoconstrictors epinephrine or mepivacaine and levonordefrin (Carbocaine® 2% with Neo-Cobefrin®)

Effects on Dental Treatment Key adverse event(s) related to dental treatment: Xerostomia (normal salivary flow resumes upon discontinuation)

Effects on Bleeding No information available to require special precautions

Adverse Reactions Percentages as reported in children and adults; some adverse reactions may be increased in "poor metabolizers" (CYP2D6). Frequency not always defined.

>10%:

Central nervous system: Headache (19%; children and adolescents), insomnia (1% to 19%), drowsiness (8% to 11%)

Dermatologic: Hyperhidrosis (4% to 15%)

Gastrointestinal: Xerostomia (17% to 35%), nausea (7% to 26%), decreased appetite (15% to 23%), abdominal pain (7% to 18%), vomiting (4% to 11%), constipation (1% to 11%)

Genitourinary: Erectile dysfunction (8% to 21%)

1% to 10%:

Cardiovascular: Increased diastolic blood pressure (5% to 9%; ≥15 mm Hg), systolic hypertension (4% to 5%), palpitations (3%), cold extremities (1% to 3%), syncope (≤3%), flushing (≥2%), orthostatic hypotension (≤2%), tachycardia (≤2%), prolonged Q-T interval on ECG

Central nervous system: Fatigue (6% to 10%), dizziness (5% to 8%), depression (4% to 7%), disturbed sleep (3% to 7%), irritability (5% to 6%), jitteriness (2% to 5%), abnormal dreams (4%), chills (3%), paresthesia (adults 3%; postmarketing observation in children), anxiety (≥2%), hostility (children and adolescents 2%), emotional lability (1% to 2%), agitation, restlessness, sensation of cold

Dermatologic: Excoriation (2% to 4%), skin rash (2%), pruritus, urticaria

Endocrine & metabolic: Weight loss (2% to 7%), decreased libido (3%), hot flash (3%), increased thirst (2%), menstrual disease

Gastrointestinal: Dyspepsia (4%), anorexia (3%), dysgeusia, flatulence

Genitourinary: Ejaculatory disorder (2% to 6%), urinary retention (1% to 6%), dysmenorrhea (3%), dysuria (2%), orgasm abnormal, pollakiuria, prostatitis, testicular pain, urinary frequency

Neuromuscular & skeletal: Tremor (1% to 5%), muscle spasm, weakness

Ophthalmic: Blurred vision (1% to 4%), conjunctivitis (1% to 3%), mydriasis
Respiratory: Pharyngolaryngeal pain
Miscellaneous: Therapeutic response unexpected (2%)
<1%, postmarketing, and/or case reports: Aggressive behavior, akathisia, anaphylaxis, angioedema, cerebrovascular accident, change in libido, delusions, growth suppression (children), hallucination, hepatotoxicity, hypersensitivity reaction, hypoesthesia, hypomania, impulsivity, jaundice, lethargy, mania, myocardial infarction, panic attack, pelvic pain, priapism, Raynaud's phenomenon, rhabdomyolysis, seizure (including patients with no prior history or known risk factors for seizure), severe hepatic disease, suicidal ideation, tics

General Dosage Range Dosage adjustment recommended in patients with hepatic impairment or on concomitant therapy.

Oral:

Children ≥6 years and ≤70 kg: Initial: 0.5 mg/kg/day in 1-2 divided doses; Maintenance: 0.5-1.4 mg/kg/day in 1-2 divided doses (maximum: 1.4 mg/kg/day **or** 100 mg/day, whichever is less)

Children ≥6 years and >70 kg and Adults: Initial: 40 mg/day in 1-2 divided doses; Maintenance: 40-100 mg/day in 1-2 divided doses (maximum: 100 mg/day)

Mechanism of Action Selectively inhibits the reuptake of norepinephrine (Ki 4.5 nM) with little to no activity at the other neuronal reuptake pumps or receptor sites.

Pharmacodynamics/Kinetics

Half-life Elimination Atomoxetine: 5 hours (up to 24 hours in poor metabolizers); Active metabolites: 4-hydroxyatomoxetine: 6-8 hours; N-desmethylatomoxetine: 6-8 hours (34-40 hours in poor metabolizers)

Time to Peak Plasma: 1-2 hours; delayed 3 hours by high-fat meal

Pregnancy Risk Factor C

Pregnancy Considerations Adverse events have been observed in animal reproduction studies. Information related to atomoxetine use in pregnancy is limited; appropriate contraception is recommended for sexually active women of childbearing potential (Heiligenstein, 2003).

AtorvaSTATin (a TORE va sta tin)

Related Information

Cardiovascular Diseases *on page 1752*

Brand Names: US Lipitor

Brand Names: Canada ACT Atorvastatin; Apo-Atorvastatin; Auro-Atorvastatin; Ava-Atorvastatin; Dom-Atorvastatin; GD-Atorvastatin; JAMP-Atorvastatin; Lipitor; Mylan-Atorvastatin; Novo-Atorvastatin; PMS-Atorvastatin; RAN-Atorvastatin; ratio-Atorvastatin; Reedy-Atorvastatin; Riva-Atorvastatin; Sandoz-Atorvastatin

Generic Availability (US) Yes

Pharmacologic Category Antilipemic Agent, HMG-CoA Reductase Inhibitor

Use

Dyslipidemias:

Dysbetalipoproteinemia: Treatment of primary dysbetalipoproteinemia (Fredrickson type III).

Heterozygous familial and nonfamilial hypercholesterolemia and mixed dyslipidemia: To reduce elevated total cholesterol (total-C), low-density lipoprotein cholesterol (LDL-C), apolipoprotein B (apo B), and triglyceride levels, and to increase HDL-C in patients with primary hypercholesterolemia (heterozygous familial and nonfamilial) and mixed dyslipidemia (Fredrickson type IIa and IIb).

Heterozygous familial hypercholesterolemia: To reduce total-C, LDL-C, and apo B levels in boys and postmenarche girls 10 to 17 years of age with heterozygous familial hypercholesterolemia with LDL-C ≥190 mg/dL, LDL-C ≥160 mg/dL with positive family history of premature cardiovascular disease (CVD), or LDL-C ≥160 mg/dL with two or more other CVD risk factors.

Homozygous familial hypercholesterolemia: To reduce total-C and LDL-C in patients with homozygous familial hypercholesterolemia as an adjunct to other lipid-lowering treatments (eg, LDL apheresis) or if such treatments are unavailable.

Hypertriglyceridemia: Treatment of elevated serum triglyceride levels (Fredrickson type IV).

Limitations of use: Has not been studied in conditions where the major lipid abnormality is elevation of chylomicrons (Fredrickson types I and V).

Prevention of cardiovascular disease (CVD):

Primary prevention of cardiovascular disease (high-risk for CVD): To reduce the risk of MI, stroke, and revascularization procedures and angina in adult patients without clinically evident coronary heart disease (CHD) who have multiple CHD risk factors (eg, age, smoking, hypertension, low high-density lipoprotein cholesterol [HDL-C], family history of early CHD); to reduce the risk of MI and stroke in patients with type 2 diabetes and without clinically evident CHD but with multiple risk factors for CHD (eg, retinopathy, albuminuria, smoking, hypertension).

Secondary prevention of cardiovascular disease: To reduce the risk of nonfatal MI, fatal and nonfatal stroke, revascularization procedures, hospitalization for decompensated heart failure, and angina in patients with clinically evident CHD.

Guideline recommendations: Primary and secondary prevention of atherosclerotic cardiovascular disease (ASCVD) to reduce the risk of ASCVD in select adult patients (ACC/AHA [Stone 2013]; NLA [Jacobson 2015]). Refer to respective guideline for specific recommendations.

Local Anesthetic/Vasoconstrictor Precautions No information available to require special precautions

Effects on Dental Treatment Key adverse event(s) related to dental treatment: Assess unusual presentations of muscle weakness or myopathy resulting from lipid therapy such as patient having a difficult time brushing teeth or weakness with chewing. Refer patient back to their physician for evaluation and adjustment of lipid therapy.

Effects on Bleeding No information available to require special precautions

Adverse Reactions

>10%:
Gastrointestinal: Diarrhea (7% to 14%)
Neuromuscular & skeletal: Arthralgia (9% to 12%)
Respiratory: Nasopharyngitis (13%)

2% to 10%:
Cardiovascular: Hemorrhagic stroke (2%)
Central nervous system: Insomnia (5%)
Endocrine & metabolic: Diabetes mellitus (6%)
Gastrointestinal: Nausea (7%), dyspepsia (6%)
Genitourinary: Urinary tract infection (7% to 8%), cystitis (interstitial; Huang 2015)
Hepatic: Increased serum transaminases (≤2%)

Neuromuscular & skeletal: Limb pain (9%), myalgia (4% to 8%), musculoskeletal pain (5%), muscle spasm (4% to 5%)

Respiratory: Pharyngolaryngeal pain (3% to 4%)

<2%, postmarketing, and/or case reports: Abdominal distress, abdominal pain, abnormal hepatic function tests, alopecia, amnesia (reversible), anaphylaxis, anemia, angioedema, anorexia, back pain, blurred vision, bullous rash, chest pain, cholestasis, cholestatic jaundice, cognitive dysfunction (reversible), confusion (reversible), depression, dizziness, dysgeusia, elevated glycosylated hemoglobin (HbA_{1c}), epistaxis, eructation, erythema multiforme, fatigue, fever, flatulence, gynecomastia, hematuria, hepatic failure, hepatitis, hyperglycemia, hypoesthesia, increased creatinine phosphokinase, increased serum alkaline phosphatase, increased serum glucose, jaundice, joint swelling, malaise, memory impairment (reversible), muscle fatigue, myasthenia, myopathy, myositis, neck pain, neck stiffness, nightmares, pancreatitis, paresthesia, peripheral edema, peripheral neuropathy, pruritus, rhabdomyolysis, rupture of tendon, Stevens-Johnson syndrome, thrombocytopenia, tinnitus, toxic epidermal necrolysis, urticaria, vomiting, weight gain

Dosing

Adult & Geriatric

Primary prevention: Note: Doses should be individualized according to the baseline LDL-cholesterol concentrations and patient response; adjustments should be made at intervals of 2 to 4 weeks

Hypercholesterolemia (heterozygous familial and nonfamilial) and mixed hyperlipidemia (Fredrickson types IIa and IIb): Oral: Initial: 10 or 20 mg once daily; patients requiring >45% reduction in LDL-C may be started at 40 mg once daily; range: 10 to 80 mg once daily

Homozygous familial hypercholesterolemia: Oral: 10 to 80 mg once daily

Prevention of cardiovascular disease/reduce the risk of ASCVD:

ACC/AHA Blood Cholesterol Guideline recommendations (ACC/AHA [Stone 2013]): Adults ≥21 years:

Primary Prevention:

LDL-C ≥190 mg/dL: High-intensity therapy: 80 mg once daily; if unable to tolerate, may reduce dose to 40 mg once daily

Type 1 or 2 diabetes and age 40 to 75 years: Moderate-intensity therapy: 10 to 20 mg once daily

Type 1 or 2 diabetes, age 40 to 75 years, and an estimated 10-year ASCVD risk ≥7.5%: High-intensity therapy: 80 mg once daily; if unable to tolerate, may reduce dose to 40 mg once daily

Age 40 to 75 years and an estimated 10-year ASCVD risk ≥7.5%: Moderate- to high-intensity therapy: 10 to 80 mg once daily

Secondary prevention:

Patient has clinical ASCVD (eg, coronary heart disease, stroke/TIA, or peripheral arterial disease presumed to be of atherosclerotic origin) or is post-CABG (AHA [Kulik 2015]) **and:**

Age ≤75 years: High-intensity therapy: 80 mg once daily; if unable to tolerate, may reduce dose to 40 mg once daily

Age >75 years or not a candidate for high intensity therapy: Moderate-intensity therapy: 10 to 20 mg once daily

NLA Dyslipidemia Guideline recommendations (NLA [Jacobson 2015]): Adults ≥20 years:

Primary or secondary prevention: Note: Treatment initiation using either moderate- or high-intensity statin therapy is recommended in qualifying patients based on ASCVD risk assessment criteria and baseline non-HDL-C and LDL-C values. Dosage should be individualized based on patient characteristics, tolerance to therapy, and with consideration for non-HDL-C and LDL-C treatment goals.

Moderate-intensity therapy (30 to 50% reduction of LDL-C generally): 10 to 20 mg once daily

High-intensity therapy (≥50% reduction of LDL-C generally): 40 to 80 mg once daily

Intensive lipid-lowering after an ACS event regardless of baseline LDL (off-label use): Oral: Initial: 80 mg once daily; adjust based on patient tolerability (Cannon 2004; Pederson 2005; Schwartz 2001). **Note:** Currently, the ACC/AHA guidelines for Non-ST-Elevation ACS do not specify which statin to use (ACC/AHA [Amsterdam 2014]).

Noncardioembolic stroke/TIA (off-label use): Oral: Initial: 80 mg once daily; adjust based on patient tolerability (Adams 2008; Amarenco 2006). Also consider the ACC/AHA Blood Cholesterol Guideline recommendations (Stone 2013).

Dosage adjustment for atorvastatin with concomitant medications:

Boceprevir, nelfinavir: Use lowest effective atorvastatin dose (not to exceed 40 mg daily)

Clarithromycin, itraconazole, fosamprenavir, ritonavir (plus darunavir, fosamprenavir, or saquinavir): Use lowest effective atorvastatin dose (not to exceed 20 mg daily)

Lomitapide: Consider atorvastatin dose reduction (per lomitapide manufacturer).

Pediatric

Note: Doses should be individualized according to the baseline LDL-cholesterol concentrations and patient response; adjustments should be made at intervals of 4 weeks

Heterozygous familial hypercholesterolemia: Children ≥10 years and Adolescents (females postmenarche): Oral: 10 mg once daily (maximum: 20 mg/day)

Dosage adjustment for atorvastatin with concomitant medications: Refer to adult dosing.

Renal Impairment

No dosage adjustment necessary.

Dialysis: Due to the high protein binding, atorvastatin is not expected to be cleared by dialysis (not studied)

Hepatic Impairment

Contraindicated in active liver disease or in patients with unexplained persistent elevations of serum transaminases.

Adjustment for Toxicity

Severe muscle symptoms or fatigue: Promptly discontinue use; evaluate CPK, creatinine, and urinalysis for myoglobinuria (Stone 2013).

Mild to moderate muscle symptoms: Discontinue use until symptoms can be evaluated; evaluate patient for conditions that may increase the risk for muscle symptoms (eg, hypothyroidism, reduced renal or hepatic function, rheumatologic disorders such as polymyalgia rheumatica, steroid myopathy, vitamin D deficiency, or primary muscle diseases). Upon resolution, resume the original or lower dose of atorvastatin. If muscle symptoms recur, discontinue atorvastatin use. After muscle symptom resolution, may then use a low dose of a different statin; gradually increase if tolerated. In the absence of continued statin use, if muscle symptoms or elevated CPK continues after 2 months, consider other causes of muscle symptoms. If determined to be due to another condition aside from statin use, may resume statin therapy at the original dose (Stone 2013).

Mechanism of Action Inhibitor of 3-hydroxy-3-methylglutaryl coenzyme A (HMG-CoA) reductase, the rate-limiting enzyme in cholesterol synthesis (reduces the production of mevalonic acid from HMG-CoA); this then results in a compensatory increase in the expression of LDL receptors on hepatocyte membranes and a stimulation of LDL catabolism. In addition to the ability of HMG-CoA reductase inhibitors to decrease levels of high-sensitivity C-reactive protein (hsCRP), they also possess pleiotropic properties including improved endothelial function, reduced inflammation at the site of the coronary plaque, inhibition of platelet aggregation, and anticoagulant effects (de Denus 2002; Ray 2005).

Contraindications

Hypersensitivity to atorvastatin or any component of the formulation; active liver disease; unexplained persistent elevations of serum transaminases; pregnancy or women who may become pregnant; breastfeeding

Canadian labeling: Additional contraindications (not in US labeling): Telaprevir Canadian product monograph contraindicates use with atorvastatin.

Warnings/Precautions Secondary causes of hyperlipidemia should be ruled out prior to therapy. Drug therapy should be only one component of multiple risk factor intervention in patients at significantly increased risk for atherosclerotic vascular disease due to hypercholesterolemia. In patients with CHD or multiple risk factors for CHD, initiate therapy simultaneously with diet. Rhabdomyolysis with acute renal failure secondary to myoglobinuria and/or myopathy has been reported; patients should be monitored closely. This risk is dose-related and is increased with concurrent use of strong CYP3A4 inhibitors (eg, clarithromycin, itraconazole, protease inhibitors), cyclosporine, fibric acid derivatives (eg, gemfibrozil), or niacin (doses ≥1 g/day); if concurrent use is warranted, consider lower starting and maintenance doses of atorvastatin. Use caution in patients with inadequately treated hypothyroidism, and those taking other drugs associated with myopathy (eg, colchicine); these patients are predisposed to myopathy. Uncomplicated myalgia immune-mediated necrotizing myopathy (IMNM) associated with HMG-CoA reductase inhibitors use has also been reported. Patients should be instructed to report unexplained muscle pain, tenderness, weakness, or brown urine, particularly if accompanied by malaise or fever. Discontinue therapy if markedly elevated CPK levels occur or myopathy is diagnosed/suspected.

Persistent elevations in serum transaminases have been reported; upon dose reduction, drug interruption, or discontinuation, transaminase levels returned to or near pretreatment levels. Postmarketing reports of fatal and nonfatal hepatic failure have been reported and are rare. If serious hepatotoxicity with clinical symptoms and/or hyperbilirubinemia or jaundice occurs during treatment, interrupt therapy promptly. If an alternate etiology is not identified, do not restart atorvastatin. Liver enzyme tests should be obtained at baseline and as clinically indicated and if signs/symptoms of liver injury occur. Ethanol may enhance the potential of adverse hepatic effects; instruct patients to avoid excessive ethanol consumption. Increases in HbA_{1c} and fasting blood glucose have been reported. Use with caution in patients who consume large amounts of ethanol or have a history of liver disease; use is contraindicated in patients with active liver disease or unexplained persistent elevations of serum transaminases. Use with caution in patients with renal impairment and the elderly; these patients are predisposed to myopathy.

Patients with recent stroke or TIA receiving long-term therapy with high-dose (ie, 80 mg/day) atorvastatin may be at increased risk for hemorrhagic stroke (SPARCL Investigators 2006). A subsequent post-hoc analysis demonstrated that patients with lacunar or hemorrhagic stroke may be at higher risk of hemorrhagic stroke; however, this finding was determined to be hypothesis generating. The overall benefit of treatment with atorvastatin (ie, reduced risk of stroke and cardiovascular events) in this population seems to outweigh the increased risk of hemorrhagic stroke if one truly exists (Goldstein 2008). The manufacturer recommends temporary discontinuation for elective major surgery, acute medical or surgical conditions, or in any patient experiencing an acute, serious condition suggestive of a myopathy or having a risk factor predisposing to the development of renal failure secondary to rhabdomyolysis (eg, sepsis, hypotension, trauma, uncontrolled seizures, severe metabolic, endocrine, or electrolyte disorders). Based on current research and clinical guidelines, HMG-CoA reductase inhibitors should be continued in the perioperative period (ACC/AHA [Fleisher 2014). Postoperative discontinuation of statin therapy is associated with an increased risk of cardiac morbidity and mortality. Potentially significant interactions may exist, requiring dose or frequency adjustment, additional monitoring, and/or selection of alternative therapy. Consult drug interactions database for more detailed information.

Some dosage forms may contain polysorbate 80 (also known as Tweens). Hypersensitivity reactions, usually a delayed reaction, have been reported following exposure to pharmaceutical products containing polysorbate 80 in certain individuals (Isaksson 2002; Lucente 2000; Shelley 1995).

Drug Interactions

Metabolism/Transport Effects Substrate of CYP3A4 (major), P-glycoprotein, SLCO1B1; **Note:** Assignment of Major/Minor substrate status based on clinically relevant drug interaction potential; **Inhibits** CYP3A4 (weak)

Avoid Concomitant Use

Avoid concomitant use of AtorvaSTATin with any of the following: Antihepaciviral Combination Products; Conivaptan; CycloSPORINE (Systemic); Fusidic Acid (Systemic); Gemfibrozil; Idelalisib; PAZOPanib; Pimozide; Posaconazole; Red Yeast Rice; Telaprevir; Tipranavir

Increased Effect/Toxicity

AtorvaSTATin may increase the levels/effects of: Aliskiren; ARIPiprazole; Cimetidine; DAPTOmycin; Digoxin; DilTIAZem; Dofetilide; Flibanserin; HYDROcodone; Ketoconazole (Systemic); Lomitapide; Midazolam; NiMODipine; PAZOPanib; Pimozide; Repaglinide; Spironolactone; Trabectedin; Verapamil

The levels/effects of AtorvaSTATin may be increased by: Acipimox; Amiodarone; Antihepaciviral Combination Products; Aprepitant; Asunaprevir; Azithromycin (Systemic); Bezafibrate; Boceprevir; Ciprofibrate; Clarithromycin; Cobicistat; Colchicine; Conivaptan; CycloSPORINE (Systemic); CYP3A4 Inhibitors (Moderate); CYP3A4 Inhibitors (Strong); Cyproterone;

Daclatasvir; Danazol; Dasatinib; DilTIAZem; Dronedarone; Elbasvir; Eltrombopag; Erythromycin (Systemic); Fenofibrate and Derivatives; Fluconazole; Fosaprepitant; Fusidic Acid (Systemic); Gemfibrozil; Grapefruit Juice; Grazoprevir; Idelalisib; Itraconazole; Ivacaftor; Ketoconazole (Systemic); MiFEPRIStone; Netupitant; Niacin; Niacinamide; Palbociclib; P-glycoprotein/ABCB1 Inhibitors; Posaconazole; Protease Inhibitors; QuiNINE; Raltegravir; Ranolazine; Red Yeast Rice; Rupatadine; Simeprevir; Stiripentol; Telaprevir; Telithromycin; Teriflunomide; Ticagrelor; Tipranavir; Velpatasvir; Verapamil; Voriconazole

Decreased Effect

AtorvaSTATin may decrease the levels/effects of: Dabigatran Etexilate; Lanthanum

The levels/effects of AtorvaSTATin may be decreased by: Antacids; Bexarotene (Systemic); Bile Acid Sequestrants; Bosentan; CYP3A4 Inducers (Moderate); CYP3A4 Inducers (Strong); Dabrafenib; Deferasirox; Efavirenz; Enzalutamide; Etravirine; Fosphenytoin; Mitotane; Phenytoin; Rifamycin Derivatives; Siltuximab; St John's Wort; Tocilizumab

Food Interactions Atorvastatin serum concentrations may be increased by grapefruit juice. Management: Avoid concurrent intake of large quantities of grapefruit juice (>1 quart/day).

Dietary Considerations Before initiation of therapy, patients should be placed on a standard cholesterol-lowering diet for 3 to 6 months and the diet should be continued during drug therapy. Atorvastatin serum concentration may be increased when taken with grapefruit juice; avoid concurrent intake of large quantities (>1 quart/day).

Red yeast rice contains variable amounts of several compounds that are structurally similar to HMG-CoA reductase inhibitors, primarily monacolin K (or mevinolin) which is structurally identical to lovastatin; concurrent use of red yeast rice with HMG-CoA reductase inhibitors may increase the incidence of adverse and toxic effects (Lapi 2008; Smith 2003).

Pharmacodynamics/Kinetics

Onset of Action Initial changes: 3 to 5 days; Maximal reduction in plasma cholesterol and triglycerides: 2 to 4 weeks; LDL reduction: 10 mg/day: 39% (for each doubling of this dose, LDL is lowered approximately 6%)

Half-life Elimination Parent drug: ~14 hours; Equipotent metabolites: 20 to 30 hours

Time to Peak Serum: 1 to 2 hours

Pregnancy Risk Factor X

Pregnancy Considerations Studies in animals and pregnant women have shown evidence of fetal abnormalities and use is contraindicated in women who are or may become pregnant. There are reports of congenital anomalies following maternal use of HMG-CoA reductase inhibitors in pregnancy; however, maternal disease, differences in specific agents used, and the low rates of exposure limit the interpretation of the available data (Godfrey 2012; Lecarpentier 2012). Cholesterol biosynthesis may be important in fetal development; serum cholesterol and triglycerides increase normally during pregnancy. The discontinuation of lipid lowering medications temporarily during pregnancy is not expected to have significant impact on the long term outcomes of primary hypercholesterolemia treatment.

HMG-CoA reductase inhibitors should be discontinued prior to pregnancy (ADA 2013). If treatment of dyslipidemias is needed in pregnant women or in women of reproductive age, other agents are preferred (Berglund 2012; Stone 2013). The manufacturer recommends administration to women of childbearing potential only when conception is highly unlikely and patients have been informed of potential hazards.

Breastfeeding Considerations It is not known if atorvastatin is excreted in breast milk. Due to the potential for serious adverse reactions in a nursing infant, use while breastfeeding is contraindicated by the manufacturer.

Dosage Forms

Tablet, Oral:

Lipitor: 10 mg, 20 mg, 40 mg, 80 mg
Generic: 10 mg, 20 mg, 40 mg, 80 mg

Atovaquone (a TOE va kwone)

Related Information

Systemic Viral Diseases *on page 1806*

Brand Names: US Mepron

Brand Names: Canada Mepron

Pharmacologic Category Antiprotozoal

Use

Pneumocystis jirovecii pneumonia (PCP), prophylaxis: Prevention of PCP in adults and adolescents 13 years and older who are intolerant to trimethoprim-sulfamethoxazole (TMP-SMZ)

Pneumocystis jirovecii pneumonia (PCP), treatment: Acute oral treatment of mild-to moderate PCP in adults and adolescents 13 years and older who are intolerant to TMP-SMZ

Local Anesthetic/Vasoconstrictor Precautions No information available to require special precautions

Effects on Dental Treatment Key adverse event(s) related to dental treatment: Oral *Candida* infection

Effects on Bleeding No information available to require special precautions

Adverse Reactions Frequency not always defined. Adverse reaction statistics have been compiled from studies including patients with advanced HIV disease. Consequently, it is difficult to distinguish reactions attributed to atovaquone from those caused by the underlying disease or a combination thereof.

>10%:

Central nervous system: Headache (16% to 31%), insomnia (10% to 19%), depression, pain

Dermatologic: Skin rash (22% to 46%), pruritus (5% to ≥10%), diaphoresis

Gastrointestinal: Diarrhea (19% to 42%), nausea (21% to 32%), vomiting (14% to 22%), abdominal pain (4% to 21%)

Infection: Infection (18% to 22%)

Neuromuscular & skeletal: Weakness (8% to 31%), myalgia

Respiratory: Cough (14% to 25%), rhinitis (5% to 24%), dyspnea (15% to 21%), sinusitis (7% to ≥10%), flu-like symptoms

Miscellaneous: Fever (14% to 40%)

1% to 10%:

Cardiovascular: Hypotension (≤1%)

Central nervous system: Dizziness (3% to 8%), anxiety (≤7%)

Endocrine & metabolic: Hyponatremia (7% to 10%), hyperglycemia (≤9%), increased amylase (7% to 8%), hypoglycemia (≤1%)

Gastrointestinal: Oral candidiasis (5% to 10%), anorexia (≤7%), dyspepsia (≤5%), constipation (≤3%), dysgeusia (≤3%)

Hematologic & oncologic: Anemia (4% to 6%), neutropenia (3% to 5%)
Hepatic: Increased liver enzymes (4% to 8%)
Renal: Increased blood urea nitrogen (≤1%), increased serum creatinine (≤1%)
Respiratory: Bronchospasm (2% to 4%)

<1%, postmarketing, and/or case reports: Acute renal failure, angioedema, constriction of the pharynx, corneal disease (vortex keratopathy), desquamation, erythema multiforme, hepatic failure (rare), hepatitis (rare), hypersensitivity reaction, methemoglobinemia, pancreatitis, Stevens-Johnson syndrome, thrombocytopenia, urticaria

General Dosage Range Oral: *Adolescents ≥13 years and Adults:* 1500 mg daily in 1-2 divided doses

Mechanism of Action Inhibits electron transport in mitochondria resulting in the inhibition of key metabolic enzymes responsible for the synthesis of nucleic acids and ATP

Pharmacodynamics/Kinetics

Half-life Elimination Children (4 months to 12 years): 60 hours (range: 31-163 hours); Adults: 2.9 days; Adults with AIDS: 2.2 days

Time to Peak Dual peak serum concentrations at 1 to 8 hours and at 24 to 96 hours after dose due to enterohepatic cycling

Pregnancy Risk Factor C

Pregnancy Considerations Adverse events were observed in animal reproduction studies. Diagnosis and treatment of *Pneumocystis jirovecii* pneumonia (PCP) in pregnant women is the same as in nonpregnant women; however, information specific to the use of atovaquone in pregnancy is limited (HHS [OI adult 2015]).

Atovaquone and Proguanil

(a TOE va kwone & pro GWA nil)

Related Information

Atovaquone *on page 185*

Brand Names: US Malarone®

Brand Names: Canada Malarone®; Malarone® Pediatric

Pharmacologic Category Antimalarial Agent

Use

Malaria prevention: Prophylaxis of *Plasmodium falciparum* malaria, including areas where chloroquine resistance has been reported

Malaria treatment: Treatment of acute, uncomplicated *P. falciparum* malaria

Local Anesthetic/Vasoconstrictor Precautions No information available to require special precautions

Effects on Dental Treatment No significant effects or complications reported

Effects on Bleeding No information available to require special precautions

Adverse Reactions The following adverse reactions were reported in patients being treated for malaria. When used for prophylaxis, reactions are similar to those seen with placebo.

>10%:

Gastrointestinal: Abdominal pain (17%), nausea (12%), vomiting (children: 10% to 13%; adults: 12%)
Hepatic: Increased serum ALT (27%; increased liver function test values typically normalized after ~4 weeks), increased serum AST (17%; increased liver function test values typically normalized after ~4 weeks)

1% to 10%:

Central nervous system: Headache (10%), dizziness (5%)
Dermatologic: Pruritus (children: 6%)
Gastrointestinal: Diarrhea (children: 6%; adults: 8%), anorexia (5%)
Neuromuscular & skeletal: Weakness (8%)

<1%, postmarketing, and/or case reports: Anaphylaxis (rare), anemia (rare), angioedema, cholestasis, erythema multiforme (rare), hallucination, hepatic failure (case report), hepatitis (rare), neutropenia, pancytopenia (with severe renal impairment), psychotic reaction (rare), seizure (rare), skin photosensitivity, skin rash, Stevens-Johnson syndrome (rare), stomatitis, urticaria, vasculitis (rare)

General Dosage Range Oral:

Children 5-8 kg: Treatment: 125 mg/50 mg as a single daily dose
Children 9-10 kg: Treatment: 187.5 mg/75 mg as a single daily dose
Children 11-20 kg: Prophylaxis: 62.5 mg/25 mg; Treatment: 250 mg/100 mg as a single daily dose
Children 21-30 kg: Prophylaxis: 125 mg/50 mg; Treatment: 500 mg/200 mg as a single daily dose
Children 31-40 kg: Prophylaxis: 187.5 mg/75 mg; Treatment: 750 mg/300 mg as a single daily dose
Children >40 kg, Adolescents, and Adults: Prophylaxis: 250 mg/100 mg; Treatment: 1000 mg/400 mg as a single daily dose

Mechanism of Action

Atovaquone: Selectively inhibits parasite mitochondrial electron transport.

Proguanil: The metabolite cycloguanil inhibits dihydrofolate reductase, disrupting deoxythymidylate synthesis. Together, atovaquone/cycloguanil affect the erythrocytic and exoerythrocytic stages of development.

Pharmacodynamics/Kinetics

Half-life Elimination

Atovaquone: 2-3 days (adults), 1-2 days (children)
Proguanil: 12-21 hours

Pregnancy Risk Factor C

Pregnancy Considerations Adverse events were not observed with the combination of atovaquone/proguanil in animal reproduction studies. The pharmacokinetics of atovaquone and proguanil may be altered during pregnancy (Wilby 2011). Malaria infection in pregnant women may be more severe than in nonpregnant women. Because *P. falciparum* malaria can cause maternal death and fetal loss, pregnant women traveling to malaria-endemic areas must use personal protection against mosquito bites. Atovaquone/proguanil may be used as an alternative treatment of malaria in pregnant women; consult current CDC guidelines (CDC 2013).

Atropine (Systemic)

(A troe peen)

Brand Names: US AtroPen

Pharmacologic Category Anticholinergic Agent; Antidote; Antispasmodic Agent, Gastrointestinal

Use

Antidote: Antidote for anticholinesterase poisoning (carbamate insecticides, nerve agents, organophosphate insecticides); antidote for muscarine-containing mushroom poisoning.

Adjuvant use with anticholinesterases (eg, edrophonium, neostigmine) to decrease their adverse effects during reversal of neuromuscular blockade.

Cardiovascular conditions: Treatment of symptomatic sinus bradycardia, atrioventricular (AV) nodal block.

Note: Likely not effective for type II second-degree or third-degree AV block (AHA [Hazinski 2015]). Use is no longer recommended in the management of asystole or pulseless electrical activity (PEA) (ACLS 2010).

Respiratory tract: Preoperative/preanesthetic medication to inhibit salivation and secretions.

Local Anesthetic/Vasoconstrictor Precautions No information available to require special precautions

Effects on Dental Treatment Key adverse event(s) related to dental treatment: Xerostomia and changes in salivation (normal salivary flow resumes upon discontinuation), dry throat, and nasal dryness

Effects on Bleeding No information available to require special precautions

Adverse Reactions Frequency not always defined. Severity and frequency of adverse reactions are dose related.

Cardiovascular: Asystole, atrial arrhythmia, atrial fibrillation, atrioventricular dissociation (transient), bigeminy, bradycardia, cardiac dilatation, chest pain, decreased blood pressure, ECG changes (prolonged P wave, shortened PR segment, R on T phenomenon, shortened RT duration, prolonged QT interval, widening of QRS Complex, flattened T wave, repolarization abnormalities, ST segment elevation, retrograde conduction), ectopic beats (atrial), extrasystoles (nodal, ventricular, supraventricular), flushing, increased blood pressure, left heart failure, myocardial infarction, nodal arrhythmia (no P wave on ECG), palpitations, sinus tachycardia, supraventricular tachycardia (including junctional tachycardia), tachycardia, trigeminy, ventricular arrhythmia, ventricular fibrillation, ventricular flutter, ventricular premature contractions, ventricular tachycardia, weak pulse (or impalpable peripheral pulses)

Central nervous system: Abnormal electroencephalogram (runs of alpha waves, increase in photic stimulation, and signs of drowsiness), agitation (children), amnesia, anxiety, ataxia, behavioral changes, coma, confusion, decreased deep tendon reflex, delirium, dizziness, drowsiness, dysarthria, dysmetria, emotional disturbance, excitement, feeling hot, hallucination (visual or aural), headache, hyperpyrexia, hyperreflexia, hypertonia, insomnia, intoxicated feeling, irritability (children), lack of concentration, lethargy (children), mania, myoclonus, neurologic abnormality, nocturnal enuresis, opisthotonus, paranoia, positive Babinski sign, restlessness, seizure (generally tonic-clonic), stupor, vertigo

Dermatologic: Anhidrosis, cold skin, dermatitis, dry and hot skin, erythematous rash, hyperhidrosis, macular eruption, maculopapular rash, papular rash, scarlatiniform rash, skin rash

Endocrine & metabolic: Dehydration, hyperglycemia, hypoglycemia, hypokalemia, hyponatremia, increased thirst, loss of libido

Gastrointestinal: Abdominal and bladder distension, abdominal pain, constipation, delayed gastric emptying, diminished bowel sounds, dry mucous membranes, dysphagia, malabsorption, nausea, oral lesion, paralytic ileus, salivation, vomiting, xerostomia

Genitourinary: Difficulty in micturition, impotence, urinary hesitancy, urinary retention, urinary urgency

Hematologic & oncologic: Decreased hemoglobin, increased hemoglobin, increased red blood cell count, leukocytosis, petechiae

Hypersensitivity: Hypersensitivity reaction

Local: Injection site reaction

Neuromuscular & skeletal: Laryngospasm, muscle twitching, weakness

Ophthalmic: Abnormal eye movements (cyclophoria and heterophoria), angle-closure glaucoma (acute), blepharitis, blindness, blurred vision, conjunctivitis, crusted of eyelid, cycloplegia, decreased accommodation, decreased visual acuity, dry eye syndrome, eye irritation, keratoconjunctivitis sicca, lacrimation, mydriasis, photophobia, strabismus

Renal: Increased blood urea nitrogen

Respiratory: Bradypnea, changes in respiration (labored respiration), cyanosis, dyspnea, laryngitis, pulmonary edema, respiratory failure, stridor (inspiratory), tachypnea

Miscellaneous: Failure to thrive, fever (secondary to decreased sweat gland activity), swelling (children), tongue biting

General Dosage Range

IM; SubQ:

Children <5 kg: 0.02 mg/kg/dose every 4 to 6 hours as needed

Children ≥5 kg: 0.01 to 0.02 mg/kg/dose every 4 to 6 hours as needed (maximum: 0.4 mg/dose; minimum: 0.1 mg/dose)

Adults: 0.4 to 0.6 mg every 4 to 6 hours as needed

IM (AtroPen):

Children <6.8 kg: 0.25 mg/dose (maximum: 3 doses)

Children 6.8 to 18 kg: 0.5 mg/dose (maximum: 3 doses)

Children 18 to 41 kg: 1 mg/dose (maximum: 3 doses)

Children >41 kg and Adults: 2 mg/dose (maximum: 3 doses)

IV: *Children and Adults:* Dosage varies greatly depending on indication

Mechanism of Action Blocks the action of acetylcholine at parasympathetic sites in smooth muscle, secretory glands, and the CNS; increases cardiac output, dries secretions. Atropine reverses the muscarinic effects of cholinergic poisoning due to agents with acetylcholinesterase inhibitor activity by acting as a competitive antagonist of acetylcholine at muscarinic receptors. The primary goal in cholinergic poisonings is reversal of bronchorrhea and bronchoconstriction. Atropine has no effect on the nicotinic receptors responsible for muscle weakness, fasciculations, and paralysis.

Pharmacodynamics/Kinetics

Onset of Action

Inhibition of salivation: IM: Within 30 minutes; maximum effect: 30 to 60 minutes (Mirakhur 1980; Volz-Zang 1995)

Increased heart rate:

IM: Within 15 to 30 minutes (Kentala 1990; Volz-Zang 1995); maximum effect: 45 to 60 minutes (Mirakhur 1980; Volz-Zang 1995)

IV: Immediate; maximum effect: 0.7 to 4 minutes (Lonnerholm 1975; Santini 1999)

Duration of Action Inhibition of salivation: IM: ≤4 hours

Half-life Elimination Children <2 years: 6.9 ± 3 hours; Children >2 years: 2.5 ± 1.2 hours; Adults: 3 ± 0.9 hours; Elderly 65 to 75 years of age: 10 ± 7.3 hours

Time to Peak IM: Auto-injector: 3 minutes

Pregnancy Risk Factor B/C (manufacturer specific)

Pregnancy Considerations Adverse events were not observed in animal reproduction studies (studies not conducted by all manufacturers). Atropine has been found to cross the human placenta (Kanto 1981). In general, medications used as antidotes should take into consideration the health and prognosis of the mother; antidotes should be administered to pregnant women if there is a clear indication for use and should not be withheld because of fears of teratogenicity (Bailey 2003). Medications used for the treatment of cardiac arrest in pregnancy are the same as in the non-pregnant woman. Doses and indications should follow current Advanced Cardiovascular Life Support guidelines. Appropriate medications should not be withheld due to concerns of fetal teratogenicity (Jeejeebhoy [AHA] 2015).

Prescribing and Access Restrictions The AtroPen formulation is available for use primarily by the Department of Defense.

Atropine (Ophthalmic) (A troe peen)

Brand Names: US Atropine-Care [DSC]; Isopto Atropine [DSC]

Brand Names: Canada Dioptic's Atropine Solution; Isopto Atropine

Pharmacologic Category Anticholinergic Agent, Ophthalmic; Ophthalmic Agent, Mydriatic

Use

Amblyopia, healthy eye penalization (solution only): Penalization of the healthy eye in the treatment of amblyopia.

Mydriasis, Cycloplegia: Produce mydriasis and/or cycloplegia.

Local Anesthetic/Vasoconstrictor Precautions No information available to require special precautions

Effects on Dental Treatment Key adverse event(s) related to dental treatment: Xerostomia and changes in salivation (normal salivary flow resumes upon discontinuation), dry throat, and nasal dryness

Effects on Bleeding No information available to require special precautions

Adverse Reactions Frequency not defined. Severity and frequency of adverse reactions are dose related.

Cardiovascular: Delirium, flushing, hypotension, increased blood pressure

Central nervous system: Irritability, restlessness

Dermatologic: Contact dermatitis, xeroderma

Gastrointestinal: Xerostomia

Ophthalmic: Blurred vision, decreased lacrimation, eye irritation, eyelid edema, eye pain, papillary conjunctivitis, photophobia, stinging of eyes, superficial keratitis

Respiratory: Dry throat, respiratory depression

General Dosage Range

Ophthalmic:

Ointment: *Infants, Children, Adolescents, and Adults:* Apply a small amount in the conjunctival sac 1 to 2 times daily.

Solution:

Infants ≥3 months and Children <3 years: Instill 1 drop in the conjunctiva prior to maximal dilation time; maximum dose: 1 drop per eye per day.

Children ≥3 years, Adolescents, and Adults: Instill 1 drop in the conjunctiva prior to maximal dilation time; may repeat up to twice daily as needed.

Mechanism of Action Blocks the action of acetylcholine that induces mydriasis and allows the radial pupillary dilator muscle to contract resulting in dilation of the pupil; induces cycloplegia by paralysis of the ciliary muscle.

Pharmacodynamics/Kinetics

Onset of Action Ophthalmic solution: Within minutes; maximum effect: within hours

Duration of Action Multiple days

Half-life Elimination 2.5 ± 0.8 hours

Time to Peak 28 ± 27 minutes (range: 3 to 60 minutes)

Pregnancy Considerations Atropine crosses the placenta following systemic maternal use (Shutt 1979). Atropine is systemically available following ophthalmic administration. If ophthalmic agents are needed during pregnancy, the minimum effective dose should be used in combination with punctual occlusion to decrease potential exposure to the fetus (Samples 1988).

Attapulgite (at a PULL gite)

Related Information

Ulcerative, Erosive, and Painful Oral Mucosal Disorders *on page 1853*

Brand Names: Canada Kaopectate Children's [OTC]; Kaopectate Extra Strength [OTC]; Kaopectate [OTC]

Pharmacologic Category Antidiarrheal

Use Note: Not approved in the US

Symptomatic treatment of diarrhea and cramps

Local Anesthetic/Vasoconstrictor Precautions No information available to require special precautions

Effects on Dental Treatment No significant effects or complications reported

Effects on Bleeding No information available to require special precautions

General Dosage Range Oral:

Children 3-6 years: 300 mg/dose (maximum dose: 2100 mg/day)

Children 6-12 years: 600-750 mg/dose (maximum dose: 4500 mg/day)

Children >12 years and Adults: 1200-1500 mg/dose (maximum dose: 8400 mg/day)

Mechanism of Action Nonselectively absorbs excess intestinal fluid, thereby reducing stool liquidity. May interfere with absorption of nutrients and other drugs as well.

Product Availability Not available in the US

Avanafil (a VAN a fil)

Brand Names: US Stendra

Pharmacologic Category Phosphodiesterase-5 Enzyme Inhibitor

Use Erectile dysfunction: Treatment of erectile dysfunction

Local Anesthetic/Vasoconstrictor Precautions No information available to require special precautions

Effects on Dental Treatment No significant effects or complications reported

Effects on Bleeding No information available to require special precautions

Adverse Reactions

>10%: Central nervous system: Headache (1% to 12%)

2% to 10%:

Cardiovascular: Flushing (3% to 10%), ECG abnormality (1% to 3%)

Central nervous system: Dizziness (1% to 2%)

Gastrointestinal: Viral gastroenteritis (≤2%)

Neuromuscular & skeletal: Back pain (1% to 3%)

Respiratory: Nasopharyngitis (1% to 5%), nasal congestion (1% to 3%), upper respiratory tract infection (1% to 3%)

<2%, postmarketing, and/or case reports: Abdominal distress, angina pectoris, anterior ischemic optic neuropathy (nonarteritic), arthralgia, balanitis, bronchitis, constipation, cough, deep vein thrombosis, depression, diarrhea, drowsiness, dyspepsia, dyspnea on exertion, epistaxis, fatigue, gastritis, gastroesophageal reflux disease, hearing loss, hematuria, hyperglycemia, hypertension, hypoglycemia, hypotension, increased serum ALT, influenza, insomnia, limb pain, muscle spasm, musculoskeletal pain, myalgia, nausea, nephrolithiasis, oropharyngeal pain, palpitations, peripheral edema, pollakiuria, priapism, pruritus, sinus congestion, sinusitis, skin rash, tinnitus, urinary tract infection, vertigo, vision color changes, vision loss (temporary or permanent), vomiting, wheezing

General Dosage Range Dosage adjustment recommended in patients on concomitant therapy.

Oral: *Adults:* Initial: 100 mg taken ~15 minutes prior to sexual activity; taken as one single dose and not more than once daily; dose may be increased to 200 mg ~15 minutes prior to sexual activity or decreased to 50 mg ~30 minutes prior to sexual activity using the lowest dose that provides benefit; maximum: 200 mg daily

Mechanism of Action Does not directly cause penile erections, but affects the response to sexual stimulation. The physiologic mechanism of erection of the penis involves release of nitric oxide (NO) in the corpus cavernosum during sexual stimulation. NO then activates the enzyme guanylate cyclase, which results in increased levels of cyclic guanosine monophosphate (cGMP), producing smooth muscle relaxation and inflow of blood to the corpus cavernosum. Avanafil enhances the effect of NO by inhibiting phosphodiesterase type 5 (PDE-5), which is responsible for degradation of cGMP in the corpus cavernosum; when sexual stimulation causes local release of NO, inhibition of PDE-5 by avanafil causes increased levels of cGMP in the corpus cavernosum, resulting in smooth muscle relaxation and inflow of blood to the corpus cavernosum; at recommended doses, it has no effect in the absence of sexual stimulation.

Pharmacodynamics/Kinetics

Half-life Elimination Terminal: ~5 hours

Time to Peak Plasma: 30 to 45 minutes (fasting); 1.12 to 1.25 hours (high-fat meal)

Pregnancy Risk Factor C

Pregnancy Considerations Based on data from animal reproduction studies, avanafil is predicted to have a low risk for major developmental abnormalities in humans. This product is not indicated for use in women.

Axitinib (ax I ti nib)

Brand Names: US Inlyta

Brand Names: Canada Inlyta

Pharmacologic Category Antineoplastic Agent, Tyrosine Kinase Inhibitor; Antineoplastic Agent, Vascular Endothelial Growth Factor (VEGF) Inhibitor

Use Renal cell carcinoma, advanced: Treatment of advanced renal cell carcinoma after failure of one prior systemic therapy.

Local Anesthetic/Vasoconstrictor Precautions Significant hypertension can occur with the use of this drug; monitor for hypertension prior to using local anesthetic with vasoconstrictor; medical consult if necessary

Effects on Dental Treatment Key adverse event(s) related to dental treatment: Oral mucosal inflammation, stomatitis, and taste alteration have been reported

Effects on Bleeding Chemotherapy may result in significant myelosuppression, potentially including significant reduction in platelet counts and altered hemostasis. Hemorrhagic events have been reported. In patients who are under active treatment with axitinib, medical consult is suggested.

Adverse Reactions

>10%:

Cardiovascular: Hypertension (40%; grades 3/4: 16%)

Central nervous system: Fatigue (39%), voice disorder (31%), headache (14%)

Dermatologic: Palmar-plantar erythrodysesthesia (27%; grades 3/4: 5%), skin rash (13%; grades 3/4: <1%)

Endocrine & metabolic: Decreased serum bicarbonate (44%), hypocalcemia (39%), hyperglycemia (28%), weight loss (25%), hypothyroidism (19%; grades 3/4: <1%), hypernatremia (17%), hyperkalemia (15%), hypoalbuminemia (15%), hyponatremia (13%), hypophosphatemia (13%), hypoglycemia (11%)

Gastrointestinal: Diarrhea (55%; grades 3/4: 11%), decreased appetite (34%), nausea (32%; grades 3/4: 3%), increased serum lipase (3% to 27%), increased serum amylase (25%), vomiting (24%; grades 3/4: 3%), constipation (20%), mucosal inflammation (15%), stomatitis (15%), abdominal pain (8% to 14%), dysgeusia (11%)

Genitourinary: Proteinuria (11%; grade 3: 3%)

Hematologic and oncologic: Anemia (4% to 35%; grades 3/4: <1%), lymphocytopenia (33%; grades 3/4: 3%), hemorrhage (16%; grades 3/4 1%), thrombocytopenia (15%; grades 3/4: <1%), leukopenia (11%)

Hepatic: Increased serum alkaline phosphatase (30%), increased serum ALT (22%; grades 3/4: <1%), increased serum AST (20%; grades 3/4: <1%)

Neuromuscular & skeletal: Weakness (21%), arthralgia (15%), limb pain (13%)

Renal: Increased serum creatinine (55%)

Respiratory: Cough (15%), dyspnea (15%)

1% to 10%:

Cardiovascular: Venous thrombosis (grades 3/4: 3%), arterial thrombosis (2%; grade 3/4: 1%), pulmonary embolism (2%) deep vein thrombosis (1%), transient ischemic attack (1%), retinal vein occlusion (≤1%), retinal thrombosis (≤1%)

Central nervous system: Dizziness (9%)

Dermatologic: Xeroderma (10%), pruritus (7%), alopecia (4%), erythema (2%)

Endocrine & metabolic: Dehydration (6%), hyperthyroidism (1%)

Gastrointestinal: Dyspepsia (10%), hemorrhoids (4%), gastrointestinal fistula (1%), gastrointestinal perforation (≤1%)

Genitourinary: Hematuria (3%)

Hematologic and Oncologic: Increased hemoglobin (9%), rectal hemorrhage (2%), polycythemia (1%)

Neuromuscular & skeletal: Myalgia (7%)

Otic: Tinnitus (3%)

Respiratory: Epistaxis (6%), hemoptysis (2%)

<1%, postmarketing, and/or case reports: Cardiac failure, cerebral hemorrhage, cerebrovascular accident, fever, hypertensive crisis, neutropenia, reversible posterior leukoencephalopathy syndrome

General Dosage Range Dosage adjustment recommended in patients with hepatic impairment, on concomitant therapy, or who develop toxicities.

Oral: *Adults:* 5 mg every 12 hours; maximum: 10 mg every 12 hours

Mechanism of Action Axitinib is a selective second generation tyrosine kinase inhibitor which blocks angiogenesis and tumor growth by inhibiting vascular endothelial growth factor receptors (VEGFR-1, VEGFR-2, and VEGFR-3).

Pharmacodynamics/Kinetics

Half-life Elimination 2.5 to 6.1 hours

Time to Peak 2.5 to 4 hours

Pregnancy Risk Factor D

Pregnancy Considerations Teratogenic, embryotoxic, and fetotoxic events were observed in animal reproduction studies when administered in doses less than the normal human dose. Based on its mechanism of action and because axitinib inhibits angiogenesis (a critical component of fetal development), adverse effects on pregnancy would be expected. Women of childbearing potential should be advised to avoid pregnancy during therapy.

Prescribing and Access Restrictions Available from select specialty pharmacies. Further information may be obtained at 877-744-5675 or www.inlytahcp.com.

AzaCITIDine (ay za SYE ti deen)

Brand Names: US Vidaza

Brand Names: Canada Vidaza

Pharmacologic Category Antineoplastic Agent, Antimetabolite; Antineoplastic Agent, DNA Methylation Inhibitor

Use Myelodysplastic syndromes: Treatment of myelodysplastic syndromes (MDS) in patients with the following French-American-British (FAB) classification subtypes: Refractory anemia or refractory anemia with ringed sideroblasts (if accompanied by neutropenia or thrombocytopenia or requiring transfusions), refractory anemia with excess blasts, refractory anemia with excess blasts in transformation, and chronic myelomonocytic leukemia.

Local Anesthetic/Vasoconstrictor Precautions No information available to require special precautions

Effects on Dental Treatment Key adverse event(s) related to dental treatment: Mucositis, gingival bleeding, oral mucosal petechiae, stomatitis, oral hemorrhage, and tongue ulceration.

Effects on Bleeding Gingival bleeding is reported in 10% of patients. Thrombocytopenia is reported in 66% to 70% of patients receiving azacitidine subcutaneously.

Adverse Reactions

>10%:

Cardiovascular: Peripheral edema (7% to 19%), chest pain (16%)

Central nervous system: Fatigue (13% to 36%), rigors (26%), headache (22%), dizziness (19%), anxiety (5% to 13%), depression (12%), malaise (11%), pain (11%), insomnia (9% to 11%)

Dermatologic: Erythema (7% to 17%), pallor (16%), skin lesion (15%), skin rash (10% to 14%), pruritus (12%), diaphoresis (11%)

Endocrine & metabolic: Weight loss (≤16%), pitting edema (15%), hypokalemia (6% to 13%)

Gastrointestinal: Nausea (48% to 71%), vomiting (27% to 54%), constipation (34% to 50%), diarrhea (36%), anorexia (13% to 21%), abdominal pain (11% to 16%), abdominal tenderness (12%)

Hematologic & oncologic: Thrombocytopenia (66% to 70%; grades 3/4: 58%), anemia (51% to 70%; grades 3/4: 14%), neutropenia (32% to 66%; grades 3/4: 61%), leukopenia (18% to 48%; grades 3/4: 15%), bruise (19% to 31%), petechia (11% to 24%), febrile neutropenia (14% to 16%; grades 3/4: 13%), bone marrow depression (nadir: days 10 to 17; recovery: days 28 to 31)

Local: Injection site reactions (14% to 29%): Erythema (35% to 43%; more common with IV administration), pain (19% to 23%; more common with IV administration), bruising (5% to 14%)

Neuromuscular & skeletal: Weakness (29%), arthralgia (22%), limb pain (20%), back pain (19%), myalgia (16%)

Respiratory: Cough (11% to 30%), dyspnea (5% to 29%), pharyngitis (20%), epistaxis (16%), nasopharyngitis (15%), upper respiratory infection (9% to 13%), pneumonia (11%), rales (9% to 11%)

Miscellaneous: Fever (30% to 52%)

5% to 10%:

Cardiovascular: Heart murmur (10%), tachycardia (9%), hypertension (≤9%), hypotension (7%), syncope (6%), chest wall pain (5%)

Central nervous system: Lethargy (7% to 8%), hypoesthesia (5%), postoperative pain (5%)

Dermatologic: Night sweats (9%), cellulitis (8%), rash at injection site (6%), urticaria (6%), skin nodules (5%), xeroderma (5%)

Gastrointestinal: Gingival hemorrhage (10%), stomatitis (8%), hemorrhoids (7%), dyspepsia (6% to 7%), abdominal distention (6%), loose stools (6%), dysphagia (5%), tongue ulcer (5%)

Genitourinary: Urinary tract infection (8% to 9%), dysuria (8%), hematuria (≤6%)

Hematologic & oncologic: Lymphadenopathy (10%), hematoma (9%), oral mucosal petechiae (8%), postprocedural hemorrhage (6%), oral hemorrhage (5%)

Hypersensitivity: Transfusion reaction (7%)

Infection: Herpes simplex infection (9%)

Local: Itching at injection site (7%), hematoma at injection site (6%), induration at injection site (5%), injection site granuloma (5%), skin discoloration at injection site (5%), swelling at injection site (5%)

Neuromuscular & skeletal: Muscle cramps (6%)

Respiratory: Rhinorrhea (10%), wheezing (9%), abnormal breath sounds (8%), nasal congestion (6%), pharyngolaryngeal pain (6%), pleural effusion (6%), post nasal drip (6%), rhinitis (6%), rhonchi (6%), atelectasis (5%), sinusitis (5%)

Miscellaneous: Lymphadenopathy (10%), herpes simplex (9%), night sweats (9%), transfusion reaction (7%), mouth hemorrhage (5%)

<5%, postmarketing, and/or case reports: Abscess (limb, perirectal), aggravated bone pain, agranulocytosis, anaphylactic shock, atrial fibrillation, azotemia, bacterial infection, blastomycosis, bone marrow failure, cardiac failure, catheter site hemorrhage, cellulitis, cerebral hemorrhage, cholecystectomy, cholecystitis, congestive cardiomyopathy, decreased serum bicarbonate, dehydration, diverticulitis, fibrosis (interstitial and alveolar), gastrointestinal hemorrhage, glycosuria, hemophthalmos, hemoptysis, hepatic coma, hypersensitivity reaction, hypophosphatemia, increased serum creatinine, injection site infection, interstitial pulmonary disease, intracranial hemorrhage, leukemia cutis, melena, necrotizing fasciitis, neutropenic sepsis, orthostatic hypotension, pancytopenia, pneumonitis, polyuria, pulmonary infiltrates, pyoderma gangrenosum, renal failure, renal tubular acidosis, respiratory distress, seizure, sepsis, sepsis syndrome, septic shock, splenomegaly, Sweet's

syndrome, tissue necrosis at injection site, toxoplasmosis, tumor lysis syndrome

General Dosage Range Dosage adjustment recommended in patients who develop toxicities

IV, SubQ: *Adults:* 75 to 100 mg/m^2/day for 7 days every 4 weeks

Mechanism of Action Antineoplastic effects may be a result of azacitidine's ability to promote hypomethylation of DNA, restoring normal gene differentiation and proliferation. Azacitidine also exerts direct toxicity to abnormal hematopoietic cells in the bone marrow.

Pharmacodynamics/Kinetics

Half-life Elimination IV, SubQ: ~4 hours

Time to Peak SubQ: 30 minutes

Pregnancy Considerations Adverse events were observed in animal reproduction studies. Based on its mechanism of action, azacitidine may cause fetal harm if administered during pregnancy. Women of childbearing potential should be advised to avoid pregnancy during treatment; verify pregnancy status prior to therapy initiation. In addition, males should be advised to avoid fathering a child while on azacitidine therapy and should use effective contraception during therapy.

AzaTHIOprine (ay za THYE oh preen)

Brand Names: US Azasan; Imuran

Brand Names: Canada Apo-Azathioprine; Imuran; Mylan-Azathioprine; Teva-Azathioprine

Pharmacologic Category Immunosuppressant Agent

Use

Renal transplantation: Adjunctive therapy in prevention of rejection of kidney transplants

Rheumatoid arthritis: Treatment of active rheumatoid arthritis (RA), to reduce signs and symptoms

Local Anesthetic/Vasoconstrictor Precautions No information available to require special precautions

Effects on Dental Treatment No significant effects or complications reported

Effects on Bleeding Thrombocytopenia and bleeding may occur.

Adverse Reactions Frequency not always defined; dependent upon dose, duration, indication, and concomitant therapy.

Central nervous system: Malaise

Gastrointestinal: Nausea and vomiting (rheumatoid arthritis: 12%), diarrhea

Hematologic & oncologic: Leukopenia (renal transplant: >50%; rheumatoid arthritis: 28%), neoplasia (renal transplant 3% [other than lymphoma], 0.5% [lymphoma]), thrombocytopenia

Hepatic: Hepatotoxicity, increased serum alkaline phosphatase, increased serum bilirubin, increased serum transaminases

Infection: Increased susceptibility to infection (renal transplant 20%; rheumatoid arthritis <1%; includes bacterial, fungal, protozoal, viral, opportunistic, and reactivation of latent infections)

Neuromuscular & skeletal: Myalgia

Miscellaneous: Fever

<1%, postmarketing and/or case reports: Abdominal pain, acute myelocytic leukemia, alopecia, anemia, arthralgia, bone marrow depression, hemorrhage, hepatic veno-occlusive disease, hepatosplenic T-cell lymphomas, hepatotoxicity (idiosyncratic) (Chalasani, 2014), hypersensitivity, hypotension, interstitial pneumonitis (reversible), JC virus infection, macrocytic anemia, malignant lymphoma, malignant neoplasm of skin, negative nitrogen balance, pancreatitis, pancytopenia, progressive multifocal leukoencephalopathy, skin rash, steatorrhea, Sweet's syndrome (acute febrile neutrophilic dermatosis)

General Dosage Range Dosage adjustment recommended in patients with renal impairment, on concomitant therapy, or who develop toxicities.

Oral, IV: *Adults:*

Renal transplantation: Initial: 3 to 5 mg/kg/day in 1 to 2 divided doses; Maintenance: 1 to 3 mg/kg/day in 1 to 2 divided doses

Rheumatoid arthritis: Initial: 1 mg/kg/day (50 to 100 mg) in 1 to 2 divided doses; Maintenance: 0.5 to 2.5 mg/kg/day in 1 to 2 divided doses

Mechanism of Action Azathioprine is an imidazolyl derivative of mercaptopurine; metabolites are incorporated into replicating DNA and halt replication; also block the pathway for purine synthesis (Taylor 2005). The 6-thioguanine nucleotide metabolites appear to mediate the majority of azathioprine's immunosuppressive and toxic effects.

Pharmacodynamics/Kinetics

Onset of Action Immune thrombocytopenia (oral): Initial response: 30 to 90 days; Peak response: 30 to 120 days (Neunert 2011)

Half-life Elimination Azathioprine and mercaptopurine: Variable: ~2 hours (Taylor 2005)

Time to Peak Oral: 1 to 2 hours (including metabolites)

Pregnancy Risk Factor D

Pregnancy Considerations Adverse events have been observed in animal reproduction studies. Azathioprine crosses the placenta in humans; congenital anomalies, immunosuppression, hematologic toxicities (lymphopenia, pancytopenia), and intrauterine growth retardation have been reported. Women of childbearing potential should avoid becoming pregnant during treatment.

Intrauterine growth retardation and preterm delivery are also reported in pregnancies following a kidney transplant. Stable immunosuppression is required in pregnant women who have had a kidney transplant and an increased risk of fetal malformations has not been observed with azathioprine; doses ≤2 mg/kg/day are recommended (Durst 2015; Hou 2013).

Although contraindicated by the manufacturer, available guidelines suggest that use of azathioprine is acceptable for the treatment of rheumatoid arthritis (Flint 2016). Azathioprine may also be used for the adjunctive treatment of lupus nephritis in pregnant women (Hahn 2012). Both guidelines recommend doses ≤2 mg/kg/day during pregnancy (Flint 2016; Hahn 2012). Agents other than azathioprine are recommended for the treatment of immune thrombocytopenia (Neunert 2011) and inflammatory bowel disease (van der Woude 2015) in pregnant women.

The National Transplantation Pregnancy Registry (NTPR) is a registry which follows pregnancies which occur in maternal transplant recipients or those fathered by male transplant recipients. The NTPR encourages reporting of pregnancies following solid organ transplant by contacting them at 877-955-6877 or NTPR@giftoflifeinstitute.org.

Azelaic Acid (a zeh LAY ik AS id)

Brand Names: US Azelex; Finacea

Brand Names: Canada Finacea

Pharmacologic Category Topical Skin Product, Acne

Use

Acne vulgaris (cream): Treatment of mild to moderate inflammatory acne vulgaris.

Guideline recommendations: The American Association of Dermatology (AAD) acne guidelines support azelaic acid use as an adjunctive treatment option and, in particular, recommend its use in the treatment of postinflammatory dyspigmentation (AAD [Zaenglein 2016]).

Rosacea (foam, gel): Treatment of inflammatory papules and pustules of mild to moderate rosacea.

Limitations of use: Efficacy for treatment of erythema in rosacea in the absence of papules and pustules has not been evaluated.

Local Anesthetic/Vasoconstrictor Precautions No information available to require special precautions

Effects on Dental Treatment No significant effects or complications reported

Effects on Bleeding No information available to require special precautions

Adverse Reactions

>10%: Dermatologic: Burning sensation of skin (≤16%), stinging of skin (≤16%), tingling of skin (≤16%)

1% to 10%:

Dermatologic: Pruritus (1% to 6%), erythema (≤2%), skin irritation (≤2%), acne (gel: ≤1%), contact dermatitis (≤1%), desquamation (≤1%), xeroderma (≤1%), xerosis (≤1%)

Local: Application site pain (6%), application site pruritus (3%)

<1%, postmarketing, and/or case reports: Angioedema, application site erythema, dermatitis, dyspnea, edema, exacerbation of asthma, exacerbation of herpes labialis, facial edema, hypersensitivity reaction, hypertrichosis, hypopigmentation, iridocyclitis, local dryness, skin depigmentation (small spots), skin rash, swelling of eye, urticaria, vitiligo, wheezing

General Dosage Range

Topical: *Children ≥12 years, Adolescents, and Adults:* Apply to the affected area(s) twice daily.

Mechanism of Action Azelaic acid is a dietary constituent normally found in whole grain cereals; can be formed endogenously. Exact mechanism is not known. *In vitro*, azelaic acid possesses antimicrobial activity against *Propionibacterium acnes* and *Staphylococcus epidermidis*. May decrease microcomedo formation.

Pharmacodynamics/Kinetics

Onset of Action Cream: Within 4 weeks

Half-life Elimination Topical: Healthy subjects: 12 hours

Pregnancy Risk Factor B

Pregnancy Considerations Adverse events have been observed in animal reproduction studies following oral administration. The amount of azelaic acid available systemically following topical administration is minimal (<4%).

Azelastine (Nasal) (a ZEL as teen)

Brand Names: US Astelin [DSC]; Astepro

Brand Names: Canada Astelin

Pharmacologic Category Histamine H_1 Antagonist; Histamine H_1 Antagonist, Second Generation

Use

Perennial allergic rhinitis (Astepro 0.1% and 0.15% solution only): Relief of symptoms of perennial allergic rhinitis in adults and pediatric patients ≥6 months.

Seasonal allergic rhinitis: Relief of symptoms of seasonal allergic rhinitis in adults and pediatric patients ≥2 years (Astepro 0.1% and 0.15% solution) and ≥5 years (azelastine [generic] 0.1% solution).

Vasomotor rhinitis (azelastine [generic] 0.1% solution): Relief of symptoms of vasomotor rhinitis in adults and adolescents ≥12 years.

Local Anesthetic/Vasoconstrictor Precautions No information available to require special precautions

Effects on Dental Treatment Key adverse event(s) related to dental treatment: Bitter taste, xerostomia (normal salivary flow resumes upon discontinuation), aphthous stomatitis, glossitis, and burning sensation in throat. Chronic use of antihistamines will inhibit salivary flow, particularly in elderly patients. May contribute to periodontal disease and oral discomfort.

Effects on Bleeding No information available to require special precautions

Adverse Reactions Adverse reactions may be dose-, indication-, or product-dependent:

>10%:

Central nervous system: Bitter taste (4% to 20%), headache (1% to 15%), drowsiness (≤12%)

Infection: Cold symptoms (children ≤17%)

Respiratory: Rhinitis (exacerbation; ≤17%), cough (children: 11%; infants and children: ≥2%)

2% to 10%:

Central nervous system: Dysesthesia (8%), dizziness (2%), fatigue (2%)

Dermatologic: Contact dermatitis

Endocrine & metabolic: Weight gain (2%)

Gastrointestinal: Dysgeusia (children: 2% to 4%), nausea (3%), xerostomia (3%), vomiting

Infection: Upper respiratory tract infection (children: ≥2% to 3%)

Neuromuscular & skeletal: Myalgia (≤2%)

Ophthalmic: Conjunctivitis (<2% to 5%)

Otic: Otitis media (infants & children: ≥2%)

Respiratory: Epistaxis (2% to 7%), asthma (5%), sinusitis (3% to >5%), burning sensation of the nose (4%), pharyngitis (4%), nasal discomfort (≤4%), sneezing (1% to 3%), sore nose (infants and children: ≥2%), nasal mucosa ulcer (≤2%), pharyngolaryngeal pain

Miscellaneous: Fever

<2%:

Cardiovascular: Flushing, hypertension, tachycardia

Central nervous system: Abnormality in thinking, anxiety, depersonalization, depression, hypoesthesia, malaise, nervousness, sleep disorder, vertigo

Dermatologic: Eczema, folliculitis, furunculosis

Endocrine & metabolic: Albuminuria, amenorrhea

Gastrointestinal: Abdominal pain, ageusia, aphthous stomatitis, constipation, diarrhea, gastroenteritis, glossitis, increased appetite, toothache

Genitourinary: Hematuria, mastalgia

Hepatic: Increased serum ALT

Hypersensitivity: Hypersensitivity reaction

Infection: Herpes simplex infection, viral infection

Neuromuscular & skeletal: Back pain, dislocation of temporomandibular joint, hyperkinesia, limb pain, rheumatoid arthritis

Ophthalmic: Eye pain, watery eyes

Renal: Polyuria

Respiratory: Bronchitis, bronchospasm, laryngitis, nasal congestion, paranasal sinus hypersecretion, paroxysmal nocturnal dyspnea, postnasal drip, sore throat

Miscellaneous: Laceration

<1%, postmarketing, and/or case reports: Altered sense of smell, anaphylactoid reaction, anosmia, application site irritation, atrial fibrillation, blurred vision, chest

pain, confusion, drug tolerance, dyspnea, facial edema, increased serum transaminases, insomnia, muscle spasm, nasal sores, palpitations, paresthesia, pruritus, skin rash, urinary retention, visual disturbance, xerophthalmia

General Dosage Range Intranasal:

Infants ≥6 months and Children <12 years: One spray in each nostril twice daily

Children ≥12 years, Adolescents, and Adults: One or two sprays in each nostril twice daily or two sprays in each nostril once daily

Mechanism of Action Competes with histamine for H_1-receptor sites on effector cells and inhibits the release of histamine and other mediators involved in the allergic response; when used intranasally, reduces hyper-reactivity of the airways; increases the motility of bronchial epithelial cilia, improving mucociliary transport

Pharmacodynamics/Kinetics

Onset of Action 30 minutes (Wallace 2008); maximum effect: 3 hours

Duration of Action 12 hours

Half-life Elimination Azelastine: 22 hours (0.1% solution), 25 hours (0.15% solution); Desmethylazelastine: 52 hours (0.1% solution), 57 hours (0.15% solution)

Time to Peak 2 to 3 hours (Azelastine [generic] 0.1% solution); 3 to 4 hours (Astepro)

Pregnancy Risk Factor C

Pregnancy Considerations Adverse events have been observed in some animal reproduction studies. Azelastine is systemically absorbed following nasal inhalation and may have side effects similar to other antihistamines. However, data related to the use of azelastine in pregnancy is limited; if treatment for rhinitis in a pregnant woman is needed, other agents are preferred (Wallace 2008).

Azilsartan (ay zil SAR tan)

Related Information

Cardiovascular Diseases *on page 1752*

Brand Names: US Edarbi

Brand Names: Canada Edarbi

Pharmacologic Category Angiotensin II Receptor Blocker; Antihypertensive

Use

Hypertension: Treatment of hypertension; may be used alone or in combination with other antihypertensives

Guideline recommendations:

Hypertension: The 2014 guideline for the management of high blood pressure in adults (Eighth Joint National Committee [JNC 8]) recommends initiation of pharmacologic treatment to lower blood pressure for the following patients:

- Patients ≥60 years of age with systolic blood pressure (SBP) ≥150 mm Hg or diastolic blood pressure (DBP) ≥90 mm Hg. Goal of therapy is SBP <150 mm Hg and DBP <90 mm Hg.
- Patients <60 years of age with SBP ≥140 mm Hg or DBP is ≥90 mm Hg. Goal of therapy is SBP <140 mm Hg and DBP <90 mm Hg.
- Patients ≥18 years of age with diabetes and SBP ≥140 mm Hg or DBP ≥90 mm Hg. Goal of therapy is SBP <140 mm Hg and DBP <90 mm Hg.
- Patients ≥18 years of age with chronic kidney disease (CKD) and SBP ≥140 mm Hg or DBP ≥90 mm Hg. Goal of therapy is SBP <140 mm Hg and DBP <90 mm Hg.

Chronic kidney disease (CKD) and hypertension: Regardless of race or diabetes status, the use of an ACE inhibitor (ACEI) or angiotensin receptor blocker (ARB) as initial therapy is recommended to improve kidney outcomes. In the general nonblack population (without CKD) including those with diabetes, initial antihypertensive treatment should consist of a thiazide-type diuretic, calcium channel blocker, ACEI, or ARB. In the general black population (without CKD) including those with diabetes, initial antihypertensive treatment should consist of a thiazide-type diuretic or a calcium channel blocker instead of an ACEI or ARB.

Coronary artery disease and hypertension: The American Heart Association, American College of Cardiology and American Society of Hypertension (AHA/ACC/ASH) 2015 scientific statement for the treatment of hypertension in patients with coronary artery disease (CAD) recommends the use of an ARB (or ACE inhibitor) as part of a regimen in patients with hypertension and chronic stable angina if there is prior MI, LV systolic dysfunction, diabetes mellitus, or CKD. A BP target of <140/90 mm Hg is reasonable for the secondary prevention of cardiovascular events. A lower target BP (<130/80 mm Hg) may be appropriate in some individuals with CAD, previous MI, stroke or transient ischemic attack, or CAD risk equivalents (AHA/ACC/ASH [Rosendorff 2015]).

Local Anesthetic/Vasoconstrictor Precautions No information available to require special precautions

Effects on Dental Treatment Key adverse event(s) related to dental treatment: Patients may experience orthostatic hypotension as they stand up after treatment; especially if lying in dental chair for extended periods of time. Use caution with sudden changes in position during and after dental treatment.

Effects on Bleeding No information available to require special precautions

Adverse Reactions Frequency not always defined.

Cardiovascular: Hypotension, orthostatic hypotension

Central nervous system: Dizziness, fatigue

Gastrointestinal: Diarrhea (2%), nausea

Hematologic & oncologic: Decreased hemoglobin, decreased hematocrit, decreased red blood cells, leukopenia (rare), thrombocytopenia (rare)

Neuromuscular & skeletal: Muscle spasm, weakness

Renal: Increased serum creatinine

Respiratory: Cough

<1%, postmarketing, and/or case reports: Angioedema, pruritus, skin rash

General Dosage Range Oral: *Adults:* 40-80 mg once daily

Mechanism of Action Angiotensin II (which is formed by enzymatic conversion from angiotensin I) is the primary pressor agent of the renin-angiotensin system. Effects of angiotensin II include vasoconstriction, stimulation of aldosterone synthesis/release, cardiac stimulation, and renal sodium reabsorption. Azilsartan inhibits angiotensin II's vasoconstrictor and aldosterone-secreting effects by selectively blocking the binding of angiotensin II to the AT_1 receptor in vascular smooth muscle and adrenal gland tissues (azilsartan has a stronger affinity for the AT_1 receptor than the AT_2 receptor). The action is independent of the angiotensin II synthesis pathways. Azilsartan does not inhibit ACE (kininase II), therefore it does not affect the response to bradykinin (the clinical relevance of this is unknown) and does not bind to or inhibit other receptors or ion channels of importance in cardiovascular regulation.

Pharmacodynamics/Kinetics

Half-life Elimination ~11 hours

Time to Peak Serum: 1.5-3 hours

Pregnancy Risk Factor D

Pregnancy Considerations [US Boxed Warning]: Drugs that act on the renin-angiotensin system can cause injury and death to the developing fetus. Discontinue as soon as possible once pregnancy is detected. The use of drugs which act on the renin-angiotensin system are associated with oligohydramnios. Oligohydramnios, due to decreased fetal renal function, may lead to fetal lung hypoplasia and skeletal malformations. Use is also associated with anuria, hypotension, renal failure, skull hypoplasia, and death in the fetus/neonate. The exposed fetus should be monitored for fetal growth, amniotic fluid volume, and organ formation. Infants exposed *in utero* should be monitored for hyperkalemia, hypotension, and oliguria (exchange transfusions or dialysis may be needed). These adverse events are generally associated with maternal use in the second and third trimesters.

Untreated chronic maternal hypertension is also associated with adverse events in the fetus, infant, and mother. The use of angiotensin II receptor blockers is not recommended to treat chronic uncomplicated hypertension in pregnant women and should generally be avoided in women of reproductive potential (ACOG, 2013). The Canadian labeling contraindicates use in pregnant women.

Azithromycin (Systemic) (az ith roe MYE sin)

Related Information

Antibiotic Prophylaxis *on page 1812*

Bacterial Infections *on page 1835*

Clinical Risk Related to Drugs Prolonging QT Interval *on page 1772*

Periodontal Diseases *on page 1844*

Sexually-Transmitted Diseases *on page 1804*

Related Sample Prescriptions

Bacterial Infections and Periodontal Diseases - Sample Prescriptions *on page 32*

Prevention of Endocarditis and to Reduce the Risk of Late Infections of Joint Prostheses - Sample Prescriptions *on page 37*

Sinus Infection Treatment - Sample Prescriptions *on page 38*

Brand Names: US Zithromax; Zithromax Tri-Pak; Zithromax Z-Pak; Zmax

Brand Names: Canada ACT-Azithromycin; Apo-Azithromycin; Apo-Azithromycin Z; Azithromycin for Injection; Azithromycin for Injection, USP; Dom-Azithromycin; GD-Azithromycin; Mylan-Azithromycin; Novo-Azithromycin; PHL-Azithromycin; PMS-Azithromycin; PRO-Azithromycine; Riva-Azithromycin; Sandoz-Azithromycin; Zithromax; Zithromax For Intravenous Injection; Zmax SR

Generic Availability (US) Yes

Pharmacologic Category Antibiotic, Macrolide

Dental Use Alternate oral antibiotic for prevention of infective endocarditis in individuals allergic to penicillins or ampicillin, when amoxicillin cannot be used; alternate antibiotic in the treatment of common orofacial infections caused by aerobic gram-positive cocci and susceptible anaerobes

Use

Oral, IV:

Acute bacterial exacerbations of chronic obstructive pulmonary disease: Treatment of acute bacterial exacerbations of chronic obstructive pulmonary disease (COPD) due to *Haemophilus influenzae, Moraxella catarrhalis*, or *Streptococcus pneumoniae*

Acute otitis media: Treatment of acute otitis media due to *H. influenzae, M. catarrhalis*, or *S. pneumoniae*

Bacterial sinusitis, acute: Treatment of acute bacterial sinusitis due to *H. influenzae, M. catarrhalis,* or *S. pneumoniae*

Chancroid: Treatment of genital ulcer disease (in men) due to *Haemophilus ducreyi* (chancroid)

***Mycobacterium avium* complex (MAC):** Prevention of MAC (alone or in combination with rifabutin) in patients with advanced HIV infection; treatment of disseminated MAC (in combination with ethambutol) in patients with advanced HIV infection

Pelvic inflammatory disease: Treatment of pelvic inflammatory disease (PID) due to *Chlamydia trachomatis, Neisseria gonorrhoeae*, or *Mycoplasma hominis*

Pharyngitis/tonsillitis: Treatment of pharyngitis/tonsillitis due to *Streptococcus pyogenes* as an alternative to first-line therapy

Pneumonia, community-acquired: Treatment of community-acquired pneumonia due to *Chlamydophila pneumoniae, H. influenzae, Legionella pneumophila, Moraxella catarrhalis, Mycoplasma pneumoniae*, or *S. pneumoniae*

Skin and skin structure infection, uncomplicated: Treatment of uncomplicated skin and skin structure infections due to *Staphylococcus aureus, S. pyogenes*, or *Streptococcus agalactiae*

Urethritis/cervicitis: Treatment of urethritis and cervicitis due to *C. trachomatis* or *N. gonorrhoeae*

Limitations of use (tablets, oral suspension, Zmax only): Not recommended for use in patients with moderate to severe pneumonia who are judged to be inappropriate for oral therapy with any of the following concomitant conditions: Cystic fibrosis, nosocomial infections, known or suspected bacteremia, hospitalized, elderly or debilitated or significant health problems that affect the ability to respond to illness (eg, immunodeficiency, functional asplenia)

Local Anesthetic/Vasoconstrictor Precautions Azithromycin is one of the drugs confirmed to prolong the QT interval and is accepted as having a risk of causing torsade de pointes. The risk of drug-induced torsade de pointes is extremely low when a single QT interval prolonging drug is prescribed. In terms of epinephrine, it is not known what effect vasoconstrictors in the local anesthetic regimen will have in patients with a known history of congenital prolonged QT interval or in patients taking any medication that prolongs the QT interval. Until more information is obtained, it is suggested that the clinician consult with the physician prior to the use of a vasoconstrictor in suspected patients, and that the vasoconstrictor (epinephrine, mepivacaine and levonordefrin [Carbocaine® 2% with Neo-Cobefrin®]) be used with caution. See Dental Comment.

Effects on Dental Treatment No significant effects or complications reported

Effects on Bleeding No information available to require special precautions

Adverse Reactions

>10%: Gastrointestinal: Loose stools (≤14%; single-dose regimens tend to be associated with increased

incidence), vomiting (children, single-dose regimens tend to be associated with increased incidence: 1% to 14%; adults: ≤2%; adults, single 2 g dose: 1% to 7%), diarrhea (2% to 9%; single-dose regimens 4% to 14%), nausea (≤7%; high single-dose regimens 4% to 18%)

1% to 10%:

Cardiovascular: Chest pain (≤1%), palpitations (≤1%)

Central nervous system: Dizziness (≤1%), drowsiness (≤1%), fatigue (≤1%), headache (≤1%), vertigo (≤1%)

Dermatologic: Skin rash (≤5%; single-dose regimens tend to be associated with increased incidence), dermatitis (children: ≤2%), pruritus (≤2%), skin photosensitivity (≤1%)

Endocrine & metabolic: Increased lactate dehydrogenase (1% to 3%), increased gamma-glutamyl transferase (1% to 2%), increased serum potassium (1% to 2%), decreased serum bicarbonate (adults: ≥1%), decreased serum glucose (adults: >1%)

Gastrointestinal: Abdominal pain (1% to 7%; single-dose regimens tend to be associated with increased incidence), anorexia (≤2%), dysgeusia (≤1%), dyspepsia (≤1%), flatulence (≤1%), gastritis (≤1%), melena (adults, multiple-dose regimens: ≤1%), mucositis (≤1%), oral candidiasis (≤1%)

Genitourinary: Vaginitis (≤3%), genital candidiasis (adults, multiple-dose regimens: ≤1%)

Hematologic & oncologic: Decrease in absolute neutrophil count (children: 15% to 16%; 500 to 1500 cells/mm^3), decreased hematocrit (adults: >1%), decreased hemoglobin (adults: >1%), increased neutrophils (adults: >1%), thrombocythemia (adults: >1%), change in neutrophil count (children: ≥1%), eosinophilia (≥1%), lymphocytopenia (≥1%)

Hepatic: Increased serum ALT (≤6%), increased serum AST (≤6%), increased serum bilirubin (≤3%), cholestatic jaundice (≤1%)

Local (adults with IV administration): Pain at injection site (7%), local inflammation (3%)

Neuromuscular & skeletal: Increased creatine phosphokinase (1% to 2%)

Renal: Increased serum creatinine (≤6%), increased blood urea nitrogen (≤1%), nephritis (adults, multiple-dose regimens: ≤1%)

Respiratory: Bronchospasm (≤1%)

Miscellaneous: Fever (children: (≤2%)

<1%, postmarketing, and/or case reports: Abnormal stools, acute renal failure, ageusia, aggressive behavior, agitation, alteration in sodium, altered sense of smell, altered serum glucose, anaphylaxis, anemia, angioedema, anosmia, anxiety, arthralgia, asthma, basophilia, bronchitis, cardiac arrhythmia, change in serum potassium, chills, *Clostridium difficile* associated diarrhea, conjunctivitis (children), constipation, convulsions, cough, deafness, decreased serum potassium, decreased serum sodium, diaphoresis, DRESS syndrome, dyspnea, dysuria, eczema, edema, emotional lability, enteritis, erythema multiforme, exacerbation of myasthenia gravis, facial edema, flu-like symptoms, fungal dermatitis, fungal infection, gastrointestinal disease, hearing loss, hepatic failure, hepatic insufficiency, hepatic necrosis, hepatitis, hepatotoxicity (idiosyncratic) (Chalasani 2014), hostility, hyperactivity, hyperkinesia, hypersensitivity reaction, hypotension, increased monocytes, increased serum alkaline phosphatase, increased serum bicarbonate, increased serum glucose, increased serum phosphate, interstitial nephritis, insomnia, irritability, jaundice, Lambert-Eaton syndrome, leukopenia, maculopapular rash, malaise, nervousness, neutropenia, otitis media, pain, pancreatitis, paresthesia, pharyngitis, pleural effusion, prolonged Q-T interval on ECG, pseudomembranous colitis, pyloric stenosis, pyloric stenosis (infantile hypertrophic), rhinitis, seizure, Stevens-Johnson syndrome, syncope, thrombocytopenia, tinnitus, tongue discoloration, torsades de pointes toxic epidermal necrolysis, urticaria, ventricular tachycardia, vesiculobullous dermatitis, weakness

Dental Usual Dosage

Prophylaxis against infective endocarditis (off-label use): Oral:

Children: 15 mg/kg 30-60 minutes before procedure (maximum: 500 mg). **Note:** American Heart Association (AHA) guidelines now recommend prophylaxis only in patients undergoing invasive procedures and in whom underlying cardiac conditions may predispose to a higher risk of adverse outcomes should infection occur. As of April 2007, routine prophylaxis for GI/GU procedures is no longer recommended by the AHA.

Adolescents ≥16 years and Adults: 500 mg 30-60 minutes prior to the procedure. **Note:** American Heart Association (AHA) guidelines now recommend prophylaxis only in patients undergoing invasive procedures and in whom underlying cardiac conditions may predispose to a higher risk of adverse outcomes should infection occur. As of April 2007, routine prophylaxis for GI/GU procedures is no longer recommended by the AHA.

Bacterial sinusitis: Oral:

Children ≥6 months: 10 mg/kg once daily for 3 days (maximum: 500 mg/day)

Adolescents ≥16 years and Adults: 500 mg/day for a total of 3 days

Extended release suspension (Zmax): 2 g as a single dose

Orofacial infections: Adolescents ≥16 years and Adults: Oral: 500 mg/day, then 250 mg days 2-5

Treatment of periodontal disease: 500 mg once daily for 4-7 days

Dosing

Adult & Geriatric Note: Extended release suspension (Zmax) is not interchangeable with immediate release formulations. Use should be limited to approved indications. All doses are expressed as immediate release azithromycin unless otherwise specified

Acne vulgaris (off-label use): Oral: Dosing regimens used in clinical trials have varied greatly. All trials used pulse-dosing regimens; regimens included: 500 mg once daily for 4 consecutive days per month for 3 consecutive months (Babaeinejad 2011; Parsad 2001) **or** 500 mg once daily for 3 days in the first week, followed by 500 mg once weekly until week 10 (Maleszka 2011) **or** 500 mg once daily for 3 consecutive days each week in month 1, followed by 500 mg once daily for 2 consecutive days each week in month 2, then 500 mg once daily for 1 day each week in month 3 (Kus 2005). The shortest possible duration should be used to minimize development of bacterial resistance; re-evaluate at 3 to 4 months (AAD [Zaenglein 2016]).

Babesiosis (off-label use): Oral: 500 to 1,000 mg on day 1, followed by 250 mg once daily for 7 to 10 days with atovaquone; higher doses may be required in immunocompromised patients (600 to 1,000 mg daily). **Note:** Relapsing infection may require at least

6 weeks of therapy (Krause 2000; Vannier 2012; IDSA [Wormser 2006]).

Bacterial sinusitis, acute: Oral: 500 mg daily for a total of 3 days

Extended release suspension (Zmax): 2 g as a single dose

Bronchiolitis obliterans syndrome (off-label use): Oral: 250 mg daily for 5 days, followed by 250 mg 3 times per week for a minimum of 3 months (Meyer 2014). **Note:** It is unclear whether azithromycin should be continued long-term if a benefit is observed or if it should be discontinued if lung function does not improve (Meyer 2014).

Cat scratch disease (off-label use): Oral: ≥45.5 kg: 500 mg as a single dose, then 250 mg once daily for 4 additional days (Bass 1998; Stevens 2014)

Cesarean section (nonelective), prophylaxis (preoperative) (off-label use): IV: 500 mg as a single dose 1 hour prior to surgical incision; used in conjunction with standard preoperative antibiotics (Tita 2016)

Chancroid due to *H. ducreyi*: Oral: 1 g as a single dose. **Note:** Data are limited concerning the efficacy in HIV infected patients (CDC [Workowski 2015]).

***Chlamydia trachomatis* infection:** Oral: 1 g as a single dose (CDC [Workowski 2015])

Cholera (off-label use): Oral: 1 g as a single dose (Saha 2006)

Community-acquired pneumonia:

Oral: 500 mg on day 1 followed by 250 mg once daily on days 2 to 5

Extended release suspension (Zmax): 2 g as a single dose

IV: 500 mg as a single dose for at least 2 days, follow IV therapy by the oral route with a single daily dose of 500 mg to complete a 7- to 10-day course of therapy. **Note:** Guidelines recommend a duration of ≥5 days dosing (IDSA/ATS [Mandell 2007])

Gonococcal infection, conjunctivitis (off-label use): Oral: 1 g as a single dose in combination with ceftriaxone (CDC [Workowski 2015])

Gonococcal infection, disseminated (arthritis, arthritis-dermatitis, meningitis, endocarditis) (off-label use): Oral: 1 g as a single dose in combination with ceftriaxone (CDC [Workowski 2015])

Gonococcal infection, expedited partner therapy (off-label use): Oral: 1 g as a single dose in combination with cefixime (CDC [Workowski 2015]). **Note:** To be used only for heterosexual partners with gonorrhea if health department partner-management strategies are impractical/unavailable and there is concern by the provider for the prompt evaluation and treatment of the partner; medication may be delivered to partner by patient, collaborating pharmacy, or disease investigation specialist as permitted by law; written materials to educate partners about their exposure to gonorrhea, importance of therapy, and when to seek clinical evaluation for adverse reactions/complications must also be provided with the medication (CDC [Workowski 2015]).

Gonococcal infection, uncomplicated (cervix, rectum [off-label use], urethra) (off-label regimen): Oral: 1 g as a single dose in combination with ceftriaxone (preferred) or cefixime (only if ceftriaxone unavailable) (CDC [Workowski 2015])

Patients with severe cephalosporin allergy (off-label regimen): 2 g as a single dose in combination with gemifloxacin or gentamicin IM (CDC [Workowski 2015])

Gonococcal infection, uncomplicated (pharynx) (off-label use): Oral: 1 g as a single dose in combination with ceftriaxone (CDC [Workowski 2015])

Granuloma inguinale (donovanosis) (off-label use): Oral: 1 g once weekly **or** 500 mg once daily for at least 3 weeks and until lesions have healed. **Note:** If symptoms do not improve within the first few days of therapy, the addition of gentamicin may be considered (CDC [Workowski 2015]).

***Helicobacter pylori* infection (off-label use):** Oral: 500 mg once daily for 3 to 7 days in combination with an acid-reducing drug and other antibiotics (Laine 1999; Trevisani 1998)

Infection prophylaxis in neutropenia (off-label use): Oral: 250 mg once daily; initiate at the time of stem cell infusion and continue until recovery from neutropenia or initiation of empiric antibiotics for neutropenic fever (IDSA [Freifeld 2011]; Tomblyn 2009)

Lyme disease (erythema migrans or borrelial lymphocytoma) (off-label use): Oral: 500 mg once daily for 7 to 10 days (IDSA [Wormser 2009])

Mild to moderate respiratory tract, skin, and soft tissue infections: Oral: 500 mg in a single loading dose on day 1 followed by 250 mg daily as a single dose on days 2 to 5

Alternative regimen: Bacterial exacerbation of COPD: 500 mg daily for a total of 3 days

***Mycobacterium avium* complex (MAC) infection:** Oral:

Disseminated disease in HIV-infected patients (HHS [OI adult 2016]):

Treatment: 500 to 600 mg daily in combination with ethambutol

Primary prophylaxis: 1,200 mg once weekly (preferred) **or** 600 mg twice weekly; may discontinue prophylaxis when CD4 count >100 cells/mm^3 for ≥3 months in response to antiretroviral therapy (ART)

Secondary prophylaxis: 500 to 600 mg daily in combination with ethambutol; may discontinue when patient has completed ≥12 months of therapy, has no signs/symptoms of MAC disease, and has sustained (>6 months) CD4 count >100 cells/mm^3 in response to ART

Pulmonary disease (nodular/bronchiectatic disease) in non-HIV-infected patients (off-label use): 500 to 600 mg 3 times weekly in combination with rifampin and ethambutol; continue treatment until patient is culture negative on therapy for 1 year (ATS/IDSA [Griffith 2007])

Pulmonary disease (severe nodular/bronchiectatic or cavitary disease) in non-HIV-infected patients (off-label use): 250 to 300 mg once daily in combination with a rifamycin plus ethambutol; continue treatment until patient is culture negative on therapy for 1 year. May also consider addition of 3-times-weekly amikacin or streptomycin early in therapy (ATS/IDSA [Griffith 2007]).

Pulmonary disease in patients with cystic fibrosis (off-label use): 250 to 500 mg once daily in combination with rifampin and ethambutol; continue for 12 months beyond culture conversion. **Note:** Intermitted dosing (3 times weekly) is not recommended for patients with cystic fibrosis (Floto 2016)

***Mycoplasma genitalium* (off-label use)** (Falk 2015; CDC [Workowski 2015]): Oral:

Single-dose regimen: 1 g as a single dose

Extended-dose regimen: 500 mg on day 1, followed by 250 mg once daily on days 2 through 5

Nontuberculous mycobacterial disease (off-label use): Oral:

Mycobacterium abscessus pulmonary disease in patients with cystic fibrosis: 250 to 500 mg once daily in combination with amikacin plus one or more additional IV antibiotic based on tolerability and drug susceptibility for 3 to 12 weeks, followed by a continuation phase of azithromycin 250 to 500 mg once daily in combination with inhaled amikacin with 2 to 3 additional antibiotics (eg, minocycline, clofazimine, moxifloxacin, linezolid) (Floto 2016)

M. abscessus skin, soft tissue, or bone infections: 250 mg once daily in combination with an IV antibiotic (eg, amikacin, cefoxitin, imipenem); duration depends on severity and site of infection (ATS/IDSA [Griffith 2007])

Pelvic inflammatory disease (PID): IV: 500 mg as a single dose for 1 to 2 days, follow IV therapy by the oral route with a single daily dose of 250 mg to complete a 7-day course of therapy

Pertussis (off-label use) (CDC 2005): Oral: 500 mg on day 1 followed by 250 mg daily on days 2 to 5 (maximum: 500 mg daily)

Pharyngitis (including susceptible group A streptococci), tonsillitis (as an alternative agent in penicillin-allergic patients): Oral: 12 mg/kg (maximum: 500 mg) on day 1 followed by 6 mg/kg (maximum: 250 mg) once daily on days 2 through 5. **Note:** Regimen is also recommended by the Infectious Disease Society of America (IDSA) (Shulman 2012).

Prevention of exacerbations of chronic obstructive pulmonary disease (COPD) (off-label use): Oral: 250 mg once daily (Albert 2011) or 500 mg 3 times weekly (Uzun 2014). **Note:** Duration of prophylaxis in clinical studies was 1 year (Albert 2011; Uzun 2014).

Prevention of pulmonary exacerbations in patients with noncystic fibrosis bronchiectasis (off-label use): Oral: 500 mg 3 days per week. **Note:** Duration of treatment in clinical trial was 6 months; durations >6 months have not been evaluated. Trial patients had ≥1 exacerbation in the past year, no macrolide treatment for >3 months in the past 6 months, and were screened for nontuberculous mycobacterial infection prior to treatment (Wong 2012). A more selective approach for patients with functionally mild disease has been suggested (Wilson 2012).

Prophylaxis against infective endocarditis (off-label use): Oral: 500 mg 30 to 60 minutes prior to the procedure. **Note:** American Heart Association (AHA) guidelines now recommend prophylaxis only in patients undergoing invasive procedures and in whom underlying cardiac conditions may predispose to a higher risk of adverse outcomes should infection occur. As of April 2007, routine prophylaxis for GI/GU procedures is no longer recommended by the AHA.

Prophylaxis against sexually transmitted diseases following sexual assault (off-label use): Oral: 1 g as a single dose in combination with ceftriaxone (plus metronidazole or tinidazole) (CDC [Workowski 2015])

Shigella dysentery type 1 (off-label use): Oral: 1,000 to 1,500 mg once daily for 1 to 5 days (WHO 2005)

Syphilis, primary and secondary (off-label use): Oral: 2,000 mg as a single dose. **Note:** Because of the possibility of resistance and treatment failure, azithromycin should be used with caution and should not be used to treat syphilis in patients with HIV, pregnant women, or in the MSM population (CDC [Workowski 2015]).

***Toxoplasma gondii* encephalitis (treatment) in HIV-infected patients (off- label use):** Oral: 900 to 1,200 mg once daily in combination with pyrimethamine and leucovorin for at least 6 weeks, followed by a chronic maintenance therapy regimen (HHS [OI adult 2016])

Traveler's diarrhea (off-label use): Oral: 1,000 mg as a single dose **or** 500 mg once daily for 1 to 3 days with or without concomitant loperamide (ACG [Riddle 2016]; CDC 2015; Ericsson 2007; Tribble 2007). **Note:** Increased nausea may occur with the 1,000 mg single dose regimen (Tribble 2007). Three-day course of 500 mg is the preferred regimen for dysentery or febrile diarrhea (ACG [Riddle 2016]).

Urethritis/cervicitis (nongonococcal): Oral: 1 g as a single dose

Pediatric Note: Extended release suspension (Zmax) is not interchangeable with immediate release formulations. Use should be limited to approved indications. All doses are expressed as immediate release azithromycin unless otherwise specified.

Note: Adolescents ≥16 years: Refer to adult dosing.

Acne vulgaris (off-label use): Adolescents ≥13 years: Oral: Dosing regimens used in clinical trials have varied greatly. All trials used pulse-dosing regimens; regimens include: 500 mg once daily for 4 consecutive days per month for 3 consecutive months (Babaeinejad 2011) **or** 500 mg once daily for 3 days in the first week, followed by 500 mg once weekly until week 10 (Maleszka 2011). The shortest possible duration should be used to minimize development of bacterial resistance; re-evaluate at 3 to 4 months (AAD [Zaenglein 2016]).

Bacterial sinusitis: Children ≥6 months: Oral: 10 mg/kg once daily for 3 days (maximum: 500 mg daily)

Cat scratch disease (off-label use) (Bass 1998; Stevens 2014): Oral:

<45.5 kg: 10 mg/kg as a single dose, then 5 mg/kg once daily for 4 additional days

≥45.5 kg: Refer to adult dosing.

***Chlamydia trachomatis* infection (off-label use):** Oral: Children ≥45 kg: 1 g as a single dose (CDC [Workowski 2015])

Community-acquired pneumonia (CAP) (IDSA/PIDS 2011): Infants >3 months and Children: **Note:** A beta-lactam antibiotic should be added if typical bacterial pneumonia cannot be ruled out.

Presumed mild infection or step-down therapy, atypical *(M. pneumoniae, Chlamydophila* [also known as *Chlamydia*] *pneumoniae, C. trachomatis)* (preferred): Oral: 10 mg/kg (maximum dose: 500 mg) as a single dose on the first day, followed by 5 mg/kg/day (maximum dose: 250 mg) on days 2 through 5

Presumed moderate to severe infection, atypical *(M. pneumoniae, Chlamydophila* [also known as *Chlamydia*] *pneumoniae, C. trachomatis)*: IV: 10 mg/kg/day on days 1 and 2, then switch to oral azithromycin therapy if possible to finish the 5-day course

Alternative regimens for community-acquired pneumonia: Oral: 10 mg/kg (maximum dose: 500 mg) once daily for 3 days (Kogan 2003)

Extended release suspension (Zmax): Infants ≥6 months and Children: Oral:

<75 lbs (34 kg): 60 mg/kg as a single dose

≥75 lbs (34 kg): Refer to adult dosing

Disseminated *M. avium* complex disease in patients with advanced HIV infection (off-label use) (DHHS 2013): Oral:

Treatment: 10 to 12 mg/kg/day (maximum: 500 mg) in combination with ethambutol; patients with severe disease should also receive rifabutin

Primary prophylaxis: 20 mg/kg (maximum: 1,200 mg) once weekly (preferred) or alternatively, 5 mg/kg/day once daily (maximum: 250 mg daily)

Secondary prophylaxis: 5 mg/kg/day once daily (maximum: 250 mg daily) in combination with ethambutol, with or without rifabutin

Gonococcal infection, conjunctivitis (off-label use): Adolescents: Refer to adult dosing.

Gonococcal infection, disseminated (arthritis, arthritis-dermatitis, meningitis, endocarditis) (off-label use): Adolescents: Refer to adult dosing.

Gonococcal infection, uncomplicated (cervix, rectum [off-label use], urethra) (off-label regimen): Adolescents: Refer to adult dosing.

Gonococcal infection, uncomplicated (pharynx) (off-label use): Adolescents: Refer to adult dosing.

Otitis media: Children ≥6 months: Oral:

1-day regimen: 30 mg/kg as a single dose (maximum dose: 1,500 mg)

3-day regimen: 10 mg/kg once daily for 3 days (maximum: 500 mg daily)

5-day regimen: 10 mg/kg on day 1 (maximum: 500 mg daily) followed by 5 mg/kg/day once daily on days 2 to 5 (maximum: 250 mg daily)

Pertussis (off-label use) (CDC 2005): Oral:

Children <6 months: 10 mg/kg/day for 5 days

Children ≥6 months: 10 mg/kg on day 1 (maximum: 500 mg daily) followed by 5 mg/kg/day once daily on days 2 to 5 (maximum: 250 mg daily)

Pharyngitis (including susceptible group A streptococci), tonsillitis (as an alternative agent in penicillin allergic patients):

Manufacturer's labeling and AHA/AAP recommendations: Children ≥2 years and Adolescents: Oral: 12 mg/kg/dose once daily for 5 days (maximum: 500 mg daily) (AHA guidelines [Gerber 2009]; *Red Book* [AAP 2012])

Alternative recommendations:

Children and Adolescents (off-label dose/regimen): Oral: Suspension: 20 mg/kg once daily for 3 days (maximum dose/day: 1,000 mg) (Cohen 2004; O'Doherty 1996)

Children and Adolescents: Oral: 12 mg/kg (maximum: 500 mg) on day 1 followed by 6 mg/kg/dose (maximum: 250 mg) once daily on days 2 through 5 (IDSA guidelines [Shulman 2012])

Prophylaxis against infective endocarditis (off-label use): Oral: 15 mg/kg 30 to 60 minutes before procedure. **Note:** American Heart Association (AHA) guidelines now recommend prophylaxis only in patients undergoing invasive procedures and in whom underlying cardiac conditions may predispose to a higher risk of adverse outcomes should infection occur. As of April 2007, routine prophylaxis for GI/GU procedures is no longer recommended by the AHA.

Prophylaxis against sexually transmitted diseases following sexual assault (off-label use): Adolescents: Refer to adult dosing.

Shigella dysentery type 1 (off-label use): Oral: 6 to 20 mg/kg/day for 1 to 5 days (WHO 2005)

Renal Impairment

Use with caution in patients with GFR <10 mL/minute (AUC increased by 35% compared to patients with normal renal function); however, no dosage adjustment is provided in the manufacturer's labeling.

No supplemental dose or dosage adjustment necessary, including patients on intermittent hemodialysis, peritoneal dialysis, or continuous renal replacement therapy (eg, CVVHD) (Aronoff 2007; Heintz 2009).

Hepatic Impairment Azithromycin is predominantly hepatically eliminated; however, there is no dosage adjustment provided in the manufacturer's labeling. Use with caution due to potential for hepatotoxicity (rare); discontinue immediately for signs or symptoms of hepatitis.

Mechanism of Action Inhibits RNA-dependent protein synthesis at the chain elongation step; binds to the 50S ribosomal subunit resulting in blockage of transpeptidation

Contraindications

Hypersensitivity to azithromycin, erythromycin, other macrolide (eg, azalide or ketolide) antibiotics, or any component of the formulation; history of cholestatic jaundice/hepatic dysfunction associated with prior azithromycin use

Note: The manufacturer does not list concurrent use of pimozide as a contraindication; however, azithromycin is listed as a contraindication in the manufacturer's labeling for pimozide.

Warnings/Precautions Use with caution in patients with preexisting liver disease; hepatocellular and/or cholestatic hepatitis, with or without jaundice, hepatic necrosis, failure and death have occurred. Discontinue immediately if symptoms of hepatitis occur (malaise, nausea, vomiting, abdominal colic, fever). Allergic (hypersensitivity) reactions (eg, angioedema, anaphylaxis, Stevens-Johnson syndrome, toxic epidermal necrolysis and drug reaction with eosinophilia and systemic symptoms [DRESS]) have been reported (rare), including fatalities; reappearance of allergic reaction may occur shortly after discontinuation without further azithromycin exposure. May mask or delay symptoms of incubating gonorrhea or syphilis, so appropriate culture and susceptibility tests should be performed prior to initiating a treatment regimen. Prolonged use may result in fungal or bacterial superinfection, including *C. difficile*-associated diarrhea (CDAD); CDAD has been observed >2 months postantibiotic treatment. Use caution with renal dysfunction. Macrolides (especially erythromycin) have been associated with rare QT_c prolongation and ventricular arrhythmias, including torsade de pointes; consider avoiding use in patients with prolonged QT interval, congenital long QT syndrome, history of torsade de pointes, bradyarrhythmias, uncorrected hypokalemia or hypomagnesemia, clinically significant bradycardia, uncompensated heart failure, or concurrent use of Class IA (eg, quinidine, procainamide) or Class III (eg, amiodarone, dofetilide, sotalol) antiarrhythmic agents or other drugs known to prolong the QT interval. Use with caution in patients with myasthenia gravis. Use of azithromycin in neonates and infants (treatment up to 42 days of life) has been associated with infantile hypertrophic pyloric stenosis (IHPS); observe for non-bilious vomiting or irritability with feeding (Eberly 2015).

Oral suspensions (immediate release and extended release) are not interchangeable.

Drug Interactions

Metabolism/Transport Effects **Substrate** of CYP3A4 (minor); **Note:** Assignment of Major/Minor substrate status based on clinically relevant drug interaction potential; **Inhibits** CYP1A2 (weak), P-glycoprotein

Avoid Concomitant Use

Avoid concomitant use of Azithromycin (Systemic) with any of the following: Amiodarone; BCG (Intravesical); Cholera Vaccine; Cisapride; Highest Risk QTc-Prolonging Agents; Hydroxychloroquine; Ivabradine; MiFEPRIStone; PAZOPanib; Pimozide; Probucol; Promazine; QuiNINE; Silodosin; Terfenadine; Topotecan; VinCRIStine (Liposomal); Vinflunine

Increased Effect/Toxicity

Azithromycin (Systemic) may increase the levels/ effects of: Afatinib; Amiodarone; AtorvaSTATin; Bilastine; Brentuximab Vedotin; Cardiac Glycosides; Cisapride; Colchicine; CycloSPORINE (Systemic); Dabigatran Etexilate; DOXOrubicin (Conventional); Edoxaban; Everolimus; Highest Risk QTc-Prolonging Agents; Ivermectin (Systemic); Lovastatin; Moderate Risk QTc-Prolonging Agents; Naldemedine; Naloxegol; PAZOPanib; P-glycoprotein/ABCB1 Substrates; Pimozide; Prucalopride; QuiNINE; Ranolazine; RifAXIMin; Silodosin; Simvastatin; Tacrolimus (Systemic); Tacrolimus (Topical); Terfenadine; TiZANidine; Topotecan; Venetoclax; VinCRIStine (Liposomal); Vitamin K Antagonists

The levels/effects of Azithromycin (Systemic) may be increased by: Hydroxychloroquine; Ivabradine; MiFEPRIStone; Nelfinavir; Probucol; Promazine; QTc-Prolonging Agents (Indeterminate Risk and Risk Modifying); Vinflunine

Decreased Effect

Azithromycin (Systemic) may decrease the levels/ effects of: BCG (Intravesical); BCG Vaccine (Immunization); Cholera Vaccine; Lactobacillus and Estriol; Sodium Picosulfate; Typhoid Vaccine

Food Interactions Rate and extent of GI absorption may be altered depending upon the formulation. Azithromycin suspension, not tablet form, has significantly increased absorption (46%) with food. Management: Immediate release suspension and tablet may be taken without regard to food; extended release suspension should be taken on an empty stomach (at least 1 hour before or 2 hours following a meal).

Dietary Considerations

Some products may contain sodium and/or sucrose.

Oral suspension, immediate release, may be administered with or without food.

Oral suspension, extended release, should be taken on an empty stomach (at least 1 hour before or 2 hours following a meal).

Tablet may be administered with food to decrease GI effects.

Pharmacodynamics/Kinetics

Half-life Elimination Terminal: Oral, IV: Infants and Children 4 months to 15 years: 54.5 hours; Adults: Immediate release: 68-72 hours; Extended release: 59 hours

Time to Peak Oral: Serum: Immediate release: ~2 to 3 hours; Extended release: 3 to 5 hours

Pregnancy Risk Factor B

Pregnancy Considerations Adverse events were not observed in animal reproduction studies. Azithromycin crosses the placenta (Ramsey 2003). The maternal serum half-life of azithromycin is unchanged in early pregnancy and decreased at term; however, high concentrations of azithromycin are sustained in the myometrium and adipose tissue (Fischer 2012; Ramsey 2003). Azithromycin is recommended for the treatment of several infections, including chlamydia, gonococcal infections, and *Mycobacterium avium* complex (MAC) in pregnant patients (consult current guidelines) (CDC [Workowski 2015]; HHS [opportunistic; adult] 2015).

Breastfeeding Considerations Azithromycin is excreted in breast milk.

The relative infant dose (RID) of azithromycin is 4% to 8% when calculated using the highest breast milk concentration located and compared to an infant therapeutic dose of 5 to 10 mg/kg/day. In general, breastfeeding is considered acceptable when the RID is <10% (Anderson 2016; Ito 2000). Using the highest milk concentration (2.8 mcg/mL), the estimated daily infant dose via breast milk is 0.42 mg/kg/day. This milk concentration was obtained following maternal administration of oral azithromycin as a 1 g loading dose followed in 48 hours by azithromycin 500 mg for 3 days; milk concentrations increased over time and reached a peak 30 hours after the last oral dose (Kelsey 1994).

Following a single dose of IV azithromycin 500 mg, azithromycin was measurable in breast milk for up to 48 hours. The median half-life in breast milk was 15.6 hours (Sutton 2015).

Decreased appetite, diarrhea, rash, and somnolence have been reported in nursing infants exposed to macrolide antibiotics (Goldstein 2009). In general, antibiotics that are present in breast milk may cause non-dose-related modification of bowel flora. Monitor infants for GI disturbances (WHO 2002). In addition, an increased risk for infantile hypertrophic pyloric stenosis (IHPS) may be present in infants who are exposed to macrolides via breast milk, especially during the first 2 weeks of life (Lund 2014); however, data is conflicting (Goldstein 2009). The manufacturer recommends that caution be exercised when administering azithromycin to breastfeeding women.

The CDC's Sexually Transmitted Diseases Treatment Guidelines state that azithromycin is one of the recommended agents for the treatment of granuloma inguinale in lactating women. For lymphogranuloma venereum, azithromycin may be considered as an alternative agent in this patient population (CDC [Workowski 2015]).

Dosage Forms

Packet, Oral:

Zithromax: 1 g (3 ea, 10 ea)

Generic: 1 g (3 ea, 10 ea)

Solution Reconstituted, Intravenous:

Zithromax: 500 mg (1 ea)

Generic: 500 mg (1 ea)

Solution Reconstituted, Intravenous [preservative free]:

Generic: 500 mg (1 ea)

Suspension Reconstituted, Oral:

Zithromax: 100 mg/5 mL (15 mL); 200 mg/5 mL (15 mL, 22.5 mL, 30 mL)

Zmax: 2 g (1 ea)

Generic: 100 mg/5 mL (15 mL); 200 mg/5 mL (15 mL, 22.5 mL, 30 mL)

Tablet, Oral:

Zithromax: 250 mg, 500 mg, 600 mg

Zithromax Tri-Pak: 500 mg

Zithromax Z-Pak: 250 mg

Generic: 250 mg, 500 mg, 600 mg

Dental Comment There is evidence that azithromycin is proarrhythmic (see Local Anesthetic/Vasoconstrictor Precautions)

A recent large retrospective review of the cardiovascular risks of azithromycin was published. Researchers reviewed a Tennessee Medicaid cohort of patients to evaluate cardiovascular mortality in patients taking azithromycin, amoxicillin, ciprofloxacin, levofloxacin, or no antibiotic. The cohort included patients who took azithromycin (347,795 prescriptions); propensity-score-matched persons who took no antibiotics (1,391,180 control periods); and patients who took amoxicillin (1,348,672 prescriptions), ciprofloxacin (264,626 prescriptions), or levofloxacin (193,906 prescriptions). The risk of cardiovascular death was greater with azithromycin than with ciprofloxacin, but similar to levofloxacin. Amoxicillin showed no increase in risk of cardiovascular death. The estimated risk for azithromycin was 47 additional cardiovascular deaths per million courses of treatment (Ray 2012).

Aztreonam (Systemic) (AZ tree oh nam)

Brand Names: US Azactam; Azactam in Dextrose

Pharmacologic Category Antibiotic, Monobactam

Use Treatment of patients with urinary tract infections, lower respiratory tract infections, septicemia, skin/skin structure infections, intra-abdominal infections, and gynecological infections caused by susceptible gram-negative bacilli

Local Anesthetic/Vasoconstrictor Precautions No information available to require special precautions

Effects on Dental Treatment No significant effects or complications reported

Effects on Bleeding No information available to require special precautions

Adverse Reactions

>10%:

Hematologic & oncologic: Neutropenia (children 3% to 11%; adults <1%)

Hepatic: Increased serum transaminases (children, high dose: >3 times ULN: 15% to 20%; children, standard dose: increased serum AST 4%, increased serum ALT 7%)

Local: Pain at injection site (children 12%, adults 2%)

1% to 10%:

Cardiovascular: Phlebitis (intravenous: ≤2%), thrombophlebitis (intravenous: ≤2%)

Dermatologic: Skin rash (children 4%, adults ≤1%)

Gastrointestinal: Diarrhea (≤1%), nausea (≤1%), vomiting (≤1%)

Hematologic & oncologic: Eosinophilia (children 6%, adults <1%), thrombocythemia (children 4%, adults <1%)

Local: Erythema at injection site (intravenous: Children 3%, adults <1%), discomfort at injection site (intramuscular: ≤2%), swelling at injection site (intramuscular: ≤2%)

Renal: Increased serum creatinine (children 6%)

Miscellaneous: Fever (≤1%)

<1%, postmarketing, and/or case reports: Abdominal cramps, anaphylaxis, anemia, angioedema, breast tenderness, bronchospasm, chest pain, *Clostridium difficile* associated diarrhea, confusion, diaphoresis, diplopia, dizziness, dysgeusia, dyspnea, erythema multiforme, exfoliative dermatitis, flushing, gastrointestinal hemorrhage, halitosis, headache, hepatitis, hepatobiliary disease, hypotension, increased serum alkaline phosphatase, increased serum ALT (adults), increased serum AST (adults), induration at injection site, insomnia, jaundice, leukocytosis, malaise, myalgia, nasal congestion, numbness of tongue, oral mucosa ulcer, pancytopenia, paresthesia, petechia, positive direct Coombs test, prolonged partial thromboplastin time, prolonged prothrombin time, pruritus, pseudomembranous colitis, purpura, seizure, sneezing, thrombocytopenia, tinnitus, toxic epidermal necrolysis, urticaria, vaginitis, ventricular bigeminy (transient), ventricular premature contractions (transient), vertigo, vulvovaginal candidiasis, weakness, wheezing

General Dosage Range Dosage adjustment recommended in patients with renal impairment

IM: *Adults:* 500 mg to 1 g every 8 to 12 hours

IV:

Infants ≥9 months, Children, and Adolescents: 30 to 50 mg/kg/dose every 6 to 8 hours (maximum: 8 g daily)

Adults: 1 to 2 g every 6 to 12 hours (maximum: 8 g daily)

Mechanism of Action Inhibits bacterial cell wall synthesis by binding to one or more of the penicillin-binding proteins (PBPs) which in turn inhibits the final transpeptidation step of peptidoglycan synthesis in bacterial cell walls, thus inhibiting cell wall biosynthesis. Bacteria eventually lyse due to ongoing activity of cell wall autolytic enzymes (autolysins and murein hydrolases) while cell wall assembly is arrested. Monobactam structure makes cross-allergenicity with beta-lactams unlikely.

Pharmacodynamics/Kinetics

Half-life Elimination Injection:Neonates: <7 days, ≤2.5 kg: 5.5 to 9.9 hours; <7 days, >2.5 kg: 2.6 hours; 1 week to 1 month: 2.4 hours

Children 2 months to 12 years: 1.7 hours

Children with cystic fibrosis: 1.3 hours

Adults: Normal renal function: 1.7 to 2.9 hours

End-stage renal disease: 6 to 8 hours

Time to Peak IM, IV push: Within 60 minutes; IV infusion: 1.5 hours

Pregnancy Risk Factor B

Pregnancy Considerations Adverse events have not been observed in animal reproduction studies. Aztreonam crosses the placenta and can be detected in the fetus.

Aztreonam (Oral Inhalation) (AZ tree oh nam)

Brand Names: US Cayston

Brand Names: Canada Cayston

Pharmacologic Category Antibiotic, Miscellaneous

Use Cystic fibrosis: Improve respiratory symptoms in cystic fibrosis (CF) patients with pulmonary *Pseudomonas aeruginosa* infections

Local Anesthetic/Vasoconstrictor Precautions No information available to require special precautions

Effects on Dental Treatment No significant effects or complications reported

Effects on Bleeding No information available to require special precautions

Adverse Reactions

>10%:

Gastrointestinal: Pharyngolaryngeal pain (12%)

Respiratory: Cough (54%), nasal congestion (16%), wheezing (16%)

Miscellaneous: Fever (13%; more common in children)

1% to 10%:
- Cardiovascular: Chest discomfort (8%)
- Dermatologic: Skin rash (2%)
- Gastrointestinal: Abdominal pain (7%), vomiting (6%)
- Respiratory: Bronchospasm (3%; patients experienced ≥15% reduction in FEV_1)

<1%, postmarketing, and/or case reports: Arthralgia, facial rash, facial swelling, hypersensitivity reaction, joint swelling, pharyngeal edema

General Dosage Range

Oral inhalation: *Children ≥7 years, Adolescents, and Adults:* 75 mg 3 times daily

Mechanism of Action Inhibits bacterial cell wall synthesis by binding to one or more of the penicillin-binding proteins (PBPs), which in turn inhibits the final transpeptidation step of peptidoglycan synthesis in bacterial cell walls, thus inhibiting cell wall biosynthesis. Bacteria eventually lyse due to ongoing activity of cell wall autolytic enzymes (autolysins and murein hydrolases), while cell wall assembly is arrested. Monobactam structure makes cross-allergenicity with beta-lactams unlikely.

Pharmacodynamics/Kinetics

Half-life Elimination Adults: 2.1 hours

Pregnancy Risk Factor B

Pregnancy Considerations Animal reproduction studies have not been conducted with aztreonam solution for inhalation; however, adverse events were not observed in animal reproduction studies conducted with the injection. Aztreonam crosses the placenta and reaches the fetal circulation following IV administration; however, peak plasma concentrations following inhalation of aztreonam are significantly less than those observed following aztreonam IV.

Prescribing and Access Restrictions Cayston (aztreonam inhalation solution) is only available through a select group of specialty pharmacies and cannot be obtained through a retail pharmacy. Because Cayston may only be used with the Altera Nebulizer System, it can only be obtained from the following specialty pharmacies; IV Solutions/Maxor; Foundation Care; Pharmaceutical Specialties Inc; TLCRx/ ModernHEALTH; and Walgreens Specialty Pharmacy. This network of specialty pharmacies ensures proper access to both the drug and device. To obtain the medication and proper nebulizer, contact the Cayston Access Program at 1-877-7CAYSTON (1-877-722-9786) or at www.cayston.com. In Canada, Cayston is distributed by Innomar Solutions specialty pharmacy; Canadian healthcare providers and patients may obtain additional information at http://cayston.ca/

Bacitracin (Systemic) (bas i TRAY sin)

Brand Names: US BACiiM

Brand Names: Canada BaciJect

Pharmacologic Category Antibiotic, Miscellaneous

Use Pneumonia and empyema: Treatment of pneumonia and empyema in infants caused by susceptible staphylococci; due to toxicity risks, systemic uses of bacitracin should be limited to situations where less toxic alternatives would not be effective

Local Anesthetic/Vasoconstrictor Precautions No information available to require special precautions

Effects on Dental Treatment No significant effects or complications reported

Effects on Bleeding No information available to require special precautions

Adverse Reactions

Frequency not defined.
- Dermatologic: Skin rash
- Endocrine & metabolic: Albuminuria
- Gastrointestinal: Nausea, vomiting
- Genitourinary: Azotemia, casts in urine, nephrotoxicity
- Local: Pain at injection site
- Renal: Renal failure

Postmarketing and/or case reports: Anaphylaxis (intraoperative exposure [Damm, 2011])

General Dosage Range

IM:

Infants ≤2.5 kg: 900 units/kg/day in 2 to 3 divided doses

Infants >2.5 kg: 1000 units/kg/day in 2 to 3 divided doses

Mechanism of Action Inhibits bacterial cell wall synthesis by preventing transfer of mucopeptides into the growing cell wall

Pregnancy Considerations This product is not indicated for use in women of reproductive age.

Bacitracin (Ophthalmic) (bas i TRAY sin)

Pharmacologic Category Antibiotic, Ophthalmic

Use Superficial ocular infections: Treatment of superficial ocular infections involving the conjunctiva or cornea due to susceptible organisms

Local Anesthetic/Vasoconstrictor Precautions No information available to require special precautions

Effects on Dental Treatment No significant effects or complications reported

Effects on Bleeding No information available to require special precautions

Adverse Reactions

1% to 10%: Hypersensitivity: Hypersensitivity reaction (7% [Hätinen, 1985])

Postmarketing and/or case reports: Contact dermatitis (Pichichero, 2011)

General Dosage Range Ophthalmic: *Children, Adolescents, and Adults:* Apply 1 to 3 times daily

Mechanism of Action Inhibits bacterial cell wall synthesis by preventing transfer of mucopeptides into the growing cell wall

Pregnancy Considerations Bacitracin is not absorbed systemically following ophthalmic administration (Robert, 2001). If ophthalmic agents are needed during pregnancy, the minimum effective dose should be used in combination with punctual occlusion to decrease potential exposure to the fetus (Samples, 1988).

Bacitracin (Topical) (bas i TRAY sin)

Brand Names: Canada Bacitin

Pharmacologic Category Antibiotic, Topical

Use Topical infection prevention: Prevention of infection in minor cuts, scrapes, or burns.

Local Anesthetic/Vasoconstrictor Precautions No information available to require special precautions

Effects on Dental Treatment No significant effects or complications reported

Effects on Bleeding No information available to require special precautions

Adverse Reactions Postmarketing and/or case reports: Anaphylaxis (Elsner, 1990; Farley, 1995)

General Dosage Range Topical: *Children, Adolescents, and Adults:* Apply 1 to 3 times daily

Mechanism of Action Inhibits bacterial cell wall synthesis by preventing transfer of mucopeptides into the growing cell wall

Pregnancy Considerations Although large studies have not been conducted, absorption is limited following topical application; use during pregnancy has not been associated with an increased risk of adverse fetal events (Leachman, 2006; Murase, 2014).

Baclofen (BAK loe fen)

Brand Names: US EnovaRX-Baclofen; Equipto-Baclofen; First-Baclofen 1; First-Baclofen 5; Gablofen; Lioresal

Brand Names: Canada Apo-Baclofen; Dom-Baclofen; Lioresal; Lioresal D.S.; Lioresal Intrathecal; Mylan-Baclofen; Novo-Baclofen; PHL-Baclofen; PMS-Baclofen; ratio-Baclofen; Riva-Baclofen; VPI-Baclofen Intrathecal

Pharmacologic Category Skeletal Muscle Relaxant

Use

Spasticity:

Oral: Management of reversible spasticity associated with multiple sclerosis or spinal cord lesions

Intrathecal: Management of severe spasticity of spinal cord origin (eg, spinal cord injury, multiple sclerosis) or cerebral origin (eg, cerebral palsy, traumatic brain injury) in patients ≥4 years; may be considered as an alternative to destructive neurosurgical procedures.

Limitations of use: Patients should first respond to a screening dose of intrathecal baclofen prior to consideration for long term infusion via an implantable pump. For spasticity of spinal cord origin, chronic infusion via an implantable pump should be reserved for patients unresponsive to oral baclofen therapy, or those who experience intolerable CNS side effects at effective doses. Patients with spasticity due to traumatic brain injury should wait at least one year after the injury before consideration of long term intrathecal baclofen therapy.

Local Anesthetic/Vasoconstrictor Precautions No information available to require special precautions

Effects on Dental Treatment No significant effects or complications reported

Effects on Bleeding No information available to require special precautions

Adverse Reactions

>10%:

Central nervous system: Hypotonia (2% to 35%), drowsiness (6% to 21%), confusion (1% to 11%), headache (2% to 11%)

Gastrointestinal: Nausea (1% to 12%), vomiting (2% to 11%)

1% to 10%:

Cardiovascular: Hypotension (≤9%), peripheral edema (≤3%)

Central nervous system: Seizure (≤10%), dizziness (2% to 8%), insomnia (≤7%), paresthesia (≤7%), hypertonia (≤6%), pain (≤4%), speech disturbance (≤4%), depression (2%), coma (≤2%), abnormality in thinking (≤1%), agitation (≤1%), chills (≤1%)

Dermatologic: Pruritus (4%), urticaria (≤1%)

Gastrointestinal: Constipation (≤6%), sialorrhea (≤3%), xerostomia (≤3%), diarrhea (≤2%)

Genitourinary: Urinary retention (≤8%), urinary frequency (≤6%), difficulty in micturition (2%), impotence (≤2%), urinary incontinence (≤2%)

Neuromuscular & skeletal: Back pain (≤2%), weakness (≤2%), tremor (≤1%)

Ophthalmic: Ambylopia (≤2%)

Respiratory: Hypoventilation (≤4%), pneumonia (≤2%), dyspnea (≤1%)

Miscellaneous: Accidental injury (≤4%)

<1%, postmarketing, and/or case reports: Abdominal pain, accommodation disturbance, akathisia, albuminuria, alopecia, amnesia, ankle edema, anorexia, anxiety, apnea, ataxia, blurred vision, bradycardia, carcinoma, chest pain, contact dermatitis, decreased libido, deep vein thrombophlebitis, dehydration, dermal ulcer, diaphoresis, diplopia, dysarthria, dysautonomia, dysgeusia, dysphagia, dystonia, dysuria, epilepsy, erectile dysfunction, euphoria, excitement, facial edema, fecal incontinence, fever, gastrointestinal hemorrhage, hallucination, hematuria, hyperglycemia, hyperhidrosis, hypertension, hyperventilation, hypothermia, hysteria, inhibited ejaculation, intestinal obstruction, leukocytosis, loss of postural reflex, malaise, miosis, muscle rigidity, myalgia, mydriasis, nasal congestion, nephrolithiasis, nocturia, nystagmus, occult blood in stools, oliguria, opisthotonus, orgasm disturbance, pallor, palpitations, paranoia, personality disorder, petechial rash, priapism, pulmonary embolism, scoliosis, scoliosis progression, sedation, sexual disorder, skin rash, slurred speech, strabismus, suicidal ideation, syncope, taste disorder, tinnitus, tongue irritation, vaginitis, vasodilatation, weight gain, weight loss

General Dosage Range

Intrathecal:

Children ≥4 years and Adolescents: Screening dose: 25 to 100 mcg; Initial infusion: Infuse at a 24-hourly rate dosed at twice the test dose or equivalent to the screening dose if efficacy of screening dose was maintained >8 hours

Adults: Screening dose: 50 to 100 mcg; Initial infusion: Infuse at a 24-hourly rate dosed at twice the test dose or equivalent to the screening dose if efficacy of screening dose was maintained >8 hours

Oral:

Children ≥12 years, Adolescents, and Adults: Initial: 5 mg 3 times daily; usual dose range: 40 to 80 mg daily; maximum: 80 mg daily (20 mg 4 times daily)

Mechanism of Action Inhibits the transmission of both monosynaptic and polysynaptic reflexes at the spinal cord level, possibly by hyperpolarization of primary afferent fiber terminals, with resultant relief of muscle spasticity

Pharmacodynamics/Kinetics

Onset of Action

Intrathecal bolus: 30 minutes to 1 hour; Continuous infusion: 6 to 8 hours after infusion initiation

Peak effect: Intrathecal bolus: 4 hours (effects may last 4 to 8 hours); Continuous infusion: 24 to 48 hours

Half-life Elimination

Oral:

Pediatric patients with cerebral palsy (age range: 2 to 17 years): 4.5 hours (He 2014)

Adults: 3.75 ± 0.96 hours (Brunton 2011)

Intrathecal: CSF elimination half-life: 1.5 hours over the first 4 hours

Time to Peak Serum: Oral: 1 hour (0.5 to 4 hours) (Brunton 2011)

Pregnancy Risk Factor C

Pregnancy Considerations Adverse events have been observed in animal reproduction studies. Withdrawal symptoms in the neonate were noted in a case report following the maternal use of oral baclofen 20 mg 4 times/day throughout pregnancy (Ratnayaka 2001).

Plasma concentrations following administration of intrathecal baclofen are significantly less than those with oral doses; exposure to the fetus is expected to be limited (Morton 2009).

Balsalazide (bal SAL a zide)

Brand Names: US Colazal; Giazo

Pharmacologic Category 5-Aminosalicylic Acid Derivative; Anti-inflammatory Agent

Use Treatment of mildly- to moderately-active ulcerative colitis

Giazo™: Only approved in males ≥18 years; effectiveness in females was not demonstrated

Local Anesthetic/Vasoconstrictor Precautions No information available to require special precautions

Effects on Dental Treatment No significant effects or complications reported

Effects on Bleeding No information available to require special precautions

Adverse Reactions

>10%:

Central nervous system: Headache (children: 15%; adults: 8%)

Gastrointestinal: Abdominal pain (children: 12% to 13%; adults: ≤6%)

1% to 10%:

Central nervous system: Fatigue (children: 4%; adults: ≤2%), insomnia (adults: 2%)

Gastrointestinal: Vomiting (children: 10%; adults: ≤4%), diarrhea (children: 9%; adults: ≤5%), exacerbation of ulcerative colitis (children: 6%; adults: 1%), nausea (adults: 5%; children: 4%), hematochezia (children: 4%), stomatitis (children: 3%), anorexia (adults: 2%), dyspepsia (adults: 2%), flatulence (adults: ≤2%), abdominal cramps (adults: 1%), constipation (adults: ≤1%), xerostomia (adults: ≤1%)

Genitourinary: Urinary tract infection (adults: 1% to 4%), dysmenorrhea (children: 3%)

Hematologic & oncologic: Anemia (4%)

Neuromuscular & skeletal: Arthralgia (adults: ≤4%), musculoskeletal pain (adults: 2%), myalgia (adults: ≤1%)

Respiratory: Pharyngitis (children: 6%; adults: 2%), flu-like symptoms (children: 4%; adults: 1%), respiratory infection (adults: ≤4%), cough (children: 3%; adults: 2%), pharyngolaryngeal pain (adults: 4%, children: 3%), rhinitis (adults: 2%)

Miscellaneous: Fever (children: 6%; adults: 2%)

<1%, postmarketing, and/or case reports: Alopecia, back pain, bowel urgency, bronchopneumonia, cholestatic jaundice, dizziness, dyspnea, edema, erythema nodosum, facial edema, fecal impaction, gastroenteritis, gastroesophageal reflux disease, hepatic cirrhosis, hepatic failure, hepatic injury, hepatic necrosis, hepatotoxicity, hyperbilirubinemia, hypersensitivity reaction, increased blood pressure, increased heart rate, increased liver enzymes, increased serum AST, interstitial nephritis, jaundice, Kawasaki-like syndrome, lethargy, malaise, myocarditis, pain, pancreatitis, pericarditis, pleural effusion, pneumonia (with and without eosinophilia), pruritus, renal failure, skin rash, vasculitis

General Dosage Range Oral:

Capsule:

Children ≥5 years: 750 mg **or** 2.25 g 3 times daily

Adults: 2.25 g 3 times daily

Tablet: *Adults: Males:* 3.3 g twice daily

Mechanism of Action Balsalazide is a prodrug, converted by bacterial azoreduction to 5-aminosalicylic acid (mesalamine, active), 4-aminobenzoyl-β-alanine (inert), and their metabolites. 5-aminosalicylic acid may decrease inflammation by blocking the production of arachidonic acid metabolites topically in the colon mucosa.

Pharmacodynamics/Kinetics

Onset of Action Delayed; may require several days to weeks (2 weeks); similar in adults and children

Half-life Elimination Primary effect is topical (colonic mucosa); therapeutic effect appears not to be influenced by the systemic half-life of balsalazide (1.9 hours) or its metabolites (5-ASA [9.5 hours], N-Ac-5-ASA [10.4 hours])

Time to Peak Balsalazide: Capsule: 1 to 2 hours; Tablet: 0.5 hours

Pregnancy Risk Factor B

Pregnancy Considerations Adverse events have not been observed in animal reproduction studies. Mesalamine (5-aminosalicylic acid) is the active metabolite of balsalazide; mesalamine is known to cross the placenta. Refer to the mesalamine monograph for additional information.

Basiliximab (ba si LIK si mab)

Brand Names: US Simulect

Brand Names: Canada Simulect

Pharmacologic Category Immunosuppressant Agent; Monoclonal Antibody

Use

Renal transplant (prophylaxis of acute rejection): Prophylaxis of acute organ rejection in renal transplantation in combination with cyclosporine (modified) and corticosteroids

Guideline recommendations: While basiliximab is FDA-approved for prophylaxis of acute organ rejection in renal transplantation in combination with cyclosporine (modified) and corticosteroids, cyclosporine is no longer recommended as the first line agent of choice. The Kidney Disease: Improving Global Outcomes (KDIGO) clinical practice guidelines for care of kidney transplant recipients recommend induction as part of the initial immunosuppressive regimen for all kidney transplants to reduce the risk of acute rejection. KDIGO recommends an interleukin 2 receptor antagonist (eg, basiliximab) as the first line induction agent for acute rejection prophylaxis except in those patients at high immunologic risk. (KDIGO [Kasiske 2009]).

Local Anesthetic/Vasoconstrictor Precautions No information available to require special precautions

Effects on Dental Treatment Key adverse event(s) related to dental treatment: Facial edema and ulcerative stomatitis. Causes gingival hypertrophy (GH) similar to that caused by cyclosporine; early reports indicate that frequency/incidence of basiliximab-induced GH not as high as cyclosporine-induced GH.

Effects on Bleeding No information available to require special precautions

Adverse Reactions Frequency not defined. Administration of basiliximab did not appear to increase the incidence or severity of adverse effects in clinical trials. Adverse events were reported in 96% of both the placebo and basiliximab groups.

>10%:

Cardiovascular: Hypertension, peripheral edema

Central nervous system: Headache, insomnia, pain

Dermatologic: Acne vulgaris, wound complication

Endocrine & metabolic: Hypercholesterolemia, hyperglycemia, hyperkalemia, hyperuricemia, hypokalemia, hypophosphatemia
Gastrointestinal: Abdominal pain, constipation, diarrhea, dyspepsia, nausea, vomiting
Genitourinary: Urinary tract infection
Hematologic & oncologic: Anemia
Infection: Viral infection
Neuromuscular & skeletal: Tremor
Respiratory: Dyspnea, upper respiratory infection
Miscellaneous: Fever

3% to 10%:
Cardiovascular: Abnormal heart sounds, angina pectoris, atrial fibrillation, cardiac arrhythmia, cardiac failure, chest pain, hypotension, tachycardia, thrombosis
Central nervous system: Agitation, anxiety, depression, dizziness, fatigue, hypoesthesia, malaise, rigors
Dermatologic: Dermal ulcer, dermatological disease, hypertrichosis, pruritus, skin rash
Endocrine & metabolic: Acidosis, albuminuria, anasarca, dehydration, diabetes mellitus, hypercalcemia, hyperlipidemia, hypertriglyceridemia, hypervolemia, hypocalcemia, hypoglycemia, hypomagnesemia, hyponatremia, increased nonprotein nitrogen, increased serum glucocorticoids, weight gain
Gastrointestinal: Enlargement of abdomen, esophagitis, flatulence, gastroenteritis, gastrointestinal hemorrhage, GI moniliasis, gingival hyperplasia, hernia, melena, stomatitis (including ulcerative)
Genitourinary: Bladder dysfunction, dysuria, genital edema (male), hematuria, impotence, oliguria, ureteral disease, urinary frequency, urinary retention
Hematologic & oncologic: Hematoma, hemorrhage, hypoproteinemia, leukopenia, polycythemia, purpura, thrombocytopenia
Infection: Cytomegalovirus disease, herpes virus infection (simplex and zoster), infection, sepsis
Neuromuscular & skeletal: Arthralgia, arthropathy, back pain, bone fracture, leg pain, muscle cramps, myalgia, neuropathy, paresthesia, weakness
Ophthalmic: Cataract, conjunctivitis, visual disturbance
Renal: Renal insufficiency, renal tubular necrosis
Respiratory: Bronchitis, bronchospasm, cough, pharyngitis, pneumonia, pulmonary edema, rhinitis, sinusitis
Miscellaneous: Accidental injury, cyst

<1%, postmarketing, and/or case reports: Anaphylaxis, capillary leak syndrome, cytokine release syndrome, diabetes (new onset), hypersensitivity reaction (includes bronchospasm, cardiac failure, dyspnea, hypotension, pruritus, pulmonary edema, respiratory failure, skin rash, sneezing, tachycardia, urticaria), impaired fasting glucose, impaired glucose tolerance, lymphoproliferative disorder

General Dosage Range IV:

Children <35 kg: 10 mg within 2 hours prior to transplant surgery, followed by a second 10 mg dose 4 days after transplantation

Children ≥35 kg and Adults: 20 mg within 2 hours prior to transplant surgery, followed by a second 20 mg dose 4 days after transplantation

Mechanism of Action Chimeric (murine/human) immunosuppressant monoclonal antibody which blocks the alpha-chain of the interleukin-2 (IL-2) receptor complex; this receptor is expressed on activated T lymphocytes and is a critical pathway for activating cell-mediated allograft rejection

Pharmacodynamics/Kinetics

Duration of Action Mean: 36 ± 14 days (determined by IL-2R alpha saturation in patients also on cyclosporine and corticosteroids)

Half-life Elimination Children 1 to 11 years: 9.5 ± 4.5 days; Adolescents 12 to 16 years: 9.1 ± 3.9 days; Adults: Mean: 7.2 ± 3.2 days

Pregnancy Risk Factor B

Pregnancy Considerations

Adverse effects were not observed in animal reproduction studies. Basiliximab is a monoclonal IgG antibody which targets IL-2 receptors. IgG is known to cross the placenta; IL-2 receptors play an important role in the development of the immune system.

Women of childbearing potential should use effective contraceptive measures before beginning treatment, during, and for 4 months after completion of basiliximab treatment.

The National Transplantation Pregnancy Registry (NTPR) is a registry which follows pregnancies which occur in maternal transplant recipients or those fathered by male transplant recipients. The NTPR encourages reporting of pregnancies following solid organ transplant by contacting them at 877-955-6877 or NTPR@giftoflifeinstitute.org.

Becaplermin (be KAP ler min)

Brand Names: US Regranex

Pharmacologic Category Growth Factor, Platelet-Derived; Topical Skin Product

Use Diabetic ulcers: Adjunctive treatment of lower extremity diabetic neuropathic ulcers that extend into the subcutaneous tissue or beyond and have an adequate blood supply.

Limitations of use: Efficacy has not been established for pressure and venous stasis ulcers; has not been evaluated for diabetic neuropathic ulcers that do not extend through the dermis into subcutaneous tissue (stage I or II, International Association of Enterostomal Therapy [IAET] staging classification) or ischemic diabetic ulcers.

Local Anesthetic/Vasoconstrictor Precautions No information available to require special precautions

Effects on Dental Treatment No significant effects or complications reported

Effects on Bleeding No information available to require special precautions

Adverse Reactions

1% to 10%: Dermatologic: Erythematous rash (2%)

<1%, postmarketing, and/or case reports: Connective tissue disorder (excessive granulation tissue), dermal ulcer (with or without tunneling), erythema (with purulent discharge), infected skin ulcer, local pain

General Dosage Range Topical: *Adults and Adolescents ≥16 years:* Apply appropriate amount of gel once daily; to determine the length of gel to apply to the ulcer, measure the greatest length of the ulcer by the greatest width of the ulcer. Tube size and unit of measure will determine the formula used in the calculation. Recalculate amount of gel needed every 1 to 2 weeks, depending on the rate of change in ulcer area.

Centimeters: 15 g tube: [ulcer length (cm) x width (cm)] divided by 4 = length of gel (cm); 2 g tube: [ulcer length (cm) x width (cm)] divided by 2 = length of gel (cm)

Inches: 15 g tube: [length (in) x width (in)] x 0.6 = length of gel (in); 2 g tube: [length (in) x width (in)] x 1.3 = length of gel (in)

Mechanism of Action Recombinant B-isoform homodimer of human platelet-derived growth factor (rPDGF-BB) which enhances formation of new granulation tissue, induces fibroblast proliferation and differentiation to promote wound healing; also promotes angiogenesis.

Pregnancy Risk Factor C

Pregnancy Considerations Animal reproduction studies have not been conducted.

Beclomethasone (Nasal) (be kloe METH a sone)

Brand Names: US Beconase AQ; Qnasl; Qnasl Childrens

Brand Names: Canada Apo-Beclomethasone; Mylan-Beclo AQ; Rivanase AQ

Pharmacologic Category Corticosteroid, Nasal

Use

Nasal polyps Beconase AQ only: Prevention of recurrence of nasal polyps following surgical removal

Rhinitis:

Beconase AQ: Relief of symptoms of seasonal or perennial allergic rhinitis and nonallergic (vasomotor) rhinitis

Qnasl: Treatment of the nasal symptoms associated with seasonal or perennial allergic rhinitis in patients 4 years and older.

Local Anesthetic/Vasoconstrictor Precautions No information available to require special precautions

Effects on Dental Treatment No significant effects or complications reported

Effects on Bleeding No information available to require special precautions

Adverse Reactions Frequency not always defined.

>10%: Respiratory: Nasopharyngitis (≤24%; children: 2%)

1% to 10%:

Central nervous system: Dizziness (≤5%), headache (≤5%), altered sense of smell, anosmia

Dermatologic: Skin rash, urticaria

Endocrine & metabolic: Adrenal suppression (at high doses or in susceptible individuals), hypercorticoidism(at high doses or in susceptible individuals)

Gastrointestinal: Nausea (≤5%), ageusia, oral candidiasis (rare; more likely with aqueous solution), unpleasant taste

Hypersensitivity: Anaphylactoid reaction, anaphylaxis, angioedema

Immunologic: Immunosuppression

Neuromuscular & skeletal: Decreased linear skeletal growth rate

Ophthalmic: Intraocular pressure increased (5%), lacrimation (≤3%), cataract, glaucoma

Respiratory: Epistaxis (2% to 11%), sneezing (4%), upper respiratory tract infection (children: 3%), nasal congestion (≤3%), rhinorrhea (≤3%), nasal mucosa irritation (erosion) (≤1%), bronchospasm, dry nose, nasal candidiasis (rare; more likely with aqueous solution), pharyngeal candidiasis (rare; more likely with aqueous solution), wheezing

Miscellaneous: Fever (children: 3%), wound healing impairment

<1%, postmarketing, and/or case reports: Burning sensation, nasal mucosa ulcer, nasal septum perforation

General Dosage Range Intranasal:

Children ≥4 years, Adolescents, and Adults (Qnasl): 1 or 2 inhalations each nostril once daily (maximum: 80 or 320 mcg daily)

Children ≥6 years, Adolescents, and Adults (Beconase AQ): 1 or 2 inhalations each nostril twice daily (maximum: 336 mcg daily)

Mechanism of Action Controls the rate of protein synthesis; depresses the migration of polymorphonuclear leukocytes, fibroblasts; reverses capillary permeability and lysosomal stabilization at the cellular level to prevent or control inflammation

Pharmacodynamics/Kinetics

Onset of Action Within a few days up to 2 weeks

Half-life Elimination BDP: 0.5 hours; 17-BMP: 2.7 hours

Pregnancy Risk Factor C

Pregnancy Considerations Adverse events have been observed in some animal reproduction studies. Hypoadrenalism may occur in newborns following maternal use of corticosteroids in pregnancy; monitor. Intranasal corticosteroids are recommended for the treatment of rhinitis during pregnancy; the lowest effective dose should be used (NAEPP, 2005; Wallace, 2008).

Beclomethasone (Oral Inhalation)
(be kloe METH a sone)

Related Information

Respiratory Diseases *on page* 1777

Brand Names: US Qvar

Brand Names: Canada QVAR

Generic Availability (US) No

Pharmacologic Category Corticosteroid, Inhalant (Oral)

Use

Asthma: Maintenance and prophylactic treatment of asthma in patients ≥5 years (including those who require corticosteroids and those who may benefit from a dose reduction/elimination of systemically administered corticosteroids)

Limitations of use: Not for relief of acute bronchospasm.

Guideline recommendations: A low-dose inhaled corticosteroid (in addition to an as-needed short acting beta$_2$-agonist) is the initial preferred long-term control medication for children, adolescents, and adult patients with persistent asthma who are candidates for treatment according to a step-wise treatment approach (GINA 2016; NAEPP 2007).

Local Anesthetic/Vasoconstrictor Precautions No information available to require special precautions

Effects on Dental Treatment Key adverse event(s) related to dental treatment: Oral candidiasis, xerostomia (normal salivary flow resumes upon discontinuation), nasal dryness, and dry throat. Localized infections with *Candida albicans* or *Aspergillus niger* occur frequently in the mouth and pharynx with repetitive use of an oral inhaler; may require treatment with appropriate antifungal therapy or discontinuance of inhaler use.

Effects on Bleeding No information available to require special precautions

Adverse Reactions

>10%: Central nervous system: Headache (12%)

1% to 10%:

Central nervous system: Voice disorder (1% to 3%), pain (2%)

Gastrointestinal: Nausea (1%)

Genitourinary: Dysmenorrhea (1% to 3%)

Neuromuscular & skeletal: Back pain (1%)
Respiratory: Upper respiratory tract infection (9%), pharyngitis (8%), rhinitis (6%), sinusitis (3%), cough (1% to 3%)

<1%, postmarketing, and/or case reports: Anaphylactoid reaction, anaphylaxis, behavioral changes (such as aggressiveness, depression, sleep disturbances, psychomotor hyperactivity, suicidal ideation; more common in children), dysgeusia (Tuccori 2011), sleep disturbances, psychomotor hyperactivity, suicidal ideation; more common in children), decreased linear skeletal growth rate (in children/adolescents), hypersensitivity reaction (immediate and delayed; including angioedema, bronchospasm, rash, urticaria), HPA-axis suppression

Dosing

Adult & Geriatric

Asthma: Inhalation, oral (doses should be titrated to the lowest effective dose once asthma is controlled):

US labeling:

Patients previously on bronchodilators only: Initial dose 40 to 80 mcg twice daily; maximum dose: 320 mcg twice daily

Patients previously on inhaled corticosteroids: Initial dose 40 to 160 mcg twice daily; maximum dose: 320 mcg twice daily

Canadian labeling:

Mild asthma: 50 to 100 mcg twice daily; maximum dose: 100 mcg twice daily

Moderate asthma: 100 to 250 mcg twice daily; maximum dose: 250 mcg twice daily

Severe asthma: 300 to 400 mcg twice daily; maximum dose: 400 mcg twice daily

Asthma Guidelines:

National Asthma Education and Prevention Program guidelines (NAEPP 2007): HFA inhaler (refers to Qvar 40 mcg and 80 mcg strengths available in US):

"Low" dose: 80 to 240 mcg daily
"Medium" dose: >240 to 480 mcg daily
"High" dose: >480 mcg daily

Global Initiative for Asthma guidelines (GINA 2016): HFA inhaler (refers to Qvar 50 mcg and 100 mcg strengths available in Canada):

"Low" dose: 100 to 200 mcg daily
"Medium" dose: >200 to 400 mcg daily
"High" dose: >400 mcg daily

Conversion: *Conversion from oral systemic corticosteroid to orally inhaled corticosteroid:* Initiation of oral inhalation therapy should begin in patients whose asthma is reasonably stabilized on oral corticosteroids (OCS). A gradual dose reduction of OCS should begin ~7 days after starting inhaled therapy. US labeling recommends reducing prednisone dose no more rapidly than ≤2.5 mg/day (or equivalent of other OCS) every 1 to 2 weeks. The Canadian labeling recommends decreasing the daily dose of prednisone by 1 mg (or equivalent of other OCS) every 7 days or more in closely monitored patients. If adrenal insufficiency occurs, temporarily increase the OCS dose and follow with a more gradual withdrawal. **Note:** When transitioning from systemic to inhaled corticosteroids, supplemental systemic corticosteroid therapy may be necessary during periods of stress or during severe asthma attacks.

Chronic obstructive pulmonary disease (stable) (off-label use): Inhalation, oral: 50 to 400 mcg daily in combination with a long-acting bronchodilator (GOLD, 2014).

Pediatric

Asthma: Inhalation, oral (doses should be titrated to the lowest effective dose once asthma is controlled):

US labeling:

Children 5 to 11 years: Initial: 40 mcg twice daily; maximum dose: 80 mcg twice daily

Children ≥12 years and Adolescents: Refer to adult dosing

Canadian labeling:

Children 5 to 11 years: Initial: 50 mcg twice daily; maximum dose: 100 mcg twice daily

Children ≥12 years and Adolescents: Refer to adult dosing.

Asthma Guidelines:

National Asthma Education and Prevention Program guidelines (NAEPP 2007): HFA inhaler (refers to Qvar 40 mcg and 80 mcg strengths available in US):

Children 5 to 11 years:
"Low" dose: 80 to 160 mcg daily
"Medium" dose: >160 to 320 mcg daily
"High" dose: >320 mcg daily

Children ≥12 years and Adolescents: Refer to adult dosing.

Global Initiative for Asthma guidelines (GINA 2016): HFA inhaler (refers to Qvar 50 mcg and 100 mcg strengths available in Canada):

Children ≤5 years: "Low" dose: 100 mcg daily

Children 6 to 11 years:
"Low" dose: 50 to 100 mcg daily
"Medium" dose: >100 to 200 mcg daily
"High" dose: >200 mcg daily

Children ≥12 years and Adolescents: Refer to adult dosing.

Conversion: *Conversion from oral systemic corticosteroid to orally inhaled corticosteroid:* Initiation of oral inhalation therapy should begin in patients whose asthma is reasonably stabilized on oral corticosteroids (OCS). A gradual dose reduction of OCS should begin ~7 days after starting inhaled therapy. US labeling recommends reducing prednisone dose no more rapidly than ≤2.5 mg/day (or equivalent of other OCS) every 1 to 2 weeks. The Canadian labeling recommends decreasing the daily dose of prednisone by 1 mg (or equivalent of other OCS) every 7 days or more in closely monitored patients. If adrenal insufficiency occurs, temporarily increase the OCS dose and follow with a more gradual withdrawal. **Note:** When transitioning from systemic to inhaled corticosteroids, supplemental systemic corticosteroid therapy may be necessary during periods of stress or during severe asthma attacks.

Renal Impairment There are no dosage adjustments provided in the manufacturer's labeling

Hepatic Impairment There are no dosage adjustments provided in the manufacturer's labeling

Mechanism of Action

Controls the rate of protein synthesis; depresses the migration of polymorphonuclear leukocytes, fibroblasts; reverses capillary permeability and lysosomal stabilization at the cellular level to prevent or control inflammation

Contraindications

Hypersensitivity to beclomethasone or any component of the formulation; status asthmaticus, or other acute asthma episodes requiring intensive measures

Documentation of allergenic cross-reactivity for corticosteroids is limited. However, because of similarities in chemical structure and/or pharmacologic actions, the possibility of cross-sensitivity cannot be ruled out with certainty.

Canadian labeling: Additional contraindications (not in US labeling): Moderate to severe bronchiectasis requiring intensive measures; untreated fungal, bacterial, or tubercular infections of the respiratory tract

Warnings/Precautions May cause hypercorticism or suppression of hypothalamic-pituitary-adrenal (HPA) axis, particularly in younger children or in patients receiving high doses for prolonged periods. HPA axis suppression may lead to adrenal crisis. Withdrawal and discontinuation of a corticosteroid should be done slowly and carefully. Particular care is required when patients are transferred from systemic corticosteroids to inhaled products due to possible adrenal insufficiency or withdrawal from steroids, including an increase in allergic symptoms. Patients receiving >20 mg per day of prednisone (or equivalent) may be most susceptible. Fatalities have occurred due to adrenal insufficiency in asthmatic patients during and after transfer from systemic corticosteroids to aerosol steroids; aerosol steroids do **not** provide the systemic steroid needed to treat patients having trauma, surgery, or infections (particularly gastroenteritis), or other conditions with severe electrolyte loss. Select surgical patients on long-term, high-dose, inhaled corticosteroid (ICS), should be given stress doses of hydrocortisone intravenously during the surgical period and the dose reduced rapidly within 24 hours after surgery (Expert Panel Report 3, 2007).

Bronchospasm may occur with wheezing after inhalation (possibly life-threatening); if bronchospasm occurs, discontinue steroid and treat with a fast-acting bronchodilator. Supplemental steroids (oral or parenteral) may be needed during stress or severe asthma attacks. Not to be used in status asthmaticus or for the relief of acute bronchospasm. Immediate hypersensitivity reactions may occur, including angioedema, bronchospasm, rash, and urticaria; discontinue use if reaction occurs. Corticosteroid use may cause psychiatric disturbances, including depression, euphoria, insomnia, mood swings, and personality changes. Preexisting psychiatric conditions may be exacerbated by corticosteroid use. Prolonged use of corticosteroids may also increase the incidence of secondary infection, mask acute infection (including fungal infections), prolong or exacerbate viral infections, or limit response to vaccines. Avoid use, if possible, in patients with ocular herpes, active or quiescent respiratory or untreated viral, fungal, parasitic or bacterial systemic infections (Canadian labeling contraindicates use with untreated respiratory infections). Exposure to chickenpox or measles should be avoided. Close observation is required in patients with latent tuberculosis and/or TB reactivity; restrict use in active TB. Prolonged treatment with corticosteroids has been associated with the development of Kaposi sarcoma (case reports); if noted, discontinuation of therapy should be considered. *Candida albicans* infections may occur in the mouth and pharynx; rinsing (and spitting) with water after inhaler use may decrease risk. Rare cases of vasculitis (Churg-Strauss syndrome) or other systemic eosinophilic conditions can occur; often associated with decrease and/or withdrawal of oral corticosteroid therapy following initiation of inhaled corticosteroid.

Use with caution in patients with major risk factors for decreased bone mineral count. Use with caution in patients with thyroid disease, hepatic impairment, renal impairment, cardiovascular disease, diabetes, glaucoma, cataracts, myasthenia gravis, patients at risk for seizures, or GI diseases (diverticulitis, peptic ulcer, ulcerative colitis). Use caution following acute MI (corticosteroids have been associated with myocardial rupture). Because of the risk of adverse effects, systemic corticosteroids should be used cautiously in elderly patients in the smallest possible effective dose for the shortest duration.

Orally inhaled corticosteroids may cause a reduction in growth velocity in pediatric patients (~1 centimeter per year [range: 0.3 to 1.8 cm per year] and related to dose and duration of exposure). To minimize the systemic effects of orally inhaled corticosteroids, each patient should be titrated to the lowest effective dose. Growth should be routinely monitored in pediatric patients. A gradual tapering of dose may be required prior to discontinuing therapy; there have been reports of systemic corticosteroid withdrawal symptoms (eg, joint/muscle pain, lassitude, depression) when withdrawing oral inhalation therapy. When transferring to oral inhalation therapy from systemic corticosteroid therapy; previously suppressed allergic conditions (rhinitis, conjunctivitis, eczema, arthritis, and eosinophilic conditions) may be unmasked; during transition monitor pulmonary function tests (FEV_1 or PEF), beta-agonist use, and asthma symptoms and observe for signs and symptoms of adrenal insufficiency.

Drug Interactions

Metabolism/Transport Effects None known.

Avoid Concomitant Use

Avoid concomitant use of Beclomethasone (Oral Inhalation) with any of the following: Aldesleukin; BCG (Intravesical); Desmopressin; Loxapine; Natalizumab; Pimecrolimus; Tacrolimus (Topical); Tofacitinib

Increased Effect/Toxicity

Beclomethasone (Oral Inhalation) may increase the levels/effects of: Amphotericin B; Ceritinib; Deferasirox; Desmopressin; Fingolimod; Leflunomide; Loop Diuretics; Loxapine; Natalizumab; Thiazide and Thiazide-Like Diuretics; Tofacitinib

The levels/effects of Beclomethasone (Oral Inhalation) may be increased by: Denosumab, Ocrelizumab; Pimecrolimus; Tacrolimus (Topical); Trastuzumab

Decreased Effect

Beclomethasone (Oral Inhalation) may decrease the levels/effects of: Aldesleukin; BCG (Intravesical); Coccidioides immitis Skin Test; Corticorelin; Hyaluronidase; Nivolumab; Sipuleucel-T; Tertomotide; Vaccines (Inactivated)

The levels/effects of Beclomethasone (Oral Inhalation) may be decreased by: Echinacea

Pharmacodynamics/Kinetics

Onset of Action Within 1 to 2 days in some patients; usually within 1 to 2 weeks; Maximum effect: 3 to 4 weeks

Half-life Elimination BDP: 0.5 hours; 17-BMP: 2.7 hours

Time to Peak Plasma: Oral inhalation: BDP: 0.5 hours; 17-BMP: 0.7 hours

Pregnancy Risk Factor C

Pregnancy Considerations Adverse events have been observed in animal reproduction studies. Hypoadrenalism may occur in newborns following maternal use of corticosteroids in pregnancy. Based on available data, an overall increased risk of congenital malformations or a decrease in fetal growth has not been associated with maternal use of inhaled corticosteroids during pregnancy (Bakhireva, 2005; NAEPP, 2005;

Namazy, 2004). Uncontrolled asthma is associated with adverse events in pregnancy (increased risk of perinatal mortality, pre-eclampsia, preterm birth, low birth weight infants). Inhaled corticosteroids are recommended for the treatment of asthma during pregnancy (most information available using budesonide) (ACOG, 2008; NAEPP, 2005).

Breastfeeding Considerations Other corticosteroids have been found in breast milk; however, information for beclomethasone is not available. Due to the potential for serious adverse reactions in the nursing infant, the manufacturer recommends a decision be made whether to discontinue nursing or to discontinue the drug, taking into account the importance of treatment to the mother. Use of inhaled corticosteroids is not a contraindication to breastfeeding (NAEPP, 2005).

Dosage Forms Considerations
QVAR 8.7 g canisters contain 120 inhalations.

Dosage Forms
Aerosol Solution, Inhalation:
Qvar: 40 mcg/actuation (8.7 g); 80 mcg/actuation (8.7 g)

Dosage Forms: Canada
Aerosol, for oral inhalation:
QVAR: 50 mcg/inhalation (6.5 g, 12.4 g); 100 mcg/inhalation (6.5 g, 12.4 g)

Bedaquiline (bed AK wi leen)

Related Information
Clinical Risk Related to Drugs Prolonging QT Interval *on page 1772*

Brand Names: US Sirturo

Pharmacologic Category Antitubercular Agent

Use
Multidrug-resistant pulmonary tuberculosis: Treatment of pulmonary multidrug-resistant tuberculosis (MDR-TB) in combination therapy in adults (≥18 years of age) when other alternatives are not available.
Limitations of use: Not for use in extrapulmonary TB, latent infection due to TB, drug-sensitive TB, or treatment of other mycobacteria. Clinical data in HIV-1 infected patients coinfected with MDR-TB are limited (safety and efficacy has not been established).

Local Anesthetic/Vasoconstrictor Precautions Bedaquiline is one of the drugs confirmed to prolong the QT interval and is accepted as having a risk of causing torsade de pointes. In terms of epinephrine, it is not known what effect vasoconstrictors in the local anesthetic regimen will have in patients with a known history of congenital prolonged QT interval or in patients taking any medication that prolongs the QT interval. Until more information is obtained, it is suggested that the clinician consult with the physician prior to the use of a vasoconstrictor in suspected patients, and that the vasoconstrictor (epinephrine, mepivacaine and levonordefrin [Carbocaine® 2% with Neo-Cobefrin®]) be used with caution. See Dental Comment.

Effects on Dental Treatment No significant effects or complications reported

Effects on Bleeding No information available to require special precautions

Adverse Reactions
Frequency not always defined.
>10%:
Cardiovascular: Chest pain (11%)
Central nervous system: Headache (28%)
Gastrointestinal: Nausea (38%)
Hepatic: Increased serum transaminases (9% to 11%)
Neuromuscular & skeletal: Arthralgia (33%)
Respiratory: Hemoptysis (18%)
1% to 10%:
Dermatologic: Skin rash (8%)
Gastrointestinal: Anorexia (9%), increased serum amylase
<1%, postmarketing, and/or case reports: Hepatotoxicity, prolonged Q-T interval on ECG

General Dosage Range Oral: *Adults:*
Weeks 1-2: 400 mg once daily
Weeks 3-24: 200 mg 3 times weekly (total weekly dose: 600 mg)

Mechanism of Action As a diarylquinoline antimycobacterial, inhibits the proton transfer chain of mycobacterial ATP synthase required for energy generation in *M. tuberculosis*. It is not active against human ATP synthase.

Pharmacodynamics/Kinetics
Half-life Elimination Terminal: 5.5 months (bedaquiline and M2 metabolite)
Time to Peak Serum: Oral: 5 hours

Pregnancy Risk Factor B

Pregnancy Considerations Adverse events were not observed in animal reproduction studies.

Dental Comment See Local Anesthetic/Vasoconstrictor Precautions

Belatacept (bel AT a sept)

Brand Names: US Nulojix

Pharmacologic Category Selective T-Cell Costimulation Blocker

Use
Kidney transplant: Prophylaxis of organ rejection concomitantly with basiliximab induction, mycophenolate, and corticosteroids in adult Epstein-Barr virus (EBV) seropositive kidney transplant recipients
Limitations of use: Use only in EBV seropositive patients; use for prophylaxis of organ rejection in transplanted organs other than the kidney has not been established.

Local Anesthetic/Vasoconstrictor Precautions No information available to require special precautions

Effects on Dental Treatment Key adverse event(s) related to dental treatment: Stomatitis has been reported

Effects on Bleeding No information available to require special precautions

Adverse Reactions Incidences reported as part of a combination therapy regimen.
>10%:
Cardiovascular: Peripheral edema (34%), hypertension (32%), hypotension (18%)
Central nervous system: Headache (21%), insomnia (15%)
Endocrine & metabolic: Hypokalemia (21%), hyperkalemia (20%), hypophosphatemia (19%), lipid metabolism disorder (19%), hyperglycemia (16%), hypocalcemia (13%), hypercholesterolemia (11%)
Gastrointestinal: Diarrhea (39%), constipation (33%), nausea (24%), vomiting (22%), abdominal pain (19%)
Genitourinary: Urinary tract infection (37%), dysuria (11%)
Hematologic & oncologic: Anemia (45%), leukopenia (20%)
Infection: Infection (72% to 82%, serious infection 24% to 36%), fungal infection (185), herpes virus

infection (7% to 14%), cytomegalovirus disease (11% to 13%), influenza (11%)

Neuromuscular & skeletal: Arthralgia (17%), back pain (13%)

Renal: Proteinuria (16%; up to 33% 2+ proteinuria at 1 month post-transplant), graft complications (renal: 25%), hematuria (16%), increased serum creatinine (15%)

Respiratory: Cough (24%), upper respiratory tract infection (15%), nasopharyngitis (13%), dyspnea (12%)

Miscellaneous: Fever (28%)

1% to 10%:

Cardiovascular: Arteriovenous fistula site complication (thrombosis, <10%), atrial fibrillation (<10%)

Central nervous system: Anxiety (10%), Guillain-Barré syndrome (<10%), dizziness (9%)

Dermatologic: Alopecia (<10%), hyperhidrosis (<10%), acne vulgaris (8%)

Endocrine & metabolic: Diabetes mellitus (new onset, 5% to 8%), hypomagnesemia (7%), hyperuricemia (5%)

Gastrointestinal: Stomatitis (<10%; including aphthous stomatitis), upper abdominal pain (9%)

Genitourinary: Urinary incontinence (<10%)

Hematologic & oncologic: Hematoma (<10%), lymphocele (<10%), neutropenia (<10%), malignant neoplasm (4%), malignant neoplasm of skin (nonmelanoma, 2%)

Immunologic: Antibody development (2%)

Infection: Polyoma virus infection (3% to 4%)

Neuromuscular & skeletal: Musculoskeletal pain (<10%), tremor (8%)

Renal: Acute renal failure (<10%), hydronephrosis (<10%), kidney transplant dysfunction (chronic allograft nephropathy: <10%), renal disease (renal artery stenosis: <10%), renal insufficiency (<10%), renal tubular necrosis (9%)

Respiratory: Bronchitis (10%), tuberculosis (1% to 2%)

Miscellaneous: Infusion related reaction (5%)

<1%, postmarketing, and/or case reports: Anaphylaxis, aspergillosis (cerebral; higher dosing regimen), encephalitis (Chagas, West Nile; higher dosing regimen), graft rejection (renal), lymphoproliferative disorder (post transplant; incidence is 9-fold higher in non-EBV seropositive patients), meningitis (cryptococcal), nephropathy (polyoma virus-associated mainly BK), progressive multifocal leukoencephalopathy (higher dosing regimen)

General Dosage Range IV: *Adults:* Initial phase: 10 mg/kg on day 1 (day of transplantation, prior to transplant) and day 5 (post-transplant), and at the end of week 2, 4, 8, and 12 post-transplant; maintenance phase: 5 mg/kg every 4 weeks beginning at the end of week 16 post-transplant

Mechanism of Action Fusion protein which acts as a selective T-cell (lymphocyte) costimulation blocker by binding to CD80 and CD86 receptors on antigen presenting cells (APC), blocking the required CD28 mediated interaction between APCs and T cells needed to activate T lymphocytes. T-cell stimulation results in cytokine production and proliferation, mediators in immunologic rejection associated with kidney transplantation.

Pharmacodynamics/Kinetics

Half-life Elimination ~10 days (healthy patients and kidney transplant patients)

Pregnancy Risk Factor C

Pregnancy Considerations Adverse events have been observed in animal reproduction studies.

The National Transplantation Pregnancy Registry (NTPR) is a registry which follows pregnancies which occur in maternal transplant recipients or those fathered by male transplant recipients. The NTPR encourages reporting of pregnancies following solid organ transplant by contacting them at 877-955-6877 or NTPR@giftoflifeinstitute.org.

Prescribing and Access Restrictions

The ENLiST registry has been created to further determine the safety of belatacept, particularly the incidence of post-transplant lymphoproliferative disorder (PTLD), CNS PTLD, and progressive multifocal leukoencephalopathy (PML), in U.S. adult EBV-seropositive kidney transplant patients. Transplant centers are encouraged to participate (1-800-321-1335).

Effective March 15, 2017, Bristol-Myers Squibb will not be able to supply Nulojix for new patients. To ensure existing patients continue to receive Nulojix, they must be registered in the Nulojix Distribution Program and receive a unique patient identification number which will be required when placing orders for the drug. McKesson Plasma and Biologics will be the exclusive distributor of Nulojix and may be contacted at 1-877-625-2566 or more information may be found at: http://www.nulojixhcp.bmscustomerconnect.com/servlet/servlet.FileDownload?file=00Pi000000nzpG5EAI. BMS anticipates that it will be able to supply Nulojix to new patients again in 2018.

Belimumab (be LIM yoo mab)

Brand Names: US Benlysta

Brand Names: Canada Benlysta

Pharmacologic Category Monoclonal Antibody

Use

Systemic lupus erythematosus: Treatment of adult patients with active, autoantibody-positive systemic lupus erythematosus (SLE) who are receiving standard therapy.

Limitations of use: Use is not recommended in patients with severe active lupus nephritis, severe active CNS lupus, or in combination with other biologics, including B-cell targeted therapies or intravenous (IV) cyclophosphamide.

Local Anesthetic/Vasoconstrictor Precautions No information available to require special precautions

Effects on Dental Treatment No significant effects or complications reported

Effects on Bleeding No information available to require special precautions

Adverse Reactions

>10%:

Gastrointestinal: Nausea (15%), diarrhea (12%)

Hypersensitivity: Hypersensitivity (13%)

Miscellaneous: Infusion related reaction (17%)

>3% to 10%:

Central nervous system: Insomnia (6% to 7%), depression (5% to 6%), migraine (5%), anxiety (4%), headache (≥3%)

Dermatologic: Dermatological reaction (≥3%)

Gastrointestinal: Viral gastroenteritis (3%)

Genitourinary: Urinary tract infection (site not specified >5%), cystitis (4%)

Hematologic & oncologic: Leukopenia (4%)

Infection: Influenza (>5%)

Neuromuscular & skeletal: Limb pain (6%)

Respiratory: Bronchitis (9%), nasopharyngitis (9%), sinusitis (>5%), upper respiratory tract infection (>5%), pharyngitis (5%)

Miscellaneous: Fever (10%)

<3%, postmarketing, and/or case reports: Anaphylaxis (including fatalities), angioedema, antibody development, bradycardia, cellulitis, dyspnea, eyelid edema, hypotension, myalgia, pneumonia, progressive multifocal leukoencephalopathy (immune compromised), pruritus, skin rash, suicidal tendencies, urticaria

General Dosage Range IV: *Adults:* 10 mg/kg every 2 weeks for 3 doses; Maintenance: 10 mg/kg every 4 weeks

Mechanism of Action Belimumab is an IgG1-lambda monoclonal antibody that prevents the survival of B lymphocytes by blocking the binding of soluble human B lymphocyte stimulator protein (BLyS) to receptors on B lymphocytes. This reduces the activity of B-cell mediated immunity and the autoimmune response.

Pharmacodynamics/Kinetics

Onset of Action B cells: 8 weeks; Clinical improvement (SLE Responder Index and flare reduction): 16 weeks (Navarra, 2011)

Half-life Elimination 19.4 days

Pregnancy Considerations

IgG molecules are known to cross the placenta (belimumab is an engineered IgG molecule) with increasing amounts as pregnancy progresses. Effective contraception should be used during and for at least 4 months following treatment in women of childbearing potential. If exposure occurs during pregnancy, monitor the newborn for B-cell reduction and other immune dysfunction and consider risks and benefits prior to administering live vaccines.

Healthcare providers are encouraged to enroll women exposed to belimumab during pregnancy in a pregnancy registry (877-681-6296); patients may also enroll themselves.

Belinostat (be LIN oh stat)

Brand Names: US Beleodaq

Pharmacologic Category Antineoplastic Agent, Histone Deacetylase (HDAC) Inhibitor

Use Peripheral T-cell lymphoma: Treatment of relapsed or refractory peripheral T-cell lymphoma (PTCL)

Local Anesthetic/Vasoconstrictor Precautions Belinostat is one of the drugs confirmed to prolong the QT interval and is accepted as having a risk of causing torsade de pointes. The risk of drug-induced torsade de pointes is extremely low when a single QT interval prolonging drug is prescribed. In terms of epinephrine, it is not known what effect vasoconstrictors in the local anesthetic regimen will have in patients with a known history of congenital prolonged QT interval or in patients taking any medication that prolongs the QT interval. Until more information is obtained, it is suggested that the clinician consult with the physician prior to the use of a vasoconstrictor in suspected patients, and that the vasoconstrictor (epinephrine, mepivacaine and levonordefrin [Carbocaine® 2% with Neo-Cobefrin®]) be used with caution.

Effects on Dental Treatment Key adverse event(s) related to dental treatment: Hypotension reported (10% incidence); monitor patient for dizziness when arising from dental chair

Effects on Bleeding Chemotherapy may result in significant myelosuppression, potentially including significant reduction in platelet counts (thrombocytopenia grades 3/4: 7%) and altered hemostasis. In patients who are under active treatment with these agents, medical consult is suggested.

Adverse Reactions

>10%:

Cardiovascular: Peripheral edema (20%), prolonged Q-T interval on ECG (11%; grades 3/4: 4%)

Central nervous system: Fatigue (37%; grades 3/4: 5%), chills (16%; grades 3/4: 1%), headache (15%)

Dermatologic: Skin rash (20%; grades 3/4: 1%), pruritus (16%; grades 3/4: 3%)

Endocrine & metabolic: Increased lactate dehydrogenase (16%; grades 3/4: 2%), hypokalemia (12%; grades 3/4: 4%)

Gastrointestinal: Nausea (42%; grades 3/4: 1%), vomiting (29%; grades 3/4: 1%), constipation (23%; grades 3/4: 1%), diarrhea (23%; grades 3/4: 2%), decreased appetite (15%; grades 3/4: 2%), abdominal pain (11%; grades 3/4: 1%)

Hematologic & oncologic: Anemia (32%; grades 3/4: 11%), thrombocytopenia (16%; grades 3/4: 7%)

Local: Pain at injection site (14%)

Respiratory: Dyspnea (22%; grades 3/4: 6%), cough (19%)

Miscellaneous: Fever (35%; grades 3/4: 2%)

1% to 10%:

Cardiovascular: Hypotension (10%; grades 3/4: 3%), phlebitis (10%; grades 3/4: 1%)

Central nervous system: Dizziness (10%)

Infection: Infection (>2%)

Renal: Increased serum creatinine (>2%)

Respiratory: Pneumonia (>2%)

Miscellaneous: Multi-organ failure (>2%)

<1%, postmarketing, and/or case reports: Abnormal hepatic function tests, febrile neutropenia, hepatic failure, hepatotoxicity, leukopenia, sepsis, tumor lysis syndrome, ventricular fibrillation

General Dosage Range Dosage adjustment recommended in patients who develop toxicities

IV: *Adults:* 1000 mg/m^2 daily on days 1 to 5 of a 21-day cycle

Mechanism of Action Histone deacetylase (HDAC) inhibitor which catalyzes acetyl group removal from protein lysine residues (of histone and some nonhistone proteins). Inhibition of histone deacetylase results in accumulation of acetyl groups, leading to cell cycle arrest and apoptosis. Belinostat has preferential cytotoxicity toward tumor cells versus normal cells.

Pharmacodynamics/Kinetics

Half-life Elimination 1.1 hours

Time to Peak At end of infusion (Steele, 2011)

Pregnancy Risk Factor D

Pregnancy Considerations Animal reproduction studies have not been conducted. Belinostat is a genotoxic drug that targets dividing cells; embryofetal toxicity is expected if exposure occurs during pregnancy. Based on animal data, belinostat may also impair male fertility. Women of reproductive potential should avoid pregnancy during treatment with belinostat.

Dental Comment This drug is known to prolong the QT interval (see Local Anesthetic/Vasocontrictor Precautions)

Benazepril (ben AY ze pril)

Related Information

Cardiovascular Diseases *on page 1752*

Brand Names: US Lotensin

Brand Names: Canada Lotensin

Pharmacologic Category Angiotensin-Converting Enzyme (ACE) Inhibitor; Antihypertensive

Use

Hypertension: Treatment of hypertension, either alone or in combination with other antihypertensive agents

Guideline recommendations:

Hypertension: The 2014 guideline for the management of high blood pressure in adults (Eighth Joint National Committee [JNC 8]) recommends initiation of pharmacologic treatment to lower blood pressure for the following patients:

- Patients ≥60 years of age with systolic blood pressure (SBP) ≥150 mm Hg or diastolic blood pressure (DBP) ≥90 mm Hg. Goal of therapy is SBP <150 mm Hg and DBP <90 mm Hg.
- Patients <60 years of age with SBP ≥140 mm Hg or DBP is ≥90 mm Hg. Goal of therapy is SBP <140 mm Hg and DBP <90 mm Hg.
- Patients ≥18 years of age with diabetes and SBP ≥140 mm Hg or DBP ≥90 mm Hg. Goal of therapy is SBP <140 mm Hg and DBP <90 mm Hg.
- Patients ≥18 years of age with chronic kidney disease (CKD) and SBP ≥140 mm Hg or DBP ≥90 mm Hg. Goal of therapy is SBP <140 mm Hg and DBP <90 mm Hg.

Chronic kidney disease (CKD) and hypertension: Regardless of race or diabetes status, the use of an ACE inhibitor (ACEI) or angiotensin receptor blocker (ARB) as initial therapy is recommended to improve kidney outcomes. In the general nonblack population (without CKD) including those with diabetes, initial antihypertensive treatment should consist of a thiazide-type diuretic, calcium channel blocker, ACEI, or ARB. In the general black population (without CKD) including those with diabetes, initial antihypertensive treatment should consist of a thiazide-type diuretic or a calcium channel blocker **instead of** an ACEI or ARB.

Coronary artery disease (CAD) and hypertension: The American Heart Association, American College of Cardiology and American Society of Hypertension (AHA/ACC/ASH) 2015 scientific statement for the treatment of hypertension in patients with CAD recommends the use of an ACE inhibitor (or an ARB) as part of a regimen in patients with hypertension and chronic stable angina if there is prior MI, LV systolic dysfunction, diabetes mellitus, or CKD. A BP target of <140/90 mm Hg is reasonable for the secondary prevention of cardiovascular events. A lower target BP (<130/80 mm Hg) may be appropriate in some individuals with CAD, previous MI, stroke or transient ischemic attack, or CAD risk equivalents(AHA/ACC/ASH [Rosendorff 2015]).

Local Anesthetic/Vasoconstrictor Precautions No information available to require special precautions

Effects on Dental Treatment Key adverse event(s) related to dental treatment: Patients may experience orthostatic hypotension as they stand up after treatment; especially if lying in dental chair for extended periods of time. Use caution with sudden changes in position during and after dental treatment.

An angiotensin-converting enzyme (ACE) inhibitor cough is a dry, hacking, nonproductive cough that can potentially interfere with longer dental procedures if patient has this side effect.

Effects on Bleeding No information available to require special precautions

Adverse Reactions

1% to 10%:

Central nervous system: Headache (6%), dizziness (4%), drowsiness (2%), orthostatic dizziness (2%)

Renal: Increased serum creatinine (2%), renal insufficiency (may occur in patients with bilateral renal artery stenosis or hypovolemia)

Respiratory: Cough (1% to 10%)

<1%, postmarketing, and/or case reports (Limited to important or life-threatening): Agranulocytosis, alopecia, anaphylactoid reaction, angina pectoris, angioedema (includes head, neck, and intestinal angioedema), arthralgia, arthritis, asthma, dermatitis, dyspnea, ECG changes, eosinophilia, flushing, gastritis, hemolytic anemia, hyperbilirubinemia, hyperglycemia, hyperkalemia, hypersensitivity, hypertonia, hyponatremia, hypotension, impotence, increased blood urea nitrogen (transient), increased serum transaminases, increased uric acid, insomnia, leukopenia, myalgia, neutropenia, orthostatic hypotension, palpitations, pancreatitis, paresthesia, pemphigus, peripheral edema, proteinuria, pruritus, shock, skin photosensitivity, skin rash, Stevens-Johnson syndrome, syncope, thrombocytopenia, vomiting

Eosinophilic pneumonitis, anaphylaxis, neutropenia, agranulocytosis, renal insufficiency, and renal failure have been reported with other ACE inhibitors. In addition, a syndrome including fever, myalgia, arthralgia, interstitial nephritis, vasculitis, rash, eosinophilia, and elevated ESR has been reported to be associated with ACE inhibitors.

General Dosage Range Dosage adjustment recommended in patients with renal impairment

Oral:

Children ≥6 years and Adolescents: Initial: 0.2 mg/kg/day (up to 10 mg daily); Maintenance: 0.1 to 0.6 mg/kg/day (maximum: 40 mg daily)

Adults: Initial: 5 to 10 mg daily; Maintenance: 20 to 80 mg daily in 1 to 2 divided doses

Mechanism of Action Competitive inhibition of angiotensin I being converted to angiotensin II, a potent vasoconstrictor, through the angiotensin I-converting enzyme (ACE) activity, with resultant lower levels of angiotensin II which causes an increase in plasma renin activity and a reduction in aldosterone secretion

Pharmacodynamics/Kinetics

Onset of Action

Reduction in plasma angiotensin-converting enzyme (ACE) activity: Peak effect: 1 to 2 hours after 2 to 20 mg dose (Nussberger 1987; Nussberger 1989)

Reduction in blood pressure: Peak effect: Single dose: 2 to 4 hours; Continuous therapy: 2 weeks (Fogari 1990)

Duration of Action Reduction in plasma angiotensin-converting enzyme (ACE) activity: >90% inhibition for 24 hours after 5 to 20 mg dose (Balfour 1991)

Half-life Elimination Benazeprilat: Effective: 10 to 11 hours; Terminal: Children: 5 hours, Adults: 22 hours

Time to Peak

Parent drug: 0.5 to 1 hour

Active metabolite (benazeprilat): Fasting: 1 to 2 hours; Nonfasting: 2 to 4 hours

Pregnancy Risk Factor D

Pregnancy Considerations **[U.S. Boxed Warning]: Drugs that act on the renin-angiotensin system can cause injury and death to the developing fetus. Discontinue as soon as possible once pregnancy is detected.** Benazepril crosses the placenta. Drugs that act on the renin-angiotensin system are associated with oligohydramnios. Oligohydramnios, due to decreased fetal renal function, may lead to fetal lung hypoplasia and skeletal malformations. Their use in pregnancy is also associated with anuria, hypotension, renal failure, skull hypoplasia, and death in the fetus/neonate. Teratogenic effects may occur following maternal use of an ACE inhibitor during the first trimester, although this finding may be confounded by maternal disease. Because adverse fetal events are well documented with exposure later in pregnancy, ACE inhibitor use in pregnant women is not recommended (Seely 2014; Weber 2014). Infants exposed to an ACE inhibitor in utero should be monitored for hyperkalemia, hypotension, and oliguria. Oligohydramnios may not appear until after irreversible fetal injury has occurred. Exchange transfusions or dialysis may be required to reverse hypotension or improve renal function, although data related to the effectiveness in neonates is limited.

Chronic maternal hypertension itself is also associated with adverse events in the fetus/infant and mother. ACE inhibitors are not recommended for the treatment of uncomplicated hypertension in pregnancy (ACOG 2013) and they are specifically contraindicated for the treatment of hypertension and chronic heart failure during pregnancy by some guidelines (Regitz-Zagrosek 2011). In addition, ACE inhibitors should generally be avoided in women of reproductive age (ACOG 2013). If treatment for hypertension or chronic heart failure in pregnancy is needed, other agents should be used (ACOG 2013; Regitz-Zagrosek 2011).

Bendamustine (ben da MUS teen)

Brand Names: US Bendeka; Treanda

Brand Names: Canada Treanda

Pharmacologic Category Antineoplastic Agent, Alkylating Agent; Antineoplastic Agent, Alkylating Agent (Nitrogen Mustard)

Use

Chronic lymphocytic leukemia: Treatment of chronic lymphocytic leukemia (CLL)

Non-Hodgkin lymphoma: Treatment of indolent B-cell non-Hodgkin lymphoma (NHL) which has progressed during or within 6 months of rituximab treatment or a rituximab-containing regimen

Local Anesthetic/Vasoconstrictor Precautions No information available to require special precautions

Effects on Dental Treatment Key adverse event(s) related to dental treatment: Stomatitis, xerostomia (normal salivary flow resumes upon discontinuation).

Effects on Bleeding Thrombocytopenia has been reported in 77% to 86% (grade 3/4: 11% to 25%) of patients.

Adverse Reactions

>10%:

Cardiovascular: Peripheral edema (13%)

Central nervous system: Fatigue (9% to 57%), headache (21%), dizziness (14%), chills (6% to 14%), insomnia (13%)

Dermatologic: Skin rash (8% to 16%)

Endocrine & metabolic: Weight loss (7% to 18%), dehydration (14%)

Gastrointestinal: Nausea (20% to 75%), vomiting (16% to 40%), diarrhea (9% to 37%), constipation (29%), anorexia (23%), stomatitis (15%), abdominal pain (13%), decreased appetite (13%), dyspepsia (11%)

Hematologic & oncologic: Lymphocytopenia (68% to 99%; grades 3/4: 47% to 94%), bone marrow depression (grades 3/4: 98%; nadir: in week 3), leukopenia (61% to 94%; grades 3/4: 28% to 56%), decreased hemoglobin (88% to 89%; grades 3/4: 11% to 13%), decreased neutrophils (75% to 86%; grades 3/4: 43% to 60%), thrombocytopenia (77% to 86%; grades 3/4: 11% to 25%)

Hepatic: Increased serum bilirubin (34%)

Neuromuscular & skeletal: Back pain (14%), weakness (8% to 11%)

Respiratory: Cough (4% to 22%), dyspnea (16%)

Miscellaneous: Fever (24% to 34%)

1% to 10%:

Cardiovascular: Tachycardia (7%), chest pain (6%), hypotension (6%), exacerbation of hypertension (3%)

Central nervous system: Anxiety (8%), depression (6%), pain (6%)

Dermatologic: Pruritus (5% to 6%), hyperhidrosis (5%), night sweats (5%), xeroderma (5%)

Endocrine & metabolic: Hypokalemia (9%), hyperuricemia (7%), hyperglycemia (grades 3/4: 3%), hypocalcemia (grades 3/4: 2%), hyponatremia (grades 3/4: 2%)

Gastrointestinal: Gastroesophageal reflux disease (10%), xerostomia (9%), dysgeusia (7%), oral candidiasis (6%), abdominal distention (5%), upper abdominal pain (5%)

Genitourinary: Urinary tract infection (10%)

Hematologic & oncologic: Febrile neutropenia (grades 3/4: 6%)

Hepatic: Increased serum ALT (grades 3/4: 3%), increased serum AST (grades 3/4: 1%)

Hypersensitivity: Hypersensitivity (5%)

Infection: Herpes zoster (10%), infection (6%), herpes simplex infection (3%)

Local: Infusion site pain (6%), catheter pain (5%)

Neuromuscular & skeletal: Arthralgia (6%), limb pain (5%), ostealgia (5%)

Renal: Increased serum creatinine (grades 3/4: 2%)

Respiratory: Upper respiratory tract infection (10%), sinusitis (9%), pharyngolaryngeal pain (8%), pneumonia (8%), nasopharyngitis (6% to 7%), nasal congestion (5%), wheezing (5%)

Frequency not defined:

Central nervous system: Drowsiness, malaise

Dermatologic: Dermatitis, skin necrosis

Gastrointestinal: Mucositis

Hematologic & oncologic: Hemolysis

<1%, postmarketing, and/or case reports: Acute renal failure, anaphylactoid reaction, anaphylaxis, atrial fibrillation, bronchogenic carcinoma, bullous rash, cardiac failure, dermatological reaction (toxic), DRESS syndrome, erythema, extravasation injury, hepatitis, hepatotoxicity, injection site reaction (including irritation, pain, phlebitis, pruritus, swelling), myelodysplastic syndrome, myeloid leukemia (acute), myeloproliferative disease, myocardial infarction, neutropenic sepsis, palpitations, pancytopenia, pneumonia (*Pneumocystis jiroveci*), pneumonitis, pulmonary alveolar hemorrhage (with grade 3 thrombocytopenia), pulmonary fibrosis, reactivation of disease (including, but not limited to hepatitis B, cytomegalovirus, *Mycobacterium tuberculosis*, herpes zoster), sepsis, septic shock, Stevens-Johnson syndrome, toxic epidermal necrolysis, tumor lysis syndrome

General Dosage Range Dosage adjustment recommended in patients who develop toxicities

IV: *Adults:* 100 mg/m^2 on days 1 and 2 of a 28-day treatment cycle **or** 120 mg/m^2 on days 1 and 2 of a 21-day treatment cycle

Mechanism of Action Bendamustine is an alkylating agent (nitrogen mustard derivative) with a benzimidazole ring (purine analog) which demonstrates only partial cross-resistance (*in vitro*) with other alkylating agents. It leads to cell death via single and double strand DNA cross-linking. Bendamustine is active against quiescent and dividing cells. The primary cytotoxic activity is due to bendamustine (as compared to metabolites).

Pharmacodynamics/Kinetics

Half-life Elimination Bendamustine: ~40 minutes; M3: ~3 hours; M4: ~30 minutes

Time to Peak At end of infusion

Pregnancy Risk Factor D

Pregnancy Considerations Adverse events were observed in animal reproduction studies. May cause fetal harm if administered during pregnancy. For women and men of reproductive potential, effective contraception should be used during and for 3 months after treatment.

Benzocaine (BEN zoe kane)

Related Information

Oral Pain *on page 1830*

Related Sample Prescriptions

Ulcerative and Erosive Disorders - Sample Prescriptions *on page 43*

Brand Names: US Anacaine; Anbesol Cold Sore Therapy [OTC]; Anbesol JR [OTC]; Anbesol Maximum Strength [OTC]; Anbesol [OTC]; Baby Anbesol [OTC]; Benz-O-Sthetic [OTC]; Benzocaine Oral Anesthetic [OTC] [DSC]; Bi-Zets/Benzotroches [OTC]; Blistex Medicated [OTC]; Cepacol Dual Relief [OTC] [DSC]; Cepacol Sensations Hydra [OTC] [DSC]; Cepacol Sensations Warming [OTC] [DSC]; Chiggerex [OTC]; Chiggertox [OTC]; Dent-O-Kain/20 [OTC]; Dentapaine [OTC]; Dermoplast [OTC]; Foille [OTC]; HurriCaine One [OTC]; Hurricaine [OTC]; Ivy-Rid [OTC]; Kank-A Mouth Pain [OTC]; Ora-film [OTC]; Oral Pain Relief Max St [OTC] [DSC]; Pinnacaine Otic [DSC]; Sore Throat Relief [OTC]; Topex Topical Anesthetic; Trocaine Throat [OTC]; Zilactin Baby [OTC]

Brand Names: Canada Anbesol® Baby; Zilactin Baby®; Zilactin-B®

Generic Availability (US) May be product dependent

Pharmacologic Category Analgesic, Topical; Local Anesthetic

Dental Use Ester-type topical local anesthetic for temporary relief of pain associated with toothache, minor sore throat pain, and canker sore

Use Note: Approved ages and uses for products may vary; consult product labeling for specific information:

Topical, external:

Dermal irritation: Ointment 5%, spray 5% and 20%: Temporary relief of pain and itching associated with minor skin irritations, cuts, scrapes, minor burns, sunburn, and insect bites; prevention of infection in minor cuts, scrapes and burns

Poison ivy/sumac: Spray 5% (Ivy-Rid only): Temporary relief of pain and itching associated with poison ivy/oak/sumac

Topical, oral:

Mouth and gum irritation:

Ointment 20%: Temporary relief of pain associated with fever blisters and cold sores.

Gel 10% and 20%, lozenge, spray 5%, liquid 10% and 20%: Temporary relief of pain associated with toothache, sore gums, sore throat, canker sores, braces, minor dental procedures, or minor injury of the mouth and gum caused by dentures or orthodontic appliances. **Note:** Although product is available in a gel formulation for relief of pain associated with teething in infants ≥4 months, the FDA, AAP, and American Academy of Pediatric Dentistry do not recommend use due to safety concerns related to increased methemoglobinemia risk in infants and children <2 years (AAP 2011a; FDA 2012).

Sore throat/mouth, gag reflex suppression: Spray 20%: Topical anesthetic for oral or mucosal areas; temporary relief of occasional minor irritation and pain associated with sore mouth and throat; temporary suppression of gag reflex.

Topical anesthetic: Gel or liquid 20% (Topex only): Topical anesthetic for use on oral mucosa prior to local anesthetic injections, scaling and prophylaxis; to relieve discomfort associated with taking impressions and intraoral radiographs.

Local Anesthetic/Vasoconstrictor Precautions No information available to require special precautions

Effects on Dental Treatment A patient history of allergy to ester-type local anesthetics contraindicates the use of this product.

Effects on Bleeding No information available to require special precautions

Adverse Reactions Frequency not defined.

Central nervous system: Localized burning, stinging sensation

Dermatologic: Contact dermatitis, localized erythema, localized rash, urticaria

Hematologic & oncologic: Methemoglobinemia

Hypersensitivity: Hypersensitivity

Local: Local pruritus, localized edema, localized tenderness

Dental Usual Dosage Relief of pain (toothache, minor sore throat pain, and canker sore): Children ≥2 years and Adults: Topical (oral): 10% to 20%: Apply thin layer to affected area up to 4 times daily

Dosing

Adult & Geriatric Note: General dosing guidelines provided; refer to specific product labeling for dosing instructions.

Dermal irritation: Topical (external): Spray 5% and 20%, ointment 5%: Apply to affected area or use 1 spray up to 4 times daily as needed. In cases of bee stings, remove stinger before treatment.

Mouth and gum irritation: Topical (oral): Gel 10% or 20%, liquid 10% or 20%, ointment 20%, spray 5%: Apply thin layer to affected area or use 1 spray up to 4 times daily as needed.

Poison ivy/sumac: Topical (external): Spray 5% (Ivy-Rid only). Spray affected area until wet.

Sore throat/mouth, gag reflex suppression: Topical (oral):

Lozenge: Allow 1 lozenge to dissolve slowly in mouth; may repeat every 2 hours as needed.

Spray 20%:

Benz-O-Sthetic: Spray 2 to 3 times or as needed. Repeat if needed for larger areas.

Hurricaine: Spray on affected area or throat up to 4 times daily.

Topical anesthetic: Topical (oral): Gel or liquid 20% (Topex only): Apply a small amount to mucosa to achieve topical anesthesia.

Pediatric Note: General dosing guidelines provided; refer to specific product labeling for dosing instructions.

Dermal irritation: Topical (external): Spray 5% and 20%, ointment 5%: Children ≥2 years and Adolescents: Refer to adult dosing.

Mouth and gum irritation: Topical (oral):

Gel 10% or 20%, liquid 10% or 20%, ointment 20%: Children ≥2 years and Adolescents: Refer to adult dosing.

Spray 5%: Children ≥6 years and Adolescents: Refer to adult dosing.

Sore throat/mouth, gag reflex suppression: Topical (oral):

Lozenge: Children ≥5 years and Adolescents: Refer to adult dosing.

Spray 20%:

Benz-O-Sthetic: Children ≥6 years and Adolescents: Refer to adult dosing.

Hurricaine: Children ≥2 years and Adolescents: Refer to adult dosing.

Teething pain: Note: Use not recommended by AAP, FDA, and the American Academy of Pediatric Dentistry (AAP 2011; AAPD 2012): Manufacturer's labeling: Infants ≥4 months and Children: Topical (oral): Gel 7.5%: Apply pea-size amount to affected gum area up to 4 times daily.

Topical anesthetic: Topical (oral): Gel or liquid 20% (Topex only): Refer to adult dosing.

Renal Impairment There are no dosage adjustments provided in the manufacturer's labeling.

Hepatic Impairment There are no dosage adjustments provided in the manufacturer's labeling.

Mechanism of Action Blocks both the initiation and conduction of nerve impulses by decreasing the neuronal membrane's permeability to sodium ions, which results in inhibition of depolarization with resultant blockade of conduction

Contraindications

Hypersensitivity to benzocaine, para-aminobenzoic acid (PABA), or any component of the formulation

OTC labeling: When used for self-medication, do not use if you have allergy to local anesthetics (procaine, butacaine, benzocaine, or other "caine" anesthetics). Do not use over deep or puncture wounds, infections, serious burns, or lacerations.

Warnings/Precautions Methemoglobinemia has been reported following topical use, particularly with higher concentration (14% to 20%) spray formulations applied to the mouth or mucous membranes. When applied as a spray to the mouth or throat, multiple sprays (or sprays of longer than indicated duration) are not recommended. Use caution with breathing problems (asthma, bronchitis, emphysema, in smokers), inflamed/damaged mucosa, heart disease, children <6 months of age, and hemoglobin or enzyme abnormalities (glucose-6-phosphate dehydrogenase deficiency, hemoglobin-M disease, NADH-methemoglobin reductase deficiency, pyruvate-kinase deficiency). Alternatives to benzocaine sprays, such as topical lidocaine preparations, should be considered for patients at higher risk of this reaction. The classical clinical finding of methemoglobinemia is chocolate brown-colored arterial blood. However, suspected cases should be confirmed by co-oximetry, which yields a direct and accurate measure of methemoglobin levels. Standard pulse oximetry readings or arterial blood gas values are not reliable. Clinically significant methemoglobinemia requires immediate treatment (Anderson 1988; Cooper 1997; Moore 2004). Due to the heightened risk of methemoglobinemia, not recommended for use in patients <2 years unless under the advice and supervision by a health care professional. The FDA recommends against using topical OTC medications for teething pain as some products may cause harm; the use of OTC topical anesthetics (eg, benzocaine) for teething pain is also discouraged by AAP, and The American Academy of Pediatric Dentistry (AAP 2011; AAPD 2012).

Some dosage forms may contain benzyl alcohol; large amounts of benzyl alcohol (≥99 mg/kg/day) have been associated with a potentially fatal toxicity ("gasping syndrome") in neonates; the "gasping syndrome" consists of metabolic acidosis, respiratory distress, gasping respirations, CNS dysfunction (including convulsions, intracranial hemorrhage), hypotension and cardiovascular collapse (AAP ["Inactive" 1997]; CDC 1982); some data suggests that benzoate displaces bilirubin from protein binding sites (Ahlfors 2001); avoid or use dosage forms containing benzyl alcohol with caution in neonates. See manufacturer's labeling. Some dosage forms may contain propylene glycol; large amounts are potentially toxic and have been associated hyperosmolality, lactic acidosis, seizures and respiratory depression; use caution (AAP 1997; Zar 2007). See manufacturer's labeling.

When used for self-medication, notify healthcare provider if condition worsens, or does not improve within 7 days; clears up and occurs again within a few days; or if accompanied by additional symptoms (eg, swelling, rash, headache, nausea, vomiting, or fever). Do not use topical products on open wounds; avoid contact with the eyes. Do not use for a prolonged time and/or on large portions of the body. When topical anesthetics are used prior to cosmetic or medical procedures, the lowest amount of anesthetic necessary for pain relief should be applied. High systemic levels and toxic effects (eg, methemoglobinemia, irregular heartbeats, respiratory depression, seizures, death) have been reported in patients who (without supervision of a trained professional) have applied topical anesthetics in large amounts (or to large areas of the skin), left these products on for prolonged periods of time, or have used wraps/dressings to cover the skin following application.

Drug Interactions

Metabolism/Transport Effects None known.

Avoid Concomitant Use There are no known interactions where it is recommended to avoid concomitant use.

Increased Effect/Toxicity

Benzocaine may increase the levels/effects of: Prilocaine; Sodium Nitrite

The levels/effects of Benzocaine may be increased by: Dapsone (Topical); Nitric Oxide; Tetracaine (Topical)

Decreased Effect There are no known significant interactions involving a decrease in effect.

Pharmacodynamics/Kinetics

Onset of Action Anesthetic effect: Spray: 15 to 30 seconds.

Dosage Forms

Aerosol, External:

Dermoplast [OTC]: Benzocaine 20% and menthol 0.5% (56 g)

Ivy-Rid [OTC]: 2% (82.5 mL)

Aerosol, Mouth/Throat:

Hurricaine [OTC]: 20% (57 g)

Topex Topical Anesthetic: 20% (57 g)

Gel, Mouth/Throat:

Anbesol [OTC]: 10% (9 g)

Anbesol JR [OTC]: 10% (9 g)
Anbesol Maximum Strength [OTC]: 20% (9 g)
Baby Anbesol [OTC]: 7.5% (9 g)
Benz-O-Sthetic [OTC]: 20% (15 g, 29 g)
Dentapaine [OTC]: 20% (11 g)
Hurricaine [OTC]: 20% (5.25 g, 28.4 g, 30 g)
Zilactin Baby [OTC]: 10% (9.4 g)

Liquid, External:
Chiggertox [OTC]: 2.1% (30 mL)

Liquid, Mouth/Throat:
Anbesol [OTC]: 10% (12 mL)
Anbesol Maximum Strength [OTC]: 20% (12 mL)
Benz-O-Sthetic [OTC]: 20% (56 g)
Dent-O-Kain/20 [OTC]: 20% (9 mL)

Lozenge, Mouth/Throat:
Bi-Zets/Benzotroches [OTC]: 15 mg (10 ea)
Sore Throat Relief [OTC]: 10 mg (2 ea)
Trocaine Throat [OTC]: 10 mg (1 ea)

Ointment, External:
Anacaine: 10% (30 g)
Anbesol Cold Sore Therapy [OTC]: 20% (9 g)
Blistex Medicated [OTC]: (6.3 g)
Chiggerex [OTC]: 2% (52.5 g)
Foille [OTC]: 5% (28 g)

Solution, Mouth/Throat:
Benz-O-Sthetic [OTC]: 20% (30 mL)
Hurricaine [OTC]: 20% (30 mL)
HurriCaine One [OTC]: 20% (2 ea, 25 ea)
Kank-A Mouth Pain [OTC]: 20% (9.75 mL)

Strip, Mouth/Throat:
Ora-film [OTC]: 6% (12 ea)

Swab, Mouth/Throat:
Benz-O-Sthetic [OTC]: 20% (2 ea)
Hurricaine [OTC]: 20% (72 ea)

Dental Comment Health Canada has issued a reminder to healthcare professionals that benzocaine sprays must be used judiciously to minimize the risk of methemoglobinemia. Almost all reported cases have been associated with higher concentration (14% to 20% benzocaine) spray products used in the mouth and on other mucous membranes. Alternatives to benzocaine sprays, such as topical lidocaine preparations, should be considered for patients at higher risk of this reaction.

Benzonatate (ben ZOE na tate)

Related Information
Perioral Premalignant Lesions and Management of Patients Undergoing Cancer Therapy *on page 1875*

Brand Names: US Tessalon Perles; Zonatuss [DSC]

Pharmacologic Category Antitussive

Use Cough: Symptomatic relief of cough

Local Anesthetic/Vasoconstrictor Precautions No information available to require special precautions

Effects on Dental Treatment No significant effects or complications reported

Effects on Bleeding No information available to require special precautions

Adverse Reactions Frequency not defined.
Cardiovascular: Chest numbness
Central nervous system: Chills, confusion, dizziness, hallucination, headache, sedation
Dermatologic: Pruritus, skin rash
Gastrointestinal: Constipation, gastrointestinal distress, nausea
Hypersensitivity: Hypersensitivity reaction (bronchospasm, laryngospasm, cardiovascular collapse)
Ophthalmic: Burning sensation of eyes
Respiratory: Nasal congestion

General Dosage Range Oral: *Children >10 years, Adolescents, and Adults:* 100 to 200 mg 3 times/day as needed for cough (maximum single dose: 200 mg; maximum dose: 600 mg/day)

Mechanism of Action Tetracaine congener with antitussive properties; suppresses cough by topical anesthetic action on the respiratory stretch receptors

Pharmacodynamics/Kinetics
Onset of Action Therapeutic: 15 to 20 minutes
Duration of Action 3 to 8 hours

Pregnancy Risk Factor C

Pregnancy Considerations Animal reproduction studies have not been conducted.

Benztropine (BENZ troe peen)

Related Information
Dentin Hypersensitivity, Acid Erosion, High Caries Index, Management of Alveolar Osteitis, and Xerostomia *on page 1857*

Brand Names: US Cogentin

Brand Names: Canada Benztropine Omega; Kynesia; PMS-Benztropine

Pharmacologic Category Anti-Parkinson Agent, Anticholinergic; Anticholinergic Agent

Use
Extrapyramidal disorders: Aid in the control of extrapyramidal disorders (except tardive dyskinesia) due to neuroleptic drugs (eg, phenothiazines).
Parkinsonism: Adjunctive therapy of all forms of parkinsonism.

Local Anesthetic/Vasoconstrictor Precautions No information available to require special precautions

Effects on Dental Treatment Key adverse event(s) related to dental treatment: Xerostomia and changes in salivation (normal salivary flow resumes upon discontinuation), dry throat, and nasal dryness (very prevalent).

Effects on Bleeding No information available to require special precautions

Adverse Reactions Frequency not defined.
Cardiovascular: Tachycardia
Central nervous system: Confusion, depression, disorientation, heatstroke, hyperthermia, lethargy, memory impairment, nervousness, numbness of fingers, psychotic symptoms (exacerbation of pre-existing symptoms), toxic psychosis, visual hallucination
Dermatologic: Skin rash
Gastrointestinal: Constipation, nausea, paralytic ileus, vomiting, xerostomia
Genitourinary: Dysuria, urinary retention
Ophthalmic: Blurred vision, mydriasis

General Dosage Range IM, IV, Oral: *Adults:* Range: 0.5-8 mg daily

Mechanism of Action Possesses both anticholinergic and antihistaminic effects. *In vitro* anticholinergic activity approximates that of atropine; *in vivo* it is only about half as active as atropine. Animal data suggest its antihistaminic activity and duration of action approach that of pyrilamine maleate.

Pharmacodynamics/Kinetics
Onset of Action
IM, IV: Within a few minutes; there is no significant difference between onset of effect after intravenous or intramuscular injection
Oral: Within 1 hour
Time to Peak Plasma: Oral: 7 hours (Brocks 1999)

Pregnancy Considerations Animal reproduction studies have not been conducted. Paralytic ileus (which resolved rapidly) was reported in two newborns exposed to a combination of benztropine and chlorpromazine during the second and third trimesters and the last 6 weeks of pregnancy, respectively (Falterman, 1980).

Benzydamine (ben ZID a meen)

Brand Names: Canada Apo-Benzydamine; Dom-Benzydamine; Novo-Benzydamine; Pharixia; Tantum

Pharmacologic Category Anti-inflammatory, Locally Applied; Local Anesthetic, Oral

Use Note: Not approved in the US

Mucositis: Symptomatic relief of oropharyngeal mucositis due to radiation therapy

Pharyngitis (acute): Relief of acute sore throat pain

Local Anesthetic/Vasoconstrictor Precautions No information available to require special precautions

Effects on Dental Treatment Key adverse event(s) related to dental treatment: Numbness, burning/stinging sensation, and xerostomia (normal salivary flow resumes upon discontinuation).

Effects on Bleeding No information available to require special precautions

Adverse Reactions

Frequency not always defined.

Central nervous system: Localized numbness (10%), drowsiness, headache

Dermatologic: Burning sensation of skin (≤8%), stinging of the skin (≤8%)

Gastrointestinal: Nausea (≤2%), vomiting (≤2%), xerostomia

Respiratory: Cough, pharyngitis

General Dosage Range Oral rinse: *Adults:* Gargle with 15 mL every 1½ to 3 hours until symptoms resolve **or** 3 or 4 times daily

Mechanism of Action Nonsteroidal anti-inflammatory drug; inhibits production of proinflammatory cytokines to reduce local pain and inflammation (Lalla, 2014). Also has local anesthetic activity.

Pharmacodynamics/Kinetics

Time to Peak 2 hours

Pregnancy Considerations Adverse effects were observed in animal reproduction studies. Safety has not been established in pregnant women.

Product Availability Not available in the US

Bepotastine (be poe TAS teen)

Brand Names: US Bepreve

Brand Names: Canada Bepreve

Pharmacologic Category Histamine H_1 Antagonist; Histamine H_1 Antagonist, Second Generation; Mast Cell Stabilizer

Use Treatment of itching associated with allergic conjunctivitis

Local Anesthetic/Vasoconstrictor Precautions No information available to require special precautions

Effects on Dental Treatment Key adverse event(s) related to dental treatment: Taste abnormalities reported in ≤25% of patients

Effects on Bleeding No information available to require special precautions

Adverse Reactions

>10%: Gastrointestinal: Dysgeusia (25%)

1% to 10%:

Central nervous system: Headache (2% to 5%)

Ophthalmic: Eye irritation (2% to 5%)

Respiratory: Nasopharyngitis (2% to 5%)

<1%, postmarketing, and/or case reports: Hypersensitivity reaction, pharyngeal edema, pruritus, skin rash, swelling of lips, swollen tongue

General Dosage Range Ophthalmic: *Children ≥2 years and Adults:* Instill 1 drop into the affected eye(s) twice daily

Mechanism of Action Direct H_1-receptor antagonist and inhibits release of histamine from mast cells

Pharmacodynamics/Kinetics

Onset of Action Within 3 minutes (Macejko, 2010)

Duration of Action Up to 16 hours (Williams, 2011)

Time to Peak Serum: 1-2 hours

Pregnancy Risk Factor C

Pregnancy Considerations Teratogenic effects were not observed in most animal reproduction studies following oral administration; however, a decrease in fetal weight and a decrease in live births were observed in some studies. In humans, plasma concentrations are below the limit of quantification (<2 ng/mL) 24 hours after ophthalmic administration.

Beractant (ber AKT ant)

Brand Names: US Survanta

Brand Names: Canada Survanta

Pharmacologic Category Lung Surfactant

Use Respiratory distress syndrome: Prevention of respiratory distress syndrome (RDS) in premature neonates with birth weight <1,250 g or with evidence of surfactant deficiency (administer within 15 minutes of birth); treatment of RDS in neonates with x-ray confirmation of RDS and requiring mechanical ventilation (administer within 8 hours of birth).

Local Anesthetic/Vasoconstrictor Precautions No information available to require special precautions

Effects on Dental Treatment No significant effects or complications reported

Effects on Bleeding No information available to require special precautions

Adverse Reactions Frequency not defined. The following occurred during the dosing procedure:

>10%: Cardiovascular: Bradycardia (transient)

1% to 10%: Respiratory: Oxygen desaturation

<1%, postmarketing, and/or case reports: Apnea, hypercapnia, hypertension, hypotension, increased susceptibility to infection (post-treatment nosocomial sepsis), low blood CO2, obstruction of endotracheal tube, pallor, pulmonary air leak, pulmonary interstitial emphysema, vasoconstriction

General Dosage Range Endotracheal: *Premature neonates:* 4 mL/kg (100 mg phospholipids/kg); may repeat if needed, no more frequently than every 6 hours to a maximum of 4 doses during the first 48 hours of life

Mechanism of Action Replaces deficient or ineffective endogenous lung surfactant in neonates with respiratory distress syndrome (RDS) or in neonates at risk of developing RDS. Surfactant prevents the alveoli from collapsing during expiration by lowering surface tension between air and alveolar surfaces.

Pharmacodynamics/Kinetics

Onset of Action Improved oxygenation: Within minutes

Pregnancy Considerations Beractant is only indicated for use in premature neonates

Besifloxacin (be si FLOX a sin)

Brand Names: US Besivance

Brand Names: Canada Besivance

Pharmacologic Category Antibiotic, Fluoroquinolone; Antibiotic, Ophthalmic

Use Bacterial conjunctivitis: Treatment of bacterial conjunctivitis caused by susceptible isolates of the following bacteria: *Aerococcus viridans*, CDC coryneform group G, *Haemophilus influenzae*, *Staphylococcus aureus*, *Staphylococcus epidermidis*, *Streptococcus mitis* group, *Streptococcus oralis*, *Streptococcus pneumoniae*, *Corynebacterium pseudodiphtheriticum*, *Corynebacterium striatum*, *Moraxella lacunata*, *Moraxella catarrhalis*, *Pseudomonas aeruginosa*, *Staphylococcus hominis*, *Staphylococcus lugdunensis*, *Staphylococcus warneri*, *Streptococcus salivarius*.

Local Anesthetic/Vasoconstrictor Precautions No information available to require special precautions

Effects on Dental Treatment No significant effects or complications reported

Effects on Bleeding No information available to require special precautions

Adverse Reactions Frequency not always defined.

1% to 2%:

Central nervous system: Headache

Ophthalmic: Conjunctival erythema (2%), blurred vision, eye irritation, eye pain, eye pruritus

General Dosage Range Ophthalmic: *Children ≥1 year, Adolescents and Adults:* 1 drop into affected eye(s) 3 times daily (4 to 12 hours apart)

Mechanism of Action Inhibits both DNA gyrase and topoisomerase IV. DNA gyrase is an essential bacterial enzyme required for DNA replication, transcription, and repair. Topoisomerase IV is an essential bacterial enzyme required for decatenation during cell division. Inhibition effect is bactericidal.

Pharmacodynamics/Kinetics

Half-life Elimination ~7 hours

Pregnancy Risk Factor C

Pregnancy Considerations Adverse events were observed in some animal reproduction studies. Systemic concentrations of besifloxacin following ophthalmic administration are low. If ophthalmic agents are needed during pregnancy, the minimum effective dose should be used in combination with punctual occlusion for 3 to 5 minutes after application to decrease potential exposure to the fetus (Samples 1988).

Beta-Carotene (BAY ta KARE oh teen)

Brand Names: US A-Caro-25 [OTC]; B-Caro-T [OTC]; Caroguard [OTC]

Pharmacologic Category Vitamin, Fat Soluble

Use Prophylaxis against photosensitivity reactions in erythropoietic protoporphyria (EPP)

Local Anesthetic/Vasoconstrictor Precautions No information available to require special precautions

Effects on Dental Treatment No significant effects or complications reported

Effects on Bleeding No information available to require special precautions

Adverse Reactions Frequency not defined.

Central nervous system: Dizziness

Dermatologic: Carotenoderma (yellowing of palms, hands, or soles of feet, and to a lesser extent the face)

General Dosage Range Oral:

Children <14 years: 30-150 mg/day

Adults: 30-300 mg/day

Mechanism of Action The exact mechanism of action in erythropoietic protoporphyria has not as yet been elucidated; although patient must become carotenemic before effects are observed, there appears to be more than a simple internal light screen responsible for the drug's action. A protective effect was achieved when beta-carotene was added to blood samples. The concentrations of solutions used were similar to those achieved in treated patients. Topically applied beta-carotene is considerably less effective than systemic therapy.

Pregnancy Considerations Maternal intake of beta carotene influences cord blood concentrations (Scaife, 2006).

Betaine (BAY ta een)

Brand Names: US Cystadane

Brand Names: Canada Cystadane

Pharmacologic Category Homocystinuria, Treatment Agent

Use Homocystinuria: Treatment of homocystinuria including deficiencies or defects in cystathionine beta-synthase (CBS), 5,10-methylene tetrahydrofolate reductase (MTHFR), and cobalamin cofactor metabolism (CBL).

Local Anesthetic/Vasoconstrictor Precautions No information available to require special precautions

Effects on Dental Treatment No significant effects or complications reported

Effects on Bleeding No information available to require special precautions

Adverse Reactions

Frequency not defined.

Gastrointestinal: Diarrhea, dysgeusia, gastrointestinal distress, nausea

<1%, postmarketing, and/or case reports: Abnormal skin odor, agitation, alopecia, anorexia, cerebral edema (associated with hypermethioninemia), dental disease, depression, glossitis, irritability, personality disorder, sleep disorder, urinary incontinence, urticaria, vomiting

General Dosage Range Oral:

Infants and Children <3 years: Initial: 100 mg/kg/day, then increase weekly by 50 mg/kg increments, as needed

Children ≥3 years, Adolescents, and Adults: 3 g twice daily

Mechanism of Action Betaine is an endogenous metabolite of choline. Betaine acts as a methyl group donor in the remethylation of homocysteine to methionine. Homocystinuria is an inborn error of metabolism in which elevated plasma homocysteine levels can lead to mental retardation, ocular abnormalities, osteoporosis, premature atherosclerosis and thromboembolic disease. Remethylation is one of the two divergent pathways in the metabolism of homocysteine. The second pathway involves transulfuration of homocysteine to produce cysteine. A number of enzymes and cofactors are also involved in these pathways.

Pregnancy Risk Factor C

Pregnancy Considerations Animal reproduction studies have not been conducted.

Prescribing and Access Restrictions Cystadane may be obtained by contacting AnovoRx at wholesale@anovorx.com.

Betamethasone (Systemic)

(bay ta METH a sone)

Related Information

Respiratory Diseases *on page 1777*

Brand Names: US Celestone Soluspan; Celestone [DSC]; ReadySharp Betamethasone

Brand Names: Canada Betaject; Celestone Soluspan

Generic Availability (US) May be product dependent

Pharmacologic Category Corticosteroid, Systemic

Dental Use Treatment of a variety of oral diseases of allergic, inflammatory, or autoimmune origin

Use

Intramuscular:

Allergic states: Control of severe or incapacitating allergic conditions intractable to adequate trials of conventional treatment in asthma, atopic dermatitis, contact dermatitis, drug hypersensitivity reactions, perennial or seasonal allergic rhinitis, serum sickness, transfusion reactions

Dermatologic diseases: Bullous dermatitis herpetiformis, exfoliative erythroderma, mycosis fungoides, pemphigus, severe erythema multiforme (Stevens-Johnson syndrome)

Endocrine disorders: Congenital adrenal hyperplasia, hypercalcemia associated with cancer, nonsuppurative thyroiditis. Hydrocortisone or cortisone is the drug of choice in primary or secondary adrenocortical insufficiency. Synthetic analogs may be used in conjunction with mineralocorticoids where applicable; in infancy mineralocorticoid supplementation is of particular importance

Gastrointestinal diseases: To tide the patient over a critical period of the disease in regional enteritis and ulcerative colitis

Hematologic disorders: Acquired (autoimmune) hemolytic anemia, Diamond-Blackfan anemia, pure red cell aplasia, selected cases of secondary thrombocytopenia

Neoplastic diseases: Palliative management of leukemias and lymphomas

Nervous system: Acute exacerbations of multiple sclerosis; cerebral edema associated with primary or metastatic brain tumor or craniotomy. **Note**: Treatment guidelines recommend the use of high-dose IV or oral methylprednisolone for acute exacerbations of multiple sclerosis (AAN [Scott 2011]; NICE 2014).

Ophthalmic diseases: Sympathetic ophthalmia, temporal arteritis, uveitis and ocular inflammatory conditions unresponsive to topical corticosteroids

Renal diseases: To induce diuresis or remission of proteinuria in idiopathic nephrotic syndrome or that due to lupus erythematosus

Respiratory diseases: Berylliosis, fulminating or disseminated pulmonary tuberculosis when used concurrently with appropriate antituberculous chemotherapy, idiopathic eosinophilic pneumonias, symptomatic sarcoidosis

Rheumatic disorders: Adjunctive therapy for short-term administration (to tide the patient over an acute episode or exacerbation) in acute gouty arthritis; acute rheumatic carditis; ankylosing spondylitis; psoriatic arthritis; rheumatoid arthritis, including juvenile rheumatoid arthritis (selected cases may require low-dose maintenance therapy); treatment of dermatomyositis, polymyositis, and systemic lupus erythematosus.

Miscellaneous: Trichinosis with neurologic or myocardial involvement, tuberculous meningitis with subarachnoid block or impending block when used with appropriate antituberculous chemotherapy

Intra-articular or soft tissue administration:

Adjunctive therapy for short-term administration (to tide the patient over an acute episode or exacerbation) in acute gouty arthritis, acute and subacute bursitis, acute nonspecific tenosynovitis, epicondylitis, rheumatoid arthritis, synovitis of osteoarthritis

Intralesional:

Treatment of alopecia areata; discoid lupus erythematosus; keloids; localized hypertrophic, infiltrated, inflammatory lesions of granuloma annulare, lichen planus, lichen simplex chronicus (neurodermatitis), and psoriatic plaques; necrobiosis lipoidica diabeticorum

Local Anesthetic/Vasoconstrictor Precautions No information available to require special precautions

Effects on Dental Treatment No significant effects or complications reported

Effects on Bleeding Variable effects on anticoagulant therapy are observed with glucocorticoids such as betamethasone.

Adverse Reactions

Frequency not defined.

Cardiovascular: Cardiac failure, edema, hypertension, hypotension

Central nervous system: Dizziness, headache, increased intracranial pressure, insomnia, myasthenia, nervousness, pseudotumor cerebri, seizure, vertigo

Dermatologic: Atrophic striae, diaphoresis, ecchymoses, facial erythema, fragile skin, hyperpigmentation, hypopigmentation, perioral dermatitis (oral)

Endocrine & metabolic: Amenorrhea, Cushing's syndrome, diabetes mellitus, fluid retention growth suppression, hirsutism, HPA-axis suppression, hyperglycemia, hypokalemia, menstrual disease, protein catabolism, sodium retention

Gastrointestinal: Abdominal distention, dyspepsia, hiccups, increased appetite, pancreatitis, peptic ulcer, ulcerative esophagitis

Hematologic & oncologic: Petechia

Hypersensitivity: Anaphylactoid reaction, hypersensitivity reaction

Infection: Secondary infection, sterile abscess

Local: Injection site reaction (intra-articular use)

Neuromuscular & skeletal: Amyotrophy, arthralgia, bone fracture, myopathy, osteonecrosis (femoral and humeral heads), osteoporosis

Ophthalmic: Cataract, glaucoma, increased intraocular pressure

Miscellaneous: Wound healing impairment

Dosing

Adult Note: Dosages expressed as combined amount of betamethasone sodium phosphate and betamethasone acetate; 1 mg is equivalent to betamethasone sodium phosphate 0.5 mg and betamethasone acetate 0.5 mg. Base dosage on severity of disease and patient response.

Usual dosage range: IM: Initial: 0.25 to 9 mg daily

Indication-specific dosing:

Antenatal fetal maturation (off-label use): IM: 12 mg every 24 hours for a total of 2 doses (ACOG 171 2016). A single course of betamethasone is recommended for women between 24 and 34 weeks of gestation, including those with ruptured membranes or multiple gestations, who are at risk of delivering within 7 days. A single course may be appropriate in some women beginning at 23 weeks gestation or late preterm (between 34 0/7 weeks and 36 6/7 weeks gestation). A single repeat course may be considered in some women with pregnancies less than 34 weeks gestation at risk for delivery within 7 days and who had a course of antenatal corticosteroids >14 days prior (ACOG 171 2016; ACOG 172 2016; ACOG 677 2016).

Bursitis (other than of foot), tenosynovitis, peritendinitis: Intrabursal: 3 to 6 mg (0.5 to 1 mL) for one dose; several injections may be required for acute exacerbations or chronic conditions; reduced doses may be warranted for repeat injections.

Dermatologic: Intralesional: 1.2 mg/cm^2 (0.2 mL/cm^2) for one dose (maximum: 6 mg [1 mL] weekly).

Foot disorders: Intra-articular: 1.5 mg to 6 mg (0.25 to 1 mL) per dose at 3 to 7 day intervals. Dose is based upon condition:

Bursitis: 1.5 mg to 3 mg (0.25 to 0.5 mL)

Tenosynovitis: 3 mg (0.5 mL)

Acute gouty arthritis: 3 mg to 6 mg (0.5 to 1 mL)

Multiple sclerosis: Note: Treatment guidelines recommend the use of high-dose IV or oral methylprednisolone for acute exacerbations of multiple sclerosis (AAN [Scott 2011]; NICE 2014).

IM: 30 mg daily for 1 week, followed by 12 mg every other day for 4 weeks.

Rheumatoid and osteoarthritis: Intra-articular: 3 mg to 12 mg (0.5 to 2 mL) for one dose. Dose is based upon the joint size:

Very large (eg, hip): 6 to 12 mg (1 to 2 mL)

Large (eg, knee, ankle, shoulder): 6 mg (1 mL)

Medium (eg, elbow, wrist): 3 mg to 6 mg (0.5 to 1 mL)

Small (eg, inter- or metacarpophalangeal, sternoclavicular): 1.5 mg to 3 mg (0.25 to 0.5 mL)

Geriatric Refer to adult dosing. Use the lowest effective dose.

Pediatric Note: Dosages expressed as combined amount of betamethasone sodium phosphate and betamethasone acetate; 1 mg is equivalent to betamethasone sodium phosphate 0.5 mg and betamethasone acetate 0.5 mg. Base dosage on severity of disease and patient response.

Inflammatory conditions: Children and Adolescents: IM: 0.02 to 0.3 mg/kg/day (0.6 to 9 mg/m^2/day) in 3 or 4 divided doses

Renal Impairment There are no dosage adjustments provided in the manufacturer's labeling.

Hepatic Impairment There are no dosage adjustments provided in the manufacturer's labeling.

Mechanism of Action Controls the rate of protein synthesis; depresses the migration of polymorphonuclear leukocytes, fibroblasts; reverses capillary permeability and lysosomal stabilization at the cellular level to prevent or control inflammation

Contraindications

Hypersensitivity to any component of the formulation; IM administration contraindicated in idiopathic thrombocytopenic purpura.

Documentation of allergenic cross-reactivity for glucocorticoids is limited. However, because of similarities in chemical structure and/or pharmacologic actions, the possibility of cross-sensitivity cannot be ruled out with certainty.

Warnings/Precautions Avoid concurrent use of other corticosteroids.

May cause hypercorticism or suppression of hypothalamic-pituitary-adrenal (HPA) axis, particularly in younger children or in patients receiving high doses for prolonged periods. HPA axis suppression may lead to adrenal crisis. Withdrawal and discontinuation of a corticosteroid should be done slowly and carefully. Particular care is required when patients are transferred from systemic corticosteroids to inhaled products due to possible adrenal insufficiency or withdrawal from steroids, including an increase in allergic symptoms. Patients receiving >20 mg per day of prednisone (or equivalent) may be most susceptible. Fatalities have occurred due to adrenal insufficiency in asthmatic patients during and after transfer from systemic corticosteroids to aerosol steroids; aerosol steroids do not provide the systemic steroid needed to treat patients having trauma, surgery, or infections. In stressful situations, HPA axis-suppressed patients should receive adequate supplementation with natural glucocorticoids (hydrocortisone or cortisone) rather than betamethasone (due to lack of mineralocorticoid activity).

Acute myopathy has been reported with high-dose corticosteroids, usually in patients with neuromuscular transmission disorders; may involve ocular and/or respiratory muscles; monitor creatine kinase; recovery may be delayed. Corticosteroid use may cause psychiatric disturbances, including depression, euphoria, insomnia, mood swings, and personality changes. Preexisting psychiatric conditions may be exacerbated by corticosteroid use. Prolonged use of corticosteroids may also increase the incidence of secondary infection, mask acute infection (including fungal infections), prolong or exacerbate viral infections, or limit response to killed or inactivated vaccines. Special pathogens (*Amoeba*, *Candida*, *Cryptococcus*, *Mycobacterium*, *Nocardia*, *Pneumocystis*, *Strongyloides*, or *Toxoplasma*) may be activated or an infection exacerbation may occur (may be fatal). Amebiasis or *Strongyloides* infections should be particularly ruled out. Exposure to varicella zoster (chickenpox) should be avoided; corticosteroids should not be used to treat ocular herpes simplex. Corticosteroids should not be used for cerebral malaria or viral hepatitis. Close observation is required in patients with latent tuberculosis and/or TB reactivity; restrict use in active TB (only in conjunction with antituberculosis treatment). Prolonged treatment with corticosteroids has been associated with the development of Kaposi sarcoma (case reports); if noted, discontinuation of therapy should be considered. High-dose corticosteroids should not be used to manage acute head injury. Rare cases of anaphylactoid reactions have been observed in patients receiving corticosteroids.

Use with caution in patients with thyroid disease, hepatic impairment, renal impairment, cardiovascular disease, diabetes, glaucoma, cataracts, myasthenia gravis, patients at risk for osteoporosis, patients at risk for seizures, or GI diseases (diverticulitis, fresh intestinal anastomoses, peptic ulcer, ulcerative colitis) due to perforation risk. Use caution following acute MI (corticosteroids have been associated with myocardial rupture). Use with caution in patients with HF and/or hypertension; long-term use has been associated with fluid retention and electrolyte disturbances. Dietary modifications may be necessary. Use with caution in patients with a recent history of myocardial infarction (MI); left ventricular free wall rupture has been reported after the use of corticosteroids. Use with caution in patients with renal impairment; fluid and sodium retention and increased potassium and calcium excretion may occur. Dietary modifications may be necessary. Not recommended for the treatment of optic neuritis; may increase frequency of new episodes. Intra-articular injection may result in joint tissue damage. Injection into an infected site should be avoided. Injection into a previously infected join is usually not recommended. If infection is suspected, joint fluid examination is recommended. If septic arthritis occurs after injection, institute appropriate antimicrobial therapy. Suspension for injection is for intramuscular, intra-articular or intralesional use only, do not administer intravenously. Corticosteroids are not approved for epidural injection. Serious neurologic events (eg, spinal cord infarction, paraplegia, quadriplegia, cortical blindness, stroke), some resulting in death, have been reported with epidural injection of corticosteroids, with and without use of fluoroscopy. Intra-articular injected corticosteroids may be systemically absorbed. May produce systemic as well as local effects. Appropriate examination of any joint fluid present is necessary to exclude a septic process. Avoid injection into an infected site. Do not inject into unstable joints. Intra-articular injection may result in damage to joint tissues. Potentially significant drug-drug interactions may exist, requiring dose or frequency adjustment, additional monitoring, and/or selection of alternative therapy. Because of the risk of adverse effects, systemic corticosteroids should be used cautiously in the elderly in the smallest possible effective dose for the shortest duration. Withdraw therapy with gradual tapering of dose.

Prolonged use in children may affect growth velocity; growth should be routinely monitored in pediatric patients.

Drug Interactions

Metabolism/Transport Effects None known.

Avoid Concomitant Use

Avoid concomitant use of Betamethasone (Systemic) with any of the following: Aldesleukin; BCG (Intravesical); Desmopressin; Indium 111 Capromab Pendetide; MiFEPRIStone; Natalizumab; Pimecrolimus; Tacrolimus (Topical); Tofacitinib

Increased Effect/Toxicity

Betamethasone (Systemic) may increase the levels/effects of: Acetylcholinesterase Inhibitors; Amphotericin B; Androgens; Ceritinib; Deferasirox; Desirudin; Desmopressin; Fingolimod; Leflunomide; Loop Diuretics; Natalizumab; Nicorandil; NSAID (COX-2 Inhibitor); NSAID (Nonselective); Quinolone Antibiotics; Thiazide and Thiazide-Like Diuretics; Tofacitinib; Vaccines (Live); Warfarin

The levels/effects of Betamethasone (Systemic) may be increased by: Aprepitant; CYP3A4 Inhibitors (Strong); Denosumab; DilTIAZem; Estrogen Derivatives; Fosaprepitant; Indacaterol; MiFEPRIStone; Neuromuscular-Blocking Agents (Nondepolarizing); Ocrelizumab; Pimecrolimus; Roflumilast; Salicylates; Tacrolimus (Topical); Telaprevir; Trastuzumab

Decreased Effect

Betamethasone (Systemic) may decrease the levels/effects of: Aldesleukin; Antidiabetic Agents; BCG (Intravesical); Calcitriol (Systemic); Coccidioides immitis Skin Test; Corticorelin; Hyaluronidase; Indium 111 Capromab Pendetide; Isoniazid; Nivolumab; Salicylates; Sipuleucel-T; Telaprevir; Tertomotide; Urea Cycle Disorder Agents; Vaccines (Inactivated); Vaccines (Live)

The levels/effects of Betamethasone (Systemic) may be decreased by: CYP3A4 Inducers (Strong); Echinacea; MiFEPRIStone; Mitotane

Pharmacodynamics/Kinetics

Half-life Elimination

6.5 hours (Peterson 1983)

Time to Peak Serum: IV: 10 to 36 minutes (Peterson 1983)

Pregnancy Risk Factor C

Pregnancy Considerations Adverse events have been observed with corticosteroids in animal reproduction studies. Betamethasone crosses the placenta (Brownfoot 2013); and is partially metabolized by placental enzymes to an inactive metabolite (Murphy 2007). Some studies have shown an association between first trimester systemic corticosteroid use and oral clefts (Park-Wyllie 2000; Pradat 2003). Systemic corticosteroids may have an effect on fetal growth (decreased birth weight); however, information is conflicting (Lunghi 2010). Hypoadrenalism may occur in newborns following maternal use of corticosteroids during pregnancy; monitor.

Because antenatal corticosteroid administration may reduce the incidence of intraventricular hemorrhage, necrotizing enterocolitis, neonatal mortality, and respiratory distress syndrome, the injection is often used for antenatal fetal lung maturation in patients with preterm premature rupture of membranes or preterm labor who are at risk of preterm delivery. A single course of betamethasone is recommended for women between 24 and 34 weeks gestation who are at risk of delivering within 7 days, including those with ruptured membranes or multiple gestations. A single course of betamethasone may be considered for women beginning at 23 weeks gestation, who are at risk of delivering within 7 days, in consultation with the family. In addition, a single course of betamethasone may be given to women between 34 0/7 weeks and 36 6/7 weeks who are at risk of preterm delivery within 7 days and who have not previously received corticosteroids; use of concomitant tocolytics is not currently recommended and administration of late preterm corticosteroids has not been evaluated in women with intrauterine infection, multiple gestations, pregestational diabetes, or women who delivered previously by cesarean section at term. Multiple repeat courses are not recommended. However, in women with pregnancies less than 34 weeks gestation at risk for delivery within 7 days and who had a course of antenatal corticosteroids >14 days prior, a single repeat course may be considered; use of a repeat course in women with premature rupture of membranes is controversial (ACOG 171 2016; ACOG 172 2016; ACOG 677 2016).

When systemic corticosteroids are needed in pregnancy, it is generally recommended to use the lowest effective dose for the shortest duration of time, avoiding high doses during the first trimester (Leachman 2006; Lunghi 2010; Makol 2011; Østensen 2009).

Breastfeeding Considerations Corticosteroids are excreted in human milk. The onset of milk secretion after birth may be delayed and the volume of milk produced may be decreased by antenatal betamethasone therapy; this affect was seen when delivery occurred 3-9 days after the betamethasone dose in women between 28 and 34 weeks gestation. Antenatal betamethasone therapy did not affect milk production when birth occurred <3 days or >10 days of treatment (Henderson, 2008).

The manufacturer notes that when used systemically, maternal use of corticosteroids have the potential to cause adverse events in a nursing infant (eg, growth suppression, interfere with endogenous corticosteroid production) and therefore recommends that caution be exercised when administering betamethasone to nursing women. If there is concern about exposure to the infant, some guidelines recommend waiting 4 hours after the maternal dose of an oral systemic corticosteroid before breastfeeding in order to decrease potential exposure to the infant (based on a study using prednisolone) (Bae, 2011; Leachman, 2006; Makol, 2011; Ost, 1985).

Dosage Forms

Kit, Injection:

ReadySharp Betamethasone: Betamethasone sodium phosphate 3 mg and betamethasone acetate 3 mg per 1 mL

Suspension, Injection:

Celestone Soluspan: Betamethasone sodium phosphate 3 mg and betamethasone acetate 3 mg per 1 mL (5 mL)

Generic: Betamethasone sodium phosphate 3 mg and betamethasone acetate 3 mg per 1 mL (5 mL)

Betamethasone (Topical) (bay ta METH a sone)

Related Sample Prescriptions

Ulcerative and Erosive Disorders - Sample Prescriptions *on page 43*

Brand Names: US AlphaTrex; Diprolene; Diprolene AF; Luxiq; Sernivo

Brand Names: Canada Betaderm; Beteflam; Betnesol; Celestoderm V; Celestoderm V/2; Diprolene; Diprosone; Luxiq; Prevex B; ratio-Ectosone; Ratio-Topilene; Ratio-Topisone; Rivasone; Rolene; Rosone; Taro-Sone; Valisone Scalp Lotion

Generic Availability (US) May be product dependent

Pharmacologic Category Corticosteroid, Topical

Dental Use Treatment of a variety of oral diseases of allergic, inflammatory, or autoimmune origin

Use

Dermatoses: Relief of inflammatory and pruritic manifestations of corticosteroid-responsive dermatoses.

Dermatoses of the scalp (foam): Relief of inflammatory and pruritic manifestations of corticosteroid-responsive dermatoses of the scalp.

Plaque psoriasis (spray; patch [Canadian product]): Treatment of mild to moderate plaque psoriasis in patients 18 years and older.

Local Anesthetic/Vasoconstrictor Precautions No information available to require special precautions

Effects on Dental Treatment No significant effects or complications reported

Effects on Bleeding Variable effects on anticoagulant therapy are observed with glucocorticoids such as betamethasone.

Adverse Reactions

>10%: Local: Application site reactions (2% to 44%; includes burning, stinging, and itching; most reactions were mild)

1% to 10%:

Central nervous system: Tingling (2%; paresthesia at application site)

Dermatologic: Skin atrophy (children: 10%), acneiform eruption (2%), alopecia (2%), pruritus (≤2%), dermatitis (<1%)

Ophthalmic: Conjunctivitis (2%)

Frequency not defined: Endocrine & metabolic: HPA axis suppression

<1%, postmarketing, and/or case reports: Application-site infection, atrophic striae, bullous dermatitis, capillary fragility, contact dermatitis, dermal ulcer (of psoriatic lesions), dysgeusia, dyshidrotic eczema, eczema, edema, epidermolysis, erythema, exacerbation of psoriasis, folliculitis, herpes zoster, hirsutism, hyperglycemia, hypersensitivity reaction, localized vesiculation, pain, skin discoloration, skin hypertrophy, skin rash, telangiectasia

Dental Usual Dosage Allergic or inflammatory diseases: Topical: Gel: Apply small quantity with cotton swab to affected area 3-4 times/day

Dosing

Adult Note: Base dosage on severity of disease and patient response. Use lowest dose possible for shortest period of time to avoid HPA axis suppression. Therapy should be discontinued when control is achieved.

Corticosteroid-responsive dermatoses: Topical:

Cream, augmented formulation: Betamethasone dipropionate 0.05%: Apply once or twice daily (maximum: 50 g weekly).

Cream, unaugmented formulation:

Betamethasone dipropionate 0.05%: Apply once daily; may increase to twice daily if needed

Betamethasone valerate 0.1%: Apply 1 to 3 times daily. **Note:** Once- or twice-daily applications are usually effective.

Foam: Apply to the scalp twice daily, once in the morning and once at night. **Note:** Reassess if no improvement after 2 weeks of treatment.

Gel, augmented formulation: Apply once or twice daily; rub in gently (maximum: 50 g weekly). **Note:** Reassess if no improvement after 2 weeks of treatment.

Lotion, augmented formulation: Betamethasone dipropionate 0.05%: Apply a few drops once or twice daily (maximum: 50 mL weekly). **Note:** Reassess if no improvement after 2 weeks of treatment.

Lotion, unaugmented formulation:

Betamethasone dipropionate 0.05%: Apply a few drops twice daily

Betamethasone valerate 0.1%: Apply a few drops twice daily; may consider increasing dose for resistant cases. Following improvement, may apply once daily.

Ointment, augmented formulation: Betamethasone dipropionate 0.05%: Apply once or twice daily (maximum: 50 g weekly). **Note:** Reassess if no improvement after 2 weeks of treatment.

Ointment, unaugmented formulation:

Betamethasone dipropionate 0.05%: Apply once daily; may increase to twice daily if needed

Betamethasone valerate 0.1%: Apply 1 to 3 times daily. **Note:** Once- or twice-daily applications are usually effective.

Plaque psoriasis: Topical:

Patch [Canadian product]: Betamethasone valerate: Apply 1 patch (2.25 mg) to each affected area once daily [up to 5 patches (11.25 mg) may be applied daily]; maximum duration of therapy: 30 days.

Spray, unaugmented formulation: Betamethasone dipropionate 0.05%: Apply twice daily for up to 4 weeks

Geriatric Refer to adult dosing. Use the lowest effective dose.

Pediatric Note: Base dosage on severity of disease and patient response. Use lowest dose possible for shortest period of time to avoid HPA axis suppression. Therapy should be discontinued when control is achieved.

Corticosteroid-responsive dermatoses: Topical:

Children: Cream, lotion or ointment: Unaugmented formulation: Refer to adult dosing.

Adolescents: Cream, gel, lotion, or ointment: Augmented formulation: Refer to adult dosing.

Renal Impairment There are no dosage adjustments provided in the manufacturer's labeling.

Hepatic Impairment There are no dosage adjustments provided in the manufacturer's labeling.

Mechanism of Action Topical corticosteroids have anti-inflammatory, antipruritic, and vasoconstrictive properties. May depress the formation, release, and activity of endogenous chemical mediators of inflammation (kinins, histamine, liposomal enzymes, prostaglandins) through the induction of phospholipase A_2 inhibitory proteins (lipocortins) and sequential inhibition of the release of arachidonic acid. Betamethasone has intermediate to very high range potency (dosage-form dependent).

Contraindications Hypersensitivity to betamethasone, other corticosteroids, or any component of the formulation

Patch [Canadian product]: Additional contraindications: Viral (eg, herpes or varicella) lesions of the skin, bacterial or fungal skin infections, parasitic infections, skin manifestations relating to tuberculosis or syphilis, eruptions following vaccinations; <18 years of age

Warnings/Precautions Very high potency topical products are not for treatment of rosacea, perioral dermatitis; not for use on face, groin, or axillae; not for use in a diapered area. Avoid concurrent use of other corticosteroids.

May cause hypercorticism or suppression of hypothalamic-pituitary-adrenal (HPA) axis, particularly in younger children or in patients receiving high doses for prolonged periods. HPA axis suppression may lead to adrenal crisis.

Topical corticosteroids may be absorbed percutaneously. Absorption of topical corticosteroids may cause manifestations of Cushing syndrome (rare), hyperglycemia, or glycosuria. Absorption is increased by the use of occlusive dressings, application to denuded skin, application to large surface areas, or prolonged use. Potentially significant interactions may exist, requiring dose or frequency adjustment, additional monitoring, and/or selection of alternative therapy.

Discontinue if skin irritation or contact dermatitis should occur; do not use in patients with decreased skin circulation. Withdraw therapy with gradual tapering of dose by reducing the frequency of application or substitution of a less potent steroid. Allergic contact dermatitis can occur and is usually diagnosed by failure to heal rather than clinical exacerbation; discontinue use if irritation occurs and treat appropriately.

Augmented (eg,very high potency) product use in patients <13 years of age is not recommended. Not for treatment of rosacea, perioral dermatitis, or if skin atrophy is present at treatment site; not for facial, groin, axillary, oral, ophthalmic, or intravaginal use. Children may absorb proportionally larger amounts after topical application and may be more prone to systemic effects. HPA axis suppression, intracranial hypertension, and Cushing syndrome have been reported in children receiving topical corticosteroids. Prolonged use may affect growth velocity; growth should be routinely monitored in pediatric patients. Use lowest dose possible for shortest period of time to avoid HPA axis suppression.

Foam contains flammable propellants. Avoid fire, flame, and smoking during and immediately following administration. Patch [Canadian product] has not been studied in psoriasis of the face, scalp or intertriginous areas; contains methyl and propyl parahydroxybenzoate, which may cause hypersensitivity (sometimes delayed).

Drug Interactions

Metabolism/Transport Effects None known.

Avoid Concomitant Use

Avoid concomitant use of Betamethasone (Topical) with any of the following: Aldesleukin

Increased Effect/Toxicity

Betamethasone (Topical) may increase the levels/effects of: Ceritinib; Deferasirox

Decreased Effect

Betamethasone (Topical) may decrease the levels/effects of: Aldesleukin; Corticorelin; Hyaluronidase

Pregnancy Risk Factor C

Pregnancy Considerations Adverse events have been observed with corticosteroids in animal reproduction studies. Topical corticosteroids are preferred over systemic for treating conditions, such as psoriasis or atopic dermatitis in pregnant women; high potency corticosteroids are not recommended during the first trimester. Topical products are not recommended for extensive use, in large quantities, or for long periods of time in pregnant women (Bae, 2011; Koutroulis, 2011; Leachman, 2006). Refer to the Betamethasone systemic monograph for additional information.

Breastfeeding Considerations Corticosteroids are excreted in human milk. It is not known if systemic absorption following topical administration results in detectable quantities in human milk. Do not apply topical corticosteroids to nipples; hypertension was noted in a nursing infant exposed to a topical corticosteroid while nursing (Leachman, 2006).

The manufacturer notes that when used systemically, maternal use of corticosteroids have the potential to cause adverse events in a nursing infant (eg, growth suppression, interfere with endogenous corticosteroid production) and therefore recommends that caution be exercised when administering betamethasone to nursing women.

Dosage Forms

Cream, External:

Diprolene AF: 0.05% (15 g, 50 g)

Generic: 0.05% (15 g, 45 g, 50 g); 0.1% (15 g, 45 g)

Emulsion, External:

Sernivo: 0.05% (120 mL)

Foam, External:

Luxiq: 0.12% (50 g, 100 g)

Generic: 0.12% (50 g, 100 g)

Gel, External:

AlphaTrex: 0.05% (15 g, 50 g)

Generic: 0.05% (15 g, 50 g)

Lotion, External:

Diprolene: 0.05% (30 mL, 60 mL)

Generic: 0.05% (30 mL, 60 mL); 0.1% (60 mL)

Ointment, External:

Diprolene: 0.05% (15 g, 50 g)

Generic: 0.05% (15 g, 45 g, 50 g); 0.1% (15 g, 45 g)

Betamethasone and Salicylic Acid

Brand Names: Canada Diprosalic; Ratio-Topisalic

Pharmacologic Category Corticosteroid, Topical; Keratolytic Agent

Use Note: Not approved in the US

Dermatoses: Topical management of subacute and chronic hyperkeratotic and dry dermatosis responsive to corticosteroid therapy.

Local Anesthetic/Vasoconstrictor Precautions No information available to require special precautions

Effects on Dental Treatment No significant effects or complications reported

Effects on Bleeding No information available to require special precautions

Adverse Reactions See individual agents.

Mechanism of Action Refer to individual agents.

Pregnancy Considerations Refer to individual agents.

Product Availability Not available in the US

Betaxolol (Systemic) (be TAKS oh lol)

Related Information

Cardiovascular Diseases *on page* 1752

Brand Names: US Kerlone [DSC]

Pharmacologic Category Antihypertensive; Beta-Blocker, Beta-1 Selective

Use

Hypertension: Management of hypertension

Guideline recommendations:

Hypertension: The 2014 guideline for the management of high blood pressure in adults (Eighth Joint National Committee [JNC 8]) recommends initiation of pharmacologic treatment to lower blood pressure for the following patients (JNC8 [James, 2013]):

- Patients ≥60 years of age, with systolic blood pressure (SBP) ≥150 mm Hg or diastolic blood pressure (DBP) ≥90 mm Hg. Goal of therapy is SBP <150 mm Hg and DBP <90 mm Hg.
- Patients <60 years of age, with SBP ≥140 mm Hg or DBP ≥90 mm Hg. Goal of therapy is SBP <140 mm Hg and DBP <90 mm Hg.
- Patients ≥18 years of age with diabetes, with SBP ≥140 mm Hg or DBP ≥90 mm Hg. Goal of therapy is SBP <140 mm Hg and DBP <90 mm Hg.
- Patients ≥18 years of age with chronic kidney disease (CKD), with SBP ≥140 mm Hg or DBP ≥90 mm Hg. Goal of therapy is SBP <140 mm Hg and DBP <90 mm Hg.

Chronic kidney disease (CKD) and hypertension: Regardless of race or diabetes status, the use of an ACE inhibitor (ACEI) or angiotensin receptor blocker (ARB) as initial therapy is recommended to improve kidney outcomes. In the general nonblack population (without CKD) including those with diabetes, initial antihypertensive treatment should consist of a thiazide-type diuretic, calcium channel blocker, ACEI, or ARB. In the general black population (without CKD) including those with diabetes, initial antihypertensive treatment should consist of a thiazide-type diuretic or a calcium channel blocker **instead of** an ACEI or ARB.

Coronary artery disease (CAD) and hypertension: The American Heart Association, American College of Cardiology and American Society of Hypertension (AHA/ACC/ASH) 2015 scientific statement for the treatment of hypertension in patients with coronary artery disease (CAD) recommends the use of a beta blocker as part of a regimen in patients with hypertension and chronic stable angina with a history of prior MI. A BP target of <140/90 mm Hg is reasonable for the secondary prevention of cardiovascular events. A lower target BP (<130/80 mm Hg) may be appropriate in some individuals with CAD, previous MI, stroke or transient ischemic attack, or CAD risk equivalents (AHA/ACC/ASH [Rosendorff 2015]).

Local Anesthetic/Vasoconstrictor Precautions No information available to require special precautions

Effects on Dental Treatment Betaxolol is a cardioselective beta-blocker. Local anesthetic with vasoconstrictor can be safely used in patients medicated with betaxolol. Nonselective beta-blockers (ie, propranolol, nadolol) enhance the pressor response to epinephrine or levonordefrin, resulting in hypertension and bradycardia; this has not been reported for betaxolol. Many nonsteroidal anti-inflammatory drugs, such as ibuprofen and indomethacin, can reduce the hypotensive effect of beta-blockers after 3 or more weeks of therapy with the NSAID. Short-term NSAID use (ie, 3 days) requires no special precautions in patients taking beta-blockers.

Effects on Bleeding No information available to require special precautions

Adverse Reactions

2% to 10%:

Cardiovascular: Bradycardia (6% to 8%; symptomatic bradycardia: ≤2%; dose-dependent), chest pain (2% to 7%), cold extremities (2%), palpitations (2%), edema (≤2%; similar to placebo)

Central nervous system: Fatigue (3% to 10%), insomnia (1% to 5%), lethargy (3%), paresthesia (2%)

Gastrointestinal: Nausea (2% to 6%), dyspepsia (4% to 5%), diarrhea (2%)

Hematologic & oncologic: Positive ANA titer (5%)

Neuromuscular & skeletal: Arthralgia (3% to 5%)

Respiratory: Dyspnea (2%), pharyngitis (2%)

<2%, postmarketing, and/or case reports: Abnormal dreams, abnormality in thinking, acidosis, alopecia, amnesia, anemia, angina pectoris, anorexia, arthropathy, ataxia, atrioventricular block, blepharitis, breast fibroadenosis, bronchitis, bronchospasm, cardiac arrhythmia, cardiac failure, cataract, cerebrovascular disease, conjunctivitis, constipation, cough, cystitis, deafness, decreased libido, depression, diabetes mellitus, diaphoresis, dysgeusia, dysphagia, dysuria, emotional lability, epistaxis, erythematous rash, exacerbation of psoriasis, fever, flushing, hallucination, hemophthalmos, hypercholesterolemia, hyperglycemia, hyperkalemia, hyperlipidemia, hypersensitivity reaction, hypertension, hypertrichosis, hyperuricemia, hypoglycemia, hypokalemia, hypotension, impotence, increased lactate dehydrogenase, increased serum ALT, increased serum AST, influenza, intermittent claudication, iritis, labyrinth disease, leukocytosis, lymphadenopathy, malaise, menstrual disease, muscle cramps, myocardial infarction, nervousness, neuralgia, neuropathy, numbness, oliguria, peripheral ischemia, Peyronie's disease, pneumonia, prostatitis, proteinuria, pruritus, purpura, renal insufficiency, rhinitis, rigors, scotoma, sinusitis, skin rash, stupor, syncope, tendonitis, thrombocytopenia, thrombophlebitis, thrombosis, tinnitus, tremor, twitching, visual disturbance, vomiting, weight gain, weight loss, xerostomia

General Dosage Range Dosage adjustment recommended in patients with renal impairment

Oral:

Adults: 5 to 20 mg once daily

Elderly: Initial dose: 5 mg once daily

Mechanism of Action Competitively blocks beta$_1$-receptors, with little or no effect on beta$_2$-receptors

Pharmacodynamics/Kinetics

Onset of Action 1 to 1.5 hours

Half-life Elimination 14 to 22 hours; prolonged in hepatic disease and/or chronic renal failure. In patients with chronic renal failure undergoing dialysis, the half-life and AUC are approximately doubled.

Time to Peak 1.5 to 6 hours

Pregnancy Risk Factor C

Pregnancy Considerations Adverse events were observed in some animal reproduction studies. Betaxolol crosses the placenta and can be detected in the amniotic fluid as well as umbilical cord blood. Measurable concentrations of betaxolol can also be found in the newborn blood and urine (Morselli 1990). Following maternal use of betaxolol, the beta-blocker effects may persist in the neonate for several days after birth. The risk of cardiac and pulmonary complications is increased in the neonate. Bradycardia, hypoglycemia, and respiratory distress have been reported and monitoring of the neonate for 3 to 5 days after birth is recommended. Reduced birth weight has also been observed following in utero exposure to beta-blockers as a class.

The maternal half-life and serum concentration of betaxolol immediately postpartum are not significantly different than what is observed in nonpregnant women (Boutroy 1990; Morselli 1990). Untreated chronic maternal hypertension and preeclampsia are also associated with adverse events in the fetus, infant, and mother (ACOG 2015; Magee 2014). Although beta-blockers may be used when treatment of hypertension in pregnancy is indicated, agents other than betaxolol are preferred (ACOG 2013; Magee 2014; Regitz-Zagrosek 2011).

Bethanechol (be THAN e kole)

Brand Names: US Urecholine

Brand Names: Canada Duvoid; PHL-Bethanechol; PMS-Bethanechol

Pharmacologic Category Cholinergic Agonist

Use

Neurogenic bladder: Treatment of neurogenic atony of the urinary bladder with retention

Urinary retention: Treatment of acute postoperative and postpartum nonobstructive (functional) urinary retention

Local Anesthetic/Vasoconstrictor Precautions No information available to require special precautions

Effects on Dental Treatment This is a cholinergic agent similar to pilocarpine; expect to see salivation and sweating in patients.

Effects on Bleeding No information available to require special precautions

Adverse Reactions Frequency not defined.

Cardiovascular: Flushing, hypotension, tachycardia

Central nervous system: Colic, headache, malaise, seizure

Dermatologic: Diaphoresis

Gastrointestinal: Abdominal cramps, borborygmi, diarrhea, eructation, nausea, salivation, vomiting

Genitourinary: Urinary urgency

Ophthalmic: Lacrimation, miosis

Respiratory: Asthma, bronchoconstriction

General Dosage Range Oral: *Adults:* 10 to 50 mg 3 to 4 times daily

Mechanism of Action Due to stimulation of the parasympathetic nervous system, bethanechol increases bladder muscle tone causing contractions which initiate urination. Bethanechol also stimulates gastric motility, increases gastric tone and may restore peristalsis.

Pharmacodynamics/Kinetics

Onset of Action 30 to 90 minutes

Duration of Action ~1 hour (with therapeutic doses); up to 6 hours with large doses

Pregnancy Risk Factor C

Pregnancy Considerations Animal reproduction studies have not been conducted.

Bevacizumab (be vuh SIZ uh mab)

Related Information

Osteonecrosis of the Jaw *on page 1796*

Brand Names: US Avastin

Brand Names: Canada Avastin

Pharmacologic Category Antineoplastic Agent, Monoclonal Antibody; Antineoplastic Agent, Vascular Endothelial Growth Factor (VEGF) Inhibitor; Vascular Endothelial Growth Factor (VEGF) Inhibitor

Use

Cervical cancer, persistent/recurrent/metastatic: Treatment of persistent, recurrent, or metastatic cervical cancer (in combination with paclitaxel and either cisplatin or topotecan).

Colorectal cancer, metastatic: First- or second-line treatment of metastatic colorectal cancer (CRC) (in combination with fluorouracil-based chemotherapy); second-line treatment of metastatic CRC (in combination with fluoropyrimidine-irinotecan- or fluoropyrimidine-oxaliplatin-based chemotherapy) after progression on a first-line treatment containing bevacizumab.

Limitations of use: Not indicated for the adjuvant treatment of colon cancer.

Glioblastoma: Treatment of progressive glioblastoma (as a single agent).

Non-small cell lung cancer, nonsquamous: First-line treatment of unresectable, locally advanced, recurrent or metastatic nonsquamous non-small cell lung cancer (NSCLC) (in combination with carboplatin and paclitaxel).

Ovarian (epithelial), fallopian tube, or primary peritoneal cancer (platinum-resistant recurrent): Treatment of platinum-resistant recurrent epithelial ovarian, fallopian tube, or primary peritoneal cancer (in combination with paclitaxel, doxorubicin [liposomal], or topotecan) in patients who received no more than 2 prior chemotherapy regimens.

Ovarian (epithelial), fallopian tube, or primary peritoneal cancer (platinum-sensitive recurrent): Treatment of platinum-sensitive recurrent epithelial ovarian, fallopian tube, or primary peritoneal cancer (in combination with carboplatin and paclitaxel or with carboplatin and gemcitabine and then followed by single-agent bevacizumab).

Renal cell carcinoma, metastatic: Treatment of metastatic renal cell carcinoma (RCC) (in combination with interferon alfa).

Local Anesthetic/Vasoconstrictor Precautions No information available to require special precautions

Effects on Dental Treatment Key adverse event(s) related to dental treatment: Xerostomia (normal salivary flow resumes upon discontinuation), stomatitis, taste disorder, and gingival bleeding.

Cases of osteonecrosis of the jaw (ONJ) have been associated with bevacizumab exposure. ONJ presents clinically as exposed necrotic bone of at least 8 weeks duration with or without the presence of pain, infection, or previous trauma in a patient who has not received radiation to the jaw. Since ONJ is also associated with bisphosphonate exposure and bisphosphonates are known to have antiangiogenic properties, inhibition of angiogenesis may play a role in ONJ associated with these two classes of drugs. Patients developing ONJ while on bevacizumab therapy should receive care by an oral surgeon. See Dental Comment.

Effects on Bleeding Minor gum bleeding has been reported in 2% to 4% of patients. Thrombocytopenia has been reported. A medical consult is suggested.

Adverse Reactions Percentages reported as monotherapy and as part of combination chemotherapy regimens. Some studies only reported hematologic toxicities grades ≥4 and nonhematologic toxicities grades ≥3.

>10%:

Cardiovascular: Hypertension (12% to 34%; grades 3/4: 5% to 18%), venous thromboembolism (secondary: 21%; with oral anticoagulants), peripheral edema (15%), hypotension (7% to 15%), venous thromboembolism (8% to 14%; grades 3/4: 5% to 15%), arterial thrombosis (6%; grades 3/4: 3%)

Central nervous system: Fatigue (33% to 80%; grades 3/4: 4% to 19%), pain (8% to 62%; grades 3/4: 8%), headache (22% to 37%; grades 3/4: 3% to 4%), dizziness (19% to 26%), taste disorder (14% to 21%), peripheral sensory neuropathy (17% to 18%), anxiety (17%)

Dermatologic: Alopecia (6% to 32%), palmar-plantar erythrodysesthesia (11%), exfoliative dermatitis (>10%), xeroderma (>10%)

Endocrine & metabolic: Ovarian failure (34%), hyperglycemia (26%), hypomagnesemia (24%), weight loss (15% to 21%), hyponatremia (19%; grades 3/4: 4%), hypoalbuminemia (16%)

Gastrointestinal: Abdominal pain (50% to 61%; grades 3/4: 8%), vomiting (47% to 52%; grades 3/4: 11%), anorexia (35% to 43%), constipation (40%; grades 3/4: 4%), decreased appetite (34%), diarrhea (21%; grades 3/4: 1% to 34%), stomatitis (15% to 32%), gastrointestinal hemorrhage (19% to 24%), dyspepsia (17% to 24%), mucosal inflammation (13%), nausea (grades 3/4: 12%)

Genitourinary: Proteinuria (4% to 36%; grades >2%: grades 3/4: ≤7%; median onset: 5.6 months; median time to resolution: 6.1 months), urinary tract infection (22%; grades 3/4: 8%), pelvic pain (14%; grades 3/4: 6%)

Hematologic & oncologic: Hemorrhage (40%; grades 3/4: ≤7%), leukopenia (grades 3/4: 37%), pulmonary hemorrhage (4% to 31%), neutropenia (12%; grades ≥3: 8% to 27%, grade 4: 27%), lymphocytopenia (12%; grades 3/4: 6%)

Infection: Infection (55%; serious: 7% to 14%; pneumonia, catheter infection, or wound infection)

Neuromuscular & skeletal: Myalgia (19%), back pain (12%; grades 3/4: 6%)

Renal: Increased serum creatinine (16%)

Respiratory: Upper respiratory tract infection (40% to 47%), epistaxis (17% to 35%), dyspnea (25% to 26%), rhinitis (3% to >10%)

Miscellaneous: Postoperative wound complication (including dehiscence, 1% to 15%)

1% to 10%:

Cardiovascular: Thrombosis (8% to 10%), deep vein thrombosis (6% to 9%; grades 3/4: 9%), syncope (grades 3/4: 3%), intra-abdominal thrombosis (venous, grades 3/4: 3%), left ventricular dysfunction (grades 3/4: 1%), pulmonary embolism (1%)

Central nervous system: Voice disorder (5% to 9%)

Dermatologic: Dermal ulcer (6%), cellulitis (grades 3/4: 3%), acne vulgaris (1%)

Endocrine & metabolic: Dehydration (grades 3/4: 4% to 10%), hypokalemia (grades 3/4: 7%)

Gastrointestinal: Xerostomia (4% to 7%), rectal pain (6%), colitis (1% to 6%), intestinal obstruction (grades 3/4: 4%), gingival hemorrhage (minor, 2% to 4%), gastrointestinal perforation (≤ 3%), gastroesophageal reflux disease (2%), gastrointestinal fistula (≤2%), gingivitis (2%), oral mucosa ulcer (2%), gastritis (1%), gingival pain (1%)

Genitourinary: Vaginal hemorrhage (4%)

Hematologic & oncologic: Febrile neutropenia (5%), neutropenic infection (grades 3/4: 5%), thrombocytopenia (5%), hemorrhage (CNS; 5%; grades 3/4: 1%)

Infection: Abscess (tooth, 2%)

Neuromuscular & skeletal: Weakness (grades 3/4: 10%), dysarthria (8%)

Ophthalmic: Blurred vision (2%)

Otic: Tinnitus (2%), deafness (1%)

Respiratory: Pneumonitis (grades 3/4: 5%),

Miscellaneous: Fistula (gastrointestinal-vaginal; 8%), fistula (anal; 6%; grades 3/4: 4%), infusion related reaction (<3%), fistula (≤2%)

<1%, postmarketing, and/or case reports: Anaphylaxis, anastomotic ulcer, angina pectoris, antibody development (anti-bevacizumab and neutralizing), bladder fistula, bronchopleural fistula, cerebral infarction, conjunctival hemorrhage, endophthalmitis (infectious and sterile), eye discomfort, eye pain, fistula of bile duct, fulminant necrotizing fasciitis, gallbladder perforation, gastrointestinal ulcer, hemolytic anemia (microangiopathic; when used in combination with sunitinib), hemoptysis, hemorrhagic stroke, hypersensitivity, hypertensive crisis, hypertensive encephalopathy, increased intraocular pressure, inflammation of anterior segment of eye (toxic anterior segment syndrome) (Sato 2010), intestinal necrosis, intraocular inflammation (iritis, vitritis), mesenteric thrombosis, myocardial infarction, nasal septum perforation, nephrotic syndrome, ocular hyperemia, osteonecrosis of the jaw, pancytopenia, permanent vision loss, polyserositis, pulmonary hypertension, rectal fistula, renal failure, renal fistula, renal thrombotic microangiopathy, retinal detachment, retinal hemorrhage, reversible posterior leukoencephalopathy syndrome, sepsis, tracheoesophageal fistula, transient ischemic attacks, vaginal fistula, visual disturbance, vitreous hemorrhage, vitreous opacity

General Dosage Range IV: *Adults:* 5 or 10 mg/kg every 2 weeks **or** 7.5 or 15 mg/kg every 3 weeks

Mechanism of Action Bevacizumab is a recombinant, humanized monoclonal antibody which binds to, and neutralizes, vascular endothelial growth factor (VEGF), preventing its association with endothelial receptors, Flt-1 and KDR. VEGF binding initiates angiogenesis (endothelial proliferation and the formation of new blood vessels). The inhibition of microvascular growth is believed to retard the growth of all tissues (including metastatic tissue).

Pharmacodynamics/Kinetics

Half-life Elimination

IV:

Pediatric patients (age: 1 to 21 years): Median: 11.8 days (range: 4.4 to 14.6 days) (Glade Bender 2008)

Adults: ~20 days (range: 11 to 50 days)

Intravitreal: ~5 to 10 days (Bakri 2007; Krohne 2008)

Pregnancy Considerations Based on its mechanism of action, bevacizumab would be expected to cause fetal harm if administered to a pregnant woman. Information from postmarketing reports following exposure in pregnancy is limited. Women of reproductive potential should use effective contraception during therapy and for 6 months following the last dose (due to the long half-life of bevacizumab). Bevacizumab treatment may also increase the risk of ovarian failure and impair fertility; long term effects on fertility are not known.

Dental Comment Three case reports describe the development of ONJ in association with bevacizumab therapy. All three cases were cancer patients treated with bevacizumab 10 mg/kg every 2 weeks and 15 mg/kg every 3 weeks (Estilo 2009; Greuter 2008). Another report showed that a combination of bisphosphonates and antiangiogenic factors (primarily bevacizumab) induces ONJ more frequently than bisphosphonates alone. Of the 25 patients receiving concurrent treatment with bisphosphonates and the antiangiogenic drug bevacizumab, four developed ONJ (16%). Of the 91 patients receiving bisphosphonates without antiangiogenic factors, one developed ONJ (1.1%), a significant statistical difference (Christodoulou 2009).

Bexarotene (Systemic) (beks AIR oh teen)

Brand Names: US Targretin

Pharmacologic Category Antineoplastic Agent, Retinoic Acid Derivative

Use Cutaneous T-cell lymphoma, refractory: Treatment of cutaneous manifestations of cutaneous T-cell lymphoma in patients who are refractory to at least one prior systemic therapy

Local Anesthetic/Vasoconstrictor Precautions No information available to require special precautions

Effects on Dental Treatment Key adverse event(s) related to dental treatment: Xerostomia (normal salivary flow resumes upon discontinuation) and gingivitis.

Effects on Bleeding No information available to require special precautions

Adverse Reactions

Frequency not always defined.

>10%:

Cardiovascular: Peripheral edema (11% to 13%)

Central nervous system: Headache (30% to 42%), chills (10% to 13%), insomnia (5% to 11%)

Dermatologic: Exfoliative dermatitis (10% to 28%), skin rash (17% to 23%), xeroderma (9% to 11%), alopecia (4% to 11%)

Endocrine & metabolic: Hyperlipidemia (79%), hypercholesterolemia (32% to 62%), hypothyroidism (29% to 53%), increased lactate dehydrogenase (7% to 13%)

Gastrointestinal: Diarrhea (7% to 42%), anorexia (2% to 23%), nausea (8% to 16%), vomiting (4% to 13%), abdominal pain (4% to 11%)

Hematologic & oncologic: Leukopenia (17% to 47%), anemia (6% to 25%), hypochromic anemia (4% to 13%)

Infection: Infection (13% to 23%; bacterial infection: 1% to 13%)

Neuromuscular & skeletal: Weakness (20% to 45%), back pain (2% to 11%)

Respiratory: Flu-like symptoms (4% to 13%)

Miscellaneous: Fever (5% to 17%)

1% to 10%:

Cardiovascular: Angina pectoris, cardiac failure (right), cerebrovascular accident, chest pain, hypertension, subdural hematoma, syncope, tachycardia

Central nervous system: Agitation, ataxia, confusion, depression, dizziness, hyperesthesia, myasthenia, neuropathy

Dermatologic: Acne vulgaris, allergic skin reaction, cellulitis, cheilitis, cutaneous nodule, maculopapular rash, skin photosensitivity, pustular rash, skin rash, sunburn, vesiculobullous dermatitis

Endocrine & metabolic: Albuminuria, hyperglycemia, weight gain, weight loss

Gastrointestinal: Colitis, constipation, dyspepsia, flatulence, gastroenteritis, gingivitis, increased serum amylase, melena, pancreatitis, xerostomia

Genitourinary: Dysuria, hematuria, mastalgia, urinary incontinence, urinary tract infection, urinary urgency

Hematologic & oncologic: Acquired blood coagulation disorder, eosinophilia, hemorrhage, hypoproteinemia, lymphocytosis, thrombocythemia, thrombocytopenia

Hepatic: Hepatic failure, increased serum ALT, increased serum AST, increased serum bilirubin

Infection: Candidiasis, sepsis

Neuromuscular & skeletal: Arthralgia, arthrosis, myalgia, ostealgia

Ophthalmic: Blepharitis, cataract (new and worsening), conjunctivitis, corneal lesion, keratitis, visual field defect, xerophthalmia

Otic: Otalgia, otitis externa

Renal: Increased serum creatinine, renal function abnormality

Respiratory: Bronchitis, cough, dyspnea, hemoptysis, hypoxia, pharyngitis, pleural effusion, pneumonia, pulmonary edema, rhinitis

Miscellaneous: Serous drainage

General Dosage Range Dosage adjustment recommended in patients who develop toxicities.

Oral: *Adults:* 300 to 400 mg/m^2 once daily

Mechanism of Action Selectively binds to and activates retinoid X receptors (RXRs). Once activated, RXRs function as transcription factors to regulate the expression of genes which control cellular differentiation and proliferation. Bexarotene inhibits the growth *in vitro* of some tumor cell lines of hematopoietic and squamous cell origin and induces tumor regression *in vivo* in some animal models.

Pharmacodynamics/Kinetics

Half-life Elimination ~7 hours

Time to Peak ~2 hours

Pregnancy Considerations [U.S. Boxed Warning]: Bexarotene is a retinoid, a drug class associated with birth defects in humans; do not administer during pregnancy. Bexarotene caused birth defects when administered orally to pregnant rats. It must not be given to a pregnant woman or a woman who intends to become pregnant. If a woman becomes pregnant while taking the drug, it must be stopped immediately and appropriate counseling be given. In women of childbearing potential, therapy should be started on the second or third day of a normal menstrual period. Either abstinence or 2 forms of reliable contraception (one should be nonhormonal) must be used for at least 1 month before initiating therapy, during therapy, and for 1 month following discontinuation of bexarotene. A negative pregnancy test (sensitivity of at least 50 milliunits/mL) within 1 week prior to beginning therapy, and monthly thereafter is required for women of childbearing potential. A maximum 1 month supply is recommended so that pregnancy tests may be evaluated. Male patients must use a condom during any sexual contact with women of childbearing age during therapy, and for at least 1 month following discontinuation of bexarotene.

Bicalutamide (bye ka LOO ta mide)

Brand Names: US Casodex

Brand Names: Canada ACH-Bicalutamide; ACT Bicalutamide; Apo-Bicalutamide; Casodex; Dom-Bicalutamide; JAMP-Bicalutamide; Mylan-Bicalutamide; PHL-Bicalutamide; PMS-Bicalutamide; PRO-Bicalutamide; RAN-Bicalutamide; Sandoz-Bicalutamide; Teva-Bicalutamide

Pharmacologic Category Antineoplastic Agent, Antiandrogen

Use

Prostate cancer, metastatic: Treatment of stage D_2 metastatic prostate cancer (in combination with an LHRH agonist)

Limitation of use: Bicalutamide 150 mg daily is not approved for use alone or with other treatments

Local Anesthetic/Vasoconstrictor Precautions No information available to require special precautions

Effects on Dental Treatment Key adverse event(s) related to dental treatment: Xerostomia (normal salivary flow resumes upon discontinuation).

Effects on Bleeding No information available to require special precautions

Adverse Reactions Adverse reaction percentages reported as part of combination regimen with an LHRH analogue unless otherwise noted.

>10%:

Cardiovascular: Peripheral edema (13%)

Central nervous system: Pain (35%)

Endocrine & metabolic: Hot flash (53%), gynecomastia (9%; monotherapy [150 mg]: 38% to 73% [McLeod 2006])

Gastrointestinal: Constipation (22%), nausea (15%), diarrhea (12%), abdominal pain (11%)

Genitourinary: Mastalgia (6%; monotherapy [150 mg]: 39% to 85% [McLeod 2006]), pelvic pain (21%), hematuria (12%), nocturia (12%)

Hematologic & oncologic: Anemia (11%)

Infection: Infection (18%)

Neuromuscular & skeletal: Back pain (25%), weakness (22%)

Respiratory: Dyspnea (13%)

≥2% to 10%:

Cardiovascular: Chest pain (8%), hypertension (8%), angina pectoris (2% to <5%), cardiac arrest (2% to <5%), cardiac failure (2% to <5%), coronary artery disease (2% to <5%), edema (2% to <5%), myocardial infarction (2% to <5%), syncope (2% to <5%)

Central nervous system: Dizziness (10%), paresthesia (8%), headache (7%), insomnia (7%), myasthenia (7%), anxiety (5%), chills (2% to <5%), confusion (2% to <5%), drowsiness (2% to <5%), hypertonia (2% to <5%), nervousness (2% to <5%), neuropathy (2% to <5%), depression (4%)

Dermatologic: Skin rash (9%), diaphoresis (6%), alopecia (2% to <5%), pruritus (2% to <5%), xeroderma (2% to <5%)

Endocrine & metabolic: Weight loss (7%), hyperglycemia (6%), weight gain (5%), decreased libido (2% to <5%), dehydration (2% to <5%), gout (2% to <5%), hypercholesterolemia (2% to <5%)

Gastrointestinal: Dyspepsia (7%), anorexia (6%), flatulence (6%), vomiting (6%), dysphagia (2% to <5%), hernia (2% to <5%), melena (2% to <5%), periodontal abscess (2% to <5%), xerostomia (2% to <5%)

Genitourinary: Urinary tract infection (9%), impotence (7%), difficulty in micturition (5%), urinary retention (5%), dysuria (2% to <5%), urinary urgency (2% to <5%), urinary incontinence (4%)

Hematologic & oncologic: Gastrointestinal carcinoma (2% to <5%), rectal hemorrhage (2% to <5%), skin carcinoma (2% to <5%)

Hepatic: Increased liver enzymes (7%), increased serum alkaline phosphatase (5%)

Infection: Herpes zoster (2% to <5%), sepsis (2% to <5%)

Neuromuscular & skeletal: Ostealgia (9%), arthritis (5%), leg cramps (2% to <5%), myalgia (2% to <5%), neck pain (2% to <5%), pathological fracture (4%)

Ophthalmic: Cataract (2% to <5%)

Renal: Polyuria (6%), hydronephrosis (2% to <5%), increased blood urea nitrogen (2% to <5%), increased serum creatinine (2% to <5%)

Respiratory: Cough (8%), pharyngitis (8%), flu-like symptoms (7%), bronchitis (6%), asthma (2% to <5%), epistaxis (2% to <5%), sinusitis (2% to <5%), pneumonia (4%), rhinitis (4%)

Miscellaneous: Cyst (2% to <5%), fever (2% to <5%)

<1%, postmarketing, and/or case reports: Decreased glucose tolerance, decreased hemoglobin, decreased white blood cell count, hepatic failure, hepatitis, hepatotoxicity, hypersensitivity (including angioedema and urticaria), increased serum ALT, increased serum AST, increased serum bilirubin, interstitial pneumonitis, interstitial pulmonary disease (most often at doses >50 mg), pulmonary fibrosis, skin photosensitivity

General Dosage Range Oral: *Adults: Males:* 50 mg once daily

Mechanism of Action Androgen receptor inhibitor; pure nonsteroidal antiandrogen that binds to androgen receptors; specifically a competitive inhibitor for the binding of dihydrotestosterone and testosterone; prevents testosterone stimulation of cell growth in prostate cancer

Pharmacodynamics/Kinetics

Half-life Elimination

Active enantiomer: ~6 days (~10 days in severe hepatic impairment)

Time to Peak Active enantiomer: ~31 hours

Pregnancy Considerations Bicalutamide is contraindicated in women. Androgen receptor inhibition during pregnancy may affect fetal development. In addition, male fertility may be impaired. Males with female partners of reproductive potential should use effective contraception during therapy and for 130 days after the last dose.

Bimatoprost (bi MAT oh prost)

Brand Names: US Latisse; Lumigan

Brand Names: Canada Latisse; Lumigan; Lumigan RC; Vistitan

Pharmacologic Category Ophthalmic Agent, Antiglaucoma; Prostaglandin, Ophthalmic

Use

Elevated intraocular pressure (Lumigan; Vistitan [Canadian product]): Reduction of elevated intraocular pressure (IOP) in patients with open-angle glaucoma or ocular hypertension

Hypotrichosis of the eyelashes (Latisse): Treatment of hypotrichosis of the eyelashes

Local Anesthetic/Vasoconstrictor Precautions No information available to require special precautions

Effects on Dental Treatment No significant effects or complications reported

Effects on Bleeding No information available to require special precautions

Adverse Reactions Adverse reactions and percentages are for Lumigan unless noted:

>10%:

Dermatologic: Increased growth in number of eyelashes

Ophthalmic: Conjunctival hyperemia (25% to 45%; Latisse: <4%), eye pruritus (>10%; Latisse: <4%)

1% to 10%:

Central nervous system: Headache (1% to 5%), foreign body sensation of eye

Dermatologic: Erythema of eyelid (1% to 10%; Latisse: <4%), skin hyperpigmentation (Latisse: <4%), hyperpigmentation of eyelashes, pigmentation of the periocular skin

Endocrine & metabolic: Hirsutism

Hepatic: Abnormal hepatic function tests (1% to 5%)

Infection: Infection (10% [primarily colds and upper respiratory tract infections])

Neuromuscular & skeletal: Weakness (1% to 5%)

Ophthalmic: Dry eye syndrome (1% to 10%; Latisse: <4%), eye irritation (1% to 10%; Latisse: <4%), allergic conjunctivitis, asthenopia, blepharitis, burning sensation of eyes, cataract, conjunctival edema, conjunctival hemorrhage, eye discharge, eye pain, iris hyperpigmentation (may be delayed), lacrimation, photophobia, superficial punctate keratitis, visual disturbance

<1%, postmarketing, and/or case reports: Bacterial keratitis (caused by inadvertent contamination of multiple-dose ophthalmic solutions), blurred vision, cystoid macular edema, dizziness, eyelid edema, hair breakage, hypersensitivity reaction, hypertension, iritis, macular edema, madarosis, nausea, skin rash (including macular and erythematous), uveitis

General Dosage Range

Ophthalmic (Lumigan): *Adolescents ≥16 years and Adults:* Instill 1 drop into affected eye(s) once daily in the evening

Ophthalmic, topical: (Latisse): *Children ≥5 years, Adolescents, and Adults:* Place 1 drop on applicator and apply evenly along the skin of the upper eyelid at base of eyelashes once daily at bedtime

Mechanism of Action As a synthetic analog of prostaglandin with ocular hypotensive activity, bimatoprost decreases intraocular pressure by increasing the outflow of aqueous humor. Bimatoprost may increase the percent and duration of hairs in the growth phase, resulting in eyelash growth.

Pharmacodynamics/Kinetics

Onset of Action Reduction of IOP: ~4 hours; Peak effect: Maximum reduction of IOP: ~8 to 12 hours

Half-life Elimination IV: ≤45 minutes

Time to Peak ≤10 minutes

Pregnancy Risk Factor C

Pregnancy Considerations Adverse events have been observed in animal reproduction studies.

Bisacodyl (bis a KOE dil)

Brand Names: US Bisac-Evac [OTC]; Bisacodyl EC [OTC]; Bisacodyl Laxative [OTC]; Biscolax [OTC]; Correct [OTC]; Ducodyl [OTC]; Dulcolax [OTC]; Ex-Lax Ultra [OTC]; Fleet Bisacodyl [OTC]; Fleet Laxative [OTC]; Gentle Laxative [OTC]; Laxative [OTC]; Stimulant Laxative [OTC]; The Magic Bullet [OTC]; Womens Laxative [OTC]

Brand Names: Canada Apo-Bisacodyl [OTC]; Bisacodyl-Odan [OTC]; Carter's Little Pills [OTC]; Codulax [OTC]; Dulcolax For Women [OTC]; Dulcolax [OTC]; PMS-Bisacodyl [OTC]; ratio-Bisacodyl [OTC]; Silver Bullet Suppository [OTC]; Soflax EX [OTC]; The Magic Bullet [OTC]; Woman's Laxative [OTC]

Pharmacologic Category Laxative, Stimulant

Use

Bowel cleansing (enema only): Bowel cleansing prior to rectal examination.

Constipation: Temporary relief of occasional constipation and irregularity.

Local Anesthetic/Vasoconstrictor Precautions No information available to require special precautions

Effects on Dental Treatment No significant effects or complications reported

Effects on Bleeding No information available to require special precautions

Adverse Reactions <1%: Abdominal cramps (mild), electrolyte disturbance (metabolic acidosis or alkalosis, hypocalcemia), nausea, rectal irritation (burning), vertigo, vomiting

General Dosage Range

Oral:

Children 6 years to <12 years: 5 mg once daily

Children ≥12 years, Adolescents, and Adults: 5 to 15 mg once daily

Rectal:

Suppository:

Children 6 to <12 years: 5 mg (1/2 suppository) once daily

Children ≥12 years, Adolescents, and Adults: 10 mg (1 suppository) once daily

Enema: *Children ≥12 years, Adolescents, and Adults:* 10 mg (1 enema) once daily

Mechanism of Action Stimulates peristalsis by directly irritating the smooth muscle of the intestine, possibly the colonic intramural plexus; alters water and electrolyte secretion producing net intestinal fluid accumulation and laxation

Pharmacodynamics/Kinetics

Onset of Action Oral: 6 to 12 hours; Rectal: 0.25 to 1 hour (suppository), 5 to 20 minutes (enema)

Half-life Elimination BHPM: ~8 hours (Friedrich 2011)

Pregnancy Considerations Plasma concentrations of BHPM (the active metabolite of bisacodyl) are low (median: 61 ng/mL; range: 21 to 194 ng/mL) following doses of 10 mg/day for 7 days (Friedrich, 2011). Although not first choice for the treatment of constipation in pregnant women, short-term use of stimulant laxatives is generally considered safe in pregnancy; long-term use should be avoided (Cullen, 2007; Prather, 2004; Wald, 2003).

Bismuth Subcitrate, Metronidazole, and Tetracycline

(BIZ muth sub CIT rate, me troe NI da zole, & tet ra SYE kleen)

Brand Names: US Pylera

Pharmacologic Category Antibiotic, Miscellaneous; Antibiotic, Tetracycline Derivative; Antidiarrheal

Use Duodenal ulcer associated with *Helicobacter pylori* infection: In combination with omeprazole for the treatment of patients with *H. pylori* infection and duodenal ulcer disease (active or history of within the past 5 years) to eradicate *H. pylori*.

Local Anesthetic/Vasoconstrictor Precautions No information available to require special precautions

Effects on Dental Treatment Tetracyclines are not recommended for use during pregnancy since they can cause enamel hypoplasia and permanent teeth discoloration; long-term use associated with oral candidiasis; taste perversion has been reported.

Effects on Bleeding No information available to require special precautions

Adverse Reactions Also see individual agents. Adverse reactions are associated with concomitant administration of omeprazole.

>10%: Gastrointestinal: Abnormal stools (16%)

1% to 10%:

Central nervous system: Headache (5%), dizziness (3%)

Dermatologic: Maculopapular rash (1%)

Gastrointestinal: Nausea (8%), diarrhea (7%), abdominal pain (5%), dysgeusia (4%), dyspepsia (3%), constipation (1%), xerostomia (1%)

Genitourinary: Vaginitis (3%), urine abnormality (1%)

Hepatic: Increased serum ALT (1%), increased serum AST (1%)

Neuromuscular & skeletal: Weakness (3%)

Miscellaneous: Laboratory test abnormality (2%)

<1%, postmarketing, and/or case reports: Abdominal distention, anxiety, back pain, candidiasis, chest discomfort, chest pain, drowsiness, duodenal ulcer, eructation, fatigue, flatulence, gastritis, gastroenteritis, increased appetite, increased creatine phosphokinase, malaise, myalgia, skin rash, tachycardia, tongue discoloration (darkening), visual disturbance, vomiting, weight gain

General Dosage Range Oral: *Adults:* Three capsules 4 times daily after meals and at bedtime

Mechanism of Action

Bismuth: Has both antisecretory and antimicrobial action; may provide some anti-inflammatory action as well.

Metronidazole: After diffusing into the organism, interacts with DNA to cause a loss of helical DNA structure and strand breakage resulting in inhibition of protein synthesis and cell death in susceptible organisms.

Tetracycline: Inhibits bacterial protein synthesis by binding with the 30S and possibly the 50S ribosomal subunit(s) of susceptible bacteria; may also cause alterations in the cytoplasmic membrane.

Bismuth, metronidazole, and tetracycline individually have demonstrated *in vitro* activity against most susceptible strains of *H. pylori* isolated from patients with duodenal ulcers.

Pregnancy Considerations This combination is contraindicated in women who are pregnant. Metronidazole and tetracycline both cross the human placenta and may have adverse effects to the fetus. See individual agents.

Bismuth Subgallate (BIZ muth sub GAL ate)

Brand Names: US Devrom [OTC]

Pharmacologic Category Gastrointestinal Agent, Miscellaneous

Use Flatulence and feces deodorizer: Eliminating or reducing odor from flatulence and feces

Local Anesthetic/Vasoconstrictor Precautions No information available to require special precautions

Effects on Dental Treatment No significant effects or complications reported

Effects on Bleeding No information available to require special precautions

Adverse Reactions Frequency not defined.

Gastrointestinal: Darkening of stools, melanoglossia

General Dosage Range Oral: *Children ≥12 years, Adolescents, and Adults:* Oral: 1 to 2 capsules or chewable tablets up to 4 times daily (maximum: 8 capsules or chewable tablets per 24 hours).

Mechanism of Action Adsorbs extra water in large intestine, as well as toxins; forms a protective coat on the intestinal mucosa.

Bismuth Subsalicylate (BIZ muth sub sa LIS i late)

Related Information

Gastrointestinal Disorders *on page 1775*

Brand Names: US Bismatrol Maximum Strength [OTC]; Bismatrol [OTC]; Diotame [OTC]; Geri-Pectate [OTC]; Kao-Tin [OTC]; Peptic Relief [OTC]; Pepto-Bismol To-Go [OTC]; Pepto-Bismol [OTC]; Pink Bismuth [OTC]; Stomach Relief Max St [OTC]; Stomach Relief Plus [OTC]; Stomach Relief [OTC]

Pharmacologic Category Antidiarrheal

Use

Diarrhea: To control diarrhea, reduce number of bowel movements, and firm stool.

Dyspepsia: Relief of gas, upset stomach, indigestion, heartburn, and nausea.

Local Anesthetic/Vasoconstrictor Precautions No information available to require special precautions

Effects on Dental Treatment No significant effects or complications reported

Effects on Bleeding No information available to require special precautions

Adverse Reactions Frequency not defined; subsalicylate formulation:

Central nervous system: Anxiety, confusion, depression, headache, slurred speech

Gastrointestinal: Fecal discoloration (grayish black; impaction may occur in infants and debilitated patients), tongue discoloration (darkening)

Neuromuscular & skeletal: Muscle spasm, weakness

Otic: Hearing loss, tinnitus

General Dosage Range Oral: *Children ≥12 years, Adolescents, and Adults:* ~525 mg every 30 to 60 minutes or 1,050 mg every 60 minutes (maximum: ~4,200 mg [8 doses (regular strength); 4 doses (maximum strength)]/24 hours)

Mechanism of Action Bismuth subsalicylate exhibits both antisecretory and antimicrobial action. This agent may provide some anti-inflammatory action as well. The salicylate moiety provides antisecretory effect and the bismuth exhibits antimicrobial directly against bacterial and viral gastrointestinal pathogens.

Pharmacodynamics/Kinetics

Half-life Elimination Terminal: Bismuth: 21 to 72 days; Salicylate: 2 to 5 hours

Pregnancy Considerations Following oral administration, bismuth and salicylates cross the placenta. The use of salicylates in pregnancy may adversely affect the newborn (Lione, 1988). Use during pregnancy is not recommended (Mahadevan 2007).

Bisoprolol (bis OH proe lol)

Related Information

Cardiovascular Diseases *on page 1752*

Brand Names: US Zebeta

Brand Names: Canada Apo-Bisoprolol; Ava-Bisoprolol; Mylan-Bisoprolol; Novo-Bisoprolol; PHL-Bisoprolol; PMS-Bisoprolol; PRO-Bisoprolol; Sandoz-Bisoprolol; Teva-Bisoprolol

Pharmacologic Category Antihypertensive; Beta-Blocker, Beta-1 Selective

Use

Hypertension: Treatment of hypertension, alone or in combination with other agents

Guideline recommendations:

Hypertension: The 2014 guideline for the management of high blood pressure in adults (Eighth Joint National Committee [JNC 8]) recommends initiation of pharmacologic treatment to lower blood pressure for the following patients (JNC8 [James, 2013]):

- Patients ≥60 years of age, with systolic blood pressure (SBP) ≥150 mm Hg or diastolic blood pressure (DBP) ≥90 mm Hg. Goal of therapy is SBP <150 mm Hg and DBP <90 mm Hg.
- Patients <60 years of age, with SBP ≥140 mm Hg or DBP ≥90 mm Hg. Goal of therapy is SBP <140 mm Hg and DBP <90 mm Hg.
- Patients ≥18 years of age with diabetes, with SBP ≥140 mm Hg or DBP ≥90 mm Hg. Goal of therapy is SBP <140 mm Hg and DBP <90 mm Hg.
- Patients ≥18 years of age with chronic kidney disease (CKD), with SBP ≥140 mm Hg or DBP ≥90 mm Hg. Goal of therapy is SBP <140 mm Hg and DBP <90 mm Hg.

Chronic kidney disease (CKD) and hypertension: Regardless of race or diabetes status, the use of an ACE inhibitor (ACEI) or angiotensin receptor blocker (ARB) as initial therapy is recommended to improve kidney outcomes. In the general nonblack population (without CKD) including those with diabetes, initial antihypertensive treatment should consist of a thiazide-type diuretic, calcium channel blocker, ACEI, or ARB. In the general black population (without CKD) including those with diabetes, initial antihypertensive treatment should consist of a thiazide-type diuretic or a calcium channel blocker **instead of** an ACEI or ARB.

Coronary artery disease (CAD) and hypertension: The American Heart Association, American College of Cardiology and American Society of Hypertension (AHA/ACC/ASH) 2015 scientific statement for the treatment of hypertension in patients with coronary artery disease (CAD) recommends the use of a beta blocker as part of a regimen in patients with hypertension and chronic stable angina with a history of prior MI. A BP target of <140/90 mm Hg is reasonable for the secondary prevention of cardiovascular events. A lower target BP (<130/80 mm Hg) may be appropriate in some individuals with CAD, previous MI, stroke or transient ischemic attack, or CAD risk equivalents (AHA/ACC/ASH [Rosendorff 2015]).

Local Anesthetic/Vasoconstrictor Precautions No information available to require special precautions

Effects on Dental Treatment Bisoprolol is a cardioselective beta-blocker. Local anesthetic with vasoconstrictor can be safely used in patients medicated with bisoprolol. Nonselective beta-blockers (ie, propranolol, nadolol) enhance the pressor response to epinephrine, resulting in hypertension and bradycardia; this has not been reported for bisoprolol. Many nonsteroidal anti-inflammatory drugs, such as ibuprofen and indomethacin, can reduce the hypotensive effect of beta-blockers after 3 or more weeks of therapy with the NSAID. Short-term NSAID use (ie, 3 days) requires no special precautions in patients taking beta-blockers.

Effects on Bleeding No information available to require special precautions

Adverse Reactions

1% to 10%:

Cardiovascular: Chest pain (1% to 2%)

Central nervous system: Fatigue (dose related; 6% to 8%), insomnia (2% to 3%), hypoesthesia (1% to 2%)

Gastrointestinal: Diarrhea (dose related; 3% to 4%), nausea (2%), vomiting (1% to 2%)

Neuromuscular & skeletal: Arthralgia (2% to 3%), weakness (dose related; ≤2%)

Respiratory: Upper respiratory infection (5%), rhinitis (3% to 4%), sinusitis (2%), dyspnea (1% to 2%)

<1%, postmarketing, and/or case reports (limited to important or life-threatening): Abdominal pain, abnormal lacrimation, acne vulgaris, alopecia, amnesia, angioedema, anxiety, asthma, back pain, bradycardia (dose related), bronchitis, bronchospasm, cardiac arrhythmia, claudication, cold extremities, confusion (especially in the elderly), congestive heart failure, constipation, cough, cystitis, decreased libido, depression, dermatitis, dizziness, drowsiness, dysgeusia, dyspepsia, dyspnea on exertion, eczema, edema, exfoliative dermatitis, eye pain, flushing, gastritis, gout, hallucination, headache, hearing loss, hyperesthesia, hyperglycemia, hyperkalemia, hyperphosphatemia, hypersensitivity angiitis, hypertriglyceridemia, hypotension, impotence, increased blood urea nitrogen, increased serum creatinine, increased serum transaminases, increased uric acid, insomnia, leukopenia, malaise, muscle cramps, myalgia, neck pain, nervousness, orthostatic hypotension, palpitations, paresthesia, peptic ulcer, Peyronie's disease, pharyngitis, polyuria, positive ANA titer, pruritus, psoriasiform eruption, psoriasis, purpura, renal colic, restlessness, sensation of eye pressure, skin rash, syncope, thrombocytopenia, tinnitus, tremor, twitching, vasculitis, vertigo, visual disturbance, weight gain, xerostomia

General Dosage Range Dosage adjustment recommended in patients with renal impairment

Oral: *Adults and Elderly:* Initial: 2.5 to 5 mg once daily; Maintenance: 2.5 to 20 mg once daily

Mechanism of Action Selective inhibitor of $beta_1$-adrenergic receptors; competitively blocks $beta_1$-receptors, with little or no effect on $beta_2$-receptors at doses ≤20 mg

Pharmacodynamics/Kinetics

Onset of Action 1 to 2 hours

Half-life Elimination Normal renal function: 9 to 12 hours; CrCl <40 mL/minute: 27 to 36 hours; Hepatic cirrhosis: 8 to 22 hours

Time to Peak 2 to 4 hours

Pregnancy Risk Factor C

Pregnancy Considerations Adverse events were observed in animal reproduction studies. Adverse events, such as fetal/neonatal bradycardia, hypoglycemia, and reduced birth weight have been observed following in utero exposure to beta-blockers as a class. Adequate facilities for monitoring infants at birth are generally recommended.

Untreated chronic maternal hypertension and preeclampsia are also associated with adverse events in the fetus, infant, and mother (ACOG 2015; Magee 2014). Although beta-blockers may be used when treatment of hypertension or heart failure in pregnancy is indicated, agents other than bisoprolol are preferred (ACOG 2013; ESC [Regitz-Zagrosek 2011]; Magee 2014;).

Bivalirudin (bye VAL i roo din)

Related Information

Cardiovascular Diseases *on page 1752*

Brand Names: US Angiomax

Brand Names: Canada Angiomax

Pharmacologic Category Anticoagulant; Anticoagulant, Direct Thrombin Inhibitor

Use

Percutaneous coronary intervention: Anticoagulant used in conjunction with aspirin with provisional glycoprotein IIb/IIIa inhibitor as described in the REPLACE-2 trial in patients undergoing percutaneous coronary intervention (PCI) (see **Note**); used in conjunction with aspirin for patients undergoing PCI with (or at risk of) heparin-induced thrombocytopenia (HIT)/ thrombosis syndrome (HITTS). **Note:** Patients requiring immediate catheter-based reperfusion for STEMI were excluded from the REPLACE-2 trial (Lincoff 2004).

Percutaneous transluminal coronary angioplasty: Anticoagulant used in conjunction with aspirin for patients with unstable angina undergoing percutaneous transluminal coronary angioplasty (PTCA).

Limitations of use: Safety and effectiveness have not been established in patients with acute coronary syndromes who are not undergoing PTCA or PCI.

Local Anesthetic/Vasoconstrictor Precautions No information available to require special precautions

Effects on Dental Treatment Key adverse event(s) related to dental treatment: Bleeding is the major adverse effect of bivalirudin. Additional adverse effects are often related to idiosyncratic reactions, the frequency is difficult to estimate. Adverse reactions reported were generally less than those seen with heparin. See Effects on Bleeding.

Effects on Bleeding As with all anticoagulants, bleeding is a potential adverse effect of bivalirudin during dental surgery; risk is dependent on multiple variables, including the intensity of anticoagulation and patient susceptibility. Medical consult is suggested. It is unlikely that ambulatory patients presenting for dental treatment will be taking intravenous anticoagulant therapy such as bivalirudin.

Adverse Reactions As with all anticoagulants, bleeding is the major adverse effect of bivalirudin. Hemorrhage may occur at virtually any site. Risk is dependent on multiple variables, including the intensity of anticoagulation, concurrent use of a glycoprotein IIb/IIIa inhibitor, and patient susceptibility. Additional adverse effects are often related to idiosyncratic reactions, and the frequency is difficult to estimate. Adverse reactions reported were generally less than those seen with heparin.

>10%:

- Cardiovascular: Hypotension (≤12%)
- Central nervous system: Pain (≤15%), headache (≤12%)
- Gastrointestinal: Nausea (≤15%)
- Hematologic & oncologic: Minor hemorrhage (Protocol defined: 14%; heparin 26%; TIMI defined: 1%; heparin 3% [Lincoff, 2003])
- Neuromuscular & skeletal: Back pain (9% to 42%)

1% to 10%:

- Cardiovascular: Hypertension (6%), bradycardia (5%), angina pectoris (≤5%), thrombosis (1%; <4 hours, in patients with STEMI undergoing primary PCI)
- Central nervous system: Insomnia (7%), anxiety (6%), nervousness (5%)
- Gastrointestinal: Vomiting (≤6%), abdominal pain (5%), dyspepsia (5%)
- Genitourinary: Pelvic pain (6%), urinary retention (4%)
- Hematologic & oncologic: Major hemorrhage (Protocol defined: 2% to 4%; heparin 4% to 9%; TIMI defined: 0.6%; heparin 0.9%; transfusion required: 1% to 2%; heparin 2% to 6% [Lincoff, 2003])
- Local: Pain at injection site (≤8%)
- Miscellaneous: Fever (5%)

<1%, postmarketing, and/or case reports: Cardiac tamponade, cerebral ischemia, confusion, facial paralysis, hemorrhage (fatal), hypersensitivity reaction (including anaphylaxis), increased INR, increased susceptibility to infection, intracranial hemorrhage, oliguria, pulmonary edema, pulmonary hemorrhage, renal failure, retroperitoneal hemorrhage, sepsis, syncope, thrombocytopenia, vascular disease, venous thrombosis (during PCI, including intracoronary brachytherapy), ventricular fibrillation

General Dosage Range

Dosage adjustment recommended in patients with renal impairment.

IV: *Adults:* Bolus: 0.75 mg/kg; may repeat at 0.3 mg/kg if necessary; Infusion: 1.75 mg/kg/hour for duration of procedure and up to 4 hours postprocedure if needed; after 4 hours may continue 0.2 mg/kg/hour for up to 20 hours if needed

Mechanism of Action Bivalirudin acts as a specific and reversible direct thrombin inhibitor; it binds to the catalytic and anionic exosite of both circulating and clot-bound thrombin. Catalytic binding site occupation functionally inhibits coagulant effects by preventing thrombin-mediated cleavage of fibrinogen to fibrin monomers, and activation of factors V, VIII, and XIII. Shows linear dose- and concentration-dependent prolongation of ACT, aPTT, PT, and TT.

Pharmacodynamics/Kinetics

Onset of Action Immediate

Duration of Action Coagulation times return to baseline ~1 hour following discontinuation of infusion

Half-life Elimination

Normal renal function (CrCl ≥90 mL/minute): 25 minutes

Severe renal impairment (CrCl 10 to 29 mL/minute): 57 minutes

Dialysis-dependent patients (off dialysis): 3.5 hours

Pregnancy Risk Factor B

Pregnancy Considerations Adverse events have not been observed in animal reproduction studies. Bivalirudin is used in conjunction with aspirin, which may lead to maternal or fetal adverse effects, especially during the third trimester. Use of parenteral direct thrombin inhibitors in pregnancy should be limited to those women who have severe allergic reactions to heparin, including heparin-induced thrombocytopenia, and who cannot receive danaparoid (Guyatt, 2012).

Bleomycin (blee oh MYE sin)

Brand Names: Canada Blenoxane; Bleomycin Injection, USP

Pharmacologic Category Antineoplastic Agent, Antibiotic

Use

Head and neck cancers: Treatment of squamous cell carcinomas of the head and neck

Hodgkin lymphoma: Treatment of Hodgkin lymphoma

Malignant pleural effusion: Sclerosing agent for malignant pleural effusion

Testicular cancer: Treatment of testicular cancer

Local Anesthetic/Vasoconstrictor Precautions No information available to require special precautions

Effects on Dental Treatment Key adverse event(s) related to dental treatment: Stomatitis and mucositis.

Effects on Bleeding No information available to require special precautions

Adverse Reactions

Frequency not always defined. The pathogenesis of respiratory adverse effects is not certain, but may be due to damage of pulmonary, vascular, or connective tissue. Response to steroid therapy is variable and somewhat controversial.

>10%:

Cardiovascular: Phlebitis

Central nervous system: Tumor pain

Dermatologic: Hyperpigmentation (50%), atrophic striae (≤50%), erythema (≤50%), exfoliation of the skin (≤50%; particularly on the palmar and plantar surfaces of the hands and feet), hyperkeratosis (≤50%), localized vesiculation (≤50%), skin rash (≤50%), skin sclerosis (≤50%), alopecia (may be dose-related and reversible with discontinuation), nailbed changes (may be dose-related and reversible with discontinuation)

Endocrine & metabolic: Weight loss

Gastrointestinal: Stomatitis (≤30%), mucositis (≤30%), anorexia

Miscellaneous: Febrile reaction (25% to 50%; acute)

1% to 10%:

Dermatologic: Onycholysis, pruritus, thickening of skin

Hypersensitivity: Anaphylactoid reaction (including chills, confusion, fever, hypotension, wheezing; onset may be immediate or delayed for several hours)

Neuromuscular & skeletal: Scleroderma (diffuse)

Respiratory: Tachypnea (≤5% to 10%), rales (≤5% to 10%), interstitial pneumonitis (acute or chronic: ≤5% to 10%), pulmonary fibrosis (≤5% to 10%), hypoxia (1%)

Miscellaneous: Adverse drug effect (idiosyncratic reaction: 1% in lymphoma patients)

<1%, postmarketing, and/or case reports: Angioedema, bone marrow depression (rare), cerebrovascular accident, cerebral arteritis, chest pain, coronary artery disease, hepatotoxicity, hyperpigmentation (flagellate), ischemic heart disease, malaise, myocardial infarction, nausea, nephrotoxicity, pericarditis, Raynaud's phenomenon, scleroderma-like skin changes, Stevens-Johnson syndrome, thrombotic thrombocytopenic purpura, toxic epidermal necrolysis, vomiting

General Dosage Range Dosage adjustment recommended in patients with renal impairment or who develop toxicities.

IV: *Adults:* Dosage varies greatly depending on indication

Intrapleural: *Adults:* 60 units as a single instillation

Mechanism of Action Inhibits synthesis of DNA; binds to DNA leading to single- and double-strand breaks; also inhibits (to a lesser degree) RNA and protein synthesis

Pharmacodynamics/Kinetics

Half-life Elimination Terminal: IV: 2 hours

Time to Peak Serum: IM, SubQ, Intrapleural: 30 to 60 minutes

Pregnancy Risk Factor D

Pregnancy Considerations Adverse effects were observed in animal reproduction studies. According to the manufacturer, women of childbearing potential should avoid becoming pregnant during bleomycin treatment. The European Society for Medical Oncology has published guidelines for diagnosis, treatment, and follow-up of cancer during pregnancy; the guidelines recommend referral to a facility with expertise in cancer during pregnancy and encourage a multidisciplinary team (obstetrician, neonatologist, oncology team). In general, if chemotherapy is indicated, it should be avoided in the first trimester and there should be a 3-week time period between the last chemotherapy dose and anticipated delivery, and chemotherapy should not be administered beyond week 33 of gestation (Peccatori 2013). When multiagent therapy is needed to treat Hodgkin lymphoma during pregnancy, bleomycin (as a component of the ABVD [doxorubicin, bleomycin, vinblastine, and dacarbazine] regimen) may be used, starting with the second trimester (Follows 2014; Peccatori 2013).

Blinatumomab (blin a TOOM oh mab)

Brand Names: US Blincyto

Brand Names: Canada Blincyto

Pharmacologic Category Antineoplastic Agent, Anti-CD19/CD3; Antineoplastic Agent, Monoclonal Antibody

Use Acute lymphoblastic leukemia: Treatment of Philadelphia chromosome-negative (Ph-) relapsed or refractory B-cell precursor acute lymphoblastic leukemia (ALL)

Local Anesthetic/Vasoconstrictor Precautions No information available to require special precautions

Effects on Dental Treatment No significant effects or complications reported

Effects on Bleeding Neutropenia and neutropenic fever, including life-threatening episodes, have been reported. Anemia and thrombocytopenia may also occur. In patients under active treatment with this agent, medical consult is suggested.

Adverse Reactions

>10%:

Cardiovascular: Peripheral edema (25%; ≥ grade 3: <1%), chest pain (11%; ≥ grade 3: 1%), hypotension (11%; ≥ grade 3: 2%)

Central nervous system: Neurotoxicity (50%; ≥ grade 3: 15%; incidence increased in older adults), headache (36%; ≥ grade 3: 3%), fatigue (17%; ≥ grade 3: 1%), chills (15%), insomnia (15%), dizziness (14%; ≥ grade 3: <1%)

Dermatologic: Skin rash (21%; ≥ grade 3: 2%)

Endocrine & metabolic: Hypokalemia (23%; ≥ grade 3: 6%), hypomagnesemia (12%), hyperglycemia (11%; ≥ grade 3: 7%), weight gain (11%)

Gastrointestinal: Nausea (25%), constipation (20%; ≥ grade 3: <1%), diarrhea (20%; ≥ grade 3: 1%), abdominal pain (15%; ≥ grade 3: 2%), vomiting (13%)

Hematologic & oncologic: Febrile neutropenia (25%; ≥ grade 3: 23%), anemia (18%; ≥ grade 3: 13%), neutropenia (16%; ≥ grade 3: 15%), thrombocytopenia (11%; ≥ grade 3: 8%)

Hepatic: Increased serum ALT (12%; ≥ grade 3: 6%), increased serum AST (11%; ≥ grade 3: 4%)

Hypersensitivity: Cytokine release syndrome (including cytokine storms) (11%; ≥ grade 3: 1%)
Infection: Infection (44%; ≥ grade 3: 25%), bacterial infection (19%; ≥ grade 3: 12%), fungal infection (15%; ≥ grade 3: 7%), viral infection (13%; ≥ grade 3: 4%)
Neuromuscular & skeletal: Tremor (20%; ≥ grade 3: 1%), back pain (14%; ≥ grade 3: 2%), limb pain (12%; ≥ grade 3: 1%), ostealgia (11%; ≥ grade 3: 3%)
Respiratory: Cough (19%), dyspnea (15%; ≥ grade 3: 5%)
Miscellaneous: Fever (62%; ≥ grade 3: 7%)

1% to 10%:
Cardiovascular: Hypertension (8%; ≥ grade 3: 5%), tachycardia (8%), edema (5%)
Central nervous system: Confusion (7%), brain disease (5%), paresthesia (5%), aphasia (4%), disorientation (3%), convulsions (2%), memory impairment (2%), cognitive dysfunction (1%), loss of consciousness
Endocrine & metabolic: Hypophosphatemia (6%; ≥ grade 3: 5%), increased gamma-glutamyl transferase (6%), hypoalbuminemia (4%)
Gastrointestinal: Decreased appetite (10%; ≥ grade 3: 3%)
Hematologic & oncologic: Decreased serum immunoglobulins (9%), leukopenia (9%; ≥ grade 3: 8%), tumor lysis syndrome (4%), leukocytosis (2%), lymphocytopenia (1%)
Hepatic: Increased serum bilirubin (8%), increased liver enzymes (1%)
Hypersensitivity: Cytokine storm (1%), hypersensitivity (1%)
Infection: Sepsis (7%; ≥ grade 3: 6%)
Neuromuscular & skeletal: Arthralgia (10%; ≥ grade 3: 2%)
Respiratory: Pneumonia (9%; ≥ grade 3: 8%)

<1%, postmarketing, and/or case reports: Bronchospasm, capillary leak syndrome, leukoencephalopathy, pancreatitis, speech disturbance

General Dosage Range Dosage adjustment recommended in patients who develop toxicities.

IV: *Pediatrics and Adults:* Cycle 1: 9 **mcg** daily (or 5 **mcg**/m^2/day if <45 kg) on days 1 to 7, followed by 28 **mcg** daily (or 15 **mcg**/m^2/day if <45 kg) on days 8 to 28 of a 6-week treatment cycle; Cycles 2 through 5: 28 **mcg** daily (or 15 **mcg**/m^2/day if <45 kg) on days 1 to 28 of a 6-week treatment cycle

Mechanism of Action Blinatumomab is a bispecific T-cell engager (BiTE) which binds to CD19 expressed on B-cells and CD3 expressed on T-cells. It activates endogenous T cells by connecting CD3 in the T-cell receptor complex with CD19 on B-cells (malignant and benign), thus forming a cytolytic synapse between a cytotoxic T-cell and the cancer target B-cell (Topp 2014). Blinatumomab mediates the production of cytolytic proteins, release of inflammatory cytokines, and proliferation of T cells, which result in lysis of CD19-positive cells.

Pharmacodynamics/Kinetics

Half-life Elimination Pediatrics: 2.19 hours; Adults: 2.11 hours

Pregnancy Considerations Animal reproductions studies have not been conducted. Based on the mechanism of action, blinatumomab may cause fetal harm when administered to a pregnant woman. Newborns exposed in utero may develop B-cell lymphocytopenia; monitor B-lymphocytes prior to administering live virus vaccines. Verify pregnancy status of women of reproductive potential prior to initiating treatment; effective contraception should be used during treatment and for at least 48 hours after the last dose.

Boceprevir (boe SE pre vir)

Related Information

Dentin Hypersensitivity, Acid Erosion, High Caries Index, Management of Alveolar Osteitis, and Xerostomia *on page 1857*
Systemic Viral Diseases *on page 1806*

Brand Names: US Victrelis [DSC]

Brand Names: Canada Victrelis [DSC]

Pharmacologic Category Antihepaciviral, Protease Inhibitor (Anti-HCV); NS3/4A Inhibitor

Use

Chronic hepatitis C: Treatment of chronic hepatitis C (CHC) genotype 1 (in combination with peginterferon alfa and ribavirin) in adult patients with compensated liver disease (including cirrhosis) who were previously untreated or have failed prior therapy with peginterferon alfa and ribavirin therapy including prior null responders, partial responders, and relapsers

Guideline recommendations: Boceprevir-containing regimens are **not** recommended in HCV treatment guidelines for treatment naïve or treatment-experienced patients with hepatitis C virus (HCV), regardless of genotype (AASLD/IDSA 2015). Hepatitis C treatment guidelines are constantly changing with the advent of new treatment therapies and information; consult current clinical practice guidelines for the most recent treatment recommendations.

Local Anesthetic/Vasoconstrictor Precautions No information available to require special precautions

Effects on Dental Treatment Key adverse event(s) related to dental treatment: Xerostomia (normal salivary flow resumes upon discontinuation) and abnormal taste.

Effects on Bleeding No information available to require special precautions

Adverse Reactions

Frequency not always defined.

>10%:
Central nervous system: Fatigue (55% to 58%), chills (33% to 34%), insomnia (30% to 34%), irritability (21% to 22%), dizziness (16% to 19%), headache
Dermatologic: Alopecia (22% to 27%), xeroderma (18% to 22%), skin rash (16% to 17%)
Gastrointestinal: Nausea (43% to 46%), dysgeusia (35% to 44%), decreased appetite (25% to 26%), diarrhea (24% to 25%), vomiting (15% to 20%), xerostomia (11% to 15%)
Hematologic & oncologic: Anemia (45% to 50%), neutropenia (14% to 31%)
Neuromuscular & skeletal: Arthralgia (19% to 23%), weakness (15% to 21%)
Respiratory: Dyspnea (8% to 11%)

1% to 10%: Hematologic & oncologic: Thrombocytopenia

<1%, postmarketing, and/or case reports: Agranulocytosis, angioedema, DRESS syndrome, exfoliative dermatitis, oral mucosa ulcer, pancytopenia, pneumonia, sepsis, skin toxicity, Stevens-Johnson syndrome, stomatitis, thromboembolism, toxoderma, urticaria

General Dosage Range Oral: *Adults:* 800 mg 3 times daily

Mechanism of Action Binds reversibly to nonstructural protein 3 (NS 3) serine protease and inhibits replication of the hepatitis C virus. Considered a direct-acting antiviral treatment for HCV, also called a specifically targeted antiviral therapy for HCV (STAT-C).

Pharmacodynamics/Kinetics

Half-life Elimination Plasma: Adults: ~3.4 hours

Time to Peak Serum: 2 hours

Pregnancy Risk Factor B / X (in combination with ribavirin and peginterferon alfa)

Pregnancy Considerations

Use is contraindicated in pregnant women and males whose female partners are pregnant.

Adverse events were not observed with boceprevir in animal reproduction studies; however, boceprevir must not be used as monotherapy (must be used in combination with peginterferon alfa and ribavirin according to the manufacturer's labeling). Adverse events have been observed with ribavirin and interferons (specific studies with peginterferon alfa-2a have not been conducted) in animal reproduction studies. Use of ribavirin in combination with peginterferon alfa-2a is contraindicated in pregnant women and males whose female partners are pregnant. A negative pregnancy test is required before initiation of therapy and pregnancy testing should be conducted monthly during treatment and for 6 months after therapy has ended. Women of childbearing potential and males must use at least 2 effective forms of contraception during treatment and continue contraceptive measures for at least 6 months after completion of therapy. One of the two forms of effective contraception may be a combined oral contraceptive product with at least 1 mg of norethindrone; oral contraceptives with <1 mg of norethindrone and other forms of hormonal contraception are contraindicated because they have not been studied. If patient or female partner becomes pregnant during treatment, she should be counseled about potential risks of exposure. Mother-to-child transmission of HCV does not occur if the woman is not viremic, therefore, HCV-infected women of childbearing potential should postpone pregnancy until therapy is complete. Treatment of HCV is not recommended for women who are already pregnant (AASLD/IDSA 2015).

Product Availability Note: Victrelis is no longer available in the US.

Bortezomib (bore TEZ oh mib)

Brand Names: US Velcade

Brand Names: Canada Bortezomib For Injection; Velcade

Pharmacologic Category Antineoplastic Agent, Proteasome Inhibitor

Use

Mantle cell lymphoma: Treatment of mantle cell lymphoma

Multiple myeloma: Treatment of multiple myeloma

Local Anesthetic/Vasoconstrictor Precautions No information available to require special precautions

Effects on Dental Treatment Key adverse event(s) related to dental treatment: Abnormal taste and stomatitis.

Effects on Bleeding Dose-related thrombocytopenia (~35%; nadir: day 11; recovery: by day 21) is most common hematological event with platelet counts usually returning to baseline following active therapy each cycle. A medical consult is suggested.

Adverse Reactions Incidences reported are associated with monotherapy. Additional adverse reactions reported with mono- or combination therapy; frequency not defined.

Cardiovascular: Hypotension (8% to 9%; grades 3/4: ≤2%), cardiac disease (treatment emergent; 8%), acute pulmonary edema (≤1%), cardiac failure (≤1%), cardiogenic shock (≤1%), pulmonary edema (≤1%), aggravated atrial fibrillation, angina pectoris, atrial flutter, atrioventricular block, bradycardia, cerebrovascular accident, deep vein thrombosis, edema, embolism (peripheral), facial edema, hemorrhagic stroke, hypertension, ischemic heart disease, myocardial infarction, pericardial effusion, pericarditis, peripheral edema, phlebitis, portal vein thrombosis, pulmonary embolism, septic shock, sinoatrial arrest, subdural hematoma, torsades de pointes, transient ischemic attacks, ventricular tachycardia

Central nervous system: Peripheral neuropathy (IV: 35% to 54%; SubQ: 37%; grade ≥2: 24% to 39%; grade ≥3: SubQ: 5% to 6%; IV: 7% to 15%; grade 4: <1%), fatigue (7% to 52%), neuralgia (23%), headache (10% to 19%), paresthesia (7% to 19%), dizziness (10% to 18%; excludes vertigo), agitation, anxiety, ataxia, brain disease, cerebral hemorrhage, chills, coma, confusion, cranial nerve palsy, dysarthria, dysautonomia, dysesthesia, insomnia, malaise, mental status changes, motor dysfunction, paralysis, psychosis, seizure, spinal cord compression, suicidal ideation, vertigo

Dermatologic: Skin rash (12% to 23%), pruritus, urticaria

Endocrine & metabolic: Dehydration (2%), amyloid heart disease, hyperglycemia (diabetic patients), hyperkalemia, hypernatremia, hyperuricemia, hypocalcemia, hypoglycemia (diabetic patients), hypokalemia, hyponatremia, weight loss

Gastrointestinal: Diarrhea (19% to 52%), nausea (14% to 52%), constipation (24% to 34%), vomiting (9% to 29%), anorexia (14% to 21%), abdominal pain (11%), decreased appetite (11%), cholestasis, duodenitis (hemorrhagic), dysphagia, fecal impaction, gastritis (hemorrhagic), gastroenteritis, gastroesophageal reflux disease, hematemesis, intestinal obstruction, intestinal perforation, melena, oral candidiasis, pancreatitis, paralytic ileus, peritonitis, stomatitis

Genitourinary: Bladder spasm, hematuria, hemorrhagic cystitis, urinary incontinence, urinary retention, urinary tract infection

Hematologic & oncologic: Thrombocytopenia (16% to 52%; grade 3: 5% to 24%; grade 4: 3% to 7%; nadir: Day 11; recovery: By day 21), neutropenia (5% to 27%; grade 3: 8% to 18%; grade 4: 2% to 4%; nadir: Day 11; recovery: By day 21), anemia (12% to 23%; grade 3: 4% to 6%; grade 4: <1%). leukopenia (18% to 20%; grade 3: 5%; grade 4: ≤1%), hemorrhage (≥grade 3: 2%), disseminated intravascular coagulation, febrile neutropenia, lymphocytopenia, oral mucosal petechiae

Hepatic: Ascites, hepatic failure, hepatic hemorrhage, hepatitis, hyperbilirubinemia

Hypersensitivity: Anaphylaxis, angioedema, hypersensitivity, hypersensitivity angiitis

Infection: Herpes zoster (reactivation; 6% to 11%), herpes simplex infection (1% to 3%), herpes zoster (1% to 2%), aspergillosis, bacteremia, listeriosis, toxoplasmosis

Local: Injection site reaction (mostly redness; SubQ: 6%), irritation at injection site (IV 5%), catheter infection

Neuromuscular & skeletal: Weakness (7% to 16%), arthralgia, back pain, bone fracture, limb pain, myalgia, ostealgia

Ophthalmic: Blurred vision, conjunctival infection, conjunctival irritation, diplopia

Otic: Auditory impairment

Renal: Bilateral hydronephrosis, nephrolithiasis, proliferative glomerulonephritis, renal failure

Respiratory: Dyspnea (11%), pneumonia (1% to 3%), adult respiratory distress syndrome, aspiration pneumonia, atelectasis, bronchitis, chronic obstructive pulmonary disease (exacerbation), cough, epistaxis, hemoptysis, hypoxia, laryngeal edema, nasopharyngitis, pleural effusion, pneumonitis, pulmonary hypertension, pulmonary infiltrates (including diffuse), respiratory tract infection, sinusitis

Miscellaneous: Fever (8% to 23%)

<1%, postmarketing, and/or case reports: Acute ischemic stroke, amyloidosis, autonomic neuropathy, blindness, cardiac tamponade, chalazion (Fraunfelder 2016), deafness (bilateral), decreased left ventricular ejection fraction, dysgeusia, dyspepsia, hemolytic-uremic syndrome, herpes meningoencephalitis, increased gamma-glutamyl transferase, increased serum alkaline phosphatase, increased serum transaminases, interstitial pneumonitis, intestinal obstruction, ischemic colitis, ocular herpes simplex, optic neuritis, optic neuropathy, progressive multifocal leukoencephalopathy, prolonged Q-T interval on ECG, pulmonary disease, respiratory insufficiency, reversible posterior leukoencephalopathy syndrome, sepsis, SIADH, Stevens-Johnson syndrome, subarachnoid hemorrhage, Sweet syndrome, syncope, tachycardia, toxic epidermal necrolysis, tumor lysis syndrome

General Dosage Range Dosage adjustment recommended in patients with hepatic impairment or who develop toxicities.

IV, SubQ: *Adults:* 1.3 mg/m^2; frequency and duration vary depending on indication

Mechanism of Action Bortezomib inhibits proteasomes, enzyme complexes which regulate protein homeostasis within the cell. Specifically, it reversibly inhibits chymotrypsin-like activity at the 26S proteasome, leading to activation of signaling cascades, cell-cycle arrest, and apoptosis.

Pharmacodynamics/Kinetics

Half-life Elimination Single dose: IV: 9 to 15 hours; Multiple dosing: 1 mg/m^2: 40 to 193 hours; 1.3 mg/m^2: 76 to 108 hour

Pregnancy Risk Factor D

Pregnancy Considerations Adverse effects (fetal loss and decreased fetal weight) were observed in animal reproduction studies at doses less than the equivalent human dose (based on BSA). Women of reproductive potential should avoid becoming pregnant and should use effective contraception during treatment.

Bosentan (boe SEN tan)

Brand Names: US Tracleer

Brand Names: Canada ACT Bosentan; Mylan-Bosentan; PMS-Bosentan; Sandoz-Bosentan; Teva-Bosentan; Tracleer

Pharmacologic Category Endothelin Receptor Antagonist; Vasodilator

Use Pulmonary arterial hypertension: Treatment of pulmonary artery hypertension (PAH) (WHO Group I) in patients with WHO/NYHA Class II, III, or IV symptoms to improve exercise capacity and decrease the rate of clinical deterioration. **Note:** According to treatment guidelines from the Fifth World Symposium on Pulmonary Hypertension (WSPH), only a small number of PAH patients with WHO-FC IV symptoms (ie, severely ill patients) were included in clinical trials, therefore, most experts consider bosentan second-line therapy in these patients (WSPH [Gailè 2013]).

Local Anesthetic/Vasoconstrictor Precautions No information available to require special precautions

Effects on Dental Treatment Key adverse event(s) related to dental treatment: Endothelin antagonists have caused bleeding gums; there have been no specific reports for bosentan

Effects on Bleeding No information available to require special precautions

Adverse Reactions

>10%:

Cardiovascular: Edema (≤11%)

Central nervous system: Headache (15%)

Hematologic & oncologic: Decreased hemoglobin (typically in first 6 weeks of therapy; ≥1 g/dL: ≤57%; <11 g/dL: 3% to 6%)

Hepatic: Increased serum ALT (≥3 times ULN: ≤12%; 8 times ULN: ≤2%; dose-related), increased serum AST (≥3 times ULN: ≤12%; 8 times ULN: ≤2%; dose-related)

Respiratory: Respiratory tract infection (22%)

1% to 10%:

Cardiovascular: Chest pain (5%), syncope (5%), flushing (4%), hypotension (4%), palpitations (4%)

Endocrine & metabolic: Fluid retention (≤2%)

Hematologic & oncologic: Anemia (3%)

Neuromuscular & skeletal: Arthralgia (4%)

Respiratory: Sinusitis (4%)

<1%, postmarketing, and/or case reports: Anaphylaxis, angioedema, DRESS syndrome, hepatic cirrhosis (prolonged therapy), hepatic failure (rare), hypersensitivity reaction, jaundice, leukopenia, nasal congestion, neutropenia, peripheral edema, severe anemia, skin rash, thrombocytopenia

General Dosage Range Dosage adjustment recommended in patients with hepatic impairment or on concomitant therapy

Oral:

Children >12 years, Adolescents, and Adults <40 kg: Initial: 62.5 mg twice daily; Maintenance: 62.5 mg twice daily

Children >12 years, Adolescents, and Adults ≥40 kg: Initial: 62.5 mg twice daily for 4 weeks; Maintenance: 125 mg twice daily

Mechanism of Action Endothelian receptor antagonist that blocks endothelin receptors on endothelium and vascular smooth muscle (stimulation of these receptors is associated with vasoconstriction). Bosentan blocks both ET_A and ET_B receptors, with a slightly higher affinity for the A subtype.

Pharmacodynamics/Kinetics

Half-life Elimination ~5 hours; prolonged with heart failure, possibly with PAH

Time to Peak Plasma: 3 to 5 hours

Pregnancy Risk Factor X

Pregnancy Considerations **[US Boxed Warning]: May cause birth defects (based on animal data); use in pregnancy is contraindicated. Exclude pregnancy prior to initiation of therapy and obtain pregnancy tests monthly during treatment. Reliable contraception must be used during therapy and for 1 month after stopping treatment. Hormonal contraceptives (oral, injectable, transdermal, or implantable) should not be used as the sole means of contraception because they may not be effective in patients receiving bosentan. Patients with an intrauterine device (IUD) or tubal ligation do not**

need additional contraceptive measures. When a hormonal or barrier contraceptive is used, one additional method of contraception is still needed if a male partner has had a vasectomy. When initiating treatment for women of reproductive potential, a negative pregnancy test should be documented within the first 5 days of a normal menstrual period and ≥11 days after the last unprotected intercourse. A missed menses or suspected pregnancy should be reported to a healthcare provider and prompt immediate pregnancy testing. Sperm counts may be reduced in men during treatment. Women with pulmonary arterial hypertension (PAH) are encouraged to avoid pregnancy (McLaughlin 2009; Taichman 2014).

Prescribing and Access Restrictions As a requirement of the REMS program, access to this medication is restricted. Bosentan (Tracleer) is only available through Tracleer REMS Program. Only prescribers and pharmacies registered with Tracleer REMS Program may prescribe and dispense bosentan. Further information may be obtained from the manufacturer, Actelion Pharmaceuticals (1-866-228-3546 or http://www.tracleer.com/hcp/prescribing-tracleer.asp).

Brentuximab Vedotin (bren TUX i mab ve DOE tin)

Brand Names: US Adcetris

Brand Names: Canada Adcetris

Pharmacologic Category Antineoplastic Agent, Anti-CD30; Antineoplastic Agent, Antibody Drug Conjugate; Antineoplastic Agent, Monoclonal Antibody

Use

Anaplastic large cell lymphoma (systemic): Treatment of systemic anaplastic large cell lymphoma after failure of at least 1 prior multiagent chemotherapy regimen

Hodgkin lymphoma, relapsed or refractory: Treatment of classical Hodgkin lymphoma after failure of at least 2 prior multiagent chemotherapy regimens (in patients who are not autologous hematopoietic stem cell transplant [HSCT] candidates) or after failure of autologous HSCT

Hodgkin lymphoma (post-autologous hematopoietic stem cell transplantation): Treatment of classical Hodgkin lymphoma in patients at high risk of relapse or progression as post–autologous HSCT consolidation

Local Anesthetic/Vasoconstrictor Precautions No information available to require special precautions

Effects on Dental Treatment No significant effects or complications reported

Effects on Bleeding Thrombocytopenia occurred in 16% to 28% of patients. A medical consult is suggested.

Adverse Reactions

>10%:

Cardiovascular: Peripheral edema (4% to 16%)

Central nervous system: Peripheral neuropathy (54% to 67%), peripheral sensory neuropathy (2% to 56%; grade 3: 8% to 10%), fatigue (24% to 49%), pain (7% to 28%), peripheral motor neuropathy (4% to 23%; grade 3: 3% to 6%), headache (11% to 19%), insomnia (14% to 16%), dizziness (11% to 16%), chills (10% to 13%), anxiety (7% to 11%)

Dermatologic: Skin rash (27% to 31%), pruritus (12% to 19%), alopecia (13% to 14%), night sweats (9% to 12%)

Endocrine & metabolic: Weight loss (6% to 19%)

Gastrointestinal: Nausea (2% to 42%), diarrhea (20% to 36%), abdominal pain (3% to 25%), vomiting (3% to 22%), constipation (13% to 19%), decreased appetite (11% to 16%)

Hematologic & oncologic: Neutropenia (54% to 78%; grade 3: 12% to 30%; grade 4: 6% to 9%), anemia (27% to 52%; grade 3: 2% to 8%; grade 4: 4%), thrombocytopenia (16% to 41%; grade 3: 5% to 7%; grade 4: 2% to 5%), lymphadenopathy (10% to 11%)

Immunologic: Antibody development (antibrentuximab; transient: 30%; persistent: 7%)

Neuromuscular & skeletal: Arthralgia (9% to 19%), myalgia (11% to 17%), back pain (10% to 14%), muscle spasm (9% to 11%)

Respiratory: Upper respiratory tract infection (12% to 47%), cough (17% to 25%), dyspnea (13% to 19%), oropharyngeal pain (9% to 11%)

Miscellaneous: Fever (2% to 38%), infusion related reaction (12% to 15%)

1% to 10%:

Cardiovascular: Septic shock (3%), supraventricular cardiac arrhythmia (3%), pulmonary embolism (2%)

Dermatologic: Xeroderma (4% to 10%)

Genitourinary: Urinary tract infection (3%)

Hepatic: Hepatotoxicity (2%)

Neuromuscular & skeletal: Limb pain (3% to 10%)

Renal: Pyelonephritis (2%)

Respiratory: Pulmonary toxicity (5%, noninfectious; including interstitial pulmonary disease, adult respiratory distress syndrome), pneumonia (4%), pneumonitis (2%), pneumothorax (2%)

Frequency not defined: Progressive multifocal leukoencephalopathy, Stevens-Johnson syndrome, tumor lysis syndrome

<1%, postmarketing, and/or case reports: Anaphylaxis, enterocolitis, febrile neutropenia, gastrointestinal erosion, gastrointestinal perforation, gastrointestinal ulcer, hyperglycemia, intestinal obstruction, JC virus infection, neutropenic colitis, opportunistic infection, pancreatitis, serious infection, toxic epidermal necrolysis

General Dosage Range Dosage adjustment recommended in patients who develop toxicities or with hepatic impairment.

IV: *Adults:* 1.8 mg/kg every 3 weeks (maximum dose: 180 mg)

Mechanism of Action Brentuximab vedotin is an antibody drug conjugate (ADC) directed at CD30 consisting of 3 components: 1) a CD30-specific chimeric IgG1 antibody cAC10; 2) a microtubule-disrupting agent, monomethylauristatin E (MMAE); and 3) a protease cleavable dipeptide linker (which covalently conjugates MMAE to cAC10). The conjugate binds to cells which express CD30, and forms a complex which is internalized within the cell and releases MMAE. MMAE binds to the tubules and disrupts the cellular microtubule network, inducing cell cycle arrest (G2/M phase) and apoptosis.

Pharmacodynamics/Kinetics

Half-life Elimination Terminal: ADC: ~4 to 6 days

Time to Peak ADC: At end of infusion; MMAE: ~1 to 3 days

Pregnancy Considerations Adverse events were observed in animal reproduction studies. Based on the mechanism of action and on animal data, brentuximab vedotin may cause fetal harm if administered to a pregnant woman. In women of reproductive potential, verify pregnancy prior to treatment initiation. Women of reproductive potential and men with female partners of reproductive potential should avoid pregnancy during treatment and for at least 6 months after the final dose.

Brentuximab vedotin treatment may compromise fertility in males.

Brexpiprazole (breks PIP ray zole)

Brand Names: US Rexulti

Pharmacologic Category Second Generation (Atypical) Antipsychotic

Use

Major depressive disorder: Adjunctive treatment of major depressive disorder (MDD)

Schizophrenia: Treatment of schizophrenia

Local Anesthetic/Vasoconstrictor Precautions No information available to require special precautions

Effects on Dental Treatment Key adverse event(s) related to dental treatment: Drug-induced extrapyramidal reaction has been reported

Effects on Bleeding No information available to require special precautions

Adverse Reactions

>10%:

Central nervous system: Akathisia (4% to 14%; dose-related)

Endocrine & metabolic: Increased serum triglycerides (<500 mg/dL: 8% to 13%; ≥500 mg/dL: <1%), weight gain (3% to 11%)

1% to 10%:

Central nervous system: Headache (major depressive disorder: 9%), drug-induced extrapyramidal reaction (5% to 6%), drowsiness (4% to 6%), fatigue (major depressive disorder: 3% to 5%), dizziness (major depressive disorder: 2% to 5%), anxiety (major depressive disorder: 2% to 4%), restlessness (major depressive disorder: 2% to 4%; dose-related), sedation (2% to 3%), abnormal dreams (≥1%), insomnia (≥1%)

Dermatologic: Hyperhidrosis (≥1%)

Endocrine & metabolic: Decreased cortisol (major depressive disorder: 3% to 4%), increased serum prolactin (≥1%)

Gastrointestinal: Dyspepsia (schizophrenia: 3% to 6%), increased appetite (major depressive disorder: 3%), constipation (major depressive disorder: 2% to 3%), diarrhea (schizophrenia: 2%), abdominal pain (≥1%), flatulence (≥1%), nausea (≥1%), sialorrhea (≥1%), xerostomia (≥1%)

Genitourinary: Urinary tract infection (≥1%)

Neuromuscular & skeletal: Tremor (2% to 5%), increased creatine phosphokinase (schizophrenia: 2% to 4%), myalgia (≥1%)

Ophthalmic: Blurred vision (≥1%)

Respiratory: Nasopharyngitis (major depressive disorder: 3% to 7%)

<1%, postmarketing, and/or case reports: Dystonia (excluding akathisia), orthostatic hypotension, syncope

General Dosage Range

Dosage adjustment recommended in patients with renal or hepatic impairment, on concomitant therapy with CYP3A4 or CYP2D6 inhibitors or with CYP2D6 poor metabolizer status

Oral: *Adults:* 0.5 to 1 mg once daily; maximum daily dose: 3 to 4 mg

Mechanism of Action Brexpiprazole exhibits partial agonist activity for 5-HT_{1A} and D_2 receptors and antagonist activity for 5-HT_{2A} receptors.

Pharmacodynamics/Kinetics

Half-life Elimination Terminal: Brexpiprazole: 91 hours; DM-3411: 86 hours

Time to Peak Plasma: Within 4 hours

Pregnancy Considerations Adverse events were observed in some animal reproduction studies. Antipsychotic use during the third trimester of pregnancy has a risk for abnormal muscle movements (extrapyramidal symptoms [EPS]) and/or withdrawal symptoms in newborns following delivery. Symptoms in the newborn may include agitation, feeding disorder, hypertonia, hypotonia, respiratory distress, somnolence, and tremor; these effects may be self-limiting or require hospitalization.

Treatment algorithms have been developed by the ACOG and the APA for the management of depression in women prior to conception and during pregnancy (Yonkers 2009). The ACOG recommends that therapy during pregnancy be individualized; treatment with psychiatric medications during pregnancy should incorporate the clinical expertise of the mental health clinician, obstetrician, primary health care provider, and pediatrician. Safety data related to atypical antipsychotics during pregnancy is limited and routine use is not recommended. However, if a woman is inadvertently exposed to an atypical antipsychotic while pregnant, continuing therapy may be preferable to switching to a typical antipsychotic that the fetus has not yet been exposed to; consider risk:benefit (ACOG 2008).

Health care providers are encouraged to enroll women exposed to brexpiprazole during pregnancy in the National Pregnancy Registry for Atypical Antipsychotics (866-961-2388 or http://www.womensmentalhealth.org/clinical-and-research-programs/pregnancyregistry/).

Brimonidine (Ophthalmic) (bri MOE ni deen)

Brand Names: US Alphagan P

Brand Names: Canada Alphagan; Alphagan P; Apo-Brimonidine; Brimonidine P; PMS-Brimonidine; ratio-Brimonidine; Sandoz Brimonidine

Pharmacologic Category $Alpha_2$ Agonist, Ophthalmic; Ophthalmic Agent, Antiglaucoma

Use Elevated intraocular pressure: Reduction of elevated intraocular pressure (IOP) in patients with open-angle glaucoma or ocular hypertension

Local Anesthetic/Vasoconstrictor Precautions No information available to require special precautions

Effects on Dental Treatment No significant effects or complications reported

Effects on Bleeding No information available to require special precautions

Adverse Reactions Actual frequency of adverse reactions may be formulation dependent; percentages reported with Alphagan P:

>10%:

Central nervous system: Drowsiness (children 25% to 83%; adults 1% to 4%)

Ophthalmic: Allergic conjunctivitis, conjunctival hyperemia, eye pruritus

1% to 10% (unless otherwise noted 1% to 4%):

Cardiovascular: Hypertension (5% to 9%), hypotension

Central nervous system: Dizziness, fatigue, foreign body sensation of eye, headache, impaired consciousness (children), insomnia

Dermatologic: Erythema of eyelid, skin rash

Endocrine & metabolic: Hypercholesterolemia

Gastrointestinal: Xerostomia (5% to 9%), dyspepsia

Hypersensitivity: Local ocular hypersensitivity reaction (5% to 9%), hypersensitivity reaction

Infection: Infection
Neuromuscular & skeletal: Weakness
Ophthalmic: Burning sensation of eyes (5% to 9%), follicular conjunctivitis (5% to 9%), visual disturbance (5% to 9%), blepharitis, blepharoconjunctivitis, blurred vision, cataract, conjunctival edema, conjunctival hemorrhage, conjunctivitis, decreased visual acuity, dry eye syndrome, epiphora, eye discharge, eye irritation, eyelid disease, eyelid edema, eye pain, keratitis, photophobia, stinging of eyes, superficial punctate keratitis, visual field defect, vitreous detachment, vitreous opacity, watery eyes
Respiratory: Bronchitis, cough, dyspnea, flu-like symptoms, pharyngitis, rhinitis, sinus infection, sinusitis

<1%, postmarketing, and/or case reports: Anterior uveitis, apnea (infants), bradycardia, corneal erosion, depression, dermatological reaction (erythema, eyelid pruritus, vasodilatation), dry nose, dysgeusia, hordeolum, hypothermia (infants), hypotonia (infants), iritis, keratoconjunctivitis sicca, miosis, nausea, tachycardia

General Dosage Range Ophthalmic: *Children ≥2 years, Adolescents, and Adults:* Instill 1 drop in affected eye(s) 3 times/day

Mechanism of Action A relatively selective alpha-2 adrenergic agonist; causes reduction of aqueous humor formation and increased uveoscleral outflow

Pharmacodynamics/Kinetics

Half-life Elimination ~2 to 3 hours

Time to Peak Plasma: 0.5 to 4 hours

Pregnancy Risk Factor B

Pregnancy Considerations Teratogenic effects were not observed in animal reproduction studies.

Brimonidine (Topical) (bri MOE ni deen)

Brand Names: US Mirvaso

Pharmacologic Category $Alpha_2$-Adrenergic Agonist

Use Rosacea: Topical treatment of persistent (nontransient) erythema of rosacea in adults 18 years and older.

Local Anesthetic/Vasoconstrictor Precautions No information available to require special precautions

Effects on Dental Treatment No significant effects or complications reported

Effects on Bleeding No information available to require special precautions

Adverse Reactions

1% to 10%:
Cardiovascular: Flushing (3%)
Central nervous system: Burning sensation of skin (2%), localized warm feeling (1%), paresthesia (1%)
Dermatologic: Erythema (4%), acne vulgaris (1%), allergic contact dermatitis (1%; due to active ingredient [1 case] or preservative [1 case]), contact dermatitis (1%), dermatitis (1%), skin pain (1%)
Ophthalmic: Blurred vision (1%)
Respiratory: Nasal congestion (1%)

<1%, postmarketing, and/or case reports: Angioedema, bradycardia, dizziness, facial erythema, hypersensitivity reaction, hypotension (including orthostatic), pallor, pharyngeal edema, swelling of lips, swollen tongue, urticaria

General Dosage Range Topical: *Adults:* Apply a pea-size amount once daily as a thin layer across the entire face covering the central forehead, each cheek, nose, and chin.

Mechanism of Action Relatively selective $alpha_2$-receptor agonist that when applied topically may decrease erythema through direct vasoconstriction.

Pharmacodynamics/Kinetics

Time to Peak Maximum plasma concentrations observed after 15 days

Pregnancy Risk Factor B

Pregnancy Considerations Adverse events were not observed in animal reproduction studies.

Brinzolamide (brin ZOH la mide)

Brand Names: US Azopt

Brand Names: Canada Azopt

Pharmacologic Category Carbonic Anhydrase Inhibitor (Ophthalmic); Ophthalmic Agent, Antiglaucoma

Use Elevated intraocular pressure: Treatment of elevated intraocular pressure (IOP) in patients with ocular hypertension or open-angle glaucoma

Local Anesthetic/Vasoconstrictor Precautions No information available to require special precautions

Effects on Dental Treatment Key adverse event(s) related to dental treatment: Taste disturbances.

Effects on Bleeding No information available to require special precautions

Adverse Reactions

1% to 10%:
Cardiovascular: Hyperemia (1% to 5%)
Central nervous system: Foreign body sensation of eye (1% to 5%), headache (1% to 5%)
Dermatologic: Dermatitis (1% to 5%)
Gastrointestinal: Dysgeusia (5% to 10%)
Ophthalmic: Blurred vision (5% to 10%), blepharitis (1% to 5%), eye discharge (1% to 5%), eye discomfort (1% to 5%), eye pain (1% to 5%), eye pruritus (1% to 5%), keratitis (1% to 5%), xerophthalmia (1% to 5%)
Respiratory: Rhinitis (1% to 5%)

<1%, postmarketing, and/or case reports: Alopecia, asthenopia, chest pain, conjunctivitis, corneal disease, crusting of eyelid, diarrhea, diplopia, dizziness, dyspepsia, dyspnea, hypersensitivity reaction, hypertonia, keratoconjunctivitis, lacrimation, nausea, pharyngitis, renal pain, urticaria, xerostomia

General Dosage Range Ophthalmic: *Adults:* Instill 1 drop in affected eye(s) 3 times daily

Mechanism of Action Brinzolamide inhibits carbonic anhydrase, leading to decreased aqueous humor secretion. This results in a reduction of intraocular pressure.

Pregnancy Risk Factor C

Pregnancy Considerations Adverse events have been observed in animal reproduction studies.

Brivaracetam (briv a RA se tam)

Brand Names: US Briviact

Brand Names: Canada Brivlera

Pharmacologic Category Anticonvulsant, Miscellaneous

Use Partial-onset seizures: Adjunctive therapy in the treatment of partial-onset seizures in adults and adolescents 16 years of age and older with epilepsy.

Local Anesthetic/Vasoconstrictor Precautions No information available to require special precautions

Effects on Dental Treatment Key adverse event(s) related to dental treatment: Incidence of sedation and equilibrium disturbances in patients taking brivaracetam reported; monitor for symptoms, particularly for equilibrium problems, as patient arises from dental chair, and assist as necessary.

Effects on Bleeding No information available to require special precautions

Adverse Reactions Frequency not always defined.

Central nervous system: Fatigue (≤20% to ≤27%; dose-dependent), hypersomnia (≤20% to ≤27%; dose-dependent), lethargy (≤20% to ≤27%), malaise (≤20% to ≤27%; dose-dependent), drowsiness (≤16% to ≤27%; dose-dependent), sedation (≤16% to ≤27%; dose-dependent), dizziness (12% to ≤16%), equilibrium disturbance (≤3% to ≤16%), abnormal gait (≤16%), ataxia (≤16%), vertigo (≤16%), psychiatric disturbance (13%; includes psychotic and nonpsychotic), euphoria (IV: ≥3%), feeling drunk (IV: ≥3%), infusion-site pain (IV: ≥3%), irritability (3%), suicidal ideation

Gastrointestinal: Nausea and vomiting (5%), dysgeusia (IV:≥3%), constipation (2%)

Hematologic & oncologic: Decreased white blood cell count (2%)

Hypersensitivity: Hypersensitivity reaction

Neuromuscular & skeletal: Weakness (≤20% to ≤27%)

Ophthalmic: Nystagmus (≤16%)

<1%, postmarketing, and/or case reports: Angioedema, bronchospasm, decreased neutrophils

General Dosage Range

Dosage adjustment recommended in patients with hepatic impairment or on concomitant therapy.

Oral, IV: *Adolescents ≥16 years and Adults:* Initial: 50 mg 2 times daily (maximum: 200 mg/day)

Mechanism of Action The precise mechanism by which brivaracetam exerts its antiepileptic activity is unknown. Brivaracetam displays a high and selective affinity for synaptic vesicle protein 2A (SV2A) in the brain, which may contribute to the antiepileptic effect.

Pharmacodynamics/Kinetics

Half-life Elimination ~9 hours

Time to Peak Oral: 1 hour (fasting, range: 0.25 to 3 hours).

Pregnancy Risk Factor C

Pregnancy Considerations

Adverse events have been observed in animal reproduction studies.

Females exposed to brivaracetam during pregnancy are encouraged to enroll themselves into the North American Antiepileptic Drug (NAAED) Pregnancy Registry by calling 1-888-233-2334. Additional information is available at http://www.aedpregnancyregistry.org.

Controlled Substance

C-V

Bromazepam (broe MA zo pam)

Brand Names: Canada Apo-Bromazepam; Lectopam; Teva-Bromazepam

Pharmacologic Category Benzodiazepine

Use Note: Not approved in the US.

Anxiety: Short-term, symptomatic treatment of severe anxiety

Local Anesthetic/Vasoconstrictor Precautions No information available to require special precautions

Effects on Dental Treatment Key adverse event(s) related to dental treatment: Xerostomia (normal salivary flow resumes upon discontinuation).

Effects on Bleeding No information available to require special precautions

Adverse Reactions Frequency not defined.

Cardiovascular: Cardiac arrest, hypotension, palpitations, tachycardia

Central nervous system: Ataxia, confusion, depression, dizziness, drowsiness, emotional lability, euphoria, fatigue, headache, impaired consciousness, myasthenia, seizure

Dermatologic: Pruritus, skin rash

Endocrine & metabolic: Change in libido, decreased serum glucose, increased serum glucose

Gastrointestinal: Gastrointestinal distress, increased serum alanine aminotransferase, increased serum aspartate aminotransferase, nausea, vomiting, xerostomia

Genitourinary: Urinary incontinence

Hematologic: Decreased hematocrit, decreased hemoglobin, decreased white blood cell count, increased WBC count

Hepatic: Increased serum alkaline phosphatase, increased serum bilirubin

Neuromuscular & skeletal: Muscle spasm

Ocular: Blurred vision, diplopia

Respiratory: Respiratory depression

General Dosage Range Oral:

Adults: Initial: 6 to 18 mg/day in divided doses; Maintenance: 6 to 30 mg/day in divided doses. Limited experience with doses up to 60 mg/day.

Elderly/debilitated: Initial: 3 mg/day in divided doses

Mechanism of Action Benzodiazepines bind to stereospecific benzodiazepine receptors on the postsynaptic GABA neuron at several sites within the central nervous system, including the limbic system, reticular formation. Enhancement of the inhibitory effect of GABA on neuronal excitability results by increased neuronal membrane permeability to chloride ions. This shift in chloride ions results in hyperpolarization (a less excitable state) and stabilization. Benzodiazepine receptors and effects appear to be linked to the GABA-A receptors. Benzodiazepines do not bind to GABA-B receptors (Brunton, 2011).

Pharmacodynamics/Kinetics

Half-life Elimination 20 hours (may be prolonged in the elderly)

Time to Peak Serum: ≤2 hours (may be delayed by food)

Pregnancy Considerations Adverse events were observed in animal reproduction studies. Benzodiazepines have the potential to cause harm to the fetus. An increased risk of fetal malformations may be associated with first trimester exposure (malformations of the heart, cleft lip/palate). Maternal use later in pregnancy may be associated with adverse events in the fetus (irregular heart beat) and neonate (hypothermia, hypotonia, respiratory depression, poor feeding, withdrawal).

Product Availability Not available in the US

Bromfenac (BROME fen ak)

Brand Names: US Bromday [DSC]; Prolensa

Pharmacologic Category Nonsteroidal Anti-inflammatory Drug (NSAID), Ophthalmic

Use Postoperative ocular inflammation/pain: Treatment of postoperative inflammation and reduction of ocular pain following cataract surgery.

Local Anesthetic/Vasoconstrictor Precautions No information available to require special precautions

Effects on Dental Treatment The dentist should be aware of the potential of abnormal coagulation. Caution should also be exercised in the use of NSAIDs in patients already on anticoagulant therapy with drugs such as warfarin (Coumadin®). See Effects on Bleeding.

Effects on Bleeding Bromfenac is marketed in the U.S. only as an ophthalmic drop. It is a nonselective NSAID which is known to reversibly inhibit platelet aggregation. However, there is no scientific evidence to warrant discontinuation of topical NSAIDs prior to dental surgery.

Adverse Reactions

1% to 10%:

Central nervous system: Headache (≥1% to ≤8%)

Ophthalmic: Anterior chamber inflammation (1% to 8%), iritis (1% to 8%), ocular hypertension (1% to 8%), vitreous opacity (1% to 8%), eye pain (≤1% to ≤8%), abnormal sensation in eyes (2% to 7%), conjunctival hyperemia (2% to 7%), eye irritation (burning/stinging; 2% to 7%), eye pruritus (2% to 7%), eye redness (2% to 7%)

Frequency not defined:

Hematologic & oncologic: Prolonged bleeding time

Miscellaneous: Wound healing impairment

<1%, postmarketing and/or case reports: Corneal erosion, corneal perforation, corneal thinning, epithelial keratopathy

General Dosage Range Ophthalmic: *Adults:* Instill 1 drop into affected eye(s) once or twice daily

Mechanism of Action Inhibits prostaglandin synthesis by decreasing the activity of the enzyme, cyclooxygenase 1 and 2, which results in decreased formation of prostaglandin precursors.

Pharmacodynamics/Kinetics

Half-life Elimination 0.5 to 4 hours (following oral administration)

Pregnancy Risk Factor C

Pregnancy Considerations Adverse events have been observed in animal reproduction studies. Exposure to nonsteroidal anti-inflammatory drugs late in pregnancy may lead to premature closure of the ductus arteriosus and may inhibit uterine contractions; some manufacturers recommend avoiding use in late pregnancy.

Bromocriptine (broe moe KRIP teen)

Brand Names: US Cycloset; Parlodel

Brand Names: Canada Dom-Bromocriptine; PMS-Bromocriptine

Pharmacologic Category Anti-Parkinson Agent, Dopamine Agonist; Antidiabetic Agent, Dopamine Agonist; Ergot Derivative

Use

Acromegaly (excluding Cycloset): Treatment of acromegaly

Hyperprolactinemia (excluding Cycloset): Treatment of prolactin-secreting pituitary adenoma or disorders associated with hyperprolactinemia including amenorrhea with or without galactorrhea, hypogonadism, or infertility

Parkinson disease (excluding Cycloset): Treatment of the signs and symptoms of idiopathic or postencephalitic Parkinson disease; as adjunctive treatment to levodopa (alone or with a peripheral decarboxylase inhibitor)

Type 2 diabetes mellitus (Cycloset only): To improve glycemic control in adults with type 2 diabetes mellitus (noninsulin dependent, NIDDM) as an adjunct to diet and exercise

Local Anesthetic/Vasoconstrictor Precautions Bromocriptine is a semisynthetic ergot alkaloid derivative; there is a possibility that it has vasoconstricting effects; use vasoconstrictor with caution

Effects on Dental Treatment Key adverse event(s) related to dental treatment: Patients may experience orthostatic hypotension as they stand up after treatment; especially if lying in dental chair for extended periods of time. Use caution with sudden changes in position during and after dental treatment.

Effects on Bleeding No information available to require special precautions

Adverse Reactions Note: Frequency of adverse effects may vary by dose and/or indication.

>10%:

Central nervous system: Dizziness, fatigue, headache

Gastrointestinal: Constipation, nausea

Neuromuscular & skeletal: Weakness

Respiratory: Rhinitis

1% to 10%:

Cardiovascular: Hypotension (including postural/orthostatic), Raynaud's phenomenon, syncope, vasospasm (digital)

Central nervous system: Drowsiness, lightheadedness

Endocrine & metabolic: Hypoglycemia (4%; in combination with sulfonylureas or other antidiabetic agents: 7% to 9%)

Gastrointestinal: Abdominal cramps, anorexia, diarrhea, dyspepsia, gastrointestinal hemorrhage, vomiting, xerostomia

Infection: Increased susceptibility to infection

Ophthalmic: Amblyopia

Respiratory: Flu-like symptoms, nasal congestion, sinusitis

Postmarketing and/or case reports: Abdominal distress, acquired valvular heart disease, alopecia, anxiety, ataxia, blepharospasm, blurred vision, bradycardia, cardiac arrhythmia, cerebrovascular accident (postpartum), cold extremities, cold intolerance, confusion, constrictive pericarditis, delusions, depression, dyskinesia, dysphagia, dyspnea, epileptiform seizures, ergot alkaloids toxicity, erythromelalgia, gastrointestinal ulcer, hallucination, heavy headedness, hypersensitivity reaction, hypertension (postpartum), increased cerebrospinal fluid pressure, increased libido, insomnia, lassitude, lethargy, muscle cramps, myocardial infarction (postpartum), narcolepsy, nervousness, nightmares, on-off phenomenon, pallor, paranoia, paresthesia, pericardial effusion, peripheral edema, pleural effusion, pleurisy, psychomotor agitation, psychosis, pulmonary fibrosis, retroperitoneal fibrosis, seizure (postpartum), skin mottling, skin rash, sleep disorder, status epilepticus (postpartum), tachycardia, tingling of the ears, tinnitus, transient blindness, urinary frequency, urinary incontinence, urinary retention, vasodepressor syncope, ventricular tachycardia, vertigo, visual disturbance

General Dosage Range Oral:

Children and Adolescents 11 to 15 years: Initial: 1.25 to 2.5 mg daily; Maintenance: 2.5 to 10 mg daily

Adolescents ≥16 years: Initial: 1.25 to 2.5 mg daily; Maintenance: 2.5 to 15 mg daily

Adults: Dosage varies greatly depending on indication

Mechanism of Action Semisynthetic ergot alkaloid derivative and a sympatholytic dopamine D_2 receptor agonist which activates postsynaptic dopamine receptors in the tuberoinfundibular (inhibiting pituitary prolactin secretion) and nigrostriatal pathways (enhancing coordinated motor control).

In the treatment of type 2 diabetes mellitus, the mechanism of action is unknown; however, bromocriptine is believed to affect circadian rhythms which are mediated, in part, by dopaminergic activity, and are believed to play a role in obesity and insulin resistance. It is postulated that bromocriptine (when administered during the morning and released into the systemic circulation in a rapid, 'pulse-like' dose) may reset hypothalamic circadian activities which have been altered by obesity, thereby resulting in the reversal of insulin resistance and decreases in glucose production, without increasing serum insulin concentrations (Gaziano 2010; Pijl 2000).

Pharmacodynamics/Kinetics

Duration of Action 8 to12 hours

Half-life Elimination Cycloset: ~6 hours; Parlodel: 4.85 hours

Time to Peak Serum: Cycloset: 53 minutes; Parlodel: 2.5 ± 2 hours

Pregnancy Risk Factor B

Pregnancy Considerations Bromocriptine crosses the placenta (Molitch 2015). Data collected from women taking bromocriptine during pregnancy suggest the incidence of birth defects is not increased with use. However, the majority of women discontinued use within 8 weeks of pregnancy.

Women with hyperprolactinemia may be infertile, have amenorrhea and galactorrhea. A mechanical contraceptive should be used during therapy until normal ovulatory menses is established. Contraception can then be discontinued if pregnancy is desired. Bromocriptine should be discontinued if pregnancy is confirmed unless needed for treatment of a rapidly expanding macroadenoma. When used for the treatment of acromegaly or Parkinson disease, consider discontinuing therapy during pregnancy. If treatment is withdrawn, monitor for signs and symptoms of an enlarging prolactin secreting tumor. Regardless of indication, if bromocriptine is needed in a pregnant woman, monitor closely for hypertensive disorders during pregnancy and immediately postpartum.

During treatment with bromocriptine, fertility may occur prior to restoration of menses in infertile women, therefore a pregnancy test is recommended every 4 weeks during the amenorrheic period. Once menses resume, pregnancy tests should be done any time a menstrual period is missed. Women not seeking pregnancy should be advised to use appropriate contraception.

Brompheniramine (brome fen IR a meen)

Brand Names: US J-Tan PD [OTC] [DSC], Respa-BR [DSC]

Pharmacologic Category Alkylamine Derivative; Histamine H_1 Antagonist; Histamine H_1 Antagonist, First Generation

Use Upper respiratory allergies: Temporary relief of sneezing; itchy, watery eyes; itchy nose or throat; and runny nose caused by hay fever (allergic rhinitis) or other upper respiratory allergies.

Local Anesthetic/Vasoconstrictor Precautions No information available to require special precautions

Effects on Dental Treatment Key adverse event(s) related to dental treatment: Xerostomia (normal salivary flow resumes upon discontinuation). Chronic use of antihistamines will inhibit salivary flow, particularly in elderly patients; this may contribute to periodontal disease and oral discomfort.

Effects on Bleeding No information available to require special precautions

Adverse Reactions Frequency not defined.

Cardiovascular: Angina pectoris, chest tightness, circulatory shock, extrasystoles, hypotension, increased blood pressure, palpitations, tachycardia

Central nervous system: Anxiety, ataxia, central nervous system stimulation, chills, confusion, dizziness, drowsiness, euphoria, excitement, fatigue, headache, hysteria, insomnia, irritability, nervousness, neuritis, paresthesia, restlessness, sedation, seizure, tension, vertigo

Dermatologic: Diaphoresis, skin photosensitivity, skin rash, urticaria

Gastrointestinal: Abdominal cramps, anorexia, constipation, diarrhea, epigastric distress, heartburn, nausea, vomiting, xerostomia

Genitourinary: Dysuria, early menses, urinary retention

Hematologic & oncologic: Agranulocytosis, hemolytic anemia, hypoplastic anemia, thrombocytopenia

Hypersensitivity: Anaphylactic shock

Neuromuscular & skeletal: Tremor, weakness

Ophthalmic: Blurred vision, diplopia, mydriasis

Otic: Acute labyrinthitis, tinnitus

Renal: Polyuria

Respiratory: Dry nose, dry throat, nasal congestion, thickening of bronchial secretions, wheezing

General Dosage Range Oral:

Children 2 to <6 years: 1 mg (1 mL) every 4 to 6 hours (maximum: 6 mg [6 mL] per 24 hours)

Children 6 to <12 years: 2 mg (2 mL) every 4 to 6 hours (maximum: 12 mg [12 mL] per 24 hours)

Mechanism of Action Competes with histamine for H_1-receptor sites on effector cells

Pharmacodynamics/Kinetics

Half-life Elimination Children: ~12 hours (Simons, 1999); Adults: ~25 hours (Simons, 1982)

Time to Peak Serum: Children: 3-3.5 hours (Simons, 1999); Adults: 2-4 hours (Simons, 1982)

Pregnancy Considerations Maternal first-generation antihistamine use has generally not resulted in an increased risk of birth defects (Babalola, 2013; Murase, 2014); however, information specific to brompheniramine is limited (Heinonen, 1977; Seto, 1993). Antihistamines may be used for the treatment of rhinitis, urticaria, systemic pruritus or atopic dermatitis in pregnant women (although agents other than brompheniramine or second generation antihistamines may be preferred) (Babalola, 2013; Murase, 2014; Wallace, 2008; Zuberbier, 2014). Antihistamines are not recommended for treatment of pruritus associated with intrahepatic cholestasis in pregnancy (Ambros-Rudolph, 2011; Kremer, 2011).

Budesonide (Systemic) (byoo DES oh nide)

Brand Names: US Entocort EC; Uceris

Brand Names: Canada Cortiment; Entocort

Generic Availability (US) May be product dependent

Pharmacologic Category Corticosteroid, Systemic

Use

Crohn disease (capsules): Treatment of active Crohn disease (mild to moderate) involving the ileum and/or the ascending colon in patients 8 years and older; maintenance of clinical remission (for up to 3 months) of Crohn disease (mild to moderate) involving the ileum and/or the ascending colon in adults.

Ulcerative colitis (tablets): Induction of remission in patients with active ulcerative colitis (mild to moderate).

Local Anesthetic/Vasoconstrictor Precautions No information available to require special precautions

Effects on Dental Treatment Key adverse event(s) related to dental treatment: Xerostomia (normal salivary flow resumes upon discontinuation), dry throat, abnormal taste, and herpes simplex. Localized infections with *Candida albicans* or *Aspergillus niger* have occurred frequently in the mouth and pharynx with repetitive use of oral inhaler of corticosteroids. These infections may require treatment with appropriate antifungal therapy or discontinuance of treatment with corticosteroid inhaler.

Effects on Bleeding Variable effects on anticoagulant therapy are observed with glucocorticoids such as budesonide (systemic, oral inhalation).

Adverse Reactions

>10%:

Central nervous system: Headache (15% to 21%)

Dermatologic: Acne vulgaris (15%)

Endocrine & metabolic: Decreased cortisol (foam 17%; tablets 2% to 4%), bruise (15%), moon face (11%)

Gastrointestinal: Nausea (2% to 11%)

Respiratory: Respiratory tract infection (11%)

1% to 10%:

Cardiovascular: Chest pain (<5%), edema (<5%), facial edema (<5%), flushing (<5%), hypertension (<5%), palpitations (<5%), tachycardia (<5%)

Central nervous system: Dizziness (<5% to 7%), fatigue (3% to 5%), agitation (<5%), amnesia (<5%), confusion (<5%), drowsiness (<5%), insomnia (<5%), malaise (<5%), nervousness (<5%), paresthesia (<5%), sleep disorder (<5%), vertigo (<5%)

Dermatologic: Alopecia (<5%), dermatitis (<5%), dermatological disease (<5%), diaphoresis (<5%), eczema (<5%)

Endocrine & metabolic: Hirsutism (≤5%), hypokalemia (1% to <5%), intermenstrual bleeding (<5%), menstrual disease (<5%), weight gain (<5%), adrenocortical insufficiency (foam 4%; capsules >1%), redistribution of body fat (1%)

Gastrointestinal: Diarrhea (10%), dyspepsia (6%), anal disease (<5%), enteritis (<5%), epigastric pain (<5%), exacerbation of Crohn's disease (<5%), gastrointestinal fistula (<5%), glossitis (<5%), hemorrhoids (<5%), increased appetite (<5%), intestinal obstruction (<5%), oral candidiasis (<5%), upper abdominal pain (3% to 4%), flatulence (3%), abdominal distention (2%), constipation (2%)

Genitourinary: Urinary tract infection (2% to <5%), dysuria (<5%), nocturia (<5%), urinary frequency (<5%), hematuria (≥1%), pyuria (≥1%)

Hematologic & oncologic: C-reactive protein increased (1% to <5%), leukocytosis (1% to <5%), purpura (<5%), abnormal neutrophils (≥1%), anemia (≥1%), increased erythrocyte sedimentation rate (≥1%)

Hepatic: Increased serum alkaline phosphatase (≥1%)

Hypersensitivity: Tongue edema (<5%)

Infection: Viral infection (6%), abscess (<5%)

Neuromuscular & skeletal: Ankle edema (7%), arthralgia (5%), arthritis (≤5%), hyperkinesia (<5%), muscle cramps (<5%), myalgia (<5%), tremor (<5%), weakness (<5%)

Ophthalmic: Eye disease (<5%), visual disturbance (<5%)

Otic: Otic infection (<5%)

Respiratory: Sinusitis (8%), bronchitis (<5%), dyspnea (<5%), flu-like symptoms (<5%), pharyngeal disease (<5%), rhinitis (<5%)

Miscellaneous: Fever (<5%)

<1%, postmarketing, and/or case reports: Allergic dermatitis, anaphylaxis, emotional lability, hyperglycemia, maculopapular rash, pancreatitis, peripheral edema, pruritus, pseudotumor cerebri, rectal bleeding, skin rash

Dosing

Adult & Geriatric

Crohn disease (active): Oral: Capsule: 9 mg once daily in the morning for up to 8 weeks; recurring episodes may be treated with a repeat 8-week course of treatment.

Maintenance of remission: Following treatment of active disease (control of symptoms with Crohn Disease Activity Index [CDAI] <150), treatment may be continued at a dosage of 6 mg once daily for up to 3 months. If symptom control is maintained for 3 months, tapering of the dosage to complete cessation is recommended. Continued dosing beyond 3 months has not been demonstrated to result in substantial benefit.

Ulcerative colitis (active): Oral: Tablet: 9 mg once daily in the morning for up to 8 weeks

Eosinophilic esophagitis (off-label use): Oral: 2 mg/day as an oral budesonide viscous liquid/suspension. Dose may be divided into 2 doses. Avoid ingesting any solid or liquid food for 30 minutes after budesonide administration. (Dellon 2013; Dohil 2010; Liacouras 2011; Rubinstein 2014).

Pediatric

Crohn disease (active): Children ≥8 years and Adolescents ≤17 years (weighing >25 kg): Oral: Capsule: 9 mg once daily in the morning for up to 8 weeks, then 6 mg once daily for 2 weeks.

Eosinophilic esophagitis (off-label use):

Children ≥10 years of age or ≥5 ft in height: 2 mg/day as an oral budesonide viscous liquid/suspension. Dose may be divided into 2 doses. Avoid ingesting any solid or liquid food for 30 minutes after budesonide administration. (Dellon, 2013; Dohil, 2010; Liacouras, 2011; Rubinstein 2014).

Children <10 years or <5 ft in height: 1 mg/day as an oral budesonide viscous liquid/suspension. Avoid ingesting any solid or liquid food for 30 minutes after budesonide administration. (Dellon, 2013; Dohil, 2010; Liacouras, 2011; Rubinstein, 2014).

Renal Impairment There are no dosage adjustments provided in the manufacturer's labeling; use with caution.

Hepatic Impairment Oral capsule:

Mild hepatic impairment (Child-Pugh class A): No dosage adjustment necessary.

Moderate hepatic impairment (Child-Pugh class B): Consider reduced dosage to 3 mg once daily and monitor for hypercorticism.

Severe hepatic impairment (Child-Pugh class C): Avoid use.

Oral tablet:

Mild hepatic impairment: There are no specific dosage adjustments provided in the manufacturer's labeling; use with caution.

Moderate to severe hepatic impairment: There are no specific dosage adjustments provided in the manufacturer's labeling (has not been studied);

monitor for hypercorticism; consider discontinuing use.

Mechanism of Action Controls the rate of protein synthesis; depresses the migration of polymorphonuclear leukocytes, fibroblasts; reverses capillary permeability and lysosomal stabilization at the cellular level to prevent or control inflammation. Has potent glucocorticoid activity and weak mineralocorticoid activity.

Contraindications

Hypersensitivity to budesonide or any component of the formulation.

Documentation of allergenic cross-reactivity for corticosteroids is limited. However, because of similarities in chemical structure and/or pharmacologic actions, the possibility of cross-sensitivity cannot be ruled out with certainty.

Canadian labeling: Additional contraindications (not in US labeling): Active tuberculosis; systemic or local bacterial, fungal or viral infections; hypersensitivity to soya or peanut (Cortiment)

Warnings/Precautions May cause hypercorticism or suppression of hypothalamic-pituitary-adrenal (HPA) axis, particularly in younger children, or in patients receiving high doses for prolonged periods. HPA axis suppression may lead to adrenal crisis. Withdrawal and discontinuation of a corticosteroid should be done slowly and carefully. Particular care is required when patients are transferred from systemic corticosteroids to inhaled products or corticosteroids with lower systemic effect due to possible adrenal insufficiency or withdrawal from steroids, including an increase in allergic symptoms. Patients receiving >20 mg per day of prednisone (or equivalent) may be most susceptible. Fatalities have occurred due to adrenal insufficiency in asthmatic patients during and after transfer from systemic corticosteroids to aerosol steroids; aerosol steroids do not provide the systemic steroid needed to treat patients having trauma, surgery, or infections.

Acute myopathy has been reported with high-dose corticosteroids, usually in patients with neuromuscular transmission disorders; may involve ocular and/or respiratory muscles; monitor creatine kinase; recovery may be delayed. Corticosteroid use may cause psychiatric disturbances, including euphoria, insomnia, mood swings, personality changes, severe depression or psychotic manifestations. Preexisting psychiatric conditions may be exacerbated by corticosteroid use. Prolonged use of corticosteroids may increase the incidence of secondary infection, mask acute infection (including fungal infections), prolong or exacerbate viral infections, or limit response to killed or inactivated vaccines. Exposure to chickenpox or measles should be avoided; corticosteroids should not be used to treat ocular herpes simplex. Corticosteroids should not be used for cerebral malaria, fungal infections, viral hepatitis. Close observation is required in patients with latent tuberculosis and/or TB reactivity; restrict use in active TB (only fulminating or disseminated TB in conjunction with antituberculosis treatment). Amebiasis should be ruled out in any patient with recent travel to tropic climates or unexplained diarrhea prior to initiation of corticosteroids. Use with extreme caution in patients with *Strongyloides* infections; hyperinfection, dissemination and fatalities have occurred. Prolonged treatment with corticosteroids has been associated with the development of Kaposi sarcoma (case reports); if noted, discontinuation of therapy should be considered (Goedert 2002).

Avoid use in patients with severe hepatic impairment (Child-Pugh class C). Consider reduced dosage in patients with moderate hepatic impairment (Child-Pugh Class B); monitor for hypercorticism. Long-term use of corticosteroids in patients with hepatic impairment, including cirrhosis, has been associated with fluid retention. Use with caution in patients with thyroid disease, renal impairment, diabetes, glaucoma, cataracts, myasthenia gravis, osteoporosis, patients at risk for seizures or seizure disorder, or GI diseases (diverticulitis, fresh intestinal anastomoses, active or latent, peptic ulcer, ulcerative colitis, abscess or other pyogenic infection). Use with caution in patients with HF and/or hypertension; use has been associated with fluid retention, electrolyte disturbances, and hypertension. Use caution following acute MI (corticosteroids have been associated with myocardial rupture).

Rare cases of anaphylactoid reactions have been observed in patients receiving corticosteroids. Potentially significant interactions may exist, requiring dose or frequency adjustment, additional monitoring, and/or selection of alternative therapy.

Some dosage forms may contain polysorbate 80 (also known as Tweens). Hypersensitivity reactions, usually a delayed reaction, have been reported following exposure to pharmaceutical products containing polysorbate 80 in certain individuals (Isaksson 2002; Lucente 2000; Shelley 1995). Thrombocytopenia, ascites, pulmonary deterioration, and renal and hepatic failure have been reported in premature neonates after receiving parenteral products containing polysorbate 80 (Alade 1986; CDC 1984). See manufacturer's labeling

Drug Interactions

Metabolism/Transport Effects Substrate of CYP3A4 (major); **Note:** Assignment of Major/Minor substrate status based on clinically relevant drug interaction potential

Avoid Concomitant Use

Avoid concomitant use of Budesonide (Systemic) with any of the following: Aldesleukin; BCG (Intravesical); Conivaptan; CYP3A4 Inhibitors (Moderate); CYP3A4 Inhibitors (Strong); Fusidic Acid (Systemic); Grapefruit Juice; Idelalisib; Natalizumab; Pimecrolimus; Tacrolimus (Topical); Tofacitinib

Increased Effect/Toxicity

Budesonide (Systemic) may increase the levels/ effects of: Deferasirox; Fingolimod; Leflunomide; Natalizumab; Tofacitinib

The levels/effects of Budesonide (Systemic) may be increased by: Conivaptan; CYP3A4 Inhibitors (Moderate); CYP3A4 Inhibitors (Strong); Dasatinib; Denosumab; Fosaprepitant; Fusidic Acid (Systemic); Grapefruit Juice; Idelalisib; Ivacaftor; Ocrelizumab; Palbociclib; Pimecrolimus; Roflumilast; Simeprevir; Stiripentol; Tacrolimus (Topical); Trastuzumab

Decreased Effect

Budesonide (Systemic) may decrease the levels/ effects of: Aldesleukin; BCG (Intravesical); Coccidioides immitis Skin Test; Corticorelin; Hyaluronidase; Nivolumab; Sipuleucel-T; Tertomotide; Vaccines (Inactivated)

The levels/effects of Budesonide (Systemic) may be decreased by: Antacids; Bile Acid Sequestrants; Echinacea

Food Interactions Grapefruit juice may double systemic exposure of orally administered budesonide. Administration of capsule or tablet with a high-fat meal delays peak concentrations (but does not alter the extent of absorption. Management: Avoid grapefruit juice with oral capsules or tablets.

Dietary Considerations Avoid grapefruit juice.

Pharmacodynamics/Kinetics

Half-life Elimination IV:

Children 9 to 14 years: 1.9 hours

Adults: 2 to 3.6 hours

Time to Peak Capsule: 0.5 to 10 hours; Tablet (extended release): 13.3 ± 5.9 hours

Pregnancy Risk Factor C (tablet)

Pregnancy Considerations Some studies have shown an association between first trimester systemic corticosteroid use and oral clefts (Park-Wyllie 2000; Pradat 2003). Systemic corticosteroids may also influence fetal growth (decreased birth weight); however, information is conflicting (Lunghi 2010). Hypoadrenalism may occur in newborns following maternal use of corticosteroids in pregnancy (monitor). When systemic corticosteroids are needed in pregnancy, it is generally recommended to use the lowest effective dose for the shortest duration of time, avoiding high doses during the first trimester (Leachman 2006; Lunghi 2010). Budesonide may be used for the induction of remission in pregnant women with inflammatory bowel disease (Habal 2012; Nguyen 2016).

Breastfeeding Considerations Budesonide is excreted in breast milk. According to the manufacturer, the decision to breast-feed during therapy should take into account the risk of exposure to the infant and the benefits of treatment to the mother. If there is concern about exposure to the infant, some guidelines recommend waiting 4 hours after the maternal dose of an oral systemic corticosteroid before breastfeeding in order to decrease potential exposure to the nursing infant (based on a study using prednisolone) (Habal 2012; Ost 1985).

Dosage Forms

Capsule Delayed Release Particles, Oral:

Entocort EC: 3 mg

Generic: 3 mg

Tablet Extended Release 24 Hour, Oral:

Uceris: 9 mg

Dosage Forms: Canada

Tablet Extended Release 24 Hour, Oral:

Cortiment: 9 mg

Budesonide (Nasal) (byoo DES oh nide)

Brand Names: US Rhinocort Allergy [OTC]; Rhinocort Aqua

Brand Names: Canada Mylan-Budesonide AQ; Rhinocort Aqua; Rhinocort Turbuhaler

Generic Availability (US) Yes

Pharmacologic Category Corticosteroid, Nasal

Use

US labeling:

Rx: Allergic rhinitis: Management of symptoms of seasonal or perennial allergic rhinitis in adults and children ≥6 years.

OTC: Upper respiratory symptoms: Relief of symptoms of hay fever or other upper respiratory allergies (eg, nasal congestion, runny nose, itchy nose, sneezing) in adults and children ≥6 years.

Canadian labeling:

Nasal polyps: Treatment of nasal polyps; prevention of nasal polyps after polypectomy.

Rhinitis: Management of symptoms of seasonal allergic, perennial, and vasomotor rhinitis unresponsive to conventional therapy.

Local Anesthetic/Vasoconstrictor Precautions No information available to require special precautions

Effects on Dental Treatment No significant effects or complications reported

Effects on Bleeding No information available to require special precautions

Adverse Reactions

1% to 10%: Respiratory: Epistaxis (8%), pharyngitis (4%), bronchospasm (2%), cough (2%), nasal mucosa irritation (2%)

<1%, postmarketing, and/or case reports: Anosmia, cataract, crusting of nose, dizziness, fatigue, glaucoma, growth suppression, headache, hypersensitivity reaction, increased intraocular pressure, mucous membrane ulceration, nasal septum perforation, nausea, pharyngeal disease (irritation, itchy throat, throat pain), wheezing

Dosing

Adult & Geriatric

US labeling:

Rx: Allergic rhinitis: Intranasal: One spray (32 mcg) in each nostril once daily (total daily dose: 64 mcg/day). Some patients who do not achieve adequate control may benefit from increased dosage. A reduced dosage may be effective after initial control is achieved (maximum dose: 4 sprays [128 mcg] in each nostril once daily [total daily dose: 256 mcg/day]).

OTC: Upper respiratory symptoms: Intranasal: Two sprays (64 mcg) in each nostril once daily (total daily dosage: 128 mcg/day); once symptoms improve, reduce to 1 spray (32 mcg) in each nostril once daily (total daily dosage: 64 mcg/day)

Canadian labeling: **Note:** Discontinue therapy if significant improvement is not observed within 3 weeks

Nasal polyps: Intranasal:

Rhinocort Aqua: One spray (64 mcg) in each nostril twice daily; total daily dose: 256 mcg/day

Rhinocort Turbuhaler: One application (100 mcg) in each nostril twice daily; total daily dose: 400 mcg/day

Rhinitis: Intranasal: **Note:** If possible initiate therapy prior to allergen exposure.

Rhinocort Aqua: Initial: Two sprays (128 mcg) in each nostril once daily **or** 1 spray (64 mcg) in each nostril twice daily (total daily dose: 256 mcg/day); Maintenance: Individualize, use lowest effective dose.

Rhinocort Turbuhaler: Initial: Two applications (200 mcg) in each nostril once daily (total daily dose: 400 mcg/day); Maintenance: Individualize; use lowest effective dose.

Pediatric

Nasal polyps: Children ≥6 years and Adolescents: Intranasal: *Canadian labeling:* Refer to adult dosing.

Allergic rhinitis (Rx):

US labeling:

Children ≥6 years to <12 years: Intranasal: One spray (32 mcg) in each nostril once daily (total daily dosage: 64 mcg/day). Some patients who do not achieve adequate control may benefit from increased dosage. A reduced dosage may be effective after initial control is achieved (maximum dose: 2 sprays [64 mcg] in each nostril once daily [total daily dosage: 128 mcg/day]).

Children ≥12 years and Adolescents: Refer to adult dosing.

Canadian labeling: Children ≥6 years and Adolescents: Refer to adult dosing.

Upper respiratory symptoms (OTC):

Children ≥12 years and Adolescents: Intranasal: Refer to adult dosing.

Children 6 years to <12 years: Intranasal: One spray (32 mcg) in each nostril once daily (total daily dosage: 64 mcg/day). If symptoms do not improve, may increase to 2 sprays (64 mcg) in each nostril once daily (total daily dosage: 128 mcg/day); once symptoms improve, reduce to 1 spray (32 mcg) in each nostril once daily (total daily dosage: 64 mcg/day).

Renal Impairment There are no dosage adjustments provided in the manufacturer's labeling (has not been studied).

Hepatic Impairment There are no dosage adjustments provided in manufacturer's labeling (has not been studied). Systemic availability of budesonide may be increased in patients with hepatic impairment; monitor closely for signs and symptoms of hypercorticism.

Mechanism of Action Controls the rate of protein synthesis; depresses the migration of polymorphonuclear leukocytes, fibroblasts; reverses capillary permeability and lysosomal stabilization at the cellular level to prevent or control inflammation. Has potent glucocorticoid activity and weak mineralocorticoid activity.

Contraindications

Hypersensitivity to budesonide or any component of the formulation

OTC labeling: When used for self-medication, do not use in children <6 years of age.

Canadian labeling: Additional contraindications (not in US labeling): Tuberculosis (active or quiescent); untreated bacterial, fungal, or viral infections; use in children <6 years of age

Warnings/Precautions Hypersensitivity reactions (eg, anaphylactic reactions, angioedema, pruritus, urticaria, rash, dermatitis) may occur. Nasal septal perforation, nasal ulceration, epistaxis, and localized *Candida albicans* infections of the nose and/or pharynx may occur. Monitor patients periodically for adverse nasal effects; discontinuation of therapy may be necessary if an infection occurs. May delay wound healing; avoid nasal corticosteroid use in patients with recent nasal septal ulcers, nasal surgery or nasal trauma until healing has occurred. Prolonged use of corticosteroids may also increase the incidence of secondary infection, mask acute infection (including fungal infections), prolong or exacerbate viral infections, or limit response to vaccines. Exposure to chickenpox should be avoided. Avoid use or use with caution in patients with latent/active tuberculosis, untreated bacterial or fungal infections (local or systemic), viral or parasitic infections, or ocular herpes simplex. The Canadian labeling contraindicates use in patients with active or quiescent TB or with untreated bacterial, fungal, or viral infections. Use with caution in patients with cataracts and/or glaucoma; increased intraocular pressure, glaucoma, and cataracts have occurred with prolonged use. Consider routine eye exams in chronic users or in patients who report visual changes.

Avoid using higher than recommended dosages; suppression of linear growth (ie, reduction of growth velocity), reduced bone mineral density, hypercorticism (Cushing syndrome) or suppression of hypothalamic-pituitary-adrenal (HPA) axis may occur; titrate to lowest effective dose. Reduction in growth velocity may occur when corticosteroids are administered to pediatric patients, even at recommended doses via intranasal route (monitor growth). Withdrawal and discontinuation of a corticosteroid should be done slowly and carefully. Potentially significant drug-drug interactions may exist, requiring dose or frequency adjustment, additional monitoring, and/or selection of alternative therapy.

Self-medication (OTC use): Consult a health care provider before use if you have had recent nose ulcers or nose surgery; have a nose injury that has not healed; are using a steroid medicine for asthma, allergies or skin rash; have an eye infection; and/or have or had glaucoma or cataracts. When using this product, symptoms may get better on the first day of treatment; however, it may take up to 2 weeks of daily use to feel the most relief. Discontinue use and consult a health care provider if symptoms do not improve after 2 weeks, or if an infection (eg, persistent fever), changes in vision, or frequent nosebleeds occur. Do not spray into eyes or mouth or use more than directed or for the common cold.

Drug Interactions

Metabolism/Transport Effects Substrate of CYP3A4 (minor); **Note:** Assignment of Major/Minor substrate status based on clinically relevant drug interaction potential

Avoid Concomitant Use

Avoid concomitant use of Budesonide (Nasal) with any of the following: Desmopressin

Increased Effect/Toxicity

Budesonide (Nasal) may increase the levels/effects of: Ceritinib; Desmopressin

The levels/effects of Budesonide (Nasal) may be increased by: Cobicistat; CYP3A4 Inhibitors (Strong); Telaprevir

Decreased Effect There are no known significant interactions involving a decrease in effect.

Pharmacodynamics/Kinetics

Onset of Action Rhinocort Aqua: Within 10 hours; Peak effect: Up to 2 weeks

Half-life Elimination 2 to 3 hours

Time to Peak Plasma: Nasal: 30 minutes

Pregnancy Risk Factor B

Pregnancy Considerations Adverse events have been observed with corticosteroids in animal reproduction studies. Hypoadrenalism may occur in newborns following maternal use of corticosteroids in pregnancy; monitor. Studies of pregnant women using intranasal budesonide have not demonstrated an increased risk of abnormalities. Intranasal corticosteroids are recommended for the treatment of rhinitis during pregnancy; the lowest effective dose should be used (NAEPP, 2005; Wallace, 2008); budesonide is preferred (Wallace, 2008).

Breastfeeding Considerations Following use of budesonide powder for oral inhalation, ~0.3% to 1% of the maternal dose was found in breast milk. The maximum concentration appeared within 45 minutes of dosing. Plasma budesonide levels obtained from infants ~90 minutes after breastfeeding (~140 minutes after maternal dose) were below the limit of quantification. Milk concentrations following the use of the nasal inhaler are expected to be similar. The use of inhaled corticosteroids is not considered a contraindication to breastfeeding (NAEPP, 2005). The manufacturer recommends using only when clinically appropriate, at the lowest effective dose, and administering the dose following a feeding in order to minimize potential exposure to the nursing infant.

Dosage Forms Considerations

Rhinocort Aqua: 8.6 g bottles contain 120 sprays.

Rhinocort Allergy: 5 mL bottles contain 60 sprays, 8.43 mL bottles contain 120 sprays

Dosage Forms

Suspension, Nasal:

Rhinocort Allergy [OTC]: 32 mcg/actuation (5 mL, 8.43 mL)

Rhinocort Aqua: 32 mcg/actuation (8.6 g)

Generic: 32 mcg/actuation (8.6 g, 8.43 mL)

Dosage Forms: Canada

Powder for nasal inhalation:

Rhinocort Turbuhaler: 100 mcg/inhalation

Suspension, intranasal [spray]:

Rhinocort Aqua: 64 mcg/inhalation

Budesonide (Oral Inhalation)

(byoo DES oh nide)

Brand Names: US Pulmicort; Pulmicort Flexhaler

Brand Names: Canada Pulmicort Turbuhaler

Generic Availability (US) May be product dependent

Pharmacologic Category Corticosteroid, Inhalant (Oral)

Use

Nebulization: Maintenance and prophylactic treatment of asthma

Oral inhalation: Maintenance and prophylactic treatment of asthma; includes patients who require oral corticosteroids and those who may benefit from systemic dose reduction/elimination

Guideline recommendations: Asthma: A low-dose inhaled corticosteroid (*in addition to an as-needed short acting beta$_2$-agonist*) is the initial preferred long term control medication for children, adolescents, and adult patients with persistent asthma who are candidates for treatment according to a step-wise treatment approach (GINA 2016; NAEPP 2007).

Local Anesthetic/Vasoconstrictor Precautions No information available to require special precautions

Effects on Dental Treatment Key adverse event(s) related to dental treatment: Xerostomia (normal salivary flow resumes upon discontinuation), dry throat, abnormal taste, and herpes simplex. Localized infections with *Candida albicans* or *Aspergillus niger* have occurred frequently in the mouth and pharynx with repetitive use of oral inhaler of corticosteroids. These infections may require treatment with appropriate antifungal therapy or discontinuance of treatment with corticosteroid inhaler.

Effects on Bleeding Variable effects on anticoagulant therapy are observed with glucocorticoids such as budesonide (systemic, oral inhalation).

Adverse Reactions

Frequencies are for both formulations unless otherwise indicated.

>10%:

Otic: Otitis media (suspension: 12%; powder: 1%)

Respiratory: Respiratory infection (suspension: 38%; powder: ≥3%), rhinitis (5% to 12%)

1% to 10%:

Cardiovascular: Syncope (powder: 1% to 3%), chest pain (suspension: 1% to <3%)

Central nervous system: Headache (powder: ≥3%; suspension: <1%), pain (powder: ≥3%), hypertonia (powder: 1% to 3%), insomnia (powder: 1% to 3%), voice disorder (powder: 1% to 3%), emotional lability (suspension: 1% to <3%), fatigue (suspension: 1% to <3%)

Dermatologic: Skin rash (suspension: 4%; powder: <1%), contact dermatitis (suspension: 1% to <3%), eczema (suspension: 1% to <3%), pruritus (suspension: 1% to <3%), pustular rash (suspension: 1% to <3%)

Endocrine & metabolic: Weight gain (1% to 3%)

Gastrointestinal: Dyspepsia (≥5%), nausea (2% to ≥5%), gastroenteritis (suspension: 5%), diarrhea (suspension: 4%), vomiting (1% to 4%), abdominal pain (1% to 3%), dysgeusia (powder: 1% to 3%), xerostomia (powder: 1% to 3%), anorexia (suspension: 1% to <3%), viral gastroenteritis (powder: 2%), oral candidiasis (powder: 1%)

Hematologic & oncologic: Ecchymosis (powder: 1% to 3%), cervical lymphadenopathy (suspension: 1% to <3%), purpura (suspension: 1% to <3%)

Hypersensitivity: Hypersensitivity reaction (1% to <3%)

Infection: Candidiasis (suspension: 4% to 5%), viral infection (suspension: 4% to 5%), infection (1% to 3%), herpes simplex infection (suspension: 1% to <3%)

Neuromuscular & skeletal: Arthralgia (≥5%), weakness (≥5%), back pain (powder: ≥3%), bone fracture (1% to 3%), myalgia (1% to 3%), neck pain (powder: 1% to 3%), hyperkinesia (suspension: 1% to <3%)

Ophthalmic: Conjunctivitis (suspension: 4%), eye infection (suspension: 1% to <3%)

Otic: Otic infection (suspension: 5%), otalgia (suspension: 1% to <3%), otitis externa (suspension: 1% to <3%)

Respiratory: Nasopharyngitis (powder: 9%), cough (5% to 9%), epistaxis (suspension: 2% to 4%), respiratory tract infection (powder: ≥3%), sinusitis (powder: ≥3%; suspension: <1%), nasal congestion (powder: 3%), pharyngitis (powder: 3%; suspension: <1%), flu-like symptoms (suspension: 1% to <3%), stridor (suspension: 1% to <3%), allergic rhinitis (powder: 2%), viral upper respiratory tract infection (powder: 2%)

Miscellaneous: Fever (≥3%)

Postmarketing and/or case reports: Adrenocortical insufficiency, aggressive behavior, anxiety, avascular necrosis of femoral head, bronchitis, bruise, cataract, depression, glaucoma, growth suppression, hypercorticoidism, increased intraocular pressure, irritability, nervousness, osteoporosis, pain, psychosis, restlessness, skin irritation (facial), throat irritation, wheezing

Dosing

Adult & Geriatric

Asthma: Oral inhalation: Titrate to lowest effective dose once patient is stable.

Pulmicort Flexhaler: Initial: 360 mcg twice daily (selected patients may be initiated at 180 mcg twice daily); maximum: 720 mcg twice daily; **Note:** May increase dose after 1 to 2 weeks of therapy in patients who are not adequately controlled

Pulmicort Turbuhaler [Canadian product]:

Initial (or during periods of severe asthma or when switching from oral corticosteroid therapy): 400 to 2,400 mcg daily in 2 to 4 divided doses

Maintenance: 200 to 400 mcg twice daily (higher doses may be needed for some patients). Patients taking 400 mcg/day may take as a single daily dose.

Asthma guidelines:

National Asthma Education and Prevention Program guidelines (NAEPP 2007): Dry powder inhaler (refers to the Pulmicort Flexhaler available in US). **Note:** Administer in divided doses twice daily.

"Low" dose: 180 to 600 mcg/day

"Medium" dose: >600 to 1,200 mcg/day

"High" dose: >1,200 mcg/day

Global Initiative for Asthma guidelines (GINA 2016): Dry powder inhaler (refers to the Pulmicort Turbuhaler available in Canada):

"Low" dose: 200 to 400 mcg daily

"Medium" dose: >400 to 800 mcg daily

"High" dose: >800 mcg daily

Conversion: *Conversion from oral systemic corticosteroid to orally inhaled corticosteroid:* Initiation of oral inhalation therapy should begin in patients whose asthma is reasonably stabilized on oral corticosteroids (OCS). A gradual dose reduction of OCS should begin ~7 to 10 days after starting inhaled therapy. The manufacturer labeling recommends reducing prednisone dose by 2.5 mg/day (or equivalent of other OCS) on a weekly basis (patients using oral inhaler) or by ≤25% every 1 to 2 weeks (patients using respules). **Note:** When transitioning from systemic to inhaled corticosteroids, supplemental systemic corticosteroid therapy may be necessary during periods of stress or during severe asthma attacks.

Chronic obstructive pulmonary disease (acute exacerbation) (off-label use): Nebulization: 2 mg every 6 hours (Maltais 2002)

Chronic obstructive pulmonary disease (stable) (off-label use): Oral inhalation: 100 to 400 mcg daily in combination with a long-acting bronchodilator (COLD 2014)

Eosinophilic esophagitis (off-label use): Oral: 2 mg/day as an oral budesonide viscous liquid/suspension. Dose may be divided into 2 doses. Avoid ingesting any solid or liquid food for 30 minutes after budesonide administration. (Dellon 2013; Dohil 2010; Liacouras 2011; Rubinstein 2014).

Pediatric

Asthma: Titrate to lowest effective dose once patient is stable.

Oral inhalation:

Pulmicort Flexhaler: Children ≥6 years: Initial: 180 mcg twice daily (some patients may be initiated at 360 mcg twice daily); maximum: 360 mcg twice daily; **Note:** May increase dose after 1 to 2 weeks of therapy in patients who are not adequately controlled.

Pulmicort Turbuhaler [Canadian product]:

Children 6 to 11 years:

Initial (or during periods of severe asthma or when switching from oral corticosteroid therapy): 200 to 400 mcg daily in 2 divided doses

Maintenance: Individualized, lowest effective dose in 2 divided doses

Children ≥12 years: Refer to adult dosing.

Asthma guidelines:

National Asthma Education and Prevention Program guidelines (NAEPP 2007): Dry powder inhaler (refers to the Pulmicort Flexhaler available in US). **Note:** Administer in divided doses twice daily.

Children 5 to 11 years:

"Low" dose: 180 to 400 mcg/day

"Medium" dose: >400 to 800 mcg/day

"High" dose: >800 mcg/day

Children ≥12 years and Adolescents: Refer to adult dosing.

Global Initiative for Asthma guidelines (GINA 2016): Dry powder inhaler (refers to the Pulmicort Turbuhaler available in Canada):

Children 6 to 11 years:

"Low" dose: 100 to 200 mcg daily

"Medium" dose: >200 to 400 mcg daily

"High" dose: >400 mcg daily

Children ≥12 years and Adolescents: Refer to adult dosing.

Conversion: *Conversion from oral systemic corticosteroid to orally inhaled corticosteroid:* Initiation of oral inhalation therapy should begin in patients whose asthma is reasonably stabilized on oral corticosteroids (OCS). A gradual dose reduction of OCS should begin ~7 to 10 days after starting inhaled therapy. The manufacturer labeling recommends reducing prednisone dose by 2.5 mg/day (or equivalent of other OCS) on a weekly basis (patients using oral inhaler) or by ≤25% every 1 to 2 weeks (patients using respules). **Note:** When transitioning from systemic to inhaled corticosteroids, supplemental systemic corticosteroid therapy may be necessary during periods of stress or during severe asthma attacks.

Nebulization: Pulmicort Respules: Children 12 months to 8 years: Titrate to lowest effective dose once patient is stable; start at 0.25 mg/day or use as follows:

Previous therapy of bronchodilators alone: 0.5 mg/day administered as a single dose or divided twice daily (maximum daily dose: 0.5 mg)

Previous therapy of inhaled corticosteroids: 0.5 mg/day administered as a single dose or divided twice daily (maximum daily dose: 1 mg)

Previous therapy of oral corticosteroids: 1 mg/day administered as a single dose or divided twice daily (maximum daily dose: 1 mg)

Asthma guidelines:

National Asthma Education and Prevention Program guidelines (NAEPP 2007):

Children 0 to 4 years:

"Low" dose: 0.25 to 0.5 mg/day

"Medium" dose: >0.5 to 1 mg/day

"High" dose: >1 mg/day

Children 5 to 11 years:

"Low" dose: 0.5 mg/day

"Medium" dose: 1 mg/day

"High" dose: 2 mg/day

Global Initiative for Asthma guidelines (GINA 2016):

Children ≤5 years: "Low" dose: 0.5 mg daily

Children 6 to 11 years:

"Low" dose: 0.25 to 0.5 mg daily

"Medium" dose: >0.5 to 1 mg daily

"High" dose: >1 mg daily

Oral: Eosinophilic esophagitis (off-label use):

Children ≥10 years of age or ≥5 ft in height: 2 mg/day as an oral budesonide viscous liquid/suspension. Dose may be divided into 2 doses. Avoid ingesting any solid or liquid food for 30 minutes after budesonide administration. (Dellon 2013; Dohil 2010; Liacouras 2011; Rubinstein 2014).

Children <10 years or <5 ft in height: 1 mg/day as an oral budesonide viscous liquid/suspension. Avoid ingesting any solid or liquid food for 30 minutes after budesonide administration. (Dellon 2013; Dohil 2010; Liacouras 2011; Rubinstein 2014).

Renal Impairment There are no dosage adjustments provided in the manufacturer's labeling (has not been studied).

Hepatic Impairment There are no dosage adjustments provided in the manufacturer's labeling (has not been studied). However, budesonide undergoes hepatic metabolism; drug may accumulate with hepatic impairment; use with caution; monitor closely for signs and symptoms of hypercorticism.

Mechanism of Action Controls the rate of protein synthesis; depresses the migration of polymorphonuclear leukocytes, fibroblasts; reverses capillary permeability and lysosomal stabilization at the cellular level to prevent or control inflammation. Has potent glucocorticoid activity and weak mineralocorticoid activity.

Contraindications

Hypersensitivity to budesonide or any component of the formulation; severe hypersensitivity to milk proteins (Pulmicort Flexhaler); primary treatment of status asthmaticus or other acute episodes of asthma requiring intensive measures

Canadian labeling: Additional contraindications (not in US labeling): Moderate-to-severe bronchiectasis, pulmonary tuberculosis (active or quiescent), untreated respiratory infection (bacterial, fungal, or viral)

Warnings/Precautions May cause hypercorticism or suppression of hypothalamic-pituitary-adrenal (HPA) axis, particularly in younger children, in patients receiving high doses for prolonged periods, or with concomitant CYP3A4 inhibitor use. HPA axis suppression may lead to adrenal crisis. Withdrawal and discontinuation of a corticosteroid should be done slowly and carefully. Particular care is required when patients are transferred from systemic corticosteroids to inhaled products or corticosteroids with lower systemic effect due to possible adrenal insufficiency or withdrawal from steroids, including an increase in allergic symptoms. Adult patients receiving >20 mg per day of prednisone (or equivalent) may be most susceptible. Fatalities have occurred due to adrenal insufficiency in asthmatic patients during and after transfer from systemic corticosteroids to aerosol steroids; aerosol steroids do not provide the systemic steroid needed to treat patients having trauma, surgery, or infections. Do not use this product to transfer patients directly from oral corticosteroid therapy. Select surgical patients on long-term, high-dose, inhaled corticosteroid (ICS), should be given stress doses of hydrocortisone intravenously during the surgical period and the dose reduced rapidly within 24 hours after surgery (NAEPP 2007). Rare cases of vasculitis (Churg-Strauss syndrome) or other systemic eosinophilic conditions can occur; often associated with decrease and/or withdrawal of oral corticosteroid therapy following initiation of inhaled corticosteroid.

Bronchospasm may occur with wheezing after inhalation; if this occurs stop steroid and treat with a fast-acting bronchodilator (eg, albuterol). Supplemental steroids (oral or parenteral) may be needed during stress or severe asthma attacks. Not to be used in status asthmaticus or for the relief of acute bronchospasm. Acute myopathy has been reported with high-dose corticosteroids, usually in patients with neuromuscular transmission disorders; may involve ocular and/or respiratory muscles; monitor creatine kinase; recovery may be delayed. Corticosteroid use may cause psychiatric disturbances, including depression, euphoria, insomnia, mood swings, and personality changes. Preexisting psychiatric conditions may be exacerbated by corticosteroid use. Prolonged use of corticosteroids may also increase the incidence of secondary infection, mask acute infection (including fungal infections), prolong or exacerbate viral infections, or limit response to vaccines. Exposure to chickenpox should be avoided; corticosteroids should not be used to treat ocular herpes simplex. Corticosteroids should not be used for viral hepatitis. Close observation is required in patients with latent tuberculosis and/or TB reactivity; restrict use in active TB (only in conjunction with antituberculosis treatment). *Candida albicans* infections may occur in the mouth and pharynx; rinsing (and spitting) with water after inhaler use may decrease risk. Prolonged treatment with corticosteroids has been associated with the development of Kaposi sarcoma (case reports); if noted, discontinuation of therapy should be considered.

Use with caution in patients with thyroid disease, hepatic impairment, cardiovascular disease, diabetes, glaucoma, cataracts, myasthenia gravis, patients at risk for osteoporosis, patients at risk for seizures, or GI diseases (diverticulitis, peptic ulcer, ulcerative colitis) due to perforation risk. Use caution following acute MI (corticosteroids have been associated with myocardial rupture).

Potentially significant interactions may exist, requiring dose or frequency adjustment, additional monitoring, and/or selection of alternative therapy.

Orally-inhaled corticosteroids may cause a reduction in growth velocity in pediatric patients (~1 centimeter per year [range: 0.3 to 1.8 cm per year] and related to dose and duration of exposure). To minimize the systemic effects of orally-inhaled corticosteroids, each patient should be titrated to the lowest effective dose. Growth should be routinely monitored in pediatric patients. Withdraw systemic therapy with gradual tapering of dose. There have been reports of systemic corticosteroid withdrawal symptoms (eg, joint/muscle pain, lassitude, depression) when withdrawing oral inhalation therapy. Pulmicort Flexhaler contains lactose; very rare anaphylactic reactions have been reported in patients with severe milk protein allergy. Some dosage forms may contain polysorbate 80 (also known as Tweens). Hypersensitivity reactions, usually a delayed reaction, have been reported following exposure to pharmaceutical products containing polysorbate 80 in certain individuals (Isaksson 2002; Lucente 2000; Shelley 1995). Thrombocytopenia, ascites, pulmonary deterioration, and renal and hepatic failure have been reported in premature neonates after receiving parenteral products containing polysorbate 80 (Alade 1986; CDC 1984). See manufacturer's labeling.

Drug Interactions

Metabolism/Transport Effects None known.

Avoid Concomitant Use

Avoid concomitant use of Budesonide (Oral Inhalation) with any of the following: Aldesleukin; Desmopressin; Loxapine

Increased Effect/Toxicity

Budesonide (Oral Inhalation) may increase the levels/effects of: Amphotericin B; Ceritinib; Deferasirox; Desmopressin; Loop Diuretics; Loxapine; Thiazide and Thiazide-Like Diuretics

The levels/effects of Budesonide (Oral Inhalation) may be increased by: CYP3A4 Inhibitors (Strong); Telaprevir

Decreased Effect

Budesonide (Oral Inhalation) may decrease the levels/effects of: Aldesleukin; Corticorelin; Hyaluronidase

Pharmacodynamics/Kinetics

Onset of Action Nebulization: 2 to 8 days; Inhalation: 24 hours

Peak effect: Nebulization: 4 to 6 weeks; Inhalation: 1 to 2 weeks

Half-life Elimination

Children 4 to 6 years: 2.3 hours (after nebulization)

Children and Adolescents 10 to 14 years: 1.5 hours

Adults: 2 to 3.6 hours

Time to Peak

Nebulization: Pulmicort Respules: Children: 20 minutes

Oral inhalation: Pulmicort Flexhaler:

Children and Adolescents: 15 to 30 minutes

Adults: 10 minutes

Pregnancy Risk Factor B (inhalation)

Pregnancy Considerations Adverse events have been observed with corticosteroids in animal reproduction studies. Some studies have shown an association between first trimester systemic corticosteroid use and oral clefts (Park-Wyllie 2000; Pradat 2003). Systemic corticosteroids may also influence fetal growth (decreased birth weight); however, information is conflicting (Lunghi 2010). Hypoadrenalism may occur in newborns following maternal use of corticosteroids in pregnancy; monitor. When systemic corticosteroids are needed in pregnancy, it is generally recommended to use the lowest effective dose for the shortest duration of time, avoiding high doses during the first trimester (Leachman 2006; Lunghi 2010). Budesonide may be used for the induction of remission in pregnant women with inflammatory bowel disease (Habal 2012).

Based on available data, an overall increased risk of congenital malformations or a decrease in fetal growth has not been associated with maternal use of inhaled corticosteroids during pregnancy (Bakhireva 2005; NAEPP 2005; Namazy 2004). In addition, studies of pregnant women specifically using inhaled budesonide have not demonstrated an increased risk of congenital abnormalities. Uncontrolled asthma is associated with adverse events on pregnancy (increased risk of perinatal mortality, pre-eclampsia, preterm birth, low birth weight infants). Inhaled corticosteroids are recommended for the treatment of asthma during pregnancy; budesonide is preferred (ACOG 2008; NAEPP 2005).

Breastfeeding Considerations Following use of the powder for oral inhalation, ~0.3% to 1% of the maternal dose was found in breast milk. The maximum concentration appeared within 45 minutes of dosing. Plasma budesonide levels obtained from infants ~90 minutes after breastfeeding (~140 minutes after maternal dose) were below the limit of quantification. Concentrations of budesonide in breast milk are expected to be higher following administration of oral capsules/tablets than after an inhaled dose.

According to the manufacturer of the product for inhalation, the decision to continue or discontinue breastfeeding during therapy should take into account the risk of minimal exposure to the infant and the benefits of breastfeeding to the mother. The use of inhaled corticosteroids is not considered a contraindication to breastfeeding (NAEPP 2005).

Dosage Forms Considerations

Pulmicort Flexhaler 180 mcg/actuation canisters contain 120 actuations and the 90 mcg/actuation canisters contain 60 inhalations.

Dosage Forms

Aerosol Powder Breath Activated, Inhalation:

Pulmicort Flexhaler: 90 mcg/actuation (1 ea); 180 mcg/actuation (1 ea)

Suspension, Inhalation:

Pulmicort: 0.25 mg/2 mL (2 mL); 0.5 mg/2 mL (2 mL); 1 mg/2 mL (2 mL)

Generic: 0.25 mg/2 mL (2 mL); 0.5 mg/2 mL (2 mL); 1 mg/2 mL (2 mL)

Dosage Forms: Canada

Powder for oral inhalation:

Pulmicort Turbuhaler: 100 mcg/inhalation, 200 mcg/inhalation, 400 mcg/inhalation

Budesonide (Topical) (byoo DES oh nide)

Brand Names: US Uceris

Brand Names: Canada Entocort Enema

Pharmacologic Category Corticosteroid, Rectal

Use

Ulcerative colitis: Remission induction in patients with active mild to moderate distal ulcerative colitis extending up to 40 cm from the anal verge

Entocort Enema [Canadian product]: Management of distal ulcerative colitis (rectum, sigmoid, and descending colon)

Local Anesthetic/Vasoconstrictor Precautions No information available to require special precautions

Effects on Dental Treatment No significant effects or complications reported

Effects on Bleeding No information available to require special precautions

Adverse Reactions Frequency not always defined.

>10%: Endocrine & metabolic: Decreased plasma cortisol (17%)

1% to 10%:

Endocrine & metabolic: Adrenocortical insufficiency (4%), hpa-axis suppression, hypercorticism

Gastrointestinal: Nausea (2%)

<1%, postmarketing, and/or case reports: Acne vulgaris, adrenal cortex hypofunction, agitation, allergic dermatitis, anaphylaxis, anxiety, depression, diarrhea, dizziness, drowsiness, dysphoria, emotional lability, exacerbation of diabetes mellitus, fever, flatulence, hyperacidity (peptic ulcer), hyperglycemia, hypertension, insomnia, maculopapular rash, pancreatitis, peripheral edema, pruritus, pseudotumor cerebri, skin rash, sleep disorder, urticaria

General Dosage Range Rectal: *Adults:* Initial: 2 mg (one metered dose) 2 times/day for 2 weeks; Maintenance: 2 mg (one metered dose) once daily for 4 weeks

Mechanism of Action Controls the rate of protein synthesis; depresses the migration of polymorphonuclear leukocytes, fibroblasts; reverses capillary permeability and lysosomal stabilization at the cellular level to prevent or control inflammation. Has potent glucocorticoid activity and weak mineralocorticoid activity.

Pharmacodynamics/Kinetics

Half-life Elimination Rectal enema [Canadian product]: 2 to 3 hours

Time to Peak Rectal enema [Canadian product]: 1.5 hours

Pregnancy Risk Factor C

Pregnancy Considerations Adverse events were observed in some animal reproduction studies. Hypoadrenalism may occur in newborns following maternal use of corticosteroids in pregnancy; monitor. Oral budesonide has been used for the induction of remission in pregnant women with inflammatory bowel disease (Habal, 2012).

Budesonide and Formoterol

(byoo DES oh nide & for MOH te rol)

Related Information

Budesonide (Oral Inhalation) *on page 246*
Formoterol *on page 767*

Brand Names: US Symbicort

Brand Names: Canada Symbicort

Pharmacologic Category Beta$_2$ Agonist; Beta$_2$-Adrenergic Agonist, Long-Acting; Corticosteroid, Inhalant (Oral)

Use Treatment of asthma in patients ≥12 years of age where combination therapy is indicated; maintenance treatment of airflow obstruction associated with chronic obstructive pulmonary disease (COPD; including chronic bronchitis and emphysema)

Local Anesthetic/Vasoconstrictor Precautions No information available to require special precautions

Effects on Dental Treatment Key adverse event(s) related to dental treatment: Formoterol: Xerostomia (normal salivary flow resumes upon discontinuation). Localized infections with *Candida albicans* or *Aspergillus niger* have occurred frequently in the mouth and pharynx with repetitive use of oral inhaler of corticosteroids. These infections may require treatment with appropriate antifungal therapy or discontinuance of treatment with corticosteroid inhaler.

Effects on Bleeding No information available to require special precautions

Adverse Reactions Note: Percentage of adverse events may be dose related; causation not established. Also see individual agents.

>10%:

Central nervous system: Headache (7% to 11%)

Respiratory: Nasopharyngitis (7% to 11%), upper respiratory tract infection (4% to 11%)

1% to 10%:

Central nervous system: Dizziness (<3%)

Gastrointestinal: Abdominal distress (1% to 7%), oral candidiasis (1% to 6%), vomiting (1% to 3%)

Infection: Influenza (2% to 3%)

Neuromuscular & skeletal: Back pain (2% to 3%)

Respiratory: Pharyngolaryngeal pain (6% to 9%), lower respiratory tract infection (3% to 8%), sinusitis (4% to 6%), bronchitis (5%), nasal congestion (3%)

<1%, postmarketing, and/or case reports: Agitation, anaphylaxis, angina pectoris, angioedema, anxiety, atrial arrhythmia, behavioral changes, bronchospasm, bruise, cataract, cough, decreased linear skeletal growth rate (pediatric patients), depression, dermatitis, extrasystoles, glaucoma, hypercorticoidism signs and symptoms, hyperglycemia, hypersensitivity reaction, hypertension, hypokalemia, hypotension, immunosuppression, increased intraocular pressure, insomnia, muscle cramps, nausea, nervousness, palpitations, pruritus, restlessness, skin rash, tachycardia, throat irritation, tremor, urticaria, ventricular arrhythmia, voice disorder

General Dosage Range Inhalation:

Children ≥12 years: 2 inhalations once or twice daily (maximum: 4 inhalations/day)

Adults: 2 inhalations twice daily (maximum: 4 inhalations/day)

Mechanism of Action Formoterol relaxes bronchial smooth muscle by selective action on beta$_2$ receptors with little effect on heart rate. Formoterol has a long-acting effect. Budesonide is a corticosteroid which controls the rate of protein synthesis, depresses the migration of polymorphonuclear leukocytes/fibroblasts, and reverses capillary permeability and lysosomal stabilization at the cellular level to prevent or control inflammation.

Pharmacodynamics/Kinetics

Onset of Action Asthma: 15 minutes; maximum benefit: May take ≥2 weeks

Pregnancy Risk Factor C

Pregnancy Considerations Adverse events were observed in animal reproduction studies using this combination. Refer to individual agents.

Bumetanide (byoo MET a nide)

Related Information

Cardiovascular Diseases *on page 1752*

Brand Names: US Bumex

Brand Names: Canada Burinex

Pharmacologic Category Antihypertensive; Diuretic, Loop

Use Management of edema secondary to heart failure or hepatic or renal disease (including nephrotic syndrome)

Local Anesthetic/Vasoconstrictor Precautions No information available to require special precautions

Effects on Dental Treatment No significant effects or complications reported

Effects on Bleeding No information available to require special precautions

Adverse Reactions

>10%:

Endocrine & metabolic: Hyperuricemia (18%), hypochloremia (15%), hypokalemia (15%)

Genitourinary: Azotemia (11%)

1% to 10%:

Central nervous system: Dizziness (1%)

Endocrine & metabolic: Hyponatremia (9%), hyperglycemia (7%), phosphorus change (5%), variations in bicarbonate (3%), abnormal serum calcium (2%), abnormal lactate dehydrogenase (1%)

Neuromuscular & skeletal: Muscle cramps (1%)

Renal: Increased serum creatinine (7%)

Respiratory: Variations in CO_2 content (4%)

<1%, postmarketing, and/or case reports: Abdominal pain, abnormal alkaline phosphatase, abnormal bilirubin levels, abnormal hematocrit, abnormal hemoglobin level, abnormal transaminase, arthritic pain, asterixis, auditory impairment, blood cholesterol abnormal, brain disease (in patients with preexisting liver disease), change in creatinine clearance, change in prothrombin time, change in WBC count, chest pain, dehydration, diaphoresis, diarrhea, dyspepsia, ECG changes, erectile dysfunction, fatigue, glycosuria, headache, hyperventilation, hypotension, musculoskeletal pain, nausea, nipple tenderness, orthostatic hypotension, otalgia, ototoxicity, premature ejaculation, proteinuria, pruritus, renal failure, skin rash, Stevens-Johnson syndrome, thrombocytopenia, toxic epidermal necrolysis, urticaria, vertigo, vomiting, weakness, xerostomia

General Dosage Range

IM, IV:

Infants and Children: 0.015 to 0.1 mg/kg/dose every 6 to 24 hours (maximum: 10 mg/day)

Adults: 0.5 to 1 mg/dose; may repeat in 2 to 3 hours for up to 2 doses (maximum: 10 mg/day)

Oral:

Infants and Children: 0.015 to 0.1 mg/kg/dose every 6 to 24 hours (maximum: 10 mg/day)

Adults: 0.5 to 2 mg 1 to 2 times daily; may repeat in 4 to 5 hours for up to 2 doses (maximum: 10 mg/day)

Mechanism of Action Inhibits reabsorption of sodium and chloride in the ascending loop of Henle and proximal renal tubule, interfering with the chloride-binding cotransport system, thus causing increased excretion of water, sodium, chloride, magnesium, phosphate, and calcium; it does not appear to act on the distal tubule

Pharmacodynamics/Kinetics

Onset of Action Oral, IM: 0.5 to 1 hour; IV: 2 to 3 minutes

Peak effect: Oral: 1 to 2 hours; IV: 15 to 30 minutes

Duration of Action Oral: 4 to 6 hours; IV: 2 to 3 hours

Half-life Elimination

Premature and full term neonates: 6 hours (range up to 15 hours)

Infants <2 months: 2.5 hours

Infants 2 to 6 months: 1.5 hours

Adults: 1 to 1.5 hours

Pregnancy Risk Factor C

Pregnancy Considerations Adverse events have been observed in some animal reproduction studies.

Bupivacaine (byoo PIV a kane)

Related Information

Oral Pain *on page 1830*

Brand Names: US Bupivacaine Spinal; Marcaine; Marcaine Preservative Free; Marcaine Spinal; ReadySharp Bupivacaine; Sensorcaine; Sensorcaine-MPF; Sensorcaine-MPF Spinal

Brand Names: Canada Marcaine®; Sensorcaine®

Pharmacologic Category Local Anesthetic

Use Local or regional anesthesia; spinal anesthesia (0.75% in dextrose 8.25% injection); diagnostic and therapeutic procedures; obstetrical procedures (only 0.25% and 0.5% concentrations)

0.25%: Local infiltration, peripheral nerve block, sympathetic block, caudal or epidural block

0.5%: Peripheral nerve block, caudal and epidural block

0.75% **(not for obstetrical anesthesia)**: Retrobulbar block, epidural block. **Note:** Reserve for surgical procedures where a high degree of muscle relaxation and prolonged effect are necessary

Local Anesthetic/Vasoconstrictor Precautions No information available to require special precautions

Effects on Dental Treatment No significant effects or complications reported

Effects on Bleeding No information available to require special precautions

Adverse Reactions Note: Incidence of adverse reactions is difficult to define. Most effects are dose related, and are often due to accelerated absorption from the injection site, unintentional intravascular injection, or slow metabolic degradation. The development of any central nervous system symptoms may be an early indication of more significant toxicity (seizure).

Cardiovascular: Bradycardia, cardiac arrest, heart block, hypotension, palpitations, ventricular arrhythmia

Central nervous system: Anxiety, dizziness, restlessness

Gastrointestinal: Nausea, vomiting

Hypersensitivity: Anaphylactoid reaction, hypersensitivity reaction (urticaria, pruritus, angioedema)

Neuromuscular & skeletal: Chondrolysis (continuous intra-articular administration), weakness

Ophthalmic: Blurred vision, miosis

Otic: Tinnitus

Respiratory: Apnea, hypoventilation (usually associated with unintentional subarachnoid injection during high spinal anesthesia)

<1%, postmarketing, and/or case reports: Seizure; usually associated with unintentional subarachnoid injection during high spinal anesthesia: cranial nerve palsy, fecal incontinence, headache, loss of anal sphincter control, loss of perineal sensation, paralysis, paresthesia, persistent anesthesia, septic meningitis, sexual disorder (loss of function), urinary incontinence

General Dosage Range

Caudal block: *Children >12 years and Adults:* 15-30 mL of 0.25% or 0.5%

Epidural block: *Children >12 years and Adults:* 10-20 mL of 0.25% or 0.5% in 3-5 mL increments **or** 10-20 mL of 0.75% if high degree of muscle relaxation and prolonged effects needed

Infiltration (local): *Children >12 years and Adults:* 0.25% (maximum: 175 mg)

Nerve block: *Children >12 years and Adults:*

Peripheral: 5 mL of 0.25% or 0.5% (maximum: 400 mg/day)

Sympathetic: 20-50 mL of 0.25%

Retrobulbar anesthesia: *Children >12 years and Adults:* 2-4 mL of 0.75%

Spinal: *Adults:* Preservative free solution of 0.75% bupivacaine in 8.25% dextrose:

Cesarean section: 1-1.4 mL

Lower abdominal procedures: 1.6 mL

Lower extremity and perineal procedures: 1 mL

Normal vaginal delivery: 0.8 mL (higher doses may be required in some patients)

Mechanism of Action Blocks both the initiation and conduction of nerve impulses by decreasing the neuronal membrane's permeability to sodium ions, which results in inhibition of depolarization with resultant blockade of conduction

Pharmacodynamics/Kinetics

Onset of Action Anesthesia (route and dose dependent):

Epidural: Up to 17 minutes to spread to T6 dermatome (Scott 1980)

Infiltration: Fast (Barash 2009); Dental injection: 2 to 10 minutes

Spinal: Within 1 minute; maximum dermatome level achieved within 15 minutes in most cases

Duration of Action Route and dose dependent:

Epidural: 2 to 7.7 hours (Barash 2009)

Infiltration: 2 to 8 hours (Barash 2009); Dental injection: Up to 7 hours

Spinal: 1.5 to 2.5 hours (Hadzic 2007)

Half-life Elimination Age dependent: Neonates: 8.1 hours; Adults: 2.7 hours

Time to Peak Plasma: Caudal, epidural, or peripheral nerve block: 30 to 45 minutes

Pregnancy Risk Factor C

Pregnancy Considerations Adverse events were observed in animal reproduction studies. Bupivacaine crosses the placenta. Bupivacaine is approved for use at term in obstetrical anesthesia or analgesia. **[U.S. Boxed Warning]: The 0.75% is not recommended for obstetrical anesthesia.** Bupivacaine 0.75% solutions have been associated with cardiac arrest following epidural anesthesia in obstetrical patients and use of this concentration is not recommended for this purpose.

Use in obstetrical paracervical block anesthesia is contraindicated.

Bupivacaine and Epinephrine

(byoo PIV a kane & ep i NEF rin)

Related Information

Bupivacaine *on page 251*
EPINEPHrine (Systemic) *on page 580*
Oral Pain *on page 1830*

Brand Names: US Marcaine® with Epinephrine; Sensorcaine® with Epinephrine; Sensorcaine®-MPF with Epinephrine; Vivacaine™

Brand Names: Canada Sensorcaine® with Epinephrine

Generic Availability (US) Yes

Pharmacologic Category Local Anesthetic

Dental Use Local anesthesia

Use Local anesthetic (injectable) for peripheral nerve block, infiltration, sympathetic block, caudal or epidural block, retrobulbar block

Local Anesthetic/Vasoconstrictor Precautions No information available to require special precautions

Effects on Dental Treatment It is common to misinterpret psychogenic responses to local anesthetic injection as an allergic reaction. Intraoral injections are perceived by many patients as a stressful procedure in dentistry. Common symptoms to this stress are diaphoresis, palpitations, and hyperventilation. Patients may exhibit hypersensitivity to bisulfites contained in local anesthetic solution to prevent oxidation of epinephrine. In general, patients reacting to bisulfites have a history of asthma and their airways are hyper-reactive to asthmatic syndrome.

Degree of adverse effects in the CNS and cardiovascular system is directly related to the blood levels of bupivacaine: Bradycardia, hypersensitivity reactions (rare; may be manifest as dermatologic reactions and edema at injection site), asthmatic syndromes.

High blood levels: Anxiety, restlessness, disorientation, confusion, dizziness, tremors, seizures, CNS depression (resulting in somnolence, unconsciousness and possible respiratory arrest), nausea, and vomiting.

Effects on Bleeding No information available to require special precautions

Adverse Reactions See individual agents.

Dental Usual Dosage

Infiltration and nerve block in maxillary and mandibular area: Children >12 years and Adults: 9 mg (1.8 mL) of bupivacaine as a 0.5% solution with epinephrine 1:200,000 per injection site. A second dose may be administered if necessary to produce adequate anesthesia after allowing up to 10 minutes for onset. Up to a maximum of 90 mg of bupivacaine hydrochloride per dental appointment. The effective anesthetic dose varies with procedure, intensity of anesthesia needed, duration of anesthesia required, and physical condition of the patient; always use the lowest effective dose along with careful aspiration.

The following numbers of dental carpules (1.8 mL) provide the indicated amounts of bupivacaine hydrochloride 0.5% and vasoconstrictor (epinephrine 1:200,000). See table.

# of Cartridges (1.8 mL)	mg Bupivacaine (0.5%)	mg Vasoconstrictor (Epinephrine 1:200,000)
1	9	0.009
2	18	0.018
3	27	0.027
4	36	0.036
5	45	0.045
6	54	0.054
7	63	0.063
8	72	0.072
9	81	0.081
10	90	0.090

Note: Adult and children doses of bupivacaine hydrochloride with epinephrine cited from USP Dispensing Information (USP DI), 17th ed, The United States Pharmacopeial Convention, Inc, Rockville, MD, 1997, 134.

Dosing

Adult & Geriatric Dose varies with procedure, depth of anesthesia, vascularity of tissues, duration of anesthesia, and condition of patient. Do not use solutions containing preservatives for caudal or epidural block.

Caudal block (preservative free): 15-30 mL of 0.25% or 0.5%

Epidural block (other than caudal block, preservative free): 10-20 mL of 0.25% or 0.5%. Administer in 3-5 mL increments, allowing sufficient time to detect toxic manifestations of inadvertent IV or intrathecal administration.

Surgical procedures requiring a high degree of muscle relaxation and prolonged effects only: 10-20 mL of 0.75% (**Note:** Not to be used in obstetrical cases)

Local anesthesia: Infiltration: 0.25% infiltrated locally (maximum: 175 mg of bupivacaine)

Peripheral nerve block: 5 mL of 0.25% or 0.5% (maximum: 400 mg/day of bupivacaine)

Retrobulbar anesthesia: 2-4 mL of 0.75%

Sympathetic nerve block: 20-50 mL of 0.25%

Infiltration and nerve block in maxillary and mandibular area: 9 mg (1.8 mL) of bupivacaine as a 0.5% solution with epinephrine 1:200,000 per injection site. A second dose may be administered if necessary to produce adequate anesthesia after allowing up to 10 minutes for onset. Up to a maximum of 90 mg of bupivacaine hydrochloride per dental appointment. The effective anesthetic dose varies with procedure, intensity of anesthesia needed, duration of anesthesia required, and physical condition of the patient; always use the lowest effective dose along with careful aspiration.

Pediatric

Children >12 years: Refer to adult dosing.

Renal Impairment No dosage adjustments provided in manufacturer's labeling; use with caution.

Hepatic Impairment No dosage adjustments provided in manufacturer's labeling; use with caution.

Mechanism of Action Local anesthetics bind selectively to the intracellular surface of sodium channels to block influx of sodium into the axon. As a result, depolarization necessary for action potential propagation and subsequent nerve function is prevented. The block at the sodium channel is reversible. When drug diffuses away from the axon, sodium channel function is restored and nerve propagation returns.

Epinephrine prolongs the duration of the anesthetic actions of bupivacaine by causing vasoconstriction (alpha-adrenergic receptor agonist) of the vasculature surrounding the nerve axons. This prevents the diffusion of bupivacaine away from the nerves resulting in a longer retention in the axon

Contraindications Hypersensitivity to bupivacaine, epinephrine, amide-type local anesthetics, or any component of the formulation

Warnings/Precautions Some commercially available formulations contain sodium metabisulfite, which may cause allergic-type reactions. Do not use solutions containing preservatives for caudal or epidural block. Intravascular injections should be avoided. Local anesthetics have been associated with rare occurrences of sudden respiratory arrest. Convulsions due to systemic toxicity leading to cardiac arrest have also been reported, presumably following unintentional intravascular injection. **[U.S. Boxed Warning]: The 0.75% is not recommended for obstetrical anesthesia.** A test dose is recommended prior to epidural administration and all reinforcing doses with continuous catheter technique. Use caution with cardiovascular dysfunction, hepatic impairment, or patients with compromised blood supply. Bupivacaine-containing products have been associated with rare occurrences of arrhythmias, cardiac arrest, and death. Use caution in debilitated, elderly, or acutely ill patients; dose reduction may be required. Dental practitioners and/or clinicians using local anesthetic agents should be well trained in diagnosis and management of emergencies that may arise from the use of these agents. Resuscitative equipment, oxygen, and other resuscitative drugs should be available for immediate use. Not recommended for use in children <12 years of age.

Continuous intra-articular infusion of local anesthetics after arthroscopic or other surgical procedures is **not** an approved use; chondrolysis (primarily shoulder joint) has occurred following infusion, with some requiring arthroplasty or shoulder replacement.

Drug Interactions

Metabolism/Transport Effects Refer to individual components.

Avoid Concomitant Use

Avoid concomitant use of Bupivacaine and Epinephrine with any of the following: Blonanserin; Ergot Derivatives; Iobenguane I 123; Lurasidone

Increased Effect/Toxicity

Bupivacaine and Epinephrine may increase the levels/effects of: Amifostine; Antipsychotic Agents (Second Generation [Atypical]); Bupivacaine (Liposomal); Doxofylline; Hypotension-Associated Agents; Levodopa; Lurasidone; Neuromuscular-Blocking Agents; Nitroprusside; Sympathomimetics

The levels/effects of Bupivacaine and Epinephrine may be increased by: Alfuzosin; AtoMOXetine; Barbiturates; Beta-Blockers; Blood Pressure Lowering Agents; Brimonidine (Topical); Cannabinoid-Containing Products; Cocaine; COMT Inhibitors; Diazoxide; Ergot Derivatives; Herbs (Hypotensive Properties); Hyaluronidase; Inhalational Anesthetics; Linezolid; Lormetazepam; MAO Inhibitors; Molsidomine; Naftopidil; Nicergoline; Nicorandil; Obinutuzumab; Pentoxifylline; Phosphodiesterase 5 Inhibitors; Prostacyclin Analogues; Quinagolide; Serotonin/Norepinephrine Reuptake Inhibitors; Tedizolid; Tricyclic Antidepressants

Decreased Effect

Bupivacaine and Epinephrine may decrease the levels/effects of: Antidiabetic Agents; Benzylpenicilloyl Polylysine; Iobenguane I 123; Technetium Tc 99m Tilmanocept

The levels/effects of Bupivacaine and Epinephrine may be decreased by: Alpha1-Blockers; Benperidol; Blonanserin; CloZAPine; Promethazine; Spironolactone

Pregnancy Risk Factor C

Pregnancy Considerations See individual agents.

Dosage Forms

Injection, solution [preservative free]: Bupivacaine 0.25% and epinephrine 1:200,000 (10 mL, 30 mL); bupivacaine 0.5% and epinephrine 1:200,000 (10 mL, 30 mL)

Marcaine® with Epinephrine: Bupivacaine 0.25% and epinephrine 1:200,000 (10 mL, 30 mL); bupivacaine 0.5% and epinephrine 1:200,000 (10 mL, 30 mL)

Sensorcaine® MPF with Epinephrine: Bupivacaine 0.25% and epinephrine 1:200,000 (10 mL, 30 mL); bupivacaine 0.5% and epinephrine 1:200,000 (10 mL, 30 mL); bupivacaine 0.75% and epinephrine 1:200,000 (30 mL)

Injection, solution: Bupivacaine 0.25% and epinephrine 1:200,000 (50 mL); bupivacaine 0.5% and epinephrine 1:200,000 (50 mL)

Marcaine® with Epinephrine, Sensorcaine® with Epinephrine: Bupivacaine 0.25% and epinephrine 1.200,000 (50 mL); bupivacaine 0.5% and epinephrine 1:200,000 (50 mL)

Injection, solution [for dental use]:

Marcaine® with Epinephrine, Vivacaine™: Bupivacaine 0.5% and epinephrine 1:200,000 (1.8 mL)

Dental Comment A 2010 report, reviewed adverse events submitted voluntarily over a 10-year period involving the dental local anesthetics articaine, bupivacaine, lidocaine, mepivacaine, and prilocaine in the United States. Bupivacaine reported incidence: One case per 124,286,050 cartridges sold. The reported incidence of paresthesia was one case for 13,800,970 cartridges of all local anesthetics sold in the U.S. (Garisto, 2010).

Bupivacaine (Liposomal)

(byoo PIV a kane lye po SO mal)

Brand Names: US Exparel

Pharmacologic Category Local Anesthetic

Use Postsurgical analgesia: Injection into the surgical site to provide postsurgical analgesia.

Local Anesthetic/Vasoconstrictor Precautions No information available to require special precautions

Effects on Dental Treatment No significant effects or complications reported

Effects on Bleeding No information available to require special precautions

Adverse Reactions

Frequency not always defined.

>10%: Gastrointestinal: Nausea (2% to 40%), vomiting (28%), constipation (2% to ≥10%)

1% to 10%:

Cardiovascular: Hypotension (2% to 10%), peripheral edema (2% to 10%), tachycardia (4%), bradycardia (2%), edema (<2%), hypertension (<2%), palpitations (<2%), sinus bradycardia (<2%), supraventricular extrasystole (<2%), syncope (<2%), ventricular premature contractions (<2%), ventricular tachycardia (<2%), heart block

Central nervous system: Insomnia (2% to 10%), dizziness (6%), drowsiness (2% to 5%), headache (4%), flushing sensation (2%), hypoesthesia (2%), agitation (<2%), anxiety (<2%), chills (<2%), confusion (<2%), depression (<2%), pain (<2%), paresthesia (<2%), restlessness (<2%), lethargy (1%), paralysis, persistent anesthesia, seizure

Dermatologic: Pruritus (3%), diaphoresis (<2%), erythema (<2%), hyperhidrosis (<2%), pallor (<2%), pruritic rash (<2%), urticaria (<2%)

Genitourinary: Urinary incontinence (<2%), urinary retention (<2%)

Hematologic & oncologic: Acute posthemorrhagic anemia (2% to 10%; postoperative)

Hepatic: Increased serum AST (3%), increased serum ALT (1%)

Hypersensitivity: Anaphylactoid reaction (<2%), hypersensitivity reaction (<2%)

Infection: Fungal infection (2%)

Local: Localized edema (incision site: 2%)

Neuromuscular & skeletal: Back pain (2% to 10%), muscle spasm (2% to 10%), laryngospasm (<2%), neck pain (<2%), tremor (<2%), weakness (<2%), chondrolysis (continuous intra-articular administration; develops months after surgery)

Ophthalmic: Blurred vision (<2%), miosis

Otic: Tinnitus (<2%)

Renal: Increased serum creatinine (2%)

Respiratory: Apnea (<2%), hypoxia (<2%), respiratory depression (<2%), respiratory failure (<2%)

Miscellaneous: Fever (2%)

General Dosage Range Infiltration (local): *Adults:* Maximum single-dose infiltration for any postsurgical site: 266 mg (20 mL)

Mechanism of Action Blocks both the initiation and conduction of nerve impulses by decreasing the neuronal membrane's permeability to sodium ions, which results in inhibition of depolarization with resultant blockade of conduction.

Pharmacodynamics/Kinetics

Duration of Action Local: Systemic: 96 hours

Half-life Elimination 24 to 34 hours

Time to Peak 0.5 to 2 hours

Pregnancy Considerations Adverse events have been observed in animal reproduction studies. Bupivacaine crosses the placenta. Not recommended for use in pregnancy. Use in obstetrical paracervical block anesthesia is contraindicated; may cause fetal bradycardia and death.

Buprenorphine (byoo pre NOR feen)

Brand Names: US Belbuca; Buprenex; Butrans; Probuphine Implant Kit

Brand Names: Canada Butrans

Generic Availability (US) May be product dependent

Pharmacologic Category Analgesic, Opioid; Analgesic, Opioid Partial Agonist

Use

Opioid dependence:

Subdermal implant: Maintenance treatment of opioid dependence in patients who have achieved and sustained prolonged clinical stability on low to moderate doses (≤8 mg/day) of a transmucosal buprenorphine-containing product for 3 months or longer with no need for supplemental dosing or adjustments

Sublingual tablet: Treatment of opioid dependence

Pain management:

Buccal film, transdermal patch: Management of pain severe enough to require around-the-clock, long-term opioid treatment and for which alternative treatment options are inadequate

Injection: Management of pain severe enough to require an opioid analgesic and for which treatments are inadequate

Limitations of use: Reserve buprenorphine for use in patients for whom alternative treatment options (eg, nonopioid analgesics, opioid combination products, immediate-release opioids) are ineffective, not tolerated, or would be otherwise inadequate to provide sufficient management of pain. Buprenorphine buccal film and transdermal patch are not indicated as an as needed analgesic.

Local Anesthetic/Vasoconstrictor Precautions No information available to require special precautions

Effects on Dental Treatment No significant effects or complications reported

Effects on Bleeding No information available to require special precautions

Adverse Reactions

Buccal film:

1% to 10%:

Cardiovascular: Hypertension (≥1% to <5%), peripheral edema (≥1% to <5%)

Central nervous system: Fatigue (≥5%), anxiety (≥1% to <5%), depression (≥1% to <5%), falling (≥1% to <5%), insomnia (≥1% to <5%), withdrawal syndrome (≥1% to <5%), headache (4%), dizziness (2%), drowsiness (1%)

Dermatologic: Hyperhidrosis (≥1% to <5%), pruritus (≥1% to <5%), skin rash (≥1% to <5%)

Endocrine & metabolic: Hot flash (≥1% to <5%)

Gastrointestinal: Nausea (9% to 10%; incidence may be increased during dose titration), diarrhea (≥5%), xerostomia (≥5%), vomiting (4% to 5%), abdominal pain (≥1% to <5%), decreased appetite (≥1% to <5%), gastroenteritis (≥1% to <5%), constipation (3% to 4%)

Genitourinary: Urinary tract infection (≥1% to <5%)

Hematologic & oncologic: Anemia (≥1% to <5%), bruise (≥1% to <5%)

Neuromuscular & skeletal: Back pain (≥1% to <5%), muscle spasm (≥1% to <5%)

Respiratory: Upper respiratory tract infection (≥5%), bronchitis (≥1% to <5%), nasopharyngitis (≥1% to <5%), oropharyngeal pain (≥1% to <5%), sinus congestion (≥1% to <5%), sinusitis (≥1% to <5%)

Miscellaneous: Fever (≥1% to <5%)

Implant:

>10%:

Central nervous system: Headache (13%)

Dermatologic: Pruritus (12%; at implant site)

Miscellaneous: Pain at medication pump site (4% to 13%)

1% to 10%:

Cardiovascular: Edema (5%; at implant site), chest pain (1%)

Central nervous system: Depression (6%), dizziness (4%), drowsiness (3%), fatigue (3%), chills (2%), migraine (2%), paresthesia (1%), sedation (1%), sensation of cold (1%)

Dermatologic: Erythema (10%; at implant site), skin rash (2%), excoriation (1% to 2%; including scratch), skin lesion (1%)

Gastrointestinal: Constipation (6%), nausea (6%), vomiting (6%), toothache (5%), upper abdominal pain (3%), flatulence (1%)
Hematologic & oncologic: Hemorrhage (7%; at implant site)
Local: Local swelling (1%)
Neuromuscular & skeletal: Back pain (6%), limb pain (3%), weakness (2%)
Respiratory: Oropharyngeal pain (5%), cough (3%), dyspnea (1%)
Miscellaneous: Fever (3%), laceration (3%)

Injection:
>10%: Central nervous system: Sedation (≤66%)
1% to 10%:
Cardiovascular: Hypotension (1% to 5%)
Central nervous system: Dizziness (5% to 10%), vertigo (5% to 10%), headache (1% to 5%)
Dermatologic: Diaphoresis (1% to 5%)
Gastrointestinal: Nausea (5% to 10%), vomiting (1% to 5%)
Ophthalmic: Miosis (1% to 5%)
Respiratory: Hypoventilation (1% to 5%)

Sublingual Tablet:
>10%:
Central nervous system: Headache (29%), insomnia (21%)
Dermatologic: Diaphoresis (13%)
Gastrointestinal: Nausea (14%), abdominal pain (12%), constipation (8%)
Infection: Infection (12%)
1% to 10%: Gastrointestinal: Vomiting (8%)

Transdermal patch:
>10%:
Central nervous system: Dizziness (2% to 15%), headache (3% to 14%), drowsiness (2% to 13%)
Gastrointestinal: Nausea (6% to 23%), constipation (3% to 13%)
Local: Local pruritus (4% to 15%)
1% to 10%:
Cardiovascular: Chest pain (1% to <5%), hypertension (1% to <5%), peripheral edema (1% to <5%)
Central nervous system: Anxiety (1% to <5%), depression (1% to <5%), falling (1% to <5%), fatigue (1% to <5%), hypoesthesia (1% to <5%), insomnia (1% to <5%), migraine (1% to <5%), pain (1% to <5%), paresthesia (1% to <5%)
Dermatologic: Diaphoresis (1% to <5%), pruritus (1% to <5%), skin rash (1% to <5%)
Gastrointestinal: Vomiting (4% to 9%), xerostomia (6%), anorexia (1% to <5%), diarrhea (1% to <5%), dyspepsia (1% to <5%), upper abdominal pain (1% to <5%), abdominal distress (2%)
Genitourinary: Urinary tract infection (1% to <5%)
Local: Application site erythema (3% to 10%), application site rash (3% to 8%), application site irritation (1% to 6%)
Neuromuscular & skeletal: Arthralgia (1% to <5%), back pain (1% to <5%), joint swelling (1% to <5%), limb pain (1% to <5%), muscle spasm (1% to <5%), musculoskeletal pain (1% to <5%), myalgia (1% to <5%), neck pain (1% to <5%), tremor (1% to <5%), weakness (1% to <5%)
Respiratory: Bronchitis (1% to <5%), cough (1% to <5%), dyspnea (1% to <5%), flu-like symptoms (1% to <5%), nasopharyngitis (1% to <5%), pharyngolaryngeal pain (1% to <5%), sinusitis (1% to <5%), upper respiratory tract infection (1% to <5%)
Miscellaneous: Fever (1% to <5%)

<1%, postmarketing, and/or case reports: Abdominal discomfort, abdominal distention, abnormal dreams, abnormal hepatic function tests, acute sinusitis, agitation, amblyopia, anaphylactic shock, angina pectoris, angioedema, apathy, apnea, application site dermatitis, ataxia, blurred vision, bradycardia, bronchospasm, cellulitis, chills, coma, confusion, conjunctivitis, constipation, contact dermatitis, cough, cyanosis, decreased appetite, decreased libido, decreased serum testosterone, dehydration, depersonalization, depression, diarrhea, diplopia, disorientation, diverticulitis, dry eye syndrome, dysarthria, dysgeusia, dyspepsia, dysphagia, dysphoria, dyspnea, emotional lability, euphoria, exacerbation of asthma, excoriation, facial edema, fatigue, flatulence, flushing, hallucination, hepatic encephalopathy, hepatic failure, hepatic necrosis, hepatitis (including cytolytic), hepatorenal syndrome, hiccups, hot flash, hypersensitivity reaction, hypertension, hyperventilation, hypoesthesia, hypogonadism (Brennan 2013; Debono 2011), hypotension, hypoventilation, increased blood pressure, increased serum ALT, increased serum AST, increased serum transaminases, injection site reaction, intestinal obstruction, jaundice, laceration, lack of concentration, lethargy, loss of consciousness, malaise, memory impairment, mental deficiency, mental status changes, migraine, miosis, musculoskeletal pain, myasthenia, nasal congestion, neck pain, nervousness, nightmares, orthostatic hypotension, pallor, palpitations, paresthesia, prolonged Q-T interval on ECG, pruritus, psychosis, respiratory depression, respiratory distress, restlessness, rhinitis, rhinorrhea, sedation, seizure, sexual disorder, skin rash, slurred speech, syncope, tachycardia, tinnitus, tooth abscess, toothache, tremor, unsteady gait, urinary hesitancy, urinary incontinence, urinary retention, urticaria, vasodilatation, vertigo, visual disturbance, weakness, weight loss, Wenckebach period on ECG, wheezing, withdrawal syndrome, xeroderma

Dosing

Adult

Acute pain (moderate to severe): Note: Long-term use is not recommended. The following recommendations are guidelines and do not represent the maximum doses that may be required in all patients. Doses should be titrated to pain relief/prevention. Buprenorphine has an analgesic ceiling.

IM: Initial: 0.3 mg every 6 to 8 hours as needed; initial dose (up to 0.3 mg) may be repeated once in 30 to 60 minutes after the initial dose if needed

Slow IV: Initial: 0.3 mg every 6 to 8 hours as needed; initial dose (up to 0.3 mg) may be repeated once in 30 to 60 minutes after the initial dose if needed

Chronic pain (moderate to severe):

Buccal film: **Note:** Buprenorphine buccal film doses of 600, 750, and 900 mcg are only for use following titration from lower doses (maximum dose: 900 mcg every 12 hours).

Opioid-naive patients and opioid-non-tolerant patients: Initial: 75 mcg once daily or, if tolerated, every 12 hours for at least 4 days, then increase to 150 mcg every 12 hours.

Opioid-experienced patients (conversion from other opioids to buprenorphine): Discontinue all other around-the-clock opioids when buprenorphine is initiated. Taper patient's current opioid to no more than 30 mg oral morphine sulfate equivalents daily before initiating buprenorphine. Following analgesic taper, base the initial buprenorphine dose on the patient's daily opioid dose prior to taper. Patients may require additional short-acting analgesics during the taper period.

Patients who were receiving daily dose of <30 mg of oral morphine equivalents: Initial: 75 mcg once daily or every 12 hours

Patients who were receiving daily dose of 30 to 89 mg of oral morphine equivalents: Initial: 150 mcg every 12 hours

Patients who were receiving daily dose of 90 to 160 mg of oral morphine equivalents: Initial: 300 mcg every 12 hours

Patients who were receiving daily dose of >160 mg of oral morphine equivalents: Buprenorphine buccal film may not provide adequate analgesia; **consider the use of an alternate analgesic.**

Conversion from methadone: Close monitoring is required when converting methadone to another opioid. Ratio between methadone and other opioid agonists varies widely according to previous dose exposure. Methadone has a long half-life and can accumulate in the plasma.

Dose titration (opioid-naive or opioid-experienced patients): Individually titrate in increments of 150 mcg every 12 hours, no more frequently than every 4 days, to a dose that provides adequate analgesia and minimizes adverse reactions (maximum dose: 900 mcg every 12 hours; doses up to 450 mcg every 12 hours were studied in opioid naive patients). Patients may require additional short-acting analgesics during titration.

Discontinuation of therapy: Use a gradual downward titration of the dose to prevent withdrawal; do not abruptly discontinue.

Patients with oral mucositis: Reduce the starting dose and titration incremental dose by 50%.

Transdermal patch:

Opioid-naive patients: Initial: 5 **mcg**/hour applied once every 7 days

Opioid-experienced patients (conversion from other opioids to buprenorphine): Discontinue all other around-the-clock opioid drugs when buprenorphine therapy is initiated. Short-acting analgesics as needed may be continued until analgesia with transdermal buprenorphine is attained. There is a potential for buprenorphine to precipitate withdrawal in patients already receiving opioids.

Patients who were receiving daily dose of <30 mg of oral morphine equivalents: Initial: 5 **mcg**/hour applied once every 7 days

Patients who were receiving daily dose of 30 to 80 mg of oral morphine equivalents: Taper the current around-the-clock opioid for up to 7 days to ≤30 mg/day of oral morphine or equivalent before initiating therapy. Initial: 10 **mcg**/hour applied once every 7 days

Patient who were receiving daily dose of >80 mg of oral morphine equivalents: Buprenorphine transdermal patch, even at the maximum dose of 20 **mcg**/hour applied once every 7 days, may not provide adequate analgesia; **consider the use of an alternate analgesic.**

Dose titration (opioid-naive or opioid-experienced patients): May increase dose in 5 mcg/hour, 7.5 mcg/hour, or 10 mcg/hour increments (using no more than two patches), based on patient's supplemental short-acting analgesic requirements, with a minimum titration interval of 72 hours (maximum dose: 20 mcg/hour applied once every 7 days; risk for QTc prolongation increases with doses >20 mcg/hour patch).

Discontinuation of therapy: Taper dose gradually every 7 days to prevent withdrawal in the physically dependent patient; consider initiating immediate-release opioids, if needed.

Opioid withdrawal in heroin-dependent hospitalized patients (off-label use): IV infusion: 0.3 to 0.9 mg (diluted in 50 to 100 mL of NS) over 20 to 30 minutes every 6 to 12 hours (Welsh 2002)

Opioid dependence:

Subdermal implant: Insert 4 implants subdermally in the inner side of the upper arm. Remove no later than 6 months after the date of insertion; if continued treatment is desired, insert 4 new implants subdermally in the inner side of the contralateral arm. After one insertion in each arm, discontinue treatment with subdermal implants.

Converting back to sublingual tablet: On day of implant removal, resume buprenorphine treatment at previous sublingual dose.

Sublingual tablet: **Note:** The combination product, buprenorphine and naloxone, is preferred therapy over buprenorphine monotherapy for induction treatment (and stabilization/maintenance treatment) for short-acting opioid dependence (US Department of Health and Human Services 2005).

Manufacturer's labeling:

Induction: Day 1: 8 mg; Day 2 and subsequent induction days: 16 mg; usual induction dosage range: 12 to 16 mg/day (induction usually accomplished over 3 to 4 days). Treatment should begin at least 4 hours after last use of heroin or other short-acting opioids, preferably when first signs of withdrawal appear. Titrating dose to clinical effectiveness should be done as rapidly as possible to prevent undue withdrawal symptoms and patient drop-out during the induction period. There is little controlled experience with induction in patients on methadone or other long-acting opioids; consult expert physician experienced with this procedure.

Maintenance: Target dose: 16 mg/day; in some patients 12 mg/day may be effective; patients should be switched to the buprenorphine/naloxone combination product for maintenance and unsupervised therapy.

Alternate dosing (Kampman [ASAM 2015]):

Induction: 2 to 4 mg; if no signs of precipitated withdrawal after 60 to 90 minutes, may increase in increments of 2 to 4 mg. Once initial dose is tolerated, may increase to a dose that is clinically effective and provides 24 hours of stabilization. Buprenorphine treatment initiation should begin after mild to moderate opioid withdrawal signs appear (to avoid precipitated withdrawal), which is generally at least 6 to 12 hours after last use of short-acting opioids (eg, heroin, oxycodone) and 24 to 72 hours after last use of long-acting opioids (methadone).

After induction and titration, daily dose usually ≥8 mg/day. In patients continuing to use opioids, consider increasing the dose by 4 to 8 mg to a daily dose of ≥12 to 16 mg/day.

Geriatric

Acute pain (moderate to severe): IM, slow IV: Refer to adult dosing; use with caution.

Chronic pain (moderate to severe): Buccal film, transdermal patch: No specific dosage adjustments required; use caution and titrate slowly due to potential for increased risk of adverse events.

Opioid dependence: Subdermal implant: No specific dosage adjustments required; use caution due to potential for increased risk of adverse events and inability to adjust dosage.

Pediatric

Acute pain (moderate to severe):

Children 2 to 12 years: IM, slow IV: 2 to 6 **mcg**/kg every 4 to 6 hours

Adolescents ≥13 years: Refer to adult dosing.

Opioid dependence: Adolescents ≥16 years: Refer to adult dosing.

Renal Impairment There are no dosage adjustments provided in the manufacturer's labeling (has not been adequately studied); use with caution. In pharmacokinetic studies, renal impairment (including administration pre- or post-hemodialysis) was not associated with increased buprenorphine plasma concentrations.

Hepatic Impairment

Buccal film:

Mild impairment (Child-Pugh class A): No dosage adjustment necessary.

Moderate impairment (Child-Pugh class B): No dosage adjustment necessary; use caution and monitor for signs and symptoms of toxicity or overdose.

Severe impairment (Child-Pugh class C): Reduce starting dose and reduce titration dose by 50% (ie, from 150 mcg to 75 mcg).

Injection:

Mild or moderate impairment: There are no dosage adjustments provided in the manufacturer's labeling; however, need for dosage adjustment is unlikely as systemic exposure following IV buprenorphine in these patients was similar to healthy subjects.

Severe impairment: There are no dosage adjustments provided in the manufacturer's labeling; use with caution.

Subdermal implant:

Mild impairment: There are no dosage adjustments provided in the manufacturer's labeling (has not been studied).

Moderate or severe impairment: Use is not recommended.

Sublingual:

Mild impairment: No dosage adjustment necessary.

Moderate impairment: No dosage adjustment necessary; use caution and monitor for signs and symptoms of toxicity or overdose.

Severe impairment: Consider reducing initial and titration incremental dose by 50%; monitor for signs and symptoms of toxicity or overdose.

Transdermal patch:

Mild or moderate impairment: There are no dosage adjustments provided in the manufacturer's labeling; however, need for dosage adjustment is unlikely as systemic exposure following IV buprenorphine in these patients was similar to that observed in healthy subjects.

Severe impairment: There are no dosage adjustments provided in the manufacturer's labeling (has not been studied); consider alternative therapy with more flexibility for dosing adjustments.

Mechanism of Action Buprenorphine exerts its analgesic effect via high-affinity binding to mu opiate receptors in the CNS; displays partial mu agonist and weak kappa antagonist activity. Due to it being a partial mu agonist, its analgesic effects plateau at higher doses and it then behaves like an antagonist.

Contraindications

Hypersensitivity (eg, anaphylaxis) to buprenorphine or any component of the formulation.

Buccal film, injection, transdermal patch: Additional contraindications: Significant respiratory depression; acute or severe asthma in an unmonitored setting or in the absence of resuscitative equipment; GI obstruction, including paralytic ileus (known or suspected).

Documentation of allergenic cross-reactivity for opioids is limited. However, because of similarities in chemical structure and/or pharmacologic actions, the possibility of cross-sensitivity cannot be ruled out with certainty.

Canadian labeling: Transdermal patch (Additional contraindications; not in US labeling): Hypersensitivity to other opioids; suspected surgical abdomen (eg, acute appendicitis or pancreatitis); mild, intermittent or short duration pain that can otherwise be managed; management of acute pain, including use in outpatient or day surgeries; management of peri-operative pain relief, or in other situations characterized by rapidly varying analgesic requirements; acute respiratory depression; hypercapnia; cor pulmonale; obstructive airway (other than asthma); status asthmaticus; acute alcoholism or alcohol dependence; delirium tremens; convulsive disorders; severe CNS depression; increased cerebrospinal or intracranial pressure; head injury; concurrent use or use within 14 days of monoamine oxidase inhibitors (MAOIs); myasthenia gravis; severe hepatic insufficiency; opioid dependent patients and for narcotic withdrawal treatment; pregnancy or during labor and delivery; breastfeeding

Warnings/Precautions An opioid-containing analgesic regimen should be tailored to each patient's needs and based upon the type of pain being treated (acute versus chronic), the route of administration, degree of tolerance for opioids (naive versus chronic user), age, weight, and medical condition. The optimal analgesic dose varies widely among patients. Doses should be titrated to pain relief/prevention. When switching patients from buprenorphine to naltrexone, do not initiate naltrexone until 7 to 14 days after buprenorphine discontinuation. No time delay is required when switching patients from buprenorphine to methadone (Kampman [ASAM 2015]).

May cause CNS depression, which may impair physical or mental abilities; patients must be cautioned about performing tasks that require mental alertness (eg, operating machinery, driving). **[US Boxed Warning]: Serious, life-threatening, or fatal respiratory depression may occur. Monitor closely for respiratory depression, especially during initiation or dose escalation. Misuse or abuse by chewing, swallowing, snorting, or injecting buprenorphine extracted from the buccal film or transdermal system will result in the uncontrolled delivery of buprenorphine and pose a significant risk of overdose and death. Carbon dioxide retention from opioid-induced respiratory depression can exacerbate the sedating effects of opioids. Accidental exposure to even one dose, especially in children, can result in a fatal overdose.** Use with caution and monitor for respiratory depression in patients with significant chronic obstructive pulmonary disease or cor pulmonale and those with a substantially decreased respiratory reserve, hypoxia, hypercapnia, or preexisting respiratory depression, particularly when initiating and titrating therapy; critical respiratory depression may occur, even at therapeutic dosages. Consider the use of alternative nonopioid analgesics in these patients. Use opioids with caution for chronic pain and titrate dosage cautiously in patients with risk factors for sleep-disordered breathing, including HF and obesity. Avoid opioids in patients with moderate to severe sleep-disordered breathing (Dowell [CDC 2016]). When using buprenorphine for treatment of opioid dependence, treat acute pain with nonopioid analgesics whenever possible. If treatment with a high-affinity full opioid analgesic is required, monitor closely for respiratory depression, as high doses may be necessary to achieve pain relief. Use with caution in elderly patients; may be more sensitive to adverse effects (eg, life-threatening respiratory depression). In chronic pain, monitor opioid use closely in this age group due to an increased potential for risks, including certain risks such as falls/fracture, cognitive impairment, and constipation (Dowell [CDC 2016]). Consider the use of alternative nonopioid analgesics in these patients. Also use with caution in debilitated or cachectic patients; there is a greater potential for life-threatening respiratory depression, even at therapeutic dosages. Consider the use of alternative nonopioid analgesics in these patients.

Hypersensitivity reactions, including bronchospasm, angioneurotic edema, and anaphylactic shock, have been reported.

Hepatitis has been reported; hepatic events ranged from transient, asymptomatic transaminase elevations to hepatic failure; in many cases, patients had preexisting hepatic impairment. Monitor liver function tests in patients at increased risk for hepatotoxicity (eg, history of alcohol abuse, preexisting hepatic dysfunction, IV drug abusers) prior to and during therapy. Remove buprenorphine subdermal implant if signs and symptoms of buprenorphine toxicity develop concurrent with hepatic impairment. Use buccal film and sublingual tablet with caution in patients with moderate hepatic impairment; dosage adjustment recommended in severe hepatic impairment. Subdermal implants should not be used in patients with preexisting moderate to severe hepatic impairment. Transdermal patch should not be used in patients with severe hepatic impairment; consider alternative therapy with more flexibility for dosing adjustments.

Avoid use in patients with CNS depression or coma as these patients are susceptible to intracranial effects of CO_2 retention. Use with extreme caution in patients with head injury, intracranial lesions, or elevated intracranial pressure; exaggerated elevation of ICP may occur. Buprenorphine can produce miosis and changes in the level of consciousness that may interfere with patient evaluation. May cause severe hypotension, including orthostatic hypotension and syncope; use with caution in patients with hypovolemia, cardiovascular disease (including acute MI), or drugs that may exaggerate hypotensive effects (including phenothiazines or general anesthetics). Monitor for symptoms of hypotension following initiation or dose titration. Avoid use in patients with circulatory shock. May obscure diagnosis or clinical course of patients with acute abdominal conditions. Use with caution in patients with a history of ileus or bowel obstruction; buccal film, injection, and transdermal patch are contraindicated in patients with known or suspected GI obstruction, including paralytic ileus. Use with caution in patients with biliary tract dysfunction, including acute pancreatitis; may cause constriction of sphincter of Oddi. Use with caution in patients with a history of seizure disorders; may cause or exacerbate preexisting seizures. Use with caution in patients with adrenal insufficiency, including Addison disease. Long-term opioid use may cause secondary hypogonadism, which may lead to sexual dysfunction, infertility, mood disorders, and osteoporosis (Brennan 2013). Use with caution in patients with renal impairment, morbid obesity, toxic psychosis, thyroid dysfunction, or prostatic hyperplasia and/or urinary stricture. Potentially significant drug-drug interactions may exist, requiring dose or frequency adjustment, additional monitoring, and/or selection of alternative therapy. **[US Boxed Warning]: Concomitant use of benzodiazepines or other CNS depressants, including alcohol and opioids, may result in profound sedation, respiratory depression, coma, and death. Reserve concomitant prescribing of opioids and benzodiazepines or other CNS depressants for use in patients for whom alternative treatment options are inadequate. Limit dosages and durations to the minimum required. Follow patients for signs and symptoms of respiratory depression and sedation.**

[US Boxed Warning]: Use exposes patients and other users to the risks of addiction, abuse, and misuse, potentially leading to overdose and death. Assess each patient's risk before prescribing; monitor all patients regularly for development of these behaviors or conditions. Use with caution in patients with a history of drug abuse or acute alcoholism; potential for drug dependency exists. Other factors associated with increased risk for misuse include younger age and psychotropic medication use. Consider offering naloxone prescriptions in patients with factors associated with an increased risk for overdose, such as history of overdose or substance use disorder, higher opioid dosages (≥50 morphine milligram equivalents/day orally), and concomitant benzodiazepine use (Dowell [CDC 2016]). The misuse of buccal film by swallowing or of transdermal patch by placing it in the mouth, chewing it, swallowing it, or using it in ways other than indicated may cause choking, overdose, and death. Use with caution in patients with delirium tremens. Buccal film and transdermal patch are indicated for the management of pain severe enough to require daily, around-the-clock, long-term opioid treatment; should not be used for as-needed pain relief. Therapy with the buccal film or transdermal patch is not appropriate for use in the management of addictions. Handle removed implants with adequate security, accountability, and proper disposal, per facility procedure for a Schedule III drug product, and per applicable federal, state, and local regulations. To properly dispose of transdermal patch, fold it over on itself and flush down the toilet; alternatively, seal the used patch in the provided Patch-Disposal Unit and dispose of in the trash. When used for chronic pain (outside of end-of-life or palliative care, active cancer treatment, sickle cell disease, or medication-assisted treatment for opioid use disorder) in outpatient setting in adults, opioids should not be used as first-line therapy for chronic pain management (pain >3-month duration or beyond time of normal tissue healing) due to limited short-term benefits, undetermined long-term benefits, and association with serious risks (eg, overdose, MI, auto accidents, risk of developing opioid use disorder). Preferred management includes nonpharmacologic therapy and nonopioid therapy (eg, NSAIDs, acetaminophen, certain anticonvulsants and antidepressants). If opioid therapy is initiated, it should be combined with nonpharmacologic and nonopioid therapy, as appropriate. Prior to initiation, known risks of opioid therapy should be discussed and realistic treatment goals for pain/function should be established, including consideration for discontinuation if benefits do not outweigh risks. Therapy should be continued only if clinically meaningful improvement in pain/function outweighs risks. Therapy should be initiated at the lowest effective dosage using immediate-release opioids (instead of extended-release/long-acting opioids). Risk associated with use increases with higher opioid dosages. Risks and benefits should be re-evaluated when increasing dosage to ≥50 morphine milligram equivalents (MME)/day orally; dosages ≥90 MME/day orally should be avoided unless carefully justified (Dowell [CDC 2016]).

Do not exceed a dose of 900 mcg every 12 hours buccal film or one 20 **mcg**/hour transdermal patch due to the risk of QTc-interval prolongation. Avoid using in patients with a personal or family history of long QT syndrome or in patients taking concurrent class IA or III antiarrhythmics or other medications that prolong the QT interval. Use with caution in patients with hypokalemia, hypomagnesemia, or clinically unstable cardiac disease, including unstable heart failure, unstable atrial fibrillation, symptomatic bradycardia, or active MI. Avoid exposure of transdermal patch application site and surrounding area to direct external heat sources (eg, heating pads, electric blankets, heat or tanning lamps, hot baths/saunas, hot water bottles, or direct sunlight). Buprenorphine release from the patch is temperature-dependent and may result in overdose. Patients who experience fever or increase in core temperature should be monitored closely and adjust dose if signs or respiratory depression or CNS depression occur. Application-site reactions, including rare cases of severe reactions (eg, vesicles, discharge, "burns"), have been observed with transdermal patch use; onset varies from days to months after initiation; patients should be instructed to report severe reactions promptly and discontinue therapy. Oral mucositis may result in more rapid absorption and higher buprenorphine plasma levels in patients using buccal film; reduce dose in patients with oral mucositis and monitor closely for signs and symptoms of toxicity or overdose. **[US Boxed Warning]: Prolonged use during pregnancy can cause neonatal withdrawal syndrome, which may be life-threatening if not recognized and treated according to according to protocols developed by neonatology experts. If opioid use is required for a prolonged period in a pregnant woman, advise the patient of the risk of neonatal withdrawal syndrome and ensure that appropriate treatment will be available.** Signs and symptoms include irritability, hyperactivity and abnormal sleep pattern, high-pitched cry, tremor, vomiting, diarrhea, and failure to gain weight. Onset, duration, and severity depend on the drug used, duration of use, maternal dose, and rate of drug elimination by the newborn.

Reversal of partial opioid agonists or mixed opioid agonist/antagonists (eg, buprenorphine, pentazocine) may be incomplete and large doses of naloxone may be required. Concurrent use of opioid agonist/antagonist analgesics may precipitate withdrawal symptoms and/or reduced analgesic efficacy in patients following prolonged therapy with mu opioid agonists. Abrupt discontinuation following prolonged use may also lead to withdrawal symptoms and is not recommended; taper dose gradually when discontinuing.

Tablets, which are used for induction treatment of opioid dependence, should not be started until effects of withdrawal are evident. If subdermal implants are not immediately replaced in contralateral arm after removal, maintain patients on their previous dosage of sublingual buprenorphine.

In patients undergoing elective surgery (excluding caesarean section), discontinuation of buprenorphine 24 to 36 hours before anticipated need for surgical anesthesia may be considered. Short-acting opioids may be given during and/or after surgery. In patients unable to abruptly discontinue buprenorphine prior to surgery, full opioid agonists may be added to the buprenorphine to maintain proper anesthesia; however, increased doses may be required to overcome buprenorphine receptor blockade. The decision whether to discontinue buprenorphine prior to elective surgery should be made in consultation with the surgeon and anesthesiologist (Kampman [ASAM 2015]).

[US Boxed Warning]: Insertion and removal of implant are associated with the risk of implant migration, protrusion, and expulsion. Rare but serious complications including nerve damage and migration resulting in embolism and death may result from improper insertion in the upper arm. Additional complications may include local migration, protrusion, and expulsion. Incomplete insertions or infections may lead to protrusion or expulsion. Because of the risks associated with insertion and removal, buprenorphine implant is available only through a restricted program. All health care providers must successfully complete a live training program on the insertion and removal procedures and become certified, prior to performing insertions or prescribing buprenorphine implants. Patients must be monitored to ensure that the implant is removed by a health care provider certified to perform insertions. Infection may occur at site of insertion or removal, with excessive palpation shortly after insertion and improper removal increasing the risk. Examine the insertion site one week following insertion for signs of infection or problems with wound healing. Use subdermal implants with caution in patients with a history of keloid formation, connective tissue disease (ie, scleroderma) or history of recurrent MRSA infections. Subdermal implant is not appropriate for patients who are new to treatment or have not sustained prolonged clinical stability on buprenorphine 8 mg/day or less.

Drug Interactions

Metabolism/Transport Effects

Substrate of CYP3A4 (major); **Note:** Assignment of Major/Minor substrate status based on clinically relevant drug interaction potential; **Inhibits** CYP1A2 (weak), CYP2A6 (weak)

Avoid Concomitant Use

Avoid concomitant use of Buprenorphine with any of the following: Analgesics (Opioid); Atazanavir; Azelastine (Nasal); Conivaptan; Eluxadoline; Fusidic Acid (Systemic); Idelalisib; MAO Inhibitors; Mixed Agonist / Antagonist Opioids; Orphenadrine; Oxomemazine; Paraldehyde; Thalidomide

Increased Effect/Toxicity

Buprenorphine may increase the levels/effects of: Alvimopan; Azelastine (Nasal); Blonanserin; Desmopressin; Diuretics; Eluxadoline; Flunitrazepam; Highest Risk QTc-Prolonging Agents; MAO Inhibitors; Methotrimeprazine; MetyroSINE; Orphenadrine; Paraldehyde; Piribedil; Pramipexole; Ramosetron; ROPINIRole; Rotigotine; Selective Serotonin Reuptake Inhibitors; Serotonin Modulators; Suvorexant; Thalidomide; TiZANidine; Zolpidem

The levels/effects of Buprenorphine may be increased by: Alcohol (Ethyl); Amphetamines; Anticholinergic Agents; Aprepitant; Atazanavir; Boceprevir; Brimonidine (Topical); Cannabis; Ceritinib; Chlormethiazole; Chlorphenesin Carbamate; CNS Depressants; Cobicistat; Conivaptan; CYP3A4 Inhibitors (Moderate); CYP3A4 Inhibitors (Strong); Daclatasvir; Dasatinib; Dimethindene (Topical); Dronabinol; Droperidol; Fosaprepitant; Fusidic Acid (Systemic); Idelalisib; Ivacaftor; Kava Kava; Lofexidine; Magnesium Sulfate; Methotrimeprazine; MiFEPRIStone; Minocycline; Nabilone; Netupitant; Ombitasvir, Paritaprevir, and Ritonavir; Ombitasvir, Paritaprevir, Ritonavir, and Dasabuvir; Oxomemazine; Palbociclib; Perampanel; Rufinamide; Simeprevir; Sodium Oxybate; Stiripentol; Succinylcholine; Tetrahydrocannabinol

Decreased Effect

Buprenorphine may decrease the levels/effects of: Analgesics (Opioid); Atazanavir; Diuretics; Gastrointestinal Agents (Prokinetic); Pegvisomant

The levels/effects of Buprenorphine may be decreased by: Boceprevir; Bosentan; CYP3A4 Inducers (Moderate); CYP3A4 Inducers (Strong); Dabrafenib; Deferasirox; Efavirenz; Enzalutamide; Etravirine; Mitotane; Mixed Agonist / Antagonist Opioids; Nalmefene; Naltrexone; Siltuximab; St John's Wort; Tocilizumab

Pharmacodynamics/Kinetics

Onset of Action Analgesic: IM: ≥15 minutes; Peak effect: IM: ~1 hour

Duration of Action IM: ≥6 hours

Half-life Elimination

Premature neonates (GA: 27 to 32 weeks): IV: 20 ± 8 hours (Barrett 1993)

Children 4 to 7 years: IV: ~1 hour (Olkkola 1989)

Adults: IV: 2.2 to 3 hours; Buccal film: 27.6 ± 11.2 hours; Apparent terminal half-life: Sublingual tablet: ~37 hours; Transdermal patch: ~26 hours. **Note:** Extended elimination half-life for sublingual administration may be due to depot effect (Kuhlman 1996)

Time to Peak Plasma: Buccal film: 2.5 to 3 hours; Subdermal implant: 12 hours after insertion, with steady state achieved by week 4; Sublingual: 30 minutes to 1 hour (Kuhlman 1996); Transdermal patch: Steady state achieved by day 3

Pregnancy Risk Factor C

Pregnancy Considerations Adverse effects have been observed in some animal reproduction studies. Buprenorphine crosses the placenta; buprenorphine and norbuprenorphine can be detected in newborn serum, urine, and meconium following in utero exposure (CSAT 2004). Based on available data, an increased risk of major malformations has not been observed. **[US Boxed Warning]: Prolonged use of opioids during pregnancy can result in neonatal opioid withdrawal syndrome, which may be life-threatening if not recognized and requires management according to protocols developed by neonatology experts. If opioid use is required for a prolonged period in a pregnant woman, advise the patient of the risk of neonatal opioid withdrawal syndrome and ensure appropriate treatment will be available.** Following chronic opioid therapy in pregnancy, adverse events in the newborn (including withdrawal) may occur; monitoring of the neonate is recommended. The minimum effective dose should be used if opioids are needed (Chou 2009). The onset of withdrawal in infants of women receiving buprenorphine during pregnancy ranged from day 1 to day 8 of life, most occurring on day 1. Symptoms of withdrawal may include agitation, apnea, bradycardia, convulsions, hypertonia, myoclonus, respiratory depression, and tremor. Based on available data, there does not appear to be a dose-response relationship with the incidence of neonatal abstinence syndrome.

Buprenorphine is currently considered an alternate treatment for pregnant women who need therapy for opioid addiction (CSAT 2004; Dow 2012; Kampman [ASAM 2015]); however, use in pregnancy for this purpose is increasing (ACOG 2012; Soyka 2013). Because dose adjustments cannot be made, it may not be appropriate to initiate use of the implant in pregnant women; women who become pregnant while using the implant should be closely monitored. Buprenorphine should not be used to treat pain during labor. Women receiving buprenorphine for the treatment of addiction should be maintained on their daily dose of buprenorphine in addition to receiving the same pain management options during labor and delivery as opioid-naive women; maintenance doses of buprenorphine will not provide adequate pain relief. Opioid agonist-antagonists should be avoided for the treatment of labor pain in women maintained on buprenorphine due to the risk of precipitating acute withdrawal. In addition, buprenorphine should not be given to women in labor taking methadone (ACOG 2012).

Amenorrhea may develop secondary to substance abuse; pregnancy may occur following the initiation of buprenorphine maintenance treatment. Contraception counseling is recommended to prevent unplanned pregnancies (Dow 2012). Long-term opioid use may cause secondary hypogonadism, which may lead to sexual dysfunction or infertility (Brennan 2013).

Breastfeeding Considerations Buprenorphine is excreted in breast milk. Based on data from six women taking a median oral dose of buprenorphine 0.29 mg/kg/day, 5 to 8 days postpartum, the concentrations of buprenorphine and its metabolite in breast milk were low (0.2% and 0.12% of the weight adjusted maternal dose, respectively). Using data from seven women taking an average oral dose of buprenorphine 7 mg/day, ~1 month postpartum, the concentrations of buprenorphine and its metabolite in breast milk were also low (0.38% and 0.18% of the weight adjusted maternal dose, respectively). When used for pain management (injection, patch), the manufacturers do not recommend use in breastfeeding women. When used for opioid addiction (sublingual tablet), the manufacturer recommends that caution be used if breastfeeding. Nursing infants exposed to large doses of opioids should be monitored for apnea and sedation (Montgomery 2012).

When buprenorphine is used to treat opioid addiction in nursing women, most guidelines allow breastfeeding as long as the infant is tolerant to the dose and other contraindications do not exist (eg, not using additional drugs or alcohol, HIV negative); caution should be used when nursing infants not previously exposed (ACOG 2012; CSAT 2004; Kampman [ASAM 2015]; Montgomery 2012). If additional illicit substances are being abused, women treated with buprenorphine should pump and discard breast milk until sobriety is established (ACOG 2012; Dow 2012).

Controlled Substance C-III

Prescribing and Access Restrictions

Subdermal implant: Prescribing of implants and inserting or removing implants are limited to healthcare providers who have completed a live training program. Additionally, inserting or removing implants is limited to healthcare providers who have demonstrated procedural competency. As a prerequisite for participating in the live training program, the healthcare provider must have performed at least one qualifying surgical procedure in the last 3 months. Qualifying procedures are those performed under local anesthesia using aseptic technique and include, at a minimum, making skin incisions or placing sutures. Buprenorphine subdermal implant will only be distributed to certified prescribers through a restricted distribution program. Information concerning the insertion and removal procedures can be obtained by calling 1-844-859-6341.

Sublingual tablet: Prescribing of tablets for opioid dependence is limited to physicians who have met the qualification criteria and have received a DEA number specific to prescribing this product. Tablets will be available through pharmacies and wholesalers which normally provide controlled substances.

Dosage Forms Considerations Note: Subdermal implant and subcutaneous implant both refer to Probuphine.

Dosage Forms

Film, Buccal:

Belbuca: 75 mcg (60 ea); 150 mcg (60 ea); 300 mcg (60 ea); 450 mcg (60 ea); 600 mcg (60 ea); 750 mcg (60 ea); 900 mcg (60 ea)

Implant, Subcutaneous:

Probuphine Implant Kit: 74.2 mg (4 ea)

Patch Weekly, Transdermal:

Butrans: 5 mcg/hr (4 ea); 7.5 mcg/hr (4 ea); 10 mcg/hr (4 ea); 15 mcg/hr (4 ea); 20 mcg/hr (4 ea)

Solution, Injection:

Buprenex: 0.3 mg/mL (1 mL)

Generic: 0.3 mg/mL (1 mL)

Tablet Sublingual, Sublingual:

Generic: 2 mg, 8 mg

Buprenorphine and Naloxone

(byoo pre NOR feen & nal OKS one)

Related Information

Buprenorphine *on page 254*

Naloxone *on page 1164*

Brand Names: US Bunavail; Suboxone; Zubsolv

Brand Names: Canada Mylan-Buprenorphine/Naloxone; Suboxone; Teva-Buprenorphine/Naloxone

Pharmacologic Category Analgesic, Opioid; Analgesic, Opioid Partial Agonist

Use

Opioid dependence: Treatment of opioid dependence.

General information: Buprenorphine/naloxone should be used as part of a complete treatment plan to include counseling and psychosocial support.

Local Anesthetic/Vasoconstrictor Precautions No information available to require special precautions

Effects on Dental Treatment No significant effects or complications reported

Effects on Bleeding No information available to require special precautions

Adverse Reactions Also see individual agents.

>10%:

Central nervous system: Headache (36%), withdrawal syndrome (25%; placebo 37%), pain (22%)

Dermatologic: Diaphoresis (14%)

Gastrointestinal: Glossodynia (film), oral hypoesthesia (film), oral mucosa erythema (film)

1% to 10%:

Cardiovascular: Vasodilatation (9%)

Gastrointestinal: Vomiting (8%)

General Dosage Range

Buccal: *Adolescents ≥16 years and Adults:* Buprenorphine 2.1 to 12.6 mg/naloxone 0.3 to 2.1 mg once daily (target dose: Buprenorphine 8.4 mg/naloxone 1.4 mg once daily)

Sublingual:

Sublingual film: *Adolescents ≥16 years and Adults:* Buprenorphine 2 to 24 mg/naloxone 0.5 to 6 mg once daily (target dose: Buprenorphine 16 mg/naloxone 4 mg once daily)

Sublingual tablet: *Adolescents ≥16 years and Adults:* Buprenorphine 2.9 to 17.2 mg/naloxone 0.71 to 4.2 mg once daily (target dose: Buprenorphine 11.4 mg/naloxone 2.9 mg once daily)

Mechanism of Action

Buprenorphine: Buprenorphine exerts its analgesic effect via high affinity binding to mu opiate receptors in the CNS; displays partial mu agonist and weak kappa antagonist activity

Naloxone: Pure opioid antagonist that competes and displaces opioids at opioid receptor sites

Pharmacodynamics/Kinetics

Half-life Elimination Suboxone: Buprenorphine 24 to 42 hours; Naloxone 2 to 12 hours; Bunavail: Buprenorphine 16.4 to 27.5 hours; Naloxone 1.9 to 2.4 hours

Pregnancy Considerations Neonatal opioid withdrawal syndrome may occur after chronic maternal exposure to opioids. In the treatment of addiction involving opioid use in pregnant women, the buprenorphine/naloxone combination product is not recommended for use (insufficient evidence); however, the buprenorphine monoproduct is a reasonable and recommended option for use (Kampman [ASAM 2015]). Women who become pregnant while on this combination should generally be transitioned to the single agent (buprenorphine) product (ACOG 2012). See individual agents.

Controlled Substance C-III

Prescribing and Access Restrictions

In the US prescribing of tablets for opioid dependence is limited to physicians who have met the qualification criteria and have received a DEA number specific to prescribing this product. Tablets will be available through pharmacies and wholesalers which normally provide controlled substances.

In Canada, buprenorphine/naloxone sublingual tablets may be prescribed only by physicians experienced in substitution treatment in opioid dependence and who have completed a recognized buprenorphine/naloxone education program. Components of the program include: Training of physicians in the use of buprenorphine/naloxone; maintenance of a list of physicians who have completed training; daily dosing supervision by a health care professional until the patient is clinically stable and able to safely store buprenorphine/naloxone. Take-home doses should be assessed and reviewed regularly. Further information about the program may be obtained by contacting the manufacturer.

BuPROPion (byoo PROE pee on)

Related Information

Cardiovascular Diseases *on page 1752*

Dentin Hypersensitivity, Acid Erosion, High Caries Index, Management of Alveolar Osteitis, and Xerostomia *on page 1857*

Vasoconstrictor Interactions With Antidepressants *on page 1913*

Brand Names: US Aplenzin; Budeprion SR [DSC]; Buproban [DSC]; Forfivo XL; Wellbutrin SR; Wellbutrin XL; Wellbutrin [DSC]; Zyban

Brand Names: Canada Bupropion SR; Mylan-Bupropion XL; Novo-Bupropion SR; PMS-Bupropion SR; ratio-Bupropion SR; Sandoz-Bupropion SR; Wellbutrin SR; Wellbutrin XL; Zyban

Generic Availability (US) Yes

Pharmacologic Category Antidepressant, Dopamine/Norepinephrine-Reuptake Inhibitor; Smoking Cessation Aid

Use

Major depressive disorder (Aplenzin, Forfivo XL, Wellbutrin, Wellbutrin SR, Wellbutrin XL): Treatment of major depressive disorder (MDD).

Seasonal affective disorder (Aplenzin, Wellbutrin XL): Prevention of seasonal major depressive episodes in patients with a diagnosis of seasonal affective disorder (SAD).

Smoking cessation (Buproban and Zyban): As an aid to smoking cessation treatment.

Local Anesthetic/Vasoconstrictor Precautions Part of the mechanism of bupropion is to block reuptake of norepinephrine along with dopamine. Because of the potential for norepinephrine elevation within CNS synapses, it is suggested that vasoconstrictor be administered with caution and to monitor vital signs in dental patients taking antidepressants that affect norepinephrine in this way.

Effects on Dental Treatment Key adverse event(s) related to dental treatment: Abnormal taste, significant xerostomia (normal salivary flow resumes with discontinuation).

Effects on Bleeding Thrombocytopenia (<1%) as been reported.

Adverse Reactions

>10%:

Cardiovascular: Tachycardia (≤11%)

Central nervous system: Insomnia (11% to 40%), headache (25% to 34%), agitation (2% to 32%), dizziness (6% to 22%)

Dermatologic: Diaphoresis (5% to 22%)

Endocrine & metabolic: Weight loss (14% to 23%)

Gastrointestinal: Xerostomia (10% to 28%), constipation (8% to 26%), nausea and vomiting (23%), nausea (1% to 18%)

Neuromuscular & skeletal: Tremor (1% to 21%)

Ophthalmic: Blurred vision (3% to 15%)

Respiratory: Nasopharyngitis (13%), pharyngitis (3% to 13%), rhinitis (12%)

1% to 10%:

Cardiovascular: Palpitations (2% to 6%), cardiac arrhythmia (5%), chest pain (≤4%), flushing (≤4%), hypertension (1% to 4%; may be severe), hypotension (3%)

Central nervous system: Lack of concentration (9%), confusion (≤8%), anxiety (3% to 8%), hostility (≤6%), nervousness (4% to 5%), abnormal dreams (3% to 5%), sensory disturbance (4%), sleep disorder (4%), migraine (≤4%), irritability (3%), memory impairment (≤3%), drowsiness (2% to 3%), pain (3%), akathisia (≤2%), central nervous system stimulation (≤2%), paresthesia (≤2%), twitching (≤2%), dystonia (≥1%), abnormality in thinking (1%), depression

Dermatologic: Skin rash (1% to 8%), pruritus (2% to 4%), xeroderma (2%), urticaria (1% to 2%)

Endocrine & metabolic: Weight gain (9%), menstrual disease (2% to 5%), decreased libido (≤3%), hot flash (1% to 3%)

Gastrointestinal: Abdominal pain (2% to 9%), diarrhea (4% to 7%), flatulence (6%), anorexia (1% to 5%), dysgeusia (2% to 4%), increased appetite (2% to 4%), vomiting (≥1% to 4%), dyspepsia (3%), oral mucosa ulcer (2%), dysphagia (≤2%)

Genitourinary: Urinary frequency (≥1% to 5%), urinary urgency (≤2%), vaginal hemorrhage (≤2%), urinary tract infection (≤1%)

Hypersensitivity: Hypersensitivity reaction (1%)

Infection: Infection (8% to 9%)

Neuromuscular & skeletal: Myalgia (2% to 6%), arthralgia (4% to 5%), weakness (4%), neck pain (2%), arthritis (≤2%), dyskinesia (≥1%)

Otic: Tinnitus (1% to 6%), auditory disturbance (5%)

Renal: Polyuria (≤1%)

Respiratory: Upper respiratory infection (9%), sinusitis (2% to 5%), cough (2% to 4%), increased cough (2% to 3%), epistaxis (2%), bronchitis (≤2%)

Miscellaneous: Accidental injury (2%), fever (1% to 2%)

Frequency not defined: Ophthalmic: Diplopia (≤3%)

<1%, postmarketing, and/or case reports: Abnormal accommodation, abnormal stools, aggressive behavior, akinesia, alopecia, amnesia, anaphylactic shock, anaphylactoid reaction, anaphylaxis, anemia, angioedema, angle-closure glaucoma, aphasia, ataxia, atrioventricular block, bronchospasm, bruxism, cerebrovascular accident, change in prothrombin time, chills, colitis, coma, complete atrioventricular block, cystitis, deafness, delayed hypersensitivity, delirium, delusions, depersonalization, derealization, drug-induced Parkinson disease, dry eye syndrome, dysarthria, dyspareunia, dysphoria, dysuria, ecchymoses, edema, EEG pattern changes, ejaculatory disorder, emotional lability, erythema multiforme, esophagitis, euphoria, exfoliative dermatitis, extrapyramidal reaction, extrasystoles, facial edema, gastric ulcer, gastroesophageal reflux disease, gastrointestinal hemorrhage, gingival hemorrhage, gingivitis, glossitis, glycosuria, gynecomastia, hallucination, hepatic injury, hepatic insufficiency, hepatitis, hirsutism, homicidal ideation, hyperglycemia, hyperkinesia, hypertonia, hypoesthesia, hypoglycemia, hypokinesia, hypomania, impotence, increased intraocular pressure, increased libido, increased thirst, inguinal hernia, intestinal perforation, jaundice, leg cramps, leukocytosis, leukopenia, lymphadenopathy, maculopapular rash, malaise, manic behavior, menopause, muscle rigidity, musculoskeletal chest pain, myasthenia, mydriasis, myocardial infarction, myoclonus, neuralgia, neuropathy, orthostatic hypotension, painful erection, pancreatitis, pancytopenia, panic, paranoia, peripheral edema, phlebitis, pneumonia, prostatic disease, psychiatric signs and symptoms, psychosis, pulmonary embolism, restlessness, rhabdomyolysis, salpingitis, sciatica, seizure (dose-related), serum sickness-like reaction, SIADH, sialorrhea, skin photosensitivity, Stevens-Johnson syndrome, stomatitis, suicidal ideation, syncope, tardive dyskinesia, thrombocytopenia, tongue edema, urinary incontinence, urinary retention, vaginitis, vasodilatation, vertigo

Dosing

Adult

Depression: Oral: **Note:** Treatment should be periodically evaluated at appropriate intervals to ensure lowest effective dose is used.

Immediate release hydrochloride salt: Initial: 100 mg twice daily; after 3 days may increase to the usual dose of 100 mg 3 times a day; if no clinical improvement after several weeks, may increase to a maximum dose of 450 mg daily in 3 or 4 divided doses; do not exceed 150 mg in a single dose

Sustained release hydrochloride salt: Initial: 150 mg daily in the morning; if tolerated, after 3 days, may increase to a target dose of 150 mg twice daily; if no clinical improvement after several weeks, may increase to a maximum dose of 200 mg twice daily

Extended release:

Hydrochloride salt (Wellbutrin XL): Initial: 150 mg once daily in the morning; if tolerated, as early as day 4, may increase to 300 mg once daily (maximum dose: 300 mg/day; however, guidelines suggest up to 450 mg/day may be used [APA 2010]). **Note:** Forfivo XL may only be used after initial dose titration with other bupropion products.

Hydrochloride salt (Forfivo XL): *Switching from Wellbutrin immediate release, SR, or XL to Forfivo XL:* Patients receiving 300 mg daily of bupropion hydrochloride for at least 2 weeks and requiring a dose increase or patients already taking 450 mg daily of bupropion hydrochloride may switch to Forfivo XL 450 mg once daily.

Hydrobromide salt (Aplenzin): Initial: 174 mg once daily in the morning; may increase as early as day 4 of dosing to 348 mg once daily (target dose); maximum dose: 522 mg daily.

Switching from hydrochloride salt formulation (eg, Wellbutrin immediate release, SR, XL, or Forfivo XL) to hydrobromide salt formulation (Aplenzin):

Bupropion hydrochloride 150 mg daily is equivalent to bupropion hydrobromide 174 mg once daily

Bupropion hydrochloride 300 mg daily is equivalent to bupropion hydrobromide 348 mg once daily

Bupropion hydrochloride 450 mg daily is equivalent to bupropion hydrobromide 522 mg once daily

Seasonal affective disorder (SAD): Initial: 150 mg once daily (Wellbutrin XL) or 174 mg once daily (Aplenzin) in the morning; if tolerated, may increase after 1 week to 300 mg once daily (Wellbutrin XL) or 348 mg once daily (Aplenzin) in the morning.

Note: Prophylactic treatment should be reserved for those patients with frequent depressive episodes and/or significant impairment. Initiate treatment in the Autumn prior to symptom onset, and discontinue in early Spring with dose tapering. Doses >300 mg daily (Wellbutrin XL) or >348 mg daily (Aplenzin) have not been studied in SAD (maximum: Wellbutrin XL 300 mg daily; Aplenzin 522 mg daily).

Smoking cessation (Zyban, Buproban): Initial: 150 mg once daily for 3 days; increase to 150 mg twice daily; treatment should continue for 7 to 12 weeks (maximum dose: 300 mg daily).

Note: Therapy should begin at least 1 week before target quit date. Target quit dates are generally in the second week of treatment. If patient successfully quits smoking after 7 to 12 weeks, may consider ongoing maintenance therapy based on individual patient risk:benefit. Efficacy of maintenance therapy (300 mg daily) has been demonstrated for up to 6 months. Conversely, if significant progress has not been made by the seventh week of therapy, success is unlikely and treatment discontinuation should be considered.

Dosing conversion between hydrochloride salt immediate (Wellbutrin), sustained (Wellbutrin SR), and extended release (Wellbutrin XL, Forfivo XL) products: Convert using same total daily dose (up to the maximum recommended dose for a given dosage form), but adjust frequency as indicated for sustained (twice daily) or extended (once daily) release products.

Discontinuation of therapy: Upon discontinuation of antidepressant therapy, gradually taper the dose to allow for the detection of re-emerging symptoms. Withdrawal symptoms resulting from abrupt discontinuation are unlikely because bupropion has minimal serotonergic activity (APA 2010).

Manufacturer's labeling:

Aplenzin: In patients receiving 348 mg once daily, taper dose down to 174 mg once daily for 2 weeks prior to discontinuing.

Forfivo XL: Because the 450 mg tablet is the only available dose formulation, use another bupropion formulation for tapering the dose prior to discontinuation.

Wellbutrin XL: In patients receiving 300 mg once daily, taper dose down to 150 mg once daily for 2 weeks prior to discontinuing.

MAO inhibitor recommendations:

Switching to or from an MAO inhibitor antidepressant:

Allow 14 days to elapse between discontinuing an MAO inhibitor intended to treat depression and initiation of bupropion.

Allow 14 days to elapse between discontinuing bupropion and initiation of an MAO inhibitor intended to treat depression.

Attention-deficit/hyperactivity disorder (off-label use): Oral:

Sustained release: Initial: 100 mg once daily in the morning; increase weekly in 100 mg/day increments based on response and tolerability up to 200 mg twice daily (Reimherr 2005; Wilens 2001)

Extended release: Initial: 150 mg once daily in the morning for 1 week; increase to 300 mg once daily for 3 weeks; may further increase dose based on response and tolerability up to 450 mg once daily (Wilens 2005).

Depression associated with bipolar disorder (off-label use): Oral: Initial: 100 mg/day; increase based on response and tolerability at 2-week intervals up to 450 mg/day (average dose in clinical trials was 250 mg/day) (Grossman 1999; McIntyre 2002).

Obesity (off-label use): Oral: *Sustained release:* Initial: 150 mg once daily in the morning; increase to 150 mg twice daily after 3 days; may further increase dose after 2 weeks based on response and tolerability to 200 mg twice daily (dose-dependent responses were identified in one clinical trial) (Anderson 2002; Gadde 2001; Jain 2002).

Geriatric

Depression: Oral (hydrochloride salt): Initial: 37.5 mg of immediate release tablets twice daily or 100 mg daily of sustained release tablets; increase by 37.5 to 100 mg every 3 to 4 days as tolerated to a maximum dose of 300 mg daily (in divided doses). There is evidence that the elderly respond at 150 mg daily in divided doses, but some may require a higher dose. **Note:** Patients with Alzheimer's dementia-related depression may require a lower starting dosage of 37.5 mg once or twice daily (100 mg daily sustained release), increased as needed up to 300 mg daily in divided doses (300 mg daily for sustained release) (Rabins 2007).

Smoking cessation: Refer to adult dosing.

Discontinuation of therapy: Refer to adult dosing.

MAO inhibitor recommendations: Refer to adult dosing.

Pediatric ADHD (off-label use): Children and Adolescents: Oral:

Immediate release: Initial: 3 mg/kg/**day** in 2 to 3 divided doses; maximum initial dose 150 mg/**day**; increase dose as needed to a maximum daily dose of 6 mg/kg/**day** or 300 mg/**day** with no single dose >150 mg. (AACAP [Pliszka 2007])

Sustained release and extended release: May use in place of immediate-release tablets, once the daily dose is increased using the immediate release product and the 12-hour dosage corresponds to a sustained-release tablet size or the 24-hour dosage corresponds to an extended release tablet size.

MAO inhibitor recommendations: Refer to adult dosing.

Renal Impairment

Use with caution; manufacturer's labeling suggests a reduction in dose and/or frequency be considered but does not provide specific dosing recommendations. Aplenzin, Wellbutrin, Wellbutrin SR, Wellbutrin XL, and Zyban product labeling defines renal impairment as GFR <90 mL/minute.

Forfivo XL: Use is not recommended.

Hepatic Impairment

Mild impairment (Child-Pugh score 5 to 6): Use with caution; manufacturer's labeling suggests a reduction in dose and/or frequency be considered but does not provide specific dosing recommendations.

Forfivo XL: Use is not recommended.

Moderate to severe impairment, including severe hepatic cirrhosis (Child-Pugh score 7 to 15): Use with extreme caution; maximum dose:

Aplenzin: 174 mg every other day

Buproban: Severe hepatic cirrhosis: 150 mg every other day

Forfivo XL: Use is not recommended.

Wellbutrin: 75 mg once daily

Wellbutrin SR: 100 mg once daily or 150 mg every other day

Wellbutrin XL, Zyban: 150 mg every other day

Mechanism of Action Aminoketone antidepressant structurally different from all other marketed antidepressants; like other antidepressants the mechanism of bupropion's activity is not fully understood. Bupropion is a relatively weak inhibitor of the neuronal uptake of norepinephrine and dopamine, and does not inhibit monoamine oxidase or the reuptake of serotonin. Metabolite inhibits the reuptake of norepinephrine. The primary mechanism of action is thought to be dopaminergic and/or noradrenergic.

Contraindications

Hypersensitivity to bupropion or any component of the formulation; seizure disorder; history of anorexia/bulimia; patients undergoing abrupt discontinuation of ethanol or sedatives, including benzodiazepines, barbiturates, or antiepileptic drugs; use of MAO inhibitors (concurrently or within 14 days of discontinuing either bupropion or the MAO inhibitor); initiation of bupropion in a patient receiving linezolid or intravenous methylene blue

Aplenzin, Forfivo XL, Wellbutrin XL: Additional contraindications: Other conditions that increase seizure risk, including arteriovenous malformation, severe head injury, severe stroke, CNS tumor, CNS infection

Forfivo XL: Additional contraindications: Patients receiving other dosage forms of bupropion

Canadian labeling: Additional contraindications (not in US labeling): Concurrent use or use within 14 days of thioridazine; concurrent use with other dosage forms of bupropion

Warnings/Precautions [US Boxed Warning]: Antidepressants increase the risk of suicidal thinking and behavior in children, adolescents, and young adults in short-term trials. These trials did not show an increased risk in patients >65 years of age. In patients of all ages who are started on antidepressant therapy, monitor closely for worsening and for emergence of suicidal thoughts and behaviors, particularly during the initial 1 to 2 months of therapy or during periods of dosage adjustments (increases or decreases); **advise families and caregivers of the need for close observation and communication with the prescriber.** A medication guide concerning the use of antidepressants should be dispensed with each prescription.

The possibility of a suicide attempt is inherent in major depression and may persist until remission occurs. Worsening depression and severe abrupt suicidality that are not part of the presenting symptoms may require discontinuation or modification of drug therapy. Use caution in high-risk patients during initiation of therapy. Prescriptions should be written for the smallest quantity consistent with good patient care. The patient's family or caregiver should be alerted to monitor patients for the emergence of suicidality and associated behaviors such as anxiety, agitation, panic attacks, insomnia, irritability, hostility, impulsivity, akathisia, hypomania, and mania; patients should be instructed to notify their healthcare provider if any of these symptoms or worsening depression or psychosis occur.

[US Boxed Warning]: Serious neuropsychiatric events have occurred in patients taking bupropion for smoking cessation, including changes in mood (eg, depression, mania), psychosis, hallucinations, paranoia, delusions, homicidal ideation, hostility, agitation, aggression, anxiety, panic, suicidal ideation, suicide attempt and completed suicide. **The majority occurred during bupropion treatment; some occurred during treatment discontinuation. A causal relationship is uncertain as depressed mood may be a symptom of nicotine withdrawal. Some cases also occurred in patients taking bupropion who continued to smoke.** However, subsequent controlled trials in patients with or without psychiatric disorders have not identified significant differences in neuropsychiatric effects for patients taking bupropion, varenicline, nicotine patches, or placebo (Anthenelli 2016; Cinciripini 2013). **Observe all patients taking bupropion for neuropsychiatric reactions. Instruct patients to contact a health care provider.**

May cause delusions, hallucinations, psychosis, concentration disturbance, paranoia, and confusion; most common in depressed patients and patients with a diagnosis of bipolar disorder. Symptoms may abate with dose reduction and/or withdrawal of treatment. May precipitate a manic, mixed, or hypomanic episode; risk is increased in patients with bipolar disorder or who have risk factors for bipolar disorder. Screen patients for a history of bipolar disorder and the presence of risk factors including a family history of bipolar disorder, suicide, or depression. **Bupropion is not FDA approved for bipolar depression.**

May cause a dose-related risk of seizures. Use is contraindicated in patients with a history of seizures or certain conditions with high seizure risk (eg, history of anorexia/bulimia or patients undergoing abrupt discontinuation of ethanol, benzodiazepines, barbiturates, or antiepileptic drugs). Aplenzin, Forfivo XL, and Wellbutrin XL are also contraindicated in patients with certain conditions with high seizure risk (eg, arteriovenous malformation, severe head injury, severe stroke, CNS tumor, and CNS infection). Use caution with concurrent use of antipsychotics, antidepressants, theophylline, systemic corticosteroids, stimulants (including cocaine), anorexiants, or hypoglycemic agents, or with excessive use of ethanol, benzodiazepines, sedative/hypnotics, or opioids. Use with caution in seizure-potentiating metabolic disorders (hypoglycemia, hyponatremia, severe hepatic impairment, and hypoxia). The dose-dependent risk of seizures may be reduced by gradual dose increases and by not exceeding the maximum daily dose. Do not coadminister with other bupropion-containing formulations; Forfivo XL is contraindicated in patients receiving other dosage forms of bupropion. Permanently discontinue if seizure occurs during therapy. Chewing, crushing, injecting, or dividing long-acting products may increase seizure risk.

May cause CNS stimulation (restlessness, anxiety, insomnia) or anorexia. May increase the risks associated with electroconvulsive therapy (ECT); consider discontinuing, when possible, prior to ECT treatment (APA 2010). May cause weight loss; use caution in patients where weight loss is not desirable. The incidence of sexual dysfunction with bupropion is generally lower than with SSRIs.

May elevate blood pressure and cause hypertension. Events have been observed in patients with or without evidence of preexisting hypertension. The risk is increased when used concomitantly with monoamine oxidase inhibitors, nicotine replacement, or other drugs that increase dopaminergic or noradrenergic activity. Assess blood pressure before treatment and monitor periodically. Use caution in patients with cardiovascular disease, hypertension, or coronary artery disease; treatment-emergent hypertension (including some severe cases) has been reported, both with bupropion alone and in combination with nicotine transdermal systems. All children diagnosed with ADHD (off-label use of bupropion) who may be candidates for stimulant medications should have a thorough cardiovascular assessment to identify risk factors for sudden cardiac death prior to initiation of drug therapy. Use with caution in patients with hepatic or renal dysfunction and in elderly patients; reduced dose and/or frequency may be recommended; Forfivo XL is not recommended in patients with hepatic or renal impairment. Elderly patients may be at greater risk of accumulation during chronic dosing. May cause motor or cognitive impairment in some patients; use with caution if tasks requiring alertness such as operating machinery or driving are undertaken. May cause mild pupillary dilation, which in susceptible individuals can lead to an episode of narrow-angle glaucoma. Consider evaluating patients who have not had an iridectomy for narrow-angle glaucoma risk factors. Anaphylactoid/anaphylactic reactions have occurred, with symptoms of pruritus, urticaria, angioedema, and dyspnea. Serious reactions have been (rarely) reported, including erythema multiforme, Stevens-Johnson syndrome and anaphylactic shock. Arthralgia, myalgia, and fever with rash and other symptoms suggestive of delayed hypersensitivity resembling serum sickness have been reported. Potentially significant drug-drug interactions may exist, requiring dose or frequency adjustment, additional monitoring, and/or selection of alternative therapy. Using doses higher than prescribed may result in increased motor activity, agitation/excitement and euphoria. Inhalation of crushed tablets or injection of dissolved bupropion has been reported, some resulting in seizures and death.

Extended release tablet: Insoluble tablet shell may remain intact and be visible in the stool.

Drug Interactions

Metabolism/Transport Effects **Substrate** of CYP1A2 (minor), CYP2A6 (minor), CYP2B6 (major), CYP2C9 (minor), CYP2D6 (minor), CYP2E1 (minor), CYP3A4 (minor); **Note:** Assignment of Major/Minor substrate status based on clinically relevant drug interaction potential; **Inhibits** CYP2D6 (moderate), OCT2

Avoid Concomitant Use

Avoid concomitant use of BuPROPion with any of the following: MAO Inhibitors; Thioridazine

Increased Effect/Toxicity

BuPROPion may increase the levels/effects of: Ajmaline; Alcohol (Ethyl); ARIPiprazole; Brexpiprazole; Citalopram; CloZAPine; CYP2D6 Substrates; DOXOrubicin (Conventional); Eliglustat; Fesoterodine; FLUoxetine; FluvoxaMINE; Indoramin; Iohexol; Iomeprol; Iopamidol; Lorcaserin; Metoprolol; Nebivolol; OCT2 Substrates; PARoxetine; Perhexiline; Propafenone; Thioridazine; Tricyclic Antidepressants; Vortioxetine

The levels/effects of BuPROPion may be increased by: Alcohol (Ethyl); Anti-Parkinson Agents (Dopamine Agonist); CYP2B6 Inhibitors (Weak); MAO Inhibitors; MiFEPRIStone; Thiotepa

Decreased Effect

BuPROPion may decrease the levels/effects of: Codeine; Ioflupane I 123; Tamoxifen; TraMADol

The levels/effects of BuPROPion may be decreased by: Antihepaciviral Combination Products; CYP2B6 Inducers (Moderate); Dabrafenib; Efavirenz; Isavuconazonium Sulfate; Lopinavir; Lumacaftor; Nilotinib; Ritonavir

Pharmacodynamics/Kinetics

Onset of Action 1 to 2 weeks

Duration of Action 1 to 2 days

Half-life Elimination

Distribution: 3 to 4 hours

Elimination: ~21 hours after chronic dosing (range: 12 to 30 hours); Metabolites (after a single dose): Hydroxybupropion: 20 ± 5 hours; Erythrohydrobupropion: 33 ± 10 hours; Threohydrobupropion: 37 ± 13 hours

Extended release (Aplenzin): 21 ± 7 hours; Metabolites: Hydroxybupropion: 24 ± 5 hours; Erythrohydrobupropion: 31 ± 8 hours; Threohydrobupropion: 51 ± 9 hours

Time to Peak

Bupropion: Immediate release: Within 2 hours; Sustained release: Within 3 hours; Extended release: ~5 hours (Forfivo XL: 5 hours [fasting]; 12 hours [fed])

Metabolite: Hydroxybupropion: Immediate release: ~3 hours; Extended release, sustained release: ~6 to 7 hours

Pregnancy Risk Factor C

Pregnancy Considerations Adverse events have been observed in some animal reproduction studies. Bupropion and its metabolites were found to cross the placenta in in vitro studies (Earhart 2012). An increased risk of congenital malformations has not been observed following maternal use of bupropion during pregnancy; however, data specific to cardiovascular malformations is inconsistent. The long-term effects on development and behavior have not been studied. The ACOG recommends that antidepressant therapy during pregnancy be individualized; treatment of depression during pregnancy should incorporate the clinical expertise of the mental health clinician, obstetrician, primary health care provider, and pediatrician. According to the American Psychiatric Association (APA), the risks of medication treatment should be weighed against other treatment options and untreated depression. For women who discontinue antidepressant medications during pregnancy and who may be at high risk for postpartum depression, the medications can be restarted following delivery. Treatment algorithms have been developed by the ACOG and the APA for the management of depression in women prior to conception and during pregnancy (ACOG 2008; APA 2010; Yonkers 2009). There is insufficient information related to the use of bupropion to recommend use in pregnancy (ACOG 2010).

Pregnant women exposed to antidepressants during pregnancy are encouraged to enroll in the National Pregnancy Registry for Antidepressants (NPRAD). Women 18 to 45 years of age or their health care providers may contact the registry by calling 844-405-6185. Enrollment should be done as early in pregnancy as possible.

Breastfeeding Considerations Bupropion and its metabolites are excreted into breast milk. The estimated dose to a nursing infant varies by study and has been reported as ~2% of the weight-adjusted maternal dose (range: 1.4% to 10.6%) (Davis 2009; Haas 2004). Adverse events have been reported with some antidepressants and a seizure was noted in one 6-month-old nursing infant exposed to bupropion (a causal effect could not be confirmed) (Chaudron 2004; Hale 2010; Neuman 2014). Recommendations for use in nursing women vary by manufacturer labeling.

Dosage Forms

Tablet, Oral:
- Generic: 75 mg, 100 mg

Tablet Extended Release 12 Hour, Oral:
- Wellbutrin SR: 100 mg, 150 mg, 200 mg
- Zyban: 150 mg
- Generic: 100 mg, 150 mg, 200 mg

Tablet Extended Release 24 Hour, Oral:
- Aplenzin: 174 mg, 348 mg, 522 mg
- Forfivo XL: 450 mg
- Wellbutrin XL: 150 mg, 300 mg
- Generic: 150 mg, 300 mg

Dosage Forms: Canada Refer to Dosage Forms. **Note:** Aplenzin, Buproban, and Forfivo XL are not available in Canada.

Buserelin (BYOO se rel in)

Brand Names: Canada Suprefact; Suprefact Depot

Pharmacologic Category Gonadotropin Releasing Hormone Agonist

Use Note: Not approved in the US

Endometriosis: Nasal solution: Treatment of endometriosis in women who do not require surgical intervention as first-line therapy (length of therapy is usually 6 months, and should not exceed 9 months)

Prostate cancer, advanced: Injection, nasal solution: Palliative treatment in patients with hormone-dependent advanced prostate cancer (stage D)

Local Anesthetic/Vasoconstrictor Precautions Buserelin may cause hypertension and palpitations. Monitor blood pressure prior to dental procedures if using local anesthesia with vasoconstrictor. There have been no reports of any direct interaction with buserelin and vasoconstrictor.

Effects on Dental Treatment No significant effects or complications reported

Effects on Bleeding No information available to require special precautions

Adverse Reactions Note: Adverse reaction profile differs based on population/medication and route of administration.

>10%:
- Central nervous system: Headache (20% to 29%)
- Endocrine & metabolic: Loss of libido (prostatic cancer 75% to 85%), hot flash (14% to 72%), hypermenorrhea (endometriosis 24%), decreased libido (endometriosis 12%, prostatic cancer 2% to 5%)
- Gastrointestinal: Flatulence (≤15%)
- Genitourinary: Impotence (prostatic cancer 2% to 79%), vaginal dryness (endometriosis 29%)
- Neuromuscular & skeletal: Back pain (4% to 28%), weakness (≤14%)
- Respiratory: Nasal mucosa irritation (intranasal 13%)

1% to 10%:
- Cardiovascular: Edema (≤6%), hypertension (2% to 5%), peripheral edema (2%), palpitations (≤1%)
- Central nervous system: Dizziness (9%), depression (8%), malaise (≤8%), emotional lability (7%), insomnia (≤5%), nervousness (≤2%), pain (≤2%), anxiety (1%), hostility (1%), sleep disorder (1%)
- Dermatologic: Acne vulgaris (endometriosis 5%), dermatological reaction (2%), urticaria at injection site (subcutaneous 2%), xeroderma (2%), diaphoresis (≤2%), pruritus (≤2%)
- Endocrine & metabolic: Gynecomastia (prostatic cancer ≤3%), weight gain (≤3%), premenstrual syndrome (endometriosis 2%), weight loss (≤2%), menstrual disease (endometriosis 1%), hirsutism (endometriosis ≤1%), increased testosterone level (clinical flare; prostatic cancer ≤1%)
- Gastrointestinal: Diarrhea (≤8%), nausea (≤7%), increased appetite (≤5%), sore throat (≤5%), vomiting (1% to 4%), gastrointestinal fullness (3%), xerostomia (1% to 3%), gastrointestinal distress (≤3%), dysgeusia (2%), constipation (≤1%)
- Genitourinary: Leukorrhea (endometriosis 4%), mastalgia (endometriosis 3%), dyspareunia (endometriosis 2%), vaginal discharge (endometriosis 2%), vaginitis (endometriosis 2%), pelvic pain (endometriosis ≤2%), vaginal discomfort (endometriosis 1%)
- Hematologic & oncologic: Purpura (1%)
- Infection: Infection (7%)
- Local: Application site reaction (intranasal 8%), pain at injection site (subcutaneous 5%), injection site reaction (subcutaneous ≤5%), application site irritation (intranasal 4%), irritation at injection site (subcutaneous 3%), swelling at injection site (subcutaneous 3%)

Neuromuscular & skeletal: Arthralgia (≤5%), myalgia (2% to 5%), limb pain (2%), neck stiffness (1%)
Respiratory: Dry nose (intranasal 2%), rhinitis (2%), upper respiratory tract infection (1%)
<1%, postmarketing, and/or case reports: Abdominal pain, abnormality in thinking, accommodation disturbance, altered sense of smell, amnesia, anaphylactic shock, anaphylactoid reaction, anemia, anorexia, arthralgia, arthritis, bleeding at injection site, breast atrophy (endometriosis), breast hypertrophy (endometriosis), cardiac failure, change in appetite, decreased bone mineral density, decreased glucose tolerance, drowsiness, dry eye syndrome, dyslipidemia, dyspnea, ear disease, eczema, ejaculatory disorder (prostatic cancer), epistaxis, exacerbation of diabetes mellitus, extrinsic asthma, eye disease, eye irritation, fatigue, fecal incontinence, feminization (prostatic cancer), fever, gastrointestinal pain, genital pain (prostatic cancer; male), genitourinary disease, hyperalgesia, hypercholesterolemia, hyperglycemia, hyperlipidemia, hypersensitivity reaction, increased acid phosphatase (transient), increased plasma estradiol concentration (endometriosis; transient), increased serum bilirubin, increased serum transaminases, increased thirst, lack of concentration, lactation (endometriosis; female), leukopenia, loss of body hair, loss of scalp hair, memory impairment, muscle cramps, musculoskeletal pain, myelofibrosis, myopathy, onychia sicca, oral mucosa ulcer, otalgia, ovarian cyst (endometriosis; during initial phase of therapy), pharyngitis, pituitary neoplasm, rhinorrhea, sensation of eye pressure, skin photosensitivity, skin rash, suicidal tendencies, syncope, tachycardia, testicular atrophy (prostatic cancer), thrombocytopenia, thrombophlebitis, thrombosis, tinnitus, transient blindness (one eye), tremor, urinary retention, vaginal hemorrhage (endometriosis), vasodilatation, vertigo, visual disturbance

General Dosage Range

Intranasal: *Adults:* 400 mcg (200 mcg into each nostril) 3 times daily

SubQ: *Adults:*

Implants: 6.3 mg every 2 months **or** 9.45 mg every 3 months

Injection: Initial: 500 mcg every 8 hours for 7 days; maintenance: 200 mcg once daily

Mechanism of Action Synthetic peptide analog of gonadotropin hormone releasing hormone (GnRH) with a magnified GnRH agonist effect and an extended duration of activity. Following an initial rise in the pituitary gonadotropins luteinizing hormone (LH) and follicle-stimulating hormone (FSH), chronic administration of buserelin results in a sustained suppression of LH and FSH and interferes with the production of ovarian and testicular steroids. Eventually, a decline in gonadal steroids to castration levels is observed.

Pharmacodynamics/Kinetics

Onset of Action 3-month depot implant: Mean time until testosterone reached castrate levels: 10 days

Half-life Elimination SubQ: Immediate release: 80 minutes; Depot implants: 20 to 30 days; Nasal: 1 to 2 hours

Time to Peak 3-month depot: <1 day

Pregnancy Considerations

Buserelin is contraindicated in pregnant women.

Patients should employ a nonhormonal method of contraception during therapy. To exclude preexisting pregnancy, begin treatment on the first or second day of menses; if there is doubt, a pregnancy test is recommended. Ovulation may occur with a missed dose; in the event a patient conceives, therapy should be discontinued.

Product Availability Not available in the US

BusPIRone (byoo SPYE rone)

Related Information

Management of the Patient With Anxiety or Depression *on page 1873*

Brand Names: Canada Apo-Buspirone; Dom-Buspirone; PMS-Buspirone; Riva-Buspirone; Teva-Buspirone

Pharmacologic Category Antianxiety Agent, Miscellaneous

Use Generalized anxiety disorder: Management of generalized anxiety disorder (GAD)

Local Anesthetic/Vasoconstrictor Precautions No information available to require special precautions

Effects on Dental Treatment Key adverse event(s) related to dental treatment: Xerostomia (normal salivary flow resumes upon discontinuation).

Effects on Bleeding No information available to require special precautions

Adverse Reactions

>10%: Central nervous system: Dizziness (3% to 12%)
1% to 10%:
Cardiovascular: Chest pain (≥1%)
Central nervous system: Drowsiness (10%), headache (6%), nervousness (5%), confusion (2%), excitement (2%), numbness (2%), outbursts of anger (2%), abnormal dreams (≥1%), ataxia (1%) paresthesia (1%)
Dermatologic: Diaphoresis (1%), skin rash (1%)
Gastrointestinal: Nausea (8%), diarrhea (2%), sore throat (≥1%)
Neuromuscular & skeletal: Weakness (2%), musculoskeletal pain (1%), tremor (1%)
Ophthalmic: Blurred vision (2%)
Otic: Tinnitus (≥1%)
Respiratory: Nasal congestion (≥1%)
<1%, postmarketing, and/or case reports: Acne vulgaris, akathisia, alcohol abuse, alopecia, altered sense of smell, amenorrhea, angioedema, anorexia, apathy, arthralgia, bradycardia, bruise, cardiac failure, cardiomyopathy, cerebrovascular accident, change in libido, claustrophobia, cogwheel rigidity, cold intolerance, conjunctivitis, delayed ejaculation, depersonalization, dissociative reaction, dysgeusia, dyskinesia, dysphoria, dyspnea, dystonia, dysuria, edema, emotional lability, eosinophilia, epistaxis, euphoria, extrapyramidal reaction, eye pain, facial edema, fear, fever, flatulence, flushing, galactorrhea, glossopyrosis, hallucination, hemorrhagic diathesis, hiccups, hyperacusis, hypersensitivity reaction, hypertension, hyperventilation, hypotension, impotence, increased appetite, increased intraocular pressure, increased serum ALT, increased serum AST, increased serum transaminases, inner ear disturbance, involuntary muscle movements, irritable bowel syndrome, laryngitis, leukopenia, malaise, memory impairment, menstrual disease, muscle cramps, muscle spasm, myocardial infarction, nocturia, parkinsonian-like syndrome, pelvic inflammatory disease, personality disorder, photophobia, pruritus, psychosis, rectal hemorrhage, restless leg syndrome, restlessness, roaring sensation in head, salivation, seizure, serotonin syndrome, skin blister, slowed reaction time, slurred speech, stiffness, stupor, suicidal ideation, syncope, thinning of nails, thrombocytopenia, thyroid disease, urinary frequency, urinary hesitancy, urinary

incontinence, urinary retention, urticaria, vertigo, visual disturbance (tunnel vision), weight gain, weight loss, xeroderma

General Dosage Range Oral: *Adults:* Initial: 7.5 mg twice daily; Maintenance: Up to 30 mg twice daily (usual dose: 10-15 mg twice daily)

Mechanism of Action The mechanism of action of buspirone is unknown. Buspirone has a high affinity for serotonin 5-HT_{1A} and 5-HT_2 receptors, without affecting benzodiazepine-GABA receptors. Buspirone has moderate affinity for dopamine D_2 receptors.

Pharmacodynamics/Kinetics

Onset of Action Within 2 weeks

Half-life Elimination 2 to 3 hours; increased with renal or hepatic impairment

Time to Peak Serum: 40 to 90 minutes

Pregnancy Risk Factor B

Pregnancy Considerations Adverse events have not been observed in animal reproduction studies.

Busulfan (byoo SUL fan)

Brand Names: US Busulfex; Myleran

Brand Names: Canada Busulfex; Myleran

Pharmacologic Category Antineoplastic Agent, Alkylating Agent

Use

Chronic myeloid leukemia (CML):

Injection: Conditioning regimen prior to allogeneic hematopoietic progenitor cell transplantation for CML (in combination with cyclophosphamide)

Tablets: Palliative treatment of CML

Local Anesthetic/Vasoconstrictor Precautions No information available to require special precautions

Effects on Dental Treatment Key adverse event(s) related to dental treatment: Xerostomia (normal salivary flow resumes upon discontinuation), mucositis/stomatitis.

Effects on Bleeding Thrombocytopenia is a dose-limiting toxicity of busulfan. A medical consult is suggested.

Adverse Reactions

Intravenous:

>10%:

Cardiovascular: Edema (28% to 36%), tachycardia (44%), hypertension (36%), thrombosis (33%), chest pain (26%), vasodilatation (25%), hepatic veno-occlusive disease (hepatic sinusoidal obstruction syndrome; children: 21%; adults: 8% to 12%)

Central nervous system: Insomnia (84%), anxiety (72%), headache (69%), chills (46%), pain (44%), dizziness (30%), depression (23%)

Dermatologic: Skin rash (57%), pruritus (28%)

Endocrine & metabolic: Hypomagnesemia (77%), hyperglycemia (66%), hypokalemia (64%), hypocalcemia (49%)

Gastrointestinal: Vomiting (95% to 100%), nausea (adults 98%; children 83%), mucositis (≤97%), stomatitis (adults ≤97%; children 79%), anorexia (85%), diarrhea (84%; grades 3/4: 5%), abdominal pain (72%), dyspepsia (44%), constipation (38%), xerostomia (26%), rectal disease (25%), gastrointestinal fullness (23%)

Hematologic & oncologic: Neutropenia (100%; onset: 4 days; median recovery: 13 days [with G-CSF support]), bone marrow depression (≤100%), thrombocytopenia (98%; median onset: 5 to 6 days), lymphocytopenia (children: 79%), anemia (69%)

Hepatic: Hyperbilirubinemia (49%), increased serum ALT (31%)

Hypersensitivity: Hypersensitivity reaction (26%)

Immunologic: Graft versus host disease (children: 25%)

Local: Inflammation at injection site (25%)

Neuromuscular & skeletal: Weakness (51%), back pain (23%)

Renal: Increased serum creatinine (21%)

Respiratory: Rhinitis (44%), pulmonary disease (34%), cough (28%), dyspnea (25%), epistaxis (25%), pneumonia (children: 21%)

Miscellaneous: Fever (80%)

1% to 10%: Cardiovascular: Cardiac tamponade (children with thalassemia: 2%)

Frequency not defined:

Cardiovascular: Atrial fibrillation, cardiac arrhythmia, cardiomegaly, catheter site thrombosis (central venous catheter), complete atrioventricular block, ECG abnormality, flushing, hypotension, left heart failure, pericardial effusion, ventricular premature contractions

Central nervous system: Agitation, brain disease, cerebral hemorrhage, coma, confusion, delirium, drowsiness, hallucination, lethargy

Dermatologic: Acne vulgaris, alopecia, erythema nodosum, exfoliative dermatitis, maculopapular rash, skin discoloration, vesicular eruption, vesiculobullous dermatitis

Endocrine & metabolic: Hot flash, hypervolemia, hyponatremia, hypophosphatemia, weight gain

Gastrointestinal: Esophagitis, hematemesis, hiccups, intestinal obstruction, pancreatitis, rectal pain

Genitourinary: Dysuria, hematuria, hemorrhagic cystitis, oliguria

Hematologic & oncologic: Prolonged prothrombin time

Hepatic: Hepatomegaly, increased serum alkaline phosphatase, jaundice

Immunologic: Graft versus host disease (adults)

Infection: Infection

Local: Pain at injection site

Neuromuscular & skeletal: Arthralgia, myalgia

Otic: Ear disease

Renal: Increased blood urea nitrogen

Respiratory: Asthma, atelectasis, hemoptysis, hyperventilation, hypoxia, pharyngitis, pleural effusion, pulmonary alveolar hemorrhage, pulmonary interstitial fibrosis, sinusitis

Oral:

1% to 10%:

Central nervous system: Seizure (2%; despite prophylactic seizure therapy)

Dermatologic: Skin hyperpigmentation (5% to 10%)

Frequency not defined:

Endocrine & metabolic: Amenorrhea, ovarian failure

Hematologic & oncologic: Bone marrow depression (including anemia, leukopenia, thrombocytopenia), pancytopenia

Respiratory: Pulmonary interstitial fibrosis

IV and/or Oral: <1%, postmarketing, and/or case reports: Acute leukemia, adrenocortical insufficiency, alopecia (permanent), anhidrosis, aplastic anemia (may be irreversible), azoospermia, capillary leak syndrome, cataract (rare), cheilosis, cholestatic jaundice, corneal thinning, dry mucous membranes, enamel hypoplasia, myocardiopathy (endocardial fibrosis of left ventricle), erythema multiforme, esophageal varices (with continuous busulfan and thioguanine therapy), febrile neutropenia, fragile skin, gynecomastia, hepatic fibrosis (centrilobular sinus), hepatic disease (hepatocellular atrophy), hepatic necrosis, hepatic veno-occlusive disease (oral), lens changes, malignant neoplasm, myasthenia gravis, porphyria cutanea tarda, pulmonary fibrosis (with bronchopulmonary dysplasia), recall skin sensitization (skin rash), sepsis, sterility, testicular atrophy, thrombotic thrombocytopenic purpura, tumor lysis syndrome, urticaria, xeroderma

General Dosage Range

IV:

Children ≤12 kg: **HSCT:** 1.1 mg/kg (actual body weight) every 6 hours for 16 doses

Children >12 kg: **HSCT:** 0.8 mg/kg (actual body weight) every 6 hours for 16 doses

Adults: **HSCT:** 0.8 mg/kg every 6 hours for 16 doses (use ideal body weight or actual body weight, whichever is lower; use adjusted body weight if obese)

Oral: Dosage adjustment is recommended in patients who experience toxicity:

Children: Induction: 60 mcg/kg/day **or** 1.8 mg/m^2/day; Maintenance: Resume induction dose **or** 1 to 3 mg/day

Adults: Induction: 60 mcg/kg/day **or** 1.8 mg/m^2/day; usual range: 4 to 8 mg/day; Maintenance: Resume induction dose **or** 1 to 3 mg/day

Mechanism of Action Busulfan is an alkylating agent which reacts with the N-7 position of guanosine and interferes with DNA replication and transcription of RNA. Busulfan has a more marked effect on myeloid cells than on lymphoid cells and is also very toxic to hematopoietic stem cells. Busulfan exhibits little immunosuppressive activity. Interferes with the normal function of DNA by alkylation and cross-linking the strands of DNA.

Pharmacodynamics/Kinetics

Half-life Elimination 2 to 3 hours

Time to Peak Serum: Oral: ~1 hour; IV: Within 5 minutes

Pregnancy Risk Factor D

Pregnancy Considerations Adverse events were observed in animal reproduction studies. May cause fetal harm if administered during pregnancy. The solvent in IV busulfan, DMA, is also associated with teratogenic effects and may impair fertility. Women and men of childbearing potential should use effective contraception to avoid pregnancy during and after busulfan treatment.

Butalbital, Acetaminophen, Caffeine, and Codeine

(byoo TAL bi tal, a seet a MIN oh fen, KAF een, & KOE deen)

Related Information

Acetaminophen *on page 56*

Caffeine *on page 276*

Codeine *on page 410*

Brand Names: US Fioricet with Codeine

Generic Availability (US) Yes

Pharmacologic Category Analgesic Combination (Opioid); Analgesic, Opioid; Barbiturate

Use

Tension or muscle contraction headache: Management of the symptom complex of tension (muscle contraction) headache when nonopioid analgesic and alternative treatments are inadequate.

Limitations of use: Reserve for use in patients for whom alternative treatment options (eg, nonopioid, non-barbiturate analgesics) are ineffective, not tolerated, or would be otherwise inadequate to provide sufficient management of pain.

Local Anesthetic/Vasoconstrictor Precautions No information available to require special precautions

Effects on Dental Treatment No significant effects or complications reported (see Dental Comment)

Effects on Bleeding As a single agent, acetaminophen does not appear to affect bleeding or platelet aggregation. Acetaminophen may prolong the INR and increase bleeding in patients taking warfarin (Coumadin). For patients taking warfarin, single acetaminophen doses or acetaminophen therapy of short duration should be safe, but if large (>1.3 g/day) doses are administered for longer than 10-14 days, then the INR should be monitored (see Dental Comment).

Adverse Reactions Frequency not defined.

Cardiovascular: Syncope, tachycardia

Central nervous system: Agitation, confusion, depression, dizziness, drowsiness, euphoria, excitement, fatigue, headache, increased energy, intoxicated feeling, lethargy, numbness, paresthesia, sedation, seizure, shakiness

Dermatologic: Hyperhidrosis, pruritus

Endocrine & metabolic: Hot flash

Gastrointestinal: Abdominal pain, constipation, dysphagia, flatulence, heartburn, nausea, vomiting, xerostomia

Genitourinary: Diuresis

Hypersensitivity: Hypersensitivity reaction

Neuromuscular & skeletal: Leg pain, muscle fatigue

Otic: Otalgia, tinnitus

Respiratory: Dyspnea, nasal congestion

Miscellaneous: Fever, heavy eyelids

Postmarketing and/or case reports: Hypogonadism (Brennan, 2013; Debono 2011)

Note: Potential reactions associated with components of Fioricet with Codeine include agranulocytosis, cardiac stimulation, dependence, erythema multiforme, hyperglycemia, irritability, nephrotoxicity, rash, thrombocytopenia, toxic epidermal necrolysis, tremor

Dosing

Adult

Tension or muscle contraction headache: Oral:

Butalbital 50 mg/acetaminophen 300 mg/caffeine 40 mg/codeine 30 mg: 1 to 2 capsules every 4 hours as needed; maximum dose: 6 capsules (butalbital 300 mg/acetaminophen 1,800 mg/caffeine 240 mg/codeine 180 mg) per day

Butalbital 50 mg/acetaminophen 325 mg/caffeine 40 mg/codeine 30 mg: 1 to 2 capsules every 4 hours as needed; maximum dose: 6 capsules (butalbital 300 mg/acetaminophen 1,950 mg/caffeine 240 mg/codeine 180 mg) per day

Discontinuation of therapy: Decrease dose by 25% to 50% every 2 to 4 days; monitor carefully for signs/symptoms of withdrawal. If patient displays withdrawal symptoms, increase dose to previous level and then reduce dose more slowly by increasing interval between dose reductions, decreasing amount of daily dose reduction, or both.

Geriatric Refer to adult dosing. Initiate dosing at the lower end of the dosage range; monitor closely.

Renal Impairment There are no specific dosage adjustments provided in the manufacturer's labeling; initiate with a low dose or with longer dosing intervals and titrate slowly; use with caution and monitor carefully.

Hepatic Impairment There are no specific dosage adjustments provided in the manufacturer's labeling (has not been studied); initiate with a low dose or with longer dosing intervals and titrate slowly; use with caution and monitor carefully.

Mechanism of Action

Acetaminophen: Inhibits the synthesis of prostaglandins in the central nervous system and peripherally blocks pain impulse generation; produces antipyresis from inhibition of hypothalamic heat-regulating center.

Butalbital: Short- to intermediate-acting barbiturate; depresses the sensory cortex, decreases motor activity, alters cerebellar function, and produces drowsiness, sedation, hypnosis, and dose-dependent respiratory depression.

Caffeine: CNS stimulant; use with acetaminophen and dihydrocodeine increases the level of analgesia provided by each agent.

Codeine: Binds to opiate receptors in the CNS, causing inhibition of ascending pain pathways, altering the perception of and response to pain; produces generalized CNS depression.

Contraindications

Known intolerance or hypersensitivity to butalbital, codeine, caffeine, acetaminophen, or any component of the formulation; significant respiratory depression; postoperative pain management in children who have undergone tonsillectomy and/or adenoidectomy; acute or severe bronchial asthma in an unmonitored setting or in the absence of resuscitative equipment; concurrent use of monoamine oxidase inhibitors (MAOIs) or use of MAOIs within the last 14 days; GI obstruction, including paralytic ileus (known or suspected); porphyria.

Documentation of allergenic cross-reactivity for opioids is limited. However, because of similarities in chemical structure and/or pharmacologic actions, the possibility of cross-sensitivity cannot be ruled out with certainty.

Warnings/Precautions [US Boxed Warning]: Respiratory depression and death have occurred in children who received codeine following tonsillectomy and/or adenoidectomy and had evidence of being ultra-rapid metabolizers of codeine due to a CYP2D6 polymorphism. Deaths have also occurred in nursing infants after being exposed to high concentrations of morphine because the mothers were ultra-rapid metabolizers. Use is contraindicated in the postoperative pain management of children who have undergone tonsillectomy and/or adenoidectomy. **[US Boxed Warning]: Serious, life-threatening, or fatal respiratory depression may occur with use. Monitor for respiratory depression, especially during initiation of therapy or following a dose increase.** Carbon dioxide retention from opioid-induced respiratory depression can exacerbate the sedating effects of opioids. Use with caution and monitor for respiratory depression in patients with significant chronic obstructive pulmonary disease or cor pulmonale, and those having a substantially decreased respiratory reserve, hypoxia, hypercarbia, or preexisting respiratory depression, particularly when initiating therapy and titrating therapy; critical respiratory depression may occur, even at therapeutic dosages. Consider the use of alternative nonopioid analgesics in these patients.

[US Boxed Warning]: Prolonged use of opioids during pregnancy can cause neonatal withdrawal syndrome, which may be life-threatening if not recognized and treated according to protocols developed by neonatology experts. If opioid use is required for a prolonged period in a pregnant woman, advise the patient of the risk of neonatal opioid withdrawal syndrome and ensure that appropriate treatment will be available. Signs and symptoms include irritability, hyperactivity and abnormal sleep pattern, high-pitched cry, tremor, vomiting, diarrhea, and failure to gain weight. Onset, duration, and severity depend on the drug used, duration of use, maternal dose, and rate of drug elimination by the newborn.

Use caution in patients with two or more copies of the variant CYP2D6*2 allele; may have extensive conversion from codeine to morphine and thus increased opioid-mediated effects. Avoid the use of codeine in these patients; consider alternative analgesics such as morphine or a nonopioid agent (Crews, 2012). The occurrence of this phenotype is seen in 0.5% to 1% of Chinese and Japanese, 0.5% to 1% of Hispanics, 1% to 10% of Caucasians, 3% of African-Americans, and 16% to 28% of North Africans, Ethiopians, and Arabs.

May cause CNS depression, which may impair physical or mental abilities; patients must be cautioned about performing tasks which require mental alertness (eg, operating machinery or driving). **[US Boxed Warning]: Acetaminophen has been associated with cases of acute liver failure, at times resulting in liver transplant and death. Most of the cases of liver injury are associated with the use of acetaminophen at doses that exceed 4 g/day, and often involve more than one acetaminophen-containing product.** Risk is increased with alcohol use, preexisting liver disease, and intake of more than one source of acetaminophen-containing medications. Chronic daily dosing in adults has also resulted in liver damage in some patients. Hypersensitivity and anaphylactic reactions have been reported with acetaminophen use; discontinue immediately if symptoms of allergic or hypersensitivity reactions occur.

Serious and potentially fatal skin reactions such as acute generalized exanthematous pustulosis, Stevens-Johnson syndrome (SJS), and toxic epidermal necrolysis (TEN) have occurred rarely with acetaminophen. Discontinue treatment at the first appearance of skin rash (or any other sign of hypersensitivity). Concurrent use of mixed agonist/antagonist analgesics (eg, pentazocine, nalbuphine, butorphanol) or partial agonist analgesics (eg, buprenorphine) may precipitate withdrawal symptoms and/or reduced analgesic efficacy in patients following prolonged therapy with mu opioid agonists. Abrupt discontinuation following prolonged use may also lead to withdrawal symptoms; taper dose gradually when discontinuing. May cause severe hypotension (including orthostatic hypotension and syncope); use with caution in patients with hypovolemia, cardiovascular disease (including acute myocardial infarction [MI]), or drugs that may exaggerate hypotensive effects (including phenothiazines or general anesthetics). Monitor for symptoms of hypotension following initiation or dose titration. Avoid use in patients with circulatory shock.

[US Boxed Warning]: Use exposes patients and other users to the risks of opioid addiction, abuse, and misuse, which can lead to overdose and death. Assess each patient's risk prior to prescribing; monitor all patients regularly for the development of these behaviors or conditions. Use with caution in patients with a history of drug abuse or acute alcoholism; potential for drug dependency exists. Other factors associated with increased risk for misuse include younger age, concomitant depression (major), and psychotropic medication use. **[US Boxed Warning]: Accidental ingestion of even one dose, especially**

in children, can result in a fatal overdose of codeine.

[US Boxed Warning]: Concomitant use of opioids with benzodiazepines or other CNS depressants, including alcohol, may result in profound sedation, respiratory depression, coma, and death. Reserve concomitant prescribing of butalbital/acetaminophen/caffeine/codeine and benzodiazepines or other CNS depressants for use in patients for whom alternative treatment options are inadequate. Limit dosage and durations to the minimum required and follow patients for signs and symptoms of respiratory depression and sedation. [US Boxed Warning]: The effects of concomitant use or discontinuation of cytochrome P450 3A4 inducers, 3A4 inhibitors, or 2D6 inhibitors with codeine are complex. Use of cytochrome P450 3A4 inducers, 3A4 inhibitors, or 2D6 inhibitors with butalbital/acetaminophen/caffeine/codeine requires careful consideration of the effects on codeine, and the active metabolite, morphine. Potentially significant interactions may exist, requiring dose or frequency adjustment, additional monitoring, and/or selection of alternative therapy.

Use with caution in patients with hypersensitivity reactions to other phenanthrene-derivative opioid agonists (eg, morphine, hydrocodone, oxycodone). Use caution with Addison disease, known G6PD deficiency, renal or hepatic impairment. Use caution in patients with head injury or other intracranial lesions, acute abdominal conditions, adrenal insufficiency, biliary tract impairment, pancreatitis, urethral stricture of BPH, thyroid dysfunction, toxic psychosis, delirium tremens, morbidly obese, or in patients with respiratory diseases. Use caution in patients with two or more copies of the variant CYP2D6*2 allele; may have extensive conversion from codeine to morphine and thus increased opioid-mediated effects. Tolerance or drug dependence may result from extended use. Avoid use in patients with impaired consciousness or coma as these patients are susceptible to intracranial effects of CO_2 retention. Caffeine may cause CNS and cardiovascular stimulation, as well as GI irritation in high doses. Use with caution in elderly, cachectic or debilitated patients; there is a greater potential for critical respiratory depression, even at therapeutic dosages. Consider the use of alternative nonopioid analgesics in these patients. Use with caution in patients with a history of seizure disorder; may cause or exacerbate preexisting seizures. Opioids may cause or aggravate constipation.

Drug Interactions

Metabolism/Transport Effects Refer to individual components.

Avoid Concomitant Use

Avoid concomitant use of Butalbital, Acetaminophen, Caffeine, and Codeine with any of the following: Acebrophylline; Azelastine (Nasal); Doxofylline; Eluxadoline; Hemin; Iobenguane I 123; Methoxyflurane; Mianserin; Mixed Agonist / Antagonist Opioids; Orphenadrine; Oxomemazine; Paraldehyde; Somatostatin Acetate; Stiripentol; Thalidomide; Ulipristal; Voriconazole

Increased Effect/Toxicity

Butalbital, Acetaminophen, Caffeine, and Codeine may increase the levels/effects of: Alvimopan; Analgesics (Opioid); Azelastine (Nasal); Blonanserin; Blood Pressure Lowering Agents; Busulfan; Dasatinib; Desmopressin; Diuretics; Doxofylline; Eluxadoline; Flunitrazepam; Formoterol; HYDROcodone; Imatinib; Indacaterol; Iohexol; Iomeprol; Iopamidol; Methotrimeprazine; Methoxyflurane; MetyroSINE; Mipomersen; Olodaterol; Orphenadrine; OxyCODONE; Paraldehyde; Phenylephrine (Systemic); Piribedil; Pramipexole; Prilocaine; Ramosetron; ROPINIRole; Rotigotine; Selective Serotonin Reuptake Inhibitors; Serotonin Modulators; Sodium Nitrite; SORAfenib; Suvorexant; Sympathomimetics; Thalidomide; Thiazide and Thiazide-Like Diuretics; TiZANidine; Zolpidem

The levels/effects of Butalbital, Acetaminophen, Caffeine, and Codeine may be increased by: Abiraterone Acetate; Acebrophylline; Amphetamines; Anticholinergic Agents; AtoMOXetine; Brimonidine (Topical); Cannabis; Chloramphenicol; Chlormethiazole; Chlorphenesin Carbamate; Ciprofloxacin (Systemic); CNS Depressants; Cocaine; CYP1A2 Inhibitors (Moderate); CYP1A2 Inhibitors (Strong); Dapsone (Topical); Dasatinib; Deferasirox; Dimethindene (Topical); Dronabinol; Droperidol; HydrOXYzine; Isoniazid; Kava Kava; Linezolid; Lofexidine; Magnesium Sulfate; MAO Inhibitors; Methotrimeprazine; MetyraPONE; Mianserin; Minocycline; Nabilone; Nitric Oxide; Norfloxacin; Obeticholic Acid; Oxomemazine; Peginterferon Alfa-2b; Perampanel; Probenecid; Rufinamide; Sodium Oxybate; Somatostatin Acetate; Somatostatin Analogs; SORAfenib; Stiripentol; Succinylcholine; Tapentadol; Tedizolid; Tetracaine (Topical); Tetrahydrocannabinol; Valproate Products; Vemurafenib

Decreased Effect

Butalbital, Acetaminophen, Caffeine, and Codeine may decrease the levels/effects of: Adenosine; Beta-Blockers; Calcium Channel Blockers; Chloramphenicol; Contraceptives (Estrogens); Contraceptives (Progestins); CycloSPORINE (Systemic); Diuretics; Doxycycline; Gastrointestinal Agents (Prokinetic); Griseofulvin; Hemin; Iobenguane I 123; LamoTRIgine; Lithium; Methoxyflurane; Mianserin; Pegvisomant; Propacetamol; Regadenoson; Teniposide; Theophylline Derivatives; Tricyclic Antidepressants; Ulipristal; Valproate Products; Vitamin K Antagonists; Voriconazole

The levels/effects of Butalbital, Acetaminophen, Caffeine, and Codeine may be decreased by: Cholestyramine Resin; CYP2D6 Inhibitors (Moderate); CYP2D6 Inhibitors (Strong); Mianserin; Mixed Agonist / Antagonist Opioids; Multivitamins/Minerals (with ADEK, Folate, Iron); Nalmefene; Naltrexone; Pyridoxine; Rifamycin Derivatives; Teriflunomide

Pregnancy Considerations Animal reproduction studies have not been conducted with this combination. Withdrawal seizures were reported in an infant 2 days after birth following maternal use of a butalbital product during the last 2 months of pregnancy; butalbital was detected in the newborns serum. **[US Boxed Warning]: Prolonged use of opioids during pregnancy can cause neonatal withdrawal syndrome, which may be life-threatening if not recognized and treated according to protocols developed by neonatology experts. If opioid use is required for a prolonged period in a pregnant woman, advise the patient of the risk of neonatal opioid withdrawal syndrome and ensure that appropriate treatment will be available.** Refer to the acetaminophen, caffeine, or codeine monographs for additional information.

Breastfeeding Considerations Barbiturates, acetaminophen, caffeine, and codeine are excreted in breast milk. Due to the potential for serious adverse reactions in the nursing infant, the manufacturer recommends a decision be made whether to discontinue nursing or to discontinue the drug, taking into account the importance of treatment to the mother. Refer to Acetaminophen, Caffeine, or Codeine monographs for additional information.

Controlled Substance C-III

Dosage Forms

Capsule, oral: Butalbital 50 mg, acetaminophen 300 mg, caffeine 40 mg, and codeine phosphate 30 mg; Butalbital 50 mg, acetaminophen 325 mg, caffeine 40 mg, and codeine 30 mg

Fioricet with Codeine: Butalbital 50 mg, acetaminophen 300 mg, caffeine 40 mg, and codeine 30 mg

Dental Comment Although the ***OTC product labeling*** for acetaminophen products state to limit the maximum dose to 3,000 mg daily (for extra strength) or 3,250 mg (for regular strength) (see this site for details: http://www.tylenolprofessional.com/extra-strength-tylenol-dosage-faq.html), it is still appropriate for patients to take up to 4,000 mg daily "under the direction of a healthcare provider" (http://www.tylenolprofessional.com/assets/v4/faqs-new-dosing.pdf).

The acetaminophen component requires use with caution in patients who use alcohol, with preexisting liver disease, and those receiving more than one source of acetaminophen-containing medication.

Hepatotoxicity caused by acetaminophen is potentiated by chronic alcohol consumption. People who are taking acetaminophen, even at therapeutic doses, and consume alcohol are at risk of developing hepatotoxicity.

Acetaminophen may increase the levels and enhance the anticoagulant effects of vitamin K antagonists acenocoumarol and warfarin (Coumadin). Studies have reported that acetaminophen has increased the INR in warfarin treated patients with daily acetaminophen doses as low as 2 g, particularly when taking acetaminophen for >1 week (Antlitz, 1968; Boeijinga, 1982; Gebauer, 2003; Hylek, 1998; Rubin, 1984). In addition, case reports of bleeding as a result of increased INR have been published (Bagheri, 1999; Bartle, 1991). There is no known mechanism of the interaction; furthermore, some studies have failed to demonstrate this interaction (Gadisseur, 2003; Kwan, 1995; van den Bemt, 2002). In terms of risk, the data suggest that acetaminophen and warfarin could interact in some clinically significant manner but that the benefits of concomitant use of acetaminophen for pain control in dental patients taking warfarin usually outweigh the risks. An appropriate monitoring plan should be in place to identify potential negative effects and dosage adjustments may be necessary in a minority of patients. The interaction may be more likely to occur with daily acetaminophen doses of >1.3 g for >1 week.

There are no reports of acetaminophen interacting with antiplatelet drugs such as aspirin, clopidogrel (Plavix), or prasugrel (Effient). Also, there are no reports of acetaminophen in combination with hydrocodone, codeine, or oxycodone interacting with warfarin (Coumadin).

Butalbital and Acetaminophen

(byoo TAL bi tal & a seet a MIN oh fen)

Related Information

Acetaminophen *on page 56*

PHENobarbital *on page 1325*

Brand Names: US Allzital; Bupap; Marten-Tab; Orviban CF [DSC]; Phrenilin Forte [DSC]; Promacet [DSC]

Pharmacologic Category Analgesic, Nonopioid; Barbiturate

Use Tension or muscle contraction headache: Relief of the symptomatic complex of tension or muscle contraction headache

Local Anesthetic/Vasoconstrictor Precautions No information available to require special precautions

Effects on Dental Treatment No significant effects or complications reported (see Dental Comment)

Effects on Bleeding As a single agent, acetaminophen does not appear to affect bleeding or platelet aggregation. Acetaminophen may prolong the INR and increase bleeding in patients taking warfarin (Coumadin). For patients taking warfarin, single acetaminophen doses or acetaminophen therapy of short duration should be safe, but if large (>1.3 g/day) doses are administered for longer than 10-14 days, then the INR should be monitored (see Dental Comment).

Adverse Reactions Frequency not defined.

Cardiovascular: Tachycardia

Central nervous system: Agitation, confusion, depression, dizziness, drowsiness, euphoria, excitement, headache, increased energy, intoxicated feeling, lethargy, numbness, paresthesia, sedation, seizure, shakiness

Dermatologic: Hyperhidrosis, pruritus

Endocrine & metabolic: Hot flash

Gastrointestinal: Abdominal pain, constipation, dysphagia, flatulence, heartburn, nausea, vomiting, xerostomia

Genitourinary: Diuresis

Hypersensitivity: Hypersensitivity reaction

Neuromuscular & skeletal: Leg pain, muscle fatigue

Otic: Otalgia, tinnitus

Respiratory: Dyspnea, nasal congestion

Miscellaneous: Fever, heavy eyelids

<1%, postmarketing, and/or case reports: Erythema multiforme, toxic epidermal necrolysis

General Dosage Range Oral: *Children ≥12 years, Adolescents, and Adults:* 1 or 2 tablets every 4 hours as needed. Maximum: Butalbital 25 mg/acetaminophen 325 mg: 12 tablets (butalbital 300 mg/acetaminophen 3,900 mg) per 24 hours; butalbital 50 mg/acetaminophen 300 to 325 mg: 6 tablets (butalbital 300 mg/acetaminophen 1,950 mg) per 24 hours

Mechanism of Action

Butalbital: Short- to intermediate-acting barbiturate; depresses the sensory cortex, decreases motor activity, alters cerebellar function, and produces drowsiness, sedation, hypnosis, and dose-dependent respiratory depression.

Acetaminophen: Inhibits the synthesis of prostaglandins in the central nervous system and peripherally blocks pain impulse generation.

Pharmacodynamics/Kinetics

Half-life Elimination Butalbital: ~35 hours

Pregnancy Risk Factor C

Pregnancy Considerations Animal reproduction studies have not been conducted with this combination. Withdrawal seizures were reported in an infant 2 days after birth following maternal use of a butalbital product during the last 2 months of pregnancy; butalbital was detected in the newborns serum. Also refer to acetaminophen monograph for information specific to acetaminophen.

Dental Comment Although the ***OTC product labeling*** for acetaminophen products state to limit the maximum dose to 3,000 mg daily (for extra strength) or 3,250 mg (for regular strength) (see this site for details: http://www.tylenolprofessional.com/extra-strength-tylenol-dosage-faq.html), it is still appropriate for patients to take up to 4,000 mg daily "under the direction of a healthcare provider" (http://www.tylenolprofessional.com/assets/v4/faqs-new-dosing.pdf).

The acetaminophen component requires use with caution in patients who use alcohol, with preexisting liver disease, and those receiving more than one source of acetaminophen-containing medication.

Hepatotoxicity caused by acetaminophen is potentiated by chronic alcohol consumption. People who are taking acetaminophen, even at therapeutic doses, and consume alcohol are at risk of developing hepatotoxicity.

Acetaminophen may increase the levels and enhance the anticoagulant effects of vitamin K antagonists acenocoumarol and warfarin (Coumadin). Studies have reported that acetaminophen has increased the INR in warfarin treated patients with daily acetaminophen doses as low as 2 g, particularly when taking acetaminophen for >1 week (Antlitz, 1968; Boeijinga, 1982; Gebauer, 2003; Hylek, 1998; Rubin, 1984). In addition, case reports of bleeding as a result of increased INR have been published (Bagheri, 1999; Bartle, 1991). There is no known mechanism of the interaction; furthermore, some studies have failed to demonstrate this interaction (Gadisseur, 2003; Kwan, 1995; van den Bemt, 2002). In terms of risk, the data suggest that acetaminophen and warfarin could interact in some clinically significant manner but that the benefits of concomitant use of acetaminophen for pain control in dental patients taking warfarin usually outweigh the risks. An appropriate monitoring plan should be in place to identify potential negative effects and dosage adjustments may be necessary in a minority of patients. The interaction may be more likely to occur with daily acetaminophen doses of >1.3 g for >1 week.

There are no reports of acetaminophen interacting with antiplatelet drugs such as aspirin, clopidogrel (Plavix), or prasugrel (Effient). Also, there are no reports of acetaminophen in combination with hydrocodone, codeine, or oxycodone interacting with warfarin (Coumadin).

Butenafine (byoo TEN a feen)

Brand Names: US Lotrimin Ultra [OTC]; Mentax

Pharmacologic Category Antifungal Agent, Topical

Use

Topical infections: Topical treatment of tinea (pityriasis) versicolor due to *Malassezia furfur*

OTC labeling: Topical treatment of tinea pedis (athlete's foot), tinea cruris (jock itch), and tinea corporis (ringworm)

Local Anesthetic/Vasoconstrictor Precautions No information available to require special precautions

Effects on Dental Treatment No significant effects or complications reported

Effects on Bleeding No information available to require special precautions

Adverse Reactions ≥1%: Dermatologic: Burning sensation of skin, contact dermatitis, erythema, pruritus, skin irritation, stinging of the skin

General Dosage Range Topical: *Children ≥12 years, Adolescents, and Adults:* Apply to affected area once or twice daily

Mechanism of Action Butenafine exerts fungicidal activity against dermatophytes (eg,trichophyton, epidermophyton) by blocking squalene epoxidation, resulting in inhibition of ergosterol synthesis and subsequent weakening of fungal cell membranes.

Pharmacodynamics/Kinetics

Half-life Elimination Biphasic: Alpha: 35 hours; Beta: >150 hours

Time to Peak Serum: 6 to 15 hours

Pregnancy Risk Factor C

Pregnancy Considerations Adverse effects were not observed in animal reproduction studies.

Butoconazole (byoo toe KOE na zole)

Brand Names: US Gynazole-1

Pharmacologic Category Antifungal Agent, Imidazole Derivative; Antifungal Agent, Vaginal

Use Vulvovaginal candidiasis: Local treatment of vulvovaginal candidiasis due to *Candida albicans*

Local Anesthetic/Vasoconstrictor Precautions No information available to require special precautions

Effects on Dental Treatment No significant effects or complications reported

Effects on Bleeding No information available to require special precautions

Adverse Reactions Frequency not defined.

Gastrointestinal: Abdominal cramps, abdominal pain

Genitourinary: Pelvic pain, vulvovaginal burning, vulvovaginal disease (soreness), vulvovaginal pruritus, vulvovaginal swelling

General Dosage Range Intravaginal: *Adults:* Insert 1 applicatorful as a single dose

Mechanism of Action Inhibits biosynthesis of ergosterol, damaging the fungal cell wall membrane, which increases permeability in susceptible fungi (*Candida*), causing leaking of nutrients

Pharmacodynamics/Kinetics

Time to Peak Plasma: 12 to 24 hours

Pregnancy Risk Factor C

Pregnancy Considerations Adverse events have been observed in some animal reproduction studies. Following vaginal administration, small amounts are absorbed systemically. Single dose, topical azole regimens are not recommended for the treatment of vulvovaginal candidiasis; only topical azole therapies with 7 day regimens are recommended in pregnant women with vulvovaginal candidiasis. This product may weaken latex or rubber condoms or diaphragms (CDC [Workowski 2015]).

Butorphanol (byoo TOR fa nole)

Brand Names: Canada Butorphanol (Nasal Spray); PMS-Butorphanol

Pharmacologic Category Analgesic, Opioid; Analgesic, Opioid Partial Agonist

Use

Pain management: Management of pain severe enough to require an opioid analgesic and for which alternative treatments are inadequate

Limitations of use: Reserve for use in patients for whom alternative treatment options (eg, nonopioid analgesics, opioid combination products) are ineffective, not tolerated, or would be otherwise inadequate to provide sufficient management of pain.

Pain during labor (injection only): Management of pain during labor.

Preoperative medication (injection only): Preoperative or preanesthetic medication

Supplement to balanced anesthesia (injection only): Supplement to balanced anesthesia

Local Anesthetic/Vasoconstrictor Precautions No information available to require special precautions

Effects on Dental Treatment Key adverse event(s) related to dental treatment: Xerostomia (normal salivary flow resumes upon discontinuation) and unpleasant aftertaste.

Effects on Bleeding No information available to require special precautions

Adverse Reactions

>10%:

Central nervous system: Drowsiness (43%), dizziness (19%), insomnia (nasal spray 11%)

Gastrointestinal: Nausea and vomiting (13%)

Respiratory: Nasal congestion (nasal spray 13%)

1% to 10%:

Cardiovascular: Palpitations, vasodilatation

Central nervous system: Anxiety, burning sensation, confusion, euphoria, floating feeling, headache, lethargy, nervousness, paresthesia

Dermatologic: Cold and clammy skin, diaphoresis, pruritus

Gastrointestinal: Anorexia, constipation, stomach pain, unpleasant taste, xerostomia

Neuromuscular & skeletal: Tremor, weakness

Ophthalmic: Blurred vision

Otic: Otalgia, tinnitus

Respiratory: Bronchitis, cough, dyspnea, epistaxis, nasal discomfort, pharyngitis, rhinitis, sinus congestion, sinusitis, upper respiratory tract infection

<1%, postmarketing, and/or case reports: Abnormal dreams, agitation, apnea, chest pain, convulsions, delusions, depression, drug dependence, dysphoria, edema, hallucination, hostility, hypertension, hypogonadism (Brennan, 2013; Debono, 2011), hypotension, respiratory depression, seizure, shallow respiration, skin rash, speech disturbance, syncope, tachycardia, urination disorder, urticaria, vertigo, withdrawal syndrome

General Dosage Range Dosage adjustment recommended in patients with hepatic or renal impairment

IM:

Adults: Initial: 2 mg, may repeat every 3 to 4 hours as needed; Usual range: 1 to 4 mg every 3 to 4 hours as needed **or** 2 mg prior to surgery

Elderly: Initial: 1 mg, repeated dosing generally should be at least 6 hours apart

IV:

Adults: Initial: 1 mg, may repeat every 3 to 4 hours as needed; Usual range: 0.5 to 2 mg every 3 to 4 hours as needed **or** 2 mg and/or an incremental dose of 0.5 to 1 mg (up to 0.06 mg/kg) as supplement to surgery

Elderly: Initial: 0.5 mg, repeated dosing generally should be at least 6 hours apart

Intranasal:

Adults: Initial: One spray (1 mg per spray) in 1 nostril, may repeat in 60 to 90 minutes, then repeat initial dose sequence in 3 to 4 hours after last dose as needed; may use initial dose of 1 spray in each nostril (2 mg) in patients who will remain recumbent

Elderly: Initial: One spray (1 mg per spray) in 1 nostril, may repeat after 90 to 120 minutes; repeated dosing generally should be at least 6 hours apart

Mechanism of Action Agonist of kappa opiate receptors and partial agonist of mu opiate receptors in the CNS, causing inhibition of ascending pain pathways, altering the perception of and response to pain; produces analgesia, respiratory depression, and sedation similar to opioids

Pharmacodynamics/Kinetics

Onset of Action IM, Nasal: ≤15 minutes; IV: Within a few minutes

Peak effect: IM, IV: 0.5 to 1 hour; Nasal: 1 to 2 hours

Duration of Action IM, IV: 3 to 4 hours; Nasal: 4 to 5 hours

Half-life Elimination

IV, nasal: ~2 to 9 hours; Hydroxybutorphanol: ~18 hours

Elderly: IV, nasal: ~3 to 9 hours

Renal impairment (CrCl <30 mL/minute): ~10.5 hours

Hepatic impairment: ~16.8 hours

Time to Peak Plasma: IM: 20 to 40 minutes; Nasal: 30 to 60 minutes

Pregnancy Risk Factor C

Pregnancy Considerations

Adverse events have been observed in some animal reproduction studies. Butorphanol crosses the placenta. Butorphanol injection is approved for the management of pain during labor; apnea or respiratory distress in the newborn may occur. When used for pain relief during labor, opioids may temporarily affect the heart rate of the fetus (ACOG 2002). The manufacturer recommends that caution be used if abnormal fetal heart rate patterns are present.

[US Boxed Warning]: Prolonged use of opioids during pregnancy can cause neonatal withdrawal syndrome, which may be life-threatening if not recognized and treated according to protocols developed by neonatology experts. If opioid use is required for a prolonged period in a pregnant woman, advise the patient of the risk of neonatal opioid withdrawal syndrome and ensure that appropriate treatment will be available. If chronic opioid exposure occurs in pregnancy, adverse events in the newborn (including withdrawal) may occur; monitoring of the neonate is recommended. The minimum effective dose should be used if opioids are needed (Chou 2009). Neonatal abstinence syndrome following opioid exposure may present with autonomic (eg, fever, temperature instability), gastrointestinal (eg, diarrhea, vomiting, poor feeding/weight gain), or neurologic (eg, high pitched crying, increased muscle tone, irritability, seizure, tremor) symptoms (Dow 2012; Hudak 2012).

Controlled Substance C-IV

Cabazitaxel (ca baz i TAKS el)

Brand Names: US Jevtana

Brand Names: Canada Jevtana

Pharmacologic Category Antineoplastic Agent, Antimicrotubular; Antineoplastic Agent, Taxane Derivative

Use Prostate cancer, metastatic: Treatment of hormone-refractory metastatic prostate cancer (in combination with prednisone) in patients previously treated with a docetaxel-containing regimen

Local Anesthetic/Vasoconstrictor Precautions No information available to require special precautions

Effects on Dental Treatment Key adverse event(s) related to dental treatment: Taste alteration

Effects on Bleeding Thrombocytopenia has been reported in ≤48% of patients. A medical consult is suggested.

Adverse Reactions Adverse reactions reported for combination therapy with prednisone.

>10%:

Central nervous system: Fatigue (37%), peripheral neuropathy (13%; grades 3/4: <1%)

Gastrointestinal: Diarrhea (47%), nausea (34%), vomiting (22%), constipation (20%), abdominal pain (17%), anorexia (16%), dysgeusia (11%)

Genitourinary: Hematuria (17%)

Hematologic & oncologic: Anemia (98%; grades 3/4: 11%), leukopenia (96%; grades 3/4: 69%), neutropenia (94%; grades 3/4: 82%), thrombocytopenia (48%; grades 3/4: 4%)

Neuromuscular & skeletal: Weakness (20%), back pain (16%), arthralgia (11%)

Respiratory: Dyspnea (12%), cough (11%)

Miscellaneous: Fever (12%)

1% to 10%:

Cardiovascular: Peripheral edema (9%), cardiac arrhythmia (5%), hypotension (5%)

Central nervous system: Dizziness (8%), headache (8%), pain (5%)

Dermatologic: Alopecia (10%)

Endocrine & metabolic: Weight loss (9%), dehydration (5%)

Gastrointestinal: Dyspepsia (10%), mucosal inflammation (6%)

Genitourinary: Urinary tract infection (8%), dysuria (7%)

Hematologic & oncologic: Febrile neutropenia (7%; grades 3/4: 7%)

Hepatic: Increased serum ALT, increased serum AST, increased serum bilirubin

Neuromuscular & skeletal: Muscle spasm (7%)

Renal: Renal failure (4%)

Frequency not defined:

Endocrine & metabolic: Electrolyte disturbance

<1%, postmarketing, and/or case reports: Adult respiratory distress syndrome, enterocolitis, gastritis, gastrointestinal hemorrhage, gastrointestinal perforation, hypersensitivity reaction (includes bronchospasm, erythema, hypotension, skin rash), interstitial pneumonitis, interstitial pulmonary disease, intestinal obstruction, neutropenic enterocolitis, sepsis, septic shock

General Dosage Range Dosage adjustment recommended in patients with hepatic impairment or who develop toxicities

IV: *Adults:* 25 mg/m^2 once every 3 weeks

Mechanism of Action Cabazitaxel is a taxane derivative which is a microtubule inhibitor; it binds to tubulin promoting assembly into microtubules and inhibiting disassembly which stabilizes microtubules. This inhibits microtubule depolymerization and cell division, arresting the cell cycle and inhibiting tumor proliferation. Unlike other taxanes, cabazitaxel has a poor affinity for multidrug resistance (MDR) proteins, therefore conferring activity in resistant tumors.

Pharmacodynamics/Kinetics

Half-life Elimination Terminal: 95 hours

Pregnancy Risk Factor D

Pregnancy Considerations Adverse events have been observed in animal reproduction studies. Cabazitaxel is not indicated for use in women. May cause fetal harm if administered during pregnancy. Pregnant women should avoid exposure to cabazitaxel.

Cabergoline (ca BER goe leen)

Brand Names: Canada ACT Cabergoline; Dostinex

Pharmacologic Category Ergot Derivative

Use

Hyperprolactinemic disorders: Treatment of hyperprolactinemic disorders, either idiopathic or caused by pituitary adenomas.

Limitations of use: Not indicated for inhibition or suppression of physiologic lactation.

Canadian labeling: Additional use (not in U.S. labeling): Prevention of the onset of physiological lactation in the puerperium when clinically indicated (eg, still born baby or neonatal death, conditions that interfere with suckling, severe acute or chronic mental illness, maternal disease which may be transmitted to the baby that require medications which are excreted in the milk).

Limitations of use: Not indicated for suppression of already established postpartum lactation.

Local Anesthetic/Vasoconstrictor Precautions Cabergoline is a semisynthetic ergot alkaloid derivative; there is a possibility that it has vasoconstricting effects; use vasoconstrictor with caution

Effects on Dental Treatment Key adverse event(s) related to dental treatment: Xerostomia (normal salivary flow resumes upon discontinuation), throat irritation, and toothache.

Effects on Bleeding No information available to require special precautions

Adverse Reactions

>10%:

Central nervous system: Headache (26%), dizziness (15% to 17%)

Gastrointestinal: Nausea (27% to 29%)

1% to 10%:

Cardiovascular: Orthostatic hypotension (4%), hypotension (1%), palpitations (1%), peripheral edema (1%), syncope (1%)

Central nervous system: Fatigue (5% to 7%), drowsiness (2% to 5%), vertigo (1% to 4%), depression (3%), pain (2%), nervousness (1% to 2%), paresthesia (1% to 2%), anxiety (1%), insomnia (1%), lack of concentration (1%), malaise (1%)

Dermatologic: Acne vulgaris (1%), pruritus (1%)

Endocrine & metabolic: Hot flash (1% to 3%), dependent edema (1%)

Gastrointestinal: Constipation (7% to 10%), abdominal pain (5%), dyspepsia (2% to 5%), vomiting (2% to 4%), diarrhea (2%), flatulence (2%), xerostomia (2%), anorexia (1%), toothache (1%)

Genitourinary: Mastalgia (1% to 2%), dysmenorrhea (1%)

Neuromuscular & skeletal: Weakness (6% to 9%), arthralgia (1%)

Ophthalmic: Periorbital edema (1%), visual disturbance (1%)

Respiratory: Flu-like symptoms (1%), rhinitis (1%), throat irritation (1%)

<1%, postmarketing, and/or case reports: Aggressive behavior, alopecia, cardiac failure (in Parkinson's disease [PD] patients), confusion (in PD patients), constrictive pericarditis (in PD patients), duodenal ulcer (in PD patients), dyskinesia (in PD patients), epistaxis, facial edema, gastric ulcer (in PD patients), hallucination (in PD patients), heart valve disease, hypersexuality, increased libido, pathological gambling, pericardial fibrotic disorder, pleural effusion (in PD patients), psychosis, pulmonary fibrosis (in PD patients), weight gain, weight loss

General Dosage Range Oral: *Adults:* Initial: 0.25 mg twice weekly; Maintenance: Up to 1 mg twice weekly

Mechanism of Action Cabergoline is a long acting dopamine receptor agonist with a high affinity for D_2 receptors; prolactin secretion by the anterior pituitary is predominantly under hypothalamic inhibitory control exerted through the release of dopamine. It is a potent 5-HT_{2B}-receptor agonist, which may contribute to observed fibrotic/valvulopathic events.

Pharmacodynamics/Kinetics

Half-life Elimination 63 to 69 hours

Time to Peak Plasma: 2 to 3 hours

Pregnancy Risk Factor B

Pregnancy Considerations

Adverse events have not been observed in most animal reproduction studies. Treatment of hyperprolactinemia may restore fertility in previously infertile women. Although available evidence suggests cabergoline use early in pregnancy does not cause harm to the fetus, it is recommended that therapy be discontinued once pregnancy is discovered. If treatment during pregnancy is required, other agents are preferred. Monitoring of prolactin levels should be suspended during pregnancy (Melmed 2011). Not recommended for use in women with pregnancy-induced hypertension (eg, preeclampsia, eclampsia, postpartum hypertension) unless benefit outweighs potential risk.

Canadian labeling (not in US labeling): Exclude pregnancy prior to use; prevent pregnancy for ≥1 month following discontinuation of treatment.

Caffeine (KAF een)

Brand Names: US Cafcit; Keep Alert [OTC]; No Doz Maximum Strength [OTC]; Stay Awake Maximum Strength [OTC]; Stay Awake [OTC]; Vivarin [OTC]

Pharmacologic Category Central Nervous System Stimulant; Phosphodiesterase Enzyme Inhibitor, Nonselective

Use

Caffeine citrate: Treatment of idiopathic apnea of prematurity

Caffeine and sodium benzoate: Treatment of acute respiratory depression (not a preferred agent)

Caffeine [OTC labeling]: Restore mental alertness or wakefulness when experiencing fatigue

Local Anesthetic/Vasoconstrictor Precautions No information available to require special precautions

Effects on Dental Treatment Key adverse event(s) related to dental treatment: Caffeine causes tachycardia, increases in blood pressure, and palpitations. Consider monitoring blood pressure prior to using local anesthetic with a vasoconstrictor. Symptoms associated with bruxism have been observed in some patients.

Effects on Bleeding No information available to require special precautions

Adverse Reactions Frequency not specified; primarily serum-concentration related.

Cardiovascular: Angina pectoris, chest pain, flushing, palpitations, sinus tachycardia, supraventricular tachycardia, vasodilatation, ventricular arrhythmia

Central nervous system: Agitation, delirium, dizziness, hallucination, headache, insomnia, irritability, psychosis, restlessness

Dermatologic: Urticaria

Gastrointestinal: Esophageal motility disorder (sphincter tone decreased), gastritis

Genitourinary: Diuresis

Neuromuscular & skeletal: Fasciculations

Ophthalmic: Increased intraocular pressure (>180 mg caffeine), miosis

General Dosage Range

IM (caffeine and sodium benzoate):

Children: 8 mg/kg every 4 hours as needed

Adults: 250 mg as a single dose; may repeat as needed (maximum: 500 mg/dose; 2500 mg/day)

IV:

Neonates (caffeine citrate): Loading dose: 10-20 mg/kg; Maintenance: 5 mg/kg once daily

Children (caffeine and sodium benzoate): 8 mg/kg every 4 hours as needed

Adults (caffeine and sodium benzoate): 250 mg as a single dose; may repeat as needed (maximum: 500 mg/dose; 2500 mg/day) **or** 300-2000 mg (electroconvulsive therapy)

Oral:

Neonates (caffeine citrate): Loading dose: 10-20 mg/kg; Maintenance: 5 mg/kg once daily

Children ≥12 years and Adults: 100-200 mg every 3-4 hours as needed (OTC labeling)

SubQ (caffeine and sodium benzoate): *Children:* 8 mg/kg every 4 hours as needed

Mechanism of Action Increases levels of 3'5' cyclic AMP by inhibiting phosphodiesterase; CNS stimulant which increases medullary respiratory center sensitivity to carbon dioxide, stimulates central inspiratory drive, and improves skeletal muscle contraction (diaphragmatic contractility); prevention of apnea may occur by competitive inhibition of adenosine

Pharmacodynamics/Kinetics

Half-life Elimination

Neonates: 72-96 hours (range: 40-230 hours)

Children >9 months and Adults: 5 hours

Time to Peak Serum: Oral: Within 30 minutes to 2 hours

Pregnancy Risk Factor C

Pregnancy Considerations Adverse events were observed in animal reproduction studies. Caffeine crosses the placenta; serum concentrations in the fetus are similar to those in the mother (Grosso, 2005). Based on current studies, usual dietary exposure to caffeine is unlikely to cause congenital malformations (Brent, 2011). However, available data shows conflicting results related to maternal caffeine use and the risk of other adverse events, such as spontaneous abortion or growth retardation (Brent, 2011; Jahanfar, 2013). The half-life of caffeine is prolonged during the second and third trimesters of pregnancy and maternal and fetal exposure is also influenced by maternal smoking or drinking (Brent, 2011; Koren, 2000). Current guidelines recommend limiting caffeine intake from all sources to ≤200 mg/day (ACOG, 2010).

Calcifediol (kal si fe DYE ole)

Brand Names: US Rayaldee

Pharmacologic Category Vitamin D Analog

Use

Secondary hyperparathyroidism: Treatment of secondary hyperparathyroidism in adults with stage 3 or 4 chronic kidney disease and serum total 25-hydroxyvitamin D levels less than 30 ng/mL.

Limitations of use: Not indicated for the treatment of secondary hyperparathyroidism in patients with stage 5 chronic kidney disease or in patients with end-stage renal disease (ESRD) on dialysis.

Local Anesthetic/Vasoconstrictor Precautions No information available to require special precautions

Effects on Dental Treatment Key adverse event(s) related to dental treatment: Nasopharyngitis has been reported

Effects on Bleeding No information available to require special precautions

Adverse Reactions

>10%: Hematologic & oncologic: Abnormal phosphorus levels (increased: 45%; hyperphosphatemia: <1%)

1% to 10%:

Cardiovascular: Congestive heart failure (4%)

Endocrine & metabolic: Hypercalcemia (4%; patients requiring dose reduction for hypercalcemia: 2%), hyperkalemia (3%), hyperuricemia (2%)

Hematologic & oncologic: Anemia (5%), bruise (2%)

Neuromuscular & skeletal: Osteoarthritis (2%)

Renal: Increased serum creatinine (5%)

Respiratory: Nasopharyngitis (5%), cough (4%), dyspnea (4%), bronchitis (3%), chronic obstructive pulmonary disease (1%), pneumonia (1%)

Mechanism of Action Calcifediol, a prohormone of the active form of vitamin D_3, calcitriol (1,25 dihydroxyvitamin D_3), is catalyzed to calcitriol by the 1-alpha-hydroxylase enzyme, CYP27B1, primarily in the kidney. Calcitriol binds to vitamin D receptors in target tissues activating vitamin D responsive pathways resulting in increased intestinal absorption of calcium and phosphorus and reduced parathyroid hormone synthesis.

Pharmacodynamics/Kinetics

Onset of Action ~2 weeks; maximum effect: ~3 months

Half-life Elimination Healthy adults: ~11 days; Stage 3 and 4 CKD: ~25 days

Pregnancy Risk Factor C

Pregnancy Considerations Adverse events were observed in animal reproduction studies. Endogenous calcifediol crosses the placenta in concentrations generally lower than those in the maternal plasma; supplementation increases cord blood 25OHD concentrations (IOM 2011).

Calcipotriene (kal si POE try een)

Brand Names: US Calcitrene; Dovonex; Sorilux

Brand Names: Canada Dovonex

Pharmacologic Category Topical Skin Product; Vitamin D Analog

Use Plaque psoriasis: Treatment of plaque psoriasis of the body (cream, foam, ointment) or of the scalp (foam, solution)

Local Anesthetic/Vasoconstrictor Precautions No information available to require special precautions

Effects on Dental Treatment No significant effects or complications reported

Effects on Bleeding No information available to require special precautions

Adverse Reactions Frequency may vary with site of application. Frequency not always defined.

Central nervous system: Tingling of skin (≤23%)

Dermatologic: Burning sensation of skin (≤23%), stinging of the skin (≤23%), skin rash (1% to 11%), dermatitis, desquamation, erythema, exacerbation of psoriasis, pruritus, skin irritation, xeroderma

Local: Application site pain (3%), application site erythema (2%)

<1%, postmarketing, and/or case reports: Allergic contact dermatitis, contact dermatitis, hypercalcemia, hyperpigmentation, folliculitis, skin atrophy

General Dosage Range Topical: *Adults:* Cream: Apply a thin film to affected area twice daily; Foam: Apply a thin film to the affected skin or scalp twice daily; Ointment: Apply a thin film to affected area 1 or 2 times daily; Solution: Apply to affected scalp twice daily

Mechanism of Action Synthetic vitamin D_3 analog which regulates skin cell production and proliferation. Binds to vitamin D receptors and inhibits keratinocyte proliferation and enhances keratinocyte differentiation (Menter 2009).

Pharmacodynamics/Kinetics

Onset of Action Improvement begins after 2 weeks; marked improvement seen after 8 weeks

Pregnancy Risk Factor C

Pregnancy Considerations Adverse events have been observed in some animal reproduction studies. If treatment during pregnancy is needed, other agents may be preferred (Hsu 2012; Zeichner 2010).

Calcitonin (kal si TOE nin)

Brand Names: US Fortical [DSC]; Miacalcin

Brand Names: Canada Calcimar

Pharmacologic Category Antidote; Hormone

Use

Injection:

Hypercalcemia: Adjunctive therapy for hypercalcemia

Paget disease: Treatment of symptomatic Paget disease of bone (osteitis deformans) in patients who are nonresponsive or intolerant to alternative therapy

Postmenopausal osteoporosis: Treatment of osteoporosis in women more than 5 years postmenopause

Intranasal:

Postmenopausal osteoporosis: Treatment of postmenopausal osteoporosis in women more than 5 years postmenopause

Local Anesthetic/Vasoconstrictor Precautions No information available to require special precautions

Effects on Dental Treatment No significant effects or complications reported

Effects on Bleeding No information available to require special precautions

Adverse Reactions Unless otherwise noted, frequencies reported are with nasal spray.

>10%: Respiratory: Rhinitis (<12%, including ulcerative)

1% to 10%:

Cardiovascular: Flushing (injection: 2% to 5%, hands or face; nasal spray: <1%)

Central nervous system: Depression (1% to 3%), dizziness (1% to 3%), paresthesia (1% to 3%)

Dermatologic: Erythematous rash (1% to 3%)

Gastrointestinal: Nausea (injection: 10%; nasal spray: 1% to 3%), abdominal pain (1% to 3%)

Hematologic & oncologic: Malignant neoplasm (5%), lymphadenopathy (1% to 3%)

Infection: Infection (1% to 3%)

Local: Injection site reaction (injection: 10%)

Neuromuscular & skeletal: Back pain (5%), myalgia (1% to 3%), osteoarthritis (1% to 3%)

Ophthalmic: Abnormal lacrimation (1% to 3%), conjunctivitis (1% to 3%)

Respiratory: Bronchospasm (1% to 3%), flu-like symptoms (1% to 3%), sinusitis (1% to 3%), upper respiratory tract infection (1% to 3%)

<1%, postmarketing, and/or case reports (all routes): Alopecia, altered sense of smell, anaphylactic shock, anaphylactoid reaction, anaphylaxis, anorexia, antibody development (drug efficacy can be affected),

arthralgia, casts in urine, cough, decreased appetite (injection), diaphoresis, diarrhea, dysgeusia, dyspnea, earlobe pruritus (injection), edema, excoriation (nasal mucosa), eye pain, facial edema, fever, headache, hearing loss, hypersensitivity reaction, hypertension, hypocalcemia, musculoskeletal pain, nasal mucosa ulcer, nocturia, pedal edema, peripheral edema, polyuria, pruritus, salty taste (injection), skin rash, sneezing, tachycardia, tinnitus, tremor, urine abnormality, urticaria (injection), visual disturbance, vomiting

General Dosage Range

IM, SubQ: *Adults:* Paget's disease/osteoporosis: 100 units daily; Hypercalcemia: 4 to 8 units/kg every 12 hours (maximum: 8 units/kg every 6 hours)

Intranasal: *Adults:* 200 units (1 spray) in one nostril once daily

Mechanism of Action Peptide sequence similar to human calcitonin; functionally antagonizes the effects of parathyroid hormone. Directly inhibits osteoclastic bone resorption; promotes the renal excretion of calcium, phosphate, sodium, magnesium, and potassium by decreasing tubular reabsorption; increases the jejunal secretion of water, sodium, potassium, and chloride

Pharmacodynamics/Kinetics

Onset of Action

Hypercalcemia: IM, SubQ: ~2 hours

Paget's disease: Within a few months; may take up to 1 year for neurologic symptom improvement

Duration of Action Hypercalcemia: IM, SubQ: 6 to 8 hours; following multiple doses, hypercalcemic effect diminishes within 24 to 48 hours (Nilsson 1978; Stevenson 1988)

Half-life Elimination Terminal: IM 58 minutes; SubQ 59 to 64 minutes; Nasal: ~18 to 23 minutes

Time to Peak Plasma: SubQ ~23 minutes; Nasal: ~10 to 13 minutes

Pregnancy Risk Factor C

Pregnancy Considerations Adverse events have been observed in animal reproduction studies. Calcitonin does not cross the placenta.

Calcitriol (Systemic) (kal si TRYE ole)

Brand Names: US Rocaltrol

Brand Names: Canada Calcijex; Calcitriol Injection; Calcitriol-Odan; Rocaltrol

Pharmacologic Category Vitamin D Analog

Use

Management of hypocalcemia in patients on chronic renal dialysis (oral, injection); management of secondary hyperparathyroidism in patients with chronic kidney disease (CKD) not yet on dialysis (predialysis patients) (oral); management of hypocalcemia in patients with hypoparathyroidism and pseudohypoparathyroidism (oral)

Canadian labeling: Additional uses (not in US labeling): Vitamin D-resistant rickets (oral)

Local Anesthetic/Vasoconstrictor Precautions No information available to require special precautions

Effects on Dental Treatment Key adverse event(s) related to dental treatment: Metallic taste and xerostomia (normal salivary flow resumes upon discontinuation).

Effects on Bleeding No information available to require special precautions

Adverse Reactions

>10%: Endocrine & metabolic: Hypercalcemia

1% to 10%:

Central nervous system: Headache

Dermatologic: Skin rash

Endocrine & metabolic: Polydipsia

Gastrointestinal: Abdominal pain, nausea

Genitourinary: Urinary tract infection

Frequency not defined:

Cardiovascular: Cardiac arrhythmia, hypertension

Central nervous system: Apathy, drowsiness, hyperthermia, metallic taste, psychosis, sensory disturbance

Dermatologic: Erythema, erythema multiforme, pruritus, urticaria

Endocrine & metabolic: Albuminuria, calcinosis, decreased libido, dehydration, growth suppression, hypercholesterolemia, weight loss

Gastrointestinal: Anorexia, constipation, pancreatitis, stomach pain, vomiting, xerostomia

Genitourinary: Hypercalciuria, nocturia

Hepatic: Increased serum ALT, increased serum AST

Hypersensitivity: Hypersensitivity reaction

Local: Pain at injection site (mild)

Neuromuscular & skeletal: Dystrophy, myalgia, ostealgia, weakness

Ophthalmic: Conjunctivitis, photophobia

Renal: Calcium nephrolithiasis, increased blood urea nitrogen, increased serum creatinine, polyuria

Respiratory: Rhinorrhea

<1%, postmarketing and/or case reports: Agitation, anaphylaxis, apprehension, hypermagnesemia, hyperphosphatemia, hypervitaminosis D, increased hematocrit, increased hemoglobin, increased neutrophils, increased serum alkaline phosphatase, insomnia, limb pain, lymphocytosis

General Dosage Range Dosage adjustment recommended in patients who develop toxicities

IV: *Adults:* 0.5 to 4 mcg 3 times weekly

Oral:

Children 1 to <3 years: 0.25 to 0.75 mcg daily **or** 0.01 to 0.015 mcg/kg/day (maximum: 0.5 mcg daily)

Children ≥3 to 5 years: 0.25 to 0.75 mcg daily

Children ≥6 years: 0.25 to 2 mcg daily

Adults: 0.25 mcg every other day to 2 mcg once daily

Mechanism of Action Calcitriol, the active form of vitamin D (1,25 hydroxyvitamin D_3), binds to and activates the vitamin D receptor in kidney, parathyroid gland, intestine, and bone, stimulating intestinal calcium transport and absorption. It reduces PTH levels and improves calcium and phosphate homeostasis by stimulating bone resorption of calcium and increasing renal tubular reabsorption of calcium. Decreased renal conversion of vitamin D to its primary active metabolite (1,25 hydroxyvitamin D) in chronic renal failure leads to reduced activation of vitamin D receptor, which subsequently removes inhibitory suppression of parathyroid hormone (PTH) release; increased serum PTH (secondary hyperparathyroidism) reduces calcium excretion and enhances bone resorption.

Pharmacodynamics/Kinetics

Onset of Action Oral: 2 hours; maximum effect: 10 hours

Duration of Action Oral, IV: 3 to 5 days

Half-life Elimination Children 1.8 to 16 years undergoing peritoneal dialysis: 27.4 hours; Healthy adults: 5 to 8 hours; Hemodialysis: 16 to 22 hours

Time to Peak Serum: Oral: 3 to 6 hours; Hemodialysis: 8 to 12 hours

Pregnancy Risk Factor C

Pregnancy Considerations Adverse effects have been observed in some animal reproduction studies. Maternal calcitriol may be detected in the fetal circulation. Mild hypercalcemia has been reported in a newborn following maternal use of calcitriol during pregnancy. Adverse effects on fetal development were not observed with use of calcitriol during pregnancy in women (N=9) with pseudovitamin D-dependent rickets. Doses were adjusted every 4 weeks to keep calcium concentrations within normal limits (Edouard 2011). If calcitriol is used for the management of hypoparathyroidism in pregnancy, dose adjustments may be needed as pregnancy progresses and again following delivery. Vitamin D and calcium levels should be monitored closely and kept in the lower normal range (Callies 1998).

Calcitriol (Topical) (kal si TRYE ole)

Brand Names: US Vectical

Brand Names: Canada Silkis

Pharmacologic Category Vitamin D Analog

Use Plaque psoriasis: Management of mild-to-moderate plaque psoriasis

Local Anesthetic/Vasoconstrictor Precautions No information available to require special precautions

Effects on Dental Treatment Key adverse event(s) related to dental treatment: Metallic taste and xerostomia (normal salivary flow resumes upon discontinuation).

Effects on Bleeding No information available to require special precautions

Adverse Reactions

>10%: Endocrine: Hypercalcemia (24%)

1% to 10%:

Dermatologic: Psoriasis (4%), pruritus (1% to 3%), skin discomfort

Genitourinary: Urine abnormality (4%), hypercalciuria (3%)

<1%, postmarketing, and/or case reports: Burning sensation of skin, dermatitis (acute; blistering), eczema (including extensive flare up), erythema, nephrolithiasis, skin atrophy

General Dosage Range Topical: *Adults:* Apply to affected areas twice daily (maximum: 200 g weekly)

Mechanism of Action The mechanism by which calcitriol is beneficial in the treatment of psoriasis has not been established.

Pharmacodynamics/Kinetics

Duration of Action Oral, IV: 3 to 5 days

Half-life Elimination Children 1.8-16 years undergoing peritoneal dialysis: 27.4 hours; Healthy adults: 5 to 8 hours; Hemodialysis: 16 to 22 hours

Time to Peak Oral: 3 to 6 hours; Hemodialysis: 8 to 12 hours

Pregnancy Risk Factor C

Pregnancy Considerations Adverse effects have been observed in some animal reproduction studies. When treatment for psoriasis in pregnancy is needed, the use of other agents is generally preferred (Babalola 2013; Bae 2012).

Calcium and Vitamin D
(KAL see um & VYE ta min dee)

Brand Names: US Cal-CYUM [OTC] [DSC]; Calcet Petites [OTC]; Calcitrate [OTC]; Caltrate 600+D [OTC]; Caltrate 600+D3 Soft [OTC]; Caltrate 600+Soy [OTC]; Caltrate ColonHealth [OTC]; Caltrate Gummy Bites [OTC]; Citracal Maximum [OTC]; Citracal Petites [OTC]; Citracal Regular [OTC]; Os-Cal Calcium + D3 [OTC]; Os-Cal Extra D3 [OTC]; Os-Cal [OTC]; Oysco 500+D [OTC]; Oysco D [OTC] [DSC]

Generic Availability (US) Yes

Pharmacologic Category Calcium Salt; Electrolyte Supplement, Oral; Vitamin, Fat Soluble

Use Dietary supplement, antacid

Local Anesthetic/Vasoconstrictor Precautions No information available to require special precautions

Effects on Dental Treatment No significant effects or complications reported

Effects on Bleeding No information available to require special precautions

Adverse Reactions Frequency not defined; also see individual agents

Central nervous system: Headache

Endocrine & metabolic: Hypercalcemia

Gastrointestinal: Gastrointestinal distress

Genitourinary: Hypercalciuria

Dosing

Adult & Geriatric Calcium supplement, hyperphosphatemia: Oral: Refer to individual monographs for dietary reference intake.

Renal Impairment Use caution in severe renal impairment.

Contraindications Hypersensitivity to any component of the formulation; hypophosphatemia, hypercalcemia, evidence of vitamin D toxicity; history of kidney stones

Warnings/Precautions Constipation, bloating, and gas are common with calcium supplements. Use with caution patients with respiratory failure, renal impairment or respiratory acidosis. Use with caution in patients with renal failure to avoid hypercalcemia; frequent monitoring of serum calcium and phosphorus is necessary. Use caution when administering calcium supplements to patients with a history of kidney stones. Hypercalcemia and hypercalciuria are most likely to occur in hypoparathyroid patients receiving high doses of vitamin D. Calcium absorption is impaired in achlorhydria; common in elderly, use an alternate salt (eg, citrate) and administer with food. Calcium administration interferes with absorption of some minerals and drugs; use with caution. Taking calcium (≤500 mg) with food improves absorption.

Some products may contain soy, tartrazine, or phenylalanine, or may be derived from shellfish.

Drug Interactions

Metabolism/Transport Effects None known.

Avoid Concomitant Use

Avoid concomitant use of Calcium Carbonate and Vitamin D with any of the following: Calcium Acetate

Increased Effect/Toxicity

Calcium Carbonate and Vitamin D may increase the levels/effects of: Amphetamines; Calcium Acetate; Calcium Polystyrene Sulfonate; Cardiac Glycosides; Dexmethylphenidate; Methylphenidate; QuiNIDine; Sodium Polystyrene Sulfonate; Vitamin D Analogs

The levels/effects of Calcium Carbonate and Vitamin D may be increased by: Multivitamins/Fluoride (with ADE); Thiazide and Thiazide-Like Diuretics

Decreased Effect

Calcium Carbonate and Vitamin D may decrease the levels/effects of: Allopurinol; Alpha-Lipoic Acid; Antipsychotic Agents (Phenothiazines); Atazanavir; Bisacodyl; Bismuth Subcitrate; Bisphosphonate Derivatives; Bosutinib; Calcium Channel Blockers; Captopril; Cefditoren; Cefpodoxime; Cefuroxime; Chloroquine; Corticosteroids (Oral); Cysteamine (Systemic); Dabigatran Etexilate; Dabrafenib; Dasatinib; Deferiprone; Delavirdine; Diacerein; DOBUTamine; Dolutegravir; Eltrombopag; Elvitegravir; Erlotinib;

Estramustine; Fosinopril; Gabapentin; Gefitinib; HMG-CoA Reductase Inhibitors; Hyoscyamine; Iron Salts; Isoniazid; Itraconazole; Ketoconazole (Systemic); Ledipasvir; Mesalamine; Methenamine; Multivitamins/Fluoride (with ADE); Multivitamins/Minerals (with ADEK, Folate, Iron); Mycophenolate; Nilotinib; PAZOPanib; PenicillAMINE; Phosphate Supplements; Potassium Acid Phosphate; Quinolone Antibiotics; Rilpivirine; Riociguat; Sotalol; Strontium Ranelate; Sulpiride; Tetracycline Derivatives; Thyroid Products; Trientine; Velpatasvir

The levels/effects of Calcium Carbonate and Vitamin D may be decreased by: Alpha-Lipoic Acid; Trientine

Food Interactions Food may increase calcium absorption. Calcium may decrease iron absorption. Bran, foods high in oxalates, or whole grain cereals may decrease calcium absorption. Management: Administer preferably with food.

Dietary Considerations Take (preferably with food) 2 hours before or after other medications to minimize GI upset. Some products may contain phenylalanine (avoid use in phenylketonurics).

Pregnancy Considerations Available evidence suggests safe use during pregnancy.

Breastfeeding Considerations Available evidence suggests safe use during lactation.

Dosage Forms

Caplet, oral:

Citracal Maximum [OTC]: Calcium 315 mg and vitamin D 250 units

Os-Cal Calcium + D3 [OTC]: Calcium 500 mg and vitamin D 200 units

Os-Cal Extra D3 [OTC]: Calcium 500 mg and vitamin D 600 units

Capsule, oral:

Generic: Calcium 600 mg and vitamin D 100 units, Calcium 600 mg and vitamin D 400 units, Calcium 600 mg and vitamin D 500 units, Calcium 600 mg and vitamin D 1000 units

Tablet, oral:

Calcet Petites [OTC]: Calcium 200 mg and vitamin D 250 units

Calcitrate [OTC]: Calcium 315 mg and vitamin D 250 units

Caltrate 600+D [OTC]: Calcium 600 mg and vitamin D 400 units, calcium 600 mg and vitamin D 800 units

Caltrate 600+Soy [OTC]: Calcium 600 mg and vitamin D 200 units

Caltrate ColonHealth [OTC]: Calcium 600 mg and vitamin D 200 units

Citracal Petites [OTC]: Calcium 200 mg and vitamin D 250 units

Citracal Regular [OTC]: Calcium 250 mg and vitamin D 200 units

Oysco 500+D [OTC]: Calcium 500 mg and vitamin D 200 units

Generic: Calcium 250 mg and vitamin D 125 units; calcium 315 mg and vitamin D 200 units; calcium 315 mg and vitamin D 250 units; calcium 500 mg and vitamin D 125 units; calcium 500 mg and vitamin D 200 units; calcium 500 mg and vitamin D 400 units; calcium 500 mg and vitamin D 600 units; calcium 600 mg and vitamin D 125 units; calcium 600 mg and vitamin D 200 units; calcium 600 mg and vitamin D 400 units; calcium 600 mg and vitamin D 800 units

Tablet, chewable:

Caltrate Gummy Bites [OTC]: Calcium 250 mg and vitamin D 400 units

Caltrate 600+D3 Soft [OTC]: Calcium 600 mg and vitamin D 800 units

Os-Cal [OTC]: Calcium 500 mg and vitamin D 600 units

Generic: Calcium 500 mg and vitamin D 100 units; calcium 500 mg and vitamin D 200 units; calcium 500 mg and vitamin D 600 units; calcium 600 mg and vitamin D 400 units

Calcium Carbonate (KAL see um KAR bun ate)

Related Information

Rheumatoid Arthritis, Osteoarthritis, and Osteoporosis *on page 1792*

Brand Names: US Alcalak [OTC] [DSC]; Antacid Calcium Extra Strength [OTC]; Antacid Calcium [OTC]; Antacid Extra Strength [OTC]; Antacid [OTC]; Cal-Carb Forte [OTC]; Cal-Gest Antacid [OTC]; Cal-Mint [OTC]; Calcarb 600 [OTC] [DSC]; Calci-Chew [OTC]; Calci-Mix [OTC] [DSC]; Calcium 600 [OTC]; Calcium Antacid Extra Strength [OTC]; Calcium Antacid Ultra Max St [OTC]; Calcium Antacid [OTC]; Calcium High Potency [OTC]; Caltrate 600 [OTC]; Florical [OTC]; Maalox Childrens [OTC]; Maalox [OTC]; Os-Cal [OTC] [DSC]; Oysco 500 [OTC]; Titralac [OTC]; Tums Chewy Bites [OTC]; Tums Chewy Delights [OTC]; Tums E-X 750 [OTC]; Tums Freshers [OTC]; Tums Kids [OTC]; Tums Lasting Effects [OTC]; Tums Smoothies [OTC]; Tums Ultra 1000 [OTC]; Tums [OTC]

Brand Names: Canada Apo-Cal; Calcite-500; Caltrate; Caltrate Select; Os-Cal; Tums Chews Extra Strength; Tums Extra Strength; Tums Regular Strength; Tums Smoothies; Tums Ultra Strength

Pharmacologic Category Antacid; Antidote; Calcium Salt; Electrolyte Supplement, Oral; Phosphate Binder

Use

Antacid: For the relief of acid indigestion, heartburn, sour stomach, and GI upset associated with these symptoms

Calcium supplementation: For use as a dietary supplement when calcium intake may be inadequate (eg, osteoporosis, osteomalacia, hypocalcemic rickets) (IOM, 2011)

Local Anesthetic/Vasoconstrictor Precautions No information available to require special precautions

Effects on Dental Treatment Key adverse event(s) related to dental treatment: Xerostomia (normal salivary flow resumes upon discontinuation).

Effects on Bleeding No information available to require special precautions

Adverse Reactions Well tolerated

1% to 10%:

Central nervous system: Headache, laxative effect

Endocrine & metabolic: Hypercalcemia, hypophosphatemia, milk-alkali syndrome (with very high, chronic dosing and/or renal failure [headache, nausea, irritability, and weakness or alkalosis, hypercalcemia, renal impairment])

Gastrointestinal: Abdominal pain, anorexia, constipation, flatulence, hyperacidity (acid rebound), nausea, vomiting, xerostomia

General Dosage Range Oral:

Dietary Reference Intake for Calcium:

Children 0 to <6 months: Adequate intake: 200 mg **elemental calcium** daily

Children 6 to 12 months: Adequate intake: 260 mg **elemental calcium** daily

Children 1 to 3 years: RDA: 700 mg **elemental calcium** daily

Children 4 to 8 years: RDA: 1,000 mg **elemental calcium** daily
Children 9 to 18 years: RDA: 1,300 mg **elemental calcium** daily
Adults 19 to 50 years: RDA: 1,000 mg **elemental calcium** daily
Adults ≥51 years, females: RDA: 1,200 mg **elemental calcium** daily
Adults 51 to 70 years, males: RDA: 1,000 mg **elemental calcium** daily
Adults >70 years, males: RDA: 1,200 mg **elemental calcium** daily

Antacid:
Children 2 to 5 years (10.9 to 21.3 kg): 375 to 400 mg as symptoms occur; maximum: 1,500 mg daily for up to 2 weeks
Children 6 to 11 years (≥21.8 kg): 750 to 800 mg as symptoms occur; maximum: 3,000 mg daily for up to 2 weeks
Children ≥12 years and Adults ≤51 years: 500 to 3,000 mg as symptoms occur for up to 2 weeks; maximum: 7,500 mg daily for up to 2 weeks
Adults >51 years: 1 to 4 tablets as symptoms occur; maximum: 8,000 mg daily for up to 2 weeks

Calcium supplementation:
Children 2 to 4 years: 750 mg twice daily
Children ≥4 years and Adolescents: 750 mg 3 times daily

Mechanism of Action As dietary supplement, used to prevent or treat negative calcium balance; in osteoporosis, it helps to prevent or decrease the rate of bone loss. Calcium is an integral component of the skeleton and also moderates nerve and muscle performance and allows normal cardiac function. Also used to treat hyperphosphatemia in patients with chronic kidney disease by combining with dietary phosphate to form insoluble calcium phosphate, which is excreted in feces. Calcium salts as antacids neutralize gastric acidity resulting in increased gastric and duodenal bulb pH; they additionally inhibit proteolytic activity of pepsin if the pH is increased >4 and increase lower esophageal sphincter tone (IOM, 2011).

Pregnancy Considerations Calcium crosses the placenta. Intestinal absorption of calcium increases during pregnancy. The amount of calcium reaching the fetus is determined by maternal physiological changes. Calcium requirements are the same in pregnant and nonpregnant females (IOM, 2011). Calcium-based antacids are considered low risk during pregnancy; excessive use should be avoided (Mahadevan, 2006).

Calcium Carbonate and Magnesium Hydroxide

(KAL see um KAR bun ate & mag NEE zhum hye DROKS ide)

Related Information
Calcium Carbonate *on page 280*
Magnesium Hydroxide *on page 1035*

Brand Names: US Geri-Lanta Supreme [OTC]; Mi-Acid Double Strength [OTC]; Mylanta Supreme [OTC]; Mylanta Ultra [OTC] [DSC]

Pharmacologic Category Antacid

Use Antacid: Relief of heartburn, acid indigestion, sour stomach and GI upset associated with these symptoms

Local Anesthetic/Vasoconstrictor Precautions No information available to require special precautions

Effects on Dental Treatment No significant effects or complications reported

Effects on Bleeding No information available to require special precautions

General Dosage Range Oral: *Adults:* 2 to 4 tablets (maximum: 8 tablets per 24 hours) **or** 10 to 20 mL 4 times daily (maximum: 90 mL per 24 hours)

Pregnancy Considerations Calcium-based antacids are considered low risk during pregnancy; excessive use should be avoided (Mahadevan 2006). Most magnesium-containing antacids are considered low risk during pregnancy (Mahadevan 2006).

Calcium Citrate (KAL see um SIT rate)

Related Information
Rheumatoid Arthritis, Osteoarthritis, and Osteoporosis *on page 1792*

Brand Names: US Cal-Citrate [OTC]; Calcitrate [OTC]

Brand Names: Canada Osteocit®

Pharmacologic Category Calcium Salt

Use Dietary supplement

Local Anesthetic/Vasoconstrictor Precautions No information available to require special precautions

Effects on Dental Treatment No significant effects or complications reported

Effects on Bleeding No information available to require special precautions

Adverse Reactions Frequency not defined. Mild hypercalcemia (calcium: >10.5 mg/dL) may be asymptomatic or manifest as anorexia, constipation, nausea, and vomiting. More severe hypercalcemia (calcium: >12 mg/dL) is associated with coma, confusion, delirium, and stupor.
Central nervous system: Headache
Endocrine & metabolic: Hypercalcemia, hypophosphatemia, increased thirst
Gastrointestinal: Abdominal pain, anorexia, constipation, nausea, vomiting

General Dosage Range Oral:
Children 1-6 months: Adequate intake: 200 mg/day
Children 7-12 months: Adequate intake: 260 mg/day
Children 1-3 years: RDA: 700 mg/day
Children 4-8 years: RDA: 1000 mg/day
Children 9-18 years: RDA: 1300 mg/day
Adults: 500-2000 mg divided 2-4 times/day
Adults 19-50 years: RDA: 1000 mg/day
Adults ≥51 years, females: RDA: 1200 mg/day
Adults 51-70 years, males: RDA: 1000 mg/day
Adults >70 years, males: RDA: 1200 mg/day

Mechanism of Action Moderates nerve and muscle performance via action potential excitation threshold regulation

Pregnancy Considerations Calcium crosses the placenta. Intestinal absorption of calcium increases during pregnancy. The amount of calcium reaching the fetus is determined by maternal physiological changes. Calcium requirements are the same in pregnant and nonpregnant females (IOM, 2011).

Calcium Glubionate (KAL see um gloo BYE oh nate)

Related Information
Rheumatoid Arthritis, Osteoarthritis, and Osteoporosis *on page 1792*

Brand Names: US Calcionate [OTC]

Pharmacologic Category Calcium Salt

Use Dietary supplement

Local Anesthetic/Vasoconstrictor Precautions No information available to require special precautions

Effects on Dental Treatment No significant effects or complications reported

Effects on Bleeding No information available to require special precautions

Adverse Reactions Frequency not defined. Symptoms reported with hypercalcemia.

Endocrine & metabolic: Increased thirst
Gastrointestinal: Abdominal pain, anorexia, constipation, nausea, vomiting, xerostomia
Renal: Polyuria

General Dosage Range Oral:

Children 1-6 months: Adequate intake: 200 mg/day
Children 7-12 months: Adequate intake: 260 mg/day
Children 1-3 years: RDA: 700 mg/day
Children 4-8 years: RDA: 1000 mg/day
Children 9-18 years: RDA: 1300 mg/day
Adults 19-50 years: RDA: 1000 mg/day
Adults ≥51 years, females: RDA: 1200 mg/day
Adults 51-70 years, males: RDA: 1000 mg/day
Adults >70 years, males: RDA: 1200 mg/day

Mechanism of Action As dietary supplement, used to prevent or treat negative calcium balance. The calcium in calcium salts moderates nerve and muscle performance and allows normal cardiac function.

Pregnancy Considerations Calcium crosses the placenta. Intestinal absorption of calcium increases during pregnancy. The amount of calcium reaching the fetus is determined by maternal physiological changes. Calcium requirements are the same in pregnant and nonpregnant females (IOM, 2011).

Calcium Gluconate (KAL see um GLOO koe nate)

Related Information

Rheumatoid Arthritis, Osteoarthritis, and Osteoporosis *on page 1792*

Brand Names: US Cal-Glu [OTC]

Pharmacologic Category Calcium Salt; Electrolyte Supplement, Oral; Electrolyte Supplement, Parenteral

Use

IV: Treatment of hypocalcemia and conditions secondary to hypocalcemia (eg, tetany, seizures, arrhythmias); treatment of cardiac disturbances secondary to hyperkalemia; adjunctive treatment of rickets, osteomalacia, and magnesium sulfate overdose; decrease capillary permeability in allergic conditions, nonthrombocytopenic purpura, and exudative dermatoses (eg, dermatitis herpetiformis, pruritus secondary to certain drugs); treatment of black widow spider bites to relieve muscle cramping

Oral: Dietary calcium supplementation

Local Anesthetic/Vasoconstrictor Precautions No information available to require special precautions

Effects on Dental Treatment No significant effects or complications reported

Effects on Bleeding No information available to require special precautions

Adverse Reactions Frequency not defined.

IV:

Cardiovascular (with rapid IV injection): Arrhythmia, bradycardia, cardiac arrest, hypotension, syncope, vasodilation
Central nervous system: Sense of oppression (with rapid IV injection)
Endocrine & metabolic: Hypercalcemia
Gastrointestinal: Chalky taste
Neuromuscular & skeletal: Tingling sensation (with rapid IV injection)
Miscellaneous: Heat waves (with rapid IV injection)
Postmarketing and/or case reports: Calcinosis cutis

Oral: Gastrointestinal: Constipation

General Dosage Range

IV: *Children, Adolescents, and Adults:* Dosage varies greatly depending on indication

Oral (IOM, 2011):

Children 1 to 6 months: Adequate intake: 200 mg **elemental calcium** daily
Children 7 to 12 months: Adequate intake: 260 mg **elemental calcium** daily
Children 1 to 3 years: RDA: 700 mg **elemental calcium** daily
Children 4 to 8 years: RDA: 1000 mg **elemental calcium** daily
Children 9 to 18 years: RDA: 1300 mg **elemental calcium** daily
Adults 19 to 50 years: RDA: 1000 mg **elemental calcium** daily
Adults ≥51 years, females: RDA: 1200 mg **elemental calcium** daily
Adults 51 to 70 years, males: RDA: 1000 mg **elemental calcium** daily
Adults >70 years, males: RDA: 1200 mg **elemental calcium** daily

Mechanism of Action Moderates nerve and muscle performance via action potential threshold regulation.

In hydrogen fluoride exposures, calcium gluconate provides a source of calcium ions to complex free fluoride ions and prevent or reduce toxicity; administration also helps to correct fluoride-induced hypocalcemia.

Pregnancy Risk Factor C

Pregnancy Considerations Animal reproduction studies have not been conducted. Calcium crosses the placenta. The amount of calcium reaching the fetus is determined by maternal physiological changes. Calcium requirements are the same in pregnant and nonpregnant females (IOM 2011). Information related to use as an antidote in pregnancy is limited. In general, medications used as antidotes should take into consideration the health and prognosis of the mother; antidotes should be administered to pregnant women if there is a clear indication for use and should not be withheld because of fears of teratogenicity (Bailey 2003). Medications used for the treatment of cardiac arrest in pregnancy are the same as in the non-pregnant woman. Doses and indications should follow current Advanced Cardiovascular Life Support guidelines. Appropriate medications should not be withheld due to concerns of fetal teratogenicity (Jeejeebhoy [AHA] 2015).

Calcium Lactate (KAL see um LAK tate)

Related Information

Rheumatoid Arthritis, Osteoarthritis, and Osteoporosis *on page 1792*

Brand Names: US Cal-Lac [OTC]

Pharmacologic Category Calcium Salt

Use Treatment and prevention of calcium depletion

Local Anesthetic/Vasoconstrictor Precautions No information available to require special precautions

Effects on Dental Treatment No significant effects or complications reported

Effects on Bleeding No information available to require special precautions

Adverse Reactions <1%, postmarketing, and/or case reports: Confusion, constipation, dizziness, headache, hypercalcemia, hypercalciuria, hypomagnesemia, hypophosphatemia, milk-alkali syndrome, nausea, vomiting, xerostomia

General Dosage Range Oral:

Children 1-6 months: Adequate intake: 200 mg/day
Children 7-12 months: Adequate intake: 260 mg/day
Children 1-3 years: RDA: 700 mg/day
Children 4-8 years: RDA: 1000 mg/day
Children 9-18 years: RDA: 1300 mg/day
Adults 19-50 years: RDA: 1000 mg/day
Adults ≥51 years, females: RDA: 1200 mg/day
Adults 51-70 years, males: RDA: 1000 mg/day
Adults >70 years, males: RDA: 1200 mg/day

Mechanism of Action As dietary supplement, used to prevent or treat negative calcium balance; in osteoporosis, it helps to prevent or decrease the rate of bone loss. The calcium in calcium salts moderates nerve and muscle performance and allows normal cardiac function.

Pregnancy Considerations Calcium crosses the placenta. Intestinal absorption of calcium increases during pregnancy. The amount of calcium reaching the fetus is determined by maternal physiological changes. Calcium requirements are the same in pregnant and nonpregnant females (IOM, 2011).

Calfactant (kaf AKT ant)

Brand Names: US Infasurf

Pharmacologic Category Lung Surfactant

Use Prevention of respiratory distress syndrome (RDS) in premature infants at high risk for RDS and for the treatment ("rescue") of premature infants who develop RDS

Prophylaxis: Therapy at birth with calfactant is indicated for premature infants <29 weeks of gestational age at significant risk for RDS. Should be administered as soon as possible, preferably within 30 minutes after birth.

Treatment: For infants ≤72 hours of age with RDS (confirmed by clinical and radiologic findings) and requiring endotracheal intubation.

Local Anesthetic/Vasoconstrictor Precautions No information available to require special precautions

Effects on Dental Treatment No significant effects or complications reported

Effects on Bleeding No information available to require special precautions

Adverse Reactions

>10%:

- Cardiovascular: Bradycardia (34%)
- Gastrointestinal: Endotracheal tube reflux (21%)
- Respiratory: Cyanosis (65%), airway obstruction (39%)
- Miscellaneous: Mechanical ventilation (16%; manual ventilation required)

1% to 10%:

- Miscellaneous: Endotracheal intubation (3%; reintubation needed)

General Dosage Range Intratracheal: *Premature infants:* 3 mL/kg (body weight at birth) every 12 hours for a total of 3 doses

Mechanism of Action Endogenous lung surfactant is essential for effective ventilation because it modifies alveolar surface tension, thereby stabilizing the alveoli. Lung surfactant deficiency is the cause of respiratory distress syndrome (RDS) in premature infants and lung surfactant restores surface activity to the lungs of these infants.

Canagliflozin (kan a gli FLOE zin)

Brand Names: US Invokana

Brand Names: Canada Invokana

Generic Availability (US) No

Pharmacologic Category Antidiabetic Agent, Sodium-Glucose Cotransporter 2 (SGLT2) Inhibitor; Sodium-Glucose Cotransporter 2 (SGLT2) Inhibitor

Use Diabetes mellitus, type 2: Treatment of type 2 diabetes mellitus (noninsulin dependent, NIDDM) as an adjunct to diet and exercise to improve glycemic control

Local Anesthetic/Vasoconstrictor Precautions No information available to require special precautions

Effects on Dental Treatment Key adverse event(s) related to dental treatment: Hypoglycemia reported; patients should be appointed for dental treatment in the morning in order to minimize chance of stress-induced hypoglycemia. Dizziness and syncope have been reported; patients may experience orthostatic hypotension as they stand up after treatment; especially if lying in dental chair for extended periods of time. Use caution with sudden changes in position during and after dental treatment.

Canagliflozin-dependent patients with diabetes (noninsulin dependent, type 2) should be questioned by the dental professional at each dental visit to assess their risk for stress induced hypoglycemia. The dental professional should inquire about the patient's routine (ie, work, sleep schedule, eating patterns), history of hypoglycemia, time of last medication dose, last meal, and most recent blood sugar assessment. Keep a supply of glucose tablets and other carbohydrates in the office to prepare for a hypoglycemic event. Seek medical attention when necessary (American Diabetes Association 2016).

Effects on Bleeding No information available to require special precautions

Adverse Reactions

>10%:

- Endocrine & metabolic: Increased serum potassium (>5.4 mEq/mL: 9% to 27%, ≥6.5 mEq/mL: 1% to 2%; dose-related; more risk in patients with moderate renal impairment)
- Genitourinary: Genitourinary infection (females: 11% to 12%; including vulvovaginal candidiasis, vulvovaginal mycotic infection, vulvovaginitis, vaginal infection, vulvitis; males: 4%; including balanitis/balanoposthitis, balanitis candida, fungal genital infection)

1% to 10%:

- Central nervous system: Falling (1% to 2%), fatigue (2%)
- Endocrine & metabolic: Hypoglycemia (4%; monotherapy), increased thirst (2% to 3%)
- Gastrointestinal: Abdominal pain (2%), constipation (2%)
- Genitourinary: Urinary tract infection (6%), polyuria (5%), vulvovaginal pruritus (2% to 3%)
- Hypersensitivity: Hypersensitivity (4%)
- Neuromuscular & skeletal: Bone fracture (1% to 2%), weakness (≤1%)
- Renal: Renal insufficiency (2% to 4%; 18% to 23% in patients with baseline eGFR 30 to <50 mL/minute/1.73 m^2)

Frequency not defined:

Endocrine & metabolic: Hypermagnesemia, increased LDL cholesterol, increased serum cholesterol (non-HDL), increased serum phosphate

Hematologic & oncologic: Increased hemoglobin

Neuromuscular & skeletal: Decreased bone mineral density

Renal: Acute renal failure

<1%, postmarketing, and/or case reports: Anaphylaxis, angioedema, ketoacidosis, pancreatitis, pyelonephritis, skin photosensitivity, urosepsis

Dosing

Adult & Geriatric Note: If present, correct volume depletion prior to initiation.

Diabetes mellitus, type 2: Oral: Initial: 100 mg once daily prior to first meal of the day; may increase to 300 mg once daily (**only** in patients with eGFR ≥60 mL/minute/1.73 m^2)

Dosing adjustment for concomitant therapy with UDP-glucuronosyl transferase (UGT) inducers (eg, rifampin, phenytoin, phenobarbital, ritonavir): Consider increasing the canagliflozin dose to 300 mg once daily in patients currently tolerating canagliflozin 100 mg once daily who have eGFR ≥60 mL/minute/1.73 m^2 and require additional glycemic control. If patient is receiving concurrent UGT enzyme inducers **and** has eGFR 45 to <60 mL/minute/1.73 m^2, consider alternate antihyperglycemic therapy.

Renal Impairment

US labeling:

eGFR ≥60 mL/minute/1.73 m^2: No dosage adjustment necessary.

eGFR 45 to <60 mL/minute/1.73 m^2: Maximum dose: 100 mg once daily. If patient receiving concurrent UDP-glucuronosyl transferase (UGT) enzyme inducers (eg, rifampin, phenytoin, phenobarbital, ritonavir) and eGFR 45 to <60 mL/minute/1.73 m^2 at baseline, consider the use of another antidiabetic agent.

eGFR ≥30 to <45 mL/minute/1.73 m^2: Use not recommended for initiation of therapy or when eGFR is persistently <45 mL/minute/1.73 m^2.

eGFR <30 mL/minute/1.73 m^2: Use is contraindicated.

End-stage renal disease (ESRD): Use is contraindicated.

Hemodialysis: Use is contraindicated.

Canadian labeling:

eGFR ≥60 mL/minute/1.73 m^2: No dosage adjustment necessary.

eGFR 45 to <60 mL/minute/1.73 m^2: Avoid initiating therapy if eGFR <60 mL/minute/1.73 m^2 at baseline. If eGFR persistently falls to 45 to <60 mL/minute/1.73 m^2 during therapy, do not exceed 100 mg once daily. If patient receiving concurrent UDP-glucuronosyl transferase (UGT) enzyme inducers (eg, rifampin, phenytoin, phenobarbital, ritonavir) and eGFR 45 to <60 mL/minute/1.73 m^2 at baseline, consider the use of another antidiabetic agent.

eGFR <45 mL/minute/1.73 m^2: Use is contraindicated.

ESRD: Use is contraindicated.

Hemodialysis: Use is contraindicated.

Hepatic Impairment

Mild-to-moderate impairment (Child-Pugh class A, B): No dosage adjustment necessary.

Severe impairment (Child-Pugh class C): Use not recommended (has not been studied).

Mechanism of Action By inhibiting sodium-glucose cotransporter 2 (SGLT2) in the proximal renal tubules, canagliflozin reduces reabsorption of filtered glucose from the tubular lumen and lowers the renal threshold for glucose (RT_G). SGLT2 is the main site of filtered glucose reabsorption; reduction of filtered glucose reabsorption and lowering of RT_G result in increased urinary excretion of glucose, thereby reducing plasma glucose concentrations.

Contraindications

History of serious hypersensitivity to canagliflozin or any component of the formulation; severe renal impairment (eGFR <30 mL/minute/1.73 m^2); end-stage renal disease or patients on dialysis.

Canadian labeling: Additional contraindications (not in US labeling): eGFR <45 mL/minute/1.73 m^2

Warnings/Precautions Potentially significant drug-drug interactions may exist, requiring dose or frequency adjustment, additional monitoring, and/or selection of alternative therapy. Patients may experience hypersensitivity reactions (eg, urticaria) with some being severe; generally occurs within hours to days after therapy initiation. Discontinue canagliflozin if hypersensitivity occurs and treat as appropriate. Acute kidney injury has been reported; may require hospitalization and dialysis; has occurred in patients <65 years of age. Prior to initiation, consider risk factors for acute kidney injury (eg, hypovolemia, chronic renal insufficiency, heart failure, use of concomitant medications including diuretics, ACE inhibitors, ARBs, and NSAIDs). Temporarily discontinue use with reduced oral intake or fluid losses; discontinue use if acute kidney injury occurs. Additional abnormalities in renal function (decreased eGFR, increased serum creatinine) may occur upon initiation and are dose dependent. Monitor renal function frequently in patients with an eGFR <60 mL/minute/1.73 m^2 and discontinue therapy if eGFR is persistently <45 mL/minute/1.73 m^2. May cause symptomatic hypotension due to intravascular volume depletion especially in patients with renal impairment (ie, eGFR <60 mL/minute/1.73 m^2), elderly, patients on other antihypertensives (eg, diuretics, ACE inhibitors, or angiotensin receptor blockers [ARBs]), or those with low systolic blood pressure. Assess volume status prior to initiation in patients at risk of hypotension and correct if depleted; monitor signs and symptoms of hypotension after initiation. May cause hyperkalemia. Patients predisposed to hyperkalemia (including patients with renal impairment or taking potassium-sparing diuretics, ACE inhibitors, and ARBs) are more likely to develop hyperkalemia; monitor serum potassium after initiation in those who are predisposed. May cause dose-related LDL-cholesterol (C) elevation; monitor LDL-C and treat as needed. May increase the risk of genital mycotic infections (eg, vulvovaginal mycotic infection, vulvovaginal candidiasis, vulvovaginitis, candida balanitis, balanoposthitis). Patients with a history of these infections or uncircumcised males are at greater risk. Increased incidence of bone fractures may occur as early as 12 weeks after treatment initiation. Consider patient's risk of fracture prior to initiation. According to the American Diabetes Association guidelines, sodium glucose co-transporter-2 (SGLT2) inhibitors should be avoided in patients with fracture risk factors (ADA 2016a). An increased incidence of leg and foot amputations (mostly affecting toes) has been observed in patients receiving canagliflozin compared to those receiving placebo in an ongoing clinical trial; causal relationship has not yet been established. Further investigation is ongoing (FDA safety communication May 2016).

Glycemic efficacy may be less and adverse reactions may be higher with moderate renal impairment (eGFR 30 to <50 mL/minute/1.73 m^2). Incidence of hyperkalemia may be higher with the 300 mg dose. Dosage adjustment may be necessary in patients with preexisting renal impairment. Safety and efficacy in severe renal impairment (<30 mL/minute/1.73 m^2), ESRD, and in patients receiving dialysis are not established and canagliflozin is contraindicated in these patients. Not recommended for use in severe hepatic impairment (has not been studied). Dose adjustment is not necessary in mild or moderate hepatic impairment.

Not for use in patients with diabetic ketoacidosis (DKA) **or** patients with type 1 diabetes mellitus (insulin-dependent, IDDM). Elderly patients (≥65 years) may have an increased risk of symptoms related to intravascular volume depletion (eg, hypotension, orthostatic hypotension, dizziness, syncope, and dehydration) during therapy, especially with the 300 mg dose; elderly patients ≥75 years may experience a more pronounced risk. HbA_{1c} reductions may be less in patients >65 years compared to younger patients.

Serious urinary infections including urosepsis and pyelonephritis requiring hospitalization have been reported; treatment with SGLT2 inhibitors increase the risk for urinary tract infections (UTI); monitor for signs and symptoms of UTI and treat as needed. Cases of ketoacidosis, a serious and life-threatening condition resulting in urgent hospitalization, have been reported in patients with type 1 and type 2 diabetes mellitus receiving sodium glucose cotransporter 2 (SGLT2) inhibitors; in some cases, patients have presented with normal or only modestly elevated blood glucose (<250 mg/dL) (Bobart 2016; FDA 2015; Handelsman 2016). Before initiating treatment, consider risk factors that may predispose to ketoacidosis (eg, pancreatic insulin deficiency, dose decreases or discontinuation of insulin, caloric restriction, alcohol abuse, extensive exercise, MI, stroke, severe infection, surgery, any other extreme stress event) (Handlelsman 2016). The American Association of Clinical Endocrinologists and American College of Endocrinology recommend considering withholding of SGLT2 inhibitors for at least 24 hours prior to events that may precipitate diabetic ketoacidosis (Handelsman 2016), while others have suggested withholding for 3 to 5 days (Bobart 2016). Patients presenting with nausea/vomiting, abdominal pain, generalized malaise, and/or shortness of breath should be assessed immediately for ketoacidosis; if indicated, consider interruption or discontinuation of therapy.

Drug Interactions

Metabolism/Transport Effects **Substrate** of CYP3A4 (minor), MRP2, P-glycoprotein, UGT1A9, UGT2B4; **Note:** Assignment of Major/Minor substrate status based on clinically relevant drug interaction potential; **Inhibits** CYP2C8 (weak), CYP2C9 (weak)

Avoid Concomitant Use

Avoid concomitant use of Canagliflozin with any of the following: Amodiaquine

Increased Effect/Toxicity

Canagliflozin may increase the levels/effects of: ACE Inhibitors; Aliskiren; Amodiaquine; Angiotensin II Receptor Blockers; Eplerenone; Hypoglycemia-Associated Agents; Insulin; Loop Diuretics; Potassium-Sparing Diuretics; Sulfonylureas

The levels/effects of Canagliflozin may be increased by: Alpha-Lipoic Acid; Androgens; Heparin; Heparin (Low Molecular Weight); MAO Inhibitors; Pegvisomant; Prothionamide; Quinolone Antibiotics; Salicylates; Selective Serotonin Reuptake Inhibitors

Decreased Effect

The levels/effects of Canagliflozin may be decreased by: CarBAMazepine; Efavirenz; Fosphenytoin; Hyperglycemia-Associated Agents; PHENobarbital; Phenytoin; Primidone; Quinolone Antibiotics; RifAMPin; Ritonavir; St John's Wort; Thiazide and Thiazide-Like Diuretics

Dietary Considerations Individualized medical nutrition therapy (MNT) based on ADA recommendations is an integral part of therapy.

Pharmacodynamics/Kinetics

Onset of Action Within 24 hours (dose-dependent)

Duration of Action Suppression of the renal threshold for glucose (RT_G) occurs throughout the 24-hour dosing interval; maximal RT_G suppression occurred with the 300 mg dose (RT_G decreased from baseline of ~240 mg/dL to a mean of 70 to 90 mg/dL over 24 hours).

Half-life Elimination Apparent terminal half-life: 100 mg dose: 10.6 hours; 300 mg dose: 13.1 hours

Time to Peak Plasma: 1 to 2 hours

Pregnancy Risk Factor C

Pregnancy Considerations Adverse events have been observed in animal reproduction studies. Based on animal data, adverse fetal effects on renal development may occur in humans following in utero exposure during the second and third trimesters.

In women with diabetes, maternal hyperglycemia can be associated with congenital malformations as well as adverse effects in the fetus, neonate, and the mother (ACOG 2005; ADA 2016d; Kitzmiller 2008; Metzger 2007). To prevent adverse outcomes, prior to conception and throughout pregnancy, maternal blood glucose and HbA_{1c} should be kept as close to target goals as possible but without causing significant hypoglycemia (ACOG 2013; ADA 2016d; Blumer 2013; Kitzmiller 2008). Agents other than canagliflozin are currently recommended to treat diabetes in pregnant women (ACOG 2013; Blumer 2013).

Breastfeeding Considerations It is not known if canagliflozin is excreted in breast milk. Due to the potential for serious adverse reactions in the nursing infant, the manufacturer recommends a decision be made whether to discontinue nursing or to discontinue the drug, taking into account the importance of treatment to the mother.

Dosage Forms

Tablet, Oral:

Invokana: 100 mg, 300 mg

Canakinumab (can a KIN ue mab)

Brand Names: US Ilaris

Brand Names: Canada Ilaris

Pharmacologic Category Interleukin-1 Beta Inhibitor; Interleukin-1 Inhibitor; Monoclonal Antibody

Use

Periodic fever syndromes:

Cryopyrin-associated periodic syndromes: Treatment of cryopyrin-associated periodic syndromes (CAPS) in adults and children 4 years and older, including familial cold autoinflammatory syndrome (FCAS) and Muckle-Wells syndrome (MWS). **Note:** Has also been studied in Neonatal-onset multisystem inflammatory disease (Ilaris Canadian product labeling 2014; Sibley 2015).

Familial Mediterranean fever: Treatment of familial Mediterranean fever in adult and pediatric patients.

Hyperimmunoglobulin D Syndrome (HIDS)/Mevalonate Kinase Deficiency (MKD): Treatment of hyperimmunoglobulin D (Hyper-IgD) Syndrome (HIDS)/Mevalonate Kinase Deficiency (MKD) in adult and pediatric patients.

Tumor necrosis factor (TNF) receptor associated periodic syndrome: Treatment of TNF receptor associated periodic syndrome (TRAPS) in adult and pediatric patients.

Systemic juvenile idiopathic arthritis: Treatment of active systemic juvenile idiopathic arthritis (SJIA) in patients 2 years and older.

Local Anesthetic/Vasoconstrictor Precautions No information available to require special precautions

Effects on Dental Treatment No significant effects or complications reported

Effects on Bleeding No information available to require special precautions

Adverse Reactions

>10%:

Central nervous system: Headache (14%), vertigo (9% to 14%)

Endocrine & metabolic: Weight gain (11%)

Gastrointestinal: Diarrhea (20%), upper abdominal pain (7% to 16%), nausea (14%), gastroenteritis (3% to 11%)

Infection: Infection (30% to 54%; serious infection: 2% to 5%), influenza (17%)

Local: Injection site reaction (≤12%)

Neuromuscular and skeletal: Musculoskeletal pain (11%)

Respiratory: Nasopharyngitis (11% to 34%), rhinitis (5% to 17%), bronchitis (11%), pharyngitis (3% to 11%)

1% to 10%:

Endocrine & metabolic: Decreased serum calcium (8% [Lachmann 2009])

Genitourinary: Proteinuria (8% [Lachmann 2009])

Hematologic & oncologic: Decreased white blood cell count (10%), eosinophilia (7% [Lachmann 2009]), decreased neutrophils (transient: ≤7%), decreased platelet count (mild and transient: ≤6%)

Hepatic: Increased serum bilirubin (7% [Lachmann 2009]), increased serum AST (≤4%), increased serum ALT (≤4%)

Immunologic: Antibody development (non-neutralizing: ≤3%)

Renal: Decreased creatinine clearance (8% [Lachmann 2009])

Respiratory: Upper respiratory tract infection (7%)

Frequency not defined: Hepatic: Increased serum transaminases

<1%, postmarketing, and/or case reports: Hypersensitivity reaction

General Dosage Range SubQ:

Children, Adolescents, and Adults ≤40 kg: FMF, HIDS/MKD, TRAPS: 2 to 4 mg/kg every 4 weeks.

Children, Adolescents, and Adults >40 kg: FMF, HIDS/MKD, TRAPS: 150 mg to 300 mg every 4 weeks.

Children ≥2 years and ≥7.5 kg and Adolescents: SJIA: 4 mg/kg every 4 weeks (maximum: 300 mg per dose)

Children ≥4 years and Adolescents 15 to 40 kg: CAPS: 2 to 3 mg/kg every 8 weeks

Children ≥4 years, Adolescents, and Adults >40 kg: CAPS: 150 mg every 8 weeks

Mechanism of Action Canakinumab reduces inflammation by binding to interleukin-1 beta (IL-1beta) (no binding to IL-1 alpha or IL-1 receptor antagonist [IL-1ra]) and preventing interaction with cell surface receptors. Cryopyrin-associated periodic syndromes (CAPS) refers to rare genetic syndromes caused by mutations in the nucleotide-binding domain, leucine rich family (NLR), pyrin domain containing 3 (NLRP-3) gene or the cold-induced autoinflammatory syndrome-1 (CIAS1) gene. Cryopyrin, a protein encoded by this gene, regulates IL-1beta activation. Deficiency of cryopyrin results in excessive inflammation.

Pharmacodynamics/Kinetics

Onset of Action Maximum effect: Within 8 days CRP and serum amyloid normalization

Half-life Elimination Children ≥4 years: 22.9 to 25.7 days; Adults: 26 days

Time to Peak Serum: Children ≥4 years: 2 to 7 days; Adults: ~7 days

Pregnancy Considerations Adverse events have been observed in animal reproduction studies. Canakinumab is a recombinant IgG monoclonal antibody; IgG is known to cross the placenta in a linear fashion as pregnancy progresses; potential fetal exposure is likely to be greater during the second and third trimesters.

Candesartan (kan de SAR tan)

Related Information

Cardiovascular Diseases *on page 1752*

Brand Names: US Atacand

Brand Names: Canada ACH Candesartan; Apo-Candesartan; Atacand; CO Candesartan; DOM-Candesartan; JAMP-Candesartan; Mylan-Candesartan; PMS-Candesartan; Ran-Candesartan; Sandoz-Candesartan; Teva-Candesartan

Pharmacologic Category Angiotensin II Receptor Blocker; Antihypertensive

Use

Heart failure: Treatment of heart failure (NYHA class II-IV)

Hypertension: Alone or in combination with other antihypertensive agents in treating hypertension

Guideline recommendations:

Heart failure: The ACCF/AHA 2013 heart failure guidelines recommend the use of ARBs (ie, candesartan, losartan, and valsartan) in patients with HF with reduced ejection fraction who cannot tolerate ACE inhibitors (due to cough) to reduce morbidity and mortality. They also suggest that ARBs are reasonable first-line alternatives to ACE inhibitors in patients already maintained on an ARB for other indications (ACCF/AHA [Yancy, 2013]).

Hypertension: The 2014 guideline for the management of high blood pressure in adults (Eighth Joint National Committee [JNC 8; James, 2013]) recommends initiation of pharmacologic treatment to lower blood pressure for the following patients:

- Patients ≥60 years of age with systolic blood pressure (SBP) ≥150 mm Hg or diastolic blood pressure (DBP) ≥90 mm Hg. Goal of therapy is SBP <150 mm Hg and DBP <90 mm Hg.
- Patients <60 years of age with SBP ≥140 mm Hg or DBP ≥90 mm Hg. Goal of therapy is SBP <140 mm Hg and DBP <90 mm Hg.
- Patients ≥18 years of age with diabetes and SBP ≥140 mm Hg or DBP ≥90 mm Hg. Goal of therapy is SBP <140 mm Hg and DBP <90 mm Hg.
- Patients ≥18 years of age with chronic kidney disease (CKD) and SBP ≥140 mm Hg or DBP

≥90 mm Hg. Goal of therapy is SBP <140 mm Hg and DBP <90 mm Hg.

Chronic kidney disease (CKD) and hypertension: Regardless of race or diabetes status, the use of an ACE inhibitor (ACEI) or angiotensin receptor blocker (ARB) as initial therapy is recommended to improve kidney outcomes. In the general non-black population (without CKD), including those with diabetes, initial antihypertensive treatment should consist of a thiazide-type diuretic, calcium channel blocker, ACEI, or ARB. In the general black population (without CKD), including those with diabetes, initial antihypertensive treatment should consist of a thiazide-type diuretic or a calcium channel blocker instead of an ACEI or ARB.

Coronary artery disease and hypertension: The American Heart Association, American College of Cardiology and American Society of Hypertension (AHA/ACC/ASH) 2015 scientific statement for the treatment of hypertension in patients with coronary artery disease (CAD) recommends the use of an ARB (or ACE inhibitor) as part of a regimen in patients with hypertension and chronic stable angina if there is prior MI, LV systolic dysfunction, diabetes mellitus, or CKD. A BP target of <140/90 mm Hg is reasonable for the secondary prevention of cardiovascular events. A lower target BP (<130/80 mm Hg) may be appropriate in some individuals with CAD, previous MI, stroke or transient ischemic attack, or CAD risk equivalents (AHA/ACC/ASH [Rosendorff 2015]).

Local Anesthetic/Vasoconstrictor Precautions No information available to require special precautions

Effects on Dental Treatment Key adverse event(s) related to dental treatment: Patients may experience orthostatic hypotension as they stand up after treatment; especially if lying in dental chair for extended periods of time. Use caution with sudden changes in position during and after dental treatment.

Effects on Bleeding No information available to require special precautions

Adverse Reactions Frequency not always defined.

Cardiovascular: Hypotension (heart failure 19%), angina pectoris, myocardial infarction, palpitations, tachycardia

Central nervous system: Anxiety, depression, dizziness, drowsiness, headache, paresthesia, vertigo

Dermatologic: Diaphoresis, skin rash

Endocrine & metabolic: Hyperkalemia (heart failure <1% to 6%), hyperglycemia, hypertriglyceridemia, hyperuricemia

Gastrointestinal: Dyspepsia, gastroenteritis

Genitourinary: Hematuria

Neuromuscular & skeletal: Back pain, increased creatine phosphokinase, myalgia, weakness

Renal: Increased serum creatinine (≤13% in patients with heart failure with drug discontinuation required in 6%)

Respiratory: Dyspnea, epistaxis, pharyngitis, rhinitis, upper respiratory tract infection

Miscellaneous: Fever

<1%, postmarketing, and/or case reports: Agranulocytosis, anemia, angioedema, atrial fibrillation, bradycardia, cardiac failure, cerebrovascular accident, chest pain, confusion, cough, falling, hepatic insufficiency, hepatitis, hypersensitivity, hyponatremia, leukopenia, loss of consciousness, malaise, myasthenia, myositis, neutropenia, pancreatitis, pneumonia, presyncope, pruritus, pulmonary edema, renal failure, renal insufficiency, rhabdomyolysis, sinusitis, thrombocytopenia, urticaria

General Dosage Range Dosage adjustment recommended in patients with hepatic impairment.

Oral:

Children 1 to <6 years: Initial: 0.2 mg/kg/day in 1 to 2 divided doses; Maintenance: 0.05 to 0.4 mg/kg/day in 1 to 2 divided doses (maximum daily dose: 0.4 mg/kg/day)

Children ≥6 years and Adolescents <17 years: Initial: <50 kg: 4 to 8 mg daily in 1 to 2 divided doses; ≥50 kg: 8 to 16 mg daily in 1 to 2 divided doses; Maintenance: 2 to 32 mg daily in 1 to 2 divided doses (maximum daily dose: 32 mg daily)

Adults: Initial: 4 to 16 mg once daily; Maintenance: 4 to 32 mg daily in 1 to 2 divided doses

Mechanism of Action Candesartan is an angiotensin receptor antagonist. Angiotensin II acts as a vasoconstrictor. In addition to causing direct vasoconstriction, angiotensin II also stimulates the release of aldosterone. Once aldosterone is released, sodium as well as water are reabsorbed. The end result is an elevation in blood pressure. Candesartan binds to the AT1 angiotensin II receptor. This binding prevents angiotensin II from binding to the receptor thereby blocking the vasoconstriction and the aldosterone secreting effects of angiotensin II.

Pharmacodynamics/Kinetics

Onset of Action

2 to 3 hours; antihypertensive effect: Within 2 weeks; Peak effect: 6 to 8 hours; maximum antihypertensive effect: 4 to 6 weeks

Duration of Action >24 hours

Half-life Elimination Dose dependent: 5 to 9 hours

Time to Peak Children (1 to 17 years); Adults: 3 to 4 hours

Pregnancy Risk Factor D

Pregnancy Considerations [US Boxed Warning]: Drugs that act on the renin-angiotensin system can cause injury and death to the developing fetus. Discontinue as soon as possible once pregnancy is detected. The use of drugs which act on the renin-angiotensin system are associated with oligohydramnios. Oligohydramnios, due to decreased fetal renal function, may lead to fetal lung hypoplasia and skeletal malformations. Use is also associated with anuria, hypotension, renal failure, skull hypoplasia, and death in the fetus/neonate. The exposed fetus should be monitored for fetal growth, amniotic fluid volume, and organ formation. Infants exposed *in utero* should be monitored for hyperkalemia, hypotension, and oliguria (exchange transfusions or dialysis may be needed). These adverse events are generally associated with maternal use in the second and third trimesters.

Untreated chronic maternal hypertension is also associated with adverse events in the fetus, infant, and mother. The use of angiotensin II receptor blockers is not recommended to treat chronic uncomplicated hypertension in pregnant women and should generally be avoided in women of reproductive potential (ACOG, 2013).

Cangrelor (KAN grel or)

Brand Names: US Kengreal

Pharmacologic Category Antiplatelet Agent; Antiplatelet Agent, Non-thienopyridine

Use Percutaneous coronary intervention (PCI): Adjunct to PCI to reduce the risk of periprocedural myocardial infarction (MI), repeat coronary revascularization, and stent thrombosis in patients who have not been treated with a $P2Y_{12}$ platelet inhibitor and are not being given a glycoprotein IIb/IIIa inhibitor

Local Anesthetic/Vasoconstrictor Precautions No information available to require special precautions

Effects on Dental Treatment No significant effects or complications reported

Effects on Bleeding Cangrelor increases the risk of bleeding. However, it is indicated as an intravenous infusion prior to and during percutaneous coronary intervention and has a short elimination half-life. No antiplatelet effect is observed an hour after discontinuation. There is no information to require any special precautions for dental procedures in patients previously exposed to Cangrelor.

Adverse Reactions

Hematologic & oncologic: Hemorrhage (GUSTO: 16%; TIMI: <1%)

Renal: Renal insufficiency (3%; severe; creatinine clearance <30 mL/minute)

Respiratory: Dyspnea (1%)

<1%, postmarketing, and/or case reports: Hypersensitivity reaction

General Dosage Range IV: *Adults:* Initial: 30 mcg/kg; Maintenance: 4 mcg/kg/minute continued for at least 2 hours or for the duration of the PCI

Mechanism of Action Cangrelor, a nonthienopyridine adenosine triphosphate analogue, is a direct $P2Y_{12}$ platelet receptor inhibitor that blocks adenosine diphosphate (ADP)-induced platelet activation and aggregation. Cangrelor binds selectively and reversibly to the $P2Y_{12}$ receptor, preventing further signaling and platelet activation.

Pharmacodynamics/Kinetics

Onset of Action Platelet inhibition occurs within 2 minutes

Duration of Action Antiplatelet effect is maintained throughout duration of infusion. After discontinuation, platelet function returns to normal within 1 hour

Half-life Elimination ~3 to 6 minutes

Time to Peak Within 2 minutes

Pregnancy Risk Factor C

Pregnancy Considerations Adverse events were observed in some animal reproduction studies.

Capecitabine (ka pe SITE a been)

Related Information

Fluorouracil (Systemic) *on page 737*

Brand Names: US Xeloda

Brand Names: Canada Teva-Capecitabine; Xeloda

Pharmacologic Category Antineoplastic Agent, Antimetabolite; Antineoplastic Agent, Antimetabolite (Pyrimidine Analog)

Use

Breast cancer, metastatic:

Monotherapy: Treatment of metastatic breast cancer resistant to both paclitaxel and an anthracycline-containing regimen or resistant to paclitaxel in patients for whom further anthracycline therapy is not indicated

Combination therapy: Treatment of metastatic breast cancer (in combination with docetaxel) after failure of a prior anthracycline-containing regimen

Colorectal cancer: First-line treatment of metastatic colorectal cancer when treatment with a fluoropyrimidine alone is preferred; adjuvant therapy of Dukes' C colon cancer after complete resection of the primary tumor when fluoropyrimidine therapy alone is preferred

Local Anesthetic/Vasoconstrictor Precautions No information available to require special precautions

Effects on Dental Treatment Key adverse event(s) related to dental treatment: Stomatitis, abnormal taste, and taste disturbance.

Effects on Bleeding Bleeding has been reported in <6% of patients. Thrombocytopenia has been reported in 24% of patients and is severe (grade 4) in 1%. A medical consult is suggested.

Adverse Reactions Frequency listed derived from monotherapy trials. Incidence reported for all indications and usage, unless otherwise noted. Frequency not always defined.

>10%:

Cardiovascular: Edema (≤15%)

Central nervous system: Fatigue (≤42%), paresthesia (stage IV breast cancer: 21%; grades 3/4: 1%), pain (≤12%)

Dermatologic: Palmar-plantar erythrodysesthesia (54% to 60%; grades ≥3: 11% to 17%), dermatitis (27% to 37%, grades ≥3: 1%)

Gastrointestinal: Diarrhea (47% to 57%, grades 3/4: 2% to 13%), nausea (34% to 43%; stage IV breast cancer: 53%), vomiting (metastatic colorectal cancer, stage IV breast cancer: 27% to 37%; Dukes' C colon cancer: 15%), abdominal pain (metastatic colorectal cancer: 35%; stage IV breast cancer: 20%; Dukes' C colon cancer: 14%), decreased appetite (26%), stomatitis (22% to 25%), anorexia (stage IV breast cancer: 23%; Dukes' C colon cancer: 9%), constipation (9% to 15%)

Hematologic & oncologic: Lymphocytopenia (stage IV breast cancer: 94%; stage IV breast cancer, grades 3/4: 15% to 44%), anemia (72% to 80%, grades 3/4: ≤3%), neutropenia (≤26%, grades 3/4: ≤3%), thrombocytopenia (stage IV breast cancer: 24%; all: grades 3/4: 1% to 3%)

Hepatic: Hyperbilirubinemia (Metastatic colorectal cancer: 48%; stage IV breast cancer: 22%; all: grades 3/4: 2% to 23%)

Neuromuscular & skeletal: Weakness (≤42%)

Ophthalmic: Eye irritation (13% to 15%)

Miscellaneous: Fever (7% to 18%)

1% to 10%:

Cardiovascular: Venous thrombosis (8%), chest pain (≤6%), atrial fibrillation (<5%), bradycardia (<5%), collapse (<5%), extrasystoles (<5%), pericardial effusion (<5%), ventricular premature contractions (<5%), angina pectoris, cardiac arrest, cardiac arrhythmia, cardiac failure, cardiomyopathy, ECG changes, ischemic heart disease, myocardial infarction

Central nervous system: Lethargy (10%), peripheral sensory neuropathy (10%), headache (5% to 10%), insomnia (≤8%), dizziness (6% to 8%), ataxia (<5%), depression (≤5%), mood changes (5%), abnormal gait (<5%), brain disease (<5%), dysarthria (<5%), dysphasia (<5%), equilibrium disturbance (<5%), irritability (<5%), myasthenia (<5%), sedation (<5%), vertigo (<5%)

Dermatologic: Nail disease (≤7%), skin discoloration (7%), skin rash (7%), alopecia (6%), erythema (6%), dermal ulcer (<5%), pruritus (<5%)

Endocrine & metabolic: Dehydration (7%), hot flash (<5%), hypokalemia (<5%), hypomagnesemia (<5%), increased thirst (<5%), weight gain (<5%), decreased serum calcium (Dukes' C colon cancer: grades 3/4: 2%), increased serum calcium (Dukes' C colon cancer: grades 3/4: 1%)

Gastrointestinal: Gastrointestinal motility disorder (10%), GI inflammation (upper: 8%), oral discomfort (grades 3/4: 10%), dyspepsia (6% to 8%), upper abdominal pain (7%), intestinal obstruction (≤6%), dysgeusia (6%), gastrointestinal hemorrhage (6%), abdominal distention (<5%), dysphagia (<5%), rectal pain (<5%), toxic dilation of intestine (<5%), increased serum alanine aminotransferase (Dukes' C colon cancer: grades 3/4: 2%), sore throat (2%), necrotizing enterocolitis

Hematologic & oncologic: Hemorrhage (<5%), lymphedema (<5%), granulocytopenia (Dukes' C colon cancer: grades 3/4: 3%), immune thrombocytopenia (1%)

Hepatic: Abnormal hepatic function tests (<5%)

Hypersensitivity: Drug-induced hypersensitivity (<5%)

Infection: Viral infection (metastatic colorectal cancer: 5%)

Neuromuscular & skeletal: Back pain (10%), myalgia (≤9%), arthralgia (8%), limb pain (stage IV breast cancer: 6%), tremor (<5%)

Ophthalmic: Visual disturbance (metastatic colorectal cancer: 5%), conjunctivitis (≤5%), keratoconjunctivitis (<5%)

Respiratory: Cough (≤7%), chest mass (<5%), dyspnea (<5%), flu-like symptoms (<5%), hemoptysis (<5%), hoarseness (<5%), pharyngeal disease (metastatic colorectal cancer: 5%), epistaxis (≤3%), laryngitis (1%)

<1%, postmarketing, and/or case reports (limited to important or life-threatening): Acute renal failure, arthritis, ascites, asthma, blood coagulation disorder, bone marrow depression, bronchitis, bronchopneumonia, bronchospasm, cachexia, cerebrovascular accident, cholestatic hepatitis, confusion, cutaneous lupus erythematosus, diaphoresis, ecchymoses, esophagitis, fibrosis, flu-like symptoms, fungal infection, gastric ulcer, gastroenteritis, gastrointestinal perforation, hepatic failure, hepatic fibrosis, hepatitis, hypersensitivity, hypertension, hypertriglyceridemia, hypotension, jaundice, keratitis, lacrimal stenosis, leukoencephalopathy, leukopenia, loss of consciousness, myocarditis, nocturia, ostealgia, pancytopenia, phlebitis (venous), photophobia, pneumonia, pulmonary embolism, radiation recall phenomenon, renal insufficiency, respiratory distress, sepsis, Stevens-Johnson syndrome, syncope, tachycardia, toxic epidermal necrolysis

General Dosage Range Dosage adjustment recommended in patients with renal impairment or who develop toxicities

Oral: *Adults:* 1,250 mg/m^2 twice daily for 2 weeks, every 21 days

Mechanism of Action Capecitabine is a prodrug of fluorouracil. It undergoes hydrolysis in the liver and tissues to form fluorouracil which is the active moiety. Fluorouracil is a fluorinated pyrimidine antimetabolite that inhibits thymidylate synthetase, blocking the methylation of deoxyuridylic acid to thymidylic acid, interfering with DNA, and to a lesser degree, RNA synthesis. Fluorouracil appears to be phase specific for the G_1 and S phases of the cell cycle.

Pharmacodynamics/Kinetics

Half-life Elimination ~0.75 hour

Time to Peak 1.5 hours; Fluorouracil: 2 hours

Pregnancy Considerations Based on animal reproduction studies and its mechanism of action, fetal harm may occur if capecitabine is administered during pregnancy. Pregnancy testing is recommended prior to therapy initiation. Women of reproductive potential should use effective contraception during treatment and for 6 months after the last dose. Males with female partners of reproductive potential should use effective contraception during treatment and for 3 months after the last dose.

Capreomycin (kap ree oh MYE sin)

Brand Names: US Capastat Sulfate

Pharmacologic Category Antibiotic, Miscellaneous; Antitubercular Agent

Use Tuberculosis, pulmonary: Treatment of pulmonary infections caused by capreomycin-susceptible strains of *Mycobacterium tuberculosis*, in combination with other appropriate antituberculosis agents, when the primary agents (eg, isoniazid, rifampin, ethambutol, pyrazinamide) have been ineffective or cannot be used because of toxicity or the presence of resistant tubercle bacilli.

Local Anesthetic/Vasoconstrictor Precautions No information available to require special precautions

Effects on Dental Treatment No significant effects or complications reported

Effects on Bleeding No information available to require special precautions

Adverse Reactions

Frequency not always defined.

>10%:

Otic: Ototoxicity (subclinical hearing loss: 11%; clinical loss: 3%)

Genitourinary: Nephrotoxicity (36%, increased blood urea nitrogen)

1% to 10%: Hematologic: Eosinophilia (dose-related, mild)

<1%, postmarketing, and/or case reports: Bartter's syndrome, hepatic insufficiency (decreased sulfobromophthalein excretion), hypersensitivity (includes fever, maculopapular rash, urticaria), hypocalcemia, hypokalemia, hypomagnesemia, increased serum creatinine, injection site reaction (includes abscess at injection site, bleeding at injection site, induration at injection site, and pain at injection site), kidney damage, leukocytosis, leukopenia, nephritis (toxic), renal tubular necrosis, thrombocytopenia (rare), tinnitus, urine sedimentation abnormality, vertigo

General Dosage Range Dosage adjustment recommended in patients with renal impairment.

IM, IV: *Adults:* 1 g once daily (maximum: 20 mg/kg/dose) for 60 to 120 days, followed by 1 g 2 to 3 times weekly

Mechanism of Action Capreomycin is a cyclic polypeptide antimicrobial. It is administered as a mixture of capreomycin IA and capreomycin IB. The mechanism of action of capreomycin is not well understood. Mycobacterial species that have become resistant to other agents are usually still sensitive to the action of capreomycin. However, significant cross-resistance with viomycin, kanamycin, and neomycin occurs.

Pharmacodynamics/Kinetics

Half-life Elimination CrCl 100 to 110 mL/minute: 5 to 6 hours; CrCl 50 to 80 mL/minute: 7 to 10 hours; CrCl 20 to 40 mL/minute: 12 to 20 hours; CrCl 10 mL/minute: 29 hours; CrCl 0 mL/minute: 55 hours

Time to Peak Serum: IM: 1 to 2 hours

Pregnancy Risk Factor C

Pregnancy Considerations Adverse events have been reported in animal reproduction studies. **[US**

Boxed Warning]: Safety has not been established in pregnant women; avoid use during pregnancy because of the risk of fetal nephrotoxicity and congenital hearing loss (MMWR 2003).

Capsaicin (kap SAY sin)

Related Information

Capsicum Peppers *on page 1702*

Brand Names: US Aflexeryl-MC [OTC] [DSC]; Aleveer [OTC] [DSC]; Allevess [OTC]; Captracin [DSC]; Capzasin-HP [OTC]; Capzasin-P [OTC]; DiabetAid Pain and Tingling Relief [OTC]; Flexin; Levatio; MaC Patch [DSC]; MenCaps [OTC]; Neuvaxin [DSC]; Qroxin [DSC]; Qutenza; Releevia; Releevia MC; RelyyT [DSC]; Renovo; Salonpas Gel-Patch Hot [OTC]; Salonpas Hot [OTC] [DSC]; Sinelee [DSC]; Solaice [DSC]; Trixaicin HP [OTC]; Trixaicin [OTC] [DSC]; Zostrix Arthritis Pain Relief [OTC]; Zostrix Diabetic Foot Pain [OTC] [DSC]; Zostrix Diabetic Pain Relief [OTC] [DSC]; Zostrix Foot Pain Relief [OTC] [DSC]; Zostrix [OTC] [DSC]; Zostrix-HP [OTC]

Brand Names: Canada Zostrix; Zostrix H.P.

Generic Availability (US) Yes: Cream

Pharmacologic Category Analgesic, Topical; Topical Skin Product; Transient Receptor Potential Vanilloid 1 (TRPV1) Agonist

Dental Use Potential use as topical agent in burning mouth syndrome and oral mucositis

Use

Muscle/Joint pain: Temporary relief of minor aches and pain of muscles and joints associated with backache, strains, sprains, arthritis, bruises, cramps, or muscle stiffness or soreness.

Neuropathic pain: Management of neuropathic pain associated with diabetic neuropathy or postherpetic neuralgia.

Local Anesthetic/Vasoconstrictor Precautions No information available to require special precautions

Effects on Dental Treatment No significant effects or complications reported

Effects on Bleeding No information available to require special precautions

Adverse Reactions The following adverse events occurred with topical patch administration.

>10%: Local: Localized erythema (63%), local pain (42%)

1% to 10%:

Cardiovascular: Hypertension (2%; transient)

Dermatologic: Papule (6%), local dryness (2%), pruritus (2%)

Gastrointestinal: Nausea (5%), vomiting (3%)

Local: Local pruritus (6%), localized edema (4%), local swelling (2%)

Respiratory: Nasopharyngitis (4%), sinusitis (3%), bronchitis (2%)

<1%, postmarketing, and/or case reports: Abnormal skin odor, application site reactions (includes bruise, dermatitis, desquamation, excoriation, hyperesthesia, inflammation, paresthesia, urticaria), burning sensation of skin, cough, dizziness, dysgeusia, headache, hypoesthesia, peripheral edema, peripheral sensory neuropathy, throat irritation

Dental Usual Dosage Topical: Apply cream or gel to affected area 3-4 times/day

Dosing

Adult & Geriatric

Muscle/joint pain: Topical:

Cream, gel, liquid, lotion: Apply thin film to affected areas 3 to 4 times daily.

Patch:

0.025%, 0.03%, 0.0375%, 0.05% (Sinelee only): Apply 1 patch to affected area for up to 8 hours (maximum: 4 patches/day); do not use for >5 consecutive days (product specific)

0.05% (Solaice only): Apply 1 patch to affected area for up to 8 hours (maximum: 4 patches/day)

Neuropathic pain: Topical: Patch (Qutenza): Apply patch to most painful area for 60 minutes. Up to 4 patches may be applied in a single application. Treatment may be repeated ≥3 months as needed for return of pain (do not apply more frequently than every 3 months). Area should be pretreated with a topical anesthetic prior to patch application.

Diabetic neuropathy (off-label use): Topical: Cream (0.075%): Apply 4 times/day (Bril 2011)

Pediatric

Muscle/joint pain: Topical: Patch:

0.025%, 0.03%, 0.0375%, 0.05% (Sinelee only): Children ≥12 years and Adolescents: Refer to adult dosing.

0.05% (Solaice only): Adolescents ≥16 years: Refer to adult dosing.

Renal Impairment There are no dosage adjustments provided in the manufacturer's labeling.

Hepatic Impairment There are no dosage adjustments provided in the manufacturer's labeling.

Mechanism of Action Capsaicin, a transient receptor potential vanilloid 1 receptor (TRPV1) agonist, activates TRPV1 ligand-gated cation channels on nociceptive nerve fibers, resulting in depolarization, initiation of action potential, and pain signal transmission to the spinal cord; capsaicin exposure results in subsequent desensitization of the sensory axons and inhibition of pain transmission initiation. In arthritis, capsaicin induces release of substance P, the principal chemomediator of pain impulses from the periphery to the CNS, from peripheral sensory neurons; after repeated application, capsaicin depletes the neuron of substance P and prevents reaccumulation. The functional link between substance P and the capsaicin receptor, TRPV1, is not well understood.

Contraindications

Hypersensitivity to capsaicin, menthol, or any component of the formulation.

OTC labeling: When used for self-medication, do not use on wounds, damaged, broken, or irritated skin; do not cover with bandage; do not use in combination with external heat source (eg, heating pad).

Warnings/Precautions May cause serious burns (eg, first- to third-degree chemical burns) at the application site. In some cases, hospitalization has been required. Discontinue use and seek medical attention if signs of skin injury (eg, pain, swelling, or blistering) occur following application (FDA Drug Safety Communication, 2012). May cause CNS depression, which may impair physical or mental abilities; patients must be cautioned about performing tasks that require mental alertness (eg, operating machinery or driving). Use with caution in patients with uncontrolled hypertension, or a history of cardiovascular or cerebrovascular events; transient increases in blood pressure due to treatment-related pain have occurred during and after application of RX patch.

For external use only; avoid contact with eyes, mouth, genitals, or any or other mucous membranes. Do not use immediately before or after activities such as bathing, swimming, showering, sun bathing, strenuous exercise, steam bath, sauna, or other heat or sunlight exposure to the treated area. Stop use and consult a healthcare provider if excessive redness, blistering burning or irritation develops, symptoms get worse, symptoms persist for >7 days, symptoms resolve and then recur, or if difficulty breathing or swallowing occurs. Do not handle contact lenses for 1 hour after handling, applying, or removing capsaicin (product specific).

RX labeling: Do not cover with bandage or compression. Use only on intact skin; do not use on wounds, damaged, broken, infected, sensitive or inflamed skin. Do not apply to face or scalp. Do not use concurrently with other external pain-relieving products.

OTC labeling: Transient burning may occur and generally disappears after several days.

Patch: Avoid inhaling airborne material from dried residue. Remove patches gently and slowly to decrease risk of aerosolization; inhalation of airborne capsaicin may result in coughing or sneezing.

Qutenza: If skin not intended to be treated comes in contact with capsaicin, apply provided cleansing gel for one minute and wipe off with dry gauze; then wash the area with soap and water. Post-application pain should be treated with local cooling methods (ice pack) and/or analgesics.

Benzyl alcohol and derivatives: Some dosage forms may contain benzyl alcohol; large amounts of benzyl alcohol (≥99 mg/kg/day) have been associated with a potentially fatal toxicity ("gasping syndrome") in neonates; the "gasping syndrome" consists of metabolic acidosis, respiratory distress, gasping respirations, CNS dysfunction (including convulsions, intracranial hemorrhage), hypotension and cardiovascular collapse (AAP ["Inactive" 1997]; CDC, 1982); some data suggests that benzoate displaces bilirubin from protein binding sites (Ahlfors, 2001); avoid or use dosage forms containing benzyl alcohol with caution in neonates. See manufacturer's labeling.

Drug Interactions

Metabolism/Transport Effects Substrate of CYP2E1 (minor); **Note:** Assignment of Major/Minor substrate status based on clinically relevant drug interaction potential

Avoid Concomitant Use There are no known interactions where it is recommended to avoid concomitant use.

Increased Effect/Toxicity There are no known significant interactions involving an increase in effect.

Decreased Effect There are no known significant interactions involving a decrease in effect.

Pharmacodynamics/Kinetics

Onset of Action

OTC products (capsaicin 0.025% to 0.1%): 2 to 4 weeks of continuous therapy; Qutenza patch: 1 week after application

Half-life Elimination Topical patch (capsaicin 8%): 1.64 hours (Babbar 2009)

Pregnancy Risk Factor B

Pregnancy Considerations Adverse events have not been observed in animal reproduction studies with capsaicin patch or liquid. Systemic absorption is limited following topical administration of the patch; plasma concentrations are below the limit of detection 3 to 6 hours after the patch is removed.

Breastfeeding Considerations It is not known if capsaicin is excreted in breast milk following topical administration. Some manufacturers recommend not breastfeeding on the day of treatment after the patch has been applied to reduce any potential infant exposure.

Dosage Forms

Cream, topical: 0.025% (60 g)
Capzasin-HP [OTC]: 0.1% (42.5 g)
Capzasin-P [OTC]: 0.035% (42.5 g)
Trixaicin HP [OTC]: 0.075% (60 g)
Zostrix Arthritis Pain Relief [OTC]: 0.025% (56.6 g)
Zostrix-HP [OTC]: 0.1% (60 g)

Gel, topical:
Capzasin-P [OTC]: 0.025% (42.5 g) [contains menthol]

Liquid, topical:
Capzasin-P [OTC]: 0.15% (29.5 mL)

Lotion, topical:
DiabetAid Pain and Tingling Relief [OTC]: 0.025% (120 mL)

Patch, topical:
Allevess [OTC]: 0.05% (15s) [contains menthol 5%]
Flexin: 0.0375% (15s) [contains menthol 5%]
Levatio: 0.03% (15s) [contains menthol 5%]
MenCaps [OTC]: 0.0225% (15s) [contains menthol 4.5%]
Qutenza: 8% (1s, 2s)
Releevia: 0.0375% (15s) [contains menthol 5%]
Releevia MC: 0.0375% (15s) [contains menthol 5%]
RelyyT: 0.025% (15s) [contains menthol 5%]
Renovo: 0.0375% (15s) [contains menthol 5%]
Salonpas Gel-Patch Hot [OTC]: 0.025% (3s, 6s)

Captopril (KAP toe pril)

Related Information

Cardiovascular Diseases *on page 1752*

Brand Names: Canada Apo-Capto; Dom-Captopril; Mylan-Captopril; PMS-Captopril; Teva-Captopril

Pharmacologic Category Angiotensin-Converting Enzyme (ACE) Inhibitor; Antihypertensive

Use

Diabetic nephropathy: Treatment of diabetic nephropathy (proteinuria more than 500 mg daily) in patients with type 1 insulin-dependent diabetes mellitus and retinopathy

Heart failure: Treatment of congestive heart failure

Hypertension: Management of hypertension

Left ventricular dysfunction after myocardial infarction: To improve survival following myocardial infarction in clinically stable patients with left ventricular dysfunction manifested as an ejection fraction of 40% or less, and to reduce the incidence of overt heart failure and subsequent hospitalizations for congestive heart failure in these patients.

Guideline recommendations:

Heart failure: The American College of Cardiology Foundation/American Heart Association (ACCF/AHA) 2013 heart failure guidelines recommend the use of angiotensin-converting enzyme (ACE) inhibitors, along with other guideline directed medical therapies, to prevent heart failure in patients with a reduced ejection fraction who have a history of myocardial infarction (stage B heart failure), to prevent heart failure in any patient with a reduced ejection fraction (stage B heart failure), or to treat those with heart failure and reduced ejection fraction (stage C heart failure) (Yancy, 2013).

Hypertension: The 2014 guideline for the management of high blood pressure in adults (Eighth Joint National Committee [JNC 8]) recommends initiation of pharmacologic treatment to lower blood pressure for the following patients:

- Patients ≥60 years of age with systolic blood pressure (SBP) ≥150 mm Hg or diastolic blood pressure (DBP) ≥90 mm Hg. Goal of therapy is SBP <150 mm Hg and DBP <90 mm Hg.
- Patients <60 years of age with SBP ≥140 mm Hg or DBP is ≥90 mm Hg. Goal of therapy is SBP <140 mm Hg and DBP <90 mm Hg.
- Patients ≥18 years of age with diabetes and SBP ≥140 mm Hg or DBP ≥90 mm Hg. Goal of therapy is SBP <140 mm Hg and DBP <90 mm Hg.
- Patients ≥18 years of age with chronic kidney disease (CKD) and SBP ≥140 mm Hg or DBP ≥90 mm Hg. Goal of therapy is SBP <140 mm Hg and DBP <90 mm Hg.

Chronic kidney disease (CKD) and hypertension: Regardless of race or diabetes status, the use of an ACE inhibitor (ACEI) or angiotensin receptor blocker (ARB) as initial therapy is recommended to improve kidney outcomes. In the general nonblack population (without CKD) including those with diabetes, initial antihypertensive treatment should consist of a thiazide-type diuretic, calcium channel blocker, ACEI, or ARB. In the general black population (without CKD) including those with diabetes, initial antihypertensive treatment should consist of a thiazide-type diuretic or a calcium channel blocker **instead of** an ACEI or ARB.

Coronary artery disease (CAD) and hypertension: The American Heart Association, American College of Cardiology and American Society of Hypertension (AHA/ACC/ASH) 2015 scientific statement for the treatment of hypertension in patients with CAD recommends the use of an ACE inhibitor (or an ARB) as part of a regimen in patients with hypertension and chronic stable angina if there is prior MI, LV systolic dysfunction, diabetes mellitus, or CKD. A BP target of <140/90 mm Hg is reasonable for the secondary prevention of cardiovascular events. A lower target BP (<130/80 mm Hg) may be appropriate in some individuals with CAD, previous MI, stroke or transient ischemic attack, or CAD risk equivalents (AHA/ACC/ASH [Rosendorff 2015]).

STEMI: The 2013 American College of Cardiology Foundation/American Heart Association guidelines for the management of patients with ST-elevation myocardial infarction (STEMI) states that an ACE inhibitor (eg, captopril) should be initiated within the first 24 hours after STEMI in patients with anterior MI, heart failure, or left ventricular ejection fraction ≤40%. It is also reasonable to initiate an ACE inhibitor in all patients with STEMI (ACCF/AHA [O'Gara, 2013]).

Local Anesthetic/Vasoconstrictor Precautions
No information available to require special precautions

Effects on Dental Treatment Key adverse event(s) related to dental treatment: Loss or diminished perception of taste; Patients may experience orthostatic hypotension as they stand up after treatment; especially if lying in dental chair for extended periods of time. Use caution with sudden changes in position during and after dental treatment.

An angiotensin-converting enzyme (ACE) Inhibitor cough is a dry, hacking, nonproductive cough that can potentially interfere with longer dental procedures if patient has this side effect.

Effects on Bleeding No information available to require special precautions

Adverse Reactions

Frequency not defined:

Cardiovascular: Angina pectoris, cardiac arrest, cardiac arrhythmia, cardiac failure, flushing, myocardial infarction, orthostatic hypotension, Raynaud's phenomenon, syncope

Central nervous system: Ataxia, cerebrovascular insufficiency, confusion, depression, drowsiness, myasthenia, nervousness

Dermatologic: Bullous pemphigoid, erythema multiforme, exfoliative dermatitis, pallor, Stevens-Johnson syndrome

Endocrine & metabolic: Gynecomastia, hyponatremia (symptomatic)

Gastrointestinal: Cholestasis, dyspepsia, glossitis, pancreatitis

Genitourinary: Impotence, nephrotic syndrome, oliguria, urinary frequency

Hematologic & oncologic: Agranulocytosis, anemia, pancytopenia, thrombocytopenia

Hepatic: Hepatic necrosis (rare), hepatitis, increased serum alkaline phosphatase, increased serum bilirubin, increased serum transaminases, jaundice

Hypersensitivity: Anaphylactoid reaction, angioedema

Neuromuscular & skeletal: Myalgia, weakness

Ophthalmic: Blurred vision

Renal: Polyuria, renal failure, renal insufficiency

Respiratory: Bronchospasm, eosinophilic pneumonitis, rhinitis

1% to 10%:

Cardiovascular: Hypotension (1% to 3%), chest pain (1%), palpitations (1%), tachycardia (1%)

Dermatologic: Skin rash (maculopapular or urticarial [4% to 7%]; in patients with rash, a positive ANA and/or eosinophilia has been noted in 7% to 10%), pruritus (2%)

Endocrine & metabolic: Hyperkalemia (1% to 11%)

Gastrointestinal: Dysgeusia (2% to 4%; loss of taste or diminished perception)

Genitourinary: Proteinuria (1%)

Hematologic & oncologic: Neutropenia (≤4%; in patients with renal insufficiency or collagen-vascular disease)

Hypersensitivity: Hypersensitivity reaction (rash, pruritus, fever, arthralgia, and eosinophilia: 4% to 7%; depending on dose and renal function)

Renal: Increased serum creatinine, renal insufficiency (worsening; may occur in patients with bilateral renal artery stenosis or hypovolemia)

Respiratory: Cough (<1% to 2%)

Miscellaneous: Hypersensitivity reactions (rash, pruritus, fever, arthralgia, and eosinophilia) have occurred in 4% to 7% of patients (depending on dose and renal function); dysgeusia - loss of taste or diminished perception (2% to 4%)

<1%, postmarketing, and/or case reports: Abdominal pain, alopecia, angina pectoris, anorexia, aphthous stomatitis, aplastic anemia, arthralgia, cholestatic jaundice, constipation, diarrhea, dizziness, dyspnea, eosinophilia, fatigue, fever, gastric irritation, glomerulonephritis, Guillain-Barre syndrome, headache, hemolytic anemia, Huntington's chorea (exacerbation), hyperthermia, increased erythrocyte sedimentation rate, insomnia, interstitial nephritis, Kaposi's

sarcoma, malaise, myalgia, nausea, paresthesia, peptic ulcer, pericarditis, psoriasis, seizure (in premature infants), systemic lupus erythematosus, vasculitis, visual hallucination (Doane, 2013), vomiting, xerostomia

General Dosage Range Dosage adjustment recommended in patients with renal impairment

Oral:

Infants: Initial: 0.15 to 0.3 mg/kg/dose; Maximum: 6 mg/kg/day in 1 to 4 divided doses

Children: Initial: 0.3 to 0.5 mg/kg/dose; Maximum: 6 mg/kg/day in 2 to 4 divided doses

Older Children: Initial: 6.25 to 12.5 mg every 12 to 24 hours; Maximum: 6 mg/kg/day

Adolescents: Initial: 12.5 to 25 mg; Maximum: 450 mg daily

Adults: Initial: 6.25 to 25 mg 2 to 3 times daily; Maintenance: 25 to 450 mg daily in 2 to 3 divided doses; maximum: 450 mg daily

Mechanism of Action Competitive inhibitor of angiotensin-converting enzyme (ACE); prevents conversion of angiotensin I to angiotensin II, a potent vasoconstrictor; results in lower levels of angiotensin II which causes an increase in plasma renin activity and a reduction in aldosterone secretion

Pharmacodynamics/Kinetics

Onset of Action Within 15 minutes; Peak effect: Blood pressure reduction: 1 to 1.5 hours after dose; Maximum effect: Antihypertensive: 60-90 minutes; may require several weeks of therapy before full hypotensive effect is seen

Duration of Action Dose related, may require several weeks of therapy before full hypotensive effect

Half-life Elimination

Infants with CHF: 3.3 hours; range: 1.2-12.4 hours (Pereira 1991)

Children: 1.5 hours; range: 0.98-2.3 hours (Levy 1991)

Adults: Healthy volunteers: ~1.7 hours (Duchin 1982). In two studies, patients with chronic renal failure demonstrated approximately 2-fold longer half-lives as compared to normal subjects (Giudicelli 1984; Onoyama 1981). Half-life was up to 21 hours in patients with severe renal impairment and up to 32 hours in patients on chronic hemodialysis in another study (Duchin 1984)

Time to Peak Within 1-2 hours

Pregnancy Risk Factor D

Pregnancy Considerations [U.S. Boxed Warning]: Drugs that act on the renin-angiotensin system can cause injury and death to the developing fetus. Discontinue as soon as possible once pregnancy is detected. Captopril crosses the placenta (Hurault de Lingy 1987). Drugs that act on the renin-angiotensin system are associated with oligohydramnios. Oligohydramnios, due to decreased fetal renal function, may lead to fetal lung hypoplasia and skeletal malformations. Their use in pregnancy is also associated with anuria, hypotension, renal failure, skull hypoplasia, and death in the fetus/neonate. Teratogenic effects may occur following maternal use of an ACE inhibitor during the first trimester, although this finding may be confounded by maternal disease. Because adverse fetal events are well documented with exposure later in pregnancy, ACE inhibitor use in pregnant women is not recommended (Seely 2014; Weber 2014). Infants exposed to an ACE inhibitor in utero should be monitored for hyperkalemia, hypotension, and oliguria. Oligohydramnios may not appear until after irreversible fetal injury has occurred. Exchange transfusions or dialysis may be required to reverse hypotension or improve renal function, although data related to the effectiveness in neonates is limited.

Chronic maternal hypertension itself is also associated with adverse events in the fetus/infant and mother. ACE inhibitors are not recommended for the treatment of uncomplicated hypertension in pregnancy (ACOG 2013) and they are specifically contraindicated for the treatment of hypertension and chronic heart failure during pregnancy by some guidelines (Regitz-Zagrosek 2011). In addition, ACE inhibitors should generally be avoided in women of reproductive age (ACOG 2013). If treatment for hypertension or chronic heart failure in pregnancy is needed, other agents should be used (ACOG 2013; Regitz-Zagrosek 2011).

CarBAMazepine (kar ba MAZ e peen)

Related Information

Temporomandibular Dysfunction (TMD), Chronic Pain, and Fibromyalgia *on page 1868*

Brand Names: US Carbatrol; Epitol; Equetro; TEGretol; TEGretol-XR

Brand Names: Canada Apo-Carbamazepine; Dom-Carbamazepine; Mazepine; Mylan-Carbamazepine CR; PMS-Carbamazepine; Sandoz-Carbamazepine; Taro-Carbamazepine Chewable; Tegretol; Teva-Carbamazepine

Generic Availability (US) Yes

Pharmacologic Category Anticonvulsant, Miscellaneous

Dental Use Pain relief of trigeminal or glossopharyngeal neuralgia

Use

Bipolar 1 disorder (Equetro only): Treatment of acute manic or mixed episodes associated with bipolar 1 disorder

Epilepsy: Treatment of partial seizures with complex symptomatology (psychomotor, temporal lobe), generalized tonic-clonic seizures (grand mal), or mixed seizure patterns

Limitations of use: Carbamazepine is not indicated for the treatment of absence seizures (petit mal); it has been associated with increased frequency of generalized convulsions in these patients.

Trigeminal or glossopharyngeal neuralgia (oral only): Treatment of pain associated with trigeminal or glossopharyngeal neuralgia

Local Anesthetic/Vasoconstrictor Precautions No information available to require special precautions

Effects on Dental Treatment Key adverse event(s) related to dental treatment: Xerostomia (normal salivary flow resumes upon discontinuation).

Effects on Bleeding No information available to require special precautions

Adverse Reactions

>10%:

Central nervous system: Dizziness (oral: 44%; intravenous: 9%), drowsiness (oral: 32%; intravenous: 5%), ataxia (15%)

Gastrointestinal: Nausea (oral: 29%), vomiting (oral: 18%)

1% to 10%:

Cardiovascular: Hypertension (oral: 3%), atrial tachycardia (intravenous: <2%), inversion T wave on ECG (intravenous: <2%)

Central nervous system: Speech disturbance (oral: 6%), abnormality in thinking (oral: 2%), paresthesia (oral: 2%), twitching (oral: 2%), vertigo (oral: 2%)

Dermatologic: Pruritus (oral: 8%), skin rash (oral: 7%)

Endocrine & metabolic: Hyponatremia (intravenous: <2%)
Gastrointestinal: Constipation (oral: 10%), xerostomia (oral: 8%)
Hematologic & oncologic: Anemia (intravenous: 7%)
Neuromuscular & skeletal: Weakness (oral: 8%), tremor (oral: 3%)
Ophthalmic: Blurred vision (5% to 6%), diplopia (intravenous: 5%; oral: <1%)

Frequency not defined:
Cardiovascular: Atrioventricular block, cardiac arrhythmia, cardiac failure, coronary artery disease (aggravation), edema, hypotension, syncope, thromboembolism, thrombophlebitis
Central nervous system: Agitation, amnesia, chills, depression, fatigue, hallucination, headache, hyperacusis, neuroleptic malignant syndrome (NMS), peripheral neuritis, talkativeness
Dermatologic: Acute generalized exanthematous pustulosis, alopecia, diaphoresis, dyschromia, erythema multiforme, erythema nodosum, exfoliative dermatitis, maculopapular rash, onychomadesis, skin photosensitivity, Stevens-Johnson syndrome, toxic epidermal necrolysis, urticaria
Endocrine & metabolic: Albuminuria, glycosuria, porphyria, SIADH
Gastrointestinal: Glossitis, pancreatitis, stomatitis
Genitourinary: Azotemia, impotence, microscopic urine deposits, oliguria, urinary frequency, urinary retention
Hematologic & oncologic: Agranulocytosis, aplastic anemia, bone marrow depression, eosinophilia, leukocytosis, leukopenia, lymphadenopathy, pancytopenia, purpura, thrombocytopenia
Hepatic: Abnormal hepatic function tests, hepatitis, jaundice
Hypersensitivity: Hypersensitivity reaction, multi-organ hypersensitivity
Neuromuscular & skeletal: Arthralgia, exacerbation of systemic lupus erythematosus, leg cramps, myalgia, osteoporosis
Ophthalmic: Cataract, conjunctivitis, increased intraocular pressure
Renal: Increased blood urea nitrogen, renal failure
Respiratory: Dry throat, pneumonia, pulmonary hypersensitivity
Miscellaneous: Fever

<1%, postmarketing, and/or case reports: Abdominal pain, abnormal thyroid function test, aseptic meningitis, anorexia, confusion, decreased serum calcium, defective spermatogenesis, diarrhea, diplopia, dysgeusia (Syed 2016), gastric distress, hepatic failure, hepatotoxicity (idiosyncratic) (Chalasani 2014), hirsutism, increased liver enzymes, intrahepatic cholestasis, involuntary body movements, lupus-like syndrome, nystagmus, oculomotor disturbances, paralysis, reduced fertility (male), suicidal ideation, tinnitus

Dental Usual Dosage Trigeminal or glossopharyngeal neuralgia: Oral:
Adults: Initial: 200 mg/day in 2 divided doses (tablets, extended release tablets, or extended release capsules) or 4 divided doses (oral suspension) with food, gradually increasing in increments of 200 mg/day as needed
Maintenance: Usual: 400-800 mg daily in 2 divided doses (tablets, extended release tablets, or extended release capsules) or 4 divided doses (oral suspension); maximum dose: 1200 mg/day

Dosing

Adult & Geriatric Dosage must be adjusted according to patient's response and serum concentrations. When converting from an immediate-release formulation to an extended-release formulation, the same total daily mg dose of carbamazepine should be administered, divided into twice daily dosing. Avoid abrupt withdrawal.

Epilepsy:
IV:
Note: IV carbamazepine is a replacement therapy for oral carbamazepine; therapy should generally be initiated with oral formulation. Convert back to oral therapy at previous total daily oral dose as soon as clinically appropriate. Use longer than 7 days is not recommended.
Total daily IV dose should be equivalent to 70% of previous total daily oral dose; divide total daily IV dose into 4 infusions (every 6 hours) over 30 minutes.
Oral:
Initial: 400 mg/day in 2 divided doses or 4 divided doses (oral suspension only); increase by up to 200 mg/day at weekly intervals using a twice daily regimen of extended-release capsule or tablet, or a 3 to 4 times/day regimen of other formulations until optimal response and therapeutic levels are achieved; usual dose: 800 to 1,200 mg/day.
Maximum recommended dose: 1,600 mg/day.

Trigeminal or glossopharyngeal neuralgia: Oral:
Initial: 200 mg/day in a single dose (extended-release capsule), 2 divided doses (tablet forms) or 4 divided doses (oral suspension), gradually increasing in increments of 200 mg/day as needed. Administer extended-release capsule in 2 divided doses if total daily dose exceeds 200 mg.
Maintenance: Usual: 400 to 800 mg daily in 2 divided doses or 4 divided doses (oral suspension only); maximum dose: 1,200 mg/day.

Bipolar disorder: Equetro: Oral: Initial: 400 mg/day in 2 divided doses; may adjust by 200 mg/day increments; maximum dose: 1,600 mg/day.

Neuropathic pain, critically ill patients (off-label use): Oral: Initial: 50 to 100 mg twice daily in combination with IV opioids; Maintenance: 100 to 200 mg every 4 to 6 hours; maximum dose: 1,200 mg daily (Barr 2013).

Restless legs syndrome (off-label use): Oral: 100 to 600 mg daily for up to 5 weeks have been studied (Lundvall 1983; Telstad 1984). Doses of 100 to 300 mg at bedtime have been shown to reduce RLS attacks (Telstad 1984). Additional data is necessary to further define the role of carbamazepine in the treatment of this condition.

Pediatric Dosage must be adjusted according to patient's response and serum concentrations. Children <12 years who receive ≥400 mg/day of carbamazepine may be converted to extended-release capsules (Carbatrol) using the same total daily dosage divided twice daily. Avoid abrupt withdrawal.

Epilepsy: Oral:
Children <6 years: Initial: 10 to 20 mg/kg/day in 2 or 3 divided doses (tablet forms) or 4 divided doses (oral suspension only); increase dose every week until optimal response and therapeutic levels are achieved; maximum recommended dose: 35 mg/kg/day.
Children 6 to 12 years: Initial: 200 mg/day in 2 divided doses (tablet forms) or 4 divided doses (oral

suspension only); increase by up to 100 mg/day at weekly intervals using a twice daily regimen of extended-release tablets or 3 to 4 times daily regimen of other formulations until optimal response and therapeutic levels are achieved.

Maintenance: Usual: 400 to 800 mg/day; maximum recommended dose: 1,000 mg/day (all tablet forms and oral suspension) or 35 mg/kg/day (capsule forms).

Children >12 years: Refer to adult dosing.

Maximum recommended doses:

Children 12 to 15 years: 1,000 mg/day.

Children >15 years: 1,200 mg/day.

Renal Impairment

IV: Adults:

CrCl ≥60 mL/minute: No dosage adjustment necessary; monitor closely.

CrCl 15 to 59 mL/minute: Avoid use.

CrCl <15 mL/minute: No dosage adjustment provided in manufacturer's labeling (has not been studied).

Oral: There are no dosage adjustments provided in the manufacturer's labeling; however, the following recommendations have been used by some clinicians:

Children and Adults:

GFR <10 mL/minute: Administer 75% of dose (Aronoff 2007)

Hemodialysis, peritoneal dialysis: Administer 75% of dose (postdialysis) (Aronoff 2007)

Continuous renal replacement therapy (CRRT):

Adults: No dosage adjustment recommended (Aronoff 2007)

Children: Administer 75% of dose (Aronoff 2007)

Hepatic Impairment There are no dosage adjustments provided in the manufacturer's labeling. Use with caution and consider dose reduction; carbamazepine is metabolized primarily in the liver.

Mechanism of Action In addition to anticonvulsant effects, carbamazepine has anticholinergic, antineuralgic, antidiuretic, muscle relaxant, antimanic, antidepressive, and antiarrhythmic properties; may depress activity in the nucleus ventralis of the thalamus or decrease synaptic transmission or decrease summation of temporal stimulation leading to neural discharge by limiting influx of sodium ions across cell membrane or other unknown mechanisms; stimulates the release of ADH and potentiates its action in promoting reabsorption of water; chemically related to tricyclic antidepressants

Contraindications

Hypersensitivity to carbamazepine, tricyclic antidepressants, or any component of the formulation; bone marrow depression; with or within 14 days of MAO inhibitor use; concomitant use of nefazodone or boceprevir; concomitant use of delavirdine or other nonnucleoside reverse transcriptase inhibitors that are substrate of CYP3A4

Canadian labeling: Additional contraindications (not in US labeling): Atrioventricular (AV) heart block; hepatic disease; history of hepatic porphyria (acute intermittent porphyria, variegate porphyria, porphyria cutanea tarda); serious blood disorder; concurrent use with itraconazole and voriconazole

Warnings/Precautions

[US Boxed Warning]: The risk of developing anemia or agranulocytosis is increased during treatment. Monitor CBC, platelets, and differential prior to and during therapy; discontinue if significant bone marrow suppression occurs. A spectrum of hematologic effects has been reported with use (eg, agranulocytosis, aplastic anemia, neutropenia, leukopenia, thrombocytopenia, pancytopenia, and anemias); patients with a previous history of adverse hematologic reaction to any drug may be at increased risk. Early detection of hematologic change is important; advise patients of early signs and symptoms including fever, sore throat, mouth ulcers, infections, easy bruising, and petechial or purpuric hemorrhage.

[US Boxed Warning]: Severe and sometimes fatal dermatologic reactions, including toxic epidermal necrolysis (TENS) and Stevens-Johnson syndrome (SJS), may occur during therapy. The risk is increased in patients with the variant HLA-B*1502 allele, found most often in patients of Asian ancestry. Patients with an increased likelihood of carrying this allele should be screened prior to initiating therapy. Avoid use in patients testing positive for the allele; discontinue therapy in patients who have a serious dermatologic reaction. The risk of SJS or TENS may also be increased if carbamazepine is used in combination with other antiepileptic drugs associated with these reactions. Presence of the *HLA-B*1502* allele has not been found to predict the risk of less serious dermatologic reactions such as anticonvulsant hypersensitivity syndrome or nonserious rash. **[US Boxed Warning]: Patients with an increased likelihood of carrying the HLA-B*1502 allele,** such as those of Asian descent, **should be screened for the variant HLA-B*1502 allele prior to initiating therapy. This genetic variant has been associated with a significantly increased risk of developing Stevens-Johnson syndrome and/or toxic epidermal necrolysis. Patients with a positive result should not be started on carbamazepine.** The risk of developing a hypersensitivity reaction may be increased in patients with the variant *HLA-A*3101* allele. These hypersensitivity reactions include SJS/TEN, maculopapular eruptions, and drug reaction with eosinophilia and systemic symptoms (DRESS/multiorgan hypersensitivity). The *HLA-A*3101* allele may occur more frequently patients of African-American, Arabic, Asian, European, Indian, Latin American, and Native American ancestry. Hypersensitivity has also been reported in patients experiencing reactions to other anticonvulsants; the history of hypersensitivity reactions in the patient or their immediate family members should be reviewed. Approximately 25% to 30% of patients allergic to carbamazepine will also have reactions with oxcarbazepine. Potentially serious, sometimes fatal multiorgan hypersensitivity reactions (also known as drug reaction with eosinophilia and systemic symptoms [DRESS]) have been reported with some antiepileptic drugs including carbamazepine; monitor for signs and symptoms of possible disparate manifestations associated with lymphatic, hepatic, renal, and/or hematologic organ systems; gradual discontinuation and conversion to alternate therapy may be required.

Antiepileptics are associated with an increased risk of suicidal behavior/thoughts with use (regardless of indication); risk observed as early as 1 week after initiation and continued through duration of trials (most trials ≤24 weeks. Monitor all patients for signs/symptoms of depression, suicidal tendencies, and other unusual behavior changes during therapy and instructed to inform their healthcare provider immediately if symptoms occur.

Administer carbamazepine with caution to patients with history of cardiac damage or ECG abnormalities (or at risk for ECG abnormalities). Use with caution in patients with hepatic impairment; avoid use in patients with hepatic porphyria (eg, acute intermittent porphyria, variegate porphyria, porphyria cutanea tarda). Use with caution in patients with renal impairment. Avoid use of IV product in moderate or severe renal impairment. Renal toxicity has been reported; monitor renal function at baseline and periodically thereafter. Hepatotoxicity ranging from slight elevations in liver enzymes to rare hepatic failure has been reported and may occur concomitantly with other immunoallergenic syndromes such as multiorgan hypersensitivity (DRESS syndrome) and serious dermatologic reactions including Stevens-Johnson syndrome; monitor baseline and periodic liver function, particularly in patients with a history of liver disease; discontinue carbamazepine immediately in cases of aggravated liver dysfunction or active liver disease. In some cases, hepatic effects may progress despite discontinuation of carbamazepine. Rare cases of a hepatic failure and vanishing bile duct syndrome involving destruction and disappearance of the intrahepatic bile ducts have been reported. Clinical courses of vanishing bile duct syndrome have been variable ranging from fulminant to indolent. May activate latent psychosis and/or cause confusion or agitation; elderly patients may be at an increased risk for psychiatric effects.

Carbamazepine is not effective in absence, myoclonic, or akinetic seizures; carbamazepine administration may increase the frequency of seizures in patients with these types of seizures, Exacerbation of certain seizure types have been seen after initiation of carbamazepine therapy in children with mixed seizure disorders. Anticonvulsants should not be discontinued abruptly because of the possibility of increasing seizure frequency; therapy should be withdrawn gradually to minimize the potential of increased seizure frequency, unless safety concerns require a more rapid withdrawal. May cause CNS depression, which may impair physical or mental abilities; patients must be cautioned about performing tasks which require alertness (eg, operating machinery or driving). Potentially significant interactions may exist, requiring dose or frequency adjustment, additional monitoring, and/or selection of alternative therapy. Carbamazepine has mild anticholinergic activity; use with caution in patients with increased intraocular pressure, or sensitivity to anticholinergic effects. Hyponatremia caused by the syndrome of inappropriate antidiuretic hormone secretion (SIADH) may occur during therapy. Risk may be increased in the elderly or in patients also taking diuretics and may be dose-dependent. Consider discontinuing therapy in patients with symptomatic hyponatremia.

Administration of the suspension will yield higher peak and lower trough serum levels than an equal dose of the tablet form; consider a lower starting dose given more frequently (same total daily dose) when using the suspension. The suspension may contain sorbitol; avoid use in patents with hereditary fructose intolerance. Vials of the injectable product contain the excipient cyclodextrin (sulfobutylether beta-cyclodextrin), which may accumulate in patients with renal insufficiency, although the clinical significance of this finding is uncertain (Luke 2010).

Drug Interactions

Metabolism/Transport Effects **Substrate** of CYP2C8 (minor), CYP3A4 (major); **Note:** Assignment of Major/Minor substrate status based on clinically relevant drug interaction potential; **Induces** CYP1A2 (strong), CYP2B6 (moderate), CYP2C8 (strong), CYP2C9 (strong), CYP3A4 (strong), UGT1A1

Avoid Concomitant Use

Avoid concomitant use of CarBAMazepine with any of the following: Abiraterone Acetate; Antihepaciviral Combination Products; Apixaban; Apremilast; Aprepitant; Artemether; Asunaprevir; Axitinib; Azelastine (Nasal); BCG (Intravesical); Bedaquiline; Boceprevir; Bortezomib; Bosutinib; Cariprazine; Ceritinib; CloZAPine; Cobicistat; Cobimetinib; Conivaptan; Crizotinib; Dabrafenib; Daclatasvir; Dasabuvir; Deferiprone; Deflazacort; Delamanid; Delavirdine; Dienogest; Dipyrone; Dronedarone; Efavirenz; Eliglustat; Elvitegravir; Enzalutamide; Etravirine; Everolimus; Flibanserin; Fusidic Acid (Systemic); Grazoprevir; Ibrutinib; Idelalisib; Irinotecan Products; Isavuconazonium Sulfate; Itraconazole; Ivabradine; Ivacaftor; Ixazomib; Lapatinib; Ledipasvir; Lumefantrine; Lurasidone; Macitentan; MAO Inhibitors; MiFEPRIStone; Naldemedine; Naloxegol; Nefazodone; Netupitant; Nevirapine; NIFEdipine; Nilotinib; NiMODipine; Nisoldipine; Olaparib; Ombitasvir, Paritaprevir, Ritonavir, and Dasabuvir; Orphenadrine; Oxomemazine; Palbociclib; Panobinostat; Paraldehyde; PAZOPanib; Pirfenidone; PONATinib; Praziquantel; Ranolazine; Regorafenib; Ribociclib; Rilpivirine; Rivaroxaban; Roflumilast; RomiDEPsin; Simeprevir; Sofosbuvir; Sonidegib; SORAfenib; Stiripentol; Suvorexant; Tasimelteon; Telaprevir; Tenofovir Alafenamide; Thalidomide; Ticagrelor; Tofacitinib; Tolvaptan; Toremifene; Trabectedin; TraMADol; Ulipristal; Vandetanib; Velpatasvir; Vemurafenib; Venetoclax; VinCRIStine (Liposomal); Vinflunine; Vorapaxar; Voriconazole

Increased Effect/Toxicity

CarBAMazepine may increase the levels/effects of: Adenosine; Alcohol (Ethyl); Analgesics (Opioid); Azelastine (Nasal); Blonanserin; Buprenorphine; Clarithromycin; ClomiPRAMINE; CloZAPine; CNS Depressants; Deferiprone; Desmopressin; Doxercalciferol; Eslicarbazepine; Flunitrazepam; Fosphenytoin; HYDROcodone; Ifosfamide; Isoniazid; Lacosamide; Lithium; MAO Inhibitors; Methotrimeprazine; MetyroSINE; Orphenadrine; OxyCODONE; Paraldehyde; Phenytoin; Piribedil; Pramipexole; Rotigotine; Selective Serotonin Reuptake Inhibitors; Thalidomide

The levels/effects of CarBAMazepine may be increased by: Allopurinol; Brimonidine (Topical); Brivaracetam; Calcium Channel Blockers (Nondihydropyridine); Cannabis; Carbonic Anhydrase Inhibitors; Chlorphenesin Carbamate; Cimetidine; Ciprofloxacin (Systemic); Clarithromycin; Conivaptan; CYP3A4 Inhibitors (Moderate); CYP3A4 Inhibitors (Strong); Danazol; Darunavir; Dimethindene (Topical); Dipyrone; Doxylamine; Dronabinol; Droperidol; Erythromycin (Systemic); Fluconazole; FLUoxetine; FluvoxaMINE; Fusidic Acid (Systemic); Grapefruit Juice; HydrOXYzine; Idelalisib; Isoniazid; Kava Kava; LamoTRIgine; LevETIRAcetam; Lofexidine; Loxapine; Magnesium Sulfate; Methotrimeprazine; Minocycline; Nabilone; Nefazodone; Oxomemazine; Promazine; Protease Inhibitors; QUEtiapine; QuiNINE; Resveratrol; Sodium Oxybate; Stiripentol; Tapentadol; Telaprevir; Tetrahydrocannabinol; Thiazide and Thiazide-Like Diuretics; TraMADol; Trimeprazine; Valproate Products; Zolpidem

Decreased Effect

CarBAMazepine may decrease the levels/effects of: Abiraterone Acetate; Acetaminophen; Afatinib; Albendazole; Antihepaciviral Combination Products; Apixaban; Apremilast; Aprepitant; ARIPiprazole;

ARIPiprazole Lauroxil; Artemether; Asunaprevir; Axitinib; Bazedoxifene; BCG (Intravesical); Bedaquiline; Bendamustine; Benperidol; Boceprevir; Bortezomib; Bosutinib; Brentuximab Vedotin; Brexpiprazole; Brivaracetam; Cabozantinib; Calcifediol; Calcium Channel Blockers (Dihydropyridine); Calcium Channel Blockers (Nondihydropyridine); Canagliflozin; Cannabidiol; Cannabis; Cariprazine; Caspofungin; Ceritinib; Chlormethiazole; Citalopram; Clarithromycin; Clindamycin (Systemic); CloZAPine; Cobicistat; Cobimetinib; Contraceptives (Estrogens); Contraceptives (Progestins); Corticosteroids (Systemic); Crizotinib; CycloSPORINE (Systemic); CYP1A2 Substrates; CYP2B6 Substrates; CYP2C8 Substrates; CYP2C9 Substrates; CYP3A4 Substrates; Dabigatran Etexilate; Dabrafenib; Daclatasvir; Dasabuvir; Dasatinib; Deflazacort; Delamanid; Delavirdine; Dexamethasone (Systemic); Diclofenac (Systemic); Dienogest; Diethylstilbestrol; Dolutegravir; DOXOrubicin (Conventional); Doxycycline; Dronabinol; Dronedarone; Efavirenz; Eliglustat; Elvitegravir; Enzalutamide; Erlotinib; Eslicarbazepine; Estriol (Systemic); Estriol (Topical); Etizolam; Etoposide; Etoposide Phosphate; Etravirine; Everolimus; Exemestane; Ezogabine; Felbamate; Fingolimod; Flibanserin; Flunarizine; Fosphenytoin; Gefitinib; Gestrinone; Grazoprevir; GuanFACINE; Haloperidol; Hydrocortisone (Systemic); Ibrutinib; Idelalisib; Ifosfamide; Imatinib; Irinotecan Products; Isavuconazonium Sulfate; Itraconazole; Ivabradine; Ivacaftor; Ixabepilone; Ixazomib; Lacosamide; LamoTRIgine; Lapatinib; Ledipasvir; LevETIRAcetam; Linagliptin; Lopinavir; Lumefantrine; Lurasidone; Macitentan; Manidipine; Maraviroc; Mebendazole; Methadone; MethylPREDNISolone; Mianserin; MiFEPRIStone; Mirodenafil; Naldemedine; Naloxegol; Nefazodone; Netupitant; Neuromuscular-Blocking Agents (Nondepolarizing); Nevirapine; NIFEdipine; Nilotinib; NiMODipine; Nisoldipine; Olaparib; Ombitasvir, Paritaprevir, Ritonavir, and Dasabuvir; Osimertinib; OXcarbazepine; Palbociclib; Paliperidone; Panobinostat; PAZOPanib; Perampanel; Phenytoin; Pimavanserin; Pirfenidone; PONATinib; Praziquantel; PrednisoLONE (Systemic); PredniSONE; Propacetamol; Propafenone; Protease Inhibitors; QUEtiapine; QuiNINE; Radotinib; Ramelteon; Ranolazine; Reboxetine; Regorafenib; Ribociclib; Rilpivirine; RisperiDONE; Rivaroxaban; Roflumilast; Rolapitant; RomiDEPsin; Rufinamide; SAXagliptin; Sertraline; Simeprevir; Sirolimus; Sofosbuvir; Sonidegib; SORAfenib; Sulthiame; SUNItinib; Suvorexant; Tadalafil; Tasimelteon; Telaprevir; Temsirolimus; Tenofovir Alafenamide; Tetrahydrocannabinol; Theophylline Derivatives; Thyroid Products; TiaGABine; Ticagrelor; Tofacitinib; Tolvaptan; Topiramate; Toremifene; Trabectedin; TraMADol; Treprostinil; Tricyclic Antidepressants; Tropisetron; Udenafil; Ulipristal; Valproate Products; Vandetanib; Vecuronium; Velpatasvir; Vemurafenib; Venetoclax; Vilazodone; VinCRIStine (Liposomal); Vinflunine; Vitamin K Antagonists; Vorapaxar; Voriconazole; Vortioxetine; Zaleplon; Ziprasidone; Zolpidem; Zuclopenthixol

The levels/effects of CarBAMazepine may be decreased by: Bosentan; CYP3A4 Inducers (Moderate); CYP3A4 Inducers (Strong); Deferasirox; Efavirenz; Felbamate; Fosphenytoin; Mefloquine; Methylfolate; Mianserin; Mitotane; Orlistat; Phenytoin; Rufinamide; Siltuximab; St John's Wort; Theophylline Derivatives; Tocilizumab; TraMADol

Food Interactions Carbamazepine serum levels may be increased if taken with food and/or grapefruit juice. Management: Avoid concurrent ingestion of grapefruit juice. Maintain adequate hydration, unless instructed to restrict fluid intake.

Dietary Considerations Folate and vitamin B: Carbamazepine use has been associated with low serum concentrations of folate, vitamin B_2 (riboflavin), B_6 (pyridoxine) and B_{12} (cyanocobalamin), which may contribute to hyperhomocysteinemia. Hyperhomocysteinemia may contribute to cardiovascular disease, venous thromboembolic disease, dementia, neuropsychiatric symptoms, and poor seizure control. Some health care providers recommend administering folic acid, riboflavin, pyridoxine, and cyanocobalamin supplements in patients taking carbamazepine (Apeland 2003; Apeland 2008; Belcastro 2012; Bochyńska 2012).

Pharmacodynamics/Kinetics

Half-life Elimination Half-life is variable because of autoinduction which is usually complete 3 to 5 weeks after initiation of a fixed carbamazepine regimen.

Carbamazepine: Initial: 25 to 65 hours; Extended release: 35 to 40 hours; Multiple doses: Children: 8 to 14 hours; Adults: 12 to 17 hours

Epoxide metabolite: Initial: 34 ± 9 hours

Time to Peak Unpredictable:

Immediate release: Suspension: Multiple doses: 1.5 hour; tablet: 4 to 5 hours

Extended release: Carbatrol, Equetro: 12 to 26 hours (single dose), 4 to 8 hours (multiple doses); Tegretol®-XR: 3 to 12 hours

Pregnancy Risk Factor D (product specific)

Pregnancy Considerations Studies in pregnant women have demonstrated a risk to the fetus. Carbamazepine and its metabolites can be found in the fetus and may be associated with teratogenic effects, including spina bifida, craniofacial defects, cardiovascular malformations, and hypospadias. The risk of teratogenic effects is higher with anticonvulsant polytherapy than monotherapy.

Developmental delays have also been observed following *in utero* exposure to carbamazepine (per manufacturer); however, socioeconomic factors, maternal and paternal IQ, and polytherapy may contribute to these findings. Pregnancy may cause small decreases of carbamazepine plasma concentrations in the second and third trimesters; monitoring should be considered. When used for the treatment of bipolar disorder, use of carbamazepine should be avoided during the first trimester of pregnancy if possible. The use of a single medication for the treatment of bipolar disorder or epilepsy in pregnancy is preferred. Carbamazepine may decrease plasma concentrations of hormonal contraceptives; breakthrough bleeding or unintended pregnancy may occur and alternate or back-up methods of contraception should be considered.

Patients exposed to carbamazepine during pregnancy are encouraged to enroll themselves into the AED Pregnancy Registry by calling 1-888-233-2334. Additional information is available at www.aedpregnancyregistry.org.

Breastfeeding Considerations Carbamazepine and its active epoxide metabolite are found in breast milk. Carbamazepine can also be detected in the serum of nursing infants. Transient hepatic dysfunction has been observed in some case reports. Nursing should be discontinued if adverse events are observed. According to the manufacturer, the decision to continue or discontinue breastfeeding during therapy should take into account the risk of exposure to the infant and the benefits of treatment to the mother. Respiratory depression, seizures, nausea, vomiting, diarrhea, and/or decreased feeding have been observed in neonates exposed to carbamazepine *in utero* and may represent a neonatal withdrawal syndrome.

Product Availability Carnexiv (carbamazepine injection): FDA approved October 2016; anticipated availability in early 2017. Information pertaining to this product within the monograph is pending revision. Consult the prescribing information for additional information.

Dosage Forms

Capsule Extended Release 12 Hour, Oral:
Carbatrol: 100 mg, 200 mg, 300 mg
Equetro: 100 mg, 200 mg, 300 mg
Generic: 100 mg, 200 mg, 300 mg

Suspension, Oral:
TEGretol: 100 mg/5 mL (450 mL)
Generic: 100 mg/5 mL (450 mL)

Tablet, Oral:
Epitol: 200 mg
TEGretol: 200 mg
Generic: 200 mg

Tablet Chewable, Oral:
Generic: 100 mg

Tablet Extended Release 12 Hour, Oral:
TEGretol-XR: 100 mg, 200 mg, 400 mg
Generic: 100 mg, 200 mg, 400 mg

Carbamide Peroxide (KAR ba mide per OKS ide)

Brand Names: US Auraphene-B [OTC]; Debrox [OTC] [DSC]; E-R-O Ear Drops [OTC]; E-R-O Ear Wax Removal System [OTC]; Ear Drops Earwax Aid [OTC] [DSC]; Ear Drops [OTC]; Ear Wax Remover [OTC] [DSC]; Earwax Treatment Drops [OTC]; Gly-Oxide [OTC]; Thera-Ear [OTC] [DSC]

Pharmacologic Category Anti-inflammatory, Locally Applied; Otic Agent, Cerumenolytic

Use

Oral: Temporary use in cleansing of canker sore and minor wounds or gum inflammation due to minor dental procedures, dentures, orthodontic appliances, accidental injury, or other irritations of mouth and gums; aids in removal of phlegm, mucus, or other secretions associated with occasional sore mouth.

Otic: Aid to soften, loosen, and remove excessive earwax.

Local Anesthetic/Vasoconstrictor Precautions No information available to require special precautions

Effects on Dental Treatment No significant effects or complications reported (see Dental Comment)

Effects on Bleeding No information available to require special precautions

Adverse Reactions Frequency not defined.

Dermatologic: Localized erythema, skin rash
Infection: Superinfection
Local: Local irritation, redness

General Dosage Range

Otic: *Children ≥12 years, Adolescents, and Adults:* Instill 5 to 10 drops twice daily

Topical (oral): *Children ≥2 years. Adolescents, and Adults:* Apply several drops on affected area, expectorate after 2 to 3 minutes 4 times/day **or** place 10 to 20 drops on tongue, swish for ≥1 minute, then expectorate 4 times/day.

Mechanism of Action Carbamide peroxide releases hydrogen peroxide which serves as a source of nascent oxygen upon contact with catalase; deodorant action is probably due to inhibition of odor-causing bacteria; softens impacted cerumen due to its foaming action

Pharmacodynamics/Kinetics

Onset of Action ~24 hours

Dental Comment When used as tooth whitening product, most common side effect is tooth sensitivity.

Carbidopa (kar bi DOE pa)

Brand Names: US Lodosyn

Pharmacologic Category Anti-Parkinson Agent, Decarboxylase Inhibitor

Use

Parkinsonism: Given with carbidopa/levodopa in the treatment of idiopathic Parkinson disease, postencephalitic parkinsonism, and symptomatic parkinsonism, which may follow injury to the nervous system by carbon monoxide and/or manganese intoxication.

Note: Administration of carbidopa allows use of a lower dosage of levodopa, more rapid titration, and a decrease in nausea and vomiting associated with levodopa; use with carbidopa/levodopa in patients requiring additional carbidopa; has no effect without levodopa.

Local Anesthetic/Vasoconstrictor Precautions No information available to require special precautions

Effects on Dental Treatment Key adverse event(s) related to dental treatment: Dopaminergic therapy in Parkinson's disease includes the use of carbidopa in combination with levodopa. Carbidopa/levodopa combination is associated with orthostatic hypotension. Patients may experience orthostatic hypotension as they stand up after treatment; especially if lying in dental chair for extended periods of time. Use caution with sudden changes in position during and after dental treatment.

Effects on Bleeding No information available to require special precautions

Adverse Reactions Adverse reactions are associated with concomitant administration with levodopa.

Cardiovascular: Cardiac arrhythmia, chest pain, edema, flushing, hypertension, hypotension, myocardial infarction, orthostatic hypotension, palpitation, phlebitis, syncope

Central nervous system: Abnormal dreams, abnormal gait, agitation, anxiety, ataxia, confusion, decreased mental acuity, delusions, dementia, depression (with or without suicidal tendencies), disorientation, dizziness, drowsiness, euphoria, extrapyramidal reaction, falling, fatigue, glossopyrosis, hallucination, headache, Horner's syndrome, impulse control disorder, insomnia, malaise, memory impairment, nervousness, neuroleptic malignant syndrome, nightmares, numbness, on-off phenomenon, paranoia, paresthesia, pathological gambling, peripheral neuropathy, psychosis, seizure (causal relationship not established), trismus

Dermatologic: Alopecia, bulla, diaphoresis, discoloration of sweat, skin rash

Endocrine & metabolic: Abnormal lactate dehydrogenase, glycosuria, hot flash, hyperglycemia, hypokalemia, increased libido (including hypersexuality), increased uric acid, weight changes

Gastrointestinal: Abdominal distress, abdominal pain, anorexia, bruxism, constipation, diarrhea, discoloration of saliva, duodenal ulcer, dysgeusia, dyspepsia, dysphagia, flatulence, gastrointestinal hemorrhage, heartburn, hiccups, nausea, sialorrhea, sore throat, vomiting, xerostomia

Genitourinary: Priapism, proteinuria, urinary frequency, urinary incontinence, urinary retention, urinary tract infection, urine discoloration

Hematologic & oncologic: Abnormal Coombs' test, agranulocytosis, anemia, decreased hematocrit, decreased hemoglobin, hemolytic anemia, leukopenia, malignant melanoma, thrombocytopenia

Hepatic: Abnormal alanine aminotransferase, abnormal alkaline phosphatase, abnormal aspartate transaminase, abnormal bilirubin levels, abnormal lactate dehydrogenase

Hypersensitivity: Angioedema, hypersensitivity reaction (bulla, IgA vasculitis, pruritus, urticaria)

Neuromuscular & skeletal: Back pain, dyskinesia (including choreiform, dystonic, and other involuntary movements), leg pain, muscle cramps, muscle twitching, shoulder pain, tremor, weakness

Ophthalmic: Blepharospasm, blurred vision, diplopia, mydriasis, oculogyric crisis (may be associated with acute dystonic reactions)

Renal: Increased blood urea nitrogen, increased serum creatinine

Respiratory: Cough, dyspnea, hoarseness, upper respiratory tract infection

General Dosage Range Oral: *Adults:* 25 mg 3-4 times/day (maximum: 200 mg carbidopa/day)

Mechanism of Action Carbidopa is a peripheral decarboxylase inhibitor with little or no pharmacological activity when given alone in usual doses. It inhibits the peripheral decarboxylation of levodopa to dopamine; and as it does not cross the blood-brain barrier, unlike levodopa, effective brain concentrations of dopamine are produced with lower doses of levodopa. At the same time, reduced peripheral formation of dopamine reduces peripheral side-effects, notably nausea and vomiting, and cardiac arrhythmias, although the dyskinesias and adverse mental effects associated with levodopa therapy tend to develop earlier.

Pregnancy Risk Factor C

Pregnancy Considerations Adverse events have not been observed in animal reproduction studies. Carbidopa can be detected in the umbilical cord but absorption in fetal tissue is minimal (Merchant, 1995). The incidence of Parkinson's disease in pregnancy is relatively rare and information related to the use of carbidopa in pregnant women is limited to use with other agents. Refer to the carbidopa and levodopa monograph for additional information.

Carbidopa and Levodopa

(kar bi DOE pa & lee voe DOE pa)

Related Information

Carbidopa *on page 298*

Brand Names: US Duopa; Parcopa [DSC]; Rytary; Sinemet; Sinemet CR

Brand Names: Canada Apo-Levocarb; Apo-Levocarb CR; Dom-Levo-Carbidopa; Duodopa; Levocarb CR; PMS-Levocarb CR; PRO-Levocarb; Sinemet; Sinemet CR; Teva-Levocarbidopa

Pharmacologic Category Anti-Parkinson Agent, Decarboxylase Inhibitor; Anti-Parkinson Agent, Dopamine Precursor

Use Parkinson disease: Treatment of Parkinson disease, postencephalitic parkinsonism, and symptomatic parkinsonism that may follow carbon monoxide and/or manganese intoxication; treatment of motor fluctuations in advanced Parkinson disease (intestinal suspension [Duopa] only).

Local Anesthetic/Vasoconstrictor Precautions No information available to require special precautions

Effects on Dental Treatment Key adverse event(s) related to dental treatment: Xerostomia (normal salivary flow resumes upon discontinuation) and taste alterations; Dopaminergic therapy in Parkinson's disease (ie, treatment with levodopa and carbidopa combination) is associated with orthostatic hypotension. Patients may experience orthostatic hypotension as they stand up after treatment; especially if lying in dental chair for extended periods of time. Use caution with sudden changes in position during and after dental treatment.

Effects on Bleeding No information available to require special precautions

Adverse Reactions

>10%:

Cardiovascular: Orthostatic hypotension (≤73%)

Central nervous system: Dizziness (6% to 19%), headache (13% to 17%; oral 1% to 5%), depression (with or without suicidal tendencies; Duopa 11%)

Gastrointestinal: Nausea (3% to 30%), constipation (≤22%)

Local: Erythema at injection site (Duopa 19%), application site discharge (Duopa 11%)

Neuromuscular & skeletal: Dyskinesia (12% to 17%; Rytary 2% to 5%; including choreiform, dystonic and other involuntary movements), increased creatine phosphokinase (≤17%)

Renal: Increased blood urea nitrogen (≤13%)

Miscellaneous: Procedural complications (from device insertion; Duopa 57%)

1% to 10%:

Cardiovascular: Peripheral edema (Duopa 8%), hypertension (≤8%), Ischemia (≤2%)

Central nervous system: Insomnia (6% to 9%), anxiety (2% to 8%), confusion (2% to 8%), abnormal dreams (2% to 6%), polyneuropathy (Duopa 5%), sleep disorder (Duopa 5%), hallucination (1% to 5%), psychosis (1% to 5%)

Dermatologic: Wound healing impairment (excessive granulation tissue; Duopa 5%), skin rash (≤5%)

Gastrointestinal: Hiatal hernia (6% to 8%), xerostomia (7%), intestinal obstruction (Duopa 5%), diarrhea (≤5%), dyspepsia (≤5%), ileus (≤5%), vomiting (≤5%)

Genitourinary: Bacteriuria (1% to 5%)

Hematologic & oncologic: Leukocyturia (1% to 5%)

Respiratory: Atelectasis (Duopa 8%), oropharyngeal pain (Duopa 8%), upper respiratory tract infection (Duopa 8%; Sinemet and Sinemet CR ≤2%)

Miscellaneous: Fever (≤5%)

Frequency not defined:

Cardiovascular: Cardiac arrhythmia, chest pain, edema, flushing, hypotension, myocardial infarction, palpitations, phlebitis, syncope

Central nervous system: Abnormal behavior, abnormal gait, abnormality in thinking, agitation, ataxia, decreased mental acuity, delirium, delusions, dementia, disorientation, drowsiness, euphoria, extrapyramidal reaction, falling, fatigue, glossopyrosis, Horner syndrome (reactivation), impulse control disorder, malaise, memory impairment, narcolepsy, nervousness, neuroleptic malignant syndrome, nightmares, numbness, on-off phenomenon, pain (naso-jejunal insertion), paranoia, paresthesia, pathological gambling, peripheral neuropathy, seizure (causal relationship not established), trismus

Dermatologic: Alopecia, diaphoresis, discoloration of sweat

Endocrine & metabolic: Abnormal alanine aminotransferase, abnormal alkaline phosphatase, abnormal aspartate transaminase, abnormal lactate dehydrogenase, glycosuria, hot flash, hyperglycemia, hypokalemia, increased libido (including hypersexuality), increased uric acid, weight gain, weight loss

Gastrointestinal: Abdominal distention (PEG-J and naso-jejunal insertion), abdominal distress (PEG-J and naso-jejunal insertion), abdominal pain (PEG-J and naso-jejunal insertion), anorexia, bruxism, discoloration of saliva, duodenal ulcer (PEG-J and naso-jejunal insertion), duodenitis (erosive, PEG-J and naso-jejunal insertion), dysgeusia, dysphagia (naso-jejunal insertion), esophageal hemorrhage (naso-jejunal insertion), flatulence (PEG-J insertion), gastritis (erosive; PEG-J and naso-jejunal insertion), gastrointestinal hemorrhage (PEG-J and naso-jejunal insertion), heartburn, hiccups, intussusception (PEG-J and naso-jejunal insertion), peritonitis (PEG-J and naso-jejunal insertion), sialorrhea, sore throat (naso-jejunal insertion), upper abdominal pain (PEG-J and naso-jejunal insertion)

Genitourinary: Difficulty in micturition, priapism, proteinuria, urinary frequency, urinary incontinence, urinary retention, urinary tract infection, urine discoloration

Hematologic & oncologic: Agranulocytosis, anemia, decreased hematocrit, decreased hemoglobin, hemolytic anemia, IgA vasculitis, leukopenia, malignant melanoma

Hepatic: Abnormal bilirubin levels

Hypersensitivity: Hypersensitivity reaction (angioedema, bullous lesions [including pemphigus-like reactions], pruritus, urticaria)

Immunologic: Abnormal Coombs test

Infection: Abscess (postoperative; PEG-J and naso-jejunal insertion)

Neuromuscular & skeletal: Back pain, excessive tremors, leg pain, muscle cramps, muscle twitching, shoulder pain, weakness

Ophthalmic: Blepharospasm, blurred vision, diplopia, glaucoma, increased intraocular pressure, mydriasis, oculogyric crisis (may be associated with acute dystonic reactions)

Respiratory: Cough, dyspnea, hoarseness

General Dosage Range

Oral: *Adults:*

Immediate release: Initial: Carbidopa 25 mg/levodopa 100 mg 3 times/day (maximum: 8 tablets of any strength/day **or** 200 mg of carbidopa and 2,000 mg of levodopa)

Controlled release: Initial: Carbidopa 50 mg/levodopa 200 mg 2 times daily, at intervals not <6 hours (maximum: 8 tablets/day)

Extended-release: Initial: Carbidopa 23.75 mg/levodopa 95 mg 3 times daily (maximum: Carbidopa 612.5 mg/levodopa 2,450 mg).

Intestinal suspension: *Adults:* Dosage varies (maximum: 2,000 mg of the levodopa component (ie, one cassette per day).

Mechanism of Action Parkinson disease symptoms are due to a lack of striatal dopamine; levodopa circulates in the plasma to the blood-brain-barrier (BBB), where it crosses, to be converted by striatal enzymes to dopamine; carbidopa inhibits the peripheral plasma breakdown of levodopa by inhibiting its decarboxylation, and thereby increases available levodopa at the BBB

Pharmacodynamics/Kinetics

Half-life Elimination Immediate release: Levodopa (in presence of carbidopa): 1.5 hours; Half-life may be prolonged with controlled and extended release formulations due to continuous absorption.

Time to Peak Immediate release: 0.5 hours; Controlled and extended release: 2 hours; Intestinal gel [Canadian product]: Therapeutic plasma levels reached 10 to 30 minutes following morning bolus dose; Intestinal suspension: 2.5 hours

Pregnancy Risk Factor C

Pregnancy Considerations Adverse events have been observed in some animal reproduction studies using this combination. Carbidopa can be detected in the umbilical cord, but absorption in fetal tissue is minimal. Levodopa crosses the placenta and can be metabolized by the fetus and detected in fetal tissue (Merchant 1995). The incidence of Parkinson disease in pregnancy is relatively rare, and information related to the use of carbidopa/levodopa in pregnant women is limited (Ball 1995; Cook 1985; Golbe 1987; Serikawa 2011; Shulman 2000). Current guidelines note that the available information is insufficient to make a recommendation for the treatment of restless legs syndrome in pregnant women (Aurora 2012).

Prescribing and Access Restrictions Duodopa intestinal gel [Canadian product]: In Canada, the Duodopa Education Program is a risk mitigation program established to provide safe and effective use of Duodopa in advanced Parkinson patients. The program involves:

- Education of prescribing neurologists and other health care providers on suitable candidates for treatment, surgical procedures (PEG tube placement), and follow-up care including infusion device education.
- Distribution of educational materials to patients and caregivers describing Duodopa intestinal gel and its proper use, PEG tube placement, and complications associated with the mode of administration and/or PEG tube placement.

Carbinoxamine (kar bi NOKS a meen)

Brand Names: US Arbinoxa [DSC]; Karbinal ER; Palgic [DSC]; RyVent

Pharmacologic Category Ethanolamine Derivative; Histamine H_1 Antagonist; Histamine H_1 Antagonist, First Generation

Use Allergies: For the symptomatic treatment of seasonal and perennial allergic rhinitis; vasomotor rhinitis; allergic conjunctivitis caused by inhalant allergens and foods; mild, uncomplicated allergic skin manifestations of urticaria and angioedema; dermatographism; as therapy for anaphylactic reactions adjunctive to epinephrine and other standard measures after the acute manifestations have been controlled; amelioration of the severity of allergic reactions to blood or plasma.

Local Anesthetic/Vasoconstrictor Precautions No information available to require special precautions

Effects on Dental Treatment Key adverse event(s) related to dental treatment: Xerostomia (normal salivary flow resumes upon discontinuation).

Effects on Bleeding No information available to require special precautions

Adverse Reactions Frequency not defined.

Cardiovascular: Chest tightness, extrasystoles, hypotension, palpitations, tachycardia

Central nervous system: Ataxia (most frequent), chills, confusion, dizziness (most frequent), drowsiness (most frequent), euphoria, excitability, fatigue, headache, hysteria, insomnia, irritability, nervousness,

neuritis, paresthesia, restlessness, sedation (most frequent), seizure, vertigo
Dermatologic: Diaphoresis, skin photosensitivity, skin rash, urticaria
Endocrine & metabolic: Increased uric acid
Gastrointestinal: Anorexia, constipation, diarrhea, epigastric distress (most frequent), nausea, vomiting, xerostomia
Genitourinary: Difficulty in micturition, early menses, urinary frequency, urinary retention
Hematologic & oncologic: Agranulocytosis, hemolytic anemia, thrombocytopenia
Hypersensitivity: Anaphylactic shock, hypersensitivity reaction
Neuromuscular & skeletal: Tremor
Ophthalmic: Blurred vision, diplopia
Otic: Labyrinthitis, tinnitus
Respiratory: Dry nose, dry throat, nasal congestion, thickening of bronchial secretions (most frequent), wheezing

General Dosage Range

Oral, extended release:
Children 2 to <4 years: 3-4 mg every 12 hours
Children 4 to <6 years: 3-8 mg every 12 hours
Children 6 to <12 years: 6-12 mg every 12 hours
Children ≥12 years, Adolescents, and Adults: 6-16 mg every 12 hours

Oral, immediate release:
Children 2 to <6 years: 0.2-0.4 mg/kg/day divided into 3-4 doses (weight-based dosing preferred) **or** 1-2 mg 3-4 times daily
Children 6 to <12 years: 2-4 mg 3-4 times daily
Children ≥12 years, Adolescents, and Adults: 4-8 mg 3-4 times daily

Mechanism of Action Carbinoxamine competes with histamine for H_1-receptor sites on effector cells in the gastrointestinal tract, blood vessels, and respiratory tract.

Pharmacodynamics/Kinetics

Duration of Action ~4 hours (immediate release)

Half-life Elimination
17 hours (extended release)

Time to Peak Serum: 1.5 to 5 hours

Pregnancy Risk Factor C

Pregnancy Considerations Animal reproduction studies have not been conducted. Maternal antihistamine use has generally not resulted in an increased risk of birth defects; however, information specific for the use of carbinoxamine during pregnancy has not been located. Although antihistamines are recommended for some indications in pregnant women, the use of other agents with specific pregnancy data may be preferred.

CARBOplatin (KAR boe pla tin)

Brand Names: Canada Carboplatin Injection; Carboplatin Injection BP

Pharmacologic Category Antineoplastic Agent, Alkylating Agent; Antineoplastic Agent, Platinum Analog

Use Ovarian cancer, advanced: Initial treatment of advanced ovarian cancer in combination with other established chemotherapy agents; palliative treatment of recurrent ovarian cancer after prior chemotherapy, including cisplatin-based treatment

Local Anesthetic/Vasoconstrictor Precautions No information available to require special precautions

Effects on Dental Treatment Key adverse event(s) related to dental treatment: Stomatitis, mucositis, and taste dysgeusia.

Effects on Bleeding Hemorrhagic complication (ie, bleeding) has been reported in 5% of patients. Thrombocytopenia is one of the dose-limiting complications of carboplatin's myelosuppression. A medical consult is suggested.

Adverse Reactions Percentages reported with single-agent therapy.

>10%:
Central nervous system: Pain (23%)
Endocrine & metabolic: Hyponatremia (29% to 47%), hypomagnesemia (29% to 43%), hypocalcemia (22% to 31%), hypokalemia (20% to 28%)
Gastrointestinal: Vomiting (65% to 81%), abdominal pain (17%), nausea (without vomiting: 10% to 15%)
Hematologic & oncologic: Bone marrow depression (dose related and dose limiting; nadir at ~21 days with single-agent therapy), anemia (71% to 90%; grades 3/4: 21%), leukopenia (85%; grades 3/4: 15% to 26%), neutropenia (67%; grades 3/4: 16% to 21%), thrombocytopenia (62%; grades 3/4: 25% to 35%)
Hepatic: Increased serum alkaline phosphatase (24% to 37%), increased serum AST (15% to 19%)
Hypersensitivity: Hypersensitivity (2% to 16%)
Neuromuscular & skeletal: Weakness (11%)
Renal: Decreased creatinine clearance (27%), increased blood urea nitrogen (14% to 22%)

1% to 10%:
Central nervous system: Peripheral neuropathy (4% to 6%), neurotoxicity (5%)
Dermatologic: Alopecia (2% to 3%)
Gastrointestinal: Constipation (6%), diarrhea (6%), dysgeusia (1%), mucositis (≤1%), stomatitis (≤1%)
Hematologic & oncologic: Bleeding complications (5%), hemorrhage (5%)
Hepatic: Increased serum bilirubin (5%)
Infection: Infection (5%)
Ophthalmic: Visual disturbance (1%)
Otic: Ototoxicity (1%)
Renal: Increased serum creatinine (6% to 10%)

<1%, postmarketing, and/or case reports (Limited to important or life-threatening): Anaphylaxis, anorexia, bronchospasm, cardiac failure, cerebrovascular accident, dehydration, embolism, erythema, febrile neutropenia, hemolytic anemia (acute), hemolytic-uremic syndrome, hypertension, hypotension, injection site reaction (pain, redness, swelling), limb ischemia (acute), malaise, metastases, pruritus, skin rash, tissue necrosis (associated with extravasation), urticaria, vision loss

General Dosage Range Dosage adjustment recommended in renal impairment or who develop toxicities

IV: *Adults:* 300 to 360 mg/m² every 4 weeks **or** AUC of 4 to 6 (using Calvert formula)

Mechanism of Action Carboplatin is a platinum compound alkylating agent which covalently binds to DNA; interferes with the function of DNA by producing interstrand DNA cross-links. Carboplatin is apparently not cell-cycle specific.

Pharmacodynamics/Kinetics

Half-life Elimination CrCl >60 mL/minute: Carboplatin: 2.6 to 5.9 hours (based on a dose of 300 to 500 mg/m²); Platinum (from carboplatin): ≥5 days

Pregnancy Risk Factor D

Pregnancy Considerations Adverse events have been observed in animal reproduction studies. May cause fetal harm if administered during pregnancy.

Women of childbearing potential should avoid becoming pregnant during treatment.

Carboprost Tromethamine

(KAR boe prost tro METH a meen)

Brand Names: US Hemabate

Brand Names: Canada Hemabate

Pharmacologic Category Abortifacient; Prostaglandin

Use

Termination of pregnancy: For aborting pregnancy between week 13 and 20 of gestation as calculated from the first day of the last normal menstrual period and in the following conditions related to second trimester abortion: Failure of expulsion of the fetus during the course of treatment by another method; premature rupture of membranes in intrauterine methods with loss of drug and insufficient or absent uterine activity; requirement of a repeat intrauterine instillation of drug for expulsion of the fetus; inadvertent or spontaneous rupture of membranes in the presence of a previable fetus and absence of adequate activity for expulsion.

Refractory postpartum uterine hemorrhage: Treatment of postpartum hemorrhage due to uterine atony that has not responded to conventional methods of management. Prior treatment should include the use of intravenously (IV) administered oxytocin, manipulative techniques such as uterine massage and, unless contraindicated, intramuscular ergot preparations.

Local Anesthetic/Vasoconstrictor Precautions No information available to require special precautions

Effects on Dental Treatment No significant effects or complications reported

Effects on Bleeding No information available to require special precautions

Adverse Reactions Frequency not always defined. Effects due to increased smooth muscle contractility are most common and are generally transient and reversible upon discontinuation of therapy.

Cardiovascular: Chest pain, chest tightness, flushing, hypertension, palpitations, septic shock syncope, tachycardia, vasodepressor syncope

Central nervous system: Anxiety, chills, choking sensation, disturbed sleep, dizziness, drowsiness, dystonia, headache, increased body temperature (may be drug-induced or due to postabortion endometritis), lethargy, nervousness, paresthesia, shivering, vertigo

Dermatologic: Diaphoresis, skin rash

Endocrine & metabolic: Fullness of throat, hot flash, increased thirst, thyroid storm

Gastrointestinal: Diarrhea (approximately 67%), vomiting (approximately 67%), nausea (approximately 33%), dysgeusia, epigastric pain, gag reflex, hematemesis, hiccups, retching, xerostomia

Genitourinary: Breast tenderness, cervical perforation (posterior), endometritis (from intrauterine device [IUD]), gynecological pain (dysmenorrhea-like pain), menometrorrhagia, retained placenta (fragment), urinary tract infection, uterine perforation, uterine rupture, sacculation of uterus

Local: Pain at injection site

Neuromuscular & skeletal: Back pain, leg cramps, myalgia, torticollis, weakness

Ophthalmic: Blepharospasm, blurred vision, eye pain

Otic: Tinnitus

Respiratory: Asthma, bronchospasm, cough, dry throat, dyspnea, epistaxis, hyperventilation, pulmonary edema, respiratory distress, upper respiratory tract infection, wheezing

<1%, postmarketing, and/or case reports: Hypersensitivity reaction (includes anaphylactic shock, anaphylactoid reaction, anaphylaxis, angioedema)

General Dosage Range IM: *Adults (females):* Termination of pregnancy: 250 mcg at 1.5- to 3.5-hour intervals, a 500 mcg dose may be given if uterine response is not adequate after several 250 mcg doses (maximum total dose: 12 mg); Postpartum bleeding: 250 mcg; may repeat if needed (maximum total dose: 2 mg [8 doses])

Mechanism of Action Carboprost is an analog of naturally occurring prostaglandin F_2 alpha (dinoprost); carboprost stimulates uterine contractility which usually results in expulsion of the products of conception and is used to induce abortion between 13-20 weeks of pregnancy. When used postpartum, hemostasis at the placentation site is achieved through the myometrial contractions produced by carboprost.

Pharmacodynamics/Kinetics

Time to Peak Serum: IM: 30 minutes

Pregnancy Risk Factor C

Pregnancy Considerations Teratogenic effects were not observed in animal reproduction studies. When used for termination of pregnancy, carboprost is not considered feticidal, but is used to terminate pregnancy due to its ability to stimulate uterine contractions; use is not indicated if the fetus has reached a stage of viability *in utero*. Complete termination of pregnancy may not be induced in ~20% of cases and should therefore be completed in another way.

Cariprazine (kar IP ra zeen)

Brand Names: US Vraylar

Pharmacologic Category Second Generation (Atypical) Antipsychotic

Use

Schizophrenia: Treatment of schizophrenia

Bipolar I disorder: Acute treatment of manic or mixed episodes associated with bipolar I disorder

Local Anesthetic/Vasoconstrictor Precautions No information available to require special precautions

Effects on Dental Treatment

Key adverse event(s) related to dental treatment: Toothache and xerostomia has been reported

Effects on Bleeding No information available to require special precautions

Adverse Reactions Note: Reactions reported with doses up to 6 mg daily as doses greater than this do not result in significant therapeutic benefit but do increase adverse reactions.

>10%:

Central nervous system: Drug-induced extrapyramidal reaction (excluding akathisia and restlessness: 15% to 26%), Parkinsonian-like syndrome (13% to 21%), akathisia (9% to 20%), headache (14%), insomnia (9% to 13%)

Gastrointestinal: Nausea (7% to 13%)

1% to 10%:

Cardiovascular: Hypertension (2% to 5%), tachycardia (2%)

Central nervous system: Drowsiness (7% to 8%), restlessness (4% to 7%), dizziness (3% to 7%), anxiety (5% to 6%), agitation (5%), dystonia (2% to 5%), fatigue (3% to 4%)

Dermatologic: Skin rash (2%)

Endocrine & metabolic: Weight gain (2% to 3%)

Gastrointestinal: Vomiting (4% to 10%), dyspepsia (5% to 7%), abdominal pain (6%), constipation (6%), diarrhea (4%), toothache (4%), decreased appetite (3%), xerostomia (3%)

Hepatic: Increased liver enzymes (1%)

Neuromuscular & skeletal: Leg pain (4%), back pain (3%), musculoskeletal stiffness (2% to 3%), arthralgia (2%), increased creatine phosphokinase (2%)

Ophthalmic: Blurred vision (4%)

General Dosage Range

Dosage adjustment recommended in patients on concomitant therapy with CYP3A4 inhibitors.

Oral: *Adults:* 1.5 to 6 mg once daily (maximum: 6 mg daily)

Mechanism of Action Cariprazine is a second generation antipsychotic which displays partial agonist activity at dopamine D_2 and serotonin 5-HT_{1A} receptors and antagonist activity at serotonin 5-HT_{2A} receptors. It exhibits high affinity for dopamine (D_2 and D_3) and serotonin (5-HT_{1A}) receptors and has low affinity for serotonin 5-HT_{2C} and alpha$_{1A}$-adrenergic receptors. Cariprazine functions as an antagonist for 5-HT_{2B} (high affinity) and 5-HT_{2A} receptors (moderate affinity), binds to histamine H_1 receptors, and has no affinity for muscarinic (cholinergic) receptors.

Pharmacodynamics/Kinetics

Half-life Elimination Cariprazine: 2 to 4 days; DDCAR: 1 to 3 weeks

Time to Peak Plasma: Cariprazine: 3 to 6 hours

Pregnancy Considerations Antipsychotic use during the third trimester of pregnancy has a risk for abnormal muscle movements (extrapyramidal symptoms [EPS]) and/or withdrawal symptoms in newborns following delivery. Symptoms in the newborn may include agitation, feeding disorder, hypertonia, hypotonia, respiratory distress, somnolence, and tremor; these effects may be self-limiting or require hospitalization.

The ACOG recommends that therapy during pregnancy be individualized; treatment with psychiatric medications during pregnancy should incorporate the clinical expertise of the mental health clinician, obstetrician, primary health care provider, and pediatrician. Safety data related to atypical antipsychotics during pregnancy are limited and routine use is not recommended. However, if a woman is inadvertently exposed to an atypical antipsychotic while pregnant, continuing therapy may be preferable to switching to a typical antipsychotic that the fetus has not yet been exposed to; consider risk: benefit (ACOG 2008).

Health care providers are encouraged to enroll women exposed to cariprazine during pregnancy in the National Pregnancy Registry for Atypical Antipsychotics (866-961-2388 or http://www.womensmentalhealth.org/clinical-and-research-programs/pregnancyregistry/).

Carisoprodol (kar eye soe PROE dole)

Brand Names: US Soma

Pharmacologic Category Skeletal Muscle Relaxant

Use

Musculoskeletal conditions: Short-term (2 to 3 weeks) treatment of discomfort associated with acute painful musculoskeletal conditions.

Limitations of use: Carisoprodol should only be used for short periods (up to 2 or 3 weeks); adequate evidence of effectiveness for more prolonged use has not been established and acute, painful musculoskeletal conditions are generally of short duration.

Local Anesthetic/Vasoconstrictor Precautions No information available to require special precautions

Effects on Dental Treatment No significant effects or complications reported

Effects on Bleeding No information available to require special precautions

Adverse Reactions

>10%: Central nervous system: Drowsiness (13% to 17%)

1% to 10%: Central nervous system: Dizziness (7% to 8%), headache (3% to 5%)

Postmarketing and/or case reports: Abdominal cramps, agitation, allergic dermatitis, anaphylaxis, angioedema, ataxia, burning sensation of eyes, depression, drug dependence, dyspnea, epigastric pain, eosinophilia, erythema multiforme, exacerbation of asthma, fixed drug eruption, hallucination, headache, hiccups, hypersensitivity reaction, idiosyncratic reaction (symptoms may include agitation, ataxia, confusion, diplopia, disorientation, dysarthria, euphoria, extreme weakness, muscle twitching, mydriasis, temporary vision loss, and/or transient quadriplegia); insomnia, irritability, leukopenia, nausea, orthostatic hypotension, pancytopenia, paradoxical central nervous system stimulation, pruritus, psychosis, seizure, skin rash, syncope, tachycardia, transient flushing of face, tremor, urticaria, vertigo, vomiting, weakness, withdrawal syndrome (abdominal cramps, headache, insomnia, nausea, seizure)

General Dosage Range Oral: *Adolescents ≥16 years and Adults:* 250-350 mg 3 times daily and at bedtime

Mechanism of Action Precise mechanism is not yet clear, but many effects have been ascribed to its central depressant actions. In animals, carisoprodol blocks interneuronal activity and depresses polysynaptic neuron transmission in the spinal cord and reticular formation of the brain. It is also metabolized to meprobamate, which has anxiolytic and sedative effects.

Pharmacodynamics/Kinetics

Onset of Action Rapid

Duration of Action 4 to 6 hours

Half-life Elimination Carisoprodol: ~2 hours; Meprobamate: ~10 hours

Time to Peak Plasma: 1.5 to 2 hours

Pregnancy Risk Factor C

Pregnancy Considerations Adverse events have been observed in animal reproduction studies. Limited postmarketing data with meprobamate (the active metabolite) do not show a consistent association between maternal use and an increased risk for congenital malformations.

Controlled Substance C-IV

Carmustine (kar MUS teen)

Brand Names: US BiCNU; Gliadel Wafer

Brand Names: Canada BiCNU; Gliadel Wafer

Pharmacologic Category Antineoplastic Agent, Alkylating Agent; Antineoplastic Agent, Alkylating Agent (Nitrosourea)

Use

Brain tumors:

Injection: Palliative treatment of brain tumors including glioblastoma, brainstem glioma, medulloblastoma, astrocytoma, ependymoma, and metastatic brain tumors

Wafer (implant): Treatment of newly-diagnosed high-grade malignant glioma (as an adjunct to surgery and radiation); treatment of recurrent glioblastoma multiforme (as adjunct to surgery)

Hodgkin lymphoma, relapsed/refractory: Injection: Palliative treatment (secondary) of Hodgkin lymphoma (in combination with other antineoplastics) that has relapsed with or was refractory to primary therapy

Multiple myeloma: Injection: Palliative treatment of multiple myeloma (in combination with prednisone)

Non-Hodgkin lymphomas, relapsed/refractory: Injection: Palliative treatment (secondary) of non-Hodgkin lymphoma (in combination with other antineoplastics) that has relapsed with or was refractory to primary therapy

Local Anesthetic/Vasoconstrictor Precautions No information available to require special precautions

Effects on Dental Treatment Key adverse event(s) related to dental treatment: Stomatitis.

Effects on Bleeding Bone marrow suppression, notably thrombocytopenia, may contribute to bleeding. A medical consult is suggested.

Adverse Reactions

IV: Frequency not defined:

Cardiovascular: Cardiac arrhythmia (with high doses), chest pain, flushing (with rapid infusion), hypotension, tachycardia

Central nervous system: Dizziness, headache

Dermatologic: Burning sensation of skin (after skin contact), hyperpigmentation (after skin contact)

Gastrointestinal: Nausea (common; dose related), vomiting (common; dose related)

Hematologic & oncologic: Leukopenia (common; onset: 5 to 6 weeks; recovery: After 1 to 2 weeks), thrombocytopenia (common: onset: ~4 weeks; recovery: After 1 to 2 weeks), anemia, febrile neutropenia, malignant neoplasm (secondary; acute leukemia, bone marrow dysplasias)

Hepatic: Increased serum alkaline phosphatase, increased serum bilirubin, increased serum transaminases

Hypersensitivity: Hypersensitivity reaction

Infection: Infection (with high doses)

Local: Burning sensation at injection site, erythema at injection site, pain at injection site, swelling at injection site, tissue necrosis at injection site, venous thrombosis at injection site (rare)

Ophthalmic: Neuroretinitis, suffusion of the conjunctiva (with rapid infusion)

Renal: Azotemia (progressive; with long-term therapy), nephron atrophy (with long-term therapy), nephrotoxicity, renal failure (with long-term therapy)

Respiratory: Interstitial pneumonitis (with high doses), lung hypoplasia, pulmonary fibrosis (occurring up to 17 years after treatment), pulmonary infiltrates

Wafer:

>10%:

Central nervous system: Seizure (37%; new or worsening: 20%), cerebral edema (4% to 23%), depression (16%)

Dermatologic: Skin rash (5% to 12%)

Gastrointestinal: Nausea (22%), vomiting (21%), constipation (19%)

Genitourinary: Urinary tract infection (21%)

Neuromuscular & skeletal: Weakness (22%)

Miscellaneous: Wound healing impairment (14% to 16%), fever (12%)

1% to 10%:

Cardiovascular: Chest pain (5%)

Central nervous system: Intracranial hypertension (9%), cerebral hemorrhage (6%), meningitis (4%)

Gastrointestinal: Abdominal pain (8%)

Infection: Abscess (local 6%)

Neuromuscular & skeletal: Back pain (7%)

<1%, postmarketing, and/or case reports: Sepsis

General Dosage Range Dosage adjustment recommended in patients with renal impairment or who develop toxicity.

IV: *Adults:* 150 to 200 mg/m^2 every 6 to 8 weeks **or** 75 to 100 mg/m^2/day for 2 days every 6-8 weeks

Implantation: *Adults:* 8 wafers placed in the resection cavity (total dose: 61.6 mg)

Mechanism of Action Interferes with the normal function of DNA and RNA by alkylation and cross-linking the strands of DNA and RNA, and by possible protein modification; may also inhibit enzyme processes by carbamylation of amino acids in protein

Pharmacodynamics/Kinetics

Half-life Elimination IV: Biphasic: Initial: 1.4 minutes; Secondary: 22 minutes (active metabolites: Plasma half-life of 67 hours)

Pregnancy Risk Factor D

Pregnancy Considerations Adverse events have been observed in animal reproduction studies. Carmustine may cause fetal harm if administered to a pregnant woman. Women of childbearing potential should use effective contraception to avoid becoming pregnant while on treatment. May impair fertility. Advise males of potential risk of infertility and to seek fertility/family planning counseling prior to receiving carmustine wafer implants.

Carvedilol (KAR ve dil ole)

Related Information

Cardiovascular Diseases *on page 1752*

Brand Names: US Coreg; Coreg CR

Brand Names: Canada Apo-Carvedilol; Auro-Carvedilol; Dom-Carvedilol; JAMP-Carvedilol; Mylan-Carvedilol; Novo-Carvedilol; PMS-Carvedilol; RAN-Carvedilol; ratio-Carvedilol

Generic Availability (US) May be product dependent

Pharmacologic Category Antihypertensive; Beta-Blocker With Alpha-Blocking Activity

Use

Hypertension: Management of hypertension.

The 2014 guideline for the management of high blood pressure in adults (Eighth Joint National Committee [JNC 8]) recommends initiation of pharmacologic treatment to lower blood pressure for the following patients (JNC 8 [James, 2013]):

- Patients ≥60 years of age, with systolic blood pressure (SBP) ≥150 mm Hg or diastolic blood pressure (DBP) ≥90 mm Hg. Goal of therapy is SBP <150 mm Hg and DBP <90 mm Hg.
- Patients <60 years of age, with SBP ≥140 mm Hg or DBP ≥90 mm Hg. Goal of therapy is SBP <140 mm Hg and DBP <90 mm Hg.
- Patients ≥18 years of age with diabetes, with SBP ≥140 mm Hg or DBP ≥90 mm Hg. Goal of therapy is SBP <140 mm Hg and DBP <90 mm Hg.
- Patients ≥18 years of age with chronic kidney disease (CKD), with SBP ≥140 mm Hg or DBP ≥90 mm Hg. Goal of therapy is SBP <140 mm Hg and DBP <90 mm Hg.

In patients with CKD, regardless of race or diabetes status, the use of an ACE inhibitor (ACEI) or angiotensin receptor blocker (ARB) as initial therapy is recommended to improve kidney outcomes. In the general non-black population (without CKD) including those with diabetes, initial antihypertensive treatment should consist of a thiazide-type diuretic, calcium channel blocker, ACEI, or ARB. In the general black population (without CKD) including those with diabetes, initial antihypertensive treatment should consist of a thiazide-type diuretic or a calcium channel blocker **instead of** an ACEI or ARB.

Heart failure: Mild to severe chronic heart failure of ischemic or cardiomyopathic origin (usually in addition to standard therapy [eg, diuretics, ACE inhibitors]).

The ACCF/AHA 2013 heart failure guidelines recommend the use of 1 of the 3 beta blockers (ie, bisoprolol, carvedilol, or extended-release metoprolol succinate) for all patients with recent or remote history of MI or ACS and reduced ejection fraction (rEF) to reduce mortality, for all patients with rEF to prevent symptomatic HF (even if no history of MI), and for all patients with current or prior symptoms of HF with reduced ejection fraction (HFrEF), unless contraindicated, to reduce morbidity and mortality (Yancy, 2013).

Left ventricular dysfunction following myocardial infarction (MI): Left ventricular dysfunction following MI (clinically stable with LVEF ≤40%)

Local Anesthetic/Vasoconstrictor Precautions Carvedilol is a nonselective beta-blocker, but also has alpha-adrenergic blocking actions. No intrinsic sympathomimetic activity has been documented for carvedilol. Unlike other nonselective beta-blockers such as propranolol, with which epinephrine has interacted with to result in initial hypertensive episode followed by tachycardia, any interaction with carvedilol and vasoconstrictor to result in hypertensive episode would not be expected. There is no information available to require special precautions.

Effects on Dental Treatment Key adverse event(s) related to dental treatment: Patients may experience orthostatic hypotension as they stand up after treatment; especially if lying in dental chair for extended periods of time. Use caution with sudden changes in position during and after dental treatment. Periodontitis has been reported in product labeling for carvedilol; no other reports have confirmed this effect; any possible mechanism for this effect is unknown. Many nonsteroidal anti-inflammatory drugs, such as ibuprofen and indomethacin, can reduce the hypotensive effect of beta-blockers after 3 or more weeks of therapy with the NSAID. Short-term NSAID use (ie, 3 days) requires no special precautions in patients taking beta-blockers.

Effects on Bleeding No information available to require special precautions

Adverse Reactions Note: Frequency ranges include data from hypertension and heart failure trials. Higher rates of adverse reactions have generally been noted in patients with heart failure. However, the frequency of adverse effects associated with placebo is also increased in this population.

>10%:

Cardiovascular: Hypotension (9% to 20%)

Central nervous system: Dizziness (2% to 32%), fatigue (4% to 24%)

Endocrine & metabolic: Hyperglycemia (5% to 12%)

Gastrointestinal: Weight gain (10% to 12%), diarrhea (1% to 12%)

Neuromuscular & skeletal: Weakness (7% to 11%)

1% to 10%:

Cardiovascular: Bradycardia (2% to 10%), syncope (3% to 8%), peripheral edema (1% to 7%), generalized edema (5% to 6%), angina (1% to 6%), dependent edema (≤4%), AV block, cerebrovascular accident, hypertension, hyper-/hypovolemia, orthostatic hypotension, palpitation

Central nervous system: Headache (5% to 8%), depression, fever, hypoesthesia, hypotonia, insomnia, malaise, somnolence, vertigo

Endocrine & metabolic: Hypercholesterolemia (1% to 4%), hypertriglyceridemia (1%), diabetes mellitus, gout, hyperkalemia, hyperuricemia, hypoglycemia, hyponatremia

Gastrointestinal: Nausea (2% to 9%), vomiting (1% to 6%), abdominal pain, melena, periodontitis, weight loss

Genitourinary: Impotence

Hematologic: Anemia, prothrombin decreased, purpura, thrombocytopenia

Hepatic: Alkaline phosphatase increased (1% to 3%), GGT increased, transaminases increased

Neuromuscular & skeletal: Back pain (2% to 7%), arthralgia (1% to 6%), arthritis, muscle cramps, paresthesia

Ocular: Blurred vision (1% to 5%)

Renal: BUN increased (≤6%), nonprotein nitrogen increased (6%), albuminuria, creatinine increased, glycosuria, hematuria, renal insufficiency

Respiratory: Cough (5% to 8%), nasopharyngitis (4%), rales (4%), dyspnea (>3%), pulmonary edema (>3%), rhinitis (2%), nasal congestion (1%), sinus congestion (1%)

Miscellaneous: Injury (3% to 6%), allergy, flu-like syndrome, sudden death

<1%, postmarketing, and/or case reports (limited to important or life-threatening): Anaphylactoid reaction, alopecia, angioedema, aplastic anemia, amnesia, asthma, bronchospasm, bundle branch block, cholestatic jaundice, concentration decreased, diaphoresis, erythema multiforme, exfoliative dermatitis, GI hemorrhage, HDL decreased, hearing decreased, hyperbilirubinemia, hypersensitivity reaction, hypokalemia, hypokinesia, interstitial pneumonitis, leukopenia, libido decreased, migraine, myocardial ischemia, nervousness, neuralgia, nightmares, pancytopenia, paresis, peripheral ischemia, photosensitivity, pruritus, rash (erythematous, maculopapular, and psoriaform), respiratory alkalosis, seizure, Stevens-Johnson syndrome, tachycardia, tinnitus, toxic epidermal necrolysis, urinary incontinence, urticaria, xerostomia

Dosing

Adult Reduce dosage if heart rate drops to <55 beats/minute.

Hypertension: Oral:

Immediate release: 6.25 mg twice daily; if tolerated, dose should be maintained for 1 to 2 weeks, then increased to 12.5 mg twice daily. If necessary, dosage may be increased to a maximum of 25 mg twice daily after 1 to 2 weeks. Usual dosage range (ASH/ISH [Weber, 2014]): 6.25 to 25 mg twice daily.

Extended release: Initial: 20 mg once daily, if tolerated, dose should be maintained for 1 to 2 weeks then increased to 40 mg once daily if necessary; if this dose is tolerated, maintain for 1 to 2 weeks then, if necessary, increase to 80 mg once daily; maximum dose: 80 mg once daily

Heart failure: Oral: **Note:** Initiate only in stable patients or hospitalized patients after volume status has been optimized and IV diuretics, vasodilators, and inotropic agents have all been successfully discontinued. Caution should be used when initiating in patients who required inotropes during their hospital course. Increase dose gradually and monitor for congestive signs and symptoms of HF making every effort to achieve target dose shown to be effective (HFSA [Lindenfeld, 2010]; Packer, 1996; ACCF/AHA [Yancy, 2013])

Immediate release: 3.125 mg twice daily for 2 weeks; if this dose is tolerated, may increase to 6.25 mg twice daily. Double the dose every 2 weeks to the highest dose tolerated by patient. (Prior to initiating therapy, other heart failure medications should be stabilized and fluid retention minimized.)

Maximum recommended dose:

Mild-to-moderate heart failure:

<85 kg: 25 mg twice daily

>85 kg: 50 mg twice daily

Severe heart failure: 25 mg twice daily (Packer, 2001)

Extended release: Initial: 10 mg once daily for 2 weeks; if the dose is tolerated, increase dose to 20 mg, 40 mg, and 80 mg over successive intervals of at least 2 weeks. Maintain on lower dose if higher dose is not tolerated. **Note:** The 2013 ACCF/AHA heart failure guidelines recommend a maximum dose of 80 mg once daily (Yancy, 2013).

Left ventricular dysfunction following MI: Oral: **Note:** Should be initiated only after patient is hemodynamically stable and fluid retention has been minimized.

Immediate release: Initial 3.125 to 6.25 mg twice daily; increase dosage incrementally (ie, from 6.25 to 12.5 mg twice daily) at intervals of 3 to 10 days, based on tolerance, to a target dose of 25 mg twice daily. **Note:** The 2013 ACCF/AHA heart failure guidelines recommend a maximum dose of 50 mg twice daily (Yancy, 2013].

Extended release: Initial: Extended release: Initial: 10 to 20 mg once daily; increase dosage incrementally at intervals of 3 to 10 days, based on tolerance, to a target dose of 80 mg once daily.

Angina pectoris (off-label use): Oral: *Immediate release:* 25 to 50 mg twice daily

Atrial fibrillation (rate control) (off-label use): Usual maintenance dose: 3.125 to 25 mg twice daily (AHA/ACC/HRS [January, 2014]). In patients with heart failure, the initial dose of 3.125 mg twice daily may be increased at 2-week intervals to a target dose of 25 mg twice daily (50 mg twice daily for patients weighing >85 kg) (Khand, 2003)

Gastroesophageal varices (off- label use): Oral: Initial: 6.25 mg **once** daily; may increase after 1 week to 12.5 mg **once** daily if heart rate ≥55 bpm (LaBrecque 2014; Tripathi 2009). Increasing doses beyond 12.5 mg daily increases unwanted adverse effects without additional benefit (Reiberger 2012).

Conversion from immediate release to extended release (Coreg CR):

Current dose immediate release tablets 3.125 mg twice daily: Convert to extended release capsules 10 mg once daily

Current dose immediate release tablets 6.25 mg twice daily: Convert to extended release capsules 20 mg once daily

Current dose immediate release tablets 12.5 mg twice daily: Convert to extended release capsules 40 mg once daily

Current dose immediate release tablets 25 mg twice daily: Convert to extended release capsules 80 mg once daily

Geriatric Refer to adult dosing. In the management of hypertension, consider lower initial doses and titrate to response (Aronow, 2011).

Renal Impairment No dosage adjustment necessary; not significantly cleared by hemodialysis

Hepatic Impairment

Mild to moderate impairment: There are no dosage adjustments provided in the manufacturer's labeling.

Severe impairment: Use is contraindicated.

Mechanism of Action As a racemic mixture, carvedilol has nonselective beta-adrenoreceptor and alpha-adrenergic blocking activity. No intrinsic sympathomimetic activity has been documented. Associated effects in hypertensive patients include reduction of cardiac output, exercise- or beta-agonist-induced tachycardia, reduction of reflex orthostatic tachycardia, vasodilation, decreased peripheral vascular resistance (especially in standing position), decreased renal vascular resistance, reduced plasma renin activity, and increased levels of atrial natriuretic peptide. In CHF, associated effects include decreased pulmonary capillary wedge pressure, decreased pulmonary artery pressure, decreased heart rate, decreased systemic vascular resistance, increased stroke volume index, and decreased right atrial pressure (RAP).

Contraindications

Serious hypersensitivity to carvedilol or any component of the formulation; decompensated cardiac failure requiring intravenous inotropic therapy; bronchial asthma or related bronchospastic conditions; second- or third-degree AV block, sick sinus syndrome, and severe bradycardia (except in patients with a functioning artificial pacemaker); cardiogenic shock; severe hepatic impairment

Documentation of allergenic cross-reactivity for drugs alpha/beta adrenergic blocking agents is limited. However, because of similarities in chemical structure and/or pharmacologic actions, the possibility of cross-sensitivity cannot be ruled out with certainty.

Warnings/Precautions Heart failure patients may experience a worsening of renal function (rare); risk factors include ischemic heart disease, diffuse vascular disease, underlying renal dysfunction, and/or systolic BP <100 mm Hg. Initiate cautiously and monitor for possible deterioration in patient status (eg, symptoms of HF). Worsening heart failure or fluid retention may occur during upward titration; dose reduction or temporary discontinuation may be necessary. Adjustment of other medications (ACE inhibitors and/or diuretics) may also be required. Bradycardia may occur; reduce dosage if heart rate drops to <55 beats/minute. Bradycardia may be observed more frequently in elderly patients (>65 years of age); dosage reductions may be necessary.

Symptomatic hypotension with or without syncope may occur with carvedilol (usually within the first 30 days of therapy); close monitoring of patient is required especially with initial dosing and dosing increases; blood pressure must be lowered at a rate appropriate for the patient's clinical condition. Initiation with a low dose, gradual up-titration, and administration with food may help to decrease the occurrence of hypotension or syncope. Advise patients to avoid driving or other hazardous tasks during initiation of therapy due to the risk of syncope. Beta-blocker therapy should not be withdrawn abruptly (particularly in patients with CAD), but gradually tapered to avoid acute tachycardia, hypertension, and/or ischemia. Chronic beta-blocker therapy should not be routinely withdrawn prior to major surgery.

In general, patients with bronchospastic disease should not receive beta-blockers; if used at all, should be used cautiously with close monitoring. May precipitate or aggravate symptoms of arterial insufficiency in patients with PVD; use with caution and monitor for progression of arterial obstruction. Use with caution in patients with diabetes; may potentiate hypoglycemia and/or mask signs and symptoms (eg, sweating, anxiety, tachycardia). In patients with heart failure and diabetes, use of carvedilol may worsen hyperglycemia; may require adjustment of antidiabetic agents. May mask signs of hyperthyroidism (eg, tachycardia); if hyperthyroidism is suspected, carefully manage and monitor; abrupt withdrawal may exacerbate symptoms of hyperthyroidism or precipitate thyroid storm. May induce or exacerbate psoriasis. Use with caution in patients suspected of having Prinzmetal variant angina. Use with caution in patients with myasthenia gravis. Use with caution in patients with mild to moderate hepatic impairment; use is contraindicated in patients with severe impairment. Use with caution in patients with pheochromocytoma; adequate alpha-blockade is required prior to use. Use caution with history of severe anaphylaxis to allergens; patients taking beta-blockers may become more sensitive to repeated challenges. Treatment of anaphylaxis (eg, epinephrine) in patients taking beta-blockers may be ineffective or promote undesirable effects.

Intraoperative floppy iris syndrome has been observed in cataract surgery patients who were on or were previously treated with alpha$_1$-blockers; there appears to be no benefit in discontinuing alpha blocker therapy prior to surgery. Instruct patients to inform ophthalmologist of carvedilol use when considering eye surgery. Potentially significant interactions may exist, requiring dose or frequency adjustment, additional monitoring, and/or selection of alternative therapy.

Some dosage forms may contain polysorbate 80 (also known as Tweens). Hypersensitivity reactions, usually a delayed reaction, have been reported following exposure to pharmaceutical products containing polysorbate 80 in certain individuals (Isaksson, 2002; Lucente 2000; Shelley, 1995). Thrombocytopenia, ascites, pulmonary deterioration, and renal and hepatic failure have been reported in premature neonates after receiving parenteral products containing polysorbate 80 (Alade, 1986; CDC, 1984). See manufacturer's labeling.

Drug Interactions

Metabolism/Transport Effects Substrate of CYP1A2 (minor), CYP2C9 (minor), CYP2D6 (major), CYP2E1 (minor), CYP3A4 (minor), P-glycoprotein; **Note:** Assignment of Major/Minor substrate status based on clinically relevant drug interaction potential; **Inhibits** P-glycoprotein

Avoid Concomitant Use

Avoid concomitant use of Carvedilol with any of the following: Beta2-Agonists; Ceritinib; Floctafenine; Methacholine; PAZOPanib; Rivastigmine; Silodosin; Topotecan; VinCRIStine (Liposomal)

Increased Effect/Toxicity

Carvedilol may increase the levels/effects of: Afatinib; Alpha-/Beta-Agonists (Direct-Acting); Alpha1-Blockers; Alpha2-Agonists; Amifostine; Antipsychotic Agents (Phenothiazines); Antipsychotic Agents (Second Generation [Atypical]); Bilastine; Bradycardia-Causing Agents; Brentuximab Vedotin; Bupivacaine; Cardiac Glycosides; Ceritinib; Cholinergic Agonists; Colchicine; CycloSPORINE (Systemic); Dabigatran Etexilate; Digoxin; Disopyramide; DOXOrubicin (Conventional); DULoxetine; Edoxaban; Ergot Derivatives; Everolimus; Fingolimod; Grass Pollen Allergen Extract (5 Grass Extract); Hypotension-Associated Agents; Insulin; Ivabradine; Lacosamide; Levodopa; Lidocaine (Systemic); Lidocaine (Topical); Mepivacaine; Methacholine; Midodrine; Naldemedine; Naloxegol; Nitroprusside; PAZOPanib; Perhexiline; P-glycoprotein/ABCB1 Substrates; Prucalopride; Ranolazine; RifAXIMin; Silodosin; Sulfonylureas; Topotecan; Venetoclax; VinCRIStine (Liposomal)

The levels/effects of Carvedilol may be increased by: Abiraterone Acetate; Acetylcholinesterase Inhibitors; Ajmaline; Alfuzosin; Alpha2-Agonists; Aminoquinolines (Antimalarial); Amiodarone; Anilidopiperidine Opioids; Antipsychotic Agents (Phenothiazines); Asunaprevir; Barbiturates; Benperidol; Bretylium; Brimonidine (Topical); Calcium Channel Blockers (Nondihydropyridine); Cimetidine; Cobicistat; CYP2C9 Inhibitors (Moderate); CYP2C9 Inhibitors (Strong); CYP2D6 Inhibitors (Moderate); CYP2D6 Inhibitors (Strong); Darunavir; Diazoxide; Digoxin; Dipyridamole; Disopyramide; Dronedarone; Floctafenine; Herbs (Hypotensive Properties); Imatinib; Lormetazepam; Lumacaftor; Lumefantrine; Methoxyflurane; Molsidomine; Naftopidil; NiCARdipine; Nicergoline; Nicorandil; NIFEdipine; Obinutuzumab; Panobinostat; Peginterferon Alfa-2b; Pentoxifylline; Perhexiline; P-glycoprotein/ABCB1 Inhibitors; Phosphodiesterase 5 Inhibitors; Propafenone; Prostacyclin Analogues; Quinagolide; QuiNINE; Ranolazine; Regorafenib; Reserpine; Rivastigmine; Ruxolitinib; Selective Serotonin Reuptake Inhibitors; Tofacitinib

Decreased Effect

Carvedilol may decrease the levels/effects of: Beta2-Agonists; Theophylline Derivatives

The levels/effects of Carvedilol may be decreased by: Amphetamines; Barbiturates; Herbs (Hypertensive Properties); Lumacaftor; Methylphenidate; Nonsteroidal Anti-Inflammatory Agents; Peginterferon Alfa-2b; P-glycoprotein/ABCB1 Inducers; Rifamycin Derivatives; Yohimbine

Food Interactions Food decreases rate but not extent of absorption. Management: Administration with food minimizes risks of orthostatic hypotension.

Dietary Considerations Should be taken with food to minimize the risk of orthostatic hypotension.

Pharmacodynamics/Kinetics

Onset of Action Antihypertensive effect: Alpha-blockade: Within 30 minutes; Beta-blockade: Within 1 hour. Peak antihypertensive effect: ~1 to 2 hours

Half-life Elimination

Infants and Children 6 weeks to 3.5 years (n=8): 2.2 hours (Laer 2002)

Children and Adolescents 5.5 to 19 years (n=7): 3.6 hours (Laer 2002)

Adults 7 to 10 hours; some have reported lower values: Adults 24 to 37 years (n=9): 5.2 hours (Laer 2002)

R(+)-carvedilol: 5 to 9 hours

S(-)-carvedilol: 7 to 11 hours

Time to Peak Extended release: ~5 hours

Pregnancy Risk Factor C

Pregnancy Considerations Adverse events have been observed in animal reproduction studies. Adverse events, such as fetal/neonatal bradycardia, hypoglycemia, and reduced birth weight, have been observed following in utero exposure to beta-blockers as a class. Adequate facilities for monitoring infants at birth is generally recommended.

Untreated chronic maternal hypertension and preeclampsia are also associated with adverse events in the fetus, infant, and mother (ACOG 2015; Magee 2014). Although beta-blockers may be used when treatment of hypertension or heart failure in pregnancy is indicated, agents other than carvedilol are preferred (ACOG 2013; ESC [Regitz-Zagrosek 2011]; Magee 2014).

Breastfeeding Considerations It is not known if carvedilol is excreted in breast milk. Due to the potential for serious adverse reactions in the nursing infant (including bradycardia), the manufacturer recommends a decision be made whether to discontinue nursing or to discontinue the drug, taking into account the importance of treatment to the mother. breastfeeding is not recommended for women with heart failure related to peripartum cardiomyopathy due to the high metabolic demands of lactation and breastfeeding (ESC [Regitz-Zagrosek 2011]; Sliwa 2010).

Dosage Forms

Capsule Extended Release 24 Hour, Oral:
Coreg CR: 10 mg, 20 mg, 40 mg, 80 mg

Tablet, Oral:
Coreg: 3.125 mg, 6.25 mg, 12.5 mg, 25 mg
Generic: 3.125 mg, 6.25 mg, 12.5 mg, 25 mg

Dosage Forms: Canada Note: Refer to Dosage Forms. Extended-release capsules are not available in Canada.

Caspofungin (kas poe FUN jin)

Related Information
Fungal Infections *on page 1847*

Brand Names: US Cancidas

Brand Names: Canada Cancidas

Pharmacologic Category Antifungal Agent, Parenteral; Echinocandin

Use

Aspergillosis, invasive: Treatment of invasive aspergillosis in patients 3 months and older who are refractory to or intolerant of other therapies (eg, amphotericin B, lipid formulations of amphotericin B, itraconazole).

Candidemia and other *Candida* infections: Treatment of candidemia and the following *Candida* infections in patients 3 months and older: intra-abdominal abscesses, peritonitis, and pleural space infections.

Candidiasis, esophageal: Treatment of esophageal candidiasis in patents 3 months and older.

Fungal infections, empiric therapy (neutropenic patients): Empiric therapy for presumed fungal infections in febrile, neutropenic patients 3 months and older.

Local Anesthetic/Vasoconstrictor Precautions No information available to require special precautions

Effects on Dental Treatment No significant effects or complications reported

Effects on Bleeding No information available to require special precautions

Adverse Reactions

>10%:

Cardiovascular: Hypotension (adults: 3% to 20%; infants, children, and adolescents: 9%), peripheral edema (adults: 6% to 11%), tachycardia (7% to 11%)

Central nervous system: Chills (adults: 9% to 23%; infants, children, and adolescents: 13%), headache (9% to 15%)

Dermatologic: Skin rash (4% to 23%)

Gastrointestinal: Diarrhea (adults: 6% to 27%; infants, children, and adolescents: 7%), vomiting (6% to 17%), nausea (adults: 5% to 15%; infants, children, and adolescents: 4%)

Hematologic & oncologic: Decreased hemoglobin (adults: 18% to 21%), decreased hematocrit (adults: 13% to 18%), decreased white blood cell count (adults: 12%), anemia (adults: 11%)

Hepatic: Increased serum alkaline phosphatase (adults: 9% to 22%), increased serum ALT (adults: 4% to 18%; infants, children, and adolescents: 5%), increased serum AST (adults: 6% to 16%; infants, children, and adolescents: 2%), increased serum bilirubin (adults: 5% to 13%)

Local: Localized phlebitis (adults: 18%)

Renal: Increased serum creatinine (adults: 3% to 11%)

Respiratory: Respiratory failure (adults: 2% to 20%), cough (adults: 6% to 11%), pneumonia (adults: 4% to 11%)

Miscellaneous: Infusion related reaction (20% to 35%), fever (6% to 30%), septic shock (adults: 11% to 14%)

1% to 10%:

Cardiovascular: Hypertension (5% to 9%), atrial fibrillation (<5%), bradycardia (<5%), cardiac arrhythmia (<5%), edema (<5%), flushing (<5%), myocardial infarction (<5%)

Central nervous system: Anxiety (<5%), confusion (<5%), depression (<5%), dizziness (<5%), drowsiness (<5%), fatigue (<5%), insomnia (<5%), seizure (<5%)

Dermatologic: Erythema (5% to 9%), pruritus (infants, children, and adolescents: 6%), skin lesion (<5%), urticaria (<5%), decubitus ulcer (adults: 3% to 5%)

Endocrine & metabolic: Hypomagnesemia (adults: 7%), hyperglycemia (adults: 6%), hypokalemia (5% to 6%), hypercalcemia (<5%), hypervolemia (<5%)

Gastrointestinal: Abdominal pain (4% to 9%), mucosal inflammation (4% to 6%), abdominal distention (<5%), anorexia (<5%), constipation (<5%), decreased appetite (<5%), dyspepsia (<5%), upper abdominal pain (<5%)

Genitourinary: Urinary tract infection (<5%), nephrotoxicity (adults: 3%; serum creatinine ≥2 x baseline value or ≥1 mg/dL in patients with serum creatinine above ULN range)

Hematologic & oncologic: Blood coagulation disorder (<5%), febrile neutropenia (<5%), neutropenia (<5%), petechia (<5%), thrombocytopenia (<5%)

Hepatic: Decreased serum albumin (adults: 7%), hepatic failure (<5%), hepatomegaly (<5%), hepatotoxicity (<5%), hyperbilirubinemia (<5%), jaundice (<5%)

Infection: Sepsis (adults: 5% to 7%), bacteremia (<5%)

Local: Catheter infection (infants, children, and adolescents: 9%), infusion site reaction (<5%; pain/pruritus/swelling)

Neuromuscular & skeletal: Arthralgia (<5%), back pain (<5%), limb pain (<5%), tremor (<5%), weakness (<5%)

Renal: Hematuria (adults: 10%), increased blood urea nitrogen (adults: 4% to 9%), renal failure (<5%)

Respiratory: Dyspnea (adults: 9%), pleural effusion (adults: 9%), respiratory distress (adults: ≤8%), rales (adults: 7%), epistaxis (<5%), hypoxia (<5%), tachypnea (<5%)

<1%, postmarketing, and/or case reports: Anaphylaxis, erythema multiforme, exfoliation of skin, hepatic necrosis, hepatitis, histamine release (including facial

swelling, bronchospasm, sensation of warmth), increased gamma-glutamyl transferase, pancreatitis, renal insufficiency, Stevens-Johnson syndrome, swelling, toxic epidermal necrolysis

General Dosage Range Dosage adjustment recommended in patients with hepatic impairment or on concomitant therapy

IV:

Infants ≥3 months, Children, and Adolescents ≤17 years: 70 mg/m² on day 1, subsequent dosing: 50 to 70 mg/m² once daily (maximum daily dose, loading or maintenance: 70 mg daily)

Adults: Initial: 50 to 70 mg on day 1; subsequent dose: 50 to 70 mg once daily

Mechanism of Action Inhibits synthesis of β(1,3)-D-glucan, an essential component of the cell wall of susceptible fungi. Highest activity is in regions of active cell growth. Mammalian cells do not require β(1,3)-D-glucan, limiting potential toxicity.

Pharmacodynamics/Kinetics

Half-life Elimination Beta (distribution): 9 to 11 hours (~8 hours in children <12 years); Terminal: 40 to 50 hours; beta phase half-life is 32% to 43% lower in pediatric patients than in adult patients

Pregnancy Risk Factor C

Pregnancy Considerations Adverse events have been observed in animal reproduction studies. When treatment of invasive *Aspergillus* or *Candida* infections is needed during pregnancy, other agents are preferred (DHHS [adult] 2014; IDSA [Pappas 2016]). Use may be considered in HIV-infected pregnant women with invasive *Aspergillus* or *Candida* infections when refractory to other agents (DHHS [adult] 2014)

Cefaclor (SEF a klor)

Related Information

Antibiotic Prophylaxis *on page 1812*
Bacterial Infections *on page 1835*

Brand Names: Canada Apo-Cefaclor; Ceclor; Novo-Cefaclor; Nu-Cefaclor; PMS-Cefaclor

Generic Availability (US) Yes

Pharmacologic Category Antibiotic, Cephalosporin (Second Generation)

Dental Use Alternative antibiotic for treatment of orofacial infections in patients allergic to penicillins; susceptible bacteria including aerobic gram-positive bacteria and anaerobes

Use

Acute bacterial exacerbations of chronic bronchitis (extended-release tablets only): Treatment of acute bacterial exacerbations of chronic bronchitis due to *Haemophilus influenzae* (excluding beta-lactamase-negative, ampicillin-resistant strains only), *Moraxella catarrhalis*, or *Streptococcus pneumoniae*.

Lower respiratory tract infections (capsules and oral suspension only): Treatment of lower respiratory tract infections, including pneumonia, caused by *S. pneumoniae*, *H. influenzae*, and *Streptococcus pyogenes*.

Otitis media (capsules and oral suspension only): Treatment of otitis media caused by *S. pneumoniae*, *H. influenzae*, staphylococci, and *S. pyogenes*.

Pharyngitis and tonsillitis: Treatment of pharyngitis and tonsillitis due to *S. pyogenes*.

Secondary bacterial infections of acute bronchitis (extended-release tablets only): Treatment of secondary bacterial infections of acute bronchitis due to *H. influenzae* (excluding beta-lactamase negative, ampicillin-resistant strains), *M. catarrhalis*, or *S. pneumoniae*.

Skin and skin structure infections, uncomplicated: Treatment of uncomplicated skin and skin structure infections due to *Staphylococcus aureus* (methicillin-susceptible) or *S. pyogenes* (capsules and oral suspension only).

Urinary tract infections (capsules and oral suspension only): Treatment of urinary tract infections, including pyelonephritis and cystitis, caused by *Escherichia coli*, *Proteus mirabilis*, *Klebsiella* spp, and coagulase-negative staphylococci.

Local Anesthetic/Vasoconstrictor Precautions No information available to require special precautions

Effects on Dental Treatment No significant effects or complications reported (see Dental Comment)

Effects on Bleeding No information available to require special precautions

Adverse Reactions

1% to 10%:

Dermatologic: Rash (1% to 2%; includes erythematous rash, maculopapular rash, or morbilliform rash)

Gastrointestinal: Diarrhea (3%)

Genitourinary: Vaginitis (2%), vulvovaginal candidiasis (2%)

Hematologic & oncologic: Eosinophilia (2%)

Hepatic: Increased serum transaminases (3%)

<1%, postmarketing, and/or case reports: Agitation, agranulocytosis, anaphylaxis, angioedema, aplastic anemia, arthralgia, cholestatic jaundice, confusion, dizziness, drowsiness, hallucination, hemolytic anemia, hepatitis, hyperactivity, insomnia, interstitial nephritis, irritability, nausea, nervousness, neutropenia, paresthesia, prolonged prothrombin time, pruritus, pseudomembranous colitis, seizure, serum sickness, Stevens-Johnson syndrome, thrombocytopenia, toxic epidermal necrolysis, urticaria, vomiting

Dental Usual Dosage Orofacial infections: Adults: Oral: Dosing range: 250-500 mg every 8 hours

Dosing

Adult & Geriatric

Treatment of susceptible infections: Oral:

Immediate-release: 250 to 500 mg every 8 hours

Extended-release: 500 mg every 12 hours

Indication-specific dosing: Note: An extended-release tablet dose of 500 mg twice daily is clinically equivalent to an immediate-release capsule dose of 250 mg 3 times daily; an extended-release tablet dose of 500 mg twice daily is **NOT** clinically equivalent to 500 mg 3 times daily of other cefaclor formulations.

Acute bacterial exacerbations of chronic bronchitis: Oral: Extended-release: 500 mg every 12 hours for 7 days

Secondary bacterial infection of acute bronchitis: Oral: Extended-release: 500 mg every 12 hours for 7 days

Pediatric

Treatment of susceptible infections: Usual dosage range:

Infants ≥1 month, Children, and Adolescents: Oral: Immediate-release: 20 to 40 mg/kg/day divided every 8 to 12 hours; maximum dose: 1,000 mg/day

Adolescents ≥16 years: Oral: Extended-release: 500 mg every 12 hours

Indication-specific dosing:

Infants >1 month, Children, and Adolescents:

Lower respiratory tract infections: Oral: Immediate-release: 20 to 40 mg/kg/day divided every 8 hours (maximum dose: 1,000 mg/day). If beta-hemolytic streptococcus/*S. pyogenes* suspected, treat for at least 10 days.

Otitis media: Oral: Immediate-release: 40 mg/kg/day divided every 12 hours (maximum dose: 1,000 mg/day). If beta-hemolytic streptococcus/S. pyogenes suspected, treat for at least 10 days.

Pharyngitis/tonsillitis: Oral: Immediate-release: 20 mg/kg/day divided every 12 hours (maximum dose: 1,000 mg/day). If beta-hemolytic streptococcus/*S. pyogenes* confirmed, treat for at least 10 days. **Note:** Not a preferred drug (Shulman 2012).

Skin and skin structure infections, uncomplicated: Oral: Immediate-release: 20 to 40 mg/kg/day divided every 8 hours (maximum dose: 1,000 mg/day). If due to beta-hemolytic streptococcus/*S. pyogenes*, treat for at least 10 days.

Urinary tract infections: Oral: Immediate-release: 20 to 40 mg/kg/day divided every 8 hours (maximum dose: 1,000 mg/day).

Adolescents ≥16 years: **Note:** An extended-release tablet dose of 500 mg twice daily is clinically equivalent to an immediate-release capsule dose of 250 mg 3 times daily; an extended-release tablet dose of 500 mg twice daily is **NOT** clinically equivalent to 500 mg 3 times daily of other cefaclor formulations.

Acute bacterial exacerbations of chronic bronchitis: Oral: Extended-release: 500 mg every 12 hours for 7 days

Secondary bacterial infection of acute bronchitis: Oral: Extended-release: 500 mg every 12 hours for 7 days

Renal Impairment

Manufacturer's labeling:

Oral, immediate-release: There are no dosage adjustments provided in the manufacturer's labeling; however, half-life is increased in anuric patients; use with caution.

Oral, extended-release: There are no dosage adjustments provided in the manufacturer's labeling.

Dialysis: Moderately dialyzable (20% to 50%)

Alternative recommendations (off-label dosing) (Aronoff 2007):

Adults: Oral, immediate-release:

Mild to severe impairment: No dosage adjustment necessary.

End-stage renal disease (ESRD) on intermittent hemodialysis (IHD) (administer after hemodialysis on dialysis days): Supplement with 250 to 500 mg after dialysis.

Peritoneal dialysis: Administer 250 to 500 mg every 8 hours.

Infants, Children and Adolescents: Oral, immediate-release:

GFR ≥10 mL/minute: No dosage adjustment necessary.

GFR <10 mL/minute: Administer 50% of the recommended dose (based on indication)

End-stage renal disease (ERD) on intermittent hemodialysis (IHD) (supplemental dose post-hemodialysis needed): Administer 50% of the recommended dose (based on indication).

Peritoneal dialysis: Administer 50% of the recommended dose (based on indication).

Hepatic Impairment There are no dosage adjustments provided in the manufacturer's labeling.

Mechanism of Action Inhibits bacterial cell wall synthesis by binding to one or more of the penicillin-binding proteins (PBPs), which in turn inhibits the final transpeptidation step of peptidoglycan synthesis in bacterial cell walls, thus inhibiting cell wall biosynthesis. Bacteria eventually lyse due to ongoing activity of cell wall autolytic enzymes (autolysins and murein hydrolases) while cell wall assembly is arrested.

Contraindications Hypersensitivity to cefaclor, any component of the formulation, or other cephalosporins

Warnings/Precautions Anaphylactic reactions have occurred. If a serious hypersensitivity reaction occurs, discontinue and institute emergency supportive measures, including airway management and treatment (eg, epinephrine, antihistamines and/or corticosteroids). Use with caution in patients with a history of gastrointestinal disease, particularly colitis. Use with caution in patients with renal impairment. Prolonged use may result in fungal or bacterial superinfection, including *C. difficile*-associated diarrhea (CDAD) and pseudomembranous colitis; CDAD has been observed >2 months postantibiotic treatment. Use with caution in patients with a history of penicillin allergy. An extended-release tablet dose of 500 mg twice daily is clinically equivalent to an immediate-release capsule dose of 250 mg 3 times daily; an extended-release tablet dose of 500 mg twice daily is **NOT** clinically equivalent to 500 mg 3 times daily of other cefaclor formulations. Potentially significant interactions may exist, requiring dose or frequency adjustment, additional monitoring, and/or selection of alternative therapy.

Benzyl alcohol and derivatives: Some dosage forms may contain sodium benzoate/benzoic acid; benzoic acid (benzoate) is a metabolite of benzyl alcohol; large amounts of benzyl alcohol (≥99 mg/kg/day) have been associated with a potentially fatal toxicity ("gasping syndrome") in neonates; the "gasping syndrome" consists of metabolic acidosis, respiratory distress, gasping respirations, CNS dysfunction (including convulsions, intracranial hemorrhage), hypotension, and cardiovascular collapse (AAP ["Inactive" 1997]; CDC, 1982); some data suggests that benzoate displaces bilirubin from protein binding sites (Ahlfors, 2001); avoid or use dosage forms containing benzyl alcohol derivative with caution in neonates. See manufacturer's labeling.

Drug Interactions

Metabolism/Transport Effects Substrate of OAT3

Avoid Concomitant Use

Avoid concomitant use of Cefaclor with any of the following: BCG (Intravesical); Cholera Vaccine

Increased Effect/Toxicity

Cefaclor may increase the levels/effects of: Aminoglycosides; Vitamin K Antagonists

The levels/effects of Cefaclor may be increased by: Probenecid; Teriflunomide

Decreased Effect

Cefaclor may decrease the levels/effects of: BCG (Intravesical); BCG Vaccine (Immunization); Cholera Vaccine; Lactobacillus and Estriol; Sodium Picosulfate; Typhoid Vaccine

Food Interactions The bioavailability of cefaclor extended-release tablets is decreased 23% and the maximum concentration is decreased 67% when taken on an empty stomach. Management: Administer with food.

Dietary Considerations Extended release tablets should be taken with or within 1 hour of food.

Pharmacodynamics/Kinetics

Half-life Elimination 0.6 to 0.9 hours; prolonged with renal impairment (2.3 to 2.8 hours in anuria)

Time to Peak Capsules, oral suspension: 30 to 60 minutes; Extended-release tablets: 2.5 hours

Pregnancy Risk Factor B

Pregnancy Considerations Adverse events were not observed in animal reproduction studies. An increased risk of teratogenic effects has not been observed following maternal use of cefaclor.

Breastfeeding Considerations Small amounts of cefaclor are excreted in breast milk. The manufacturer recommends that caution be exercised when administering cefaclor to nursing women. Nondose-related effects could include modification of bowel flora.

Dosage Forms

Capsule, Oral:
Generic: 250 mg, 500 mg

Suspension Reconstituted, Oral:
Generic: 125 mg/5 mL (150 mL); 250 mg/5 mL (150 mL); 375 mg/5 mL (100 mL)

Tablet Extended Release 12 Hour, Oral:
Generic: 500 mg

Dental Comment Cefaclor is effective against anaerobic bacteria, but the sensitivity of alpha-hemolytic Streptococcus vary; approximately 10% of strains are resistant. Nearly 70% are intermediately sensitive. Patients allergic to penicillins can use a cephalosporin; the incidence of cross-reactivity between penicillins and cephalosporins is 1% to 5% when the allergic reaction to penicillin is delayed. If the patient has a history of anaphylaxis to penicillin, cephalosporins are contraindicated in these patients.

Cefadroxil (sef a DROKS il)

Related Information

Antibiotic Prophylaxis *on page 1812*
Bacterial Infections *on page 1835*

Brand Names: Canada Apo-Cefadroxil; PRO-Cefadroxil; Teva-Cefadroxil

Generic Availability (US) Yes

Pharmacologic Category Antibiotic, Cephalosporin (First Generation)

Dental Use Alternative antibiotic for treatment of orofacial infections in patients allergic to penicillins; susceptible bacteria including aerobic gram-positive bacteria and anaerobes

Use

Pharyngitis and/or tonsillitis: Treatment of pharyngitis and/or tonsillitis caused by *Streptococcus pyogenes* (group A beta-hemolytic streptococci).

Skin and skin structure infections: Treatment of skin and skin structure infections caused by staphylococci and/or streptococci.

Urinary tract infection: Treatment of urinary tract infections caused by *Escherichia coli*, *Proteus mirabilis*, and *Klebsiella* species.

Local Anesthetic/Vasoconstrictor Precautions No information available to require special precautions

Effects on Dental Treatment No significant effects or complications reported

Effects on Bleeding No information available to require special precautions

Adverse Reactions

1% to 10%: Gastrointestinal: Diarrhea

<1%: postmarketing, and/or case reports: Abdominal pain, agranulocytosis, anaphylaxis, angioedema, arthralgia, cholestasis, *Clostridium difficile* associated diarrhea, dyspepsia, erythema multiforme, erythematous rash, fever, genital candidiasis, hepatic failure, increased serum transaminases, maculopapular rash, nausea, neutropenia, pruritus, pseudomembranous colitis, serum sickness, Stevens-Johnson syndrome, thrombocytopenia, urticaria, vaginitis, vomiting

Dental Usual Dosage Orofacial infections: Oral: Adults: Dosage range: 250-500 mg every 8 hours

Dosing

Adult & Geriatric

Pharyngitis: Oral:

Manufacturer's labeling: 1 g/day in a single or 2 divided doses for 10 days

Alternate dosing: 30 mg/kg/dose once daily (maximum: 1 g daily) for 10 days (Shulman 2012). **Note:** Recommended as an alternative agent in penicillin-allergic patients; however, avoid in patients with immediate type hypersensitivity to penicillin.

Prosthetic joint infection, staphylococci (oxacillin-susceptible), chronic oral antimicrobial suppression (off-label use): 500 mg every 12 hours (Osmon 2013)

Skin and skin structure infections: Oral: 1 g daily in a single or 2 divided doses

Tonsillitis: Oral: 1 g daily in a single or 2 divided doses for 10 days

Urinary tract infections: Oral: 1 g twice daily. For uncomplicated cystitis: 1 or 2 g daily in a single or 2 divided doses

Pediatric

Pharyngitis: Children and Adolescents: Oral:

Manufacturer's labeling: 30 mg/kg/day in a single dose or divided every 12 hours

Alternate dosing: Refer to adult dosing

Skin and skin structure infections: Children and Adolescents: Oral: 30 mg/kg/day in divided doses every 12 hours. For impetigo: 30 mg/kg/day in a single dose or divided every 12 hours.

Tonsillitis: Children and Adolescents: Oral: 30 mg/kg/day in a single dose or divided every 12 hours

Urinary tract infections: Children and Adolescents: Oral: 30 mg/kg/day in divided doses every 12 hours

Renal Impairment

Initial: 1 g as a single dose.

Maintenance:

CrCl >50 mL/minute: No dosage adjustment necessary.
CrCl 25 to 50 mL/minute: 500 mg every 12 hours.
CrCl 10 to 25 mL/minute: 500 mg every 24 hours.
CrCl <10 mL/minute: 500 mg every 36 hours.

Hepatic Impairment There are no dosage adjustments provided in the manufacturer's labeling.

Mechanism of Action Inhibits bacterial cell wall synthesis by binding to one or more of the penicillin-binding proteins (PBPs) which in turn inhibits the final transpeptidation step of peptidoglycan synthesis in bacterial cell walls, thus inhibiting cell wall biosynthesis. Bacteria eventually lyse due to ongoing activity of cell wall autolytic enzymes (autolysins and murein hydrolases) while cell wall assembly is arrested.

Contraindications Hypersensitivity to cefadroxil, any component of the formulation, or other cephalosporins

Warnings/Precautions Use with caution in patients with renal impairment (CrCl <50 mL/minute/1.73 m^2); dosage adjustment may be needed. Hypersensitivity reactions, including anaphylaxis, may occur. If an allergic reaction occurs, discontinue treatment and institute appropriate supportive measures. Use with caution in patients with a history of penicillin allergy. Use with caution in patients with a history of gastrointestinal disease, particularly colitis. Prolonged use may result in fungal or bacterial superinfection, including *C. difficile*-associated diarrhea (CDAD) and pseudomembranous colitis; CDAD has been observed >2 months postantibiotic treatment. Only IM penicillin has been shown to be effective in the prophylaxis of rheumatic fever. Cefadroxil is generally effective in the eradication of streptococci from the oropharynx; efficacy data for cefadroxil in the prophylaxis of subsequent rheumatic fever episodes are not available. Potentially significant drug-drug interactions may exist, requiring dose or frequency adjustment, additional monitoring, and/or selection of alternative therapy.

Suspension may contain sulfur dioxide (sulfite); hypersensitivity reactions, including anaphylaxis and/or asthmatic exacerbations, may occur (may be life threatening).

Dosage form specific issues: Some dosage forms may contain sodium benzoate/benzoic acid; benzoic acid (benzoate) is a metabolite of benzyl alcohol; large amounts of benzyl alcohol (≥99 mg/kg/day) have been associated with a potentially fatal toxicity ("gasping syndrome") in neonates; the "gasping syndrome" consists of metabolic acidosis, respiratory distress, gasping respirations, CNS dysfunction (including convulsions, intracranial hemorrhage), hypotension, and cardiovascular collapse (AAP ["Inactive" 1997]; CDC 1982); some data suggests that benzoate displaces bilirubin from protein binding sites (Ahlfors, 2001); avoid or use dosage forms containing benzyl alcohol derivative with caution in neonates. Some dosage forms may contain propylene glycol; large amounts are potentially toxic and have been associated with hyperosmolality, lactic acidosis, seizures, and respiratory depression; use caution (AAP 1997; Zar 2007). See manufacturer's labeling.

Drug Interactions

Metabolism/Transport Effects None known.

Avoid Concomitant Use

Avoid concomitant use of Cefadroxil with any of the following: BCG (Intravesical); Cholera Vaccine

Increased Effect/Toxicity

Cefadroxil may increase the levels/effects of: Vitamin K Antagonists

The levels/effects of Cefadroxil may be increased by: Probenecid

Decreased Effect

Cefadroxil may decrease the levels/effects of: BCG (Intravesical); BCG Vaccine (Immunization); Cholera Vaccine; Lactobacillus and Estriol; Sodium Picosulfate; Typhoid Vaccine

Pharmacodynamics/Kinetics

Half-life Elimination 1 to 2 hours; 20 to 24 hours in renal failure

Time to Peak

Serum: Within 70 to 90 minutes

Pregnancy Risk Factor B

Pregnancy Considerations Adverse events have not been observed in animal reproduction studies. Cefadroxil crosses the placenta. Limited data is available concerning the use of cefadroxil in pregnancy; however, adverse fetal effects were not noted in a small clinical trial.

Breastfeeding Considerations Very small amounts of cefadroxil are excreted in breast milk. The manufacturer recommends that caution be exercised when administering cefadroxil to nursing women. Nondose-related effects could include modification of bowel flora.

Dosage Forms

Capsule, Oral:

Generic: 500 mg

Suspension Reconstituted, Oral:

Generic: 250 mg/5 mL (50 mL, 100 mL); 500 mg/5 mL (75 mL, 100 mL)

Tablet, Oral:

Generic: 1 g

CeFAZolin (sef A zoe lin)

Related Information

Antibiotic Prophylaxis *on page 1812*

Brand Names: Canada Cefazolin For Injection; Cefazolin For Injection, USP

Generic Availability (US) Yes

Pharmacologic Category Antibiotic, Cephalosporin (First Generation)

Dental Use Alternative antibiotic for prevention of infective endocarditis when parenteral administration is needed. Individuals allergic to amoxicillin (penicillins) may receive cefazolin provided they have not had an immediate, local, or systemic IgE-mediated anaphylactic allergic reaction to penicillin. Alternate antibiotic for premedication in patients not allergic to penicillin who may be at potential increased risk of hematogenous total joint infection when parenteral administration is needed.

Use

Biliary tract infections: Treatment of biliary tract infections due to *Escherichia coli*, various strains of streptococci, *Proteus mirabilis*, *Klebsiella* species and *Staphylococcus aureus*.

Bone and joint infections: Treatment of bone and joint infections due to *S. aureus*.

Endocarditis, treatment: Treatment of endocarditis due to *S. aureus* (penicillin-sensitive and penicillin-resistant) and group A beta-hemolytic streptococci (*S. pyogenes*).

Genital infections: Treatment of genital infections (ie, prostatitis, epididymitis) due to *E. coli*, *P. mirabilis*, and *Klebsiella* species.

Perioperative prophylaxis: To reduce the incidence of certain postoperative infections in patients undergoing surgical procedures.

Respiratory tract infections: Treatment of respiratory tract infections due to *S. pneumoniae*, *Klebsiella* species, *Haemophilus influenzae*, *S. aureus* (penicillin-sensitive and penicillin-resistant) and group A beta-hemolytic streptococci.

Septicemia: Treatment of septicemia due to *Streptococcus pneumoniae*, *S. aureus* (penicillin-sensitive and penicillin-resistant), *P. mirabilis*, *E. coli* and *Klebsiella* species.

Skin and skin structure infections: Treatment of skin and skin structure infections due to *S. aureus* (penicillin-sensitive and penicillin-resistant), group A beta-hemolytic streptococci and other strains of streptococci.

Urinary tract infections: Treatment of urinary tract infections due to *E. coli*, *P. mirabilis*, *Klebsiella* species and some strains of enterobacter.

Local Anesthetic/Vasoconstrictor Precautions No information available to require special precautions

Effects on Dental Treatment No significant effects or complications reported

Effects on Bleeding May potentiate the anticoagulant effects of vitamin K anticoagulants (ie, warfarin) due to alterations of gut flora.

Adverse Reactions Frequency not defined.

Cardiovascular: Localized phlebitis

Central nervous system: Seizure

Dermatologic: Pruritus, skin rash, Stevens-Johnson syndrome

Gastrointestinal: Abdominal cramps, anorexia, diarrhea, nausea, oral candidiasis, pseudomembranous colitis, vomiting

Genitourinary: Vaginitis

Hepatic: Hepatitis, increased serum transaminases

Hematologic: Eosinophilia, leukopenia, neutropenia, thrombocythemia, thrombocytopenia

Hypersensitivity: Anaphylaxis

Local: Pain at injection site

Renal: Increased blood urea nitrogen, increased serum creatinine, renal failure

Miscellaneous: Fever

Dental Usual Dosage

Infective endocarditis prophylaxis (off-label use): IM, IV:

Infants and Children: 50 mg/kg 30 to 60 minutes before procedure; maximum dose: 1 g

Adults: 1 g 30 to 60 minutes before procedure.

Note: Intramuscular injections should be avoided in patients who are receiving anticoagulant therapy. In these circumstances, orally administered regimens should be given whenever possible. Intravenously administered antibiotics should be used for patients who are unable to tolerate or absorb oral medications.

Note: American Heart Association (AHA) guidelines now recommend prophylaxis only in patients undergoing invasive procedures and in whom underlying cardiac conditions may predispose to a higher risk of adverse outcomes should infection occur. As of April 2007, routine prophylaxis for GI/GU procedures is no longer recommended by the AHA.

Prophylaxis in total joint replacement patient: IM, IV: Adults: 1 g 1 hour prior to the procedure

Note: In general, patients with prosthetic joint implants do not require prophylactic antibiotics prior to dental procedures. In planning an invasive oral procedure, dental consultation with the patient's orthopedic surgeon may be advised to review the risks of infection.

Dosing

Adult & Geriatric

Usual dosage range: IM, IV: 1 to 1.5 g every 8 hours, depending on severity of infection; maximum: 12 g daily

Catheter-related bloodstream infections (off-label use): IV: 2 g every 8 hours (IDSA [Mermel 2009])

Cholecystitis, mild-to-moderate: IV: 1 to 2 g every 8 hours for 4 to 7 days (provided source controlled)

Endocarditis, treatment: IV:

Manufacturer's labeling: 1 to 1.5 g every 6 hours

Alternate dosing (AHA [Baddour 2015]): MSSA in penicillin-allergic (nonanaphylactoid) patients:

Native valve: 2 g every 8 hours for 6 weeks

Prosthetic valve: 2 g every 8 hours for a minimum of 6 weeks (in combination with rifampin for entire course of therapy and gentamicin for the first 2 weeks)

Group B streptococcus (neonatal prophylaxis): IV: 2 g once, then 1 g every 8 hours until delivery (CDC 2010)

Intra-abdominal infection, complicated, community-acquired, mild-to-moderate (in combination with metronidazole): IV: 1 to 2 g every 8 hours for 4 to 7 days (provided source controlled)

Moderate to severe infections: IV: 500 mg to 1 g every 6 to 8 hours

Mild infection with gram-positive cocci: IV: 250 to 500 mg every 8 hours

Osteomyelitis, native vertebral (off-label dose): Staphylococci (oxacillin-susceptible): IV: 1 to 2 g every 8 hours for 6 weeks (IDSA [Berbari 2015])

Perioperative prophylaxis:

Manufacturer's labeling: IM, IV: 1 to 2 g initiated 30 to 60 minutes prior to surgery; may repeat after 2 hours if procedure is lengthy with 500 mg to 1 g intraoperatively, followed by 500 mg to 1 g every 6 to 8 hours for 24 hours postoperatively.

Guideline recommendations (off-label): IV: **Note:** For most surgical procedures, joint clinical practice guidelines from the American Society of Health-System Pharmacists, Infectious Diseases Society of America, Surgical Infection Society, and Society for Healthcare Epidemiology of America (ASHP/IDSA/SIS/SHEA) recommend a dose of 2 g within 60 minutes prior to surgical incision (for nonobese patients weighing <120 kg). For procedures requiring anaerobic coverage (eg, appendectomy, small bowel surgery with intestinal obstruction, colon procedures), combine cefazolin with metronidazole as an alternative to a second generation cephalosporin with anaerobic activity (eg, cefoxitin or cefotetan). Cefazolin doses may be repeated intraoperatively in 4 hours if procedure is lengthy or if there is excessive blood loss (Bratzler 2013).

Obesity: The ASHP/IDSA/SIS/SHEA guidelines recommend that for patients weighing ≥120 kg, a dose of 3 g within 60 minutes prior to surgical incision should be administered (Bratzler 2013). Alternatively, for patients with BMI >40 kg/m^2, a single 2 g dose may be sufficient for common general surgical procedures lasting <5 hours; patients enrolled in this multigroup study had a BMI up to a group mean of 55.7 kg/m^2 (Ho 2012).

Cardiothoracic surgery: IV: 1 g (see "**Note**") initiated 30 to 60 minutes prior to surgery (usually at the time of anesthetic induction); repeat dose if the duration of operation exceeds 3 hours (Hillis 2011). The ASHP/IDSA/SIS/SHEA guidelines recommend the use of 2 g (single dose) administered within 60 minutes prior to surgical incision (Bratzler 2013). May either continue for ≤48 hours postoperatively or administer as a single dose preoperatively (may be preferred due to reduced cost and potential for antimicrobial resistance) (Bratzler 2013; Bucknell 2000; Douglas 2011; Edwards 2006; Hillis 2011).

Note: For patients weighing >60 kg, the Society of Thoracic Surgeons recommends a preoperative dose of 2 g administered within 60 minutes of skin incision. If the surgical incision remains open in the operating room, follow with 1 g every 3 to 4 hours unless cardiopulmonary bypass is to be discontinued within 4 hours then delay administration (Engelman 2007).

Peritonitis, treatment (off-label route; Li 2010):

Intraperitoneal:

Intermittent exchange: 15 mg/kg per exchange every 24 hours in the long dwell (≥6 hours)

Continuous exchange: Loading dose: 500 mg per liter of dialysate. Maintenance: 125 mg per liter of dialysate.

Note: If patient has residual renal function (eg, >100 mL/day urine output), empirically increase each dose by 25%

Automated peritoneal dialysis: 20 mg/kg every 24 hours in the long day dwell; **Note:** Guidelines suggest nighttime levels of intraperitoneal cefazolin may fall below the MIC of most organisms and adding cefazolin to each exchange may be warranted

Pneumococcal pneumonia: IV: 500 mg every 12 hours

Prophylaxis against infective endocarditis (off-label use): IM, IV: 1 g 30 to 60 minutes before procedure. Intramuscular injections should be avoided in patients who are receiving anticoagulant therapy. In these circumstances, orally administered regimens should be given whenever possible. Intravenously administered antibiotics should be used for patients who are unable to tolerate or absorb oral medications.

Note: American Heart Association (AHA) guidelines now recommend prophylaxis only in patients undergoing invasive procedures and in whom underlying cardiac conditions may predispose to a higher risk of adverse outcomes should infection occur. As of April 2007, routine prophylaxis for GI/GU procedures is no longer recommended by the AHA.

Prophylaxis in total joint replacement patients undergoing dental procedures which produce bacteremia (off-label use): IM, IV: 1 g 1 hour prior to procedure (ADA/AAOS 2003). **Note:** In general, patients with prosthetic joint implants do not require prophylactic antibiotics prior to dental procedures. In planning an invasive oral procedure, dental consultation with the patient's orthopedic surgeon may be advised to review the risks of infection (Sollecito 2015).

Prosthetic joint infection, *Staphylococcal* (oxacillin-susceptible): IV: 1 to 2 g every 8 hours for 2 to 6 weeks (in combination with rifampin) followed by oral antibiotic treatment and suppressive regimens (Osmon 2013)

Severe infection: IV: 1 to 1.5 g every 6 hours

Skin and soft tissue infection due to MSSA, including pyomyositis: IV: 1 g every 8 hours for 7 to 14 days; treat pyomyositis for 14 to 21 days (IDSA [Stevens 2014])

Skin and soft tissue necrotizing infection due to MSSA (off-label use): IV: 1 g every 8 hours; continue until further debridement is not necessary, patient has clinically improved, and patient is afebrile for 48 to 72 hours (IDSA [Stevens 2014])

Streptococcal skin infections: IV: 1 g every 8 hours (IDSA [Stevens 2014])

Surgical site infection (trunk or extremity [away from axilla or perineum]) (off-label use): IV: 500 mg to 1 g every 8 hours (IDSA [Stevens 2014])

UTI (uncomplicated): IM, IV: 1 g every 12 hours

Pediatric

Usual dosage range: IM, IV: Infants >1 month, Children, and Adolescents: 25 to 100 mg/kg/day divided every 6 to 8 hours; maximum: 6 **g** daily

Community-acquired pneumonia (CAP) (IDSA/PIDS 2011), moderate-to-severe infection, *S. aureus* (methicillin-susceptible) (preferred): Infants >3 months and Children: IM, IV: 150 mg/kg/day divided every 8 hours

Perioperative prophylaxis (off-label use): Children ≥1 year: IV: **Note:** For most surgical procedures, joint clinical practice guidelines from the American Society of Health-System Pharmacists, Infectious Diseases Society of America, Surgical Infection Society, and Society for Healthcare Epidemiology of America (ASHP/IDSA/SIS/SHEA) recommend a dose of 30 mg/kg (maximum dose: 2,000 mg) administered within 60 minutes prior to surgical incision. For procedures requiring anaerobic coverage (eg, appendectomy, small bowel surgery with intestinal obstruction, colon procedures), combine cefazolin with metronidazole as an alternative to a second generation cephalosporin with anaerobic activity (eg, cefoxitin or cefotetan). Cefazolin doses may be repeated intraoperatively in 4 hours if procedure is lengthy or if there is excessive blood loss (Bratzler 2013).

Peritonitis, treatment (off-label route; Warady 2012): Infants, Children, and Adolescents: Intraperitoneal:

Intermittent exchange: 20 mg/kg every 24 hours in the long dwell

Continuous exchange: Loading dose: 500 mg per liter of dialysate. Maintenance: 125 mg per liter of dialysate.

Prophylaxis against infective endocarditis (off-label use): Infants and Children: IM, IV: 50 mg/kg 30 to 60 minutes before procedure; maximum dose: 1,000 mg. Intramuscular injections should be avoided in patients who are receiving anticoagulant therapy. In these circumstances, orally administered regimens should be given whenever possible. Intravenously administered antibiotics should be used for patients who are unable to tolerate or absorb oral medications.

Note: American Heart Association (AHA) guidelines now recommend prophylaxis only in patients undergoing invasive procedures and in whom underlying cardiac conditions may predispose to a higher risk of adverse outcomes should infection occur. As of April 2007, routine prophylaxis for GI/GU procedures is no longer recommended by the AHA.

Skin and soft tissue infection due to MSSA, including pyomyositis: Infants and Children: IV: 50 mg/kg/day divided every 8 hours for 7 to 14 days; treat pyomyositis for 14 to 21 days (IDSA [Stevens 2014])

Skin and soft tissue necrotizing infections due to MSSA (off-label use): Infants and Children: IV: 33 mg/kg every 8 hours; continue until further debridement is not necessary, patient has clinically improved, and patient is afebrile for 48 to 72 hours (IDSA [Stevens 2014])

Streptococcal skin infections: Infants and Children: IV: 33 mg/kg every 8 hours (IDSA [Stevens 2014])

Renal Impairment

Adults:

CrCl ≥55 mL/minute: No dosage adjustment necessary

CrCl 35 to 54 mL/minute: Administer full dose in intervals of ≥8 hours

CrCl 11 to 34 mL/minute: Administer 50% of usual dose every 12 hours

CrCl ≤10 mL/minute: Administer 50% of usual dose every 18 to 24 hours

Intermittent hemodialysis (IHD) (administer after hemodialysis on dialysis days): Dialyzable (20% to 50%): 500 mg to 1 g every 24 hours **or** use 1 to 2 g every 48 to 72 hours (Heintz 2009) **or** 15 to 20 mg/kg (maximum dose: 2 g) after dialysis 3 times weekly (Ahern 2003; Sowinski 2001) **or** 2 g after dialysis if next dialysis expected in 48 hours or 3 g after dialysis if next dialysis is expected in 72 hours (Stryjewski 2007).

Note: Dosing dependent on the assumption of 3 times weekly, complete IHD sessions.

Peritoneal dialysis (PD): IV: 500 mg every 12 hours

Continuous renal replacement therapy (CRRT) (Heintz 2009; Trotman 2005): Drug clearance is highly dependent on the method of renal replacement, filter type, and flow rate. Appropriate dosing requires close monitoring of pharmacologic response, signs of adverse reactions due to drug accumulation, as well as drug concentrations in relation to target trough (if appropriate). The following are general recommendations only (based on dialysate flow/ultrafiltration rates of 1 to 2 L/hour and minimal residual renal function) and should not supersede clinical judgment:

CVVH: Loading dose of 2 g followed by 1 to 2 g every 12 hours

CVVHD/CVVHDF: Loading dose of 2 g followed by either 1 g every 8 hours **or** 2 g every 12 hours. **Note:** Dosage of 1 g every 8 hours results in similar steady-state concentrations as 2 g every 12 hours and is more cost effective (Heintz 2009).

Infants >1 month, Children, and Adolescents:

CrCl >70 mL/minute: No dosage adjustment necessary.

CrCl 40 to 70 mL/minute: 60% of usual daily dose divided every 12 hours

CrCl 20 to 40 mL/minute: 25% of usual daily dose divided every 12 hours

CrCl 5 to 20 mL/minute: 10% of usual daily dose every 24 hours

Intermittent hemodialysis (IHD): 25 mg/kg per dose every 24 hours (Aronoff 2007)

Peritoneal dialysis (PD): 25 mg/kg per dose every 24 hours (Aronoff 2007)

Continuous renal replacement therapy (CRRT): 25 mg/kg per dose every 8 hours (Aronoff 2007)

Hepatic Impairment There are no dosage adjustments provided in the manufacturer's labeling.

Obesity Refer to indication-specific dosing for obesity-related information (may not be available for all indications).

Mechanism of Action Inhibits bacterial cell wall synthesis by binding to one or more of the penicillin-binding proteins (PBPs) which in turn inhibits the final transpeptidation step of peptidoglycan synthesis in bacterial cell walls, thus inhibiting cell wall biosynthesis. Bacteria eventually lyse due to ongoing activity of cell wall autolytic enzymes (autolysins and murein hydrolases) while cell wall assembly is arrested.

Contraindications Hypersensitivity to cefazolin, other cephalosporin antibiotics, penicillins, other beta-lactams, or any component of the formulation.

Warnings/Precautions Hypersensitivity reactions, including anaphylaxis, may occur. If an allergic reaction occurs, discontinue treatment and institute appropriate supportive measures. Use with caution in patients with a history of penicillin allergy. Use with caution in patients with renal impairment; dosage adjustment required. Prolonged use may result in fungal or bacterial superinfection, including *C. difficile*-associated diarrhea (CDAD) and pseudomembranous colitis; CDAD has been observed >2 months postantibiotic treatment. May be associated with increased INR, especially in nutritionally-deficient patients, prolonged treatment, hepatic or renal disease. Use with caution in patients with a history of seizure disorder; high levels, particularly in the presence of renal impairment, may increase risk of seizures. Potentially significant drug-drug interactions may exist, requiring dose or frequency adjustment, additional monitoring, and/or selection of alternative therapy.

Drug Interactions

Metabolism/Transport Effects None known.

Avoid Concomitant Use

Avoid concomitant use of CeFAZolin with any of the following: BCG (Intravesical); Cholera Vaccine

Increased Effect/Toxicity

CeFAZolin may increase the levels/effects of: Fosphenytoin; Phenytoin; Vitamin K Antagonists

The levels/effects of CeFAZolin may be increased by: Probenecid

Decreased Effect

CeFAZolin may decrease the levels/effects of: BCG (Intravesical); BCG Vaccine (Immunization); Cholera Vaccine; Lactobacillus and Estriol; Sodium Picosulfate; Typhoid Vaccine

Dietary Considerations Some products may contain sodium.

Pharmacodynamics/Kinetics

Half-life Elimination IM or IV: Neonates: 3 to 5 hours; Adults: 1.8 hours (IV); ~2 hours (IM) (prolonged with renal impairment)

Time to Peak Serum: IM: 0.5 to 2 hours; IV: Within 5 minutes

Pregnancy Risk Factor B

Pregnancy Considerations Adverse effects have not been observed in animal reproduction studies. Cefazolin crosses the placenta. Adverse events have not been reported in the fetus following administration of cefazolin prior to cesarean section. Cefazolin is recommended for group B streptococcus prophylaxis in pregnant patients with a nonanaphylactic penicillin allergy. It is also one of the antibiotics recommended for prophylactic use prior to cesarean delivery and may be used in certain situations prior to vaginal delivery in women at high risk for endocarditis.

Due to pregnancy-induced physiologic changes, the pharmacokinetics of cefazolin are altered. The half-life is shorter, the AUC is smaller, and the clearance and volume of distribution are increased.

Breastfeeding Considerations Small amounts of cefazolin are excreted in breast milk. The manufacturer recommends that caution be exercised when administering cefazolin to nursing women. Nondose-related effects could include modification of bowel flora.

Dosage Forms

Solution, Intravenous:

Generic: 1 g (50 mL); 2 g (100 mL)

Solution Prefilled Syringe, Intravenous:

Generic: 2 g/20 mL (20 mL)

Solution Reconstituted, Injection:

Generic: 500 mg (1 ea); 1 g (1 ea); 10 g (1 ea); 20 g (1 ea); 100 g (1 ea); 300 g (1 ea)

Solution Reconstituted, Injection [preservative free]:

Generic: 500 mg (1 ea); 1 g (1 ea); 10 g (1 ea)

Solution Reconstituted, Intravenous:

Generic: 1 g (1 ea); 2 g (1 ea)

Cefdinir (SEF di ner)

Pharmacologic Category Antibiotic, Cephalosporin (Third Generation)

Use

Acute bacterial otitis media: Treatment of acute bacterial otitis media in pediatric patients caused by *Haemophilus influenzae* (including beta-lactamase-producing strains), *Streptococcus pneumoniae* (penicillin-susceptible strains only) and *Moraxella catarrhalis* (including beta-lactamase-producing strains).

Acute exacerbations of chronic bronchitis: Treatment of acute exacerbations of chronic bronchitis in adults and adolescents caused by *H. influenzae* (including beta-lactamase producing strains), *H. parainfluenzae* (including beta-lactamase-producing strains), *S. pneumoniae* (penicillin-susceptible strains only) and *M. catarrhalis* (including beta-lactamase-producing strains).

Acute maxillary sinusitis: Treatment of acute maxillary sinusitis in adults and adolescents caused by *H. influenzae* (including beta-lactamase-producing strains), *S. pneumoniae* (penicillin-susceptible strains only) and *M. catarrhalis* (including beta-lactamase-producing strains). **Note:** Limitations of use: According to the IDSA guidelines for acute bacterial rhinosinusitis, cefdinir is no longer recommended as monotherapy for initial empiric treatment (Chow 2012).

Community-acquired pneumonia: Treatment of community-acquired pneumonia in adults and adolescents caused by *H. influenzae* (including beta-lactamase-producing strains), *H. parainfluenzae* (including beta-lactamase-producing strains), *S. pneumoniae* (penicillin-susceptible strains only) and *M. catarrhalis* (including beta-lactamase-producing strains).

Pharyngitis/Tonsillitis: Treatment of pharyngitis/tonsillitis in adults, adolescents, and pediatric patients caused by *S. pyogenes*.

Skin and skin structure infections, uncomplicated: Treatment of uncomplicated skin and skin structure infections in adults, adolescents, and pediatric patients caused by *Staphylococcus aureus* (including beta-lactamase-producing strains) and *S. pyogenes*.

Local Anesthetic/Vasoconstrictor Precautions No information available to require special precautions

Effects on Dental Treatment No significant effects or complications reported

Effects on Bleeding No information available to require special precautions

Adverse Reactions

>10%: Gastrointestinal: Diarrhea (8% to 15%)

1% to 10%:

Central nervous system: Headache (2%)

Dermatologic: Skin rash (≤3%)

Endocrine & metabolic: Decreased serum bicarbonate (≤1%), glycosuria (≤1%), hyperglycemia (≤1%), hyperphosphatemia (≤1%), increased gamma-glutamyl transferase (≤1%), increased lactate dehydrogenase (≤1%)

Gastrointestinal: Nausea (≤3%), abdominal pain (≤1%), vomiting (≤1%)

Genitourinary: Vulvovaginal candidiasis (≤4%), proteinuria (1% to 2%), occult blood in urine (≤1%), urine alkalinization (≤1%), vaginitis (≤1%)

Hematologic & oncologic: Elevated urine leukocytes (≤2%), lymphocytosis (≤2%), eosinophilia (1%), lymphocytopenia (1%), functional disorder of polymorphonuclear neutrophils (≤1%), thrombocythemia (≤1%), change in WBC count (≤1%)

Hepatic: Increased serum alkaline phosphatase (≤1%), increased serum ALT (≤1%)

Renal: Increased urine specific gravity (≤1%)

<1%, postmarketing, and/or case reports: Abnormal stools, anaphylaxis, anorexia, asthma, blood coagulation disorder, bloody diarrhea, candidiasis, cardiac failure, chest pain, cholestasis, conjunctivitis, constipation, cutaneous candidiasis, decreased hemoglobin, decreased urine specific gravity, disseminated intravascular coagulation, dizziness, drowsiness, dyspepsia, enterocolitis (acute), eosinophilic pneumonitis, erythema multiforme, erythema nodosum, exfoliative dermatitis, facial edema, fever, flatulence, fulminant hepatitis, granulocytopenia, hemolytic anemia, hemorrhagic colitis, hemorrhagic diathesis, hepatic failure, hepatitis (acute), hyperkalemia, hyperkinesia, hypersensitivity angiitis, hypertension, hypocalcemia, hypophosphatemia, immune thrombocytopenia, increased amylase, increased blood urea nitrogen, increased monocytes, increased serum AST, increased serum bilirubin, insomnia, interstitial pneumonitis (idiopathic), intestinal obstruction, involuntary body movements, jaundice, laryngeal edema, leukopenia, leukorrhea, loss of consciousness, maculopapular rash, melena, myocardial infarction, pancytopenia, peptic ulcer, pneumonia (drug-induced), pruritus, pseudomembranous colitis, renal disease, renal failure (acute), respiratory failure (acute), rhabdomyolysis, serum sickness, shock, Stevens-Johnson syndrome, stomatitis, thrombocytopenia, toxic epidermal necrolysis, upper gastrointestinal hemorrhage, weakness, xerostomia

General Dosage Range Dosage adjustment recommended in patients with renal impairment

Oral:

Infants ≥6 months and Children: 14 mg/kg/day in 1 to 2 divided doses (maximum: 600 mg/day)

Adolescents and Adults: 600 mg/day in 1 to 2 divided doses

Mechanism of Action Inhibits bacterial cell wall synthesis by binding to one or more of the penicillin-binding proteins (PBPs) which in turn inhibits the final transpeptidation step of peptidoglycan synthesis in bacterial cell walls, thus inhibiting cell wall biosynthesis. Bacteria eventually lyse due to ongoing activity of cell wall autolytic enzymes (autolysins and murein hydrolases) while cell wall assembly is arrested.

Pharmacodynamics/Kinetics

Half-life Elimination 1.7 (± 0.6) hours with normal renal function

Time to Peak 2 to 4 hours

Pregnancy Risk Factor B

Pregnancy Considerations Teratogenic events have not been observed in animal reproduction studies. An increase in most types of birth defects was not found following first trimester exposure to cephalosporins.

Cefditoren (sef de TOR en)

Related Information

Bacterial Infections *on page 1835*

Brand Names: US Spectracef

Pharmacologic Category Antibiotic, Cephalosporin (Third Generation)

Use Treatment of acute bacterial exacerbation of chronic bronchitis or community-acquired pneumonia (due to susceptible organisms including *Haemophilus influenzae*, *Haemophilus parainfluenzae*, *Streptococcus pneumoniae*-penicillin susceptible only, *Moraxella catarrhalis*); pharyngitis or tonsillitis (*Streptococcus pyogenes*); and uncomplicated skin and skin-structure infections (*Staphylococcus aureus* - not MRSA, *Streptococcus pyogenes*)

Local Anesthetic/Vasoconstrictor Precautions No information available to require special precautions

Effects on Dental Treatment No significant effects or complications reported

Effects on Bleeding No information available to require special precautions

Adverse Reactions

>10%: Gastrointestinal: Diarrhea (11% to 15%)

1% to 10%:

Central nervous system: Headache (2% to 3%)

Endocrine & metabolic: Increased serum glucose (1% to 2%)

Gastrointestinal: Nausea (4% to 6%), abdominal pain (2%), dyspepsia (1% to 2%), vomiting (1%)

Genitourinary: Vulvovaginal candidiasis (3% to 6%), hematuria (3%)

Hematologic & oncologic: Decreased hematocrit (2%), elevated urine leukocytes (2%)

<1%, postmarketing, and/or case reports: Abnormal dreams, acute renal failure, decreased serum albumin, anorexia, arthralgia, asthma, change in WBC count (decrease or increase), coagulation time increased, constipation, decreased hemoglobin, decreased neutrophils, decreased serum calcium, decreased serum sodium, diaphoresis, dizziness, drowsiness, dysgeusia, eosinophilic pneumonitis, eosinophilia, eructation, erythema multiforme, facial edema, fever, flatulence, fungal infection, gastritis, gastrointestinal disease, hyperglycemia, hypersensitivity reaction, hypochloremia, hypophosphatemia, increased appetite, increased blood urea nitrogen, increased serum ALT, increased serum AST, increased serum cholesterol, increased serum potassium, increased thirst, insomnia, interstitial pneumonitis, leukopenia, leukorrhea, lymphocytosis, myalgia, nervousness, oral candidiasis, oral mucosa ulcer, pain, peripheral edema, pharyngitis, positive direct Coombs test, pseudomembranous colitis, proteinuria, pruritus, rhinitis, sinusitis, skin rash, Stevens-Johnson syndrome, stomatitis, thrombocythemia, thrombocytopenia, toxic epidermal necrolysis, urinary frequency, urticaria, vaginitis, weakness, weight loss, xerostomia

General Dosage Range Dosage adjustment recommended in patients with renal impairment

Oral: *Children ≥12 years, Adolescents, and Adults:* 200 to 400 mg twice daily

Mechanism of Action Inhibits bacterial cell wall synthesis by binding to one or more of the penicillin-binding proteins (PBPs) which in turn inhibits the final transpeptidation step of peptidoglycan synthesis in bacterial cell walls, thus inhibiting cell wall biosynthesis. Bacteria eventually lyse due to ongoing activity of cell wall autolytic enzymes (autolysins and murein hydrolases) while cell wall assembly is arrested.

Pharmacodynamics/Kinetics

Half-life Elimination 1.6 ± 0.4 hours; increased with moderate (2.7 hours) and severe (4.7 hours) renal impairment

Time to Peak 1.5 to 3 hours

Pregnancy Risk Factor B

Pregnancy Considerations Adverse events have not been observed in animal reproduction studies. An increase in most types of birth defects was not found following first trimester exposure to cephalosporins.

Cefepime (SEF e pim)

Brand Names: US Maxipime

Brand Names: Canada Maxipime

Pharmacologic Category Antibiotic, Cephalosporin (Fourth Generation)

Use

Febrile neutropenia: Empiric treatment of febrile neutropenic patients.

Intra-abdominal infections: Treatment of complicated intra-abdominal infections, in combination with metronidazole, caused by *Escherichia coli*, viridans group streptococci, *Pseudomonas aeruginosa*, *Klebsiella pneumoniae*, *Enterobacter* species, or *Bacteroides fragilis*.

Pneumonia (moderate to severe): Treatment of moderate to severe pneumonia caused by *Streptococcus pneumoniae*, including cases associated with concurrent bacteremia, *P. aeruginosa*, *K. pneumoniae*, or *Enterobacter* species.

Skin and skin structure infections: Treatment of moderate to severe uncomplicated skin and skin structure infections caused by *Staphylococcus aureus* (methicillin-susceptible isolates only) or *Streptococcus pyogenes*.

Urinary tract infections (including pyelonephritis): Treatment of complicated and uncomplicated urinary tract infections, including pyelonephritis, caused by *E. coli* or *K. pneumoniae*, when the infection is severe, or caused by *E. coli*, *K. pneumoniae*, or *Proteus mirabilis*, when the infection is mild to moderate, including cases associated with concurrent bacteremia with these microorganisms.

Local Anesthetic/Vasoconstrictor Precautions No information available to require special precautions

Effects on Dental Treatment No significant effects or complications reported

Effects on Bleeding No information available to require special precautions

Adverse Reactions

>10%: Hematologic & oncologic: Positive direct Coombs test (without hemolysis: 16%)

1% to 10%:

Cardiovascular: Localized phlebitis (1%)

Central nervous system: Headache (≤1%)

Dermatologic: Skin rash (1% to 4%), pruritus (≤1%)

Endocrine & metabolic: Hypophosphatemia (3%)

Gastrointestinal: Diarrhea (≤3%), nausea (≤2%), vomiting (≤1%)

Hematologic & oncologic: Eosinophilia (2%)

Hepatic: Increased serum ALT (3%), abnormal partial thromboplastin time (2%), increased serum AST (2%), abnormal prothrombin time (1%)

Hypersensitivity: Hypersensitivity (in patients with a history of penicillin allergy: ≤10%)

Miscellaneous: Fever (≤1%)

<1%, postmarketing, and/or case reports: Agranulocytosis, anaphylactic shock, anaphylaxis, anemia, aphasia, brain disease, *Clostridium difficile* associated diarrhea, colitis, coma, confusion, decreased hematocrit, erythema, hallucination, hypercalcemia, hyperkalemia, hyperphosphatemia, hypocalcemia, increased blood urea nitrogen, increased serum alkaline phosphatase, increased serum bilirubin, increased serum creatinine, leukopenia, local inflammation, local pain, myoclonus, neurotoxicity, neutropenia, oral candidiasis, pseudomembranous colitis, seizure, status epilepticus (nonconvulsive), stupor, thrombocytopenia, urticaria, vaginitis

General Dosage Range Dosage adjustment recommended in patients with renal impairment

IM:

Infants ≥2 months, Children, and Adolescents ≤16 years (≤40 kg): 50 mg/kg/dose every 12 hours (maximum dose: 1 g/dose)

Children >40 kg, Adolescents >16 years, and Adults: 500 to 1000 mg every 12 hours

IV:

Infants ≥2 months, Children, and Adolescents ≤16 years (≤40 kg): 50 mg/kg/dose every 8 to 12 hours (maximum dose: 2 g/dose)

Children >40 kg, Adolescents >16 years, and Adults: 1 to 2 g every 8 to 12 hours

Mechanism of Action Inhibits bacterial cell wall synthesis by binding to one or more of the penicillin-binding proteins (PBPs) which in turn inhibits the final transpeptidation step of peptidoglycan synthesis in bacterial cell walls, thus inhibiting cell wall biosynthesis. Bacteria eventually lyse due to ongoing activity of cell wall autolytic enzymes (autolysis and murein hydrolases) while cell wall assembly is arrested.

Pharmacodynamics/Kinetics

Half-life Elimination

Neonates: 4 to 5 hours (Lima-Rogel 2008)
Children 2 months to 6 years: 1.77 to 1.96 hours
Adults: 2 hours
Hemodialysis: 13.5 hours
Continuous peritoneal dialysis: 19 hours

Time to Peak IM: 1 to 2 hours; IV: 0.5 hours

Pregnancy Risk Factor B

Pregnancy Considerations Adverse events were not observed in animal reproduction studies. Cefepime crosses the placenta.

Cefixime (sef IKS eem)

Related Information

Sexually-Transmitted Diseases *on page 1804*

Brand Names: US Suprax

Brand Names: Canada Auro-Cefixime; Suprax

Pharmacologic Category Antibiotic, Cephalosporin (Third Generation)

Use

Treatment of uncomplicated urinary tract infections (due to *Escherichia coli* and *Proteus mirabilis*), otitis media (due to *Haemophilus influenzae, Moraxella catarrhalis,* and *Streptococcus pyogenes*), pharyngitis and tonsillitis (due to *Streptococcus pyogenes*), acute exacerbations of chronic bronchitis (due to *Streptococcus pneumoniae* and *Haemophilus influenzae*); uncomplicated cervical/urethral gonorrhea (due to *N. gonorrhoeae* [penicillinase- and nonpenicillinase-producing])

Canadian labeling (not in US labeling): Treatment of uncomplicated urinary tract infections also due to *Klebsiella* spp., otitis media, acute exacerbations of chronic bronchitis, pharyngitis and tonsillitis or sinusitis also due to *Moroxella catarrhalis* (beta-lactamase positive and negative strains), or sinusitis caused by *S. pneumoniae*, *H influenzae* (beta-lactamase positive and negative strains) and *S. pyogenes.*

Note: Due to concerns of resistance, the CDC no longer recommends use of cefixime as a first-line regimen in the treatment of uncomplicated gonorrhea in the US; ceftriaxone is the preferred cephalosporin in combination with azithromycin (CDC 2012; CDC [Workowski 2015]).

Local Anesthetic/Vasoconstrictor Precautions No information available to require special precautions

Effects on Dental Treatment No significant effects or complications reported

Effects on Bleeding No information available to require special precautions

Adverse Reactions

>10%: Gastrointestinal: Diarrhea (16%)

2% to 10%: Gastrointestinal: Abdominal pain, nausea, dyspepsia, flatulence, loose stools

<2%: Acute renal failure, anaphylactoid reaction, anaphylaxis, angioedema, candidiasis, dizziness, drug fever, eosinophilia, erythema multiforme, facial edema, fever, headache, hepatitis, hyperbilirubinemia, increased blood urea nitrogen, increased serum creatinine, increased serum transaminases, jaundice, leukopenia, neutropenia, prolonged prothrombin time, pruritus, pseudomembranous colitis, seizure, serum sickness-like reaction, skin rash, Stevens-Johnson syndrome, thrombocytopenia, toxic epidermal necrolysis, urticaria, vaginitis, vomiting

General Dosage Range Dosage adjustment recommended in patients with renal impairment

Oral:

Children ≥6 months to 12 years or ≤45 kg: 8 mg/kg/day divided every 12-24 hours (maximum: 400 mg daily)

Children >12 years or >45 kg, Adolescents, and Adults: 400 mg daily divided every 12-24 hours

Mechanism of Action Inhibits bacterial cell wall synthesis by binding to one or more of the penicillin-binding proteins (PBPs); which in turn inhibits the final transpeptidation step of peptidoglycan synthesis in bacterial cell walls, thus inhibiting cell wall biosynthesis. Bacteria eventually lyse due to ongoing activity of cell wall autolytic enzymes (autolysins and murein hydrolases) while cell wall assembly is arrested.

Pharmacodynamics/Kinetics

Half-life Elimination Normal renal function: 3 to 4 hours; Moderate impairment (CrCl 20 to 40 mL/minute): 6.4 hours; Renal failure: Up to 11.5 hours

Time to Peak Serum: Tablet, suspension: 2 to 6 hours; Capsule: 3 to 8 hours; Delayed with food

Pregnancy Risk Factor B

Pregnancy Considerations Teratogenic effects were not observed in animal reproduction studies. Cefixime crosses the placenta and can be detected in the amniotic fluid (Ozyüncü 2010).

Product Availability Suprax 400 mg tablets have been discontinued in the US for more than 1 year.

Cefotaxime (sef oh TAKS eem)

Brand Names: US Claforan in D5W [DSC]; Claforan [DSC]

Brand Names: Canada Cefotaxime Sodium For Injection; Claforan

Pharmacologic Category Antibiotic, Cephalosporin (Third Generation)

Use

Bacteremia/Septicemia: Treatment of bacteremia/septicemia caused by *Escherichia coli*, *Klebsiella* species, and *Serratia marcescens*, *Staphylococcus aureus* and *Streptococcus* species (including *Streptococcus pneumoniae*).

Bone or joint infections: Treatment of bone or joint infections caused by *S. aureus* (penicillinase and nonpenicillinase producing strains), *Streptococcus* species (including *Streptococcus pyogenes*), *Pseudomonas* species (including *Pseudomonas aeruginosa*), and *Proteus mirabilis*.

CNS infections: Treatment of CNS infections (eg, meningitis, ventriculitis) caused by *Neisseria meningitidis*, *Haemophilus influenzae*, *S. pneumoniae*, *Klebsiella pneumoniae*, and *E. coli*.

Genitourinary infections: Treatment of genitourinary infections, including urinary tract infections (UTIs), caused by *Enterococcus* species, *Staphylococcus epidermidis*, *S. aureus* (penicillinase and nonpenicillinase producing), *Citrobacter* species, *Enterobacter* species, *E. coli*, *Klebsiella* species, *P. mirabilis*,

Proteus vulgaris, Providencia stuartii, Morganella morganii, Providencia rettgeri, S. marcescens, and *Pseudomonas* species (including *P. aeruginosa*). Also, uncomplicated gonorrhea (cervical/urethral and rectal) caused by *Neisseria gonorrhoeae*, including penicillinase-producing strains. **Note:** CDC STD guidelines do not recommend cefotaxime as a treatment option for uncomplicated gonorrhea; ceftriaxone is the preferred cephalosporin (CDC [Workowski 2015]).

Gynecologic infections: Treatment of gynecologic infections, including pelvic inflammatory disease, endometritis, and pelvic cellulitis, caused by *S. epidermidis, Streptococcus* species, *Enterococcus* species, *Enterobacter* species, *Klebsiella* species, *E. coli, P. mirabilis, Bacteroides* species (including *Bacteroides fragilis*), *Clostridium* species, and anaerobic cocci (including *Peptostreptococcus* and *Peptococcus* species) and *Fusobacterium* species (including *Fusobacterium nucleatum*).

Intra-abdominal infections: Treatment of intra-abdominal infections, including peritonitis caused by *Streptococcus* species, *E. coli, Klebsiella* species, *Bacteroides* species, and anaerobic cocci (including *Peptostreptococcus* species and *Peptococcus* species), *P. mirabilis*, and *Clostridium* species.

Lower respiratory tract infections: Treatment of lower respiratory tract infections, including pneumonia, caused by *S. pneumoniae, S. pyogenes* (group A streptococci) and other streptococci (excluding enterococci, [eg, *Enterococcus faecalis*]), *S. aureus* (penicillinase and nonpenicillinase producing), *E. coli, Klebsiella* species, *H. influenzae* (including ampicillin-resistant strains), *H. parainfluenzae, P. mirabilis, S. marcescens, Enterobacter* species, and indole-positive *Proteus* and *Pseudomonas* species (including *P. aeruginosa*).

Skin and skin structure infections: Treatment of skin and skin structure infections caused by *S. aureus* (penicillinase and nonpenicillinase producing), *S. epidermidis, S. pyogenes* (group A streptococci) and other streptococci, *Enterococcus* species, *Acinetobacter* species, *E. coli, Citrobacter* species (including *Citrobacter freundii*), *Enterobacter* species, *Klebsiella* species, *P. mirabilis, P. vulgaris, M. morganii, P. rettgeri, Pseudomonas* species, *S. marcescens, Bacteroides* species, and anaerobic cocci (including *Peptostreptococcus* species and *Peptococcus* species).

Surgical prophylaxis: Reduce the incidence of certain infections in patients undergoing surgical procedures (eg, abdominal or vaginal hysterectomy, GI and GU tract surgery) that may be classified as contaminated or potentially contaminated; reduce the incidence of certain postoperative infections in patients undergoing cesarean section.

Local Anesthetic/Vasoconstrictor Precautions No information available to require special precautions

Effects on Dental Treatment No significant effects or complications reported

Effects on Bleeding No information available to require special precautions

Adverse Reactions

1% to 10%:

Dermatologic: Pruritus (≤2%), skin rash (≤2%)

Gastrointestinal: Colitis (≤1%), diarrhea (≤1%), nausea (≤1%), vomiting (≤1%)

Hematologic & oncologic: Eosinophilia (≤2%)

Local: Induration at injection site (IM ≤4%), inflammation at injection site (IV ≤4%), pain at injection site (IM ≤4%), tenderness at injection site (IM ≤4%)

Miscellaneous: Fever (≤2%)

<1%, postmarketing and/or case reports: Acute generalized exanthematous pustulosis, acute renal failure, agranulocytosis, anaphylaxis, bone marrow failure, brain disease, candidiasis, cardiac arrhythmia (after rapid IV injection via central catheter), cholestasis, *Clostridium difficile* associated diarrhea, dizziness, erythema multiforme, granulocytopenia, headache, hemolytic anemia, hepatitis, increased blood urea nitrogen, increased gamma-glutamyl transferase, increased lactate dehydrogenase, increased serum alkaline phosphatase, increased serum ALT, increased serum AST, increased serum bilirubin, increased serum creatinine, injection site phlebitis, interstitial nephritis, jaundice, leukopenia, local irritation, neutropenia, pancytopenia, positive direct Coombs test, pseudomembranous colitis, Stevens-Johnson syndrome, thrombocytopenia, toxic epidermal necrolysis, urticaria, vaginitis

General Dosage Range Dosage adjustment recommended in patients with renal impairment

IM:

Infants and Children 1 month to 12 years and <50 kg: 50 to 180 mg/kg/day in divided doses every 4 to 6 hours (maximum: 12 g daily)

Children ≥50 kg, Children >12 years, and Adults: 1 to 2 g every 8 to 12 hours **or** 0.5 to 1 g as a single dose (maximum: 12 g per day)

IV:

Infants and Children 1 month to 12 years and <50 kg: 50 to 180 mg/kg/day in divided doses every 4 to 6 hours (maximum: 12 g daily)

Children ≥50 kg, Adolescents, and Adults: 1 to 2 g every 4 to 12 hours (maximum: 12 g daily)

Mechanism of Action Inhibits bacterial cell wall synthesis by binding to one or more of the penicillin-binding proteins (PBPs) which in turn inhibits the final transpeptidation step of peptidoglycan synthesis in bacterial cell walls, thus inhibiting cell wall biosynthesis. Bacteria eventually lyse due to ongoing activity of cell wall autolytic enzymes (autolysins and murein hydrolases) while cell wall assembly is arrested. Cefotaxime has activity in the presence of some beta-lactamases, both penicillinases and cephalosporinases, of gram-negative and gram-positive bacteria. *Enterococcus* species may be intrinsically resistant to cefotaxime. Most extended-spectrum beta-lactamase (ESBL)-producing and carbapenemase-producing isolates are resistant to cefotaxime.

Pharmacodynamics/Kinetics

Half-life Elimination

Cefotaxime: Infants ≤1500 g: 4.6 hours; Infants >1500 g: 3.4 hours; Children: 1.5 hours; Adults: 1 to 1.5 hours; prolonged with renal and/or hepatic impairment

Desacetylcefotaxime: 1.3 to 1.9 hours; prolonged with renal impairment (Ings 1982)

Time to Peak Serum: IM: Within 30 minutes

Pregnancy Risk Factor B

Pregnancy Considerations Adverse events have not been observed in animal reproduction studies. Cefotaxime crosses the human placenta and can be found in fetal tissue. An increase in most types of birth defects was not found following first trimester exposure to cephalosporins. During pregnancy, peak cefotaxime serum concentrations are decreased and the serum half-life is shorter. Cefotaxime is approved for use in women undergoing cesarean section (consult current guidelines for appropriate use).

CefoTEtan (SEF oh tee tan)

Brand Names: US Cefotan

Pharmacologic Category Antibiotic, Cephalosporin (Second Generation)

Use

Bone and joint infections: Treatment of bone and joint infections caused by *Staphylococcus aureus*.

Gynecologic infections: Treatment of gynecologic infections caused by *S. aureus*, (including penicillinase- and non-penicillinase-producing strains), *Staphylococcus epidermidis*, *Streptococcus* spp. (excluding enterococci), *Streptococcus agalactiae*, *Escherichia coli*, *Proteus mirabilis*, *Neisseria gonorrhoeae*, *Bacteroides* spp. (excluding *Bacteroides distasonis*, *Bacteroides ovatus*, *Bacteroides thetaiotaomicron*), *Fusobacterium* spp., and gram-positive anaerobic cocci (including *Peptococcus* and *Peptostreptococcus* spp.).

Limitations of use: Cefotetan has no activity against *Chlamydia (Chlamydophila) trachomatis*. When treating pelvic inflammatory disease, add appropriate antichlamydial coverage.

Intra-abdominal infections: Treatment of intra-abdominal infections caused by *E. coli*, *Klebsiella* spp. (including *K. pneumoniae*), *Streptococcus* spp. (excluding enterococci) and *Clostridium* spp.

Lower respiratory tract infections: Treatment of lower respiratory tract infections caused by *Streptococcus pneumoniae*, *S. aureus* (penicillinase- and non-penicillinase-producing strains), *Haemophilus influenzae* (including ampicillin-resistant strains), *Klebsiella* spp. (including *K. pneumoniae*), *E. coli*, *P. mirabilis*, and *Serratia marcescens*.

Serious infections: Treatment of confirmed or suspected gram-positive or gram-negative sepsis or in patients with other serious infections (often administered with concomitant aminoglycosides).

Skin and skin structure infections: Treatment of skin and skin structure infections due to *S. aureus* (penicillinase- and non-penicillinase-producing strains), *Staphylococcus epidermidis*, *Streptococcus pyogenes*, *Streptococcus* spp. (excluding enterococci), *E. coli*, *K. pneumoniae*, *Peptococcus niger*, *Peptostreptococcus* spp.

Surgical (perioperative) prophylaxis: Preoperative administration in surgical procedures that are classified as clean contaminated or potentially contaminated (eg, cesarean section, abdominal or vaginal hysterectomy, transurethral surgery, biliary tract surgery, GI surgery).

Urinary tract infections: Treatment of urinary tract infections caused by *E. coli*, *Klebsiella* spp. (including *K. pneumoniae*), *P. mirabilis* and *Proteus* spp. (which may include the organisms now called *Proteus vulgaris*, *Providencia rettgeri*, and *Morganella morganii*).

Local Anesthetic/Vasoconstrictor Precautions No information available to require special precautions

Effects on Dental Treatment No significant effects or complications reported

Effects on Bleeding May potentiate the anticoagulant effects of vitamin K anticoagulants (ie, warfarin) due to alterations of gut flora. Cefotetan may have additional hypoprothrombinemic activity.

Adverse Reactions

1% to 10%:

Gastrointestinal: Diarrhea (1%)

Hepatic: Increased serum transaminases (1%)

Hypersensitivity: Hypersensitivity reaction (1%)

<1%, postmarketing, and/or case reports: Agranulocytosis, anaphylaxis, eosinophilia, fever, hemolytic anemia, hemorrhage, increased blood urea nitrogen, increased serum creatinine, leukopenia, nausea, nephrotoxicity, phlebitis, prolonged prothrombin time, pruritus, pseudomembranous colitis, skin rash, thrombocythemia, thrombocytopenia, urticaria, vomiting

General Dosage Range Dosage adjustment recommended in patients with renal impairment

IM: *Adults:* 1 to 4 g daily divided every 12 hours **or** 1 to 2 g every 24 hours

IV: *Adults:* 1 to 6 g daily divided every 12 hours **or** 1 to 2 g every 24 hours **or** 1 to 2 g prior to surgery

Mechanism of Action Inhibits bacterial cell wall synthesis by binding to one or more of the penicillin-binding proteins (PBPs) which in turn inhibits the final transpeptidation step of peptidoglycan synthesis in bacterial cell walls, thus inhibiting cell wall biosynthesis. Bacteria eventually lyse due to ongoing activity of cell wall autolytic enzymes (autolysins and murein hydrolases) while cell wall assembly is arrested.

Pharmacodynamics/Kinetics

Half-life Elimination 3 to 4.6 hours, prolonged in patients with moderately impaired renal function (up to 10 hours)

Time to Peak Serum: IM: 1 to 3 hours

Pregnancy Risk Factor B

Pregnancy Considerations Adverse events have not been observed in animal reproduction studies. Cefotetan crosses the placenta and produces therapeutic concentrations in the amniotic fluid and cord serum. Cefotetan is one of the antibiotics recommended for use with cesarean delivery.

CefOXitin (se FOKS i tin)

Brand Names: US Mefoxin [DSC]

Brand Names: Canada Cefoxitin For Injection

Pharmacologic Category Antibiotic, Cephalosporin (Second Generation)

Use

Bone and joint infections: Treatment of bone and joint infections caused by *Staphylococcus aureus* (including penicillinase-producing strains).

Gynecological infections: Treatment of endometritis, pelvic cellulitis, and pelvic inflammatory disease caused by *Escherichia coli*, *Neisseria gonorrhoeae* (including penicillinase-producing strains), *Bacteroides* species including *Bacteroides fragilis*, *Clostridium* species, *P. niger*, *Peptostreptococcus* species, and *Streptococcus agalactiae*.

Intra-abdominal infections: Treatment of peritonitis and intra-abdominal infections or abscess, caused by *E. coli*, *Klebsiella* species, *Bacteroides* species (including *B. fragilis*), and *Clostridium* species.

Lower respiratory tract infections: Treatment of pneumonia and lung abscess, caused by *Streptococcus pneumoniae*, other streptococci (excluding enterococci; eg, *Enterococcus faecalis* [formerly *Streptococcus faecalis*]), *S. aureus* (including penicillinase-producing strains), *E. coli*, *Klebsiella* species, *Haemophilus influenzae*, and *Bacteroides* species.

Perioperative prophylaxis: Prophylaxis of infection in patients undergoing uncontaminated GI surgery, abdominal or vaginal hysterectomy, or cesarean section.

Septicemia: Treatment of septicemia caused by *S. pneumoniae*, *S. aureus* (including penicillinase-producing strains), *E. coli*, *Klebsiella* species, and *Bacteroides* species including *B. fragilis*.

Skin and skin structure infections: Treatment of skin and skin structure infections caused by *S. aureus* (including penicillinase-producing strains), *Staphylococcus epidermidis*, *Streptococcus pyogenes* and other streptococci (excluding enterococci [eg, *E. faecalis*] [formerly *S. faecalis*]), *E. coli*, *Proteus mirabilis*, *Klebsiella* species, *Bacteroides* species including *B. fragilis*, *Clostridium* species, *P. niger*, and *Peptostreptococcus* species.

Urinary tract infections: Treatment of UTIs caused by *E. coli*, *Klebsiella* species, *P. mirabilis*, *Morganella morganii*, *Proteus vulgaris*, and *Providencia* species (including *Providencia rettgeri*).

Limitations of use: Cefoxitin does not have activity against *Chlamydia trachomatis*. When cefoxitin is used to treat pelvic inflammatory disease, add appropriate antichlamydial coverage.

Local Anesthetic/Vasoconstrictor Precautions No information available to require special precautions

Effects on Dental Treatment No significant effects or complications reported

Effects on Bleeding May potentiate the anticoagulant effects of vitamin K anticoagulants (ie, warfarin) due to alterations of gut flora.

Adverse Reactions

1% to 10%: Gastrointestinal: Diarrhea

<1%: Anaphylaxis, angioedema, bone marrow depression, dyspnea, eosinophilia, exacerbation of myasthenia gravis, exfoliative dermatitis, fever, hemolytic anemia, hypotension, increased blood urea nitrogen, increased serum creatinine, increased serum transaminases, interstitial nephritis, jaundice, leukopenia, nausea, nephrotoxicity (increased; with aminoglycosides), phlebitis, prolonged prothrombin time, pruritus, pseudomembranous colitis, skin rash, thrombocytopenia, thrombophlebitis, toxic epidermal necrolysis, urticaria, vomiting

General Dosage Range Dosage adjustment recommended in patients with renal impairment

IV:

Children >3 months: 80 to 160 mg/kg/day divided every 4 to 6 hours (maximum: 12 **g daily) or** 30 to 40 mg/kg prior to surgery

Adolescents: 80 to 160 mg/kg/day divided every 4 to 6 hours (maximum: 12 **g daily) or** 1 to 2 g prior to surgery

Adults: 1 to 2 g every 4 to 8 hours (maximum: 12 g daily) **or** 2 g prior to surgery

Mechanism of Action Inhibits bacterial cell wall synthesis by binding to one or more of the penicillin-binding proteins (PBPs) which in turn inhibits the final transpeptidation step of peptidoglycan synthesis in bacterial cell walls, thus inhibiting cell wall biosynthesis. Bacteria eventually lyse due to ongoing activity of cell wall autolytic enzymes (autolysins and murein hydrolases) while cell wall assembly is arrested.

Pharmacodynamics/Kinetics

Half-life Elimination Neonates and Infants (PNA: 10-53 days): 1.4 hours (Regazzi 1983); Adults: 41-59 minutes; prolonged with renal impairment

Time to Peak Serum: IM: Within 20-30 minutes

Pregnancy Considerations Adverse events have not been observed in animal reproduction studies. Cefoxitin crosses the placenta and reaches the cord serum and amniotic fluid. Peak serum concentrations of cefoxitin during pregnancy may be similar to or decreased compared to nonpregnant values. Maternal half-life may be shorter at term. Pregnancy-induced hypertension increases trough concentrations in the immediate postpartum period. Cefoxitin is one of the antibiotics recommended for prophylactic use prior to cesarean delivery.

Cefpodoxime (sef pode OKS eem)

Pharmacologic Category Antibiotic, Cephalosporin (Third Generation)

Use

Chronic bronchitis, acute bacterial exacerbation: Treatment of acute bacterial exacerbation of chronic bronchitis caused by *Streptococcus pneumoniae*, *Haemophilus influenzae* (non-beta-lactamase-producing strains only), or *Moraxella catarrhalis*.

Gonorrhea:

Acute, uncomplicated anorectal infections in women: Treatment of acute, uncomplicated anorectal infections in women due to *N. gonorrhoeae* (including penicillinase-producing strains). **Note:** Due to issues of resistance, cefpodoxime is no longer recommended for the treatment of acute, uncomplicated anorectal infections in women.

Acute, uncomplicated urethral and cervical: Treatment of acute, uncomplicated urethral and cervical gonorrhea caused by *Neisseria gonorrhoeae* (including penicillinase-producing strains). **Note:** Due to issues of resistance, cefpodoxime is no longer recommended for the treatment of acute, uncomplicated urethral and cervical gonorrhea.

Otitis media, acute: Treatment of acute otitis media caused by *S. pneumoniae*, (excluding penicillin-resistant strains), *Streptococcus pyogenes*, *H. influenzae* (including beta-lactamase-producing strains), or *M. catarrhalis* (including beta-lactamase producing strains).

Pharyngitis or tonsillitis: Treatment of pharyngitis or tonsillitis caused by *S. pyogenes*.

Pneumonia, community-acquired: Treatment of community-acquired pneumonia caused by *S. pneumoniae* or *H. influenzae* (including beta-lactamase-producing strains).

Sinusitis, acute maxillary: Treatment of acute maxillary sinusitis caused by *H. influenzae* (including beta lactamase producing strains), *S. pneumoniae*, and *M. catarrhalis*. **Note:** According to the Infectious Diseases Society of America (IDSA) guidelines for acute bacterial rhinosinusitis, cefpodoxime is no longer recommended as monotherapy for initial empiric treatment.

Skin and skin structure infections, uncomplicated: Treatment of uncomplicated skin and skin structure infections caused by *S. aureus* (including penicillinase-producing strains) or *S. pyogenes*.

Urinary tract infections (cystitis), uncomplicated: Treatment of cystitis caused by *Escherichia coli*, *Klebsiella pneumoniae*, *Proteus mirabilis*, or *Staphylococcus saprophyticus*.

Local Anesthetic/Vasoconstrictor Precautions No information available to require special precautions

Effects on Dental Treatment No significant effects or complications reported

Effects on Bleeding No information available to require special precautions

Adverse Reactions

>10%:

Dermatologic: Diaper rash (12%)

Gastrointestinal: Diarrhea (infants and toddlers 15%)
1% to 10%:
Central nervous system: Headache (1%)
Dermatologic: Skin rash (1%)
Gastrointestinal: Diarrhea (7%), nausea (4%), abdominal pain (2%), vomiting (1% to 2%)
Genitourinary: Vaginal infection (3%)
<1%: Anaphylaxis, anxiety, chest pain, cough, decreased appetite, dizziness, dysgeusia, epistaxis, eye pruritus, fatigue, fever, flatulence, flushing, fungal skin infection, hypotension, insomnia, malaise, nightmares, pruritus, pseudomembranous colitis, purpuric nephritis, tinnitus, vulvovaginal candidiasis, weakness, xerostomia

General Dosage Range Dosage adjustment recommended in patients with renal impairment

Oral:

Infants ≥ 2 months and Children <12 years: 10 mg/kg/day divided every 12 hours (maximum: 200 mg/dose)

Children ≥12 years, Adolescents, and Adults: 100 to 400 mg every 12 hours **or** 200 mg as a single dose

Mechanism of Action Inhibits bacterial cell wall synthesis by binding to one or more of the penicillin-binding proteins (PBPs) which in turn inhibits the final transpeptidation step of peptidoglycan synthesis in bacterial cell walls, thus inhibiting cell wall biosynthesis. Bacteria eventually lyse due to ongoing activity of cell wall autolytic enzymes (autolysins and murein hydrolases) while cell wall assembly is arrested.

Pharmacodynamics/Kinetics

Half-life Elimination ~2 to 3 hours; prolonged with renal impairment (~10 hours for CrCl <30 mL/minute)

Time to Peak Tablets: Within 2 to 3 hours; Oral suspension: Slower in presence of food, 48% increase in T_{max}

Pregnancy Risk Factor B

Pregnancy Considerations Teratogenic events were not observed in animal reproduction studies. An increase in most types of birth defects was not found following first trimester exposure to cephalosporins.

Cefprozil (sef PROE zil)

Related Information

Antibiotic Prophylaxis *on page 1812*

Brand Names: Canada Apo-Cefprozil; Auro-Cefprozil; Ava-Cefprozil; Cefzil; RAN-Cefprozil; Sandoz-Cefprozil

Pharmacologic Category Antibiotic, Cephalosporin (Second Generation)

Use

Acute bacterial exacerbation of chronic bronchitis: Treatment of mild to moderate acute bacterial exacerbations of chronic bronchitis caused by *S. pneumoniae*, *H. influenzae* (including beta-lactamase–producing strains), and *M. catarrhalis* (including beta-lactamase–producing strains).

Otitis media: Treatment of mild to moderate otitis media caused by *S. pneumoniae*, *Haemophilus influenzae* (including beta-lactamase–producing strains), and *Moraxella (Branhamella) catarrhalis* (including beta-lactamase–producing strains).

Pharyngitis/tonsillitis: Treatment of mild to moderate pharyngitis/tonsillitis caused by *Streptococcus pyogenes.*

Limitations of use: Cefprozil is generally effective in the eradication of *S. pyogenes* from the nasopharynx; however, substantial data establishing the efficacy of cefprozil in the subsequent prevention of rheumatic fever are not available at present.

Skin and skin-structure infections, uncomplicated: Treatment of mild to moderate uncomplicated skin and skin-structure infections caused by *Staphylococcus aureus* (including penicillinase-producing strains) and *S. pyogenes.*

Local Anesthetic/Vasoconstrictor Precautions No information available to require special precautions

Effects on Dental Treatment No significant effects or complications reported

Effects on Bleeding No information available to require special precautions

Adverse Reactions

Frequency not always defined.
1% to 10%:
Central nervous system: Dizziness (1%)
Dermatologic: Diaper rash (2%), genital pruritus (2%)
Gastrointestinal: Nausea (4%), diarrhea (3%), abdominal pain (1%), vomiting (1%)
Genitourinary: Vaginitis
Hepatic: Increased serum transaminases (2%)
Infection: Superinfection
<1%, postmarketing, and/or case reports: Anaphylaxis, angioedema, arthralgia, cholestatic jaundice, confusion, drowsiness, eosinophilia, erythema multiforme, fever, headache, hyperactivity, increased blood urea nitrogen, increased serum creatinine, insomnia, leukopenia, pseudomembranous colitis, serum sickness, skin rash, Stevens-Johnson syndrome, thrombocytopenia, urticaria

General Dosage Range Dosage adjustment recommended in patients with renal impairment

Oral:

Infants and Children ≥6 months to 2 years: 7.5 to 15 mg/kg/dose every 12 hours

Children ≥2 to 12 years: 15 to 30 mg/kg/day divided every 12 hours **or** 20 mg/kg every 24 hours (maximum: 1,000 mg/day)

Children >12 years, Adolescents, and Adults: 250 to 500 mg every 12 hours **or** 500 mg every 24 hours

Mechanism of Action Inhibits bacterial cell wall synthesis by binding to one or more of the penicillin-binding proteins (PBPs) which in turn inhibits the final transpeptidation step of peptidoglycan synthesis in bacterial cell walls, thus inhibiting cell wall biosynthesis. Bacteria eventually lyse due to ongoing activity of cell wall autolytic enzymes (autolysins and murein hydrolases) while cell wall assembly is arrested.

Pharmacodynamics/Kinetics

Half-life Elimination

Infants and Children (6 months to 12 years): 1.5 hours
Adults:
Normal renal function: 1.3 hours
Renal impairment: 5.2 hours
Renal failure: 5.9 hours
Hepatic impairment: 2 hours

Time to Peak Serum: Fasting: 1.5 hours

Pregnancy Risk Factor B

Pregnancy Considerations Adverse events were not observed in animal reproduction studies.

Ceftaroline Fosamil (sef TAR oh leen FOS a mil)

Brand Names: US Teflaro

Pharmacologic Category Antibiotic, Cephalosporin (Fifth Generation)

Use

Pneumonia, community-acquired: Treatment of community-acquired bacterial pneumonia in adults and pediatric patients 2 months of age and older caused by *Streptococcus pneumoniae* (including cases with concurrent bacteremia), *Staphylococcus aureus* (methicillin-susceptible isolates only), *Haemophilus influenzae*, *Klebsiella pneumoniae*, *Klebsiella oxytoca*, and *Escherichia coli*.

Skin and skin structure infections: Treatment of acute bacterial skin and skin structure infections in adults and pediatric patients 2 months of age and older caused by *Staphylococcus aureus* (including methicillin-susceptible and methicillin-resistant isolates), *Streptococcus pyogenes*, *Streptococcus agalactiae*, *Escherichia coli*, *Klebsiella pneumoniae*, and *Klebsiella oxytoca*.

Local Anesthetic/Vasoconstrictor Precautions No information available to require special precautions

Effects on Dental Treatment No significant effects or complications reported

Effects on Bleeding No information available to require special precautions

Adverse Reactions The following reactions occurred in all indicated populations unless otherwise specified.

>10%: Hematologic & oncologic: Positive direct Coombs test (infants, children, and adolescents: 18%; adults: 10% to 11%; no evidence of hemolysis in any treatment group)

1% to 10%:

Cardiovascular: Bradycardia (adults: <2%), palpitations (adults: <2%), phlebitis (adults: 2%)

Central nervous system: Insomnia (adults: 3% to 4%), headache (infants, children, and adolescents: <3%), dizziness (adults: <2%), seizure (adults: <2%)

Dermatologic: Skin rash (3% to 7%), pruritus (infants, children, and adolescents: <3%), urticaria (adults: <2%)

Endocrine & metabolic: Hypokalemia (adults: 2%), hyperglycemia (adults: <2%), hyperkalemia (adults: <2%)

Gastrointestinal: Diarrhea (5% to 8%), vomiting (2% to 5%), nausea (3% to 4%), constipation (adults: 2%), abdominal pain (adults: <2%), pseudomembranous colitis (adults: <2%)

Hematologic & oncologic: Anemia (adults: <2%), eosinophilia (adults: <2%), neutropenia (adults: <2%), thrombocytopenia (adults: <2%)

Hepatic: Increased serum ALT (infants, children, and adolescents: <3%), increased serum AST (infants, children, and adolescents: <3%), increased serum transaminases (adults: 2%), hepatitis (adults: <2%)

Hypersensitivity: Anaphylaxis (adults: <2%), hypersensitivity (adults: <2%)

Renal: Renal failure (adults: <2%)

Miscellaneous: Fever (adults: <2% to 3%)

<1%, postmarketing, and/or case reports: Agranulocytosis (adults), leukopenia (adults)

General Dosage Range Dosage adjustment recommended in patients with renal impairment.

IV:

Infants ≥2 months and Children <2 years: 8 mg/kg/dose every 8 hours

Children ≥2 years and Adolescents <18 years weighing ≤33 kg: 12 mg/kg/dose every 8 hours

Children ≥ 2 years and Adolescents <18 years weighing >33 kg: 400 mg every 8 hours or 600 mg every 12 hours

Adolescents ≥18 years and Adults: 600 mg every 12 hours

Mechanism of Action Inhibits bacterial cell wall synthesis by binding to penicillin-binding proteins (PBPs) 1 through 3. This action blocks the final transpeptidation step of peptidoglycan synthesis in bacterial cell walls and inhibits cell wall biosynthesis. Bacteria eventually lyse due to ongoing activity of cell wall autolytic enzymes (autolysis and murein hydrolases) while cell wall assembly is arrested. Ceftaroline has a strong affinity for PBP2a, a modified PBP in MRSA, and PBP2x in *S. pneumoniae*, contributing to its spectrum of activity against these bacteria.

Pharmacodynamics/Kinetics

Half-life Elimination ~1.6 hours (single dose); ~2.66 hours (multiple dose)

Time to Peak ~1 hour

Pregnancy Considerations Adverse events have been observed in some animal reproduction studies.

CefTAZidime (SEF tay zi deem)

Brand Names: US Fortaz; Fortaz in D5W; Tazicef

Brand Names: Canada Ceftazidime For Injection; Fortaz

Pharmacologic Category Antibiotic, Cephalosporin (Third Generation)

Use

Bacterial septicemia: Treatment of septicemia caused by *Pseudomonas aeruginosa*, *Klebsiella* spp., *Haemophilus influenzae*, *Escherichia coli*, *Serratia* spp., *Streptococcus pneumoniae*, and *Staphylococcus aureus* (methicillin-susceptible strains).

Bone and joint infections: Treatment of bone and joint infections caused by *Pseudomonas aeruginosa*, *Klebsiella* spp., *Enterobacter* spp., and *Staphylococcus aureus* (methicillin-susceptible strains).

CNS infections: Treatment of meningitis caused by *Haemophilus influenzae* and *Neisseria meningitidis*. Ceftazidime has also been used successfully in cases of meningitis due to *Pseudomonas aeruginosa* and *Streptococcus pneumoniae*.

Empiric therapy in the immunocompromised patient: Empiric treatment of infections in immunocompromised patients.

Gynecologic infections: Treatment of endometritis, pelvic cellulitis, and other infections of the female genital tract caused by *Escherichia coli*.

Intra-abdominal infections: Treatment of peritonitis caused by *Escherichia coli*, *Klebsiella* spp., and *Staphylococcus aureus* (methicillin-susceptible strains) and polymicrobial intra-abdominal infections caused by aerobic and anaerobic organisms and some *Bacteroides* spp. (many strains of *Bacteroides fragilis* are resistant).

Lower respiratory tract infections: Treatment of lower respiratory tract infections, including pneumonia, caused by *Pseudomonas aeruginosa* and other *Pseudomonas* spp.; *Haemophilus influenzae*, including ampicillin-resistant strains; *Klebsiella* spp.; *Enterobacter* spp.; *Proteus mirabilis*; *Escherichia coli*; *Serratia* spp.; *Citrobacter* spp.; *Streptococcus pneumoniae*; and *Staphylococcus aureus* (methicillin-susceptible strains).

Skin and skin-structure infections: Treatment of skin and skin-structure infections caused by *Pseudomonas aeruginosa*; *Klebsiella* spp.; *Escherichia coli*; *Proteus* spp.; including *Proteus mirabilis* and indole-positive *Proteus*; *Enterobacter* spp.; *Serratia* spp.; *Staphylococcus aureus* (methicillin-susceptible strains); and *Streptococcus pyogenes* (group A beta-hemolytic streptococci).

Urinary tract infections (UTI): Treatment of complicated and uncomplicated UTIs caused by *Pseudomonas aeruginosa*; *Enterobacter* spp.; *Proteus* spp., including *Proteus mirabilis* and indole-positive *Proteus*; *Klebsiella* spp.; and *Escherichia coli*.

Local Anesthetic/Vasoconstrictor Precautions No information available to require special precautions

Effects on Dental Treatment No significant effects or complications reported

Effects on Bleeding No information available to require special precautions

Adverse Reactions

1% to 10%:

Cardiovascular: Phlebitis (1%)

Endocrine & metabolic: Increased lactate dehydrogenase (6%), increased gamma-glutamyl transferase (5%)

Gastrointestinal: Diarrhea (1%)

Hematologic & oncologic: Eosinophilia (8%), positive direct Coombs test (4%; without hemolysis), thrombocythemia (2%)

Hepatic: Increased serum ALT (7%), increased serum AST (6%), increased serum alkaline phosphatase (4%)

Hypersensitivity: Hypersensitivity reactions (2%)

Local: Inflammation at injection site (1%), pain at injection site (1%)

<1%: Abdominal pain, agranulocytosis, anaphylaxis (severe in rare instances, including cardiopulmonary arrest), angioedema, asterixis, brain disease, candidiasis, *Clostridium difficile* associated diarrhea, dizziness, erythema multiforme, fever, headache, hemolytic anemia, hyperbilirubinemia, increased blood urea nitrogen, increased serum creatinine, jaundice, leukopenia, lymphocytosis, myoclonus, nausea, neuromuscular excitability, neutropenia, paresthesia, pruritus, pseudomembranous colitis, renal disease (may be severe, including renal failure), renal insufficiency, seizure, skin rash, Stevens-Johnson syndrome, thrombocytopenia, toxic epidermal necrolysis, urticaria, vaginitis, vomiting

General Dosage Range Dosage adjustment recommended in patients with renal impairment

IM: *Adults:* 500 mg to 2 g every 8 to 12 hours

IV:

Children 1 month to 12 years: 30 to 50 mg/kg every 8 hours (maximum: 6 g daily)

Children ≥12 years, Adolescents, and Adults: 500 mg to 2 g every 8 to 12 hours (maximum: 6 g daily)

Mechanism of Action Inhibits bacterial cell wall synthesis by binding to one or more of the penicillin-binding proteins (PBPs), which in turn inhibits the final transpeptidation step of peptidoglycan synthesis in bacterial cell walls, thus inhibiting cell wall biosynthesis. Bacteria eventually lyse due to ongoing activity of cell wall autolytic enzymes (autolysins and murein hydrolases) while cell wall assembly is arrested.

Pharmacodynamics/Kinetics

Half-life Elimination 1 to 2 hours, prolonged with renal impairment

Time to Peak Serum: IM: ~1 hour

Pregnancy Risk Factor B

Pregnancy Considerations Adverse events have not been observed in animal reproduction studies. Ceftazidime crosses the placenta and reaches the cord serum and amniotic fluid. An increase in most types of birth defects was not found following first trimester exposure to cephalosporins. Maternal peak serum concentration is unchanged in the first trimester. After the first trimester, serum concentrations decrease by approximately 50% of those in nonpregnant patients. Renal clearance is increased during pregnancy.

Ceftazidime and Avibactam

(SEF tay zi deem & a vi BAK tam)

Brand Names: US Avycaz

Pharmacologic Category Cephalosporin Combination

Use

Intra-abdominal infections, complicated: Treatment of complicated intra-abdominal infections (cIAI) in patients 18 years and older, in combination with metronidazole, caused by *Citrobacter freundii* complex, *Enterobacter cloacae*, *Escherichia coli*, *Klebsiella oxytoca*, *K. pneumoniae*, *Proteus mirabilis*, and *Pseudomonas aeruginosa*.

Urinary tract infections, complicated (including pyelonephritis): Treatment of complicated urinary tract infections (cUTI) (including pyelonephritis) in patients 18 years and older, caused by *Citrobacter freundii* complex, *E. cloacae*, *Escherichia coli*, *Klebsiella pneumoniae*, *Proteus mirabilis*, and *Pseudomonas aeruginosa*.

Local Anesthetic/Vasoconstrictor Precautions No information available to require special precautions

Effects on Dental Treatment No significant effects or complications reported

Effects on Bleeding No information available to require special precautions

Adverse Reactions

1% to 10%:

Gastrointestinal: Diarrhea (3%), nausea (3%), constipation (2%), upper abdominal pain (1%)

Hematologic & oncologic: Positive direct coombs test (3%; no hemolytic anemia reactions reported)

<1%, postmarketing, and/or case reports: Acute renal failure, anxiety, candidiasis, *Clostridium difficile*-associated diarrhea, dysgeusia, hypokalemia, increased gamma-glutamyl transferase, increased serum ALT, increased serum AST, injection site phlebitis, maculopapular rash, nephrolithiasis, pruritus, renal insufficiency, skin rash, thrombocytopenia, urticaria

General Dosage Range Note: Dosage recommendations are expressed as total grams of the ceftazidime/avibactam combination

Dosage adjustment recommended in patients with renal impairment.

IV: *Adults:* 2.5 g every 8 hours

Mechanism of Action

Ceftazidime inhibits bacterial cell wall synthesis by binding to one or more of the penicillin-binding proteins (PBPs) which in turn inhibits the final transpeptidation step of peptidoglycan synthesis in bacterial cell walls, thus inhibiting cell wall biosynthesis. Bacteria eventually lyse due to ongoing activity of cell wall autolytic enzymes (autolysins and murein hydrolases) while cell wall assembly is arrested.

Avibactam inactivates some beta-lactamases and protects ceftazidime from degradation.

Pharmacodynamics/Kinetics

Half-life Elimination Ceftazidime: 2.76 hours; Avibactam: 2.71 hours

Pregnancy Considerations Adverse events have not been observed in animal reproduction studies conducted with ceftazidime; adverse events have been observed in some animal reproduction studies conducted with avibactam.

Ceftibuten (sef TYE byoo ten)

Related Information

Bacterial Infections *on page* 1835

Brand Names: US Cedax

Pharmacologic Category Antibiotic, Cephalosporin (Third Generation)

Use

Acute bacterial exacerbations of chronic bronchitis: Treatment of mild to moderate acute bacterial exacerbations of chronic bronchitis due to *Haemophilus influenzae* (including beta-lactamase-producing strains), *Moraxella catarrhalis* (including beta-lactamase-producing strains), or *Streptococcus pneumoniae* (penicillin-susceptible strains only).

Limitations of use: In acute bacterial exacerbations of chronic bronchitis clinical trials where *M. catarrhalis* was isolated from infected sputum at baseline, ceftibuten clinical efficacy was 22% less than control.

Acute bacterial otitis media: Treatment of mild to moderate acute bacterial otitis media due to *H. influenzae* (including beta-lactamase-producing strains), *M. catarrhalis* (including beta-lactamase-producing strains), or *Streptococcus pyogenes*.

Limitations of use: Although ceftibuten used empirically was equivalent to comparators in the treatment of clinically and/or microbiologically documented acute otitis media, the efficacy against *S. pneumoniae* was 23% less than control. Therefore, ceftibuten should be given empirically only when adequate antimicrobial coverage against *S. pneumoniae* has been previously administered.

Pharyngitis/tonsillitis: Treatment of mild to moderate pharyngitis and tonsillitis due to *S. pyogenes*.

Local Anesthetic/Vasoconstrictor Precautions No information available to require special precautions

Effects on Dental Treatment No significant effects or complications reported

Effects on Bleeding No information available to require special precautions

Adverse Reactions

1% to 10%:

Central nervous system: Headache (≤3%), dizziness (≤1%)

Gastrointestinal: Nausea (≤4%), diarrhea (3% to 4%), dyspepsia (≤2%), loose stools (≤2%), abdominal pain (1% to 2%), vomiting (1% to 2%)

Hematologic & oncologic: Eosinophilia (3%), decreased hemoglobin (1% to 2%), change in platelet count (increase: ≤1%)

Hepatic: Increased serum ALT (≤1%), increased serum bilirubin (≤1%)

Renal: Increased blood urea nitrogen (2% to 4%)

<1%, postmarketing, and/or case reports: Agitation, anorexia, aphasia, candidiasis, constipation, dehydration, diaper rash, drowsiness, dysgeusia, dyspnea, dysuria, eructation, fatigue, fever, flatulence, hematuria, hyperkinesia, increased serum alkaline phosphatase, increased serum AST, increased serum creatinine, insomnia, irritability, jaundice, leukopenia, melena, nasal congestion, paresthesia, pruritus, pseudomembranous colitis, psychosis, rigors, serum sickness, skin rash, Stevens-Johnson syndrome, stridor, thrombocytopenia, toxic epidermal necrolysis, urticaria, vaginitis, xerostomia

General Dosage Range Dosage adjustment recommended in patients with renal impairment

Oral:

Infants and Children 6 months to <12 years: 9 mg/kg/dose once daily (maximum: 400 mg/day)

Children ≥12 years, Adolescents, and Adults: 400 mg once daily

Mechanism of Action Inhibits bacterial cell wall synthesis by binding to one or more of the penicillin-binding proteins (PBPs) which in turn inhibits the final transpeptidation step of peptidoglycan synthesis in bacterial cell walls, thus inhibiting cell wall biosynthesis. Bacteria eventually lyse due to ongoing activity of cell wall autolytic enzymes (autolysins and murein hydrolases) while cell wall assembly is arrested.

Pharmacodynamics/Kinetics

Half-life Elimination Children: 2 hours; Adults: 2.4 hours; CrCl 30 to 49 mL/minute: 7.1 hours; CrCl 5 to 29 mL/minute: 13.4 hours; CrCl <5 mL/minute: 22.3 hours

Time to Peak 2 to 2.6 hours

Pregnancy Risk Factor B

Pregnancy Considerations Adverse events have not been observed in animal reproduction studies. An increase in most types of birth defects was not found following first trimester exposure to cephalosporins (Crider 2009).

Ceftolozane and Tazobactam

(sef TOL oh zane & taz oh BAK tam)

Brand Names: US Zerbaxa

Brand Names: Canada Zerbaxa

Pharmacologic Category Cephalosporin Combination

Use

Intra-abdominal infections: Treatment of complicated intra-abdominal infections in adults, in combination with metronidazole, caused by *Enterobacter cloacae*, *Escherichia coli*, *Klebsiella oxytoca*, *K. pneumoniae*, *Proteus mirabilis*, *Pseudomonas aeruginosa*, *Bacteroides fragilis*, *Streptococcus anginosus*, *Streptococcus constellatus*, and *Streptococcus salivarius*.

Urinary tract infections: Treatment of complicated urinary tract infections, including pyelonephritis, in adults caused by *Escherichia coli*, *Klebsiella pneumoniae*, *Proteus mirabilis*, and *Pseudomonas aeruginosa*.

Local Anesthetic/Vasoconstrictor Precautions No information available to require special precautions

Effects on Dental Treatment No significant effects or complications reported

Effects on Bleeding No information available to require special precautions

Adverse Reactions

1% to 10%:

Cardiovascular: Hypotension (≤2%), atrial fibrillation (≤1%)

Central nervous system: Headache (3% to 6%), insomnia (complicated intra-abdominal infections: 4%; complicated UTIs: 1%), anxiety (≤2%), dizziness (≤1%)

Dermatologic: Skin rash (≤2%)

Endocrine: Hypokalemia (complicated intra-abdominal infections: 3%; complicated UTIs: <1%)

Gastrointestinal: Nausea (3% to 8%), diarrhea (complicated intra-abdominal infections: 6%; complicated UTIs: 2%), constipation (2% to 4%), vomiting (complicated intra-abdominal infections: 3%, complicated UTIs: 1%), abdominal pain (≤1%)

Hematologic & oncologic: Anemia (≤2%), thrombocythemia (≤2%)

Hepatic: Increased serum ALT (2%), increased serum AST (1% to 2%)

Miscellaneous: Fever (complicated intra-abdominal infections: 6%; complicated UTIs: 2%)

<1%, postmarketing, and/or case reports: Abdominal distention, angina pectoris, candidiasis, *Clostridium difficile* associated diarrhea, dyspepsia, dyspnea, flatulence, fungal urinary tract infection, gastritis, hyperglycemia, hypomagnesemia, hypophosphatemia, increased gamma-glutamyl transferase, increased serum alkaline phosphatase, infusion site reaction, nonhemorrhagic stroke, oropharyngeal candidiasis, paralytic ileus, positive direct Coombs test, renal failure, renal insufficiency, tachycardia, urticaria, venous thrombosis, vulvovaginal candidiasis

General Dosage Range Dosage adjustment recommended in patients with renal impairment

IV: *Adults:* 1.5 g ceftolozane/tazobactam (ceftolozane 1 g and tazobactam 500 mg) every 8 hours

Mechanism of Action Ceftolozane inhibits bacterial cell wall synthesis by binding to one or more of the penicillin-binding proteins (PBPs); which in turn inhibits the final transpeptidation step of peptidoglycan synthesis in bacterial cell walls, thus inhibiting cell wall biosynthesis. Ceftolozane is an inhibitor of PBPs of *Pseudomonas aeruginosa* (eg, PBP1b, PBP1c, and PBP3) and *Escherichia coli* (eg, PBP3). Tazobactam irreversibly inhibits many beta-lactamases (eg, certain penicillinases and cephalosporinases), and can covalently bind to some plasmid-mediated and chromosomal bacterial beta-lactamases.

Pharmacodynamics/Kinetics

Half-life Elimination Ceftolozane: ~3 hours; Tazobactam: ~1 hour

Time to Peak Plasma: Immediately following completion of 60-minute infusion

Pregnancy Risk Factor B

Pregnancy Considerations Adverse events were observed in some animal reproduction studies. Tazobactam crosses the placenta (Bourget, 1998).

CefTRIAXone (sef trye AKS one)

Related Information

Antibiotic Prophylaxis *on page 1812*

Sexually-Transmitted Diseases *on page 1804*

Brand Names: US Rocephin [DSC]

Brand Names: Canada Ceftriaxone for Injection; Ceftriaxone for Injection USP; Ceftriaxone Sodium for Injection; Ceftriaxone Sodium for Injection BP

Pharmacologic Category Antibiotic, Cephalosporin (Third Generation)

Use

Acute bacterial otitis media: Caused by *Streptococcus pneumoniae*, *Haemophilus influenzae* (including beta-lactamase-producing strains), or *Moraxella catarrhalis* (including beta-lactamase-producing strains).

Bacterial septicemia: Caused by *Staphylococcus aureus*, *S. pneumoniae*, *Escherichia coli*, *H. influenzae*, or *Klebsiella pneumoniae*.

Bone and joint infections: Caused by *S. aureus*, *S. pneumoniae*, *E. coli*, *Proteus mirabilis*, *K. pneumoniae*, or *Enterobacter* spp.

Intra-abdominal infections: Caused by *E. coli*, *K. pneumoniae*, *Bacteroides fragilis*, *Clostridium* spp., or *Peptostreptococcus* spp.

Lower respiratory tract infections: Caused by *S. pneumoniae*, *S. aureus*, *H. influenzae*, *Haemophilus parainfluenzae*, *K. pneumoniae*, *E. coli*, *Enterobacter aerogenes*, *P. mirabilis*, or *Serratia marcescens*.

Meningitis: Caused by *H. influenzae*, *Neisseria meningitidis*, or *S. pneumoniae*. Ceftriaxone has also been used successfully in a limited number of cases of meningitis and shunt infection caused by *Staphylococcus epidermidis* and *E. coli* (efficacy for these 2 organisms in this organ system was studied in fewer than 10 infections).

Pelvic inflammatory disease: Caused by *N. gonorrhoeae*. Ceftriaxone, like other cephalosporins, has no activity against *Chlamydia trachomatis*. Therefore, when cephalosporins are used in the treatment of patients with pelvic inflammatory disease and *C. trachomatis* is one of the suspected pathogens, appropriate antichlamydial coverage should be added.

Skin and skin structure infections: Caused by *S. aureus*, *S. epidermidis*, *Streptococcus pyogenes*, viridans group streptococci, *E. coli*, *Enterobacter cloacae*, *Klebsiella oxytoca*, *K. pneumoniae*, *P. mirabilis*, *Morganella morganii* (efficacy for this organism in this organ system was studied in fewer than 10 infections), *Pseudomonas aeruginosa*, *S. marcescens*, *Acinetobacter calcoaceticus*, or *B. fragilis* (efficacy for this organism in this organ system was studied in fewer than 10 infections), or *Peptostreptococcus* spp.

Surgical prophylaxis: Reduce the incidence of postoperative infections in patients undergoing surgical procedures classified as contaminated or potentially contaminated (eg, vaginal or abdominal hysterectomy or cholecystectomy for chronic calculous cholecystitis in high-risk patients, such as those older than 70 years, with acute cholecystitis not requiring therapeutic antimicrobials, obstructive jaundice, or common duct bile stones) and in surgical patients for whom infection at the operative site would present serious risk (eg, during coronary artery bypass surgery).

Uncomplicated gonorrhea (cervical/urethral and rectal): Caused by *N. gonorrhoeae*, including both penicillinase- and nonpenicillinase-producing strains, and pharyngeal gonorrhea caused by nonpenicillinase-producing strains of *N. gonorrhoeae*.

Urinary tract infections (complicated and uncomplicated): Caused by *E. coli*, *P. mirabilis*, *Proteus vulgaris*, *M. morganii*, or *K. pneumoniae*.

Local Anesthetic/Vasoconstrictor Precautions No information available to require special precautions

Effects on Dental Treatment No significant effects or complications reported

Effects on Bleeding May potentiate the anticoagulant effects of vitamin K anticoagulants (ie, warfarin) due to alterations of gut flora.

Adverse Reactions

>10%:

Dermatologic: Skin tightness (IM: ≤5% to ≤17%; local)

Local: Induration at injection site (≤5% to ≤17%; incidence higher with IM), warm sensation at injection site (IM: ≤5% to ≤17%)

1% to 10%:

Dermatologic: Skin rash (2%)

Gastrointestinal: Diarrhea (3%)

Hematologic & oncologic: Eosinophilia (6%), thrombocythemia (5%), leukopenia (2%)

Hepatic: Increased serum transaminases (3%)

Local: Pain at injection site (≤1%), tenderness at injection site (≤1%)

Renal: Increased blood urea nitrogen (1%)

<1%, postmarketing and/or case reports: Abdominal pain, acute generalized exanthematous pustulosis, acute renal failure (post-renal), agranulocytosis, allergic dermatitis, anaphylactoid reaction, anaphylaxis, anemia, basophilia, blood coagulation disorder, bronchospasm, candidiasis, casts in urine, chills, choledocholithiasis, cholelithiasis, clostridium difficile associated diarrhea, colitis, decreased prothrombin time, diaphoresis, dizziness, dysgeusia, dyspepsia, edema, epistaxis, erythema multiforme, fever, flatulence, flushing, gallbladder sludge, glossitis, glycosuria, granulocytopenia, headache, hematuria, hemolytic anemia, hypersensitivity pneumonitis, increased monocytes, increased serum alkaline phosphatase, increased serum bilirubin, increased serum creatinine, jaundice, kernicterus, leukocytosis, lymphocytopenia, lymphocytosis, nausea, nephrolithiasis, neutropenia, oliguria, palpitations, pancreatitis, phlebitis, prolonged prothrombin time, pruritus, pseudomembranous colitis, seizure, serum sickness, Stevens-Johnson syndrome, stomatitis, thrombocytopenia, toxic epidermal necrolysis, ureteral obstruction, urogenital fungal infection, urolithiasis, urticaria, vaginitis, vomiting

General Dosage Range

IM:

Children: 50 to 100 mg/kg/day divided every 12 to 24 hours (maximum: 4,000 mg daily) **or** 125 mg or 50 mg/kg as a single dose

Adults: 1 to 2 g every 12 to 24 hours **or** 125 to 250 mg as a single dose

IV:

Children: 50 to 100 mg/kg/day divided every 12 to 24 hours (maximum: 4,000 mg daily)

Adults: 1 to 2 g every 12 to 24 hours (maximum: 4,000 mg daily)

Mechanism of Action Inhibits bacterial cell wall synthesis by binding to one or more of the penicillin-binding proteins (PBPs) which in turn inhibits the final transpeptidation step of peptidoglycan synthesis in bacterial cell walls, thus inhibiting cell wall biosynthesis. Bacteria eventually lyse due to ongoing activity of cell wall autolytic enzymes (autolysins and murein hydrolases) while cell wall assembly is arrested.

Pharmacodynamics/Kinetics

Half-life Elimination

Neonates (Martin 1984): 1 to 4 days: 16 hours; 9 to 30 days: 9 hours

Children (age not specified): 4.1 to 6.6 hours (Richards 1984)

Adults: Normal renal and hepatic function: ~5 to 9 hours

Adults: Renal impairment (mild-to-severe): ~12 to 16 hours

Time to Peak Serum: IM: 2 to 3 hours

Pregnancy Risk Factor B

Pregnancy Considerations Adverse events have not been observed in animal reproduction studies. Ceftriaxone crosses the placenta. Pregnancy was found to influence the single dose pharmacokinetics of ceftriaxone when administered prior to delivery (Popović 2007). The pharmacokinetics of ceftriaxone following multiple doses in the third trimester are similar to those of nonpregnant patients (Bourget Fernandez 1993). Ceftriaxone is recommended for use in pregnant women for the treatment of gonococcal infections, Lyme disease, and may be used in certain situations prior to vaginal delivery in women at high risk for endocarditis (consult current guidelines) (ACOG 120, 2011; CDC [Workowski 2015]; Wormser 2006).

Cefuroxime (se fyoor OKS eem)

Related Information

Antibiotic Prophylaxis *on page 1812*
Bacterial Infections *on page 1835*

Brand Names: US Ceftin; Zinacef; Zinacef in D5W [DSC]; Zinacef in Sterile Water

Brand Names: Canada Apo-Cefuroxime; Auro-Cefuroxime; Ceftin; Cefuroxime For Injection; Cefuroxime For Injection, USP; PRO-Cefuroxime; ratio-Cefuroxime

Pharmacologic Category Antibiotic, Cephalosporin (Second Generation)

Use

Acute bacterial maxillary sinusitis (tablets and oral suspension only): Treatment of mild to moderate acute bacterial maxillary sinusitis in adults and pediatric patients ≥3 months caused by *Streptococcus pneumoniae, Haemophilus influenzae* (non-beta-lactamase-producing strains only).

Limitations of use: Effectiveness for sinus infections caused by beta-lactamase–producing *H. influenzae* or *M. catarrhalis* in patients with acute bacterial maxillary sinusitis has not been established. **Note**: According to the IDSA guidelines for acute bacterial rhinosinusitis, cefuroxime is no longer recommended as monotherapy for initial empiric treatment (Chow 2012).

Acute bacterial exacerbations of chronic bronchitis (tablets only): Treatment of mild to moderate acute bacterial exacerbations of chronic bronchitis in adults and adolescents ≥13 years caused by *S. pneumoniae, H. influenzae* (beta-lactamase negative strains), or *Haemophilus parainfluenzae* (beta-lactamase negative strains).

Acute otitis media (tablets and oral suspension only): Treatment of pediatric patients ≥3 months with acute bacterial otitis media caused by *S. pneumoniae, H. influenzae* (including beta-lactamase-producing strains), *Moraxella catarrhalis* (including beta-lactamase-producing strains), or *Streptococcus pyogenes*.

Bone and joint infections (injection only): Treatment of bone and joint infections caused by *Staphylococcus aureus* (penicillinase- and non-penicillinase-producing strains).

Lower respiratory tract infections (injection only): Treatment of lower respiratory tract infections, including pneumonia, caused by *S. pneumoniae, H. influenzae* (including ampicillin-resistant strains), *Klebsiella* spp., *S. aureus* (penicillinase- and non-penicillinase-producing strains), *S. pyogenes*, and *Escherichia coli*.

Lyme disease (early) (tablets only): Treatment of adults and adolescents ≥13 years with early Lyme disease caused by *Borrelia burgdorferi*.

Pharyngitis/tonsillitis (tablets and oral suspension only): Treatment of mild to moderate pharyngitis/tonsillitis caused by *S. pyogenes* in adults and pediatric patients ≥3 months

Limitations of use: The efficacy in the prevention of rheumatic fever has not been established in clinical trials. Efficacy in the treatment of penicillin-resistant strains of *S. pyogenes* has not been demonstrated.

Septicemia (injection only): Treatment of septicemia caused by *S. aureus* (penicillinase- and non-penicillinase-producing strains), *S. pneumoniae, E. coli, H. influenzae* (including ampicillin-resistant strains), and *Klebsiella* spp.

Skin and skin structure infection (impetigo) (oral suspension only): Treatment of pediatric patients 3 months to 12 years of age with skin or skin structure infections (impetigo) caused by *S. aureus* (including beta-lactamase-producing strains) or *S. pyogenes*.

Skin and skin structure infection (injection; tablets [uncomplicated infections only]): Treatment of adults and pediatric patients >3 months with skin and skin-structure infections (including impetigo) caused by *S. aureus* (penicillinase- and non-penicillinase-producing strains), *S. pyogenes*, *E. coli*, *Klebsiella* spp., and *Enterobacter* spp.

Surgical (perioperative) prophylaxis (injection only): Prophylaxis of infection in patients undergoing surgical procedures (eg, vaginal hysterectomy) that are classified as clean-contaminated or potentially contaminated procedures.

Urinary tract infections (tablets and injection only): Treatment of adults and pediatric patients >3 months with urinary tract infections caused by *E. coli* and *Klebsiella* spp.

Local Anesthetic/Vasoconstrictor Precautions No information available to require special precautions

Effects on Dental Treatment No significant effects or complications reported

Effects on Bleeding No information available to require special precautions

Adverse Reactions

>10%: Gastrointestinal: Diarrhea (4% to 11%, duration dependent)

1% to 10%:

Cardiovascular: Local thrombophlebitis (2%)

Dermatologic: Diaper rash (children 3%)

Endocrine & metabolic: Increased lactate dehydrogenase (1%)

Gastrointestinal: Nausea and vomiting (3% to 7%), unpleasant taste (children 5%)

Genitourinary: Vaginitis (≤5%)

Hematologic & oncologic: Decreased hematocrit (≤10%), decreased hemoglobin (≤10%), eosinophilia (1% to 7%)

Hepatic: Increased serum transaminases (2% to 4%), increased serum alkaline phosphatase (2%)

Immunologic: Jarisch-Herxheimer reaction (6%)

<1%, postmarketing, and/or case reports (Limited to important or life-threatening): Abdominal pain, anaphylaxis, angioedema, anorexia, arthralgia, brain disease, candidiasis, chest pain, chest tightness, chills, cholestasis, *Clostridium difficile* associated diarrhea, colitis, cough, decreased creatinine clearance, dizziness, drowsiness, drug fever, dyspepsia, dyspnea, dysuria, erythema, erythema multiforme, fever, flatulence, gastrointestinal hemorrhage, gastrointestinal infection, glossitis, headache, hearing loss, hemolytic anemia, hepatitis, hyperactivity, hyperbilirubinemia, hypersensitivity, hypersensitivity angiitis, increased blood urea nitrogen, increased liver enzymes, increased serum creatinine, increased thirst, interstitial nephritis, irritability, jaundice, joint swelling, leukopenia, muscle cramps, muscle rigidity, muscle spasm (neck), neutropenia, oral mucosa ulcer, pancytopenia, positive direct Coombs test, prolonged prothrombin time, pruritus, pseudomembranous colitis, renal insufficiency, renal pain, seizure, serum sickness-like reaction, sialorrhea, sinusitis, skin rash, Stevens-Johnson syndrome, stomach cramps, tachycardia, thrombocytopenia (rare), toxic epidermal necrolysis, trismus, upper respiratory tract infection, urethral bleeding, urethral pain, urinary tract infection, urticaria, vaginal discharge, vaginal irritation, viral infection, vulvovaginal candidiasis, vulvovaginal pruritus

General Dosage Range Dosage adjustment recommended in patients with renal impairment

IM, IV:

Infants ≥3 months and Children ≤12 years: 75 to 150 mg/kg/day divided every 8 hours (maximum: 6 g/day)

Children >12 years, Adolescents and Adults: 750 mg to 1.5 g every 6 to 8 hours (maximum: 6 g/day) **or** 1.5 g as a single dose

Oral:

Infants ≥3 months and Children ≤12 years: 20 to 30 mg/kg/day in 2 divided doses **or** 125 to 250 mg every 12 hours (maximum: 1,000 mg/day)

Children >12 years, Adolescents, and Adults: 250 to 500 mg every 12 hours **or** 1 g as a single dose

Mechanism of Action Inhibits bacterial cell wall synthesis by binding to one or more of the penicillin-binding proteins (PBPs) which in turn inhibits the final transpeptidation step of peptidoglycan synthesis in bacterial cell walls, thus inhibiting cell wall biosynthesis. Bacteria eventually lyse due to ongoing activity of cell wall autolytic enzymes (autolysins and murein hydrolases) while cell wall assembly is arrested.

Pharmacodynamics/Kinetics

Half-life Elimination

Premature neonates:

PNA ≤3 days: Median: 5.8 hours (de Louvois 1982)

PNA ≥8 days: Median: 1.6-3.8 hours (de Louvois 1982)

Children and Adolescents: 1.4-1.9 hours

Adults: ~1 to 2 hours; prolonged with renal impairment

Time to Peak Serum: IM: ~15 to 60 minutes; IV: 2 to 3 minutes; Oral: Children: ~3 to 4 hours; Adults: ~2 to 3 hours

Pregnancy Risk Factor B

Pregnancy Considerations Adverse events were not observed in animal reproduction studies. Cefuroxime crosses the placenta and reaches the cord serum and amniotic fluid. Placental transfer is decreased in the presence of oligohydramnios. Several studies have failed to identify an increased teratogenic risk to the fetus following maternal cefuroxime use.

During pregnancy, mean plasma concentrations of cefuroxime are 50% lower, the AUC is 25% lower, and the plasma half-life is shorter than nonpregnant values. At term, plasma half-life is similar to nonpregnant values and peak maternal concentrations after IM administration are slightly decreased. Pregnancy does not alter the volume of distribution. Cefuroxime is one of the antibiotics recommended for prophylactic use prior to cesarean delivery.

Celecoxib (se le KOKS ib)

Related Information

Oral Pain *on page 1830*

Rheumatoid Arthritis, Osteoarthritis, and Osteoporosis *on page 1792*

Brand Names: US CeleBREX

Brand Names: Canada ACCEL-Celecoxib; ACT Celecoxib; Apo-Celecoxib; Bio-Celecoxib; Celebrex; GD-Celecoxib; JAMP-Celecoxib; Mar-Celecoxib; Mint-Celecoxib; Mylan-Celecoxib; PMS-Celecoxib; Priva-Celecoxib; RAN-Celecoxib; Riva-Celecoxib; Sandoz-Celecoxib; Teva-Celecoxib

Generic Availability (US) Yes

Pharmacologic Category Analgesic, Nonopioid; Nonsteroidal Anti-inflammatory Drug (NSAID), COX-2 Selective

Dental Use Management of acute dental pain

Use

Acute pain: Management of acute pain.

Ankylosing spondylitis: Relief of the signs/symptoms of ankylosing spondylitis.

Juvenile idiopathic arthritis: Relief of the signs/symptoms of juvenile idiopathic arthritis (JIA) in patients 2 years and older.

Osteoarthritis: Relief of the signs/symptoms of osteoarthritis.

Primary dysmenorrhea: Treatment of primary dysmenorrhea.

Rheumatoid arthritis: Relief of the signs/symptoms of rheumatoid arthritis.

Local Anesthetic/Vasoconstrictor Precautions No information available to require special precautions

Effects on Dental Treatment Key adverse event(s) related to dental treatment: Stomatitis, abnormal taste, and xerostomia (normal salivary flow resumes upon discontinuation).

Effects on Bleeding No effects on bleeding or platelet function have been reported. See Dental Comment.

Adverse Reactions

≥2%:

Cardiovascular: Peripheral edema (2%)

Gastrointestinal: Diarrhea (6%), dyspepsia (9%), abdominal pain (4%), flatulence (2%), gastroesophageal reflux disease, vomiting

Hepatic: Increased liver enzymes (<3x ULN: ≤6%)

Renal: Nephrolithiasis (3%)

Respiratory: Upper respiratory tract infection (8%), sinusitis (5%), pharyngitis (2%), rhinitis (2%), dyspnea

Miscellaneous: Accidental injury (3%)

Frequency not defined:

Dermatologic: Acute generalized exanthematous pustulosis, exfoliative dermatitis

Gastrointestinal: Gastrointestinal perforation, gastrointestinal ulcer, GI inflammation, intestinal perforation

Hypersensitivity: Anaphylaxis

Immunologic: DRESS syndrome

Respiratory: Local alveolar osteitis (post oral surgery patients)

<2%, postmarketing, and/or case reports: Acute renal failure, ageusia, agranulocytosis, albuminuria, alopecia, anaphylactoid reaction, anemia, angina pectoris, angioedema, anorexia, anosmia, anxiety, aplastic anemia, arthralgia, aseptic meningitis, ataxia, bronchitis, bronchospasm, bronchospasm (aggravated), cellulitis, cerebrovascular accident, chest pain, cholelithiasis, colitis (with bleeding), constipation, contact dermatitis, coronary artery disease, cough, cyst, cyst (NOS), cystitis, deafness, decreased hemoglobin, deep vein thrombosis, depression, dermatitis, diaphoresis, diverticulitis, drowsiness, dysphagia, dysuria, ecchymoses, edema, epistaxis, eructation, erythema multiforme, erythematous rash, esophageal perforation, esophagitis, exacerbation of hypertension, facial edema, fatigue, fever, flu-like symptoms, gangrene of skin or other tissue, gastritis, gastroenteritis, gastroesophageal reflux disease, gastrointestinal hemorrhage, hematuria, hemorrhoids, hepatic failure, hepatic necrosis, hepatitis, hiatal hernia, hot flash, hypercholesterolemia, hyperglycemia, hypersensitivity exacerbation, hypersensitivity reaction, hypertonia, hypoesthesia, hypoglycemia, hypokalemia, hyponatremia, increased appetite, increased blood urea nitrogen, increased creatine phosphokinase, increased nonprotein nitrogen, increased serum alkaline phosphatase, interstitial nephritis, intestinal obstruction, intracranial hemorrhage, jaundice, laryngitis, leg cramps, leukopenia, maculopapular rash, melena, migraine, myalgia, myocardial infarction, nervousness, osteoarthritis, pain, palpitations, pancreatitis, pancytopenia, paresthesia, peripheral pain, pneumonia, pruritus, pulmonary embolism, skin changes, skin photosensitivity, Stevens-Johnson syndrome, stomatitis, syncope, synovitis, tachycardia, tendonitis, tenesmus, thrombocythemia, thrombocytopenia, thrombophlebitis, tinnitus, toxic epidermal necrolysis, urinary frequency, urticaria, vasculitis, ventricular fibrillation, vertigo, weight gain, xeroderma, xerostomia

Dental Usual Dosage Acute dental pain: Adults: Oral: 400 mg, followed by an additional 200 mg if needed on day 1; maintenance dose: 200 mg twice daily as needed

Dosing

Adult Note: Use the lowest effective dose for the shortest duration of time, consistent with individual patient treatment goals.

Acute pain or primary dysmenorrhea: Oral: Initial dose: 400 mg, followed by an additional 200 mg if needed on day 1; maintenance dose: 200 mg twice daily as needed

Ankylosing spondylitis: Oral: 200 mg once daily or 100 mg twice daily; if no effect after 6 weeks, may increase to 400 mg/day. If no response following 6 weeks of treatment with 400 mg/day, consider discontinuation and alternative treatment.

Osteoarthritis: Oral: 200 mg once daily **or** 100 mg twice daily

Rheumatoid arthritis: Oral: 100 to 200 mg twice daily

Acute gout (off-label use): 800 mg once followed by 400 mg on day 1; then 400 mg twice daily for one week (ACR guidelines [Khanna 2012]; Schumacker 2012)

Dosing adjustment in poor CYP2C9 metabolizers (ie, CYP2C9*3/*3): Reduce initial dose by 50%; consider alternative treatment in patients with JIA who are poor CYP2C9 metabolizers.

Geriatric Initiate at the lowest recommended dose. The AUC in elderly patients (especially females and patients weighing <50 kg) may be increased by 50% compared with younger subjects.

Pediatric Note: Use the lowest effective dose for the shortest duration of time, consistent with individual patient treatment goals.

Juvenile idiopathic arthritis (JIA): Oral: Children ≥2 years:

≥10 kg to ≤25 kg: 50 mg twice daily

>25 kg: 100 mg twice daily

*Dosing adjustment in poor CYP2C9 metabolizers (eg, CYP2C9*3/*3):* Consider alternative therapy.

Renal Impairment

Mild or moderate impairment: There are no dosage adjustments provided in the manufacturer's labeling; however, since <1% of the drug is excreted in the urine, dosage adjustment is not necessary (Davies 2000). Based on unpublished data, AUC was ~40% *lower* in patients with chronic renal insufficiency (GFR 35 to 60 mL/minute) compared with subjects with normal renal function due to a higher apparent clearance.

Severe impairment: Use is not recommended.

Advanced renal disease: Use is not recommended; however, if celecoxib treatment cannot be avoided, monitor renal function closely.

Abnormal renal function tests (persistent or worsening): Discontinue use.

Hepatic Impairment

Mild impairment (Child-Pugh class A): No dosage adjustment necessary; AUC increased ~40% in mild hepatic impairment compared with healthy subjects.

Moderate impairment (Child-Pugh class B): Reduce dose by 50%.

Severe impairment (Child-Pugh class C): Use is not recommended.

Abnormal liver function tests (persistent or worsening): Discontinue use.

Mechanism of Action Inhibits prostaglandin synthesis by decreasing the activity of the enzyme, cyclooxygenase-2 (COX-2), which results in decreased formation of prostaglandin precursors; has antipyretic, analgesic, and anti-inflammatory properties. Celecoxib does not inhibit cyclooxygenase-1 (COX-1) at therapeutic concentrations.

Contraindications

Hypersensitivity to celecoxib, sulfonamides, aspirin, other NSAIDs, or any component of the formulation; patients who have experienced asthma, urticaria, or allergic-type reactions after taking aspirin or other NSAIDs; use in the setting of CABG surgery.

Note: Although the FDA approved product labeling states this medication is contraindicated with other sulfonamide-containing drug classes, the scientific basis of this statement has been challenged. See "Warnings/Precautions" for more detail.

Canadian labeling: Additional contraindications (not in US labeling): Pregnancy (third trimester); women who are breastfeeding; severe, uncontrolled heart failure; active gastrointestinal ulcer (gastric, duodenal, peptic); active gastrointestinal bleeding; inflammatory bowel disease; cerebrovascular bleeding; severe liver impairment or active hepatic disease; severe renal impairment (CrCl <30 mL/minute) or deteriorating renal disease; known hyperkalemia; use in patients <18 years of age

Warnings/Precautions **[US Boxed Warning]: NSAIDs cause an increased risk of serious (and potentially fatal) adverse cardiovascular thrombotic events, including MI and stroke. Risk may occur early during treatment and may increase with duration of use.** Relative risk appears to be similar in those with and without known cardiovascular disease or risk factors for cardiovascular disease; however, absolute incidence of cardiovascular events (which may occur early during treatment) was higher in patients with known cardiovascular disease or risk factors. New onset hypertension or exacerbation of hypertension may occur (NSAIDs may also impair response to ACE inhibitors, thiazide diuretics, or loop diuretics); may contribute to cardiovascular events; monitor blood pressure; use with caution in patients with hypertension. May cause sodium and fluid retention, use with caution in patients with edema. Avoid use in patients with heart failure (ACCF/AHA [Yancy 2013]). Avoid use in patients with recent MI unless benefits outweigh risk of cardiovascular thrombotic events. Long-term cardiovascular risk in children has not been evaluated. Use the lowest effective dose for the shortest duration of time, consistent with individual patient goals, to reduce risk of cardiovascular events; alternate therapies should be considered for patients at high risk.

[US Boxed Warning]: Celecoxib is contraindicated in the setting of coronary artery bypass graft surgery (CABG). Risk of MI and stroke may be increased with use following CABG surgery.

[US Boxed Warning]: NSAIDs cause an increased risk of serious gastrointestinal inflammation, ulceration, bleeding, and perforation (may be fatal); elderly patients and patients with history of peptic ulcer disease and/or GI bleeding are at greater risk for serious GI events. These events may occur at any time during therapy and without warning. Avoid use in patients with active GI bleeding. Use caution with a history of GI ulcers, concurrent therapy known to increase the risk of GI bleeding (eg, aspirin, anticoagulants and/or corticosteroids, selective serotonin reuptake inhibitors), smoking, use of alcohol, or in the elderly or debilitated patients. Use the lowest effective dose for the shortest duration of time, consistent with individual patient goals, to reduce risk of GI adverse events; alternate therapies should be considered for patients at high risk. When used concomitantly with aspirin, a substantial increase in the risk of gastrointestinal complications (eg, ulcer) occurs; concomitant gastroprotective therapy (eg, proton pump inhibitors) is recommended (Bhatt 2008).

NSAIDs may cause serious skin adverse events including exfoliative dermatitis, Stevens-Johnson syndrome (SJS), and toxic epidermal necrolysis (TEN); may occur without warning and in patients without prior known sulfa allergy. Anaphylactoid reactions may occur, even without prior exposure; patients with "aspirin triad" (bronchial asthma, aspirin intolerance, rhinitis) may be at increased risk. Contraindicated in patients who have experienced an anaphylactic reaction with NSAID or aspirin therapy. The manufacturer's labeling states to not administer to patients with aspirin-sensitive asthma due to severe and potentially fatal bronchospasm that has been reported in such patients having received aspirin and the potential for cross reactivity with other NSAIDs. The manufacturer also states to use with caution in patients with other forms of asthma. However, in patients with known aspirin-exacerbated respiratory disease (AERD), the use of celecoxib initiated at a low dose with gradual titration in patients with stable, mild to moderate persistent asthma has been used without incident (Morales 2013).

Use with caution in patients with decreased hepatic (dosage adjustments are recommended for moderate hepatic impairment; not recommended for patients with severe hepatic impairment) or renal function. Transaminase elevations have been reported with use; closely monitor patients with any abnormal LFT. Rare (sometimes fatal), severe hepatic reactions (eg, fulminant hepatitis, hepatic necrosis, hepatic failure) have occurred with NSAID use, rarely; discontinue if signs or symptoms of liver disease develop, if systemic manifestations occur, or with persistent or worsening abnormal hepatic function tests. NSAID use may compromise existing renal function; dose-dependent decreases in prostaglandin synthesis may result from NSAID use, causing a reduction in renal blood flow which may cause renal decompensation (usually reversible). Patients with impaired renal function, dehydration, hypovolemia, heart failure, liver dysfunction, those taking diuretics, ACE inhibitors, angiotensin II receptor blockers, and the elderly are at greater risk for renal toxicity. Rehydrate patient before starting therapy; monitor renal function closely. Avoid use in patients with advanced renal disease; discontinue use with persistent or worsening abnormal renal function tests. Long-term NSAID use may result in renal papillary necrosis.

Use with caution in patients with known or suspected deficiency of cytochrome P450 isoenzyme 2C9; poor metabolizers may have higher plasma levels due to reduced metabolism; consider reduced initial doses. Alternate therapies should be considered in patients with JIA who are poor metabolizers of CYP2C9.

Anemia may occur with use; monitor hemoglobin or hematocrit in patients on long-term treatment. Celecoxib does not affect PT, PTT or platelet counts; does not inhibit platelet aggregation at approved doses. Potentially significant drug-drug interactions may exist, requiring dose or frequency adjustment, additional monitoring, and/or selection of alternative therapy.

Use with caution in pediatric patients with systemic-onset juvenile idiopathic arthritis (JIA); serious adverse reactions, including disseminated intravascular coagulation, may occur.

Sulfonamide ("sulfa") allergy: The FDA-approved product labeling for many medications containing a sulfonamide chemical group includes a broad contraindication in patients with a prior allergic reaction to sulfonamides. There is a potential for cross-reactivity between members of a specific class (eg, two antibiotic sulfonamides). However, concerns for cross-reactivity have previously extended to all compounds containing the sulfonamide structure (SO_2NH_2). An expanded understanding of allergic mechanisms indicates cross-reactivity between antibiotic sulfonamides and nonantibiotic sulfonamides may not occur or at the very least this potential is extremely low (Brackett 2004; Johnson 2005; Slatore 2004; Tornero 2004). In particular, mechanisms of cross-reaction due to antibody production (anaphylaxis) are unlikely to occur with nonantibiotic sulfonamides. T-cell-mediated (type IV) reactions (eg, maculopapular rash) are less well understood and it is not possible to completely exclude this potential based on current insights. In cases where prior reactions were severe (Stevens-Johnson syndrome/TEN), some clinicians choose to avoid exposure to these classes.

Drug Interactions

Metabolism/Transport Effects **Substrate** of CYP2C9 (major), CYP3A4 (minor); **Note:** Assignment of Major/Minor substrate status based on clinically relevant drug interaction potential; **Inhibits** CYP2C8 (moderate), CYP2D6 (weak)

Avoid Concomitant Use

Avoid concomitant use of Celecoxib with any of the following: Amodiaquine; Dexketoprofen; Floctafenine; Ketorolac (Nasal); Ketorolac (Systemic); Mecamylamine; Morniflumate; Nonsteroidal Anti-Inflammatory Agents; NSAID (COX-2 Inhibitor); Omacetaxine; Pelubiprofen; Phenylbutazone; Talniflumate; Tenoxicam; Zaltoprofen

Increased Effect/Toxicity

Celecoxib may increase the levels/effects of: 5-ASA Derivatives; Ajmaline; Aliskiren; Aminoglycosides; Aminolevulinic Acid; Amodiaquine; Anticoagulants; ARIPiprazole; Bisphosphonate Derivatives; CycloSPORINE (Systemic); CYP2C8 Substrates; Deferasirox; Desmopressin; Digoxin; Drospirenone; Eplerenone; Estrogen Derivatives; Haloperidol; Lithium; Mecamylamine; Methotrexate; NSAID (COX-2 Inhibitor); Omacetaxine; Perhexiline; Porfimer; Potassium-Sparing Diuretics; PRALAtrexate; Prilocaine; Quinolone Antibiotics; Sodium Nitrite; Tacrolimus (Systemic); Tenofovir Products; Tolperisone; Triflusal; Vancomycin; Verteporfin; Vitamin K Antagonists

The levels/effects of Celecoxib may be increased by: ACE Inhibitors; Alcohol (Ethyl); Angiotensin II Receptor Blockers; Antidepressants (Tricyclic, Tertiary Amine); Aspirin; Ceritinib; Corticosteroids (Systemic); CycloSPORINE (Systemic); CYP2C9 Inhibitors (Moderate); CYP2C9 Inhibitors (Strong); Dapsone (Topical); Dexketoprofen; Felbinac; Floctafenine; Herbs (Anticoagulant/Antiplatelet Properties); Ketorolac (Nasal); Ketorolac (Systemic); Loop Diuretics; Lumacaftor; MiFEPRIStone; Morniflumate; Naftazone; Nitric Oxide; Nonsteroidal Anti-Inflammatory Agents; Pelubiprofen; Phenylbutazone; Probenecid; Selective Serotonin Reuptake Inhibitors; Sodium Phosphates; Talniflumate; Tenoxicam; Tetracaine (Topical); Thiazide and Thiazide-Like Diuretics; Tolperisone; Triflusal; Zaltoprofen

Decreased Effect

Celecoxib may decrease the levels/effects of: ACE Inhibitors; Aliskiren; Angiotensin II Receptor Blockers; Beta-Blockers; Eplerenone; HydrALAZINE; Loop Diuretics; Potassium-Sparing Diuretics; Prostaglandins (Ophthalmic); Selective Serotonin Reuptake Inhibitors; Thiazide and Thiazide-Like Diuretics

The levels/effects of Celecoxib may be decreased by: Bile Acid Sequestrants; CYP2C9 Inducers (Strong); Dabrafenib; Enzalutamide; Lumacaftor

Food Interactions Peak concentrations are delayed and AUC is increased by 10% to 20% when taken with a high-fat meal. Management: Administer without regard to meals.

Pharmacodynamics/Kinetics

Half-life Elimination Children and Adolescents ~7-16 years (steady-state): 6 ± 2.7 hours (range: 3-10 hours) (Stempak 2002); Adults: ~11 hours (fasted)

Time to Peak Children: Median: 3 hours (range: 1-5.8 hours) (Stempak 2002); Adults: ~3 hours

Pregnancy Risk Factor C (prior to 30 weeks gestation)/D (≥30 weeks gestation)

Pregnancy Considerations Teratogenic effects have been observed in some animal studies; therefore, celecoxib is classified as pregnancy category C. Celecoxib is a NSAID that primarily inhibits COX-2 whereas other currently available NSAIDs are nonselective for COX-1 and COX-2. The effects of this selective inhibition to the fetus have not been well studied and limited information is available specific to celecoxib. NSAID exposure during the first trimester is not strongly associated with congenital malformations; however, cardiovascular anomalies and cleft palate have been observed following NSAID exposure in some studies. The use of a NSAID close to conception may be associated with an increased risk of miscarriage. Nonteratogenic effects have been observed following NSAID administration during the third trimester including: Myocardial degenerative changes, prenatal constriction of the ductus arteriosus, fetal tricuspid regurgitation, failure of the ductus arteriosus to close postnatally; renal dysfunction or failure, oligohydramnios; gastrointestinal bleeding or perforation, increased risk of necrotizing enterocolitis; intracranial bleeding (including intraventricular hemorrhage), platelet dysfunction with resultant bleeding; pulmonary hypertension. Because it may cause premature closure of the ductus arteriosus, the use of celecoxib is not recommended ≥30 weeks gestation. The chronic use of NSAIDs in women of reproductive age may be associated with infertility that is reversible upon discontinuation of the medication. A registry is available for pregnant women exposed to autoimmune medications including celecoxib. For additional information contact the Organization of Teratology Information Specialists, OTIS Autoimmune Diseases Study, at 877-311-8972.

Breastfeeding Considerations Small amounts of celecoxib are found in breast milk. The manufacturer recommends that caution be exercised when administering celecoxib to nursing women.

Dosage Forms

Capsule, Oral:

CeleBREX: 50 mg, 100 mg, 200 mg, 400 mg

Generic: 50 mg, 100 mg, 200 mg, 400 mg

Dental Comment The product labeling for **all** prescription nonsteroidal anti-inflammatory agents (NSAIDs) now include boxed warnings regarding an increased risk of cardiovascular (CV) events and gastrointestinal (GI) bleeding associated with their use and a contraindication for use in patients who have recently undergone coronary artery bypass graft (CABG) surgery. Medication guides are also now required for these products. Manufacturers of over-the-counter products are to include warnings about potential skin reactions, which are already included in prescription labeling.

The FDA encourages physicians to consider this information in risk-to-benefit evaluations while considering the use of the COX-2 selective celecoxib (CeleBREX®) in patients. Similar COX-2 selective drugs, including rofecoxib (Vioxx®) and valdecoxib (Bextra®), were pulled from the market due to increased risks of adverse CV events associated with their use. In addition, the FDA advises an evaluation of alternative therapy. If physicians determine that continued use is appropriate for individual patients, the lowest effective dose of celecoxib should be prescribed.

The association between selective COX-2 inhibitors and increased cardiovascular risk has been noted previously and prompted by publication of a meta-analysis entitled "Risk of Cardiovascular Events Associated With Selective COX-2 Inhibitors" in the August 22, 2001, edition of the *Journal of the American Medical Association (JAMA)*. The researchers re-evaluated four previously published trials, assessing cardiovascular events in patients receiving either celecoxib or rofecoxib. They found an association between the use of COX-2 inhibitors and cardiovascular events (including MI and ischemic stroke). The annualized MI rate was found to be significantly higher in patients receiving celecoxib or rofecoxib than in the control (placebo) group from a recent meta-analysis of primary prevention trials. Although cause and effect cannot be established (these trials were originally designed to assess GI effects, not cardiovascular ones), the authors believe the available data raise a cautionary flag concerning the risk of cardiovascular events with the use of COX-2 inhibitors.

Cross-reactivity, including bronchospasm, is a concern with aspirin and other NSAIDs, in aspirin-sensitive patients. The manufacturer suggests that celecoxib should not be administered to patients with this type of aspirin sensitivity and should be used with caution in patients with preexisting asthma.

The manufacturer studied the effect of celecoxib on the anticoagulant effect of warfarin and found no alteration of anticoagulant effect, as determined by prothrombin time, in patients taking 2-5 mg daily. However, the manufacturer has issued a caution when using celecoxib with warfarin since those patients are at increased risk of bleeding complications.

Cellulose (Oxidized/Regenerated)

(SEL yoo lose, OKS i dyzed re JEN er aye ted)

Related Information

Antiplatelet and Anticoagulation Considerations in Dentistry *on page 1764*

Brand Names: US Interceed; Surgicel SNoW 1"x2"; Surgicel SNoW 2"x4"; Surgicel SNoW 4"x4"

Generic Availability (US) No

Pharmacologic Category Hemostatic Agent

Dental Use To control bleeding created during a dental procedure

Use Hemostatic; temporary packing for the control of capillary, venous, or small arterial hemorrhage

Local Anesthetic/Vasoconstrictor Precautions No information available to require special precautions

Effects on Dental Treatment No significant effects or complications reported

Effects on Bleeding No information available to require special precautions

Adverse Reactions Frequency not defined.

Central nervous system: Headache

Dermatologic: Burning sensation of the nose

Local: Application site edema (encapsulation)

Respiratory: Sneezing (rhinological procedures), stinging sensation of the nose

Miscellaneous: Foreign body reaction (with or without) infection

1%, postmarketing, and/or case reports: Numbness, pain, paralysis

Dental Usual Dosage Control bleeding created during a dental procedure: Topical: Minimal amounts of the fabric strip are laid on the bleeding site or held firmly against the tissues until hemostasis occurs; remove excess material

Dosing

Adult & Geriatric Bleeding: Topical: Minimal amounts of the fabric strip are laid on the bleeding site or held firmly against the tissues until hemostasis occurs; remove excess material

Mechanism of Action Cellulose, oxidized regenerated is saturated with blood at the bleeding site and swells into a brownish or black gelatinous mass which aids in the formation of a clot. When used in small amounts, it is absorbed from the sites of implantation with little or no tissue reaction. In addition to providing hemostasis, oxidized regenerated cellulose also has been shown *in vitro* to have bactericidal properties.

Contraindications Hypersensitivity to any component of the formulation; implantation into bone defects; hemorrhage from large arteries; nonhemorrhagic oozing; use as an adhesion product

Warnings/Precautions Pain, numbness, or paralysis have been reported if used near a bony or neural space and left inside patient; use minimum amount necessary to achieve hemostasis. Remove as much of agent as possible after hemostasis is achieved. Do not leave in a contaminated or infected space. Always remove completely following hemostasis if applied in proximity to foramina in bone, areas of bony confine, the spinal cord or optic nerve and chasm; product may swell and exert unwanted pressure. The material should not be moistened before insertion since the hemostatic effect is greater when applied dry. The material should not be impregnated with anti-infective agents. Its hemostatic effect is not enhanced by the addition of thrombin.

Drug Interactions

Metabolism/Transport Effects None known.

Avoid Concomitant Use There are no known interactions where it is recommended to avoid concomitant use.

Increased Effect/Toxicity There are no known significant interactions involving an increase in effect.

Decreased Effect There are no known significant interactions involving a decrease in effect.

Pregnancy Considerations Has been evaluated for use in gynecologic surgeries (Sharma, 2003; Sharma, 2006).

Dosage Forms

Pad, External:

Interceed: (10 ea)
Surgicel SNoW 1"x2": (10 ea)
Surgicel SNoW 2"x4": (10 ea)
Surgicel SNoW 4"x4": (10 ea)

Cephalexin (sef a LEKS in)

Related Information

Antibiotic Prophylaxis *on page 1812*
Bacterial Infections *on page 1835*

Related Sample Prescriptions

Bacterial Infections and Periodontal Diseases - Sample Prescriptions *on page 32*
Prevention of Endocarditis and to Reduce the Risk of Late Infections of Joint Prostheses - Sample Prescriptions *on page 37*

Brand Names: US Daxbia; Keflex

Brand Names: Canada Apo-Cephalex; Dom-Cephalexin; Keflex; PMS-Cephalexin; Teva-Cephalexin

Generic Availability (US) Yes

Pharmacologic Category Antibiotic, Cephalosporin (First Generation)

Dental Use Prophylaxis in total joint replacement patients undergoing dental procedures; alternative oral antibiotic for prevention of infective endocarditis in individuals allergic to penicillins or ampicillin

Note: Individuals allergic to amoxicillin (penicillins) may receive cephalexin provided they have not had an immediate, local, or systemic IgE-mediated anaphylactic allergic reaction to penicillin.

Use

Bone infections: Treatment of bone infections caused by *Staphylococcus aureus* and/or *Proteus mirabilis*.

Genitourinary tract infections: Treatment of genitourinary tract infections, including acute prostatitis, caused by *Escherichia coli*, *P. mirabilis*, and *Klebsiella pneumoniae*.

Otitis media: Treatment of otitis media caused by *Streptococcus pneumoniae*, *Haemophilus influenzae*, *S. aureus*, *Streptococcus pyogenes*, and *Moraxella catarrhalis*.

Respiratory tract infections: Treatment of respiratory tract infections caused by *S. pneumoniae* and *S. pyogenes*.

Skin and skin structure infections: Treatment of skin and skin structure infections caused by *S. aureus* and/or *S. pyogenes*.

Local Anesthetic/Vasoconstrictor Precautions No information available to require special precautions

Effects on Dental Treatment No significant effects or complications reported (see Dental Comment)

Effects on Bleeding No information available to require special precautions

Adverse Reactions Frequency not defined.

Central nervous system: Agitation, confusion, dizziness, fatigue, hallucination, headache

Dermatologic: Erythema multiforme (rare), genital pruritus, skin rash, Stevens-Johnson syndrome (rare), toxic epidermal necrolysis (rare), urticaria

Gastrointestinal: Abdominal pain, diarrhea, dyspepsia, gastritis, nausea (rare), pseudomembranous colitis, vomiting (rare)

Genitourinary: Genital candidiasis, vaginal discharge, vaginitis

Hematologic & oncologic: Eosinophilia, hemolytic anemia, neutropenia, thrombocytopenia

Hepatic: Cholestatic jaundice (rare), hepatitis (transient, rare), increased serum ALT, increased serum AST

Hypersensitivity: Anaphylaxis, angioedema, hypersensitivity reaction

Neuromuscular & skeletal: Arthralgia, arthritis, arthropathy

Renal: Interstitial nephritis (rare)

Dental Usual Dosage

Prophylaxis against infective endocarditis (dental, oral, or respiratory tract procedures): Oral:

Children >1 year: 50 mg/kg 30 to 60 minutes prior to procedure; maximum: 2 g

Children >15 years and Adults: 2 g 30 to 60 minutes prior to procedure

Note: American Heart Association (AHA) guidelines now recommend prophylaxis only in patients undergoing invasive procedures and in whom underlying cardiac conditions may predispose to a higher risk of adverse outcomes should infection occur.

Prophylaxis in total joint replacement patients undergoing dental procedures which produce bacteremia: Oral: Adults: 2 g 1 hour prior to procedure

Note: In general, patients with prosthetic joint implants do not require prophylactic antibiotics prior to dental procedures. In planning an invasive oral procedure, dental consultation with the patient's orthopedic surgeon may be advised to review the risks of infection.

Dosing

Adult & Geriatric

Dosing range: Oral: 250 to 1,000 mg every 6 hours or 500 mg every 12 hours (maximum: 4 g/day)

Indication-specific dosing:

Impetigo: Oral: 250 mg every 6 hours; continue for 7 days, depending upon clinical response (IDSA [Stevens 2014])

Infective endocarditis, prophylaxis (dental, oral, or respiratory tract procedures) (off-label use): Oral: 2 g 30 to 60 minutes prior to procedure. **Note:** American Heart Association (AHA) guidelines now recommend prophylaxis only in patients undergoing invasive procedures and in whom underlying cardiac conditions may predispose to a higher risk of adverse outcomes should infection occur (AHA [Wilson 2007]).

Prophylaxis in patients with prosthetic joint implants undergoing dental procedures which produce bacteremia (off-label use): Oral: 2 g 1 hour prior to procedure (ADA/AAOS 2003). **Note:** In general, patients with prosthetic joint implants do not require prophylactic antibiotics prior to dental procedures. In planning an invasive oral procedure, dental consultation with the patient's orthopedic surgeon may be advised to review the risks of infection (Sollecito 2015).

Prosthetic joint infection, chronic oral antimicrobial suppression (off-label use): Oral:

Propionibacterium spp (alternative to penicillin or amoxicillin): 500 mg every 6 to 8 hours (Osmon 2013)

Staphylococci, oxacillin-susceptible (preferred): 500 mg every 6 to 8 hours (Osmon 2013)

Streptococci, beta-hemolytic (alternative to penicillin or amoxicillin): 500 mg every 6 to 8 hours (Osmon 2013)

Skin and skin structure infections: Oral:

Manufacturer's labeling: 250 mg every 6 hours or 500 mg every 12 hours

Alternate recommendations: 500 mg every 6 hours (IDSA [Stevens 2014])

Streptococcal pharyngitis: Oral: 500 mg every 12 hours. **Note:** Recommended by the Infectious Disease Society of America (IDSA) as an alternative agent for group A streptococcal pharyngitis in penicillin-allergic patients (avoid in patients with immediate-type hypersensitivity to penicillin) with a duration of 10 days (Shulman 2012).

Streptococcal skin infections: 500 mg every 6 hours (IDSA [Stevens 2014])

Surgical site infection (trunk or extremity [away from axilla or perineum]) (off-label use): Oral: 500 mg every 6 hours (IDSA [Stevens 2014])

Uncomplicated cystitis: Oral: 250 mg every 6 hours or 500 mg every 12 hours for 7 to 14 days

Pediatric

Usual dose:

Children >1 year and Adolescents <15 years: Oral: 25 to 100 mg/kg/day in divided doses every 6 to 8 hours (maximum: 4 g/day)

Adolescents ≥ 15 years: Oral: 250 to 1,000 mg every 6 hours; maximum daily dose: 4 g/day

Indication-specific dosing:

Community-acquired pneumonia (CAP) (IDSA/PIDS 2011), *S. aureus* (methicillin-susceptible), mild infection or step-down therapy (preferred) (off-label use): Infants >3 months and Children: Oral: 75 to 100 mg/kg/day in 3 to 4 divided doses

Impetigo: Children: Oral: 25 to 50 mg/kg/day in 3 to 4 divided doses; continue for 7 days, depending upon clinical response (IDSA [Stevens 2014])

Infective endocarditis, prophylaxis (dental, oral, or respiratory tract procedures) (off-label use): Infants, Children, and Adolescents: Oral: 50 mg/kg 30 to 60 minutes prior to procedure (maximum dose: 2 g). **Note:** American Heart Association (AHA) guidelines now recommend prophylaxis only in patients undergoing invasive procedures and in whom underlying cardiac conditions may predispose to a higher risk of adverse outcomes should infection occur (AHA [Wilson 2007]).

Otitis media: Children: 75 to 100 mg/kg/day in 4 divided doses

Prophylaxis in total joint replacement patients undergoing dental procedures which produce bacteremia (off-label use): Adolescents ≥15 years: Refer to adult dosing.

Severe infections: Children: Oral: 50 to 100 mg/kg/day in divided doses every 6 to 8 hours

Skin and skin structure infections:

Manufacturer's labeling:

Children >1 year and Adolescents <15 years: Oral: 25 to 50 mg/kg/day in divided doses every 6 to 12 hours

Adolescents ≥15 years: Refer to adult dosing.

Alternate recommendations: Children: 25 to 50 mg/kg/day divided every 6 hours (IDSA [Stevens 2014])

Streptococcal pharyngitis: Children >1 year: Oral: 25 to 50 mg/kg/day divided every 12 hours. **Note:** Recommended by the Infectious Disease Society of America (IDSA) as an alternative agent for group A streptococcal pharyngitis in penicillin-allergic patients (avoid in patients with immediate-type hypersensitivity to penicillin) at a dose of 40 mg/kg/day divided twice daily (maximum: 1000 mg daily) for 10 days (Shulman 2012).

Uncomplicated cystitis: Adolescents ≥15 years: Refer to adult dosing.

Renal Impairment Adolescents >15 years and Adults:

CrCl ≥60 mL/minute: No dosage adjustment necessary.

CrCl 30 to 59 mL/minute: There are no specific dosage adjustments provided in the manufacturer's labeling; maximum recommended daily dose: 1,000 mg/day.

CrCl 15 to 29 mL/minute: 250 mg every 8 to 12 hours

CrCl 5 to 14 mL/minute (not yet on dialysis): 250 every 24 hours

CrCl 1 to 4 mL/minute (not yet on dialysis): 250 mg every 48 to 60 hours

End stage renal disease (ESRD) on intermittent hemodialysis: There are no dosage adjustments provided in the manufacturer's labeling; however the following guidelines have been used by some clinicians (Aronoff 2007): Oral: 250 to 500 mg every 12 to 24 hours; moderately dialyzable (20% to 50%); give dose after dialysis session.

Peritoneal dialysis: There are no dosage adjustments provided in the manufacturer's labeling; however, the following guidelines have been used by some clinicians (Aronoff 2007): Oral: 250 to 500 mg every 12 to 24 hours.

Hepatic Impairment There are no dosage adjustments provided in the manufacturer's labeling.

Mechanism of Action Inhibits bacterial cell wall synthesis by binding to one or more of the penicillin-binding proteins (PBPs) which in turn inhibits the final transpeptidation step of peptidoglycan synthesis in bacterial cell walls, thus inhibiting cell wall biosynthesis. Bacteria eventually lyse due to ongoing activity of cell wall autolytic enzymes (autolysins and murein hydrolases) while cell wall assembly is arrested.

Contraindications Hypersensitivity to cephalexin, other cephalosporins, or any component of the formulation

Warnings/Precautions Allergic reactions (eg, rash, urticaria, angioedema, anaphylaxis, erythema multiforme, Stevens-Johnson syndrome, toxic epidermal necrolysis [TEN]) have been reported. If an allergic reaction occurs, discontinue immediately and institute appropriate treatment. Use with caution in patients with a history of seizure disorder; high levels, particularly in the presence of renal impairment, may increase risk of seizures. Modify dosage in patients with severe renal impairment. Use with caution in patients with a history of penicillin allergy, especially IgE-mediated reactions (eg, anaphylaxis, urticaria). Positive direct Coombs tests and acute intravascular hemolysis has been reported. If anemia develops during or after therapy, discontinue use and work up for drug-induced hemolytic anemia. Prolonged use may result in fungal or bacterial superinfection, including *C. difficile*-associated diarrhea (CDAD) and pseudomembranous colitis; CDAD has been observed >2 months postantibiotic treatment. May be associated with increased INR, especially in nutritionally-deficient patients, prolonged treatment, hepatic or renal disease. Potentially significant interactions may exist, requiring dose or frequency adjustment, additional monitoring, and/or selection of alternative therapy.

Drug Interactions

Metabolism/Transport Effects None known.

Avoid Concomitant Use

Avoid concomitant use of Cephalexin with any of the following: BCG (Intravesical); Cholera Vaccine

Increased Effect/Toxicity

Cephalexin may increase the levels/effects of: MetFORMIN; Vitamin K Antagonists

The levels/effects of Cephalexin may be increased by: Probenecid

Decreased Effect

Cephalexin may decrease the levels/effects of: BCG (Intravesical); BCG Vaccine (Immunization); Cholera Vaccine; Lactobacillus and Estriol; Sodium Picosulfate; Typhoid Vaccine

The levels/effects of Cephalexin may be decreased by: Multivitamins/Minerals (with ADEK, Folate, Iron); Multivitamins/Minerals (with AE, No Iron); Zinc Salts

Food Interactions Peak antibiotic serum concentration is lowered and delayed, but total drug absorbed is not affected. Cephalexin serum levels may be decreased if taken with food. Management: Administer without regard to food.

Pharmacodynamics/Kinetics

Half-life Elimination Neonates: 5 hours; Children 3-12 months: 2.5 hours; Adults: 0.5 to 1.2 hours (prolonged with renal impairment)

Time to Peak Serum: ~1 hour

Pregnancy Risk Factor B

Pregnancy Considerations Adverse events were not observed in animal reproduction studies. Cephalexin crosses the placenta and produces therapeutic concentrations in the fetal circulation and amniotic fluid (Creatsas 1980). Peak concentrations in pregnant patients are similar to those in nonpregnant patients. Prolonged labor may decrease oral absorption (Griffith 1983; Paterson 1972).

Breastfeeding Considerations Cephalexin is excreted in breast milk.

The relative infant dose (RID) of cephalexin is 0.13% to 0.52% when compared to an infant therapeutic dose of 25 to 100 mg/kg/day. In general, breastfeeding is considered acceptable when the relative infant dose is <10%; when an RID is >25% breastfeeding should generally be avoided (Anderson 2016; Ito 2000). Using a milk concentration of 0.85 mcg/mL, the estimated daily infant dose via breast milk is 0.13 mg/kg/day. This milk concentration was obtained following a single maternal dose of cephalexin 1,000 mg orally on the third postpartum day (Kafetzis 1981).

The mean peak milk concentration occurred 4 to 5 hours after the dose (Kafetzis 1981). Slightly higher concentrations of cephalexin were detected in the breast milk of a lactating woman also administered probenecid and cephalexin for ≥16 days (Ilett 2006).

Diarrhea has been reported in breastfeeding infants (Ilett 2006; Ito 1993). In general, antibiotics that are present in breast milk may cause nondose-related modification of bowel flora. Monitor infants for GI disturbances (WHO 2002).

When an antibiotic is needed, cephalexin may be used to treat mastitis in breastfeeding women allergic to preferred agents (Amir 2014; Berens 2015). The manufacturer recommends that caution be exercised when administering cephalexin to nursing women.

Dosage Forms

Capsule, Oral:

Daxbia: 333 mg

Keflex: 250 mg, 500 mg, 750 mg

Generic: 250 mg, 500 mg, 750 mg

Suspension Reconstituted, Oral:

Generic: 125 mg/5 mL (100 mL, 200 mL); 250 mg/5 mL (100 mL, 200 mL)

Tablet, Oral:

Generic: 250 mg, 500 mg

Dental Comment Cephalexin is effective against anaerobic bacteria, but the sensitivity of alpha-hemolytic Streptococcus vary; approximately 10% of strains are resistant. Nearly 70% are intermediately sensitive. Patients allergic to penicillins can use a cephalosporin; the incidence of cross-reactivity between penicillins and cephalosporins is 1% to 5% when the allergic reaction to penicillin is delayed. If the patient has a history of anaphylaxis to penicillin, cephalosporins are contraindicated in these patients.

Ceritinib (se RI ti nib)

Brand Names: US Zykadia

Brand Names: Canada Zykadia

Pharmacologic Category Antineoplastic Agent, Anaplastic Lymphoma Kinase Inhibitor; Antineoplastic Agent, Tyrosine Kinase Inhibitor

Use Non-small cell lung cancer, metastatic: Treatment of patients with anaplastic lymphoma kinase (ALK)-positive metastatic non-small cell lung cancer (NSCLC) who have progressed on or are intolerant to crizotinib.

Local Anesthetic/Vasoconstrictor Precautions Ceritinib is one of the drugs confirmed to prolong the QT interval and is accepted as having a risk of causing torsade de pointes. The risk of drug-induced torsade de pointes is extremely low when a single QT interval prolonging drug is prescribed. In terms of epinephrine, it is not known what effect vasoconstrictors in the local anesthetic regimen will have in patients with a known history of congenital prolonged QT interval or in patients taking any medication that prolongs the QT interval. Until more information is obtained, it is suggested that the clinician consult with the physician prior to the use of a vasoconstrictor in suspected patients, and that the vasoconstrictor (epinephrine, mepivacaine and levonordefrin [Carbocaine® 2% with Neo-Cobefrin®]) be used with caution.

Effects on Dental Treatment No significant effects or complications reported (see Dental Comment)

Effects on Bleeding No information available to require special precautions

Adverse Reactions

>10%:

Central nervous system: Fatigue (52%), neuropathy (17%; including paresthesia, muscular weakness, gait disturbance, peripheral neuropathy, hypoesthesia, peripheral sensory neuropathy, dysesthesia, neuralgia, peripheral motor neuropathy, hypotonia, polyneuropathy)

Dermatologic: Skin rash (16%; including maculopapular rash, acneiform dermatitis)

Endocrine & metabolic: Increased serum glucose (49%; grades 3/4: 13%), decreased serum phosphate (36%)

Gastrointestinal: Diarrhea (86%; grades 3/4: 6%), nausea (80%; grades 3/4: 4%), vomiting (60%; grades 3/4: 4%), abdominal pain (54%), decreased appetite (34%), constipation (29%), increased serum lipase (28%), disease of esophagus (16%; including dyspepsia, gastroesophageal reflux disease, dysphagia)

Hematologic & oncologic: Decreased hemoglobin (84%)

Hepatic: Increased serum ALT (80%; grades 3/4: 27%), increased serum AST (75%; grades 3/4: 13%), increased serum bilirubin (15%; grades 3/4: 1%)

Renal: Increased serum creatinine (58%)

1% to 10%:

Cardiovascular: Prolonged Q-T interval on ECG (4%; >60 msec increase from baseline: 3%; >500 msec: <1%), bradycardia (3%), sinus bradycardia (1%)

Ophthalmic: Visual disturbance (9%; including vision impairment, blurred vision, photopsia, accommodation disorder, presbyopia, reduced visual acuity)

Respiratory: Interstitial pulmonary disease (4%; grades 3/4: 3%)

General Dosage Range Dosage adjustment recommended in patients on concomitant therapy or who develop toxicities.

Oral: *Adults:* 750 mg once daily

Mechanism of Action Potent inhibitor of anaplastic lymphoma kinase (ALK), a tyrosine kinase involved in the pathogenesis of non-small cell lung cancer. ALK gene abnormalities due to mutations or translocations may result in expression of oncogenic fusion proteins (eg, ALK fusion protein) which alter signaling and expression and result in increased cellular proliferation and survival in tumors which express these fusion proteins. ALK inhibition reduces proliferation of cells expressing the genetic alteration. Ceritinib also inhibits insulin-like growth factor 1 receptor (IGF-1R), insulin receptor (InsR), and ROS1. Ceritinib has demonstrated activity in crizotinib-resistant tumors in NSCLC xenograft models.

Pharmacodynamics/Kinetics

Half-life Elimination 41 hours

Time to Peak ~4 to 6 hours

Pregnancy Risk Factor D

Pregnancy Considerations Adverse events were observed in animal reproduction studies. Based on its mechanism of action, ceritinib may cause fetal harm if administered to a pregnant woman. Women of reproductive potential should use effective contraception during treatment and for at least 2 weeks following therapy discontinuation.

Dental Comment See Local Anesthetic/Vasoconstrictor Precautions

Certolizumab Pegol (cer to LIZ u mab PEG ol)

Related Information

Rheumatoid Arthritis, Osteoarthritis, and Osteoporosis *on page 1792*

Brand Names: US Cimzia; Cimzia Prefilled; Cimzia Starter Kit

Brand Names: Canada Cimzia

Pharmacologic Category Antirheumatic, Disease Modifying; Gastrointestinal Agent, Miscellaneous; Tumor Necrosis Factor (TNF) Blocking Agent

Use

Ankylosing spondylitis: Treatment of adults with active ankylosing spondylitis (AS)

Crohn disease: Treatment of moderately to severely active Crohn disease in patients who have inadequate response to conventional therapy

Psoriatic arthritis: Treatment of adult patients with active psoriatic arthritis

Rheumatoid arthritis: Treatment of adults with moderately to severely active rheumatoid arthritis (RA) (as monotherapy or in combination with nonbiological disease-modifying antirheumatic drugs [DMARDS])

Local Anesthetic/Vasoconstrictor Precautions No information available to require special precautions

Effects on Dental Treatment Key adverse event(s) related to dental treatment: Aphthous ulcers reported in <1% of patients.

Effects on Bleeding No information available to require special precautions

Adverse Reactions

>10%:

Gastrointestinal: Nausea (≤11% [Schreiber 2005])

Immunologic: Antibody development (7% to 23%)

Infection: Infection (38%; serious: 3%)

Respiratory: Upper respiratory tract infection (6% to 20%)

1% to 10%:

Cardiovascular: Hypertension (≤5%), angina pectoris (<5%), atrial fibrillation (<5%), cardiac arrhythmia (<5%), cardiac failure (<5%; new or worsening), cerebrovascular accident (<5%), hypertensive heart disease (<5%), ischemic heart disease (<5%), myocardial infarction (<5%), pericardial effusion (<5%), pericarditis (<5%), transient ischemic attacks (<5%), vasculitis (<5%)

Central nervous system: Headache (5%), anxiety (<5%), bipolar mood disorder (<5%), suicidal tendencies (<5%), fatigue (≤3%)

Dermatologic: Skin rash (≤9%), alopecia (<5%), dermatitis (<5%), erythema nodosum (<5%), urticaria (<5%)

Endocrine & metabolic: Menstrual disease (<5%)

Genitourinary: Urinary tract infection (≤8%), nephrotic syndrome (<5%)

Hematologic & oncologic: Anemia (<5%), hemorrhage (<5%), hypercoagulability state (<5%), leukopenia (<5%), lymphadenopathy (<5%), pancytopenia (<5%), thrombophlebitis (<5%), positive ANA titer (≤4%)

Hepatic: Hepatitis (<5%), increased serum transaminases (<5%)

Neuromuscular & skeletal: Arthralgia (6% to 7%), back pain (≤4%)

Ophthalmic: Optic neuritis (<5%), retinal hemorrhage (<5%), uveitis (<5%)

Renal: Renal failure (<5%)

Respiratory: Cough (≤6%), nasopharyngitis (5%), tuberculosis (<5%; peritoneal, pulmonary, and disseminated), bronchitis (≤3%), pharyngitis (≤3%)

Miscellaneous: Fever (3%)

<1%, postmarketing, and/or case reports: Abdominal pain, aplastic anemia, autoimmune hepatitis (Shelton 2015), cytopenia, demyelinating disease (exacerbation), diarrhea, fistula, hepatosplenic T-cell lymphoma, herpes virus infection, hypersensitivity reaction (eg, allergic dermatitis, angioedema, dizziness [postural], dyspnea, hepatotoxicity (idiosyncratic) (Chalasani 2014), hot flush, hypotension, injection site reactions, malaise, serum sickness, syncope), intestinal obstruction, leukemia, limb pain, lupus erythematosus, lupus-like syndrome, lymphoma, malignant melanoma, malignant neoplasm, Merkel cell carcinoma, neoplasm (benign, malignant, and unspecified; including cysts

and polyps), opportunistic infection (rare), peripheral edema, peripheral neuropathy, pneumonia, psoriasis (including new onset, palmoplantar, pustular, or exacerbation), pyelonephritis, reactivation of HBV, sarcoidosis, seizure, sensory disturbance, thrombocytopenia, viral infection, weakness

General Dosage Range SubQ: Adults: Initial: 400 mg, repeat dose 2 and 4 weeks after initial dose; Maintenance: 400 mg every 4 weeks **or** 200 mg every other week

Mechanism of Action Certolizumab is a pegylated humanized antibody Fab' fragment of tumor necrosis factor alpha (TNF-alpha) monoclonal antibody. Certolizumab binds to and selectively neutralizes human TNF-alpha activity. (Elevated levels of TNF-alpha have a role in the inflammatory process associated with Crohn disease and in joint destruction associated with rheumatoid arthritis.) Since it is not a complete antibody (lacks Fc region), it does not induce complement activation, antibody-dependent cell-mediated cytotoxicity, or apoptosis. Pegylation of certolizumab allows for delayed elimination and therefore an extended half-life.

Pharmacodynamics/Kinetics

Half-life Elimination ~14 days

Time to Peak Plasma: 54 to 171 hours

Pregnancy Considerations Adverse effects have not been observed in animal reproduction studies. Certolizumab was found to cross the human placenta. Serum concentrations in 12 infants of 10 mothers were ≥75% lower than the maternal serum at delivery (last maternal dose of 400 mg given 5 to 42 days prior to birth). Although placental transfer was low, infants may have a slower rate of elimination than adults. In 1 infant, certolizumab serum concentrations decreased from 1.02 to 0.84 mcg/mL over 4 weeks. Adverse events were not reported. The safety of administering live or live-attenuated vaccines to exposed infants is not known. If a biologic agent such as certolizumab is needed to treat inflammatory bowel disease during pregnancy, it is recommended to hold therapy after 30 weeks gestation (Habal 2012).

Health care providers are encouraged to enroll women exposed to certolizumab during pregnancy in the MotherToBaby Pregnancy Studies by contacting the Organization of Teratology Information Specialists (OTIS) (877-311-8972) or http://mothertobaby.org/pregnancy-studies/.

Cetirizine (se TI ra zeen)

Brand Names: US All Day Allergy Childrens [OTC]; All Day Allergy [OTC]; Cetirizine HCl Allergy Child [OTC]; Cetirizine HCl Childrens Alrgy [OTC]; Cetirizine HCl Childrens [OTC]; Cetirizine HCl Hives Relief [OTC]; ZyrTEC Allergy Childrens [OTC]; ZyrTEC Allergy [OTC]; ZyrTEC Childrens Allergy [OTC]; ZyrTEC Childrens Hives Relief [OTC] [DSC]; ZyrTEC Hives Relief [OTC] [DSC]

Brand Names: Canada Aller-Relief [OTC]; Apo-Cetirizine [OTC]; Extra Strength Allergy Relief [OTC]; PMS-Cetirizine; Reactine; Reactine [OTC]

Generic Availability (US) May be product dependent

Pharmacologic Category Histamine H_1 Antagonist; Histamine H_1 Antagonist, Second Generation; Piperazine Derivative

Use

Upper respiratory allergies: Temporarily relieves symptoms of upper respiratory allergies.

Urticaria: Relieves itching due to urticaria.

Local Anesthetic/Vasoconstrictor Precautions No information available to require special precautions

Effects on Dental Treatment Key adverse event(s) related to dental treatment: Xerostomia and decreased salivation (normal salivary flow resumes upon discontinuation).

Effects on Bleeding No information available to require special precautions

Adverse Reactions

>10%: Central nervous system: Drowsiness (adults 14%; children 2% to 4%), headache (children 11% to 14%, placebo 12%)

2% to 10%:

Central nervous system: Insomnia (children 9%; adults <2%), fatigue (adults 6%), malaise (4%), dizziness (adults 2%)

Gastrointestinal: Abdominal pain (children 4% to 6%), xerostomia (adults 5%), diarrhea (children 2% to 3%), nausea (children 2% to 3%; placebo 2%), vomiting (children 2% to 3%)

Respiratory: Pharyngitis (children 3% to 6%; placebo 3%), epistaxis (children 2% to 4%; placebo 3%), bronchospasm (children 2% to 3%; placebo 2%)

<2% (as reported in adults and/or children): Abnormality in thinking, accommodation disturbance, acne vulgaris, ageusia, alopecia, altered sense of smell, amnesia, anaphylaxis, angioedema, anorexia, anxiety, aphthous stomatitis, arthralgia, arthritis, ataxia, back pain, blepharoptosis, blindness, bronchitis, bullous rash, cardiac failure, chest pain, cholestasis, confusion, conjunctivitis, constipation, cutaneous nodules, cystitis, deafness, decreased libido, dehydration, depersonalization, depression, dermatitis, dermatological disease, diabetes mellitus, diaphoresis, dysgeusia, dysmenorrhea, dyspepsia, dyspnea, dysuria, eczema, edema, emotional lability, enlargement of abdomen, eructation, erythematous rash, euphoria, eye pain, facial edema, fever, flatulence, flushing, furunculosis, fussiness, gastritis, glaucoma, glomerulonephritis, hematuria, hemolytic anemia, hemophthalmos, hemorrhoids, hepatic insufficiency, hepatitis, hot flash, hyperesthesia, hyperkeratosis, hyperkinesia, hypermenorrhea, hypertension, hypertonia, hypertrichosis, hyperventilation, hypoesthesia, hypotension, increased appetite, increased bronchial secretions, increased liver enzymes (transient), increased serum bilirubin, increased thirst, intermenstrual bleeding, irritability, lack of concentration, leg cramps, leukorrhea, lower extremity edema, lymphadenopathy, maculopapular rash, mastalgia (female), melena, migraine, myalgia, myasthenia, myelitis, myocardial infarction, nasal polyposis, nervousness, nightmares, orofacial dyskinesia, osteoarthritis, otalgia, ototoxicity, pain, pallor, palpitations, paralysis, paresthesia, periorbital edema, pneumonia, polyuria, pruritus, purpura, rectal hemorrhage, respiratory tract disease, rhinitis, rigors, seborrhea, sialorrhea, sinusitis, skin photosensitivity, skin rash, sleep disorder, stomatitis, syncope, tachycardia, thrombocytopenia, tinnitus, tongue discoloration, tongue edema, tremor, twitching, upper respiratory tract infection, urinary frequency, urinary incontinence, urinary retention, urinary tract infection, urticaria, vaginitis, vertigo, visual field defect, voice disorder, weakness, weight gain, xeroderma, xerophthalmia

Postmarketing and/or case reports: Aggressive behavior, convulsions, hallucination, hypotension (severe), suicidal ideation

Dosing

Adult Upper respiratory allergies, urticaria: Oral: 5 to 10 mg once daily, depending upon symptom severity (maximum dose: 10 mg daily)

Geriatric Upper respiratory allergies, urticaria: Oral: 5 mg once daily (maximum dose: 5 mg daily). The previously available prescription product recommended a maximum dose of 10 mg once daily in patients <77 years of age or 5 mg once daily in patients ≥77 years of age (Zyrtec Prescribing Information, 2006).

Pediatric

Upper respiratory allergies, urticaria: Oral:

Infants 6 to <12 months: 2.5 mg once daily

Children 12 months to <2 years: 2.5 mg once daily; may increase to a maximum dose of 2.5 mg every 12 hours if needed

Children 2 to 5 years: Initial: 2.5 mg once daily; may be increased to a maximum dose of 2.5 mg every 12 hours **or** 5 mg once daily

Children ≥6 years and Adolescents: Refer to adult dosing.

Renal Impairment There are no dosage adjustments provided in the manufacturer's labeling; however, the following adjustments have been recommended (Aronoff, 2007):

Adults:

GFR >50 mL/minute: No dosage adjustment necessary.

GFR ≤50 mL/minute: 5 mg once daily

Intermittent hemodialysis: 5 mg once daily; 5 mg 3 times per week may also be effective.

Peritoneal dialysis: 5 mg once daily.

Infants, Children, and Adolescents:

GFR ≥30 mL/minute/1.73 m^2: No dosage adjustment necessary.

GFR 10 to 29 mL/minute/1.73 m^2: Decrease dose by 50%.

GFR <10 mL/minute/1.73 m^2: Not recommended.

Intermittent hemodialysis or peritoneal dialysis: Decrease dose by 50%.

Hepatic Impairment There are no dosage adjustments provided in the manufacturer's labeling.

Mechanism of Action Competes with histamine for H_1-receptor sites on effector cells in the gastrointestinal tract, blood vessels, and respiratory tract

Contraindications Hypersensitivity to cetirizine, hydroxyzine, or any component of the formulation

Warnings/Precautions Cetirizine should be used cautiously in patients with hepatic or renal impairment; consider dosage adjustment in patients with renal impairment. Use with caution in elderly patients; may be more sensitive to adverse effects. May cause drowsiness; use caution performing tasks which require alertness (eg, operating machinery or driving). Potentially significant drug-drug interactions may exist, requiring dose or frequency adjustment, additional monitoring, and/or selection of alternative therapy. Effects may be potentiated when used with other sedative drugs or ethanol.

Drug Interactions

Metabolism/Transport Effects Substrate of CYP3A4 (minor), P-glycoprotein; **Note:** Assignment of Major/Minor substrate status based on clinically relevant drug interaction potential

Avoid Concomitant Use

Avoid concomitant use of Cetirizine with any of the following: Aclidinium; Azelastine (Nasal); Cimetropium; Eluxadoline; Glucagon; Glycopyrrolate (Oral Inhalation); Ipratropium (Oral Inhalation); Levosulpiride; Nitroglycerin; Orphenadrine; Oxatomide; Oxomemazine; Paraldehyde; Potassium Chloride; Thalidomide; Tiotropium; Umeclidinium

Increased Effect/Toxicity

Cetirizine may increase the levels/effects of: AbobotulinumtoxinA; Alcohol (Ethyl); Analgesics (Opioid); Anticholinergic Agents; Azelastine (Nasal); Blonanserin; Buprenorphine; Cimetropium; CNS Depressants; Eluxadoline; Flunitrazepam; Glucagon; Glycopyrrolate (Oral Inhalation); HYDROcodone; Methotrimeprazine; MetyroSINE; Mirabegron; Mirtazapine; OnabotulinumtoxinA; Orphenadrine; OxyCODONE; Paraldehyde; Pilsicainide; Piribedil; Potassium Chloride; Pramipexole; Ramosetron; RimabotulinumtoxinB; ROPINIRole; Rotigotine; Selective Serotonin Reuptake Inhibitors; Suvorexant; Thalidomide; Thiazide and Thiazide-Like Diuretics; Tiotropium; Topiramate; Zolpidem

The levels/effects of Cetirizine may be increased by: Aclidinium; Brimonidine (Topical); Cannabis; Chloral Betaine; Chlormethiazole; Chlorphenesin Carbamate; Dimethindene (Topical); Doxylamine; Dronabinol; Droperidol; HydrOXYzine; Ipratropium (Oral Inhalation); Kava Kava; Lofexidine; Lumacaftor; Magnesium Sulfate; Methotrimeprazine; Mianserin; Minocycline; Nabilone; Oxatomide; Oxomemazine; Perampanel; P-glycoprotein/ABCB1 Inhibitors; Pilsicainide; Pramlintide; Ranolazine; Rufinamide; Sodium Oxybate; Tapentadol; Tetrahydrocannabinol; Trimeprazine; Umeclidinium

Decreased Effect

Cetirizine may decrease the levels/effects of: Acetylcholinesterase Inhibitors; Benzylpenicilloyl Polylysine; Betahistine; Gastrointestinal Agents (Prokinetic); Hyaluronidase; Itopride; Levosulpiride; Nitroglycerin; Secretin

The levels/effects of Cetirizine may be decreased by: Acetylcholinesterase Inhibitors; Amphetamines; Lumacaftor; P-glycoprotein/ABCB1 Inducers

Food Interactions Cetirizine's absorption and maximal concentration are reduced when taken with food. Management: May be taken without regard to meals.

Pharmacodynamics/Kinetics

Onset of Action Suppression of skin wheal and flare: 0.7 hours (Simons, 1999)

Duration of Action Suppression of skin wheal and flare: ≥24 hours (Simons, 1999)

Half-life Elimination Children: 6.2 hours; Adults: 8 hours

Time to Peak Serum: 1 hour

Pregnancy Considerations Maternal use of cetirizine has not been associated with an increased risk of major malformations. Cetirizine may be used for the treatment of rhinitis and urticaria during pregnancy (NAEPP 2005; Wallace 2008; Zuberbier 2014).

Breastfeeding Considerations Cetirizine is present in breast milk.

Drowsiness and irritability have been reported in breastfed infants exposed to antihistamines (Ito 1993). In general, second generation antihistamines (eg, cetirizine) are less sedating as compared to their first generation counterparts. If a breastfed infant is exposed to a second generation antihistamine via breast milk, they should be monitored for irritability, jitteriness, or drowsiness (Butler 2014).

When treatment with an antihistamine is needed in breastfeeding women, second generation antihistamines are preferred (Butler 2014; Powell 2015; Zuberier 2014).

Antihistamines may decrease maternal serum prolactin concentrations when administered prior to the establishment of nursing (Messinis 1985).

Dosage Forms

Capsule, Oral:
ZyrTEC Allergy [OTC]: 10 mg

Solution, Oral:
All Day Allergy Childrens [OTC]: 5 mg/5 mL (118 mL)
Cetirizine HCl Allergy Child [OTC]: 5 mg/5 mL (120 mL)
Cetirizine HCl Childrens [OTC]: 5 mg/5 mL (118 mL)
Cetirizine HCl Hives Relief [OTC]: 5 mg/5 mL (120 mL)
Generic: 5 mg/5 mL (120 mL, 473 mL)

Syrup, Oral:
Cetirizine HCl Childrens Alrgy [OTC]: 5 mg/5 mL (118 mL, 120 mL)
ZyrTEC Childrens Allergy [OTC]: 5 mg/5 mL (118 mL)
Generic: 5 mg/5 mL (5 mL, 120 mL, 473 mL, 480 mL)

Tablet, Oral:
All Day Allergy [OTC]: 10 mg
ZyrTEC Allergy [OTC]: 10 mg
Generic: 5 mg, 10 mg

Tablet Chewable, Oral:
All Day Allergy Childrens [OTC]: 10 mg
Generic: 5 mg, 10 mg

Tablet Dispersible, Oral:
ZyrTEC Allergy [OTC]: 10 mg
ZyrTEC Allergy Childrens [OTC]: 10 mg

Cetrorelix (set roe REL iks)

Brand Names: US Cetrotide
Brand Names: Canada Cetrotide
Pharmacologic Category Gonadotropin Releasing Hormone Antagonist
Use Controlled ovarian stimulation: Inhibits premature luteinizing hormone (LH) surges in women undergoing controlled ovarian stimulation.
Local Anesthetic/Vasoconstrictor Precautions No information available to require special precautions
Effects on Dental Treatment No significant effects or complications reported
Effects on Bleeding No information available to require special precautions
Adverse Reactions

1% to 10%:
Central nervous system: Headache (1%)
Endocrine & metabolic: Ovarian hyperstimulation syndrome (WHO grade II or III: 4%), Increased gamma-glutamyl transferase (≤1% to 2%)
Gastrointestinal: Nausea (1%)
Hepatic: Increased serum alkaline phosphatase (≤1% to 2%), increased serum ALT (≤1% to 2%), increased serum AST (≤1% to 2%)

<1%, postmarketing and/or case reports: Anaphylaxis (includes cough, hypotension, skin rash), injection site reactions (bruising at injection site, erythema at injection site, injection site pruritus, local swelling)

General Dosage Range SubQ: *Adults (females):* 0.25 mg once daily **or** 3 mg as a single dose
Mechanism of Action Competes with naturally-occurring GnRH for binding on receptors of the pituitary. This delays luteinizing hormone surge, preventing ovulation until the follicles are of adequate size.
Pharmacodynamics/Kinetics
Onset of Action 0.25 mg dose: 2 hours; 3 mg dose: 1 hour
Duration of Action 0.25 mg dose: 24 hours; 3 mg dose (single dose): 4 days
Half-life Elimination 0.25 mg dose: 5 hours; 0.25 mg multiple doses: 20.6 hours; 3 mg dose: 62.8 hours
Time to Peak 1 to 2 hours
Pregnancy Risk Factor X
Pregnancy Considerations Studies in animals or pregnant women have shown evidence of fetal abnormalities and use is contraindicated in women who are or may become pregnant. Resorption resulting in fetal loss would be expected if used in a pregnant woman. Exclude pregnancy before beginning treatment.

Cetuximab (se TUK see mab)

Brand Names: US Erbitux
Brand Names: Canada Erbitux
Pharmacologic Category Antineoplastic Agent, Epidermal Growth Factor Receptor (EGFR) Inhibitor; Antineoplastic Agent, Monoclonal Antibody
Use

Colorectal cancer, metastatic: Treatment of *KRAS* wild-type (without mutation), epidermal growth factor receptor (EGFR)-expressing metastatic colorectal cancer as determined by approved tests (in combination with FOLFIRI [irinotecan, fluorouracil, and leucovorin] as first line treatment, in combination with irinotecan [in patients refractory to irinotecan-based chemotherapy], or as a single agent in patients who have failed irinotecan- and oxaliplatin-based chemotherapy or who are intolerant to irinotecan).

Limitation of use: Cetuximab is not indicated for the treatment of *RAS*-mutant colorectal cancer or when results of the *RAS* mutation tests are unknown.

Head and neck cancer, squamous cell: Treatment of squamous cell cancer of the head and neck (as a single agent for recurrent or metastatic disease after platinum-based chemotherapy failure; in combination with radiation therapy as initial treatment of locally or regionally advanced disease; in combination with platinum and fluorouracil-based chemotherapy as first-line treatment of locoregional or metastatic disease).

Local Anesthetic/Vasoconstrictor Precautions No information available to require special precautions
Effects on Dental Treatment No significant effects or complications reported
Effects on Bleeding No information available to require special precautions
Adverse Reactions

>10%:
Central nervous system: Fatigue (91%), malaise (≤73%), pain (59%), peripheral sensory neuropathy (45%; grades 3/4: 1%), headache (19% to 38%), insomnia (27%), confusion (18%), chills (≤16%), rigors (≤16%), anxiety (14%), depression (14%)
Dermatologic: Desquamation (95%), acneiform eruption (15% to 88%; grades 3/4: 1% to 18%), radiodermatitis (86%), xeroderma (14% to 57%), pruritus (14% to 47%), skin rash (28% to 44%), changes in nails (31%), acne vulgaris (14% to 22%), paronychia (20%), palmar-plantar erythrodysesthesia (19%), skin fissure (19%), alopecia (12%)
Endocrine & metabolic: Weight loss (15% to 84%), hypomagnesemia (6% to 55%), dehydration (13% to 25%), hypocalcemia (12%), hypokalemia (12%)

Gastrointestinal: Diarrhea (19% to 72%), nausea (49% to 64%), abdominal pain (59%), constipation (53%), vomiting (40%), stomatitis (31% to 32%), anorexia (25% to 30%), dyspepsia (14% to 16%), xerostomia (12%)

Hematologic & oncologic: Neutropenia (49%; grades 3/4: 31%), leukopenia (grades 3/4: 17%)

Hepatic: Increased serum alanine aminotransferase (43%), increased serum aspartate aminotransferase (38%), increased serum alkaline phosphatase (33%)

Infection: Infection (13% to 44%), infection without neutropenia (38%)

Local: Application site reaction (18%)

Neuromuscular & skeletal: Weakness (≤73%), ostealgia (15%), arthralgia (14%)

Ophthalmic: Conjunctivitis (10% to 18%)

Respiratory: Dyspnea (49%), cough (30%), pharyngitis (26%)

Miscellaneous: Fever (22% to 29%), infusion related reaction (10% to 18%; grades 3/4: 2% to 5%)

1% to 10%:

Cardiovascular: Cardiorespiratory arrest (2% to 3%), ischemic heart disease (2%)

Dermatologic: Hypertrichosis

Gastrointestinal: Dysgeusia (10%)

Immunologic: Antibody development (5%)

Infection: Sepsis (1% to 4%)

Renal: Renal failure (1%: colorectal cancer patients; frequency not defined in other populations)

<1%, postmarketing, and/or case reports: Abscess, aseptic meningitis, blepharitis, bronchospasm, bullous pemphigoid, cardiac arrhythmia, cellulitis, cheilitis, corneal ulcer, electrolyte disturbance, hoarseness, hypotension, interstitial pulmonary disease, keratitis, loss of consciousness, mucosal inflammation, myocardial infarction, pulmonary embolism, shock, skin infection, Stevens-Johnson syndrome, stridor, toxic epidermal necrolysis

General Dosage Range Dosage adjustment recommended in patients who develop toxicities

IV: *Adults:* Loading dose: 400 mg/m^2; Maintenance: 250 mg/m^2 weekly

Mechanism of Action Recombinant human/mouse chimeric monoclonal antibody which binds specifically to the epidermal growth factor receptor (EGFR, HER1, c-ErbB-1) and competitively inhibits the binding of epidermal growth factor (EGF) and other ligands. Binding to the EGFR blocks phosphorylation and activation of receptor-associated kinases, resulting in inhibition of cell growth, induction of apoptosis, and decreased matrix metalloproteinase and vascular endothelial growth factor production. EGFR signal transduction results in *RAS* wild-type activation; cells with *RAS* mutations appear to be unaffected by EGFR inhibition.

Pharmacodynamics/Kinetics

Half-life Elimination ~112 hours (range: 63 to 230 hours)

Pregnancy Risk Factor C

Pregnancy Considerations Adverse events were observed in animal reproduction studies. Human IgG is known to cross the placenta. Because cetuximab inhibits epidermal growth factor (EGF), a component of fetal development, adverse effects on pregnancy would be expected. The manufacturer recommends that males and females use effective contraception during therapy and for 6 months following the last dose of cetuximab.

Cetylpyridinium (SEE til peer i DI nee um)

Brand Names: US Antiseptic Oral Rinse [OTC]; Breath Rx [OTC] [DSC]; Cepacol Antibacterial [OTC]; Clean Zing [OTC]; Larynex [OTC]

Generic Availability (US) Yes

Pharmacologic Category Antiseptic, Oral Mouthwash

Dental Use Antiseptic to aid in the prevention and reduction of plaque and gingivitis, and to freshen breath

Use Antiseptic to aid in the prevention and reduction of plaque and gingivitis, and to freshen breath

Local Anesthetic/Vasoconstrictor Precautions No information available to require special precautions

Effects on Dental Treatment Key adverse event(s) related to dental treatment: Tooth and tongue staining and oral irritation.

Effects on Bleeding No information available to require special precautions

Adverse Reactions Frequency not defined. Gastrointestinal: Dental discoloration, mouth irritation, tongue discoloration

Dental Usual Dosage Prevention and reduction of plaque and gingivitis, and to freshen breath: Children ≥6 years and Adults: Oral (OTC labeling): Rinse or gargle as directed; may be used before or after brushing (2 times/day)

Dosing

Adult & Geriatric Antiseptic (OTC labeling): Oral: Swish 20 mL thoroughly between teeth for 30 seconds then spit; use twice daily; may be used before or after brushing; do not swallow.

Pediatric Antiseptic (OTC labeling): Children ≥6 years: Refer to adult dosing.

Contraindications Hypersensitivity to cetylpyridinium or any component of the formulation

Warnings/Precautions If an amount greater than used for rinsing is swallowed, seek professional assistance or contact a poison control center immediately. Stop use and consult a healthcare professional if symptoms or condition worsens or persists; if gingivitis, bleeding, or redness persists for more than 2 weeks; if gums are painful and swollen; if pus from the gum line, loose teeth, or increased spacing between the teeth occurs. Avoid contact with eyes.

Drug Interactions

Metabolism/Transport Effects None known.

Avoid Concomitant Use There are no known interactions where it is recommended to avoid concomitant use.

Increased Effect/Toxicity There are no known significant interactions involving an increase in effect.

Decreased Effect There are no known significant interactions involving a decrease in effect.

Pregnancy Considerations Cetylpyridinium chloride mouthwash (alcohol free) has been associated with a reduction in preterm births in pregnant women with periodontal disease (Jeffcoat, 2011).

Dosage Forms

Liquid, Mouth/Throat:

Antiseptic Oral Rinse [OTC]: 0.05% (44 mL)

Cepacol Antibacterial [OTC]: 0.05% (710 mL)

Clean Zing [OTC]: 0.06% (480 mL)

Lozenge, Mouth/Throat:

Larynex [OTC]: (500 ea)

Dental Comment Numerous mouthwashes contain cetylpyridinium, review product labeling for additional information.

Cevimeline (se vi ME leen)

Related Information

Dentin Hypersensitivity, Acid Erosion, High Caries Index, Management of Alveolar Osteitis, and Xerostomia *on page 1857*

Perioral Premalignant Lesions and Management of Patients Undergoing Cancer Therapy *on page 1875*

Brand Names: US Evoxac

Brand Names: Canada Evoxac

Generic Availability (US) Yes

Pharmacologic Category Cholinergic Agonist

Dental Use Treatment of symptoms of dry mouth in patients with Sjögren's syndrome

Use Xerostomia (associated with Sjögren's syndrome): Treatment of symptoms of dry mouth in patients with Sjögren's syndrome.

Local Anesthetic/Vasoconstrictor Precautions No information available to require special precautions

Effects on Dental Treatment Key adverse event(s) related to dental treatment: Excessive salivation, salivary gland pain

Effects on Bleeding No information available to require special precautions

Adverse Reactions

Frequency not always defined.

>10%:

Dermatologic: Diaphoresis (19%)

Gastrointestinal: Nausea (14%)

Respiratory: Sinusitis (12%), rhinitis (11%), upper respiratory tract infection (11%)

1% to 10%:

Cardiovascular: Chest pain, edema, palpitations, peripheral edema

Central nervous system: Fatigue (3%), insomnia (2%), depression, hypertonia, hypoesthesia, hyporeflexia, migraine, vertigo

Dermatologic: Dermatological disease, erythematous rash, pruritus

Endocrine & metabolic: Hot flash (2%), increased amylase

Gastrointestinal: Abdominal pain (8%), vomiting (5%), sialorrhea (2%), anorexia, aphthous stomatitis, constipation, eructation, flatulence, gastroesophageal reflux disease, hiccups, salivary gland pain, sialadenitis, toothache, xerostomia

Genitourinary: Urinary tract infection (6%), cystitis, vaginitis

Hematologic & oncologic: Anemia

Hypersensitivity: Hypersensitivity reaction

Infection: Abscess, candidiasis, fungal infection, infection

Neuromuscular & skeletal: Back pain (5%), arthralgia (4%), skeletal pain (3%), weakness (1%), leg cramps, myalgia, tremor

Ophthalmic: Eye disease, eye infection, eye pain, visual disturbance, xerophthalmia

Otic: Otalgia, otitis media

Respiratory: Cough (6%), bronchitis (4%), epistaxis, flu-like symptoms, pneumonia

Miscellaneous: Fever

<1%, postmarketing, and/or case reports: acute exacerbations of multiple sclerosis, aggressive behavior, alopecia, angina pectoris, anterior chamber eye hemorrhage, aphasia, apnea, arthropathy, avascular necrosis of femoral head, bronchospasm, bullous rash, bundle branch block, cardiac arrhythmia, cardiac disease, cholecystitis, cholelithiasis, cholinergic syndrome, deafness, dehydration, delirium, dementia, depersonalization, diabetes mellitus, dyskinesia, ECG abnormality, emotional lability, eosinophilia, esophageal stenosis, esophagitis, extrasystoles, facial edema, gastric ulcer, gastrointestinal hemorrhage, gingival hyperplasia, glaucoma, granulocytopenia, hallucination, hematoma, hematuria, hepatic insufficiency, hyperglycemia, hyperkalemia, hypertension, hypoglycemia, hypotension, hypothyroidism, immune thrombocytopenia, impotence, increased liver enzymes, intestinal obstruction, inversion T wave on ECG, irritable bowel syndrome, leukopenia, lymphocytosis, manic reaction, menstrual disease, myocardial infarction, nephrolithiasis, neuropathy, paralysis, paranoia, paresthesia, peptic ulcer, pericarditis, peripheral ischemia, skin photosensitivity reaction, pleural effusion, pulmonary embolism, pulmonary fibrosis, rectal disease, renal insufficiency, seizure, sepsis, supraventricular tachycardia, syncope, systemic lupus erythematosus, tachycardia, tenosynovitis, thrombocytopenia, thrombophlebitis, ulcerative colitis, urinary retention, urination disorder, vasculitis

Dental Usual Dosage Dry mouth (in Sjögren's syndrome): Adults: Oral: 30 mg 3 times/day

Dosing

Adult & Geriatric Xerostomia (associated with Sjögren's syndrome): Oral: 30 mg 3 times/day

Renal Impairment There are no dosage adjustment provided in the manufacturer's labeling.

Hepatic Impairment There are no dosage adjustment provided in the manufacturer's labeling.

Mechanism of Action Binds to muscarinic (cholinergic) receptors, causing an increase in secretion of exocrine glands (such as salivary and sweat glands) and increase tone of smooth muscle in gastrointestinal and urinary tracts

Contraindications Hypersensitivity to cevimeline or any component of the formulation; uncontrolled asthma; when miosis is undesirable (eg, narrow-angle glaucoma, acute iritis)

Warnings/Precautions May alter cardiac conduction and/or heart rate; use caution in patients with significant cardiovascular disease, including angina, or myocardial infarction. Cevimeline has the potential to increase bronchial smooth muscle tone, airway resistance, and bronchial secretions; use with caution in patients with controlled asthma, COPD, or chronic bronchitis. May cause blurred vision, decreased visual acuity (particularly at night and in patients with central lens changes) and impaired depth perception. Patients should be cautioned about driving at night or performing hazardous activities in reduced lighting. Use with caution in patients with a history of cholelithiasis; may induce contractions of the gallbladder or biliary smooth muscle, precipitating complications such as cholangitis, cholecystitis, or biliary obstruction.

Use with caution in patients with a history of cholelithiasis, may induce contractions of the gallbladder or biliary smooth muscle, precipitating complications such as cholangitis, cholecystitis, or biliary obstruction. Use with caution in patients with a history of nephrolithiasis; may induce smooth muscle spasms, precipitating renal colic or ureteral reflux in patients with nephrolithiasis. Patients with a known or suspected deficiency of CYP2D6 may be at higher risk of adverse effects.

Drug Interactions

Metabolism/Transport Effects Substrate of CYP2D6 (minor), CYP3A4 (minor); **Note:** Assignment of Major/Minor substrate status based on clinically relevant drug interaction potential

Avoid Concomitant Use There are no known interactions where it is recommended to avoid concomitant use.

Increased Effect/Toxicity

The levels/effects of Cevimeline may be increased by: Acetylcholinesterase Inhibitors; Beta-Blockers

Decreased Effect

Cevimeline may decrease the levels/effects of: Cimetropium

Pharmacodynamics/Kinetics

Half-life Elimination 5 ± 1 hours

Time to Peak 1.5 to 2 hours

Pregnancy Risk Factor C

Pregnancy Considerations Adverse effects were observed in animal reproduction studies.

Breastfeeding Considerations It is not known if cevimeline is excreted in breast milk. Due to the potential for serious adverse reactions in the nursing infant, the manufacturer recommends a decision be made whether to discontinue nursing or to discontinue the drug, taking into account the importance of treatment to the mother.

Dosage Forms

Capsule, Oral:

Evoxac: 30 mg

Generic: 30 mg

Dental Comment Patient may experience sweating and/or facial flushing when beginning treatment.

Chlophedianol and Dexbrompheniramine

(kloe fe DYE a nol & deks brom fen EER a meen)

Brand Names: US Chlo Hist [OTC]

Pharmacologic Category Alkylamine Derivative; Antitussive; Histamine H_1 Antagonist; Histamine H_1 Antagonist, First Generation

Use Cough and cold symptoms: Temporary relief of cough due to minor throat and bronchial irritation; runny nose; sneezing; itching of the nose or throat; and itchy, watery eyes.

Local Anesthetic/Vasoconstrictor Precautions No information available to require special precautions

Effects on Dental Treatment Key adverse event(s) related to dental treatment: Dexbrompheniramine has anticholinergic properties and may cause xerostomia; normal salivary flow will resume with discontinuance.

Effects on Bleeding No information available to require special precautions

Adverse Reactions As reported with combination product; frequency not defined.

Central nervous system: Drowsiness, excitability (more common in children)

General Dosage Range Oral:

Children 6 to <12 years: Chlophedianol 12.5 mg/dexbrompheniramine 1 mg (5 mL) every 6 hours (Maximum: Chlophedianol 50 mg/dexbrompheniramine 4 mg (20 mL) per 24 hours.

Children ≥12 years, Adolescents, and Adults: Chlophedianol 25 mg/dexbrompheniramine 2 mg (10 mL) every 6 hours (Maximum: Chlophedianol 100 mg/dexbrompheniramine 8 mg (40 mL) per 24 hours.

Mechanism of Action Chlophedianol is an antitussive; dexbrompheniramine is an antihistamine.

Chloral Hydrate (KLOR al HYE drate)

Brand Names: Canada Chloral Hydrate-Odan; PMS-Chloral Hydrate

Pharmacologic Category Hypnotic, Miscellaneous

Use Note: Not approved in the US

Procedural sedation: Sedative/hypnotic for surgeries and diagnostic procedures; sedative prior to EEG evaluations

Note: The manufacturer labeling includes indications for pain control; alcohol, opioid or barbiturate withdrawal; and short-term treatment of insomnia; however, chloral hydrate is no longer recommended to be used this way (Schutte-Rodin 2008; VA/DoD 2015).

Local Anesthetic/Vasoconstrictor Precautions No information available to require special precautions

Effects on Dental Treatment No significant effects or complications reported

Effects on Bleeding No information available to require special precautions

Adverse Reactions Frequency not defined.

Cardiovascular: Atrial arrhythmia, depression of myocardial contractility, hypotension, shortening of refractory periods, torsades de pointes, ventricular arrhythmia

Central nervous system: Abnormal gait, ataxia, confusion, delirium, dizziness, drowsiness, drug dependence (physical and psychological; with prolonged use or large doses), hallucinations, hangover effect, malaise, nightmares, paradoxical excitation, somnambulism, vertigo

Dermatologic: Skin rash (including erythema, eczematoid dermatitis, urticaria, scarlatiniform exanthems)

Endocrine & metabolic: Acute porphyria, ketonuria

Gastrointestinal: Diarrhea, flatulence, gastric irritation, nausea, vomiting

Hematologic & oncologic: Acute porphyria, eosinophilia, leukopenia

Ophthalmic: Allergic conjunctivitis, blepharoptosis, keratoconjunctivitis

Otic: Increased middle ear pressure (infants and children)

Respiratory: Airway obstruction (young children), laryngeal edema (children)

Miscellaneous: Drug tolerance

General Dosage Range Oral:

Children and Adolescents: 25 to 50 mg/kg/dose (maximum single dose: 1,000 mg); may repeat once using half the dose

Adults: 500 to 1,000 mg prior to procedure

Mechanism of Action Central nervous system depressant effects are due to its active metabolite trichloroethanol, mechanism unknown

Pharmacodynamics/Kinetics

Onset of Action 10-20 minutes; Maximum effect (time to sleep): 0.5-1 hour

Duration of Action 4-8 hours

Half-life Elimination

Chloral hydrate: Infants: 1 hour

Active metabolite (trichloroethanol):

Neonates: Range: 8.5-66 hours

Half-life decreases with increasing postmenstrual age (PMA):

Preterm infants (PMA 31-37 weeks): Mean half-life: 40 hours

Term infants (PMA 38-42 weeks): Mean half-life: 28 hours

Older children (PMA 57-708 weeks): Mean half-life: 10 hours

Adults: 8-10 hours

Trichloroacetic acid: Adults: 67.2 hours

Pregnancy Considerations Animal reproduction studies have not been conducted. Chloral hydrate crosses the placenta, and long-term use may lead to withdrawal symptoms in the neonate.

Product Availability Not available in the US

Chlorambucil (klor AM byoo sil)

Brand Names: US Leukeran

Brand Names: Canada Leukeran

Pharmacologic Category Antineoplastic Agent, Alkylating Agent; Antineoplastic Agent, Alkylating Agent (Nitrogen Mustard)

Use

Chronic lymphocytic leukemia: Management of chronic lymphocytic leukemia (CLL)

Lymphomas: Management of Hodgkin lymphoma (HL) and non-Hodgkin lymphomas (NHL)

Local Anesthetic/Vasoconstrictor Precautions No information available to require special precautions

Effects on Dental Treatment Key adverse event(s) related to dental treatment: Stomatitis.

Effects on Bleeding Thrombocytopenia has been reported to occur 1-2 weeks after a short course of therapy and persist for up to 4 weeks.

Adverse Reactions Frequency not defined.

Central nervous system: Drug fever, peripheral neuropathy

Dermatologic: Allergic skin reaction, skin rash, urticaria

Endocrine & metabolic: Amenorrhea

Gastrointestinal: Diarrhea (infrequent), nausea (infrequent), oral mucosa ulcer (infrequent), vomiting (infrequent)

Genitourinary: Azoospermia, cystitis (sterile), infertility

Hematologic & oncologic: Anemia, bone marrow depression, bone marrow failure (irreversible), leukemia (secondary), leukopenia, lymphocytopenia, malignant neoplasm (secondary), neutropenia (onset: 3 weeks; recovery: 10 days after last dose), pancytopenia, thrombocytopenia

Hepatic: Hepatotoxicity, jaundice

Hypersensitivity: Angioedema, hypersensitivity reaction

Respiratory: Interstitial pneumonitis, pulmonary fibrosis

Miscellaneous: Fever

1%, postmarketing, and/or case reports: Agitation, ataxia, confusion, erythema multiforme, flaccid paresis, seizure (focal/generalized), hallucination, muscle twitching, myoclonus, SIADH (syndrome of inappropriate antidiuretic hormone secretion), Stevens-Johnson syndrome, toxic epidermal necrolysis, tremor

General Dosage Range Dosage adjustment recommended in patients with hepatic impairment or who develop toxicities

Oral: *Adults:* 0.1 to 0.2 mg/kg/day for 3 to 6 weeks **or** 0.4 mg/kg intermittently, biweekly, or monthly (may increase by 0.1 mg/kg/dose)

Mechanism of Action Alkylating agent; interferes with DNA replication and RNA transcription by alkylation and cross-linking the strands of DNA

Pharmacodynamics/Kinetics

Half-life Elimination ~1.5 hours; Phenylacetic acid mustard: ~1.8 hours

Time to Peak Within 1 hour; Phenylacetic acid mustard: Within 1.9 ± 0.7 hours

Pregnancy Risk Factor D

Pregnancy Considerations Animal reproduction studies have demonstrated teratogenicity. Chlorambucil crosses the human placenta. Following exposure during the first trimester, case reports have noted adverse renal effects (unilateral agenesis). Women of childbearing potential should avoid becoming pregnant while receiving treatment. **[U.S. Boxed Warning]: Affects human fertility; probably mutagenic and teratogenic as well**; chromosomal damage has been documented. Reversible and irreversible sterility (when administered to prepubertal and pubertal males), azoospermia (in adult males) and amenorrhea (in females) have been observed. Fibrosis, vasculitis and depletion of primordial follicles have been noted on autopsy of the ovaries.

Chloramphenicol (klor am FEN i kole)

Brand Names: Canada Chloromycetin; Chloromycetin Succinate; Diochloram; Pentamycetin

Pharmacologic Category Antibiotic, Miscellaneous

Use Serious infections: Treatment of serious infections, including cystic fibrosis exacerbations, bacterial meningitis, and bacteremia, caused by *Chlamydiaceae, Hemophilus influenzae, Rickettsia, Salmonella* spp. (acute infections), and other organisms when other less toxic agents are ineffective or contraindicated.

Local Anesthetic/Vasoconstrictor Precautions No information available to require special precautions

Effects on Dental Treatment Key adverse event(s) related to dental treatment: Glossitis and stomatitis.

Effects on Bleeding Thrombocytopenia has been reported with short or long courses of therapy due to bone marrow suppression.

Adverse Reactions Frequency not defined.

Central nervous system: Confusion, delirium, depression, headache

Dermatologic: Skin rash, urticaria

Gastrointestinal: Diarrhea, enterocolitis, glossitis, nausea, stomatitis, vomiting

Hematologic & oncologic: Aplastic anemia, bone marrow depression, granulocytopenia, hypoplastic anemia, pancytopenia, thrombocytopenia

Hypersensitivity: Anaphylaxis, angioedema, hypersensitivity reaction

Ophthalmic: Optic neuritis

Miscellaneous: Fever, Gray syndrome

General Dosage Range IV: *Infants, Children, Adolescents, and Adults:* 50 to 100 mg/kg/day divided every 6 hours (maximum: 4 g/day)

Mechanism of Action Reversibly binds to 50S ribosomal subunits of susceptible organisms preventing amino acids from being transferred to growing peptide chains thus inhibiting protein synthesis

Pharmacodynamics/Kinetics

Half-life Elimination

Neonates: 1 to 2 days: 24 hours; 10 to 16 days: 10 hours

Chloramphenicol: Infants: Significantly prolonged (Powell 1982); Children 4 to 6 hours; Adults: ~4 hours (Ambrose 1984)

Hepatic disease: Prolonged (Ambrose 1984)

Pregnancy Considerations Chloramphenicol crosses the placenta producing cord concentrations approaching maternal serum concentrations. An increased risk of teratogenic effects has not been associated with the use of chloramphenicol in pregnancy (Czeizel 2000; Heinonen 1977). "Gray Syndrome" has occurred in premature infants and newborns receiving chloramphenicol. The manufacturer recommends caution if used in a pregnant patient near term or during labor. Chloramphenicol may be used as an alternative agent for the treatment of Rocky Mountain Spotted Fever in pregnant women although caution should be used when administration occurs during the third trimester (Biggs 2015).

ChlordiazePOXIDE (klor dye az e POKS ide)

Related Information

Dentin Hypersensitivity, Acid Erosion, High Caries Index, Management of Alveolar Osteitis, and Xerostomia *on page 1857*

Pharmacologic Category Benzodiazepine

Use

Acute alcohol withdrawal: Management of acute alcohol withdrawal

Anxiety: Management of anxiety disorders or short-term relief of anxiety symptoms

Preoperative anxiety: Management of preoperative apprehension and anxiety

Local Anesthetic/Vasoconstrictor Precautions No information available to require special precautions

Effects on Dental Treatment Key adverse event(s) related to dental treatment: Xerostomia (normal salivary flow resumes upon discontinuation).

Effects on Bleeding No information available to require special precautions

Adverse Reactions Frequency not defined

Cardiovascular: Edema, syncope

Central nervous system: Abnormal electroencephalogram, ataxia, confusion, drowsiness, drug-induced extrapyramidal reaction

Dermatologic: Skin rash

Endocrine & metabolic: Change in libido, menstrual disease

Gastrointestinal: Constipation, nausea

Hematologic & oncologic: Agranulocytosis, bone marrow depression

Hepatic: Hepatic insufficiency, jaundice

Miscellaneous: Paradoxical reaction

General Dosage Range

Oral:

Children ≥6 years and Adolescents: 10 to 30 mg daily in 2 to 4 divided doses

Adults: 15 to 300 mg daily in 3 to 4 divided doses

Elderly: 10 to 20 mg daily in 2 to 4 divided doses

Mechanism of Action Binds to stereospecific benzodiazepine receptors on the postsynaptic GABA neuron at several sites within the CNS, including the limbic system, reticular formation. Enhancement of the inhibitory effect of GABA on neuronal excitability results by increased neuronal membrane permeability to chloride ions. This shift in chloride ions results in hyperpolarization (a less excitable state) and stabilization. Benzodiazepine receptors and effects appear to be linked to the GABA-A receptors. Benzodiazepines do not bind to GABA-B receptors (Vinkers 2012).

Pharmacodynamics/Kinetics

Half-life Elimination Parent: 24 to 48 hours; demoxepam 14 to 95 hours (Schwartz 1971)

Time to Peak Serum: 0.5 to 2 hours (Baskin, 1982)

Pregnancy Considerations Adverse events have been observed in some animal reproduction studies. Chlordiazepoxide crosses the human placenta and fetal serum concentrations are similar to those in the mother. Teratogenic effects have been observed with some benzodiazepines (including chlordiazepoxide); however, additional studies are needed. The incidence of premature birth and low birth weights may be increased following maternal use of benzodiazepines; hypoglycemia and respiratory problems in the neonate may occur following exposure late in pregnancy. Neonatal withdrawal symptoms may occur within days to weeks after birth and "floppy infant syndrome" (which also includes withdrawal symptoms) has been reported with some benzodiazepines (Bergman 1992; Iqbal 2002; Wikner 2007).

Controlled Substance C-IV

Chlorhexidine Gluconate
(klor HEKS i deen GLOO koe nate)

Related Information

Bacterial Infections *on page 1835*

Dentin Hypersensitivity, Acid Erosion, High Caries Index, Management of Alveolar Osteitis, and Xerostomia *on page 1857*

Osteonecrosis of the Jaw *on page 1796*

Periodontal Diseases *on page 1844*

Perioral Premalignant Lesions and Management of Patients Undergoing Cancer Therapy *on page 1875*

Ulcerative, Erosive, and Painful Oral Mucosal Disorders *on page 1853*

Related Sample Prescriptions

Antimicrobial Oral Rinse - Sample Prescriptions *on page 31*

Brand Names: US Antiseptic Skin Cleanser [OTC]; Betasept Surgical Scrub [OTC]; ChloraPrep One Step [OTC]; Dyna-Hex 2 [OTC]; Hibiclens [OTC]; Hibistat [OTC] [DSC]; Paroex; Peridex; Periogard; Tegaderm CHG Dressing [OTC]

Brand Names: Canada Apo-Chlorhexidine Oral Rinse; Denti-Care Chlorhexidine Gluconate Oral Rinse; GUM Paroex; ORO-Clense; Perichlor; Peridex Oral Rinse; Periogard; X-Pur Chlorhexidine

Generic Availability (US) May be product dependent

Pharmacologic Category Antibiotic, Oral Rinse; Antibiotic, Topical

Dental Use

Antibacterial dental rinse; chlorhexidine is active against gram-positive and gram-negative organisms, facultative anaerobes, aerobes, and yeast

Chip, for periodontal pocket insertion: Indicated as an adjunct to scaling and root planing procedures for reduction of pocket depth in patients with adult periodontitis; may be used as part of a periodontal maintenance program

Use

Oral rinse: Antibacterial dental rinse for gingivitis treatment

Periodontal chip: Adjunctive therapy to reduce pocket depth in patients with periodontitis

Topical: Skin cleanser for preoperative skin preparation, skin wound and general skin cleanser for patients; surgical scrub and antiseptic hand rinse for healthcare personnel

Local Anesthetic/Vasoconstrictor Precautions No information available to require special precautions

Effects on Dental Treatment Key adverse event(s) related to dental treatment: Increased tartar on teeth, altered taste perception, staining of oral surfaces (mucosa, teeth, dorsum of tongue), and oral/tongue irritation. Staining may be visible as soon as 1 week after therapy begins and is more pronounced when there is a heavy accumulation of unremoved plaque and when teeth fillings have rough surfaces. Stain does not have a clinically adverse effect but because removal may not be possible, patient with anterior restorations should be advised of the potential permanency of the stain.

Effects on Bleeding No information available to require special precautions

Adverse Reactions

Oral:

>10%: Gastrointestinal: Dysgeusia, increased tartar formation, mouth discoloration

1% to 10%: Gastrointestinal: Mouth irritation, tongue irritation

Topical:

Dermatologic: Allergic sensitization, erythema, hypersensitivity reaction, rough skin, xeroderma

<1%, postmarketing, and/or case reports: Anaphylaxis (Health Canada May 2016), dyspnea, facial edema, nasal congestion

Dental Usual Dosage Adults:

Oral rinse (Peridex, PerioGard):

Floss and brush teeth, completely rinse toothpaste from mouth and swish 15 mL (one capful) undiluted oral rinse around in mouth for 30 seconds, then expectorate. Caution patient not to swallow the medicine and instruct not to eat for 2-3 hours after treatment (cap on bottle measures 15 mL).

Treatment of gingivitis: Oral prophylaxis: Swish for 30 seconds with 15 mL chlorhexidine, then expectorate; repeat twice daily (morning and evening). Patient should have a re-evaluation followed by a dental prophylaxis every 6 months.

Periodontal chip: One chip is inserted into a periodontal pocket with a probing pocket depth ≥5 mm. Up to 8 chips may be inserted in a single visit. Treatment is recommended every 3 months in pockets with a remaining depth ≥5 mm. If dislodgment occurs 7 days or more after placement, the subject is considered to have had the full course of treatment. If dislodgment occurs within 48 hours, a new chip should be inserted. The chip biodegrades completely and does not need to be removed. Patients should avoid dental floss at the site of periochip® insertion for 10 days after placement because flossing might dislodge the chip.

Insertion of periodontal chip: Pocket should be isolated and surrounding area dried prior to chip insertion. The chip should be grasped using forceps with the rounded edges away from the forceps. The chip should be inserted into the periodontal pocket to its maximum depth. It may be maneuvered into position using the tips of the forceps or a flat instrument.

Dosing

Adult & Geriatric

Gingivitis: *Oral rinse:* Swish for 30 seconds with 15 mL (one capful) of undiluted oral rinse after toothbrushing, then expectorate; repeat twice daily (morning and evening). Therapy should be initiated immediately following a dental prophylaxis. Patient should be reevaluated and given a dental prophylaxis at intervals no longer than every 6 months.

Periodontitis: *Periodontal chip:* One chip is inserted into a periodontal pocket with a probing pocket depth ≥5 mm. Up to 8 chips may be inserted in a single visit. Treatment is recommended every 3 months in pockets with a remaining depth ≥5 mm. If dislodgment occurs 7 days or more after placement, the subject is considered to have had the full course of treatment. If dislodgment occurs within 48 hours, a new chip should be inserted. The chip biodegrades completely and does not need to be removed. Patients should avoid dental floss at the site of periodontal chip insertion for 10 days after placement because flossing might dislodge the chip.

Insertion of periodontal chip: Pocket should be isolated and surrounding area dried prior to chip insertion. The chip should be grasped using forceps with the rounded edges away from the forceps. The chip should be inserted into the periodontal pocket to its maximum depth. It may be maneuvered into position using the tips of the forceps or a flat instrument.

Skin cleanser for preoperative skin preparation, skin wound and general skin cleanser for patients; surgical scrub and antiseptic hand rinse for healthcare personnel: *Topical:*

Surgical scrub: Scrub hands and forearms for 3 minutes paying close attention to nails, cuticles, and interdigital spaces, and rinse thoroughly, wash for an additional 3 minutes, rinse, and dry thoroughly.

Surgical hand antiseptic: Lotion: Dispense 1 pumpful in palm of 1 hand; dip fingertips of opposite hand into solution and work it under nails. Spread remainder evenly over hand and just above elbow, covering all surfaces. Repeat on other hand. Dispense another pumpful in each hand and reapply to each hand up to the wrist. Allow to dry before gloving.

Healthcare personnel hand antiseptic:

Liquid or solution: Wash with ~5 mL for 15 seconds; rinse thoroughly with water and dry

Lotion: Apply to clean, dry hands and nails. Dispense 1 pumpful (2 mL) into the palm of 1 hand; apply evenly to cover both hands up to the wrists; allow to dry without wiping.

Towelette: Rub 15 seconds paying close attention to nails and interdigital spaces; no watering or toweling necessary

Preoperative skin preparation:

Solution: Apply liberally to surgical site and swab for at least 2 minutes. Dry with sterile towel. Repeat procedure (swab for additional 2 minutes and dry with sterile towel).

Applicator (ChloraPrep One-Step):

Dry surgical sites (eg, abdomen, arm): Completely wet treatment area; use gentle back and forth strokes for ~30 seconds. Allow solution to air dry for ~30 seconds. If using an ignition source (eg, electrocautery), allow solution to completely dry for a minimum of 3 minutes for hairless skin and up to 1 hour in hair; do not blot or wipe away. **Note:** Prior to use with electrocautery procedures, consult specific product labeling to determine if the ChloraPrep product may be used near an ignition source.

Moist surgical sites (eg, inguinal area): Completely wet treatment area; use gentle back and forth strokes for ~2 minutes. Allow solution to air dry for ~1 minute. If using an ignition source (eg, electrocautery), allow solution to completely dry for a minimum of 3 minutes for hairless skin and up to 1 hour in hair; do not blot or wipe away. **Note:** Prior to use with electrocautery procedures, consult specific product labeling to determine if the ChloraPrep product may be used near an ignition source.

Preparation of skin prior to an injection: Swab: Apply swab to procedure site for 15 seconds; allow to air dry for 30 seconds (do not blot or wipe dry). **Note:** Maximum treatment area for 1 swab is ~2.5 inches x 2.5 inches.

Wound care and general skin cleansing: Rinse area with water, then apply minimum amount necessary to cover skin or wound area and wash gently. Rinse again thoroughly.

Renal Impairment There are no dosage adjustments provided in the manufacturer's labeling.

Hepatic Impairment There are no dosage adjustments provided in the manufacturer's labeling.

Mechanism of Action Chlorhexidine has activity against gram-positive and gram-negative organisms, facultative anaerobes, aerobes, and yeast; it is both bacteriostatic and bactericidal, depending on its concentration. The bactericidal effect of chlorhexidine is a result of the binding of this cationic molecule to negatively charged bacterial cell walls and extramicrobial complexes. At low concentrations, this causes an alteration of bacterial cell osmotic equilibrium and leakage of potassium and phosphorous resulting in a bacteriostatic effect. At high concentrations of chlorhexidine, the cytoplasmic contents of the bacterial cell precipitate and result in cell death.

Contraindications Hypersensitivity to chlorhexidine or any component of the formulation

Warnings/Precautions Serious allergic reactions, including anaphylaxis, have been reported with use.

Oral rinse: Staining of oral surfaces (teeth, tooth restorations, dorsum of tongue) may occur; patients exhibited a measurable increase of staining in the facial anterior after six months of therapy that is more pronounced when there is a heavy accumulation of unremoved plaque. Stain does not adversely affect health of the gingivae or other oral tissues, and most stain can be removed from most tooth surfaces by dental prophylaxis. Because removal may not be possible, patients with anterior facial restorations with rough surfaces or margins should be advised of the potential permanency of the stain. An increase in supragingival calculus has been observed with use; it is not known if the incidence of subgingival calculus is increased. Dental prophylaxis to remove calculus deposits should be performed at least every 6 months. May alter taste perception during use; has rarely been associated with permanent taste alteration.

Effect on periodontitis has not been determined; has not been tested in patients with acute necrotizing ulcerative gingivitis.

Periodontal chip: Infectious events (eg, abscesses, cellulitis) have been observed rarely with adjunctive chip placement post scaling and root planing; use with caution in patients with periodontal disease and concomitant diseases potentially decreasing immune status (eg, diabetes, cancer). Use in acute periodontal abscess pocket is not recommended.

Topical: For topical use only. Keep out of eyes, ears, and the mouth; if contact occurs, rinse with cold water immediately; permanent eye injury may result if agent enters and remains in the eye. Deafness has been reported following instillation in the middle ear through perforated ear drums. Avoid applying to wounds that involve more than the superficial skin layers. Avoid repeated use as general skin cleansing of large surfaces (unless necessary for condition). Not for preoperative preparation of face or head; avoid contact with meninges (do not use on lumbar puncture sites). Avoid applying to genital areas; generalized allergic reactions, irritation, and sensitivity have been reported. Solutions may be flammable (products may contain alcohol); avoid exposure to open flame and/or ignition source (eg, electrocautery) until completely dry; avoid application to hairy areas which may significantly delay drying time. Use with caution in children <2 months of age due to potential for increased absorption, and risk of irritation or chemical burns. May cause staining of fabrics (brown stain) due to a chemical reaction between chlorhexidine gluconate bound to fabric and chlorine (if sufficient chlorine is present from certain laundry detergents used during laundering process). When used as a topical antiseptic, improper use may lead to product contamination. Although infrequent, product contamination has been associated with reports of localized and systemic infections. To reduce the risk of infection, ensure antiseptic products are used according to the labeled instructions; avoid diluting products after opening; and apply single-use containers only one time to one patient and discard any unused solution (FDA Drug Safety Communication, 2013).

Drug Interactions

Metabolism/Transport Effects None known.

Avoid Concomitant Use There are no known interactions where it is recommended to avoid concomitant use.

Increased Effect/Toxicity There are no known significant interactions involving an increase in effect.

Decreased Effect There are no known significant interactions involving a decrease in effect.

Pharmacodynamics/Kinetics

Duration of Action Serum concentrations: Detectable levels are not present in the plasma 12 hours after administration

Pregnancy Risk Factor B/C (manufacturer specific)

Pregnancy Considerations Adverse events have not been observed in animal reproduction studies following use of the oral rinse; use of periodontal chip has not been studied. Chlorhexidine oral rinse is poorly absorbed from the GI tract.

Breastfeeding Considerations It is not known if chlorhexidine is excreted in breast milk. The manufacturer recommends that caution be exercised when administering chlorhexidine oral rinse to nursing women. However, oral rinse is not intended for ingestion; patient should expectorate after rinsing.

Dosage Forms

Liquid, External:

Betasept Surgical Scrub [OTC]: 4% (118 mL, 237 mL, 473 mL, 946 mL)

Hibiclens [OTC]: 4% (15 mL, 118 mL, 236 mL, 473 mL, 946 mL, 3790 mL)

Generic: 2% (118 mL); 4% (118 mL, 237 mL, 473 mL, 946 mL, 3800 mL)

Miscellaneous, External:

Tegaderm CHG Dressing [OTC]: (Dressing) (1 ea)

Pad, External:

Generic: 2% (2 ea, 6 ea)

Solution, External:

Antiseptic Skin Cleanser [OTC]: 4% (118 mL, 237 mL)

ChloraPrep One Step [OTC]: 2% (3 mL, 10.5 mL)

Dyna-Hex 2 [OTC]: 2% (473 mL)

Solution, Mouth/Throat:

Paroex: 0.12% (473 mL)

Peridex: 0.12% (118 mL, 473 mL, 1893 mL)

Periogard: 0.12% (473 mL)

Generic: 0.12% (15 mL, 118 mL, 473 mL)

Chloroprocaine (klor oh PROE kane)

Related Information

Oral Pain *on page 1830*

Brand Names: US Nesacaine; Nesacaine-MPF

Pharmacologic Category Local Anesthetic

Use

Local anesthesia: Production of local anesthesia by infiltration and peripheral nerve block (chloroprocaine with preservatives); production of local anesthesia by infiltration and peripheral and central nerve block, including lumbar and caudal epidural blocks (chloroprocaine without preservatives).

Limitations of use: Do not use chloroprocaine with or without preservatives for subarachnoid administration. Do not use chloroprocaine with preservatives for lumbar or caudal epidural anesthesia.

Local Anesthetic/Vasoconstrictor Precautions No information available to require special precautions

Effects on Dental Treatment No significant effects or complications reported

Effects on Bleeding No information available to require special precautions

Adverse Reactions

Frequency not defined.

Cardiovascular: Bradycardia, hypotension, ventricular arrhythmia

Central nervous system: Anxiety, dizziness, loss of consciousness, restlessness

Dermatologic: Erythema, pruritus, urticaria

Hypersensitivity: Anaphylactoid reaction, angioedema, hypersensitivity reaction

Neuromuscular & skeletal: Chondrolysis (continuous intra-articular administration)

Ophthalmic: Blurred vision

Otic: Tinnitus

<1%, postmarketing, and/or case reports: Seizure (0.1%)

General Dosage Range

Caudal block: *Adults:* Preservative-free: 2% or 3%: 15-25 mL; may repeat at 40- to 60-minute intervals

Infiltration and peripheral nerve block:

Children >3 years and Adolescents: Infiltration: Concentrations of 0.5% to 1% (maximum without epinephrine: 11 mg/kg); Nerve block: Concentrations of 1% to 1.5% (maximum without epinephrine: 11 mg/kg)

Adults: Dosage varies greatly depending on indication

Lumbar epidural block: *Adults:* Preservative-free: 2% or 3%: 2 to 2.5 mL per segment; usual total volume: 15 to 25 mL, may repeat with doses that are 2-6 mL less than total initial dose every 40 to 50 minutes

Mechanism of Action Chloroprocaine is an ester-type local anesthetic, which stabilizes the neuronal membranes and prevents initiation and transmission of nerve impulses thereby affecting local anesthetic actions. Chloroprocaine reversibly prevents generation and conduction of electrical impulses in neurons by decreasing the transient increase in permeability to sodium. The differential sensitivity generally depends on the size of the fiber; small fibers are more sensitive than larger fibers and require a longer period for recovery. Sensory pain fibers are usually blocked first, followed by fibers that transmit sensations of temperature, touch, and deep pressure. High concentrations block sympathetic somatic sensory and somatic motor fibers. The spread of anesthesia depends upon the distribution of the solution. This is primarily dependent on the volume of drug injected.

Pharmacodynamics/Kinetics

Onset of Action 6 to 12 minutes

Duration of Action Up to 60 minutes (patient, type of block, concentration, and method of anesthesia dependent)

Half-life Elimination In vitro, plasma: Neonates: 43 ± 2 seconds; Adults: 21 ± 2 seconds (males), 25 ± 1 second (females)

Pregnancy Risk Factor C

Pregnancy Considerations Animal reproduction studies have not been conducted. Local anesthetics rapidly cross the placenta and may cause varying degrees of maternal, fetal, and neonatal toxicity. Close maternal and fetal monitoring (heart rate and electronic fetal monitoring advised) are required during obstetrical use. Maternal hypotension has resulted from regional anesthesia. Positioning the patient on her left side and elevating the legs may help. Epidural, paracervical, or pudendal anesthesia may alter the forces of parturition through changes in uterine contractility or maternal expulsive efforts. The use of some local anesthetic drugs during labor and delivery may diminish muscle strength and tone for the first day or two of life. Administration as a paracervical block is not recommended with toxemia of pregnancy, fetal distress, or prematurity. Administration of a paracervical block early in pregnancy has resulted in maternal seizures and cardiovascular collapse. Fetal bradycardia and acidosis also have been reported. Fetal depression has occurred following unintended fetal intracranial injection while administering a paracervical and/or pudendal block.

Chloroquine (KLOR oh kwin)

Related Information

Clinical Risk Related to Drugs Prolonging QT Interval *on page 1772*

Brand Names: US Aralen [DSC]

Brand Names: Canada Aralen; Novo-Chloroquine

Pharmacologic Category Aminoquinoline (Antimalarial); Antimalarial Agent

Use

Malaria: Suppressive treatment and acute attacks of malaria due to *Plasmodium vivax*, *P. malariae*, *P. ovale*, and susceptible strains of *P. falciparum*.

Extraintestinal amebiasis: Treatment of extraintestinal amebiasis.

Local Anesthetic/Vasoconstrictor Precautions Chloroquine is one of the drugs confirmed to prolong the QT interval and is accepted as having a risk of causing torsade de pointes. The risk of drug-induced torsade de pointes is extremely low when a single QT interval prolonging drug is prescribed. In terms of epinephrine, it is not known what effect vasoconstrictors in the local anesthetic regimen will have in patients with a known history of congenital prolonged QT interval or in patients taking any medication that prolongs the QT interval. Until more information is obtained, it is suggested that the clinician consult with the physician prior to the use of a vasoconstrictor in suspected patients, and that the vasoconstrictor (epinephrine, mepivacaine and levonordefrin [Carbocaine® 2% with Neo-Cobefrin®]) be used with caution.

Effects on Dental Treatment Key adverse event(s) related to dental treatment: Stomatitis.

Effects on Bleeding Thrombocytopenia has been reported.

Adverse Reactions Frequency not defined.

Cardiovascular: Cardiomyopathy, ECG changes (rare; including prolonged QRS and QT_c intervals, T wave inversion or depression), hypotension (rare), torsade de pointes (rare)

Central nervous system: Agitation, anxiety, confusion, decreased deep tendon reflex, delirium, depression, extrapyramidal reaction (dystonia, dyskinesia, protrusion of the tongue, torticollis), hallucination, headache, insomnia, personality changes, polyneuropathy, psychosis, seizure

Dermatologic: Alopecia, bleaching of hair, blue gray skin pigmentation, erythema multiforme (rare), exacerbation of psoriasis, exfoliative dermatitis (rare), lichen planus, pleomorphic rash, pruritus, skin photosensitivity, Stevens-Johnson syndrome (rare), toxic epidermal necrolysis (rare), urticaria

Gastrointestinal: Abdominal cramps, anorexia, diarrhea, nausea, vomiting

Hematologic & oncologic: Agranulocytosis (rare; reversible), aplastic anemia, neutropenia, pancytopenia, thrombocytopenia

Hepatic: Hepatitis, increased liver enzymes

Hypersensitivity: Anaphylactoid reaction, anaphylaxis, angioedema

Immunologic: DRESS syndrome

Neuromuscular & skeletal: Myopathy, neuromuscular disease, proximal myopathy

Ophthalmic: Accommodation disturbances, blurred vision, corneal opacity (reversible), macular degeneration (may be irreversible), maculopathy (may be irreversible), nocturnal amblyopia, retinopathy (including irreversible changes in some patients long-term or high-dose therapy), visual field defects

Otic: Deafness (nerve), hearing loss (risk increased in patients with pre-existing auditory damage), tinnitus

General Dosage Range Dosage adjustment recommended in patients with renal impairment

Oral: *Children and Adults:* Dosage varies greatly depending on indication

Mechanism of Action Binds to and inhibits DNA and RNA polymerase; interferes with metabolism and hemoglobin utilization by parasites; inhibits prostaglandin effects; chloroquine concentrates within parasite acid vesicles and raises internal pH resulting in inhibition of parasite growth; may involve aggregates of ferriprotoporphyrin IX acting as chloroquine receptors causing membrane damage; may also interfere with nucleoprotein synthesis

Pharmacodynamics/Kinetics

Half-life Elimination 3-5 days

Time to Peak Serum: Oral: Within 1-2 hours

Pregnancy Considerations In animal reproduction studies, drug accumulated in fetal ocular tissues and remained for several months following drug elimination from the rest of the body. Chloroquine and its metabolites cross the placenta and can be detected in the cord blood and urine of the newborn infant (Akintonwa, 1988; Essien, 1982; Law, 2008). In one study, chloroquine and its metabolites were measurable in the cord blood 89 days (mean) after the last maternal dose (Law, 2008).

Malaria infection in pregnant women may be more severe than in nonpregnant women and has a high risk of maternal and perinatal morbidity and mortality. Therefore, pregnant women and women who are likely to become pregnant are advised to avoid travel to malaria-risk areas. Chloroquine is recommended for the treatment of pregnant women for uncomplicated malaria in chloroquine-sensitive regions; when caused by chloroquine-sensitive *P. vivax* or *P. ovale*, pregnant women should be maintained on chloroquine prophylaxis for the duration of their pregnancy (refer to current guidelines) (CDC, 2011; CDC, 2012).

Dental Comment See Local Anesthetic/Vasoconstrictor Precautions

Chlorothiazide (klor oh THYE a zide)

Related Information

Cardiovascular Diseases *on page 1752*

Brand Names: US Diuril; Sodium Diuril

Pharmacologic Category Antihypertensive; Diuretic, Thiazide

Use Management of hypertension; adjunctive treatment of edema

Guideline recommendations:

Hypertension: The 2014 guideline for the management of high blood pressure in adults (Eighth Joint National Committee [JNC 8]) recommends initiation of pharmacologic treatment to lower blood pressure for the following patients:

- Patients ≥60 years of age with systolic blood pressure (SBP) ≥150 mm Hg or diastolic blood pressure (DBP) ≥90 mm Hg. Goal of therapy is SBP <150 mm Hg and DBP <90 mm Hg.
- Patients <60 years of age with SBP ≥140 mm Hg or DBP is ≥90 mm Hg. Goal of therapy is SBP <140 mm Hg and DBP <90 mm Hg.
- Patients ≥18 years of age with diabetes and SBP ≥140 mm Hg or DBP ≥90 mm Hg. Goal of therapy is SBP <140 mm Hg and DBP <90 mm Hg.
- Patients ≥18 years of age with chronic kidney disease (CKD) and SBP ≥140 mm Hg or DBP ≥90 mm Hg. Goal of therapy is SBP <140 mm Hg and DBP <90 mm Hg.

Chronic kidney disease (CKD) and hypertension: Regardless of race or diabetes status, the use of an ACE inhibitor (ACEI) or angiotensin receptor blocker (ARB) as initial therapy is recommended to improve kidney outcomes. In the general non-black population (without CKD) including those with diabetes, initial antihypertensive treatment should consist of a thiazide-type diuretic, calcium channel blocker, ACEI, or ARB. In the general black population (without CKD), including those with diabetes, initial antihypertensive treatment should consist of a thiazide-type diuretic or a calcium channel blocker **instead of** an ACEI or ARB.

Coronary artery disease (CAD) and hypertension: The American Heart Association, American College of Cardiology and American Society of Hypertension (AHA/ACC/ASH) 2015 scientific statement for the treatment of hypertension in patients with coronary artery disease (CAD) recommends the use of a thiazide (or thiazide-like diuretic) as part of a regimen in patients with hypertension and chronic stable angina. A BP target of <140/90 mm Hg is reasonable for the secondary prevention of cardiovascular events. A lower target BP (<130/80 mm Hg) may be appropriate in some individuals with CAD, previous MI, stroke or transient ischemic attack, or CAD risk equivalents (AHA/ACC/ASH [Rosendorff 2015]).

Local Anesthetic/Vasoconstrictor Precautions No information available to require special precautions

Effects on Dental Treatment Key adverse event(s) related to dental treatment: Patients may experience orthostatic hypotension as they stand up after treatment; especially if lying in dental chair for extended periods of time. Use caution with sudden changes in position during and after dental treatment.

Effects on Bleeding No information available to require special precautions

Adverse Reactions Frequency not defined.

Cardiovascular: Hypotension, necrotizing angiitis, orthostatic hypotension
Central nervous system: Dizziness, headache, paresthesia, restlessness, vertigo
Dermatologic: Alopecia, erythema multiforme, exfoliative dermatitis, skin photosensitivity, skin rash, Stevens-Johnson syndrome, toxic epidermal necrolysis, urticaria
Endocrine & metabolic: Glycosuria, hypercalcemia, hyperglycemia, hyperuricemia, hypochloremic alkalosis, hypokalemia, hypomagnesemia, hyponatremia, increased serum cholesterol, increased serum triglycerides
Gastrointestinal: Abdominal cramps, anorexia, constipation, diarrhea, gastric irritation, nausea, pancreatitis, sialadenitis, vomiting
Genitourinary: Hematuria (IV), impotence
Hematologic & oncologic: Agranulocytosis, aplastic anemia, hemolytic anemia, leukopenia, purpura, thrombocytopenia
Hepatic: Jaundice
Hypersensitivity: Anaphylaxis
Neuromuscular & skeletal: Muscle spasm, systemic lupus erythematosus, weakness
Ophthalmic: Blurred vision, xanthopsia
Renal: Interstitial nephritis, renal failure, renal insufficiency
Respiratory: Pneumonitis, pulmonary edema, respiratory distress
Miscellaneous: Fever

General Dosage Range

IV: *Adults:* 250 to 1000 mg once or twice daily (maximum: 1000 mg daily)

Oral:

Children <6 months: 10 to 30 mg/kg/day in 2 divided doses (maximum: 375 mg daily)

Children ≥6 months: 10 to 20 mg/kg/day in 1 to 2 divided doses (maximum: 375 mg daily)

Adults: 250 to 2000 mg daily in 1 to 2 divided doses (maximum: 1000 mg daily [CHF])

Mechanism of Action Inhibits sodium and chloride reabsorption in the distal tubules causing increased excretion of sodium, chloride, and water resulting in diuresis. Loss of potassium, hydrogen ions, magnesium, phosphate, and bicarbonate also occurs.

Pharmacodynamics/Kinetics

Onset of Action Diuresis: Oral: Within 2 hours; IV: 15 minutes; Peak effect: Oral: ~4 hours; IV: 30 minutes

Duration of Action Diuretic action: Oral: ~6 to 12 hours; IV: 2 hours

Half-life Elimination 45 to 120 minutes

Pregnancy Risk Factor C

Pregnancy Considerations Adverse events were not observed in animal reproduction studies; however, studies were not complete. Chlorothiazide crosses the placenta and is found in cord blood. Maternal use may cause may cause fetal or neonatal jaundice, thrombocytopenia, or other adverse events observed in adults. Use of thiazide diuretics to treat edema during normal pregnancies is not appropriate; use may be considered when edema is due to pathologic causes (as in the nonpregnant patient); monitor. Untreated chronic maternal hypertension is associated with adverse events in the fetus, infant, and mother (ACOG, 2013). Women who required thiazide diuretics for the treatment of hypertension prior to pregnancy may continue their use (ACOG, 2013).

Chlorpheniramine (klor fen IR a meen)

Related Information

Bacterial Infections *on page 1835*

Related Sample Prescriptions

Sinus Infection Treatment - Sample Prescriptions *on page 38*

Brand Names: US Aller-Chlor [OTC]; Allergy-Time [OTC]; Chlor-Trimeton Allergy [OTC]; Chlor-Trimeton [OTC]; Chlorphen [OTC] [DSC]; Ed Chlorped Jr [OTC]; Ed ChlorPed [OTC]; Ed-Chlortan [OTC]; Pharbechlor [OTC]

Brand Names: Canada Chlor-Tripolon®; Novo-Pheniram

Generic Availability (US) May be product dependent

Pharmacologic Category Alkylamine Derivative; Histamine H_1 Antagonist; Histamine H_1 Antagonist, First Generation

Dental Use Treatment of histamine-induced allergic symptoms

Use Allergic symptoms, allergic rhinitis, urticaria, pruritus: Perennial and seasonal allergic rhinitis and other allergic symptoms including urticaria, pruritus

Local Anesthetic/Vasoconstrictor Precautions No information available to require special precautions

Effects on Dental Treatment Key adverse event(s) related to dental treatment: Xerostomia (normal salivary flow resumes upon discontinuation). Chronic use of antihistamines will inhibit salivary flow, particularly in elderly patients; this may contribute to periodontal disease, tooth decay, and oral discomfort.

Effects on Bleeding No information available to require special precautions

Adverse Reactions

>10%:
Central nervous system: Drowsiness (slight to moderate)
Respiratory: Thickening of bronchial secretions

1% to 10%:
Central nervous system: Dizziness, excitability, fatigue, headache, nervousness
Endocrine & metabolic: Weight gain
Gastrointestinal: Abdominal pain, diarrhea, increased appetite, nausea, xerostomia
Genitourinary: Urinary retention
Neuromuscular & skeletal: Arthralgia, weakness
Ophthalmic: Diplopia
Renal: Polyuria
Respiratory: Pharyngitis

Dosing

Adult

Allergic symptoms, allergic rhinitis, urticaria, pruritus: Oral: **Chlorpheniramine maleate:**

Immediate release: 4 mg every 4 to 6 hours; do not exceed 24 mg/24 hours

Extended release: 12 mg every 12 hours; do not exceed 24 mg/24 hours

Motion sickness (off-label use): Immediate release: 4 to 12 mg administered 3 hours prior to initiating stimulus for motion sickness (Buckey 2004). **Note:** Avoid use if it is unsafe for patient to be sedated.

Pediatric Allergic symptoms, allergic rhinitis, urticaria, pruritus: Oral: **Chlorpheniramine maleate:**

Immediate release:

Children 6 to 11 years: 2 mg every 4 to 6 hours; do not exceed 12 mg/24 hours

Children ≥12 years: Refer to adult dosing.

Extended release: Children ≥12 years: Refer to adult dosing.

Renal Impairment There are no dosage adjustments provided in manufacturer's labeling.

Hepatic Impairment There are no dosage adjustments provided in the manufacturer's labeling; however, chlorpheniramine is metabolised via the liver; therefore, a dose adjustment may be necessary.

Mechanism of Action Competes with histamine for H_1-receptor sites on effector cells in the gastrointestinal tract, blood vessels, and respiratory tract

Contraindications Hypersensitivity to chlorpheniramine maleate or any component of the formulation; narrow-angle glaucoma; bladder neck obstruction; symptomatic prostate hypertrophy; during acute asthmatic attacks; stenosing peptic ulcer; pyloroduodenal obstruction. Avoid use in premature and term newborns due to possible association with SIDS.

OTC labeling: When used for self-medication, do not use to make a child sleep

Warnings/Precautions Causes sedation, caution must be used in performing tasks that require alertness (eg, operating machinery, driving). Sedative effects of CNS depressants or ethanol are potentiated. Use with caution in patients with urinary tract obstruction, symptomatic prostatic hyperplasia, thyroid dysfunction, increased intraocular pressure, and cardiovascular disease (including hypertension and ischemic heart disease). Antihistamines may cause excitation in young children. Not for OTC use in children <2 years of age.

Benzyl alcohol and derivatives: Some dosage forms may contain sodium benzoate/benzoic acid; benzoic acid (benzoate) is a metabolite of benzyl alcohol; large amounts of benzyl alcohol (≥99 mg/kg/day) have been associated with a potentially fatal toxicity ("gasping syndrome") in neonates; the "gasping syndrome" consists of metabolic acidosis, respiratory distress, gasping respirations, CNS dysfunction (including convulsions, intracranial hemorrhage), hypotension, and cardiovascular collapse (AAP ["Inactive" 1997]; CDC, 1982); some data suggests that benzoate displaces bilirubin from protein binding sites (Ahlfors, 2001); avoid or use dosage forms containing benzyl alcohol derivative with caution in neonates. See manufacturer's labeling.

Drug Interactions

Metabolism/Transport Effects **Substrate** of CYP2D6 (major), CYP3A4 (minor); **Note:** Assignment of Major/Minor substrate status based on clinically relevant drug interaction potential

Avoid Concomitant Use

Avoid concomitant use of Chlorpheniramine with any of the following: Aclidinium; Azelastine (Nasal); Cimetropium; Eluxadoline; Glucagon; Glycopyrrolate (Oral Inhalation); Ipratropium (Oral Inhalation); Levosulpiride; Nitroglycerin; Orphenadrine; Oxatomide; Oxomemazine; Paraldehyde; Potassium Chloride; Thalidomide; Tiotropium; Umeclidinium

Increased Effect/Toxicity

Chlorpheniramine may increase the levels/effects of: AbobotulinumtoxinA; Alcohol (Ethyl); Analgesics (Opioid); Anticholinergic Agents; Azelastine (Nasal); Blonanserin; Buprenorphine; Cimetropium; CNS Depressants; Eluxadoline; Flunitrazepam; Fosphenytoin-Phenytoin; Glucagon; Glycopyrrolate (Oral Inhalation); HYDROcodone; Methotrimeprazine; MetyroSINE; Mirabegron; Mirtazapine; OnabotulinumtoxinA; Orphenadrine; OxyCODONE; Paraldehyde; Perhexiline; Piribedil; Potassium Chloride; Pramipexole; Ramosetron; RimabotulinumtoxinB; ROPINIRole; Rotigotine; Selective Serotonin Reuptake Inhibitors; Suvorexant; Thalidomide; Thiazide and Thiazide-Like Diuretics; Thioridazine; Tiotropium; Topiramate; Zolpidem

The levels/effects of Chlorpheniramine may be increased by: Abiraterone Acetate; Aclidinium; Ajmaline; Asunaprevir; Brimonidine (Topical); Cannabis; Chloral Betaine; Chlormethiazole; Chlorphenesin Carbamate; Cobicistat; CYP2D6 Inhibitors (Moderate); CYP2D6 Inhibitors (Strong); Darunavir; Dimethindene (Topical); Doxylamine; Dronabinol; Droperidol; HydrOXYzine; Imatinib; Ipratropium (Oral Inhalation); Kava Kava; Lofexidine; Lumefantrine; Magnesium Sulfate; Methotrimeprazine; Mianserin; Minocycline; Nabilone; Oxatomide; Oxomemazine; Panobinostat; Peginterferon Alfa-2b; Perampanel; Perhexiline; Pramlintide; QuiNINE; Rufinamide; Sodium Oxybate; Tapentadol; Tetrahydrocannabinol; Thioridazine; Trimeprazine; Umeclidinium

Decreased Effect

Chlorpheniramine may decrease the levels/effects of: Acetylcholinesterase Inhibitors; Benzylpenicilloyl Polylysine; Betahistine; Gastrointestinal Agents (Prokinetic); Hyaluronidase; Itopride; Levosulpiride; Nitroglycerin; Secretin

The levels/effects of Chlorpheniramine may be decreased by: Acetylcholinesterase Inhibitors; Amphetamines; Peginterferon Alfa-2b

Dietary Considerations Some products may contain phenylalanine.

Pharmacodynamics/Kinetics

Half-life Elimination

Serum: Children and Adolescents 6 to 16 years: 13.1 ± 6.6 hours (range: 6.3 to 23.1 hours) (Simons 1982); Adults: 14-24 hours (Paton 1985)

Time to Peak

Children and Adolescents 6 to 16 years: Oral: 2.5 ± 1.5 hours (range: 1 to 6 hours) (Simons 1982); Adults: 2-3 hours (Sharma 2003)

Pregnancy Considerations Maternal chlorpheniramine use has generally not resulted in an increased risk of birth defects (Aselton 1985; Gilboa 2009; Heinonen 1977; Jick 1981). Antihistamines may be used for the treatment of rhinitis, urticaria, and pruritus with rash in pregnant women (although second generation antihistamines may be preferred) (Angier 2010; Murase 2014; Wallace 2008; Zuberbier 2014). Antihistamines are not recommended for treatment of pruritus associated with intrahepatic cholestasis in pregnancy (Ambros-Rudolph 2011; Kremer 2011).

Breastfeeding Considerations Chlorpheniramine is excreted into breast milk. In general, first generation antihistamines should be used with caution in breastfeeding women and nursing infants should be monitored for irritability or drowsiness. Second generation antihistamines are preferred (Butler 2014). Antihistamines may temporarily decrease maternal serum prolactin concentrations when administered prior to the establishment of nursing (Messinis 1985).

Dosage Forms

Liquid, Oral:

Ed ChlorPed [OTC]: 2 mg/mL (60 mL)

Syrup, Oral:

Aller-Chlor [OTC]: 2 mg/5 mL (120 mL)
Chlor-Trimeton [OTC]: 2 mg/5 mL (120 mL)
Ed Chlorped Jr [OTC]: 2 mg/5 mL (118 mL, 473 mL)

Tablet, Oral:

Aller-Chlor [OTC]: 4 mg
Allergy-Time [OTC]: 4 mg

Chlor-Trimeton [OTC]: 4 mg
Ed-Chlortan [OTC]: 4 mg
Pharbechlor [OTC]: 4 mg
Generic: 4 mg

Tablet Extended Release, Oral:
Chlor-Trimeton Allergy [OTC]: 12 mg
Generic: 12 mg

Chlorpheniramine and Pseudoephedrine

(klor fen IR a meen & soo doe e FED rin)

Related Information

Chlorpheniramine *on page 349*
Pseudoephedrine *on page 1404*

Brand Names: US Dicel Chewable [OTC] [DSC]; LoHist-D [OTC]; Maxichlor PSE [OTC]; Neutrahist Pediatric [OTC] [DSC]; SudoGest Sinus & Allergy [OTC]

Brand Names: Canada Triaminic Cold & Allergy

Pharmacologic Category Alkylamine Derivative; Alpha/Beta Agonist; Decongestant; Histamine H_1 Antagonist; Histamine H_1 Antagonist, First Generation

Use Relief of nasal congestion associated with the common cold, hay fever, allergic rhinitis, and other allergies

Local Anesthetic/Vasoconstrictor Precautions Use with caution since pseudoephedrine is a sympathomimetic amine which could interact with epinephrine to cause a pressor response

Effects on Dental Treatment Key adverse event(s) related to dental treatment:

Chlorpheniramine: Prolonged use will cause significant xerostomia (normal salivary flow resumes upon discontinuation).

Pseudoephedrine: Xerostomia (prolonged use worsens; normal salivary flow resumes upon discontinuation).

Effects on Bleeding No information available to require special precautions

Adverse Reactions See individual agents.

General Dosage Range Oral: *Children ≥6 years and Adults:* Dosage varies greatly depending on product.

Mechanism of Action

Chlorpheniramine competes with histamine for H_1-receptor sites on effector cells in the gastrointestinal tract, blood vessels, and respiratory tract.

Pseudoephedrine is a sympathomimetic amine and isomer of ephedrine; acts as a decongestant in respiratory tract mucous membranes with less vasoconstrictor action than ephedrine in normotensive individuals.

Pregnancy Risk Factor C

Pregnancy Considerations Reproduction studies have not been conducted with this combination product. See individual agents.

Chlorpheniramine, Pseudoephedrine, and Codeine

(klor fen IR a meen, soo doe e FED rin, & KOE deen)

Related Information

Chlorpheniramine *on page 349*
Codeine *on page 410*
Pseudoephedrine *on page 1404*

Brand Names: US Phenylhistine DH [OTC]; Tricode AR [DSC]

Pharmacologic Category Alkylamine Derivative; Alpha/Beta Agonist; Analgesic, Opioid; Antitussive; Decongestant; Histamine H_1 Antagonist; Histamine H_1 Antagonist, First Generation

Use Cough and upper respiratory allergy symptoms: Temporary relief of symptoms (runny nose, sneezing, itching of nose or throat, itchy/watery eyes, cough due to minor throat and bronchial irritation, nasal congestion, reduces swelling of nasal passages) associated with the common cold, allergic rhinitis, or other upper respiratory allergies.

Local Anesthetic/Vasoconstrictor Precautions Use with caution since pseudoephedrine is a sympathomimetic amine which could interact with epinephrine to cause a pressor response

Effects on Dental Treatment Key adverse event(s) related to dental treatment:

Chlorpheniramine: Significant xerostomia with prolonged use (normal salivary flow resumes upon discontinuation).

Pseudoephedrine: Xerostomia (normal salivary flow resumes upon discontinuation).

Effects on Bleeding No information available to require special precautions

Adverse Reactions Also see individual agents.

<1%, postmarketing, and/or case reports: Hypogonadism (Brennan 2013; Debono 2011)

General Dosage Range Oral:

Children 6 to <12 years: Chlorpheniramine 2 mg/codeine 8 to 10 mg/pseudoephedrine 30 mg per 5 mL: 5 mL every 4 to 6 hours (maximum: 20 mL [chlorpheniramine 8 mg/codeine 32 to 40 mg/pseudoephedrine 120 mg] per 24 hours)

Children ≥12 years, Adolescents, and Adults: Chlorpheniramine 2 mg/codeine 8 to 10 mg/pseudoephedrine 30 mg per 5 mL: 10 mL every 4 to 6 hours (maximum: 40 mL [chlorpheniramine 16 mg/codeine 64 to 80 mg/pseudoephedrine 240 mg] per 24 hours)

Mechanism of Action

Codeine: Binds to opioid receptors in the CNS, causing inhibition of ascending pain pathways, altering the perception of and response to pain; causes cough suppression by direct central action in the medulla; produces generalized CNS depression.

Chlorpheniramine: A propylamine derivative antihistamine drug (H_1 receptor antagonist) that also possesses anticholinergic and sedative activity. It prevents released histamine from dilating capillaries and causing edema of the respiratory mucosa.

Pseudoephedrine: Directly stimulates alpha-adrenergic receptors of respiratory mucosa causing vasoconstriction; directly stimulates beta-adrenergic receptors causing bronchial relaxation.

Controlled Substance C-V

ChlorproMAZINE (klor PROE ma zeen)

Related Information

Clinical Risk Related to Drugs Prolonging QT Interval *on page 1772*

Brand Names: Canada Chlorpromazine Hydrochloride Inj; Teva-Chlorpromazine

Pharmacologic Category Antimanic Agent; First Generation (Typical) Antipsychotic; Phenothiazine Derivative

Use

Behavioral problems: Treatment of severe behavioral problems in children 1 to 12 years of age marked by combativeness and/or explosive hyperexcitable behavior (out of proportion to immediate provocations).

Bipolar disorder: Treatment of manic episodes associated with bipolar disorder.

Hiccups: Treatment of intractable hiccups.

Hyperactivity: Short-term treatment of hyperactive children who show excessive motor activity with accompanying conduct disorders consisting of some or all of the following symptoms: impulsivity, difficulty sustaining attention, aggressiveness, mood lability, and poor frustration tolerance.

Nausea/Vomiting: Management of nausea and vomiting.

Porphyria, acute intermittent: Treatment of acute intermittent porphyria.

Schizophrenia/Psychotic disorders: Treatment of schizophrenia and psychotic disorders.

Surgery: Management of restlessness and apprehension prior to surgery.

Tetanus: Adjunctive therapy in the treatment of tetanus.

Local Anesthetic/Vasoconstrictor Precautions Chlorpromazine is one of the drugs confirmed to prolong the QT interval and is accepted as having a risk of causing torsade de pointes. The risk of drug-induced torsade de pointes is extremely low when a single QT interval prolonging drug is prescribed. In terms of epinephrine, it is not known what effect vasoconstrictors in the local anesthetic regimen will have in patients with a known history of congenital prolonged QT interval or in patients taking any medication that prolongs the QT interval. Until more information is obtained, it is suggested that the clinician consult with the physician prior to the use of a vasoconstrictor in suspected patients, and that the vasoconstrictor (epinephrine, mepivacaine and levonordefrin [Carbocaine® 2% with Neo-Cobefrin®]) be used with caution.

Effects on Dental Treatment Key adverse event(s) related to dental treatment:

Xerostomia (normal salivary flow resumes upon discontinuation).

Significant hypotension may occur, especially when the drug is administered parenterally. Patients may experience orthostatic hypotension as they stand up after treatment; especially if lying in dental chair for extended periods of time. Use caution with sudden changes in position during and after dental treatment. Orthostatic hypotension is due to alpha-receptor blockade; elderly are at greater risk.

Tardive dyskinesia: Prevalence rate may be 40% in elderly; development of the syndrome and the irreversible nature are proportional to duration and total cumulative dose over time. Extrapyramidal reactions are more common in elderly with up to 50% developing these reactions after 60 years of age. Drug-induced Parkinson's syndrome occurs often; akathisia is the most common extrapyramidal reaction in elderly.

Increased confusion, memory loss, psychotic behavior, and agitation frequently occur as a consequence of anticholinergic effects. Antipsychotic-associated sedation in nonpsychotic patients is extremely unpleasant due to feelings of depersonalization, derealization, and dysphoria.

Effects on Bleeding No information available to require special precautions

Adverse Reactions Frequency not defined.

Cardiovascular: ECG abnormality (nonspecific QT changes), orthostatic hypotension, tachycardia

Central nervous system: Akathisia, dizziness, drowsiness, dystonia, neuroleptic malignant syndrome, parkinsonian-like syndrome, seizure, tardive dyskinesia

Dermatologic: Dermatitis, skin photosensitivity, skin pigmentation (slate gray)

Endocrine & metabolic: Amenorrhea, gynecomastia, hyperglycemia, hypoglycemia

Gastrointestinal: Constipation, nausea, xerostomia

Genitourinary: Breast engorgement, ejaculatory disorder, false positive pregnancy test, impotence, lactation, urinary retention

Hematologic & oncologic: Agranulocytosis, aplastic anemia, eosinophilia, hemolytic anemia, immune thrombocytopenia, leukopenia

Hepatic: Jaundice

Ophthalmic: Blurred vision, corneal changes, epithelial keratopathy, retinitis pigmentosa

General Dosage Range IM, IV, Oral: *Infants ≥6 months, Children, Adolescents, and Adults:* Dosage varies greatly depending on indication.

Mechanism of Action Chlorpromazine is an aliphatic phenothiazine antipsychotic which blocks postsynaptic mesolimbic dopaminergic receptors in the brain; exhibits a strong alpha-adrenergic blocking effect and depresses the release of hypothalamic and hypophyseal hormones; believed to depress the reticular activating system, thus affecting basal metabolism, body temperature, wakefulness, vasomotor tone, and emesis

Pharmacodynamics/Kinetics

Onset of Action IM: 15 minutes; Oral: 30 to 60 minutes; Antipsychotic effects: Gradual, may take up to several weeks; Maximum antipsychotic effect: 6 weeks to 6 months

Duration of Action Oral: 4 to 6 hours

Half-life Elimination Biphasic: Initial: Children: 1.1 hours; Adults: ~2 hours; Terminal: Children: 7.7 hours; Adults: ~30 hours

Pregnancy Considerations Embryotoxicity was observed in animal reproduction studies. Jaundice or hyper- or hyporeflexia have been reported in newborn infants following maternal use of phenothiazines. Antipsychotic use during the third trimester of pregnancy has a risk for abnormal muscle movements (extrapyramidal symptoms [EPS]) and withdrawal symptoms in newborns following delivery. Symptoms in the newborn may include agitation, feeding disorder, hypertonia, hypotonia, respiratory distress, somnolence, and tremor; these effects may be self-limiting or require hospitalization.

Dental Comment See Local Anesthetic/Vasoconstrictor Precautions

ChlorproPAMIDE (klor PROE pa mide)

Related Information

Endocrine Disorders and Pregnancy *on page 1781*

Brand Names: Canada Apo-Chlorpropamide

Pharmacologic Category Antidiabetic Agent, Sulfonylurea

Use Management of blood sugar in type 2 diabetes mellitus (noninsulin dependent, NIDDM) as an adjunct to diet and exercise to lower blood glucose

Local Anesthetic/Vasoconstrictor Precautions No information available to require special precautions

Effects on Dental Treatment Key adverse event(s) related to dental treatment: Patients with diabetes should be questioned by the dental professional at each dental visit to assess their risk for stress-induced hypoglycemia. The dental professional should inquire about the patient's routine (ie, work, sleep schedule, eating patterns), history of hypoglycemia, time of last medication dose, last meal, and most recent blood sugar assessment. Keep a supply of glucose tablets and other carbohydrates in the office to prepare for a hypoglycemic event. Seek medical attention when necessary (American Diabetes Association, 2014).

Effects on Bleeding No information available to require special precautions

Adverse Reactions Frequency not always defined.

Central nervous system: Disulfiram-like reaction, dizziness, headache

Dermatologic: Pruritus (<3%), maculopapular rash (≤1%), urticaria (≤1%), erythema multiforme, exfoliative dermatitis, skin photosensitivity

Endocrine & metabolic: Hepatic porphyria, hypoglycemia, porphyria cutanea tarda, SIADH (syndrome of inappropriate antidiuretic hormone secretion), weight gain

Gastrointestinal: Nausea (<5%), anorexia (<2%), diarrhea (<2%), hunger (<2%), vomiting (<2%)

Hematologic & oncologic: Agranulocytosis, aplastic anemia, eosinophilia, hemolytic anemia, leukopenia, pancytopenia, thrombocytopenia

Hepatic: Cholestatic jaundice, hepatic failure, hepatitis

<1%, postmarketing, and/or case reports: Proctocolitis

General Dosage Range Oral:

Adults: Initial: 250 mg daily; Maintenance: 100-500 mg daily (maximum: 750 mg daily)

Elderly: Initial: 100-125 mg daily

Mechanism of Action Stimulates insulin release from the pancreatic beta cells; reduces glucose output from the liver; insulin sensitivity is increased at peripheral target sites

Pharmacodynamics/Kinetics

Onset of Action 1 hour; Peak effect: 3-6 hours

Duration of Action 24 hours

Half-life Elimination ~36 hours, prolonged in elderly or with renal impairment; End-stage renal disease: 50-200 hours

Time to Peak Serum: 2-4 hours

Pregnancy Risk Factor C

Pregnancy Considerations Animal reproduction studies have not been conducted. Chlorpropamide crosses the placenta and measurable serum concentrations can be found in infants exposed in utero. Severe hypoglycemia lasting 4 to 10 days has been noted in infants born to mothers taking a sulfonylurea (including chlorpropamide) at the time of delivery; additional adverse events have also been reported and may be influenced by maternal glycemic control (Jackson 1962; Kemball 1970; Uhrig 1983; Zucker 1968).

In women with diabetes, maternal hyperglycemia can be associated with congenital malformations as well as adverse effects in the fetus, neonate, and the mother (ACOG 2005; ADA 2016c; Kitzmiller 2008; Metzger 2007). To prevent adverse outcomes, prior to conception and throughout pregnancy maternal blood glucose and HbA_{1c} should be kept as close to target goals as possible but without causing significant hypoglycemia (ACOG 2013; ADA 2016c; Blumer 2013; Kitzmiller 2008). Agents other than chlorpropamide are currently recommended to treat diabetes in pregnant women (ACOG 2013; Blumer 2013). The manufacturer recommends if chlorpropamide is used during pregnancy, it should be discontinued at least 1 month before the expected delivery date.

Chlorthalidone (klor THAL i done)

Related Information

Cardiovascular Diseases *on page 1752*

Brand Names: Canada Apo-Chlorthalidone

Pharmacologic Category Antihypertensive; Diuretic, Thiazide-Related

Use

Edema: Adjunctive treatment of edema associated with heart failure, renal impairment, hepatic cirrhosis, or corticosteroid and estrogen therapy.

Hypertension: Management of hypertension (monotherapy or in combination with other antihypertensives).

Guideline recommendations:

Hypertension: The 2014 guideline for the management of high blood pressure in adults (Eighth Joint National Committee [JNC 8]) recommends initiation of pharmacologic treatment to lower blood pressure for the following patients:

- Patients ≥60 years of age with systolic blood pressure (SBP) ≥150 mm Hg or diastolic blood pressure (DBP) ≥90 mm Hg. Goal of therapy is SBP <150 mm Hg and DBP <90 mm Hg.
- Patients <60 years of age with SBP ≥140 mm Hg or DBP is ≥90 mm Hg. Goal of therapy is SBP <140 mm Hg and DBP <90 mm Hg.
- Patients ≥18 years of age with diabetes and SBP ≥140 mm Hg or DBP ≥90 mm Hg. Goal of therapy is SBP <140 mm Hg and DBP <90 mm Hg.
- Patients ≥18 years of age with chronic kidney disease (CKD) and SBP ≥140 mm Hg or DBP ≥90 mm Hg. Goal of therapy is SBP <140 mm Hg and DBP <90 mm Hg.

Chronic kidney disease (CKD) and hypertension: In patients with CKD, regardless of race or diabetes status, the use of an ACE inhibitor (ACEI) or angiotensin receptor blocker (ARB) as initial therapy is recommended to improve kidney outcomes. In the general nonblack population (without CKD) including those with diabetes, initial antihypertensive treatment should consist of a thiazide-type diuretic, calcium channel blocker, ACEI, or ARB. In the general black population (without CKD), including those with diabetes, initial antihypertensive treatment should consist of a thiazide-type diuretic or a calcium channel blocker **instead of** an ACEI or ARB.

Coronary artery disease (CAD) and hypertension: The American Heart Association, American College of Cardiology and American Society of Hypertension (AHA/ACC/ASH) 2015 scientific statement for the treatment of hypertension in patients with coronary artery disease (CAD) recommends the use of a thiazide (or thiazide-like diuretic) as part of a regimen in patients with hypertension and chronic stable angina. A BP target of <140/90 mm Hg is reasonable for the secondary prevention of cardiovascular events. A lower target BP (<130/80 mm Hg) may be appropriate in some individuals with CAD, previous MI, stroke or transient ischemic attack, or CAD risk equivalents (AHA/ACC/ASH [Rosendorff 2015]).

Local Anesthetic/Vasoconstrictor Precautions No information available to require special precautions

Effects on Dental Treatment No significant effects or complications reported

Effects on Bleeding No information available to require special precautions

Adverse Reactions Frequency not defined.

Dermatologic: Skin photosensitivity
Endocrine & metabolic: Hypokalemia
Gastrointestinal: Anorexia, dyspepsia
<1%, postmarketing, and/or case reports: Agranulocytosis, aplastic anemia, cholecystitis, constipation, decreased protein-bound iodine, decreased sexual activity, diabetes mellitus, diarrhea, dizziness, glycosuria, gout, headache, hepatic insufficiency, hypercalcemia, hyperglycemia, hypersensitivity reaction, hyperuricemia, hypochloremic alkalosis, hyponatremia, hypophosphatemia, impotence, insomnia, jaundice, leukopenia, muscle cramps, muscle spasm, nausea, necrotizing angiitis, orthostatic hypotension, pancreatitis, paresthesia, polyuria, purpura, renal insufficiency, restlessness, skin rash, thrombocytopenia, toxic epidermal necrolysis, urticaria, vasculitis, vertigo, vomiting, weakness, xanthopsia

General Dosage Range Oral: *Adults:* 25 to 100 mg once daily (maximum: 200 mg/day)

Mechanism of Action Sulfonamide-derived diuretic that inhibits sodium and chloride reabsorption in the cortical-diluting segment of the ascending loop of Henle

Pharmacodynamics/Kinetics

Onset of Action ~2.6 hours; Peak effect: 2 to 6 hours (Carter 2004)

Duration of Action Single dose: 24 to 48 hours; Long-term dosing: 48 to 72 hours (Carter 2004)

Half-life Elimination Single dose: 40 hours; Long-term dosing: 45 to 60 hours (Carter 2004); may be prolonged with renal impairment

Pregnancy Risk Factor B

Pregnancy Considerations Adverse events have not been observed in animal reproduction studies. Chlorthalidone crosses the placenta and can be detected in cord blood. Maternal use may cause fetal or neonatal jaundice, thrombocytopenia, or other adverse events observed in adults. Use of thiazide diuretics to treat edema during normal pregnancies is not appropriate; use may be considered when edema is due to pathologic causes (as in the nonpregnant patient); monitor. Untreated chronic maternal hypertension is associated with adverse events in the fetus, infant, and mother. Women who require thiazide diuretics for the treatment of hypertension prior to pregnancy may continue their use (ACOG 2013).

Chlorzoxazone (klor ZOKS a zone)

Related Information

Temporomandibular Dysfunction (TMD), Chronic Pain, and Fibromyalgia *on page 1868*

Brand Names: US Lorzone; Parafon Forte DSC

Pharmacologic Category Skeletal Muscle Relaxant

Use Musculoskeletal conditions: Adjunct to rest, physical therapy, and other measures for the relief of discomfort associated with acute, painful musculoskeletal conditions

Local Anesthetic/Vasoconstrictor Precautions No information available to require special precautions

Effects on Dental Treatment No significant effects or complications reported

Effects on Bleeding No information available to require special precautions

Adverse Reactions Frequency not defined.

Central nervous system: Dizziness, drowsiness, malaise, paradoxical central nervous system stimulation
Genitourinary: Urine discoloration
<1%, postmarketing, and/or case reports: Allergic skin rash, anaphylaxis (very rare), angioedema (very rare), ecchymoses, gastrointestinal hemorrhage, hepatotoxicity, petechia

General Dosage Range Oral: *Adults:* 250 to 750 mg 3 to 4 times daily

Mechanism of Action Centrally acting agent; acts on the spinal cord and subcortical areas of the brain to inhibit polysynaptic reflex arcs involved in causing and maintaining skeletal muscle spasms

Pharmacodynamics/Kinetics

Onset of Action Within 1 hour (Desiraju 1983)

Duration of Action Up to 6 hours (Desiraju 1983)

Half-life Elimination ~1 hour (Desiraju 1983)

Time to Peak ~1 to 2 hours

Pregnancy Considerations Animal reproduction studies have not been conducted.

Cholecalciferol (kole e kal SI fer ole)

Brand Names: US Aqueous Vitamin D [OTC]; Bio-D-Mulsion Forte [OTC]; Bio-D-Mulsion [OTC]; BProtected Pedia D-Vite [OTC]; D-3-5 [OTC]; D-Vi-Sol [OTC]; D-Vita [OTC]; D3-50 [OTC]; Decara [OTC]; Delta D3 [OTC]; Dialyvite Vitamin D 5000 [OTC]; Dialyvite Vitamin D3 Max [OTC]; Pronutrients Vitamin D3 [OTC]; Vitamin D3 Super Strength [OTC]

Brand Names: Canada D-Vi-Sol

Pharmacologic Category Vitamin D Analog

Use

Dietary supplement: As a vitamin D dietary supplement

Vitamin D deficiency: Prevention and treatment of vitamin D deficiency

Local Anesthetic/Vasoconstrictor Precautions No information available to require special precautions

Effects on Dental Treatment Key adverse event(s) related to dental treatment: Metallic taste and xerostomia (normal salivary flow resumes upon discontinuation).

Effects on Bleeding No information available to require special precautions

Adverse Reactions No adverse reactions listed in the manufacturer's labeling.

General Dosage Range Oral:

Children 0 to 12 months: Adequate intake: 400 units/day (IOM 2011)

Children 1 year to Adults ≤70 years: RDA: 600 units/day (IOM 2011)

Elderly >70 years: RDA: 800 units/day (IOM 2011)

Mechanism of Action Cholecalciferol (vitamin D_3) is a provitamin. The active metabolite, 1,25-dihydroxyvitamin D (calcitriol), stimulates calcium and phosphate absorption from the small intestine, promotes secretion of calcium from bone to blood; promotes renal tubule phosphate resorption (IOM 2011)

Pharmacodynamics/Kinetics

Half-life Elimination Circulating: 25(OH)D: 2 to 3 weeks; 1,25-dihydroxyvitamin D: ~4 hours (Holick 2011)

Pregnancy Considerations The cholecalciferol metabolite, 25(OH)D, crosses the placenta; maternal serum concentrations correlate with fetal concentrations at birth (Misra 2008; Wagner 2008). Vitamin D requirements are the same in pregnant and nonpregnant females (IOM 2011).

Vitamin D deficiency in a pregnant woman may lead to a vitamin D deficiency in the neonate (Misra 2008;

Wagner 2008). Serum 25(OH)D concentrations should be measured in pregnant women considered to be at increased risk of deficiency (ACOG 2011). The amount of vitamin D contained in prenatal vitamins may not be adequate to treat a deficiency during pregnancy; although larger doses may be needed, current guidelines recommend a total of 1,000 to 2,000 units/day until more safety data is available (ACOG 2011; Holick 2011). In women not at risk for deficiency, doses larger than the RDA should be avoided during pregnancy (ACOG 2011).

Cholestyramine Resin

(koe LES teer a meen REZ in)

Related Information

Cardiovascular Diseases *on page 1752*

Brand Names: US Prevalite; Questran; Questran Light

Brand Names: Canada Novo-Cholamine; Novo-Cholamine Light; Olestyr; PMS-Cholestyramine; Questran; Questran Light Sugar Free; ZYM-Cholestyramine-Light; ZYM-Cholestyramine-Regular

Pharmacologic Category Antilipemic Agent, Bile Acid Sequestrant

Use Adjunct in the management of primary hypercholesterolemia; pruritus associated with elevated levels of bile acids; regression of arteriolosclerosis

Local Anesthetic/Vasoconstrictor Precautions No information available to require special precautions

Effects on Dental Treatment No significant effects or complications reported

Effects on Bleeding No information available to require special precautions

Adverse Reactions Frequency not defined.

Cardiovascular: Edema, syncope

Central nervous system: Anxiety, dizziness, drowsiness, fatigue, headache, neuralgia, paresthesia, vertigo

Dermatologic: Perianal skin irritation, skin irritation, skin rash, urticaria

Endocrine & metabolic: Hyperchloremic metabolic acidosis (children), increased libido, weight gain, weight loss

Gastrointestinal: Abdominal pain, anorexia, biliary colic, constipation, dental bleeding, dental caries, dental discoloration, diarrhea, diverticulitis, duodenal ulcer with hemorrhage, dysgeusia, dysphagia, eructation, flatulence, gallbladder calcification, gastric ulcer, gastrointestinal hemorrhage, hemorrhoidal bleeding, hiccups, intestinal obstruction (rare), melena, nausea, pancreatitis, rectal pain, steatorrhea, tongue irritation, tooth enamel damage (dental erosion), vomiting

Genitourinary: Diuresis, dysuria, hematuria

Hematologic & oncologic: Adenopathy, anemia, bruise, hemorrhage, hypoprothrombinemia, prolonged prothrombin time, rectal hemorrhage

Hepatic: Abnormal hepatic function tests

Neuromuscular & skeletal: Arthralgia, arthritis, back pain, myalgia, osteoporosis

Ophthalmic: Nocturnal amblyopia (rare), uveitis

Otic: Tinnitus

Respiratory: Asthma, dyspnea, wheezing

General Dosage Range Oral: *Adults:* 4-24 g/day in 1-6 divided doses

Mechanism of Action Forms a nonabsorbable complex with bile acids in the intestine, releasing chloride ions in the process; inhibits enterohepatic reuptake of intestinal bile salts and thereby increases the fecal loss of bile salt-bound low density lipoprotein cholesterol

Pharmacodynamics/Kinetics

Onset of Action Peak effect: 21 days

Pregnancy Risk Factor C

Pregnancy Considerations Cholestyramine is not absorbed systemically, but may interfere with vitamin absorption; therefore, regular prenatal supplementation may not be adequate. There are no studies in pregnant women; use with caution.

Cholic Acid (KOE lik AS id)

Brand Names: US Cholbam

Pharmacologic Category Bile Acid

Use

Bile acid synthesis disorders: Treatment of bile acid synthesis disorders due to single enzyme defects (SEDs).

Peroxisomal disorders: Treatment (adjunctive) of peroxisomal disorders (PDs), including Zellweger spectrum disorders, in patients who exhibit manifestations of hepatic disease, steatorrhea, or complications from decreased fat soluble vitamin absorption.

Limitations of use: The safety and effectiveness of cholic acid on extrahepatic manifestations of bile acid synthesis disorders due to SEDs or PDs, including Zellweger spectrum disorders, have not been established.

Local Anesthetic/Vasoconstrictor Precautions No information available to require special precautions

Effects on Dental Treatment No significant effects or complications reported

Effects on Bleeding No information available to require special precautions

Adverse Reactions

>10%:

Gastrointestinal: Cholestasis (≤14%, exacerbation)

Hepatic: increased serum bilirubin (≤14%), increased serum transaminases (≤14%)

1% to 10%:

Central nervous system: Malaise (≤1%), peripheral neuropathy (≤1%)

Dermatologic: Skin lesion (≤1%)

Gastrointestinal: Diarrhea (1% to 2%), abdominal pain (≤1%), intestinal polyps (≤1%), nausea (≤1%), reflux esophagitis (≤1%)

Genitourinary: Urinary tract infection (≤1%)

Hepatic: Hepatic disease (6%, exacerbation), jaundice (≤1%)

<1%, postmarketing, and/or case reports: Cholelithiasis (3β-HSD deficienct patient)

General Dosage Range Oral: *Neonates ≥3 weeks, Infants, Children, Adolescents, and Adults:* 10 to 15 mg/kg (once daily or in 2 divided doses).

Mechanism of Action Cholic acid, a primary bile acid, enhances bile flow and provides the physiologic feedback inhibition of bile acid synthesis to maintain bile acid homeostasis.

Pregnancy Considerations Animal reproduction studies have not been conducted. Information related to the use of cholic acid during pregnancy is limited. Tests of hepatic function should be monitored closely.

A registry is available for women exposed to cholic acid during pregnancy. Patients or their health care provider should call 844-202-6262 to enroll.

Prescribing and Access Restrictions Cholbam is only available through an exclusive pharmacy provider, Dohmen Life Science Services, Inc. For additional information, call 844.CHOLBAM (844.246.5226) or visit http://www.cholbam.com/support-and-resources/cholbam-4-u/.

Choline Magnesium Trisalicylate

(KOE leen mag NEE zhum trye sa LIS i late)

Related Information

Temporomandibular Dysfunction (TMD), Chronic Pain, and Fibromyalgia *on page 1868*

Pharmacologic Category Salicylate

Use

Acute painful shoulder: Management of acute painful shoulder

Analgesia: Relief of mild to moderate pain

Antipyresis: Management of pyrexia

Arthritis: Relief of signs/symptoms of osteoarthritis, rheumatoid arthritis, and other arthritis (long-term management and acute flares)

Juvenile idiopathic arthritis: Anti-inflammatory or analgesic management (in children) of juvenile idiopathic arthritis and other appropriate conditions

Local Anesthetic/Vasoconstrictor Precautions

No information available to require special precautions

Effects on Dental Treatment The dentist should be aware of the potential of abnormal coagulation. Caution should also be exercised in the use of NSAIDs in patients already on anticoagulant therapy with drugs such as warfarin (Coumadin®). See Effects on Bleeding.

Effects on Bleeding Nonacetylated salicylates, such as choline salicylate or magnesium salicylate, do not affect platelet aggregation and do not increase bleeding time. There have been rare reports of thrombocytopenia with salicylates.

Adverse Reactions

Frequency not defined.

<20%:

Gastrointestinal: Constipation, diarrhea, dyspepsia, epigastric pain, heartburn, nausea, vomiting

Otic: Tinnitus

<2%:

Central nervous system: Dizziness, drowsiness, headache, lethargy

Otic: Auditory impairment

<1%, postmarketing, and/or case reports: Anorexia, asthma, bruise, confusion, duodenal ulcer, dysgeusia, edema, epistaxis, erythema multiforme, esophagitis, gastric ulcer, hallucination, hearing loss (irreversible), increased blood urea nitrogen, increased liver enzymes, increased serum creatinine, occult blood in stools, pruritus, skin rash, weight gain

General Dosage Range Oral:

Children and Adolescents ≤37 kg: 50 mg/kg daily in 2 divided doses

Children and Adolescents >37 kg: 2250 mg daily in 2 divided doses

Adults: 1500 mg twice daily **or** 3000 mg once daily at bedtime **or** 2000 mg to 3000 mg daily in 2 or 3 divided doses.

Elderly: 750 mg 3 times daily

Mechanism of Action Weakly inhibits cyclooxygenase enzymes, which results in decreased formation of prostaglandin precursors; antipyretic, analgesic, and anti-inflammatory properties.

Other proposed mechanisms not fully elucidated (and possibly contributing to the anti-inflammatory effect to varying degrees) include inhibiting chemotaxis, altering lymphocyte activity, inhibiting neutrophil aggregation/activation, and decreasing proinflammatory cytokine levels.

Pharmacodynamics/Kinetics

Half-life Elimination Dose dependent: Tablet: 9 to 17 hours

Time to Peak Serum: Liquid: 1 to 2 hours

Pregnancy Risk Factor C

Pregnancy Considerations Animal reproduction studies have not been conducted. Due to the known effects of other salicylates on the fetal cardiovascular system (closure of ductus arteriosus), use during late pregnancy should be avoided.

Chorionic Gonadotropin (Human)

(kor ee ON ik goe NAD oh troe pin, HYU man)

Related Information

Chorionic Gonadotropin (Recombinant) *on page 357*

Brand Names: US Novarel; Pregnyl

Brand Names: Canada Chorionic Gonadotropin for Injection; Pregnyl

Pharmacologic Category Gonadotropin; Ovulation Stimulator

Use

Hypogonadotrophic hypogonadism: Treatment of hypogonadism secondary to a pituitary deficiency in males.

Ovulation induction: Induction of ovulation and pregnancy in the anovulatory, infertile woman in whom the cause of anovulation is secondary and not caused by primary ovarian failure, and who has been appropriately pretreated with human menotropins.

Prepubertal cryptorchidism: Treatment of prepubertal cryptorchidism not caused by anatomic obstruction.

Local Anesthetic/Vasoconstrictor Precautions

No information available to require special precautions

Effects on Dental Treatment No significant effects or complications reported

Effects on Bleeding No information available to require special precautions

Adverse Reactions Frequency not defined.

Cardiovascular: Edema

Central nervous system: Depression, fatigue, headache, irritability, restlessness

Endocrine & metabolic: Gynecomastia

Genitourinary: Precocious puberty

Hypersensitivity: Hypersensitivity reaction (local or systemic)

Local: Injection site reaction, pain at injection site

<1%, postmarketing, and/or case reports: Arterial thrombosis, ovarian hyperstimulation syndrome, rupture of ovarian cyst

General Dosage Range IM:

Children ≥4 years and Adolescents (males): Dosage varies greatly depending on indication

Adults (females): 5,000 to 10,000 units 1 day following last dose of menotropins

Adults (males): 500 to 4,000 units 3 times/week

Mechanism of Action Human chorionic gonadotropin (hCG) is produced by the human placenta; available preparations provide purified luteinizing hormone obtained from the urine of pregnant women. hCG stimulates production of gonadal steroid hormones by causing production of androgen by the testes and the development of secondary sex characteristics in males. In females, hCG acts as a substitute for luteinizing hormone (LH) to stimulate ovulation.

Pharmacodynamics/Kinetics

Duration of Action IM: ~36 hours

Half-life Elimination Biphasic: Initial: 6 to 11 hours; Terminal: 23 to 37 hours

Time to Peak Plasma: IM: Within 6 hours

Pregnancy Risk Factor X

Pregnancy Considerations Studies in animals have shown evidence of fetal abnormalities at doses intended to induce superovulation (used in combination regimens). Testicular tumors in otherwise healthy men have been reported when treating secondary infertility. The incidence of ectopic pregnancy and increased pregnancy loss may be increased in women undergoing assisted reproductive therapy. Congenital abnormalities have also been observed, however a causal association has not been established. In women undergoing ovulation induction, discontinue use after pregnancy is established.

Chorionic Gonadotropin (Recombinant)

(kor ee ON ik goe NAD oh troe pin ree KOM be nant)

Related Information

Chorionic Gonadotropin (Human) *on page 356*

Brand Names: US Ovidrel

Brand Names: Canada Ovidrel®

Pharmacologic Category Gonadotropin; Ovulation Stimulator

Use As part of an assisted reproductive technology (ART) program, induces ovulation in infertile females who have been pretreated with follicle stimulating hormones (FSH); induces ovulation and pregnancy in infertile females when the cause of infertility is functional

Local Anesthetic/Vasoconstrictor Precautions No information available to require special precautions

Effects on Dental Treatment No significant effects or complications reported

Effects on Bleeding No information available to require special precautions

Adverse Reactions

2% to 10%:

Endocrine & metabolic: Ovarian cyst (3%), ovarian hyperstimulation (<2% to 3%)

Gastrointestinal: Abdominal pain (3% to 4%), nausea (3%), vomiting (3%)

Local: Pain at injection site (8%), bruising at injection site (3% to 5%), injection site reaction (<2% to 3%), inflammation at injection site (≤2%)

Miscellaneous: Postoperative pain (5%)

<2%, postmarketing, and/or case reports: Abdominal swelling, albuminuria, back pain, breast pain, cardiac arrhythmia, cervical carcinoma, cervical lesion, cough, diarrhea, dizziness, dysuria, ectopic pregnancy, emotional lability, fever, flatulence, headache, heart murmur, herpes genitalis, hiccups, hot flash, hyperglycemia, hypersensitivity reaction, insomnia, intermenstrual bleeding, leukocytosis, leukorrhea, malaise, mastalgia, paresthesia, pharyngitis, pruritus, skin rash, upper respiratory tract infection, urinary incontinence, urinary tract infection, vaginal discomfort, vaginal hemorrhage, vaginitis, vulvovaginal candidiasis

General Dosage Range SubQ: *Adults (females):* 250 mcg given 1 day following last dose of follicle stimulating agent

Mechanism of Action Luteinizing hormone analogue produced by recombinant DNA techniques; stimulates late follicular maturation and initiates rupture of the ovarian follicle once follicular development has occurred

Pharmacodynamics/Kinetics

Half-life Elimination Initial: 4 hours; Terminal: 29 hours

Time to Peak 12-24 hours

Pregnancy Risk Factor X

Pregnancy Considerations Adverse events were observed in animal reproduction studies. Ectopic pregnancy, premature labor, postpartum fever, and spontaneous abortion have been reported in clinical trials. Congenital abnormalities have also been observed, however, the incidence is similar during natural conception.

Ciclesonide (Nasal) (sye KLES oh nide)

Brand Names: US Omnaris; Zetonna

Brand Names: Canada Drymira; Omnaris; Omnaris HFA

Pharmacologic Category Corticosteroid, Nasal

Use Management of seasonal and perennial allergic rhinitis

Local Anesthetic/Vasoconstrictor Precautions No information available to require special precautions

Effects on Dental Treatment No significant effects or complications reported

Effects on Bleeding No information available to require special precautions

Adverse Reactions

>10%:

Respiratory: Epistaxis (≤11%)

1% to 10%:

Central nervous system: Headache (3% to 7%)

Gastrointestinal: Nausea (≥2%)

Genitourinary: Urinary tract infection (≥2%)

Infection: Influenza (≥2%)

Neuromuscular & skeletal: Back pain (≥2%), strain (≥2%)

Otic: Otalgia (2%)

Respiratory: Nasopharyngitis (2% to 7%), nasal discomfort (3% to 6%), pharyngolaryngeal pain (≥3%), bronchitis (≥2%), cough (≥2%; may be dose-responsive), nasal septum disorder (≥2%; may be dose-responsive), oropharyngeal pain (≥2%), sinusitis (≥2%), streptococcal pharyngitis (≥2%), viral upper respiratory tract infection (≥2%), upper respiratory infection (≤2%)

<1%, postmarketing, and/or case reports: Angioedema (with angioedema of the lips, angioedema of the oropharynx, and angioedema of the tongue), dizziness, dysgeusia, dyspepsia, leukocytosis, nasal candidiasis, nasal congestion, nasal mucosa ulcer, pharyngeal candidiasis, rhinorrhea, throat irritation, xerostomia

General Dosage Range Intranasal:

Omnaris®: *Children ≥6 years and Adults:* 2 sprays (50 mcg/spray) per nostril once daily (maximum: 200 mcg/day)

Zetonna™: *Children ≥12 years and Adults:* 1 spray (37 mcg/spray) per nostril once daily (maximum: 74 mcg/day)

Pharmacodynamics/Kinetics

Onset of Action 24-48 hours; further improvement observed over 1-2 weeks in seasonal allergic rhinitis or 5 weeks in perennial allergic rhinitis

Pregnancy Risk Factor C

Pregnancy Considerations Adverse events were observed in some animal reproduction studies. Hypoadrenalism may occur in newborns following maternal use of corticosteroids in pregnancy; monitor. Intranasal corticosteroids may be used in the treatment of rhinitis during pregnancy; the lowest effective dose should be used (NAEPP, 2005; Wallace, 2008).

Ciclesonide (Oral Inhalation)

(sye KLES oh nide)

Related Information

Respiratory Diseases *on page* 1777

Brand Names: US Alvesco

Brand Names: Canada Alvesco

Generic Availability (US) No

Pharmacologic Category Corticosteroid, Inhalant (Oral)

Use

Bronchial asthma: Prophylactic management of bronchial asthma

Guideline recommendations: A low-dose inhaled corticosteroid *(in addition to an as-needed short acting beta$_2$-agonist)* is the initial preferred long term control medication for children, adolescents, and adult patients with persistent asthma who are candidates for treatment according to a step-wise treatment approach (GINA 2016; NAEPP 2007).

Local Anesthetic/Vasoconstrictor Precautions No information available to require special precautions

Effects on Dental Treatment Key adverse event(s) related to dental treatment: Dysphonia has been reported with use of this medication. Localized infections with *Candida albicans* or *Aspergillus niger* occur frequently in the mouth and pharynx with repetitive use of an oral inhaler; may require treatment with appropriate antifungal therapy or discontinuance of inhaler use.

Effects on Bleeding No information available to require special precautions

Adverse Reactions

>10%:

- Central nervous system: Headache (≤11%)
- Respiratory: Nasopharyngitis (≤11%)

1% to 10%:

- Cardiovascular: Facial edema (≥3%)
- Central nervous system: Dizziness (≥3%), fatigue (≥3%), voice disorder (1%)
- Dermatologic: Urticaria (≥3%)
- Gastrointestinal: Gastroenteritis (≥3%), oral candidiasis (≥3%)
- Infection: Influenza (≥3%)
- Neuromuscular & skeletal: Arthralgia (≥3%), back pain (≥3%), limb pain (≥3%), musculoskeletal chest pain (≥3%)
- Ophthalmic: Conjunctivitis (≥3%)
- Otic: Otalgia (2%)
- Respiratory: Upper respiratory tract infection (≤9%), nasal congestion (≤6%), pharyngolaryngeal pain (≤5%), hoarseness (≥3%), pneumonia (≥3%), sinusitis (≥3%), paradoxical bronchospasm (2%)

<1%, postmarketing, and/or case reports: Angioedema (with swelling of lip/pharynx/tongue), cataract, chest discomfort, increased gamma-glutamyl transferase, increased intraocular pressure, increased serum ALT, nausea, palpitations, pharyngeal candidiasis, skin rash, weight gain, xerostomia

Dosing

Adult & Geriatric Asthma: Oral inhalation (Alvesco): **Note:** Titrate to the lowest effective dose once asthma stability is achieved:

US labeling:

- Prior therapy with bronchodilators alone: Initial: 80 mcg twice daily (maximum dose: 320 mcg/day)
- Prior therapy with inhaled corticosteroids: Initial: 80 mcg twice daily (maximum dose: 640 mcg/day)
- Prior therapy with oral corticosteroids: Initial: 320 mcg twice daily (maximum dose: 640 mcg/day)

Canadian labeling: Initial: 400 mcg once daily; maintenance: 100-800 mcg/day (1-2 puffs once daily; more severe asthma may require 400 mcg twice daily). **Note:** Canadian Thoracic Society 2010 Asthma Management guidelines recommendation: Doses >200 mcg/day may provide minimal additional benefit while increasing risks for adverse events; add-on therapy should be considered prior to dose increases >200 mcg/day (Lougheed 2010).

Asthma guidelines: Global Initiative for Asthma guidelines (GINA 2016): HFA inhaler (refers to Alvesco 80 mcg and 160 mcg strengths available in the US):

- "Low" dose: 80 to 160 mcg daily
- "Medium" dose: >160 to 320 mcg daily
- "High" dose: >320 mcg daily

Conversion: *Conversion from oral to orally-inhaled steroid:* Initiation of oral inhalation therapy should begin in patients who have previously been stabilized on oral corticosteroids (OCS). A gradual dose reduction of OCS should begin ~7-10 days after starting inhaled therapy. U.S. labeling recommends reducing prednisone dose no more rapidly than ≤2.5 mg/day on a weekly basis. The Canadian labeling recommends decreasing the daily dose of prednisone by 1 mg (or equivalent of other OCS) every 7 days in closely monitored patients, and every 10 days in patients whom close monitoring is not possible. In the presence of withdrawal symptoms, resume previous OCS dose for 1 week before attempting further dose reductions.

Pediatric Asthma: Oral inhalation (Alvesco): **Note:** Titrate to the lowest effective dose once asthma stability is achieved:

US labeling: Children ≥12 years and Adolescents: Refer to adult dosing.

Canadian labeling:

- Children 6 to 11 years: Initial: 100-200 mcg once daily; maintenance: 100-200 mcg/day (1-2 puffs once daily). **Note:** Canadian Thoracic Society 2010 Asthma Management guidelines recommend dose titration in children 6-11 years who fail to achieve an adequate response in spite of adherence to therapy and/or lack of alternative factors (eg, environmental triggers) which might impair response (Lougheed 2010).
- Children ≥12 years and Adolescents: Refer to adult dosing.

Asthma guidelines: Global Initiative for Asthma guidelines (GINA 2016): HFA inhaler (refers to Alvesco 80 mcg and 160 mcg strengths available in the US):

- Children ≤5 years: "Low" dose: 160 mcg daily
- Children 6 to 11 years:
  - "Low" dose: 80 mcg daily
  - "Medium" dose: >80 to 160 mcg daily
  - "High" dose: >160 mcg daily
- Children ≥12 years and Adolescents: Refer to adult dosing.

Renal Impairment There are no dosage adjustments provided in the manufacturer labeling (has not been studied); however, dose adjustments may not be necessary as ≤20% of drug is eliminated renally.

Hepatic Impairment Dosage adjustments are not necessary.

Mechanism of Action Ciclesonide is a nonhalogenated, glucocorticoid prodrug that is hydrolyzed to the pharmacologically active metabolite des-ciclesonide following administration. Des-ciclesonide has a high affinity for the glucocorticoid receptor and exhibits anti-inflammatory activity. The mechanism of action for corticosteroids is believed to be a combination of three important properties - anti-inflammatory activity, immunosuppressive properties, and antiproliferative actions.

Contraindications

Hypersensitivity to ciclesonide or any component of the formulation; primary treatment of acute asthma or status asthmaticus

Canadian labeling: Additional contraindications (not in U.S. labeling): Untreated fungal, bacterial, or tuberculosis infections of the respiratory tract; moderate-to-severe bronchiectasis

Warnings/Precautions May cause hypercorticism or suppression of hypothalamic-pituitary-adrenal (HPA) axis, particularly in younger children or in patients receiving high doses for prolonged periods. HPA axis suppression may lead to adrenal crisis. Withdrawal and discontinuation of a corticosteroid should be done slowly and carefully. Particular care is required when patients are transferred from systemic corticosteroids to inhaled products due to possible adrenal insufficiency or withdrawal from steroids, including an increase in allergic symptoms. Adult patients receiving >20 mg per day of prednisone (or equivalent) may be most susceptible. Fatalities have occurred due to adrenal insufficiency in asthmatic patients during and after transfer from systemic corticosteroids to aerosol steroids; aerosol steroids do **not** provide the systemic steroid needed to treat patients having trauma, surgery, or infections. Select surgical patients on long-term, high-dose, inhaled corticosteroid (ICS), should be given stress doses of hydrocortisone intravenously during the surgical period and the dose reduced rapidly within 24 hours after surgery (NAEPP, 2007).

Bronchospasm may occur with wheezing after inhalation; if this occurs stop steroid and treat with a fast-acting bronchodilator. Supplemental steroids (oral or parenteral) may be needed during stress or severe asthma attacks. Not to be used in status asthmaticus or for the relief of acute bronchospasm. Oropharyngeal thrush due to candida albicans infection may occur with use. Prolonged use of corticosteroids may also increase the incidence of secondary infection, mask acute infection (including fungal infections), prolong or exacerbate viral infections, or limit response to vaccines. Exposure to chickenpox and measles should be avoided; corticosteroids should not be used to treat ocular herpes simplex. Close observation is required in patients with latent tuberculosis and/or TB reactivity; restrict use in active TB (only in conjunction with antituberculosis treatment). Use in patients with TB is contraindicated in the Canadian labeling. Prolonged treatment with corticosteroids has been associated with the development of Kaposi's sarcoma (case reports); if noted, discontinuation of therapy should be considered.

Use with caution in patients with cardiovascular disease, diabetes, severe hepatic impairment, thyroid disease, psychiatric disturbances, myasthenia gravis, glaucoma, cataracts, patients at risk for osteoporosis, and patients at risk for seizures. Use in renally-impaired patients has not been studied; however, ≤20% of drug is eliminated renally. Use with caution in elderly patients.

Orally inhaled corticosteroids may cause a reduction in growth velocity in pediatric patients (~1 cm per year [range: 0.3-1.8 cm per year] and related to dose and duration of exposure). To minimize the systemic effects of orally inhaled corticosteroids, each patient should be titrated to the lowest effective dose. Growth should be routinely monitored in pediatric patients.

Drug Interactions

Metabolism/Transport Effects Substrate of CYP3A4 (minor); **Note:** Assignment of Major/Minor substrate status based on clinically relevant drug interaction potential

Avoid Concomitant Use

Avoid concomitant use of Ciclesonide (Oral Inhalation) with any of the following: Aldesleukin; Desmopressin; Loxapine

Increased Effect/Toxicity

Ciclesonide (Oral Inhalation) may increase the levels/effects of: Amphotericin B; Ceritinib; Deferasirox; Desmopressin; Loop Diuretics; Loxapine; Thiazide and Thiazide-Like Diuretics

Decreased Effect

Ciclesonide (Oral Inhalation) may decrease the levels/effects of: Aldesleukin; Corticorelin; Hyaluronidase

Pharmacodynamics/Kinetics

Onset of Action >4 weeks for maximum benefit

Half-life Elimination Ciclesonide: 0.7 hours; des-ciclesonide: 6-7 hours

Time to Peak ~1 hour (des-ciclesonide)

Pregnancy Risk Factor C

Pregnancy Considerations Adverse events were observed in some animal reproduction studies. Hypoadrenalism may occur in infants born to mothers receiving corticosteroids during pregnancy. Based on available data, an overall increased risk of congenital malformations or a decrease in fetal growth has not been associated with maternal use of inhaled corticosteroids during pregnancy (Bakhireva, 2005; NAEPP, 2005; Namazy, 2004). Uncontrolled asthma is associated with adverse events in pregnancy (increased risk of perinatal mortality, pre-eclampsia, preterm birth, low birth weight infants). Inhaled corticosteroids are recommended for the treatment of asthma during pregnancy (most information available using budesonide) (ACOG, 2008; NAEPP, 2005).

Breastfeeding Considerations Systemic corticosteroids are excreted in human milk. It is not known if sufficient quantities of ciclesonide are absorbed following oral inhalation to produce detectable amounts in breast milk; however, oral absorption is limited (<1%). The manufacturer recommends that caution be exercised when administering ciclesonide to nursing women. The use of inhaled corticosteroids is not considered a contraindication to breastfeeding (NAEPP, 2005).

Dosage Forms Considerations Alvesco 6.1 g canisters contain 60 inhalations.

Dosage Forms

Aerosol Solution, Inhalation:

Alvesco: 80 mcg/actuation (6.1 g); 160 mcg/actuation (6.1 g)

Dosage Forms: Canada

Aerosol for oral inhalation:

Alvesco: 100 mcg/inhalation; 200 mcg/inhalation

Ciclopirox (sye kloe PEER oks)

Brand Names: US Ciclodan; Ciclodan Cream; Ciclodan Solution; Ciclopirox Treatment; CNL8 Nail [DSC]; Loprox; Pedipirox-4 Nail [DSC]; Penlac

Brand Names: Canada Apo-Ciclopirox; Loprox; Penlac; PMS-Ciclopirox; Stieprox; Taro-Ciclopirox

Pharmacologic Category Antifungal Agent, Topical

Use

Dermatologic conditions (infectious and seborrheal):

Cream, suspension: Topical treatment of tinea pedis, tinea cruris, and tinea corporis due to *Trichophyton rubrum*, *Trichophyton mentagrophytes*, *Epidermophyton floccosum*, and *Microsporum canis*; candidiasis (moniliasis) due to *Candida albicans*; tinea (pityriasis) versicolor due to *Malassezia furfur.*

Gel: Topical treatment of interdigital tinea pedis and tinea corporis due to *T. rubrum*, *T. mentagrophytes*, or *E. floccosum*; seborrheic dermatitis of the scalp.

Nail lacquer topical solution: Topical treatment of immunocompetent patients with mild to moderate onychomycosis of fingernails and toenails, without lunula involvement, due to *Trichophyton rubrum*, as a component of a comprehensive management program.

Shampoo: Topical treatment of seborrheic dermatitis of the scalp in adults.

Local Anesthetic/Vasoconstrictor Precautions No information available to require special precautions

Effects on Dental Treatment No significant effects or complications reported

Effects on Bleeding No information available to require special precautions

Adverse Reactions Frequency not always defined.

Cardiovascular: Facial edema, ventricular tachycardia (shampoo)

Central nervous system: Headache

Dermatologic: Acne vulgaris, alopecia, contact dermatitis, erythema, hair discoloration (rare; shampoo formulation in light-haired individuals), localized erythema, nail disease (shape or color change with lacquer), pruritus, skin rash, xeroderma

Local: Application site burning (gel: 7% to 34%; other dose forms: ≤1%), local irritation, local pain

Ophthalmic: Eye pain

General Dosage Range Topical:

Cream, suspension: *Children >10 years, Adolescents, and Adults:* Apply twice daily

Gel: *Adolescents ≥16 years and Adults:* Apply twice daily

Lacquer: *Children ≥12 years, Adolescents, and Adults:* Apply to adjacent skin and affected nails daily; remove with alcohol every 7 days

Shampoo: *Adolescents ≥16 years and Adults:* Apply 5 to 10 mL to wet hair, lather, and leave on hair and scalp for ~3 minutes, rinse; repeat twice weekly (allow minimum of 3 days between applications)

Mechanism of Action Inhibiting transport of essential elements in the fungal cell disrupting the synthesis of DNA, RNA, and protein

Pharmacodynamics/Kinetics

Half-life Elimination Biologic: Cream, suspension: 1.7 hours; Elimination: Gel: 5.5 hours

Pregnancy Risk Factor B

Pregnancy Considerations Adverse events were not observed in animal reproduction studies.

Cidofovir (si DOF o veer)

Related Information

Systemic Viral Diseases *on page 1806*

Brand Names: US Vistide [DSC]

Pharmacologic Category Antiviral Agent

Use

Cytomegalovirus retinitis: Treatment of cytomegalovirus (CMV) retinitis in patients with AIDS.

Limitations of use: Safety and efficacy have not been established for treatment of other CMV infections (eg, pneumonitis, gastroenteritis), congenital or neonatal CMV disease, or CMV disease in non-HIV infected individuals.

Local Anesthetic/Vasoconstrictor Precautions No information available to require special precautions

Effects on Dental Treatment Key adverse event(s) related to dental treatment: Stomatitis and abnormal taste.

Effects on Bleeding No reports of bleeding or thrombocytopenia with cidofovir alone.

Adverse Reactions

Frequency not defined. *Incidence not specifically defined, but reported in the range of >10%. **Incidence not specifically defined, but reported in the range of 1% to 10%.

Cardiovascular: Cardiac failure, cardiomyopathy, cardiovascular disease, edema, orthostatic hypotension, shock, syncope, tachycardia

Central nervous system: Chills,* headache,* pain,* agitation, amnesia, anxiety, confusion, convulsions, dizziness, hallucination, insomnia, malaise, vertigo

Dermatologic: Alopecia,* skin rash,* skin discoloration, skin photosensitivity, urticaria

Endocrine & metabolic: Decreased serum bicarbonate,* Fanconi's syndrome,** adrenocortical insufficiency

Gastrointestinal: Anorexia,* diarrhea,* nausea,* oral candidiasis,* vomiting,* abdominal pain, aphthous stomatitis, colitis, constipation, dysphagia, fecal incontinence, gastritis, gastrointestinal hemorrhage, gingivitis, melena, proctitis, stomatitis, tongue discoloration

Genitourinary: Nephrotoxicity,* proteinuria,* urinary incontinence

Hematologic & oncologic: Anemia,* neutropenia,* hypochromic anemia, immune thrombocytopenia, leukocytosis, leukopenia, lymphadenopathy, pancytopenia, pseudolymphoma, splenomegaly, thrombocytopenia

Hepatic: Abnormal liver function tests, hepatic disease, hepatic necrosis, hepatomegaly, hepatosplenomegaly, jaundice

Hypersensitivity: Hypersensitivity reaction

Infection: Infection,* sepsis

Local: Injection site reaction

Neuromuscular & skeletal: Weakness,* tremor

Ophthalmic: Decreased intraocular pressure,* iritis,* uveitis,* amblyopia, blindness, cataract, conjunctivitis, corneal lesion, diplopia, visual disturbance

Otic: Hearing loss

Renal: Increased serum creatinine*

Respiratory: Cough,* dyspnea,* pneumonia**

Miscellaneous: Fever*

<1%, postmarketing, and/or case reports: Hepatic failure, metabolic acidosis, pancreatitis

General Dosage Range Dosage adjustment recommended in patients with renal impairment

IV: *Adults:* Induction: 5 mg/kg once weekly for 2 consecutive weeks; Maintenance: 5 mg/kg once every 2 weeks

Mechanism of Action Cidofovir is converted to cidofovir diphosphate (the active intracellular metabolite); cidofovir diphosphate suppresses CMV replication by selective inhibition of viral DNA synthesis. Incorporation of cidofovir diphosphate into growing viral DNA chain results in viral DNA synthesis rate reduction.

Pharmacodynamics/Kinetics

Half-life Elimination Plasma: ~2.6 hours; intracellular elimination half-lives of metabolites are longer (range: 24 to 87 hours) (Lea, 1996)

Pregnancy Risk Factor C

Pregnancy Considerations

[US Boxed Warning]: Possibly carcinogenic and teratogenic based on animal data. May cause hypospermia. Women of childbearing potential should use effective contraception during therapy and for 1 month following treatment. Males should use a barrier contraceptive during therapy and for 3 months following treatment.

The indications for treating CMV retinitis during pregnancy are the same as in nonpregnant HIV infected woman; however systemic therapy should be avoided during the first trimester when possible. When therapy is needed to treat maternal infection, agents other than cidofovir are recommended (DHHS [Adult OI 2014]).

Cilazapril (sye LAY za pril)

Brand Names: Canada Apo-Cilazapril; CO Cilazapril; Inhibace; Mylan-Cilazapril; PHL-Cilazapril; PMS-Cilazapril; Teva-Cilazapril

Pharmacologic Category Angiotensin-Converting Enzyme (ACE) Inhibitor; Antihypertensive

Use Note: Not approved in the US

Heart failure: Adjunctive treatment of heart failure (HF)

Note: The ACCF/AHA 2013 heart failure guidelines recommend the use of ACE inhibitors, along with other guideline directed medical therapies, to prevent heart failure in patients with a reduced ejection fraction who have a history of MI (Stage B HF), to prevent heart failure in any patient with a reduced ejection fraction (Stage B HF), or to treat those with heart failure and reduced ejection fraction (Stage C HFrEF) (ACCF/AHA [Yancy, 2013]).

Hypertension: Management of hypertension

Local Anesthetic/Vasoconstrictor Precautions No information available to require special precautions

Effects on Dental Treatment Key adverse event(s) related to dental treatment: Patients may experience orthostatic hypotension as they stand up after treatment; especially if lying in dental chair for extended periods of time. Use caution with sudden changes in position during and after dental treatment.

An angiotensin-converting enzyme (ACE) inhibitor cough is a dry, hacking, nonproductive cough that can potentially interfere with longer dental procedures if patient has this side effect.

Effects on Bleeding No information available to require special precautions

Adverse Reactions

Frequency not always defined.

1% to 10%:

Cardiovascular: Orthostatic hypotension (2%), palpitations (≤1%), symptomatic hypotension (heart failure patients: ≤1%)

Central nervous system: Dizziness (3% to 8%), headache (3% to 5%), fatigue (2% to 3%)

Gastrointestinal: Nausea (1% to 3%)

Neuromuscular & skeletal: Weakness (≤2%)

Renal: Increased serum creatinine

Respiratory: Cough (hypertension patients: 2%; heart failure patients: ≤8%; sometimes severe)

1%, postmarketing, and/or case reports: Abdominal pain, agranulocytosis (rare), alopecia, anaphylaxis (rare), anemia, angina pectoris, angioedema (including facial edema), anorexia, anxiety, arthralgia, ataxia, atrial fibrillation, atrioventricular block, bradycardia, bronchitis, bronchospasm, bullous dermatitis (rare), cardiac arrhythmia, cardiac decompensation, cardiac failure, cerebrovascular accident (rare), chest pain, confusion, conjunctivitis, constipation, decreased libido, depression, dermatitis, diarrhea, diaphoresis, drowsiness, dysgeusia, dyspepsia, dyspnea, dysuria, epistaxis, erythema multiforme (rare), exacerbation of psoriasis (rare), exfoliative dermatitis (rare), extrasystoles, fatigue, flatulence, flushing, gastrointestinal hemorrhage, gout, hemolytic anemia, hyperbilirubinemia, hyperglycemia, hyperkalemia (more common in renal patients), hypoesthesia, immune thrombocytopenia (rare), impotence, increased liver enzymes (rare), increased serum transaminases, insomnia, leg cramps, leukopenia, lichen planus (rare), lupus-like syndrome (rare), malaise, migraine, myalgia, myocardial infarction (rare), nausea, nervousness, neutropenia (rare), pancreatitis (rare), paresthesia, pemphigus, pharyngitis, photophobia, polyuria, proteinuria, pruritus, psoriasiform eruption (rare), purpura (rare), rectal hemorrhage, renal failure (rare), respiratory tract infection, rhinitis, rigors, sinusitis, skin rash (rare; including erythematous rash and maculopapular rash), Stevens-Johnson syndrome (rare), syncope, tachycardia, tinnitus, toxic epidermal necrolysis, transient ischemic attacks (rare), tremor, uremia, urinary frequency, urticaria (rare), vertigo, visual disturbance, visual hallucination (Doane 2013), voice disorder, vomiting, xerostomia

General Dosage Range Dosage adjustment recommended in patients with hepatic or renal impairment

Oral:

Adults: Initial: 0.5 to 2.5 mg once daily (maximum: 5 mg/day [CHF]; 10 mg/day [HTN])

Elderly: Initial: 0.5 to 1.25 mg once daily (maximum: 2.5 mg/day [CHF]; 10 mg/day [HTN])

Mechanism of Action Cilazapril is a prodrug that is rapidly converted to cilazaprilat (active metabolite), a competitive inhibitor of angiotensin-converting enzyme (ACE); prevents conversion of angiotensin I to angiotensin II, a potent vasoconstrictor; results in lower levels of angiotensin II which causes an increase in plasma renin activity and a reduction in aldosterone secretion.

Pharmacodynamics/Kinetics

Onset of Action ~1 to 2 hours; Peak effect: Antihypertensive effect: 3 to 7 hours; Heart failure (reduction of systemic vascular resistance and pulmonary capillary wedge pressure): 2 to 4 hours

Duration of Action Therapeutic effect: Up to 24 hours

Half-life Elimination Cilazaprilat: Terminal: Single dose: 36 to 49 hours; Multidose: ~54 hours

Time to Peak Cilazaprilat: Within 2 hours

Pregnancy Considerations [Canadian Boxed Warning]: Use of cilazapril is contraindicated during pregnancy. Drugs that act on the renin-angiotensin system can cause injury and death to the developing fetus. Discontinue as soon as possible once pregnancy is detected. Females planning pregnancy should be switched to alternative therapy that has been proven safe during pregnancy.

Teratogenic effects may occur following maternal use during pregnancy. Drugs that act on the renin-angiotensin system are associated with oligohydramnios. Oligohydramnios, due to decreased fetal renal function, may lead to fetal lung hypoplasia and skeletal malformations. Their use in pregnancy is also associated with anuria, hypotension, renal failure, skull hypoplasia, and death in the fetus/neonate. Chronic maternal hypertension itself is also associated with adverse events in the mother and fetus/infant. However, ACE inhibitors are not recommended during pregnancy to treat maternal hypertension or heart failure. Use of an ACE inhibitor should also be avoided in any woman of reproductive age. The exposed fetus should be monitored for fetal growth, amniotic fluid volume, and organ formation. Infants exposed to an ACE inhibitor *in utero* should be monitored for hyperkalemia, hypotension, and oliguria.

Product Availability Not available in the US

Cilostazol (sil OH sta zol)

Related Information

Antiplatelet and Anticoagulation Considerations in Dentistry *on page 1764*

Cardiovascular Diseases *on page 1752*

Brand Names: US Pletal [DSC]

Pharmacologic Category Antiplatelet Agent; Phosphodiesterase-3 Enzyme Inhibitor; Vasodilator

Use Intermittent claudication: Reduction of symptoms of intermittent claudication, as indicated by an increased walking distance.

Local Anesthetic/Vasoconstrictor Precautions No information available to require special precautions

Effects on Dental Treatment No significant effects or complications reported

Effects on Bleeding Cilostazol causes reversible inhibition of platelet aggregation. To restore platelet function, cilostazol should be discontinued for 96 hours (4 days). A medical consult is recommended to determine the benefit:risk of continuing or discontinuing cilostazol for invasive dental procedures.

Adverse Reactions

>10%:

Central nervous system: Headache (27% to 34%)

Gastrointestinal: Diarrhea (12% to 19%), abnormal stools (12% to 15%)

Infection: Infection (10% to 14%)

Respiratory: Rhinitis (7% to 12%)

1% to 10%:

Cardiovascular: Palpitations (5% to 10%), peripheral edema (7% to 9%), tachycardia (4%), atrial fibrillation (<2%), atrial flutter (<2%), cardiac arrest (<2%), cardiac failure (<2%), cerebral infarction (<2%), edema (<2%), facial edema (<2%), hypotension (<2%), myocardial infarction (<2%), nodal arrhythmia (<2%), orthostatic hypotension (<2%), supraventricular tachycardia (<2%), syncope (<2%), varicose veins (<2%), ventricular premature contractions (<2%), ventricular tachycardia (<2%)

Central nervous system: Dizziness (9% to 10%), vertigo (3%), anxiety (<2%), chills (<2%), insomnia (<2%), malaise (<2%), neuralgia (<2%)

Dermatologic: Ecchymoses (<2%), furunculosis (eye: <2%), skin hypertrophy (<2%), urticaria (<2%), xeroderma (<2%)

Endocrine & metabolic: Albuminuria (<2%), diabetes mellitus (<2%), gout (<2%), hyperlipidemia (<2%), hyperuricemia (<2%), increased gamma-glutamyl transferase (<2%)

Gastrointestinal: Nausea (7%), dyspepsia (6%), abdominal pain (4% to 5%), flatulence (3%), anorexia (<2%), cholelithiasis (<2%), colitis (<2%), duodenal ulcer (<2%), duodenitis (<2%), esophageal hemorrhage (<2%), esophagitis (<2%), gastric ulcer (<2%), gastritis (<2%), gastroenteritis (<2%), gingival hemorrhage (<2%), hematemesis (<2%), melena (<2%), peptic ulcer (<2%), periodontal abscess (<2%)

Genitourinary: Cystitis (<2%), pelvic pain (<2%), urinary frequency (<2%), vaginal hemorrhage (<2%), vaginitis (<2%)

Hematologic & oncologic: Anemia (<2%), hemorrhage (<2%), hemorrhage (eye, <2%), iron deficiency anemia (<2%), polycythemia (<2%), purpura (<2%), rectal hemorrhage (<2%), retroperitoneal hemorrhage (<2%)

Hypersensitivity: Tongue edema (<2%)

Neuromuscular & skeletal: Back pain (7%), myalgia (3%), arthralgia (<2%), bursitis (<2%), neck stiffness (<2%), ostealgia (<2%)

Ophthalmic: Amblyopia (<2%), blindness (<2%), conjunctivitis (<2%), diplopia (<2%), retinal hemorrhage (<2%)

Otic: Otalgia (<2%), tinnitus (<2%)

Renal: Increased serum creatinine (<2%)

Respiratory: Pharyngitis (10%), cough (3% to 4%), asthma (<2%), epistaxis (<2%), hemoptysis (<2%), pneumonia (<2%), sinusitis (<2%)

Miscellaneous: Fever (<2%)

Postmarketing and/or case reports: Abnormal hepatic function tests, agranulocytosis, anaphylaxis, angina pectoris, angioedema, aplastic anemia, cerebrovascular accident, cerebral hemorrhage, chest pain, coronary thrombosis (stent), fixed drug eruption, gastrointestinal hemorrhage, granulocytopenia, hematoma (extradural), hematuria, hemorrhagic diathesis, hepatic insufficiency, hot flash, hyperglycemia, hypersensitivity, hypertension, increased blood pressure, increased blood urea nitrogen, interstitial pneumonitis, intracranial hemorrhage, jaundice, leukopenia, pain, pancytopenia, pulmonary hemorrhage, pruritus, prolonged Q-T interval on ECG, skin rash, Stevens-Johnson syndrome, subcutaneous hemorrhage, subdural hematoma, thrombocytopenia, thrombosis, torsades de pointes, vasodilatation, vomiting

General Dosage Range Dosage adjustment recommended in patients on concomitant therapy

Oral: *Adults:* 100 mg twice daily

Mechanism of Action Cilostazol and its metabolites are inhibitors of phosphodiesterase III. As a result, cyclic AMP is increased leading to reversible inhibition of platelet aggregation, vasodilation, and inhibition of vascular smooth muscle cell proliferation.

Pharmacodynamics/Kinetics

Onset of Action Effect on walking distance: 2 to 4 weeks; may require up to 12 weeks

Half-life Elimination ~11 to 13 hours

Pregnancy Risk Factor C

Pregnancy Considerations Adverse events have been observed in animal reproduction studies.

Cimetidine (sye MET i deen)

Related Information

Gastrointestinal Disorders *on page 1775*

Brand Names: US Cimetidine Acid Reducer [OTC]; Tagamet HB [OTC] [DSC]

Brand Names: Canada Apo-Cimetidine; Dom-Cimetidine; Mylan-Cimetidine; Novo-Cimetidine; Nu-Cimet; PMS-Cimetidine

Pharmacologic Category Histamine H_2 Antagonist

Use

Duodenal ulcer: Short-term treatment of active duodenal ulcer and maintenance therapy after the healing of active ulcer.

Gastric ulcer: Short-term treatment of active, benign gastric ulcer.

Gastroesophageal reflux disease: Treatment of erosive gastroesophageal reflux disease (GERD).

Pathological hypersecretory conditions: Treatment of pathological hypersecretory conditions (eg, Zollinger-Ellison syndrome, systemic mastocytosis, multiple endocrine adenomas).

Heartburn (OTC only): Relief and prevention of heartburn associated with acid indigestion and sour stomach.

Local Anesthetic/Vasoconstrictor Precautions No information available to require special precautions

Effects on Dental Treatment No significant effects or complications reported

Effects on Bleeding No information available to require special precautions

Adverse Reactions

1% to 10%:

Central nervous system: Headache (2% to 4%), dizziness (1%), drowsiness (1%), agitation

Endocrine & metabolic: Gynecomastia (<1% to 4%)

Gastrointestinal: Diarrhea (1%)

Frequency not defined:

Cardiovascular: Atrioventricular block, bradycardia, hypotension, tachycardia, vasculitis

Central nervous system: Confusion, decreased sexual activity

Dermatologic: Alopecia, erythema multiforme, exfoliative dermatitis, skin rash, Stevens-Johnson syndrome, toxic epidermal necrolysis

Gastrointestinal: Nausea, pancreatitis, vomiting

Genitourinary: Breast swelling

Hematologic & oncologic: Agranulocytosis, aplastic anemia, hemolytic anemia (immune-based), neutropenia, pancytopenia, thrombocytopenia

Hepatic: Hepatic fibrosis (case report), increased serum ALT, increased serum AST

Hypersensitivity: Anaphylaxis

Neuromuscular & skeletal: Arthralgia, myalgia, polymyositis

Renal: Increased serum creatinine, interstitial nephritis

Respiratory: Pneumonia (causal relationship not established)

Miscellaneous: Fever

General Dosage Range Dosage adjustment recommended in patients with renal impairment

Oral:

Children <12 years: 20 to 40 mg/kg/day

Children ≥12 years and Adolescents: 20 to 40 mg/kg/day **or** 200 mg 1 to 2 times daily [OTC]

Adults: 300 mg 4 times daily **or** 400 to 800 mg 1 to 2 times daily **or** 200 mg 1 to 2 times daily [OTC]

Mechanism of Action Competitive inhibition of histamine at H_2 receptors of the gastric parietal cells resulting in reduced gastric acid secretion, gastric volume and hydrogen ion concentration reduced

Pharmacodynamics/Kinetics

Onset of Action 1 hour

Duration of Action 80% reduction in gastric acid secretion for 4 to 5 hours after 300 mg dose

Half-life Elimination Neonates: 3.6 hours; Children: 1.4 hours; Adults: ~2 hours

Time to Peak Serum: Oral: 0.75 to 1.5 hours

Pregnancy Risk Factor B

Pregnancy Considerations Adverse events have not been observed in animal reproduction studies. Cimetidine crosses the placenta (Howe 1981). Histamine H_2 antagonists have been evaluated for the treatment of gastroesophageal reflux disease (GERD), as well as gastric and duodenal ulcers during pregnancy (Cappell 2003; Richter 2003). Histamine H_2 antagonists may be used for aspiration prophylaxis prior to cesarean delivery (ASA 2007).

Cinacalcet (sin a KAL cet)

Brand Names: US Sensipar

Brand Names: Canada Sensipar

Pharmacologic Category Calcimimetic

Use

Hyperparathyroidism, primary: Treatment of severe hypercalcemia in adult patients with primary hyperparathyroidism for whom parathyroidectomy would be indicated on the basis of serum calcium levels, but who are unable to undergo parathyroidectomy

Hyperparathyroidism, secondary: Treatment of secondary hyperparathyroidism in adult patients with chronic kidney disease (CKD) on dialysis.

Limitation of use: Not indicated for use in patients with CKD who are not on dialysis (due to the increased risk of hypocalcemia)

Parathyroid carcinoma: Treatment of hypercalcemia in adult patients with parathyroid carcinoma

Local Anesthetic/Vasoconstrictor Precautions No information available to require special precautions

Effects on Dental Treatment No significant effects or complications reported

Effects on Bleeding No information available to require special precautions

Adverse Reactions

>10%:

Cardiovascular: Hypotension (12%)

Central nervous system: Paresthesia (14% to 29%), headache (≤21%), fatigue (12% to 21%), depression (10% to 18%)

Endocrine & metabolic: Hypocalcemia (<8.4 mg/dL: 6% to 75%; <7.5 mg/dL: 29% to 33%), dehydration (≤24%), hypercalcemia (12% to 21%), hypoparathyroidism (intact parathyroid hormone <100 pg/mL: ≤11%)

Gastrointestinal: Nausea (30% to 66%), vomiting (26% to 52%), diarrhea (21%), anorexia (6% to 21%), constipation (5% to 18%), abdominal pain (11%)

Hematologic & oncologic: Anemia (6% to 17%)

Neuromuscular & skeletal: Bone fracture (12% to 21%), muscle spasm (11% to 18%), arthralgia (6% to 17%), weakness (5% to 17%), myalgia (15%), back pain (12%), limb pain (10% to 12%)

Respiratory: Dyspnea (13%), cough (12%), upper respiratory tract infection (8% to 12%)

1% to 10%:

Cardiovascular: Hypertension (7%)

Central nervous system: Dizziness (7% to 10%), noncardiac chest pain (6%), seizure (≤3%)

Endocrine & metabolic: Hyperkalemia (8%)

Gastrointestinal: Upper abdominal pain (8%), dyspepsia (7%), decreased appetite (6%)

Hypersensitivity: Hypersensitivity reaction (9%)

Infection: Localized infection (dialysis access site; 5%)

Postmarketing and/or case reports: Adynamic bone disease, angioedema, cardiac arrhythmia, cardiac failure, hypotension (idiosyncratic), prolonged Q-T interval on ECG (secondary to hypocalcemia), skin rash, urticaria, ventricular arrhythmia (secondary to hypocalcemia)

General Dosage Range Dosage adjustment recommended in patients on concomitant therapy or who develop toxicities

Oral: *Adults:* Initial: 30 mg once or twice daily; Maintenance: Increase dose incrementally every 2 to 4 weeks up to 180 mg once daily or 90 mg 4 times daily to normalize calcium levels or maintain iPTH level

Mechanism of Action Increases the sensitivity of the calcium-sensing receptor on the parathyroid gland thereby, concomitantly lowering parathyroid hormone (PTH), serum calcium, and serum phosphorus levels, preventing progressive bone disease and adverse events associated with mineral metabolism disorders.

Pharmacodynamics/Kinetics

Half-life Elimination Terminal: 30 to 40 hours; moderate hepatic impairment: 65 hours; severe hepatic impairment: 84 hours

Time to Peak ~2 to 6 hours; increased with food

Pregnancy Risk Factor C

Pregnancy Considerations Adverse events have been observed in animal reproduction studies. Women who become pregnant during cinacalcet treatment are encouraged to enroll in Amgen's Pregnancy Surveillance Program (1-800-772-6436).

Ciprofloxacin (Systemic) (sip roe FLOKS a sin)

Related Information

Periodontal Diseases *on page 1844*

Related Sample Prescriptions

Bacterial Infections and Periodontal Diseases - Sample Prescriptions *on page 32*

Brand Names: US Cipro; Cipro in D5W; Cipro XR

Brand Names: Canada ACT Ciprofloxacin; Apo-Ciproflox; Auro-Ciprofloxacin; Cipro; Cipro XL; Ciprofloxacin Injection; Ciprofloxacin Injection USP; Ciprofloxacin Intravenous Infusion; Ciprofloxacin Intravenous Infusion BP; Dom-Ciprofloxacin; JAMP-Ciprofloxacin; Mar-Ciprofloxacin; Mint-Ciproflox; Mint-Ciprofloxacin; Mylan-Ciprofloxacin; PHL-Ciprofloxacin; PMS-Ciprofloxacin; PMS-Ciprofloxacin XL; PRO-Ciprofloxacin; RAN-Ciproflox; ratio-Ciprofloxacin; Riva-Ciprofloxacin; Sandoz-Ciprofloxacin; Septa-Ciprofloxacin; Taro-Ciprofloxacin; Teva-Ciprofloxacin

Generic Availability (US) Yes

Pharmacologic Category Antibiotic, Fluoroquinolone

Use

Children: Treatment of complicated urinary tract infections and pyelonephritis due to *E. coli.* **Note:** Although effective, ciprofloxacin is not the drug of first choice in children.

Children and Adults: Prophylaxis to reduce incidence or progression of disease following exposure to aerosolized *Bacillus anthracis*; prophylaxis and treatment of plague, including pneumonic and septicemic plague, due to *Yersinia pestis*.

Adults: Treatment of the following infections when caused by susceptible bacteria: Urinary tract infections; acute uncomplicated cystitis in females; chronic bacterial prostatitis; bone and joint infections due to *Enterobacter cloacae*, *Serratia marcescens*, or *Pseudomonas aeruginosa*; complicated intra-abdominal infections (in combination with metronidazole); infectious diarrhea; typhoid fever due to *Salmonella typhi* (eradication of chronic typhoid carrier state has not been proven); hospital-acquired (nosocomial) pneumonia.

Limitations of use: Because fluoroquinolones have been associated with disabling and potentially irreversible serious adverse reactions (eg, tendinitis and tendon rupture, peripheral neuropathy, CNS effects), reserve ciprofloxacin for use in patients who have no alternative treatment options for acute uncomplicated cystitis.

Local Anesthetic/Vasoconstrictor Precautions No information available to require special precautions

Effects on Dental Treatment No significant effects or complications reported

Effects on Bleeding No information available to require special precautions

Adverse Reactions

1% to 10%:

Central nervous system: Neurological signs and symptoms (children 2%; includes dizziness, insomnia, nervousness, somnolence), headache (IV administration), restlessness (IV administration)

Dermatologic: Skin rash (children 2%, adults 1%)

Gastrointestinal: Diarrhea (children 5%; adults 2%), vomiting (children 5%; adults 1%), abdominal pain (children 3%; adults <1%), dyspepsia (children 3%; adults <1%), nausea (3%)

Hepatic: Increased serum AST (adults 1%), increased serum ALT

Local: Injection site reactions (IV administration)

Respiratory: Rhinitis (children 3%)

Miscellaneous: Fever (children 2%; adults <1%)

<1%, postmarketing, and/or case reports: Abnormal gait, acute generalized exanthematous pustulosis, acute gout attack, acute renal failure, ageusia, agitation, agranulocytosis, albuminuria, anaphylactic shock, anaphylaxis, anemia, angina pectoris, angioedema, anorexia, anosmia, anxiety, arthralgia, ataxia, atrial flutter, bone marrow depression (life-threatening), bronchospasm, candidiasis, candiduria, cardiorespiratory arrest, casts in urine, cerebral thrombosis, chills, cholestatic jaundice, chromatopsia, *Clostridium difficile*-associated diarrhea, confusion, constipation, crystalluria (particularly in alkaline urine), decreased hematocrit, decreased hemoglobin, decreased prothrombin time, delirium, depersonalization, depression (including self-injurious behavior), dizziness, drowsiness, dyspepsia (adults), dysphagia, dysphasia, dyspnea, edema, eosinophilia, erythema multiforme, erythema nodosum, exacerbation of myasthenia gravis, exfoliative dermatitis, fixed drug eruption, flatulence, gastrointestinal hemorrhage, hallucination, headache (oral), hematuria, hemolytic anemia, hepatic failure, hepatic necrosis, hepatotoxicity (idiosyncratic) (Chalasani 2014), hyperesthesia, hyperglycemia, hyperpigmentation, hypersensitivity reaction, hypertension, hypertonia, hypoglycemia, hypotension, increased blood urea nitrogen, increased creatine phosphokinase, increased INR (in patients treated with vitamin K antagonists), increased intracranial pressure, increased lactate dehydrogenase, increased serum alkaline phosphatase, increased serum bilirubin, increased serum cholesterol, increased serum creatinine, increased serum glucose, increased serum lipase, increased serum triglycerides, increased uric acid, insomnia, interstitial nephritis, intestinal perforation, irritability, jaundice,

laryngeal edema, lethargy, lymphadenopathy, malaise, manic behavior, mastalgia, methemoglobinemia, migraine, myalgia, myocardial infarction, myoclonus, nephritis, nephrolithiasis, nightmares, nystagmus, orthostatic hypotension, palpitations, pancreatitis, pancytopenia (life-threatening), paranoia, paresthesia, peripheral neuropathy, petechia, phobia, phototoxicity, pneumonitis, polyneuropathy, prolonged prothrombin time (in patients treated with vitamin K antagonists), pseudotumor cerebri, pulmonary edema, rupture of tendon, seizure (including grand mal), serum sickness-like reaction, skin photosensitivity, status epilepticus, Stevens-Johnson syndrome, suicidal ideation, suicidal tendencies, syncope, tachycardia, tendonitis, thrombocythemia, thrombocytopenia, thrombophlebitis, tinnitus, torsades de pointes, toxic epidermal necrolysis, toxic psychosis, tremor, twitching, unresponsive to stimuli, urethral bleeding, vaginitis, vasculitis, ventricular arrhythmia, ventricular ectopy, visual disturbance, vulvovaginal candidiasis, weakness

Dosing

Adult & Geriatric

Note: Extended release tablets and immediate release formulations are not interchangeable. Unless otherwise specified, oral dosing reflects the use of immediate release formulations.

Anthrax:

Inhalational (postexposure prophylaxis):

Oral: 500 mg every 12 hours for 60 days

IV: 400 mg every 12 hours for 60 days

Cutaneous (without systemic involvement), treatment (off-label use) (Hendricks 2014): Oral: Immediate release formulation: 500 mg every 12 hours for 7 to 10 days after naturally acquired infection; 60 days following biological weapon-related event

Systemic (including meningitis), treatment (off-label use) (Hendricks 2014): IV: 400 mg every 8 hours; use in combination with a protein synthesis inhibitor (eg, clindamycin, linezolid); If meningitis is suspected or cannot be ruled out, use in combination with another bactericidal antimicrobial (eg, beta-lactam) and a protein synthesis inhibitor (eg, clindamycin, linezolid). Duration of therapy is 2 weeks when meningitis has been excluded; ≥2 to 3 weeks for possible/confirmed meningitis. Patients exposed to aerosolized spores require prophylaxis to complete an antimicrobial course of 60 days from illness onset.

Bacterial enteric infections in HIV-infected patients (empiric treatment) (off-label use; HHS [OI adult 2015]):

Oral: 500 to 750 mg every 12 hours

IV: 400 mg every 12 hours

Bacterial meningitis (off-label use): IV: 400 mg every 8 to 12 hours (IDSA [Tunkel 2004])

Bite wounds (animal, human) (off-label use) (IDSA [Stevens 2014]): Note: Recommended as an alternative therapy for human bite wound in patients hypersensitive to beta-lactams.

Oral: 500 to 750 mg twice daily; in combination with metronidazole

IV: 400 mg every 12 hours; in combination with metronidazole

Bone/joint infections:

Oral: 500 to 750 mg twice daily for 4 to 8 weeks

IV:

Mild/moderate: 400 mg every 12 hours for 4 to 8 weeks

Severe/complicated: 400 mg every 8 hours for 4 to 8 weeks

Cat scratch disease (off-label use): Oral: 500 mg twice daily (Holley 1991). Additional data may be necessary to further define the role of ciprofloxacin in this condition.

Chancroid (off-label use): Oral: 500 mg twice daily for 3 days (CDC [Workowski 2015])

Diabetic foot infections, moderate to severe (off-label use): Note: Initial treatment should begin with an IV regimen for severe infections; moderate infections may initially be treated with IV or oral regimen. Use in combination with clindamycin; there is limited evidence supporting clindamycin for severe *S. aureus* infections (IDSA [Lipsky 2012]).

Oral: 500 to 750 mg every 12 hours (Nix 1987; Peterson 1989)

Endocarditis due to HACEK organisms (off-label use) (AHA [Baddour 2015]):

Oral: 500 mg every 12 hours for 4 weeks (native valve) or 6 weeks (prosthetic valve)

IV: 400 mg every 12 hours for 4 weeks (native valve) or 6 weeks (prosthetic valve)

Febrile neutropenia, low-risk cancer patients (empiric) (off-label use): Oral: 750 mg every 12 hours until resolution of neutropenia; use in combination with amoxicillin and clavulanate or clindamycin if penicillin allergy (ASCO [Flowers 2013]; ISDA [Freifeld 2011]; Kern 1999)

Granuloma inguinale (donovanosis) (alternative to preferred therapy) (off-label use): Oral: 750 mg twice daily for at least 3 weeks (and until lesions have healed) (CDC [Workowski 2015]). **Note:** If symptoms do not improve within the first few days of therapy, the addition of gentamicin may be considered (CDC [Workowski 2015]).

Infectious diarrhea: Oral:

Salmonella: 500 mg twice daily for 5 to 7 days

Shigella (including Shigella dysentery type 1) (off-label regimen): 500 mg twice daily for 3 days (IDSA 2001)

Traveler's diarrhea (off-label regimen): Mild: 750 mg as a single dose (CDC 2012; de la Cabada Bauch 2011); Severe: 500 mg twice daily for 3 days (IDSA 2001)

Vibrio cholerae (off-label regimen): 1 g as a single (CDC 2011)

Infectious diarrhea due to *Salmonella, Shigella,* or *Campylobacter* in HIV-infected patients (off-label use; HHS [OI adult 2015]). Note: Patients with bacteremia due to *Campylobacter* should receive additional therapy with an aminoglycoside

Oral: 500 to 750 mg every 12 hours

IV: 400 mg every 12 hours

Duration of therapy: Oral, IV.

Salmonella: Without bacteremia: 7 to 14 days (CD4 count ≥200 cells/mm^3) or 2 to 6 weeks (CD4 count <200 cells/mm^3); With bacteremia: 14 days or longer based on clinical condition (CD4 count ≥200 cells/mm^3) or 2 to 6 weeks (CD4 count <200 cells/mm^3)

Shigella or *Campylobacter*: Gastroenteritis: 7 to 10 days; Bacteremia: ≥14 days; Recurrent infections: *Campylobacter*: 2 to 6 weeks; *Shigella*: ≤6 weeks

Intra-abdominal infection, complicated, community-acquired (in combination with metronidazole): Note: Avoid using in settings where *E. coli* susceptibility to fluoroquinolones is <90%:

Oral: 500 mg every 12 hours for 7 to 14 days

IV: 400 mg every 12 hours for 7 to 14 days; **Note:** Guidelines recommend treatment duration of 4 to 7 days (provided source controlled) (IDSA [Solomkin 2010])

Meningococcal meningitis prophylaxis (off-label use): Oral: 500 mg as a single dose (CDC 2005)

Osteomyelitis, native vertebral (IDSA [Berbari 2015]):

Enterobacteriaceae (off-label dose; alternative therapy):

Oral: 500 to 750 mg every 12 hours for 6 weeks

IV: 400 mg every 12 hours for 6 weeks

Pseudomonas aeruginosa (off-label dose; alternative therapy): **Note:** Double coverage may be considered (ie, ciprofloxacin plus a beta-lactam):

Oral: 750 mg every 12 hours for 6 weeks

IV: 400 mg every 8 hours for 6 weeks

Salmonella (off-label use):

Oral: 500 mg every 12 hours for 6 to 8 weeks

IV: 400 mg every 12 hours for 6 to 8 weeks

Peritoneal dialysis catheter, exit site or tunnel infection (off-label use): Oral: 250 mg twice daily (Li [ISPD 2010])

Peritonitis, treatment (off-label use): Intraperitoneal: Continuous ambulatory peritoneal dialysis (CAPD): Continuous method: All exchanges: Loading dose: 50 mg/L of dialysate; maintenance dose: 25 mg/L (Li [ISPD 2010])

Plague (CDC [plague] 2015):

Postexposure prophylaxis: Oral: 500 mg twice daily for 7 days

Treatment: ***Note:*** *Duration of therapy is 10 to 14 days (or until 2 days after patient is afebrile).*

Oral: 500 to 750 mg every 12 hours

IV: 400 mg every 8 to 12 hours

Pneumonia, hospital-acquired (nosocomial) including ventilator-associated: IV: 400 mg every 8 hours as part of a combination regimen (dependent on patient and institution-specific risk factors) (IDSA [Kalil 2016]).

Prevention of bacterial infections in hematopoietic cell transplant (off-label use): Oral: 500 mg twice daily; begin at the time of stem cell infusion and continue until recovery of neutropenia or until initiation of empiric antibiotic therapy for febrile neutropenia (Tomblyn 2009)

Prostatitis (chronic, bacterial):

Oral: 500 mg every 12 hours for 28 days

IV: 400 mg every 12 hours for 28 days

Prosthetic joint infection (off-label use; IDSA [Osmon 2013]):

Chronic suppression: Oral: 250 to 500 mg twice daily.

Treatment: **Note:** Duration of therapy is 4 to 6 weeks; consider addition of an aminoglycoside in patients with infection caused by *Pseudomonas aeruginosa*.

Oral: 750 mg twice daily

IV: 400 mg every 12 hours

Skin and soft tissue necrotizing infection due to *Aeromonas hydrophila* (off-label use): IV: 400 mg every 12 hours; in combination with doxycycline. Continue treatment until further debridement is not necessary, patient has clinically improved, and patient is afebrile for 48 to 72 hours (IDSA [Stevens 2014]).

Spontaneous bacterial peritonitis (prevention) (off-label use): Oral: Long-term prophylaxis: 500 mg once daily (preferred) (Terg 2008). Weekly dosing of 750 mg orally for long-term prophylaxis has been studied, but concerns regarding quinolone bacterial resistance limit use (AASLD [Runyon 2012]; Roulachon 1995). American Association for the Study of Liver Diseases (AASLD) guidelines note that intermittent dosing (ie, 5 days/week, weekly) of antibiotics, although shown to be effective in SBP prevention, may be inferior to daily dosing due to development of bacterial resistance. Daily dosing regimens are preferred (AASLD [Runyon 2012]).

Surgical (preoperative) prophylaxis (off-label use): IV: 400 mg within 120 minutes prior to surgical incision (Bratzler 2013)

Surgical site infection (intestinal or GU tract, perineum, or axilla) (off-label use) (IDSA [Stevens 2014]):

Oral: 750 mg every 12 hours, in combination with metronidazole

IV: 400 mg every 12 hours, in combination with metronidazole

Tularemia (off-label use):

Contained casualty management: IV: 400 mg twice daily for 10 days. Can switch to oral administration when clinically indicated (Dennis 2001).

Mass casualty management or postexposure prophylaxis: Oral: 500 or 750 mg twice daily for 14 days. At least 14 days of therapy is recommended in oral regimens (Bossi [tularemia] 2004; Dennis 2001; Stevens 2014).

Typhoid fever: Oral: 500 mg every 12 hours for 10 days

Urinary tract infection:

Cystitis, acute uncomplicated: **Note:** Use as empiric therapy for uncomplicated urinary tract infections is discouraged due to significant *E. coli* resistance and safety issues; reserve for clinical situations where other appropriate treatment options cannot be used (Bidell 2016; IDSA [Gupta 2011]).

Oral, immediate release: 250 mg every 12 hours for 3 days

Oral, extended release (Cipro XR): 500 mg every 24 hours for 3 days

Complicated (including pyelonephritis):

Oral, immediate release: 250 to 500 mg every 12 hours for 7 to 14 days

Oral, extended release (Cipro XR): 1,000 mg every 24 hours for 7 to 14 days

IV: 200 to 400 mg every 8 to 12 hours for 7 to 14 days

Pediatric

Note: In pediatric patients, ciprofloxacin is not routinely first-line therapy, but after assessment of risks and benefits, can be considered a reasonable alternative for some situations [eg, anthrax, resistance (cystic fibrosis)] or in situations where the only alternative is parenteral therapy and ciprofloxacin offers an oral therapy option (Bradley 2011b).

Note: Extended release tablets and immediate release formulations are not interchangeable. Unless otherwise specified, oral dosing reflects the use of immediate release formulations.

Usual dosage range (*Red Book* [AAP 2015]): Infants, Children, and Adolescents:

Mild to moderate infections: Oral: 10 mg/kg/dose twice daily (maximum dose: 500 mg/dose)

Severe infections:

Oral: 15 to 20 mg/kg/dose twice daily (maximum dose: 750 mg/dose)

IV: 10 mg/kg/dose every 8 to 12 hours (maximum dose: 400 mg/dose)

Anthrax: Infants, Children, and Adolescents:
Inhalational (postexposure prophylaxis):
Oral: 15 mg/kg/dose every 12 hours for 60 days (maximum dose: 500 mg/dose)
IV: 10 mg/kg/dose every 12 hours for 60 days; do **not** exceed 400 mg/dose (800 mg/day)
Cutaneous, treatment (without systemic involvement) (off-label use) (AAP [Bradley 2014]): Oral: 15 mg/kg/dose every 12 hours (maximum dose: 500 mg/dose). Duration: 7 to 10 days for naturally acquired infection, up to 60 days for biological weapon-related event.
Systemic, treatment (including meningitis) (off-label use) (AAP [Bradley 2014]): IV: Initial: 10 mg/kg/dose every 8 hours (maximum dose: 400 mg/dose) as part of combination therapy; continue until clinical criteria for stability are met, then may switch to oral therapy (15 mg/kg/dose orally twice daily) to complete a 60-day course

Bacterial enteric infections in HIV-infected patients (empiric treatment) (off-label use): Adolescents: Refer to adult dosing

Chancroid (off-label use): Adolescents: Oral: 500 mg twice daily for 3 days (*Red Book* [AAP 2015])

Endocarditis, culture negative, empiric therapy (off-label use): Note: Administer in combination with other antibiotics: Children and Adolescents (AHA [Baltimore 2015]):
Oral: 10 to 15 mg/kg/dose twice daily for 4 to 6 weeks; maximum dose: 750 mg/dose
IV: 10 to 15 mg/kg/dose twice daily for 4 to 6 weeks; maximum dose: 400 mg/dose

Infectious diarrhea due to *Salmonella*, *Shigella*, or *Campylobacter* in HIV-infected patients (off-label dose): Adolescents: Refer to adult dosing.

Intra-abdominal infection, complicated (off-label use): Infants, Children, and Adolescents: IV: 10 to 15 mg/kg/dose every 12 hours; maximum dose: 400 mg/dose (IDSA [Solomkin 2010])

Meningococcal invasive disease prophylaxis, high-risk contacts (off-label use): Infants, Children, and Adolescents: Oral: 20 mg/kg as a single dose; maximum dose: 500 mg/dose (*Red Book* [AAP 2015])

***Mycobacterium avium* complex, severe or disseminated disease, HIV-exposed/-infected (off-label use):** Infants and Children: Oral: 10 to 15 mg/kg/dose twice daily in addition to other antibiotics; maximum dose: 750 mg/dose (HHS [pediatric] 2013)

Peritoneal dialysis catheter, exit site or tunnel infection (off-label use): Infants, Children, and Adolescents: 10 to15 mg/kg/dose once daily (maximum dose: 500 mg/dose) (Warady [ISPD 2012])

Peritonitis, treatment (off-label use): Infants, Children, and Adolescents: Intraperitoneal: Continuous ambulatory peritoneal dialysis (CAPD): Continuous method: All exchanges: Loading dose: 50 mg/L of dialysate; maintenance dose: 25 mg/L (Warady [ISPD 2012])

Plague:
Manufacturer's labeling: Infants, Children, and Adolescents:
Oral: 15 mg/kg/dose every 8 to 12 hours for 10 to 21 days; maximum: 500 mg/dose
IV: 10 mg/kg/dose every 8 to 12 hours for 10 to 21 days; maximum: 400 mg/dose
Alternate dosing (CDC [plague] 2015): Children and Adolescents:
Treatment:
Initial treatment: IV: 15 mg/kg/dose every 12 hours; maximum dose: 400 mg/dose; continue until 2 days after fever subsides, then may change to oral therapy.
Oral step down to complete a 10 to 14 day course: Oral: 20 mg/kg/dose twice daily; maximum dose: 500 mg/dose.
Postexposure prophylaxis: Oral: 20 mg/kg/dose twice daily for 7 days; maximum dose: 500 mg/dose)

Pneumonia, community-acquired (*H. influenzae*) (off-label use): Infants >3 months and Children: IV: 15 mg/kg/dose every 12 hours (IDSA/PIDS [Bradley 2011a])

Surgical (preoperative) prophylaxis (off-label use): Children and Adolescents: IV: 10 mg/kg/dose within 120 minutes prior to surgical incision (maximum dose: 400 mg/dose) (Bratzler 2013)

Urinary tract infection:
Cystitis, acute uncomplicated: Adolescents ≥18 years: Oral, extended release: Refer to adult dosing
Complicated, including pyelonephritis:
Oral, immediate release: Children and Adolescents ≤17 years: 10 to 20 mg/kg/dose every 12 hours for 10 to 21 days; maximum dose: 750 mg/dose.
Oral, extended release: Adolescents ≥18 years: Refer to adult dosing
IV: 6 to 10 mg/kg/dose every 8 hours for 10 to 21 days (maximum dose: 400 mg/dose)

Renal Impairment Adults:
Manufacturer's labeling:
Oral, immediate release:
CrCl >50 mL/minute: No dosage adjustment necessary.
CrCl 30 to 50 mL/minute: 250 to 500 mg every 12 hours
CrCl 5 to 29 mL/minute: 250 to 500 mg every 18 hours
ESRD on intermittent hemodialysis (IHD)/peritoneal dialysis (PD) (administer after dialysis on dialysis days): 250 to 500 mg every 24 hours
Oral, extended release:
CrCl ≥30 mL/minute: No dosage adjustment necessary.
CrCl <30 mL/minute: 500 mg every 24 hours
ESRD on intermittent hemodialysis (IHD)/peritoneal dialysis (PD) (administer after dialysis on dialysis days): 500 mg every 24 hours
IV:
CrCl ≥30 mL/minute: No dosage adjustment necessary.
CrCl 5 to 29 mL/minute: 200 to 400 mg every 18 to 24 hours
Alternate recommendations: Oral (immediate release), IV:
CrCl >50 mL/minute: No dosage adjustment necessary (Aronoff 2007).
CrCl 10 to 50 mL/minute: Administer 50% to 75% of usual dose every 12 hours (Aronoff 2007).
CrCl <10 mL/minute: Administer 50% of usual dose every 12 hours (Aronoff 2007).
Intermittent hemodialysis (IHD) (administer after hemodialysis on dialysis days): Minimally dialyzable (<10%): Oral: 250 to 500 mg every 24 hours **or** IV: 200 to 400 mg every 24 hours (Heintz 2009). **Note:** Dosing dependent on the assumption of 3 times weekly, complete IHD sessions.

Continuous renal replacement therapy (CRRT) (Heintz 2009; Trotman 2005): Drug clearance is highly dependent on the method of renal replacement, filter type, and flow rate. Appropriate dosing requires close monitoring of pharmacologic response, signs of adverse reactions due to drug accumulation, as well as drug concentrations in relation to target trough (if appropriate). The following are general recommendations only (based on dialysate flow/ultrafiltration rates of 1 to 2 L/hour and minimal residual renal function) and should not supersede clinical judgment:

CVVH/CVVHD/CVVHDF: IV: 200 to 400 mg every 12 to 24 hours

Hepatic Impairment There are no dosage adjustments provided in manufacturer's labeling. Use with caution in severe impairment.

Mechanism of Action Inhibits DNA-gyrase in susceptible organisms; inhibits relaxation of supercoiled DNA and promotes breakage of double-stranded DNA

Contraindications Hypersensitivity to ciprofloxacin, any component of the formulation, or other quinolones; concurrent administration of tizanidine

Warnings/Precautions [US Boxed Warning]: Fluoroquinolones are associated with disabling and potentially irreversible serious adverse reactions that may occur together, including tendinitis and tendon rupture, peripheral neuropathy, and CNS effects. Discontinue ciprofloxacin immediately and avoid use of fluoroquinolones in patients who experience any of these serious adverse reactions. Patients of any age or without preexisting risk factors have experienced these reactions; may occur within hours to weeks after initiation. **[US Boxed Warning]: Reserve use of ciprofloxacin for treatment of acute bacterial sinusitis, acute bacterial exacerbation of chronic bronchitis, or acute uncomplicated cystitis for patients who have no alternative treatment options because of the risk of disabling and potentially serious adverse reactions (eg, tendinitis and tendon rupture, peripheral neuropathy, CNS effects).**

Fluoroquinolones have been associated with an increased risk of tendonitis and tendon rupture in all ages; risk may be increased with concurrent corticosteroids, solid organ transplant recipients, and in patients >60 years of age, but has also occurred in patients without these risk factors. Rupture of the Achilles tendon has been reported most frequently; but other tendon sites (eg, rotator cuff, biceps, hand) have also been reported. Inflammation and rupture may occur bilaterally. Cases have been reported within hours or days of initiation, and up to several months after discontinuation of therapy. Strenuous physical activity, renal failure, and previous tendon disorders may be independent risk factor for tendon rupture. Discontinue at first sign of tendon pain, swelling, inflammation or rupture. Avoid use in patients with a history of tendon disorders or who have experienced tendinitis or tendon rupture. Use with caution in patients with rheumatoid arthritis; may increase risk of tendon rupture. Fluoroquinolones have been associated with an increased risk of CNS effects including seizures, increased intracranial pressure (including pseudotumor cerebri), and toxic psychosis; may also cause nervousness, agitation, insomnia, anxiety, nightmares, paranoia, dizziness, confusion, tremors, hallucinations, depression, and suicidal thoughts or actions. May occur following the first dose; discontinue immediately and avoid further use of fluoroquinolones in patients who experience these reactions. Use with caution in patients with known or suspected CNS disorder, or risk factors that may predispose to seizures or lower the seizure threshold. Fluoroquinolones have been associated with an increased risk of peripheral neuropathy; may occur soon after initiation of therapy and may be irreversible; discontinue if symptoms of sensory or sensorimotor neuropathy occur. Avoid use in patients who have previously experienced peripheral neuropathy.

Fluoroquinolones may prolong QT_c interval; avoid use in patients with a history of or at risk for QT_c prolongation, torsade de pointes, uncorrected hypokalemia, hypomagnesemia, cardiac disease (heart failure, myocardial infarction, bradycardia) or concurrent administration of other medications known to prolong the QT interval (including Class Ia and Class III antiarrhythmics, cisapride, erythromycin, antipsychotics, and tricyclic antidepressants). Hepatocellular, cholestatic, or mixed liver injury has been reported, including hepatic necrosis, life-threatening hepatic events, and fatalities. Acute liver injury can be rapid onset (range: 1 to 39 days), often associated with hypersensitivity. Most fatalities occurred in patients >55 years of age. Discontinue immediately if signs/symptoms of hepatitis (abdominal tenderness, dark urine, jaundice, pruritus) occur. Additionally, temporary increases in transaminases or alkaline phosphatase or cholestatic jaundice may occur (highest risk in patients with previous liver damage).

Prolonged use may result in fungal or bacterial superinfection, including *C. difficile*-associated diarrhea (CDAD) and pseudomembranous colitis; CDAD has been observed >2 months postantibiotic treatment. Rarely crystalluria has occurred; urine alkalinity may increase the risk. Ensure adequate hydration during therapy. Adverse effects, including those related to joints and/or surrounding tissues, are increased in pediatric patients and therefore, ciprofloxacin should not be considered as drug of choice in children (exception is anthrax treatment).

Fluoroquinolones have been associated with the development of serious, and sometimes fatal, hypoglycemia, most often in elderly diabetics but also in patients without diabetes. Prompt identification and treatment of hypoglycemia is essential. Individual quinolones may differ in their potential to cause this effect. It was most evident with gatifloxacin (no longer marketed as a systemic formulation). Hyperglycemia has also been associated with the use of fluoroquinolones. Patients should be monitored closely for signs/symptoms of disordered glucose regulation.

Severe hypersensitivity reactions, including anaphylaxis, have occurred with quinolone therapy. Reactions may present as typical allergic symptoms after a single dose, or may manifest as severe idiosyncratic dermatologic, vascular, pulmonary, renal, hepatic, and/or hematologic events, usually after multiple doses. Prompt discontinuation of drug should occur if skin rash or other symptoms arise. **[US Boxed Warning]: May exacerbate myasthenia gravis; avoid use in patients with a known history of myasthenia gravis.** Cases of severe exacerbations, including the need for ventilatory support and deaths have been reported. Use caution in renal impairment. Use with caution in elderly patients; adverse effects (eg, tendon rupture, QT changes) may be increased. Avoid excessive sunlight and take precautions to limit exposure (eg, loose fitting clothing, sunscreen); may cause moderate to severe photosensitivity/phototoxicity reactions. Discontinue use if photosensitivity occurs. Since ciprofloxacin is ineffective in the treatment of syphilis and may mask symptoms, all patients should be tested for syphilis at the time of gonorrheal diagnosis and 3 months later. Hemolytic reactions may (rarely) occur with quinolone use in patients with latent or actual glucose-6-phosphate dehydrogenase (G6PD) deficiency.

Potentially significant interactions may exist, requiring dose or frequency adjustment, additional monitoring, and/or selection of alternative therapy. Serious and fatal reactions including seizures, status epilepticus, cardiac arrest and respiratory failure have been reported with concomitant administration of theophylline. If concurrent use is unavoidable, monitor serum theophylline levels and adjust theophylline dose as warranted.

Drug Interactions

Metabolism/Transport Effects **Substrate** of OAT3, P-glycoprotein; **Inhibits** CYP1A2 (strong), CYP3A4 (weak)

Avoid Concomitant Use

Avoid concomitant use of Ciprofloxacin (Systemic) with any of the following: Agomelatine; BCG (Intravesical); Cholera Vaccine; CloZAPine; DULoxetine; Highest Risk QTc-Prolonging Agents; Hydroxychloroquine; Ivabradine; Lomitapide; Meptazinol; MiFEPRIStone; Nadifloxacin; Pimozide; Pomalidomide; Probucol; Promazine; Strontium Ranelate; Tasimelteon; TiZANidine; Vinflunine

Increased Effect/Toxicity

Ciprofloxacin (Systemic) may increase the levels/effects of: Agomelatine; Aminolevulinic Acid; ARIPiprazole; Bendamustine; Blood Glucose Lowering Agents; Caffeine; CarBAMazepine; CloZAPine; CYP1A2 Substrates; Delamanid; DULoxetine; Erlotinib; Flibanserin; Heroin; Highest Risk QTc-Prolonging Agents; HYDROcodone; Kola Nut; Lomitapide; Methotrexate; Moderate Risk QTc-Prolonging Agents; NiMODipine; Pentoxifylline; Pimozide; Pirfenidone; Pomalidomide; Porfimer; Rasagiline; Roflumilast; ROPINIRole; Ropivacaine; Tasimelteon; Theophylline Derivatives; TiZANidine; Varenicline; Verteporfin; Vitamin K Antagonists; Zolpidem

The levels/effects of Ciprofloxacin (Systemic) may be increased by: ACE Inhibitors; Angiotensin II Receptor Blockers; Corticosteroids (Systemic); Fosphenytoin; Hydroxychloroquine; Ivabradine; MiFEPRIStone; Nadifloxacin; Nonsteroidal Anti-Inflammatory Agents; Probenecid; Probucol; Promazine; QTc-Prolonging Agents (Indeterminate Risk and Risk Modifying); Spironolactone; Teriflunomide; Vinflunine

Decreased Effect

Ciprofloxacin (Systemic) may decrease the levels/effects of: BCG (Intravesical); BCG Vaccine (Immunization); Blood Glucose Lowering Agents; Cholera Vaccine; Didanosine; Fosphenytoin; Lactobacillus and Estriol; Mycophenolate; Phenytoin; Sodium Picosulfate; Thyroid Products; Typhoid Vaccine

The levels/effects of Ciprofloxacin (Systemic) may be decreased by: Antacids; Calcium Salts; Didanosine; Iron Salts; Lanthanum; Magnesium Salts; Meptazinol; Multivitamins/Minerals (with ADEK, Folate, Iron); Multivitamins/Minerals (with AE, No Iron); Patiromer; Quinapril; Sevelamer; Strontium Ranelate; Sucralfate; Zinc Salts

Food Interactions Food decreases rate, but not extent, of absorption. Ciprofloxacin serum levels may be decreased if taken with divalent or trivalent cations. Rarely, crystalluria may occur. Enteral feedings may decrease plasma concentrations of ciprofloxacin probably by >30% inhibition of absorption. Management: May administer with food to minimize GI upset. Avoid or take ciprofloxacin 2 hours before or 6 hours after antacids, dairy products, or calcium-fortified juices alone or in a meal containing >800 mg calcium, oral multivitamins, or mineral supplements containing divalent and/or trivalent cations. Ensure adequate hydration during therapy. Ciprofloxacin should not be administered with enteral feedings. The feeding would need to be discontinued for 1-2 hours prior to and after ciprofloxacin administration. Nasogastric administration produces a greater loss of ciprofloxacin bioavailability than does nasoduodenal administration.

Dietary Considerations Food: Drug may cause GI upset; take without regard to meals (manufacturer prefers that immediate release tablet is taken 2 hours after meals). Extended release tablet may be taken with meals that contain dairy products (calcium content <800 mg), but not with dairy products alone.

Dairy products, calcium-fortified juices, oral multivitamins, and mineral supplements: Absorption of ciprofloxacin is decreased by divalent and trivalent cations. The manufacturer states that the usual dietary intake of calcium (including meals which include dairy products) has not been shown to interfere with ciprofloxacin absorption. Immediate release ciprofloxacin and Cipro XR may be taken 2 hours before or 6 hours after any of these products.

Caffeine: Patients consuming regular large quantities of caffeinated beverages may need to restrict caffeine intake if excessive cardiac or CNS stimulation occurs.

Pharmacodynamics/Kinetics

Half-life Elimination Children: 4 to 5 hours; Adults: Normal renal function: 3 to 5 hours

Time to Peak Oral:

Immediate release tablet: 0.5 to 2 hours

Extended release tablet: Cipro XR: 1 to 2.5 hours

Pregnancy Risk Factor C

Pregnancy Considerations Adverse events have been observed in some animal reproduction studies. Ciprofloxacin crosses the placenta and produces measurable concentrations in the amniotic fluid and cord serum (Ludlam 1997). Based on available data, an increased risk of teratogenic effects has not been observed following ciprofloxacin use during pregnancy (Bar-Oz 2009; Padberg 2014). Ciprofloxacin is recommended for prophylaxis and treatment of pregnant women exposed to anthrax (Meaney-Delman 2014). Serum concentrations of ciprofloxacin may be lower during pregnancy than in nonpregnant patients (Giamarellou 1989).

Breastfeeding Considerations Ciprofloxacin is present in breast milk.

The relative infant dose (RID) of ciprofloxacin is 2.8% when calculated using the highest average breast milk concentration located and compared to an infant therapeutic dose of 20 mg/kg/day. In general, breastfeeding is considered acceptable when the relative infant dose is <10%; when an RID is >25% breastfeeding should generally be avoided (Anderson 2016; Ito 2000). Using the highest average milk concentration (3.79 mcg/mL), the estimated daily infant dose via breast milk is 0.569 mg/kg/day. This milk concentration was obtained following a maternal dose of ciprofloxacin 750 mg every 12 hours for 3 doses (n=10) (Giamarellou 1989).

There is a case report of perforated pseudomembranous colitis in a breastfeeding infant whose mother was taking ciprofloxacin (Harmon 1992). In general, antibiotics that are present in breast milk may cause nondose-related modification of bowel flora. Monitor infants for GI disturbances (WHO 2002).

Ciprofloxacin is recommended for the prophylaxis and treatment of *Bacillus anthracis* in breastfeeding women (Meaney-Delman 2014). Alternative agents are recommended in nursing women for the treatment of chancroid (CDC [Workowski 2015]). The manufacturer does not recommend use of ciprofloxacin in breastfeeding women due to concerns of potential articular damage; however, this risk is considered low even in children receiving high therapeutic doses. Therefore, some sources do not consider maternal use of ciprofloxacin to be a reason to discontinue nursing as long as the infant is monitored for gastrointestinal symptoms (eg, diarrhea) which could occur following antibiotic exposure (Kaplan 2015). Other sources recommend avoiding quinolone antibiotics if alternative agents are available (WHO 2002).

Dosage Forms

Solution, Intravenous:
Generic: 200 mg/100 mL (100 mL); 400 mg/200 mL (200 mL)

Solution, Intravenous [preservative free]:
Cipro in D5W: 400 mg/200 mL (200 mL)
Generic: 200 mg/100 mL (100 mL); 400 mg/200 mL (200 mL); 200 mg/20 mL (20 mL); 400 mg/40 mL (40 mL)

Suspension Reconstituted, Oral:
Cipro: 250 mg/5 mL (100 mL); 500 mg/5 mL (100 mL)
Generic: 250 mg/5 mL (100 mL); 500 mg/5 mL (100 mL)

Tablet, Oral:
Cipro: 250 mg, 500 mg
Generic: 100 mg, 250 mg, 500 mg, 750 mg

Tablet Extended Release 24 Hour, Oral:
Cipro XR: 500 mg, 1000 mg
Generic: 500 mg, 1000 mg

Ciprofloxacin and Fluocinolone

(sip roe FLOKS a sin & floo oh SIN oh lone)

Brand Names: US Otovel

Pharmacologic Category Antibiotic, Fluoroquinolone; Antibiotic, Otic; Antibiotic/Corticosteroid, Otic; Corticosteroid, Otic

Use Acute otitis media: Treatment of acute otitis media with tympanostomy tubes (AOMT) due to susceptible isolates of *Staphylococcus aureus, Streptococcus pneumoniae, Haemophilus influenza, Moraxella catarrhalis,* and *Pseudomonas aeruginosa* in pediatric patients 6 months and older.

Local Anesthetic/Vasoconstrictor Precautions No information available to require special precautions

Effects on Dental Treatment No significant effects or complications reported

Effects on Bleeding No information available to require special precautions

Adverse Reactions

1% to 10%:
Dermatologic: Connective tissue disorder (excessive granulation tissue;1%)
Local: Application site discharge (otorrhea: 5%)

Frequency not defined: Infection: Bacterial superinfection

<1%, postmarketing, and/or case reports: Auricular edema, candidiasis, dizziness, dysgeusia, equilibrium disturbance, eustachian tube congestion, exfoliation of skin, flushing, headache, hypersensitivity reaction, hypoacusis, otalgia, otic infection, paresthesia, pruritus of ear, tinnitus, tympanic membrane disease, tympanostomy tube blockage (device occlusion)

General Dosage Range Otic: *Infants ≥6 months, Children, and Adolescents:* 0.25 mL twice daily

Mechanism of Action

Ciprofloxacin: Inhibits DNA-gyrase in susceptible organisms; inhibits relaxation of supercoiled DNA and promotes breakage of double-stranded DNA.

Fluocinolone: Topical corticosteroids have anti-inflammatory, antipruritic, and vasoconstrictive properties. May depress the formation, release, and activity of endogenous chemical mediators of inflammation (kinins, histamine, liposomal enzymes, prostaglandins) through the induction of phospholipase A_2 inhibitory proteins (lipocortins) and sequential inhibition of the release of arachidonic acid.

Pregnancy Considerations Due to limited systemic absorption, exposure of ciprofloxacin or fluocinolone to the fetus is not expected following maternal otic administration.

Cisapride (SIS a pride)

Brand Names: US Propulsid®

Pharmacologic Category Gastrointestinal Agent, Prokinetic

Use Treatment of nocturnal symptoms of gastroesophageal reflux disease (GERD); has demonstrated effectiveness for gastroparesis, refractory constipation, and nonulcer dyspepsia

Local Anesthetic/Vasoconstrictor Precautions Cisapride is one of the drugs confirmed to prolong the QT interval and is accepted as having a risk of causing torsade de pointes. The risk of drug-induced torsade de pointes is extremely low when a single QT interval prolonging drug is prescribed. In terms of epinephrine, it is not known what effect vasoconstrictors in the local anesthetic regimen will have in patients with a known history of congenital prolonged QT interval or in patients taking any medication that prolongs the QT interval. Until more information is obtained, it is suggested that the clinician consult with the physician prior to the use of a vasoconstrictor in suspected patients, and that the vasoconstrictor (epinephrine, mepivacaine and levonordefrin [Carbocaine® 2% with Neo-Cobefrin®]) be used with caution.

Effects on Dental Treatment Key adverse event(s) related to dental treatment: Xerostomia (normal salivary flow resumes upon discontinuation).

Effects on Bleeding No information available to require special precautions

Adverse Reactions

Frequency not defined.

>5%:
Central nervous system: Headache
Dermatologic: Skin rash
Gastrointestinal: Abdominal cramps, diarrhea, dyspepsia, flatulence, nausea, xerostomia
Respiratory: Rhinitis

<5%:
Cardiovascular: Tachycardia
Central nervous system: Anxiety, drowsiness, extrapyramidal reaction, fatigue, insomnia, seizure
Hematologic & oncologic: Aplastic anemia, granulocytopenia, leukopenia, pancytopenia, thrombocytopenia
Hepatic: Increased liver enzymes
Infection: Viral infection (increased incidence)

Respiratory: Cough, sinusitis, upper respiratory tract infection

<1%, postmarketing, and/or case reports: Apnea, bronchospasm, gynecomastia, hyperprolactinemia, methemoglobinemia, psychiatric disturbance, skin photosensitivity

General Dosage Range

Oral:

Children: 0.15-0.3 mg/kg 3-4 times/day (maximum: 10 mg/dose)

Adults: Initial: 5-10 mg 4 times/day, may increase to 20 mg 4 times/day if needed

Mechanism of Action Enhances the release of acetylcholine at the myenteric plexus. *In vitro* studies have shown cisapride to have serotonin-4 receptor agonistic properties which may increase gastrointestinal motility and cardiac rate; increases lower esophageal sphincter pressure and lower esophageal peristalsis; accelerates gastric emptying of both liquids and solids.

Pharmacodynamics/Kinetics

Onset of Action 0.5-1 hour

Half-life Elimination 6-12 hours

Pregnancy Risk Factor C

Pregnancy Considerations Adverse events were observed in animal reproduction studies.

Prescribing and Access Restrictions In U.S., available via limited-access protocol only. Call 877-795-4247 for more information.

Dental Comment See Local Anesthetic/Vasoconstrictor Precautions

CISplatin (SIS pla tin)

Brand Names: Canada Cisplatin Injection; Cisplatin Injection BP; Cisplatin Injection, Mylan STD

Pharmacologic Category Antineoplastic Agent, Alkylating Agent; Antineoplastic Agent, Platinum Analog

Use

Bladder cancer, advanced: Treatment (as a single agent) of advanced bladder cancer (transitional cell) in patients who are no longer candidates for local therapy including surgery and/or radiation therapy

Ovarian cancer, metastatic: Treatment of metastatic ovarian cancer (in combination with other chemotherapy agents) in patients who have previously received appropriate surgery and/or radiation therapy, or as a single agent for refractory tumors in patients who have not previously received cisplatin

Testicular cancer, metastatic: Treatment of metastatic testicular cancer (in combination with other chemotherapy agents) in patients who have previously received appropriate surgery and/or radiation therapy

Local Anesthetic/Vasoconstrictor Precautions No information available to require special precautions

Effects on Dental Treatment No significant effects or complications reported

Effects on Bleeding Cisplatin causes relatively less bone marrow suppression than many other antineoplastic agents. Thrombocytopenia may occur 18-23 days following treatment.

Adverse Reactions

>10%:

Central nervous system: Neurotoxicity (peripheral neuropathy is dose and duration dependent)

Gastrointestinal: Nausea and vomiting (76% to 100%)

Genitourinary: Nephrotoxicity (28% to 36%; acute renal failure and chronic renal insufficiency)

Hematologic & oncologic: Anemia (≤40%), leukopenia (25% to 30%; nadir: Day 18 to 23; recovery: By day 39; dose related), thrombocytopenia (25% to 30%; nadir: Day 18 to 23; recovery: By day 39; dose related)

Hepatic: Increased liver enzymes

Otic: Ototoxicity (children 40% to 60%; adults 10% to 31%; as tinnitus, high frequency hearing loss)

1% to 10%: Local: Local irritation

<1%, postmarketing, and/or case reports: Alopecia (mild), ageusia, anaphylaxis, aortic thrombosis (Fernandes 2011), autonomic neuropathy, bradycardia (Schlumbrecht 2015), bronchoconstriction, cardiac arrhythmia, cardiac failure, cerebral arteritis, cerebrovascular accident, dehydration, diarrhea, extravasation, heart block, hemolytic anemia (acute), hemolytic-uremic syndrome, hiccups, hypercholesterolemia, hyperuricemia, hypocalcemia, hypokalemia, hypomagnesemia, hyponatremia, hypophosphatemia, hypotension, increased serum amylase, ischemic heart disease, leukoencephalopathy, Lhermitte's sign, myocardial infarction, neutropenic enterocolitis (Furonaka 2005), optic neuritis, pancreatitis (Trivedi 2005), papilledema, peripheral ischemia (acute), phlebitis (Tokuda 2014), reversible posterior leukoencephalopathy syndrome, seizure, SIADH, skin rash, tachycardia, tetany, thrombotic thrombocytopenic purpura, vision color changes, vision loss

General Dosage Range Dosage adjustment recommended in patients with renal impairment

IV: *Adults:* 50 to 70 mg/m^2 every 3 to 4 weeks **or** 75 to 100 mg/m^2/day every 3 to 4 weeks **or** 20 mg/m^2/day for 5 days every 3 weeks

Mechanism of Action Inhibits DNA synthesis by the formation of DNA cross-links; denatures the double helix; covalently binds to DNA bases and disrupts DNA function; may also bind to proteins; the *cis*-isomer is 14 times more cytotoxic than the *trans*-isomer; both forms cross-link DNA but cis-platinum is less easily recognized by cell enzymes and, therefore, not repaired. Cisplatin can also bind two adjacent guanines on the same strand of DNA producing intrastrand cross-linking and breakage.

Pharmacodynamics/Kinetics

Half-life Elimination

Children: Free drug: 1.3 hours; Total platinum: 44 hours

Adults: Initial: 14 to 49 minutes; Beta: 0.7 to 4.6 hours; Gamma: 24 to 127 hours (O'Dwyer 2000)

Pregnancy Risk Factor D

Pregnancy Considerations Adverse effects have been observed in animal reproduction studies. Women of childbearing potential should be advised to avoid pregnancy during treatment. May case fetal harm if administered during pregnancy.

Citalopram (sye TAL oh pram)

Related Information

Clinical Risk Related to Drugs Prolonging QT Interval *on page 1772*

Escitalopram *on page 599*

Vasoconstrictor Interactions With Antidepressants *on page 1913*

Brand Names: US CeleXA

Brand Names: Canada Abbott-Citalopram; Accell-Citalopram; ACT Citalopram; AG-Citalopram; Apo-Citalopram; Auro-Citalopram; Celexa; Citalopram-Odan; CTP 30; Dom-Citalopram; ECL-Citalopram; JAMP-Citalopram; Mar-Citalopram; Mint-Citalopram; Mylan-Citalopram; Nat-Citalopram; PHL-Citalopram; PMS-Citalopram; Q-Citalopram; RAN-Citalo; Riva-Citalopram; Sandoz-Citalopram; Septa-Citalopram; Teva-Citalopram

Generic Availability (US) Yes

Pharmacologic Category Antidepressant, Selective Serotonin Reuptake Inhibitor

Use Depression: Treatment of depression

Local Anesthetic/Vasoconstrictor Precautions Although caution should be used in patients taking tricyclic antidepressants, no interactions have been reported with vasoconstrictors and citalopram, a nontricyclic antidepressant which acts to increase serotonin; no precautions appear to be needed

Citalopram is one of the drugs confirmed to prolong the QT interval and is accepted as having a risk of causing torsade de pointes. The risk of drug-induced torsade de pointes is extremely low when a single QT interval prolonging drug is prescribed. In terms of epinephrine, it is not known what effect vasoconstrictors in the local anesthetic regimen will have in patients with a known history of congenital prolonged QT interval or in patients taking any medication that prolongs the QT interval. Until more information is obtained, it is suggested that the clinician consult with the physician prior to the use of a vasoconstrictor in suspected patients, and that the vasoconstrictor (epinephrine, mepivacaine and levonordefrin [Carbocaine® 2% with Neo-Cobefrin®]) be used with caution.

Effects on Dental Treatment Key adverse event(s) related to dental treatment: Xerostomia (normal salivary flow resumes upon discontinuation). Premarketing trials reported abnormal taste. See Effects on Bleeding and Dental Comment.

Effects on Bleeding Selective serotonin reuptake inhibitors, such as citalopram, may impair platelet aggregation due to platelet serotonin depletion, possibly increasing the risk of a bleeding complication. The risk of a bleeding complication can be increased by coadministration of other antiplatelet agents, such as NSAIDs and aspirin.

Adverse Reactions

>10%:

Central nervous system: Drowsiness (18%; dose related), insomnia (15%; dose related)

Dermatologic: Diaphoresis (11%; dose related)

Gastrointestinal: Nausea (21%), xerostomia (20%)

1% to 10%:

Cardiovascular: Prolonged Q-T interval on ECG (2%), hypotension (≥1%), orthostatic hypotension (≥1%), tachycardia (≥1%), bradycardia (1%)

Central nervous system: Fatigue (5%; dose related), anxiety (4%), agitation (3%), yawning (2%; dose related), amnesia (≥1%), apathy (≥1%), confusion (≥1%), depression (≥1%), lack of concentration (≥1%), migraine (≥1%), paresthesia (≥1%)

Dermatologic: Skin rash (≥1%), pruritus (≥1%)

Endocrine & metabolic: Decreased libido (1% to 4%), amenorrhea (≥1%), weight gain (≥1%), weight loss (≥1%)

Gastrointestinal: Diarrhea (8%), dyspepsia (5%), anorexia (4%), vomiting (4%), abdominal pain (3%), dysgeusia (≥1%), flatulence (≥1%), increased appetite (≥1%), sialorrhea (≥1%)

Genitourinary: Ejaculatory disorder (6%), dysmenorrhea (3%), impotence (3%; dose related)

Neuromuscular & skeletal: Tremor (8%), arthralgia (2%), myalgia (2%)

Ophthalmic: Accommodation disturbance (≥1%)

Renal: Polyuria (≥1%)

Respiratory: Rhinitis (5%), upper respiratory tract infection (5%), sinusitis (3%), cough (≥1%)

Miscellaneous: Fever (2%)

<1%, postmarketing, and/or case reports: Abnormal gait, abnormal lacrimation, abnormal serum prolactin levels, acne vulgaris, acute renal failure, aggressive behavior, akathisia, alopecia, altered serum glucose, anaphylaxis, anemia, angina pectoris, angioedema, angle-closure glaucoma, arthritis, asthma, ataxia, atrial fibrillation, blepharoptosis, blood coagulation disorder, breast hypertrophy, bronchitis, bronchospasm, bruxism, bundle branch block, bursitis, cardiac arrest, cardiac failure, cataract, catatonia, cellulitis, cerebrovascular accident, cholecystitis, cholelithiasis, choreoathetosis, colitis, conjunctivitis, dehydration, delirium, delusions, depersonalization, dermatitis, diplopia, diverticulitis, drug dependence, dry eye syndrome, duodenal ulcer, dyskinesia, dysphagia, dyspnea, dystonia, dysuria, ecchymoses, eczema, emotional lability, epistaxis, eructation, erythema multiforme, esophagitis, euphoria, extrapyramidal reaction, extrasystoles, eye pain, facial edema, flu-like symptoms, flushing, galactorrhea, gastric ulcer, gastritis, gastroenteritis, gastroesophageal reflux disease, gastrointestinal hemorrhage, gingival hemorrhage, gingivitis, glossitis, goiter, granulocytopenia, gynecomastia, hallucination, hematuria, hemolytic anemia, hemorrhoids, hepatic necrosis, hepatitis, hiccups, hot flash, hyperbilirubinemia, hyperesthesia, hyperkinesia, hypersensitivity reaction, hypertension, hypertonia, hypertrichosis, hypochromic anemia, hypoesthesia, hypoglycemia, hypohidrosis, hypokalemia, hypokinesia, hyponatremia, hypoprothrombinemia, hypothyroidism, increased libido, increased liver enzymes, increased serum alkaline phosphatase, increased thirst, involuntary muscle movements, ischemic heart disease, jaundice, keratitis, laryngitis, leg cramps, leukocytosis, leukopenia, lymphadenopathy, lymphocytopenia, lymphocytosis, mastalgia, melanosis, myasthenia, mydriasis, myocardial infarction, myoclonus, nephrolithiasis, neuralgia, neuroleptic malignant syndrome (Stevens 2008), nightmares, nystagmus, obesity, oliguria, osteoporosis, pancreatitis, panic attack, paranoia, peripheral edema, phlebitis, photophobia, pneumonia, pneumonitis, priapism, pruritus ani, psoriasis, psychosis, pulmonary embolism, purpura, pyelonephritis, Raynaud's phenomenon (Khouri 2016; Peiró 2007), renal pain, rhabdomyolysis, rigors, seasonal allergic rhinitis, seizure, serotonin syndrome, skeletal pain, skin discoloration, skin photosensitivity, stomatitis, stupor, syncope, thrombocytopenia, thrombosis, tinnitus, tonic-clonic seizures, torsades de pointes, toxic epidermal necrolysis, transient ischemic attacks, urinary incontinence, urinary retention, urticaria, vaginal hemorrhage, ventricular arrhythmia, vertigo, withdrawal syndrome, xeroderma

Dosing

Adult Note: Doses >40 mg daily are not recommended due to the risk of QT prolongation.

Depression: Adults <60 years: Oral: Initial: 20 mg once daily; increase the dose by 20 mg at an interval of ≥1 week to a maximum dose of 40 mg daily. Additional efficacy with doses >40 mg daily has not been demonstrated in clinical trials.

Poor metabolizers of CYP2C19 or concurrent use of moderate-to-strong CYP2C19 inhibitors (eg, cimetidine, omeprazole): Maximum dose: 20 mg daily

Binge eating disorder (off-label use): Oral: Initial: 20 mg once daily; may increase to 40 mg once daily. Doses up to 60 mg daily were evaluated; however, according to the manufacturer, dosing should not exceed 40 mg/day (McElroy 2003). Additional data are necessary to further define the role of citalopram in this condition.

Generalized anxiety disorder (off-label use): Oral: Initial: 10 mg once daily; may progressively increase dose to 40 mg daily (Blank 2006; Lenze 2005). Additional data are necessary to further define the role of citalopram in this condition.

Hot flashes (off-label use): Oral: Initial: 10 mg once daily; increase dose to 20 mg after 1 to 4 weeks. Doses as high as 40 mg daily have been studied (Kalay 2007; Suvanto-Luukkonen 2005)

Obsessive compulsive disorder (off-label use): Oral: Initial: 20 mg once daily; may increase to target dose of 40 mg daily. Doses up to 60 mg daily were evaluated; however, according to the manufacturer, dosing should not exceed 40 mg/day (APA [Koran 2007]; Montgomery 2001).

Panic disorder (off-label use): Oral: Initial: 10 mg daily for 7 days, then increase dose to 20 mg daily (Perna 2003; Stahl 2003). Consider further dosage adjustments based on response and tolerability. Mean dose in flexible dose clinical trials was 20 to 40 mg daily; doses up to 60 mg daily have been evaluated (Leinonen 2000; Perna 2003, Seedat 2003; Stahl 2003; Wade 1997).

Pathological gambling (off-label use): Oral: Initial: 10 mg once daily; may progressively increase to 40 mg daily. Doses up to 60 mg daily were evaluated; however, according to the manufacturer, dosing should not exceed 40 mg/day (Zimmerman 2002). Additional data are necessary to further define the role of citalopram in this condition.

Premature Ejaculation (off-label use): Oral: Initial: 20 mg once daily; may increase dose based on response and tolerability up to 40 mg/day (Althof 2014; Safarinejad 2006). Additional data may be necessary to further define the role of citalopram in this condition.

Discontinuation of therapy: Upon discontinuation of antidepressant therapy, gradually taper the dose to minimize the incidence of withdrawal symptoms and allow for the detection of re-emerging symptoms. Evidence supporting ideal taper rates is limited. APA and NICE guidelines suggest tapering therapy over at least several weeks with consideration to the half-life of the antidepressant; antidepressants with a shorter half-life may need to be tapered more conservatively. In addition for long-term treated patients, WFSBP guidelines recommend tapering over 4-6 months. If intolerable withdrawal symptoms occur following a dose reduction, consider resuming the previously prescribed dose and/or decrease dose at a more gradual rate (APA 2010; Bauer 2002; Haddad 2001; NCCMH 2010; Schatzberg 2006; Shelton 2001; Warner 2006).

MAO inhibitor recommendations:

Switching to or from an MAO inhibitor intended to treat psychiatric disorders:

Allow 14 days to elapse between discontinuing an MAO inhibitor intended to treat psychiatric disorders and initiation of citalopram.

Allow 14 days to elapse between discontinuing citalopram and initiation of an MAO inhibitor intended to treat psychiatric disorders.

Use with other MAO inhibitors (linezolid or IV methylene blue):

Do not initiate citalopram in patients receiving linezolid or IV methylene blue; consider other interventions for psychiatric condition.

If urgent treatment with linezolid or IV methylene blue is required in a patient already receiving citalopram and potential benefits outweigh potential risks, discontinue citalopram promptly and administer linezolid or IV methylene blue. Monitor for serotonin syndrome for 2 weeks or until 24 hours after the last dose of linezolid or IV methylene blue, whichever comes first. May resume citalopram 24 hours after the last dose of linezolid or IV methylene blue.

Geriatric Depression: Elderly ≥60 years: Oral: Initial: 20 mg once daily; maximum dose in adults ≥60 years: 20 mg daily due to increased exposure and the risk of QT prolongation. Refer to adult dosing.

Discontinuation of therapy: Refer to adult dosing.

MAO inhibitor recommendations: Refer to adult dosing.

Pediatric Obsessive-compulsive disorder (off-label use): Children and Adolescents: Oral: 10-40 mg/day (Mukaddes 2003; Thomsen 1997; Thomsen 2001)

Discontinuation of therapy: Refer to adult dosing.

MAO inhibitor recommendations: Refer to adult dosing.

Renal Impairment

Mild-to-moderate impairment: No dosage adjustment necessary.

Severe impairment: CrCl <20 mL/minute: No dosage adjustment provided in manufacturer's labeling (has not been studied); use caution.

Hepatic Impairment Initial: 20 mg once daily; maximum recommended dose: 20 mg daily due to decreased clearance and the risk of QT prolongation

Mechanism of Action A racemic bicyclic phthalane derivative, citalopram selectively inhibits serotonin reuptake in the presynaptic neurons and has minimal effects on norepinephrine or dopamine. Uptake inhibition of serotonin is primarily due to the *S*-enantiomer of citalopram. Displays little to no affinity for serotonin, dopamine, adrenergic, histamine, GABA, or muscarinic receptor subtypes.

Contraindications

Hypersensitivity to citalopram or any component of the formulation; use of MAO inhibitors intended to treat psychiatric disorders (concurrently or within 14 days of discontinuing either citalopram or the MAO inhibitor); initiation of citalopram in a patient receiving linezolid or intravenous methylene blue; concomitant use with pimozide

Canadian labeling: Additional contraindications (not in US labeling): Known QT interval prolongation or congenital long QT syndrome

Warnings/Precautions [US Boxed Warning]: Antidepressants increase the risk of suicidal thinking and behavior in children, adolescents, and young adults (18 to 24 years of age) with major depressive disorder (MDD) and other psychiatric disorders; consider risk prior to prescribing. Short-term studies did not show an increased risk in patients >24 years of age and showed a decreased risk in patients ≥65 years. Closely monitor patients for clinical worsening, suicidality, or unusual changes in behavior, particularly during the initial 1-2 months of therapy or during periods of dosage adjustments (increases or decreases); the patient's family or caregiver should be instructed to closely observe the patient and communicate condition with healthcare provider. A medication guide concerning the use of antidepressants should be dispensed with each prescription. **Citalopram is not FDA approved for use in children.**

The possibility of a suicide attempt is inherent in major depression and may persist until remission occurs. Use caution in high-risk patients. Worsening depression and severe abrupt suicidality that are not part of the presenting symptoms may require discontinuation or modification of drug therapy. The patient's family or caregiver should be alerted to monitor patients for the emergence of suicidality and associated behaviors (such as agitation, irritability, hostility, impulsivity, and hypomania) and call healthcare provider.

May worsen psychosis in some patients or precipitate a shift to mania or hypomania in patients with bipolar disorder. Patients presenting with depressive symptoms should be screened for bipolar disorder. Monotherapy in patients with bipolar disorder should be avoided. **Citalopram is not FDA approved for the treatment of bipolar depression.**

Potentially life-threatening serotonin syndrome (SS) has occurred with serotonergic agents (eg, SSRIs, SNRIs), particularly when used in combination with other serotonergic agents (eg, triptans, TCAs, fentanyl, lithium, tramadol, buspirone, St. John's wort, tryptophan) or agents that impair metabolism of serotonin (eg, MAO inhibitors intended to treat psychiatric disorders, other MAO inhibitors [ie, linezolid and intravenous methylene blue]). Discontinue treatment (and any concomitant serotonergic agent) immediately if signs/symptoms arise. May increase the risks associated with electroconvulsive therapy. Has a low potential to impair cognitive or motor performance; caution operating hazardous machinery or driving. Bone fractures have been associated with antidepressant treatment. Consider the possibility of a fragility fracture if an antidepressant-treated patient presents with unexplained bone pain, point tenderness, swelling, or bruising (Rabenda 2013; Rizzoli 2012).

Citalopram causes dose-dependent QTc prolongation; torsade de pointes, ventricular tachycardia, and sudden death have been reported. Use is not recommended in patients with congenital long QT syndrome, bradycardia, recent MI, uncompensated heart failure, hypokalemia, and/or hypomagnesemia, or patients receiving concomitant medications which prolong the QT interval; if use is essential and cannot be avoided in these patients, ECG monitoring is recommended. Discontinue therapy in any patient with persistent QTc measurements >500 msec. Serum electrolytes, particularly potassium and magnesium, should be monitored prior to initiation and periodically during therapy in any patient at increased risk for significant electrolyte disturbances; hypokalemia and/or hypomagnesemia should be corrected prior to use. Due to the QT prolongation risk, doses >40 mg/day are not recommended. In a scientific statement from the American Heart Association, citalopram has been determined to be an agent that may exacerbate underlying myocardial dysfunction (magnitude: major) (AHA [Page 2016]). Additionally, the maximum daily dose should not exceed 20 mg/day in certain populations (eg, CYP2C19 poor metabolizers, patients with hepatic impairment, elderly patients). Potentially significant interactions may exist, requiring dose or frequency adjustment, additional monitoring, and/or selection of alternative therapy. Consult drug interactions database for more detailed information.

Use with caution in patients with a previous seizure disorder or condition predisposing to seizures such as brain damage or alcoholism. May cause or exacerbate sexual dysfunction. Pharmacokinetics are altered in patients ≥60 years of age; a lower maximum dose of 20 mg/day is recommended in this population because of the risk of QT prolongation. May cause mild pupillary dilation, which in susceptible individuals can lead to an episode of narrow-angle glaucoma. Consider evaluating patients who have not had an iridectomy for narrow-angle glaucoma risk factors. Citalopram is not FDA-approved for use in children; however, if used, monitor weight and growth regularly during therapy due to the potential for decreased appetite and weight loss with SSRI use.

Abrupt discontinuation or interruption of antidepressant therapy has been associated with a discontinuation syndrome. Symptoms arising may vary with antidepressant however commonly include nausea, vomiting, diarrhea, headaches, light-headedness, dizziness, diminished appetite, sweating, chills, tremors, paresthesias, fatigue, somnolence, and sleep disturbances (eg, vivid dreams, insomnia). Greater risks for developing a discontinuation syndrome have been associated with antidepressants with shorter half-lives, longer durations of treatment, and abrupt discontinuation. For antidepressants of short or intermediate half-lives, symptoms may emerge within 2-5 days after treatment discontinuation and last 7-14 days (APA 2010; Fava 2006; Haddad 2001; Shelton 2001; Warner 2006).

Drug Interactions

Metabolism/Transport Effects Substrate of CYP2C19 (major), CYP2D6 (minor), CYP3A4 (major); **Note:** Assignment of Major/Minor substrate status based on clinically relevant drug interaction potential; **Inhibits** CYP1A2 (weak), CYP2D6 (weak)

Avoid Concomitant Use

Avoid concomitant use of Citalopram with any of the following: Conivaptan; Dapoxetine; Dosulepin; Fluconazole; Fusidic Acid (Systemic); Highest Risk QTc-Prolonging Agents; Hydroxychloroquine; Idelalisib; Iobenguane I 123; Ivabradine; Linezolid; MAO Inhibitors; Methylene Blue; MiFEPRIStone; Moderate Risk QTc-Prolonging Agents; Pimozide; Probucol; Promazine; Tryptophan; Urokinase; Vinflunine

Increased Effect/Toxicity

Citalopram may increase the levels/effects of: Agents with Antiplatelet Properties; Anticoagulants; Antidepressants (Serotonin Reuptake Inhibitor/Antagonist); Antipsychotic Agents; Apixaban; Aspirin; Blood Glucose Lowering Agents; BusPIRone; Cephalothin; Collagenase (Systemic); Dabigatran Etexilate; Deoxycholic Acid; Desmopressin; Dextromethorphan; Dosulepin; Edoxaban; Highest Risk QTc-Prolonging Agents; Ibritumomab; Methylene Blue; Mexiletine; NSAID (COX-2 Inhibitor); NSAID (Nonselective); Obinutuzumab; Perhexiline; Pimozide; Rivaroxaban; Salicylates; Serotonin Modulators; Thiazide and Thiazide-Like Diuretics; Thrombolytic Agents; TiZANidine; Tositumomab and Iodine I 131 Tositumomab; TraMADol; Tricyclic Antidepressants; Urokinase; Vitamin K Antagonists

The levels/effects of Citalopram may be increased by: Alcohol (Ethyl); Analgesics (Opioid); Antiemetics (5HT3 Antagonists); Antipsychotic Agents; Aprepitant;

Bilastine; Buprenorphine; BuPROPion; BusPIRone; Cimetidine; CNS Depressants; Conivaptan; CYP2C19 Inhibitors (Moderate); CYP3A4 Inhibitors (Moderate); CYP3A4 Inhibitors (Strong); Dapoxetine; Fluconazole; Fosaprepitant; Fusidic Acid (Systemic); Glucosamine; Herbs (Anticoagulant/Antiplatelet Properties); Hydroxychloroquine; Ibrutinib; Idelalisib; Indapamide; Ivabradine; Ivacaftor; Limaprost; Linezolid; Lithium; MAO Inhibitors; Metaxalone; Methylene Blue; Methylphenidate; Metoclopramide; MetyroSINE; MiFEPRIStone; Moderate Risk QTc-Prolonging Agents; Multivitamins/Fluoride (with ADE); Multivitamins/Minerals (with ADEK, Folate, Iron); Multivitamins/Minerals (with AE, No Iron); Netupitant; Omega-3 Fatty Acids; Omeprazole; Palbociclib; Pentosan Polysulfate Sodium; Pentoxifylline; Probucol; Promazine; Prostacyclin Analogues; QTc-Prolonging Agents (Indeterminate Risk and Risk Modifying); Simeprevir; Stiripentol; Tedizolid; Teneligliptin; Tipranavir; TraMADol; Tricyclic Antidepressants; Tryptophan; Vinflunine; Vitamin E (Systemic)

Decreased Effect

Citalopram may decrease the levels/effects of: Iobenguane I 123; Ioflupane I 123; Thyroid Products

The levels/effects of Citalopram may be decreased by: Bosentan; CarBAMazepine; CYP3A4 Inducers (Moderate); CYP3A4 Inducers (Strong); Cyproheptadine; Dabrafenib; Deferasirox; Enzalutamide; Mitotane; NSAID (COX-2 Inhibitor); NSAID (Nonselective); RifAMPin; Siltuximab; St John's Wort; Tocilizumab

Dietary Considerations May be taken without regard to food.

Pharmacodynamics/Kinetics

Onset of Action Depression: The onset of action is 1-4 weeks; however, individual response varies greatly and full response may not be seen until 8-12 weeks after initiation of treatment.

Duration of Action 1-2 days

Half-life Elimination 24-48 hours (average: 35 hours); doubled with hepatic impairment and increased by 30% (following multiple doses) to 50% (following single dose) in elderly patients (≥60 years)

Time to Peak Serum: 1-6 hours, average within 4 hours

Pregnancy Risk Factor C

Pregnancy Considerations Adverse events have been observed in animal reproduction studies. Citalopram and its metabolites cross the human placenta. An increased risk of teratogenic effects, including cardiovascular defects, may be associated with maternal use of citalopram or other SSRIs; however, available information is conflicting. Nonteratogenic effects in the newborn following SSRI/SNRI exposure late in the third trimester include respiratory distress, cyanosis, apnea, seizures, temperature instability, feeding difficulty, vomiting, hypoglycemia, hypo- or hypertonia, hyper-reflexia, jitteriness, irritability, constant crying, and tremor. Symptoms may be due to the toxicity of the SSRIs/SNRIs or a discontinuation syndrome and may be consistent with serotonin syndrome associated with SSRI treatment. Persistent pulmonary hypertension of the newborn (PPHN) has also been reported with SSRI exposure. The long-term effects of in utero SSRI exposure on infant development and behavior are not known.

Due to pregnancy-induced physiologic changes, women who are pregnant may require adjusted doses of citalopram to achieve euthymia. The ACOG recommends that therapy with SSRIs or SNRIs during pregnancy be individualized; treatment of depression during pregnancy should incorporate the clinical expertise of the mental health clinician, obstetrician, primary health care provider, and pediatrician. According to the American Psychiatric Association (APA), the risks of medication treatment should be weighed against other treatment options and untreated depression. For women who discontinue antidepressant medications during pregnancy and who may be at high risk for postpartum depression, the medications can be restarted following delivery. Treatment algorithms have been developed by the ACOG and the APA for the management of depression in women prior to conception and during pregnancy.

Pregnant women exposed to antidepressants during pregnancy are encouraged to enroll in the National Pregnancy Registry for Antidepressants (NPRAD). Women 18 to 45 years of age or their health care providers may contact the registry by calling 844-405-6185. Enrollment should be done as early in pregnancy as possible.

Breastfeeding Considerations Citalopram and its metabolites are excreted in breast milk. According to the manufacturer, the decision to continue or discontinue breastfeeding during therapy should take into account the risk of exposure to the infant and the benefits of treatment to the mother. Excessive somnolence, decreased feeding, colic, irritability, restlessness, and weight loss have been reported in breast-fed infants. The long-term effects on development and behavior have not been studied; therefore, citalopram should be prescribed to a mother who is breastfeeding only when the benefits outweigh the potential risks. Maternal use of an SSRI during pregnancy may cause delayed milk secretion.

Dosage Forms

Solution, Oral:

Generic: 10 mg/5 mL (240 mL)

Tablet, Oral:

CeleXA: 10 mg, 20 mg, 40 mg

Generic: 10 mg, 20 mg, 40 mg

Dental Comment Problems with SSRI-induced bruxism have been reported and may preclude their use; clinicians attempting to evaluate any patient with bruxism or involuntary muscle movement, who is simultaneously being treated with an SSRI drug, should be aware of the potential association.

Also see Local Anesthetic/Vasoconstrictor Precautions

Citric Acid, Magnesium Carbonate, and Glucono-Delta-Lactone

(SI trik AS id, mag NEE see um KAR bo nate, and GLOO kon o DEL ta LAK tone)

Brand Names: US Renacidin

Pharmacologic Category Genitourinary Irrigant; Urinary Tract Product

Use Dissolution or prevention of calcifications: Dissolution of struvite or apatite type bladder calculi; to prevent encrustations of indwelling urethral catheters and cystostomy tubes.

Local Anesthetic/Vasoconstrictor Precautions No information available to require special precautions

Effects on Dental Treatment No significant effects or complications reported

Effects on Bleeding No information available to require special precautions

Adverse Reactions Frequency not always defined.

*Frequency not specifically defined, but reported within range of incidence rates.

>10%:

Central nervous system: Fever (20% to 40%), flank pain (transient)

Genitourinary: Urothelial ulceration (≤13%)

Local: Localized edema (urothelial; ≤13%)

1% to 10%:

Endocrine & metabolic: Hypermagnesemia*, hyperphosphatemia*

Gastrointestinal: Nausea*

Genitourinary: Dysuria*, hematuria*, irritable bladder*, nausea*, urinary tract infection*

Infection: Candidiasis* (1% to 10%)

Neuromuscular & skeletal: Back pain* (1% to 10%)

Renal: Increased serum creatinine* (1% to 10%)

<1%, postmarketing and/or case reports: Intestinal obstruction, septicemia, thrombophlebitis, vomiting

General Dosage Range Irrigation (indwelling urethral catheter or cystostomy tube): *Adults:* 30 mL into catheter 3 times daily **or** 30 mL into bladder, retained for 30 to 60 minutes then drained 4 to 6 times daily

Mechanism of Action Magnesium from the irrigating solution is exchanged for calcium in the stone matrix. The magnesium stones are soluble and are able to dissolve in the acidic pH of the solution.

Pregnancy Risk Factor C

Pregnancy Considerations Animal reproduction studies have not been conducted.

Citric Acid, Sodium Citrate, and Potassium Citrate

(SIT rik AS id, SOW dee um SIT rate, & poe TASS ee um SIT rate)

Brand Names: US Cytra-3 [DSC]; Virtrate-3

Pharmacologic Category Alkalinizing Agent

Use Conditions where long-term maintenance of an alkaline urine is desirable as in control and dissolution of uric acid and cystine calculi of the urinary tract

Local Anesthetic/Vasoconstrictor Precautions No information available to require special precautions

Effects on Dental Treatment No significant effects or complications reported

Effects on Bleeding No information available to require special precautions

Adverse Reactions Frequency not defined.

Cardiovascular: Cardiac abnormalities

Endocrine & metabolic: Metabolic alkalosis, calcium levels, hyperkalemia, hypernatremia

Gastrointestinal: Diarrhea

Neuromuscular & skeletal: Tetany

General Dosage Range Oral:

Children: 5-15 mL after meals and at bedtime

Adults: 15-30 mL after meals and at bedtime

Pregnancy Risk Factor Not established

Pregnancy Considerations Use caution with toxemia of pregnancy.

Cladribine (KLA dri been)

Brand Names: Canada Cladribine Injection

Pharmacologic Category Antineoplastic Agent, Antimetabolite; Antineoplastic Agent, Antimetabolite (Purine Analog)

Use Treatment of active hairy cell leukemia

Local Anesthetic/Vasoconstrictor Precautions No information available to require special precautions

Effects on Dental Treatment No significant effects or complications reported

Effects on Bleeding The major dose-limiting adverse effect of cladribine is bone marrow suppression including severe (grade 4) thrombocytopenia in ~12% of patients receiving repeated courses of therapy; recovery is usually by day 12.

Adverse Reactions

>10%:

Central nervous system: Fatigue (11% to 45%), headache (7% to 22%)

Dermatologic: Skin rash (10% to 27%)

Gastrointestinal: Nausea (22% to 28%), decreased appetite (8% to 17%), vomiting (9% to 13%)

Hematologic & oncologic: Neutropenia (grade 4: 70%; recovery by week 5), febrile neutropenia (8% to 47%; severe: 32%), anemia (1% to 37%; recovery by week 8), bone marrow depression (34%; prolonged), thrombocytopenia (grade 4: 12%; recovery by day 12)

Infection: Infection (month 1: 28% [serious: 6%]; month 2: 6%)

Local: Injection site reaction (9% to 19%)

Respiratory: Abnormal breath sounds (4% to 11%)

Miscellaneous: Fever (33% to 69%; ≥100°F: 67%; ≥104°F: 11%)

1% to 10%:

Cardiovascular: Edema (2% to 6%), tachycardia (2% to 6%), phlebitis (2%), thrombosis (2%)

Central nervous system: Dizziness (6% to 9%), chills (2% to 9%), malaise (5% to 7%), insomnia (3% to 7%), pain (6%), anxiety (1%), myasthenia (1%)

Dermatologic: Diaphoresis (9%), erythema (6%), pruritus (2% to 6%), hyperhidrosis (3%)

Gastrointestinal: Diarrhea (7% to 10%), constipation (4% to 9%), abdominal pain (4% to 6%), flatulence (1%)

Hematologic & oncologic: Purpura (10%), petechia (2% to 8%), bruise (1% to 2%)

Neuromuscular & skeletal: Weakness (6% to 9%), myalgia (6% to 7%), arthralgia (3% to 5%)

Respiratory: Cough (7% to 10%), dyspnea (5% to 7%), epistaxis (5%), rales (1%)

<1%, postmarketing, and/or case reports: Aplastic anemia, bacteremia, cellulitis, cerebrovascular accident, confusion, conjunctivitis, decreased CD-4 cell count (nadir: 4 to 6 months), hemolytic anemia, hypereosinophilia, hypersensitivity reaction, impaired consciousness, increased serum bilirubin, increased serum transaminases, lower extremity weakness, myelodysplastic syndrome, opportunistic infection (cytomegalovirus disease, fungal infection, herpes virus infection, listeriosis, *Pneumocystis jirovecii*), pancytopenia (prolonged), pneumonia, polyneuropathy (with high doses), progressive multifocal leukoencephalopathy, pulmonary infiltrates (interstitial), quadriparesis (reported at high doses), reactivated tuberculosis, renal failure, renal insufficiency (with high doses), septic shock, Stevens-Johnson syndrome, toxic epidermal necrolysis, tumor lysis syndrome, urticaria

General Dosage Range Dosage adjustment recommended in patients with renal impairment

IV: *Adults:* Continuous infusion: 0.09 mg/kg/day for 7 days

Mechanism of Action A purine nucleoside analogue; prodrug which is activated via phosphorylation by deoxycytidine kinase to a 5'-triphosphate derivative (2-CaAMP). This active form incorporates into DNA to result in the breakage of DNA strand and shutdown of

DNA synthesis and repair. This also results in a depletion of nicotinamide adenine dinucleotide and adenosine triphosphate (ATP). Cladribine is cell-cycle nonspecific.

Pharmacodynamics/Kinetics

Half-life Elimination Children 8 months to 18 years: 19.7 ± 3.4 hours (Kearns, 1994); Adults: After a 2-hour infusion (with normal renal function): 5.4 hours

Pregnancy Risk Factor D

Pregnancy Considerations Teratogenic effects and fetal mortality were observed in animal reproduction studies. May cause fetal harm if administered during pregnancy. Women of reproductive potential should use highly effective contraception during treatment.

Clarithromycin (kla RITH roe mye sin)

Related Information

Antibiotic Prophylaxis *on page 1812*
Bacterial Infections *on page 1835*
Clinical Risk Related to Drugs Prolonging QT Interval *on page 1772*
Gastrointestinal Disorders *on page 1775*

Brand Names: US Biaxin; Biaxin XL; Biaxin XL Pac

Brand Names: Canada Accel-Clarithromycin; Apo-Clarithromycin; Apo-Clarithromycin XL; Biaxin; Biaxin BID; Biaxin XL; Dom-Clarithromycin; Mylan-Clarithromycin; PMS-Clarithromycin; RAN-Clarithromycin; Riva-Clarithromycin; Sandoz-Clarithromycin; Teva-Clarithromycin

Generic Availability (US) Yes

Pharmacologic Category Antibiotic, Macrolide

Dental Use Alternate oral antibiotic for prevention of infective endocarditis in individuals allergic to penicillins or ampicillin, when amoxicillin cannot be used

Use

Infants and Children 6 months and older:

Acute maxillary sinusitis due to susceptible *H. influenzae, S. pneumoniae,* or *Moraxella catarrhalis*

Acute otitis media due to susceptible *H. influenzae, M. catarrhalis,* or *S. pneumoniae*

Community-acquired pneumonia due to susceptible *Mycoplasma pneumoniae, S. pneumoniae,* or *Chlamydophila pneumoniae*

Disseminated mycobacterial infections due to *M. avium* or *M. intracellulare*

Pharyngitis/tonsillitis due to susceptible *S. pyogenes*

Prevention of disseminated mycobacterial infections due to *M. avium* complex (MAC) disease in patients with advanced HIV infection (20 months of age and older)

Uncomplicated skin/skin structure infection due to susceptible *S. aureus* or *S. pyogenes*

Adults:

Pharyngitis/tonsillitis due to susceptible *S. pyogenes*

Acute maxillary sinusitis due to susceptible *H. influenzae, M. catarrhalis,* or *S. pneumoniae*

Acute exacerbation of chronic bronchitis due to susceptible *H. influenzae, H. parainfluenzae, M. catarrhalis,* or *S. pneumoniae*

Community-acquired pneumonia due to susceptible *H. influenzae, H. parainfluenzae, M. catarrhalis, Mycoplasma pneumoniae, S. pneumoniae,* or *Chlamydophila pneumoniae*

Uncomplicated skin/skin structure infections due to susceptible *S. aureus* or *S. pyogenes*

Disseminated mycobacterial infections due to *M. avium* or *M. intracellulare*

Prevention of disseminated mycobacterial infections due to MAC disease in patients with advanced HIV infection

Duodenal ulcer disease due to *H. pylori* in regimens with other drugs including amoxicillin and lansoprazole or omeprazole, or in combination with omeprazole. **Note:** Regimens that contain clarithromycin as the single antibacterial agent are more likely to be associated with the development of clarithromycin resistance.

Local Anesthetic/Vasoconstrictor Precautions Clarithromycin is one of the drugs confirmed to prolong the QT interval and is accepted as having a risk of causing torsade de pointes. In terms of epinephrine, it is not known what effect vasoconstrictors in the local anesthetic regimen will have in patients with a known history of congenital prolonged QT interval or in patients taking any medication that prolongs the QT interval. Until more information is obtained, it is suggested that the clinician consult with the physician prior to the use of a vasoconstrictor in suspected patients, and that the vasoconstrictor (epinephrine, mepivacaine and levonordefrin [Carbocaine® 2% with Neo-Cobefrin®]) be used with caution. See Dental Comment.

Effects on Dental Treatment Key adverse event(s) related to dental treatment: Abnormal taste.

Effects on Bleeding No information available to require special precautions

Adverse Reactions

1% to 10%:

Central nervous system: Headache (2%), insomnia

Dermatologic: Skin rash (children 3%)

Gastrointestinal: Dysgeusia (adults 3% to 7%), vomiting (children 6%), diarrhea (3% to 6%), nausea (adults 3%), abdominal pain (2% to 3%), dyspepsia (adults 2%)

Hematologic & oncologic: Prolonged prothrombin time (adults 1%)

Hepatic: Abnormal hepatic function tests

Hypersensitivity: Anaphylactoid reaction

Infection: Candidiasis (including oral)

Renal: Increased blood urea nitrogen (4%)

<1%, postmarketing, and/or case reports (Limited to important or life-threatening): Abdominal distension, abnormal albumin-globulin ratio, acne vulgaris, ageusia, agranulocytosis, altered sense of smell, anaphylaxis, angioedema, anorexia, anosmia, anxiety, asthma, atrial fibrillation, behavioral changes, bullous dermatitis, cardiac arrest, cellulitis, chest pain, chills, cholestasis, cholestatic hepatitis, *Clostridium difficile* associated diarrhea, *Clostridium difficile* (colitis), confusion, constipation, dark urine (abnormal urine color associated with liver injury), decreased appetite, decreased white blood cell count, dental discoloration (reversible with dental cleaning), depersonalization, depression, disorientation, dizziness, DRESS syndrome, drowsiness, dyskinesia, eosinophilia, epistaxis, eructation, esophagitis, extrasystoles, fatigue, fever, flatulence, gastritis, gastroenteritis, gastroesophageal reflux disease, glossitis, hallucination, hearing loss (reversible), hemorrhage, hepatic failure, hepatic insufficiency, hepatitis, hepatotoxicity (idiosyncratic) (Chalasani 2014), hyperhidrosis, hypersensitivity, hypoglycemia, IgA vasculitis, increased gamma-glutamyl transferase, increased INR, increased lactate dehydrogenase, increased serum alkaline phosphatase, increased serum ALT, increased serum AST, increased serum bilirubin, increased serum creatinine, infection, interstitial nephritis, jaundice, leukopenia, loss of consciousness, maculopapular rash, malaise,

manic behavior, muscle spasm, myalgia, myopathy, neck stiffness, nervousness, neutropenia, nightmares, palpitations, pancreatitis, parasominas, paresthesia, prolonged QT interval on ECG, pruritus, pseudomembranous colitis, psychosis, pulmonary embolism, rectal pain, renal failure, rhabdomyolysis, seizure, Stevens-Johnson syndrome, stomatitis, thrombocytopenia, tinnitus, tongue discoloration, torsades de pointes, toxic epidermal necrolysis, tremor, urticaria, vaginal infection, ventricular arrhythmia, ventricular tachycardia, vertigo, weakness, xerostomia

Dental Usual Dosage Prophylaxis against infective endocarditis (off-label use): Oral:

Children: 15 mg/kg 30-60 minutes before procedure

Adults: 500 mg 30-60 minutes prior to procedure

Dosing

Adult & Geriatric

Usual dosage range: Oral: 250 to 500 mg every 12 hours **or** 1000 mg (two 500 mg extended-release tablets) once daily for 7 to 14 days

Acute exacerbation of chronic bronchitis: Oral:

M. catarrhalis and *S. pneumoniae*: 250 mg every 12 hours for 7 to 14 days **or** 1,000 mg (two 500 mg extended-release tablets) once daily for 7 days

H. influenzae: 500 mg every 12 hours for 7 to 14 days **or** 1,000 mg (two 500 mg extended-release tablets) once daily for 7 days

H. parainfluenzae: 500 mg every 12 hours for 7 days **or** 1,000 mg (two 500 mg extended-release tablets) once daily for 7 days

Acute maxillary sinusitis: Oral: 500 mg every 12 hours for 14 days **or** 1,000 mg (two 500 mg extended-release tablets) once daily for 14 days

Bartonellosis in HIV-infected patients (excluding CNS infections and endocarditis) (off-label use; HHS [OI adult 2015]): Oral:

Treatment (alternative to preferred): 500 mg twice daily for at least 3 months

Long-term suppressive therapy: 500 mg twice daily; may discontinue if completed 3 to 4 months therapy and CD4 >200 cells/mm^3 for at least 6 months. **Note:** Some clinicians would discontinue only if Bartonella titers have also decreased four-fold

Lyme disease (off-label use): Oral: 500 mg twice daily for 14 to 21 days (not recommended for pregnant women) (Wormser 2006)

Mycobacterial infection, disseminated (prevention and treatment): Oral:

Manufacturer's labeling: 500 mg twice daily (use with other antimycobacterial drugs, eg, ethambutol or rifampin). Continue therapy if clinical response is observed; may discontinue when patient is considered at low risk of disseminated infection.

Alternate dosing: *Mycobacterium avium* complex disease (MAC) in HIV-infected patients (HHS [OI adult 2015]):

Primary prophylaxis: 500 mg twice daily; may discontinue when CD4 count >100 cells/mm^3 for ≥3 months in response to ART

Treatment and chronic maintenance therapy: 500 mg twice daily plus ethambutol; consider additional agents (eg, rifabutin, aminoglycoside, fluoroquinolone) for CD4 <50 cells/mm^3, high mycobacterial load, or ineffective antiretroviral therapy; may discontinue chronic maintenance if no signs/symptoms of MAC disease, have maintained a CD4 count >100 cells/mm^3 for >6 months in response to ART, and completed at least 12 months of therapy

Peptic ulcer disease: Eradication of *Helicobacter pylori*: Dual or triple combination regimens with bismuth subsalicylate, amoxicillin, an H_2-receptor antagonist, or proton-pump inhibitor: Oral: 500 mg every 8 to 12 hours for 10 to 14 days

Pertussis (off-label use): Oral: 500 mg twice daily for 7 days (CDC 2005)

Pharyngitis, tonsillitis: Oral: 250 mg every 12 hours for 10 days. **Note:** Recommended by the Infectious Disease Society of America (IDSA) as an alternative agent for group A streptococcal pharyngitis in penicillin-allergic patients (Shulman 2012).

Pneumonia, community-acquired: Oral:

Manufacturer's labeling:

C. pneumoniae, *M. pneumoniae*, and *S. pneumoniae*: 250 mg every 12 hours for 7 to 14 days **or** 1,000 mg (two 500 mg extended-release tablets) once daily for 7 days

H. influenzae: 250 mg every 12 hours for 7 days **or** 1,000 mg (two 500 mg extended-release tablets) once daily for 7 days

H. parainfluenzae and *M. catarrhalis*: 1000 mg (two 500 mg extended-release tablets) once daily for 7 days

Alternate dosing:

Outpatient empiric therapy: 500 mg twice daily for 5 days, in combination with a beta-lactam (Lim 2009; Mandell 2007)

Prophylaxis against infective endocarditis (off-label use): Oral: 500 mg 30 to 60 minutes prior to procedure. **Note:** American Heart Association (AHA) guidelines now recommend prophylaxis only in patients undergoing invasive procedures and in whom underlying cardiac conditions may predispose to a higher risk of adverse outcomes should infection occur. As of April 2007, routine prophylaxis for GI/GU procedures is no longer recommended by the AHA (Wilson 2007).

Skin and skin structure infection, uncomplicated: Oral: 250 mg every 12 hours for 7 to 14 days

Dosage adjustment for concomitant therapy: Atazanavir: Decrease clarithromycin dose by 50%.

Pediatric

Usual dosage range: Note: All pediatric dosing recommendations based on immediate release product formulations (tablet and oral suspension):

Infants ≥6 months, Children, and Adolescents: Oral: 7.5 mg/kg every 12 hours (maximum: 500 mg/dose) for 10 days

Acute otitis media: Infants ≥6 months, Children, and Adolescents: Oral: 7.5 mg/kg/dose (maximum: 500 mg/dose) every 12 hours for 10 days. **Note:** Due to increased *S. pneumoniae* and *H. influenzae* resistance, macrolides are not routinely recommended as a treatment option (Lieberthal 2013)

Bartonellosis in (treatment/long-term suppressive therapy) HIV-infected patients (excluding CNS infections and endocarditis) (off-label use): Adolescents: Oral: Refer to adult dosing.

Lyme disease (off-label use): Infants, Children, and Adolescents: Oral: 7.5 mg/kg/dose (maximum dose: 500 mg) twice daily for 14-21 days (Wormser 2006)

Mycobacterial infection, disseminated (prevention and treatment): Oral:

Manufacturer's labeling: 7.5 mg/kg/dose (maximum: 500 mg/dose) twice daily; use in combination with other antimycobacterial agents for the treatment of disseminated MAC. **Note:** Safety of clarithromycin for MAC not studied in children <20 months.

Alternative recommendations: Disseminated *Mycobacterium avium* complex (MAC) disease in HIV-exposed/-positive patients:

Infants and children (CDC 2009):

Primary prophylaxis: 7.5 mg/kg/dose (maximum: 500 mg/dose) twice daily

Secondary prophylaxis: 7.5 mg/kg/dose (maximum: 500 mg/dose) twice daily, plus ethambutol, with or without rifabutin

Treatment: 7.5-15 mg/kg/dose (maximum: 500 mg/dose) twice daily plus ethambutol, plus rifabutin (for severe disease)

Adolescents: Refer to adult dosing.

Pertussis (off-label use): Infants ≥1 month, Children, and Adolescents: Oral: 7.5 mg/kg/dose (maximum: 500 mg/dose) every 12 hours for 7 days (CDC 2005)

Pharyngitis/tonsillitis: Oral: 7.5 mg/kg/dose (maximum: 250 mg/dose) every 12 hours for 10 days. **Note:** Recommended by the Infectious Disease Society of America (IDSA) as an alternative agent for group A streptococcal pharyngitis in penicillin-allergic patients (Shulman 2012).

Pneumonia, community-acquired: Infants >3 months and Children: Oral: **Note:** A beta-lactam antibiotic should be added if typical bacterial pneumonia cannot be ruled out.

Presumed atypical *(M. pneumoniae, C. pneumoniae, C. trachomatis)* infection, mild-to-severe atypical infection or step-down therapy (alternative to azithromycin): 7.5 mg/kg/dose (maximum dose: 500 mg) every 12 hours (Bradley 2011)

Prophylaxis against infective endocarditis (off-label use): Children and Adolescents: Oral: 15 mg/kg/dose (maximum: 500 mg/dose) 30-60 minutes before procedure (maximum: 500 mg). **Note:** American Heart Association (AHA) guidelines now recommend prophylaxis only in patients undergoing invasive procedures and in whom underlying cardiac conditions may predispose to a higher risk of adverse outcomes should infection occur. As of April 2007, routine prophylaxis for GI/GU procedures is no longer recommended by the AHA (Wilson 2007).

Sinusitis: Infants ≥6 months, Children, and Adolescents: Oral: 7.5 mg/kg/dose (maximum: 500 mg/dose) every 12 hours for 10 days

Skin/skin structure infections, uncomplicated: Infants ≥6 months, Children, and Adolescents: Oral: 7.5 mg/kg/dose (maximum: 250 mg dose) every 12 hours for 10 days

Renal Impairment

CrCl ≥30 mL/minute: No dosage adjustment necessary.

CrCl <30 mL/minute: Decrease clarithromycin dose by 50%

Hemodialysis: Administer after HD session is completed (Aronoff 2007)

In combination with atazanavir or ritonavir:

CrCl 30 to 60 mL/minute: Decrease clarithromycin dose by 50%.

CrCl <30 mL/minute: Decrease clarithromycin dose by 75%.

Hepatic Impairment No dosing adjustment necessary if renal function is normal; however, in patients with hepatic impairment and concomitant severe renal impairment, a dosage reduction or prolonged dosing intervals may be appropriate.

Mechanism of Action Exerts its antibacterial action by binding to 50S ribosomal subunit resulting in inhibition of protein synthesis. The 14-OH metabolite of clarithromycin is twice as active as the parent compound against certain organisms.

Contraindications

Hypersensitivity to clarithromycin, erythromycin, any of the macrolide antibiotics, or any component of the formulation; history of cholestatic jaundice/hepatic dysfunction associated with prior use of clarithromycin; concomitant use with cisapride, pimozide, ergot alkaloids (eg, ergotamine, dihydroergotamine), or HMG-CoA reductase inhibitors extensively metabolized by CYP3A4 (eg, lovastatin, simvastatin); concomitant use with colchicine in patients with renal or hepatic impairment

Canadian labeling: Additional contraindications (not in US labeling): Severe hepatic failure in combination with renal impairment; history of QT prolongation (congenital or documented acquired QT prolongation or ventricular cardiac arrhythmia, including torsades de pointes; hypokalemia; concomitant use with saquinavir, midazolam (oral), colchicine (regardless of hepatic/renal impairment), ticagrelor; concomitant use with astemizole, terfenadine, or ranolazine (not available in Canada)

Warnings/Precautions Use has been associated with QT prolongation and infrequent cases of arrhythmias, including torsade de pointes (may be fatal). Systemic exposure is increased in the elderly; may be at increased risk of torsades de pointes, particularly if concurrent severe renal impairment. Avoid use in patients with known prolongation of the QT interval, ventricular cardiac arrhythmia (including torsades de pointes), uncorrected hypokalemia or hypomagnesemia, clinically significant bradycardia, and patients receiving Class IA (eg, quinidine, procainamide) or Class III (eg, amiodarone, dofetilide, sotalol) antiarrhythmic agents. Use caution in patients with coronary artery disease; postmarketing safety trial suggests increased risk of cardiovascular mortality with short-term clarithromycin use (vs placebo) in patients with stable CAD. However, more smokers were randomized to the clarithromycin arm (Jespersen 2006).

Elevated liver function tests and hepatitis (hepatocellular and/or cholestatic with or without jaundice) have been reported; usually reversible after discontinuation of clarithromycin. May lead to hepatic failure or death (rarely), especially in the presence of preexisting diseases and/or concomitant use of medications. Discontinue immediately if symptoms of hepatitis (eg, anorexia, jaundice, abdominal tenderness, pruritus, dark urine) occur. Use with caution in patients with myasthenia gravis; exacerbation of symptoms and new onset of symptoms has occurred. Use with caution in severe renal impairment; dosage adjustment required.

Potentially significant drug-drug interactions may exist, requiring dose or frequency adjustment, additional monitoring, and/or selection of alternative therapy. Prolonged use may result in fungal or bacterial superinfection, including *C. difficile*-associated diarrhea (CDAD) and pseudomembranous colitis; CDAD has been observed >2 months postantibiotic treatment. Decreased *H. pylori* eradication rates have been observed with short-term (≤7 days) combination therapy. Current guidelines recommend 10 to 14 days of therapy (triple or quadruple) for eradication of *H. pylori* in pediatric and adult patients (Chey 2007; NASPHGAN [Koletzko 2011]). Decreased survival has been observed in HIV patients with *Mycobacterium avium* complex (MAC) receiving clarithromycin doses above the maximum recommended dose; maximum recommended dosing should not be exceeded in this population. Development of resistance to clarithromycin has been observed when used as prophylaxis and treatment of MAC infection (Biaxin Canadian product labeling 2016).

Severe acute reactions have (rarely) been reported, including anaphylaxis, Stevens-Johnson syndrome (SJS), toxic epidermal necrolysis (TEN), drug rash with eosinophilia and systemic symptoms (DRESS), and Henoch-Schönlein purpura (IgA vasculitis); discontinue therapy and initiate treatment immediately for severe acute hypersensitivity reactions. The presence of extended release tablets in the stool has been reported, particularly in patients with anatomic (eg, ileostomy, colostomy) or functional GI disorders with decreased transit times. Consider alternative dosage forms (eg, suspension) or an alternative antimicrobial for patients with tablet residue in the stool and no signs of clinical improvement. Some dosage forms may contain propylene glycol; large amounts are potentially toxic and have been associated hyperosmolality, lactic acidosis, seizures, and respiratory depression; use caution (AAP 1997; Zar 2007). Some dosage forms may contain lactose or sucrose; consider sucrose content when administering to diabetic patients.

Drug Interactions

Metabolism/Transport Effects Substrate of CYP3A4 (major); **Note:** Assignment of Major/Minor substrate status based on clinically relevant drug interaction potential; **Inhibits** CYP1A2 (weak), CYP3A4 (strong), P-glycoprotein

Avoid Concomitant Use

Avoid concomitant use of Clarithromycin with any of the following: Ado-Trastuzumab Emtansine; Alfuzosin; Aprepitant; Astemizole; Asunaprevir; Avanafil; Axitinib; Barnidipine; BCG (Intravesical); Blonanserin; Bosutinib; Bromocriptine; Budesonide (Systemic); Ceritinib; Cholera Vaccine; Cisapride; Cobimetinib; Conivaptan; Crizotinib; Dabrafenib; Dapoxetine; Dihydroergotamine; Disopyramide; Domperidone; Dronedarone; Eletriptan; Eplerenone; Ergotamine; Everolimus; Flibanserin; FLUoxetine; Fusidic Acid (Systemic); Halofantrine; Highest Risk QTc-Prolonging Agents; Hydroxychloroquine; Ibrutinib; Idelalisib; Irinotecan Products; Isavuconazonium Sulfate; Ivabradine; Lapatinib; Lercanidipine; Lomitapide; Lopinavir; Lovastatin; Lurasidone; Macitentan; MiFEPRIStone; Naloxegol; Nilotinib; NiMODipine; Nisoldipine; Olaparib; Palbociclib; PAZOPanib; Pimozide; Probucol; Promazine; QUEtiapine; QuiNINE; Radotinib; Ranolazine; Red Yeast Rice; Regorafenib; Rupatadine; Salmeterol; Silodosin; Simeprevir; Simvastatin; Sonidegib; Suvorexant; Tamsulosin; Terfenadine; Ticagrelor; Tolvaptan; Topotecan; Toremifene; Trabectedin; Udenafil; Ulipristal; Vemurafenib; VinCRIStine (Liposomal); Vinflunine; Vorapaxar

Increased Effect/Toxicity

Clarithromycin may increase the levels/effects of: Ado-Trastuzumab Emtansine; Afatinib; Alfentanil; Alfuzosin; Alitretinoin (Systemic); Almotriptan; Alosetron; ALPRAZolam; Antineoplastic Agents (Vinca Alkaloids); Apixaban; Aprepitant; ARIPiprazole; ARIPiprazole Lauroxil; Astemizole; Asunaprevir; AtorvaSTATin; Avanafil; Axitinib; Barnidipine; Bedaquiline; Bilastine; Blonanserin; Boceprevir; Bortezomib; Bosentan; Bosutinib; Brentuximab Vedotin; Brexpiprazole; Brinzolamide; Bromocriptine; Budesonide (Nasal); Budesonide (Oral Inhalation); Budesonide (Systemic); Budesonide (Topical); Buprenorphine; BusPIRone; Cabazitaxel; Cabergoline; Cabozantinib; Calcifediol; Calcium Channel Blockers; Cannabidiol; Cannabis; CarBAMazepine; Cardiac Glycosides; Cariprazine; Ceritinib; Cilostazol; Cisapride; Cobicistat; Cobimetinib; Colchicine; Conivaptan; Corticosteroids (Orally Inhaled); Corticosteroids (Systemic); Crizotinib; CycloSPORINE (Systemic); CYP3A4 Inducers (Strong); CYP3A4 Substrates; Dabigatran Etexilate; Dabrafenib; Daclatasvir; Dapoxetine; Dasatinib; Deflazacort; Delamanid; Dienogest; Dihydroergotamine; Disopyramide; DOCEtaxel; Domperidone; DOXOrubicin (Conventional); Dronabinol; Dronedarone; Drospirenone; Dutasteride; Edoxaban; Eletriptan; Eplerenone; Ergot Derivatives; Ergotamine; Erlotinib; Estazolam; Eszopiclone; Etizolam; Everolimus; FentaNYL; Fesoterodine; Flibanserin; FLUoxetine; Fluticasone (Nasal); Fluticasone (Oral Inhalation); Gefitinib; GlipiZIDE; GlyBURIDE; GuanFACINE; Halofantrine; Highest Risk QTc-Prolonging Agents; HYDROcodone; HydrOXYzine; Ibrutinib; Imatinib; Imidafenacin; Irinotecan Products; Isavuconazonium Sulfate; Ivabradine; Ivacaftor; Ixabepilone; Lacosamide; Lapatinib; Lercanidipine; Levobupivacaine; Levomilnacipran; Lomitapide; Lopinavir; Lovastatin; Lurasidone; Macitentan; Manidipine; Maraviroc; MedroxyPROGESTERone; MethylPREDNISolone; Midazolam; Mirodenafil; Moderate Risk QTc-Prolonging Agents; Naldemedine; Naloxegol; Nilotinib; NiMODipine; Nintedanib; Nisoldipine; Olaparib; Ospemifene; Oxybutynin; OxyCODONE; Palbociclib; Panobinostat; Parecoxib; Paricalcitol; PARoxetine; PAZOPanib; P-glycoprotein/ABCB1 Substrates; Pimecrolimus; Pimozide; Pitavastatin; PONATinib; Pranlukast; Pravastatin; Praziquantel; PrednisoLONE (Systemic); PredniSONE; Protease Inhibitors; Prucalopride; QUEtiapine; QuiNINE; Radotinib; Ramelteon; Ranolazine; Reboxetine; Red Yeast Rice; Regorafenib; Repaglinide; Retapamulin; RifAXIMin; Rilpivirine; Rivaroxaban; RomiDEPsin; Rupatadine; Ruxolitinib; Salmeterol; SAXagliptin; Sildenafil; Silodosin; Simeprevir; Simvastatin; Sirolimus; Sonidegib; SORAfenib; Suvorexant; Tacrolimus (Systemic); Tacrolimus (Topical); Tadalafil; Tamsulosin; Tasimelteon; Telaprevir; Temsirolimus; Terfenadine; Tetrahydrocannabinol; Theophylline Derivatives; Ticagrelor; TiZANidine; Tofacitinib; Tolterodine; Tolvaptan; Topotecan; Toremifene; Trabectedin; TraMADol; TraZODone; Triazolam; Udenafil; Ulipristal; Vardenafil; Vemurafenib; Venetoclax; Vilazodone; VinCRIStine (Liposomal); Vinflunine; Vitamin K Antagonists; Vorapaxar; Zidovudine; Zopiclone

The levels/effects of Clarithromycin may be increased by: Antihepaciviral Combination Products; Boceprevir; Bosentan; CarBAMazepine; Cobicistat; Conivaptan; CYP3A4 Inducers (Moderate); CYP3A4 Inducers (Strong); CYP3A4 Inhibitors (Moderate); CYP3A4 Inhibitors (Strong); Fusidic Acid (Systemic); Hydroxychloroquine; Idelalisib; Ivabradine; Lopinavir; MiFEPRIStone; Netupitant; Probucol; Promazine; Protease Inhibitors; QTc-Prolonging Agents (Indeterminate Risk and Risk Modifying); Stiripentol; Telaprevir; TraZODone; Vinflunine

Decreased Effect

Clarithromycin may decrease the levels/effects of: BCG (Intravesical); BCG Vaccine (Immunization); Cholera Vaccine; Doxercalciferol; Ifosfamide; Lactobacillus and Estriol; Prasugrel; Sodium Picosulfate; Ticagrelor; Typhoid Vaccine; Zidovudine

The levels/effects of Clarithromycin may be decreased by: Bosentan; CarBAMazepine; CYP3A4 Inducers

(Moderate); CYP3A4 Inducers (Strong); Deferasirox; Efavirenz; Enzalutamide; Etravirine; Lopinavir; Mitotane; Protease Inhibitors; Siltuximab; St John's Wort; Tocilizumab

Food Interactions Immediate release: Food delays rate, but not extent of absorption; Extended release: Food increases clarithromycin AUC by ~30% relative to fasting conditions. Management: Administer immediate release products without regard to meals. Administer extended release products with food.

Dietary Considerations Extended release tablets should be taken with food.

Pharmacodynamics/Kinetics

Half-life Elimination Immediate release: Clarithromycin: 3-7 hours; 14-OH-clarithromycin: 5-9 hours

Time to Peak Immediate release: 2-3 hours; Extended release: 5-8 hours

Pregnancy Risk Factor C

Pregnancy Considerations Adverse events have been documented in some animal reproduction studies. Clarithromycin crosses the placenta (Witt 2003). The manufacturer recommends that clarithromycin not be used in a pregnant woman unless there are no alternative therapies. Clarithromycin is generally not recommended for the treatment or prophylaxis of *Mycobacterium avium* complex (MAC) or bacterial respiratory disease in HIV-infected pregnant patients (HHS [opportunistic; adult] 2015).

Breastfeeding Considerations Clarithromycin and its active metabolite (14-hydroxy clarithromycin) are excreted into breast milk. The manufacturer recommends that caution be used if administered to nursing women. Decreased appetite, diarrhea, rash, and somnolence have been noted in nursing infants exposed to macrolide antibiotics (Goldstein 2009).

Dosage Forms

Suspension Reconstituted, Oral:
Biaxin: 250 mg/5 mL (50 mL, 100 mL)
Generic: 125 mg/5 mL (50 mL, 100 mL); 250 mg/5 mL (50 mL, 100 mL)

Tablet, Oral:
Biaxin: 250 mg, 500 mg
Generic: 250 mg, 500 mg

Tablet Extended Release 24 Hour, Oral:
Biaxin XL: 500 mg
Biaxin XL Pac: 500 mg
Generic: 500 mg

Dental Comment The FDA issued a special alert in December 2005 stating that short-term therapy with clarithromycin in patients with stable coronary artery disease may cause significantly higher cardiovascular mortality. The use of 500 mg clarithromycin daily for 14 days in patients with the above condition resulted in significantly higher all-cause mortality compared to patients taking placebo. This information is provided to the dental practitioner on the possible association between short-term use of clarithromycin for infections and increases in mortality in patients with a history of stable coronary artery disease.

Also see Local Anesthetic/Vasoconstrictor Precautions

Clemastine (KLEM as teen)

Brand Names: US Dayhist Allergy 12 Hour Relief [OTC]; Tavist Allergy [OTC]

Pharmacologic Category Ethanolamine Derivative; Histamine H_1 Antagonist; Histamine H_1 Antagonist, First Generation

Use

Allergic rhinitis: Relief of symptoms associated with allergic rhinitis or other upper respiratory allergies (eg, sneezing, rhinorrhea, pruritus, and lacrimation) in children ≥12 years of age and adults (tablets and syrup) and in children 6 to 12 years (syrup only)

Urticaria/angioedema: Relief of mild, uncomplicated allergic skin manifestations of urticaria and angioedema in children ≥12 years of age and adults (tablets and syrup) and in children 6 to 12 years (syrup only)

***OTC Labeling:* Common cold/hay fever/upper respiratory allergies:** Relief of symptoms associated with the common cold (eg, rhinorrhea, sneezing, throat/nose pruritus, lacrimation) in children ≥12 years of age and adults

Local Anesthetic/Vasoconstrictor Precautions No information available to require special precautions

Effects on Dental Treatment Key adverse event(s) related to dental treatment: Xerostomia (normal salivary flow resumes upon discontinuation).

Effects on Bleeding No information available to require special precautions

Adverse Reactions Frequency not defined.

Cardiovascular: Hypotension, palpitations, tachycardia
Central nervous system: Ataxia, confusion, dizziness, drowsiness (slight to moderate), fatigue, headache, insomnia, irritability, nervousness, restlessness, sedation
Dermatologic: Skin photosensitivity, skin rash
Gastrointestinal: Constipation, diarrhea, epigastric distress, nausea, vomiting, xerostomia
Genitourinary: Difficulty in micturition, urinary frequency, urinary retention
Hematologic & oncologic: Agranulocytosis, hemolytic anemia, thrombocytopenia
Hypersensitivity: Anaphylaxis
Ophthalmic: Blurred vision
Otic: Tinnitus
Respiratory: Thickening of bronchial secretions

General Dosage Range Oral:

Children 6 to <12 years: Clemastine fumarate 0.67 to 1.34 mg (0.5 to 1 mg base) twice daily (maximum: clemastine fumarate 4.02 mg/**day** [3 mg/**day** base])

Children ≥12 years, Adolescents, and Adults: Clemastine fumarate 1.34 to 2.68 mg (1 to 2 mg base) 1 to 3 times daily (maximum: clemastine fumarate 2.68 to 8.04 mg/**day** [2 to 6 mg/**day** base])

Mechanism of Action Competes with histamine for H_1-receptor sites on effector cells in the gastrointestinal tract, blood vessels, and respiratory tract; anticholinergic and sedative effects are also seen.

Pharmacodynamics/Kinetics

Onset of Action 2 hours after administration; Peak effect: Therapeutic: 5 to 7 hours

Duration of Action 10 to 12 hours; may persist for up to 24 hours

Half-life Elimination ~21 hours (range: 10 to 33 hours) (Sharma 2003)

Time to Peak 2 to 4 hours

Pregnancy Risk Factor B

Pregnancy Considerations Maternal clemastine use has generally not resulted in an increased risk of birth defects. Antihistamines are recommended for the treatment of rhinitis, urticaria, and pruritus with rash in pregnant women (although second generation antihistamines may be preferred). Antihistamines are not recommended for treatment of pruritus associated with intrahepatic cholestasis in pregnancy.

Clevidipine (klev ID i peen)

Related Information

Calcium Channel Blockers and Gingival Hyperplasia *on page 1908*

Brand Names: US Cleviprex

Brand Names: Canada Cleviprex

Pharmacologic Category Antihypertensive; Calcium Channel Blocker; Calcium Channel Blocker, Dihydropyridine

Use Hypertension: Management of hypertension when oral therapy is not feasible or not desirable.

Local Anesthetic/Vasoconstrictor Precautions No information available to require special precautions

Effects on Dental Treatment Key adverse event(s) related to dental treatment: Although other calcium channel blockers (eg, nifedipine, diltiazem) have been associated with gingival hyperplasia, there are no reports that clevidipine has caused this adverse effect.

Effects on Bleeding No information available to require special precautions

Adverse Reactions

>10%:

Cardiovascular: Atrial fibrillation (21%)

Central nervous system: Insomnia (12%)

Gastrointestinal: Nausea (5% to 21%)

Miscellaneous: Fever (19%)

1% to 10%:

Central nervous system: Headache (6%)

Gastrointestinal: Vomiting (3%)

Hematologic & oncologic: Postprocedural hemorrhage (3%)

Renal: Acute renal failure (9%)

Respiratory: Pneumonia (3%), respiratory failure (3%)

<1%, postmarketing, and/or case reports: Dyspnea, hypersensitivity reaction, hypotension, increased serum triglycerides, intestinal obstruction, myocardial infarction, oxygen saturation decreased, syncope, tachycardia (reflex), thrombophlebitis

General Dosage Range IV: *Adults:* Initial: 1 to 2 mg/hour; Usual maintenance: 4 to 6 mg/hour; Maximum: 21 mg/hour (1,000 mL/24 hours)

Mechanism of Action Dihydropyridine calcium channel blocker with potent arterial vasodilating activity. Inhibits calcium ion influx through the L-type calcium channels during depolarization in arterial smooth muscle, producing a decrease in mean arterial pressure (MAP) by reducing systemic vascular resistance.

Pharmacodynamics/Kinetics

Onset of Action 2 to 4 minutes after start of infusion

Duration of Action IV: 5 to 15 minutes

Half-life Elimination Biphasic: Initial: 1 minute (predominant); Terminal: ~15 minutes

Pregnancy Risk Factor C

Pregnancy Considerations Adverse events have been observed in animal reproduction studies. Untreated chronic maternal hypertension is associated with adverse events in the fetus, infant, and mother. If treatment for hypertension during pregnancy is needed, other agents are preferred (ACOG 2012).

Clidinium and Chlordiazepoxide

(kli DI nee um & klor dye az e POKS ide)

Related Information

ChlordiazePOXIDE *on page 344*

Brand Names: US Librax

Brand Names: Canada Chlorax; Librax

Pharmacologic Category Antispasmodic Agent, Gastrointestinal; Benzodiazepine

Use

Emotional and somatic factors in gastrointestinal disorders: Control emotional and somatic factors in gastrointestinal disorders.

Irritable bowel syndrome: Adjunctive therapy for treatment of irritable bowel syndrome (eg, irritable colon, spastic colon, mucous colitis) and acute enterocolitis

Peptic ulcer: Adjunctive therapy for treatment of peptic ulcer

Local Anesthetic/Vasoconstrictor Precautions No information available to require special precautions

Effects on Dental Treatment Key adverse event(s) related to dental treatment: Xerostomia and changes in salivation (normal salivary flow resumes upon discontinuation).

Effects on Bleeding No information available to require special precautions

Adverse Reactions

Frequency not defined.

1% to 10%:

Central nervous system: Ataxia, confusion, drowsiness

Gastrointestinal: Constipation, nausea, xerostomia

Miscellaneous: Anticholinergic side effects

<1%, postmarketing, and/or case reports: Agranulocytosis, extrapyramidal reaction, hematologic disease, hepatic insufficiency, jaundice, syncope

General Dosage Range Oral: *Adults:* 1 to 2 capsules 3 to 4 times daily

Mechanism of Action

Clidinium: Synthetic anticholinergic that has an antispasmodic and antisecretory effect on the GI tract

Chlordiazepoxide: Benzodiazepine with anxiolytic and sedative properties. Binds to benzodiazepine receptors on the postsynaptic gamma-aminobutyric acid (GABA) neuron at several sites within the CNS, including the limbic system. Benzodiazepine receptors and effects appear to be linked to the GABA-A receptors. Benzodiazepines do not bind to GABA-B receptors.

Pregnancy Considerations Adverse events were not observed in animal reproduction studies with this combination. Refer to the chlordiazepoxide monograph for details related to chlordiazepoxide exposure in pregnant women.

Controlled Substance

C-IV or nonscheduled (DEA exemption status dependent)

Clindamycin (Systemic) (klin da MYE sin)

Related Information

Antibiotic Prophylaxis *on page 1812*

Bacterial Infections *on page 1835*

Osteonecrosis of the Jaw *on page 1796*

Periodontal Diseases *on page 1844*

Related Sample Prescriptions

Bacterial Infections and Periodontal Diseases - Sample Prescriptions *on page 32*

Prevention of Endocarditis and to Reduce the Risk of Late Infections of Joint Prostheses - Sample Prescriptions *on page 37*

Brand Names: US Cleocin; Cleocin in D5W; Cleocin Phosphate; CLIN Single Use

Brand Names: Canada Apo-Clindamycin; Auro-Clindamycin; Ava-Clindamycin; Clindamycin Injection; Clindamycin Injection SDZ; Clindamycin Injection, USP; Clindamycin IV Infusion; Clindamycine; Dalacin C;

Mylan-Clindamycin; PMS-Clindamycin; Riva-Clindamycin; Teva-Clindamycin

Generic Availability (US) May be product dependent

Pharmacologic Category Antibiotic, Lincosamide

Dental Use Alternate oral antibiotic for prevention of infective endocarditis in individuals allergic to penicillins or ampicillin, when amoxicillin cannot be used; alternate IM or IV antibiotic for prevention of infective endocarditis in patients allergic to penicillins or ampicillin and unable to take oral medication; alternate oral antibiotic for prophylaxis for dental patients with total joint replacement who are allergic to penicillin; alternate IV antibiotic for prophylaxis for dental patients with total joint replacement who are allergic to penicillin and unable to take oral medications; alternate antibiotic in the treatment of common orofacial infections caused by aerobic gram-positive cocci and susceptible anaerobes; treatment of periodontal disease

Use

Bone and joint infections: Treatment of bone and joint infections, including acute hematogenous osteomyelitis caused by *Staphylococcus aureus* and as adjunctive therapy in the surgical treatment of chronic bone and joint infections caused by susceptible organisms.

Gynecological infections: Treatment of gynecologic infections, including endometritis, nongonococcal tubo-ovarian abscess, pelvic cellulitis, and postsurgical vaginal cuff infection caused by susceptible anaerobes.

Intra-abdominal infections: Treatment of intra-abdominal infections, including peritonitis and intra-abdominal abscess caused by susceptible anaerobic organisms.

Lower respiratory tract infections: Treatment of lower respiratory tract infections, including pneumonia, empyema, and lung abscess caused by anaerobes, *Streptococcus pneumoniae*, other streptococci (except *Enterococcus faecalis*), and *S. aureus*.

Septicemia: Treatment of septicemia caused by *S. aureus*, streptococci (except *E. faecalis*), and susceptible anaerobes.

Skin and skin structure infections: Treatment of skin and skin structure infections caused by *Streptococcus pyogenes*, *S. aureus*, and anaerobes.

Local Anesthetic/Vasoconstrictor Precautions No information available to require special precautions

Effects on Dental Treatment No significant effects or complications reported (See Dental Comment)

Effects on Bleeding No information available to require special precautions

Adverse Reactions Frequency not defined.

Cardiovascular: Hypotension (rare; IV administration), thrombophlebitis (IV)

Central nervous system: Metallic taste (IV)

Dermatologic: Acute generalized exanthematous pustulosis, erythema multiforme (rare), exfoliative dermatitis (rare), maculopapular rash, pruritus, skin rash, Stevens-Johnson syndrome (rare), toxic epidermal necrolysis, urticaria, vesiculobullous dermatitis

Gastrointestinal: Abdominal pain, antibiotic-associated colitis, *Clostridium difficile* associated diarrhea, diarrhea, esophageal ulcer, esophagitis, nausea, pseudomembranous colitis, unpleasant taste (IV), vomiting

Genitourinary: Azotemia, oliguria, proteinuria, vaginitis

Hematologic & oncologic: Agranulocytosis, eosinophilia (transient), neutropenia (transient), thrombocytopenia

Hepatic: Abnormal hepatic function tests, jaundice

Hypersensitivity: Anaphylactic shock, anaphylactoid reaction (rare), anaphylaxis, angioedema, hypersensitivity reaction

Immunologic: DRESS syndrome

Local: Abscess at injection site (IM), induration at injection site (IM), irritation at injection site (IM), pain at injection site (IM)

Neuromuscular & skeletal: Polyarthritis (rare)

Renal: Renal insufficiency (rare)

Dental Usual Dosage

Orofacial infection:

Children:

Oral: 10-20 mg/kg/day in 3-4 equally divided doses

IV: 15-25 mg/kg/day in 3-4 equally divided doses

Adults:

Oral: 150-450 mg/dose for 7 days; maximum dose: 1.8 g/day

IV: 600-900 mg every 8 hours

Treatment of periodontal disease: Oral: 300 mg every 8 hours for 8 days

Infective endocarditis prophylaxis:

Children:

Oral: 20 mg/kg 30-60 minutes before procedure

IM, IV: 20 mg/kg 30-60 minutes before procedure. **Note:** Intramuscular injections should be avoided in patients who are receiving anticoagulant therapy. In these circumstances, orally administered regimens should be given whenever possible. Intravenously administered antibiotics should be used for patients who are unable to tolerate or absorb oral medications.

Adults:

Oral: 600 mg 30-60 minutes before procedure

IM, IV: 600 mg 30-60 minutes before procedure. **Note:** Intramuscular injections should be avoided in patients who are receiving anticoagulant therapy. In these circumstances, orally administered regimens should be given whenever possible. Intravenously administered antibiotics should be used for patients who are unable to tolerate or absorb oral medications.

Prophylaxis in total joint replacement patients undergoing dental procedures which produce bacteremia:

Adults:

Oral: 600 mg 1 hour prior to procedure

IV: 600 mg 1 hour prior to procedure (for patients unable to take oral medication)

Note: In general, patients with prosthetic joint implants do not require prophylactic antibiotics prior to dental procedures. In planning an invasive oral procedure, dental consultation with the patient's orthopedic surgeon may be advised to review the risks of infection.

Dosing

Adult & Geriatric

Usual dose:

Oral: 150 to 450 mg every 6 hours

IM, IV: 600 to 2,700 mg daily in 2 to 4 divided doses; up to 4,800 mg IV daily may be used in life-threatening infections (maximum: 600 mg/dose IM)

Anthrax (off-label use) (Hendricks 2014):

Postexposure prophylaxis: Oral: 600 mg every 8 hours for 60 days after exposure

Cutaneous, treatment: Oral: 600 mg every 8 hours for 7 to 10 days after naturally acquired infection; 60 days following biological weapon related event

Systemic, treatment: IV: 900 mg every 8 hours; use in combination with a bactericidal antimicrobial (eg, fluoroquinolone, penicillin G); if meningitis is suspected or cannot be ruled out, use in combination with 2 bactericidal antimicrobials (eg, fluoroquinolone **and** beta-lactam). Duration of therapy is 2 weeks when meningitis has been excluded; ≥2 to 3 weeks for possible/confirmed meningitis. Patients exposed to aerosolized spores require prophylaxis to complete an antimicrobial course of 60 days from illness onset.

Injectional: IV: 600 mg every 8 hours in combination with ciprofloxacin and other antibiotics (eg, a 5-drug combination) (Hicks 2012)

Babesiosis (off-label use):

Oral: 600 mg every 8 hours for 7 to 10 days with quinine (IDSA [Wormser 2006]; Vannier 2012)

IV: 300 to 600 mg every 6 hours for 7 to 10 days with quinine (IDSA [Wormser 2006]; Vannier 2012)

Note: Relapsing infection may require at least 6 weeks of therapy (Vannier 2012)

Bacterial vaginosis (alternative to preferred therapy) (off-label use): Oral: 300 mg twice daily for 7 days (CDC [Workowski 2015])

Bite wounds (animal) (off-label use):

Oral: 300 mg 3 times daily; in combination with a second- or third-generation cephalosporin, levofloxacin, or sulfamethoxazole and trimethoprim (IDSA [Stevens 2014])

IV: 600 mg every 6 to 8 hours; in combination with a second- or third-generation cephalosporin, levofloxacin, or sulfamethoxazole and trimethoprim (IDSA [Stevens 2014])

Diabetic foot infection, mild to moderate (off-label use): Oral: 300 to 450 mg every 6 to 8 hours (Bader 2008; Lipsky 1990). **Note:** For moderate infection, use in combination with ciprofloxacin or levofloxacin (limited evidence supporting clindamycin for severe *S. aureus* infections). Check macrolide sensitivity and consider ordering a "D-test" before using for MRSA (IDSA [Lipsky 2012]).

Group B streptococci (neonatal prophylaxis) (off-label use): IV: 900 mg every 8 hours until delivery (CDC 2010)

Impetigo: Oral: 300 to 450 mg 4 times daily for 7 days, depending on response (IDSA [Stevens 2014])

Malaria, severe (off-label use): IV: Load: 10 mg/kg followed by 5 mg/kg every 8 hours *plus* IV quinidine gluconate; switch to oral therapy (clindamycin *plus* quinine) when able for total clindamycin treatment duration of 7 days. **Note:** Quinine duration is region specific, consult CDC for current recommendations (CDC 2013).

Malaria, uncomplicated treatment (off-label use): Oral: 20 mg/kg/day divided every 8 hours for 7 days *plus* quinine (CDC 2013)

Osteomyelitis due to MRSA (off-label use): IV, Oral: 600 mg 3 times daily for a minimum of 8 weeks. **Note:** Some experts combine with rifampin (IDSA [Liu 2011]).

Osteomyelitis, native vertebral (off- label dose) (IDSA [Berbari 2015]):

Staphylococci (oxacillin-susceptible) (alternative therapy):

IV: 600 to 900 mg every 8 hours for 6 weeks

Oral: 300 to 450 mg four times daily

Propionibacterium acnes (alternative therapy): IV: 600 to 900 mg every 8 hours for 6 weeks

Pelvic inflammatory disease: IV: 900 mg every 8 hours with gentamicin (conventional or single daily dosing); transition from parenteral to clindamycin 450 mg orally 4 times daily (or oral doxycycline) can usually be initiated after 24 to 48 hours of clinical improvement to complete 14 days of total therapy. **Note:** If tubo-ovarian abscess is present, oral clindamycin in combination with doxycycline is a preferred regimen to complete 14 days of therapy (CDC [Workowski 2015]).

Pharyngitis, group A streptococci (GAS) (off-label use): Oral:

Acute treatment in penicillin-allergic patients: 300 mg every 8 hours for 10 days (IDSA [Shulman 2012])

Chronic carrier treatment: 300 mg every 8 hours for 10 days (IDSA [Shulman 2012]).

***Pneumocystis* pneumonia (PCP) in HIV-infected patients (alternative to preferred therapy) (off-label use):**

IV: 600 mg every 6 hours or 900 mg every 8 hours with primaquine for 21 days (HHS [OI adult 2016])

Oral: 450 mg every 6 hours or 600 mg every 8 hours with primaquine for 21 days (HHS [OI adult 2016])

Pneumonia due to MRSA (off-label use): IV, Oral: 600 mg 3 times daily for 7 to 21 days (IDSA [Liu 2011])

Prophylaxis against infective endocarditis (off-label use):

Oral: 600 mg 30 to 60 minutes before procedure with no follow-up dose needed (Wilson 2007)

IM, IV: 600 mg 30 to 60 minutes before procedure. Intramuscular injections should be avoided in patients who are receiving anticoagulant therapy. In these circumstances, orally administered regimens should be given whenever possible. Intravenously administered antibiotics should be used for patients who are unable to tolerate or absorb oral medications (Wilson 2007).

Note: American Heart Association (AHA) guidelines now recommend prophylaxis only in patients undergoing invasive procedures and in whom underlying cardiac conditions may predispose to a higher risk of adverse outcomes should infection occur. As of April 2007, routine prophylaxis for GI/GU procedures is no longer recommended by the AHA.

Prophylaxis in total joint replacement in patients undergoing dental procedures which produce bacteremia (off-label use): Note: In general, patients with prosthetic joint implants do not require prophylactic antibiotics prior to dental procedures. In planning an invasive oral procedure, dental consultation with the patient's orthopedic surgeon may be advised to review the risks of infection (Sollecito 2015).

Oral: 600 mg 1 hour prior to procedure (ADA 2003)

IV: 600 mg 1 hour prior to procedure (for patients unable to take oral medication) (ADA 2003)

Prosthetic joint infection (off-label use) (IDSA [Osmon 2013]):

Chronic antimicrobial suppression, Staphylococci (oxacillin-susceptible) (alternative to cephalexin or cefadroxil) (off-label use): Oral: 300 mg every 6 hours

Propionibacterium acnes, treatment (alternative to penicillin G or ceftriaxone):

Oral: 300 to 450 mg every 6 hours for 4 to 6 weeks

IV: 600 to 900 mg every 8 hours for 4 to 6 weeks

Septic arthritis due to MRSA (off-label use): IV, Oral: 600 mg 3 times daily for 3 to 4 weeks (IDSA [Liu 2011])

Skin and soft tissue infections due to MSSA:

Oral: 300 to 450 mg 4 times daily for 7 to 14 days (IDSA [Stevens 2014])

IV: 600 mg every 8 hours for 7 to 14 days (IDSA [Stevens 2014])

Skin and soft tissue infections due to MRSA (off-label use):

Oral: 300 to 450 mg 4 times daily for 7 to 14 days (IDSA [Stevens 2014])

IV: 600 mg every 8 hours for 7 to 14 days (IDSA [Stevens 2014])

Complicated infections: IV, Oral: 600 mg 3 times daily for 7 to 14 days (IDSA [Liu 2011])

Cellulitis: Oral: 300 to 450 mg 3 times daily for 5 to 10 days (IDSA [Liu 2011])

Skin and soft tissue necrotizing infections (off-label use): IV: 600 to 900 mg every 8 hours, in combination with cefotaxime or ceftriaxone for empiric therapy of polymicrobial infections **or** in combination with penicillin IV for the treatment of group A streptococcal or *Clostridium* species necrotizing infections. May give as monotherapy for MSSA. Continue until further debridement is not necessary, patient has clinically improved, and patient is afebrile for 48 to 72 hours (IDSA [Stevens 2014])

Streptococcal skin infections: IV: 600 to 900 mg every 8 hours (IDSA [Stevens 2014])

Surgical (perioperative) prophylaxis (off-label use): IV: 900 mg within 60 minutes prior to surgical incision. Doses may be repeated in 6 hours if procedure is lengthy (Bratzler 2013).

Toxic shock syndrome: IV: 900 mg every 8 hours with additional concomitant therapy (Lappin 2009; Wong 2013)

***Toxoplasma gondii* encephalitis in HIV-infected patients (off label use):**

Treatment (alternative to preferred regimen): IV, Oral: 600 mg every 6 hours in combination with pyrimethamine and leucovorin. Continue therapy for at least 6 weeks; longer duration may be required if incomplete response or extensive disease (HHS [OI adult 2016]).

Chronic maintenance therapy (alternative to preferred regimen): Oral: 600 mg every 8 hours in combination with pyrimethamine and leucovorin; may discontinue when asymptomatic and CD4 count >200 cells/mm^3 for 6 months in response to ART (HHS [OI adult 2016])

Pediatric

Usual dose:

Neonates: IM, IV: Manufacturer's labeling: 15 to 20 mg/kg/day divided every 6 to 8 hours.

Infants, Children, and Adolescents:

Oral: 8 to 40 mg/kg/day in 3 to 4 divided doses; Manufacturer's labeling: 8 to 20 mg/kg/day (as hydrochloride) or 8 to 25 mg/kg/day (as palmitate) in 3 to 4 divided doses; minimum dose of palmitate: 37.5 mg 3 times daily

IM, IV: Manufacturer's labeling: 20 to 40 mg/kg/day or 350 to 450 mg/m^2/day in 3 to 4 divided doses

Acute bacterial rhinosinusitis (off-label use): Oral: 30 to 40 mg/kg/day divided every 8 hours with concomitant cefixime or cefpodoxime for 10 to 14 days. **Note:** Recommended in patients with non-type I penicillin allergy, after failure of initial therapy or in patients at risk for antibiotic resistance (eg, daycare attendance, age <2 years, recent hospitalization, antibiotic use within the past month) (Chow 2012).

Acute otitis media (off-label use): Oral: 30 to 40 mg/kg/day in 3 divided doses for 5 to 10 days. Use with or without concomitant third-generation cephalosporin for failure of initial antibiotic therapy; use with a third-generation cephalosporin is recommended for failure of a second course of antibiotics. Duration depends upon illness severity and patient age: Severe illness or <2 years: 10 days; 2 to 5 years: 7 days; children ≥6 years: 5 to 7 days (Lieberthal 2013).

Anthrax (off-label use) (Bradley 2014):

Postexposure prophylaxis: Oral: 30 mg/kg/day divided every 8 hours for 60 days after exposure (maximum: 900 mg/dose)

Cutaneous, treatment: Oral: 30 mg/kg/day divided every 8 hours for 7 to 10 days after naturally acquired infection; up to 60 days following biological weapon related event (maximum: 900 mg/dose)

Systemic, treatment: IV: 40 mg/kg/day divided every 8 hours for ≥14 days (maximum: 900 mg/dose); use in combination with a bactericidal antimicrobial (eg, fluoroquinolone, penicillin G); if meningitis is suspected or cannot be ruled out, use in combination with 2 bactericidal antimicrobials (eg, fluoroquinolone **and** beta-lactam or glycopeptide). Continue with prophylaxis therapy for up to 60 days from onset of illness.

Babesiosis (off-label use): Oral: 20 to 40 mg/kg/day divided every 8 hours for 7 to 10 days *plus* quinine (*Red Book* [AAP 2015])

Impetigo: Oral: 20 mg/kg/day divided every 8 hours for 7 days, depending on response (IDSA [Stevens 2014])

Malaria, severe (off-label use): IV: Load: 10 mg/kg followed by 15 mg/kg/day divided every 8 hours *plus* IV quinidine gluconate; switch to oral therapy (clindamycin *plus* quinine) when able for total clindamycin treatment duration of 7 days (**Note:** Quinine duration is region specific, consult CDC for current recommendations) (CDC 2013)

Malaria, uncomplicated treatment (off-label use): Oral: 20 mg/kg/day divided every 8 hours for 7 days *plus* quinine (CDC 2013)

Osteomyelitis due to MRSA (off-label use): IV, Oral: 10 to 13 mg/kg/dose every 6 to 8 hours for a minimum of 4 to 6 weeks (maximum: 40 mg/kg/day) (IDSA [Liu 2011])

Pharyngitis, group A streptococci (IDSA recommendations): Oral:

Acute treatment in penicillin-allergic patients: 21 mg/kg/day divided every 8 hours (maximum: 300 mg per dose) for 10 days (IDSA [Shulman 2012])

Chronic carrier treatment: 20 to 30 mg/kg/day divided every 8 hours (maximum: 300 mg per dose) for 10 days (IDSA [Shulman 2012])

Pneumocystis pneumonia (PCP) in HIV-infected patients (alternative to preferred therapy) (off-label use): Adolescents: Refer to adult dosing.

Pneumonia:

Community-acquired pneumonia (CAP) (IDSA/PIDS [Bradley 2011]): Infants >3 months and Children: **Note:** In children ≥5 years, a macrolide antibiotic should be added if atypical pneumonia cannot be ruled out.

Group A *Streptococcus:*

Moderate to severe infection (alternative to ampicillin/penicillin): IV: 40 mg/kg/day divided every 6 to 8 hours

Mild infection, step-down therapy (alternative to amoxicillin/penicillin): Oral: 40 mg/kg/day divided every 8 hours

Presumed bacterial (in addition to recommended antibiotic therapy), *S. pneumoniae* moderate to severe (MICs to penicillin ≤2.0 mcg/mL) (alternative to ampicillin/penicillin): IV: 40 mg/kg/day divided every 6 to 8 hours

S. pneumoniae:
Moderate to severe infection (MICs to penicillin ≥4.0 mcg/mL) (alternative to ceftriaxone): IV: 40 mg/kg/day divided every 6 to 8 hours
Mild infection, step-down therapy (MICs to penicillin ≥4.0 mcg/mL) (alternative to levofloxacin or linezolid): Oral: 30 to 40 mg/kg/day divided every 8 hours
S. aureus (methicillin-susceptible):
Moderate to severe infection (alternative to cefazolin or oxacillin): IV: 40 mg/kg/day divided every 6 to 8 hours
Mild infection, step-down therapy (alternative to cephalexin): Oral: 30 to 40 mg/kg/day divided every 6 to 8 hours
S. aureus (methicillin-resistant/clindamycin-susceptible):
Moderate to severe infection (preferred): IV: 40 mg/kg/day divided every 6 to 8 hours; recommended duration: 7 to 21 days (IDSA [Liu 2011])
Mild infection, step-down therapy (preferred): Oral: 30 to 40 mg/kg/day divided every 6 to 8 hours; recommended duration: 7 to 21 days (IDSA [Liu 2011])

Health care-associated pneumonia (HAP) (methicillin-resistant/clindamycin-susceptible): Children: Oral, IV: 30 to 40 mg/kg/day divided every 6 to 8 hours for 7 to 21 days (IDSA [Liu 2011])

Prophylaxis against infective endocarditis (off-label use):
Oral: 20 mg/kg 30 to 60 minutes before procedure (Wilson 2007)
IM, IV: 20 mg/kg 30 to 60 minutes before procedure. Intramuscular injections should be avoided in patients who are receiving anticoagulant therapy. In these circumstances, orally administered regimens should be given whenever possible. Intravenously administered antibiotics should be used for patients who are unable to tolerate or absorb oral medications (Wilson 2007).
Note: American Heart Association (AHA) guidelines now recommend prophylaxis only in patients undergoing invasive procedures and in whom underlying cardiac conditions may predispose to a higher risk of adverse outcomes should infection occur. As of April 2007, routine prophylaxis for GI/GU procedures is no longer recommended by the AHA.

Septic arthritis due to MRSA (off-label use): IV, Oral: 10 to 13 mg/kg/dose every 6 to 8 hours for minimum of 3 to 4 weeks (maximum: 40 mg/kg/day) (IDSA [Liu 2011])

Skin and soft tissue infections due to MSSA:
Oral: 25 to 30 mg/kg/day divided every 8 hours for 7 to 14 days (IDSA [Stevens 2014])
IV: 25 to 40 mg/kg/day divided every 8 hours for 7 to 14 days (IDSA [Stevens 2014])

Skin and soft tissue infections due to MRSA (off-label use):
Oral: 30 to 40 mg/kg/day divided every 8 hours for 7 to 14 days (IDSA [Stevens 2014])
IV: 25 to 40 mg/kg/day divided every 8 hours for 7 to 14 days (IDSA [Stevens 2014])
Complicated infections: Oral, IV: 10 to 13 mg/kg/dose every 6 to 8 hours for 7 to 14 days (maximum: 40 mg/kg/day) (IDSA [Liu 2011])
Cellulitis: Oral: 10 to 13 mg/kg/dose every 6 to 8 hours for 5 to 10 days (maximum: 40 mg/kg/day) (IDSA [Liu 2011])

Skin and soft tissue necrotizing infections (off-label use): IV: 10 to 13 mg/kg/dose every 8 hours, in combination with cefotaxime for empiric therapy of polymicrobial infections **or** in combination with penicillin IV for the treatment of group A streptococcal or *Clostridium* species necrotizing infections. May give as monotherapy for MSSA. Continue until further debridement is not necessary, patient has clinically improved, and patient is afebrile for 48 to 72 hours (IDSA [Stevens 2014])

Streptococcal skin infections: IV: 10 to 13 mg/kg/dose every 8 hours (IDSA [Stevens 2014])

Surgical (perioperative) prophylaxis (off-label use): IV: 10 mg/kg within 60 minutes prior to surgical incision. Doses may be repeated in 6 hours if procedure is lengthy (maximum single dose: 900 mg) (Bratzler 2013).

***Toxoplasma gondii* encephalitis in HIV-exposed/-positive patients (off-label use):**
Children:
Treatment: IV, Oral: 5 to 7.5 mg/kg/dose (maximum dose: 600 mg) every 6 hours (plus pyrimethamine and leucovorin) (HHS [pediatric] 2016).
Secondary prevention: Oral: 7 to 10 mg/kg/dose (maximum dose: 600 mg) every 8 hours (plus pyrimethamine and leucovorin) (HHS [pediatric] 2016).
Adolescents: Refer to adult dosing.

Renal Impairment Mild to severe impairment: No dosage adjustment necessary
End-stage renal disease (ESRD) on hemodialysis or peritoneal dialysis: Not removed from serum (eg, poorly dialyzed); no supplemental dose or dosage adjustment necessary (Aronoff 2007).
Continuous renal replacement therapy (CRRT) (eg, CVVH, CVVHD, CVVHDF): No supplemental dose or dosage adjustment necessary (Heintz 2009).

Hepatic Impairment Mild impairment: There are no dosage adjustments provided in the manufacturer's labeling.
Moderate to severe impairment: There are no dosage adjustments provided in the manufacturer's labeling; in studies of patients with moderate or severe liver disease, half-life is prolonged, however, when administered on an every 8 hour schedule, accumulation should rarely occur. In severe liver disease, use caution and monitor liver enzymes periodically during therapy.

Mechanism of Action Reversibly binds to 50S ribosomal subunits preventing peptide bond formation thus inhibiting bacterial protein synthesis; bacteriostatic or bactericidal depending on drug concentration, infection site, and organism

Contraindications
Hypersensitivity to clindamycin, lincomycin, or any component of the formulation.
Canadian labeling: Additional contraindications (not in US labeling): Oral clindamycin: Infants <30 days of age.

Warnings/Precautions Dosage adjustment may be necessary in patients with severe hepatic dysfunction. **[US Boxed Warning]: Can cause severe and possibly fatal colitis. Should be reserved for serious infections where less toxic antimicrobial agents are inappropriate. It should not be used in patients with nonbacterial infections such as most upper respiratory tract infections. Hypertoxin-producing strains of *C. difficile* cause increased morbidity and mortality, as these infections can be refractory to antimicrobial therapy and may require colectomy. *C. difficile* -associated diarrhea (CDAD) must be considered in all patients who present with**

diarrhea following antibiotic use. CDAD has been observed >2 months postantibiotic treatment. If CDAD is suspected or confirmed, ongoing antibiotic use not directed against *C. difficile* may need to be discontinued. Institute appropriate fluid and electrolyte management, protein supplementation, antibiotic treatment of C. difficile, and surgical evaluation as clinically indicated. Use with caution in patients with a history of gastrointestinal disease, particularly colitis. Use may result in overgrowth of nonsusceptible organisms, particularly yeast. Should superinfection occur, appropriate measures should be taken as indicated by the clinical situation. Severe hypersensitivity reactions, including severe skin reactions (eg, drug reaction with eosinophilia and systemic symptoms [DRESS], Stevens-Johnson syndrome [SJS], and toxic epidermal necrolysis [TEN]), some fatal, and anaphylactic reactions, including anaphylactic shock, have been reported. Permanently discontinue treatment and institute appropriate therapy if these reactions occur. Some products may contain tartrazine (FD&C yellow no. 5), which may cause allergic reactions in certain individuals. Allergy is frequently seen in patients who also have an aspirin hypersensitivity. Use caution in atopic patients. A subgroup of older patients with associated severe illness may tolerate diarrhea less well. Monitor carefully for changes in bowel frequency. Not appropriate for use in the treatment of meningitis due to inadequate penetration into the CSF. Do not inject IV undiluted as a bolus. Product should be diluted in compatible fluid and infused over 10 to 60 minutes. Potentially significant interactions may exist, requiring dose or frequency adjustment, additional monitoring, and/or selection of alternative therapy.

Benzyl alcohol and derivatives: Some dosage forms may contain benzyl alcohol; large amounts of benzyl alcohol (≥99 mg/kg/day) have been associated with a potentially fatal toxicity ("gasping syndrome") in neonates; the "gasping syndrome" consists of metabolic acidosis, respiratory distress, gasping respirations, CNS dysfunction (including convulsions, intracranial hemorrhage), hypotension and cardiovascular collapse (AAP ["Inactive" 1997]; CDC 1982); some data suggests that benzoate displaces bilirubin from protein binding sites (Ahlfors 2001); avoid or use dosage forms containing benzyl alcohol with caution in neonates. See manufacturer's labeling.

Drug Interactions

Metabolism/Transport Effects Substrate of CYP3A4 (minor); **Note:** Assignment of Major/Minor substrate status based on clinically relevant drug interaction potential

Avoid Concomitant Use

Avoid concomitant use of Clindamycin (Systemic) with any of the following: BCG (Intravesical); Cholera Vaccine; Erythromycin (Systemic); Mecamylamine

Increased Effect/Toxicity

Clindamycin (Systemic) may increase the levels/effects of: Mecamylamine; Neuromuscular-Blocking Agents

Decreased Effect

Clindamycin (Systemic) may decrease the levels/effects of: BCG (Intravesical); BCG Vaccine (Immunization); Cholera Vaccine; Erythromycin (Systemic); Lactobacillus and Estriol; Sodium Picosulfate; Typhoid Vaccine

The levels/effects of Clindamycin (Systemic) may be decreased by: CYP3A4 Inducers (Strong); Kaolin

Pharmacodynamics/Kinetics

Half-life Elimination Neonates: Premature: 8.7 hours; Full-term: 3.6 hours; Infants 1 month to 1 year: 3 hours; Children: ~2.5 hours; Adults: 3 hours; Elderly (oral) ~4 hours (range: 3.4 to 5.1 hours)

Time to Peak Serum: Oral: Within 60 minutes; IM: 1 to 3 hours

Pregnancy Risk Factor B

Pregnancy Considerations Adverse events were not observed in animal reproduction studies. Clindamycin crosses the placenta and can be detected in the cord blood and fetal tissue (Philipson 1973; Weinstein 1976). Clindamycin injection contains benzyl alcohol which may also cross the placenta. Clindamycin pharmacokinetics are not affected by pregnancy (Philipson 1976; Weinstein 1976). Clindamycin is recommended for use in pregnant women for the prophylaxis of group B streptococcal disease in newborns (alternative therapy) (ACOG 485, 2011); prophylaxis and treatment of *Toxoplasma gondii* encephalitis (alternative therapy), or *Pneumocystis pneumonia* (PCP) (alternative therapy) (HHS [OI adult 2015]); bacterial vaginosis (CDC [Workowski 2015]); anthrax (Meaney-Delman 2014); or malaria (CDC 2013). Clindamycin is also one of the antibiotics recommended for prophylactic use prior to cesarean delivery and may be used in certain situations prior to vaginal delivery in women at high risk for endocarditis (ACOG 120, 2011).

Breastfeeding Considerations Clindamycin is excreted in breast milk.

The relative infant dose (RID) of clindamycin is 1.2% to 4.7% when calculated using the highest verifiable breast milk concentration located and compared to an infant therapeutic dose of 10 to 40 mg/kg/day. In general, breastfeeding is considered acceptable when the RID is <10%; when an RID is >25% breastfeeding should generally be avoided (Anderson 2016; Ito 2000). Using the highest verifiable milk concentration (3.1 mcg/mL), the estimated daily infant dose via breast milk is 0.465 mg/kg/day. This milk concentration was obtained following maternal administration of oral clindamycin 150 mg three times daily for at least 1 week (Stéen 1982). The manufacturer reports that clindamycin breast milk concentrations range from 0.7 to 3.8 mcg/mL (maternal dose, route, and duration not specified).

One case of bloody stools in an infant occurred after a mother received clindamycin while breastfeeding; however, a causal relationship was not confirmed (Mann 1980). In general, antibiotics that are present in breast milk may cause nondose-related modification of bowel flora. Due to the potential for serious adverse reactions in the breastfeeding infant, breastfeeding is not recommended by the manufacturer. Additional guidelines recommend to avoid clindamycin in breastfeeding women if possible; monitor breastfeeding infants for GI disturbances, diarrhea, and bloody stools if maternal treatment is required (WHO 2002).

Dosage Forms

Capsule, Oral:

Cleocin: 75 mg, 150 mg, 300 mg

Generic: 75 mg, 150 mg, 300 mg

Kit, Injection:

CLIN Single Use: 300 mg/2 mL

Solution, Injection:

Cleocin Phosphate: 300 mg/2 mL (2 mL); 600 mg/4 mL (4 mL); 900 mg/6 mL (6 mL); 9 g/60 mL (60 mL) ▶

Generic: 300 mg/2 mL (2 mL); 600 mg/4 mL (4 mL); 900 mg/6 mL (6 mL); 9000 mg/60 mL (60 mL); 9 g/60 mL (60 mL)

Solution, Intravenous:

Cleocin in D5W: 300 mg/50 mL (50 mL); 600 mg/50 mL (50 mL); 900 mg/50 mL (50 mL)

Cleocin Phosphate: 300 mg/2 mL (2 mL); 600 mg/4 mL (4 mL); 900 mg/6 mL (6 mL)

Generic: 300 mg/50 mL (50 mL); 600 mg/50 mL (50 mL); 900 mg/50 mL (50 mL); 150 mg/mL (2 mL); 900 mg/6 mL (6 mL)

Solution Reconstituted, Oral:

Cleocin: 75 mg/5 mL (100 mL)

Generic: 75 mg/5 mL (100 mL)

Dental Comment About 1% of clindamycin users develop pseudomembranous colitis. Symptoms may occur 2 to 9 days after initiation of therapy; however, it has never occurred with the 1-dose regimen of clindamycin used to prevent bacterial endocarditis.

Clindamycin (Topical) (klin da MYE sin)

Brand Names: US Cleocin; Cleocin-T; Clindacin ETZ; Clindacin Pac; Clindacin-P; Clindagel; ClindaMax; Clindesse; Evoclin

Brand Names: Canada Clinda-T; Clindasol; Clindets; Dalacin T; Dalacin Vaginal; Taro-Clindamycin

Pharmacologic Category Antibiotic, Lincosamide; Topical Skin Product, Acne

Use Treatment of bacterial vaginosis (vaginal cream, vaginal suppository); topically in treatment of severe acne

Local Anesthetic/Vasoconstrictor Precautions No information available to require special precautions

Effects on Dental Treatment No significant effects or complications reported

Effects on Bleeding No information available to require special precautions

Adverse Reactions

Topical: >10%: Dermatologic: Xeroderma (18% to 23%; gel, lotion, solution), oily skin (gel, lotion: 10% to 18%; solution: 1%), erythema (7% to 16%; gel, lotion, solution), burning sensation of skin (10% to 11%; gel, lotion, solution), exfoliation of skin (7% to 11%; lotion, solution), pruritus (7% to 11%; gel, lotion, solution)

Vaginal:

>10%: Genitourinary: Vaginal moniliasis (≤13%)

1% to 10%:

Dermatologic: Pruritus (≤1% nonapplication site; <1% application site)

Genitourinary: Vulvovaginal disease (3% to 9%), vulvovaginitis (≤7%), vaginal pain (2%), trichomonal vaginitis (≤1%)

Infection: Fungal infection (≤1%)

<1%, postmarketing, and/or case reports (all routes): Abdominal cramps, abdominal pain, application site pain, bacterial infection, bloody diarrhea, colitis, constipation, contact dermatitis, diarrhea (hemorrhagic or severe), dizziness, dysgeusia, dyspepsia, dysuria, edema, endometriosis, epistaxis, erythema, eye pain, fever, flank pain, flatulence, folliculitis, folliculitis (gram-negative infection), gastrointestinal disease, gastrointestinal distress, halitosis, headache, hypersensitivity reaction, hyperthyroidism, maculopapular rash, menstrual disease, nausea, pain, pseudomembranous colitis, pyelonephritis, severe colitis, skin rash, upper respiratory infection, urinary tract infection, urticaria, uterine hemorrhage, vaginal discharge, vertigo, vomiting, vulvovaginal pruritus

General Dosage Range

Intravaginal: *Adults:* Insert 1 suppository or applicatorful once daily **or** 1 applicatorful as a single dose (Clindesse)

Topical: *Children ≥12 years, Adolescents, and Adults:* Apply once or twice daily

Mechanism of Action Reversibly binds to 50S ribosomal subunits preventing peptide bond formation thus inhibiting bacterial protein synthesis; bacteriostatic or bactericidal depending on drug concentration, infection site, and organism

Pharmacodynamics/Kinetics

Half-life Elimination Vaginal cream: 1.5-2.6 hours following repeated dosing; Vaginal suppository: 11 hours (range: 4-35 hours, limited by absorption rate)

Time to Peak Vaginal cream: ~10-14 hours (range: 4-24 hours); Vaginal suppository: ~5 hours (range: 1-10 hours)

Pregnancy Risk Factor B

Pregnancy Considerations Adverse effects were not observed in animal reproduction studies. Clindamycin has been shown to cross the placenta following oral and parenteral dosing (Philipson 1973; Weinstein 1976). The amount of clindamycin available systemically is less following topical and vaginal application than with IV or oral administration.

Various clindamycin vaginal products are available for the treatment of bacterial vaginosis. Recommendations for use in pregnant woman vary by product labeling. Current guidelines note that the same oral or vaginal regimens used in nonpregnant women may be used during pregnancy, including oral or vaginal clindamycin (CDC [Workowski 2015]).

If treatment for acne is needed during pregnancy, topical clindamycin may be considered if an antibiotic is needed. To decrease systemic exposure, pregnant women should avoid application to inflamed skin for long periods of time, or to large body surface areas (Kong 2013).

Clindamycin and Benzoyl Peroxide
(klin da MYE sin & BEN zoe il peer OKS ide)

Related Information

Clindamycin (Topical) *on page 388*

Brand Names: US Acanya; BenzaClin; Duac; Neuac; Onexton

Brand Names: Canada BenzaClin; Clindoxyl

Pharmacologic Category Acne Products; Topical Skin Product; Topical Skin Product, Acne

Use Acne: Topical treatment of acne vulgaris

Local Anesthetic/Vasoconstrictor Precautions No information available to require special precautions

Effects on Dental Treatment No significant effects or complications reported

Effects on Bleeding No information available to require special precautions

Adverse Reactions Also see individual agents.

>10%:

Dermatologic: Application site scaling (≤21%), local dryness (≤16%)

Local: Application site erythema (<31%), local desquamation (2% to 19%), application site itching (≤17%)

1% to 10%:

Dermatologic: Stinging of the skin (application site: ≤7%), sunburn (local; 1%)

Local: Application site burning (≤10%), application site reaction (3%)

<1%, postmarketing, and/or case reports: Anaphylaxis, application site irritation, application site pain, contact dermatitis, hypersensitivity reaction, local discoloration, local skin exfoliation, skin rash, urticaria

General Dosage Range Topical: *Children ≥12 years, Adolescents, and Adults:* Apply once or twice daily to affected area.

Mechanism of Action Clindamycin and benzoyl peroxide have activity against *Propionibacterium acnes in vitro*. This organism has been associated with acne vulgaris. Benzoyl peroxide releases free-radical oxygen which oxidizes bacterial proteins in the sebaceous follicles decreasing the number of anaerobic bacteria and decreasing irritating-type free fatty acids. Clindamycin reversibly binds to 50S ribosomal subunits preventing peptide bond formation thus inhibiting bacterial protein synthesis; it is bacteriostatic or bactericidal depending on drug concentration, infection site, and organism.

Pregnancy Risk Factor C

Pregnancy Considerations Animal reproduction studies have not been conducted with this combination. Refer to individual monographs.

CloBAZam (KLOE ba zam)

Brand Names: US Onfi

Brand Names: Canada Apo-Clobazam; Clobazam-10; Dom-Clobazam; Frisium; Novo-Clobazam; PMS-Clobazam

Pharmacologic Category Anticonvulsant, Benzodiazepine; Benzodiazepine

Use

US labeling: **Lennox-Gastaut syndrome:** Adjunctive treatment of seizures associated with Lennox-Gastaut syndrome in patients ≥2 years

Canadian labeling: **Epilepsy:** Adjunctive treatment of epilepsy

Local Anesthetic/Vasoconstrictor Precautions No information available to require special precautions

Effects on Dental Treatment Key adverse event(s) related to dental treatment: Xerostomia (normal salivary flow resumes upon discontinuation). Paradoxical reactions (including excitation, agitation, hallucinations, and psychosis) are known to occur with benzodiazepines.

Effects on Bleeding No information available to require special precautions

Adverse Reactions

>10%:

Central nervous system: Drowsiness (16% to 25%), lethargy (10% to 15%), aggressive behavior (8% to 14%), irritability (3% to 11%)

Gastrointestinal: Sialorrhea (13% to 14%)

Respiratory: Upper respiratory tract infection (13% to 14%)

Miscellaneous: Fever (10% to 17%)

1% to 10%:

Central nervous system: Ataxia (10%), sedation (9%), insomnia (5% to 7%), psychomotor agitation (5%), fatigue (3% to 5%), dysarthria (2% to 5%), dysarthria (2% to 5%)

Gastrointestinal: Constipation (2% to 10%), vomiting (7% to 9%), decreased appetite (7%), increased appetite (2% to 5%), dysphagia (5%)

Genitourinary: Urinary tract infection (2% to 5%)

Respiratory: Cough (3% to 7%), pneumonia (3% to 7%), bronchitis (2% to 5%)

Postmarketing and/or case reports: Abdominal distention, agitation, anemia, angioedema, anxiety, apathy, aspiration, behavioral changes, blurred vision, confusion, delirium, delusions, depression, diplopia, eosinophilia, facial edema, hallucination, hypothermia, increased liver enzymes, leukopenia, lip edema, mood changes, muscle spasm, respiratory depression, skin rash, Stevens-Johnson syndrome, suicidal ideation, suicidal tendencies, thrombocytopenia, toxic epidermal necrolysis, urinary retention, urticaria, withdrawal syndrome

General Dosage Range Dosage adjustment recommended in patients with hepatic impairment or CYP2C19 poor metabolizers.

Oral: *Children ≥2 years, Adolescents, and Adults:* Initial: 5 to 10 mg/day; Maintenance: Up to 40 mg/day

Mechanism of Action Clobazam is a 1,5 benzodiazepine which binds to stereospecific benzodiazepine receptors on the postsynaptic GABA neuron at several sites within the central nervous system, including the limbic system, reticular formation. Enhancement of the inhibitory effect of GABA on neuronal excitability results by increased neuronal membrane permeability to chloride ions. This shift in chloride ions results in hyperpolarization (a less excitable state) and stabilization. Benzodiazepine receptors and effects appear to be linked to the GABA-A receptors. Benzodiazepines do not bind to GABA B receptors (Vinkers 2012).

Pharmacodynamics/Kinetics

Onset of Action Maximum effect: 5 to 9 days

Half-life Elimination Children: Clobazam: 16 hours (Ng 2007); Adults: Clobazam: 36 to 42 hours; N-desmethyl (active): 71 to 82 hours

Time to Peak Tablet: 0.5 to 4 hours; Oral suspension: 0.5 to 2 hours

Pregnancy Risk Factor C

Pregnancy Considerations Adverse events were observed in animal reproduction studies. Clobazam crosses the placenta. An increased risk of fetal malformations may be associated with first trimester exposure. Exposure to benzodiazepines immediately prior to or during birth may result in hypothermia, hypotonia, respiratory depression, and difficulty feeding in the neonate; neonates exposed to benzodiazepines late in pregnancy may develop dependence and withdrawal. The incidence of premature birth and low birth weights may be increased following maternal use of benzodiazepines; hypoglycemia and respiratory problems in the neonate may occur following exposure late in pregnancy. Neonatal withdrawal symptoms may occur within days to weeks after birth and "floppy infant syndrome" (which also includes withdrawal symptoms) has been reported with some benzodiazepines (Bergman 1992; Iqbal 2002; Wikner 2007). A combination of factors influences the potential teratogenicity of anticonvulsant therapy. When treating women with epilepsy, monotherapy with the lowest effective dose and avoidance medications known to have a high incidence of teratogenic effects is recommended (Harden 2009; Wlodarczyk 2012).

Patients exposed to clobazam during pregnancy are encouraged to enroll themselves into the North American Antiepileptic Drug (NAAED) Pregnancy Registry by calling 1-888-233-2334. Additional information is available at www.aedpregnancyregistry.org.

Controlled Substance C-IV

Clobetasol (kloe BAY ta sol)

Related Information

Ulcerative, Erosive, and Painful Oral Mucosal Disorders *on page 1853*

Related Sample Prescriptions

Ulcerative and Erosive Disorders - Sample Prescriptions *on page 43*

Brand Names: US Clobetasol Propionate E; Clobex; Clobex Spray; Clodan; Cormax Scalp Application; Olux; Olux-E; Temovate; Temovate E

Brand Names: Canada Clobex; Dermovate; Mylan-Clobetasol; Novo-Clobetasol; Olux-E; PMS-Clobetasol; ratio-Clobetasol; Taro-Clobetasol

Generic Availability (US) May be product dependent

Pharmacologic Category Corticosteroid, Topical

Dental Use Short-term relief of oral mucosal inflammation

Use **Steroid-responsive dermatoses:** Short-term relief of inflammation and pruritic manifestations of moderate to severe corticosteroid-responsive dermatoses

Local Anesthetic/Vasoconstrictor Precautions No information available to require special precautions

Effects on Dental Treatment No significant effects or complications reported

Effects on Bleeding No information available to require special precautions

Adverse Reactions Frequency not always defined; may depend upon formulation used, length of application, surface area covered, and the use of occlusive dressings.

Central nervous system: Localized burning (5% to 40%), numbness of fingers (<2%), intracranial hypertension (children; systemic effect reported with topical corticosteroids)

Dermatologic: Stinging of skin (<2% to 5%), pruritus (<2% to 3%), pruritus hiemalis (2%), xeroderma (≤2%), erythema (<2%), folliculitis (<2%), skin atrophy (<2%), skin fissure (<2%), telangiectasia (<2%), atrophic striae (children)

Endocrine & metabolic: Adrenal suppression, Cushing's syndrome, glycosuria, growth suppression, HPA-axis suppression, hyperglycemia

Local: Local irritation (1%), local pain (1%)

Respiratory: Upper respiratory tract infection (8%), nasopharyngitis (5%), streptococcal pharyngitis (1%)

<1%, postmarketing, and/or case reports: Alopecia, exfoliation of skin, skin rash, urticaria

Dental Usual Dosage Oral mucosal inflammation: Children ≥12 years and Adults: Cream: Apply twice daily for up to 2 weeks (maximum dose: 50 g/week); discontinue application when control is achieved; if no improvement is seen, reassessment of diagnosis may be necessary

Dosing

Adult & Geriatric Note: Discontinue when control achieved; if improvement not seen within 2 weeks, reassessment of diagnosis may be necessary.

Oral mucosal inflammation (off-label use): Topical: *Cream:* Apply twice daily for up to 2 weeks (maximum dose: 50 g/week); discontinue application when control is achieved; if no improvement is seen, reassessment of diagnosis may be necessary

Steroid-responsive dermatoses: Topical: *Cream, emollient cream, foam, gel, lotion, ointment, solution:* Apply twice daily for up to 2 weeks (maximum dose: 50 g/week or 50 mL/week)

Mild to moderate plaque-type psoriasis of non-scalp areas: Topical: *Foam:* Apply twice daily for up to 2 weeks (maximum dose: 50 g/week)

Moderate to severe plaque-type psoriasis: Topical: *Emollient cream, lotion:* Apply twice daily for up to 2 weeks; can be used for up to 4 weeks when application is <10% of body surface area (maximum dose: 50 g/week or 50 mL/week). Treatment with lotion beyond 2 weeks should be limited to localized lesions (<10% body surface area) which have not improved sufficiently.

Spray: Apply by spraying directly onto affected area twice daily and gently rub into skin. Limit treatment to 4 consecutive weeks; treatment beyond 2 weeks should be limited to localized lesions which have not improved sufficiently. Maximum total dose: 50 g/week or 59 mL/week. Do not use more than 26 sprays per application or 52 sprays per day.

Scalp psoriasis, moderate to severe: Topical:

Foam: Apply twice daily for up to 2 weeks (maximum dose: 50 g/week)

Shampoo: Apply thin film to dry scalp once daily (maximum dose: 50 g/week or 50 mL/week); leave in place for 15 minutes, then add water, lather; rinse thoroughly. Limit treatment to 4 consecutive weeks.

Pediatric Note: Discontinue when control achieved; if improvement not seen within 2 weeks, reassessment of diagnosis may be necessary. Use in children <12 years is not recommended.

Mild to moderate plaque-type psoriasis of non-scalp areas: Topical: *Foam:* Children ≥12 years and Adolescents: Refer to adult dosing.

Moderate to severe plaque-type psoriasis: Topical:

Emollient cream: Adolescents ≥16 years: Refer to adult dosing.

Lotion, spray: Adolescents ≥18 years: Refer to adult dosing.

Scalp psoriasis, moderate to severe: Topical:

Foam: Children ≥12 years and Adolescents: Refer to adult dosing.

Shampoo: Adolescents ≥18 years: Refer to adult dosing.

Steroid-responsive dermatoses: Topical:

Cream, emollient cream, foam, gel, ointment, solution: Children ≥12 years and Adolescents: Refer to adult dosing.

Lotion: Adolescents ≥18 years: Refer to adult dosing.

Oral mucosal inflammation (off-label use): Topical: *Cream:* Children ≥12 years and Adolescents: Refer to adult dosing.

Renal Impairment There are no dosage adjustments provided in the manufacturer's labeling.

Hepatic Impairment There are no dosage adjustments provided in the manufacturer's labeling.

Mechanism of Action Topical corticosteroids have anti-inflammatory, antipruritic, and vasoconstrictive properties. May depress the formation, release, and activity of endogenous chemical mediators of inflammation (kinins, histamine, liposomal enzymes, prostaglandins) through the induction of phospholipase A_2 inhibitory proteins (lipocortins) and sequential inhibition of the release of arachidonic acid. Clobetasol has very high range potency.

Contraindications Hypersensitivity to clobetasol, other corticosteroids, or any component of the formulation; primary infections of the scalp (scalp solution only)

Warnings/Precautions Systemic absorption of topical corticosteroids may cause hypothalamic-pituitary-adrenal (HPA) axis suppression particularly in younger children. HPA axis suppression may lead to adrenal crisis.

Allergic contact dermatitis may occur; it is usually diagnosed by failure to heal rather than clinical exacerbation. Prolonged treatment with corticosteroids has been associated with the development of Kaposi sarcoma (case reports); if noted, discontinuation of therapy should be considered. Local effects may occur, including folliculitis, acneiform eruptions, hypopigmentation, perioral dermatitis, allergic contact dermatitis, secondary infection, striae, miliaria, skin atrophy and telangiectasia; may be irreversible. Adverse systemic effects including Cushing syndrome, hyperglycemia, glycosuria, and HPA suppression may occur when used on large surface areas, denuded skin, or with an occlusive dressing. Use in children <12 years of age is not recommended. Children may absorb proportionally larger amounts after topical application and may be more prone to systemic effects. Prolonged use may affect growth velocity; growth should be routinely monitored in pediatric patients. Clobex lotion, Clobex shampoo, Clobex spray, and Clodan shampoo are not recommended for use in pediatric patients ≤17 years.

Do not use on the face, axillae, or groin or for the treatment of rosacea or perioral dermatitis. Emollient cream contains imidurea; may cause allergic sensitization or irritation upon skin contact with the skin. Foam and spray are flammable; do not use near open flame.

Drug Interactions

Metabolism/Transport Effects None known.

Avoid Concomitant Use

Avoid concomitant use of Clobetasol with any of the following: Aldesleukin

Increased Effect/Toxicity

Clobetasol may increase the levels/effects of: Ceritinib; Deferasirox

Decreased Effect

Clobetasol may decrease the levels/effects of: Aldesleukin; Corticorelin; Hyaluronidase

Pregnancy Risk Factor C

Pregnancy Considerations Adverse events have been observed in animal reproduction studies. Extensive use in pregnant women is not recommended.

Breastfeeding Considerations It is not known if topical application will result in detectable quantities in breast milk. The manufacturer recommends that caution be exercised when administering clobetasol to nursing women.

Dosage Forms

Cream, External:
- Clobetasol Propionate E: 0.05% (15 g, 30 g, 60 g)
- Temovate: 0.05% (30 g, 60 g)
- Temovate E: 0.05% (60 g)
- Generic: 0.05% (15 g, 30 g, 45 g, 60 g)

Foam, External:
- Olux: 0.05% (50 g, 100 g)
- Olux-E: 0.05% (50 g, 100 g)
- Generic: 0.05% (50 g, 100 g)

Gel, External:
- Temovate: 0.05% (60 g)
- Generic: 0.05% (15 g, 30 g, 60 g)

Kit, External:
- Clodan: 0.05%

Liquid, External:
- Clobex Spray: 0.05% (59 mL, 125 mL)
- Generic: 0.05% (59 mL, 125 mL)

Lotion, External:
- Clobex: 0.05% (59 mL, 118 mL)
- Generic: 0.05% (59 mL, 118 mL)

Ointment, External:
- Temovate: 0.05% (15 g, 30 g)
- Generic: 0.05% (15 g, 30 g, 45 g, 60 g)

Shampoo, External:
- Clobex: 0.05% (118 mL)
- Clodan: 0.05% (118 mL)
- Generic: 0.05% (118 mL)

Solution, External:
- Cormax Scalp Application: 0.05% (50 mL)
- Temovate: 0.05% (50 mL)
- Generic: 0.05% (25 mL, 50 mL)

Clodronate (KLOE droh nate)

Related Information

Osteonecrosis of the Jaw *on page 1796*

Brand Names: Canada Bonefos; Clasteon

Pharmacologic Category Bisphosphonate Derivative

Use Note: Not approved in the US

Hypercalcemia of malignancy: Management of hypercalcemia of malignancy

Osteolytic bone metastases: Management of osteolysis due to bone metastases of malignancy

Local Anesthetic/Vasoconstrictor Precautions No information available to require special precautions

Effects on Dental Treatment Osteonecrosis of the jaw (ONJ), generally associated with local infection and/or tooth extraction and often with delayed healing, has been reported in patients taking bisphosphonates. Symptoms included nonhealing extraction socket or an exposed jawbone. Most reported cases of bisphosphonate-associated osteonecrosis have been in cancer patients treated with intravenous bisphosphonates. However, some have occurred in patients with postmenopausal osteoporosis taking oral bisphosphonates. Dental surgery, particularly tooth extraction, may increase the risk for ONJ. Patients who develop ONJ while on bisphosphonate therapy should receive care by an oral surgeon. See Dental Comment.

Effects on Bleeding No information available to require special precautions

Adverse Reactions

>10%: Hepatic: Increased serum transaminases (postmenopausal osteopenic women: 18%; >2 x ULN: 2%)

1% to 10%:
- Endocrine & metabolic: Hypocalcemia (2% to 3%)
- Gastrointestinal: Gastrointestinal disease (≤10%; includes stomach pain), vomiting (intravenous: 4%), nausea (1% to 3%), diarrhea (≤2%), anorexia (oral: 1%)
- Renal: Increased serum creatinine (oral: 1%)

<1%, postmarketing, and/or case reports: Arthralgia (severe), bronchospasm (patients with aspirin-sensitive asthma), conjunctivitis, dysphagia, erythematous rash, femur fracture (atypical subtrochanteric and diaphyseal), hypersensitivity reactions (angioedema, dyspnea [in patients with aspirin-sensitive asthma], pruritus, respiratory disorder, skin rash, urticaria), hypophosphatemia (transient), increased liver enzymes, increased parathyroid hormone, leukemia (rare), maculopapular rash, mouth irritation, myalgia (severe), myelodysplasia (rare), oliguria, oropharyngeal ulcer, ostealgia (severe), osteonecrosis (jaw or external auditory canal), proteinuria, renal failure, renal insufficiency, uveitis

General Dosage Range Dosage adjustment recommended in patients with renal impairment

IV: *Adults:* 1,500 mg as single dose (Clasteon) **or** 300 mg/day (Clasteon, Bonefos)

Oral: *Adults:* 1,600 to 2,400 mg/day in 1 to 2 divided doses (maximum: 3,200 mg/day)

Mechanism of Action A bisphosphonate that lowers serum calcium by inhibition of bone resorption via actions on osteoclasts or on osteoclast precursors; may also have indirect inhibitory effects through osteoblastic cells, which control recruitment and activity of osteoclasts.

Pharmacodynamics/Kinetics

Onset of Action Calcium-lowering effects: IV: Within 48 hours

Duration of Action Calcium-lowering effects: 5 days to 3 weeks following discontinuation

Half-life Elimination Terminal: Oral: ~6 hours; IV: 13 hours (serum); prolonged in bone tissue

Time to Peak Plasma: Oral: 30 minutes

Pregnancy Considerations Use is contraindicated during pregnancy. Adverse events have been observed in animal reproduction studies. It is not known if bisphosphonates cross the placenta, but fetal exposure is expected (Djokanovic 2008; Stathopoulos 2011). Available data have not shown that exposure to bisphosphonates during pregnancy significantly increases the risk of adverse fetal events (Djokanovic 2008; Levy 2009; Stathopoulos 2011). However until additional data is available, most sources recommend discontinuing bisphosphonate therapy in women of reproductive potential as early as possible prior to a planned pregnancy; use in premenopausal women should be reserved for special circumstances when rapid bone loss is occurring (Bhalla 2010; Pereira 2012; Stathopoulos 2011). Because hypocalcemia has been described following *in utero* bisphosphonate exposure, exposed infants should be monitored for hypocalcemia after birth (Djokanovic 2008; Stathopoulos 2011).

Product Availability Not available in the US

Dental Comment A review of 2,408 published cases of bisphosphonate-associated osteonecrosis of the jaw bone (BP-associated ONJ) was done by Filleul 2010. BP therapy was associated with 89% of the cases to treat malignancies and 11% of the cases to treat nonmalignant conditions. Information on the specific bisphosphonate used was available for 1,694 of the patients. Intravenous therapy (primarily zoledronic acid) was received by 88% of the patients and 12% received oral treatment (primarily alendronate). Of all the cases of BP-associated ONJ, 67% were preceded by tooth extraction and for 26% of patients, there was no predisposing factor identified.

A 2010 retrospective case review reported the prevalence of BP-associated ONJ in patients using alendronate-type drugs was 1 out of 952 patients or ~0.1% (Lo 2010). Of the 8,572 respondents, nine cases of ONJ were identified; five had developed ONJ spontaneously and four developed ONJ after tooth extraction. When extrapolated to patient-years of bisphosphonate exposure, this prevalence rate of 0.1% equates to a frequency of 28 cases per 100,000 person-years of oral bisphosphonate treatment. An Australian group (Mavrokokki 2007), identified the frequency of BP-associated ONJ in osteoporotic patients, mainly taking weekly oral alendronate, was 1 in 8,470 to 1 in 2,260 (0.01% to 0.04%) patients. If extractions were carried out, the calculated frequency was 1 in 1,130 to 1 in 296 (0.09% to 0.34%) patients. The median time to onset of ONJ in alendronate patients was 24 months.

According to the 2011 report by the American Dental Association (ADA), the incidence of BP-associated ONJ remains low and the benefits of using oral bisphosphonates significantly outweighs the risk of developing BP-associated ONJ for treatment and prevention of osteoporosis and cancer treatment (Hellstein 2011). The full 47-page report can be accessed at http://www.ada.org/~/media/ADA/Member%20Center/FIles/topics_ARONJ_report.ashx.

The ADA review of 2011 stated the incidence of oral BP-associated ONJ was one case for every 1,000 individuals exposed to oral bisphosphonates (0.1%) (Hellstein 2011).

The most comprehensive review to date on osteonecrosis of the jaw bone (ONJ) has been published in the *Journal of Bone and Mineral Research* (Khan 2015), and written by an International Task Force of authors, totaling 34, from academe; industry; clinical medical and dental practice; oral and maxillofacial surgery; bone and mineral research; epidemiology; medical and dental oncology; orthopedic surgery; osteoporosis research; muscle and bone research; endocrinology and diagnostic sciences. The work provides a systematic review of the literature and international consensus on the classification, incidence, pathophysiology, diagnosis, and management of ONJ in both oncology and osteoporosis patient populations. This review of the literature from January 2003 to April 2014, with 299 references, offers recommendations for management of ONJ based on multidisciplinary international consensus.

Prevalence and incidence of ONJ in osteoporosis patients from the Task Force report:

Prevalence – the percent of osteoporotic population affected with ONJ

After reviewing all literature reports on this subject, the Task Force concluded that the prevalence of ONJ in patients prescribed oral BPs for the treatment of osteoporosis ranges from 0% to 0.04% with the majority being below 0.001%. However, the Task Force does cite the study of (Lo et al) that evaluated the Kaiser Permanente database and found the prevalence of ONJ in those receiving BPs for more than 2 years to range from 0.05% to 0.21% and appeared to be related to duration of exposure. As mentioned above, the American Dental Association has previously reported that the prevalence of ONJ in osteoporosis patients using oral BPs to be 1 out of 1,000 or 0.1% (Hellstein 2011).

Incidence - the rate at which ONJ occurs or the number of times it happens

From currently available data, the incidence of ONJ in the osteoporosis patient population appears to be low ranging from 0.15% to less than 0.001% person-years drug exposure. In terms of the osteoporosis patient population taking oral BPs, the incidence ranges from 1.04 to 69 per 100,000 patient years of drug exposure.

Clofarabine (klo FARE a been)

Brand Names: US Clolar

Brand Names: Canada Clolar

Pharmacologic Category Antineoplastic Agent, Antimetabolite; Antineoplastic Agent, Antimetabolite (Purine Analog)

Use Acute lymphoblastic leukemia, relapsed or refractory: Treatment of relapsed or refractory acute lymphoblastic leukemia (ALL) in patients 1 to 21 years of age (after at least 2 prior regimens)

Local Anesthetic/Vasoconstrictor Precautions No information available to require special precautions

Effects on Dental Treatment Key adverse event(s) related to dental treatment: Mucosal inflammation and gingival bleeding.

Effects on Bleeding Chemotherapy may result in significant myelosuppression, potentially including significant reduction in platelet counts and altered hemostasis. In patients who are under active treatment with these agents, medical consult is suggested.

Due to the thrombocytopenic effects of clofarabine, an increased risk of bleeding may be seen in patients receiving concomitant NSAIDs (including aspirin).

Adverse Reactions Incidences include off-label use in the treatment of AML.

>10%:

Cardiovascular: Tachycardia (35%), hypotension (29%), flushing (19%), hypertension (13%), edema (12%)

Central nervous system: Headache (43%), chills (34%), fatigue (34%), anxiety (21%), pain (15%)

Dermatologic: Pruritus (43%), skin rash (38%), palmar-plantar erythrodysesthesia (16%), erythema (11%)

Gastrointestinal: Vomiting (78%), nausea (73%), diarrhea (56%), abdominal pain (35%), anorexia (30%), gingival bleeding (17%), mucosal inflammation (16%), oral candidiasis (11%)

Genitourinary: Hematuria (13%)

Hematologic & oncologic: Leukopenia (88%; grades 3/4: 88%), anemia (83%, grades 3/4: 75%), lymphocytopenia (82%; grades 3/4: 82%), thrombocytopenia (81%; grades 3/4: 80%), neutropenia (10% to 64%; grades 3/4: 64%; grade 4: 7%), febrile neutropenia (55%; grade 3: 51%; grade 4: 3%), petechia (26%; grade 3: 6%)

Hepatic: Increased serum ALT (81%), increased serum AST (74%), increased bilirubin (45%)

Infection: Infection (83%; includes bacterial, fungal, and viral), sepsis (including septic shock; 17%)

Local: Catheter infection (12%)

Neuromuscular & skeletal: Limb pain (30%), myalgia (14%)

Renal: Increased serum creatinine (50%)

Respiratory: Epistaxis (27%), dyspnea (13%), pleural effusion (12%)

Miscellaneous: Fever (39%)

1% to 10%:

Cardiovascular: Pericardial effusion (8%), capillary leak syndrome (4%), hepatic veno-occlusive disease (2%)

Central nervous system: Drowsiness (10%), irritability (10%), lethargy (10%), agitation (5%), mental status changes (1% to 4%)

Dermatologic: Cellulitis (8%), pruritic rash (8%)

Gastrointestinal: Rectal pain (8%), upper abdominal pain (8%), pseudomembranous colitis (7%), stomatitis (7%), pancreatitis (1% to 4%), typhlitis (1% to 4%)

Hematologic & oncologic: Tumor lysis syndrome (6%; grade 3: 6%), oral mucosal petechiae (5%; grade 3: 4%)

Hepatic: Jaundice (8%), hyperbilirubinemia (1% to 4%)

Hypersensitivity: Hypersensitivity (1% to 4%)

Infection: Herpes simplex infection (10%), bacteremia (9%), candidiasis (7%), herpes zoster (7%), staphylococcal bacteremia (6%), staphylococcal sepsis (5%), influenza (1% to 4%), sepsis syndrome (2%)

Neuromuscular & skeletal: Back pain (10%), ostealgia (10%), weakness (10%), arthralgia (9%)

Renal: Acute renal failure

Respiratory: Pneumonia (10%), respiratory distress (10%), tachypnea (9%), upper respiratory tract infection (5%), pulmonary edema (1% to 4%), sinusitis (1% to 4%)

<1%, postmarketing, and/or case reports: Enterocolitis (occurs more frequently within 30 days of treatment and with combination chemotherapy), exfoliative dermatitis, gastrointestinal hemorrhage, hallucination (Jeha 2006), hepatic failure, hepatitis, hepatomegaly (Jeha 2006), hypokalemia (Jeha 2006), hyponatremia, hypophosphatemia, increased right ventricular pressure (Jeha 2006), left ventricular systolic dysfunction (Jeha 2006), major hemorrhage (including cerebral and pulmonary; majority of cases associated with thrombocytopenia), Stevens-Johnson syndrome, toxic epidermal necrolysis

General Dosage Range Dosage adjustment recommended in patients with renal impairment or who develop toxicities.

IV: *Children >1 year, Adolescents and Adults ≤21 years:* 52 mg/m^2/day days 1 through 5; repeat every 2 to 6 weeks

Mechanism of Action Clofarabine, a purine (deoxyadenosine) nucleoside analog, is metabolized to clofarabine 5'-triphosphate. Clofarabine 5'-triphosphate decreases cell replication and repair as well as causing cell death. To decrease cell replication and repair, clofarabine 5'-triphosphate competes with deoxyadenosine triphosphate for the enzymes ribonucleotide reductase and DNA polymerase. Cell replication is decreased when clofarabine 5'-triphosphate inhibits ribonucleotide reductase from reacting with deoxyadenosine triphosphate to produce deoxynucleotide triphosphate which is needed for DNA synthesis. Cell replication is also decreased when clofarabine 5'-triphosphate competes with DNA polymerase for incorporation into the DNA chain; when done during the repair process, cell repair is affected. To cause cell death, clofarabine 5'-triphosphate alters the mitochondrial membrane by releasing proteins, an inducing factor and cytochrome C.

Pharmacodynamics/Kinetics

Half-life Elimination Children and Adolescents 2 to 19 years: 5.2 hours; Children and Adults: 7 hours; may be prolonged in in the elderly and in patients with renal impairment (Bonate, 2011)

Pregnancy Risk Factor D

Pregnancy Considerations Adverse events were observed in animal reproduction studies. May cause fetal harm if administered to a pregnant woman. Women of childbearing potential should avoid becoming pregnant during therapy. All patients should use effective contraception to prevent pregnancy during treatment.

ClomiPHENE (KLOE mi feen)

Brand Names: US Serophene [DSC]

Brand Names: Canada Clomid; Serophene

Pharmacologic Category Ovulation Stimulator; Selective Estrogen Receptor Modulator (SERM)

Use Treatment of ovulatory dysfunction in women desiring pregnancy

Local Anesthetic/Vasoconstrictor Precautions No information available to require special precautions

Effects on Dental Treatment No significant effects or complications reported

Effects on Bleeding No information available to require special precautions

Adverse Reactions

>10%: Endocrine & metabolic: Ovary enlargement (14%)

1% to 10%:

Central nervous system: Headache (1%)

Endocrine & metabolic: Hot flash (10%)

Gastrointestinal: Abdominal distention (≤6%), abdominal distress (≤6%), bloating (≤6%), nausea (2%), vomiting (2%)

Genitourinary: Breast disease (discomfort: 2%), abnormal uterine bleeding (1%)

Ophthalmic: Visual disturbance (2%, includes blurred vision, diplopia, phosphene, photophobia, photopsia, scotomata, seeing visual waves, vitreous opacity)

<1%, postmarketing/case reports: Accommodation disturbance, acne vulgaris, acute surgical abdomen, alopecia, anxiety, arthralgia, back pain, cardiac arrhythmia, cataract, cerebrovascular accident, chest pain, constipation, depression, dermatitis, diarrhea, dizziness, dry hair, dyspnea, ectopic pregnancy, edema, endometriosis, erythema multiforme, erythema nodosum, eye pain, fatigue, fever, hepatitis, hypersensitivity reaction, hypertension, hypertrichosis, increased appetite, increased serum transaminases, increased urine output, insomnia, irritability, leukocytosis, macular edema, migraine, mood changes, myalgia, neoplasm, nervousness, optic neuritis, ovarian cyst, ovarian hemorrhage, palpitations, paresthesia, phlebitis, pruritus, psychosis, pulmonary embolism, retinal hemorrhage, retinal thrombosis, retinal vascular spasm, seizure, skin rash, syncope, tachycardia, thrombophlebitis, thyroid disease, tinnitus, urinary frequency, urticaria, uterine hemorrhage, vaginal dryness, vertigo, vision loss (temporary/prolonged), vitreous detachment (posterior), weakness, weight gain, weight loss

General Dosage Range Oral: *Adults (females):* 50 to 100 mg daily for 5 days

Mechanism of Action Clomiphene is a racemic mixture consisting of zuclomiphene (~38%) and enclomiphene (~62%), each with distinct pharmacologic properties. Clomiphene acts at the level of the hypothalamus, occupying cell surface and intracellular estrogen receptors (ERs) for longer durations than estrogen. This interferes with receptor recycling, effectively depleting hypothalamic ERs and inhibiting normal estrogenic negative feedback. Impairment of the feedback signal results in increased pulsatile GnRH secretion from the hypothalamus and subsequent pituitary gonadotropin (FSH, LH) release, causing growth of the ovarian follicle, followed by follicular rupture (ASRM 2013; Dickey, 1996).

Pharmacodynamics/Kinetics

Onset of Action Ovulation: 5 to 10 days following course of treatment

Duration of Action Effects are cumulative; ovulation may occur in the cycle following the last treatment (Dickey, 1996)

Half-life Elimination ~5 days (Goldstein 2000)

Time to Peak ~6 hours (Goldstein 2000)

Pregnancy Risk Factor X

Pregnancy Considerations Adverse events were observed in animal reproduction studies. The incidence of adverse fetal effects following maternal use of clomiphene for ovulation induction is similar to those seen in the general population. Clomiphene is not indicated for use in women who are already pregnant.

ClomiPRAMINE (kloe MI pra meen)

Related Information

Dentin Hypersensitivity, Acid Erosion, High Caries Index, Management of Alveolar Osteitis, and Xerostomia *on page 1857*

Vasoconstrictor Interactions With Antidepressants *on page 1913*

Brand Names: US Anafranil

Brand Names: Canada Anafranil; Apo-Clomipramine; CO Clomipramine; Dom-Clomipramine; Novo-Clomipramine

Pharmacologic Category Antidepressant, Tricyclic (Tertiary Amine)

Use Treatment of obsessive-compulsive disorder (OCD)

Local Anesthetic/Vasoconstrictor Precautions Use with caution; epinephrine and levonordefrin have been shown to have an increased pressor response in combination with TCAs. Clomipramine is one of the drugs confirmed to prolong the QT interval and is accepted as having a risk of causing torsade de pointes. The risk of drug-induced torsade de pointes is extremely low when a single QT interval prolonging drug is prescribed. In terms of epinephrine, it is not known what effect vasoconstrictors in the local anesthetic regimen will have in patients with a known history of congenital prolonged QT interval or in patients taking any medication that prolongs the QT interval. Until more information is obtained, it is suggested that the clinician consult with the physician prior to the use of a vasoconstrictor in suspected patients, and that the vasoconstrictor (epinephrine, mepivacaine and levonordefrin [Carbocaine® 2% with Neo-Cobefrin®]) be used with caution.

Effects on Dental Treatment Key adverse event(s) related to dental treatment: Xerostomia and changes in salivation (normal salivary flow resumes upon discontinuation). Long-term treatment with TCAs, such as clomipramine, increases the risk of caries by reducing salivation and salivary buffer capacity.

Effects on Bleeding No information available to require special precautions

Adverse Reactions Data shown for children reflects both children and adolescents studied in clinical trials.

>10%:

Central nervous system: Dizziness (adults 54%; children & adolescents 41%), drowsiness (46% to 54%), headache (adults 52%), fatigue (35% to 39%), insomnia (adults 25%; children & adolescents 11%), nervousness (adults 18%; children & adolescents 4%), myoclonus (adults 13%; children & adolescents 2%)

Dermatologic: Diaphoresis (adults 29%; children & adolescents 9%)

Endocrine & metabolic: Change in libido (adults 21%), weight gain (adults 18%; children & adolescents 2%)

Gastrointestinal: Xerostomia (adults 84%, children & adolescents 63%), constipation (adults 47%; children & adolescents 22%), nausea (adults 33%), dyspepsia (13% to 22%), anorexia (12% to 22%), diarrhea (7% to 13%), abdominal pain (adults 11%), increased appetite (adults 11%)

Genitourinary: Ejaculation failure (adults 42%, children & adolescents 6%), impotence (adults 20%), difficulty in micturition (adults 14%; children & adolescents 4%)

Neuromuscular & skeletal: Tremor (adults 54%; children & adolescents 33%), myalgia (adults 13%)

Ophthalmic: Visual disturbance (adults 18%; children & adolescents 7%)
Respiratory: Pharyngitis (adults 14%), rhinitis (adults 12%)

1% to 10%:

Cardiovascular: Flushing (7% to 8%), chest pain (children & adolescents 7%), orthostatic hypotension (children, adolescents, and adults 4% to 6%), palpitations (4%), tachycardia (children, adolescents, and adults 2% to 4%), ECG abnormality (2%), syncope (children & adolescents 2%)

Central nervous system: Anxiety (adults 9%; children & adolescents 2%), paresthesia (adults 9%), memory impairment (7% to 9%), sleep disorder (4% to 9%), twitching (adults 7%), depression (adults 5%), lack of concentration (adults 5%), pain (3% to 4%), hypertonia (2% to 4%), abnormal dreams (adults 3%), agitation (adults 3%), confusion (adults 3%; children & adolescents 2%), migraine (adults 3%), psychosomatic disorder (adults 3%), speech disturbance (adults 3%), yawning (adults 3%), aggressive behavior (children & adolescents 2%), chills (adults 2%), depersonalization (2%), emotional lability (adults 2%), irritability (children & adolescents 2%), paresis (children & adolescents 2%), myasthenia (1% to 2%), panic attack (1% to 2%), abnormality in thinking (≥1%), vertigo (≥1%)

Dermatologic: Skin rash (4% to 8%), pruritus (adults 6%), body odor (children & adolescents 2%), dermatitis (adults 2%), xeroderma (adults 2%), urticaria (adults 1%)

Endocrine & metabolic: Weight loss (children & adolescents 7%), hot flash (2% to 5%), menstrual disease (adults 4%), amenorrhea (adults 1%)

Gastrointestinal: Dysgeusia (4% to 8%), vomiting (7%), flatulence (adults 6%), aphthous stomatitis (children & adolescents 2%), dysphagia (adults 2%), gastrointestinal disease (adults 2%), halitosis (children & adolescents 2%), esophagitis (adults 1%)

Genitourinary: Urinary retention (children & adolescents 7%; adults 2%), urinary tract infection (adults 6%), urinary frequency (adults 5%), lactation (nonpuerperal; adults 4%), breast hypertrophy (adults 2%), cystitis (adults 2%), leukorrhea (adults 2%), vaginitis (adults 2%), mastalgia (adults 1%)

Hematologic & oncologic: Purpura (adults 3%)

Hepatic: Increased serum ALT (>3 x ULN: 3%), increased serum AST (>3 x ULN: 1%)

Hypersensitivity: Hypersensitivity reaction (children & adolescents 7%)

Neuromuscular & skeletal: Weakness (children & adolescents 2%; adults 1%)

Ophthalmic: Abnormal lacrimation (adults 3%), anisocoria (children & adolescents 2%), blepharospasm (children & adolescents 2%), mydriasis (adults 2%), ocular allergy (children & adolescents 2%), conjunctivitis (adults 1%)

Otic: Tinnitus (4% to 6%)

Respiratory: Bronchospasm (children & adolescents 7%; adults 2%), sinusitis (adults 6%), dyspnea (children & adolescents 2%), epistaxis (adults 2%), laryngitis (children & adolescents 2%)

Miscellaneous: Fever (adults 4%)

<1%, postmarketing, and/or case reports: Abnormal electroencephalogram, accommodation disturbance, agranulocytosis, albuminuria, alopecia, altered sense of smell, anemia, aneurysm, angle-closure glaucoma, anticholinergic syndrome, apathy, aphasia, apraxia, ataxia, atrial flutter, blepharitis, bloody stools, bone marrow depression, bradycardia, brain disease, breast fibroadenosis, bronchitis, bundle branch block, cardiac arrest, cardiac arrhythmia, cardiac failure, catatonic-like state, cellulitis, cerebral hemorrhage, cervical dysplasia, cheilitis, chloasma, cholinergic syndrome, choreoathetosis, chromatopsia, chronic enteritis, colitis, coma, conjunctival hemorrhage, cyanosis, deafness, dehydration, delirium, delusions, dental caries, dermal ulcer, diabetes mellitus, diplopia, duodenitis, dyskinesia, dystonia, eczema, edema, edema (oral), endometrial hyperplasia, endometriosis, enlargement of salivary glands, epididymitis, erythematous rash, exophthalmos, exostosis, extrapyramidal reaction, extrasystoles, gastric dilation, gastric ulcer, gastroesophageal reflux disease, glycosuria, goiter, gout, gynecomastia, hallucination, heart block, hematuria, hemiparesis, hemoptysis, hepatic injury (severe), hepatitis, hostility, hyperacusis, hypercholesterolemia, hyperesthesia, hyperglycemia, hyperkinesia, hyperreflexia, hyperthermia, hyperthyroidism, hyperuricemia, hyperventilation, hypnogenic hallucinations, hypoesthesia, hypokalemia, hypokinesia, hypothyroidism, hypoventilation, intestinal obstruction, irritable bowel syndrome, ischemic heart disease, keratitis, laryngismus, leukemoid reaction, leukopenia, local inflammation (uterine), lupus erythematous-like rash, lymphadenopathy, maculopapular rash, manic reaction, muscle spasm, mutism, myocardial infarction, myopathy, myositis, nephrolithiasis, neuralgia, neuropathy, nocturnal amblyopia, oculogyric crisis, oculomotor nerve paralysis, ovarian cyst, pancytopenia, paralytic ileus, paranoia, peptic ulcer, periarteritis nodosa, peripheral ischemia, pharyngeal edema, phobia, photophobia, pneumonia, premature ejaculation, pseudolymphoma, psoriasis, psychosis, pyelonephritis, pyuria, rectal hemorrhage, renal cyst, schizophreniform disorder, scleritis, seizure, sensory disturbance, serotonin syndrome, skin hypertrophy, skin photosensitivity, somnambulism, strabismus, stupor, suicidal ideation, thrombocytopenia, thrombophlebitis, tongue ulcer, torticollis, urinary incontinence, uterine hemorrhage, vaginal hemorrhage, vasospasm, ventricular tachycardia, visual field defect, voice disorder, withdrawal syndrome

General Dosage Range Oral:

Children ≥10 years and Adolescents: Initial: 25 mg daily; Maintenance: Up to 3 mg/kg/day (maximum: 200 mg daily)

Adults: Initial: 25 mg daily; Maintenance: Up to 250 mg daily

Mechanism of Action Clomipramine appears to affect serotonin uptake while its active metabolite, desmethylclomipramine, affects norepinephrine uptake

Pharmacodynamics/Kinetics

Onset of Action Onset of action: 1-2 weeks; maximum effect: 8-12 weeks

Duration of Action 1-2 days

Half-life Elimination Adults (following a 150 mg dose): Clomipramine 19-37 hours (mean: 32 hours); DMI: 54-77 hours (mean: 69 hours)

Time to Peak 2-6 hours

Pregnancy Risk Factor C

Pregnancy Considerations Adverse events were observed in some animal reproduction studies. Clomipramine and its metabolite desmethylclomipramine cross the placenta and can be detected in cord blood and neonatal serum at birth (Loughhead 2006; ter Horst 2011). Data from five newborns found the half-life for clomipramine in the neonate to be 42 ± 16 hours following in utero exposure. Serum concentrations were not found to correlate to withdrawal symptoms (ter Horst 2011). Withdrawal symptoms (including jitteriness, tremor, and seizures) have been observed in neonates whose mothers took clomipramine up to delivery.

The ACOG recommends that therapy for depression during pregnancy be individualized; treatment should incorporate the clinical expertise of the mental health clinician, obstetrician, primary health care provider, and pediatrician (ACOG 2008). According to the American Psychiatric Association (APA), the risks of medication treatment should be weighed against other treatment options and untreated depression. For women who discontinue antidepressant medications during pregnancy and who may be at high risk for postpartum depression, the medications can be restarted following delivery (APA 2010). Treatment algorithms have been developed by the ACOG and the APA for the management of depression in women prior to conception and during pregnancy (Yonkers 2009).

Pregnant women exposed to antidepressants during pregnancy are encouraged to enroll in the National Pregnancy Registry for Antidepressants (NPRAD). Women 18 to 45 years of age or their health care providers may contact the registry by calling 844-405-6185. Enrollment should be done as early in pregnancy as possible.

Dental Comment See Local Anesthetic/Vasoconstrictor Precautions

ClonazePAM (kloe NA ze pam)

Related Information

Dentin Hypersensitivity, Acid Erosion, High Caries Index, Management of Alveolar Osteitis, and Xerostomia *on page 1857*

Brand Names: US KlonoPIN

Brand Names: Canada Apo-Clonazepam; Clonapam; Clonazepam-R; CO Clonazepam; Dom-Clonazepam; Dom-Clonazepam-R; Mylan-Clonazepam; PHL-Clonazepam; PHL-Clonazepam-R; PMS-Clonazepam; PMS-Clonazepam-R; PRO-Clonazepam; ratio-Clonazepam; Riva-Clonazepam; Rivotril; Sandoz-Clonazepam; Teva-Clonazepam; ZYM-Clonazepam

Generic Availability (US) Yes

Pharmacologic Category Anticonvulsant, Benzodiazepine; Benzodiazepine

Dental Use Burning mouth syndrome

Use

Panic disorder: Treatment of panic disorder, with or without agoraphobia.

Seizure disorders: Mono- or adjunctive therapy in the treatment of the Lennox-Gastaut syndrome (petit mal variant), akinetic, and myoclonic seizures; absence seizures (petit mal) unresponsive to succinimides.

Local Anesthetic/Vasoconstrictor Precautions No information available to require special precautions

Effects on Dental Treatment Key adverse event(s) related to dental treatment: Xerostomia and changes in salivation (normal salivary flow resumes upon discontinuation), gum soreness, and coated tongue.

Effects on Bleeding No information available to require special precautions

Adverse Reactions Reactions reported in patients with seizure disorder, unless otherwise noted. Frequency not always defined.

>10%: Central nervous system: Drowsiness (seizure disorder: ~50%; panic disorder: 26% to 50%), ataxia (seizure disorder: ~30%; panic disorder: 1% to 9%), behavioral problems (seizure disorder: ~25%), dizziness (panic disorder: 5% to 12%)

1% to 10%:

Central nervous system: Fatigue (panic disorder: 6% to 9%), depression (panic disorder: 6% to 8%), memory impairment (panic disorder: 4% to 5%), nervousness (panic disorder: 3% to 4%), dysarthria (panic disorder: ≤4%), reduced intellectual ability (panic disorder: ≤4%), emotional lability (panic disorder: 2%), confusion (panic disorder: ≤2%), delayed ejaculation (panic disorder ≤2%)

Endocrine & metabolic: Decreased libido (panic disorder: ≤3%)

Gastrointestinal: Constipation (panic disorder: 3% to 5%), decreased appetite (panic disorder: 3%), abdominal pain (panic disorder: 2%)

Genitourinary: Dysmenorrhea (panic disorder: 3% to 6%), vaginitis (panic disorder: 2% to 4%), impotence (panic disorder: ≤3%), urinary tract infection (panic disorder: ≤2%), urinary frequency (panic disorder: 1% to 2%)

Hypersensitivity: Hypersensitivity (panic disorder: 2% to 4%)

Neuromuscular & skeletal: Myalgia (panic disorder: 2% to 4%)

Ophthalmic: Blurred vision (panic disorder: 2% to 3%)

Respiratory: Upper respiratory tract infection (panic disorder: 6% to 10%), sinusitis (panic disorder: 4% to 8%), influenza (panic disorder: 4% to 5%), cough (panic disorder: ≤4%), rhinitis (panic disorder: 2% to 4%), pharyngitis (panic disorder: 2% to 3%), bronchitis (panic disorder: 2%)

Frequency not defined:

Cardiovascular: Edema (ankle or facial), palpitations

Central nervous system: Amnesia, aphonia, choreiform movements, coma, glassy-eyed appearance, hallucination, headache, hemiparesis, hypotonia, hysteria, insomnia, myasthenia, psychosis, slurred speech, vertigo

Dermatologic: Alopecia, skin rash

Endocrine & metabolic: Dehydration, hirsutism, increased libido, weight gain, weight loss

Gastrointestinal: Anorexia, coated tongue, diarrhea, encopresis, gastritis, gingival pain, increased appetite, nausea, xerostomia

Genitourinary: Dysuria, nocturia, urinary incontinence, urinary retention

Hematologic & oncologic: Anemia, eosinophilia, leukopenia, lymphadenopathy, thrombocytopenia

Hepatic: Hepatomegaly, increased serum alkaline phosphatase (transient), increased serum transaminases (transient)

Neuromuscular & skeletal: Dysdiadochokinesia, tremor

Ophthalmic: Abnormal eye movements, diplopia, nystagmus

Respiratory: Chest congestion, dyspnea, respiratory depression, rhinorrhea, upper respiratory complaint (hypersecretion)

Miscellaneous: Fever, paradoxical reactions (including aggressive behavior, agitation, anxiety excitability, hostility, irritability, nervousness, nightmares, sleep disturbance, vivid dreams), physical health deterioration

<1%, postmarketing, and/or case reports (any indication): Abdominal distress, abnormal behavior (increased oppositional behavior), accidental injury, acne flare, ageusia, aggressive behavior, alcohol intoxication, anxiety, apathy, arthralgia, back pain,

bladder dysfunction, bone fracture, burn, burning sensation of skin, candidiasis, cellulitis, chest pain, contact dermatitis, cystitis, depersonalization, dermal hemorrhage, dermatological reaction, disinhibition (organic), dyspepsia, ejaculatory disorder, epistaxis, exacerbation of asthma, excitement, excoriation, eye irritation, falling, flatulence, flushing, foot pain, frequent bowel movements, fungal infection, gastric distress, gout, heartburn, heavy headedness, hemorrhoids, herpes simplex infection, hoarseness, hordeolum, hyperactivity, hypertonia, hypoesthesia, hunger, illusion, increased dream activity, increased thirst, infectious mononucleosis, irregular menses, irritability, jaw pain, knee effusion, knee pain, lack of concentration, leg pain, leg thrombophlebitis, local inflammation, lower back pain, malaise, mastalgia, migraine, motion sickness, orthostatic hypotension, otalgia, otitis, pain, paresis, paresthesia, pedal edema, pelvic pain, periorbital edema, pleurisy, pneumonia, polyuria, pruritus, pustular rash, shivering, shoulder pain, sialorrhea, sleep disorder, slowed reaction time, sneezing, sprain, strain, streptococcal infection, suicidal ideation, suicidal tendencies, tendonitis, tongue edema, toothache, twitching, twitching of eye, urinary tract hemorrhage, urine discoloration, viral infection, visual disturbance, visual field defect, xeroderma, xerophthalmia, yawning

Dental Usual Dosage Burning mouth syndrome (off-label use): Adults: Oral: 0.25-3 mg/day in 2 divided doses, in morning and evening

Dosing

Adult

Panic disorder: Oral: 0.25 mg twice daily; increase in increments of 0.125 to 0.25 mg twice daily every 3 days; target dose: 1 mg daily (maximum: 4 mg/day).

Discontinuation of treatment: To discontinue, treatment should be withdrawn gradually. Decrease dose by 0.125 mg twice daily every 3 days until medication is completely withdrawn.

Seizure disorders: Oral:

Initial daily dose not to exceed 1.5 mg given in 3 divided doses; may increase by 0.5 to 1 mg every third day until seizures are controlled or adverse effects seen (maximum: 20 mg/day).

Usual maintenance dose: 2 to 8 mg daily in 1 to 2 divided doses (Brodie 1997); do not exceed 20 mg/day.

Bipolar disorder, mixed or manic episodes (off-label use): Oral: 2 to 8 mg daily, in 2 to 4 divided doses; total daily doses as high as 16 mg have been studied (Bottai 1995; Chouinard 1983; Clark 1997; Edwards 1991; WFSBP [Grunze 2009]).

Burning mouth syndrome (off-label use):

Oral: Initial: 0.25 at bedtime for 1 week; increase dose by ≤0.25 mg every week; maximum dose: 3 mg daily in 3 divided doses. **Note:** Use should be limited (Buchanan 2008; Grushka 1998).

Topical: May administer topically with 1 mg 3 times daily (after each meal). **Note:** Patient should be instructed to suck on the tablet, retain saliva in mouth near the pain sites without swallowing for 3 minutes, and then expectorate saliva (Gremeau-Richard 2004).

Essential tremor (off-label use): Oral: Initial: 0.5 mg at bedtime; increase dose by 0.5 mg every 3 to 4 days; maximum dose: 6 mg daily (Biary 1987; Thompson 1984; Zesiewicz 2005; Zesiewicz 2011).

REM sleep behavior disorder (off-label use): 0.25 to 2 mg 30 minutes prior to bedtime (maximum: 4 mg 30 minutes prior to bedtime). **Note:** Use with caution in patients with dementia, gait disorders, or obstructive sleep apnea (Aurora 2010).

Restless leg syndrome (off-label use): Oral: Initial: 1 mg 30 minutes prior to bedtime; increase dose by 0.5 to 1 mg at weekly intervals. Doses up to 2 mg once daily have been used in clinical trials (Montagna 1984; Peled 1987; Saletu 2001). Additional data may be necessary to further define the role of clonazepam in the treatment of this condition.

Tardive dyskinesia (off-label use): Oral: Initial: 1 mg/day; adjust dosage based on response and tolerability by 1 mg/day every 3 to 4 days up to a maximum dose of 4.5 mg/day (Thaker 1990).

Tic disorders (off-label use): Oral: Initial: 0.5 mg at bedtime; adjust dose by 0.5 mg every 2 weeks based on response and tolerability. Dosing range in clinical studies was 1 to 12 mg/day (Merikangas 1985; Troung 1988).

Geriatric Refer to adult dosing. Initiate with low doses and observe closely.

Pediatric

Seizure disorders: Oral:

Infants, Children ≤10 years or ≤30 kg:

Initial daily dose: 0.01 to 0.03 mg/kg/day (maximum initial dose: 0.05 mg/kg/day) given in 2 to 3 divided doses; increase by no more than 0.25 to 0.5 mg every third day until seizures are controlled or adverse effects seen.

Usual maintenance dose: 0.1 to 0.2 mg/kg/day divided 3 times daily.

Children >10 years or >30 kg and Adolescents: Refer to adult dosing.

Renal Impairment There are no dosage adjustments provided in the manufacturer's labeling; use with caution. Clonazepam metabolites may accumulate in patients with renal impairment.

Hepatic Impairment There are no dosage adjustments provided in the manufacturer's labeling; use with caution. Clonazepam undergoes hepatic metabolism. Contraindicated in patients with significant hepatic impairment.

Mechanism of Action The exact mechanism is unknown, but believed to be related to its ability to enhance the activity of GABA; suppresses the spike-and-wave discharge in absence seizures by depressing nerve transmission in the motor cortex.

Contraindications Hypersensitivity to clonazepam, other benzodiazepines, or any component of the formulation; significant liver disease; acute narrow-angle glaucoma

Warnings/Precautions Pooled analysis of trials involving various antiepileptics (regardless of indication) showed an increased risk of suicidal thoughts/behavior (incidence rate: 0.43% treated patients compared to 0.24% of patients receiving placebo); risk observed as early as 1 week after initiation and continued through duration of trials (most trials ≤24 weeks). Monitor all patients for notable changes in behavior that might indicate suicidal thoughts or depression; notify healthcare provider immediately if symptoms occur. Use caution in patients with depression, particularly if suicidal risk may be present.

Benzodiazepines have been associated with anterograde amnesia (Nelson 1999). May cause CNS depression, which may impair physical or mental abilities; patients must be cautioned about performing tasks which require mental alertness (eg, operating machinery or driving). Paradoxical reactions, including hyperactive or aggressive behavior, have been reported with benzodiazepines, particularly in adolescent/pediatric or psychiatric patients (Mancuso 2004). Clonazepam may cause respiratory depression and may produce an increase in salivation; use with caution in patients with compromised respiratory function and in patients who have difficulty handling secretions. May be used in patients with open angle glaucoma who are receiving appropriate therapy; contraindicated in acute narrow angle glaucoma. Use with caution in patients with a history of drug abuse or acute alcoholism; potential for drug dependency exists. Tolerance, psychological and physical dependence may occur with prolonged use. Use with caution in patients with hepatic impairment; accumulation likely to occur. Contraindicated in patients with significant hepatic impairment. Use with caution in patients with renal impairment; clonazepam metabolites are renally eliminated. Use with caution in debilitated patients. Use with extreme caution in patients who are at risk of falls; benzodiazepines have been associated with falls and traumatic injury. Use with caution in patients with porphyria; may have a porphyrogenic effect.

Does not have analgesic, antidepressant, or antipsychotic properties. Worsening of seizures may occur when added to patients with multiple seizure types. Periodically reevaluate the long-term usefulness of clonazepam for the individual patient. Clonazepam is a long half-life benzodiazepine. Duration of action after a single dose is determined by redistribution rather than metabolism. Tolerance develops to the anticonvulsant effects. It does not develop to the anxiolytic effects (Vinkers 2012). Chronic use of this agent may increase the perioperative benzodiazepine dose needed to achieve desired effect. Rebound or withdrawal symptoms may occur following abrupt discontinuation or large decreases in dose. Use caution when reducing dose or withdrawing therapy; decrease slowly and monitor for withdrawal symptoms. Flumazenil may cause withdrawal in patients receiving long-term benzodiazepine therapy (Brogden 1988). Potentially significant drug-drug interactions may exist, requiring dose or frequency adjustment, additional monitoring, and/or selection of alternative therapy. **[US Boxed Warning]: Concomitant use of benzodiazepines and opioids may result in profound sedation, respiratory depression, coma, and death. Reserve concomitant prescribing of these drugs for use in patients for whom alternative treatment options are inadequate. Limits dosages to the minimum required. Follow patients for signs and symptoms of respiratory depression and sedation.**

Drug Interactions

Metabolism/Transport Effects **Substrate** of CYP3A4 (major); **Note:** Assignment of Major/Minor substrate status based on clinically relevant drug interaction potential

Avoid Concomitant Use

Avoid concomitant use of ClonazePAM with any of the following: Azelastine (Nasal); Conivaptan; Fusidic Acid (Systemic); Idelalisib; Methadone; OLANZapine; Orphenadrine; Oxomemazine; Paraldehyde; Sodium Oxybate; Thalidomide

Increased Effect/Toxicity

ClonazePAM may increase the levels/effects of: Alcohol (Ethyl); Analgesics (Opioid); Azelastine (Nasal); Blonanserin; Buprenorphine; CloZAPine; CNS Depressants; Flunitrazepam; HYDROcodone; Methadone; Methotrimeprazine; MetyroSINE; Mirtazapine; Orphenadrine; OxyCODONE; Paraldehyde; Piribedil; Pramipexole; ROPINIRole; Rotigotine; Selective Serotonin Reuptake Inhibitors; Sodium Oxybate; Suvorexant; Thalidomide; Zolpidem

The levels/effects of ClonazePAM may be increased by: Aprepitant; Brimonidine (Topical); Cannabis; Chlormethiazole; Chlorphenesin Carbamate; Cobicistat; Conivaptan; Cosyntropin; CYP3A4 Inhibitors (Moderate); CYP3A4 Inhibitors (Strong); Dasatinib; Dimethindene (Topical); Doxylamine; Dronabinol; Droperidol; Fosaprepitant; Fusidic Acid (Systemic); HydrOXYzine; Idelalisib; Ivacaftor; Kava Kava; Lofexidine; Magnesium Sulfate; Methotrimeprazine; MiFEPRIStone; Minocycline; Nabilone; Netupitant; OLANZapine; Oxomemazine; Palbociclib; Perampanel; Rufinamide; Simeprevir; Stiripentol; Tapentadol; Teduglutide; Tetrahydrocannabinol; Trimeprazine; Vigabatrin

Decreased Effect

The levels/effects of ClonazePAM may be decreased by: Bosentan; CYP3A4 Inducers (Moderate); CYP3A4 Inducers (Strong); Dabrafenib; Deferasirox; Enzalutamide; Mitotane; Siltuximab; St John's Wort; Theophylline Derivatives; Tocilizumab; Yohimbine

Pharmacodynamics/Kinetics

Onset of Action ~20 to 40 minutes (Hanson 1972)

Duration of Action Infants and young children: 6 to 8 hours (Hanson 1972); Adults: ≤12 hours (Hanson 1972)

Half-life Elimination Children: 22 to 33 hours (Walson 1996); Adults: 17 to 60 hours (Walson 1996)

Time to Peak Serum: 1 to 4 hours

Pregnancy Risk Factor D

Pregnancy Considerations Adverse events have been observed in some animal reproduction studies. Clonazepam crosses the placenta. Teratogenic effects have been observed with some benzodiazepines; however, additional studies are needed. The incidence of premature birth and low birth weights may be increased following maternal use of benzodiazepines; hypoglycemia and respiratory problems in the neonate may occur following exposure late in pregnancy. Neonatal withdrawal symptoms may occur within days to weeks after birth and "floppy infant syndrome" (which also includes withdrawal symptoms) has been reported with some benzodiazepines, including clonazepam (Bergman 1992; Iqbal 2002; Wikner 2007). A combination of factors influences the potential teratogenicity of anticonvulsant therapy. When treating women with epilepsy, monotherapy with the lowest effective dose and avoidance medications known to have a high incidence of teratogenic effects is recommended (Harden 2009; Wlodarczyk 2012).

Patients exposed to clonazepam during pregnancy are encouraged to enroll themselves into the AED Pregnancy Registry by calling 1-888-233-2334. Additional information is available at www.aedpregnancyregistry.org.

Breastfeeding Considerations Clonazepam is excreted in breast milk. Drowsiness, lethargy, or weight loss in nursing infants have been observed in case reports following maternal use of some benzodiazepines (Iqbal 2002). breastfeeding is not recommended by the manufacturer.

Controlled Substance C-IV

Dosage Forms

Tablet, Oral:

KlonoPIN: 0.5 mg, 1 mg, 2 mg
Generic: 0.5 mg, 1 mg, 2 mg

Tablet Dispersible, Oral:

Generic: 0.125 mg, 0.25 mg, 0.5 mg, 1 mg, 2 mg

CloNIDine (KLON i deen)

Related Information

Cardiovascular Diseases *on page 1752*

Dentin Hypersensitivity, Acid Erosion, High Caries Index, Management of Alveolar Osteitis, and Xerostomia *on page 1857*

Brand Names: US Catapres; Catapres-TTS-1; Catapres-TTS-2; Catapres-TTS-3; Duraclon; Kapvay

Brand Names: Canada Apo-Clonidine; Catapres; Dixarit; Dom-Clonidine; Novo-Clonidine

Pharmacologic Category $Alpha_2$-Adrenergic Agonist; Antihypertensive

Use

Oral:

Immediate release: Management of hypertension (monotherapy or as adjunctive therapy)

Extended release (Kapvay): Treatment of attention-deficit/hyperactivity disorder (ADHD) (monotherapy or as adjunctive therapy)

Epidural (Duraclon): For continuous epidural administration as adjunctive therapy with opioids for treatment of severe cancer pain in patients tolerant to or unresponsive to opioids alone; epidural clonidine is generally more effective for neuropathic pain and less effective (or possibly ineffective) for somatic or visceral pain

Transdermal patch: Management of hypertension (monotherapy or as adjunctive therapy)

Note: According to the Eighth Joint National Committee (JNC 8) guidelines, clonidine is **not** recommended for the initial treatment of hypertension (James 2013). According to the AHA/ACC/ASH 2015 scientific statement for the treatment of hypertension in patients with coronary artery disease (CAD), clonidine should be avoided for the treatment of hypertension in patients with heart failure (with reduced ejection fraction) of ischemic origin (AHA/ACC/ASH [Rosendorff 2015]).

Local Anesthetic/Vasoconstrictor Precautions No information available to require special precautions

Effects on Dental Treatment Key adverse event(s) related to dental treatment: Significant xerostomia (normal salivary flow resumes upon discontinuation) and abnormal taste; Patients may experience orthostatic hypotension as they stand up after treatment; especially if lying in dental chair for extended periods of time. Use caution with sudden changes in position during and after dental treatment.

Effects on Bleeding No information available to require special precautions

Adverse Reactions Frequency not always defined.

Oral, Transdermal: Incidence of adverse events may be less with transdermal compared to oral due to the lower peak/trough ratio.

>10%:

Central nervous system: Drowsiness (2% to 38%), headache (1% to 29%), fatigue (4% to 16%), dizziness (2% to 16%)

Dermatologic: Transient skin rash (localized; characterized by pruritus and erythema; transdermal 15% to 50%), contact dermatitis (transdermal 8% to 34%)

Gastrointestinal: Xerostomia (≤40%), upper abdominal pain (15%)

1% to 10%:

Cardiovascular: Bradycardia (≤4%), edema (3%), localized blanching (transdermal 1%), palpitations (1%), tachycardia (≤3%), atrioventricular block, cardiac arrhythmia, cardiac failure, cerebrovascular accident, chest pain, ECG abnormality, flushing, orthostatic hypotension, prolonged Q-T Interval on ECG, Raynaud's phenomenon, syncope

Central nervous system: Sedation (3% to 10%), irritability (5% to 9%), nightmares (4% to 9%), insomnia (≤6%), emotional disturbance (4%), lethargy (3%), nervousness (1% to 3%), depression (1%), throbbing (transdermal 1%), withdrawal syndrome (1%), aggressive behavior, agitation, anxiety, behavioral changes, delirium, delusions, hallucination (visual and auditory), malaise, numbness (localized; transdermal), paresthesia, parotid pain (oral), restlessness, vivid dream

Dermatologic: Localized vesiculation (transdermal 7%), allergic contact sensitivity (transdermal 5%), hyperpigmentation (transdermal 5%), burning sensation of skin (transdermal 3%), excoriation (transdermal 3%), macular eruption (1%), papule (transdermal 1%), alopecia, hypopigmentation (localized; transdermal), pallor, skin rash, urticaria

Endocrine & metabolic: Gynecomastia (1%), weight gain (<1%), decreased libido, hyperglycemia (transient; oral), increased thirst

Gastrointestinal: Constipation (1% to 10%), viral gastrointestinal infection (5%), anorexia (1%), abdominal pain (oral), diarrhea, gastrointestinal pseudo-obstruction (oral), nausea, parotitis (oral), sore throat, vomiting

Genitourinary: Urinary incontinence (4%), sexual disorder (3%), erectile dysfunction (2% to 3%), nocturia (1%), pollakiuria, urinary retention

Hematologic & oncologic: Thrombocytopenia (oral)

Hepatic: Abnormal hepatic function tests (mild transient abnormalities; <1%), hepatitis

Hypersensitivity: Angioedema

Neuromuscular & skeletal: Weakness (10%), tremor (1% to 4%), arthralgia (1%), myalgia (1%), leg cramps (<1%), increased creatine phosphokinase (transient; oral), limb pain

Ophthalmic: Accommodation disturbance, blurred vision, burning sensation of eyes, decreased lacrimation, dry eye syndrome, increased lacrimation

Otic: Otitis media (≤3%), otalgia

Respiratory: Asthma, dry nose, epistaxis, flu-like symptoms, nasal congestion, nasopharyngitis, respiratory tract infection, rhinorrhea

Miscellaneous: Crying (1% to 3%), fever

Epidural: Note: The following adverse events occurred more often than placebo in cancer patients with intractable pain being treated with concurrent epidural morphine.

>10%:

Cardiovascular: Hypotension (45%), orthostatic hypotension (32%)

Central nervous system: Confusion (13%), dizziness (13%)

Gastrointestinal: Xerostomia (13%)

1% to 10%:

Cardiovascular: Chest pain (5%)

Central nervous system: Hallucination (5%)

Dermatologic: Diaphoresis (5%)

Gastrointestinal: Nausea and vomiting (8%)

Otic: Tinnitus (5%)

General Dosage Range Note: Dosing is expressed as the salt (clonidine hydrochloride) unless otherwise noted.

Epidural:

Children: Initial: 0.5 mcg/kg/**hour**

Adults: Initial: 30 mcg/hour; Maintenance: Up to 40 mcg/hour

Oral, immediate release:
Adults: Initial: 0.1 mg twice daily; Maintenance: 0.1 to 0.8 mg/day in 2 divided doses (maximum: 2.4 mg/day)
Elderly: Initial: 0.1 mg once daily
Oral, extended release: *Children ≥6 years:* (Kapvay): Initial: 0.1 mg at bedtime; maximum: 0.4 mg/day [ADHD use]
Transdermal: *Adults:* Initial: 0.1 mg/24 hour patch applied once every 7 days; Maintenance: 0.1 to 0.3 mg/24 hour patch applied once every 7 days (maximum: 0.6 mg/24 hours)

Mechanism of Action Stimulates alpha$_2$-adrenoceptors in the brain stem, thus activating an inhibitory neuron, resulting in reduced sympathetic outflow from the CNS, producing a decrease in peripheral resistance, renal vascular resistance, heart rate, and blood pressure; epidural clonidine may produce pain relief at spinal presynaptic and postjunctional alpha$_2$-adrenoceptors by preventing pain signal transmission; pain relief occurs only for the body regions innervated by the spinal segments where analgesic concentrations of clonidine exist. For the treatment of ADHD, the mechanism of action is unknown; it has been proposed that postsynaptic alpha$_2$-agonist stimulation regulates subcortical activity in the prefrontal cortex, the area of the brain responsible for emotions, attentions, and behaviors and causes reduced hyperactivity, impulsiveness, and distractibility. Epidurally administered clonidine produces dose-dependent analgesia not antagonized by opiate antagonists. The analgesia is limited to the body regions innervated by the spinal segments where analgesic concentrations of clonidine are present. Clonidine is thought to produce analgesia at presynaptic and postjunctional alpha-2-adrenoceptors in the spinal cord by preventing pain signal transmission to the brain.

Pharmacodynamics/Kinetics

Onset of Action

Antihypertensive effect: Transdermal: Steady state reached in ~3 days

Attention-deficit/hyperactivity disorder: Oral: Extended release (Kapvay): Onset of action: 1 to 2 weeks (AAP 2011)

Half-life Elimination

Children: 6.13 ± 1.33 hours (Lonnqvist 1993)

Adults: Normal renal function: 12 to 16 hours; Renal impairment: ≤41 hours

Epidural administration: CSF half-life elimination: 1.3 ± 0.5 hours; plasma half-life elimination: 22 ± 15 hours

Transdermal: Half-life elimination (after patch removal): ~20 hours (due to skin depot effect; increase in plasma clonidine concentrations may occur after patch removal [MacGregor 1985])

Time to Peak Plasma: Oral: Immediate release: 1 to 3 hours; Extended release (Kapvay): 7 to 8 hours

Pregnancy Risk Factor C

Pregnancy Considerations Adverse events have been observed in some animal reproduction studies. Clonidine crosses the placenta; concentrations in the umbilical cord plasma are similar to those in the maternal serum and concentrations in the amniotic fluid may be 4 times those in the maternal serum. The pharmacokinetics of clonidine may be altered during pregnancy (Buchanan 2009). Untreated chronic maternal hypertension is associated with adverse events in the fetus, infant, and mother. If treatment for hypertension during pregnancy is needed, other agents are preferred (ACOG 2012). **[U.S. Boxed Warning]: Epidural clonidine is not recommended for obstetrical or postpartum pain** due to risk of hemodynamic instability.

Clopidogrel (kloh PID oh grel)

Related Information

Antiplatelet and Anticoagulation Considerations in Dentistry *on page 1764*

Cardiovascular Diseases *on page 1752*

Brand Names: US Plavix

Brand Names: Canada Abbott-Clopidogrel; Accel-Clopidogrel; ACT Clopidogrel; Apo-Clopidogrel; Auro-Clopidogrel; Dom-Clopidogrel; JAMP-Clopidogrel; Mar-Clopidogrel; Mint-Clopidogrel; Mylan-Clopidogrel; Plavix; PMS-Clopidogrel; RAN-Clopidogrel; Riva-Clopidogrel; Sandoz-Clopidogrel; Teva-Clopidogrel

Generic Availability (US) Yes

Pharmacologic Category Antiplatelet Agent; Antiplatelet Agent, Thienopyridine

Use

Acute coronary syndrome:

Acute ST-segment elevation myocardial infarction: To reduce the rate of myocardial infarction and stroke in conjunction with aspirin in patients with acute ST-elevation MI (STEMI) who are to be managed medically.

Unstable angina/non-ST-segment elevation myocardial infarction: To decrease the rate of MI and stroke in conjunction with aspirin in patients with non-ST-segment elevation acute coronary syndrome (unstable angina/non-ST-elevation myocardial infarction [UA/NSTEMI]), including patients who are to be managed medically and those who are to be managed with coronary revascularization.

Recent myocardial infarction, recent stroke, or established peripheral arterial disease: To reduce the rate of MI and stroke in patients with a history of recent MI, recent stroke, or established peripheral arterial disease.

Local Anesthetic/Vasoconstrictor Precautions

No information available to require special precautions

Effects on Dental Treatment Aspirin in combination with clopidogrel (Plavix®), prasugrel (Effient®), or ticagrelor (Brilinta™) is the primary prevention strategy against stent thrombosis after placement of drug-eluting metal stents in coronary patients. Premature discontinuation of combination antiplatelet therapy (ie, dual antiplatelet therapy) strongly increases the risk of a catastrophic event of stent thrombosis leading to myocardial infarction and/or death, so says a science advisory issued in January 2007 from the American Heart Association in collaboration with the American Dental Association and other professional healthcare organizations. The advisory stresses a 12-month therapy of dual antiplatelet therapy after placement of a drug-eluting stent in order to prevent thrombosis at the stent site. Any elective surgery should be postponed for 1 year after stent implantation, and if surgery must be performed, consideration should be given to continuing the antiplatelet therapy during the perioperative period in high-risk patients with drug-eluting stents.

This advisory was issued from a science panel made up of representatives from the American Heart Association (AHA), the American College of Cardiology, the Society for Cardiovascular Angiography and Interventions, the American College of Surgeons, the American Dental Association (ADA), and the American College of Physicians (Grines, 2007).

Effects on Bleeding Clopidogrel irreversibly inhibits platelet aggregation which persists for the life of the platelet (7-10 days) and until new platelets are released. Clopidogrel should **not** be discontinued in patients with cardiac stents that have not completed their full course of dual antiplatelet therapy (eg, aspirin and clopidogrel [prasugrel or ticagrelor]); patient-specific situations need to be discussed with cardiologist. If normal platelet function is desired, clopidogrel should be discontinued for at least 5 days. A medical consult is recommended to determine the benefit:risk of continuing or discontinuing clopidogrel therapy for invasive dental procedures.

Adverse Reactions As with all drugs that may affect hemostasis, bleeding is associated with clopidogrel. Hemorrhage may occur at virtually any site. Risk is dependent on multiple variables, including the concurrent use of multiple agents that alter hemostasis and patient susceptibility. Frequency not always defined.

Dermatologic: Pruritus

Gastrointestinal: Gastrointestinal hemorrhage (2%)

Hematologic & oncologic: Hematoma

Respiratory: Epistaxis

<1%, postmarketing, and/or case reports: Abdominal pain, abnormal hepatic function tests, acute generalized exanthematous pustulosis, acute hepatic failure, agranulocytosis, anaphylactoid reaction, anasarca, angioedema, aplastic anemia, arthralgia, arthritis, bronchospasm, bullous rash, colitis (including ulcerative or lymphocytic), confusion, constipation, decreased neutrophils, decreased platelet count, dermal hemorrhage, diarrhea, dizziness, DRESS syndrome, drug-induced hypersensitivity (to other thienopyridines [eg, ticlopidine, prasugrel]), duodenal ulcer, dyspepsia, eczema, eosinophilia, eosinophilic pneumonitis, erythema multiforme, erythematous rash, exfoliative dermatitis, fever, flatulence, gastric ulcer, gastritis, glomerulopathy, granulocytopenia, gynecomastia, hallucination, headache, hemarthrosis, hematuria, hemophilia A (acquired), hemophthalmos (including conjunctival and retinal), hemoptysis, hemothorax, hepatitis (noninfectious), hepatitis A, hyperbilirubinemia, hypermenorrhea, hypersensitivity reaction, hypochromic anemia, hypotension, IgA vasculitis, increased serum creatinine, interstitial pneumonitis, intracranial hemorrhage, ischemic necrosis, leukopenia, lichen planus, liver steatosis, maculopapular rash, major hemorrhage (requiring hospitalization), musculoskeletal disease (bleeding), myalgia, nausea, pancreatitis, pancytopenia, paresthesia, peripheral ischemia (potentially leading to necrosis), prolonged bleeding time, pulmonary embolism, pulmonary hemorrhage, purpura, renal function abnormality, respiratory tract hemorrhage, retroperitoneal hemorrhage, serum sickness, Stevens-Johnson syndrome, stomatitis, taste disorder, thrombotic thrombocytopenic purpura, toxic epidermal necrolysis, upper gastrointestinal tract ulcer (hemorrhagic), urticaria, vasculitis, vertigo, vomiting, wound hemorrhage

Dosing

Adult & Geriatric

Acute coronary syndrome (ACS): Oral:

Unstable angina, non-ST-segment elevation myocardial infarction (UA/NSTEMI) (also referred to as NSTE-ACS): Initial: 300 mg or 600 mg loading dose, followed by 75 mg once daily for up to 12 months in combination with aspirin, followed by aspirin indefinitely (ACC/AHA [Amsterdam 2014]). **Note:** If patient is to undergo PCI, see *Percutaneous coronary intervention (PCI) for acute coronary syndrome* dosing.

ST-segment elevation myocardial infarction (STEMI): receiving fibrinolytic therapy (in combination with aspirin and appropriate anticoagulant) (ACCF/AHA [O'Gara 2013]): **Note:** If patient is to undergo primary PCI, see *Percutaneous coronary intervention (PCI) for acute coronary syndrome* dosing.

Age ≤75 years: Loading dose of 300 mg followed by 75 mg once daily for at least 14 days up to 1 year (in the absence of bleeding).

Age >75 years: 75 mg once daily (no loading dose) for at least 14 days up to 1 year (in the absence of bleeding).

Percutaneous coronary intervention (PCI) for acute coronary syndrome (eg, NSTE-ACS or STEMI) (off-label use): 600 mg (loading dose) given as early as possible before or at the time of PCI, followed by 75 mg once daily (in combination with aspirin) for at least 12 months (bare metal or drug-eluting stent) (ACC/AHA [Amsterdam 2014]); ACC/AHA [Levine 2016]; ACCF/AHA/SCAI [Levine 2011]; ACCF/AHA [O'Gara 2013]).

PCI after fibrinolytic therapy (ACCF/AHA [O'Gara 2013]):

Fibrinolytic administered **with** a loading dose of clopidogrel: Continue 75 mg once daily and do not administer an additional loading dose.

Fibrinolytic administered within previous 24 hours **without** a loading dose of clopidogrel: Administer 300 mg loading dose before or at the time of PCI.

Fibrinolytic administered more than 24 hours ago without a loading dose of clopidogrel: Administer 600 mg loading dose before or at the time of PCI.

Higher versus standard maintenance dosing: May consider a maintenance dose of 150 mg once daily for 6 days, then 75 mg once daily thereafter in patients not at high risk for bleeding (CURRENT-OASIS 7 Investigators 2010); however, in another study, in patients with high on-treatment platelet reactivity, the use of 150 mg once daily for 6 months did not demonstrate a difference in 6-month incidence of death from cardiovascular causes, nonfatal MI, or stent thrombosis compared to standard dose therapy (Price 2011).

Duration of clopidogrel (in combination with aspirin) after stent placement for ACS: **Premature interruption of therapy may result in stent thrombosis with subsequent fatal and nonfatal MI.** According to the ACC/AHA Duration of Dual Antiplatelet Therapy (DAPT) guidelines, at least 12 months of a $P2Y_{12}$ inhibitor (eg, clopidogrel) is recommended for those with ACS receiving either stent type (bare metal [BMS] or drug eluting stent [DES]). The DAPT score may be useful in determining whether to prolong or extend DAPT in patients with stent placement (Yeh 2016). In patients with DES placement with a high risk of bleeding or significant overt bleeding on DAPT, it may be reasonable to discontinue clopidogrel after 6 months of therapy (ACC/AHA [Levine 2016]).

CYP2C19 poor metabolizers (ie, *CYP2C19*2* or *3 carriers): Although routine genetic testing is not recommended in patients treated with clopidogrel undergoing PCI, testing may be considered to identify poor metabolizers who would be at risk for poor outcomes while receiving clopidogrel; if identified, these patients may be considered for an alternative $P2Y_{12}$ inhibitor (Levine 2011). An appropriate regimen for this patient population has not been established in clinical outcome trials. Although a 600 mg loading dose, followed by 150 mg once daily produced greater active metabolite exposure and antiplatelet response compared to the 300 mg/ 75 mg regimen, it does not appear that this dosing strategy improves outcomes for this patient population (Price 2011; Simon 2011).

Atrial fibrillation (off-label use): Oral: 75 mg once daily (in combination with aspirin 75-100 mg once daily) (ACTIVE Investigators 2009). **Note:** Oral anticoagulation is preferred due to better outcomes; clopidogrel and aspirin may be used in patients who cannot take oral anticoagulation and are at low bleeding risk (ACCP [You 2012]).

Carotid artery stenosis, symptomatic (including recent carotid endarterectomy) (off-label use): Oral: 75 mg once daily (ACCP [Guyatt 2012])

Coronary artery bypass graft surgery (secondary prevention) (off-label use) (AHA [Kulik 2015]):

Following off-pump CABG: 75 mg once daily (in combination with aspirin) for 1 year

Aspirin-allergic or -intolerant patients: 75 mg once daily; continue indefinitely

Coronary artery disease (CAD), established (off-label use): Oral: 75 mg once daily. **Note:** Established CAD defined as patients 1-year post ACS, with prior revascularization, coronary stenosis >50% by angiogram, and/or evidence for cardiac ischemia on diagnostic testing (includes patients after the first year post-ACS and/or with prior CABG surgery) (ACCP [Guyatt 2012]).

Percutaneous coronary intervention (PCI), non-acute coronary syndrome (ie, stable ischemic heart disease) (off-label use): 600 mg (loading dose) given as early as possible before or at the time of PCI, followed by 75 mg once daily (in combination with aspirin) for at least 1 month (bare metal stent) or for at least 6 months (drug-eluting stent) (ACC/AHA [Levine 2016]; ACCF/AHA/SCAI [Levine 2011]).

Duration of clopidogrel (in combination with aspirin) after stent placement for stable ischemic heart disease (SIHD): **Premature interruption of therapy may result in stent thrombosis with subsequent fatal and nonfatal MI.** According to the ACC/AHA Duration of Dual Antiplatelet Therapy (DAPT) guidelines, those receiving a newer generation DES, at least 6 months of clopidogrel therapy is recommended. Those receiving a BMS should be given clopidogrel for a minimum of 1 month. The DAPT score may be useful in determining whether to prolong or extend DAPT in patients with stent placement (Yeh 2016). In patients with DES placement with a high risk of bleeding or significant overt bleeding on DAPT, it may be reasonable to discontinue clopidogrel after 3 months of therapy (ACC/AHA [Levine 2016]).

Peripheral artery percutaneous transluminal angioplasty (with or without stenting) or peripheral artery bypass graft surgery, postprocedure (off-label use): Oral: 75 mg once daily. **Note:** For below-knee bypass graft surgery with prosthetic grafts, combine with aspirin 75-100 mg/day (ACCP [Guyatt 2012]).

Recent MI, recent stroke, or established peripheral arterial disease (PAD): Oral: 75 mg once daily. **Note:** The ACCF/AHA guidelines for PAD recommend clopidogrel as an alternative to aspirin (Class Ib recommendation) or in conjunction with aspirin for those who are not at an increased risk of bleeding but are of high cardiovascular risk (Class IIb recommendation). These recommendations also pertain to those with intermittent claudication or critical limb ischemia, prior lower extremity revascularization, or prior amputation for lower extremity ischemia (ACCF/AHA [Rooke 2011]).

Secondary prevention of cardioembolic stroke (patient not candidate for oral anticoagulation) (off-label use): Oral: 75 mg once daily (in combination with aspirin) (ACCP [Guyatt 2012])

Renal Impairment No dosage adjustment necessary (Basra 2011). **Note:** GFR stage 5 (ie, ESRD or an eGFR <15 mL/minute) is associated with higher residual platelet reactivity with maintenance dosing (Muller 2012).

Hepatic Impairment No dosage adjustment necessary.

Mechanism of Action Clopidogrel requires *in vivo* biotransformation to an active thiol metabolite. The active metabolite irreversibly blocks the $P2Y_{12}$ component of ADP receptors on the platelet surface, which prevents activation of the GPIIb/IIIa receptor complex, thereby reducing platelet aggregation. Platelets blocked by clopidogrel are affected for the remainder of their lifespan (~7-10 days).

Contraindications

Hypersensitivity (eg, anaphylaxis) to clopidogrel or any component of the formulation; active pathological bleeding (eg,, peptic ulcer, intracranial hemorrhage).

Canadian labeling: Additional contraindications (not in U.S. labeling): Significant liver impairment or cholestatic jaundice; concomitant use of repaglinide

Warnings/Precautions [US Boxed Warning]: Effectiveness of clopidogrel results from its antiplatelet activity, which is dependent on its conversion to an active metabolite by the CYP-450 system, principally CYP2C19. In patients who are homozygous for nonfunctional alleles of the CYP2C19 genes (termed "CYP2C19 poor metabolizers"), clopidogrel at recommended doses forms less of the active metabolite and has a reduced effect on platelet activity. Tests are available to identify patients who are CYP2C19 poor metabolizers. Consider use of another platelet P2Y12 inhibitor in patients identified as CYP2C19 poor metabolizers. Genetic testing may be considered prior to initiating clopidogrel in patients at moderate or high risk for poor outcomes (eg, PCI in patients with extensive and/or very complex disease). The optimal dose for CYP2C19 poor metabolizers has yet to be determined. After initiation of clopidogrel, functional testing (eg, VerifyNow® P2Y12 assay) may also be done to determine clopidogrel responsiveness (Holmes 2010).

In patients with coronary stents, premature interruption of therapy may result in stent thrombosis with subsequent fatal and nonfatal MI. Duration of therapy, in general, is determined by the type of stent placed (bare metal or drug eluting) and whether an ACS event was ongoing at the time of placement (ACC/AHA [Levine 2016]; AHA/ACC/SCAI/ACS/ADA [Grines 2007]). Consider discontinuing 5 days before elective surgery (except in patients with cardiac stents that have not completed their full course of dual antiplatelet therapy; patient-specific situations need to be discussed with cardiologist; AHA/ACC/SCAI/ACS/ADA Science Advisory provides recommendations). Discontinue at least

5 days before elective CABG; when urgent CABG is necessary, the ACCF/AHA CABG guidelines recommend discontinuation for at least 24 hours prior to surgery (ACCF/AHA [Hillis 2011]). The ACCF/AHA STEMI guidelines recommend discontinuation for at least 24 hours prior to on-pump CABG if possible; off-pump CABG may be performed within 24 hours of clopidogrel administration if the benefits of prompt revascularization outweigh the risks of bleeding (ACCF/AHA [O'Gara 2013]).

Because of structural similarities, cross-reactivity has been reported among the thienopyridines (clopidogrel, prasugrel, and ticlopidine); use with caution or avoid in patients with hypersensitivity or hematologic reactions to previous thienopyridine use. Use of clopidogrel is contraindicated in patients with hypersensitivity to clopidogrel. Although desensitization may be considered for mild-to-moderate hypersensitivity, do not desensitize patients with prior life-threatening allergic reactions to clopidogrel (eg, toxic epidermal necrolysis, exfoliative dermatitis, Stevens-Johnson syndrome, TTP) (Lokhandwala 2011). Use with caution in patients with moderate to severe renal impairment (experience is limited).

Clopidogrel increases the risk of bleeding. Use is contraindicated in patients with active pathological bleeding (eg, peptic ulcer, intracranial hemorrhage). Additional risk factors for bleeding include age ≥75 years, propensity to bleed (eg, recent trauma or surgery, recent or recurrent GI bleeding, active peptic ulcer disease, severe hepatic impairment), body weight <60 kg, CABG or other surgical procedure, concomitant use of medications that increase risk of bleeding (eg, warfarin, NSAIDs). Use with caution in patients with platelet disorders, bleeding disorders and/or at increased risk for bleeding. Bleeding should be suspected if patient becomes hypotensive after undergoing recent coronary angiography, PCI, CABG, or other surgical procedure even if overt signs of bleeding do not exist. It may be possible to restore hemostasis by administering exogenous platelets; however, platelet transfusions within 4 hours of the loading dose or 2 hours of the maintenance dose may be less effective. Cases of TTP (usually occurring within the first 2 weeks of therapy), resulting in some fatalities, have been reported; urgent plasmapheresis is required. In patients with recent lacunar stroke (within 180 days), the use of clopidogrel in addition to aspirin did not significantly reduce the incidence of the primary outcome of stroke recurrence (any ischemic stroke or intracranial hemorrhage) compared to aspirin alone; the use of clopidogrel in addition to aspirin did however increase the risk of major hemorrhage and the rate of all-cause mortality (SPS3 Investigators 2012). Potentially significant interactions may exist, requiring dose or frequency adjustment, additional monitoring, and/or selection of alternative therapy.

Drug Interactions

Metabolism/Transport Effects **Substrate** of CYP2C19 (major), CYP3A4 (minor); **Note:** Assignment of Major/Minor substrate status based on clinically relevant drug interaction potential; **Inhibits** CYP2B6 (weak), CYP2C8 (moderate), CYP2C9 (weak), SLCO1B1

Avoid Concomitant Use

Avoid concomitant use of Clopidogrel with any of the following: Amodiaquine; Urokinase

Increased Effect/Toxicity

Clopidogrel may increase the levels/effects of: Agents with Antiplatelet Properties; Amodiaquine; Anticoagulants; Apixaban; BuPROPion; Cephalothin; Collagenase (Systemic); CYP2C8 Substrates; Dabigatran Etexilate; Deoxycholic Acid; Edoxaban; Ibritumomab; Obinutuzumab; Pioglitazone; Repaglinide; Rivaroxaban; Rosuvastatin; Salicylates; Thrombolytic Agents; Tositumomab and Iodine I 131 Tositumomab; Urokinase; Warfarin

The levels/effects of Clopidogrel may be increased by: Dasatinib; FluvoxaMINE; Glucosamine; Herbs (Anticoagulant/Antiplatelet Properties); Ibrutinib; Limaprost; Multivitamins/Fluoride (with ADE); Multivitamins/Minerals (with ADEK, Folate, Iron); Multivitamins/Minerals (with AE, No Iron); Omega-3 Fatty Acids; Pentosan Polysulfate Sodium; Pentoxifylline; Prostacyclin Analogues; Rifamycin Derivatives; Tipranavir; Vitamin E (Systemic)

Decreased Effect

The levels/effects of Clopidogrel may be decreased by: Amiodarone; Calcium Channel Blockers; Cangrelor; CYP2C19 Inhibitors (Moderate); CYP2C19 Inhibitors (Strong); Dexlansoprazole; Erythromycin (Systemic); Esomeprazole; FluvoxaMINE; Grapefruit Juice; Lansoprazole; Morphine (Liposomal); Morphine (Systemic); Omeprazole; Pantoprazole; RABEprazole

Food Interactions Consumption of three 200 mL glasses of grapefruit juice a day may substantially reduce clopidogrel antiplatelet effects. Management: Avoid or minimize the consumption of grapefruit or grapefruit juice (Holmberg, 2013).

Dietary Considerations Avoid or minimize the consumption of grapefruit juice (Holmberg, 2013).

Pharmacodynamics/Kinetics

Onset of Action

Onset of action: Inhibition of platelet aggregation (IPA): Dose-dependent:

- 300-600 mg loading dose: Detected within 2 hours
- 50-100 mg/day: Detected by the second day of treatment

Peak effect: Time to maximal IPA: Dose-dependent: **Note:** Degree of IPA based on adenosine diphosphate (ADP) concentration used during light aggregometry:

- 300-600 mg loading dose:
  - ADP 5 micromole/L: 20% to 30% IPA at 6 hours post administration (Montelescot, 2006)
  - ADP 20 micromole/L: 30% to 37% IPA at 6 hours post administration (Montelescot, 2006)
- 50-100 mg/day: ADP 5 micromole/L: 50% to 60% IPA at 5-7 days (Herbert, 1993)

Duration of Action Platelet aggregation and bleeding time gradually return to baseline after ~5 days after discontinuation.

Half-life Elimination Parent drug: ~6 hours; Thiol derivatiove (active metabolite) ~30 minutes; carboxylic acid derivative (inactive; main circulating metabolite): ~8 hours; **Note:** A clopidogrel radiolabeled study has shown that covalent binding to platelets accounts for 2% of radiolabel and has a half-life of 11 days.

Time to Peak Serum: ~0.75 hours

Pregnancy Risk Factor B

Pregnancy Considerations Adverse events have not been observed in animal reproduction studies. Information related to use during pregnancy is limited (Bauer 2012; DeSantis 2011; Myers 2011).

Breastfeeding Considerations It is not known if clopidogrel is excreted in breast milk. Due to the potential for serious adverse reactions in the nursing infant, the manufacturer recommends a decision be made whether to discontinue nursing or to discontinue the drug, taking into account the importance of treatment to the mother.

Dosage Forms

Tablet, Oral:

Plavix: 75 mg, 300 mg

Generic: 75 mg, 300 mg

Dental Comment There is no scientific evidence to warrant the discontinuance of clopidogrel prior to dental surgery. Patients taking one clopidogrel tablet daily as an antithrombotic and who require dental surgery should be given special consideration in consultation with physician.

Clorazepate (klor AZ e pate)

Related Information

Dentin Hypersensitivity, Acid Erosion, High Caries Index, Management of Alveolar Osteitis, and Xerostomia *on page 1857*

Brand Names: US Tranxene-T

Brand Names: Canada Clorazepate

Pharmacologic Category Anticonvulsant, Benzodiazepine; Benzodiazepine

Use

Alcohol withdrawal: Symptomatic relief of acute alcohol withdrawal.

Anxiety disorders: Management of anxiety disorders and short-term relief of the symptoms of anxiety.

Partial seizures: Adjunct therapy in the management of partial seizures.

Local Anesthetic/Vasoconstrictor Precautions No information available to require special precautions

Effects on Dental Treatment Key adverse event(s) related to dental treatment: Xerostomia (normal salivary flow resumes upon discontinuation); drowsiness; Patients may experience orthostatic hypotension as they stand up after treatment; especially if lying in dental chair for extended periods of time. Use caution with sudden changes in position during and after dental treatment. It is suggested that opioid analgesics not be given for pain control to patients taking clorazepate due to enhanced sedation.

Effects on Bleeding No information available to require special precautions

Adverse Reactions Frequency not defined.

Cardiovascular: Hypotension

Central nervous system: Anxiety, ataxia, confusion, depression, dizziness, drowsiness, dysarthria, fatigue, headache, insomnia, irritability, memory impairment, nervousness, slurred speech

Dermatologic: Skin rash

Endocrine & metabolic: Decreased libido

Gastrointestinal: Constipation, decreased appetite, diarrhea, increased appetite, nausea, vomiting, xerostomia

Hepatic: Increased serum transaminases, jaundice

Neuromuscular & skeletal: Tremor

Ophthalmic: Blurred vision, diplopia

General Dosage Range Oral:

Children 9 to 12 years: Initial: Up to 7.5 mg twice daily; maximum dose: 60 mg/day.

Children >12 years, Adolescents, and Adults: Initial: Up to 7.5 mg 3 times daily; maximum dose: 90 mg/day.

Elderly: Anxiety: Initial: 7.5 mg to 15 mg/day

Mechanism of Action Binds to stereospecific benzodiazepine receptors on the postsynaptic GABA neuron at several sites within the central nervous system, including the limbic system and reticular formation. Enhancement of the inhibitory effect of GABA on neuronal excitability results by increased neuronal membrane permeability to chloride ions. This shift in chloride ions results in hyperpolarization (a less excitable state) and stabilization. Benzodiazepine receptors and effects appear to be linked to the GABA-A receptors. Benzodiazepines do not bind to GABA-B receptors (Nelson 1999).

Pharmacodynamics/Kinetics

Half-life Elimination Nordiazepam: 20 to 160 hours; Oxazepam: 6 to 24 hours (Riss, 2008)

Time to Peak Serum: ~0.5 to 2 hour (Carrigan, 1977; Riss, 2008)

Pregnancy Considerations Nordiazepam, the active metabolite of clorazepate, crosses the placenta and is measurable in cord blood and amniotic fluid. Teratogenic effects have been observed with some benzodiazepines (including clorazepate); however, additional studies are needed. The incidence of premature birth and low birth weights may be increased following maternal use of benzodiazepines; hypoglycemia and respiratory problems in the neonate may occur following exposure late in pregnancy. Neonatal withdrawal symptoms may occur within days to weeks after birth and "floppy infant syndrome" (which also includes withdrawal symptoms) has been reported with some benzodiazepines (Bergman 1992; Iqbal 2002; Patel 1980; Rey 1979; Wikner 2007). A combination of factors influences the potential teratogenicity of anticonvulsant therapy. When treating women with epilepsy, monotherapy with the lowest effective dose and avoidance of medications known to have a high incidence of teratogenic effects is recommended (Harden 2009; Wlodarczyk 2012).

Patients exposed to clorazepate during pregnancy are encouraged to enroll themselves into the AED Pregnancy Registry by calling 1-888-233-2334. Additional information is available at www.aedpregnancyregistry.org.

Controlled Substance C-IV

Clotrimazole (Oral) (kloe TRIM a zole)

Related Information

Fungal Infections *on page 1847*

Related Sample Prescriptions

Fungal Infections - Sample Prescriptions *on page 35*

Generic Availability (US) Yes

Pharmacologic Category Antifungal Agent, Imidazole Derivative; Antifungal Agent, Oral Nonabsorbed

Dental Use Treatment of susceptible fungal infections, including oropharyngeal candidiasis; limited data suggest that clotrimazole troches may be effective for prophylaxis against oropharyngeal candidiasis in neutropenic patients

Use

Oropharyngeal candidiasis (treatment): Local treatment of oropharyngeal candidiasis.

Oropharyngeal candidiasis (prophylaxis): To reduce the incidence of oropharyngeal candidiasis in immunocompromised patients undergoing chemotherapy, radiotherapy, or steroid therapy utilized in the treatment of leukemia, solid tumors, or renal transplantation.

Local Anesthetic/Vasoconstrictor Precautions No information available to require special precautions

Effects on Dental Treatment No significant effects or complications reported

Effects on Bleeding No information available to require special precautions

Adverse Reactions

>10%: Hepatic: Abnormal liver function tests

Frequency not defined:

Dermatologic: Pruritus

Gastrointestinal: Nausea, vomiting

Dental Usual Dosage Oropharyngeal candidiasis: Children >3 years and Adults: Oral:

Prophylaxis: 10 mg troche dissolved 3 times/day for the duration of chemotherapy or until steroids are reduced to maintenance levels

Treatment: 10 mg troche dissolved slowly 5 times/day for 14 consecutive days

Dosing

Adult & Geriatric

Oropharyngeal candidiasis (prophylaxis): Oral: 10 mg dissolved slowly 3 times daily for the duration of chemotherapy or until steroids are reduced to maintenance levels.

Oropharyngeal candidiasis (treatment): Oral: 10 mg dissolved slowly 5 times daily for 14 consecutive days. Note: When used for initial treatment in patients with HIV-1, duration of therapy is 7 to 14 days (DHHS [adult] 2014; DHHS [pediatric] 2013).

Pediatric Oropharyngeal candidiasis (treatment): Children ≥3 years and Adolescents: Refer to adult dosing.

Renal Impairment There are no dosage adjustments provided in the manufacturer's labeling.

Hepatic Impairment There are no dosage adjustments provided in the manufacturer's labeling.

Mechanism of Action Binds to phospholipids in the fungal cell membrane altering cell wall permeability resulting in loss of essential intracellular elements

Contraindications

Hypersensitivity to clotrimazole or any component of the formulation

Documentation of allergenic cross-reactivity for antifungals is limited. However, because of similarities in chemical structure and/or pharmacologic actions, the possibility of cross-sensitivity can not be ruled out with certainty.

Warnings/Precautions Clotrimazole should not be used for treatment of systemic fungal infection. Abnormal LFTs have been reported, including abnormal aspartate aminotransferase (AST). Elevations are usually minimal. Monitor LFTs periodically, especially in patients with preexisting hepatic impairment. Clotrimazole must be slowly dissolved in the mouth for maximum efficacy. Potentially significant drug-drug interactions may exist, requiring dose or frequency adjustment, additional monitoring, and/or selection of alternative therapy.

Drug Interactions

Metabolism/Transport Effects Inhibits CYP1A2 (weak), CYP2A6 (weak), CYP2C8 (weak), CYP2C9 (weak), CYP2E1 (weak), CYP3A4 (weak)

Avoid Concomitant Use

Avoid concomitant use of Clotrimazole (Oral) with any of the following: Amodiaquine; Pimozide

Increased Effect/Toxicity

Clotrimazole (Oral) may increase the levels/effects of: Amodiaquine; ARIPiprazole; CloZAPine; Dofetilide; Flibanserin; HYDROcodone; Lomitapide; NiMODipine; Pimozide; Tacrolimus (Systemic); TiZANidine

Decreased Effect There are no known significant interactions involving a decrease in effect.

Pregnancy Risk Factor C

Pregnancy Considerations Adverse events have been observed in animal reproduction studies.

Breastfeeding Considerations

It is not known if clotrimazole is excreted in breast milk following oral (troche) administration (data not located); however, systemic absorption is low (Sawyer 1975).

Dosage Forms

Lozenge, Mouth/Throat:

Generic: 10 mg (70 ea, 140 ea)

Troche, Mouth/Throat:

Generic: 10 mg

Clotrimazole (Topical) (kloe TRIM a zole)

Brand Names: US 3 Day Vaginal [OTC]; Alevazol [OTC]; Clotrimazole 3 Day [OTC]; Clotrimazole GRx [OTC]; Desenex [OTC]; Gyne-Lotrimin 3 [OTC]; Gyne-Lotrimin [OTC]; Lotrimin AF For Her [OTC]; Lotrimin AF [OTC]; Pro-Ex Antifungal [OTC]; Shopko Athletes Foot [OTC]

Brand Names: Canada Canesten Topical; Canesten Vaginal; Clotrimaderm; Trivagizole-3

Generic Availability (US) Yes

Pharmacologic Category Antifungal Agent, Imidazole Derivative; Antifungal Agent, Oral Nonabsorbed/Partially Absorbed; Antifungal Agent, Topical; Antifungal Agent, Vaginal

Use Treatment of susceptible fungal infections, including dermatophytoses, superficial mycoses, and cutaneous candidiasis, as well as vulvovaginal candidiasis

Local Anesthetic/Vasoconstrictor Precautions

No information available to require special precautions

Effects on Dental Treatment No significant effects or complications reported

Effects on Bleeding No information available to require special precautions

Adverse Reactions Vaginal:

1% to 10%: Genitourinary: Vulvovaginal burning

<1% (Limited to important or life-threatening): Burning sensation of the penis (of sexual partner), polyuria, pruritus vulvae, vaginal discharge, vulvar pain, vulvar swelling

Dental Usual Dosage Cutaneous candidiasis: Children >3 years and Adults: Topical (cream, solution): Apply twice daily; if no improvement occurs after 4 weeks of therapy, re-evaluate diagnosis.

Dosing

Adult & Geriatric

Dermatophytosis, cutaneous candidiasis: Topical (cream, solution): Apply twice daily; if no improvement occurs after 4 weeks of therapy, re-evaluate diagnosis.

Vulvovaginal candidiasis: Intravaginal:

Cream (1%): Insert 1 applicatorful of 1% vaginal cream daily (preferably at bedtime) for 7 consecutive days. **Note:** Guidelines recommend a duration of 7 to 14 days (CDC [Workowski 2015]).

Cream (2%): Insert 1 applicatorful of 2% vaginal cream daily (preferably at bedtime) for 3 consecutive days.

Dermatologic infection (superficial): Topical (cream, solution): Apply to affected area twice daily (morning and evening) for 7 consecutive days.

Pediatric Vaginal, topical infections: Children >12 years: Refer to adult dosing.

Mechanism of Action Binds to phospholipids in the fungal cell membrane altering cell wall permeability resulting in loss of essential intracellular elements

Contraindications Hypersensitivity to clotrimazole or any component of the formulation

Warnings/Precautions Avoid contact with eyes.

Benzyl alcohol and derivatives: Some dosage forms may contain benzyl alcohol; large amounts of benzyl alcohol (≥99 mg/kg/day) have been associated with a potentially fatal toxicity ("gasping syndrome") in neonates; the "gasping syndrome" consists of metabolic acidosis, respiratory distress, gasping respirations, CNS dysfunction (including convulsions, intracranial hemorrhage), hypotension and cardiovascular collapse (AAP ["Inactive" 1997]; CDC, 1982); some data suggests that benzoate displaces bilirubin from protein binding sites (Ahlfors, 2001); avoid or use dosage forms containing benzyl alcohol with caution in neonates. See manufacturer's labeling.

Drug Interactions

Metabolism/Transport Effects None known.

Avoid Concomitant Use

Avoid concomitant use of Clotrimazole (Topical) with any of the following: Progesterone

Increased Effect/Toxicity

Clotrimazole (Topical) may increase the levels/effects of: Sirolimus; Tacrolimus (Systemic)

Decreased Effect

Clotrimazole (Topical) may decrease the levels/effects of: Progesterone

Pharmacodynamics/Kinetics

Time to Peak Serum: Vaginal cream: ~24 hours

Pregnancy Considerations Following topical and vaginal administration, small amounts of imidazoles are absorbed systemically (Duhm 1974). Vaginal topical azole products (7-day therapies only) are the preferred treatment of vulvovaginal candidiasis in pregnant women. This product may weaken latex condoms and diaphragms (CDC [Workowski 2015]).

Dosage Forms

Cream, External:
- Clotrimazole GRx [OTC]: 1% (14 g)
- Desenex [OTC]: 1% (30 g)
- Lotrimin AF [OTC]: 1% (12 g, 24 g)
- Lotrimin AF For Her [OTC]: 1% (24 g)
- Pro-Ex Antifungal [OTC]: 1% (42 g)
- Shopko Athletes Foot [OTC]: 1% (28.4 g)
- Generic: 1% (15 g, 30 g, 45 g)

Cream, Vaginal:
- 3 Day Vaginal [OTC]: 2% (21 g)
- Clotrimazole 3 Day [OTC]: 2% (22.2 g)
- Gyne-Lotrimin [OTC]: 1% (45 g)
- Gyne-Lotrimin 3 [OTC]: 2% (21 g)
- Generic: 1% (45 g)

Ointment, External:
- Alevazol [OTC]: 1% (56.7 g)

Solution, External:
- Generic: 1% (10 mL, 30 mL)

Cloxacillin (kloks a SIL in)

Brand Names: Canada Apo-Cloxi; Cloxacillin for injection; Novo-Cloxin

Pharmacologic Category Antibiotic, Penicillin

Use Note: Not approved in the US

Bacterial infections: Treatment of bacterial infections including endocarditis, pneumonia, bone and joint infections, skin and soft-tissue infections, and sepsis that are caused by susceptible strains of penicillinase-producing staphylococci.

Limitations of use: Exhibits good activity against *Staphylococcus aureus*; has activity against many streptococci, but is less active than penicillin and is generally not used in clinical practice to treat streptococcal infections. Not effective against methicillin-resistant staphylococci.

Local Anesthetic/Vasoconstrictor Precautions No information available to require special precautions

Effects on Dental Treatment Key adverse event(s) related to dental treatment: Prolonged use of penicillins may lead to development of oral candidiasis.

Effects on Bleeding No information available to require special precautions

Adverse Reactions Frequency not defined. Adverse effects may be reported as class effects rather than specific to cloxacillin.

Cardiovascular: Hypotension, thrombophlebitis

Central nervous system: Confusion, lethargy, myoclonus, seizure (high doses and/or renal failure), twitching

Dermatologic: Pruritus, skin rash, urticaria

Gastrointestinal: Abdominal pain, diarrhea, epigastric distress, flatulence, hairy tongue, loose stools, melanoglossia, nausea, oral candidiasis, pseudomembranous colitis, stomatitis, vomiting

Genitourinary: Hematuria, proteinuria

Hematologic & oncologic: Agranulocytosis, anemia, bone marrow depression, eosinophilia, granulocytopenia, hemolytic anemia, immune thrombocytopenia, leukopenia, neutropenia, thrombocytopenia

Hepatic: Increased serum alkaline phosphatase, increased serum ALT, increased serum AST, hepatotoxicity

Hypersensitivity: Anaphylaxis, angioedema, hypersensitivity reaction (immediate and delayed)

Immunologic: Serum sickness-like reaction

Neuromuscular & skeletal: Laryngospasm

Renal: Interstitial nephritis, renal insufficiency, renal tubular disease

Respiratory: Bronchospasm, laryngeal edema, sneezing, wheezing

Miscellaneous: Fever

General Dosage Range

Oral:

Children ≤20 kg: 25 to 50 mg/kg/day in divided doses every 6 hours

Children >20 kg and Adults: 250 to 500 mg every 6 hours

IM:

Children ≤20 kg: 25 to 50 mg/kg/day in divided doses every 6 hours

Children >20 kg and Adults: 250 to 500 mg every 6 hours

IV:

Children ≤20 kg: 25 to 50 mg/kg/day in divided doses every 6 hours

Children >20 kg and Adults: 250 to 500 mg every 6 hours (maximum adult dose: 6 g/day)

Mechanism of Action Inhibits bacterial cell wall synthesis by binding to one or more of the penicillin-binding proteins (PBPs) which in turn inhibit the final transpeptidation step of peptidoglycan synthesis in bacterial cell walls, thus inhibiting cell wall biosynthesis. Bacteria eventually lyse due to ongoing activity of cell wall autolytic enzymes (autolysins and murein hydrolases) while cell wall assembly is arrested.

Pharmacodynamics/Kinetics

Half-life Elimination 0.5 to 1.5 hours; prolonged with renal impairment and in neonates

Time to Peak Oral: Serum: ~1 hour

Pregnancy Considerations Cloxacillin crosses the placenta and distributes into fetal tissue

Product Availability Not available in the US

CloZAPine (KLOE za peen)

Brand Names: US Clozaril; FazaClo; Versacloz

Brand Names: Canada AA-Clozapine; Clozaril; Gen-Clozapine

Pharmacologic Category Second Generation (Atypical) Antipsychotic

Use

Schizophrenia, treatment resistant: Treatment of severely ill patients with schizophrenia who fail to respond adequately to antipsychotic treatment.

Suicidal behavior in schizophrenia or schizoaffective disorder: To reduce the risk of suicidal behavior in patients with schizophrenia or schizoaffective disorder who are judged to be at chronic risk for reexperiencing suicidal behavior, based on history and recent clinical state.

Local Anesthetic/Vasoconstrictor Precautions Most pharmacology textbooks state that in presence of phenothiazines, systemic doses of epinephrine paradoxically decrease the blood pressure. This is the so called "epinephrine reversal" phenomenon. This has never been observed when epinephrine is given by infiltration as part of the local anesthesia procedure.

Effects on Dental Treatment Key adverse event(s) related to dental treatment: Sialorrhea and xerostomia (normal salivary flow resumes upon discontinuation); Patients may experience orthostatic hypotension as they stand up after treatment; especially if lying in dental chair for extended periods of time. Use caution with sudden changes in position during and after dental treatment. Do not use atropine-like drugs for xerostomia in patients taking clozapine due to significant potentiation.

Effects on Bleeding No information available to require special precautions

Adverse Reactions

>10%:

Cardiovascular: Tachycardia (17% to 25%), hypotension (9% to 13%), hypertension (4% to 12%)

Central nervous system: Drowsiness (≤39% to 46%), sedation (≤39%), dizziness (14% to 27%), insomnia (2% to 20%), vertigo (≤19%)

Gastrointestinal: Sialorrhea (13% to 48%), weight gain (4% to 31%), constipation (14% to 25%), nausea (5% to 17%), vomiting (3% to 17%), dyspepsia (14%)

Miscellaneous: Fever (5% to 13%)

1% to 10%:

Cardiovascular: Syncope (6%)

Central nervous system: Headache (7% to 10%), agitation (4%), restlessness (4%), akinesia (≤4%), disturbed sleep (≤4%), nightmares (≤4%), akathisia (3%), confusion (3%), seizure (3%; dose related), fatigue (2%)

Dermatologic: Diaphoresis (6%), skin rash (2%)

Gastrointestinal: Xerostomia (5% to 6%), abdominal distress (≤4%), heartburn (≤4%), diarrhea (2%)

Genitourinary: Urine abnormality (2%)

Hematologic & oncologic: Leukopenia (≤3%), neutropenia (≤3%), eosinophilia (1%)

Neuromuscular & skeletal: Tremor (6%), hypokinesia (≤4%), muscle rigidity (3%)

Ophthalmic: Visual disturbance (5%)

<1%, postmarketing, and/or case reports: Abnormal electrocephalogram, agranulocytosis, angioedema, aspiration, bradycardia, cardiac arrhythmia (atrial or ventricular), cardiac failure, cardiomyopathy (usually dilated), cataplexy, cerebrovascular accident, cholestasis, colitis, deep vein thrombosis, delirium, diabetes mellitus, dyschromia, dysphagia, enlargement of salivary glands, erythema multiforme, esophageal dysmotility, fecal impaction, gastroenteritis, granulocytopenia, hepatic cirrhosis, hepatic fibrosis, hepatic insufficiency, hepatic necrosis, hepatitis, hepatotoxicity, hyperglycemia, hyperosmolar coma, hypersensitivity reaction, hyperuricemia, hyponatremia, increased creatine, increased erythrocyte sedimentation rate, increased hematocrit, increased hemoglobin, increased serum cholesterol, increased serum triglycerides, interstitial nephritis (acute), intestinal obstruction, jaundice, ketoacidosis, leukocytosis, liver injury, liver steatosis, lower respiratory tract infection, mitral valve insufficiency, myasthenia syndrome, myocardial infarction, myocarditis, myoclonus, neuroleptic malignant syndrome, nocturnal enuresis, obsessive compulsive disorder, obstructive sleep apnea syndrome (Shirani 2011), orthostatic hypotension, palpitations, pancreatitis (acute), paralytic ileus, paresthesia, periorbital edema, pheochromocytoma (pseudo), pleural effusion, pneumonia, priapism, prolonged QT interval on ECG, psychosis (exacerbated), pulmonary embolism, renal failure, retrograde ejaculation, rhabdomyolysis, sialadenitis, sepsis, skin photosensitivity, status epilepticus, Stevens-Johnson syndrome, syncope, systemic lupus erythematosus, tardive dyskinesia, thrombocytopenia, thrombocytosis, torsade de pointes, vasculitis, weight loss

General Dosage Range Oral: *Adults:* Initial: 12.5 mg once or twice daily; Usual maintenance: 300 to 450 mg daily (maximum: 900 mg daily)

Mechanism of Action The therapeutic efficacy of clozapine (dibenzodiazepine antipsychotic) is proposed to be mediated through antagonism of the dopamine type 2 (D_2) and serotonin type 2A (5-HT_{2A}) receptors. In addition, it acts as an antagonist at alpha-adrenergic, histamine H_1, cholinergic, and other dopaminergic and serotonergic receptors.

Pharmacodynamics/Kinetics

Onset of Action Within 1 week for sedation, improvement in sleep; 6 to 12 weeks for antipsychotic effects; Adequate trial: 6 to 12 weeks at a therapeutic dose and blood level; Maximum effect: 6 to 12 months; improvement may continue 6 to 12 months after clozapine initiation (Meltzer 2003)

Duration of Action Variable

Half-life Elimination Steady state: 12 hours (range: 4 to 66 hours)

Time to Peak Suspension: 2.2 hours (range: 1 to 3.5 hours); Tablets: 2.5 hours (range: 1 to 6 hours); Dispersible tablets: 2.3 hours (range: 1 to 6 hours)

Pregnancy Risk Factor B

Pregnancy Considerations Adverse events were not observed in animal reproduction studies. Clozapine crosses the placenta and can be detected in the fetal blood and amniotic fluid (Barnas, 1994). Antipsychotic use during the third trimester of pregnancy has a risk for abnormal muscle movements (extrapyramidal symptoms [EPS]) and/or withdrawal symptoms in newborns following delivery. Symptoms in the newborn may include agitation, feeding disorder, hypertonia, hypotonia, respiratory distress, somnolence, and tremor; these effects may be self-limiting or require hospitalization.

Clozapine may theoretically cause agranulocytosis in the fetus and should not routinely be used in pregnancy (NICE 2007). The American College of Obstetricians and Gynecologists recommends that therapy during pregnancy be individualized; treatment with psychiatric medications during pregnancy should incorporate the clinical expertise of the mental health clinician, obstetrician, primary healthcare provider, and pediatrician. Safety data related to atypical antipsychotics during pregnancy is limited and routine use is not recommended. However, if a woman is inadvertently exposed to an atypical antipsychotic while pregnant, continuing therapy may be preferable to switching to a typical antipsychotic that the fetus has not yet been exposed to; consider risk:benefit (ACOG 2008). An increased risk of exacerbation of psychosis should be considered when discontinuing or changing treatment during pregnancy and postpartum.

Healthcare providers are encouraged to enroll women 18 to 45 years of age exposed to clozapine during pregnancy in the Atypical Antipsychotics Pregnancy Registry (1-866-961-2388 or http://www.womensmentalhealth.org/pregnancyregistry).

Women with amenorrhea associated with use of other antipsychotic agents may return to normal menstruation when switching to clozapine therapy. Reliable contraceptive measures should be employed by women of childbearing potential switching to clozapine therapy.

Prescribing and Access Restrictions

US: Clozapine is only available through the Clozapine REM Program because of the risk of severe neutropenia. Health care professionals must be certified with the program by enrolling and completing training in order to prescribe clozapine. Patients must be enrolled in the program and comply with ANC testing and monitoring requirements in order to receive clozapine. Pharmacies must be certified with the program by enrolling and completing training in order to dispense to patients who are eligible to receive clozapine.

Further information is available at http://www.clozapinerems.com or 1-844-267-8678.

Canada: Currently, there are multiple manufacturers that distribute clozapine and each manufacturer has its own registry and distribution system. Patients must be registered in a database that includes their location, prescribing physician, testing laboratory, and dispensing pharmacist before using clozapine. Patients may not be switched from one brand of clozapine to another without completion of a new registry-specific patient registration form by signed by the prescribing physician. Information specific to each monitoring program is available from the individual manufacturers.

Cobicistat (koe BIK i stat)

Brand Names: US Tybost

Pharmacologic Category Cytochrome P-450 Inhibitor

Use

HIV-1 infection: Treatment of HIV-1 infection to increase systemic exposure of atazanavir or darunavir (once-daily dosing regimen) in combination with other antiretroviral agents

Limitations of use: Cobicistat is **not** interchangeable with ritonavir to increase systemic exposure of darunavir 600 mg twice daily, fosamprenavir, saquinavir, or tipranavir due to lack of exposure data. The use of cobicistat is not recommended with darunavir 600 mg twice daily, fosamprenavir, saquinavir, or tipranavir.

Local Anesthetic/Vasoconstrictor Precautions No information available to require special precautions

Effects on Dental Treatment No significant effects or complications reported

Effects on Bleeding No information available to require special precautions

Adverse Reactions All adverse reactions are from trials using cobicistat coadministered with atazanavir, emtricitabine + tenofovir unless otherwise noted. Frequency not always defined.

Central nervous system: Headache (2%), abnormal dreams (<2%), depression (<2%), fatigue (<2%), insomnia (<2%)

Dermatologic: Skin rash (5%)

Endocrine & metabolic: Increased gamma-glutamyl transferase (>5 x ULN: 4%), glycosuria (3%), Fanconi's syndrome (<2%), increased HDL cholesterol, increased LDL cholesterol, increased serum cholesterol, increased serum triglycerides

Gastrointestinal: Increased serum amylase (>2 x ULN: 4% to 7%), diarrhea (2%), nausea (2%), upper abdominal pain (<2%), vomiting (<2%)

Genitourinary: Hematuria (6%), proximal tubular nephropathy (2%)

Hepatic: Hyperbilirubinemia (>2.5 x ULN: 73%), increased serum ALT (>5 x ULN: 6%), jaundice (6%), increased serum AST (>5 x ULN: 4%)

Neuromuscular & skeletal: Increased creatine phosphokinase (8%), rhabdomyolysis (<2%)

Ophthalmic: Scleral icterus (4%)

Renal: Nephrolithiasis (<2%), renal disease (<2%), decreased creatinine clearance (no effect on renal glomerular function in patients with normal renal function), increased serum creatinine, renal insufficiency

General Dosage Range Oral: *Adults:* 150 mg once daily.

Mechanism of Action Cobicistat is a mechanism-based inhibitor of cytochrome P450 3A (CYP3A). Inhibition of CYP3A-mediated metabolism by cobicistat and increases the systemic exposure of CYP3A substrates atazanavir and darunavir.

Pharmacodynamics/Kinetics

Half-life Elimination Terminal: ~3 to 4 hours

Time to Peak ~3.5 hours

Pregnancy Considerations It is not known if cobicistat crosses the placenta. Data collected by the antiretroviral pregnancy registry are insufficient to evaluate human teratogenic risk. Maternal antiretroviral therapy may increase the risk of preterm delivery, although available information is conflicting possibly due to variability of maternal factors (disease severity; initiation of therapy); however, maternal antiretroviral medication should not be withheld due to concerns of preterm birth. Information related to stillbirth, low birth weight, and small for gestational age infants is limited. Long-term follow-up is recommended for all infants exposed to antiretroviral medications; children who develop significant organ system abnormalities of unknown etiology (particularly of the CNS or heart) should be evaluated for potential mitochondrial dysfunction.

Combination antiretroviral therapy (cART) therapy is recommended for all HIV-infected pregnant women to keep the viral load below the limit of detection and reduce the risk of perinatal transmission. When HIV is diagnosed during pregnancy in a woman who has never received antiretroviral therapy, cART should begin as soon as possible after diagnosis. The Health and Human Services (HHS) Perinatal HIV Guidelines note, due to insufficient data, cobicistat cannot be recommended as initial therapy in antiretroviral-naive pregnant women. Pharmacokinetic data are insufficient to make dosing recommendations during pregnancy. In general, women who become pregnant on a stable cART regimen may continue that regimen if viral suppression is effective, appropriate drug exposure can be achieved, contraindications for use in pregnancy are not present, and the regimen is well tolerated. Monitoring during pregnancy is more frequent than in nonpregnant adults; cART should also be continued postpartum.

For HIV-infected couples planning a pregnancy, maximum viral suppression with combination antiretroviral therapy (cART) is recommended prior to conception for the HIV-infected partner(s) and expert consultation is recommended; modification of therapy (if needed) and optimization of the woman's health should be done prior to conception. HIV-infected women not planning a pregnancy may use any available type of contraception, considering possible drug interactions and contraindications of the specific method. In addition, consistent use of condoms is also recommended (even during pregnancy) to prevent transmission of HIV or other sexually transmitted diseases.

Health care providers are encouraged to enroll pregnant women exposed to antiretroviral medications as early in pregnancy as possible in the Antiretroviral Pregnancy Registry (1-800-258-4263 or www.-APRegistry.com). Health care providers caring for HIV-infected women and their infants may contact the National Perinatal HIV Hotline (888-448-8765) for clinical consultation (HHS [perinatal] 2016).

Cobimetinib (koe bi ME ti nib)

Brand Names: US Cotellic

Brand Names: Canada Cotellic

Pharmacologic Category Antineoplastic Agent, MEK Inhibitor

Use Melanoma, unresectable or metastatic: Treatment of unresectable or metastatic melanoma in patients with a BRAF V600E or V600K mutation (In combination with vemurafenib)

Local Anesthetic/Vasoconstrictor Precautions Hypertension can occur with the use of this drug. Monitor for hypertension prior to using local anesthetic with vasoconstrictor; medical consult if necessary.

Effects on Dental Treatment Key adverse event(s) related to dental treatment: Stomatitis (14%; includes aphthous stomatitis, mucositis, and oral mucosa ulcer) has been observed

Effects on Bleeding Hemorrhage may occur with cobimetinib; Grade 3 to 4 bleeding has occurred. In patients who are under active treatment with these agents, medical consult is suggested.

Adverse Reactions

Percentages reported as part of combination chemotherapy regimens.

>10%:

Cardiovascular: Decreased left ventricular ejection fraction (grades 2/3: 26%), hypertension (15%)

Dermatologic: Skin photosensitivity (46% to 47%, grades 3/4: 4%; includes solar dermatitis and sunburn), acneiform eruption (16%, grades 3/4: 2%)

Endocrine & metabolic: Hypophosphatemia (68%), increased gamma-glutamyl transferase (65%; grades 3/4: 21%), hypoalbuminemia (42%), hyponatremia (38%), hyperkalemia (26%), hypokalemia (25%), hypocalcemia (24%)

Gastrointestinal: Diarrhea (60%), nausea (41%), vomiting (24%), stomatitis (14%; includes aphthous stomatitis, mucositis, and oral mucosa ulcer)

Hematologic & oncologic: Lymphocytopenia (73%, grades 3/4: 10%), anemia (69%; grades 3/4: 3%), thrombocytopenia (18%), hemorrhage (13%, grades 3/4: 1%; includes bruise, ecchymoses, epistaxis, gingival hemorrhage, hematemesis, hematochezia, hemoptysis, hemorrhoidal bleeding, hypermenorrhea, melena, menometrorrhagia, nail bed bleeding, pulmonary hemorrhage, purpura, rectal hemorrhage, rupture of ovarian cyst, subarachnoid hemorrhage, subgaleal hematoma, traumatic hematoma, uterine hemorrhage, and vaginal hemorrhage)

Hepatic: Increased serum AST (73%, grades 3/4: 7% to 8%), increased serum alkaline phosphatase (71%, grades 3/4: 7%), increased serum ALT (68%, grades 3/4: 11%)

Neuromuscular & skeletal: Increased creatine phosphokinase (79%, grades 3/4: 12% to 14%)

Ophthalmic: Visual impairment (15%, grades 3/4: <1%; includes blurred vision, decreased visual acuity), chorioretinopathy (13%, grades 3/4: <1%), retinal detachment (12%, grades 3/4: 2%; includes detachment of macular retinal pigment epithelium and retinal pigment epithelium detachment)

Renal: Increased serum creatinine (100%; grades 3/4: 3%)

Miscellaneous: Fever (28%)

1% to 10%:

Central nervous system: Chills (10%)

Dermatologic: Skin rash (grades 3/4: 16%; grade 4: 2%; rash resulting in hospitalization: 3%)

Gastrointestinal: Gastrointestinal hemorrhage (4%)

Genitourinary: Genitourinary tract hemorrhage (2%), hematuria (2%)

Hematologic & oncologic: Keratoacanthoma (≤6%), squamous cell carcinoma of skin (≤6%), basal cell carcinoma (5%)

Hepatic: Abnormal bilirubin levels (grades 3/4: 2%)

<1%, postmarketing, and/or case reports: Cerebral hemorrhage, malignant melanoma (second primary), malignant neoplasm (noncutaneous)

General Dosage Range Dosage adjustment recommended in patients who develop toxicities or are on concomitant therapy. **Oral:** *Adults:* 60 mg once daily days 1 to 21 of each 28-day treatment cycle

Mechanism of Action

Cobimetinib is a potent and selective inhibitor of the mitogen-activated extracellular kinase (MEK) pathway (Larkin 2014); it reversibly inhibits MEK1 and MEK2, which are upstream regulators of the extracellular signal-related kinase (ERK) pathway. The ERK pathway promotes cellular proliferation. MEK1 and MEK2 are part of the BRAF pathway, which is activated by BRAF V600E and K mutations. Vemurafenib targets a different kinase in the RAS/RAF/MEK/ERK pathway; when cobimetinib and vemurafenib are used in combination, increased apoptosis and reduced tumor growth occurs.

Pharmacodynamics/Kinetics

Half-life Elimination Mean: 44 hours (range: 23 to 70 hours)

Time to Peak Median: 2.4 hours (range: 1 to 24 hours)

Pregnancy Considerations Adverse events were observed in animal reproduction studies. Based on the mechanism of action, cobimetinib would be expected to cause fetal harm. Women of reproductive potential should use effective contraception during therapy and for 2 weeks after the final dose. The study protocol recommended the use of two forms of effective contraception during therapy and for at least 6 months following discontinuation for women of reproductive potential and for males with partners of reproductive potential (Larkin 2013 [Protocol GO28141]).

Prescribing and Access Restrictions Available through specialty pharmacies. Further information may be obtained from the manufacturer, Genentech, at 1-888-249-4918, or at http://www.cotellic.com.

Cocaine (koe KANE)

Related Information

Management of the Chemically Dependent Patient *on page 1821*

Pharmacologic Category Local Anesthetic

Use Topical anesthesia (and vasoconstriction) for mucous membranes of the oral, laryngeal, or nasal cavities.

Local Anesthetic/Vasoconstrictor Precautions Although plain local anesthetic is not contraindicated, vasoconstrictor is absolutely contraindicated in any patient under the influence of or within 2 hours of cocaine use

Effects on Dental Treatment Key adverse event(s) related to dental treatment: Loss of taste perception. See Dental Comment.

Effects on Bleeding No information available to require special precautions

Adverse Reactions Note: Use of the topical solution may produce systemic reactions from excessive and rapid absorption.

Frequency not defined:

Cardiovascular: Decreased heart rate (low doses), myocardial infarction (Lenders 2013; Makaryus 2006), tachycardia (moderate doses), vasoconstriction, ventricular arrhythmia (Lenders 2013)

Central nervous system: Central nervous system depression (may follow CNS excitation), central nervous system stimulation, excitation, nervousness, restlessness, tonic-clonic seizures

Gastrointestinal: Vomiting

Neuromuscular & skeletal: Tremor

Ophthalmic: Corneal membrane sloughing, corneal ulcer, mydriasis

Miscellaneous: Fever

General Dosage Range Topical: *Children, Adolescents, and Adults:* Dosage depends on the area to be anesthetized, tissue vascularity, technique of anesthesia, and individual patient tolerance; the lowest dose necessary to produce adequate anesthesia should be used.

Mechanism of Action Ester local anesthetic blocks both the initiation and conduction of nerve impulses by decreasing the neuronal membrane's permeability to sodium ions, which results in inhibition of depolarization with resultant blockade of conduction; interferes with the uptake of norepinephrine by adrenergic nerve terminals producing vasoconstriction

Pharmacodynamics/Kinetics

Onset of Action ~1 minute; Peak effect: ~5 minutes

Duration of Action Dose dependent: ≥30 minutes; cocaine metabolites may appear in urine of neonates up to 5 days after birth due to maternal cocaine use shortly before birth

Half-life Elimination 75 minutes

Pregnancy Risk Factor C

Pregnancy Considerations Animal reproduction studies have not been conducted with this product. Cocaine rapidly crosses the placenta in concentrations equal to those in the mother. Adverse events occur in the fetus (eg, congenital malformations, growth restriction), infant (neonatal abstinence syndrome), and mother (eg, preterm labor, placental abruption) following maternal abuse (Fajemirokun-Odudeyi, 2004).

Controlled Substance C-II

Dental Comment The cocaine user, regardless of how the cocaine was administered, presents a potential life-threatening situation in the dental operatory. A patient under the influence of cocaine could be compared to a car going 100 mph. Blood pressure is elevated, heart rate is likely increased, and the use of a local anesthetic with epinephrine may result in a medical emergency. Such patients can be identified by their jitteriness, irritability, talkativeness, tremors, and short, abrupt speech patterns. These same signs and symptoms may also be seen in a normal dental patient with preoperative dental anxiety; therefore, the dentist must be particularly alert in order to identify the potential cocaine abuser. If cocaine use is suspected, the patient should never be given a local anesthetic with vasoconstrictor, for fear of exacerbating the cocaine-induced sympathetic response. Life-threatening episodes of cardiac arrhythmias and hypertensive crises have been reported when local anesthetic with vasoconstrictor was administered to a patient under the influence of cocaine. No local anesthetic, used by any dentist, can interfere with, nor test positive by cocaine in any urine testing screen. Therefore, the dentist does not need to be concerned with any false drug-use accusations associated with dental anesthesia.

Codeine (KOE deen)

Related Information

Oral Pain *on page 1830*

Brand Names: Canada Codeine Contin; PMS-Codeine; ratio-Codeine

Generic Availability (US) Yes

Pharmacologic Category Analgesic, Opioid; Antitussive

Dental Use Treatment of postoperative pain

Use Pain: Management of mild-to-moderately-severe pain

Local Anesthetic/Vasoconstrictor Precautions No information available to require special precautions

Effects on Dental Treatment No significant effects or complications reported (see Dental Comment)

Effects on Bleeding No information available to require special precautions

Adverse Reactions Frequency not defined.

Cardiovascular: Bradycardia, cardiac arrest, circulatory depression, flushing, hypertension, hypotension, palpitations, shock, syncope, tachycardia

Central nervous system: Abnormal dreams, agitation, anxiety, apprehension, ataxia, chills, depression, disorientation, dizziness, drowsiness, dysphoria, euphoria, fatigue, hallucination, headache, increased intracranial pressure, insomnia, nervousness, paresthesia, sedation, shakiness, taste disorder, vertigo

Dermatologic: Diaphoresis, pruritus, skin rash, urticaria

Gastrointestinal: Abdominal cramps, abdominal pain, anorexia, biliary tract spasm, constipation, diarrhea, nausea, pancreatitis, vomiting, xerostomia

Genitourinary: Urinary hesitancy, urinary retention

Hypersensitivity: Hypersensitivity reaction

Neuromuscular & skeletal: Laryngospasm, muscle rigidity, tremor, weakness

Ophthalmic: Blurred vision, diplopia, miosis, nystagmus, visual disturbance

Respiratory: Bronchospasm, dyspnea, respiratory arrest, respiratory depression

<1%, postmarketing, and/or case reports: Hypogonadism (Brennan 2013; Debono 2011)

Dental Usual Dosage Postoperative pain: Adults: Oral (immediate release): 30 mg every 4 to 6 hours as needed; patients with prior opioid exposure may require higher initial doses. Usual range: 15 to 120 mg every 4 to 6 hours as needed

Dosing

Adult Note: Codeine 30 mg per 5 mL oral solution has been discontinued in the US for more than 1 year.

Cough (off-label use in the US): Oral: Reported doses vary; range: 7.5 to 120 mg/day as a single dose or in divided doses (Bolser 2006; Smith 2010); **Note:** The American College of Chest Physicians does not recommend the routine use of codeine as an antitussive in patients with upper respiratory infections (Bolser 2006).

Pain management (analgesic): Oral: **Note:** These are guidelines and do not represent the maximum doses that may be required in all patients. Doses should be titrated to pain relief/prevention.

Immediate release (tablet, oral solution): Initial: 15 to 60 mg every 4 hours as needed; maximum total daily dose: 360 mg/day; patients with prior opioid exposure may require higher initial doses. **Note:** The American Pain Society recommends an initial dose of 30 to 60 mg for adults with moderate pain (American Pain Society 2008).

Controlled release: Codeine Contin [Canadian product]: **Note:** Titrate at intervals of ≥48 hours until adequate analgesia has been achieved. Daily doses >600 mg/day should not be used; patients requiring higher doses should be switched to an opioid approved for use in severe pain. In patients who receive both Codeine Contin and an immediate release or combination codeine product for breakthrough pain, the rescue dose of immediate release codeine product should be ≤12.5% of the total daily Codeine Contin dose.

Opioid-naive patients: Initial: 50 mg every 12 hours

Conversion from immediate release codeine preparations: Immediate release codeine preparations contain ~75% codeine base. Therefore, patients who are switching from immediate release codeine preparations may be transferred to a ~25% lower total daily dose of Codeine Contin, equally divided into 2 daily doses every 12 hours.

*Conversion from a combination codeine product (eg, codeine with acetaminophen **or** aspirin):* See table:

Number of 30 mg Codeine Combination Tablets Daily	Initial Dose of Codeine Contin	Maintenance Dose of Codeine Contin
≤6	50 mg every 12 h	100 mg every 12 h
7-9	100 mg every 12 h	150 mg every 12 h
10-12	150 mg every 12 h	200 mg every 12 h
>12	200 mg every 12 h	200-300 every 12 h (maximum: 300 mg every 12 h)

Conversion from another opioid analgesic: Using the patient's current opioid dose, calculate an equivalent daily dose of immediate release codeine. A ~25% lower dose of Codeine Contin should then be initiated, equally divided into 2 daily doses.

Discontinuation of therapy: **Note:** Gradual dose reduction is recommended if clinically appropriate. Initially reduce the total daily dose by 50% and administer equally divided into 2 daily doses for 2 days followed by a 25% reduction every 2 days thereafter.

Restless leg syndrome (off-label use): Oral: Initial: 30 mg once daily at bedtime or during the night; may increase to 60 mg if needed; maximum dose: 180 mg in 2 to 3 divided doses. May be used alone or in combination with other medications used to treat RLS (Earley 2003; Sandyk 1987; Silbers 2013; Walters 2001). Additional data may be necessary to further define the role of codeine in this condition.

Geriatric Refer to adult dosing. Use with caution and consider initiation at the low end of the dosing range; reduced initial dosages may be necessary.

Pediatric Note: Codeine 30 mg per 5 mL oral solution has been discontinued in the US for more than 1 year.

Pain management (analgesic) (off-label population): Oral: **Note:** These are guidelines and do not represent the maximum doses that may be required in all patients. Doses should be titrated to pain relief/prevention.)

Immediate release (tablet, oral solution): Initial: 0.5 to 1 mg/kg/dose every 4 hours as needed; maximum: 60 mg/dose (American Pain Society 2008)

Controlled-release tablet [Canadian product]: Use is not recommended (has not been studied)

Renal Impairment

US labeling: There are no specific dosage adjustments provided in the manufacturers labeling; however, clearance may be reduced; active metabolites may accumulate. Initiate at lower doses or longer dosing intervals followed by careful titration.

Canadian labeling:

Immediate release (tablet, oral solution):

CrCl >50 mL/minute: No dosage adjustment necessary.

CrCl 10 to 50 mL/minute: Administer 75% of dose and titrate carefully as needed.

CrCl <10 mL/minute: Administer 50% of dose and titrate carefully as needed.

Controlled release: There are no dosage adjustments provided in the manufacturer labeling; however, a reduced dosage is recommended

Alternate recommendations: The following guidelines have been used by some clinicians (Aronoff 2007):
CrCl 10 to 50 mL/minute: Administer 75% of dose
CrCl <10 mL/minute: Administer 50% of dose

Hepatic Impairment There are no dosage adjustments provided in the manufacturer's labeling (has not been studied); however, initial lower doses or longer dosing intervals followed by careful titration are recommended.

Mechanism of Action Binds to opioid receptors in the CNS, causing inhibition of ascending pain pathways, altering the perception of and response to pain; causes cough suppression by direct central action in the medulla; produces generalized CNS depression

Contraindications

Hypersensitivity to codeine or any component of the formulation; respiratory depression in the absence of resuscitative equipment; acute or severe bronchial asthma or hypercarbia; presence or suspicion of paralytic ileus; postoperative pain management in children who have undergone tonsillectomy and/or adenoidectomy

Canadian labeling: Additional contraindications (not in US labeling): Hypersensitivity to other opioid analgesics; cor pulmonale; acute alcoholism; delirium tremens; severe CNS depression; convulsive disorders; increased cerebrospinal or intracranial pressure; head injury; obstructive airway disease (in addition to asthma); known or suspected mechanical GI obstruction or any disease that affects bowel transit; suspected surgical abdomen (eg, acute appendicitis or pancreatitis); use with or within 14 days of MAO inhibitors; pregnancy and during labor and delivery; children <12 years of age; Additional product specific contraindications: Codeine Contin: acute pain; intermittent or short duration pain that can be managed with alternative pain medication; breastfeeding

Warnings/Precautions [US Boxed Warning]: Respiratory depression and death have occurred in children who received codeine following tonsillectomy and/or adenoidectomy and were found to have evidence of being ultra-rapid metabolizers of codeine due to a CYP2D6 polymorphism. Deaths have also occurred in nursing infants after being exposed to high concentrations of morphine because the mothers were ultra-rapid metabolizers. Use is contraindicated in the postoperative pain management of children who have undergone tonsillectomy and/or adenoidectomy. Use caution in patients with two or more copies of the variant CYP2D6*2 allele; may have extensive conversion to morphine and thus increased opioid-mediated effects. Avoid the use of codeine in these patients; consider alternative analgesics such as morphine or a nonopioid agent (Crews 2012). The occurrence of this phenotype is seen in 0.5% to 1% of Chinese and Japanese, 0.5% to 1% of Hispanics, 1% to 10% of Caucasians, 3% of African-Americans, and 16% to 28% of North Africans, Ethiopians, and Arabs.

May cause dose-related respiratory depression. The risk is increased in elderly patients, debilitated patients, and patients with conditions associated with hypoxia, hypercapnia, or upper airway obstruction. Use with caution in the elderly; may be more sensitive to adverse effects. Use opioids for chronic pain with caution in this age group; monitor closely due to an increased potential for risks, including certain risks such as falls/fracture, cognitive impairment, and constipation. Clearance may also be reduced in older adults (with or without renal impairment) resulting in a narrow therapeutic window and increasing the risk for respiratory depression or overdose (Dowell [CDC 2016]). Use with caution in patients with preexisting respiratory compromise (hypoxia), COPD or other obstructive pulmonary disease, and kyphoscoliosis or other skeletal disorder which may alter respiratory function; critical respiratory depression may occur, even at therapeutic dosages. Use opioids with caution for chronic pain and titrate dosage cautiously in patients with risk factors for sleep-disordered breathing, including HF and obesity. Avoid opioids in patients with moderate to severe sleep-disordered breathing (Dowell [CDC 2016]).

After chronic maternal exposure to opioids, neonatal withdrawal syndrome may occur in the newborn; monitor neonate closely. Signs and symptoms include irritability, hyperactivity and abnormal sleep pattern, high pitched cry, tremor, vomiting, diarrhea and failure to gain weight. Onset, duration and severity depend on the drug used, duration of use, maternal dose, and rate of drug elimination by the newborn. Opioid withdrawal syndrome in the neonate, unlike in adults, may be life-threatening and should be treated according to protocols developed by neonatology experts.

Use may cause or aggravate constipation; chronic use may result in obstructive bowel disease, particularly in those with underlying intestinal motility disorders. Constipation may also be problematic in patients with unstable angina or those patients post-myocardial infarction. Avoid use in patients with gastrointestinal obstruction, particularly paralytic ileus. May cause hypotension; use with caution in patients with hypovolemia, cardiovascular disease (including acute MI), or drugs which may exaggerate hypotensive effects (including phenothiazines or general anesthetics). May cause CNS depression, which may impair physical or mental abilities; patients must be cautioned about performing tasks which require mental alertness (eg, operating machinery or driving).

Use with extreme caution in patients with head injury, intracranial lesions, or elevated intracranial pressure; exaggerated elevation of ICP may occur. Use with caution in patients with hypersensitivity reactions to other phenanthrene-derivative opioid agonists (hydrocodone, hydromorphone, levorphanol, oxycodone, oxymorphone), adrenal insufficiency (including Addison's disease), biliary tract dysfunction, pancreatitis, thyroid dysfunction, morbid obesity, prostatic hyperplasia and/or urinary stricture, or severe hepatic or renal impairment. Use may obscure diagnosis or clinical course of patients with acute abdominal conditions. May induce or aggravate seizures; use with caution in patients with seizure disorders. Avoid use in patients with CNS depression or coma as these patients are susceptible to intracranial effects of CO_2 retention.

Potential for drug dependency exists. Use in patients with a history of drug abuse or acute alcoholism is contraindicated in the Canadian labeling. Use opioids for chronic pain with caution in patients at increased risk for misuse; factors associated with increased risk include previous substance use disorder, younger age, concomitant depression (major), and psychotropic medication use. Consider offering naloxone prescriptions in patients with factors associated with an increased risk for overdose, such as history of overdose or substance use disorder, higher opioid dosages (≥50 morphine milligram equivalents/day orally), and concomitant benzodiazepine use (Dowell [CDC 2016]). Use opioids with caution for chronic pain in patients with mental health conditions (eg, depression, anxiety disorders, post-traumatic stress disorder) due to increased risk for opioid use disorder and overdose; more frequent monitoring is recommended (Dowell [CDC 2016]). Potentially significant drug interactions may exist, requiring dose or frequency adjustment, additional monitoring, and/or selection of alternative therapy. Effects may be potentiated when used with other sedative drugs or ethanol. In the chronic pain setting, avoid prescribing opioids and benzodiazepines concurrently whenever possible; epidemiologic studies suggest there is an increased risk for potentially fatal overdose with concurrent use (Dowell [CDC 2016]). Concurrent use of agonist/antagonist analgesics may precipitate withdrawal symptoms and/or reduced analgesic efficacy in patients following prolonged therapy with mu opioid agonists. Abrupt discontinuation following prolonged use may also lead to withdrawal symptoms.

Some preparations contain sulfites which may cause allergic reactions. Healthcare provider should be alert to the potential for abuse, misuse, and diversion. Opioids should **not** be used as first-line therapy for chronic pain management (pain >3-month duration or beyond time of normal tissue healing) due to limited short-term benefits, undetermined long-term benefits, and association with serious risks (eg, overdose, MI, auto accidents, risk of developing opioid use disorder). Preferred management includes nonpharmacologic therapy and nonopioid therapy (eg, NSAIDs, acetaminophen, certain anticonvulsants and antidepressants). If opioid therapy is initiated, it should be combined with nonpharmacologic and non-opioid therapy, as appropriate. Prior to initiation, known risks of opioid therapy should be discussed and realistic treatment goals for pain/function should be established, including consideration for discontinuation if benefits do not outweigh risks. Therapy should be continued only if clinically meaningful improvement in pain/function outweighs risks. Therapy should be initiated at the lowest effective dosage using immediate-release opioids (instead of extended-release/long-acting opioids). Risk associated with use increases with higher opioid dosages. Risks and benefits should be re-evaluated when increasing dosage to ≥50 morphine milligram equivalents (MME)/day orally; dosages ≥90 MME/day orally should be avoided unless carefully justified (Dowell [CDC 2016]).

Drug Interactions

Metabolism/Transport Effects **Substrate** of CYP2D6 (major); **Note:** Assignment of Major/Minor substrate status based on clinically relevant drug interaction potential

Avoid Concomitant Use

Avoid concomitant use of Codeine with any of the following: Azelastine (Nasal); Eluxadoline; Mixed Agonist / Antagonist Opioids; Orphenadrine; Oxomemazine; Paraldehyde; Thalidomide

Increased Effect/Toxicity

Codeine may increase the levels/effects of: Alvimopan; Analgesics (Opioid); Azelastine (Nasal); Blonanserin; Desmopressin; Diuretics; Eluxadoline; Flunitrazepam; HYDROcodone; Methotrimeprazine; MetyroSINE; Orphenadrine; OxyCODONE; Paraldehyde; Piribedil; Pramipexole; Ramosetron; ROPINIRole; Rotigotine; Selective Serotonin Reuptake Inhibitors; Serotonin Modulators; Suvorexant; Thalidomide; Zolpidem

The levels/effects of Codeine may be increased by: Amphetamines; Anticholinergic Agents; Brimonidine (Topical); Cannabis; Chlormethiazole; Chlorphenesin Carbamate; CNS Depressants; Dimethindene (Topical); Dronabinol; Droperidol; Kava Kava; Lofexidine; Magnesium Sulfate; MAO Inhibitors; Methotrimeprazine; Minocycline; Nabilone; Oxomemazine; Perampanel; Rufinamide; Sodium Oxybate; Somatostatin Analogs; Succinylcholine; Tapentadol; Tetrahydrocannabinol

Decreased Effect

Codeine may decrease the levels/effects of: Diuretics; Gastrointestinal Agents (Prokinetic); Pegvisomant

The levels/effects of Codeine may be decreased by: CYP2D6 Inhibitors (Moderate); CYP2D6 Inhibitors (Strong); Mixed Agonist / Antagonist Opioids; Nalmefene; Naltrexone

Pharmacodynamics/Kinetics

Onset of Action Oral: Immediate release: 0.5-1 hour; Peak effect: Oral: Immediate release: 1-1.5 hours

Duration of Action Immediate release: 4-6 hours

Half-life Elimination 2.5-3.5 hours

Time to Peak Plasma: Immediate release: 1 hour; Controlled release [Canadian product]: 3.3 hours

Pregnancy Risk Factor C

Pregnancy Considerations Adverse events have been observed in animal reproduction studies. Opioid analgesics cross the placenta. In humans, birth defects (including some heart defects) have been associated with maternal use of codeine during the first trimester of pregnancy (Broussard 2011). If chronic opioid exposure occurs in pregnancy, adverse events in the newborn (including withdrawal) may occur; monitoring of the neonate is recommended. The minimum effective dose should be used if opioids are needed (Chou 2009). Neonatal abstinence syndrome following opioid exposure may present with autonomic (eg, fever, temperature instability), gastrointestinal (eg, diarrhea, vomiting, poor feeding/weight gain), or neurologic (eg, high pitched crying, increased muscle tone, irritability, seizure, tremor) symptoms (Dow 2012; Hudak 2012).

Breastfeeding Considerations Codeine and its active metabolite morphine are excreted in breast milk (Meny 1993).

Concentrations of codeine and morphine are dependent upon the mother's CYP2D6 metabolism. In women with normal CYPD2D6 metabolism, the amount detected in breast milk is expected to be dose-dependent; however, deaths have occurred in nursing infants exposed to high concentrations of morphine because the mothers were ultrarapid metabolizers.

Adverse events in the infant may include drowsiness, sedation, decreased tone, or breathing difficulties; in addition breastfeeding may be difficult for the infant. Codeine and morphine can also be detected in the serum of nursing infants (Meny 1993).

Current guidelines note that nonopioid analgesics are preferred for postpartum pain in breastfeeding women (Montgomery 2012). If an oral opioid is needed to treat maternal pain, agents other than codeine are preferred (Sachs 2013); codeine should be used with caution (Montgomery 2012). Because adverse CNS events appear to worsen in the nursing infant after 4 days likely due to morphine accumulation, use of codeine should be limited to no more than 4 days in breastfeeding women (Kahan 2011; Madadi 2009). Mothers should closely monitor their nursing infants for adverse effects. In general, a single occasional dose of an opioid analgesic may be compatible with breastfeeding (WHO 2002).

Product Availability Codeine 30 mg per 5 mL oral solution has been discontinued in the US for more than 1 year.

Controlled Substance C-II

Dosage Forms

Tablet, Oral:

Generic: 15 mg, 30 mg, 60 mg

Dosage Forms: Canada

Solution, Oral, as phosphate: 25 mg/5 mL

Tablet, controlled release:

Codeine Contin: 50 mg, 100 mg, 150 mg, 200 mg

Dental Comment It is recommended that codeine not be used as the sole entity for analgesia because of moderate efficacy along with relatively high incidence of nausea, sedation, and constipation. In addition, codeine has some opioid addiction liability. Codeine in combination with acetaminophen or aspirin is recommended. Maximum effective analgesic dose of codeine is 60 mg (1 grain). Beyond 60 mg increases respiratory depression only.

Codeine and Chlorpheniramine

(KOE deen & klor fen IR a meen)

Brand Names: US Codar AR; Lexuss 210; Tuzistra XR; Z-Tuss AC [OTC]

Pharmacologic Category Analgesic, Opioid; Antitussive; Histamine H_1 Antagonist; Histamine H_1 Antagonist, First Generation

Use Cough and upper respiratory allergy symptoms: Relief of cough and symptoms associated with upper respiratory allergies or a common cold in adults ≥18 years.

Local Anesthetic/Vasoconstrictor Precautions No information available to require special precautions

Effects on Dental Treatment Key adverse event(s) related to dental treatment: Xerostomia (normal salivary flow resumes upon discontinuation).

Effects on Bleeding No information available to require special precautions

Adverse Reactions Frequency not defined; reactions reported with combination product and/or individual agents. Also see individual agents.

Cardiovascular: Decreased heart rate, facial flushing, hypertension, hypotension, increased heart rate, orthostatic hypotension, palpitations, shock, syncope

Central nervous system: Agitation, confusion, depression, dizziness, drowsiness, euphoria, excitability, false sense of well-being, fatigue, headache, insomnia, irritability, malaise, nervousness, relaxation, restlessness, sedation, vertigo

Dermatologic: Dermatitis, diaphoresis, erythema, facial swelling, pruritus, skin rash, urticaria

Endocrine & metabolic: Altered serum glucose (change in glucose utilization), glycosuria, gynecomastia, hypoglycemia, increased libido, pheochromocytoma crisis

Gastrointestinal: Abdominal distention, abdominal pain, acute pancreatitis, anorexia, constipation, decreased gastrointestinal motility, diarrhea, dyspepsia, epigastric distress, gastroesophageal reflux disease, hiccups, increased appetite, nausea and vomiting, xerostomia

Genitourinary: Decreased lactation, dysuria, early menses, irritable bladder, ureteral spasm, urinary frequency, urinary hesitancy, urinary retention

Neuromuscular & skeletal: Dyskinesia, facial dyskinesia, laryngospasm (allergic), tremor, weakness

Ophthalmic: Blurred vision, diplopia, hypermetropia, increased lacrimation, mydriasis, photophobia, visual disturbance

Otic: Labyrinthitis, tinnitus

Respiratory: Allergic bronchospasm, atelectasis, dry nose, dry throat, laryngismus, nasal congestion, respiratory depression, respiratory distress, wheezing

General Dosage Range Oral: *Adults:* 10 mL every 12 hours; maximum dose: 20 mL per 24 hours

Mechanism of Action

Codeine: Binds to opioid receptors in the CNS, causing inhibition of ascending pain pathways, altering the perception of and response to pain; causes cough suppression by direct central action in the medulla; produces generalized CNS depression.

Chlorpheniramine: H_1 receptor antagonist that also possesses anticholinergic and sedative activity. It prevents released histamine from dilating capillaries and causing edema of the respiratory mucosa.

Pregnancy Risk Factor C

Pregnancy Considerations Animal reproduction studies have not been conducted with this combination. See individual agents.

Controlled Substance

Extended Release Suspension: C-III; Liquid products: C-V

Colchicine (KOL chi seen)

Brand Names: US Colcrys; Mitigare

Brand Names: Canada Jamp-Colchicine; PMS-Colchicine

Pharmacologic Category Antigout Agent

Use

Familial Mediterranean fever (tablet [eg, Colcrys] only): Treatment of familial Mediterranean fever in adults and children 4 years and older.

Gout flares: Prophylaxis and the treatment of acute gout flares when taken at the first sign of a flare. **Note:** Mitigare is only approved for prophylaxis of gout flares.

Local Anesthetic/Vasoconstrictor Precautions No information available to require special precautions

Effects on Dental Treatment No significant effects or complications reported

Effects on Bleeding No information available to require special precautions

Adverse Reactions Frequency not always defined.

>10%: Gastrointestinal: Gastrointestinal disease (26% to 77%), diarrhea (23% to 77%), vomiting (17%), nausea (4% to 17%)

1% to 10%:

Central nervous system: Fatigue (1% to 4%), headache (1% to 2%)

Endocrine & metabolic: Gout (4%)

Gastrointestinal: Abdominal cramps, abdominal pain

Respiratory: Pharyngolaryngeal pain (2% to 3%)

<1%, postmarketing, and/or case reports: Alopecia, aplastic anemia, azoospermia, bone marrow, dermatitis, depression, disseminated intravascular coagulation, dysgeusia (Syed 2016), granulocytopenia, hepatotoxicity, hypersensitivity reaction, increased creatine phosphokinase, increased serum ALT, increased serum AST, lactose intolerance, leukopenia, maculopapular rash, myalgia, myasthenia, myopathy, myotonia, neuropathy, oligospermia, pancytopenia, peripheral neuritis, purpura, rhabdomyolysis, skin rash, thrombocytopenia, toxic neuromuscular disease

General Dosage Range Dosage adjustment recommended in patients with renal impairment or on concomitant therapy

Oral:

Children 4 to 6 years: 0.3 to 1.8 mg daily in 1 to 2 divided doses

Children 6 to 12 years: 0.9 to 1.8 mg daily in 1 to 2 divided doses

Children 12 to 16 years: 1.2 to 2.4 mg daily in 1 to 2 divided doses

Adolescents >16 years and Adults: 0.6 to 2.4 mg daily in 1 to 2 divided doses **or** Initial: 1.2 mg; repeat with 0.6 mg in 1 hour (maximum total therapy: 1.8 mg within 1 hour)

Mechanism of Action Disrupts cytoskeletal functions by inhibiting β-tubulin polymerization into microtubules, preventing activation, degranulation, and migration of neutrophils associated with mediating some gout symptoms. In familial Mediterranean fever, may interfere with intracellular assembly of the inflammasome complex present in neutrophils and monocytes that mediate activation of interleukin-1β.

Pharmacodynamics/Kinetics

Onset of Action Oral: Pain relief: ~18 to 24 hours

Half-life Elimination 27 to 31 hours (multiple oral doses; young, healthy volunteers)

Time to Peak Serum: Oral: 0.5 to 3 hours

Pregnancy Risk Factor C

Pregnancy Considerations Adverse events were observed in animal reproduction studies. Colchicine crosses the human placenta. Use during pregnancy in the treatment of familial Mediterranean fever has not shown an increase in miscarriage, stillbirth, or teratogenic effects (limited data).

Colchicine and Probenecid

(KOL chi seen & proe BEN e sid)

Related Information

Colchicine *on page 414*

Probenecid *on page 1387*

Pharmacologic Category Anti-inflammatory Agent; Antigout Agent; Uricosuric Agent

Use Treatment of chronic gouty arthritis when complicated by frequent, recurrent acute attacks of gout

Local Anesthetic/Vasoconstrictor Precautions No information available to require special precautions

Effects on Dental Treatment No significant effects or complications reported

Effects on Bleeding No information available to require special precautions

Adverse Reactions See individual agents.

General Dosage Range Dosage adjustment recommended in patients with renal impairment

Oral: *Adults:* Initial: One tablet daily; Maintenance: 1 tablet twice daily

Pregnancy Considerations See individual agents.

Colesevelam (koh le SEV a lam)

Related Information

Cardiovascular Diseases *on page 1752*

Brand Names: US Welchol

Brand Names: Canada Lodalis

Generic Availability (US) No

Pharmacologic Category Antilipemic Agent, Bile Acid Sequestrant

Use

Diabetes mellitus, type 2: Improve glycemic control in adults with type 2 diabetes mellitus (noninsulin dependent, NIDDM) in conjunction with diet and exercise

Heterozygous familial hypercholesterolemia: Management of heterozygous familial hypercholesterolemia (heFH) in adolescent patients (males and postmenarcheal females 10-17 years of age) used alone or in combination with a 3-hydroxy-3-methylglutaryl coenzyme A (HMG-CoA) reductase inhibitor when after an adequate trial of dietary therapy patient continues to have low-density lipoprotein-cholesterol (LDL-C) ≥190 mg/dL or LDL-C ≥160 mg/dL with positive family history of premature cardiovascular disease (CVD) or with two or more CVD risk factors.

Hyperlipidemia:

U.S. labeling: Management of elevated LDL-C in adults with primary hyperlipidemia (Fredrickson type IIa) when used alone or in combination with an HMG-CoA reductase inhibitor in conjunction with diet and exercise

Canadian labeling (Lodalis): Adjunct to diet and lifestyle modifications in the management of primary hypercholesterolemia (Fredrickson type IIa) as monotherapy or in combination with an HMG-CoA reductase inhibitor

Limitations of use: Should not be used for the treatment of type 1 diabetes or diabetic ketoacidosis. Colesevelam has not been studied in Fredrickson Type I, III, IV, and V dyslipidemias; type 2 diabetes in combination with a dipeptidyl peptidase 4 inhibitor; pediatric patients with type 2 diabetes; children <10 years of age or in premenarchal girls. No effect on cardiovascular morbidity and mortality has been established. There is no evidence of macrovascular disease risk reduction with colesevelam use.

Local Anesthetic/Vasoconstrictor Precautions No information available to require special precautions

Effects on Dental Treatment No significant effects or complications reported

Effects on Bleeding No information available to require special precautions

Adverse Reactions Actual frequency may be dependent upon indication. Unless otherwise noted, frequency of adverse effects is reported for adult patients.

>10%: Gastrointestinal: Constipation (3% to 11%)

1% to 10%:

Cardiovascular: Cardiovascular toxicity (2%, including myocardial infarction, aortic stenosis, bradycardia), hypertension (2% to 3%)

Central nervous system: Headache (children and adults 4% to 8%), fatigue (children 4%)

Endocrine & metabolic: Hypertriglyceridemia (4% to 5%; >500 mg/dL: <1%; >1,000 mg/dL: <1%), hyperglycemia (3%), hypoglycemia (3%)

Gastrointestinal: Dyspepsia (3% to 8%), diarrhea (4%), nausea (children and adults 3% to 4%), gastroesophageal reflux disease (2%), periodontal abscess (2%), vomiting (children 2%)

Hematologic & oncologic: C-reactive protein increased (3%)

Neuromuscular & skeletal: Weakness (4%), back pain (2%), increased creatine phosphokinase (children and adults 2%), myalgia (2%)

Respiratory: Nasopharyngitis (children 5% to 6%), upper respiratory tract infection (children and adults 3% to 5%), flu-like symptoms (children 4%), pharyngitis (3%), rhinitis (children 2%)

<1%, postmarketing, and/or case reports: Abdominal distension, dysphagia, esophageal obstruction, fecal impaction, flatulence, worsening of hemorrhoids, increased serum transaminases, infection, intestinal obstruction, pancreatitis, unstable angina pectoris

Dosing

Adult & Geriatric *U.S. labeling:* Hyperlipidemia, type 2 diabetes mellitus: Oral:

Once-daily dosing: 3.75 g (oral suspension or 6 tablets)

Twice-daily dosing: 1.875 g (3 tablets)

***Canadian labeling:* Hyperlipidemia:** Oral:

Combination therapy: 2.5 to 3.75 g (4 to 6 tablets) daily; maximum dose: 3.75 g (6 tablets) given once daily or 1.875 g (3 tablets) given twice daily

Monotherapy: Initial: 1.875 g (3 tablets) twice daily or 3.75 g (6 tablets) once daily; maximum dose: 4.375 g (7 tablets) daily

Pediatric Heterozygous familial hypercholesterolemia: Children 10 to 17 years (males and postmenarchal females): Oral: 3.75 g once daily (oral suspension). **Note:** Due to large tablet size, oral suspension is recommended in pediatric patients.

Renal Impairment No dosage adjustments necessary; not absorbed from the gastrointestinal tract.

Hepatic Impairment No dosage adjustments necessary; not absorbed from the gastrointestinal tract.

Mechanism of Action Cholesterol is the major precursor of bile acid. Colesevelam binds with bile acids in the intestine to form an insoluble complex that is eliminated in feces. This increased excretion of bile acids results in an increased oxidation of cholesterol to bile acid and a lowering of the serum cholesterol.

Contraindications

History of bowel obstruction; serum TG concentrations of more than 500 mg/dL; history of hypertriglyceridemia-induced pancreatitis.

Canadian labeling: Hypersensitivity to colesevelam or any component of the formulation; bowel or biliary obstruction

Warnings/Precautions Use with caution in treating patients with serum triglyceride concentrations >300 mg/dL and in patients using insulin, thiazolidinediones, or sulfonylureas (may cause increased concentrations) or in patients susceptible to fat-soluble vitamin deficiencies. Discontinue if triglyceride concentrations exceed 500 mg/dL or hypertriglyceridemia-induced pancreatitis occurs. The American College of Cardiology/American Heart Association recommends to avoid use in patients with baseline fasting triglyceride levels ≥300 mg/dL or type III hyperlipoproteinemia since severe triglyceride elevations may occur. Use bile acid sequestrants with caution in patients with triglyceride levels 250-299 mg/dL and evaluate a fasting lipid panel in 4-6 weeks after initiation; discontinue use if triglycerides are >400 mg/dL (Stone, 2013). Use is not recommended in patients with gastroparesis, other severe GI motility disorders, or a history of major GI tract surgery or patients at risk for bowel obstruction. Use tablets with caution in patients with dysphagia or swallowing disorders; use the oral suspension form of colesevelam due to large tablet size and risk for esophageal obstruction.

Minimal effects are seen on HDL-C and triglyceride levels. Secondary causes of hypercholesterolemia should be excluded before initiation. Colesevelam has not been studied in Fredrickson Type I, III, IV, or V dyslipidemias. Colesevelam is not indicated for the management of type 1 diabetes, particularly in the acute management (eg, DKA). It is also not indicated in type 2 diabetes mellitus as monotherapy and must be used as an adjunct to diet, exercise, and glycemic control with insulin or oral antidiabetic agents. The use of colesevelam in pediatric patients with type 2 diabetes has not been evaluated. Combination with dipeptidyl peptidase 4 inhibitors or thiazolidinediones has not been studied extensively. There is no evidence of macrovascular disease risk reduction with colesevelam.

Use with caution in patients susceptible to fat-soluble vitamin deficiencies. Absorption of fat soluble vitamins A, D, E, and K may be decreased; patients should take vitamins ≥4 hours before colesevelam. Potentially significant drug-drug interactions may exist, requiring dose or frequency adjustment, additional monitoring, and/or selection of alternative therapy. Some products may contain phenylalanine.

Drug Interactions

Metabolism/Transport Effects None known.

Avoid Concomitant Use

Avoid concomitant use of Colesevelam with any of the following: Mycophenolate

Increased Effect/Toxicity There are no known significant interactions involving an increase in effect.

Decreased Effect

Colesevelam may decrease the levels/effects of: Amiodarone; AtorvaSTATin; Chenodiol; Cholic Acid; Contraceptives (Estrogens); Contraceptives (Progestins); Corticosteroids (Oral); CycloSPORINE (Systemic); Deferasirox; Ethinyl Estradiol; Ezetimibe; Glimepiride; GlipiZIDE; GlyBURIDE; Leflunomide; Lomitapide; Loop Diuretics; Methotrexate; Multivitamins/Fluoride (with ADE); Multivitamins/Minerals (with ADEK, Folate, Iron); Multivitamins/Minerals (with AE, No Iron); Mycophenolate; Niacin; Nonsteroidal Anti-Inflammatory Agents; Norethindrone; Obeticholic Acid; Olmesartan; Phenytoin; Pravastatin; Propranolol; Raloxifene; Teriflunomide; Tetracycline Derivatives; Thiazide and Thiazide-Like Diuretics; Thyroid Products; Ursodiol; Vancomycin; Vitamin D Analogs; Vitamin K Antagonists

Dietary Considerations Should be taken with meal(s) and a liquid. Follow dietary guidelines. Some products may contain phenylalanine.

Pharmacodynamics/Kinetics

Onset of Action

Lipid lowering: Therapeutic: ~2 weeks

Reduction of hemoglobin A_{1C} (Type II diabetes): 4-6 weeks initial onset; 12-18 weeks maximal effect

Pregnancy Risk Factor B

Pregnancy Considerations Adverse effects have not been observed in animal reproduction studies. Colesevelam is not absorbed systemically, but may interfere with vitamin absorption; therefore, regular supplementation may not be adequate.

Breastfeeding Considerations Due to lack of systemic absorption, colesevelam is not expected to be excreted in breast milk; however, the tendency of colesevelam to interfere with the vitamin absorption may have an effect on the nursing infant.

Dosage Forms Considerations

Welchol contains phenylalanine 27 mg per 3.75 gram packet

Dosage Forms

Packet, Oral:

Welchol: 3.75 g (30 ea)

Tablet, Oral:

Welchol: 625 mg

Dosage Forms: Canada

Tablet, oral:

Lodalis: 625 mg

Colestipol (koe LES ti pole)

Related Information

Cardiovascular Diseases *on page 1752*

Brand Names: US Colestid; Colestid Flavored

Brand Names: Canada Colestid

Pharmacologic Category Antilipemic Agent, Bile Acid Sequestrant

Use Primary hypercholesterolemia: Adjunctive therapy to diet in patients with primary hypercholesterolemia

Local Anesthetic/Vasoconstrictor Precautions No information available to require special precautions

Effects on Dental Treatment No significant effects or complications reported

Effects on Bleeding Because colestipol can bind with and impair the absorption of dietary vitamin K, hypoprothrombinemia can occur

Adverse Reactions Frequency not defined.

Cardiovascular: Angina, chest pain, peripheral edema, tachycardia

Central nervous system: Dizziness, fatigue, headache (including migraine and sinus headache), insomnia

Dermatologic: Dermatitis, skin rash, urticaria

Gastrointestinal: Abdominal cramps, abdominal pain, anorexia, bloating, constipation, cholecystitis, cholelithiasis, diarrhea, dyspepsia, dysphagia, esophageal obstruction, flatulence, heartburn, hemorrhoidal bleeding, nausea, peptic ulcer, vomiting

Hepatic: Increased serum alkaline phosphatase, increased serum ALT, increased serum AST

Neuromuscular & skeletal: Arthralgia, arthritis, back pain, myalgia, weakness

Respiratory: Dyspnea

General Dosage Range Oral: *Adults:* Granules: Initial: 5 g once or twice daily; Maintenance: 5 to 30 g per day, once daily or in divided doses; Tablets: Initial: 2 g once or twice daily; Maintenance: 2 to 16 g per day, once daily or in divided doses

Mechanism of Action Binds with bile acids to form an insoluble complex that is eliminated in feces; it thereby increases the fecal loss of bile acid-bound low density lipoprotein cholesterol

Pharmacodynamics/Kinetics

Onset of Action Lowering of serum cholesterol: ~1 month; LDL-C reduction: ~19%

Pregnancy Considerations Colestipol is not absorbed systemically (<0.17%), but may interfere with vitamin absorption; therefore, regular prenatal supplementation may not be adequate. There are no studies in pregnant women; use with caution.

Colistimethate (koe lis ti METH ate)

Brand Names: US Coly-Mycin M

Brand Names: Canada Coly-Mycin M

Pharmacologic Category Antibiotic, Miscellaneous

Use Treatment of acute or chronic infections due to sensitive strains of certain gram-negative bacilli (particularly *Pseudomonas aeruginosa*) which are resistant to other antibacterials or in patients allergic to other antibacterials

Local Anesthetic/Vasoconstrictor Precautions No information available to require special precautions

Effects on Dental Treatment No significant effects or complications reported

Effects on Bleeding No information available to require special precautions

Adverse Reactions Frequency not always defined.

Central nervous system: Neurotoxicity (7%; higher incidence with high-dose IV use in cystic fibrosis [Boss 1991; Koch-Weser 1970]), dizziness, headache, oral paresthesia, peripheral paresthesia, slurred speech, vertigo

Dermatologic: Pruritus, skin rash, urticaria

Gastrointestinal: Gastric distress

Genitourinary: Decreased urine output, nephrotoxicity (18% to 26% [Dalfino 2012; Oliveira 2009]), proteinuria

Neuromuscular & skeletal: Lower extremity weakness

Renal: Acute renal failure (33% to 60% [Akajagbor 2013; Deryke 2010]), increased blood urea nitrogen, increased serum creatinine

Respiratory: Apnea, respiratory distress

Miscellaneous: Fever

Postmarketing and/or case reports: Pulmonary toxicity (acute respiratory tract failure following inhalation, bronchoconstriction, bronchospasm, chest tightness, respiratory distress)

General Dosage Range Dosage adjustment recommended in patients with renal impairment or who develop toxicities.

IM, IV: *Children and Adults:* 2.5 to 5 mg/kg/day **colistin base activity** in 2 to 4 divided doses; maximum: 5 mg/kg/day

Mechanism of Action Colistimethate (or the sodium salt [colistimethate sodium]) is the inactive prodrug which is hydrolyzed to colistin, which acts as a cationic detergent and damages the bacterial cytoplasmic membrane causing leaking of intracellular substances and cell death

Pharmacodynamics/Kinetics

Half-life Elimination IM, IV: Colistimethate: 2 to 3 hours

Critically ill: Infants (including premature infants), Children, Adolescents, and Adults: IV: Colistimethate: 2.3 hours; Colistin: 14.4 hours (Plachouras 2009)

Cystic fibrosis: IV: Colistin: ~3.5 hours (Li 2003)

ESRD patients receiving CAPD: IV: Colistin: 13.2 hours (Koomanachai 2014)

Time to Peak

Healthy volunteers: IV: Colistin: 2 hours (range: 1 to 4 hours) (Couet 2011)

Critically ill: IV: Colistin: ~7 hours (Plachouras 2009)

Pregnancy Risk Factor C

Pregnancy Considerations Adverse events have been observed in animal reproduction studies. Colistimethate crosses the placenta in humans.

Collagen (Absorbable) (KOL la jen, ab SORB able)

Related Information

Antiplatelet and Anticoagulation Considerations in Dentistry *on page 1764*

Brand Names: US CollaCote; CollaPatch; CollaPlug; HeliCote; HeliPlug; HeliTape

Generic Availability (US) Yes

Pharmacologic Category Hemostatic Agent

Dental Use Control of bleeding created during dental surgery

Use Hemostatic

Local Anesthetic/Vasoconstrictor Precautions No information available to require special precautions

Effects on Dental Treatment No significant effects or complications reported

Effects on Bleeding No information available to require special precautions

Adverse Reactions Frequency not defined. Reactions listed are based on reports for other agents in this same pharmacologic class and may not be specifically reported for collagen (adsorbable/dental).

Hypersensitivity: Hypersensitivity reaction

Miscellaneous: Foreign body reaction, wound healing impairment (adhesion formation)

<1%, postmarketing, and/or case reports: Seroma (subgaleal)

Dental Usual Dosage Control of bleeding: Children and Adults: Topical: A sufficiently large dressing should be selected so as to completely cover the oral wound

Dosing

Adult & Geriatric Control of bleeding: Topical: A sufficiently large dressing should be selected so as to completely cover the oral wound

Pediatric Refer to adult dosing.

Mechanism of Action The highly porous sponge structure absorbs blood and wound exudate. The collagen component causes aggregation of platelets which bind to collagen fibrils. The aggregated platelets degranulate, releasing coagulation factors that promote the formation of fibrin.

Contraindications There are no contraindications listed in the manufacturer's labeling.

Warnings/Precautions Should not be used on infected or contaminated wounds

Drug Interactions

Metabolism/Transport Effects None known.

Avoid Concomitant Use There are no known interactions where it is recommended to avoid concomitant use.

Increased Effect/Toxicity There are no known significant interactions involving an increase in effect.

Decreased Effect There are no known significant interactions involving a decrease in effect.

Dosage Forms

Wound dressing:

Generics:

3/8" x 3/4"

3/4" x 1 1/2"

1" x 3"

Brands:

CollaCote®, CollaPlug®, CollaTape®:

3/8" x 3/4"

3/4" x 1 1/2"

1" x 3"

Collagenase (Systemic) (KOL la je nase)

Brand Names: US Xiaflex

Brand Names: Canada Xiaflex

Pharmacologic Category Enzyme

Use

Dupuytren contracture: Treatment of adults with Dupuytren contracture with a palpable cord

Peyronie disease: Treatment of adult men with Peyronie disease with a palpable plaque and curvature deformity of at least 30 degrees at the start of therapy

Adverse Reactions

Dupuytren's contracture:

>10%:

Cardiovascular: Peripheral edema (primarily as swelling of injected hand: 73% to 77%)

Dermatologic: Pruritus (4% to 15%), hemorrhagic blister (12%)

Hematologic & oncologic: Bruise (59% to 70%), lymphadenopathy (13%)

Immunologic: Antibody development (≥86%; neutralizing antibodies: AUX-I: 10%; AUX-II: 21%)

Local: Bleeding at injection site (6% to 38%), injection site reaction (35%; includes erythema, inflammation, irritation), swelling at injection site (5% to 24%), tenderness at injection site (24%), pain at injection site (14%)

Neuromuscular & skeletal: Limb pain (35% to 51%)

Miscellaneous: Laceration (9% to 22%)

1% to 10%:

Central nervous system: Lymph node pain (8%), axillary pain (6% to 7%)

Dermatologic: Erythema (6%), ecchymoses (5%)

Local: Hematoma at injection site (8%)

<1%, postmarketing, and/or case reports: Anaphylaxis, antibody development (IgE; increased with successive injections), causalgia, ligament disorder, pulley rupture, rupture of tendon, sensory disturbance, vasodepressor syncope

Peyronie disease:

>10%:

Genitourinary: Penile hematoma (66%; severe: 4% to 6%), penile swelling (55%), penile pain (45%), penile ecchymoses (15%), penile popping sensation (13%)

Immunologic: Antibody development (55% to >99%; neutralizing antibodies: AUX-I: 60%; AUX-II: 52%; no correlation to clinical response or adverse reaction)

1% to 10%:

Central nervous system: Procedural pain (2%), suprapubic pain (1%)

Dermatologic: Hemorrhagic blister (5%), genital pruritus (3%), skin discoloration (2%), localized vesiculation (injection site, 1%)

Genitourinary: Blisters on penis (3%), painful erection (3%), erectile dysfunction (2%), dyspareunia (1%)

Local: Itching at injection site (1% to 4%), localized edema (1%)

Miscellaneous: Nodule (1%)

<1%, postmarketing, and/or case reports: Penile fracture, sudden penile detumescence

General Dosage Range Intralesional: *Adults:* 0.58 mg per cord or plaque

Mechanism of Action Collagenase clostridium histolyticum contains two forms of microbial collagenase (Collagenase AUX-I and Collagenase AUX-II) isolated and purified from the fermentation of *Clostridium histolyticum* bacteria; collagenase lyses collagen, leading to enzymatic disruption of contracted Dupuytren cord or Peyronie plaque (both comprised primarily of collagen).

Pregnancy Risk Factor B

Pregnancy Considerations Adverse events have not been observed in animal reproduction studies. Pharmacokinetic studies in humans did not show quantifiable systemic levels following intralesional injection into a Dupuytren cord; however, low levels were quantifiable in the plasma following administration into the penile plaque. IgE-anti-drug antibodies commonly develop in treated patients; effects to the fetus are unknown.

Prescribing and Access Restrictions As a requirement of the Risk Evaluation and Mitigation Strategy (REMS) program, access to this medication is restricted. Because of the risks of corporal rupture or other serious penile injury, collagenase (for the treatment of Peyronie disease) is available only through a restricted program under a REMS called the XIAFLEX REMS Program. Prescribers and healthcare sites must be certified with the program. Call 1-877-313-1235 or visit www.Xiaflexrems.com for more information.

Collagenase (Topical) (KOL la je nase)

Brand Names: US Santyl
Brand Names: Canada Santyl
Pharmacologic Category Enzyme, Topical Debridement
Use Dermal ulcers: Debriding chronic dermal ulcers and severely burned areas.
Local Anesthetic/Vasoconstrictor Precautions No information available to require special precautions
Effects on Dental Treatment No significant effects or complications reported
Effects on Bleeding No information available to require special precautions
Adverse Reactions Frequency not defined.
Local: Application site burning, application site irritation, application site pain
<1%, postmarketing and/or case reports: Hypersensitivity reaction
General Dosage Range Topical: *Adults:* Apply once daily
Mechanism of Action Collagenase is an enzyme derived from the fermentation by *Clostridium histolyticum* and differs from other proteolytic enzymes in that its enzymatic action has a high specificity for native and denatured collagen in necrotic tissue; collagenase will not attack collagen in healthy tissue or newly formed granulation tissue. Therefore, collagenase is effective for the removal of detritus, formation of granulation tissue, and subsequent epithelization of dermal ulcers and severely burned areas.
Pregnancy Considerations It is not known if collagenase is absorbed systemically following topical application.

Collagen Hemostat (KOL la jen HEE moe stat)

Related Information
Antiplatelet and Anticoagulation Considerations in Dentistry *on page 1764*
Brand Names: US Actifoam Collagen Sponge; Avitene; Avitene Flour; Endo Avitene; Syringe Avitene; Ultrafoam Sponge 2x6.25x7CM; Ultrafoam Sponge 8x12.5x1CM; Ultrafoam Sponge 8x12.5x3CM; Ultrafoam Sponge 8x25x1CM; Ultrafoam Sponge 8x6.25x1CM
Brand Names: Canada Avitene
Generic Availability (US) No
Pharmacologic Category Hemostatic Agent
Dental Use Adjunct to hemostasis when control of bleeding by ligature is ineffective or impractical
Use Hemostasis: Adjunct to hemostasis in surgical procedures when control of bleeding by ligature or conventional procedures is ineffective or impractical.
Local Anesthetic/Vasoconstrictor Precautions No information available to require special precautions
Effects on Dental Treatment No significant effects or complications reported
Effects on Bleeding Used in surgical procedures as an adjunct to hemostasis when control of bleeding by ligature or conventional procedures is ineffective or impractical.
Adverse Reactions Frequency not defined.
Miscellaneous: Adhesion formation, allergic reaction, edema, foreign body reaction, hematoma, inflammation, potentiation of infection
Postmarketing and/or case reports: Numbness, pain, paralysis, subgaleal seroma; alveolalgia and transient laryngospasm with dental use
Dental Usual Dosage Hemostasis: Adults: Topical: Apply dry directly to source of bleeding; remove excess material after ~10-15 minutes
Dosing
Adult & Geriatric
Hemostasis: Topical: Apply dry directly to source of bleeding; remove excess material after ~5 to 10 minutes. If breakthrough bleeding occurs in areas of thin application, additional product may be applied depending on the severity of bleeding (in capillary bleeding, 1 g will usually be sufficient for a 50 cm^2 area; thicker coverage will be required for more brisk bleeding).
Renal Impairment There are no dosage adjustments provided in the manufacturer's labeling.
Hepatic Impairment There are no dosage adjustments provided in the manufacturer's labeling.
Mechanism of Action Collagen hemostat is an absorbable topical hemostatic agent prepared from purified bovine corium collagen and shredded into fibrils. Physically, microfibrillar collagen hemostat yields a large surface area. Chemically, it is collagen with hydrochloric acid noncovalently bound to some of the available amino groups in the collagen molecules. When in contact with a bleeding surface, collagen hemostat attracts platelets which adhere to its fibrils and undergo the release phenomenon. This triggers aggregation of the platelets into thrombi in the interstices of the fibrous mass, initiating the formation of a physiologic platelet plug.
Contraindications
Closure of skin incisions; application to bone surfaces to which prosthetic materials are attached with methylmethacrylate adhesives.
Instat MCH: There are no contraindications listed in the manufacturer's labeling.
Warnings/Precautions Pain, numbness, or paralysis have been reported if used near a bony or neural space and left inside patient; use minimum amount necessary to achieve hemostasis (FDA, 2004). Contains bovine serum protein; increases in anti-BSA titer have been observed. Use is not recommended in patients sensitive to bovine derived collagen. Use in contaminated wounds may enhance infection; do not leave MCH in a contaminated or infected space.

Not for injection, intraocular, or intravascular use. Do not use as a surface dressing except for immediate control of bleeding; use minimum amount necessary to achieve hemostasis. Avoid spillage on nonbleeding surfaces particularly in abdominal or thoracic viscera. Remove as much of agent as possible after hemostasis is achieved. Do not use in conjunction with autologous blood salvage circuits because fragments of MCH may pass through filters of blood scavenging systems; avoid reintroduction of blood from operative sites treated with MCH. Not intended to treat systemic coagulation disorders. Do not reuse, reprocess, resterilize, or repackage because doing so may lead to device failure or create a risk of contamination of the device and/or cause patient infection or cross infection.

Sponge: Do not use in instances of pumping arterial hemorrhage, where blood or other fluids have pooled, or where the point of hemorrhage is submerged as it may mask an underlying source of bleeding, resulting in hematoma.

Drug Interactions

Metabolism/Transport Effects None known.

Avoid Concomitant Use There are no known interactions where it is recommended to avoid concomitant use.

Increased Effect/Toxicity There are no known significant interactions involving an increase in effect.

Decreased Effect There are no known significant interactions involving a decrease in effect.

Pharmacodynamics/Kinetics

Onset of Action Hemostasis: 2 to 5 minutes

Dosage Forms

Miscellaneous, External:

Actifoam Collagen Sponge: (10 ea)
Endo Avitene: (1 ea)
Syringe Avitene: (1 g)
Ultrafoam Sponge 2x6.25x7CM: 2 cm x 6.25 cm x 7 cm (1 ea)
Ultrafoam Sponge 8x12.5x1CM: 8 cm x 12.5 cm x 1 cm (1 ea)
Ultrafoam Sponge 8x12.5x3CM: 8 cm x 12.5 cm x 3 cm (1 ea)
Ultrafoam Sponge 8x25x1CM: 8 cm x 25 cm x 1 cm (1 ea)
Ultrafoam Sponge 8x6.25x1CM: 8 cm x 6.25 cm x 1 cm (1 ea)

Pad, External:

Avitene: (1 ea)

Powder, External:

Avitene Flour: (6 ea, 1 g, 5 g)

Conivaptan (koe NYE vap tan)

Brand Names: US Vaprisol

Pharmacologic Category Vasopressin Antagonist

Use

Euvolemic or hypervolemic hyponatremia: Treatment of euvolemic and hypervolemic hyponatremia in hospitalized patients.

Limitations of use: Conivaptan is not approved for use in heart failure; however, conivaptan has been shown to be effective in improving sodium levels and intracardiac pressures, and increasing urine output (especially in combination with loop diuretics) in patients with heart failure (Goldsmith 2008; Goldsmith 2011; Udelsen 2001). Conivaptan has not been shown to be effective for treating symptoms of heart failure.

Local Anesthetic/Vasoconstrictor Precautions No information available to require special precautions

Effects on Dental Treatment Key adverse event(s) related to dental treatment: Dry mouth, oral candidiasis; Patients may experience orthostatic hypotension as they stand up after treatment; especially if lying in dental chair for extended periods of time. Use caution with sudden changes in position during and after dental treatment.

Effects on Bleeding No information available to require special precautions

Adverse Reactions

>10%:

Cardiovascular: Orthostatic hypotension (6% to 14%)
Endocrine & metabolic: Hypokalemia (10% to 22%)
Local: Injection site reaction (63% to 73%; including erythema at injection site, injection site pain, injection site phlebitis, swelling at injection site)
Miscellaneous: Fever (5% to 11%)

1% to 10%:

Cardiovascular: Hypertension (6% to 8%), hypotension (5% to 8%), peripheral edema (3% to 8%), phlebitis (5%), atrial fibrillation (2% to 5%), ECG abnormality (≤5%)
Central nervous system: Headache (8% to 10%), insomnia (4% to 5%), confusion (≤5%), pain (2%)
Dermatologic: Pruritus (1% to 5%), erythema (3%)
Endocrine & metabolic: Hyponatremia (6% to 8%), increased thirst (3% to 6%), hypomagnesemia (2% to 5%), hyperglycemia (≤3%), hypoglycemia (≤3%), dehydration (2%)
Gastrointestinal: Constipation (6% to 8%), vomiting (5% to 7%), diarrhea (≤7%), nausea (3% to 5%), xerostomia (4%), oral candidiasis (2%)
Genitourinary: Urinary tract infection (4% to 5%), hematuria (2%)
Hematologic & oncologic: Anemia (5% to 6%)
Renal: Polyuria (5% to 6%)
Respiratory: Pneumonia (2% to 5%), pharyngolaryngeal pain (1% to 5%)

<1%, postmarketing, and/or case reports: Atrial arrhythmia, sepsis

General Dosage Range Dosage adjustment recommended in patients with hepatic impairment

IV: *Adults:* 20 mg loading dose, followed by 20 mg over 24 hours; (maximum: 40 mg over 24 hours)

Mechanism of Action Conivaptan is an arginine vasopressin (AVP) receptor antagonist with affinity for AVP receptor subtypes V_{1A} and V_2. The antidiuretic action of AVP is mediated through activation of the V_2 receptor, which functions to regulate water and electrolyte balance at the level of the collecting ducts in the kidney. Serum levels of AVP are commonly elevated in euvolemic or hypervolemic hyponatremia, which results in the dilution of serum sodium and the relative hyponatremic state. Antagonism of the V_2 receptor by conivaptan promotes the excretion of free water (without loss of serum electrolytes) resulting in net fluid loss, increased urine output, decreased urine osmolality, and subsequent restoration of normal serum sodium concentrations.

Pharmacodynamics/Kinetics

Half-life Elimination 5.3 to 8.1 hours

Pregnancy Considerations Adverse events have been observed in animal reproduction studies.

Copper IUD (KOP er eye uh dee)

Brand Names: US Paragard Intrauterine Copper

Pharmacologic Category Contraceptive

Use Contraception: For prevention of pregnancy, intrauterine device (IUD) may be in place for up to 10 years

Local Anesthetic/Vasoconstrictor Precautions No information available to require special precautions

Effects on Dental Treatment No significant effects or complications reported

Effects on Bleeding No information available to require special precautions

Adverse Reactions Frequency not defined.

Dermatologic: Urticaria (allergic)
Endocrine & metabolic: Hypermenorrhea, spotty menstruation
Genitourinary: Abnormal vaginal hemorrhage, cervical perforation, dysmenorrhea, dyspareunia, ectopic pregnancy, embedment of intrauterine system in the myometrium, leukorrhea, pelvic cramps, pelvic pain, spontaneous migration of the IUD, uterine perforation, vaginitis

Hematologic & oncologic: Anemia
Miscellaneous: Device expulsion
Neuromuscular & skeletal: Back pain

Mechanism of Action The mechanism of action is not well defined but may involve interfering with sperm transport, fertilization, and prevention of implantation. A copper IUD may prevent fertilization by interfering with the ability of sperm to reach the fallopian tube, or decrease the sperm's ability to fertilize by causing a foreign body reaction and chemical changes that may be toxic. Implantation can rarely occur with a copper IUD; however, the number of fertilized ova is decreased when compared to sexually active women not using a contraceptive. When fertilized ova are present, they do not develop normally (Rivera, 1999). The number of women with a copper IUD who have an unintended pregnancy within the first year of insertion following typical use and perfect use is <1%.

Pregnancy Considerations Use during pregnancy is contraindicated. An increased risk of birth defects has not been observed from the copper released from the device. However, the risk of spontaneous abortion, premature delivery, sepsis, septic shock, and death (rare) are increased if an intrauterine pregnancy occurs with the IUD in place. Premature labor and delivery may also occur.

Corticorelin (kor ti koe REL in)

Brand Names: US Acthrel

Pharmacologic Category Diagnostic Agent

Use Cushing syndrome, differential diagnosis: Used as a diagnostic aid to differentiate between pituitary and ectopic production of ACTH in patients with ACTH-dependent disease

Local Anesthetic/Vasoconstrictor Precautions No information available to require special precautions

Effects on Dental Treatment No significant effects or complications reported

Effects on Bleeding No information available to require special precautions

Adverse Reactions Frequency not always defined. Incidence of adverse effects is dependent upon dose.

Cardiovascular: Decreased blood pressure (7%), asystole, flushing (face, neck, and upper chest), palpitations (Corticorelin 2004)
Central nervous system: Tonic-clonic seizures (1%), dizziness, (Corticorelin 2004), metallic taste (Corticorelin 2004)
Gastrointestinal: Vomiting (Corticorelin 2004), xerostomia (Corticorelin 2004)
Respiratory: Dyspnea (urge to inspire)
<1%, postmarketing, and/or case reports: Angioedema, chest tightness, hypotension (severe), increased heart rate, loss of consciousness, tachycardia (severe), wheezing

General Dosage Range IV: *Children, Adolescents, and Adults:* 1 mcg/kg

Mechanism of Action Corticorelin ovine, a peptide of ovine corticotropin-releasing hormone (oCRH) and an analogue of human CRH (hCRH), stimulates adrenocorticotropic hormone (ACTH) release from the anterior pituitary. ACTH stimulates the adrenal cortex to produce cortisol. Depending on the plasma ACTH and cortisol response following the corticorelin stimulation test, the results aid the clinician in the differentiation between the source of ACTH-dependent hypercortisolism (pituitary vs ectopic).

Pharmacodynamics/Kinetics

Onset of Action IV:
Plasma ACTH concentration: Increases 2 minutes after injection
Plasma cortisol concentration: Increases within 10 minutes after injection
Peak effect: Response to injection is biphasic with a second lower peak 2 to 3 hours postinjection; basal and peak response levels vary depending on AM or PM administration. In general, baseline ACTH and cortisol concentrations are higher in the AM.
Plasma ACTH concentration: Initial peak: 15 to 60 minutes after injection
Plasma cortisol concentration: Initial peak at 30 to 120 minutes after injection

Duration of Action IV: Plasma ACTH and cortisol concentrations remain elevated for up to 2 hours after injection.

Half-life Elimination
$t_{1/2}$: Exhibits biexponential decay; Fast component: 11.6 ± 1.5 minutes; slow component: 73 ± 8 minutes

Pregnancy Risk Factor C

Pregnancy Considerations Animal reproduction studies have not been conducted.

Corticotropin (kor ti koe TROE pin)

Brand Names: US HP Acthar

Pharmacologic Category Corticosteroid, Systemic

Use

Collagen diseases: Treatment of exacerbations or as maintenance therapy of systemic lupus erythematosus, or systemic dermatomyositis (polymyositis).

Dermatologic diseases: Treatment of severe erythema multiforme or Stevens-Johnson syndrome.

Diuresis in nephrotic syndrome: To induce a diuresis or remission of proteinuria in patients with nephrotic syndrome without idiopathic uremia or due to lupus erythematosus.

Infantile spasms: Treatment of infantile spasms in infants and children younger than 2 years.

Multiple sclerosis: Treatment of acute exacerbations of multiple sclerosis in adults. **Note**: Treatment guidelines recommend the use of high dose IV or oral methylprednisolone for acute exacerbations of multiple sclerosis (AAN [Scott 2011]; NICE 2014).

Ophthalmic diseases: Treatment of severe acute and chronic allergic and inflammatory processes involving the eye and its adnexa (eg, keratitis, iritis, iridocyclitis, diffuse posterior uveitis, choroiditis, optic neuritis, chorioretinitis, anterior segment inflammation).

Rheumatic disorders: As adjunctive therapy for acute episodes/exacerbations of psoriatic arthritis, rheumatoid arthritis, including juvenile rheumatoid arthritis (select cases may require low-dose maintenance therapy) and/or ankylosing spondylitis.

Serum sickness: Treatment of serum sickness.

Symptomatic sarcoidosis: Treatment of symptomatic sarcoidosis.

Local Anesthetic/Vasoconstrictor Precautions No information available to require special precautions

Effects on Dental Treatment No significant effects or complications reported

Effects on Bleeding No information available to require special precautions

Adverse Reactions Frequency not always defined. Adverse events associated with infantile spasm treatment unless otherwise indicated. Other adverse events associated with corticosteroids may also occur.

Cardiovascular: Hypertension (11%), cardiac hypertrophy (3%), increased blood pressure (associated with cortisol elevation)
Central nervous system: Seizure (12%), irritability (7%), behavioral changes (associated with cortisol elevation), mood changes (associated with cortisol elevation)
Endocrine & metabolic: Cushingoid state (3%), decreased glucose tolerance (associated with cortisol elevation), fluid retention (associated with cortisol elevation)
Gastrointestinal: Decreased appetite (3%), diarrhea (3%), vomiting (3%), weight gain (1%; associated with cortisol elevation), increased appetite (associated with cortisol elevation)
Infection: Infection (20%)
Respiratory: Nasal congestion (1%)
Miscellaneous: Fever (5%)
<1%, postmarketing and/or case reports: Abdominal distention, carbohydrate intolerance (infants), cardiac failure, diaphoresis (adults), epidermal thinning (adults), facial erythema, headache (adults), hirsutism, hypersensitivity reaction, hypokalemic alkalosis (infants), intracranial hemorrhage (adults), myasthenia, necrotizing angiitis (adults), pancreatitis (adults), reversible cerebral atrophy (infants; secondary to hypertension), subdural hematoma, ulcerative esophagitis, vertebral compression fracture (infants), vertigo (adults)

General Dosage Range

IM:

Infants and Children <2 years: 75 units/m²/dose twice daily (infantile spasms) followed by gradual downward titration of dose

IM/SubQ:

Children >2 years and Adolescents: 40 to 80 units every 24 to 72 hours

Adults: 80 to 120 units/day for 2 to 3 weeks (acute exacerbation of multiple sclerosis [MS]) **or** 40 to 80 units every 24 to 72 hours (indications other than MS)

Mechanism of Action Stimulates the adrenal cortex to secrete adrenal steroids (including cortisol), weakly androgenic substances, and aldosterone

Pharmacodynamics/Kinetics

Onset of Action Maximum effect: Cortisol serum concentration: IM, SubQ: 3-12 hours

Duration of Action Repository: 10-25 hours, up to 3 days

Half-life Elimination ACTH: 15 minutes

Pregnancy Risk Factor

C

Pregnancy Considerations Adverse events were observed in animal reproduction studies. Endogenous corticotropin concentrations are increased near delivery (Smith, 2007).

Some studies have shown an association between first trimester systemic corticosteroid use and oral clefts (Park-Wyllie, 2000; Pradat, 2003). Systemic corticosteroids may also influence fetal growth (decreased birth weight); however, information is conflicting (Lunghi, 2010). When systemic corticosteroids are needed in pregnancy, it is generally recommended to use the lowest effective dose for the shortest duration of time, avoiding high doses during the first trimester (Leachman, 2006; Lunghi, 2010; Makol, 2011; Østensen, 2009).

Prescribing and Access Restrictions H.P. Acthar® Gel is only available through specialty pharmacy distribution and not through traditional distribution sources (eg, wholesalers, retail pharmacies). Hospitals wishing to acquire H.P. Acthar® Gel should contact CuraScript Specialty Distribution (1-877-599-7748).

After treatment is initiated, discharge or outpatient prescriptions should be submitted to the Acthar Support and Access Program (A.S.A.P.) in order to ensure an uninterrupted supply of the medication. The Acthar Referral/Prescription form is available online at http://www.acthar.com/files/Acthar-Prescription-Referral-Form.pdf.

Additional information is available for the A.S.A.P. at http://www.acthar.com/healthcare-professionals/physician-patient-referrals or by calling 1-888-435-2284.

Cortisone (KOR ti sone)

Related Information

Respiratory Diseases *on page 1777*
Triamcinolone (Systemic) *on page 1600*

Pharmacologic Category Corticosteroid, Systemic

Use

Allergic states: Control of severe or incapacitating allergic conditions intractable to adequate trials of conventional treatment of atopic dermatitis, bronchial asthma, contact dermatitis, drug hypersensitivity reactions, seasonal or perennial allergic rhinitis, and serum sickness.

Dermatologic diseases: Bullous dermatitis herpetiformis, exfoliative dermatitis, mycosis fungoides, pemphigus, severe erythema multiforme (Stevens-Johnson syndrome), severe psoriasis, severe seborrheic dermatitis.

Endocrine disorders: Congenital adrenal hyperplasia, hypercalcemia associated with cancer, nonsuppurative thyroiditis, primary or secondary adrenocortical insufficiency (hydrocortisone or cortisone is the first choice; synthetic analogs may be used in conjunction with mineralocorticoids when applicable; in infancy, mineralocorticoid supplementation is of particular importance).

Gastrointestinal diseases: To tide the patient over a critical period of the disease in regional enteritis and ulcerative colitis.

Hematologic disorders: Acquired (autoimmune) hemolytic anemia, congenital (erythroid) hypoplastic anemia, erythroblastopenia (red blood cell [RBC] anemia), idiopathic thrombocytopenic purpura in adults, secondary thrombocytopenia in adults.

Neoplastic diseases: Palliative management of leukemias and lymphomas in adults; acute leukemia of childhood.

Ophthalmic diseases: Severe acute and chronic allergic and inflammatory processes involving the eye and its adnexa (eg, allergic conjunctivitis, allergic corneal marginal ulcers, anterior segment inflammation, chorioretinitis, diffuse posterior uveitis and choroiditis, keratitis, herpes zoster ophthalmicus, iritis and iridocyclitis, optic neuritis, sympathetic ophthalmia).

Renal diseases: To induce diuresis or remission of proteinuria in nephrotic syndrome, without uremia, of the idiopathic type or that is caused by lupus erythematosus.

Respiratory diseases: Aspiration pneumonitis, berylliosis, fulminating or disseminated pulmonary tuberculosis when used concurrently with appropriate antituberculosis chemotherapy, Loeffler syndrome not manageable by other means, symptomatic sarcoidosis.

Rheumatic disorders: Adjunctive therapy for short-term administration (to tide the patient over an acute episode or exacerbation) in acute and subacute bursitis; acute gouty arthritis; acute nonspecific tenosynovitis; ankylosing spondylitis; epicondylitis; posttraumatic osteoarthritis; psoriatic arthritis; rheumatoid arthritis (RA), including juvenile RA (select cases may require low-dose maintenance therapy); and synovitis of osteoarthritis. During an exacerbation or as maintenance therapy in select cases of acute rheumatic carditis, systemic dermatomyositis (polymyositis), and systemic lupus erythematosus.

Miscellaneous: Tuberculous meningitis with subarachnoid block or impending block when used concurrently with appropriate antituberculous chemotherapy; trichinosis with neurologic or myocardial involvement.

Local Anesthetic/Vasoconstrictor Precautions No information available to require special precautions

Effects on Dental Treatment A compromised immune response may occur if patient has been taking systemic cortisone. The need for corticosteroid coverage in these patients should be considered before any dental treatment; consult with physician.

Effects on Bleeding Variable effects on anticoagulant therapy are observed with glucocorticoids, such as cortisone.

Adverse Reactions Frequency not defined.

>10%:

Central nervous system: Insomnia, nervousness

Gastrointestinal: Dyspepsia, increased appetite

1% to 10%:

Endocrine & metabolic: Diabetes mellitus, hirsutism

Neuromuscular & skeletal: Arthralgia

Ophthalmic: Cataract, glaucoma

Respiratory: Epistaxis

<1%, postmarketing, and/or case reports: Abdominal distention, acne vulgaris, alkalosis, amenorrhea, amyotrophy, bone fracture, bruise, Cushing's syndrome, decreased glucose tolerance, delirium, edema, emotional lability, euphoria, fluid retention, growth suppression, hallucination, headache, HPA-axis suppression, hyperglycemia, hyperpigmentation, hypersensitivity reaction, hypertension, hypokalemia, myalgia, nausea, osteoporosis, pancreatitis, peptic ulcer, pseudotumor cerebri, psychosis, seizure, skin atrophy, sodium retention, ulcerative esophagitis, vertigo, vomiting

General Dosage Range Oral:

Children: 0.5 to 10 mg/kg/day **or** 20 to 300 mg/m^2/day divided every 6 to 8 hours

Adults: 25 to 300 mg/day

Mechanism of Action Decreases inflammation by suppression of migration of polymorphonuclear leukocytes and reversal of increased capillary permeability

Pharmacodynamics/Kinetics

Half-life Elimination ~0.5 hours

Time to Peak ~2 hours

Pregnancy Considerations Adverse events have been observed with corticosteroids in animal reproduction studies. Cortisone crosses the placenta (Migeon 1957). Some studies have shown an association between first trimester systemic corticosteroid use and oral clefts (Park-Wyllie 2000; Pradat 2003). Systemic corticosteroids may also influence fetal growth (decreased birth weight); however, information is conflicting (Lunghi 2010). Hypoadrenalism may occur in newborns following maternal use of corticosteroids in pregnancy (monitor). When systemic corticosteroids are needed in pregnancy, it is generally recommended to use the lowest effective dose for the shortest duration of time, avoiding high doses during the first trimester (Leachman 2006; Lunghi 2010; Makol 2011; Østensen 2009). Cortisone may be used (alternative agent) to treat primary adrenal insufficiency (PAI) in pregnant women. Pregnant women with PAI should be monitored at least once each trimester (Bornstein 2016).

Cosyntropin (koe sin TROE pin)

Brand Names: US Cortrosyn

Brand Names: Canada Cortrosyn; Synacthen Depot

Pharmacologic Category Corticosteroid, Systemic; Diagnostic Agent

Use

Diagnostic test to differentiate primary adrenal insufficiency from secondary (pituitary) adrenocortical insufficiency

Synacthen Depot [Canadian product]: Additional indications: Treatment of various disease states (eg, collagen, dermatologic, endocrine, ocular, hemolytic). Consult manufacturer labeling for detailed list.

Local Anesthetic/Vasoconstrictor Precautions No information available to require special precautions

Effects on Dental Treatment No significant effects or complications reported

Effects on Bleeding No information available to require special precautions

Adverse Reactions Frequency not defined. Adverse events associated with other corticosteroids may be observed when Synacthen Depot (Canadian product) is used for therapeutic purposes. Refer to corticosteroid monographs for comprehensive lists.

Cardiovascular: Bradycardia, hypertension, peripheral edema, tachycardia

Dermatologic: Skin rash, urticaria at injection site (with erythema)

Hypersensitivity: Anaphylaxis, hypersensitivity reaction

<1%, postmarketing and/or case reports: Adrenal hemorrhage (Synacthen Depot)

General Dosage Range IM, IV:

Children ≤2 years: 0.125 mg

Children >2 years and Adults: 0.25 mg

Mechanism of Action Stimulates the adrenal cortex to secrete adrenal steroids (including hydrocortisone, cortisone), androgenic substances, and a small amount of aldosterone

Pharmacodynamics/Kinetics

Onset of Action Onset of action: IM, IV: Within 5 minutes increases in plasma cortisol concentrations are observed in healthy individuals; Maximum effect: IM, IV: 45-60 minutes peak plasma cortisol concentration

Duration of Action Synacthen Depot [Canadian product]: IM: Plasma concentrations of 200-300 pg/mL maintained for 12 hours

Half-life Elimination Synacthen Depot [Canadian product]: 7 minutes

Time to Peak Serum: IM, IV push: ~1 hour; plasma cortisol levels rise in healthy individuals within 5 minutes

Pregnancy Risk Factor C

Pregnancy Considerations Animal reproduction studies have not been conducted with cosyntropin; adverse events have been observed with corticosteroids in animal reproduction studies. Some studies have shown an association between first trimester systemic corticosteroid use and oral clefts (Park-Wyllie 2000; Pradat 2003). Systemic corticosteroids may also influence fetal growth (decreased birth weight);

however, information is conflicting (Lunghi 2010). When systemic corticosteroids are needed in pregnancy, it is generally recommended to use the lowest effective dose for the shortest duration of time, avoiding high doses during the first trimester (Leachman 2006; Lunghi 2010; Makol 2011; Østensen 2009). Cosyntropin is the recommended test to diagnose primary adrenal insufficiency during pregnancy. Pregnancy may alter cortisol levels, and higher concentrations are used to interpret the results based on trimester (Bornstein 2016).

Crisaborole (kris a BOR ole)

Brand Names: US Eucrisa

Pharmacologic Category Phosphodiesterase-4 Enzyme Inhibitor, Topical; Topical Skin Product

Use Atopic dermatitis: Topical treatment of mild to moderate atopic dermatitis in patients ≥2 years of age

Local Anesthetic/Vasoconstrictor Precautions No information available to require special precautions

Effects on Dental Treatment No significant effects or complications reported

Effects on Bleeding No information available to require special precautions

Adverse Reactions

1% to 10%: Local: Application site pain (4%)

<1%, postmarketing, and/or case reports: Hypersensitivity reaction, urticaria

General Dosage Range Topical: *Children ≥2 years, Adolescents, and Adults:* Apply a thin film to affected area(s) 2 times daily.

Mechanism of Action Inhibits phosphodiesterase 4 (PDE-4) and results in increased intracellular cyclic adenosine monophosphate (cAMP) levels.

Pregnancy Considerations Adverse effects were not observed in animal reproduction studies, except with high oral doses which also produced maternal toxicity.

Crizotinib (kriz OH ti nib)

Related Information

Clinical Risk Related to Drugs Prolonging QT Interval *on page 1772*

Brand Names: US Xalkori

Brand Names: Canada Xalkori

Pharmacologic Category Antineoplastic Agent, Anaplastic Lymphoma Kinase Inhibitor; Antineoplastic Agent, Tyrosine Kinase Inhibitor

Use Non-small cell lung cancer, metastatic: Treatment of patients with metastatic non-small cell lung cancer (NSCLC) whose tumors are anaplastic lymphoma kinase (ALK)-positive (as detected by an approved test) or are ROS1-positive

Local Anesthetic/Vasoconstrictor Precautions Crizotinib is one of the drugs confirmed to prolong the QT interval and is accepted as having a risk of causing torsade de pointes. The risk of drug-induced torsade de pointes is extremely low when a single QT interval prolonging drug is prescribed. In terms of epinephrine, it is not known what effect vasoconstrictors in the local anesthetic regimen will have in patients with a known history of congenital prolonged QT interval or in patients taking any medication that prolongs the QT interval. Until more information is obtained, it is suggested that the clinician consult with the physician prior to the use of a vasoconstrictor in suspected patients, and that the vasoconstrictor (epinephrine, mepivacaine, and levonordefrin [Carbocaine® 2% with Neo-Cobefrin®]) be used with caution.

Effects on Dental Treatment Key adverse event(s) related to dental treatment: Stomatitis and taste alteration have been reported

Effects on Bleeding No reports of bleeding or thrombocytopenia

Adverse Reactions

>10%:

Cardiovascular: Edema (31% to 49%), bradycardia (5% to 14%)

Central nervous system: Fatigue (27% to 29%), neuropathy (19% to 25%; includes dysesthesia, gait disturbance, hypoesthesia, muscular weakness, neuralgia, peripheral neuropathy, parasthesia, peripheral sensory neuropathy, polyneuropathy, burning sensation in skin), headache (22%), dizziness (18% to 22%)

Dermatologic: Skin rash (9% to 11%)

Endocrine & metabolic: Hypophosphatemia (28% to 32%), hypokalemia (18%)

Gastrointestinal: Diarrhea (60% to 61%), nausea (55% to 56%), vomiting (46% to 47%), constipation (42% to 43%), decreased appetite (30%), abdominal pain (26%), dysgeusia (26%), dyspepsia (8% to 14%)

Genitourinary: Decreased estimated GFR (eGFR) (<90 mL/min/1.73 m^2: 76%; <60 mL/min/1.73 m^2: 38%; <30 mL/min/1.73 m^2: 4%)

Hematologic & oncologic: Neutropenia (49% to 52%; grades 3/4: 11% to 12%), lymphocytopenia (48% to 51%; grades 3/4: 7% to 9%)

Hepatic: Increased serum ALT (76% to 79%), increased serum AST (61% to 66%)

Neuromuscular & skeletal: Limb pain (16%)

Ophthalmic: Visual disturbance (60% to 71%; onset: <2 weeks; includes blurred vision, diplopia, photophobia, photopsia, visual acuity decreased, visual brightness, visual field defect, visual impairment, vitreous floaters)

Respiratory: Upper respiratory tract infection (26% to 32%)

Miscellaneous: Fever (19%)

1% to 10%:

Cardiovascular: Pulmonary embolism (6%), prolonged Q-T interval on ECG (5% to 6%), syncope (1% to 3%)

Endocrine & metabolic: Weight loss (10%), weight gain (8%), diabetic ketoacidosis (≤2%), decreased plasma testosterone (1%; hypogonadism)

Gastrointestinal: Dysphagia (10%), esophagitis (2% to 6%)

Hepatic: Hepatic failure (1%)

Infection: Sepsis (≤5%)

Neuromuscular & skeletal: Muscle spasm (8%)

Renal: Renal cyst (3% to 5%)

Respiratory: Adult respiratory distress syndrome (≤5%), interstitial pulmonary disease (≤5%; grades 3/4: 1%; includes acute respiratory distress syndrome, pneumonitis), pneumonia (≤5%), respiratory failure (≤5%), dyspnea (2%)

Frequency not defined:

Cardiovascular: Cardiac arrhythmia, septic shock

<1%, postmarketing, and/or case reports: Hepatotoxicity

General Dosage Range Dosage adjustment recommended in patients with renal impairment or who develop toxicities.

Oral: *Adults:* 250 mg twice daily

Mechanism of Action Tyrosine kinase receptor inhibitor, which inhibits anaplastic lymphoma kinase (ALK),

Hepatocyte Growth Factor Receptor (HGFR, c-MET), ROS1 (c-ros), and Recepteur d'Origine Nantais (RON). ALK gene abnormalities due to mutations or translocations may result in expression of oncogenic fusion proteins (eg, ALK fusion protein) which alter signaling and expression and result in increased cellular proliferation and survival in tumors which express these fusion proteins. Approximately 2% to 7% of patients with NSCLC have the abnormal echinoderm microtubule-associated protein-like 4, or EML4-ALK gene (which has a higher prevalence in never smokers or light smokers and in patients with adenocarcinoma). Inhibition of ALK, ROS1, and c-Met phosphorylation is concentration-dependent. Crizotinib selectively inhibits ALK tyrosine kinase, which reduces proliferation of cells expressing the genetic alteration.

Pharmacodynamics/Kinetics

Half-life Elimination Terminal: 42 hours

Time to Peak 4 to 6 hours

Pregnancy Considerations Adverse events have been observed in animal reproduction studies. Based on the mechanism of action, crizotinib may cause fetal harm if administered during pregnancy. Women of child-bearing potential should use adequate contraception during treatment and for at least 45 days after the last crizotinib dose; males with female partners of reproductive potential should use condoms during treatment and for at least 90 days after the final dose. The Canadian labeling recommends adequate contraception during treatment and for at least 90 days after the last dose for both males and females.

Prescribing and Access Restrictions Available through specialty pharmacies. Further information may be obtained from the manufacturer, Pfizer, at 1-877-744-5675, or at http://www.pfizerpro.com

Dental Comment See Local Anesthetic/Vasoconstrictor Precautions

Cromolyn (Systemic) (KROE moe lin)

Brand Names: US Gastrocrom

Brand Names: Canada Nalcrom

Pharmacologic Category Mast Cell Stabilizer

Use Systemic mastocytosis

Local Anesthetic/Vasoconstrictor Precautions No information available to require special precautions

Effects on Dental Treatment Key adverse event(s) related to dental treatment:

Systemic: Glossitis, stomatitis, and unpleasant taste.

Effects on Bleeding No information available to require special precautions

Adverse Reactions

Cardiovascular: Chest pain, edema, flushing, palpitations, tachycardia, ventricular premature contractions

Central nervous system: Headache (5%), irritability (2%), malaise (1%), anxiety, behavioral changes, burning sensation, convulsions, depression, dizziness, dizziness (postprandial), fatigue, hallucination, hypoesthesia, insomnia, lethargy, migraine, nervousness, paresthesia, psychosis

Dermatologic: Pruritus (3%), skin rash (2%), erythema, skin photosensitivity, urticaria

Gastrointestinal: Diarrhea (5%), nausea (3%), abdominal pain (2%), constipation, dyspepsia, dysphagia, esophageal spasm, flatulence, glossitis, stomatitis, unpleasant taste, vomiting

Genitourinary: Dysuria, urinary frequency

Hematologic & oncologic: Neutropenia, pancytopenia, polycythemia, purpura

Hepatic: Abnormal hepatic function tests

Hypersensitivity: Anaphylaxis, angioedema

Neuromuscular & skeletal: Myalgia (3%), arthralgia, lower extremity weakness, lupus erythematosus, stiffness of legs

Otic: Tinnitus

Respiratory: Dyspnea, pharyngitis

General Dosage Range

Oral:

Children 2 to 12 years: 100 mg 4 times/day (maximum: 40 mg/kg/day)

Children >12 years, Adolescents, and Adults: 200 mg 4 times/day (maximum: 40 mg/kg/day)

Mechanism of Action Prevents the mast cell release of histamine, leukotrienes, and slow-reacting substance of anaphylaxis by inhibiting degranulation after contact with antigens

Pharmacodynamics/Kinetics

Onset of Action Response to treatment: Oral: May occur within 2 to 6 weeks

Half-life Elimination 80 to 90 minutes

Pregnancy Risk Factor B

Pregnancy Considerations Adverse events were not observed in animal reproduction studies following oral administration. Systemic absorption following oral administration is <1%.

Cromolyn (Oral Inhalation) (KROE moe lin)

Brand Names: Canada Nu-Cromolyn; PMS-Sodium Cromoglycate

Pharmacologic Category Mast Cell Stabilizer

Use Prophylactic agent used for long-term (chronic) control of asthma; prevention of exercise-induced bronchospasm

Local Anesthetic/Vasoconstrictor Precautions No information available to require special precautions

Effects on Dental Treatment Key adverse event(s) related to dental treatment:

Inhalation: Unpleasant taste.

Effects on Bleeding No information available to require special precautions

Adverse Reactions Frequency not always defined.

Central nervous system: Drowsiness

Dermatologic: Burning sensation of the nose, pruritus of nose

Gastrointestinal: Nausea, stomach pain

Hypersensitivity: Serum sickness

Respiratory: Cough (20%; transient), wheezing (4%; mild), epistaxis, nasal congestion, sneezing

<1%, postmarketing, and/or case reports: Anaphylaxis, anemia, angioedema, arthralgia, bronchospasm, dizziness, dysuria, exfoliative dermatitis, headache, hemoptysis, hoarseness, joint swelling, lacrimation, laryngeal edema, nephrosis, myalgia, parotid gland enlargement, pericarditis, peripheral neuritis, photodermatitis, polymyositis, pulmonary infiltrates (with eosinophilia), skin rash, urinary frequency, urticaria, vasculitis (periarteritis), vertigo

General Dosage Range Inhalation: *Children ≥2 years, Adolescents, and Adults:* Initial: 20 mg 4 times/day; Maintenance: 20 mg 3 to 4 times/day **or** 20 mg prior to exercise or allergen exposure

Mechanism of Action Prevents the mast cell release of histamine, leukotrienes, and slow-reacting substance of anaphylaxis by inhibiting degranulation after contact with antigens

Pharmacodynamics/Kinetics

Half-life Elimination 80 to 90 minutes

Time to Peak Serum: Inhalation: ~15 minutes

Pregnancy Risk Factor B

Pregnancy Considerations Adverse events were not observed in animal reproduction studies following SubQ administration. Limited data suggest little or no placental transfer (Brogden 1974). Uncontrolled asthma is associated with adverse events on pregnancy. Although cromolyn sodium is considered to have a good safety profile, due to decreased efficacy, other agents are preferred for the control of asthma in pregnancy (GINA 2016).

Crotamiton (kroe TAM i tonn)

Brand Names: US Eurax

Brand Names: Canada Eurax Cream

Pharmacologic Category Scabicidal Agent

Use Treatment of scabies (*Sarcoptes scabiei*) and symptomatic treatment of pruritus

Local Anesthetic/Vasoconstrictor Precautions No information available to require special precautions

Effects on Dental Treatment No significant effects or complications reported

Effects on Bleeding No information available to require special precautions

Adverse Reactions Frequency not defined.

Central nervous system: Localized warm feeling
Dermatologic: Contact dermatitis, pruritus, skin rash
Hypersensitivity: Local hypersensitivity reaction
Local: Local irritation

General Dosage Range **Topical:** *Adults:* Pruritus: Massage into affected areas as needed; Scabies: Apply a thin layer from the neck to the toes; repeat in 24 hours.

Mechanism of Action Crotamiton has scabicidal activity against *Sarcoptes scabiei*; mechanism of action unknown. Antipruritic effects mediated by inhibition of histamine, serotonin, and PAR-2 (Sekine 2012).

Pregnancy Risk Factor C

Pregnancy Considerations Animal reproduction studies have not been conducted; use during pregnancy only if clearly needed.

Cyanocobalamin (sye an oh koe BAL a min)

Brand Names: US B-12 Compliance Injection; Nascobal; Physicians EZ Use B-12; Vitamin Deficiency System-B12

Pharmacologic Category Vitamin, Water Soluble

Use Treatment of pernicious anemia; vitamin B_{12} deficiency due to dietary deficiencies or malabsorption diseases, inadequate secretion of intrinsic factor, and inadequate utilization of B_{12} (eg, during neoplastic treatment); increased B_{12} requirements due to pregnancy, thyrotoxicosis, hemorrhage, malignancy, liver or kidney disease

Local Anesthetic/Vasoconstrictor Precautions No information available to require special precautions

Effects on Dental Treatment No significant effects or complications reported

Effects on Bleeding No information available to require special precautions

Adverse Reactions Frequency not defined.

Cardiovascular: Congestive heart failure, peripheral vascular disease, thrombosis (peripheral)
Central nervous system: Abnormal gait, anxiety, ataxia, dizziness, headache, hypoesthesia, nervousness, pain, paresthesia
Dermatologic: Pruritus, skin rash (transient), urticaria
Gastrointestinal: Diarrhea, dyspepsia, glossitis, nausea, sore throat, vomiting
Hematologic & Oncologic: Polycythemia vera
Hypersensitivity: Anaphylaxis (parenteral)
Infection: Infection
Neuromuscular & skeletal: Arthritis, back pain, myalgia, weakness
Respiratory: Dyspnea, pulmonary edema, rhinitis

General Dosage Range

IM, SubQ: *Children and Adults:* Dosage varies greatly depending on indication

Intranasal: *Adults:* Nascobal: 500 mcg in one nostril once weekly

Oral: *Adults:* 250-2000 mcg daily

Mechanism of Action Coenzyme for various metabolic functions, including fat and carbohydrate metabolism and protein synthesis, used in cell replication and hematopoiesis

Pharmacodynamics/Kinetics

Onset of Action

Megaloblastic anemia: IM:
Conversion of megaloblastic to normoblastic erythroid hyperplasia within bone marrow: 8 hours
Increased reticulocytes: 2 to 5 days
Complicated vitamin B_{12} deficiency: IM, SubQ: Resolution of:
Psychiatric sequelae: 24 hours
Thrombocytopenia: 10 days
Granulocytopenia: 2 weeks

Time to Peak Serum: IM, SubQ: 30 minutes to 2 hours; Intranasal: 1.6 hours

Pregnancy Considerations Animal reproduction studies have not been conducted. Water soluble vitamins cross the placenta. Absorption of vitamin B_{12} may increase during pregnancy. Vitamin B_{12} requirements may be increased in pregnant women compared to nonpregnant women. Serum concentrations of vitamin B_{12} are higher in the neonate at birth than the mother (IOM, 1998).

Cyclizine (SYE kli zeen)

Brand Names: US Cyclivert [OTC] [DSC]

Pharmacologic Category Histamine H_1 Antagonist; Histamine H_1 Antagonist, First Generation; Piperazine Derivative

Use Prevention and treatment of nausea, vomiting, and vertigo associated with motion sickness

Local Anesthetic/Vasoconstrictor Precautions No information available to require special precautions

Effects on Dental Treatment Key adverse event(s) related to dental treatment: Xerostomia (normal salivary flow resumes upon discontinuation).

Effects on Bleeding No information available to require special precautions

Adverse Reactions Frequency not defined.

>10%:
Central nervous system: Drowsiness
Gastrointestinal: Xerostomia

1% to 10%:
Central nervous system: Headache
Dermatologic: Dermatitis
Gastrointestinal: Nausea
Genitourinary: Urinary retention
Ophthalmic: Diplopia
Renal: Polyuria

Mechanism of Action Cyclizine is a piperazine derivative with properties of histamines. The precise mechanism of action in inhibiting the symptoms of motion sickness is not known. It may have effects directly on the labyrinthine apparatus and central actions on the labyrinthine apparatus and on the chemoreceptor trigger zone. Cyclizine exerts a central anticholinergic action.

Pharmacodynamics/Kinetics

Half-life Elimination Cyclizine: ~14 hours; Norcyclizine: ~24 hours; Norchlorcyclizine: ~6 days (Paton, 1985; Walker, 1996)

Pregnancy Considerations Although cyclizine is approved for the prevention and treatment of nausea and vomiting, other agents are currently recommended for the treatment of nausea and vomiting in pregnancy (ACOG 2015).

Product Availability All products have been discontinued in the US for more than 1 year.

Cyclobenzaprine (sye kloe BEN za preen)

Related Information

Dentin Hypersensitivity, Acid Erosion, High Caries Index, Management of Alveolar Osteitis, and Xerostomia *on page 1857*

Temporomandibular Dysfunction (TMD), Chronic Pain, and Fibromyalgia *on page 1868*

Brand Names: US Active-Cyclobenzaprine; Amrix; Cyclophene RapidPaq; EnovaRX-Cyclobenzaprine HCl; Fexmid; Flexeril [DSC]; Tabradol FusePaq; Tabradol RapidPaq

Brand Names: Canada Apo-Cyclobenzaprine; Auro-Cyclobenzaprine; Ava-Cyclobenzaprine; Dom-Cyclobenzaprine; JAMP-Cyclobenzaprine; Mylan-Cyclobenzaprine; Novo-Cycloprine; PHL-Cyclobenzaprine; PMS-Cyclobenzaprine; Q-Cyclobenzaprine; ratio-Cyclobenzaprine; Riva-Cycloprine; ZYM-Cyclobenzaprine

Generic Availability (US) May be product dependent

Pharmacologic Category Skeletal Muscle Relaxant

Dental Use Treatment of muscle spasm associated with acute temporomandibular joint pain (TMJ)

Use Muscle spasm: As an adjunct to rest and physical therapy for short-term (2 to 3 weeks) relief of muscle spasm associated with acute, painful musculoskeletal conditions.

Local Anesthetic/Vasoconstrictor Precautions No information available to require special precautions

Effects on Dental Treatment Key adverse event(s) related to dental treatment: Xerostomia and changes in salivation (normal salivary flow resumes upon discontinuation).

Effects on Bleeding No information available to require special precautions

Adverse Reactions

>10%:

- Central nervous system: Drowsiness (1% to 39%), dizziness (1% to 11%)
- Gastrointestinal: Xerostomia (6% to 32%)

1% to 10%:

- Central nervous system: Fatigue (1% to 6%), headache (1% to 5%), confusion (1% to 3%), decreased mental acuity (1% to 3%), irritability (1% to 3%), nervousness (1% to 3%)
- Gastrointestinal: Dyspepsia (≤4%), abdominal pain (1% to 3%), acid regurgitation (1% to 3%), constipation (1% to 3%), diarrhea (1% to 3%), nausea (1% to 3%), unpleasant taste (1% to 3%)
- Neuromuscular & skeletal: Weakness (1% to 3%)
- Ophthalmic: Blurred vision (1% to 3%)
- Respiratory: Pharyngitis (1% to 3%), upper respiratory tract infection (1% to 3%)

<1%, postmarketing, and/or case reports: Abnormal dreams, abnormal hepatic function tests, abnormality in thinking, ageusia, agitation, anaphylaxis, angioedema, anorexia, anxiety, ataxia, cardiac arrhythmia, cholestasis, convulsions,depression, diaphoresis, diplopia, disorientation, dysarthria, excitement (paradoxical, children), facial edema, flatulence, gastritis, gastrointestinal pain, hallucination, hepatitis (rare), hypertonia, hypotension, increased thirst, insomnia, jaundice, malaise, muscle twitching, palpitations, paresthesia, pruritus, psychosis, seizure, serotonin syndrome, skin rash, syncope, tachycardia, tinnitus, tongue edema, tremor, urinary frequency, urinary retention, urticaria, vasodilation, vertigo, vomiting

Dental Usual Dosage Treatment of muscle spasm associated with acute TMJ pain (Burket, 2008) (**Note:** Do not use longer than 2-3 weeks): Oral:

Adults: Initial: 5 mg 3 times/day; may increase to 7.5-10 mg 3 times/day if needed

Elderly: 5 mg 3 times/day; plasma concentration and incidence of adverse effects are increased in the elderly; dose should be titrated slowly

Dosing

Adult Muscle spasm: Oral: **Note:** Do not use longer than 2 to 3 weeks

Capsule, extended release: Usual: 15 mg once daily; some patients may require up to 30 mg once daily

Tablet, immediate release: Initial: 5 mg 3 times daily; may increase up to 10 mg 3 times daily if needed

Geriatric

Capsule, extended release: Use not recommended.

Tablet, immediate release: Initial: 5 mg; titrate dose slowly and consider less frequent dosing.

Pediatric Muscle spasm: Oral: Tablet, immediate release: Children ≥15 years: Refer to adult dosing.

Renal Impairment There are no dosage adjustment provided in the manufacturer's labeling.

Hepatic Impairment

Capsule, extended release: Mild to severe impairment: Use not recommended.

Tablet, immediate release:

Mild impairment: Initial: 5 mg; use with caution; titrate slowly and consider less frequent dosing

Moderate to severe impairment: Use not recommended.

Mechanism of Action Centrally-acting skeletal muscle relaxant pharmacologically related to tricyclic antidepressants; reduces tonic somatic motor activity influencing both alpha and gamma motor neurons

Contraindications Hypersensitivity to cyclobenzaprine or any component of the formulation; during or within 14 days of MAO inhibitors; hyperthyroidism; heart failure; arrhythmias; heart block or conduction disturbances; acute recovery phase of MI

Warnings/Precautions May cause CNS depression, which may impair physical or mental abilities; ethanol and/or other CNS depressants may enhance these effects. Patients must be cautioned about performing tasks which require mental alertness (eg, operating machinery or driving). Cyclobenzaprine shares the toxic potentials of the tricyclic antidepressants (including arrhythmias, tachycardia, and conduction time prolongation) and the usual precautions of tricyclic antidepressant therapy should be observed; use with caution in patients with urinary hesitancy or retention, angle-closure glaucoma or increased intraocular pressure, hepatic impairment, or in the elderly.

Potentially life-threatening serotonin syndrome has occurred with cyclobenzaprine when used in combination with other serotonergic agents (eg, SSRIs, SNRIs, TCAs, meperidine, tramadol, buspirone, MAO inhibitors), bupropion, and verapamil. Monitor patients closely especially during initiation/dose titration for signs/symptoms of serotonin syndrome such as mental status changes (eg, agitation, hallucinations); autonomic instability (eg, tachycardia, labile blood pressure, diaphoresis); neuromuscular changes (eg, tremor, rigidity, myoclonus); GI symptoms (eg, nausea, vomiting, diarrhea); and/or seizures. Discontinue cyclobenzaprine and any concomitant serotonergic agent immediately if signs/symptoms arise. Concomitant use or use within 14 days of discontinuing an MAO inhibitor is contraindicated.

Extended release capsules not recommended for use in mild-to-severe hepatic impairment or in the elderly. Potentially significant drug-drug interactions may exist, requiring dose or frequency adjustment, additional monitoring, and/or selection of alternative therapy. Effects may be potentiated when used with other CNS depressants or ethanol.

Drug Interactions

Metabolism/Transport Effects **Substrate** of CYP1A2 (major), CYP2D6 (minor), CYP3A4 (minor); **Note:** Assignment of Major/Minor substrate status based on clinically relevant drug interaction potential

Avoid Concomitant Use

Avoid concomitant use of Cyclobenzaprine with any of the following: Aclidinium; Azelastine (Nasal); Cimetropium; Dapoxetine; Eluxadoline; Glucagon; Glycopyrrolate (Oral Inhalation); Ipratropium (Oral Inhalation); Levosulpiride; MAO Inhibitors; Methylene Blue; Nitroglycerin; Orphenadrine; Oxatomide; Oxomemazine; Paraldehyde; Potassium Chloride; Thalidomide; Tiotropium; Umeclidinium

Increased Effect/Toxicity

Cyclobenzaprine may increase the levels/effects of: AbobotulinumtoxinA; Alcohol (Ethyl); Analgesics (Opioid); Anticholinergic Agents; Antipsychotic Agents; Azelastine (Nasal); Blonanserin; Buprenorphine; Cimetropium; CNS Depressants; Eluxadoline; Flunitrazepam; Glucagon; Glycopyrrolate (Oral Inhalation); HYDROcodone; MAO Inhibitors; Methotrimeprazine; Metoclopramide; MetyroSINE; Mirabegron; Mirtazapine; OnabotulinumtoxinA; Orphenadrine; OxyCODONE; Paraldehyde; Piribedil; Potassium Chloride; Pramipexole; Ramosetron; RimabotulinumtoxinB; ROPINIRole; Rotigotine; Selective Serotonin Reuptake Inhibitors; Serotonin Modulators; Suvorexant; Thalidomide; Thiazide and Thiazide-Like Diuretics; Tiotropium; Topiramate; Zolpidem

The levels/effects of Cyclobenzaprine may be increased by: Abiraterone Acetate; Aclidinium; Antiemetics (5HT3 Antagonists); Antipsychotic Agents; Brimonidine (Topical); Cannabis; Chloral Betaine; Chlormethiazole; Chlorphenesin Carbamate; CYP1A2 Inhibitors (Moderate); CYP1A2 Inhibitors (Strong); Dapoxetine; Deferasirox; Dimethindene (Topical); Doxylamine; Dronabinol; Droperidol; HydrOXYzine; Ipratropium (Oral Inhalation); Kava Kava; Lofexidine; Magnesium Sulfate; Metaxalone; Methotrimeprazine; Methylene Blue; Methylphenidate; Mianserin; Minocycline; Nabilone; Obeticholic Acid; Oxatomide; Oxomemazine; Peginterferon Alfa-2b; Perampanel; Pramlintide; Rufinamide; Sodium Oxybate; Tapentadol; Tetrahydrocannabinol; Tolperisone; Trimeprazine; Umeclidinium; Vemurafenib

Decreased Effect

Cyclobenzaprine may decrease the levels/effects of: Acetylcholinesterase Inhibitors; Gastrointestinal Agents (Prokinetic); Itopride; Levosulpiride; Nitroglycerin; Secretin

The levels/effects of Cyclobenzaprine may be decreased by: Acetylcholinesterase Inhibitors; Ombitasvir, Paritaprevir, and Ritonavir; Ombitasvir, Paritaprevir, Ritonavir, and Dasabuvir

Food Interactions Food increases bioavailability (peak plasma concentrations increased by 35% and area under the curve by 20%) of the extended release capsule. Management: Monitor for increased effects if taken with food.

Pharmacodynamics/Kinetics

Onset of Action Immediate release tablet: Within 1 hour

Duration of Action Immediate release tablet: 12 to 24 hours

Half-life Elimination Normal hepatic function: Range: 8 to 37 hours; Immediate release tablet: 18 hours; Extended release capsule: 32 hours; Impaired hepatic function: 46.2 hours (range: 22.4 to 188 hours) (Winchell 2002)

Time to Peak Immediate release tablet: ~4 hours (Winchell 2002); Extended release capsule: 7 to 8 hours

Pregnancy Risk Factor B

Pregnancy Considerations Adverse events have not been observed in animal reproduction studies. The manufacturer recommends avoiding use during pregnancy unless clearly needed.

Breastfeeding Considerations It is not known if cyclobenzaprine is excreted in breast milk. Because cyclobenzaprine is closely related to tricyclic antidepressants, some of which are excreted in breast milk, the manufacturer recommends that caution be exercised when administering cyclobenzaprine to breastfeeding women.

Dosage Forms Considerations

EnovaRX-Cyclobenzaprine and Active-Cyclobenzaprine creams are compounded from kits. Refer to manufacturer's labeling for compounding instructions.

Tabradol FusePaq is a compounding kit for the preparation of an oral suspension in a vehicle containing methylsulfonylmethane. Refer to manufacturer's labeling for compounding instructions.

Dosage Forms

Capsule Extended Release 24 Hour, Oral:
Amrix: 15 mg, 30 mg

Cream, Transdermal:
Active-Cyclobenzaprine: 5% (120 g)
Cyclophene RapidPaq: 5% (100 g)
EnovaRX-Cyclobenzaprine HCl: 20 mg/g (120 g)

Suspension, Oral:
Tabradol FusePaq: 1 mg/mL (250 mL)
Tabradol RapidPaq: 1 mg/mL (250 mL)

Tablet, Oral:
Fexmid: 7.5 mg
Generic: 5 mg, 7.5 mg, 10 mg

Cyclopentolate (sye kloe PEN toe late)

Brand Names: US Cyclogyl

Brand Names: Canada AK Pentolate Oph Soln; Cyclogyl; Diopentolate; Minims Cyclopentolate; PMS-Cyclopentolate

Pharmacologic Category Anticholinergic Agent, Ophthalmic

Use Mydriasis/Cycloplegia: Produce mydriasis and cycloplegia.

Local Anesthetic/Vasoconstrictor Precautions No information available to require special precautions

Effects on Dental Treatment No significant effects or complications reported

Effects on Bleeding No information available to require special precautions

Adverse Reactions Frequency not defined.

1% to 10%:

Cardiovascular: Tachycardia

Central nervous system: Ataxia, hallucination, hyperactivity, incoherent speech, psychosis, restlessness, seizure

Dermatologic: Burning sensation of skin

Hypersensitivity: Hypersensitivity reaction

Ophthalmic: Accommodation disturbance (loss), increased intraocular pressure

General Dosage Range Ophthalmic:

Infants: Instill 1 drop of 0.5% solution as a single dose

Children and Adolescents: Instill 1 or 2 drops of 0.5%, 1%, or 2% solution; may repeat with 0.5% or 1% solution in 5 to 10 minutes

Adults: Instill 1 or 2 drops of 0.5%, 1%, or 2% solution; may repeat in 5 to 10 minutes

Mechanism of Action Prevents the muscle of the ciliary body and the sphincter muscle of the iris from responding to cholinergic stimulation, causing mydriasis and cycloplegia

Pharmacodynamics/Kinetics

Onset of Action Peak effect: Cycloplegia: 25 to 75 minutes; Mydriasis: Within 15-60 minutes, with recovery taking up to 24 hours

Duration of Action Cycloplegia: ≤24 hours

Pregnancy Risk Factor C

Pregnancy Considerations Animal reproduction studies have not been conducted.

Cyclophosphamide (sye kloe FOS fa mide)

Brand Names: Canada Procytox

Pharmacologic Category Antineoplastic Agent, Alkylating Agent; Antineoplastic Agent, Alkylating Agent (Nitrogen Mustard); Antirheumatic Miscellaneous; Immunosuppressant Agent

Use

Oncology uses: Treatment of acute lymphoblastic leukemia (ALL), acute myelocytic leukemia (AML), breast cancer, chronic lymphocytic leukemia (CLL), chronic myeloid leukemia (CML), Hodgkin lymphoma, mycosis fungoides, multiple myeloma, neuroblastoma, non-Hodgkin lymphomas (including Burkitt lymphoma), ovarian adenocarcinoma, and retinoblastoma

Limitations of use: Although potentially effective as a single-agent in susceptible malignancies, cyclophosphamide is more frequently used in combination with other chemotherapy drugs

Nononcology uses: Nephrotic syndrome: Treatment of minimal change nephrotic syndrome (biopsy proven) in children who are unresponsive or intolerant to corticosteroid therapy

Limitations of use: The safety and efficacy for the treatment of nephrotic syndrome in adults or in other renal diseases has not been established.

Local Anesthetic/Vasoconstrictor Precautions No information available to require special precautions

Effects on Dental Treatment Key adverse event(s) related to dental treatment: Mucositis and stomatitis.

Effects on Bleeding Hematologic toxicities including thrombocytopenia are among the important dose-limiting effects of cyclophosphamide. A medical consult is recommended.

Adverse Reactions Frequency not defined.

Dermatologic: Alopecia (reversible; onset: 3 to 6 weeks after start of treatment)

Endocrine & metabolic: Amenorrhea, increased gonadotropin secretion

Gastrointestinal: Abdominal pain, anorexia, diarrhea, mucositis, nausea and vomiting (dose-related), stomatitis

Genitourinary: Azoospermia, defective oogenesis, hemorrhagic cystitis, oligospermia, sterility

Hematologic & oncologic: Anemia, bone marrow depression, febrile neutropenia, leukopenia (dose-related; recovery: 7 to 10 days after cessation), neutropenia, thrombocytopenia

Infection: Infection

<1%, postmarketing, and/or case reports: Acute respiratory distress, anaphylaxis, auditory disturbance, blurred vision, cardiac arrhythmia (with high-dose [HSCT] therapy), cardiac failure (with high-dose [HSCT] therapy), cardiac tamponade (with high-dose [HSCT] therapy), cardiotoxicity, confusion, C-reactive protein increased, dizziness, dyschromia (skin/fingernails), dyspnea, erythema multiforme, gastrointestinal hemorrhage, heart block, hematuria, hemopericardium, hemorrhagic colitis, hemorrhagic myocarditis (with high-dose [HSCT] therapy), hemorrhagic ureteritis, hepatic veno-occlusive disease (also called hepatic sinusoidal obstruction syndrome), hepatitis, hepatotoxicity, hypersensitivity reaction, hyperuricemia, hypokalemia, hyponatremia, increased lactate dehydrogenase, interstitial pneumonitis, ischemia (acute; mesenteric), jaundice, malaise, metastases, methemoglobinemia (with high-dose [HSCT] therapy), multi-organ failure, myocardial necrosis (with high-dose [HSCT] therapy), neurotoxicity, neutrophilic eccrine hidradenitis, ovarian fibrosis, pancreatitis, pericarditis, pneumonia, pulmonary hypertension, pulmonary infiltrates, pulmonary interstitial fibrosis (with high doses), pulmonary veno-occlusive disease, pyelonephritis, radiation recall phenomenon, reactivation of disease, reduced ejection fraction, renal tubular necrosis, reversible posterior leukoencephalopathy syndrome, rhabdomyolysis, sepsis, septic shock, SIADH, skin rash, Stevens-Johnson syndrome, testicular atrophy, thrombocytopenia (immune mediated), thrombosis (arterial and venous), toxic epidermal necrolysis, toxic megacolon, tumor lysis syndrome, urinary fibrosis, weakness, wound healing impairment

General Dosage Range Dosage adjustment recommended in patients with hepatic or renal impairment or who develop toxicities.

IV: *Children and Adults:* Dosage varies greatly depending on indication.

Oral: *Children and Adults:* Dosage varies greatly depending on indication.

Mechanism of Action Cyclophosphamide is an alkylating agent that prevents cell division by cross-linking DNA strands and decreasing DNA synthesis. It is a cell cycle phase nonspecific agent. Cyclophosphamide also possesses potent immunosuppressive activity. Cyclophosphamide is a prodrug that must be metabolized to active metabolites in the liver.

Pharmacodynamics/Kinetics

Half-life Elimination IV: 3 to 12 hours; Children: 4 hours; Adults: 6 to 8 hours

Time to Peak Oral: ~1 hour; IV: Metabolites: 2 to 3 hours

Pregnancy Risk Factor D

Pregnancy Considerations Cyclophosphamide crosses the placenta and can be detected in amniotic fluid (D'Incalci 1982). Based on the mechanism of action, cyclophosphamide may cause fetal harm if administered during pregnancy. Adverse events (including ectrodactylia) were observed in human studies following exposure to cyclophosphamide. Women of childbearing potential should avoid pregnancy while receiving cyclophosphamide and for up to 1 year after completion of treatment. Males with female partners who are or may become pregnant should use a condom during and for at least 4 months after cyclophosphamide treatment. Cyclophosphamide may cause sterility in males and females (may be irreversible) and amenorrhea in females. When treatment is needed for lupus nephritis, cyclophosphamide should be avoided in women who are pregnant or those who wish to preserve their fertility (Hahn 2012).

Chemotherapy, if indicated, may be administered to pregnant women with breast cancer as part of a combination chemotherapy regimen (common regimens administered during pregnancy include doxorubicin (or epirubicin), cyclophosphamide, and fluorouracil); chemotherapy should not be administered during the first trimester, after 35 weeks gestation, or within 3 weeks of planned delivery (Amant 2010; Loibl 2006). The European Society for Medical Oncology has published guidelines for diagnosis, treatment, and follow-up of cancer during pregnancy. The guidelines recommend referral to a facility with expertise in cancer during pregnancy and encourage a multidisciplinary team (obstetrician, neonatologist, oncology team). In general, if chemotherapy is indicated, it should be avoided during in the first trimester, there should be a 3-week time period between the last chemotherapy dose and anticipated delivery, and chemotherapy should not be administered beyond week 33 of gestation (Peccatori 2013).

CycloSERINE (sye kloe SER een)

Brand Names: US Seromycin [DSC]

Pharmacologic Category Antibiotic, Miscellaneous; Antitubercular Agent

Use

Tuberculosis: Treatment of active pulmonary or extrapulmonary tuberculosis, in combination with other agents, when treatment with primary tuberculosis therapy has proved inadequate

Urinary tract infections: May be effective in treatment of acute urinary tract infections caused by susceptible strains of gram-positive and gram-negative bacteria, especially *Enterobacter* spp. and *Escherichia coli*. **Note:** Should be considered only when more conventional therapy has failed and when the organism has been demonstrated to be susceptible to the drug.

Local Anesthetic/Vasoconstrictor Precautions No information available to require special precautions

Effects on Dental Treatment No significant effects or complications reported

Effects on Bleeding No information available to require special precautions

Adverse Reactions Frequency not defined.

Cardiovascular: Cardiac arrhythmia, cardiac failure

Central nervous system: Coma, confusion, dizziness, drowsiness, dysarthria, headache, hyperreflexia, paresis, paresthesia, psychosis, restlessness, seizure, vertigo

Dermatologic: Skin rash

Endocrine & metabolic: Cyanocobalamin deficiency, folate deficiency

Hepatic: Increased liver enzymes

Hypersensitivity: Hypersensitivity reaction

Neuromuscular & skeletal: Tremor

General Dosage Range Dosage adjustment recommended in patients with renal impairment

Oral: *Adults:* Initial: 250 mg every 12 hours for 14 days; Maintenance: 500 to 1,000 mg/day in 2 divided doses

Mechanism of Action Inhibits bacterial cell wall synthesis by competing with amino acid (D-alanine) for incorporation into the bacterial cell wall; bacteriostatic or bactericidal

Pharmacodynamics/Kinetics

Half-life Elimination Normal renal function: 12 hours

Time to Peak Serum: 4 to 8 hours

Pregnancy Risk Factor C

Pregnancy Considerations Adverse events have not been observed in animal reproduction studies. Cycloserine crosses the placenta and can be detected in the fetal blood and amniotic fluid. The American Thoracic Society recommends use in pregnant women only if there are no alternatives (CDC 2003).

CycloSPORINE (Systemic) (SYE kloe spor een)

Brand Names: US Gengraf; Neoral; SandIMMUNE

Brand Names: Canada Apo-Cyclosporine; Neoral; Sandimmune I.V.; Sandoz-Cyclosporine

Generic Availability (US) Yes

Pharmacologic Category Calcineurin Inhibitor; Immunosuppressant Agent

Dental Use Used as an immunosuppressive agent

Use

Cyclosporine modified:

Transplant rejection prophylaxis: Prophylaxis of organ rejection in kidney, liver, and heart transplants (has been used with azathioprine and/or corticosteroids)

Rheumatoid arthritis: Treatment of severe, active rheumatoid arthritis (RA) not responsive to methotrexate alone

Psoriasis: Treatment of severe, recalcitrant plaque psoriasis in nonimmunocompromised adults unresponsive to or unable to tolerate other systemic therapy

Cyclosporine non-modified: Transplant rejection (prophylaxis/treatment): Prophylaxis of organ rejection in kidney, liver, and heart transplants (has been used with azathioprine and/or corticosteroids; treatment of chronic organ rejection)

Canadian labeling: Additional uses (not in US labeling):

Cyclosporine modified: Nephrotic syndrome: Induction and maintenance of remission in steroid dependent/resistant nephrotic syndrome due to glomerular disease (eg, minimal change nephropathy, membranous glomerulonephritis, focal and segmental glomerulosclerosis); maintenance of steroid induced remission allowing for steroid dose reduction or withdrawal.

Cyclosporine modified/non-modified: Bone marrow transplantation: Prophylaxis of graft rejection following bone marrow transplantation; prophylaxis or treatment of graft-versus-host disease (GVHD)

Local Anesthetic/Vasoconstrictor Precautions No information available to require special precautions

Effects on Dental Treatment Key adverse event(s) related to dental treatment: Mouth sores, swallowing difficulty, gingivitis, gum hyperplasia, xerostomia (normal salivary flow resumes upon discontinuation), abnormal taste, tongue disorder, and gingival bleeding (see Dental Comment)

Effects on Bleeding No information available to require special precautions

Adverse Reactions Adverse reactions reported with systemic use, including rheumatoid arthritis, psoriasis, and transplantation (kidney, liver, and heart). Percentages noted include the highest frequency regardless of indication/dosage. Frequencies may vary for specific conditions or formulation.

>10%:

Cardiovascular: Hypertension (8% to 53%), edema (5% to 14%)
Central nervous system: Headache (2% to 25%), paresthesia (1% to 11%)
Dermatologic: Hypertrichosis (5% to 19%)
Endocrine & metabolic: Hirsutism (21% to 45%), increased serum triglycerides (15%), female genital tract disease (9% to 11%)
Gastrointestinal: Nausea (2% to 23%), diarrhea (3% to 13%), gingival hyperplasia (2% to 16%), abdominal distress (<1% to 15%), dyspepsia (2% to 12%)
Genitourinary: Urinary tract infection (kidney transplant: 21%)
Infection: Increased susceptibility to infection (3% to 25%), viral infection (kidney transplant: 16%)
Neuromuscular & skeletal: Tremor (7% to 55%), leg cramps (2% to 12%)
Renal: Increased serum creatinine (16% to ≥50%), renal insufficiency (10% to 38%)
Respiratory: Upper respiratory tract infection (1% to 14%)

Kidney, liver, and heart transplant only (≤2% unless otherwise noted):

Cardiovascular: Chest pain (≤4%), flushing (<1% to 4%), glomerular capillary thrombosis, myocardial infarction
Central nervous system: Convulsions (1% to 5%), anxiety, confusion, lethargy, tingling sensation
Dermatologic: Skin infection (7%), acne vulgaris (1% to 6%), nail disease (brittle fingernails), hair breakage, night sweats, pruritus
Endocrine & metabolic: Gynecomastia (<1% to 4%), hyperglycemia, hypomagnesemia, weight loss
Gastrointestinal: Vomiting (2% to 10%), anorexia, aphthous stomatitis, constipation, dysphagia, gastritis, hiccups, pancreatitis
Genitourinary: Hematuria
Hematologic & oncologic: Leukopenia (<1% to 6%), lymphoma (<1% to 6%), anemia, thrombocytopenia, upper gastrointestinal hemorrhage
Hepatic: Hepatotoxicity (<1% to 7%)
Infection: Localized fungal infection (8%), cytomegalovirus disease (5%), septicemia (5%), abscess (4%), fungal infection (systemic: 2%)
Neuromuscular & skeletal: Arthralgia, myalgia, weakness
Ophthalmic: Conjunctivitis, visual disturbance
Otic: Hearing loss, tinnitus
Respiratory: Sinusitis (<1% to 7%), pneumonia (6%)
Miscellaneous: Fever

Rheumatoid arthritis only (1% to <3% unless otherwise noted):

Cardiovascular: Chest pain (4%), cardiac arrhythmia (2%), abnormal heart sounds, cardiac failure, myocardial infarction, peripheral ischemia
Central nervous system: Dizziness (8%), pain (6%), insomnia (4%), depression (3%), migraine (2% to 3%), anxiety, drowsiness, emotional lability, hypoesthesia, lack of concentration, malaise, neuropathy, nervousness, paranoia, vertigo
Dermatologic: Cellulitis, dermatological reaction, dermatitis, diaphoresis, dyschromia, eczema, enanthema, folliculitis, nail disease, pruritus, urticaria, xeroderma
Endocrine & metabolic: Menstrual disease (3%), decreased libido, diabetes mellitus, goiter, hot flash, hyperkalemia, hyperuricemia, hypoglycemia, increased libido, weight gain, weight loss
Gastrointestinal: Vomiting (9%), flatulence (5%), gingivitis (4%), constipation, dysgeusia, dysphagia, enlargement of salivary glands, eructation, esophagitis, gastric ulcer, gastritis, gastroenteritis, gingival hemorrhage, glossitis, peptic ulcer, tongue disease, xerostomia
Genitourinary: Leukorrhea (1%), breast fibroadenosis, hematuria, mastalgia, nocturia, urine abnormality, urinary incontinence, urinary urgency, uterine hemorrhage
Hematologic & oncologic: Purpura (3% to 4%), anemia, carcinoma, leukopenia, lymphadenopathy
Hepatic: Hyperbilirubinemia
Infection: Abscess (including renal), bacterial infection, candidiasis, fungal infection, herpes simplex infection, herpes zoster, viral infection
Neuromuscular & skeletal: Arthralgia, bone fracture, dislocation, myalgia, stiffness, synovial cyst, tendon disease, weakness
Ophthalmic: Cataract, conjunctivitis, eye pain, visual disturbance
Otic: Tinnitus, deafness, vestibular disturbance
Renal: Abscess (renal), increased blood urea nitrogen, polyuria, pyelonephritis
Respiratory: Cough (5%), dyspnea (5%), sinusitis (4%), abnormal breath sounds, bronchospasm, epistaxis, tonsillitis

Psoriasis only (1% to <3% unless otherwise noted):

Cardiovascular: Chest pain, flushing
Central nervous system: Psychiatric disturbance (4% to 5%), pain (3% to 4%), dizziness, insomnia, nervousness, vertigo
Dermatologic: Acne vulgaris, folliculitis, hyperkeratosis, pruritus, skin rash, xeroderma
Endocrine & metabolic: Hot flash
Gastrointestinal: Abdominal distention, constipation, gingival hemorrhage, increased appetite
Genitourinary: Urinary frequency
Hematologic & oncologic: Abnormal erythrocytes, altered platelet function, blood coagulation disorder, carcinoma, hemorrhagic diathesis
Hepatic: Hyperbilirubinemia
Neuromuscular & skeletal: Arthralgia (1% to 6%)
Ophthalmic: Visual disturbance
Respiratory: Flu-like symptoms (8% to 10%), bronchospasm (5%), cough (5%), dyspnea (5%), rhinitis (5%), respiratory tract infection
Miscellaneous: Fever

Postmarketing and/or case reports (any indication):

Anaphylaxis/anaphylactoid reaction (possibly associated with Cremophor EL vehicle in injection formulation), brain disease, central nervous system toxicity, cholestasis, cholesterol increased, exacerbation of psoriasis (transformation to erythrodermic or pustular psoriasis), fatigue, gout, haemolytic uremic syndrome, hepatic insufficiency, hepatitis, hyperbilirubinemia, hyperkalemia, hyperlipidemia, hypertrichosis, hyperuricemia, hypomagnesemia, impaired consciousness, increased susceptibility to infection (including JC virus and BK virus), jaundice, leg pain (possibly a manifestation of Calcineurin-Inhibitor Induced Pain Syndrome), malignant lymphoma, migraine, myalgia, myopathy, myositis, papilledema, progressive multifocal leukoencephalopathy, pseudotumor cerebri, pulmonary edema (noncardiogenic), renal disease (polyoma virus-associated), reversible posterior leukoencephalopathy syndrome, rhabdomyolysis, thrombotic microangiopathy

Dental Usual Dosage Note: Neoral/Gengraf and Sandimmune are not bioequivalent and cannot be used interchangeably.

Autoimmune diseases: Adults: 1-3 mg/kg/day

Dosing

Adult Neoral/Gengraf and Sandimmune are not bioequivalent and cannot be used interchangeably.

Psoriasis: Oral: Cyclosporine (modified): Initial dose: 2.5 mg/kg daily, divided twice daily

Titration:

US labeling: Increase by 0.5 mg/kg daily if insufficient response is seen after 4 weeks of treatment. Additional dosage increases may be made every 2 weeks if needed (maximum dose: 4 mg/kg daily)

Canadian labeling: Increase by 0.5 to 1 mg/kg daily if insufficient response is seen after 4 weeks of treatment. Additional dosage increases may be made every 4 weeks if needed (maximum dose: 5 mg/kg daily)

Discontinue if no benefit is seen by 6 weeks of therapy at the maximum dose. Once patients are adequately controlled, the dose should be decreased to the lowest effective dose. Doses lower than 2.5 mg/kg daily may be effective. The Canadian labeling recommends attempting to wean patients off therapy if no relapse occurs within 6 months of achieving remission. Treatment longer than 1 year is not recommended.

Note: Increase the frequency of blood pressure monitoring after each alteration in dosage of cyclosporine. Cyclosporine dosage should be decreased by 25% to 50% in patients with no history of hypertension who develop sustained hypertension during therapy and, if hypertension persists, treatment with cyclosporine should be discontinued.

Rheumatoid arthritis: Oral: Cyclosporine (modified): Initial dose: 2.5 mg/kg daily, divided twice daily; salicylates, NSAIDs, and oral glucocorticoids may be continued (refer to Drug Interactions)

Titration:

US labeling: Dose may be increased by 0.5 to 0.75 mg/kg daily if insufficient response is seen after 8 weeks of treatment; additional dosage increases may be made again at 12 weeks (maximum dose: 4 mg/kg daily). Discontinue if no benefit is seen by 16 weeks of therapy.

Canadian labeling: If insufficient response to initial dose after 6 weeks, may increase dose gradually as tolerated (maximum dose: 5 mg/kg daily); maintenance therapy should be individualized to the lowest effective and tolerable dose; may take up to 12 weeks before full effect is achieved.

Note: Increase the frequency of blood pressure monitoring after each alteration in dosage of cyclosporine. Cyclosporine dosage should be decreased by 25% to 50% in patients with no history of hypertension who develop sustained hypertension during therapy and, if hypertension persists, treatment with cyclosporine should be discontinued.

Solid organ transplant (newly transplanted patients): Adjunct therapy with corticosteroids is recommended. Initial dose should be given 4 to 12 hours prior to transplant or may be given postoperatively; adjust initial dose to achieve desired plasma concentration.

Oral: Dose is dependent upon type of transplant and formulation:

Cyclosporine (modified):

Renal: 9 ± 3 mg/kg daily, in 2 divided doses

Liver: 8 ± 4 mg/kg daily, in 2 divided doses

Heart: 7 ± 3 mg/kg daily, in 2 divided doses

Cyclosporine (non-modified): Initial doses of 10 to 14 mg/kg daily have been used for renal transplants (the manufacturer's labeling includes dosing from initial clinical trials of 15 mg/kg daily [range: 14 to 18 mg/kg daily]; however, this higher dosing level is rarely used any longer). Continue initial dose daily for 1 to 2 weeks; taper by 5% per week to a maintenance dose of 5 to 10 mg/kg daily; some renal transplant patients may be dosed as low as 3 mg/kg daily

Note: When using the non-modified formulation, cyclosporine levels may increase in liver transplant patients when the T-tube is closed; dose may need decreased

IV: Cyclosporine (non-modified): Manufacturer's labeling: Initial dose: 5 to 6 mg/kg daily or one-third of the oral dose as a single dose, infused over 2 to 6 hours; use should be limited to patients unable to take capsules or oral solution; patients should be switched to an oral dosage form as soon as possible.

Note: Many transplant centers administer cyclosporine as "divided dose" infusions (in 2 to 3 doses daily) or as a continuous (24-hour) infusion; dosages range from 3 to 7.5 mg/kg daily. Specific institutional protocols should be consulted.

Note: Conversion to cyclosporine (modified) from cyclosporine (non-modified): Start with daily dose previously used and adjust to obtain preconversion cyclosporine trough concentration. Plasma concentrations should be monitored every 4 to 7 days and dose adjusted as necessary, until desired trough level is obtained. When transferring patients with previously poor absorption of cyclosporine (non-modified), monitor trough levels at least twice weekly (especially if initial dose exceeds 10 mg/kg daily); high plasma levels are likely to occur.

Acute graft versus host disease (GVHD), prevention (off-label use in the US): IV followed by oral:

Initial: IV: 3 mg/kg daily 1 day prior to transplant; may convert to oral therapy when tolerated; titrate dose to appropriate cyclosporine trough concentration (in combination with methotrexate); taper per protocol (refer to specific references for tapering and target trough details); discontinue 6 months post-transplant in the absence of acute GVHD (Ratanatharathorn 1998; Ruutu 2013; Storb 1986a; Storb 1986b)

or

Initial: IV: 5 mg/kg (continuous infusion over 20 hours) each day for 6 days (loading dose) starting

2 days prior to transplant, then 3 mg/kg over 20 hours each day for 11 days starting on post-transplant day 4, then 3.75 mg/kg over 20 hours each day for 21 days starting on day 15, then **oral** (in 2 divided daily doses): 10 mg/kg daily days 36 to 83, then 8 mg/kg daily days 84 to 97, then 6 mg/kg daily days 98 to 119, then 4 mg/kg daily days 120 to 180, then discontinue (in combination with methotrexate +/- corticosteroid) (Chao 1993; Chao 2000)

Bone marrow transplantation *(Canadian labeling):* **Note:** IV administration is preferred for initial therapy.

Oral: Cyclosporine (modified): Initial: 12.5 to 15 mg/kg daily in 2 divided doses beginning 1 day prior to transplant; Maintenance: ~12.5 mg/kg daily in 2 divided doses every 12 hours for at least 3 to 6 months (higher doses may be required in patients with gastrointestinal conditions which may decrease absorption); decrease dose gradually to zero by 1 year following transplant. Patients who develop GVHD after discontinuation of cyclosporine may be reinitiated on therapy with a loading dose of 10 to 12.5 mg/kg followed by the previously established maintenance dose. Patients with mild, chronic GVHD should be treated with lowest effective dose.

IV: Cyclosporine (non-modified): Initial: 3 to 5 mg/kg daily or one-third of the oral dose as a single dose (infused over 2 to 6 hours) beginning 1 day prior to transplant; Maintenance: May continue initial dose for up to 2 weeks; however, patients should be switched to an oral dosage form as soon as possible.

Focal segmental glomerulosclerosis (off-label use in the US): Oral: Initial: 3.5 to 5 mg/kg daily divided every 12 hours (in combination with oral prednisone) (Braun 2008; Cattran 1999)

Immune thrombocytopenia, refractory (off-label use): Oral: 5 mg/kg daily divided every 12 hours for 6 days, followed by 2.5 to 3 mg/kg daily (titrate to serum levels of 100 to 200 ng/mL); time to response in clinical trials was ~3 to 4 weeks (Provan 2010). Additional studies have used initial doses of 2.5 to 5 mg/kg daily in 2 divided doses; maintenance doses were adjusted to maintain serum levels between 150 and 400 ng/mL (Choudhary 2008; Emilia 2002; Zver 2006).

Interstitial cystitis (bladder pain syndrome) (off-label use): Oral: Initial: 2 to 3 mg/kg/day in 2 divided doses (maximum of 300 mg daily). Once symptom relief is established, the dose can be tapered as tolerated (to as low as 1 mg/kg as a single daily dose) and in some cases can be stopped with continued benefit. Treatment duration was at least 6 months to more than 1 year in some patients (Forrest 2012; Sairanen 2004; Sairanen 2005; Sairanen 2008).

Nephrotic syndrome *(Canadian labeling):* Oral: Cyclosporine (modified):

Initial: 3.5 mg/kg daily in 2 divided doses every 12 hours; titrate for induction of remission and renal function. Adjunct therapy with low-dose oral corticosteroids is recommended for patients with an inadequate response to cyclosporine (particularly if steroid-resistant).

Maintenance: Dose is individualized based on proteinuria, serum creatinine, and tolerability but should be maintained at lowest effective dose; maximum dose: 5 mg/kg daily. Discontinue if no improvement is observed after 3 months.

Lupus nephritis (off-label use): Oral: Cyclosporine (modified): Initial: 4 mg/kg daily for 1 month (reduce dose if trough concentrations >200 ng/mL); reduce dose by 0.5 mg/kg every 2 weeks to a maintenance dose of 2.5 to 3 mg/kg daily (Moroni 2006)

Ulcerative colitis, severe (steroid-refractory) (off-label use):

IV: Cyclosporine (non-modified): 2 to 4 mg/kg daily, infused continuously over 24 hours. (Lichtiger 1994; Van Assche 2003). **Note:** Some studies suggest no therapeutic difference between low-dose (2 mg/kg) and high-dose (4 mg/kg) cyclosporine regimens (Van Assche 2003).

Oral: Cyclosporine (modified): 2.3 to 3 mg/kg every 12 hours (De Saussure 2005; Weber 2006)

Note: Patients responsive to IV therapy should be switched to oral therapy when possible.

Uveitis (off-label dose): Oral: 2.5 to 5 mg/kg daily in 2 divided doses; gradually decrease to maintenance dose; used alone or in conjunction with other corticosteroids (Isnard Bagnis 2002; Matthews 2010; Murphy 2005; Ozdal 2002; Zaghetto 2010). An expert panel recommends initial dose of 3 to 5 mg/kg daily; reducing dose, once inflammation was under control, to 2 to 3 mg/kg daily until a maintenance dose of 1 mg/kg daily is achieved (Diaz-Llopis 2009).

Geriatric Refer to adult dosing. **Sandimmune and Neoral/Gengraf are not bioequivalent and cannot be used interchangeably.**

Pediatric

Bone marrow transplantation ***(Canadian labeling)*:** **Note:** IV administration is preferred for initial therapy.

Oral: Cyclosporine (modified): Initial: 12.5 to 15 mg/kg daily in 2 divided doses beginning 1 day prior to transplant; Maintenance: ~12.5 mg/kg daily in 2 divided doses every 12 hours for at least 3 to 6 months (higher doses may be required in patients with gastrointestinal conditions which may decrease absorption); decrease dose gradually to zero by 1 year following transplant. Patients who develop graft versus host disease (GVHD) after discontinuation of cyclosporine may be reinitiated on therapy with a loading dose of 10 to 12.5 mg/kg followed by the previously established maintenance dose. Patients with mild, chronic GVHD should be treated with lowest effective dose.

IV: Cyclosporine (non-modified): Initial: 3 to 5 mg/kg daily or one-third of the oral dose as a single dose (infused over 2 to 6 hours) beginning 1 day prior to transplant; Maintenance: may continue initial dose for up to 2 weeks; however, patients should be switched to an oral dosage form as soon as possible.

Nephrotic syndrome ***(Canadian labeling)*:** Oral: Cyclosporine (modified):

Initial: 4.2 mg/kg daily in 2 divided doses every 12 hours; titrate for induction of remission and renal function. Adjunct therapy with low-dose oral corticosteroids is recommended for patients with an inadequate response to cyclosporine (particularly if steroid-resistant).

Maintenance: Dose is individualized based on proteinuria, serum creatinine, and tolerability but should be maintained at lowest effective dose; maximum dose: 6 mg/kg daily. Discontinue if no improvement is observed after 3 months.

Solid organ transplant: Refer to adult dosing. Children may require, and are able to tolerate, larger doses than adults.

Renal Impairment

Nephrotic syndrome: *Canadian labeling:* Initial: 2.5 mg/kg daily

Serum creatinine levels >30% above pretreatment levels: Take another sample within 2 weeks; if the level remains >30% above pretreatment levels, decrease dosage of cyclosporine (modified) by 25% to 50%.

Psoriasis (severe):

Abnormal renal function prior to treatment: Use is contraindicated.

Abnormal renal function during treatment:

US labeling:

Serum creatinine levels ≥25% above pretreatment levels: Take another sample within 2 weeks; if the level remains ≥25% above pretreatment levels, decrease dosage of cyclosporine (modified) by 25% to 50%. If two dosage adjustments do not reverse the increase in serum creatinine levels, treatment should be discontinued.

Serum creatinine levels ≥50% above pretreatment levels: Decrease cyclosporine dosage by 25% to 50%. If two dosage adjustments do not reverse the increase in serum creatinine levels, treatment should be discontinued.

Canadian labeling: Serum creatinine levels >30% above pretreatment levels: Decrease dosage of cyclosporine (modified) by 25% to 50%. If dosage adjustment does not reverse the increase in serum creatinine levels within 30 days, discontinue treatment.

Rheumatoid arthritis:

Abnormal renal function prior to treatment: Use is contraindicated.

Abnormal renal function during treatment: *Canadian labeling:*

Serum creatinine levels >30% above pretreatment levels: Take another sample within 2 weeks; if the level remains ≥30% above pretreatment levels, manufacturer labeling recommends reducing dose but does not provide specific dosing recommendation. If dosage adjustment does not reverse the increase in serum creatinine levels within 30 days, discontinue treatment.

Serum creatinine levels >50% above pretreatment levels: Reduce dose by 50%; if dosage adjustment does not reverse the increase in serum creatinine levels within 30 days, discontinue treatment.

Hemodialysis: Supplemental dose is not necessary.

Peritoneal dialysis: Supplemental dose is not necessary.

Hepatic Impairment

Mild-to-moderate impairment: There are no dosage adjustments provided in the manufacturer's labeling; monitor blood concentrations.

Severe impairment: There are no dosage adjustments provided in the manufacturer's labeling; however, metabolism is extensively hepatic (exposure is increased). Monitor blood concentrations; may require dose reduction.

Mechanism of Action Inhibition of production and release of interleukin II and inhibits interleukin II-induced activation of resting T-lymphocytes.

Contraindications

Hypersensitivity to cyclosporine or any component of the formulation. IV cyclosporine is contraindicated in hypersensitivity to polyoxyethylated castor oil (Cremophor EL).

Rheumatoid arthritis and psoriasis patients with abnormal renal function, uncontrolled hypertension, or malignancies. Concomitant treatment with PUVA or UVB therapy, methotrexate, other immunosuppressive agents, coal tar, or radiation therapy are also contraindications for use in patients with psoriasis.

Canadian labeling: Additional contraindications (not in US labeling): Concurrent use with bosentan; rheumatoid arthritis and psoriasis patients with primary or secondary immunodeficiency excluding autoimmune disease, uncontrolled infection, or malignancy (excluding non-melanoma skin cancer).

Warnings/Precautions

[US Boxed Warning]: Increased risk of lymphomas and other malignancies (including fatal outcomes), **particularly skin cancers;** risk is related to intensity/duration of therapy and the use of more than one immunosuppressive agent; all patients should avoid excessive sun/UV light exposure. **[US Boxed Warning]: May cause hypertension; risk is increased with increasing doses/duration.** Use caution when changing dosage forms.

[US Boxed Warning]: Renal impairment, including structural kidney damage has occurred (when used at high doses); risk is increased with increasing doses/duration; monitor renal function closely. Elevations in serum creatinine and BUN generally respond to dosage reductions. Use caution with other potentially nephrotoxic drugs (eg, acyclovir, aminoglycoside antibiotics, amphotericin B, ciprofloxacin); monitor renal function closely with concomitant use. If significant renal impairment occurs, reduce the dose of the coadministered medication or consider alternative treatment. Elevations in serum creatinine and BUN associated with nephrotoxicity generally respond to dosage reductions. In renal transplant patients with rapidly rising BUN and creatinine, carefully evaluate to differentiate between cyclosporine-associated nephrotoxicity and renal rejection episodes. In cases of severe rejection that fail to respond to pulse steroids and monoclonal antibodies, switching to an alternative immunosuppressant agent may be preferred to increasing cyclosporine to excessive blood concentrations.

[US Boxed Warning]: Increased risk of infection with use; serious and fatal infections have been reported. Bacterial, viral, fungal, and protozoal infections (including opportunistic infections) have occurred. Polyoma virus infections, such as the JC virus and BK virus, may result in serious and sometimes fatal outcomes. The JC virus is associated with progressive multifocal leukoencephalopathy (PML), and PML has been reported in patients receiving cyclosporine. PML may be fatal and presents with hemiparesis, apathy, confusion, cognitive deficiencies, and ataxia; consider neurologic consultation as indicated. The BK virus is associated with nephropathy, and polyoma virus-associated nephropathy (PVAN) has been reported in patients receiving cyclosporine. PVAN is associated with serious adverse effects including renal dysfunction and renal graft loss. If PML or PVAN occur in transplant patients, consider reducing immunosuppression therapy as well as the risk that reduced immunosuppression poses to grafts.

Hepatotoxicity (transaminase and bilirubin elevations) and liver injury, including cholestasis, jaundice, hepatitis, and liver failure, has been reported. These events were mainly in patients with confounding factors including infections, coadministration with other potentially hepatotoxic medications, underlying conditions, and significant comorbidities. Fatalities have also been reported rarely, primarily in transplant patients. Increased hepatic enzymes and bilirubin have occurred, usually in the first month and when used at high doses; improvement is usually seen with dosage reduction.

Should be used initially with corticosteroids in transplant patients. Significant hyperkalemia (with or without hyperchloremic metabolic acidosis) and hyperuricemia have occurred with therapy. Syndromes of microangiopathic hemolytic anemia and thrombocytopenia have occurred and may result in graft failure; it is accompanied by platelet consumption within the graft. Syndrome may occur without graft rejection. Although management of the syndrome is unclear, discontinuation or reduction of cyclosporine, in addition to streptokinase and heparin administration or plasmapheresis, has been associated with syndrome resolution. However, resolution seems to be dependent upon early detection of the syndrome via indium 111 labeled platelet scans.

May cause seizures, particularly if used with high-dose corticosteroids. Encephalopathy (including posterior reversible encephalopathy syndrome [PRES]) has also been reported; predisposing factors include hypertension, hypomagnesemia, hypocholesterolemia, high-dose corticosteroids, high cyclosporine serum concentration, and graft-versus-host disease (GVHD). Encephalopathy may be more common in patients with liver transplant compared to kidney transplant. Other neurotoxic events, such as optic disc edema (including papilloedema and potential visual impairment), have been rarely reported primarily in transplant patients.

[US Boxed Warning]: The modified/non-modified formulations are not bioequivalent; cyclosporine (modified) has increased bioavailability as compared to cyclosporine (non-modified) and the products cannot be used interchangeably without close monitoring. Cyclosporine (modified) refers to the oral solution and capsule dosage formulations of cyclosporine in an aqueous dispersion (previously referred to as "microemulsion"). Potentially significant drug-drug/drug-food interactions may exist, requiring dose or frequency adjustment, additional monitoring, and/or selection of alternative therapy. Gingival hyperplasia may occur; avoid concomitant nifedipine in patients who develop gingival hyperplasia (may increase frequency of hyperplasia). Monitor cyclosporine concentrations closely following the addition, modification, or deletion of other medication. Live, attenuated vaccines may be less effective; vaccination should be avoided. Make dose adjustments based on cyclosporine blood concentrations. **[US Boxed Warning]: Cyclosporine non-modified absorption is erratic; monitor blood concentrations closely. [US Boxed Warning]: Prescribing and dosage adjustment should only be under the direct supervision of an experienced physician. Adequate laboratory/medical resources and follow-up are necessary.** Anaphylaxis has been reported with IV use; reserve for patients who cannot take oral form. **[US Boxed Warning]: Risk of skin cancer may be increased in transplant patients.** Due to the increased risk for nephrotoxicity in renal transplantation, avoid using standard doses of cyclosporine in combination with everolimus; reduced cyclosporine doses are recommended; monitor cyclosporine concentrations closely. Cyclosporine and everolimus combination therapy may increase the risk for proteinuria. Cyclosporine combined with either everolimus or sirolimus may increase the risk for thrombotic microangiopathy/thrombotic thrombocytopenic purpura/hemolytic uremic syndrome (TMA/TTP/HUS). Cyclosporine has extensive hepatic metabolism and exposure is increased in patients with severe hepatic impairment; may require dose reduction.

Patients with psoriasis should avoid excessive sun exposure. **[US Boxed Warning]: Risk of skin cancer may be increased with a history of PUVA and possibly methotrexate or other immunosuppressants, UVB, coal tar, or radiation.**

Psoriasis: If receiving other immunosuppressive agents, radiation or UV therapy, concurrent use of cyclosporine is not recommended.

Products may contain corn oil, ethanol (consider alcohol content in certain patient populations, including pregnant or breastfeeding women, patients with liver disease, seizure disorders, alcohol dependency, or pediatrics), or propylene glycol; injection also contains the vehicle Cremophor EL (polyoxyethylated castor oil), which has been associated with hypersensitivity (anaphylactic) reactions. Due to the risk for anaphylaxis, IV cyclosporine should be reserved for use in patients unable to take an oral formulation. Some dosage forms may contain propylene glycol; large amounts are potentially toxic and have been associated hyperosmolality, lactic acidosis, seizures, and respiratory depression; use caution (AAP 1997; Zar 2007).

Drug Interactions

Metabolism/Transport Effects Substrate of CYP3A4 (major), P-glycoprotein; **Note:** Assignment of Major/Minor substrate status based on clinically relevant drug interaction potential; **Inhibits** BCRP, BSEP, CYP2C9 (weak), CYP3A4 (weak), P-glycoprotein, SLCO1B1

Avoid Concomitant Use

Avoid concomitant use of CycloSPORINE (Systemic) with any of the following: Aliskiren; Asunaprevir; AtorvaSTATin; BCG (Intravesical); Bosentan; Cholic Acid; Conivaptan; Crizotinib; Dronedarone; Enzalutamide; Eplerenone; Foscarnet; Fusidic Acid (Systemic); Grazoprevir; Idelalisib; Lercanidipine; Lovastatin; MiFEPRIStone; Natalizumab; PAZOPanib; Pimecrolimus; Pimozide; Pitavastatin; Potassium-Sparing Diuretics; Silodosin; Simeprevir; Simvastatin; Tacrolimus (Systemic); Tacrolimus (Topical); Tofacitinib; Topotecan; Vaccines (Live); VinCRIStine (Liposomal)

Increased Effect/Toxicity

CycloSPORINE (Systemic) may increase the levels/effects of: Afatinib; Aliskiren; Ambrisentan; ARIPiprazole; Asunaprevir; AtorvaSTATin; Bilastine; Boceprevir; Bosentan; Brentuximab Vedotin; Calcium Channel Blockers (Dihydropyridine); Calcium Channel Blockers (Nondihydropyridine); Caspofungin; Cholic Acid; Colchicine; Dabigatran Etexilate; Dexamethasone (Systemic); Digoxin; Dofetilide; DOXOrubicin (Conventional); Dronedarone; Edoxaban; Eluxadoline; Etoposide; Etoposide Phosphate; Everolimus; Ezetimibe; Fibric Acid Derivatives; Fimasartan; Fingolimod; Flibanserin; Fluvastatin; Grazoprevir; HYDROcodone; Imipenem; Leflunomide; Lercanidipine; Lomitapide; Loop Diuretics; Lovastatin; Methotrexate; MethylPREDNISolone; Minoxidil (Systemic); Minoxidil (Topical); MitoXANTRONE; Naldemedine; Naloxegol; Natalizumab; Neuromuscular-Blocking Agents; NiMODipine; Nonsteroidal Anti-Inflammatory Agents; PAZOPanib; P-glycoprotein/ABCB1 Substrates; Pimozide; Pitavastatin; Pravastatin; PrednisoLONE (Systemic); PredniSONE; Protease Inhibitors;

Prucalopride; Ranolazine; Repaglinide; RifAXIMin; Rosuvastatin; Silodosin; Simeprevir; Simvastatin; Sirolimus; Tacrolimus (Systemic); Tacrolimus (Topical); Ticagrelor; Tofacitinib; Topotecan; Vaccines (Live); Venetoclax; VinCRIStine (Liposomal)

The levels/effects of CycloSPORINE (Systemic) may be increased by: AcetaZOLAMIDE; Aminoglycosides; Amiodarone; Amphotericin B; Androgens; Angiotensin II Receptor Blockers; Antifungal Agents (Azole Derivatives, Systemic); Aprepitant; Azithromycin (Systemic); Boceprevir; Bromocriptine; Calcium Channel Blockers (Dihydropyridine); Calcium Channel Blockers (Nondihydropyridine); Carvedilol; Chloramphenicol; Clarithromycin; Conivaptan; Crizotinib; Cyclophosphamide; CYP3A4 Inhibitors (Moderate); CYP3A4 Inhibitors (Strong); Dasatinib; Denosumab; Dexamethasone (Systemic); Dronabinol; Eplerenone; Erythromycin (Systemic); Ezetimibe; Fluconazole; Fosaprepitant; Foscarnet; Fusidic Acid (Systemic); GlyBURIDE; Grapefruit Juice; Idelalisib; Imatinib; Imipenem; Isavuconazonium Sulfate; Ivacaftor; Lercanidipine; Melphalan; Methotrexate; MethylPREDNISolone; Metoclopramide; Metreleptin; MiFEPRIStone; Netupitant; Nonsteroidal Anti-Inflammatory Agents; Norfloxacin; Ocrelizumab; Ombitasvir, Paritaprevir, and Ritonavir; Ombitasvir, Paritaprevir, Ritonavir, and Dasabuvir; Omeprazole; Palbociclib; P-glycoprotein/ABCB1 Inhibitors; Pimecrolimus; Potassium-Sparing Diuretics; Pravastatin; PrednisoLONE (Systemic); PredniSONE; Protease Inhibitors; Quinupristin; Ranolazine; Ritonavir; Roflumilast; Simeprevir; Sirolimus; Stiripentol; Sulfonamide Derivatives; Tacrolimus (Systemic); Tacrolimus (Topical); Telaprevir; Telithromycin; Temsirolimus; Trastuzumab

Decreased Effect

CycloSPORINE (Systemic) may decrease the levels/effects of: BCG (Intravesical); Coccidioides immitis Skin Test; Eltrombopag; GlyBURIDE; Mycophenolate; Nivolumab; Sipuleucel-T; Tertomotide; Vaccines (Inactivated); Vaccines (Live)

The levels/effects of CycloSPORINE (Systemic) may be decreased by: Adalimumab; Armodafinil; Ascorbic Acid; Barbiturates; Bosentan; CarBAMazepine; Colesevelam; Cyclophosphamide; CYP3A4 Inducers (Moderate); CYP3A4 Inducers (Strong); Dabrafenib; Deferasirox; Dexamethasone (Systemic); Echinacea; Efavirenz; Enzalutamide; Fibric Acid Derivatives; Fosphenytoin; Griseofulvin; Imipenem; MethylPREDNISolone; Metreleptin; Mitotane; Modafinil; Multivitamins/Fluoride (with ADE); Multivitamins/Minerals (with ADEK, Folate, Iron); Multivitamins/Minerals (with AE, No Iron); Nafcillin; Orlistat; Phenytoin; PrednisoLONE (Systemic); PredniSONE; Probucol; Pyrazinamide; Rifamycin Derivatives; Sevelamer; Siltuximab; Somatostatin Analogs; St John's Wort; Sulfinpyrazone; Sulfonamide Derivatives; Tocilizumab; Vitamin E (Systemic)

Food Interactions Grapefruit juice increases cyclosporine serum concentrations. Management: Avoid grapefruit juice.

Dietary Considerations Avoid grapefruit juice with oral cyclosporine use.

Pharmacodynamics/Kinetics

Half-life Elimination Oral: May be prolonged with hepatic impairment and shorter in pediatric patients due to the higher metabolism rate

Cyclosporine (non-modified): Biphasic: Alpha: 1.4 hours; Terminal: 19 hours (range: 10-27 hours)

Cyclosporine (modified): Biphasic: Terminal: 8.4 hours (range: 5-18 hours)

Time to Peak Serum: Oral:

Cyclosporine (non-modified): 2-6 hours; some patients have a second peak at 5-6 hours

Cyclosporine (modified): Renal transplant: 1.5-2 hours

Pregnancy Risk Factor C

Pregnancy Considerations Adverse events were not observed following the use of oral cyclosporine in animal reproduction studies (using doses that were not maternally toxic). In humans, cyclosporine crosses the placenta; maternal concentrations do not correlate with those found in the umbilical cord. Cyclosporine may be detected in the serum of newborns for several days after birth (Claris 1993). Based on clinical use, premature births and low birth weight were consistently observed in pregnant transplant patients (additional pregnancy complications also present). Formulations may contain alcohol; the alcohol content should be taken into consideration in pregnant women.

The pharmacokinetics of cyclosporine may be influenced by pregnancy (Grimer 2007). Cyclosporine may be used in pregnant renal, liver, or heart transplant patients (Cowan 2012; EBPG Expert Group on Renal Transplantation 2002; McGuire 2009; Parhar 2012). If therapy is needed for psoriasis, other agents are preferred; however, cyclosporine may be used as an alternative agent along with close clinical monitoring; use should be avoided during the first trimester if possible (Bae 2012). If treatment is needed for lupus nephritis, other agents are recommended to be used in pregnant women (Hahn 2012).

Following transplant, normal menstruation and fertility may be restored within months; however, appropriate contraception is recommended to prevent pregnancy until 1-2 years following the transplant to improve pregnancy outcomes (Cowan 2012; EBPG Expert Group on Renal Transplantation 2002; McGuire 2009; Parhar 2012).

The National Transplantation Pregnancy Registry (NTPR) is a registry which follows pregnancies which occur in maternal transplant recipients or those fathered by male transplant recipients. The NTPR encourages reporting of pregnancies following solid organ transplant by contacting them at 877-955-6877 or NTPR@giftoflifeinstitute.org.

Breastfeeding Considerations Cyclosporine is excreted in breast milk. Concentrations of cyclosporine in milk vary widely and breastfeeding during therapy is generally not recommended (Bae 2012; Cowan 2012). Due to the potential for serious adverse in the breastfeeding infant, a decision should be made to discontinue cyclosporine or to discontinue breastfeeding, taking into account the importance of treatment to the mother. Formulations may contain alcohol which may be present in breast milk and could be absorbed orally by the breastfeeding infant.

Dosage Forms Considerations

Cyclosporine (modified): Gengraf and Neoral

Cyclosporine (non-modified): SandIMMUNE

Cyclosporine injection contains polyoxyethylated castor oil (Cremophor EL)

Dosage Forms

Capsule, Oral:

Gengraf: 25 mg, 50 mg, 100 mg

Neoral: 25 mg, 100 mg

SandIMMUNE: 25 mg, 100 mg

Generic: 25 mg, 50 mg, 100 mg

Solution, Intravenous:
SandIMMUNE: 50 mg/mL (5 mL)
Generic: 50 mg/mL (5 mL)
Solution, Oral:
Gengraf: 100 mg/mL (50 mL)
Neoral: 100 mg/mL (50 mL)
SandIMMUNE: 100 mg/mL (50 mL)
Generic: 100 mg/mL (50 mL)

Dosage Forms: Canada
Capsule, Oral:
Neoral: 10 mg, 25 mg, 50 mg, 100 mg
Solution, Intravenous:
SandIMMUNE IV: 50 mg/mL (1 mL, 5 mL)
Solution, Oral:
Neoral: 100 mg/mL (50 mL)

Dental Comment Consider a medical consultation prior to any invasive dental procedure in patients who have received an organ transplant; delayed wound healing due to the immunosuppressive effects and an increased potential for postoperative infection may be of concern.

CycloSPORINE (Ophthalmic)

(SYE kloe spor een)

Brand Names: US Restasis; Restasis Multidose

Brand Names: Canada Restasis

Pharmacologic Category Calcineurin Inhibitor; Immunosuppressant Agent

Use Keratoconjunctivitis sicca: Increase tear production when suppressed tear production is presumed to be due to keratoconjunctivitis sicca-associated ocular inflammation (in patients not already using topical anti-inflammatory drugs or punctal plugs)

Local Anesthetic/Vasoconstrictor Precautions No information available to require special precautions

Effects on Dental Treatment No significant effects or complications reported

Effects on Bleeding No information available to require special precautions

Adverse Reactions Frequency not always defined.
>10%: Ophthalmic: Burning sensation of eyes (17%)
1% to 10%:
Central nervous system: Foreign body sensation of eye
Ophthalmic: Blurred vision, conjunctival hyperemia, epiphora, eye discharge, eye pain, eye pruritus, stinging of eyes, visual disturbance
<1%, postmarketing and/or case reports: Eye injury (from bottle tip during administration), hypersensitivity reaction (including angioedema, dyspnea, facial swelling, pharyngeal edema, swelling of eye, swollen tongue, urticaria)

General Dosage Range Ophthalmic: *Adolescents ≥16 years and Adults:* Instill 1 drop in each eye twice daily (approximately 12 hours apart)

Pregnancy Risk Factor C

Pregnancy Considerations Adverse events were not observed following the use of oral cyclosporine in animal reproduction studies. Serum concentrations are below the limit of detection (<0.1 ng/mL) following ophthalmic use; fetal exposure following ophthalmic administration is not expected.

Cyproheptadine (si proe HEP ta deen)

Brand Names: Canada Euro-Cyproheptadine; PMS-Cyproheptadine

Pharmacologic Category Histamine H_1 Antagonist; Histamine H_1 Antagonist, First Generation; Piperidine Derivative

Use Allergic conditions: Perennial and seasonal allergic rhinitis; vasomotor rhinitis; allergic conjunctivitis caused by inhalant allergens and foods; mild, uncomplicated allergic skin manifestations of urticaria and angioedema; amelioration of allergic reactions to blood or plasma; cold urticaria; dermatographism; adjunctive anaphylactic therapy.

Local Anesthetic/Vasoconstrictor Precautions No information available to require special precautions

Effects on Dental Treatment Key adverse event(s) related to dental treatment: Xerostomia (normal salivary flow resumes upon discontinuation)

Effects on Bleeding No information available to require special precautions

Adverse Reactions Frequency not defined.
Cardiovascular: Extrasystoles, hypotension, palpitations, tachycardia
Central nervous system: Ataxia, chills, confusion, dizziness, drowsiness, euphoria, excitement, fatigue, hallucination, headache, hysteria, insomnia, irritability, nervousness, neuritis, paresthesia, restlessness, sedation, seizure, vertigo
Dermatologic: Diaphoresis, skin photosensitivity, skin rash, urticaria
Gastrointestinal: Abdominal pain, anorexia, cholestasis, constipation, diarrhea, increased appetite, nausea, vomiting, xerostomia
Genitourinary: Difficulty in micturition, urinary frequency, urinary retention
Hematologic & oncologic: Agranulocytosis, hemolytic anemia, leukopenia, thrombocytopenia
Hepatic: Hepatic failure, hepatitis, jaundice
Hypersensitivity: Anaphylactic shock, angioedema, hypersensitivity reaction
Neuromuscular & skeletal: Tremor
Ophthalmic: Blurred vision, diplopia
Otic: Labyrinthitis (acute), tinnitus
Respiratory: Nasal congestion, pharyngitis, thickening of bronchial secretions

General Dosage Range
Oral:
Children 2 to 6 years: 2 mg 2 or 3 times daily; maximum: 12 mg/day
Children 7 to 14 years: 4 mg 2 or 3 times daily; maximum: 16 mg/day
Adolescents >14 years and Adults: 4 to 20 mg daily in divided doses; maximum: 0.5 mg/kg/day

Mechanism of Action A potent antihistamine and serotonin antagonist with anticholinergic effects; competes with histamine for H_1 receptor sites on effector cells in the gastrointestinal tract, blood vessels, and respiratory tract (Paton 1985).

Pharmacodynamics/Kinetics
Half-life Elimination Metabolites: ~16 hours (Paton 1985)
Time to Peak Plasma: 6 to 9 hours (Paton 1985)

Pregnancy Risk Factor B

Pregnancy Considerations Adverse events were observed in some animal reproduction studies. Per the product labeling, an increased risk of congenital abnormalities was not observed following maternal use of cyproheptadine during the first, second, or third trimesters in two studies of pregnant women; however the possibility of harm cannot be ruled out. Although cyproheptadine is approved for the treatment of allergic conditions such as rhinitis and uritcaria, other agents are preferred for use in pregnant women (Scadding

2008; Wallace 2008; Zuberbier 2014). Antihistamines are not recommended for treatment of pruritus associated with intrahepatic cholestasis in pregnancy (Ambros-Rudolph 2011; Kremer 2014).

Cysteamine (Systemic) (sis TEE a meen)

Brand Names: US Cystagon; Procysbi

Pharmacologic Category Anticystine Agent; Urinary Tract Product

Use Nephropathic cystinosis: Treatment of nephropathic cystinosis in adults and pediatric patients

Local Anesthetic/Vasoconstrictor Precautions No information available to require special precautions

Effects on Dental Treatment No significant effects or complications reported

Effects on Bleeding No information available to require special precautions

Adverse Reactions Frequency not always defined. Immediate release as reported in children. Delayed release as reported in children, adolescents, and adults.

Cardiovascular: Hypertension (immediate release: ≤5%)

Central nervous system: Lethargy (immediate release: 11%), headache (5% to 9%), fatigue (delayed release: >5%), abnormality in thinking (immediate release: ≤5%), ataxia (immediate release: ≤5%), brain disease (immediate release: ≤5%), confusion (immediate release: ≤5%), depression (immediate release: ≤5%), dizziness (≤5%), drowsiness (immediate release: ≤5%), emotional lability (immediate release: ≤5%), hallucination (immediate release: ≤5%), jitteriness (immediate release: ≤5%), nervousness (immediate release: ≤5%), nightmares (immediate release: ≤5%), seizure (immediate release: ≤5%)

Dermatologic: Skin rash (>5% to 7%), abnormal skin odor (delayed release: >5%), urticaria (immediate release: ≤5%)

Endocrine & metabolic: Dehydration (immediate release: ≤5%)

Gastrointestinal: Vomiting (immediate release: 35%; delayed release: 19%), anorexia (immediate release: 31%; delayed release: 2%), diarrhea (immediate release: 16%; delayed release: >5%), nausea (delayed release: 16%; immediate release: ≤5%), abdominal discomfort (delayed release: ≤14%), abdominal pain (≤14%), constipation (immediate release: ≤5%), duodenitis (immediate release: ≤5%), dyspepsia (immediate release: ≤5%), gastroenteritis (immediate release: ≤5%), gastrointestinal hemorrhage (immediate release: ≤5%), gastrointestinal ulcer (immediate release: ≤5%), halitosis

Hematologic & oncologic: Anemia (immediate release: ≤5%), leukopenia (immediate release: ≤5%)

Hepatic: Abnormal hepatic function tests (immediate release: ≤5%)

Hypersensitivity: Anaphylaxis, hypersensitivity reaction

Neuromuscular & skeletal: Hyperkinesia (immediate release: ≤5%), tremor (immediate release: ≤5%)

Otic: Hearing loss (immediate release: ≤5%)

Renal: Interstitial nephritis (immediate release: ≤5%), renal failure (immediate release: ≤5%)

Miscellaneous: Fever (immediate release: 22%)

<1%, postmarketing, and/or case reports: Atrophic striae, connective tissue disorder (Ehlers Danlos-like syndrome), erythema multiforme, fragile skin, genu valgum, intracranial hypertension (benign), joint hyperextension, leg pain, molluscoid pseudotumors, osteopenia, papilledema, pseudotumor cerebri, scoliosis, skin lesion, toxic epidermal necrolysis, vertebral compression fracture

General Dosage Range Dosage adjustment recommended in patients who develop toxicities.

Oral:

Immediate release:

Children and Adolescents weighing ≤50 kg: Initial: 1/6 to 1/4 of maintenance dose; Maintenance: 1.3 g/m^2/day in 4 divided doses (maximum dose: 1.95 g/m^2/day)

Adolescents and Adults weighing >50 kg: Initial: 1/6 to 1/4 of maintenance dose; Maintenance: 2 g/day in 4 divided doses (maximum: 1.95 g/m^2/day)

Delayed release: *Children ≥2 years, Adolescents, and Adults:* Initial: 1/6 to 1/4 of maintenance dose; Maintenance: 1.3 g/m^2/day divided every 12 hours (maximum: 1.95 g/m^2/day) **or** Maintenance weight-based dosing range of 400 to 2,000 mg/day in 2 divided doses.

Mechanism of Action Reacts with cystine within the lysosome to convert it to cysteine and to a cysteine-cysteamine mixed disulfide, both of which can then exit the lysosome in patients with cystinosis, an inherited defect of lysosomal transport

Pharmacodynamics/Kinetics

Onset of Action Immediate release: 1.8 ± 0.8 hours; Delayed release: 3 to 3.5 hours

Duration of Action Immediate release: 6 hours; Delayed release: ~12 hours

Half-life Elimination Immediate release: Children and Adolescents: 1.5 ± 0.4 hours (Langman 2012); Adults:1.5 hours; Delayed release: Children and Adolescents: 4.2 ± 6.8 hours (Langman 2012); Adults: 4.2 hours

Time to Peak Immediate release: Children and Adolescents: Mean range: 1.2 to 1.4 hours (range 1 to 2 hours) (Belldina 2003; Langman 2012); Adults: ~1.4 hours; Delayed release: Children and Adolescents: 3.1 ± 1.5 hours (Langman 2012); Adults: 3 to 4.6 hours

Pregnancy Considerations Adverse events were observed in animal reproduction studies

Cysteine (SIS te een)

Brand Names: US Cystech [OTC]

Pharmacologic Category Nutritional Supplement

Use Nutritional supplement: Additive to crystalline amino acid solutions to meet the intravenous (IV) amino acid nutritional requirements of infants receiving total parenteral nutrition (TPN)

Local Anesthetic/Vasoconstrictor Precautions No information available to require special precautions

Effects on Dental Treatment No significant effects or complications reported

Effects on Bleeding No information available to require special precautions

Adverse Reactions Frequency not defined.

Cardiovascular: Flushing, phlebitis, thrombosis

Central nervous system: Localized warm feeling

Dermatologic: Localized erythema

Endocrine & metabolic: Metabolic acidosis

Gastrointestinal: Nausea

Genitourinary: Azotemia

Renal: Increased blood urea nitrogen

Miscellaneous: Fever

General Dosage Range IV: *Infants (receiving PN):* 40 mg cysteine per 1 g of amino acids; dosage will vary with the daily amino acid dosage

Mechanism of Action Cysteine is a sulfur-containing amino acid synthesized from methionine via the transsulfuration pathway. It is a precursor of the tripeptide glutathione and also of taurine. Newborn infants have a relative deficiency of the enzyme necessary to affect this conversion. Cysteine may be considered an essential amino acid in infants.

Pregnancy Considerations Cysteine is generally considered to be a nonessential amino acid in adults because it can be synthesized from methionine (an essential amino acid). The RDA for methionine + cysteine is increased in pregnant women (IOM, 2005).

Cytarabine (Conventional)

(sye TARE a been con VEN sha nal)

Brand Names: Canada Cytarabine Injection; Cytosar

Pharmacologic Category Antineoplastic Agent, Antimetabolite; Antineoplastic Agent, Antimetabolite (Pyrimidine Analog)

Use

Acute myeloid leukemia: Remission induction (in combination with other chemotherapy medications) in acute myeloid leukemia (AML)

Acute lymphocytic leukemia: Treatment of acute lymphocytic leukemia (ALL)

Chronic myeloid leukemia: Treatment of chronic myeloid leukemia (CML; blast phase)

Meningeal leukemia: Prophylaxis and treatment of meningeal leukemia

Local Anesthetic/Vasoconstrictor Precautions No information available to require special precautions

Effects on Dental Treatment Key adverse event(s) related to dental treatment: Mucositis

Effects on Bleeding Hematologic effects depend on dose and schedule of treatment. Platelets are one of the primary cell lines affected. Patients will develop thrombocytopenia on approximately day 7 which resolves about day 21-28. A medical consult is recommended.

Adverse Reactions Frequency not always defined. CNS, gastrointestinal, ophthalmic, and pulmonary toxicities are more common with high-dose regimens.

Cardiovascular: Angina pectoris, chest pain, hepatic veno-occlusive disease (also called hepatic sinusoidal obstruction syndrome), local thrombophlebitis, pericarditis

Central nervous system: Aseptic meningitis, cerebral dysfunction, dizziness, headache, neuritis, neurotoxicity, paralysis (intrathecal and IV combination therapy), reversible posterior leukoencephalopathy syndrome

Dermatologic: Acute generalized exanthematous pustulosis, alopecia, dermal ulcer, ephelis, pruritus, skin rash, urticaria

Endocrine & metabolic: Hyperuricemia

Gastrointestinal: Abdominal pain, anal fissure, anal inflammation, anorexia, diarrhea, esophageal ulcer, esophagitis, increased serum amylase, increased serum lipase, intestinal necrosis, mucositis, nausea, pancreatitis, sore throat, toxic megacolon, vomiting

Genitourinary: Urinary retention

Hematologic & oncologic: Anemia, bone marrow depression, hemorrhage, leukopenia, megaloblastosis, neutropenia (onset: 1 to 7 days; nadir [biphasic]: 7 to 9 days and at 15 to 24 days; recovery [biphasic]: 9 to 12 days and at 24 to 34 days), reticulocytopenia, thrombocytopenia (onset: 5 days; nadir: 12 to 15 days; recovery 15 to 25 days)

Hepatic: Hepatic insufficiency, increased serum transaminases (acute), jaundice

Hypersensitivity: Allergic edema, anaphylaxis

Infection: Sepsis

Local: Cellulitis at injection site, inflammation at injection site (SC injection), pain at injection site (SC injection)

Neuromuscular & skeletal: Rhabdomyolysis

Ophthalmic: Conjunctivitis

Renal: Renal insufficiency

Respiratory: Acute respiratory distress, dyspnea, interstitial pneumonitis

Miscellaneous: Drug toxicity (cytarabine syndrome; chest pain, conjunctivitis, fever, maculopapular rash, malaise, myalgia, ostealgia), fever

Adverse events associated with high-dose cytarabine

Cardiovascular: Cardiomegaly, cardiomyopathy (in combination with cyclophosphamide)

Central nervous system: Neurotoxicity (patients with renal impairment: ≤55%), coma, drowsiness, neurocerebellar toxicity, peripheral neuropathy (motor and sensory), personality changes

Dermatologic: Alopecia (complete), desquamation, skin rash (severe)

Gastrointestinal: Gastrointestinal ulcer, necrotizing enterocolitis, pancreatitis, peritonitis, pneumatosis cystoides intestinalis

Hepatic: Hepatic abscess, hepatic injury, hyperbilirubinemia

Infection: Sepsis

Ophthalmic: Corneal toxicity, hemorrhagic conjunctivitis

Respiratory: Acute respiratory distress, pulmonary edema

Adverse events associated with intrathecal cytarabine administration

Central nervous system: Aphonia, leukoencephalopathy (necrotizing; with concurrent cranial irradiation, intrathecal methotrexate, and intrathecal hydrocortisone), nerve palsy (accessory nerve), neurotoxicity, paraplegia

Gastrointestinal: Dysphagia, nausea, vomiting

Ophthalmic: Blindness (with concurrent systemic chemotherapy and cranial irradiation), diplopia

Respiratory: Cough, hoarseness

Miscellaneous: Fever

General Dosage Range Dosage adjustment recommended in patients with hepatic or renal impairment

IV: *Children and Adults:* AML Induction: 100 to 200 mg/m²/day for 7 days

Mechanism of Action Inhibits DNA synthesis. Cytarabine gains entry into cells by a carrier process, and then must be converted to its active compound, aracytidine triphosphate. Cytarabine is a pyrimidine analog and is incorporated into DNA; however, the primary action is inhibition of DNA polymerase resulting in decreased DNA synthesis and repair. The degree of cytotoxicity correlates linearly with incorporation into DNA; therefore, incorporation into the DNA is responsible for drug activity and toxicity. Cytarabine is specific for the S phase of the cell cycle (blocks progression from the G_1 to the S phase).

Pharmacodynamics/Kinetics

Half-life Elimination IV: Initial: 7 to 20 minutes; Terminal: 1 to 3 hours; Intrathecal: 2 to 6 hours

Time to Peak IM, SubQ: 20 to 60 minutes

Pregnancy Risk Factor D

Pregnancy Considerations Adverse effects were demonstrated in animal reproduction studies. Limb and ear defects have been noted in case reports of cytarabine exposure during the first trimester of pregnancy. The following have also been noted in the neonate: Pancytopenia, WBC depression, electrolyte abnormalities, prematurity, low birth weight, decreased hematocrit or platelets. Risk to the fetus is decreased if treatment can be avoided during the first trimester; however, women of childbearing potential should be advised of the potential risks.

Cytarabine (Liposomal)

(sye TARE a been lye po SO mal)

Brand Names: US DepoCyt

Brand Names: Canada DepoCyt

Pharmacologic Category Antineoplastic Agent, Antimetabolite; Antineoplastic Agent, Antimetabolite (Pyrimidine Analog)

Use Lymphomatous meningitis: Intrathecal treatment of lymphomatous meningitis

Local Anesthetic/Vasoconstrictor Precautions No information available to require special precautions

Effects on Dental Treatment No significant effects or complications reported

Effects on Bleeding Hematologic effects depend on dose and schedule of treatment. Platelets are one of the primary cell lines affected. Patients will develop thrombocytopenia on approximately day 7 which resolves about day 21-28. A medical consult is recommended.

Adverse Reactions

>10%:

Cardiovascular: Peripheral edema (11%)

Central nervous system: Chemical arachnoiditis (without dexamethasone premedication: 100%; with dexamethasone premedication: 33% to 42%; grade 4: 19% to 30%; onset: ≤5 days), headache (56%), confusion (33%), fatigue (25%), abnormal gait (23%), seizure (20% to 22%), dizziness (18%), lethargy (16%), insomnia (14%), memory impairment (14%), pain (14%)

Endocrine & metabolic: Dehydration (13%)

Gastrointestinal: Nausea (46%), vomiting (44%), constipation (25%), diarrhea (12%), decreased appetite (11%)

Genitourinary: Urinary tract infection (14%)

Hematologic & oncologic: Anemia (12%), thrombocytopenia (3% to 11%)

Neuromuscular & skeletal: Weakness (40%), back pain (24%), limb pain (15%), neck pain (14%), arthralgia (11%), neck stiffness (11%)

Ophthalmic: Blurred vision (11%)

Miscellaneous: Fever (32%)

1% to 10%:

Cardiovascular: Tachycardia (9%), hypotension (8%), hypertension (6%), syncope (3%), edema (2%)

Central nervous system: Agitation (10%), hypoesthesia (10%), myasthenia (10%), depression (8%), anxiety (7%), peripheral neuropathy (3% to 4%), abnormal reflexes (3%), sensorimotor neuropathy (3%)

Dermatologic: Diaphoresis (2%), pruritus (2%)

Endocrine & metabolic: Hypokalemia (7%), hyponatremia (7%), hyperglycemia (6%)

Gastrointestinal: Abdominal pain (9%), dysphagia (8%), anorexia (5%), hemorrhoids (3%), mucosal inflammation (3%)

Genitourinary: Urinary incontinence (7%), urinary retention (5%)

Hematologic & oncologic: Neutropenia (10%), bruise (2%)

Neuromuscular & skeletal: Tremor (9%)

Otic: Hypoacusis (6%)

Respiratory: Dyspnea (10%), cough (7%), pneumonia (6%)

<1%, postmarketing, and/or case reports: Anaphylaxis, bladder disease (bladder control impaired), blindness, brain disease, cauda equina syndrome, cranial nerve palsy, deafness, drowsiness, elevated spinal fluid protein, fecal incontinence, hemiplegia, hydrocephalus, increased intracranial pressure, leukocytosis (in CSF), meningitis (infectious), myelopathy, nervous system disease (neurologic deficit), numbness, papilledema, visual disturbance

General Dosage Range Dosage adjustment recommended in patients who develop toxicities

Intrathecal: *Adults:* Induction: 50 mg every 14 days for a total of 2 doses (weeks 1 and 3); Consolidation: 50 mg every 14 days for 3 doses (weeks 5, 7, and 9), followed by 50 mg at week 13; Maintenance: 50 mg every 28 days for 4 doses (weeks 17, 21, 25, and 29)

Mechanism of Action Cytarabine liposomal is a sustained-release formulation of the active ingredient cytarabine, an antimetabolite which acts through inhibition of DNA synthesis and is cell cycle-specific for the S phase of cell division. Cytarabine is converted intracellularly to its active metabolite cytarabine-5'-triphosphate (ara-CTP). Ara-CTP also appears to be incorporated into DNA and RNA; however, the primary action is inhibition of DNA polymerase, resulting in decreased DNA synthesis and repair. The liposomal formulation allows for gradual release, resulting in prolonged exposure.

Pharmacodynamics/Kinetics

Half-life Elimination CSF: 6 to 82 hours

Time to Peak CSF: Intrathecal: <1 hour

Pregnancy Risk Factor D

Pregnancy Considerations Adverse effects were observed in animal reproductive studies with conventional cytarabine. Conventional cytarabine has been associated with fetal malformations when given as a component of systemic combination chemotherapy during the first trimester. Systemic exposure following intrathecal administration of cytarabine liposomal is negligible; however, women of childbearing potential should avoid becoming pregnant during treatment.

Dabigatran Etexilate (da BIG a tran ett EX ill ate)

Related Information

Antiplatelet and Anticoagulation Considerations in Dentistry *on page 1764*

Cardiovascular Diseases *on page 1752*

Brand Names: US Pradaxa

Brand Names: Canada Pradaxa

Pharmacologic Category Anticoagulant; Anticoagulant, Direct Thrombin Inhibitor; Direct Oral Anticoagulant (DOAC)

Use

Deep venous thrombosis and pulmonary embolism treatment and prevention: Treatment of deep venous thrombosis (DVT) and pulmonary embolism in patients who have been treated with a parenteral anticoagulant for 5 to 10 days; to reduce the risk of recurrence of DVT and pulmonary embolism in patients who have been previously treated.

Nonvalvular atrial fibrillation (to reduce the risk of stroke and systemic embolism): Reduce the risk of stroke and systemic embolism in patients with nonvalvular atrial fibrillation (AF)

Note: The 2014 American Heart Association/American College of Cardiology/Heart Rhythm Society guidelines for the management of AF recommend oral anticoagulation for patients with nonvalvular AF or atrial flutter with prior stroke, TIA, or a CHA_2DS_2-VASc score ≥2. As an alternative to warfarin, dabigatran may also be used for 3 weeks prior and 4 weeks after cardioversion in patients with AF or atrial flutter of ≥48 hours duration or when the duration is unknown (January 2014).

Postoperative thromboprophylaxis:

US labeling: Prophylaxis of deep vein thrombosis (DVT) and pulmonary embolism in patients who have undergone hip replacement surgery.

Canadian labeling: Postoperative thromboprophylaxis in patients who have undergone total hip or knee replacement procedures

Local Anesthetic/Vasoconstrictor Precautions No information available to require special precautions

Effects on Dental Treatment Dabigatran etexilate is converted *in vivo* to the active dabigatran, a specific, reversible, direct thrombin inhibitor. It causes bleeding by preventing thrombin-mediated effects, and by inhibiting thrombin-induced platelet aggregation.

Effects on Bleeding Dabigatran etexilate inhibits clot formation via direct inhibition of thrombin (factor IIa). Dabigatran increases the risk of bleeding and can cause significant and sometimes fatal bleeding. Hemorrhage may occur at virtually any site; risk is depenedent on multiple variables, including the intensity of anticoagulation and patient susceptibility. Medical consult is suggested.

Adverse Reactions

>10%:

Gastrointestinal: Gastrointestinal symptoms (eg, dyspepsia, gastritis-like symptoms; 25% to 40%; dose dependent)

Hematologic & oncologic: Hemorrhage (11% to 19%; major hemorrhage: ≤3%; hemorrhage [life-threatening]: 2%)

1% to 10%:

Gastrointestinal: Dyspepsia (8%; includes abdominal pain, abdominal discomfort, epigastric discomfort), gastrointestinal hemorrhage (≤6%; major: ≤2%), gastritis (3%; includes gastroesophageal reflux disease, esophagitis, erosive gastritis, gastrointestinal hemorrhage, hemorrhagic gastritis, gastrointestinal ulcer)

<1%, postmarketing, and/or case reports: Allergic edema, anaphylactic shock, anaphylaxis, angioedema, catheter site hemorrhage, cerebrovascular accident (in patients with prosthetic heart valve), decreased hematocrit, epidural hematoma (with spinal puncture or spinal/epidural anesthesia), esophageal ulcer, genitourinary tract hemorrhage, hemarthrosis, hypersensitivity reaction, intracranial hemorrhage (includes hemorrhagic stroke, subarachnoid bleeding, subdural hematoma), muscle hemorrhage, myocardial infarction, pericardial effusion (severe hemorrhagic; occurred postoperatively in patients with prosthetic heart valve; required intervention for hemodynamic compromise), retroperitoneal hemorrhage, spinal hematoma (with spinal puncture or spinal/epidural anesthesia), thrombocytopenia, thromboembolism (in patients with prosthetic heart valve), transient ischemic attacks (in patients with prosthetic heart valve)

General Dosage Range Dosage adjustment recommended in patients with renal impairment or patients on concomitant therapy.

Oral: *Adults:* 150 mg twice daily or 220 mg once daily

Mechanism of Action Prodrug lacking anticoagulant activity that is converted *in vivo* to the active dabigatran, a specific, reversible, direct thrombin inhibitor that inhibits both free and fibrin-bound thrombin. Inhibits coagulation by preventing thrombin-mediated effects, including cleavage of fibrinogen to fibrin monomers, activation of factors V, VIII, XI, and XIII, and inhibition of thrombin-induced platelet aggregation.

Pharmacodynamics/Kinetics

Half-life Elimination 12-17 hours; Elderly: 14-17 hours; Mild-to-moderate renal impairment: 15-18 hours; Severe renal impairment: 28 hours (Stangier 2010)

Time to Peak Plasma: Dabigatran: 1 hour; delayed 2 hours by food (no effect on bioavailability)

Pregnancy Risk Factor C

Pregnancy Considerations Adverse events were observed in some animal reproduction studies. An *ex vivo* human placenta dual perfusion model illustrated that dabigatran crossed the placenta at term; dabigatran etexilate mesylate (prodrug) had limited placental transfer (Bapat 2014). Data are insufficient to evaluate the safety of direct thrombin inhibitors during pregnancy; use of oral agents during pregnancy should be avoided (Guyatt 2012). Consider the risks of bleeding and stroke if used during pregnancy.

Dental Comment At recommended therapeutic doses, dabigatran etexilate prolongs the activated partial thromboplastin time (aPTT). With an oral dose of 150 mg twice daily, the median peak aPTT is approximately twice that of control values. Twelve hours after the last dose, the median aPTT is 1.5 x control. The INR test is relatively insensitive to the activity of dabigatran etexilate and may not be elevated in patients on dabigatran etexilate.

Dacarbazine (da KAR ba zeen)

Brand Names: Canada Dacarbazine for Injection, BP

Pharmacologic Category Antineoplastic Agent, Alkylating Agent (Triazene)

Use

Hodgkin lymphoma: Treatment of Hodgkin lymphoma (in combination with other chemotherapy agents)

Metastatic malignant melanoma: Treatment of metastatic malignant melanoma

Local Anesthetic/Vasoconstrictor Precautions No information available to require special precautions

Effects on Dental Treatment Key adverse event(s) related to dental treatment: Metallic taste.

Effects on Bleeding Hematopoietic suppression (including platelets) is the most common toxicity of dacarbazine. Risk of thrombocytopenia, which can be life-threatening, reaches a nadir at 7-10 days. A medical consult is recommended.

Adverse Reactions Frequency not always defined.

Central nervous system: Infusion-site pain

Dermatologic: Alopecia

Gastrointestinal: Nausea and vomiting (>90%), anorexia

Hematologic & oncologic: Bone marrow depression (onset: 5 to 7 days; nadir: 7 to 10 days; recovery: 21 to 28 days), leukopenia, thrombocytopenia

<1%, postmarketing, and/or case reports: Anaphylaxis, anemia, diarrhea, dysgeusia, eosinophilia, erythema, facial flushing, facial paresthesia, flu-like symptoms (fever, myalgia, malaise), hepatic necrosis, increased liver enzymes (transient), paresthesia, renal function test abnormality, skin photosensitivity, skin rash, urticaria, venous obstruction (hepatic vein)

General Dosage Range Dosage adjustment recommended in patients with renal impairment

IV:

Pediatrics: 375 mg/m^2 on days 1 and 15, repeat every 28 days

Adults: 375 mg/m^2 days 1 and 15 every 4 weeks **or** 250 mg/m^2 days 1 to 5 every 3 weeks

Mechanism of Action Alkylating agent which is converted to the active alkylating metabolite MTIC [(methyltriazene-1-yl)-imidazole-4-carboxamide] via the cytochrome P450 system. The cytotoxic effects of MTIC are manifested through alkylation (methylation) of DNA at the O^6, N^7 guanine positions which lead to DNA double strand breaks and apoptosis. Dacarbazine is non-cell cycle specific (Marchesi 2007).

Pharmacodynamics/Kinetics

Half-life Elimination Biphasic: Initial: 19 minutes, Terminal: 5 hours

Pregnancy Risk Factor C

Pregnancy Considerations [US Boxed Warning]: Studies have demonstrated this agent to be carcinogenic and/or teratogenic when used in animals; adverse effects have been observed in animal reproduction studies. Women of reproductive potential should avoid becoming pregnant during treatment. The European Society for Medical Oncology has published guidelines for diagnosis, treatment, and follow-up of cancer during pregnancy. The guidelines recommend referral to a facility with expertise in cancer during pregnancy and encourage a multidisciplinary team (obstetrician, neonatologist, oncology team). In general, if chemotherapy is indicated, it should be avoided during in the first trimester, there should be a 3-week time period between the last chemotherapy dose and anticipated delivery, and chemotherapy should not be administered beyond week 33 of gestation (Peccatori 2013). An international consensus panel has published guidelines for hematologic malignancies during pregnancy. Dacarbazine is a component of the ABVD regimen, which is used for the treatment of Hodgkin lymphoma. If treatment cannot be deferred until after delivery in patients with early stage Hodgkin lymphoma, ABVD may be administered safely and effectively in the latter phase of pregnancy (based on limited data); for patients with advanced-stage disease, ABVD can be administered in the second and third trimesters (Lishner 2016).

Daclatasvir (dak LAT as vir)

Brand Names: US Daklinza

Brand Names: Canada Daklinza

Pharmacologic Category Antihepaciviral, NS5A Inhibitor; NS5A Inhibitor

Use

Chronic hepatitis C: Treatment of chronic hepatitis C virus (HCV) genotype 1 or genotype 3 infection in combination with sofosbuvir, with or without ribavirin

Limitations of use: Sustained virologic response rates are reduced in HCV genotype 3-infected patients with cirrhosis receiving daclatasvir in combination with sofosbuvir for 12 weeks.

Local Anesthetic/Vasoconstrictor Precautions No information available to require special precautions

Effects on Dental Treatment No significant effects or complications reported

Effects on Bleeding No information available to require special precautions

Adverse Reactions All adverse drug reactions are from combination therapy trials with sofosbuvir.

>10%:

Central nervous system: Fatigue (14% to 15%), headache (12% to 14%)

Gastrointestinal: Nausea (8% to 15%)

Hematologic & Oncologic: Anemia (20%)

1% to 10%:

Central nervous system: Drowsiness (5%), insomnia (3%)

Dermatologic: Skin rash (8%)

Gastrointestinal: Diarrhea (3% to 5%), increased serum lipase (>3x ULN, transient)

<1%, postmarketing, and/or case reports: Reactivation of HBV (FDA Safety Alert Dec. 8, 2016)

General Dosage Range Dosage adjustment recommended in patients on concomitant therapy

Oral: *Adults:* 60 mg once daily with concomitant antihepacivirals (based on genotype and patient characteristics)

Mechanism of Action Daclatasvir binds to the N-terminus within Domain 1 of HCV nonstructural protein 5A (NS5A) and inhibits viral RNA replication and virion assembly.

Pharmacodynamics/Kinetics

Half-life Elimination ~12 to 15 hours

Time to Peak Plasma: ≤2 hours

Pregnancy Considerations If used in combination with ribavirin, all warnings related to the use of ribavirin and pregnancy and/or contraception should be followed. Mother-to-child transmission of HCV does not occur if the woman is not viremic, therefore, HCV-infected women of childbearing potential should postpone pregnancy until therapy is complete. Treatment of HCV is not recommended for women who are already pregnant (AASLD/IDSA 2015).

Daclizumab (dac KLYE zue mab)

Brand Names: US Zinbryta

Brand Names: Canada Zinbryta

Pharmacologic Category Immunosuppressant Agent; Interleukin-2 Inhibitor; Monoclonal Antibody

Use Multiple sclerosis, relapsing: Treatment of relapsing forms of multiple sclerosis (MS) in adult patients. Daclizumab should generally be reserved for patients who have had an inadequate response to 2 or more medications indicated for the treatment of MS.

Local Anesthetic/Vasoconstrictor Precautions No information available to require special precautions

Effects on Dental Treatment Key adverse event(s) related to dental treatment: Oropharyngeal pain, bronchitis, pharyngitis, rhinitis, tonsillitis have been reported

Effects on Bleeding No information available to require special precautions

Adverse Reactions

>10%:

Dermatologic: Allergic skin reaction (18% to 37%), skin rash (7% to 11%)

Immunologic: Autoimmune disease (13% to 32%)

Infection: Infection (50% to 65%)

Respiratory: Nasopharyngitis (25%), upper respiratory tract infection (9% to 17%)

1% to 10%:

Central nervous system: Depression (7% to 10%), seizure (1%)

Dermatologic: Dermatitis (3% to 9%), eczema (5%), acne vulgaris (3%)

Hematologic & oncologic: Lymphadenopathy (5%), anemia (3%)

Hepatic: Increased serum ALT (5% to 6%), increased serum AST (3% to 6%), hepatic injury (≤1%)
Infection: Influenza (9%)
Respiratory: Oropharyngeal pain (8%), bronchitis (7%), pharyngitis (6%), rhinitis (4%), tonsillitis (4%)
Miscellaneous: Fever (3%)

Frequency not defined:
Dermatologic: Desquamation, erythema, folliculitis, pruritus, psoriasis, skin photosensitivity, skin rash (toxic), xeroderma
Gastrointestinal: Diarrhea
Hematologic & oncologic: Decreased absolute lymphocyte count, lymphadenitis
Hepatic: Abnormal hepatic function tests, increased liver enzymes
Hypersensitivity: Hypersensitivity reaction (including anaphylaxis, angioedema, and urticaria)
Infection: Viral infection
Respiratory: Laryngitis, pneumonia, respiratory tract infection

<1%, postmarketing, and/or case reports: Autoimmune hepatitis, colitis (serious; noninfectious), increased serum alkaline phosphatase (<2 x ULN), increased serum bilirubin (≥2 x ULN), increased serum transaminases (≥3 x ULN), malignant neoplasm of breast (more common in women), suicidal ideation

General Dosage Range SubQ: *Adults:* 150 mg once monthly

Mechanism of Action Daclizumab is a humanized monoclonal antibody which binds to the CD25 subunit of the high-affinity interleukin-2 (IL-2) receptor to prevent signaling at the high-affinity IL-2 receptor while allowing increased IL-2 availability for signaling at the intermediate-affinity IL-2 receptor (Gold 2013, Kappos 2015). Because IL-2 has a role in activating and regulating the immune system; CD25 antagonism may result in therapeutic benefit in multiple sclerosis (Gold 2013).

Pharmacodynamics/Kinetics

Half-life Elimination SubQ: 21 days

Time to Peak SubQ: 5 to 7 days

Pregnancy Considerations Adverse events were observed in animal reproduction studies. Daclizumab is a monoclonal antibody; monoclonal antibodies are known to cross the placenta, with increasing amounts during the second and third trimesters. Use of similar agents is not recommended for the treatment of multiple sclerosis in pregnant women (Coyle 2016, Pozzilli 2015).

Prescribing and Access Restrictions

Access is restricted to pharmacies/distributors enrolled in the Zinbryta REMS program. Further information is available at 1-800-456-2255.

In Canada, Zinbryta is available through a controlled distribution program called the Biogen One Support Program (1-855-676-6300).

DACTINomycin (dak ti noe MYE sin)

Brand Names: US Cosmegen

Brand Names: Canada Cosmegen

Pharmacologic Category Antineoplastic Agent, Antibiotic

Use

Ewing sarcoma: Treatment of Ewing sarcoma (as part of a combination chemotherapy and/or multimodality treatment regimen)

Gestational trophoblastic neoplasia: Treatment of gestational trophoblastic neoplasia (as a single agent or in combination with other chemotherapy agents)

Rhabdosarcoma: Treatment of childhood rhabdosarcoma (as part of a combination chemotherapy and/or multimodality treatment regimen)

Solid tumors: Palliative and/or adjunctive treatment of locally recurrent or locoregional solid malignancies (as a component of regional perfusion)

Testicular cancer, metastatic (nonseminomatous): Treatment of metastatic nonseminomatous testicular cancer

Wilms tumor: Treatment of Wilms tumor (as part of a combination chemotherapy and/or multimodality treatment regimen)

Local Anesthetic/Vasoconstrictor Precautions No information available to require special precautions

Effects on Dental Treatment Key adverse event(s) related to dental treatment: Stomatitis and mucositis

Effects on Bleeding Onset of thrombocytopenia, which can be severe, occurs at 7 days with the nadir at 14-21 days. A medical consult is recommended.

Adverse Reactions Frequency not defined.
Cardiovascular: Hepatic veno-occlusive disease (hepatic sinusoidal obstruction syndrome)
Central nervous system: Fatigue, lethargy, malaise
Dermatologic: Acne vulgaris, alopecia (reversible), cheilitis, dermal ulcer (following extravasation), epidermolysis, erythema (of previously irradiated skin), erythema multiforme, exfoliation of skin, localized erythema, skin pigmentation (of previously irradiated skin), skin rash, Stevens-Johnson syndrome, toxic epidermal necrolysis
Endocrine & metabolic: Growth suppression, hyperuricemia, hypocalcemia
Gastrointestinal: Abdominal pain, anorexia, diarrhea, dysphagia, esophagitis, gastrointestinal ulcer, mucositis, nausea, proctitis, stomatitis, vomiting
Hematologic & oncologic: Agranulocytosis, anemia, aplastic anemia, bone marrow depression (onset: 7 days; nadir: 14 to 21 days; recovery: 21 to 28 days), febrile neutropenia, leukopenia, neutropenia, pancytopenia, reticulocytopenia, thrombocytopenia, thrombocytopenia (immune-mediated)
Hepatic: Abnormal hepatic function tests, ascites, hepatic failure, hepatitis, hepatomegaly, hepatopathy thrombocytopenia syndrome, hepatotoxicity, increased serum bilirubin
Hypersensitivity: Anaphylactoid reaction
Infection: Infection, sepsis (including neutropenic sepsis)
Local: Localized edema, local pain
Neuromuscular & skeletal: Myalgia
Renal: Renal function abnormality
Respiratory: Pharyngitis, pneumonitis
Miscellaneous: Fever, tissue necrosis

General Dosage Range

IV:

Children >6 months: 15 mcg/kg/day **or** 400 to 600 mcg/m²/day for 5 days every 3 to 6 weeks

Adults: 12 to 15 mcg/kg/day **or** 400 to 600 mcg/m²/day for 5 days every 3 to 6 weeks **or** 1,000 mcg/m² on day 1 **or** 500 mcg/dose days 1 and 2

Regional perfusion: *Adults:* Lower extremity or pelvis: 50 mcg/kg; Upper extremity: 35 mcg/kg

Mechanism of Action Binds to the guanine portion of DNA intercalating between guanine and cytosine base pairs inhibiting DNA and RNA synthesis and protein synthesis

Pharmacodynamics/Kinetics

Half-life Elimination ~36 hours; Children: Range: 14 to 43 hours (Veal 2005)

Pregnancy Risk Factor D

Pregnancy Considerations [US Boxed Warning]: Avoid exposure during pregnancy. Adverse effects have been observed in animal reproduction studies. Women of childbearing potential are advised not to become pregnant. When used for gestational trophoblastic neoplasm, unfavorable outcomes have been reported when subsequent pregnancies occur within 6 months of treatment. It is recommended to use effective contraception for 6 months to 1 year after therapy (Matsui 2004; Seckl 2013)

Dalbavancin (dal ba VAN sin)

Brand Names: US Dalvance

Pharmacologic Category Glycopeptide

Use Acute bacterial skin and skin structure infections: Treatment of adult patients with acute bacterial skin and skin structure infections (ABSSSI) caused by susceptible isolates of the following gram-positive microorganisms: *Staphylococcus aureus* (including methicillin-susceptible and methicillin-resistant strains), *Streptococcus pyogenes*, *Streptococcus agalactiae*, *S. dysgalactiae*, *Streptococcus anginosus* group (including *S. anginosus*, *S. intermedius*, *S. constellatus*), and *Enterococcus faecalis* (vancomycin-susceptible strains)

Local Anesthetic/Vasoconstrictor Precautions No information available to require special precautions

Effects on Dental Treatment Key adverse event(s) related to dental treatment: Use may result in fungal superinfection including *Candida albicans* in the oral cavity.

Effects on Bleeding Dalbavancin may affect bleeding times including spontaneous hematoma and wound hemorrhage; may interfere with test used to monitor coagulation such as INR.

Adverse Reactions

1% to 10%:

Cardiovascular: Flushing (<2%), phlebitis (<2%)

Central nervous system: Headache (5%), dizziness (<2%)

Dermatologic: Skin rash (3%), pruritus (2%), urticaria (<2%)

Endocrine & metabolic: Hypoglycemia (<2%)

Gastrointestinal: Nausea (6%), diarrhea (4%), vomiting (3%), abdominal pain (<2%), gastrointestinal hemorrhage (<2%), hematochezia (<2%), melena (<2%), oral candidiasis (<2%), pseudomembranous colitis (<2%)

Hematologic & oncologic: Acute posthemorrhagic anemia (<2%), anemia (<2%), eosinophilia (<2%), hematoma (spontaneous; <2%), increased INR (<2%), leukopenia (<2%), neutropenia (<2%), petechia (<2%), thrombocythemia (<2%), thrombocytopenia (<2%), wound hemorrhage (<2%)

Hepatic: Hepatotoxicity (<2%)

Hepatic: Increased serum alkaline phosphatase (<2%), increased serum transaminases (<2%)

Hypersensitivity: Anaphylactoid reaction (<2%)

Infection: Vulvovaginal infection (mycotic; <2%)

Respiratory: Bronchospasm (<2%)

Miscellaneous: Infusion related reaction (<2%)

<1%, postmarketing, and/or case reports: Anaphylaxis, *Clostridium difficile*-associated diarrhea, hypersensitivity reaction, increased serum ALT (>3 x ULN)

General Dosage Range Dosage adjustment recommended in renal impairment

IV: *Adults:* 1,500 mg as a single dose **or** 1,000 mg as a single dose initially, followed by 500 mg as a single dose 1 week later

Mechanism of Action Dalbavancin is a lipoglycopeptide which binds to the D-alanyl-D-alanine terminus of the stem pentapeptide in nascent cell wall peptidoglycan, preventing cross-linking and interfering with cell wall synthesis. It is bactericidal in vitro against *Staphylococcus aureus* and *Streptococcus pyogenes*

Pharmacodynamics/Kinetics

Half-life Elimination 346 hours

Pregnancy Considerations Adverse events have been observed in animal reproduction studies. The long half-life of dalbavancin should be considered when evaluating potential exposure to the fetus.

Dalfampridine (dal FAM pri deen)

Brand Names: US Ampyra

Brand Names: Canada Fampyra

Pharmacologic Category Potassium Channel Blocker

Use Treatment to improve walking in patients with multiple sclerosis (MS)

Local Anesthetic/Vasoconstrictor Precautions No information available to require special precautions

Effects on Dental Treatment No significant effects or complications reported

Effects on Bleeding No information available to require special precautions

Adverse Reactions

>10%: Genitourinary: Urinary tract infection (12%)

1% to 10%:

Central nervous system: Insomnia (9%), dizziness (7%), headache (7%), equilibrium disturbance (5%), paresthesia (4%)

Gastrointestinal: Nausea (7%), constipation (3%), dyspepsia (2%)

Neuromuscular & skeletal: Weakness (7%), back pain (5%), acute exacerbations of multiple sclerosis (4%)

Respiratory: Nasopharyngitis (4%), pharyngolaryngeal pain (2%)

<1%, postmarketing and/or case reports: Hypersensitivity reaction, seizure, vomiting

General Dosage Range Oral: Extended release: *Adults:* 10 mg every 12 hours

Mechanism of Action Nonspecific potassium channel blocker which improves conduction in focally demyelinated axons by delaying repolarization and prolonging the duration of action potentials. Enhanced neuronal conduction is thought to strengthen skeletal muscle fiber twitch activity, thereby, improving peripheral motor neurologic function.

Pharmacodynamics/Kinetics

Half-life Elimination 5.2-6.5 hours; prolonged in severe renal impairment (~3 times longer)

Time to Peak Plasma: 3-4 hours

Pregnancy Risk Factor C

Pregnancy Considerations Adverse events have been observed in animal reproduction studies, including decreased growth and death.

Dalteparin (dal TE pa rin)

Related Information

Cardiovascular Diseases *on page 1752*

Brand Names: US Fragmin

Brand Names: Canada Fragmin

Pharmacologic Category Anticoagulant; Anticoagulant, Low Molecular Weight Heparin

Use

Deep vein thrombosis prophylaxis: Prevention of deep vein thrombosis (DVT) which may lead to pulmonary embolism (PE), in patients requiring abdominal surgery who are at risk for thromboembolism complications (eg, >40 years of age, obesity, patients with malignancy, history of DVT or PE, and surgical procedures requiring general anesthesia and lasting >30 minutes); patients undergoing hip-replacement surgery; or in patients who are at risk for thromboembolism complications due to severe immobility during an acute illness.

Unstable angina/non-Q-wave myocardial infarction: Prevention of ischemic complications in patients with unstable angina or non-Q-wave myocardial infarction on concurrent aspirin therapy.

Venous thromboembolism, extended treatment in cancer patients: Extended treatment (6 months) of acute symptomatic venous thromboembolism (DVT and/or PE) to reduce the recurrence of venous thromboembolism in cancer patients.

Canadian labeling: Additional use (off-label use in US): Treatment of acute DVT; prevention of venous thromboembolism (VTE) in patients at risk of VTE undergoing general surgery; anticoagulant in extracorporeal circuit during hemodialysis and hemofiltration

Local Anesthetic/Vasoconstrictor Precautions No information available to require special precautions

Effects on Dental Treatment Key adverse event(s) related to dental treatment: Bleeding is the major adverse effect of dalteparin. Adverse reactions reported were generally less than those seen with heparin. See Effects on Bleeding.

Effects on Bleeding The risk of bleeding and thrombocytopenia is high with low molecular weight heparin anticoagulants such as dalteparin. The use of NSAIDs and aspirin should be avoided. A medical consult is recommended.

Adverse Reactions

Note: As with all anticoagulants, bleeding is the major adverse effect of dalteparin. Hemorrhage may occur at virtually any site. Risk is dependent on multiple variables.

>10%: Hematologic & oncologic: Hemorrhage (3% to 14%), thrombocytopenia (including heparin-induced thrombocytopenia, <1%; cancer clinical trials: ~11%)

1% to 10%:

Hematologic & oncologic: Major hemorrhage (≤6%), wound hematoma (3%)

Hepatic: Increased serum ALT (>3 x ULN: 4% to 10%), increased serum AST (>3 x ULN: 5% to 9%)

Local: Pain at injection site (≤12%), hematoma at injection site (≤7%)

<1% (Limited to important or life-threatening): Alopecia, anaphylactoid reaction, gastrointestinal hemorrhage, hemoptysis, hypersensitivity reaction (fever, pruritus, rash, injections site reaction, bullous eruption), postoperative wound bleeding, skin necrosis, subdural hematoma, thrombosis (associated with heparin-induced thrombocytopenia). Spinal or epidural hematomas can occur following neuraxial anesthesia or spinal puncture, resulting in paralysis.

General Dosage Range SubQ: *Adults:* Prophylaxis: 2,500 to 5,000 units daily; Treatment: 120 units/kg every 12 hours (maximum: 10,000 units/dose) **or** ~150 to 200 units/kg (maximum: 18,000 units/dose) once daily.

Mechanism of Action Low molecular weight heparin analog with a molecular weight of 4,000 to 6,000 daltons; the commercial product contains 3% to 15% heparin with a molecular weight <3,000 daltons, 65% to 78% with a molecular weight of 3,000 to 8,000 daltons and 14% to 26% with a molecular weight >8,000 daltons; while dalteparin has been shown to inhibit both factor Xa and factor IIa (thrombin), the antithrombotic effect of dalteparin is characterized by a higher ratio of antifactor Xa to antifactor IIa activity (ratio = 4)

Pharmacodynamics/Kinetics

Onset of Action Anti-Xa activity: Within 1 to 2 hours

Duration of Action >12 hours

Half-life Elimination Route dependent: Anti-Xa activity:

IV: 2.1 ± 0.3 (40 unit/kg/dose) to 2.3 ± 0.4 (60 unit/kg/dose); prolonged in chronic renal impairment requiring hemodialysis

SubQ: 3 to 5 hours

Time to Peak Serum: SubQ: Anti-Xa activity: ~4 hours

Pregnancy Risk Factor B

Pregnancy Considerations Adverse effects have not been observed in animal reproduction studies. Low molecular weight heparin (LMWH) does not cross the placenta; increased risks of fetal bleeding or teratogenic effects have not been reported (Bates 2012).

LMWH is recommended over unfractionated heparin for the treatment of acute venous thromboembolism (VTE) in pregnant women. LMWH is also recommended over unfractionated heparin for VTE prophylaxis in pregnant women with certain risk factors. LMWH should be discontinued at least 24 hours prior to induction of labor or a planned cesarean delivery. For women undergoing cesarean section and who have additional risk factors for developing VTE, the prophylactic use of LMWH may be considered. For women who require long-term anticoagulation with warfarin and who are considering pregnancy, LMWH substitution should be done prior to conception when possible. When choosing therapy, fetal outcomes (ie, pregnancy loss, malformations), maternal outcomes (ie, VTE, hemorrhage), burden of therapy, and maternal preference should be considered (Guyatt 2012). LMWH may also be used in women with mechanical heart valves (consult current guidelines for details) (Bates 2012; Nishimura 2014).

Multiple-dose vials contain benzyl alcohol (avoid in pregnant women due to association with gasping syndrome in premature infants); use of preservative-free formulation is recommended.

Danaparoid (da NAP a roid)

Brand Names: Canada Orgaran

Pharmacologic Category Anticoagulant; Anticoagulant, Heparinoid

Use Note: Not approved in the US

Catheter patency: Intermittent flushing to maintain patency of catheters/IV lines and/or access ports

Deep vein thrombosis: Prevention of postoperative deep vein thrombosis (DVT) following orthopedic or major abdominal and thoracic surgery; prevention of DVT in patients with confirmed diagnosis of non-hemorrhagic stroke

Heparin-induced thrombocytopenia: Management of heparin-induced thrombocytopenia (HIT)

Local Anesthetic/Vasoconstrictor Precautions No information available to require special precautions

Effects on Dental Treatment Key adverse event(s) related to dental treatment: Bleeding is the major adverse effect of danaparoid. See Effects on Bleeding.

Effects on Bleeding As with all anticoagulants, bleeding is the major adverse effect of danaparoid. Hemorrhage may occur at virtually any site; risk is dependent on multiple variables including the intensity of anticoagulation and patient susceptibility. At the recommended doses, LMWHs do not significantly influence platelet aggregation or affect global clotting time (ie, PT or aPTT). Medical consult is suggested.

Adverse Reactions Frequency not always defined. As with all anticoagulants, bleeding is the major adverse effect of danaparoid. Hemorrhage may occur at virtually any site. Risk is dependent on multiple variables.

1% to 10%:

Central nervous system: Pain (5%)
Dermatologic: Skin rash (1%)
Gastrointestinal: Nausea (3%), constipation (2%)
Genitourinary: Urinary retention (1%)
Hematologic & oncologic: Leukocytosis (1%)
Infection: Infection (2%)
Local: Hematoma at injection site (≤5%)
Respiratory: Pneumonia (1%)
Miscellaneous: Fever (2% to 5%)

Frequency not defined:

Cardiovascular: Atrial fibrillation, cerebral infarction, decreased blood pressure (arterial), deep vein thrombosis, hypotension, peripheral edema
Central nervous system: Cerebral hemorrhage, confusion, fatigue, hemiparesis, insomnia, loss of consciousness, restlessness
Genitourinary: Hematuria, urinary incontinence, urinary tract hemorrhage (including microscopic), urine abnormality
Hematologic & oncologic: Bruise, hematoma, hemorrhage (dose-related), thrombocytopenia
Hypersensitivity: Hypersensitivity reaction
Infection: Sepsis
Neuromuscular & skeletal: Muscle spasm, tremor
Respiratory: Apnea, asthma

<1%, postmarketing, and/or case reports: Increased serum alkaline phosphatase, increased serum ALT (transient), increased serum AST (transient)

General Dosage Range Dosage adjustment recommended in patients with renal impairment

SubQ:

Children: 10 units/kg every 12 hours
Adults: Dosage varies greatly depending on indication

IV:

Children: Initial bolus: 30 units/kg; maintenance: 1.2-4 units/kg/hour
Adults: Dosage varies greatly depending on indication

Mechanism of Action Inhibits factor Xa and IIa (anti-Xa effects >20 times anti-IIa effects). Prevents fibrin formation in the coagulation pathway via thrombin generation inhibition.

Pharmacodynamics/Kinetics

Onset of Action Peak effect: SubQ: Maximum anti-factor Xa activities occur in 4-5 hours

Half-life Elimination Anti-Xa activity: ~25 hours (renal impairment: 29-35 hours); Thrombin generation inhibition activity: ~7 hours

Pregnancy Considerations Adverse events have not been observed in animal reproduction studies. The manufacturer labeling states that incidental observations in pregnant women during the last trimesters, gave no indication that use during pregnancy results in fetal abnormalities or exacerbation of bleeding in the mother or infant during delivery. Use in pregnant women however is generally not recommended unless deemed medically necessary and alternative therapy is unavailable. Danaparoid does not cross the placenta and is the preferred anticoagulant in pregnant women with HIT (Guyatt 2012).

Product Availability Not available in the US

Danazol (DA na zole)

Brand Names: Canada Cyclomen

Pharmacologic Category Androgen

Use

Endometriosis: Treatment of endometriosis amenable to hormonal management.

Fibrocystic breast disease: Management of symptoms (pain, tenderness, nodularity) of fibrocystic breast disease which are not reduced by simple measures (including padded brassieres and analgesics) and require suppression of ovarian function.

Hereditary angioedema: Prevention of attacks of angioedema of all types (cutaneous, abdominal, laryngeal) in males and females.

Local Anesthetic/Vasoconstrictor Precautions No information available to require special precautions

Effects on Dental Treatment No significant effects or complications reported

Effects on Bleeding Thrombocytopenia and thrombotic events have been reported.

Adverse Reactions Frequency not defined.

Cardiovascular: Edema, flushing, hypertension, myocardial infarction, palpitations, syncope, tachycardia
Central nervous system: Depression, dizziness, emotional lability, fatigue, headache, nervousness, paresthesia, sleep disorder, voice disorder (deepening of the voice, hoarseness, instability, sore throat)
Dermatologic: Acne vulgaris, alopecia, diaphoresis, maculopapular rash, papular rash, pruritus, seborrhea, urticaria, vesicular eruption
Endocrine & metabolic: Amenorrhea (may continue post-therapy), change in libido, decreased glucose tolerance (and glucagon changes), decreased HDL cholesterol, decreased thyroxine binding globulin, hirsutism (mild), increased LDL cholesterol, increased thyroxine binding globulin, menstrual disease (altered timing of cycle, spotting), weight gain
Gastrointestinal: Constipation, gastroenteritis, nausea, vomiting
Genitourinary: Abnormalities in semen viscosity, abnormalities in semen volume, abnormalities in sperm motility, breast atrophy, hematuria, inhibition of spermatogenesis, spermatozoa disorder (sperm count changes), vaginal dryness, vaginal irritation
Hematologic & oncologic: Decreased sex hormone binding globulin, eosinophilia, increased red blood cell count, increased sex hormone-binding globulin, leukocytosis, leukopenia, malignant neoplasm (after prolonged use), petechial rash, polycythemia, purpuric rash, secondary polycythemia (reversible), thrombocythemia, thrombocytopenia
Hepatic: Cholestatic jaundice, hepatic adenoma, hepatic neoplasm (malignant; after prolonged use), increased liver enzymes, jaundice, peliosis hepatitis
Neuromuscular & skeletal: Ankylosis, arthralgia, back pain, increased creatine phosphokinase, joint swelling, limb pain, muscle cramps, muscle spasm, neck pain, tremor, weakness
Ophthalmic: Visual disturbance
Respiratory: Interstitial pneumonitis

<1%, postmarketing, and/or case reports: Anxiety, carpal tunnel syndrome, cataract, change in appetite, chills, clitoromegaly, convulsions, erythema multiforme, fever, gingival hemorrhage, Guillain-Barre syndrome, hepatotoxicity (idiosyncratic) (Chalasani 2014), nasal congestion, nipple discharge, pancreatitis, pelvic pain, pseudotumor cerebri, purpura (splenic peliosis), skin photosensitivity, Stevens-Johnson syndrome

General Dosage Range Oral: *Adults:* Initial: 100 to 800 mg/day in 2 to 3 divided doses; Maintenance: Titrate dose

Mechanism of Action Suppresses pituitary output of follicle-stimulating hormone (FSH) and luteinizing hormone (LH), resulting in regression and atrophy of normal and ectopic endometrial tissue; decreases rate of growth of abnormal breast tissue; reduces attacks associated with hereditary angioedema by increasing levels of C4 component of complement

Pharmacodynamics/Kinetics

Onset of Action

Fibrocystic breast disease: Onset of pain/tenderness relief: 1 month (usually significantly relieved at 2 to 3 months); nodule elimination: 4 to 6 months

Immune thrombocytopenia (off-label use): Initial response: 14 to 90 days; Peak response: 28 to 180 days (Neunert 2011)

Half-life Elimination ~10 hours (variable; up to 24 hours following long term use for endometriosis)

Time to Peak Serum: 4 hours (range: 2 to 8 hours)

Pregnancy Risk Factor X

Pregnancy Considerations [US Boxed Warning]: Danazol use is contraindicated in pregnancy. Pregnancy should be ruled out immediately prior to starting treatment using a sensitive test (eg, beta subunit test if available) capable of determining early pregnancy. A nonhormonal method of contraception should also be used during therapy. If a patient becomes pregnant during danazol treatment, discontinue danazol and apprise the patient of the potential risk to the fetus. Exposure to danazol in utero may result in androgenic effects on the female fetus; reports of clitoral hypertrophy, labial fusion, urogenital sinus defect, vaginal atresia, and ambiguous genitalia have been received. Therapy should be discontinued for 2 months prior to attempting pregnancy (Caballero 2012).

Dantrolene (DAN troe leen)

Brand Names: US Dantrium; Revonto; Ryanodex

Brand Names: Canada Dantrium

Pharmacologic Category Skeletal Muscle Relaxant

Use

IV: Management of malignant hyperthermia (MH); prevention of MH in susceptible individuals (preoperative/postoperative administration)

Oral: Treatment of spasticity associated with upper motor neuron disorders (eg, spinal cord injury, stroke, cerebral palsy, or multiple sclerosis); management of MH; prevention of MH in susceptible individuals (preoperative/postoperative administration)

Note: Dantrolene prophylaxis is not recommended for most MH-susceptible patients, provided nontriggering anesthetics are used and an adequate supply of dantrolene is available.

Local Anesthetic/Vasoconstrictor Precautions No information available to require special precautions

Effects on Dental Treatment No significant effects or complications reported

Effects on Bleeding No information available to require special precautions

Adverse Reactions Frequency not always defined.

Cardiovascular: Flushing (intravenous: 27%), atrioventricular block (intravenous: 3%), tachycardia (3%), cardiac failure, phlebitis, variable blood pressure

Central nervous system: Drowsiness (17%; drowsiness may persist for 48 hours post dose), voice disorder (intravenous: 13%), feeling abnormal (intravenous: 10%), dizziness (3%), headache (3%), myasthenia (3%), chills, choking sensation, confusion, depression, fatigue, insomnia, malaise, nervousness, seizure, speech disturbance

Dermatologic: Acneiform eruption (capsules), diaphoresis, eczematous rash, erythema (intravenous), hair disease (abnormal growth), pruritus, urticaria

Gastrointestinal: Dysphagia (10%; use caution at meal time on day of administration as swallowing may be difficult), nausea (10%), vomiting (3%), abdominal cramps, anorexia, constipation, diarrhea, dysgeusia, gastric irritation, gastrointestinal hemorrhage, sialorrhea

Genitourinary: Crystalluria, difficulty in micturition, erectile dysfunction, hematuria, nocturia, urinary frequency, urinary incontinence, urinary retention

Hematologic & oncologic: Anemia, aplastic anemia, leukopenia, lymphocytic lymphoma, thrombocytopenia

Hepatic: Hepatitis

Hypersensitivity: Anaphylaxis

Local: Injection site reaction (intravenous: 3%; pain, erythema, swelling), local tissue necrosis (with extravasation due to high product pH)

Neuromuscular & skeletal: Limb pain (intravenous: 3%), back pain, myalgia

Ophthalmic: Blurred vision (intravenous: 3%), diplopia, epiphora, visual disturbance

Respiratory: Dyspnea (intravenous), pleural effusion (with pericarditis), pulmonary edema (rare), respiratory depression

Miscellaneous: Fever

<1%, postmarketing, and/or case reports: Decrease in forced vital capacity (intravenous), dyspnea (intravenous), hepatic disease, hepatotoxicity (oral), increased liver enzymes (oral), respiratory muscle failure (intravenous)

General Dosage Range

IV: *Infants, Children, Adolescents, and Adults:* 1 to 2.5 mg/kg; may repeat up to cumulative dose of 10 mg/kg **or** 2.5 mg/kg as a single dose

Oral:

Infants, Children, and Adolescents: 4 to 8 mg/kg/day in 4 divided doses **or** 0.5 to 2 mg/kg/dose 1 to 4 times daily (maximum: 400 mg daily)

Adults: 4 to 8 mg/kg/day in 4 divided doses **or** 25 to 100 mg 1 to 4 times daily (maximum: 400 mg daily)

Mechanism of Action Acts directly on skeletal muscle by interfering with release of calcium ion from the sarcoplasmic reticulum; prevents or reduces the increase in myoplasmic calcium ion concentration that activates the acute catabolic processes associated with malignant hyperthermia

Pharmacodynamics/Kinetics

Half-life Elimination

Neonates (at birth): ~20 hours (Shime 1988)

Children 2 to 7 years: 10 hours (range: 8.1 to 14.8 hours) (Lerman 1989)

Adults: 4 to 11 hours

Pregnancy Risk Factor C

Pregnancy Considerations Adverse events have been observed in animal reproduction studies. Dantrolene crosses the human placenta. Cord blood concentrations are similar to those in the maternal plasma at term. and dantrolene can be detected in the newborn serum at delivery. Adverse events were not observed in the newborn following maternal doses of 100 mg/day administered orally prior to delivery (Shime, 1988). Uterine atony has been reported following dantrolene injection after delivery; however, this may be due in part to the mannitol contained in the IV preparation (Shin, 1995; Weingarten, 1987). Prophylactic use of dantrolene is not routinely recommended in pregnant women susceptible to MH prior to obstetric surgery, if use is needed, close monitoring of the mother and newborn is recommended (Krause 2004; Norman 1995).

Dapagliflozin (dap a gli FLOE zin)

Brand Names: US Farxiga

Brand Names: Canada Forxiga

Pharmacologic Category Antidiabetic Agent, Sodium-Glucose Cotransporter 2 (SGLT2) Inhibitor; Sodium-Glucose Cotransporter 2 (SGLT2) Inhibitor

Use Diabetes mellitus, type 2: As an adjunct to diet and exercise to improve glycemic control in adults with type 2 diabetes mellitus

Local Anesthetic/Vasoconstrictor Precautions No information available to require special precautions

Effects on Dental Treatment Key adverse event(s) related to dental treatment: Dizziness and syncope have been reported; patients may experience orthostatic hypotension as they stand up after treatment; especially if lying in dental chair for extended periods of time. Use caution with sudden changes in position during and after dental treatment.

Dapagliflozin-dependent patients with diabetes (non-insulin dependent, type 2) should be questioned by the dental professional at each dental visit to assess their risk for stress-induced hypoglycemia. The dental professional should inquire about the patient's routine (ie, work, sleep schedule, eating patterns), history of hypoglycemia, time of last medication dose, last meal, and most recent blood sugar assessment. Keep a supply of glucose tablets and other carbohydrates in the office to prepare for a hypoglycemic event. Seek medical attention when necessary (American Diabetes Association 2016).

Effects on Bleeding No information available to require special precautions

Adverse Reactions

1% to 10%:

Endocrine & metabolic: Dyslipidemia (3%), hyperphosphatemia (2%), hypovolemia (1%)

Gastrointestinal: Nausea (3%)

Genitourinary: Fungal vaginosis (7% to 8%; includes [in order of frequency] vulvovaginal mycotic infection, vaginal infection, vulvovaginal candidiasis, vulvovaginitis, genital infection, genital candidiasis, fungal genital infection, vulvitis, genitourinary tract infection, vulval abscess, vaginitis bacterial), urinary tract infection (6%), increased urine output (3% to 4%: includes [in order of frequency] pollakiuria, polyuria, and urine output increased), genitourinary fungal infections (mycotic; in males: 3%; includes [in order of frequency] balanitis, fungal genital infection, balanitis candida, genital candidiasis, genital infection, penile infection, balanoposthitis, balanoposthitis infective, genital infection, posthitis), dysuria (2%)

Hematologic & oncologic: Increased hematocrit (1%)

Infection: Influenza (2% to 3%)

Neuromuscular & skeletal: Bone fracture (8%; in patients with moderate renal impairment), back pain (4%), limb pain (2%)

Respiratory: Nasopharyngitis (7%)

Frequency not defined:

Endocrine & metabolic: Increased LDL cholesterol

Renal: Decreased estimated GFR (eGFR), increased serum creatinine

<1%, postmarketing, and/or case reports: Acute renal failure, allergic skin reaction (severe), anaphylaxis, angioedema, bladder neoplasm, hypersensitivity reaction (including urticaria), ketoacidosis, pyelonephritis, skin rash, urosepsis

General Dosage Range Oral: *Adults:* 5 to 10 mg once daily

Mechanism of Action By inhibiting sodium-glucose cotransporter 2 (SGLT2) in the proximal renal tubules, dapagliflozin reduces reabsorption of filtered glucose from the tubular lumen and lowers the renal threshold for glucose (RT_G). SGLT2 is the main site of filtered glucose reabsorption; reduction of filtered glucose reabsorption and lowering of RT_G result in increased urinary excretion of glucose, thereby reducing plasma glucose concentrations.

Pharmacodynamics/Kinetics

Half-life Elimination ~12.9 hours

Time to Peak 2 hours

Pregnancy Risk Factor C

Pregnancy Considerations Adverse events were observed in some animal reproduction studies. Based on animal data, adverse fetal effects on renal development may occur in humans following *in utero* exposure during the second and third trimesters.

In women with diabetes, maternal hyperglycemia can be associated with congenital malformations as well as adverse effects in the fetus, neonate, and the mother (ACOG 2005; ADA 2016d; Kitzmiller 2008; Metzger 2007). To prevent adverse outcomes, prior to conception and throughout pregnancy maternal blood glucose and HbA_{1c} should be kept as close to target goals as possible but without causing significant hypoglycemia (ACOG 2013; ADA 2016d; Blumer 2013; Kitzmiller 2008). Agents other than dapagliflozin are currently recommended to treat diabetes in pregnant women (ACOG 2013; Blumer 2013).

Dapagliflozin and Metformin

(dap a gli FLOE zin & met FOR min)

Brand Names: US Xigduo XR

Brand Names: Canada Xigduo

Pharmacologic Category Antidiabetic Agent, Biguanide; Antidiabetic Agent, Sodium-Glucose Cotransporter 2 (SGLT2) Inhibitor; Sodium-Glucose Cotransporter 2 (SGLT2) Inhibitor

Use Diabetes mellitus, type 2: As an adjunct to diet and exercise to improve glycemic control in adults with type 2 diabetes mellitus (noninsulin dependent, NIDDM) when treatment with both dapagliflozin and metformin is appropriate.

Local Anesthetic/Vasoconstrictor Precautions No information available to require special precautions

Effects on Dental Treatment Key adverse event(s) related to dental treatment: Dizziness and syncope have been reported; patients may experience

orthostatic hypotension as they stand up after treatment; especially if lying in dental chair for extended periods of time. Use caution with sudden changes in position during and after dental treatment.

Dapagliflozin-dependent patients with diabetes (non-insulin dependent, type 2) should be questioned by the dental professional at each dental visit to assess their risk for stress-induced hypoglycemia. The dental professional should inquire about the patient's routine (ie, work, sleep schedule, eating patterns), history of hypoglycemia, time of last medication dose, last meal, and most recent blood sugar assessment. Keep a supply of glucose tablets and other carbohydrates in the office to prepare for a hypoglycemic event. Seek medical attention when necessary (American Diabetes Association 2016).

Effects on Bleeding No information available to require special precautions

Adverse Reactions

See individual monographs for additional adverse effects reported with each agent

1% to 10%:

Central nervous system: Headache (5%), dizziness (3%)

Endocrine & metabolic: Dyslipidemia (2% to 3%)

Infection: Genitourinary fungal infection (female: 9%, includes bacterial vaginosis, female genital tract infection, genital abscess, vaginal infection, vulvovaginal candidiasis; male: 4%, includes balanitis, balanitis [candida], balanoposthitis, posthitis), influenza (3% to 4%)

Gastrointestinal: Nausea (3% to 4%), constipation (3%)

Genitourinary: Urinary tract infection (6%), increased urine output (2% to 3%), dysuria (2%)

Respiratory: Cough (3%), pharyngitis (2% to 3%)

<1%, postmarketing, and/or case reports: Ketoacidosis (FDA Safety Communication, December 4, 2015), pyelonephritis (FDA Safety Communication, December 4, 2015), urosepsis (FDA Safety Communication, December 4, 2015)

General Dosage Range Oral: *Adults:* Initial: Individualize based on patient's current antidiabetic regimen; range: dapagliflozin 5 mg/metformin 500 mg once daily to dapagliflozin 10 mg/metformin 2,000 mg once daily. Maximum: dapagliflozin 10 mg/metformin 2,000 mg once daily.

Mechanism of Action

Dapagliflozin: By inhibiting sodium-glucose cotransporter 2 (SGLT2) in the proximal renal tubules, dapagliflozin reduces reabsorption of filtered glucose from the tubular lumen and lowers the renal threshold for glucose (RTG). SGLT2 is the main site of filtered glucose reabsorption; reduction of filtered glucose reabsorption and lowering of RTG result in increased urinary excretion of glucose, thereby reducing plasma glucose concentrations.

Metformin: Decreases hepatic glucose production, decreases intestinal absorption of glucose, improves insulin sensitivity by increasing peripheral glucose uptake and utilization.

Pregnancy Risk Factor C

Pregnancy Considerations

The Canadian labeling contraindicates use during pregnancy.

Animal reproduction studies have not been conducted with this combination. Metformin crosses the placenta. Refer to individual monographs.

Dapsone (Systemic) (DAP sone)

Related Information

HIV Infection and AIDS *on page 1785*

Pharmacologic Category Antibiotic, Miscellaneous

Use Treatment of leprosy (due to susceptible strains of *Mycobacterium leprae*) and dermatitis herpetiformis

Local Anesthetic/Vasoconstrictor Precautions No information available to require special precautions

Effects on Dental Treatment No significant effects or complications reported

Effects on Bleeding No information available to require special precautions

Adverse Reactions Frequency not always defined.

>10%: Hematologic: Reticulocyte increase (2% to 12%), hemolysis (>10%; dose related; seen in patients with and without G6PD deficiency), hemoglobin decrease (>10%; 1-2 g/dL; almost all patients), methemoglobinemia (>10%), red cell life span shortened (>10%), Agranulocytosis, anemia, leukopenia, pure red cell aplasia (case report)

Cardiovascular: Tachycardia

Central nervous system: Fever, headache, insomnia, psychosis, vertigo

Dermatologic: Bullous and exfoliative dermatitis, erythema nodosum, exfoliative dermatitis, morbilliform and scarlatiniform reactions, phototoxicity, Stevens-Johnson syndrome, toxic epidermal necrolysis, urticaria

Endocrine & metabolic: Hypoalbuminemia (without proteinuria), male infertility

Gastrointestinal: Abdominal pain, nausea, pancreatitis, vomiting

Hepatic: Cholestatic jaundice, hepatitis

Neuromuscular & skeletal: Lower motor neuron toxicity (prolonged therapy), lupus-like syndrome, peripheral neuropathy (rare, nonleprosy patients)

Ocular: Blurred vision

Otic: Tinnitus

Renal: Albuminuria, nephrotic syndrome, renal papillary necrosis

Respiratory: Interstitial pneumonitis, pulmonary eosinophilia

Miscellaneous: Infectious mononucleosis-like syndrome (rash, fever, lymphadenopathy, hepatic dysfunction)

General Dosage Range Oral: *Adults:* 50 to 300 mg once daily

Mechanism of Action Competitive antagonist of para-aminobenzoic acid (PABA) and prevents normal bacterial utilization of PABA for the synthesis of folic acid

Pharmacodynamics/Kinetics

Half-life Elimination Children: 15.1 hours (Mirochnick 1993); Adults: 28 hours (range: 10 to 50 hours)

Time to Peak 4 to 8 hours

Pregnancy Risk Factor C

Pregnancy Considerations Dapsone crosses the placenta (Brabin 2004). Per the manufacturer, dapsone has not shown an increased risk of congenital anomalies when given during all trimesters of pregnancy. Several reports have described adverse effects in the newborn after in utero exposure to dapsone, including neonatal hemolytic disease, methemoglobinemia, and hyperbilirubinemia (Hocking 1968; Kabra 1998; Thornton 1989). Dapsone may be used in pregnant women requiring maintenance therapy of either leprosy or dermatitis herpetiformis. Dapsone may be used as an alternative agent for management of *Pneumocystis jirovecii* pneumonia (PCP) or *Toxoplasma gondii* encephalitis in pregnant, HIV-infected patients (HHS [OI

Adult] 2016). Because of the theoretical increased risk for hyperbilirubinemia and kernicterus, neonatal care providers should be informed if maternal dapsone is used near term (HHS [OI Adult] 2016).

Dapsone (Topical) (DAP sone)

Brand Names: US Aczone

Brand Names: Canada Aczone

Pharmacologic Category Topical Skin Product, Acne

Use Acne vulgaris: Topical treatment of acne vulgaris

Guideline recommendations: American Academy of Dermatology (AAD) acne guidelines recommend dapsone 5% topical gel for inflammatory acne, particularly in adult females with acne (AAD [Zaenglein 2016]).

Local Anesthetic/Vasoconstrictor Precautions No information available to require special precautions

Effects on Dental Treatment No significant effects or complications reported

Effects on Bleeding No information available to require special precautions

Adverse Reactions Frequency not always defined.

Central nervous system: Suicidal tendencies, tonic-clonic movements

Gastrointestinal: Abdominal pain, pancreatitis, severe vomiting

Respiratory: Sinusitis (2%), pharyngitis

<1%, postmarketing, and/or case reports: Depression, erythema, facial edema, methemoglobinemia (Swartzentruber 2015), psychosis

General Dosage Range Topical: *Children ≥12 years, Adolescents, and Adults:* Apply pea-sized amount in thin layer to affected areas once (7.5% gel) or twice (5% gel) daily

Pregnancy Risk Factor C

Pregnancy Considerations Adverse events were observed in some animal reproduction studies. The amount of dapsone available systemically is less following topical application than with oral administration. If treatment for acne is deemed necessary during pregnancy, topical agents are currently recommended; information specific to dapsone is lacking (Gollnick 2003; Kong 2013; Meredith 2013).

DAPTOmycin (DAP toe mye sin)

Brand Names: US Cubicin; Cubicin RF

Brand Names: Canada Cubicin

Pharmacologic Category Antibiotic, Cyclic Lipopeptide

Use

Skin and skin structure infections, complicated: Treatment of complicated skin and skin structure infections caused by *Staphylococcus aureus* (including methicillin-resistant isolates), *Streptococcus pyogenes*, *Streptococcus agalactiae*, *Streptococcus dysgalactiae* subspecies *equisimilis*, and *Enterococcus faecalis* (vancomycin-susceptible strains only).

***S. aureus* bloodstream infections:** Treatment of *S. aureus* bloodstream infections (bacteremia), including those with right-sided infective endocarditis, caused by methicillin-susceptible and methicillin-resistant isolates.

Limitations of use: Not indicated for the treatment of pneumonia.

Local Anesthetic/Vasoconstrictor Precautions No information available to require special precautions

Effects on Dental Treatment No significant effects or complications reported

Effects on Bleeding No information available to require special precautions

Adverse Reactions

1% to 10%:

Cardiovascular: Chest pain (7%), edema (7%), hypertension (6%), hypotension (2%)

Central nervous system: Insomnia (9%), headache (5%), dizziness (2%)

Dermatologic: Pruritus (6%), diaphoresis (5%), skin rash (4%)

Gastrointestinal: Abdominal pain (6%), diarrhea (5%)

Genitourinary: Urinary tract infection (2%)

Hepatic: Abnormal hepatic function tests (3%), increased serum alkaline phosphatase (2%)

Infection: Gram-negative organism infection (8%), bacteremia (5%), sepsis (5%)

Neuromuscular & skeletal: Increased creatine phosphokinase (3% to 9%)

Respiratory: Pharyngolaryngeal pain (8%), dyspnea (2%)

Frequency not defined:

Cardiovascular: Atrial fibrillation, atrial flutter

Central nervous system: Hallucination, hypoesthesia (including oral)

Endocrine & metabolic: Increased serum phosphate

Gastrointestinal: Decreased appetite, epigastric distress, gingival pain, oral candidiasis, xerostomia

Genitourinary: Fungal urinary tract infection, proteinuria, vulvovaginal candidiasis

Hematologic & oncologic: Lymphadenopathy

Hepatic: Increased serum ALT, increased serum AST

Infection: Candidiasis, fungal septicemia

Neuromuscular & skeletal: Dyskinesia

Ophthalmic: Blurred vision

Otic: Tinnitus

Renal: Renal insufficiency

<1%, postmarketing, and/or case reports: Abdominal distension, acute generalized exanthematous pustulosis, acute renal failure, anaphylaxis, anemia, arthralgia, *Clostridium difficile*-associated diarrhea, cough, decreased appetite, dysgeusia, eczema, electrolyte disturbance, eosinophilia, eosinophilic pneumonitis, eye irritation, fatigue, fever, flushing, hypomagnesemia, hypersensitivity reaction (including angioedema, drug rash with eosinophilia and systemic symptoms [DRESS], dysphagia, hives, pulmonary eosinophilia, truncal erythema), increased lactate dehydrogenase, increased myoglobin, increased serum bicarbonate, jaundice, leukocytosis, mental status changes, muscle cramps, myalgia, myasthenia, myopathy, nausea, neutropenia (Knoll 2013), paresthesia, peripheral neuropathy, renal failure, rhabdomyolysis, rigors, Stevens-Johnson syndrome, stomatitis, supraventricular cardiac arrhythmia, thrombocytopenia, thrombocythemia, vertigo, vesiculobullous dermatitis, visual disturbance, vomiting, weakness

General Dosage Range Dosage adjustment recommended in patients with renal impairment

IV: *Adults:* 4 to 6 mg/kg once daily

Mechanism of Action Daptomycin binds to components of the cell membrane of susceptible organisms and causes rapid depolarization, inhibiting intracellular synthesis of DNA, RNA, and protein. Daptomycin is bactericidal in a concentration-dependent manner.

Pharmacodynamics/Kinetics

Half-life Elimination

Neonates and Infants <3 months: Median: 6.2 hours (range: 3.7 to 9 hours) (Cohen-Wolkowiez 2012)

Children 2 to 6 years: Mean range: 5.3 to 5.7 hours (Abdel-Rahman 2008; Abdel-Rahman 2011)

Children 7 to 11 years: 5.6 ± 2.2 hours (Abdel-Rahman 2008)
Children 12 to 17 years: 6.7 ± 2.2 hours (Abdel-Rahman 2008)
Adults: 8 to 9 hours (up to 28 hours in renal impairment)

Pregnancy Risk Factor B

Pregnancy Considerations Adverse events were not observed in animal reproduction studies. Successful use of daptomycin during the second and third trimesters of pregnancy has been described; however, only limited information is available from case reports.

Daratumumab (dar a TOOM ue mab)

Brand Names: US Darzalex

Brand Names: Canada Darzalex

Pharmacologic Category Antineoplastic Agent, Anti-CD38; Antineoplastic Agent, Monoclonal Antibody

Use Multiple myeloma, relapsed/refractory: Treatment of multiple myeloma (in combination with dexamethasone and either lenalidomide or bortezomib) in patients who have received at least one prior therapy; treatment of multiple myeloma (as monotherapy) in patients who have received at least 3 prior lines of therapy, including a proteasome inhibitor and an immunomodulatory agent or who are double refractory to a proteasome inhibitor and an immunomodulatory agent.

Local Anesthetic/Vasoconstrictor Precautions No information available to require special precautions

Effects on Dental Treatment No significant effects or complications reported

Effects on Bleeding Chemotherapy may result in significant myelosuppression, including thrombocytopenia. In patients under active treatment a medical consult is suggested.

Adverse Reactions Some incidences may include data from combination therapy trials.

>10%:

Central nervous system: Fatigue (39%), headache (12%)
Gastrointestinal: Nausea (27%), diarrhea (16%), constipation (15%), decreased appetite (15%), vomiting (14%)
Hematologic & oncologic: Lymphocytopenia (72%; grade: 3: 30%; grade 4: 10%), neutropenia (60%; grade 3: 17%; grade 4: 3%), thrombocytopenia (48%; grade 3: 10%; grade 4: 8%), anemia (45%; grade 3: 19%)
Infection: Herpes zoster (3%)
Neuromuscular & skeletal: Back pain (23%), arthralgia (17%), leg pain (15%), musculoskeletal chest pain (12%)
Respiratory: Cough (21%), upper respiratory (20%), nasal congestion (17%), dyspnea (15%), nasopharyngitis (15%), pneumonia (6% to 11%)
Miscellaneous: Infusion related reaction (first infusion: 46% to 48%; second infusion: 2%; subsequent infusions: 4%), fever (3% to 21%)

1% to 10%:

Cardiovascular: Hypertension (10%)
Central nervous system: Chills (10%)
Miscellaneous: Physical health deterioration (3%)

General Dosage Range

IV: *Adults:* 16 mg/kg once weekly (weeks 1 to 8 or weeks 1 to 9), every 2 weeks (weeks 9 to 24 or weeks 10 to 24), and then every 4 weeks until disease progression (weeks 25 and beyond)

Mechanism of Action Daratumumab is an IgG1κ human monoclonal antibody directed against CD38. CD38 is a cell surface glycoprotein which is highly expressed on myeloma cells, yet is expressed at low levels on normal lymphoid and myeloid cells (Lokhorst 2015). By binding to CD38, daratumumab inhibits the growth of CD38 expressing tumor cells by inducing apoptosis directly through Fc mediated cross linking as well as by immune-mediated tumor cell lysis through complement dependent cytotoxicity, antibody dependent cell mediated cytotoxicity, and antibody dependent cellular phagocytosis.

Pharmacodynamics/Kinetics

Half-life Elimination Monotherapy: 18 ± 9 days; Combination therapy: 23 ± 12 days

Pregnancy Considerations Animal reproduction studies have not been conducted. Daratumumab is a monoclonal antibody; monoclonal antibodies are known to cross the placenta. Based on the mechanism of action, daratumumab may cause myeloid or lymphoid cell depletion and decreased bone density in the fetus. Females of reproduction potential should use effective contraception during therapy and for 3 months after treatment is complete. The administration of live vaccines should be deferred for neonates and infants exposed to daratumumab in utero until a hematology evaluation can be completed.

Darbepoetin Alfa (dar be POE e tin AL fa)

Brand Names: US Aranesp (Albumin Free)

Brand Names: Canada Aranesp

Pharmacologic Category Colony Stimulating Factor; Erythropoiesis-Stimulating Agent (ESA); Hematopoietic Agent

Use

Anemia: Treatment of anemia due to concurrent myelosuppressive chemotherapy in patients with cancer (nonmyeloid malignancies) receiving chemotherapy (palliative intent) for a planned minimum of 2 additional months of chemotherapy; treatment of anemia due to chronic kidney disease (including patients on dialysis and not on dialysis)

Limitations of use: In clinical trials, darbepoetin alfa has not demonstrated improved quality of life, fatigue, or well-being. Darbepoetin alfa is **not** indicated for use under the following conditions:

- Cancer patients receiving hormonal therapy, therapeutic biologic products, or radiation therapy unless also receiving concurrent myelosuppressive chemotherapy
- Cancer patients receiving myelosuppressive chemotherapy when the expected outcome is curative
- As a substitute for red blood cell (RBC) transfusion in patients requiring immediate correction of anemia

Local Anesthetic/Vasoconstrictor Precautions No information available to require special precautions

Effects on Dental Treatment No significant effects or complications reported

Effects on Bleeding Erythropoiesis-stimulating agents have been associated with thromboembolic events.

Adverse Reactions

>10%:

Cardiovascular: Hypertension (31%), peripheral edema (17%), edema (6% to 13%)
Gastrointestinal: Abdominal pain (10% to 13%)
Respiratory: Dyspnea (17%), cough (12%)

1% to 10%:

Cardiovascular: Angina pectoris, hypotension, myocardial infarction, pulmonary embolism, thromboembolism, thrombosis of vascular graft (arteriovenous), vascular injury (vascular access complications)

Central nervous system: Cerebrovascular disease

Dermatologic: Erythema, skin rash

Endocrine & metabolic: Hypervolemia

<1%, postmarketing, and/or case reports: Anaphylaxis, anemia (associated with neutralizing antibodies; severe; with or without other cytopenias), angioedema, bronchospasm, cerebrovascular accident, hypersensitivity reaction, hypertensive encephalopathy, pure red cell aplasia, seizure, tumor growth (progression/recurrence; cancer patients), urticaria

General Dosage Range

IV:

Children 1 to 18 years: 0.45 mcg/kg once weekly **or** 0.75 mcg/kg once every 2 weeks **or** 6.25 to 200 mcg/week

Adults: 0.45 mcg/kg once weekly **or** every 4 weeks **or** 0.75 mcg/kg once every 2 weeks **or** 6.25 to 200 mcg/week

SubQ:

Children 1 to 18 years: 0.45 mcg/kg once weekly **or** 0.75 mcg/kg once every 2 weeks **or** 6.25 to 200 mcg/week

Adults: 0.45 to 4.5 mcg/kg/week **or** 0.45 mcg/kg every 4 weeks **or** 0.75 mcg/kg once every 2 weeks **or** 500 mcg once every 3 weeks **or** 6.25 to 200 mcg/week

Mechanism of Action Induces erythropoiesis by stimulating the division and differentiation of committed erythroid progenitor cells; induces the release of reticulocytes from the bone marrow into the bloodstream, where they mature to erythrocytes. There is a dose-response relationship with this effect. This results in an increase in reticulocyte counts followed by a rise in hematocrit and hemoglobin levels. When administered SubQ or IV, darbepoetin alfa's half-life is ~3 times that of epoetin alfa concentrations.

Pharmacodynamics/Kinetics

Onset of Action Increased hemoglobin levels not generally observed until 2 to 6 weeks after initiating treatment

Half-life Elimination Note: Darbepoetin alfa half-life is approximately 3-fold longer than epoetin alfa following IV administration

Children:

IV: Terminal: 22.1 hours (range: 12 to 30 hours)

SubQ: Terminal: 42.8 hours (range: 16 to 86 hours); Children with cancer: 49.4 hours

Adults:

CKD:

IV: 21 hours

SubQ: Nondialysis patients: 70 hours (range: 35 to 139 hours); Dialysis patients: 46 hours (range: 12 to 89 hours)

Cancer: SubQ: 74 hours (range: 24 to 144 hours)

Time to Peak SubQ:

CKD: Adults: 48 hours (range: 12 to 72 hours; independent of dialysis); Children: 36 hours (range: 10 to 58 hours)

Cancer: Adults: 71 to 90 hours (range: 28 to 123 hours); Children: 71 hours (range: 21 to 143 hours)

Pregnancy Risk Factor C

Pregnancy Considerations Adverse events were observed in animal reproduction studies. Women who become pregnant during treatment with darbepoetin alfa are encouraged to enroll in Amgen's Pregnancy Surveillance Program (800-772-6436).

Prescribing and Access Restrictions As a requirement of the REMS program, access to this medication is restricted. Healthcare providers and hospitals must be enrolled in the ESA APPRISE (Assisting Providers and Cancer Patients with Risk Information for the Safe use of ESAs) Oncology Program (866-284-8089; http://www.esa-apprise.com) to prescribe or dispense ESAs (ie, darbepoetin alfa, epoetin alfa) to patients with cancer.

Darifenacin (dar i FEN a sin)

Brand Names: US Enablex

Brand Names: Canada Enablex

Pharmacologic Category Anticholinergic Agent

Use Overactive bladder: Treatment of overactive bladder with symptoms of urinary frequency, urgency, or urge incontinence.

Local Anesthetic/Vasoconstrictor Precautions No information available to require special precautions

Effects on Dental Treatment Key adverse event(s) related to dental treatment: Xerostomia (normal salivary flow resumes upon discontinuation). Prolonged xerostomia may contribute to discomfort and dental disease (eg, caries, periodontal disease, and oral candidiasis).

Effects on Bleeding No information available to require special precautions

Adverse Reactions

>10%: Gastrointestinal: Xerostomia (19% to 35%), constipation (15% to 21%)

1% to 10%:

Cardiovascular: Hypertension (≥1%), peripheral edema (≥1%)

Central nervous system: Headache (7%), dizziness (<2%), pain (≥1%)

Dermatological: Pruritus (≥1%), skin rash (≥1%), xeroderma (≥1%)

Endocrine & metabolic: Weight gain (≥1%)

Gastrointestinal: Dyspepsia (3% to 8%), abdominal pain (2% to 4%), nausea (2% to 4%), vomiting (≥1%)

Genitourinary: Urinary tract infection (4% to 5%), vaginitis (≥1%), urinary retention (acute)

Neuromuscular & skeletal: Weakness (<3%), arthralgia (≥1%), back pain (≥1%)

Ophthalmic: Dry eye syndrome (2%), visual disturbance (≥1%)

Respiratory: Flu-like symptoms (1% to 3%), bronchitis (≥1%), pharyngitis (≥1%), rhinitis (≥1%), sinusitis (≥1%)

Postmarketing and/or case reports: Anaphylaxis, angioedema, confusion, erythema multiforme, granuloma (annulare), hallucination, hypersensitivity reaction, palpitations

General Dosage Range Dosage adjustment recommended in patients with hepatic impairment or on concomitant therapy

Oral: *Adults:* Initial: 7.5 mg once daily; Maintenance: 7.5 to 15 mg once daily

Mechanism of Action Selective antagonist of the M3 muscarinic (cholinergic) receptor subtype. Blockade of the receptor limits bladder contractions, reducing the symptoms of bladder irritability/overactivity (urge incontinence, urgency and frequency).

Pharmacodynamics/Kinetics

Half-life Elimination ~13 to 19 hours

Time to Peak Plasma: ~7 hours

Pregnancy Risk Factor C

Pregnancy Considerations Adverse events have been observed in animal reproduction studies.

Darunavir (dar OO na veer)

Related Information

HIV Infection and AIDS *on page 1785*

Brand Names: US Prezista

Brand Names: Canada Prezista

Pharmacologic Category Antiretroviral, Protease Inhibitor (Anti-HIV)

Use HIV-1 infection: Treatment of HIV-1 infection, coadministered with ritonavir and other antiretroviral agents, in adults and pediatric patients 3 years and older

Local Anesthetic/Vasoconstrictor Precautions No information available to require special precautions

Effects on Dental Treatment No significant effects or complications reported

Effects on Bleeding Increased bleeding has been noted with protease inhibitors, such as darunavir, in patients with hemophilia A or B. No other information is available to require special precautions in other patients.

Adverse Reactions As a class, protease inhibitors potentially cause dyslipidemias which includes elevated cholesterol and triglycerides and a redistribution of body fat centrally to cause increased abdominal girth, buffalo hump, facial atrophy, and breast enlargement. These agents also cause hyperglycemia. Frequency of adverse events is reported for darunavir/ritonavir in both treatment-naive and experienced patients. Frequency, type, and severity of adverse events in pediatric patients are comparable to adult patients unless otherwise noted. See also Ritonavir monograph.

>10%:

Dermatologic: Skin rash (children: 5% to 19%; adults: 6% to 7%)

Endocrine & metabolic: Hypercholesterolemia (adults: grade 2: 23% to 25%; grade 3: 1% to 10%; children: grade 3: 1%), increased LDL cholesterol (adults: grade 2: 14%; grade 3: 8% to 9%; children: grade 3: 3%), hyperglycemia (grade 2: 10% to 11%; grade 3: 1%; grade 4: <1%)

Gastrointestinal: Vomiting (children: 13% to 33%; adults: 2% to 5%), nausea (children: 4% to 25%; adults: 4% to 7%), diarrhea (children: 11% to 24%; adults: 8% to 14%)

2% to 10%:

Central nervous system: Headache (children: 9%, adults: 3% to 7%), fatigue (children: 3%; adults: ≤2%)

Dermatologic: Pruritus (children: 8%; adults: <2%)

Endocrine & metabolic: Increased serum triglycerides (grade 2: 3% to 10%; grade 3: 2% to 7%; grade 4: 1% to 3%), increased amylase (adults: grade 2: 5% to 6%, grade 3: 5% to 7%; children: grade 3: 4%, grade 4: 1%), diabetes mellitus (2%)

Gastrointestinal: Abdominal pain (children: 5% to 10%; adults: 5% to 6%), decreased appetite (children: 8%; adults: 2%), anorexia (children: 5%; adults: 2%), increased serum lipase (adults: grade 2: 3%; grade 3: ≤2%; grade 4: <1%; children: grade 3: 1%), abdominal distention (2%), dyspepsia (2%)

Hepatic: Increased serum ALT (adults: grade 2: 7%, grade 3: 2% to 3%; grade 4: ≤1%; children: grade 3: 3%; grade 4: 1%), increased serum AST (adults: grade 2: 6%; grade 3: 2% to 4%; grade 4: ≤1%; children: grade 3: 1%)

Neuromuscular & skeletal: Weakness (≤3%)

<2%, postmarketing, and/or case reports: Abnormal dreams, absence seizures, acute generalized exanthematous pustulosis, acute renal failure, acute respiratory distress, allergic dermatitis, alopecia, anemia, angioedema, anxiety, arthralgia, arthritis, arthropathy, biliary obstruction, blurred vision, bradycardia, cerebral infarction, cerebrovascular accident, decreased serum creatinine, dehydration, depression, dermatitis (including dermatitis medicamentosa), dizziness, DRESS syndrome, drowsiness, dyspnea, epistaxis, erythema multiforme, facial edema, facial paralysis, feeling of heaviness, fever, flatulence, folliculitis, gastritis, gynecomastia, hematuria, hepatic cirrhosis, hepatic failure, hepatic neoplasm (malignant), hepatitis (acute and cytolytic), hepatotoxicity, hiccups, hyperbilirubinemia, hyperhidrosis, hyperkalemia, hyperlipidemia, hypersensitivity, hypertension, hyperthermia, hypoesthesia, immune reconstitution syndrome, impaired consciousness, increased serum alkaline phosphatase, infection (including clostridium infection, parasitic infection [cryptosporidiosis], cytomegalovirus disease [encephalitis], hepatitis B, esophageal candidiasis), jaundice, limb pain, lipoatrophy, maculopapular rash, malignant lymphoma, mean glomerular filtration rate decreased, metabolic acidosis, myalgia, myocardial infarction, myocarditis, myositis, neoplasm (diffuse large B-cell), nephrolithiasis, neuromuscular disease, neutropenia, nightmares, night sweats, obesity, oropharyngeal ulcer, osteonecrosis, osteopenia, osteoporosis, pancreatitis, pancytopenia, paresthesia, peripheral edema, peripheral neuropathy, pneumothorax, polydipsia, polyuria, progressive multifocal leukoencephalopathy, proteinuria, pulmonary edema, rectal hemorrhage, redistribution of body fat (eg, buffalo hump, increased abdominal girth, breast engorgement, facial atrophy), renal insufficiency, renal tubular necrosis, respiratory failure, rhabdomyolysis (coadministration with HMG-CoA reductase inhibitors), rigors, seizure, sepsis, skin rash (toxic), Stevens-Johnson syndrome, swelling of eye, tachycardia, thrombocytopenia, toxic epidermal necrolysis, transient ischemic attacks, urticaria, uveitis, vertigo, xerostomia

General Dosage Range Dosage adjustment recommended in patients who develop toxicities.

Oral:

Children ≥3 years and Adolescents:

≥10 kg to <11 kg: Darunavir 350 mg (tablet) to 360 mg (suspension) once daily with ritonavir 64 mg once daily **or** Darunavir 200 mg twice daily with ritonavir 32 mg twice daily

≥11 kg to <12 kg: Darunavir 385 mg (tablet) to 400 mg (suspension) once daily with ritonavir 64 mg once daily **or** Darunavir 220 mg twice daily with ritonavir 32 mg twice daily

≥12 kg to <13 kg: Darunavir 420 mg once daily with ritonavir 80 mg once daily **or** Darunavir 240 mg twice daily with ritonavir 40 mg twice daily

≥13 kg to <14 kg: Darunavir 455 mg (tablet) to 460 mg (suspension) once daily with ritonavir 80 mg once daily **or** Darunavir 260 mg twice daily with ritonavir 40 mg twice daily

≥14 kg to <15 kg: Darunavir 490 mg (tablet) to 500 mg (suspension) once daily with ritonavir 96 mg once daily **or** Darunavir 280 mg twice daily with ritonavir 48 mg twice daily

≥15 kg to <30 kg: Darunavir 600 mg once daily with ritonavir 100 mg once daily **or** Darunavir 375 mg (tablet) or 380 mg (suspension) twice daily with ritonavir 48 mg twice daily

≥30 kg to <40 kg: Darunavir 675 mg (tablet) to 500 mg (suspension) once daily with ritonavir 100 mg once daily **or** Darunavir 450 mg (tablet) to 460 mg (suspension) twice daily with ritonavir 60 mg twice daily

≥40 kg: Darunavir 800 mg once daily with ritonavir 100 mg once daily **or** Darunavir: 600 mg twice daily with ritonavir 100 mg twice daily

Adults: Darunavir: 600 mg twice daily; Ritonavir: 100 mg twice daily **or** Darunavir: 800 mg once daily; Ritonavir: 100 mg once daily

Pregnant patients: 600 mg twice daily with ritonavir 100 mg twice daily.

Mechanism of Action Binds to the site of HIV-1 protease activity and inhibits cleavage of viral Gag-Pol polyprotein precursors into individual functional proteins required for infectious HIV. This results in the formation of immature, noninfectious viral particles.

Pharmacodynamics/Kinetics

Half-life Elimination ~15 hours

Pregnancy Considerations Darunavir has a low level of transfer across the human placenta. No increased risk of overall birth defects has been observed following first trimester exposure according to data collected by the antiretroviral pregnancy registry. A small increased risk of preterm birth has been associated with maternal use of protease inhibitor-based combination antiretroviral (ARV) therapy during pregnancy; however, the benefits of use generally outweigh this risk and PIs should not be withheld if otherwise recommended. Information related to stillbirth, low birth weight, and small for gestational age infants is limited. Long-term follow-up is recommended for all infants exposed to antiretroviral medications; children who develop significant organ system abnormalities of unknown etiology (particularly of the CNS or heart) should be evaluated for potential mitochondrial dysfunction. Hyperglycemia, new onset of diabetes mellitus, or diabetic ketoacidosis have been reported with PIs; it is not clear if pregnancy increases this risk.

Combination antiretroviral therapy (cART) therapy is recommended for all HIV-infected pregnant women to keep the viral load below the limit of detection and reduce the risk of perinatal transmission. When HIV is diagnosed during pregnancy in a woman who has never received antiretroviral therapy, cART should begin as soon as possible after diagnosis. The Health and Human Services (HHS) Perinatal HIV Guidelines recommend darunavir as a preferred protease inhibitor (PI) for initial use in antiretroviral-naive pregnant patients when combined with low-dose ritonavir boosting. Serum concentrations are decreased during pregnancy; therefore, once-daily dosing is not recommended; ritonavir-boosted twice-daily dosing should be used. In general, women who become pregnant on a stable cART regimen may continue that regimen if viral suppression is effective, appropriate drug exposure can be achieved, contraindications for use in pregnancy are not present, and the regimen is well tolerated. **Note:** Once-daily dosing of darunavir should only be considered in women who are already pregnant, and virologically stable on a once daily dose, and in whom changing to a twice daily regimen would compromise tolerability or compliance. Monitoring during pregnancy is more frequent than in non-pregnant adults; cART should be continued postpartum.

For HIV-infected couples planning a pregnancy, maximum viral suppression with combination antiretroviral therapy (cART) is recommended prior to conception for the HIV-infected partner(s) and expert consultation is recommended; modification of therapy (if needed) and optimization of the woman's health should be done prior to conception. HIV-infected women not planning a pregnancy may use any available type of contraception, considering possible drug interactions and contraindications of the specific method. In addition, consistent use of condoms is also recommended (even during pregnancy) to prevent transmission of HIV or other sexually transmitted diseases.

Health care providers are encouraged to enroll pregnant women exposed to antiretroviral medications as early in pregnancy as possible in the Antiretroviral Pregnancy Registry (1-800-258-4263 or www.APRegistry.com). Health care providers caring for HIV-infected women and their infants may contact the National Perinatal HIV Hotline (888-448-8765) for clinical consultation (HHS [perinatal], 2016).

Dasatinib (da SA ti nib)

Brand Names: US Sprycel

Brand Names: Canada Sprycel

Pharmacologic Category Antineoplastic Agent, BCR-ABL Tyrosine Kinase Inhibitor; Antineoplastic Agent, Tyrosine Kinase Inhibitor

Use

Acute lymphoblastic leukemia: Treatment of Philadelphia chromosome-positive (Ph+) acute lymphoblastic leukemia (ALL) with resistance or intolerance to prior therapy.

Chronic myeloid leukemia: Treatment of newly diagnosed Ph+ chronic myeloid leukemia (CML) in chronic phase; treatment of chronic, accelerated, or myeloid or lymphoid blast phase Ph+ CML with resistance or intolerance to prior therapy, including imatinib.

Local Anesthetic/Vasoconstrictor Precautions Dasatinib is one of the drugs confirmed to prolong the QT interval and is accepted as having a risk of causing torsade de pointes. The risk of drug-induced torsade de pointes is extremely low when a single QT interval prolonging drug is prescribed. In terms of epinephrine, it is not known what effect vasoconstrictors in the local anesthetic regimen will have in patients with a known history of congenital prolonged QT interval or in patients taking any medication that prolongs the QT interval. Until more information is obtained, it is suggested that the clinician consult with the physician prior to the use of a vasoconstrictor in suspected patients, and that the vasoconstrictor (epinephrine, mepivacaine and levonordefrin [Carbocaine® 2% with Neo-Cobefrin®]) be used with caution.

Effects on Dental Treatment Key adverse event(s) related to dental treatment: Mucositis/stomatitis, taste perversion.

Effects on Bleeding Bleeding was experienced in ≤9% of patients with ≤7% severe. Thrombocytopenia is prevalent. A medical consult is recommended.

Adverse Reactions

≥10%:

Cardiovascular: Facial edema, peripheral edema

Central nervous system: Headache (12% to 33%), fatigue (8% to 26%), pain (11%)

Dermatologic: Skin rash (11% to 21%; includes drug eruption, erythema, erythema multiforme, erythematous rash, erythrosis, exfoliative rash, follicular rash, heat rash, macular rash, maculopapular rash, milia, papular rash, pruritic rash, pustular rash, skin exfoliation, skin irritation, urticaria vesiculosa, vesicular rash), pruritus (12%)

Endocrine & metabolic: Fluid retention (19% to 48%; grades 3/4: 1% to 8%; cardiac-related: 9%)

Gastrointestinal: Diarrhea (17% to 31%), nausea (8% to 24%), vomiting (5% to 16%), abdominal pain (7% to 12%)

Hematologic & oncologic: Thrombocytopenia (grades 3/4: 22% to 85%), neutropenia (grades 3/4: 29% to 79%), anemia (grades 3/4: 13% to 74%), hemorrhage (8% to 26%; grades 3/4: 1% to 9%), febrile neutropenia (4% to 12%; grades 3/4: 4% to 12%)

Infection: Infection (9% to 14%; includes bacterial, fungal, viral)

Local: Localized edema (3% to 22%; grades 3/4: ≤1%; superficial)

Neuromuscular & skeletal: Musculoskeletal pain (<22%), myalgia (7% to 13%), arthralgia (≤13%)

Respiratory: Pleural effusion (5% to 28%; grades 3/4: ≤7%), dyspnea (3% to 24%)

Miscellaneous: Fever (6% to 18%)

1% to <10%:

Cardiovascular: Cardiac conduction disturbance (7%), ischemic heart disease (4%), cardiac disease (≤4%; includes cardiac failure, cardiomyopathy, diastolic dysfunction, ejection fraction decreased, left ventricular dysfunction, ventricular failure), edema (≤4%; generalized), pericardial effusion (≤4%; grades 3/4: ≤1%), prolonged Q-T interval on ECG (≤1%), cardiac arrhythmia, chest pain, flushing, hypertension, palpitations, tachycardia

Central nervous system: Chills, depression, dizziness, drowsiness, insomnia, myasthenia, neuropathy, peripheral neuropathy

Dermatologic: Acne vulgaris, alopecia, dermatitis, eczema, hyperhidrosis, urticaria, xeroderma

Endocrine & metabolic: Hyperuricemia, weight gain, weight loss

Gastrointestinal: Constipation (10%), gastrointestinal hemorrhage (2% to 9%; grades 3/4: 1% to 7%), abdominal distention, change in appetite, colitis (including neutropenic colitis), dysgeusia, dyspepsia, enterocolitis, gastritis, mucositis, stomatitis

Hematologic & oncologic: Intracranial hemorrhage (≤3%; grades 3/4: ≤3%), bruise

Hepatic: Increased serum bilirubin (grades 3/4: ≤6%), increased serum ALT (grades 3/4: ≤5%), increased serum AST (grades 3/4: ≤4%), ascites (≤1%)

Infection: Herpes virus infection, sepsis

Neuromuscular & skeletal: Muscle spasm (5%), stiffness, weakness

Ophthalmic: Blurred vision, decreased visual acuity, dry eye syndrome, visual disturbance

Otic: Tinnitus

Renal: Increased serum creatinine (grades 3/4: ≤8%)

Respiratory: Pulmonary hypertension (≤5%; grades 3/4: ≤1%), pulmonary edema (≤4%; grades 3/4: ≤3%), cough, pneumonia (bacterial, viral, or fungal), pneumonitis, pulmonary infiltrates, upper respiratory tract infection

Miscellaneous: Soft tissue injury (oral)

<1%, postmarketing, and/or case reports: Abnormal gait, abnormal platelet aggregation, abnormal T waves on ECG, acute coronary syndrome, acute pancreatitis, acute respiratory distress, amnesia, anal fissure, angina pectoris, anxiety, arthritis, asthma, ataxia, atrial fibrillation, atrial flutter, bronchospasm, bullous skin disease, cardiomegaly, cerebrovascular accident, cholecystitis, cholestasis, confusion, conjunctivitis, convulsions, coronary artery disease, cor pulmonale, cranial nerve palsy (facial), decreased libido, deep vein thrombosis, dehydration, dementia, dermal ulcer, diabetes mellitus, dyschromia, dysphagia, embolism, emotional lability, epistaxis, equilibrium disturbance, erythema nodosum, esophagitis, fibrosis (dermal), fistula (anal), gastroesophageal reflux disease, gastrointestinal disease (protein wasting), gingival hemorrhage, gynecomastia, hearing loss, hematoma, hematuria, hemoptysis, hemorrhage (ocular), hepatitis, hypercholesterolemia, hypersensitivity, hypersensitivity angiitis, hyperthyroidism, hypoalbuminemia, hypotension, hypothyroidism, increased creatine phosphokinase, increased gamma-glutamyl transferase, increased lacrimation, increased pulmonary artery pressure, increased troponin, inflammation (panniculitis), interstitial pulmonary disease, intestinal obstruction, livedo reticularis, lymphadenopathy, lymphocytopenia, malaise, menstrual disease, myocarditis, nail disease, optic neuritis, osteonecrosis, ototoxicity (hemorrhage), palmar-plantar erythrodysesthesia, pancreatitis, pericarditis, petechia, photophobia, pleuropericarditis, prolongation P-R interval on ECG, proteinuria, pulmonary embolism, pure red cell aplasia, reactivation of HBV, renal failure, renal insufficiency, rhabdomyolysis, skin photosensitivity, Stevens-Johnson syndrome, Sweet syndrome, syncope, tendonitis, thrombophlebitis, thrombosis, thyroiditis, transient ischemic attacks, tremor, tumor lysis syndrome, upper gastrointestinal tract ulcer, urinary frequency, uterine hemorrhage, vaginal hemorrhage, ventricular arrhythmia, ventricular tachycardia, vertigo, voice disorder

General Dosage Range Dosage adjustment recommended in patients on concomitant therapy or who develop toxicities

Oral: *Adults:* 100 to 180 mg once daily

Mechanism of Action BCR-ABL tyrosine kinase inhibitor; targets most imatinib-resistant BCR-ABL mutations (except the T315I and F317V mutants) by distinctly binding to active and inactive ABL-kinase. Kinase inhibition halts proliferation of leukemia cells. Also inhibits SRC family (including SRC, LKC, YES, FYN); c-KIT, EPHA2 and platelet derived growth factor receptor (PDGFRβ)

Pharmacodynamics/Kinetics

Half-life Elimination Terminal: 3 to 5 hours

Time to Peak 0.5 to 6 hours

Pregnancy Considerations Dasatinib crosses the placenta, with fetal plasma and amniotic concentrations comparable to maternal concentrations. Adverse effects, including hydrops fetalis and fetal leukopenia and thrombocytopenia have been reported following maternal exposure to dasatinib. Women of reproductive potential should use effective contraception during and for 30 days after the final dose to avoid becoming pregnant. Pregnant women are advised to avoid contact with crushed or broken tablets.

Dental Comment See Local Anesthetic/Vasoconstrictor Precautions

DAUNOrubicin (Conventional)

(daw noe ROO bi sin con VEN sha nal)

Brand Names: Canada Cerubidine; Daunorubicin Hydrochloride for Injection

Pharmacologic Category Antineoplastic Agent, Anthracycline; Antineoplastic Agent, Topoisomerase II Inhibitor

Use

Acute lymphocytic leukemia: Treatment (remission induction) of acute lymphocytic leukemia (ALL) in children and adults (in combination with other chemotherapy)

Acute myeloid leukemia: Treatment (remission induction) of acute myeloid leukemia (AML) in adults (in combination with other chemotherapy)

Local Anesthetic/Vasoconstrictor Precautions No information available to require special precautions

Effects on Dental Treatment Key adverse event(s) related to dental treatment: Stomatitis and discoloration of saliva.

Effects on Bleeding Thrombocytopenia occurs with the nadir in 10-14 days and recovery in 21-28 days. A medical consult is suggested.

Adverse Reactions

Frequency not defined.

>10%:

Cardiovascular: Cardiac failure (dose-related, may be delayed for 7 to 8 years after treatment), ECG abnormality (transient, generally asymptomatic and self-limiting; includes atrial premature contractions, ST segment changes on ECG, supraventricular tachycardia, ventricular premature contractions)

Dermatologic: Alopecia (reversible)

Gastrointestinal: Nausea (mild), stomatitis, vomiting (mild)

Genitourinary: Red urine discoloration

Hematologic & oncologic: Bone marrow depression (onset: 7 days; nadir: 10 to 14 days; recovery: 21 to 28 days; primarily leukopenia; anemia, thrombocytopenia)

Miscellaneous: Radiation recall phenomenon

1% to 10%:

Dermatologic: Discoloration of sweat

Endocrine & metabolic: Hyperuricemia

Gastrointestinal: Abdominal pain, diarrhea, discoloration of saliva, gastrointestinal ulcer

Local: Post-injection flare

Ophthalmic: Discoloration of tears

<1%, postmarketing, and/or case reports: Anaphylactoid reaction, cardiac arrhythmia, cardiomyopathy, hepatitis, hypersensitivity reaction (systemic; includes angioedema, dysphagia, dyspnea, pruritus, urticaria), increased serum bilirubin, increased serum transaminases, infertility, injection site reaction (includes injection site cellulitis, local thrombophlebitis, pain at injection site), leukemia (secondary), myocardial infarction, myocarditis, nail bed changes (pigmentation), nail disease (banding), onycholysis, pericarditis, skin rash, sterility, typhlitis (neutropenic)

General Dosage Range Dosage adjustment recommended in patients with hepatic or renal impairment

IV:

Children <2 years or BSA <0.5 m²: 1 mg/kg on day 1 every week for 4 to 6 cycles (maximum cumulative dose: 10 mg/kg)

Children ≥2 years and BSA ≥0.5 m²: 25 mg/m² on day 1 every week for 4 to 6 cycles (maximum cumulative dose: 300 mg/m²)

Adults <60 years: 30 to 60 mg/m²/day for 2 to 3 days (maximum cumulative dose: 550 mg/m²; 400 mg/m² with chest irradiation)

Adults ≥60 years: 30 mg/m²/day for 2 to 3 days (maximum cumulative dose: 550 mg/m²; 400 mg/m² with chest irradiation)

Mechanism of Action Inhibits DNA and RNA synthesis by intercalation between DNA base pairs and by steric obstruction. Daunomycin intercalates at points of local uncoiling of the double helix. Although the exact mechanism is unclear, it appears that direct binding to DNA (intercalation) and inhibition of DNA repair (topoisomerase II inhibition) result in blockade of DNA and RNA synthesis and fragmentation of DNA.

Pharmacodynamics/Kinetics

Half-life Elimination Initial: 45 minutes; Terminal: 18.5 hours; Daunorubicinol plasma half-life: ~27 hours

Pregnancy Risk Factor D

Pregnancy Considerations Adverse events have been observed in animal reproduction studies. Daunorubicin crosses the placenta. Women of reproductive potential should avoid pregnancy.

DAUNOrubicin (Liposomal)

(daw noe ROO bi sin lye po SO mal)

Brand Names: US DaunoXome [DSC]

Pharmacologic Category Antineoplastic Agent, Anthracycline; Antineoplastic Agent, Topoisomerase II Inhibitor

Use

Kaposi sarcoma: First-line treatment of advanced HIV-associated Kaposi sarcoma

Limitation of use: Daunorubicin (liposomal) is not recommended in HIV-related Kaposi sarcoma which is less than advanced.

Local Anesthetic/Vasoconstrictor Precautions No information available to require special precautions

Effects on Dental Treatment Key adverse event(s) related to dental treatment: Stomatitis.

Effects on Bleeding Thrombocytopenia occurs with the nadir in 14 days and recovery in 21 days. A medical consult is recommended.

Adverse Reactions Frequency not always defined.

Cardiovascular: Edema (11%), chest pain (10%), angina pectoris (≤5%), atrial fibrillation (≤5%), cardiac arrest (≤5%), cardiac tamponade (≤5%), hypertension (≤5%), myocardial infarction (≤5%), palpitations (≤5%), pericardial effusion (≤5%), pulmonary hypertension (≤5%), sinus tachycardia (≤5%), supraventricular tachycardia (≤5%), syncope (≤5%), tachycardia (≤5%), ventricular premature contractions (≤5%), decreased left ventricular ejection fraction (3%; reduction of 20% to 25%), cardiomyopathy (cumulative, dose-related; total dose above 300 mg/m²)

Central nervous system: Fatigue (49%), headache (25%), rigors (19%), neuropathy (13%), depression (10%), malaise (10%), dizziness (8%), insomnia (6%), abnormality in thinking (≤5%), amnesia (≤5%), anxiety (≤5%), ataxia (≤5%), confusion (≤5%), drowsiness (≤5%), emotional lability (≤5%), hallucination (≤5%), hypertonia (≤5%), meningitis (≤5%), seizure (≤5%)

Dermatologic: Diaphoresis (14%), alopecia (8%), pruritus (7%), folliculitis (≤5%), seborrhea (≤5%), xeroderma (≤5%)

Endocrine & metabolic: Dehydration (≤5%), hot flash (≤5%), increased thirst (≤5%)

Gastrointestinal: Nausea (54%), diarrhea (38%), abdominal pain (23%), anorexia (23%), vomiting (23%), stomatitis (10%), constipation (7%), tenesmus (5%), dental caries (≤5%), dysgeusia (≤5%), dysphagia (≤5%), gastritis (≤5%), gastrointestinal hemorrhage (≤5%), gingival hemorrhage (≤5%), hemorrhoids (≤5%), hiccups (≤5%), increased appetite (≤5%), melena (≤5%), xerostomia (≤5%)

Genitourinary: Dysuria (≤5%), nocturia (≤5%)

Hematologic & oncologic: Neutropenia (<1,000 cells/mm³: 36%; grade 4: 15%), lymphadenopathy (≤5%),

splenomegaly (≤5%), bone marrow depression (especially granulocytes; platelets and erythrocytes less effected), severe granulocytopenia (may be associated with fever and result in infection)
Hepatic: Hepatomegaly (≤5%)
Hypersensitivity: Hypersensitivity reaction (24%)
Infection: Opportunistic infection (40%; median time to first infection/illness: 214 days)
Local: Inflammation at injection site (≤5%)
Neuromuscular & skeletal: Back pain (16%), arthralgia (7%), myalgia (7%), abnormal gait (≤5%), hyperkinesia (≤5%), tremor (≤5%)
Ophthalmic: Visual disturbance (5%), conjunctivitis (≤5%), eye pain (≤5%)
Otic: Deafness (≤5%), otalgia (≤5%), tinnitus (≤5%)
Renal: Polyuria (≤5%)
Respiratory: Cough (28%), dyspnea (26%), rhinitis (12%), sinusitis (8%), flu-like symptoms (5%), hemoptysis (≤5%), increased bronchial secretions (≤5%), pulmonary infiltrates (≤5%)
Miscellaneous: Fever (47%), infusion-related reaction (14%; includes back pain, flushing, chest tightness)

General Dosage Range Dosage adjustment recommended in patients with hepatic or renal impairment or who develop toxicities.

IV: *Adults:* 40 mg/m^2 once every 2 weeks

Mechanism of Action Liposomal preparation of daunorubicin; liposomes have been shown to penetrate solid tumors more effectively, possibly because of their small size and longer circulation time. Once in tissues, daunorubicin is released (over time). Daunorubicin inhibits DNA and RNA synthesis by intercalation between DNA base pairs and by steric obstruction; and intercalates at points of local uncoiling of the double helix. Although the exact mechanism is unclear, it appears that direct binding to DNA (intercalation) and inhibition of DNA repair (topoisomerase II inhibition) result in blockade of DNA and RNA synthesis and fragmentation of DNA.

Pharmacodynamics/Kinetics

Half-life Elimination Distribution: 4.4 hours

Pregnancy Risk Factor D

Pregnancy Considerations Adverse events were observed in animal reproduction studies. May cause fetal harm if administered during pregnancy. Women of childbearing potential should avoid becoming pregnant while receiving treatment.

Decitabine (de SYE ta been)

Brand Names: US Dacogen

Pharmacologic Category Antineoplastic Agent, Antimetabolite; Antineoplastic Agent, DNA Methylation Inhibitor

Use Myelodysplastic syndromes: Treatment of myelodysplastic syndromes (MDS), including previously treated and untreated, de novo and secondary MDS of all French-American-British (FAB) subtypes (refractory anemia, refractory anemia with ringed sideroblasts, refractory anemia with excess blasts, refractory anemia with excess blasts in transformation, and chronic myelomonocytic leukemia) and intermediate-1, intermediate-2, and high-risk International Prognostic Scoring System (IPSS) groups

Local Anesthetic/Vasoconstrictor Precautions No information available to require special precautions

Effects on Dental Treatment Key adverse event(s) related to dental treatment: Oral mucosal petechiae, stomatitis, gingival bleeding, tongue ulceration, oral candidiasis, lip ulceration, mucosal inflammation, gingival pain have been reported.

Effects on Bleeding Gingival bleeding and oral mucosal petechiae have been reported with decitabine therapy as well as a high incidence (27% to 89%) of thrombocytopenia. A medical consult is recommended.

Adverse Reactions

>10%:
Cardiovascular: Peripheral edema (25% to 27%), edema (5% to 18%), heart murmur (16%), hypotension (6% to 11%)
Central nervous system: Fatigue (46%), headache (23% to 28%), insomnia (14% to 28%), rigors (22%), dizziness (18% to 21%), chills (16%), pain (5% to 13%), confusion (8% to 12%), lethargy (12%), hypoesthesia (11%), anxiety (9% to 11%)
Dermatologic: Pallor (23%), skin rash (11% to 19%), erythema (5% to 14%), cellulitis (9% to 12%), pruritus (9% to 11%)
Endocrine & metabolic: Hyperglycemia (6% to 33%), hypoalbuminemia (7% to 24%), hypomagnesemia (5% to 24%), hypokalemia (12% to 22%), hyponatremia (19%), hyperkalemia (13%)
Gastrointestinal: Nausea (40% to 42%), constipation (30% to 35%), diarrhea (28% to 34%), vomiting (16% to 25%), anorexia (≤8% to 23%), decreased appetite (≤8% to 23%), abdominal pain (5% to 14%), stomatitis (11% to 12%), dyspepsia (10% to 12%)
Hematologic & oncologic: Neutropenia (38% to 90%; grades 3/4: 37% to 87%; recovery 28 to 50 days), thrombocytopenia (27% to 89%; grades 3/4: 24% to 85%), anemia (31% to 82%; grades 3/4: 22%), petechia (12% to 39%), febrile neutropenia (20% to 29%; grades 3/4: 23%), leukopenia (6% to 28%; grades 3/4: 22%), bruise (9% to 22%), oral mucosal petechiae (13%), lymphadenopathy (12%)
Hepatic: Hyperbilirubinemia (6% to 14%), increased serum alkaline phosphatase (11%)
Local: Localized tenderness (11%)
Neuromuscular & skeletal: Arthralgia (17% to 20%), limb pain (18% to 19%), back pain (17% to 18%), weakness (15%)
Respiratory: Cough (27% to 40%), dyspnea (29%), pneumonia (20% to 22%), pharyngitis (16%), rales (8% to 14%), epistaxis (13%)
Miscellaneous: Fever (6% to 53%), lesion (5% to 11%)

5% to 10%:
Cardiovascular: Tachycardia (8%), chest wall pain (7%), chest pain (≤6% to 7%), chest discomfort (≤6% to 7%), facial edema (6%), hypertension (6%), cardiac failure (5%)
Central nervous system: Depression (9%), falling (8%), malaise (5%), mouth pain (5%)
Dermatologic: Alopecia (8%), xeroderma (8%), urticaria (6%), catheter site erythema (5%), night sweats (5%)
Endocrine & metabolic: Hyperuricemia (10%), weight loss (9%), increased lactate dehydrogenase (8%), dehydration (6% to 8%), hypochloremia (6%), increased serum bicarbonate (6%), decreased serum bicarbonate (5%), hypoproteinemia (5%)
Gastrointestinal: Mucosal inflammation (9%), gingival hemorrhage (8%), hemorrhoids (8%), loose stools (7%), tongue ulcer (7%), oral candidiasis (6%), toothache (6%), dysphagia (5% to 6%), abdominal distention (5%), gastroesophageal reflux disease (5%), glossalgia (5%), oral mucosa ulcer (lip: 5%)
Genitourinary: Urinary tract infection (7%), dysuria (6%)

Hematologic & oncologic: Hematoma (5%), pancytopenia (5%), thrombocythemia (5%)
Hepatic: Ascites (10%), increased serum AST (10%), decreased serum bilirubin (5%)
Hypersensitivity: Transfusion reaction (7%)
Infection: Candidiasis (10%), bacteremia (5% to 8%), staphylococcal infection (7%), tooth abscess (5%)
Local: Catheter infection (8%), catheter pain (5%), swelling at injection site (5%)
Neuromuscular & skeletal: Myalgia (5% to 9%), muscle spasm (7%), ostealgia (6%), musculoskeletal discomfort (≤5% to 6%), musculoskeletal pain (≤5% to 6%), crepitations (5%)
Ophthalmic: Blurred vision (6%)
Otic: Otalgia (6%)
Renal: Polyuria (5%)
Respiratory: Hypoxia (10%), upper respiratory tract infection (10%), abnormal breath sounds (5% to 10%), pharyngolaryngeal pain (8%), pulmonary edema (6%), sinusitis (5% to 6%), pleural effusion (5%), post nasal drip (5%), sinus congestion (5%)

<5%, postmarketing, and/or case reports: Abscess (peridiverticular), acute cardiorespiratory failure, anaphylaxis, atrial fibrillation, cardiomyopathy, catheter site hemorrhage, cholecystitis, fungal infection, gastrointestinal hemorrhage, gingival pain, hemoptysis, hypersensitivity reaction, intracranial hemorrhage, mental status change, myocardial infarction, mycobacterium avium complex, pseudomonal lung infection, pulmonary aspergillosis, pulmonary embolism, pulmonary infiltrates, pulmonary mass, renal failure, sepsis, splenomegaly, supraventricular tachycardia, Sweet's syndrome (acute febrile neutrophilic dermatosis), urethral bleeding

General Dosage Range Dosage adjustment recommended in patients who develop toxicities

IV: *Adults:* 15 mg/m^2 every 8 hours for 3 days every 6 weeks **or** 20 mg/m^2 daily for 5 days every 28 days

Mechanism of Action After phosphorylation, decitabine is incorporated into DNA and inhibits DNA methyltransferase causing hypomethylation and subsequent cell death (within the S-phase of the cell cycle).

Pharmacodynamics/Kinetics

Half-life Elimination ~30 to 35 minutes

Pregnancy Risk Factor D

Pregnancy Considerations Adverse events were observed in animal reproduction studies. Based on the mechanism of action, decitabine may cause fetal harm if administered during pregnancy. Women of childbearing potential should be advised to use effective contraception to avoid pregnancy during treatment and for 1 month after treatment. In addition, males should be advised to avoid fathering a child while on decitabine therapy and for 2 months after treatment.

Deferasirox (de FER a sir ox)

Brand Names: US Exjade; Jadenu

Brand Names: Canada Exjade; Jadenu

Pharmacologic Category Chelating Agent

Use

Chronic iron overload due to transfusions: Treatment of chronic iron overload caused by blood transfusions (transfusional hemosiderosis) in patients 2 years and older.

Chronic iron overload in nontransfusion-dependent thalassemia syndromes: Treatment of chronic iron overload in patients 10 years and older with nontransfusion-dependent thalassemia syndromes and with a liver iron concentration (LIC) of at least 5 mg of iron per gram of liver dry weight (mg Fe/g dw) and a serum ferritin greater than 300 mcg/L

Limitations of use: Safety and efficacy of deferasirox in combination with other iron chelation therapies have not been established. Controlled studies of deferasirox in myelodysplastic syndromes and chronic iron overload due to transfusions have not been conducted.

Local Anesthetic/Vasoconstrictor Precautions No information available to require special precautions

Effects on Dental Treatment No significant effects or complications reported

Effects on Bleeding Thrombocytopenia (<1%) has been reported.

Adverse Reactions

>10%:
Dermatologic: Skin rash (dose related; 6% to 11%)
Gastrointestinal: Abdominal pain (dose related; 21% to 28%), nausea (dose related; 11% to 23%), vomiting (dose related; 10% to 21%), diarrhea (dose related; 5% to 20%)
Genitourinary: Proteinuria (19%)
Renal: Increased serum creatinine (dose related; 2% to 38%)

1% to 10%: Hepatic: Increased serum ALT (2% to 8%)

Frequency not defined:
Central nervous system: Headache (Phatak 2010; Vichinsky 2007)
Gastrointestinal: Constipation (Vichinsky 2007)
Hepatic: Increased serum bilirubin (Vichinsky 2007)
Infection: Viral infection (Vichinsky 2007)
Neuromuscular & skeletal: Arthralgia (Vichinsky 2007), back pain (Vichinsky 2007)
Respiratory: Cough (Vichinsky 2007), nasopharyngitis (Vichinsky 2007), pharyngitis (Vichinsky 2007), respiratory tract infection (Vichinsky 2007)

<1%, postmarketing, and/or case reports: Abnormal hepatic function tests, acute pancreatitis, acute renal failure, agranulocytosis, alopecia, anaphylaxis, anemia (worsening), angioedema, anxiety, cataract, cholelithiasis, dizziness, drug fever, duodenal ulcer, dyschromia, edema, erythema multiforme, esophagitis, Fanconi syndrome, fatigue, fever, gastric ulcer, gastritis, gastrointestinal hemorrhage, gastrointestinal perforation, glycosuria, hearing loss (including high frequency), hepatic failure, hepatic insufficiency, hepatitis, hyperactivity, hypersensitivity angiitis, hypersensitivity reaction, IgA vasculitis, increased intraocular pressure, insomnia, interstitial nephritis, maculopathy, neutropenia, nontuberculous mycobacterial infection, optic neuritis, pancreatitis (associated with gallstones), pharyngolaryngeal pain, purpura, renal tubular disease, renal tubular necrosis, retinopathy, sleep disorder, Stevens-Johnson syndrome, thrombocytopenia, toxic epidermal necrolysis, urticaria, visual disturbance

General Dosage Range Dosage adjustment recommended in patients with renal or hepatic impairment, on concomitant therapy, or who develop toxicities

Oral:
Exjade: *Children ≥2 years, Adolescents, and Adults:* Initial: 20 mg/kg once daily; Maintenance (usual): 20 to 30 mg/kg once daily (maximum: 40 mg/kg/day)
Jadenu: Children ≥2 years, Adolescents, and Adults: Initial: 7 mg/kg once daily; Maintenance (usual): 7 to 14 mg/kg once daily (maximum: 28 mg/kg/day)

Mechanism of Action Selectively binds iron, forming a complex that is excreted primarily through the feces.

Pharmacodynamics/Kinetics

Half-life Elimination 8 to 16 hours

Time to Peak Plasma: Tablets and tablets for oral suspension: ~1.5 to 4 hours

Pregnancy Risk Factor C

Pregnancy Considerations Adverse events were observed in animal reproduction studies. Information related to the use of deferasirox in pregnant women is limited (Vini 2011).

Deferiprone (de FER i prone)

Brand Names: US Ferriprox

Pharmacologic Category Chelating Agent

Use

Transfusional iron overload: Treatment of transfusional iron overload due to thalassemia syndromes with inadequate response to other chelation therapy.

Limitation of use: Safety and effectiveness have not been established for the treatment of transfusional iron overload in patients with other chronic anemias.

Local Anesthetic/Vasoconstrictor Precautions Deferiprone is one of the drugs confirmed to prolong the QT interval and is accepted as having a risk of causing torsade de pointes. The risk of drug-induced torsade de pointes is extremely low when a single QT interval prolonging drug is prescribed. In terms of epinephrine, it is not known what effect vasoconstrictors in the local anesthetic regimen will have in patients with a known history of congenital prolonged QT interval or in patients taking any medication that prolongs the QT interval. Until more information is obtained, it is suggested that the clinician consult with the physician prior to the use of a vasoconstrictor in suspected patients, and that the vasoconstrictor (epinephrine, mepivacaine and levonordefrin [Carbocaine® 2% with Neo-Cobefrin®]) be used with caution.

Effects on Dental Treatment No significant effects or complications reported

Effects on Bleeding No information available to require special precautions

Adverse Reactions

>10%:

Gastrointestinal: Nausea (13%)

Genitourinary: Urine discoloration (15%)

1% to 10%:

Central nervous system: Headache (3%)

Gastrointestinal: Vomiting (10%), abdominal distress (≤10%), abdominal pain (≤10%), increased appetite (4%), diarrhea (3%), dyspepsia (2%), weight gain (2%), decreased appetite (1%)

Hematologic & oncologic: Neutropenia (6% to 7%), agranulocytosis (2%)

Hepatic: Increased serum ALT (8%), increased serum AST (1%)

Neuromuscular and skeletal: Arthralgia (10%), back pain (2%), limb pain (2%), arthropathy (1%)

<1%, postmarketing, and/or case reports: Abnormal gait, acute respiratory distress, anaphylactic shock, atrial fibrillation, bruxism, cardiac failure, cartilage disease, cerebellar syndrome, cerebral hemorrhage, chills, cryptococcosis (cutaneous infection), decreased serum zinc, dehydration, depression, diaphoresis, diplopia, drowsiness, encephalitis (enteroviral), enterocolitis, epistaxis, fever, furuncle, gastric ulcer, glycosuria, hemoglobinuria, hemoptysis, hepatitis A, hepatomegaly, hypersensitivity reaction, hypertension, hypospadias, hypotension, IgA vasculitis, increased creatine phosphokinase, increased intracranial pressure, increased serum bilirubin, jaundice, metabolic acidosis, multi-organ failure, myositis, obsessive compulsive disorder, pancreatitis, pancytopenia, papilledema, parotid gland enlargement, periorbital edema, peripheral edema, pharyngitis, pneumonia, pruritus, psychomotor disturbance, pulmonary embolism, pustular rash, pyramidal tract syndrome, rectal hemorrhage, retinal toxicity, seizure, sepsis, skin photosensitivity, skin rash, subcutaneous abscess, thrombocythemia, torsades de pointes, trismus, urticaria

General Dosage Range Oral: *Adults:* 25 to 33 mg/kg 3 times/day (maximum: 99 mg/kg/day)

Mechanism of Action Iron-chelating agent with affinity for ferric ion (iron III); binds to ferric ion and forms a 3:1 (deferiprone:iron) complex which is excreted in the urine. Has a lower affinity for other metals such as copper, aluminum, and zinc.

Pharmacodynamics/Kinetics

Half-life Elimination ~2 hours

Time to Peak ~1-2 hours

Pregnancy Risk Factor D

Pregnancy Considerations Adverse effects have been observed in animal reproduction studies. Although there is limited data in humans, deferiprone may cause fetal harm if administered during pregnancy. During treatment with deferiprone in women of reproductive potential, pregnancy should be avoided.

Dental Comment See Local Anesthetic/Vasoconstrictor Precautions

Deferoxamine (de fer OKS a meen)

Brand Names: US Desferal

Brand Names: Canada Deferoxamine Mesylate for Injection; Desferal; PMS-Deferoxamine

Pharmacologic Category Antidote; Chelating Agent

Use Adjunct in the treatment of acute iron intoxication; treatment of chronic iron overload secondary to multiple transfusions

Local Anesthetic/Vasoconstrictor Precautions No information available to require special precautions

Effects on Dental Treatment No significant effects or complications reported

Effects on Bleeding No information available to require special precautions

Adverse Reactions Frequency not defined.

Cardiovascular: Flushing, hypotension, shock, tachycardia

Central nervous system: Brain disease (aluminum toxicity/dialysis-related), dizziness, headache, neuropathy (peripheral, sensory, motor, or mixed), paresthesia, seizure

Dermatologic: Skin rash, urticaria

Endocrine & metabolic: Growth suppression (children), hyperparathyroidism (aggravated), hypocalcemia

Gastrointestinal: Abdominal distress, abdominal pain, diarrhea, nausea, vomiting

Genitourinary: Dysuria, urine discoloration (reddish color)

Hematologic & oncologic: Dysplasia (metaphyseal; children <3 years; dose related), leukopenia, thrombocytopenia

Hepatic: Hepatic insufficiency, increased serum transaminases

Hypersensitivity: Anaphylaxis (with or without shock), angioedema, hypersensitivity

Infection: Infection (*Yersinia*, mucormycosis)

Local: Injection site reaction (burning, crust, edema, erythema, eschar, induration, infiltration, irritation, pain, pruritus, swelling, vesicles, wheal formation)

Neuromuscular & skeletal: Arthralgia, muscle spasm, myalgia

Ophthalmic: Blurred vision, cataract, chromatopsia, corneal opacity, decreased peripheral vision, decreased visual acuity, nocturnal amblyopia, optic neuritis, retinal pigment changes, scotoma, vision loss, visual field defect

Otic: Hearing loss, tinnitus

Renal: Acute renal failure, increased serum creatinine, renal tubular disease

Respiratory: Acute respiratory distress (dyspnea, cyanosis, and/or interstitial infiltrates), asthma

Miscellaneous: Fever

General Dosage Range Dosage adjustment recommended in patients with renal impairment

IM:

Children and Adolescents: 90 mg/kg/dose every 8 hours (maximum: 6,000 mg/24 hours)

Adults: Initial: 1,000 mg, followed by 500 mg every 4 hours for 2 doses; Maintenance: 500 mg every 4 to 12 hours **or** 500 to 1000 mg once daily (maximum: 6,000 mg/day)

IV:

Children and Adolescents: 20 to 40 mg/kg/day 5 to 7 days per week; dose should not exceed 40 mg/kg/day until growth has ceased

Adults: Initial: 1,000 mg, followed by 500 mg every 4 hours for 2 doses; Maintenance: 500 mg every 4 to 12 hours (maximum: 6,000 mg/day) **or** 40 to 50 mg/kg/day (maximum: 60 mg/kg/day) 5 to 7 days per week

SubQ:

Children ≥3 years and Adolescents: 20 to 40 mg/kg/day (maximum: 1,000 to 2,000 mg/day)

Adults: 1,000 to 2,000 mg/day **or** 20 to 40 mg/kg/day

Mechanism of Action Complexes with trivalent ions (ferric ions), primarily in the vascular space, to form ferrioxamine, which is eliminated in the urine by the kidneys. One hundred milligrams of deferoxamine will bind about 8.5 mg of free circulating elemental iron (85 mg per 1,000 mg dose) but does not remove iron from transferrin or hemoglobin. Binding of cytoplasmic free iron reduces the free iron-induced disruption of mitochondrial cell membranes and enzyme systems. Ferrioxamine may create a pink- to red- or orange-colored urine as it is being excreted.

Pharmacodynamics/Kinetics

Half-life Elimination 14 hours; plasma: 20 to 30 minutes (Brittenham 2011)

Pregnancy Risk Factor C

Pregnancy Considerations Adverse events have been observed in animal reproduction studies. Toxic amounts of iron or deferoxamine have not been noted to cross the placenta; however, the metabolic effects of a maternal overdose may adversely affect the fetus. In case of acute iron toxicity, treatment during pregnancy should not be withheld (Chang 2011).

Defibrotide (DE fib ro tide)

Brand Names: US Defitelio

Pharmacologic Category Antiplatelet Agent; Thrombolytic Agent

Use Hepatic sinusoidal obstruction syndrome (treatment): Treatment of hepatic sinusoidal obstruction syndrome (SOS; formerly called veno-occlusive disease [VOD]) with renal or pulmonary dysfunction following hematopoietic stem cell transplant (HSCT).

Local Anesthetic/Vasoconstrictor Precautions No information available to require special precautions

Effects on Dental Treatment Key adverse event(s) related to dental treatment: Increased bleeding with invasive procedures (see Effects on Bleeding)

Effects on Bleeding Defibrotide has antiplatelet and fibrinolytic properties; expect increased bleeding with invasive dental procedures; medical consult is recommended

Adverse Reactions

>10%:

Cardiovascular: Hypotension (11% to 37%)

Gastrointestinal: Diarrhea (24%), vomiting (18%), nausea (16%)

Hematologic & oncologic: Hemorrhage (59%; any type)

Respiratory: Epistaxis (14%)

1% to 10%:

Central nervous system: Intracranial hemorrhage (3%), cerebral hemorrhage (2%)

Endocrine & metabolic: Hyperuricemia (2%)

Gastrointestinal: Gastrointestinal hemorrhage (9%)

Hematologic & oncologic: Pulmonary hemorrhage (4%)

Hypersensitivity: Hypersensitivity reaction (<2%)

Immunologic: Graft versus host disease (6%)

Infection: Sepsis (7%), infection (3%)

Respiratory: Pulmonary alveolar hemorrhage (7% to 9%), pulmonary infiltrates (6%), pneumonia (5%)

Frequency not defined:

Cardiovascular: Thrombophlebitis

Endocrine & metabolic: Hot flash

Gastrointestinal: Abdominal cramps, abdominal pain, bloody diarrhea, hematemesis

Genitourinary: Hematuria

Hematologic & oncologic: Oral hemorrhage

Renal: Renal failure

Miscellaneous: Fever

Mechanism of Action Defibrotide augments plasmin enzymatic activity to hydrolyze fibrin clots. It reduces endothelial cell (EC) activation and increases EC-mediated fibrinolysis by increasing tissue plasminogen activator and thrombomodulin expression, as well as by decreasing von Willebrand factor and plasminogen activator inhibitor-1 expression.

Pharmacodynamics/Kinetics

Half-life Elimination <2 hours

Pregnancy Considerations Adverse effects have been observed in animal reproduction studies.

Product Availability

Defitelio: FDA approved March 2016; anticipated availability is currently unknown.

Deflazacort (de FLAZE a kort)

Brand Names: US Emflaza

Pharmacologic Category Corticosteroid, Systemic

Use Duchenne muscular dystrophy: Treatment of Duchenne muscular dystrophy (DMD) in patients ≥5 years of age

Local Anesthetic/Vasoconstrictor Precautions No information available to require special precautions

Effects on Dental Treatment No significant effects or complications reported

Effects on Bleeding No information available to require special precautions

Adverse Reactions

>10%:

Dermatologic: Erythema (8% to 28%)

Endocrine & metabolic: Cushingoid appearance (33% to 60%), hirsutism (10% to 35%), weight gain (20% to 28%), obesity (central, 10% to 25%)
Gastrointestinal: Abdominal pain (including upper abdominal pain: 18%), increased appetite (14%)
Genitourinary: Pollakiuria (12% to 15%)
Respiratory: Cough (12%), upper respiratory tract infection (12%)

1% to 10%:

Cardiovascular: Cardiac arrhythmia (≥1%)
Central nervous system: Irritability (8% to 10%), abnormal behavior (9%), psychomotor agitation (6%), aggressive behavior (≥1%), depression (≥1%), dizziness (≥1%), emotional disturbance (≥1%), emotional lability (≥1%), heat exhaustion (≥1%), hypertonia (≥1%, hypertonic bladder), insomnia (≥1%), mood changes (≥1%), sleep disorder (≥1%)
Dermatologic: Skin rash (7%), atrophic striae (6%), acneiform eruption (≥1%), acne vulgaris (≥1%), alopecia (≥1%), impetigo (≥1%)
Endocrine & metabolic: Glycosuria (≥1%), hot flash (≥1%), increased thirst (≥1%)
Gastrointestinal: Constipation (10%), abdominal distress (6%), nausea (6%), dyspepsia (≥1%), gastrointestinal disease (≥1%)
Genitourinary: Dysuria (≥1%), testicular pain (≥1%), urinary tract infection (≥1%), urine discoloration (≥1%)
Hematologic & oncologic: Bruise (6%)
Infection: Influenza (≥1%), tooth abscess (≥1%), viral infection (≥1%)
Neuromuscular & skeletal: Back pain (7%), back injury (≥1%), limb pain (≥1%), muscle spasm (≥1%), myalgia (≥1%), neck pain (≥1%)
Ophthalmic: Hordeolum (≥1%), increased lacrimation (≥1%)
Otic: Otitis externa (≥1%)
Respiratory: Nasopharyngitis (10%), rhinorrhea (8%), epistaxis (6%), hypoventilation (≥1%), pharyngitis (≥1%)
Miscellaneous: Fever (9%), accidental injury (≥1%, face), mass (≥1%, neck)

Frequency not defined.

Central nervous system: Myasthenia (associated with long-term use)
Neuromuscular & skeletal: Bone fracture (long bones including the fibula as well as greenstick fractures), decreased bone mineral density, osteopenia (associated with long-term use), tendon disease (associated with long-term use)

<1%, postmarketing, and/or case reports: Abnormal serum calcium (negative calcium balance), acute pancreatitis (especially in children), acute peptic ulcer with hemorrhage and perforation, amyotrophy, anaphylaxis, anxiety, avascular necrosis of bones, carbohydrate intolerance, change in serum protein (negative protein balance), chorioretinitis, cognitive dysfunction (including confusion, amnesia, delusions, hallucinations, mania, or suicidal thoughts), corneal thinning, decreased serum potassium, edema, exacerbation of epilepsy, hemorrhage, hypersensitivity, hypokalemic alkalosis, increased intracranial pressure (with papilledema in children), leukocytosis, negative nitrogen balance, peptic ulcer, pseudotumor cerebri, scleral thinning, thromboembolism (especially in patients with underlying conditions associated with increased thrombotic tendency), toxic epidermal necrolysis, vertebral compression fracture, vertigo, wound healing impairment

Mechanism of Action Concentration-dependent, anti-inflammatory and immunomodulatory effects from inhibition of leucocyte function; deflazacort has been shown to inhibit IL-1-beta-stimulated IL-6 production from human osteoblast-like cells and chondrocytes (Markham, 1994).

Pregnancy Considerations Deflazacort crosses the placenta. Orofacial clefts, intrauterine growth restriction, and decreased birth weight have been reported following maternal use. Hypoadrenalism may occur in newborns following maternal use of corticosteroids in pregnancy; monitor.

Product Availability Emflaza: FDA approved February 2017; anticipated availability is currently undetermined

Degarelix (deg a REL ix)

Brand Names: US Firmagon

Brand Names: Canada Firmagon

Pharmacologic Category Antineoplastic Agent, Gonadotropin-Releasing Hormone Antagonist; Gonadotropin Releasing Hormone Antagonist

Use Prostate cancer, advanced: Treatment of advanced prostate cancer

Local Anesthetic/Vasoconstrictor Precautions Degarelix may prolong QT interval; it is suggested that the clinician consult with the physician prior to use of vasoconstrictor in suspected patients; use vasoconstrictor (epinephrine, mepivacaine and levonordefrin [Carbocaine® 2% with Neo Cobefrin®]) with caution.

Effects on Dental Treatment No significant effects or complications reported

Effects on Bleeding No information available to require special precautions

Adverse Reactions

>10%:

Central nervous system: Fatigue (3% to ≥10%)
Endocrine & metabolic: Hot flash (26%), increased gamma-glutamyl transferase (≥10%), weight loss (≥10%), weight gain (9% to ≥10%)
Hepatic: Increased serum transaminases (47%)
Local: Injection site reactions (35%, grade 3: ≤2%; pain at injection site [28%], erythema at injection site [17%], swelling at injection site [6%], induration at injection site [4%], injection site nodule [3%], injection site infection [including abscess, 1%])
Miscellaneous: Fever (1% to ≥10%)

1% to 10%:

Cardiovascular: Hypertension (6%)
Central nervous system: Chills (5%), dizziness (1% to 5%), headache (1% to 5%), insomnia (1% to 5%)
Dermatologic: Diaphoresis
Endocrine & metabolic: Hypercholesterolemia (3%), gynecomastia
Gastrointestinal: Constipation (5%), nausea (1% to 5%), diarrhea
Genitourinary: Urinary tract infection (5%), erectile dysfunction, testicular atrophy
Hepatic: Increased serum ALT (10%; grade 3: <1%), increased serum AST (5%; grade 3: <1%)
Immunologic: Antibody development (antidegarelix: 10%)
Neuromuscular & skeletal: Back pain (6%), arthralgia (5%), weakness (1% to 5%)
Miscellaneous: Night sweats (1% to 5%)

<1%, postmarketing, and/or case reports: Bone metastases (worsening), cerebrovascular accident, depression, hypersensitivity reaction (including anaphylaxis, urticaria, and angioedema), itching at injection site,

local soreness/soreness at injection site, malignant lymphoma, mental status changes, myocardial infarction, osteoarthritis, prolonged Q-T interval on ECG, squamous cell carcinoma, unstable angina pectoris

General Dosage Range SubQ: *Adults:* Loading dose: 240 mg; Maintenance dose: 80 mg every 28 days

Mechanism of Action Gonadotropin-releasing hormone (GnRH) antagonist which reversibly binds to GnRH receptors in the anterior pituitary gland, blocking the receptor and decreasing secretion of luteinizing hormone (LH) and follicle stimulation hormone (FSH), resulting in rapid androgen deprivation by decreasing testosterone production, thereby decreasing testosterone levels. Testosterone levels do not exhibit an initial surge, or flare, as is typical with GnRH agonists (Crawford 2011).

Pharmacodynamics/Kinetics

Onset of Action Rapid; ~96% of patients had testosterone levels ≤50 ng/dL within 3 days (Klotz 2008)

Half-life Elimination Loading dose: SubQ: ~53 days; Maintenance dose: SubQ: ~31 days (Canadian labeling)

Time to Peak Plasma: Loading dose: SubQ: Within 2 days

Pregnancy Risk Factor X

Pregnancy Considerations

Use is contraindicated in women who are or may become pregnant.

Adverse events were observed in animal reproduction studies.

Dental Comment See Local Anesthetic/Vasoconstrictor Precautions

Delavirdine (de la VIR deen)

Related Information

HIV Infection and AIDS *on page 1785*

Brand Names: US Rescriptor

Brand Names: Canada Rescriptor

Pharmacologic Category Antiretroviral, Reverse Transcriptase Inhibitor, Non-nucleoside (Anti-HIV)

Use Treatment of HIV-1 infection in combination with at least two additional antiretroviral agents

Local Anesthetic/Vasoconstrictor Precautions No information available to require special precautions

Effects on Dental Treatment No significant effects or complications reported

Effects on Bleeding No reports of bleeding or thrombocytopenia.

Adverse Reactions

Frequency not always defined. Frequency of adverse reactions reported from occurrence in clinical trials with delavirdine when used as part of combination antiretroviral therapy.

Cardiovascular: Cardiac arrhythmia, cardiac insufficiency, cardiac rate disturbance, cardiomyopathy, hypersensitivity angiitis, hypertension, orthostatic hypotension, peripheral vascular disease

Central nervous system: Headache (19% to 20%), depression (10% to 15%), anxiety (6% to 8%), cognitive dysfunction, confusion, emotional lability, hallucination, paralysis, vertigo

Dermatologic: Skin rash (16% to 32%), desquamation, erythema multiforme, fungal dermatitis, Stevens-Johnson syndrome

Endocrine & metabolic: Increased serum transaminases (2% to 5%), increased amylase (3%), increased serum bilirubin (2%), hyperglycemia, hyperkalemia, hypertriglyceridemia, hyperuricemia, hypocalcemia, hyponatremia, hypophosphatemia, increased gamma-glutamyl transferase, menstrual disease, redistribution of body fat

Gastrointestinal: Nausea (20% to 25%), vomiting (3% to 11%), abdominal pain (4% to 6%), anorexia, bloody stools, colitis, diarrhea, diverticulitis, fecal incontinence, gastroenteritis, gastrointestinal hemorrhage, gingival hemorrhage, increased serum lipase, pancreatitis, vomiting

Genitourinary: Hematuria, urinary tract infection

Hematologic & oncologic: Decreased hemoglobin (1% to 3%), prolonged prothrombin time (2%), adenopathy, bruise, eosinophilia, granulocytosis, leukopenia, pancytopenia, purpura, spleen disease, thrombocytopenia

Hepatic: Hepatomegaly, increased serum alkaline phosphatase, jaundice

Hypersensitivity: Angioedema, hypersensitivity reaction

Infection: Abscess, candidiasis (oral/vaginal), infection

Neuromuscular & skeletal: Ostealgia, tetany

Ophthalmic: Conjunctivitis

Renal: Increased serum creatinine, nephrolithiasis, renal pain

Respiratory: Bronchitis (6% to 8%), chest congestion, dyspnea, pneumonia

Miscellaneous: Fever (4% to 12%)

<1%, postmarketing and/or case reports: Acute renal failure, hemolytic anemia, hepatic failure, immune reconstitution syndrome, rhabdomyolysis

General Dosage Range Oral: *Children ≥16 years and Adults:* 400 mg 3 times/day

Mechanism of Action Delavirdine binds directly to reverse transcriptase, blocking RNA-dependent and DNA-dependent DNA polymerase activities

Pharmacodynamics/Kinetics

Half-life Elimination 5.8 hours (range: 2-11 hours)

Time to Peak Plasma: 1 hour

Pregnancy Risk Factor C

Pregnancy Considerations Adverse events were observed in some animal reproduction studies. Hypersensitivity reactions (including hepatic toxicity and rash) are more common in women on NNRTI therapy; it is not known if pregnancy increases this risk.

Combination antiretroviral therapy (cART) therapy is recommended for all HIV-infected pregnant women. The goal of therapy is to keep the viral load below the limit of detection and prevent perinatal transmission. Therapy must be individualized. In general, women who become pregnant on a stable cART regimen may continue that regimen if viral suppression is effective, contraindications for use in pregnancy are not present, and the regimen is well tolerated. For HIV infected couples planning a pregnancy, maximum viral suppression with cART is recommended prior to conception for the HIV-infected partner(s). When HIV is diagnosed during pregnancy in a woman who has never received antiretroviral therapy, cART should be considered as soon as possible after diagnosis to reduce the risk of perinatal transmission. If antiretroviral drug-resistance testing is done, treatment may be started prior to obtaining results, then adjusted accordingly. Monitoring during pregnancy is more frequent than in non-pregnant adults. If cART must be interrupted for <24 hours, stop then restart all medications simultaneously in order to decrease the chance of developing resistance. Long-term follow-up is recommended for all infants exposed to antiretroviral medications; children who develop significant organ system abnormalities (particularly of the CNS or heart) should be evaluated for potential mitochondrial dysfunction.

HIV infected women not planning a pregnancy may use any available type of contraception, considering possible drug interactions and contraindications of the specific method. In addition, consistent use of condoms is also recommended (even during pregnancy) to prevent transmission of HIV or other sexually transmitted diseases.

Health care providers are encouraged to enroll pregnant women exposed to antiretroviral medications as early in pregnancy as possible in the Antiretroviral Pregnancy Registry (1-800-258-4263 or www.APRegistry.com). Health care providers caring for HIV-infected women and their infants may contact the National Perinatal HIV Hotline (888-448-8765) for clinical consultation (HHS [perinatal] 2016).

Delmopinol (del MOE pi nol)

Brand Names: US Decapinol

Pharmacologic Category Antibacterial, Oral Rinse

Local Anesthetic/Vasoconstrictor Precautions No information available to require special precautions

Effects on Dental Treatment No significant effects or complications reported

Mechanism of Action Reduces adhesion of plaque-causing bacteria, reducing the formation of new plaque and promoting the removal of deposits with normal mechanical disruption (brushing and flossing). Ultimately causes a reduction in both plaque and gingivitis. Decapinol® is regulated as a medical device because the primary mode of action is to serve as a physical barrier without chemical activity.

Pregnancy Risk Factor The manufacturer does not recommend use in pregnant women.

Demeclocycline (dem e kloe SYE kleen)

Pharmacologic Category Antibiotic, Tetracycline Derivative

Use

Note: Use of demeclocycline as an antibacterial agent is uncommon; alternative tetracycline agents (eg, doxycycline, minocycline, tetracycline) are generally preferred.

Acne: Adjunctive therapy in severe acne.

Actinomycosis: Treatment of actinomycosis caused by *Actinomyces israelii* when penicillin is contraindicated.

Acute intestinal amebiasis: Adjunct to amebicides in acute intestinal amebiasis.

Anthrax: Treatment of anthrax due to *Bacillus anthracis* when penicillin is contraindicated.

Cholera: Treatment of cholera caused by *Vibrio cholerae*.

Clostridium: Treatment of clostridial disease caused by *Clostridium* spp. when penicillin is contraindicated.

Gram-negative infections: Treatment of infections caused by *Escherichia coli*, *Enterobacter aerogenes*, *Shigella* species, and *Acinetobacter* species.

Listeriosis: Treatment of listeriosis due to *Listeria monocytogenes* when penicillin is contraindicated.

Ophthalmic infections: Treatment of inclusion conjunctivitis or trachoma caused by *Chlamydia trachomatis*.

Plague: Treatment of plague due to *Yersinia pestis*.

Relapsing fever: Treatment of relapsing fever caused by *Borrelia recurrentis*.

Respiratory tract infections: Treatment of respiratory tract infections caused by *Haemophilus influenzae*, *Klebsiella* species, or *Mycoplasma pneumoniae*; treatment of upper respiratory tract infections caused by *Streptococcus pneumoniae*.

Rickettsial infections: Treatment of Rocky Mountain spotted fever, typhus fever, and the typhus group, Q fever, rickettsialpox and tick fevers caused by *Rickettsiae*.

Sexually transmitted diseases:

Treatment of lymphogranuloma venereum caused by *Chlamydia trachomatis*; granuloma inguinale caused by *Klebsiella granulomatis*; chancroid caused by *Haemophilus ducreyi*; nongonococcal urethritis caused by *Ureaplasma urealyticum* or *Chlamydia trachomatis*; when penicillin is contraindicated, uncomplicated urethritis in men caused by *Neisseria gonorrhea* and other uncomplicated gonococcal infections, infections in women caused by *N. gonorrhea*, and syphilis caused by *Treponema pallidum* subspecies pallidum.

Demeclocycline is not a recommended alternative for gonorrhea according to the Centers for Disease Control and Prevention (CDC) sexually transmitted diseases guidelines. Consult current guidelines for recommendations (Workowski 2015).

Skin and skin structure infections: Treatment of skin and skin structure infections caused by *Staphylococcus aureus*.

Urinary tract infections: Treatment of urinary tract infections caused by *Klebsiella* species

Vincent infection: Treatment of Vincent infection caused by *Fusobacterium fusiforme* when penicillin is contraindicated.

Yaws: Treatment of yaws caused by *Treponema pallidum* subspecies pertenue when penicillin is contraindicated.

Zoonotic infections: Treatment of psittacosis (ornithosis) caused by *Chlamydophila psittaci*; tularemia caused by *Francisella tularensis*; brucellosis caused by *Brucella* species (in conjunction with streptomycin); bartonellosis caused by *Bartonella bacilliformis*; infections caused by *Campylobacter fetus*.

Local Anesthetic/Vasoconstrictor Precautions No information available to require special precautions

Effects on Dental Treatment Tetracyclines are not recommended for use during pregnancy or in children ≤8 years of age since they have been reported to cause enamel hypoplasia and permanent teeth discoloration. Tetracyclines should only be used in these patients if other agents are contraindicated or alternative antimicrobials will not eradicate the organism. Long-term use associated with oral candidiasis.

Effects on Bleeding No information available to require special precautions

Adverse Reactions Frequency not defined.

Cardiovascular: Pericarditis

Central nervous system: Bulging fontanel (infants), dizziness, headache, pseudotumor cerebri (adults)

Dermatologic: Erythema multiforme, erythematous rash, maculopapular rash, skin photosensitivity, skin pigmentation, urticaria

Endocrine & metabolic: Microscopic thyroid discoloration (brown/black), nephrogenic diabetes insipidus

Gastrointestinal: Anorexia, dental discoloration (children <8 years, rare in adults), diarrhea, dysphagia, enterocolitis, esophageal ulcer, glossitis, nausea, pancreatitis, vomiting

Genitourinary: Balanitis, inflammatory anogenital lesion (with monilial overgrowth)

Hematologic & oncologic: Eosinophilia, hemolytic anemia, IgA vasculitis, neutropenia, thrombocytopenia

Hepatic: Increased liver enzymes
Hypersensitivity: Anaphylaxis, angioedema
Infection: Superinfection
Neuromuscular & skeletal: Exacerbation of systemic lupus erythematosus, Lambert-Eaton syndrome, lupus-like syndrome, polyarthralgia
Ophthalmic: Visual disturbance
Otic: Tinnitus
Renal: Acute renal failure, increased blood urea nitrogen
Respiratory: Pulmonary infiltrates
<1%, postmarketing, and/or case reports: Exfoliative dermatitis, fixed drug eruption, hepatic failure, hepatitis, hepatotoxicity, Stevens-Johnson syndrome, thyroid dysfunction

General Dosage Range Dosage adjustment recommended in patients with renal and hepatic impairment

Oral:

Children >8 years and Adolescents: 7 to 13 mg/kg/day (maximum: 600 mg/day) divided every 6 to 12 hours

Adults: 600 mg/day in 2 or 4 divided doses

Mechanism of Action Inhibits protein synthesis by binding with the 30S and possibly the 50S ribosomal subunit(s) of susceptible bacteria; may also cause alterations in the cytoplasmic membrane; inhibits the action of ADH in patients with chronic SIADH

Pharmacodynamics/Kinetics

Onset of Action SIADH: 2 to 5 days (Sherlock 2010)

Half-life Elimination 10 to 16 hours

Time to Peak Serum: ~4 hours

Pregnancy Risk Factor D

Pregnancy Considerations Demeclocycline crosses the placenta (Gibbons 1960). Tetracyclines accumulate in developing teeth and long tubular bones (Mylonas 2011). Permanent discoloration of teeth (yellow, gray, brown) can occur following in utero exposure and is more likely to occur following long-term or repeated exposure.

As a class, tetracyclines are generally considered second-line antibiotics in pregnant women and their use should be avoided (Mylonas 2011). Demeclocycline is not recommended for the treatment of Rocky Mountain Spotted Fever (Biggs 2016), Q fever (Anderson 2013), or anthrax infection (Meaney-Delman 2014) in pregnant women. When systemic antibiotics are needed for dermatologic conditions in pregnant women, other agents are preferred (Kong 2013; Murase 2014).

Denosumab (den OH sue mab)

Related Information

Osteonecrosis of the Jaw *on page* *1796*

Brand Names: US Prolia; Xgeva

Brand Names: Canada Prolia; Xgeva

Generic Availability (US) No

Pharmacologic Category Bone-Modifying Agent; Monoclonal Antibody

Use

Hypercalcemia of malignancy (Xgeva): Treatment of hypercalcemia of malignancy refractory to bisphosphonate therapy

Osteoporosis/bone loss (Prolia): Treatment of osteoporosis in postmenopausal women at high risk of fracture; treatment of osteoporosis (to increase bone mass) in men at high risk of fracture; treatment of bone loss in men receiving androgen-deprivation therapy (ADT) for nonmetastatic prostate cancer; treatment of bone loss in women receiving aromatase inhibitor (AI) therapy for breast cancer

Tumors (Xgeva): Prevention of skeletal-related events (eg, fracture, spinal cord compression, bone pain requiring surgery/radiation therapy) in patients with bone metastases from solid tumors; treatment of giant cell tumor of the bone in adults and skeletally mature adolescents that is unresectable or where surgical resection is likely to result in severe morbidity

Limitation of use: Denosumab is NOT indicated for prevention of skeletal-related events in patients with multiple myeloma

Local Anesthetic/Vasoconstrictor Precautions No information available to require special precautions

Effects on Dental Treatment Cases of osteonecrosis of the jaw bone (ONJ) have been associated with denosumab exposure. ONJ presents clinically as exposed necrotic bone of at least 8 weeks duration with or without the presence of pain, infection, or previous trauma in a patient who has not received radiation to the jaws. Since ONJ is also associated with bisphosphonate exposure, and osteoclasts are the common targets of bisphosphonates and denosumab, osteoclastic inhibition may play a central role in ONJ associated with these two classes of drugs. Patients developing ONJ while on denosumab therapy should receive care by an oral surgeon. See Warnings/Precautions and Dental Comment.

Effects on Bleeding No information available to require special precautions

Adverse Reactions A postmarketing safety program for Prolia is available to collect information on adverse events; more information is available at http://www.proliasafety.com. To report adverse events for either Prolia or Xgeva, prescribers may also call Amgen at 800-772-6436 or FDA at 800-332-1088.

Percentages noted with Prolia (60 mg every 6 months) unless specified as Xgeva (120 mg every 4 weeks):

>10%:
Cardiovascular: Hypertension (11%, Lewiecki 2007)
Central nervous system: Fatigue (Xgeva: ≤45%), headache (Xgeva: 13% to 24%), peripheral edema (5%; Xgeva: 24%)
Dermatologic: Dermatitis (4% to 11%), eczema (4% to 11%), skin rash (3% to 11%)
Endocrine & metabolic: Hypophosphatemia (Xgeva: 32%; grade 3: 10% to 15%), hypocalcemia (2%; Xgeva: 3% to 18%; grade 3: 3%)
Gastrointestinal: Nausea (Xgeva: 31%), decreased appetite (Xgeva: 24%), vomiting (Xgeva: 24%), constipation (Xgeva: 21%), diarrhea (Xgeva: 20%)
Hematologic & oncologic: Anemia (Xgeva: 21%)
Infection: Influenza (11%, Lewiecki 2007)
Neuromuscular & skeletal: Weakness (Xgeva: ≤45%), arthralgia (7% to 14%), limb pain (10% to 12%), back pain (8% to 12%)
Respiratory: Dyspnea (Xgeva: 21% to 27%), cough (Xgeva: 15%)

1% to 10%:
Cardiovascular: Angina pectoris (3%)
Central nervous system: Sciatica (5%)
Endocrine & metabolic: Hypercholesterolemia (7%)
Gastrointestinal: Flatulence (2%)
Hematologic & oncologic: Malignant neoplasm (new; 3% to 5%)
Infection: Serious infection (4%)
Neuromuscular & skeletal: Musculoskeletal pain (6%), ostealgia (4%), myalgia (3%), osteonecrosis (jaw; ≤2%; Xgeva ≤2%)
Ophthalmic: Cataract (≤5%)
Respiratory: Nasopharyngitis (7%), upper respiratory tract infection (5%)

<1%, postmarketing, and/or case reports: Anaphylaxis (both formulations), antibody development (both formulations), endocarditis, erythema, facial swelling, femur fracture (both formulations; diaphyseal, subtrochanteric), hearing loss (FDA Safety Alert June 6, 2016), hypercalcemia (Xgeva, following discontinuation), hypersensitivity (both formulations), hypotension, pancreatitis, severe hypocalcemia (symptomatic; both formulations), urticaria

Dosing

Adult & Geriatric Note: Administer calcium and vitamin D as necessary to prevent or treat hypocalcemia

Hypercalcemia of malignancy (Xgeva): SubQ: 120 mg every 4 weeks; during the first month, give an additional 120 mg on days 8 and 15 (Hu 2014)

Prevention of skeletal-related events in bone metastases from solid tumors (Xgeva): SubQ: 120 mg every 4 weeks (Fizazi 2011; Henry 2011; Stopeck 2010)

Treatment of androgen deprivation-induced bone loss in men with prostate cancer (Prolia): SubQ: 60 mg as a single dose, once every 6 months (Smith 2009)

Treatment of aromatase inhibitor-induced bone loss in women with breast cancer (Prolia): SubQ: 60 mg as a single dose, once every 6 months (Ellis 2008)

Treatment of giant cell tumor of the bone (Xgeva): SubQ: 120 mg once every 4 weeks; during the first month, give an additional 120 mg on days 8 and 15 (Blay 2011; Thomas 2010)

Treatment of osteoporosis in men or postmenopausal women (Prolia): SubQ: 60 mg as a single dose, once every 6 months

Bone destruction caused by rheumatoid arthritis (off-label use): SubQ: 60 mg or 180 mg as a single one time dose and repeated at 6 months (in combination with continued methotrexate); a total of 2 doses was administered in the study (Cohen 2008). Additional data may be necessary to further define the role of denosumab in this condition.

Pediatric Note: Administer calcium and vitamin D as necessary to prevent or treat hypocalcemia

Treatment of giant cell tumor of the bone (Xgeva): Adolescents (skeletally mature) 13 to 17 years: SubQ: 120 mg once every 4 weeks; during the first month, give an additional 120 mg on days 8 and 15

Renal Impairment Monitor patients with severe impairment (CrCl <30 mL/minute or on dialysis) closely due to increased risk of hypocalcemia.

Prolia: No dosage adjustment necessary.

Xgeva: There are no dosage adjustments provided in the manufacturer's labeling. Guidelines suggest dosage adjustment is not necessary; close monitoring for hypocalcemia is recommended (Gravalos 2016; Van Poznak 2011).

Hepatic Impairment There are no dosage adjustments provided in the manufacturer's labeling (has not been studied).

Mechanism of Action Denosumab is a monoclonal antibody with affinity for nuclear factor-kappa ligand (RANKL). Osteoblasts secrete RANKL; RANKL activates osteoclast precursors and subsequent osteolysis which promotes release of bone-derived growth factors, such as insulin-like growth factor-1 (IGF1) and transforming growth factor-beta (TGF-beta), and increases serum calcium levels. Denosumab binds to RANKL, blocks the interaction between RANKL and RANK (a receptor located on osteoclast surfaces), and prevents osteoclast formation, leading to decreased bone resorption and increased bone mass in osteoporosis. In solid tumors with bony metastases, RANKL inhibition decreases osteoclastic activity leading to decreased skeletal related events and tumor-induced bone destruction. In giant cell tumors of the bone (which express RANK and RANKL), denosumab inhibits tumor growth by preventing RANKL from activating its receptor (RANK) on the osteoclast surface, osteoclast precursors, and osteoclast-like giant cells.

Contraindications Hypersensitivity to denosumab or any component of the formulation; preexisting hypocalcemia; pregnancy (Prolia only)

Warnings/Precautions Clinically significant hypersensitivity (including anaphylaxis) has been reported. May include throat tightness, facial edema, upper airway edema, lip swelling, dyspnea, pruritus, rash, urticaria, and hypotension. If anaphylaxis or clinically significant hypersensitivity occurs, initiate appropriate management and permanently discontinue. Denosumab may cause or exacerbate hypocalcemia; severe symptomatic cases (including fatalities) have been reported. An increased risk has been observed with increasing renal dysfunction, most commonly severe dysfunction (creatinine clearance <30 mL/minute and/or on dialysis), and with inadequate/no calcium supplementation. Monitor calcium levels; correct preexisting hypocalcemia prior to therapy. Monitor levels more frequently when denosumab is administered with other drugs that can also lower calcium levels. Use caution in patients with a history of hypoparathyroidism, thyroid surgery, parathyroid surgery, malabsorption syndromes, excision of small intestine, severe renal impairment/dialysis, or other conditions which would predispose the patient to hypocalcemia; monitor calcium, phosphorus, and magnesium closely during therapy (the manufacturer recommends monitoring within 14 days of injection [Prolia] or during the first weeks of therapy initiation [Xgeva]). Hypocalcemia lasting weeks to months (and requiring frequent monitoring) has been reported in postmarketing analyses. Administer calcium, vitamin D, and magnesium as necessary. Patients with severe renal impairment (CrCl <30 mL/minute) or those on dialysis may also develop marked elevations of serum parathyroid hormone (PTH). Hypercalcemia (clinically significant) may occur in patients with growing skeletons weeks to months following discontinuation of denosumab therapy. Monitor for signs/symptoms of hypercalcemia (eg, nausea, vomiting, headache, decreased alertness) and treat accordingly. Incidence of infections may be increased, including serious skin infections, abdominal, urinary, ear, or periodontal infections. Endocarditis has also been reported following use. Patients should be advised to contact their healthcare provider if signs or symptoms of severe infection or cellulitis develop. Use with caution in patients with impaired immune systems or using concomitant immunosuppressive therapy; may be at increased risk for serious infections. Evaluate the need for continued treatment with serious infection.

Atypical femur fractures have been reported in patients receiving denosumab. The fractures may occur anywhere along the femoral shaft (may be bilateral) and commonly occur with minimal to no trauma to the area. Some patients experience prodromal pain weeks or months before the fracture occurs. Because these fractures also occur in osteoporosis patients not treated with denosumab, it is unclear if denosumab therapy is the cause for the fractures; concomitant glucocorticoids may contribute to fracture risk. Advise patients to report new/unusual hip, thigh, or groin pain; and if so, evaluate for atypical/incomplete fracture. Contralateral limb should be assessed if atypical fracture occurs. Consider interrupting therapy in patients who develop an atypical femoral fracture. Following treatment discontinuation (in patients being treated for osteoporosis), the fracture risk increases, including risk of multiple vertebral fractures; vertebral fractures occurred as early as 7 months (average: 19 months) after the last dose of denosumab. Evaluate benefit/risk before initiating denosumab treatment for osteoporosis, especially in patients with prior vertebral fracture. If denosumab is discontinued, consider transitioning to an alternative osteoporosis therapy.

Osteonecrosis of the jaw (ONJ), also referred to as medication-related osteonecrosis of the jaw (MRONJ), has been reported in patients receiving denosumab. ONJ may manifest as jaw pain, osteomyelitis, osteitis, bone erosion, tooth/periodontal infection, toothache, gingival ulceration/erosion. Risk factors include invasive dental procedures (eg, tooth extraction, dental implants, oral surgery), cancer diagnosis, immunosuppressive therapy, angiogenesis inhibitor therapy, chemotherapy, systemic corticosteroids, poor oral hygiene, use of a dental appliance, ill-fitting dentures, periodontal and/or other pre-existing dental disease, diabetes and gingival infections, local infection with delayed healing, anemia, and/or coagulopathy. In studies of patients with osseous metastasis, a longer duration of denosumab exposure was associated with a higher incidence of ONJ, although a majority of patients had predisposing factors, including a history of poor oral hygiene, tooth extraction, or the use of a dental appliance. Patients should maintain good oral hygiene during treatment. A dental exam and appropriate preventive dentistry should be performed prior to therapy. The manufacturer's labeling recommends avoiding invasive dental procedures in patients with bone metastases receiving denosumab for prevention of skeletal-related events and to consider temporary discontinuation of therapy in these patients if invasive dental procedure is required. According to a position paper by the American Association of Maxillofacial Surgeons (AAOMS), MRONJ has been associated with bisphosphonates and other antiresorptive agents (denosumab), and antiangiogenic agents (eg, bevacizumab, sunitinib) used for the treatment of osteoporosis or malignancy; risk is significantly higher in cancer patients receiving antiresorptive therapy compared to patients receiving osteoporosis treatment (regardless of medication used or dosing schedule). MRONJ risk is increased with intravenous antiresorptive therapy compared to the minimal risk associated with oral bisphosphonate use, although risk appears to increase with oral bisphosphonates when duration of therapy exceeds 4 years. The AAOMS suggests that if medically permissible, initiation of denosumab for cancer therapy should be delayed until optimal dental health is attained (if extractions are required, antiresorptive therapy should delayed until the extraction site has mucosalized or until after adequate osseous healing). Once denosumab is initiated for oncologic disease, procedures that involve direct osseous injury and placement of dental implants should be avoided. Patients developing ONJ during therapy should receive care by an oral surgeon (AAOMS [Ruggiero 2014]). According to the manufacturer, discontinuation of denosumab should be considered (based on risk/benefit evaluation) in patients who develop ONJ.

Postmenopausal osteoporosis: For use in women at high risk for fracture which is defined as a history of osteoporotic fracture or multiple risk factors for fracture. May also be used in women who failed or did not tolerate other therapies.

Bone metastases: Denosumab is not indicated for the prevention of skeletal-related events in patients with multiple myeloma. In trials of with multiple myeloma patients, denosumab was noninferior to zoledronic acid in delaying time to first skeletal-related event and mortality was increased in a subset of the denosumab-treated group.

Breast cancer: The American Society of Clinical Oncology (ASCO) updated guidelines on the role of bone-modifying agents (BMAs) in the prevention and treatment of skeletal-related events for metastatic breast cancer patients (Van Poznak 2011). The guidelines recommend initiating a BMA (denosumab, pamidronate, zoledronic acid) in patients with metastatic breast cancer to the bone. There is currently no literature indicating the superiority of one particular BMA. Optimal duration is not defined; however, the guidelines recommend continuing therapy until substantial decline in patient's performance status. The ASCO guidelines are in alignment with package insert guidelines for dosing, renal dose adjustments, infusion times, prevention and management of osteonecrosis of the jaw, and monitoring of laboratory parameter recommendations. BMAs are not the first-line therapy for pain. BMAs are to be used as adjunctive therapy for cancer-related bone pain associated with bone metastasis, demonstrating a modest pain control benefit. BMAs should be used in conjunction with agents such as NSAIDs, opioid and nonopioid analgesics, corticosteroids, radiation/surgery, and interventional procedures.

Denosumab therapy results in significant suppression of bone turnover; the long term effects of treatment are not known but may contribute to adverse outcomes such as ONJ, atypical fractures, or delayed fracture healing; monitor. Use with caution in patients with renal impairment (CrCl <30 mL/minute) or patients on dialysis; risk of hypocalcemia is increased. Dose adjustment is not needed when administered at 60 mg every 6 months (Prolia); once-monthly dosing has not been evaluated in patients with renal impairment (Xgeva). Dermatitis, eczema, and rash (which are not necessarily specific to the injection site) have been reported; consider discontinuing if severe symptoms occur. Packaging may contain natural latex rubber. May impair bone growth in children with open growth plates or inhibit eruption of dentition. In pediatrics, indicated only for the treatment of giant cell tumor of the bone in adolescents who are skeletally mature. Do not administer Prolia and Xgeva to the same patient for different indications. Denosumab is intended for subcutaneous route only and should not be administered intravenously, intramuscularly, or intradermally. Potentially significant interactions may exist, requiring dose or frequency adjustment, additional monitoring, and/or selection of alternative therapy.

Drug Interactions

Metabolism/Transport Effects None known.

Avoid Concomitant Use

Avoid concomitant use of Denosumab with any of the following: Belimumab

Increased Effect/Toxicity

Denosumab may increase the levels/effects of: Belimumab; Immunosuppressants

Decreased Effect There are no known significant interactions involving a decrease in effect.

Dietary Considerations Ensure adequate calcium and vitamin D intake to prevent or treat hypocalcemia. Calcium 1000 mg/day and vitamin D ≥400 units/day is recommended in product labeling (Prolia). If dietary intake is inadequate, dietary supplementation is recommended. Women and men should consume:

Calcium: 1000 mg/day (men: 50 to 70 years) **or** 1200 mg/day (women ≥51 years and men ≥71 years) (IOM 2011; NOF 2014)

Vitamin D: 800 to 1000 units/day (men and women ≥50 years) (NOF 2014). Recommended Dietary Allowance (RDA): 600 units/day (men and women ≤70 years) **or** 800 units/day (men and women ≥71 years) (IOM 2011).

Pharmacodynamics/Kinetics

Onset of Action Decreases markers of bone resorption by ~85% within 3 days; maximal reductions observed within 1 month

Hypercalcemia of malignancy: Time to response (median): 9 days; Time to complete response (median): 23 days (Hu 2014)

Duration of Action Markers of bone resorption return to baseline within 12 months of discontinuing therapy

Hypercalcemia of malignancy: Duration of response (median): 104 days; Duration of complete response (median): 34 days (Hu 2014)

Half-life Elimination ~25 to 28 days

Time to Peak Serum: 10 days (range: 3 to 21 days)

Pregnancy Risk Factor D (Xgeva)/X (Prolia)

Pregnancy Considerations Use of Prolia is contraindicated in pregnant women. Adverse events were observed in animal reproduction studies. Specifically, increased fetal loss, stillbirths, postnatal mortality, absent lymph nodes, abnormal bone growth, and decreased neonatal growth was observed in cynomolgus monkeys exposed to denosumab throughout pregnancy. Denosumab was measurable in the offspring at one month of age. Fetal exposure to monoclonal antibodies is expected to increase as pregnancy progresses. Women of reproductive potential should be advised to use effective contraception during denosumab treatment and for at least 5 months following the last dose. Studies of denosumab when used for osteoporosis/bone loss in men demonstrated that it is unlikely that a female partner or fetus would be exposed during unprotected sex to pharmacologically relevant denosumab concentrations via seminal fluid; however, exposure from seminal fluid of men receiving denosumab for other indications and higher doses is unknown and therefore their pregnant partners should be counseled regarding this potential risk.

Women exposed to denosumab during pregnancy should contact the Amgen Pregnancy Surveillance Program (800-772-6436).

Breastfeeding Considerations It is not known if denosumab is excreted in breast milk. According to the manufacturer, the decision to discontinue denosumab or discontinue breastfeeding should take into account the benefits of treatment to the mother. In some animal studies, mammary gland development was impaired following exposure to denosumab during pregnancy, resulting in impaired lactation postpartum.

Dosage Forms

Solution, Subcutaneous [preservative free]:

Prolia: 60 mg/mL (1 mL)

Xgeva: 120 mg/1.7 mL (1.7 mL)

Dental Comment In head-to-head comparison trials of denosumab and zoledronate (a bisphosphonate) for the treatment of bone metastasis in patients with cancer, 20 cases of ONJ were detected out of a total of 1026 subjects (2.0%) exposed to denosumab. There were 14 cases of ONJ observed out of a total of 1020 subjects (1.4%) exposed to zoledronate (Kyrgidis, 2010). The case of a 60-year old male cancer patient who developed ONJ after treatment with denosumab has been published (Taylor, 2010). In that report, the patient participated in a trial for a phase 3 study of denosumab. The patient had never been prescribed a bisphosphonate medication before treatment with denosumab. Clinical and radiological features of the lesion were diagnostic of probable ONJ. After discontinuation of the denosumab, the patient was treated with antibiotics and chlorhexidine rinses for a week. The necrotic bone sequestered 12 months later, and 15 months after initial presentation, the mucosa had healed with no further symptoms. Another case reported the development of ONJ in a 65-year old women being treated for giant cell tumor with denosumab. Although the patient was medically compromised and on multiple medications, the authors proposed that a common thread in ONJ development is inhibition of osteoclastic activity, mediated in this case by denosumab.

Deoxycholic Acid (dee ox i KOE lik AS id)

Brand Names: US Kybella

Pharmacologic Category Lipolytic

Use

Submental convexity/fullness: Improvement in the appearance of moderate to severe convexity or fullness associated with submental fat in adults.

Limitations of use: The safe and effective use for the treatment of subcutaneous fat outside the submental region has not been established and is not recommended.

Local Anesthetic/Vasoconstrictor Precautions No information available to require special precautions

Effects on Dental Treatment No significant effects or complications reported

Effects on Bleeding No information available to require special precautions

Adverse Reactions Frequency not always defined.

Cardiovascular: Hypertension (3%), presyncope, syncope

Central nervous system: Paresthesia (14%), headache (8%), neuropathy (4%, marginal mandibular)

Dermatologic: Injection site pruritus (12%), skin tightness (5% injection site), skin discoloration at injection site, urticaria at injection site

Gastrointestinal: Dysphagia (2%), nausea (2%)

Hematologic & oncologic: Lymphadenopathy

Local: Injection site reaction (96%), swelling at injection site (20% to 87%), bruising at injection site (72%), hematoma at injection site (72%), pain at injection site (16% to 70%), injection site numbness (42% to 66%), erythema at injection site (27%), induration at injection site (23%), injection site nodule (13%), warm sensation at injection site (4%), bleeding at injection site

Neuromuscular & skeletal: Neck pain

Respiratory: Oropharyngeal pain (3%)

Mechanism of Action Deoxycholic acid is a cytolytic drug that physically destroys the cell membrane causing lysis when injected into tissue.

Pharmacodynamics/Kinetics

Duration of Action Post treatment deoxycholic plasma levels return to endogenous range within 24 hours

Time to Peak 18 minutes

Pregnancy Considerations Adverse events have been observed in some animal reproduction studies. Pregnant women and women of reproductive potential not using effective contraception were excluded from initial studies (McDiarmid, 2014; Rzany, 2014).

Desipramine (des IP ra meen)

Related Information

Dentin Hypersensitivity, Acid Erosion, High Caries Index, Management of Alveolar Osteitis, and Xerostomia *on page 1857*

Vasoconstrictor Interactions With Antidepressants *on page 1913*

Brand Names: US Norpramin

Brand Names: Canada Dom-Desipramine; Novo-Desipramine; Nu-Desipramine; PMS-Desipramine

Pharmacologic Category Antidepressant, Tricyclic (Secondary Amine)

Use Depression: Treatment of depression

Local Anesthetic/Vasoconstrictor Precautions Use with caution; epinephrine and levonordefrin have been shown to have an increased pressor response in combination with TCAs. Desipramine is one of the drugs confirmed to prolong the QT interval and is accepted as having a risk of causing torsade de pointes. The risk of drug-induced torsade de pointes is extremely low when a single QT interval prolonging drug is prescribed. In terms of epinephrine, it is not known what effect vasoconstrictors in the local anesthetic regimen will have in patients with a known history of congenital prolonged QT interval or in patients taking any medication that prolongs the QT interval. Until more information is obtained, it is suggested that the clinician consult with the physician prior to the use of a vasoconstrictor in suspected patients, and that the vasoconstrictor (epinephrine, mepivacaine and levonordefrin [Carbocaine® 2% with Neo-Cobefrin®]) be used with caution.

Effects on Dental Treatment Key adverse event(s) related to dental treatment: Xerostomia and changes in salivation (normal salivary flow resumes upon discontinuation), unpleasant taste, stomatitis, and black tongue. Long-term treatment with TCAs increases the risk of caries by reducing salivation and salivary buffer capacity.

Effects on Bleeding Thrombocytopenia has been reported.

Adverse Reactions Frequency not defined. Some reactions listed are based on reports for other agents in this same pharmacologic class, and may not be specifically reported for desipramine.

Cardiovascular: Cardiac arrhythmia, cerebrovascular accident, edema, flushing, heart block, hypertension, hypotension, myocardial infarction, palpitations, premature ventricular contractions, tachycardia, ventricular fibrillation, ventricular tachycardia

Central nervous system: Agitation, anxiety, ataxia, confusion, delusions, disorientation, dizziness, drowsiness, drug fever, EEG pattern changes, extrapyramidal reaction, falling, fatigue, hallucination, headache, hypomania, insomnia, neuroleptic malignant syndrome, nightmares, numbness, peripheral neuropathy, psychosis (exacerbation), restlessness, seizure, tingling of extremities, tingling sensation, withdrawal syndrome

Dermatologic: Alopecia, diaphoresis (excessive), pruritus, skin photosensitivity, skin rash, urticaria

Endocrine & metabolic: Decreased libido, decreased serum glucose, galactorrhea, gynecomastia, increased libido, increased serum glucose, SIADH, weight gain, weight loss

Gastrointestinal: Abdominal cramps, anorexia, constipation, diarrhea, epigastric distress, increased pancreatic enzymes, melanoglossia, nausea, paralytic ileus, parotid gland enlargement, stomatitis, sublingual adenitis, unpleasant taste, vomiting, xerostomia

Genitourinary: Breast hypertrophy, impotence, nocturia, painful ejaculation, testicular swelling, urinary hesitancy, urinary retention, urinary tract dilation

Hematologic & oncologic: Agranulocytosis, eosinophilia, petechia, purpura, thrombocytopenia

Hepatic: Abnormal hepatic function tests, cholestatic jaundice, hepatitis, increased liver enzymes, increased serum alkaline phosphatase

Neuromuscular & skeletal: Tremor, weakness

Ophthalmic: Accommodation disturbance, blurred vision, increased intraocular pressure, mydriasis

Otic: Tinnitus

Renal: Polyuria

Miscellaneous: Fever

Postmarketing and/or case reports: Angle-closure glaucoma, serotonin syndrome, suicidal ideation, suicidal tendencies

General Dosage Range Oral:

Adolescents: 25-100 mg/day in single or divided doses (maximum: 150 mg/day)

Adults: 100-200 mg/day in single or divided doses (maximum: 300 mg/day)

Elderly: 25-100 mg/day in single or divided doses (maximum: 150 mg/day)

Mechanism of Action Traditionally believed to increase the synaptic concentration of norepinephrine (and to a lesser extent, serotonin) in the central nervous system by inhibition of its reuptake by the presynaptic neuronal membrane. However, additional receptor effects have been found including desensitization of adenyl cyclase, down regulation of beta-adrenergic receptors, and down regulation of serotonin receptors.

Pharmacodynamics/Kinetics

Onset of Action Depression: Individual responses vary; however, 4 to 8 weeks of treatment is needed before determining if a patient is partially or nonresponsive (APA, 2010).

Half-life Elimination Adults: 15 to 24 hours (Weiner, 1981)

Time to Peak Plasma: ~6 hours (Weiner, 1981)

Pregnancy Considerations Animal reproduction studies are inconclusive. Tricyclic antidepressants may be associated with irritability, jitteriness, and convulsions (rare) in the neonate (Yonkers 2009).

The ACOG recommends that therapy for depression during pregnancy be individualized; treatment should incorporate the clinical expertise of the mental health clinician, obstetrician, primary health care provider, and pediatrician (ACOG 2008). According to the American Psychiatric Association (APA), the risks of medication treatment should be weighed against other treatment options and untreated depression. For women who discontinue antidepressant medications during pregnancy and who may be at high risk for postpartum depression, the medications can be restarted following delivery (APA 2010). Treatment algorithms have been developed by the ACOG and the APA for the management of depression in women prior to conception and during pregnancy (Yonkers 2009).

Pregnant women exposed to antidepressants during pregnancy are encouraged to enroll in the National Pregnancy Registry for Antidepressants (NPRAD). Women 18 to 45 years of age or their health care providers may contact the registry by calling 844-405-6185. Enrollment should be done as early in pregnancy as possible.

Dental Comment See Local Anesthetic/Vasoconstrictor Precautions

Desirudin (des i ROO din)

Related Information

Cardiovascular Diseases *on page 1752*

Brand Names: US Iprivask

Pharmacologic Category Anticoagulant; Anticoagulant, Direct Thrombin Inhibitor

Use Deep vein thrombosis, prophylaxis: Prophylaxis of deep vein thrombosis (DVT) in patients undergoing hip-replacement surgery

Local Anesthetic/Vasoconstrictor Precautions No information available to require special precautions

Effects on Dental Treatment No significant effects or complications reported

Effects on Bleeding As with all anticoagulants, bleeding is a potential adverse effect of desirudin during dental surgery; risk is dependent on multiple variables, including the intensity of anticoagulation and patient susceptibility. Medical consult is suggested. It is unlikely that ambulatory patients presenting for dental treatment will be taking intravenous anticoagulant therapy such as desirudin.

Adverse Reactions As with all anticoagulants, bleeding is the major adverse effect. Hemorrhage may occur at any site.

2% to 10%:

Cardiovascular: Deep vein thrombophlebitis (2%)

Dermatologic: Wound secretion (4%)

Gastrointestinal: Nausea (2%)

Hematologic & oncologic: Hematoma (6%), anemia (3%), major hemorrhage (≤3%; may include hemophthalmos, intracranial hemorrhage, intraspinal hemorrhage, prosthetic joint hemorrhage, or retroperitoneal hemorrhage)

Local: Residual mass at injection site (4%)

<2%, postmarketing, and/or case reports: Anaphylactoid reaction, anaphylaxis, cerebrovascular disease, decreased hemoglobin, dizziness, epistaxis, fever, hematemesis, hematuria, hemorrhage (fatal), hypersensitivity reaction, hypotension, leg pain, lower extremity edema, thrombosis, vomiting, wound healing impairment

General Dosage Range Dosage adjustment recommended in patients with renal impairment

SubQ: *Adults:* 15 mg every 12 hours

Mechanism of Action Desirudin is a direct, highly selective thrombin inhibitor. Reversibly binds to the active thrombin site of free and clot-associated thrombin. Inhibits fibrin formation, activation of coagulation factors V, VII, and XIII, and thrombin-induced platelet aggregation resulting in a dose-dependent prolongation of the activated partial thromboplastin time (aPTT).

Pharmacodynamics/Kinetics

Half-life Elimination ~2 hours; Prolonged with renal impairment (CrCl <31 mL/minute/1.73 m^2: Up to 12 hours)

Time to Peak Plasma: 1 to 3 hours

Pregnancy Risk Factor C

Pregnancy Considerations Adverse events have been observed in animal reproduction studies. Data are insufficient to evaluate the safety of thrombin inhibitors during pregnancy (Guyatt, 2012).

Desloratadine (des lor AT a deen)

Brand Names: US Clarinex; Clarinex Reditabs [DSC]

Brand Names: Canada Aerius; Aerius Kids; Desloratadine Allergy Control

Generic Availability (US) May be product dependent

Pharmacologic Category Histamine H_1 Antagonist; Histamine H_1 Antagonist, Second Generation; Piperidine Derivative

Use Relief of nasal and non-nasal symptoms of seasonal allergic rhinitis (SAR) and perennial allergic rhinitis (PAR); treatment of chronic idiopathic urticaria (CIU)

Local Anesthetic/Vasoconstrictor Precautions No information available to require special precautions

Effects on Dental Treatment Key adverse event(s) related to dental treatment: Xerostomia (normal salivary flow resumes upon discontinuation)

Effects on Bleeding No information available to require special precautions

Adverse Reactions Note: Frequency reported in children, unless otherwise noted.

>10%:

Central nervous system: Headache (adults 14%), irritability (12%)

Gastrointestinal: Diarrhea (15% to 20%)

Respiratory: Upper respiratory tract infection (11% to 21%), cough (11%)

Miscellaneous: Fever (12% to 17%)

1% to 10%:

Central nervous system: Drowsiness (children 9%; adults 2%), insomnia (5%), fatigue (adults 2% to 5%), dizziness (adults 4%), emotional lability (3%)

Dermatologic: Erythema (3%), maculopapular rash (3%)

Gastrointestinal: Vomiting (6%), anorexia (5%), nausea (children 3%; adults 5%), dyspepsia (adults 3%), increased appetite (3%), xerostomia (adults 3%)

Genitourinary: Urinary tract infection (4%), dysmenorrhea (adults 2%)

Infection: Varicella (4%), parasitic infection (3%)

Neuromuscular & skeletal: Myalgia (adults 2% to 3%)

Otic: Otitis media (children 6%)

Respiratory: Bronchitis (6%), rhinorrhea (5%), pharyngitis (children 3% to 5%; adults 3% to 4%), epistaxis (3%)

Postmarketing and/or case reports: Hepatitis (rare), hyperbilirubinemia, hypersensitivity reactions (including anaphylaxis, dyspnea, edema, pruritus, rash, urticaria), increased liver enzymes, movement disorder (including dystonia, tics, and extrapyramidal symptoms), palpitations, psychomotor agitation, seizure, tachycardia

Dosing

Adult & Geriatric

Chronic idiopathic urticaria: Oral: 5 mg once daily. In one clinical trial, the titrated use of higher doses (up to 10 mg twice daily) in adults demonstrated clinical improvement (Staevska, 2010).

Seasonal or perennial allergic rhinitis: Oral: 5 mg once daily

Pediatric

Perennial allergic rhinitis, chronic idiopathic urticaria: Oral:

Children:

6 to 11 months: 1 mg once daily

12 months to 5 years: 1.25 mg once daily

6 to 11 years: 2.5 mg once daily

Children ≥12 years and Adolescents: Refer to adult dosing.

Seasonal allergic rhinitis: Oral:

Children:

2 to 5 years: 1.25 mg once daily

6 to 11 years: 2.5 mg once daily

Children ≥12 years and Adolescents: Refer to adult dosing.

Renal Impairment

Adults: Mild to severe impairment: 5 mg every other day.

Children: There are no dosage adjustments provided in manufacturer's labeling (has not been studied).

Hepatic Impairment

Adults: Mild to severe impairment: 5 mg every other day.

Children: There are no dosage adjustments provided in manufacturer's labeling (has not been studied).

Mechanism of Action Desloratadine, a major active metabolite of loratadine, is a long-acting tricyclic antihistamine with selective peripheral histamine H_1 receptor antagonistic activity.

Contraindications Hypersensitivity to desloratadine, loratadine, or any component of the formulation

Warnings/Precautions Hypersensitivity reactions (including anaphylaxis) have been reported with use; discontinue therapy immediately with signs/symptoms of hypersensitivity. Dose should be adjusted in patients with liver or renal impairment. Use with caution in patients known to be slow metabolizers of desloratadine (incidence of side effects may be increased). Some products may contain phenylalanine.

Benzyl alcohol and derivatives: Some dosage forms may contain sodium benzoate/benzoic acid; benzoic acid (benzoate) is a metabolite of benzyl alcohol; large amounts of benzyl alcohol (≥99 mg/kg/day) have been associated with a potentially fatal toxicity ("gasping syndrome") in neonates; the "gasping syndrome" consists of metabolic acidosis, respiratory distress, gasping respirations, CNS dysfunction (including convulsions, intracranial hemorrhage), hypotension, and cardiovascular collapse (AAP ["Inactive" 1997]; CDC, 1982); some data suggests that benzoate displaces bilirubin from protein binding sites (Ahlfors, 2001); avoid or use dosage forms containing benzyl alcohol derivative with caution in neonates. See manufacturer's labeling.

Drug Interactions

Metabolism/Transport Effects Substrate of P-glycoprotein

Avoid Concomitant Use

Avoid concomitant use of Desloratadine with any of the following: Aclidinium; Azelastine (Nasal); Cimetropium; Eluxadoline; Glucagon; Glycopyrrolate (Oral Inhalation); Ipratropium (Oral Inhalation); Levosulpiride; Nitroglycerin; Orphenadrine; Oxatomide; Oxomemazine; Paraldehyde; Potassium Chloride; Thalidomide; Tiotropium; Umeclidinium

Increased Effect/Toxicity

Desloratadine may increase the levels/effects of: AbobotulinumtoxinA; Alcohol (Ethyl); Analgesics (Opioid); Anticholinergic Agents; Azelastine (Nasal); Blonanserin; Buprenorphine; Cimetropium; CNS Depressants; Eluxadoline; Flunitrazepam; Glucagon; Glycopyrrolate (Oral Inhalation); HYDROcodone; Methotrimeprazine; MetyroSINE; Mirabegron; Mirtazapine; OnabotulinumtoxinA; Orphenadrine; OxyCODONE; Paraldehyde; Piribedil; Potassium Chloride; Pramipexole; Ramosetron; RimabotulinumtoxinB; ROPINIRole; Rotigotine; Selective Serotonin Reuptake Inhibitors; Suvorexant; Thalidomide; Thiazide and Thiazide-Like Diuretics; Tiotropium; Topiramate; Zolpidem

The levels/effects of Desloratadine may be increased by: Aclidinium; Brimonidine (Topical); Cannabis; Chloral Betaine; Chlormethiazole; Chlorphenesin Carbamate; Dimethindene (Topical); Doxylamine; Dronabinol; Droperidol; HydrOXYzine; Ipratropium (Oral Inhalation); Kava Kava; Lofexidine; Lumacaftor; Magnesium Sulfate; Methotrimeprazine; Mianserin; Minocycline; Nabilone; Oxatomide; Oxomemazine; Perampanel; P-glycoprotein/ABCB1 Inhibitors; Pramlintide; Ranolazine; Rufinamide; Sodium Oxybate; Tapentadol; Tetrahydrocannabinol; Trimeprazine; Umeclidinium

Decreased Effect

Desloratadine may decrease the levels/effects of: Acetylcholinesterase Inhibitors; Benzylpenicilloyl Polylysine; Betahistine; Gastrointestinal Agents (Prokinetic); Hyaluronidase; Itopride; Levosulpiride; Nitroglycerin; Secretin

The levels/effects of Desloratadine may be decreased by: Acetylcholinesterase Inhibitors; Amphetamines; Lumacaftor; P-glycoprotein/ABCB1 Inducers

Food Interactions Food does not affect bioavailability.

Dietary Considerations May be taken with or without food. Some products may contain phenylalanine.

Pharmacodynamics/Kinetics

Onset of Action Within 1 hour

Duration of Action 24 hours

Half-life Elimination 27 hours

Time to Peak 3 hours

Pregnancy Risk Factor C

Pregnancy Considerations Adverse events have been observed in animal reproduction studies; therefore, the manufacturer classifies desloratadine as pregnancy category C. The use of antihistamines for the treatment of rhinitis during pregnancy is generally considered to be safe at recommended doses. Information related to the use of desloratadine during pregnancy is limited; therefore, other agents may be preferred. Desloratadine is the primary metabolite of loratadine; refer to the Loratadine monograph for additional information.

Breastfeeding Considerations Desloratadine is excreted into breast milk. According to the manufacturer, the decision to continue or discontinue breastfeeding during therapy should take into account the risk of exposure to the infant and the benefits of treatment to the mother.

Dosage Forms

Syrup, Oral:

Clarinex: 0.5 mg/mL (473 mL)

Tablet, Oral:

Clarinex: 5 mg

Generic: 5 mg

Tablet Dispersible, Oral:

Generic: 2.5 mg, 5 mg

Desmopressin (des moe PRES in)

Brand Names: US DDAVP; DDAVP Rhinal Tube; Stimate

Brand Names: Canada Apo-Desmopressin; DDAVP; DDAVP Melt; DDAVP Rhinyle; Nocdurna; Octostim; PMS-Desmopressin; Teva-Desmopressin

Pharmacologic Category Antihemophilic Agent; Hemostatic Agent; Hormone, Posterior Pituitary; Vasopressin Analog, Synthetic

Use

Injection:

Diabetes insipidus: Antidiuretic replacement therapy in the management of central (cranial) diabetes insipidus; management of the temporary polyuria and polydipsia following head trauma or surgery in the pituitary region.

Limitations of use: Desmopressin is ineffective for the treatment of nephrogenic diabetes insipidus.

Hemophilia A: For use in patients with hemophilia A with factor VIII coagulant activity levels >5% to maintain hemostasis during surgical procedures and postoperatively when administered 30 minutes prior to the scheduled procedure and to also stop bleeding due to spontaneous or trauma-induced injuries, such as hemarthroses, intramuscular hematomas, or mucosal bleeding.

Limitations of use: Not indicated for the treatment of homophilia A with factor VIII coagulant activity levels ≤5%, for the treatment of hemophilia B, or in patients who have factor VIII antibodies. In certain clinical situations, it may be justified to try desmopressin with careful monitoring in patients with factor VIII levels between 2% and 5%.

Von Willebrand disease (type 1): For use in patients with mild to moderate classic von Willebrand disease (type 1) with factor VIII coagulant activity levels >5% to maintain hemostasis during surgical procedures and postoperatively when administered 30 minutes prior to the scheduled procedure and to stop bleeding due to spontaneous or trauma-induced injuries, such as hemarthroses, intramuscular hematomas, or mucosal bleeding.

Limitations of use: Patients with von Willebrand disease who are least likely to respond are those with severe homozygous von Willebrand disease with factor VIII coagulant activity and factor VIII von Willebrand factor antigen levels <1%; other patients may respond (variable) depending on the type of molecular defect they have. Check bleeding time and factor VIII coagulant activity, ristocetin cofactor activity, and von Willebrand factor antigen during administration of desmopressin to ensure that adequate levels are being achieved. Not indicated for the treatment of severe classic von Willebrand disease (type I) or when there is evidence of an abnormal molecular form of factor VIII antigen.

Uremic bleeding (Octostim [Canadian product]): Prevention or treatment of bleeding in patients with uremia.

Intranasal:

Diabetes insipidus (DDAVP Rhinal tube): Antidiuretic replacement therapy in the management of central (cranial) diabetes insipidus; management of the temporary polyuria and polydipsia following head trauma or surgery in the pituitary region.

Limitation of use: Desmopressin is ineffective for the treatment of nephrogenic diabetes insipidus.

Hemophilia A (Stimate; Octostim [Canadian product]): For use in patients with hemophilia A with factor VIII coagulant activity levels >5% and to stop bleeding due to spontaneous or trauma-induced injuries, such as hemarthroses, intramuscular hematomas, or mucosal bleeding.

Limitations of use: Not indicated for the treatment of hemophilia A with factor VIII coagulant activity levels ≤5%, for the treatment of hemophilia B, or in patients who have factor VIII antibodies.

von Willebrand disease (type 1) (Stimate; Octostim [Canadian product]): For use in patients with mild to moderate classic von Willebrand disease (type 1) with factor VIII coagulant activity levels >5% and to stop bleeding due to spontaneous or trauma-induced injuries, such as hemarthroses, intramuscular hematomas, mucosal bleeding, or menorrhagia.

Limitations of use: Not indicated for the treatment of severe classic von Willebrand disease (type 1) or when there is evidence of an abnormal molecular form of factor VIII antigen.

Tablets:

Diabetes insipidus: Antidiuretic replacement therapy in the management of central diabetes insipidus; management of the temporary polyuria and polydipsia following head trauma or surgery in the pituitary region.

Limitation of use: Desmopressin is ineffective for the treatment of nephrogenic diabetes insipidus.

Nocturia (Nocdurna [Canadian product] only): Treatment of nocturia in adults with four or less nocturnal voids.

Primary nocturnal enuresis: Management of primary nocturnal enuresis, either alone or as an adjunct to behavioral conditioning or other nonpharmacologic intervention.

Local Anesthetic/Vasoconstrictor Precautions No information available to require special precautions

Effects on Dental Treatment No significant effects or complications reported

Effects on Bleeding Rare reports of thrombotic events including thromboembolism have been associated with desmopressin, although no causality has been determined.

Adverse Reactions Frequency may not be defined (may be dose or route related).

Cardiovascular: Decreased blood pressure (IV), increased blood pressure (IV), flushing (facial)

Central nervous system: Headache (2% to 5%), dizziness (intranasal; ≤3%), chills (intranasal; 2%), nostril pain (intranasal; ≤2%)

Dermatologic: Skin rash

Endocrine & metabolic: Hyponatremia, water intoxication

Gastrointestinal: Abdominal pain (intranasal; 2%) gastrointestinal disease (intranasal; ≤2%), nausea (intranasal; ≤2%), abdominal cramps, sore throat

Hepatic: Increased serum transaminases (transient; associated primarily with tablets)

Local: Burning sensation at injection site, erythema at injection site, swelling at injection site

Neuromuscular & skeletal: Weakness (intranasal; ≤2%)

Ophthalmic: Abnormal lacrimation (intranasal; ≤2%), conjunctivitis (intranasal; ≤2%), ocular edema (intranasal; ≤2%)

Respiratory: Rhinitis (intranasal; 3% to 8%), epistaxis (intranasal; ≤3%), cough, nasal congestion, upper respiratory tract infection

<1%, postmarketing, and/or case reports: Abnormality in thinking, agitation, anaphylaxis (rare), balanitis,

cerebral thrombosis (IV; acute), chest pain, coma, diarrhea, drowsiness, dyspepsia, edema, eye pruritus, hypersensitivity reaction (rare), insomnia, localized warm feeling, myocardial infarction (IV), pain, palpitations, photophobia, seizure, tachycardia, vomiting, vulvar pain

General Dosage Range

IV:

Infants ≥3 months, Children, and Adolescents: 0.3 mcg/kg as a single dose, may repeat dose if needed

Children ≥12 years and Adolescents: 2 to 4 mcg daily in 2 divided doses **or** one-tenth (1/10) of the intranasal maintenance dose.

Adults: 2 to 4 mcg daily in 2 divided doses **or** one-tenth (1/10) of the intranasal maintenance dose **or** 0.3 mcg/kg as a single dose

Intranasal:

Infants ≥3 months and Children ≤12 years: Usual dose range: 5 to 30 mcg daily (0.05 to 0.3 mL daily) in 1 to 2 divided doses

Infants ≥11 months and Children ≤12 years (<50 kg): 150 mcg (1 spray in 1 nostril of high concentration) as a single dose

Adolescents and Adults: 10 to 40 mcg daily as a single dose or divided 2 to 3 times daily

Adolescents (<50 kg) and Adults (<50 kg): 150 mcg (1 spray in 1 nostril of high concentration spray) as a single dose

Adolescents (≥50 kg) and Adults (≥50 kg): 300 mcg (1 spray in each nostril of high concentration spray) as a single dose in each nostril

Oral:

Children 4 to 5 years: Initial: 0.05 mg twice daily; Maintenance: 0.1 to 1.2 mg daily in 2 to 3 divided doses

Children ≥6 years and Adolescents: Initial: 0.05 mg twice daily **or** 0.2 mg at bedtime; Maintenance: 0.1 to 1.2 mg daily in 2 to 3 divided doses **or** 0.2 to 0.6 mg at bedtime

Adults: 0.2 to 0.6 mg at bedtime **or** 0.1 to 1.2 mg daily in 2 to 3 divided doses

SubQ: *Children ≥12 years, Adolescents, and Adults:* 2 to 4 mcg daily in 2 divided doses **or** one-tenth (1/10) of the intranasal maintenance dose

Mechanism of Action Synthetic analogue of the antidiuretic hormone arginine vasopressin. In a dose dependent manner, desmopressin increases cyclic adenosine monophosphate (cAMP) in renal tubular cells which increases water permeability resulting in decreased urine volume and increased urine osmolality; increases plasma levels of von Willebrand factor, factor VIII, and t-PA contributing to a shortened activated partial thromboplastin time (aPTT) and bleeding time.

Pharmacodynamics/Kinetics

Onset of Action

Intranasal: Antidiuretic: 15 to 30 minutes; Increased factor VIII and von Willebrand factor (vWF) activity (dose related): 30 minutes

Peak effect: Antidiuretic: 1 hour; Increased factor VIII and vWF activity: 1.5 hours

IV infusion: Increased factor VIII and vWF activity: 30 minutes (dose related)

Peak effect: 1.5 to 2 hours

Oral tablet: Antidiuretic: ~1 hour

Peak effect: 4 to 7 hours

Duration of Action Intranasal, Injection, Oral tablet: ~6 to 14 hours

Half-life Elimination 2 to 4 hours; Renal impairment: 9 hours

Pregnancy Risk Factor B

Pregnancy Considerations Adverse events were not observed in animal reproduction studies. Anecdotal reports suggest congenital anomalies and low birth weight. However, causal relationship has not been established. Desmopressin has been used safely throughout pregnancy for the treatment of diabetes insipidus (Brewster 2005; Schrier 2010). The use of desmopressin is limited for the treatment of von Willebrand disease in pregnant women (NHLBI 2007).

Product Availability Noctiva nasal spray: FDA approved March 2017; anticipated availability is currently undetermined. Information pertaining to this product within the monograph is pending revision. Noctiva is indicated for the treatment of nocturia due to nocturnal polyuria in adults; consult the prescribing information for additional information.

Desonide (DES oh nide)

Brand Names: US Desonate; DesOwen; DesOwen Cream w/Cetaphil Lot [DSC]; DesOwen Lot w/Cetaphil Cream [DSC]; DesOwen Oint w/Cetaphil Lot [DSC]; LoKara; Tridesilon; Verdeso

Brand Names: Canada Desocort; PDP-Desonide; Tridesilon; Verdeso

Pharmacologic Category Corticosteroid, Topical

Use

Atopic dermatitis (foam and gel): Treatment of mild to moderate atopic dermatitis in patients 3 months and older

Corticosteroid-responsive dermatoses (cream, ointment, and lotion): Relief of inflammatory and pruritic manifestations of corticosteroid-responsive dermatoses.

Local Anesthetic/Vasoconstrictor Precautions No information available to require special precautions

Effects on Dental Treatment No significant effects or complications reported

Effects on Bleeding No information available to require special precautions

Adverse Reactions Frequency not defined.

Cardiovascular: Hypertension

Central nervous system: Headache, irritability

Dermatologic: Erythema (transient, intense), exfoliation of skin, pruritus, skin rash, telangiectasia, xeroderma

Endocrine & metabolic: HPA-axis suppression, hyperglycemia

Infection: Increased susceptibility to infection

Local: Application site: Atrophic striae, dermatitis, dyschromia, local irritation, local pruritus, localized burning, skin atrophy, stinging of the skin

Respiratory: Asthma, cough, pharyngitis, upper respiratory tract infection

Postmarketing and/or case reports: Localized erythema, dermatological reaction, facial swelling

General Dosage Range Topical:

Infants ≥3 months, Children, and Adolescents: Foam, gel: Apply 2 times daily sparingly

Adults: Apply 2 to 4 times daily sparingly

Mechanism of Action Topical corticosteroids have anti-inflammatory, antipruritic, and vasoconstrictive properties. May depress the formation, release, and activity of endogenous chemical mediators of inflammation (kinins, histamine, liposomal enzymes, prostaglandins) through the induction of phospholipase A_2 inhibitory proteins (lipocortins) and sequential inhibition of the release of arachidonic acid. Desonide has low range potency.

Pregnancy Risk Factor C

Pregnancy Considerations Adverse events have been observed in animal reproduction studies.

Desoximetasone (des oks i MET a sone)

Brand Names: US Topicort; Topicort Spray

Brand Names: Canada Desoxicream; Topicort®; Topicort® Gel; Topicort® Mild; Topicort® Ointment

Pharmacologic Category Corticosteroid, Topical

Use

Cream, gel, ointment: Relief of inflammation and pruritic symptoms of corticosteroid-responsive dermatosis

Spray: Plaque psoriasis treatment

Local Anesthetic/Vasoconstrictor Precautions No information available to require special precautions

Effects on Dental Treatment No significant effects or complications reported

Effects on Bleeding No information available to require special precautions

Adverse Reactions

>10%: Endocrine & metabolic: HPA-axis suppression (psoriasis patients: spray: 8% to 22%)

<1%: Acneiform eruption, allergic contact dermatitis, atrophic striae, burning sensation, erythema, folliculitis (including folliculopustular lesions), hypertrichosis, hypopigmentation, local irritation, localized burning, localized vesiculation, maceration of the skin, miliaria, perioral dermatitis, pruritus, secondary infection, skin atrophy, xeroderma

General Dosage Range Topical:

Children and Adolescents: Cream, gel, ointment: Apply a thin film to affected area twice daily

Adults: Cream, gel, ointment, spray: Apply a thin film to affected area twice daily

Mechanism of Action Topical corticosteroids have anti-inflammatory, antipruritic, and vasoconstrictive properties. May depress the formation, release, and activity of endogenous chemical mediators of inflammation (kinins, histamine, liposomal enzymes, prostaglandins) through the induction of phospholipase A_2 inhibitory proteins (lipocortins) and sequential inhibition of the release of arachidonic acid. Desoximetasone has intermediate to high range potency (dosage-form dependent).

Pregnancy Risk Factor C

Pregnancy Considerations Corticosteroids were found to be teratogenic following topical application in animal reproduction studies. In general, the use of topical corticosteroids during pregnancy is not considered to have significant risk; however, intrauterine growth retardation in the infant has been reported (rare). The use of large amounts or for prolonged periods of time should be avoided (Reed, 1997).

Desvenlafaxine (des ven la FAX een)

Related Information

Dentin Hypersensitivity, Acid Erosion, High Caries Index, Management of Alveolar Osteitis, and Xerostomia *on page 1857*

Vasoconstrictor Interactions With Antidepressants *on page 1913*

Brand Names: US Khedezla; Pristiq

Brand Names: Canada Pristiq

Pharmacologic Category Antidepressant, Serotonin/Norepinephrine Reuptake Inhibitor

Use Major depressive disorder: Treatment of major depressive disorder (MDD)

Local Anesthetic/Vasoconstrictor Precautions Part of the mechanism of desvenlafaxine is to block reuptake of norepinephrine along with dopamine. Because of the potential for norepinephrine elevation within CNS synapses, it is suggested that vasoconstrictor be administered with caution and to monitor vital signs in dental patients taking antidepressants that affect norepinephrine in this way. This is particularly important in patients taking desvenlafaxine, which has been noted to cause a sustained increase in blood pressure or heart rate. Dose-related increase in systolic and diastolic blood pressure have also been reported.

Effects on Dental Treatment Key adverse event(s) related to dental treatment: Significant xerostomia (normal salivary flow resumes upon discontinuation). See Effects on Bleeding.

Effects on Bleeding Platelet dysfunction (ie, impaired platelet aggregation) may occur during treatment with serotonin norepinephrine reuptake inhibitors (SNRIs), such as desvenlafaxine, due to platelet serotonin depletion, possibly increasing the risk of a bleeding complication. NSAIDs may increase this risk.

Adverse Reactions Reported for 50 to 100 mg/day.

>10%:

Central nervous system: Dizziness (10% to 13%), insomnia (9% to 12%)

Dermatologic: Hyperhidrosis (10% to 11%)

Gastrointestinal: Nausea (22% to 26%), xerostomia (11% to 17%)

1% to 10%:

Cardiovascular: Orthostatic hypotension (elderly 8%), syncope (<2%), tachycardia (<2%), hypertension (dose related; ≤1% of patients taking 50 to 100 mg daily had sustained diastolic BP ≥90 mm Hg)

Central nervous system: Drowsiness (≤9%), fatigue (7%), anxiety (3% to 5%), delayed ejaculation (1% to 5%), abnormal dreams (2% to 3%), anorgasmia (males ≤3%; females 1%), jitteriness (2%), depersonalization (<2%), dystonia (<2%), vertigo (≤2%), yawning (1%), disturbance in attention (≤1%), male sexual disorder (≤1%)

Dermatologic: Alopecia (<2%), skin photosensitivity (<2%), skin rash (<2%)

Endocrine & metabolic: Decreased libido (males 4% to 5%), increased serum cholesterol (increased by ≥50 mg/dL and ≥261 mg/dL: 3% to 4%), increased serum prolactin (<2%), weight gain (<2%), hot flash (1%), increased LDL cholesterol (increased by ≥50 mg/dL and ≥190 mg/dL: ≤1%)

Gastrointestinal: Constipation (9%), decreased appetite (5% to 8%), vomiting (≤4%), bruxism (<2%)

Genitourinary: Proteinuria (6% to 8%), erectile dysfunction (3% to 6%), urinary retention (<2%), ejaculation failure (≤1%), urinary hesitancy (≤1%)

Hepatic: Abnormal hepatic function tests (<2%)

Hypersensitivity: Angioedema (<2%)

Neuromuscular & skeletal: Tremor (≤3%), stiffness (<2%), weakness (<2%)

Ophthalmic: Blurred vision (3% to 4%), mydriasis (2%)

Otic: Tinnitus (≤2%)

Frequency not defined: Cardiovascular: Coronary occlusion, ischemic heart disease, myocardial infarction

<1%, postmarketing, and/or case reports: Acute pancreatitis, angle-closure glaucoma, seizure, Stevens-Johnson syndrome

General Dosage Range Dosage adjustment recommended in patients with hepatic or renal impairment

Oral: *Adults:* Initial: 50 mg once daily

Mechanism of Action Desvenlafaxine is a potent and selective serotonin and norepinephrine reuptake inhibitor.

Pharmacodynamics/Kinetics

Half-life Elimination ~10 to 11 hours; prolonged in renal failure and hepatic failure

Pregnancy Risk Factor C

Pregnancy Considerations Adverse events have been observed in some animal reproduction studies. Nonteratogenic effects in the newborn following SSRI/SNRI exposure late in the third trimester include respiratory distress, cyanosis, apnea, seizures, temperature instability, feeding difficulty, vomiting, hypoglycemia, hyper- or hypotonia, hyper-reflexia, jitteriness, irritability, constant crying, and tremor. Symptoms may be due to the toxicity of the SNRIs/SSRIs or a discontinuation syndrome and may be consistent with serotonin syndrome associated with treatment. The long-term effects of in utero SNRI/SSRI exposure on infant development and behavior are not known.

The ACOG recommends that therapy with SSRIs or SNRIs during pregnancy be individualized; treatment of depression during pregnancy should incorporate the clinical expertise of the mental health clinician, obstetrician, primary health care provider, and pediatrician. According to the American Psychiatric Association (APA), the risks of medication treatment should be weighed against other treatment options and untreated depression. For women who discontinue antidepressant medications during pregnancy and who may be at high risk for postpartum depression, the medications can be restarted following delivery. Treatment algorithms have been developed by the ACOG and the APA for the management of depression in women prior to conception and during pregnancy.

Desvenlafaxine is the major active metabolite of venlafaxine; also refer to the Venlafaxine monograph.

Pregnant women exposed to antidepressants during pregnancy are encouraged to enroll in the National Pregnancy Registry for Antidepressants (NPRAD). Women 18 to 45 years of age or their health care providers may contact the registry by calling 844-405-6185. Enrollment should be done as early in pregnancy as possible.

Dexamethasone (Systemic)

(deks a METH a sone)

Related Information

Respiratory Diseases *on page 1777*

Ulcerative, Erosive, and Painful Oral Mucosal Disorders *on page 1853*

Related Sample Prescriptions

Ulcerative and Erosive Disorders - Sample Prescriptions *on page 43*

Brand Names: US Active Injection D; Baycadron [DSC]; Dexamethasone Intensol; DexPak 10 Day; DexPak 13 Day; DexPak 6 Day; DoubleDex; LoCort 11-Day; LoCort 7-Day; ReadySharp Dexamethasone; ZonaCort 11 Day; ZonaCort 7 Day

Brand Names: Canada Apo-Dexamethasone; Dexasone; Dom-Dexamethasone; PHL-Dexamethasone; PMS-Dexamethasone; PRO-Dexamethasone; ratio-Dexamethasone

Generic Availability (US) May be product dependent

Pharmacologic Category Anti-inflammatory Agent; Antiemetic; Corticosteroid, Systemic

Dental Use Treatment of a variety of oral diseases of allergic, inflammatory or autoimmune origin; aphthous stomatitis (systemic dexamethasone used topically); lichen planus (erosive) and other oral vesiculoerosive diseases

Use Note: Treatment guidelines recommend the use of high dose IV or oral methylprednisolone for acute exacerbations of multiple sclerosis (AAN [Scott 2011], NICE 2014).

Oral, IV or IM injection:

Allergic states: Control of severe or incapacitating allergic conditions intractable to adequate trials of conventional treatment: seasonal or perennial allergic rhinitis, bronchial asthma, contact dermatitis, atopic dermatitis, serum sickness, drug hypersensitivity reactions; acute noninfectious laryngeal edema, urticarial transfusion reactions (injection only).

Collagen diseases: During an exacerbation or as maintenance therapy in selected cases of systemic lupus erythematosus or acute rheumatic carditis.

Dermatologic diseases: Pemphigus; bullous dermatitis herpetiformis; severe erythema multiforme (Stevens-Johnson syndrome); exfoliative dermatitis; exfoliative erythroderma; mycosis fungoides; severe psoriasis; severe seborrheic dermatitis.

Diagnostic testing: Diagnostic testing of adrenocortical hyperfunction.

Edematous states: To induce a diuresis or remission of proteinuria in idiopathic nephrotic syndrome or that because of systemic lupus erythematosus.

Endocrine disorders: Primary, secondary, or acute (injection only) adrenocortical insufficiency (hydrocortisone or cortisone is the first choice); preoperatively, and in the event of serious trauma or illness, in adrenal insufficiency or when adrenocortical reserve is doubtful (injection only); shock unresponsive to conventional therapy if adrenocortical insufficiency exists or is suspected (injection only); congenital adrenal hyperplasia; nonsuppurative thyroiditis; hypercalcemia associated with cancer.

GI diseases: To tide the patient over a critical period of the disease in ulcerative colitis or regional enteritis.

Hematologic disorders: Idiopathic thrombocytopenic purpura in adults (not IM); secondary thrombocytopenia in adults (select cases); acquired (autoimmune) hemolytic anemia; pure red cell aplasia; congenital (erythroid) hypoplastic anemia (Diamond Blackfan anemia).

Neoplastic diseases: Palliative management of leukemias and lymphomas in adults and acute leukemia of childhood.

Nervous system: Acute exacerbations of multiple sclerosis; cerebral edema associated with primary or metastatic brain tumor or craniotomy.

Ophthalmic diseases: Severe acute and chronic allergic and inflammatory processes involving the eye and its adnexa such as allergic conjunctivitis; keratitis; allergic corneal marginal ulcers; herpes zoster ophthalmicus; iritis and iridocyclitis; chorioretinitis; anterior segment inflammation; diffuse posterior uveitis and choroiditis; optic neuritis; sympathetic ophthalmia; temporal arteritis; uveitis; ocular inflammatory conditions unresponsive to topical corticosteroids.

Respiratory diseases: Symptomatic sarcoidosis; Loeffler syndrome not manageable by other means; berylliosis; fulminating or disseminated pulmonary tuberculosis when used concurrently with appropriate antituberculous chemotherapy; aspiration pneumonitis; idiopathic eosinophilic pneumonias.

Rheumatic disorders: As adjunctive therapy for short-term administration in psoriatic arthritis, rheumatoid arthritis (RA), juvenile RA, ankylosing spondylitis, acute and subacute bursitis, acute nonspecific tenosynovitis, acute gouty arthritis, posttraumatic osteoarthritis, synovitis of osteoarthritis, epicondylitis; treatment of dermatomyositis, polymyositis, and systemic lupus erythematosus.

Miscellaneous: Tuberculous meningitis with subarachnoid block or impending block when used with appropriate antituberculous chemotherapy; trichinosis with neurologic or myocardial involvement.

Intraarticular or soft tissue injection: As adjunctive therapy for short-term administration in synovitis of osteoarthritis, RA, acute and subacute bursitis, acute gouty arthritis, epicondylitis, acute nonspecific tenosynovitis, posttraumatic osteoarthritis

Intralesional injection: Keloids; localized hypertrophic, infiltrated, inflammatory lesions of lichen planus, psoriatic plaques, granuloma annulare, and lichen simplex chronicus (neurodermatitis); discoid lupus erythematosus; necrobiosis lipoidica diabeticorum; alopecia areata; cystic tumors of an aponeurosis or tendon (ganglia)

Local Anesthetic/Vasoconstrictor Precautions No information available to require special precautions

Effects on Dental Treatment No significant effects or complications reported

Effects on Bleeding No information available to require special precautions

Adverse Reactions Some reactions listed are based on reports for other agents in this same pharmacologic class and may not be specifically reported for dexamethasone.

Frequency not defined:

Cardiovascular: Bradycardia, cardiac arrhythmia, cardiac failure, cardiomegaly, circulatory shock, edema, embolism (fat), hypertension, hypertrophic cardiomyopathy (premature infants), myocardial rupture (post-MI), syncope, tachycardia, thromboembolism, thrombophlebitis, vasculitis

Central nervous system: Depression, emotional lability, euphoria, headache, increased intracranial pressure, insomnia, malaise, myasthenia, neuritis, neuropathy, paresthesia, personality changes, pseudotumor cerebri (usually following discontinuation), psychic disorder, seizure, vertigo

Dermatologic: Acne vulgaris, allergic dermatitis, alopecia, atrophic striae, diaphoresis, ecchymoses, erythema, facial erythema, fragile skin, hyperpigmentation, hypertrichosis, hypopigmentation, perianal skin irritation (itching, burning, tingling; following IV injection), petechiae, skin atrophy, skin rash, subcutaneous atrophy, suppression of skin test reaction, urticaria, xeroderma

Endocrine & metabolic: Adrenal suppression, carbohydrate intolerance, Cushing syndrome, decreased glucose tolerance, decreased serum potassium, diabetes mellitus, fluid retention, glycosuria, growth suppression (children), hirsutism, HPA-axis suppression, hyperglycemia, hypokalemic alkalosis, menstrual disease, moon face, negative nitrogen balance, protein catabolism, redistribution of body fat, sodium retention, weight gain

Gastrointestinal: Abdominal distention, gastrointestinal hemorrhage, gastrointestinal perforation, hiccups, increased appetite, nausea, pancreatitis, peptic ulcer, pruritus ani (following IV injection), ulcerative esophagitis

Genitourinary: Defective (increased or decreased) spermatogenesis

Hematologic & oncologic: Kaposi sarcoma, petechial, tumor lysis syndrome

Hepatic: Hepatomegaly, increased serum transaminases

Hypersensitivity: Anaphylactoid reaction, anaphylaxis, angioedema, hypersensitivity

Infection: Infection, sterile abscess

Local: Postinjection flare (intra-articular use)

Neuromuscular & skeletal: Amyotrophy, aseptic necrosis of bones (femoral and humoral heads), bone fractures, Charcot-like arthropathy, myasthenia, myopathy (particularly in conjunction with neuromuscular disease or neuromuscular-blocking agents), osteoporosis, rupture of tendon, steroid myopathy, vertebral compression fracture

Ophthalmic: Exophthalmos, glaucoma, increased intraocular pressure, subcapsular posterior cataract

Respiratory: Pulmonary edema

Miscellaneous: Wound healing impairment

Dental Usual Dosage

Erosive lichen planus and major aphthae: Oral: For 3 days, rinse with 15 mL dexamethasone (0.5 mg/5 mL) oral elixir 4 times/day and swallow; then for 3 days, rinse with 5 mL 4 times/day and swallow; then for 3 days, rinse with 5 mL 4 times/day and swallow every other time. Then for 3 days rinse with 5 mL 4 times/day and expectorate. Continue the rinse and expectorate mode for 2 minutes, but discontinue medication when mouth becomes completely comfortable.

Recurrent aphthous stomatitis: Rinse with 5 mL dexamethasone (0.5 mg/5 mL) oral elixir for 2 minutes 4 times/day and expectorate

Dosing

Adult

Adrenal crisis (shock due to adrenal insufficiency and unresponsive to conventional therapy) (off-label dose): IV: 4 to 10 mg as a single dose, which may be repeated if necessary. **Note:** Hydrocortisone is the preferred agent in this setting (ES [Bornstein 2016]).

Anti-inflammatory/immunosuppressive/endocrine disorders:

Oral, IM, IV: 0.5 to 9 mg/day in divided doses every 6 to 12 hours; dose depends upon condition being treated and response of patient.

Intra-articular, intralesional, or soft tissue injection: Dosage and frequency depend on the condition and the site of injection; frequency range: once every 3 to 5 days to once every 2 to 3 weeks

Large joints (eg, knee): Single dose: 2 to 4 mg

Small joints (eg, interphalangeal, temporomandibular): Single dose: 0.8 to 1 mg

Bursae: Single dose: 2 to 4 mg

Tendon Sheaths: Single dose: 0.4 to 1 mg

Soft tissue infiltration: Single dose: 2 to 6 mg

Ganglia: 1 to 2 mg

Brain tumor (palliative management of cerebral edema or neurological deficits associated with recurrent or inoperable brain tumors): Oral, IV: 2 mg 2 to 3 times daily may be effective; individualize dose based on disease response and patient tolerance.

Cerebral edema (associated with brain tumor or craniotomy): IM, IV: 10 mg IV immediately, followed by 4 mg IM every 6 hours until cerebral edema subsides, then switch to oral regimen; dosage may be reduced after 2 to 4 days and gradually discontinued over 5 to 7 days

Cushing syndrome, diagnostic (low dose): Oral: 1 mg at 11 PM, draw blood at 8 AM; greater accuracy for Cushing syndrome may be achieved with 0.5 mg every 6 hours for 48 hours (with 24-hour urine collection for 17-hydroxycorticosteroid excretion)

Differentiation of Cushing syndrome due to ACTH excess from Cushing due to other causes: Oral: 2 mg every 6 hours for 48 hours (with 24-hour urine collection for 17-hydroxycorticosteroid excretion)

Immune thrombocytopenia (primary), initial therapy: Oral: 40 mg once daily for 4 consecutive days; if platelet count continues to remain <30,000/mm^3 or bleeding symptoms occur by day 10, may administer an additional 4-day course of 40 mg once daily (Wei 2016) **or** 40 mg once daily for 4 consecutive days, if platelets fall below 30,000/mm^3 within 6 months a second course may be administered, followed by a prednisone taper (Cheng 2003). Pulsed dexamethasone dosing of 40 mg once daily for 4 days every 14 or 28 days for 4 to 6 cycles has also been used (Mazzucconi 2007; Provan 2010).

Multiple sclerosis (acute exacerbation):

Note: Treatment guidelines recommend the use of high dose IV or oral methylprednisolone for acute exacerbations of multiple sclerosis (AAN [Scott 2011], NICE 2014).

Oral: 30 mg/day for 1 week, followed by 4 to 12 mg every other day for 1 month

Acute mountain sickness (AMS)/high altitude cerebral edema (HACE) (off-label use):

Prevention: Oral: 2 mg every 6 hours **or** 4 mg every 12 hours starting on the day of ascent; may be discontinued after staying at the same elevation for 2 to 3 days or if descent is initiated; do not exceed a 10 day duration (Luks 2010). **Note:** In situations of rapid ascent to altitudes >3500 meters (such as rescue or military operations), 4 mg every 6 hours may be considered (Luks 2010).

Treatment: Oral, IM, IV:

AMS: 4 mg every 6 hours (Luks 2010)

HACE: Initial: 8 mg as a single dose; Maintenance: 4 mg every 6 hours until symptoms resolve (Luks 2010)

Accelerated fetal lung maturation (off-label use): IM: 6 mg every 12 hours for a total of 4 doses (ACOG 171 2016). A single course is recommended for women between 24 and 34 weeks of gestation, including those with ruptured membranes or multiple gestations, who are at risk of delivering within 7 days. A single course may be appropriate in some women beginning at 23 weeks gestation or late preterm (between 34 0/7 weeks and 36 6/7 weeks gestation). A single repeat course may be considered in some women with pregnancies less than 34 weeks gestation at risk for delivery within 7 days and who had a course of antenatal corticosteroids >14 days prior (ACOG 171 2016; ACOG 172 2016; ACOG 677 2016).

Airway edema or extubation (off-label use): IV: 0.5 mg/kg/dose (maximum dose: 10 mg/dose) 6 to 12 hours prior to extubation then every 6 hours for 5 doses (Khemani 2009) **or** 5 mg every 6 hours for 4 doses with extubation performed 24 hours after last injection (Lee 2007).

Chemotherapy-associated nausea and vomiting, prevention (off-label use):

High emetic potential chemotherapy: Oral, IV: 12 mg on day 1 prior to chemotherapy (in combination with aprepitant or fosaprepitant and a 5HT$_3$ antagonist on day 1) followed by 8 mg on days 2 to 3 or days 2 to 4 (with aprepitant on days 2 and 3 if aprepitant used on day 1) (Basch 2011; Roila 2016) **or** (if aprepitant/fosaprepitant not used): 20 mg day 1 (in combination with a 5HT$_3$ antagonist on day 1) followed by 8 mg twice daily for 3 to 4 days (Roila 2016)

Moderate emetic potential chemotherapy: Oral, IV: 8 mg on day 1 prior to chemotherapy (in combination with a 5HT$_3$ antagonist on day 1) and 8 mg on days 2 and 3; may be administered as 4 mg twice daily (Basch 2011; Roila 2016)

Low emetic potential chemotherapy: Oral, IV: 4 to 8 mg prior to chemotherapy (Basch 2011; Roila 2016)

Dosing when used in combination with extended-release granisetron (Raftopoulos 2015):

Day 1: IV: 20 mg (for highly emetic chemotherapy) **or** 8 mg (for moderately emetic chemotherapy)

Days 2, 3, and 4: Oral: 8 mg twice daily (for highly emetic chemotherapy)

Dexamethasone suppression test (depression/suicide indicator) (off-label use): Oral: 1 mg at 11 PM, draw blood at 8 AM the following day for plasma cortisol determination

Glucocorticoid remediable aldosteronism, treatment (off-label use): Oral: Initial: 0.125 to 0.25 mg once daily, preferably at bedtime to suppress early morning ACTH surge (Funder 2016)

Multiple myeloma (off-label use): Note: Multiple dexamethasone-containing regimens are available for the treatment of multiple myeloma. Refer to appropriate literature/guidelines for additional details.

Oral: 40 mg once daily on days 1 to 4, 9 to 12, and 17 to 20 (as induction therapy) in combination with bortezomib and doxorubicin for 3 cycles (Sonneveld 2012) **or** 40 mg once weekly on days 1, 8, 15, and 22 every 28 days (in combination with lenalidomide) until disease progression (Rajkumar 2010) or 40 mg once weekly on days 1, 8, 15, and 22 every 28 days (in combination with pomalidomide) until disease progression or unacceptable toxicity (San Miguel 2013) **or** 40 mg once weekly on days 1, 8, 15, and 22 every 28 days (in combination with ixazomib and lenalidomide) until disease progression or unacceptable toxicity (Moreau 2015) **or** 28 mg orally plus 8 mg IV (prior to elotuzumab) on days 1, 8, 15, and 22 every 28 days for 2 cycles, followed by 28 mg orally plus 8 mg IV (prior to elotuzumab) on days 1 and 15 and 40 mg orally on days 8 and 22 every 28 days thereafter until disease progression or unacceptable toxicity (in combination with elotuzumab and lenalidomide) (Lonial 2015).

Oral or IV: 20 mg once daily days 1, 2, 4, 5, 8, 9, 11, and 12 every 21 days (in combination with daratumumab and bortezomib) for 8 cycles (Palumbo 2016) **or** 20 mg on days 1 (prior to daratumumab infusion) and 2 each week (in combination with daratumumab and lenalidomide) until disease progression or unacceptable toxicity (Dimopoulos 2016a); for patients >75 years of age, BMI <18.5, poorly controlled diabetes, or corticosteroid intolerance a reduced dexamethasone dose of 20 mg once a week was used (Dimopoulous 2016a; Palumbo 2016).

Geriatric Refer to adult dosing. Use cautiously in the elderly in the smallest possible dose.

Pediatric

Anti-inflammatory/immunosuppressive/endocrine disorders: Infants, Children, and Adolescents: Oral, IM, IV: Initial dose range: 0.02 to 0.3 mg/kg/**day** (0.6 to 9 mg/m^2/**day**) in divided doses every 6 to 12 hours; dose depends upon condition being treated and response of patient; dosage for infants and children should be based on disease severity and patient response

Asthma exacerbation: Limited data available: Infants, Children, and Adolescents: Oral, IM, IV: 0.6 mg/kg once daily as a single dose or once daily for 2 days; maximum dose: 16 mg/dose (Hegenbarth 2008; Keeney 2014; Quereshi 2001); single dose regimens as low as 0.3 mg/kg/dose and as high as 1.7 mg/kg/dose have also been reported (Keeney 2014; Qureshi 2001; Shefrin 2009). **Note:** Duration greater than 2 days is not recommended due to increased risk of metabolic effects (GINA 2014).

Cerebral edema: Infants, Children, and Adolescents: Oral, IM, IV: Loading dose: 1 to 2 mg/kg/dose as a single dose; maintenance: 1 to 1.5 mg/kg/**day** in divided doses every 4 to 6 hours; maximum: 16 mg/**day** (Kleigman 2007).

Congenital adrenal hyperplasia: Adolescents (fully grown): Oral: 0.25 to 0.5 mg once daily (AAP 2010; Speiser 2010). **Note:** For younger patients who are still growing, hydrocortisone or fludrocortisone are preferred.

Physiologic replacement: Infants, Children, and Adolescents: Oral, IM, IV: 0.03 to 0.15 mg/kg/**day** in divided doses every 6 to 12 hours (Kleigman 2007) or 0.2 to 0.25 mg/m^2/**day** once daily; some patients may require 0.3 mg/m^2/**day** (Gupta 2008)

Acute mountain sickness (AMS) (moderate)/high altitude cerebral edema (HACE) (off-label use): Limited data available: Infants, Children, and Adolescents: Oral, IM, IV: 0.15 mg/kg/dose every 6 hours; maximum dose: 4 mg/dose; consider using for high altitude pulmonary edema because of associated HACE with this condition (Luks 2010; Pollard 2001)

Airway edema or extubation (off-label use): Limited data available: Infants, Children, and Adolescents: IV: 0.5 mg/kg/dose (maximum dose: 10 mg/dose) 6 to 12 hours prior to extubation then every 6 hours for 5 doses (total dexamethasone dose: 3 mg/kg) (Anene 1996; Khemani 2009; Tellez 1991)

Bacterial meningitis (*H. influenzae* type b) (off-label use): Limited data available: Infants >6 weeks and Children: IV: 0.15 mg/kg/dose every 6 hours for the first 2 to 4 days of antibiotic treatment; start dexamethasone 10 to 20 minutes before or with the first dose of antibiotic; if antibiotics have already been administered, dexamethasone use has not been shown to improve patient outcome and is not recommended (Tunkel 2004).

Chemotherapy-associated nausea and vomiting, prevention (off-label use): Pediatric Oncology Group of Ontario guideline recommendations (Dupuis 2013): Infants, Children, and Adolescents:

High emetic potential chemotherapy: Oral, IV: 6 mg/m^2/dose every 6 hours (in combination with a $5HT_3$ antagonist and aprepitant [if no interaction with aprepitant and if ≥12 years]); reduce dexamethasone dose by 50% if administered concomitantly with aprepitant

Moderate emetic potential chemotherapy: Oral, IV:

BSA ≤0.6 m^2: 2 mg every 12 hours (in combination with a $5HT_3$ antagonist)

BSA >0.6 m^2: 4 mg every 12 hours (in combination with a $5HT_3$ antagonist)

Croup (laryngotracheobronchitis) (off-label use): Limited data available: Infants and Children: Oral, IM, IV: 0.6 mg/kg once; usual maximum dose: 16 mg (doses as high as 20 mg have been used) (Bjornson 2004; Hegenbarth 2008; Rittichier 2000). **Note:** a single oral dose of 0.15 mg/kg has been shown effective in children with mild to moderate croup (Russell 2004; Sparrow 2006).

Immune thrombocytopenia (primary), second-line treatment (off-label use): Children and Adolescents: Oral: 0.6 mg/kg/**day** for 4 days every 4 weeks up to 6 cycles (Neunert 2011). Consider a maximum daily dose cap (eg, 24 mg or 40 mg) based on response, individual tolerance and/or institutional policy.

Immune thrombocytopenia, chronic (refractory) (off-label use): Children and Adolescents: Oral: 0.6 mg/kg/**day** for 4 days every 4 weeks for 6 cycles (Hedlund-Treutiger 2003; Neunert 2011) **or** 28 to 40 mg/m^2/**day** for 4 days every 4 weeks for 6 cycles (response usually observed within 3 days); maximum dose: 40 mg/**day** (Chen 1997; Khune 1997; Provan 2010]). Consider a maximum daily dose cap (eg, 24 mg or 40 mg) based on response, individual tolerance and/or institutional policy.

Renal Impairment There are no dosage adjustments provided in the manufacturer's labeling; use with caution.

Hemodialysis: Supplemental dose is not necessary (Aronoff 2007).

Peritoneal dialysis: Supplemental dose is not necessary (Aronoff 2007).

International Myeloma Working Group (IMWG) Recommendations: The International Myeloma Working Group (IMWG) recommendations suggest that dexamethasone may be administered without dosage adjustment in multiple myeloma patients with renal impairment, including those on dialysis. The IMWG recommends the use of the Chronic Kidney Disease Epidemiology Collaboration (CKD-EPI) equation (preferred) or the Modification of Diet in Renal Disease (MDRD) formula to evaluate renal function estimation in multiple myeloma patients with a stable serum creatinine (Dimopoulos 2016b).

Hepatic Impairment There are no dosage adjustments provided in the manufacturer's labeling.

Mechanism of Action A long acting corticosteroid with minimal sodium-retaining potential. Decreases inflammation by suppression of neutrophil migration, decreased production of inflammatory mediators, and reversal of increased capillary permeability; suppresses normal immune response. Dexamethasone's mechanism of antiemetic activity is unknown.

Contraindications

Hypersensitivity to dexamethasone or any component of the formulation; systemic fungal infections

Documentation of allergenic cross-reactivity for corticosteroids is limited. However, because of similarities in chemical structure and/or pharmacologic actions, the possibility of cross-sensitivity cannot be ruled out with certainty.

Warnings/Precautions Corticosteroids are not approved for epidural injection. Serious neurologic events (eg, spinal cord infarction, paraplegia, quadriplegia, cortical blindness, stroke), some resulting in death, have been reported with epidural injection of corticosteroids, with and without use of fluoroscopy. Intra-articular injection may produce systemic as well as local effects. Appropriate examination of any joint fluid present is necessary to exclude a septic process. Avoid injection into an infected site. Do not inject into unstable joints. Patients should not overuse joints in which symptomatic benefit has been obtained as long as the inflammatory process remains active. Frequent intra-articular injection may result in damage to joint tissues.

Use with caution in patients with thyroid disease, hepatic impairment, renal impairment, cardiovascular disease, diabetes, glaucoma, cataracts, myasthenia gravis, osteoporosis, seizures, or GI diseases (diverticulitis, fresh intestinal anastomoses, active or latent peptic ulcer, ulcerative colitis, abscess or other pyogenic infection) due to perforation risk. Use caution following acute MI (corticosteroids have been associated with myocardial rupture). Use with caution in patients with a history of ocular herpes simplex; corneal perforation has occurred; do not use in active ocular herpes simplex. Not recommended for the treatment of optic neuritis; may increase frequency of new episodes. Use with caution in the elderly with the smallest possible effective dose for the shortest duration. May affect growth velocity; growth should be routinely monitored in pediatric patients. Withdraw therapy with gradual tapering of dose.

May cause hypercorticism or suppression of hypothalamic-pituitary-adrenal (HPA) axis, particularly in younger children or in patients receiving high doses for prolonged periods. HPA axis suppression may lead to adrenal crisis. Withdrawal and discontinuation of a corticosteroid should be done slowly and carefully. Particular care is required when patients are transferred from systemic corticosteroids to inhaled products due to possible adrenal insufficiency or withdrawal from steroids, including an increase in allergic symptoms. Adult patients receiving >20 mg per day of prednisone (or equivalent) may be most susceptible. Fatalities have occurred due to adrenal insufficiency in asthmatic patients during and after transfer from systemic corticosteroids to aerosol steroids; aerosol steroids do not provide the systemic steroid needed to treat patients having trauma, surgery, or infections. Dexamethasone does not provide adequate mineralocorticoid activity in adrenal insufficiency (may be employed as a single dose while cortisol assays are performed). In the management/prevention of adrenal crisis in patients with known primary adrenal insufficiency, the Endocrine Society practice guidelines state dexamethasone (intravenous) is the least preferred alternative agent and should be used only if no other glucocorticoid is available. For the treatment of chronic primary adrenal insufficiency (ie, physiologic replacement), dexamethasone (oral) is not recommended due to the risk of Cushingoid side effects (ES [Bornstein 2016]). Rare cases of anaphylactoid reactions have been observed in patients receiving corticosteroids. Patients may require higher doses when subject to stress (ie, trauma, surgery, severe infection).

Acute myopathy has been reported with high dose corticosteroids, usually in patients with neuromuscular transmission disorders; may involve ocular and/or respiratory muscles; monitor creatine kinase; recovery may be delayed. Perineal burning, tingling, pain and pruritus have been reported with IV administration. May occur more commonly in females, with higher doses, and with rapid administration. Symptom onset is sudden and usually resolves in <1 minute (Allan 1986; Neff 2002; Perron 2003; Singh 2011). Corticosteroid use may cause psychiatric disturbances, including depression, euphoria, insomnia, mood swings, severe depression to psychotic manifestations. Preexisting psychiatric conditions may be exacerbated by corticosteroid use. Prolonged use of corticosteroids may increase the incidence of secondary infection, cause activation of latent infections, mask acute infection (including fungal infections), prolong or exacerbate viral infections, or limit response to killed or inactivated vaccines. Exposure to chickenpox or measles should be avoided; corticosteroids should not be used to treat ocular herpes simplex. Corticosteroids should not be used for cerebral malaria, fungal infections, or viral hepatitis. Close observation is required in patients with latent tuberculosis and/or TB reactivity; restrict use in active TB (only fulminating or disseminated TB in conjunction with antituberculosis treatment). Amebiasis should be ruled out in any patient with recent travel to tropic climates or unexplained diarrhea prior to initiation of corticosteroids. Use with extreme caution in patients with Strongyloides infections; hyperinfection, dissemination and fatalities have occurred.

Prolonged treatment with corticosteroids has been associated with the development of Kaposi sarcoma (case reports); if noted, discontinuation of therapy should be considered (Goedert 2002). High-dose corticosteroids should not be used to manage acute head injury (BTF [Carney 2016]). Some products may contain sodium sulfite, a sulfite that may cause allergic-type reactions including anaphylaxis and life-threatening or less severe asthmatic episodes in susceptible patients. Potentially significant drug-drug interactions may exist, requiring dose or frequency adjustment, additional monitoring, and/or selection of alternative therapy. Some dosage forms may contain propylene glycol; large amounts are potentially toxic and have been associated hyperosmolality, lactic acidosis, seizures, and respiratory depression; use caution (AAP ["Inactive" 1997]; Zar 2007).

Benzyl alcohol and derivatives: Some dosage forms may contain sodium benzoate/benzoic acid; benzoic acid (benzoate) is a metabolite of benzyl alcohol; large amounts of benzyl alcohol (≥99 mg/kg/day) have been associated with a potentially fatal toxicity ("gasping syndrome") in neonates; the "gasping syndrome" consists of metabolic acidosis, respiratory distress, gasping respirations, CNS dysfunction (including convulsions, intracranial hemorrhage), hypotension, and cardiovascular collapse (AAP ["Inactive" 1997]; CDC 1982); some data suggests that benzoate displaces bilirubin from protein binding sites (Ahlfors 2001); avoid or use dosage forms containing benzyl alcohol derivative with caution in neonates. See manufacturer's labeling.

Drug Interactions

Metabolism/Transport Effects **Substrate** of CYP3A4 (major), P-glycoprotein; **Note:** Assignment of Major/Minor substrate status based on clinically relevant drug interaction potential; **Induces** CYP2A6 (weak/moderate), CYP2C9 (weak/moderate), CYP3A4 (weak), UGT1A1

Avoid Concomitant Use

Avoid concomitant use of Dexamethasone (Systemic) with any of the following: Aldesleukin; BCG (Intravesical); Conivaptan; Desmopressin; Fusidic Acid

(Systemic); Idelalisib; Indium 111 Capromab Pendetide; Lapatinib; MiFEPRIStone; Natalizumab; Nilotinib; Pimecrolimus; Rilpivirine; RomiDEPsin; Simeprevir; Tacrolimus (Topical); Tofacitinib; VinCRIStine (Liposomal)

Increased Effect/Toxicity

Dexamethasone (Systemic) may increase the levels/effects of: Acetylcholinesterase Inhibitors; Amphotericin B; Androgens; CycloSPORINE (Systemic); Deferasirox; Desirudin; Desmopressin; Fingolimod; Fosphenytoin; Leflunomide; Lenalidomide; Loop Diuretics; Natalizumab; Nicorandil; NSAID (COX-2 Inhibitor); NSAID (Nonselective); Phenytoin; Quinolone Antibiotics; Thalidomide; Thiazide and Thiazide-Like Diuretics; Tofacitinib; Vaccines (Live); Warfarin

The levels/effects of Dexamethasone (Systemic) may be increased by: Aprepitant; Asparaginase (E. coli); Asparaginase (Erwinia); Conivaptan; CycloSPORINE (Systemic); CYP3A4 Inhibitors (Moderate); CYP3A4 Inhibitors (Strong); Denosumab; DilTIAZem; Estrogen Derivatives; Fosamprenavir; Fosaprepitant; Fusidic Acid (Systemic); Idelalisib; Indacaterol; Ivacaftor; MiFEPRIStone; Netupitant; Neuromuscular-Blocking Agents (Nondepolarizing); Ocrelizumab; Palbociclib; P-glycoprotein/ABCB1 Inhibitors; Pimecrolimus; Ranolazine; Roflumilast; Salicylates; Stiripentol; Tacrolimus (Topical); Telaprevir; Trastuzumab

Decreased Effect

Dexamethasone (Systemic) may decrease the levels/effects of: Aldesleukin; Antidiabetic Agents; BCG (Intravesical); Calcitriol (Systemic); Caspofungin; CloZAPine; Cobicistat; Coccidioides immitis Skin Test; Corticorelin; CycloSPORINE (Systemic); Daclatasvir; Dasatinib; Elvitegravir; Fosamprenavir; Fosphenytoin; Hyaluronidase; HYDROcodone; Imatinib; Indium 111 Capromab Pendetide; Isoniazid; Ixabepilone; Lapatinib; Nalmefene; Nilotinib; NiMODipine; Nivolumab; Phenytoin; Rilpivirine; RomiDEPsin; Salicylates; Simeprevir; Sipuleucel-T; SUNItinib; Telaprevir; Tertomotide; Triazolam; Urea Cycle Disorder Agents; Vaccines (Inactivated); Vaccines (Live); VinCRIStine (Liposomal); Voriconazole

The levels/effects of Dexamethasone (Systemic) may be decreased by: Antacids; Bile Acid Sequestrants; Bosentan; CYP3A4 Inducers (Moderate); CYP3A4 Inducers (Strong); Dabrafenib; Deferasirox; Echinacea; Enzalutamide; Fosphenytoin; MiFEPRIStone; Mitotane; Phenytoin; Siltuximab; St John's Wort; Tocilizumab

Dietary Considerations May be taken with meals to decrease GI upset. May need diet with increased potassium, pyridoxine, vitamin C, vitamin D, folate, calcium, and phosphorus.

Pharmacodynamics/Kinetics

Onset of Action

Acetate: IV: Rapid

Immune thrombocytopenia: Oral: Initial response: 2 to 14 days; Peak response: 4 to 28 days (Neunert 2011)

Duration of Action IV: Short

Half-life Elimination

Extremely low birth-weight infants with BPD: 9.26 ± 3.34 hours (range: 5.85 to 16.1 hours) (Charles 1993)

Children 4 months to 16 years: 4.34 ± 4.14 hours (range: 2.33 to 9.54 hours) (Richter 1983)

Adults: Oral: 4 ± 0.9 hours (Czock 2005); IV: ~1 to 5 hours (Hochhaus 2001; Miyabo 1991; Rohdewald 1987; Toth 1999)

Time to Peak Serum: Oral: 1 to 2 hours (Czock 2005); IM: ~30 to 120 minutes (Egerman 1997; Hochhaus 2001); IV: 5 to 10 minutes (free dexamethasone) (Miyabo 1991; Rohdewald 1987)

Pregnancy Risk Factor C

Pregnancy Considerations Adverse events have been observed with corticosteroids in animal reproduction studies. Dexamethasone crosses the placenta (Brownfoot 2013); and is partially metabolized by placental enzymes to an inactive metabolite (Murphy 2007). Some studies have shown an association between first trimester systemic corticosteroid use and oral clefts (Park-Wyllie 2000; Pradat 2003). Systemic corticosteroids may have an effect on fetal growth (decreased birth weight); however, information is conflicting (Lunghi 2010). Hypoadrenalism may occur in newborns following maternal use of corticosteroids during pregnancy; monitor.

Because antenatal corticosteroid administration may reduce the incidence of intraventricular hemorrhage, necrotizing enterocolitis, neonatal mortality, and respiratory distress syndrome, the injection is often used for antenatal fetal lung maturation in patients with preterm premature rupture of membranes or preterm labor who are at risk of preterm delivery (most data is available for betamethasone). A single course of corticosteroids is recommended for women between 24 and 34 weeks gestation who are at risk of delivering within 7 days, including those with ruptured membranes or multiple gestations. A single course of corticosteroids may be considered for women beginning at 23 weeks gestation, who are at risk of delivering within 7 days, in consultation with the family. In addition, a single course of corticosteroids may be given to women between 34 0/7 weeks and 36 6/7 weeks who are at risk of preterm delivery within 7 days and who have not previously received corticosteroids; use of concomitant tocolytics is not currently recommended and administration of late preterm corticosteroids has not been evaluated in women with intrauterine infection, multiple gestations, pregestational diabetes, or women who delivered previously by cesarean section at term. Multiple repeat courses are not recommended. However, in women with pregnancies less than 34 weeks gestation at risk for delivery within 7 days and who had a course of antenatal corticosteroids >14 days prior, a single repeat course may be considered; use of a repeat course in women with premature rupture of membranes is controversial (ACOG 171 2016; ACOG 172 2016; ACOG 677 2016).

When systemic corticosteroids are needed in pregnancy, it is generally recommended to use the lowest effective dose for the shortest duration of time, avoiding high doses during the first trimester (Leachman 2006; Lunghi 2010; Makol 2011; Østensen 2009). Dexamethasone should not be used to treat primary adrenal insufficiency in pregnant women (Bornstein 2016).

Breastfeeding Considerations Corticosteroids are excreted in breast milk; information specific to dexamethasone has not been located. The manufacturer notes that when used systemically, maternal use of corticosteroids have the potential to cause adverse events in a nursing infant (eg, growth suppression, interfere with endogenous corticosteroid production). Due to the potential for serious adverse reactions in the nursing infant, the manufacturer recommends a decision be made whether to discontinue nursing or to discontinue the drug, taking into account the importance of treatment to the mother. If there is concern about exposure to the infant, some guidelines recommend waiting 4 hours after the maternal dose of an oral systemic corticosteroid before breastfeeding in order to decrease potential exposure to the nursing infant (based on a study using prednisolone) (Bae 2011; Leachman 2006; Makol 2011; Ost 1985).

Dosage Forms

Concentrate, Oral:
Dexamethasone Intensol: 1 mg/mL (30 mL)

Elixir, Oral:
Generic: 0.5 mg/5 mL (237 mL)

Kit, Injection:
ReadySharp Dexamethasone: 10 mg/mL

Kit, Injection [preservative free]:
Active Injection D: 10 mg/mL
DoubleDex: 10 mg/mL

Solution, Injection:
Generic: 4 mg/mL (1 mL); 20 mg/5 mL (5 mL); 120 mg/30 mL (30 mL); 10 mg/mL (1 mL); 100 mg/10 mL (10 mL)

Solution, Injection [preservative free]:
Generic: 4 mg/mL (1 mL); 10 mg/mL (1 mL)

Solution, Oral:
Generic: 0.5 mg/5 mL (240 mL, 500 mL)

Tablet, Oral:
DexPak 10 Day: 1.5 mg
DexPak 13 Day: 1.5 mg
DexPak 6 Day: 1.5 mg
Generic: 0.5 mg, 0.75 mg, 1 mg, 1.5 mg, 2 mg, 4 mg, 6 mg

Tablet Therapy Pack, Oral:
LoCort 11-Day: 1.5 mg (41 ea)
LoCort 7-Day: 1.5 mg (27 ea)
ZonaCort 11 Day: 1.5 mg (41 ea)
ZonaCort 7 Day: 1.5 mg (27 ea)

Dexchlorpheniramine (deks klor fen EER a meen)

Pharmacologic Category Alkylamine Derivative; Histamine H_1 Antagonist; Histamine H_1 Antagonist, First Generation

Use Hypersensitivity reactions: For the treatment of perennial and seasonal allergic rhinitis; vasomotor rhinitis; allergic conjunctivitis; mild, uncomplicated allergic skin manifestations of urticaria and angioedema; amelioration of allergic reactions to blood or plasma; dermatographism; adjunctive therapy for the management of anaphylactic reactions.

Local Anesthetic/Vasoconstrictor Precautions No information available to require special precautions

Effects on Dental Treatment Key adverse event(s) related to dental treatment: Significant xerostomia (normal salivary flow resumes upon discontinuation)

Effects on Bleeding No information available to require special precautions

Adverse Reactions Frequency not defined.

Cardiovascular: Chest tightness
Central nervous system: Ataxia, chills, confusion, convulsions, dizziness, drowsiness (slight to moderate), euphoria, excitement, fatigue, hysteria, insomnia, irritability, nervousness, neuritis, paresthesia, restlessness, sedation, vertigo
Dermatologic: Diaphoresis, skin photosensitivity, skin rash (due to drug), urticaria
Gastrointestinal: Anorexia, constipation, diarrhea, epigastric distress, nausea, vomiting, xerostomia
Genitourinary: Difficulty in micturition, early menses, urinary frequency, urinary retention
Hematologic & oncologic: Agranulocytosis, hemolytic anemia, thrombocytopenia
Hypersensitivity: Anaphylactic shock
Neuromuscular & skeletal: Tremor
Ophthalmic: Blurred vision, diplopia
Otic: Acute labyrinthitis, tinnitus
Respiratory: Dry nose, dry throat, nasal congestion, thickening of bronchial secretions, wheezing

General Dosage Range Oral:
Children 2 to 5 years: 0.5 mg every 4 to 6 hours
Children 6 to 11 years: 1 mg every 4 to 6 hours
Children ≥12 years, Adolescents, and Adults: 2 mg every 4 to 6 hours

Mechanism of Action Dexchlorpheniramine competes with histamine for H_1-receptor sites on effector cells in the gastrointestinal tract, blood vessels, and respiratory tract. Dexchlorpheniramine is the predominant active isomer of chlorpheniramine and is approximately twice as active as the racemic compound (Moreno 2010).

Pharmacodynamics/Kinetics

Half-life Elimination 20 to 30 hours (Moreno 2010)

Time to Peak ~3 hours (Moreno 2010)

Pregnancy Considerations Maternal antihistamine use has generally not resulted in an increased risk of birth defects; however, information specific to dexchlorpheniramine is limited (Källén 2002). Dexchlorpheniramine is the *dextro*-isomer of chlorpheniramine. Antihistamines may be used for the treatment of rhinitis, urticaria, and pruritus with rash in pregnant women (although second generation antihistamines may be preferred) (Murase 2014; Wallace 2008; Zuberbier 2014). Antihistamines are not recommended for treatment of pruritus associated with intrahepatic cholestasis in pregnancy (Ambros-Rudolph 2011; Kremer 2011).

Dexchlorpheniramine and Pseudoephedrine

(deks klor fen EER a meen & soo doe e FED rin)

Brand Names: US Rescon [OTC]

Pharmacologic Category Alkylamine Derivative; Alpha/Beta Agonist; Decongestant; Histamine H_1 Antagonist; Histamine H_1 Antagonist, First Generation

Use Upper respiratory allergies: Temporary relief of nasal congestion, runny nose, sneezing, itching of nose or throat and itchy, watery eyes caused by hay fever or other upper respiratory allergies.

Local Anesthetic/Vasoconstrictor Precautions Use with caution since pseudoephedrine is a sympathomimetic amine which could interact with epinephrine to cause a pressor response

Effects on Dental Treatment Key adverse event(s) related to dental treatment: Xerostomia (normal salivary flow resumes upon discontinuation)

Effects on Bleeding No information available to require special precautions

Adverse Reactions There are no adverse reactions listed in the manufacturer's labeling. See individual agents.

General Dosage Range Oral: *Children ≥12 years, Adolescents, and Adults:* Dexchlorpheniramine 2 mg/pseudoephedrine 60 mg (1 tablet) every 4 to 6 hours (maximum: dexchlorpheniramine 8 mg/pseudoephedrine 240 mg [4 tablets] per 24 hours)

Mechanism of Action

Dexchlorpheniramine: Competes with histamine for H_1-receptor sites on effector cells in the gastrointestinal tract, blood vessels, and respiratory tract. Dexchlorpheniramine is the predominant active isomer of chlorpheniramine and is approximately twice as active as the racemic compound (Moreno 2010).

Pseudoephedrine: Directly stimulates alpha-adrenergic receptors of respiratory mucosa causing vasoconstriction; directly stimulates beta-adrenergic receptors causing bronchial relaxation, increased heart rate and contractility.

Pregnancy Considerations Refer to individual agents.

Dexlansoprazole (deks lan SOE pra zole)

Related Information

Gastrointestinal Disorders *on page 1775*

Brand Names: US Dexilant

Brand Names: Canada Dexilant

Pharmacologic Category Proton Pump Inhibitor; Substituted Benzimidazole

Use

Erosive esophagitis: Healing of all grades of erosive esophagitis in patients ≥12 years for up to 8 weeks (capsules only); to maintain healing of erosive esophagitis and relief of heartburn for up to 6 months in adults and 16 weeks in patients 12 to 17 years of age.

Gastroesophageal reflux disease: Treatment of heartburn associated with symptomatic nonerosive gastroesophageal reflux disease (GERD) in patients ≥12 years for 4 weeks.

Local Anesthetic/Vasoconstrictor Precautions No information available to require special precautions

Effects on Dental Treatment Key adverse event(s) related to dental treatment: Xerostomia (normal salivary flow resumes upon discontinuation) and taste alteration has been reported in <2% of patients.

Effects on Bleeding No information available to require special precautions

Adverse Reactions Incidence reported for adults unless otherwise specified.

≥2%:

Central nervous system: Headache (<2%; adolescents: ≥5%)

Gastrointestinal: Diarrhea (adolescents and adults: ≥5%), abdominal pain (adolescents: ≥5%), flatulence (1% to 3%), vomiting (1% to 2%)

Respiratory: Nasopharyngitis (adults: <2%; adolescents: ≥5%), oropharyngeal pain (adolescents: ≥5%), upper respiratory tract infection (2% to 3%)

<2%, postmarketing, and/or case reports: Abdominal distress, abdominal tenderness, abnormal bowel sounds, abnormal dreams, abnormal hepatic function tests, abnormal stools, acne vulgaris, acute renal failure, anaphylaxis, anemia, angina pectoris, anorectal pain, anxiety, arthralgia, arthritis, aspiration, asthma, autoimmune hemolytic anemia, Barrett esophagus, bezoar formation, biliary colic, blurred vision, bone fracture, bradycardia, bronchitis, candidiasis, cardiac arrhythmia, cerebrovascular accident, change in appetite, change in libido, chest pain, chills, cholelithiasis, chronic renal insufficiency (Lazarus 2016), *Clostridium difficile*-associated diarrhea, colitis (microscopic), colonic polyps, constipation, constriction of the pharynx, cough, deafness, decreased platelet count, decreased serum bilirubin, deep vein thrombosis, delayed gastric emptying, depression, dermatitis, dizziness, duodenitis, dysgeusia, dysmenorrhea, dyspareunia, dyspepsia, dysphagia, dyspnea, dysuria, edema (including oral, facial, and pharyngeal), enteritis, eructation, erythema, esophagitis, exfoliative dermatitis, eye irritation, falling, feeling abnormal, fever, gastric polyp, gastritis, gastroenteritis, gastroesophageal reflux disease, gastrointestinal disease, gastrointestinal hypermotility, gastrointestinal perforation, gastrointestinal ulcer, goiter, halitosis, hematemesis, hematochezia, hemorrhoids, hepatitis, hepatomegaly, hepatotoxicity (idiosyncratic) (Chalasani 2014), hiccups, hot flash, hypercalcemia, hypermenorrhea, hypersensitivity angiitis, hypersensitivity reaction, hypertension, hyperventilation, hypokalemia, hypomagnesemia, hyponatremia, immune thrombocytopenia, increased gastrin, increased serum alkaline phosphatase, increased serum ALT, increased serum AST, increased serum bilirubin, increased serum creatinine, increased serum glucose, increased serum potassium, increased serum total protein, inflammation, influenza, insomnia, irritable bowel syndrome, joint sprain, lymphadenopathy, memory impairment, menstrual disease, migraine, mucosal inflammation, mucus stools, muscle cramps, musculoskeletal pain, myalgia, myocardial infarction, nodule, oral bullae, oral herpes, otalgia, pain, painful defecation, palpitations, pancreatitis, paresthesia (oral), pharyngitis, procedural pain, proctitis, pruritus, psychomotor agitation, rectal hemorrhage, respiratory congestion, retching, seizure, sinusitis, skin lesion, skin rash, sore throat, Stevens-Johnson syndrome, sunburn, swelling of eye, tachycardia, tinnitus, toxic epidermal necrolysis, transient ischemic attacks, tremor, trigeminal neuralgia, urinary urgency, urticaria, vertigo, viral infection, vulvovaginal infection, weakness, weight gain, xerostomia

General Dosage Range Dosage adjustment recommended in patients with hepatic impairment

Oral: *Children ≥12 years, Adolescents, and Adults:* 30 to 60 mg once daily

Mechanism of Action Proton pump inhibitor; decreases acid secretion in gastric parietal cells through inhibition of (H+, K+)-ATPase enzyme system, blocking the final step in gastric acid production

Pharmacodynamics/Kinetics

Half-life Elimination ~1 to 2 hours

Time to Peak Serum:

Capsules: **Note:** Two distinct peaks secondary to dual release formulation: Initial peak between 1 and 2 hours and a second higher peak between 4 and 5 hours.

Orally disintegrating tablets: 1 to 6 hours.

Pregnancy Considerations Adverse events have not been observed in animal reproduction studies. Dexlansoprazole is the R-enantiomer of lansoprazole. Information related to dexlansoprazole in pregnancy has not been located. Refer to the lansoprazole monograph for additional information. When treating GERD in pregnancy, PPIs may be used when clinically indicated (Katz 2013).

Product Availability

Dexilant SoluTab: FDA approved January 2016; anticipated availability is currently unknown. Consult the prescribing information for additional information.

Dexmedetomidine (deks MED e toe mi deen)

Brand Names: US Precedex

Brand Names: Canada Precedex

Pharmacologic Category $Alpha_2$-Adrenergic Agonist; Sedative

Use

Intensive care unit sedation: Sedation of initially-intubated and mechanically-ventilated patients during treatment in an intensive care setting

Procedural sedation: Procedural sedation prior to and/or during awake fiberoptic intubation; sedation prior to and/or during surgical or other procedures of non-intubated patients

Local Anesthetic/Vasoconstrictor Precautions No information available to require special precautions

Effects on Dental Treatment Key adverse event(s) related to dental treatment: Xerostomia and changes in salivation (normal salivary flow resumes upon discontinuation)

Effects on Bleeding No information available to require special precautions

Adverse Reactions Frequency dependent upon dose, duration, and indication.

>10%:

Cardiovascular: Hypotension (24% to 56%), bradycardia (5% to 42%), systolic hypertension (28%), tachycardia (25%), hypertension (diastolic; 12%), hypertension (11%)

Central nervous system: Agitation (5% to 14%)

Gastrointestinal: Constipation (6% to 14%), nausea (3% to 11%)

Respiratory: Respiratory depression (37%; placebo 32%)

1% to 10%:

Cardiovascular: Atrial fibrillation (2% to 9%), peripheral edema (3% to 7%), hypovolemia (3%), edema (2%)

Central nervous system: Anxiety (5% to 9%)

Endocrine & metabolic: Hypokalemia (9%), hyperglycemia (7%), hypoglycemia (5%), increased thirst (2%), hypocalcemia (1%), hypomagnesemia (1%)

Gastrointestinal: Xerostomia (3% to 4%)

Genitourinary: Oliguria (2%)

Hematologic & oncologic: Anemia (3%)

Renal: Acute renal failure (2% to 3%), decreased urine output (1%)

Respiratory: Respiratory failure (2% to 10%), adult respiratory distress syndrome (1% to 9%), pleural effusion (2%), wheezing (≤1%)

Miscellaneous: Fever (5% to 7%), withdrawal syndrome (ICU sedation; 3% to 5%)

Postmarketing and/or case reports: Abdominal pain, acidosis, apnea, atrioventricular block, bronchospasm, cardiac arrhythmia, cardiac disease, chills, confusion, convulsions, decreased visual acuity, delirium, diaphoresis, diarrhea, dizziness, drug tolerance (use >24 hours), dyspnea, extrasystoles, hallucination, headache, heart block, hemorrhage, hepatic insufficiency, hyperbilirubinemia, hypercapnia, hyperkalemia, hypernatremia, hyperpyrexia, hypoventilation, hypoxia, illusion, increased blood urea nitrogen, increased gamma-glutamyl transferase, increased serum alkaline phosphatase, increased serum ALT, increased serum AST, inversion T-wave on ECG, myocardial infarction, neuralgia, neuritis, pain, photopsia, polyuria, prolonged Q-T interval on ECG, pulmonary congestion, respiratory acidosis, rigors, seizure, sinoatrial arrest, speech disturbance, supraventricular tachycardia, tachyphylaxis (use >24 hours), variable blood pressure, ventricular arrhythmia, ventricular tachycardia, visual disturbance, vomiting

General Dosage Range IV: *Adults:* Loading infusion: 0.5 to 1 mcg/kg; Maintenance infusion: 0.2 to 1 mcg/kg/**hour**

Mechanism of Action Selective alpha$_2$-adrenoceptor agonist with anesthetic and sedative properties thought to be due to activation of G-proteins by alpha$_{2a}$-adrenoceptors in the brainstem resulting in inhibition of norepinephrine release; peripheral alpha$_{2b}$-adrenoceptors are activated at high doses or with rapid IV administration resulting in vasoconstriction.

Pharmacodynamics/Kinetics

Onset of Action IV Bolus: 5 to 10 minutes; Peak effect: 15 to 30 minutes

Duration of Action Dose dependent: 60 to 120 minutes

Half-life Elimination Distribution: ~6 minutes; Terminal: ~up to 3 hours (Venn 2002); significantly prolonged in patients with severe hepatic impairment (Cunningham, 1999)

Pregnancy Risk Factor C

Pregnancy Considerations Adverse effects have been observed in some animal reproduction studies. Dexmedetomidine is expected to cross the placenta. Information related to use during pregnancy is limited (El-Tahan 2012).

Dexmethylphenidate (dex meth il FEN i date)

Brand Names: US Focalin; Focalin XR

Pharmacologic Category Central Nervous System Stimulant

Use Attention-deficit/hyperactivity disorder: Treatment of attention-deficit/hyperactivity disorder (ADHD) in patients ≥6 years

Local Anesthetic/Vasoconstrictor Precautions No information available to require special precautions

Effects on Dental Treatment Key adverse event(s) related to dental treatment: Dexmethylphenidate causes tachycardia, increases in blood pressure, and palpitations. Consider monitoring blood pressure prior to using local anesthetic with a vasoconstrictor. Symptoms associated with bruxism have been observed in some patients.

Effects on Bleeding No information available to require special precautions

Adverse Reactions Actual frequency may be dependent upon dose and/or formulation.

>10%:

Central nervous system: Headache (25% to 39%), insomnia (children 5% to 17%), restlessness (adults 12%), anxiety (5% to 11%)

Gastrointestinal: Appetite decreased (children 30%), xerostomia (adults 7% to 20%), abdominal pain (children 15%)

1% to 10%:

Central nervous system: Dizziness (adults 6%), fever (children 5%), irritability (children ≤5%), depression (children ≤3%), mood swings (children ≤3%)

Dermatologic: Pruritus (children ≤3%)

Gastrointestinal: Nausea (children 9%), dyspepsia (5% to 9%), vomiting (children 2% to 9%), anorexia (children 5% to 7%), pharyngolaryngeal pain (adults 4% to 7%)

Respiratory: Nasal congestion (children ≤5%)

Postmarketing and/or case reports: Accommodation difficulties, anaphylaxis, angioedema, blurred vision, hypersensitivity reactions

Also refer to Methylphenidate for adverse effects seen with other methylphenidate products.

General Dosage Range Oral:
Extended release:
Children ≥6 years and Adolescents: Initial: 5 mg once daily (maximum dose: 30 mg/day)
Adults: Initial: 10 mg once daily (maximum dose: 40 mg/day)
Immediate release: *Children ≥6 years, Adolescents, and Adults:* Initial: 2.5 mg twice daily (maximum dose: 20 mg/day)

Mechanism of Action Dexmethylphenidate is the more active, *d-threo*-enantiomer, of racemic methylphenidate. It is a CNS stimulant; blocks the reuptake of norepinephrine and dopamine, and increases their release into the extraneuronal space.

Pharmacodynamics/Kinetics

Onset of Action Rapid, within 1 to 2 hours of an effective dose

Duration of Action Immediate release: 3 to 5 hours; extended release: 9 to 12 hours (Dopheide 2009)

Half-life Elimination Immediate release: Children: 2 to 3 hours; Adults: 2 to 4.5 hours (**Note:** A few subjects displayed a half-life between 5 to 7 hours)

Time to Peak Fasting:
Immediate release: 1 to 1.5 hours; after a high-fat meal: 2.9 hours
Extended release: First peak: 1.5 hours (range: 1 to 4 hours); Second peak: 6.5 hours (range: 4.5 to 7 hours)

Pregnancy Risk Factor C

Pregnancy Considerations Adverse events have been observed in animal reproduction studies. Dexmethylphenidate is the more active *d-threo*-enantiomer of racemic methylphenidate; refer to Methylphenidate monograph for additional information

Controlled Substance C-II

Dexpanthenol (deks PAN the nole)

Brand Names: US Panthoderm [OTC]

Pharmacologic Category Gastrointestinal Agent, Stimulant; Topical Skin Product

Use

Injection: Prophylactic use (immediately after major abdominal surgery) to minimize paralytic ileus; intestinal atony causing abdominal distention; postoperative or postpartum retention of flatus, or postoperative delay in resumption of intestinal motility; paralytic ileus

Topical: Relieves itching and aids healing of minor dermatoses

Local Anesthetic/Vasoconstrictor Precautions No information available to require special precautions

Effects on Dental Treatment No significant effects or complications reported

Effects on Bleeding No information available to require special precautions

Adverse Reactions Frequency not defined.
Cardiovascular: Decreased blood pressure (slight)
Central nervous system: Agitation, paresthesia
Dermatologic: Dermatitis, pruritus, skin irritation, urticaria
Gastrointestinal: Diarrhea, increased peristalsis, vomiting
Hypersensitivity: Hypersensitivity reaction
Respiratory: Dyspnea

General Dosage Range IM, IV: *Adults:* Initial: 250 or 500 mg; repeat in 2 hours, and then every 6 hours as needed

Topical: *Children, Adolescents, and Adults:* Apply to affected area once or twice daily

Mechanism of Action A pantothenic acid B vitamin analog that is converted to coenzyme A internally; coenzyme A is essential to normal fatty acid synthesis, amino acid synthesis and acetylation of choline in the production of the neurotransmitter, acetylcholine

Pregnancy Risk Factor C

Pregnancy Considerations Animal reproduction studies have not been conducted.

Product Availability Dexpanthenol injection has been discontinued in the US for more than 1 year.

Dexrazoxane (deks ray ZOKS ane)

Brand Names: US Totect [DSC]; Zinecard

Brand Names: Canada Zinecard

Pharmacologic Category Antidote; Antidote, Extravasation; Chemoprotective Agent

Use

Prevention of cardiomyopathy associated with doxorubicin (Zinecard, generic products): To reduce the incidence and severity of cardiomyopathy associated with doxorubicin administration in women with metastatic breast cancer who have received a cumulative doxorubicin dose of 300 mg/m^2 and will benefit from continuing doxorubicin therapy to maintain tumor control. Not recommended for use with initial doxorubicin therapy.

Extravasation of anthracyclines (Totect): Treatment of extravasation resulting from intravenous anthracycline chemotherapy.

Local Anesthetic/Vasoconstrictor Precautions No information available to require special precautions

Effects on Dental Treatment No significant effects or complications reported

Effects on Bleeding Thrombocytopenia has been reported in patients who are under active treatment with dexrazoxane. A medical consult is suggested

Adverse Reactions Note: Most adverse reactions are thought to be attributed to chemotherapy, except for increased myelosuppression, pain at injection site, and phlebitis.

Prevention of doxorubicin cardiomyopathy (reactions listed are those which were greater in the dexrazoxane arm in a comparison of chemotherapy plus dexrazoxane vs chemotherapy alone):
Cardiovascular: Phlebitis (6%)
Central nervous system: Fatigue (61%), neurotoxicity (17%)
Dermatologic: Erythema (5%)
Hematologic & oncologic: Bone marrow depression, granulocytopenia, leukopenia, thrombocytopenia
Infection: Infection (23%), sepsis (17%)
Local: Pain at injection site pain (12%)
Miscellaneous: Fever (34%)
Postmarketing, and/or case reports: Metastases (including acute myeloid leukemia, myelodysplastic syndrome)

Anthracycline extravasation:
Cardiovascular: Peripheral edema (10%), localized phlebitis (6%)
Central nervous system: Fatigue (13%), dizziness (11%), depression (8%), headache (6%), insomnia (5%)
Dermatologic: Alopecia (14%)
Endocrine & metabolic: Hypercalcemia (7%), hyponatremia (6%), increased lactate dehydrogenase (5%)

Gastrointestinal: Nausea (43%), vomiting (19%), diarrhea (11%), abdominal pain (6%), constipation (6%), anorexia (5%)

Hematologic & oncologic: Decreased white blood cell count (73%; grade 3: 25%; grade 4: 20%), decreased neutrophils (61%; grade 3: 22%; grade 4: 24%), decreased hemoglobin (43%; grade 3: 3%), anemia (6%), febrile neutropenia (3%), neutropenia (3%), leukopenia, thrombocytopenia

Hepatic: Increased serum AST (28%), increased serum ALT (22%), increased serum bilirubin (11%), increased serum alkaline phosphatase (4%)

Infection: Postoperative infection (16%)

Local: Pain at injection site (16%)

Renal: Increased serum creatinine (14%)

Respiratory: Dyspnea (8%), pneumonia (6%), cough (5%)

Miscellaneous: Fever (21%)

General Dosage Range Dosage adjustment recommended in patients with renal impairment or hepatic impairment

IV: *Adults:* A 10:1 ratio of dexrazoxane:doxorubicin (dexrazoxane 500 mg/m^2:doxorubicin 50 mg/m^2) (prevention of cardiomyopathy) **or** 1000 mg/m^2 on days 1 and 2 (maximum dose: 2000 mg), followed by 500 mg/m^2 on day 3 (maximum dose: 1000 mg) (anthracycline extravasation)

Mechanism of Action Derivative of ethylenediaminetetraacetic acid (EDTA); a potent intracellular chelating agent. As a cardioprotectant, dexrazoxane appears to be converted intracellularly to a ring-opened chelating agent that interferes with iron-mediated oxygen free radical generation thought to be responsible, in part, for anthracycline-induced cardiomyopathy. In the management of anthracycline extravasation, dexrazoxane may act by reversibly inhibiting topoisomerase II, protecting tissue from anthracycline cytotoxicity, thereby decreasing tissue damage.

Pharmacodynamics/Kinetics

Half-life Elimination 2.1 to 2.5 hours

Pregnancy Risk Factor D

Pregnancy Considerations Adverse events were observed in animal reproduction studies using doses less than the equivalent human dose (based on BSA). May cause fetal harm if administered during pregnancy. Women of childbearing potential should use highly effective contraception to prevent pregnancy during treatment.

Dextroamphetamine (deks troe am FET a meen)

Brand Names: US Dexedrine; ProCentra; Zenzedi

Brand Names: Canada Dexedrine

Pharmacologic Category Central Nervous System Stimulant

Use

Attention-deficit/hyperactivity disorder: Treatment of attention-deficit/hyperactivity disorder (ADHD) as part of a total treatment program that typically includes other remedial measures (psychological, educational, social) for a stabilizing effect in children 3 to 16 years of age.

Narcolepsy: Treatment of narcolepsy.

Local Anesthetic/Vasoconstrictor Precautions Use vasoconstrictor with caution in patients taking dextroamphetamine. Amphetamines enhance the sympathomimetic response of epinephrine and norepinephrine leading to potential hypertension and cardiotoxicity.

Effects on Dental Treatment Key adverse event(s) related to dental treatment: Dextroamphetamine causes tachycardia, increases in blood pressure, and palpitations. Consider monitoring blood pressure prior to using local anesthetic with a vasoconstrictor. Symptoms associated with bruxism have been observed in some patients.

Effects on Bleeding No information available to require special precautions

Adverse Reactions Frequency not defined.

Cardiovascular: Cardiomyopathy, hypertension, palpitations, tachycardia

Central nervous system: Aggressive behavior, dizziness, dysphoria, euphoria, exacerbation of tics, Gilles de la Tourette's syndrome, headache, insomnia, mania, overstimulation, psychosis, restlessness

Dermatologic: Urticaria

Endocrine & metabolic: Change in libido, weight loss

Gastrointestinal: Anorexia, constipation, diarrhea, unpleasant taste, xerostomia

Genitourinary: Frequent erections, impotence, prolonged erection

Neuromuscular & skeletal: Dyskinesia, rhabdomyolysis, tremor

Ophthalmic: Accommodation disturbances, blurred vision

General Dosage Range Oral:

ADHD:

Children 3 to 5 years: Immediate release tablets or oral solution: Initial: 2.5 mg once daily (maximum dose: 40 mg daily)

Children ≥6 years and Adolescents: Initial 5 mg once or twice daily (maximum dose: 40 mg daily)

Narcolepsy:

Children 6 to 12 years: Initial: 5 mg once daily; Usual dosage: 5 to 60 mg daily in divided doses.

Children >12 years, Adolescents and Adults: Initial: 10 mg once daily; Usual dosage: 5 to 60 mg daily in divided doses.

Mechanism of Action Amphetamines are noncatecholamine, sympathomimetic amines that promote release of catecholamines (primarily dopamine and norepinephrine) from their storage sites in the presynaptic nerve terminals. A less significant mechanism may include their ability to block the reuptake of catecholamines by competitive inhibition.

Pharmacodynamics/Kinetics

Duration of Action Immediate release: 4 to 6 hours; extended release: 8 hours (Dopheide 2009)

Half-life Elimination Adults: 10 to 12 hours

Time to Peak Serum: Immediate release: ~3 hours; Sustained release: ~8 hours

Pregnancy Risk Factor C

Pregnancy Considerations Adverse effects have been observed in animal reproduction studies. The majority of human data is based on illicit amphetamine/methamphetamine exposure and not from therapeutic maternal use (Golub, 2005). Use of amphetamines during pregnancy may lead to an increased risk of premature birth and low birth weight; newborns may experience symptoms of withdrawal. Behavioral problems may also occur later in childhood (LaGasse, 2012).

Controlled Substance C-II

Dextroamphetamine and Amphetamine

(deks troe am FET a meen & am FET a meen)

Related Information

Dextroamphetamine *on page 484*

Brand Names: US Adderall; Adderall XR

Brand Names: Canada Adderall XR

Generic Availability (US) Yes

Pharmacologic Category Central Nervous System Stimulant

Use

Attention-deficit/hyperactivity disorder: Treatment of attention-deficit/hyperactivity disorder (ADHD) as part of a total treatment program that typically includes other remedial measures (psychological, educational, social) for a stabilizing effect.

Narcolepsy (immediate release only): Treatment of narcolepsy.

Local Anesthetic/Vasoconstrictor Precautions Use vasoconstrictor with caution in patients taking dextroamphetamine. Amphetamines enhance the sympathomimetic response of epinephrine and norepinephrine leading to potential hypertension and cardiotoxicity.

Effects on Dental Treatment Key adverse event(s) related to dental treatment: Dextroamphetamine and amphetamine causes tachycardia, increases in blood pressure, and palpitations. Consider monitoring blood pressure prior to using local anesthetic with a vasoconstrictor. Symptoms associated with bruxism have been observed in some patients.

Effects on Bleeding No information available to require special precautions

Adverse Reactions

Frequency not always defined.

Cardiovascular: Systolic hypertension (extended release; adolescents: 12% to 35%; dose related; transient), tachycardia (extended release; adults: ≤6%), palpitations (extended release: 2% to 4%), increased blood pressure, myocardial infarction, Raynaud's phenomenon

Central nervous system: Insomnia (extended release: 12% to 27%), headache (extended release; adults: ≤26%), emotional lability (extended release: 2% to 9%), anxiety (extended release; adults: 8%), agitation (extended release; adults: ≤8%), dizziness (extended release: 2% to 7%), nervousness (extended release: 6%), fatigue (extended release: 2% to 6%), drowsiness (extended release: 2% to 4%), speech disturbance (extended release: 2% to 4%), twitching (extended release: 2% to 4%), aggressive behavior, depression, dysphoria, euphoria, exacerbation of vocal tics, formication, irritability, outbursts of anger, overstimulation, paresthesia, psychosis, restlessness, talkativeness

Dermatologic: Diaphoresis (extended release: 2% to 4%), skin photosensitivity (extended release: 2% to 4%), alopecia, dermatillomania, skin rash, urticaria

Endocrine & metabolic: Weight loss (extended release: 4% to 10%), decreased libido (extended release: 2% to 4%), dysmenorrhea (extended release: 2% to 4%)

Gastrointestinal: Decreased appetite (extended release: 22% to 36%), xerostomia (extended release: 2% to 35%), abdominal pain (extended release: 11% to 14%), nausea (extended release: 2% to 8%), vomiting (extended release: 2% to 7%), diarrhea (extended release: 2% to 6%), constipation (extended release: 2% to 4%), dyspepsia (extended release: 2% to 4%), teeth clenching (extended release: ≤4%), tooth infection (extended release: ≤4%), anorexia (extended release: 2%), bruxism, unpleasant taste

Genitourinary: Urinary tract infection (extended release: 5%), impotence (extended release: 2% to 4%), frequent erections, prolonged erections

Hypersensitivity: Anaphylaxis, angioedema, hypersensitivity reaction

Infection: Infection (extended release: 2% to 4%)

Neuromuscular & skeletal: Dyskinesia, rhabdomyolysis, tremor

Ophthalmic: Blurred vision, mydriasis

Respiratory: Dyspnea (extended release: 2% to 4%)

Miscellaneous: Fever (extended release: 5%)

<1%, postmarketing, and/or case reports: Cardiomyopathy, cerebrovascular accident, exacerbation of Gilles de la Tourette's syndrome, exacerbation of vocal tics, peripheral vascular disease, seizure, Stevens-Johnson syndrome, toxic epidermal necrolysis

Dosing

Adult & Geriatric Note: Use lowest effective individualized dose; administer first dose as soon as awake.

ADHD: Oral:

Note: Interrupt therapy occasionally to determine if there is a recurrence of behavioral symptoms sufficient to require continued therapy.

Immediate release: Initial: 5 mg once or twice daily; may increase daily dose in 5 mg increments at weekly intervals until optimal response is obtained; usual dosage range: 5 to 40 mg/day in 1 to 3 divided doses.

Extended release: Initial: 20 mg once daily in the morning; higher doses (up to 60 mg/day) have been evaluated; however, there is not adequate evidence that higher doses afforded additional benefit. The Canadian labeling recommends a maximum dose of 30 mg/day.

Narcolepsy: *Immediate release*: Oral: Initial: 10 mg once daily in the morning; may increase daily dose in 10 mg increments at weekly intervals until optimal response is obtained; usual dosage range: 5 to 60 mg/day in 1 to 3 divided doses.

Pediatric

Note: Use lowest effective individualized dose; administer first dose as soon as awake.

ADHD: Oral:

Note: Interrupt therapy occasionally to determine if there is a recurrence of behavioral symptoms sufficient to require continued therapy.

Children <3 years: Use is not recommended.

Children 3 to 5 years: Immediate release: Initial 2.5 mg once daily in the morning; may increase daily dose in 2.5 mg increments at weekly intervals until optimal response is obtained; usual dosage range: 2.5 to 40 mg/day in 1 to 3 divided doses.

Children ≥6 years:

Immediate release: Refer to adult dosing.

Extended release: 5 to 10 mg once daily in the morning; may increase daily dose in 5 to 10 mg increments at weekly intervals until optimal response is obtained; maximum: 30 mg/day.

Adolescents:

Immediate release: Refer to adult dosing.

Extended release: 10 mg once daily in the morning; may increase to 20 mg daily after 1 week if needed; higher doses (up to 60 mg/day) have been evaluated; however, there is not adequate evidence that higher doses afforded additional benefit. The Canadian labeling recommends a maximum dose of 30 mg/day.

Narcolepsy: *Immediate release*: Oral:

Children ≥6 years: Initial: 5 mg daily; may increase daily dose in 5 mg increments at weekly intervals until optimal response is obtained; usual dosage: 5 to 60 mg/day in 1 to 3 divided doses.

Adolescents: Refer to adult dosing.

Renal Impairment

US labeling: There are no dosage adjustments provided in the manufacturer's labeling; use with caution.

Canadian labeling:

Mild or moderate impairment: There are no dosage adjustments provided in the manufacturer's labeling.

Severe impairment: (GFR 15 to <30 mL/minute/1.73 m^2): Maximum dose: 20 mg/day.

Hemodialysis: There are no specific dosage adjustments provided in the manufacturer's labeling; however, the manufacturer recommends considering further dosage reductions (compared to that recommended for severe impairment). Dextroamphetamine is not dialyzable.

Hepatic Impairment There are no dosage adjustments provided in the manufacturer's labeling; use with caution.

Mechanism of Action Amphetamines are noncatecholamine, sympathomimetic amines that promote release of catecholamines (primarily dopamine and norepinephrine) from their storage sites in the presynaptic nerve terminals. A less significant mechanism may include their ability to block the reuptake of catecholamines by competitive inhibition.

Contraindications

Hypersensitivity (eg, angioedema, anaphylaxis) or idiosyncrasy to amphetamine, sympathomimetic amines or any component of the formulation; advanced arteriosclerosis; symptomatic cardiovascular disease; moderate-to-severe hypertension; hyperthyroidism; glaucoma; agitated states; patients with a history of drug abuse; during or within 14 days following MAO inhibitor (including linezolid or methylene blue).

Documentation of allergenic cross-reactivity for amphetamines is limited. However, because of similarities in chemical structure and/or pharmacologic actions, the possibility of cross-sensitivity cannot be ruled out with certainty.

Warnings/Precautions Recommended to be used as part of a comprehensive treatment program for attention deficit disorders. **[US Boxed Warning]: Use has been associated with serious cardiovascular events including sudden death in patients with preexisting structural cardiac abnormalities or other serious heart problems (sudden death in children and adolescents; sudden death, stroke and MI in adults.** These products should be avoided in the patients with known serious structural cardiac abnormalities, cardiomyopathy, serious heart rhythm abnormalities, or other serious cardiac problems that could increase the risk of sudden death. Patients should be carefully evaluated for cardiac disease prior to initiation of therapy. Patients who develop exertional chest pain, unexplained syncope, or other symptoms suggestive of cardiac disease during treatment should undergo a prompt cardiac evaluation. CNS stimulants may increase heart rate (mean increase: 3 to 6 bpm) and blood pressure (mean increase: 2 to 4 mm Hg). Use with caution in patients with cardiovascular conditions that may be exacerbated by increases in blood pressure or heart rate (eg, hypertension, heart failure, recent myocardial infarction, ventricular arrhythmia). Stimulants are associated with peripheral vasculopathy, including Raynaud phenomenon; signs/symptoms are usually mild and intermittent, and generally improve with dose reduction or discontinuation. Digital ulceration and/or soft tissue breakdown have been observed rarely; monitor for digital changes during therapy and seek further evaluation (eg, rheumatology) if necessary. Amphetamines may impair the ability to engage in potentially hazardous activities; patients must be cautioned about performing tasks which require mental alertness (eg, operating machinery or driving). Difficulty in accommodation and blurred vision has been reported with the use of stimulants.

Limited information exists regarding amphetamine use in seizure disorder (Cortese 2013). The manufacturer recommends use with caution in patients with a history of seizure disorder; may lower seizure threshold leading to new onset or breakthrough seizure activity. If seizures occur, discontinue therapy. Use with caution in patients with preexisting psychosis or bipolar disorder. May exacerbate symptoms of behavior and thought disorder in psychotic patients; new-onset psychosis or mania may occur with stimulant use; consider discontinuation if such symptoms (eg, delusional thinking, hallucinations, mania) occur. May be associated with aggressive behavior or hostility (causal relationship not established); monitor for development or worsening of these behaviors. Screen patients with comorbid depressive symptoms prior to initiating treatment to determine if they are at risk for bipolar disorder. Use with caution in patients with Tourette syndrome or other tic disorders. Stimulants may exacerbate tics (motor and phonic) and Tourette syndrome; however, evidence demonstrating increased tics is limited. Evaluate for tics and Tourette syndrome prior to therapy initiation (AACAP [Murphy 2013; Pliszka 2007]). **[US Boxed Warning]: Has high potential for abuse. Administration for prolonged periods may lead to drug dependence and must be avoided. Particular attention should be paid to the possibility of subjects obtaining dextroamphetamine/amphetamine for nontherapeutic use or distribution to others, and the drug should be prescribed or dispensed sparingly.** Use with caution in patients with history of ethanol or drug abuse. Prescriptions should be written for the smallest quantity consistent with good patient care to minimize possibility of overdose. Abrupt discontinuation following high doses or for prolonged periods may result in symptoms for withdrawal.

Hypersensitivity reactions, including anaphylaxis, Stevens-Johnson syndrome, toxic epidermal necrolysis, angioedema, and urticaria have been observed. Use with caution in patients with hepatic or renal impairment; elimination is reduced.

Appetite suppression may occur, particularly in children. Use of stimulants has been associated with weight loss and slowing growth rate; monitor growth rate and weight during treatment. Treatment interruption may be necessary in patients who are not increasing in height or gaining weight as expected. Use caution in elderly patients due to CNS stimulant adverse effects.

Potentially significant interactions may exist, requiring dose or frequency adjustment, additional monitoring, and/or selection of alternative therapy. Potentially life-threatening serotonin syndrome (SS) may occur when dextroamphetamine/amphetamine is used in combination with other serotonergic agents (eg, selective serotonin reuptake inhibitors, serotonin norepinephrine reuptake inhibitors, triptans, tricyclic antidepressants, fentanyl, lithium, tramadol, buspirone, St. John's wort, tryptophan), agents that impair metabolism of serotonin (eg, monoamine oxidase inhibitors) or CYP2D6 inhibitors that impair metabolism of dextroamphetamine/amphetamine. Concomitant use with monoamine oxidase inhibitors is contraindicated. If concomitant use of dextroamphetamine/amphetamine with serotonergic drugs or CYP2D6 inhibitors is indicated, initiate dextroamphetamine/amphetamine at a low dose and monitor patient closely for signs and symptoms of SS. Discontinue treatment (and any concomitant serotonergic agent) immediately if signs/symptoms arise.

Drug Interactions

Metabolism/Transport Effects Refer to individual components.

Avoid Concomitant Use

Avoid concomitant use of Dextroamphetamine and Amphetamine with any of the following: Acebrophylline; Iobenguane I 123; MAO Inhibitors

Increased Effect/Toxicity

Dextroamphetamine and Amphetamine may increase the levels/effects of: Analgesics (Opioid); Doxofylline; Iohexol; Iomeprol; Iopamidol; Sympathomimetics

The levels/effects of Dextroamphetamine and Amphetamine may be increased by: Acebrophylline; Alkalinizing Agents; Antacids; AtoMOXetine; Cannabinoid-Containing Products; Carbonic Anhydrase Inhibitors; Cocaine; Linezolid; MAO Inhibitors; Proton Pump Inhibitors; Tedizolid; Tricyclic Antidepressants

Decreased Effect

Dextroamphetamine and Amphetamine may decrease the levels/effects of: Antihistamines; Antihypertensive Agents; Ethosuximide; Iobenguane I 123; Ioflupane I 123; PHENobarbital; Phenytoin

The levels/effects of Dextroamphetamine and Amphetamine may be decreased by: Ammonium Chloride; Antipsychotic Agents; Ascorbic Acid; Gastrointestinal Acidifying Agents; Lithium; Methenamine; Multivitamins/Fluoride (with ADE); Multivitamins/Minerals (with ADEK, Folate, Iron); Multivitamins/Minerals (with AE, No Iron); Urinary Acidifying Agents

Food Interactions Amphetamine serum levels may be reduced if taken with acidic food, juices, or vitamin C. Management: Monitor response when taken concurrently.

Pharmacodynamics/Kinetics

Duration of Action Tablet: 4 to 6 hours (Dopheide 2009)

Half-life Elimination

Children 6 to 12 years: d-amphetamine: 9 hours; l-amphetamine: 11 hours

Adolescents 13 to 17 years: d-amphetamine: 11 hours; l-amphetamine: 13 to 14 hours

Adults: d-amphetamine: 10 hours; l-amphetamine: 13 hours

Time to Peak Immediate release: 3 hours; Extended release: 7 hours

Pregnancy Risk Factor C

Pregnancy Considerations Adverse events have been observed in animal reproduction studies. The majority of human data is based on illicit amphetamine/methamphetamine exposure and not from therapeutic maternal use (Golub 2005). Use of amphetamines during pregnancy may lead to an increased risk of premature birth and low birth weight; newborns may experience symptoms of withdrawal. Behavioral problems may also occur later in childhood (LaGasse 2012).

Breastfeeding Considerations The majority of human data is based on illicit amphetamine/methamphetamine exposure and not from therapeutic maternal use (Golub 2005). Amphetamines are excreted into breast milk and use may decrease milk production. Increased irritability, agitation, and crying have been reported in nursing infants (ACOG 2011). A case report describes maternal use of amphetamine 20 mg/day throughout pregnancy and while breastfeeding. Milk concentrations were higher in breast milk than the maternal serum. The milk/plasma ratio ranged from 2.8 to 7.5 when measured on days 10 and 42 following delivery (Steiner 1984). The manufacturer recommends that mothers taking dextroamphetamine/amphetamine refrain from nursing.

Controlled Substance C-II

Dosage Forms

Capsule, extended release, oral:

Adderall XR:

5 mg [dextroamphetamine 1.25 mg, dextroamphetamine saccharate 1.25 mg, amphetamine aspartate monohydrate 1.25 mg, amphetamine sulfate 1.25 mg]

10 mg [dextroamphetamine sulfate 2.5 mg, dextroamphetamine saccharate 2.5 mg, amphetamine aspartate monohydrate 2.5 mg, amphetamine sulfate 2.5 mg]

15 mg [dextroamphetamine sulfate 3.75 mg, dextroamphetamine saccharate 3.75 mg, amphetamine aspartate monohydrate 3.75 mg, amphetamine sulfate 3.75 mg]

20 mg [dextroamphetamine sulfate 5 mg, dextroamphetamine saccharate 5 mg, amphetamine aspartate monohydrate 5 mg, amphetamine sulfate 5 mg]

25 mg [dextroamphetamine sulfate 6.25 mg, dextroamphetamine saccharate 6.25 mg, amphetamine aspartate monohydrate 6.25 mg, amphetamine sulfate 6.25 mg]

30 mg [dextroamphetamine sulfate 7.5 mg, dextroamphetamine saccharate 7.5 mg, amphetamine aspartate monohydrate 7.5 mg, amphetamine sulfate 7.5 mg]

Generic:

5 mg [dextroamphetamine sulfate 1.25 mg, dextroamphetamine saccharate 1.25 mg, amphetamine aspartate monohydrate 1.25 mg, amphetamine sulfate 1.25 mg (equivalent to amphetamine base 3.1 mg)]

10 mg [dextroamphetamine sulfate 2.5 mg, dextroamphetamine saccharate 2.5 mg, amphetamine aspartate monohydrate 2.5 mg, amphetamine sulfate 2.5 mg (equivalent to amphetamine base 6.3 mg)]

15 mg [dextroamphetamine sulfate 3.75 mg, dextroamphetamine saccharate 3.75 mg, amphetamine aspartate monohydrate 3.75 mg, amphetamine sulfate 3.75 mg (equivalent to amphetamine base 9.4 mg)]

20 mg [dextroamphetamine sulfate 5 mg, dextroamphetamine saccharate 5 mg, amphetamine aspartate monohydrate 5 mg, amphetamine sulfate 5 mg (equivalent to amphetamine base 12.5 mg)]

25 mg [dextroamphetamine sulfate 6.25 mg, dextroamphetamine saccharate 6.25 mg, amphetamine aspartate monohydrate 6.25 mg, amphetamine sulfate 6.25 mg (equivalent to amphetamine base 15.6 mg)]

30 mg [dextroamphetamine sulfate 7.5 mg, dextroamphetamine saccharate 7.5 mg, amphetamine

aspartate monohydrate 7.5 mg, amphetamine sulfate 7.5 mg (equivalent to amphetamine base 18.8 mg)]

Tablet, oral:

Adderall:

5 mg [dextroamphetamine sulfate 1.25 mg, dextroamphetamine saccharate 1.25 mg, amphetamine aspartate monohydrate 1.25 mg, amphetamine sulfate 1.25 mg]

7.5 mg [dextroamphetamine sulfate 1.875 mg, dextroamphetamine saccharate 1.875 mg, amphetamine aspartate monohydrate 1.875 mg, amphetamine sulfate 1.875 mg]

10 mg [dextroamphetamine sulfate 2.5 mg, dextroamphetamine saccharate 2.5 mg, amphetamine aspartate monohydrate 2.5 mg, amphetamine sulfate 2.5 mg]

12.5 mg [dextroamphetamine sulfate 3.125 mg, dextroamphetamine saccharate 3.125 mg, amphetamine aspartate monohydrate 3.125 mg, amphetamine sulfate 3.125 mg]

15 mg [dextroamphetamine sulfate 3.75 mg, dextroamphetamine saccharate 3.75 mg, amphetamine aspartate monohydrate 3.75 mg, amphetamine sulfate 3.75 mg]

20 mg [dextroamphetamine sulfate 5 mg, dextroamphetamine saccharate 5 mg, amphetamine aspartate monohydrate 5 mg, amphetamine sulfate 5 mg]

30 mg [dextroamphetamine sulfate 7.5 mg, dextroamphetamine saccharate 7.5 mg, amphetamine aspartate monohydrate 7.5 mg, amphetamine sulfate 7.5 mg]

Generic:

5 mg [dextroamphetamine sulfate 1.25 mg, dextroamphetamine saccharate 1.25 mg, amphetamine aspartate monohydrate 1.25 mg, amphetamine sulfate 1.25 mg (equivalent to amphetamine base 3.13 mg)]

7.5 mg [dextroamphetamine sulfate 1.875 mg, dextroamphetamine saccharate 1.875 mg, amphetamine aspartate monohydrate 1.875 mg, amphetamine sulfate 1.875 mg (equivalent to amphetamine base 4.7 mg)]

10 mg [dextroamphetamine sulfate 2.5 mg, dextroamphetamine saccharate 2.5 mg, amphetamine aspartate monohydrate 2.5 mg, amphetamine sulfate 2.5 mg (equivalent to amphetamine base 6.3 mg)]

12.5 mg [dextroamphetamine sulfate 3.125 mg, dextroamphetamine saccharate 3.125 mg, amphetamine aspartate monohydrate 3.125 mg, amphetamine sulfate 3.125 mg (equivalent to amphetamine base 7.8 mg)]

15 mg [dextroamphetamine sulfate 3.75 mg, dextroamphetamine saccharate 3.75 mg, amphetamine aspartate monohydrate 3.75 mg, amphetamine sulfate 3.75 mg (equivalent to amphetamine base 9.4 mg)]

20 mg [dextroamphetamine sulfate 5 mg, dextroamphetamine saccharate 5 mg, amphetamine aspartate monohydrate 5 mg, amphetamine sulfate 5 mg (equivalent to amphetamine base 12.6 mg)]

30 mg [dextroamphetamine sulfate 7.5 mg, dextroamphetamine saccharate 7.5 mg, amphetamine aspartate monohydrate 7.5 mg, amphetamine sulfate 7.5 mg (equivalent to amphetamine base 18.8 mg)]

Dextromethorphan (deks troe meth OR fan)

Brand Names: US Buckleys Cough [OTC]; Cough DM [OTC]; Creomulsion Adult [OTC]; Creomulsion for Children [OTC]; Delsym Cough Childrens [OTC]; Delsym [OTC]; ElixSure Cough [OTC]; Hold [OTC]; Little Colds Cough Formula [OTC]; PediaCare Childrens Long-Act [OTC]; Robafen Cough [OTC]; Robitussin 12 Hour Cough Child [OTC]; Robitussin 12 Hour Cough [OTC]; Robitussin Childrens Cough LA [OTC]; Robitussin CoughGels [OTC] [DSC]; Robitussin Lingering CoughGels [OTC]; Robitussin Lingering LA Cough [OTC]; Robitussin Maximum Strength [OTC] [DSC]; Scot-Tussin Diabetes CF [OTC]; Silphen DM Cough [OTC]; Simply Cough [OTC] [DSC]; Triaminic Long Acting Cough [OTC]; Trocal Cough Suppressant [OTC]; Vicks Nature Fusion Cough [OTC] [DSC]

Pharmacologic Category Antitussive; N-Methyl-D-Aspartate Receptor Antagonist

Use Cough (suppressant): Temporary control of cough due to minor throat and bronchial irritation associated with the common cold or inhaled irritants; temporary relief of cough impulse to improve sleep (extended release formulations)

Local Anesthetic/Vasoconstrictor Precautions No information available to require special precautions

Effects on Dental Treatment No significant effects or complications reported

Effects on Bleeding No information available to require special precautions

Adverse Reactions Frequency not defined.

Central nervous system: Confusion, excitement, irritability, nervousness, serotonin syndrome

General Dosage Range Oral:

Extended release:

Children 4 to 6 years: 15 mg twice daily (maximum: 30 mg/day)

Children 6 to 12 years: 30 mg twice daily (maximum: 60 mg/day)

Children >12 years and Adults: 60 mg twice daily (maximum: 120 mg/day)

Immediate release:

Children 4 to 6 years: 2.5 to 7.5 mg every 4-8 hours (maximum: 30 mg/day)

Children 6 to 12 years: 5 to 10 mg every 4 hours **or** 15 mg every 6 to 8 hours (maximum: 60 mg/day)

Children >12 years and Adults: 10 to 20 mg every 4 hours **or** 30 mg every 6 to 8 hours (maximum: 120 mg/day)

Mechanism of Action Decreases the sensitivity of cough receptors and interrupts cough impulse transmission by depressing the medullary cough center through sigma receptor stimulation; structurally related to codeine

Pharmacodynamics/Kinetics

Onset of Action Antitussive: 15-30 minutes

Duration of Action ≤6 hours

Half-life Elimination Dextromethorphan: Extensive metabolizers: 2-4 hours; poor metabolizers: 24 hours

Time to Peak 2-3 hours

Pregnancy Considerations Maternal use of standard OTC doses of dextromethorphan when used as an antitussive during the first trimester of pregnancy has not been found to increase the risk of teratogenic effects. Dextromethorphan is metabolized in the liver via CYP2D6 and CYP3A enzymes. The activity of both enzymes is increased in the mother during pregnancy. In the fetus, CYP2D6 activity is low in the fetal liver and CYP3A4 activity is present by ~17 weeks gestation.

Dextromethorphan and Phenylephrine

(deks troe meth OR fan & fen il EF rin)

Related Information

Dextromethorphan *on page 488*

Phenylephrine (Systemic) *on page 1330*

Brand Names: US PediaCare® Children's Multi-Symptom Cold [OTC]; Safetussin® CD [OTC]; Sudafed PE® Children's Cold & Cough [OTC]; Triaminic® Day Time Cold & Cough [OTC]

Pharmacologic Category Antitussive; Decongestant

Use Temporary relief of symptoms of hay fever, the common cold, and upper respiratory allergies including sinus/nasal congestion, minor bronchial/throat irritation, and cough

Local Anesthetic/Vasoconstrictor Precautions Use with caution since phenylephrine is a sympathomimetic amine which could interact with epinephrine to cause a pressor response

Effects on Dental Treatment No significant effects or complications reported

Effects on Bleeding No information available to require special precautions

Adverse Reactions See individual agents.

General Dosage Range Oral:

Children ≥4-12 years: Dosage varies greatly depending on product

Children ≥12 years and Adults: Safetussin® CD: 10 mL every 6 hours as needed (maximum: 40 mL/24 hours)

Mechanism of Action See individual agents.

Dextromethorphan and Quinidine

(deks troe meth OR fan & KWIN i deen)

Related Information

Dextromethorphan *on page 488*

QuiNIDine *on page 1413*

Brand Names: US Nuedexta

Pharmacologic Category N-Methyl-D-Aspartate Receptor Antagonist

Use Pseudobulbar affect: Treatment of pseudobulbar affect (PBA)

Local Anesthetic/Vasoconstrictor Precautions See individual agents

Effects on Dental Treatment See individual agents

Effects on Bleeding See individual agents

Adverse Reactions Also see individual agents.

>10%: Gastrointestinal: Diarrhea (13%)

1% to 10%:

- Cardiovascular: Peripheral edema (5%)
- Central nervous system: Dizziness (10%)
- Endocrine & metabolic: Increased gamma-glutamyl transferase (3%)
- Gastrointestinal: Vomiting (5%), flatulence (3%)
- Genitourinary: Urinary tract infection (4%)
- Infection: Influenza (4%)
- Neuromuscular & skeletal: Weakness (5%)
- Respiratory: Cough (5%)

General Dosage Range Oral: *Adults:* Initial: Dextromethorphan 20 mg/quinidine 10 mg once daily for 7 days; Maintenance: Dextromethorphan 20 mg/quinidine 10 mg every 12 hour; Maximum: dextromethorphan 40 mg/quinidine 20 mg in a 24-hour period.

Mechanism of Action Dextromethorphan may relieve the symptoms of PBA by binding to sigma-1 receptors in the brain which may be involved in behavior, however the exact mechanism of action is not known. Quinidine is used to block the rapid metabolism of dextromethorphan, thereby increasing serum concentrations. The dose of quinidine in this combination product provides serum concentrations 1% to 3% of those needed to treat cardiac arrhythmias.

Pharmacodynamics/Kinetics

Half-life Elimination Dextromethorphan: 13 hours in extensive metabolizers; Quinidine: 7 hours in extensive metabolizers

Time to Peak Dextromethorphan: 3 to 4 hours; Quinidine: 1 to 2 hours

Pregnancy Risk Factor C

Pregnancy Considerations Adverse events were observed in animal reproduction studies using this combination. See individual agents.

Dental Comment See individual agents

Diatrizoate Meglumine

(dye a tri ZOE ate MEG loo meen)

Brand Names: US Cystografin; Cystografin-Dilute

Pharmacologic Category Iodinated Contrast Media; Radiological/Contrast Media, Ionic (High Osmolality)

Use Retrograde cystourethrography: Diagnostic agent for retrograde cystourethrography

Local Anesthetic/Vasoconstrictor Precautions No information available to require special precautions

Effects on Dental Treatment No significant effects or complications reported

Effects on Bleeding No information available to require special precautions

Adverse Reactions Frequency not defined.

- Endocrine & metabolic: Altered thyroid hormone levels (transient suppression), hypothyroidism
- Hypersensitivity: Anaphylactoid reactions (risk if intravasation of drug occurs), hypersensitivity reaction (risk if intravasation of drug occurs; reactions reported include facial edema, glottis edema, respiratory distress, convulsions, shock)
- <1%, postmarketing, and/or case reports: Thyroid dysfunction (underactive; premature infants and infants with underlying medical conditions are more vulnerable; FDA Safety Alert, 2015)

General Dosage Range Bladder instillation: *Children, Adolescents, and Adults:* 25 to 300 mL

Mechanism of Action Radiopaque contrast agent.

Pregnancy Risk Factor C

Pregnancy Considerations Animal reproduction studies have not been conducted. In general, iodinated contrast media agents may cross the placenta; use should be avoided unless absolutely required to obtain diagnostic information that will influence the care of the mother or fetus during pregnancy (ACOG 2016; ACR 2015).

Diatrizoate Meglumine and Diatrizoate Sodium

(dye a tri ZOE ate MEG loo meen & dye a tri ZOE ate SOW dee um)

Related Information

Diatrizoate Meglumine *on page 489*

Brand Names: US Gastrografin; MD-76 R; MD-Gastroview

Pharmacologic Category Iodinated Contrast Media; Radiological/Contrast Media, Ionic (High Osmolality)

Use

Oral/rectal: Radiographic examination of GI tract; adjunct to contrast enhancement in computed tomography of the torso (in conjunction with an IV radiopaque contrast agent)

Injection: Angiocardiography (pediatric), aortography, contrast enhancement of brain or body computed tomographic (CT), digital subtraction angiography, excretory urography, peripheral arteriography, selective coronary arteriography (with or without left ventriculography), selective renal arteriography, selective visceral arteriography

Local Anesthetic/Vasoconstrictor Precautions No information available to require special precautions

Effects on Dental Treatment No significant effects or complications reported

Effects on Bleeding No information available to require special precautions

Adverse Reactions

Frequency not defined. Some reactions listed are based on reports for other agents in this same pharmacologic class, and may not be specifically reported for diatrizoate meglumine and diatrizoate sodium.

Oral/rectal:

Cardiovascular: Tachyarrhythmia
Dermatologic: Erythema, urticaria
Gastrointestinal: Diarrhea, nausea, vomiting
Hypersensitivity: Anaphylaxis
Respiratory: Dyspnea, hypoxia

Injection: Specific procedure-related adverse events may also occur:

Cardiovascular: Arterial thrombosis at injection site (with peripheral arteriography), brachial plexopathy (palsy following axillary artery injections [with peripheral arteriography]), cardiac arrhythmia (with pediatric angiocardiography, aortography, or coronary arteriography), cardiovascular signs and symptoms (severe including cardiac arrest; with excretion urography), chest pain (with coronary arteriography), choking sensation, ECG changes (transient, with coronary angiography), edema, flushing, hypertension, hypotension, myocardial infarction (with coronary arteriography), partial collapse of the injected vein, peripheral vasodilation, venospasm (injection site), venous pain (injection site), ventricular fibrillation (with excretion urography or coronary angiography)

Central nervous system: Chills, dizziness, feeling hot, headache

Dermatologic: Diaphoresis, pallor, pruritus, skin rash, urticaria

Endocrine & metabolic: Hypothyroidism, altered thyroid hormone levels (transient suppression)

Gastrointestinal: Nausea, retching, vomiting

Genitourinary: Nephrotoxicity (with aortography, including renal infarction, acute tubular necrosis with oliguria and anuria)

Hematologic & Oncologic: Disseminated intravascular coagulation, facial petechiae, neutropenia, retroperitoneal hemorrhage (with aortography, translumbar approach)

Hypersensitivity: Anaphylactoid reaction, anaphylaxis (with severe asthmatic reaction [with excretion urography]), hypersensitivity reaction

Local: Bleeding at injection site (with peripheral arteriography), burning sensation at injection site, injection site numbness, pain at injection site, inflammation at injection site, tissue necrosis at injection site (with extravasation)

Neuromuscular & skeletal: Muscle cramps, spinal cord injury (with aortography), tremors, weakness

Ophthalmic: Conjunctival petechiae, lacrimation

Renal: Acute renal failure

Respiratory: Sneezing, wheezing

Miscellaneous: Fever, procedural complications (injury to aorta and neighboring organs [with aortography]; hemorrhage, thrombosis, pseudoaneurysms at the puncture site, dislodgment of arteriosclerotic plaques [with coronary arteriography])

<1%, postmarketing, and/or case reports: Thyroid dysfunction (underactive; premature infants and infants with underlying medicals conditions are more vulnerable; FDA Safety Alert, 2015)

General Dosage Range

Intra-arterial: Dosage varies greatly depending on indication.

IV: Dosage varies greatly depending on indication.

Oral:

Infants and Children <5 years: 30 mL, may dilute 1:1 (if <10 kg or debilitated, dilute 1:3 in water)

Children 5 to 10 years: 60 mL, may dilute 1:1 (if <10 kg or debilitated, dilute 1:3 in water)

Children >10 year and Adolescents: Dosage varies.

Adults: 30 to 90 mL **or** 25 to 77 mL in 1000 mL tap water (administer 240 mL of solution); dosage depends on indication

Rectal:

Children <5 years: Dosage varies. Dilute 1:5 in tap water

Children ≥5 years: Dilute 90 mL in 500 mL tap water

Adults: Dilute 240 mL in 1000 mL tap water

Mechanism of Action Radiopaque contrast agent; opacifies vessels or tissues in the path of the flow of the contrast medium, permitting radiographic visualization of the internal structures of the body.

Pharmacodynamics/Kinetics

Half-life Elimination Injection: Initial: 10 minutes; Terminal: 100 minutes

Pregnancy Risk Factor B

Pregnancy Considerations Adverse events were not observed in animal reproduction studies. Following IV administration, diatrizoate salts cross the placenta and may enter fetal circulation. In general, use of iodinated contrast media agents should be avoided unless absolutely required to obtain diagnostic information that will influence the care of the mother or fetus during pregnancy (ACOG 2016; ACR 2015).

Diatrizoate Meglumine and Iodipamide Meglumine

(dye a tri ZOE ate MEG loo meen & eye oh DI pa mide MEG loo meen)

Related Information

Diatrizoate Meglumine *on page* 489
Iodipamide Meglumine *on page* 912

Brand Names: US Sinografin

Pharmacologic Category Contrast Agent; Iodinated Contrast Media; Radiological/Contrast Media, Ionic (Low Osmolality)

Use Hysterosalpingography: Contrast enhancement for hysterosalpingography.

Local Anesthetic/Vasoconstrictor Precautions No information available to require special precautions

Effects on Dental Treatment No significant effects or complications reported

Effects on Bleeding No information available to require special precautions

Adverse Reactions Frequency not defined.

Cardiovascular: Bradycardia (rare), hypotension, syncope

Central nervous system: Chills, dizziness

Endocrine & metabolic: Thyroid dysfunction (underactive; premature infants and infants with underlying medical conditions are more vulnerable; FDA Safety Alert 2015)

Gastrointestinal: Abdominal pain, abdominal tenderness, nausea, vomiting

Hypersensitivity: Anaphylactoid reaction, hypersensitivity reaction (including arthralgia, circulatory collapse, flushing, pruritus, respiratory distress, skin rash, sweating, urticaria)

Miscellaneous: Fever

General Dosage Range Intrauterine: *Adults:* Usual dose: 3 to 4 mL; Total dosage range: 1.5 to 10 mL

Mechanism of Action Opacification of vessels and anatomical structures in the path of flow of the contrast media which allows for radiographic visualization

Pregnancy Considerations The procedure for which this product is indicated is contraindicated during or within 6 months of pregnancy termination. Diatrizoate meglumine crosses the placenta and enters the fetal circulation. Also refer to individual agents.

DiazePAM (dye AZ e pam)

Related Information

Dentin Hypersensitivity, Acid Erosion, High Caries Index, Management of Alveolar Osteitis, and Xerostomia *on page 1857*

Management of the Patient With Anxiety or Depression *on page 1873*

Temporomandibular Dysfunction (TMD), Chronic Pain, and Fibromyalgia *on page 1868*

Related Sample Prescriptions

Sedation (Prior to Dental Treatment) - Sample Prescriptions *on page 42*

Brand Names: US Diastat AcuDial; Diastat Pediatric; DiazePAM Intensol; Valium

Brand Names: Canada Apo-Diazepam; Bio-Diazepam; Diastat; Diazemuls; Diazepam Auto Injector; Diazepam Injection SDZ; Diazepam Injection USP; Novo-Dipam; PMS-Diazepam; Valium

Generic Availability (US) Yes

Pharmacologic Category Anticonvulsant, Benzodiazepine; Benzodiazepine

Dental Use Oral medication for preoperative dental anxiety; sedative component in IV conscious sedation in oral surgery patients; skeletal muscle relaxant

Use

Acute ethanol withdrawal (oral and injection): May be useful in symptomatic relief of acute agitation, tremor, impending or acute delirium, tremens, and hallucinosis.

Anxiety (oral and injection): Management of anxiety disorders; short-term relief of the symptoms of anxiety.

Muscle spasm (oral and injection): As an adjunct for the relief of skeletal muscle spasm due to reflex spasm caused by local pathology (eg, inflammation of muscles or joints, secondary to trauma); spasticity caused by upper motor neuron disorders (eg, cerebral palsy, paraplegia); athetosis; stiff-man syndrome; tetanus.

Preoperative (injection): Relief of anxiety and tension in patients undergoing surgical procedures; prior to cardioversion for the relief of anxiety and tension and to diminish patient's recall (IV only); as an adjunct prior to endoscopic procedures for apprehension, anxiety, or acute stress reactions and to diminish patient's recall.

Note: Use of diazepam in patients undergoing cardioversion or endoscopic procedures has been superseded by agents with a more pharmacokinetically favorable profile (eg, midazolam) (Thomas 2014; Triantafillidis 2013)

Seizures: Adjunct in convulsive disorders (oral); management of select, refractory epilepsy patients on stable regimens of antiepileptic drugs requiring intermittent use of diazepam to control episodes of increased seizure activity (rectal); adjunct in severe recurrent convulsive seizures (injection).

Status epilepticus (injection): Adjunct in status epilepticus.

Local Anesthetic/Vasoconstrictor Precautions No information available to require special precautions

Effects on Dental Treatment Key adverse event(s) related to dental treatment: Xerostomia and changes in salivation (normal salivary flow resumes upon discontinuation) (see Dental Comment)

Effects on Bleeding No information available to require special precautions

Adverse Reactions Frequency not defined. Adverse reactions may vary by route of administration.

Cardiovascular: Hypotension, localized phlebitis, vasodilatation

Central nervous system: Amnesia, ataxia, confusion, depression, drowsiness, dysarthria, fatigue, headache, slurred speech, vertigo

Dermatologic: Skin rash

Endocrine & metabolic: Change in libido

Gastrointestinal: Altered salivation (dry mouth or hypersalivation), constipation, diarrhea, nausea

Genitourinary: Urinary incontinence, urinary retention

Hepatic: Jaundice

Local: Pain at injection site

Neuromuscular & skeletal: Tremor, weakness

Ophthalmic: Blurred vision, diplopia

Respiratory: Apnea, asthma, bradypnea

Miscellaneous: Paradoxical reaction (eg, aggressiveness, agitation, anxiety, delusions, hallucinations, inappropriate behavior, increased muscle spasms, insomnia, irritability, psychoses, rage, restlessness, sleep disturbances, stimulation)

Dental Usual Dosage

Anxiety/sedation/skeletal muscle relaxant: Adults:

Oral: 2 to 10 mg 2 to 4 times daily

IM, IV: 2 to 10 mg, may repeat in 3 to 4 hours if needed

Anxiety: Elderly: Oral: Initial: 1 to 2 mg 1 to 2 times daily; increase gradually as needed, rarely need to use >10 mg daily (watch for hypotension and excessive sedation)

Skeletal muscle relaxant: Elderly: Oral: Initial: 2 to 5 mg 2 to 4 times daily

Dosing

Adult Note: Oral absorption is more reliable than IM

Acute ethanol withdrawal:

IV, IM: 10 mg initially; may administer 5 to 10 mg 3 to 4 hours later, if needed

Oral: 10 mg 3 to 4 times during first 24 hours, then decrease to 5 mg 3 to 4 times daily as needed

Anxiety (symptoms/disorders):

Oral: 2 to 10 mg 2 to 4 times daily if needed

IM, IV: 2 to 10 mg; may repeat in 3 to 4 hours, if needed

Muscle spasm:

Oral: 2 to 10 mg 3 or 4 times daily

IV, IM: Initial: 5 to 10 mg; then 5 to 10 mg in 3 to 4 hours, if necessary. Larger doses may be required if associated with tetanus.

Preoperative: Anxiety: IM: 10 mg prior to surgery

Sedation in the ICU patient: *IV:* Loading dose: 5 to 10 mg; Maintenance dose: 0.03 to 0.1 mg/kg every 30 minutes to 6 hours (Barr 2013)

Seizures:

Adjunctive maintenance therapy: Oral: 2 to 10 mg 2 to 4 times daily.

Intermittent management of seizures: Rectal gel (Diastat): 0.2 mg/kg; may be repeated in 4 to 12 hours if needed; do not use for more than 5 episodes per month or more than one episode every 5 days. **Note:** Round dose to the nearest 2.5 mg increment.

Status epilepticus:

IV:

American Epilepsy Society recommendations: 0.15 to 0.2 mg/kg (maximum dose: 10 mg); may repeat once (AES [Glauser 2016])

Neurocritical Care Society recommendations: 0.15 mg/kg (maximum dose: 10 mg) given at a rate of ≤5 mg/minute; may repeat in 5 minutes (NCS [Brophy 2012]).

Rectal (formulation not specified) (off-label use): **Note:** The parenteral formulation of diazepam may be given rectally if rectal gel (Diastat) is not available (Arif 2008).

American Epilepsy Society recommendations: 0.2 to 0.5 mg/kg (maximum dose: 20 mg) (AES [Glauser 2016])

Premonitory/Out-of-hospital treatment: 10 mg once; may repeat once if necessary (Kälviäinen 2007)

Skeletal muscle relaxant (adjunct therapy): *Oral:* 2 to 10 mg 3 to 4 times daily

Geriatric Oral absorption is more reliable than IM

Elderly and/or debilitated patients:

Oral: 2 to 2.5 mg 1 to 2 times daily initially; increase gradually as needed and tolerated.

Rectal gel: Due to the increased half-life in elderly and debilitated patients, consider reducing dose.

Pediatric

Conscious sedation for procedures:

Oral:

Children: 0.2 to 0.3 mg/kg (maximum dose: 10 mg) 45 to 60 minutes prior to procedure

Adolescents: 10 mg

IV: Adolescents: 5 mg; may repeat with 2.5 mg if needed (Zeltzer 1990)

Febrile seizure prophylaxis: *Oral:* Children: 1 mg/kg/day divided every 8 hours; initiate therapy at first sign of fever and continue for 24 hours after fever is gone

Muscle spasm associated with tetanus: *IV, IM:*

Infants >30 days and Children <5 years: 1 to 2 mg/dose every 3 to 4 hours as needed

Children ≥5 years: 5 to 10 mg/dose every 3 to 4 hours as needed

Sedation or muscle relaxation or anxiety: *Oral:* Children: 0.12 to 0.8 mg/kg/day in divided doses every 6 to 8 hours

Seizures: *Rectal gel (Diastat):* Round dose to the nearest 2.5 mg increment; dose may be repeated in 4 to 12 hours if needed; do not use for more than 5 episodes per month or more than one episode every 5 days.

Children 2 to 5 years: 0.5 mg/kg (maximum dose: 20 mg)

Children 6 to 11 years: 0.3 mg/kg (maximum dose: 20 mg)

Children ≥12 years and Adolescents: 0.2 mg/kg (maximum dose: 20 mg)

Status epilepticus:

IV:

American Academy of Pediatrics recommendations: 0.1 to 0.3 mg/kg (maximum dose: 10 mg) given over ~2 minutes; may repeat dose after 5 to 10 minutes (AAP [Hegenbarth 2008])

American Epilepsy Society recommendations: Infants, Children, and Adolescents: 0.15 to 0.2 mg/kg (maximum dose: 10 mg); may repeat once (AES [Glauser 2016])

Neurocritical Care Society recommendations: 0.15 mg/kg (maximum dose: 10 mg) given at a rate of ≤5 mg/minute; may repeat in 5 minutes (NCS [Brophy 2012])

Rectal (formulation not specified) (off-label use): **Note:** The parenteral formulation of diazepam may be given rectally if rectal gel (Diastat) is not available (Arif 2008; Dieckmann 1994). Maximum recommended dose according to the manufacturer: 20 mg/dose

American Academy of Pediatrics recommendations (AAP [Hegenbarth 2008]): Initial: 0.5 mg/kg (maximum dose: 20 mg).

American Epilepsy Society recommendations (AES [Glauser 2016]): Infants, Children and Adolescents: 0.2 to 0.5 mg/kg (maximum dose: 20 mg).

Neurocritical Care Society recommendations (NCS [Brophy 2012]):

Children 2 to 5 years: 0.5 mg/kg

Children 6 to 11 years: 0.3 mg/kg

Children >12 years and Adolescents: 0.2 mg/kg

Spasticity in cerebral palsy (off-label use): *Oral:* Dose should be individualized:

Children ≤5 years: <8.5 kg: 0.5 to 1 mg at bedtime; 8.5 to 15 kg: 1 to 2 mg at bedtime (Mathew 2005)

Children 5 to 16 years: 1.25 mg 3 times daily to 5 mg 4 times daily (Engle 1966)

Renal Impairment There are no dosage adjustments provided in the manufacturer's labeling; use with caution.

Hemodialysis: Not dialyzable (0% to 5%); supplemental dose is not necessary.

Hepatic Impairment There are no dosage adjustments provided in the manufacturer's labeling; use with caution. The oral tablets are contraindicated in severe hepatic impairment.

Mechanism of Action Binds to stereospecific benzodiazepine receptors on the postsynaptic GABA neuron at several sites within the central nervous system, including the limbic system, reticular formation. Enhancement of the inhibitory effect of GABA on neuronal excitability results by increased neuronal membrane permeability to chloride ions. This shift in chloride ions results in hyperpolarization (a less excitable state) and stabilization. Benzodiazepine receptors and effects appear to be linked to the GABA-A receptors. Benzodiazepines do not bind to GABA-B receptors.

Contraindications

Hypersensitivity to diazepam or any component of the formulation; acute narrow-angle glaucoma; untreated open-angle glaucoma; infants <6 months of age (oral); myasthenia gravis, severe respiratory impairment, severe hepatic impairment, sleep apnea syndrome (oral tablet).

Documentation of allergenic cross-reactivity for benzodiazepines is limited. However, because of similarities in chemical structure and/or pharmacologic actions, the possibility of cross-sensitivity cannot be ruled out with certainty.

Warnings/Precautions When used as an adjunct in treating convulsive disorders, an increase in frequency/severity of tonic-clonic seizures may occur and require dose adjustment of anticonvulsant. Abrupt withdrawal may result in a temporary increase in the frequency and/or severity of seizures. Use with caution in debilitated patients, obese patients, patients with hepatic disease, or renal impairment. Oral tablet is contraindicated in patients with severe hepatic impairment, severe respiratory impairment, or sleep apnea syndrome. Use with caution in patients with respiratory disease or impaired gag reflex.

Use caution in patients with depression or anxiety associated with depression, particularly if suicidal risk may be present. Use with extreme caution in patients with a history of drug abuse or acute alcoholism; potential for drug dependency exists. Tolerance and psychological and physical dependence may occur with prolonged use (generally >10 days). Use with extreme caution in patients who are at risk of falls; benzodiazepines have been associated with falls and traumatic injury. Rebound or withdrawal symptoms may occur following abrupt discontinuation or large decreases in dose. Use caution when reducing dose or withdrawing therapy; decrease slowly and monitor for withdrawal symptoms. The benzodiazepine receptor antagonist flumazenil may cause withdrawal in patients receiving long-term benzodiazepine therapy. Diazepam is a long half-life benzodiazepine. Tolerance develops to the sedative, hypnotic, and anticonvulsant effects. It does not develop to the anxiolytic or skeletal muscle relaxing effects (Vinkers 2012). Chronic use of this agent may increase the perioperative benzodiazepine dose needed to achieve desired effect.

Benzodiazepines have been associated with anterograde amnesia. Paradoxical reactions, including hyperactive or aggressive behavior, hallucinations, and psychoses, have been reported with benzodiazepines, particularly in adolescent/pediatric or elderly patients. Diazepam should be discontinued if such reactions occur. Does not have analgesic, antidepressant, or antipsychotic properties. May be used in patients with open-angle glaucoma who are receiving appropriate therapy; contraindicated in acute narrow-angle glaucoma and untreated open-angle glaucoma. Potentially significant interactions may exist, requiring dose or frequency adjustment, additional monitoring, and/or selection of alternative therapy. **[US Boxed Warning]: Concomitant use of benzodiazepines and opioids may result in profound sedation, respiratory depression, coma, and death; reserve concomitant prescribing of these drugs for use in patients for whom alternative treatment options are inadequate, and limit dosages and durations to the minimum required. Follow patients for signs and symptoms of respiratory depression and sedation.**

May cause CNS depression, which may impair physical or mental abilities; patients must be cautioned about performing tasks that require mental alertness (eg, operating machinery, driving).

Parenteral: Vesicant; ensure proper needle or catheter placement prior to and during administration; avoid extravasation. Acute hypotension, muscle weakness, apnea, and/or cardiac arrest have occurred with parenteral administration. Acute effects may be more prevalent in patients receiving concurrent barbiturates, opioids, or ethanol. Appropriate resuscitative equipment and qualified personnel should be available during administration and monitoring. Avoid use of the injection in patients in shock, coma, or in acute ethanol intoxication with depression of vital signs. Intra-arterial injection should be avoided. Tonic status epilepticus has been precipitated in patients treated with diazepam IV for absence status or absence variant status.

Rectal gel: Administration of rectal gel should only be performed by individuals trained to recognize characteristic seizure activity and monitor response. Not recommended for chronic, daily use. Use with caution in patients with neurologic damage.

Some dosage forms may contain benzyl alcohol and/or sodium benzoate/benzoic acid; benzoic acid (benzoate) is a metabolite of benzyl alcohol; large amounts of benzyl alcohol (≥99 mg/kg/day) have been associated with a potentially fatal toxicity ("gasping syndrome") in neonates; the "gasping syndrome" consists of metabolic acidosis, respiratory distress, gasping respirations, CNS dysfunction (including convulsions, intracranial hemorrhage), hypotension, and cardiovascular collapse (AAP 1997; CDC 1982); some data suggest that benzoate displaces bilirubin from protein binding sites (Ahlfors 2001); avoid or use dosage forms containing benzyl alcohol and/or benzyl alcohol derivative with caution in neonates. See manufacturer's labeling.

Some dosage forms may contain propylene glycol; large amounts are potentially toxic and have been associated with hyperosmolality, lactic acidosis, seizures, and respiratory depression; use caution (AAP 1997; Zar 2007).

Drug Interactions

Metabolism/Transport Effects Substrate of CYP1A2 (minor), CYP2B6 (minor), CYP2C19 (major), CYP2C9 (minor), CYP3A4 (major); **Note:** Assignment of Major/Minor substrate status based on clinically relevant drug interaction potential

Avoid Concomitant Use

Avoid concomitant use of DiazePAM with any of the following: Azelastine (Nasal); Conivaptan; Fusidic Acid (Systemic); Idelalisib; Methadone; OLANZapine; Orphenadrine; Oxomemazine; Paraldehyde; Sodium Oxybate; Thalidomide

Increased Effect/Toxicity

DiazePAM may increase the levels/effects of: Ajmaline; Alcohol (Ethyl); Alfentanil; Analgesics (Opioid); Azelastine (Nasal); Blonanserin; Buprenorphine; CloZAPine; CNS Depressants; Flunitrazepam; HYDROcodone; Methadone; Methotrimeprazine; MetyroSINE; Mirtazapine; Orphenadrine; OxyCODONE; Paraldehyde; Piribedil; Pramipexole; ROPINIRole; Rotigotine; Selective Serotonin Reuptake Inhibitors; Sodium Oxybate; Suvorexant; Thalidomide; Zolpidem

The levels/effects of DiazePAM may be increased by: Aprepitant; Brimonidine (Topical); Cannabis; Chlormethiazole; Chlorphenesin Carbamate; Conivaptan; Cosyntropin; CYP2C19 Inhibitors (Moderate); CYP2C19 Inhibitors (Strong); CYP3A4 Inhibitors (Moderate); CYP3A4 Inhibitors (Strong); Dasatinib; Dimethindene (Topical); Disulfiram; Doxylamine; Dronabinol; Droperidol; Etravirine; Fosamprenavir; Fosaprepitant; Fusidic Acid (Systemic); HydrOXYzine; Idelalisib; Ivacaftor; Kava Kava; Lofexidine; Magnesium Sulfate; Methotrimeprazine; MiFEPRIStone; Minocycline; Nabilone; Netupitant; OLANZapine; Oxomemazine; Palbociclib; Perampanel; Ritonavir;

Rufinamide; Saquinavir; Simeprevir; Stiripentol; Tapentadol; Teduglutide; Tetrahydrocannabinol; Trimeprazine

Decreased Effect

The levels/effects of DiazePAM may be decreased by: Bosentan; CYP2C19 Inducers (Strong); CYP3A4 Inducers (Moderate); CYP3A4 Inducers (Strong); Dabrafenib; Deferasirox; Enzalutamide; Etravirine; Mitotane; Ombitasvir, Paritaprevir, and Ritonavir; Ombitasvir, Paritaprevir, Ritonavir, and Dasabuvir; Siltuximab; St John's Wort; Theophylline Derivatives; Tocilizumab; Yohimbine

Pharmacodynamics/Kinetics

Onset of Action

Sedation: Pediatric patients: IV: 4 to 5 minutes (Krauss 2006)

Status epilepticus: IV: 1 to 3 minutes; Rectal: 2 to 10 minutes

Duration of Action

Sedation: Pediatric patients: 60 to 120 minutes (Krauss 2006)

Status epilepticus: 15 to 30 minutes

Half-life Elimination Note: Diazepam accumulates upon multiple dosing and the terminal elimination half-life is slightly prolonged.

IM:

Premature neonates (GA: 28 to 34 weeks): 54 hours

Infants: ~30 hours (Morselli 1973)

Children 3 to 8 years: 18 hours (Morselli 1973)

Adults: Parent: ~60 to 72 hours; Desmethyldiazepam: ~152 to 174 hours (Lamson 2011)

IV: Parent: 33 to 45 hours; Desmethyldiazepam: 87 hours (Cloyd 1998; Greenblatt 1989a)

Oral: Parent: 44 to 48 hours; Desmethyldiazepam: 100 hours (Greenblatt 1989b)

Rectal: Parent: 45 to 46 hours; Desmethyldiazepam: 71 to 99 hours (Cloyd 1998)

Time to Peak

IM: Median: 1 hour (range: 0.25 to 2 hours) (Lamson 2011)

IV: ~1 minute (Cloyd 1998)

Oral: 15 minutes to 2.5 hours (1.25 hours when fasting; 2.5 hours with food) (Greenblatt 1989b)

Rectal: 1.5 hours

Pregnancy Risk Factor D

Pregnancy Considerations Adverse events have been observed in animal reproduction studies. In humans, diazepam and its metabolites (N-desmethyldiazepam, temazepam, and oxazepam) cross the placenta. Teratogenic effects have been observed with diazepam; however, additional studies are needed. The incidence of premature birth and low birth weights may be increased following maternal use of benzodiazepines; hypoglycemia and respiratory problems in the neonate may occur following exposure late in pregnancy. Neonatal withdrawal symptoms may occur within days to weeks after birth and "floppy infant syndrome" (which also includes withdrawal symptoms) has been reported with some benzodiazepines (including diazepam) (Bergman 1992; Iqbal 2002; Wikner 2007). A combination of factors influences the potential teratogenicity of anticonvulsant therapy. When treating women with epilepsy, monotherapy with the lowest effective dose and avoidance of medications known to have a high incidence of teratogenic effects is recommended (Harden 2009; Wlodarczyk 2012).

Breastfeeding Considerations Diazepam and its metabolites are excreted in breast milk in concentrations approximately one-tenth of those in maternal plasma (days 3 to 9 postpartum). Drowsiness, lethargy, or weight loss in breastfeeding infants have been observed in case reports following maternal use of some benzodiazepines, including diazepam (Iqbal 2002). breastfeeding is not recommended (Iqbal 2002). Because diazepam and its metabolites may be present in breast milk for prolonged periods following administration of the rectal gel, the manufacturer recommends discontinuing breastfeeding for an appropriate period of time.

Controlled Substance C-IV

Dosage Forms

Concentrate, Oral:

DiazePAM Intensol: 5 mg/mL (30 mL)

Generic: 5 mg/mL (30 mL)

Gel, Rectal:

Diastat AcuDial: 10 mg (1 ea); 20 mg (1 ea)

Diastat Pediatric: 2.5 mg (1 ea)

Generic: 2.5 mg (1 ea); 10 mg (1 ea); 20 mg (1 ea)

Solution, Injection:

Generic: 5 mg/mL (2 mL, 10 mL)

Solution, Oral:

Generic: 1 mg/mL (5 mL, 500 mL)

Solution Auto-injector, Intramuscular:

Generic: 10 mg/2 mL (2 mL)

Tablet, Oral:

Valium: 2 mg, 5 mg, 10 mg

Generic: 2 mg, 5 mg, 10 mg

Dental Comment An adult companion should accompany the patient to and from dental office.

Diazoxide (dye az OKS ide)

Brand Names: US Proglycem

Brand Names: Canada Proglycem

Pharmacologic Category Antidote, Hypoglycemia; Vasodilator, Direct-Acting

Use

Hyperinsulinemic hypoglycemia: Management of hypoglycemia due to hyperinsulinism due to the following conditions in adults (ie, inoperable islet cell adenoma or carcinoma, or extrapancreatic malignancy) and infants and children (ie, leucine sensitivity, islet cell hyperplasia, nesidioblastosis, extrapancreatic malignancy, islet cell adenoma, or adenomatosis; may be used preoperatively as a temporary measure, and postoperatively, if hypoglycemia persists).

Note: Consider treatment with diazoxide when other specific medical therapy or surgical management for hypoglycemia due to the above conditions either has been unsuccessful or is not feasible.

Local Anesthetic/Vasoconstrictor Precautions No information available to require special precautions

Effects on Dental Treatment No significant effects or complications reported

Effects on Bleeding No information available to require special precautions

Adverse Reactions Frequency not defined.

Cardiovascular: Cardiac failure (due to sodium and water retention), hyperosmolar coma (nonketotic), hypertension (transient), hypotension, palpitations, tachycardia

Central nervous system: Anxiety, dizziness, extrapyramidal reaction, headache, insomnia, malaise, paresthesia, peripheral neuritis (poly)

Dermatologic: Cutaneous candidiasis, loss of scalp hair, pruritus, purpura, skin rash

Endocrine & metabolic: Albuminuria, diabetic ketoacidosis, fluid retention, galactorrhea, glycosuria, gout, hirsutism, hyperglycemia, sodium retention

Gastrointestinal: Abdominal pain, acute pancreatitis, ageusia (transient), anorexia, diarrhea, intestinal obstruction, nausea, pancreatic necrosis, vomiting

Genitourinary: Azotemia, decreased urine output, hematuria, lump in breast (enlargement), nephrotic syndrome (reversible), uricosuria

Hematologic & oncologic: Decreased hematocrit, decreased hemoglobin, decreased serum immunoglobulins (IgG), eosinophilia, hemorrhage (excessive), lymphadenopathy, neutropenia (transient), thrombocytopenia

Hepatic: Increased serum alkaline phosphatase, increased serum AST

Infection: Herpes virus infection

Neuromuscular & skeletal: Accelerated bone maturation, craniofacial abnormality (children with chronic use), weakness

Ophthalmic: Blurred vision, cataract (transient), diplopia, lacrimation, scotoma (ring), subconjunctival hemorrhage

Renal: Decreased creatinine clearance

Miscellaneous: Fever

<1%, postmarketing, and/or case reports: Chest pain, pulmonary hypertension (infants and neonates)

General Dosage Range Oral:

Neonates and Infants: 8 to 15 mg/kg/day in divided doses every 8 to 12 hours

Children, Adolescents, and Adults: 3 to 8 mg/kg/day in divided doses every 8 to 12 hours

Mechanism of Action Opens ATP-dependent potassium channels on pancreatic beta cells in the presence of ATP and Mg^{2+}, resulting in hyperpolarization of the cell and inhibition of insulin release. Diazoxide binds to a different site on the potassium channel than the sulfonylureas (Doyle, 2003).

Pharmacodynamics/Kinetics

Onset of Action Hyperglycemic: Oral: Within 1 hour

Duration of Action Hyperglycemic: Oral: Normal renal function: ≤8 hours

Half-life Elimination Oral: Children: 9.5 to 24 hours; Adults: 24 to 36 hours

Pregnancy Risk Factor C

Pregnancy Considerations Adverse events have been observed in animal studies. Diazoxide crosses the human placenta and appears in cord blood. Altered carbohydrate metabolism, hyperbilirubinemia, and thrombocytopenia have been reported in the fetus or neonate. Alopecia and hypertrichosis lanuginosa have also been reported in infants following maternal use of diazoxide during the last 19 to 60 days of pregnancy.

Dibucaine (DYE byoo kane)

Brand Names: US Nupercainal [OTC]

Generic Availability (US) Yes

Pharmacologic Category Antihemorrhoidal Agent; Local Anesthetic

Dental Use Amide derivative local anesthetic for minor skin conditions

Use

Dermal pain/itching: Temporary relief of pain and itching caused by sunburn, minor burns, minor cuts, scrapes, insect bites or minor skin irritation.

Hemorrhoids/anorectal disorders; rectal pain/itching: Temporary relief of pain and itching due to hemorrhoids and other anorectal disorders.

Local Anesthetic/Vasoconstrictor Precautions No information available to require special precautions

Effects on Dental Treatment No significant effects or complications reported

Effects on Bleeding No information available to require special precautions

Adverse Reactions Frequency not defined.

1% to 10%:

Central nervous system: Localized burning

Dermatologic: Contact dermatitis

Hypersensitivity: Angioedema

Dental Usual Dosage Local pain (local anesthetic): Children and Adults: Topical: Apply gently to the affected areas; no more than 30 g for adults or 7.5 g for children should be used in any 24-hour period

Dosing

Adult & Geriatric

Dermal pain/itching: Topical: Apply to affected area up to 3 or 4 times daily. Maximum daily dose: 30 g/day

Hemorrhoids/anorectal disorders; rectal pain/itching: Topical: Apply to affected external anal area up to 3 or 4 times daily.

Pediatric

Dermal pain/itching: Children ≥2 years (weight ≥16 kg) and Adolescents: Topical: Apply to affected area up to 3 or 4 times daily. Maximum daily dose: 7.5 g/day

Hemorrhoids/anorectal disorders; rectal pain/itching: Children ≥12 years and Adolescents: Topical: Refer to adult dosing.

Renal Impairment There are no dosage adjustments provided in the manufacturer's labeling.

Hepatic Impairment There are no dosage adjustments provided in the manufacturer's labeling.

Mechanism of Action Blocks both the initiation and conduction of nerve impulses by decreasing the neuronal membrane's permeability to sodium ions, which results in inhibition of depolarization with resultant blockade of conduction.

Contraindications OTC labeling: When used for self-medication, do not use in or near the eyes or in children <2 years or weight <16 kg.

Documentation of allergenic cross-reactivity for amide local anesthetics limited. However, because of similarities in chemical structure and/or pharmacologic actions, the possibility of cross-sensitivity cannot be ruled out with certainty.

Warnings/Precautions When topical anesthetics are used prior to cosmetic or medical procedures, the lowest amount of anesthetic necessary for pain relief should be applied. High systemic levels and toxic effects (eg, methemoglobinemia, irregular heart beats, respiratory depression, seizures, death) have been reported in patients who (without supervision of a trained professional) have applied topical anesthetics in large amounts (or to large areas of the skin), left these products on for prolonged periods of time, or have used wraps/dressings to cover the skin following application.

Self-medication (OTC use): For external use only. When used for self-medication, notify healthcare provider and discontinue use if condition worsens, does not improve within 7 days, or if redness, irritation, swelling, bleeding or other symptoms develop or increase. Do not put this product into the rectum using fingers or any mechanical device or applicator; do not exceed recommended dose unless directed by a healthcare provider. Do not use in large quantities, particularly over raw surfaces or blistered areas.

Drug Interactions

Metabolism/Transport Effects None known.

Avoid Concomitant Use There are no known interactions where it is recommended to avoid concomitant use.

Increased Effect/Toxicity There are no known significant interactions involving an increase in effect.

Decreased Effect There are no known significant interactions involving a decrease in effect.

Pharmacodynamics/Kinetics

Onset of Action Within 15 minutes

Duration of Action 2 to 4 hours

Dosage Forms

Ointment, External:

Nupercainal [OTC]: 1% (56.7 g)

Generic: 1% (28 g, 28.35 g)

Ointment, Rectal:

Nupercainal [OTC]: 1% (28.4 g, 60 g)

Diclofenac (Systemic) (dye KLOE fen ak)

Related Information

Rheumatoid Arthritis, Osteoarthritis, and Osteoporosis *on page 1792*

Temporomandibular Dysfunction (TMD), Chronic Pain, and Fibromyalgia *on page 1868*

Brand Names: US Cambia; Cataflam [DSC]; Dyloject; Voltaren-XR [DSC]; Zipsor; Zorvolex

Brand Names: Canada Apo-Diclo; Apo-Diclo Rapide; Apo-Diclo SR; Cambia; Diclofenac EC; Diclofenac ECT; Diclofenac K; Diclofenac SR; Diclofenac-SR; Dom-Diclofenac; Dom-Diclofenac SR; PMS-Diclofenac; PMS-Diclofenac K; PMS-Diclofenac-SR; PRO-Diclo-Rapide; Sandoz-Diclofenac; Sandoz-Diclofenac Rapide; Sandoz-Diclofenac SR; Teva-Diclofenac; Teva-Diclofenac EC; Teva-Diclofenac K; Teva-Diclofenac SR; Voltaren; Voltaren Rapide; Voltaren SR

Generic Availability (US) May be product dependent

Pharmacologic Category Analgesic, Nonopioid; Nonsteroidal Anti-inflammatory Drug (NSAID); Nonsteroidal Anti-inflammatory Drug (NSAID), Oral

Dental Use Immediate-release tablets: Acute treatment of mild-to-moderate pain

Use

Ankylosing spondylitis (delayed-release tablets only): Acute or long-term use in the relief of signs and symptoms of ankylosing spondylitis.

Dysmenorrhea (immediate-release tablets only): Treatment of primary dysmenorrhea.

Migraine (powder for oral solution only): Acute treatment of migraine attacks with or without aura in adults.

Osteoarthritis (immediate-release, extended-release, and delayed-release tablets; capsules [Zorvolex]; and suppositories [Canadian product] only): Relief of signs and symptoms of osteoarthritis.

Pain

Capsules/immediate-release tablets only: Relief of mild to moderate acute pain.

Injection only: Management of mild to moderate pain and moderate to severe pain (alone or in combination with opioid analgesics) in adults.

Rheumatoid arthritis (immediate-release, extended-release, and delayed-release tablets; and suppositories [Canadian product] only): Relief of signs and symptoms of rheumatoid arthritis.

Local Anesthetic/Vasoconstrictor Precautions No information available to require special precautions

Effects on Dental Treatment The dentist should be aware of the potential of abnormal coagulation. Caution should also be exercised in the use of NSAIDs in patients already on anticoagulant therapy with drugs such as warfarin (Coumadin®). See Effects on Bleeding.

Effects on Bleeding Nonselective NSAIDs such as diclofenac (systemic) inhibit platelet aggregation and prolong bleeding time in some patients. Unlike aspirin, the NSAID effect on platelet function is quantitatively less, of shorter duration, and reversible. Normal platelet function should occur in ~5 elimination half-lives or in <10 hours after discontinuation of diclofenac (systemic). Concomitant use of other NSAIDs should be avoided.

Adverse Reactions

Injection: Frequency not always defined.

Cardiovascular: Edema (≤10%), cerebrovascular accident, hypertension, myocardial infarction, significant cardiovascular event

Central nervous system: Headache (≤10%), dizziness (8%)

Dermatologic: Pruritus (≤10%), skin rash (≤10%), exfoliative dermatitis, Stevens-Johnson syndrome, toxic epidermal necrolysis

Endocrine & metabolic: Fluid retention

Gastrointestinal: Constipation (13%), abdominal pain (≤10%), diarrhea (≤10%), dyspepsia (≤10%), esophageal perforation (≤10%), flatulence (≤10%), gastrointestinal ulcer (≤10%; including gastric/duodenal), heartburn (≤10%), intestinal perforation (≤10%), nausea (≤10%), vomiting (≤10%)

Hematologic & oncologic: Anemia (≤10%), hemorrhage (≤10%), prolonged bleeding time (≤10%)

Hepatic: Increased liver enzymes (≤10%), increased serum transaminases (15%), increased serum ALT (≤4%; >8X ULN: ≤1%), increased serum AST (2% to ≤4%; >8X ULN: ≤1%)

Hypersensitivity: Anaphylactoid reaction

Local: Infusion site reaction (10%), extravasation (3%)

Otic: Tinnitus (≤10%)

Renal: Renal insufficiency (≤10%)

Miscellaneous: Wound healing impairment (8%), gastrointestinal inflammation

<1%, postmarketing, and/or case reports: Abnormal Dreams, agranulocytosis, alopecia, anaphylaxis, angioedema, anxiety, aplastic anemia, asthma, auditory impairment, blurred vision, cardiac arrhythmia, change in appetite, colitis, coma, confusion, congestive heart failure, conjunctivitis, convulsions, cystitis, depression, diaphoresis, drowsiness, dyspnea, dysuria, ecchymoses, eosinophilia, eructation, erythema multiforme, esophagitis, exfoliative dermatitis, fever, fulminant hepatitis, gastritis, gastrointestinal hemorrhage, glossitis, hallucination, hematemesis, hematuria, hemolytic anemia, hepatic failure, hepatic necrosis, hepatitis, hepatotoxicity, hyperglycemia, hypertension, hypotension, infection, insomnia, interstitial nephritis, jaundice, leukopenia, lymphadenopathy, malaise, melena, meningitis, nervousness, oliguria, palpitations, pancreatitis, pancytopenia, paresthesia, pneumonia, polyuria, proteinuria, purpura, rectal hemorrhage, renal failure, respiratory depression, sepsis, skin photosensitivity, stomatitis, syncope, tachycardia, thrombocytopenia, toxic epidermal necrolysis, tremor, urticaria, vasculitis, vertigo, weakness, weight changes

Oral: Frequency not always defined.

>10%:

Cardiovascular: Edema (33%)

Hepatic: Increased serum transaminases (≤3 x ULN; 15%)

1% to 10%:

Cardiovascular: Hypertension (2% to 3%)

Central nervous system: Headache (4% to 8%), procedural pain (3%), dizziness (2%), falling (2%)

Dermatologic: Pruritus (7%), skin rash

Gastrointestinal: Constipation (5% to 8%), nausea (6% to 7%), diarrhea (6%), GI adverse effects (gastric ulcer, hemorrhage, and perforation; ≤4%, risk increases with therapy duration), abdominal pain (2% to 3%), vomiting (3%), dyspepsia (2% to 3%), flatulence (2% to 3%), heartburn, abdominal discomfort (2%), duodenal ulcer

Genitourinary: Urinary tract infection (7%)

Hematologic & oncologic: Bruise (3%), anemia, prolonged bleeding time

Hepatic: Increased serum ALT (>3 x ULN: ≤4%; >8 x ULN: ≤1%), increased serum AST (>3 x ULN; ≤4%; >8 x ULN: ≤1%)

Infection: Influenza (3%)

Neuromuscular & skeletal: Osteoarthritis (5%), arthralgia (3%), back pain (3%), limb pain (3%)

Renal: Renal function abnormality

Otic: Tinnitus

Renal: Increased serum creatinine (2%), renal function abnormality

Respiratory: Upper respiratory tract infection (8%), nasopharyngitis (6%), sinusitis (3% to 5%), cough (4%), bronchitis (3%)

<1%, postmarketing, and/or case reports: Abnormal dreams, agranulocytosis, alopecia, anaphylactoid reaction, anaphylaxis, angioedema, anxiety, aplastic anemia, aseptic meningitis, asthma, auditory impairment, azotemia (Gurwitz, 1990), blurred vision, cardiac arrhythmia, cardiac failure, cerebrovascular accident, change in appetite, chest pain, colitis, coma, confusion, conjunctivitis, cystitis, decreased hemoglobin (Goldstein, 2011), depression, diaphoresis, diplopia, disorientation, drowsiness, dyspnea, dysuria, ecchymoses, eosinophilia, eructation, erythema multiforme, esophageal ulcer, esophagitis, exfoliative dermatitis, fever, fluid retention, fulminant hepatitis, gastritis, glossitis, hallucination, hearing loss, hematemesis, hematuria, hemolytic anemia, hepatic failure, hepatic necrosis, hepatitis, hepatotoxicity, hyperglycemia, hypotension, infection, insomnia, interstitial nephritis, intestinal perforation, jaundice, leukopenia, lymphadenopathy, malaise, melena, memory impairment, meningitis, myocardial infarction, nephrotic syndrome, nervousness, oliguria, palpitations, pancreatitis, pancytopenia, paresthesia, peptic ulcer, pneumonia, polyuria, proteinuria, psychotic reaction, purpura, rectal hemorrhage, renal failure, renal papillary necrosis, respiratory depression, seizure, sepsis, skin photosensitivity, Stevens-Johnson syndrome, stomatitis, syncope, tachycardia, taste disorder, thrombocytopenia, toxic epidermal necrolysis, tremor, urticaria, vasculitis, vertigo, weakness, weight changes, xerostomia

Rectal suppository [Canadian product]:

Also refer to adverse reactions associated with oral formulations.

<1%, postmarketing, and/or case reports: Hemorrhoids (exacerbation), local hemorrhage, proctitis, rectal irritation

Dental Usual Dosage Pain: Adults: Oral: Starting dose: 50 mg 3 times/day; maximum dose: 150 mg/day

Dosing

Adult

Ankylosing spondylitis: Oral: Delayed-release tablet: 25 mg 4 times daily and 25 mg at bedtime as needed

Migraine: Oral: Powder for oral solution: 50 mg (one packet) as a single dose; safety and efficacy of a second dose have not been established.

Osteoarthritis:

Oral:

Immediate-release tablet: 50 mg 2 to 3 times daily; Delayed-release tablet: 50 mg 2 to 3 times daily or 75 mg twice daily; Extended-release tablet: 100 mg once daily

Canadian labeling: Enteric-coated tablet: 50 mg every 8 hours (maximum: 100 mg/day); Slow-release tablet: 75 to 100 mg daily (maximum: 100 mg/day)

Immediate-release capsule: Zorvolex (diclofenac acid): 35 mg 3 times daily.

Rectal suppository [Canadian product]: Insert 50 mg or 100 mg rectally as single dose to substitute for final oral daily dose (maximum combined dose [rectal and oral]: 100 mg/day)

Pain:

Oral:

Immediate-release tablet: 50 mg 3 times daily; may administer 100 mg as an initial dose, followed by 50 mg 3 times daily

Canadian labeling: 50 mg every 6 to 8 hours for up to 7 days (maximum: 100 mg/day)

Immediate-release capsule:

Zipsor (diclofenac potassium): 25 mg 4 times daily

Zorvolex (diclofenac acid): 18 mg or 35 mg 3 times daily

IV: 37.5 mg every 6 hours as needed; adjust frequency according to patient response (maximum: 150 mg/day).

Primary dysmenorrhea: Oral: Immediate-release tablet: 50 mg 3 times daily; may administer 100 mg as an initial dose, followed by 50 mg 3 times daily

Canadian labeling: Immediate release tablet: Day 1: Initial: 100 mg then 50 mg every 6 to 8 hours (maximum: 200 mg/day); Day 2 and beyond (up to 7 days): 50 mg every 6 to 8 hours (maximum: 100 mg/day)

Rheumatoid arthritis:

Oral: Immediate-release tablet: 50 mg 3 to 4 times daily; Delayed-release tablet: 50 mg 3 to 4 times daily or 75 mg twice daily; Extended-release tablet: 100 mg once daily; may increase to 100 mg twice daily

Canadian labeling: Enteric-coated tablet: 50 mg every 8 hours (maximum: 100 mg/day); Slow-release tablet: 75 to 100 mg daily (maximum: 100 mg/day)

Rectal suppository [Canadian product]: Insert 50 mg or 100 mg rectally as single dose to substitute for final oral daily dose (maximum combined dose [rectal and oral]: 100 mg/day

Geriatric Refer to adult dosing. Use with caution; initiate using lowest recommended dose and frequency.

Pediatric Juvenile idiopathic arthritis (off-label use): Children ≥3 years and Adolescents: Oral: Delayed-release tablet (diclofenac sodium): 2 to 3 mg/kg/day in divided doses (Haapasaari, 1983; Hashkes, 2005)

Renal Impairment

Oral:

Mild or moderate impairment: No dosage adjustment necessary.

Significant impairment or advanced renal disease: Use is not recommended.

Injection:

Mild impairment: There are no dosage adjustments provided in the manufacturer's labeling.

Moderate to severe impairment: Use is not recommended; contraindicated in patients in the perioperative period and who are at risk for volume depletion.

KDIGO 2012 guidelines provide the following recommendations for NSAIDs:

eGFR 30 to <60 mL/minute/1.73 m^2: Temporarily discontinue in patients with intercurrent disease that increases risk of acute kidney injury.

eGFR <30 mL/minute/1.73 m^2: Avoid use.

Hepatic Impairment There are no dosage adjustments provided in the manufacturer's labeling; however, may require dosage adjustment due to extensive hepatic metabolism. Additional product-specific recommendations:

Cambia: Use the lowest effective dose for the shortest duration possible.

Zipsor/Zorvolex: Initial: Initiate treatment at the lowest dose; if efficacy is not achieved with the lowest dose, discontinue use.

Injection:

Mild impairment: No dosage adjustment necessary.

Moderate to severe impairment: Use is not recommended (has not been studied).

Mechanism of Action Reversibly inhibits cyclooxygenase-1 and 2 (COX-1 and 2) enzymes, which results in decreased formation of prostaglandin precursors; has antipyretic, analgesic, and anti-inflammatory properties

Other proposed mechanisms not fully elucidated (and possibly contributing to the anti-inflammatory effect to varying degrees), include inhibiting chemotaxis, altering lymphocyte activity, inhibiting neutrophil aggregation/ activation, and decreasing proinflammatory cytokine levels.

Contraindications

Hypersensitivity to diclofenac (eg, anaphylactoid reactions, serious skin reactions) or bovine protein (Zipsor only) or any component of the formulation; history of asthma, urticaria, or other allergic-type reactions after taking aspirin or other NSAIDs; use in the setting of CABG surgery; patients with moderate to severe renal impairment in the perioperative period and who are at risk for volume depletion (injection only).

Canadian labeling: Additional contraindications (not in U.S. labeling): Severe uncontrolled heart failure, active gastric/duodenal/peptic ulcer; active GI bleed or perforation; regional ulcer, gastritis, or ulcerative colitis; cerebrovascular bleeding or other bleeding disorders; inflammatory bowel disease; severe hepatic impairment; active hepatic disease; severe renal impairment (CrCl <30 mL/minute) or deteriorating renal disease; known hyperkalemia; patients <16 years of age; breastfeeding; pregnancy (third trimester); use of diclofenac suppository if recent history of bleeding or inflammatory lesions of rectum/anus.

Warnings/Precautions [US Boxed Warning]: NSAIDs cause an increased risk of serious (and potentially fatal) adverse cardiovascular thrombotic events, including MI and stroke. Risk may occur early during treatment and may increase with duration of use. Relative risk appears to be similar in those with and without known cardiovascular disease or risk factors for cardiovascular disease; however, absolute incidence of serious cardiovascular thrombotic events (which may occur early during treatment) was higher in patients with known cardiovascular disease or risk factors and in those receiving higher doses. New onset hypertension or exacerbation of hypertension may occur (NSAIDs may also impair response to ACE inhibitors, thiazide diuretics, or loop diuretics); may contribute to cardiovascular events; monitor blood pressure; use with caution in patients with hypertension. May cause sodium and fluid retention; use with caution in patients with edema. Avoid use in heart failure (ACCF/AHA [Yancy 2013]). Avoid use in patients with recent MI unless benefits outweigh risk of cardiovascular thrombotic events. Use the lowest effective dose for the shortest duration of time, consistent with individual patient goals, to reduce risk of cardiovascular events; alternate therapies should be considered for patients at high risk. **[US Boxed Warning]: Use is contraindicated in the setting of coronary artery bypass graft (CABG) surgery.** Risk of MI and stroke may be increased with use following CABG surgery.

NSAID use may compromise existing renal function; dose-dependent decreases in prostaglandin synthesis may result from NSAID use, reducing renal blood flow which may cause renal decompensation (usually reversible). Patients with impaired renal function, dehydration, hypovolemia, heart failure, hepatic impairment, those taking diuretics and ACE inhibitors, and the elderly are at greater risk of renal toxicity. Rehydrate patient before starting therapy; monitor function closely. Long-term NSAID use may result in renal papillary necrosis and other renal injury. NSAID use may increase the risk for hyperkalemia, particularly in elderly patients, diabetic patients, those with renal disease, and with concomitant use of other agents capable of inducing hyperkalemia (eg, ACE inhibitors). Monitor potassium closely. Avoid use in patients with advanced renal disease unless benefits are expected to outweigh risk of worsening renal function; monitor closely if therapy must be initiated. Injection is not recommended in patients with moderate to severe renal impairment and is contraindicated in patients with moderate to severe renal impairment in the perioperative period and who are at risk for volume depletion.

[US Boxed Warning]: NSAIDs cause an increased risk of serious gastrointestinal inflammation, ulceration, bleeding, and perforation (may be fatal); elderly patients and patients with history of peptic ulcer disease and/or GI bleeding are at greater risk for serious GI events. These events may occur at any time during therapy and without warning. Avoid use in patients with active GI bleeding. Use caution with a history of GI ulcers, concurrent therapy known to increase the risk of GI bleeding (eg, aspirin, anticoagulants and/or corticosteroids, selective serotonin reuptake inhibitors), advanced hepatic disease, coagulopathy, smoking, use of alcohol, or in elderly or debilitated patients. Use the lowest effective dose for the shortest duration of time, consistent with individual patient goals, to reduce risk of GI adverse events; alternate therapies should be considered for patients at high risk. When used concomitantly with aspirin, a substantial increase in the risk of gastrointestinal complications (eg, ulcer) occurs; concomitant gastroprotective therapy (eg, proton pump inhibitors) is recommended (Bhatt 2008).

Use the lowest effective dose for the shortest duration of time, consistent with individual patient goals, to reduce risk of cardiovascular or GI adverse events. Alternate therapies should be considered for patients at high risk. Elderly patients are at greater risk for serious GI, cardiovascular, and/or renal adverse events.

NSAIDs may cause potentially fatal serious skin adverse events including exfoliative dermatitis, Stevens-Johnson syndrome (SJS), and toxic epidermal necrolysis (TEN); may occur without warning; discontinue use at first sign of skin rash (or any other hypersensitivity).

Anaphylactoid reactions may occur, even without prior exposure; patients with "aspirin triad" (bronchial asthma, aspirin intolerance, rhinitis) may be at increased risk. Use is contraindicated in patients who experience bronchospasm, asthma, rhinitis, or urticaria with NSAID or aspirin therapy. Use caution in other forms of asthma. Platelet adhesion and aggregation may be decreased; may prolong bleeding time; patients with coagulation disorders or who are receiving anticoagulants should be monitored closely. Anemia may occur; patients on long-term NSAID therapy should be monitored for anemia. Rarely, NSAID use may cause severe blood dyscrasias (eg, agranulocytosis, aplastic anemia, thrombocytopenia).

Use with caution in patients with hepatic impairment; reduced doses may be required due to extensive hepatic metabolism. Patients with advanced hepatic disease are at an increased risk of GI bleeding with NSAIDs. Transaminase elevations have been reported with use; closely monitor patients with any abnormal LFT. Rare, sometimes fatal, severe hepatic reactions (eg, fulminant hepatitis, hepatic necrosis, hepatic failure) have occurred with NSAID use; discontinue immediately if clinical signs or symptoms of liver disease develop or if systemic manifestations occur.

NSAIDS may cause drowsiness, dizziness, blurred vision, and other neurologic effects which may impair physical or mental abilities; patients must be cautioned about performing tasks which require mental alertness (eg, operating machinery or driving). Discontinue use with blurred or diminished vision and perform ophthalmologic exam. Monitor vision with long-term therapy. May increase the risk of aseptic meningitis, especially in patients with systemic lupus erythematosus (SLE) and mixed connective tissue disorders.

Withhold for at least 4 to 6 half-lives prior to surgical or dental procedures.

Different formulations of oral diclofenac are not bioequivalent, even if the milligram strength is the same; do not interchange products.

Zipsor (capsule) contains gelatin; use is contraindicated in patients with history of hypersensitivity to bovine protein.

Injection is not indicated for long-term use.

Oral solution: Indicated only for the acute treatment of migraine (not indicated for migraine prophylaxis or cluster headache). Acute migraine agents (eg, NSAIDs, triptans, opioids, ergotamine, or a combination of the agents) used for 10 or more days per month may lead to worsening of headaches (medication overuse headache); withdrawal treatment may be necessary in the setting of overuse. Product may contain phenylalanine.

Drug Interactions

Metabolism/Transport Effects **Substrate** of CYP1A2 (minor), CYP2B6 (minor), CYP2C19 (minor), CYP2C8 (minor), CYP2C9 (minor), CYP2D6 (minor), CYP3A4 (minor); **Note:** Assignment of Major/Minor substrate status based on clinically relevant drug interaction potential; **Inhibits** CYP1A2 (weak), CYP2C9 (weak), CYP2E1 (weak), UGT1A6

Avoid Concomitant Use

Avoid concomitant use of Diclofenac (Systemic) with any of the following: Dexketoprofen; Floctafenine; Ketorolac (Nasal); Ketorolac (Systemic); Morniflumate; NSAID (COX-2 Inhibitor); Omacetaxine; Pelubiprofen; Phenylbutazone; Talniflumate; Tenoxicam; Urokinase; Zaltoprofen

Increased Effect/Toxicity

Diclofenac (Systemic) may increase the levels/effects of: 5-ASA Derivatives; Agents with Antiplatelet Properties; Aliskiren; Aminoglycosides; Aminolevulinic Acid; Anticoagulants; Apixaban; Bisphosphonate Derivatives; Cephalothin; CloZAPine; Collagenase (Systemic); CycloSPORINE (Systemic); Dabigatran Etexilate; Deferasirox; Deferiprone; Deoxycholic Acid; Desmopressin; Digoxin; Drospirenone; Edoxaban; Eplerenone; Haloperidol; Ibritumomab; Lithium; Methotrexate; Nalmefene; Nonsteroidal Anti-Inflammatory Agents; NSAID (COX-2 Inhibitor); Obinutuzumab; Omacetaxine; PEMEtrexed; Porfimer; Potassium-Sparing Diuretics; PRALAtrexate; Quinolone Antibiotics; Rivaroxaban; Salicylates; Tacrolimus (Systemic); Tenofovir Products; Thrombolytic Agents; TiZANidine; Tolperisone; Tositumomab and Iodine I 131 Tositumomab; Urokinase; Vancomycin; Verteporfin; Vitamin K Antagonists

The levels/effects of Diclofenac (Systemic) may be increased by: ACE Inhibitors; Alcohol (Ethyl); Angiotensin II Receptor Blockers; Antidepressants (Tricyclic, Tertiary Amine); Corticosteroids (Systemic); CycloSPORINE (Systemic); CYP2C9 Inhibitors (Strong); Dasatinib; Dexketoprofen; Felbinac; Floctafenine; Glucosamine; Herbs (Anticoagulant/Antiplatelet Properties); Ibrutinib; Ketorolac (Nasal); Ketorolac (Systemic); Limaprost; Loop Diuretics; Morniflumate; Multivitamins/Fluoride (with ADE); Multivitamins/Minerals (with ADEK, Folate, Iron); Multivitamins/Minerals (with AE, No Iron); Naftazone; Omega-3 Fatty Acids; Pelubiprofen; Pentosan Polysulfate Sodium; Pentoxifylline; Phenylbutazone; Probenecid; Prostacyclin Analogues; Resveratrol; Selective Serotonin Reuptake Inhibitors; Serotonin/Norepinephrine Reuptake Inhibitors; Sodium Phosphates; Talniflumate; Tenoxicam; Thiazide and Thiazide-Like Diuretics; Tipranavir; Tolperisone; Vitamin E (Systemic); Voriconazole; Zaltoprofen

Decreased Effect

Diclofenac (Systemic) may decrease the levels/effects of: ACE Inhibitors; Aliskiren; Angiotensin II Receptor Blockers; Beta-Blockers; Eplerenone; HydrALAZINE; Loop Diuretics; Potassium-Sparing Diuretics; Prostaglandins (Ophthalmic); Salicylates; Selective Serotonin Reuptake Inhibitors; Thiazide and Thiazide-Like Diuretics

The levels/effects of Diclofenac (Systemic) may be decreased by: Bile Acid Sequestrants; CYP2C9 Inducers (Strong); Salicylates

Dietary Considerations Oral immediate-release formulations may be taken with food to decrease GI distress. However, food may reduce effectiveness of oral solution and diclofenac acid (capsule). Some products may contain phenylalanine.

Pharmacodynamics/Kinetics

Half-life Elimination Oral: ~2 hours, ~1 hour (liquid filled capsule [Zipsor]); Injection: ~1.4 hours

Time to Peak Serum: **Note:** Fasted values reported for oral products; may be delayed with food.

Cambia: ~0.25 hours
Cataflam, Zorvolex: ~1 hour
Zipsor: ~0.47 ± 0.17 hour
Injection: ~5 minutes
Tablet, delayed release (diclofenac sodium): 2.3 hours
Tablet, extended release (diclofenac sodium): 5.3 hours

Pregnancy Risk Factor C (oral, injection)/D (≥30 weeks gestation [oral, injection])

Pregnancy Considerations Adverse events have not been observed in animal reproduction studies. Diclofenac crosses the placenta and can be detected in fetal tissue and amniotic fluid. NSAID exposure during the first trimester is not strongly associated with congenital malformations; however, cardiovascular anomalies and cleft palate have been observed following NSAID exposure in some studies. The use of a NSAID close to conception may be associated with an increased risk of miscarriage. Nonteratogenic effects have been observed following NSAID administration during the third trimester including: Myocardial degenerative changes, prenatal constriction of the ductus arteriosus, fetal tricuspid regurgitation, failure of the ductus arteriosus to close postnatally; renal dysfunction or failure, oligohydramnios; gastrointestinal bleeding or perforation, increased risk of necrotizing enterocolitis; intracranial bleeding (including intraventricular hemorrhage), platelet dysfunction with resultant bleeding; pulmonary hypertension. Because they may cause premature closure of the ductus arteriosus, use of NSAIDs in pregnancy (particularly late pregnancy) should be avoided. The manufacturer's labeling specifically notes that use at ≥30 weeks' gestation should be avoided. The chronic use of NSAIDs in women of reproductive age may be associated with infertility that is reversible upon discontinuation of the medication. A registry is available for pregnant women exposed to autoimmune medications including diclofenac. For additional information contact the Organization of Teratology Information Specialists, OTIS Autoimmune Diseases Study, at 877-311-8972

Breastfeeding Considerations Low concentrations of diclofenac can be found in breast milk. breastfeeding is not recommended by most manufacturers. The manufacturers of the injection recommend that caution be exercised when administering diclofenac to breastfeeding women.

Dosage Forms

Capsule, Oral:
Zipsor: 25 mg
Zorvolex: 18 mg, 35 mg

Packet, Oral:
Cambia: 50 mg (1 ea, 9 ea)

Solution, Intravenous:
Dyloject: 37.5 mg/mL (1 mL)

Tablet, Oral:
Generic: 50 mg

Tablet Delayed Release, Oral:
Generic: 25 mg, 50 mg, 75 mg

Tablet Extended Release 24 Hour, Oral:
Generic: 100 mg

Dosage Forms: Canada Note: Refer also to Dosage Forms; Zipsor and Zorvolex capsules are not currently available in Canada.

Suppository:
Voltaren: 50 mg, 100 mg

Diclofenac (Topical) (dye KLOE fen ak)

Brand Names: US Diclo Gel with Xrylix Sheets; Diclozor; DSG Pak [DSC]; DST Plus Pak; EnovaRX-Diclofenac Sodium; Flector; Klofensaid II; Lexixryl; Pennsaid; Rexaphenac; Solaraze; Voltaren; Vopac MDS; Xrylix

Brand Names: Canada Pennsaid; Voltaren Emulgel

Pharmacologic Category Nonsteroidal Anti-inflammatory Drug (NSAID); Nonsteroidal Anti-inflammatory Drug (NSAID), Topical

Use

Gel 1%: Relief of osteoarthritis pain in joints amenable to topical therapy (eg, ankle, elbow, foot, hand, knee, wrist)

Canadian labeling (not in US labeling): Relief of pain associated with acute, localized joint/muscle injuries (eg, sports injuries, strains) in patients ≥16 years of age

Gel 3%: Treatment of actinic keratosis (AK) in conjunction with sun avoidance

Patch: Treatment of acute pain due to minor strains, sprains, and contusions

Solution: Treatment of osteoarthritis pain of the knee

Local Anesthetic/Vasoconstrictor Precautions No information available to require special precautions

Effects on Dental Treatment No significant effects or complications reported

Effects on Bleeding No information available to require special precautions

Adverse Reactions

Topical gel:

>10%:

Dermatologic: Pruritus (≤52%), application site rash (35% to 46%), contact dermatitis (2% to 33%), xeroderma (3% to 27%), application site pain (15% to 26%), desquamation (application site 6% to 24%)

Hepatic: Increased serum transaminases (<3 x ULN: 15%; >3 x ULN: 2% to 4%; >8 x ULN: 1%)

1% to 10%:

Cardiovascular: Chest pain (1% to 2%), hypertension (1% to 2%)

Central nervous system: Headache (7%), hyperesthesia (3%), paresthesia (2%), pain (1% to 2%), migraine (1%)

Dermatologic: Application site paresthesia (≤8%), vesiculobullous dermatitis (application site 4%), skin rash (4%), alopecia (application site 2%), skin photosensitivity (application site 3%), dermal ulcer (1% to 2%), acne vulgaris (application site 1%)

Endocrine & metabolic: Application site edema (3% to 4%), hypercholesterolemia (1%), hyperglycemia (1%)

Gastrointestinal: Diarrhea (2%), dyspepsia (2%), abdominal pain (1% to 2%)

Genitourinary: Hematuria (2%)

Hepatic: Increased serum ALT (2% to 4%), increased serum AST (2% to 4%), increased liver enzymes

Neuromuscular and skeletal: Back pain (4%), increased creatine phosphokinase (4%), myalgia (2% to 3%), arthralgia (2%), arthropathy (2%), hypokinesia (2%), neck pain (2%), weakness (2%)

Ophthalmic: Conjunctivitis (2% to 4%), eye pain (2%)

Respiratory: Flu-like symptoms (10%), asthma (2%), dyspnea (2%), pneumonia (2%), sinusitis (2%)
Miscellaneous: Accidental injury (4%)

<1%, postmarketing, and/or case reports: Application site irritation, application site papules, application site reaction (skin carcinoma, hypertonia, skin hypertrophy lacrimation disorder, maculopapular rash, purpuric rash, vasodilation), application site vesicles, edema, hepatic failure, hepatic necrosis, hepatitis (fulfillment; with and without jaundice), hepatotoxicity, jaundice, paresthesia, seborrhea, skin hypertrophy, urticaria

Topical solution:

>10%: Dermatologic: Xeroderma (application site 22% to 32%; nonapplication site 2%)

1% to 10%:

Cardiovascular: Edema (3%)

Dermatologic: Contact dermatitis (2% to 9%), desquamation (application site 7%), application site erythema (4%), pruritus (application site 2% to 4%; nonapplication site 2%); skin rash (3%), application site induration (2%), application site pain (2%), application site rash (2%)

Gastrointestinal: Dyspepsia (8%), abdominal pain (6%), diarrhea (4%), flatulence (4%), nausea (2% to 4%), constipation (3%), halitosis (1%)

Genitourinary: Urinary tract infection (3%)

Hematologic & oncologic: Bruise (2%)

Infection: Infection (3%)

Respiratory: Sinus congestion (2%), sinusitis (1%)

Postmarketing and/or case reports: Accidental injury, aphthous stomatitis, asthma, back pain, blurred vision, body odor, burning sensation of skin, cardiovascular disease, cataract, chest pain, decreased appetite, depression, dizziness, drowsiness, dysgeusia, dyspnea, eczema, eye disease, eye pain, facial edema, gastroenteritis, headache, hypersensitivity reaction, hypertension, increased blood pressure, increased serum creatinine, laryngismus, laryngitis, leg cramps, lethargy, lip edema, myalgia, neck stiffness, oral mucosa ulcer, otalgia, palpitations, pharyngeal edema, pharyngitis, rectal hemorrhage, scabbing, skin discoloration, tongue edema, urticaria, visual disturbance, weakness, xerostomia

Transdermal patch:

1% to 10%:

Central nervous system: Dizziness (<1%), hypoesthesia (<1%)

Dermatologic: Hyperhidrosis (<4%), local dryness (<4%), localized erythema (<4%), localized vesiculation (<4%), skin discoloration (<4%), dermatitis (2%), hypersensitivity reaction (dermal)

Gastrointestinal: Nausea (3%), upper abdominal pain (<3%), constipation (<3%), diarrhea (<3%), gastritis (<3%), vomiting (<3%), xerostomia (<3%), dysgeusia (2%)

Local: Application site atrophy (<4%), local irritation (<4%), localized edema, local pruritus

Neuromuscular & skeletal: Hyperkinesia (<1%)

Postmarketing and/or case reports: Cerebrovascular accident, edema, exfoliative dermatitis, fluid retention, myocardial infarction, Stevens-Johnson syndrome, toxic epidermal necrolysis

General Dosage Range Topical: *Adults:*

1% gel: Apply 2 to 4 g to affected joint 4 times daily (maximum: 16 g daily single joint of lower extremity, 8 g daily single joint of upper extremity); Maximum total body dose of 1% gel should not exceed 32 g per day.

3% gel: Apply to lesion area twice daily

Patch: Apply 1 patch twice daily

1.5% solution: Apply 40 drops to each affected knee 4 times daily

2% solution: Apply 2 pump actuations to each affected knee twice daily

Mechanism of Action

Reversibly inhibits cyclooxygenase-1 and 2 (COX-1 and 2) enzymes, which results in decreased formation of prostaglandin precursors; has antipyretic, analgesic, and anti-inflammatory properties

Other proposed mechanisms not fully elucidated (and possibly contributing to the anti-inflammatory effect to varying degrees), include inhibiting chemotaxis, altering lymphocyte activity, inhibiting neutrophil aggregation/activation, and decreasing proinflammatory cytokine levels.

Pharmacodynamics/Kinetics

Half-life Elimination Patch: ~12 hours; Solution 1.5%: 36.7 ± 20.8 hours (single application)

Time to Peak Serum: Patch: 10 to 20 hours; Solution 1.5%: 11 ± 6.4 hours (single application); Gel 3%: 4.5 ± 8 hours; Gel 1%: 10 to 14 hours

Pregnancy Risk Factor

B (gel 3%)

C (gel 1%, solution, patch)

D (≥30 weeks gestation [gel 1%, patch, solution])

Pregnancy Considerations Adverse events have been observed in some animal reproduction studies. When administered orally, diclofenac crosses the placenta. The amount of diclofenac available systemically following topical application is less in comparison to oral doses. Reversible constriction of the ductus arteriosus in utero has been observed following topical application of diclofenac. Additional adverse fetal and maternal effects have been observed following oral use of diclofenac. Because they may cause premature closure of the ductus arteriosus, US product labeling notes that the use of NSAIDs late in pregnancy should be avoided; the product labeling for most products specifically states use should be avoided starting at 30 weeks gestation.

Diclofenac and Misoprostol

(dye KLOE fen ak & mye soe PROST ole)

Related Information

Diclofenac (Systemic) *on page 496*

MiSOPROStol *on page 1133*

Rheumatoid Arthritis, Osteoarthritis, and Osteoporosis *on page 1792*

Brand Names: US Arthrotec

Brand Names: Canada ACT Diclo-Miso; Arthrotec; GD-Diclofenac/Misoprostol

Pharmacologic Category Analgesic, Nonopioid; Nonsteroidal Anti-inflammatory Drug (NSAID), Oral; Prostaglandin

Use Osteoarthritis/rheumatoid arthritis: Treatment of the signs and symptoms of osteoarthritis or rheumatoid arthritis in patients at high risk for NSAID-induced gastric and duodenal ulcers and their complications.

Local Anesthetic/Vasoconstrictor Precautions No information available to require special precautions

Effects on Dental Treatment The dentist should be aware of the potential of abnormal coagulation. Caution should also be exercised in the use of NSAIDs in patients already on anticoagulant therapy with drugs such as warfarin (Coumadin). See Effects on Bleeding.

Effects on Bleeding Nonselective NSAIDs, such as diclofenac, inhibit platelet aggregation and prolong bleeding time in some patients. Unlike aspirin, the NSAID effect on platelet function is quantitatively less, of shorter duration, and reversible.

Adverse Reactions Percentages reported with combination product. Also see individual agents.

>10%: Gastrointestinal: Abdominal pain (21%), diarrhea (19%), dyspepsia (14%), nausea (11%)

1% to 10%:

Gastrointestinal: Flatulence (9%)

Hepatic: Increased serum ALT (2%)

Frequency not defined:

Central nervous system: Anxiety, depression, dizziness, drowsiness, fatigue, headache, insomnia, irritability, lack of concentration, malaise, paresthesia, vertigo

Dermatologic: Alopecia, diaphoresis, eczema, pemphigoid reaction, pruritus, skin photosensitivity

Endocrine & metabolic: Dehydration, hypermenorrhea, hyponatremia, menstrual disease

Gastrointestinal: Anorexia, benign gastrointestinal neoplasm, change in appetite, constipation, dysgeusia, dysphagia, eructation, esophageal ulcer, esophagitis, gastritis, gastroesophageal reflux disease, melena, peptic ulcer, tenesmus, vomiting, xerostomia

Genitourinary: Dysmenorrhea, dysuria, mastalgia, nocturia, proteinuria, urinary tract infection, vaginal hemorrhage

Hematologic & oncologic: Decreased hematocrit, leukopenia, purpura

Hepatic: Increased serum AST

Neuromuscular & skeletal: Arthralgia, increased serum alkaline phosphatase, myalgia, weakness

Ophthalmic: Diplopia

Otic: Tinnitus

Renal: Polyuria

Respiratory: Asthma, cough, epistaxis, hyperventilation

<1%, postmarketing, and/or case reports: Abnormal dreams, abnormal lacrimation, acne vulgaris, ageusia, agranulocytosis, amblyopia, anaphylactoid reaction, anaphylaxis, anemia, angioedema, aphthous stomatitis, aplastic anemia, aseptic meningitis, atrial fibrillation, auditory impairment, blurred vision, bruise, bullous rash, cardiac arrhythmia, cerebral hemorrhage, cerebrovascular accident, chills, coma, confusion, conjunctivitis, cystitis, decreased platelet aggregation, dermal ulcer, disorientation, dyspnea, ecchymosis, edema, enteritis, eosinophilia, erythema multiforme, exfoliative dermatitis, fever, fluid retention, fulminant hepatitis, gastrointestinal hemorrhage, gastrointestinal perforation, gastrointestinal ulcer, GI inflammation, glaucoma, glomerulonephritis, glomerulopathy (glomerulonephritis minimal lesion), glossitis, glycosuria, gout, hallucination, heartburn, hematemesis, hematuria, hemolytic anemia, hemorrhoids, hepatic failure, hepatic insufficiency, hepatic necrosis, hepatitis, hepatotoxicity (idiosyncratic) (Chalasani 2014), hyperbilirubinemia, hypercholesterolemia, hyperesthesia, hyperglycemia, hypersensitivity reaction, hypertension, hypertonia, hyperuricemia, hypoesthesia, hypoglycemia, hypotension, impotence, increased blood urea nitrogen, increased coagulation time, increased creatine phosphokinase, increased lactate dehydrogenase, infection, intermenstrual bleeding, interstitial nephritis, intestinal perforation, iritis, jaundice, laryngeal edema, leukocytosis, leukorrhea, lymphadenopathy, membranous glomerulonephritis, meningitis, migraine, mood changes, mucocutaneous eruptions, myocardial infarction, nephrotic syndrome, nervousness, neuralgia, nightmares, nocturnal amblyopia, oliguria, palpitations, pancreatitis, pancytopenia, paranoia, perineal pain, periorbital edema, pharyngeal edema, phlebitis, pneumonia, porphyria, pruritus ani, psychotic reaction, pulmonary embolism, rectal bleeding, reduced fertility (female), renal failure, renal insufficiency, renal papillary necrosis, respiratory depression, seizure, sepsis, skin rash, Stevens-Johnson syndrome, stomatitis, syncope, tachycardia, thrombocythemia, thrombocytopenia, toxic epidermal necrolysis, transient ischemic attacks, tremor, urinary frequency, urticaria, uterine cramps, uterine hemorrhage, vaginitis, vasculitis, ventricular premature contractions, visual disturbance, weight changes

General Dosage Range Oral: *Adults:* Diclofenac 50 mg/misoprostol 200 mcg: One tablet 2 to 4 times daily; Diclofenac 75 mg/misoprostol 200 mcg: One tablet twice daily

Mechanism of Action

Diclofenac: Reversibly inhibits cyclooxygenase-1 and 2 (COX-1 and 2) enzymes, which results in decreased formation of prostaglandin precursors; has antipyretic, analgesic, and anti-inflammatory properties.

Misoprostol: Synthetic prostaglandin E1 analog that replaces the protective prostaglandins consumed with prostaglandin-inhibiting therapies (eg, NSAIDs).

Pregnancy Considerations Adverse events have not been observed in animal reproduction studies with this combination; however, adverse fetal events have been observed following in utero exposure to both diclofenac and misoprostol in human pregnancy. **[US Boxed Warning]: Use is contraindicated in pregnant women; administration of misoprostol to pregnant women may cause abortion, premature birth, or birth defects; uterine rupture has been reported. Do not use in women of childbearing potential unless the woman requires NSAID therapy and is at high risk of developing gastric or duodenal ulceration or for developing complications from gastric or duodenal ulcers associated with NSAID use. May be prescribed to women of childbearing potential if the patient is capable of complying with effective contraceptive measures; has a negative serum pregnancy test within 2 weeks prior to starting therapy; has received both oral and written communication of the potential risks of misoprostol, the risk of possible contraception failure, and danger to other women of childbearing potential should the drug be taken by mistake; and will start diclofenac/misoprostol only on the second or third day of the next normal menstrual period.** In addition, diclofenac can cause premature closure of the ductus arteriosus and use should be avoided in pregnancy (particularly late pregnancy). Women should also avoid pregnancy through one menstrual cycle or one month after therapy is complete. See individual agents.

Dicloxacillin (dye kloks a SIL in)

Related Information

Bacterial Infections *on page 1835*

Pharmacologic Category Antibiotic, Penicillin

Use Staphylococcal infections: Treatment of infections caused by penicillinase-producing staphylococci.

Local Anesthetic/Vasoconstrictor Precautions

No information available to require special precautions

Effects on Dental Treatment Key adverse event(s) related to dental treatment: Prolonged use of penicillins may lead to development of oral candidiasis.

Effects on Bleeding Thrombocytopenia has been reported.

Adverse Reactions Frequency not defined.

1% to 10%: Gastrointestinal: Abdominal pain diarrhea, nausea

<1%, postmarketing, and/or case reports: Agranulocytosis, anemia, eosinophilia, fever, hematuria, hemolytic anemia, hepatotoxicity, hypersensitivity reaction, increased blood urea nitrogen, increased liver enzymes (transient), increased serum creatinine, interstitial nephritis, leukopenia, neutropenia, prolonged prothrombin time, pseudomembranous colitis, seizure (with extremely high doses and/or renal failure), serum sickness-like reaction, skin rash (maculopapular rash to exfoliative dermatitis), thrombocytopenia, vaginitis, vomiting

General Dosage Range Oral:

Infants, Children, and Adolescents <40 kg: 12.5 to 25 mg/kg/day divided every 6 hours

Children and Adolescents ≥40 kg and Adults: 125 to 250 mg every 6 hours

Mechanism of Action Inhibits bacterial cell wall synthesis by binding to one or more of the penicillin-binding proteins (PBPs) which in turn inhibits the final transpeptidation step of peptidoglycan synthesis in bacterial cell walls, thus inhibiting cell wall biosynthesis. Bacteria eventually lyse due to ongoing activity of cell wall autolytic enzymes (autolysins and murein hydrolases) while cell wall assembly is arrested.

Pharmacodynamics/Kinetics

Half-life Elimination ~0.7 hours; prolonged with renal impairment (Nauta 1976)

Time to Peak Serum: 1 to 1.5 hours

Pregnancy Risk Factor B

Pregnancy Considerations Adverse events have not been observed in animal reproduction studies. Dicloxacillin crosses the placenta (Depp 1970). Maternal use of penicillins has generally not resulted in an increased risk of birth defects.

Dicyclomine (dye SYE kloe meen)

Related Information

Dentin Hypersensitivity, Acid Erosion, High Caries Index, Management of Alveolar Osteitis, and Xerostomia *on page* 1857

Brand Names: US Bentyl

Brand Names: Canada Bentylol; Dicyclomine Hydrochloride Injection; Formulex; Jamp-Dicyclomine; Protylol; Riva-Dicyclomine

Pharmacologic Category Anticholinergic Agent

Use Treatment of functional bowel/irritable bowel syndrome

Local Anesthetic/Vasoconstrictor Precautions

No information available to require special precautions

Effects on Dental Treatment Key adverse event(s) related to dental treatment: Xerostomia and changes in salivation (normal salivary flow resumes upon discontinuation)

Effects on Bleeding No information available to require special precautions

Adverse Reactions

>10%:

Central nervous system: Dizziness (40%)

Gastrointestinal: Xerostomia (33%), nausea (14%)

Ophthalmic: Blurred vision (27%)

1% to 10%:

Central nervous system: Drowsiness (9%), nervousness (6%)

Neuromuscular & skeletal: Weakness (7%)

Postmarketing and/or case reports: Abdominal distention, abdominal pain, anaphylactic shock, angioedema, confusion, constipation, cycloplegia, decreased lactation, delirium, dermatitis (allergic), dyspepsia, dyspnea, erythema, facial edema, fatigue, hallucination, headache, hypersensitivity, insomnia, malaise, mydriasis, nasal congestion, palpitations, skin rash, syncope, tachyarrhythmia, vomiting

General Dosage Range

IM: *Adults:* 10-20 mg 4 times daily

Oral: *Adults:* Initial: 20 mg 4 times daily; may increase to 40 mg 4 times daily

Mechanism of Action Blocks the action of acetylcholine at parasympathetic sites in smooth muscle, secretory glands and the CNS

Pharmacodynamics/Kinetics

Onset of Action 1 to 2 hours

Duration of Action Up to 4 hours

Half-life Elimination Initial phase: ~1.8 hours; Terminal phase: Undetermined, but somewhat longer than the initial phase

Time to Peak Oral: 60-90 minutes

Pregnancy Risk Factor B

Pregnancy Considerations Adverse events have not been observed in animal reproduction studies. In epidemiologic studies, birth defects were not observed in pregnant women taking doses up to 40 mg daily throughout the first trimester; information has not been located when used in pregnant women at recommended doses (80-160 mg daily). Use for the treatment of irritable bowel syndrome (IBS) is not recommended during pregnancy (Mahadevan, 2006).

Didanosine (dye DAN oh seen)

Related Information

HIV Infection and AIDS *on page* 1785

Brand Names: US Videx; Videx EC

Brand Names: Canada Videx EC

Pharmacologic Category Antiretroviral, Reverse Transcriptase Inhibitor, Nucleoside (Anti-HIV)

Use HIV infection: Treatment of HIV-1 infection in combination with other antiretroviral agents.

Local Anesthetic/Vasoconstrictor Precautions

No information available to require special precautions

Effects on Dental Treatment Key adverse event(s) related to dental treatment: Xerostomia (normal salivary flow resumes upon discontinuation).

Effects on Bleeding Thrombocytopenia has been reported in <1% of patients treated.

Adverse Reactions As reported in monotherapy studies; risk of toxicity may increase when combined with other agents.

>10%:

Central nervous system: Peripheral neuropathy (17% to 20%)

Endocrine & metabolic: Increased amylase (15% to 17%)

Gastrointestinal: Diarrhea (19% to 28%), abdominal pain (7% to 13%)

1% to 10%:

Dermatologic: Pruritus (≤7% to 9%), skin rash (≤7% to 9%)

Endocrine & metabolic: Increased uric acid (2% to 3%)

Gastrointestinal: Pancreatitis (1% to 7%; dose-dependent; >65 years of age: 10%; younger patients: 5%)

Hepatic: Increased serum AST (7% to 9%), increased serum ALT (6% to 9%), increased serum alkaline phosphatase (1% to 4%)

<1%, postmarketing, and/or case reports: Alopecia, anaphylactoid reaction, anemia, anorexia, arthralgia, chills, diabetes mellitus, dyspepsia, fever, flatulence, granulocytopenia, hepatic failure, hepatitis, hepatomegaly, hyperglycemia, hypersensitivity reaction, hypoglycemia, immune reconstitution syndrome, lactic acidosis, leukopenia, lipodystrophy, liver steatosis, myalgia, myopathy, optic neuritis, pain, parotid gland enlargement, portal hypertension (noncirrhotic), renal insufficiency (acute), retinal pigment changes (depigmentation), rhabdomyolysis, sialadenitis, Stevens-Johnson syndrome, symptomatic hyperlactatemia, thrombocytopenia, weakness, xerophthalmia, xerostomia

General Dosage Range Dosage adjustment recommended in patients with renal impairment

Oral:

Delayed release:

Children ≥6 years and 20 kg to <25 kg: 200 mg once daily

Children ≥6 years and 25 kg to <60 kg and Adults <60 kg: 250 mg once daily

Children and Adults ≥60 kg: 400 mg once daily

Pediatric powder for oral solution (Videx):

Infants 2 weeks to 8 months: 100 mg/m^2 twice daily

Children >8 months to 18 years: 120 mg/m^2 twice daily

Adolescents and Adults <60 kg: 125 mg twice daily **or** 250 mg once daily

Adolescents and Adults ≥60 kg: 200 mg twice daily **or** 400 mg once daily

Mechanism of Action Didanosine, a purine nucleoside (adenosine) analog and the deamination product of dideoxyadenosine (ddA), inhibits HIV replication *in vitro* in both T cells and monocytes. Didanosine is converted within the cell to the mono-, di-, and triphosphates of ddA. These ddA triphosphates act as substrate and inhibitor of HIV reverse transcriptase substrate and inhibitor of HIV reverse transcriptase thereby blocking viral DNA synthesis and suppressing HIV replication.

Pharmacodynamics/Kinetics

Half-life Elimination

Plasma:

Newborns (1 day old): 2 ± 0.7 hours

Infants 2 weeks to 4 months: 1.2 ± 0.3 hours

Infants 8 months to Adolescents 19 years: 0.8 ± 0.3 hours

Adults with normal renal function: 1.5 ± 0.4 hours

Intracellular: Adults: 25 to 40 hours

Elimination: Increased as CrCl decreased

Children 20 kg to <25 kg: 0.75 ± 0.13 hours

Children 25 kg to <60 kg: 0.92 ± 0.09 hours

Children ≥60 kg: 1.26 ± 0.19 hours

Adults ≥60 kg: 1.19 ± 0.21 hours; 2 ± 0.3 hours (renal impairment [CrCl <30 mL/minute]); 4.1 ± 1.2 hours (dialysis)

Time to Peak Delayed release capsules: 2 hours; Powder for suspension: 0.25 to 1.5 hours

Pregnancy Risk Factor B

Pregnancy Considerations Adverse events have not been observed in animal reproduction studies. Didanosine has a low to moderate level of transfer across the human placenta. Based on data from the Antiretroviral Pregnancy Registry, an increased rate of birth defects has been observed following maternal use of didanosine during the first trimester and later during pregnancy; no pattern of defects has been observed and clinical relevance is uncertain. Maternal antiretroviral therapy may increase the risk of preterm delivery, although available information is conflicting possibly due to maternal factors (disease severity; initiation of therapy); maternal medication should not be withheld due to concerns of preterm birth. Information related to stillbirth, low birth weight, and small for gestational age infants is limited. Long-term follow-up is recommended for all infants exposed to antiretroviral medications; children who develop significant organ system abnormalities (particularly of the CNS or heart) should be evaluated for potential mitochondrial dysfunction.

[US Boxed Warning]: Fatal lactic acidosis has been reported in pregnant women using didanosine and stavudine in combination with other antiretroviral agents. Cases of lactic acidosis and hepatic steatosis related to mitochondrial toxicity have been reported with use of nucleoside reverse transcriptase inhibitors (NRTIs). These adverse events are similar to other rare but life-threatening syndromes that occur during pregnancy (eg, HELLP syndrome). In general, nucleoside reverse transcriptase inhibitors are well tolerated and the benefits of use generally outweigh potential risk. However, due to reports of potentially fatal lactic acidosis, didanosine and stavudine should not be used in combination during pregnancy. Combination antiretroviral therapy (cART) therapy is recommended for all HIV-infected pregnant women to keep the viral load below the limit of detection and reduce the risk of perinatal transmission. When HIV is diagnosed during pregnancy in a woman who has never received antiretroviral therapy, cART should begin as soon as possible after diagnosis. The Health and Human Services (HHS) Perinatal HIV Guidelines do not recommend didanosine for initial therapy in antiretroviral-naive pregnant women due to toxicity. Pharmacokinetics are not significantly altered during pregnancy; dose adjustments of didanosine are not needed. In general, women who become pregnant on a stable cART regimen may continue that regimen if viral suppression is effective, appropriate drug exposure can be achieved, contraindications for use in pregnancy are not present, and the regimen is well tolerated. However, because didanosine has a high risk of toxicity, pregnant women should be switched to a preferred or alternative regimen. Monitoring during pregnancy is more frequent than in non-pregnant adults; cART should be continued postpartum.

For HIV-infected couples planning a pregnancy, maximum viral suppression with combination antiretroviral therapy (cART) is recommended prior to conception for the HIV-infected partner(s) and expert consultation is recommended; modification of therapy (if needed) and optimization of the woman's health should be done prior to conception. HIV-infected women not planning a pregnancy may use any available type of contraception, considering possible drug interactions and contraindications of the specific method. In addition, consistent use of condoms is also recommended (even during pregnancy) to prevent transmission of HIV or other sexually transmitted diseases.

Health care providers are encouraged to enroll pregnant women exposed to antiretroviral medications as early in pregnancy as possible in the Antiretroviral Pregnancy Registry (1-800-258-4263 or www.APRegistry.com). Health care providers caring for

HIV-infected women and their infants may contact the National Perinatal HIV Hotline (888-448-8765) for clinical consultation (HHS [perinatal] 2016).

Dienogest (dye EN oh jest)

Brand Names: Canada Visanne

Pharmacologic Category Antiandrogen

Use Note: Not approved in the US

Endometriosis: Management of pelvic pain associated with endometriosis

Local Anesthetic/Vasoconstrictor Precautions No information available to require special precautions

Effects on Dental Treatment No significant effects or complications reported

Effects on Bleeding No information available to require special precautions

Adverse Reactions

1% to 10%:

Central nervous system: Headache (7%), depression (3%), disturbed sleep (2%), irritability (1%), migraine (1%), nervousness (1%)

Dermatologic: Acne vulgaris (2%), alopecia (1%)

Endocrine & metabolic: Breast changes (discomfort: 5%), weight gain (4%), ovarian cyst (3%), decreased libido (2%)

Gastrointestinal: Nausea (4%), abdominal pain (2%)

Genitourinary: Vaginal hemorrhage (1%)

Neuromuscular & skeletal: Weakness (2%)

<1%, postmarketing, and/or case reports: Abdominal distress, anemia, anxiety, back pain, breast induration, constipation, decreased glucose tolerance, dermatitis, diarrhea, disturbance in attention, dysautonomia, edema, fibrocystic breast disease, flatulence, genital discharge, GI inflammation, heaviness in limbs, hot flash, increased appetite, limb pain, lump in breast, mood changes, muscle spasm, onychoclasis, ostealgia, palpitations, pelvic pain, pruritus, skin pigmentation, skin photosensitivity, tinnitus, urinary tract infection, vulvovaginal candidiasis, vomiting, vulvar dryness, xeroderma, xerophthalmia

General Dosage Range Oral: *Females: Children ≥12 years and Adolescents (postmenarche) and Adults:* 2 mg once daily

Mechanism of Action Dienogest is a steroid with antiandrogen properties that lacks androgen, mineralocorticoid or glucocorticoid activity. Exhibits strong progestogenic effects although it binds uterine progesterone receptors with an affinity much lower (about one-tenth) than that of progesterone. Decreases estradiol production and thus suppresses estradiol's trophic effects on eutopic and ectopic endometrium. Inhibits cellular proliferation via direct antiproliferative, immunologic, and antiangiogenic effects.

Pharmacodynamics/Kinetics

Half-life Elimination ~9 to 10 hours

Time to Peak ~1.5 hours

Pregnancy Considerations Use is contraindicated during pregnancy and pregnancy should be ruled out prior to initiating therapy. Based on limited data, inadvertent exposure in pregnancy has not shown adverse effects to the fetus. Use of hormonal contraceptives is not recommended during dienogest therapy. Nonhormonal contraceptives should be employed during treatment. Ovulation is often inhibited during therapy although normal menstruation usually returns within 2 months of therapy discontinuation.

Product Availability Not available in the US

Diethylpropion (dye eth il PROE pee on)

Pharmacologic Category Anorexiant; Central Nervous System Stimulant; Sympathomimetic

Use Short-term (few weeks) adjunct in the management of exogenous obesity

Pharmacotherapy for weight loss is recommended only for obese patients with a body mass index ≥30 kg/m^2, or ≥27 kg/m^2 in the presence of other risk factors such as hypertension, diabetes, and/or dyslipidemia or a high waist circumference; therapy should be used in conjunction with a comprehensive weight management program.

Local Anesthetic/Vasoconstrictor Precautions Use vasoconstrictor with caution in patients taking diethylpropion. Amphetamine-like drugs such as diethylpropion enhance the sympathomimetic response of epinephrine and norepinephrine leading to potential hypertension and cardiotoxicity.

Effects on Dental Treatment Key adverse event(s) related to dental treatment: Diethylpropion causes tachycardia, increases in blood pressure, and palpitations. Consider monitoring blood pressure prior to using local anesthetic with a vasoconstrictor. Symptoms associated with bruxism have been observed in some patients.

Effects on Bleeding No information available to require special precautions

Adverse Reactions Frequency not defined.

Cardiovascular: Cardiac arrhythmia, cerebrovascular accident, ECG changes, heart valve disease, hypertension, palpitations, tachycardia

Central nervous system: Anxiety, depression, dizziness, drowsiness, dysphoria, euphoria, headache, insomnia, jitteriness, malaise, nervousness, overstimulation, precordial pain, psychosis, restlessness, seizure

Dermatologic: Alopecia, diaphoresis, ecchymoses, erythema, skin rash, urticaria

Endocrine & metabolic: Changes in libido, gynecomastia, menstrual disease

Gastrointestinal: Abdominal distress, constipation, diarrhea, dysgeusia, nausea, vomiting, xerostomia

Genitourinary: Dysuria, impotence

Hematologic & oncologic: Agranulocytosis, bone marrow depression, leukopenia

Neuromuscular & skeletal: Dyskinesia, myalgia, tremor

Ophthalmic: Blurred vision, mydriasis

Renal: Polyuria

Respiratory: Dyspnea, pulmonary hypertension

Miscellaneous: Tachyphylaxis

General Dosage Range Oral:

Controlled release: *Children >16 years and Adults:* 75 mg once daily

Immediate release: *Children >16 years and Adults:* 25 mg 3 times daily

Mechanism of Action Diethylpropion is a sympathomimetic amine with pharmacologic properties similar to the amphetamines. It is also structurally similar to bupropion. The mechanism of action in reducing appetite appears to be secondary to CNS effects, including stimulation of the hypothalamus to release norepinephrine

Pharmacodynamics/Kinetics

Half-life Elimination Aminoketone metabolites: ~4-6 hours

Pregnancy Risk Factor B

Pregnancy Considerations Adverse events have not been observed in animal reproduction studies. Crosses the human placenta; spontaneous reports of congenital malformations have been reported, but an association with diethylpropion has not been established. Withdrawal symptoms may occur in the neonate following maternal use of diethylpropion.

Controlled Substance C-IV

Diflorasone (dye FLOR a sone)

Brand Names: US ApexiCon; ApexiCon E; Psorcon

Pharmacologic Category Corticosteroid, Topical

Use Dermatoses: Treatment of inflammation and pruritic symptoms of corticosteroid-responsive dermatoses (high to very high potency topical corticosteroid)

Local Anesthetic/Vasoconstrictor Precautions No information available to require special precautions

Effects on Dental Treatment No significant effects or complications reported

Effects on Bleeding No information available to require special precautions

Adverse Reactions Frequency not defined. Reactions listed are based on reports for other agents in this same pharmacologic class and may not be specifically reported for diflorasone. Diflorasone is classified as a potent topical steroid.

Central nervous system: Burning sensation

Dermatologic: Acneiform eruption, allergic contact dermatitis, atrophic striae, folliculitis, hypertrichosis, hypopigmentation, maceration of the skin, miliaria, perioral dermatitis, pruritus, skin atrophy, skin irritation, xeroderma

Endocrine & metabolic: HPA-axis suppression (children at greater risk)

Infection: Secondary infection

Postmarketing and/or case reports: Acne rosacea (Hengge 2006), aggravation reaction (cutaneous candidiasis, herpes, dermodex) (Hengge 2006), cataract (Hengge 2006), dermal ulcer (Hengge 2006), glaucoma (Hengge 2006), granuloma gluteale infantum (Hengge 2006), hirsutism (Hengge 2006), hyperpigmentation (Hengge 2006), Kaposi's sarcoma (reactivation) (Hengge 2006), masking of infection (tinea incognito) (Hengge 2006), nonthrombocytopenic purpura (Hengge 2006), ocular hypertension (Hengge 2006), psoriasis flare (rebound) (Hengge 2006), purpura (Hengge 2006), skin photosensitivity (Hengge 2006), spontaneous star-shaped scar-like lesions (Hengge 2006), telangiectasia (Hengge 2006)

General Dosage Range Topical: *Adults:* Apply 1 to 3 times daily

Mechanism of Action Topical corticosteroids have anti-inflammatory, antipruritic, and vasoconstrictive properties. May depress the formation, release, and activity of endogenous chemical mediators of inflammation (kinins, histamine, liposomal enzymes, prostaglandins) through the induction of phospholipase A_2 inhibitory proteins (lipocortins) and sequential inhibition of the release of arachidonic acid. Diflorasone has high range potency.

Pregnancy Risk Factor C

Pregnancy Considerations Adverse events have been observed in animal reproduction studies. Topical products are not recommended for extensive use, in large quantities, or for long periods of time in pregnant women.

Diflunisal (dye FLOO ni sal)

Related Information

Oral Pain *on page 1830*

Rheumatoid Arthritis, Osteoarthritis, and Osteoporosis *on page 1792*

Temporomandibular Dysfunction (TMD), Chronic Pain, and Fibromyalgia *on page 1868*

Related Sample Prescriptions

Oral Pain - Sample Prescriptions *on page 28*

Brand Names: Canada Apo-Diflunisal; Novo-Diflunisal

Generic Availability (US) Yes

Pharmacologic Category Analgesic, Nonopioid; Nonsteroidal Anti-inflammatory Drug (NSAID), Oral

Dental Use Treatment of postoperative pain

Use

Osteoarthritis/Rheumatoid arthritis (RA): Treatment of osteoarthritis and RA

Pain, mild to moderate: Treatment of mild to moderate pain

Local Anesthetic/Vasoconstrictor Precautions No information available to require special precautions

Effects on Dental Treatment The dentist should be aware of the potential of abnormal coagulation. Caution should also be exercised in the use of NSAIDs in patients already on anticoagulant therapy with drugs such as warfarin (Coumadin®). See Effects on Bleeding.

Effects on Bleeding As an inhibitor of prostaglandin synthetase, diflunisal has a dose-related effect on platelet function and bleeding time. In healthy volunteers, 250 mg twice daily for 8 days had no effect on platelet function, and 500 mg twice daily (the usual recommended dose) had a slight effect. However, at 1000 mg twice daily (which exceeds the maximum recommended dosage), diflunisal inhibited platelet function. In contrast with aspirin, these effects of diflunisal were reversible because diflunisal is a salicylic acid derivative.

Adverse Reactions Frequency not always defined.

1% to 10%:

Central nervous system: Headache (3% to 9%), dizziness (1% to 3%), drowsiness (1% to 3%), fatigue (1% to 3%), insomnia (1% to 3%)

Dermatologic: Skin rash (3% to 9%)

Gastrointestinal: Diarrhea (3% to 9%), dyspepsia (3% to 9%), gastrointestinal pain (3% to 9%), nausea (3% to 9%), constipation (1% to 3%), flatulence (1% to 3%), vomiting (1% to 3%), gastrointestinal ulcer

Otic: Tinnitus (1% to 3%)

<1%, postmarketing, and/or case reports: Agranulocytosis, anaphylactic reaction (acute), angioedema, anorexia, auditory impairment, blurred vision, bronchospasm, chest pain, cholestasis, confusion, cystitis, depression, diaphoresis, disorientation, DRESS syndrome, dry mucous membranes, dyspnea, dysuria, edema, eructation, erythema multiforme, esophagitis, exfoliative dermatitis, flushing, gastritis, gastrointestinal hemorrhage, gastrointestinal perforation, hallucination, hearing loss, hematuria, hemolytic anemia, hepatitis, hepatotoxicity (idiosyncratic; Chalasani 2014), hypersensitivity angiitis, hypersensitivity reaction, interstitial nephritis, jaundice, muscle cramps, necrotizing fasciitis, nephrotic syndrome, nervousness, palpitations, paresthesia, peptic ulcer, peripheral neuropathy, proteinuria, pruritus, renal failure, renal insufficiency, seizure, skin photosensitivity, Stevens-Johnson syndrome, stomatitis, syncope,

tachycardia, thrombocytopenia, toxic epidermal necrolysis, tremor, urticaria, vasculitis, vertigo, weakness, wheezing

Dental Usual Dosage Mild-to-moderate pain: Adults: Oral: Initial: 500-1000 mg followed by 250-500 mg every 8-12 hours; maximum daily dose: 1.5 g

Dosing

Adult

Osteoarthritis/Rheumatoid arthritis: Oral: 500 mg to 1,000 mg daily in 2 divided doses; maximum dose: 1,500 mg/day

Pain, mild to moderate: Oral: Initial: 1,000 mg, followed by 500 mg every 12 hours; maintenance doses of 500 mg every 8 hours may be necessary in some patients; maximum dose: 1,500 mg/day

Dosage adjustments: A lower dosage may be appropriate depending on pain severity, patient response, or weight; Initial: 500 mg, followed by 250 mg every 8 to 12 hours; maximum dose: 1,500 mg/day

Geriatric

Osteoarthritis/Rheumatoid arthritis: Refer to adult dosing.

Pain, mild to moderate: Oral: Initial: 500 mg, followed by 250 mg every 8 to 12 hours; maximum dose: 1,500 mg/day

Pediatric

Osteoarthritis/Rheumatoid arthritis: Adolescents ≥12 years: Oral: Refer to adult dosing

Pain, mild to moderate: Adolescents ≥12 years: Oral: Refer to adult dosing

Renal Impairment There are no dosage adjustments provided in the manufacturer's labeling; avoid use in patients with advanced renal disease.

The following adjustments have been used by some clinicians (Aronoff, 2007):

CrCl ≤50 mL/minute: Administer 50% of normal dose.

Hemodialysis: No supplement required.

CAPD: No supplement required.

KDIGO 2012 guidelines provide the following recommendations for NSAIDs:

eGFR 30 to <60 mL/minute/1.73 m^2: Temporarily discontinue in patients with intercurrent disease that increases risk of acute kidney injury.

eGFR <30 mL/minute/1.73 m^2: Avoid use.

Hepatic Impairment There are no dosage adjustments provided in the manufacturer's labeling; use with caution.

Mechanism of Action Reversibly inhibits cyclooxygenase-1 and 2 (COX-1 and 2) enzymes, which results in decreased formation of prostaglandin precursors; has antipyretic, analgesic, and anti-inflammatory properties.

Other proposed mechanisms not fully elucidated (and possibly contributing to the anti-inflammatory effect to varying degrees) include inhibiting chemotaxis, altering lymphocyte activity, inhibiting neutrophil aggregation/activation, and decreasing proinflammatory cytokine levels.

Contraindications Known hypersensitivity to diflunisal or any component of the formulation; in the setting of coronary artery bypass graft (CABG) surgery; history of asthma, urticaria, or allergic-type reactions after taking aspirin or other NSAIDs.

Warnings/Precautions [US Boxed Warning]: NSAIDs cause an increased risk of serious (and potentially fatal) adverse cardiovascular thrombotic events, including MI and stroke. Risk may occur early during treatment and may increase with duration of use. Relative risk appears to be similar in those with and without known cardiovascular disease or risk factors for cardiovascular disease; however, absolute incidence of serious cardiovascular thrombotic events (which may occur early during treatment) was higher in patients with known cardiovascular disease or risk factors and in those receiving higher doses. New onset hypertension or exacerbation of hypertension may occur (NSAIDs may also impair response to ACE inhibitors, thiazide diuretics, or loop diuretics); may contribute to cardiovascular events; monitor blood pressure; use with caution in patients with hypertension. May cause sodium and fluid retention; use with caution in patients with edema. Avoid use in heart failure (ACCF/AHA [Yancy 2013]). Avoid use in patients with recent MI unless benefits outweigh risk of cardiovascular thrombotic events. Use the lowest effective dose for the shortest duration of time, consistent with individual patient goals, to reduce risk of cardiovascular events; alternate therapies should be considered for patients at high risk.

[US Boxed Warning]: Use is contraindicated in the setting of coronary artery bypass graft (CABG) surgery. Risk of MI and stroke may be increased with use following CABG surgery.

[US Boxed Warning]: NSAIDs cause an increased risk of serious gastrointestinal inflammation, ulceration, bleeding, and perforation (may be fatal); elderly patients and patients with history of peptic ulcer disease and/or GI bleeding are at greater risk of serious GI events. These events may occur at any time during therapy and without warning. Avoid use in patients with active GI bleeding. Use caution with a history of GI ulcers, concurrent therapy known to increase the risk of GI bleeding (eg, aspirin, anticoagulants and/or corticosteroids, selective serotonin reuptake inhibitors), advanced hepatic disease, coagulopathy, smoking, use of alcohol, or in elderly or debilitated patients. Use the lowest effective dose for the shortest duration of time, consistent with individual patient goals, to reduce risk of GI adverse events; alternate therapies should be considered for patients at high risk. When used concomitantly with aspirin, a substantial increase in the risk of gastrointestinal complications (eg, ulcer) occurs; concomitant gastroprotective therapy (eg, proton pump inhibitors) is recommended (Bhatt 2008).

Platelet adhesion and aggregation may be decreased; may prolong bleeding time; patients with coagulation disorders or who are receiving anticoagulants should be monitored closely. Anemia may occur; patients on long-term NSAID therapy should be monitored for anemia. Rarely, NSAID use has been associated with potentially severe blood dyscrasias (eg, agranulocytosis, thrombocytopenia, aplastic anemia).

NSAID use may compromise existing renal function; dose-dependent decreases in prostaglandin synthesis may result from NSAID use, reducing renal blood flow which may cause renal decompensation (usually reversible). Patients with impaired renal function, dehydration, hypovolemia, heart failure, hepatic impairment, those taking diuretics and ACE inhibitors, and elderly patients are at greater risk of renal toxicity. Rehydrate patient before starting therapy; monitor renal function closely. Long-term NSAID use may result in renal papillary necrosis and other renal injury. Avoid use in patients with advanced renal disease unless benefits are expected to outweigh risk of worsening renal function; monitor renal function closely if therapy must be initiated. NSAID use may increase the risk of ▶

hyperkalemia, particularly in the elderly, diabetics, renal disease, and with concomitant use of other agents capable of inducing hyperkalemia (eg, ACE-inhibitors). Monitor potassium closely.

Use with caution in patients with hepatic impairment; patients with advanced hepatic disease are at an increased risk of GI bleeding with NSAIDs. Transaminase elevations have been reported with use; closely monitor patients with any abnormal LFT. Rare, sometimes fatal severe hepatic reactions (eg, fulminant hepatitis, hepatic necrosis, hepatic failure) have occurred with NSAID use; discontinue immediately if clinical signs or symptoms of hepatic disease develop or if systemic manifestations occur.

Contraindicated in patients with aspirin-sensitive asthma; severe, potentially fatal bronchospasm may occur. Use caution in patients with other forms of asthma. May cause drowsiness, dizziness, blurred vision, and other neurologic effects which may impair physical or mental abilities; patients must be cautioned about performing tasks which require mental alertness (eg, operating machinery or driving). Blurred vision has been reported; refer for ophthalmologic evaluation if symptoms occur.

NSAIDs may cause potentially fatal, serious skin adverse events including exfoliative dermatitis, Stevens-Johnson syndrome (SJS), and toxic epidermal necrolysis (TEN); may occur without warning; discontinue use at first sign of skin rash (or any other hypersensitivity). A potentially life-threatening, hypersensitivity syndrome has been reported; monitor for constitutional symptoms and cutaneous findings; other organ dysfunction may be involved. Even in patients without prior exposure anaphylactoid reactions may occur; patients with "aspirin triad" (bronchial asthma, aspirin intolerance, rhinitis) may be at increased risk. Contraindicated in patients who experience bronchospasm, asthma, rhinitis, or urticaria with NSAID or aspirin therapy.

Diflunisal is a derivative of acetylsalicylic acid and therefore may be associated with Reye's syndrome. Elderly patients are at greater risk for serious GI, cardiovascular, and/or renal adverse events; use with caution. Withhold for at least 4 to 6 half-lives prior to surgical or dental procedures. Potentially significant interactions may exist, requiring dose or frequency adjustment, additional monitoring, and/or selection of alternative therapy.

Drug Interactions

Metabolism/Transport Effects None known.

Avoid Concomitant Use

Avoid concomitant use of Diflunisal with any of the following: Dexketoprofen; Floctafenine; Ketorolac (Nasal); Ketorolac (Systemic); Morniflumate; NSAID (COX-2 Inhibitor); Omacetaxine; Pelubiprofen; Phenylbutazone; Talniflumate; Tenoxicam; Urokinase; Zaltoprofen

Increased Effect/Toxicity

Diflunisal may increase the levels/effects of: 5-ASA Derivatives; Agents with Antiplatelet Properties; Aliskiren; Aminoglycosides; Aminolevulinic Acid; Anticoagulants; Apixaban; Bisphosphonate Derivatives; Cephalothin; Collagenase (Systemic); CycloSPORINE (Systemic); Dabigatran Etexilate; Deferasirox; Deoxycholic Acid; Desmopressin; Digoxin; Drospirenone; Edoxaban; Eplerenone; Haloperidol; Ibritumomab; Lithium; Methotrexate; Nonsteroidal Anti-Inflammatory Agents; NSAID (COX-2 Inhibitor); Obinutuzumab; Omacetaxine; PEMEtrexed; Porfimer; Potassium-Sparing Diuretics; PRALAtrexate; Quinolone Antibiotics; Rivaroxaban; Salicylates; Tacrolimus (Systemic); Tenofovir Products; Thrombolytic Agents; Tolperisone; Tositumomab and Iodine I 131 Tositumomab; Urokinase; Vancomycin; Verteporfin; Vitamin K Antagonists

The levels/effects of Diflunisal may be increased by: ACE Inhibitors; Alcohol (Ethyl); Angiotensin II Receptor Blockers; Antidepressants (Tricyclic, Tertiary Amine); Corticosteroids (Systemic); CycloSPORINE (Systemic); Dasatinib; Dexketoprofen; Diclofenac (Systemic); Felbinac; Floctafenine; Glucosamine; Herbs (Anticoagulant/Antiplatelet Properties); Ibrutinib; Ketorolac (Nasal); Ketorolac (Systemic); Limaprost; Loop Diuretics; Morniflumate; Multivitamins/Fluoride (with ADE); Multivitamins/Minerals (with ADEK, Folate, Iron); Multivitamins/Minerals (with AE, No Iron); Naftazone; Omega-3 Fatty Acids; Pelubiprofen; Pentosan Polysulfate Sodium; Pentoxifylline; Phenylbutazone; Probenecid; Prostacyclin Analogues; Selective Serotonin Reuptake Inhibitors; Serotonin/Norepinephrine Reuptake Inhibitors; Sodium Phosphates; Talniflumate; Tenoxicam; Thiazide and Thiazide-Like Diuretics; Tipranavir; Tolperisone; Vitamin E (Systemic); Zaltoprofen

Decreased Effect

Diflunisal may decrease the levels/effects of: ACE Inhibitors; Aliskiren; Angiotensin II Receptor Blockers; Beta-Blockers; Eplerenone; HydrALAZINE; Loop Diuretics; Potassium-Sparing Diuretics; Prostaglandins (Ophthalmic); Salicylates; Selective Serotonin Reuptake Inhibitors; Thiazide and Thiazide-Like Diuretics

The levels/effects of Diflunisal may be decreased by: Bile Acid Sequestrants; Salicylates

Dietary Considerations May administer with food or milk to decrease GI upset.

Pharmacodynamics/Kinetics

Onset of Action Analgesic: ~1 hour; maximal effect: 2 to 3 hours

Duration of Action 8 to 12 hours

Half-life Elimination 8 to 12 hours; prolonged with renal impairment (Brogden 1980)

Time to Peak Serum: 2 to 3 hours

Pregnancy Risk Factor C

Pregnancy Considerations Adverse events were observed in animal reproduction studies. Nonteratogenic effects have been observed following NSAID administration during the third trimester including: Myocardial degenerative changes, prenatal constriction of the ductus arteriosus, fetal tricuspid regurgitation, failure of the ductus arteriosus to close postnatally; renal dysfunction or failure, oligohydramnios; gastrointestinal bleeding or perforation, increased risk of necrotizing enterocolitis; intracranial bleeding (including intraventricular hemorrhage), platelet dysfunction with resultant bleeding; pulmonary hypertension. Because they may cause premature closure of the ductus arteriosus, use of NSAIDs late in pregnancy should be avoided.

Breastfeeding Considerations Diflunisal is excreted into breast milk at levels of 2% to 7% of those in maternal plasma. According to the manufacturer, the decision to breast-feed during therapy should take into account the risk of exposure to the infant and the benefits of treatment to the mother.

Dosage Forms

Tablet, Oral:

Generic: 500 mg

Dosage Forms: Canada
Tablet, Oral: 250 mg

Dental Comment The advantage of diflunisal as a pain reliever is its 12-hour duration of effect. In many cases, this long effect will ensure a full night sleep during the postoperative pain period.

Difluprednate (dye floo PRED nate)

Brand Names: US Durezol

Brand Names: Canada Durezol

Pharmacologic Category Corticosteroid, Ophthalmic

Use

Inflammation/pain: Treatment of inflammation and pain following ocular surgery.

Uveitis: Treatment of endogenous anterior uveitis.

Local Anesthetic/Vasoconstrictor Precautions No information available to require special precautions

Effects on Dental Treatment No significant effects or complications reported

Effects on Bleeding No information available to require special precautions

Adverse Reactions

>10%: Ophthalmic: Anterior chamber inflammation, blepharitis, cataract (secondary), conjunctival edema, corneal edema, eye pain, ocular hyperemia (ciliary, conjunctival, limbal), photophobia

1% to 10%:

Central nervous system: Headache

Ophthalmic: Blurred vision, decreased visual acuity, dry eye syndrome, eye irritation, increased intraocular pressure, iridocyclitis, iritis, ophthalmic inflammation (postoperative), punctate keratitis, uveitis

<1%, postmarketing, and/or case reports: Corneal changes (pigmentation and striae), crusting of eyelid, episcleritis, eye pruritus, foreign body sensation of eye, increased lacrimation, injected sclera, local discomfort, local irritation, macular edema

General Dosage Range Ophthalmic:

Endogenous anterior uveitis: Adults: Instill 1 drop in affected eye(s) 4 times daily for 14 days, then taper

Inflammation/pain associated with ocular surgery: Infants, Children, Adolescents, and Adults: Instill 1 drop in affected eye(s) 4 times daily for 2 weeks, then 2 times daily for 1 week, then taper

Mechanism of Action Corticosteroids inhibit the inflammatory response including edema, capillary dilation, leukocyte migration, and scar formation. Difluprednate penetrates cells readily to induce the production of lipocortins. These proteins modulate the activity of prostaglandins and leukotrienes.

Pregnancy Risk Factor C

Pregnancy Considerations Adverse events have been observed in animal reproduction studies. The amount of difluprednate absorbed systemically following ophthalmic administration is below the limit of quantification (<50 ng/mL).

Digoxin (di JOKS in)

Related Information

Cardiovascular Diseases *on page 1752*

Brand Names: US Digitek; Digox; Lanoxin; Lanoxin Pediatric

Brand Names: Canada Apo-Digoxin; Digoxin Injection CSD; Lanoxin; Pediatric Digoxin CSD; PMS-Digoxin; Toloxin

Pharmacologic Category Antiarrhythmic Agent, Miscellaneous; Cardiac Glycoside

Use

Atrial fibrillation: Control of ventricular response rate in adults with chronic atrial fibrillation.

Heart failure: Treatment of mild-to-moderate (or stage C as recommended by the ACCF/AHA) heart failure (HF) in adults; to increase myocardial contractility in pediatric patients with heart failure

Note: In treatment of atrial fibrillation (AF), use is not considered first-line in patients with AF; digoxin may be considered for rate control in patients with heart failure with reduced ejection fraction (HFrEF) without pre-excitation or in sedentary patients (AHA/ACC/HRS [January 2014]). In the treatment of heart failure, digoxin should be considered for use only in HF with reduced ejection fraction (HFrEF) when symptoms remain despite guideline-directed medical therapy or as initial therapy in patients with severe symptoms yet to respond to guideline-directed medical therapy (ACCF/AHA [Yancy 2013]).

Local Anesthetic/Vasoconstrictor Precautions Use vasoconstrictor with caution due to risk of cardiac arrhythmias with digoxin

Effects on Dental Treatment Sensitive gag reflex may cause difficulty in taking a dental impression.

Effects on Bleeding No information available to require special precautions

Adverse Reactions Incidence not always reported.

Cardiovascular: Accelerated junctional rhythm, asystole, atrial tachycardia with or without block, AV dissociation, first-, second- (Wenckebach), or third-degree heart block, facial edema, PR prolongation, PVCs (especially bigeminy or trigeminy), ST segment depression, ventricular tachycardia or ventricular fibrillation

Central nervous system: Dizziness (6%), mental disturbances (5%), headache (4%), apathy, anxiety, confusion, delirium, depression, fever, hallucinations

Dermatologic: Rash (erythematous, maculopapular [most common], papular, scarlatiniform, vesicular or bullous), pruritus, urticaria, angioneurotic edema

Gastrointestinal: Nausea (4%), vomiting (2%), diarrhea (4%), abdominal pain, anorexia

Neuromuscular & skeletal: Weakness

Ocular: Visual disturbances (blurred or yellow vision)

Respiratory: Laryngeal edema

<1%, postmarketing, and/or case reports (limited to important or life-threatening): Asymmetric chorea, gynecomastia, thrombocytopenia, palpitation, intestinal ischemia, hemorrhagic necrosis of the intestines, vaginal cornification, eosinophilia, sexual dysfunction, diaphoresis

General Dosage Range Dosage adjustment recommended in patients with renal impairment

IM, IV:

Preterm infants: Digitalizing dose: 15 to 25 mcg/kg; Maintenance: 4 to 6 mcg/kg/day in divided doses every 12 hours

Full-term infants: Digitalizing dose: 20 to 30 mcg/kg; Maintenance: 5 to 8 mcg/kg/day in divided doses every 12 hours

Children 1 month to 2 years: Digitalizing dose: 30 to 50 mcg/kg; Maintenance: 7.5 to 12 mcg/kg/day in divided doses every 12 hours

Children 2 to 5 years: Digitalizing dose: 25 to 35 mcg/kg; Maintenance: 6 to 9 mcg/kg/day in divided doses every 12 hours

Children 5 to 10 years: Digitalizing dose: 15 to 30 mcg/kg; Maintenance: 4 to 8 mcg/kg/day in divided doses every 12 hours

Children >10 years: Digitalizing dose: 8 to 12 mcg/kg; Maintenance: 2 to 3 mcg/kg once daily

Adults: Digitalizing dose: 0.5 to 1 mg; Maintenance: 0.1 to 0.4 mg once daily

Oral:

Preterm infants: Digitalizing dose: 20 to 30 mcg/kg; Maintenance: 5 to 7.5 mcg/kg/day in divided doses every 12 hours

Full-term infants: Digitalizing dose: 25 to 35 mcg/kg; Maintenance: 6 to 10 mcg/kg/day in divided doses every 12 hours

Children 1 month to 2 years: Digitalizing dose: 35 to 60 mcg/kg; Maintenance: 10 to 15 mcg/kg/day in divided doses every 12 hours

Children 2 to 5 years: Digitalizing dose: 30 to 40 mcg/kg; Maintenance: 7.5 to 10 mcg/kg/day in divided doses every 12 hours

Children 5 to 10 years: Digitalizing dose: 20 to 35 mcg/kg; Maintenance: 5 to 10 mcg/kg/day in divided doses every 12 hours

Children >10 years: Digitalizing dose: 10 to 15 mcg/kg; Maintenance: 2.5 to 5 mcg/kg once daily

Adults: Digitalizing dose: 0.75 to 1.5 mg; Maintenance: 0.125 to 0.5 mg once daily

Mechanism of Action

Heart failure: Inhibition of the sodium/potassium ATPase pump in myocardial cells results in a transient increase of intracellular sodium, which in turn promotes calcium influx via the sodium-calcium exchange pump leading to increased contractility. May improve baroreflex sensitivity (Gheorghiade 1991).

Supraventricular arrhythmias: Direct suppression of the AV node conduction to increase effective refractory period and decrease conduction velocity - positive inotropic effect, enhanced vagal tone, and decreased ventricular rate to fast atrial arrhythmias. Atrial fibrillation may decrease sensitivity and increase tolerance to higher serum digoxin concentrations.

Pharmacodynamics/Kinetics

Onset of Action

Heart rate control: Oral: 1 to 2 hours; IV: 5 to 60 minutes

Peak effect: Heart rate control: Oral: 2 to 8 hours; IV: 1 to 6 hours; **Note:** In patients with atrial fibrillation, median time to ventricular rate control in one study was 6 hours (range: 3 to 15 hours) (Siu, 2009)

Duration of Action Adults: 3 to 4 days

Half-life Elimination

Age, renal and cardiac function dependent:

- Neonates: Premature: 61 to 170 hours; Full-term: 35 to 45 hours
- Infants: 18 to 25 hours
- Children: 18 to 36 hours
- Adults: 36 to 48 hours
- Adults, anephric: 3.5 to 5 days

Parent drug: 38 hours; Metabolites: Digoxigenin: 4 hours; Monodigitoxoside: 3 to 12 hours

Time to Peak Serum: Oral: 1 to 3 hours

Pregnancy Risk Factor C

Pregnancy Considerations Animal reproduction studies have not been conducted. Digoxin crosses the placenta and serum concentrations are similar in the mother and fetus at delivery. Digoxin is recommended in the treatment of fetal tachycardia determined to be SVT. In pregnant women, use of digoxin is recommended as a first-line agent for chronic treatment of highly symptomatic SVT; the lowest effective dose is recommended (Page [ACC/AHA/HRS 2015]).

Dihydroergotamine (dye hye droe er GOT a meen)

Brand Names: US D.H.E. 45; Migranal

Brand Names: Canada Migranal

Pharmacologic Category Antimigraine Agent; Ergot Derivative

Use

Cluster headaches (injection): Acute treatment of cluster headaches.

Migraines (intranasal; injection): Acute treatment of migraine headaches with or without aura; not intended for the prophylactic therapy of migraine or for the management of hemiplegic or basilar migraine.

Local Anesthetic/Vasoconstrictor Precautions

Use vasoconstrictor with caution in patients taking dihydroergotamine; this ergot alkaloid derivative directly stimulates vascular smooth muscle resulting in vasoconstriction of peripheral vasculature

Effects on Dental Treatment Key adverse event(s) related to dental treatment: Rhinitis and abnormal taste.

Effects on Bleeding No information available to require special precautions

Adverse Reactions

>10%: Nasal spray: Respiratory: Rhinitis (26%)

1% to 10%: Nasal spray:

- Central nervous system: Taste disorder (8%), dizziness (4%), drowsiness (3%)
- Endocrine & metabolic: Hot flash (1%)
- Gastrointestinal: Nausea (10%), vomiting (4%), diarrhea (2%)
- Local: Application site reaction (6%)
- Neuromuscular & skeletal: Stiffness (1%), weakness (1%)
- Respiratory: Pharyngitis (3%)

<1%, postmarketing, and/or case reports (Limited to important or life-threatening): Injection and nasal spray: Abdominal pain, anxiety, cerebral hemorrhage, cerebrovascular accident, coronary artery vasospasm, diaphoresis, diarrhea, dizziness, dyspnea, edema, fibrothorax (prolonged use), flushing, headache, hyperkinesia, hypertension, ischemic heart disease, muscle cramps, myalgia, myasthenia, myocardial infarction, palpitations, paresthesia, peripheral cyanosis, peripheral ischemia, retroperitoneal fibrosis (prolonged use), skin rash, subarachnoid hemorrhage, tremor, valvular sclerosis (associated with ergot alkaloids), ventricular fibrillation, ventricular tachycardia (transient)

General Dosage Range

IM, SubQ: *Adults:* 1 mg initially, may repeat hourly up to 3 mg total (maximum: 6 mg/week)

IV: *Adults:* 1 mg initially, may repeat hourly up to 2 mg total (maximum: 6 mg/week)

Intranasal: *Adults:* 1 spray (0.5 mg) in each nostril initially, repeat after 15 minutes for a total of 4 sprays (2 mg)

Mechanism of Action Efficacy in migraine is attributed to the activation of $5\text{-}HT_{1D}$ receptors located on intracranial blood vessels resulting in vasoconstriction and/or activation of $5\text{-}HT_{1D}$ receptors on sensory nerve endings of the trigeminal system resulting in the inhibition of pro-inflammatory neuropeptide release. Dihydroergotamine binds with high affinity to serotonin $5\text{-}HT_{1D\alpha}$, $5\text{-}HT_{1D\beta}$, $5\text{-}HT_{1A}$, $5\text{-}HT_{2A}$, and $5\text{-}HT_{2C}$ receptors, noradrenaline α_{2A}, α_{2B} and α_1 receptors, and dopamine D_{2L} and D_3 receptors. Dihydroergotamine also possesses oxytocic properties.

Pharmacodynamics/Kinetics

Half-life Elimination ~9 to 10 hours

Time to Peak Serum: IM: 24 minutes; IV: 1 to 2 minutes; Intranasal: 30 to 60 minutes (Saper 2006); SubQ 15 to 45 minutes (Schran 1985)

Pregnancy Risk Factor X

Pregnancy Considerations Dihydroergotamine is oxytocic and should not be used during pregnancy.

DilTIAZem (dil TYE a zem)

Related Information

Calcium Channel Blockers and Gingival Hyperplasia *on page 1908*

Cardiovascular Diseases *on page 1752*

Brand Names: US Cardizem; Cardizem CD; Cardizem LA; Cartia XT; Dilacor XR [DSC]; Dilt-CD [DSC]; Dilt-XR; DilTIAZem CD; Diltzac [DSC]; Matzim LA; Taztia XT; Tiazac

Brand Names: Canada ACT Diltiazem CD; ACT Diltiazem T; Apo-Diltiaz; Apo-Diltiaz CD; Apo-Diltiaz SR; Apo-Diltiaz TZ; Cardizem CD; Diltiazem Hydrochloride Injection; Diltiazem TZ; Diltiazem-CD; PMS-Diltiazem CD; Sandoz-Diltiazem CD; Sandoz-Diltiazem T; Teva-Diltiazem; Teva-Diltiazem CD; Teva-Diltiazem HCL ER Capsules; Tiazac; Tiazac XC

Generic Availability (US) Yes

Pharmacologic Category Antianginal Agent; Antiarrhythmic Agent, Class IV; Antihypertensive; Calcium Channel Blocker; Calcium Channel Blocker, Nondihydropyridine

Use

Oral: Management of hypertension (monotherapy or in combination with other antihypertensives); management of chronic stable angina or angina from coronary artery spasm.

Guideline recommendations:

Hypertension: The 2014 guideline for the management of high blood pressure in adults (JNC 8) recommends initiation of pharmacologic treatment to lower blood pressure for the following patients (JNC8 [James 2013]):

- Patients ≥60 years of age, with systolic blood pressure (SBP) ≥150 mm Hg or diastolic blood pressure (DBP) ≥90 mm Hg. Goal of therapy is SBP <150 mm Hg and DBP <90 mm Hg.
- Patients <60 years of age, with SBP ≥140 mm Hg or DBP ≥90 mm Hg. Goal of therapy is SBP <140 mm Hg and DBP <90 mm Hg.
- Patients ≥18 years of age with diabetes, with SBP ≥140 mm Hg or DBP ≥90 mm Hg. Goal of therapy is SBP <140 mm Hg and DBP <90 mm Hg.
- Patients ≥18 years of age with chronic kidney disease (CKD), with SBP ≥140 mm Hg or DBP ≥90 mm Hg. Goal of therapy is SBP <140 mm Hg and DBP <90 mm Hg.

Chronic kidney disease (CKD) and hypertension: Regardless of race or diabetes status, the use of an ACE inhibitor (ACEI) or angiotensin receptor blocker (ARB) as initial therapy is recommended to improve kidney outcomes. In the general nonblack population (without CKD) including those with diabetes, initial antihypertensive treatment should consist of a thiazide-type diuretic, calcium channel blocker, ACEI, or ARB. In the general black population (without CKD) including those with diabetes, initial antihypertensive treatment should consist of a thiazide-type diuretic or a calcium channel blocker **instead of** an ACEI or ARB.

Coronary artery disease (CAD) and hypertension: The American Heart Association, American College of Cardiology and American Society of Hypertension (AHA/ACC/ASH) 2015 scientific statement for the treatment of hypertension in patients with coronary artery disease (CAD) recommends that a non-dihydropyridine CCB (verapamil, diltiazem) may be used as a substitute for a beta blocker in patients who have an intolerance or contraindication to beta blockers with ongoing ischemia, hypertension and chronic stable angina, or if angina or hypertension continues to be uncontrolled while receiving standard therapies (eg, beta blocker). However, a non-dihydropyridine CCB (eg, verapamil, diltiazem) should be avoided in patients with LV dysfunction or heart failure (with reduced ejection fraction). A BP target of <140/90 mm Hg is reasonable for the secondary prevention of cardiovascular events. A lower target BP (<130/80 mm Hg) may be appropriate in some individuals with CAD, previous MI, stroke or transient ischemic attack, or CAD risk equivalents (AHA/ACC/ASH [Rosendorff 2015]).

Injection: Control of rapid ventricular rate in patients with atrial fibrillation or atrial flutter; conversion of paroxysmal supraventricular tachycardia (PSVT)

Guideline recommendations: ACC/AHA/HRS supraventricular tachycardia (SVT) guidelines recommends IV diltiazem as a therapeutic option for the acute treatment (ie, conversion) of a variety of SVTs (AVNRT, AVRT, and focal AT) in hemodynamically stable patients. Diltiazem is not appropriate for patients with suspected systolic heart failure or pre-excitation on ECG (ACC/AHA/HRS [Page 2015])

Local Anesthetic/Vasoconstrictor Precautions No information available to require special precautions

Effects on Dental Treatment Key adverse event(s) related to dental treatment: Diltiazem has been reported to cause >10% incidence of gingival hyperplasia; usually disappears with discontinuation (consultation with physician is suggested).

Effects on Bleeding No information available to require special precautions

Adverse Reactions Note: Frequencies represent ranges for various dosage forms. Patients with impaired ventricular function and/or conduction abnormalities may have higher incidence of adverse reactions.

>10%:

Cardiovascular: Edema (2% to 15%)

Central nervous system: Headache (5% to 12%)

2% to 10%:

Cardiovascular: Atrioventricular block (2% to 8%; first degree), edema (2% to 8%; lower limb), bradycardia (2% to 6%), hypotension (<2% to 4%), vasodilatation (2% to 3%), extrasystoles (2%), flushing (1% to 2%), palpitations (1% to 2%)

Central nervous system: Dizziness (3% to 10%), pain (6%), nervousness (2%)

Dermatologic: Skin rash (1% to 4%)

Endocrine & metabolic: Gout (1% to 2%)

Gastrointestinal: Dyspepsia (1% to 6%), constipation (<2% to 4%), vomiting (2%), diarrhea (1% to 2%)

Local: Injection site reaction (4%; itching, burning)

Neuromuscular & skeletal: Weakness (1% to 4%), myalgia (2%)

Respiratory: Rhinitis (<2% to 10%), pharyngitis (2% to 6%), dyspnea (1% to 6%), bronchitis (1% to 4%), cough (≤3), sinus congestion (1% to 2%)

<2%, postmarketing, and/or case reports: Abnormal dreams, abnormal gait, albuminuria, alopecia, amblyopia, amnesia, angina pectoris, angioedema, anorexia, asystole, atrioventricular block (second or third

degree), bruise, bundle branch block, cardiac arrhythmia, cardiac failure, crystalluria, depression, drowsiness, dysgeusia, ECG abnormality, epistaxis, erythema multiforme, exfoliative dermatitis, extrapyramidal reaction, gingival hyperplasia, gynecomastia, hallucination, hemolytic anemia, hyperglycemia, hypersensitivity angiitis, hypersensitivity reaction, hyperuricemia, impotence, increased creatine phosphokinase, increased lactate dehydrogenase, increased serum alkaline phosphatase, increased serum ALT, increased serum AST, increased serum bilirubin, increased thirst, insomnia, leukopenia, muscle cramps, myopathy, nausea, neck stiffness, nocturia, pain, paresthesia, personality changes, petechia, polyuria, prolonged bleeding time, pruritus, purpura, retinopathy, skin photosensitivity, Stevens-Johnson syndrome, syncope, tachycardia, thrombocytopenia, tinnitus, toxic epidermal necrolysis, tremor, urticaria, ventricular premature contractions, weight gain, xerostomia

Dosing

Adult

Angina: Oral:

Capsule, extended release:

Dilacor XR, Dilt-XR: Initial: 120 mg once daily; titrate over 7 to 14 days; usual dose range (ACC/AHA [Gibbons 2002]): 120 to 320 mg daily: maximum: 480 mg/day.

Cardizem CD, Cartia XT: Initial: 120 to 180 mg once daily; titrate over 7 to 14 days; usual dose range (ACC/AHA [Gibbons 2002]): 120 to 320 mg daily; maximum: 480 mg/day.

Tiazac, Taztia XT: Initial: 120 to 180 mg once daily; titrate over 7 to 14 days; usual dose range (ACC/AHA [Gibbons 2002]): 120 to 320 mg daily; maximum: 540 mg/day.

Tablet, extended release (Cardizem LA, Matzim LA, Tiazac XC [Canadian product]): Initial: 180 mg once daily; may increase at 7- to 14-day intervals; usual dose range (ACC/AHA [Gibbons 2002]): 120 to 320 mg/day; maximum: 360 mg/day.

Tablet, immediate release (Cardizem): Initial: 30 mg 4 times daily; titrate dose gradually at 1- to 2-day intervals; usual dose range (ACC/AHA [Gibbons 2002]): 120 to 320 mg daily in 4 divided doses.

Hypertension: Oral:

Capsule, extended release (once-daily dosing):

Cardizem CD, Cartia XT: Initial: 180 to 240 mg once daily; dose adjustment may be made after 14 days; usual dose range (ASH/ISH [Weber 2014]): 240 to 360 mg daily; maximum: 480 mg/day.

Dilacor XR, Dilt-XR: Initial: 180 to 240 mg once daily; dose adjustment may be made after 14 days; usual dose range (ASH/ISH [Weber 2014]): 240 to 360 mg daily; maximum: 540 mg/day.

Tiazac, Taztia XT: Initial: 120 to 240 mg once daily; dose adjustment may be made after 14 days; usual dose range (ASH/ISH [Weber 2014]): 240 to 360 mg daily; maximum: 540 mg/day.

Capsule, extended release (twice-daily dosing): Initial: 60 to 120 mg twice daily; dose adjustment may be made after 14 days; usual range: 240 to 360 mg daily.

Note: Diltiazem is available as a generic intended for either once- or twice-daily dosing, depending on the formulation; verify appropriate extended release capsule formulation is administered.

Tablet, extended release (Cardizem LA, Matzim LA, Tiazac XC [Canadian product]): Initial: 180 to 240 mg once daily; dose adjustment may be made after 14 days; usual dose range (ASH/ISH [Weber 2014]): 240 to 360 mg daily; maximum: 540 mg/day.

Atrial fibrillation, atrial flutter, PSVT (acute treatment): IV:

Control of rapid ventricular rate in atrial fibrillation or atrial flutter or conversion of PSVT:

Initial bolus dose: 0.25 mg/kg actual body weight over 2 minutes (average adult dose: 20 mg); ACLS guideline recommends 15 to 20 mg

Repeat bolus dose (may be administered after 15 minutes if the response is inadequate): 0.35 mg/kg actual body weight over 2 minutes (average adult dose: 25 mg); ACLS guideline recommends 20 to 25 mg

Continuous infusion (infusions >24 hours or infusion rates >15 mg/hour are not recommended): Initial infusion rate of 10 mg/hour; rate may be increased in 5 mg/hour increments up to 15 mg/hour as needed; some patients may respond to an initial rate of 5 mg/hour.

If diltiazem injection is administered by continuous infusion for >24 hours, the possibility of decreased diltiazem clearance, prolonged elimination half-life, and increased diltiazem and/or diltiazem metabolite plasma concentrations should be considered.

Atrial fibrillation (rate control) (off-label use): Oral: Extended release (capsule or tablet): Usual maintenance dose: 120 to 360 mg once daily (AHA/ACC/HRS [January 2014]).

Supraventricular tachycardia (ongoing management) (off-label use): Oral:

Extended release (capsule or tablet): Initial: 120 mg daily in divided doses or once daily; usual maintenance dose: 360 mg daily in divided doses or once daily (ACC/AHA/HRS [Page 2015]).

Immediate release: Initial: 120 mg daily in divided doses; usual maintenance dose: 360 mg daily in divided doses (ACC/AHA/HRS [Page 2015]).

Conversion from IV diltiazem to oral diltiazem:

Oral dose (mg daily) is approximately equal to [rate (mg/hour) x 3 + 3] x 10.

3 mg/hour = 120 mg daily
5 mg/hour = 180 mg daily
7 mg/hour = 240 mg daily
11 mg/hour = 360 mg daily

Geriatric Refer to adult dosing. In the management of hypertension, consider lower initial doses (eg, 120 mg once daily using extended release capsule) and titrate to response (Aronow 2011).

Pediatric

Hypertension (off-label use): Children and Adolescents: Minimal information available: Oral: Initial: 1.5 to 2 mg/kg/day in 3 to 4 divided doses (extended release formulations may be dosed once or twice daily); maximum dose: 3.5 mg/kg/day; some centers use a maximum dose of 6 mg/kg/day up to 360 mg/day (Flynn 2000).

Renal Impairment There are no dosage adjustments provided in the manufacturer's labeling; use with caution.

Dialysis: Not removed by hemo- or peritoneal dialysis; supplemental dose is not necessary.

Hepatic Impairment There are no dosage adjustment provided in the manufacturer's labeling; use with caution; extensively metabolized by the liver; half-life is increased in patients with cirrhosis.

Mechanism of Action Inhibits calcium ion from entering the "slow channels" or select voltage-sensitive areas of vascular smooth muscle and myocardium during depolarization; produces relaxation of coronary vascular smooth muscle and coronary vasodilation; increases myocardial oxygen delivery in patients with vasospastic angina

Contraindications

Oral: Hypersensitivity to diltiazem or any component of the formulation; sick sinus syndrome (except in patients with a functioning artificial pacemaker); second- or third-degree AV block (except in patients with a functioning artificial pacemaker); hypotension (systolic <90 mm Hg); acute MI and pulmonary congestion

Intravenous (IV): Hypersensitivity to diltiazem or any component of the formulation; sick sinus syndrome (except in patients with a functioning artificial pacemaker); second- or third-degree AV block (except in patients with a functioning artificial pacemaker); severe hypotension; cardiogenic shock; administration concomitantly or within a few hours of the administration of IV beta-blockers; atrial fibrillation or flutter associated with accessory bypass tract (eg, Wolff-Parkinson-White syndrome, short PR syndrome); ventricular tachycardia (with wide-complex tachycardia [QRS ≥0.12 seconds], must determine whether origin is supraventricular or ventricular)

Canadian labeling: Additional contraindications (not in US labeling): Pregnancy; use in women of childbearing potential; concurrent use with intravenous dantrolene; concurrent use with ivabradine.

Warnings/Precautions May cause first-, second-, and third-degree AV block or sinus bradycardia and risk increases with agents known to slow cardiac conduction. Symptomatic hypotension with or without syncope can rarely occur; blood pressure must be lowered at a rate appropriate for the patient's clinical condition. Use caution in left ventricular dysfunction (may exacerbate condition). The ACCF/AHA heart failure guidelines recommend to avoid use in patients with heart failure due to lack of benefit and/or worse outcomes with calcium channel blockers in general (ACCF/AHA [Yancy 2013]). Use with caution with hypertrophic obstructive cardiomyopathy; routine use is currently not recommended due to insufficient evidence (Maron 2003). Mild elevations of transaminases with and without concomitant elevation in alkaline phosphatase and bilirubin have been observed and frequently resolve spontaneously. Significant elevations in hepatic transaminases (eg, alkaline phosphatase, LDH, AST, ALT) and signs of acute hepatic injury have also been observed 1 to 8 weeks after therapy initiation and have been reversible upon discontinuation. Use with caution in hepatic or renal impairment. Transient dermatologic reactions have been observed with use; if reaction persists, discontinue. Stevens-Johnson syndrome, toxic epidermal necrolysis, erythema multiforme, and/or exfoliative dermatitis have been reported. Potentially significant interactions may exist, requiring dose or frequency adjustment, additional monitoring, and/or selection of alternative therapy.

Unless otherwise contraindicated, appropriate vagal maneuvers should be attempted prior to administration of IV diltiazem. Use with caution in patients hemodynamically compromised; continuously monitor ECG and blood pressure during administration (especially during continuous IV infusion). Initial use should be, if possible, in a setting where monitoring and resuscitation equipment, including DC cardioversion/defibrillation, are present.

Drug Interactions

Metabolism/Transport Effects Substrate of CYP2C9 (minor), CYP2D6 (minor), CYP3A4 (major), P-glycoprotein; **Note:** Assignment of Major/Minor substrate status based on clinically relevant drug interaction potential; **Inhibits** CYP2C9 (weak), CYP2D6 (weak), CYP3A4 (moderate)

Avoid Concomitant Use

Avoid concomitant use of DilTIAZem with any of the following: Aprepitant; Asunaprevir; Bosutinib; Budesonide (Systemic); Ceritinib; Cobimetinib; Conivaptan; Dantrolene; Domperidone; Flibanserin; Fusidic Acid (Systemic); Ibrutinib; Idelalisib; Ivabradine; Lomitapide; Naloxegol; Olaparib; Pimozide; RifAMPin; Simeprevir; Tolvaptan; Trabectedin; Ulipristal

Increased Effect/Toxicity

DilTIAZem may increase the levels/effects of: Alfentanil; Amifostine; Amiodarone; AmLODIPine; Antipsychotic Agents (Second Generation [Atypical]); Apixaban; Aprepitant; ARIPiprazole; Aspirin; Asunaprevir; AtorvaSTATin; Atosiban; Avanafil; Beta-Blockers; Blonanserin; Bosentan; Bosutinib; Bradycardia-Causing Agents; Brexpiprazole; Bromocriptine; Budesonide (Systemic); Budesonide (Topical); BusPIRone; Calcium Channel Blockers (Dihydropyridine); Cannabis; CarBAMazepine; Cardiac Glycosides; Ceritinib; Cilostazol; Cobimetinib; Colchicine; Corticosteroids (Systemic); CycloSPORINE (Systemic); CYP3A4 Substrates; Dapoxetine; Deflazacort; Dofetilide; Domperidone; DOXOrubicin (Conventional); Dronabinol; Dronedarone; DULoxetine; Eletriptan; Eliglustat; Eplerenone; Esmolol; Everolimus; FentaNYL; Fingolimod; Flibanserin; Fosaprepitant; Fosphenytoin; GuanFACINE; Halofantrine; HYDROcodone; HydrOXYzine; Hypotension-Associated Agents; Ibrutinib; Imatinib; Ivabradine; Ivacaftor; Lacosamide; Levodopa; Lithium; Lomitapide; Lovastatin; Lurasidone; Magnesium Salts; Manidipine; Midodrine; Mirodenafil; Naldemedine; Naloxegol; Neuromuscular-Blocking Agents (Nondepolarizing); NiMODipine; Nitroprusside; Olaparib; OxyCODONE; Perhexiline; Phenytoin; Pimecrolimus; Pimozide; Propafenone; QuiNIDine; Ranolazine; Red Yeast Rice; Rupatadine; Salmeterol; SAXagliptin; Sildenafil; Simeprevir; Simvastatin; Sonidegib; Suvorexant; Tacrolimus (Systemic); Tacrolimus (Topical); Tetrahydrocannabinol; Ticagrelor; Tolvaptan; Trabectedin; Udenafil; Ulipristal; Venetoclax; Vilazodone; Vindesine; Zopiclone; Zuclopenthixol

The levels/effects of DilTIAZem may be increased by: Alfuzosin; Alpha1-Blockers; Anilidopiperidine Opioids; Antifungal Agents (Azole Derivatives, Systemic); AtorvaSTATin; Barbiturates; Benperidol; Bretylium; Brimonidine (Topical); Calcium Channel Blockers (Dihydropyridine); Cimetidine; CloNIDine; Conivaptan; CycloSPORINE (Systemic); CYP3A4 Inhibitors (Moderate); CYP3A4 Inhibitors (Strong); Dantrolene; Dasatinib; Diazoxide; Dronedarone; Fluconazole; Fosaprepitant; Fusidic Acid (Systemic); Grapefruit Juice; Herbs (Hypotensive Properties); Idelalisib; Ivabradine; Lormetazepam; Lovastatin; Macrolide Antibiotics; Magnesium Salts; MiFEPRIStone; Molsidomine; Naftopidil; Netupitant; Nicergoline; Nicorandil; Obinutuzumab; Palbociclib; Pentoxifylline; P-glycoprotein/ABCB1 Inhibitors; Phosphodiesterase 5 Inhibitors; Prostacyclin Analogues; Protease Inhibitors; Quinagolide; Regorafenib; Ruxolitinib; Simvastatin; Stiripentol; Tofacitinib

Decreased Effect

DilTIAZem may decrease the levels/effects of: Clopidogrel; Ifosfamide

The levels/effects of DilTIAZem may be decreased by: Amphetamines; Barbiturates; Bosentan; Calcium Salts; CarBAMazepine; Colestipol; CYP3A4 Inducers (Moderate); CYP3A4 Inducers (Strong); Dabrafenib; Deferasirox; Efavirenz; Enzalutamide; Herbs (Hypertensive Properties); Methylphenidate; Mitotane; Phenytoin; RifAMPin; Rifamycin Derivatives; Siltuximab; St John's Wort; Tocilizumab; Yohimbine

Food Interactions Grapefruit juice may increase the serum concentration of diltiazem. Management: Monitor response to diltiazem with concurrent use.

Pharmacodynamics/Kinetics

Onset of Action Oral: Immediate release tablet: 30 to 60 minutes; IV: Bolus: 3 minutes

Duration of Action IV: Bolus: 1 to 3 hours; Continuous infusion (after discontinuation): 0.5 to 10 hours

Half-life Elimination Immediate release tablet: 3 to 4.5 hours; Extended release tablet: 6 to 9 hours; Extended release capsules: 4 to 9.5 hours; IV: single dose: ~3.4 hours; continuous infusion: 4 to 5 hours

Time to Peak Serum: Immediate release tablet: 2 to 4 hours; Extended release tablet: 11 to 18 hours; Extended release capsule: 10 to 14 hours

Pregnancy Risk Factor C

Pregnancy Considerations Adverse events have been observed in animal reproduction studies. Untreated chronic maternal hypertension is associated with adverse events in the fetus, infant, and mother. If treatment for hypertension during pregnancy is needed, other agents are preferred (ACOG 2013). Women with hypertrophic cardiomyopathy who are controlled with diltiazem prior to pregnancy may continue therapy, but increased fetal monitoring is recommended (Gersh 2011).

Breastfeeding Considerations Diltiazem is excreted in breast milk in concentrations similar to those in the maternal plasma (Okada 1985). breastfeeding is not recommended by the manufacturer.

Dosage Forms

Capsule Extended Release 12 Hour, Oral:

Generic: 60 mg, 90 mg, 120 mg

Capsule Extended Release 24 Hour, Oral:

Cardizem CD: 120 mg, 180 mg, 240 mg, 360 mg

Cartia XT: 120 mg, 180 mg, 240 mg, 300 mg

Dilt-XR: 120 mg, 180 mg, 240 mg

DilTIAZem CD: 120 mg, 180 mg, 240 mg, 300 mg

Taztia XT: 120 mg, 180 mg, 240 mg, 300 mg, 360 mg

Tiazac: 120 mg, 180 mg, 240 mg, 300 mg, 360 mg, 420 mg

Generic: 120 mg, 180 mg, 240 mg, 300 mg, 360 mg, 420 mg

Solution, Intravenous:

Generic: 25 mg/5 mL (5 mL); 50 mg/10 mL (10 mL); 125 mg/25 mL (25 mL)

Solution Reconstituted, Intravenous:

Generic: 100 mg (1 ea)

Tablet, Oral:

Cardizem: 30 mg, 60 mg, 120 mg

Generic: 30 mg, 60 mg, 90 mg, 120 mg

Tablet Extended Release 24 Hour, Oral:

Cardizem LA: 120 mg, 180 mg, 240 mg, 300 mg, 360 mg, 420 mg

Matzim LA: 180 mg, 240 mg, 300 mg, 360 mg, 420 mg

Generic: 180 mg, 240 mg, 300 mg, 360 mg, 420 mg

Dosage Forms: Canada Note: Also refer to Dosage Forms.

Tablet, Extended Release, Oral:

Tiazac XC: 120 mg, 180 mg, 240 mg, 300 mg, 360 mg

DimenhyDRINATE (dye men HYE dri nate)

Brand Names: US Dramamine [OTC]; Driminate [OTC]; Motion Sickness [OTC]

Brand Names: Canada Apo-Dimenhydrinate [OTC]; Children's Motion Sickness Liquid [OTC]; Dimenhydrinate Injection; Dinate [OTC]; Gravol IM; Gravol [OTC]; Jamp-Dimenhydrinate [OTC]; Nauseatol [OTC]; PMS-Dimenhydrinate [OTC]; Sandoz-Dimenhydrinate [OTC]; Teva-Dimenate; Travel Tabs [OTC]

Pharmacologic Category Ethanolamine Derivative; Histamine H_1 Antagonist; Histamine H_1 Antagonist, First Generation

Use

US labeling: **Motion sickness:** Treatment and prevention of nausea, vertigo, and vomiting associated with motion sickness.

Canadian labeling: **Nausea, vomiting and/or vertigo:** Treatment and prevention of nausea, vomiting and/or vertigo associated with motion sickness, radiation sickness, postoperative recovery, use of other drugs, Mènière disease and other labyrinthine disturbances.

Local Anesthetic/Vasoconstrictor Precautions No information available to require special precautions

Effects on Dental Treatment Key adverse event(s) related to dental treatment: Significant xerostomia (normal salivary flow resumes upon discontinuation).

Effects on Bleeding No information available to require special precautions

Adverse Reactions Frequency not defined.

Cardiovascular: Tachycardia

Central nervous system: Dizziness, drowsiness, excitement, headache, insomnia, lassitude, nervousness, restlessness

Dermatologic: Skin rash

Gastrointestinal: Anorexia, epigastric distress, nausea, xerostomia

Genitourinary: Dysuria

Ophthalmic: Blurred vision

Respiratory: Thickening of bronchial secretions

General Dosage Range

Oral:

Children 2 to 5 years: 12.5 to 25 mg every 6 to 8 hours (maximum: 75 mg daily)

Children 6 to 12 years: 25 to 50 mg every 6 to 8 hours (maximum: 150 mg daily)

IM:

Children: 1.25 mg/kg **or** 37.5 mg/m^2 4 times daily (maximum: 300 mg daily)

Adults: 50 to 100 mg every 4 hours

IV: *Adults:* 50 to 100 mg every 4 hours

Mechanism of Action Competes with histamine for H_1-receptor sites on effector cells in the gastrointestinal tract, blood vessels, and respiratory tract; blocks chemoreceptor trigger zone, diminishes vestibular stimulation, and depresses labyrinthine function through its central anticholinergic activity

Pharmacodynamics/Kinetics

Onset of Action Antiemetic: IV: immediate; IM: 20 to 30 minutes; Oral: 15 to 30 minutes (Gravol Canadian labeling 2016)

Duration of Action 4 to 6 hours (Gravol Canadian labeling 2016)

Half-life Elimination 5 to 8 hours (Gravol Canadian labeling 2016)

Pregnancy Risk Factor B

Pregnancy Considerations Adverse events have not been observed in animal reproduction studies. Dimenhydrinate crosses the placenta. The risk of fetal abnormalities was not increased following maternal use of dimenhydrinate during any trimester of pregnancy. Dimenhydrinate may be used for the adjunctive treatment of nausea and vomiting of pregnancy (Arsenault 2002); other agents are preferred for initial therapy (ACOG 2015). Dimenhydrinate may have an oxytocic effect if used during labor.

Dimercaprol (dye mer KAP role)

Brand Names: US Bal in Oil

Pharmacologic Category Antidote

Use Antidote to gold, arsenic (except arsine), or acute mercury poisoning (except nonalkyl mercury); adjunct to edetate CALCIUM disodium in acute lead poisoning

Local Anesthetic/Vasoconstrictor Precautions No information available to require special precautions

Effects on Dental Treatment No significant effects or complications reported

Effects on Bleeding No information available to require special precautions

Adverse Reactions Frequency not always defined.

Cardiovascular: Chest pain, hypertension (dose-related), tachycardia (dose-related)

Central nervous system: Anxiety, burning sensation (lips, mouth, throat), headache, nervousness, paresthesia (hand)

Dermatologic: Diaphoresis

Gastrointestinal: Abdominal pain, nausea, salivation, sore throat, vomiting

Genitourinary: Burning sensation of the penis

Hematologic & oncologic: Leukopenia (polymorphonuclear)

Infection: Abscess

Local: Pain at injection site

Neuromuscular & skeletal: Weakness

Ophthalmic: Blepharospasm, conjunctivitis, lacrimation

Renal: Renal insufficiency (acute)

Respiratory: Pharyngeal edema, rhinorrhea, throat irritation

Miscellaneous: Fever (children ~30%)

General Dosage Range IM: *Children and Adults:* Dosage varies greatly depending on indication

Mechanism of Action Sulfhydryl group combines with ions of various heavy metals to form relatively stable, nontoxic, soluble chelates which are excreted in urine

Pharmacodynamics/Kinetics

Time to Peak Serum: 0.5-1 hour

Pregnancy Risk Factor C

Pregnancy Considerations Animal reproduction studies have not been conducted. There are no adequate and well-controlled studies in pregnant women.

Lead poisoning: Lead is known to cross the placenta in amounts related to maternal plasma levels. Prenatal lead exposure may be associated with adverse events such as spontaneous abortion, preterm delivery, decreased birth weight, and impaired neurodevelopment. Some adverse outcomes may occur with maternal blood lead levels <10 mcg/dL. In addition, pregnant women exposed to lead may have an increased risk of gestational hypertension. Consider chelation therapy in pregnant women with confirmed blood lead levels ≥45 mcg/dL (pregnant women with blood lead levels ≥70 mcg/dL should be considered for chelation regardless of trimester). There are alternatives to the use of dimercaprol and consultation with experts in lead poisoning and high-risk pregnancy is recommended. Encephalopathic pregnant women should be chelated regardless of trimester (CDC, 2010).

Dimethyl Fumarate (dye meth il FYOO ma rate)

Brand Names: US Tecfidera

Brand Names: Canada Tecfidera

Pharmacologic Category Fumaric Acid Derivative; Immunomodulator, Systemic

Use Multiple sclerosis: Treatment of patients with relapsing forms of multiple sclerosis

Local Anesthetic/Vasoconstrictor Precautions No information available to require special precautions

Effects on Dental Treatment No significant effects or complications reported

Effects on Bleeding No information available to require special precautions

Adverse Reactions

>10%:

Cardiovascular: Flushing (40%)

Gastrointestinal: Abdominal pain (18%), diarrhea (14%), nausea (12%)

Infection: Infection (60%; placebo: 58%)

1% to 10%:

Dermatologic: Pruritus (8%), skin rash (8%), erythema (5%)

Gastrointestinal: Vomiting (9%), dyspepsia (5%)

Genitourinary: Proteinuria (6%)

Hematologic: Lymphocytopenia (2% to 6%)

Hepatic: Increased serum AST (4%)

<1%, postmarketing, and/or case reports: Anaphylaxis, angioedema, eosinophilia (transient), progressive multifocal leukoencephalopathy

General Dosage Range Oral: *Adults:* Initial: 120 mg twice daily; Maintenance: 240 mg twice daily

Mechanism of Action DMF and its active metabolite, monomethyl fumarate (MMF), have been shown to activate the nuclear factor (erythroid-derived 2)-like 2 (Nrf2) pathway, which is involved in cellular response to oxidative stress. The mechanism by which dimethyl fumarate (DMF) exerts a therapeutic effect in MS is unknown, although it is believed to result from its anti-inflammatory and cytoprotective properties via activation of the Nrf2 pathway (Fox, 2012; Gold, 2012).

Pharmacodynamics/Kinetics

Half-life Elimination MMF: ~1 hour

Time to Peak 2 to 2.5 hours; delayed to 5.5 hours with food

Pregnancy Risk Factor C

Pregnancy Considerations

Adverse events were observed in animal reproduction studies.

Women exposed to dimethyl fumarate during pregnancy are encouraged to enroll in the Pregnancy Registry by calling 866-810-1462 or visiting www.tecfiderapregnancyregistry.com.

Dinoprostone (dye noe PROST one)

Brand Names: US Cervidil; Prepidil; Prostin E2

Brand Names: Canada Cervidil®; Prepidil®; Prostin E_2®

Pharmacologic Category Abortifacient; Prostaglandin

Use

Endocervical gel (Prepidil): Promote cervical ripening in patients at or near term in whom there is a medical or obstetrical indication for the induction of labor

Suppositories (Prostin E_2): Terminate pregnancy from 12th through 20th week of gestation; evacuate uterus in cases of missed abortion or intrauterine fetal death up to 28 weeks of gestation; manage benign hydatidiform mole (nonmetastatic gestational trophoblastic disease)

Tablet (oral) (Prostin E_2; [Canadian product]): Elective induction of labor; when indications for induction of labor exist (eg, premature rupture of amniotic membranes, toxemia of pregnancy, Rh incompatibility, diabetes mellitus, hypertension, postmaturity, intrauterine death or fetal growth retardation)

Vaginal gel (Prostin E_2; [Canadian product]): Induction of labor in patients at or near term with singleton pregnancy, vertex presentation, and favorable induction features

Vaginal insert (Cervidil): Initiation and/or continuation of cervical ripening in patients at or near term in whom there is a medical or obstetrical indication for the induction of labor

Local Anesthetic/Vasoconstrictor Precautions No information available to require special precautions

Effects on Dental Treatment No significant effects or complications reported

Effects on Bleeding No information available to require special precautions

Adverse Reactions

Endocervical gel:

1% to 10%:

Central nervous system: Localized warm feeling (vagina; 2%)

Gastrointestinal: Gastrointestinal distress (6%)

Genitourinary: Uterine contractions (abnormal 7%)

Neuromuscular & skeletal: Back pain (3%)

<1%, postmarketing and/or case reports: Amnionitis, amniotic fluid embolism (anaphylactoid syndrome of pregnancy), disseminated intravascular coagulation (postpartum), hypersensitivity reaction (including anaphylaxis, anaphylactic shock, and anaphylactoid reaction), premature rupture of membranes, uterine rupture (with intracervical administration)

Suppository:

Frequency not defined:

Cardiovascular: Cardiac arrhythmia, chest pain, chest tightness, hypotension, syncope

Central nervous system: Chills, dizziness, headache, paresthesia, shivering, tension

Dermatologic: Diaphoresis, skin discoloration, skin rash

Endocrine & metabolic: Dehydration, hot flash

Gastrointestinal: Diarrhea, endometritis, nausea, vomiting

Genitourinary: Breast tenderness, urinary retention, uterine rupture, vaginal pain, vaginismus, vaginitis, vulvitis

Neuromuscular & skeletal: Arthralgia, arthritis (new or exacerbated), back pain, leg cramps (nocturnal), muscle cramps, myalgia, neck stiffness, tremor, weakness

Ophthalmic: Blurred vision, eye pain

Otic: Auditory impairment

Respiratory: Cough, dyspnea, laryngitis, pharyngitis, wheezing

Miscellaneous: Fever

<1%, postmarketing and/or case reports: Myocardial infarction

Tablets (oral) [Canadian product]:

Frequency not always defined:

Cardiovascular: Amniotic fluid embolism (pulmonary), cardiac arrest

Central nervous system: Malaise (transient vasovagal symptoms)

Gastrointestinal: Vomiting (with or without nausea/diarrhea: 21% to 50%; dose dependent)

Genitourinary: Hypertonic uterine contractions (3%), cervical dilation (rapid), placental abruption, uterine contractions (abnormal), uterine rupture

Hypersensitivity: Hypersensitivity reaction (including anaphylaxis, anaphylactic shock, and nonimmunologic anaphylaxis [formerly known as anaphylactoid reaction])

Neuromuscular & skeletal: Back pain

Respiratory: Asthma

<1%, postmarketing and/or case reports: Bronchospasm, chills, disseminated intravascular coagulation, dizziness, dyspnea, fever, flushing, headache, hiccups, hypertension, hypotension, postpartum hemorrhage, skin rash, tachycardia

Vaginal gel [Canadian product]:

Frequency not always defined:

Cardiovascular: Cardiac arrest

Central nervous system: Localized warm feeling (vagina)

Gastrointestinal: Diarrhea, nausea, vomiting

Genitourinary: Hypertonic uterine contractions (3%), uterine contractions (abnormal), uterine rupture

Hypersensitivity: Hypersensitivity reaction (including anaphylaxis, anaphylactic shock, and nonimmunologic anaphylaxis [formerly known as anaphylactoid reaction])

Neuromuscular & skeletal: Back pain

Miscellaneous: Fever

<1%, postmarketing and/or case reports: Disseminated intravascular coagulation

Vaginal insert:

1% to 10%:

Genitourinary: Hypertonic uterine contractions (*without* fetal distress 2% to 5%, *with* fetal distress 3%)

<1% postmarketing and/or case reports: Abdominal pain, amniotic fluid embolism (anaphylactoid syndrome of pregnancy), diarrhea, disseminated intravascular coagulation (postpartum), fever, hypersensitivity reaction, hypotension, nausea, uterine rupture, vomiting

General Dosage Range

Endocervical: *Children (females of reproductive age) and Adults (females):* 0.5 mg; may repeat every 6 hours if needed. Maximum cumulative dose: 1.5 mg/24 hours

Intravaginal: *Children (females of reproductive age) and Adults (females):* Insert: 10 mg; remove at onset of active labor or after 12 hours; Suppository: 20 mg every 3-5 hours until abortion occurs

Mechanism of Action Dinoprostone (prostaglandin E_2) is an endogenous hormone found in low concentrations in most tissues of the body. When administered as an abortifacient, it stimulates uterine contractions similar to those seen during natural labor. When administered for labor induction, it relaxes the smooth muscle of the cervix allowing dilation and passage of the fetus through the birth canal.

Pharmacodynamics/Kinetics

Onset of Action Uterine contractions: Vaginal suppository: Within 10 minutes

Duration of Action Vaginal insert: 0.3 mg/hour over 12 hours; Vaginal suppository: Up to 2-3 hours

Half-life Elimination 2.5-5 minutes

Time to Peak Endocervical gel: 30-45 minutes

Pregnancy Risk Factor C

Pregnancy Considerations Skeletal anomalies and embryotoxicity have been observed in animal reproduction studies. Although these effects would not be expected in humans when administered after the period of organogenesis, a sustained increase in uterine tone may have increased risks of adverse events to the fetus.

Fetal distress without corresponding maternal uterine hyperstimulation was observed in 3% to 4% of infants exposed to Cervidil *in utero*. No adverse effects on physical or psychomotor function were observed in a 3 year follow-up study of exposed infants. Abnormal fetal heart rates were observed in 17% of infants exposed to Prepidil gel *in utero*. Deceleration, intrauterine fetal sepsis, fetal depression and fetal acidosis have also been reported with administration of the endocervical gel. Still births, abnormal fetal heart rate and fetal distress have been reported with administration of Prostin E_2 vaginal gel and oral tablets [Canadian product].

When used for termination of pregnancy, dinoprostone is not considered feticidal, but is used to terminate pregnancy due to its ability to stimulate uterine contractions; do not use if fetus has reached the stage of viability.

DiphenhydrAMINE (Systemic)

(dye fen HYE dra meen)

Related Information

Bacterial Infections *on page 1835*

Perioral Premalignant Lesions and Management of Patients Undergoing Cancer Therapy *on page 1875*

Ulcerative, Erosive, and Painful Oral Mucosal Disorders *on page 1853*

Viral Infections *on page 1849*

Related Sample Prescriptions

Ulcerative and Erosive Disorders - Sample Prescriptions *on page 43*

Brand Names: US Aler-Dryl [OTC]; Allergy Relief Childrens [OTC]; Allergy Relief [OTC]; Altaryl [OTC]; Anti-Hist Allergy [OTC]; Banophen [OTC]; Benadryl Allergy Childrens [OTC]; Benadryl Allergy [OTC]; Benadryl Dye-Free Allergy [OTC]; Benadryl [OTC] [DSC]; Complete Allergy Medication [OTC]; Complete Allergy Relief [OTC]; Dicopanol FusePaq; Dicopanol RapidPaq; Diphen [OTC]; Diphenhist [OTC]; Genahist [OTC]; Geri-Dryl [OTC]; GoodSense Allergy Relief [OTC]; Naramin [OTC]; Nighttime Sleep Aid [OTC]; Nytol Maximum Strength [OTC]; Nytol [OTC]; Ormir [OTC]; PediaCare Childrens Allergy [OTC]; Pharbedryl; Pharbedryl [OTC]; Q-Dryl [OTC]; QlearQuil Nighttime Allergy [OTC] [DSC]; Quenalin [OTC] [DSC]; Scot-Tussin Allergy Relief [OTC]; Siladryl Allergy [OTC]; Silphen Cough [OTC]; Simply Allergy [OTC] [DSC]; Simply Sleep [OTC]; Sleep Tabs [OTC]; Sominex Maximum Strength [OTC] [DSC]; Sominex [OTC]; Tetra-Formula Nighttime Sleep [OTC]; Total Allergy Medicine [OTC]; Total Allergy [OTC]; Triaminic Cough/Runny Nose [OTC]; ZzzQuil [OTC]

Brand Names: Canada Allerdryl; Allernix; Benadryl; Nytol; Nytol Extra Strength; PMS-Diphenhydramine; Simply Sleep; Sominex

Generic Availability (US) May be product dependent

Pharmacologic Category Ethanolamine Derivative; Histamine H_1 Antagonist; Histamine H_1 Antagonist, First Generation

Dental Use Symptomatic relief of nasal mucosal congestion; symptomatic relief of oral erosions (systemic diphenhydramine used topically) including aphthous stomatitis

Use Symptomatic relief of allergic symptoms caused by histamine release including nasal allergies and allergic dermatosis; adjunct to epinephrine in the treatment of anaphylaxis; insomnia, occasional; prevention or treatment of motion sickness; antitussive; management of Parkinsonian syndrome including drug-induced extrapyramidal symptoms (dystonic reactions) alone or in combination with centrally acting anticholinergic agents

Local Anesthetic/Vasoconstrictor Precautions No information available to require special precautions

Effects on Dental Treatment Key adverse event(s) related to dental treatment: Xerostomia (normal salivary flow resumes upon discontinuation) and dry mucous membranes. Chronic use of antihistamines will inhibit salivary flow, particularly in elderly patients; may contribute to periodontal disease and oral discomfort. See Dental Comment.

Effects on Bleeding No information available to require special precautions

Adverse Reactions Frequency not defined.

Cardiovascular: Chest tightness, extrasystoles, hypotension, palpitations, tachycardia

Central nervous system: Ataxia, chills, confusion, dizziness, drowsiness, euphoria, excitement, fatigue, headache, insomnia, irritability, nervousness, neuritis, paradoxical excitation, paresthesia, restlessness, sedation, seizure, vertigo

Dermatologic: Diaphoresis

Endocrine & metabolic: Menstrual disease (early menses)

Gastrointestinal: Anorexia, constipation, diarrhea, dry mucous membranes, epigastric distress, nausea, vomiting, xerostomia

Genitourinary: Difficulty in micturition, urinary frequency, urinary retention

Hematologic & oncologic: Agranulocytosis, hemolytic anemia, thrombocytopenia

Hypersensitivity: Anaphylactic shock

Neuromuscular & skeletal: Tremor

Ophthalmic: Blurred vision, diplopia

Otic: Labyrinthitis (acute), tinnitus

Respiratory: Constriction of the pharynx, nasal congestion, thickening of bronchial secretions, wheezing

Dental Usual Dosage

Symptomatic relief of nasal mucosal congestion: Adults: Oral: 25 to 50 mg every 6 to 8 hours

Symptomatic relief of oral erosions (used topically): Adults: Rinse with 5 to 10 mL every 2 hours and expectorate

Dosing

Adult

Allergic reactions:

Oral: 25 to 50 mg every 4 to 8 hours; maximum: 300 mg daily

IM, IV: 10 to 50 mg per dose; single doses up to 100 mg may be used if needed; not to exceed 400 mg daily

Antitussive: Oral: 25 mg every 4 hours; maximum: 150 mg daily

Motion sickness: Note: When used for prophylaxis, administer 30 minutes before motion.

Oral (treatment or prophylaxis): 25 to 50 mg every 6 to 8 hours

IM, IV (treatment): 10 to 50 mg per dose; single doses up to 100 mg may be used if needed; maximum: 400 mg daily

Insomnia, occasional: Oral: 50 mg at bedtime

Parkinsonism:

Oral: 25 to 50 mg 3 or 4 times daily

IM, IV: 10 to 50 mg per dose; single doses up to 100 mg may be used if needed; maximum: 400 mg daily

Rhinitis, sneezing due to common cold: Oral: 25 to 50 mg every 4 to 6 hours; maximum: 300 mg daily

Pediatric

Allergic reactions: Infants, Children, and Adolescents: IM, IV, Oral: 5 mg/kg/day in divided doses every 6 to 8 hours: maximum: 300 mg daily

Alternate dosing by age: Oral:

2 to <6 years (off-label use): 6.25 mg every 4 to 6 hours; maximum: 37.5 mg daily (Kleigman, 2011)

6 to <12 years: 12.5 to 25 mg every 4 to 6 hours; maximum: 150 mg daily

≥12 years: Refer to adult dosing.

Anaphylaxis (adjunct to epinephrine)/allergic reaction (off-label use): Infants, Children, and Adolescents: IM, IV, Oral: 1 to 2 mg/kg/dose; maximum: 50 mg/dose (Hegenbarth, 2008; Kliegman, 2011; Liberman, 2008; Lieberman, 2010; Simons, 2011)

Antitussive: Children ≥12 years: Refer to adult dosing.

Dystonic reactions (off-label use): Infants, Children, and Adolescents: IM, IV: 1 to 2 mg/kg/dose; maximum single dose: 50 mg (Hegenbarth, 2008; Kliegman, 2011)

Insomnia, occasional: Oral:

Children 2 to 12 years, weighing 10 to 50 kg (off-label use): Limited data available: 1 mg/kg administered 30 minutes before bedtime; maximum single dose: 50 mg (Russo, 1976)

Children ≥12 years and Adolescents: Refer to adult dosing.

Motion sickness:

Prophylaxis: Oral:

Manufacturer's labeling: Infants, Children, and Adolescents: **Note:** Administer 30 minutes before motion

Weight-directed dosing: 5 mg/kg/day divided into 3 to 4 doses; maximum: 300 mg daily

Fixed dosing: 12.5 to 25 mg 3 to 4 times daily

Alternate dosing: Children 2 to 12 years: Limited data available: 0.5 to 1 mg/kg/dose every 6 hours; maximum single dose: 25 mg. First dose should be administered 1 hour before travel (CDC, 2014).

Treatment: Infants, Children, and Adolescents:

IV, IM: 5 mg/kg/day divided into 4 doses; maximum: 300 mg daily

Oral:

Weight-directed dosing: 5 mg/kg/day divided into 3 to 4 doses; maximum: 300 mg daily

Fixed dosing: 12.5 to 25 mg 3 to 4 times daily

Rhinitis, sneezing due to common cold: Oral:

Children 6 to <12 years: 12.5 to 25 mg every 4 to 6 hours; maximum: 150 mg daily

Children ≥12 years and Adolescents: Refer to adult dosing.

Renal Impairment There are no dosage adjustments provided in the manufacturer's labeling.

Hepatic Impairment There are no dosage adjustments provided in the manufacturer's labeling.

Mechanism of Action Competes with histamine for H_1-receptor sites on effector cells in the gastrointestinal tract, blood vessels, and respiratory tract; anticholinergic and sedative effects are also seen

Contraindications Hypersensitivity to diphenhydramine, other structurally related antihistamines, or any component of the formulation; neonates or premature infants; breastfeeding

Additional contraindications: Parenteral: Use as a local anesthetic

OTC labeling: When used for self-medication, do not use in children <6 years, to make a child sleep, or with any other diphenhydramine-containing products (including topical products)

Warnings/Precautions Causes sedation, caution must be used in performing tasks which require alertness (eg, operating machinery or driving). Potentially significant drug-drug interactions may exist, requiring dose or frequency adjustment, additional monitoring, and/or selection of alternative therapy. Sedative effects of CNS depressants or ethanol are potentiated. Antihistamines may cause excitation in young children. Toxicity (overdose) in pediatric patients may result in hallucinations, convulsions, or death; neonates and young children are highly sensitive to depressive effects of diphenhydramine; use is contraindicated in neonates. Use with caution in patients with angle-closure glaucoma, pyloroduodenal obstruction (including stenotic peptic ulcer), urinary tract obstruction (including bladder neck obstruction and symptomatic prostatic hyperplasia), asthma, hyperthyroidism, increased intraocular pressure, and cardiovascular disease (including hypertension and tachycardia).

Some preparations contain soy protein; avoid use in patients with soy protein or peanut allergies. Some products may contain phenylalanine. Some products may contain alcohol. Some dosage forms may contain propylene glycol; large amounts are potentially toxic and have been associated hyperosmolality, lactic acidosis, seizures, and respiratory depression; use caution (AAP ["Inactive" 1997]; Zar, 2007).

Benzyl alcohol and derivatives: Some dosage forms may contain sodium benzoate/benzoic acid; benzoic acid (benzoate) is a metabolite of benzyl alcohol; large amounts of benzyl alcohol (≥99 mg/kg/day) have been associated with a potentially fatal toxicity ("gasping syndrome") in neonates; the "gasping syndrome" consists of metabolic acidosis, respiratory distress, gasping respirations, CNS dysfunction (including convulsions, intracranial hemorrhage), hypotension, and cardiovascular collapse (AAP ["Inactive" 1997]; CDC, 1982); some data suggests that benzoate displaces bilirubin from protein binding sites (Ahlfors, 2001); avoid or use dosage forms containing benzyl alcohol derivative with caution in neonates. See manufacturer's labeling.

Some dosage forms may contain polysorbate 80 (also known as Tweens). Hypersensitivity reactions, usually a delayed reaction, have been reported following exposure to pharmaceutical products containing polysorbate 80 in certain individuals (Isaksson, 2002; Lucente 2000; Shelley, 1995). Thrombocytopenia, ascites, pulmonary deterioration, and renal and hepatic failure have been reported in premature neonates after receiving parenteral products containing polysorbate 80 (Alade, 1986; CDC, 1984). See manufacturer's labeling.

Oral products: Oral solutions are available in two concentrations (ie, 12.5 mg/5 mL and 50 mg/30 mL [eg, ZzzQuil]); precautions should be taken to verify and avoid confusion between the different concentrations; dose should be clearly presented as "mg"; the 50 mg/30 mL oral solution is indicated for the occasional treatment of insomnia.

Parenteral products: Subcutaneous or intradermal use has been associated with tissue necrosis; administer IV or IM only.

Drug Interactions

Metabolism/Transport Effects **Inhibits** CYP2D6 (weak)

Avoid Concomitant Use

Avoid concomitant use of DiphenhydrAMINE (Systemic) with any of the following: Aclidinium; Azelastine (Nasal); Cimetropium; Eluxadoline; Glucagon; Glycopyrrolate (Oral Inhalation); Ipratropium (Oral Inhalation); Levosulpiride; Nitroglycerin; Orphenadrine; Oxatomide; Oxomemazine; Paraldehyde; Potassium Chloride; Thalidomide; Tiotropium; Umeclidinium

Increased Effect/Toxicity

DiphenhydrAMINE (Systemic) may increase the levels/effects of: AbobotulinumtoxinA; Alcohol (Ethyl); Analgesics (Opioid); Anticholinergic Agents; ARIPiprazole; Azelastine (Nasal); Blonanserin; Buprenorphine; Cimetropium; CNS Depressants; Eluxadoline; Flunitrazepam; Glucagon; Glycopyrrolate (Oral Inhalation); Highest Risk QTc-Prolonging Agents; HYDROcodone; Methotrimeprazine; MetyroSINE; Mirabegron; Mirtazapine; Moderate Risk QTc-Prolonging Agents; OnabotulinumtoxinA; Orphenadrine; OxyCODONE; Paraldehyde; Perhexiline; Piribedil; Potassium Chloride; Pramipexole; Ramosetron; RimabotulinumtoxinB; ROPINIRole; Rotigotine; Selective Serotonin Reuptake Inhibitors; Suvorexant; Thalidomide; Thiazide and Thiazide-Like Diuretics; Tiotropium; Topiramate; Zolpidem

The levels/effects of DiphenhydrAMINE (Systemic) may be increased by: Aclidinium; Brimonidine (Topical); Cannabis; Chloral Betaine; Chlormethiazole; Chlorphenesin Carbamate; Dimethindene (Topical); Doxylamine; Dronabinol; Droperidol; HydrOXYzine; Ipratropium (Oral Inhalation); Kava Kava; Lofexidine; Magnesium Sulfate; Methotrimeprazine; Mianserin; MiFEPRIStone; Minocycline; Nabilone; Oxatomide; Oxomemazine; Perampanel; Pramlintide; Rufinamide; Sodium Oxybate; Tapentadol; Tetrahydrocannabinol; Trimeprazine; Umeclidinium

Decreased Effect

DiphenhydrAMINE (Systemic) may decrease the levels/effects of: Acetylcholinesterase Inhibitors; Benzylpenicilloyl Polylysine; Betahistine; Gastrointestinal Agents (Prokinetic); Hyaluronidase; Itopride; Levosulpiride; Nitroglycerin; Secretin

The levels/effects of DiphenhydrAMINE (Systemic) may be decreased by: Acetylcholinesterase Inhibitors; Amphetamines

Dietary Considerations Some products may contain sodium and/or phenylalanine.

Pharmacodynamics/Kinetics

Duration of Action

Histamine-induced wheal suppression: ≤10 hours (Simons, 1990)

Histamine-induced flare suppression: ≤12 hours (Simons, 1990)

Half-life Elimination Children: 5 hours (range: 4 to 7 hours); Adults: 9 hours (range: 7 to 12 hours); Elderly: 13.5 hours (range: 9 to 18 hours) (Blyden, 1986; Simons, 1990)

Time to Peak Serum: ~2 hours (Blyden, 1986; Simons, 1990)

Pregnancy Risk Factor B

Pregnancy Considerations Adverse events have not been observed in animal reproduction studies. Diphenhydramine crosses the placenta (Miller 2000; Parkin 1974). In general, the use of first generation antihistamines immediately before parturition may cause respiratory depression in the newborn (Zuberbier 2014). Diphenhydramine may be used for the treatment of allergic conditions in pregnant women when a first generation antihistamine is indicated (Babalola 2013; Murase 2014; Zuberbier 2014). Antihistamines are not recommended for treatment of pruritus associated with intrahepatic cholestasis in pregnancy (Ambros-Rudolph 2011; Kremer 2014).

Breastfeeding Considerations Breastfeeding is contraindicated by the manufacturer.

Diphenhydramine is present in breast milk (Rindi 1951).

Drowsiness and irritability have been reported in breastfed infants exposed to antihistamines; of these effects, drowsiness was reported in infants exposed to diphenhydramine (Ito 1993). The manufacturer warns that premature infants and newborns have a higher risk of intolerance to antihistamines. In general, if a breastfed infant is exposed to a first generation antihistamine via breast milk, they should be monitored for irritability or drowsiness (Butler 2014).

When treatment with an antihistamine is needed in breastfeeding women, second generation antihistamines are preferred (Butler 2014; Powell 2015; Zuberbier 2014).

Antihistamines may decrease maternal serum prolactin concentrations when administered prior to the establishment of lactation (Messinis 1985).

Dosage Forms Considerations Dicopanol FusePaq is a compounding kit for the preparation of an oral suspension. Refer to manufacturer's labeling for compounding instructions.

Dosage Forms

Capsule, Oral:

Allergy Relief [OTC]: 25 mg
Banophen [OTC]: 25 mg, 50 mg
Benadryl Allergy [OTC]: 25 mg
Benadryl Dye-Free Allergy [OTC]: 25 mg
Diphenhist [OTC]: 25 mg
Genahist [OTC]: 25 mg
Geri-Dryl [OTC]: 25 mg
GoodSense Allergy Relief [OTC]: 25 mg
Ormir [OTC]: 50 mg
Pharbedryl [OTC]: 25 mg, 50 mg, 50 mg
Q-Dryl [OTC]: 25 mg
ZzzQuil [OTC]: 25 mg
Generic: 25 mg, 50 mg

Elixir, Oral:

Altaryl [OTC]: 12.5 mg/5 mL (120 mL, 480 mL, 3840 mL)
Generic: 12.5 mg/5 mL (5 mL, 10 mL)

Liquid, Oral:

Allergy Relief Childrens [OTC]: 12.5 mg/5 mL (118 mL, 480 mL)
Banophen [OTC]: 12.5 mg/5 mL (118 mL, 473 mL)
Benadryl Allergy Childrens [OTC]: 12.5 mg/5 mL (118 mL, 236 mL)

Diphenhist [OTC]: 12.5 mg/5 mL (118 mL, 473 mL)
Naramin [OTC]: 12.5 mg/5 mL (5 mL)
PediaCare Childrens Allergy [OTC]: 12.5 mg/5 mL (118 mL)
Q-Dryl [OTC]: 12.5 mg/5 mL (118 mL, 237 mL, 473 mL)
Scot-Tussin Allergy Relief [OTC]: 12.5 mg/5 mL (118.3 mL, 240 mL, 480 mL, 3780 mL)
Siladryl Allergy [OTC]: 12.5 mg/5 mL (118 mL, 237 mL, 473 mL)
Total Allergy Medicine [OTC]: 12.5 mg/5 mL (118 mL)
ZzzQuil [OTC]: 50 mg/30 mL (177 mL, 354 mL)

Solution, Injection:
Generic: 50 mg/mL (1 mL, 10 mL)

Solution, Injection [preservative free]:
Generic: 50 mg/mL (1 mL)

Strip, Oral:
Triaminic Cough/Runny Nose [OTC]: 12.5 mg (14 ea, 16 ea)

Suspension Reconstituted, Oral:
Dicopanol FusePaq: 5 mg/mL (150 mL)
Dicopanol RapidPaq: 5 mg/mL (150 mL)

Syrup, Oral:
Altaryl [OTC]: 12.5 mg/5 mL (120 mL, 480 mL, 3785 mL)
Silphen Cough [OTC]: 12.5 mg/5 mL (118 mL, 237 mL, 473 mL)

Tablet, Oral:
Aler-Dryl [OTC]: 50 mg
Allergy Relief [OTC]: 25 mg
Anti-Hist Allergy [OTC]: 25 mg
Banophen [OTC]: 25 mg
Benadryl Allergy [OTC]: 25 mg
Complete Allergy Medication [OTC]: 25 mg
Complete Allergy Relief [OTC]: 25 mg
Diphen [OTC]: 25 mg
Diphenhist [OTC]: 25 mg
Geri-Dryl [OTC]: 25 mg
Nighttime Sleep Aid [OTC]: 25 mg
Nytol [OTC]: 25 mg
Nytol Maximum Strength [OTC]: 50 mg
Simply Sleep [OTC]: 25 mg
Sleep Tabs [OTC]: 25 mg
Sominex [OTC]: 25 mg
Tetra-Formula Nighttime Sleep [OTC]: 50 mg
Total Allergy [OTC]: 25 mg
Generic: 25 mg

Tablet Chewable, Oral:
Benadryl Allergy Childrens [OTC]: 12.5 mg

Dental Comment 25-50 mg of diphenhydramine orally every 4-6 hours can be used to treat mild dermatologic manifestations of allergic reactions to penicillin and other antibiotics. Diphenhydramine is not recommended as local anesthetic for either infiltration route or nerve block since the vehicle has caused local necrosis upon injection. A 50:50 mixture of diphenhydramine liquid (12.5 mg/5 mL) in Kaopectate® or Maalox® is used as a local application for recurrent aphthous ulcers; swish 15 mL for 2 minutes 4 times/day.

DiphenhydrAMINE (Topical)

(dye fen HYE dra meen)

Brand Names: US Anti-Itch Maximum Strength [OTC]; Anti-Itch [OTC]; Banophen [OTC]; Benadryl Itch Relief [OTC]; Benadryl Itch Stopping [OTC]; Benadryl Maximum Strength [OTC] [DSC]; Itch Relief [OTC]

Brand Names: Canada Benadryl® Cream; Benadryl® Itch Relief Stick; Benadryl® Spray

Pharmacologic Category Ethanolamine Derivative; Histamine H_1 Antagonist; Histamine H_1 Antagonist, First Generation; Topical Skin Product

Use Topically for relief of pain and itching associated with insect bites, minor cuts and burns, or rashes due to poison ivy, poison oak, and poison sumac

Local Anesthetic/Vasoconstrictor Precautions No information available to require special precautions

Effects on Dental Treatment No significant effects or complications reported

Effects on Bleeding No information available to require special precautions

Adverse Reactions Frequency not defined.
Dermatologic: Photosensitivity, rash, urticaria

General Dosage Range Topical: *Children ≥2 years and Adults:* Apply 1% or 2% up to 3-4 times/day

Pregnancy Considerations When administered orally, diphenhydramine crosses the placenta. Diphenhydramine can also be measurable in the serum following topical administration to large areas of the body. Refer to the diphenhydramine (systemic) monograph.

Diphenoxylate and Atropine

(dye fen OKS i late & A troe peen)

Related Information
Atropine (Systemic) *on page 186*
Dentin Hypersensitivity, Acid Erosion, High Caries Index, Management of Alveolar Osteitis, and Xerostomia *on page 1857*

Brand Names: US Lomotil

Brand Names: Canada Lomotil

Pharmacologic Category Antidiarrheal

Use Diarrhea: Adjunctive management of diarrhea

Local Anesthetic/Vasoconstrictor Precautions No information available to require special precautions

Effects on Dental Treatment Key adverse event(s) related to dental treatment: Significant xerostomia (normal salivary flow resumes upon discontinuation).

Effects on Bleeding No information available to require special precautions

Adverse Reactions Frequency not defined.
Cardiovascular: Flushing, tachycardia
Central nervous system: Confusion, depression, dizziness, drowsiness, euphoria, headache, hyperthermia, lethargy, malaise, numbness, restlessness, sedation
Dermatologic: Pruritus, urticaria, xeroderma
Gastrointestinal: Abdominal distress, anorexia, gingival swelling, nausea, pancreatitis, paralytic ileus, toxic megacolon, vomiting, xerostomia
Genitourinary: Urinary retention
Hypersensitivity: Anaphylaxis, angioedema

General Dosage Range Oral:
Children ≥2 years and <13 years (liquid only): Initial: Diphenoxylate 0.3 to 0.4 mg/kg/day in 4 divided doses; Maintenance: Reduce as needed, may be as low as 25% of the initial daily dose
Adults: Initial: Diphenoxylate 5 mg 4 times daily (maximum: 20 mg/day); Maintenance: Reduce as needed, may be as low as 5 mg/day

Mechanism of Action Diphenoxylate inhibits excessive GI motility and GI propulsion; commercial preparations contain a subtherapeutic amount of atropine to discourage abuse

Pharmacodynamics/Kinetics
Onset of Action Within 45 to 60 minutes
Half-life Elimination Diphenoxylate: 2.5 hours; Diphenoxylic acid: 12 to 14 hours
Time to Peak Diphenoxylate: Serum: ~2 hours

Pregnancy Risk Factor C

Pregnancy Considerations Animal reproduction studies have not been conducted with this combination. Refer to individual agents.

Controlled Substance C-V

Dipivefrin (dye PI ve frin)

Brand Names: Canada Ophtho-Dipivefrin™; PMS-Dipivefrin; Propine®

Pharmacologic Category Alpha/Beta Agonist; Ophthalmic Agent, Antiglaucoma; Ophthalmic Agent, Vasoconstrictor

Use Reduces elevated intraocular pressure in chronic open-angle glaucoma; also used to treat ocular hypertension, low tension, and secondary glaucomas

Local Anesthetic/Vasoconstrictor Precautions No information available to require special precautions

Effects on Dental Treatment No significant effects or complications reported

Effects on Bleeding No information available to require special precautions

Adverse Reactions Frequency not defined.

1% to 10%:

Central nervous system: Headache

Ophthalmic: Blepharoconjunctivitis, blurred vision, burning sensation of eyes, cystoid macular edema, eye pain, follicular conjunctivitis, mydriasis, ocular hyperemia, photophobia, stinging of eyes

<1%, postmarketing, and/or case reports: Cardiac arrhythmia, hypertension

General Dosage Range Ophthalmic: *Adults:* Instill 1 drop every 12 hours

Mechanism of Action Dipivefrin is a prodrug of epinephrine which is the active agent that stimulates alpha- and/or beta-adrenergic receptors increasing aqueous humor outflow

Pharmacodynamics/Kinetics

Onset of Action

Ocular pressure: ~30 minutes

Mydriasis: ~30 minutes

Duration of Action

Ocular pressure effect: ≥12 hours

Mydriasis: Several hours

Pregnancy Risk Factor B

Pregnancy Considerations Adverse events have not been observed in animal reproduction studies when administered orally. Systemic adverse events (eg, arrhythmias, hypertension) have been reported following ophthalmic application; use is not recommended in pregnancy (Razeghinejad, 2011).

Dipyridamole (dye peer ID a mole)

Brand Names: US Persantine [DSC]

Brand Names: Canada Apo-Dipyridamole FC; Dipyridamole For Injection; Persantine

Pharmacologic Category Antiplatelet Agent; Vasodilator

Use

Oral: Used with warfarin to decrease thrombosis in patients after artificial heart valve replacement

IV: Diagnostic agent in CAD

Local Anesthetic/Vasoconstrictor Precautions No information available to require special precautions

Effects on Dental Treatment No significant effects or complications reported

Effects on Bleeding Dipyridamole inhibits platelet aggregation and may increase the risk of bleeding.

Adverse Reactions

Oral: Frequency not always defined.

Cardiovascular: Angina pectoris, flushing

Central nervous system: Dizziness (14%), headache (2%)

Dermatologic: Skin rash (2%), pruritus

Gastrointestinal: Abdominal distress (6%), diarrhea, vomiting

Hepatic: Hepatic insufficiency

Postmarketing and/or case reports: Alopecia, arthritis, cholelithiasis, dyspepsia, fatigue, hepatitis, hypersensitivity reaction, hypotension, laryngeal edema, malaise, myalgia, nausea, palpitations, paresthesia, tachycardia, thrombocytopenia

IV:

>10%:

Cardiovascular: Exacerbation of angina pectoris (20%)

Central nervous system: Dizziness (12%), headache (12%)

1% to 10%:

Cardiovascular: ECG abnormality (5% to 8%; ST-T changes, extrasystoles), hypotension (5%), flushing (3%), tachycardia (3%), altered blood pressure (2%), hypertension (2%)

Central nervous system: Pain (3%), fatigue (1%), paresthesia (1%)

Gastrointestinal: Nausea (5%)

Respiratory: Dyspnea (3%)

<1%, postmarketing, and/or case reports (Limited to important or life-threatening): Abdominal pain, arthralgia, ataxia, back pain, bronchospasm, cardiac arrhythmia (ventricular tachycardia, bradycardia, AV block, SVT, atrial fibrillation, asystole), cardiomyopathy, cough, depersonalization, diaphoresis, dysgeusia, dyspepsia, dysphagia, ECG abnormality (unspecified), edema, eructation, flatulence, hypersensitivity reaction, hypertonia, hyperventilation, increased appetite, increased thirst, injection site reaction, leg cramps (intermittent claudication), malaise, mastalgia, muscle rigidity, myalgia, myocardial infarction, orthostatic hypotension, otalgia, palpitations, perineal pain, pharyngitis, pleuritic chest pain, pruritus, renal pain, rhinitis, skin rash, syncope, tenesmus, tinnitus, tremor, urticaria, vertigo, visual disturbance, vomiting, weakness, xerostomia

General Dosage Range

IV: *Adults:* 0.56 mg/kg over 4 minutes (maximum: 70 mg)

Oral: *Children ≥12 years and Adults:* 75 to 100 mg 4 times/day

Mechanism of Action Inhibits the activity of adenosine deaminase and phosphodiesterase, which causes an accumulation of adenosine, adenine nucleotides, and cyclic AMP; these mediators then inhibit platelet aggregation and may cause vasodilation; may also stimulate release of prostacyclin or PGD_2; causes coronary vasodilation

Pharmacodynamics/Kinetics

Half-life Elimination Terminal: 10-12 hours

Time to Peak Serum: 2-2.5 hours

Pregnancy Risk Factor B

Pregnancy Considerations Adverse events have not been observed in animal reproduction studies.

Disopyramide (dye soe PEER a mide)

Related Information

Clinical Risk Related to Drugs Prolonging QT Interval *on page 1772*

Brand Names: US Norpace; Norpace CR

Brand Names: Canada Rythmodan

Pharmacologic Category Antiarrhythmic Agent, Class Ia

Use Life-threatening ventricular arrhythmias (eg, sustained ventricular tachycardia)

Local Anesthetic/Vasoconstrictor Precautions Disopyramide is one of the drugs confirmed to prolong the QT interval and is accepted as having a risk of causing torsade de pointes. The risk of drug-induced torsade de pointes is extremely low when a single QT interval prolonging drug is prescribed. In terms of epinephrine, it is not known what effect vasoconstrictors in the local anesthetic regimen will have in patients with a known history of congenital prolonged QT interval or in patients taking any medication that prolongs the QT interval. Until more information is obtained, it is suggested that the clinician consult with the physician prior to the use of a vasoconstrictor in suspected patients, and that the vasoconstrictor (epinephrine, mepivacaine and levonordefrin [Carbocaine® 2% with Neo-Cobefrin®]) be used with caution.

Effects on Dental Treatment Key adverse event(s) related to dental treatment: Xerostomia (normal salivary flow resumes upon discontinuation).

Effects on Bleeding No information available to require special precautions

Adverse Reactions Frequency not always defined. The most common adverse effects are related to cholinergic blockade. The most serious adverse effects of disopyramide are hypotension and cardiac failure.

>10%:

Gastrointestinal: Xerostomia (32%), constipation (11%)

Genitourinary: Urinary hesitancy (14% to 23%)

1% to 10%:

Cardiovascular: Cardiac conduction disturbance, cardiac failure, chest pain, edema, hypotension, syncope

Central nervous system: Dizziness, fatigue, headache, malaise, myasthenia, nervousness

Dermatologic: Generalized dermatosis, pruritus, skin rash

Endocrine & metabolic: Hypokalemia, increased serum cholesterol, increased serum triglycerides, weight gain

Gastrointestinal: Abdominal distention, anorexia, bloating, diarrhea, flatulence, nausea, vomiting

Genitourinary: Impotence (1% to 3%), urinary frequency, urinary retention, urinary urgency

Neuromuscular & skeletal: Myalgia

Ophthalmic: Blurred vision, xerophthalmia

Respiratory: Dry throat, dyspnea

<1%, postmarketing, and/or case reports: Agranulocytosis, atrioventricular block, cardiac arrhythmia (new or worsened; proarrhythmic effect), cholestatic jaundice, decreased hematocrit, decreased hemoglobin, depression, dysuria, fever, gynecomastia, hepatotoxicity, hypoglycemia, increased blood urea nitrogen, increased serum creatinine, increased serum transaminases, insomnia, mydriasis, numbness, paresthesia, peripheral neuropathy, psychosis, psychotic reaction, respiratory distress, skin blister (toxic), systemic lupus erythematosus (rare; generally in patients previously receiving procainamide), thrombocytopenia, tingling sensation

General Dosage Range Dosage adjustment recommended in patients with hepatic or renal impairment

Oral:

Controlled release:

Adults <50 kg: 200 mg every 12 hours

Adults ≥50 kg: 300 mg every 12 hours

Immediate release:

Children <1 year: 10 to 30 mg/kg/day in 4 divided doses

Children 1 to 4 years: 10 to 20 mg/kg/day in 4 divided doses

Children 4 to 12 years: 10 to 15 mg/kg/day in 4 divided doses

Children 12 to 18 years: 6 to 15 mg/kg/day in 4 divided doses

Adults <50 kg: 100 mg every 6 hours

Adults ≥50 kg: 150 mg every 6 hours

Mechanism of Action Class Ia antiarrhythmic: Decreases myocardial excitability and conduction velocity; reduces disparity in refractory between normal and infarcted myocardium; possesses anticholinergic, peripheral vasoconstrictive, and negative inotropic effects

Pharmacodynamics/Kinetics

Onset of Action 0.5-3.5 hours

Duration of Action Immediate release: 1.5-8.5 hours

Half-life Elimination Children: 3.15 hours; Adults: 4-10 hours (prolonged with heart failure and hepatic or renal impairment)

Time to Peak Serum: Immediate release: Within 2 hours; Controlled release: 4-7 hours

Pregnancy Risk Factor C

Pregnancy Considerations Adverse events have been observed in animal reproduction studies. Disopyramide levels have been reported in human fetal blood. Disopyramide may stimulate contractions in pregnant women. In a case report, disopyramide use in the third trimester resulted in painful uterine contractions after the first dose and hemorrhage after the second dose (Abbi, 1999).

Dental Comment See Local Anesthetic/Vasoconstrictor Precautions

Disulfiram (dye SUL fi ram)

Brand Names: US Antabuse

Pharmacologic Category Aldehyde Dehydrogenase Inhibitor

Use Alcoholism: Management of chronic alcoholism

Local Anesthetic/Vasoconstrictor Precautions No information available to require special precautions

Effects on Dental Treatment No significant effects or complications reported

Effects on Bleeding No information available to require special precautions

Adverse Reactions Frequency not defined.

Central nervous system: Aftertaste (metallic or garlic-like), drowsiness, fatigue, headache, peripheral neuritis, peripheral neuropathy, polyneuropathy, psychosis

Dermatologic: Acneiform eruption, allergic dermatitis, skin rash

Genitourinary: Impotence

Hepatic: Cholestatic hepatitis, fulminant hepatitis, hepatic failure (multiple case reports)

Ophthalmic: Optic neuritis

General Dosage Range Oral: *Adults:* Initial: 500 mg once daily; Maintenance: 125 to 500 mg once daily (maximum: 500 mg/day)

Mechanism of Action Disulfiram is a thiuram derivative which blocks the oxidation of alcohol at the acetaldehyde stage. When taken concomitantly with alcohol, there is an increase in serum acetaldehyde levels. High acetaldehyde causes uncomfortable symptoms including flushing, throbbing in head and neck, nausea, vomiting, diaphoresis, thirst, palpitations, chest pain, dyspnea, hyperventilation, tachycardia, syncope, weakness, blurred vision, confusion, vertigo, and hypotension. This reaction is the basis for disulfiram use in post-withdrawal long-term care of alcoholism.

Pharmacodynamics/Kinetics

Onset of Action Full effect: 12 hours

Duration of Action ~1 to 2 weeks after last dose

Pregnancy Considerations Safety in pregnancy has not been established; there is limited data on maternal use during pregnancy (Reitnauer,1997).

DOBUTamine (doe BYOO ta meen)

Brand Names: Canada Dobutamine Injection, USP; Dobutrex

Pharmacologic Category Adrenergic Agonist Agent; Inotrope

Use

Cardiac decompensation: Short-term management of patients with cardiac decompensation

American College of Cardiology/American Heart Association heart failure (HF) guideline recommendations (ACCF/AHA [Yancy 2013]): To maintain systemic perfusion and preserve end-organ performance in patients with cardiogenic shock; bridge therapy in stage D HF unresponsive to guideline-directed medical therapy and device therapy in patients awaiting heart transplant or mechanical circulatory support; short-term management of hospitalized patients with severe systolic dysfunction presenting with low blood pressure and significantly depressed cardiac output; long-term management (palliative therapy) in select patients with stage D HF unresponsive to guideline-directed medical therapy and device therapy who are not candidates for heart transplant or mechanical circulatory support.

Local Anesthetic/Vasoconstrictor Precautions No information available to require special precautions

Effects on Dental Treatment No significant effects or complications reported

Effects on Bleeding No information available to require special precautions

Adverse Reactions Incidence of adverse events is not always reported.

Cardiovascular: Ventricular premature contractions (5%; dose related), angina pectoris (1% to 3%), chest pain (1% to 3%; nonspecific), palpitations (1% to 3%), hypotension, increased blood pressure, increased heart rate, localized phlebitis, ventricular ectopy (increased)

Central nervous system: Headache (1% to 3%), paresthesia

Dermatologic: Skin necrosis (isolated cases)

Endocrine & metabolic: Decreased serum potassium (slight)

Gastrointestinal: Nausea (1% to 3%)

Hematologic & oncologic: Thrombocytopenia (isolated cases)

Local: Local inflammation, local pain (from infiltration)

Neuromuscular & skeletal: Leg cramps (mild)

Respiratory: Dyspnea (1% to 3%)

Miscellaneous: Fever (1% to 3%)

General Dosage Range IV: *Children and Adults:* 0.5 to 20 mcg/kg/minute (maximum: 40 mcg/kg/minute)

Mechanism of Action Dobutamine, a racemic mixture, stimulates myocardial $beta_1$-adrenergic receptors primarily by the (+) enantiomer and some $alpha_1$ receptor agonism by the (-) enantiomer, resulting in increased contractility and heart rate, and stimulates both $beta_2$- and $alpha_1$-receptors in the vasculature. Although $beta_2$ and $alpha_1$ adrenergic receptors are also activated, the effects of $beta_2$ receptor activation may equally offset or be slightly greater than the effects of $alpha_1$ stimulation, resulting in some vasodilation in addition to the inotropic and chronotropic actions (Leier 1988; Majerus 1989; Ruffolo 1987). Lowers central venous pressure and wedge pressure, but has little effect on pulmonary vascular resistance (Leier 1977; Leier 1978).

Pharmacodynamics/Kinetics

Onset of Action IV: 1-10 minutes; Peak effect: 10-20 minutes

Half-life Elimination 2 minutes

Pregnancy Risk Factor B

Pregnancy Considerations Adverse events have not been observed in animal reproduction studies. Dobutamine should not be used as a diagnostic agent during stress testing in pregnant women (Regitz-Zagrosek 2011). Medications used for the treatment of cardiac arrest in pregnancy are the same as in the non-pregnant woman. Appropriate medications should not be withheld due to concerns of fetal teratogenicity. Dobutamine use during the post-resuscitation phase may be considered; however, the effects of inotropic support on the fetus should also be considered. Doses and indications should follow current Advanced Cardiovascular Life Support (ACLS) guidelines (Jeejeebhoy [AHA] 2015).

DOCEtaxel (doe se TAKS el)

Brand Names: US Docefrez [DSC]; Taxotere

Brand Names: Canada Docetaxel for Injection; Docetaxel Injection; Taxotere

Pharmacologic Category Antineoplastic Agent, Antimicrotubular; Antineoplastic Agent, Taxane Derivative

Use

Docefrez:

Breast cancer: Treatment of breast cancer (locally advanced/metastatic) after prior chemotherapy failure

Non-small cell lung cancer: Treatment of locally advanced or metastatic non–small cell lung cancer (NSCLC) after prior platinum-based chemotherapy failure; treatment of previously untreated unresectable locally advanced or metastatic NSCLC (in combination with cisplatin)

Prostate cancer: Treatment of hormone-refractory metastatic prostate cancer (in combination with prednisone)

Taxotere (and various generic brands):

Breast cancer: Treatment of breast cancer (locally advanced/metastatic) after prior chemotherapy failure; adjuvant treatment (in combination with doxorubicin and cyclophosphamide) of operable node-positive breast cancer

Gastric cancer: Treatment of advanced gastric adenocarcinoma, including gastroesophageal junction adenocarcinoma (in combination with cisplatin and fluorouracil) in patients who have not received prior chemotherapy for advanced disease

Head and neck cancer: Treatment (induction) of locally advanced squamous cell head and neck cancer (in combination with cisplatin and fluorouracil)

NSCLC: Treatment of locally advanced or metastatic NSCLC after failure of prior platinum-based chemotherapy; treatment of previously untreated unresectable locally advanced or metastatic NSCLC (in combination with cisplatin)

Prostate cancer: Treatment of androgen-independent (hormone refractory) metastatic prostate cancer (in combination with prednisone)

Local Anesthetic/Vasoconstrictor Precautions No information available to require special precautions

Effects on Dental Treatment Key adverse event(s) related to dental treatment: Mucositis, stomatitis, and taste perversion.

Effects on Bleeding Thrombocytopenia (8% to 14%) and bleeding episodes have been reported. A medical consult is recommended.

Adverse Reactions Percentages reported for docetaxel monotherapy; frequency may vary depending on diagnosis, dose, liver function, prior treatment, and premedication.

>10%:

Central nervous system: Central nervous system toxicity (20% to 58%; severe: ≤6%; including neuropathy)

Dermatologic: Alopecia (56% to 76%), dermatological reaction (20% to 48%; severe: ≤5%), nail disease (11% to 41%)

Endocrine & metabolic: Fluid retention (includes edema and effusion; 13% to 60%; severe: 7% to 9%; dose dependent)

Gastrointestinal: Stomatitis (19% to 53%; severe 1% to 8%), diarrhea (23% to 43%; severe: 5% to 6%), nausea (34% to 42%), vomiting (22% to 23%)

Hematologic & oncologic: Neutropenia (84% to 99%; grade 4: 75% to 86%; nadir [median]: 7 days, duration [severe neutropenia]: 7 days; dose dependent), leukopenia (84% to 99%; grade 4: 32% to 44%), anemia (65% to 97%; dose dependent; grades 3/4: 8% to 9%), thrombocytopenia (8% to 14%; grade 4: 1%; dose dependent), febrile neutropenia (≤14%; dose dependent)

Hepatic: Increased serum transaminases (4% to 19%)

Hypersensitivity: Hypersensitivity (1% to 21%; with premedication 15%)

Infection: Infection (1% to 34%; dose dependent)

Neuromuscular & skeletal: Weakness (53% to 66%; severe: ≤18%), myalgia (3% to 23%), neuromuscular reaction (16%)

Respiratory: Pulmonary reaction (41%)

Miscellaneous: Fever (31% to 35%)

1% to 10%:

Cardiovascular: Decreased left ventricular ejection fraction (8%), hypotension (3%)

Central nervous system: Peripheral motor neuropathy (4%; severe; mainly distal extremity weakness)

Gastrointestinal: Dysgeusia (6%)

Hepatic: Increased serum bilirubin (9%), increased serum alkaline phosphatase (4% to 7%)

Infection: Severe infection (6%)

Local: Infusion site reactions (4%, including hyperpigmentation, inflammation, redness, dryness, phlebitis, extravasation, swelling of the vein)

Neuromuscular and skeletal: Arthralgia (3% to 9%)

<1%, postmarketing, and/or case reports: Abdominal pain, acute myelocytic leukemia, acute respiratory distress, alopecia (permanent), anaphylactic shock, anorexia, ascites, atrial fibrillation, atrial flutter, back pain, bronchospasm, cardiac arrhythmia, cardiac tamponade, chest pain, chest tightness, chills, colitis, confusion, conjunctivitis, constipation, cystoid macular edema, deep vein thrombosis, dehydration, disease of the lacrimal apparatus (duct obstruction), disseminated intravascular coagulation, drug fever, duodenal ulcer, dyspnea, ECG abnormality, epiphora (more common with weekly administration [Kintzel 2006]), erythema multiforme, esophagitis, flushing, gastrointestinal hemorrhage, gastrointestinal obstruction, gastrointestinal perforation, hearing loss, hemorrhagic diathesis, hepatitis, hypertension, hyponatremia, intestinal obstruction, interstitial pulmonary disease, ischemic colitis, lacrimation, localized erythema of the extremities, loss of consciousness (transient), lymphedema (peripheral), multiorgan failure, myelodysplastic syndrome, myocardial infarction, neutropenic enterocolitis, ototoxicity, pain, palmar-plantar erythrodysesthesia, pneumonia, pneumonitis, pruritus, pulmonary edema, pulmonary embolism, pulmonary fibrosis, radiation pneumonitis, radiation recall phenomenon, renal failure, renal insufficiency, respiratory failure, skin changes (scleroderma-like), seizure, sepsis, sinus tachycardia, skin rash, Stevens-Johnson syndrome, subacute cutaneous lupus erythematosus, syncope, tachycardia, thrombophlebitis, toxic epidermal necrolysis, unstable angina pectoris, visual disturbance (transient)

General Dosage Range Dosage adjustment recommended in patients with hepatic impairment, on concomitant therapy, or who develop toxicities.

IV: *Adults:* 60 to 100 mg/m^2 every 3 weeks

Mechanism of Action Docetaxel promotes the assembly of microtubules from tubulin dimers, and inhibits the depolymerization of tubulin which stabilizes microtubules in the cell. This results in inhibition of DNA, RNA, and protein synthesis. Most activity occurs during the M phase of the cell cycle.

Pharmacodynamics/Kinetics

Half-life Elimination Terminal: ~11 hours

Pregnancy Risk Factor D

Pregnancy Considerations Adverse events have been observed in animal reproduction studies. An *ex vivo* human placenta perfusion model illustrated that docetaxel crossed the placenta at term. Placental transfer was low and affected by the presence of albumin; higher albumin concentrations resulted in lower docetaxel placental transfer (Berveiller, 2012). Some pharmacokinetic properties of docetaxel may be altered in pregnant women (van Hasselt 2014). Women of childbearing potential should avoid becoming pregnant during therapy. A pregnancy registry is available for all cancers diagnosed during pregnancy at Cooper Health (877-635-4499).

Docosanol (doe KOE san ole)

Related Sample Prescriptions

Viral Infections - Sample Prescriptions *on page 40*

Brand Names: US Abreva [OTC]

Generic Availability (US) No

Pharmacologic Category Antiviral Agent, Topical

Dental Use Treatment of herpes simplex of the face or lips

Use Cold sore/fever blister: Treatment of cold sores/fever blisters on the face or lips.

Local Anesthetic/Vasoconstrictor Precautions No information available to require special precautions

Effects on Dental Treatment No significant effects or complications reported (see Dental Comment)

Effects on Bleeding No information available to require special precautions

Adverse Reactions Frequency not defined.

Hypersensitivity: Hypersensitivity reaction

Dental Usual Dosage Herpes simplex (face/lips): Children ≥12 years and Adults: Topical: Apply 5 times/day to affected area of face or lips. Start at first sign of cold sore or fever blister and continue until healed.

Dosing

Adult & Geriatric

Cold sore/fever blister: Topical: Apply 5 times daily to affected area of face or lips. Start at first sign of cold sore or fever blister and continue until healed. If not healed within 10 days, discontinue use and contact health care provider.

Pediatric

Cold sore/fever blister: Children ≥12 years and Adolescents: Refer to adult dosing.

Renal Impairment There are no dosage adjustments provided in the manufacturer's labeling.

Hepatic Impairment There are no dosage adjustments provided in the manufacturer's labeling.

Mechanism of Action Prevents viral entry and replication at the cellular level

Contraindications OTC labeling: When used for self-medication, do not use if you have hypersensitivity to docosanol or any component of the formulation

Warnings/Precautions For external use only; do not apply to inside of mouth or around eyes. Apply at the first sign of cold sore/fever blister (tingle); early treatment ensures best results. Do not share product with others. Discontinue use and contact a health care provider if the condition gets worse or is not healed within 10 days. Severe allergic reactions (eg, hives, facial swelling, wheezing/difficulty breathing, rash, shock) may occur with use; discontinue and seek medical attention immediately if an allergic reaction occurs.

Some dosage forms may contain benzyl alcohol; large amounts of benzyl alcohol (≥99 mg/kg/day) have been associated with a potentially fatal toxicity ("gasping syndrome") in neonates; the "gasping syndrome" consists of metabolic acidosis, respiratory distress, gasping respirations, CNS dysfunction (including convulsions, intracranial hemorrhage), hypotension and cardiovascular collapse (AAP ["Inactive" 1997]; CDC, 1982); some data suggests that benzoate displaces bilirubin from protein binding sites (Ahlfors, 2001); avoid or use dosage forms containing benzyl alcohol with caution in neonates. See manufacturer's labeling.

Drug Interactions

Metabolism/Transport Effects None known.

Avoid Concomitant Use There are no known interactions where it is recommended to avoid concomitant use.

Increased Effect/Toxicity There are no known significant interactions involving an increase in effect.

Decreased Effect

Docosanol may decrease the levels/effects of: Talimogene Laherparepvec

Dosage Forms

Cream, External:

Abreva [OTC]: 10% (2 g)

Dental Comment Wash hands before and after applying cream. Begin treatment at first tingle of cold sore or fever blister. Rub into area gently, but completely. Do not apply directly to inside of mouth or around eyes. Contact healthcare provider if sore gets worse or does not heal within 10 days. Do not share this product with others, may spread infection. Notify healthcare professional if pregnant or breastfeeding.

Docusate (DOK yoo sate)

Brand Names: US Colace Clear [OTC]; Colace [OTC]; D.O.S. [OTC] [DSC]; Diocto [OTC]; DocQLace [OTC]; Docu Soft [OTC]; Docu [OTC]; Docuprene [OTC]; Docusil [OTC]; DocuSol Kids [OTC]; DocuSol Mini [OTC]; DOK [OTC]; Dulcolax Stool Softener [OTC]; Enemeez Mini [OTC]; Healthy Mama Move It Along [OTC]; Kao-Tin [OTC]; KS Stool Softener [OTC]; Laxa Basic [OTC]; Pedia-Lax [OTC]; Promolaxin [OTC]; Silace [OTC]; Sof-Lax [OTC]; Stool Softener Laxative DC [OTC] [DSC]; Stool Softener [OTC]; Sur-Q-Lax [OTC] [DSC]; Vacuant Mini-Enema [OTC] [DSC]

Brand Names: Canada Apo-Docusate Calcium [OTC]; Apo-Docusate Sodium [OTC]; Calax [OTC]; Colace [OTC]; Docusate Sodium Odan [OTC]; Dom-Docusate Sodium [OTC]; Dosolax [OTC]; Dulcocomfort Stool Softener [OTC]; Euro-Docusate C [OTC]; Jamp-Docusate [OTC]; Novo-Docusate Calcium [OTC]; Novo-Docusate Sodium [OTC]; PHL-Docusate Sodium [OTC]; PMS-Docusate Calcium [OTC]; PMS-Docusate Sodium [OTC]; ratio-Docusate Sodium [OTC]; Selax [OTC]; Silace [OTC]; Sirop Docusate De Sodium [OTC]; Soflax C [OTC]; Soflax [OTC]; Taro-Docusate [OTC]; Teva-Docusate Calcium [OTC]; Teva-Docusate Sodium [OTC]

Pharmacologic Category Stool Softener

Use Stool softener: Prevention of straining during defecation and constipation associated with hard, dry stools; relief of occasional constipation

Local Anesthetic/Vasoconstrictor Precautions No information available to require special precautions

Effects on Dental Treatment Key adverse event(s) related to dental treatment: Throat irritation.

Effects on Bleeding No information available to require special precautions

Adverse Reactions 1% to 10%: Respiratory: Throat irritation (liquid)

General Dosage Range

Oral:

Children 2 to <12 years: 50 to 150 mg once daily or in divided doses

Children ≥12 years, Adolescents, and Adults: 50 to 360 mg once daily or in divided doses

Rectal:

Children 2 to <12 years: 1 enema (100 or 283 mg) daily

Children ≥12 years, Adolescents, and Adults: 1 to 3 enemas (283 to 849 mg) daily

Mechanism of Action Reduces surface tension of the oil-water interface of the stool resulting in enhanced incorporation of water and fat allowing for stool softening (Roering, 2010)

Pharmacodynamics/Kinetics

Onset of Action Oral: 12 to 72 hours; Rectal: 2 to 15 minutes

Pregnancy Considerations The short-term use of docusate for the treatment of constipation is generally considered safe during pregnancy (Mahadevan 2006). Hypomagnesemia was reported in a newborn following chronic maternal overuse throughout pregnancy (Schindler 1984).

Dofetilide (doe FET il ide)

Related Information

Cardiovascular Diseases *on page 1752*

Clinical Risk Related to Drugs Prolonging QT Interval *on page 1772*

Brand Names: US Tikosyn

Pharmacologic Category Antiarrhythmic Agent, Class III

Use Atrial fibrillation/atrial flutter: Maintenance of normal sinus rhythm in patients with chronic atrial fibrillation/atrial flutter of longer than 1-week duration who have been converted to normal sinus rhythm; conversion of atrial fibrillation and atrial flutter to normal sinus rhythm.

Local Anesthetic/Vasoconstrictor Precautions Dofetilide is one of the drugs confirmed to prolong the QT interval and is accepted as having a risk of causing torsade de pointes. The risk of drug-induced torsade de pointes is extremely low when a single QT interval prolonging drug is prescribed. In terms of epinephrine, it is not known what effect vasoconstrictors in the local anesthetic regimen will have in patients with a known history of congenital prolonged QT interval or in patients taking any medication that prolongs the QT interval. Until more information is obtained, it is suggested that the clinician consult with the physician prior to the use of a vasoconstrictor in suspected patients, and that the vasoconstrictor (epinephrine, mepivacaine and levonordefrin [Carbocaine® 2% with Neo-Cobefrin®]) be used with caution.

Effects on Dental Treatment No significant effects or complications reported

Effects on Bleeding No information available to require special precautions

Adverse Reactions

>10%:

- Cardiovascular: Torsades de pointes (patients receiving doses in excess of those recommended: ≤11%; cardiac failure patients: 3%; patients with recent myocardial infarction: <1%; occurs most frequently within the first 3 days of therapy)
- Central nervous system: Headache (11%)

1% to 10%:

- Cardiovascular: Chest pain (10%), ventricular fibrillation (≤5%), ventricular tachycardia (3% to 4%), bradycardia (≤2%), cardiac arrest (≤2%), cerebral ischemia (≤2%), cerebrovascular accident (≤2%), edema (≤2%), myocardial infarction (≤2%), syncope (≤2%), atrioventricular block (<2%), heart block (1%)
- Central nervous system: Dizziness (8%), insomnia (4%), facial paralysis (≤2%), flaccid paralysis (≤2%), migraine (≤2%), paralysis (≤2%), paresthesia (≤2%)
- Dermatologic: Skin rash (3%)
- Gastrointestinal: Nausea (5%), abdominal pain (3%), diarrhea (3%)
- Hepatic: Hepatotoxicity (≤2%), hepatic injury (<2%)
- Hypersensitivity: Angioedema (≤2%)
- Neuromuscular & skeletal: Back pain (3%)
- Respiratory: Respiratory tract infection (7%), dyspnea (6%), flu-like symptoms (4%), increased cough (≤2%), cough (<2%)
- Miscellaneous: Accidental injury (3%), surgery (3%)

<1%, postmarketing, and/or case reports: Bundle branch block

General Dosage Range Dosage adjustment required in patients with renal impairment

Oral: *Adults:* Initial: 500 mcg twice daily; Maintenance: 125 to 500 mcg twice daily **or** 125 mcg once daily (maximum: 500 mcg twice daily).

Mechanism of Action Vaughan Williams Class III antiarrhythmic activity. Blockade of the cardiac ion channel carrying the rapid component of the delayed rectifier potassium current. Dofetilide has no effect on sodium channels, adrenergic alpha-receptors, or adrenergic beta-receptors. It increases the monophasic action potential duration due to delayed repolarization. The increase in the QT interval is a function of prolongation of both effective and functional refractory periods in the His-Purkinje system and the ventricles. Changes in cardiac conduction velocity and sinus node function have not been observed in patients with or without structural heart disease. PR and QRS width remain the same in patients with preexisting heart block and or sick sinus syndrome.

Pharmacodynamics/Kinetics

Half-life Elimination ~10 hours; prolonged with renal impairment

Time to Peak Serum: Fasting: 2 to 3 hours

Pregnancy Risk Factor C

Pregnancy Considerations Adverse events have been observed in animal reproduction studies.

Dental Comment See Local Anesthetic/Vasoconstrictor Precautions

Dolasetron (dol A se tron)

Related Information

Clinical Risk Related to Drugs Prolonging QT Interval *on page 1772*

Brand Names: US Anzemet

Pharmacologic Category Antiemetic; Selective 5-HT_3 Receptor Antagonist

Use

Injection: Prevention and treatment of postoperative nausea and vomiting in adults and children ≥2 years

Oral: Prevention of nausea and vomiting associated with moderately emetogenic cancer chemotherapy (initial and repeat courses) in adults and children ≥2 years

Local Anesthetic/Vasoconstrictor Precautions Dolasetron is one of the drugs confirmed to prolong the QT interval and is accepted as having a risk of causing torsade de pointes. The risk of drug-induced torsade de pointes is extremely low when a single QT interval prolonging drug is prescribed. In terms of epinephrine, it is not known what effect vasoconstrictors in the local anesthetic regimen will have in patients with a known history of congenital prolonged QT interval or in patients taking any medication that prolongs the QT interval. Until more information is obtained, it is suggested that the clinician consult with the physician prior to the use of a vasoconstrictor in suspected patients, and that the vasoconstrictor (epinephrine, mepivacaine and levonordefrin [Carbocaine® 2% with Neo-Cobefrin®]) be used with caution.

Effects on Dental Treatment Key adverse event(s) related to dental treatment: Taste alterations.

Effects on Bleeding No information available to require special precautions

Adverse Reactions Adverse events may vary according to indication and route of administration.

>10%: Central nervous system: Headache (oral: 18% to 23%; IV: 9%)

1% to 10%:
Cardiovascular: Bradycardia (4% to 5%; may be severe after IV administration), tachycardia (≤3%), edema (<2%), facial edema (<2%), flushing (<2%), hypotension (<2%; may be severe after IV administration), orthostatic hypotension (<2%), peripheral edema (<2%), peripheral ischemia (<2%), phlebitis (<2%), sinus arrhythmia (<2%), thrombophlebitis (<2%)
Central nervous system: Fatigue (oral: 3% to 6%), dizziness (1% to 6%), pain (≤3%), abnormal dreams (<2%), agitation (<2%), anxiety (<2%), ataxia (<2%), chills (≤2%), confusion (<2%), depersonalization (<2%), paresthesia (<2%), shivering (≤2%), sleep disorder (<2%), twitching (<2%), vertigo (<2%)
Dermatologic: Diaphoresis (<2%), skin rash (<2%), urticaria (<2%)
Endocrine & metabolic: Increased gamma-glutamyl transferase (<2%)
Gastrointestinal: Diarrhea (oral: 2% to 5%), dyspepsia (≤3%), abdominal pain (<2%), anorexia (<2%), constipation (<2%), dysgeusia (<2%), pancreatitis (<2%)
Genitourinary: Dysuria (<2%), hematuria (<2%)
Hematologic and oncologic: Anemia (<2%), hematoma (<2%), prolonged prothrombin time (<2%), prolonged partial thromboplastin time (<2%), purpura (<2%), thrombocytopenia (<2%)
Hepatic: Hyperbilirubinemia (<2%), increased serum alkaline phosphatase (<2%)
Hypersensitivity: Anaphylaxis (<2%)
Local: Burning sensation at injection site (IV: <2%), pain at injection site (IV: <2%)
Neuromuscular & skeletal: Arthralgia (<2%), myalgia (<2%), tremor (<2%)
Ophthalmic: Photophobia (<2%), visual disturbance (<2%)
Otic: Tinnitus (<2%)
Renal: Acute renal failure (<2%), polyuria (<2%)
Respiratory: Bronchospasm (<2%), dyspnea (<2%), epistaxis (<2%)
<1%, postmarketing, and/or case reports: Abnormal T waves on ECG, appearance of U waves on ECG, atrial fibrillation, atrial flutter, atrioventricular block, bundle branch block (left and right), cardiac arrest, chest pain, extrasystoles (APCs or VPCs), increased serum ALT (transient), increased serum AST (transient), ischemic heart disease, nodal arrhythmia, palpitations, prolongation P-R interval on ECG (dose dependent), prolonged Q-T interval on ECG, serotonin syndrome, slow R wave progression, ST segment changes on ECG, syncope (may be severe after IV administration), torsades de pointes, ventricular arrhythmia, ventricular fibrillation cardiac arrest (IV), ventricular tachycardia (IV), wide complex tachycardia (IV), widened QRS complex on ECG (dose-dependent)

General Dosage Range

IV:

Children 2-16 years: 0.35 mg/kg as a single dose (maximum: 12.5 mg/dose)

Adults: 12.5 mg as a single dose (maximum: 12.5 mg)

Oral:

Children 2-16 years: 1.2 or 1.8 mg/kg as a single dose (maximum: 100 mg/dose)

Adults: 100 mg as single dose

Mechanism of Action Selective serotonin receptor (5-HT_3) antagonist, blocking serotonin both peripherally (primary site of action) and centrally at the chemoreceptor trigger zone

Pharmacodynamics/Kinetics

Half-life Elimination
Dolasetron: IV: ≤10 minutes
Hydrodolasetron:
Oral: Children: 5.5 hours; Adolescents: 6.4 hours; Adults: 8.1 hours
IV: Children: 4.8 hours; Adults: 7.3 hours
Severe renal impairment: 11 hours
Severe hepatic impairment: 11 hours

Time to Peak Hydrodolasetron: IV: 0.6 hours; Oral: ~1 hour

Pregnancy Risk Factor B

Pregnancy Considerations Adverse events have not been observed in animal reproduction studies.

Dental Comment See Local Anesthetic/Vasoconstrictor Precautions

Dolutegravir (doe loo TEG ra vir)

Brand Names: US Tivicay

Brand Names: Canada Tivicay

Pharmacologic Category Antiretroviral, Integrase Inhibitor (Anti-HIV)

Use

HIV-1 infection: Treatment of HIV-1 infection in combination with other antiretroviral agents in adult and pediatric patients weighing at least 30 kg.

Limitations of use: Use in integrase strand transfer inhibitor (INSTI)-experienced patients should be guided by the number and type of baseline INSTI substitutions. Efficacy with 50 mg twice daily is reduced in patients with an INSTI-resistance Q148 substitution plus 2 or more additional INSTI-resistance substitutions, including T66A, L74I/M, E138A/K/T, G140S/A/C, Y143R/C/H, E157Q, G163S/E/K/Q, or G193E/R.

Local Anesthetic/Vasoconstrictor Precautions No information available to require special precautions

Effects on Dental Treatment No significant effects or complications reported

Effects on Bleeding No information available to require special precautions

Adverse Reactions Adverse reactions reported with combination therapy.
>10%:
Endocrine & metabolic: Hyperglycemia (≤14%)
Hepatic: Increased serum ALT (≤18%; includes patients with hepatitis B and/or C infections)
1% to 10%:
Central nervous system: Insomnia (≤7%), fatigue (≤2%), headache (≤2%), suicidal ideation (<2%), suicidal tendencies (<2%), depression (≤1%)
Dermatologic: Pruritus (<2%)
Gastrointestinal: Increased serum lipase (2% to 10%), diarrhea (≤2%), abdominal distress (<2%), abdominal pain (<2%), flatulence (<2%), upper abdominal pain (<2%), vomiting (<2%), nausea (≤1%)
Hematologic & oncologic: Neutropenia (3% to 4%; grades 3/4: 2%), leukopenia (2% to 3%)
Hepatic: Increased serum AST (≤8%), hyperbilirubinemia (≤3%), hepatitis (<2%)
Hypersensitivity: Hypersensitivity reaction (≤1%)
Neuromuscular & skeletal: Increased creatine phosphokinase (1% to 7%), myositis (<2%)
Renal: Renal insufficiency (<2%)
<1%, postmarketing, and/or case reports: Abnormal dreams, dizziness, immune reconstitution syndrome, increased serum creatinine, skin rash

General Dosage Range Dosage adjustment recommended in patients on concomitant therapy.

Oral:

Children and Adolescents (30 to <40 kg): 35 mg once daily

Children and Adolescents (≥40 kg): 50 mg once daily

Adults: 50 mg once or twice daily

Mechanism of Action Binds to the integrase active site and inhibits the strand transfer step of HIV-1 DNA integration necessary for the HIV replication cycle.

Pharmacodynamics/Kinetics

Half-life Elimination ~14 hours

Time to Peak 2 to 3 hours

Pregnancy Considerations It is not known if dolutegravir crosses the placenta. Data collected by the antiretroviral pregnancy registry are insufficient to evaluate human teratogenic risk. Maternal antiretroviral therapy may increase the risk of preterm delivery, although available information is conflicting possibly due to variability of maternal factors (disease severity; initiation of therapy); however, maternal antiretroviral medication should not be withheld due to concerns of preterm birth. Information related to stillbirth, low birth weight, and small for gestational age infants is limited. Long-term follow-up is recommended for all infants exposed to antiretroviral medications; children who develop significant organ system abnormalities of unknown etiology (particularly of the CNS or heart) should be evaluated for potential mitochondrial dysfunction.

Combination antiretroviral therapy (cART) therapy is recommended for all HIV-infected pregnant women to keep the viral load below the limit of detection and reduce the risk of perinatal transmission. When HIV is diagnosed during pregnancy in a woman who has never received antiretroviral therapy, cART should begin as soon as possible after diagnosis. The Health and Human Services (HHS) Perinatal HIV Guidelines note data are insufficient to recommend dolutegravir as initial therapy in antiretroviral-naive pregnant women. Pharmacokinetic data are insufficient to make dosing recommendations during pregnancy. In general, women who become pregnant on a stable cART regimen may continue that regimen if viral suppression is effective, appropriate drug exposure can be achieved, contraindications for use in pregnancy are not present, and the regimen is well tolerated. Monitoring during pregnancy is more frequent than in non-pregnant adults; cART should be continued postpartum.

For HIV-infected couples planning a pregnancy, maximum viral suppression with combination antiretroviral therapy (cART) is recommended prior to conception for the HIV-infected partner(s) and expert consultation is recommended; modification of therapy (if needed) and optimization of the woman's health should be done prior to conception. HIV-infected women not planning a pregnancy may use any available type of contraception, considering possible drug interactions and contraindications of the specific method. In addition, consistent use of condoms is also recommended (even during pregnancy) to prevent transmission of HIV or other sexually transmitted diseases.

Health care providers are encouraged to enroll pregnant women exposed to antiretroviral medications as early in pregnancy as possible in the Antiretroviral Pregnancy Registry (1-800-258-4263 or www.APRegistry.com). Health care providers caring for HIV-infected women and their infants may contact the National Perinatal HIV Hotline (888-448-8765) for clinical consultation (HHS [perinatal] 2016).

Donepezil (doh NEP e zil)

Brand Names: US Aricept; Aricept ODT [DSC]

Brand Names: Canada Accel-Donepezil; ACT-Donepezil; ACT-Donepezil ODT; Apo-Donepezil; Aricept; Aricept RDT; Auro-Donepezil; Bio-Donepezil; JAMP-Donepezil; Mar-Donepezil; Mylan-Donepezil; PMS-Donepezil; RAN-Donepezil; Riva-Donepezil; Sandoz-Donepezil; Sandoz-Donepezil ODT; Septa Donepezil; Teva-Donepezil

Pharmacologic Category Acetylcholinesterase Inhibitor (Central)

Use Alzheimer disease: Treatment of mild, moderate, or severe dementia of the Alzheimer type

Local Anesthetic/Vasoconstrictor Precautions No information available to require special precautions

Effects on Dental Treatment No significant effects or complications reported

Effects on Bleeding No information available to require special precautions

Adverse Reactions

>10%:

Central nervous system: Insomnia (2% to 14%)

Gastrointestinal: Nausea (3% to 19%; dose related), diarrhea (5% to 15%; dose related)

Infection: Infection (11%)

Miscellaneous: Accidental injury (7% to 13%)

≥1% to 10%:

Cardiovascular: Hypertension (3%), chest pain (2%), syncope (2%), atrial fibrillation (≥1%), bradycardia (≥1%), cardiac failure (≥1%), ECG abnormality (≥1%), edema (≥1%), hypotension (≥1%), peripheral edema (≥1%), vasodilation (≥1%)

Central nervous system: Headache (3% to 10%), pain (3% to 9%), dizziness (2% to 8%), fatigue (1% to 8%), abnormal dreams (3%), hallucination (3%), hostility (3%), depression (2% to 3%), nervousness (1% to 3%), confusion (2%), drowsiness (2%), emotional lability (2%; including crying), personality disorder (2%), abnormal gait (≥1%), aggressive behavior (≥1%), agitation (≥1%), anxiety (≥1%), aphasia (≥1%), ataxia (≥1%), convulsions (≥1%), delusions (≥1%), irritability (≥1%), paresthesia (≥1%), restlessness (≥1%), vertigo (≥1%), wandering (≥1%)

Dermatologic: Ecchymosis (4% to 5%), eczema (3%), dermal ulcer (≥1%), diaphoresis (≥1%), pruritus (≥1%), skin rash (≥1%), urticaria (≥1%)

Endocrine & metabolic: Weight loss (3% to 5%; dose related), hyperlipidemia (2%), dehydration (1% to 2%), glycosuria (≥1%), hot flash (≥1%), increased lactate dehydrogenase (≥1%), increased libido (≥1%)

Gastrointestinal: Vomiting (3% to 9%; dose related), anorexia (2% to 8%), abdominal pain (≥1%), bloating (≥1%), constipation (≥1%), dyspepsia (≥1%), epigastric pain (≥1%), fecal incontinence (≥1%), gastroenteritis (≥1%), gastrointestinal hemorrhage (≥1%), sore throat (≥1%), toothache (≥1%)

Genitourinary: Urinary incontinence (1% to 3%), urinary frequency (2%), cystitis (≥1%), hematuria (≥1%), nocturia (≥1%), urinary tract infection (≥1%)

Hematologic & oncologic: Bruise (2%), hemorrhage (2%), anemia (≥1%)

Hepatic: Increased serum alkaline phosphatase (≥1%)

Infection: Fungal infection (≥1%), influenza (≥1%)

Neuromuscular & skeletal: Muscle cramps (3% to 8%), back pain (3%), increased creatine phosphokinase (3%), arthritis (1% to 2%), weakness (1% to 2%), bone fracture (≥1%), tremor (≥1%)

Ophthalmic: Blurred vision (≥1%), cataract (≥1%), eye irritation (≥1%)

Respiratory: Bronchitis (≥1%), dyspnea (≥1%), flu-like symptoms (≥1%), increased cough (≥1%), pharyngitis (≥1%), pneumonia (≥1%)

Miscellaneous: Fever (2%)

≤1%, postmarketing, and/or case reports: Abnormal hepatic function tests, abnormal lacrimation, abnormal vision, abscess, acute rhinitis, albuminuria, alopecia, angina pectoris, apathy, arteritis, arthralgia, arthropathy, asthma, atelectasis, atrophic striae, benign prostatic hypertrophy, blepharitis, breast fibroadenosis, cachexia, cardiomegaly, cellulitis, cerebral hemorrhage, cerebral infarction, cerebral ischemia, cerebrovascular accident, chills, cholecystitis, cholelithiasis, conjunctival hemorrhage, conjunctivitis, convulsions, decreased libido, deep vein thrombosis, dementia, dermatitis, diabetes mellitus, diverticulitis, duodenal ulcer, dysarthria, dysgeusia, dysphagia, dysphoria, dysuria, emotional disturbance, eosinophilia, epigastric distress, epistaxis, eructation, erythema, erythrocytopenia, esophagitis, euphoria, extrapyramidal reaction, facial edema, fasciculations, fibrocystic breast changes, first degree atrioventricular block, flatulence, fungal dermatitis, gastritis, gastric ulcer, gingivitis, glaucoma, goiter, gout, hearing loss, heart block, hemiplegia, hemolytic anemia, hemorrhoids, hepatitis, hernia, herpes zoster, hiatal hernia, hirsutism, hyperbilirubinemia, hyperglycemia, hyperkeratosis, hypersensitivity reaction, hypertonia, hypokalemia, hypokinesia, hyponatremia, hypoproteinemia, hypoxia, increased appetite, increased blood urea nitrogen, increased gamma-glutamyl transferase, increased post-void residual urine volume, increased serum ALT, increased serum AST, increased serum creatinine, increased serum transaminases, increased thirst, intestinal obstruction, intracranial hemorrhage, iron deficiency anemia, irritable bowel syndrome, jaundice, leg cramps, leukocytosis, localized coldness, malaise, mastitis, melena, motion sickness, muscle spasm, myalgia, myasthenia, myocardial infarction, neuralgia, neurodermatitis, neuroleptic malignant syndrome, night sweats, nystagmus, orthostatic hypotension, osteoporosis, otalgia, otitis externa, otitis media, pacing, pancreatitis, paranoia, peptic ulcer disease, periodontal abscess, periodontitis, periorbital edema, peripheral vascular disease, pernicious anemia, pleurisy, polydipsia, post nasal drip, prolonged Q-T interval on ECG, psoriasis, pulmonary congestion, pyelonephritis, pyuria, rectal hemorrhage, renal failure, retinal hemorrhage, rhabdomyolysis, rhinitis, seeing spots, sensation of cold, sepsis, severe depression, sialorrhea, skin discoloration, sleep apnea, snoring, supraventricular extrasystole, supraventricular tachycardia, thrombocythemia, thrombocytopenia, tinnitus, tongue edema, tonic-clonic seizures, torsades de pointes, transient ischemic attacks, urinary urgency, uterine hemorrhage, vaginitis, vasodilation, ventricular premature contractions, ventricular tachycardia, vertigo, vesiculobullous dermatitis, weight gain, wheezing, xeroderma, xerophthalmia, xerostomia

General Dosage Range Oral: *Adults:* Initial: 5 mg once daily; Maintenance: 5 to 23 mg once daily

Mechanism of Action Alzheimer's disease is characterized by cholinergic deficiency in the cortex and basal forebrain, which contributes to cognitive deficits. Donepezil reversibly and noncompetitively inhibits centrally-active acetylcholinesterase, the enzyme responsible for hydrolysis of acetylcholine. This appears to result in increased concentrations of acetylcholine available for synaptic transmission in the central nervous system.

Pharmacodynamics/Kinetics

Half-life Elimination 70 hours; time to steady-state: 15 days

Time to Peak Plasma: Tablet, 10 mg: 3 hours; Tablet, 23 mg: ~8 hours; **Note:** Peak plasma concentrations almost twofold higher for the 23 mg tablet compared to the 10 mg tablet

Pregnancy Risk Factor C

Pregnancy Considerations Adverse events have been observed in some animal reproduction studies.

Doripenem (dore i PEN em)

Brand Names: US Doribax

Pharmacologic Category Antibiotic, Carbapenem

Use

Intra-abdominal infections, complicated: Treatment of complicated intra-abdominal infections caused by *Bacteroides caccae, Bacteroides fragilis, Bacteroides thetaiotaomicron, Bacteroides uniformis, Bacteroides vulgatus, Escherichia coli, Klebsiella pneumoniae, Peptostreptococcus micros, Pseudomonas aeruginosa, Streptococcus intermedius,* and *Streptococcus constellatus.*

Urinary tract infections, complicated (including pyelonephritis): Treatment of complicated urinary tract infections (UTIs), including pyelonephritis, caused by *E. coli* (including cases with concurrent bacteremia), *Acinetobacter baumannii, K. pneumoniae, Proteus mirabilis,* and *P. aeruginosa.*

Local Anesthetic/Vasoconstrictor Precautions No information available to require special precautions

Effects on Dental Treatment Prolonged use of doripenem may lead to development of oral candidiasis.

Effects on Bleeding Thrombocytopenia has been reported through postmarketing surveillance

Adverse Reactions

>10%:

Central nervous system: Headache (3% to 16%)

Gastrointestinal: Diarrhea (6% to 12%), nausea (4% to 12%)

1% to 10%:

Cardiovascular: Phlebitis (2% to 8%)

Dermatologic: Skin rash (1% to 6%; includes allergic/bullous dermatitis, erythema, macular/papular eruptions, urticaria, and erythema multiforme), pruritus (1% to 3%)

Gastrointestinal: Oral candidiasis (1% to 3%), *Clostridium difficile* associated diarrhea (≤1%)

Genitourinary: Vaginal infection (1% to 2%)

Hematologic & oncologic: Anemia (2% to 10%)

Hepatic: Increased serum transaminases (2% to 7%)

<1%, postmarketing, and/or case reports: Anaphylaxis, interstitial pneumonitis, leukopenia, neutropenia, renal failure, renal insufficiency, seizure, Stevens-Johnson syndrome, thrombocytopenia, toxic epidermal necrolysis

General Dosage Range Dosage adjustment recommended in patients with renal impairment

IV: *Adults:* 500 mg every 8 hours

Mechanism of Action Inhibits bacterial cell wall synthesis by binding to several of the penicillin-binding proteins (PBP-2, PBP-3, PBP-4), which in turn inhibits the final transpeptidation step of peptidoglycan synthesis in bacterial cell walls, thus inhibiting cell wall biosynthesis; bacteria eventually lyse due to ongoing activity of cell wall autolytic enzymes (autolysins and murein hydrolases) while cell wall assembly is arrested.

Pharmacodynamics/Kinetics

Half-life Elimination ~1 hour

Pregnancy Risk Factor B

Pregnancy Considerations Adverse events have not been observed in animal reproduction studies. Information related to use during pregnancy has not been located.

Dornase Alfa (DOOR nase AL fa)

Brand Names: US Pulmozyme

Brand Names: Canada Pulmozyme

Pharmacologic Category Enzyme; Mucolytic Agent

Use Cystic fibrosis: Management of cystic fibrosis patients, in conjunction with standard therapies, to improve pulmonary function; reduce the risk of respiratory tract infections requiring parenteral antibiotics in patients with a forced vital capacity (FVC) ≥40% of predicted.

Local Anesthetic/Vasoconstrictor Precautions No information available to require special precautions

Effects on Dental Treatment Key adverse event(s) related to dental treatment: Pharyngitis

Effects on Bleeding No information available to require special precautions

Adverse Reactions Adverse events were similar in children using the PARI BABY nebulizer (facemask as opposed to mouthpiece) with the addition of cough.

>10%:

- Cardiovascular: Chest pain (18% to 25%)
- Central nervous system: Voice disorder (12% to 18%)
- Dermatologic: Skin rash (3% to 12%)
- Respiratory: Cough (PARI-BABY nebulizer facemask: children 3 months to <5 years: 45%; children 5 to ≤10 years: 30%), pharyngitis (32% to 40%), rhinitis (30%; in patients with FVC: <40%), decrease in forced vital capacity (≥10% decrease of predicted: 22%; in patients with FVC: <40%), dyspnea (17%; in patients with FVC: <40%)
- Miscellaneous: Fever (32% in patients with FVC <40%)

1% to 10%:

- Gastrointestinal: Dyspepsia (≤3%)
- Immunologic: Antibody development (to dornase alfa: 2% to 4%)
- Ophthalmic: Conjunctivitis (1% to 5%)
- Respiratory: Laryngitis (3% to 4%)

<1%, postmarketing and/or case reports: Headache, urticaria

General Dosage Range Inhalation: *Children >5 years and Adults:* 2.5 mg once daily

Mechanism of Action The hallmark of cystic fibrosis lung disease is the presence of abundant, purulent airway secretions composed primarily of highly polymerized DNA. The principal source of this DNA is the nuclei of degenerating neutrophils, which is present in large concentrations in infected lung secretions. The presence of this DNA produces a viscous mucous that may contribute to the decreased mucociliary transport and persistent infections that are commonly seen in this population. Dornase alfa is a deoxyribonuclease (DNA) enzyme produced by recombinant gene technology. Dornase selectively cleaves DNA, thus reducing mucous viscosity and as a result, airflow in the lung is improved and the risk of bacterial infection may be decreased.

Pharmacodynamics/Kinetics

Onset of Action Nebulization: Enzyme levels are measured in sputum in ~15 minutes and decline rapidly thereafter

Duration of Action Sputum concentrations decline within 2 hours of inhalation

Pregnancy Considerations Adverse events have not been observed in animal reproduction studies.

Dorzolamide (dor ZOLE a mide)

Brand Names: US Trusopt

Brand Names: Canada Sandoz-Dorzolamide; Trusopt

Pharmacologic Category Carbonic Anhydrase Inhibitor (Ophthalmic); Ophthalmic Agent, Antiglaucoma

Use Elevated intraocular pressure: Treatment of elevated intraocular pressure (IOP) in patients with ocular hypertension or open-angle glaucoma

Local Anesthetic/Vasoconstrictor Precautions No information available to require special precautions

Effects on Dental Treatment No significant effects or complications reported

Effects on Bleeding No information available to require special precautions

Adverse Reactions Frequency not always defined.

- Dermatologic: Skin rash
- Gastrointestinal: Bitter taste (~25% following administration), fatigue, headache, nausea
- Genitourinary: Urolithiasis
- Hypersensitivity: Local ocular hypersensitivity reaction (~10%)
- Neuromuscular & skeletal: Weakness
- Ocular: Burning sensation of eyes (~33%), eye discomfort (~33%), stinging of eyes (~33%), superficial punctate keratitis (10% to 15%), blurred vision (1% to 5%), conjunctivitis (1% to 5%), eyelid irritation (1% to 5%), eye redness (1% to 5%), lacrimation (1% to 5%), photophobia (1% to 5%), xerophthalmia (1% to 5%), iridocyclitis

<1%, postmarketing and/or case reports: Angioedema, bronchospasm, choriodal detachment (following filtration procedures), contact dermatitis, crusting of eyelid, dizziness, dyspnea, epistaxis, myopia (transient), ocular pain, paresthesia, pruritus, Stevens-Johnson syndrome, throat irritation, toxic epidermal necrolysis, urticaria, xerostomia

General Dosage Range Ophthalmic: *Children, Adolescents, and Adults:* Instill 1 drop into affected eye(s) 3 times daily

Mechanism of Action Reversible inhibition of the enzyme carbonic anhydrase resulting in reduction of hydrogen ion secretion at renal tubule and an increased renal excretion of sodium, potassium, bicarbonate, and water to decrease production of aqueous humor; also inhibits carbonic anhydrase in central nervous system to retard abnormal and excessive discharge from CNS neurons

Pharmacodynamics/Kinetics

Duration of Action 8 to 12 hours

Half-life Elimination Terminal RBC half-life: 147 days; washes out of RBCs nonlinearly, resulting in a rapid decline of drug concentration initially, followed by a slower elimination phase with a half-life of about 4 months

Pregnancy Risk Factor C

Pregnancy Considerations Adverse events have been observed in animal reproduction studies following systemic administration. IOP is usually lower during pregnancy. If topical medications for the treatment of glaucoma in pregnant women cannot be discontinued because small increases in IOP cannot be tolerated, the minimum effective dose should be used in combination with punctual occlusion to decrease exposure to the fetus (Johnson, 2001).

Dorzolamide and Timolol

(dor ZOLE a mide & TYE moe lole)

Related Information

Dorzolamide *on page 530*

Timolol (Ophthalmic) *on page 1568*

Brand Names: US Cosopt; Cosopt PF

Brand Names: Canada Apo-Dorzo-Timop; Cosopt; Cosopt Preservative Free; Sandoz-Dorzolamide/Timolol

Pharmacologic Category Beta-Adrenergic Blocker, Nonselective; Carbonic Anhydrase Inhibitor (Ophthalmic); Ophthalmic Agent, Antiglaucoma

Use Elevated intraocular pressure: Reduction of elevated intraocular pressure (IOP) in patients with open-angle glaucoma or ocular hypertension who are insufficiently responsive to beta-blockers

Local Anesthetic/Vasoconstrictor Precautions Epinephrine has interacted with nonselective beta-blockers, such as propranolol, to result in initial hypertensive episode followed by bradycardia. Timolol is also a nonselective beta-blocker. The significance of a potential systemic interaction with epinephrine is unknown. However, it is suggested that cautionary procedures be used, particularly if vasoconstrictor is used immediately following a dose of timolol taken by the patient.

Effects on Dental Treatment Key adverse event(s) related to dental treatment: Taste perversion.

Effects on Bleeding No information available to require special precautions

Adverse Reactions Frequency not always defined. Percentages as reported with combination product. Also see individual agents.

>5%:

Gastrointestinal: Dysgeusia (≤30%)

Ophthalmic: Burning sensation of eyes (≤30%), stinging of eyes (≤30%), blurred vision (5% to 15%), conjunctival hyperemia (5% to 15%), eye pruritus (5% to 15%), superficial punctate keratitis (5% to 15%)

1% to 5%:

Cardiovascular: Hypertension

Central nervous system: Dizziness, headache

Dermatologic: Erythema of eyelid

Gastrointestinal: Abdominal pain, dyspepsia, nausea

Genitourinary: Urinary tract infection

Infection: Influenza

Neuromuscular & skeletal: Back pain

Ophthalmic: Blepharitis, cataract (including post-subcapsular), cloudy vision, conjunctival discharge, conjunctival edema, conjunctivitis, corneal erosion, corneal staining, dry eye syndrome, eye discharge (including eyelid), eye disease (debris in eye), eye pain (includes eyelid), eyelid edema, follicular conjunctivitis, foreign body sensation of eye, lacrimation, lens nucleus discoloration, ocular exudate (eyelid), optic disk cupping (glaucomatous), scaling of eyelid, visual field defect, vitreous detachment

Respiratory: Bronchitis, cough, pharyngitis, sinusitis, upper respiratory tract infection

<1%, postmarketing, and/or case reports: Bradycardia, cardiac failure, cerebrovascular accident, chest pain, choroidal detachment (following filtration procedures), depression, diarrhea, dyspnea, heart block, hypotension, iridocyclitis, myocardial infarction, nasal congestion, paresthesia, photophobia, respiratory failure, skin rash, Stevens-Johnson syndrome, toxic epidermal necrolysis, urolithiasis, vomiting, xerostomia

General Dosage Range Ophthalmic: *Children ≥2 years and Adults:* Instill 1 drop into affected eye(s) twice daily

Mechanism of Action

Dorzolamide: Inhibits carbonic anhydrase in the ciliary processes of the eye resulting decreased bicarbonate ion formation which decreases sodium and fluid transport, thus decreasing aqueous humor secretion and reduces intraocular pressure.

Timolol: Blocks both $beta_1$- and $beta_2$-adrenergic receptors, reduces intraocular pressure by reducing aqueous humor production or possibly increases the outflow of aqueous humor

Pregnancy Risk Factor C

Pregnancy Considerations Reproductive studies have not been conducted with this combination. Refer to individual agents.

Doxapram (DOKS a pram)

Brand Names: US Dopram

Pharmacologic Category Respiratory Stimulant

Use Respiratory stimulant for respiratory depression secondary to anesthesia, mild-to-moderate drug-induced respiratory and CNS depression; acute hypercapnia secondary to COPD

Note: In general, the use of doxapram as a respiratory stimulant in adults is limited; alternate therapies are preferred.

Local Anesthetic/Vasoconstrictor Precautions No information available to require special precautions

Effects on Dental Treatment No significant effects or complications reported

Effects on Bleeding No information available to require special precautions

Adverse Reactions Frequency not defined.

Cardiovascular: Cardiac arrhythmia, change in heart rate, chest pain, chest tightness, flattened T wave on ECG, flushing, increased blood pressure, phlebitis, ventricular fibrillation, ventricular tachycardia

Central nervous system: Apprehension, clonus, disorientation, dizziness, hallucination, headache, hyperactivity, hyperreflexia, involuntary muscle movements, paresthesia, positive Babinski sign, seizure

Dermatologic: Burning sensation of skin, diaphoresis, pruritus

Endocrine & metabolic: Albuminuria

Gastrointestinal: Bowel urgency, diarrhea, hiccups, nausea, vomiting

Genitourinary: Urinary incontinence, urinary retention

Hematologic & oncologic: Decreased hematocrit, decreased hemoglobin, hemolysis, decreased red blood cells

Neuromuscular & skeletal: Fasciculations, laryngospasm, muscle spasm

Ophthalmic: Mydriasis

Renal: Increased blood urea nitrogen

Respiratory: Bronchospasm, cough, dyspnea, hyperventilation, hypoventilation (rebound), tachypnea

Miscellaneous: Fever

<1%, postmarketing, and/or case reports: Agitation (emergence), prolonged Q-T interval on ECG (premature neonates), second degree atrioventricular block (premature neonates)

General Dosage Range IV: *Children ≥12 years, Adolescents, and Adults:* Initial: 0.5-1 mg/kg as an intermittent injection every 5 minutes until response (maximum total dose: 2 mg/kg) **or** 1-5 mg/minute as an IV infusion until response; should not be continued >2 hours (maximum total dose: 4 mg/kg [3000 mg daily])

Mechanism of Action Stimulates respiration through action on peripheral carotid chemoreceptors; respiratory center in medulla is also directly stimulated as dosage is increased

Pharmacodynamics/Kinetics

Onset of Action Respiratory stimulation: Single IV injection: 20 to 40 seconds; Peak effect: Single IV injection: 1 to 2 minutes

Duration of Action Single IV injection: 5 to 12 minutes

Half-life Elimination Serum: Neonates, premature: 6.6 to 12 hours; Adults: Mean: 3.4 hours (range: 2.4 to 4.1 hours)

Pregnancy Risk Factor B

Pregnancy Considerations Adverse events have not been observed in animal reproduction studies.

Doxazosin (doks AY zoe sin)

Related Information

Cardiovascular Diseases *on page 1752*

Brand Names: US Cardura; Cardura XL

Brand Names: Canada Apo-Doxazosin; Cardura-1; Cardura-2; Cardura-4; Dom-Doxazosin; Doxazosin-1; Doxazosin-2; Doxazosin-4; Mylan-Doxazosin; PMS-Doxazosin; Teva-Doxazosin

Pharmacologic Category Alpha$_1$ Blocker; Antihypertensive

Use

Benign prostatic hyperplasia: Treatment of signs and symptoms of benign prostatic hyperplasia (BPH).

Hypertension (immediate release only): Management of hypertension (monotherapy or in combination with other antihypertensives).

Note: The 2014 guideline for the management of high blood pressure in adults (Eighth Joint National Committee [JNC 8]) does **not** recommend the use of doxazosin in the treatment of hypertension (JNC8 [James 2013]). According to the AHA/ACC/ASH 2015 scientific statement for the treatment of hypertension in patients with coronary artery disease (CAD), doxazosin should only be used if other drugs for the management of hypertension and heart failure do not achieve BP control at maximum tolerated doses (AHA/ACC/ASH [Rosendorff 2015]).

Local Anesthetic/Vasoconstrictor Precautions No information available to require special precautions

Effects on Dental Treatment Key adverse event(s) related to dental treatment: Xerostomia (normal salivary flow resumes upon discontinuation); Patients may experience orthostatic hypotension as they stand up after treatment; especially if lying in dental chair for extended periods of time. Use caution with sudden changes in position during and after dental treatment.

Effects on Bleeding No information available to require special precautions

Adverse Reactions

>10%: Central nervous system: Dizziness (5% to 19%), malaise (≤12%), fatigue (8% to ≤12%), headache (6% to 10%)

1% to 10%:

Cardiovascular: Edema (3% to 4%), hypotension (1% to 2%), orthostatic hypotension (<1% to 2%), cardiac arrhythmia (1%), facial edema (1%), flushing (1%), palpitations (1%)

Central nervous system: Drowsiness (1% to 5%), vertigo (2% to 4%), pain (2%), anxiety (1%), ataxia (1%), hypertonia (1%), insomnia (1%), movement disorder (1%), myasthenia (1%)

Endocrine & metabolic: Sexual disorder (2%)

Gastrointestinal: Abdominal pain (2%), nausea (1% to 2%), dyspepsia (1%), xerostomia (1%)

Genitourinary: Urinary incontinence (1%), urinary tract infection (1%)

Neuromuscular & skeletal: Weakness (4% to 7%), muscle cramps (1%), myalgia (1%), arthralgia (≤1%), arthritis (≤1%)

Ophthalmic: Visual disturbance (2%)

Otic: Tinnitus (1%)

Renal: Polyuria (2%)

Respiratory: Respiratory tract infection (5%), rhinitis (3%), dyspnea (1% to 3%), epistaxis (1%)

<1%, postmarketing, and/or case reports: Abnormal hepatic function tests, abnormal lacrimation, abnormality in thinking, agitation, alopecia, altered sense of smell, amnesia, angina pectoris, anorexia, back pain, blurred vision, bradycardia, bronchospasm (aggravated), cerebrovascular accident, chest pain, cholestasis, cholestatic hepatitis, confusion, cough, decreased libido, depersonalization, diaphoresis, diarrhea, dysgeusia, dysuria, eczema, emotional lability, fecal incontinence, fever, flu-like symptoms, gastroenteritis, gastrointestinal obstruction, gout, gynecomastia, hematuria, hepatitis, hot flash, hypersensitivity reaction, hypoesthesia, hypokalemia, impotence, increased appetite, increased thirst, infection, intraoperative floppy iris syndrome (cataract surgery), jaundice, lack of concentration, leukopenia, lymphadenopathy, mastalgia, migraine, myocardial infarction, nephrolithiasis, nervousness, neutropenia, nocturia, orthostatic dizziness, otalgia, pallor, paranoia, paresis, paresthesia, peripheral ischemia, pharyngitis, photophobia, priapism, pruritus, purpura, rigors, sinusitis, skin rash, syncope, tachycardia, thrombocytopenia, tremor, twitching, urinary frequency, urination disorder, urticaria, vomiting, weight gain, weight loss, xeroderma

General Dosage Range Oral:

Extended release: *Adults:* Initial: 4 mg once daily (maximum: 8 mg/day)

Immediate release: *Adults:* Initial: 1 mg once daily (maximum: 8 mg/day [BPH]; 16 mg/day [hypertension])

Mechanism of Action

Hypertension: Competitively inhibits postsynaptic alpha$_1$-adrenergic receptors which results in vasodilation of veins and arterioles and a decrease in total peripheral resistance and blood pressure; ~50% as potent on a weight by weight basis as prazosin.

BPH: Competitively inhibits postsynaptic alpha$_1$-adrenergic receptors in prostatic stromal and bladder neck tissues. This reduces the sympathetic tone-induced urethral stricture causing BPH symptoms.

Pharmacodynamics/Kinetics

Duration of Action >24 hours

Half-life Elimination Immediate release: ~22 hours; Extended release: 15 to 19 hours

Time to Peak Serum: Immediate release: 2 to 3 hours; Extended release: 8 ± 3.7 to 9 ± 4.7 hours

Pregnancy Considerations Adverse events were observed in some animal reproduction studies. Doxazosin crosses the placenta (Versmissen 2016). Untreated chronic maternal hypertension is associated with adverse events in the fetus, infant, and mother. If treatment for hypertension during pregnancy is needed, other agents are generally preferred (ACOG, 2013).

Doxepin (Systemic) (DOKS e pin)

Related Information

Dentin Hypersensitivity, Acid Erosion, High Caries Index, Management of Alveolar Osteitis, and Xerostomia *on page 1857*

Management of the Patient With Anxiety or Depression *on page 1873*

Vasoconstrictor Interactions With Antidepressants *on page 1913*

Brand Names: US Silenor

Brand Names: Canada Apo-Doxepin; Novo-Doxepin; Silenor; Sinequan; Zonalon

Generic Availability (US) May be product dependent

Pharmacologic Category Antidepressant, Tricyclic (Tertiary Amine)

Use

Depression and/or anxiety: Treatment of psychoneurotic patients with depression and/or anxiety; depression and/or anxiety associated with alcoholism; depression and/or anxiety associated with organic disease; psychotic depressive disorders with associated anxiety, including involutional depression and manic-depressive disorders.

Insomnia (Silenor only): Treatment of insomnia characterized by difficulty with sleep maintenance.

Local Anesthetic/Vasoconstrictor Precautions Doxepin is one of the drugs confirmed to prolong the QT interval and is accepted as having a risk of causing torsade de pointes. In terms of epinephrine, it is not known what effect vasoconstrictors in the local anesthetic regimen will have in patients with a known history of congenital prolonged QT interval or in patients taking any medication that prolongs the QT interval. Until more information is obtained, it is suggested that the clinician consult with the physician prior to the use of a vasoconstrictor in suspected patients, and that the vasoconstrictor (epinephrine, mepivacaine, and levonordefrin [Carbocaine® 2% with Neo-Cobefrin®]) be used with caution. See Dental Comment.

Effects on Dental Treatment Key adverse event(s) related to dental treatment: Xerostomia and changes in salivation (normal salivary flow resumes upon discontinuation)

Oral: Aphthous stomatitis, unpleasant taste, trouble with gums

Long-term treatment with TCAs increases the risk of caries by reducing salivation and salivary buffer capacity.

Effects on Bleeding No information available to require special precautions

Adverse Reactions Actual frequency may be dependent on diagnosis.

Cardiovascular: Hypertension (chronic insomnia patients ≤3%), edema, flushing, hypotension, tachycardia

Central nervous system: Sedation (chronic insomnia patients 6% to 9%), dizziness (chronic insomnia patients ≥1%), ataxia, chills, confusion, disorientation, drowsiness, extrapyramidal reaction, fatigue, hallucination, headache, numbness, paresthesia, seizure, tardive dyskinesia

Dermatologic: Alopecia, diaphoresis (excessive), pruritus, skin photosensitivity, skin rash

Endocrine & metabolic: Altered serum glucose, change in libido, galactorrhea, gynecomastia, SIADH, weight gain

Gastrointestinal: Nausea (chronic insomnia patients 2%), gastroenteritis (chronic insomnia patients ≤2%), anorexia, aphthous stomatitis, constipation, diarrhea, dysgeusia, dyspepsia, vomiting, xerostomia

Genitourinary: Breast hypertrophy, testicular swelling, urinary retention

Hematologic & oncologic: Agranulocytosis, eosinophilia, leukopenia, purpura, thrombocytopenia

Hepatic: Jaundice

Neuromuscular & skeletal: Tremor, weakness

Ophthalmic: Blurred vision

Otic: Tinnitus

Respiratory: Upper respiratory tract infection (chronic insomnia patients 4%), exacerbation of asthma

<1%, postmarketing, and/or case reports: Abdominal pain, abnormal dreams, abnormal gait, acne rosacea, adenocarcinoma (lung, stage I), adjustment disorder, ageusia, altered blood pressure (inadequately controlled), anemia, angle-closure glaucoma, anxiety, arthralgia, atrioventricular block, back injury, back pain, blepharospasm, bone fracture, breast cyst, bronchitis, cerebrovascular accident, change in appetite, chest pain, confusion, cough, decreased heart rate, decreased lacrimation, decreased neutrophils, decreased performance on neuropsychometrics, decreased range of motion (joints), depression, dermatitis, diplopia, disturbance in attention, dysmenorrhea, dyspnea, dysuria, ECG abnormality (ST-T segment, QRS complex, QRS axis), erythema, eye infection, eye pain, eye redness, falling, feeling of heaviness, folliculitis, fungal infection, gastroesophageal reflux disease, gum line erosion, hematochezia, hematoma, hemoglobinuria, herpes zoster, hot flash, hyperbilirubinemia, hyperhidrosis, hyperkalemia, hypermagnesemia, hypersensitivity, hypoacusis, hypokalemia, increased serum ALT, increased serum transaminases, influenza, joint sprain, laceration, laryngitis, lethargy, limb pain, lip blister, lower respiratory tract infection, malignant melanoma, migraine, mood elevation, motion sickness, muscle cramps, myalgia, nasal congestion, nasopharyngeal disorder, neck pain, nightmares, nocturia, onychomycosis, otalgia, pallor, palpitations, perforated tympanic membrane, peripheral edema, pharyngitis, pharyngolaryngeal pain, pneumonia, rales, rhinorrhea, sinus congestion, sinusitis, skin irritation, sleep paralysis, somnambulism (complex sleep-related behavior [sleep-driving, cooking or eating food, making phone calls]), staphylococcal cellulitis, syncope, tenosynovitis, tooth infection, urinary incontinence, urinary tract infection, vasodepressor syncope, ventricular premature contractions, viral infection, wheezing

Dosing

Adult

Depression and/or anxiety: Oral: Initial: 25 to 50 mg as a single dose at bedtime or in divided doses; gradually increase based on response and tolerability to a usual dose of 100-300 mg daily (APA 2010; Bauer 2013)

Insomnia (Silenor): Oral: 3 to 6 mg once daily within 30 minutes of bedtime; maximum dose: 6 mg daily

Chronic urticaria (off-label use): Oral: Adults: 10 mg 3 times daily (Greene, 1985) **or** 10 mg to 30 mg once daily at bedtime (Yadav 2009)

Discontinuation of therapy: Upon discontinuation of antidepressant therapy, gradually taper the dose to minimize the incidence of withdrawal symptoms and allow for the detection of re-emerging symptoms. Evidence supporting ideal taper rates is limited. APA and NICE guidelines suggest tapering therapy over at least several weeks with consideration to the half-life of the antidepressant; antidepressants with a shorter half-life may need to be tapered more conservatively. In addition for long-term treated patients, WFSBP guidelines recommend tapering over 4 to 6 months. If intolerable withdrawal symptoms occur following a dose reduction, consider resuming the previously prescribed dose and/or decrease dose at a more gradual rate (APA, 2010; Bauer 2002; Haddad 2001; NCCMH 2010; Schatzberg 2006; Shelton 2001; Warner 2006).

MAO inhibitor recommendations:

Switching to or from an MAO inhibitor intended to treat psychiatric disorders:

Allow 14 days to elapse between discontinuing an MAO inhibitor intended to treat psychiatric disorders and initiation of doxepin.

Allow 14 days to elapse between discontinuing doxepin and initiation of an MAO inhibitor intended to treat psychiatric disorders.

Use with other MAO inhibitors (such as linezolid or IV methylene blue):

Do not initiate doxepin in patients receiving linezolid or IV methylene blue; consider other interventions for psychiatric condition.

If urgent treatment with linezolid or IV methylene blue is required in a patient already receiving doxepin and potential benefits outweigh potential risks, discontinue doxepin promptly and administer linezolid or IV methylene blue. Monitor for serotonin syndrome for 2 weeks or until 24 hours after the last dose of linezolid or IV methylene blue, whichever comes first. May resume doxepin 24 hours after the last dose of linezolid or IV methylene blue.

Geriatric

Depression and/or anxiety: Oral: Carefully adjust the use of doxepin on a once-a-day dosage regimen in elderly patients based on the patient's condition; elderly patients generally should be started on low doses of doxepin and observed closely. Avoid doses >6 mg/day (Beers Criteria [AGS 2015]).

Insomnia: Oral: 3 mg once daily within 30 minutes of bedtime; increase to 6 mg once daily if clinically needed; maximum dose: 6 mg daily. Avoid doses >6 mg/day (Beers Criteria [AGS 2015]).

Discontinuation of therapy: Refer to adult dosing.

MAO inhibitor recommendations: Refer to adult dosing.

Renal Impairment There are no dosage adjustments provided in manufacturer's labeling.

Hepatic Impairment Silenor: Initial: 3 mg once daily

Mechanism of Action

Increases the synaptic concentration of serotonin and norepinephrine in the central nervous system by inhibition of their reuptake by the presynaptic neuronal membrane (Pinder, 1977); antagonizes the histamine (H_1) receptor for sleep maintenance.

Efficacy of doxepin in the off-label use of chronic urticaria is believed to be related to its potent H_1 and H_2 receptor antagonist activity (Kozel 2004).

Contraindications

Hypersensitivity to doxepin, dibenzoxepins, or any component of the formulation; glaucoma; urinary retention; use of MAO inhibitors within 14 days

Documentation of allergenic cross-reactivity for tricyclic antidepressants is limited. However, because of similarities in chemical structure and/or pharmacologic actions, the possibility of cross-sensitivity cannot be ruled out with certainty.

Warnings/Precautions

[US Boxed Warning]: Antidepressants increase the risk of suicidal thinking and behavior in children, adolescents, and young adults (18-24 years of age) with major depressive disorder (MDD) and other psychiatric disorders; consider risk prior to prescribing. Short-term studies did not show an increased risk in patients >24 years of age and showed a decreased risk in patients ≥65 years. Closely monitor for clinical worsening, suicidality, or unusual changes in behavior, particularly during the initial 1 to 2 months of therapy or during periods of dosage adjustments (increases or decreases); the patient's family or caregiver should be instructed to closely observe the patient and communicate condition with healthcare provider. A medication guide should be dispensed with each prescription. **Doxepin is not approved for use in pediatric patients.**

The possibility of a suicide attempt is inherent in major depression and may persist until remission occurs. Use caution in high-risk patients. Worsening depression and severe abrupt suicidality that are not part of the presenting symptoms may require discontinuation or modification of drug therapy. The patient's family or caregiver should be alerted to monitor patients for the emergence of suicidality and associated behaviors (such as agitation, irritability, hostility, impulsivity, and hypomania) and call healthcare provider.

Risk of suicidal behavior may be increased regardless of doxepin dose; antidepressant doses of doxepin are 10- to 100-fold higher than doses for insomnia.

May precipitate a shift to mania or hypomania in patients with bipolar disorder. Patients presenting with depressive symptoms should be screened for bipolar disorder. Monotherapy in patients with bipolar disorder should be avoided. **Doxepin is not FDA approved for the treatment of bipolar depression.**

Should only be used for insomnia after evaluation of potential causes of sleep disturbance. Failure of sleep disturbance to resolve after 7 to 10 days may indicate psychiatric or medical illness. An increased risk for hazardous sleep-related activities has been noted; discontinue use with any sleep-related episodes. The risks of sedative and anticholinergic effects are high relative to other antidepressant agents. Anxiety, psychosis, and other neuropsychiatric symptoms may occur unpredictably. May cause CNS depression, which may impair physical or mental abilities; patients must be cautioned about performing tasks that require mental alertness (eg, operating machinery or driving). Also use caution in patients with benign prostatic hyperplasia, xerostomia, visual problems, constipation, or history of bowel obstruction.

May cause orthostatic hypotension or conduction disturbances (risks are moderate relative to other antidepressants). Use with caution in patients with a history of cardiovascular disease (including previous MI, stroke, tachycardia, or conduction abnormalities). In a scientific statement from the American Heart Association, doxepin has been determined to be an agent that may exacerbate underlying myocardial dysfunction (magnitude: moderate) (AHA [Page 2016]). Use with caution in patients with respiratory compromise or sleep apnea; use of Silenor is generally not recommended with severe sleep apnea.

Use caution in patients with a previous seizure disorder or condition predisposing to seizures such as brain damage, alcoholism, or concurrent therapy with other drugs which lower the seizure threshold (APA 2010). Bone fractures have been associated with antidepressant treatment. Consider the possibility of a fragility fracture if an antidepressant-treated patient presents with unexplained bone pain, point tenderness, swelling, or bruising (Rabenda 2013; Rizzoli 2012). Use with caution in patients with hepatic dysfunction. May cause mild pupillary dilation which in susceptible individuals can lead to an episode of narrow-angle glaucoma. Consider evaluating patients who have not had an iridectomy for narrow-angle glaucoma risk factors. Potentially significant drug-drug interactions may exist, requiring dose or frequency adjustment, additional monitoring, and/or selection of alternative therapy.

May cause confusion and over sedation in the elderly.

Abrupt discontinuation or interruption of antidepressant therapy has been associated with a discontinuation syndrome. Symptoms arising may vary with antidepressant however commonly include nausea, vomiting, diarrhea, headaches, lightheadedness, dizziness, diminished appetite, sweating, chills, tremors, paresthesias, fatigue, somnolence, and sleep disturbances (eg, vivid dreams, insomnia). Greater risks for developing a discontinuation syndrome have been associated with antidepressants with shorter half-lives, longer durations of treatment, and abrupt discontinuation. For antidepressants of short or intermediate half-lives, symptoms may emerge within 2-5 days after treatment discontinuation and last 7 to 14 days (APA 2010; Fava 2006; Haddad 2001; Shelton 2001; Warner 2006).

Drug Interactions

Metabolism/Transport Effects Substrate of CYP1A2 (minor), CYP2C19 (minor), CYP2D6 (major), CYP3A4 (minor); **Note:** Assignment of Major/Minor substrate status based on clinically relevant drug interaction potential

Avoid Concomitant Use

Avoid concomitant use of Doxepin (Systemic) with any of the following: Aclidinium; Azelastine (Nasal); Cimetropium; Dapoxetine; Dronedarone; Eluxadoline; Glucagon; Glycopyrrolate (Oral Inhalation); Iobenguane I 123; Ipratropium (Oral Inhalation); Levosulpiride; Linezolid; MAO Inhibitors; Methylene Blue; Moxonidine; Nitroglycerin; Orphenadrine; Oxatomide; Oxomemazine; Paraldehyde; Potassium Chloride; Thalidomide; Tiotropium; Umeclidinium

Increased Effect/Toxicity

Doxepin (Systemic) may increase the levels/effects of: AbobotulinumtoxinA; Alcohol (Ethyl); Alpha-/Beta-Agonists (Direct-Acting); Alpha1-Agonists; Amphetamines; Analgesics (Opioid); Anticholinergic Agents; Antipsychotic Agents; Aspirin; Azelastine (Nasal); Beta2-Agonists; Blonanserin; Buprenorphine; Cimetropium; Citalopram; CNS Depressants; Desmopressin; Dronedarone; Eluxadoline; Escitalopram; Flunitrazepam; Glucagon; Glycopyrrolate (Oral Inhalation); Highest Risk QTc-Prolonging Agents; HYDROcodone; Iohexol; Iomeprol; Iopamidol; Methotrimeprazine; Methylene Blue; MetyroSINE; Mirabegron; Mirtazapine; Moderate Risk QTc-Prolonging Agents; Nicorandil; NSAID (COX-2 Inhibitor); NSAID (Nonselective); OnabotulinumtoxinA; Orphenadrine; OxyCODONE; Paraldehyde; Perhexiline; Piribedil; Potassium Chloride; Pramipexole; QuiNIDine; Ramosetron; RimabotulinumtoxinB; ROPINIRole; Rotigotine; Selective Serotonin Reuptake Inhibitors; Serotonin Modulators; Sodium Phosphates; Sulfonylureas; Suvorexant; Thalidomide; Thiazide and Thiazide-Like Diuretics; Tiotropium; Topiramate; Vitamin K Antagonists; Yohimbine; Zolpidem

The levels/effects of Doxepin (Systemic) may be increased by: Abiraterone Acetate; Aclidinium; Altretamine; Antiemetics (5HT3 Antagonists); Antipsychotic Agents; Asunaprevir; Brimonidine (Topical); BuPROPion; Cannabis; Chloral Betaine; Chlormethiazole; Chlorphenesin Carbamate; Cimetidine; Cinacalcet; Citalopram; Cobicistat; CYP2D6 Inhibitors (Moderate); CYP2D6 Inhibitors (Strong); Dapoxetine; Darunavir; Dexmethylphenidate; Dimethindene (Topical); Doxylamine; Dronabinol; Droperidol; DULoxetine; Escitalopram; FLUoxetine; FluvoxaMINE; HydrOXYzine; Imatinib; Ipratropium (Oral Inhalation); Kava Kava; Linezolid; Lithium; Magnesium Sulfate; MAO Inhibitors; Metaxalone; Methotrimeprazine; Methylene Blue; Methylphenidate; Metoclopramide; MetyroSINE; Mianserin; MiFEPRIStone; Minocycline; Nabilone; Oxatomide; Oxomemazine; Panobinostat; PARoxetine; Peginterferon Alfa-2b; Perampanel; Perhexiline; Pramlintide; Protease Inhibitors; QuiNIDine; Rufinamide; Sertraline; Sodium Oxybate; Tapentadol; Tedizolid; Tetrahydrocannabinol; Thyroid Products; Trimeprazine; Umeclidinium; Valproate Products

Decreased Effect

Doxepin (Systemic) may decrease the levels/effects of: Acetylcholinesterase Inhibitors; Alpha1-Agonists; Alpha2-Agonists; Alpha2-Agonists (Ophthalmic); Gastrointestinal Agents (Prokinetic); Iobenguane I 123; Itopride; Levosulpiride; Moxonidine; Nitroglycerin; Secretin

The levels/effects of Doxepin (Systemic) may be decreased by: Acetylcholinesterase Inhibitors; Barbiturates; CarBAMazepine; Peginterferon Alfa-2b; St John's Wort

Food Interactions Administration with a high-fat meal increases the bioavailability of Silenor and delays the peak plasma concentration by ~3 hours. Management: Silenor should not be taken during or within 3 hours of a meal.

Pharmacodynamics/Kinetics

Onset of Action Individual responses may vary; 4-8 weeks of treatment are needed before determining if a patient with depression is partially or nonresponsive (APA 2010); onset of anxiolytic effects may have a latency of 2-6 weeks (Bandelow 2008)

Half-life Elimination Adults: Doxepin: ~15 hours; N-desmethyldoxepin: 31 hours

Time to Peak Serum: Fasting: Silenor: 3.5 hours

Pregnancy Risk Factor C

Pregnancy Considerations Adverse events were observed in animal reproduction studies. Tricyclic antidepressants may be associated with irritability, jitteriness, and convulsions (rare) in the neonate (Yonkers 2009).

The ACOG recommends that therapy for depression during pregnancy be individualized; treatment should incorporate the clinical expertise of the mental health clinician, obstetrician, primary health care provider, and pediatrician (ACOG 2008). According to the American Psychiatric Association (APA), the risks of medication treatment should be weighed against other treatment options and untreated depression. For women who discontinue antidepressant medications during pregnancy and who may be at high risk for postpartum depression, the medications can be restarted following delivery (APA 2010). Treatment algorithms have been developed by the ACOG and the APA for the management of depression in women prior to conception and during pregnancy (Yonkers 2009).

Pregnant women exposed to antidepressants during pregnancy are encouraged to enroll in the National Pregnancy Registry for Antidepressants (NPRAD). Women 18 to 45 years of age or their health care providers may contact the registry by calling 844-405-6185. Enrollment should be done as early in pregnancy as possible.

Breastfeeding Considerations Doxepin and N-desmethyldoxepin are excreted into breast milk (Frey, 1999; Kemp, 1985). Drowsiness, vomiting, poor feeding, and muscle hypotonia were noted in a nursing infant following maternal use of doxepin. Symptoms began to resolve 24 hours after feedings with breast milk were discontinued (Frey, 1999). In addition, product labeling notes that drowsiness and apnea have been reported in a nursing infant following maternal use of doxepin for depression. The manufacturer recommends that caution be used if administered to a nursing woman.

Dosage Forms

Capsule, Oral:

Generic: 10 mg, 25 mg, 50 mg, 75 mg, 100 mg, 150 mg

Concentrate, Oral:

Generic: 10 mg/mL (118 mL, 120 mL)

Tablet, Oral:

Silenor: 3 mg, 6 mg

Dosage Forms: Canada Note: Refer to Dosage Forms. Oral concentrate is not available in Canada.

Dental Comment See Local Anesthetic/Vasoconstrictor Precautions

Doxepin (Topical) (DOKS e pin)

Brand Names: US Prudoxin; Zonalon

Brand Names: Canada Zonalon

Generic Availability (US) Yes

Pharmacologic Category Topical Skin Product

Dental Use Cream: Treatment of burning mouth syndrome and neuropathic pain

Use Pruritus: Short-term (≤8 days) management of moderate pruritus in adults with atopic dermatitis or lichen simplex chronicus.

Local Anesthetic/Vasoconstrictor Precautions No information available to require special precautions

Effects on Dental Treatment Key adverse event(s) related to dental treatment: Xerostomia and changes in salivation (normal salivary flow resumes upon discontinuation)

Topical: Taste alteration

Long-term treatment with TCAs increases the risk of caries by reducing salivation and salivary buffer capacity.

Effects on Bleeding No information available to require special precautions

Adverse Reactions

>10%:

Central nervous system: Drowsiness (22%)

Dermatologic: Burning sensation of skin (≤23%), stinging of the skin (≤23%)

1% to 10%:

Cardiovascular: Edema (1%)

Central nervous system: Dizziness (2%), emotional lability (2%)

Gastrointestinal: Xerostomia (10%), dysgeusia (2%)

<1%, postmarketing, and/or case reports: Anxiety, contact dermatitis, numbness of tongue

Dental Usual Dosage Treatment of burning mouth syndrome and neuropathic pain (off-label uses): Adults: Oral: Topical: Cream: Apply 3-4 times daily

Dosing

Adult

Pruritus: Topical: Apply a thin film 4 times/day with at least 3- to 4-hour interval between applications; not recommended for use >8 days.

Note: Risk of systemic side effects is greater when applying to over 10% of body surface area. If excessive drowsiness occurs it may be necessary to decrease the BSA treated, decrease the frequency of applications and/or the amount of cream applied or discontinue therapy.

Neuropathic pain (off-label use): Topical: 3.3% cream (extemporaneous preparation): Apply a thin film to painful area 3 times daily (McCleane 2000).

Geriatric

Refer to adult dosing; use with caution.

Renal Impairment There are no dosage adjustments provided in the manufacturer's labeling (has not been studied); higher doxepin concentrations may occur with renal impairment.

Hepatic Impairment There are no dosage adjustments provided in the manufacturer's labeling.

Mechanism of Action Doxepin has H_1 and H_2 histamine receptor blocking actions, the exact mechanism by which it exerts its antipruritic effect is unknown.

Contraindications

Hypersensitivity to doxepin or any component of the formulation; untreated narrow-angle glaucoma; tendency to urinary retention

Canadian labeling: Additional contraindications (not in US labeling): Hypersensitivity to other dibenzoxepins compounds; use in children <12 years of age

Warnings/Precautions For external use only (not for ophthalmic, vaginal, or oral use); avoid contact with eyes. Doxepin is significantly absorbed following topical administration; plasma levels may be similar to those achieved with oral administration. May cause CNS depression, which may impair physical or mental abilities; patients must be cautioned about performing tasks that require mental alertness (eg, operating machinery or driving). Drowsiness has been reported in >20% of patients; risk is increased with greater body surface area (>10%) application.

Also use caution in patients with benign prostatic hyperplasia, xerostomia, visual problems, constipation, or history of bowel obstruction. May cause anticholinergic effects (dry mouth, thirst, taste changes, dry eyes).

May cause contact sensitization; use for >8 days may increase risk. Use with caution in patients with renal impairment; higher doxepin concentrations may occur. May cause confusion and oversedation in the elderly; use with caution; monitor closely.

Some dosage forms may contain benzyl alcohol; large amounts of benzyl alcohol (≥99 mg/kg/day) have been associated with a potentially fatal toxicity ("gasping syndrome") in neonates; the "gasping syndrome" consists of metabolic acidosis, respiratory distress, gasping respirations, CNS dysfunction (including convulsions, intracranial hemorrhage), hypotension and cardiovascular collapse (AAP 1997; CDC 1982); some data suggests that benzoate displaces bilirubin from protein binding sites (Ahlfors 2001); avoid or use dosage forms containing benzyl alcohol with caution in neonates. See manufacturer's labeling. Potentially significant interactions may exist, requiring dose or frequency adjustment, additional monitoring, and/or selection of alternative therapy.

Drug Interactions

Metabolism/Transport Effects Substrate of CYP1A2 (minor), CYP2C19 (minor), CYP2D6 (major), CYP3A4 (minor); **Note:** Assignment of Major/Minor substrate status based on clinically relevant drug interaction potential

Avoid Concomitant Use

Avoid concomitant use of Doxepin (Topical) with any of the following: Aclidinium; Azelastine (Nasal); Cimetropium; Dapoxetine; Dronedarone; Eluxadoline; Glucagon; Glycopyrrolate (Oral Inhalation); Iobenguane I 123; Ipratropium (Oral Inhalation); Levosulpiride; Linezolid; MAO Inhibitors; Methylene Blue; Moxonidine; Nitroglycerin; Orphenadrine; Oxatomide; Oxomemazine; Paraldehyde; Potassium Chloride; Thalidomide; Tiotropium; Umeclidinium

Increased Effect/Toxicity

Doxepin (Topical) may increase the levels/effects of: AbobotulinumtoxinA; Alcohol (Ethyl); Alpha-/Beta-Agonists (Direct-Acting); Alpha1-Agonists; Amphetamines; Analgesics (Opioid); Anticholinergic Agents; Antipsychotic Agents; Aspirin; Azelastine (Nasal); Beta2-Agonists; Blonanserin; Buprenorphine; Cimetropium; Citalopram; CNS Depressants; Desmopressin; Dronedarone; Eluxadoline; Escitalopram; Flunitrazepam; Glucagon; Glycopyrrolate (Oral Inhalation); Highest Risk QTc-Prolonging Agents; HYDROcodone; Iohexol; Iomeprol; Iopamidol; Methotrimeprazine; Methylene Blue; MetyroSINE; Mirabegron; Mirtazapine; Moderate Risk QTc-Prolonging Agents; Nicorandil; NSAID (COX-2 Inhibitor); NSAID (Nonselective); OnabotulinumtoxinA; Orphenadrine; OxyCODONE; Paraldehyde; Perhexiline; Piribedil; Potassium Chloride; Pramipexole; QuiNIDine; Ramosetron; RimabotulinumtoxinB; ROPINIRole; Rotigotine; Selective Serotonin Reuptake Inhibitors; Serotonin Modulators; Sodium Phosphates; Sulfonylureas; Suvorexant; Thalidomide; Thiazide and Thiazide-Like Diuretics; Tiotropium; Topiramate; Vitamin K Antagonists; Yohimbine; Zolpidem

The levels/effects of Doxepin (Topical) may be increased by: Abiraterone Acetate; Aclidinium; Altretamine; Antiemetics (5HT3 Antagonists); Antipsychotic Agents; Asunaprevir; Brimonidine (Topical); BuPROPion; Cannabis; Chloral Betaine; Chlormethiazole; Chlorphenesin Carbamate; Cimetidine; Cinacalcet; Citalopram; Cobicistat; CYP2D6 Inhibitors (Moderate); CYP2D6 Inhibitors (Strong); Dapoxetine; Darunavir; Dexmethylphenidate; Dimethindene (Topical); Doxylamine; Dronabinol; Droperidol; DULoxetine; Escitalopram; FLUoxetine; FluvoxaMINE; HydrOXYzine; Imatinib; Ipratropium (Oral Inhalation); Kava Kava; Linezolid; Lithium; Magnesium Sulfate; MAO Inhibitors; Metaxalone; Methotrimeprazine; Methylene Blue; Methylphenidate; Metoclopramide; MetyroSINE; Mianserin; MiFEPRIStone; Minocycline; Nabilone; Oxatomide; Oxomemazine; Panobinostat; PARoxetine; Peginterferon Alfa-2b; Perampanel; Perhexiline; Pramlintide; Protease Inhibitors; QuiNIDine; Rufinamide; Sertraline; Sodium Oxybate; Tapentadol; Tedizolid; Tetrahydrocannabinol; Thyroid Products; Trimeprazine; Umeclidinium; Valproate Products

Decreased Effect

Doxepin (Topical) may decrease the levels/effects of: Acetylcholinesterase Inhibitors; Alpha1-Agonists; Alpha2-Agonists; Alpha2-Agonists (Ophthalmic); Gastrointestinal Agents (Prokinetic); Iobenguane I 123; Itopride; Levosulpiride; Moxonidine; Nitroglycerin; Secretin

The levels/effects of Doxepin (Topical) may be decreased by: Acetylcholinesterase Inhibitors; Barbiturates; CarBAMazepine; Peginterferon Alfa-2b; St John's Wort

Pharmacodynamics/Kinetics

Half-life Elimination 28 to 52 hours (desmethyldoxepin)

Pregnancy Risk Factor B

Pregnancy Considerations Adverse effects were not observed in animal reproduction studies. Following topical application, plasma levels may be similar to those achieved with oral administration. Also refer to the doxepin (systemic) monograph.

Breastfeeding Considerations Doxepin is excreted into breast milk following oral administration. Following topical application, plasma levels may be similar to those achieved with oral administration. Due to the potential for serious adverse reactions in the nursing infant, the manufacturer recommends a decision be made whether to discontinue nursing or to discontinue the drug, taking into account the importance of treatment to the mother. Also refer to the doxepin (systemic) monograph.

Dosage Forms

Cream, External:

Prudoxin: 5% (45 g)

Zonalon: 5% (30 g, 45 g)

Generic: 5% (45 g)

Doxercalciferol (doks er kal si fe FEER ole)

Brand Names: US Hectorol

Brand Names: Canada Hectorol

Pharmacologic Category Vitamin D Analog

Use

Secondary hyperparathyroidism (dialysis): Injection, oral: Treatment of secondary hyperparathyroidism in patients with chronic kidney disease on dialysis

Secondary hyperparathyroidism (predialysis patients): Oral: Treatment of secondary hyperparathyroidism in patients with stage 3 or 4 chronic kidney disease

Local Anesthetic/Vasoconstrictor Precautions No information available to require special precautions

Effects on Dental Treatment No significant effects or complications reported

Effects on Bleeding No information available to require special precautions

Adverse Reactions

Adverse events as reported in dialysis patients.

>10%:

Cardiovascular: Edema (34%)

Central nervous system: Headache (28%), malaise (28%), dizziness (12%)

Gastrointestinal: Nausea and vomiting (21%)

Respiratory: Dyspnea (12%)

1% to 10%:

Cardiovascular: Bradycardia (7%)

Central nervous system: Sleep disorder (3%)

Dermatologic: Pruritus (8%)

Endocrine & metabolic: Weight gain (5%), hyperphosphatemia (2% to 4%), hypercalcemia (1%)

Gastrointestinal: Anorexia (5%), dyspepsia (5%)

Infection: Abscess (3%)

Neuromuscular & skeletal: Arthralgia (5%)

<1%, postmarketing, and/or case reports: Hypersensitivity reaction (including anaphylaxis, angioedema, hypotension, unresponsive to stimuli, chest discomfort, dyspnea, pruritus, burning sensation of skin)

General Dosage Range

IV: *Adults:* Initial: 4 mcg 3 times/week at the end of dialysis; Titrate to response; Maintenance: Up to 18 mcg/week

Oral:

Adults (dialysis patients): Initial: 10 mcg 3 times/week at dialysis; Maintenance: Up to 60 mcg/week

Adults (predialysis patients): Initial: 1 mcg/day; Maintenance: Up to 3.5 mcg/day

Mechanism of Action Doxercalciferol is metabolized to the active form of vitamin D. The active form of vitamin D controls the intestinal absorption of dietary calcium, the tubular reabsorption of calcium by the kidneys, and in conjunction with PTH, the mobilization of calcium from the skeleton.

Pharmacodynamics/Kinetics

Half-life Elimination Major metabolite: ~32 to 37 hours (range: up to 96 hours)

Time to Peak Major metabolite: 2.1 to 13.9 hours (injection); 11 to 12 hours (oral).

Pregnancy Risk Factor B

Pregnancy Considerations Adverse events have not been observed in animal reproduction studies

DOXOrubicin (Conventional)

(doks oh ROO bi sin con VEN sha nal)

Related Information

DOXOrubicin (Liposomal) *on page 539*

Brand Names: US Adriamycin

Brand Names: Canada Adriamycin PFS; Doxorubicin Hydrochloride For Injection, USP; Doxorubicin Hydrochloride Injection

Pharmacologic Category Antineoplastic Agent, Anthracycline; Antineoplastic Agent, Topoisomerase II Inhibitor

Use

Breast cancer: Treatment component of adjuvant therapy in women with evidence of axillary lymph node involvement following resection of primary breast cancer

Metastatic cancers or disseminated neoplastic conditions: Treatment of acute lymphoblastic leukemia, acute myeloid leukemia, Wilms tumor, neuroblastoma, soft tissue and bone sarcomas, breast cancer, ovarian cancer, transitional cell bladder carcinoma, thyroid carcinoma, gastric carcinoma, Hodgkin lymphoma, non-Hodgkin lymphoma, and bronchogenic carcinoma in which the small cell histologic type is the most responsive compared with other cell types

Local Anesthetic/Vasoconstrictor Precautions No information available to require special precautions

Effects on Dental Treatment Key adverse event(s) related to dental treatment: Stomatitis and mucositis.

Effects on Bleeding Severe myelosuppression with thrombocytopenia and anemia occur. Medical consult suggested.

Adverse Reactions Frequency not always defined.

Cardiovascular:

Acute cardiotoxicity: Atrioventricular block, bradycardia, bundle branch block, ECG abnormality, extrasystoles (atrial or ventricular), nonspecific ST or T wave changes on ECG, sinus tachycardia, supraventricular tachycardia, tachyarrhythmia, ventricular tachycardia

Delayed cardiotoxicity: Cardiac failure (manifestations include ascites, cardiomegaly, dyspnea, edema, gallop rhythm, hepatomegaly, oliguria, pleural effusion, pulmonary edema, tachycardia), decreased left ventricular ejection fraction, myocarditis, pericarditis

Central nervous system: Malaise

Dermatologic: Alopecia, discoloration of sweat, pruritus, skin photosensitivity, skin rash; urticaria

Endocrine & metabolic: Amenorrhea, dehydration, hyperuricemia

Gastrointestinal: Abdominal pain, anorexia, diarrhea, discoloration of saliva, gastrointestinal ulcer, mucositis, nausea, vomiting

Genitourinary: Urine discoloration, infertility (may be temporary)

Hematologic & oncologic: Leukopenia (≤75%; nadir: 10 to 14 days; recovery: by day 21), neutropenia (≤75%; nadir: 10 to 14 days; recovery: by day 21), anemia, thrombocytopenia

Local: Post-injection flare

Neuromuscular & skeletal: Weakness

Ophthalmic: Discoloration of tears

Miscellaneous: Necrosis (colon), radiation recall phenomenon

<1%, postmarketing, and/or case reports: Acute myelocytic leukemia (secondary), anaphylaxis, azoospermia, chills, coma (when in combination with cisplatin or vincristine), conjunctivitis, febrile neutropenia, fever, gonadal disease (gonadal impairment; children), growth suppression (prepubertal), hepatitis, hyperpigmentation (nail, oral mucosa, skin), hypersensitivity reaction (systemic; including angioedema, dysphagia, and dyspnea, pruritus, urticaria), increased serum bilirubin, increased serum transaminases, infection, keratitis, lacrimation, myelodysplastic syndrome, oligospermia, onycholysis, peripheral neurotoxicity (with intra-arterial doxorubicin), phlebosclerosis, pneumonitis (radiation recall; children), seizure (when in combination with cisplatin or vincristine), sepsis, shock, Stevens-Johnson syndrome, toxic epidermal necrolysis, typhlitis (neutropenic)

General Dosage Range Dosage adjustment recommended in patients with hepatic impairment or who develop toxicities

IV: *Children, Adolescents, and Adults:* Dosage varies greatly depending on indication

Mechanism of Action Inhibition of DNA and RNA synthesis by intercalation between DNA base pairs by inhibition of topoisomerase II and by steric obstruction. Doxorubicin intercalates at points of local uncoiling of the double helix. Although the exact mechanism is unclear, it appears that direct binding to DNA (intercalation) and inhibition of DNA repair (topoisomerase II inhibition) result in blockade of DNA and RNA synthesis and fragmentation of DNA. Doxorubicin is also a powerful iron chelator; the iron-doxorubicin complex can bind DNA and cell membranes and produce free radicals that immediately cleave the DNA and cell membranes.

Pharmacodynamics/Kinetics

Half-life Elimination

Distribution: ~5 minutes

Terminal: 20 to 48 hours

Male: 54 hours; Female: 35 hours

Pregnancy Risk Factor D

Pregnancy Considerations Adverse events have been observed in animal reproduction studies. Based on the mechanism of action, doxorubicin may cause fetal harm if administered during pregnancy (according to the manufacturer's labeling). Advise patients (females of reproductive potential and males with female partners of reproductive potential) to use effective nonhormonal contraception during and for 6 months following therapy. Limited information is available from a retrospective study of women who received doxorubicin (in combination with cyclophosphamide) during the second or third (prior to week 35) trimester for the treatment of pregnancy-associated breast cancer (Ring 2005). Some pharmacokinetic properties of doxorubicin may be altered in pregnant women (van Hasselt 2014). The European Society for Medical Oncology (ESMO) has published guidelines for diagnosis, treatment, and follow-up of cancer during pregnancy (Peccatori 2013); the guidelines recommend referral to a facility with expertise in cancer during pregnancy and encourage a multidisciplinary team (obstetrician, neonatologist, oncology team). If chemotherapy is indicated, it should **not** be administered in the first trimester, but may begin in the second trimester. There should be a 3-week time period between the last chemotherapy dose and anticipated delivery, and chemotherapy should not be administered beyond week 33 of gestation.

A pregnancy registry is available for all cancers diagnosed during pregnancy at Cooper Health (877-635-4499).

DOXOrubicin (Liposomal)

(doks oh ROO bi sin lye po SO mal)

Related Information

DOXOrubicin (Conventional) *on page 538*

Brand Names: US Doxil; Lipodox 50; Lipodox [DSC]

Brand Names: Canada Caelyx

Pharmacologic Category Antineoplastic Agent, Anthracycline; Antineoplastic Agent, Topoisomerase II Inhibitor

Use

AIDS-related Kaposi sarcoma: Treatment of AIDS-related Kaposi sarcoma (after failure of or intolerance to prior systemic therapy)

Multiple myeloma: Treatment of multiple myeloma (in combination with bortezomib) in patients who are bortezomib-naïve and have received at least 1 prior therapy

Ovarian cancer, advanced: Treatment of progressive or recurrent ovarian cancer (after platinum-based treatment)

Local Anesthetic/Vasoconstrictor Precautions No information available to require special precautions

Effects on Dental Treatment Key adverse event(s) related to dental treatment: Xerostomia (normal salivary flow resumes upon discontinuation), mucositis, gingivitis, glossitis, mouth ulceration, taste perversion, and stomatitis.

Effects on Bleeding Severe myelosuppression with thrombocytopenia and anemia occur. Medical consult suggested.

Adverse Reactions Frequency not always defined.

>10%:

Cardiovascular: Cardiomyopathy (dose related: 11%; Kaposi sarcoma: <1%), cardiotoxicity (11%), chest tightness (11%), flushing (11%), hypotension (1% to 11%)

Central nervous system: Fatigue (>20%), headache (≤11%)

Dermatologic: Palmar-plantar erythrodysesthesia (ovarian cancer: ≤51%; grades 3/4: 24%), skin rash (grades 3/4: 29%, Kaposi sarcoma: 1% to 5%), alopecia (9% to 19%), facial swelling (11%)

Gastrointestinal: Nausea (ovarian cancer: 46%; Kaposi sarcoma: 17% to 18%; grades 3/4: 5%), stomatitis (grades 3/4: 41%, Kaposi sarcoma: 5% to 8%), vomiting (grades 3/4: 33%; Kaposi sarcoma: 8%), constipation (>20%), diarrhea (grades 3/4: 21%; Kaposi sarcoma: 3% to 8%), anorexia (20%; Kaposi sarcoma: 1% to 5%), mucous membrane disease (14%; grades 3/4: 4%), dyspepsia 12%; grades 3/4: <1%)

Hematologic & oncologic: Thrombocytopenia (dose related, Kaposi sarcoma: 1% to 61%), neutropenia (dose related: 4% to 49%), leukopenia (37%), anemia (16% to 58%; dose related <1% to 5%)

Neuromuscular & skeletal: Weakness (grades 3/4: 40%; Kaposi sarcoma: 7% to 10%), back pain (grades 3/4: 11% to 12%; Kaposi sarcoma: 1% to 5%)

Respiratory: Pharyngitis (16%; Kaposi sarcoma <1%), dyspnea (1% to 15%)

Miscellaneous: Fever (21%; Kaposi sarcoma: 8% to 9%; grades 3/4: <1%), infusion related reaction (7% to 11%)

1% to 10%:

Cardiovascular: Cardiac arrest (≤10%), chest pain (Kaposi sarcoma: 1% to 5%), deep thrombophlebitis (ovarian cancer: 1% to 10%), tachycardia (1% to 10%), vasodilation (ovarian cancer: 1% to 10%)

Central nervous system: Depression (ovarian cancer: 1% to 10%), dizziness (1% to 10%), drowsiness (1% to 10%), chills (Kaposi sarcoma: 1% to 5%)

Dermatologic: Acne vulgaris (ovarian cancer: 1% to 10%), ecchymoses (ovarian cancer: 1% to 10%), exfoliative dermatitis (ovarian cancer: 1% to 10%), fungal dermatitis (ovarian cancer: 1% to 10%), furunculosis (ovarian cancer: 1% to 10%), herpes simplex dermatitis (1% to 10%), pruritus (1% to 10%), skin discoloration (ovarian cancer: 1% to 10%), vesiculobullous dermatitis (ovarian cancer: 1% to 10%), xeroderma (ovarian cancer: 1% to 10%), maculopapular rash (≤10%)

Endocrine & metabolic: Hypercalcemia (ovarian cancer: 1% to 10%), hypokalemia (ovarian cancer: 1% to 10%), hyponatremia (ovarian cancer: 1% to 10%), weight loss (1% to 10%), dehydration (≤10%), hyperglycemia (1% to 5%)

Gastrointestinal: Dysphagia (1% to 10%), esophagitis (ovarian cancer: 1% to 10%), intestinal obstruction (ovarian cancer: 1% to 10%), oral candidiasis (1% to 10%), oral mucosa ulcer (1% to 10%), dysgeusia (1% to ≤10%), abdomen enlarged (ovarian cancer 1% to 5%), glossitis (1% to 5%), increased serum alanine aminotransferase (Kaposi sarcoma 1% to 5%), cachexia

Genitourinary: Hematuria (ovarian cancer: 1% to 10%), hemorrhagic cystitis, urinary tract infection (ovarian cancer: 1% to 10%), vulvovaginal candidiasis (ovarian cancer 1% to 10%)

Hematologic & oncologic: Rectal hemorrhage (ovarian cancer: 1% to 10%), hemolysis (1% to 5%), prolonged prothrombin time (1% to 5%), bone marrow depression (Kaposi sarcoma), progression of cancer (Kaposi sarcoma)

Hepatic: Hyperbilirubinemia (1% to 10%), increased serum alkaline phosphatase (Kaposi sarcoma 1% to 8%)

Hypersensitivity: Hypersensitivity reaction (Kaposi sarcoma 1% to 5%)

Infection: Infection (1% to 12%), herpes zoster (≤10%), paresthesia (5%), myalgia (ovarian cancer: 1% to 5%), neuropathy (ovarian cancer 1% to 5%), toxoplasmosis (Kaposi sarcoma)

Ocular: Dry eye syndrome (ovarian cancer: 1% to 10%), conjunctivitis (≤10%), retinitis (Kaposi sarcoma 1% to 5%) optic neuritis (Kaposi sarcoma)

Respiratory: Epistaxis (ovarian cancer: 1% to 10%), pneumonia (1% to 10%), rhinitis (ovarian cancer: 1% to 10%), sinusitis (ovarian cancer: 1% to 10%), increased cough (≤10%), cough (Kaposi sarcoma)

<1%, postmarketing, and/or case reports (Limited to important or life-threatening): Abnormal vision, abscess, acute brain syndrome, albuminuria, alkaline phosphatase increased anaphylactic reaction, anxiety, arthralgia, asthma, balanitis, blindness, bone pain, bronchitis, bundle branch block (Kaposi sarcoma), BUN increased, candidiasis (Kaposi sarcoma), cardiomegaly, cardiomyopathy, cellulitis, CHF, colitis, confusion, congestive heart failure (Kaposi sarcoma), creatinine increased, cryptococcosis, cryptococcosis (Kaposi sarcoma), diabetes mellitus, dysuria,edema, emotional lability, erythema multiforme, erythema nodosum, eosinophilia, fecal impaction, flatulence, flu-like syndrome, gastritis, hemorrhage, hepatic failure, hepatitis (Kaposi sarcoma), hepatosplenomegaly, hyperkalemia, hyperlipidemia, hypernatremia, hyperuricemia, hyperventilation, hypoglycemia, hypomagnesemia, hypophosphatemia, hypoproteinemia, hypothermia, injection site hemorrhage, injection site pain, insomnia, jaundice, ketosis, lactic dehydrogenase increased, lymphadenopathy, lymphangitis, migraine, myositis, muscle spasm, optic neuritis, pain, pallor, palpitations (Kaposi sarcoma), pancreatitis, pericardial effusion, petechia, pneumothorax, peripheral edema, pleural effusion, pulmonary embolism, radiation injury, sclerosing cholangitis, seizure, secondary acute myelocytic leukemia, sepsis (Kaposi sarcoma), skin necrosis, skin ulcer, syncope, squamous cell carcinoma, Stevens-Johnson syndrome, tenesmus, thrombophlebitis (Kaposi sarcoma), thromboplastin decreased, thrombosis (Kaposi sarcoma), tinnitus, toxic epidermal necrolysis, urticaria, vertigo (Kaposi sarcoma), ventricular arrhythmia (Kaposi sarcoma)

General Dosage Range Dosage adjustment recommended in patients with hepatic impairment or who develop toxicities

IV: *Adults:* 20 to 30 mg/m^2 every 3 weeks **or** 50 mg/m^2 every 4 weeks

Mechanism of Action Doxorubicin inhibits DNA and RNA synthesis by intercalating between DNA base pairs causing steric obstruction and inhibits topoisomerase-II at the point of DNA cleavage. Doxorubicin is also a powerful iron chelator. The iron-doxorubicin complex can bind DNA and cell membranes, producing free hydroxyl (OH) radicals that cleave DNA and cell membranes. Active throughout entire cell cycle. Doxorubicin liposomal is a pegylated formulation which protects the liposomes, and thereby increases blood circulation time.

Pharmacodynamics/Kinetics

Half-life Elimination Terminal: Distribution: ~4.7 to 5.2 hours, Elimination: ~52 to 55 hours

Pregnancy Considerations Adverse events were observed in animal reproduction studies. May cause fetal harm if administered during pregnancy. Women and men of reproductive potential should use effective contraception during therapy and for 6 months after treatment. Doxorubicin liposomal may damage spermatozoa and testicular tissue in males and may result in oligospermia, azoospermia, and permanent loss of fertility. May cause amenorrhea, infertility, and premature menopause in females.

Doxycycline (doks i SYE kleen)

Related Information

Periodontal Diseases *on page 1844*

Sexually-Transmitted Diseases *on page 1804*

Related Sample Prescriptions

Bacterial Infections and Periodontal Diseases - Sample Prescriptions *on page 32*

Brand Names: US Acticlate; Adoxa; Adoxa Pak 1/100; Adoxa Pak 1/150; Adoxa Pak 2/100; Alodox Convenience [DSC]; Avidoxy; Doryx; Doryx MPC; Doxy 100; Mondoxyne NL; Monodox; Morgidox; NicAzelDoxy 30 [DSC]; NicAzelDoxy 60 [DSC]; Ocudox [DSC]; Oracea; Oraxyl [DSC]; TargaDOX; Vibramycin

Brand Names: Canada Apo-Doxy; Apo-Doxy Tabs; Apprilon; Dom-Doxycycline; Doxycin; Doxytab; Periostat; PHL-Doxycycline; PMS-Doxycycline; Teva-Doxycycline; Vibramycin

Generic Availability (US) May be product dependent

Pharmacologic Category Antibiotic, Tetracycline Derivative

Dental Use Treatment of periodontitis associated with presence of *Actinobacillus actinomycetemcomitans* (AA); adjunct to scaling and root planing to promote attachment level gain and to reduce pocket depth in adult periodontitis (systemic levels are subinhibitory against bacteria)

Use

Acne: Adjunctive therapy in severe acne.

Actinomycosis: Treatment of actinomycosis caused by *Actinomyces israelii* when penicillin is contraindicated.

Acute intestinal amebiasis: Adjunct to amebicides in acute intestinal amebiasis.

Anthrax, including inhalational anthrax (postexposure): Treatment of anthrax caused by *Bacillus anthracis*, including inhalational (postexposure) prophylaxis; to reduce the incidence or progression of disease following exposure to aerosolized *B. anthracis*.

Cholera: Treatment of cholera infections caused by *Vibrio cholerae*.

***Clostridium*:** Treatment of infections caused by *Clostridium* spp. when penicillin is contraindicated.

Gram-negative infections: Treatment of infections caused by *Escherichia coli*, *Enterobacter aerogenes*, *Shigella* spp., *Acinetobacter* spp., *Klebsiella* spp. (respiratory and urinary infections), and *Bacteroides* spp.; *Neisseria meningitidis* (when penicillin is contraindicated).

Gram-positive infections: Treatment of infections caused by *Streptococcus* spp., when susceptible.

Listeriosis: Treatment of listeriosis due to *Listeria monocytogenes* when penicillin is contraindicated.

Malaria prophylaxis: Prophylaxis of malaria due to *Plasmodium falciparum* in short-term travelers (under 4 months) to areas with chloroquine and/or pyrimethamine-sulfadoxine-resistant strains.

Mycoplasma pneumoniae: Treatment of infections caused by *Mycoplasma pneumoniae*.

Ophthalmic infections: Treatment of inclusion conjunctivitis or trachoma caused by *Chlamydia trachomatis*.

Periodontitis (Periostat [Canadian product] only): Adjunct to scaling and root planing to promote attachment level gain and to reduce pocket depth in patients with adult periodontitis.

Relapsing fever: Treatment of relapsing fever caused by *Borrelia recurrentis*.

Respiratory tract infections: Treatment of respiratory infections caused by *Haemophilus influenzae*, *Klebsiella* spp., or *Mycoplasma pneumoniae*; treatment of upper respiratory tract infections caused by *Streptococcus pneumoniae*; respiratory infections caused by *Staphylococcus aureus* (doxycycline is not the drug of choice in the treatment of any type of staphylococcal infections).

Rickettsial infections: Treatment of Rocky Mountain spotted fever, typhus fever and the typhus group, Q fever, rickettsialpox, and tick fevers caused by *Rickettsiae*.

Rosacea (Oracea, Apprilon [Canadian product] only): Treatment of only inflammatory lesions (papules and pustules) of rosacea in adults.

Sexually transmitted diseases: Treatment of lymphogranuloma venereum and uncomplicated urethral, endocervical, or rectal infections caused by *Chlamydia trachomatis*; granuloma inguinale (donovanosis) caused by *Klebsiella granulomatis*; chancroid caused by *Haemophilus ducreyi*; nongonococcal urethritis caused by *Ureaplasma urealyticum*; when penicillin is contraindicated, uncomplicated gonorrhea caused by *Neisseria gonorrhea* and syphilis caused by *Treponema pallidum*.

Note: The Centers for Disease Control and Prevention (CDC) sexually transmitted disease guidelines recommend dual antimicrobial therapy be used for uncomplicated gonorrhea due to *N. gonorrhea* resistance concerns; ceftriaxone is the preferred cephalosporin and doxycycline is an alternate option for the second antimicrobial only in cases azithromycin allergy (CDC [Workowski 2015]).

Skin and skin structure infections (Avidoxy only): Treatment of skin and skin structure infections caused by *Staphylococcus aureus* (doxycycline is not the drug of choice in the treatment of any type of staphylococcal infections).

Vincent infection: Treatment of Vincent infection caused by *Fusobacterium fusiforme* when penicillin is contraindicated.

Yaws: Treatment of yaws caused by *Treponema pallidum* subspecies *pertenue* when penicillin is contraindicated.

Zoonotic infections: Treatment of psittacosis (ornithosis) caused by *Chlamydophila psittaci*; plague due to *Yersinia pestis*; tularemia caused by *Francisella tularensis*; brucellosis caused by *Brucella* spp. (in conjunction with streptomycin); bartonellosis caused by *Bartonella bacilliformis*; infections caused by *Campylobacter fetus*.

Local Anesthetic/Vasoconstrictor Precautions

No information available to require special precautions

Effects on Dental Treatment Key adverse event(s) related to dental treatment: Glossitis and tooth discoloration (children). Opportunistic "superinfection" with *Candida albicans*; tetracyclines are not recommended for use during pregnancy or in children ≤8 years of age since they have been reported to cause enamel hypoplasia and permanent teeth discoloration. The use of tetracyclines should only be used in these patients if other agents are contraindicated or alternative antimicrobials will not eradicate the organism.

Effects on Bleeding Hemolytic anemia and thrombocytopenia have been reported

Adverse Reactions

>10%: Infection: Common cold (22%)

1% to 10%:

- Cardiovascular: Hypertension (3%), increased blood pressure (2%)
- Central nervous system: Pain (2% to 4%), anxiety (2%)
- Dermatologic: Skin rash (4%)
- Endocrine & metabolic: Increased lactate dehydrogenase (2%), increased serum glucose (1%)
- Gastrointestinal: Nausea (8%), dyspepsia (6%), diarrhea (5% to 6%), acid indigestion (4%), upper abdominal pain (2%), abdominal distention (1%), abdominal pain (1%), xerostomia (1%)
- Genitourinary: Dysmenorrhea (4%)
- Hepatic: Increased serum AST (2%)
- Infection: Fungal infection (2%), influenza (2%)
- Neuromuscular & skeletal: Arthralgia (6%), back pain (1%)
- Respiratory: Nasopharyngitis (5%), bronchitis (3%), sinusitis (3%), nasal congestion (2%), sinus headache (1%)

Frequency not defined:

- Cardiovascular: Flushing
- Dermatologic: Skin hyperpigmentation
- Endocrine & metabolic: Thyroid disease (brown/black discoloration; no dysfunction reported)
- Gastrointestinal: Anorexia
- Genitourinary: Vulvovaginal candidiasis
- Hematologic & oncologic: Leukopenia
- Immunologic: DRESS syndrome
- Neuromuscular & skeletal: Myalgia
- Otic: Tinnitus

<1%, postmarketing, and/or case reports: Anaphylactoid reaction, anaphylaxis, angioedema, bulging fontanel (infants), *Clostridium difficile* associated diarrhea, decreased appetite, dental discoloration (children), dysphagia, dyspnea, enamel hypoplasia, enterocolitis, eosinophilia, erythema multiforme, erythematous rash, esophageal ulcer, esophagitis, exacerbation of systemic lupus erythematosus, exfoliative dermatitis, glossitis, headache, hemolytic anemia, hepatic dysfunction, hepatotoxicity (rare; including hepatic failure, autoimmune hepatitis, cholestasis), hypersensitivity reaction, hypotension, IgA vasculitis, increased blood urea nitrogen (dose related), increased serum ALT, inflammatory anogenital lesion, intracranial hypertension (adults), maculopapular rash, neutropenia, pericarditis, peripheral edema, permanent vision loss, proctitis, pseudomembranous colitis, serum sickness, skin photosensitivity, Stevens-Johnson syndrome, stomatitis, tachycardia, thrombocytopenia, tinnitus, toxic epidermal necrolysis, urticaria, vomiting

Dental Usual Dosage

Adults: Oral: Treatment of periodontitis (refractory): 100-200 mg once daily for 21 days (Jolkovsky 2006).

Note: A specific formulation (Periostat [available in

Canada]) containing a subantimicrobial dosage is also available for use as an adjunct to scaling and root planing. In addition, doxycycline gel (Atridox) is available for subgingival application (see Doxycycline Hyclate Periodontal Extended-Release Liquid monograph).

Dosing

Adult & Geriatric

Note: Doryx MPC 120 mg is equivalent to Doryx (doxycycline hyclate delayed-release tablets) 100 mg

Acute bacterial rhinosinusitis (off-label use): Oral: 200 mg/day in 1 to 2 divided doses for 5 to 7 days (Chow 2012)

Anthrax:

Inhalational (postexposure prophylaxis): Oral (immediate and delayed-release), IV (use oral route when possible): 100 mg every 12 hours for 60 days (CDC [Hendricks 2014])

Doryx MPC: Oral: 120 mg every 12 hours for 60 days

Cutaneous (without systemic involvement), treatment: Oral: 100 mg every 12 hours for 7 to 10 days after naturally acquired infection; 60 days for bioterrorism-related cases (CDC [Hendricks 2014].

Systemic (penicillin susceptible strains; excluding meningitis), treatment: IV: Initial: 200 mg as a single dose, then 100 mg every 12 hours in combination with penicillin G or ampicillin; duration of therapy is 2 weeks or until clinically stable. Patients exposed to aerosolized spores require prophylaxis to complete an antimicrobial course of 60 days from illness onset (CDC [Hendricks 2014])

Bacillary angiomatosis, cutaneous (off-label use): Oral: 100 mg twice daily. **Note:** Duration of initial therapy should be for 2 weeks to 2 months, although treatment durations are not standardized (IDSA [Stevens 2014])

***Bartonella* infection in HIV-infected patients (off-label use) (HHS [OI adult 2015]): Note:** Duration of therapy is at least 3 months; continuation of therapy depends on relapse occurrence and clinical condition

Bacillary Angiomatosis, Peliosis Hepatis, Bacteremia, and Osteomyelitis: Oral, IV: 100 mg every 12 hours

Infections Involving the CNS: Oral, IV: 100 mg every 12 hours; may add rifampin therapy

Confirmed Bartonella Endocarditis: 100 mg IV every 12 hours in combination with gentamicin for 2 weeks, then continue with doxycycline 100 mg IV or orally every 12 hours

Other Severe Infections: Oral, IV: 100 mg every 12 hours in combination with rifampin

Bite wounds (animal/human) (off-label use) (IDSA [Stevens 2014]):

Animal bite: Oral, IV: 100 mg twice daily

Human bite: Oral: 100 mg twice daily

Brucellosis: Oral: 100 mg twice daily for 6 weeks with rifampin or streptomycin (Ariza 2007). **Note:** In the treatment of brucellar native vertebral osteomyelitis, 3 months of doxycycline therapy is recommended (usually with 2 to 3 weeks of concomitant streptomycin or 3 months of concomitant rifampin) (IDSA [Berbari 2015]).

Cellulitis (purulent) due to community-acquired MRSA (off-label use): Oral: 100 mg twice daily for 5 to 10 days (Liu 2011)

Cervicitis due to *Chlamydia trachomatis* (off-label use): Oral: 100 mg twice daily for 7 days; consider concurrent treatment for gonorrhea if patient at risk for contracting or lives in an area with high prevalence of gonorrhea (CDC [Workowski 2015])

***Chlamydia trachomatis*, uncomplicated urethral, endocervical or rectal infections:** Oral: (immediate and delayed-release): 100 mg twice daily for 7 days; alternatively, for endocervical or urethral infections, may give 200 mg delayed-release tablet once daily for 7 days (CDC [Workowski 2015])

Doryx MPC: Oral: 120 mg twice daily for 7 days

Community-acquired pneumonia, bronchitis: Oral, IV: 100 mg twice daily (Ailani 1999; Mandell 2007)

Epididymitis (most likely caused by *C. trachomatis* or *N. gonorrhoeae*) (off-label use): Oral (immediate and delayed-release): 100 mg twice daily for 10 days (in combination with ceftriaxone); sexual partners should also be referred for treatment (CDC [Workowski 2015])

Doryx MPC: Oral: 120 mg twice daily for at least 10 days

Gonococcal (uncomplicated) infection of the cervix, rectum (off-label use) or urethra: Oral: (immediate and delayed-release): 100 mg twice daily for 7 days; must be given in combination with ceftriaxone (preferred) or cefixime (only if ceftriaxone is not available) (CDC [Workowski 2015]). **Note:** Azithromycin is preferred over doxycycline as the second antimicrobial in combination with ceftriaxone in uncomplicated infections due to a high prevalence of tetracycline resistance in isolates and the convenience/compliance advantages of single dose azithromycin therapy; doxycycline should only be used in cases of azithromycin allergy (CDC [Workowski 2015]).

Alternatively, manufacturer's labeling recommends a single-visit dose in nonanorectal infections in men: 300 mg initially, repeat dose in 1 hour (total dose: 600 mg); of note, this dosing is not mentioned in the CDC STD 2015 treatment guidelines.

Doryx MPC: Oral: 120 mg twice daily for 7 days. **Note:** Not for anorectal infections in men

Alternatively, manufacturer's labeling recommends a single-visit dose: 360 mg initially, repeat dose in 1 hour (total dose: 720 mg); of note, this dosing is not mentioned in the CDC STD 2015 treatment guidelines.

Granuloma inguinale (donovanosis) (alternative to preferred therapy): Oral: 100 mg twice daily for at least 3 weeks (and until lesions have healed) (CDC [Workowski 2015]). **Note:** If symptoms do not improve within the first few days of therapy, the addition of gentamicin may be considered (CDC [Workowski 2015]).

Human granulocytic anaplasmosis (off-label use): Oral, IV: 100 mg twice daily for 10 days (IDSA [Wormser 2006])

Lyme disease (off-label use): Oral (Halperin 2007; IDSA [Wormser 2006]):

Prevention: Initiate within 72 hours of tick removal: 200 mg administered as a single dose

Treatment (early Lyme disease without neurologic manifestations): 100 mg twice daily for 10 to 21 days

Treatment (meningitis or other early neurologic manifestations): 100 to 200 mg twice daily for 14 days (range: 10 to 28 days)

Lymphogranuloma venereum: Oral: 100 mg twice daily for 21 days (CDC [Workowski 2015])

Malaria chemoprophylaxis: Start 1 to 2 days prior to travel to endemic area; continue daily during travel and for 4 weeks after leaving endemic area

Oral (immediate and delayed-release): 100 mg/day
Doryx MPC: Oral: 120 mg daily

Malaria, severe, treatment (off-label use): Oral, IV: 100 mg every 12 hours for 7 days with quinidine gluconate. **Note:** Quinidine gluconate duration is region specific; consult CDC for current recommendations (CDC 2013).

Malaria, uncomplicated, treatment (off-label use): Oral: 100 mg twice daily for 7 days with quinine sulfate (and primaquine for *Plasmodium vivax*). **Note:** Quinine sulfate duration is region specific; consult CDC for current recommendations (CDC 2013).

Nongonococcal urethritis: Oral (immediate and delayed-release): 100 mg twice daily for 7 days
Doryx MPC: Oral: 120 mg twice daily for 7 days

Pelvic inflammatory disease (off-label use):

Treatment, inpatient: IV: 100 mg twice daily (in combination with cefoxitin [preferred] or cefotetan [preferred] or ampicillin/sulbactam [alternative]); transition from parenteral to oral doxycycline therapy can usually be initiated within 24 to 48 hours of clinical improvement for a total treatment duration of 14 days. If tubo-ovarian abscess is present, oral clindamycin or oral metronidazole in combination with doxycycline is preferred to complete 14 days of therapy (CDC [Workowski 2015])

Treatment, outpatient: Oral: 100 mg twice daily for 14 days (with or without metronidazole); must be preceded by a single IM dose of cefoxitin (plus oral probenecid) or ceftriaxone or other parenteral third-generation cephalosporin (eg, cefotaxime) (CDC [Workowski 2015])

Periodontitis: Oral (Periostat [Canadian product]): 20 mg twice daily as an adjunct following scaling and root planing; may treat for up to 9 months

Periodontitis, refractory (off-label use): Oral: 100 to 200 mg daily (Jolkovsky 2006)

Proctitis, proctocolitis, enteritis (off-label use): Oral: 100 mg twice daily for 7 days (in combination with ceftriaxone) (CDC [Workowski 2015]). **Note:** Consider 21 days of treatment for presumptive lymphogranuloma venereum in those with HIV infection or positive rectal chlamydial amplification test (NAAT).

Prosthetic joint infection (off-label use): Oral:

Chronic oral antimicrobial suppression:

Propionibacterium spp (alternative to penicillin or amoxicillin): 100 mg twice daily (Osmon 2013)

Staphylococci (oxacillin-resistant): 100 mg twice daily (Osmon 2013)

Staphylococci (oxacillin-sensitive or –resistant) oral phase treatment (after completion of pathogen-specific IV) following 1-stage exchange:

Total ankle, elbow, hip, or shoulder arthroplasty: 100 mg twice daily for 3 months; **Note:** Must be used in combination with rifampin (Osmon 2013)

Total knee arthroplasty: 100 mg twice daily for 6 months; **Note:** Must be used in combination with rifampin (Osmon 2013)

Q fever: Oral:

Acute: 100 mg every 12 hours for 14 days (CDC 2013); **Note:** In patients who have valvular heart disease, consider increasing the duration of therapy to 1 year and adding hydroxychloroquine to the regimen to prevent endocarditis; consultation with an infectious disease expert is recommended (CDC 2002; Fenollar 2001).

Chronic (CDC 2013):

Endocarditis or vascular infection: 100 mg every 12 hours in combination with hydroxychloroquine for ≥18 months

Noncardiac organ disease: 100 mg every 12 hours in combination with hydroxychloroquine (duration based on serologic response; ID consult recommended)

Postpartum with serologic evidence present >12 months after delivery: 100 mg every 12 hours in combination with hydroxychloroquine for 12 months

Rosacea: Oral: Oracea, Apprilon [Canadian product]: 40 mg once daily in the morning

Sclerosing agent for pleural effusion (off-label use): Intrapleural: 500 mg as a single dose in 100 mL NS (Porcel 2006); may require a repeat dose (Kvale 2007)

Skin and soft tissue infections (off-label use) (IDSA [Stevens 2014]):

Due to MSSA or MRSA: Oral: 100 mg twice daily

Necrotizing infection due to Aeromonas hydrophila or Vibrio vulnificus: IV: 100 mg every 12 hours; in combination with ciprofloxacin or ceftriaxone for *Aeromonas hydrophila* or in combination with ceftriaxone or cefotaxime for *Vibrio vulnificus*. Continue treatment until further debridement is not necessary, patient has clinically improved, and patient is afebrile for 48 to 72 hours.

Syphilis, penicillin-allergic patients: Note: Data to support the use of alternatives to penicillin alternatives in primary and secondary syphilis and limited and also are not well documented in the treatment of latent syphilis (CDC [Workowski 2015]).

Primary/secondary: Oral (immediate and delayed-release): 100 mg twice daily for 14 days
Doryx MPC: Oral: 120 mg twice daily for 14 days

Latent: Oral (immediate and delayed-release): 100 mg twice daily for 28 days
Doryx MPC: Oral: 120 mg twice daily for 28 days

Tickborne rickettsial disease: Oral, IV: 100 mg twice daily for 5 to 7 days; severe or complicated disease may require longer treatment

Tularemia:

Mild to moderate infections: Oral: 100 mg twice daily for ≥14 days (IDSA [Stevens 2014])

Mass casualty management or postexposure prophylaxis (when used as a biological weapon): Oral: 100 mg twice daily for 14 days (Dennis 2001)

Contained casualty management (when used as a biological weapon): IV (may transition to oral if clinically appropriate): 100 mg every 12 hours for 14-21 days (Dennis 2001)

Vibrio cholerae: Oral: 300 mg as a single dose (WHO 2004)

***Yersinia pestis* (plague):** Oral, IV: 200 mg initially then 100 mg twice daily **or** 200 mg once daily for 10 to 14 days, or until 2 days after fever subsides (CDC 2015; Daya 2005; Inglesby 2000; IDSA [Stevens 2014])

Pediatric

Usual dosage range:

Immediate and delayed-release:

Children >8 years and Adolescents (<45 kg): Oral, IV: 2 to 4 mg/kg/day in 1 to 2 divided doses, not to exceed 200 mg/day (AAP [Red Book] 2015)

Children >8 years and Adolescents (≥45 kg): Oral, IV: Refer to adult dosing.

Doryx MPC: Oral:
Mild-to-moderate infections:
Children >8 years and Adolescents (<45 kg): 5.3 mg/kg/day in 2 divided doses on day 1, followed by 2.6 mg/kg/day in 1 to 2 divided doses
Children >8 years and Adolescents (≥45 kg): Refer to adult dosing.
Severe or life-threatening infections (eg, anthrax, tickborne rickettsial disease):
Children >8 years and Adolescents (<45 kg): 2.6 mg/kg/**dose** every 12 hours
Children >8 years and Adolescents (≥45 kg): Refer to adult dosing.

Anthrax:
Inhalational (postexposure prophylaxis) (ACIP 2010): Oral (immediate and delayed-release), IV (use oral route when possible):
≤8 years: 2.2 mg/kg every 12 hours for 60 days
>8 years and ≤45 kg: 2.2 mg/kg every 12 hours for 60 days
>8 years and >45 kg: 100 mg every 12 hours for 60 days
Doryx MPC: Oral:
Children >8 years and Adolescents (<45 kg): 2.6 mg/kg/**dose** twice daily for 60 days
Children >8 years and Adolescents (≥45 kg): Refer to adult dosing.
Cutaneous (treatment): Oral: See dosing for "Inhalational (postexposure prophylaxis)"
Note: In the presence of systemic involvement, extensive edema, and/or lesions on head/neck, doxycycline should initially be administered IV
Inhalational/gastrointestinal/oropharyngeal (treatment): IV: Refer to dosing for inhalational anthrax (postexposure prophylaxis); switch to oral therapy when clinically appropriate.
Note: Initial treatment should include two or more agents predicted to be effective (CDC 2001). Agents suggested for use in conjunction with doxycycline or ciprofloxacin include rifampin, vancomycin, imipenem, penicillin, ampicillin, chloramphenicol, clindamycin, and clarithromycin. May switch to oral antimicrobial therapy when clinically appropriate. Continue combined therapy for 60 days

***Bartonella* infection in HIV-infected patients (off-label use):** Refer to adult dosing

Community-acquired pneumonia (CAP) (IDSA/PIDS 2011): Children >7 years: Oral: **Note:** A beta-lactam antibiotic should be added if typical bacterial pneumonia cannot be ruled out.
Presumed atypical, mild atypical (*M. pneumoniae, C. pneumoniae, C. trachomatis*) infection or step-down therapy (alternative to azithromycin): 2 to 4 mg/kg/day in 2 divided doses (maximum: 200 mg/day)

Cellulitis (purulent) due to community-acquired MRSA (off-label use): Children >8 years and ≤45 kg: Oral: 2 mg/kg/dose every 12 hours for 5 to 10 days; >45 kg: Refer to adult dosing (Liu 2011)

Chlamydial infections, uncomplicated: Children ≥8 years (and >45 kg) and Adolescents: Oral: *US labeling:* 100 mg twice daily for 7 days; alternatively, for endocervical or urethral infections, may give 200 mg delayed-release tablet once daily for 7 days (CDC [Workowski 2015])

Human granulocytic anaplasmosis (off-label use): Children ≥8 years and Adolescents: Oral, IV: 4 mg/kg/day in 2 divided doses (maximum: 100 mg/dose) for 10 days (IDSA [Wormser 2006])

Localized juvenile periodontitis (LJP) (off-label use): Oral: 50 to 100 mg/day

Lyme disease (off-label use): Children ≥8 years: Oral (Halperin 2007; Wormser 2006):
Prevention: 4 mg/kg (maximum: 200 mg) administered as a single dose; **Note:** Initiate within 72 hours of tick removal
Treatment (early Lyme disease without neurologic manifestations): 1 to 2 mg/kg twice daily for 10 to 21 days (maximum: 100 mg/dose)
Treatment (meningitis and other early neurologic manifestations): 4 to 8 mg/kg/day in 2 divided doses for 10 to 28 days (maximum: 200 mg/dose)

Malaria chemoprophylaxis: Start 1 to 2 days prior to travel to endemic area; continue daily during travel and for 4 weeks after leaving endemic area
Children ≥8 years and Adolescents: Oral (immediate and delayed-release):
Manufacturer's labeling:
<45 kg: 2 mg/kg/dose once daily (maximum: 100 mg/day)
≥45 kg: 100 mg once daily
Alternative recommendation: 2.2 mg/kg/dose once daily (maximum: 100 mg/day) (Arguin [CDC 2016]).
Doryx MPC: Oral:
Children >8 years and Adolescents (<45 kg): 2.4 mg/kg/dose once daily
Children >8 years and Adolescents (≥45 kg): Refer to adult dosing.

Malaria, severe, treatment (off-label use): Children ≥8 years: Oral, IV:
<45 kg: 2.2 mg/kg (maximum dose: 100 mg) every 12 hours for 7 days with quinidine gluconate. **Note:** Quinidine gluconate duration is region specific; consult CDC for current recommendations (CDC 2011).
≥45 kg: 100 mg every 12 hours for 7 days with quinidine gluconate. **Note:** Quinidine gluconate duration is region specific; consult CDC for current recommendations (CDC 2011).

Malaria, uncomplicated, treatment (off-label use): Children ≥8 years: Oral: 2.2 mg/kg (maximum dose: 100 mg) every 12 hours for 7 days with quinine sulfate. **Note:** Quinine sulfate duration is region specific, consult CDC for current recommendations (CDC 2011).

Q fever: Oral:
Acute:
Children <8 years with high-risk criteria (eg, hospitalized or have severe illness, with preexisting heart valvulopathy, immunocompromised, or with delayed Q fever diagnosis who have experienced illness for >14 days without resolution of symptoms): 2.2 mg/kg/dose (maximum: 100 mg per dose) twice daily for 14 days (CDC 2013).
Children <8 years with mild or uncomplicated illness: 2.2 mg/kg/dose (maximum: 100 mg per dose) twice daily for 5 days. If patient remains febrile past 5 days of treatment, switch to sulfamethoxazole and trimethoprim (CDC 2013). **Note:** Some clinicians may recommend initial treatment with sulfamethoxazole and trimethoprim for children <8 years with mild or uncomplicated illness (Hartzell 2008; CDC 2013).

Children ≥8 years and Adolescents: 2.2 mg/kg/ dose (maximum: 100 mg per dose) twice daily for 14 days (CDC 2013).

Chronic: ID consult recommended for treatment of chronic Q fever (CDC 2013)

Skin and soft tissue infections due to MSSA or MRSA (off-label use): Children ≥ 8 years: Oral:

≤45 kg: 2 mg/kg every 12 hours (IDSA [Lui 2011])

>45 kg: 100 mg twice daily (IDSA [Lui 2011]; IDSA [Stevens 2014])

Tickborne rickettsial disease (eg, Rocky Mountain spotted fever): Children and Adolescents: Oral, IV:

<45 kg: 2.2 mg/kg (maximum dose: 100 mg) every 12 hours for 5 to 7 days; severe or complicated disease may require longer treatment (CDC 2006)

≥45 kg: Refer to adult dosing.

Tularemia (when used as a biological weapon) (off-label use) (Dennis 2001):

Mass casualty management or postexposure prophylaxis: Oral:

Children <45 kg: 2.2 mg/kg twice daily for 14 days

Children ≥45 kg: 100 mg twice daily for 14 days

Contained casualty management: IV (may transition to oral if clinically indicated):

Children <45 kg: 2.2 mg/kg twice daily for 14 to 21 days

Children ≥45 kg: 100 mg every 12 hours for 14 to 21 days

Renal Impairment

No dosage adjustment necessary.

Dialysis: Poorly dialyzed (0% to 5%); no supplemental dose or dosage adjustment necessary, including patients on intermittent hemodialysis, peritoneal dialysis, or continuous renal replacement therapy (eg, CVVHD).

Hepatic Impairment There are no dosage adjustments provided in the manufacturer's labeling.

Mechanism of Action

Inhibits protein synthesis by binding with the 30S and possibly the 50S ribosomal subunit(s) of susceptible bacteria; may also cause alterations in the cytoplasmic membrane

Periostat capsules [Canadian product]: Proposed mechanism: Has been shown to inhibit collagenase activity *in vitro*. Also has been noted to reduce elevated collagenase activity in the gingival crevicular fluid of patients with periodontal disease. Systemic levels do not reach inhibitory concentrations against bacteria.

Contraindications

Hypersensitivity to doxycycline, other tetracyclines, or any component of the formulation

Periostat, Apprilon [Canadian products]: Additional contraindications: Use in infants and children <8 years of age or during second or third trimester of pregnancy; breastfeeding

Warnings/Precautions Photosensitivity reaction may occur with this drug; discontinue at first sign of skin erythema. Use skin protection and avoid prolonged exposure to sunlight and ultraviolet light. May be associated with increases in BUN secondary to antianabolic effects; this does not occur with use of doxycycline in patients with renal impairment. Hypersensitivity syndromes have been reported, including drug rash with eosinophilia and systemic symptoms (DRESS), urticaria, angioneurotic edema, anaphylaxis, anaphylactoid purpura, serum sickness, pericarditis, and systemic lupus erythematosus exacerbation; discontinue use for serious hypersensitivity reactions. Hepatotoxicity rarely occurs; if symptomatic, assess LFTs and discontinue drug. Intracranial hypertension (eg, pseudotumor cerebri [PCI]) has been associated with use; headache, blurred vision, diplopia, vision loss, and/or papilledema may occur. Women of childbearing age who are overweight or have a history of intracranial hypertension are at greater risk. Intracranial hypertension typically resolves after discontinuation of treatment; however, permanent visual loss is possible. If visual symptoms develop during treatment, prompt ophthalmologic evaluation is warranted. Intracranial pressure can remain elevated for weeks after drug discontinuation; monitor patient until stable. Esophagitis and ulcerations (sometimes severe) may occur; patients with dysphagia and/ or retrosternal pain may require assessment for esophageal lesions.

Prolonged use may result in fungal or bacterial superinfection, including *Clostridium difficile*-associated diarrhea (CDAD) and pseudomembranous colitis; CDAD has been observed >2 months postantibiotic treatment. May induce hyperpigmentation in many organs, including nails, bone, skin (diffuse pigmentation as well as over sites of scars and injury), eyes, thyroid, visceral tissue, oral cavity (teeth, mucosa, alveolar bone), sclerae, and heart valves independently of time or amount of drug administration. May cause tissue hyperpigmentation, tooth enamel hypoplasia, or permanent tooth discoloration (more common with long-term use, but observed with repeated, short courses) when used during tooth development (last half of pregnancy, infancy, and childhood <8 years); manufacturer states to use in children <8 years only when the potential benefits outweigh the risks in severe or life-threatening conditions (eg, anthrax, Rocky Mountain spotted fever), particularly when there are no alternative therapies. Limited use between age 6 to 7 years has minimal effect on the color of permanent incisors (CDC 2006). Recommended in treatment of anthrax exposure (CDC 2001), tickborne rickettsial diseases (CDC 2006), and Q fever (CDC 2013). When used for malaria prophylaxis, does not completely suppress asexual blood stages of *Plasmodium* strains. Doxycycline does not suppress *P. falciparum*'s sexual blood stage gametocytes. Patients completing a regimen may still transmit the infection to mosquitoes outside endemic areas. Potentially significant drug-drug interactions may exist, requiring dose or frequency adjustment, additional monitoring, and/or selection of alternative therapy.

Acne: The American Academy of Dermatology acne guidelines recommend doxycycline as adjunctive treatment for moderate and severe acne and forms of inflammatory acne that are resistant to topical treatments. Concomitant topical therapy with benzoyl peroxide or a retinoid should be administered with systemic antibiotic therapy (eg, doxycycline) and continued for maintenance after the antibiotic course is completed (AAD [Zaenglein 2016]).

Oracea or Apprilon (Canadian product): Do not be use for the treatment or prophylaxis of bacterial infections (dose may be subefficacious and promote resistance).

Syrup contains sodium metabisulfite, which may cause allergic reactions in certain individuals (eg, asthmatic patients).

Drug Interactions

Metabolism/Transport Effects None known.

Avoid Concomitant Use

Avoid concomitant use of Doxycycline with any of the following: BCG (Intravesical); Cholera Vaccine;

Mecamylamine; Methoxyflurane; Retinoic Acid Derivatives; Strontium Ranelate

Increased Effect/Toxicity

Doxycycline may increase the levels/effects of: Aminolevulinic Acid; Mecamylamine; Methoxyflurane; Mipomersen; Neuromuscular-Blocking Agents; Porfimer; Retinoic Acid Derivatives; Verteporfin; Vitamin K Antagonists

Decreased Effect

Doxycycline may decrease the levels/effects of: BCG (Intravesical); BCG Vaccine (Immunization); Cholera Vaccine; Iron Salts; Lactobacillus and Estriol; Penicillins; Sodium Picosulfate; Typhoid Vaccine

The levels/effects of Doxycycline may be decreased by: Antacids; Barbiturates; Bile Acid Sequestrants; Bismuth Subcitrate; Bismuth Subsalicylate; Calcium Salts; CarBAMazepine; Fosphenytoin; Iron Salts; Lanthanum; Magnesium Salts; Multivitamins/Minerals (with ADEK, Folate, Iron); Multivitamins/Minerals (with AE, No Iron); Phenytoin; Quinapril; RifAMPin; Strontium Ranelate; Sucralfate; Sucroferric Oxyhydroxide

Food Interactions

Ethanol: Chronic ethanol ingestion may reduce the serum concentration of doxycycline.

Food: Doxycycline serum levels may be slightly decreased if taken with high fat meal or milk. Administration with iron or calcium may decrease doxycycline absorption. May decrease absorption of calcium, iron, magnesium, zinc, and amino acids. Management: Administer Doryx and Doryx MPC without regard to meals. Administer Oracea on an empty stomach 1 hour before or 2 hours after meals.

Dietary Considerations

Tetracyclines (in general): Take with food if gastric irritation occurs. While administration with food may decrease GI absorption of doxycycline by up to 20%, administration on an empty stomach is not recommended due to GI intolerance. Of currently available tetracyclines, doxycycline has the least affinity for calcium.

Oracea, Apprilon [Canadian product]: Take on an empty stomach 1 hour before or 2 hours after meals.

Periostat [Canadian product]: Take at least 1 hour before morning and evening meals.

Some products may contain sodium.

Pharmacodynamics/Kinetics

Half-life Elimination

18 to 22 hours; End-stage renal disease: 18 to 25 hours

Oracea, Apprilon [Canadian product]: Single dose: 21 hours

Periostat [Canadian product]: Single dose: 18 hours

Time to Peak Serum: Oral: Immediate release: 1.5 to 4 hours; delayed-release tablets: 2.8 to 3 hours

Pregnancy Risk Factor D

Pregnancy Considerations Tetracyclines cross the placenta (Mylonas 2011). Therapeutic doses of doxycycline during pregnancy are unlikely to produce substantial teratogenic risk, but data are insufficient to say that there is no risk. In general, reports of exposure have been limited to short durations of therapy in the first trimester. Tetracyclines accumulate in developing teeth and long tubular bones (Mylonas 2011). Permanent discoloration of teeth (yellow, gray, brown) can occur following in utero exposure and is more likely to occur following long-term or repeated exposure.

Doxycycline is the recommended agent for the treatment of Rocky Mountain Spotted Fever in pregnant women (Biggs 2016). For other indications, many guidelines consider use of doxycycline to be contraindicated during pregnancy, or to be a relative contraindication in pregnant women if other agents are available and appropriate for use (Anderson 2013; CDC 2011; HHS [OI adult 2015]; Stevens 2014; Workowski [CDC 2015]; Wormser 2006). Doxycycline should not be used for the treatment of rosacea in pregnant women. When systemic antibiotics are needed for dermatologic conditions, other agents are preferred (Kong 2013; Murase 2014). As a class, tetracyclines are generally considered second-line antibiotics in pregnant women and their use should be avoided (Mylonas 2011).

Breastfeeding Considerations Doxycycline is excreted in breast milk.

The relative infant dose (RID) of doxycycline is 6.14% when calculated using the highest average breast milk concentration located and compared to an infant therapeutic dose of 4.4 mg/kg/day. In general, breastfeeding is considered acceptable when the RID is <10%; when an RID is >25% breastfeeding should generally be avoided (Anderson 2016; Ito 2000). Using the highest average milk concentration (1.8 mcg/mL), the estimated daily infant dose via breast milk is 0.27 mg/kg/day. This milk concentration was obtained following maternal administration of a single oral dose of doxycycline 200 mg (Tokuda 1969). Concentrations of doxycycline in breast milk may increase with duration of therapy (Anderson 1991).

Oral absorption of doxycycline is not markedly influenced by simultaneous ingestion of milk; therefore, oral absorption of doxycycline by the breastfeeding infant would not be expected to be diminished by the calcium in the maternal milk.

The therapeutic use of doxycycline should be avoided during tooth development (children <8 years of age) unless there are no alternative therapies due to the potential for tissue hyperpigmentation, tooth enamel hypoplasia, or permanent tooth discoloration. Theoretically, this risk is also present in breastfeeding infants exposed to doxycycline via breast milk. Although nursing is not specifically contraindicated, the effects of long-term exposure via breast milk are not known. According to the manufacturer, the decision to continue or discontinue breastfeeding during therapy should take into account the risk of infant exposure, the benefits of breastfeeding to the infant, and benefits of treatment to the mother. The World Health Organization (WHO) states that maternal use of doxycycline should be avoided if possible but that a single dose or the short-term use of doxycycline is probably safe; there exists a possibility of dental staining and inhibition of bone growth in the infant, especially with prolonged use (WHO 2002). In general, antibiotics that are present in breast milk may cause nondose-related modification of bowel flora. Monitor infants for GI disturbances, such as thrush and diarrhea (WHO 2002).

Current guidelines note that the short-term use of doxycycline for the treatment of RMSF is considered compatible with breastfeeding (Biggs 2016). However, breastfeeding is a relative contraindication for the use of doxycycline in the treatment of Lyme disease (Wormser 2006). If used for the treatment or prophylaxis of malaria, breastfeeding during doxycycline therapy is considered compatible; however, the theoretical risk of dental staining and inhibition of long bone growth in the breastfeeding infant should be considered (WHO 2002).

Long-term use of tetracyclines (eg, for the treatment of acne) should be avoided in breastfeeding women (Pugashetti 2013).

Dosage Forms Considerations

Alodox Convenience kits contain doxycycline tablets 20 mg, plus eyelid cleanser

Morgidox kits contain doxycycline capsules 100 mg, plus AcuWash moisturizing Daily Cleanser

NizAzel Doxy kits contain doxycycline tablets 100 mg, plus NicAzel FORTE dietary supplement tablets

Ocudox kits contain doxycycline capsules 50 mg, plus eyelid cleanser and Tears Again Advanced eyelid spray

Dosage Forms

Capsule, Oral:
- Adoxa: 150 mg
- Mondoxyne NL: 50 mg, 75 mg, 100 mg
- Monodox: 75 mg, 100 mg
- Morgidox: 50 mg, 100 mg
- Vibramycin: 100 mg
- Generic: 50 mg, 75 mg, 100 mg, 150 mg

Capsule Delayed Release, Oral:
- Oracea: 40 mg
- Generic: 40 mg

Kit, Combination:
- Morgidox: 1 x 50 mg, 1 x 100 mg, 2 x 100 mg

Solution Reconstituted, Intravenous [preservative free]:
- Doxy 100: 100 mg (1 ea)
- Generic: 100 mg (1 ea)

Suspension Reconstituted, Oral:
- Vibramycin: 25 mg/5 mL (60 mL)
- Generic: 25 mg/5 mL (60 mL)

Syrup, Oral:
- Vibramycin: 50 mg/5 mL (473 mL)

Tablet, Oral:
- Acticlate: 75 mg, 150 mg
- Adoxa: 50 mg, 75 mg, 100 mg
- Adoxa Pak 1/100: 100 mg
- Adoxa Pak 2/100: 100 mg
- Adoxa Pak 1/150: 150 mg
- Avidoxy: 100 mg
- TargaDOX: 50 mg
- Generic: 20 mg, 50 mg, 75 mg, 100 mg, 150 mg

Tablet Delayed Release, Oral:
- Doryx: 50 mg, 150 mg, 200 mg
- Doryx MPC: 120 mg
- Generic: 50 mg, 75 mg, 100 mg, 150 mg, 200 mg

Dosage Forms: Canada

Capsule, oral:
- Apprilon: 40 mg [30 mg (immediate release) and 10 mg (delayed release)]
- Periostat: 20 mg

Doxycycline Hyclate Periodontal Extended-Release Liquid

(doks i SYE kleen HI klayt per ee oh DON tal ik STEN did ri LES LIK wid)

Related Information

Doxycycline *on page 540*

Periodontal Diseases *on page 1844*

Brand Names: US Atridox

Brand Names: Canada Atridox

Generic Availability (US) No

Pharmacologic Category Antibiotic, Tetracycline Derivative

Dental Use Treatment of chronic adult periodontitis for gain in clinical attachment, reduction in probing depth, and reduction in bleeding upon probing

Use Periodontitis: Treatment of chronic adult periodontitis for a gain in clinical attachment, reduction in probing depth, and reduction in bleeding on probing.

Local Anesthetic/Vasoconstrictor Precautions No information available to require special precautions

Effects on Dental Treatment Key adverse event(s) related to dental treatment: Discoloration of teeth (in children), gum discomfort, toothache, periodontal abscess, tooth sensitivity, broken tooth, tooth mobility, endodontic abscess, and jaw pain

Mechanical oral hygiene procedures (ie, tooth brushing, flossing) should be avoided in any treated area for 7 days.

Effects reported in clinical trials were similar in incidence between doxycycline-containing product and vehicle alone; comparable to standard therapies including scaling and root planing or oral hygiene. Although there is no known relationship between doxycycline and hypertension, unspecified primary hypertension was noted in 1.6% of the doxycycline gel group, as compared to 0.2% in the vehicle group (allergic reactions to the vehicle were also reported in two patients).

Effects on Bleeding No information available to require special precautions

Adverse Reactions

>10%:
- Central nervous system: Headache (27%)
- Gastrointestinal: Minor gum irritation (18%), toothache (14%; pressure sensitivity)

1% to 10%:
- Cardiovascular: Hypertension (<1% to 2%)
- Central nervous system: Local discomfort (sensitive teeth: 8%), sore mouth (4%; soft tissue erythema, unspecified pain), insomnia (3%), tension headache (2%)
- Dermatologic: Dermatitis (1%), skin infection (1%)
- Endocrine & metabolic: Premenstrual syndrome (4%)
- Gastrointestinal: Periodontal abscess (10%), sore throat (6%), injury of tooth (5%), dyspepsia (4%), gingivitis (4%), diarrhea (3%), nausea (2%), periodontal abscess (2%; lesion), vomiting (2%), dental bleeding (1%)
- Infection: Common cold (26%), influenza (3% to 6%), tooth abscess (2%; pulpitis)
- Neuromuscular & skeletal: Myalgia (6%), back pain (4%), arm pain (2%), leg pain (2%), lower back pain (2%), muscle tenderness (2%), jaw pain (1%), neck pain (1%), shoulder pain (1%)
- Respiratory: Sinus congestion (6%), sinus infection (5%), cough (4%), bronchitis (2%), ENT infection (2%), allergic rhinitis (1%)
- Miscellaneous: Fever (1%)

<1%, postmarketing, and/or case reports: Aphthous stomatitis, enamel hypoplasia, fistula, hypersensitivity reaction, permanent dental discoloration, skin photosensitivity, tooth loss

Dental Usual Dosage Oral, subgingival: Dose depends on size, shape and number of pockets treated. Application may be repeated four months after initial treatment. The delivery system consists of 2 separate syringes in a single pouch. Syringe A contains 450 mg of a bioabsorbable polymer gel; syringe B contains doxycycline hyclate 50 mg. To prepare for instillation, couple syringe A to syringe B. Inject contents of syringe A (purple stripe) into syringe B, then push contents back into syringe A. Repeat this mixing cycle at a rate of one cycle per second for 100 cycles. If syringes are stored prior to use (a maximum of 3 days), repeat mixing cycle 10 times before use. After appropriate mixing, contents should be in syringe A. Holding syringes vertically, with syringe A at the bottom, pull back on the syringe A plunger, allowing contents to flow down barrel for several seconds. Uncouple syringes and attach enclosed blunt cannula to syringe A. Local anesthesia is not required for placement. Cannula tip may be bent to resemble periodontal probe and used to explore pocket. Express product from syringe until pocket is filled. To separate tip from formulation, turn tip towards the tooth and press against tooth surface to achieve separation. An appropriate dental instrument may be used to pack gel into the pocket. Pockets may be covered with either Coe-pak or Octyldentdental adhesive.

Dosing

Adult & Geriatric

Periodontitis: Subgingival application: Dose depends on size, shape and number of pockets treated. Contains 50 mg doxycycline hyclate per 500 mg of formulation in each final blended syringe product.

Atridox subgingival controlled-release product: Local anesthesia is not required for placement. Cannula tip may be bent to resemble periodontal probe and used to explore pocket. Express product from syringe until pocket is filled. To separate tip from formulation, turn tip towards the tooth and press against tooth surface to achieve separation. An appropriate dental instrument may be used to pack gel into the pocket. Pockets may be covered with either Coe-Pak or Octyldent dental adhesive. Application may be repeated 4 months after initial treatment.

Mechanism of Action Inhibits protein synthesis by binding with the 30S and possibly the 50S ribosomal subunit(s) of susceptible bacteria; may also cause alterations in the cytoplasmic membrane

Doxycycline inhibits collagenase *in vitro* and has been shown to inhibit collagenase in the gingival crevicular fluid in adults with periodontitis

Contraindications

Hypersensitivity to doxycycline, tetracycline or any component of the formulation; children <8 years of age

Canadian labeling: Additional contraindications (not in U.S. labeling): Children <12 years of age; pregnancy; breastfeeding

Warnings/Precautions Photosensitivity reaction may occur with this drug; avoid prolonged exposure to sunlight or tanning equipment. Prolonged use may result in fungal or bacterial superinfection, including *C. difficile*-associated diarrhea (CDAD) and pseudomembranous colitis; CDAD has been observed >2 months postantibiotic treatment. May cause tissue hyperpigmentation, enamel hypoplasia, or permanent tooth discoloration; use of tetracyclines should be avoided during tooth development (children <8 years of age) unless other drugs are not likely to be effective or are contraindicated. The Canadian labeling contraindicates use in children <12 years of age.

Additional specific warnings for doxycycline gel (Atridox) for subgingival application: This product has not been evaluated or tested in immunocompromised patients, in patients with oral candidiasis, or in conditions characterized by severe periodontal defects with little remaining periodontium. May result in overgrowth of nonsusceptible organisms, including fungi. Effects of treatment >9 months have not been evaluated. Has not been evaluated for use in regeneration of alveolar bone

Drug Interactions

Metabolism/Transport Effects None known.

Avoid Concomitant Use There are no known interactions where it is recommended to avoid concomitant use.

Increased Effect/Toxicity There are no known significant interactions involving an increase in effect.

Decreased Effect There are no known significant interactions involving a decrease in effect.

Pregnancy Risk Factor D

Pregnancy Considerations Exposure to tetracyclines during the second or third trimester may cause permanent discoloration of the teeth. Most reports do not show an increase risk for teratogenicity with the exception of a potential small increased risk for cleft palate or esophageal atresia/stenosis. Serum concentrations following subgingival use are significantly less than with oral tablets. The Canadian labeling contraindicates use in pregnant women.

Breastfeeding Considerations Tetracyclines, including oral doxycycline, are excreted in breast milk and therefore, breastfeeding is not recommended. The Canadian labeling contraindicates use in breastfeeding women.

Doxycycline is less bound to the calcium in maternal milk which may lead to increased absorption compared to other tetracyclines. Only minimal amounts of oral doxycycline are excreted in human milk and the relative amount of tooth staining has been reported to be lower when compared to other tetracycline analogs. Non-dose-related effects could include modification of bowel flora. Serum concentrations following subgingival use are significantly less than with oral tablets.

Dosage Forms

Liquid, subgingival:

Atridox: 10%

Doxylamine (dox IL a meen)

Brand Names: US Doxytex [DSC]; Nitetime Sleep-Aid [OTC]; Sleep Aid [OTC]

Brand Names: Canada Unisom-2

Pharmacologic Category Ethanolamine Derivative; Histamine H_1 Antagonist; Histamine H_1 Antagonist, First Generation

Use

Allergic rhinitis or other respiratory allergies (oral liquid only): Temporary relief of rhinorrhea, sneezing, itchy nose or throat, and itchy, watery eyes due to hay fever or other respiratory allergies

Insomnia (tablets only): Reduce difficulty falling asleep

Local Anesthetic/Vasoconstrictor Precautions No information available to require special precautions

Effects on Dental Treatment Key adverse event(s) related to dental treatment: Dry mucous membranes and significant xerostomia (normal salivary flow resumes upon discontinuation)

Effects on Bleeding No information available to require special precautions

Adverse Reactions Frequency not defined.

Cardiovascular: Palpitations, tachycardia

Central nervous system: Disorientation, dizziness, drowsiness, headache, paradoxical central nervous system stimulation, vertigo

Gastrointestinal: Anorexia, constipation, diarrhea, dry mucous membranes, epigastric pain, xerostomia

Genitourinary: Dysuria, urinary retention
Ophthalmic: Blurred vision, diplopia

General Dosage Range

Children 2 to <6 years: 2.5 mg every 4 to 6 hours; maximum: 15 mg in 24 hours.

Children ≥12 years, Adolescents, and Adults: 25 mg once daily 30 minutes before bedtime.

Mechanism of Action Doxylamine competes with histamine for H_1-receptor sites on effector cells; blocks chemoreceptor trigger zone, diminishes vestibular stimulation, and depresses labyrinthine function through its central anticholinergic activity.

Pharmacodynamics/Kinetics

Half-life Elimination 10-12 hours (Paton, 1985; Friedman, 1985); may be increased in the elderly (Friedman, 1989)

Time to Peak 2-4 hours (Paton, 1985; Friedman, 1985; Friedman, 1989)

Pregnancy Risk Factor C

Pregnancy Considerations Animal reproduction studies were not conducted by the manufacturer. Maternal use of doxylamine in combination with pyridoxine during pregnancy has not been shown to increase the baseline risk of major malformations. Doxylamine is recommended for the treatment of nausea and vomiting of pregnancy (ACOG 2015). When an antihistamine is needed for the treatment of allergic rhinitis during pregnancy, other agents may be preferred (Scadding 2008; Wallace 2008).

Dronabinol (droe NAB i nol)

Brand Names: US Marinol

Pharmacologic Category Antiemetic; Appetite Stimulant

Use

Appetite stimulation in AIDS patients: Treatment of anorexia associated with weight loss in patients with AIDS.

Chemotherapy-induced nausea and vomiting: Treatment of nausea and vomiting associated with cancer chemotherapy in patients who have failed to respond adequately to conventional antiemetic treatments.

Local Anesthetic/Vasoconstrictor Precautions No information available to require special precautions

Effects on Dental Treatment Key adverse event(s) related to dental treatment: Xerostomia (normal salivary flow resumes upon discontinuation); Patients may experience orthostatic hypotension as they stand up after treatment; especially if lying in dental chair for extended periods of time. Use caution with sudden changes in position during and after dental treatment.

Effects on Bleeding No information available to require special precautions

Adverse Reactions Frequency not always defined.

>1%:

Cardiovascular: Facial flushing, palpitations, tachycardia, vasodilatation

Central nervous system: Euphoria (antimetic: 24%; appetite stimulant: 8%), abnormality in thinking (3% to 10%), dizziness (3% to 10%), drowsiness (3% to 10%), paranoia (3% to 10%), amnesia, anxiety, ataxia, confusion, depersonalization, hallucination, nervousness

Gastrointestinal: Abdominal pain (3% to 10%), nausea (3% to 10%), vomiting (3% to 10%)

Neuromuscular & skeletal: Weakness

<1%, postmarketing, and/or case reports: Anorexia, burning sensation of skin, chills, conjunctival injection, conjunctivitis, cough, delirium, depression, diaphoresis, diarrhea, disorientation, exacerbation of depression, falling, fatigue, fecal incontinence, flushing, headache, hypotension, increased liver enzymes, insomnia, loss of consciousness, malaise, mental status change (exacerbation of mania or schizophrenia), movement disorder, myalgia, nightmares, oral lesion, panic attack, pharyngeal edema, rhinitis, seizure, sinusitis, skin rash, speech disturbance, swelling of lips, syncope, tinnitus, urticaria, visual disturbance

General Dosage Range Dosage reduction recommended in patients who develop toxicities.

Oral:

Capsules:

Children and Adolescents: Initial: 5 mg/m^2 as a single dose; Maintenance: 5 mg/m^2/dose every 2 to 4 hours for a total of 4 to 6 doses/day (maximum: 15 mg/m^2/dose)

Adults: Initial: 5 mg/m^2 as a single dose; Maintenance: 5 mg/m^2/dose every 2 to 4 hours for a total of 4 to 6 doses/day (maximum: 15 mg/m^2/dose) **or** 5 mg 3 to 4 times daily **or** Initial: 2.5 mg once or twice daily; Maintenance: Titrate up to 20 mg/day in divided doses

Oral solution:

Adults <65 years: Initial: 2.1 mg twice daily; maximum: 8.4 mg twice a day **or** 4.2 mg/m^2 1 to 3 hours prior to chemotherapy and then every 2 to 4 hours after chemotherapy; maximum: 12.6 mg/m^2/dose and 4 to 6 doses/day.

Adults ≥65 years: Initial: 2.1 mg once daily; maximum: 8.4 mg twice a day **or** 2.1 mg/m^2 1 to 3 hours prior to chemotherapy; maximum: 12.6 mg/m^2/dose and 4 to 6 doses/day.

Mechanism of Action Dronabinol (synthetic delta-9-tetrahydrocannabinol [delta-9-THC]), an active cannabinoid and natural occurring component of *Cannabis sativa L.* (marijuana), activates cannabinoid receptors CB_1 and CB_2. Activation of the CB_1 receptor produces marijuana-like effects on psyche and circulation, whereas activation of the CB_2 receptor does not. Dronabinol has approximately equal affinity for the CB_1 and CB_2 receptors; however, efficacy is less at CB_2 receptors. Activation of the cannabinoid system with dronabinol causes psychological effects that can be divided into 4 groups: affective (euphoria and easy laughter); sensory (increased perception of external stimuli and of the person's own body); somatic (feeling of the body floating or sinking in the bed); and cognitive (distortion of time perception, memory lapses, difficulty in concentration). Most effects (eg, analgesia, appetite enhancement, muscle relaxation, hormonal actions) are mediated by central cannabinoid receptors (CB_1), their distribution reflecting many of the medicinal benefits and adverse effects (Grotenhermen 2003).

Pharmacodynamics/Kinetics

Onset of Action ~0.5 to 1 hour; Peak effect: 2 to 4 hours

Duration of Action 4 to 6 hours (psychoactive effects); ≥24 hours (appetite stimulation)

Half-life Elimination Biphasic: Alpha: 4 to 5 hours; Terminal: 25 to 36 hours

Time to Peak Serum: 0.5 to 4 hours

Pregnancy Risk Factor C

Pregnancy Considerations Adverse events have been observed in animal reproduction studies. Although information related to the use of synthetic cannabinoids during pregnancy is limited, cannabinoids cross the placenta. Maternal use may increase the risk of adverse fetal/neonatal outcomes including growth restriction, low birth weight, preterm birth, and stillbirth. Some dosage forms also contain a significant amount of alcohol.

Product Availability Syndros (dronabinol oral solution): FDA approved July 2016; anticipated availability is currently undetermined.

Controlled Substance C-III

Dronedarone (droe NE da rone)

Related Information

Cardiovascular Diseases *on page 1752*

Clinical Risk Related to Drugs Prolonging QT Interval *on page 1772*

Brand Names: US Multaq

Brand Names: Canada Multaq

Pharmacologic Category Antiarrhythmic Agent, Class III

Use Paroxysmal or persistent atrial fibrillation: To reduce the risk of hospitalization for atrial fibrillation (AF) in patients in sinus rhythm with a history of paroxysmal or persistent AF

Local Anesthetic/Vasoconstrictor Precautions Dronedarone is one of the drugs confirmed to prolong the QT interval and is accepted as having a risk of causing torsade de pointes. The risk of drug-induced torsade de pointes is extremely low when a single QT interval prolonging drug is prescribed. In terms of epinephrine, it is not known what effect vasoconstrictors in the local anesthetic regimen will have in patients with a known history of congenital prolonged QT interval or in patients taking any medication that prolongs the QT interval. Until more information is obtained, it is suggested that the clinician consult with the physician prior to the use of a vasoconstrictor in suspected patients, and that the vasoconstrictor (epinephrine, mepivacaine and levonordefrin [Carbocaine® 2% with Neo-Cobefrin®]) be used with caution.

Effects on Dental Treatment No significant effects or complications reported (see Dental Comment)

Effects on Bleeding No information available to require special precautions

Adverse Reactions

>10%:

Cardiovascular: Prolonged Q-T interval on ECG (Bazett; 28% [placebo: 19%]; defined as >450 msec in males or >470 msec in female)

Renal: Increased serum creatinine (51%; increased >10%; occurred 5 days after initiation)

1% to 10%:

Cardiovascular: Bradycardia (3%)

Dermatologic: Allergic dermatitis (≤5%), dermatitis (≤5%), eczema (≤5%), pruritus (≤5%), skin rash (≤5%; described as generalized, macular, maculopapular, erythematous)

Gastrointestinal: Diarrhea (9%), nausea (5%), abdominal pain (4%), dyspepsia (2%), vomiting (2%)

Neuromuscular & skeletal: Weakness (7%)

<1%, postmarketing, and/or case reports: Acute hepatic failure (requiring transplant), anaphylaxis, angioedema, atrial flutter (with 1:1 atrioventricular conduction), cardiac failure (new or worsened), dysgeusia, hepatic injury, hyperbilirubinemia, hypersensitivity angiitis, increased blood urea nitrogen, increased liver enzymes, interstitial pulmonary disease, pneumonitis, pulmonary fibrosis, skin photosensitivity, vasculitis

General Dosage Range Oral: *Adults:* 400 mg twice daily

Mechanism of Action A noniodinated antiarrhythmic agent structurally related to amiodarone exhibiting properties of all 4 antiarrhythmic classes. Dronedarone inhibits sodium (I_{Na}) and potassium (I_{Kr}, I_{KS}, I_{K1}, and I_{K-ACh}) channels resulting in prolongation of the action potential and refractory period in myocardial tissue without reverse-use dependent effects; decreases AV conduction and sinus node function through inhibition of calcium (I_{Ca-L}) channels and beta$_1$-receptor blocking activity. Similar to amiodarone, dronedarone also inhibits alpha$_1$-receptor mediated increases in blood pressure.

Pharmacodynamics/Kinetics

Half-life Elimination 13-19 hours

Time to Peak Plasma: 3-6 hours

Pregnancy Risk Factor X

Pregnancy Considerations Studies in animals have shown evidence of fetal abnormalities and use is contraindicated in women who are or may become pregnant

Dental Comment See Local Anesthetic/Vasoconstrictor Precautions

Droperidol (droe PER i dole)

Related Information

Clinical Risk Related to Drugs Prolonging QT Interval *on page 1772*

Brand Names: Canada Droperidol Injection, USP

Pharmacologic Category Antiemetic; First Generation (Typical) Antipsychotic

Use Postoperative nausea/vomiting (PONV): Prevention and/or treatment of nausea and vomiting from surgical and diagnostic procedures

Local Anesthetic/Vasoconstrictor Precautions Droperidol is one of the drugs confirmed to prolong the QT interval and is accepted as having a risk of causing torsade de pointes. The risk of drug-induced torsade de pointes is extremely low when a single QT interval prolonging drug is prescribed. In terms of epinephrine, it is not known what effect vasoconstrictors in the local anesthetic regimen will have in patients with a known history of congenital prolonged QT interval or in patients taking any medication that prolongs the QT interval. Until more information is obtained, it is suggested that the clinician consult with the physician prior to the use of a vasoconstrictor in suspected patients, and that the vasoconstrictor (epinephrine, mepivacaine and levonordefrin [Carbocaine® 2% with Neo-Cobefrin®]) be used with caution.

Effects on Dental Treatment See Warnings/Precautions. Key adverse event(s) related to dental treatment: Patients may experience orthostatic hypotension as they stand up after treatment; especially if lying in dental chair for extended periods of time. Use caution with sudden changes in position during and after dental treatment.

Effects on Bleeding No information available to require special precautions

Adverse Reactions Frequency not defined.

Cardiovascular: Cardiac arrest, hypertension, hypotension (especially orthostatic), QT_c prolongation (dose dependent), tachycardia, torsade de pointes, ventricular tachycardia

Central nervous system: Anxiety, chills, depression (postoperative, transient), dizziness, drowsiness (postoperative) increased, dysphoria, extrapyramidal symptoms (akathisia, dystonia, oculogyric crisis),

hallucinations (postoperative), hyperactivity, neuroleptic malignant syndrome (NMS) (rare), restlessness
Respiratory: Bronchospasm, laryngospasm
Miscellaneous: Anaphylaxis, shivering

General Dosage Range IM, IV:
Children 2 to 12 years: Maximum: 0.1 mg/kg; additional doses may be repeated
Adults: Maximum initial dose: 2.5 mg; additional doses of 1.25 mg may be administered

Mechanism of Action Droperidol is a butyrophenone antipsychotic; antiemetic effect is a result of blockade of dopamine stimulation of the chemoreceptor trigger zone. Other effects include alpha-adrenergic blockade, peripheral vascular dilation, and reduction of the pressor effect of epinephrine resulting in hypotension and decreased peripheral vascular resistance; may also reduce pulmonary artery pressure

Pharmacodynamics/Kinetics
Onset of Action 3-10 minutes; Peak effect: Within 30 minutes
Duration of Action 2-4 hours, may extend to 12 hours
Half-life Elimination ~2.3 hours

Pregnancy Risk Factor C

Pregnancy Considerations Adverse events were observed in some animal reproduction studies. Although use in pregnancy has been reported, due to cases of QT prolongation and torsade de pointes (some fatal), use of other agents in pregnant women is recommended (ACOG 2015).

Dental Comment See Local Anesthetic/Vasoconstrictor Precautions

Drospirenone and Estradiol
(droh SPYE re none & es tra DYE ole)

Related Information
Estradiol (Systemic) *on page 609*

Brand Names: US Angeliq
Brand Names: Canada Angeliq
Pharmacologic Category Estrogen and Progestin Combination

Use Treatment of moderate-to-severe vasomotor symptoms associated with menopause; treatment of vulvar and vaginal atrophy associated with menopause

Local Anesthetic/Vasoconstrictor Precautions No information available to require special precautions

Effects on Bleeding No information available to require special precautions related to hemostasis in dental procedures.

Adverse Reactions
>10%:
Genitourinary: Mastalgia (6% to 18%), genital bleeding (3% to 14%)
1% to 10%:
Central nervous system: Emotional lability (1%), migraine (≤1%)
Gastrointestinal: Abdominal pain (≤4% to 7%), gastrointestinal pain (≤4% to 7%)
Genitourinary: Cervical polyp (≤1%)
<1%, postmarketing, and/or case reports: Cerebral infarction, cerebrovascular accident, embolism, hypersensitivity reaction, malignant neoplasm of breast, myocardial infarction, pulmonary vascular occlusion, pruritus, skin rash, thromboembolism, urticaria, venous obstruction (peripheral deep vein)

General Dosage Range Oral: *Adults (females):* 1 tablet daily

Mechanism of Action
Drospirenone is a synthetic progestin and spironolactone analog with antimineralocorticoid and antiandrogenic activity. Counteracts estrogen effects causing endometrial thinning.
Estrogens are responsible for the development and maintenance of the female reproductive system and secondary sexual characteristics. Estradiol is the principal intracellular human estrogen and is more potent than estrone and estriol at the receptor level; it is the primary estrogen secreted prior to menopause. Following menopause, estrone and estrone sulfate are more highly produced. Estrogens modulate the pituitary secretion of gonadotropins, luteinizing hormone, and follicle-stimulating hormone through a negative feedback system; estrogen replacement reduces elevated levels of these hormones in postmenopausal women.

Pharmacodynamics/Kinetics
Half-life Elimination Drospirenone: ~36-42 hours
Time to Peak Plasma: Drospirenone: 1 hour; Estradiol: ~2 hours (range 0.3-10 hours)

Pregnancy Considerations Use is contraindicated during pregnancy

Droxidopa (drox i DOE pa)

Brand Names: US Northera
Pharmacologic Category Alpha/Beta Agonist

Use Neurogenic orthostatic hypotension: Treatment of orthostatic dizziness, light-headedness, or the "feeling that you are about to black out" in adults with symptomatic neurogenic orthostatic hypotension (NOH) caused by primary autonomic failure (Parkinson disease [PD], multiple system atrophy [MSA], and pure autonomic failure [PAF]), dopamine beta-hydroxylase deficiency, and nondiabetic autonomic neuropathy.

Local Anesthetic/Vasoconstrictor Precautions
Droxidopa is converted to norepinephrine in tissues to result in possible hypertension; use vasoconstrictor with caution since epinephrine or levonordefrin may increase the hypertensive effects of Droxidopa.

Effects on Dental Treatment Key adverse event(s) related to dental treatment: Dizziness, syncope, falling have all been observed; special precautions should be taken when patient suddenly arises from the dental chair

Effects on Bleeding No information available to require special precautions

Adverse Reactions
>10%: Central nervous system: Headache (6% to 13%)
1% to 10%:
Cardiovascular: Hypertension (2% to 7%)
Central nervous system: Dizziness (4% to 10%)
Gastrointestinal: Nausea (9%)
Postmarketing and/or case reports: Abdominal pain, agitation, blurred vision, chest pain, confusion, delirium, diarrhea, fatigue, hallucination, hyperpyrexia, hypersensitivity reaction (including anaphylaxis, angioedema, bronchospasm, skin rash, urticaria), memory impairment, pancreatitis, psychosis, vomiting

General Dosage Range Oral: *Adults:* Initial: 100 mg 3 times daily (maximum dose: 1,800 mg/day)

Mechanism of Action A synthetic amino acid analog that is directly metabolized to norepinephrine by dopadecarboxylase. Droxidopa is believed to exert its pharmacological effects through norepinephrine. Norepinephrine increases blood pressure by inducing peripheral arterial and venous vasoconstriction.

Pharmacodynamics/Kinetics
Half-life Elimination ~2.5 hours
Time to Peak
Plasma: 1 to 4 hours
Pregnancy Considerations Adverse events have been observed in some animal reproduction studies.

DULoxetine (doo LOX e teen)

Related Information

Dentin Hypersensitivity, Acid Erosion, High Caries Index, Management of Alveolar Osteitis, and Xerostomia *on page 1857*

Vasoconstrictor Interactions With Antidepressants *on page 1913*

Brand Names: US Cymbalta; Irenka [DSC]

Brand Names: Canada Apo-Duloxetine; Auro-Duloxetine; Cymbalta; Duloxetine DR; JAMP-Duloxetine; Mint-Duloxetine; PMS-Duloxetine; RAN-Duloxetine; Riva-Duloxetine; Sandoz Duloxetine

Pharmacologic Category Antidepressant, Serotonin/Norepinephrine Reuptake Inhibitor

Use

Chronic musculoskeletal pain: Management of chronic musculoskeletal pain.

Diabetic peripheral neuropathic pain: Management of diabetic peripheral neuropathy.

Fibromyalgia (except Irenka): Management of fibromyalgia.

Generalized anxiety disorder: Treatment of generalized anxiety disorder (GAD).

Major depressive disorder: Treatment of major depressive disorder (MDD).

Local Anesthetic/Vasoconstrictor Precautions Although duloxetine is not a tricyclic antidepressant, it does block norepinephrine reuptake within the CNS synapses as part of its mechanism. It has been suggested that vasoconstrictors be administered with caution and to monitor vital signs in dental patients taking antidepressants that affect norepinephrine in this way.

Effects on Dental Treatment Key adverse event(s) related to dental treatment: Xerostomia and changes in salivation (normal salivary flow resumes upon discontinuation). See Effects on Bleeding.

Effects on Bleeding Platelet dysfunction (ie, impaired platelet aggregation) may occur during treatment with serotonin norepinephrine reuptake inhibitors (SNRIs) such as duloxetine due to platelet serotonin depletion, possibly increasing the risk of a bleeding complication. Concurrent NSAID use may increase this risk.

Adverse Reactions

>10%:

Central nervous system: Headache (13% to 14%), drowsiness (9% to 11%; dose related), fatigue (7% to 11%; dose related)

Gastrointestinal: Nausea (18% to 23%), xerostomia (adults: 11% to 14%; dose related, children and adolescents: 2%), abdominal pain (children and adolescents: 13%, adults: 5%)

Endocrine & metabolic: Weight loss (children and adolescents: 14%, adults: ≥1%)

Neuromuscular & skeletal: Weakness (≤7% to ≤11%; dose related)

1% to 10%:

Cardiovascular: Flushing (3%), increased blood pressure (2%), palpitations (≥1% to 2%)

Central nervous system: Insomnia (7% to 10%; dose related), dizziness (8% to 9%), agitation (3% to 4%), anxiety (3%), delayed ejaculation (2%; dose related), yawning (≥1% to 2%), abnormal dreams (≥1%), anorgasmia (≥1%), chills (≥1%), hypoesthesia (≥1%), lethargy (≥1%), paresthesia (≥1%), rigors (≥1%), sleep disorder (≥1%), vertigo (≥1%)

Dermatologic: Diaphoresis (6%), pruritus (≥1%)

Endocrine & metabolic: Decreased libido (3%), orgasm abnormal (≥1% to 2%), hot flash (≥1%), weight gain (≥1%)

Gastrointestinal: Constipation (9% to 10%; dose related), decreased appetite (6% to 10%; dose related), vomiting (children and adolescents: 9%; adults: 3% to 4%), diarrhea (6% to 9%), dyspepsia (2%), dysgeusia (≥1%), flatulence (≥1%)

Genitourinary: Erectile dysfunction (4%), ejaculatory disorder (2%), urinary frequency (≥1%)

Hepatic: Increased serum ALT (>3 x ULN: 1%)

Neuromuscular & skeletal: Tremor (2% to 3%; dose related), musculoskeletal pain (≥1%)

Ophthalmic: Blurred vision (≥1% to 3%)

Respiratory: Oropharyngeal pain (children and adolescents: 4%; adults: ≥1%), cough (children and adolescents: 3%)

<1%, postmarketing, and/or case reports: Abnormal gait, acute pancreatitis, aggressive behavior (particularly early in treatment or after treatment discontinuation), akathisia, anaphylaxis, angioedema, angle-closure glaucoma, apathy, bruxism, cholestatic jaundice, cold extremities, confusion, contact dermatitis, dehydration, diplopia, disorientation, disturbance in attention, dry eye syndrome, dysarthria, dyskinesia, dyslipidemia, dysphagia, dysuria, ecchymoses, elevated glycosylated hemoglobin (diabetic neuropathic pain), emotional lability, epistaxis, eructation, erythema, erythema multiforme, extrapyramidal reaction, falling, feeling abnormal, galactorrhea, gastric ulcer, gastritis, gastroenteritis, gastrointestinal hemorrhage, gynecological bleeding, halitosis, hallucination, hematoma, hepatic failure, hepatitis, hepatomegaly, hostility, hyperbilirubinemia, hypercholesterolemia, hyperglycemia, hyperkalemia, hyperlipidemia, hyperprolactinemia, hypersensitivity angiitis, hypersensitivity reaction, hypertensive crisis, hypertonia, hypokalemia, hypomania, hyponatremia, hypothyroidism, impulsivity, increased blood pressure, increased creatinine phosphokinase, increased diastolic blood pressure, increased serum alkaline phosphatase, increased serum AST, increased serum bicarbonate, increased serum transaminases, increased thirst, irritability, jaundice, laryngitis, lymphocytic colitis, malaise, malodorous urine, mania, menopausal symptoms, menstrual disease, myocardial infarction, muscle spasm, muscle twitching, myoclonus, night sweats, nocturia, orthostatic hypotension, otalgia, outbursts of anger (particularly early in treatment or after treatment discontinuation), panic attack, petechia, pharyngeal edema, polyuria, restless leg syndrome, seizure, sensation of cold, serotonin syndrome, sexual disorder, SIADH, skin photosensitivity, skin rash, Stevens-Johnson syndrome, stomatitis, suicidal ideation, supraventricular cardiac arrhythmia, syncope, tachycardia, testicular pain, tinnitus, trismus, urinary retention, urinary urgency, urticaria, visual disturbance

General Dosage Range Oral:

Adults: 30 to 60 mg daily in 1 to 2 divided doses (maximum: 120 mg daily)

Children and Adolescents 7 to 17 years: 30 to 60 mg once daily (maximum: 120 mg daily)

Mechanism of Action Duloxetine is a potent inhibitor of neuronal serotonin and norepinephrine reuptake and a weak inhibitor of dopamine reuptake. Duloxetine has no significant activity for muscarinic cholinergic, H_1-histaminergic, or alpha$_2$-adrenergic receptors. Duloxetine does not possess MAO-inhibitory activity.

Pharmacodynamics/Kinetics

Half-life Elimination ~12 hours (range: 8 to 17 hours); ~4 hours longer in elderly women

Time to Peak 6 hours; 10 hours when ingested with food

Pregnancy Risk Factor C

Pregnancy Considerations Adverse events have been observed in animal reproduction studies. Nonteratogenic effects in the newborn following SSRI/SNRI exposure late in the third trimester include respiratory distress, cyanosis, apnea, seizures, temperature instability, feeding difficulty, vomiting, hypoglycemia, hyper- or hypotonia, hyper-reflexia, jitteriness, irritability, constant crying, and tremor. Symptoms may be due to the toxicity of the SNRIs/SSRIs or a discontinuation syndrome and may be consistent with serotonin syndrome associated with SSRI treatment. The long-term effects of in utero SNRI/SSRI exposure on infant development and behavior are not known.

The ACOG recommends that therapy with SSRIs or SNRIs during pregnancy be individualized; treatment of depression during pregnancy should incorporate the clinical expertise of the mental health clinician, obstetrician, primary health care provider, and pediatrician. According to the American Psychiatric Association (APA), the risks of medication treatment should be weighed against other treatment options and untreated depression. For women who discontinue antidepressant medications during pregnancy and who may be at high risk for postpartum depression, the medications can be restarted following delivery. Treatment algorithms have been developed by the ACOG and the APA for the management of depression in women prior to conception and during pregnancy.

Health care providers are encouraged to enroll women exposed to duloxetine during pregnancy in the Cymbalta Pregnancy Registry (866-814-6975 or http://cymbaltapregnancyregistry.com).

Pregnant women exposed to antidepressants during pregnancy are encouraged to enroll in the National Pregnancy Registry for Antidepressants (NPRAD). Women 18 to 45 years of age or their health care providers may contact the registry by calling 844-405-6185. Enrollment should be done as early in pregnancy as possible.

Dutasteride (doo TAS teer ide)

Brand Names: US Avodart

Brand Names: Canada ACT-Dutasteride; Apo-Dutasteride; Avodart; Med-Dutasteride; Mint-Dutasteride; PMS-Dutasteride; Riva-Dutasteride; Sandoz-Dutasteride; Teva-Dutasteride

Pharmacologic Category 5 Alpha-Reductase Inhibitor

Use

Benign prostatic hyperplasia: Treatment of symptomatic benign prostatic hyperplasia (BPH) as monotherapy (to improve symptoms, reduce the risk of acute urinary retention, and to reduce the risk of need for BPH-related surgery) or combination therapy with tamsulosin

Limitations of use: Not approved for the prevention of prostate cancer.

Local Anesthetic/Vasoconstrictor Precautions No information available to require special precautions

Effects on Dental Treatment No significant effects or complications reported

Effects on Bleeding No information available to require special precautions

Adverse Reactions Frequency of most adverse events (except prostate cancer high grade) tends to decrease with continued use (>6 months). Frequency not always defined.

1% to 10%:

Endocrine & metabolic: Decreased libido (≤3%; incidence highest during first 6 months of therapy), gynecomastia (including breast tenderness, breast enlargement; ≤1%), increased luteinizing hormone, increased testosterone level, increased thyroid stimulating hormone level

Genitourinary: Impotence (≤5%; incidence highest during first 6 months of therapy), ejaculatory disorder (≤2%)

Hematologic & oncologic: Prostate cancer high grade (≤1%)

<1%, postmarketing, and/or case reports: Angioedema, cardiac failure, depressed mood, dermatological reaction (serious), dizziness, hypersensitivity, localized edema, malignant neoplasm of breast (males), pruritus, skin rash, testicular pain, testicular swelling, urticaria

General Dosage Range Oral: *Adults (males):* 0.5 mg once daily

Mechanism of Action Dutasteride is a 4-azo analog of testosterone and is a competitive, selective inhibitor of both reproductive tissues (type 2) and skin and hepatic (type 1) 5α-reductase. This results in inhibition of the conversion of testosterone to dihydrotestosterone and markedly suppresses serum dihydrotestosterone levels.

Pharmacodynamics/Kinetics

Half-life Elimination Terminal: ~5 weeks

Time to Peak 2-3 hours

Pregnancy Risk Factor X

Pregnancy Considerations Abnormalities of external male genitalia were reported in animal reproduction studies. Use is not indicated in women. Pregnant women are advised to avoid contact with crushed or broken tablets and the semen from a male partner exposed to dutasteride.

Dutasteride and Tamsulosin

(doo TAS teer ide & tam SOO loe sin)

Related Information

Dutasteride *on page* 553

Tamsulosin *on page* 1525

Brand Names: US Jalyn

Brand Names: Canada Jalyn

Pharmacologic Category 5 Alpha-Reductase Inhibitor; Alpha$_1$ Blocker

Use

Benign prostatic hyperplasia: Treatment of symptomatic benign prostatic hyperplasia (BPH) in men with an enlarged prostate.

Limitations of use: Dutasteride-containing products are not approved for the prevention of prostate cancer.

Local Anesthetic/Vasoconstrictor Precautions No information available to require special precautions

Effects on Dental Treatment Key adverse event(s) related to dental treatment: Tamsulosin: Patients may experience orthostatic hypotension as they stand up after treatment; especially if lying in dental chair for extended periods of time. Use caution with sudden changes in position during and after dental treatment.

Effects on Bleeding No information available to require special precautions

Adverse Reactions Frequencies reported for when products used in combination. Also see individual agents.

1% to 10%:

Central nervous system: Dizziness (2%)

Endocrine & metabolic: Decreased libido (5% to 6%), breast changes (3% to 5%, including breast hypertrophy, breast swelling, breast tenderness, gynecomastia, mastalgia, nipple pain, nipple swelling)

Genitourinary: Ejaculatory disorder (10% to 11%), impotence (8% to 10%)

<1%, postmarketing, and/or case reports: Malignant neoplasm of prostate (high-grade)

General Dosage Range Oral: *Adults (males):* 1 capsule (0.5 mg dutasteride/0.4 mg tamsulosin) once daily

Mechanism of Action

Dutasteride is a 4-azo analog of testosterone and is a competitive, selective inhibitor of both reproductive tissues (type 2) and skin and hepatic (type 1) 5α-reductase. This results in inhibition of the conversion of testosterone to dihydrotestosterone and markedly suppresses serum dihydrotestosterone levels.

Tamsulosin is an antagonist of $alpha_{1A}$-adrenoreceptors in the prostate. Smooth muscle tone in the prostate is mediated by $alpha_{1A}$-adrenoreceptors; blocking them leads to relaxation of smooth muscle in the bladder neck and prostate, causing an improvement of urine flow and decreased symptoms of BPH. Approximately 75% of the $alpha_1$-receptors in the prostate are of the $alpha_{1A}$subtype.

Pregnancy Risk Factor X

Pregnancy Considerations Use contraindicated in pregnancy. Not indicated for use in women. See individual agents.

Dyphylline (DYE fi lin)

Brand Names: US Lufyllin [DSC]

Pharmacologic Category Phosphodiesterase Enzyme Inhibitor, Nonselective

Use Bronchodilator in reversible airway obstruction due to asthma, chronic bronchitis, or emphysema

Local Anesthetic/Vasoconstrictor Precautions No information available to require special precautions

Effects on Dental Treatment Do not prescribe any erythromycin product to patients taking theophylline products. Erythromycin will delay the normal metabolic inactivation of theophyllines leading to increased blood levels; this has resulted in nausea, vomiting and CNS restlessness.

Effects on Bleeding No information available to require special precautions

Adverse Reactions Frequency not defined. Reactions reported with other xanthine derivatives and may be dose-related.

Cardiovascular: Circulatory shock, extrasystoles, flushing, hypotension, palpitations, tachycardia, ventricular arrhythmia

Central nervous system: Agitation, headache, hyperexcitability, insomnia, irritability, restlessness, seizure

Endocrine & metabolic: Albuminuria, hyperglycemia, SIADH

Gastrointestinal: Diarrhea, epigastric pain, hematemesis, nausea, vomiting

Genitourinary: Diuresis, hematuria

Neuromuscular & skeletal: Muscle twitching

Respiratory: Tachypnea

General Dosage Range Oral: *Adults:* Up to 15 mg/kg 4 times daily

Mechanism of Action Causes bronchodilatation, through phosphodiesterase inhibition which increases concentrations of cyclic adenine monophosphate (cAMP) and produces relaxation of bronchial smooth muscle.

Pharmacodynamics/Kinetics

Half-life Elimination ~2 hours (may be increased in renal impairment)

Time to Peak Plasma: ~45 minutes; Anuric patients: may be increased 3 to 4 times normal

Pregnancy Risk Factor C

Pregnancy Considerations Animal reproduction studies have not been conducted.

Echothiophate Iodide

(ek oh THYE oh fate EYE oh dide)

Brand Names: US Phospholine Iodide

Pharmacologic Category Acetylcholinesterase Inhibitor; Ophthalmic Agent, Antiglaucoma; Ophthalmic Agent, Miotic

Use

Accommodative esotropia: Concomitant esotropias with a significant accommodative component.

Glaucoma: Treatment of chronic open-angle glaucoma; subacute or chronic angle-closure glaucoma (postiridectomy or where surgery is refused or contraindicated); certain nonuveitic secondary types of glaucoma, especially glaucoma following cataract surgery.

Local Anesthetic/Vasoconstrictor Precautions No information available to require special precautions

Effects on Dental Treatment No significant effects or complications reported

Effects on Bleeding No information available to require special precautions

Adverse Reactions Frequency not defined.

Cardiovascular: Bradycardia, cardiac abnormality, flushing, hypotension

Central nervous system: Brow ache, myasthenia

Dermatologic: Diaphoresis

Gastrointestinal: Diarrhea, nausea, vomiting

Ophthalmic: Blepharospasm, blurred vision, burning sensation of eyes, cataract, conjunctival erythema, conjunctival thickening, eye redness, increased intraocular pressure (paradoxical), iris cyst, iritis (latent), lacrimal duct obstruction (nasolacrimal canal), lacrimation, miosis, myopia, retinal detachment, stinging of eyes, uveitis (activation)

Respiratory: Dyspnea

General Dosage Range Ophthalmic:

Children and Adolescents: Diagnosis: Instill 1 drop of (0.125%) into both eyes at bedtime for 2 to 3 weeks; Treatment: Instill 1 drop of 0.06% once daily **or** 0.125% every other day (maximum: 0.125%day)

Adults: Initial: 1 drop (0.03%) twice daily; Maintenance: 1 to 2 doses daily or every other day

Mechanism of Action Long-acting inhibition of cholinesterase enhances activity of endogenous acetylcholine. Reduced degradation of acetylcholine leads to continuous stimulation of the ciliary muscle producing miosis; other effects include potentiation of accommodation and facilitation of aqueous humor outflow, with attendant reduction in intraocular pressure.

Pharmacodynamics/Kinetics

Onset of Action Miosis: ≤60 minutes; Peak effect: Intraocular pressure decrease: 24 hours

Duration of Action Miosis: 1 to 4 weeks; Intraocular pressure: Days to weeks.

Pregnancy Risk Factor C

Pregnancy Considerations Animal reproduction studies have not been conducted.

Econazole (e KONE a zole)

Brand Names: US Ecoza

Pharmacologic Category Antifungal Agent, Imidazole Derivative; Antifungal Agent, Topical

Use Fungal infection:

Cream: Treatment of tinea pedis, tinea cruris, and tinea corporis caused by *Trichophyton rubrum*, *Trichophyton mentagrophytes*, *Trichophyton tonsurans*, *Microsporum canis*, *Microsporum audouini*, *Microsporum gypseum*, and *Epidermophyton floccosum* in the treatment of cutaneous candidiasis, and in the treatment of tinea versicolor.

Foam: Treatment of interdigital tinea pedis caused by *Trichophyton rubrum*, *Trichophyton mentagrophytes*, and *Epidermophyton floccosum* in patients 12 years and older

Local Anesthetic/Vasoconstrictor Precautions No information available to require special precautions

Effects on Dental Treatment No significant effects or complications reported

Effects on Bleeding No information available to require special precautions

Adverse Reactions

1% to 10%: Dermatologic: Burning sensation of skin (3%), erythema (3%), pruritus (3%), stinging of the skin (3%)

<1%, postmarketing, and/or case reports: Application site reaction, pruritic rash

General Dosage Range Topical: *Children ≥12 years, Adolescents, and Adults:* Apply sufficient quantity once or twice daily

Mechanism of Action Alters fungal cell wall membrane permeability; may interfere with RNA and protein synthesis, and lipid metabolism

Pharmacodynamics/Kinetics

Time to Peak Foam: 6.8 ± 5.1 hours

Pregnancy Risk Factor C

Pregnancy Considerations Adverse events were observed in some animal reproduction studies. The manufacturer recommends avoiding use during pregnancy, especially during the first trimester.

Eculizumab (e kue LIZ oo mab)

Brand Names: US Soliris

Brand Names: Canada Soliris

Pharmacologic Category Monoclonal Antibody; Monoclonal Antibody, Complement Inhibitor

Use

Atypical hemolytic uremic syndrome: Treatment of atypical hemolytic uremic syndrome (aHUS) to inhibit complement-mediated thrombotic microangiopathy.

Limitation of use: Eculizumab is not indicated for the treatment of patients with Shiga toxin *Escherichia coli*-related hemolytic uremic syndrome.

Paroxysmal nocturnal hemoglobinuria: Treatment of paroxysmal nocturnal hemoglobinuria (PNH) to reduce hemolysis.

Local Anesthetic/Vasoconstrictor Precautions No information available to require special precautions

Effects on Dental Treatment No significant effects or complications reported

Effects on Bleeding No information available to require special precautions

Adverse Reactions Frequency reported for adolescent and adult patients ≥13 years unless otherwise noted.

>10%:

Cardiovascular: Hypertension (aHUS: 17% to 59%; infants, children, and adolescents 5 months through 17 years: 18%), peripheral edema (20% to 29%), tachycardia (aHUS: children 21%), hypotension (12% to 20%)

Central nervous system: Headache (37% to 50%; serious: 2%; infants, children, and adolescents 5 months through 17 years: 18%), insomnia (10% to 24%), fatigue (7% to 20%)

Dermatologic: Skin rash (infants ≥5 months, children, adolescents, and adults 12% to 18%), pruritus (6% to 15%)

Endocrine & metabolic: Hypokalemia (10% to 18%)

Gastrointestinal: Diarrhea (32% to 47%; infants, children, and adolescents 2 months through 17 years: 32%), vomiting (15% to 47%; infants, children, and adolescents 2 months through 17 years: 21% to 27%), nausea (12% to 40%), abdominal pain (15% to 30%), gastroenteritis (5% to 18%), dyspepsia (infants, children, and adolescents 5 months through 17 years: 14%)

Genitourinary: Urinary tract infection (15% to 35%; infants, children, and adolescents 5 months through 17 years: 18%), uropathy (infants, children, and adolescents 5 months through 17 years: 18%), proteinuria (5% to 12%)

Hematologic & oncologic: Anemia (17% to 35%; serious: 2%), neoplasm (6% to 30%), leukopenia (16% to 24%)

Local: Catheter infection (infants, children, and adolescents 5 months through 17 years: 14%)

Neuromuscular & skeletal: Weakness (15% to 20%), back pain (5% to 19%), arthralgia (6% to 17%), muscle spasm (infants, children, and adolescents 5 months through 17 years: 14%), limb pain (7% to 11%)

Ophthalmic: Eye disease (10% to 29%; infants, children, and adolescents 5 months through 17 years: 14%)

Renal: Renal insufficiency (15% to 20%)

Respiratory: Nasopharyngitis (18% to 55%; infants, children, and adolescents 5 months through 17 years: 27%), upper respiratory tract infection (infants ≥2 months, children, adolescents, and adults 5% to 40%), cough (infants ≥5 months, children, adolescents, and adults 12% to 36%), nasal congestion (aHUS: children 21%), rhinitis (infants, children, and adolescents 5 months through 17 years: 18%), bronchitis (10% to 18%), oropharyngeal pain (infants, children, and adolescents 5 months through 17 years: 14%)

Miscellaneous: Fever (infants, children, and adolescents 2 months through 17 years: 47% to 50%; adults 17% to 25%)

1% to 10%:

Gastrointestinal: Constipation (7%)

Immunologic: Antibody development (2% to 3%; neutralizing: 1%)

Infection: Herpes virus infection (7%), viral infection (serious: 2%), meningococcal infection (≤1%)

Neuromuscular & skeletal: Myalgia (7%)
Respiratory: Respiratory tract infection (7%), sinusitis (7%), flu-like symptoms (5%)

<1%, postmarketing, and/or case reports: Abdominal distention, anxiety, aspergillosis, cholangitis, dizziness, dysgeusia, endometritis, hematoma (mild), infusion related reaction, pyelonephritis

General Dosage Range IV:

Infants ≥2 months, Children, and Adolescents:

5 kg to <10 kg: Induction: 300 mg weekly for 1 dose; Maintenance: 300 mg at week 2, then 300 mg every 3 weeks

10 kg to <20 kg: Induction: 600 mg weekly for 1 dose; Maintenance: 300 mg at week 2, then 300 mg every 2 weeks

20 kg to <30 kg: Induction: 600 mg weekly for 2 doses; Maintenance: 600 mg at week 3, then 600 mg every 2 weeks

30 kg to <40 kg: Induction: 600 mg weekly for 2 doses; Maintenance: 900 mg at week 3, then 900 mg every 2 weeks

≥40 kg: Induction: 900 mg weekly for 4 doses; Maintenance: 1,200 mg at week 5, then 1200 mg every 2 weeks

Adults: aHUS: Induction: 900 mg weekly for 4 doses; Maintenance: 1,200 mg at week 5, then 1,200 mg every 2 weeks **or** PNH: Induction: 600 mg weekly for 4 doses; Maintenance: 900 mg at week 5, then 900 mg every 2 weeks

Mechanism of Action Terminal complement-mediated intravascular hemolysis is a key clinical feature of paroxysmal nocturnal hemoglobinuria (PNH); blocking the formation of membrane attack complex (MAC) results in stabilization of hemoglobin and a reduction in the need for RBC transfusions. Impairment of complement activity regulation leads to uncontrolled complement activation in atypical hemolytic uremic syndrome (aHUS). Eculizumab is a humanized monoclonal IgG antibody that binds to complement protein C5, preventing cleavage into C5a and C5b. Blocking the formation of C5b inhibits the subsequent formation of terminal complex C5b-9 or MAC.

Pharmacodynamics/Kinetics

Onset of Action PNH: Reduced hemolysis: ≤1 week

Half-life Elimination PNH: ~11 days (range: ~8 to 15 days); aHUS: ~12 days (during plasma exchange the half-life is reduced to 1.26 hours)

Pregnancy Risk Factor C

Pregnancy Considerations Adverse events were observed in animal reproduction studies. Eculizumab crosses the placenta and can be detected in cord blood. Pregnant women with PNH and their fetuses have high rates of morbidity and mortality during pregnancy and the postpartum period. Treatment of PNH with eculizumab has been shown to increase fetal survival and decrease maternal complications (Kelly 2015). Use of eculizumab for the treatment of a HUS in pregnancy has also been described (Ardissino 2013).

Prescribing and Access Restrictions Patients and providers must enroll with Soliris REMS OneSource Safety Program (1-888-765-4747) or at solirisrems.com prior to treatment initiation.

Edetate CALCIUM Disodium

(ED e tate KAL see um dye SOW dee um)

Pharmacologic Category Chelating Agent

Use Treatment of symptomatic acute and chronic lead poisoning

Local Anesthetic/Vasoconstrictor Precautions No information available to require special precautions

Effects on Dental Treatment No significant effects or complications reported

Effects on Bleeding No information available to require special precautions

Adverse Reactions Frequency not defined.

Cardiovascular: Cardiac arrhythmia, ECG changes, hypotension, local thrombophlebitis (IV infusion when concentration >5 mg/mL)
Central nervous system: Chills, fatigue, headache, malaise, numbness, paresthesia
Dermatologic: Cheilosis, dermatitis, skin rash
Endocrine & metabolic: Glycosuria, hypercalcemia, hypokalemia, iron deficiency (with chronic therapy), magnesium deficiency (with chronic therapy), polydipsia, zinc deficiency (with chronic therapy)
Gastrointestinal: Anorexia, gastrointestinal irritation, nausea, vomiting
Genitourinary: Nephrosis, nephrotoxicity, occult blood in urine, proteinuria, urinary frequency, urinary urgency
Hematologic & oncologic: Anemia, bone marrow depression (transient)
Hepatic: Decreased serum alkaline phosphatase, increased liver enzymes (mild)
Local: Pain at injection site (intramuscular)
Neuromuscular & skeletal: Arthralgia, myalgia, tremor
Ophthalmic: Lacrimation
Renal: Renal tubular necrosis
Respiratory: Nasal congestion, sneezing
Miscellaneous: Fever

General Dosage Range Dosage adjustment recommended in patients with renal impairment

IM, IV: *Children and Adults:* 1000-1500 mg/m^2/day (25-75 mg/kg/day)

Mechanism of Action Calcium is displaced by divalent and trivalent heavy metals, forming a nonionizing soluble complex with lead that is excreted in the urine.

Pharmacodynamics/Kinetics

Onset of Action Chelation of lead: IV: 1 hour; Maximum excretion of chelated lead with IV administration: 24 to 48 hours

Half-life Elimination 20-60 minutes

Pregnancy Risk Factor B

Pregnancy Considerations Adverse events were observed in some animal reproduction studies; there are no well controlled studies of edetate CALCIUM disodium in pregnant women. Lead is known to cross the placenta in amounts related to maternal plasma levels. Prenatal lead exposure may be associated with adverse events such as spontaneous abortion, preterm delivery, decreased birth weight, and impaired neurodevelopment. Some adverse outcomes may occur with maternal blood lead levels <10 mcg/dL. In addition, pregnant women exposed to lead may have an increased risk of gestational hypertension. Consider chelation therapy in pregnant women with confirmed blood lead levels ≥45 mcg/dL (pregnant women with blood lead levels ≥70 mcg/dL should be considered for chelation regardless of trimester). Alternatives to edetate CALCIUM disodium may be indicated and consultation with experts in lead poisoning and high-risk pregnancy is recommended. Encephalopathic pregnant women should be chelated regardless of trimester (CDC 2010).

Edoxaban (e DOX a ban)

Related Information

Antiplatelet and Anticoagulation Considerations in Dentistry *on page 1764*

Brand Names: US Savaysa

Brand Names: Canada Lixiana

Pharmacologic Category Anticoagulant; Anticoagulant, Factor Xa Inhibitor; Direct Oral Anticoagulant (DOAC)

Use

Deep vein thrombosis and pulmonary embolism: Treatment of deep vein thrombosis (DVT) and pulmonary embolism (PE) following 5 to 10 days of initial therapy with a parenteral anticoagulant.

Nonvalvular atrial fibrillation: To reduce the risk of stroke and systemic embolism (SE) in patients with nonvalvular atrial fibrillation (NVAF)

Limitations of use: Do not use in NVAF patients with CrCl >95 mL/minute because of an increased risk of ischemic stroke compared to warfarin

Local Anesthetic/Vasoconstrictor Precautions

No information available to require special precautions

Effects on Dental Treatment

Key adverse event(s) related to dental treatment: Surgical site bleeding may occur. See effects on bleeding.

Effects on Bleeding Edoxaban inhibits platelet activation and fibrin clot formation via direct, selective, and reversible inhibition of factor Xa. As with all anticoagulants, bleeding is the major adverse effect of edoxaban. Hemorrhage may occur at virtually any site; risk is dependent on multiple variables including the intensity of anticoagulation and patient susceptibility. Medical consult is suggested.

Adverse Reactions

>10%:

Hematologic and oncologic: Hemorrhage (22%)

1% to 10%:

Dermatologic: Dermal hemorrhage (6%), skin rash (4%)

Gastrointestinal: Gastrointestinal hemorrhage (4%), lower GI bleeding (3%)

Genitourinary: Vaginal hemorrhage (9%), gross hematuria (≤2%), urethral bleeding (≤2%)

Hematologic and oncologic: Major hemorrhage, non-life-threatening (7% to 9%; noncritical organ: 1%; critical organ: <1%), major hemorrhage (1%), oral hemorrhage (<3%), anemia (2%), decreased hemoglobin (≥ 2 g/dL: 1%), puncture site bleeding (1%)

Hepatic: Abnormal hepatic function tests (5% to 8%)

Respiratory: Epistaxis (5%), pharyngeal bleeding (≤3%)

<1%, postmarketing, and/or case reports: Hemorrhagic stroke, interstitial pulmonary disease (confounded by concomitant amiodarone therapy and infectious pneumonia), intracranial hemorrhage (includes epidural hematoma, nonhemorrhagic stroke with major hemorrhagic conversion, primary hemorrhagic stroke, subarachnoid hemorrhage, subdural hematoma)

General Dosage Range

Dosage adjustment recommended in patients with renal impairment.

Adults: Oral: 60 mg once daily

Mechanism of Action Edoxaban, a selective factor Xa inhibitor, inhibits free factor Xa and prothrombinase activity and inhibits thrombin-induced platelet aggregation. Inhibition of factor Xa in the coagulation cascade reduces thrombin generation and thrombus formation.

Pharmacodynamics/Kinetics

Half-life Elimination 10 to 14 hours

Time to Peak 1 to 2 hours

Pregnancy Risk Factor C

Pregnancy Considerations Adverse events have been observed in some animal reproduction studies. Ten pregnancies were reported in a study using edoxaban for the treatment of DVT or PE. Estimated exposure occurred during the first trimester with duration of exposure ~6 weeks; outcomes included six live births (two preterm), one first-trimester spontaneous abortion, and three elective terminations of pregnancy.

Edrophonium (ed roe FOE nee um)

Brand Names: US Enlon

Brand Names: Canada Enlon; Tensilon

Pharmacologic Category Acetylcholinesterase Inhibitor; Antidote; Diagnostic Agent

Use Diagnosis of myasthenia gravis; differentiation of cholinergic crises from myasthenia crises; reversal of nondepolarizing neuromuscular blockers

Note: Although the onset of action of neostigmine is delayed, the use of neostigmine (with glycopyrrolate) is usually preferred over edrophonium for the reversal of nondepolarizing neuromuscular blockers due to a longer duration of action (Barash 2009; Morgan 2013).

Local Anesthetic/Vasoconstrictor Precautions

No information available to require special precautions

Effects on Dental Treatment No significant effects or complications reported

Effects on Bleeding No information available to require special precautions

Adverse Reactions Frequency not defined. Some reactions listed are based on reports for other agents in this same pharmacologic class and may not be specifically reported for edrophonium.

Cardiovascular: Atrioventricular block, cardiac arrhythmia (especially bradycardia), cardiac arrest, ECG changes (nonspecific), flushing, hypotension, syncope, tachycardia, thrombophlebitis (IV)

Central nervous system: Convulsions, dizziness, drowsiness, dysarthria, headache, loss of consciousness, voice disorder

Dermatologic: Diaphoresis, skin rash, urticaria

Gastrointestinal: Diarrhea, dysphagia, flatulence, increased peristalsis, nausea, salivation, stomach cramps, vomiting

Genitourinary: Urinary frequency, urinary urgency

Hypersensitivity: Anaphylaxis, hypersensitivity reaction

Neuromuscular & skeletal: Fasciculations, laryngospasm, weakness

Ophthalmic: Conjunctival hyperemia, diplopia, lacrimation, miosis, spasm of accommodation

Respiratory: Bronchoconstriction, increased bronchial secretions, respiratory arrest, respiratory paralysis

Miscellaneous: Increased gastric secretions, increased intestinal secretions

General Dosage Range

IM:

Children ≤34 kg: 2 mg

Children >34 kg: 5 mg

Adults: 10 mg, if cholinergic reaction occurs, administer 2 mg 30 minutes later to rule out false-negative reaction.

IV:

Infants: 0.5 mg

Children ≤34 kg: 1 mg, followed by 1 mg every 30 to 45 seconds if no response (maximum total dose: 5 mg)

Children >34 kg: 2 mg, followed by 1 mg every 30 to 45 seconds if no response (maximum total dose: 10 mg)

Adults: 2 mg test dose, followed by 8 mg if no response **or** 10 mg every 5 to 10 minutes up to 40 mg **or** 1 mg; may repeat after 1 minute **or** 1 to 2 mg given 1 hour after oral dose of anticholinesterase

Mechanism of Action Inhibits destruction of acetylcholine by acetylcholinesterase. This facilitates transmission of impulses across myoneural junction and results in increased cholinergic responses such as miosis, increased tonus of intestinal and skeletal muscles, bronchial and ureteral constriction, bradycardia, and increased salivary and sweat gland secretions.

Pharmacodynamics/Kinetics

Onset of Action IM: 2 to 10 minutes; IV: 30 to 60 seconds

Duration of Action IM: 5 to 30 minutes: IV: 10 minutes

Half-life Elimination Infants: 73 ± 30 minutes; Children: 99 ± 31 minutes; Adults: 126 ± 59 minutes; Anephric patients: 2.4 to 4.4 hours

Pregnancy Considerations Due to the theoretical potential for complications, consider a lower initial dose when using edrophonium for the diagnosis of myasthenia gravis during pregnancy (Varner, 2013).

Efavirenz (e FAV e renz)

Related Information

HIV Infection and AIDS *on page 1785*

Brand Names: US Sustiva

Brand Names: Canada Mylan-Efavirenz; Sustiva; Teva-Efavirenz

Pharmacologic Category Antiretroviral, Reverse Transcriptase Inhibitor, Non-nucleoside (Anti-HIV)

Use HIV-1 infection: Treatment of HIV-1 infection in combination with other antiretroviral agents in adults and pediatric patients at least 3 months old and weighing at least 3.5 kg

Local Anesthetic/Vasoconstrictor Precautions No information available to require special precautions

Effects on Dental Treatment Key adverse event(s) related to dental treatment: Abnormal taste

Effects on Bleeding No information available to require special precautions related to hemostasis.

Adverse Reactions Unless otherwise noted, frequency of adverse events is as reported in adults receiving combination antiretroviral therapy.

>10%:

Central nervous system: Dizziness (2% to 28%; children: 16%), fever (children: 21%), depression (≤19%; severe: 1% to 2%), insomnia (≤16%), pain (1% to 13%; children: 14%), anxiety (2% to 13%), headache (2% to 8%; children: 11%)

Dermatologic: Skin rash (5% to 26%, grades 3/4: <1%; children: ≤46%, grades 3/4: 2% to 4%)

Endocrine & metabolic: Increased serum cholesterol (20% to 40%), increased HDL cholesterol (25% to 35%), increased serum triglycerides (≥751 mg/dL: 6% to 11%)

Gastrointestinal: Diarrhea (3% to 14%; children: ≤39%), nausea (2% to 10%; children: 12%), vomiting (3% to 6%; children 12%)

Respiratory: Cough (children: 16%)

1% to 10%:

Central nervous system: Fatigue (≤8%), lack of concentration (≤8%), drowsiness (≤7%), nervousness (2% to 7%), abnormal dreams (1% to 6%), hallucination (1%)

Dermatologic: Pruritus (≤9%)

Endocrine & metabolic: Increased amylase (grades 3/4: ≤6%), hyperglycemia (>250 mg/dL: 2% to 5%)

Gastrointestinal: Dyspepsia (≤4%), abdominal pain (2% to 3%), anorexia (≤2%)

Hematologic & oncologic: Neutropenia (grades 3/4: 2% to 10%)

Hepatic: Increased serum AST (grades 3/4: 5% to 8%; incidence higher with hepatitis B and/or C coinfection), increased serum ALT (grades 3/4: 2% to 8%; incidence higher with hepatitis B and/or C coinfection)

<1%, postmarketing, and/or case reports: Aggressive behavior, agitation, arthralgia, ataxia, attempted suicide, cerebellar ataxia, constipation, delusions, dyspnea, emotional lability, erythema multiforme, flushing, gynecomastia, hepatic failure, hepatitis, hypersensitivity reaction, hypoesthesia, immune reconstitution syndrome, lipotrophy, loss of balance, malabsorption, mania, myalgia, myopathy, neuropathy, palpitations, pancreatitis, paranoia, paresthesia, photodermatitis, psychoneurosis, psychosis, redistribution of body fat, seizure, Stevens-Johnson syndrome, suicidal ideation, tinnitus, tremor, vertigo, visual disturbance, weakness

General Dosage Range Dosage adjustment recommended in patients on concomitant therapy

Oral:

Infants ≥3 months, Children, and Adolescents:

3.5 kg to <5 kg: 100 mg once daily

5 kg to <7.5 kg: 150 mg once daily

7.5 kg to <15 kg: 200 mg once daily

15 kg to <20 kg: 250 mg once daily

20 kg to <25 kg: 300 mg once daily

25 kg to <32.5 kg: 350 mg once daily

32.5 kg to <40 kg: 400 mg once daily

≥40 kg: 600 mg once daily

Adults: 600 mg once daily

Mechanism of Action As a non-nucleoside reverse transcriptase inhibitor, efavirenz has activity against HIV-1 by binding to reverse transcriptase. It consequently blocks the RNA-dependent and DNA-dependent DNA polymerase activities including HIV-1 replication. It does not require intracellular phosphorylation for antiviral activity.

Pharmacodynamics/Kinetics

Half-life Elimination Single dose: 52 to 76 hours; Multiple doses: 40 to 55 hours

Time to Peak 3 to 5 hours

Pregnancy Considerations Efavirenz has a moderate level of transfer across the human placenta. Based on data from the Antiretroviral Pregnancy Registry, an increased risk of overall birth defects has not been observed following first trimester exposure to efavirenz. Neural tube and other CNS defects have been reported; however, a meta-analysis has shown that the risk for neural tube defects after efavirenz exposure in the first trimester are not greater than those in the general population. Maternal antiretroviral therapy may increase the risk of preterm delivery, although, available information is conflicting possibly due to variability of maternal factors (disease severity; initiation of therapy); however, maternal antiretroviral medication should not be withheld due to concerns of preterm birth. Information related to stillbirth, low birth weight, and small for gestational age infants is limited. Long-term follow-up is recommended for all infants exposed to antiretroviral medications; children who develop significant organ system abnormalities of unknown etiology (particularly of the CNS or heart) should be evaluated for potential mitochondrial dysfunction. Hypersensitivity reactions (including hepatic toxicity and rash) are more common in women on NNRTI therapy; it is not known if pregnancy increases this risk.

Combination antiretroviral therapy (cART) therapy is recommended for all HIV-infected pregnant women to keep the viral load below the limit of detection and reduce the risk of perinatal transmission. When HIV is diagnosed during pregnancy in a woman who has never received antiretroviral therapy, cART should begin as soon as possible after diagnosis. The Health and Human Services (HHS) Perinatal HIV Guidelines consider efavirenz to be a component of an alternative regimen for initial use in antiretroviral-naive pregnant women. Use may be considered for women having drug interactions with other medications or who require the convenience of once daily dosing; screening for antenatal and postpartum depression is recommended. Pharmacokinetic data from available studies do not suggest dose alterations are needed during pregnancy. In general, women who become pregnant on a stable cART regimen may continue that regimen if viral suppression is effective, appropriate drug exposure can be achieved, contraindications for use in pregnancy are not present, and the regimen is well tolerated. Although not recommended by the manufacturer, HHS guidelines do not restrict the use of efavirenz in the first trimester. For women who present in the first trimester already on an efavirenz-containing regimen and who have adequate viral suppression, efavirenz may be continued (additional fetal monitoring, such as second trimester ultrasound, should be considered to evaluate fetal anatomy). Monitoring during pregnancy is more frequent than in non-pregnant adults; cART should be continued postpartum. If an efavirenz containing regimen must be discontinued for more than a few days due to toxicity, consider evaluating for rebound viremia and drug resistance; consult current guidelines.

For HIV-infected couples planning a pregnancy, maximum viral suppression with combination antiretroviral therapy (cART) is recommended prior to conception for the HIV-infected partner(s) and expert consultation is recommended, modification of therapy (if needed) and optimization of the woman's health should be done prior to conception. HIV-infected women not planning a pregnancy may use any available type of contraception, considering possible drug interactions and contraindications of the specific method. In addition, consistent use of condoms is also recommended (even during pregnancy) to prevent transmission of HIV or other sexually transmitted diseases.

Health care providers are encouraged to enroll pregnant women exposed to antiretroviral medications as early in pregnancy as possible in the Antiretroviral Pregnancy Registry (1-800-258-4263 or www.APRegistry.com). Health care providers caring for HIV-infected women and their infants may contact the National Perinatal HIV Hotline (888-448-8765) for clinical consultation (HHS [perinatal] 2016).

Prescribing and Access Restrictions Efavirenz oral solution is available only through an expanded access (compassionate use) program. Enrollment information may be obtained by calling 877-372-7097.

Efavirenz, Emtricitabine, and Tenofovir Disoproxil Fumarate

(e FAV e renz, em trye SYE ta been, & ten OF oh vir dye soe PROX il FUE ma rate)

Related Information

Efavirenz *on page 558*
Emtricitabine *on page 568*
HIV Infection and AIDS *on page 1785*
Tenofovir Disoproxil Fumarate *on page 1539*

Brand Names: US Atripla

Brand Names: Canada Atripla

Pharmacologic Category Antiretroviral, Reverse Transcriptase Inhibitor, Non-nucleoside (Anti-HIV); Antiretroviral, Reverse Transcriptase Inhibitor, Nucleoside (Anti-HIV); Antiretroviral, Reverse Transcriptase Inhibitor, Nucleotide (Anti-HIV)

Use Treatment of HIV-1 infection

Local Anesthetic/Vasoconstrictor Precautions No information available to require special precautions

Effects on Dental Treatment Key adverse event(s) related to dental treatment: Efavirenz alone has caused xerostomia (normal salivary flow resumes upon discontinuation) and abnormal taste (see individual monograph). No significant effects or complications reported with combination drug.

Effects on Bleeding No information available to require special precautions related to hemostasis.

Adverse Reactions Frequency not always defined. The complete adverse reaction profile of combination therapy has not been established. See individual agents. The following adverse effects were noted in clinical trials with combination therapy.

>10%: Endocrine & metabolic: Hypercholesterolemia (22%)

1% to 10%:

Central nervous system: Depression (9%), fatigue (9%), dizziness (8%), headache (6%), anxiety (5%), insomnia (5%), drowsiness (4%), abnormal dreams

Dermatologic: Skin rash (7%)

Endocrine & metabolic: Increased serum triglycerides (4%), hyperglycemia (2%)

Gastrointestinal: Diarrhea (9%), nausea (9%), increased serum amylase (8%), vomiting (2%)

Genitourinary: Hematuria (3%)

Hematologic & oncologic: Neutropenia (3%)

Hepatic: Increased serum AST (3%), increased serum ALT (2%), increased serum alkaline phosphatase (1%)

Neuromuscular & skeletal: Increased creatine phosphokinase (9%)

Respiratory: Sinusitis (8%), upper respiratory tract infection (8%), nasopharyngitis (5%)

<1%, postmarketing, and/or case reports: Glycosuria

General Dosage Range Oral: *Children ≥12 years and ≥40 kg, Adolescents, and Adults:* 1 tablet (efavirenz 600 mg/emtricitabine 200 mg/tenofovir 300 mg) once daily

Mechanism of Action See individual agents.

Pregnancy Risk Factor D

Pregnancy Considerations

Adverse events have been observed in some animal reproduction studies.

The manufacturer's labeling of this combination product recommends pregnancy testing prior to therapy, and effective contraception in women of reproductive potential during treatment and for 12 weeks after therapy is discontinued.

In general, women who become pregnant on a stable combination antiretroviral therapy (cART) regimen may continue that regimen if viral suppression is effective, appropriate drug exposure can be achieved, contraindications for use in pregnancy are not present, and the regimen is well tolerated. The Health and Human Services (HHS) Perinatal HIV Guidelines consider efavirenz in combination with emtricitabine and tenofovir disoproxil fumarate as an alternative initial regimen in antiretroviral-naive pregnant women; it may be preferred in women who require co-administration of drugs without significant interactions with protease inhibitors, or for the convenience of once-daily dosing (HHS [perinatal] 2016). See individual agents.

Efinaconazole (ef in a KON a zole)

Brand Names: US Jublia

Brand Names: Canada Jublia

Pharmacologic Category Antifungal Agent, Topical

Use Onychomycosis: Topical treatment of onychomycosis of the toenail(s) due to *Trichophyton rubrum* and *Trichophyton mentagrophytes*

Local Anesthetic/Vasoconstrictor Precautions No information available to require special precautions

Effects on Dental Treatment No significant effects or complications reported

Effects on Bleeding No information available to require special precautions

Adverse Reactions 1% to 10%:

Dermatologic: Ingrown nail (2%)

Local: Application site dermatitis (2%), application site vesicles (2%), application site pain (1%)

General Dosage Range Topical: *Adults:* Apply to affected toenail(s) once daily for 48 weeks.

Mechanism of Action An azole antifungal; inhibits fungal lanosterol 14alpha-demethylase involved in the biosynthesis of ergosterol, a constituent of fungal cell membranes, resulting in fungal cell death.

Pharmacodynamics/Kinetics

Half-life Elimination 29.9 hours.

Pregnancy Risk Factor C

Pregnancy Considerations Adverse events were observed in some animal reproduction studies following SubQ administration. Small amounts of efinaconazole are absorbed systemically following topical administration.

Eflornithine (ee FLOR ni theen)

Brand Names: US Vaniqa

Brand Names: Canada Vaniqa®

Pharmacologic Category Antiprotozoal; Topical Skin Product

Use Reduce unwanted hair from face and adjacent areas under the chin

Local Anesthetic/Vasoconstrictor Precautions No information available to require special precautions

Effects on Dental Treatment No significant effects or complications reported

Effects on Bleeding No information available to require special precautions

Adverse Reactions

Injection (Priotto 2009):

>10%:

Cardiovascular: Cardiac arrhythmia (22%), hypertension (13%), chest pain (11%)

Central nervous system: Headache (46%), dizziness (17%)

Dermatologic: Pruritus (19%), skin rash (14%)

Gastrointestinal: Abdominal pain (30%), diarrhea (29%), nausea (20%), vomiting (20%), anorexia (14%)

Hematologic & oncologic: Neutropenia (33%)

Infection: Infection (2% to 16%)

Local: Injection site reaction (11%)

Neuromuscular & skeletal: Arthralgia (≤30%), myalgia (≤30%), weakness (20%)

Miscellaneous: Fever (43%)

1% to 10%:

Cardiovascular: Edema (4%), hypotension (≤3%), shock (≤3%)

Central nervous system: Insomnia (10%), seizure (9%), anxiety (8%), peripheral neuropathy (1% to 4%), coma (2%), amnesia (1%), ataxia (1%), confusion (1%), depression (1%), hallucination (1%), lethargy (1%)

Endocrine & metabolic: Dehydration (2%)

Gastrointestinal: Dysphagia (9%), xerostomia (5%), constipation (4%), changes in ALT (3%), dysgeusia (2%), hiccups (2%)

Genitourinary: Urinary frequency (≤4%), urinary urgency (≤4%), urinary incontinence (3%), change in creatinine (1%)

Hematologic & oncologic: Anemia (9%), leukopenia (4%), thrombocytopenia (4%)

Hepatic: Abnormal bilirubin levels (5%)

Local: Extravasation (8%)

Neuromuscular & skeletal: Tremor (1%)

Otic: Inner ear disturbance (5%)

Respiratory: Cough (10%), epistaxis (2%), dyspnea (1%), respiratory distress (1%)

Topical:

>10%: Dermatologic: Acne vulgaris (11% to 21%), pseudofolliculitis barbae (5% to 16%)

1% to 10%:

Central nervous system: Headache (4%), tingling of skin (2% to 4%), dizziness (1% to 2%)

Dermatologic: Stinging of the skin (4% to 8%), burning sensation of skin (4%), pruritus (3% to 4%), skin rash (2% to 3%), xeroderma (2% to 3%), erythema (1% to 3%), alopecia (1% to 2%), skin irritation (1% to 2%), folliculitis (≤1%), ingrown hair (≤1%)

Gastrointestinal: Dyspepsia (2% to 3%), anorexia (1%)

<1%, postmarketing, and/or case reports: Acne rosacea, cheilitis, contact dermatitis, dermal hemorrhage, facial edema, herpes simplex infection, nausea, numbness, swelling of lips, vertigo, weakness

General Dosage Range

Topical: *Children and Adults:* Apply thin layer to affected areas twice daily

Mechanism of Action

Cream: Eflornithine inhibits the enzyme ornithine decarboxylase (ODC) which inhibits cell division and synthetic functions and thereby affects the rate of hair growth.

Injection: Eflornithine exerts antitumor and antiprotozoal effects through specific, irreversible ("suicide") inhibition of the enzyme ornithine decarboxylase (ODC). ODC is the rate-limiting enzyme in the biosynthesis of putrescine, spermine, and spermidine, the major polyamines in nucleated cells. Polyamines are necessary for the synthesis of DNA, RNA, and proteins and are, therefore, necessary for cell growth and differentiation. Although many microorganisms and higher plants are able to produce polyamines from alternate biochemical pathways, all mammalian cells depend on ornithine decarboxylase to produce polyamines. Eflornithine inhibits ODC and rapidly depletes animal cells of putrescine and spermidine; the concentration of spermine remains the same or may even increase. Rapidly dividing cells appear to be most susceptible to the effects of eflornithine.

Pharmacodynamics/Kinetics

Onset of Action Decreased hair growth: 4-8 weeks

Duration of Action Decreased hair growth: Continues until ~8 weeks after discontinuing treatment

Half-life Elimination IV: 3-3.5 hours; Topical: 8 hours

Pregnancy Risk Factor C

Pregnancy Considerations When administered topically, teratogenic effects were not observed in animal reproduction studies. Discontinuation or not initiating therapy should be considered since information related to topical use in pregnancy is limited.

Prescribing and Access Restrictions Injectable eflornithine is donated to World Health Organization (WHO) by the manufacturer. Further information may be found on WHO website at http://www.who.int/trypanosomiasis_african/diagnosis/en/index.html or by contacting the CDC Drug Service (404-639-3670).

Elbasvir and Grazoprevir
(ELB as vir & graz OH pre vir)

Brand Names: US Zepatier

Brand Names: Canada Zepatier

Pharmacologic Category Antihepaciviral, NS5A Inhibitor; Antihepaciviral, Protease Inhibitor (Anti-HCV); NS5A Inhibitor

Use Chronic hepatitis C: Treatment of chronic hepatitis C virus (HCV) genotype 1 or 4 infection in adults; used with ribavirin in certain patient populations.

Local Anesthetic/Vasoconstrictor Precautions No information available to require special precautions

Effects on Dental Treatment Key adverse event(s) related to dental treatment: Xerostomia; normal salivary flow resumes upon discontinuation

Effects on Bleeding No information available to require special precautions

Adverse Reactions

>10%:

Central nervous system: Fatigue (7% to 11%), headache (11%)

Gastrointestinal: Nausea (5% to 11%)

1% to 10%:

Central nervous system: Insomnia (3% to 5%), dizziness (2% to 3%), irritability (1% to 2%), anxiety (1%), depression (1%)

Dermatologic: Night sweats (2%), pruritus (2%), alopecia (1%)

Gastrointestinal: Diarrhea (2% to 5%), abdominal pain (2%), constipation (2%), decreased appetite (2%), dyspepsia (2%), flatulence (2%), upper abdominal pain (2%), vomiting (1% to 2%), xerostomia (1% to 2%)

Hepatic: Increased serum bilirubin (≤2%), increased serum ALT (≤1%; may be increased in females, patients of Asian descent, and older adults)

Neuromuscular & skeletal: Weakness (4%), increased creatine phosphokinase (2%), myalgia (2%), arthralgia (≤2%)

Otic: Tinnitus (2%)

<1%, postmarketing, and/or case reports: Reactivation of HBV (FDA Safety Alert Dec. 8, 2016)

General Dosage Range Oral: *Adults:* One tablet (elbasvir 50 mg/grazoprevir 100 mg) once daily.

Mechanism of Action

Elbasvir is an inhibitor of HCV NS5A, which is essential for viral replication and virion assembly.

Grazoprevir is an inhibitor of HCV NS3/4A protease, necessary for the proteolytic cleavage of the HCV-encoded polyprotein (into mature forms of the NS3, NS4A, NS4B, NS5A, and NS5B proteins) and is essential for viral replication.

Pharmacodynamics/Kinetics

Half-life Elimination Elbasvir: ~24 hours; Grazoprevir: ~31 hours

Time to Peak Elbasvir: Median: 3 hours (range: 3 to 6 hours); Grazoprevir: Median: 2 hours (range: 30 minutes to 3 hours)

Pregnancy Considerations Adverse events have not been observed in animal reproduction studies. The safety of treating hepatitis C during pregnancy has not been established; current guidelines recommend delaying pregnancy until HCV antiviral treatment is completed (AASLD/IDSA 2016).

Eletriptan (el e TRIP tan)

Related Information

Temporomandibular Dysfunction (TMD), Chronic Pain, and Fibromyalgia *on page 1868*

Brand Names: US Relpax

Brand Names: Canada Relpax®

Pharmacologic Category Antimigraine Agent; Serotonin 5-$HT_{1B,\ 1D}$ Receptor Agonist

Use Migraines: Acute treatment of migraine, with or without aura in adults

Local Anesthetic/Vasoconstrictor Precautions No information available to require special precautions

Effects on Dental Treatment Key adverse event(s) related to dental treatment: Xerostomia (normal salivary flow resumes upon discontinuation)

Effects on Bleeding No information available to require special precautions

Adverse Reactions

1% to 10%:

Cardiovascular: Chest pain (2% to 4%; chest tightness, pain, and pressure), palpitations

Central nervous system: Dizziness (6% to 7%), drowsiness (6% to 7%), headache (4%), paresthesia (3% to 4%), chills, hypertonia, hypoesthesia, pain, vertigo

Dermatologic: Diaphoresis

Gastrointestinal: Nausea (8%), xerostomia (3% to 4%), abdominal pain (2%; pain, discomfort, stomach pain, cramps, and pressure), dyspepsia (2%), dysphagia (1% to 2%)

Neuromuscular & skeletal: Weakness (4% to 10%), back pain

Respiratory: Pharyngitis

<1%, postmarketing, and/or case reports (limited to important or life-threatening): Abnormal dreams, abnormal hepatic function tests, agitation, alopecia, amnesia, anaphylactoid reaction, anaphylaxis, anemia, angina pectoris, angioedema, aphasia, ataxia, cardiac arrhythmia, confusion, constipation, depersonalization, depression, diarrhea, diplopia, dysgeusia, dyspnea, dystonia, edema, emotional lability, esophagitis, euphoria, gingivitis, hallucination, hyperesthesia, hyperglycemia, hyperkinesia, hypersensitivity reaction, hypertension, impotence, increased creatine phosphokinase, insomnia, ischemic colitis, lacrimation, manic behavior, myalgia, myasthenia, myocardial

infarction, nervousness, paralysis, peripheral edema, peripheral vascular disorder, photophobia, polyuria, Prinzmetal angina, pruritus, purpura, seizure, sensation of pressure (chest/neck/throat/jaw), shock, sialorrhea, skin discoloration, skin rash, speech disturbance, stupor, syncope, tachycardia, thrombophlebitis, tinnitus, tongue edema, tremor, twitching, urinary frequency, urticaria, vasospasm, ventricular fibrillation, visual disturbance, vomiting

General Dosage Range Oral: *Adults:* 20 to 40 mg as a single dose, may repeat after 2 hours have elapsed (maximum: 80 mg daily)

Mechanism of Action Selective agonist for serotonin (5-HT_{1B}, 5-HT_{1D}, and 5-HT_{1F} receptors) in cranial arteries; causes vasoconstriction and reduces sterile inflammation associated with antidromic neuronal transmission correlating with relief of migraine

Pharmacodynamics/Kinetics

Half-life Elimination ~4 hours (Elderly: 4.4-5.7 hours); Metabolite: ~13 hours

Time to Peak Plasma: 1.5-2 hours

Pregnancy Risk Factor C

Pregnancy Considerations Adverse events were observed in animal reproduction studies. Information related to eletriptan use in pregnancy is limited (Källén, 2011; Nezvalová-Henriksen, 2010; Nezvalová-Henriksen, 2012). Until additional information is available, other agents are preferred for the initial treatment of migraine in pregnancy (Da Silva, 2012; MacGregor, 2012; Williams, 2012).

Eliglustat (el i GLOO stat)

Brand Names: US Cerdelga

Pharmacologic Category Enzyme Inhibitor; Glucosylceramide Synthase Inhibitor

Use

Gaucher disease: Treatment of adult patients with Gaucher disease type 1 (GD1) who are CYP2D6 extensive metabolizers (EMs), intermediate metabolizers (IMs), or poor metabolizers (PMs).

Limitations of use: Patients who are CYP2D6 ultra-rapid metabolizers (URMs) may not achieve adequate concentrations of eliglustat to achieve a therapeutic effect. A specific dosage cannot be recommended for those patients whose CYP2D6 genotype cannot be determined (IMs).

Local Anesthetic/Vasoconstrictor Precautions
No information available to require special precautions

Effects on Dental Treatment
Key adverse event(s) related to dental treatment: Oropharyngeal pain has been reported in up to 10% of patients receiving the drug

Effects on Bleeding No information available to require special precautions

Adverse Reactions

>10%:

Central nervous system: Headache (13% to 40%), fatigue (14%)

Gastrointestinal: Diarrhea (12%), nausea (10% to 12%)

Neuromuscular & skeletal: Arthralgia (45%), back pain (12%), limb pain (11%)

1% to 10%:

Cardiovascular: Palpitations (5%)

Central nervous system: Migraine (10%), dizziness (8%)

Dermatologic: Skin rash (5%)

Gastrointestinal: Flatulence (10%), upper abdominal pain (10%), dyspepsia (7%), gastroesophageal reflux disease (7%), constipation (5%)

Neuromuscular & skeletal: Weakness (8%)

Respiratory: Oropharyngeal pain (10%), cough (7%)

General Dosage Range Dosage adjustments recommended for patients taking concomitant therapy.

Oral: *Adults:* 84 mg once or twice daily.

Mechanism of Action Eliglustat inhibits the enzyme needed to produce glycosphingolipids and decreases the rate of glycosphingolipid glucosylceramide formation. Glucosylceramide accumulates in type 1 Gaucher disease, causing complications specific to this disease.

Pharmacodynamics/Kinetics

Half-life Elimination EMs: 6.5 hours; PMs: 8.9 hours.

Time to Peak EMs: 1.5 to 2 hours; PMs: 3 hours

Pregnancy Risk Factor C

Pregnancy Considerations

Adverse events were observed in some animal reproduction studies.

Uncontrolled type 1 Gaucher disease is associated with an increased risk of spontaneous abortion; maternal hepatosplenomegaly and thrombocytopenia may also occur and lead to adverse pregnancy outcomes.

Elosulfase Alfa (el oh SUL fase AL fa)

Brand Names: US Vimizim

Brand Names: Canada Vimizim

Pharmacologic Category Enzyme

Use Mucopolysaccharidosis type IVA: Treatment of mucopolysaccharidosis type IVA (MPS IVA; Morquio A syndrome)

Local Anesthetic/Vasoconstrictor Precautions
No information available to require special precautions

Effects on Dental Treatment No significant effects or complications reported

Effects on Bleeding No information available to require special precautions

Adverse Reactions

>10%:

Central nervous system: Headache (26%)

Gastrointestinal: Vomiting (31%), nausea (24%), abdominal pain (21%)

Hypersensitivity: Hypersensitivity reaction (19%)

Miscellaneous: Fever (33%)

1% to 10%:

Central nervous system: Chills (10%), fatigue (10%)

Hypersensitivity: Anaphylaxis (8%; presenting as cough, erythema, throat tightness, urticaria, flushing, cyanosis, hypotension, rash, dyspnea, chest discomfort, and gastrointestinal symptoms)

Immunologic: Immunogenicity

General Dosage Range IV: *Children ≥5 years, Adolescents, and Adults:* 2 mg/kg once weekly

Mechanism of Action Elosulfase alfa is a recombinant form of N-acetylgalactosamine-6-sulfatase, produced in Chinese hamster cells. A deficiency of this enzyme leads to accumulation of the glycosaminoglycan (GAG) substrates (keratan sulfate and chondroitin-6-sulfate) in tissues, causing cellular, tissue and organ dysfunction. Elosulfase alfa provides the exogenous enzyme (N-acetylgalactosamine-6-sulfatase) that is taken into lysosomes and thereby increases the catabolism of the GAG substrates (eg, keratan sulfate and chondroitin-6-sulfate).

Pharmacodynamics/Kinetics

Half-life Elimination Week 0: ~8 minutes; Week 22: ~36 minutes

Time to Peak Week 0: 172 minutes; Week 22: 202 minutes

Pregnancy Risk Factor C

Pregnancy Considerations Adverse events were observed in some animal reproduction studies. Mucopolysaccharidosis type IVA (MPS IVA) has the potential to cause adverse events in both the mother and fetus. A pregnancy registry is available for women who may be exposed to elosulfase alfa for the treatment of MPS IVA during pregnancy (MARS@bmrn.com or 1-800-983-4587).

Elotuzumab (el oh TOOZ ue mab)

Brand Names: US Empliciti

Brand Names: Canada Empliciti

Pharmacologic Category Antineoplastic Agent, Anti-SLAMF7; Antineoplastic Agent, Monoclonal Antibody

Use Multiple myeloma, relapsed/refractory: Treatment of multiple myeloma (in combination with lenalidomide and dexamethasone) in patients who have received 1 to 3 prior therapies

Local Anesthetic/Vasoconstrictor Precautions No information available to require special precautions

Effects on Dental Treatment No significant effects or complications reported

Effects on Bleeding Cytopenias including thrombocytopenia (grades 3/4, 19%) has been reported. Medical consult is recommended.

Adverse Reactions

All incidences reported in combination with lenalidomide and dexamethasone.

>10%:

Cardiovascular: Decreased heart rate (66%; <60 bpm), increased heart rate (48%; ≥100 bpm), altered blood pressure (systolic ≥160 mmHg: 33%; systolic <90 mmHg: 29%; diastolic ≥100 mmHg: 17%)

Central nervous system: Fatigue (62%), peripheral neuropathy (27%; grades 3/4: 4%), headache (15%)

Endocrine & metabolic: Hyperglycemia (89%), hypocalcemia (78%), hypoalbuminemia (73%), decreased serum bicarbonate (63%), hyperkalemia (32%), weight loss (14%)

Gastrointestinal: Diarrhea (47%), constipation (36%), decreased appetite (21%), vomiting (15%)

Hematologic & oncologic: Lymphocytopenia (13% to 99%; grades 3/4: 9% to 77%), leukopenia (91%; grades 3/4: 32%), thrombocytopenia (84%; grades 3/4: 19%)

Hepatic: Increased serum alkaline phosphatase (39%; grades 3/4: 1%)

Immunologic: Immunogenicity (19%; neutralizing: 6%)

Infection: Infection (81%; grades 3/4: 28%), opportunistic infection (22%), herpes zoster (14%), fungal infection (10%)

Neuromuscular & skeletal: Limb pain (16%)

Ophthalmic: Cataract (12%)

Respiratory: Cough (34%), nasopharyngitis (25%), upper respiratory tract infection (23%), pneumonia (15% to 20%), oropharyngeal pain (10%)

Miscellaneous: Fever (7% to 37%), infusion related reaction (10%; grade 3: 1%)

1% to 10%:

Cardiovascular: Chest pain (≥5%), pulmonary embolism (3%)

Central nervous system: Hypoesthesia (≥5%), mood changes (≥5%)

Dermatologic: Night sweats (≥5%)

Hematologic & oncologic: Second primary malignant neoplasm (9%), malignant neoplasm of skin (4%), solid tumor (4%), anemia (3%), malignant neoplasm (hematologic: 2%)

Hepatic: Hepatotoxicity (3%)

Hypersensitivity: Hypersensitivity (≥5%)

Renal: Acute renal failure (3%)

Respiratory: Respiratory tract infection (3%)

General Dosage Range IV: *Adults:* 10 mg/kg once weekly for 2 cycles, then 10 mg/kg once every 2 weeks for cycle 3 and beyond

Mechanism of Action Elotuzumab is a humanized IgG1 immunostimulatory monoclonal antibody directed against signaling lymphocytic activation molecule family member 7 (SLAMF7, also called CS1 [cell surface glycoprotein CD2 subset 1). SLAMF7 is expressed on most myeloma and natural killer cells, but not on normal tissues; more than 95% of bone marrow myeloma cells express SLAMF7 (Lonial, 2015). Elotuzumab directly activates natural killer cells through both the SLAMF7 pathway and Fc receptors. It also targets SLAMF7 on myeloma cells and mediates antibody-dependent cellular cytotoxicity (ADCC) through the CD16 pathway (Lonial, 2015). This immunostimulatory activity, through the increased activation of natural killer cells, increases anti-tumor activity.

Pharmacodynamics/Kinetics

Half-life Elimination ~97% of the maximum steady-state concentration is expected to be eliminated with a geometric mean (CV%) of 82.4 days.

Pregnancy Considerations Animal reproduction studies have not been conducted. Elotuzumab is indicted for use in combination with lenalidomide. Due to its potential to cause fetal harm, lenalidomide is only available through a REMS program. Males and females of reproductive potential using this combination must be able to comply with pregnancy testing and contraception requirements for lenalidomide. Refer to the lenalidomide monograph for additional information.

Eltrombopag (el TROM boe pag)

Brand Names: US Promacta

Brand Names: Canada Revolade

Pharmacologic Category Colony Stimulating Factor; Hematopoietic Agent; Thrombopoietic Agent

Use

Aplastic anemia, severe: Treatment of severe aplastic anemia in patients who have had an insufficient response to immunosuppressive therapy.

Chronic hepatitis C infection-associated thrombocytopenia: Treatment of thrombocytopenia in patients with chronic hepatitis C (CHC) to allow the initiation and maintenance of interferon based therapy.

Chronic immune (idiopathic) thrombocytopenia: Treatment of thrombocytopenia in adult and pediatric patients ≥1 year of age with chronic immune (idiopathic) thrombocytopenia (ITP) who have had insufficient response to corticosteroids, immune globulin, or splenectomy.

Limitations of use: For ITP, eltrombopag should only be used if the degree of thrombocytopenia and clinical condition increase the risk for bleeding. For chronic hepatitis C (CHC), eltrombopag should only be used if the degree of thrombocytopenia prevents initiation of or limits the ability to maintain interferon-based therapy. For CHC, safety and efficacy have not been established when used in combination with direct-acting antiviral agents without interferon for treatment of CHC infection.

Local Anesthetic/Vasoconstrictor Precautions No information available to require special precautions

Effects on Dental Treatment Key adverse event(s) related to dental treatment: Risk of bleeding in soft tissues upon discontinuation of therapy due to rebound thrombocytopenia; monitor for at least 4 weeks after discontinuation of treatment.

Effects on Bleeding Eltrombopag is used in the management of severe thrombocytopenia. Medical consultation is warranted.

Adverse Reactions Adverse reactions and incidences reported are associated with adults unless otherwise indicated.

>10%:

Central nervous system: Fatigue (ITP: 4%; chronic hepatitis C: 28%; aplastic anemia: 28%), headache (ITP: 10%; chronic hepatitis C: 21%; aplastic anemia 21%), insomnia (chronic hepatitis C: 16%), chills (chronic hepatitis C: 14%), dizziness (aplastic anemia: 14%)

Dermatologic: Pruritus (chronic hepatitis C: 15%), ecchymosis (aplastic anemia: 12%)

Gastrointestinal: Nausea (ITP: 4% to 9%; chronic hepatitis C: 19%; aplastic anemia 33%), diarrhea (aplastic anemia: 21%; chronic hepatitis C: 19%; ITP: 9%; children: 9%), appetite decreased (chronic hepatitis C: 18%), abdominal pain (aplastic anemia 12%; children: 8%)

Hematologic & oncologic: Anemia (chronic hepatitis C: 40%), febrile neutropenia (aplastic anemia: 14%)

Hepatic: Hyperbilirubinemia (total bilirubin ≥1.5 x ULN: 76%; ITP and chronic hepatitis C: 6% to 8%), increased serum transaminases (aplastic anemia: 12%), abnormal hepatic function (ITP: 11%), increased serum ALT (children: 6%; ITP: 5% to 6%), increased serum AST (ITP: 4%; children: 4%)

Neuromuscular & skeletal: Limb pain (aplastic anemia: 19%), weakness (chronic hepatitis C: 16%), arthralgia (aplastic anemia: 12%), muscle spasm (aplastic anemia: 12%), myalgia (ITP and chronic hepatitis C: 5% to 12%)

Respiratory: Cough (aplastic anemia: 23%; chronic hepatitis C: 15%; children: 9%), flu-like syndrome (chronic hepatitis C: 18%), upper respiratory infection (children: 17%; ITP: 7%), dyspnea (aplastic anemia: 14%), oropharyngeal pain (aplastic anemia: 14%; children: 8%; ITP: 4%), nasopharyngitis (children: 12%), rhinorrhea (aplastic anemia: 12%, children: 4%)

Miscellaneous: Fever (chronic hepatitis C: 30%; aplastic anemia: 14%; children: 9%)

1% to 10%:

Cardiovascular: Peripheral edema (chronic hepatitis C: 10%), thrombosis (chronic hepatitis C: 3%)

Dermatologic: Alopecia (ITP: 2%; chronic hepatitis C: 10%), skin rash (children: 5%; ITP: 3%)

Gastrointestinal: Toothache (children: 6%), vomiting (ITP: 6%), xerostomia (ITP: 2%)

Genitourinary: Urinary tract infection (ITP: 5%)

Hematologic & oncologic: Thrombocytopenia (chronic hepatitis C: 3%)

Hepatic: Alkaline phosphatase increased (ITP: 2%)

Infection: Influenza (ITP: 3%)

Neuromuscular & skeletal: Back pain (ITP: 3%), paresthesia (ITP: 3%), musculoskeletal pain (ITP: 2%)

Ophthalmic: Cataract (ITP and chronic hepatitis C: 4% to 8%)

Respiratory: Rhinitis (children: 9%), pharyngitis (ITP: 4%)

<1%, postmarketing, and/or case reports: Abdominal distension, constipation, decreased visual acuity, deep vein thrombosis, desquamation, drowsiness, dry eye syndrome, dysesthesia, dysgeusia, dyspepsia, eye pain, facial swelling, fecal discoloration, foreign body sensation, glossalgia, hemorrhage, hemorrhoids, hot flash, hyperhidrosis, hypoesthesia, hypokalemia, increased hemoglobin, increased lacrimation, increased serum albumin, increased serum creatinine, increased serum total protein, lesion (hepatic), local inflammation (wound), malaise, malignant neoplasm (rectosigmoid), night sweats, oral herpes, oropharyngeal blistering, ostealgia, portal vein thrombosis, pulmonary embolism, pulmonary infarct, retinal hemorrhage, retinal pigment changes, sinus tachycardia, sleep disorder, superficial thrombophlebitis, tachycardia, thromboembolic complications, thrombotic microangiopathy (with acute renal failure), upper abdominal pain, urticaria, vertigo

General Dosage Range Dosage adjustment recommended in patients with hepatic impairment, of East-Asian ethnicity, or who develop toxicities

Oral: *Children ≥1 year, Adolescents, and Adults* Initial: 25 to 50 mg once daily (maximum: 75 mg once daily for ITP; 100 mg once daily for chronic hepatitis C-associated thrombocytopenia; 150 mg once daily for severe aplastic anemia)

Mechanism of Action Thrombopoietin (TPO) nonpeptide agonist which increases platelet counts by binding to and activating the human TPO receptor. Activates intracellular signal transduction pathways to increase proliferation and differentiation of marrow progenitor cells.

Pharmacodynamics/Kinetics

Onset of Action Platelet count increase: Within 1 to 2 weeks

Duration of Action Platelets return to baseline: 1 to 2 weeks after last dose

Half-life Elimination ~21 to 32 hours in healthy individuals; ~26 to 35 hours in patients with ITP

Time to Peak 2 to 6 hours

Pregnancy Risk Factor C

Pregnancy Considerations Adverse effects were observed in animal reproduction studies. A Promacta pregnancy registry has been established to monitor outcomes of women exposed to eltrombopag during pregnancy (1-888-825-5249).

Product Availability Promacta oral suspension: FDA approved August 2015; anticipated availability is currently unknown.

Eluxadoline (el ux AD oh leen)

Brand Names: US Viberzi

Pharmacologic Category Gastrointestinal Agent, Miscellaneous

Use Irritable bowel syndrome with diarrhea: Treatment of irritable bowel syndrome with diarrhea (IBS-D) in adults

Local Anesthetic/Vasoconstrictor Precautions No information available to require special precautions

Effects on Dental Treatment No significant effects or complications reported

Effects on Bleeding No information available to require special precautions

Adverse Reactions

1% to 10%:

Central nervous system: Dizziness (3%), fatigue (3%), drowsiness (≤2%), euphoria (≤2%), intoxicated feeling (≤2%), sedation (≤2%)

Dermatologic: Skin rash (3%)

Gastrointestinal: Constipation (7% to 8%), nausea (7% to 8%), abdominal pain (6% to 7%), vomiting (4%), spasm of sphincter of Oddi (<1%; 1% to 4% in patients without a gallbladder), abdominal distention (3%), flatulence (3%), viral gastroenteritis (3%), gastroesophageal reflux disease (≤2%)

Hepatic: Increased serum ALT (2% to 3%), increased serum AST (≤2%)

Respiratory: Upper respiratory tract infection (5%), nasopharyngitis (4%), bronchitis (3%), asthma (≤2%), bronchospasm (≤2%), respiratory failure (≤2%), wheezing (≤2%)

<1%, postmarketing, and/or case reports: Increased liver enzymes, pancreatitis

Mechanism of Action Eluxadoline is a mixed mu-opioid receptor agonist, delta opioid receptor antagonist, and kappa opioid receptor agonist which acts locally to reduce abdominal pain and diarrhea in patients with IBS-D without constipating side effects.

Pharmacodynamics/Kinetics

Half-life Elimination 3.7 to 6 hours

Time to Peak 1.5 hours (range: 1 to 8 hours) under fed conditions; 2 hours (range: 0.5 to 6 hours) under fasting conditions

Pregnancy Considerations Adverse events have not been observed in animal reproduction studies.

Controlled Substance C-IV

Elvitegravir (el vi TEG ra vir)

Brand Names: US Vitekta [DSC]

Pharmacologic Category Antiretroviral, Integrase Inhibitor (Anti-HIV)

Use HIV-1 infection: In combination with an HIV protease inhibitor coadministered with ritonavir and with other antiretroviral drug(s) for the treatment of HIV-1 infection in antiretroviral treatment-experienced adults

Local Anesthetic/Vasoconstrictor Precautions No information available to require special precautions

Effects on Dental Treatment No significant effects or complications reported

Effects on Bleeding No information available to require special precautions

Adverse Reactions Percentages are reported for antiretroviral treatment experienced adults.

1% to 10%:

Central nervous system: Headache (3%), depression (<2%), fatigue (<2%), insomnia (<2%), suicidal ideation (<2%)

Dermatologic: Skin rash (<2%)

Gastrointestinal: Diarrhea (7%), nausea (4%), abdominal pain (<2%), dyspepsia (<2%), vomiting (<2%)

Immunologic: Immune reconstitution syndrome

General Dosage Range Dosage adjustment recommended in patients with hepatic impairment.

Oral: *Adults:* 85 to 150 mg once daily

Mechanism of Action Integrase is an HIV-1 encoded enzyme that is required for viral replication. Inhibition of integrase prevents the integration of HIV-1 DNA into host genomic DNA, blocking the formation of the HIV-1 provirus and propagation of the viral infection. Elvitegravir does not inhibit human topoisomerases I or II.

Pharmacodynamics/Kinetics

Half-life Elimination Terminal: ~9 hours

Time to Peak Plasma: ~4 hours

Pregnancy Risk Factor B

Pregnancy Considerations Adverse events were not observed in animal reproduction studies. Data collected by the antiretroviral pregnancy registry are insufficient to evaluate placental transfer or human teratogenic risk. Maternal antiretroviral therapy may increase the risk of preterm delivery, although available information is conflicting possibly due to variability of maternal factors (disease severity; initiation of therapy); however, maternal antiretroviral medication should not be withheld due to concerns of preterm birth. Information related to stillbirth, low birth weight, and small for gestational age infants is limited. Long-term follow-up is recommended for all infants exposed to antiretroviral medications; children who develop significant organ system abnormalities of unknown etiology (particularly of the CNS or heart) should be evaluated for potential mitochondrial dysfunction.

Combination antiretroviral therapy (cART) therapy is recommended for all HIV-infected pregnant women to keep the viral load below the limit of detection and reduce the risk of perinatal transmission. When HIV is diagnosed during pregnancy in a woman who has never received antiretroviral therapy, cART should begin as soon as possible after diagnosis. The Health and Human Services (HHS) Perinatal HIV Guidelines note that due to a lack of data, elvitegravir cannot be recommended as initial therapy in antiretroviral-naive pregnant women. Pharmacokinetic data are insufficient to make dosing recommendations during pregnancy. In general, women who become pregnant on a stable cART regimen may continue that regimen if viral suppression is effective, appropriate drug exposure can be achieved, contraindications for use in pregnancy are not present, and the regimen is well tolerated. Monitoring during pregnancy is more frequent than in non-pregnant adults; cART should be continued postpartum.

For HIV-infected couples planning a pregnancy, maximum viral suppression with combination antiretroviral therapy (cART) is recommended prior to conception for the HIV-infected partner(s) and expert consultation is recommended; modification of therapy (if needed) and optimization of the woman's health should be done prior to conception. HIV-infected women not planning a pregnancy may use any available type of contraception, considering possible drug interactions and contraindications of the specific method. In addition, consistent use of condoms is also recommended (even during pregnancy) to prevent transmission of HIV or other sexually transmitted diseases.

Health care providers are encouraged to enroll pregnant women exposed to antiretroviral medications as early in pregnancy as possible in the Antiretroviral Pregnancy Registry (1-800-258-4263 or www.APRegistry.com). Health care providers caring for HIV-infected women and their infants may contact the National Perinatal HIV Hotline (888-448-8765) for clinical consultation (HHS [perinatal] 2016).

Elvitegravir, Cobicistat, Emtricitabine, and Tenofovir Alafenamide

(el vi TEG ra vir, koe BIK i stat, em trye SYE ta been, & ten OF oh vir al a FEN a mide)

Brand Names: US Genvoya

Brand Names: Canada Genvoya

Pharmacologic Category Antiretroviral, Integrase Inhibitor (Anti-HIV); Antiretroviral, Reverse Transcriptase Inhibitor, Nucleoside (Anti-HIV); Antiretroviral, Reverse Transcriptase Inhibitor, Nucleotide (Anti-HIV); Cytochrome P-450 Inhibitor

Use HIV-1 infection: Treatment of HIV-1 infection in adults and pediatric patients 12 years and older weighing ≥35 kg who have no antiretroviral treatment history or to replace the current antiretroviral regimen in those who are virologically-suppressed (HIV-1 RNA <50 copies per mL) on a stable antiretroviral regimen for ≥6 months with no history of treatment failure and no known substitutions associated with resistance to elvitegravir, cobicistat, emtricitabine, or tenofovir alafenamide.

Local Anesthetic/Vasoconstrictor Precautions No information available to require special precautions

Effects on Dental Treatment No significant effects or complications reported

Effects on Bleeding No information available to require special precautions

Adverse Reactions Includes data from both treatment-naive and treatment-experienced patients. Also see individual agents.

1% to 10%:

- Central nervous system: Headache (6%), fatigue (5%)
- Endocrine & metabolic: Increased LDL cholesterol, increased serum cholesterol
- Gastrointestinal: Nausea (10%), diarrhea (7%)
- Neuromuscular & skeletal: Decreased bone mineral density (≥5% decrease at lumbar spine: 12%; ≥7% decrease at femoral neck: 11%)

Frequency not defined:

- Endocrine & metabolic: Increased HDL cholesterol, increased serum triglycerides
- Hepatic: Exacerbation of hepatitis B
- Renal: Increased serum creatinine (mean increase 0.1 mg/dL)

General Dosage Range Oral: *Children and Adolescents ≥12 years and ≥35 kg, and Adults:* One tablet once daily

Mechanism of Action Integrase strand transfer inhibitor, CYP3A enzyme inhibitor plus nucleoside and nucleotide reverse transcriptase inhibitor combination; the viral cDNA strand produced by reverse transcriptase is processed and inserted into the human genome by the enzyme HIV-1 integrase. Elvitegravir inhibits the catalytic activity of integrase, thus preventing integration of the proviral gene into human DNA. Cobicistat inhibits enzymes of the CYP3A subfamily and enhances systemic exposure to elvitegravir. Emtricitabine is a cytosine analogue and tenofovir alafenamide is converted to tenofovir in vivo; tenofovir is an analog of adenosine 5'-monophosphate. Emtricitabine and tenofovir interfere with HIV viral RNA dependent DNA polymerase activities resulting in inhibition of viral replication.

Pharmacodynamics/Kinetics

Half-life Elimination Elvitegravir: 12.9 hours; Cobicistat: 3.5 hours; Emtricitabine: 10 hours; Tenofovir alafenamide: 0.51 hours

Time to Peak Elvitegravir: 4 hours; Cobicistat: 3 hours; Emtricitabine: 3 hours; Tenofovir alafenamide: 1 hour

Pregnancy Considerations In general, women who become pregnant on a stable combination antiretroviral therapy (cART) regimen may continue that regimen if viral suppression is effective, appropriate drug exposure can be achieved, contraindications for use in pregnancy are not present, and the regimen is well tolerated. The Health and Human Services (HHS) Perinatal HIV Guidelines note there are insufficient data to recommend use of this combination product as an initial regimen in antiretroviral-naive pregnant women (HHS [perinatal] 2016). Refer to individual monographs.

Elvitegravir, Cobicistat, Emtricitabine, and Tenofovir Disoproxil Fumarate

(el vi TEG ra vir, koe BIK i stat, em trye SYE ta been, & ten OF oh vir dye soe PROX il FUE ma rate)

Related Information

HIV Infection and AIDS *on page 1785*

Brand Names: US Stribild

Brand Names: Canada Stribild

Pharmacologic Category Antiretroviral, Integrase Inhibitor (Anti-HIV); Antiretroviral, Reverse Transcriptase Inhibitor, Nucleoside (Anti-HIV); Antiretroviral, Reverse Transcriptase Inhibitor, Nucleotide (Anti-HIV); Cytochrome P-450 Inhibitor

Use HIV-1 infection: Treatment of HIV-1 infection in adults and pediatric patients ≥12 years weighing ≥35 kg who are antiretroviral treatment-naïve; as a replacement for the current antiretroviral regimen in patients who are virologically-suppressed (HIV-1 RNA <50 copies/mL) on a stable antiretroviral regimen for ≥6 months with no history of treatment failure and no known substitutions associated with resistance to elvitegravir, cobicistat, emtricitabine, or tenofovir.

Local Anesthetic/Vasoconstrictor Precautions No information available to require special precautions

Effects on Dental Treatment No significant effects or complications reported

Effects on Bleeding No information available to require special precautions

Adverse Reactions

>10%:

- Gastrointestinal: Nausea (4% to 16%), diarrhea (12%)
- Genitourinary: Proteinuria (52%)
- Renal: Increased serum creatinine (12%)

1% to 10%:

- Central nervous system: Abnormal dreams (9%), headache (2% to 7%), fatigue (4%), dizziness (3%), insomnia (3%), drowsiness (1%)
- Dermatologic: Skin rash (4%)
- Endocrine & metabolic: Increased amylase (3%)
- Gastrointestinal: Flatulence (2%)
- Genitourinary: Hematuria (4%)
- Hepatic: Increased serum AST (3%), increased serum ALT (2%)
- Neuromuscular & skeletal: Increased creatine phosphokinase (8%), bone fracture (4%)

Frequency not defined:

- Endocrine & metabolic: Increased serum cholesterol, increased serum triglycerides
- Gastrointestinal: Increased serum lipase

<1%, postmarketing, and/or case reports: Acute renal failure, Fanconi syndrome, immune reconstitution syndrome, renal failure, renal tubular disease (proximal), scleral icterus, suicidal ideation

General Dosage Range Oral: *Children and Adolescents ≥12 years and weighing ≥35 kg and Adults:* One tablet once daily

Mechanism of Action Integrase strand transfer inhibitor, CYP3A enzyme inhibitor plus nucleoside and nucleotide reverse transcriptase inhibitor combination; the viral cDNA strand produced by reverse transcriptase is processed and inserted into the human genome by the enzyme HIV-1 integrase. Elvitegravir inhibits the catalytic activity of integrase, thus preventing integration of the proviral gene into human DNA. Cobicistat inhibits enzymes of the CYP3A subfamily and enhances systemic exposure to elvitegravir. Emtricitabine is a cytosine analogue and tenofovir disoproxil fumarate (TDF) is an analog of adenosine 5'-monophosphate. Emtricitabine and tenofovir interfere with HIV viral RNA dependent DNA polymerase activities resulting in inhibition of viral replication.

Pharmacodynamics/Kinetics

Half-life Elimination Elvitegravir: 12.9 hours; Cobicistat: 3.5 hours; Emtricitabine: 10 hours; Tenofovir: 12 to 18 hours

Time to Peak Plasma: Elvitegravir: 4 hours; Cobicistat: 3 hours; Emtricitabine: 3 hours; Tenofovir: 2 hours

Pregnancy Considerations In general, women who become pregnant on a stable combination antiretroviral therapy (cART) regimen may continue that regimen if viral suppression is effective, appropriate drug exposure can be achieved, contraindications for use in pregnancy are not present, and the regimen is well tolerated. The Health and Human Services (HHS) Perinatal HIV Guidelines note there are insufficient data to recommend use of this combination product as an initial regimen in antiretroviral-naive pregnant women (HHS [perinatal] 2016). Refer to individual monographs.

Emedastine (em e DAS teen)

Brand Names: US Emadine

Pharmacologic Category Histamine H_1 Antagonist; Histamine H_1 Antagonist, Second Generation

Use Allergic conjunctivitis: For the temporary relief of the signs and symptoms of allergic conjunctivitis

Local Anesthetic/Vasoconstrictor Precautions No information available to require special precautions

Effects on Dental Treatment No significant effects or complications reported

Effects on Bleeding No information available to require special precautions

Adverse Reactions

Frequency not always defined.

>10%: Central nervous system: Headache (11%)

1% to 10%:

- Cardiovascular: Hyperemia
- Central nervous system: Abnormal dreams
- Dermatologic: Dermatitis, pruritus
- Gastrointestinal: Dysgeusia
- Neuromuscular & skeletal: Weakness
- Ophthalmic: Blurred vision, corneal infiltrates, corneal staining, keratitis, lacrimation, transient burning or stinging in the eyes, xerophthalmia
- Respiratory: Rhinitis, sinusitis

General Dosage Range Ophthalmic: *Children ≥3 years, Adolescents, and Adults:* Instill 1 drop in affected eye up to 4 times daily

Mechanism of Action Selective histamine H_1-receptor antagonist for topical ophthalmic use

Pharmacodynamics/Kinetics

Half-life Elimination Oral: Plasma: 3 to 4 hours

Pregnancy Risk Factor B

Pregnancy Considerations Adverse events have not been observed in animal reproduction studies. Systemic absorption is limited following ocular administration. Use during pregnancy is not expected to result in significant exposure to the fetus.

Empagliflozin (em pa gli FLOE zin)

Brand Names: US Jardiance

Brand Names: Canada Jardiance

Pharmacologic Category Antidiabetic Agent, Sodium-Glucose Cotransporter 2 (SGLT2) Inhibitor; Sodium-Glucose Cotransporter 2 (SGLT2) Inhibitor

Use Diabetes mellitus, type 2: Treatment of type 2 diabetes mellitus (noninsulin dependent, NIDDM) as an adjunct to diet and exercise to improve glycemic control; risk reduction of cardiovascular mortality in adults with type 2 diabetes mellitus and established cardiovascular disease

Local Anesthetic/Vasoconstrictor Precautions No information available to require special precautions

Effects on Dental Treatment Key adverse event(s) related to dental treatment: Dizziness and syncope have been reported; patients may experience orthostatic hypotension as they stand up after treatment; especially if lying in dental chair for extended periods of time. Use caution with sudden changes in position during and after dental treatment.

Empagliflozin-dependent patients with diabetes (noninsulin dependent, type 2) should be questioned by the dental professional at each dental visit to assess their risk for stress-induced hypoglycemia. The dental professional should inquire about the patient's routine (ie, work, sleep schedule, eating patterns), history of hypoglycemia, time of last medication dose, last meal, and most recent blood sugar assessment. Keep a supply of glucose tablets and other carbohydrates in the office to prepare for a hypoglycemic event. Seek medical attention when necessary (American Diabetes Association 2016).

Effects on Bleeding No information available to require special precautions

Adverse Reactions

>10%:

- Endocrine & metabolic: Hypoglycemia (combination therapy with insulin: 28%, severe hypoglycemia: ≤1%; combination therapy with metformin and a sulfonylurea: 12% to 16%; combination therapy with metformin: 1% to 2%)
- Genitourinary: Urinary tract infection (9%; females: 18%; males: 4%), increased urine output (includes polyuria, pollakiuria, nocturia: 3%)

1% to 10%:

- Endocrine & metabolic: Increased LDL cholesterol (5% to 7%), dyslipidemia (4%), increased thirst (including polydipsia: 2%)
- Gastrointestinal: Nausea (2%)
- Hematologic & oncologic: Increased hematocrit (3% to 4%)
- Infection: Genitourinary fungal infection (4%; females: 5% to 6% [includes bacterial vaginosis, cervicitis, vulvitis, vulvovaginal candidiasis, vulvovaginal infection, vulvovaginitis]; males: 2% to 3% [includes balanitis, balanoposthitis, genitourinary fungal infection, penile infection, scrotal abscess])

<1%, postmarketing, and/or case reports: Decreased estimated GFR (eGFR), hypotension, hypovolemia, increased serum creatinine, ketoacidosis (FDA Safety Communication, December 4, 2015), phimosis, pyelonephritis (FDA Safety Communication, December 4, 2015), urosepsis (FDA Safety Communication, December 4, 2015)

General Dosage Range Oral: *Adults:* 10 to 25 mg once daily

Mechanism of Action By inhibiting sodium-glucose cotransporter 2 (SGLT2) in the proximal renal tubules, empagliflozin reduces reabsorption of filtered glucose from the tubular lumen and lowers the renal threshold for glucose (RT_G). SGLT2 is the main site of filtered glucose reabsorption; reduction of filtered glucose reabsorption and lowering of RT_G result in increased urinary excretion of glucose, thereby reducing plasma glucose concentrations.

Pharmacodynamics/Kinetics

Half-life Elimination 12.4 hours

Time to Peak 1.5 hours

Pregnancy Considerations Adverse events were observed in some animal reproduction studies. Use is not recommended during the second and third trimesters.

In women with diabetes, maternal hyperglycemia can be associated with congenital malformations as well as adverse effects in the fetus, neonate, and the mother (ACOG 2005; ADA 2016d; Kitzmiller 2008; Metzger 2007). To prevent adverse outcomes, prior to conception and throughout pregnancy maternal blood glucose and HbA_{1c} should be kept as close to target goals as possible but without causing significant hypoglycemia (ACOG 2013; ADA 2016d; Blumer 2013; Kitzmiller 2008). Agents other than empaglifozin are currently recommended to treat diabetes in pregnant women (ACOG 2013; Blumer 2013).

Emtricitabine (em trye SYE ta been)

Related Information

HIV Infection and AIDS *on page 1785*

Brand Names: US Emtriva

Brand Names: Canada Emtriva

Pharmacologic Category Antiretroviral, Reverse Transcriptase Inhibitor, Nucleoside (Anti-HIV)

Use Treatment of HIV infection in combination with at least two other antiretroviral agents

Local Anesthetic/Vasoconstrictor Precautions No information available to require special precautions

Effects on Dental Treatment No significant effects or complications reported

Effects on Bleeding No information available to require special precautions related to hemostasis.

Adverse Reactions Clinical trials were conducted in patients receiving other antiretroviral agents, and it is not possible to correlate frequency of adverse events with emtricitabine alone. The range of frequencies of adverse events is generally comparable to comparator groups, with the exception of hyperpigmentation, which occurred more frequently in patients receiving emtricitabine. Unless otherwise noted, percentages are as reported in adults.

>10%:

Central nervous system: Dizziness (4% to 25%), headache (6% to 22%), insomnia (5% to 16%), abnormal dreams (2% to 11%)

Dermatologic: Hyperpigmentation (children: 32%; adults: 2% to 4%; primarily of palms and/or soles but may include tongue, arms, lip and nails; generally mild and nonprogressive without associated local reactions such as pruritus or rash), skin rash (17% to 30%; includes hypersensitivity reaction, maculopapular rash, pruritus, pustular rash, vesiculobullous rash)

Gastrointestinal: Diarrhea (children: 20%; adults: 9% to 23%), vomiting (children: 23%; adults: 9%), nausea (13% to 18%), abdominal pain (8% to 14%), gastroenteritis (children: 11%)

Infection: Infection (children: 44%)

Neuromuscular & skeletal: Weakness (12% to 16%), increased creatine phosphokinase (grades 3/4: 11% to 12%)

Otic: Otitis media (children: 23%)

Respiratory: Cough (children: 28%; adults; 14%), rhinitis (children: 20%; adults: 12% to 18%), pneumonia (children: 15%)

Miscellaneous: Fever (children: 18%)

1% to 10%:

Central nervous system: Depression (6% to 9%), paresthesia (5% to 6%), neuritis (≤4%), neuropathy (≤4%)

Endocrine & metabolic: Increased serum triglycerides (grades 3/4: 4% to 10%), increased amylase (grades 3/4: children: 9%; adults: 2% to 5%), dysglycemia (grades 3/4: 2% to 3%)

Gastrointestinal: Dyspepsia (4% to 8%), increased serum lipase (grades 3/4: ≤1%)

Genitourinary: Hematuria (grades 3/4: 3%)

Hematologic & oncologic: Anemia (children: 7%), neutropenia (grades 3/4: children: 2%; adults: 5%)

Hepatic: Increased serum transaminases (grades 3/4: 2% to 6%), increased serum alkaline phosphatase (>550 units/L: 1%), increased serum bilirubin (grades 3/4: 1%)

Neuromuscular & skeletal: Myalgia (4% to 6%), arthralgia (3% to 5%)

Respiratory: Sinusitis (8%), upper respiratory tract infection (8%), pharyngitis (5%)

<1%, postmarketing, and/or case reports: Immune reconstitution syndrome

General Dosage Range Dosage adjustment recommended in patients with renal impairment

Oral:

Capsule: *Children 3 months to 17 years and >33 kg and Adults:* 200 mg once daily

Solution:

Children <3 months: 3 mg/kg/day

Children 3 months to 17 years: 6 mg/kg once daily (maximum: 240 mg/day)

Adults: 240 mg once daily

Mechanism of Action Nucleoside reverse transcriptase inhibitor; emtricitabine is a cytosine analogue which is phosphorylated intracellularly to emtricitabine 5'-triphosphate which interferes with HIV viral RNA dependent DNA polymerase resulting in inhibition of viral replication.

Pharmacodynamics/Kinetics

Half-life Elimination Normal renal function:

Infants, Children, and Adolescents: Elimination half-life (emtricitabine):

Single dose: 11 hours

Multiple dose: 7.9 to 9.5 hours

Infants 0 to 3 months (n=20; median age: 26 days): 12.1 ± 3.1 hours

Infants 3 to 24 months (n=14): 8.9 ± 3.2 hours

Children 25 months to 6 years (n=19): 11.3 ± 6.4 hours

Children 7 to 12 years (n=17): 8.2 ± 3.2 hours

Adolescents 13 to 17 years (n=27): 8.9 ± 3.3 hours

Adults: Emtricitabine: 10 hours; Intracellular half-life (emtricitabine 5'-triphosphate): 39 hours

Time to Peak Plasma: 1-2 hours

Pregnancy Risk Factor B

Pregnancy Considerations Adverse events were not observed in animal reproduction studies. Emtricitabine has a high level of transfer across the human placenta;

no increased risk of overall birth defects has been observed according to data collected by the antiretroviral pregnancy registry. Maternal antiretroviral therapy may increase the risk of preterm delivery, although available information is conflicting possibly due to variability of maternal factors (disease severity; initiation of therapy); however, maternal antiretroviral medication should not be withheld due to concerns of preterm birth. Information related to stillbirth, low birth weight, and small for gestational age infants is limited. Long-term follow-up is recommended for all infants exposed to antiretroviral medications; children who develop significant organ system abnormalities of unknown etiology (particularly of the CNS or heart) should be evaluated for potential mitochondrial dysfunction. Cases of lactic acidosis and hepatic steatosis related to mitochondrial toxicity have been reported with use of nucleoside reverse transcriptase inhibitors (NRTIs). These adverse events are similar to other rare but life-threatening syndromes which occur during pregnancy (eg, HELLP syndrome). In general nucleoside reverse transcriptase inhibitors are well tolerated and the benefits of use generally outweigh potential risk.

Combination antiretroviral therapy (cART) therapy is recommended for all HIV-infected pregnant women to keep the viral load below the limit of detection and reduce the risk of perinatal transmission. When HIV is diagnosed during pregnancy in a woman who has never received antiretroviral therapy, cART should begin as soon as possible after diagnosis. The Health and Human Services (HHS) Perinatal HIV Guidelines consider emtricitabine with tenofovir disoproxil fumarate to be a preferred NRTI backbone for initial therapy in antiretroviral-naive pregnant women. The guidelines also consider emtricitabine plus tenofovir disoproxil fumarate a recommended dual NRTI backbone in regimens for HIV/HBV-coinfected pregnant women. Use caution with hepatitis B coinfection; hepatitis B flare may occur if emtricitabine is discontinued. The pharmacokinetics of emtricitabine are not significantly altered during pregnancy. In general, women who become pregnant on a stable cART regimen may continue that regimen if viral suppression is effective, appropriate drug exposure can be achieved, contraindications for use in pregnancy are not present, and the regimen is well tolerated. Monitoring during pregnancy is more frequent than in non-pregnant adults; cART should be continued postpartum.

For HIV-infected couples planning a pregnancy, maximum viral suppression with cART is recommended prior to conception for the HIV-infected partner(s) and expert consultation is recommended; modification of therapy (if needed) and optimization of the woman's health should be done prior to conception. HIV-infected women not planning a pregnancy may use any available type of contraception, considering possible drug interactions and contraindications of the specific method. In addition, consistent use of condoms is also recommended (even during pregnancy) to prevent transmission of HIV or other sexually transmitted diseases.

Health care providers are encouraged to enroll pregnant women exposed to antiretroviral medications as early in pregnancy as possible in the Antiretroviral Pregnancy Registry (1-800-258-4263 or www.APRegistry.com). Health care providers caring for HIV-infected women and their infants may contact the National Perinatal HIV Hotline (888-448-8765) for clinical consultation (HHS [perinatal] 2016).

Emtricitabine and Tenofovir Alafenamide

(em trye SYE ta been & ten OF oh vir al a FEN a mide)

Brand Names: US Descovy

Pharmacologic Category Antiretroviral, Reverse Transcriptase Inhibitor, Nucleoside (Anti-HIV); Antiretroviral, Reverse Transcriptase Inhibitor, Nucleotide (Anti-HIV)

Use

HIV-1 infection: Treatment of HIV-1 infection (in combination with other antiretroviral agents) in adults and pediatric patients 12 years of age and older

Limitations of use: Not indicated for use as pre-exposure prophylaxis (PrEP) to reduce the risk of sexually acquired HIV-1 in adults at high risk.

Local Anesthetic/Vasoconstrictor Precautions No information available to require special precautions

Effects on Dental Treatment Key adverse event(s) related to dental treatment: Nausea reported in 10% of patients

Effects on Bleeding No information available to require special precautions

Adverse Reactions All adverse drug reactions are from combination therapy with cobistat plus elvitegravir in treatment-naïve and treatment-experienced patients. Also see individual agents.

1% to 10%:

Gastrointestinal: Nausea (10%)

Neuromuscular & skeletal: Decreased bone mineral density (≥5% decrease at lumbar spine: 1% to 10%; ≥7% decrease at femoral neck: 1% to 7%), bone fracture (≤1%; excluding fingers and toes)

Frequency not defined:

Endocrine & metabolic: Increased HDL cholesterol, increased LDL cholesterol, increased serum cholesterol, increased serum triglycerides

Hepatic: Exacerbation of hepatitis B

Renal: Increased serum creatinine (mean increase 0.1 mg/dL)

<1%, postmarketing, and/or case reports: Acute renal failure, renal disease

General Dosage Range Oral: *Children and Adolescents ≥12 years and ≥35 kg and Adults:* One tablet once daily

Mechanism of Action Nucleoside and nucleotide reverse transcriptase inhibitor combination; emtricitabine is a cytosine analogue while tenofovir alafenamide fumarate (TAF) is an analog of adenosine 5'-monophosphate. Each drug interferes with HIV viral RNA dependent DNA polymerase activities resulting in inhibition of viral replication.

Pharmacodynamics/Kinetics

Half-life Elimination Emtricitabine: 10 hours; TAF: 0.51 hours

Pregnancy Considerations The Health and Human Services (HHS) Perinatal HIV Guidelines note there are insufficient data to recommend use of this combination product as an initial regimen in antiretroviral-naive pregnant women. In general, women who become pregnant on a stable cART regimen may continue that regimen if viral suppression is effective, appropriate drug exposure can be achieved, contraindications for use in pregnancy are not present, and the regimen is well tolerated. Monitoring during pregnancy is more frequent than in non-pregnant adults; cART should be continued postpartum (HHS [perinatal] 2016). Refer to individual monographs.

Emtricitabine and Tenofovir Disoproxil Fumarate

(em trye SYE ta been & ten OF oh vir dye soe PROX il FUE ma rate)

Related Information

Emtricitabine *on page 568*

HIV Infection and AIDS *on page 1785*

Tenofovir Disoproxil Fumarate *on page 1539*

Brand Names: US Truvada

Brand Names: Canada Truvada

Pharmacologic Category Antiretroviral, Reverse Transcriptase Inhibitor, Nucleoside (Anti-HIV); Antiretroviral, Reverse Transcriptase Inhibitor, Nucleotide (Anti-HIV)

Use

HIV-1 infection, treatment: Treatment of HIV-1 infection in combination with other antiretroviral agents in adults and pediatric patients [age not specified] weighing ≥17 kg (US labeling) or in adult patients (Canadian labeling)

HIV-1 infection, prophylaxis: Pre-exposure prophylaxis (PrEP) for prevention of HIV-1 infection in adults who are at high risk for acquiring HIV

Local Anesthetic/Vasoconstrictor Precautions No information available to require special precautions

Effects on Dental Treatment No significant effects or complications reported

Effects on Bleeding No information available to require special precautions related to hemostasis.

Adverse Reactions The adverse reaction profile of combination therapy has not been established. See individual agents.

General Dosage Range Dosage adjustment recommended in patients with renal impairment

Oral:

Children and Adolescents 17 to <22 kg: 1 tablet (emtricitabine 100 mg/tenofovir 150 mg) once daily

Children and Adolescents 22 to <28 kg: 1 tablet (emtricitabine 133 mg/tenofovir 200 mg) once daily

Children and Adolescents 28 to <35 kg: 1 tablet (emtricitabine 167 mg/tenofovir 250 mg) once daily

Children and Adolescents ≥35 kg and Adults: 1 tablet (emtricitabine 200 mg and tenofovir 300 mg) once daily

Mechanism of Action Nucleoside and nucleotide reverse transcriptase inhibitor combination; emtricitabine is a cytosine analogue while tenofovir is an analog of adenosine 5'-monophosphate. Each drug interferes with HIV viral RNA dependent DNA polymerase resulting in inhibition of viral replication.

Pregnancy Risk Factor B

Pregnancy Considerations

Animal reproduction studies have not been conducted with this combination.

An increased risk of birth defects has not been observed following use of this combination for pre-exposure prophylaxis (PrEP). Although pregnancy is not a contraindication to PrEP when used for the prevention of HIV-1 infection in adults who are at high risk for infection, long term use in pregnancy is not well studied.

In general, women who become pregnant on a stable combination antiretroviral therapy (cART) regimen may continue that regimen if viral suppression is effective, appropriate drug exposure can be achieved, contraindications for use in pregnancy are not present, and the regimen is well tolerated. The Health and Human Services (HHS) Perinatal HIV Guidelines consider emtricitabine with tenofovir disoproxil fumarate to be a preferred NRTI backbone for initial therapy in antiretroviral-naive pregnant women. The guidelines also consider emtricitabine plus tenofovir disoproxil fumarate a recommended dual NRTI backbone in regimens for HIV/HBV-coinfected pregnant women (HHS [perinatal] 2016). Refer to individual monographs.

Emtricitabine, Rilpivirine, and Tenofovir Alafenamide

(em trye SYE ta been, ril pi VIR een, & ten OF oh vir al a FEN a mide)

Brand Names: US Odefsey

Pharmacologic Category Antiretroviral, Reverse Transcriptase Inhibitor, Non-nucleoside (Anti-HIV); Antiretroviral, Reverse Transcriptase Inhibitor, Nucleoside (Anti-HIV); Antiretroviral, Reverse Transcriptase Inhibitor, Nucleotide (Anti-HIV)

Use HIV-1 infection: Treatment of HIV-1 infection (as a complete regimen) in patients 12 years of age and older as initial therapy in those with no antiretroviral treatment history with HIV-1 RNA ≤100,000 copies/mL; or to replace a stable antiretroviral regimen in those who are virologically-suppressed (HIV-1 RNA <50 copies/mL) for at least 6 months with no history of treatment failure and no known substitutions associated with resistance to the individual components.

Local Anesthetic/Vasoconstrictor Precautions No information available to require special precautions

Effects on Dental Treatment No significant effects or complications reported

Effects on Bleeding No information available to require special precautions

Adverse Reactions See individual agents.

General Dosage Range Oral: *Children and Adolescents ≥12 years and ≥35 kg and Adults:* One tablet once daily

Mechanism of Action Non-nucleoside, nucleoside, and nucleotide reverse transcriptase inhibitor combination; rilpivirine binds to reverse transcriptase and does not require intracellular phosphorylation for antiviral activity; emtricitabine is a cytosine analogue while tenofovir alafenamide fumarate (TAF) is an analog of adenosine 5'-monophosphate. Each drug interferes with HIV viral RNA dependent DNA polymerase activities resulting in inhibition of viral replication.

Pregnancy Considerations In general, women who become pregnant on a stable combination antiretroviral therapy (cART) regimen may continue that regimen if viral suppression is effective, appropriate drug exposure can be achieved, contraindications for use in pregnancy are not present, and the regimen is well tolerated. The Health and Human Services (HHS) Perinatal HIV Guidelines note there are insufficient data to recommend use of this combination product as an initial regimen in antiretroviral-naive pregnant women (HHS [perinatal] 2016). Refer to individual monographs.

Product Availability Odefsey: FDA approved March 2016; anticipated availability is currently undetermined

Emtricitabine, Rilpivirine, and Tenofovir Disoproxil Fumarate

(em trye SYE ta been, ril pi VIR een, & ten OF oh vir dye soe PROX il FUE ma rate)

Related Information

HIV Infection and AIDS *on page 1785*

Brand Names: US Complera

Brand Names: Canada Complera

Pharmacologic Category Antiretroviral, Reverse Transcriptase Inhibitor, Non-nucleoside (Anti-HIV); Antiretroviral, Reverse Transcriptase Inhibitor, Nucleoside (Anti-HIV); Antiretroviral, Reverse Transcriptase Inhibitor, Nucleotide (Anti-HIV)

Use

US labeling: Treatment of HIV-1 infection (as a complete regimen) in antiretroviral treatment-naive patients 12 years or older with HIV-1 RNA ≤100,000 copies/mL at the start of therapy, and in certain virologically suppressed (HIV-1 RNA <50 copies/mL) patients on a stable antiretroviral regimen at start of therapy in order to replace their current antiretroviral treatment regimen.

Canadian labeling: Treatment of HIV-1 infection (as a complete regimen) in adults with no known mutations associated with resistance to non-nucleoside reverse transcriptase inhibitors (NNRTIs), emtricitabine, or tenofovir and with HIV-1 RNA ≤100,000 copies/mL.

Local Anesthetic/Vasoconstrictor Precautions No information available to require special precautions

Effects on Dental Treatment No significant effects or complications reported

Effects on Bleeding No information available to require special precautions

Adverse Reactions Observed in patients receiving the same doses of emtricitabine, rilpivirine, and tenofovir as the combination product; **also see** individual agents.

>10%:

Endocrine & metabolic: Increased serum cholesterol (≤14%), increased LDL cholesterol (1% to 13%)

Hepatic: Increased serum ALT (1% to 19%), increased serum AST (1% to 16%)

2% to 10%:

Central nervous system: Depression (2% to 9%), headache (2%), insomnia (2%)

Endocrine & metabolic: Adrenocortical insufficiency (7%; not associated with any serious events)

Hepatic: Increased serum bilirubin (1% to 6%)

Renal: Increased serum creatinine (≤6%)

<2%, postmarketing, and/or case reports: Abdominal pain, abnormal dreams, anxiety, cholecystitis, cholelithiasis, decreased appetite, diarrhea, dizziness, DRESS syndrome, drowsiness, fatigue, glomerulonephritis (membranous and mesangioproliferative), hypersensitivity reaction, immune reconstitution syndrome, increased serum triglycerides (≥500 mg/dL), nausea, nephrolithiasis, nephrotic syndrome, skin rash, sleep disorder, vomiting, weight gain

General Dosage Range Dosage adjustment recommended in patients on concomitant therapy.

Oral: *Children and Adolescents ≥12 years and ≥35 kg and Adults:* One tablet once daily

Mechanism of Action Non-nucleoside, nucleoside, and nucleotide reverse transcriptase inhibitor combination; rilpivirine binds to reverse transcriptase and does not require intracellular phosphorylation for antiviral activity; emtricitabine is a cytosine analogue while tenofovir disoproxil fumarate (TDF) is an analog of adenosine 5'-monophosphate. Each drug interferes with HIV viral RNA dependent DNA polymerase activities resulting in inhibition of viral replication.

Pregnancy Risk Factor B

Pregnancy Considerations

Animal reproduction studies have not been conducted with this combination.

In general, women who become pregnant on a stable combination antiretroviral therapy (cART) regimen may continue that regimen if viral suppression is effective, appropriate drug exposure can be achieved, contraindications for use in pregnancy are not present, and the regimen is well tolerated. The Health and Human Services (HHS) Perinatal HIV Guidelines consider emtricitabine in combination with rilpivirine and tenofovir disoproxil fumarate to be an alternative NNRTI regimen for initial use in antiretroviral-naive pregnant women with a pre-treatment HIV RNA ≤100,000 copies/mL or CD4 cell count ≥200 cells/mm^3 (HHS [perinatal] 2016). Refer to individual monographs.

Enalapril (e NAL a pril)

Related Information

Cardiovascular Diseases *on page 1752*

Brand Names: US Epaned; Vasotec

Brand Names: Canada ACT-Enalapril; Apo-Enalapril; Mylan-Enalapril; PMS-Enalapril; PRO-Enalapril; RAN-Enalapril; Riva-Enalapril; Sandoz-Enalapril; Sig-Enalapril; Taro-Enalapril; Teva-Enalapril; Vasotec

Generic Availability (US) May be product dependent

Pharmacologic Category Angiotensin-Converting Enzyme (ACE) Inhibitor; Antihypertensive

Use

Asymptomatic left ventricular dysfunction: Treatment of asymptomatic left ventricular dysfunction

Heart failure: Treatment of symptomatic heart failure (HF)

Hypertension: Management of hypertension

Guideline recommendations:

Hypertension: The 2014 guideline for the management of high blood pressure in adults (Eighth Joint National Committee [JNC 8]) recommends initiation of pharmacologic treatment to lower blood pressure for the following patients:

- Patients ≥60 years of age with systolic blood pressure (SBP) ≥150 mm Hg or diastolic blood pressure (DBP) ≥90 mm Hg. Goal of therapy is SBP <150 mm Hg and DBP <90 mm Hg.
- Patients <60 years of age with SBP ≥140 mm Hg or DBP is ≥90 mm Hg. Goal of therapy is SBP <140 mm Hg and DBP <90 mm Hg.
- Patients ≥18 years of age with diabetes and SBP ≥140 mm Hg or DBP ≥90 mm Hg. Goal of therapy is SBP <140 mm Hg and DBP <90 mm Hg.
- Patients ≥18 years of age with chronic kidney disease (CKD) and SBP ≥140 mm Hg or DBP ≥90 mm Hg. Goal of therapy is SBP <140 mm Hg and DBP <90 mm Hg.

Chronic kidney disease (CKD) and hypertension: Regardless of race or diabetes status, the use of an ACE inhibitor (ACEI) or angiotensin receptor blocker (ARB) as initial therapy is recommended to improve kidney outcomes. In the general nonblack population (without CKD) including those with diabetes, initial antihypertensive treatment should consist of a thiazide-type diuretic, calcium channel blocker, ACEI, or ARB. In the general black population (without CKD) including those with diabetes, initial antihypertensive treatment should consist of a thiazide-type diuretic or a calcium channel blocker **instead of** an ACEI or ARB.

Coronary artery disease (CAD) and hypertension: The American Heart Association, American College of Cardiology and American Society of Hypertension (AHA/ACC/ASH) 2015 scientific statement for the treatment of hypertension in patients with CAD recommends the use of an ACE inhibitor (or an ARB) as part of a regimen in patients with hypertension and chronic stable angina if there is prior MI, LV systolic dysfunction, diabetes mellitus, or CKD. A BP target of <140/90 mm Hg is reasonable for the secondary prevention of cardiovascular events. A lower target BP (<130/80 mm Hg) may be appropriate in some individuals with CAD, previous MI, stroke or transient ischemic attack, or CAD risk equivalents (AHA/ACC/ASH [Rosendorff 2015]).

Heart failure: The ACCF/AHA 2013 heart failure guidelines recommend the use of ACE inhibitors, along with other guideline directed medical therapies, to prevent heart failure in patients with a reduced ejection fraction who have a history of MI (Stage B HF), to prevent heart failure in any patient with a reduced ejection fraction (Stage B HF), or to treat those with heart failure and reduced ejection fraction (Stage C HFrEF) (ACCF/AHA [Yancy 2013]).

Local Anesthetic/Vasoconstrictor Precautions No information available to require special precautions

Effects on Dental Treatment Key adverse event(s) related to dental treatment: Abnormal taste; Patients may experience orthostatic hypotension as they stand up after treatment; especially if lying in dental chair for extended periods of time. Use caution with sudden changes in position during and after dental treatment.

An angiotensin-converting enzyme (ACE) Inhibitor cough is a dry, hacking, nonproductive cough that can potentially interfere with longer dental procedures if patient has this side effect.

Effects on Bleeding No information available to require special precautions

Adverse Reactions Note: Frequency ranges include data from hypertension and heart failure trials. Higher rates of adverse reactions have generally been noted in patients with CHF. However, the frequency of adverse effects associated with placebo is also increased in this population.

>10%: Renal: Increased serum creatinine (≤20%)

1% to 10%:

Cardiovascular: Hypotension (1% to 7%), chest pain (2%), orthostatic effect (1% to 2%), orthostatic hypotension (2%), syncope (≤2%)

Central nervous system: Dizziness (4% to 8%), headache (2% to 5%), fatigue (2% to 3%)

Dermatologic: Skin rash (1% to 2%)

Gastrointestinal: Abdominal pain, anorexia, constipation, diarrhea, dysgeusia, nausea, vomiting

Neuromuscular & skeletal: Weakness

Renal: Renal insufficiency (in patients with bilateral renal artery stenosis or hypovolemia)

Respiratory: Bronchitis (1% to 2%), cough (1% to 2%), dyspnea (1% to 2%)

<1%, postmarketing, and/or case reports: Abnormal dreams, acute generalized exanthematous pustulosis, agranulocytosis, alopecia, anaphylactoid reaction, angina pectoris, angioedema, anosmia, arthralgia, arthritis, asthma, ataxia, atrial fibrillation, atrial tachycardia, blurred vision, bone marrow depression, bradycardia, bronchospasm, cardiac arrest, cardiac arrhythmia, cerebrovascular accident, cholestatic jaundice, confusion, conjunctivitis, depression, diaphoresis, drowsiness, dry eye syndrome, dyspepsia, eosinophilia, eosinophilic pneumonitis, erythema multiforme, exfoliative dermatitis, fever, flank pain, flushing, giant-cell arteritis, glossitis, gynecomastia, hallucination, hemolysis (with G6PD), hepatitis, herpes zoster, hoarseness, IgA vasculitis, increased erythrocyte sedimentation rate, intestinal obstruction, impotence, insomnia, interstitial nephritis, jaundice, lacrimation, leukocytosis, lichenoid eruption, melena, muscle cramps, myocardial infarction, myalgia, myositis, nervousness, neutropenia, ototoxicity, palpitations, pancreatitis, paresthesia, pemphigus, pemphigus foliaceus, peripheral neuropathy, positive ANA titer, pruritus, psychosis, pulmonary edema, pulmonary embolism, pulmonary infarct, pulmonary infiltrates, Raynaud's phenomenon, rhinorrhea, serositis, Sjogren's syndrome, skin photosensitivity, sore throat, Stevens-Johnson syndrome, stomatitis, systemic lupus erythematosus, thrombocytopenia, tinnitus, toxic epidermal necrolysis, upper respiratory tract infection, urticaria, vasculitis, vertigo, visual hallucination (Doane, 2013), xerostomia

Dosing

Adult & Geriatric Use lower listed initial dose in patients with hyponatremia, hypovolemia, severe heart failure, decreased renal function, or in those receiving diuretics.

Asymptomatic left ventricular dysfunction: Oral: 2.5 mg twice daily, titrated as tolerated to 10 mg twice daily (maximum: 20 mg/day).

Heart failure: Oral: Initial: 2.5 mg twice daily; usual range: 5 to 40 mg daily in 2 divided doses (maximum: 40 mg/day); titrate slowly at 1- to 2-week intervals. Target dose: 10 to 20 mg twice daily (ACCF/AHA [Yancy 2013]).

Hypertension: Oral: Initial: 5 mg once daily (2.5 mg once daily in patients taking diuretics); titrate upward, usually at 1- to 2-week intervals; usual dose range (ASH/ISH [Weber 2014]): 10 to 40 mg daily. Target dose (JNC 8 [James 2013]): 20 mg daily in 1 or 2 divided doses. Maximum: 40 mg/day. **Note:** May add a diuretic if blood pressure cannot be controlled with enalapril alone.

Conversion from IV **enalaprilat** to oral **enalapril** therapy: If not concurrently receiving diuretics, initiate enalapril 5 mg once daily; if concurrently receiving diuretics and responding to enalaprilat 0.625 mg IV every 6 hours, initiate with enalapril 2.5 mg once daily; subsequent titration as needed.

Pediatric

Use lower listed initial dose in patients with hyponatremia, hypovolemia, severe heart failure, decreased renal function, or in those receiving diuretics.

Hypertension: Infants, Children, and Adolescents: Oral: Initial: 0.08 mg/kg once daily (maximum: 5 mg/dose); adjust dosage based on patient response; doses >0.58 mg/kg (or >40 mg) have not been studied.

Heart failure (off-label dosing): Infants, Children, and Adolescents: Oral: Initial: 0.1 mg/kg/day in 1 to 2 divided doses; increase as required over 2 weeks to maximum of 0.5 mg/kg/day. **Note:** Mean dose required for CHF improvement in 39 children (9 days to 17 years) was 0.36 mg/kg/day; select individuals have been treated with doses up to 0.94 mg/kg/day (Leversha 1994; Momma 2006).

Renal Impairment

Adults:

Manufacturer's labeling:

CrCl >30 mL/minute: No dosage adjustment necessary.

CrCl ≤30 mL/minute: Initial: 2.5 mg once daily; titrate upward as needed (maximum: 40 mg/day)

Heart failure patients with serum creatinine >1.6 mg/dL: Initial: 2.5 mg once daily, increasing to twice daily as needed. Increase further in increments of 2.5 mg/dose at >4-day intervals to a maximum dose of 40 mg/day.

Intermittent hemodialysis (IHD): Moderately dialyzable (20% to 50%): Initial: 2.5 mg after dialysis on dialysis days; adjust dose on nondialysis days depending on blood pressure response

Conversion from IV **enalaprilat** to oral **enalapril** therapy:

CrCl >30 mL/minute: May initiate enalapril 5 mg once daily.

CrCl ≤30 mL/minute: May initiate enalapril 2.5 mg once daily.

Alternate recommendations (Aronoff 2007):

GFR >50 mL/minute: No dosage adjustment necessary

GFR 10 to 50 mL/minute: Administer 50% to 100% of usual dose.

GFR <10 mL/minute: Administer 25% of usual dose.

Peritoneal dialysis: Administer 25% of usual dose.

Infants, Children, and Adolescents:

Manufacturer's labeling: Use in infants and children ≤16 years of age with GFR <30 mL/minute/1.73 m^2 is not recommended (no dosing data available).

Alternate recommendations (Aronoff 2007):

GFR >50 mL/minute/1.73 m^2: No dosage adjustment necessary.

GFR 10 to 50 mL/minute/1.73 m^2: Administer 75% of usual dose.

GFR <10 mL/minute/1.73 m^2: Administer 50% of usual dose.

Hepatic Impairment No dosage adjustment necessary. Hydrolysis of enalapril to enalaprilat may be delayed and/or impaired in patients with severe hepatic impairment, but the pharmacodynamic effects of the drug do not appear to be significantly altered.

Mechanism of Action Competitive inhibitor of angiotensin-converting enzyme (ACE); prevents conversion of angiotensin I to angiotensin II, a potent vasoconstrictor; results in lower levels of angiotensin II which causes an increase in plasma renin activity and a reduction in aldosterone secretion

Contraindications

Hypersensitivity to enalapril or any component of the formulation; angioedema related to previous treatment with an ACE inhibitor; idiopathic or hereditary angioedema; concomitant use with aliskiren in patients with diabetes mellitus

Documentation of allergenic cross-reactivity for ACE inhibitors is limited. However, because of similarities in chemical structure and/or pharmacologic actions, the possibility of cross-sensitivity cannot be ruled out with certainty.

Canadian labeling: Additional contraindications (not in US labeling): Concomitant use with aliskiren-containing drugs in patients with moderate-to-severe renal impairment (GFR <60 mL/minute/1.73 m^2)

Warnings/Precautions Anaphylactic reactions may occur rarely with ACE inhibitors. At any time during treatment (especially following first dose) angioedema may occur rarely with ACE inhibitors; it may involve the head and neck (potentially compromising airway) or the intestine (presenting with abdominal pain). African-Americans may be at an increased risk. Risk may also be increased with concomitant use of mTOR inhibitor (eg, everolimus) therapy. Prolonged frequent monitoring may be required especially if tongue, glottis, or larynx are involved as they are associated with airway obstruction. Patients with a history of airway surgery may have a higher risk of airway obstruction. Aggressive early and appropriate management is critical. Use in patients with idiopathic or hereditary angioedema or previous angioedema associated with ACE inhibitor therapy is contraindicated. Severe anaphylactoid reactions may be seen during hemodialysis (eg, CVVHD) with high-flux dialysis membranes (eg, AN69), and rarely, during low density lipoprotein apheresis with dextran sulfate cellulose. Rare cases of anaphylactoid reactions have been reported in patients undergoing sensitization treatment with hymenoptera (bee, wasp) venom while receiving ACE inhibitors.

Symptomatic hypotension with or without syncope can occur with ACE inhibitors (usually with the first several doses); effects are most often observed in volume depleted patients; correct volume depletion prior to initiation; close monitoring of patient is required especially with initial dosing and dosing increases; blood pressure must be lowered at a rate appropriate for the patient's clinical condition. Initiation of therapy in patients with ischemic heart disease or cerebrovascular disease warrants close observation due to the potential consequences posed by falling blood pressure (eg, MI, stroke). Use with caution in severe aortic stenosis. Use with caution in patients with HCM and outflow tract obstruction; reduction in afterload may worsen symptoms associated with this condition (ACCF/AHA [Gersh 2011]). In patients on chronic ACE inhibitor therapy, intraoperative hypotension may occur with induction and maintenance of general anesthesia; use with caution before, during, or immediately after major surgery. Cardiopulmonary bypass, intraoperative blood loss, or vasodilating anesthesia increases endogenous renin release. Use of ACE inhibitors perioperatively will blunt angiotensin II formation and may result in hypotension. However, discontinuation of therapy prior to surgery is controversial. If continued preoperatively, avoidance of hypotensive agents during surgery is prudent (Hillis 2011). **[US Boxed Warning]: Drugs that act on the renin-angiotensin system can cause injury and death to the developing fetus. Discontinue as soon as possible once pregnancy is detected.**

Hyperkalemia may occur with ACE inhibitors; risk factors include renal dysfunction, diabetes mellitus, concomitant use of potassium-sparing diuretics, potassium supplements, and/or potassium-containing salts. Use cautiously, if at all, with these agents and monitor potassium closely. Cough may occur with ACE inhibitors. Other causes of cough should be considered (eg, pulmonary congestion in patients with heart failure) and excluded prior to discontinuation.

May be associated with deterioration of renal function and/or increases in serum creatinine, particularly in patients with low renal blood flow (eg, renal artery stenosis, heart failure) whose glomerular filtration rate (GFR) is dependent on efferent arteriolar vasoconstriction by angiotensin II; deterioration may result in oliguria, acute renal failure, and progressive azotemia. Small increases in serum creatinine may occur following initiation; consider discontinuation only in patients with progressive and/or significant deterioration in renal function (Bakris 2000). Use with caution in patients with unstented unilateral/bilateral renal artery stenosis. When unstented bilateral renal artery stenosis is present, use is generally avoided due to the elevated risk of deterioration in renal function unless possible benefits outweigh risks. ACE inhibitors effectiveness is less in black patients than in non-blacks. In addition, ACE inhibitors cause a higher rate of angioedema in black than in non-black patients. Potentially significant drug-drug interactions may exist, requiring dose or frequency adjustment, additional monitoring, and/or selection of alternative therapy.

A rare toxicity associated with ACE inhibitors is cholestatic jaundice (which may progress to fulminant hepatic necrosis). Another ACE inhibitor, captopril, has been associated with neutropenia with myeloid hypoplasia and agranulocytosis; anemia and thrombocytopenia have also occurred. Patients with collagen vascular diseases (especially with concomitant renal impairment) or renal impairment alone may be at increased risk for hematologic toxicity; periodically monitor CBC with differential in these patients.

Oral solution may contain sodium benzoate/benzoic acid; benzoic acid (benzoate) is a metabolite of benzyl alcohol. Large amounts of benzyl alcohol (≥99 mg/kg/day) have been associated with a potentially fatal toxicity ("gasping syndrome") in neonates; the "gasping syndrome" consists of metabolic acidosis, respiratory distress, gasping respirations, CNS dysfunction (including convulsions, intracranial hemorrhage), hypotension, and cardiovascular collapse (AAP 1997; CDC 1982). Some data suggest that benzoate displaces bilirubin from protein binding sites (Ahlfors 2001); avoid or use dosage forms containing benzyl alcohol derivative with caution in neonates. See manufacturer's labeling.

Drug Interactions

Metabolism/Transport Effects None known.

Avoid Concomitant Use

Avoid concomitant use of Enalapril with any of the following: Sacubitril

Increased Effect/Toxicity

Enalapril may increase the levels/effects of: Allopurinol; Amifostine; Antipsychotic Agents (Second Generation [Atypical]); AzaTHIOprine; Ciprofloxacin (Systemic); Drospirenone; DULoxetine; Ferric Gluconate; Ferric Hydroxide Polymaltose Complex; Gold Sodium Thiomalate; Grass Pollen Allergen Extract (5 Grass Extract); Hypotension-Associated Agents; Iron Dextran Complex; Levodopa; Lithium; Nitroprusside; Nonsteroidal Anti-Inflammatory Agents; Pregabalin; Sacubitril; Sodium Phosphates

The levels/effects of Enalapril may be increased by: Alfuzosin; Aliskiren; Angiotensin II Receptor Blockers; Barbiturates; Benperidol; Brimonidine (Topical); Canagliflozin; Dapoxetine; Diazoxide; DPP-IV Inhibitors; Eplerenone; Everolimus; Heparin; Heparin (Low Molecular Weight); Herbs (Hypotensive Properties); Loop Diuretics; Lormetazepam; Molsidomine; Naftopidil; Nicergoline; Nicorandil; Obinutuzumab; Pentoxifylline; Phosphodiesterase 5 Inhibitors; Potassium Salts; Potassium-Sparing Diuretics; Prostacyclin Analogues; Quinagolide; Salicylates; Sirolimus; Temsirolimus; Thiazide and Thiazide-Like Diuretics; TiZANidine; Tolvaptan; Trimethoprim

Decreased Effect

The levels/effects of Enalapril may be decreased by: Amphetamines; Aprotinin; Herbs (Hypertensive Properties); Icatibant; Lanthanum; Methylphenidate; Nonsteroidal Anti-Inflammatory Agents; Salicylates; Yohimbine

Dietary Considerations Limit salt substitutes or potassium-rich diet.

Pharmacodynamics/Kinetics

Onset of Action ~1 hour; Peak effect: 4 to 6 hours

Duration of Action 12 to 24 hours

Half-life Elimination

Enalapril: CHF: Neonates (n=3, PNA: 10-19 days): 10.3 hours (range: 4.2-13.4 hours) (Nakamura, 1994); CHF: Infants and Children ≤6.5 years of age (n=11): 2.7 hours (range: 1.3-6.3 hours) (Nakamura, 1994); Adults: Healthy: 2 hours; Congestive heart failure: 3.4 to 5.8 hours

Enalaprilat: CHF: Neonates (n=3, PNA: 10-19 days): 11.9 hours (range: 5.9-15.6 hours) (Nakamura, 1994); CHF: Infants and Children ≤6.5 years of age (n=11): 11.1 hours (range: 5.1-20.8 hours) (Nakamura, 1994); Infants 6 weeks to 8 months of age: 6 to 10 hours (Lloyd, 1989); Adults: ~35 hours (Till, 1984; Ulm, 1982)

Time to Peak Serum: Oral: Enalapril: 0.5 to 1.5 hours; Enalaprilat (active metabolite): 3 to 4.5 hours

Pregnancy Risk Factor D

Pregnancy Considerations **[US Boxed Warning]: Drugs that act on the renin-angiotensin system can cause injury and death to the developing fetus. Discontinue as soon as possible once pregnancy is detected.** Enalapril crosses the placenta; the active metabolite enalaprilat can be detected in the newborn (Schubiger 1988).

Drugs that act on the renin-angiotensin system are associated with oligohydramnios. Oligohydramnios, due to decreased fetal renal function, may lead to fetal lung hypoplasia and skeletal malformations. The use of these drugs in pregnancy is also associated with anuria, hypotension, renal failure, skull hypoplasia, and death in the fetus/neonate. Teratogenic effects may occur following maternal use of an ACE inhibitor during the first trimester, although this finding may be confounded by maternal disease. Because adverse fetal events are well documented with exposure later in pregnancy, ACE inhibitor use in pregnant women is not recommended (Seely 2014; Weber 2014). Infants exposed to an ACE inhibitor in utero should be monitored for hyperkalemia, hypotension, and oliguria. Oligohydramnios may not appear until after irreversible fetal injury has occurred. Exchange transfusions or dialysis may be required to reverse hypotension or improve renal function, although data related to the effectiveness in neonates is limited.

Chronic maternal hypertension itself is also associated with adverse events in the fetus/infant and mother. ACE inhibitors are not recommended for the treatment of uncomplicated hypertension in pregnancy (ACOG 2013) and they are specifically contraindicated for the treatment of hypertension and chronic heart failure during pregnancy by some guidelines (Regitz-Zagrosek 2011). In addition, ACE inhibitors should generally be avoided in women of reproductive age (ACOG 2013). If treatment for hypertension or chronic heart failure in pregnancy is needed, other agents should be used (ACOG 2013; Regitz-Zagrosek 2011).

Breastfeeding Considerations Enalapril and enalaprilat are excreted in breast milk. Due to the potential for serious adverse reactions in the nursing infant, the manufacturer recommends a decision be made whether to discontinue nursing or to discontinue the drug, taking into account the importance of treatment to the mother. Some guidelines consider enalapril to be acceptable for use in breastfeeding women. Monitoring of the nursing child's weight for the first 4 weeks is recommended (Regitz-Zagrosek 2011).

Dosage Forms

Solution, Oral:

Epaned: 1 mg/mL (150 mL)

Solution Reconstituted, Oral:

Epaned: 1 mg/mL (150 mL)

Tablet, Oral:

Vasotec: 2.5 mg, 5 mg, 10 mg, 20 mg

Generic: 2.5 mg, 5 mg, 10 mg, 20 mg

Dosage Forms: Canada Note: Refer to Dosage Forms. Oral powder for reconstitution is not available in Canada.

Tablet, Oral, as maleate: 40 mg

Enalaprilat (en AL a pril at)

Brand Names: Canada Vasotec IV

Pharmacologic Category Angiotensin-Converting Enzyme (ACE) Inhibitor; Antihypertensive

Use Treatment of hypertension when oral therapy is not practical

Local Anesthetic/Vasoconstrictor Precautions No information available to require special precautions

Effects on Dental Treatment Key adverse event(s) related to dental treatment: Abnormal taste; Patients may experience orthostatic hypotension as they stand up after treatment; especially if lying in dental chair for extended periods of time. Use caution with sudden changes in position during and after dental treatment.

An angiotensin-converting enzyme (ACE) Inhibitor cough is a dry, hacking, nonproductive cough that can potentially interfere with longer dental procedures if patient has this side effect.

Effects on Bleeding No information available to require special precautions

Adverse Reactions Since enalapril is converted to enalaprilat, adverse reactions associated with enalapril may also occur with enalaprilat (also refer to Enalapril monograph). Frequency ranges include data from hypertension and cardiac failure trials. Higher rates of adverse reactions have generally been noted in patients with cardiac failure. However, the frequency of adverse effects associated with placebo is also increased in this population.

1% to 10%:

Cardiovascular: Hypotension (2% to 5%)

Central nervous system: Headache (3%)

Gastrointestinal: Nausea (1%)

<1%, postmarketing, and/or case reports: Angioedema, constipation, cough, dizziness, fatigue, fever, myocardial infarction, skin rash

General Dosage Range Dosage adjustment recommended in patients with renal impairment.

IV: *Adults:* 0.625-5 mg every 6 hours

Mechanism of Action Competitive inhibitor of angiotensin-converting enzyme (ACE); prevents conversion of angiotensin I to angiotensin II, a potent vasoconstrictor; results in lower levels of angiotensin II which causes an increase in plasma renin activity and a reduction in aldosterone secretion

Pharmacodynamics/Kinetics

Onset of Action IV: ≤15 minutes; Peak effect: IV: 1-4 hours

Duration of Action IV: ~6 hours (dose-dependent)

Half-life Elimination CHF: Neonates (n=3; PNA: 10-19 days): 11.9 hours (range: 5.9-15.6 hours) (Nakamura, 1994); CHF: Infants and Children ≤6.5 years of age (n=11): 11.1 hours (range: 5.1-20.8 hours) (Nakamura, 1994); Infants 6 weeks to 8 months of age: 6-10 hours (Lloyd, 1989); Adults: ~35 hours (Till, 1984; Ulm, 1982)

Pregnancy Risk Factor C (1st trimester); D (2nd and 3rd trimesters)

Pregnancy Considerations [U.S. Boxed Warning]: Drugs that act on the renin-angiotensin system can cause injury and death to the developing fetus. Discontinue as soon as possible once pregnancy is detected. Enalapril crosses the placenta; the active metabolite enalaprilat can be detected in the newborn (Schubiger 1988).

Drugs that act on the renin-angiotensin system are associated with oligohydramnios. Oligohydramnios, due to decreased fetal renal function, may lead to fetal lung hypoplasia and skeletal malformations. The use of these drugs in pregnancy is also associated with anuria, hypotension, renal failure, skull hypoplasia, and death in the fetus/neonate. Teratogenic effects may occur following maternal use of an ACE inhibitor during the first trimester, although this finding may be confounded by maternal disease. Because adverse fetal events are well documented with exposure later in pregnancy, ACE inhibitor use in pregnant women is not recommended (Seely 2014; Weber 2014). Infants exposed to an ACE inhibitor in utero should be monitored for hyperkalemia, hypotension, and oliguria. Oligohydramnios may not appear until after irreversible fetal injury has occurred. Exchange transfusions or dialysis may be required to reverse hypotension or improve renal function, although data related to the effectiveness in neonates is limited

Chronic maternal hypertension itself is also associated with adverse events in the fetus/infant and mother. ACE inhibitors are not recommended for the treatment of uncomplicated hypertension in pregnancy (ACOG 2013) and they are specifically contraindicated for the treatment of hypertension and chronic heart failure during pregnancy by some guidelines (Regitz-Zagrosek 2011). In addition, ACE inhibitors should generally be avoided in women of reproductive age (ACOG 2013). If treatment for hypertension in pregnancy is needed, other agents should be used (ACOG 2013; Regitz-Zagrosek 2011).

Enfuvirtide (en FYOO vir tide)

Related Information

HIV Infection and AIDS *on page* 1785

Brand Names: US Fuzeon

Brand Names: Canada Fuzeon

Pharmacologic Category Antiretroviral, Fusion Protein Inhibitor (Anti-HIV)

Use HIV-1 infection: Treatment of HIV-1 infection in combination with other antiretroviral agents in treatment-experienced patients with evidence of HIV-1 replication despite ongoing antiretroviral therapy

Local Anesthetic/Vasoconstrictor Precautions No information available to require special precautions

Effects on Dental Treatment Key adverse event(s) related to dental treatment: Xerostomia (normal salivary flow resumes upon discontinuation) and taste disturbance

Effects on Bleeding No information available to require special precautions related to hemostasis.

Adverse Reactions

>10%:

Central nervous system: Fatigue (20%), insomnia (11%)

Gastrointestinal: Diarrhea (32%), nausea (23%)

Local: Injection site reaction (98%; may include cyst at injection site, erythema at injection site, induration at injection site, injection site ecchymosis, injection site nodule, injection site pruritus, pain at injection site), injection site infection (children: 11%, adults: 2%)

1% to 10%:

Dermatologic: Folliculitis (2%)

Endocrine & metabolic: Weight loss (7%)

Gastrointestinal: Abdominal pain (4%), decreased appetite (3%), pancreatitis (3%), anorexia (2%), xerostomia (2%)

Hematologic & oncologic: Eosinophilia (2% to 9%)

Hepatic: Increased serum transaminases (4%, grade 4: 1%)

Infection: Infection (4% to 6%), herpes simplex infection (4%)

Neuromuscular & skeletal: Increased creatine phosphokinase (3% to 7%), limb pain (3%), myalgia (3%)

Ophthalmic: Conjunctivitis (2%)

Respiratory: Sinusitis (6%), cough (4%), bacterial pneumonia (3%), flu-like symptoms (2%)

<1%, postmarketing, and/or case reports: Amyloidosis (cutaneous; at the injection site), angina pectoris, anxiety, constipation, depression, dysgeusia, glomerulonephritis, Guillain-Barré syndrome, hyperglycemia; hypersensitivity exacerbation (to abacavir), hypersensitivity reaction (symptoms may include fever, hypotension, increased serum transaminases, nausea, skin rash, vomiting); increased amylase, increased gamma-glutamyl transferase, insomnia, increased serum lipase, increased serum triglycerides, liver steatosis, lymphadenopathy, neutropenia, peripheral neuropathy, pulmonary disease, renal failure, renal insufficiency, renal tubular necrosis, respiratory distress, sepsis, sixth nerve palsy, suicidal tendencies, thrombocytopenia, toxic hepatitis, weakness

General Dosage Range

SubQ:

Children and Adolescents 6 to 16 years: 2 mg/kg twice daily (maximum dose: 90 mg twice daily)

Adolescents >16 years and Adults: 90 mg twice daily

Mechanism of Action Binds to the first heptad-repeat (HR1) in the gp41 subunit of the viral envelope glycoprotein. Inhibits the fusion of HIV-1 virus with CD4 cells by blocking the conformational change in gp41 required for membrane fusion and entry into CD4 cells

Pharmacodynamics/Kinetics

Half-life Elimination 3.8 ± 0.6 hours

Time to Peak SubQ: Single dose: Median: 8 hours (range: 3 to 12 hours); Multiple dosing: Median: 4 hours (range: 4 to 8 hours)

Pregnancy Risk Factor B

Pregnancy Considerations Adverse events were not observed in animal reproduction studies. Enfuvirtide has minimal to low transfer across the human placenta. Data collected by the antiretroviral pregnancy registry is insufficient to evaluate human teratogenic risk. Maternal antiretroviral therapy may increase the risk of preterm delivery, although, available information is conflicting possibly due to variability of maternal factors (disease severity; initiation of therapy); however, maternal antiretroviral medication should not be withheld due to concerns of preterm birth. Information related to stillbirth, low birth weight, and small for gestational age infants is limited. Long-term follow-up is recommended for all infants exposed to antiretroviral medications; children who develop significant organ system abnormalities of unknown etiology (particularly of the CNS or heart) should be evaluated for potential mitochondrial dysfunction.

Combination antiretroviral therapy (cART) therapy is recommended for all HIV-infected pregnant women to keep the viral load below the limit of detection and reduce the risk of perinatal transmission. When HIV is diagnosed during pregnancy in a woman who has never received antiretroviral therapy, cART should begin as soon as possible after diagnosis. The Health and Human Services (HHS) Perinatal HIV Guidelines note that there are insufficient data to recommend use of enfuvirtide as initial therapy in antiretroviral-naive pregnant women. Pharmacokinetic data are insufficient to make dosing recommendations during pregnancy. In general, women who become pregnant on a stable cART regimen may continue that regimen if viral suppression is effective, appropriate drug exposure can be achieved, contraindications for use in pregnancy are not present, and the regimen is well tolerated. Monitoring during pregnancy is more frequent than in nonpregnant adults; cART should be continued postpartum.

For HIV-infected couples planning a pregnancy, maximum viral suppression with cART is recommended prior to conception for the HIV-infected partner(s) and expert consultation is recommended; modification of therapy (if needed) and optimization of the woman's health should be done prior to conception. HIV-infected women not planning a pregnancy may use any available type of contraception, considering possible drug interactions and contraindications of the specific method. In addition, consistent use of condoms is also recommended (even during pregnancy) to prevent transmission of HIV or other sexually transmitted diseases.

Health care providers are encouraged to enroll pregnant women exposed to antiretroviral medications as early in pregnancy as possible in the Antiretroviral Pregnancy Registry (1-800-258-4263 or www.APRegistry.com). Health care providers caring for HIV-infected women and their infants may contact the National Perinatal HIV Hotline (888-448-8765) for clinical consultation (HHS [perinatal] 2016).

Enoxaparin (ee noks a PA rin)

Related Information

Cardiovascular Diseases *on page 1752*

Brand Names: US Lovenox

Brand Names: Canada Lovenox; Lovenox HP; Lovenox With Preservative

Pharmacologic Category Anticoagulant; Anticoagulant, Low Molecular Weight Heparin

Use

Acute coronary syndromes: Unstable angina (UA), non-ST-elevation (NSTEMI), and ST-elevation myocardial infarction (STEMI)

DVT prophylaxis: Following hip or knee replacement surgery, abdominal surgery, or in medical patients with severely-restricted mobility during acute illness who are at risk for thromboembolic complications. **Note:** Patients at risk of thromboembolic complications who undergo abdominal surgery include those with one or more of the following risk factors: >40 years of age, obesity, general anesthesia lasting >30 minutes, malignancy, history of deep vein thrombosis or pulmonary embolism

DVT treatment (acute): Inpatient treatment (patients with or without pulmonary embolism) and outpatient treatment (patients without pulmonary embolism)

Local Anesthetic/Vasoconstrictor Precautions No information available to require special precautions

Effects on Dental Treatment Key adverse event(s) related to dental treatment: Bleeding is the major adverse effect of enoxaparin. See Effects on Bleeding.

Effects on Bleeding As with all anticoagulants, bleeding is the major adverse effect of enoxaparin. Hemorrhage may occur at virtually any site. Routine coagulation tests, such as prothrombin time (PT) and aPTT, are relatively insensitive measures of enoxaparin injection activity and, therefore, unsuitable for monitoring. Moderate thrombocytopenia occurred at a rate of ~1%. Medical consult is suggested.

Adverse Reactions As with all anticoagulants, bleeding is the major adverse effect of enoxaparin. Hemorrhage may occur at virtually any site. Risk is dependent on multiple variables. At the recommended doses, single injections of enoxaparin do not significantly influence platelet aggregation or affect global clotting time (ie, PT or aPTT).

>10%: Hematologic & oncologic: Anemia (≤16%), hemorrhage (4% to 13%)

1% to 10%:

Cardiovascular: Peripheral edema (6%)

Central nervous system: Confusion (2%)

Gastrointestinal: Nausea (3%)

Hematologic & oncologic: Major hemorrhage (<1% to 4%; includes cases of intracranial [up to 0.8%], retroperitoneal, or intraocular hemorrhage; incidence varies with indication/population), ecchymoses (3%), thrombocytopenia (1% to 2%)

Hepatic: Increased serum ALT (>3 x ULN: 6%), increased serum AST (>3 x ULN: 6%)

Local: Hematoma at injection site (9%), bleeding at injection site (3% to 5%), pain at injection site (2%)

Renal: Hematuria (≤2%)

Miscellaneous: Fever (≤8%)

<1%, postmarketing, and/or case reports: Acute posthemorrhagic anemia, alopecia, anaphylactoid reaction, anaphylaxis, atrial fibrillation, bruising at injection site, eosinophilia, epidural hematoma (spinal; after neuroaxial anesthesia or spinal puncture; risk may be increased with indwelling epidural catheter or concomitant use of other drugs affecting hemostasis), erythema at injection site, headache, hepatic injury (hepatocellular and cholestatic), hyperkalemia, hyperlipidemia (very rare), hypersensitivity angiitis, hypersensitivity reaction, hypertriglyceridemia, injection site reactions (including nodules, inflammation, oozing), irritation at injection site, osteoporosis (following long-term therapy), pneumonia, pruritus, pulmonary edema, purpura, shock, skin necrosis, thrombocythemia, thrombosis in heparin-induced thrombocyptopenia, thrombosis (prosthetic value [in pregnant females] or associated with enoxaparin-induced thrombocytopenia; can cause limb ischemia or organ infarction), urticaria, vesicobullous rash

General Dosage Range Dosage varies greatly depending on indication.

Mechanism of Action Standard heparin consists of components with molecular weights ranging from 4000 to 30,000 daltons with a mean of 16,000 daltons. Heparin acts as an anticoagulant by enhancing the inhibition rate of clotting proteases by antithrombin III impairing normal hemostasis and inhibition of factor Xa. Low molecular weight heparins have a small effect on the activated partial thromboplastin time and strongly inhibit factor Xa. Enoxaparin is derived from porcine heparin that undergoes benzylation followed by alkaline depolymerization. The average molecular weight of enoxaparin is 4500 daltons which is distributed as (≤20%) 2000 daltons (≥68%) 2000 to 8000 daltons, and (≤18%) >8000 daltons. Enoxaparin has a higher ratio of antifactor Xa to antifactor IIa activity than unfractionated heparin.

Pharmacodynamics/Kinetics

Onset of Action Peak effect: SubQ: Antifactor Xa and antithrombin (antifactor IIa): 3 to 5 hours

Duration of Action 40 mg dose: Antifactor Xa activity: ~12 hours

Half-life Elimination Plasma: 2 to 4 times longer than standard heparin, independent of dose; based on anti-Xa activity: 4.5 to 7 hours

Pregnancy Risk Factor B

Pregnancy Considerations Adverse events were not observed in animal reproduction studies. Low molecular weight heparin (LMWH) does not cross the placenta; increased risks of fetal bleeding or teratogenic effects have not been reported (Bates 2012).

LMWH is recommended over unfractionated heparin for the treatment of acute venous thromboembolism (VTE) in pregnant women. LMWH is also recommended over unfractionated heparin for VTE prophylaxis in pregnant women with certain risk factors (eg, homozygous factor V Leiden, antiphospholipid antibody syndrome with ≥3 previous pregnancy losses). Prophylaxis is not routinely recommended for women undergoing assisted reproduction therapy; however, LMWH therapy is recommended for women who develop severe ovarian hyperstimulation syndrome. LMWH should be discontinued at least 24 hours prior to induction of labor or a planned cesarean delivery. For women undergoing cesarean section and who have additional risk factors for developing VTE, the prophylactic use of LMWH may be considered (Bates 2012).

LMWH may also be used in women with mechanical heart valves (consult current guidelines for details) (Bates 2012; Nishimura 2014). Women who require long-term anticoagulation with warfarin and who are considering pregnancy, LMWH substitution should be done prior to conception when possible. When choosing therapy, fetal outcomes (ie, pregnancy loss, malformations), maternal outcomes (ie, VTE, hemorrhage), burden of therapy, and maternal preference should be considered (Bates 2012). Monitoring antifactor Xa levels is recommended (Bates 2012; Nishimura 2014).

Multiple-dose vials contain benzyl alcohol (avoid in pregnant women due to association with gasping syndrome in premature infants); use of preservative-free formulations is recommended.

Entacapone (en TA ka pone)

Brand Names: US Comtan

Brand Names: Canada Comtan; Mylan-Entacapone; Sandoz-Entacapone; Teva-Entacapone

Pharmacologic Category Anti-Parkinson Agent, COMT Inhibitor

Use Parkinson disease: Adjunct to levodopa/carbidopa therapy in patients with idiopathic Parkinson disease who experience "wearing-off" symptoms at the end of a dosing interval

Local Anesthetic/Vasoconstrictor Precautions No information available to require special precautions

Effects on Dental Treatment Key adverse event(s) related to dental treatment: Abnormal taste; Dopaminergic therapy in Parkinson's disease (ie, treatment with levodopa) is associated with orthostatic hypotension. Entacapone enhances levodopa bioavailability and may increase the occurrence of hypotension/syncope in the dental patient. Patients may experience orthostatic hypotension as they stand up after treatment; especially if lying in dental chair for extended periods of time. Use caution with sudden changes in position during and after dental treatment.

Effects on Bleeding No information available to require special precautions

Adverse Reactions

>10%:

Gastrointestinal: Nausea (14%)

Neuromuscular & skeletal: Dyskinesia (25%)

1% to 10%:

Cardiovascular: Syncope (1%)

Central nervous system: Dizziness (8%), fatigue (6%), anxiety (2%), drowsiness (2%), agitation (1%), hallucination (≤1%)

Dermatologic: Diaphoresis (increased; 2%)

Gastrointestinal: Diarrhea (10%), abdominal pain (8%), constipation (6%), vomiting (4%), xerostomia (3%), dyspepsia (2%), flatulence (2%), dysgeusia (1%), gastritis (1%), gastrointestinal disease (1%)

Genitourinary: Urine discoloration (brown-orange; 10%)

Hematologic & oncologic: Purpura (2%)

Infection: Bacterial infection (1%)

Neuromuscular & skeletal: Hyperkinesia (10%), hypokinesia (9%), back pain (2% to 4%), weakness (2%)

Respiratory: Dyspnea (3%)

<1%, postmarketing, and/or case reports: Behavioral changes (including psychotic-like behavior), hepatitis (mainly cholestatic features), impulse control disorder (eg, pathological gambling, hypersexuality, spending money), mental status changes, neurological signs and symptoms (hyperpyrexia and confusion [resembling neuroleptic malignant syndrome]), orthostatic hypotension, pulmonary fibrosis, retroperitoneal fibrosis, rhabdomyolysis, sudden onset of sleep

General Dosage Range Oral: *Adults:* 200 mg with each dose of levodopa/carbidopa (maximum: 1600 mg daily)

Mechanism of Action Entacapone is a reversible and selective inhibitor of catechol-O-methyltransferase (COMT). When entacapone is taken with levodopa, the pharmacokinetics are altered, resulting in more sustained levodopa serum levels compared to levodopa taken alone. The resulting levels of levodopa provide for increased concentrations available for absorption across the blood-brain barrier, thereby providing for increased CNS levels of dopamine, the active metabolite of levodopa.

Pharmacodynamics/Kinetics

Onset of Action Rapid

Half-life Elimination Beta phase: 0.4 to 0.7 hours; gamma phase: 2.4 hours

Time to Peak Serum: 1 hour

Pregnancy Risk Factor C

Pregnancy Considerations Adverse events were observed in some animal reproduction studies. The incidence of Parkinson disease in pregnancy is relatively rare and information related to the use of entacapone in pregnant women is very limited (Kranick, 2010).

Entecavir (en TE ka veer)

Related Information

HIV Infection and AIDS *on page 1785*

Systemic Viral Diseases *on page 1806*

Brand Names: US Baraclude

Brand Names: Canada Apo-Entecavir; Auro-Entecavir; Baraclude; PMS-Entecavir

Pharmacologic Category Antihepadnaviral, Reverse Transcriptase Inhibitor, Nucleoside (Anti-HBV)

Use Chronic hepatitis B: Treatment of chronic hepatitis B virus (HBV) infection in adults and pediatric patients 2 years and older with evidence of active viral replication and either evidence of persistent transaminase elevations or histologically-active disease. **Note:** In adults, indication is based on data in patients with compensated and decompensated liver disease; in children, indication is based on data in patients with compensated liver disease.

Local Anesthetic/Vasoconstrictor Precautions No information available to require special precautions

Effects on Dental Treatment No significant effects or complications reported

Effects on Bleeding No information available to require special precautions related to hemostasis.

Adverse Reactions Adverse reactions are generally similar in adult and pediatric patients.

>10%:

Cardiovascular: Peripheral edema (16% with decompensated liver disease)

Hepatic: Ascites (15% with decompensated liver disease), increased serum ALT (>5 x ULN: 11% to 12%; post-treatment flare [lamivudine refractory]: >10 x ULN and >2 x baseline: 12%)

Renal: Increased serum creatinine (11% with decompensated liver disease; 1% to 2% with compensated liver disease)

Miscellaneous: Fever (14% with decompensated liver disease)

1% to 10%:

Central nervous system: Headache (2% to 4%), fatigue (1% to 3%), dizziness

Dermatologic: Skin rash

Endocrine & metabolic: Glycosuria (4%), hyperglycemia (2% to 3%), decreased serum bicarbonate (2% with decompensated liver disease)

Gastrointestinal: Increased serum lipase (7%), increased serum amylase (2% to 3%), abdominal pain (children and adolescents >1%), diarrhea (children and adolescents >1%; adults ≤1%), unpleasant taste (children and adolescents >1%), vomiting (children and adolescents >1%; adults <1%), dyspepsia (≤1%), nausea

Genitourinary: Hematuria (9%)

Hematologic & oncologic: Hepatic carcinoma (6% with decompensated liver disease)

Hepatic: Hepatic encephalopathy (10% with decompensated liver disease), increased serum bilirubin (2% to 3%), increased serum ALT (>10 x ULN and >2 x baseline: 2%; post-treatment flare [nucleoside-naive]: >10 x ULN and >2 x baseline: 2% to 8%)

Respiratory: Upper respiratory tract infection (10% with decompensated liver disease)

<1%, postmarketing, and/or case reports: Alopecia, anaphylactoid reaction, drowsiness, hepatomegaly, hypersensitivity, hypoalbuminemia, increased serum transaminases, insomnia, lactic acidosis, leukopenia, macular edema (Muqit, 2011), neutropenia,

pancreatitis, renal failure, thrombocytopenia, upper abdominal pain

General Dosage Range Dosage adjustment recommended in patients with renal impairment.

Oral: *Children ≥2 years and Adolescents:* Weight-based dosing: 0.15-1 mg once daily

Adults: 0.5-1 mg once daily

Mechanism of Action Entecavir is intracellularly phosphorylated to guanosine triphosphate which competes with natural substrates to effectively inhibit hepatitis B viral polymerase; enzyme inhibition blocks reverse transcriptase activity thereby reducing viral DNA synthesis.

Pharmacodynamics/Kinetics

Half-life Elimination Terminal: ~5-6 days; accumulation: ~24 hours

Time to Peak 0.5-1.5 hours

Pregnancy Risk Factor C

Pregnancy Considerations Teratogenic effects have been observed in animal studies. Information related to use in pregnancy is limited; use only if other options are inappropriate (DHHS [OI], 2013). Pregnant women taking entecavir should enroll in the pregnancy registry by calling 1-800-258-4263.

Enzalutamide (en za LOO ta mide)

Brand Names: US Xtandi

Brand Names: Canada Xtandi

Pharmacologic Category Antineoplastic Agent, Antiandrogen

Use Prostate cancer, metastatic: Treatment of metastatic, castration-resistant prostate cancer

Local Anesthetic/Vasoconstrictor Precautions No information available to require special precautions

Effects on Dental Treatment No significant effects or complications reported

Effects on Bleeding Although significant myelosuppression with associated altered hemostasis has been reported for many chemotherapeutic agents, myelosuppression is not common with enzalutamide and no specific precautions appear to necessary.

Adverse Reactions

>10%:

Cardiovascular: Peripheral edema (12% to 15%), hypertension (6% to 14%)

Central nervous system: Fatigue (≤51%), falling (5% to 13%), headache (11% to 12%), dizziness (10% to 11%)

Endocrine & metabolic: Hot flash (15% to 20%), weight loss (11% to 12%)

Gastrointestinal: Constipation (13% to 23%), diarrhea (12% to 22%), decreased appetite (19%), nausea (14%)

Hematologic & oncologic: Neutropenia (15%; grades 3/4: 1%)

Neuromuscular & skeletal: Weakness (≤51%), back pain (19% to 29%), arthralgia (21%), musculoskeletal pain (15% to 16%)

Respiratory: Upper respiratory tract infection (11% to 16%), dyspnea (11%)

1% to 10%:

Central nervous system: Myasthenia (10%), insomnia (8% to 9%), anxiety (7%), paresthesia (7%), cauda equina syndrome (≤7%), spinal cord compression (≤7%), altered mental status (4% to 6%), hypoesthesia (4%), hallucination (2%), restless leg syndrome (2%)

Dermatologic: Pruritus (4%), xeroderma (4%)

Endocrine & metabolic: Gynecomastia (3%)

Gastrointestinal: Dysgeusia (8%)

Genitourinary: Hematuria (7% to 9%), pollakiuria (5%)

Hematologic & oncologic: Thrombocytopenia (6%)

Hepatic: Increased serum bilirubin (3%)

Infection: Infection (≤6%; including sepsis)

Neuromuscular & skeletal: Bone fracture (4% to 9%), stiffness (3%)

Respiratory: Lower respiratory tract infection (8% to 9%), epistaxis (3%)

<1%, postmarketing, and/or case reports: Reversible posterior leukoencephalopathy syndrome, seizure

General Dosage Range Dosage adjustment recommended in patients on concomitant therapy or who develop toxicities.

Oral: *Adults:* 160 mg once daily

Mechanism of Action Enzalutamide is a pure androgen receptor signaling inhibitor; unlike other antiandrogen therapies, it has no known agonistic properties. It inhibits androgen receptor nuclear translocation, DNA binding, and coactivator mobilization, leading to cellular apoptosis and decreased prostate tumor volume.

Pharmacodynamics/Kinetics

Half-life Elimination Parent drug: 5.8 days (range: 2.8 to 10.2 days); N-desmethyl enzalutamide: 7.8 to 8.6 days

Time to Peak 1 hour (range: 0.5 to 3 hours)

Pregnancy Considerations Enzalutamide is contraindicated in pregnant women and is not indicated for use in women. Adverse effects were observed in animal reproduction studies. Enzalutamide is an androgen receptor inhibitor; based on the mechanism of action, fetal harm and potential loss of pregnancy would be expected. Male patients with female partners of reproductive potential should use effective contraception during treatment and for 3 months after the last enzalutamide dose and should use a condom if having intercourse with a pregnant woman.

EPHEDrine (Systemic) (e FED rin)

Brand Names: US Akovaz

Pharmacologic Category Alpha/Beta Agonist

Use Hypotension, anesthesia-induced: Treatment of anesthesia-induced hypotension

Note: The use of ephedrine for the treatment of acute bronchospasm, Stokes-Adams syndrome (ie, presyncope/syncope) with complete heart block, narcolepsy, depression, or myasthenia gravis has fallen out of favor given the availability of more effective agents for these conditions.

Local Anesthetic/Vasoconstrictor Precautions Use vasoconstrictor with caution since ephedrine may enhance cardiostimulation and vasopressor effects of sympathomimetics such as epinephrine

Effects on Dental Treatment Key adverse event(s) related to dental treatment: Xerostomia (normal salivary flow resumes upon discontinuation)

Effects on Bleeding No information available to require special precautions

Adverse Reactions Frequency not defined.

Cardiovascular: Angina pectoris, bradycardia, cardiac arrhythmia, hypertension, palpitations, pulse irregularity, tachycardia, ventricular ectopy, visceral vasoconstriction (renal)

Central nervous system: Anxiety, confusion, delirium, dizziness, hallucination, headache, insomnia, intracranial hemorrhage, nervousness, precordial pain, restlessness, tension, vertigo

Dermatologic: Diaphoresis, pallor

Gastrointestinal: Anorexia, nausea, vomiting
Genitourinary: Dysuria, oliguria, urinary retention (males with prostatism)
Neuromuscular & skeletal: Tremor, vesicle sphincter spasm, weakness
Respiratory: Dyspnea
Miscellaneous: Tachyphylaxis

General Dosage Range IV: *Adults:* 5 to 25 mg/dose as needed (maximum total dose: 50 mg)

Mechanism of Action Releases tissue stores of norepinephrine and thereby produces an alpha- and beta-adrenergic stimulation; longer-acting and less potent than epinephrine

Pharmacodynamics/Kinetics

Onset of Action IM: Within 10 to 20 minutes.

Duration of Action Pressor/cardiac effects: SubQ: 1 hour

Half-life Elimination Dependent upon urinary pH; Urine pH 5: ~3 hours; Urine pH 6.3: ~6 hours

Pregnancy Risk Factor C

Pregnancy Considerations Animal reproduction studies have not been conducted. Ephedrine crosses the placenta (Hughes, 1985). Ephedrine injection is used at delivery for the prevention and/or treatment of maternal hypotension associated with spinal anesthesia in women undergoing cesarean section (ASA, 2007). Serious postpartum hypertension and possibly stroke may occur if administered with oxytocic medications. Metabolic acidosis has been reported in neonates following maternal use of ephedrine; monitor.

Epinastine (ep i NAS teen)

Brand Names: US Elestat

Pharmacologic Category Histamine H_1 Antagonist; Histamine H_1 Antagonist, Second Generation

Use Treatment of allergic conjunctivitis

Local Anesthetic/Vasoconstrictor Precautions No information available to require special precautions

Effects on Dental Treatment No significant effects or complications reported

Effects on Bleeding No information available to require special precautions

Adverse Reactions

Frequency not always defined.

1% to 10%:

Central nervous system: Headache (1% to 3%)
Infection: Infection (10%; defined as cold symptoms and upper respiratory tract infection)
Ophthalmic: Burning sensation of eyes, eye pruritus, follicular conjunctivitis, ocular hyperemia
Respiratory: Cough (1% to 3%), pharyngitis (1% to 3%), rhinitis (1% to 3%), sinusitis (1% to 3%)

<1%, postmarketing, and/or case reports: Increased lacrimation

General Dosage Range Ophthalmic: *Children ≥2 years and Adults:* Instill 1 drop into each eye twice daily

Mechanism of Action Selective H_1-receptor antagonist; inhibits release of histamine from the mast cell; also has affinity for the H_2, $alpha_1$, $alpha_2$, and the 5-HT_2 receptors

Pharmacodynamics/Kinetics

Onset of Action 3-5 minutes

Duration of Action 8 hours

Half-life Elimination 12 hours

Pregnancy Risk Factor C

Pregnancy Considerations Teratogenic effects were not observed in animal studies. There are no adequate and well-controlled studies in pregnant women.

EPINEPHrine (Systemic) (ep i NEF rin)

Brand Names: US Adrenaclick; Adrenalin; Adyphren; Adyphren Amp; Adyphren Amp II; Adyphren II; Auvi-Q; EpiPen 2-Pak; EpiPen Jr 2-Pak; EPIsnap; EPY II [DSC]; EPY [DSC]

Brand Names: Canada Adrenalin; Allerject; Anapen; Anapen Junior; EpiPen; EpiPen Jr; Twinject

Generic Availability (US) May be product dependent

Pharmacologic Category Alpha/Beta Agonist

Dental Use Emergency drug for treatment of anaphylactic reactions; used as vasoconstrictor to prolong local anesthesia

Use

Hypersensitivity: Treatment of type I allergic reactions including anaphylactic reactions.

Hypotension/shock: Treatment of hypotension associated with septic shock in adults (increase mean arterial blood pressure).

Mydriasis during intraocular surgery: Induction and maintenance of mydriasis during intraocular surgery.

Local Anesthetic/Vasoconstrictor Precautions No information available to require special precautions

Effects on Dental Treatment Key adverse event(s) related to dental treatment: Xerostomia (normal salivary flow resumes upon discontinuation) and dry throat.

Effects on Bleeding No information available to require special precautions

Adverse Reactions Frequency not defined.

Cardiovascular: Angina pectoris, cardiac arrhythmia, cerebrovascular accident, chest pain, hypertension, ischemic heart disease, limb ischemia, localized blanching, myocardial infarction, palpitations, supraventricular tachycardia, tachyarrhythmia, tachycardia, vasoconstriction, ventricular arrhythmia, ventricular ectopy, ventricular fibrillation
Central nervous system: Anxiety, apprehension, disorientation, dizziness, drowsiness, exacerbation of Parkinson's disease, excitability, headache, memory impairment, nervousness, panic, paresthesia, psychomotor agitation, restlessness, tingling sensation
Dermatologic: Diaphoresis, gangrene of skin or other tissue (at injection site), pallor, piloerection, skin necrosis (with extravasation)
Endocrine & metabolic: Hyperglycemia, hypoglycemia, hypokalemia, increased serum glucose (transient), insulin resistance, lactic acidosis
Gastrointestinal: Nausea, vomiting
Hematologic & oncologic: Hemorrhage (CNS)
Local: Injection site tissue necrosis (including necrotizing fasciitis and myonecrosis)
Neuromuscular & skeletal: Tremor, weakness
Renal: Renal insufficiency
Respiratory: Dyspnea, pulmonary edema, rales

Dental Usual Dosage Hypersensitivity reaction: Self-administration following severe allergic reactions (eg, insect stings, food): **Note:** World Health Organization (WHO) and Anaphylaxis Canada recommend the availability of 1 dose for every 10 to 20 minutes of travel time to a medical emergency facility. More than 2 sequential doses should only be administered under direct medical supervision.

Children:

Adrenaclick: IM, SubQ:
Children 15 to 29 kg: 0.15 mg
Children ≥30 kg: 0.3 mg

Auvi-Q: IM, SubQ:
Children 15 to 29 kg: 0.15 mg; if anaphylactic symptoms persist, dose may be repeated

Children ≥30 kg: 0.3 mg; if anaphylactic symptoms persist, dose may be repeated

EpiPen Jr: IM, SubQ: Children 15 to 29 kg: 0.15 mg; if anaphylactic symptoms persist, dose may be repeated in 5 to 15 minutes using an additional EpiPen Jr

EpiPen: IM, SubQ: Children ≥30 kg: 0.3 mg; if anaphylactic symptoms persist, dose may be repeated in 5 to 15 minutes using an additional EpiPen

Twinject: IM SubQ:

Children 15 to 29 kg: 0.15 mg; if anaphylactic symptoms persist, dose may be repeated in 5 to 15 minutes using the same device after partial disassembly

Children ≥30 kg: 0.3 mg; if anaphylactic symptoms persist, dose may be repeated in 5 to 15 minutes using the same device after partial disassembly

Adults:

Adrenaclick: IM, SubQ: 0.3 mg

Auvi-Q: IM, SubQ: 0.3 mg; if anaphylactic symptoms persist, dose may be repeated

EpiPen: IM, SubQ: 0.3 mg; if anaphylactic symptoms persist, dose may be repeated in 5 to 15 minutes using an additional EpiPen

Twinject: IM, SubQ: 0.3 mg; if anaphylactic symptoms persist, dose may be repeated in 5 to 15 minutes using the same device after partial disassembly

Dosing

Adult & Geriatric

Note: As of May 1, 2016, ratio expressions of epinephrine concentrations are prohibited on drug labels. Ampules, vials, and syringes of epinephrine with ratio expressions may however remain in inventory until replaced by products with revised labeling. Therefore, the ratio expression of 1:1000 is equivalent to 1 mg/mL and 1:10,000 is equivalent to 0.1 mg/mL (ISMP 2015).

Acute severe asthma unresponsive to inhaled beta-agonist (off-label use): IM, SubQ: 0.01 mg/kg divided into 3 doses of approximately 0.3 to 0.5 mg every 20 minutes; the **1 mg/mL** concentration is recommended (AHA [Vanden Hoek 2010]; Cydulka 2016; Shah 2012).

Asystole/pulseless arrest, pulseless VT/VF (ACLS [Neumar 2010]):

IV, I.O.: 1 mg every 3 to 5 minutes until return of spontaneous circulation; if this approach fails, higher doses of epinephrine (up to 0.2 mg/kg) have been used for treatment of specific problems (eg, beta-blocker or calcium channel blocker overdose)

Note: High IV dose epinephrine (ie, >1 mg per dose) has not been shown to improve survival or neurological outcomes as compared to standard dose epinephrine and is not recommended (ACLS [Neumar, 2010], ACLS [Neumar 2015]).

Endotracheal: 2 to 2.5 mg every 3 to 5 minutes until IV/I.O. access established or return of spontaneous circulation; dilute in 5 to 10 mL NS or sterile water. **Note:** Absorption may be greater with sterile water (Naganobu 2000). May cause false-negative reading with exhaled CO_2 detectors; use second method to confirm tube placement if CO_2 is not detected (ACLS [Neumar 2010]).

Bradycardia (symptomatic; unresponsive to atropine or pacing): *IV infusion:* 2 to 10 mcg/minute **or** 0.1 to 0.5 mcg/kg/minute (7 to 35 mcg/minute in a 70 kg patient); titrate to desired effect (ACLS [Neumar 2010]; AHA [Peberdy 2010]).

Hypersensitivity reaction (eg, anaphylaxis): Note: SubQ administration results in slower absorption and is less reliable. IM administration in the anterolateral aspect of the middle third of the thigh is preferred in the setting of anaphylaxis (AHA [Vanden Hoek 2010]; WAO [Kemp 2008]).

IM (preferred), SubQ: 0.2 to 0.5 mg using the **1 mg/mL** solution every 5 to 15 minutes in the absence of clinical improvement (AAAAI [Lieberman 2015]; AHA [Vanden Hoek 2010]; WAO [Kemp 2008]).

IV:

Slow IV bolus: 0.1 mg using the **0.1 mg/mL** solution (further diluted in 10 mL of NS) administered over 5 to 10 minutes (Barach 1984)

Continuous infusion: May initiate with an infusion at 2 to 15 mcg/minute (with crystalloid administration) (AAAAI [Lieberman 2015]; AHA [Vanden Hoek 2010]; Brown 2004).

Note: In general, IV administration should only be done in patients who are unresponsive or profoundly hypotensive who have failed to respond to IV fluid replacement and several epinephrine injections (WAO [Kemp, 2008]). If the patient is in cardiopulmonary arrest, use of higher IV/IO push doses (ie, 1 mg every 3 to 5 minutes) should be employed or appropriate endotracheal doses administered if an advanced airway is in place (AAAAI [Lieberman 2015]; AHA [Neumar 2010]).

Self-administration following severe allergic reactions (eg, insect stings, food): **Note:** The World Health Organization (WHO) and Anaphylaxis Canada recommend the availability of one dose for every 10 to 20 minutes of travel time to a medical emergency facility. If anaphylactic symptoms persist after first dose, may repeat dose in 5 to 15 minutes (AHA [Vanden Hoek 2010]); more than 2 sequential doses should only be administered under direct medical supervision.

Adrenaclick: IM, SubQ: 0.3 mg; if anaphylactic symptoms persist, dose may be repeated using an additional Adrenaclick injector

Allerject [Canadian product]: IM: 0.3 mg; if anaphylactic symptoms persist, dose may be repeated using an additional Allerject injector

Auvi-Q: IM, SubQ: 0.3 mg; if anaphylactic symptoms persist, dose may be repeated

EpiPen: IM, SubQ: 0.3 mg; if anaphylactic symptoms persist, dose may be repeated using an additional EpiPen

Twinject [Canadian product]: IM, SubQ: 0.3 mg; if anaphylactic symptoms persist, dose may be repeated in 5 to 15 minutes using the same device after partial disassembly

Hypotension/septic shock:

Manufacturer's labeling: Septic shock: IV infusion: Initial: 0.05 to 2 mcg/kg/minute (3.5 to 140 mcg/minute in a 70 kg patient); titrate to desired mean arterial pressure (MAP). May adjust dose every 10 to 15 minutes by 0.05 to 0.2 mcg/kg/minute to achieve desired blood pressure goal. After hemodynamic stabilization, may wean incrementally every 30 minutes over 12 to 24 hours.

American Heart Association recommendation: Severe and fluid resistant (off-label dosing): IV infusion: Initial: 0.1 to 0.5 mcg/kg/minute (7 to 35 mcg/minute in a 70 kg patient); titrate to desired response (AHA [Peberdy 2010]).

Mydriasis during intraocular surgery, induction and maintenance: Intraocular: Must dilute 1 mg/mL solution to a concentration of 1 to 10 **mcg**/mL prior to intraocular use: May use as an irrigation solution as needed during the procedure or may administer intracamerally (ie, directly into the anterior chamber of the eye) with a bolus dose of 0.1 mL of a 2.5 to 10 **mcg**/mL dilution.

Pediatric

Note: As of May 1, 2016, ratio expressions of epinephrine concentrations are prohibited on drug labels. Ampules, vials, and syringes of epinephrine with ratio expressions may however remain in inventory until replaced by products with revised labeling. Therefore, the ratio expression of 1:1000 is equivalent to 1 mg/mL and 1:10,000 is equivalent to 0.1 mg/mL (ISMP 2015).

Asystole/pulseless arrest, pulseless VT/VF (after failed defibrillation attempts) (PALS [Kleinman 2010]): Infants, Children, and Adolescents:

IV, I.O.: 0.01 mg/kg (0.1 mL/kg of **0.1 mg/mL** solution) (maximum single dose: 1 mg) every 3 to 5 minutes until return of spontaneous circulation

Endotracheal: 0.1 mg/kg (0.1 mL/kg of **1 mg/mL** solution) (maximum single dose: 2.5 mg) every 3 to 5 minutes until IV/I.O. access established or return of spontaneous circulation. **Note:** Recent clinical studies suggest that lower epinephrine concentrations delivered by endotracheal administration may produce transient $beta_2$-adrenergic effects which may be detrimental (eg, hypotension, lower coronary artery perfusion pressure). IV or I.O. are the preferred methods of administration.

Bradycardia (symptomatic; unresponsive to atropine or pacing) (PALS [Kleinman 2010]): Infants, Children, and Adolescents:

IV, I.O.: 0.01 mg/kg (0.1 mL/kg of **0.1 mg/mL** solution) (maximum single dose: 1 mg) every 3 to 5 minutes as needed

Endotracheal: 0.1 mg/kg (0.1 mL/kg of **1 mg/mL** solution) (maximum single dose: 2.5 mg) every 3 to 5 minutes as needed until IV/I.O. access established. **Note:** Recent clinical studies suggest that lower epinephrine concentrations delivered by endotracheal administration may produce transient $beta_2$-adrenergic effects which may be detrimental (eg, hypotension, lower coronary artery perfusion pressure). IV or I.O. are the preferred methods of administration.

Cardiac output maintenance/stabilization, postresuscitation (PALS [Kleinman 2010]): Infants, Children, and Adolescents: Continuous IV/I.O. infusion: 0.1 to 1 mcg/kg/minute; doses <0.3 mcg/kg/minute generally produce beta-adrenergic effects and higher doses (>0.3 mcg/kg/minute) generally produce alpha-adrenergic vasoconstriction; titrate dosage to desired effect.

Hypersensitivity reaction (eg, anaphylaxis): Infants, Children, and Adolescents: **Note:** SubQ administration results in slower absorption and is less reliable. IM administration in the anterolateral aspect of the middle third of the thigh is preferred in the setting of anaphylaxis (AAAAI [Lieberman 2015]; Campbell 2014; Simons 2011).

IM (preferred), SubQ: 0.01 mg/kg (0.01 mL/kg of **1 mg/mL** solution) not to exceed 0.3 to 0.5 mg every 5 to 15 minutes (Hegenbarth 2008; Simons 2011; Simons 2015).

Self-administration following severe allergic reactions (eg, insect stings, food): **Note:** If anaphylactic symptoms persist after first dose, may repeat dose in 5 to 15 minutes (Simons 2011); more than 2 sequential doses should only be administered under direct medical supervision.

Adrenaclick: IM, SubQ:

Children 15 to 29 kg: 0.15 mg; if anaphylactic symptoms persist, dose may be repeated using an additional Adrenaclick injector

Children ≥30 kg: 0.3 mg; if anaphylactic symptoms persist, dose may be repeated using an additional Adrenaclick injector

Allerject [Canadian product]: IM:

Children 15 to 29 kg: 0.15 mg; if anaphylactic symptoms persist, dose may be repeated using an additional Allerject injector

Children ≥30 kg: 0.3 mg; if anaphylactic symptoms persist, dose may be repeated using an additional Allerject injector

Auvi-Q: IM, SubQ:

Children 15 to 29 kg: 0.15 mg; if anaphylactic symptoms persist, dose may be repeated

Children ≥30 kg: 0.3 mg; if anaphylactic symptoms persist, dose may be repeated

EpiPen Jr: IM, SubQ: Children 15 to 29 kg: 0.15 mg; if anaphylactic symptoms persist, dose may be repeated using an additional EpiPen Jr

EpiPen: IM, SubQ: Children ≥30 kg: 0.3 mg; if anaphylactic symptoms persist, dose may be repeated using an additional EpiPen

Twinject [Canadian product]: IM, SubQ:

Children 15 to 29 kg: 0.15 mg; if anaphylactic symptoms persist, dose may be repeated in 5 to 15 minutes using the same device after partial disassembly

Children ≥30 kg: 0.3 mg; if anaphylactic symptoms persist, dose may be repeated in 5 to 15 minutes using the same device after partial disassembly

Alternate auto-injector dose: IM (Sicherer 2007):

Children 10 to 25 kg: 0.15 mg

Children >25 kg: 0.3 mg

Hypotension/shock, fluid-resistant (off-label use): Continuous IV infusion: 0.1 to 1 mcg/kg/minute; doses up to 5 mcg/kg/minute may rarely be necessary (Hegenbarth 2008)

Mydriasis during intraocular surgery, induction and maintenance: Infants, Children, and Adolescents: Intraocular: Refer to adult dosing.

Renal Impairment There are no dosage adjustment provided in the manufacturer's labeling.

Hepatic Impairment There are no dosage adjustment provided in the manufacturer's labeling.

Mechanism of Action Stimulates alpha-, $beta_1$-, and $beta_2$-adrenergic receptors resulting in relaxation of smooth muscle of the bronchial tree, cardiac stimulation (increasing myocardial oxygen consumption), and dilation of skeletal muscle vasculature; small doses can cause vasodilation via $beta_2$-vascular receptors; large doses may produce constriction of skeletal and vascular smooth muscle

Contraindications

There are no absolute contraindications to the use of injectable epinephrine (including Adrenaclick, Auvi-Q, EpiPen, EpiPen Jr, Allerject [Canadian product], and Twinject [Canadian product]) in a life-threatening situation. Some products include the following contraindications: Hypersensitivity to sympathomimetic amines; general anesthesia with halogenated hydrocarbons (eg, halothane) or cyclopropane; narrow angle glaucoma; nonanaphylactic shock; in combination with local anesthesia of certain areas such as fingers, toes, and ears; use in situations where vasopressors may be contraindicated (eg, thyrotoxicosis, diabetes, in obstetrics when maternal blood pressure is in excess of 130/80 mm Hg and in hypertension and other cardiovascular disorders)

Injectable solution (Adrenalin, Epinephrine injection, USP): There are no contraindications listed in the manufacturer's labeling.

Warnings/Precautions Use with caution in elderly patients, patients with diabetes mellitus, cardiovascular diseases (eg, coronary artery disease, arrhythmias, cerebrovascular disease, heart disease hypertension), thyroid disease, pheochromocytoma, or Parkinson disease. May precipitate or aggravate angina pectoris or induce cardiac arrhythmias; use with caution especially in patients with cardiac disease or those receiving drugs that sensitize the myocardium. Due to peripheral constriction and cardiac stimulation, pulmonary edema may occur. Due to renal blood vessel constriction, decreased urine output may occur. In hypovolemic patients, correct blood volume depletion before administering any vasopressor. Some products contain sulfites as preservatives; the presence of sulfites in some products should not deter administration during a serious allergic or other emergency situation even if the patient is sulfite-sensitive. Potentially significant drug-drug interactions may exist, requiring dose or frequency adjustment, additional monitoring, and/or selection of alternative therapy.

Hypersensitivity reactions: Do not inject into the buttock; may not effectively treat anaphylaxis and has been associated with Clostridial infections (gas gangrene). Serious skin and soft tissue infections, including necrotizing fasciitis and myonecrosis caused by Clostridia (gas gangrene), have been reported rarely at the injection site. Cleansing skin with alcohol may reduce bacteria at the injection site, but alcohol cleansing does not kill *Clostridium* spores. Preferred injection site is anterolateral aspect of the thigh. Do not administer repeated injections at the same site (tissue necrosis may occur). Monitor for signs/symptoms of injection site infection. Lacerations, bent needles, and embedded needles have been reported in young children who are uncooperative during injection for hypersensitivity reaction. To minimize risk, hold the child's leg firmly in place and limit movement prior to and during injection.

IV administration: Rapid IV administration may cause death from cerebrovascular hemorrhage or cardiac arrhythmias. However, rapid IV administration during pulseless arrest is necessary. Vesicant; ensure proper needle or catheter placement prior to and during infusion; avoid extravasation. Accidental injection into digits, hands, or feet may result in local reactions, including injection site pallor, coldness and hypoesthesia or injury, resulting in bruising, bleeding, discoloration, erythema, or skeletal injury; patient should seek immediate medical attention if this occurs.

Intraocular administration: Must dilute 1 mg/mL solution to a concentration of 1 **mcg**/mL to 10 **mcg**/mL prior to intraocular use. When used undiluted, has been associated with corneal endothelial damage. Also, products containing chlorobutanol must not be used intraocularly (may be harmful to corneal endothelium).

Drug Interactions

Metabolism/Transport Effects **Substrate** of COMT

Avoid Concomitant Use

Avoid concomitant use of EPINEPHrine (Systemic) with any of the following: Blonanserin; Ergot Derivatives; Iobenguane I 123; Lurasidone

Increased Effect/Toxicity

EPINEPHrine (Systemic) may increase the levels/effects of: Doxofylline; Lurasidone; Sympathomimetics

The levels/effects of EPINEPHrine (Systemic) may be increased by: AtoMOXetine; Beta-Blockers; Cannabinoid-Containing Products; Cocaine; COMT Inhibitors; Ergot Derivatives; Hyaluronidase; Inhalational Anesthetics; Linezolid; MAO Inhibitors; Serotonin/Norepinephrine Reuptake Inhibitors; Tedizolid; Tricyclic Antidepressants

Decreased Effect

EPINEPHrine (Systemic) may decrease the levels/effects of: Antidiabetic Agents; Benzylpenicilloyl Polylysine; Iobenguane I 123

The levels/effects of EPINEPHrine (Systemic) may be decreased by: Alpha1-Blockers; Benperidol; Blonanserin; CloZAPine; Promethazine; Spironolactone

Pharmacodynamics/Kinetics

Onset of Action Bronchodilation: SubQ: ~5 to 10 minutes

Half-life Elimination IV: <5 minutes

Pregnancy Risk Factor C

Pregnancy Considerations Adverse events have been observed in animal reproduction studies. Epinephrine crosses the placenta (Sandler 1964). Uterine vasoconstriction, decreased uterine blood flow, and fetal anoxia may occur. Epinephrine is recommended for the treatment of anaphylaxis in pregnant women. Specific dosing is not available; use with caution and monitor hemodynamic response (Hepner 2013). Medications used for the treatment of cardiac arrest in pregnancy are the same as in the non-pregnant woman. Doses and indications should follow current Advanced Cardiovascular Life Support guidelines. Appropriate medications should not be withheld due to concerns of fetal teratogenicity (Jeejeebhoy [AHA] 2015). Although epinephrine injection may be used for asthma exacerbations in pregnancy, systemic therapy has not been proven to be better than use of preferred inhaled agents (NAEPP 2005).

Breastfeeding Considerations It is not known if epinephrine is excreted in breast milk. The manufacturer recommends that caution be exercised when administering epinephrine to nursing women.

Dosage Forms

Device, Injection:

EpiPen 2-Pak: 0.3 mg/0.3 mL (2 ea)

EpiPen Jr 2-Pak: 0.15 mg/0.3 mL (2 ea)

Kit, Injection:

Adyphren: 1 mg/mL

Adyphren Amp: 1 mg/mL

Adyphren Amp II: 1 mg/mL

Adyphren II: 1 mg/mL

EPIsnap: 1 mg/mL

Solution, Injection:

Adrenalin: 1 mg/mL (1 mL); 30 mg/30 mL (30 mL)

Generic: 0.1 mg/mL (10 mL); 1 mg/mL (1 mL, 30 mL)

Solution, Intravenous [preservative free]:

Generic: 1 mg/mL (1 mL)

Solution Auto-injector, Injection:

Adrenaclick: 0.15 mg/0.15 mL (2 ea); 0.3 mg/0.3 mL (2 ea)

Auvi-Q: 0.15 mg/0.15 mL (2 ea); 0.3 mg/0.3 mL (2 ea)

Generic: 0.15 mg/0.3 mL (2 ea); 0.15 mg/0.15 mL (1 ea, 2 ea); 0.3 mg/0.3 mL (1 ea, 2 ea)

Solution Prefilled Syringe, Injection:

Generic: 0.1 mg/mL (10 mL)

Solution Prefilled Syringe, Intravenous [preservative free]:
Generic: 100 mg/10 mL (10 mL)

EPINEPHrine (Oral Inhalation) (ep i NEF rin)

Brand Names: US Asthmanefrin Refill [OTC]; Asthmanefrin Starter Kit [OTC] [DSC]; Micronefrin [OTC] [DSC]; S2 [OTC]

Brand Names: Canada S2

Generic Availability (US) No

Pharmacologic Category Alpha/Beta Agonist

Dental Use Emergency drug for treatment of anaphylactic reactions; used as vasoconstrictor to prolong local anesthesia

Use OTC labeling: Treatment of bronchospasm associated with bronchial asthma

Local Anesthetic/Vasoconstrictor Precautions No information available to require special precautions

Effects on Dental Treatment Key adverse event(s) related to dental treatment: Xerostomia (normal salivary flow resumes upon discontinuation) and dry throat.

Effects on Bleeding No information available to require special precautions

Adverse Reactions There are no adverse reactions listed in the manufacturer's labeling.

Dosing

Adult & Geriatric

Bronchospasm, relief of mild asthma symptoms: Nebulization: Racemic epinephrine (2.25% solution): OTC labeling: Hand-bulb nebulizer: Add 0.5 mL to nebulizer; 1 to 3 inhalations, may repeat dose after at least 3 hours if needed. Do not exceed 12 inhalations in 24 hours.

Pediatric

Bronchospasm, relief of mild asthma symptoms: Children ≥4 years and Adolescents: Nebulization: Racemic epinephrine (2.25% solution): OTC labeling: Hand-bulb nebulizer: Add 0.5 mL to nebulizer; 1 to 3 inhalations; may repeat dose after at least 3 hours if needed. Do not exceed 12 inhalations in 24 hours. **Note:** Not recommended for routine management and treatment of asthma (GINA 2015; NAEPP 2007)

Croup (laryngotracheobronchitis), airway edema (off-label use): Infants, Children, and Adolescents: Nebulization: **Note:** Typically relief of symptoms occurs within 10 to 30 minutes and lasts 2 to 3 hours; patients should be observed for rapid symptom recurrence and possible repeat treatment.

Racemic epinephrine (2.25% solution): 0.05 to 0.1 mL/kg (maximum dose: 0.5 mL) diluted in 2 mL NS, may repeat dose every 20 minutes; others have reported use of 0.5 mL as a fixed dose for all patients; use lower end of dosing range for younger infants (Hegenbarth 2008; Rosekrans 1998; Rotta 2003; Wright 2002)

L-epinephrine (using parenteral 1 mg/mL solution): 0.5 mL/kg of **1 mg/mL** solution (maximum dose: 5 mL) diluted in NS, may repeat dose every 20 minutes; **Note:** Racemic epinephrine 10 mg = 5 mg L-epinephrine (Hegenbarth 2008)

Renal Impairment There are no dosage adjustment provided in manufacturer's labeling.

Hepatic Impairment There are no dosage adjustment provided in manufacturer's labeling.

Mechanism of Action Stimulates alpha-, $beta_1$-, and $beta_2$-adrenergic receptors resulting in relaxation of smooth muscle of the bronchial tree, cardiac stimulation (increasing myocardial oxygen consumption), and dilation of skeletal muscle vasculature; small doses can cause vasodilation via $beta_2$-vascular receptors; large doses may produce constriction of skeletal and vascular smooth muscle

Contraindications Oral inhalation (OTC labeling): Concurrent use or within 2 weeks of MAO inhibitors

Warnings/Precautions Use with caution in patients with diabetes mellitus, cardiovascular diseases (eg, arrhythmias, coronary artery disease, hypertension), thyroid disease, cerebrovascular disease, in patients with prostate enlargement or urinary retention, or in patients with seizure disorders.

Self medication (OTC use): Prior to self-medication, patients should contact healthcare provider. The product should only be used in persons with a diagnosis of asthma. If symptoms are not relieved in 20 minutes or become worse do not continue to use the product - seek immediate medical assistance. The product should not be used more frequently or at higher doses than recommended unless directed by a health care provider. This product should not be used in patients who have required hospitalization for asthma or if a patient is taking prescription medication for asthma. Use with caution in patients with prostate enlargement or urinary retention. Do not use if you have taken a MAO inhibitor (certain drugs used for depression, Parkinson disease, or other conditions) within 2 weeks.

Drug Interactions

Metabolism/Transport Effects Substrate of COMT

Avoid Concomitant Use

Avoid concomitant use of EPINEPHrine (Oral Inhalation) with any of the following: Ergot Derivatives; Iobenguane I 123; MAO Inhibitors

Increased Effect/Toxicity

EPINEPHrine (Oral Inhalation) may increase the levels/effects of: Doxofylline; Sympathomimetics

The levels/effects of EPINEPHrine (Oral Inhalation) may be increased by: AtoMOXetine; Beta-Blockers; Cannabinoid-Containing Products; Cocaine; COMT Inhibitors; Ergot Derivatives; Inhalational Anesthetics; MAO Inhibitors; Serotonin/Norepinephrine Reuptake Inhibitors; Tricyclic Antidepressants

Decreased Effect

EPINEPHrine (Oral Inhalation) may decrease the levels/effects of: Iobenguane I 123

The levels/effects of EPINEPHrine (Oral Inhalation) may be decreased by: Alpha1-Blockers; Promethazine; Spironolactone

Pharmacodynamics/Kinetics

Onset of Action Bronchodilation: Inhalation: ~1 minute

Pregnancy Considerations Epinephrine crosses the placenta following injection (Sandler 1964). Uncontrolled asthma is associated with adverse events on pregnancy (increased risk of perinatal mortality, preeclampsia, preterm birth, low birth weight infants). The occasional use of inhaled epinephrine when needed for asthma exacerbations is not expected to cause adverse fetal events. However, when treatment of asthma is needed during pregnancy, other agents are preferred (NAEPP 2005).

Dosage Forms

Nebulization Solution, Inhalation:
Asthmanefrin Refill [OTC]: 2.25% (1 ea)

Nebulization Solution, Inhalation [preservative free]:
S2 [OTC]: 2.25% (1 ea)

Epinephrine (Racemic) and Aluminum Potassium Sulfate

(ep i NEF rin, ra SEE mik and a LOO mi num poe TASS ee um SUL fate)

Related Information

EPINEPHrine (Systemic) *on page 580*

Brand Names: US Van R Gingibraid®

Generic Availability (US) No

Pharmacologic Category Adrenergic Agonist Agent; Alpha/Beta Agonist; Astringent; Vasoconstrictor

Dental Use Gingival retraction

Use Gingival retraction

Local Anesthetic/Vasoconstrictor Precautions No information available to require special precautions

Effects on Dental Treatment Key adverse event(s) related to dental treatment: Tissue retraction around base of the tooth (therapeutic effect).

Effects on Bleeding No information available to require special precautions

Adverse Reactions No data reported.

Dental Usual Dosage Gingival retraction: Adults: Pass the impregnated cord around the neck of the tooth and place into gingival sulcus; normal tissue moisture, water, or gingival retraction solutions activate impregnated cord. Limit use to one quadrant of the mouth at a time; recommended use is for 3-8 minutes in the mouth.

Dosing

Adult & Geriatric Gingival retraction: Pass the impregnated cord around the neck of the tooth and place into gingival sulcus; normal tissue moisture, water, or gingival retraction solutions activate impregnated cord. Limit use to one quadrant of the mouth at a time; recommended use is for 3-8 minutes in the mouth.

Mechanism of Action Epinephrine stimulates $alpha_1$ adrenergic receptors to cause vasoconstriction in blood vessels in gingiva; aluminum potassium sulfate, precipitates tissue and blood proteins

Contraindications Hypersensitivity to epinephrine or any component of the formulation; cardiovascular disease, hyperthyroidism, or diabetes; do not apply to areas of heavy or deep bleeding or over exposed bone

Warnings/Precautions Caution should be exercised whenever using gingival retraction cords with epinephrine since it delivers vasoconstrictor doses of racemic epinephrine to patients; the general medical history should be thoroughly evaluated before using in any patient

Drug Interactions

Metabolism/Transport Effects None known.

Avoid Concomitant Use There are no known interactions where it is recommended to avoid concomitant use.

Increased Effect/Toxicity

The levels/effects of Epinephrine (Racemic) and Aluminum Potassium Sulfate may be increased by: MAO Inhibitors

Decreased Effect

The levels/effects of Epinephrine (Racemic) and Aluminum Potassium Sulfate may be decreased by: Promethazine

Dosage Forms

Yarn, saturated in solution of racemic epinephrine 8% and aluminum potassium sulfate 7% (Van R Gingibraid®):

Type "0e": 0.20 ± 0.10 mg epinephrine/inch; Type "1e": 0.40 ± 0.20 mg epinephrine/inch; Type "2e": 0.60 ± 0.20 mg epinephrine/inch

EpiRUBicin (ep i ROO bi sin)

Brand Names: US Ellence

Brand Names: Canada Ellence; Epirubicin for Injection; Epirubicin Hydrochloride Injection; Pharmorubicin

Pharmacologic Category Antineoplastic Agent, Anthracycline; Antineoplastic Agent, Topoisomerase II Inhibitor

Use Breast cancer, adjuvant treatment: Adjuvant therapy component for primary breast cancer in patients with evidence of axillary node involvement following tumor resection

Local Anesthetic/Vasoconstrictor Precautions No information available to require special precautions

Effects on Dental Treatment Key adverse event(s) related to dental treatment: Mucositis

Effects on Bleeding Causes severe myelosuppression, including severe thrombocytopenia (grades 3/4: <5%) and anemia. In patients who are under active treatment with this agent, medical consult is suggested.

Adverse Reactions Frequency not always defined. Percentages reported as part of combination chemotherapy regimens.

Cardiovascular: Decreased left ventricular ejection fraction (asymptomatic; delayed: 1% to 2%), cardiac failure (≤2%), atrioventricular block, bradycardia, bundle branch block, cardiac arrhythmia, cardiomyopathy, ECG abnormality, myocarditis, nonspecific ST or T wave changes on ECG, sinus tachycardia, tachyarrhythmia, thromboembolism, ventricular premature contractions, ventricular tachycardia

Central nervous system: Lethargy (1% to 46%)

Dermatologic: Alopecia (70% to 96%), skin rash (1% to 9%), skin changes (1% to 5%)

Endocrine & metabolic: Amenorrhea (69% to 72%), hot flash (5% to 39%)

Gastrointestinal: Nausea and vomiting (83% to 92%; grades 3/4: 22% to 25%), mucositis (9% to 59%; grades 3/4: ≤9%), diarrhea (7% to 25%), anorexia (2% to 3%), abdominal pain, esophagitis, neutropenic enterocolitis, stomatitis, toxic megacolon

Genitourinary: Premature menopause

Hematologic & oncologic: Neutropenia (54% to 80%; grades 3/4: 11% to 67%; nadir: 10 to 14 days; recovery: by day 21), leukopenia (50% to 80%; grades 3/4: 2% to 59%), anemia (13% to 72%; grades 3/4: ≤6%), thrombocytopenia (5% to 49%; grades 3/4: ≤5%), febrile neutropenia (grades 3/4: ≤6%), acute lymphocytic leukemia, acute myelocytic leukemia, myelodysplastic syndrome

Hepatic: Ascites, hepatomegaly, increased serum transaminases

Hypersensitivity: Hypersensitivity reaction

Infection: Infection (15% to 22%; grades 3/4: ≤2%)

Local: Injection site reaction (3% to 20%; grades 3/4: <1%)

Ophthalmic: Conjunctivitis (1% to 15%)

Respiratory: Dyspnea, pulmonary edema

Miscellaneous: Fever (1% to 5%)

<1%, postmarketing, case reports: Anaphylaxis, arterial embolism, burning sensation of gastrointestinal tract,

chills, dehydration, erythema, flushing, gastrointestinal erosion, gastrointestinal hemorrhage, gastrointestinal pain, gastrointestinal ulcer, hyperuricemia, nail hyperpigmentation, oral mucosa hyperpigmentation, phlebitis, pneumonia, pulmonary embolism, radiation recall phenomenon, red urine discoloration, sepsis, shock, skin hyperpigmentation, skin photosensitivity, thrombophlebitis, urticaria

General Dosage Range Dosage adjustment recommended in patients with hepatic or renal impairment or who develop toxicities

IV: *Adults:* 100 mg/m^2 on day 1 every 3 weeks **or** 60 mg/m^2 on days 1 and 8 every 4 weeks

Mechanism of Action Epirubicin is an anthracycline antineoplastic agent; known to inhibit DNA and RNA synthesis by steric obstruction after intercalating between DNA base pairs; active throughout entire cell cycle. Intercalation triggers DNA cleavage by topoisomerase II, resulting in cytocidal activity. Also inhibits DNA helicase, and generates cytotoxic free radicals.

Pharmacodynamics/Kinetics

Half-life Elimination Triphasic; Mean terminal: 33 hours

Pregnancy Risk Factor D

Pregnancy Considerations Adverse events were observed in animal reproduction studies. Women of childbearing potential should be advised to use effective contraception and avoid becoming pregnant during treatment. Men undergoing treatment should use effective contraception. Epirubicin may cause irreversible amenorrhea in premenopausal women.

Limited information is available from a retrospective study of women who received epirubicin (in combination with cyclophosphamide or weekly as a single-agent) during the second or third (prior to week 35) trimester for the treatment of pregnancy-associated breast cancer (Ring 2005) and from a study of women who received epirubicin (weekly as a single-agent) at gestational weeks 16 through 30 for the treatment of pregnancy-associated breast cancer (Peccatori 2009). Some pharmacokinetic properties of epirubicin may be altered in pregnant women (van Hasselt 2014). The European Society for Medical Oncology (ESMO) has published guidelines for diagnosis, treatment, and follow-up of cancer during pregnancy (Peccatori 2013); the guidelines recommend referral to a facility with expertise in cancer during pregnancy and encourage a multidisciplinary team (obstetrician, neonatologist, oncology team). If chemotherapy is indicated, it should not be administered in the first trimester, but may begin in the second trimester. There should be a 3-week time period between the last chemotherapy dose and anticipated delivery, and chemotherapy should not be administered beyond week 33 of gestation.

A pregnancy registry is available for all cancers diagnosed during pregnancy at Cooper Health (877-635-4499).

Eplerenone (e PLER en one)

Related Information

Cardiovascular Diseases *on page 1752*

Brand Names: US Inspra

Brand Names: Canada Inspra

Pharmacologic Category Antihypertensive; Diuretic, Potassium-Sparing; Mineralocorticoid (Aldosterone) Receptor Antagonists

Use

Heart failure post-myocardial infarction (MI): Treatment of heart failure (HF) (LVEF ≤40%) following acute MI

Hypertension: Management of hypertension (monotherapy or in combination with other antihypertensive agents).

Canadian labeling: Additional use (not in US labeling): **Heart failure:** Treatment of NYHA class II chronic heart failure (HF) with left ventricular systolic dysfunction

Guideline recommendations:

Heart failure: The ACCF/AHA 2013 heart failure guidelines recommend the use of aldosterone antagonists, along with other guideline directed medical therapies, to reduce morbidity and mortality in patients with an LVEF ≤40% following acute MI who develop symptoms of HF or have a history of diabetes mellitus (Yancy 2013).

Hypertension: According to the Eighth Joint National Committee (JNC 8) guidelines, aldosterone antagonists are not recommended for the initial treatment of hypertension (James 2013).

STEMI/NSTE-ACS: The 2013 ACCF/AHA guidelines for the management of ST-elevation myocardial infarction (STEMI) and the 2014 ACC/AHA guidelines for the management of non-ST-Elevation Acute Coronary Syndromes (NSTE-ACS) recommend an aldosterone antagonist be given to post-MI patients (without significant renal dysfunction) who are already on an ACE inhibitor and beta-blocker, who have an LVEF ≤40% and either symptomatic HF or diabetes mellitus (ACC/AHA [Amsterdam 2014]); ACCF/AHA [O'Gara 2013]).

Local Anesthetic/Vasoconstrictor Precautions No information available to require special precautions

Effects on Dental Treatment No significant effects or complications reported

Effects on Bleeding No information available to require special precautions

Adverse Reactions

>10%: Endocrine & Metabolic: Hyperkalemia ([cardiac failure, post-myocardial infarction: >5.5 mEq/L: 16%; ≥6 mEq/L: 6%], [hypertension, >5.5 mEq/L: at dose of 400 mg: 9%; dose ≤200 mg: ≤1%]), hypertriglyceridemia (1% to 15%; dose-related)

1% to 10%:

Central nervous system: Dizziness (3%), fatigue (2%)

Endocrine & metabolic: Hyponatremia (2%; dose-related), albuminuria (1%), gynecomastia (≤1%), hypercholesterolemia (≤1%)

Gastrointestinal: Diarrhea (2%), abdominal pain (1%)

Genitourinary: Abnormal vaginal hemorrhage (≤2%), mastalgia (males: ≤1%)

Renal: Increased serum creatinine (cardiac failure, post-myocardial infarction: 6%)

Respiratory: Cough (2%), flu-like symptoms (2%)

<1%, postmarketing, and/or case reports: Angioedema, increased blood urea nitrogen, increased liver enzymes, increased uric acid, skin rash

General Dosage Range Dosage adjustment recommended in patients on concomitant therapy or based on potassium concentrations

Oral: *Adults:* Initial: 25 to 50 mg once daily; Maintenance: 25 to 50 mg once or twice daily (maximum dose: 100 mg/day)

Mechanism of Action Aldosterone, a mineralocorticoid, increases blood pressure primarily by inducing sodium and water retention. Overexpression of aldosterone is thought to contribute to myocardial fibrosis (especially following myocardial infarction) and vascular fibrosis. Mineralocorticoid receptors are located in the kidney, heart, blood vessels, and brain. Eplerenone selectively blocks mineralocorticoid receptors reducing blood pressure in a dose-dependent manner and appears to prevent myocardial and vascular fibrosis.

Pharmacodynamics/Kinetics

Half-life Elimination ~3 to 6 hours

Time to Peak Plasma: ~1.5 to 2 hours; may take up to 4 weeks for full antihypertensive effect

Pregnancy Risk Factor B

Pregnancy Considerations Adverse events have been observed in some animal reproduction studies. Information related to eplerenone use in pregnancy is limited (Cabassi, 2012; Morton, 2011). The use of mineralocorticoid receptor antagonists is not recommended to treat chronic uncomplicated hypertension in pregnant women and should generally be avoided in women of reproductive potential (ACOG, 2013).

Epoetin Alfa (e POE e tin AL fa)

Brand Names: US Epogen; Procrit

Brand Names: Canada Eprex

Pharmacologic Category Colony Stimulating Factor; Erythropoiesis-Stimulating Agent (ESA); Hematopoietic Agent

Use

Anemia: Treatment of anemia due to concurrent myelosuppressive chemotherapy in patients with cancer (nonmyeloid malignancies) receiving chemotherapy (palliative intent) for a planned minimum of 2 additional months of chemotherapy; treatment of anemia due to chronic kidney disease (including patients on dialysis and not on dialysis) to decrease the need for RBC transfusion; treatment of anemia associated with HIV (zidovudine) therapy when endogenous erythropoietin levels ≤500 mUnits/mL; reduction of allogeneic RBC transfusion for elective, noncardiac, nonvascular surgery when perioperative hemoglobin is >10 to ≤13 g/dL and there is a high risk for blood loss

Limitations of use: Epoetin alfa has not been shown to improve quality of life, fatigue, or patient well-being. Epoetin alfa is **not** indicated for use under the following conditions:

- Cancer patients receiving hormonal therapy, therapeutic biologic products, or radiation therapy unless also receiving concurrent myelosuppressive chemotherapy
- Cancer patients receiving myelosuppressive chemotherapy when the expected outcome is curative
- Surgery patients who are willing to donate autologous blood
- Surgery patients undergoing cardiac or vascular surgery
- As a substitute for RBC transfusion in patients requiring immediate correction of anemia

Local Anesthetic/Vasoconstrictor Precautions No information available to require special precautions

Effects on Dental Treatment No significant effects or complications reported

Effects on Bleeding Although ESAs have been associated with thromboembolic events, there is no information available to require special precautions for dental procedures.

Adverse Reactions

>10%:

Cardiovascular: Hypertension (3% to 28%)

Central nervous system: Headache (5% to 18%)

Dermatologic: Pruritus (12% to 21%), skin rash (2% to 19%)

Gastrointestinal: Nausea (35% to 56%), vomiting (12% to 28%)

Local: Injection site reaction (7% to 13%)

Neuromuscular & skeletal: Arthralgia (10% to 16%)

Respiratory: Cough (4% to 26%)

Miscellaneous: Fever (10% to 42%)

1% to 10%:

Cardiovascular: Deep vein thrombosis, edema, pulmonary embolism, thrombosis

Central nervous system: Chills, depression, dizziness, insomnia

Dermatologic: Urticaria

Endocrine & metabolic: Hyperglycemia, hypokalemia, weight loss

Gastrointestinal: Dysphagia, stomatitis

Hematologic & oncologic: Leukopenia

Neuromuscular & skeletal: Muscle spasm, myalgia, ostealgia

Respiratory: Respiratory congestion, upper respiratory tract infection

Miscellaneous: Vascular access complications (clotting)

<1%, postmarketing, and/or case reports: Anaphylaxis, angioedema, antibody development (neutralizing), bronchospasm, cerebrovascular accident, erythema, hypersensitivity reaction, hypertensive encephalopathy, myocardial infarction, porphyria, pure red cell aplasia, retinal thrombosis (arterial), seizure, tachycardia, temporal thrombosis, thrombophlebitis, thrombosis (microvascular), transient ischemic attacks, tumor growth, venous thrombosis

General Dosage Range IV, SubQ: Children and Adults: Dosage varies greatly depending on indication

Mechanism of Action Induces erythropoiesis by stimulating the division and differentiation of committed erythroid progenitor cells; induces the release of reticulocytes from the bone marrow into the bloodstream, where they mature to erythrocytes. There is a dose response relationship with this effect. This results in an increase in reticulocyte counts followed by a rise in hematocrit and hemoglobin levels.

Pharmacodynamics/Kinetics

Onset of Action Several days; Peak effect: Hemoglobin level: 2 to 6 weeks

Half-life Elimination

Neonates: With high doses, nonlinear kinetics have been observed (Wu, 2012)

Anemia of prematurity:

PMA <32 week (weight: 800 ± 206 grams): IV: 8.1 ± 2.7 hours, SubQ: 7.1 ± 4.1 hours (Brown 1993)

PMA ≥32 weeks (weight range: 1330 to 1740 g): SubQ: Median: 7.9 hours (range: 5.6 to 19.4 hours) (Krishnan 1996)

Neuroprotective/hypoxic ischemia encephalopathy (HIE) (Wu, 2012): ≥36 weeks GA; IV:

250 units/kg: 7.6 ± 6.9 hours

500 units/kg: 7.2 ± 1.9 hours

1,000 units/kg: 15 ± 4.5 hours

2,500 units/kg: 18.7 ± 4.7 hours

Infants, Children, and Adolescents: Chronic kidney disease: IV: 4 to 13 hours

Adults: Cancer: SubQ: 16 to 67 hours; Chronic kidney disease: IV: 4 to 13 hours

Time to Peak Serum: Pediatric patients >1 month and Adults: Chronic kidney disease: SubQ: 5 to 24 hours

Pregnancy Risk Factor C

Pregnancy Considerations Adverse events were observed in animal reproduction studies. In vitro studies suggest that recombinant erythropoietin does not cross the human placenta (Reisenberger 1997). Polyhydramnios and intrauterine growth retardation have been reported with use in women with chronic kidney disease (adverse effects also associated with maternal disease). Hypospadias and pectus excavatum have been reported with first trimester exposure (case report).

Recombinant erythropoietin alfa has been evaluated as adjunctive treatment for severe pregnancy associated iron deficiency anemia (Breymann 2001; Krafft 2009) and has been used in pregnant women with iron-deficiency anemia associated with chronic kidney disease (CKD) (Furaz-Czerpak 2012; Josephson 2007).

Amenorrheic premenopausal women should be cautioned that menstruation may resume following treatment with recombinant erythropoietin (Furaz-Czerpak 2012). Multidose formulations containing benzyl alcohol are contraindicated for use in pregnant women; if treatment during pregnancy is needed, single dose preparations should be used.

Women who become pregnant during treatment with epoetin alfa are encouraged to enroll in Amgen's Pregnancy Surveillance Program (1-800-772-6436).

Prescribing and Access Restrictions As a requirement of the REMS program, access to this medication is restricted. Healthcare providers and hospitals must be enrolled in the ESA APPRISE (Assisting Providers and Cancer Patients with Risk Information for the Safe use of ESAs) Oncology Program (866-284-8089; http://www.esa-apprise.com) to prescribe or dispense ESAs (ie, epoetin alfa, darbepoetin alfa) to patients with cancer.

Epoprostenol (e poe PROST en ole)

Brand Names: US Flolan; Veletri

Brand Names: Canada Caripul; Flolan

Pharmacologic Category Prostacyclin; Prostaglandin; Vasodilator

Use Pulmonary arterial hypertension: Treatment of pulmonary arterial hypertension (PAH) (WHO Group I) in patients with NYHA Class III or IV symptoms to improve exercise capacity. **Note:** According to treatment guidelines from the Fifth World Symposium on Pulmonary Hypertension (WSPH) and the American College of Chest Physicians (ACCP), continuous IV epoprostenol is recommended as first-line therapy in PAH patients with WHO-FC IV symptoms (ACCP [Taichman 2014]; WSPH [Gailè 2013]).

Local Anesthetic/Vasoconstrictor Precautions No information available to require special precautions

Effects on Dental Treatment No significant effects or complications reported. Epoprostenol is an inhibitor of platelet aggregation and may enhance the risk of bleeding with other antiplatelet agents (such as aspirin and/or NSAIDs).

Effects on Bleeding Epoprostenol is a potent inhibitor of platelet aggregation and increases the risk of hemorrhagic complications. A medical consult is suggested.

Adverse Reactions

Note: Adverse events reported during dose initiation and escalation include flushing (58%), headache (49%), nausea/vomiting (32%), hypotension (16%), anxiety/nervousness/agitation (11%), chest pain (11%); dizziness, abdominal pain, bradycardia, musculoskeletal pain, dyspnea, back pain, diaphoresis, dyspepsia, hypoesthesia/paresthesia, and tachycardia are also reported. Although some adverse reactions may be related to the underlying disease state, abdominal pain, anxiety/nervousness/agitation, arthralgia, bleeding, bradycardia, diarrhea, diaphoresis, flu-like syndrome, flushing, headache, hypotension, jaw pain, nausea, pain, pulmonary edema, rash, tachycardia, thrombocytopenia, and vomiting are clearly contributed to epoprostenol. The following adverse events have been reported during chronic administration for idiopathic or heritable PAH:

>10%:

Cardiovascular: Tachycardia (35% to 43%), flushing (23% to 42%), hypotension (13%)

Central nervous system: Dizziness (83%), headache (46% to 83%), chills (25%), fever (25%), flu-like syndrome (25%), sepsis (25%), anxiety (21%), nervousness (21%), tremor (21%), agitation (11%)

Dermatologic: Dermal ulcer (39%), eczema (25%), skin rash (25%), urticaria (25%)

Gastrointestinal: Nausea (≤67%), vomiting (≤67%), anorexia (66%), diarrhea (37% to 50%)

Local: Injection site reactions: Infection (18%), pain (11%)

Neuromuscular & skeletal: Arthralgia (≤84%), neck pain (≤84%), pain (≤84%), jaw pain (54% to 75%), myalgia (44%), musculoskeletal pain (35%), hyperesthesia (≤12%), hypoesthesia (≤12%), paresthesia (≤12%)

<1%, postmarketing, and/or case reports: Abdominal pain, anemia, ascites, bradycardia, diaphoresis, dyspnea, fatigue, hemorrhage, hepatic failure, hypersplenism, hyperthyroidism, pallor, pancytopenia, pulmonary edema, pulmonary embolism, splenomegaly, thrombocytopenia

General Dosage Range IV: *Adults:* Initial: 1 to 2 ng/kg/minute; increase dose in increments of 1 to 2 ng/kg/minute every 15 minutes until response

Mechanism of Action Epoprostenol is also known as prostacyclin and PGI_2. It is a strong vasodilator of all vascular beds. In addition, it is a potent endogenous inhibitor of platelet aggregation. The reduction in platelet aggregation results from epoprostenol's activation of intracellular adenylate cyclase and the resultant increase in cyclic adenosine monophosphate concentrations within the platelets. Additionally, it is capable of decreasing thrombogenesis and platelet clumping in the lungs by inhibiting platelet aggregation.

Pharmacodynamics/Kinetics

Half-life Elimination ~6 minutes

Pregnancy Risk Factor B

Pregnancy Considerations Adverse events have not been observed in animal reproduction studies. Women with pulmonary arterial hypertension (PAH) are encouraged to avoid pregnancy (McLaughlin 2009; Taichman 2014).

Prescribing and Access Restrictions Orders for epoprostenol are distributed by two sources in the United States. Information on orders or reimbursement assistance may be obtained from either Accredo Health, Inc (1-866-344-4874) or CVS Caremark (1-877-242-2738).

Eprosartan (ep roe SAR tan)

Related Information

Cardiovascular Diseases *on page 1752*

Brand Names: US Teveten

Brand Names: Canada Teveten

Pharmacologic Category Angiotensin II Receptor Blocker; Antihypertensive

Use

Hypertension: Treatment of hypertension; may be used alone or in combination with other antihypertensives

Guideline recommendations:

Hypertension: The 2014 guideline for the management of high blood pressure in adults (Eighth Joint National Committee [JNC 8; James, 2013]) recommends initiation of pharmacologic treatment to lower blood pressure for the following patients:

- Patients ≥60 years of age with systolic blood pressure (SBP) ≥150 mm Hg or diastolic blood pressure (DBP) ≥90 mm Hg. Goal of therapy is SBP <150 mm Hg and DBP <90 mm Hg.
- Patients <60 years of age with SBP ≥140 mm Hg or DBP ≥90 mm Hg. Goal of therapy is SBP <140 mm Hg and DBP <90 mm Hg.
- Patients ≥18 years of age with diabetes and SBP ≥140 mm Hg or DBP ≥90 mm Hg. Goal of therapy is SBP <140 mm Hg and DBP <90 mm Hg.
- Patients ≥18 years of age with chronic kidney disease (CKD) and SBP ≥140 mm Hg or DBP ≥90 mm Hg. Goal of therapy is SBP <140 mm Hg and DBP <90 mm Hg.

Chronic kidney disease (CKD) and hypertension: Regardless of race or diabetes status, the use of an ACE inhibitor (ACEI) or angiotensin receptor blocker (ARB) as initial therapy is recommended to improve kidney outcomes. In the general nonblack population (without CKD), including those with diabetes, initial antihypertensive treatment should consist of a thiazide-type diuretic, calcium channel blocker, ACEI, or ARB. In the general black population (without CKD), including those with diabetes, initial antihypertensive treatment should consist of a thiazide-type diuretic or a calcium channel blocker instead of an ACEI or ARB.

Coronary artery disease (CAD) and hypertension: The American Heart Association, American College of Cardiology and American Society of Hypertension (AHA/ACC/ASH) 2015 scientific statement for the treatment of hypertension in patients with CAD recommends the use of an ACE inhibitor (or an ARB) as part of a regimen in patients with hypertension and chronic stable angina if there is prior MI, LV systolic dysfunction, diabetes mellitus, or CKD. A BP target of <140/90 mm Hg is reasonable for the secondary prevention of cardiovascular events. A lower target BP (<130/80 mm Hg) may be appropriate in some individuals with CAD, previous MI, stroke or transient ischemic attack, or CAD risk equivalents (AHA/ACC/ASH [Rosendorff 2015]).

Local Anesthetic/Vasoconstrictor Precautions No information available to require special precautions

Effects on Dental Treatment Key adverse event(s) related to dental treatment: Patients may experience orthostatic hypotension as they stand up after treatment; especially if lying in dental chair for extended periods of time. Use caution with sudden changes in position during and after dental treatment.

Effects on Bleeding No information available to require special precautions

Adverse Reactions

1% to 10%:

Central nervous system: Fatigue (2%), depression (1%)

Endocrine & metabolic: Hypertriglyceridemia (1%)

Gastrointestinal: Abdominal pain (2%)

Genitourinary: Urinary tract infection (1%)

Infection: Viral infection (2%)

Respiratory: Upper respiratory tract infection (8%), cough (4%), pharyngitis (4%), rhinitis (4%)

Miscellaneous: Accidental injury (2%)

<1%, postmarketing, and/or case reports: Albuminuria, anemia, angina pectoris, anorexia, anxiety, arthritis, arthropathy, asthma, ataxia, atrial fibrillation, back pain, bradycardia, conjunctivitis, constipation, cystitis, diabetes mellitus, diaphoresis, drowsiness, ECG abnormality, eczema, epistaxis, esophagitis, ethanol sensitization (intolerance), exacerbation of arthritis, extrasystoles, facial edema, fever, flatulence, flu-like symptoms, flushing sensation, furunculosis, gastritis, gastroenteritis, gingivitis, glycosuria, gout, hematuria, herpes simplex infection, hypercholesterolemia, hyperglycemia, hyperkalemia, hypokalemia, hyponatremia, hypotension, increased blood urea nitrogen, increased creatine phosphokinase, increased serum creatinine, increased serum transaminases, insomnia, leg cramps, leukopenia, maculopapular rash, malaise, migraine, nausea, nephrolithiasis, nervousness, neuritis, neutropenia, orthostatic hypotension, otitis externa, otitis media, pain, palpitations, paresthesia, periodontitis, peripheral edema, peripheral ischemia, polyuria, pruritus, purpura, rigors, skeletal pain, skin rash, substernal pain, tachycardia, tendonitis, thrombocytopenia, tinnitus, toothache, tremor, urinary frequency, urinary incontinence, vertigo, visual disturbance, vomiting, weakness, xerophthalmia, xerostomia

General Dosage Range Oral: *Adults:* Initial: 600 mg once daily; Maintenance: 400 to 800 mg daily in 1 to 2 divided doses

Mechanism of Action Angiotensin II is formed from angiotensin I in a reaction catalyzed by angiotensin-converting enzyme (ACE, kininase II). Angiotensin II is the principal pressor agent of the renin-angiotensin system, with effects that include vasoconstriction, stimulation of synthesis and release of aldosterone, cardiac stimulation, and renal reabsorption of sodium. Eprosartan blocks the vasoconstrictor and aldosterone-secreting effects of angiotensin II by selectively blocking the binding of angiotensin II to the AT1 receptor in many tissues, such as vascular smooth muscle and the adrenal gland. Its action is therefore independent of the pathways for angiotensin II synthesis. Blockade of the renin-angiotensin system with ACE inhibitors, which inhibit the biosynthesis of angiotensin II from angiotensin I, is widely used in the treatment of hypertension. ACE inhibitors also inhibit the degradation of bradykinin, a reaction also catalyzed by ACE. Because eprosartan does not inhibit ACE (kininase II), it does not affect the response to bradykinin. Whether this difference has clinical relevance is not yet known. Eprosartan does not bind to or block other hormone receptors or ion channels known to be important in cardiovascular regulation.

Pharmacodynamics/Kinetics

Half-life Elimination Terminal: 5 to 9 hours (Bottorff, 1999)

Time to Peak Serum: Fasting: 1 to 2 hours

Pregnancy Risk Factor D

Pregnancy Considerations [US Boxed Warning]: Drugs that act on the renin-angiotensin system can cause injury and death to the developing fetus. Discontinue as soon as possible once pregnancy is detected. The use of drugs which act on the renin-angiotensin system are associated with oligohydramnios. Oligohydramnios, due to decreased fetal renal function, may lead to fetal lung hypoplasia and skeletal malformations. Use is also associated with anuria, hypotension, renal failure, skull hypoplasia, and death in the fetus/neonate. The exposed fetus should be monitored for fetal growth, amniotic fluid volume, and organ formation. Infants exposed *in utero* should be monitored for hyperkalemia, hypotension, and oliguria (exchange transfusions or dialysis may be needed). These adverse events are generally associated with maternal use in the second and third trimesters.

Untreated chronic maternal hypertension is also associated with adverse events in the fetus, infant, and mother. The use of angiotensin II receptor blockers is not recommended to treat chronic uncomplicated hypertension in pregnant women and should generally be avoided in women of reproductive potential (ACOG, 2013).

Product Availability Teveten 400 mg tablets have been discontinued in the US more than 1 year.

Eptifibatide (ep TIF i ba tide)

Related Information

Cardiovascular Diseases *on page 1752*

Brand Names: US Integrilin

Brand Names: Canada Eptifibatide Injection; Integrilin

Pharmacologic Category Antiplatelet Agent, Glycoprotein IIb/IIIa Inhibitor

Use

Acute coronary syndrome: Treatment of patients with acute coronary syndrome (unstable angina/non-ST-segment elevation myocardial infarction [UA/NSTEMI]), including patients who are to be managed medically and those undergoing percutaneous coronary intervention (PCI)

Percutaneous coronary intervention: Treatment of patients undergoing PCI, including those undergoing intracoronary stenting.

Local Anesthetic/Vasoconstrictor Precautions No information available to require special precautions

Effects on Dental Treatment Key adverse event(s) related to dental treatment: Bleeding; patients weighing <70 kg may have an increased risk of major bleeding. See Effects on Bleeding.

Effects on Bleeding Bleeding is the most common complication. Eptifibatide inhibits platelet aggregation. Vascular and other trauma should be avoided. It is unlikely that dental work would be performed in patients undergoing treatment for acute coronary syndrome.

Adverse Reactions Frequency not always defined. Bleeding is the major drug-related adverse effect. Access site is often primary source of bleeding complications. Incidence of bleeding is also related to heparin intensity. Patients weighing <70 kg may have an increased risk of major bleeding.

>10%: Hematologic: & oncologic: Hemorrhage (major: 1% to 11%; minor: 3% to 14%; transfusion required: 2% to 13%)

1% to 10%:

Cardiovascular: Hypotension (≤7%)

Hematologic & oncologic: Thrombocytopenia (1% to 3%; includes acute profound thrombocytopenia, immune-mediated thrombocytopenia)

Local: Injection site reaction

<1%, postmarketing and/or case reports: Anaphylaxis, cerebrovascular accident, gastrointestinal hemorrhage, intracranial hemorrhage, pulmonary hemorrhage

General Dosage Range Dosage adjustment recommended in patients with renal impairment

IV: *Adults:* Bolus: 180 mcg/kg (maximum: 22.6 mg), repeat once for PCI; Infusion: 2 mcg/kg/minute (maximum: 15 mg/hour)

Mechanism of Action Eptifibatide is a cyclic heptapeptide which blocks the platelet glycoprotein IIb/IIIa receptor, the binding site for fibrinogen, von Willebrand factor, and other ligands. Inhibition of binding at this final common receptor reversibly blocks platelet aggregation and prevents thrombosis.

Pharmacodynamics/Kinetics

Onset of Action Immediate after initial bolus (>80% inhibition of ADP-induced aggregation achieved 5 minutes after bolus dose); maximal effect achieved within 1 hour (Gilchrist, 2001; Tardiff, 2001)

Duration of Action Platelet function restored ~4 to 8 hours following discontinuation (Tardiff, 2001)

Half-life Elimination ~2.5 hours

Pregnancy Risk Factor B

Pregnancy Considerations Adverse events have not been observed in animal reproduction studies.

Ergocalciferol (er goe kal SIF e role)

Brand Names: US Calcidol [OTC]; Calciferol [OTC]; Drisdol [DSC]; Drisdol [OTC] [DSC]

Brand Names: Canada D-Forte; Erdol

Pharmacologic Category Vitamin D Analog

Use

Dietary supplement: For use as a vitamin D supplement.

Familial hypophosphatemia: Treatment of familial hypophosphatemia.

Hypoparathyroidism: Treatment of hypoparathyroidism.

Rickets: Treatment of refractory rickets, also known as vitamin D-resistant rickets.

Local Anesthetic/Vasoconstrictor Precautions No information available to require special precautions

Effects on Dental Treatment Key adverse event(s) related to dental treatment: Metallic taste and xerostomia (normal salivary flow resumes upon discontinuation).

Effects on Bleeding No information available to require special precautions

Adverse Reactions Frequency not defined: Endocrine & metabolic: Hypervitaminosis D

General Dosage Range Oral:

Infants 0 to 12 months: Adequate intake: 400 units/day

Children, Adolescents, and Adults ≤70 years: RDA: 600 units/day

Children, Adolescents, and Adults: Hypoparathyroidism: 1.25 to 5 mg/day (50,000 to 200,000 units); Vitamin D-*resistant* rickets: 12,000 to 500,000 units/day

Elderly >70 years: RDA: 800 units/day

Mechanism of Action Ergocalciferol (vitamin D_2) is a provitamin. The active metabolite, 1,25-dihydroxyvitamin D (calcitriol), stimulates calcium and phosphate absorption from the small intestine, promotes secretion of calcium from bone to blood; promotes renal tubule phosphate resorption.

Pharmacodynamics/Kinetics

Onset of Action 10 to 24 hours; Maximum effect: ~1 month following daily doses

Half-life Elimination Circulating: 25(OH)D: 2 to 3 weeks; 1,25-dihydroxyvitamin D ~4 hours (Holick, 2011)

Pregnancy Risk Factor C

Pregnancy Considerations

Adverse events were observed in some animal reproduction studies. The ergocalciferol (vitamin D_2) metabolite, 25(OH)D, crosses the placenta; maternal serum concentrations correlate with fetal concentrations at birth (Misra, 2008; Wagner, 2008).

Vitamin D deficiency in a pregnant woman may lead to a vitamin D deficiency in the neonate (Misra, 2008; Wagner, 2008). Serum 25(OH)D concentrations should be measured in pregnant women considered to be at increased risk of deficiency (ACOG, 2011). The amount of vitamin D contained in prenatal vitamins may not be adequate to treat a deficiency during pregnancy; although larger doses may be needed, current guidelines recommend a total of 1000 to 2000 units/day until more safety data is available (ACOG, 2011; Holick, 2011). In women not at risk for deficiency, doses larger than the RDA should be avoided during pregnancy (ACOG, 2011).

Ergoloid Mesylates (ER goe loid MES i lates)

Brand Names: Canada Hydergine

Pharmacologic Category Ergot Derivative

Use

Mental capacity decline: Treatment of signs and symptoms of an idiopathic decline in mental capacity.

Note: Individuals who do respond come from groups of patients who would be considered clinically to suffer from some ill-defined process related to aging or to have some underlying dementing condition (ie, primary progressive dementia, Alzheimer dementia, senile onset, multi-Infarct dementia).

Local Anesthetic/Vasoconstrictor Precautions Although ergoloid mesylates are derivatives of the natural ergot alkaloids, they lack any vasoconstricting effects; there is no information available to require special precautions with vasoconstrictor

Effects on Dental Treatment Key adverse event(s) related to dental treatment: Patients may experience orthostatic hypotension as they stand up after treatment; especially if lying in dental chair for extended periods of time. Use caution with sudden changes in position during and after dental treatment.

Effects on Bleeding No information available to require special precautions

Adverse Reactions Frequency not defined. Adverse effects are minimal.

Cardiovascular: Bradycardia, flushing, orthostatic hypotension

Dermatologic: Skin rash

Gastrointestinal: Gastrointestinal distress (sublingual administration), nausea (sublingual administration; transient)

Local: Local irritation (sublingual administration)

Ophthalmic: Blurred vision

Respiratory: Nasal congestion

General Dosage Range Oral: *Adults:* 1 mg 3 times daily

Mechanism of Action Ergoloid mesylates do not have the vasoconstrictor effects of the natural ergot alkaloids; exact mechanism in dementia is unknown; originally classed as peripheral and cerebral vasodilator, now considered a "metabolic enhancer"; there is no specific evidence that clearly establishes the mechanism by which ergoloid mesylate preparations produce mental effects, nor is there conclusive evidence that the drug particularly affects cerebral arteriosclerosis or cerebrovascular insufficiency.

Pharmacodynamics/Kinetics

Half-life Elimination Serum: ~2.6 to 5.1 hours

Time to Peak Serum: 1.5 to 3 hours

Ergonovine (er goe NOE veen)

Brand Names: Canada Ergonovine Maleate Injection

Pharmacologic Category Ergot Derivative; Oxytocic Agent

Use Note: Not approved in the US

Postpartum or postabortion hemorrhage: Prevention and treatment of postpartum and postabortion hemorrhage caused by uterine atony

Local Anesthetic/Vasoconstrictor Precautions Use vasoconstrictor with caution in patients taking ergonovine; this ergot alkaloid derivative causes constriction of peripheral blood vessels

Effects on Dental Treatment No significant effects or complications reported

Effects on Bleeding Rare but significant events related to hemorrhage (cerebral hemorrhage, subarachnoid hemorrhage, and stroke) have occurred following injection of some agents in this class. However, there is no information related to special precautions associated with bleeding related to dental procedures.

Adverse Reactions Frequency not defined.

Cardiovascular: Angina pectoris (transient), bradycardia, hypertension, myocardial infarction, palpitations, shock, thrombophlebitis

Central nervous system: Dizziness, hallucination, headache, vertigo

Dermatologic: Diaphoresis

Endocrine & metabolic: Water intoxication

Gastrointestinal: Abdominal pain, diarrhea, nausea, vomiting

Genitourinary: Hematuria

Hypersensitivity: Hypersensitivity reaction

Respiratory: Dyspnea

Miscellaneous: Ergot alkaloids toxicity

General Dosage Range IM, IV: *Adults:* 0.2 mg, may repeat every 2 to 4 hours if needed, up to maximum of 5 total doses

Mechanism of Action Similar smooth muscle actions as seen with ergotamine; however, it affects primarily uterine smooth muscles producing sustained contractions and thereby shortens the third stage of labor. Has slight alpha-adrenergic blocking activity and produces less vasoconstriction than ergotamine.

Pharmacodynamics/Kinetics

Onset of Action IM: 2 to 5 minutes; IV: Immediate

Duration of Action IM: Uterine effect: ≥3 hours; IV: ~45 minute

Pregnancy Considerations Ergonovine is used in the third stage of labor for the prevention or treatment of postpartum hemorrhage and should not be used prior to delivery of the placenta. Prior to administration, the placenta should be delivered and the possibility of twin pregnancy ruled out. Administration causes hyperstimulation of the uterus and may cause uterine tetany, decreased uteroplacental blood flow, uterine rupture, cervical and perineal lacerations, amniotic fluid embolism, and possible trauma to the infant.

Product Availability Not available in the US

Ergotamine (er GOT a meen)

Related Information

Dentin Hypersensitivity, Acid Erosion, High Caries Index, Management of Alveolar Osteitis, and Xerostomia *on page 1857*

Brand Names: US Ergomar

Pharmacologic Category Antimigraine Agent; Ergot Derivative

Use Vascular headache: Abort or prevent vascular headaches, such as migraine, migraine variants, or so-called "histaminic cephalalgia"

Local Anesthetic/Vasoconstrictor Precautions Use vasoconstrictor with caution in patients taking ergotamine; this ergot alkaloid derivative causes constriction of peripheral blood vessels

Effects on Dental Treatment No significant effects or complications reported

Effects on Bleeding No information available to require special precautions

Adverse Reactions Frequency not defined.

Cardiovascular: Bradycardia, cold extremities, ECG changes, edema, hypertension, ischemia, pulselessness, tachycardia, valvular sclerosis, vasospasm

Central nervous system: Numbness, paresthesia, precordial distress, precordial pain, vertigo

Dermatologic: Gangrene of skin or other tissue, pruritus

Gastrointestinal: Nausea, vomiting

Genitourinary: Retroperitoneal fibrosis

Neuromuscular & skeletal: Myalgia, weakness

Respiratory: Cyanosis, pleuropulmonary fibrosis

General Dosage Range Sublingual: *Adults:* 2 mg (1 tablet) under tongue at first sign of migraine, then 2 mg every 30 minutes if needed (maximum dose: 6 mg per 24 hours, 10 mg per week)

Mechanism of Action Has partial agonist and/or antagonist activity against tryptaminergic, dopaminergic and alpha-adrenergic receptors depending upon their site; is a highly active uterine stimulant; it causes constriction of peripheral and cranial blood vessels and produces depression of central vasomotor centers

Pharmacodynamics/Kinetics

Half-life Elimination 2-2.5 hours (Perrin 1985)

Time to Peak Serum: Oral: 2 hours (Perrin 1985)

Pregnancy Risk Factor X

Pregnancy Considerations May cause prolonged constriction of the uterine vessels and/or increased myometrial tone leading to reduced placental blood flow. This has contributed to fetal growth retardation in animals.

Ergotamine and Caffeine

(er GOT a meen & KAF een)

Related Information

Caffeine *on page 276*

Ergotamine *on page 592*

Brand Names: US Cafergot; Migergot

Brand Names: Canada Cafergor

Pharmacologic Category Antimigraine Agent; Central Nervous System Stimulant; Ergot Derivative

Use Vascular headache: Prevention or treatment of vascular headaches, such as migraine, migraine variants, or so-called "histaminic cephalalgia"

Local Anesthetic/Vasoconstrictor Precautions Use vasoconstrictor with caution in patients taking ergotamine; this ergot alkaloid derivative causes constriction of peripheral blood vessels

Effects on Dental Treatment Key adverse event(s) related to dental treatment: Ergotamine and caffeine cause tachycardia, increases in blood pressure, and palpitations. Consider monitoring blood pressure prior to using local anesthetic with a vasoconstrictor. Symptoms associated with bruxism have been observed in some patients.

Effects on Bleeding No information available to require special precautions

Adverse Reactions Frequency not defined.

Cardiovascular: Bradycardia, cold extremities, ECG changes, edema, hypertension, ischemia, pulselessness, tachycardia, valvular sclerosis, vasospasm

Central nervous system: Numbness, paresthesia, precordial distress, precordial pain, vertigo

Dermatologic: Gangrene of skin or other tissue, pruritus

Gastrointestinal: Anal fissure (with overuse of suppository), nausea, rectal ulcer (with overuse of suppository), vomiting

Genitourinary: Retroperitoneal fibrosis

Neuromuscular & skeletal: Myalgia, weakness

Respiratory: Cyanosis, pleuropulmonary fibrosis

General Dosage Range

Use is contraindicated in renal and/or hepatic impairment.

Oral: *Adults:* Ergotamine 2 mg and caffeine 200 mg (2 tablets) at onset of attack; then ergotamine 1 mg and caffeine 100 mg (1 tablet) every 30 minutes as needed (maximum dose: Ergotamine 6 mg and caffeine 600 mg [6 tablets] per attack; do not exceed ergotamine 10 mg and caffeine 1,000 mg [10 tablets] per week)

Rectal: *Adults:* Ergotamine 2 mg and caffeine 100 mg (1 suppository) at first sign of an attack; follow with second dose after 1 hour, if needed (maximum dose: Ergotamine 4 mg and caffeine 200 mg [2 suppositories] per attack; do not exceed ergotamine 10 mg and caffeine 500 mg [5 suppositories] per week)

Mechanism of Action Has partial agonist and/or antagonist activity against tryptaminergic, dopaminergic and alpha-adrenergic receptors depending upon their site; is a highly active uterine stimulant; it causes constriction of peripheral and cranial blood vessels and produces depression of central vasomotor centers

Pharmacodynamics/Kinetics

Half-life Elimination 2 to 2.5 hours (Perrin, 1985)

Time to Peak Serum: Ergotamine: 2 hours (Perrin, 1985)

Pregnancy Risk Factor X

Pregnancy Considerations Animal reproduction studies have not been conducted with this combination. Ergotamine and caffeine both cross the placenta and may cause prolonged constriction of the uterine vessels and/or increased myometrial tone leading to reduced placental blood flow. Use is contraindicated in pregnant women.

EriBULin (er i BUE lin)

Brand Names: US Halaven

Brand Names: Canada Halaven

Pharmacologic Category Antineoplastic Agent, Antimicrotubular

Use

Breast cancer, metastatic: Treatment of metastatic breast cancer in patients who have received at least 2 prior chemotherapy regimens for the treatment of metastatic disease (prior treatment should have included an anthracycline and a taxane in either the adjuvant or metastatic setting)

Liposarcoma, unresectable or metastatic: Treatment of unresectable or metastatic liposarcoma in patients who have received a prior anthracycline-containing regimen

Local Anesthetic/Vasoconstrictor Precautions No information available to require special precautions

Effects on Dental Treatment Key adverse event(s) related to dental treatment: Xerostomia (normal salivary flow resumes upon discontinuation), stomatitis, mucosal inflammation, or taste alteration.

Effects on Bleeding Anemia is a primary adverse effect. A medical consult is suggested.

Adverse Reactions

>10%:

Cardiovascular: Peripheral edema (≥5% to 12%)

Central nervous system: Fatigue (≤62%), peripheral neuropathy (29% to 35%; grades 3/4: 3% to 8%), headache (18% to 19%)

Dermatologic: Alopecia (35% to 45%)

Endocrine & metabolic: Hypokalemia (≥5% to 30%), hypocalcemia (28%), weight loss (21%), hypophosphatemia (20%)

Gastrointestinal: Nausea (35% to 41%), constipation (25% to 32%), abdominal pain (≥5% to 29%), anorexia (20%), decreased appetite (19%), vomiting (18% to 19%), diarrhea (17% to 18%), stomatitis (≥5% to 14%)

Genitourinary: Urinary tract infection (10% to 11%)

Hematologic & oncologic: Neutropenia (63% to 82%; grade 4: 29% grades 3/4: 12% to 57%; nadir: 13 days; recovery: 8 days), anemia (58% to 70%; grades 3/4: 2% to 4%)

Hepatic: Increased serum ALT (18% to 43%), increased serum AST (36%)

Neuromuscular & skeletal: Weakness (≤62%), arthralgia (≤22%), myalgia (≤22%), back pain (16%), ostealgia (12%), limb pain (11%)

Respiratory: Cough (14% to 18%), dyspnea (16%)

Miscellaneous: Fever (21% to 28%)

1% to 10%:

Cardiovascular: Hypotension (≥5% to <10%)

Central nervous system: Anxiety (≥5% to <10%), depression (≥5% to <10%), dizziness (≥5% to <10%), insomnia (≥5% to <10%), myasthenia (≥5% to <10%)

Dermatologic: Skin rash (≥5% to <10%)

Endocrine & metabolic: Hyperglycemia (≥5% to <10%)

Gastrointestinal: Dysgeusia (≥5% to <10%), dyspepsia (≥5% to <10%), xerostomia (≥5% to <10%), mucosal inflammation (9%)

Hematologic & oncologic: Thrombocytopenia (≥5% to <10%; grades ≥3: 1%), febrile neutropenia (≤5%)

Neuromuscular & skeletal: Muscle spasm (≥5% to <10%), musculoskeletal pain (≥5% to <10%),

Ophthalmic: Increased lacrimation (≥5% to <10%)

Respiratory: Oropharyngeal pain (≥5% to <10%), upper respiratory tract infection (≥5% to <10%)

<1%, postmarketing, and/or case reports: Dehydration, drug-induced hypersensitivity, hepatotoxicity, hypomagnesemia, interstitial pulmonary disease, lymphocytopenia, neutropenic sepsis, pancreatitis, pneumonia, prolonged Q-T interval on ECG, pruritus, sepsis, Stevens-Johnson syndrome, toxic epidermal necrolysis

General Dosage Range Dosage adjustment recommended in patients with renal or hepatic impairment or who develop toxicities

IV: *Adults:* Eribulin mesylate: 1.4 mg/m^2 days 1 and 8 every 3 weeks

Mechanism of Action Eribulin is a non-taxane microtubule inhibitor which is a halichondrin B analog. It inhibits the growth phase of the microtubule by inhibiting formation of mitotic spindles causing mitotic blockage and arresting the cell cycle at the G_2/M phase; suppresses microtubule polymerization yet does not affect depolymerization.

Pharmacodynamics/Kinetics

Half-life Elimination ~40 hours

Pregnancy Considerations Adverse effects were observed in animal reproduction studies. Based on its mechanism of action, eribulin would be expected to cause fetal harm if administered during pregnancy. Women of reproductive potential should use effective contraception to avoid pregnancy during eribulin treatment and for at least 2 weeks following the last eribulin dose; males with female partners of reproductive potential should use effective contraception during eribulin treatment and for 3.5 months following the last dose. The Canadian labeling recommends effective contraception during and for at least 3 months after treatment in women of reproductive potential.

Erlotinib (er LOE tye nib)

Brand Names: US Tarceva

Brand Names: Canada Tarceva; Teva-Erlotinib

Pharmacologic Category Antineoplastic Agent, Epidermal Growth Factor Receptor (EGFR) Inhibitor; Antineoplastic Agent, Tyrosine Kinase Inhibitor

Use

Non-small cell lung cancer, metastatic: Treatment of metastatic non-small cell lung cancer (NSCLC) in tumors with epidermal growth factor receptor (EGFR) exon 19 deletions or exon 21 (L858R) substitution mutations as detected by an approved test either as first-line, maintenance, or as second or greater line treatment after progression following at least 1 prior chemotherapy regimen.

Limitations of use: Use in combination with platinum-based chemotherapy is not recommended. Safety and efficacy of treatment for metastatic NSCLC with EGFR mutations other than exon 19 deletion or exon 21 (L858R) substitution have not been established.

Pancreatic cancer: First-line treatment of locally advanced, unresectable, or metastatic pancreatic cancer (in combination with gemcitabine)

Local Anesthetic/Vasoconstrictor Precautions No information available to require special precautions

Effects on Dental Treatment Key adverse event(s) related to dental treatment: Xerostomia (normal salivary flow resumes upon discontinuation), mucositis, abnormal taste, and stomatitis.

Effects on Bleeding In treatment of pancreatic carcinoma, has been noted to cause microangiopathic hemolytic anemia with thrombocytopenia

Adverse Reactions

Adverse reactions reported with monotherapy:

>10%:

Cardiovascular: Chest pain (≤18%)

Central nervous system: Fatigue (9% to 52%)

Dermatologic: Skin rash (49% to 85%; grade 3: 5% to 13%; grade 4: <1%; median onset: 8 days), xeroderma (4% to 21%), pruritus (7% to 16%), paronychia (4% to 16%), alopecia (14% to 15%), acne vulgaris (6% to 12%)

Gastrointestinal: Diarrhea (20% to 62%; grade 3: 2% to 6%; grade 4: <1%; median onset: 12 days), anorexia (9% to 52%), nausea (23% to 33%), decreased appetite (≤28%), vomiting (13% to 23%), mucositis (≤18%), stomatitis (11% to 17%), abdominal pain (3% to 11%), constipation (≤8%)

Genitourinary: Urinary tract infection (≤4%)

Hematologic & oncologic: Anemia (≤11%; grade 4: 1%)

Infection: Increased susceptibility to infection (4% to 24%)

Miscellaneous: Fever (≤11%)

Neuromuscular & skeletal: Weakness (≤53%), back pain (19%), arthralgia (≤13%), musculoskeletal pain (11%)

Ophthalmic: Conjunctivitis (12% to 18%), keratoconjunctivitis sicca (12%)

Respiratory: Cough (33% to 48%), dyspnea (41% to 45%; grades 3/4: 8% to 28%)

1% to 10%:

Cardiovascular: Peripheral edema (≤5%)

Central nervous system: Pain (≤9%), headache (≤7%), anxiety (≤5%), dizziness (≤4%), insomnia (≤4%), neurotoxicity (≤4%), paresthesia (≤4%), voice disorder (≤4%)

Dermatologic: Folliculitis (≤8%), nail disease (≤7%), exfoliative dermatitis (5%), hypertrichosis (5%), skin fissure (5%), acneiform eruption (4% to 5%), erythema (≤5%), dermatitis (4%), erythematous rash (≤4%), palmar-plantar erythrodysesthesia (≤4%), bullous dermatitis

Endocrine & metabolic: Weight loss (4% to 5%)

Gastrointestinal: Dyspepsia (≤5%), xerostomia (≤3%), taste disorder (≤1%)

Hematologic & oncologic: Lymphocytopenia (≤4%; grade 3: 1%), leukopenia (≤3%), thrombocytopenia (≤1%)

Hepatic: Hyperbilirubinemia (7%; grade 3: ≤1%), increased serum ALT (grade 2: 2% to 4%; grade 3: 1% to 3%), increased gamma-glutamyl transferase (≤4%), hepatic failure (≤1%)

Neuromuscular & skeletal: Muscle spasm (≤4%), musculoskeletal chest pain (≤4%), ostealgia (≤4%)

Otic: Tinnitus (≤1%)

Renal: Increased serum creatinine (≤1%), renal failure (≤1%),

Respiratory: Nasopharyngitis (≤7%), epistaxis (≤4%), pulmonary embolism (≤4%), respiratory tract infection (≤4%), pneumonitis (3%), pulmonary fibrosis (3%)

<1%: Interstitial pulmonary disease

Adverse reactions reported with combination (erlotinib plus gemcitabine) therapy:

>10%:

Cardiovascular: Edema (37%), thrombosis (grades 3/4: 11%)

Central nervous system: Fatigue (73% to 79%), depression (19%), dizziness (15%), headache (15%), anxiety (13%)

Dermatologic: Skin rash (70%), alopecia (14%)

Gastrointestinal: Nausea (60%), anorexia (52%), diarrhea (48%), abdominal pain (46%), vomiting (42%), weight loss (39%), stomatitis (22%), dyspepsia (17%), flatulence (13%)

Hepatic: Increased serum ALT (grade 2: 31%, grade 3: 13%, grade 4: <1%), increased serum AST (grade 2: 24%, grade 3: 10%, grade 4 <1%), hyperbilirubinemia (grade 2: 17%, grade 3: 10%, grade 4: <1%)

Infection: Increased susceptibility to infection (39%)

Miscellaneous: Fever (36%)

Neuromuscular & skeletal: Ostealgia (25%), myalgia (21%), neuropathy (13%), rigors (12%)

Respiratory: Dyspnea (24%), cough (16%)

1% to 10%:

Cardiovascular: Cardiac arrhythmia (<5%), syncope (<5%), deep vein thrombosis (4%), cerebrovascular accident (3%; including cerebral hemorrhage), myocardial infarction (2%)

Gastrointestinal: Intestinal obstruction (<5%), pancreatitis (<5%)

Hematologic & oncologic: Hemolytic anemia (<5%), microangiopathic hemolytic anemia with thrombocytopenia (1%)

Renal: Renal insufficiency (<5%), renal failure (1%)

Respiratory: Interstitial pulmonary disease (<3%)

<1%: Bullous dermatitis, exfoliative dermatitis, hepatic failure

Mono- or combination therapy: <1%, postmarketing, and/or case reports: Acute peptic ulcer with hemorrhage, bronchiolitis, corneal perforation, corneal ulcer, decreased lacrimation, episcleritis, gastritis, gastrointestinal hemorrhage, gastrointestinal perforation, hearing loss, hematemesis, hematochezia, hepatorenal syndrome, hepatotoxicity, hirsutism, hyperpigmentation, hypokalemia, increased eyelash thickness, increased growth in number of eyelashes, keratitis, melena, misdirected growth of eyelashes, myopathy (in combination with statin therapy), ocular inflammation, peptic ulcer, rhabdomyolysis (in combination with statin therapy), skin photosensitivity, skin rash (acneiform; sparing prior radiation field), Stevens-Johnson syndrome, toxic epidermal necrolysis, tympanic membrane perforation, uveitis

General Dosage Range Dosage adjustment recommended in patients with hepatic impairment, on concomitant therapy, who smoke, or who develop toxicities

Oral: *Adults:* 100 to 150 mg daily

Mechanism of Action Reversibly inhibits overall epidermal growth factor receptor (HER1/EGFR) - tyrosine kinase activity. Intracellular phosphorylation is inhibited which prevents further downstream signaling, resulting in cell death. Erlotinib has higher binding affinity for EGFR exon 19 deletion or exon 21 L858R mutations than for the wild type receptor.

Pharmacodynamics/Kinetics

Half-life Elimination 36.2 hours

Time to Peak Plasma: 4 hours

Pregnancy Considerations Adverse events were observed in animal reproduction studies. Erlotinib crosses the placenta (Ji 2015; Jovelet 2015). Information related to the use of erlotinib in pregnancy is limited (Ji 2015; Rivas 2012; Zambelli 2008). Based on the mechanism of action, erlotinib may cause fetal harm if administered in pregnancy. Advise females of reproductive potential to use effective contraception during treatment and for at least 1 month after the last erlotinib dose.

Ertapenem (er ta PEN em)

Brand Names: US INVanz

Brand Names: Canada Invanz

Pharmacologic Category Antibiotic, Carbapenem

Use Moderate-to-severe infections:

Acute pelvic infections: For the treatment of acute pelvic infections, including postpartum endomyometritis, septic abortion, and postsurgical gynecologic infections caused by *Streptococcus agalactiae*, *Escherichia coli*, *Bacteroides fragilis*, *Porphyromonas asaccharolytica*, *Peptostreptococcus* spp, or *Prevotella bivia*.

Community-acquired pneumonia: For the treatment of community-acquired pneumonia (CAP) caused by *Streptococcus pneumoniae* (penicillin-susceptible isolates only), including cases with concurrent bacteremia; *Haemophilus influenzae* (beta-lactamase-negative isolates only); or *Moraxella catarrhalis*.

Complicated intra-abdominal infections: For the treatment of complicated intra-abdominal infections caused by *E. coli*, *Clostridium clostridioforme*, *Eubacterium lentum*, *Peptostreptococcus* spp, *B. fragilis*, *Bacteroides distasonis*, *Bacteroides ovatus*, *Bacteroides thetaiotaomicron*, or *Bacteroides uniformis*.

Complicated skin and skin structure infections: For the treatment of complicated skin and skin structure infections, including diabetic foot infections without osteomyelitis caused by *Staphylococcus aureus* (methicillin-susceptible isolates only), *S. agalactiae*, *Streptococcus pyogenes*, *E. coli*, *Klebsiella pneumoniae*, *Proteus mirabilis*, *B. fragilis*, *Peptostreptococcus* spp, *P. asaccharolytica*, or *P. bivia*. Ertapenem has not been studied in diabetic foot infections with concomitant osteomyelitis.

Complicated urinary tract infections: For the treatment of complicated urinary tract infections (UTIs), including pyelonephritis caused by *E. coli*, including cases with concurrent bacteremia or *K. pneumoniae*.

Prophylaxis of surgical-site infection in colorectal surgery: For the prophylaxis of surgical-site infection in adults following elective colorectal surgery.

Note: Methicillin-resistant *Staphylococcus aureus*, *Enterococcus* spp, penicillin-resistant strains of *Streptococcus pneumoniae*, *Acinetobacter*, and *Pseudomonas aeruginosa*, are **resistant** to ertapenem while most extended-spectrum beta-lactamase (ESBL)-producing bacteria remain sensitive to ertapenem.

Local Anesthetic/Vasoconstrictor Precautions No information available to require special precautions

Effects on Dental Treatment Key adverse event(s) related to dental treatment: Oral candidiasis

Effects on Bleeding No information available to require special precautions

Adverse Reactions

>10%: Gastrointestinal: Diarrhea (6% to 12%)

1% to 10%:

Cardiovascular: Edema (3%), chest pain (<2%), phlebitis (<2%), thrombophlebitis (<2%), hypotension (1% to 2%)

Central nervous system: Headache (2% to 7%), altered mental status (eg, agitation, confusion, disorientation, mental acuity decreased, somnolence, stupor) (3% to 5%), insomnia (3%), dizziness (2%), hypothermia (infants, children, and adolescents <2%)

Dermatologic: Diaper rash (infants and children 5%), skin rash (2% to 3%), pruritus (1% to 2%), genital rash (infants, children, and adolescents <2%), skin lesion (infants, children, and adolescents <2%)

Gastrointestinal: Vomiting (2% to 10%), nausea (6% to 9%), abdominal pain (4% to 5%), constipation (2% to 4%), decreased appetite (infants, children, and adolescents <2%)

Genitourinary: Erythrocyturia (1% to 3%), vaginitis (1% to 3%)

Hematologic & oncologic: Thrombocythemia (4% to 7%), decreased neutrophils (3% to 6%), decreased hemoglobin (5%), decreased hematocrit (3%), leukocyturia (2% to 3%), leukopenia (<2%), eosinophilia (1% to 2%)

Hepatic: Increased serum ALT (8% to 9%), increased serum AST (7% to 8%), increased serum alkaline (4% to 7%)

Infection: Herpes simplex infection (infants, children, and adolescents <2%)

Local: Infused vein complication (4% to 7%)

Neuromuscular & skeletal: Arthralgia (infants, children, and adolescents <2%)

Otic: Otic infection (infants, children, and adolescents <2%)

Respiratory: Cough (≤4%), dyspnea (1% to 3%), nasopharyngitis (infants, children, and adolescents <2%), rhinitis (infants, children, and adolescents <2%), rhinorrhea (infants, children, and adolescents <2%), upper respiratory tract infection (infants, children, and adolescents 2%), wheezing (infants, children, and adolescents <2%)

Miscellaneous: Fever (2% to 5%)

<1%, postmarketing, and/or case reports: Abdominal distention, acid regurgitation, aggressive behavior, anaphylactoid reaction, anaphylaxis, anorexia, anuria, anxiety, asthma, asystole, ataxia, atrial fibrillation, bladder dysfunction, bradycardia, bronchoconstriction, cardiac arrest, cardiac arrhythmia, cardiac failure, chills, cholelithiasis, *Clostridium difficile* associated diarrhea, decreased serum albumin, dehydration, delirium, dental discoloration, depression, dermatitis, desquamation, diaphoresis, DRESS syndrome, duodenitis, dysgeusia, dyskinesia, dyspepsia, dysphagia, epistaxis, erythema, esophagitis, extravasation, facial edema, fatigue, flank pain, flatulence, flushing, gastritis, gastrointestinal hemorrhage, gout, hallucination, heart murmur, hematoma, hemoptysis, hemorrhoids, hiccups, hyperglycemia, hyperkalemia, hypertension, hypoesthesia, hypokalemia, hypoxemia, impaired consciousness, increased blood urea nitrogen, increased serum bilirubin (total), increased serum creatinine, increased serum sodium, induration at injection site, intestinal obstruction, jaundice, leg pain, malaise, muscle spasm, myoclonus, nervousness, oliguria, oral candidiasis, oral mucosa ulcer, pain, pain at injection site, pancreatitis, paresthesia, pharyngitis, pleural effusion, pleuritic chest pain, prolonged prothrombin time, pyloric stenosis, rales, renal insufficiency, respiratory distress, rhonchi, seizure, septicemia, septic shock, sore throat, stomatitis, subdural hematoma, syncope, tachycardia, thrombocytopenia, tissue necrosis, tremor, unsteady gait, urinary retention, urticaria, ventricular tachycardia, vertigo, voice disorder, vulvovaginal candidiasis, vulvovaginal pruritus, vulvovaginitis, weakness, weight loss

General Dosage Range Dosage adjustment recommended in patients with renal impairment

IM, IV:

Infants ≥3 months and Children: 15 **mg**/kg twice daily (maximum: 1 g daily)

Adolescents and Adults: 1 g once daily or as single dose

Mechanism of Action Inhibits bacterial cell wall synthesis by binding to one or more of the penicillin-binding proteins; which in turn inhibits the final transpeptidation step of peptidoglycan synthesis in bacterial cell walls, thus inhibiting cell wall biosynthesis. Bacteria eventually lyse due to ongoing activity of cell wall autolytic enzymes (autolysins and murein hydrolases) while cell wall assembly is arrested.

Pharmacodynamics/Kinetics

Half-life Elimination

Children 3 months to 12 years: ~2.5 hours

Children ≥13 years and Adults: ~4 hours

Time to Peak IM: ~2.3 hours

Pregnancy Risk Factor B

Pregnancy Considerations Teratogenic effects were not observed in animal reproduction studies. Ertapenem is approved for the treatment of postpartum endomyometritis, septic abortion, and postsurgical infections. Information related to use during pregnancy has not been located.

Erythromycin (Systemic) (er ith roe MYE sin)

Related Information

Bacterial Infections *on page 1835*

Clinical Risk Related to Drugs Prolonging QT Interval *on page 1772*

Related Sample Prescriptions

Bacterial Infections and Periodontal Diseases - Sample Prescriptions *on page 32*

Brand Names: US E.E.S. 400; E.E.S. Granules; Ery-Tab; EryPed 200; EryPed 400; Erythrocin Lactobionate; Erythrocin Stearate; PCE

Brand Names: Canada Apo-Erythro Base; Apo-Erythro E-C; Apo-Erythro-ES; Apo-Erythro-S; EES; Erybid; Eryc; Novo-Rythro Estolate; Novo-Rythro Ethylsuccinate; Nu-Erythromycin-S; PCE

Generic Availability (US) May be product dependent

Pharmacologic Category Antibiotic, Macrolide

Dental Use Alternative to penicillin VK for treatment of orofacial infections

Use

Bacterial infections: Treatment of susceptible bacterial infections, including *S. pyogenes*, some *S. pneumoniae*, some *S. aureus*, *M. pneumoniae*, *Legionella pneumophila*, diphtheria, pertussis, *Chlamydia*, erythrasma, *N. gonorrhoeae*, *E. histolytica*, syphilis and nongonococcal urethritis, and *Campylobacter* gastroenteritis; used in conjunction with neomycin for decontaminating the bowel

Surgical (preoperative) prophylaxis (colorectal): Colorectal decontamination, in conjunction with other agents, prior to surgical intervention

Local Anesthetic/Vasoconstrictor Precautions Erythromycin is one of the drugs confirmed to prolong the QT interval and is accepted as having a risk of causing torsade de pointes. In terms of epinephrine, it is not known what effect vasoconstrictors in the local anesthetic regimen will have in patients with a known history of congenital prolonged QT interval or in patients taking any medication that prolongs the QT interval. Until more information is obtained, it is suggested that the clinician consult with the physician prior to the use of a vasoconstrictor in suspected patients, and that the vasoconstrictor (epinephrine, mepivacaine and levonordefrin [Carbocaine® 2% with Neo-Cobefrin®]) be used with caution. See Dental Comment.

Effects on Dental Treatment Key adverse event(s) related to dental treatment: Oral candidiasis.

Effects on Bleeding No information available to require special precautions

Adverse Reactions Frequency not defined. Incidence may vary with formulation.

Cardiovascular: QT_c prolongation, torsade de pointes, ventricular arrhythmia, ventricular tachycardia

Central nervous system: Seizure

Dermatologic: Erythema multiforme, pruritus, skin rash, Stevens-Johnson syndrome, toxic epidermal necrolysis, urticaria

Gastrointestinal: Abdominal pain, anorexia, diarrhea, nausea, oral candidiasis, pancreatitis, pseudomembranous colitis, pyloric stenosis (infantile hypertrophic), vomiting

Hepatic: Abnormal hepatic function tests, cholestatic jaundice (most common with estolate), hepatitis

Hypersensitivity: Anaphylaxis, hypersensitivity reaction

Local: Injection site phlebitis

Neuromuscular & skeletal: Weakness

Otic: Hearing loss

Renal: Interstitial nephritis

Postmarketing and/or case reports: Hepatotoxicity (idiosyncratic) (Chalasani 2014)

Dental Usual Dosage Treatment of orofacial infections: Adults: Oral:

Base: 250 to 500 mg every 6 to 12 hours

Ethylsuccinate: 400 to 800 mg every 6 to 12 hours

Dosing

Adult & Geriatric Note: Due to differences in absorption, 400 mg erythromycin ethylsuccinate produces the same serum levels as 250 mg erythromycin base or stearate.

Usual dosage range:

Oral:

Base: 250 to 500 mg every 6 to 12 hours; maximum: 4 g daily

Ethylsuccinate: 400 to 800 mg every 6 to 12 hours; maximum: 4 g daily

IV: Lactobionate: 15 to 20 mg/kg/day divided every 6 hours or 500 mg to 1 g every 6 hours; maximum: 4 g daily

Indication-specific dosing:

Acne vulgaris (alternative therapy) (off-label use): Oral: Initial: 250 to 500 mg (base) twice daily, followed by 250 to 500 mg (base) once daily (Tan 2003; Tan 2005). The shortest possible duration should be used to minimize development of bacterial resistance; re-evaluate at 3 to 4 months (AAD [Zaenglein 2016])

Bartonella **spp infections (bacillary angiomatosis [BA], peliosis hepatis [PH]) (off-label use):** Oral: 500 mg (base) 4 times daily for 3 months (BA) or 4 months (PH) (Koehler 1992; Rolain 2004; Stevens 2014; Tappero 1993). **Note:** IDSA skin and soft tissue infection guidelines recommend a duration of initial therapy of 2 weeks to 2 months for cutaneous BA, although treatment durations are not standardized (IDSA [Stevens 2014])

***Bartonella* spp infections in HIV-infected patients (off-label use; HHS [OI adult 2015]): Note:** Duration of therapy is at least 3 months; continuation of therapy depends on relapse occurrence and clinical condition

Bacillary angiomatosis, peliosis hepatis, bacteremia, and osteomyelitis: Oral, IV: 500 mg every 6 hours

Other severe infections (excluding CNS infections or endocarditis): Oral, IV: 500 mg every 6 hours with rifampin

Chancroid (off-label use): Oral: 500 mg (base) 3 times daily for 7 days; **Note:** Isolates with intermediate resistance have been documented (CDC [Workowski 2015])

***Chlamydia trachomatis* infection, uncomplicated:** Oral:

Manufacturer's labeling: Urethral, endocervical, or rectal infections (when tetracycline is contraindicated or not tolerated): 500 mg (base) 4 times a day or two 333 mg (base) tablets every 8 hours for at least 7 days

Alternate dosing; Urogenital infections: 500 mg (base) four times daily or 800 mg (ethylsuccinate) four times daily for 7 days (CDC [Workowski 2015])

Gastroparesis (off-label use):

IV: 3 mg/kg administered over 45 minutes every 8 hours (Camilleri 2013)

Oral: Patients refractory/intolerant to other prokinetic agents (eg, metoclopramide, domperidone): 250 to 500 mg (base) 3 times daily before meals. Limit duration of therapy, tachyphylaxis may occur after 4 weeks (Camilleri 2013).

Granuloma inguinale (donovanosis) (off-label use): Oral: 500 mg (base) 4 times daily for at least 21 days and resolution of lesions (CDC [Workowski 2015]). **Note:** If symptoms do not improve within the first few days of therapy, the addition of gentamicin may be considered (CDC [Workowski 2015]).

Impetigo (IDSA [Stevens 2014]): Oral:

Base: 250 mg 4 times daily for 7 days, depending on response

Ethylsuccinate: 400 mg 4 times daily for 7 days, depending on response

Legionnaire disease: Oral: 1.6 to 4 g (ethylsuccinate) daily or 1 to 4 g (base) daily in divided doses for 21 days. **Note:** No longer preferred therapy and only used in nonhospitalized patients.

Lymphogranuloma venereum (alternative to preferred therapy) (off-label use): Oral: 500 mg (base) 4 times daily for 21 days (CDC [Workowski 2015])

Nongonococcal urethritis: Oral:

Manufacturer's labeling:

Base: When tetracycline is contraindicated or not tolerated: 500 mg (base) 4 times daily or two 333 mg (base) tablets every 8 hours for at least 7 days

Ethylsuccinate: 800 mg (ethylsuccinate) 3 times daily for 7 days. **Note:** May use 250 mg (base) or 400 mg (ethylsuccinate) 4 times daily for 14 days if gastrointestinal intolerance.

Alternate dosing: 500 mg (base) 4 times daily or 800 mg (ethylsuccinate) 4 times daily for 7 days (CDC [Workowski 2015]).

Pertussis: Oral: 500 mg (base) every 6 hours for 14 days

Surgical (preoperative) prophylaxis (colorectal) (off-label dose): Oral: 1 g erythromycin base per dose at 1 PM, 2 PM, and 11 PM on the day before 8 AM surgery combined with mechanical cleansing of the large intestine, oral neomycin. Perioperative IV antibiotics are also given on the day of surgery (Bratzler 2013).

Pediatric Note: Due to differences in absorption, 400 mg erythromycin ethylsuccinate produces the same serum levels as 250 mg erythromycin base or stearate.

Usual dosage range: Infants and Children:

Oral:

Base: 30 to 50 mg/kg/day in 2 to 4 divided doses; maximum: 2 g daily

Ethylsuccinate: 30 to 50 mg/kg/day in 2 to 4 divided doses; dose may be increased (eg, to 60 to 100 mg/kg/day) in severe infections; maximum: 4 g/day

Stearate: 30 to 50 mg/kg/day in 2 to 4 divided doses; maximum: 2 g daily

IV: Lactobionate: 15 to 20 mg/kg/day divided every 6 hours; maximum: 4 g daily

Indication-specific dosing:

Infants and Children:

***Bartonella* spp infections (bacillary angiomatosis [BA], peliosis hepatis [PH]) (off-label use):** Oral: 40 mg/kg/day (ethylsuccinate) in 4 divided doses (maximum: 2 g daily) for 3 months (BA) or 4 months (PH) (Rolain 2004). **Note:** IDSA skin and soft tissue infection guidelines recommend a duration of initial therapy of 2 weeks to 2 months for cutaneous BA, although treatment durations are not standardized (IDSA [Stevens 2014])

***Chlamydia trachomatis* infection, uncomplicated:** Urogenital infection:

Children and Adolescents <45 kg (off-label population): 50 mg/kg/day (base or ethylsuccinate) in 4 divided doses for 14 days (CDC [Workowski 2015])

Adolescents ≥45 kg (off-label population): 500 mg (base) four times daily or 800 mg (ethylsuccinate) four times daily for 7 days (CDC [Workowski 2015])

Community-acquired pneumonia (CAP) (IDSA/PIDS 2011): Infants >3 months and Children: **Note:** A beta-lactam antibiotic should be added if typical bacterial pneumonia cannot be ruled out.

Presumed atypical *(M. pneumoniae, Chlamydophila* [also known as *Chlamydia*] *pneumoniae, C. trachomatis)* infection, mild atypical infection or step-down therapy (alternative to azithromycin): Oral: 10 mg/kg/dose every 6 hours

Moderate to severe atypical infection (alternative to azithromycin): IV: 5 mg/kg/dose every 6 hours

Impetigo: Oral: 40 mg/kg/day in 3 to 4 divided doses for 7 days, depending on response (IDSA [Stevens 2014])

Mild/moderate infection: Oral: 30 to 50 mg/kg/day in divided doses every 6 to 12 hours

Pertussis: Oral: 40 to 50 mg/kg/day in 4 divided doses for 14 days; maximum: 2 g daily (not preferred agent for infants <1 month due to IHPS)

Pharyngitis, tonsillitis (streptococcal): Oral: 20 mg (base)/kg/day or 40 mg (ethylsuccinate)/kg/day in 2 divided doses for 10 days. **Note:** No longer preferred therapy due to increased organism resistance.

Surgical (preoperative) prophylaxis (colorectal) (off-label use): Children ≥1 year: Oral: 20 mg (base)/kg (maximum dose: 1000 mg) at 1 PM, 2 PM, and 11 PM on the day before 8 AM surgery combined with mechanical cleansing of the large intestine, oral neomycin. Perioperative IV antibiotics are also given on the day of surgery (Bratzler 2013).

Severe infection: IV: 15 to 20 mg/kg/day divided every 6 hours; maximum: 4 g daily

Adolescents:

***Bartonella* spp infections in HIV-infected patients (off-label use):** Refer to adult dosing.

Renal Impairment

There are no dosage adjustments provided in the manufacturer's labeling.

Dialysis: Slightly dialyzable (5% to 20%). Supplemental dose is not necessary in hemo- or peritoneal dialysis or in continuous arteriovenous or venovenous hemofiltration (Aronoff 2007).

Hepatic Impairment There are no dosage adjustments provided in the manufacturer's labeling; use with caution.

Mechanism of Action Inhibits RNA-dependent protein synthesis at the chain elongation step; binds to the 50S ribosomal subunit resulting in blockage of transpeptidation

Contraindications Hypersensitivity to erythromycin, any macrolide antibiotics, or any component of the formulation

Concomitant use with pimozide, cisapride, ergotamine or dihydroergotamine, terfenadine, astemizole, lovastatin, or simvastatin

Warnings/Precautions Use caution in patients with preexisting liver disease; hepatic impairment with or without jaundice has occurred, it may be accompanied by malaise, nausea, vomiting, abdominal colic, and fever; discontinue use if these occur. Potentially significant drug-drug interactions may exist, requiring dose or frequency adjustment, additional monitoring, and/or selection of alternative therapy. Prolonged use may result in fungal or bacterial superinfection, including *C. difficile*-associated diarrhea (CDAD) and pseudomembranous colitis; CDAD has been observed >2 months postantibiotic treatment. Use in infants has been associated with infantile hypertrophic pyloric stenosis (IHPS); observe for nonbilious vomiting or irritability with feeding. Macrolides have been associated with rare QTc prolongation and ventricular arrhythmias, including torsade de pointes; avoid use in patients with prolonged QT interval, uncorrected hypokalemia or hypomagnesemia, clinically significant bradycardia, or concurrent use of Class IA (eg, quinidine, procainamide) or Class III (eg, amiodarone, dofetilide, sotalol) antiarrhythmic agents. Avoid concurrent use with strong CYP3A inhibitors; may increase the risk of sudden cardiac death (Ray 2004). Use caution in elderly patients; risk of adverse events, including hearing loss and/or torsades de pointes, may be increased, particularly if concurrent renal/hepatic impairment. Exacerbation of and new onset of myasthenia gravis symptoms have been reported.

Benzyl alcohol and derivatives: Some dosage forms may contain benzyl alcohol; large amounts of benzyl alcohol (≥99 mg/kg/day) have been associated with a potentially fatal toxicity ("gasping syndrome") in neonates; the "gasping syndrome" consists of metabolic acidosis, respiratory distress, gasping respirations, CNS dysfunction (including convulsions, intracranial hemorrhage), hypotension and cardiovascular collapse (AAP ["Inactive" 1997]; CDC 1982); some data suggests that benzoate displaces bilirubin from protein binding sites (Ahlfors 2001); avoid or use dosage forms containing benzyl alcohol with caution in neonates. See manufacturer's labeling.

Drug Interactions

Metabolism/Transport Effects **Substrate** of CYP2B6 (minor), CYP3A4 (major), P-glycoprotein; **Note:** Assignment of Major/Minor substrate status based on clinically relevant drug interaction potential; **Inhibits** CYP3A4 (moderate), P-glycoprotein

Avoid Concomitant Use

Avoid concomitant use of Erythromycin (Systemic) with any of the following: Aprepitant; Asunaprevir; Barnidipine; BCG (Intravesical); Bosutinib; Budesonide (Systemic); Cholera Vaccine; Cisapride; Clindamycin (Topical); Cobimetinib; Conivaptan; Disopyramide; Domperidone; Flibanserin; Fluconazole; Fusidic Acid (Systemic); Highest Risk QTc-Prolonging Agents; Hydroxychloroquine; Ibrutinib; Idelalisib; Ivabradine; Lincosamide Antibiotics; Lomitapide; Lovastatin; Mequitazine; MiFEPRIStone; Naloxegol; Olaparib; PAZOPanib; Pimozide; Probucol; Promazine; QuiNIDine; QuiNINE; Silodosin; Simeprevir; Simvastatin; Terfenadine; Tolvaptan; Topotecan; Trabectedin; Ulipristal; VinCRIStine (Liposomal); Vinflunine

Increased Effect/Toxicity

Erythromycin (Systemic) may increase the levels/effects of: Afatinib; Alfentanil; ALPRAZolam; Antineoplastic Agents (Vinca Alkaloids); Apixaban; Aprepitant; ARIPiprazole; Asunaprevir; AtorvaSTATin; Avanafil; Barnidipine; Bilastine; Blonanserin; Bosentan; Bosutinib; Brentuximab Vedotin; Brexpiprazole; Bromocriptine; Budesonide (Systemic); Budesonide (Topical); BusPIRone; Calcium Channel Blockers; Cannabis; CarBAMazepine; Cardiac Glycosides; Cilostazol; Cisapride; CloZAPine; Cobimetinib; Colchicine; CycloSPORINE (Systemic); CYP3A4 Substrates; Dabigatran Etexilate; Dapoxetine; Deflazacort; Disopyramide; Domperidone; Doxofylline; DOXOrubicin (Conventional); Dronabinol; Edoxaban; Eletriptan; Eplerenone; Ergot Derivatives; Estazolam; Everolimus; FentaNYL; Fexofenadine; Flibanserin; GuanFACINE; Highest Risk QTc-Prolonging Agents; HYDROcodone; HydrOXYzine; Ibrutinib; Imatinib; Ivabradine; Ivacaftor; Lomitapide; Lovastatin; Lurasidone; Mequitazine; Midazolam; Mirodenafil; Moderate Risk QTc-Prolonging Agents; Naldemedine; Naloxegol; Nintedanib; Olaparib; OxyCODONE; PAZOPanib; P-glycoprotein/ABCB1 Substrates; Pimecrolimus; Pimozide; Pitavastatin; Pravastatin; QuiNIDine; QuiNINE; Ranolazine; Repaglinide; Rifamycin Derivatives; RifAXIMin; Rilpivirine; Rivaroxaban; Rupatadine; Salmeterol; SAXagliptin; Sertraline; Sildenafil; Silodosin; Simeprevir; Simvastatin; Sirolimus; Sonidegib; Suvorexant; Tacrolimus (Systemic); Tacrolimus (Topical); Telaprevir; Temsirolimus; Terfenadine; Tetrahydrocannabinol; Theophylline Derivatives; Ticagrelor; Tolvaptan; Topotecan; Trabectedin; Triazolam; Udenafil; Ulipristal; Vardenafil; Venetoclax; Vilazodone; VinCRIStine (Liposomal); Vitamin K Antagonists; Zopiclone

The levels/effects of Erythromycin (Systemic) may be increased by: Conivaptan; CYP3A4 Inhibitors (Moderate); CYP3A4 Inhibitors (Strong); Dasatinib; Fluconazole; Fosaprepitant; Fusidic Acid (Systemic); Hydroxychloroquine; Idelalisib; Ivabradine; MiFEPRIStone; Netupitant; Palbociclib; P-glycoprotein/ABCB1 Inhibitors; Probucol; Promazine; QTc-Prolonging Agents (Indeterminate Risk and Risk Modifying); Simeprevir; Stiripentol; Telaprevir; Vinflunine

Decreased Effect

Erythromycin (Systemic) may decrease the levels/effects of: Amdinocillin; BCG (Intravesical); BCG Vaccine (Immunization); Cholera Vaccine; Clindamycin (Topical); Clopidogrel; Ifosfamide; Lactobacillus and Estriol; Sodium Picosulfate; Typhoid Vaccine; Zafirlukast

The levels/effects of Erythromycin (Systemic) may be decreased by: Bosentan; CYP3A4 Inducers (Moderate); CYP3A4 Inducers (Strong); Dabrafenib; Deferasirox; Enzalutamide; Etravirine; Lincosamide Antibiotics; Mitotane; Siltuximab; St John's Wort; Tocilizumab

Food Interactions

Ethanol: Ethanol may decrease absorption of erythromycin or enhance effects of ethanol. Management: Avoid ethanol.

Food: Erythromycin serum levels may be altered if taken with food (formulation-dependent). GI upset, including diarrhea, is common. Management: May be taken with food to decrease GI upset, otherwise take around-the-clock with a full glass of water. Do not give with milk or acidic beverages (eg, soda, juice).

Dietary Considerations Some products may contain sodium.

Base, PCE or stearate dosage forms should be taken on an empty stomach (2 hours before or after a meal).

Ethylsuccinate (EES) or delayed-release (ERY-TAB) dosage forms may be administered without regards to meals.

May consider administering after food to decrease GI discomfort.

Pharmacodynamics/Kinetics

Half-life Elimination Neonates (≤15 days of age): 2.1 hours; Adults: Peak: 1.5-2 hours; End-stage renal disease: 5-6 hours

Time to Peak Serum: Base: 4 hours; Ethylsuccinate: 0.5 to 2.5 hours; Stearate: 3 hours (Steigbigel 2000); delayed with food due to differences in absorption

Pregnancy Risk Factor B

Pregnancy Considerations Adverse events were not observed in animal reproduction studies. Erythromycin crosses the placenta and low concentrations are found in the fetal serum. Cardiovascular anomalies following exposure in early pregnancy have been reported in some observational studies. Serum concentrations of erythromycin may be variable in pregnant women (Kiefer 1955; Philipson 1976).

In patients with acute infections during pregnancy, erythromycin may be given if an antibiotic is required and appropriate based on bacterial sensitivity (ACOG No. 120 2011). Erythromycin is the antibiotic of choice for preterm premature rupture of membranes (with membrane rupture between 24 0/7 to 33 6/7 weeks gestation) (ACOG 2013), the treatment of lymphogranuloma venereum in pregnancy, and the treatment of or long-term suppression of Bartonella infection in HIV-infected pregnant patients. Erythromycin is one of the antibiotics that may be used for the treatment of chancroid or granuloma inguinale and during pregnancy, and may be appropriate as an alternative agent for the treatment of chlamydial infections in pregnant women (consult current guidelines) (CDC [Workowski 2015]; HHS [opportunistic; adult] 2015).

Breastfeeding Considerations Erythromycin is excreted in breast milk; therefore, the manufacturer recommends that caution be exercised when administering erythromycin to breastfeeding women. Decreased appetite, diarrhea, rash, and somnolence have been reported in nursing infants exposed to macrolide antibiotics (Goldstein 2009).

One case report and a cohort study raise the possibility for a connection with pyloric stenosis in neonates exposed to erythromycin via breast milk; an alternative antibiotic may be preferred for breastfeeding mothers of infants in this age group (Sørensen 2003; Stang 1986).

Dosage Forms

Capsule Delayed Release Particles, Oral:

Generic: 250 mg

Solution Reconstituted, Intravenous:

Erythrocin Lactobionate: 500 mg (1 ea)

Suspension Reconstituted, Oral:

E.E.S. Granules: 200 mg/5 mL (100 mL, 200 mL)

EryPed 200: 200 mg/5 mL (100 mL)

EryPed 400: 400 mg/5 mL (100 mL)

Generic: 200 mg/5 mL (100 mL, 200 mL)

Tablet, Oral:

E.E.S. 400: 400 mg

Erythrocin Stearate: 250 mg

Generic: 250 mg, 400 mg, 500 mg

Tablet Delayed Release, Oral:

Ery-Tab: 250 mg, 333 mg, 500 mg

PCE: 333 mg, 500 mg

Dental Comment Many patients cannot tolerate erythromycin because of abdominal pain and nausea; the mechanism of this adverse effect appears to be the motilin agonistic properties of erythromycin in the GI tract. For these patients, clindamycin is indicated as the alternative antibiotic for treatment of orofacial infections.

HMG-CoA reductase inhibitors, also known as the statins, effectively decrease the hepatic cholesterol biosynthesis resulting in the reduction of blood LDL-cholesterol concentrations. The AUC of atorvastatin (Lipitor®) was increased 33% by erythromycin administration. Combination of erythromycin and lovastatin (Mevacor®) has been associated with rhabdomyolysis (Ayanian, et al). The mechanism of erythromycin is inhibiting the CYP3A4 metabolism of atorvastatin, lovastatin, and cerivastatin. Simvastatin (Zocor®) would likely be affected in a similar manner by the coadministration of erythromycin. Clarithromycin (Biaxin®) may exert a similar effect as erythromycin on atorvastatin, lovastatin, cerivastatin, and simvastatin.

Also see Local Anesthetic/Vasoconstrictor Precautions

Escitalopram (es sye TAL oh pram)

Related Information

Citalopram *on page 371*

Clinical Risk Related to Drugs Prolonging QT Interval *on page 1772*

Vasoconstrictor Interactions With Antidepressants *on page 1913*

Brand Names: US Lexapro

Brand Names: Canada ACT Escitalopram; Apo-Escitalopram; Cipralex; Cipralex MELTZ; JAMP-Escitalopram; Mar-Escitalopram; Mylan-Escitalopram; PMS-Escitalopram; Priva-Escitalopram; RAN-Escitalopram; Riva-Escitalopram; Sandoz Escitalopram; Teva-Escitalopram

Generic Availability (US) Yes

Pharmacologic Category Antidepressant, Selective Serotonin Reuptake Inhibitor

Use Treatment of major depressive disorder; generalized anxiety disorders (GAD)

Canadian labeling: Additional use (not in US labeling): Treatment of obsessive-compulsive disorder (OCD)

Local Anesthetic/Vasoconstrictor Precautions Although caution should be used in patients taking tricyclic antidepressants, no interactions have been reported with vasoconstrictors and escitalopram, a non-tricyclic antidepressant which acts to increase serotonin; no precautions appear to be needed

Escitalopram is one of the drugs confirmed to prolong the QT interval and is accepted as having a risk of causing torsade de pointes. The risk of drug-induced torsade de pointes is extremely low when a single QT interval prolonging drug is prescribed. In terms of epinephrine, it is not known what effect vasoconstrictors in the local anesthetic regimen will have in patients with a known history of congenital prolonged QT interval or in patients taking any medication that prolongs the QT interval. Until more information is obtained, it is suggested that the clinician consult with the physician prior to the use of a vasoconstrictor in suspected patients, and that the vasoconstrictor (epinephrine, mepivacaine, and levonordefrin [Carbocaine® 2% with Neo-Cobefrin®]) be used with caution.

Effects on Dental Treatment Key adverse event(s) related to dental treatment: Xerostomia (normal salivary flow resumes upon discontinuation) and toothache (see Effects on Bleeding and Dental Comment)

Effects on Bleeding Selective serotonin reuptake inhibitors such as escitalopram may impair platelet aggregation due to platelet serotonin depletion, possibly increasing the risk of a bleeding complication. The risk of a bleeding complication can be increased by coadministration of other antiplatelet agents such as NSAIDs and aspirin.

Adverse Reactions

>10%:

Central nervous system: Headache (24%), insomnia (7% to 14%), drowsiness (4% to 13%)

Gastrointestinal: Nausea (15% to 18%), diarrhea (6% to 14%)

Genitourinary: Ejaculatory disorder (9% to 14%)

1% to 10%:

Central nervous system: Fatigue (2% to 8%), dizziness (4% to 7%), anorgasmia (2% to 6%), abnormal dreams (3%), lethargy (3%), paresthesia (2%), yawning (2%)

Dermatologic: Diaphoresis (3% to 8%)

Endocrine & metabolic: Decreased libido (3% to 7%), menstrual disease (2%)

Gastrointestinal: Xerostomia (4% to 9%), constipation (3% to 6%), dyspepsia (2% to 6%), decreased appetite (3%), vomiting (3%), abdominal pain (2%), flatulence (2%), toothache (2%)

Genitourinary: Impotence (2% to 3%), urinary tract infection (children ≥2%)

Neuromuscular & skeletal: Neck pain (≤3%), shoulder pain (≤3%), back pain (children ≥2%)

Respiratory: Flu-like symptoms (5%), rhinitis (5%), sinusitis (3%), nasal congestion (children ≥2%)

<1%, postmarketing, and/or case reports: Abdominal cramps, abnormal gait, acute renal failure, aggressive behavior, agitated depression, agitation, agranulocytosis, akathisia, alopecia, amnesia, anaphylaxis, anemia, angioedema, angle-closure glaucoma, anxiety, apathy, aplastic anemia, arthralgia, ataxia, atrial fibrillation, blurred vision, bradycardia, bronchitis, cardiac failure, cerebrovascular accident, chest pain, choreoathetosis, cough, deep vein thrombosis, delirium, delusions, depersonalization, dermatitis, diabetes mellitus, diplopia, dyskinesia, dysmenorrhea, dysphagia, dyspnea, dystonia, dysuria, ecchymoses, edema, epistaxis, erythema multiforme, extrapyramidal reaction, fever, flushing, gastroenteritis, gastroesophageal reflux disease, gastrointestinal hemorrhage, hallucination, heartburn, hemolytic anemia, hepatic failure, hepatic necrosis, hepatitis, hot flash, hypercholesterolemia, hyperglycemia, hypermenorrhea, hyperprolactinemia, hypersensitivity reaction, hypertension, hypertensive crisis, hypoesthesia, hypoglycemia, hypokalemia, hyponatremia, hypoprothrombinemia, hypotension, immune thrombocytopenia, increased appetite, increased INR, increased liver enzymes, increased serum bilirubin, irritability, jaw tightness, lack of concentration, leukopenia, limb pain, migraine, myalgia, myasthenia, mydriasis, myocardial infarction, myoclonus, neuroleptic malignant syndrome (Stevens 2008), nightmares, nystagmus, orthostatic hypotension, palpitations, pancreatitis, panic, paranoia, Parkinsonian-like syndrome, phlebitis, priapism, prolonged Q-T interval on ECG, psychosis, pulmonary embolism, rectal hemorrhage, restless leg syndrome, rhabdomyolysis, seizure, serotonin syndrome, SIADH, sinus congestion, sinus headache, skin photosensitivity, skin rash, spontaneous abortion, Stevens-Johnson syndrome, suicidal ideation, suicidal tendencies, syncope, tachycardia, tardive dyskinesia, thrombocytopenia, thrombosis, tinnitus, torsades de pointes, toxic epidermal necrolysis, tremor, urinary frequency, urinary retention, urticaria, ventricular arrhythmia, ventricular tachycardia, vertigo, visual disturbance, weight gain, withdrawal syndrome

Dosing

Adult

US labeling: **Major depressive disorder, generalized anxiety disorder:** Oral: Initial: 10 mg once daily; dose may be increased to a maximum of 20 mg once daily after at least 1 week

Canadian labeling: **Note:** Orodispersible tablets should only be used for doses that can be accommodated with whole tablets (ie, 10 mg or multiples of that):

Major depressive disorder, generalized anxiety disorder (GAD), obsessive compulsive disorder (OCD): Oral: Initial: 10 mg once daily (may consider 5 mg once daily where sensitivity is a concern); dose may be increased as tolerated to a maximum of 20 mg once daily. In poor CYP2C19 metabolizers, initiate at a dose of 5 mg once daily; may increase dose to a maximum of 10 mg once daily. Patients with GAD or OCD who require extended therapy should be maintained at the lowest effective dose and assessed periodically to determine the need for continued therapy.

Hot flashes (off-label use): Oral: Initial: 10 mg once daily, increase to 20 mg once daily after 4 weeks if symptoms not adequately controlled (Carpenter 2012; Freeman 2011).

Panic disorder (off-label use): Initial: 5 mg once daily for 7 days, then increase dose to 10 mg once daily. Consider further dosage adjustments based on response and tolerability up to 20 mg once daily; mean dose in clinical trials was ~10 mg once daily (Stahl 2003).

Post-traumatic stress disorder (off-label use): Initial: 10 mg once daily; after 4 weeks increase to 20 mg once daily (Robert 2006). Additional data may be necessary to further define the role of escitalopram in this condition.

Discontinuation of therapy: Upon discontinuation of antidepressant therapy, gradually taper the dose to minimize the incidence of withdrawal symptoms and allow for the detection of re-emerging symptoms. Evidence supporting ideal taper rates is limited. APA and NICE guidelines suggest tapering therapy over at least several weeks with consideration to the half-life of the antidepressant; antidepressants with a shorter half-life may need to be tapered more conservatively. In addition for long-term treated patients, WFSBP guidelines recommend tapering over 4-6 months. If intolerable withdrawal symptoms occur following a dose reduction, consider resuming the previously prescribed dose and/or decrease dose at a more gradual rate (APA 2010; Bauer 2002; Haddad 2001; NCCMH 2010; Schatzberg 2006; Shelton 2001; Warner 2006).

MAO inhibitor recommendations: *US labeling:*

Switching to or from an MAO inhibitor intended to treat psychiatric disorders:

Allow 14 days to elapse between discontinuing an MAO inhibitor intended to treat psychiatric disorders and initiation of escitalopram.

Allow 14 days to elapse between discontinuing escitalopram and initiation of an MAO inhibitor intended to treat psychiatric disorders.

Use with other MAO inhibitors (linezolid or IV methylene blue):

Do not initiate escitalopram in patients receiving linezolid or IV methylene blue; consider other interventions for psychiatric condition.

If urgent treatment with linezolid or IV methylene blue is required in a patient already receiving escitalopram and potential benefits outweigh potential risks, discontinue escitalopram promptly and administer linezolid or IV methylene blue. Monitor for serotonin syndrome for 2 weeks or until 24 hours after the last dose of linezolid or IV methylene blue, whichever comes first. May resume escitalopram 24 hours after the last dose of linezolid or IV methylene blue.

Dosage adjustment with concomitant medications: *Canadian labeling:* Escitalopram dose should not exceed 10 mg once daily in patients taking omeprazole or cimetidine.

Geriatric

Major depressive disorder, generalized anxiety disorder: *US labeling:* Oral: 10 mg once daily

Major depressive disorder, generalized anxiety disorder (GAD), obsessive compulsive disorder (OCD): *Canadian labeling:* Oral: Initial: 5 mg once daily; dose may be increased as tolerated to a maximum of 10 mg once daily.

Discontinuation of therapy: Refer to adult dosing.

MAO inhibitor recommendations: Refer to adult dosing.

Pediatric Major depressive disorder Oral: Children ≥12 years: Initial: 10 mg once daily; dose may be increased to a maximum of 20 mg once daily after at least 3 weeks

Discontinuation of therapy: Refer to adult dosing.

MAO inhibitor recommendations: Refer to adult dosing.

Renal Impairment

Mild-to-moderate impairment: No dosage adjustment is necessary

Severe impairment: CrCl <20 mL/minute (US labeling) or CrCl <30 mL/minute (Canadian labeling): Use with caution.

Hepatic Impairment

US labeling: 10 mg once daily

Canadian labeling:

Mild or moderate impairment (Child-Pugh class A or B): Initial: 5 mg once daily; dose may be increased as tolerated to 10 mg once daily (maximum dose)

Severe Impairment (Child-Pugh class C): No dosage adjustment provided in manufacturer's labeling; has not been studied. Use with caution.

Mechanism of Action Escitalopram is the S-enantiomer of the racemic derivative citalopram, which selectively inhibits the reuptake of serotonin with little to no effect on norepinephrine or dopamine reuptake. It has no or very low affinity for 5-HT_{1-7}, alpha- and beta-adrenergic, D_{1-5}, H_{1-3}, M_{1-5}, and benzodiazepine receptors. Escitalopram does not bind to or has low affinity for Na^+, K^+, Cl^-, and Ca^{++} ion channels.

Contraindications

Hypersensitivity to escitalopram, citalopram, or any component of the formulation; use of MAO inhibitors intended to treat psychiatric disorders (concurrently or within 14 days of discontinuing either escitalopram or the MAO inhibitor); initiation of escitalopram in a patient receiving linezolid or intravenous methylene blue; concurrent use of pimozide

Canadian labeling: Additional contraindications (not in US labeling): Known QT-interval prolongation or congenital long QT syndrome

Warnings/Precautions [US Boxed Warning]: Antidepressants increase the risk of suicidal thinking and behavior in children, adolescents, and young adults (18 to 24 years of age) with major depressive disorder (MDD) and other psychiatric disorders; consider risk prior to prescribing. Short-term studies did not show an increased risk in patients >24 years of age and showed a decreased risk in patients ≥65 years. Closely monitor patients for clinical worsening, suicidality, or unusual changes in behavior, particularly during the initial 1-2 months of therapy or during periods of dosage adjustments (increases or decreases); the patient's family or caregiver should be instructed to closely observe the patient and communicate condition with healthcare provider. A medication guide concerning the use of antidepressants should be dispensed with each prescription. **Escitalopram is not FDA approved for use in children <12 years of age.**

The possibility of a suicide attempt is inherent in major depression and may persist until remission occurs. Use caution in high-risk patients. Worsening depression and severe abrupt suicidality that are not part of the presenting symptoms may require discontinuation or modification of drug therapy. The patient's family or caregiver should be alerted to monitor patients for the emergence of suicidality and associated behaviors (such as agitation, irritability, hostility, impulsivity, and hypomania) and call healthcare provider.

May precipitate a shift to mania or hypomania in patients with bipolar disorder. Patients presenting with depressive symptoms should be screened for bipolar disorder. Monotherapy in patients with bipolar disorder should be avoided. Escitalopram is not FDA approved for the treatment of bipolar depression.

Potentially life-threatening serotonin syndrome (SS) has occurred with serotonergic agents (eg, SSRIs, SNRIs), particularly when used in combination with other serotonergic agents (eg, triptans, TCAs, fentanyl, lithium, tramadol, buspirone, St John's wort, tryptophan) or agents that impair metabolism of serotonin (eg, MAO inhibitors intended to treat psychiatric disorders, other MAO inhibitors [ie, linezolid and intravenous methylene blue]). Discontinue treatment (and any concomitant serotonergic agent) immediately if signs/symptoms arise. May increase the risks associated with electroconvulsive therapy. Has a low potential to impair cognitive or motor performance; caution operating hazardous machinery or driving. Bone fractures have been associated with antidepressant treatment. Consider the possibility of a fragility fracture if an antidepressant-treated patient presents with unexplained bone pain, point tenderness, swelling, or bruising (Rabenda 2013; Rizzoli 2012).

Use with caution in patients with a recent history of MI or unstable heart disease. Use has been associated with dose-dependent QT-interval prolongation with doses of 10 mg and 30 mg/day in healthy subjects (mean change from baseline: 4.3 msec and 10.7 msec, respectively); prolongation of QT interval and ventricular arrhythmia (including torsade de pointes) have been reported, particularly in females with preexisting QT prolongation or other risk factors (eg, hypokalemia, other cardiac disease).

Use caution with a previous seizure disorder or condition predisposing to seizures such as brain damage, alcoholism, or concurrent therapy with other drugs which lower the seizure threshold. May cause hyponatremia/SIADH (elderly at increased risk); volume depletion (diuretics may increase risk) may occur. Use caution in patients with metabolic disease. May cause or exacerbate sexual dysfunction. Bioavailability and half-life are increased by 50% in the elderly. Use caution with severe renal impairment or liver impairment; concomitant CNS depressants. May cause mild pupillary dilation which in susceptible individuals can lead to an episode of narrow-angle glaucoma. Consider evaluating patients who have not had an iridectomy for narrow-angle glaucoma risk factors. Use with caution in patients who are hemodynamically unstable. Potentially significant drug-drug interactions may exist, requiring dose or frequency adjustment, additional monitoring, and/or selection of alternative therapy. Escitalopram systemic exposure may be increased in CYP2C19 poor metabolizers; Canadian labeling recommends a dosage adjustment in this patient population.

Abrupt discontinuation or interruption of antidepressant therapy has been associated with a discontinuation syndrome. Symptoms arising may vary with antidepressant however commonly include nausea, vomiting, diarrhea, headaches, light-headedness, dizziness, diminished appetite, sweating, chills, tremors, paresthesias, fatigue, somnolence, and sleep disturbances (eg, vivid dreams, insomnia). Greater risks for developing a discontinuation syndrome have been associated with antidepressants with shorter half-lives, longer durations of treatment, and abrupt discontinuation. For antidepressants of short or intermediate half-lives, symptoms may emerge within 2-5 days after treatment discontinuation and last 7-14 days (APA 2010; Fava 2006; Haddad 2001; Shelton 2001; Warner 2006). Some dosage forms may contain propylene glycol; large amounts are potentially toxic and have been associated hyperosmolality, lactic acidosis, seizures, and respiratory depression; use caution (AAP, 1997; Zar 2007).

Drug Interactions

Metabolism/Transport Effects **Substrate** of CYP2C19 (major), CYP3A4 (major); **Note:** Assignment of Major/Minor substrate status based on clinically relevant drug interaction potential; **Inhibits** CYP2D6 (weak)

Avoid Concomitant Use

Avoid concomitant use of Escitalopram with any of the following: Conivaptan; Dapoxetine; Dosulepin; Fusidic Acid (Systemic); Highest Risk QTc-Prolonging Agents; Hydroxychloroquine; Idelalisib; Iobenguane I 123; Ivabradine; Linezolid; MAO Inhibitors; Methylene Blue; MiFEPRIStone; Moderate Risk QTc-Prolonging Agents; Pimozide; Probucol; Promazine; Tryptophan; Urokinase; Vinflunine

Increased Effect/Toxicity

Escitalopram may increase the levels/effects of: Agents with Antiplatelet Properties; Anticoagulants; Antidepressants (Serotonin Reuptake Inhibitor/Antagonist); Antipsychotic Agents; Apixaban; Aspirin; Blood Glucose Lowering Agents; BusPIRone; Cephalothin; Collagenase (Systemic); Dabigatran Etexilate; Deoxycholic Acid; Desmopressin; Dextromethorphan; Dosulepin; Edoxaban; Highest Risk QTc-Prolonging Agents; Ibritumomab; Methylene Blue; Mexiletine; NSAID (COX-2 Inhibitor); NSAID (Nonselective); Obinutuzumab; Perhexiline; Pimozide; Rivaroxaban; Salicylates; Serotonin Modulators; Thiazide and Thiazide-Like Diuretics; Thrombolytic Agents; Tositumomab and Iodine I 131 Tositumomab; TraMADol; Tricyclic Antidepressants; Urokinase; Vitamin K Antagonists

The levels/effects of Escitalopram may be increased by: Alcohol (Ethyl); Analgesics (Opioid); Antiemetics (5HT3 Antagonists); Antipsychotic Agents; Aprepitant; Bilastine; Buprenorphine; BusPIRone; Cimetidine; CNS Depressants; Conivaptan; CYP2C19 Inhibitors (Moderate); CYP2C19 Inhibitors (Strong); CYP3A4 Inhibitors (Moderate); CYP3A4 Inhibitors (Strong); Dapoxetine; Fosaprepitant; Fusidic Acid (Systemic); Glucosamine; Herbs (Anticoagulant/Antiplatelet Properties); Hydroxychloroquine; Ibrutinib; Idelalisib; Indapamide; Ivabradine; Ivacaftor; Limaprost; Linezolid; Lithium; MAO Inhibitors; Metaxalone; Methylene Blue; Methylphenidate; Metoclopramide; MetyroSINE; MiFEPRIStone; Moderate Risk QTc-Prolonging Agents; Multivitamins/Fluoride (with ADE); Multivitamins/Minerals (with ADEK, Folate, Iron); Multivitamins/Minerals (with AE, No Iron); Netupitant; Omega-3 Fatty Acids; Omeprazole; Palbociclib; Pentosan Polysulfate Sodium; Pentoxifylline; Probucol; Promazine; Prostacyclin Analogues; QTc-Prolonging Agents (Indeterminate Risk and Risk Modifying); Stiripentol; Tedizolid; Teneligliptin; Tipranavir; TraMADol; Tricyclic Antidepressants; Tryptophan; Vinflunine; Vitamin E (Systemic)

Decreased Effect

Escitalopram may decrease the levels/effects of: Iobenguane I 123; Ioflupane I 123; Simeprevir; Thyroid Products

The levels/effects of Escitalopram may be decreased by: Boceprevir; Bosentan; CYP2C19 Inducers (Strong); CYP3A4 Inducers (Moderate); CYP3A4 Inducers (Strong); Cyproheptadine; Dabrafenib; Deferasirox; Enzalutamide; Mitotane; NSAID (COX-2 Inhibitor); NSAID (Nonselective); Siltuximab; St John's Wort; Telaprevir; Tocilizumab

Dietary Considerations May be taken with or without food.

Pharmacodynamics/Kinetics

Onset of Action Depression: The onset of action is within a week; however, individual response varies greatly and full response may not be seen until 8-12 weeks after initiation of treatment.

Half-life Elimination Mean: Adolescents: 19 hours; Adults: ~27-32 hours (increased ~50% in the elderly and doubled in patients with hepatic impairment)

Time to Peak Escitalopram: Adolescents: 2.9 hours; Adults: ~5 hours

Pregnancy Risk Factor C

Pregnancy Considerations Adverse events have been observed in animal reproduction studies. Escitalopram crosses the placenta and is distributed into the amniotic fluid. An increased risk of teratogenic effects, including cardiovascular defects, may be associated with maternal use of escitalopram or other SSRIs; however, available information is conflicting. Nonteratogenic effects in the newborn following SSRI/SNRI exposure late in the third trimester include respiratory distress, cyanosis, apnea, seizures, temperature instability, feeding difficulty, vomiting, hypoglycemia, hypo- or hypertonia, hyper-reflexia, jitteriness, irritability, constant crying, and tremor. Symptoms may be due to the toxicity of the SSRIs/SNRIs or a discontinuation syndrome and may be consistent with serotonin syndrome associated with SSRI treatment. Persistent pulmonary hypertension of the newborn (PPHN) has also been reported with SSRI exposure. The long-term effects of in utero SSRI exposure on infant development and behavior are not known. Escitalopram is the S-enantiomer of the racemic derivative citalopram; also refer to the Citalopram monograph.

Due to pregnancy-induced physiologic changes, some pharmacokinetic parameters of escitalopram may be altered. The ACOG recommends that therapy with SSRIs or SNRIs during pregnancy be individualized; treatment of depression during pregnancy should incorporate the clinical expertise of the mental health clinician, obstetrician, primary health care provider, and pediatrician. According to the American Psychiatric Association (APA), the risks of medication treatment should be weighed against other treatment options and untreated depression. For women who discontinue antidepressant medications during pregnancy and who may be at high risk for postpartum depression, the medications can be restarted following delivery. Treatment algorithms have been developed by the ACOG and the APA for the management of depression in women prior to conception and during pregnancy.

Pregnant women exposed to antidepressants during pregnancy are encouraged to enroll in the National Pregnancy Registry for Antidepressants (NPRAD). Women 18 to 45 years of age or their health care providers may contact the registry by calling 844-405-6185. Enrollment should be done as early in pregnancy as possible.

Breastfeeding Considerations Escitalopram and its metabolite are excreted into breast milk. Limited data is available concerning the effects escitalopram may have in the nursing infant and the long-term effects on development and behavior have not been studied. Adverse effects have been reported in nursing infants exposed to some SSRIs. According to the manufacturer, the decision to continue or discontinue breastfeeding during therapy should take into account the risk of exposure to the infant and the benefits of treatment to the mother. Maternal use of an SSRI during pregnancy may cause delayed milk secretion. Escitalopram is the S-enantiomer of the racemic derivative citalopram; also refer to the Citalopram monograph.

Dosage Forms

Solution, Oral:

Lexapro: 5 mg/5 mL (240 mL)

Generic: 5 mg/5 mL (240 mL)

Tablet, Oral:

Lexapro: 5 mg, 10 mg, 20 mg

Generic: 5 mg, 10 mg, 20 mg

Dosage Forms: Canada

Tablet:

Cipralex: 10 mg, 20 mg

Tablet, Orodispersible, as base:

Cipralex MELTZ: 10 mg, 20 mg [mint flavor]

Dental Comment Problems with SSRI-induced bruxism have been reported and may preclude their use; clinicians attempting to evaluate any patient with bruxism or involuntary muscle movement, who is simultaneously being treated with an SSRI drug, should be aware of the potential association (see Local Anesthetic/Vasoconstrictor Precautions)

Eslicarbazepine (es li kar BAZ e peen)

Brand Names: US Aptiom

Brand Names: Canada Aptiom

Pharmacologic Category Anticonvulsant, Miscellaneous

Use Partial-onset seizures (epilepsy): Monotherapy or adjunctive therapy in the treatment of partial-onset seizures

Local Anesthetic/Vasoconstrictor Precautions No information available to require special precautions

Effects on Dental Treatment No significant effects or complications reported

Effects on Bleeding No information available to require special precautions

Adverse Reactions Frequency not always defined.

Cardiovascular: Hypertension (2%), peripheral edema (2%)

Central nervous system: Dizziness (20% to 28%), drowsiness (16% to 28%, including fatigue, hypersomnia, sedation, lethargy, and malaise), headache (13% to 15%), fatigue (7%), cognitive dysfunction (4% to 7%, including aphasia, lack of concentration, psychomotor retardation, speech disturbance), ataxia (4% to 6%), vertigo (2% to 6%), depression (3%), equilibrium disturbance (3%), falling (3%), abnormal gait (2%), insomnia (2%), dysarthria (1% to 2%), memory impairment (1% to 2%)

Dermatologic: Skin rash (3%)

Endocrine & metabolic: Decreased serum sodium (>10 mEq/L: 5%), hyponatremia (serum sodium <125 mEq/L: 1% to 2%), hypercholesterolemia, increased LDL cholesterol, increased serum triglycerides

Gastrointestinal: Nausea (10% to 16%), vomiting (6% to 10%), diarrhea (4%), abdominal pain (2%), constipation (2%), gastritis (2%)

Genitourinary: Urinary tract infection (2%)

Hematologic & oncologic: Decreased hematocrit, decreased hemoglobin

Neuromuscular & skeletal: Tremor (2% to 4%), weakness (3%), increased creatine phosphokinase

Ophthalmic: Diplopia (9% to 11%), blurred vision (5% to 6%), decreased visual acuity (2%), nystagmus (1% to 2%)

Respiratory: Cough (2%)

Frequency not defined, postmarketing, and/or case reports: Amnesia, anaphylaxis, angioedema, bradyphrenia, confusion, decreased T3 level, decreased T4 (free and total), disorientation, DRESS syndrome, hypochloremia (concurrent with hyponatremia), increased serum bilirubin (>2 x ULN), increased serum transaminases (>3 x ULN), prolongation P-R interval on ECG (mild [Vas-da-Silva 2012]), severe dermatological reaction, Stevens-Johnson syndrome

General Dosage Range Dosage adjustment recommended in patients with renal impairment.

Oral: *Adults:* Initial: 400 mg once daily; Maintenance: 800 mg to 1,600 mg once daily.

Mechanism of Action Eslicarbazepine acetate is extensively converted to eslicarbazepine, which is considered responsible for therapeutic effects. A precise mechanism has not been defined, but is thought to involve inhibition of voltage-gated sodium channels.

Pharmacodynamics/Kinetics

Half-life Elimination 13-20 hours

Time to Peak
Eslicarbazepine: 1-4 hours

Pregnancy Risk Factor C

Pregnancy Considerations Adverse events have been observed in animal reproduction studies. Eslicarbazepine may decrease plasma concentrations of hormonal contraceptives; additional or alternative nonhormonal contraceptives are recommended in women of reproductive potential.

Patients exposed to eslicarbazepine during pregnancy are encouraged to enroll themselves into the AED Pregnancy Registry by calling 1-888-233-2334. Additional information is available at http://www.-aedpregnancyregistry.org.

Esmolol (ES moe lol)

Brand Names: US Brevibloc; Brevibloc in NaCl

Brand Names: Canada Brevibloc; Brevibloc Premixed

Pharmacologic Category Antiarrhythmic Agent, Class II; Antihypertensive; Beta-Blocker, Beta-1 Selective

Use Treatment of supraventricular tachycardia (SVT) and atrial fibrillation/flutter (control ventricular rate); treatment of intraoperative and postoperative tachycardia and/or hypertension; treatment of noncompensatory sinus tachycardia

Local Anesthetic/Vasoconstrictor Precautions No information available to require special precautions

Effects on Dental Treatment Esmolol is a cardioselective beta-blocker. Local anesthetic with vasoconstrictor can be safely used in patients medicated with esmolol. Nonselective beta-blockers (ie, propranolol, nadolol) enhance the pressor response to epinephrine, resulting in hypertension and bradycardia; this has not been reported for esmolol. Many nonsteroidal anti-inflammatory drugs, such as ibuprofen and indomethacin, can reduce the hypotensive effect of beta-blockers after 3 or more weeks of therapy with the NSAID. Short-term NSAID use (ie, 3 days) requires no special precautions in patients taking beta-blockers.

Effects on Bleeding No information available to require special precautions

Adverse Reactions

>10%: Cardiovascular: Decreased blood pressure (20% to 50%), asymptomatic hypotension (dose related: 25%), symptomatic hypotension (dose related: 12%)

1% to 10%:

Cardiovascular: Peripheral ischemia (1%)

Central nervous system: Dizziness (3%), drowsiness (3%), agitation (2%), confusion (2%), headache (2%)

Gastrointestinal: Nausea (7%), vomiting (1%)

Local: Infusion site reaction (8%; including inflammation, irritation, and severe reactions associated with extravasation [eg, blistering, necrosis, thrombophlebitis])

<1%, postmarketing, and/or case reports: Abdominal distress, abnormality in thinking, angioedema, anorexia, anxiety, arterial spasm (coronary), asystole (rare), bradycardia, bronchospasm, cardiac failure (decompensated), constipation, depression, dizziness, dyspepsia, flushing, heart block, hyperkalemia, pallor, paresthesia, psoriasis, renal tubular acidosis, seizure, severe bradycardia (rare), syncope, urinary retention, urticaria, xerostomia

General Dosage Range IV: *Adults:* Bolus: 0.5 **mg**/kg **or** 1 **mg**/kg; Infusion: 50-200 mcg/kg/minute (maximum: 300 mcg/kg/minute)

Mechanism of Action Class II antiarrhythmic: Competitively blocks response to $beta_1$-adrenergic stimulation with little or no effect of $beta_2$-receptors except at high doses, no intrinsic sympathomimetic activity, no membrane stabilizing activity

Pharmacodynamics/Kinetics

Onset of Action Beta-blockade: IV: 2-10 minutes (quickest when loading doses are administered)

Duration of Action Hemodynamic effects: 10-30 minutes; prolonged following higher cumulative doses, extended duration of use

Half-life Elimination
Children ≥18 months and Adolescents ≤16 years: Variable; mean range: 2.7 to 4.8 minutes (reported full range: 0.2 to 9.9 minutes) (Cuneo 1994; Tabbutt 2008; Wiest 1991; Wiest 1998)
Adults: Esmolol: 9 minutes; Acid metabolite: 3.7 hours; elimination of metabolite decreases with end-stage renal disease

Pregnancy Risk Factor C

Pregnancy Considerations Adverse events were observed in some animal reproduction studies. Esmolol has been shown to cause fetal bradycardia. Adverse fetal/neonatal events have also been observed with the chronic use of beta-blockers during pregnancy; however, esmolol is a short-acting beta-blocker and not indicated for chronic use. Esmolol is approved for the treatment of supraventricular tachycardia (SVT); however, other agents are preferred in pregnant women (ACC/AHA/HRS [Page 2015]).

Esomeprazole (es oh ME pray zol)

Related Information
Gastrointestinal Disorders *on page 1775*
Omeprazole *on page 1233*

Brand Names: US NexIUM; NexIUM 24HR [OTC]; NexIUM I.V.

Brand Names: Canada Apo-Esomeprazole; Mylan-Esomeprazole; Nexium; PMS-Esomeprazole DR

Generic Availability (US) May be product dependent

Pharmacologic Category Proton Pump Inhibitor; Substituted Benzimidazole

Use

Oral:

Esomeprazole magnesium and esomeprazole strontium:

Gastroesophageal reflux disease (Rx only):

Healing of erosive esophagitis: Short-term (4 to 8 weeks) treatment of erosive esophagitis

Maintenance of healing of erosive esophagitis: Maintaining symptom resolution and healing of erosive esophagitis

Symptomatic gastroesophageal reflux disease: Short-term (4 to 8 weeks) treatment of symptomatic gastroesophageal reflux disease (GERD)

***Helicobacter pylori* eradication (Rx only):** As part of a multidrug regimen for *Helicobacter pylori* eradication in patients with duodenal ulcer disease (active or history of within the past 5 years)

Risk reduction of nonsteroidal anti-inflammatory drug-associated gastric ulcer (Rx only): Prevention of gastric ulcers associated with continuous NSAID therapy in patients at risk (age ≥60 years and/or history of gastric ulcer)

Pathological hypersecretory conditions, including Zollinger-Ellison syndrome (Rx only): Treatment (long-term) of pathological hypersecretory conditions including Zollinger-Ellison syndrome

Canadian labeling: Additional use (not in US labeling): Oral: Treatment of nonerosive reflux disease (NERD); treatment of NSAID-induced gastric ulcers

Esomeprazole magnesium:

Heartburn (OTC labeling): Treatment of frequent heartburn (≥2 days per week).

IV: Esomeprazole sodium:

Gastroesophageal reflux disease (Rx only): Short-term (≤10 days) treatment of gastroesophageal reflux disease (GERD) with erosive esophagitis in pediatric patients 1 month to 17 years of age and adults when oral therapy is not possible or appropriate

Risk reduction of ulcer rebleeding postprocedure (Rx only): Decrease the risk of rebleeding postendoscopy for acute bleeding gastric or duodenal ulcers in adults

Local Anesthetic/Vasoconstrictor Precautions No information available to require special precautions

Effects on Dental Treatment Key adverse event(s) related to dental treatment: Xerostomia (normal salivary flow resumes upon discontinuation)

Effects on Bleeding No information available to require special precautions

Adverse Reactions Unless otherwise specified, percentages represent adverse reactions identified in clinical trials evaluating the oral formulation.

>10%: Central nervous system: Headache (2% to 11%)

1% to 10%:

Central nervous system: Irritability (infants: ≥5%), dizziness (intravenous: ≤3%; oral: <1%), vertigo (intravenous: ≤3%), drowsiness (children: 2%; adults: <1%)

Dermatologic: Pruritus (intravenous: 1%; oral: <1%)

Endocrine & metabolic: Altered thyroid hormone levels (increased thyroxine: ≤1%), decreased serum potassium (≤1%), decreased serum sodium (≤1%), decreased thyroid hormones (thyroxine: ≤1%), increased gastrin (≤1%), increased serum potassium (≤1%), increased serum sodium (≤1%), increased thyroid stimulating hormone level (≤1%), increased uric acid (≤1%)

Gastrointestinal: Flatulence (intravenous: 10%; oral: ≥1%), diarrhea (2% to 4%), abdominal pain (1% to 6%), nausea (intravenous: 6%; oral: ≥1% to 2%), vomiting (infants: 1% to ≥5%; adults: <1%), xerostomia (intravenous: 4%; oral: ≥1%), constipation (intravenous: 3%; oral: ≥1%)

Hematologic & oncologic: Change in platelet count (≤1%)

Hepatic: Increased serum alkaline phosphatase (≤1%), increased serum ALT (≤1%), increased serum AST (≤1%)

Local: Injection site reaction (intravenous: 2% to 4%)

Renal: Increased serum creatinine (≤1%)

Respiratory: Cough (intravenous: 1%; oral: <1%), tachypnea (infants, oral: 1%)

Miscellaneous: Fever (intravenous: 4%; oral: <1%)

Frequency not defined:

Cardiovascular: Esophageal varices

Gastrointestinal: Barrett esophagus, duodenitis, esophageal stenosis, esophageal ulcer, esophagitis, gastritis, mucosal discoloration

Hematologic & oncologic: Benign polyp

Miscellaneous: Benign nodule

<1%, postmarketing, and/or case reports: Acne vulgaris, acute interstitial nephritis, aggressive behavior, ageusia, agitation, agranulocytosis, albuminuria, alopecia, altered sense of smell, anaphylactic shock, anaphylaxis, anemia, angioedema, anorexia, apathy, aphthous stomatitis, arthralgia, arthropathy, back pain, blurred vision, bone fracture, bronchospasm, candidiasis (urogenital), cervical lymphadenopathy, change in bowel habits, chest pain, *Clostridium difficile*-associated diarrhea, colitis (microscopic), confusion, conjunctivitis, cutaneous lupus erythematous (including exacerbations), cyanocobalamin deficiency, cystitis, depression, dermatitis, diaphoresis, dysgeusia, dysmenorrhea, dyspepsia, dysphagia, dyspnea, dysuria, edema, enlargement of abdomen, epigastric pain, epistaxis, eructation, erythema multiforme, erythematous rash, exacerbation of arthritis, exacerbation of asthma, facial edema, fatigue, fibromyalgia syndrome, flu-like symptoms, flushing, frequent bowel movements, fungal infection, gastroenteritis, gastrointestinal dysplasia, gastrointestinal hemorrhage, genital candidiasis, GI moniliasis, glycosuria, goiter, gynecomastia, hallucination, hematuria, hepatic encephalopathy, hepatic failure, hepatitis, hepatotoxicity (idiosyncratic) (Chalasani 2014), hernia, hiccups, hot flash, hyperbilirubinemia, hyperhidrosis, hypersensitivity reaction, hypertension, hypertonia, hyperuricemia, hypochromic anemia, hypoesthesia, hypomagnesemia (with or without hypocalcemia and/or hypokalemia), hyponatremia, impotence, increased appetite, increased thirst, insomnia, interstitial nephritis, jaundice, laryngeal edema, leukocytosis, leukopenia, maculopapular rash, malaise, melena, menstrual disease, migraine, mouth disease, muscle cramps, myalgia, myasthenia, nervousness, otalgia, otitis media, pain, pancreatitis, pancytopenia, paresthesia, pathological fracture due to osteoporosis, peripheral edema, pharyngeal disease, pharyngitis, polymyalgia rheumatica, polyuria, pruritus ani, rectal disease, renal disease (chronic; [Lazarus 2016]), rhinitis, rigors, sinusitis, skin photosensitivity, skin rash, sleep disorder, Stevens-Johnson syndrome, stomatitis, systemic lupus erythematosus (including exacerbations), tachycardia, thrombocytopenia, tinnitus, tongue disease, tongue edema, toxic epidermal necrolysis, tremor, urinary frequency, urine abnormality, urticaria, vaginitis, vertigo, visual disturbance, visual field defect, weakness, weight gain, weight loss

Dosing

Adult & Geriatric

Note: All dosing is expressed in terms of esomeprazole base, regardless of the salt associated with the dosing information. Esomeprazole strontium 24.65 mg is equivalent to 20 mg of esomeprazole base; esomeprazole strontium 49.3 mg is equivalent to 40 mg of esomeprazole base.

Erosive esophagitis (healing): Oral: Esomeprazole magnesium, esomeprazole strontium: Initial: 20 to 40 mg once daily for 4 to 8 weeks; if incomplete healing, may continue for an additional 4 to 8 weeks; maintenance: 20 mg once daily (controlled studies did not extend beyond 6 months)

Heartburn (OTC labeling): 20 mg once daily for 14 days (maximum: 20 mg/day); treatment may be repeated after 4 months if needed

Nonerosive reflux disease (NERD) (Canadian labeling): Oral: Esomeprazole magnesium: Initial: 20 mg once daily for 2 to 4 weeks; lack of symptom control after 4 weeks warrants further evaluation; maintenance (in patients with successful initial therapy): 20 mg once daily as needed

Symptomatic gastroesophageal reflux: Oral: Esomeprazole magnesium, esomeprazole strontium: 20 mg once daily for 4 weeks; may consider an additional 4 weeks of treatment if symptoms do not resolve

Treatment of GERD (short-term): IV: 20 mg or 40 mg once daily. **Note:** Indicated only in cases where oral therapy is inappropriate or not possible; safety/efficacy ≥10 days has not been established.

Prevention of recurrent gastric or duodenal ulcer bleeding postendoscopy: IV: 80 mg over 30 minutes, followed by 8 mg/hour continuous infusion for a total of 72 hours, then 40 mg *orally* once daily for 27 additional days (Sung, 2009) or may follow continuous infusion with any single daily-dose oral proton pump inhibitor (PPI) for a duration dictated by the underlying etiology (Barkun, 2010). **Note:** The use of intermittent PPIs was found to be comparable with the use of continuous infusion PPIs in patients with high-risk endoscopic findings and may be preferred (Sachar, 2014).

***Helicobacter pylori* eradication:** Oral:

Manufacturer labeling: Esomeprazole magnesium, esomeprazole strontium: 40 mg once daily administered with amoxicillin 1,000 mg *and* clarithromycin 500 mg twice daily for 10 days

American College of Gastroenterology guidelines (Chey, 2007):

Nonpenicillin allergy: 40 mg once daily administered with amoxicillin 1,000 mg *and* clarithromycin 500 mg twice daily for 10 to 14 days

Penicillin allergy: 40 mg once daily administered with clarithromycin 500 mg *and* metronidazole 500 mg twice daily for 10 to 14 days **or** 40 mg once daily administered with bismuth subsalicylate 525 mg *and* metronidazole 250 mg *plus* tetracycline 500 mg 4 times daily for 10 to 14 days

Canadian labeling: Esomeprazole magnesium: 20 mg twice daily for 7 days; requires combination therapy

Prevention of NSAID-induced gastric ulcers: Oral:

US labeling: Esomeprazole magnesium, esomeprazole strontium: 20 to 40 mg once daily for up to 6 months

Canadian labeling: Esomeprazole magnesium: 20 mg once daily for up to 6 months

Note: 40 mg daily did not show additional benefit over 20 mg daily in clinical trials.

Treatment of NSAID-induced gastric ulcers (Canadian labeling; off-label in US): Oral: Esomeprazole magnesium: 20 mg once daily for 4 to 8 weeks (Goldstein, 2007)

Pathological hypersecretory conditions (Zollinger-Ellison syndrome): Oral: Esomeprazole magnesium, esomeprazole strontium: 40 mg twice daily; adjust regimen to individual patient needs; doses up to 240 mg daily have been administered

Pediatric

Note: All dosing is expressed in terms of esomeprazole base, regardless of the salt associated with the dosing information. Esomeprazole strontium is not recommended for use in pediatrics.

Symptomatic GERD: Oral: Esomeprazole magnesium:

Children 1 to 11 years: 10 mg once daily for up to 8 weeks; **Note:** Safety and efficacy of doses >1 mg/kg/day and/or therapy beyond 8 weeks have not been established.

Adolescents 12 to 17 years: 20 mg once daily for up to 4 weeks

Treatment of GERD (short-term): IV: **Note:** Indicated only in cases where oral therapy is inappropriate or not possible; safety/efficacy ≥10 days has not been established.

Children 1 month to <1 year: 0.5 mg/kg once daily

Children 1 to 17 years: <55 kg: 10 mg once daily; ≥55 kg: 20 mg once daily

Erosive esophagitis (healing): Oral: Esomeprazole magnesium:

Children 1 month to <1 year: **Note:** Safety and efficacy of doses >1.33 mg/kg/day and/or therapy beyond 6 weeks have not been established.

3 to 5 kg: 2.5 mg once daily for up to 6 weeks

>5 to 7.5 kg: 5 mg once daily for up to 6 weeks

>7.5 to 12 kg: 10 mg once daily for up to 6 weeks

Children 1 to 11 years: **Note:** Safety and efficacy of doses >1 mg/kg/day and/or therapy beyond 8 weeks have not been established.

<20 kg: 10 mg once daily for 8 weeks

≥20 kg: 10 to 20 mg once daily for 8 weeks

Adolescents 12 to 17 years: 20 to 40 mg once daily for 4 to 8 weeks

Nonerosive reflux disease (NERD) (Canadian labeling): Oral: Esomeprazole magnesium:

Children 1 to 11 years: 10 mg once daily for up to 8 weeks. **Note:** Safety and efficacy of doses >1 mg/kg/day and/or therapy beyond 8 weeks have not been established.

Adolescents 12 to 17 years: 20 mg once daily for 2 to 4 weeks; lack of symptom control after 4 weeks warrants further evaluation (safety studies do not extend beyond 8 weeks)

Renal Impairment

Oral:

Esomeprazole magnesium: Mild-to-severe impairment: No dosage adjustment necessary.

Esomeprazole strontium:

Mild-to-moderate impairment: No dosage adjustment necessary.

Severe impairment: Use is not recommended (has not been studied).

IV: Mild-to-severe impairment: No dosage adjustment necessary.

Hepatic Impairment

Oral:

Safety and efficacy not established in children with hepatic impairment.

Mild to moderate impairment (Child-Pugh class A or B): No dosage adjustment necessary.

Severe impairment (Child-Pugh class C): Maximum: 20 mg daily.

IV:

Treatment of GERD (short-term):

Mild to moderate impairment (Child-Pugh class A or B): No dosage adjustment necessary.

Severe impairment (Child-Pugh class C): Dose should not exceed 20 mg daily

Prevention of recurrent gastric or duodenal ulcer bleeding postendoscopy:

Mild to moderate impairment (Child-Pugh class A or B): 80 mg over 30 minutes, followed by a maximum continuous infusion of 6 mg/hour for a total of 72 hours

Severe impairment (Child-Pugh class C): 80 mg over 30 minutes, followed by a maximum continuous infusion of 4 mg/hour for a total of 72 hour

Mechanism of Action Proton pump inhibitor suppresses gastric acid secretion by inhibition of the H^+/K^+-ATPase in the gastric parietal cell. Esomeprazole is the S-isomer of omeprazole.

Contraindications
Hypersensitivity (eg, anaphylaxis, anaphylactic shock, angioedema, bronchospasm, acute interstitial nephritis, urticaria) to esomeprazole, other substituted benzimidazole proton pump inhibitors, or any component of the formulation

OTC labeling: When used for self-medication (OTC), do not use if you have trouble or pain when swallowing food; vomiting with blood, or bloody or black stools; heartburn with lightheadedness, dizziness, or sweating; chest pain or shoulder pain with shortness of breath, sweating, pain spreading to arms, neck or shoulders, or lightheadedness; frequent chest pain

Warnings/Precautions Use of proton pump inhibitors (PPIs) may increase the risk of gastrointestinal infections (eg, *Salmonella, Campylobacter*). Relief of symptoms does not preclude the presence of a gastric malignancy. No reports of enterochromaffin-like (ECL) cell carcinoids, dysplasia, or neoplasia have occurred. Use of PPIs may increase risk of CDAD, especially in hospitalized patients; consider CDAD diagnosis in patients with persistent diarrhea that does not improve. Use the lowest dose and shortest duration of PPI therapy appropriate for the condition being treated. Safety and efficacy of IV therapy for GERD >10 days have not been established; transition from IV to oral therapy as soon possible. Bioavailability may be increased in elderly patients and patients with hepatic dysfunction. Decreased *H. pylori* eradication rates have been observed with short-term (≤7 days) combination therapy. The American College of Gastroenterology recommends 10 to 14 days of therapy (triple or quadruple) for eradication of *H. pylori* (Chey 2007).

PPIs may diminish the therapeutic effect of clopidogrel, thought to be due to reduced formation of the active metabolite of clopidogrel. The manufacturer of clopidogrel recommends either avoidance of both omeprazole (even when scheduled 12 hours apart) and esomeprazole or use of a PPI with comparatively less effect on the active metabolite of clopidogrel (eg, pantoprazole). In contrast to these warnings, others have recommended the continued use of PPIs, regardless of the degree of inhibition, in patients with a history of GI bleeding or multiple risk factors for GI bleeding who are also receiving clopidogrel since no evidence has established clinically meaningful differences in outcome; however, a clinically-significant interaction cannot be excluded in those who are poor metabolizers of clopidogrel (Abraham 2010; Levine 2011). Additionally, potentially significant drug-drug interactions may exist, requiring dose or frequency adjustment, additional monitoring, and/or selection of alternative therapy.

Increased incidence of osteoporosis-related bone fractures of the hip, spine, or wrist may occur with PPI therapy. Patients on high-dose or long-term therapy (≥1 year) should be monitored. Use the lowest effective dose for the shortest duration of time, use vitamin D and calcium supplementation, and follow appropriate guidelines to reduce risk of fractures in patients at risk. Acute interstitial nephritis has been observed in patients taking PPIs; may occur at any time during therapy and is generally due to an idiopathic hypersensitivity reaction. Discontinue if acute interstitial nephritis develops.

Hypomagnesemia, reported rarely, usually with prolonged PPI use of ≥3 months (most cases >1 year of therapy); may be symptomatic or asymptomatic; severe cases may cause tetany, seizures, and cardiac arrhythmias. Consider obtaining serum magnesium concentrations prior to beginning long-term therapy, especially if taking concomitant digoxin, diuretics, or other drugs known to cause hypomagnesemia; and periodically thereafter. Hypomagnesemia may be corrected by magnesium supplementation, although discontinuation of esomeprazole may be necessary; magnesium levels typically return to normal within 1 week of stopping.

Prolonged treatment (≥2 years) may lead to vitamin B_{12} malabsorption and subsequent vitamin B_{12} deficiency. The magnitude of the deficiency is dose-related and the association is stronger in females and those younger in age (<30 years); prevalence is decreased after discontinuation of therapy (Lam 2013). Cutaneous and systemic lupus erythematosus has been reported as new onset or exacerbation of existing autoimmune disease; most cases were cutaneous lupus erythematosus (CLE), most commonly, subacute CLE (occurring within weeks to years after continuous therapy). Systemic lupus erythematosus (SLE) is less common (typically occurs within days to years after initiating treatment) and occurred primarily in young adults up to the elderly. Discontinue therapy if signs or symptoms of CLE or SLE occur and refer to specialist for evaluation; most patients improve 4 to 12 weeks after discontinuation of esomeprazole.

Cutaneous and systemic lupus erythematosus has been reported as new onset or exacerbation of existing autoimmune disease; most cases reported were cutaneous lupus erythematosus (CLE) with onset up to 2 years after continuous therapy and occurred primarily in older patients (some cases were reported in patients as young as 7 months of age); complete recovery generally occurred within 12 weeks after discontinuation. Systemic lupus erythematosus (SLE) is less common and typically occurs within 30 days after initiation (some cases were reported days or years) and occurred primarily in older adults (some cases reported in young adults); clinical symptoms generally resolved within 8 weeks. Discontinue therapy if signs or symptoms of CLE or SLE occur and refer to specialist for evaluation.

Severe liver dysfunction may require dosage reductions. Dosage adjustments are not necessary for any degree of renal impairment when using esomeprazole magnesium or esomeprazole sodium; however, since pharmacokinetics of the strontium may be reduced in mild to moderate renal impairment, esomeprazole strontium is not recommended for use in severe impairment (has not been studied). Esomeprazole strontium competes with calcium for intestinal absorption and is incorporated into bone; use of esomeprazole strontium in pediatric patients is not recommended. When used for self-medication (OTC), do not use for >14 days.

When used for self-medication (OTC), notify health care provider before use if any of the following are present: heartburn for >3 months; frequent wheezing, particularly with heartburn; unexplained weight loss; nausea or vomiting; or stomach pain. Discontinue use and notify health care provider if heartburn continues or worsens; diarrhea occurs; if >14 days of therapy is needed; or if >1 course of therapy is needed every 4 months.

Serum chromogranin A (CgA) levels increase secondary to drug-induced decreases in gastric acid. May cause false positive results in diagnostic investigations for neuroendocrine tumors. Temporarily stop omeprazole treatment ≥14 days before CgA test; if CgA level high, repeat test to confirm. Use same commercial lab for testing to prevent variable results.

Drug Interactions

Metabolism/Transport Effects Substrate of CYP2C19 (major), CYP3A4 (minor); **Note:** Assignment of Major/Minor substrate status based on clinically relevant drug interaction potential; **Inhibits** CYP2C19 (weak)

Avoid Concomitant Use

Avoid concomitant use of Esomeprazole with any of the following: Dasatinib; Delavirdine; Erlotinib; Nelfinavir; PAZOPanib; RifAMPin; Rilpivirine; Risedronate; St John's Wort; Velpatasvir

Increased Effect/Toxicity

Esomeprazole may increase the levels/effects of: Amphetamine; Cilostazol; Dexmethylphenidate; Dextroamphetamine; Methotrexate; Methylphenidate; Raltegravir; Risedronate; Saquinavir; Tacrolimus (Systemic); Vitamin K Antagonists; Voriconazole

The levels/effects of Esomeprazole may be increased by: Fluconazole; Ketoconazole (Systemic); Voriconazole

Decreased Effect

Esomeprazole may decrease the levels/effects of: Atazanavir; Bisphosphonate Derivatives; Bosutinib; Capecitabine; Cefditoren; Clopidogrel; Cysteamine (Systemic); Dabigatran Etexilate; Dabrafenib; Dasatinib; Delavirdine; Erlotinib; Gefitinib; Indinavir; Iron Salts; Itraconazole; Ketoconazole (Systemic); Ledipasvir; Mesalamine; Multivitamins/Minerals (with ADEK, Folate, Iron); Mycophenolate; Nelfinavir; Nilotinib; PAZOPanib; Posaconazole; Rilpivirine; Riociguat; Risedronate; Velpatasvir

The levels/effects of Esomeprazole may be decreased by: Dabrafenib; Enzalutamide; Lumacaftor; RifAMPin; St John's Wort; Tipranavir

Food Interactions Prolonged treatment (≥2 years) may lead to malabsorption of dietary vitamin B_{12} and subsequent vitamin B_{12} deficiency (Lam, 2013).

Dietary Considerations Take at least 1 hour before meals; best if taken before breakfast.

Pharmacodynamics/Kinetics

Half-life Elimination

Infants: 0.93 hours
Children 1 to 5 years: 0.42 to 0.74 hours (Zhao 2006)
Children 6 to 11 years: 0.73 to 0.88 hours (Zhao 2006)
Adolescents 12 to 17 years: 0.82 to 1.22 hours (Li 2006)
Adults: ~1 to 1.5 hours

Time to Peak Oral:

Infants: Median: 3 hours
Children 1 to 5 years: 1.33 to 1.44 hours (Zhao 2006)
Children 6 to 11 years: 1.75 to 1.79 hours (Zhao 2006)
Adolescents 12 to 17 years: 1.96 to 2.04 hours (Li 2006)
Adults: 1.5 to 2 hours

Pregnancy Considerations Adverse events have been observed in some animal reproduction studies. An increased risk of hypospadias was reported following maternal use of proton pump inhibitors (PPIs) during pregnancy (Anderka, 2012), but this was based on a small number of exposures and the same association was not found in another study (Erichsen, 2012). An increased risk of major birth defects following maternal use of PPIs during pregnancy was not observed in an additional study (Pasternak, 2010). Esomeprazole is the s-isomer of omeprazole; refer to the omeprazole monograph for additional information. When treating GERD in pregnancy, PPIs may be used when clinically indicated (Katz, 2013).

Breastfeeding Considerations Esomeprazole and strontium (limited data) are excreted in breast milk. According to the manufacturer, the decision to continue or discontinue breastfeeding during therapy should take into account the risk of infant exposure, the benefits of breastfeeding to the infant, and benefits of treatment to the mother. Esomeprazole is the s-isomer of omeprazole, and omeprazole is excreted in breast milk; refer to Omeprazole monograph for additional information.

Dosage Forms Considerations

Esomeprazole strontium 49.3 mg is equivalent to 40 mg of esomeprazole base.

Dosage Forms

Capsule Delayed Release, Oral:
NexIUM: 20 mg, 40 mg
NexIUM 24HR [OTC]: 20 mg
Generic: 20 mg, 24.65 mg, 40 mg, 49.3 mg

Packet, Oral:
NexIUM: 2.5 mg (30 ea); 5 mg (30 ea); 10 mg (30 ea); 20 mg (30 ea); 40 mg (30 ea)

Solution Reconstituted, Intravenous:
NexIUM I.V.: 40 mg (1 ea)
Generic: 20 mg (1 ea); 40 mg (1 ea)

Tablet Delayed Release, Oral:
NexIUM 24HR [OTC]: 20 mg

Dosage Forms: Canada Note: Strength expressed as base.

Granules, for oral suspension, delayed release, as magnesium:
Nexium®: 10 mg/packet (28s)

Tablet, extended release, as magnesium:
Nexium®: 20 mg, 40 mg

Estazolam (es TA zoe lam)

Related Information

Dentin Hypersensitivity, Acid Erosion, High Caries Index, Management of Alveolar Osteitis, and Xerostomia *on page 1857*

Pharmacologic Category Benzodiazepine

Use Insomnia: Short-term management of insomnia characterized by difficulty in falling asleep, frequent nocturnal awakenings, and/or early morning awakenings.

Local Anesthetic/Vasoconstrictor Precautions No information available to require special precautions

Effects on Dental Treatment Key adverse event(s) related to dental treatment: Significant xerostomia (normal salivary flow resumes upon discontinuation)

Effects on Bleeding No information available to require special precautions

Adverse Reactions

>10%: Central nervous system: Drowsiness (42%)

1% to 10%:

Central nervous system: Dizziness (7%), ataxia (4%), hangover effect (3%), abnormality in thinking (2%), confusion (2%), anxiety (≥1%)

Dermatologic: Pruritus (1%)

Gastrointestinal: Constipation (≥1%), xerostomia (≥1%)

Neuromuscular & skeletal: Hypokinesia (8%), leg pain (3%), stiffness (1%)

<1%, postmarketing, and/or case reports: Acne vulgaris, adenopathy, agitation, agranulocytosis, amnesia, apathy, arm pain, arthralgia, arthritis, asthma, auditory impairment, breast swelling, cardiac arrhythmia, chills, cough, decreased appetite, decreased libido, diaphoresis, diplopia, dysgeusia, dyspnea, edema, emotional lability, enterocolitis, epistaxis, euphoria, eye irritation,

eye pain, fever, flatulence, flushing, gastritis, genital discharge, hallucination, hematuria, hostility, hypersensitivity reaction, hyperventilation, hyporeflexia, increased appetite, increased serum AST, increased thirst, jaw pain, laryngitis, leukopenia, melena, muscle spasm, myalgia, neck pain, neuritis, nocturia, nystagmus, oliguria, oral mucosa ulcer, oral paresthesia, otalgia, palpitations, paresthesia, pelvic cramps (menstrual cramps), photophobia, polyuria, purpura, rhinitis, scotoma, seizure, sinusitis, skin photosensitivity, skin rash, sleep disorder, Stevens-Johnson syndrome, stupor, swelling of eye, syncope, thyroid nodule, tinnitus, tremor, twitching, urinary hesitancy, urinary incontinence, urinary urgency, urticaria, visual disturbance, vomiting, vulvovaginal pruritus, weight gain, weight loss, xeroderma

General Dosage Range Oral: *Adults:* 1 to 2 mg at bedtime

Mechanism of Action Binds to stereospecific benzodiazepine receptors on the postsynaptic GABA neuron at several sites within the central nervous system, including the limbic system, reticular formation. Enhancement of the inhibitory effect of GABA on neuronal excitability results by increased neuronal membrane permeability to chloride ions. This shift in chloride ions results in hyperpolarization (a less excitable state) and stabilization. Benzodiazepine receptors and effects appear to be linked to the GABA-A receptors. Benzodiazepines do not bind to GABA-B receptors (Vinkers 2012).

Pharmacodynamics/Kinetics

Duration of Action Variable

Half-life Elimination 10 to 24 hours

Time to Peak Serum: ~2 hours (range: 0.5 to 6 hours)

Pregnancy Risk Factor X

Pregnancy Considerations Although information specific to estazolam has not been located, all benzodiazepines are assumed to cross the placenta. Teratogenic effects have been observed with some benzodiazepines; however, additional studies are needed. The incidence of premature birth and low birth weights may be increased following maternal use of benzodiazepines; hypoglycemia and respiratory problems in the neonate may occur following exposure late in pregnancy. Neonatal withdrawal symptoms may occur within days to weeks after birth and "floppy infant syndrome" (which also includes withdrawal symptoms) has been reported with some benzodiazepines (Bergman 1992; Iqbal 2002; Wikner 2007). The use of estazolam is contraindicated in pregnant women.

Controlled Substance C-IV

Estradiol (Systemic) (es tra DYE ole)

Related Information

Endocrine Disorders and Pregnancy *on page 1781*

Rheumatoid Arthritis, Osteoarthritis, and Osteoporosis *on page 1792*

Brand Names: US Alora; Climara; Delestrogen; Depo-Estradiol; Divigel; EC-RX Estradiol; Elestrin; Estrace; Estrasorb [DSC]; Estrogel; Evamist; Femring; Menostar; Minivelle; Vivelle-Dot

Brand Names: Canada Climara; Depo-Estradiol; Divigel; Estradot; EstroGel; Menostar; Oesclim; Sandoz-Estradiol Derm 100; Sandoz-Estradiol Derm 50; Sandoz-Estradiol Derm 75

Pharmacologic Category Estrogen Derivative

Use

Breast cancer, metastatic: Treatment of metastatic breast cancer (palliation) in appropriately selected men and postmenopausal women.

Hypoestrogenism (female): Treatment of hypoestrogenism due to hypogonadism, castration, or primary ovarian failure

Osteoporosis prevention (female): Prevention of postmenopausal osteoporosis

Limitations of use: For use only in women at significant risk of postmenopausal osteoporosis; consider use of nonestrogen medications.

Prostate cancer, advanced: Treatment of androgen dependent advanced prostatic cancer (palliation)

Vasomotor symptoms associated with menopause: Treatment of moderate to severe vasomotor symptoms associated with menopause.

Vulvar and vaginal atrophy associated with menopause: Treatment of moderate to severe vulvar and vaginal atrophy associated with menopause.

Limitations of use: When used solely for the treatment of vulvar and vaginal atrophy, topical vaginal products should be considered.

Local Anesthetic/Vasoconstrictor Precautions No information available to require special precautions

Effects on Dental Treatment No significant effects or complications reported

Effects on Bleeding No information available to require special precautions

Adverse Reactions Frequency not always defined. Some adverse reactions observed with estrogen and/or progestin combination therapy.

Cardiovascular: Edema (10% to 13%), hypertension (3% to 7%), cerebrovascular accident, deep vein thrombosis, local thrombophlebitis, myocardial infarction, pulmonary thromboembolism, retinal thrombosis, thrombophlebitis, venous thromboembolism

Central nervous system: Headache (9% to 50%), pain (6% to 13%), depression (1% to 11%), anxiety (4% to 10%), dizziness (≤8%), migraine (7%), nipple pain (1% to 7%), hypoesthesia (3%), chorea, dementia, exacerbation of epilepsy, irritability, mood disorder, nervousness

Dermatologic: Skin rash (7% to 9%), pruritus (4% to 7%), chloasma, erythema multiforme, erythema nodosum, localized erythema (transdermal patch), loss of scalp hair, skin discoloration (melasma), urticaria

Endocrine & metabolic: Weight gain (4% to 9%), hot flash (6%), hirsutism (≤5%), change in libido, change in menstrual flow (alterations in frequency and flow of bleeding patterns), exacerbation of diabetes mellitus, exacerbation of porphyria, fibrocystic breast changes, fluid retention, galactorrhea, hypocalcemia, increased serum triglycerides, weight loss

Gastrointestinal: Abdominal pain (6% to 16%), dyspepsia (3% to 9%), constipation (4% to 7%), flatulence (3% to 7%), nausea (3% to 7%), gastroenteritis (3% to 4%), diarrhea (3%), abdominal cramps, bloating, carbohydrate intolerance, gallbladder disease, pancreatitis, vomiting

Genitourinary: Mastalgia (5% to 35%), vaginal hemorrhage (33%), breast tenderness (3% to 17%), endometrium disease (15%), breakthrough bleeding (6% to 11%), leukorrhea (2% to 11%), abnormal uterine bleeding (4% to 10%), breast hypertrophy (7%), dysmenorrhea (7%), cervical polyp (6%), vulvovaginal candidiasis (6%), urinary tract infection (4% to 6%), change in cervical ectropion, change in cervical secretions, endometrial hyperplasia, nipple discharge, spotting, uterine fibroids (size increased), uterine pain,

vaginal discomfort (vaginal ring; burning, irritation, itching), vaginitis
Hematologic & oncologic: Hemorrhagic eruption, hypercoagulability state, malignant neoplasm of breast, ovarian cancer
Hepatic: Cholestatic jaundice, exacerbation of hepatic hemangioma
Hypersensitivity: Hypersensitivity reaction (4% to 5%), anaphylactoid reaction, anaphylaxis, angioedema
Infection: Infection (3% to 12%), fungal infection (3% to 10%)
Local: Application site reaction (gel, spray, transdermal patch ≤1%)
Neuromuscular & skeletal: Arthralgia (4% to 12%), back pain (3% to 11%), weakness (8%), limb pain (7% to 8%), myalgia (5% to 6%), neck pain (3% to 6%), arthropathy (4% to 5%), exacerbation of systemic lupus erythematosus, leg cramps
Ophthalmic: Conjunctivitis (3%), change in corneal curvature (steepening), contact lens intolerance
Otic: Otitis media (3%)
Respiratory: Nasopharyngitis (4% to 20%), upper respiratory tract infection (6% to 17%), flu-like symptoms (8% to 13%), sinusitis (4% to 13%), sinus headache (9% to 11%), bronchitis (6% to 8%), sinus congestion (7%), pharyngitis (2% to 7%), rhinitis (2% to 6%), cough (3% to 4%), asthma (3%), exacerbation of asthma
Miscellaneous: Accidental injury (7% to 14%), cyst (7%)
Postmarketing and/or case reports: Abnormal gait, abnormal hepatic function tests, aphasia, blindness, bowel obstruction (vaginal ring), bradyphrenia, chest pain, cholecystitis, cholelithiasis, dyspnea, emotional lability, fatigue, genitourinary complaint (inadvertent ring insertion into the bladder should be considered with unexplained urinary complaints), hemorrhage, hepatitis, hyperhidrosis, hypermenorrhea, ischemic heart disease, lip swelling, local irritation (transdermal patch), localized erythema (transdermal patch), malaise, mechanical complication of genitourinary device (ring adherence to vaginal or bladder wall), meningioma, muscle spasm, myoclonus, night sweats, oral paresthesia, ovarian cyst, palpitations, paresthesia, peripheral edema, pharyngeal edema, phlebitis, portal vein thrombosis, purpura, retinal vein occlusion, soft tissue sarcoma (malignant mesenchymoma), swollen tongue, tachyphylaxis, toxic shock syndrome (vaginal ring), transient ischemic attacks, unstable angina pectoris, uterine enlargement, uterine neoplasm, vaginal discharge

General Dosage Range

IM:

Cypionate:

Adults (females): Hypoestrogenism: 1.5 to 2 mg monthly

Adults (females): Menopause: 1 to 5 mg every 3 to 4 weeks

Valerate:

Adults (females): Menopause: 10 to 20 mg every 4 weeks

Adults (males): Prostate cancer: 30 mg or more every 1 to 2 weeks

Oral:

Adults (females): Estrace: Breast cancer: 10 mg 3 times/day; Hypoestrogenism: 1 to 2 mg/day; Menopause: 0.5 to 2 mg/day

Adults (males): Estrace: Prostate cancer: 1 to 2 mg 3 times/day; Breast cancer: 10 mg 3 times/day

Intravaginal: *Adults (females):* (Femring): 0.05 to 0.1 mg, leave in place for 3 months

Topical: *Adults (females):*

Emulsion (Estrasorb): 3.48 g applied once daily in the morning

Gel: 1.25 g/day (EstroGel) or 0.87 to 1.7 g/day (Elestrin) or 0.25 to 1 g/day (Divigel) applied at the same time each day

Spray (Evamist): 1 spray (1.53 mg) per day; dosing range: 1 to 3 sprays/day

Transdermal: *Adults (females):*

Alora, Minivelle, Vivelle-Dot: Apply twice weekly continuously or cyclically (3 weeks on, 1 week off)

Climara: Apply once weekly continuously or cyclically (3 weeks on, 1 week off)

Menostar: Apply once weekly continuously

Mechanism of Action Estrogens are responsible for the development and maintenance of the female reproductive system and secondary sexual characteristics. Estradiol is the principle intracellular human estrogen and is more potent than estrone and estriol at the receptor level; it is the primary estrogen secreted prior to menopause. Following menopause, estrone and estrone sulfate are more highly produced. Estrogens modulate the pituitary secretion of gonadotropins, luteinizing hormone, and follicle-stimulating hormone through a negative feedback system; estrogen replacement reduces elevated levels of these hormones in postmenopausal women.

Pregnancy Risk Factor X

Pregnancy Considerations In general, the use of estrogen and progestin as in combination hormonal contraceptives has not been associated with teratogenic effects when inadvertently taken early in pregnancy. These products are contraindicated for use during pregnancy.

Product Availability Estrasorb has been discontinued in the US for more than 1 year.

Estradiol and Dienogest

(es tra DYE ole & dye EN oh jest)

Related Information

Dienogest *on page 505*
Endocrine Disorders and Pregnancy *on page 1781*
Estradiol (Systemic) *on page 609*

Brand Names: US Natazia®

Pharmacologic Category Contraceptive; Estrogen and Progestin Combination

Use Prevention of pregnancy; treatment of heavy menstrual bleeding

Local Anesthetic/Vasoconstrictor Precautions No information available to require special precautions

Effects on Dental Treatment No significant effects or complications reported

Effects on Bleeding No information available to require special precautions

Adverse Reactions

>10%: Central nervous system: Headache (13%, including migraine)

1% to 10%:

Central nervous system: Mood changes (3%, including depression)
Dermatologic: Acne vulgaris (4%)
Endocrine & metabolic: Menstrual disease (≤7% to 8%), breast changes (discomfort: ≤7%), weight gain (3%)
Gastrointestinal: Nausea (≤7%), vomiting (≤7%)
Genitourinary: Uterine hemorrhage (≤7% to 8%), breast tenderness (≤7%), mastalgia (≤7%)

General Dosage Range Oral: *Children and Adults (females, postmenarche):* 1 tablet daily

Mechanism of Action Combination hormonal contraceptives inhibit ovulation and may also cause changes in the cervical mucus, rendering it unfavorable for sperm penetration even if ovulation occurs. The four-phasic formulation provides the estrogen in decreasing concentrations and the progestin in increasing concentrations over the 28-day cycle.

Pharmacodynamics/Kinetics

Half-life Elimination Estradiol: ~14 hours; Dienogest: ~11 hours

Time to Peak Estradiol: ~6 hours; Dienogest: ~1 hour

Pregnancy Considerations Pregnancy should be ruled out prior to treatment and discontinued if pregnancy occurs. In general, the use of combination hormonal contraceptives when inadvertently taken early in pregnancy has not been associated with teratogenic effects. Hormonal contraceptives may be less effective in obese patients. An increase in oral contraceptive failure was noted in women with a BMI >27.3 kg/m^2. Similar findings were noted in patients weighing ≥90 kg (198 lb) using the contraceptive patch. This product was not studied in women with a BMI >30 kg/m^2.

Due to increased risk of venous thromboembolism (VTE) postpartum, combination hormonal contraceptives should not be started in any woman <21 days following delivery. Women without risk factors for VTE and who are not breastfeeding may start combination hormonal contraceptives during 21-42 days postpartum. After 42 days postpartum, restrictions for use are not related to postpartum status and should be based on other medical conditions (CDC, 2011). The manufacturer states that combination hormonal contraceptives should not be started until ≥4 weeks after delivery in women who choose not to breastfeed, or ≥4 weeks after a second trimester abortion or miscarriage

Estradiol and Levonorgestrel

(es tra DYE ole & LEE voe nor jes trel)

Related Information

Endocrine Disorders and Pregnancy *on page* 1781
Estradiol (Systemic) *on page* 609

Brand Names: US ClimaraPro

Brand Names: Canada Climara Pro

Pharmacologic Category Estrogen and Progestin Combination

Use

Moderate to severe vasomotor symptoms: Treatment of moderate to severe vasomotor symptoms associated with menopause in women with an intact uterus

Osteoporosis prevention: Prevention of postmenopausal osteoporosis in women with an intact uterus

Limitations of use: Osteoporosis: For use only in women at significant risk of osteoporosis and for whom other nonestrogen medications are not considered appropriate

Local Anesthetic/Vasoconstrictor Precautions No information available to require special precautions

Effects on Dental Treatment No significant effects or complications reported

Effects on Bleeding No information available to require special precautions related to hemostasis in dental procedures.

Adverse Reactions Percentages reported as greater in ClimaraPro when compared to estradiol alone.

>10%:
- Central nervous system: Depression (12%)
- Genitourinary: Vaginal hemorrhage (78%), mastalgia (40%)
- Local: Application site reaction (86%)
- Neuromuscular & skeletal: Back pain (13%)
- Respiratory: Upper respiratory tract infection (28%)

1% to 10%: Cardiovascular: Edema (8%)

General Dosage Range Transdermal: *Adults (women with an intact uterus):* Apply one patch (estradiol 0.045 mg/levonorgestrel 0.015 mg) weekly

Mechanism of Action Estrogens are responsible for the development and maintenance of the female reproductive system and secondary sexual characteristics. Estradiol is the principle intracellular human estrogen and is more potent than estrone and estriol at the receptor level; it is the primary estrogen secreted prior to menopause. Following menopause, estrone and estrone sulfate are more highly produced. Estrogens modulate the pituitary secretion of gonadotropins, luteinizing hormone, and follicle-stimulating hormone through a negative feedback system; estrogen replacement reduces elevated levels of these hormones in postmenopausal women.

Levonorgestrel inhibits gonadotropin production; when used in this combination, it counteracts the proliferative effects of estradiol on the endometrium.

Pharmacodynamics/Kinetics

Half-life Elimination Estradiol: 3 ± 0.67 hours; Levonorgestrel: 28 ± 6.4 hours

Time to Peak Serum: Topical: Estradiol (mean): 2-2.5 days; Levonorgestrel: 2.5 days

Pregnancy Considerations Not for use prior to menopause; use during pregnancy is contraindicated. Refer to individual monographs.

Estradiol and Norethindrone

(es tra DYE ole & nor eth IN drone)

Related Information

Endocrine Disorders and Pregnancy *on page* 1781
Estradiol (Systemic) *on page* 609
Norethindrone *on page* 1209

Brand Names: US Activella; Amabelz; CombiPatch; Lopreeza; Mimvey; Mimvey Lo

Brand Names: Canada Activelle; Activelle LD; Estalis

Pharmacologic Category Estrogen and Progestin Combination

Use

Hypoestrogenism (female): (patch): Treatment of hypoestrogenism due to hypogonadism, castration, or primary ovarian failure

Osteoporosis prevention (females): (tablet): Prevention of postmenopausal osteoporosis

Vasomotor symptoms associated with menopause: (patch, tablet): Treatment of moderate to severe vasomotor symptoms associated with menopause

Vulvar and vaginal atrophy associated with menopause: (patch, tablet): Treatment of moderate to severe vulvar and vaginal atrophy associated with menopause

Limitations of use: These combination products are indicated for women with a uterus. When used for osteoporosis, use only in women at significant risk of postmenopausal osteoporosis; consider use of nonestrogen medications. When used solely for the treatment of vulvar and vaginal atrophy, topical vaginal products should be considered.

Local Anesthetic/Vasoconstrictor Precautions No information available to require special precautions

Effects on Dental Treatment No significant effects or complications reported

Effects on Bleeding No information available to require special precautions related to hemostasis in dental procedures.

Adverse Reactions Frequency not always defined.

Cardiovascular: Peripheral edema (transdermal: 6%)

Central nervous system: Headache (11% to 25%), pain (transdermal: 15% to 19%), depression (transdermal: 8% to 9%), insomnia (6% to 8%), dizziness (transdermal: 6% to 7%), nervousness (transdermal: 3% to 6%), emotional lability (oral: 1% to 6%)

Dermatologic: Skin rash (transdermal: 5% to 6%), acne vulgaris (transdermal: 4% to 5%)

Endocrine & metabolic: Menstrual disease (transdermal: 6% to 19%), weight gain (oral: ≤9%), ovarian cyst (oral: 3% to 7%), breast hypertrophy (transdermal: 2% to 7%), hypermenorrhea (transdermal: 2% to 5%)

Gastrointestinal: Diarrhea (transdermal: 9% to 14%), abdominal pain (transdermal: 6% to 14%), nausea (3% to 12%), dyspepsia (transdermal: 6% to 8%), flatulence (transdermal: 5% to 7%), gastroenteritis (oral: 2% to 6%), constipation (transdermal: 2% to 5%)

Genitourinary: Mastalgia (transdermal: 25% to 48%; oral: 17% to 24%), dysmenorrhea (transdermal: 20% to 31%), vaginal hemorrhage (oral: 26%; transdermal: 3% to 6%), vaginitis (transdermal: 6% to 13%), postmenopausal bleeding (oral: 5% to 11%), leukorrhea (transdermal: 5% to 10%), endometrial hyperplasia (oral: ≤1% to 10%), abnormal pap smear (transdermal: 8%), vulvovaginal candidiasis (oral: 4% to 6%)

Hematologic & oncologic: Uterine fibroids (oral: 5%)

Infection: Infection (transdermal: 3% to 5%), viral infection (oral: 4%)

Local: Application site reaction (transdermal: 6% to 23%)

Neuromuscular & skeletal: Back pain (6% to 15%), weakness (transdermal: 8% to 13%), arthralgia (transdermal: 6%), limb pain (oral: 5%)

Respiratory: Rhinitis (transdermal: 13% to 22%), nasopharyngitis (oral: 21%), upper respiratory tract infection (oral: 10% to 18%), sinusitis (7% to 15%), flu-like symptoms (transdermal: 9% to 14%), respiratory tract disease (transdermal: 9% to 13%), pharyngitis (transdermal: 4% to 10%), bronchitis (transdermal: 3% to 5%)

Miscellaneous: Accidental injury (3% to 17%)

<1%, postmarketing, and/or case reports: Alopecia, altered blood pressure, anaphylactoid reaction, anaphylaxis, angioedema, bloating, breast tenderness, carbohydrate intolerance, cerebrovascular accident, cervical polyp, change in appetite, change in cervical secretions, change in corneal curvature, change in libido, chloasma, cholelithiasis, cholestatic jaundice, chorea, contact lens intolerance, cystitis-like syndrome, dementia, edema, endometrial carcinoma, erythema multiforme, erythema nodosum, exacerbation of asthma, exacerbation of endometriosis, exacerbation of porphyria, fallopian tube disease (cyst), fatigue, fibrocystic breast changes, galactorrhea, gallbladder disease, hemorrhagic eruption, hirsutism, hypersensitivity, hypertension, increased serum transaminases, increased serum triglycerides, irregular menses, irritability, leg cramps, loss of scalp hair, malignant neoplasm of breast, migraine, mood changes, myalgia, myocardial infarction, nipple discharge, ovarian carcinoma, pancreatitis, paresthesia, premenstrual-like syndrome, pruritus, pulmonary thromboembolism, retinal thrombosis, seborrhea, significant cardiovascular event, skin discoloration, stomach cramps, thrombophlebitis, uterine fibroids (size increased), uterine spasm, varicose veins, venous thromboembolism, vertigo, vomiting, weight loss

General Dosage Range

Oral: *Adults (females):* One tablet daily

Transdermal: *Adults (females):* Apply 1 patch twice weekly

Pharmacodynamics/Kinetics

Half-life Elimination Oral tablet: Estradiol: 12 to 14 hours; Norethindrone: 8 to 11 hours

Time to Peak Oral tablet: Estradiol: 5 to 8 hours; Norethindrone: 0.5 to 1.5 hours

Pregnancy Considerations Use during pregnancy is contraindicated. Not for use prior to menopause. Refer to individual monographs

Estradiol and Norgestimate

(es tra DYE ole & nor JES ti mate)

Related Information

Endocrine Disorders and Pregnancy *on page 1781*

Estradiol (Systemic) *on page 609*

Rheumatoid Arthritis, Osteoarthritis, and Osteoporosis *on page 1792*

Brand Names: US Prefest

Pharmacologic Category Estrogen and Progestin Combination

Use

Osteoporosis prevention: Prevention of osteoporosis

Vasomotor symptoms associated with menopause: Treatment of moderate to severe vasomotor symptoms

Vulvar and vaginal atrophy associated with menopause: Treatment of moderate to severe symptoms of vulvar and vaginal atrophy

Limitations of use: For use in women with a uterus. When used solely for the treatment of vulvar and vaginal atrophy, topical vaginal products should be considered. When used for the prevention of osteoporosis, use only in women at significant risk; consider use of nonestrogen medications

Local Anesthetic/Vasoconstrictor Precautions No information available to require special precautions

Effects on Dental Treatment No significant effects or complications reported

Effects on Bleeding No information available to require special precautions related to hemostasis in dental procedures.

Adverse Reactions

>10%:

Central nervous system: Headache (23%)

Gastrointestinal: Abdominal pain (12%)

Genitourinary: Mastalgia (16%)

Neuromuscular & skeletal: Back pain (12%)

Respiratory: Upper respiratory tract infection (21%), flu-like symptoms (11%)

1% to 10%:

Central nervous system: Fatigue (6%), pain (6%), depression (5%), dizziness (5%)

Gastrointestinal: Nausea (6%), flatulence (5%)

Genitourinary: Vaginal hemorrhage (9%), dysmenorrhea (8%), vaginitis (7%)

Infection: Viral infection (6%)

Neuromuscular & skeletal: Arthralgia (9%), myalgia (5%)

Respiratory: Sinusitis (8%), pharyngitis (7%), cough (5%)

General Dosage Range Oral: *Adults (females):* 1 tablet of estradiol 1 mg once daily for 3 days, followed by 1 tablet of estradiol 1 mg and norgestimate 0.09 mg once daily for 3 days; repeat sequence continuously

Mechanism of Action Estrogens are responsible for the development and maintenance of the female reproductive system and secondary sexual characteristics. Estradiol is the principle intracellular human estrogen and is more potent than estrone and estriol at the receptor level; it is the primary estrogen secreted prior to menopause. Following menopause, estrone and estrone sulfate are more highly produced. Estrogens modulate the pituitary secretion of gonadotropins, luteinizing hormone, and follicle-stimulating hormone through a negative feedback system; estrogen replacement reduces elevated levels of these hormones in postmenopausal women.

Progestins inhibit gonadotropin production which then prevents follicular maturation and ovulation. In women with adequate estrogen, progestins transform a proliferative endometrium into a secretory endometrium; when administered with estradiol, reduces the incidence of endometrial hyperplasia and risk of adenocarcinoma.

Pharmacodynamics/Kinetics

Half-life Elimination Norgestimate: 17-deacetylnorgestimate: 37 hours

Time to Peak Norgestimate: ~2 hours

Pregnancy Considerations Use is contraindicated in pregnant women. In general, the use of estrogen and progestin as in combination hormonal contraceptives has not been associated with teratogenic effects when inadvertently taken early in pregnancy.

Estramustine (es tra MUS teen)

Brand Names: US Emcyt

Brand Names: Canada Emcyt

Pharmacologic Category Antineoplastic Agent, Alkylating Agent; Antineoplastic Agent, Antimicrotubular; Antineoplastic Agent, Hormone (Estrogen/Nitrogen Mustard)

Use

Prostate cancer: Treatment (palliative) of progressive or metastatic prostate cancer

Limitation of use: A clinical practice guideline from the American Society of Clinical Oncology (ASCO) and Cancer Care Ontario recommends that estramustine not be offered to men with metastatic castration-resistant prostate cancer due to a lack of benefit in survival or quality of life (Basch, 2014).

Local Anesthetic/Vasoconstrictor Precautions No information available to require special precautions

Effects on Dental Treatment No significant effects or complications reported

Effects on Bleeding Thrombocytopenia has been reported in a small number of patients

Adverse Reactions

Frequency not always defined.

>10%:

Cardiovascular: Edema (20%)

Endocrine & metabolic: Gynecomastia (75%), increased lactate dehydrogenase (2% to 33%), decreased libido

Gastrointestinal: Nausea (16%), diarrhea (13%), gastrointestinal irritation (12%)

Genitourinary: Breast tenderness (71%)

Hepatic: Increased serum AST (2% to 33%)

Respiratory: Dyspnea (12%)

1% to 10%:

Cardiovascular: Cardiac failure (3%), local thrombophlebitis (3%), myocardial infarction (3%), cerebrovascular accident (2%), pulmonary embolism (2%), chest pain (1%), flushing (1%)

Central nervous system: Lethargy (4%), insomnia (3%), emotional lability (2%), anxiety (1%), headache (1%)

Dermatologic: Pruritus (2%), xeroderma (2%), exfoliation of skin (1%), skin rash (1%), thinning hair (1%)

Endocrine & metabolic: Increased thirst (1%)

Gastrointestinal: Anorexia (4%), flatulence (2%), gastrointestinal hemorrhage (1%), sore throat (1%), vomiting (1%)

Hematologic & oncologic: Leukopenia (4%), bruise (3%), thrombocytopenia (1%)

Hepatic: Increased serum bilirubin (1% to 2%)

Neuromuscular & skeletal: Leg cramps (9%)

Ophthalmic: Lacrimation (1%)

Respiratory: Hoarseness (1%), rhinorrhea (1%)

<1%, postmarketing, and/or case reports: Anemia, angina pectoris, angioedema, cerebral ischemia, confusion, depression, decreased glucose tolerance, hypercalcemia, hypocalcemia, hypersensitivity reaction, hypertension, impotence, ischemic heart disease, myasthenia, venous thrombosis

General Dosage Range Oral: *Adults (males):* 14 mg/kg/day (range: 10-16 mg/kg/day) in 3 or 4 divided doses

Mechanism of Action Estradiol and nornitrogen mustard carbamate-linked combination which has antiandrogen effects (due to estradiol) and antimicrotubule effects (due to nornitrogen mustard); causes a marked decrease in plasma testosterone and an increase in estrogen levels.

Pharmacodynamics/Kinetics

Half-life Elimination Estromustine: 13.6 hours (range: 9-23 hours); Estrone: 16.5 hours (Bergenheim, 1998)

Time to Peak 2-3 hours (Bergenheim, 1998)

Pregnancy Considerations Estramustine is not indicated for use in women. Some men who were impotent on estrogen therapy have regained potency while taking estramustine; effective contraception should be used for male patients with partners of childbearing potential.

Estrogens (Conjugated B/Synthetic)

(ES troe jenz KON joo gate ed, bee, sin THET ik)

Related Information

Endocrine Disorders and Pregnancy *on page 1781*

Brand Names: US Enjuvia [DSC]

Pharmacologic Category Estrogen Derivative

Use

Vasomotor symptoms associated with menopause: Treatment of moderate to severe vasomotor symptoms associated with menopause

Vulvar and vaginal atrophy associated with menopause: Treatment of moderate to severe vaginal dryness and pain with intercourse, symptoms of vulvar and vaginal atrophy, associated with menopause

Limitations of use: When used solely for the treatment of vulvar and vaginal atrophy, topical vaginal products should be considered.

Local Anesthetic/Vasoconstrictor Precautions No information available to require special precautions

Effects on Dental Treatment No significant effects or complications reported

Effects on Bleeding No information available to require special precautions related to hemostasis in dental procedures.

Adverse Reactions

>10%:

Central nervous system: Headache (25%), pain (10% to 19%)

Gastrointestinal: Abdominal pain (4% to 15%), nausea (10% to 12%)

Genitourinary: Mastalgia (13% to 15%)

1% to 10%:

Cardiovascular: Peripheral edema (4%), chest pain (3% to 4%)

Central nervous system: Dizziness (7%), paresthesia (1% to 6%), chills (4%), depression (3% to 4%), emotional lability (3% to 4%)

Dermatologic: Pruritus (6%), fungal dermatitis (2% to 4%), acne vulgaris (1% to 4%)

Gastrointestinal: Flatulence (4% to 7%), constipation (4%)

Genitourinary: Dysmenorrhea (8%), vaginitis (7%), breast tenderness (4%)

Neuromuscular & skeletal: Back pain (4%), weakness (3% to 4%)

Respiratory: Bronchitis (7%), rhinitis (7%), flu-like symptoms (6% to 7%), sinusitis (4% to 7%), increased cough (4%), upper respiratory tract infection (4%), pharyngitis (3% to 4%)

Miscellaneous: Accidental injury (9%)

<1%, postmarketing, and/or case reports: Abdominal distention, abdominal distress, alopecia, anaphylaxis, deep vein thrombosis, dementia, exacerbation of endometriosis (including malignant transformation), gallbladder disease, hypercalcemia, hypersensitivity reaction, insomnia, muscle spasm, retinal thrombosis, skin rash, thrombosis, urticaria

General Dosage Range Oral: *Adults (females):* 0.3 to 1.25 mg once daily

Mechanism of Action Conjugated B/synthetic estrogens contain a mixture of 10 synthetic estrogen substances, including sodium estrone sulfate, sodium equilin sulfate, sodium 17-alpha-dihydroequilin, sodium 17-alpha-estradiol, and sodium 17-beta-dihydroequilin. Estrogens are responsible for the development and maintenance of the female reproductive system and secondary sexual characteristics. Estradiol is the principle intracellular human estrogen and is more potent than estrone and estriol at the receptor level; it is the primary estrogen secreted prior to menopause. Following menopause, estrone and estrone sulfate are more highly produced. Estrogens modulate the pituitary secretion of gonadotropins, luteinizing hormone, and follicle-stimulating hormone through a negative feedback system; estrogen replacement reduces elevated levels of these hormones in postmenopausal women.

Pharmacodynamics/Kinetics

Half-life Elimination Conjugated estrone: 8-20 hours; conjugated equilin: 5-17 hours

Pregnancy Considerations Use is contraindicated in pregnant women. In general, the use of estrogen and progestin as in combination hormonal contraceptives have not been associated with teratogenic effects when inadvertently taken early in pregnancy.

Estrogens (Conjugated/Equine, Systemic) (ES troe jenz KON joo gate ed, EE kwine)

Related Information

Endocrine Disorders and Pregnancy *on page 1781*

Brand Names: US Premarin

Brand Names: Canada C.E.S.; Congest; PMS-Conjugated Estrogens C.S.D.; Premarin

Generic Availability (US) No

Pharmacologic Category Estrogen Derivative

Use

Abnormal uterine bleeding (injection only): Treatment of abnormal uterine bleeding due to hormonal imbalance in the absence of organic pathology.

Limitations of use: For short term use only to provide a rapid and temporary increase in estrogen levels.

Breast cancer, metastatic: Treatment of breast cancer (palliation) in appropriately selected men and postmenopausal women.

Hypoestrogenism (female): Treatment of hypoestrogenism due to hypogonadism, castration, or primary ovarian failure.

Osteoporosis prevention (female): Prevention of postmenopausal osteoporosis.

Limitations of use: For use only in women at significant risk of osteoporosis; consider use of nonestrogen medications.

Prostate cancer, advanced: Treatment of androgen-dependent prostatic cancer (palliation).

Vasomotor symptoms associated with menopause: Treatment of moderate to severe vasomotor symptoms associated with menopause.

Vulvar and vaginal atrophy associated with menopause: Treatment of moderate to severe vulvar and vaginal atrophy due to menopause.

Limitations of use: When used solely for the treatment of vulvar and vaginal atrophy, topical vaginal products should be considered.

Local Anesthetic/Vasoconstrictor Precautions No information available to require special precautions

Effects on Dental Treatment No significant effects or complications reported

Effects on Bleeding No information available to require special precautions

Adverse Reactions Percentages reported in postmenopausal women following oral use.

>10%:

Central nervous system: Headache (26% to 32%), pain (17% to 20%)

Gastrointestinal: Abdominal pain (15% to 17%)

Genitourinary: Vaginal hemorrhage (2% to 14%), mastalgia (7% to 12%)

Neuromuscular & skeletal: Back pain (13% to 14%), arthralgia (7% to 14%)

Respiratory: Pharyngitis (10% to 12%), sinusitis (6% to 11%)

1% to 10%:

Central nervous system: Depression (5% to 8%), dizziness (4% to 6%), nervousness (2% to 5%)

Dermatologic: Pruritus (4% to 5%)

Gastrointestinal: Diarrhea (6% to 7%), flatulence (6% to 7%)

Genitourinary: Vaginitis (5% to 7%), leukorrhea (4% to 7%), vulvovaginal candidiasis (5% to 6%)

Neuromuscular & skeletal: Weakness (7% to 8%), leg cramps (3% to 7%)

Respiratory: Increased cough (4% to 7%)

Frequency not defined (injection): Local: Injection site phlebitis, pain at injection site, swelling at injection site

<1%, postmarketing, and/or case reports: Abnormal uterine bleeding, alopecia, anaphylaxis, angioedema, bloating, breast hypertrophy, breast tenderness, cerebrovascular accident, change in cervical secretions, change in libido, chloasma, cholestatic jaundice, contact lens intolerance, decreased glucose tolerance, deep vein thrombosis, dementia, dysmenorrhea, edema, endometrial carcinoma, endometrial hyperplasia, erythema multiforme, erythema nodosum, exacerbation of asthma, exacerbation of epilepsy, exacerbation of hepatic hemangioma, exacerbation of porphyria, fibrocystic breast changes, galactorrhea, gallbladder disease, growth potentiation of benign meningioma, gynecomastia, hirsutism, hypersensitivity reaction, hypertension, increased serum triglycerides, irritability, ischemic colitis, malignant neoplasm of breast, migraine, mood changes, myocardial infarction, nausea, nipple discharge, ovarian carcinoma, pancreatitis, pelvic pain, pulmonary embolism, retinal thrombosis, skin rash, superficial venous thrombosis, thrombophlebitis, urticaria, uterine fibroids (increased size), vomiting, vulvovaginal candidiasis, weight changes

Dosing

Adult & Geriatric *General dosing guidelines:* When treating postmenopausal women, use estrogens for the shortest duration possible at the lowest effective dose consistent with treatment goals. Reevaluate patients as clinically appropriate to determine if treatment is still necessary. Consider use of an estrogen with a progestin in postmenopausal women with a uterus. Women who have had a hysterectomy generally do not need a progestin; however one may be needed if there is a history of endometriosis. Dosage needs to be adjusted based upon the patient's response

Abnormal uterine bleeding: Acute/heavy bleeding: IM, IV: 25 mg, may repeat in 6-12 hours if needed (manufacturer's labeling) **or** 25 mg IV repeated every 4 to 6 hours for 24 hours (ACOG 557 2013).

Breast cancer, metastatic: Oral: Males and postmenopausal females: 10 mg 3 times/day for at least 3 months

Hypoestrogenism (female) due to castration or primary ovarian failure: Oral: 1.25 mg/day given cyclically*; adjust according to severity of symptoms and patient response. For maintenance, adjust to the lowest effective dose.

Hypoestrogenism (female) due to hypogonadism: Oral: 0.3 or 0.625 mg/day given cyclically*; dose may be titrated in 6- to 12-month intervals; progestin treatment should be added to maintain bone mineral density once skeletal maturity is achieved.

Osteoporosis prevention (females): Oral: Initial: 0.3 mg/day cyclically* or daily, depending on medical assessment of patient. Dose may be adjusted based on bone mineral density and clinical response. The lowest effective dose should be used.

Prostate cancer, advanced: Oral: 1.25 to 2.5 mg 3 times/day

Uremic bleeding (off-label use): IV: 0.6 mg/kg/day for 5 days (Heistinger 1990; Livio 1986; Viganò 1988)

Vasomotor symptoms associated with menopause: Oral: Initial: 0.3 mg/day. May be given cyclically* or daily, depending on medical assessment of patient. Adjust dose based on patient's response. The lowest dose that will control symptoms should be used.

Vulvar and vaginal atrophy associated with menopause: Oral: Initial: 0.3 mg/day. The lowest dose that will control symptoms should be used. May be given cyclically* or daily, depending on medical assessment of patient. Adjust dose based on patient's response.

***Cyclic administration:** Either 3 weeks on, 1 week off **or** 25 days on, 5 days off

Pediatric Adolescents: Refer to adult dosing.

Renal Impairment There are no dosage adjustments provided in the manufacturer's labeling (has not been studied).

Hepatic Impairment There are no dosage adjustments provided in the manufacturer's labeling (has not been studied). Use is contraindicated with hepatic dysfunction or disease.

Mechanism of Action Conjugated estrogens contain a mixture of estrone sulfate, equilin sulfate, 17 alpha-dihydroequilin, 17 alpha-estradiol and 17 beta-dihydroequilin. Estrogens are responsible for the development and maintenance of the female reproductive system and secondary sexual characteristics. Estradiol is the principle intracellular human estrogen and is more potent than estrone and estriol at the receptor level; it is the primary estrogen secreted prior to menopause. Following menopause, estrone and estrone sulfate are more highly produced. Estrogens modulate the pituitary secretion of gonadotropins, luteinizing hormone, and follicle-stimulating hormone through a negative feedback system; estrogen replacement reduces elevated levels of these hormones in postmenopausal women.

Contraindications

Angioedema or anaphylactic reaction to estrogens or any component of the formulation; undiagnosed abnormal genital bleeding; DVT or PE (current or history of); active or history of arterial thromboembolic disease (eg, stroke, MI); breast cancer (except in appropriately selected patients being treated for metastatic disease); estrogen-dependent tumor (known or suspected); hepatic impairment or disease; known protein C, protein S, antithrombin deficiency or other known thrombophilic disorders; pregnancy

Canadian labeling: Additional contraindications (not in US labeling): Endometrial hyperplasia; partial or complete vision loss due to ophthalmic vascular disease; migraine with or without aura

Warnings/Precautions

Anaphylaxis requiring emergency medical management has been reported within minutes to hours of taking conjugated estrogen (CE) tablets. Angioedema involving the face, feet, hands, larynx, and tongue has also been reported. Exogenous estrogens may exacerbate symptoms in women with hereditary angioedema.

[US Boxed Warning]: Based on data from the Women's Health Initiative (WHI) studies, an increased risk of invasive breast cancer was observed in postmenopausal women using conjugated estrogens (CE) in combination with medroxyprogesterone acetate (MPA). This risk may be associated with duration of use and declines once combined therapy is discontinued (Chlebowski 2009). The risk of invasive breast cancer was decreased in postmenopausal women with a hysterectomy using CE only, regardless of weight. However, the risk was not significantly decreased in women at high risk for breast cancer (family history of breast cancer, personal history of benign breast disease) (Anderson 2012). An increase in abnormal mammogram findings has also been reported with estrogen alone or in combination with progestin therapy. Estrogen use may lead to severe hypercalcemia in patients with breast cancer and bone metastases; discontinue estrogen if hypercalcemia occurs. Postmenopausal estrogens with or without progestins may increase the risk of ovarian cancer; however, the absolute risk to an individual woman is small. Although results from various studies are not consistent, risk does not appear to be significantly associated with the duration, route, or dose of therapy. In one study, the risk decreased after 2 years following discontinuation of therapy (Mørch 2009). Although the risk of ovarian cancer is rare, women who are at an increased risk (eg, family history) should be counseled about the association (NAMS 2012).

[US Boxed Warning]: Estrogens with or without progestin should not be used to prevent cardiovascular disease. Using data from the Women's Health Initiative (WHI) studies, an increased risk of deep vein thrombosis (DVT) and stroke has been reported with CE and an increased risk of DVT, stroke, pulmonary emboli (PE) and myocardial infarction (MI) has been reported with CE with MPA in postmenopausal women 50 to 79 years of age. Additional risk factors include diabetes mellitus, hypercholesterolemia, hypertension, SLE, obesity, tobacco use, and/or history of venous thromboembolism (VTE). Risk factors should be managed appropriately; discontinue use if adverse cardiovascular events occur or are suspected. Use is contraindicated in women with active DVT, PE, active arterial thromboembolic disease or a history of these conditions.

[US Boxed Warning]: Estrogens with or without progestin should not be used to prevent dementia. In the Women's Health Initiative Memory Study (WHIMS), an increased incidence of probable dementia was observed in women ≥65 years of age taking CE alone or in combination with MPA.

[US Boxed Warning]: The use of unopposed estrogen in women with a uterus is associated with an increased risk of endometrial cancer. The addition of a progestin to estrogen therapy may decrease the risk of endometrial hyperplasia, a precursor to endometrial cancer. Adequate diagnostic measures, including endometrial sampling if indicated, should be performed to rule out malignancy in postmenopausal women with undiagnosed abnormal vaginal bleeding. There is no evidence that the use of natural estrogens results in a different endometrial risk profile than synthetic estrogens at equivalent estrogen doses. The risk of endometrial cancer is dose and duration dependent; risk appears to be greatest with use ≥5 years and may persist following discontinuation of therapy. The use of a progestin is not generally required when low doses of estrogen are used locally for vaginal atrophy (NAMS 2012; NAMS 2013). Estrogens may exacerbate endometriosis. Malignant transformation of residual endometrial implants has been reported posthysterectomy with unopposed estrogen therapy. Consider adding a progestin in women with residual endometriosis posthysterectomy.

[US Boxed Warning]: Estrogens with or without progestin should be used for the shortest duration possible at the lowest effective dose consistent with treatment goals and risks for the individual woman. Patients should be reevaluated as clinically appropriate to determine if treatment is still necessary. Available data related to treatment risks are from Women's Health Initiative (WHI) studies, which evaluated oral CE 0.625 mg with or without MPA 2.5 mg relative to placebo in postmenopausal women. Other combinations and dosage forms of estrogens and progestins were not studied. **Outcomes reported from clinical trials using CE with or without MPA should be assumed to be similar for other doses and other dosage forms of estrogens and progestins until comparable data becomes available.** Women who are early in menopause, who are in good cardiovascular health, and who are at low risk for adverse cardiovascular events can be considered candidates for estrogen with or without progestin therapy for the relief of menopausal symptoms (ACOG 565 2013). Use of a transdermal product should be considered over an oral agent in women requiring systemic therapy who have risk factors for venous thromboembolism or coronary heart disease (ACOG 556 2013; Schenck-Gustafsson 2011; Tremollieres 2011).

Women with inherited thrombophilias (eg, protein C or S deficiency) may have increased risk of venous thromboembolism (DeSancho 2010; van Vlijmen 2011). Use is contraindicated in women with protein C, protein S, antithrombin deficiency, or other known thrombophilic disorders. Estrogen compounds are generally associated with lipid effects such as increased HDL-cholesterol and decreased LDL-cholesterol. Triglycerides may also be increased in women with preexisting hypertriglyceridemia; discontinue if pancreatitis occurs. The use of estrogens and/or progestins may change the results of some laboratory tests (eg, coagulation factors, lipids, glucose tolerance, binding proteins). The dose, route, and the specific estrogen/progestin influence these changes. In addition, personal risk factors (eg, cardiovascular disease, smoking, diabetes, age) also contribute to adverse events; use of specific products may be contraindicated in women with certain risk factors. Estrogens may increase thyroid-binding globulin (TBG) levels leading to increased circulating total thyroid hormone levels. Women on thyroid replacement therapy may require higher doses of thyroid hormone while receiving estrogens. Potentially significant interactions may exist, requiring dose or frequency adjustment, additional monitoring, and/or selection of alternative therapy.

Estrogens may cause retinal vascular thrombosis; discontinue if migraine, loss of vision, proptosis, diplopia, or other visual disturbances occur; discontinue permanently if papilledema or retinal vascular lesions are observed on examination. Use caution with asthma, epilepsy, hepatic hemangiomas, migraine, porphyria, SLE; may exacerbate disease. Canadian labeling contraindicates use in migraine with aura. May have adverse effects on glucose tolerance; use caution in women with diabetes. Use caution with diseases which may be exacerbated by fluid retention, including cardiac or renal dysfunction. Use of postmenopausal estrogen may be associated with an increased risk of gallbladder disease requiring surgery. Estrogens are poorly metabolized in patients with hepatic dysfunction. Use caution with a history of cholestatic jaundice associated with prior estrogen use or pregnancy. Discontinue if jaundice develops or if acute or chronic hepatic disturbances occur. Use is contraindicated with hepatic impairment or disease. Use caution with hypoparathyroidism; estrogen-induced hypocalcemia may occur.

Whenever possible, estrogens should be discontinued at least 4 to 6 weeks prior to elective surgery associated with an increased risk of thromboembolism or during periods of prolonged immobilization.

Prior to puberty, estrogens may cause premature closure of the epiphyses. Premature breast development, vaginal bleeding and vaginal cornification may be induced in girls. Modification of the normal puberty process may occur in boys.

Osteoporosis use: For use only in women at significant risk of osteoporosis and for who other nonestrogen medications are not considered appropriate.

Vulvar and vaginal atrophy use: Moderate-to-severe symptoms of vulvar and vaginal atrophy include vaginal dryness, dyspareunia, and atrophic vaginitis. When used solely for the treatment of vulvar and vaginal atrophy, topical vaginal products should be considered. Use caution applying topical products to severely atrophic vaginal mucosa. Use of a progestin is normally not required when low-dose estrogen is applied locally and only for this purpose (NAMS 2012; NAMS 2013).

Benzyl alcohol and derivatives: Some dosage forms may contain benzyl alcohol; large amounts of benzyl alcohol (≥99 mg/kg/day) have been associated with a potentially fatal toxicity ("gasping syndrome") in neonates; the "gasping syndrome" consists of metabolic acidosis, respiratory distress, gasping respirations, CNS dysfunction (including convulsions, intracranial hemorrhage), hypotension and cardiovascular collapse (AAP ["Inactive" 1997]; CDC, 1982); some data suggests that benzoate displaces bilirubin from protein binding sites (Ahlfors 2001); avoid or use dosage forms containing benzyl alcohol with caution in neonates. See manufacturer's labeling.

Drug Interactions

Metabolism/Transport Effects Substrate of CYP1A2 (major), CYP2A6 (minor), CYP2B6 (minor), CYP2C19 (minor), CYP2C9 (minor), CYP2D6 (minor), CYP2E1 (minor), CYP3A4 (major); **Note:** Assignment of Major/Minor substrate status based on clinically relevant drug interaction potential; **Inhibits** CYP1A2 (weak)

Avoid Concomitant Use

Avoid concomitant use of Estrogens (Conjugated/ Equine, Systemic) with any of the following: Anastrozole; Dehydroepiandrosterone; Exemestane; Hemin; Indium 111 Capromab Pendetide; Ospemifene

Increased Effect/Toxicity

Estrogens (Conjugated/Equine, Systemic) may increase the levels/effects of: Ajmaline; Anthrax Immune Globulin (Human); C1 inhibitors; CloZAPine; Corticosteroids (Systemic); Dantrolene; Immune Globulin; Lenalidomide; Ospemifene; ROPINIRole; Thalidomide; Theophylline Derivatives; Tipranavir; TiZANidine

The levels/effects of Estrogens (Conjugated/Equine, Systemic) may be increased by: Ascorbic Acid; Dehydroepiandrosterone; Herbs (Estrogenic Properties); NSAID (COX-2 Inhibitor); Pomalidomide

Decreased Effect

Estrogens (Conjugated/Equine, Systemic) may decrease the levels/effects of: Anastrozole; Anticoagulants; Antidiabetic Agents; Chenodiol; Exemestane; Hemin; Hyaluronidase; Indium 111 Capromab Pendetide; Ospemifene; Somatropin; Thyroid Products; Ursodiol

The levels/effects of Estrogens (Conjugated/Equine, Systemic) may be decreased by: Bosentan; Cannabis; CYP1A2 Inducers (Strong); CYP3A4 Inducers (Moderate); CYP3A4 Inducers (Strong); Cyproterone; Dabrafenib; Deferasirox; Enzalutamide; Mitotane; Siltuximab; St John's Wort; Teriflunomide; Tipranavir; Tocilizumab

Food Interactions Folic acid absorption may be decreased. Routine use of ethanol increases estrogen level and risk of breast cancer; may also increase the risk of osteoporosis. Management: Avoid ethanol.

Dietary Considerations Ensure adequate calcium and vitamin D intake when used for the prevention of osteoporosis. Powder for reconstitution for injection (25 mg) contains lactose 200 mg.

Pharmacodynamics/Kinetics

Half-life Elimination Total estrone: 27 hours

Time to Peak Total estrone: 7 hours

Pregnancy Considerations These products are contraindicated for use during pregnancy. Estrogens are not indicated for use during pregnancy or immediately postpartum. In general, the use of estrogen and progestin as in combination hormonal contraceptives have not been associated with teratogenic effects when inadvertently taken early in pregnancy.

Breastfeeding Considerations Estrogen has been shown to decrease the quantity and quality of human milk. The manufacturer recommends that caution be used if administered to a nursing woman.

Dosage Forms

Solution Reconstituted, Injection:

Premarin: 25 mg (1 ea)

Tablet, Oral:

Premarin: 0.3 mg, 0.45 mg, 0.625 mg, 0.9 mg, 1.25 mg

Estrogens (Conjugated/Equine, Topical) (ES troe jenz KON joo gate ed, EE kwine)

Brand Names: US Premarin

Brand Names: Canada Premarin®

Pharmacologic Category Estrogen Derivative

Use Vulvar and vaginal atrophy associated with menopause: Treatment of atrophic vaginitis and kraurosis vulvae and moderate-to-severe dyspareunia (pain during intercourse) due to vaginal/vulvar atrophy of menopause

Local Anesthetic/Vasoconstrictor Precautions No information available to require special precautions

Effects on Dental Treatment No significant effects or complications reported

Effects on Bleeding No information available to require special precautions

Adverse Reactions Due to systemic absorption, other adverse effects associated with systemic therapy may also occur. Frequency of adverse events reported with daily use.

1% to 10%:

Cardiovascular: Vasodilatation (4%)

Central nervous system: Pain (7%)

Gastrointestinal: Abdominal pain (8%)

Genitourinary: Mastalgia (6%), vaginitis (6%)

Neuromuscular & skeletal: Weakness (6%), back pain (5%)

<1%, postmarketing, and/or case reports: Abdominal cramps, abnormal uterine bleeding, acne vulgaris, alopecia, anaphylaxis, application site reaction (application site burning, application site irritation, genital pruritus), arthralgia, bloating, breast hypertrophy, breast tenderness, cerebrovascular accident, change in cervical secretions, change in libido, chloasma, contact lens intolerance, cystitis-like syndrome, decreased glucose tolerance, deep vein thrombosis, dementia, depression, dizziness, dysmenorrhea,

dysuria, edema, endometrial carcinoma, endometrial hyperplasia, exacerbation of asthma, fibrocystic breast changes, gallbladder disease, gynecomastia, headache, hirsutism, hypersensitivity reaction, hypertension, increased serum triglycerides, irritability, leg cramps, leukorrhea, malignant neoplasm of breast, migraine, mood disorder, muscle cramps, myocardial infarction, nausea, nervousness, nipple discharge, pelvic pain, polyuria, precocious puberty, pulmonary embolism, retinal thrombosis, skin rash, spotting, urinary tract infection, urinary urgency, urticaria, uterine fibroids (increase in size), vomiting, vulvovaginal disease, weight changes

General Dosage Range Intravaginal: *Adults (females):*

Atrophic vaginitis, kraurosis vulvae: 0.5 to 2 g/day given cyclically

Moderate-to-severe dyspareunia due to menopause: 0.5 g twice weekly (eg, Monday and Thursday) **or** once daily cyclically

Mechanism of Action Conjugated estrogens contain a mixture of estrone sulfate, equilin sulfate, 17 alpha-dihydroequilin, 17 alpha-estradiol and 17 beta-dihydroequilin. Estrogens are responsible for the development and maintenance of the female reproductive system and secondary sexual characteristics. Estradiol is the principle intracellular human estrogen and is more potent than estrone and estriol at the receptor level; it is the primary estrogen secreted prior to menopause. Following menopause, estrone and estrone sulfate are more highly produced. Estrogens modulate the pituitary secretion of gonadotropins, luteinizing hormone, and follicle-stimulating hormone through a negative feedback system; estrogen replacement reduces elevated levels of these hormones in postmenopausal women.

Pharmacodynamics/Kinetics

Time to Peak Total estrone: 6 hours

Pregnancy Considerations In general, the use of estrogen and progestin as in combination hormonal contraceptives have not been associated with teratogenic effects when inadvertently taken early in pregnancy. These products are contraindicated for use during pregnancy. Use of the vaginal cream may weaken latex found in condoms, diaphragms, or cervical caps.

Estrogens (Conjugated/Equine) and Bazedoxifene

(ES troe jenz, KON joo gate ed/EE kwine & ba ze DOX i feen)

Brand Names: US Duavee

Pharmacologic Category Estrogen Derivative; Selective Estrogen Receptor Modulator (SERM); Tissue-Selective Estrogen Complex (TSEC)

Use

Postmenopausal osteoporosis prophylaxis: Prevention of postmenopausal osteoporosis in women with a uterus

Vasomotor symptoms: Treatment of moderate-to-severe vasomotor symptoms associated with menopause in women with a uterus

Local Anesthetic/Vasoconstrictor Precautions No information available to require special precautions

Effects on Dental Treatment No significant effects or complications reported

Effects on Bleeding No information available to require special precautions

Adverse Reactions Percentages as reported with combination product.

1% to 10%:

Central nervous system: Dizziness (5%)

Gastrointestinal: Diarrhea (8%), nausea (8%), dyspepsia (7%), upper abdominal pain (7%)

Neuromuscular & skeletal: Muscle spasm (9%), neck pain (5%)

Respiratory: Oropharyngeal pain (7%)

General Dosage Range Oral: *Adults: Females:* One tablet daily

Mechanism of Action Conjugated estrogens contain a mixture of estrone sulfate, equilin sulfate, 17 alpha-dihydroequilin, 17 alpha-estradiol and 17 beta-dihydroequilin. Bazedoxifene is a selective estrogen receptor modulator (SERM). Conjugated estrogens act as an estrogen agonist and bazedoxifene acts as an estrogen agonist/antagonist depending on the specific tissue. The combination of a SERM and estrogen [referred to as a tissue-selective estrogen complex (TSEC)] provides relief of vasomotor symptoms and maintenance of bone mineral density in postmenopausal women with a uterus, while reducing the risk of endometrial hyperplasia observed with estrogen use alone (Pickar, 2009).

Pharmacodynamics/Kinetics

Onset of Action

Relief of vasomotor symptoms: A significant reduction in the number and severity of moderate/severe hot flashes was observed after 4 weeks of therapy (Pinkerton, 2009).

Osteoporosis: A significant increase in BMD measured at the lumbar spine and hip was observed at 12 months of therapy (Lindsay, 2009).

Half-life Elimination

Bazedoxifene: ~30 hours

Total estrone: ~17 hours

Time to Peak

Bazedoxifene: ~2.5 hours

Total estrone: ~6.5 hours

Pregnancy Risk Factor X

Pregnancy Considerations Animal reproduction studies have not been conducted with this combination. This combination product is approved for use in postmenopausal women only. Use is contraindicated in women who are or who may become pregnant.

Estrogens (Conjugated/Equine) and Medroxyprogesterone

(ES troe jenz KON joo gate ed/EE kwine & me DROKS ee proe JES te rone)

Related Information

Endocrine Disorders and Pregnancy *on page 1781*

Estrogens (Conjugated/Equine, Systemic) *on page 614*

MedroxyPROGESTERone *on page 1043*

Brand Names: US Premphase; Prempro

Pharmacologic Category Estrogen and Progestin Combination

Use

Osteoporosis prevention (female): Prevention of postmenopausal osteoporosis

Limitations of use: For use only in women at significant risk of postmenopausal osteoporosis; consider use of nonestrogen medications.

Vasomotor symptoms associated with menopause: Treatment of moderate to severe vasomotor symptoms associated with menopause.

Vulvar and vaginal atrophy associated with menopause: Treatment of moderate to severe vulvar and vaginal atrophy associated with menopause.

Limitations of use: When used solely for the treatment of vulvar and vaginal atrophy, topical vaginal products should be considered.

Local Anesthetic/Vasoconstrictor Precautions No information available to require special precautions

Effects on Dental Treatment No significant effects or complications reported

Effects on Bleeding No information available to require special precautions related to hemostasis in dental procedures.

Adverse Reactions

Also see individual agents.

>10%:

Central nervous system: Headache (15% to 19%)

Gastrointestinal: Abdominal pain (7% to 17%)

Genitourinary: Mastalgia (13% to 36%), dysmenorrhea (3% to 13%)

1% to 10%:

Cardiovascular: Edema (≤4%), peripheral edema (2% to 3%), hypertension (2%), vasodilatation (≤2%), chest pain (1%), palpitations (≤1%)

Central nervous system: Depression (7% to 8%), pain (5%), emotional lability (3%), dizziness (2% to 3%), migraine (2% to 3%), nervousness (1% to 3%), anxiety (2%), hypertonia (1% to 2%), insomnia (1% to 2%)

Dermatologic: Pruritus (2% to 6%), skin rash (2%), acne vulgaris (≤2%), alopecia (≤2%), skin discoloration (1% to 2%), diaphoresis (≤1%), xeroderma (≤1%)

Endocrine & metabolic: Weight gain (3%), decreased glucose tolerance (≤1%), hypermenorrhea (≤1%)

Gastrointestinal: Nausea (6% to 8%), flatulence (4% to 8%), diarrhea (≤6%), constipation (2%), increased appetite (≤2%), eructation (≤1%)

Genitourinary: Leukorrhea (3% to 8%), breast hypertrophy (2% to 5%), pelvic pain (2% to 5%), vaginal hemorrhage (≤5%), vaginitis (2% to 4%), breakthrough bleeding (1% to 4%), uterine spasm (1% to 4%), vulvovaginal candidiasis (1% to 4%), cervical changes (1% to 3%), abnormal Pap smear (≤2%), breast engorgement (≤1%), urinary incontinence (≤1%)

Hematologic & oncologic: Malignant neoplasm of breast (≤1%)

Infection: Candidiasis (≤2%), infection (≤1%)

Neuromuscular & skeletal: Weakness (3% to 6%), back pain (2% to 7%), leg cramps (2% to 4%)

Respiratory: Pharyngitis (>5%), sinusitis (>5%), flu-like symptoms (≤1%)

<1%, postmarketing, and/or case reports: Abnormal uterine bleeding, amenorrhea, anaphylactoid reaction, anaphylaxis, angioedema, bloating, breast tenderness, cerebrovascular accident, change in appetite, change in cervical secretions, change in libido, chloasma, cholestatic jaundice, contact lens intolerance, cough, deep vein thrombosis, dementia, endometrial carcinoma, endometrial hyperplasia, erythema multiforme, erythema nodosum, exacerbation of asthma, exacerbation of epilepsy, exacerbation of tics, fibrocystic breast changes, galactorrhea, gallbladder disease, hirsutism, hypersensitivity reaction, increased serum triglycerides, irritability, ischemic colitis, malignant neoplasm of ovary, meningioma (benign; possible growth), myalgia, myocardial infarction, nipple discharge, pancreatitis, pulmonary embolism, retinal thrombosis, rhinitis, superficial venous thrombosis, thrombophlebitis, upper respiratory tract infection, urticaria, uterine fibroids (increase in size), vomiting, vulvovaginal candidiasis, weight loss

General Dosage Range Oral: *Adults (females):* Prempro: Conjugated estrogen 0.3 to 0.625 mg/mPA 1.5 to 5 mg once daily **or** Premphase: One 0.625 mg tablet daily on days 1 through 14 and 1 conjugated estrogen 0.625 mg/mPA 5 mg tablet daily on days 15 through 28

Mechanism of Action See individual agents.

Pregnancy Considerations Use is contraindicated in pregnant women. In general, the use of estrogen and progestin as in combination hormonal contraceptives have not been associated with teratogenic effects when inadvertently taken early in pregnancy.

Estrogens (Esterified) (ES troe jenz, es TER i fied)

Related Information

Endocrine Disorders and Pregnancy *on page 1781*

Brand Names: US Menest

Brand Names: Canada Estragyn

Pharmacologic Category Estrogen Derivative

Use Treatment of moderate-to-severe vasomotor symptoms associated with menopause; treatment of moderate-to-severe vulvar and vaginal atrophy associated with menopause; hypoestrogenism (due to hypogonadism, castration, or primary ovarian failure); advanced prostatic cancer (palliation), metastatic breast cancer (palliation) in men and postmenopausal women

Local Anesthetic/Vasoconstrictor Precautions No information available to require special precautions

Effects on Dental Treatment No significant effects or complications reported

Effects on Bleeding No information available to require special precautions related to hemostasis in dental procedures.

Adverse Reactions Frequency not defined.

Cardiovascular: Cerebrovascular accident, edema, hypertension, local thrombophlebitis, myocardial infarction, pulmonary embolism, retinal thrombosis, venous thromboembolism

Central nervous system: Chorea, dementia (exacerbation), depression, dizziness, exacerbation of epilepsy, headache, irritability, migraine, mood disorder, nervousness

Dermatologic: Chloasma, erythema multiforme, erythema nodosum, pruritus, loss of scalp hair, skin rash, urticaria

Endocrine & metabolic: Change in libido, exacerbation of porphyria, fibrocystic breast changes, galactorrhea, hirsutism, hypocalcemia, menstrual disease (alterations in frequency and flow of menstrual patterns), premenstrual-like syndrome, weight gain, weight loss

Gastrointestinal: Abdominal cramps, bloating, carbohydrate intolerance, gallbladder disease, nausea, pancreatitis, vomiting

Genitourinary: Breakthrough bleeding, breast hypertrophy, breast tenderness, change in cervical ectropion, change in cervical secretions, cystitis-like syndrome, dysmenorrhea, endometrial hyperplasia, nipple discharge, vulvovaginal candidiasis, vaginitis

Hematologic & oncologic: Endometrial carcinoma, hemorrhagic eruption, malignant neoplasm of breast, malignant neoplasm of ovary, uterine fibroids (increased size)

Hepatic: Cholestatic jaundice, exacerbation of hepatic hemangioma (enlargement)

Hypersensitivity: Anaphylactoid reaction, anaphylaxis, angioedema

Neuromuscular & skeletal: Arthralgia, leg cramps

Ophthalmic: Contact lens intolerance, change in corneal curvature (steepening)

Respiratory: Exacerbation of asthma

General Dosage Range

Oral:

Adults (females): Hypogonadism: 2.5-7.5 mg/day for 20 days followed by a 10-day rest, repeat until response; Castration or ovarian failure: 1.25 mg/day, cyclically; Menopause 0.3-1.25 mg/day given cyclically; Breast cancer: 10 mg 3 times/day

Adults (males): Breast cancer: 10 mg 3 times/day; Prostate cancer: 1.25-2.5 mg 3 times/day

Mechanism of Action Esterified estrogens contain a mixture of estrogenic substances; the principle component is estrone. Preparations contain 75% to 85% sodium estrone sulfate and 6% to 15% sodium equilin sulfate such that the total is not <90%. Estrogens are responsible for the development and maintenance of the female reproductive system and secondary sexual characteristics. Estradiol is the principle intracellular human estrogen and is more potent than estrone and estriol at the receptor level; it is the primary estrogen secreted prior to menopause. In males and following menopause in females, estrone and estrone sulfate are more highly produced. Estrogens modulate the pituitary secretion of gonadotropins, luteinizing hormone, and follicle-stimulating hormone through a negative feedback system; estrogen replacement reduces elevated levels of these hormones.

Pregnancy Considerations In general, the use of estrogen and progestin as in combination hormonal contraceptives have not been associated with teratogenic effects when inadvertently taken early in pregnancy. This product is contraindicated for use during pregnancy.

Estrogens (Esterified) and Methyltestosterone

(ES troe jenz es TER i fied & meth il tes TOS te rone)

Related Information

Endocrine Disorders and Pregnancy *on page 1781*

Estrogens (Esterified) *on page 619*

MethylTESTOSTERone *on page 1103*

Brand Names: US Covaryx; Covaryx H.S.; EEMT HS [DSC]; EEMT [DSC]

Pharmacologic Category Estrogen and Androgen Combination

Use Treatment of moderate-to-severe vasomotor symptoms associated with menopause not improved by estrogens alone

Local Anesthetic/Vasoconstrictor Precautions No information available to require special precautions

Effects on Dental Treatment No significant effects or complications reported

Effects on Bleeding No information available to require special precautions related to hemostasis in dental procedures.

Adverse Reactions Refer to the Estrogens (Esterified) and the Testosterone monographs.

General Dosage Range Oral: *Adults (females):* Usual dosage range (based on esterified estrogen component): 0.625-1.25 mg every day for 3 weeks and then discontinued for 1 week off

Mechanism of Action

Conjugated estrogens: Activate estrogen receptors (DNA protein complex) located in estrogen-responsive tissues. Once activated, regulate transcription of certain genes leading to observed effects.

Testosterone: Increases synthesis of DNA, RNA, and various proteins in target tissues

Pregnancy Risk Factor X

Pregnancy Considerations [U.S. Boxed Warning]: Estrogens should not be used during pregnancy. This product is specifically contraindicated during pregnancy. Refer to the Estrogens (Esterified) monograph and the Testosterone monograph for additional information.

Controlled Substance C-III or nonscheduled (DEA exemption status dependent)

Estropipate (ES troe pih pate)

Related Information

Endocrine Disorders and Pregnancy *on page 1781*

Brand Names: US Ortho-Est 0.625 [DSC]; Ortho-Est 1.25 [DSC]

Brand Names: Canada Ogen [DSC]

Pharmacologic Category Estrogen Derivative

Use

Hypoestrogenism, female: Treatment of hypoestrogenism due to hypogonadism, castration, or primary ovarian failure.

Osteoporosis prevention: Prevention of postmenopausal osteoporosis.

Vasomotor symptoms associated with menopause: Treatment of moderate to severe vasomotor symptoms associated with menopause.

Vulval and vaginal atrophy associated with menopause: Treatment of moderate to severe symptoms of vulval and vaginal atrophy associated with menopause.

Limitations of use: When used solely for the treatment of vulvar and vaginal atrophy, topical vaginal products should be considered. When used for osteoporosis prevention, use only in women at significant risk of postmenopausal osteoporosis; consider use of nonestrogen medications

Local Anesthetic/Vasoconstrictor Precautions No information available to require special precautions

Effects on Dental Treatment No significant effects or complications reported

Effects on Bleeding No information available to require special precautions related to hemostasis in dental procedures.

Adverse Reactions Frequency not defined.

Cardiovascular: Edema, hypertension, pulmonary thromboembolism, venous thromboembolism

Central nervous system: Chorea, depression, dizziness, headache, migraine

Dermatologic: Chloasma, erythema multiforme, erythema nodosum, loss of scalp hair

Endocrine & metabolic: Change in libido, exacerbation of porphyria, hirsutism, hypercalcemia, impaired glucose tolerance, increased HDL cholesterol, decreased LDL cholesterol, increased serum triglycerides, increased T4, increased thyroxine binding globulin, menstrual disease (alterations in frequency and flow of menses), phospholipidemia, weight gain, weight loss

Gastrointestinal: Abdominal cramps, bloating, carbohydrate intolerance, cholecystitis, cholelithiasis, gallbladder disease, nausea, pancreatitis, vomiting

Genitourinary: Breast hypertrophy, breast tenderness, vulvovaginal candidiasis

Hematologic & oncologic: Change in platelet count (increase), decreased antifactor Xa, decreased antithrombin III plasma level, endometrial carcinoma, hemorrhagic eruption, increased clotting factor VII, increased clotting factor VIII, increased clotting factor

IX, increased clotting factor X, increased platelet aggregation, increased serum fibrinogen, prolonged prothrombin time, uterine fibroids (increased size)

Hepatic: Cholestatic jaundice

Ophthalmic: Change in corneal curvature (steepening), contact lens intolerance

General Dosage Range Oral: *Adults (females):* 0.75 to 6 mg once daily or cyclically [menopause] **or** 1.5 to 9 mg for the first 3 weeks, followed by a rest period of 8 to 10 days [hypoestrogenism] **or** 0.75 mg for 25 days of a 31-day cycle [osteoporosis]

Mechanism of Action Estropipate is prepared from naturally occurring estrone. Estrogens are responsible for the development and maintenance of the female reproductive system and secondary sexual characteristics. Estradiol is the principle intracellular human estrogen and is more potent than estrone and estriol at the receptor level; it is the primary estrogen secreted prior to menopause. In males and following menopause in females, estrone and estrone sulfate are more highly produced. Estrogens modulate the pituitary secretion of gonadotropins, luteinizing hormone, and follicle-stimulating hormone through a negative feedback system; estrogen replacement reduces elevated levels of these hormones. Estropipate is prepared from purified crystalline estrone that has been solubilized as the sulfate and stabilized with piperazine.

Pregnancy Considerations Use is contraindicated in pregnant women. In general, the use of estrogen and progestin as in combination hormonal contraceptives has not been associated with teratogenic effects when inadvertently taken early in pregnancy.

Eszopiclone (es zoe PIK lone)

Brand Names: US Lunesta

Generic Availability (US) Yes

Pharmacologic Category Hypnotic, Miscellaneous

Use Insomnia: Treatment of insomnia

Local Anesthetic/Vasoconstrictor Precautions No information available to require special precautions

Effects on Dental Treatment Key adverse event(s) related to dental treatment: Unpleasant taste and xerostomia (normal salivary flow resumes upon discontinuation).

Effects on Bleeding No information available to require special precautions

Adverse Reactions

>10%:

Central nervous system: Headache (15% to 21%)

Gastrointestinal: Dysgeusia (8% to 34%)

1% to 10%:

Cardiovascular: Chest pain (≥1%), peripheral edema (≥1%)

Central nervous system: Drowsiness (8% to 10%), dizziness (5% to 7%), pain (4% to 5%), nervousness (≤5%), depression (1% to 4%), confusion (≤3%), neuralgia (≤3%), abnormal dreams (1% to 3%), anxiety (1% to 3%), hallucination (1% to 3%), migraine

Dermatologic: Skin rash (3% to 4%), pruritus (1% to 4%)

Endocrine & metabolic: Decreased libido (≤3%), gynecomastia (≤3%)

Gastrointestinal: Xerostomia (3% to 7%), dyspepsia (2% to 6%), nausea (4% to 5%), diarrhea (2% to 4%), vomiting (≤3%)

Genitourinary: Dysmenorrhea (≤3%), urinary tract infection (≤3%)

Infection: Infection (5% to 10%), viral infection (3%)

Miscellaneous: Accidental injury (≤3%)

<1%, postmarketing, and/or case reports: Abnormal gait, abnormality in thinking, agitation, alopecia, altered sense of smell, amenorrhea, anaphylaxis, anemia, angioedema, anorexia, apathy, aphthous stomatitis, arthritis, asthma, ataxia, blepharoptosis, breast hypertrophy, breast neoplasm, bronchitis, bursitis, cholelithiasis, colitis, conjunctivitis, contact dermatitis, cystitis, dehydration, diaphoresis, dry eye syndrome, dysphagia, dyspnea, dysuria, eczema, emotional lability, epistaxis, erythema multiforme, euphoria, facial edema, fever, gastric ulcer, gastritis, gout, halitosis, heatstroke, hematuria, hepatic disease, hepatitis, hepatomegaly, herpes zoster, hirsutism, hostility, hypercholesterolemia, hypermenorrhea, hypersensitivity reaction, hypertension, hypokalemia, hyporeflexia, increased appetite, increased thirst, insomnia, laryngitis, lymphadenopathy, maculopapular rash, malaise, mastalgia, mastitis, melena, memory impairment, myasthenia, mydriasis, myopathy, neck stiffness, nephrolithiasis, neuritis, neuropathy, nystagmus, oliguria, paresthesia, photophobia, psychoneurosis, pyelonephritis, rectal hemorrhage, reflexes decreased, renal pain, skin discoloration, skin photosensitivity, sleep disorder (complex sleep-related behavior, including cooking or eating food, making phone calls, sleep driving), swelling, thrombophlebitis, tinnitus, tongue edema, tremor, twitching, urethritis, urinary frequency, urinary incontinence, urticaria, uterine hemorrhage, vaginal hemorrhage, vaginitis, vertigo, vesiculobullous dermatitis, vestibular disturbance

Dosing

Adult

Insomnia: Oral: **Note:** The lowest effective dose should be used.

Initial: 1 mg immediately before bedtime; dosing may be increased to 2 mg or 3 mg if clinically necessary (maximum dose: 3 mg daily)

Debilitated patients: Initial: 1 mg immediately before bedtime (maximum dose: 2 mg)

Concurrent use with strong CYP3A4 inhibitor: Initial: 1 mg immediately before bedtime (maximum dose: 2 mg)

Geriatric

Initial: 1 mg immediately before bedtime (maximum dose: 2 mg)

Renal Impairment No dosage adjustment necessary.

Hepatic Impairment

Mild to moderate impairment: No dosage adjustment necessary.

Severe impairment: Initial: 1 mg immediately before bedtime (maximum dose: 2 mg); use with caution; systemic exposure is doubled in severe impairment.

Mechanism of Action May interact with GABA-receptor complexes at binding domains located close to or allosterically coupled to benzodiazepine receptors.

Contraindications Hypersensitivity to eszopiclone or any component of the formulation.

Warnings/Precautions Symptomatic treatment of insomnia should be initiated only after careful evaluation of potential causes of sleep disturbance. Failure of sleep disturbance to resolve after 7 to 10 days may indicate psychiatric and/or medical illness. Tolerance did not develop over 6 months of use. Daytime function may be impaired in patients taking higher doses (2 mg or 3 mg) even if used as prescribed; patients taking 3 mg must be cautioned about performing tasks which require mental alertness (operating machinery or driving) the day after use. An increased risk of next-day psychomotor impairment may occur if taken with less than a full night of sleep (7 to 8 hours); if higher than recommended dose is taken; if co-administered with other CNS depressants or other drugs that increase blood concentrations of eszopiclone. Dose adjustment may be necessary if taking concomitant CNS depressants; the use of concomitant sedative-hypnotics at bedtime or in the middle of the night is not recommended. Potentially significant drug-drug interactions may exist, requiring dose or frequency adjustment, additional monitoring, and/or selection of alternative therapy.

Use with caution in patients with depression; worsening of depression, including suicidal ideation has been reported with the use of hypnotics. Intentional overdose may be an issue with this population. The minimum dose that will effectively treat the individual patient should be used. Prescriptions should be written for the smallest quantity consistent with good patient care. Use caution in patients with a history of drug dependence. Hypnotics/sedatives have been associated with abnormal thinking and behavior changes including decreased inhibition, aggression, bizarre behavior, agitation, hallucinations, and depersonalization. These changes may occur unpredictably and may indicate previously unrecognized psychiatric disorders; evaluate appropriately. An increased risk for hazardous sleep-related activities such as sleep-driving, cooking and eating food, and making phone calls while asleep has also been noted; amnesia may also occur. The use of alcohol, other CNS depressants, and exceeding the recommended maximum dose may increase the risk of these activities. Discontinue treatment in patients who report any sleep-related episodes. Use caution in patients with respiratory compromise, COPD, sleep apnea, and hepatic dysfunction (dose adjustment recommended with severe impairment). Because of the rapid onset of action, administer immediately prior to bedtime or after the patient has gone to bed and is having difficulty falling asleep. Abrupt discontinuance or rapid dose decreases may lead to withdrawal symptoms. Hypersensitivity reactions including anaphylaxis as well as angioedema have been reported, in some cases following initial dosing. Patients who develop severe reactions should not be rechallenged.

Use with caution in debilitated and elderly patients; dosage adjustment recommended. Closely monitor elderly or debilitated patients for impaired cognitive and/or motor performance, confusion, and potential for falling.

Drug Interactions

Metabolism/Transport Effects **Substrate** of CYP2E1 (minor), CYP3A4 (major); **Note:** Assignment of Major/Minor substrate status based on clinically relevant drug interaction potential

Avoid Concomitant Use

Avoid concomitant use of Eszopiclone with any of the following: Azelastine (Nasal); Conivaptan; Fusidic Acid (Systemic); Idelalisib; Orphenadrine; Oxomemazine; Paraldehyde; Sodium Oxybate; Thalidomide

Increased Effect/Toxicity

Eszopiclone may increase the levels/effects of: Alcohol (Ethyl); Analgesics (Opioid); Azelastine (Nasal); Blonanserin; Buprenorphine; CNS Depressants; Flunitrazepam; HYDROcodone; Methotrimeprazine; MetyroSINE; Mirtazapine; Orphenadrine; OxyCODONE; Paraldehyde; Piribedil; Pramipexole; ROPINIRole; Rotigotine; Selective Serotonin Reuptake Inhibitors; Sodium Oxybate; Suvorexant; Thalidomide; Zolpidem

The levels/effects of Eszopiclone may be increased by: Aprepitant; Brimonidine (Topical); Cannabis; Chlormethiazole; Chlorphenesin Carbamate; Conivaptan; CYP3A4 Inhibitors (Moderate); CYP3A4 Inhibitors (Strong); Dasatinib; Dimethindene (Topical); Doxylamine; Dronabinol; Droperidol; Fosaprepitant; Fusidic Acid (Systemic); HydrOXYzine; Idelalisib; Ivacaftor; Kava Kava; Lofexidine; Magnesium Sulfate; Methotrimeprazine; MiFEPRIStone; Minocycline; Nabilone; Netupitant; Oxomemazine; Palbociclib; Perampanel; Rufinamide; Simeprevir; Stiripentol; Tapentadol; Tetrahydrocannabinol; Trimeprazine

Decreased Effect

The levels/effects of Eszopiclone may be decreased by: Bosentan; CYP3A4 Inducers (Moderate); CYP3A4 Inducers (Strong); Dabrafenib; Deferasirox; Enzalutamide; Flumazenil; Mitotane; Siltuximab; St John's Wort; Tocilizumab

Food Interactions Onset of action may be reduced if taken with or immediately after a heavy meal. Management: Take immediately prior to bedtime, not with or immediately after a heavy or high-fat meal.

Dietary Considerations Avoid taking after a heavy meal; may delay onset.

Pharmacodynamics/Kinetics

Half-life Elimination ~6 hours; Elderly (≥65 years): ~9 hours

Time to Peak ~1 hour

Pregnancy Risk Factor C

Pregnancy Considerations Adverse effects were observed in animal reproduction studies. Eszopiclone is the S-isomer of the racemic derivative zopiclone. Available data related to zopiclone (not available in the United States) and similar medications note the potential for preterm birth, low birth weight, and/or small for gestational age infants following maternal use. Long-term use of medications in this class is not recommended during pregnancy and a planned discontinuation should be done to prevent rebound insomnia (Okun 2015).

Breastfeeding Considerations It is not known if eszopiclone is excreted in breast milk. Eszopiclone is the S-isomer of the racemic derivative zopiclone. Zopiclone is excreted in human milk (Matheson 1990).

Controlled Substance C-IV

Dosage Forms

Tablet, Oral:

Lunesta: 1 mg, 2 mg, 3 mg

Generic: 1 mg, 2 mg, 3 mg

Etanercept (et a NER sept)

Related Information

Rheumatoid Arthritis, Osteoarthritis, and Osteoporosis *on page 1792*

Brand Names: US Enbrel; Enbrel SureClick

Brand Names: Canada Brenzys; Enbrel

Generic Availability (US) No

Pharmacologic Category Antirheumatic, Disease Modifying; Tumor Necrosis Factor (TNF) Blocking Agent

Use

Ankylosing spondylitis: Reducing signs and symptoms in patients with active ankylosing spondylitis.

Plaque psoriasis: Treatment of patients ≥4 years (Enbrel) or ≥18 years (Erelzi) with chronic moderate to severe plaque psoriasis who are candidates for systemic therapy or phototherapy.

Polyarticular juvenile idiopathic arthritis: Reducing signs and symptoms of moderately to severely active polyarticular juvenile idiopathic arthritis in patients ≥2 years.

Psoriatic arthritis: Reducing signs and symptoms, inhibiting the progression of structural damage of active arthritis, and improving physical function in patients with psoriatic arthritis. Etanercept can be used with or without methotrexate.

Rheumatoid arthritis: Reducing signs and symptoms, inducing major clinical response, inhibiting the progression of structural damage, and improving physical function in patients with moderately to severely active rheumatoid arthritis (RA). Etanercept can be initiated in combination with methotrexate or used alone.

Local Anesthetic/Vasoconstrictor Precautions No information available to require special precautions

Effects on Dental Treatment No significant effects or complications reported

Effects on Bleeding No information available to require special precautions

Adverse Reactions

>10%:

Dermatologic: Skin rash (3% to 13%)

Gastrointestinal: Diarrhea (3% to 16%)

Infection: Infection (50% to 81%)

Local: Injection site reaction (adults: 15% to 43%; children: 7%; bleeding, bruising, erythema, itching, pain, or swelling; mild to moderate and usually decreases with subsequent injections)

Respiratory: Upper respiratory tract infection (38% to 65%), respiratory tract infection (21% to 54%)

Miscellaneous: Antibody development (non-neutralizing; 4% to 16%), positive ANA titer (11%)

1% to 10%:

Dermatologic: Pruritus (2% to 5%), urticaria (2%)

Hypersensitivity: Hypersensitivity reaction (1%)

Miscellaneous: Fever (2% to 3%)

Frequency not defined:

Dermatologic: Cellulitis

Gastrointestinal: Gastroenteritis

Infection: Abscess, influenza, sepsis

Neuromuscular & skeletal: Osteomyelitis, septic arthritis

Renal: Pyelonephritis

Respiratory: Bronchitis, pneumonia, sinusitis

<1%, postmarketing, and/or case reports: Anemia, angioedema, aplastic anemia, aseptic meningitis, aspergillosis, autoimmune hepatitis, cardiac failure, chest pain, cutaneous lupus erythematous, demyelinating disease of the central nervous system, erythema multiforme, fungal infection (Including histoplasmosis), Guillain-Barré syndrome, hepatotoxicity (idiosyncratic) (Chalasani 2014), herpes zoster, increased serum transaminases, inflammatory bowel disease, interstitial pulmonary disease, leukemia, leukopenia, lupus-like syndrome, lymphadenopathy, malignant lymphoma, malignant melanoma, malignant neoplasm, Merkel cell carcinoma, multiple sclerosis, neutropenia, optic neuritis, pancytopenia, paresthesia, pneumonia due to *Pneumocystis carinii*, psoriasis (including new onset, palmoplantar, pustular, or exacerbation), reactivation of HBV, sarcoidosis, scleritis, seizure, skin carcinoma, Stevens-Johnson syndrome, subcutaneous nodule, thrombocytopenia, toxic epidermal necrolysis, transverse myelitis, tuberculosis (including pulmonary and extrapulmonary), uveitis, varicella zoster infection, vasculitis (cutaneous and systemic)

Dosing

Adult & Geriatric

Note: Erelzi is approved as biosimilar to Enbrel.

Ankylosing spondylitis, psoriatic arthritis, rheumatoid arthritis: SubQ: **Note:** May continue methotrexate, glucocorticoids, salicylates, NSAIDs, or analgesics during etanercept therapy.

Once-weekly dosing: 50 mg once weekly; maximum dose (rheumatoid arthritis): 50 mg/week.

Twice-weekly dosing (off-label dose): 25 mg twice weekly (Bathon 2000; Calin 2004; Davis 2003; Genovese 2002; Mease 2000; Mease 2002)

Plaque psoriasis: SubQ:

Initial: 50 mg twice weekly for 3 months (starting doses of 25 or 50 mg once weekly have also been used successfully)

Maintenance dose: 50 mg once weekly

Acute graft-versus-host disease (GVHD), treatment (off-label use): SubQ: 0.4 mg/kg (maximum: 25 mg/dose) twice weekly for 8 weeks (in combination with methylprednisolone) (Levine 2008)

Pediatric

Note: Erelzi is approved as biosimilar to Enbrel.

Juvenile idiopathic arthritis: Children ≥2 years and Adolescents: SubQ: **Note:** May continue glucocorticoids, NSAIDs, or analgesics during etanercept therapy.

Once-weekly dosing:

<63 kg: 0.8 mg/kg (maximum: 50 mg/dose) once weekly. **Note:** There is no dosage form for Erelzi that allows weight-based dosing for pediatric patients <63 kg.

≥63 kg: 50 mg once weekly.

Twice-weekly dosing (off-label dose): 0.4 mg/kg (maximum: 25 mg/dose) twice weekly (Lovell 2006).

Plaque psoriasis (Enbrel only): Children ≥4 years and Adolescents: SubQ:

<63 kg: 0.8 mg/kg (maximum: 50 mg/dose) once weekly.

≥63 kg: 50 mg once weekly

Acute graft-versus-host disease (GVHD), treatment (off-label use): Children ≥1 year and Adolescents: SubQ: Refer to adult dosing.

Renal Impairment There are no dosage adjustments provided in the manufacturer's labeling (has not been studied).

Hepatic Impairment There are no dosage adjustments provided in the manufacturer's labeling (has not been studied).

Mechanism of Action Etanercept is a recombinant DNA-derived protein composed of tumor necrosis factor receptor (TNFR) linked to the Fc portion of human IgG1. Etanercept binds tumor necrosis factor (TNF) and blocks its interaction with cell surface receptors. TNF plays an important role in the inflammatory processes and the resulting joint pathology of rheumatoid arthritis (RA), polyarticular-course juvenile idiopathic arthritis (JIA), ankylosing spondylitis (AS), and plaque psoriasis.

Contraindications

Sepsis

Canadian labeling: Additional contraindications (not in US labeling): Hypersensitivity to etanercept or any component of the formulation.

Warnings/Precautions [US Boxed Warning]: Patients receiving etanercept are at increased risk for serious infections which may result in hospitalization and/or fatality; infections usually developed in patients receiving concomitant

immunosuppressive agents (eg, methotrexate, corticosteroids) and may present as disseminated (rather than local) disease. Active tuberculosis (including reactivation of latent tuberculosis), invasive fungal (including aspergillosis, blastomycosis, candidiasis, coccidioidomycosis, histoplasmosis, and pneumocystosis) and bacterial, viral or other opportunistic infections (including Legionellosis and Listeriosis) have been reported. Monitor closely for signs/symptoms of infection during and after treatment. Discontinue for serious infection or sepsis. Consider risks versus benefits prior to initiating therapy in patients with chronic or recurrent infection. Consider empiric antifungal therapy in patients who are at risk for invasive fungal infections who develop severe systemic illness. Caution should be exercised when considering use in the elderly, patients with chronic or recurrent infections, patients exposed to tuberculosis, patients with a history of an opportunistic infection, or in patients with conditions that predispose them to infections (eg, advanced or poorly controlled diabetes) or residence/travel from areas of endemic mycoses (blastomycosis, coccidioidomycosis, histoplasmosis), or with latent infections. Do not initiate etanercept therapy in patients with an active infection, including clinically important localized infection. Patients who develop a new infection while undergoing treatment should be monitored closely.

[US Boxed Warning]: Active tuberculosis (disseminated or extrapulmonary), including reactivation of latent tuberculosis, has been reported in patients receiving etanercept. Evaluate patients for tuberculosis risk factors and latent tuberculosis infection (with a tuberculin skin test) prior to and during therapy. Treatment for latent tuberculosis should be initiated before use. Patients with initial negative tuberculin skin tests should receive continued monitoring for tuberculosis during and after treatment. Consider antituberculosis treatment if an adequate course of treatment cannot be confirmed in patients with a history of latent or active tuberculosis or with risk factors despite negative skin test. Some patients who tested negative prior to therapy have developed active infection; tests for latent tuberculosis infection may be falsely negative while on etanercept therapy. Use with caution in patients who have traveled to or resided in regions where tuberculosis is endemic. Monitor for signs and symptoms of tuberculosis in all patients. Rare reactivation of hepatitis B virus (HBV) has occurred in chronic virus carriers, usually in patients receiving concomitant immunosuppressants; evaluate for HBV prior to initiation in all patients. Monitor during and for several months following discontinuation of treatment in HBV carriers; interrupt therapy if reactivation occurs and treat appropriately with antiviral therapy. If resumption of therapy is deemed necessary, exercise caution and monitor patient closely. Patients should be brought up to date with all immunizations before initiating therapy. Live vaccines should not be given concurrently with etanercept; there are no data available concerning secondary transmission of live vaccines in patients receiving therapy. Patients with a significant exposure to varicella virus should temporarily discontinue etanercept. Treatment with varicella zoster immune globulin should be considered.

[US Boxed Warning]: Lymphoma and other malignancies (some fatal) have been reported in children and adolescents receiving TNF-blocking agents, including etanercept. Half of the malignancies reported in children and adolescents were lymphomas (Hodgkin and non-Hodgkin) while other cases varied and included rare malignancies usually associated with immunosuppression and malignancies not typically observed in this population. The impact of etanercept on the development and course of malignancy is not fully defined. Compared to the general population, an increased risk of lymphoma has been noted in clinical trials; however, rheumatoid arthritis alone has been previously associated with an increased rate of lymphoma and leukemia. Lymphomas and other malignancies were also observed (at rates higher than expected for the general population) in adult patients receiving etanercept. Hepatosplenic T-cell lymphoma (HSTCL), a rare T-cell lymphoma, has also been associated with TNF-blocking agents, primarily reported in adolescent and young adult males with Crohn disease or ulcerative colitis. Melanoma, nonmelanoma skin cancer, and Merkel cell carcinoma have been reported. Perform periodic skin examinations in all patients during therapy, particularly those at increased risk of skin cancer. Positive antinuclear antibody titers have been detected in patients (with negative baselines). Rare cases of autoimmune disorder, including lupus-like syndrome or autoimmune hepatitis, have been reported; monitor and discontinue if symptoms develop.

Allergic reactions may occur. If an anaphylactic reaction or other serious allergic reaction occurs, administration should be discontinued immediately and appropriate therapy initiated. Use with caution in patients with preexisting or recent-onset CNS demyelinating disorders. Rare cases of new-onset or exacerbation of CNS demyelinating disorders have occurred; may present with mental status changes and some may be associated with permanent disability. Optic neuritis, transverse myelitis, multiple sclerosis, Guillain-Barré syndrome, other peripheral demyelinating neuropathies, and new-onset or exacerbation of seizures have been reported. Use with caution in patients with heart failure or decreased left ventricular function; worsening and new-onset heart failure has been reported, including in patients without known preexisting cardiovascular disease. Use caution in patients with a history of significant hematologic abnormalities; has been associated with pancytopenia and aplastic anemia (rare). Patients must be advised to seek medical attention if they develop signs and symptoms suggestive of blood dyscrasias; discontinue if significant hematologic abnormalities are confirmed. Use with caution in patients with moderate to severe alcoholic hepatitis. Compared to placebo, the mortality rate in patients treated with etanercept was similar at 1 month but significantly higher after 6 months. Use with caution in patients with a history of seizures; new-onset or exacerbation of seizures have been reported. Infection has been reported at a higher incidence in elderly patients; use caution. Malignancies have been reported among children and adolescents. Some dosage forms may contain dry natural rubber (latex).

Benzyl alcohol and derivatives: Diluent for injection may contain benzyl alcohol; large amounts of benzyl alcohol (≥99 mg/kg/day) have been associated with a potentially fatal toxicity ("gasping syndrome") in neonates; the "gasping syndrome" consists of metabolic acidosis, respiratory distress, gasping respirations, CNS dysfunction (including convulsions, intracranial hemorrhage), hypotension and cardiovascular collapse (AAP ["Inactive" 1997]; CDC 1982); some data suggest that benzoate displaces bilirubin from protein-binding sites

(Ahlfors 2001); avoid or use dosage forms containing benzyl alcohol with caution in neonates. See manufacturer's labeling. Use with caution in patients with a history of seizures; new-onset or exacerbation of seizures have been reported.

Drug Interactions

Metabolism/Transport Effects None known.

Avoid Concomitant Use

Avoid concomitant use of Etanercept with any of the following: Abatacept; Anakinra; BCG (Intravesical); Belimumab; Canakinumab; Certolizumab Pegol; Cyclophosphamide; InFLIXimab; Natalizumab; Pimecrolimus; Rilonacept; Tacrolimus (Topical); Tocilizumab; Tofacitinib; Vaccines (Live); Vedolizumab

Increased Effect/Toxicity

Etanercept may increase the levels/effects of: Abatacept; Anakinra; Belimumab; Canakinumab; Certolizumab Pegol; Cyclophosphamide; Fingolimod; InFLIXimab; Leflunomide; Natalizumab; Rilonacept; Tofacitinib; Vaccines (Live); Vedolizumab

The levels/effects of Etanercept may be increased by: Denosumab; Ocrelizumab; Pimecrolimus; Roflumilast; Tacrolimus (Topical); Tocilizumab; Trastuzumab

Decreased Effect

Etanercept may decrease the levels/effects of: BCG (Intravesical); Coccidioides immitis Skin Test; Nivolumab; Sipuleucel-T; Tertomotide; Vaccines (Inactivated); Vaccines (Live)

The levels/effects of Etanercept may be decreased by: Echinacea

Pharmacodynamics/Kinetics

Onset of Action ~2 to 3 weeks; RA: 1 to 2 weeks; Maximum effect: RA: Full effect is usually seen within 3 months

Half-life Elimination RA: SubQ: Children: 70 to 94.8 hours; Adults: 102 ± 30 hours

Time to Peak RA: SubQ: 69 ± 34 hours

Pregnancy Risk Factor B

Pregnancy Considerations Adverse events have not been observed in animal reproduction studies. Etanercept crosses the placenta. Following in utero exposure, concentrations in the newborn at delivery are 3% to 32% of the maternal serum concentration.

Breastfeeding Considerations Etanercept is excreted in breast milk in low concentrations and is minimally absorbed by a breastfeeding infant (limited data). According to the manufacturer, the decision to continue or discontinue breastfeeding during therapy should take into account the risk of infant exposure, the benefits of breastfeeding to the infant, and benefits of treatment to the mother.

Product Availability Erelzi (etanercept-szzs): FDA approved August 2016; anticipated availability is currently unknown. Erelzi is approved as biosimilar to Enbrel, but not as an interchangeable product.

Dosage Forms

Solution Auto-injector, Subcutaneous [preservative free]:

Enbrel SureClick: 50 mg/mL (0.98 mL)

Solution Prefilled Syringe, Subcutaneous [preservative free]:

Enbrel: 25 mg/0.5 mL (0.51 mL); 50 mg/mL (0.98 mL)

Solution Reconstituted, Subcutaneous [preservative free]:

Enbrel: 25 mg (1 ea)

Ethacrynic Acid (eth a KRIN ik AS id)

Brand Names: US Edecrin; Sodium Edecrin

Brand Names: Canada Edecrin; Sodium Edecrin

Pharmacologic Category Diuretic, Loop

Use Management of edema associated with congestive heart failure; hepatic cirrhosis or renal disease; short-term management of ascites due to malignancy, idiopathic edema, and lymphedema

Local Anesthetic/Vasoconstrictor Precautions No information available to require special precautions

Effects on Dental Treatment No significant effects or complications reported

Effects on Bleeding No information available to require special precautions

Adverse Reactions Frequency not defined.

Cardiovascular: Thrombophlebitis (with intravenous use)

Central nervous system: Apprehension, brain disease (patients with preexisting liver disease), chills, confusion, fatigue, headache, vertigo

Dermatologic: IgA vasculitis (in patient with rheumatic heart disease), skin rash

Endocrine & metabolic: Abnormal phosphorus levels (variations), abnormal serum calcium (variations), gout, hyperglycemia, hyperuricemia (reversible), hypoglycemia (occurred in two uremic patients who received doses above those recommended), hyponatremia, variations in bicarbonate, variations in CO2 content

Gastrointestinal: Abdominal distress, abdominal pain, anorexia, diarrhea, dysphagia, gastrointestinal hemorrhage, malaise, nausea, vomiting, acute pancreatitis (rare)

Genitourinary: Hematuria

Hematologic & oncologic: Agranulocytosis, severe neutropenia, thrombocytopenia

Hepatic: Abnormal hepatic function tests, jaundice

Local: Local irritation, local pain

Ophthalmic: Blurred vision

Otic: Deafness (temporary or permanent), tinnitus

Renal: Increased serum creatinine

Miscellaneous: Fever

General Dosage Range

IV: *Adults:* 0.5-1 mg/kg/dose (maximum: 100 mg/dose)

Oral:

Children: 1-3 mg/kg/day

Adults: 50-400 mg/day in 1-2 divided doses

Elderly: Initial: 25-50 mg/day

Mechanism of Action Inhibits reabsorption of sodium and chloride in the ascending loop of Henle and distal renal tubule, interfering with the chloride-binding cotransport system, thus causing increased excretion of water, sodium, chloride, magnesium, and calcium

Pharmacodynamics/Kinetics

Onset of Action Diuresis: Oral: ~30 minutes; IV: 5 minutes; Peak effect: Oral: 2 hours; IV: 30 minutes

Duration of Action Oral: 12 hours; IV: 2 hours

Half-life Elimination Normal renal function: 2-4 hours

Pregnancy Risk Factor B

Pregnancy Considerations Adverse events have not been observed in animal reproduction studies.

Ethambutol (e THAM byoo tole)

Brand Names: US Myambutol

Brand Names: Canada Etibi

Pharmacologic Category Antitubercular Agent

Use Treatment of pulmonary tuberculosis in conjunction with other antituberculosis agents

Local Anesthetic/Vasoconstrictor Precautions No information available to require special precautions

Effects on Dental Treatment No significant effects or complications reported

Effects on Bleeding No information available to require special precautions

Adverse Reactions Frequency not defined.

Cardiovascular: Myocarditis, pericarditis

Central nervous system: Confusion, disorientation, dizziness, hallucination, headache, malaise, peripheral neuritis

Dermatologic: Dermatitis, erythema multiforme, exfoliative dermatitis, pruritus, skin rash

Endocrine & metabolic: Acute gout attack, hyperuricemia

Gastrointestinal: Abdominal pain, anorexia, gastric distress, nausea, vomiting

Hematologic & oncologic: Eosinophilia, leukopenia, lymphadenopathy, neutropenia, thrombocytopenia

Hepatic: Abnormal hepatic function tests, hepatitis, hepatotoxicity (possibly related to concurrent therapy)

Hypersensitivity: Anaphylaxis, anaphylactoid reaction, hypersensitivity reaction (syndrome includes cutaneous reactions, eosinophilia, and organ-specific inflammation)

Neuromuscular & skeletal: Arthralgia

Ophthalmic: Color blindness, decreased visual acuity, optic neuritis, scotoma, visual disturbance (usually reversible with discontinuation; irreversible blindness has been described)

Renal: Nephritis

Respiratory: Pneumonitis, pulmonary infiltrates (with or without eosinophilia)

Miscellaneous: Fever

General Dosage Range Dosage adjustment recommended in patients with renal impairment

Oral:

Children: 15-20 mg/kg/day (maximum: 1 g/day) **or** 50 mg/kg twice weekly (maximum: 2.5 g/dose)

Adults: Daily therapy: 1.5-2.5 g/kg/day (maximum dose: 1.5-2.5 g); 3 times/week DOT: 25-30 mg/kg/dose (maximum dose: 2.4 g/dose); Twice weekly DOT: 50 mg/kg/dose (maximum dose: 4 g/dose)

Mechanism of Action Inhibits arabinosyl transferase resulting in impaired mycobacterial cell wall synthesis

Pharmacodynamics/Kinetics

Half-life Elimination 2.5-3.6 hours; End-stage renal disease: 7-15 hours

Time to Peak Serum: 2-4 hours

Pregnancy Risk Factor C

Pregnancy Considerations Teratogenic effects have been seen in animals. There are no adequate and well-controlled studies in pregnant women; there have been reports of ophthalmic abnormalities in infants born to women receiving ethambutol as a component of antituberculous therapy. Use only during pregnancy if benefits outweigh risks.

Ethanolamine Oleate

(ETH a nol a meen OH lee ate)

Brand Names: US Ethamolin

Pharmacologic Category Sclerosing Agent

Use Esophageal varices: Treatment of esophageal varices that have recently bled, to prevent rebleeding.

Local Anesthetic/Vasoconstrictor Precautions No information available to require special precautions

Effects on Dental Treatment No significant effects or complications reported

Effects on Bleeding No information available to require special precautions

Adverse Reactions

1% to 10%:

Central nervous system: Pyrexia (1.8%)

Gastrointestinal: Esophageal ulcer (2%), esophageal stricture (1.3%)

Respiratory: Pleural effusion (2%), pneumonia (1.2%)

Miscellaneous: Retrosternal pain (1.6%)

<1%: Acute renal failure, anaphylaxis, esophagitis, injection necrosis, perforation

General Dosage Range IV: *Adults:* 1.5 to 5 mL per varix (maximum: 20 mL per treatment session)

Mechanism of Action Ethanolamine oleate produces a sterile dose-related inflammatory response resulting in fibrosis and possible occlusion of the vein; a dose-related extravascular inflammatory reaction occurs when the drug diffuses through the venous wall.

Pregnancy Risk Factor C

Pregnancy Considerations Animal reproduction studies have not been conducted.

Ethinyl Estradiol and Desogestrel

(ETH in il es tra DYE ole & des oh JES trel)

Brand Names: US Apri; Azurette; Bekyree; Caziant; Cyclessa; Cyred; Desogen; Emoquette; Enskyce; Juleber; Kariva; Kimidess; Mircette; Ortho-Cept [DSC]; Pimtrea; Reclipsen; Solia [DSC]; Velivet; Viorele

Brand Names: Canada Apri; Freya; Linessa; Marvelon; Ortho-Cept; Reclipsen

Generic Availability (US) Yes

Pharmacologic Category Contraceptive; Estrogen and Progestin Combination

Use Contraception: Prevention of pregnancy.

Local Anesthetic/Vasoconstrictor Precautions No information available to require special precautions

Effects on Dental Treatment When prescribing antibiotics, patient must be warned to use additional methods of birth control if on oral contraceptives.

Effects on Bleeding No information available to require special precautions

Adverse Reactions Frequency not defined. Reactions listed are based on reports for other oral contraceptives and may not be specifically reported for ethinyl estradiol/desogestrel.

Increased risk or evidence of association with use:

Cardiovascular: Arterial thromboembolism, cerebral thrombosis, hypertension, mesenteric thrombosis, myocardial infarction, pulmonary embolism, retinal thrombosis, thrombophlebitis (may be local), venous thrombosis (with or without embolism)

Central nervous system: Cerebral hemorrhage

Gastrointestinal: Gallbladder disease

Hepatic: Hepatic adenoma, hepatic neoplasm (benign)

Adverse reactions considered drug related:

Cardiovascular: Edema, worsening of varicose veins

Central nervous system: Chorea (exacerbation), depression, migraine, mood changes

Dermatologic: Allergic skin rash, chloasma (may persist)

Endocrine & metabolic: Amenorrhea, breast changes (breast hypertrophy, breast secretion, breast tenderness, mastalgia), change in menstrual flow, decreased serum folate level, exacerbation of porphyria, fluid retention, weight changes

Gastrointestinal: Abdominal cramps, abdominal pain, bloating, carbohydrate intolerance, change in appetite, nausea, vomiting

Genitourinary: Breakthrough bleeding, change in cervical ectropion, change in cervical erosion, change in cervical secretions, decreased lactation (with use immediately postpartum), spotting, transient infertility (after discontinuation of treatment), vulvovaginal candidiasis, vulvovaginitis

Hepatic: Cholestatic jaundice

Hypersensitivity: Anaphylactoid reaction (including angioedema, circulatory collapse, respiratory collapse, urticaria), anaphylaxis (including angioedema, circulatory collapse, respiratory collapse, urticaria)

Neuromuscular & skeletal: Exacerbation of systemic lupus erythematosus

Ophthalmic: Change in corneal curvature (steepening), contact lens intolerance

Adverse reactions in which association is not confirmed or denied: Acne vulgaris, Budd-Chiari syndrome, cataract, change in libido, colitis, cystitis-like syndrome, dizziness, dysmenorrhea, erythema multiforme, erythema nodosum, headache, hemolytic-uremic syndrome, hemorrhagic eruption, hirsutism, loss of scalp hair, nervousness, optic neuritis (with or without partial or complete loss of vision), pancreatitis, premenstrual syndrome, renal insufficiency

Dosing

Adult Females: Contraception: Oral: One tablet once daily

Schedule 1 (Sunday starter): Dose begins on first Sunday after onset of menstruation; if the menstrual period starts on Sunday, take first tablet that very same day. **With a Sunday start, an additional method of contraception should be used until after the first 7 days of consecutive administration.**

Schedule 2 (Day 1 starter): Dose starts on first day of menstrual cycle taking 1 tablet daily.

If all doses have not been taken on schedule and one menstrual period is missed, the possibility of pregnancy should be considered. If two consecutive menstrual periods are missed, pregnancy test is required before new dosing cycle is started.

Missed or late doses (CDC 2013):

If one dose is late (<24 hours since dose should have been taken) or if one dose is missed (24 to <48 hours since dose should have been taken): Take dose as soon as possible. Continue remaining doses at the usual time (even if that means 2 doses on the same day).

If ≥2 consecutive doses are missed (≥48 hours since dose should have been taken): Take the most recently missed dose as soon as possible, discard any other missed doses. Continue remaining doses at the usual time (even if that means taking 2 doses on the same day); use back-up contraception until hormonal pills have been taken for 7 consecutive days. If doses were missed during the last week of hormonal (active) tablets (eg, days 15 to 21 of a 28-day pack), omit the hormone-free interval by finishing the current pack and starting a new pack. If unable to start a new pack immediately, back up contraception is needed until hormonal pills from a new pack have been taken for 7 consecutive days. Consider use of emergency contraception in some situations (refer to guidelines for details).

Also refer to prescribing information for product specific information.

Pediatric Females: Contraception: Oral: See adult dosing; not to be used prior to menarche.

Renal Impairment There are no dosage adjustments provided in manufacturer's labeling (has not been studied); use with caution and monitor blood pressure closely. Consider other forms of contraception.

Hepatic Impairment Contraindicated in patients with hepatic impairment.

Mechanism of Action Combination hormonal contraceptives inhibit ovulation via a negative feedback mechanism on the hypothalamus, which alters the normal pattern of gonadotropin secretion of a follicle-stimulating hormone (FSH) and luteinizing hormone by the anterior pituitary. The follicular phase FSH and midcycle surge of gonadotropins are inhibited. In addition, combination hormonal contraceptives produce alterations in the genital tract, including changes in the cervical mucus, rendering it unfavorable for sperm penetration even if ovulation occurs. Changes in the endometrium may also occur, producing an unfavorable environment for nidation. Combination hormonal contraceptive drugs may alter the tubal transport of the ova through the fallopian tubes. Progestational agents may also alter sperm fertility.

Contraindications

Hypersensitivity to ethinyl estradiol, desogestrel, or any component of the formulation; breast cancer, endometrial cancer, or other estrogen- or progestin-dependent neoplasms (current or a history of), hepatic tumors (benign or malignant) or hepatic disease, cholestatic jaundice of pregnancy or pregnancy with prior OCP use, pregnancy, undiagnosed abnormal genital bleeding.

Use is also contraindicated in women at high risk of arterial or venous thrombotic diseases (specifics vary by product labeling), for example, women with cerebrovascular disease, coronary artery disease, diabetes mellitus with vascular disease, DVT, thrombophlebitis, thromboembolic disorders, or thrombophilic conditions, hypertension (severe or uncontrolled; specified as systolic ≥160 mm Hg or diastolic ≥100 mm Hg in some product labeling), valvular heart disease with complications, headaches with focal neurological symptoms, major surgery with prolonged immobilization, women >35 years of age who smoke ≥15 cigarettes per day.

Canadian labeling: Additional contraindications: Ocular lesions due to ophthalmic vascular disease including partial or complete loss of vision or defect in visual fields; pancreatitis associated with severe hypertriglyceridemia (current or history of); thrombophilias (inherited or acquired); severe dyslipoproteinemia; migraine with focal neurological symptoms (eg, aura); hereditary or acquired predisposition for venous or arterial thrombosis, such as Factor V Leiden mutation and activated protein C(APC) resistance, antithrombin-III deficiency, protein C deficiency, protein S deficiency, hyperhomocysteinemia (eg, due to MTHFR C677T, A1298 mutations), prothrombin mutation G20210A, and antiphospholipid-antibodies (anticardiolipin antibodies, lupus anticoagulant).

Documentation of allergenic cross-reactivity for estrogens and progestins is limited. However, because of similarities in chemical structure and/or pharmacologic actions, the possibility of cross-sensitivity cannot be ruled out with certainty.

Warnings/Precautions

[US Boxed Warning]: The risk of cardiovascular side effects is increased in women who smoke

cigarettes; risk increases with age (especially women >35 years of age) and the number of cigarettes smoked; women who use combination hormonal contraceptives should be strongly advised not to smoke. Use is contraindicated in patients >35 years of age who smoke.

The use of combination hormonal contraceptives has not been shown to increase the risk for breast cancer. However, breast cancer is a hormonal sensitive tumor and the prognosis for women with a current or recent history of breast cancer may be worse with combination hormonal contraceptive use (CDC 2010). Use is contraindicated in women with (or history of) breast cancer. The use of combination hormonal contraceptives has been associated with a slight increased risk of cervical cancer; however, studies are not consistent and may be related to additional risk factors (Gierisch 2013). Women awaiting treatment for cervical cancer may use combination hormonal contraceptives (CDC 2013). Use of combination hormonal contraceptives is associated with hepatic adenomas (rare); fatal intra-abdominal hemorrhage may result. Risk is increased with long-term (>8 years) use. Use of this product is contraindicated in women with hepatic tumors. The risk of ovarian cancer is decreased in women using combination hormonal contraceptives (CDC 2013; Walker 2015). Oral contraceptives may be used to reduce the risk of ovarian cancer, including those women with BRACA1 and BRACA2 mutations (Walker 2015).

The risk of hypertension may be increased with age, dose, and duration of use. Combination hormonal contraceptives should not be used in women with persistent blood pressure values ≥160 mm Hg systolic or ≥100 mm Hg diastolic. Women with less severe hypertension (140 to 159 mm Hg systolic or 90 to 99 mm Hg diastolic) or those with hypertension that is adequately controlled should generally not use combination hormonal contraceptives (CDC 2013). Other risk factors for cardiovascular disease (eg, older age, smoking, diabetes) should be considered when prescribing contraceptives (CDC, 2010). The manufacturer contraindicates use in women with uncontrolled hypertension and recommends monitoring women with well-controlled hypertension; discontinue therapy if blood pressure rises significantly. Oral contraceptives may increase the risk of thromboembolism, and some studies suggest this risk may be higher with third-generation contraceptives, such as those containing desogestrel; discontinue use of combination hormonal contraceptives if an arterial or venous thrombotic event occurs. Women with inherited thrombophilias (eg, protein C or S deficiency) may have increased risk of venous thromboembolism (DeSancho 2010; van Vlijmen 2011). Use of combination hormonal contraceptives is contraindicated in women with known thrombophilic conditions. Use with caution in patients with risk factors for cardiovascular disease (eg, hypertension, hypercholesterolemia, morbid obesity, diabetes, or women who smoke); use of combination hormonal contraceptives may increase the risk of arterial or venous thrombotic events (CDC 2010). Use of combination hormonal contraceptives may be contraindicated in women at high risk of arterial or venous thrombotic diseases.

Risk of cholestasis may be increased with previous cholestatic jaundice of pregnancy or jaundice with prior oral contraceptive use; use is contraindicated. May impair glucose tolerance; use caution in women with diabetes (including women with prediabetes). Combination hormonal contraceptives, as well as sun exposure and pregnancy, are triggers for chloasma. Women with a susceptibility to chloasma or additional risk factors should avoid exposure to sun or ultraviolet radiation during therapy (Handel 2014). Combination hormonal contraceptives may adversely affect lipid levels, including serum triglycerides. The type of lipid disorder, the severity, and the presence of other cardiovascular risk factors should be considered when prescribing combination hormonal contraceptives to women with lipid disorders (CDC 2010).

Breakthrough or intracyclic bleeding and spotting may occur, especially during the first 3 months of therapy. In addition, occasional missed periods may occur. Presentation of irregular, unresolving vaginal bleeding warrants further evaluation to rule out malignancy or pregnancy. Amenorrhea or oligomenorrhea may occur after discontinuing combination hormonal contraceptives, especially when such a condition was preexistent. Discontinue use with the onset of sudden enlargement, pain, or tenderness of fibroids (leiomyomata).

Use with caution in patients with a history of migraine. Use is contraindicated in women who have headaches with focal neurologic symptoms. Evaluate new, recurrent, severe, or persistent headaches and consider discontinuing therapy if appropriate. Discontinue if unexplained loss of vision, proptosis, diplopia, papilledema, or retinal vascular lesions occur and immediately evaluate for retinal vein thrombosis. Any changes with lens tolerance or vision should be evaluated by an ophthalmologist. Use with caution in patients with depression; discontinue if serious depression recurs. Use with caution in patients with diseases which may be exacerbated by fluid retention. Estrogens may induce or exacerbate symptoms in women with hereditary angioedema (Geng 2013; Zuraw 2013). May have a dose-related risk of gallbladder disease. Combination hormonal contraceptives may be poorly metabolized in women with hepatic impairment. Discontinue if jaundice develops during therapy or if liver function becomes abnormal. Use is contraindicated in women with hepatic tumors or disease. Women with renal disease should be encouraged to use another form of contraception

Potentially significant interactions may exist, requiring dose or frequency adjustment, additional monitoring, and/or selection of alternative therapy. Consult drug interactions database for more detailed information. Estrogens may increase thyroid-binding globulin (TBG) levels, leading to increased circulating total thyroid hormone levels. Women on thyroid replacement therapy may require higher doses of thyroid hormone while receiving estrogens. The use of estrogens and/or progestins may change the results of some laboratory tests (eg, coagulation factors, lipids, glucose tolerance, binding proteins). The dose, route, and the specific estrogen/progestin influences these changes. In addition, personal risk factors (eg, cardiovascular disease, smoking, diabetes, age) also contribute to adverse events; use of specific products may be contraindicated in women with certain risk factors.

Whenever possible, should be discontinued at least 4 weeks prior to and for 2 weeks following elective surgery associated with an increased risk of thromboembolism or during periods of prolonged immobilization. Not for use prior to menarche. Use is not indicated in postmenopausal women. Some products may contain tartrazine (FD&C yellow no. 5), which may cause allergic reactions in certain individuals.

When initiating a combination oral contraceptive, consideration should be given to safety, effectiveness, availability and acceptance to the patient (CDC 2013). Consider initiating with a monthly bleeding monophasic formulation containing ethinyl estradiol 30 to 35 mcg plus a progestin and adjusting based on adverse events and patient preference (Ott 2014). The minimum dosage combination of estrogen/progestin that will effectively treat the individual patient should be used.

Combination hormonal contraceptives do not protect against HIV infection or other sexually-transmitted diseases (CDC 2013).

Drug Interactions

Metabolism/Transport Effects Refer to individual components.

Avoid Concomitant Use

Avoid concomitant use of Ethinyl Estradiol and Desogestrel with any of the following: Amodiaquine; Anastrozole; Antihepaciviral Combination Products; Dasabuvir; Dehydroepiandrosterone; Exemestane; Griseofulvin; Hemin; Indium 111 Capromab Pendetide; Ixazomib; Ospemifene; TiZANidine; Tranexamic Acid; Ulipristal

Increased Effect/Toxicity

Ethinyl Estradiol and Desogestrel may increase the levels/effects of: Agomelatine; Ajmaline; Amodiaquine; Anthrax Immune Globulin (Human); Antihepaciviral Combination Products; C1 inhibitors; CloZAPine; Corticosteroids (Systemic); CYP1A2 Substrates; Dantrolene; Dasabuvir; Flibanserin; Immune Globulin; Lenalidomide; Lomitapide; Ospemifene; Pirfenidone; Pomalidomide; ROPINIRole; Selegiline; Thalidomide; Theophylline Derivatives; Tipranavir; TiZANidine; Tranexamic Acid; Voriconazole

The levels/effects of Ethinyl Estradiol and Desogestrel may be increased by: Ascorbic Acid; Atazanavir; Boceprevir; Carfilzomib; Cobicistat; Dehydroepiandrosterone; Herbs (Estrogenic Properties); Herbs (Progestogenic Properties); Lopinavir; Metreleptin; MiFEPRIStone; NSAID (COX-2 Inhibitor); Pomalidomide; Tipranavir; Voriconazole

Decreased Effect

Ethinyl Estradiol and Desogestrel may decrease the levels/effects of: Anastrozole; Anticoagulants; Antidiabetic Agents; Chenodiol; Exemestane; Fosamprenavir; Hemin; Hyaluronidase; Indium 111 Capromab Pendetide; LamoTRIgine; Ospemifene; Thyroid Products; Ulipristal; Ursodiol; Valproate Products; Vitamin K Antagonists

The levels/effects of Ethinyl Estradiol and Desogestrel may be decreased by: Acitretin; Aprepitant; Armodafinil; Artemether; Asunaprevir; Barbiturates; Bexarotene (Systemic); Bile Acid Sequestrants; Boceprevir; Bosentan; CarBAMazepine; CloBAZam; Cobicistat; Colesevelam; CYP2C19 Inducers (Strong); CYP3A4 Inducers (Moderate); CYP3A4 Inducers (Strong); Dabrafenib; Darunavir; Deferasirox; Efavirenz; Elvitegravir; Enzalutamide; Eslicarbazepine; Exenatide; Felbamate; Fosamprenavir; Fosaprepitant; Fosphenytoin; Griseofulvin; Ixazomib; Lesinurad; Lixisenatide; Lopinavir; Lumacaftor; Metreleptin; MiFEPRIStone; Mitotane; Modafinil; Mycophenolate; Nafcillin; Nelfinavir; Nevirapine; OXcarbazepine; Perampanel; Phenytoin; Primidone; Protease Inhibitors; Prucalopride; Retinoic Acid Derivatives; Rifamycin Derivatives; Rufinamide; Saquinavir; Siltuximab; St John's Wort; Sugammadex; Telaprevir; Tipranavir; Tocilizumab; Topiramate; Ulipristal

Pharmacodynamics/Kinetics

Half-life Elimination Monophasic preparations: Etonogestrel: 38 ± 20 hours; Ethinyl estradiol: 26 ± 6.8 hours

Time to Peak Monophasic preparations: Etonogestrel: 1.4 ± 0.8 hours; Ethinyl estradiol: 1.5 ± 0.8 hours; Time to peak of etonogestrel and ethinyl estradiol varies by day in cycle for biphasic and triphasic preparations

Pregnancy Risk Factor X

Pregnancy Considerations

Pregnancy status should be evaluated prior to prescribing (CDC, 2013); treatment should be discontinued if pregnancy occurs. In general, the use of combination hormonal contraceptives, when inadvertently used early in pregnancy, have not been associated with teratogenic effects. Available evidence is inconsistent if BMI alters the efficacy of combination oral contraceptives (CDC, 2010).

Due to increased risk of venous thromboembolism (VTE) postpartum, combination hormonal contraceptives should not be started in any woman <21 days following delivery. Women without risk factors for VTE and who are not breastfeeding may start combination hormonal contraceptives during 21-42 days postpartum. After 42 days postpartum, restrictions for use are not related to postpartum status and should be based on other medical conditions (CDC, 2011). The manufacturer states that combination hormonal contraceptives should not be started until ≥4 weeks after delivery in women who choose not to breast-feed.

Breastfeeding Considerations Contraceptive steroids can be detected in breast milk. Jaundice and breast enlargement in the nursing infant have been reported following the use of combination hormonal contraceptives. May also decrease the quality and quantity of breast milk; an alternative form of contraception is recommended until the infant is weaned (per manufacturer). The theoretical concerns about decreased milk production are greatest early in the postpartum period when milk production is being established. Postpartum risk status for VTE should be considered when initiating combination hormonal contraceptives after delivery. Combined hormonal contraceptives should not be started <21 days postpartum due to increased risk of VTE. Risk of VTE is still elevated in breastfeeding women until ~42 days postpartum and is greater in women with additional risk factors. After 42 days postpartum, restrictions for use are not related to postpartum VTE risk and should be based on other medical conditions (CDC, 2011).

Dosage Forms

Tablet, oral [low dose formulation]:

Azurette:
- Day 1-21: Ethinyl estradiol 0.02 mg and desogestrel 0.15 mg [21 white tablets]
- Day 22-23: 2 inactive green tablets
- Day 24-28: Ethinyl estradiol 0.01 mg [5 blue tablets] (28s)

Bekyree:
- Day 1-21: Ethinyl estradiol 0.02 mg and desogestrel 0.15 mg [21 white tablets]
- Day 22-23: 2 inactive green tablets
- Day 24-28: Ethinyl estradiol 0.01 mg [5 yellow tablets] (28s)

Kariva:
- Day 1-21: Ethinyl estradiol 0.02 mg and desogestrel 0.15 mg [21 white tablets]
- Day 22-23: 2 inactive light green tablets

Day 24-28: Ethinyl estradiol 0.01 mg [5 light blue tablets] (28s)

Kimidess:

Day 1-21: Ethinyl estradiol 0.02 mg and desogestrel 0.15 mg [21 white tablets]

Day 22-23: 2 inactive green tablets

Day 24-28: Ethinyl estradiol 0.01 mg [5 yellow tablets] (28s)

Mircette:

Day 1-21: Ethinyl estradiol 0.02 mg and desogestrel 0.15 mg [21 white tablets]

Day 22-23: 2 inactive green tablets

Day 24-28: Ethinyl estradiol 0.01 mg [5 yellow tablets] (28s)

Pimtrea:

Day 1-21: Ethinyl estradiol 0.02 mg and desogestrel 0.15 mg [21 dark blue tablets]

Day 22-23: 2 inactive white tablets

Day 24-28: Ethinyl estradiol 0.01 mg [5 green tablets] (28s)

Viorele:

Day 1-21: Ethinyl estradiol 0.02 mg and desogestrel 0.15 mg [21 white tablets]

Day 22-23: 2 inactive green tablets

Day 24-28: Ethinyl estradiol 0.01 mg [5 yellow tablets] (28s)

Tablet, oral [monophasic formulation]:

Apri 28: Ethinyl estradiol 0.03 mg and desogestrel 0.15 mg [21 rose tablets and 7 white inactive tablets] (28s)

Cyred: Ethinyl estradiol 0.03 mg and desogestrel 0.15 mg [21 active and 7 inactive tablets] (28s)

Desogen: Ethinyl estradiol 0.03 mg and desogestrel 0.15 mg [21 white tablets and 7 green inactive tablets] (28s)

Emoquette: Ethinyl estradiol 0.03 mg and desogestrel 0.15 mg [21 white tablets and 7 light green inactive tablets] (28s)

Enskyce: Ethinyl estradiol 0.03 mg and desogestrel 0.15 mg [21 light orange tablets and 7 green inactive tablets] (28s)

Juleber: Ethinyl estradiol 0.03 mg and desogestrel 0.15 mg [21 yellow tablets and 7 white inactive tablets] (28s)

Reclipsen: Ethinyl estradiol 0.03 mg and desogestrel 0.15 mg [21 rose tablets and 7 white inactive tablets] (28s)

Solia: Ethinyl estradiol 0.03 mg and desogestrel 0.15 mg (28s)

Tablet, oral [triphasic formulation]:

Caziant:

Day 1-7: Ethinyl estradiol 0.025 mg and desogestrel 0.1 mg [7 beige tablets]

Day 8-14: Ethinyl estradiol 0.025 mg and desogestrel 0.125 mg [7 orange tablets]

Day 15-21: Ethinyl estradiol 0.025 mg and desogestrel 0.15 mg [7 pink tablets]

Day 22-28: 7 white inactive tablets (28s)

Cyclessa:

Day 1-7: Ethinyl estradiol 0.025 mg and desogestrel 0.1 mg [7 light yellow tablets]

Day 8-14: Ethinyl estradiol 0.025 mg and desogestrel 0.125 mg [7 orange tablets]

Day 15-21: Ethinyl estradiol 0.025 mg and desogestrel 0.15 mg [7 red tablets]

Day 22-28: 7 green inactive tablets (28s)

Velivet:

Day 1-7: Ethinyl estradiol 0.025 mg and desogestrel 0.1 mg [7 beige tablets]

Day 8-14: Ethinyl estradiol 0.025 mg and desogestrel 0.125 mg [7 orange tablets]

Day 15-21: Ethinyl estradiol 0.025 mg and desogestrel 0.15 mg [7 pink tablets]

Day 22-28: 7 white inactive tablets (28s)

Ethinyl Estradiol and Drospirenone

(ETH in il es tra DYE ole & droh SPYE re none)

Related Information

Endocrine Disorders and Pregnancy *on page 1781*

Brand Names: US Gianvi; Loryna; Nikki; Ocella; Syeda; Vestura; Yasmin; Yaz; Zarah

Brand Names: Canada Mya; Yasmin; Yaz; Zamine; Zarah

Generic Availability (US) Yes

Pharmacologic Category Contraceptive; Estrogen and Progestin Combination

Use

Acne vulgaris (Gianvi, Loryna, Nikki, Vestura, Yaz): Treatment of moderate acne vulgaris in women 14 years and older only if the patient desires an oral contraceptive for birth control

Contraception: Prevention of pregnancy

Premenstrual dysphoric disorder (Gianvi, Yaz): Treatment of premenstrual dysphoric disorder (PMDD) for women who choose to use an oral contraceptive for contraception

Local Anesthetic/Vasoconstrictor Precautions No information available to require special precautions

Effects on Dental Treatment When prescribing antibiotics, patient must be warned to use additional methods of birth control if on oral contraceptives.

Effects on Bleeding No information available to require special precautions

Adverse Reactions Frequency not defined. Reactions listed are based on reports for other agents in this same pharmacologic class (oral contraceptives) and may not be specifically reported for drospirenone/ethinyl estradiol.

Increased risk or evidence of association with use:

Cardiovascular: Arterial thromboembolism, cerebral thrombosis, hypertension, local thrombophlebitis, mesenteric thrombosis, myocardial infarction, pulmonary embolism, retinal thrombosis

Central nervous system: Cerebral hemorrhage

Gastrointestinal: Gallbladder disease

Hepatic: Hepatic adenoma, hepatic neoplasm (benign)

Adverse reactions considered drug related:

Cardiovascular: Edema, worsening of varicose veins

Central nervous system: Depression, exacerbation of tics, migraine

Dermatologic: Allergic skin rash, chloasma

Endocrine & metabolic: Amenorrhea, breast changes (breast hypertrophy, breast secretion, breast tenderness, mastalgia), decreased serum folate level, exacerbation of porphyria, menstrual disease (menstrual flow changes), weight changes

Gastrointestinal: Abdominal cramps, bloating, carbohydrate intolerance, nausea, vomiting

Genitourinary: Breakthrough bleeding, cervical ectropion, cervical erosion, change in cervical secretions, decreased lactation (with use immediately postpartum), infertility (temporary), spotting, vulvovaginal candidiasis

Hepatic: Cholestatic jaundice

Hypersensitivity: Anaphylaxis/anaphylactoid reaction (including angioedema, circulatory shock, respiratory collapse, urticaria)

Neuromuscular & skeletal: Exacerbation of systemic lupus erythematosus

Ophthalmic: Change in corneal curvature (steepening), contact lens intolerance

Adverse reactions in which association is not confirmed or denied:

Cardiovascular: Budd-Chiari syndrome

Central nervous system: Dizziness, headache, nervousness

Dermatologic: Acne vulgaris, erythema multiforme, erythema nodosum, loss of scalp hair

Endocrine & metabolic: Change in libido, hirsutism, porphyria, premenstrual syndrome

Gastrointestinal: Change in appetite, colitis, pancreatitis

Genitourinary: Cystitis-like syndrome, dysmenorrhea, vaginitis

Hematologic & oncologic: Hemolytic-uremic syndrome, hemorrhagic eruption

Ophthalmic: Cataract, optic neuritis (with or without partial or complete loss of vision)

Renal: Renal insufficiency

Dosing

Adult

Acne (Gianvi, Loryna, Nikki, Vestura, Yaz): Females: Oral: Refer to dosing for contraception.

PMDD (Gianvi, Yaz): Females: Oral: Refer to dosing for contraception.

Contraception: Female: Oral: Dosage is 1 tablet daily for 28 consecutive days. Dosing may be started on the first day of menstrual period (Day 1 starter) or on the first Sunday after the onset of the menstrual period (Sunday starter). **With a Sunday start, an additional method of contraception should be used until after the first 7 days of consecutive administration.**

Day 1 starter: Dose starts on first day of menstrual cycle taking 1 tablet daily.

Sunday starter: Dose begins on first Sunday after onset of menstruation; if the menstrual period starts on Sunday, take first tablet that very same day.

Switching from a different contraceptive:

Oral contraceptive: Start on the same day that a new pack of the previous oral contraceptive would have been taken

Transdermal patch, vaginal ring, injection: Start on the day the next dose would have been due

IUD or implant: Start on the day of removal

Use after childbirth (in women who are not breastfeeding) or after second trimester abortion: Therapy may be started ≥4 weeks postpartum. Pregnancy should be ruled out prior to treatment if menstrual periods have not restarted and an additional method of contraception (nonhormonal) should be used until after the first 7 days of consecutive administration.

Missed doses:

If all doses have been taken on schedule and one menstrual period is missed, continue dosing cycle. If two consecutive menstrual periods are missed, pregnancy test is required before new dosing cycle is started.

If doses have been missed during the first 3 weeks and the menstrual period is missed, pregnancy should be ruled out prior to continuing treatment.

Missed doses (monophasic formulations) (refer to package insert for complete information):

One dose missed: Take as soon as remembered or take 2 tablets next day

Two consecutive doses missed in the first 2 weeks: Take 2 tablets as soon as remembered or 2 tablets next 2 days. **An additional method of contraception should be used for 7 days after missed dose.**

Two consecutive doses missed in week 3 or three consecutive doses missed at any time: **An additional method of contraception must be used for 7 days after a missed dose.**

Day 1 starter: Current pack should be discarded, and a new pack should be started that same day.

Sunday starter: Continue dose of 1 tablet daily until Sunday, then discard the rest of the pack, and a new pack should be started that same day.

Any number of doses missed in week 4: Continue taking one pill each day until pack is empty; no back-up method of contraception is needed

Pediatric Note: Not to be used prior to menarche.

Acne (Gianvi, Loryna, Nikki, Vestura, Yaz): Females: Adolescents ≥14 years: Oral: Refer to adult dosing.

PMDD (Gianvi,Yaz): Females: Oral: Refer to adult dosing.

Contraception: Females: Oral: Refer to adult dosing.

Renal Impairment Contraindicated in patients with renal dysfunction.

Hepatic Impairment Contraindicated in patients with hepatic dysfunction.

Mechanism of Action

Combination oral contraceptives inhibit ovulation via a negative feedback mechanism on the hypothalamus, which alters the normal pattern of gonadotropin secretion of a follicle-stimulating hormone (FSH) and luteinizing hormone by the anterior pituitary. The follicular phase FSH and midcycle surge of gonadotropins are inhibited. In addition, oral contraceptives produce alterations in the genital tract, including changes in the cervical mucus, rendering it unfavorable for sperm penetration even if ovulation occurs. Changes in the endometrium may also occur, producing an unfavorable environment for nidation. Oral contraceptive drugs may alter the tubal transport of the ova through the fallopian tubes. Progestational agents may also alter sperm fertility. Drospirenone is a spironolactone analogue with antimineralocorticoid and antiandrogenic activity.

Contraindications

Adrenal insufficiency, breast cancer or other estrogen- or progestin-sensitive cancer (current or a history of), hepatic tumors (benign or malignant) or disease, pregnancy, renal impairment, undiagnosed abnormal uterine bleeding. Use is also contraindicated in women at high risk of arterial or venous thrombotic diseases including: Cerebrovascular disease, coronary artery disease, diabetes mellitus with vascular disease, DVT or PE (current or history of), hypercoagulopathies (inherited or acquired), hypertension (uncontrolled), headaches with focal neurological symptoms or migraine headaches (with or without aura) if >35 years of age, thrombogenic valvular or rhythm diseases of the heart (eg, subacute bacterial endocarditis with valvular disease or atrial fibrillation), women >35 years of age who smoke.

Canadian labeling: Additional contraindications (not in US labeling): Hypersensitivity to ethinyl estradiol, drospirenone or any other component of the formulation; history of or actual myocardial infarction (MI); major surgery associated with an increased risk of postoperative thromboembolism; prolonged immobilization; severe dyslipoproteinemia; history of or actual pancreatitis associated with severe hypertriglyceridemia; steroid-dependent jaundice, cholestatic jaundice, history of jaundice in pregnancy; ocular lesion arising from ophthalmic vascular disease, such as partial or complete loss of vision or defect in visual fields

Warnings/Precautions

[U.S. Boxed Warning]: The risk of cardiovascular side effects is increased in women who smoke cigarettes; risk increases with age (especially women >35 years of age) and the number of cigarettes smoked; women who use combination hormonal contraceptives should be strongly advised not to smoke. Use is contraindicated in patients >35 years of age who smoke. Oral contraceptives may lead to increased risk of stroke or myocardial infarction, use with caution in patients with risk factors for cardiovascular disease (eg, hypertension, hypercholesterolemia, morbid obesity, diabetes, or women who smoke). Contraceptives may increase the risk of thromboembolism; discontinue if an arterial or venous thrombotic event occurs. Risk may be greater with contraceptives containing drospirenone. Women with inherited thrombophilias (eg, protein C or S deficiency) may have increased risk of venous thromboembolism (DeSancho, 2010; van Vlijmen, 2011). Use is contraindicated in women with hypercoagulopathies (inherited or acquired). Whenever possible, combination hormonal contraceptives should be discontinued at least 4 weeks prior to and for 2 weeks following elective surgery associated with an increased risk of thromboembolism or during periods of prolonged immobilization. Oral contraceptives may have a dose-related risk of vascular disease, hypertension, and gallbladder disease. Women with hypertension should be encouraged to use another form of contraception. The use of combination hormonal contraceptives has been associated with a slight increase in frequency of breast cancer; however, studies are not consistent. Use is contraindicated in women with (or history of) breast cancer.

May have adverse effects on glucose tolerance; use caution in women with diabetes. Discontinue if unexplained loss of vision, proptosis, diplopia, papilledema, or retinal vascular lesions occur and immediately evaluate for retinal vein thrombosis. Use with caution in patients with depression, or patients with history of migraine. Evaluate new, recurrent, severe, or persistent headaches. Use with headaches with focal neurological symptoms or migraine headaches with or without aura if >35 years of age is contraindicated. Not for use prior to menarche or in postmenopausal women. Estrogens may induce or exacerbate symptoms in women with hereditary angioedema. Use caution with a history of chloasma gravidarum; women with a tendency to chloasma should avoid sun and ultraviolet radiation exposure during therapy. Use of combination hormonal contraceptives is associated with hepatic adenomas (rare); fatal intra-abdominal hemorrhage may result. Risk is increased with long-term (>8 years) use. Use of this product is contraindicated in women with hepatic tumors. Combination hormonal contraceptives may be poorly metabolized in women with hepatic impairment. Discontinue if jaundice develops during therapy or if liver function becomes abnormal. Use is contraindicated with preexisting hepatic disease. Risk of cholestasis may be increased with previous cholestatic jaundice of pregnancy or jaundice with prior oral contraceptive use. Combination hormonal contraceptives may affect lipid levels. The type of lipid disorder, the severity, and the presence of other cardiovascular risk factors should be considered when prescribing combination hormonal contraceptives to women with lipid disorders (CDC, 2010). Serum triglycerides may also be increased. Estrogens may increase thyroid-binding globulin (TBG) levels, leading to increased circulating total thyroid hormone levels. Women on thyroid replacement therapy may require higher doses of thyroid hormone while receiving estrogens. The use of estrogens and/or progestins may change the results of some laboratory tests (eg, coagulation factors, lipids, glucose tolerance, binding proteins). Drospirenone can also cause an increase in plasma renin activity and plasma aldosterone. The dose, route, and the specific estrogen/progestin influences these changes. In addition, personal risk factors (eg, cardiovascular disease, smoking, diabetes, age) also contribute to adverse events; use of specific products may be contraindicated in women with certain risk factors.

The minimum dosage combination of estrogen/progestin that will effectively treat the individual patient should be used. Unscheduled bleeding (breakthrough or intracyclic) and spotting may occur, especially during the first 3 months of therapy. In addition, occasional missed periods may occur. Presentation of irregular, unresolving vaginal bleeding warrants further evaluation, including endometrial sampling, if indicated, to rule out malignancy or pregnancy. Amenorrhea or oligomenorrhea may occur after discontinuing combination hormonal contraceptives, especially when such a condition was preexistent. Potentially significant interactions may exist, requiring dose or frequency adjustment, additional monitoring, and/or selection of alternative therapy.

Acne use: For use only in females ≥14 years who have reached menarche, who also desire combination hormonal contraceptive therapy, are unresponsive to topical treatments, and have no contraindications to combination hormonal contraceptive use.

PMDD use: For use only in females who desire combination hormonal contraceptive therapy; use for more than 3 menstrual cycles has not been evaluated. Has not been evaluated for the treatment of premenstrual syndrome

Drospirenone has antimineralocorticoid activity that may lead to hyperkalemia in patients with renal insufficiency, hepatic dysfunction, or adrenal insufficiency. Use caution with medications that may increase serum potassium.

Drug Interactions

Metabolism/Transport Effects Refer to individual components.

Avoid Concomitant Use

Avoid concomitant use of Ethinyl Estradiol and Drospirenone with any of the following: Amodiaquine; Anastrozole; Antihepaciviral Combination Products; Boceprevir; Dasabuvir; Dehydroepiandrosterone; Exemestane; Griseofulvin; Hemin; Indium 111 Capromab Pendetide; Ixazomib; Ospemifene; TiZANidine; Tranexamic Acid; Ulipristal

Increased Effect/Toxicity

Ethinyl Estradiol and Drospirenone may increase the levels/effects of: Agomelatine; Ajmaline; Aliskiren; Amodiaquine; Anthrax Immune Globulin (Human); Antihepaciviral Combination Products; C1 inhibitors; CloZAPine; Corticosteroids (Systemic); CYP1A2 Substrates; Dantrolene; Dasabuvir; Flibanserin; Immune Globulin; Lenalidomide; Lomitapide; Ospemifene;

Pirfenidone; Pomalidomide; Potassium-Sparing Diuretics; ROPINIRole; Selegiline; Thalidomide; Theophylline Derivatives; Tipranavir; TiZANidine; Tranexamic Acid; Voriconazole

The levels/effects of Ethinyl Estradiol and Drospirenone may be increased by: ACE Inhibitors; Angiotensin II Receptor Blockers; Ascorbic Acid; Atazanavir; Boceprevir; Carfilzomib; Cobicistat; CYP3A4 Inhibitors (Strong); Dehydroepiandrosterone; Herbs (Estrogenic Properties); Herbs (Progestogenic Properties); Lopinavir; Metreleptin; MiFEPRIStone; Nonsteroidal Anti-Inflammatory Agents; Pomalidomide; Tipranavir; Voriconazole

Decreased Effect

Ethinyl Estradiol and Drospirenone may decrease the levels/effects of: Anastrozole; Anticoagulants; Antidiabetic Agents; Chenodiol; Exemestane; Fosamprenavir; Hemin; Hyaluronidase; Indium 111 Capromab Pendetide; LamoTRIgine; Ospemifene; Thyroid Products; Ulipristal; Ursodiol; Valproate Products; Vitamin K Antagonists

The levels/effects of Ethinyl Estradiol and Drospirenone may be decreased by: Acitretin; Aprepitant; Armodafinil; Artemether; Asunaprevir; Barbiturates; Bexarotene (Systemic); Bile Acid Sequestrants; Bosentan; CarBAMazepine; CloBAZam; Cobicistat; Colesevelam; CYP3A4 Inducers (Moderate); CYP3A4 Inducers (Strong); Dabrafenib; Darunavir; Deferasirox; Efavirenz; Elvitegravir; Enzalutamide; Eslicarbazepine; Exenatide; Felbamate; Fosamprenavir; Fosaprepitant; Fosphenytoin; Griseofulvin; Ixazomib; Lesinurad; Lixisenatide; Lopinavir; Lumacaftor; Metreleptin; MiFEPRIStone; Mitotane; Modafinil; Mycophenolate; Nafcillin; Nelfinavir; Nevirapine; OXcarbazepine; Perampanel; Phenytoin; Primidone; Protease Inhibitors; Prucalopride; Retinoic Acid Derivatives; Rifamycin Derivatives; Rufinamide; Saquinavir; Siltuximab; St John's Wort; Sugammadex; Telaprevir; Tipranavir; Tocilizumab; Topiramate; Ulipristal

Dietary Considerations Should be taken at the same time each day; may be taken with or without a meal

Pharmacodynamics/Kinetics

Half-life Elimination Terminal: Drospirenone: ~30 hours; Ethinyl estradiol: ~24 hours

Time to Peak 1 to 2 hours

Pregnancy Considerations Pregnancy status should be evaluated prior to prescribing (CDC, 2013); treatment should be discontinued if pregnancy occurs. In general, the use of combination hormonal contraceptives, when inadvertently used early in pregnancy, have not been associated with teratogenic effects. Available evidence is inconsistent if BMI alters the efficacy of combination oral contraceptives (CDC, 2010).

Due to increased risk of venous thromboembolism (VTE) postpartum, combination hormonal contraceptives should not be started in any woman <21 days following delivery. Women without risk factors for VTE and who are not breastfeeding may start combination hormonal contraceptives during 21-42 days postpartum. After 42 days postpartum, restrictions for use are not related to postpartum status and should be based on other medical conditions (CDC, 2011). The manufacturer states that combination hormonal contraceptives should not be started until ≥4 weeks after delivery in women who choose not to breast-feed, or ≥4 weeks after a second trimester abortion or miscarriage.

Breastfeeding Considerations The amount of drospirenone excreted in breast milk is ~0.02%, resulting in a maximum of ~3 mcg/day drospirenone to the infant. Jaundice and breast enlargement in the nursing infant have been reported following the use of other oral contraceptives. In addition, may decrease the quality and quantity of breast milk. Other forms of contraception are recommended while breastfeeding (per manufacturer). The theoretical concerns about decreased milk production are greatest early in the postpartum period when milk production is being established. Postpartum risk status for VTE should be considered when initiating combination hormonal contraceptives after delivery. Combined hormonal contraceptives should not be started <21 days postpartum due to increased risk of VTE. Risk of VTE is still elevated in breastfeeding women until ~42 days postpartum and is greater in women with additional risk factors. After 42 days postpartum, restrictions for use are not related to postpartum VTE risk and should be based on other medical conditions (CDC, 2011).

Dosage Forms

Tablet, oral:

Gianvi: Ethinyl estradiol 0.03 mg and drospirenone 3 mg [24 light pink active tablets and 4 white inactive tablets] (28s)

Loryna: Ethinyl estradiol 0.02 mg and drospirenone 3 mg [24 peach active tablets and 4 white inactive tablets] (28s)

Nikki: Ethinyl estradiol 0.02 mg and drospirenone 3 mg [24 pink active tablets and 4 white inactive tablets] (28s)

Ocella, Syeda, Yasmin: Ethinyl estradiol 0.03 mg and drospirenone 3 mg [21 yellow active tablets and 7 white inactive tablets] (28s)

Vestura: Ethinyl estradiol 0.02 mg and drospirenone 3 mg [24 pink active tablets and 4 peach inactive tablets] (28s)

Yaz: Ethinyl estradiol 0.02 mg and drospirenone 3 mg [24 light pink active tablets and 4 white inactive tablets] (28s)

Zarah: Ethinyl estradiol 0.03 mg and drospirenone 3 mg [21 blue active tablets and 7 peach inactive tablets] (28s)

Generic: Ethinyl estradiol 0.02 mg and drospirenone 3 mg [21 active tablets and 7 inactive tablets] (28s); Ethinyl estradiol 0.03 mg and drospirenone 3 mg [21 active tablets and 7 inactive tablets] (28s)

Ethinyl Estradiol and Ethynodiol Diacetate

(ETH in il es tra DYE ole & e thye noe DYE ole dye AS e tate)

Related Information

Endocrine Disorders and Pregnancy *on page 1781*

Brand Names: US Kelnor; Zovia 1/35E; Zovia 1/50E

Brand Names: Canada Demulen 30

Generic Availability (US) Yes

Pharmacologic Category Contraceptive; Estrogen and Progestin Combination

Use Contraception: For the prevention of pregnancy

Limitation of use: Products containing the equivalent of estrogen 50 mcg should not be used unless medically indicated.

Local Anesthetic/Vasoconstrictor Precautions No information available to require special precautions

Effects on Dental Treatment When prescribing antibiotics, patient must be warned to use additional methods of birth control if on oral contraceptives.

Effects on Bleeding No information available to require special precautions

Adverse Reactions Frequency not defined.

Cardiovascular: Arterial thromboembolism, Budd-Chiari syndrome, cerebral thrombosis, cerebrovascular accident, edema, hypertension, local thrombophlebitis, mesenteric thrombosis, myocardial infarction, pulmonary thromboembolism, retinal thrombosis

Central nervous system: Cerebral hemorrhage, depression, dizziness, headache, migraine, nervousness

Dermatologic: Acne vulgaris, allergic skin rash, chloasma (may persist), erythema multiforme, erythema nodosum, loss of scalp hair

Endocrine & metabolic: Amenorrhea, change in libido, change in menstrual flow, decreased glucose tolerance, decreased serum folate level, hirsutism, increased serum triglycerides, increased sex hormone binding globulins, increased thyroxine binding globulin, porphyria, premenstrual syndrome, weight gain, weight loss

Gastrointestinal: Abdominal cramps, bloating, carbohydrate intolerance, change in appetite, cholestasis, colitis, gallbladder disease, nausea, vomiting

Genitourinary: Breakthrough bleeding, breast hypertrophy, breast secretion, breast tenderness, change in cervical erosion, change in cervical secretions, cystitis-like syndrome, decreased lactation (postpartum), spotting, transient infertility (following discontinuation), vaginitis, vulvovaginal candidiasis

Hematologic & oncologic: Decreased antithrombin III plasma level, hemolytic-uremic syndrome, hemorrhagic eruption, increased clotting factor VII, increased clotting factor VIII, increased clotting factor IX, increased clotting factor X, increased norepinephrine-induced platelet aggregation, prolonged prothrombin time

Hepatic: Cholestatic jaundice, hepatic adenoma, hepatic neoplasm (benign), jaundice

Ophthalmic: Cataract, change in corneal curvature (steepening), contact lens intolerance, optic neuritis

Renal: Renal insufficiency

Dosing

Adult

Females: Contraception: Oral: 1 tablet once daily

Schedule 1 (Sunday starter): Dose begins on first Sunday after onset of menstruation; if the menstrual period starts on Sunday, take first tablet that very same day. **With a Sunday start, an additional method of contraception should be used until after the first 7 days of consecutive administration:**

Schedule 2 (Day 1 starter): Dose starts on first day of menstrual cycle taking 1 tablet/day:

Missed or late doses (CDC, 2013):

If one dose is late (<24 hours since dose should have been taken) or if one dose is missed (24 to <48 hours since dose should have been taken): Take dose as soon as possible. Continue remaining doses at the usual time (even if that means 2 doses on the same day).

If ≥2 consecutive doses are missed (≥48 hours since dose should have been taken): Take the most recently missed dose as soon as possible, discard any other missed doses. Continue remaining doses at the usual time (even if that means taking 2 doses on the same day); use back-up contraception until hormonal pills have been taken for 7 consecutive days. If doses were missed during the last week of hormonal (active) tablets (eg, days 15 to 21 of a 28-day pack), omit the hormone-free interval by finishing the hormonal pills from the current pack and starting a new pack. If unable to start a new pack immediately, back up contraception is needed until hormonal pills from a new pack have been taken for 7 consecutive days. Consider use of emergency contraception in some situations (refer to guidelines for details).

Also refer to package insert for product specific information.

Pediatric Females: Contraception: Oral: Refer to adult dosing; not to be used prior to menarche.

Renal Impairment There are no dosage adjustments provided in the manufacturer's labeling (has not been studied); use with caution and monitor blood pressure closely.

Hepatic Impairment Use is contraindicated.

Mechanism of Action Combination hormonal contraceptives inhibit ovulation via a negative feedback mechanism on the hypothalamus, which alters the normal pattern of gonadotropin secretion of a follicle-stimulating hormone (FSH) and luteinizing hormone by the anterior pituitary. The follicular phase FSH and midcycle surge of gonadotropins are inhibited. In addition, combination hormonal contraceptives produce alterations in the genital tract, including changes in the cervical mucus, rendering it unfavorable for sperm penetration even if ovulation occurs. Changes in the endometrium may also occur, producing an unfavorable environment for nidation. Combination hormonal contraceptive drugs may alter the tubal transport of the ova through the fallopian tubes. Progestational agents may also alter sperm fertility.

Contraindications Breast cancer or other estrogen- or progestin-dependent neoplasms (current or a history of), hepatic tumors (benign or malignant) or hepatic disease, cholestatic jaundice of pregnancy, jaundice with prior combination hormonal contraceptive use, pregnancy, undiagnosed abnormal uterine bleeding

Use is also contraindicated in women at high risk of arterial or venous thrombotic diseases, for example, women with: Cerebrovascular disease, coronary artery disease, deep vein thrombosis, myocardial infarction, or thrombophlebitis or thromboembolic disorders (current or history of)

Canadian labeling: Additional contraindications: Hypersensitivity to any component of the formulation; ocular lesions due to ophthalmic vascular disease including partial or complete loss of vision or defect in visual fields; pancreatitis associated with severe hypertriglyceridemia (current or history of); thrombophilias (inherited or acquired); severe dyslipoproteinemia; women >35 years of age who smoke >15 cigarettes per day; major surgery with increased risk of postoperative thromboembolism; prolonged immobilization; thrombogenic valvular or rhythm diseases of the heart; headaches with focal neurological symptoms (eg, aura); diabetes mellitus with vascular disease, hypertension (uncontrolled)

Documentation of allergenic cross-reactivity for estrogens and progestins is limited. However, because of similarities in chemical structure and/or pharmacologic actions, the possibility of cross-sensitivity cannot be ruled out with certainty

Warnings/Precautions

[US Boxed Warning]: The risk of cardiovascular side effects is increased in women who smoke cigarettes; risk increases with age (especially women >35 years of age) and the number of cigarettes smoked; women who use combination

hormonal contraceptives should be strongly advised not to smoke.

The use of combination hormonal contraceptives has not been shown to increase the risk for breast cancer. However, breast cancer is a hormonal-sensitive tumor and the prognosis for women with a current or recent history of breast cancer may be worse with combination hormonal contraceptive use (CDC, 2010). Use is contraindicated in women with (or history of) breast cancer. The use of combination hormonal contraceptives has been associated with a slight increased risk of cervical cancer; however, studies are not consistent and may be related to additional risk factors (Gierisch, 2013). Women awaiting treatment for cervical cancer may use combination hormonal contraceptives (CDC, 2013). The risk of ovarian cancer is decreased in women using combination hormonal contraceptives (CDC, 2013; Walker, 2015). Oral contraceptives may be used to reduce the risk of ovarian cancer including those women with BRCA1 and BRCA2 mutations (Walker, 2015).

The risk of hypertension may be increased with age, dose, and duration of use. Combination hormonal contraceptives should not be used in women with persistent blood pressure values ≥160 mm Hg systolic or ≥100 mm Hg diastolic. Women with less severe hypertension (140 to 159 mm Hg systolic or 90 to 99 mm Hg diastolic) or those with hypertension that is adequately controlled should generally not use combination hormonal contraceptives (CDC, 2013). Other risk factors for cardiovascular disease (eg, older age, smoking, diabetes) should be considered when prescribing contraceptives (CDC, 2010). Use with caution in patients with risk factors for cardiovascular disease (eg, hypertension, hypercholesterolemia, morbid obesity, diabetes, women who smoke) (CDC, 2010); use of combination hormonal contraceptives may increase the risk of arterial or venous thrombotic events. Use is contraindicated in women at high risk of arterial or venous thrombotic diseases. May increase the risk of thromboembolism; discontinue use of combination hormonal contraceptives if an arterial or venous thrombotic event occurs. Women with inherited thrombophilias (eg, protein C or S deficiency) may have increased risk of venous thromboembolism (DeSancho, 2010; van Vlijmen, 2011). The Canadian labeling contraindicates use in patients with inherited or acquired thrombophilias.

Combination hormonal contraceptives may adversely affect lipid levels, including serum triglycerides. The type of lipid disorder, the severity, and the presence of other cardiovascular risk factors should be considered when prescribing combination hormonal contraceptives to women with lipid disorders (CDC, 2010). Women with hypertriglyceridemia or a family history of hypertriglyceridemia may be at increased risk of pancreatitis when using combination hormonal contraceptives. Consider alternative contraception for women with uncontrolled dyslipidemia. The Canadian labeling contraindicates use in patients with pancreatitis associated with severe hypertriglyceridemia (current or history of). Risk of cholestasis may be increased with previous cholestasis of pregnancy or cholestasis with prior oral contraceptive use. Use is contraindicated with cholestatic jaundice or jaundice or pregnancy. May have a risk of gallbladder disease; may worsen existing gallbladder disease. The use of estrogens and/or progestins may change the results of some laboratory tests (eg, coagulation factors, lipids, glucose tolerance, binding proteins). The dose, route, and the specific estrogen/progestin influences these changes. In addition, personal risk factors (eg, cardiovascular disease, smoking, diabetes, age) also contribute to adverse events; use of specific products may be contraindicated in women with certain risk factors.

Combination hormonal contraceptives may be poorly metabolized in women with hepatic impairment. Discontinue if jaundice develops during therapy or if liver function becomes abnormal. Use is contraindicated in women with hepatic disease. Use of combination hormonal contraceptives is associated with hepatic adenomas (rare); rupture may cause fatal intra-abdominal hemorrhage. Long-term use may be associated with an increased risk of hepatocellular carcinoma (rare). Use of this product is contraindicated in women with preexisting hepatic tumors.

Evaluate new, recurrent, severe, or persistent headaches. The Canadian labeling contraindicates use in patients with migraine headaches with focal neurological symptoms (eg, aura). Estrogens may induce or exacerbate symptoms in women with hereditary angioedema (Geng, 2013; Zuraw, 2013). Use with caution in patients with diseases that may be exacerbated by fluid retention. Oral contraceptives may impair glucose tolerance; use caution in women with diabetes or prediabetes. Use with caution in patients with a history of depression; discontinue if serious depression recurs. Discontinue if unexplained loss of vision, proptosis, diplopia, papilledema, or retinal vascular lesions occur and immediately evaluate for retinal vein thrombosis. The Canadian labeling contraindicates use in patients with ocular lesions due to ophthalmic vascular disease, including partial or complete loss of vision or defect in visual fields. Any changes with contact lens tolerance or vision should be evaluated by an ophthalmologist. Combination hormonal contraceptives, as well as sun exposure and pregnancy, are triggers for chloasma. Women with a susceptibility to chloasma or additional risk factors should avoid exposure to sun or ultraviolet radiation during therapy (Handel, 2014).

Breakthrough or intracyclic bleeding and spotting may occur, especially during the first 3 months of therapy. In addition, occasional missed periods may occur. Presentation of irregular, unresolving vaginal bleeding warrants further evaluation to rule out malignancy or pregnancy. Amenorrhea or oligomenorrhea may occur after discontinuing combination hormonal contraceptives, especially when such a condition was preexistent. When initiating a combination oral contraceptive, consideration should be given to safety, effectiveness, availability, and acceptance to the patient (CDC, 2013). Consider initiating with a monthly bleeding monophasic formulation containing ethinyl estradiol 30 to 35 mcg plus a progestin, and adjusting based on adverse events and patient preference (Ott, 2014).

Potentially significant interactions may exist, requiring dose or frequency adjustment, additional monitoring, and/or selection of alternative therapy. Estrogens may increase thyroid-binding globulin levels leading to increased circulating total thyroid hormone levels. Women on thyroid replacement therapy may require higher doses of thyroid hormone while receiving estrogens. Combination hormonal contraceptives do not protect against HIV infection or other sexually transmitted diseases (CDC, 2010; CDC, 2013). Not for use prior to menarche. Whenever possible, should be discontinued at least 4 weeks prior to and for 2 weeks following elective surgery associated with an increased risk of thromboembolism or during periods of prolonged immobilization.

Drug Interactions

Metabolism/Transport Effects Refer to individual components.

Avoid Concomitant Use

Avoid concomitant use of Ethinyl Estradiol and Ethynodiol Diacetate with any of the following: Amodiaquine; Anastrozole; Antihepaciviral Combination Products; Dasabuvir; Dehydroepiandrosterone; Exemestane; Griseofulvin; Hemin; Indium 111 Capromab Pendetide; Ixazomib; Ospemifene; TiZANidine; Tranexamic Acid; Ulipristal

Increased Effect/Toxicity

Ethinyl Estradiol and Ethynodiol Diacetate may increase the levels/effects of: Agomelatine; Ajmaline; Amodiaquine; Anthrax Immune Globulin (Human); Antihepaciviral Combination Products; C1 inhibitors; CloZAPine; Corticosteroids (Systemic); CYP1A2 Substrates; Dantrolene; Dasabuvir; Flibanserin; Immune Globulin; Lenalidomide; Lomitapide; Ospemifene; Pirfenidone; Pomalidomide; ROPINIRole; Selegiline; Thalidomide; Theophylline Derivatives; Tipranavir; TiZANidine; Tranexamic Acid; Voriconazole

The levels/effects of Ethinyl Estradiol and Ethynodiol Diacetate may be increased by: Ascorbic Acid; Atazanavir; Boceprevir; Carfilzomib; Cobicistat; Dehydroepiandrosterone; Herbs (Estrogenic Properties); Herbs (Progestogenic Properties); Lopinavir; Metreleptin; MiFEPRIStone; NSAID (COX-2 Inhibitor); Pomalidomide; Tipranavir; Voriconazole

Decreased Effect

Ethinyl Estradiol and Ethynodiol Diacetate may decrease the levels/effects of: Anastrozole; Anticoagulants; Antidiabetic Agents; Chenodiol; Exemestane; Fosamprenavir; Hemin; Hyaluronidase; Indium 111 Capromab Pendetide; LamoTRIgine; Ospemifene; Thyroid Products; Ulipristal; Ursodiol; Valproate Products; Vitamin K Antagonists

The levels/effects of Ethinyl Estradiol and Ethynodiol Diacetate may be decreased by: Acitretin; Aprepitant; Armodafinil; Artemether; Asunaprevir; Barbiturates; Bexarotene (Systemic); Bile Acid Sequestrants; Boceprevir; Bosentan; CarBAMazepine; CloBAZam; Cobicistat; Colesevelam; CYP3A4 Inducers (Moderate); CYP3A4 Inducers (Strong); Dabrafenib; Darunavir; Deferasirox; Efavirenz; Elvitegravir; Enzalutamide; Eslicarbazepine; Exenatide; Felbamate; Fosamprenavir; Fosaprepitant; Fosphenytoin; Griseofulvin; Ixazomib; Lesinurad; Lixisenatide; Lopinavir; Lumacaftor; Metreleptin; MiFEPRIStone; Mitotane; Modafinil; Mycophenolate; Nafcillin; Nelfinavir; Nevirapine; OXcarbazepine; Perampanel; Phenytoin; Primidone; Protease Inhibitors; Prucalopride; Retinoic Acid Derivatives; Rifamycin Derivatives; Rufinamide; Saquinavir; Siltuximab; St John's Wort; Sugammadex; Telaprevir; Tipranavir; Tocilizumab; Topiramate; Ulipristal

Pregnancy Risk Factor X

Pregnancy Considerations Pregnancy status should be evaluated prior to prescribing (CDC 2013); treatment should be discontinued if pregnancy occurs. In general, the use of combination hormonal contraceptives, when inadvertently used early in pregnancy, have not been associated with teratogenic effects. Available evidence is inconsistent if body mass index alters the efficacy of combination oral contraceptives (CDC 2010).

Due to increased risk of venous thromboembolism (VTE) postpartum, combination hormonal contraceptives should not be started in any woman <21 days following delivery. Women without risk factors for VTE and who are not breastfeeding may start combination hormonal contraceptives during 21 to 42 days postpartum. After 42 days postpartum, restrictions for use are not related to postpartum status and should be based on other medical conditions (CDC 2011). The manufacturer states that combination hormonal contraceptives should not be started until ≥4 to 6 weeks after delivery in women who choose not to breast-feed.

Breastfeeding Considerations Contraceptive steroids can be detected in breast milk. Jaundice and breast enlargement in the nursing infant have been reported following the use of combination hormonal contraceptives. May decrease the quality and quantity of breast milk; a nonhormonal form of contraception is recommended (per manufacturer). The theoretical concerns about decreased milk production are greatest early in the postpartum period when milk production is being established (CDC 2011).

Postpartum risk status for venous thromboembolism (VTE) should be considered when initiating combination hormonal contraceptives after delivery. Combined hormonal contraceptives should not be started <21 days postpartum due to increased risk of VTE. Risk of VTE is still elevated in breastfeeding women until ~42 days postpartum and is greater in women with additional risk factors. After 42 days postpartum, restrictions for use are not related to postpartum VTE risk and should be based on other medical conditions (CDC 2011).

Dosage Forms

Tablet, oral [monophasic formulation]:

Kelnor 1/35: Ethinyl estradiol 0.035 mg and ethynodiol diacetate 1 mg [21 light yellow tablets and 7 white inactive tablets] (28s)

Zovia 1/35-28: Ethinyl estradiol 0.035 mg and ethynodiol diacetate 1 mg [21 light yellow tablets and 7 white inactive tablets] (28s)

Zovia 1/50-28: Ethinyl estradiol 0.05 mg and ethynodiol diacetate 1 mg [21 pink tablets and 7 white inactive tablets] (28s)

Generic: Ethinyl estradiol 0.05 mg and ethynodiol diacetate 1 mg [21 active tablets and 7 inactive tablets] (28s)

Ethinyl Estradiol and Etonogestrel

(ETH in il es tra DYE ole & et oh noe JES trel)

Related Information

Endocrine Disorders and Pregnancy *on page 1781*

Etonogestrel *on page 671*

Brand Names: US NuvaRing

Brand Names: Canada NuvaRing

Generic Availability (US) No

Pharmacologic Category Contraceptive; Estrogen and Progestin Combination

Use Contraception: Prevention of pregnancy.

Local Anesthetic/Vasoconstrictor Precautions No information available to require special precautions

Effects on Dental Treatment When prescribing antibiotics, patient must be warned to use additional methods of birth control if on oral contraceptives.

Effects on Bleeding No information available to require special precautions

Adverse Reactions

The most common adverse reactions associated with NuvaRing (5% to 14%): Headache, mood changes, nausea and vomiting, sinusitis, upper respiratory tract infection, vaginal discharge, vaginitis, and weight gain.

The following reactions have been associated with combination hormonal contraceptive use:

Increased risk or evidence of association with use:

Cardiovascular: Arterial thromboembolism, cerebral thrombosis, hypertension, local thrombophlebitis, mesenteric thrombosis, myocardial infarction, pulmonary embolism, retinal thrombosis, venous thrombosis (with or without embolism)

Central nervous system: Cerebral hemorrhage

Endocrine & metabolic: Decreased glucose tolerance, increased corticosteroid-binding globulin, increased sex hormone-binding globulin, increased thyroxine-binding globulin

Gastrointestinal: Gallbladder disease

Hepatic: Hepatic adenomas, hepatic carcinoma (long-term use [>8 years]), hepatic neoplasm (benign)

Adverse reactions considered drug related:

Cardiovascular: Deep vein thrombosis, edema, worsening of varicose veins

Central nervous system: Anxiety, depression, exacerbation of tics, migraine

Dermatologic: Acne vulgaris, allergic skin rash, chloasma

Endocrine & metabolic: Amenorrhea, breast changes (enlargement, pain, secretion, tenderness), change in menstrual flow, decreased libido, decreased serum folate level, exacerbation of porphyria, fluid retention, weight changes

Gastrointestinal: Abdominal cramps, abdominal pain, bloating, change in appetite, cholelithiasis, nausea, vomiting

Genitourinary: Breakthrough bleeding, cervical ectropion, cervical erosion, change in cervical secretions, decreased lactation (with use immediately postpartum), dysmenorrhea, infertility (temporary), spotting, vaginal discomfort, vaginal ulcer, vaginitis, vulvovaginal candidiasis

Hepatic: Cholestatic jaundice

Hypersensitivity: Anaphylactoid reactions (including angioedema, circulatory collapse, respiratory collapse, urticaria), anaphylaxis

Neuromuscular & skeletal: Exacerbation of systemic lupus erythematosus

Ophthalmic: Change in corneal curvature (steepening), contact lens intolerance

Adverse reactions in which association is not confirmed or denied, postmarketing, and/or case reports: Budd-Chiari syndrome, cataract, cerebrovascular accident, cervical dysplasia, change in libido, colitis, cystitis-like syndrome, dizziness, erythema multiforme, erythema nodosum, hemolytic uremic syndrome, hemorrhagic eruption, hirsutism, hypersensitivity, loss of scalp hair, malignant neoplasm of cervix, nervousness, optic neuritis (with or without partial or complete loss of vision), pancreatitis, premenstrual syndrome, renal insufficiency, toxic shock syndrome

Dosing

Adult Contraception: Females: Vaginal: One ring, inserted vaginally and left in place for 3 consecutive weeks, then removed for 1 week. A new ring is inserted 7 days after the last was removed (even if bleeding is not complete) and should be inserted at approximately the same time of day the ring was removed the previous week.

Initial treatment should begin as follows (pregnancy should always be ruled out first):

No hormonal contraceptive use in the past month: Insert ring on the first day of menstrual cycle ("Day 1"). May also insert on days 2-5 even if bleeding is not complete, however, **a spermicide or barrier method of contraception should be used for the following 7 days.***

Switching from combination oral contraceptive: Ring can be inserted on any day within 7 days after the last **active** tablet in the cycle was taken and no later than the first day a new cycle of tablets would begin. Additional forms of contraception are not needed.

Switching from progestin-only contraceptive: **A spermicide or barrier method of contraception should be used for the following 7 days with any of the following.***

If previously using a progestin-only mini-pill, insert the ring on any day of the month; insert the vaginal ring on the day after the last mini-pill; do not skip days between the last pill and insertion of the ring.

If previously using an implant, insert the ring on the same day of implant removal.

If previously using a progestin-containing IUD, insert the ring on day of IUD removal.

If previously using a progestin injection, insert the ring on the day the next injection would be given.

Following complete 1st trimester abortion or miscarriage: Insert ring within the first 5 days of abortion or miscarriage. If not inserted within 5 days, follow instructions for "No hormonal contraceptive use within the past month" and instruct patient to use a nonhormonal contraceptive in the interim.

Following delivery or 2nd trimester abortion or miscarriage: Insert ring 4 weeks postpartum (in women who are not breastfeeding) or following 2nd trimester abortion or miscarriage. **A spermicide or barrier method of contraception should be used for the following 7 days.***

Inadvertent removal or expulsion: If the ring is accidentally removed from the vagina at any time during the 3-week period of use, it may be rinsed with cool or lukewarm water (not hot) and reinserted as soon as possible. If the ring is not reinserted within 3 hours, contraceptive effectiveness will be decreased. If the ring is accidently removed from the vagina for >3 hours during weeks 1 and 2, the ring should be reinserted as soon as the woman remembers and **a spermicide or barrier method of contraception should be used until the ring has been in place for 7 consecutive days.*** If the ring is accidently removed from the vagina for >3 hours during week 3, the ring should be discarded. A new ring may be inserted immediately, restarting a new 3-week cycle, OR a new ring may be inserted ≤7 days from the time the previous ring was removed or expelled (the second option should only be done if a vaginal ring was in continuous use for ≥7 days prior to the inadvertent expulsion/removal). With either option, **a spermicide or barrier method of contraception should be used until the ring has been in place for 7 consecutive days.*** Additional guidelines are available (CDC, 2013).

If the ring has been removed for longer than 1 week, pregnancy must be ruled out prior to restarting therapy. **A spermicide or barrier method of contraception should be used for the following 7 days.***

Prolonged use: If the ring has been left in place for up to 1 extra week (up to 4 weeks total); a new ring should be inserted following a 1-week (ring-free) interval. Protection continues during week 4, however, if the ring is left in place >4 weeks, pregnancy must be ruled out prior to insertion and **a spermicide or barrier method of contraception should be used for the following 7 days.***

Disconnected ring: In the event the ring disconnects at the weld joint, discard and replace with a new ring.

***Note:** Diaphragms may interfere with proper ring placement, and therefore, are not recommended for use as an additional form of contraception.

Pediatric Contraception: Females: Children and Adolescents: Vaginal: Refer to adult dosing; not to be used prior to menarche.

Renal Impairment There are no dosage adjustments provided in the manufacturer's labeling (has not been studied).

Hepatic Impairment Use is contraindicated.

Mechanism of Action Combination hormonal contraceptives inhibit ovulation via a negative feedback mechanism on the hypothalamus, which alters the normal pattern of gonadotropin secretion of a follicle-stimulating hormone (FSH) and luteinizing hormone by the anterior pituitary. The follicular phase FSH and midcycle surge of gonadotropins are inhibited. In addition, combination hormonal contraceptives produce alterations in the genital tract, including changes in the cervical mucus, rendering it unfavorable for sperm penetration even if ovulation occurs. Changes in the endometrium may also occur, producing an unfavorable environment for nidation. Combination hormonal contraceptive drugs may alter the tubal transport of the ova through the fallopian tubes. Progestational agents may also alter sperm fertility (Rivera, 1999).

Contraindications Hypersensitivity to ethinyl estradiol, etonogestrel, or any component of the formulation; breast cancer or other estrogen- or progestin-sensitive cancer (current or a history of); hepatic tumors (benign or malignant) or hepatic disease; pregnancy; undiagnosed abnormal uterine bleeding.

Use is also contraindicated in women at high risk of arterial or venous thrombotic diseases including: Cerebrovascular disease; coronary artery disease; diabetes mellitus with vascular disease; DVT or PE (current or history of); headaches with focal neurological symptoms; migraine headaches with aura or migraine headaches if >35 years; hypertension (uncontrolled); thrombogenic valvular or rhythm diseases of the heart (eg, subacute bacterial endocarditis with valvular disease, atrial fibrillation); women >35 years who smoke; inherited or acquired hypercoagulopathies.

Canadian labeling: Additional contraindications (not in US labeling): Prodromi of a thrombosis (eg, angina pectoris or transient ischemic attack); severe dyslipoproteinemia; major surgery with prolonged immobilization, any ocular lesion from ophthalmic vascular disease such as partial or complete loss of vision or defect in visual fields; pancreatitis or history of pancreatitis with severe hypertriglyceridemia

Documentation of allergenic cross-reactivity for progestins and estrogens is limited. However, because of similarities in chemical structure and/or pharmacologic actions, the possibility of cross-sensitivity cannot be ruled out with certainty.

Warnings/Precautions [U.S. Boxed Warning]: Cigarette smoking increases the risk of serious cardiovascular events from combination hormonal contraceptive use. This risk increases with age (especially women >35 years) and with the number of cigarettes smoked. Combination hormonal contraceptive use is contraindicated in women >35 years who smoke.

The risk of hypertension may be increased with age, dose, and duration of use. Combination hormonal contraceptives should not be used in women with persistent blood pressure values ≥160 mm Hg systolic or ≥100 mm Hg diastolic. Women with less severe hypertension (140 to 159 mm Hg systolic or 90 to 99 mm Hg diastolic) or those with hypertension that is adequately controlled should generally not use combination hormonal contraceptives (CDC 2013). Other risk factors for cardiovascular disease (eg, older age, smoking, diabetes) should be considered when prescribing contraceptives (CDC 2010). May increase the risk of thromboembolism; discontinue use of combination hormonal contraceptives if an arterial or venous thrombotic event (VTE) occurs. Women with inherited thrombophilias (eg, protein C or S deficiency) may have increased risk of venous thromboembolism (DeSancho 2010; van Vlijmen 2011). Use is contraindicated in women with hypercoagulopathies (inherited or acquired). Use with caution in patients with risk factors for cardiovascular disease (eg, hypertension, hypercholesterolemia, morbid obesity, diabetes, or women who smoke); use of combination hormonal contraceptives may increase the risk of arterial or venous thrombotic events (CDC 2010). Use is contraindicated in women at high risk of arterial or venous thrombotic diseases. The use of combination hormonal contraceptives has been associated with a slight increased risk of cervical cancer or intraepithelial neoplasia; however, studies are not consistent and may be related to additional risk factors (Gierisch 2013). Women awaiting treatment for cervical cancer may use combination hormonal contraceptives (CDC 2013).

Combination hormonal contraceptives may adversely affect lipid levels, including serum triglycerides. The type of lipid disorder, the severity, and the presence of other cardiovascular risk factors should be considered when prescribing combination hormonal contraceptives to women with lipid disorders (CDC 2010). Women with hypertriglyceridemia or a family history of hypertriglyceridemia may be at increased risk of pancreatitis when using combination hormonal contraceptives. Consider alternative contraception for women with uncontrolled dyslipidemia. Risk of cholestasis may be increased with previous cholestasis of pregnancy or cholestasis with prior oral contraceptive use. Use of combination hormonal contraceptives is associated with hepatic adenomas (rare); rupture may cause fatal intra-abdominal hemorrhage. Long-term use (>8 years) may be associated with an increased risk of hepatocellular carcinoma (rare). Use is contraindicated in women with preexisting hepatic tumors. Combination hormonal contraceptives may be poorly metabolized in women with hepatic impairment. Use is contraindicated in hepatic disease. Discontinue if jaundice develops during therapy or if liver function becomes abnormal. May have a dose-related risk of gallbladder disease; preexisting gallbladder disease may be exacerbated. The use of estrogens and/or progestins may change the results of some laboratory tests (eg, coagulation factors, lipids, glucose tolerance, binding proteins). The dose, route, and the specific estrogen/progestin influence these changes. In addition, personal risk factors (eg, cardiovascular disease, smoking, diabetes, age) also contribute to adverse events; use of specific products may be contraindicated in women with certain risk factors.

Evaluate new, recurrent, severe, or persistent headaches and consider discontinuing therapy if appropriate. Discontinue if unexplained loss of vision, proptosis, diplopia, papilledema, or retinal vascular lesions occur and immediately evaluate for retinal vein thrombosis. The use of combination hormonal contraceptives has not been shown to increase the risk for breast cancer. However, breast cancer is a hormonal sensitive tumor and the prognosis for women with a current or recent history of breast cancer may be worse with combination hormonal contraceptive use (CDC 2013). Use is contraindicated in women with (or history of) breast cancer. Estrogens may induce or exacerbate symptoms in women with hereditary angioedema (Geng 2013; Zuraw 2013). May impair glucose tolerance; use caution in women with diabetes or prediabetes. Combination hormonal contraceptives, as well as sun exposure and pregnancy, are triggers for chloasma. Women with a susceptibility to chloasma or additional risk factors should avoid exposure to sun or ultraviolet radiation during therapy (Handel 2014). Use with caution in patients with a history of depression; discontinue if serious depression recurs.

Breakthrough or intracyclic bleeding and spotting may occur, especially during the first 3 months of therapy. In addition, occasional missed periods may occur. Presentation of irregular, unresolving vaginal bleeding warrants further evaluation to rule out malignancy or pregnancy. Amenorrhea or oligomenorrhea may occur after discontinuing combination hormonal contraceptives, especially when such a condition was preexistent. Estrogens may increase thyroid-binding globulin (TBG) levels leading to increased circulating total thyroid hormone levels. Women on thyroid replacement therapy may require higher doses of thyroid hormone while receiving estrogens.

Whenever possible, discontinue at least 4 weeks prior to and for 2 weeks following major surgery or other surgeries known to have an increased risk of thromboembolism or during periods of prolonged immobilization. Use is not indicated prior to menarche or in postmenopausal women. Combination hormonal contraceptives do not protect against HIV infection or other sexually transmitted diseases (CDC 2010; CDC 2013). Use with caution in patients with diseases which may be exacerbated by fluid retention. Toxic shock syndrome has been reported (causal relationship has not been established); increased risk with tampon use.

Vaginally administered combination hormonal contraceptive agents may have similar adverse effects associated with oral contraceptive products. In order to reduce some of the possible risks, the minimum dosage combination of estrogen/progestin that will effectively treat the individual patient should be used. May not be appropriate for use in women with conditions that make the vagina susceptible to irritation or ulceration; vaginal/cervical erosion and ulceration has been reported. The patients and their sexual partners may feel the ring in the vagina during intercourse. Ensure proper vaginal placement of the ring to avoid inadvertent urinary bladder insertion.

Drug Interactions

Metabolism/Transport Effects Refer to individual components.

Avoid Concomitant Use

Avoid concomitant use of Ethinyl Estradiol and Etonogestrel with any of the following: Amodiaquine; Anastrozole; Antihepaciviral Combination Products; Dasabuvir; Dehydroepiandrosterone; Exemestane; Griseofulvin; Hemin; Indium 111 Capromab Pendetide; Ixazomib; Ospemifene; TiZANidine; Tranexamic Acid; Ulipristal

Increased Effect/Toxicity

Ethinyl Estradiol and Etonogestrel may increase the levels/effects of: Agomelatine; Ajmaline; Amodiaquine; Anthrax Immune Globulin (Human); Antihepaciviral Combination Products; C1 inhibitors; CloZAPine; Corticosteroids (Systemic); CYP1A2 Substrates; Dantrolene; Dasabuvir; Flibanserin; Immune Globulin; Lenalidomide; Lomitapide; Ospemifene; Pirfenidone; Pomalidomide; ROPINIRole; Selegiline; Thalidomide; Theophylline Derivatives; Tipranavir; TiZANidine; Tranexamic Acid; Voriconazole

The levels/effects of Ethinyl Estradiol and Etonogestrel may be increased by: Ascorbic Acid; Atazanavir; Boceprevir; Carfilzomib; Cobicistat; Dehydroepiandrosterone; Herbs (Estrogenic Properties); Herbs (Progestogenic Properties); Lopinavir; Metreleptin; MiFEPRIStone; NSAID (COX-2 Inhibitor); Pomalidomide; Tipranavir; Voriconazole

Decreased Effect

Ethinyl Estradiol and Etonogestrel may decrease the levels/effects of: Anastrozole; Anticoagulants; Antidiabetic Agents; Chenodiol; Exemestane; Fosamprenavir; Hemin; Hyaluronidase; Indium 111 Capromab Pendetide; LamoTRIgine; Ospemifene; Thyroid Products; Ulipristal; Ursodiol; Valproate Products; Vitamin K Antagonists

The levels/effects of Ethinyl Estradiol and Etonogestrel may be decreased by: Acitretin; Aprepitant; Armodafinil; Artemether; Asunaprevir; Barbiturates; Bexarotene (Systemic); Bile Acid Sequestrants; Boceprevir; Bosentan; CarBAMazepine; CloBAZam; Cobicistat; Colesevelam; CYP3A4 Inducers (Moderate); CYP3A4 Inducers (Strong); Dabrafenib; Darunavir; Deferasirox; Efavirenz; Elvitegravir; Enzalutamide; Eslicarbazepine; Exenatide; Felbamate; Fosamprenavir; Fosaprepitant; Fosphenytoin; Griseofulvin; Ixazomib; Lesinurad; Lixisenatide; Lopinavir; Lumacaftor; Metreleptin; MiFEPRIStone; Mitotane; Modafinil; Mycophenolate; Nafcillin; Nelfinavir; Nevirapine; OXcarbazepine; Perampanel; Phenytoin; Primidone; Protease Inhibitors; Prucalopride; Retinoic Acid Derivatives; Rifamycin Derivatives; Rufinamide; Saquinavir; Siltuximab; St John's Wort; Sugammadex; Telaprevir; Tipranavir; Tocilizumab; Topiramate; Ulipristal

Pharmacodynamics/Kinetics

Duration of Action Serum levels (contraceptive effectiveness) decrease after 3 weeks of continuous use

Half-life Elimination Ethinyl estradiol: 45 hours; Etonogestrel: 29 hours

Time to Peak Vaginal: Ethinyl estradiol: 59 hours; Etonogestrel: 200 hours

Pregnancy Considerations Use during pregnancy is contraindicated. Pregnancy status should be evaluated prior to prescribing (CDC, 2013); treatment should be discontinued if pregnancy occurs. In general, the use of combination hormonal contraceptives, when inadvertently used early in pregnancy, have not been associated with teratogenic effects. Hormonal contraceptives may be less effective in obese patients. An increase in oral contraceptive failure was noted in women with a BMI >27.3 kg/m^2. Similar findings were noted in patients weighing ≥90 kg (198 lb) using the contraceptive patch. In a study using the vaginal ring, ethinyl estradiol serum concentrations were decreased in obese women (BMI 30-39.9 kg/m^2; n=19) in comparison to women of normal weight (BMI 19-24.9 kg/m^2; n=18; p= 0.004); etonogestrel concentrations did not differ significantly. Bleeding and spotting were more frequent in the obese women. The study was not powered to evaluate contraceptive effectiveness (Westhoff, 2012).

Due to increased risk of venous thromboembolism (VTE) postpartum, combination hormonal contraceptives should not be started in any woman <21 days following delivery. Women without risk factors for VTE and who are not breastfeeding may start combination hormonal contraceptives during 21-42 days postpartum. After 42 days postpartum, restrictions for use are not related to postpartum status and should be based on other medical conditions (CDC, 2011). The manufacturer states that combination hormonal contraceptives should not be started until ≥4 weeks after delivery in women who choose not to breast-feed, or ≥4 weeks after a second trimester abortion or miscarriage.

Breastfeeding Considerations Contraceptive steroids can be detected in breast milk. May decrease the quality and quantity of breast milk; an alternative form of contraception is recommended until the infant is weaned (per manufacturer). The theoretical concerns about decreased milk production are greatest early in the postpartum period when milk production is being established. Postpartum risk status for VTE should be considered when initiating combination hormonal contraceptives after delivery. Combined hormonal contraceptives should not be started <21 days postpartum due to increased risk of VTE. Risk of VTE is still elevated in breastfeeding women until ~42 days postpartum and is greater in women with additional risk factors. After 42 days postpartum, restrictions for use are not related to postpartum VTE risk and should be based on other medical conditions (CDC, 2011).

Dosage Forms

Ring, vaginal:

NuvaRing: Ethinyl estradiol 0.015 mg/day and etonogestrel 0.12 mg/day (3s) [3-week duration]

Ethinyl Estradiol and Levonorgestrel

(ETH in il es tra DYE ole & LEE voe nor jes trel)

Related Information

Endocrine Disorders and Pregnancy *on page 1781*

Brand Names: US Altavera; Amethia; Amethia Lo; Amethyst; Ashlyna; Aubra; Aviane; camrese; camrese lo; Chateal; Daysee; Delyla; Enpresse; FaLessa Kit; Falmina; Fayosim; Introvale; Jolessa; Kurvelo; Larissia; Lessina; Levonest; Levora; LoSeasonique; Lutera; Marlissa; Myzilra; Orsythia; Portia; Quartette; Quasense; Rivelsa; Seasonique; Setlakin; Sronyx; Trivora; Vienva

Brand Names: Canada Alesse; Alysena; Aviane; Esme; Lutera; Min-Ovral; Ovima; Portia; Seasonale; Seasonique; Triquilar

Generic Availability (US) Yes

Pharmacologic Category Contraceptive; Estrogen and Progestin Combination

Use Prevention of pregnancy; postcoital contraception

Local Anesthetic/Vasoconstrictor Precautions No information available to require special precautions

Effects on Dental Treatment When prescribing antibiotics, patient must be warned to use additional methods of birth control if on oral contraceptives.

Effects on Bleeding No information available to require special precautions

Adverse Reactions Frequency not defined. Reactions listed are based on reports for other agents in this same pharmacologic class (oral contraceptives) and may not be specifically reported for ethinyl estradiol/levonorgestrel.

Increased risk or evidence of association with use:

Cardiovascular: Arterial thromboembolism, cerebral thrombosis, hypertension, local thrombophlebitis, mesenteric thrombosis, myocardial infarction, pulmonary embolism, retinal thrombosis, venous thrombosis (with or without embolism)

Central nervous system: Cerebral hemorrhage

Gastrointestinal: Gallbladder disease

Hepatic: Hepatic adenoma, hepatic neoplasm (benign)

Adverse reactions considered drug related:

Cardiovascular: Edema, worsening of varicose veins

Central nervous system: Depression, exacerbation of tics, migraine, mood changes

Dermatologic: Allergic skin rash, chloasma

Endocrine & metabolic: Amenorrhea, breast changes (breast hypertrophy, breast secretion, breast tenderness, mastalgia), carbohydrate intolerance, decreased lactation (with use immediately postpartum), decreased serum folate level, exacerbation of porphyria, fluid retention, menstrual disease (menstrual flow changes), weight changes

Gastrointestinal: Abdominal cramps, abdominal pain, bloating, change in appetite, nausea, vomiting

Genitourinary: Breakthrough bleeding, cervical ectropion, cervical erosion, change in cervical secretions, endocervical hyperplasia, infertility (temporary), spotting, vulvovaginal candidiasis, vaginitis

Hematologic & oncologic: Uterine fibroid enlargement

Hepatic: Cholestatic jaundice, hepatic focal nodular hyperplasia

Hypersensitivity: Anaphylaxis/Anaphylactoid reaction (including angioedema, circulatory shock, respiratory collapse, urticaria)

Neuromuscular & skeletal: Exacerbation of systemic lupus erythematosus

Ophthalmic: Change in corneal curvature (steepening), contact lens intolerance

Respiratory: Rhinitis

Adverse reactions in which association is not confirmed or denied:

Cardiovascular: Budd-Chiari syndrome

Central nervous system: Dizziness, headache, nervousness

Dermatologic: Acne vulgaris, erythema multiforme, erythema nodosum, loss of scalp hair

Endocrine & metabolic: Change in libido, hirsutism, premenstrual syndrome

Gastrointestinal: Colitis, pancreatitis

Genitourinary: Abnormal Pap smear, cystitis-like syndrome, dysmenorrhea

Hematologic & oncologic: Hemolytic-uremic syndrome, hemorrhagic eruption

Ophthalmic: Cataract, optic neuritis (with or without partial or complete loss of vision)

Otic: Auditory disturbance

Renal: Renal insufficiency

Dosing

Adult Females:

Contraception, 28-day cycle: Oral:

Schedule 1 (Sunday starter): Dose begins on first Sunday after onset of menstruation; if the menstrual period starts on Sunday, take first tablet that very same day. With a Sunday start, an additional method of contraception should be used until after the first 7 days of consecutive administration:

For 21-tablet package: 1 tablet/day for 21 consecutive days, followed by 7 days off of the medication; a new course begins on the 8th day after the last tablet is taken

For 28-tablet package: 1 tablet/day without interruption

Schedule 2 (Day-1 starter): Dose starts on first day of menstrual cycle taking 1 tablet/day:

For 21-tablet package: 1 tablet/day for 21 consecutive days, followed by 7 days off of the medication; a new course begins on the 8th day after the last tablet is taken

For 28-tablet package: 1 tablet/day without interruption

If all doses have been taken on schedule and one menstrual period is missed, continue dosing cycle. If two consecutive menstrual periods are missed, pregnancy test is required before new dosing cycle is started.

Missed doses **monophasic formulations** (refer to package insert for complete information):

One dose missed: Take as soon as remembered or take 2 tablets next day

Two consecutive doses missed in the first 2 weeks: Take 2 tablets as soon as remembered or 2 tablets next 2 days. An additional method of contraception should be used for 7 days after missed dose.

Two consecutive doses missed in week 3 or three consecutive doses missed at any time: An additional method of contraception must be used for 7 days after a missed dose:

Schedule 1 (Sunday starter): Continue dose of 1 tablet daily until Sunday, then discard the rest of the pack, and a new pack should be started that same day.

Schedule 2 (Day-1 starter): Current pack should be discarded, and a new pack should be started that same day.

Missed doses **biphasic/triphasic formulations** (refer to package insert for complete information).

One dose missed: Take as soon as remembered or take 2 tablets next day.

Two consecutive doses missed in week 1 or week 2 of the pack: Take 2 tablets as soon as remembered and 2 tablets the next day. Resume taking 1 tablet daily until the pack is empty. An additional method of contraception should be used for 7 days after a missed dose.

Two consecutive doses missed in week 3 of the pack: An additional method of contraception must be used for 7 days after a missed dose.

Schedule 1 (Sunday starter): Take 1 tablet every day until Sunday. Discard the remaining pack and start a new pack of pills on the same day.

Schedule 2 (Day-1 starter): Discard the remaining pack and start a new pack the same day.

Three or more consecutive doses missed: An additional method of contraception must be used for 7 days after a missed dose.

Schedule 1 (Sunday starter): Take 1 tablet every day until Sunday; on Sunday, discard the pack and start a new pack.

Schedule 2 (Day-1 starter): Discard the remaining pack and begin new pack of tablets starting on the same day.

Contraception, 91-day cycle (extended cycle regimen): Dose begins on first Sunday after onset of menstruation; if the menstrual period starts on Sunday, take first tablet that very same day. An additional method of contraception should be used until after the first 7 days of consecutive administration:

Introvale, Jolessa, Quasense, Seasonale [Canadian product]: One active tablet/day for 84 consecutive days, followed by 1 inactive tablet/day for 7 days; if all doses have been taken on schedule and one menstrual period is missed, pregnancy should be ruled out prior to continuing therapy.

Seasonique, LoSeasonique, Quartette: One active tablet/day for 84 consecutive days, followed by 1 low dose estrogen tablet/day for 7 days; if all doses have been taken on schedule and one menstrual period is missed, pregnancy should be ruled out prior to continuing therapy.

Missed doses:

One dose missed: Take as soon as remembered or take 2 tablets the next day

Two consecutive doses missed: Take 2 tablets as soon as remembered or 2 tablets the next 2 days. An additional nonhormonal method of contraception should be used for 7 consecutive days after the missed dose.

Three or more consecutive doses missed: Do not take the missed doses; continue taking 1 tablet/day until pack is complete. Bleeding may occur during the following week. An additional nonhormonal method of contraception should be used for 7 consecutive days after the missed dose.

Any number of pills during week 13: Throw away the missed pills and keep taking scheduled pills until the pack is finished. A back-up method of contraception is not needed

Pediatric Females: Contraception or emergency contraception: Oral: Refer to adult dosing; not to be used prior to menarche.

Renal Impairment Specific guidelines not available; use with caution and monitor blood pressure closely. Consider other forms of contraception.

Hepatic Impairment Contraindicated in patients with hepatic impairment.

Mechanism of Action Combination hormonal contraceptives inhibit ovulation via a negative feedback mechanism on the hypothalamus, which alters the normal pattern of gonadotropin secretion of a follicle-stimulating hormone (FSH) and luteinizing hormone by the anterior pituitary. The follicular phase FSH and midcycle surge of gonadotropins are inhibited. In addition, combination hormonal contraceptives produce alterations in the genital tract, including changes in the cervical mucus, rendering it unfavorable for sperm penetration even if ovulation occurs. Changes in the endometrium may also occur, producing an unfavorable environment for nidation. Combination hormonal contraceptive drugs may alter the tubal transport of the ova through the fallopian tubes. Progestational agents may also alter sperm fertility.

Contraindications Breast cancer or other estrogen- or progestin-dependent neoplasms (current or a history of), hepatic tumors or disease, pregnancy, undiagnosed abnormal uterine bleeding

Use is also contraindicated in women at high risk of arterial or venous thrombotic diseases including: Cerebrovascular disease, coronary artery disease, diabetes mellitus with vascular disease, DVT or PE (current or history of), hypercoagulopathies (inherited or acquired), headaches with focal neurological symptoms, hypertension (uncontrolled), migraine headaches if >35 years of age, thrombogenic valvular or rhythm diseases of the heart (eg, subacute bacterial endocarditis with valvular disease or atrial fibrillation), women >35 years of age who smoke.

Canadian-labeling: Additional contraindication: Ocular lesions due to ophthalmic vascular disease including partial or complete loss of vision or defect in visual fields; severe dyslipoproteinemia; hereditary or acquired predisposition for venous or arterial thrombosis

Warnings/Precautions

Combination hormonal contraceptives do not protect against HIV infection or other sexually-transmitted diseases. **[U.S. Boxed Warning]: The risk of cardiovascular side effects is increased in women who smoke cigarettes; risk increases with age (especially women >35 years of age) and the number of cigarettes smoked; women who use combination hormonal contraceptives should be strongly advised not to smoke. Use is contraindicated in patients >35 years of age who smoke.** Use with caution in patients with risk factors for coronary artery disease (eg, hypertension, hypercholesterolemia, morbid obesity, diabetes, or women who smoke); may lead to increased risk of myocardial infarction. May have a dose-related risk of vascular disease and hypertension; women with hypertension should be encouraged to use a nonhormonal form of contraception. Use is contraindicated with uncontrolled hypertension. May increase the risk of thromboembolism; discontinue use of combination hormonal contraceptives if an arterial or venous thrombotic event occurs. Women with inherited thrombophilias (eg, protein C or S deficiency) may have increased risk of venous thromboembolism (DeSancho, 2010; van Vlijmen, 2011). Use is contraindicated in women with hypercoagulopathies (inherited or acquired). Whenever possible, combination hormonal contraceptives should be discontinued at least 4 weeks prior to and for 2 weeks following elective surgery associated with an increased risk of thromboembolism or during periods of prolonged immobilization. Combination hormonal contraceptives may have a dose-related risk of gallbladder disease and may worsen existing gallbladder disease. Women with renal disease should be encouraged to use another form of contraception. May have adverse effects on glucose tolerance; use caution in women with diabetes.

Combination hormonal contraceptives may affect serum triglyceride and lipoprotein levels. Triglycerides may also be increased; use with caution in patients with familial defects of lipoprotein metabolism. The use of combination hormonal contraceptives has been associated with a slight increase in frequency of breast cancer; however, studies are not consistent. Use is contraindicated in women with (or history of) breast cancer. Use caution with conditions that may be aggravated by fluid retention, depression, or history of migraine. Evaluate new, recurrent, severe or persistent headaches. Use with migraine headaches with or without aura if >35 years of age is contraindicated. Not for use prior to menarche. Estrogens may cause retinal vascular thrombosis; discontinue if migraine, loss of vision, proptosis, diplopia or other visual disturbances occur; discontinue permanently if papilledema or retinal vascular lesions are observed on examination. Risk of chloasma may be increased with history of chloasma gravidarum. Women with history of chloasma should avoid exposure to sun or ultraviolet radiation during therapy. May induce or exacerbate symptoms of hereditary angioedema.

Presentation of irregular, unresolving vaginal bleeding warrants further evaluation including endometrial sampling, if indicated, to rule out malignancy; evaluate hypothalamic-pituitary-function in women with persistent (≥6 months) amenorrhea (especially associated with breast secretion) following discontinuation of therapy. Discontinue use with the onset of sudden enlargement, pain, or tenderness of fibroids (leiomyomata). Extremely rare adenomas and focal nodular hyperplasia resulting in fatal intra-abdominal hemorrhage have been reported in association with long-term oral contraceptive use. Presentation of an abdominal mass, acute abdominal pain, or intra-abdominal bleeding warrants further evaluation to rule out source. Combination hormonal contraceptives may be poorly metabolized in women with hepatic impairment. Discontinue if jaundice develops during therapy or if liver function becomes abnormal. Use is contraindicated with preexisting hepatic tumors or disease. Risk of cholestasis may be increased with previous cholestatic jaundice of pregnancy or jaundice with prior oral contraceptive use. Estrogens may increase thyroid-binding globulin (TBG) levels leading to increased circulating total thyroid hormone levels. Women on thyroid replacement therapy may require higher doses of thyroid hormone while receiving estrogens. The use of estrogens and/or progestins may change the results of some laboratory tests (eg, coagulation factors, lipids, glucose tolerance, binding proteins). The dose, route, and the specific estrogen/progestin influences these changes. In addition, personal risk factors (eg, cardiovascular disease, smoking, diabetes, age) also contribute to adverse events; use of specific products may be contraindicated in women with certain risk factors. Some products may contain tartrazine, which may cause allergic reactions in certain individuals.

The minimum dosage combination of estrogen/progestin that will effectively treat the individual patient should be used. New patients should be started on products containing ≤0.035 mg of estrogen per tablet. Extended cycle regimen contraceptives provide more hormonal exposure per year than conventional monthly contraceptives.

Drug Interactions

Metabolism/Transport Effects Refer to individual components.

Avoid Concomitant Use

Avoid concomitant use of Ethinyl Estradiol and Levonorgestrel with any of the following: Amodiaquine; Anastrozole; Antihepaciviral Combination Products; Dasabuvir; Dehydroepiandrosterone; Exemestane; Hemin; Indium 111 Capromab Pendetide; Ospemifene; TiZANidine; Tranexamic Acid

Increased Effect/Toxicity

Ethinyl Estradiol and Levonorgestrel may increase the levels/effects of: Agomelatine; Ajmaline; Amodiaquine; Anthrax Immune Globulin (Human); Antihepaciviral Combination Products; C1 inhibitors; CloZAPine; Corticosteroids (Systemic); CYP1A2 Substrates; Dantrolene; Dasabuvir; Flibanserin; Immune Globulin; Lenalidomide; Lomitapide; Ospemifene;

Pirfenidone; ROPINIRole; Selegiline; Thalidomide; Theophylline Derivatives; Tipranavir; TiZANidine; Tranexamic Acid; Voriconazole

The levels/effects of Ethinyl Estradiol and Levonorgestrel may be increased by: Ascorbic Acid; Carfilzomib; Dehydroepiandrosterone; Herbs (Estrogenic Properties); Metreleptin; MiFEPRIStone; NSAID (COX-2 Inhibitor); Pomalidomide; Voriconazole

Decreased Effect

Ethinyl Estradiol and Levonorgestrel may decrease the levels/effects of: Anastrozole; Anticoagulants; Antidiabetic Agents; Chenodiol; Exemestane; Hemin; Hyaluronidase; Indium 111 Capromab Pendetide; LamoTRIgine; Ospemifene; Thyroid Products; Ursodiol; Valproate Products; Vitamin K Antagonists

The levels/effects of Ethinyl Estradiol and Levonorgestrel may be decreased by: Aprepitant; Armodafinil; Artemether; Asunaprevir; Barbiturates; Bexarotene (Systemic); Bile Acid Sequestrants; Boceprevir; Bosentan; CarBAMazepine; CloBAZam; Cobicistat; Colesevelam; CYP3A4 Inducers (Moderate); CYP3A4 Inducers (Strong); Dabrafenib; Deferasirox; Elvitegravir; Enzalutamide; Eslicarbazepine; Exenatide; Felbamate; Fosaprepitant; Fosphenytoin; Griseofulvin; Ixazomib; Lesinurad; Lixisenatide; Lumacaftor; Metreleptin; MiFEPRIStone; Mitotane; Modafinil; Mycophenolate; Nafcillin; Nevirapine; OXcarbazepine; Phenytoin; Protease Inhibitors; Prucalopride; Retinoic Acid Derivatives; Rifamycin Derivatives; Rufinamide; Siltuximab; St John's Wort; Sugammadex; Telaprevir; Tipranavir; Tocilizumab; Topiramate

Dietary Considerations Should be taken at the same time each day.

Pharmacodynamics/Kinetics

Half-life Elimination Ethinyl estradiol: 12-23 hours; Levonorgestrel: 22-49 hours

Pregnancy Risk Factor X

Pregnancy Considerations Pregnancy should be ruled out prior to treatment and discontinued if pregnancy occurs. In general, the use of combination hormonal contraceptives when inadvertently taken early in pregnancy have not been associated with teratogenic effects. Hormonal contraceptives may be less effective in obese patients. An increase in oral contraceptive failure was noted in women with a BMI >27.3 kg/m^2. Similar findings were noted in patients weighing ≥90 kg (198 lb) using the contraceptive patch.

Due to increased risk of venous thromboembolism (VTE) postpartum, combination hormonal contraceptives should not be started in any woman <21 days following delivery. Women without risk factors for VTE and who are not breastfeeding may start combination hormonal contraceptives during 21-42 days postpartum. After 42 days postpartum, restrictions for use are not related to postpartum status and should be based on other medical conditions (CDC, 2011). Some manufacturers recommend waiting ≥4 weeks postpartum before starting this combination.

Breastfeeding Considerations Jaundice and breast enlargement in the nursing infant have been reported following the use of combination hormonal contraceptives. May decrease the quality and quantity of breast milk; alternative form of contraception is recommended (per manufacturer). The theoretical concerns about decreased milk production are greatest early in the postpartum period when milk production is being established. Postpartum risk status for VTE should be considered when initiating combination hormonal contraceptives after delivery. Combined hormonal contraceptives should not be started <21 days postpartum due to increased risk of VTE. Risk of VTE is still elevated in breastfeeding women until ~42 days postpartum and is greater in women with additional risk factors. After 42 days postpartum, restrictions for use are not related to postpartum VTE risk and should be based on other medical conditions (CDC, 2011). Some manufacturers recommend waiting ≥4 weeks postpartum before starting this combination.

Dosage Forms

Tablet, oral [low-dose formulation]:

Aubra: Ethinyl estradiol 0.02 mg and levonorgestrel 0.1 mg [21 light yellow tablets and 7 brown inactive tablets] (28s)

Aviane: Ethinyl estradiol 0.02 mg and levonorgestrel 0.1 mg [21 orange tablets and 7 light green inactive tablets] (28s)

Delyla: Ethinyl estradiol 0.02 mg and levonorgestrel 0.1 mg [21 white tablets and 7 yellow inactive tablets] (28s)

FaLessa Kit: Ethinyl estradiol 0.02 mg and levonorgestrel 0.1 mg [21 orange tablets and 7 white inactive tablets] (28s) [packaged with Quatrefolic folate tablets]

Falmina: Ethinyl estradiol 0.02 mg and levonorgestrel 0.1 mg [21 orange tablets and 7 white inactive tablets] (28s)

Larissia: Ethinyl estradiol 0.02 mg and levonorgestrel 0.1 mg [21 white tablets and 7 yellow inactive tablets] (28s)

Lessina: Ethinyl estradiol 0.02 mg and levonorgestrel 0.1 mg [21 pink tablets and 7 white inactive tablets] (28s)

Lutera: Ethinyl estradiol 0.02 mg and levonorgestrel 0.1 mg [21 white tablets and 7 peach inactive tablets] (28s)

Orsythia: Ethinyl estradiol 0.02 mg and levonorgestrel 0.1 mg [21 pink tablets and 7 light green inactive tablets] (28s)

Sronyx: Ethinyl estradiol 0.02 mg and levonorgestrel 0.1 mg [21 white tablets and 7 peach inactive tablets] (28s)

Vienva: Ethinyl estradiol 0.02 mg and levonorgestrel 0.1 mg [21 white tablets and 7 peach inactive tablets] (28s)

Generic: Ethinyl estradiol 0.02 mg and levonorgestrel 0.1 mg [21 tablets and 7 inactive tablets] (28s)

Tablet, oral [monophasic formulation]:

Altavera: Ethinyl estradiol 0.03 mg and levonorgestrel 0.15 mg [21 peach tablets and 7 white inactive tablets] (28s)

Chateal: Ethinyl estradiol 0.03 mg and levonorgestrel 0.15 mg [21 white tablets and 7 green inactive tablets] (28s)

Kurvelo: Ethinyl estradiol 0.03 mg and levonorgestrel 0.15 mg [21 light orange tablets and 7 pink inactive tablets] (28s)

Levora: Ethinyl estradiol 0.03 mg and levonorgestrel 0.15 mg [21 white tablets and 7 peach inactive tablets] (28s)

Marlissa: Ethinyl estradiol 0.03 mg and levonorgestrel 0.15 mg [21 light orange tablets and 7 pink inactive tablets] (28s)

Portia 28: Ethinyl estradiol 0.03 mg and levonorgestrel 0.15 mg [21 pink tablets and 7 white inactive tablets] (28s)

Generic: Ethinyl estradiol 0.03 mg and levonorgestrel 0.15 mg [21 tablets and 7 inactive tablets] (28s)

Tablet, oral [extended cycle regimen]:

Amethia: Ethinyl estradiol 0.03 mg and levonorgestrel 0.15 mg [84 white tablets] and ethinyl estradiol 0.01 mg [7 light blue tablets] (91s)

Amethia Lo: Ethinyl estradiol 0.02 mg and levonorgestrel 0.1 mg [84 orange tablets] and ethinyl estradiol 0.01 mg [7 yellow tablets] (91s)

Ashlyna: Ethinyl estradiol 0.03 mg and levonorgestrel 0.15 mg [84 blue tablets] and ethinyl estradiol 0.01 mg [7 yellow tablets] (91s)

camrese: Ethinyl estradiol 0.03 mg and levonorgestrel 0.15 mg [84 light blue-green tablets] and ethinyl estradiol 0.01 mg [7 yellow tablets] (91s)

camrese lo: Ethinyl estradiol 0.02 mg and levonorgestrel 0.1 mg [84 orange tablets] and ethinyl estradiol 0.01 mg [7 yellow tablets] (91s)

Daysee: Ethinyl estradiol 0.03 mg and levonorgestrel 0.15 mg [84 light blue tablets] and ethinyl estradiol 0.01 mg [7 mustard tablets] (91s)

Fayosim:

Day 1-42: Ethinyl estradiol 0.02 mg and levonorgestrel 0.15 mg [42 pink tablets]

Day 43-63: Ethinyl estradiol 0.025 mg and levonorgestrel 0.15 mg [21 white tablets]

Day 64-84: Ethinyl estradiol 0.03 mg and levonorgestrel 0.15 mg [21 light blue tablets]

Day 85-91: Ethinyl estradiol 0.01 mg [7 mustard tablets] (91s)

Introvale: Ethinyl estradiol 0.03 mg and levonorgestrel 0.15 mg [84 peach tablets and 7 white inactive tablets] (91s)

Jolessa: Ethinyl estradiol 0.03 mg and levonorgestrel 0.15 mg [84 pink tablets and 7 white inactive tablets] (91s)

LoSeasonique: Ethinyl estradiol 0.02 mg and levonorgestrel 0.1 mg [84 orange tablets] and ethinyl estradiol 0.01 mg [7 yellow tablets] (91s)

Quartette:

Day 1-42: Ethinyl estradiol 0.02 mg and levonorgestrel 0.15 mg [42 light pink tablets]

Day 43-63: Ethinyl estradiol 0.025 mg and levonorgestrel 0.15 mg [21 pink tablets]

Day 64-84: Ethinyl estradiol 0.03 mg and levonorgestrel 0.15 mg [21 purple tablets]

Day 85-91: Ethinyl estradiol 0.01 mg [7 yellow tablets] (91s)

Quasense: Ethinyl estradiol 0.03 mg and levonorgestrel 0.15 mg] [84 white tablets and 7 peach inactive tablets] (91s)

Rivelsa:

Day 1-42: Ethinyl estradiol 0.02 mg and levonorgestrel 0.15 mg [42 light pink tablets]

Day 43-63: Ethinyl estradiol 0.025 mg and levonorgestrel 0.15 mg [21 pink tablets]

Day 64-84: Ethinyl estradiol 0.03 mg and levonorgestrel 0.15 mg [21 purple tablets]

Day 85-91: Ethinyl estradiol 0.01 mg [7 yellow tablets] (91s)

Seasonique: Ethinyl estradiol 0.03 mg and levonorgestrel 0.15 mg [84 light blue-green tablets] and ethinyl estradiol 0.01 mg [7 yellow tablets] (91s)

Setlakin: Ethinyl estradiol 0.03 mg and levonorgestrel 0.15 mg [84 pink tablets and 7 white inactive tablets] (91s)

Generic: Ethinyl estradiol 0.02 mg and levonorgestrel 0.1 mg [84 tablets] and ethinyl estradiol 0.01 mg [7 tablets] (91s); Ethinyl estradiol 0.03 mg and levonorgestrel 0.15 mg [84 tablets] and ethinyl estradiol 0.01 mg [7 tablets] (91s); Ethinyl estradiol 0.03 mg and levonorgestrel 0.15 mg [84 tablets and 7 inactive tablets] (91s)

Tablet, oral [noncyclic regimen]:

Amethyst: Ethinyl estradiol 0.02 mg and levonorgestrel 0.09 mg [28 white tablets] (28s)

Tablet, oral [triphasic formulation]:

Enpresse:

Day 1-6: Ethinyl estradiol 0.03 mg and levonorgestrel 0.05 mg [6 pink tablets]

Day 7-11: Ethinyl estradiol 0.04 mg and levonorgestrel 0.075 mg [5 white tablets]

Day 12-21: Ethinyl estradiol 0.03 mg and levonorgestrel 0.125 mg [10 orange tablets]

Day 22-28: 7 light green inactive tablets (28s)

Levonest:

Day 1-6: Ethinyl estradiol 0.03 mg and levonorgestrel 0.05 mg [6 yellow tablets]

Day 7-11: Ethinyl estradiol 0.04 mg and levonorgestrel 0.075 mg [5 green tablets]

Day 12-21: Ethinyl estradiol 0.03 mg and levonorgestrel 0.125 mg [10 light brown tablets]

Day 22-28: 7 white inactive tablets (28s)

Myzilra:

Day 1-6: Ethinyl estradiol 0.03 mg and levonorgestrel 0.05 mg [6 beige tablets]

Day 7-11: Ethinyl estradiol 0.04 mg and levonorgestrel 0.075 mg [5 white tablets]

Day 12-21: Ethinyl estradiol 0.03 mg and levonorgestrel 0.125 mg [10 light yellow tablets]

Day 22-28: 7 light green inactive tablets (28s)

Trivora:

Day 1-6: Ethinyl estradiol 0.03 mg and levonorgestrel 0.05 mg [6 blue tablets]

Day 7-11: Ethinyl estradiol 0.04 mg and levonorgestrel 0.075 mg [5 white tablets]

Day 12-21: Ethinyl estradiol 0.03 mg and levonorgestrel 0.125 mg [10 pink tablets]

Day 22-28: 7 peach inactive tablets (28s)

Generic:

Day 1-6: Ethinyl estradiol 0.03 mg and levonorgestrel 0.05 mg [6 tablets]

Day 7-11: Ethinyl estradiol 0.04 mg and levonorgestrel 0.075 mg [5 tablets]

Day 12-21: Ethinyl estradiol 0.03 mg and levonorgestrel 0.125 mg [10 tablets]

Day 22-28: 7 inactive tablets (28s)

Ethinyl Estradiol and Norelgestromin

(ETH in il es tra DYE ole & nor el JES troe min)

Brand Names: US Ortho Evra [DSC]; Xulane

Brand Names: Canada Evra

Pharmacologic Category Contraceptive; Estrogen and Progestin Combination

Use

Contraception: For the prevention of pregnancy

Limitations of use: The topical patch may be less effective in patients weighing ≥90 kg (198 lb).

Local Anesthetic/Vasoconstrictor Precautions No information available to require special precautions

Effects on Dental Treatment When prescribing antibiotics, patient must be warned to use additional methods of birth control if on oral contraceptives.

Effects on Bleeding No information available to require special precautions

Adverse Reactions The following reactions have been reported with the contraceptive patch. Adverse reactions associated with oral combination hormonal contraceptive agents are also likely to appear with the topical contraceptive patch (frequency difficult to anticipate). See individual oral contraceptive monographs for additional information.

>10%:

Central nervous system: Headache (21%)

Endocrine & metabolic: Breast changes (22%; including breast engorgement, discomfort, mastalgia)

Gastrointestinal: Nausea (17%)

Local: Application site reaction (17%)

1% to 10%:

Cardiovascular: Increased blood pressure (<3%), pulmonary embolism (<3%)

Central nervous system: Anxiety (≤6%), mood disorder (≤6%), dizziness (3%), fatigue (3%), migraine (3%), insomnia (<3%), malaise (<3%)

Dermatologic: Acne vulgaris (3%), pruritus (3%), chloasma (<3%), contact dermatitis (<3%), erythema (<3%), skin irritation (<3%)

Endocrine & metabolic: Menstrual disease (6%), weight gain (3%), change in libido (<3%), dyslipidemia (<3%), fluid retention (<3%), galactorrhea (<3%), premenstrual syndrome (<3%)

Gastrointestinal: Abdominal pain (8%), vomiting (5%), diarrhea (4%), abdominal distention (<3%), cholecystitis (<3%)

Genitourinary: Dysmenorrhea (8%), vaginal hemorrhage (6%), vulvovaginal candidiasis (4%), genital discharge (<3%), uterine spasm (<3%), vaginal dryness (<3%), vulvar dryness (<3%)

Neuromuscular & skeletal: Muscle spasm (<3%)

<1%, postmarketing, and/or case reports: Alopecia, altered serum glucose, arterial thrombosis, benign mammary fibroadenoma, blood cholesterol abnormal, cerebrovascular accident, cervical dysplasia, cholelithiasis, cholestasis, cholestatic jaundice, colitis, contact lens intolerance (or complication), decreased lactation, deep vein thrombosis, dermatological reaction, dysgeusia, eczema, edema, emotional disturbance, erythema multiforme, erythema nodosum, frustration, hepatic adenoma, hepatic neoplasm, hyperglycemia, hypersensitivity reaction, hypertension, hypertensive crisis, increased appetite, increased LDL cholesterol, insulin resistance, intracranial hemorrhage, irritability, lesion (hepatic), malignant neoplasm of breast, malignant neoplasm of cervix, mass (breast), migraine with aura, myocardial infarction, outbursts of anger, seborrheic dermatitis, skin photosensitivity, skin rash, thrombosis, urticaria, uterine fibroids

Dosing

Adult Females: Contraception: Topical:

Apply one patch each week for 3 weeks (21 total days); followed by one week that is patch-free. Each patch should be applied on the same day each week ("patch change day") and only one patch should be worn at a time. No more than 7 days should pass during the patch-free interval.

Schedule 1 (Sunday starter): Dose begins on first Sunday after onset of menstruation; if the menstrual period starts on Sunday, apply one patch that very same day. **With a Sunday start, an additional method of contraception (nonhormonal) must be used until after the first 7 days of consecutive administration unless the menstrual period starts on Sunday.** Each patch change will then occur on Sunday.

Schedule 2 (Day 1 starter): Dose starts on first day of menstrual cycle, applying one patch during the first 24 hours of menstrual cycle. Each patch change will then occur on that same day of the week. The US labeling does not indicate that a back-up method of contraception is needed as long as the patch is applied on the first day of cycle.

Additional dosing considerations:

No bleeding during patch-free week/missed menstrual period: If patch has been applied as directed, continue treatment on usual "patch change day". If used correctly, no bleeding during patch-free week does not necessarily indicate pregnancy. However, if no withdrawal bleeding occurs for 2 consecutive cycles, pregnancy should be ruled out. If patch has not been applied as directed, and one menstrual period is missed, pregnancy should be ruled out prior to continuing treatment.

If a patch becomes partially or completely detached for <24 hours: Try to reapply to same place, or replace with a new patch immediately. Do not reapply if patch is no longer sticky, if it is sticking to itself or another surface, or if it has material sticking to it.

If a patch becomes partially or completely detached for >24 hours (or time period is unknown): Apply a new patch and use this day of the week as the new "patch change day" from this point on. **An additional method of contraception (nonhormonal) must be used until after the first 7 days of consecutive administration.**

Switching from oral contraceptives or vaginal ring: Complete current cycle and apply the first patch on the day the next pill cycle would be started or ring would be inserted. If there is no menstrual bleeding within 7 days of taking the last active tablet, the patient can initiate the first patch application; however, pregnancy must be ruled out. If patch is applied later than 7 days after the last active pill or removal of the vaginal ring, **an additional method of contraception (nonhormonal) should be used until after the first 7 days of consecutive administration**

Use after childbirth: Therapy should not be started <4 weeks after childbirth. Pregnancy should be ruled out prior to treatment if menstrual periods have not restarted. **An additional method of contraception (nonhormonal) should be used until after the first 7 days of consecutive administration.**

Use after abortion or miscarriage: Therapy may be started immediately if abortion/miscarriage occurs within the first trimester. If therapy is not started within 5 days, follow instructions for first time use. An additional method of contraception (nonhormonal) should be used until after the first 7 days of consecutive administration. If abortion/miscarriage occurs during the second trimester, therapy should not be started for at least 4 weeks. Follow directions for use after childbirth.

Pediatric Females: Contraception: Topical: Refer to adult dosing; not to be used prior to menarche.

Renal Impairment There are no dosage adjustments provided in manufacturers labeling (has not been studied); use with caution and monitor blood pressure closely.

Hepatic Impairment Contraindicated in patients with hepatic impairment.

Mechanism of Action Combination hormonal contraceptives inhibit ovulation via a negative feedback mechanism on the hypothalamus, which alters the normal pattern of gonadotropin secretion of a follicle-stimulating hormone (FSH) and luteinizing hormone by the anterior pituitary. The follicular phase FSH and midcycle surge of gonadotropins are inhibited. In addition, combination hormonal contraceptives produce alterations in the genital tract, including changes in the cervical mucus, rendering it unfavorable for sperm penetration even if ovulation occurs. Changes in the endometrium may also occur, producing an unfavorable environment for nidation. Combination hormonal contraceptive drugs may alter the tubal transport of the ova through the fallopian tubes. Progestational agents may also alter sperm fertility.

Contraindications

Breast cancer or other estrogen- or progestin-dependent neoplasms (current or a history of), hepatic tumors (benign or malignant) or hepatic disease, pregnancy, undiagnosed abnormal uterine bleeding.

Use is also contraindicated in women at high risk of arterial or venous thrombotic diseases for example, women with: Cerebrovascular disease, coronary artery disease, diabetes mellitus with vascular disease, DVT or PE (current or history of), hypercoagulopathies (inherited or acquired), hypertension (uncontrolled), headaches with focal neurological symptoms, migraine headaches with aura or migraine headaches if >35 years of age, thrombogenic valvular or rhythm diseases of the heart (eg, subacute bacterial endocarditis with valvular disease or atrial fibrillation), women >35 years of age who smoke.

Canadian-labeling: Additional contraindications (not in US labeling): Hypersensitivity to any component of the formulation; actual or history of thrombophlebitis or thromboembolic disorders; thrombophilia; myocardial infarction; carcinoma of the endometrium; steroid dependent jaundice, cholestatic jaundice, or history of jaundice of pregnancy; ocular lesions due to ophthalmic vascular disease including partial or complete loss of vision or defect in visual fields; persistent blood pressure ≥160 mm Hg systolic or ≥100 mm Hg diastolic; severe dyslipoproteinemia; hereditary or acquired predisposition for venous or arterial thrombosis; major surgery associated with an increased risk of post-operative thromboembolism; prolonged immobilization.

Documentation of allergenic cross-reactivity for estrogens and progestins is limited. However, because of similarities in chemical structure and/or pharmacologic actions, the possibility of cross-sensitivity cannot be ruled out with certainty.

Warnings/Precautions

Combination hormonal contraceptives may increase the risk of venous thromboembolism. **[US Boxed Warning]: The pharmacokinetic profile of the patch is different from oral contraceptives; steady state concentrations of ethinyl estradiol are ~60% higher following use of the patch than with oral tablets containing ethinyl estradiol 35 mcg. Peak concentrations are lower with the patch. The risk of venous thromboembolism (VTE) may be further increased with use of the contraceptive patch due to increased estrogen exposure in comparison to oral contraceptives. The increased estrogen exposure may increase the risk of adverse events, including venous thromboembolism.** Discontinue use of combination hormonal contraceptives if an arterial or venous thrombotic event occurs. Women with inherited thrombophilias (eg, protein C or S deficiency) may have increased risk of venous thromboembolism (DeSancho 2010; van Vlijmen 2011). Use is contraindicated in women with hypercoagulopathies (inherited or acquired). Use with caution in patients with risk factors for cardiovascular disease (eg, hypertension, hypercholesterolemia, morbid obesity, diabetes, or women who smoke); use of combination hormonal contraceptives may increase the risk of arterial or venous thrombotic events (CDC 2010). Use is contraindicated in women at high risk of arterial or venous thrombotic diseases. The risk of hypertension may be increased with age, dose, and duration of use. Combination hormonal contraceptives should not be used in women with persistent blood pressure values ≥160 mm Hg systolic or ≥100 mm Hg diastolic. Women with less severe hypertension (140 to 159 mm Hg systolic or 90 to 99 mm Hg diastolic) or those with hypertension that is adequately controlled should generally not use combination hormonal contraceptives (CDC 2013). Other risk factors for cardiovascular disease (eg, older age, smoking, diabetes) should be considered when prescribing contraceptives (CDC 2010). The manufacturer contraindicates use in women with uncontrolled hypertension and recommends monitoring women with well-controlled hypertension; discontinue therapy if blood pressure rises significantly.

[US Boxed Warning]: The risk of cardiovascular side effects is increased in women who smoke cigarettes; risk increases with age (especially women >35 years of age) and the number of cigarettes smoked; women who use combination hormonal contraceptives should be strongly advised not to smoke. Use is contraindicated in patients >35 years of age who smoke.

The use of combination hormonal contraceptives has not been shown to increase the risk for breast cancer. However, breast cancer is a hormonal sensitive tumor and the prognosis for women with a current or recent history of breast cancer may be worse with combination hormonal contraceptive use (CDC 2010). Use is contraindicated in women with (or history of) breast cancer. The use of combination hormonal contraceptives has been associated with a slight increased risk of cervical cancer; however, studies are not consistent and may be related to additional risk factors (Gierisch 2013). Women awaiting treatment for cervical cancer may use combination hormonal contraceptives (CDC 2013). The risk of ovarian cancer is decreased in women using combination hormonal contraceptives (CDC 2013; Walker 2015). Oral contraceptives may be used to reduce the risk of ovarian cancer including those women with BRACA1 and BRACA2 mutations (Walker 2015).

May impair glucose tolerance; use caution in women with diabetes or prediabetes. Risk of cholestasis may be increased with previous cholestasis of pregnancy or cholestasis with prior oral contraceptive use. Use of combination hormonal contraceptives is associated with hepatic adenomas (rare); rupture may cause fatal intra-abdominal hemorrhage. Long term use may be associated with an increased risk of hepatocellular carcinoma (rare). Use is contraindicated with preexisting hepatic tumors. Combination hormonal contraceptives may be poorly metabolized in women with hepatic impairment. Discontinue if jaundice develops during therapy or if liver function becomes abnormal. Combination hormonal contraceptives may adversely affect lipid levels, including serum triglycerides. The type of lipid disorder, the severity, and the presence of other cardiovascular risk factors should be considered when prescribing combination hormonal contraceptives to women with lipid disorders (CDC 2010). Women with hypertriglyceridemia or a family history of hypertriglyceridemia may be at increased risk of pancreatitis when using combination hormonal contraceptives. Consider alternative contraception for women with uncontrolled dyslipidemia. Discontinue if unexplained loss of vision, proptosis, diplopia, papilledema, or retinal vascular lesions occur and immediately evaluate for retinal vein thrombosis. Breakthrough or intracyclic bleeding and spotting may occur, especially during the first 3 months of therapy. In addition, occasional missed periods may occur. Presentation of irregular, unresolving vaginal bleeding warrants further evaluation to rule out malignancy or pregnancy. Amenorrhea or oligomenorrhea may occur after discontinuing combination hormonal contraceptives, especially when such a condition was preexistent.

Combination hormonal contraceptives do not protect against HIV infection or other sexually-transmitted diseases (CDC 2010; CDC 2013). Combination hormonal contraceptives, as well as sun exposure and pregnancy, are triggers for chloasma. Women with a susceptibility to chloasma or additional risk factors should avoid exposure to sun or ultraviolet radiation during therapy (Handel 2014). Use with caution in patients with a history of depression; discontinue if serious depression recurs. May have a risk of gallbladder disease; may worsen existing gallbladder disease. Estrogens may induce or exacerbate symptoms in women with hereditary angioedema (Geng 2013; Zuraw 2013). Evaluate new, recurrent, severe or persistent headaches. Use in patients with migraine headaches with aura, or migraine headaches of any type if >35 years of age is contraindicated. Potentially significant interactions may exist, requiring dose or frequency adjustment, additional monitoring, and/or selection of alternative therapy. Estrogens may increase thyroid-binding globulin (TBG) levels leading to increased circulating total thyroid hormone levels. Women on thyroid replacement therapy may require higher doses of thyroid hormone while receiving estrogens. The use of estrogens and/or progestins may change the results of some laboratory tests (eg, coagulation factors, lipids, glucose tolerance, binding proteins). The dose, route, and the specific estrogen/progestin influences these changes. In addition, personal risk factors (eg, cardiovascular disease, smoking, diabetes, age) also contribute to adverse events; use of specific products may be contraindicated in women with certain risk factors.

Not for use prior to menarche. Whenever possible, should be discontinued at least 4 weeks prior to and for 2 weeks following elective surgery associated with an increased risk of thromboembolism or during periods of prolonged immobilization. When initiating a combination oral contraceptive, consideration should be given to safety, effectiveness, availability and acceptance to the patient (CDC 2013). Consider initiating with a monthly bleeding monophasic formulation containing ethinyl estradiol 30 to 35 mcg plus a progestin, and adjusting based on adverse events and patient preference (Ott 2014).

Drug Interactions

Metabolism/Transport Effects Refer to individual components.

Avoid Concomitant Use

Avoid concomitant use of Ethinyl Estradiol and Norelgestromin with any of the following: Amodiaquine; Anastrozole; Antihepaciviral Combination Products; Dasabuvir; Dehydroepiandrosterone; Exemestane; Griseofulvin; Hemin; Indium 111 Capromab Pendetide; Ixazomib; Ospemifene; TiZANidine; Tranexamic Acid; Ulipristal

Increased Effect/Toxicity

Ethinyl Estradiol and Norelgestromin may increase the levels/effects of: Agomelatine; Ajmaline; Amodiaquine; Anthrax Immune Globulin (Human); Antihepaciviral Combination Products; C1 inhibitors; CloZAPine; Corticosteroids (Systemic); CYP1A2 Substrates; Dantrolene; Dasabuvir; Flibanserin; Immune Globulin; Lenalidomide; Lomitapide; Ospemifene; Pirfenidone; Pomalidomide; ROPINIRole; Selegiline; Thalidomide; Theophylline Derivatives; Tipranavir; TiZANidine; Tranexamic Acid; Voriconazole

The levels/effects of Ethinyl Estradiol and Norelgestromin may be increased by: Ascorbic Acid; Atazanavir; Boceprevir; Carfilzomib; Cobicistat; Dehydroepiandrosterone; Herbs (Estrogenic Properties); Herbs (Progestogenic Properties); Lopinavir; Metreleptin; MiFEPRIStone; NSAID (COX-2 Inhibitor); Pomalidomide; Tipranavir; Voriconazole

Decreased Effect

Ethinyl Estradiol and Norelgestromin may decrease the levels/effects of: Anastrozole; Anticoagulants; Antidiabetic Agents; Chenodiol; Exemestane; Fosamprenavir; Hemin; Hyaluronidase; Indium 111 Capromab Pendetide; LamoTRIgine; Ospemifene; Thyroid Products; Ulipristal; Ursodiol; Valproate Products; Vitamin K Antagonists

The levels/effects of Ethinyl Estradiol and Norelgestromin may be decreased by: Acitretin; Aprepitant; Armodafinil; Artemether; Asunaprevir; Barbiturates; Bexarotene (Systemic); Bile Acid Sequestrants; Boceprevir; Bosentan; CarBAMazepine; CloBAZam; Cobicistat; Colesevelam; CYP3A4 Inducers (Moderate); CYP3A4 Inducers (Strong); Dabrafenib; Darunavir; Deferasirox; Efavirenz; Elvitegravir; Enzalutamide; Eslicarbazepine; Exenatide; Felbamate; Fosamprenavir; Fosaprepitant; Fosphenytoin; Griseofulvin; Ixazomib; Lesinurad; Lixisenatide; Lopinavir; Lumacaftor; Metreleptin; MiFEPRIStone; Mitotane; Modafinil; Mycophenolate; Nafcillin; Nelfinavir; Nevirapine; OXcarbazepine; Perampanel; Phenytoin; Primidone; Protease Inhibitors; Prucalopride; Retinoic Acid Derivatives; Rifamycin Derivatives; Rufinamide; Saquinavir; Siltuximab; St John's Wort; Sugammadex; Telaprevir; Tipranavir; Tocilizumab; Topiramate; Ulipristal

Pharmacodynamics/Kinetics

Half-life Elimination Topical: Ethinyl estradiol: ~17 hours; Norelgestromin: ~28 hours

Pregnancy Considerations Pregnancy status should be evaluated prior to prescribing (CDC 2013); treatment should be discontinued if pregnancy occurs. In general, the use of combination hormonal contraceptives when inadvertently taken early in pregnancy have not been associated with teratogenic effects. The topical patch may be less effective in patients weighing ≥90 kg (198 lb).

Due to increased risk of venous thromboembolism (VTE) postpartum, combination hormonal contraceptives should not be started in any woman <21 days following delivery. Women without risk factors for VTE and who are not breastfeeding may start combination hormonal contraceptives during 21-42 days postpartum. After 42 days postpartum, restrictions for use are not related to postpartum status and should be based on other medical conditions (CDC 2011). The manufacturer states that combination hormonal contraceptives should not be started until ≥4 weeks after delivery in women who choose not to breastfeed, or ≥4 weeks after a second trimester abortion or miscarriage.

Breastfeeding Considerations Contraceptive steroids can be detected in breast milk. May decrease the quality and quantity of breast milk; a nonhormonal form of contraception is recommended (per manufacturer). The theoretical concerns about decreased milk production are greatest early in the postpartum period when milk production is being established. Postpartum risk status for VTE should be considered when initiating combination hormonal contraceptives after delivery. Combined hormonal contraceptives should not be started <21 days postpartum due to increased risk of VTE. Risk of VTE is still elevated in breastfeeding women until ~42 days postpartum and is greater in women with additional risk factors. After 42 days postpartum, restrictions for use are not related to postpartum VTE risk and should be based on other medical conditions (CDC 2011).

Dosage Forms

Patch, transdermal:

Xulane: Ethinyl estradiol 0.53 mg and norelgestromin 4.86 mg [releases ethinyl estradiol 35 mcg and norelgestromin 150 mcg per day] (3s)

Dosage Forms: Canada

Patch, transdermal:

Evra: Ethinyl estradiol 0.6 mg and norelgestromin 6 mg (1s, 3s)

Ethinyl Estradiol and Norethindrone

(ETH in il es tra DYE ole & nor eth IN drone)

Related Information

Endocrine Disorders and Pregnancy *on page 1781*
Norethindrone *on page 1209*
Rheumatoid Arthritis, Osteoarthritis, and Osteoporosis *on page 1792*

Brand Names: US Alyacen 1/35; Alyacen 7/7/7; Aranelle; Balziva; Blisovi 24 Fe; Blisovi Fe 1/20; Brevicon; Briellyn; Cyclafem 1/35; Cyclafem 7/7/7; Dasetta 1/35; Dasetta 7/7/7; Estrostep Fe; Femcon Fe; femhrt; Fyavolv; Generess Fe; Gildagia; Gildess 1.5/30 [DSC]; Gildess 1/20 [DSC]; Gildess 24 Fe [DSC]; Gildess FE 1.5/30; Gildess FE 1/20; Jevantique Lo; Jinteli; Junel 1.5/30; Junel 1/20; Junel Fe 1.5/30; Junel Fe 1/20; Junel Fe 24; Kaitlib Fe; Larin 1.5/30; Larin 1/20; Larin 24 Fe; Larin Fe 1.5/30; Larin Fe 1/20; Layolis Fe; Leena; Lo Loestrin Fe; Lo Minastrin Fe [DSC]; Loestrin 21 1.5/30; Loestrin 21 1/20; Loestrin 24 Fe; Loestrin Fe 1.5/30; Loestrin Fe 1/20; Lomedia 24 Fe; Mibelas 24 Fe; Microgestin 1.5/30; Microgestin 1/20; Microgestin 24 Fe; Microgestin Fe 1.5/30; Microgestin Fe 1/20; Minastrin 24 Fe; Modicon [DSC]; Necon 0.5/35; Necon 1/35; Necon 10/11; Necon 7/7/7; Norinyl 1+35; Nortrel 0.5/35; Nortrel 1/35; Nortrel 7/7/7; Ortho-Novum 1/35; Ortho-Novum 7/7/7; Ovcon 35; Philith; Pirmella 1/35; Pirmella 7/7/7; Tarina FE 1/20; Taytulla; Tilia Fe; Tri-Legest Fe; Tri-Norinyl; Vyfemla; Wera; Wymzya Fe; Zenchent; Zenchent Fe

Brand Names: Canada Brevicon 0.5/35; Brevicon 1/35; FemHRT; Loestrin 1.5/30; Minestrin 1/20; Ortho 0.5/35; Ortho 1/35; Ortho 7/7/7; Select 1/35; Synphasic

Generic Availability (US) Yes

Pharmacologic Category Contraceptive; Estrogen and Progestin Combination

Use

Acne vulgaris (Estrostep Fe, Tilia Fe, Tri-Legest Fe): Treatment of moderate acne vulgaris in females at least 15 years of age.

Limitations of Use: When used for acne, use only in females ≥15 years of age who have achieved menarche, who also desire combination hormonal contraceptive therapy, are unresponsive to topical treatments, have no contraindications to combination hormonal contraceptive use, and plan to stay on therapy for ≥6 months.

Contraception: Prevention of pregnancy.

Vasomotor symptoms associated with menopause (femhrt, Jevantique Lo, Jinteli): Treatment of moderate to severe vasomotor symptoms associated with menopause.

Osteoporosis prevention (female) (femhrt, Jevantique Lo, Jinteli): Prevention of postmenopausal osteoporosis.

Limitations of use: For use only in women at significant risk of postmenopausal osteoporosis; consider use of nonestrogen medications.

Local Anesthetic/Vasoconstrictor Precautions No information available to require special precautions

Effects on Dental Treatment When prescribing antibiotics, patient must be warned to use additional methods of birth control if on oral contraceptives.

Effects on Bleeding No information available to require special precautions

Adverse Reactions **The following have been associated with femhrt.** Also refer to adverse reactions observed with oral contraceptives for additional reactions observed with estrogen/progestin therapy.

>10%: Central nervous system: Headache (15% to 18%)

1% to 10%:

Central nervous system: Depression (4% to 6%), nervousness (2% to 5%)

Gastrointestinal: Abdominal pain (8% to 10%), nausea and vomiting (5% to 7%), diarrhea (4% to 6%), dyspepsia (3% to 5%)

Genitourinary: Mastalgia (8% to 9%), urinary tract infection (4% to 6%), vaginitis (5%)

Infection: Viral infection (9%)

Respiratory: Sinusitis (8% to 9%)

The following have been associated with Lo Loestrin Fe. Also refer to adverse reactions observed with oral contraceptives for additional reactions observed with estrogen/progestin therapy.

1% to 10%:

Central nervous system: Headache (7%), anxiety (2%), depression (2%), migraine (1%), mood disorder (1%, including mood swings)

Dermatologic: Acne vulgaris (3%)

Endocrine & metabolic: Menstrual disease (4% to 5%, including abnormal uterine bleeding, irregular menses, menorrhagia, uterine hemorrhage, vaginal hemorrhage), weight changes (1% to 4%)

Gastrointestinal: Nausea and vomiting (7%), abdominal pain (3%)

Genitourinary: Breast tenderness (4%), dysmenorrhea (4%)

Dosing

Adult & Geriatric

Acne: Adolescents ≥15 years and Adults: Females: Oral (Estrostep Fe, Tilia Fe, Tri-Legest Fe): Refer to dosing for contraception

Contraception: Females: One tablet once daily

Schedule 1 (Sunday starter): Dose begins on first Sunday after onset of menstruation; if the menstrual period starts on Sunday, take first tablet that very same day. (This schedule is not preferred for all products [eg, Generess Fe, Lo Loestrin Fe, Lo Minastrin Fe]). With a Sunday start, an additional method of contraception should be used until after the first 7 days of consecutive administration (all products).

Schedule 2 (Day 1 starter): Dose starts on first day of menstrual cycle taking 1 tablet daily.

Additional contraceptive dosing considerations:

Switching from a different contraceptive:

Oral contraceptive: Start on the same day that a new pack of the previous oral contraceptive would have been taken.

Transdermal patch, vaginal ring, injection: Start on the day the next dose would have been due.

IUD or implant: Start on the day of removal. A backup method of contraception should be used for the first 7 days if IUD is not removed on the first day of the menstrual cycle.

Use after first trimester abortion or miscarriage: Therapy may be started immediately. If not started within 5 days, a back-up method of contraception should be used for the first 7 days.

Use after childbirth (in women who are not breastfeeding) or after second trimester abortion or miscarriage: Therapy may be started ≥4 weeks postpartum. Pregnancy should be ruled out prior to treatment if menstrual periods have not restarted. An additional method of contraception (nonhormonal) should be used until after the first 7 days of consecutive administration.

Also refer to prescribing information for product specific information or CDC 2013 for general guidance.

Missed or late doses (CDC 2013):

If one dose is late (<24 hours since dose should have been taken) or if one dose is missed (24 to <48 hours since dose should have been taken): Take dose as soon as possible. Continue remaining doses at the usual time (even if that means 2 doses on the same day).

If ≥2 consecutive doses are missed (≥48 hours since dose should have been taken): Take the most recently missed dose as soon as possible, discard any other missed doses. Continue remaining doses at the usual time (even if that means taking 2 doses on the same day); use back-up contraception until hormonal pills have been taken for 7 consecutive days. If doses were missed during the last week of hormonal (active) tablets (eg, days 15 to 21 of a 28 day pack), omit the hormone free interval by finishing the current pack and starting a new pack. If unable to start a new pack immediately, back up contraception is needed until hormonal pills from a new pack have been taken for 7 consecutive days. Consider use of emergency contraception in some situations (refer to guidelines for details).

Also refer to prescribing information for product specific information.

Postmenopausal indications: *General dosing guidelines:* When treating postmenopausal women, use estrogens for the shortest duration possible at the lowest effective dose consistent with treatment goals. Reevaluate patients as clinically appropriate to determine if treatment is still necessary. Consider use of an estrogen with a progestin in postmenopausal women with a uterus. Women who have had a hysterectomy generally do not need a progestin; however one may be needed if there is a history of endometriosis. Dosage needs to be adjusted based upon the patient's response.

Osteoporosis prevention: Females: Oral (femhrt, Jevantique Lo, Jinteli): One tablet daily

Vasomotor symptoms associated with menopause: Females: Oral (femhrt, Jevantique Lo, Jinteli): Initial: One tablet daily; patient should be reevaluated at 3- to 6-month intervals to determine if treatment is still necessary.

Pediatric

Acne: Adolescent females ≥15 years: Oral (Estrostep Fe, Tilia Fe, Tri-Legest Fe): Refer to adult dosing for contraception; not to be used prior to menarche

Contraception: Females: Oral: Refer to adult dosing; not to be used prior to menarche.

Renal Impairment There are no dosage adjustments provided in the manufacturer's labeling (has not been studied). Use with caution and monitor blood pressure closely.

Hepatic Impairment Use is contraindicated in patients with hepatic impairment.

Mechanism of Action Combination oral contraceptives inhibit ovulation via a negative feedback mechanism on the hypothalamus, which alters the normal pattern of gonadotropin secretion of a follicle-stimulating hormone (FSH) and luteinizing hormone by the anterior pituitary. The follicular phase FSH and midcycle surge of gonadotropins are inhibited. In addition, combination hormonal contraceptives produce alterations in the genital tract, including changes in the cervical mucus, rendering it unfavorable for sperm penetration even if ovulation occurs. Changes in the endometrium may also occur, producing an unfavorable environment for nidation. Combination hormonal contraceptive drugs may alter the tubal transport of the ova through the fallopian tubes. Progestational agents may also alter sperm fertility.

In postmenopausal women, exogenous estrogen is used to replace decreased endogenous production. The addition of progestin reduces the incidence of endometrial hyperplasia and risk of endometrial cancer in women with an intact uterus.

Contraindications

Combination hormonal contraceptives: Hypersensitivity to ethinyl estradiol, norethindrone, or any component of the formulation; breast cancer, endometrial cancer or other estrogen- or progestin-sensitive cancer (current or a history of); hepatic tumors (benign or malignant) or hepatic disease; pregnancy; undiagnosed abnormal uterine bleeding; cholestatic jaundice of pregnancy or jaundice with prior contraceptive pill use

Use is also contraindicated in women at high risk of arterial or venous thrombotic diseases for example, women with: Cerebrovascular disease; coronary artery disease; diabetes mellitus with vascular disease; DVT or PE (current or history of); hypertension (uncontrolled); headaches with focal neurological symptoms; migraine headaches with aura or migraine headaches if >35 years; major surgery with prolonged immobilization; valvular heart disease with complications; thrombophlebitis or thromboembolic disorders; thrombophilic conditions; women >35 years who smoke; hypercoagulopathies (inherited or acquired); thrombogenic valvular or thrombogenic rhythm diseases of the heart (eg, subacute bacterial endocarditis with valvular disease, atrial fibrillation)

Canadian labeling: Additional contraindications (not in US labeling): Angina pectoris or myocardial infarction (current or history of), ocular lesion arising from ophthalmic vascular disease (such as partial or complete loss of vision or visual field defect), migraine with focal aura (current or history of), pancreatitis associated with severe hypertriglyceridemia (current or history of), severe dyslipoproteinemia, over 35 years of age and smoke; women with hereditary or acquired predisposition for arterial or venous thrombosis, for example: factor V Leiden mutation, activated protein C (APC-) resistance, antithrombin-III-deficiency, protein C deficiency, protein S deficiency, hyperhomocysteinemia (eg, due to MTHFR C677T, A1298 mutations), prothrombin mutation G20210A, and antiphospholipid-antibodies (anticardiolipin antibodies, lupus anticoagulant).

Products used for postmenopausal indications: Angioedema, anaphylactic reaction, or hypersensitivity to any component of the formulation; undiagnosed abnormal genital bleeding; DVT or PE (current or history of); active or history of arterial thromboembolic disease (eg, stroke, MI); breast cancer (known, suspected or history of); estrogen-dependent tumor (known or suspected); hepatic impairment or disease; known protein C, protein S, antithrombin deficiency or other known thrombophilic disorders; pregnancy.

Canadian labeling: Additional contraindications (not in US labeling): endometrial hyperplasia, classical migraine, lactation

Documentation of allergenic cross-reactivity for estrogens and progestins is limited. However, because of similarities in chemical structure and/or pharmacologic actions, the possibility of cross-sensitivity cannot be ruled out with certainty.

Warnings/Precautions

[US Boxed Warning]: Based on data from the Women's Health Initiative (WHI) studies, an increased risk of invasive breast cancer was observed in postmenopausal women using conjugated estrogens (CE) in combination with medroxyprogesterone acetate (MPA). This risk may be associated with duration of use and declines once combined therapy is discontinued (Chlebowski 2009). The risk of invasive breast cancer was decreased in postmenopausal women with a hysterectomy using CE only, regardless of weight. However, the risk was not significantly decreased in women at high risk for breast cancer (family history of breast cancer, personal history of benign breast disease) (Anderson 2012). An increase in abnormal mammogram findings has also been reported with estrogen alone or in combination with progestin therapy. Estrogen use may lead to severe hypercalcemia in patients with breast cancer and bone metastases; discontinue estrogen if hypercalcemia occurs. The use of combination hormonal contraceptives has not been shown to increase the risk for breast cancer. However, breast cancer is a hormonal sensitive tumor and the prognosis for women with a current or recent history of breast cancer may be worse with combination hormonal contraceptive use (CDC 2010). Use is contraindicated in patients with (or history of) breast cancer. The use of combination hormonal contraceptives has been associated with a slight increased risk of cervical cancer; however, studies are not consistent and may be related to additional risk factors (Gierisch 2013). Women awaiting treatment for cervical cancer may use combination hormonal contraceptives (CDC 2013). **[US Boxed Warning]: The use of unopposed estrogen in women with an intact uterus is associated with an increased risk of endometrial cancer. The addition of a progestin to estrogen therapy may decrease the risk of endometrial hyperplasia, a precursor to endometrial cancer. Adequate diagnostic measures, including endometrial sampling if indicated, should be performed to rule out malignancy in postmenopausal women with undiagnosed abnormal vaginal bleeding.** There is no evidence that the use of natural estrogens results in a different endometrial risk profile than synthetic estrogens at equivalent estrogen doses. The risk of endometrial cancer appears to be dose and duration dependent; risk appears to be greatest with use ≥5 years and may persist following discontinuation of therapy. Estrogens may exacerbate endometriosis. Malignant transformation of residual endometrial implants has been reported posthysterectomy with unopposed estrogen therapy. Consider adding a progestin in women with residual endometriosis posthysterectomy. Postmenopausal estrogens with or without progestins may increase the risk of ovarian cancer; however, the absolute risk to an individual woman is small. Although results from various studies are not consistent, risk does not appear to be significantly associated with the duration, route, or dose of therapy. In one study, the risk decreased after 2 years following discontinuation of therapy (Mørch 2009). Although the risk of ovarian cancer is rare, women who are at an increased risk (eg, family history) should be counseled about the association (NAMS 2012). The risk of ovarian cancer is decreased in women using combination hormonal contraceptives (CDC 2013; Walker 2015). Oral contraceptives may be used to reduce the risk of ovarian cancer including those women with BRCA1 and BRCA2 mutations (Walker 2015).

[US Boxed Warning]: Estrogens with or without progestin should not be used to prevent dementia. In the Women's Health Initiative Memory Study (WHIMS), an increased incidence of probable dementia was observed in women ≥65 years of age taking CE alone or in combination with MPA.

[US Boxed Warning]: Estrogens with or without progestin should not be used to prevent cardiovascular disease. Using data from the Women's Health Initiative (WHI) studies, an increased risk of deep vein thrombosis (DVT) and stroke has been reported with CE and an increased risk of DVT, stroke, pulmonary emboli (PE) and myocardial infarction (MI) has been reported with CE with MPA in postmenopausal women 50 to 79 years of age. Additional risk factors include diabetes mellitus, hypercholesterolemia, hypertension, SLE, obesity, tobacco use, and/or history of venous thromboembolism (VTE). Risk factors should be managed appropriately; discontinue use immediately if adverse cardiovascular events occur or are suspected. Use is contraindicated in women with active DVT or PE (or a history of these conditions) or in women with active or recent arterial thromboembolic disease (stroke and MI), or a history of these conditions. Use combination hormonal contraceptives with caution in patients with risk factors for cardiovascular disease (eg, hypertension, hypercholesterolemia, morbid obesity, diabetes, or women who smoke); use of combination hormonal contraceptives may increase the risk of arterial or venous thrombotic events (CDC 2010). Use of combination hormonal contraceptives may be contraindicated in women at high risk of arterial or venous thrombotic diseases. **[US Boxed Warning]: The risk of cardiovascular side effects is increased in women who smoke cigarettes; risk increases with age (especially women >35 years of age) and the number of cigarettes smoked. Use of combination hormonal**

contraceptives is contraindicated in patients >35 years of age who smoke.

[US Boxed Warning]: Estrogens with or without progestin should be used for the shortest duration possible at the lowest effective dose consistent with treatment goals and risks for the individual woman. Hormone replacement therapy for menopausal symptoms is generally initiated in healthy symptomatic women within 10 years of menopause or <60 years of age who do not have contraindications for use (Stuenkel 2015). Patients should be reevaluated as clinically appropriate to determine if treatment is still necessary. Available data related to treatment risks are from Women's Health Initiative (WHI) studies, which evaluated oral CE 0.625 mg with or without MPA 2.5 mg relative to placebo in postmenopausal women. Other combinations and dosage forms of estrogens and progestins were not studied. **Outcomes reported from clinical trials using CE with or without MPA should be assumed to be similar for other doses and other dosage forms of estrogens and progestins until comparable data becomes available.** Women who are early in menopause, who are in good cardiovascular health, and who are at low risk for adverse cardiovascular events can be considered candidates for estrogen with or without progestin therapy for the relief of menopausal symptoms (ACOG 565 2013). Women at high risk of cardiovascular disease or intermediate to high risk of breast cancer should use nonhormonal therapy to treat vasomotor symptoms of menopause (Stuenkel 2015). Use of a transdermal product should be considered over an oral agent in women requiring systemic therapy who have moderate risk factors for coronary heart disease (ACOG 556 2013; Schenck-Gustafsson 2011; Stuenkel 2015). Nonoral routes of therapy are recommended for women at increased risk for venous thromboembolism (Stuenkel 2015; Tremollieres 2011). Although hormone therapy is recommended to be initiated in healthy symptomatic women within 10 years of menopause or <60 years of age who do not have contraindications for use, symptoms may continue in women >60 years of age. The continuation of hormone therapy in women >65 years of age should consider the risks and benefits for the individual woman and should not be discontinued only because of the woman's age (NAMS 2015). When initiating a combination oral contraceptive, consideration should be given to safety, effectiveness, availability and acceptance to the patient (CDC 2013). Consider initiating with a monthly bleeding monophasic formulation containing ethinyl estradiol 30 to 35 mcg plus a progestin, and adjusting based on adverse events and patient preference (Ott 2014). Combination hormonal contraceptives do not protect against HIV infection or other sexually transmitted diseases (CDC 2010; CDC 2013).

The risk of hypertension may be increased with age, dose, and duration of use. Combination hormonal contraceptives should not be used in women with persistent blood pressure values ≥160 mm Hg systolic or ≥100 mm Hg diastolic. Women with less severe hypertension (140 to 159 mm Hg systolic or 90 to 99 mm Hg diastolic) or those with hypertension that is adequately controlled should generally not use combination hormonal contraceptives (CDC 2013). Other risk factors for cardiovascular disease (eg, older age, smoking, diabetes) should be considered when prescribing contraceptives (CDC 2010). Some products are specifically contraindicated with persistent blood pressure values ≥160 mm Hg systolic or ≥100 mm Hg diastolic. Women with inherited thrombophilias (eg, protein C or S deficiency) may have increased risk of venous thromboembolism (DeSancho 2010; van Vlijmen 2011). Use is contraindicated in women with hypercoagulopathies (inherited or acquired). Oral contraceptives may increase the risk of thromboembolism; discontinue use of combination hormonal contraceptives if an arterial or venous thrombotic event occurs. Use of combination hormonal contraceptives is contraindicated in women with known thrombophilic conditions.

Potentially significant interactions may exist with hormonal contraceptives, requiring dose or frequency adjustment, additional monitoring, and/or selection of alternative therapy. Estrogens may increase thyroid-binding globulin (TBG) levels leading to increased circulating total thyroid hormone levels. Women on thyroid replacement therapy may require higher doses of thyroid hormone while receiving estrogens. Combination hormonal contraceptives may adversely affect lipid levels, including serum triglycerides. The type of lipid disorder, the severity, and the presence of other cardiovascular risk factors should be considered when prescribing combination hormonal contraceptives to women with lipid disorders (CDC 2010). Women with hypertriglyceridemia or a family history of hypertriglyceridemia may be at increased risk of pancreatitis when using combination hormonal contraceptives. Consider alternative contraception for women with uncontrolled dyslipidemia. The use of estrogens and/or progestins may change the results of some laboratory tests (eg, coagulation factors, lipids, glucose tolerance, binding proteins). The dose, route, and the specific estrogen/progestin influences these changes. In addition, personal risk factors (eg, cardiovascular disease, smoking, diabetes, age) also contribute to adverse events; use of specific products may be contraindicated in women with certain risk factors.

Use caution in patients with asthma, epilepsy, hepatic hemangiomas, porphyria, SLE; may exacerbate disease. Use with caution in patients with a history of depression; discontinue if serious depression recurs. Use with caution in patients with diseases which may be exacerbated by fluid retention, including cardiac or renal dysfunction. Discontinue use with the onset of enlargement, pain, or tenderness of preexisting uterine fibroids (leiomyomata). May increase risk of gallbladder disease; may worsen existing gallbladder disease. Use of postmenopausal estrogen may be associated with an increased risk of gallbladder disease requiring surgery. Use of combination hormonal contraceptives is associated with hepatic adenomas (rare); rupture may cause fatal intra-abdominal hemorrhage. Long term use may be associated with an increased risk of hepatocellular carcinoma (rare). Use is contraindicated with preexisting hepatic tumors. Estrogens may be poorly metabolized in women with hepatic impairment. Discontinue if jaundice develops during therapy or if liver function becomes abnormal. Use is contraindicated with preexisting hepatic disease. Risk of cholestasis may be increased with previous cholestasis of pregnancy or cholestasis with prior oral contraceptive use; use is contraindicated with a history of these conditions. May impair glucose tolerance; use caution in women with diabetes or prediabetes. Discontinue if unexplained loss of vision, proptosis, diplopia, papilledema, or retinal vascular lesions occur and immediately evaluate for retinal vein thrombosis. Any changes with lens tolerance or vision should be evaluated by an ophthalmologist. Combination hormonal contraceptives, hormone replacement therapy, as well as sun exposure and pregnancy, are triggers for chloasma. Women with a susceptibility to chloasma or additional risk factors should avoid exposure to sun or ultraviolet radiation during therapy (Handel 2014). Exogenous estrogens may exacerbate angioedema symptoms in women with hereditary angioedema (Geng 2013; Zuraw 2013). Use caution in patients with hypoparathyroidism; estrogen-induced hypocalcemia may occur. Evaluate new, recurrent, severe, or persistent headaches. Use in patients with migraine headaches with aura, or migraine headaches of any type if >35 years of age is contraindicated. Use caution in patients with otosclerosis.

Combination hormonal contraceptives are not for use prior to menarche. Safety and efficacy of some products (eg, Generess Fe, Lo Loestrin Fe; Lo Minastrin Fe) have not been established in women with a BMI >35 kg/m^2. Breakthrough or intracyclic bleeding and spotting may occur with combination hormonal contraceptives, especially during the first 3 months of therapy. In addition, occasional missed periods may occur. Presentation of irregular, unresolving vaginal bleeding warrants further evaluation to rule out malignancy or pregnancy. Amenorrhea or oligomenorrhea may occur after discontinuing combination hormonal contraceptives, especially when such a condition was preexistent.

Whenever possible, should be discontinued at least 4 weeks prior to and for 2 weeks following major surgery or other surgeries known to have an increased risk of thromboembolism or during periods of prolonged immobilization.

Tablets may contain lactose; avoid use in patients with lactase deficiency, galactose intolerance or glucose-galactose malabsorption. Some products may contain tartrazine, which may cause allergic reactions in certain individuals.

Drug Interactions

Metabolism/Transport Effects Refer to individual components.

Avoid Concomitant Use

Avoid concomitant use of Ethinyl Estradiol and Norethindrone with any of the following: Amodiaquine; Anastrozole; Antihepaciviral Combination Products; Dasabuvir; Dehydroepiandrosterone; Exemestane; Griseofulvin; Hemin; Indium 111 Capromab Pendetide; Ixazomib; Ospemifene; TiZANidine; Tranexamic Acid; Ulipristal

Increased Effect/Toxicity

Ethinyl Estradiol and Norethindrone may increase the levels/effects of: Agomelatine; Ajmaline; Amodiaquine; Anthrax Immune Globulin (Human); Antihepaciviral Combination Products; C1 inhibitors; CloZAPine; Corticosteroids (Systemic); CYP1A2 Substrates; Dantrolene; Dasabuvir; Flibanserin; Immune Globulin; Lenalidomide; Lomitapide; Ospemifene; Pirfenidone; Pomalidomide; ROPINIRole; Selegiline; Thalidomide; Theophylline Derivatives; Tipranavir; TiZANidine; Tranexamic Acid; Voriconazole

The levels/effects of Ethinyl Estradiol and Norethindrone may be increased by: Ascorbic Acid; Atazanavir; Boceprevir; Carfilzomib; Cobicistat; Dehydroepiandrosterone; Herbs (Estrogenic Properties); Herbs (Progestogenic Properties); Lopinavir; Metreleptin; MiFEPRIStone; NSAID (COX-2 Inhibitor); Pomalidomide; Tipranavir; Voriconazole

Decreased Effect

Ethinyl Estradiol and Norethindrone may decrease the levels/effects of: Anastrozole; Anticoagulants; Antidiabetic Agents; Chenodiol; Exemestane; Fosamprenavir; Hemin; Hyaluronidase; Indium 111 Capromab Pendetide; LamoTRIgine; Ospemifene; Thyroid Products; Ulipristal; Ursodiol; Valproate Products; Vitamin K Antagonists

The levels/effects of Ethinyl Estradiol and Norethindrone may be decreased by: Acitretin; Aprepitant; Armodafinil; Artemether; Asunaprevir; Barbiturates; Bexarotene (Systemic); Bile Acid Sequestrants; Boceprevir; Bosentan; CarBAMazepine; CloBAZam; Cobicistat; Colesevelam; CYP3A4 Inducers (Moderate); CYP3A4 Inducers (Strong); Dabrafenib; Darunavir; Deferasirox; Efavirenz; Elvitegravir; Enzalutamide; Eslicarbazepine; Exenatide; Felbamate; Fosamprenavir; Fosaprepitant; Fosphenytoin; Griseofulvin; Ixazomib; Lesinurad; Lixisenatide; Lopinavir; Lumacaftor; Metreleptin; MiFEPRIStone; Mitotane; Modafinil; Mycophenolate; Nafcillin; Nelfinavir; Nevirapine; OXcarbazepine; Perampanel; Phenytoin; Primidone; Protease Inhibitors; Prucalopride; Retinoic Acid Derivatives; Rifamycin Derivatives; Rufinamide; Saquinavir; Siltuximab; St John's Wort; Sugammadex; Telaprevir; Tipranavir; Tocilizumab; Topiramate; Ulipristal

Food Interactions Routine use of ethanol increases estrogen level and risk of breast cancer. Management: Avoid ethanol.

Dietary Considerations Ensure adequate calcium and vitamin D intake when used for the prevention of osteoporosis.

Pharmacodynamics/Kinetics

Half-life Elimination Ethinyl estradiol: 19 to 24 hours

Pregnancy Risk Factor X

Pregnancy Considerations

Use is contraindicated in pregnant women. Pregnancy status should be evaluated prior to prescribing combination hormonal contraceptives (CDC 2013); treatment should be discontinued if pregnancy occurs. In general, the use of combination hormonal contraceptives, when inadvertently used early in pregnancy, have not been associated with teratogenic effects. Available evidence is inconsistent if BMI alters the efficacy of combination oral contraceptives (CDC 2010); however, the manufacturers of some products (eg, Generess Fe, Lo Loestrin Fe; Lo Minastrin Fe) note that safety and efficacy have not been established in women with a BMI >35 kg/m^2.

Due to increased risk of venous thromboembolism (VTE) postpartum, combination hormonal contraceptives should not be started in any woman <21 days following delivery. Women without risk factors for VTE and who are not breastfeeding may start combination hormonal contraceptives during 21 to 42 days postpartum. After 42 days postpartum, restrictions for use are not related to postpartum status and should be based on other medical conditions (CDC 2011). The manufacturer states that combination hormonal contraceptives should not be started until ≥4 weeks after delivery in women who choose not to breast-feed.

Breastfeeding Considerations

Contraceptive steroids can be detected in breast milk. Jaundice and breast enlargement in the nursing infant have been reported following the use of combination hormonal contraceptives. May also decrease the quality and quantity of breast milk; an alternative form of contraception is recommended until the infant is weaned (per manufacturer).

The theoretical concerns about decreased milk production are greatest early in the postpartum period when milk production is being established. Postpartum risk status for VTE should be considered when initiating combination hormonal contraceptives after delivery. Combined hormonal contraceptives should not be started <21 days postpartum due to increased risk of VTE. Risk of VTE is still elevated in breastfeeding women until ~42 days postpartum and is greater in women with additional risk factors. After 42 days postpartum, restrictions for use are not related to postpartum VTE risk and should be based on other medical conditions (CDC 2011).

Dosage Forms

Capsule, oral:

Taytulla: Ethinyl estradiol 0.02 mg and norethindrone acetate 1 mg [21 pale pink capsules] and ferrous fumarate 75 mg [7 maroon capsules] (28s)

Tablet, oral:

femhrt: Ethinyl estradiol 0.0025 mg and norethindrone acetate 0.5 mg [white tablets] (28s)

Fyavolv:

0.5/2.5: Ethinyl estradiol 0.0025 mg and norethindrone acetate 0.5 mg [white-off-white tablets] (28s, 90s)

1/5: Ethinyl estradiol 0.005 mg and norethindrone acetate 1 mg [blue tablets] (28s, 90s)

Jevantique Lo: Ethinyl estradiol 0.0025 mg and norethindrone acetate 0.5 mg [white tablets] (28s)

Jinteli: Ethinyl estradiol 0.005 mg and norethindrone acetate 1 mg [white tablets] (28s, 90s)

Generic: Ethinyl estradiol 0.0025 mg and norethindrone acetate 0.5 mg (28s); Ethinyl estradiol 0.005 mg and norethindrone acetate 1 mg (28s, 90s)

Tablet, oral [monophasic formulation]:

Alyacen 1/35: Ethinyl estradiol 0.035 mg and norethindrone 1 mg [21 peach tablets and 7 light green inactive tablets] (28s)

Balziva: Ethinyl estradiol 0.035 mg and norethindrone 0.4 mg [21 light peach tablets and 7 white inactive tablets] (28s)

Blisovi 24 Fe: Ethinyl estradiol 0.02 mg and norethindrone acetate 1 mg [24 white tablets] and ferrous fumarate 75 mg [4 brown tablets] (28s)

Blisovi Fe 1/20: Ethinyl estradiol 0.02 mg and norethindrone acetate 1 mg [21 yellow tablets] and ferrous fumarate 75 mg [7 brown tablets] (28s)

Brevicon: Ethinyl estradiol 0.035 mg and norethindrone 0.5 mg [21 blue tablets and 7 orange inactive tablets] (28s)

Briellyn: Ethinyl estradiol 0.035 mg and norethindrone 0.4 mg [21 light peach tablets and 7 white-off-white inactive tablets] (28s)

Cyclafem 1/35: Ethinyl estradiol 0.035 mg and norethindrone 1 mg [21 pink tablets and 7 light green inactive tablets] (28s)

Dasetta 1/35: Ethinyl estradiol 0.035 mg and norethindrone 1 mg [21 orange tablets and 7 white inactive tablets] (28s)

Gildagia: Ethinyl estradiol 0.035 mg and norethindrone 0.4 mg [21 peach tablets and 7 light green inactive tablets] (28s)

Gildess FE 1/20: Ethinyl estradiol 0.02 mg and norethindrone acetate 1 mg [21 white tablets] and ferrous fumarate 75 mg [7 white-speckled brown tablets] (28s)

Gildess FE 1.5/30: Ethinyl estradiol 0.03 mg and norethindrone acetate 1.5 mg [21 light green tablets] and ferrous fumarate 75 mg [7 white-speckled brown tablets] (28s)

Junel 1/20: Ethinyl estradiol 0.02 mg and norethindrone acetate 1 mg [yellow tablets] (21s)

Junel 1.5/30, Loestrin 21 1.5/30: Ethinyl estradiol 0.03 mg and norethindrone acetate 1.5 mg [pink tablets] (21s)

Junel Fe 1/20: Ethinyl estradiol 0.02 mg and norethindrone acetate 1 mg [21 yellow tablets] and ferrous fumarate 75 mg [7 brown tablets] (28s)

Junel Fe 1.5/30: Ethinyl estradiol 0.03 mg and norethindrone acetate 1.5 mg [21 pink tablets] and ferrous fumarate 75 mg [7 brown tablets] (28s)

Junel Fe 24: Ethinyl estradiol 0.02 mg and norethindrone acetate 1 mg [24 pale yellow tablets] and ferrous fumarate 75 mg [4 brown tablets] (28s)

Larin 1/20: Ethinyl estradiol 0.02 mg and norethindrone acetate 1 mg [21 pale yellow tablets] (21s)

Larin 1.5/30: Ethinyl estradiol 0.03 mg and norethindrone acetate 1.5 mg [21 green tablets] (21s)

Larin Fe 1/20: Ethinyl estradiol 0.02 mg and norethindrone acetate 1 mg [21 pale yellow tablets] and ferrous fumarate 75 mg [7 brown tablets] (28s)

Larin Fe 1.5/30: Ethinyl estradiol 0.03 mg and norethindrone acetate 1.5 mg [21 green tablets] and ferrous fumarate 75 mg [7 brown tablets] (28s) [contains soya lecithin]

Larin 24 Fe: Ethinyl estradiol 0.02 mg and norethindrone acetate 1 mg [24 pale yellow tablets] and ferrous fumarate 75 mg [4 brown tablets] (28s)

Loestrin 21 1/20: Ethinyl estradiol 0.02 mg and norethindrone acetate 1 mg [light yellow tablets] (21s)

Loestrin 24 Fe: Ethinyl estradiol 0.02 mg and norethindrone acetate 1 mg [24 white tablets] and ferrous fumarate 75 mg [4 brown tablets] (28s)

Loestrin Fe 1/20: Ethinyl estradiol 0.02 mg and norethindrone acetate 1 mg [21 light yellow tablets] and ferrous fumarate 75 mg [7 brown tablets] (28s)

Loestrin Fe 1.5/30: Ethinyl estradiol 0.03 mg and norethindrone acetate 1.5 mg [21 pink tablets] and ferrous fumarate 75 mg [7 brown tablets] (28s)

Lomedia 24 Fe: Ethinyl estradiol 0.02 mg and norethindrone acetate 1 mg [24 white tablets] and ferrous fumarate 75 mg [4 brown tablets] (28s)

Microgestin 1/20: Ethinyl estradiol 0.02 mg and norethindrone acetate 1 mg [white tablets] (21s)

Microgestin 1.5/30: Ethinyl estradiol 0.03 mg and norethindrone acetate 1.5 mg [green tablets] (21s)

Microgestin 24 Fe: Ethinyl estradiol 0.02 mg and norethindrone acetate 1 mg [24 white tablets] and ferrous fumarate 75 mg [4 brown tablets] (28s)

Microgestin Fe 1/20: Ethinyl estradiol 0.02 mg and norethindrone acetate 1 mg [21 white tablets] and ferrous fumarate 75 mg [7 brown tablets] (28s)

Microgestin Fe 1.5/30: Ethinyl estradiol 0.03 mg and norethindrone acetate 1.5 mg [21 green tablets] and ferrous fumarate 75 mg [7 brown tablets] (28s)

Necon 0.5/35, Nortrel 0.5/35: Ethinyl estradiol 0.035 mg and norethindrone 0.5 mg [21 light yellow tablets and 7 white inactive tablets] (28s)

Necon 1/35: Ethinyl estradiol 0.035 mg and norethindrone 1 mg [21 dark yellow tablets and 7 white inactive tablets] (28s)

Norinyl 1+35: Ethinyl estradiol 0.035 mg and norethindrone 1 mg [21 yellow-green tablets and 7 orange inactive tablets] (28s)

Nortrel 1/35:

Ethinyl estradiol 0.035 mg and norethindrone 1 mg [yellow tablets] (21s)

Ethinyl estradiol 0.035 mg and norethindrone 1 mg [21 yellow tablets and 7 white inactive tablets] (28s)

Ortho-Novum 1/35: Ethinyl estradiol 0.035 mg and norethindrone 1 mg [21 peach tablets and 7 green inactive tablets] (28s)

Ovcon 35: Ethinyl estradiol 0.035 mg and norethindrone 0.4 mg [21 light peach tablets and 7 green inactive tablets] (28s)
Philith: Ethinyl estradiol 0.035 mg and norethindrone 0.4 mg [21 tan tablets and 7 white inactive tablets] (28s)
Pirmella 1/35: Ethinyl estradiol 0.035 mg and norethindrone 1 mg [21 peach tablets and 7 green inactive tablets] (28s)
Tarina FE 1/20: Ethinyl estradiol 0.02 mg and norethindrone acetate 1 mg [21 white tablets] and ferrous fumarate 75 mg [7 brown tablets] (28s)
Vyfemla: Ethinyl estradiol 0.035 mg and norethindrone 0.4 mg [21 light peach tablets and 7 white inactive tablets] (28s)
Wera: Ethinyl estradiol 0.035 mg and norethindrone 0.5 mg [21 light peach tablets and 7 white inactive tablets] (28s)
Zenchent: Ethinyl estradiol 0.035 mg and norethindrone 0.4 mg [21 light peach tablets and 7 white inactive tablets] (28s)

Tablet, chewable, oral [monophasic formulation]:
Femcon Fe, Wymzya Fe: Ethinyl estradiol 0.035 mg and norethindrone 0.4 mg [21 white tablets] and ferrous fumarate 75 mg [7 brown tablets] (28s)
Generess Fe: Ethinyl estradiol 0.025 mg and norethindrone 0.8 mg [24 light green tablets] and ferrous fumarate 75 mg [4 brown tablets] (28s)
Kaitlib Fe: Ethinyl estradiol 0.025 mg and norethindrone 0.8 mg [24 light green tablets] and ferrous fumarate 75 mg [4 brown tablets]
Layolis Fe: Ethinyl estradiol 0.025 mg and norethindrone 0.8 mg [24 light green tablets] and ferrous fumarate 75 mg [4 brown tablets] (28s)
Mibelas 24 Fe: Ethinyl estradiol 0.02 mg and norethindrone 1 mg [24 white tablets] and ferrous fumarate 75 mg [4 brown tablets] (28s)
Minastrin 24 Fe: Ethinyl estradiol 0.02 mg and norethindrone 1 mg [24 white tablets] and ferrous fumarate 75 mg [4 brown tablets] (28s)
Zenchent Fe: Ethinyl estradiol 0.035 mg and norethindrone 0.4 mg [21 light yellow tablets] and ferrous fumarate 75 mg [7 brown tablets] (28s)
Generic: Ethinyl estradiol 0.025 mg and norethindrone 0.8 mg [24 tablets] and ferrous fumarate 75 mg [4 tablets] (28s); Ethinyl estradiol 0.035 mg and norethindrone 0.4 mg [21 tablets] and ferrous fumarate 75 mg [7 tablets] (28s)

Tablet, oral [biphasic formulation]:
Lo Loestrin Fe:
Day 1-24: Ethinyl estradiol 0.01 mg and norethindrone acetate 1 mg [24 blue tablets]
Day 25-26: Ethinyl estradiol 0.01 mg [2 white tablets]
Day 27-28: Ferrous fumarate 75 mg [2 brown tablets] (28s)
Necon 10/11:
Day 1-10: Ethinyl estradiol 0.035 mg and norethindrone 0.5 mg [10 light yellow tablets]
Day 11-21: Ethinyl estradiol 0.035 mg and norethindrone 1 mg [11 dark yellow tablets]
Day 22-28: 7 white inactive tablets (28s)

Tablet, oral [triphasic formulation]:
Alyacen 7/7/7:
Day 1-7: Ethinyl estradiol 0.035 mg and norethindrone 0.5 mg [7 white-off-white tablets]
Day 8-14: Ethinyl estradiol 0.035 mg and norethindrone 0.75 mg [7 light peach tablets]
Day 15-21: Ethinyl estradiol 0.035 mg and norethindrone 1 mg [7 peach tablets]
Day 22-28: 7 light green inactive tablets (28s)
Aranelle:
Day 1-7: Ethinyl estradiol 0.035 mg and norethindrone 0.5 mg [7 light yellow tablets]
Day 8-16: Ethinyl estradiol 0.035 mg and norethindrone 1 mg [9 white tablets]
Day 17-21: Ethinyl estradiol 0.035 mg and norethindrone 0.5 mg [5 light yellow tablets]
Day 22-28: 7 peach inactive tablets (28s)
Cyclafem 7/7/7:
Day 1-7: Ethinyl estradiol 0.035 mg and norethindrone 0.5 mg [7 white tablets]
Day 8-14: Ethinyl estradiol 0.035 mg and norethindrone 0.75 mg [7 light pink tablets]
Day 15-21: Ethinyl estradiol 0.035 mg and norethindrone 1 mg [7 pink tablets]
Day 22-28: 7 light green inactive tablets (28s)
Dasetta 7/7/7:
Day 1-7: Ethinyl estradiol 0.035 mg and norethindrone 0.5 mg [7 light peach tablets]
Day 8-14: Ethinyl estradiol 0.035 mg and norethindrone 0.75 mg [7 peach tablets]
Day 15-21: Ethinyl estradiol 0.035 mg and norethindrone 1 mg [7 orange tablets]
Day 22-28: 7 white inactive tablets (28s)
Estrostep Fe, Tilia Fe:
Day 1-5: Ethinyl estradiol 0.02 mg and norethindrone acetate 1 mg [5 white triangular tablets]
Day 6-12: Ethinyl estradiol 0.03 mg and norethindrone acetate 1 mg [7 white square tablets]
Day 13-21: Ethinyl estradiol 0.035 mg and norethindrone acetate 1 mg [9 white round tablets]
Day 22-28: Ferrous fumarate 75 mg [7 brown tablets] (28s)
Leena:
Day 1-7: Ethinyl estradiol 0.035 mg and norethindrone 0.5 mg [7 light blue tablets]
Day 8-16: Ethinyl estradiol 0.035 mg and norethindrone 1 mg [9 light yellow-green tablets]
Day 17-21: Ethinyl estradiol 0.035 mg and norethindrone 0.5 mg [5 light blue tablets]
Day 22-28: 7 orange inactive tablets (28s)
Necon 7/7/7, Ortho-Novum 7/7/7:
Day 1-7: Ethinyl estradiol 0.035 mg and norethindrone 0.5 mg [7 white tablets]
Day 8-14: Ethinyl estradiol 0.035 mg and norethindrone 0.75 mg [7 light peach tablets]
Day 15-21: Ethinyl estradiol 0.035 mg and norethindrone 1 mg [7 peach tablets]
Day 22-28: 7 green inactive tablets (28s)
Nortrel 7/7/7:
Day 1-7: Ethinyl estradiol 0.035 mg and norethindrone 0.5 mg [7 light yellow tablets]
Day 8-14: Ethinyl estradiol 0.035 mg and norethindrone 0.75 mg [7 blue tablets]
Day 15-21: Ethinyl estradiol 0.035 mg and norethindrone 1 mg [7 peach tablets]
Day 22-28: 7 white inactive tablets (28s)
Pirmella 7/7/7:
Day 1-7: Ethinyl estradiol 0.035 mg and norethindrone 0.5 mg [7 white tablets]
Day 8-14: Ethinyl estradiol 0.035 mg and norethindrone 0.75 mg [7 light peach tablets]
Day 15-21: Ethinyl estradiol 0.035 mg and norethindrone 1 mg [7 peach tablets]
Day 22-28: 7 green inactive tablets (28s)
Tri-Legest Fe:
Day 1-5: Ethinyl estradiol 0.02 mg and norethindrone acetate 1 mg [5 light pink tablets]

Day 6-12: Ethinyl estradiol 0.03 mg and norethindrone acetate 1 mg [7 light yellow tablets]
Day 13-21: Ethinyl estradiol 0.035 mg and norethindrone acetate 1 mg [9 light blue tablets]
Day 22-28: Ferrous fumarate 75 mg [7 brown tablets] (28s)
Tri-Norinyl:
Day 1-7: Ethinyl estradiol 0.035 mg and norethindrone 0.5 mg [7 blue tablets]
Day 8-16: Ethinyl estradiol 0.035 mg and norethindrone 1 mg [9 yellow-green tablets]
Day 17-21: Ethinyl estradiol 0.035 mg and norethindrone 0.5 mg [5 blue tablets]
Day 22-28: 7 orange inactive tablets (28s)

Dental Comment Current hormone contraceptives should not be considered a risk factor for gingival or periodontal disease (Preshaw, 2013).

Ethinyl Estradiol and Norgestimate

(ETH in il es tra DYE ole & nor JES ti mate)

Related Information

Endocrine Disorders and Pregnancy *on page 1781*

Brand Names: US Estarylla; Femynor; Mono-Linyah; MonoNessa; Ortho Tri-Cyclen; Ortho Tri-Cyclen Lo; Ortho-Cyclen; Previfem; Sprintec; Tri-Estarylla; Tri-Linyah; Tri-Lo-Estarylla; Tri-Lo-Marzia; Tri-Lo-Sprintec; Tri-Previfem; Tri-Sprintec; TriNessa; TriNessa Lo

Brand Names: Canada Cyclen; Tri-Cyclen; Tri-Cyclen Lo; Tricira Lo

Generic Availability (US) Yes

Pharmacologic Category Contraceptive, Estrogen and Progestin Combination

Use

Acne vulgaris: Treatment of moderate acne vulgaris in females at least 15 years of age

Limitations of use: When used for acne, use only in females ≥15 years of age who achieved menarche, who also desire combination hormonal contraceptive therapy, and have no contraindications to combination hormonal contraceptive use

Contraception: Prevention of pregnancy.

Local Anesthetic/Vasoconstrictor Precautions No information available to require special precautions

Effects on Dental Treatment When prescribing antibiotics, patient must be warned to use additional methods of birth control if on oral contraceptives.

Effects on Bleeding No information available to require special precautions

Adverse Reactions Frequency not defined. Reactions listed are based on reports for other agents in this same pharmacologic class (oral contraceptives) and may not be specifically reported for ethinyl estradiol/norgestimate.

Increased risk or evidence of association with use:

Cardiovascular: Arterial thromboembolism, cerebral thrombosis, hypertension, local thrombophlebitis, mesenteric thrombosis, myocardial infarction, pulmonary embolism, retinal thrombosis, venous thrombosis (with or without embolism)
Central nervous system: Cerebral hemorrhage
Gastrointestinal: Gallbladder disease
Hepatic: Hepatic adenoma, hepatic neoplasm (benign)

Adverse reactions considered drug related:

Cardiovascular: Edema, worsening of varicose veins
Central nervous system: Depression, exacerbation of tics, migraine, mood changes
Dermatologic: Allergic skin rash, chloasma (may persist)
Endocrine & metabolic: Amenorrhea, breast changes (breast hypertrophy, breast secretion, breast tenderness, mastalgia), decreased serum folate level, exacerbation of porphyria, fluid retention, menstrual disease (menstrual flow changes), weight changes
Gastrointestinal: Abdominal cramps, abdominal pain, bloating, breakthrough bleeding, change in appetite, nausea, vomiting
Genitourinary: Cervical ectropion, change in cervical secretions, decreased lactation (with use immediately postpartum), infertility (temporary after discontinuation of treatment), spotting, vaginitis, vulvovaginal candidiasis
Hepatic: Cholestatic jaundice
Hypersensitivity: Anaphylaxis/Anaphylactoid reaction (including angioedema, circulatory shock, respiratory collapse, urticaria)
Neuromuscular & skeletal: Exacerbation of systemic lupus erythematosus
Ophthalmic: Contact lens intolerance, change in corneal curvature (steepening)

Adverse reactions in which association is not confirmed or denied:

Cardiovascular: Budd-Chiari syndrome, chest pain, palpitations, syncope, tachycardia
Central nervous system: Anxiety, convulsions, dizziness, headache, insomnia, nervousness, paresthesia, vertigo
Dermatologic: Acne vulgaris, erythema multiforme, erythema nodosum, hyperhidrosis, loss of scalp hair, night sweats, pruritus, skin photosensitivity
Endocrine & metabolic: Change in libido, hirsutism, hot flash, ovarian cyst, premenstrual syndrome
Gastrointestinal: Colitis, constipation, diarrhea, flatulence, pancreatitis
Genitourinary: Benign breast nodule, benign mammary fibroadenoma, breast cyst, cystitis-like syndrome, dysmenorrhea, urinary tract infection, vaginal dryness, vaginal infection
Hematologic & oncologic: Hemolytic-uremic syndrome, hemorrhagic eruption
Hepatic: Hepatitis
Neuromuscular & skeletal: Back pain, limb pain, muscle spasm, myalgia, weakness
Ophthalmic: Cataract, decreased visual acuity, dry eye syndrome, optic neuritis (with or without partial or complete loss of vision)
Renal: Renal insufficiency
Respiratory: Dyspnea

Dosing

Adult Females:

Acne (Ortho Tri-Cyclen, Tri-Estarylla, TriNessa, Tri-Previfem, Tri-Sprintec): Oral: Refer to dosing for contraception

Contraception: Oral: 1 tablet once daily

Schedule 1 (Sunday starter): Dose begins on first Sunday after onset of menstruation; if the menstrual period starts on Sunday, take first tablet that very same day. **With a Sunday start, an additional method of contraception should be used until after the first 7 days of consecutive administration.**

Schedule 2 (Day 1 starter): Dose starts on first day of menstrual cycle taking 1 tablet daily.

Additional contraceptive dosing considerations:

Switching from a different contraceptive:

Oral contraceptive: Start on the same day that a new pack of the previous oral contraceptive would have been taken.

Transdermal patch, vaginal ring, injection: Start on the day the next dose would have been due.

IUD or implant: Start on the day of removal. A backup method of contraception should be used for the first 7 days if IUD is not removed on the first day of the menstrual cycle.

Use after first trimester abortion or miscarriage: Therapy may be started immediately. If not started within 5 days, a back-up method of contraception should be used for the first 7 days.

Use after childbirth (in women who are not breast-feeding) or after second trimester abortion or miscarriage: Therapy may be started ≥4 weeks postpartum. Pregnancy should be considered prior to treatment if menstrual periods have not restarted. An additional method of contraception (nonhormonal) should be used until after the first 7 days of consecutive administration.

Missed or late doses (CDC 2013):

If one dose is late (<24 hours since dose should have been taken) or if one dose is missed (24 to <48 hours since dose should have been taken): Take dose as soon as possible. Continue remaining doses at the usual time (even if that means 2 doses on the same day).

If ≥2 consecutive doses are missed (≥48 hours since dose should have been taken): Take the most recently missed dose as soon as possible, discard any other missed doses. Continue remaining doses at the usual time (even if that means taking 2 doses on the same day); use back-up contraception until hormonal pills have been taken for 7 consecutive days. If doses were missed during the last week of hormonal (active) tablets (eg, days 15 to 21 of a 28 day pack), omit the hormone free interval by finishing the current pack and starting a new pack. If unable to start a new pack immediately, back up contraception is needed until hormonal pills from a new pack have been taken for 7 consecutive days. Consider use of emergency contraception in some situations (refer to guidelines for details).

Also refer to package insert for product specific information.

Pediatric Females:

Acne: Oral: Adolescents ≥15 years; refer to adult dosing for contraception; not to be used prior to menarche.

Contraception: Oral: Refer to adult dosing; not to be used prior to menarche.

Renal Impairment There are no dosage adjustments provided in the manufacturer's labeling (has not been studied); use with caution and monitor blood pressure closely.

Hepatic Impairment Use is contraindicated in patients with hepatic impairment.

Mechanism of Action Combination hormonal contraceptives inhibit ovulation via a negative feedback mechanism on the hypothalamus, which alters the normal pattern of gonadotropin secretion of a follicle-stimulating hormone (FSH) and luteinizing hormone by the anterior pituitary. The follicular phase FSH and midcycle surge of gonadotropins are inhibited. In addition, combination hormonal contraceptives produce alterations in the genital tract, including changes in the cervical mucus, rendering it unfavorable for sperm penetration even if ovulation occurs. Changes in the endometrium may also occur, producing an unfavorable environment for nidation. Combination hormonal contraceptive drugs may alter the tubal transport of the ova through the fallopian tubes. Progestational agents may also alter sperm fertility.

Contraindications Breast cancer or other estrogen- or progestin-dependent neoplasms (current or a history of), hepatic tumors (benign or malignant) or hepatic disease, pregnancy, undiagnosed abnormal uterine bleeding.

Use is also contraindicated in women at high risk of arterial or venous thrombotic diseases for example, women with: Cerebrovascular disease, coronary artery disease, diabetes mellitus with vascular disease, DVT or PE (current or history of), hypercoagulopathies (inherited or acquired), hypertension (uncontrolled), headaches with focal neurological symptoms, migraine headaches with aura or migraine headaches if >35 years of age, thrombogenic valvular or rhythm diseases of the heart (eg, subacute bacterial endocarditis with valvular disease or atrial fibrillation), women >35 years of age who smoke.

Canadian-labeling: Additional contraindications: Hypersensitivity to any component of the formulation; ocular lesions due to ophthalmic vascular disease including partial or complete loss of vision or defect in visual fields; steroid dependent jaundice, cholestatic jaundice or jaundice or pregnancy; pancreatitis associated with severe hypertriglyceridemia (current or history of); severe dyslipoproteinemia; prolonged immobilization or major surgery associated with an increased risk of postoperative thromboembolism; thrombophlebitis, thromboembolic disorders, or thrombophilic conditions (current or history of); prodromi of a thrombosis (eg, TIA, angina pectoris; current or history of); hereditary or acquired predisposition for venous or arterial thrombosis, such as Factor V Leiden mutation and activated protein C(APC) resistance, antithrombin-III deficiency, protein C deficiency, protein S deficiency, hyperhomocysteinemia (eg, due to MTHFR C677T, A1298 mutations), prothrombin mutation G20210A, and antiphospholipid-antibodies (anticardiolipin antibodies, lupus anticoagulant).

Documentation of allergenic cross-reactivity for estrogens and progestins is limited. However, because of similarities in chemical structure and/or pharmacologic actions, the possibility of cross-sensitivity cannot be ruled out with certainty.

Warnings/Precautions

[U.S. Boxed Warning]: The risk of cardiovascular side effects is increased in women who smoke cigarettes; risk increases with age (especially women >35 years of age) and the number of cigarettes smoked. Use is contraindicated in patients >35 years of age who smoke.

The use of combination hormonal contraceptives has not been shown to increase the risk for breast cancer. However, breast cancer is a hormonal sensitive tumor and the prognosis for women with a current or recent history of breast cancer may be worse with combination hormonal contraceptive use (CDC 2010). Use is contraindicated in women with (or history of) breast cancer. The use of combination hormonal contraceptives has been associated with a slight increased risk of cervical cancer; however, studies are not consistent and may be related to additional risk factors (Gierisch 2013). Women awaiting treatment for cervical cancer may use combination hormonal contraceptives (CDC 2013). The risk of ovarian cancer is decreased in women using combination hormonal contraceptives (CDC 2013; Walker 2015). Oral contraceptives may be used to reduce the risk of ovarian cancer including those women with BRCA1 and BRCA2 mutations (Walker 2015).

The risk of hypertension may be increased with age, dose, and duration of use. Combination hormonal contraceptives should not be used in women with persistent blood pressure values ≥160 mm Hg systolic or ≥100 mm Hg diastolic. Women with less severe hypertension (140 to 159 mm Hg systolic or 90 to 99 mm Hg diastolic) or those with hypertension that is adequately controlled should generally not use combination hormonal contraceptives (CDC 2013). Other risk factors for cardiovascular disease (eg, older age, smoking, diabetes) should be considered when prescribing contraceptives (CDC, 2010). The manufacturer contraindicates use in women with uncontrolled hypertension and recommends monitoring women with well-controlled hypertension; discontinue therapy if blood pressure rises significantly. Use with caution in patients with risk factors for cardiovascular disease (eg, hypertension, hypercholesterolemia, morbid obesity, diabetes, or women who smoke) (CDC 2010); use of combination hormonal contraceptives may increase the risk of arterial or venous thrombotic events. Use is contraindicated in women at high risk of arterial or venous thrombotic diseases. May increase the risk of thromboembolism; discontinue use of combination hormonal contraceptives if an arterial or venous thrombotic event occurs. Women with inherited thrombophilias (eg, protein C or S deficiency) may have increased risk of venous thromboembolism (DeSancho, 2010; van Vlijmen, 2011). Use is contraindicated in women with hypercoagulopathies (inherited or acquired).

Combination hormonal contraceptives may adversely affect lipid levels, including serum triglycerides. The type of lipid disorder, the severity, and the presence of other cardiovascular risk factors should be considered when prescribing combination hormonal contraceptives to women with lipid disorders (CDC 2010). Women with hypertriglyceridemia or a family history of hypertriglyceridemia may be at increased risk of pancreatitis when using combination hormonal contraceptives. Consider alternative contraception for women with uncontrolled dyslipidemia. Risk of cholestasis may be increased with previous cholestasis of pregnancy or cholestasis with prior oral contraceptive use. Canadian labeling contraindicates use with cholestatic jaundice or jaundice or pregnancy. May have a risk of gallbladder disease; may worsen existing gallbladder disease. The use of estrogens and/or progestins may change the results of some laboratory tests (eg, coagulation factors, lipids, glucose tolerance, binding proteins). The dose, route, and the specific estrogen/progestin influences these changes. In addition, personal risk factors (eg, cardiovascular disease, smoking, diabetes, age) also contribute to adverse events; use of specific products may be contraindicated in women with certain risk factors.

Combination hormonal contraceptives may be poorly metabolized in women with hepatic impairment. Discontinue if jaundice develops during therapy or if liver function becomes abnormal. Use is contraindicated in women with hepatic disease. Use of combination hormonal contraceptives is associated with hepatic adenomas (rare); rupture may cause fatal intra-abdominal hemorrhage. Long term use may be associated with an increased risk of hepatocellular carcinoma (rare). Use of this product is contraindicated in women with preexisting hepatic tumors.

Evaluate new, recurrent, severe or persistent headaches. Use in patients with migraine headaches with aura, or migraine headaches of any type if >35 years of age is contraindicated. Estrogens may induce or exacerbate symptoms in women with hereditary angioedema (Geng, 2013; Zuraw, 2013). Oral contraceptives may impair glucose tolerance; use caution in women with diabetes or prediabetes. Use with caution in patients with a history of depression; discontinue if serious depression recurs. Discontinue if unexplained loss of vision, proptosis, diplopia, papilledema, or retinal vascular lesions occur and immediately evaluate for retinal vein thrombosis. Combination hormonal contraceptives, as well as sun exposure and pregnancy, are triggers for chloasma. Women with a susceptibility to chloasma or additional risk factors should avoid exposure to sun or ultraviolet radiation during therapy (Handel 2014).

Breakthrough or intracyclic bleeding and spotting may occur, especially during the first 3 months of therapy. In addition, occasional missed periods may occur. Presentation of irregular, unresolving vaginal bleeding warrants further evaluation to rule out malignancy or pregnancy. Amenorrhea or oligomenorrhea may occur after discontinuing combination hormonal contraceptives, especially when such a condition was preexistent. When initiating a combination oral contraceptive, consideration should be given to safety, effectiveness, availability and acceptance to the patient (CDC 2013). Consider initiating with a monthly bleeding monophasic formulation containing ethinyl estradiol 30 to 35 mcg plus a progestin, and adjusting based on adverse events and patient preference (Ott 2014).

Potentially significant interactions may exist, requiring dose or frequency adjustment, additional monitoring, and/or selection of alternative therapy. Estrogens may increase thyroid-binding globulin (TBG) levels leading to increased circulating total thyroid hormone levels. Women on thyroid replacement therapy may require higher doses of thyroid hormone while receiving estrogens. Combination hormonal contraceptives do not protect against HIV infection or other sexually-transmitted diseases (CDC 2010; CDC 2013). Not for use prior to menarche. Whenever possible, should be discontinued at least 4 weeks prior to and for 2 weeks following elective surgery associated with an increased risk of thromboembolism or during periods of prolonged immobilization.

Drug Interactions

Metabolism/Transport Effects Refer to individual components.

Avoid Concomitant Use

Avoid concomitant use of Ethinyl Estradiol and Norgestimate with any of the following: Amodiaquine; Anastrozole; Antihepaciviral Combination Products; Dasabuvir; Dehydroepiandrosterone; Exemestane; Griseofulvin; Hemin; Indium 111 Capromab Pendetide; Ixazomib; Ospemifene; TiZANidine; Tranexamic Acid; Ulipristal

Increased Effect/Toxicity

Ethinyl Estradiol and Norgestimate may increase the levels/effects of: Agomelatine; Ajmaline; Amodiaquine; Anthrax Immune Globulin (Human); Antihepaciviral Combination Products; C1 inhibitors; CloZAPine; Corticosteroids (Systemic); CYP1A2 Substrates; Dantrolene; Dasabuvir; Flibanserin; Immune Globulin; Lenalidomide; Lomitapide; Ospemifene; Pirfenidone; Pomalidomide; ROPINIRole; Selegiline;

Thalidomide; Theophylline Derivatives; Tipranavir; TiZANidine; Tranexamic Acid; Voriconazole

The levels/effects of Ethinyl Estradiol and Norgestimate may be increased by: Ascorbic Acid; Atazanavir; Boceprevir; Carfilzomib; Cobicistat; Dehydroepiandrosterone; Herbs (Estrogenic Properties); Herbs (Progestogenic Properties); Lopinavir; Metreleptin; MiFEPRIStone; NSAID (COX-2 Inhibitor); Pomalidomide; Tipranavir; Voriconazole

Decreased Effect

Ethinyl Estradiol and Norgestimate may decrease the levels/effects of: Anastrozole; Anticoagulants; Antidiabetic Agents; Chenodiol; Exemestane; Fosamprenavir; Hemin; Hyaluronidase; Indium 111 Capromab Pendetide; LamoTRIgine; Ospemifene; Thyroid Products; Ulipristal; Ursodiol; Valproate Products; Vitamin K Antagonists

The levels/effects of Ethinyl Estradiol and Norgestimate may be decreased by: Acitretin; Aprepitant; Armodafinil; Artemether; Asunaprevir; Barbiturates; Bexarotene (Systemic); Bile Acid Sequestrants; Boceprevir; Bosentan; CarBAMazepine; CloBAZam; Cobicistat; Colesevelam; CYP3A4 Inducers (Moderate); CYP3A4 Inducers (Strong); Dabrafenib; Darunavir; Deferasirox; Efavirenz; Elvitegravir; Enzalutamide; Eslicarbazepine; Exenatide; Felbamate; Fosamprenavir; Fosaprepitant; Fosphenytoin; Griseofulvin; Ixazomib; Lesinurad; Lixisenatide; Lopinavir; Lumacaftor; Metreleptin; MiFEPRIStone; Mitotane; Modafinil; Mycophenolate; Nafcillin; Nelfinavir; Nevirapine; OXcarbazepine; Perampanel; Phenytoin; Primidone; Protease Inhibitors; Prucalopride; Retinoic Acid Derivatives; Rifamycin Derivatives; Rufinamide; Saquinavir; Siltuximab; St John's Wort; Sugammadex; Telaprevir; Tipranavir; Tocilizumab; Topiramate; Ulipristal

Pharmacodynamics/Kinetics

Half-life Elimination EE: 10-16 hours; NGMN: 18-25 hours; NG: 38-45 hours

Time to Peak EE and NGM: ~2 hours

Pregnancy Considerations Pregnancy status should be evaluated prior to prescribing (CDC, 2013); treatment should be discontinued if pregnancy occurs. In general, the use of combination hormonal contraceptives, when inadvertently used early in pregnancy, have not been associated with teratogenic effects. Available evidence is inconsistent if BMI alters the efficacy of combination oral contraceptives (CDC, 2010).

Due to increased risk of venous thromboembolism (VTE) postpartum, combination hormonal contraceptives should not be started in any woman <21 days following delivery. Women without risk factors for VTE and who are not breastfeeding may start combination hormonal contraceptives during 21-42 days postpartum. After 42 days postpartum, restrictions for use are not related to postpartum status and should be based on other medical conditions (CDC, 2011). The manufacturer states that combination hormonal contraceptives should not be started until ≥4 weeks after delivery in women who choose not to breast-feed.

Breastfeeding Considerations Contraceptive steroids can be detected in breast milk. Use may decrease the quality and quantity of breast milk; an alternative form of contraception is recommended until the infant is weaned (per manufacturer).

The theoretical concerns about decreased milk production are greatest early in the postpartum period when milk production is being established. Postpartum risk status for VTE should be considered when initiating combination hormonal contraceptives after delivery. Combined hormonal contraceptives should not be started <21 days postpartum due to increased risk of VTE. Risk of VTE is still elevated in breastfeeding women until ~42 days postpartum and is greater in women with additional risk factors. After 42 days postpartum, restrictions for use are not related to postpartum VTE risk and should be based on other medical conditions (CDC, 2011).

Dosage Forms

Tablet, oral [monophasic formulation]:

Estarylla: Ethinyl estradiol 0.035 mg and norgestimate 0.25 mg [21 blue tablets and 7 green inactive tablets] (28s)

Femynor: Ethinyl estradiol 0.035 mg and norgestimate 0.25 mg [21 red tablets and 7 white inactive tablets] (28s)

MonoNessa, Ortho-Cyclen: Ethinyl estradiol 0.035 mg and norgestimate 0.25 mg [21 blue tablets and 7 dark green inactive tablets] (28s)

Previfem: Ethinyl estradiol 0.035 mg and norgestimate 0.25 mg [21 blue tablets and 7 light green inactive tablets] (28s)

Sprintec: Ethinyl estradiol 0.035 mg and norgestimate 0.25 mg [21 blue tablets and 7 white inactive tablets] (28s)

Tablet, oral [triphasic formulation]:

Ortho Tri-Cyclen:

Day 1-7: Ethinyl estradiol 0.035 mg and norgestimate 0.18 mg [7 white tablets]

Day 8-14: Ethinyl estradiol 0.035 mg and norgestimate 0.215 mg [7 light blue tablets]

Day 15-21: Ethinyl estradiol 0.035 mg and norgestimate 0.25 mg [7 blue tablets]

Day 22-28: 7 dark green inactive tablets (28s)

Ortho Tri-Cyclen Lo:

Day 1-7: Ethinyl estradiol 0.025 mg and norgestimate 0.18 mg [7 white tablets]

Day 8-14: Ethinyl estradiol 0.025 mg and norgestimate 0.215 mg [7 light blue tablets]

Day 15-21: Ethinyl estradiol 0.025 mg and norgestimate 0.25 mg [7 dark blue tablets]

Day 22-28: 7 dark green inactive tablets (28s)

Tri-Estarylla

Day 1-7: Ethinyl estradiol 0.035 mg and norgestimate 0.18 mg [7 white tablets]

Day 8-14: Ethinyl estradiol 0.035 mg and norgestimate 0.215 mg [7 light blue tablets]

Day 15-21: Ethinyl estradiol 0.035 mg and norgestimate 0.25 mg [7 blue tablets]

Day 22-28: 7 green inactive tablets (28s)

Tri-Linyah:

Day 1 to 7: Ethinyl estradiol 0.035 mg and norgestimate 0.18 mg [7 green tablets]

Day 8 to 14: Ethinyl estradiol 0.035 mg and norgestimate 0.215 mg [7 light blue tablets]

Day 15 to 21: Ethinyl estradiol 0.035 mg and norgestimate 0.25 mg [7 blue tablets]

Day 22 to 28: 7 white inactive tablets (28s)

Tri-Lo-Estarylla:

Day 1 to 7: Ethinyl estradiol 0.025 mg and norgestimate 0.18 mg [7 white tablets]

Day 8 to 14: Ethinyl estradiol 0.025 mg and norgestimate 0.215 mg [7 light blue tablets]

Day 15 to 21: Ethinyl estradiol 0.025 mg and norgestimate 0.25 mg [7 blue tablets]

Day 22 to 28: 7 green inactive tablets (28s)

Tri-Lo-Marzia:

Day 1 to 7: Ethinyl estradiol 0.025 mg and norgestimate 0.18 mg [7 white tablets]

Day 8 to 14: Ethinyl estradiol 0.025 mg and norgestimate 0.215 mg [7 light yellow tablets]
Day 15 to 21: Ethinyl estradiol 0.025 mg and norgestimate 0.25 mg [7 yellow tablets]
Day 22 to 28: 7 green inactive tablets (28s)
Tri-Lo-Sprintec:
Day 1 to 7: Ethinyl estradiol 0.025 mg and norgestimate 0.18 mg [7 gray tablets]
Day 8 to 14: Ethinyl estradiol 0.025 mg and norgestimate 0.215 mg [7 light blue tablets]
Day 15 to 21: Ethinyl estradiol 0.025 mg and norgestimate 0.25 mg [7 blue tablets]
Day 22 to 28: 7 white inactive tablets (28s)
Tri-Previfem::
Day 1-7: Ethinyl estradiol 0.035 mg and norgestimate 0.18 mg [7 white tablets]
Day 8-14: Ethinyl estradiol 0.035 mg and norgestimate 0.215 mg [7 light blue tablets]
Day 15-21: Ethinyl estradiol 0.035 mg and norgestimate 0.25 mg [7 blue tablets]
Day 22-28: 7 light green inactive tablets (28s)
Tri-Sprintec:
Day 1-7: Ethinyl estradiol 0.035 mg and norgestimate 0.18 mg [7 gray tablets]
Day 8-14: Ethinyl estradiol 0.035 mg and norgestimate 0.215 mg [7 light blue tablets]
Day 15-21: Ethinyl estradiol 0.035 mg and norgestimate 0.25 mg [7 blue tablets]
Day 22-28: 7 white inactive tablets (28s)
TriNessa:
Day 1-7: Ethinyl estradiol 0.035 mg and norgestimate 0.18 mg [7 white tablets]
Day 8-14: Ethinyl estradiol 0.035 mg and norgestimate 0.215 mg [7 light blue tablets]
Day 15-21: Ethinyl estradiol 0.035 mg and norgestimate 0.25 mg [7 blue tablets]
Day 22-28: 7 dark green inactive tablets (28s)
TriNessa Lo:
Day 1 to 7: Ethinyl estradiol 0.025 mg and norgestimate 0.18 mg [7 white tablets]
Day 8 to 14: Ethinyl estradiol 0.025 mg and norgestimate 0.215 mg [7 light blue tablets]
Day 15 to 21: Ethinyl estradiol 0.025 mg and norgestimate 0.25 mg [7 blue tablets]
Day 22 to 28: 7 dark green inactive tablets (28s)

Dental Comment Current hormone contraceptives should not be considered a risk factor for gingival or periodontal disease (Preshaw, 2013).

Ethinyl Estradiol and Norgestrel

(ETH in il es tra DYE ole & nor JES trel)

Related Information
Endocrine Disorders and Pregnancy *on page 1781*

Brand Names: US Cryselle 28; Elinest; Low-Ogestrel; Ogestrel

Generic Availability (US) Yes

Pharmacologic Category Contraceptive; Estrogen and Progestin Combination

Use Contraception: Prevention of pregnancy

Local Anesthetic/Vasoconstrictor Precautions
No information available to require special precautions

Effects on Dental Treatment When prescribing antibiotics, patient must be warned to use additional methods of birth control if on oral contraceptives.

Effects on Bleeding No information available to require special precautions

Adverse Reactions Frequency not defined.

Cardiovascular: Arterial thromboembolism, Budd-Chiari syndrome, cerebral thrombosis, cerebrovascular accident, edema, hypertension, local thrombophlebitis, mesenteric thrombosis, myocardial infarction, pulmonary thromboembolism, retinal thrombosis

Central nervous system: Cerebral hemorrhage, depression, dizziness, headache, migraine, nervousness

Dermatologic: Acne vulgaris, allergic skin rash, chloasma (may persist), erythema multiforme, erythema nodosum, loss of scalp hair

Endocrine & metabolic: Amenorrhea, change in libido, decreased glucose tolerance, decreased serum folate level, hirsutism, increased serum triglycerides, increased sex hormone binding globulin, increased thyroxine binding globulin, menstrual disease (flow changes), porphyria, premenstrual syndrome, weight gain, weight loss

Gastrointestinal: Abdominal cramps, bloating, carbohydrate intolerance, change in appetite, cholestasis, colitis, gallbladder disease, nausea, vomiting

Genitourinary: Breakthrough bleeding, breast hypertrophy, breast secretion, breast tenderness, change in cervical erosion, change in cervical secretions, cystitis-like syndrome, decreased lactation (postpartum), spotting, transient infertility (following discontinuation), vaginitis, vulvovaginal candidiasis

Hematologic & oncologic: Decreased antithrombin III plasma level, hemolytic-uremic syndrome, hemorrhagic eruption, increased clotting factor VII, increased clotting factor VIII, increased clotting factor IX, increased clotting factor X, increased norepinephrine induced platelet aggregation, prolonged prothrombin time

Hepatic: Cholestatic jaundice, hepatic adenoma, hepatic neoplasm (benign), jaundice

Ophthalmic: Cataract, change in corneal curvature (steepening), contact lens intolerance, optic neuritis

Renal: Renal insufficiency

Dosing

Adult

Females: Contraception: Oral: 1 tablet once daily

Schedule 1 (Sunday starter): Dose begins on first Sunday after onset of menstruation; if the menstrual period starts on Sunday, take first tablet that very same day. **With a Sunday start, an additional method of contraception should be used until after the first 7 days of consecutive administration.**

Schedule 2 (Day 1 starter): Dose starts on first day of menstrual cycle taking 1 tablet daily.

Missed or late doses (CDC, 2013):

If one dose is late (<24 hours since dose should have been taken) or if one dose is missed (24 to <48 hours since dose should have been taken): Take dose as soon as possible. Continue remaining doses at the usual time (even if that means 2 doses on the same day).

If ≥2 consecutive doses are missed (≥48 hours since dose should have been taken): Take the most recently missed dose as soon as possible, discard any other missed doses. Continue remaining doses at the usual time (even if that means taking 2 doses on the same day); use back-up contraception until hormonal pills have been taken for 7 consecutive days. If doses were missed during the last week of hormonal (active) tablets (eg, days 15 to 21 of a 28 day pack), omit the hormone free interval by finishing the current pack and starting a new pack. If unable to start a new pack immediately, back up contraception is needed until hormonal pills from a new pack have been taken for 7 consecutive days. Consider use of emergency contraception in some situations (refer to guidelines for details).

Also refer to package insert for product specific information.

Females: Emergency contraception: (off-label use; Federal Register, 1997): Oral:

Ethinyl estradiol 0.03 mg and norgestrel 0.3 mg formulation: 4 tablets within 72 hours of unprotected intercourse followed by 4 additional tablets 12 hours after first dose

Ethinyl estradiol 0.05 mg and norgestrel 0.5 mg formulation: 2 tablets within 72 hours of unprotected intercourse followed by 2 additional tablets 12 hours after first dose

Pediatric Females: Contraception or emergency contraception: Oral: See adult dosing; not to be used prior to menarche.

Renal Impairment There are no dosage adjustments provided in the manufacturer's labeling (has not been studied); use with caution and monitor blood pressure closely.

Hepatic Impairment Use is contraindicated in patients with hepatic impairment.

Mechanism of Action Combination hormonal contraceptives inhibit ovulation via a negative feedback mechanism on the hypothalamus, which alters the normal pattern of gonadotropin secretion of a follicle-stimulating hormone (FSH) and luteinizing hormone by the anterior pituitary. The follicular phase FSH and midcycle surge of gonadotropins are inhibited. In addition, combination hormonal contraceptives produce alterations in the genital tract, including changes in the cervical mucus, rendering it unfavorable for sperm penetration even if ovulation occurs. Changes in the endometrium may also occur, producing an unfavorable environment for nidation. Combination hormonal contraceptive drugs may alter the tubal transport of the ova through the fallopian tubes. Progestational agents may also alter sperm fertility.

Contraindications Hypersensitivity to ethinyl estradiol, norgestrel, or any component of the formulation; breast cancer or other estrogen- or progestin-dependent neoplasms (current or a history of), including endometrial cancer, hepatic tumors (benign or malignant) or hepatic disease, pregnancy, undiagnosed abnormal uterine bleeding, cholestatic jaundice of pregnancy, jaundice with prior combination hormonal contraceptive use

Use is also contraindicated in women at high risk of arterial or venous thrombotic diseases, for example, women with: Cerebrovascular disease, coronary artery disease, diabetes mellitus with vascular disease, DVT or PE (current or history of), hypercoagulopathies (inherited or acquired), hypertension (uncontrolled), headaches with focal neurological symptoms, migraine headaches with aura or migraine headaches if >35 years of age, thrombogenic valvular or rhythm diseases of the heart (eg, subacute bacterial endocarditis with valvular disease or atrial fibrillation), women >35 years of age who smoke.

Documentation of allergenic cross-reactivity for estrogens and progestins is limited. However, because of similarities in chemical structure and/or pharmacologic actions, the possibility of cross-sensitivity cannot be ruled out with certainty.

Warnings/Precautions

[US Boxed Warning]: The risk of cardiovascular side effects is increased in women who smoke cigarettes; risk increases with age (especially women >35 years of age) and the number of cigarettes smoked; women who use combination hormonal contraceptives should be strongly advised not to smoke.

The use of combination hormonal contraceptives has not been shown to increase the risk for breast cancer. However, breast cancer is a hormonal sensitive tumor and the prognosis for women with a current or recent history of breast cancer may be worse with combination hormonal contraceptive use (CDC, 2010). Use is contraindicated in women with (or history of) breast cancer. The use of combination hormonal contraceptives has been associated with a slight increased risk of cervical cancer; however, studies are not consistent and may be related to additional risk factors (Gierisch, 2013). Women awaiting treatment for cervical cancer may use combination hormonal contraceptives (CDC, 2013). The risk of ovarian cancer is decreased in women using combination hormonal contraceptives (CDC, 2013; Walker, 2015). Oral contraceptives may be used to reduce the risk of ovarian cancer including those women with BRACA1 and BRACA2 mutations (Walker, 2015).

The risk of hypertension may be increased with age, dose, and duration of use. Combination hormonal contraceptives should not be used in women with persistent blood pressure values ≥160 mm Hg systolic or ≥100 mm Hg diastolic. Women with less severe hypertension (140 to 159 mm Hg systolic or 90 to 99 mm Hg diastolic) or those with hypertension that is adequately controlled should generally not use combination hormonal contraceptives (CDC, 2013). Other risk factors for cardiovascular disease (eg, older age, smoking, diabetes) should be considered when prescribing contraceptives (CDC, 2010). Use with caution in patients with risk factors for cardiovascular disease (eg, hypertension, hypercholesterolemia, morbid obesity, diabetes, or women who smoke) (CDC, 2010); use of combination hormonal contraceptives may increase the risk of arterial or venous thrombotic events. Use is contraindicated in women at high risk of arterial or venous thrombotic diseases. May increase the risk of thromboembolism; discontinue use of combination hormonal contraceptives if an arterial or venous thrombotic event occurs. Women with inherited thrombophilias (eg, protein C or S deficiency) may have increased risk of venous thromboembolism (DeSancho, 2010; van Vlijmen, 2011).

Combination hormonal contraceptives may adversely affect lipid levels, including serum triglycerides. The type of lipid disorder, the severity, and the presence of other cardiovascular risk factors should be considered when prescribing combination hormonal contraceptives to women with lipid disorders (CDC, 2010). Women with hypertriglyceridemia or a family history of hypertriglyceridemia may be at increased risk of pancreatitis when using combination hormonal contraceptives. Consider alternative contraception for women with uncontrolled dyslipidemia. Risk of cholestasis may be increased with previous cholestasis of pregnancy or cholestasis with prior oral contraceptive use. Use is contraindicated with use with cholestatic jaundice or jaundice of pregnancy. May have a risk of gallbladder disease; may worsen existing gallbladder disease. The use of estrogens and/or progestins may change the results of some laboratory tests (eg, coagulation factors, lipids, glucose tolerance, binding proteins). The dose, route, and the specific estrogen/progestin influences these changes. In addition, personal risk factors (eg, cardiovascular disease, smoking, diabetes, age) also contribute to adverse events; use of specific products may be contraindicated in women with certain risk factors.

Combination hormonal contraceptives may be poorly metabolized in women with hepatic impairment. Discontinue if jaundice develops during therapy or if liver function becomes abnormal. Use is contraindicated in women with hepatic disease. Use of combination hormonal contraceptives is associated with hepatic adenomas (rare); rupture may cause fatal intra-abdominal hemorrhage. Long term use may be associated with an increased risk of hepatocellular carcinoma (rare).

Evaluate new, recurrent, severe or persistent headaches. Use in patients with migraine headaches with aura, or migraine headaches of any type if >35 years of age is contraindicated. Estrogens may induce or exacerbate symptoms in women with hereditary angioedema (Geng, 2013; Zuraw, 2013). Oral contraceptives may impair glucose tolerance; use caution in women with diabetes or prediabetes. Use with caution in patients with a history of depression; discontinue if serious depression recurs. Discontinue if unexplained loss of vision, proptosis, diplopia, papilledema, or retinal vascular lesions occur and immediately evaluate for retinal vein thrombosis. Combination hormonal contraceptives, as well as sun exposure and pregnancy, are triggers for chloasma. Women with a susceptibility to chloasma or additional risk factors should avoid exposure to sun or ultraviolet radiation during therapy (Handel, 2014).

Breakthrough or intracyclic bleeding and spotting may occur, especially during the first 3 months of therapy. In addition, occasional missed periods may occur. Presentation of irregular, unresolving vaginal bleeding warrants further evaluation to rule out malignancy or pregnancy. Amenorrhea or oligomenorrhea may occur after discontinuing combination hormonal contraceptives, especially when such a condition was preexistent. When initiating a combination oral contraceptive, consideration should be given to safety, effectiveness, availability and acceptance to the patient (CDC, 2013). Consider initiating with a monthly bleeding monophasic formulation containing ethinyl estradiol 30 to 35 mcg plus a progestin, and adjusting based on adverse events and patient preference (Ott, 2014).

Potentially significant interactions may exist, requiring dose or frequency adjustment, additional monitoring, and/or selection of alternative therapy. Estrogens may increase thyroid-binding globulin (TBG) levels leading to increased circulating total thyroid hormone levels. Women on thyroid replacement therapy may require higher doses of thyroid hormone while receiving estrogens. Combination hormonal contraceptives do not protect against HIV infection or other sexually-transmitted diseases (CDC, 2010; CDC, 2013). Not for use prior to menarche. Whenever possible, should be discontinued at least 4 weeks prior to and for 2 weeks following elective surgery associated with an increased risk of thromboembolism or during periods of prolonged immobilization.

Drug Interactions

Metabolism/Transport Effects Refer to individual components.

Avoid Concomitant Use

Avoid concomitant use of Ethinyl Estradiol and Norgestrel with any of the following: Amodiaquine; Anastrozole; Antihepaciviral Combination Products; Dasabuvir; Dehydroepiandrosterone; Exemestane; Griseofulvin; Hemin; Indium 111 Capromab Pendetide; Ixazomib; Ospemifene; TiZANidine; Tranexamic Acid; Ulipristal

Increased Effect/Toxicity

Ethinyl Estradiol and Norgestrel may increase the levels/effects of: Agomelatine; Ajmaline; Amodiaquine; Anthrax Immune Globulin (Human); Antihepaciviral Combination Products; C1 inhibitors; CloZAPine; Corticosteroids (Systemic); CYP1A2 Substrates; Dantrolene; Dasabuvir; Flibanserin; Immune Globulin; Lenalidomide; Lomitapide; Ospemifene; Pirfenidone; Pomalidomide; ROPINIRole; Selegiline; Thalidomide; Theophylline Derivatives; Tipranavir; TiZANidine; Tranexamic Acid; Voriconazole

The levels/effects of Ethinyl Estradiol and Norgestrel may be increased by: Ascorbic Acid; Atazanavir; Boceprevir; Carfilzomib; Cobicistat; Dehydroepiandrosterone; Herbs (Estrogenic Properties); Herbs (Progestogenic Properties); Lopinavir; Metreleptin; MiFEPRIStone; NSAID (COX-2 Inhibitor); Pomalidomide; Tipranavir; Voriconazole

Decreased Effect

Ethinyl Estradiol and Norgestrel may decrease the levels/effects of: Anastrozole; Anticoagulants; Antidiabetic Agents; Chenodiol; Exemestane; Fosamprenavir; Hemin; Hyaluronidase; Indium 111 Capromab Pendetide; LamoTRIgine; Ospemifene; Thyroid Products; Ulipristal; Ursodiol; Valproate Products; Vitamin K Antagonists

The levels/effects of Ethinyl Estradiol and Norgestrel may be decreased by: Acitretin; Aprepitant; Armodafinil; Artemether; Asunaprevir; Barbiturates; Bexarotene (Systemic); Bile Acid Sequestrants; Boceprevir; Bosentan; CarBAMazepine; CloBAZam; Cobicistat; Colesevelam; CYP3A4 Inducers (Moderate); CYP3A4 Inducers (Strong); Dabrafenib; Darunavir; Deferasirox; Efavirenz; Elvitegravir; Enzalutamide; Eslicarbazepine; Exenatide; Felbamate; Fosamprenavir; Fosaprepitant; Fosphenytoin; Griseofulvin; Ixazomib; Lesinurad; Lixisenatide; Lopinavir; Lumacaftor; Metreleptin; MiFEPRIStone; Mitotane; Modafinil; Mycophenolate; Nafcillin; Nelfinavir; Nevirapine; OXcarbazepine; Perampanel; Phenytoin; Primidone; Protease Inhibitors; Prucalopride; Retinoic Acid Derivatives; Rifamycin Derivatives; Rufinamide; Saquinavir; Siltuximab; St John's Wort; Sugammadex; Telaprevir; Tipranavir; Tocilizumab; Topiramate; Ulipristal

Pregnancy Risk Factor X

Pregnancy Considerations Pregnancy status should be evaluated prior to prescribing (CDC 2013); treatment should be discontinued if pregnancy occurs. In general, the use of combination hormonal contraceptives, when inadvertently used early in pregnancy, have not been associated with teratogenic effects. Available evidence is inconsistent if BMI alters the efficacy of combination oral contraceptives (CDC 2010).

Due to increased risk of venous thromboembolism (VTE) postpartum, combination hormonal contraceptives should not be started in any woman <21 days following delivery. Women without risk factors for VTE and who are not breastfeeding may start combination hormonal contraceptives during 21 to 42 days postpartum. After 42 days postpartum, restrictions for use are not related to postpartum status and should be based on other medical conditions (CDC 2011). The manufacturer states that combination hormonal contraceptives should not be started until ≥4 to 6 weeks after delivery in women who choose not to breast-feed.

When used for emergency contraception, a barrier contraceptive is recommended immediately following use. Any regular (nonemergency) contraceptive method can be started immediately after levonorgestrel; however, a barrier method (or abstinence from sexual intercourse) is also needed for 7 days (ACOG 2015; CDC 2013). Due to the increased risk of side effects (nausea, vomiting) and increased effectiveness and availability of other preparations (eg, levonorgestrel), agents other than ethinyl estradiol/norgestrel are preferred for use as an emergency contraceptive (AAP 2012; ACOG 2015).

Breastfeeding Considerations Contraceptive steroids can be detected in breast milk. Jaundice and breast enlargement in the nursing infant have been reported following the use of combination hormonal contraceptives. May decrease the quality and quantity of breast milk; a nonhormonal form of contraception is recommended (per manufacturer). The theoretical concerns about decreased milk production are greatest early in the postpartum period when milk production is being established. Postpartum risk status for VTE should be considered when initiating combination hormonal contraceptives after delivery. Combined hormonal contraceptives should not be started <21 days postpartum due to increased risk of VTE. Risk of VTE is still elevated in breastfeeding women until ~42 days postpartum and is greater in women with additional risk factors. After 42 days postpartum, restrictions for use are not related to postpartum VTE risk and should be based on other medical conditions (CDC 2011).

Dosage Forms

Tablet, oral [monophasic formulation]: Ethinyl estradiol 0.03 mg and norgestrel 0.3 mg [21 tablets and 7 inactive tablets] (28s)

Cryselle 28: Ethinyl estradiol 0.03 mg and norgestrel 0.3 mg [21 white tablets and 7 light green inactive tablets] (28s)

Elinest: Ethinyl estradiol 0.03 mg and norgestrel 0.3 mg [21 pale pink tablets and 7 white inactive tablets] (28s)

Low-Ogestrel: Ethinyl estradiol 0.03 mg and norgestrel 0.3 mg [21 white tablets and 7 peach inactive tablets] (28s)

Ogestrel: Ethinyl estradiol 0.05 mg and norgestrel 0.5 mg [21 white tablets and 7 peach inactive tablets] (28s)

Dental Comment Current hormone contraceptives should not be considered a risk factor for gingival or periodontal disease (Preshaw, 2013).

Ethinyl Estradiol, Drospirenone, and Levomefolate

(ETH in il es tra DYE ole, droh SPYE re none, & lee voe me FOE late)

Related Information

Endocrine Disorders and Pregnancy *on page 1781*

Brand Names: US Beyaz; Rajani; Safyral

Brand Names: Canada Yaz Plus

Pharmacologic Category Contraceptive; Estrogen and Progestin Combination

Use Prevention of pregnancy; treatment of premenstrual dysphoric disorder (PMDD); treatment of acne; folate supplementation

Local Anesthetic/Vasoconstrictor Precautions No information available to require special precautions

Effects on Dental Treatment When prescribing antibiotics, patient must be warned to use additional methods of birth control if on oral contraceptives.

Effects on Bleeding No information available to require special precautions

Adverse Reactions Frequency not always defined. Percentages reported with Beyaz. For additional adverse events and postmarketing reports, refer to the Ethinyl Estradiol and Drospirenone (Yasmin, Yaz) monograph.

Central nervous system: Headache (≤6% to 13%), migraine (≤6% to 13%), fatigue (4%), irritability (3%), emotional lability (2%)

Endocrine & metabolic: Menstrual disease (4% to 25%, including menorrhagia, spotting, uterine hemorrhage, vaginal hemorrhage), decreased libido (3%), weight gain (3%)

Gastrointestinal: Nausea (≤4% to 16%), vomiting (≤4% to 16%)

Genitourinary: Breast tenderness (≤3% to 11%), mastalgia (≤3% to 11%), cervical carcinoma (stage 0), cervical dysplasia

Dosing

Adult

Acne, PMDD: Oral: Females: (Beyaz): Refer to dosing for contraception

Contraception: Oral: Females: (Beyaz, Safyral): Dosage is 1 tablet daily

Beyaz: One pink tablet daily for 24 consecutive days, then one light orange tablet daily on days 25-28

Safyral: One orange tablet daily for 21 consecutive days, then one light orange tablet daily on days 22-28

Dose should be taken at the same time each day, either after the evening meal or at bedtime. Dosing may be started on the first day of menstrual period (Day 1 starter) or on the first Sunday after the onset of the menstrual period (Sunday starter).

Day 1 starter: Dose starts on first day of menstrual cycle taking 1 tablet daily. If first dose is taken later than the first day of the menstrual cycle, **an additional method of contraception should be used until after the first 7 days of consecutive administration.**

Sunday starter: Dose begins on first Sunday after onset of menstruation; if the menstrual period starts on Sunday, take first tablet that very same day. **With a Sunday start, an additional method of contraception should be used until after the first 7 days of consecutive administration.**

Switching from a different contraceptive:

Oral contraceptive: Start on the same day that a new pack of the previous oral contraceptive would have been taken

Transdermal patch, vaginal ring, injection: Start on the day the next dose would have been due

IUD or implant: Start on the day of removal

Use after childbirth (in women who are not breastfeeding) or after second trimester abortion: Therapy may be started ≥4 weeks postpartum. Pregnancy should be ruled out prior to treatment if menstrual periods have not restarted and an additional method of contraception (nonhormonal) should be used until after the first 7 days of consecutive administration.

Missed doses:

If all doses have been taken on schedule and one menstrual period is missed, continue dosing cycle. If two consecutive menstrual periods are missed, rule out pregnancy and discontinue if pregnancy is confirmed.

If doses have been missed during the first 3 weeks or if active tablets (pink tablets) were started later than as directed and the menstrual period is missed, pregnancy should be ruled out prior to continuing treatment.

Missed doses (monophasic formulations) (refer to package insert for complete information):

One dose missed: Take as soon as remembered or take 2 tablets next day

Two consecutive doses missed in the first 2 weeks: Take 2 tablets as soon as remembered or 2 tablets next 2 days. **An additional method of contraception should be used for 7 days after missed dose.**

Two consecutive doses missed in week 3 or three consecutive doses missed at any time: **An additional method of contraception must be used for 7 days after a missed dose.**

Day 1 starter: Current pack should be discarded, and a new pack should be started that same day.

Sunday starter: Continue dose of 1 tablet daily until Sunday, then discard the rest of the pack, and a new pack should be started that same day.

Any number of doses missed in week 4: Throw away the pills that were missed. Continue taking one pill each day until pack is empty; no back-up method of contraception is needed

Pediatric

Acne: Females: Children ≥14 years: Oral: Refer to adult dosing.

Contraception, PMDD: Females: Oral: Refer to adult dosing; not to be used prior to menarche.

Renal Impairment Contraindicated in patients with renal dysfunction.

Hepatic Impairment Contraindicated in patients with hepatic disease. Exposure to drospirenone is ~3 times higher with moderate liver impairment; information not available for severe impairment.

Mechanism of Action Combination oral contraceptives inhibit ovulation via a negative feedback mechanism on the hypothalamus, which alters the normal pattern of gonadotropin secretion of a follicle-stimulating hormone (FSH) and luteinizing hormone by the anterior pituitary. The follicular phase FSH and midcycle surge of gonadotropins are inhibited. In addition, oral contraceptives produce alterations in the genital tract, including changes in the cervical mucus, rendering it unfavorable for sperm penetration even if ovulation occurs. Changes in the endometrium may also occur, producing an unfavorable environment for nidation. Oral contraceptive drugs may alter the tubal transport of the ova through the fallopian tubes. Progestational agents may also alter sperm fertility. Drospirenone is a spironolactone analogue with antimineralocorticoid and antiandrogenic activity.

Contraindications Adrenal insufficiency, breast cancer or other estrogen- or progestin-dependent neoplasms (current or a history of), hepatic tumors or disease, pregnancy, renal impairment, undiagnosed abnormal uterine bleeding. Use is also contraindicated in women at high risk of arterial or venous thrombotic diseases including: Cerebrovascular disease, coronary artery disease, diabetes mellitus with vascular disease, DVT or PE (current or history of), hypercoagulopathies (inherited or acquired), headaches with focal neurological symptoms, hypertension (uncontrolled), migraine headaches if >35 years of age, thrombogenic valvular or rhythm diseases of the heart (eg, subacute bacterial endocarditis with valvular disease or atrial fibrillation), women >35 years of age who smoke.

Warnings/Precautions

[US Boxed Warning]: The risk of cardiovascular side effects is increased in women who smoke cigarettes; risk increases with age (especially women >35 years of age) and the number of cigarettes smoked; women who use combination hormonal contraceptives should be strongly advised not to smoke. Use is contraindicated in patients >35 years of age who smoke. Use with caution in patients with risk factors for coronary artery disease (eg, hypertension, hypercholesterolemia, morbid obesity, diabetes, or women who smoke); may lead to increased risk of myocardial infarction or stroke. May have a dose-related risk of vascular disease and hypertension; women with hypertension should be encouraged to use another form of contraception. Monitor women with well-controlled hypertension and discontinue if blood pressure rises significantly. Use is contraindicated with uncontrolled hypertension or hypertension with vascular disease. Contraceptives may increase the risk of thromboembolism. Discontinue if an arterial or deep venous thrombotic event occurs. Risk may be greater with contraceptives containing drospirenone. Women with inherited thrombophilias (eg, protein C or S deficiency) may have increased risk of venous thromboembolism (DoSancho, 2010; van Vlijmen, 2011). Use is contraindicated in women with hypercoagulopathies (inherited or acquired). Estrogens may induce or exacerbate symptoms of angioedema in women with hereditary angioedema.

Steroid hormones are poorly metabolized in patients with hepatic dysfunction. Discontinue if jaundice develops or if acute or chronic hepatic disturbances occur. Use is contraindicated with hepatic disease. Cholestasis may occur in women with a history of pregnancy related or previous oral contraceptive related cholestasis. Drospirenone has antimineralocorticoid activity that may lead to hyperkalemia in patients with renal insufficiency, hepatic dysfunction, or adrenal insufficiency; use caution with medications that may increase serum potassium. Combination hormonal contraceptives may affect serum triglyceride and lipoprotein levels. Estrogen compounds are generally associated with lipid effects such as increased HDL-cholesterol and decreased LDL-cholesterol. Progestins may be associated with decreased HDL-cholesterol. Triglycerides may also be increased; use with caution in patients with familial defects of lipoprotein metabolism. Combination hormonal contraceptives may have adverse effects on glucose tolerance; use caution in women with diabetes. Use may have a dose-related risk of gallbladder disease. Estrogens may increase thyroid-binding globulin (TBG) levels leading to increased circulating total thyroid hormone levels. Women on thyroid replacement therapy may require higher doses of thyroid hormone while receiving estrogens.

The use of combination hormonal contraceptives has been associated with a slight increase in frequency of breast cancer; however, studies are not consistent. Use is contraindicated in women with breast cancer (current or history of). Extremely rare adenomas and focal nodular hyperplasia resulting in fatal intra-abdominal hemorrhage have been reported in association with long-term oral contraceptive use. Presentation of an abdominal mass, acute abdominal pain, or intra-abdominal bleeding warrants further evaluation to rule out source.

Estrogens may cause retinal vascular thrombosis; discontinue if migraine, loss of vision, proptosis, diplopia or other visual disturbances occur; discontinue permanently if papilledema or retinal vascular lesions are observed on examination. Use with caution in patients with a history of migraine. Evaluate new, recurrent, severe, or persistent headaches. Use is contraindicated in women with headaches with focal neurological symptoms or migraine headaches if >35 years of age. Use with caution in patients with diseases which may be exacerbated by fluid retention, including asthma, epilepsy, diabetes or renal dysfunction; use with caution in patients with depression. Use caution with a history of chloasma gravidarum; women with a tendency to chloasma should avoid sun and ultraviolet radiation exposure during therapy.

Unscheduled bleeding/spotting may occur within the first 3 months of use. Presentation of irregular, unresolving vaginal bleeding following previously regular cycles warrants further evaluation including endometrial sampling, if indicated, to rule out malignancy. Inform patients that oral contraceptives do not protect against HIV infection or other sexually-transmitted diseases. The minimum dosage combination of estrogen/progestin that will effectively treat the individual patient should be used. Not for use prior to menarche. Whenever possible, should be discontinued at least 4 weeks prior to and for 2 weeks following elective surgery associated with an increased risk of thromboembolism or during periods of prolonged immobilization. The use of estrogens and/or progestins may change the results of some laboratory tests (eg, coagulation factors, lipids, glucose tolerance, binding proteins). Drospirenone also can caused an increase in plasma renin activity and plasma aldosterone. Folates may mask vitamin B12 deficiency. The dose, route, and the specific estrogen/progestin influences these changes. In addition, personal risk factors (eg, cardiovascular disease, smoking, diabetes, age) also contribute to adverse events; use of specific products may be contraindicated in women with certain risk factors.

Acne use: For use only in females ≥14 years of age who have reached menarche, who also desire combination hormonal contraceptive therapy.

PMDD use: For use only in females who desire combination hormonal contraceptive therapy; use for more than 3 menstrual cycles has not been evaluated. Has not been evaluated for the treatment of premenstrual syndrome.

Drug Interactions

Metabolism/Transport Effects Refer to individual components.

Avoid Concomitant Use

Avoid concomitant use of Ethinyl Estradiol, Drospirenone, and Levomefolate with any of the following: Amodiaquine; Anastrozole; Antihepaciviral Combination Products; Boceprevir; Dasabuvir; Dehydroepiandrosterone; Exemestane; Griseofulvin; Hemin; Indium 111 Capromab Pendetide; Ixazomib; Ospemifene; Raltitrexed; TiZANidine; Tranexamic Acid; Ulipristal

Increased Effect/Toxicity

Ethinyl Estradiol, Drospirenone, and Levomefolate may increase the levels/effects of: Agomelatine; Ajmaline; Aliskiren; Amodiaquine; Anthrax Immune Globulin (Human); Antihepaciviral Combination Products; C1 inhibitors; CloZAPine; Corticosteroids (Systemic); CYP1A2 Substrates; Dantrolene; Dasabuvir; Flibanserin; Immune Globulin; Lenalidomide; Lomitapide; Ospemifene; Pirfenidone; Pomalidomide; Potassium-Sparing Diuretics; ROPINIRole; Selegiline; Thalidomide; Theophylline Derivatives; Tipranavir; TiZANidine; Tranexamic Acid; Voriconazole

The levels/effects of Ethinyl Estradiol, Drospirenone, and Levomefolate may be increased by: ACE Inhibitors; Angiotensin II Receptor Blockers; Ascorbic Acid; Atazanavir; Boceprevir; Carfilzomib; Cobicistat; CYP3A4 Inhibitors (Strong); Dehydroepiandrosterone; Herbs (Estrogenic Properties); Herbs (Progestogenic Properties); Lopinavir; Metreleptin; MiFEPRIStone; Nonsteroidal Anti-Inflammatory Agents; Pomalidomide; Tipranavir; Voriconazole

Decreased Effect

Ethinyl Estradiol, Drospirenone, and Levomefolate may decrease the levels/effects of: Anastrozole; Anticoagulants; Antidiabetic Agents; Chenodiol; Exemestane; Fosamprenavir; Hemin; Hyaluronidase; Indium 111 Capromab Pendetide; LamoTRIgine; Ospemifene; Raltitrexed; Thyroid Products; Ulipristal; Ursodiol; Valproate Products; Vitamin K Antagonists

The levels/effects of Ethinyl Estradiol, Drospirenone, and Levomefolate may be decreased by: Acitretin; Aprepitant; Armodafinil; Artemether; Asunaprevir; Barbiturates; Bexarotene (Systemic); Bile Acid Sequestrants; Bosentan; CarBAMazepine; CloBAZam; Cobicistat; Colesevelam; CYP3A4 Inducers (Moderate); CYP3A4 Inducers (Strong); Dabrafenib; Darunavir; Deferasirox; Efavirenz; Elvitegravir; Enzalutamide; Eslicarbazepine; Exenatide; Felbamate; Fosamprenavir; Fosaprepitant; Fosphenytoin; Griseofulvin; Ixazomib; Lesinurad; Lixisenatide; Lopinavir; Lumacaftor; Metreleptin; MiFEPRIStone; Mitotane; Modafinil; Mycophenolate; Nafcillin; Nelfinavir; Nevirapine; OXcarbazepine; Perampanel; Phenytoin; Primidone; Protease Inhibitors; Prucalopride; Retinoic Acid Derivatives; Rifamycin Derivatives; Rufinamide; Saquinavir; Siltuximab; St John's Wort; Sugammadex; Telaprevir; Tipranavir; Tocilizumab; Topiramate; Ulipristal

Dietary Considerations Should be taken at the same time each day; may be taken with or without a meal. Consider other sources of folic acid and ensure supplementation continues once therapy is discontinued. The RDA for folate in women 14–50 years of age is 400 mcg/day of dietary folate equivalents. The USPSTF recommends that all women of reproductive potential should take a supplement containing folic acid 400-800 mcg/day in order to decrease the risk of neural tube defects.

Pharmacodynamics/Kinetics

Half-life Elimination Terminal: Drospirenone: ~31 hours; Ethinyl estradiol: ~24 hours; levomefolate calcium: ~4-5 hours

Time to Peak Drospirenone, ethinyl estradiol: 1-2 hours; Levomefolate calcium: 0.5-1.5 hours

Pregnancy Considerations In general, the use of oral contraceptives when inadvertently taken early in pregnancy have not been associated with teratogenic effects. The addition of levomefolate in this product is intended to decrease the risk of neural tube defects if pregnancy inadvertently occurs during therapy or shortly after discontinuation. Hormonal contraceptives may be less effective in obese patients. An increase in oral contraceptive failure was noted in women with a BMI >27.3 kg/m^2. Similar findings were noted in patients weighing ≥90 kg (198 lb) using the contraceptive patch.

Due to increased risk of venous thromboembolism (VTE) postpartum, combination hormonal contraceptives should not be started in any woman <21 days following delivery. Women without risk factors for VTE and who are not breastfeeding may start combination hormonal contraceptives during 21-42 days postpartum. After 42 days postpartum, restrictions for use are not related to postpartum status and should be based on other medical conditions (CDC, 2011). The manufacturer states that combination hormonal contraceptives should not be started until ≥4 weeks after delivery in women who choose not to breastfeed, or ≥4 weeks after a second trimester abortion or miscarriage.

Breastfeeding Considerations The amount of drospirenone excreted in breast milk is ~0.02%, resulting in a maximum of ~3 mcg/day drospirenone to the infant. Jaundice and breast enlargement in the nursing infant have been reported following the use of other oral contraceptives. In addition, may decrease the quality and quantity of breast milk. Other forms of contraception are recommended while breastfeeding (per manufacturer). The theoretical concerns about decreased milk production are greatest early in the postpartum period when milk production is being established. Postpartum risk status for VTE should be considered when initiating combination hormonal contraceptives after delivery. Combined hormonal contraceptives should not be started <21 days postpartum due to increased risk of VTE. Risk of VTE is still elevated in breastfeeding women until ~42 days postpartum and is greater in women with additional risk factors. After 42 days postpartum, restrictions for use are not related to postpartum VTE risk and should be based on other medical conditions (CDC, 2011).

Dosage Forms

Tablet, oral:

Beyaz: Ethinyl estradiol 0.02 mg, drospirenone 3 mg, and levomefolate calcium 0.451 mg [24 pink tablets] and levomefolate calcium 0.451 mg [4 light orange tablets] (28s)

Rajani: Ethinyl estradiol 0.02 mg, drospirenone 3 mg, and levomefolate calcium 0.451 mg [24 white tablets] and levomefolate calcium 0.451 mg [4 light orange tablets] (28s)

Safyral: Ethinyl estradiol 0.03 mg, drospirenone 3 mg, and levomefolate calcium 0.451 mg [21 orange tablets] and levomefolate calcium 0.451 mg [7 light orange tablets] (28s)

Ethionamide (e thye on AM ide)

Brand Names: US Trecator

Pharmacologic Category Antitubercular Agent

Use Tuberculosis: Treatment of active tuberculosis, in combination with other antituberculosis agents, in patients with *Mycobacterium tuberculosis* resistant to isoniazid or rifampin, or when there is intolerance to other drugs.

Local Anesthetic/Vasoconstrictor Precautions No information available to require special precautions

Effects on Dental Treatment Key adverse event(s) related to dental treatment: Metallic taste and stomatitis; Patients may experience orthostatic hypotension as they stand up after treatment; especially if lying in dental chair for extended periods of time. Use caution with sudden changes in position during and after dental treatment.

Effects on Bleeding No information available to require special precautions

Adverse Reactions Frequency not defined.

Cardiovascular: Orthostatic hypotension

Central nervous system: Altered sense of smell, depression, dizziness, drowsiness, headache, metallic taste, peripheral neuritis, psychiatric disturbance, restlessness, seizure

Dermatologic: Acne vulgaris, alopecia, purpura, skin photosensitivity, skin rash

Endocrine & metabolic: Goiter, gynecomastia, hypoglycemia, hypothyroidism, menstrual disease, pellagra (pellagra-like syndrome), weight loss

Gastrointestinal: Abdominal pain, anorexia, diarrhea, sialorrhea, nausea, stomatitis, vomiting

Genitourinary: Impotence

Hematologic & oncologic: Leukopenia, thrombocytopenia

Hepatic: Hepatitis, increased liver enzymes, increased serum bilirubin, jaundice

Hypersensitivity: Hypersensitivity reaction

Neuromuscular & skeletal: Arthralgia

Ophthalmic: Blurred vision, diplopia, optic neuritis

General Dosage Range

Oral:

Children and Adolescents: 10 to 20 mg/kg/day in 2 to 3 divided doses or 15 mg/kg/day as a single daily dose (maximum daily dose: 1,000 mg/day)

Adults: 15 to 20 mg/kg/day in 1 to 4 divided doses (average adult dose: 750 mg; maximum daily dose: 1 g/day)

Mechanism of Action Inhibits peptide synthesis; bacteriostatic

Pharmacodynamics/Kinetics

Half-life Elimination ~2 hours

Time to Peak Serum: ~1 hour

Pregnancy Considerations Ethionamide crosses the placenta. Use during pregnancy is not recommended (Blumberg 2003).

Ethosuximide (eth oh SUKS i mide)

Brand Names: US Zarontin

Brand Names: Canada Zarontin

Pharmacologic Category Anticonvulsant, Succinimide

Use Absence (petit mal) seizures: Management of absence (petit mal) seizures

Local Anesthetic/Vasoconstrictor Precautions No information available to require special precautions

Effects on Dental Treatment No significant effects or complications reported

Effects on Bleeding No information available to require special precautions

Adverse Reactions Frequency not defined.

Central nervous system: Aggressive behavior, ataxia, delusional paranoid disorder, depression (with cases of overt suicidal intentions), disturbed sleep dizziness, drowsiness, euphoria, fatigue, headache, hyperactivity, irritability, lack of concentration, lethargy, night terrors

Dermatologic: Pruritus, skin rash, Stevens-Johnson syndrome, urticaria

Endocrine & metabolic: Hirsutism, increased libido, weight loss

Gastrointestinal: Abdominal pain, anorexia, abdominal cramps, diarrhea, epigastric pain, gastric distress, gingival hyperplasia, hiccups, nausea, swollen tongue, vomiting

Genitourinary: Occult blood in urine, vaginal hemorrhage
Hematologic & oncologic: Agranulocytosis, eosinophilia, leukopenia, pancytopenia
Hypersensitivity: Hypersensitivity reaction
Immunologic: DRESS syndrome (drug rash with eosinophilia and systemic symptoms)
Neuromuscular & skeletal: Systemic lupus erythematosus
Ophthalmic: Myopia

General Dosage Range Oral:

Children 3 to <6 years: Initial: 250 mg/day; maintenance: 20 mg/kg/day; doses >1,500 mg/day, in divided doses, should only be used under the strict supervision of a physician

Children ≥6 years and Adolescents: Initial: 500 mg/day; maintenance: 20 mg/kg/day; doses greater than 1,500 mg/day, in divided doses, should only be used under the strict supervision of a physician

Adults: Initial: 500 mg/day; doses greater than 1,500 mg/day, in divided doses, should only be used under the strict supervision of a physician

Mechanism of Action Increases the seizure threshold and suppresses paroxysmal spike-and-wave pattern in absence seizures; depresses nerve transmission in the motor cortex

Pharmacodynamics/Kinetics

Half-life Elimination Serum: Children: 30 hours; Adults: 50 to 60 hours

Time to Peak Serum: 1 to 7 hours

Pregnancy Considerations Ethosuximide crosses the placenta. Birth defects have been reported in infants. Epilepsy itself, the number of medications, genetic factors, or a combination of these may influence the teratogenicity of anticonvulsant therapy. In general, polytherapy may increase the risk of congenital malformations; monotherapy with the lowest effective dose is recommended (Harden 2009). For women with epilepsy who are planning a pregnancy in advance, baseline serum concentrations should be measured once or twice prior to pregnancy during a period when seizure control is optimal. Monitoring can then be continued up to once a month during pregnancy in women with stable seizure control (Patsalos 2008).

Patients exposed to ethosuximide during pregnancy are encouraged to enroll themselves into the NAAED Pregnancy Registry by calling 1-888-233-2334. Additional information is available at www.-aedpregnancyregistry.org.

Ethotoin (ETH oh toyn)

Brand Names: US Peganone

Pharmacologic Category Anticonvulsant, Hydantoin

Use Seizures: Control of generalized tonic-clonic (grand mal) and complex-partial (psychomotor) seizures

Local Anesthetic/Vasoconstrictor Precautions No information available to require special precautions

Effects on Dental Treatment No significant effects or complications reported

Effects on Bleeding No information available to require special precautions

Adverse Reactions Frequency not defined.

Cardiovascular: Chest pain
Central nervous system: Ataxia, dizziness, fatigue, headache, insomnia, numbness
Dermatologic: Skin rash, Stevens-Johnson syndrome
Gastrointestinal: Diarrhea, gingival hyperplasia, nausea, vomiting
Hematologic & oncologic: Hematologic disease, lymphadenopathy
Neuromuscular & skeletal: Lupus-like syndrome
Ophthalmic: Diplopia, nystagmus
Miscellaneous: Fever

General Dosage Range Oral:

Children ≥1 year and Adolescents: Initial: ≤750 mg/day; usual maintenance: 0.5 to 1 g/day; maximum: 3 g/day

Adults: Initial: ≤1 g/day; usual maintenance: 2 to 3 g/day

Mechanism of Action Stabilizes the seizure threshold and prevents the spread of seizure activity

Pharmacodynamics/Kinetics

Half-life Elimination 3 to 9 hours

Pregnancy Considerations Adverse fetal effects may occur following maternal use of ethotoin. Cleft lip and cleft palate observed with other hydantoins has also been reported following in utero exposure to ethotoin (Zablen 1977). Maternal ingestion of antiepileptic agents has been associated with neonatal coagulation defects/bleeding usually within 24 hours of birth..

Patients exposed to ethotoin during pregnancy are encouraged to enroll themselves into the AED Pregnancy Registry by calling 1-888-233-2334. Additional information is available at www.-aedpregnancyregistry.org.

Etidronate (e ti DROE nate)

Related Information

Osteonecrosis of the Jaw *on page 1796*

Brand Names: Canada ACT Etidronate; Mylan-Etidronate

Pharmacologic Category Bisphosphonate Derivative

Use Symptomatic treatment of Paget's disease; prevention and treatment of heterotopic ossification due to spinal cord injury or after total hip replacement

Local Anesthetic/Vasoconstrictor Precautions No information available to require special precautions

Effects on Dental Treatment Key adverse event(s) related to dental treatment: Abnormal taste.

Osteonecrosis of the jaw (ONJ), generally associated with local infection and/or tooth extraction and often with delayed healing, has been reported in patients taking bisphosphonates. Symptoms included nonhealing extraction socket or an exposed jawbone. Most reported cases of bisphosphonate-associated osteonecrosis have been in cancer patients treated with intravenous bisphosphonates. However, some have occurred in patients with postmenopausal osteoporosis taking oral bisphosphonates. Dental surgery, particularly tooth extraction, may increase the risk for ONJ. Patients who develop ONJ while on bisphosphonate therapy should receive care by an oral surgeon. See Dental Comment.

Effects on Bleeding No information available to require special precautions

Adverse Reactions

Gastrointestinal: Diarrhea (≤30%; dose dependent), nausea (≤30%; dose dependent)
Neuromuscular & skeletal: Ostealgia (10% to 20%; dose dependent)
Postmarketing and/or case reports: Agranulocytosis, alopecia, amnesia, angioedema, arthralgia, arthritis, bone fracture, confusion, depression, erythema multiforme, esophagitis, exacerbation of asthma, exacerbation of peptic ulcer, folliculitis, gastritis, glossitis, glossopyrosis, hallucination, headache, hypersensitivity reaction, leg cramps, leukemia, leukopenia,

maculopapular rash, osteomalacia, osteonecrosis of the jaw, pancytopenia, paresthesia, pruritus, skin rash (macular), Stevens-Johnson syndrome, toxic epidermal necrolysis, urticaria

General Dosage Range Oral: *Adults:* 5-20 mg/kg/day

Mechanism of Action Decreases bone resorption by inhibiting osteocystic osteolysis; decreases mineral release and matrix or collagen breakdown in bone

Pharmacodynamics/Kinetics

Onset of Action 1-3 months

Duration of Action Can persist for 12 months without continuous therapy

Half-life Elimination 1-6 hours

Pregnancy Risk Factor C

Pregnancy Considerations Adverse events were observed in some animal reproduction studies. It is not known if bisphosphonates cross the placenta, but fetal exposure is expected (Djokanovic, 2008; Stathopoulos, 2011). Bisphosphonates are incorporated into the bone matrix and gradually released over time. The amount available in the systemic circulation varies by dose and duration of therapy. Theoretically, there may be a risk of fetal harm when pregnancy follows the completion of therapy; however, available data have not shown that exposure to bisphosphonates during pregnancy significantly increases the risk of adverse fetal events (Djokanovic, 2008; Levy, 2009; Stathopoulos, 2011). Until additional data is available, most sources recommend discontinuing bisphosphonate therapy in women of reproductive potential as early as possible prior to a planned pregnancy; use in premenopausal women should be reserved for special circumstances when rapid bone loss is occurring (Bhalla, 2010; Pereira, 2012; Stathopoulos, 2011). Because hypocalcemia has been described following *in utero* bisphosphonate exposure, exposed infants should be monitored for hypocalcemia after birth (Djokanovic, 2008; Stathopoulos, 2011).

Dental Comment A review of 2,408 published cases of bisphosphonate-associated osteonecrosis of the jaw bone (BP-associated ONJ) was done by Filleul 2010. BP therapy was associated with 89% of the cases to treat malignancies and 11% of the cases to treat nonmalignant conditions. Information on the specific bisphosphonate used was available for 1,694 of the patients. Intravenous therapy (primarily zoledronic acid) was received by 88% of the patients and 12% received oral treatment (primarily alendronate). Of all the cases of BP-associated ONJ, 67% were preceded by tooth extraction and for 26% of patients, there was no predisposing factor identified.

A 2010 retrospective case review reported the prevalence of BP-associated ONJ in patients using alendronate-type drugs was one out of 952 patients or ~0.1% (Lo 2010). Of the 8,572 respondents, nine cases of ONJ were identified; five had developed ONJ spontaneously and four developed ONJ after tooth extraction. When extrapolated to patient-years of bisphosphonate exposure, this prevalence rate of 0.1% equates to a frequency of 28 cases per 100,000 person-years of oral bisphosphonate treatment. An Australian group (Mavrokokki 2007), identified the frequency of BP-associated ONJ in osteoporotic patients, mainly taking weekly oral alendronate, was 1 in 8,470 to 1 in 2,260 (0.01% to 0.04%) patients. If extractions were carried out, the calculated frequency was 1 in 1,130 to 1 in 296 (0.09% to 0.34%) patients. The median time to onset of ONJ in alendronate patients was 24 months.

According to the 2011 report by the American Dental Association (ADA), the incidence of BP-associated ONJ remains low and the benefits of using oral bisphosphonates significantly outweighs the risk of developing BP-associated ONJ for treatment and prevention of osteoporosis and cancer treatment (Hellstein 2011). The full 47-page report can be accessed at http://www.ada.org/~/media/ADA/Member%20Center/FIles/topics_ARONJ_report.ashx.

The ADA review of 2011 stated the incidence of oral BP-associated ONJ was one case for every 1,000 individuals exposed to oral bisphosphonates (0.1%) (Hellstein 2011).

The most comprehensive review to date on osteonecrosis of the jaw bone (ONJ) has been published in the *Journal of Bone and Mineral Research* (Khan 2015), and written by an International Task Force of authors, totaling 34, from academe; industry; clinical medical and dental practice; oral and maxillofacial surgery; bone and mineral research; epidemiology; medical and dental oncology; orthopedic surgery; osteoporosis research; muscle and bone research; endocrinology and diagnostic sciences. The work provides a systematic review of the literature and international consensus on the classification, incidence, pathophysiology, diagnosis, and management of ONJ in both oncology and osteoporosis patient populations. This review of the literature from January 2003 to April 2014, with 299 references, offers recommendations for management of ONJ based on multidisciplinary international consensus.

Prevalence and incidence of ONJ in osteoporosis patients from the Task Force report:

Prevalence – the percent of osteoporotic population affected with ONJ

After reviewing all literature reports on this subject, the Task Force concluded that the prevalence of ONJ in patients prescribed oral BPs for the treatment of osteoporosis ranges from 0% to 0.04% with the majority being below 0.001%. However, the Task Force does cite the study of (Lo et al) that evaluated the Kaiser Permanente database and found the prevalence of ONJ in those receiving BPs for more than 2 years to range from 0.05% to 0.21% and appeared to be related to duration of exposure. As mentioned above, the American Dental Association has previously reported that the prevalence of ONJ in osteoporosis patients using oral BPs to be 1 out of 1,000 or 0.1% (Hellstein 2011).

Incidence - the rate at which ONJ occurs or the number of times it happens

From currently available data, the incidence of ONJ in the osteoporosis patient population appears to be low ranging from 0.15% to less than 0.001% person-years drug exposure. In terms of the osteoporosis patient population taking oral BPs, the incidence ranges from 1.04 to 69 per 100,000 patient years of drug exposure.

Etidronate and Calcium Carbonate

(e ti DROE nate & KAL see um KAR bun ate)

Related Information

Calcium Carbonate *on page* 280

Etidronate *on page* 666

Brand Names: Canada ACT Etidrocal; Didrocal; Etidrocal; Mylan-Eti-Cal Carepac; Novo-Etidronatecal

Pharmacologic Category Bisphosphonate Derivative; Calcium Salt

Use Note: Not approved in the US

Corticosteroid-induced osteoporosis: Prevention of corticosteroid-induced osteoporosis

Postmenopausal osteoporosis: Treatment and prevention of established postmenopausal osteoporosis

Local Anesthetic/Vasoconstrictor Precautions No information available to require special precautions

Effects on Dental Treatment Osteonecrosis of the jaw (ONJ), generally associated with local infection and/or tooth extraction and often with delayed healing, has been reported in patients taking bisphosphonates. Symptoms included nonhealing extraction socket or an exposed jawbone. Most reported cases of bisphosphonate-associated osteonecrosis have been in cancer patients treated with intravenous bisphosphonates. However, some have occurred in patients with postmenopausal osteoporosis taking oral bisphosphonates. Dental surgery, particularly tooth extraction, may increase the risk for ONJ. Patients who develop ONJ while on bisphosphonate therapy should receive care by an oral surgeon. See Dental Comment.

Effects on Bleeding No information available to require special precautions

Adverse Reactions

>10%:

Central nervous system: Dizziness (16%), headache (13%)

Gastrointestinal: Diarrhea (37%), nausea (18%), flatulence (17%), constipation (13%), dyspepsia (12%), vomiting (11%)

<1%, postmarketing, and/or case reports: Agranulocytosis, alopecia, amnesia, angioedema, arthropathy, bone fracture, confusion, depression, diaphyseal femur fractures, erythema multiforme, esophagitis, exacerbation of asthma, exacerbation of peptic ulcer, folliculitis, glossitis, glossopyrosis, hallucination, leukemia (1 in 100,000 patients), leukopenia, maculopapular rash, malignant neoplasm of esophagus, musculoskeletal pain, pancytopenia, paresthesia, Stevens-Johnson syndrome, subtrochanteric fractures (femur), urticaria

General Dosage Range Oral: *Adults:* Etidronate disodium 400 mg once daily for 14 days, followed by calcium carbonate 1250 mg (500 mg elemental calcium) once daily for 76 days

Mechanism of Action See individual agents.

Pregnancy Considerations Adverse events were observed in some animal reproduction studies. Refer to individual agents. According to the manufacturer, this product is not intended for use in pregnant women.

Product Availability Not available in the US

Dental Comment See Etidronate monograph.

Etodolac (ee toe DOE lak)

Related Information

Oral Pain *on page 1830*

Rheumatoid Arthritis, Osteoarthritis, and Osteoporosis *on page 1792*

Temporomandibular Dysfunction (TMD), Chronic Pain, and Fibromyalgia *on page 1868*

Brand Names: US Lodine

Brand Names: Canada Taro-Etodolac

Generic Availability (US) Yes

Pharmacologic Category Analgesic, Nonopioid; Nonsteroidal Anti-inflammatory Drug (NSAID), Oral

Dental Use Management of postoperative pain

Use

Acute pain: Management of acute pain (immediate release only).

Arthritis: Relief of the signs and symptoms of osteoarthritis, rheumatoid arthritis, and juvenile arthritis (ER only).

Local Anesthetic/Vasoconstrictor Precautions No information available to require special precautions

Effects on Dental Treatment The dentist should be aware of the potential of abnormal coagulation. Caution should also be exercised in the use of NSAIDs in patients already on anticoagulant therapy with drugs such as warfarin (Coumadin®). See Effects on Bleeding.

Effects on Bleeding Nonselective NSAIDs such as etodolac inhibit platelet aggregation and prolong bleeding time in some patients. Unlike aspirin, the NSAID effect on platelet function is quantitatively less, of shorter duration, and reversible.

Adverse Reactions

1% to 10%:

Central nervous system: Dizziness (3% to 9%), chills (≤3%), depression (1% to 3%), nervousness (1% to 3%)

Dermatologic: Skin rash (1% to 3%), pruritus (1% to 3%)

Gastrointestinal: Dyspepsia (10%), abdominal cramps (3% to 9%), diarrhea (3% to 9%), flatulence (3% to 9%), nausea (3% to 9%), vomiting (1% to 3%), constipation (1% to 3%), melena (1% to 3%), gastritis (1% to 3%)

Genitourinary: Dysuria (1% to 3%)

Neuromuscular & skeletal: Weakness (3% to 9%)

Ophthalmic: Blurred vision (1% to 3%)

Otic: Tinnitus (1% to 3%)

Renal: Polyuria (1% to 3%)

Miscellaneous: Fever (≤3%)

<1%: Abnormal uterine bleeding, agranulocytosis, alopecia, anaphylactoid reaction, anaphylaxis, anemia, angioedema, anorexia, aphthous stomatitis, aseptic meningitis, asthma, cardiac arrhythmia, cardiac failure, cerebrovascular accident, confusion, conjunctivitis, cystitis, duodenitis, dyspnea, ecchymosis, edema, erythema multiforme, esophagitis (+/- stricture or cardiospasm), exfoliative dermatitis, gastrointestinal ulceration, hallucination, headache, hearing loss, hematemesis, hematuria, hepatic failure, hepatitis, hepatotoxicity (idiosyncratic) (Chalasani, 2014), hyperglycemia (in controlled patients with diabetes), hyperpigmentation, hypersensitivity angiitis, hypersensitivity reaction, hypertension, increased liver function tests, infection, insomnia, interstitial nephritis, jaundice, leukopenia, myocardial infarction, necrotizing angiitis, nephrolithiasis, palpitations, pancreatitis, pancytopenia, paresthesia, peptic ulcer (+/- bleeding/perforation), peripheral neuropathy, photophobia, prolonged bleeding time, pulmonary infiltrates (eosinophilia), rectal bleeding, renal failure, renal insufficiency, shock, skin photosensitivity, Stevens-Johnson syndrome, syncope, thrombocytopenia, toxic epidermal necrolysis, urticaria, vesiculobullous dermatitis, renal papillary necrosis, visual disturbance

Dental Usual Dosage Acute pain: Adults: Oral: Immediate release formulation: 200 to 400 mg every 6 to 8 hours, as needed, not to exceed total daily doses of 1000 mg

Dosing

Adult Note: For chronic conditions, response is usually observed within 1 to 2 weeks.

Acute pain: Oral: Immediate release: 200 to 400 mg every 6 to 8 hours; maximum: 1,000 mg daily.

Osteoarthritis, rheumatoid arthritis: Oral:

Immediate release: 400 mg 2 times daily **or** 300 mg 2 to 3 times daily **or** 500 mg 2 times daily.

Extended release: Initial: 400 to 1,000 mg once daily.

Geriatric Refer to adult dosing, use with caution. The elderly are more sensitive to antiprostaglandin effects and may need dosage adjustments.

Pediatric Note: For chronic conditions, response is usually observed within 1 to 2 weeks.

Juvenile arthritis: Oral: Extended release: Children ≥6 years and Adolescents ≤16 years:

20 to 30 kg: 400 mg once daily

31 to 45 kg: 600 mg once daily

46 to 60 kg: 800 mg once daily

>60 kg: 1,000 mg once daily

Renal Impairment

CrCl >88 mL/minute: No dosage adjustment necessary.

CrCl 37 to 88 mL/minute: No dosage adjustment necessary; however, use with caution.

CrCl <37 mL/minute: There are no specific dosage adjustments provided in the manufacturer's labeling; if use must be initiated, use with caution. Avoid use in patients with advanced renal disease unless benefits are expected to outweigh risk of worsening renal function.

Hemodialysis: Not significantly removed.

KDIGO 2012 guidelines provide the following recommendations for NSAIDs:

eGFR 30 to <60 mL/minute/1.73 m^2: Temporarily discontinue in patients with intercurrent disease that increases risk of acute kidney injury.

eGFR <30 mL/minute/1.73 m^2: Avoid use.

Hepatic Impairment No dosage adjustment necessary. However, reduced doses may be required due to extensive hepatic metabolism.

Mechanism of Action Reversibly inhibits cyclooxygenase-1 and 2 (COX-1 and 2) enzymes, which results in decreased formation of prostaglandin precursors; has antipyretic, analgesic, and anti-inflammatory properties

Other proposed mechanisms not fully elucidated (and possibly contributing to the anti-inflammatory effect to varying degrees), include inhibiting chemotaxis, altering lymphocyte activity, inhibiting neutrophil aggregation/activation, and decreasing proinflammatory cytokine levels.

Contraindications Hypersensitivity to etodolac, or any component of the formulation; history of asthma, urticaria, or allergic-type reactions after taking aspirin or other NSAID agents; use in the setting of coronary artery bypass graft (CABG) surgery.

Warnings/Precautions [US Boxed Warning]: NSAIDs cause an increased risk of serious (and potentially fatal) adverse cardiovascular thrombotic events, including MI and stroke. Risk may occur early during treatment and may increase with duration of use. Relative risk appears to be similar in those with and without known cardiovascular disease or risk factors for cardiovascular disease; however, absolute incidence of serious cardiovascular thrombotic events (which may occur early during treatment) was higher in patients with known cardiovascular disease or risk factors and in those receiving higher doses. New onset hypertension or exacerbation of hypertension may occur (NSAIDs may also impair response to ACE inhibitors, thiazide diuretics, or loop diuretics); may contribute to cardiovascular events; monitor blood pressure; use with caution in patients with hypertension. May cause sodium and fluid retention; use with caution in patients with edema. Avoid use in heart failure (ACCF/AHA [Yancy, 2013]). Avoid use in patients with recent MI unless benefits outweigh risk of cardiovascular thrombotic events. Use the lowest effective dose for the shortest duration of time, consistent with individual patient goals, to reduce risk of cardiovascular events; alternate therapies should be considered for patients at high risk. **[US Boxed Warning]: Use is contraindicated in the setting of coronary artery bypass graft (CABG) surgery.** Risk of MI and stroke may be increased with use following CABG surgery.

[US Boxed Warning]: NSAIDs cause increased risk of serious gastrointestinal inflammation, ulceration, bleeding, and perforation (may be fatal); elderly patients and patients with history of peptic ulcer disease and/or GI bleeding are at greater risk for serious GI events. These events may occur at any time during therapy and without warning. Avoid use in patients with active GI bleeding. Use caution with a history of GI ulcers, concurrent therapy known to increase the risk of GI bleeding (eg, aspirin, anticoagulants and/or corticosteroids, selective serotonin reuptake inhibitors), advanced hepatic disease, coagulopathy, smoking, use of alcohol, or in elderly or debilitated patients. Use the lowest effective dose for the shortest duration of time, consistent with individual patient goals, to reduce risk of GI adverse events; alternate therapies should be considered for patients at high risk. When used concomitantly with aspirin, a substantial increase in the risk of gastrointestinal complications (eg, ulcer) occurs; concomitant gastroprotective therapy (eg, proton pump inhibitors) is recommended (Bhatt, 2008).

Platelet adhesion and aggregation may be decreased; may prolong bleeding time; patients with coagulation disorders or who are receiving anticoagulants should be monitored closely. Anemia may occur; patients on long-term NSAID therapy should be monitored for anemia. Rarely, NSAID use may cause severe blood dyscrasias (eg, agranulocytosis, aplastic anemia, thrombocytopenia). May increase the risk of aseptic meningitis, especially in patients with systemic lupus erythematosus (SLE) and mixed connective tissue disorders.

NSAID use may compromise existing renal function; dose-dependent decreases in prostaglandin synthesis may result from NSAID use, reducing renal blood flow which may cause renal decompensation (usually reversible). Patients with impaired renal function, dehydration, hypovolemia, heart failure, hepatic impairment, those taking diuretics, and ACE inhibitors, and the elderly are at greater risk of renal toxicity. Rehydrate patient before starting therapy; monitor renal function closely. Long-term NSAID use may result in renal papillary necrosis and other renal injury. Avoid use in patients with advanced renal disease unless benefits are expected to outweigh risk of worsening renal function; monitor closely if therapy must be initiated.

Elderly patients are at greater risk for serious GI, cardiovascular, and/or renal events; use with caution.

NSAIDs may cause potentially fatal serious skin adverse events including exfoliative dermatitis, Stevens-Johnson syndrome (SJS), and toxic epidermal necrolysis (TEN); may occur without warning; discontinue use at first sign of skin rash (or any other hypersensitivity). Even in patients without prior exposure anaphylactoid reactions may occur; patients with "aspirin triad" (bronchial asthma, aspirin intolerance, rhinitis) may be at increased risk. Contraindicated in patients who experience bronchospasm, asthma, rhinitis, or urticaria with NSAID or aspirin therapy. Contraindicated in patients with aspirin-sensitive asthma; severe and potentially fatal bronchospasm may occur. Use caution in patients with other forms of asthma.

Transaminase elevations have been reported with use; closely monitor patients with any abnormal LFT. Rare (sometimes fatal) severe hepatic reactions (eg, fulminant hepatitis, hepatic necrosis, hepatic failure) have occurred with NSAID use; discontinue immediately if clinical signs or symptoms of liver disease develop or if systemic manifestations occur. Use with caution in patients with hepatic impairment; reduced doses may be required due to extensive hepatic metabolism. Patients with advanced hepatic disease are at an increased risk of GI bleeding with NSAIDs. NSAIDS may cause drowsiness, dizziness, blurred vision and other neurologic effects which may impair physical or mental abilities; patients must be cautioned about performing tasks which require mental alertness (eg, operating machinery or driving).

Withhold for at least 4 to 6 half-lives prior to surgical or dental procedures. Potentially significant interactions may exist, requiring dose or frequency adjustment, additional monitoring, and/or selection of alternative therapy.

Use of extended release product consisting of a nondeformable matrix should be avoided in patients with stricture/narrowing of the GI tract; symptoms of obstruction have been associated with nondeformable products.

Drug Interactions

Metabolism/Transport Effects None known.

Avoid Concomitant Use

Avoid concomitant use of Etodolac with any of the following: Dexketoprofen; Floctafenine; Ketorolac (Nasal); Ketorolac (Systemic); Morniflumate; NSAID (COX-2 Inhibitor); Omacetaxine; Pelubiprofen; Phenylbutazone; Talniflumate; Tenoxicam; Urokinase; Zaltoprofen

Increased Effect/Toxicity

Etodolac may increase the levels/effects of: 5-ASA Derivatives; Agents with Antiplatelet Properties; Aliskiren; Aminoglycosides; Aminolevulinic Acid; Anticoagulants; Apixaban; Bisphosphonate Derivatives; Cephalothin; Collagenase (Systemic); CycloSPORINE (Systemic); Dabigatran Etexilate; Deferasirox; Deoxycholic Acid; Desmopressin; Digoxin; Drospirenone; Edoxaban; Eplerenone; Haloperidol; Ibritumomab; Lithium; Methotrexate; Nonsteroidal Anti-Inflammatory Agents; NSAID (COX-2 Inhibitor); Obinutuzumab; Omacetaxine; PEMEtrexed; Porfimer; Potassium-Sparing Diuretics; PRALAtrexate; Quinolone Antibiotics; Rivaroxaban; Salicylates; Tacrolimus (Systemic); Tenofovir Products; Thrombolytic Agents; Tolperisone; Tositumomab and Iodine I 131 Tositumomab; Urokinase; Vancomycin; Verteporfin; Vitamin K Antagonists

The levels/effects of Etodolac may be increased by: ACE Inhibitors; Alcohol (Ethyl); Angiotensin II Receptor Blockers; Antidepressants (Tricyclic, Tertiary Amine); Corticosteroids (Systemic); CycloSPORINE (Systemic); Dasatinib; Dexketoprofen; Diclofenac (Systemic); Felbinac; Floctafenine; Glucosamine; Herbs (Anticoagulant/Antiplatelet Properties); Ibrutinib; Ketorolac (Nasal); Ketorolac (Systemic); Limaprost; Loop Diuretics; Morniflumate; Multivitamins/Fluoride (with ADE); Multivitamins/Minerals (with ADEK, Folate, Iron); Multivitamins/Minerals (with AE, No Iron); Naftazone; Omega-3 Fatty Acids; Pelubiprofen; Pentosan Polysulfate Sodium; Pentoxifylline; Phenylbutazone; Probenecid; Prostacyclin Analogues; Selective Serotonin Reuptake Inhibitors; Serotonin/Norepinephrine Reuptake Inhibitors; Sodium Phosphates; Talniflumate; Tenoxicam; Thiazide and Thiazide-Like Diuretics; Tipranavir; Tolperisone; Vitamin E (Systemic); Zaltoprofen

Decreased Effect

Etodolac may decrease the levels/effects of: ACE Inhibitors; Aliskiren; Angiotensin II Receptor Blockers; Beta-Blockers; Eplerenone; HydrALAZINE; Loop Diuretics; Potassium-Sparing Diuretics; Prostaglandins (Ophthalmic); Salicylates; Selective Serotonin Reuptake Inhibitors; Thiazide and Thiazide-Like Diuretics

The levels/effects of Etodolac may be decreased by: Bile Acid Sequestrants; Salicylates

Food Interactions Etodolac peak serum levels may be decreased if taken with food. Management: Administer with food to decrease GI upset.

Pharmacodynamics/Kinetics

Onset of Action Analgesia: Immediate release: ~0.5 hour; Arthritis (chronic management): Typically within 2 weeks; Maximum effect: Analgesia: 1 to 2 hours

Duration of Action Mean range: 4 to 6 hours

Half-life Elimination Terminal:

Immediate release: Children (6 to 16 years, n=11): 6.5 hours (Boni 1999); Adults: 6.4 hours

Extended release: Children (6 to 16 years, n=72): 12 hours; Adults: 8.4 hours

Time to Peak Serum:

Immediate release: Children (6 to 16 years, n=11): 1.4 hours (Boni 1999); Adults: ~1 to 2 hours, increased 1.4 to 3.8 hours with food

Extended release: ~5 to 7 hours

Pregnancy Risk Factor C

Pregnancy Considerations Adverse events have been observed in animal reproduction studies. NSAID exposure during the first trimester is not strongly associated with congenital malformations; however, cardiovascular anomalies and cleft palate have been observed following NSAID exposure in some studies. The use of an NSAID close to conception may be associated with an increased risk of miscarriage. Nonteratogenic effects have been observed following NSAID administration during the third trimester including: Myocardial degenerative changes, prenatal constriction of the ductus arteriosus, fetal tricuspid regurgitation, failure of the ductus arteriosus to close postnatally; renal dysfunction or failure, oligohydramnios; gastrointestinal bleeding or perforation, increased risk of necrotizing enterocolitis; intracranial bleeding (including intraventricular hemorrhage), platelet dysfunction with resultant bleeding; pulmonary hypertension. Because they may cause premature closure of the ductus arteriosus, use of NSAIDs late in pregnancy should be avoided (use after 31 or 32 weeks gestation is not recommended by some clinicians). The chronic use of NSAIDs in women of reproductive age may be associated with infertility that is reversible upon discontinuation of the medication.

Breastfeeding Considerations It is not known if etodolac is excreted in breast milk. Due to the potential for serious adverse reactions in the nursing infant, the manufacturer recommends a decision be made whether to discontinue nursing or to discontinue the drug, taking into account the importance of treatment to the mother.

Dosage Forms

Capsule, Oral:

Generic: 200 mg, 300 mg

Tablet, Oral:

Lodine: 400 mg

Generic: 400 mg, 500 mg

Tablet Extended Release 24 Hour, Oral:

Generic: 400 mg, 500 mg, 600 mg

Dosage Forms: Canada Refer to Dosage Forms. **Note:** Tablets and Extended Release tablets are not available in Canada.

Etomidate (e TOM i date)

Brand Names: US Amidate

Pharmacologic Category General Anesthetic

Use General anesthesia: Induction of general anesthesia; as a supplement to subpotent anesthetic agents during maintenance of anesthesia for short operative procedures (eg, dilation and curettage, cervical conization).

Local Anesthetic/Vasoconstrictor Precautions No information available to require special precautions

Effects on Dental Treatment Key adverse event(s) related to dental treatment: Hiccups.

Effects on Bleeding No information available to require special precautions

Adverse Reactions

>10%:

Central nervous system: Myoclonus (33%)

Endocrine & metabolic: Adrenal suppression

Gastrointestinal: Nausea, vomiting (on emergence from anesthesia)

Local: Pain at injection site (30% to 80%)

Neuromuscular & skeletal: Musculoskeletal disease (transient skeletal movements)

Ophthalmic: Nystagmus

1% to 10%: Gastrointestinal: Hiccups

<1%, postmarketing, and/or case reports: Apnea, bradycardia, cardiac arrhythmia, decreased cortisol (decreased cortisol synthesis), hypertension, hyperventilation, hypotension, hypoventilation, laryngospasm, tachycardia

General Dosage Range

IV:

Children >10 years, Adolescents, and Adults: Induction: 0.3 mg/kg (range: 0.2 to 0.6 mg/kg)

Adults: Supplementation to subpotent anesthetic agents: Administer smaller increments during short operative procedures to supplement subpotent anesthetic agents, such as nitrous oxide; individualize dosage (usually smaller than the original induction dose).

Mechanism of Action Ultrashort-acting nonbarbiturate hypnotic (benzylimidazole) used for rapid induction of anesthesia with minimal cardiovascular effects; produces EEG burst suppression at high doses

Pharmacodynamics/Kinetics

Onset of Action 30 to 60 seconds; Peak effect: 1 minute

Duration of Action Dose dependent: 2-3 minutes (0.15 mg/kg dose); 4-10 minutes (0.3 mg/kg dose); rapid recovery is due to rapid redistribution

Half-life Elimination Terminal: 2.6-3.5 hours

Time to Peak Serum: 7 minutes

Pregnancy Risk Factor C

Pregnancy Considerations Adverse events have been observed in animal reproduction studies.

Etonogestrel (e toe noe JES trel)

Brand Names: US Implanon [DSC]; Nexplanon

Pharmacologic Category Contraceptive; Progestin

Use Contraception: Prevention of pregnancy

Local Anesthetic/Vasoconstrictor Precautions No information available to require special precautions

Effects on Dental Treatment Key adverse event(s) related to dental treatment: Until more is known about the mechanism of interaction, use caution in prescribing antibiotics to female patients taking progestin-only contraceptives.

Effects on Bleeding No information available to require special precautions

Adverse Reactions

>10%:

Central nervous system: Headache (25%)

Dermatologic: Acne vulgaris (14%)

Endocrine & metabolic: Menstrual disease (<3 episodes/90 days: 34%; prolonged menstrual bleeding lasting >14 days: 18%; >5 episodes/90 days: 7%), amenorrhea (no bleeding in 90 days: 22%), weight gain (14%)

Gastrointestinal: Abdominal pain (11%)

Genitourinary: Vaginitis (15%), mastalgia (13%)

Respiratory: Pharyngitis (11%)

1% to 10%:

Central nervous system: Dizziness (7%), emotional lability (7%), depression (6%), nervousness (6%), pain (6%)

Dermatologic: Localized erythema (implant site: ≤3%)

Endocrine & metabolic: Dysmenorrhea (7%)

Gastrointestinal: Nausea (6%)

Genitourinary: Leukorrhea (10%)

Hypersensitivity: Hypersensitivity reaction (5%)

Local: Application site reaction (implant site: 4% to 9%), local pain (implant site: 1% to 5%), hematoma at injection site (implant site: ≤3%), bruising at injection site (implant site: 2%)

Neuromuscular & skeletal: Back pain (7%)

Respiratory: Flu-like symptoms (8%)

<1%, postmarketing, and/or case reports: Abscess, alopecia, anaphylaxis, angioedema (including exacerbation of hereditary angioedema), anxiety, arthralgia, breast hypertrophy, cerebrovascular accident, chloasma, constipation, convulsions, decreased libido, deep vein thrombosis, diarrhea, drowsiness, dysuria, edema, fatigue, fever, fibrosis (implant site), flatulence, genital pruritus, hot flash, hypertension, hypertrichosis, increased appetite, insomnia, migraine, musculoskeletal pain, myalgia, myocardial infarction, nipple discharge, ovarian cyst, paresthesia, pruritus, pulmonary embolism, rhinitis, scarring, seborrhea, seizure, skin rash, swelling (implant site), urinary tract infection, urticaria, vaginal discomfort, vomiting, weight loss

General Dosage Range Subdermal: *Adolescents and Adults (females, postmenarche):* Insert 1 implant for up to 3 years

Mechanism of Action Etonogestrel is the active metabolite of desogestrel. It prevents pregnancy by suppressing ovulation, increasing the viscosity of cervical mucous, and inhibiting endometrial proliferation.

Pharmacodynamics/Kinetics

Duration of Action Each implant maintains etonogestrel levels sufficient to inhibit ovulation for 3 years

Half-life Elimination ~25 hours

Pregnancy Considerations Use is contraindicated in pregnant women. Pregnancy status should be evaluated prior to prescribing and implant should be removed if pregnancy occurs. In general, the use of combination hormonal contraceptives, when inadvertently used early in pregnancy, have not been associated with teratogenic effects. There is no evidence that the risk is different with etonogestrel.

Due to the risk of thromboembolism, the manufacturer does not recommend insertion <21 days postpartum. However, progestin only implants may be inserted at any time if it is reasonably certain the woman is not pregnant, including immediately postpartum or post abortion (CDC 2013).

Etonogestrel serum concentrations decrease by 1 week after removal of the implant; pregnancies have been reported as early as 7 to 14 days after removal. Restart contraception immediately after removal if continued contraception is desired.

Product Availability Implanon has been discontinued in the US for more than 1 year.

Etoposide (e toe POE side)

Brand Names: US Toposar

Brand Names: Canada Etoposide Injection; Etoposide Injection USP; Vepesid

Pharmacologic Category Antineoplastic Agent, Podophyllotoxin Derivative; Antineoplastic Agent, Topoisomerase II Inhibitor

Use

Small cell lung cancer (oral and IV): Treatment (first-line) of small cell lung cancer (SCLC)

Testicular cancer (IV): Treatment of refractory testicular tumors (injectable formulation)

Canadian labeling: Treatment of small cell lung cancer (SCLC; first- and second-line); treatment of non-small cell lung cancer (NSCLC); treatment of non-Hodgkin lymphomas (first-line); treatment of testicular cancer (first-line [injectable formulation] and refractory)

Local Anesthetic/Vasoconstrictor Precautions No information available to require special precautions

Effects on Dental Treatment Key adverse event(s) related to dental treatment: Mucositis (especially at high doses) and stomatitis.

Effects on Bleeding Myelosuppression is dose related. When thrombocytopenia occurs, platelet nadirs develop 9-16 days after drug administration. Bone marrow recovery is usually complete by day 20, and no cumulative toxicity has been reported.

Adverse Reactions The following may occur with higher doses used in stem cell transplantation: Alopecia, ethanol intoxication, hepatitis, hypotension (infusion-related), metabolic acidosis, mucositis, nausea and vomiting (severe), secondary malignancy, skin lesions (resembling Stevens-Johnson syndrome).

>10%:

Dermatologic: Alopecia (8% to 66%)

Gastrointestinal: Nausea and vomiting (31% to 43%), anorexia (10% to 13%), diarrhea (1% to 13%)

Hematologic & oncologic: Leukopenia (60% to 91%; grade 4: 3% to 17%; nadir: 7 to 14 days; recovery: by day 20), thrombocytopenia (22% to 41%; grades 3/4: 1% to 20%; nadir: 9 to 16 days; recovery: by day 20), anemia (≤33%)

1% to 10%:

Cardiovascular: Hypotension (1% to 2%; due to rapid infusion)

Central nervous system: Peripheral neuropathy (1% to 2%)

Gastrointestinal: Stomatitis (1% to 6%), abdominal pain (≤2%)

Hepatic: Hepatotoxicity (≤3%)

Hypersensitivity: Anaphylactoid reaction (intravenous: 1% to 2%; oral capsules: <1%; including bronchospasm, chills, dyspnea, fever, tachycardia)

<1%, postmarketing, and/or case reports: Amenorrhea, apnea (hypersensitivity-associated), back pain, constipation, cortical blindness (transient), cough, cyanosis, diaphoresis, drowsiness, dysphagia, erythema, esophagitis, extravasation (induration/necrosis), facial swelling, fatigue, fever, hyperpigmentation, hypersensitivity reaction, interstitial pneumonitis, ischemic heart disease, laryngospasm, maculopapular rash, malaise, metabolic acidosis, mucositis, myocardial infarction, optic neuritis, ovarian failure, perivasculitis, pruritus, pulmonary fibrosis, radiation-recall phenomenon (dermatitis), reversible posterior leukoencephalopathy syndrome (RPLS), seizure, skin rash, Stevens-Johnson syndrome, tongue edema, toxic epidermal necrolysis, toxic megacolon, urticaria, vasospasm, weakness

General Dosage Range Dosage adjustment recommended in patients with hepatic impairment, renal impairment, or who develop toxicities.

IV, oral: *Adults:* Dosage varies greatly depending on indication

Mechanism of Action Etoposide has been shown to delay transit of cells through the S phase and arrest cells in late S or early G_2 phase. The drug may inhibit mitochondrial transport at the NADH dehydrogenase level or inhibit uptake of nucleosides into HeLa cells. It is a topoisomerase II inhibitor and appears to cause DNA strand breaks. Etoposide does not inhibit microtubular assembly.

Pharmacodynamics/Kinetics

Half-life Elimination Terminal: IV: Normal renal/hepatic function: Children: 6 to 8 hours: Adults: 4 to 11 hours

Pregnancy Risk Factor D

Pregnancy Considerations Adverse events were observed in animal reproduction studies. Fetal growth restriction and newborn myelosuppression have been observed following maternal use of regimens containing etoposide during pregnancy (NTP 2013; Peccatori 2013). The European Society for Medical Oncology has published guidelines for diagnosis, treatment, and follow-up of cancer during pregnancy. The guidelines recommend referral to a facility with expertise in cancer during pregnancy and encourage a multidisciplinary team (obstetrician, neonatologist, oncology team). In general, if chemotherapy is indicated, it should be avoided during in the first trimester, there should be a 3-week time period between the last chemotherapy dose and anticipated delivery, and chemotherapy should not be administered beyond week 33 of gestation. Guidelines for the treatment of SCLC are not provided (Peccatori 2013).

In women of reproductive potential, product labeling for etoposide phosphate notes that it may cause amenorrhea, infertility, or premature menopause; effective contraception should be used during therapy and for ≥6 months after the last dose. In males, azoospermia, oligospermia, or permanent loss of fertility may occur.

In addition, spermatozoa and testicular tissue may be damaged. Males with female partners of reproductive potential should use condoms during therapy and for ≥4 months after the last dose.

Etoposide Phosphate (e toe POE side FOS fate)

Related Information

Etoposide *on page 672*

Brand Names: US Etopophos

Pharmacologic Category Antineoplastic Agent, Podophyllotoxin Derivative; Antineoplastic Agent, Topoisomerase II Inhibitor

Use

Small cell lung cancer: First-line treatment of small cell lung cancer (in combination with cisplatin)

Testicular cancer, refractory: Treatment of refractory testicular tumors (in combination with other chemotherapy agents)

Local Anesthetic/Vasoconstrictor Precautions No information available to require special precautions

Effects on Dental Treatment Key adverse event(s) related to dental treatment: Mucositis (especially at high doses), stomatitis, and taste perversion.

Effects on Bleeding Myelosuppression is dose related. When thrombocytopenia occurs, platelet nadirs develop 10-15 days after drug administration. Bone marrow recovery is usually complete by day 21, and no cumulative toxicity has been reported.

Adverse Reactions Also see adverse reactions for etoposide; etoposide phosphate is converted to etoposide, adverse reactions experienced with etoposide would also be expected with etoposide phosphate.

>10%:

Central nervous system: Malaise (≤39%), chills (≤24%)

Dermatologic: Alopecia (33% to 44%)

Gastrointestinal: Nausea and vomiting (37%), anorexia (16%), mucositis (11%)

Hematologic & oncologic: Leukopenia (91%; grade 4: 17%; nadir: day 15 to 22; recovery: usually by day 21), neutropenia (88%; grade 4: 37%, nadir: day 12 to 19; recovery: usually by day 21), anemia (72%; grades 3/4: 19%), thrombocytopenia (23%; grade 4: 9%; nadir: day 10 to 15; recovery: usually by day 21)

Neuromuscular & skeletal: Weakness (≤39%)

Miscellaneous: Fever (≤24%)

1% to 10%:

Cardiovascular: Hypotension (1% to 5%), localized phlebitis (≤5%; including cellulitis at injection site, local pain, local swelling, local tissue necrosis, tissue necrosis at injection site), hypertension (3%), facial flushing (2%)

Central nervous system: Dizziness (5%)

Dermatologic: Skin rash (3%)

Gastrointestinal: Constipation (8%), abdominal pain (7%), diarrhea (6%), dysgeusia (6%)

Hypersensitivity: Anaphylactoid reaction (3%; including bronchospasm, chills, diaphoresis, dyspnea, fever, pruritus, rigors, tachycardia)

Local: Extravasation (≤5%; including cellulitis at injection site, local pain, local swelling, local tissue necrosis, tissue necrosis at injection site)

<1%, postmarketing, and/or case reports: Acute leukemia (with/without preleukemia phase), apnea (hypersensitivity-associated), back pain, cortical blindness (transient), cough, cyanosis, diaphoresis, dysphagia, erythema, facial swelling, febrile neutropenia, hepatotoxicity, hyperpigmentation, infection, interstitial pneumonitis, laryngospasm, maculopapular rash, optic neuritis, perivasculitis, pulmonary fibrosis, radiation recall phenomenon, seizure, Stevens-Johnson syndrome, swollen tongue, toxic epidermal necrolysis, urticaria

General Dosage Range Dosage adjustment recommended in patients with hepatic or renal impairment or who develop toxicities

IV: *Adults:* 35 mg/m²/day for 4 days to 100 mg/m²/day for 5 days

Mechanism of Action Etoposide phosphate is converted *in vivo* to the active moiety, etoposide, by dephosphorylation. Etoposide inhibits mitotic activity; inhibits cells from entering prophase; inhibits DNA synthesis. Initially thought to be mitotic inhibitors similar to podophyllotoxin, but actually have no effect on microtubule assembly. However, later shown to induce DNA strand breakage and inhibition of topoisomerase II (an enzyme which breaks and repairs DNA); etoposide acts in late S or early G2 phases.

Pharmacodynamics/Kinetics

Half-life Elimination Terminal: 4 to 11 hours; Children: Normal renal/hepatic function: 6 to 8 hours

Pregnancy Considerations Based on animal reproduction studies and the mechanism of action, etoposide phosphate may cause fetal harm if administered during pregnancy. Women of reproductive potential should avoid pregnancy during treatment. Fetal growth restriction and newborn myelosuppression have been observed following maternal use of regimens containing etoposide during pregnancy (NTP 2013; Peccatori 2013). The European Society for Medical Oncology has published guidelines for diagnosis, treatment, and follow-up of cancer during pregnancy. The guidelines recommend referral to a facility with expertise in cancer during pregnancy and encourage a multidisciplinary team (obstetrician, neonatologist, oncology team). In general, if chemotherapy is indicated, it should be avoided during in the first trimester, there should be a 3-week time period between the last chemotherapy dose and anticipated delivery, and chemotherapy should not be administered beyond week 33 of gestation. Guidelines for the treatment of SCLC are not provided (Peccatori 2013).

In women of reproductive potential, etoposide phosphate may cause amenorrhea, infertility, or premature menopause; effective contraception should be used during therapy and for at least 6 months after the last dose. In males, azoospermia, oligospermia, or permanent loss of fertility may occur. In addition, spermatozoa and testicular tissue may be damaged. Males with female partners of reproductive potential should use condoms during therapy and for 4 months after the last dose.

Etravirine (et ra VIR een)

Related Information

HIV Infection and AIDS *on page 1785*

Brand Names: US Intelence

Brand Names: Canada Intelence

Pharmacologic Category Antiretroviral, Reverse Transcriptase Inhibitor, Non-nucleoside (Anti-HIV)

Use Treatment of HIV-1 infection in combination with at least two additional antiretroviral agents in treatment-experienced patients exhibiting viral replication with documented non-nucleoside reverse transcriptase inhibitor (NNRTI) resistance

Local Anesthetic/Vasoconstrictor Precautions No information available to require special precautions

Effects on Dental Treatment Key adverse event(s) related to dental treatment: Stomatitis has been reported.

Effects on Bleeding No information available to require special precautions related to hemostasis.

Adverse Reactions

Frequency not always defined.

>10%:

Dermatologic: Skin rash (≥grade 2: 10% to 15%)

Endocrine & metabolic: Hyperglycemia (≤250 mg/dL: 15%; 251 to 500 mg/dL: 4%), increased LDL cholesterol (≤190 mg/dL: 13%), increased serum cholesterol (total; ≤300 mg/dL: 20%; >300 mg/dL: 8%)

Gastrointestinal: Nausea

2% to 10%:

Central nervous system: Peripheral neuropathy (≥ grade 2: 4%)

Endocrine & metabolic: Increased serum triglycerides (≤750 mg/dL: 9%; >750 mg/dL: 4% to 6%)

Gastrointestinal: Diarrhea (children and adolescents ≥2%), increased amylase (>5 x ULN: 2%)

Hepatic: Increased serum ALT (≤5 x ULN: 6%; >5 x ULN: 3%), increased serum AST (≤5 x ULN: 6%; >5 x ULN: 3%)

Renal: Increased serum creatinine (≤1.8 x ULN: 6%; >1.8 x ULN: 2%)

<2%, postmarketing, and/or case reports: Abdominal distention, abnormal dreams, amnesia, anemia (including hemolytic), angina pectoris, angioedema, anorexia, anxiety, atrial fibrillation, blurred vision, bronchospasm, confusion, constipation, decreased white blood cell count, diabetes mellitus, disorientation, disturbance in attention, disturbed sleep, DRESS syndrome (drug rash with eosinophilia and systemic symptoms), drowsiness, dyspnea, erythema multiforme, facial edema, flatulence, gastritis, gastroesophageal reflux disease, gynecomastia, hemorrhagic stroke, hematemesis, hepatic failure, hepatitis, hepatomegaly, hyperhidrosis, hypersensitivity reaction, hypersomnia, hypoesthesia, immune reconstitution syndrome, increased serum lipase, insomnia, lethargy, lipodystrophy, lipohypertrophy, liver steatosis, myocardial infarction, nervousness, nightmares, night sweats, pancreatitis, paresthesia, renal failure, retching, rhabdomyolysis, seizure, Stevens-Johnson syndrome, stomatitis, syncope, toxic epidermal necrolysis, tremor, vertigo, xeroderma, xerostomia

General Dosage Range Oral:

Children ≥6 years and ≥16 kg to <20 kg: 100 mg twice daily

Children ≥6 years and ≥20 kg to <25 kg: 125 mg twice daily

Children ≥6 years and ≥25 kg to <30 kg: 150 mg twice daily

Children ≥6 years and ≥30 kg and Adults: 200 mg twice daily

Mechanism of Action As a non-nucleoside reverse transcriptase inhibitor, etravirine has activity against HIV-1 by binding to reverse transcriptase. It consequently blocks the RNA-dependent and DNA-dependent DNA polymerase activities, including HIV-1 replication. It does not require intracellular phosphorylation for antiviral activity.

Pharmacodynamics/Kinetics

Half-life Elimination 41 hours (± 20 hours)

Time to Peak 2.5 to 4 hours

Pregnancy Risk Factor B

Pregnancy Considerations Adverse events have not been observed in animal reproduction studies. Etravirine has a variable (moderate to high) level of transfer across the human placenta. Maternal antiretroviral therapy may increase the risk of preterm delivery, although available information is conflicting possibly due to variability of maternal factors (disease severity; initiation of therapy); however, maternal antiretroviral medication should not be withheld due to concerns of preterm birth. Information related to stillbirth, low birth weight, and small for gestational age infants is limited. Long-term follow-up is recommended for all infants exposed to antiretroviral medications; children who develop significant organ system abnormalities of unknown etiology (particularly of the CNS or heart) should be evaluated for potential mitochondrial dysfunction. Hypersensitivity reactions (including hepatic toxicity and rash) are more common in women on NNRTI therapy; it is not known if pregnancy increases this risk.

Combination antiretroviral therapy (cART) therapy is recommended for all HIV-infected pregnant women to keep the viral load below the limit of detection and reduce the risk of perinatal transmission. When HIV is diagnosed during pregnancy in a woman who has never received antiretroviral therapy, cART should begin as soon as possible after diagnosis. The Health and Human Services (HHS) Perinatal HIV Guidelines do not recommend use as initial therapy in antiretroviral-naive pregnant women. The pharmacokinetics of etravirine are not significantly altered in pregnancy and dosing adjustment is not needed. In general, women who become pregnant on a stable cART regimen may continue that regimen if viral suppression is effective, appropriate drug exposure can be achieved, contraindications for use in pregnancy are not present, and the regimen is well tolerated. Monitoring during pregnancy is more frequent than in non-pregnant adults; cART should be continued postpartum.

For HIV-infected couples planning a pregnancy, maximum viral suppression with cART is recommended prior to conception for the HIV-infected partner(s) and expert consultation is recommended; modification of therapy (if needed) and optimization of the woman's health should be done prior to conception. HIV-infected women not planning a pregnancy may use any available type of contraception, considering possible drug interactions and contraindications of the specific method. In addition, consistent use of condoms is also recommended (even during pregnancy) to prevent transmission of HIV or other sexually transmitted diseases.

Health care providers are encouraged to enroll pregnant women exposed to antiretroviral medications as early in pregnancy as possible in the Antiretroviral Pregnancy Registry (1-800-258-4263 or www.APRegistry.com). Health care providers caring for HIV-infected women and their infants may contact the National Perinatal HIV Hotline (888-448-8765) for clinical consultation (HHS [perinatal] 2016).

Everolimus (e ver OH li mus)

Related Information

Dentin Hypersensitivity, Acid Erosion, High Caries Index, Management of Alveolar Osteitis, and Xerostomia *on page 1857*

Osteonecrosis of the Jaw *on page 1796*

Brand Names: US Afinitor; Afinitor Disperz; Zortress

Brand Names: Canada Afinitor; Afinitor Disperz

Pharmacologic Category Antineoplastic Agent, mTOR Kinase Inhibitor; Immunosuppressant Agent; mTOR Kinase Inhibitor

Use

Breast cancer, advanced (Afinitor only): Treatment of advanced hormone receptor-positive, HER2-negative breast cancer in postmenopausal women (in combination with exemestane and after letrozole or anastrozole failure)

Neuroendocrine tumors (Afinitor only): Treatment of locally advanced, metastatic or unresectable progressive pancreatic neuroendocrine tumors (PNET); treatment of progressive, well-differentiated, nonfunctional GI or lung neuroendocrine tumors in patients with unresectable, locally advanced or metastatic disease

Limitations of use: Not indicated for the treatment of functional carcinoid tumors.

Renal angiomyolipoma with tuberous sclerosis complex (Afinitor only): Treatment of renal angiomyolipoma with tuberous sclerosis complex (TSC) not requiring immediate surgery

Renal cell carcinoma, advanced (Afinitor only): Treatment of advanced renal cell cancer (RCC) after sunitinib or sorafenib failure

Subependymal giant cell astrocytoma (Afinitor or Afinitor Disperz only): Treatment of subependymal giant cell astrocytoma (SEGA) associated with TSC which requires intervention, but cannot be curatively resected

Liver transplantation (Zortress only): Prophylaxis of allograft rejection in liver transplantation (in combination with corticosteroids and reduced doses of tacrolimus, everolimus should not be administered earlier than 30 days post-transplant)

Renal transplantation (Zortress only): Prophylaxis of organ rejection in renal transplant patients at low to moderate immunologic risk (in combination with basiliximab induction and concurrent with corticosteroids and reduced doses of cyclosporine)

Local Anesthetic/Vasoconstrictor Precautions

No information available to require special precautions

Effects on Dental Treatment Key adverse event(s) related to dental treatment: High incidence of mouth ulcers, mucositis, and stomatitis; xerostomia and taste alterations have been observed (normal salivary flow resumes upon discontinuation) (see Dental Comment)

Effects on Bleeding No information available to require special precautions

Adverse Reactions

Transplantation:

Reactions occur in kidney and liver transplantation unless otherwise specified.

>10%:

Cardiovascular: Peripheral edema (kidney transplant: 45%; liver transplant: 18%), hypertension (kidney transplant: 30%; liver transplant: 17%)

Central nervous system: Headache (18% to 19%), insomnia (kidney transplant: 17%), procedural pain (kidney transplant: 15%)

Endocrine & metabolic: Diabetes mellitus (new onset: liver transplant: 32%; kidney transplant: 9%), hypercholesterolemia (15% to 24%), hyperkalemia (renal transplant: 18%), hypomagnesemia (kidney transplant: 14%), hypophosphatemia (kidney transplant: 13%), hyperglycemia (kidney transplant: 12%), hypokalemia (kidney transplant: 12%)

Gastrointestinal: Constipation (kidney transplant: 38%), nausea (kidney transplant: 29%; liver transplant: 14%), diarrhea (19%), vomiting (kidney transplant: 15%), abdominal pain (13%; upper abdominal pain, kidney transplant: 2%)

Genitourinary: Urinary tract infection (kidney transplant: 22%), hematuria (kidney transplant: 12%), dysuria (kidney transplant: 11%)

Hematologic & oncologic: Anemia (kidney transplant: 26%), leukopenia (3% to 12%)

Infection: Infection (kidney transplant: 62%; liver transplant: 50%), viral infection (liver transplant: 17%; kidney transplant: 10%), bacterial infection (liver transplant: 16%), hepatitis C (liver transplant: 11%)

Local: Incisional pain (kidney transplant: 16%)

Neuromuscular & skeletal: Limb pain (kidney transplant: 12%), back pain (kidney transplant: 11%)

Renal: Increased serum creatinine (kidney transplant: 18%)

Respiratory: Upper respiratory tract infection (kidney transplant: 16%)

Miscellaneous: Postoperative wound complication (kidney transplant: 35%; liver transplant: 11%; includes incisional hernia, lymphocele, seroma, wound dehiscence), fever (13% to 19%)

1% to 10%:

Cardiovascular: Hypertensive crisis (1%), angina pectoris, atrial fibrillation, chest discomfort, chest pain, congestive heart failure, deep vein thrombosis, edema, hypotension, palpitations, pulmonary embolism, renal artery thrombosis, syncope, tachycardia, venous thromboembolism

Central nervous system: Fatigue (9%), agitation, anxiety, chills, depression, dizziness, drowsiness, hallucination, hemiparesis, hypoesthesia, lethargy, malaise, migraine, myasthenia, neuralgia, pain, paresthesia

Dermatologic: Acneiform eruption, acne vulgaris, alopecia, cellulitis, diaphoresis, folliculitis, hypertrichosis, night sweats, onychomycosis, pruritus, skin rash, tinea pedis

Endocrine & metabolic: Acidosis, amenorrhea, cushingoid appearance, cyanocobalamin deficiency, dehydration, fluid retention, gout, hirsutism, hypercalcemia, hyperparathyroidism, hypertriglyceridemia, hyperuricemia, hypocalcemia, hypoglycemia, hyponatremia, iron deficiency, ovarian cyst

Gastrointestinal: Stomatitis (kidney transplant: 8%), dyspepsia (kidney transplant: 4%), abdominal distention, anorexia, decreased appetite, dysphagia, epigastric distress, flatulence, gastroenteritis, gastroesophageal reflux disease, gingival hyperplasia, hematemesis, hemorrhoids, intestinal obstruction, oral candidiasis, oral herpes, oral mucosa ulcer, peritoneal effusion, peritonitis

Genitourinary: Erectile dysfunction (kidney transplant: 5%), bladder spasm, perinephric abscess, perinephric hematoma, pollakiuria, proteinuria, pyuria, scrotal edema, urethritis, urinary retention, urinary urgency

Hematologic & oncologic: Neoplasm (3% to 4%), leukocytosis, lymphadenopathy, lymphorrhea, neutropenia, pancytopenia, thrombocythemia, thrombocytopenia

Hepatic: Abnormal hepatic function tests (liver transplant: 7%), ascites (liver transplant: 4%), hepatitis (noninfections), increased liver enzymes, increased serum alkaline phosphatase, increased serum bilirubin

Hypersensitivity: Angioedema (<1%)

Infection: BK virus (kidney transplant: 1%), bacteremia, candidiasis, herpes virus infection, influenza, sepsis, wound infection

Neuromuscular & skeletal: Tremor (8% to 9%), arthralgia, joint swelling, muscle spasm, musculoskeletal pain, myalgia, osteomyelitis, osteonecrosis, osteoporosis, spondylitis, weakness

Ophthalmic: Blurred vision, cataract, conjunctivitis

Renal: Hydronephrosis, increased blood urea nitrogen, interstitial nephritis, polyuria, pyelonephritis, renal failure (acute), renal insufficiency, renal tubular necrosis

Respiratory: Cough (kidney transplant: 7%), atelectasis, bronchitis, dyspnea, epistaxis, lower respiratory tract infection, nasal congestion, nasopharyngitis, oropharyngeal pain, pleural effusion, pneumonia, pulmonary edema, rhinorrhea, sinus congestion, sinusitis, wheezing

Antineoplastic:

Antineoplastic indications include advanced hormone receptor-positive, advanced nonfunctional NET of gastrointestinal or lung origin, HER2-negative breast cancer (advanced HR + BC), pancreatic neuroendocrine tumors (PNET), renal cell carcinoma (RCC), renal angiomyolipoma and tuberous sclerosis complex (TSC), and subependymal giant cell astrocytoma (SEGA)

>10%:

Cardiovascular: Edema (PNET: ≤39%), peripheral edema (advanced nonfunctional NET of gastrointestinal or lung origin, PNET: ≤39%; advanced HR + BC, RCC, TSC: 13% to 25%), hypertension (PNET, RCC, SEGA: 4% to 13%)

Central nervous system: Malaise (PNET: ≤45%), fatigue (advanced HR + BC, advanced nonfunctional NET of gastrointestinal or lung origin, PNET, RCC: 31% to ≤45%; SEGA: 14%), headache (PNET: ≤30%; advanced HR + BC, RCC: 19% to 21%), migraine (PNET: ≤30%), behavioral problems (SEGA: 21%; includes abnormal behavior, aggressive behavior, agitation, anxiety, obsessive compulsive symptoms, panic attack), insomnia (advanced HR + BC, PNET, RCC, SEGA: 6% to 14%), dizziness (PNET, RCC: 7% to 12%)

Dermatologic: Skin rash (PNET: 59%; advanced HR + BC, advanced nonfunctional NET of gastrointestinal or lung origin, RCC, SEGA: 21% to 39%; may include allergic dermatitis, macular eruption, maculopapular rash, papular rash, urticaria), cellulitis (SEGA: 29%), acne vulgaris (TSC: 22%; SEGA: 10%), nail disease (PNET: 22%; RCC: 5%), pruritus (advanced HR + BC, advanced nonfunctional NET of gastrointestinal or lung origin, PNET, RCC: 13% to 21%), xeroderma (PNET, RCC: 13%)

Endocrine & metabolic: Hypercholesterolemia (TSC, SEGA: 81% to 85%; advanced nonfunctional NET of gastrointestinal or lung origin: 71%), decreased serum bicarbonate (PNET: 56%), hyperglycemia (advanced nonfunctional NET of gastrointestinal or lung origin: 55%; SEGA: 25%; advanced HR + BC: 14%), hypertriglyceridemia (TSC: 52%; advanced nonfunctional NET of gastrointestinal or lung origin, SEGA: 27% to 30%), hypophosphatemia (advanced nonfunctional NET of gastrointestinal or lung origin, TSC: 43% to 49%; SEGA: 9%), decreased serum calcium (PNET: 37%), hypokalemia (advanced nonfunctional NET of gastrointestinal or lung origin: 27%), hypoalbuminemia (advanced nonfunctional NET of gastrointestinal or lung origin: 18%), amenorrhea (TSC, SEGA: 15% to 17%)

Gastrointestinal: Stomatitis (advanced HR + BC, advanced nonfunctional NET of gastrointestinal or lung origin, PNET, SEGA, TSC: 62% to 78%; advanced nonfunctional NET of gastrointestinal or lung origin grade 3: 9%; grades 3/4: ≤9%; RCC: 44%, grades 3/4: ≤4%), diarrhea (advanced nonfunctional NET of gastrointestinal or lung origin, PNET: 41% to 50%; advanced HR + BC, RCC: 30% to 33%; TSC, SEGA: 14% to 17%; may include bowel urgency, colitis, enteritis, enterocolitis, steatorrhea), abdominal pain (PNET: 36%; RCC, SEGA: 5% to 9%), decreased appetite (advanced HR + BC, advanced nonfunctional NET of gastrointestinal or lung origin, PNET: 22% to 30%; TSC: 6%), nausea (advanced HR + BC, advanced nonfunctional NET of gastrointestinal or lung origin, RCC: 26% to 29%; SEGA: 8%), vomiting (15% to 29%), weight loss (advanced HR + BC, advanced nonfunctional NET of gastrointestinal or lung origin, PNET: 22% to 28%; RCC: 9%; SEGA: 5%), anorexia (RCC: 25%), dysgeusia (advanced HR + BC, advanced nonfunctional NET of gastrointestinal or lung origin, PNET: 18% to 22%; RCC: 10%; TSC: 5%), mucositis (RCC: 19%; grades 3/4: ≤1%), constipation (advanced HR + BC, PNET, SEGA: 10% to 14%), xerostomia (advanced HR + BC, PNET, RCC: 8% to 11%)

Genitourinary: Urinary tract infection (PNET: 16%; advanced HR + BC, RCC: 5% to 10%), irregular menses (TSC, PNET: 10% to 11%)

Hematologic & oncologic: Increase in fasting plasma glucose (PNET: 75%, grades 3/4: 17%; TSC: 14%), prolonged partial thromboplastin time (SEGA: 72%), anemia (advanced nonfunctional NET of gastrointestinal or lung origin: 81%; TSC: 61%; SEGA: 41%; advanced nonfunctional NET of gastrointestinal or lung origin grade 3: 5%), lymphocytopenia (advanced nonfunctional NET of gastrointestinal or lung origin: 66%; TSC: 20%, grade 3: 1%), thrombocytopenia (advanced nonfunctional NET of gastrointestinal or lung origin: 33%; RCC, TSC: 19%; advanced HR + BC, advanced nonfunctional NET of gastrointestinal or lung origin grade 3: 2%; advanced nonfunctional NET of gastrointestinal or lung origin grade 4: 1%), leukopenia (advanced nonfunctional NET of gastrointestinal or lung origin: 49%; TSC: 37%; advanced nonfunctional NET of gastrointestinal or lung origin grade 3: 2%), neutropenia (SEGA: 46%, grade 3: 9%; advanced nonfunctional NET of gastrointestinal or lung origin: 32%)

Hepatic: Increased serum alkaline phosphatase (PNET: 74%; TSC: 32%, grade 3: 1%), increased serum AST (advanced HR + BC: 69%; advanced nonfunctional NET of gastrointestinal or lung origin, PNET: 56% to 57%; RCC, TSC, SEGA: 23% to 33%; advanced HR + BC, advanced nonfunctional NET of gastrointestinal or lung origin, RCC, TSC grade 3: ≤4%; advanced HR + BC, advanced nonfunctional NET of gastrointestinal or lung origin, RCC grade 4: ≤1%), increased serum ALT (advanced HR + BC, advanced nonfunctional NET of gastrointestinal or lung origin, PNET: 46% to 51%, RCC, TSC, SEGA: 18% to 21%; advanced nonfunctional NET of gastrointestinal or lung origin grade 3: 5%; RCC, TSC grade 3: 1%; advanced HR + BC, advanced nonfunctional NET of gastrointestinal or lung origin grade 4: ≤1%)

Infection: Infection (advanced HR + BC, advanced nonfunctional NET of gastrointestinal or lung origin: 50% to 58%; RCC: 37%; advanced HR + BC, advanced nonfunctional NET of gastrointestinal or lung origin, RCC grade 3: 4% to 8%; advanced HR + BC, advanced nonfunctional NET of gastrointestinal or lung origin, RCC grade 4: 1% to 3%)

Neuromuscular & skeletal: Weakness (RCC: 33%; advanced nonfunctional NET of gastrointestinal or lung origin: 23%; advanced HR + BC: 13%), arthralgia (advanced HR + BC, PNET, TSC: 13% to 20%), back pain (advanced HR + BC, PNET: 14% to 15%), limb pain (PNET, RCC, SEGA: 8% to 14%)
Renal: Increased serum creatinine (RCC: 50%; advanced HR + BC, PNET: 19% to 24%, advanced HR + BC, RCC grade 3: 1% to 2%, PNET grades 3/4: 2%)
Respiratory: Respiratory tract infection (SEGA: 31%, grade 3: 1%, grade 4: 1%; includes viral respiratory tract infection), cough (advanced HR + BC, advanced nonfunctional NET of gastrointestinal or lung origin, PNET, RCC, TSC: 20% to 30%; includes productive cough), nasopharyngitis (PNET: ≤25%; advanced HR + BC, RCC: 6% to 10%), rhinitis (PNET: ≤25%), upper respiratory tract infection (PNET: ≤25%; TSC: 11%; advanced HR + BC: 5%), dyspnea (advanced HR + BC, advanced nonfunctional NET of gastrointestinal or lung origin, PNET, RCC: 20% to 24%; includes dyspnea on exertion), epistaxis (advanced HR + BC, advanced nonfunctional NET of gastrointestinal or lung origin, PNET, RCC, TSC, SEGA: 5% to 22%), pneumonitis (advanced HR + BC, advanced nonfunctional NET of gastrointestinal or lung origin, PNET, RCC: 14% to 19%; TSC, SEGA: 1%; advanced HR + BC, advanced nonfunctional NET of gastrointestinal or lung origin, PNET, RCC grade 3: 2% to 4%; advanced HR + BC, PNET grade 4: <1%; may include interstitial pulmonary disease, pulmonary alveolar hemorrhage, pulmonary alveolitis, pulmonary fibrosis, pulmonary infiltrates, pulmonary toxicity, restrictive pulmonary disease), oropharyngeal pain (PNET: 11%)
Miscellaneous: Fever (advanced HR + BC, advanced nonfunctional NET of gastrointestinal or lung origin, PNET, RCC, SEGA: 15% to 31%)

1% to 10%:

Cardiovascular: Chest pain (RCC: 5%), tachycardia (RCC: 3%), congestive heart failure (RCC: 1%), deep vein thrombosis (RCC: <1%)
Central nervous system: Depression (TSC: 5%), paresthesia (RCC: 5%), chills (RCC: 4%)
Dermatologic: Alopecia (advanced HR + BC: 10%), palmar-plantar erythrodysesthesia (RCC: 5%), erythema (RCC: 4%), onychoclasis (RCC: 4%), skin lesion (RCC: 4%), acneiform eruption (RCC: 3%)
Endocrine & metabolic: Diabetes mellitus (PNET: 10%; RCC: exacerbation of diabetes mellitus: 2%, new onset: <1%), hypermenorrhea (TSC, SEGA: 6% to 10%), menstrual disease (TSC, SEGA: 6% to 10%), decreased serum fibrinogen (SEGA: 8%), increased luteinizing hormone (TSC, SEGA: 1% to 4%), increased follicle-stimulating hormone (TSC: 3%), ovarian cyst (TSC: 3%)
Gastrointestinal: Gastroenteritis (SEGA: 10%; includes viral gastroenteritis, gastrointestinal infection), hemorrhoids (RCC: 5%), dysphagia (RCC: 4%)
Genitourinary: Vaginal hemorrhage (TSC: 8%), dysmenorrhea (SEGA: 6%), uterine hemorrhage (SEGA: 6%), cystitis (advanced HR + BC: 3%)
Hematologic & oncologic: Hemorrhage (RCC: 3%)
Hepatic: Increased serum bilirubin (RCC: 3%; grade 3: <1%, grade 4: <1%)
Hypersensitivity: Hypersensitivity reaction (TSC, SEGA: 3%; includes anaphylaxis, chest pain, dyspnea, flushing), angioedema (RCC, TSC: ≤1%)
Infection: Candidiasis (advanced HR + BC, RCC: <1%), hepatitis C (advanced HR + BC: <1%), sepsis (advanced HR + BC, RCC: <1%)
Neuromuscular & skeletal: Muscle spasm (PNET: 10%), jaw pain (RCC: 3%)
Ophthalmic: Eyelid edema (RCC: 4%), conjunctivitis (RCC: 2%)
Otic: Otitis media (TSC: 6%)
Renal: Renal failure (RCC: 3%)
Respiratory: Streptococcal pharyngitis (SEGA: 10%), pleural effusion (RCC: 7%), pneumonia (advanced HR + BC, RCC, SEGA: 4% to 6%), bronchitis (advanced HR + BC, RCC: 4%), pharyngolaryngeal pain (RCC: 4%), rhinorrhea (RCC: 3%), sinusitis (advanced HR + BC, RCC: 3%)
Miscellaneous: Postoperative wound complication (RC: <1%; wound healing impairment)

<1%, postmarketing, and/or case reports: Arterial thrombosis, aspergillosis, azoospermia, cholecystitis, cholelithiasis, complex regional pain syndrome, decreased plasma testosterone, hemolytic uremic syndrome, hypersensitivity angiitis, male infertility, nephrotoxicity, oligospermia, pancreatitis (including acute pancreatitis), pericardial effusion, pneumonia (*Pneumocystis jiroveci)*, polyoma virus infection, progressive multifocal leukoencephalopathy, reactivation of HBV, respiratory distress, thrombosis of vascular graft (kidney), thrombotic thrombocytopenic purpura

General Dosage Range Dosage adjustment recommended in patients with hepatic impairment, on concomitant therapy, or who develop toxicities

Oral: *Children ≥1 year and Adults:* Dosage varies greatly depending on indication

Mechanism of Action Everolimus is a macrolide immunosuppressant and a mechanistic target of rapamycin (mTOR) inhibitor which has antiproliferative and antiangiogenic properties, and also reduces lipoma volume in patients with angiomyolipoma. Reduces protein synthesis and cell proliferation by binding to the FK binding protein-12 (FKBP-12), an intracellular protein, to form a complex that inhibits activation of mTOR (mechanistic target of rapamycin) serine-threonine kinase activity. Also reduces angiogenesis by inhibiting vascular endothelial growth factor (VEGF) and hypoxia-inducible factor (HIF-1) expression. Angiomyolipomas may occur due to unregulated mTOR activity in TSC-associated renal angiomyolipoma (Budde 2012); everolimus reduces lipoma volume (Bissler 2012).

Pharmacodynamics/Kinetics

Half-life Elimination ~30 hours (Afinitor and Zortress); in pediatric renal transplant patients (3 to 16 years), half-life similar to adult data (Van Damme-Lombaerts 2002)

Time to Peak 1 to 2 hours (Afinitor and Zortress)

Pregnancy Risk Factor C (Zortress)

Pregnancy Considerations Adverse events were observed in animal reproduction studies with exposures lower than expected with human doses. Based on the mechanism of action, may cause fetal harm if administered during pregnancy. Women of reproductive potential should be advised to avoid pregnancy and use highly effective birth control during treatment and for up to 8 weeks after everolimus discontinuation.

Everolimus may cause infertility. In females, menstrual irregularities, secondary amenorrhea, and increases in luteinizing hormone and follicle-stimulating hormone have occurred. Azoospermia and oligospermia have been observed in males. Females of reproductive potential should consider family planning options prior to therapy.

The National Transplantation Pregnancy Registry (NTPR) is a registry which follows pregnancies which occur in maternal transplant recipients or those fathered by male transplant recipients. The NTPR encourages reporting of pregnancies following solid organ transplant by contacting them at 877-955-6877 or NTPR@giftoflifeinstitute.org.

Dental Comment Consider a medical consultation prior to any invasive dental procedure in patients who have received an organ transplant; delayed wound healing due to the immunosuppressive effects and an increased potential for postoperative infection may be of concern.

Evolocumab (e voe LOK ue mab)

Brand Names: US Repatha; Repatha Pushtronex System; Repatha SureClick

Brand Names: Canada Repatha

Pharmacologic Category Antilipemic Agent, PCSK9 Inhibitor; Monoclonal Antibody

Use

Hyperlipidemia, primary: Adjunct to diet and maximally tolerated statin therapy for the treatment of adults with heterozygous familial hypercholesterolemia (HeFH) or clinical atherosclerotic cardiovascular disease (CVD), who require additional lowering of low density lipoprotein cholesterol (LDL-C).

Homozygous familial hypercholesterolemia: Adjunct to diet and other LDL-lowering therapies (eg, statins, ezetimibe, LDL apheresis) for the treatment of patients with homozygous familial hypercholesterolemia (HoFH) who require additional lowering of LDL-C.

Limitation of use: The effect of evolocumab on cardiovascular morbidity and mortality has not been determined.

Local Anesthetic/Vasoconstrictor Precautions No information available to require special precautions

Effects on Dental Treatment Key adverse event(s) related to dental treatment: Nasopharyngitis has been reported

Effects on Bleeding No information available to require special precautions

Adverse Reactions

>10%: Respiratory: Nasopharyngitis (6% to 11%)

1% to 10%:

Cardiovascular: Hypertension (3%)

Central nervous system: Dizziness (4%), fatigue (2%)

Dermatologic: Skin rash (1%)

Gastrointestinal: Gastroenteritis (3% to 6%), nausea (2%)

Genitourinary: Urinary tract infection (5%)

Hematologic & Oncologic: Bruise (1%)

Infection: Influenza (8% to 9%)

Local: Injection site reaction (6%), erythema at injection site (3% to ≤6%)

Neuromuscular & Skeletal: Myalgia (4%)

Respiratory: Upper respiratory tract infection (9%), cough (1% to 5%), sinusitis (4%)

<1%, postmarketing, and/or case reports: Antibody development, decreased LDL cholesterol (<25 mg/dL), hypersensitivity, urticaria

General Dosage Range

SubQ:

Adolescents 13 to 17 years: 420 mg once monthly

Adults: 140 mg every 2 weeks or 420 mg once monthly

Mechanism of Action Evolocumab is a human monoclonal antibody (IgG2 isotype) that binds to proprotein convertase subtilisin kexin type 9 (PCSK9). PCSK9 binds to the low-density lipoprotein receptors (LDLR) on hepatocyte surfaces to promote LDLR degradation within the liver. LDLR is the primary receptor that clears circulating LDL; therefore, the decrease in LDLR levels by PCSK9 results in higher blood levels of LDL-cholesterol (LDL-C). By inhibiting the binding of PCSK9 to LDLR, evolocumab increases the number of LDLRs available to clear LDL from the blood, thereby lowering LDL-C levels.

Pharmacodynamics/Kinetics

Onset of Action Peak effect: Proprotein convertase subtilisin kexin type 9 (PCSK9) suppression: 4 hours

Half-life Elimination 11 to 17 days

Time to Peak SubQ: 3 to 4 days

Pregnancy Considerations Adverse events were not observed in animal reproduction studies. IgG antibodies are known to cross the placenta in increasing amounts during the second and third trimesters; exposure of the fetus to evolocumab is expected.

Exemestane (ex e MES tane)

Brand Names: US Aromasin

Brand Names: Canada Aromasin; CO Exemestane

Pharmacologic Category Antineoplastic Agent, Aromatase Inhibitor

Use Breast cancer: Treatment of advanced breast cancer in postmenopausal women whose disease has progressed following tamoxifen therapy; adjuvant treatment of postmenopausal women with estrogen receptor-positive early breast cancer following 2 to 3 years of tamoxifen (for a total of 5 consecutive years of adjuvant therapy).

Local Anesthetic/Vasoconstrictor Precautions No information available to require special precautions

Effects on Dental Treatment No significant effects or complications reported

Effects on Bleeding No information available to require special precautions

Adverse Reactions

Frequency not always defined. *Incidence not specifically defined, but reported in the range of 1% to 10%.

Cardiovascular: Hypertension (5% to 15%), edema (6% to 7%), ischemic heart disease (2%; angina pectoris, myocardial infarction), chest pain*

Central nervous system: Fatigue (8% to 22%), insomnia (11% to 14%), pain (13%), headache (7% to 13%), depression (6% to 13%), dizziness (8% to 10%), anxiety (4% to 10%), paresthesia (3%), carpal tunnel syndrome (2%), confusion,* hypoesthesia*

Dermatological: Hyperhidrosis (4% to 18%), alopecia (15%), dermatitis (8%), pruritus,* skin rash*

Endocrine & metabolic: Hot flash (13% to 33%), weight gain (8%), increased follicle-stimulating hormone, increased luteinizing hormone, increased sex hormone binding globulin (with daily doses of ≥2.5 mg; dose-dependent)

Gastrointestinal: Nausea (9% to 18%), abdominal pain (6% to 11%), diarrhea (4% to 10%), vomiting (7%), anorexia (6%), constipation (5%), increased appetite (3%), dyspepsia*

Genitourinary: Urinary tract infection (2% to 5%)

Hematologic & oncologic: Lymphedema*

Hepatic: Increased serum alkaline phosphatase (14% to 15%), increased serum bilirubin (5% to 7%)

Infection: Infection*

Neuromuscular & skeletal: Arthralgia (15% to 29%), back pain (9%), limb pain (9%), myalgia (6%), osteoarthritis (6%), weakness (6%), osteoporosis (5%), pathological fracture (4%), muscle cramps (2%)
Ophthalmic: Visual disturbance (5%)
Renal: Increased serum creatinine (6%)
Respiratory: Dyspnea (10%), cough (6%), flu-like symptoms (6%), bronchitis,* pharyngitis,* rhinitis,* sinusitis,* upper respiratory tract infection*
Miscellaneous: Fever (5%)
<1%, postmarketing, and/or case reports: Acute generalized exanthematous pustulosis, cardiac failure, cholestatic hepatitis, endometrial hyperplasia, endometrial polyps, gastric ulcer, hepatitis, hypersensitivity reaction, increased gamma-glutamyl transferase, increased serum transaminases, neuropathy, osteochondrosis, thromboembolism, trigger finger, urticaria

General Dosage Range Dosage adjustment recommended in patients on concomitant therapy

Oral: *Adults (postmenopausal females):* 25 mg once daily

Mechanism of Action Exemestane is an irreversible, steroidal aromatase inactivator. It is structurally related to androstenedione, and is converted to an intermediate that irreversibly blocks the active site of the aromatase enzyme, leading to inactivation ("suicide inhibition") and thus preventing conversion of androgens to estrogens in peripheral tissues. Significantly lowers circulating estrogens in postmenopausal breast cancers where growth is estrogen-dependent.

Pharmacodynamics/Kinetics

Half-life Elimination ~24 hours

Time to Peak Women with breast cancer: 1.2 hours

Pregnancy Considerations Exemestane is not indicated for use in premenopausal women. Based on the mechanism of action and on animal data, exemestane is expected to cause fetal harm if administered to a pregnant woman. Women of reproductive potential should use effective contraception during treatment and for 1 month after the final dose. Pregnancy testing is recommended (for females of reproductive potential) within 7 days prior to therapy initiation.

Exenatide (ex EN a tide)

Related Information

Endocrine Disorders and Pregnancy *on page 1701*

Brand Names: US Bydureon; Byetta 10 MCG Pen; Byetta 5 MCG Pen

Brand Names: Canada Bydureon; Byetta

Pharmacologic Category Antidiabetic Agent, Glucagon-Like Peptide-1 (GLP-1) Receptor Agonist

Use

Type 2 diabetes mellitus: Treatment of type 2 diabetes mellitus (noninsulin dependent, NIDDM) to improve glycemic control as an adjunct to diet and exercise.

Limitations of use: Because of the uncertain relevance of the rat thyroid C-cell tumor findings to humans, prescribe exenatide ER only to patients for whom the potential benefits are considered to outweigh the potential risks. Exenatide ER is not recommended as first-line therapy for patients who have inadequate glycemic control on diet and exercise.

Local Anesthetic/Vasoconstrictor Precautions No information available to require special precautions

Effects on Dental Treatment No significant effects or complications reported

Effects on Bleeding No information available to require special precautions

Adverse Reactions Combination therapy may include a sulfonylurea, a thiazolidinedione, insulin glargine, or a combination of oral agents unless otherwise specified. * Frequency not defined.

>10%:
Central nervous system: Headache (8% to 14%)
Endocrine & metabolic: Hypoglycemia (combination therapy with a sulfonylurea: Byetta 14% to 36%, Bydureon 20%; combination therapy without a sulfonylurea ≤11%; monotherapy ≤5%; Bydureon with metformin 1% to 4%)
Gastrointestinal: Nausea (dose-dependent and usually decreases over time; Byetta combination therapy 40% to 44%, Bydureon combination therapy 9% to 24%, monotherapy 8% to 11%), diarrhea (combination therapy 6% to 20%, Bydureon monotherapy 11%, Byetta monotherapy 1% to <2%), vomiting (combination therapy 11% to 18%, Byetta monotherapy 4%)
Local: Injection site nodule (Bydureon 6% to 77%), injection site reaction (13% to 17%)

1% to 10%:
Cardiovascular: Increased heart rate* (Robinson 2013)
Central nervous system: Dizziness (Byetta combination therapy 9%, Byetta monotherapy 1% to <2%), fatigue (Bydureon combination therapy 6%), jitteriness (Byetta combination therapy 0%)
Dermatologic: Hyperhidrosis (Byetta combination therapy 3%)
Gastrointestinal: Constipation (6% to 10%), viral gastroenteritis (6% to 9%), dyspepsia (3% to 7%), decreased appetite (1% to 5%), abdominal distension (Byetta combination therapy 4%), gastroesophageal reflux disease (Byetta combination therapy 2% to 3%), flatulence (Byetta 2%)
Immunologic: Antibody development to exenatide (2% to 6%, associated with attenuated glycemic response)
Local: Itching at injection site (Bydureon ≥5%)
Neuromuscular & skeletal: Weakness (Byetta combination therapy 4% to 5%)

<1%, postmarketing, and/or case reports (all products): Abscess at injection site, acute pancreatitis, acute renal failure, alopecia, anaphylaxis, angioedema, cellulitis at injection site, chest pain (Byetta combination therapy), chills (Byetta combination therapy), drowsiness, dysgeusia, eructation, hemorrhagic pancreatitis, hypersensitivity pneumonitis (chronic; Byetta combination therapy), increased serum creatinine, influenza, kidney transplant dysfunction, macular eruption, nasopharyngitis, necrotizing pancreatitis (sometimes resulting in death), pain (stomach, side, or abdominal pain possibly radiating to the back), papular rash, prolongation P-R interval on ECG (Linnebjerg 2011), pruritus, renal function abnormality, renal insufficiency, severe diarrhea, severe hypoglycemia (Byetta combination therapy with metformin and a sulfonylurea), severe nausea, severe vomiting, tissue necrosis at injection site, upper respiratory tract infection, urticaria

General Dosage Range SubQ: *Adults:*

Immediate release: Initial: 5 mcg twice daily; Maintenance: 5-10 mcg twice daily
Extended release: 2 mg once weekly

Mechanism of Action Exenatide is an analog of the hormone incretin (glucagon-like peptide 1 or GLP-1) which increases glucose-dependent insulin secretion, decreases inappropriate glucagon secretion, increases

B-cell growth/replication, slows gastric emptying, and decreases food intake. Exenatide administration results in decreases in hemoglobin A_{1c} by approximately 0.5% to 1% (immediate release) or 1.5% to 1.9% (extended release).

Pharmacodynamics/Kinetics

Half-life Elimination

Immediate release (daily) formulation: 2.4 hours

Extended release (weekly) formulation: ~2 weeks

Time to Peak SubQ:

Immediate release (daily) formulation: 2.1 hours

Extended release (weekly) formulation: Triphasic: Phase 1: 2-5 hours; Phase 2: ~2 weeks; Phase 3: ~7 weeks

Pregnancy Risk Factor C

Pregnancy Considerations Adverse events were observed in some animal reproduction studies. Based on in vitro data, exenatide has a low potential to cross the placenta (Hiles 2003).

In women with diabetes, maternal hyperglycemia can be associated with congenital malformations as well as adverse effects in the fetus, neonate, and the mother (ACOG 2005; ADA 2016c; Kitzmiller 2008; Metzger 2007). To prevent adverse outcomes, prior to conception and throughout pregnancy maternal blood glucose and HbA_{1c} should be kept as close to target goals as possible but without causing significant hypoglycemia (ACOG 2013; ADA 2016c; Blumer 2013; Kitzmiller 2008). Agents other than exenatide are currently recommended to treat diabetes in pregnant women (ACOG 2013; Blumer 2013).

Health care providers are encouraged to enroll women exposed to exenatide during pregnancy in the pregnancy registry (800-633-9081).

Ezetimibe (ez ET i mibe)

Related Information

Cardiovascular Diseases *on page 1752*

Brand Names: US Zetia

Brand Names: Canada ACH-Ezetimibe; ACT Ezetimibe; Apo-Ezetimibe; Bio-Ezetimibe; Ezetrol; JAMP-Ezetimibe; Mar-Ezetimibe; Mint-Ezetimibe; Mylan-Ezetimibe; PMS-Ezetimibe; Priva-Ezetimibe; RAN-Ezetimibe; Riva-Ezetimibe; Sandoz Ezetimibe; Teva-Ezetimibe

Pharmacologic Category Antilipemic Agent, 2-Azetidinone

Use

Homozygous familial hypercholesterolemia: In combination with atorvastatin or simvastatin for the reduction of elevated total cholesterol (total-C) and low-density lipoprotein cholesterol (LDL-C) levels in patients with homozygous familial hypercholesterolemia as an adjunct to other lipid-lowering treatments (eg, LDL apheresis) or if such treatments are unavailable.

Homozygous sitosterolemia: As adjunctive therapy to diet for the reduction of elevated sitosterol and campesterol levels in patients with homozygous familial sitosterolemia.

Primary hyperlipidemia:

Combination therapy with HMG-CoA reductase inhibitors: In combination with a 3-hydroxy-3-methylglutaryl-coenzyme A (HMG-CoA) reductase inhibitor (statin) as adjunctive therapy to diet for the reduction of elevated total-C, LDL-C, apolipoprotein B (apo B), and non-high-density lipoprotein cholesterol (non-HDL-C) in patients with primary (heterozygous familial and nonfamilial) hyperlipidemia.

Combination therapy with fenofibrate: In combination with fenofibrate as adjunctive therapy to diet for the reduction of elevated total-C, LDL-C, apo B, and non-HDL-C in adult patients with mixed hyperlipidemia.

Monotherapy: As adjunctive therapy to diet for the reduction of elevated total-C, LDL-C, apo B, and non-HDL-C in patients with primary (heterozygous familial and nonfamilial) hyperlipidemia.

Guideline recommendations: The National Lipid Association (NLA) recommends ezetimibe in combination with a statin to reduce the risk of atherosclerotic cardiovascular disease (ASCVD) events for at-risk patients not at non-HDL-C and/or LDL-C goals despite receiving maximally tolerated statin therapy or for those who cannot tolerate higher statin doses (eg, the elderly) (NLA [Jacobson 2015]).

Local Anesthetic/Vasoconstrictor Precautions No information available to require special precautions

Effects on Dental Treatment No significant effects or complications reported

Effects on Bleeding No information available to require special precautions

Adverse Reactions

1% to 10%:

Central nervous system: Fatigue (2%)

Gastrointestinal: Diarrhea (4%)

Hepatic: Increased serum transaminases (with HMG-CoA reductase inhibitors; ≥3 x ULN: 1%)

Infection: Influenza (2%)

Neuromuscular & skeletal: Arthralgia (3%), limb pain (3%)

Respiratory: Upper respiratory tract infection (4%), sinusitis (3%)

<1%, postmarketing, and/or case reports: Abdominal pain, anaphylaxis, angioedema, autoimmune hepatitis (Stolk 2006), cholecystitis, cholelithiasis, cholestatic hepatitis (Stolk 2006), depression, dizziness, erythema multiforme, headache, hepatitis, hypersensitivity reaction, increased creatine phosphokinase, myalgia, myopathy, nausea, pancreatitis, paresthesia, rhabdomyolysis, skin rash, thrombocytopenia, urticaria

General Dosage Range Oral: *Children ≥10 years, Adolescents, and Adults:* 10 mg once daily

Mechanism of Action Inhibits absorption of cholesterol at the brush border of the small intestine via the sterol transporter, Niemann-Pick C1-Like1 (NPC1L1). This leads to a decreased delivery of cholesterol to the liver, reduction of hepatic cholesterol stores and an increased clearance of cholesterol from the blood; decreases total C, LDL-cholesterol (LDL-C), ApoB, and triglycerides (TG) while increasing HDL-cholesterol (HDL-C).

Pharmacodynamics/Kinetics

Onset of Action Within 1 week; Maximum effect: 2-4 weeks

Half-life Elimination 22 hours (ezetimibe and metabolite)

Time to Peak Plasma: 4-12 hours (ezetimibe); 1-2 hours (active metabolite); Effects: ~2 weeks

Pregnancy Risk Factor C

Pregnancy Considerations Adverse events were observed in some animal reproduction studies. Use is contraindicated in pregnant women who require combination therapy with an HMG-CoA reductase inhibitor. If treatment for familial hypercholesterolemia is needed during pregnancy, other agents are preferred (Wiegman 2015).

Ezetimibe and Simvastatin

(ez ET i mibe & SIM va stat in)

Related Information

Ezetimibe *on page 680*

Simvastatin *on page 1479*

Brand Names: US Vytorin

Pharmacologic Category Antilipemic Agent, 2-Azetidinone; Antilipemic Agent, HMG-CoA Reductase Inhibitor

Use

Homozygous familial hypercholesterolemia: As an adjunct to diet for the reduction of elevated total cholesterol (total-C) and low-density lipoprotein cholesterol (LDL-C) in patients with homozygous familial hypercholesterolemia, as an adjunct to other lipid-lowering treatments (eg, LDL apheresis), or if such treatments are unavailable

Primary hyperlipidemia: As an adjunct to diet for the reduction of elevated total-C, LDL-C, apolipoprotein B (apo B), triglycerides, and non-high-density lipoprotein cholesterol (HDL-C), and to increase HDL-C in patients with primary (heterozygous familial and nonfamilial) hyperlipidemia or mixed hyperlipidemia

Simvastatin: Primary and secondary prevention of atherosclerotic cardiovascular disease (ASCVD) according to the American College of Cardiology/American Heart Association: To reduce the risk of ASCVD in patients with clinical ASCVD (eg, coronary heart disease, stroke/TIA, or peripheral arterial disease presumed to be of atherosclerotic origin) who are greater than 75 years of age or not a candidate for high-intensity statin therapy; in patients without clinical ASCVD if LDL-C is 190 mg/dL or greater and not a candidate for high-intensity statin therapy; in patients without clinical ASCVD who have type 1 or type 2 diabetes and are between 40 and 75 years of age; in patients with an estimated 10-year ASCVD risk 7.5% or greater and who are between 40 and 75 years of age (Stone, 2013). Specific recommendations from the Kidney Disease: Improving Global Outcomes (KDIGO) organization have also been released for patients with chronic kidney disease (KDIGO [Tonelli, 2013]).

Limitations of use: No incremental benefit of ezetimibe/simvastatin on cardiovascular morbidity and mortality over and above that demonstrated for simvastatin has been established. Ezetimibe/simvastatin has not been studied in Fredrickson type I, III, IV, and V dyslipidemias.

Local Anesthetic/Vasoconstrictor Precautions No information available to require special precautions

Effects on Dental Treatment Key adverse event(s) related to dental treatment: Assess unusual presentations of muscle weakness or myopathy resulting from lipid therapy such as patient having a difficult time brushing teeth or weakness with chewing. Refer patient back to their physician for evaluation and adjustment of lipid therapy.

Effects on Bleeding No information available to require special precautions

Adverse Reactions Incidences refer to combination, Vytorin. Also see individual agents.

1% to 10%:

Central nervous system: Headache (6%)

Gastrointestinal: Diarrhea (3%)

Hepatic: Increased serum ALT (4%)

Infection: Influenza (2%)

Neuromuscular & skeletal: Myalgia (4%), limb pain (2%), myopathy

Respiratory: Upper respiratory infection (4%)

General Dosage Range Dosage adjustment recommended in patients with renal impairment or on concomitant therapy

Oral: *Adults:* Ezetimibe 10 mg and simvastatin 10 to 40 mg once daily

Mechanism of Action

Ezetimibe: Inhibits absorption of cholesterol at the brush border of the small intestine, leading to a decreased delivery of cholesterol to the liver. Ezetimibe inhibits the enzyme Niemann-Pick C1-Like1 (NPC1L1), a sterol transporter.

Simvastatin: A methylated derivative of lovastatin that acts by competitively inhibiting 3-hydroxy-3-methylglutaryl-coenzyme A (HMG-CoA) reductase, the enzyme that catalyzes the rate-limiting step in cholesterol biosynthesis. In addition to the ability of HMG-CoA reductase inhibitors to decrease levels of high-sensitivity C-reactive protein (hsCRP), they also possess pleiotropic properties including improved endothelial function, reduced inflammation at the site of the coronary plaque, inhibition of platelet aggregation, and anticoagulant effects (de Denus, 2002; Ray, 2005).

Pregnancy Risk Factor X

Pregnancy Considerations Use is contraindicated in pregnant women or women who may become pregnant. See individual agents.

Ezogabine (e ZOG a been)

Brand Names: US Potiga

Pharmacologic Category Anticonvulsant, Neuronal Potassium Channel Opener

Use Partial-onset seizures: As adjunctive treatment for partial-onset seizures in patients ≥18 years who have responded inadequately to several alternative treatments and for whom the benefits outweigh the risk of retinal abnormalities and potential decline in visual acuity

Local Anesthetic/Vasoconstrictor Precautions Ezogabine is one of the drugs confirmed to prolong the QT interval and is accepted as having a risk of causing torsade de pointes. The risk of drug-induced torsade de pointes is extremely low when a single QT interval prolonging drug is prescribed. In terms of epinephrine, it is not known what effect vasoconstrictors in the local anesthetic regimen will have in patients with a known history of congenital prolonged QT interval or in patients taking any medication that prolongs the QT interval. Until more information is obtained, it is suggested that the clinician consult with the physician prior to the use of a vasoconstrictor in suspected patients, and that the vasoconstrictor (epinephrine, mepivacaine and levonordefrin [Carbocaine® 2% with Neo-Cobefrin®]) be used with caution.

Effects on Dental Treatment Key adverse event(s) related to dental treatment: Xerostomia and changes in salivation (normal salivary flow resumes upon discontinuation)

Effects on Bleeding No information available to require special precautions

Adverse Reactions

>10%:

Central nervous system: Dizziness (dose related; 15% to 32%), drowsiness (dose related; 15% to 27%),

fatigue (13% to 16%), confusion (dose related; 4% to 16%), ataxia (dose related; 5% to 12%)
Neuromuscular & skeletal: Tremor (dose related; 10% to 12%)
2% to 10%:
Central nervous system: Vertigo (8% to 9%), memory impairment (dose related; 6% to 9%), dysarthria (2% to 8%), lack of concentration (6% to 7%), aphasia (dose related; 1% to 7%), abnormal gait (dose related; 2% to 6%), disorientation (5%), anxiety (3% to 5%), equilibrium disturbance (dose related; 3% to 5%), paresthesia (3% to 5%), amnesia (3%), dysphasia (1% to 3%), hallucination (≤2%), psychotic symptoms (≤2%)
Dermatologic: Skin discoloration (10%)
Endocrine & metabolic: Weight gain (dose related; 2% to 3%)
Gastrointestinal: Nausea (6% to 9%), constipation (dose related; 4% to 5%), dyspepsia (3%)
Genitourinary: Dysuria (dose related; 1% to 4%), urinary hesitancy (1% to 4%), urine discoloration (dose related; 2% to 3%), urinary retention (≤2%), hematuria (1% to 2%)
Infection: Influenza (4% to 5%)
Neuromuscular & skeletal: Weakness (4% to 6%)
Ophthalmic: Blurred vision (dose related; 4% to 10%), diplopia (6% to 8%)
Frequency not defined:
Cardiovascular: Prolonged Q-T interval on ECG (mean: 7.7 msec), syncope
Central nervous system: Brain disease, coma, euphoria
Dermatologic: Alopecia, skin rash
Hematologic & oncologic: Leukopenia, neutropenia, thrombocytopenia
Neuromuscular & skeletal: Muscle spasm
Ophthalmic: Nystagmus, retinal pigment changes
Renal: Nephrolithiasis, renal colic
Respiratory: Dyspnea
<2%, postmarketing, and/or case reports: Dysphagia, hydronephrosis, hyperhidrosis, hypokinesia, increased appetite, increased liver enzymes, maculopathy (acquired vitelliform lesions), malaise, mucosal discoloration, myoclonus, nail discoloration, ocular discoloration (sclera), peripheral edema, suicidal ideation, suicidal tendencies, xerostomia

General Dosage Range Dosage adjustment recommended in patients with renal impairment or hepatic impairment.

Oral:

Adults: Initial: 100 mg 3 times daily; Maintenance: 200 to 400 mg 3 times daily (maximum: 1,200 mg per day)

Elderly: Initial: 50 mg 3 times daily; Maintenance: 250 mg 3 times daily (maximum: 750 mg per day)

Mechanism of Action Ezogabine binds the KCNQ (Kv7.2-7.5) voltage-gated potassium channels, thereby stabilizing the channels in the open formation and enhancing the M-current. As a result, neuronal excitability is regulated and epileptiform activity is suppressed. In addition, ezogabine may also exert therapeutic effects through augmentation of GABA-mediated currents.

Pharmacodynamics/Kinetics

Half-life Elimination Ezogabine and NAMR: 7 to 11 hours; increased by ~30% in elderly patients

Time to Peak Plasma: 0.5 to 2 hours; delayed by 0.75 hours when administered with high-fat food

Pregnancy Risk Factor C

Pregnancy Considerations Adverse events have been observed in animal reproduction studies. Patients exposed to ezogabine during pregnancy are encouraged to enroll themselves into the North American Antiepileptic Drug (NAAED) Pregnancy Registry by calling 1-888-233-2334. Additional information is available at www.aedpregnancyregistry.org.

Product Availability In August 2016, GlaxoSmithKline announced plans to discontinue Potiga due to limited usage and continued decline in new patient initiation. Product will no longer be commercially available after June 30, 2017.

Controlled Substance C-V

Dental Comment See Local Anesthetic/Vasoconstrictor Precautions

Factor VIIa (Recombinant)

(FAK ter SEV en aye ree KOM be nant)

Brand Names: US NovoSeven RT

Brand Names: Canada Niastase; Niastase RT

Pharmacologic Category Antihemophilic Agent

Use Bleeding episodes and perioperative management: Treatment of bleeding episodes and perioperative management in adults and children with hemophilia A or B with inhibitors, congenital factor VII (FVII) deficiency, and Glanzmann's thrombasthenia with refractoriness to platelet transfusions, with or without antibodies to platelets; treatment of bleeding episodes and perioperative management in adults with acquired hemophilia.

Local Anesthetic/Vasoconstrictor Precautions No information available to require special precautions

Effects on Dental Treatment No significant effects or complications reported

Effects on Bleeding Serious thromboembolic events are associated with use. Medical consult recommended.

Adverse Reactions

1% to 10%:
Cardiovascular: Thrombosis (4%), hypertension (2%), bradycardia (1%), edema (1%), hypotension (1%)
Central nervous system: Cerebrovascular disease (<2%), headache (1%), pain (1%)
Dermatologic: Pruritus (1%), skin rash (1%)
Endocrine & metabolic: Decreased serum fibrinogen (2%)
Gastrointestinal: Vomiting (1%)
Hematologic & oncologic: Decreased prothrombin time (1%), disseminated intravascular coagulation (1%), increased fibrinolysis (1%), purpura (1%)
Hepatic: Abnormal hepatic function tests (<2%)
Hypersensitivity: Hypersensitivity reaction (1%)
Local: Injection site reaction (1%)
Neuromuscular & skeletal: Osteoarthrosis (1%)
Renal: Renal function abnormality (1%)
Respiratory: Pneumonia (1%)
Miscellaneous: Fever (4%), decreased therapeutic response (<2%)
<1%, postmarketing, and/or case reports: Anaphylactic shock, anaphylaxis, angina pectoris, angioedema, antibody development, arterial embolism (retinal), arterial thrombosis, arterial thrombosis (limb, retinal), arthralgia bowel infarction, cerebral infarction, cerebral ischemia, cerebrovascular accident, deep vein thrombosis, flushing, hepatic artery thrombosis, hypersensitivity, immunogenicity, increased fibrin degradation products (including D-dimer elevation), intracardiac thrombus, local phlebitis, myocardial infarction,

myocardial ischemia, nausea, occlusion of cerebral arteries, pain at injection site, peripheral ischemia, portal vein thrombosis, pulmonary embolism, renal artery thrombosis, shock, thrombophlebitis, urticaria, venous thrombosis at injection site

General Dosage Range IV: *Children, Adolescents, and Adults:* Dosage varies greatly depending on indication

Mechanism of Action Recombinant factor VIIa, a vitamin K-dependent glycoprotein, promotes hemostasis by activating the extrinsic pathway of the coagulation cascade. It replaces deficient activated coagulation factor VII, which complexes with tissue factor and may activate coagulation factor X to Xa and factor IX to IXa. When complexed with other factors, coagulation factor Xa converts prothrombin to thrombin, a key step in the formation of a fibrin-platelet hemostatic plug.

Pharmacodynamics/Kinetics

Half-life Elimination

Hemophilia A or B: Half-life, terminal: Children 2 to 12 years: 2.6 hours; Adults: 2.9 to 3.1 hours

Factor VII deficiency: Half-life, terminal: 2.8 to 3.1 hours

Pregnancy Considerations Adverse events have been observed in animal reproduction studies. Factor VII concentrations may vary significantly in pregnant women with coagulation disorders. Pregnant women with hemophilia should have clotting factors monitored, particularly at 28 and 34 weeks gestation and prior to invasive procedures. Recombinant factor VIIa is recommended for the management of bleeding disorders in pregnant women with factor VII deficiency. Prophylaxis at delivery may be needed if factor VII concentrations are <10 to 20 units /dL or in women with a significant bleeding history and treatment should continue for 3 to 5 days postpartum depending on route of delivery. The neonate may also be at an increased risk of bleeding following delivery and should be tested for the coagulation disorder (Kadir 2009; Lee 2006).

Factor IX Complex (Human) [(Factors II, IX, X)]

(FAK ter nyne KOM pleks HYU man FAKter too nyne ten)

Brand Names: US Bebulin; Bebulin VH [DSC]; Profilnine; Profilnine SD

Pharmacologic Category Antihemophilic Agent; Blood Product Derivative; Prothrombin Complex Concentrate (PCC)

Use

Factor IX deficiency (hemophilia B [Christmas disease]): Prevention and control of bleeding in patients with factor IX deficiency (hemophilia B or Christmas disease)

Limitations of use: Not indicated for the treatment of other factor deficiencies (eg, factor II, VII, VIII, X), treatment of hemophilia A patients with inhibitors to factor VIII, or treatment of bleeding caused by low levels of liver-dependent coagulation factors.

Local Anesthetic/Vasoconstrictor Precautions No information available to require special precautions

Effects on Dental Treatment No significant effects or complications reported

Effects on Bleeding Associated with disseminated intravascular coagulation and thromboembolism

Adverse Reactions Frequency not defined.

Cardiovascular: Flushing, thrombosis (sometimes fatal)

Central nervous system: Chills, drowsiness, headache, lethargy, paresthesia

Dermatologic: Skin rash, urticaria

Gastrointestinal: Nausea, vomiting

Hematologic & oncologic: Disseminated intravascular coagulation, heparin-induced thrombocytopenia (with products containing heparin)

Hypersensitivity: Anaphylactic shock

Immunologic: Antibody development (to clotting factor)

Respiratory: Dyspnea

Miscellaneous: Fever

General Dosage Range IV: *Children, Adolescents, and Adults:* Dosage varies greatly depending on indication

Mechanism of Action Replaces deficient clotting factor including factor X; hemophilia B, or Christmas disease, is an X-linked recessively inherited disorder of blood coagulation characterized by insufficient or abnormal synthesis of the clotting protein factor IX. Factor IX is a vitamin K-dependent coagulation factor which is synthesized in the liver. Factor IX is activated by factor XIa in the intrinsic coagulation pathway. Activated factor IX (IXa), in combination with factor VII:C, activates factor X to Xa, resulting ultimately in the conversion of prothrombin to thrombin and the formation of a fibrin clot. The infusion of exogenous factor IX to replace the deficiency present in hemophilia B temporarily restores hemostasis.

Pharmacodynamics/Kinetics

Half-life Elimination IX component: ~19 to 25 hours

Pregnancy Risk Factor C

Pregnancy Considerations Animal reproduction studies have not been conducted. Factor IX concentrations do not change significantly in pregnant women with coagulation disorders and women with factor IX deficiency may be at increased risk of postpartum hemorrhage. Pregnant women should have clotting factors monitored, particularly at 28 and 34 weeks gestation and prior to invasive procedures. Prophylaxis may be needed if factor IX concentrations are <50 units/mL at term and treatment should continue for 3 to 5 days postpartum depending on route of delivery. Because parvovirus infection may cause hydrops fetalis or fetal death, a recombinant product is preferred if prophylaxis or treatment is needed. The neonate may also be at an increased risk of bleeding following delivery and should be tested for the coagulation disorder (Chi 2012; Kadir 2009; Lee 2006).

Factor IX (Human) (FAK ter nyne HYU man)

Brand Names: US AlphaNine SD; Mononine

Brand Names: Canada Immunine VH

Pharmacologic Category Antihemophilic Agent; Blood Product Derivative

Use Prevention and control of bleeding in patients with hemophilia B (congenital factor IX deficiency or Christmas disease)

NOTE: Contains **nondetectable levels of factors II, VII, and X**. Therefore, **NOT INDICATED** for replacement therapy of any other clotting factor besides factor IX or for reversal of anticoagulation due to either vitamin K antagonists or other anticoagulants (eg, dabigatran), for hemophilia A patients with factor VIII inhibitors, or for patients in a hemorrhagic state caused by reduced production of liver-dependent coagulation factors (eg, hepatitis, cirrhosis).

Local Anesthetic/Vasoconstrictor Precautions No information available to require special precautions

Effects on Dental Treatment No significant effects or complications reported

Effects on Bleeding Associated with disseminated intravascular coagulation and thromboembolism

Adverse Reactions Frequency not defined.

Cardiovascular: Flushing, thrombosis

Central nervous system: Burning sensation (in jaw/skull), chills, headache, lethargy, paresthesia, rigors

Dermatologic: Skin photosensitivity, urticaria

Gastrointestinal: Diarrhea, nausea, vomiting

Hematologic & oncologic: Disseminated intravascular coagulation

Hepatic: Increased serum alkaline phosphatase, increased serum ALT, increased serum AST

Hypersensitivity: Anaphylaxis, hypersensitivity reaction

Local: Discomfort at injection site (stinging, burning), injection site reaction, pain at injection site

Neuromuscular & skeletal: Neck tightness

Ophthalmic: Visual disturbance

Respiratory: Allergic rhinitis, asthma, laryngeal edema, pulmonary disease

Miscellaneous: Fever (including transient fever following rapid administration)

Postmarketing and/or case reports: Angioedema, cerebral hemorrhage (intrathalamic [Douvas, 2004]), cyanosis, decreased therapeutic response, dyspnea, factor IX inhibitor development, hypotension, myocardial infarction (high doses), pulmonary embolism (high doses), superior vena cava syndrome (neonates [Douvas, 2004])

General Dosage Range IV: *Infants, Children, Adolescents, and Adults:* Dosage varies greatly depending on indication

Mechanism of Action Replaces deficient clotting factor IX. Hemophilia B, or Christmas disease, is an X-linked inherited disorder of blood coagulation characterized by insufficient or abnormal synthesis of the clotting protein factor IX. Factor IX is a vitamin K-dependent coagulation factor which is synthesized in the liver. Factor IX is activated by factor XIa in the intrinsic coagulation pathway. Activated factor IX (IXa), in combination with factor VII:C activates factor X to Xa, resulting ultimately in the conversion of prothrombin to thrombin and the formation of a fibrin clot. The infusion of exogenous factor IX to replace the deficiency present in hemophilia B temporarily restores hemostasis.

Pharmacodynamics/Kinetics

Half-life Elimination IX component: ~21 to 25 hours

Pregnancy Risk Factor C

Pregnancy Considerations Animal reproduction studies have not been conducted. Factor IX concentrations do not change significantly in pregnant women with coagulation disorders and women with factor IX deficiency may be at increased risk of postpartum hemorrhage. Pregnant women should have clotting factors monitored, particularly at 28 and 34 weeks gestation and prior to invasive procedures. Prophylaxis may be needed if factor IX concentrations are <50 units/mL at term and treatment should continue for 3 to 5 days postpartum depending on route of delivery. Because parvovirus infection may cause hydrops fetalis or fetal death, a recombinant product is preferred if prophylaxis or treatment is needed. The neonate may also be at an increased risk of bleeding following delivery and should be tested for the coagulation disorder (Chi, 2012; Kadir, 2009; Lee, 2006).

Factor IX (Recombinant)

(FAK ter nyne ree KOM be nant)

Brand Names: US BeneFIX; Ixinity; Rixubis

Brand Names: Canada BeneFix

Pharmacologic Category Antihemophilic Agent

Use

Factor IX deficiency: Prevention and control of bleeding episodes in patients with factor IX deficiency (hemophilia B [Christmas disease]); perioperative management in patients with hemophilia B; routine prophylaxis to prevent or reduce the frequency of bleeding episodes in patients with hemophilia B (Rixubis).

Limitations of use: These products are not indicated for the treatment of other factor deficiencies (eg, factor II, VII, VIII, X), for the treatment of hemophilia A patients with inhibitors to factor VIII, the reversal of coumarin-induced anticoagulation, or for the treatment of bleeding because of low levels of liver-dependent coagulation factors. Ixinity and Rixubis are not indicated for induction of immune tolerance in patients with hemophilia B.

Local Anesthetic/Vasoconstrictor Precautions No information available to require special precautions

Effects on Dental Treatment No significant effects or complications reported

Effects on Bleeding Associated with disseminated intravascular coagulation and thromboembolism

Adverse Reactions Frequency not always defined.

Cardiovascular: Flushing (3%), chest tightness (2%), thromboembolic complications, thromboembolism

Central nervous system: Headache (2% to 11%), dizziness (≤8%), chills (2%), drowsiness (2%), apathy (1%), depression (1%), lethargy (1%)

Dermatologic: Skin rash (2% to 6%), urticaria (3% to 5%), pruritic rash (1%)

Gastrointestinal: Nausea (6%), dysgeusia (≤5%), oral paresthesia (2%), vomiting (2%)

Hematologic & oncologic: Hemophilia (lack of efficacy; 1% to 2%)

Hypersensitivity: Hypersensitivity reaction

Immunologic: Antibody development (≤30%; non-neutralizing)

Infection: Influenza (1%)

Local: Injection site reaction (2% to 8%), pain at injection site (≤6%), cellulitis at injection site (2%), injection site phlebitis (2%), discomfort at injection site (1%)

Neuromuscular & skeletal: Tremor (2%), limb pain (1%), weakness (1%)

Ophthalmic: Blurred vision (2%)

Renal: Renal infarction (2%)

Respiratory: Dyspnea (3%), cough (2%, dry), hypoxia (2%)

Miscellaneous: Fever (3%)

<1%, postmarketing, and/or case reports: Anaphylaxis, angioedema, fatigue, halitosis, hypotension, nephrotic syndrome (associated with immune tolerance induction), obstructive uropathy, palpitations, peripheral thrombophlebitis, superior vena cava syndrome (neonates), therapeutic response unexpected (inadequate)

General Dosage Range IV: *Infants, Children, Adolescents, and Adults:* Dosage varies greatly depending on indication

Mechanism of Action Replaces deficient clotting factor IX. Hemophilia B, or Christmas disease, is an X-linked inherited disorder of blood coagulation characterized by insufficient or abnormal synthesis of the clotting protein factor IX. Factor IX is a vitamin K-dependent coagulation factor which is synthesized in the liver. Factor IX is activated by factor XIa in the intrinsic coagulation pathway. Activated factor IX (IXa) in combination with factor VII:C activates factor X to Xa, resulting ultimately in the conversion of prothrombin to thrombin and the formation of a fibrin clot. The infusion of exogenous factor IX to replace the deficiency present in hemophilia B temporarily restores hemostasis.

Pharmacodynamics/Kinetics

Half-life Elimination

Children: BeneFIX: 14 to 28 hours; Rixubis: 23 to 28 hours

Children ≥12 years, Adolescents, and Adults: Ixinity: 13 to 43 hours

Children ≥12 years, Adolescents, and Adults: Rixubis: ~26 hours

Adolescents >15 years and Adults: BeneFIX: 11 to 36 hours

Pregnancy Risk Factor C

Pregnancy Considerations Animal reproduction studies have not been conducted. Factor IX concentrations do not change significantly in pregnant women with coagulation disorders and women with factor IX deficiency may be at increased risk of postpartum hemorrhage. Pregnant women should have clotting factors monitored, particularly at 28 and 34 weeks gestation and prior to invasive procedures. Prophylaxis may be needed if factor IX concentrations are <50 units/mL at term and treatment should continue for 3 to 5 days postpartum depending on route of delivery. Because parvovirus infection may cause hydrops fetalis or fetal death, a recombinant product is preferred if prophylaxis or treatment is needed. The neonate may also be at an increased risk of bleeding following delivery and should be tested for the coagulation disorder (Chi 2012; Kadir 2009; Lee 2006).

Factor X (Human) (FAK ter ten HYU man)

Brand Names: US Coagadex

Pharmacologic Category Antihemophilic Agent; Blood Product Derivative

Use

Bleeding episodes and perioperative management of bleeding: Treatment of bleeding episodes in children ≥12 years of age and adults with hereditary factor X deficiency and perioperative management of bleeding episodes in children ≥12 years of age and adults with mild hereditary factor X deficiency.

Limitations of use: Perioperative management of bleeding in major surgery in patients with moderate and severe hereditary Factor X deficiency has not been studied.

Local Anesthetic/Vasoconstrictor Precautions No information available to require special precautions

Effects on Dental Treatment No significant effects or complications reported

Effects on Bleeding No information available to require special precautions

Adverse Reactions Frequency not always defined.

Central nervous system: Fatigue (6%), infusion-site pain (6%)

Hypersensitivity: Anaphylaxis, hypersensitivity reaction

Local: Infusion site reaction (6%; erythema)

Neuromuscular & skeletal: Back pain (6%)

General Dosage Range

IV: *Children ≥12, Adolescents, and Adults:* 25 units/kg/dose (maximum daily dose: 60 units/kg/day)

Mechanism of Action Replaces deficient clotting factor X needed for effective hemostasis. Factor X, an inactive zymogen, can be activated by factor IXa via the intrinsic pathway or by factor IIa via the extrinsic pathway. Factor X is then converted from its inactive form to the active form (factor Xa) by the cleavage of a 52-residue peptide from the heavy chain. Factor Xa associates with factor Va on the phospholipid surface to form the prothrombinase complex, which actives prothrombin to thrombin in the presence of calcium ions. Thrombin then acts upon soluble fibrinogen and factor XIII to generate a cross-linked fibrin clot.

Pharmacodynamics/Kinetics

Half-life Elimination Single dose: 30.3 hours

Pregnancy Considerations Animal reproduction studies have not been conducted. Factor X concentrations may increase during pregnancy and women with factor X deficiency should have clotting factors monitored, particularly at 28 and 34 weeks gestation and prior to invasive procedures. Replacement therapy may be needed if factor X concentrations are <10 to 20 units/dL. Because parvovirus infection may cause hydrops fetalis or fetal death, a recombinant product is preferred if prophylaxis or treatment is needed. The neonate may also be at an increased risk of bleeding following delivery and should be tested for the coagulation disorder (Chi 2012; Kadir 2009; Nance 2012).

Factor XIII Concentrate (Human)

(FAK ter THIR teen KON cen trate HYU man)

Brand Names: US Corifact

Brand Names: Canada Corifact

Pharmacologic Category Antihemophilic Agent; Blood Product Derivative

Use Prophylaxis against bleeding episodes and management of perioperative surgical bleeding in patients with congenital factor XIII deficiency

Local Anesthetic/Vasoconstrictor Precautions No information available to require special precautions

Effects on Dental Treatment No significant effects or complications reported

Effects on Bleeding Thrombosis and thromboembolism reported. Consider medical consult.

Adverse Reactions

Frequency not defined.

>1%:

Central nervous system: Chills, headache

Dermatologic: Erythema, pruritus, skin rash

Endocrine & metabolic: Increased lactate dehydrogenase

Hematologic & oncologic: Elevated thrombin-antithrombin levels, hematoma

Hypersensitivity: Hypersensitivity reaction

Neuromuscular & skeletal: Arthralgia, arthritis

Miscellaneous: Fever

<1%, postmarketing, and/or case reports: Anaphylaxis, antibody development (factor XIII), infection, ischemia (acute), thromboembolism

General Dosage Range IV: *Infants, Children, Adolescents, and Adults:* Initial: 40 units/kg; Maintenance: Varies depending on desired factor XIII trough levels; Usual: 40 units/kg every 28 days

Mechanism of Action Factor XIII (FXIII) is an endogenous plasma glycoprotein found in platelets, monocytes and macrophages that is converted to activated factor XIII (FXIIIa) in the presence of calcium ions. Once activated, FXIIIa cross-links fibrin and cross-links plasmin inhibitor to protect and strengthen the hemostatic platelet plug.

Pharmacodynamics/Kinetics

Duration of Action Plasma levels of FXIII: ~28 days; FXIII activity maintained at ≥5% in ≥97% of patients and ≥10% in ≥85% of patients

Half-life Elimination Children (<16 years): 5.7 ± 1 days; Adults: 7.1 ± 2.7 days

Time to Peak 1.7 hours postinfusion

Pregnancy Risk Factor C

Pregnancy Considerations Use in pregnant women only when benefit exceeds potential risk to the fetus. Thromboembolic events have been reported with use of factor XIII; pregnant women may be at increased risk due to hypercoagulable state.

Famciclovir (fam SYE kloe veer)

Related Information

Systemic Viral Diseases *on page 1806*

Viral Infections *on page 1849*

Related Sample Prescriptions

Viral Infections - Sample Prescriptions *on page 40*

Brand Names: US Famvir [DSC]

Brand Names: Canada Apo-Famciclovir; Ava-Famciclovir; CO Famciclovir; Famvir; PMS-Famciclovir; Sandoz-Famciclovir

Generic Availability (US) Yes

Pharmacologic Category Antiviral Agent

Dental Use Management of acute herpes zoster (shingles); treatment of recurrent herpes labialis in immunocompetent patients

Use Treatment of acute herpes zoster (shingles) in immunocompetent patients; treatment and suppression of recurrent episodes of genital herpes in immunocompetent patients; treatment of herpes labialis (cold sores) in immunocompetent patients; treatment of recurrent orolabial/genital (mucocutaneous) herpes simplex in HIV-infected adult patients

Local Anesthetic/Vasoconstrictor Precautions No information available to require special precautions

Effects on Dental Treatment No significant effects or complications reported

Effects on Bleeding No information available to require special precautions

Adverse Reactions Frequencies vary with dose and duration.

>10%:

Central nervous system: Headache (9% to 23%)

Gastrointestinal: Nausea (11% to 13%)

1% to 10%:

Central nervous system: Fatigue (≤5%), migraine (≤3%), paresthesia (≤3%)

Dermatologic: Pruritus (2% to 4%), skin rash (3%)

Gastrointestinal: Diarrhea (2% to 8%), flatulence (≤5%), vomiting (≤5%)

Genitourinary: Dysmenorrhea (≤8%)

Hematologic & oncologic: Neutropenia (3%), leukopenia (1%)

Hepatic: Increased serum ALT (3%), increased serum AST (2%), increased serum bilirubin (2%)

<1%, postmarketing, and/or case reports: Abnormal hepatic function tests, anaphylactic shock, anaphylaxis, anemia, angioedema (eyelid edema, facial edema, periorbital edema, pharyngeal edema), cholestatic jaundice, confusion, delirium, disorientation, dizziness, drowsiness, erythema multiforme, hallucination, hypersensitivity angiitis, palpitations, seizure, Stevens-Johnson syndrome, thrombocytopenia, toxic epidermal necrolysis, urticaria

Dental Usual Dosage Adults: Oral:

Acute herpes zoster: 500 mg every 8 hours for 7 days (**Note:** Initiate therapy as soon as possible after diagnosis and within 72 hours of rash onset)

Recurrent herpes labialis (cold sores): 1,500 mg as a single dose; initiate therapy at first sign or symptom such as tingling, burning, or itching (initiated within 1 hour in clinical studies)

Dosing

Adult & Geriatric

Genital herpes simplex virus (HSV) infection: Oral: **Note:** Initiate therapy as soon as possible after diagnosis and within 72 hours of rash onset

Immunocompetent patients:

Initial episode (off-label use): 250 mg 3 times daily for 7 to 10 days. **Note:** Treatment can be extended if healing is incomplete after 10 days of therapy (CDC [Workowski 2015])

Recurrence:

Manufacturer's labeling: 1,000 mg twice daily for 1 day (**Note:** Initiate therapy as soon as possible and within 6 hours of symptoms/lesions onset)

Alternate dosing: 125 mg twice daily for 5 days or 500 mg as a single dose, followed by 250 mg twice daily for 2 days (CDC [Workowski 2015]).

Suppressive therapy: 250 mg twice daily. **Note:** Duration not established, but efficacy/safety have been demonstrated for 1 year (CDC [Workowski 2015]).

HIV-infected patients:

Manufacturer's labeling: Recurrent episodes: 500 mg twice daily for 7 days

Alternate dosing:

Initial or recurrent episodes: 500 mg twice daily for 5 to 10 days (HHS [OI adult 2016])

Chronic suppressive therapy (off-label use): 500 mg twice daily; suppressive therapy can be continued indefinitely regardless of CD4 count in patients with severe recurrences of genital herpes or in patients who want to minimize frequency of recurrences, or to reduce the risk of genital ulcer disease in patients with CD4 cell counts <250 cells/mm^3 who are starting antiretroviral therapy. However, continuation of therapy should be reviewed annually, particularly if immune reconstitution has occurred (HHS [OI adult 2016]).

Herpes labialis/orolabial (cold sores): Oral: **Note:** Initiate therapy as soon as possible after diagnosis and within 72 hours of rash onset

Immunocompetent patients:

Recurrent episodes: 1,500 mg as a single dose; initiate therapy at first sign or symptom such as tingling, burning, or itching (initiated within 1 hour in clinical studies)

HIV patients:

Manufacturer's labeling: Recurrent episodes: 500 mg twice daily for 7 days

Alternate dosing: Treatment: 500 mg twice daily for 5 to 10 days (HHS [OI adult 2016])

Herpes zoster (shingles): Oral: **Note:** Initiate therapy as soon as possible after diagnosis and within 1 week of rash onset or any time before full crusting of lesions

Immunocompetent patients: 500 mg every 8 hours for 7 days

HIV-infected patients with acute localized dermatomal lesion (off-label use): 500 mg 3 times daily for 7 to 10 days; consider longer duration if lesions heal slowly (HHS [OI adult 2016])

HIV- infected patients with extensive cutaneous lesion or visceral involvement (off-label use): Initial therapy with acyclovir IV may be switched to famciclovir 500 mg 3 times daily to complete a 10 to 14 day course, when formation of new lesions has ceased and signs and symptoms of visceral VZV infection are improving (HHS [OI adult 2016])

Varicella infection (chickenpox) in HIV-infected patients (uncomplicated cases) (off-label use): Oral: 500 mg 3 times daily for 5 to 7 days (HHS [OI adult 2016])

Pediatric

Genital herpes simplex virus (HSV) in HIV-infected patients: Adolescents (off-label population): Oral:

Initial or recurrent episodes: 500 mg twice daily for 5 to 10 days (HHS [OI adult 2016])

Chronic suppressive therapy (off-label use): 500 mg twice daily; suppressive therapy can be continued indefinitely regardless of CD4 count in patients with severe recurrences of genital herpes or in patients who want to minimize frequency of recurrences, or to reduce the risk of genital ulcer disease in patients with CD4 cell counts <250 cells/mm^3 who are starting antiretroviral therapy. However, continuation of therapy should be reviewed annually, particularly if immune reconstitution has occurred (HHS [OI adult 2016]).

Herpes labialis/orolabial (cold sores) in HIV-infected patients: Adolescents (off-label population): Oral: Treatment: 500 mg twice daily for 5 to 10 days (HHS [OI adult 2016])

Herpes zoster (shingles) in HIV-infected patients (off-label use) (HHS [OI adult 2016]): Adolescents: Oral:

Acute localized dermatomal lesion: 500 mg 3 times daily for 7 to 10 days; consider longer duration if lesions heal slowly

Extensive cutaneous lesion or visceral involvement (off-label use): Initial therapy with acyclovir IV may be switched to famciclovir 500 mg 3 times daily to complete a 10- to 14-day course, when formation of new lesions has ceased and signs and symptoms of visceral VZV infection are improving

Varicella infection (chickenpox) in HIV-infected patients (uncomplicated cases) (off-label use): Adolescents: Oral: 500 mg 3 times daily for 5 to 7 days (HHS [OI adult 2016])

Renal Impairment

Herpes zoster:

CrCl ≥60 mL/minute: No dosage adjustment necessary

CrCl 40 to 59 mL/minute: Administer 500 mg every 12 hours

CrCl 20 to 39 mL/minute: Administer 500 mg every 24 hours

CrCl <20 mL/minute: Administer 250 mg every 24 hours

Hemodialysis: Administer 250 mg after each dialysis session.

Recurrent genital herpes: Treatment:

Single-day regimen:

CrCl ≥60 mL/minute: No dosage adjustment necessary.

CrCl 40 to 59 mL/minute: Administer 500 mg every 12 hours for 1 day

CrCl 20 to 39 mL/minute: Administer 500 mg as a single dose

CrCl <20 mL/minute: Administer 250 mg as a single dose

Hemodialysis: Administer 250 mg as a single dose after a dialysis session.

Alternatively the following recommendations have been made (Famvir Canadian product labeling 2016):

CrCl >20 mL/minute/1.73 m^2: Administer 125 mg every 12 hours

CrCl <20 mL/minute/1.73 m^2: Administer 125 mg every 24 hours

Hemodialysis: Administer 125 mg after each dialysis session.

Recurrent genital herpes: Suppression:

CrCl ≥40 mL/minute: No dosage adjustment necessary.

CrCl 20 to 39 mL/minute: Administer 125 mg every 12 hours

CrCl <20 mL/minute: Administer 125 mg every 24 hours

Hemodialysis: Administer 125 mg after each dialysis session.

Recurrent herpes labialis: Treatment (single-dose regimen):

CrCl ≥60 mL/minute: No dosage adjustment necessary.

CrCl 40 to 59 mL/minute: Administer 750 mg as a single dose

CrCl 20 to 39 mL/minute: Administer 500 mg as a single dose

CrCl <20 mL/minute: Administer 250 mg as a single dose

Hemodialysis: Administer 250 mg as a single dose after a dialysis session.

Recurrent orolabial/genital (mucocutaneous) herpes in HIV-infected patients:

CrCl ≥40 mL/minute: No dosage adjustment necessary.

CrCl 20 to 39 mL/minute: Administer 500 mg every 24 hours

CrCl <20 mL/minute: Administer 250 mg every 24 hours

Hemodialysis: Administer 250 mg after each dialysis session.

Hepatic Impairment

Mild-to-moderate impairment: No dosage adjustment is necessary

Severe impairment: No dosage adjustment provided in manufacturer's labeling; has not been studied. However, a 44% decrease in the C_{max} of penciclovir (active metabolite) was noted in patients with mild-to-moderate impairment; impaired conversion of famciclovir to penciclovir may affect efficacy.

Mechanism of Action Famciclovir undergoes rapid biotransformation to the active compound, penciclovir (prodrug), which is phosphorylated by viral thymidine kinase in HSV-1, HSV-2, and VZV-infected cells to a monophosphate form; this is then converted to penciclovir triphosphate and competes with deoxyguanosine triphosphate to inhibit HSV-2 polymerase, therefore, herpes viral DNA synthesis/replication is selectively inhibited.

Contraindications Hypersensitivity to famciclovir, penciclovir, or any component of the formulation

Warnings/Precautions Has not been established for use in immunocompromised patients (except HIV-infected patients with orolabial or genital herpes, patients with ophthalmic or disseminated zoster or with initial episode of genital herpes, and in Black and African American patients with recurrent episodes of genital herpes. Acute renal failure has been reported with use of inappropriate high doses in patients with underlying renal disease. Dosage adjustment is required in patients with renal insufficiency. Tablets contain lactose; do not use with galactose intolerance, severe lactase deficiency, or glucose-galactose malabsorption syndromes.

Drug Interactions

Metabolism/Transport Effects None known.

Avoid Concomitant Use

Avoid concomitant use of Famciclovir with any of the following: Varicella Virus Vaccine; Zoster Vaccine

Increased Effect/Toxicity There are no known significant interactions involving an increase in effect.

Decreased Effect

Famciclovir may decrease the levels/effects of: Talimogene Laherparepvec; Varicella Virus Vaccine; Zoster Vaccine

Food Interactions Rate of absorption and/or conversion to penciclovir and peak concentration are reduced with food, but bioavailability is not affected. Management: Administer without regard to meals.

Pharmacodynamics/Kinetics

Half-life Elimination

Penciclovir: 2 to 4 hours; Prolonged in renal impairment:

CrCl 40 to 59 mL/minute: ~3.4 hours

CrCl 20 to 39 mL/minute: ~6.2 hours

CrCl <20 mL/minute: ~13.4 hours

Intracellular penciclovir triphosphate: HSV 1: 10 hours; HSV 2: 20 hours; VZV: 7 hours

Time to Peak Penciclovir: ~1 hour

Pregnancy Risk Factor B

Pregnancy Considerations Adverse events have not been observed in animal reproduction studies. Based on available data, use during pregnancy appears to be well tolerated (CDC [Workowski 2015]; HHS [opportunistic; adult] 2015).

Health care providers are encouraged to enroll women exposed to famciclovir during pregnancy in the Famvir Pregnancy reporting system (888-669-6682).

Breastfeeding Considerations It is not known if famciclovir is excreted in breast milk. breastfeeding is not recommended by the manufacturer unless the potential benefits outweigh any possible risk. If herpes lesions are on breast, breastfeeding should be avoided in order to avoid transmission to infant (AAP 2012).

Dosage Forms

Tablet, Oral:

Generic: 125 mg, 250 mg, 500 mg

Famotidine (fa MOE ti deen)

Related Information

Gastrointestinal Disorders *on page 1775*

Brand Names: US Acid Reducer Maximum Strength [OTC]; Acid Reducer [OTC]; Heartburn Relief Max St [OTC]; Heartburn Relief [OTC]; Pepcid

Brand Names: Canada Acid Control; Apo-Famotidine; Famotidine Omega; Maximum Strength Pepcid AC; Mylan-Famotidine; Pepcid AC; Pepcid Complete; Peptic guard; Teva-Famotidine; Ulcidine

Generic Availability (US) Yes

Pharmacologic Category Histamine H_2 Antagonist

Use Maintenance therapy and treatment of duodenal ulcer; treatment of gastroesophageal reflux disease (GERD), active benign gastric ulcer; pathological hypersecretory conditions

OTC labeling: Relief of heartburn, acid indigestion, and sour stomach

Local Anesthetic/Vasoconstrictor Precautions No information available to require special precautions

Effects on Dental Treatment No significant effects or complications reported

Effects on Bleeding No information available to require special precautions

Adverse Reactions

>10%:

Central nervous system: Agitation (<1 year of age: ≤14%)

Gastrointestinal: Vomiting (<1 year of age: ≤14%)

1% to 10%:

Central nervous system: Headache (5%), dizziness (1%)

Gastrointestinal: Diarrhea (2%), constipation (1%), necrotizing enterocolitis (very low birth weight neonates; Guillet 2006)

<1%, postmarketing, and/or case reports: Abdominal distress, acne vulgaris, agranulocytosis, alopecia, anaphylaxis, angioedema, anorexia, anxiety, arthralgia, atrioventricular block, bronchospasm, cardiac arrhythmia, cholestatic jaundice, confusion, conjunctival injection, decreased libido, depression, drowsiness, dysgeusia, facial edema, fatigue, fever, flushing, hallucination, hepatitis, hypersensitivity reaction, increased liver enzymes, injection site reaction, insomnia, interstitial pneumonitis, leukopenia, muscle cramps, nausea, palpitations, pancytopenia, paresthesia, prolonged Q-T interval on ECG, pruritus, rhabdomyolysis, seizure, skin rash, Stevens-Johnson syndrome, thrombocytopenia, tinnitus, torsades de pointes, toxic epidermal necrolysis, urticaria, weakness, xeroderma, xerostomia

Dosing

Adult & Geriatric

Duodenal ulcer: Oral: Acute therapy: 40 mg/day at bedtime (or 20 mg twice daily) for 4-8 weeks; maintenance therapy: 20 mg/day at bedtime

Gastric ulcer: Oral: Acute therapy: 40 mg/day at bedtime

GERD: Oral: 20 mg twice daily for 6 weeks

Hypersecretory conditions: Oral: Initial: 20 mg every 6 hours, may increase in increments up to 160 mg every 6 hours

Esophagitis and accompanying symptoms due to GERD: Oral: 20 mg or 40 mg twice daily for up to 12 weeks

Peptic ulcer disease: Eradication of *Helicobacter pylori* (off-label use): Oral: 40 mg once daily; requires combination therapy with antibiotics

Stress ulcer prophylaxis, ICU patients (off-label use): Oral, IV, or nasogastric (NG) tube: 20 mg twice daily (ASHP, 1999; Baghaie, 1995); **Note:** Intended for patients with associated risk factors (eg, coagulopathy, mechanical ventilation for >48 hours, severe sepsis); discontinue use once risk factors have resolved. The Surviving Sepsis Campaign guidelines suggest the use of proton pump inhibitors rather than H_2 antagonist therapy (Dellinger, 2013).

Patients unable to take oral medication: IV: 20 mg every 12 hours

Heartburn, indigestion, sour stomach: OTC labeling: Oral: 10-20 mg every 12 hours; dose may be taken 15-60 minutes before eating foods known to cause heartburn

Pediatric Treatment duration and dose should be individualized

Peptic ulcer: 1-16 years:

Oral: 0.5 mg/kg/day at bedtime or divided twice daily (maximum dose: 40 mg/day); doses of up to 1 mg/kg/day have been used in clinical studies

IV: 0.25 mg/kg every 12 hours (maximum dose: 40 mg/day); doses of up to 0.5 mg/kg have been used in clinical studies

GERD: Oral:

<3 months: 0.5 mg/kg once daily

3-12 months: 0.5 mg/kg twice daily

1-16 years: 1 mg/kg/day divided twice daily (maximum dose: 40 mg twice daily); doses of up to 2 mg/kg/day have been used in clinical studies

Heartburn, indigestion, sour stomach: OTC labeling: Oral: Children ≥12 years: Refer to adult dosing.

Renal Impairment CrCl <50 mL/minute: Manufacturer's labeling: Administer 50% of dose **or** increase the dosing interval to every 36 to 48 hours (to limit potential CNS adverse effects).

Mechanism of Action Competitive inhibition of histamine at H_2 receptors of the gastric parietal cells, which inhibits gastric acid secretion

Contraindications Hypersensitivity to famotidine, other H_2 antagonists, or any component of the formulation

Warnings/Precautions Modify dose in patients with moderate-to-severe renal impairment. Prolonged QT interval has been reported in patients with renal dysfunction. The FDA has received reports of torsade de pointes occurring with famotidine (Poluzzi, 2009). Relief of symptoms does not preclude the presence of a gastric malignancy. Reversible confusional states, usually clearing within 3-4 days after discontinuation, have been linked to use. Prolonged treatment (≥2 years) may lead to vitamin B_{12} malabsorption and subsequent vitamin B_{12} deficiency. The magnitude of the deficiency is dose-related and the association is stronger in females and those younger in age (<30 years); prevalence is decreased after discontinuation of therapy (Lam, 2013). Increased age (>50 years) and renal or hepatic impairment are thought to be associated.

Benzyl alcohol and derivatives: Some dosage forms may contain benzyl alcohol and/or sodium benzoate/benzoic acid; benzoic acid (benzoate) is a metabolite of benzyl alcohol; large amounts of benzyl alcohol (≥99 mg/kg/day) have been associated with a potentially fatal toxicity ("gasping syndrome") in neonates; the "gasping syndrome" consists of metabolic acidosis, respiratory distress, gasping respirations, CNS dysfunction (including convulsions, intracranial hemorrhage), hypotension, and cardiovascular collapse (AAP ["Inactive" 1997]; CDC, 1982); some data suggests that benzoate displaces bilirubin from protein binding sites (Ahlfors, 2001); avoid or use dosage forms containing benzyl alcohol and/or benzyl alcohol derivative with caution in neonates. See manufacturer's labeling.

OTC labeling: When used for self-medication, patients should be instructed not to use if they have difficulty swallowing, are vomiting blood, or have bloody or black stools. Not for use with other acid reducers.

Drug Interactions

Metabolism/Transport Effects Substrate of OCT2

Avoid Concomitant Use

Avoid concomitant use of Famotidine with any of the following: Dasatinib; Delavirdine; PAZOPanib; Risedronate

Increased Effect/Toxicity

Famotidine may increase the levels/effects of: Dexmethylphenidate; Highest Risk QTc-Prolonging Agents; Methylphenidate; Moderate Risk QTc-Prolonging Agents; Risedronate; Saquinavir; Varenicline

The levels/effects of Famotidine may be increased by: BuPROPion; MiFEPRIStone

Decreased Effect

Famotidine may decrease the levels/effects of: Atazanavir; Bosutinib; Cefditoren; Cefpodoxime; Cefuroxime; Cysteamine (Systemic); Dabrafenib; Dasatinib; Delavirdine; Erlotinib; Fosamprenavir; Gefitinib; Indinavir; Iron Salts; Itraconazole; Ketoconazole (Systemic); Ledipasvir; Mesalamine; Multivitamins/Minerals (with ADEK, Folate, Iron); Nelfinavir; Nilotinib; PAZOPanib; Posaconazole; Rilpivirine; Velpatasvir

Food Interactions Prolonged treatment (≥2 years) may lead to malabsorption of dietary vitamin B_{12} and subsequent vitamin B_{12} deficiency (Lam, 2013).

Dietary Considerations May be taken without regard to meals.

Pharmacodynamics/Kinetics

Onset of Action Antisecretory effect: Oral: Within 1 hour; IV: Within 30 minutes; Peak effect: Antisecretory effect: Oral: Within 1 to 3 hours (dose-dependent)

Duration of Action Antisecretory effect: IV, Oral: 10 to 12 hours

Half-life Elimination

Infants: 0 to 3 months: 8.1 ± 3.5 hours to 10.5 ± 5.4 hours; >3 to 12 months: 4.5 ± 1.1 hours

Children: 3.3 ± 2.5 hours

Adolescents: 2.3 ± 0.4 hours

Adults: 2.5 to 3.5 hours; prolonged with renal impairment; Oliguria: >20 hours; Anuria: 24 hours

Time to Peak Serum: Oral: ~1 to 3 hours;orally disintegrating tablet: 2.5 hours

Pregnancy Risk Factor B

Pregnancy Considerations Adverse events have not been observed in animal reproduction studies; therefore, famotidine is classified as pregnancy category B. Famotidine crosses the placenta. An increased risk of congenital malformations or adverse events in the newborn has generally not been observed following maternal use of famotidine during pregnancy. Histamine H_2 antagonists have been evaluated for the treatment of gastroesophageal reflux disease (GERD), as well as gastric and duodenal ulcers, during pregnancy. Although if needed, famotidine is not the agent of choice. Histamine H_2 antagonists may be used for aspiration prophylaxis prior to cesarean delivery.

Breastfeeding Considerations Famotidine is excreted into breast milk with peak concentrations occurring ~6 hours after the maternal dose. According to the manufacturer, the decision to continue or discontinue breastfeeding during therapy should take into account the risk of exposure to the infant and the benefits of treatment to the mother.

Dosage Forms

Solution, Intravenous:

Generic: 20 mg (50 mL); 20 mg/2 mL (2 mL); 40 mg/4 mL (4 mL); 200 mg/20 mL (20 mL)

Solution, Intravenous [preservative free]:

Generic: 20 mg/2 mL (2 mL)

Suspension Reconstituted, Oral:

Pepcid: 40 mg/5 mL (50 mL)

Generic: 40 mg/5 mL (50 mL)

Tablet, Oral:

Acid Reducer [OTC]: 10 mg

Acid Reducer Maximum Strength [OTC]: 20 mg

Heartburn Relief [OTC]: 10 mg

Heartburn Relief Max St [OTC]: 20 mg

Pepcid: 20 mg, 40 mg

Generic: 10 mg, 20 mg, 40 mg

Febuxostat (feb UX oh stat)

Brand Names: US Uloric

Brand Names: Canada Uloric

Pharmacologic Category Antigout Agent; Xanthine Oxidase Inhibitor

Use

Hyperuricemia: Chronic management of hyperuricemia in patients with gout.

Limitations of use: Not recommended for treatment of asymptomatic hyperuricemia.

Local Anesthetic/Vasoconstrictor Precautions No information available to require special precautions

Effects on Dental Treatment Key adverse event(s) related to dental treatment: Xerostomia (normal salivary flow resumes upon discontinuation) and taste alteration has been reported in <1% of patients.

Effects on Bleeding No information available to require special precautions

Adverse Reactions

1% to 10%:

Dermatologic: Rash (1% to 2%)

Gastrointestinal: Nausea (1%)

Hepatic: Liver function abnormalities (5% to 7%)

Neuromuscular & skeletal: Arthralgia (1%)

<1%, postmarketing, and/or case reports: Abnormal electroencephalogram, abnormal gait, aggressive behavior, agitation, alopecia, anaphylaxis, anaphylaxis, anemia, angina pectoris, angioedema, anorexia, anxiety, arthralgia, atrial fibrillation, atrial flutter, blurred vision, bruise, cardiac failure, cerebral infarction, cerebrovascular accident, cerebrovascular accident, cholecystitis, cholelithiasis, constipation, deafness, decreased hematocrit, decreased libido, decreased serum bicarbonate, decreased urine output, dehydration, depression, dermatitis, diabetes mellitus, DRESS syndrome, dysgeusia, dyspepsia, dyspnea, ECG abnormality, eczema, edema, epistaxis, erectile dysfunction, flu-like symptoms, flushing, gastritis, gastroesophageal reflux disease, gingival pain, Guillain-Barré syndrome, gynecomastia, hair discoloration, heart murmur, hematemesis, hematochezia, hematuria, hemiparesis, hepatic failure, hepatitis, hepatomegaly, herpes zoster, hirsutism, hot flash, hyperacidity, hypercholesterolemia, hyperglycemia, hyperhidrosis, hyperkalemia, hyperlipidemia, hypernatremia, hypersensitivity, hypertension, hypertriglyceridemia, hypokalemia, hypotension, immune thrombocytopenia, increased amylase, increased blood urea nitrogen, increased creatine phosphokinase, increased lactate dehydrogenase, increased MCV, increased serum alkaline phosphatase, increased serum creatinine, increased thyroid stimulating hormone level, increased urine output, interstitial nephritis, jaundice, joint swelling, lethargy, leukocytosis, leukopenia, liver steatosis, lymphocytopenia, migraine, muscle spasm, muscle twitching, myalgia, myocardial infarction, nephrolithiasis, neutropenia, oral mucosa ulcer, pain, palpitations, pancreatitis, pancytopenia, panic attack, paresthesia, peptic ulcer, personality changes, petechia, pharyngeal edema, pollakiuria, prolonged partial thromboplastin time, prolonged prothrombin time, prostate specific antigen increase, proteinuria, psychotic symptoms, renal failure, respiratory tract infection, rhabdomyolysis, sinus bradycardia, skin discoloration, skin photosensitivity, splenomegaly, Stevens-Johnson syndrome, tachycardia, thrombocytopenia, tinnitus, toxic epidermal necrolysis, transient ischemic attacks, tremor, urinary incontinence, urinary tract infection, urticaria, vertigo, vomiting, weakness, weight gain, weight loss

General Dosage Range Oral: *Adults:* 40 to 80 mg once daily

Mechanism of Action Selectively inhibits xanthine oxidase, the enzyme responsible for the conversion of hypoxanthine to xanthine to uric acid thereby decreasing uric acid. At therapeutic concentration does not inhibit other enzymes involved in purine and pyrimidine synthesis.

Pharmacodynamics/Kinetics

Half-life Elimination ~5 to 8 hours

Time to Peak Plasma: 1 to 1.5 hours

Pregnancy Risk Factor C

Pregnancy Considerations Animal studies have demonstrated increased neonatal mortality and reduction in weight gain, but not teratogenic effects.

Felbamate (FEL ba mate)

Brand Names: US Felbatol

Pharmacologic Category Anticonvulsant, Miscellaneous

Use Monotherapy or adjunctive therapy in the treatment of partial seizures (with and without generalization); adjunctive therapy in the treatment of partial and generalized seizures associated with Lennox-Gastaut syndrome; not indicated for use as first-line treatment

Local Anesthetic/Vasoconstrictor Precautions No information available to require special precautions

Effects on Dental Treatment Key adverse event(s) related to dental treatment: Xerostomia (normal salivary flow resumes upon discontinuation) and abnormal taste.

Effects on Bleeding Associated with marked increase in aplastic anemia and may present with signs of infection, bleeding, or anemia; therefore, incidents of abnormal bleeding should be reported to prescribing physician. Incidence of thrombocytopenia is ≤1%.

Adverse Reactions

>10%:

Central nervous system: Drowsiness (children: 48%; adults: 19%), headache (adults: 7% to 37%; children: 7%), dizziness (18%), insomnia (9% to 18%), fatigue (7% to 17%), nervousness (children: 16%; adults: 7%)

Gastrointestinal: Anorexia (children: 55%; adults: 19%), vomiting (children: 39%; adults: 9% to 17%), nausea (adults: 34%; children: 7%), dyspepsia (9% to 12%), constipation (7% to 11%)

Hematologic & oncologic: Purpura (children: 13%)

Respiratory: Upper respiratory infection (children: 45%; adults: 5% to 9%)

Miscellaneous: Fever (children: 23%; adults: 3%)

1% to 10%:

Cardiovascular: Chest pain (3%), facial edema (3%), palpitations (≥1%), tachycardia (≥1%)

Central nervous system: Abnormal gait (children: 10%; adults: 5%), abnormality in thinking (children: 7%), ataxia (children: 7%; adults: 4%), emotional lability (children: 7%), pain (children: 7%), anxiety (5%), depression (5%), paresthesia (4%), stupor (3%), aggressive behavior (≥1%), agitation (≥1%), malaise (≥1%), psychological disorder (≥1%), attempted suicide (≤1%), dystonia (≤1%), euphoria (≤1%), hallucination (≤1%), migraine (≤1%)

Dermatologic: Skin rash (children: 10%; adults: 3% to 4%), acne vulgaris (3%), pruritus (≥1%), bullous rash (≤1%), urticaria (≤1%)

Endocrine and metabolic: Menstrual disease (3%), hypophosphatemia (≤3%), hypokalemia (≤1%), hyponatremia (≤1%), increased lactate dehydrogenase (≤1%)

Gastrointestinal: Hiccups (children: 10%), weight loss (children: 7%; adults: 3%), dysgeusia (6%), abdominal pain (5%), diarrhea (5%), xerostomia (3%), weight gain (≥1%), esophagitis (≤1%), increased appetite (≤1%)

Genitourinary: Urinary tract infection (3%)

Hematologic & oncologic: Leukopenia (children: 7%; adults: ≤1%), granulocytopenia (≤1%), leukocytosis (≤1%), lymphadenopathy (≤1%), thrombocytopenia (≤1%)

Hepatic: Increased liver enzymes (1% to 5%), increased serum alkaline phosphatase (≤1%)

Neuromuscular & skeletal: Tremor (6%), myalgia (3%), weakness (≥1%)

Ophthalmic: Miosis (children: 7%), diplopia (3% to 6%), visual disturbance (5%)

Otic: Otitis media (children: 10%; adults: 3%)

Respiratory: Pharyngitis (children: 10%; adults: 3%), cough (children: 7%), rhinitis (7%), sinusitis (4%), flu-like symptoms (≥1%)

<1%, postmarketing, and/or case reports: Acute renal failure, agranulocytosis, alopecia, anaphylactoid reaction, anemia, apathy, aphthous stomatitis, aplastic anemia, atrial arrhythmia, atrial fibrillation, blood coagulation disorder, blood platelet disorder, body odor, bradycardia, brain disease, buccal mucous membrane swelling, cardiac failure, cerebral edema, cerebrovascular disease, choreoathetosis, coma, confusion, delusions, diaphoresis, disseminated intravascular coagulation (DIC), dysarthria, dyskinesia, dysphagia, dyspnea, dysuria, embolism, enteritis, eosinophilia, epistaxis, exacerbation of asthma, extrapyramidal reaction, flatulence, flushing, gastric ulcer, gastritis, gastroesophageal reflux disease, gastrointestinal hemorrhage, gingival hemorrhage, glossitis, hematemesis, hematuria, hemianopsia, hemolytic anemia, hepatic failure, hepatitis, hepatorenal syndrome, hyperammonemia, hyperglycemia, hypernatremia, hypersensitivity reaction, hypertension, hypocalcemia, hypoglycemia, hypomagnesemia, hypotension, hypoxia, IgA vasculitis, increased creatine phosphokinase, intestinal obstruction, jaundice, lack of concentration, leukemia, lichen planus, livedo reticularis, manic reaction, nephrosis, neuritis (mononeuritis), nystagmus, pancreatitis, pancytopenia, paralysis, paranoia, peripheral ischemia (potentially leading to necrosis), pleural effusion, pneumonitis, psychosis, pulmonary hemorrhage, rectal hemorrhage, renal insufficiency, respiratory depression, rhabdomyolysis, SIADH (syndrome of inappropriate antidiuretic hormone secretion), skin photosensitivity, status epilepticus, Stevens-Johnson syndrome, suicidal ideation, suicidal tendencies, supraventricular tachycardia, thrombophlebitis, torsades de pointes, toxic epidermal necrolysis, urinary retention, urticaria, vaginal hemorrhage

General Dosage Range Dosage adjustment recommended in patients with renal impairment or on concomitant therapy

Oral:

Children 2-14 years: Initial: 15 mg/kg/day in divided doses 3 or 4 times/day; Maintenance: Up to 45 mg/kg/day in divided doses 3 or 4 times/day (maximum: 3,600 mg/day)

Children >14 years and Adults: Initial: 1,200 mg/day in divided doses 3 or 4 times/day; Maintenance: Up to 3,600 mg/day in divided doses 3 or 4 times/day.

Mechanism of Action Mechanism of action is unknown but has properties in common with other marketed anticonvulsants; has weak inhibitory effects on GABA-receptor binding, benzodiazepine receptor binding, and is devoid of activity at the MK-801 receptor binding site of the NMDA receptor-ionophore complex.

Pharmacodynamics/Kinetics

Half-life Elimination 20 to 23 hours (average); prolonged by 9 to 15 hours in patients with renal impairment

Time to Peak Serum: 2 to 6 hours (Patsalos 2008)

Pregnancy Risk Factor C

Pregnancy Considerations Adverse events have not been observed in animal reproduction studies. Postmarketing case reports in humans include fetal death, genital malformation, anencephaly, encephalocele, and placental disorder.

Patients exposed to felbamate during pregnancy are encouraged to enroll themselves into the North American Antiepileptic Drug (AED) Pregnancy Registry by calling 1-888-233-2334. Additional information is available at www.aedpregnancyregistry.org.

Prescribing and Access Restrictions A patient "informed consent" form should be completed and signed by the patient and physician. Copies are available from MEDA Pharmaceuticals by calling 800-526-3840.

Felodipine (fe LOE di peen)

Related Information

Calcium Channel Blockers and Gingival Hyperplasia *on page 1908*

Cardiovascular Diseases *on page 1752*

Brand Names: Canada Plendil; Sandoz-Felodipine

Pharmacologic Category Antihypertensive; Calcium Channel Blocker; Calcium Channel Blocker, Dihydropyridine

Use

Hypertension: Treatment of hypertension

The 2014 guideline for the management of high blood pressure in adults (JNC 8) recommends initiation of pharmacologic treatment to lower blood pressure for the following patients (JNC8 [James, 2013]):

- Patients ≥ 60 years of age, with systolic blood pressure (SBP) ≥150 mm Hg or diastolic blood pressure (DBP) ≥90 mm Hg. Goal of therapy is SBP <150 mm Hg and DBP <90 mm Hg.
- Patients <60 years of age, with SBP ≥140 mm Hg or DBP ≥90 mm Hg. Goal of therapy is SBP <140 mm Hg and DBP <90 mm Hg.
- Patients ≥18 years of age with diabetes, with SBP ≥140 mm Hg or DBP ≥90 mm Hg. Goal of therapy is SBP <140 mm Hg and DBP <90 mm Hg.
- Patients ≥18 years of age with chronic kidney disease (CKD), with SBP ≥140 mm Hg or DBP ≥90 mm Hg. Goal of therapy is SBP <140 mm Hg and DBP <90 mm Hg.

In patients with chronic kidney disease (CKD), regardless of race or diabetes status, the use of an ACE inhibitor (ACEI) or angiotensin receptor blocker (ARB) as initial therapy is recommended to improve kidney outcomes. In the general nonblack population (without CKD) including those with diabetes, initial antihypertensive treatment should consist of a thiazide-type diuretic, calcium channel blocker, ACEI, or ARB. In the general black population (without CKD) including those with diabetes, initial antihypertensive treatment should consist of a thiazide-type diuretic or a calcium channel blocker **instead of** an ACEI or ARB.

Local Anesthetic/Vasoconstrictor Precautions No information available to require special precautions

Effects on Dental Treatment Key adverse event(s) related to dental treatment: Gingival hyperplasia (fewer reports than other CCBs, resolves upon discontinuation, consultation with physician is suggested).

Effects on Bleeding No information available to require special precautions

Adverse Reactions

>10%:

Cardiovascular: Peripheral edema (2% to 17%)

Central nervous system: Headache (11% to 15%)

1% to 10%: Cardiovascular: Flushing (4% to 7%), tachycardia (≤3%)

<1%, postmarketing, and/or case reports: Abdominal pain, acid regurgitation, anemia, angina pectoris, angioedema, anxiety disorder, arm pain, arthralgia, back pain, bronchitis, bruise, cardiac arrhythmia, cardiac failure, cerebrovascular accident, chest pain, constipation, decreased libido, depression, diarrhea, dizziness, drowsiness, dyspnea, dysuria, epistaxis, erythema, extrasystoles, facial edema, flatulence, flu-like symptoms, flushing, foot pain, gingival hyperplasia, gynecomastia, hip pain, hypersensitivity angiitis, hypotension, impotence, influenza, insomnia, irritability, knee pain, leg pain, muscle cramps, myalgia, myocardial infarction, nausea, nervousness, palpitations, paresthesia, pharyngitis, polyuria, respiratory tract infection, sinusitis, syncope, urinary frequency, urinary urgency, urticaria, visual disturbance, vomiting, xerostomia

General Dosage Range Dosage adjustment recommended in patients with hepatic impairment

Oral:

Adults: Initial: 5 mg once daily; Maintenance: 2.5 to 10 mg once daily

Elderly: Initial: 2.5 mg once daily

Mechanism of Action Inhibits calcium ions from entering the "slow channels" or select voltage-sensitive areas of vascular smooth muscle and myocardium during depolarization, producing a relaxation of coronary vascular smooth muscle and coronary vasodilation; increases myocardial oxygen delivery in patients with vasospastic angina

Pharmacodynamics/Kinetics

Onset of Action Antihypertensive: 2 to 5 hours

Duration of Action Antihypertensive effect: 24 hours

Half-life Elimination Immediate release: 11 to 16 hours

Time to Peak 2.5 to 5 hours

Pregnancy Risk Factor C

Pregnancy Considerations Adverse events were observed in animal reproduction studies. Untreated chronic maternal hypertension is associated with adverse events in the fetus, infant, and mother. If treatment for hypertension during pregnancy is needed, other agents are preferred (ACOG, 2013). The Canadian labeling contraindicates use in women of childbearing potential and during pregnancy.

Fenofibrate and Derivatives

(fen oh FYE brate & dah RIV ah tives)

Related Information

Cardiovascular Diseases *on page 1752*

Brand Names: US Antara; Fenoglide; Fibricor; Lipofen; Lofibra; Tricor; Triglide; Trilipix

Brand Names: Canada Apo-Feno-Micro; Apo-Feno-Super; Apo-Fenofibrate; Ava-Fenofibrate Micro; Dom-Fenofibrate Micro; Feno-Micro-200; Fenofibrate Micro; Fenofibrate-S; Lipidil EZ; Lipidil Micro; Lipidil Supra; Mylan-Fenofibrate Micro; Novo-Fenofibrate Micronized; PHL-Fenofibrate Micro; PMS-Fenofibrate Micro; PRO-Feno-Super; Q-Fenofibrate Micro; ratio-Fenofibrate MC; Riva-Fenofibrate Micro; Sandoz-Fenofibrate E; Sandoz-Fenofibrate S; Teva-Fenofibrate S

Generic Availability (US) Yes

Pharmacologic Category Antilipemic Agent, Fibric Acid

Use

Hypercholesterolemia or mixed dyslipidemia: Adjunctive therapy to diet for the reduction of low-density lipoprotein cholesterol (LDL-C), total cholesterol (total-C), triglycerides, and apolipoprotein B (apo B), and to increase high-density lipoprotein cholesterol (HDL-C) in adults with primary hypercholesterolemia or mixed dyslipidemia (Fredrickson types IIa and IIb). Use lipid-altering agents in addition to a diet restricted in saturated fat and cholesterol when response to diet and nonpharmacological interventions alone has been inadequate.

Hypertriglyceridemia: Adjunctive therapy to diet for treatment of adult patients with severe hypertriglyceridemia (Fredrickson types IV and V hyperlipidemia).

Local Anesthetic/Vasoconstrictor Precautions No information available to require special precautions

Effects on Dental Treatment Key adverse event(s) related to dental treatment: Dry mouth

Effects on Bleeding Thrombocytopenia has been reported through postmarketing surveillance.

Adverse Reactions Frequency not always defined.

Cardiovascular: Pulmonary embolism (≤5%), thrombophlebitis (≤5%)

Central nervous system: Pain (1% to 4%), dizziness (≥3%)

Dermatologic: Skin rash (1%), urticaria (1%), Stevens-Johnson syndrome, toxic epidermal necrolysis

Gastrointestinal: Abdominal pain (5%), diarrhea (≥3%), dyspepsia (≥3%), cholecystitis (requiring surgery: 2%), constipation (2%)

Hematologic & oncologic: Agranulocytosis, decreased hematocrit (acute; levels stabilize with chronic therapy), decreased hemoglobin (acute; levels stabilize with chronic therapy), decreased white blood cell count (acute; levels stabilize with chronic therapy), thrombocytopenia

Hepatic: Increased serum ALT (≤13%; >3 x ULN; dose dependent), increased serum AST (≤13%; >3 x ULN; dose dependent), abnormal hepatic function tests (8%), cholestatic hepatitis, chronic active hepatitis, hepatocellular hepatitis

Neuromuscular & skeletal: Arthralgia (≥3%), limb pain (≥3%), myalgia (≥3%), increased creatine phosphokinase (3%), myopathy, toxic myopathy

Respiratory: Nasopharyngitis (≥3%), sinusitis (≥3%), upper respiratory tract infection (≥3%), rhinitis (2%)

<1%, postmarketing, and/or case reports: Acute renal failure, anemia, arthralgia, decreased HDL cholesterol, hepatic cirrhosis, hepatitis, increased serum

creatinine, muscle spasm, myalgia, pancreatitis, renal failure, rhabdomyolysis, weakness

Dosing

Adult Note: At least 2 to 3 months of therapy is required to determine efficacy.

Hypertriglyceridemia: Oral: Initial:

Antara (micronized): 30 to 90 mg once daily; maximum dose: 90 mg/day

Fenofibrate (micronized): 43 to 130 mg once daily; maximum dose: 130 mg/day

Fenoglide: 40 to 120 mg once daily; maximum dose: 120 mg/day

Fibricor: 35 to 105 mg once daily; maximum dose: 105 mg/day

Lipidil EZ [Canadian product]: 145 mg once daily; maximum dose: 145 mg/day

Lipidil Micro [Canadian product]: 200 mg once daily; maximum dose: 200 mg/day

Lipidil Supra [Canadian product]: 160 mg once daily; maximum dose: 200 mg/day

Lipofen: 50 to 150 mg once daily; maximum dose: 150 mg/day

Lofibra (micronized): 67 to 200 mg once daily; maximum dose: 200 mg/day

Lofibra (tablets): 54 to 160 mg once daily; maximum dose: 160 mg/day

TriCor: 48 to 145 mg once daily; maximum dose: 145 mg/day

Triglide: 160 mg once daily

Trilipix: 45 to 135 mg once daily; maximum dose: 135 mg/day

Hypercholesterolemia or mixed hyperlipidemia: Oral: Initial:

Antara (micronized): 90 mg once daily; maximum dose: 90 mg/day

Fenofibrate (micronized): 130 mg once daily; maximum dose: 130 mg/day

Fenoglide: 120 mg once daily

Fibricor: 105 mg once daily

Lipidil EZ [Canadian product]: 145 mg once daily; maximum dose: 145 mg/day

Lipidil Micro [Canadian product]: 200 mg once daily; maximum dose: 200 mg/day

Lipidil Supra [Canadian product]: 160 mg once daily; maximum dose: 200 mg/day

Lipofen: 150 mg once daily

Lofibra (micronized): 200 mg once daily

Lofibra (tablets): 160 mg once daily

TriCor: 145 mg once daily

Triglide: 160 mg once daily

Trilipix: 135 mg once daily

Geriatric Oral: Initial: Adjust dosage based on renal function; additional product-specific recommendations for initial dose:

Lipidil EZ [Canadian product]: 48 mg once daily

Lofibra (micronized): 67 mg once daily

Lofibra (tablets): 54 mg once daily

Renal Impairment Monitor renal function and lipid panel before adjusting.

Antara (micronized):

CrCl >80 mL/minute or eGFR ≥60 mL/minute/1.73 m^2: No dosage adjustment necessary.

CrCl >30 to 80 mL/minute or eGFR 30 to 59 mL/minute/1.73 m^2: Initiate at 30 mg once daily

CrCl ≤30 mL/minute or eGFR <30 mL/minute/1.73 m^2: Use is contraindicated.

Dialysis: Use is contraindicated.

Fenofibrate (micronized):

CrCl >80 mL/minute or eGFR ≥60 mL/minute/1.73 m^2: No dosage adjustment necessary.

CrCl >30 to 80 mL/minute or eGFR 30 to 59 mL/minute/1.73 m^2: Initiate at 43 mg once daily

CrCl ≤30 mL/minute or eGFR <30 mL/minute/1.73 m^2: Use is contraindicated.

Dialysis: Use is contraindicated.

Fenoglide:

CrCl >80 mL/minute or eGFR ≥60 mL/minute/1.73 m^2: No dosage adjustment necessary.

CrCl >30 to 80 mL/minute or eGFR 30 to 59 mL/minute/1.73 m^2: Initiate at 40 mg once daily

CrCl ≤30 mL/minute or eGFR <30 mL/minute/1.73 m^2: Use is contraindicated.

Dialysis: Use is contraindicated.

Fibricor:

CrCl >80 mL/minute: No dosage adjustment necessary.

CrCl >30 to 80 mL/minute: Initiate at 35 mg once daily

CrCl ≤30 mL/minute: Use is contraindicated.

Dialysis: Use is contraindicated.

Lipidil EZ [Canadian product]: **Note:** Interrupt treatment in patients with an increase in creatinine concentrations >50% the upper limit of normal (ULN).

CrCl >50 mL/minute: No dosage adjustment necessary.

CrCl 20 to 50 mL/minute: Initiate at 48 mg once daily

CrCl <20 mL/minute: Use is contraindicated.

Dialysis: Use is contraindicated.

Lipidil Micro [Canadian product]: **Note:** Interrupt treatment in patients with an increase in creatinine concentrations >50% the upper limit of normal (ULN).

CrCl >85 mL/minute (women) or >95 mL/minute (men): No dosage adjustment necessary.

CrCl 20 to 85 mL/minute (women) or 20 to 95 mL/minute (men): Initiate therapy with Lipidil EZ formulation with a dose of 48 mg once daily.

CrCl <20 mL/minute: Use is contraindicated.

Dialysis: Use is contraindicated.

Lipidil Supra [Canadian product]: **Note:** Interrupt treatment in patients with an increase in creatinine concentrations >50% the upper limit of normal (ULN).

CrCl >100 mL/minute: No dosage adjustment necessary.

CrCl 20 to 100 mL/minute: Initiate at 100 mg once daily

CrCl <20 mL/minute: Use is contraindicated.

Dialysis: Use is contraindicated.

Lipofen:

eGFR ≥90 mL/minute/1.73 m^2: No dosage adjustment necessary.

eGFR 30 to 89 mL/minute/1.73 m^2: Initiate at 50 mg once daily

eGFR <30 mL/minute/1.73 m^2: Use is contraindicated.

Dialysis: Use is contraindicated.

Lofibra (micronized):

CrCl >80 mL/minute: No dosage adjustment necessary.

CrCl >30 to 80 mL/minute: Initiate at 67 mg once daily

CrCl ≤30 mL/minute: Use is contraindicated.

Dialysis: Use is contraindicated.

Lofibra (tablets):

eGFR ≥60 mL/minute/1.73 m^2: No dosage adjustment necessary.

eGFR 30 to 59 mL/minute/1.73 m^2: Initiate at 54 mg once daily

eGFR <30 mL/minute/1.73 m^2: Use is contraindicated.

Dialysis: Use is contraindicated.

TriCor:

eGFR ≥60 mL/minute/1.73 m^2: No dosage adjustment necessary.

eGFR 30 to 59 mL/minute/1.73 m^2: Initiate at 48 mg once daily

eGFR <30 mL/minute/1.73 m^2: Use is contraindicated.

Dialysis: Use is contraindicated.

Triglide:

CrCl >80 mL/minute or eGFR ≥60 mL/minute/1.73 m^2: No dosage adjustment necessary.

CrCl >30 to 80 mL/minute or eGFR 30 to 59 mL/minute/1.73 m^2: Avoid use.

CrCl ≤30 mL/minute or eGFR <30 mL/minute/1.73 m^2: Use is contraindicated.

Dialysis: Use is contraindicated.

Trilipix:

eGFR ≥60 mL/minute/1.73 m^2: No dosage adjustment necessary.

eGFR 30 to 59 mL/minute/1.73 m^2: Initiate at 45 mg once daily.

eGFR <30 mL/minute/1.73 m^2: Use is contraindicated.

Dialysis: Use is contraindicated.

Hepatic Impairment Use is contraindicated. Regular monitoring of liver function tests is required; discontinue therapy in patients whose enzyme levels persist above 3 times the upper limit of normal.

Adjustment for Toxicity

Cholelithiasis: Discontinue if gallstones are found upon gallbladder studies.

CPK elevation, myopathy, and/or myositis: Discontinue therapy if the patient develops markedly elevated CPK concentrations or if myopathy/myositis is suspected or diagnosed.

HDL-C reductions: Permanently discontinue therapy if HDL-C becomes severely depressed; monitor HDL-C concentrations until returned to baseline.

Mechanism of Action Fenofibric acid, an agonist for the nuclear transcription factor peroxisome proliferator-activated receptor-alpha (PPAR-alpha), downregulates apoprotein C-III (an inhibitor of lipoprotein lipase) and upregulates the synthesis of apolipoprotein A-I, fatty acid transport protein, and lipoprotein lipase resulting in an increase in VLDL catabolism, fatty acid oxidation, and elimination of triglyceride-rich particles; as a result of a decrease in VLDL levels, total plasma triglycerides are reduced by 30% to 60%; modest increase in HDL occurs in some hypertriglyceridemic patients.

Contraindications

Hypersensitivity to fenofibrate or fenofibric acid or any component of the formulation; active liver disease, including primary biliary cirrhosis and unexplained, persistent liver function abnormality; severe renal impairment or end-stage renal disease (ESRD), including those receiving dialysis; preexisting gallbladder disease; breastfeeding

Documentation of allergenic cross-reactivity for fibrates is limited. However, because of similarities in chemical structure and/or pharmacologic actions, the possibility of cross-sensitivity cannot be ruled out with certainty.

Canadian labeling: Additional contraindications (not in US labeling): Pregnancy; known photoallergy or phototoxic reaction during treatment with fibrates or ketoprofen

Lipidil EZ, Lipidil Micro, Lipidil Supra: Additional contraindications: Allergy to soya lecithin or peanut or arachis oil; chronic or acute pancreatitis; patients <18 years of age; coadministration with HMG-CoA reductase inhibitors in patients with a predisposition for myopathy.

Warnings/Precautions Secondary causes of hyperlipidemia should be ruled out prior to therapy. Hepatic transaminases can become significantly elevated (dose-related); hepatocellular, chronic active, and cholestatic hepatitis have been reported after weeks to several years of therapy. Baseline and regular monitoring of liver function tests is required; discontinue therapy in patients whose enzyme levels persist above 3 times the upper limit of normal. Use with caution in patients with mild to moderate renal impairment; dosage adjustment may be required. Contraindicated with severe renal impairment including those receiving dialysis. Avoid use of Triglide in patients with mild or moderate renal impairment. Contraindicated active liver disease, including primary biliary cirrhosis and unexplained persistent liver function abnormalities. Increases in serum creatinine (>2 mg/dL) have been observed with use; clinical significance unknown. These elevations tend to return to baseline following discontinuation of fenofibrate. Fenofibrate has been shown to increase creatinine production (unknown mechanism) resulting in an equal increase of creatinuria thereby demonstrating that the increase does not reflect a reduction in creatinine clearance (Hottelart 2002). Monitor renal function in patients with renal impairment and consider monitoring patients with increased risk for developing renal impairment (eg, elderly and patients with diabetes). May cause cholelithiasis.

Therapy should be discontinued in patients who develop markedly elevated CPK concentrations or if myopathy/myositis is suspected or diagnosed. No incremental benefit of combination therapy on cardiovascular morbidity and mortality over statin monotherapy has been established. In patients with type 2 diabetes mellitus, neither fenofibrate monotherapy nor the addition of fenofibrate to simvastatin compared to placebo has been shown to reduce cardiovascular disease morbidity and mortality in patients with type 2 diabetes. Potentially significant drug-drug interactions may exist, requiring dose or frequency adjustment, additional monitoring, and/or selection of alternative therapy. In combination with HMG-CoA reductase inhibitors, fenofibrate is generally regarded as safer than gemfibrozil due to limited pharmacokinetic interaction with statins. According to the 2013 ACC/AHA Blood Cholesterol Guidelines, fenofibrate may be considered in patients on low- or moderate-intensity statin therapy (ie, statin therapy intended to lower LDL-C by <30% or ~30% to 50%, respectively) only if the benefits from atherosclerotic cardiovascular disease (ASCVD) risk reduction or triglyceride lowering when triglycerides are >500 mg/dL, outweigh the potential risk for adverse effects (Stone, 2013). Therapy should be withdrawn if an adequate response is not obtained after 2 to 3 months of therapy at the maximal daily dose. In patients with severe hypertriglyceridemia, the occurrence of pancreatitis may represent a failure of efficacy, a direct effect of the drug, or obstruction of the common bile duct due to biliary tract stone or sludge formation. A paradoxical, severe, and reversible decrease in HDL-C (as low as 2 mg/dL) with a simultaneous decrease in apolipoprotein A1 has been reported within 2 weeks to years after initiation of fibrate therapy; clinical significance unknown. Monitor HDL-C within a few months of initiation of therapy and discontinue if HDL-C becomes severely depressed; do not restart therapy. The occurrence of pancreatitis may represent a failure of efficacy in patients with severely elevated triglycerides. May cause mild to moderate decreases in hemoglobin, hematocrit, and WBC upon initiation of therapy which usually stabilizes with long-term therapy. Agranulocytosis and thrombocytopenia have been reported. Periodic monitoring of blood counts is recommended during the first year of therapy.

Hypersensitivity reactions have been reported. Use has been associated with pulmonary embolism (PE) and deep vein thrombosis (DVT). Use with caution in patients with risk factors for VTE. Dose adjustment may be required for elderly patients.

Some products may contain soya lecithin or peanut or arachis oil; use is contraindicated in patients with a soya lecithin allergy or a peanut or arachis allergy for applicable formulations.

Drug Interactions

Metabolism/Transport Effects Inhibits CYP2A6 (weak), CYP2C8 (weak), CYP2C9 (weak)

Avoid Concomitant Use

Avoid concomitant use of Fenofibrate and Derivatives with any of the following: Amodiaquine; Ciprofibrate

Increased Effect/Toxicity

Fenofibrate and Derivatives may increase the levels/effects of: Amodiaquine; Colchicine; Ezetimibe; HMG-CoA Reductase Inhibitors; Sulfonylureas; Vitamin K Antagonists; Warfarin

The levels/effects of Fenofibrate and Derivatives may be increased by: Acipimox; Ciprofibrate; CycloSPORINE (Systemic); Raltegravir; Tacrolimus (Systemic)

Decreased Effect

Fenofibrate and Derivatives may decrease the levels/effects of: Chenodiol; CycloSPORINE (Systemic); Ursodiol

The levels/effects of Fenofibrate and Derivatives may be decreased by: Bile Acid Sequestrants

Food Interactions

Antara (micronized): When administered under fasted conditions or with a low-fat meal, the extent of absorption and the time to peak did not change; however peak concentrations were increased in the presence of a low-fat meal. When administered with a high fat meal, a 26% increase in the AUC and 108% increase in the peak concentration were seen in comparison to the fasted state. Management: Administer with or without food.

Fenoglide: When administered with a high-fat meal, the peak concentration was increased by 44% as compared to fasting conditions. Management: Administer with meals.

Fibricor: When administered with a high-fat meal, the peak concentration was decreased by ~35% while AUC remained unchanged as compared to fasting conditions. Management: Administer with or without food.

Lipidil EZ [Canadian product]: Bioavailability was not significantly different when administered under fasting and nonfasting conditions. Management: Administer with or without food.

Lipidil Micro [Canadian product]: In comparison with nonmicronized fenofibrate formulations, micronized fenofibrate is better absorbed when administered with a low-fat meal; absorption is less influenced by a higher fat content meal. Management: Administer with meals.

Lipidil Supra [Canadian product]: In general, fenofibrate absorption is low and variable when administered under fasting conditions; absorption is increased when administered with food. Management: Administer with meals.

Lipofen: When administered with a low-fat and high-fat meal, the extent of absorption is increased by ~25% and ~58%, respectively, as compared to fasting conditions. Management: Administer with meals.

Lofibra (micronized) capsules: Absorption is increased by ~35% under fed as compared to fasting conditions. Management: Administer with meals.

Lofibra tablets: Peak concentrations and AUC were not significantly different when a single dose was administered under fasting and nonfasting conditions. Management: Administer with or without food.

TriCor: Peak concentrations and AUC were not significantly different when a single dose was administered under fasting and nonfasting conditions. Management: Administer with or without food.

Triglide: When administered with food, the rate of absorption was increased ~55% as compared to fasting conditions; the AUC remained unchanged. Management: Administer with or without food.

Trilipix: Peak concentrations and AUC were not significantly different when a single dose was administered under fasting and nonfasting conditions. Management: Administer with or without food.

Dietary Considerations

Antara, Fibricor, Lipidil EZ [Canadian product], Lofibra tablets, TriCor, Triglide, Trilipix: May be taken with or without food.

Fenoglide, Lipidil Micro [Canadian product], Lipidil Supra [Canadian product], Lipofen, Lofibra (micronized capsules): Take with meals.

Pharmacodynamics/Kinetics

Half-life Elimination Half-life elimination: Fenofibric acid: Mean: 20 hours (range: 10 to 35 hours); half-life prolonged in patients with renal impairment

Time to Peak 2 to 8 hours

Pregnancy Risk Factor C

Pregnancy Considerations Maternal toxicity was observed in pregnant rats at doses approximately equivalent to the human dose; adverse events have not been observed in animal reproduction studies done in rabbits. Reports of using fenofibrate during pregnancy are limited (Goldberg, 2012; Sunman, 2012; Whitten, 2011). Other agents are generally preferred if treatment for hypertriglyceridemia during pregnancy (Berglund, 2012) or treatment of lipid disorders in women of reproductive age (NCEP, 2001) is required. Use during pregnancy is specifically contraindicated in Canadian product labeling; some products recommend using effective birth control when treating women of reproductive age and discontinuing therapy several months prior to conception if planning a pregnancy.

Breastfeeding Considerations It is not known if fenofibrate is excreted in breast milk. Use is contraindicated in nursing women. The manufacturer recommends a decision be made whether to discontinue nursing or to discontinue the drug, taking into account the importance of treatment to the mother.

Dosage Forms Considerations

Micronized formulations: Antara, Lofibra capsules

Strength of choline fenofibrate products are expressed in terms of fenofibric acid.

Dosage Forms

Capsule, Oral:

Antara: 30 mg, 90 mg

Lipofen: 50 mg, 150 mg

Lofibra: 67 mg, 134 mg, 200 mg

Generic: 43 mg, 50 mg, 67 mg, 130 mg, 134 mg, 150 mg, 200 mg

Capsule Delayed Release, Oral:
Trilipix: 45 mg, 135 mg
Generic: 45 mg, 135 mg
Tablet, Oral:
Fenoglide: 40 mg, 120 mg
Fibricor: 35 mg, 105 mg
Lofibra: 54 mg, 160 mg
Tricor: 48 mg, 145 mg
Triglide: 160 mg
Generic: 35 mg, 40 mg, 48 mg, 54 mg, 105 mg, 120 mg, 145 mg, 160 mg

Fenoldopam (fe NOL doe pam)

Brand Names: US Corlopam

Pharmacologic Category Antihypertensive; Dopamine Agonist

Use Severe hypertension: Short-term treatment of severe hypertension (up to 48 hours in adults while in hospital), including patients with malignant hypertension with deteriorating end-organ function; short-term (up to 4 hours while in hospital) blood pressure reduction in pediatric patients while in hospital

Local Anesthetic/Vasoconstrictor Precautions
No information available to require special precautions

Effects on Dental Treatment Key adverse event(s) related to dental treatment: Xerostomia and changes in salivation (normal salivary flow resumes upon discontinuation).

Effects on Bleeding No information available to require special precautions

Adverse Reactions
Frequency not defined.
≥5%:
Cardiovascular: Flushing, hypotension
Central nervous system: Headache
Gastrointestinal: Nausea
<5%:
Cardiovascular: Angina pectoris, bradycardia, cardiac failure, chest pain, ECG abnormality (ST-T abnormalities), extrasystoles, inversion T wave on ECG, myocardial infarction, orthostatic hypotension, palpitations, tachycardia
Central nervous system: Anxiety, dizziness, insomnia
Dermatologic: Diaphoresis
Endocrine & metabolic: Hyperglycemia, hypokalemia, increased lactate dehydrogenase
Gastrointestinal: Abdominal fullness, abdominal pain, constipation, diarrhea, vomiting
Genitourinary: Oliguria, urinary tract infection
Hematologic & oncologic: Hemorrhage, leukocytosis
Hepatic: Increased serum transaminases
Local: Injection site reaction
Neuromuscular & skeletal: Back pain, muscle cramps (limbs)
Ophthalmic: Increased intraocular pressure
Renal: Increased blood urea nitrogen, increased serum creatinine
Respiratory: Dyspnea, nasal congestion
Miscellaneous: Fever

General Dosage Range IV:
Children: Initial: 0.2 mcg/kg/minute, may increase in increments of 0.3 to 0.5 mcg/kg/minute every 20 to 30 minutes (maximum dose: 0.8 mcg/kg/minute)
Adults: Initial: 0.01 to 0.3 mcg/kg/minute, may increase in increments of 0.05 to 0.1 mcg/kg/minute every 15 minutes (maximum dose: 1.6 mcg/kg/minute [reported in clinical studies])

Mechanism of Action A selective postsynaptic dopamine agonist (D_1-receptors) which exerts hypotensive effects by decreasing peripheral vasculature resistance with increased renal blood flow, diuresis, and natriuresis; 6 times as potent as dopamine in producing renal vasodilatation; has minimal adrenergic effects

Pharmacodynamics/Kinetics
Onset of Action IV: Children: 5 minutes; Adults: 10 minutes; **Note:** Majority of effect of a given infusion rate is attained within 15 minutes.
Duration of Action IV: 1 hour
Half-life Elimination IV: Children: 3 to 5 minutes; Adults: ~5 minutes

Pregnancy Risk Factor B

Pregnancy Considerations Fetal harm was not observed in animal studies; however, safety and efficacy have not been established for use during pregnancy. Use during pregnancy only if clearly needed.

Fenoprofen (fen oh PROE fen)

Related Information
Rheumatoid Arthritis, Osteoarthritis, and Osteoporosis *on page 1792*
Temporomandibular Dysfunction (TMD), Chronic Pain, and Fibromyalgia *on page 1868*

Brand Names: US Fenortho; Nalfon

Generic Availability (US) Yes

Pharmacologic Category Analgesic, Nonopioid; Nonsteroidal Anti-inflammatory Drug (NSAID), Oral

Use
Osteoarthritis: Relief of the signs and symptoms of osteoarthritis.
Pain: Relief of mild to moderate pain in adult patients.
Rheumatoid arthritis (RA): Relief of the signs and symptoms of RA.

Local Anesthetic/Vasoconstrictor Precautions
No information available to require special precautions

Effects on Dental Treatment The dentist should be aware of the potential of abnormal coagulation. Caution should also be exercised in the use of NSAIDs in patients already on anticoagulant therapy with drugs such as warfarin (Coumadin®). See Effects on Bleeding.

Effects on Bleeding Nonselective NSAIDs such as fenoprofen inhibit platelet aggregation and prolong bleeding time in some patients. Unlike aspirin, the NSAID effect on platelet function is quantitatively less, of shorter duration, and reversible.

Adverse Reactions
1% to 10%:
Cardiovascular: Peripheral edema (5%), palpitations (3%)
Central nervous system: Drowsiness (9%), headache (9%), dizziness (7%), nervousness (6%), fatigue (2%), confusion (1%)
Dermatologic: Diaphoresis (5%), pruritus (4%), skin rash (4%)
Gastrointestinal: Dyspepsia (10%), nausea (8%), constipation (7%), vomiting (3%), abdominal pain (2%)
Neuromuscular & skeletal: Weakness (5%), tremor (2%)
Ophthalmic: Blurred vision (2%)
Otic: Tinnitus (5%), auditory impairment (2%)
Respiratory: Dyspnea (3%), nasopharyngitis (1%)
<1%, postmarketing, and/or case reports: Agranulocytosis, alopecia, anaphylaxis, anemia, angioedema (angioneurotic edema), anorexia, anuria, aphthous stomatitis, aplastic anemia, atrial fibrillation, azotemia,

bloody stools, bruise, cholestatic hepatitis, cystitis, depression, diplopia, disorientation, dysgeusia, dysuria, ECG changes, exfoliative dermatitis, fever, flatulence, gastritis, gastrointestinal hemorrhage, gastrointestinal perforation, gastrointestinal ulcer, glossopyrosis, hematuria, hemolytic anemia, hemorrhage, hepatotoxicity (idiosyncratic; Chalasani, 2014), hypertension, increased lactate dehydrogenase, increased serum alkaline phosphatase, increased serum AST, insomnia, interstitial nephritis, jaundice, lymphadenopathy, malaise, mastalgia, nephrosis, oliguria, optic neuritis, pancreatitis, pancytopenia, peptic ulcer, pulmonary edema, purpura, renal failure, renal papillary necrosis, seizure, Stevens-Johnson syndrome, supraventricular tachycardia, tachycardia, thrombocytopenia, toxic epidermal necrolysis, trigeminal neuralgia, urticaria, xerostomia

Dosing

Adult & Geriatric

Rheumatoid arthritis, osteoarthritis: Oral: 400 to 600 mg 3 to 4 times daily; maximum dose: 3.2 g/day

Mild to moderate pain: Oral: 200 mg every 4 to 6 hours as needed

Renal Impairment There are no dosage adjustments provided in the manufacturer's labeling. Not recommended in patients with advanced renal disease. Not removed by hemodialysis.

Hepatic Impairment There are no dosage adjustments provided in the manufacturer's labeling.

Mechanism of Action Reversibly inhibits cyclooxygenase-1 and 2 (COX-1 and 2) enzymes, which results in decreased formation of prostaglandin precursors; has antipyretic, analgesic, and anti-inflammatory properties

Other proposed mechanisms not fully elucidated (and possibly contributing to the anti-inflammatory effect to varying degrees), include inhibiting chemotaxis, altering lymphocyte activity, inhibiting neutrophil aggregation/activation, and decreasing proinflammatory cytokine levels.

Contraindications Hypersensitivity to fenoprofen or any component of the formulation; history of asthma, urticaria, or allergic-type reaction to aspirin or other NSAIDs; in the setting of coronary artery bypass graft (CABG) surgery

Warnings/Precautions **[US Boxed Warning]: NSAIDs cause an increased risk of serious (and potentially fatal) adverse cardiovascular thrombotic events, including MI and stroke. Risk may occur early during treatment and may increase with duration of use.** Relative risk appears to be similar in those with and without known cardiovascular disease or risk factors for cardiovascular disease; however, absolute incidence of cardiovascular events (which may occur early during treatment) was higher in patients with known cardiovascular disease or risk factors. New onset hypertension or exacerbation of hypertension may occur (NSAIDs may also impair response to ACE inhibitors, thiazide diuretics, or loop diuretics); may contribute to cardiovascular events; monitor blood pressure; use with caution in patients with hypertension. May cause sodium and fluid retention, use with caution in patients with edema. Avoid use in patients with heart failure (ACCF/AHA [Yancy 2013]). Avoid use in patients with recent MI unless benefits outweigh risk of cardiovascular thrombotic events. Use the lowest effective dose for the shortest duration of time, consistent with individual patient goals, to reduce risk of cardiovascular events; alternate therapies should be considered for patients at high risk. **[US Boxed Warning]: Use is contraindicated in the setting of coronary artery bypass graft (CABG) surgery.** Risk of MI and stroke may be increased with use following CABG surgery.

NSAID use may compromise existing renal function; dose-dependent decreases in prostaglandin synthesis may result from NSAID use, reducing renal blood flow which may cause renal decompensation. NSAID use may increase the risk for hyperkalemia. Patients with impaired renal function, dehydration, hypovolemia, heart failure, liver dysfunction, those taking diuretics, and ACE inhibitors, and the elderly are at greater risk of renal toxicity and hyperkalemia. Rehydrate patient before starting therapy; monitor renal function closely. Avoid use in patients with advanced renal disease; discontinue use with persistent or worsening abnormal renal function tests. Long-term NSAID use may result in renal papillary necrosis.

[US Boxed Warning]: NSAIDs cause an increased risk of serious gastrointestinal inflammation, ulceration, bleeding, and perforation (may be fatal); elderly patients and patients with history of peptic ulcer disease and/or GI bleeding are at greater risk for serious GI events. These events may occur at any time during therapy and without warning. Avoid use in patients with active GI bleeding. Use caution with a history of GI ulcers, concurrent therapy known to increase the risk of GI bleeding (eg, aspirin, anticoagulants and/or corticosteroids, selective serotonin reuptake inhibitors), smoking, use of alcohol, or in the elderly or debilitated patients. Use the lowest effective dose for the shortest duration of time, consistent with individual patient goals, to reduce risk of GI adverse events; alternate therapies should be considered for patients at high risk. When used concomitantly with aspirin, a substantial increase in the risk of gastrointestinal complications (eg, ulcer) occurs; concomitant gastroprotective therapy (eg, proton pump inhibitors) is recommended (Bhatt, 2008).

Platelet adhesion and aggregation may be decreased; may prolong bleeding time; patients with coagulation disorders or who are receiving anticoagulants should be monitored closely. Anemia may occur; patients on long-term NSAID therapy should be monitored for anemia. Rarely, NSAID use has been associated with potentially severe blood dyscrasias (eg, agranulocytosis, thrombocytopenia, aplastic anemia).

Use the lowest effective dose for the shortest duration of time, consistent with individual patient goals, to reduce risk of cardiovascular or GI adverse events. Alternate therapies should be considered for patients at high risk.

NSAIDs may cause serious skin adverse events including exfoliative dermatitis, Stevens-Johnson syndrome (SJS), and toxic epidermal necrolysis (TEN); discontinue use at first sign of skin rash or hypersensitivity. Anaphylactoid reactions may occur, even without prior exposure; patients with "aspirin triad" (bronchial asthma, aspirin intolerance, rhinitis) may be at increased risk. Do not use in patients who experience bronchospasm, asthma, rhinitis, or urticaria with NSAID or aspirin therapy. Use caution in other forms of asthma.

Use with caution in patients with decreased hepatic function. Closely monitor patients with any abnormal LFT. Rare (sometimes fatal) severe hepatic reactions (eg, fatal fulminant hepatitis, hepatic necrosis, hepatic failure) have occurred with NSAID use; discontinue if signs or symptoms of liver disease develop, if systemic manifestations (eg, eosinophilia, rash) occur, or with persistent or worsening abnormal hepatic function tests.

NSAIDs may cause drowsiness, dizziness, blurred vision and other neurologic effects which may impair physical or mental abilities; patients must be cautioned about performing tasks which require mental alertness (eg, operating machinery or driving). If visual disturbances occur, preform ophthalmologic exam.

Periodically monitor auditory function in patients with hearing impairment during prolonged therapy. Potentially significant interactions may exist, requiring dose or frequency adjustment, additional monitoring, and/or selection of alternative therapy

Withhold for at least 4 to 6 half-lives prior to surgical or dental procedures.

Drug Interactions

Metabolism/Transport Effects None known.

Avoid Concomitant Use

Avoid concomitant use of Fenoprofen with any of the following: Dexketoprofen; Floctafenine; Ketorolac (Nasal); Ketorolac (Systemic); Morniflumate; NSAID (COX-2 Inhibitor); Omacetaxine; Pelubiprofen; Phenylbutazone; Talniflumate; Tenoxicam; Urokinase; Zaltoprofen

Increased Effect/Toxicity

Fenoprofen may increase the levels/effects of: 5-ASA Derivatives; Agents with Antiplatelet Properties; Aliskiren; Aminoglycosides; Aminolevulinic Acid; Anticoagulants; Apixaban; Bisphosphonate Derivatives; Cephalothin; Collagenase (Systemic); CycloSPORINE (Systemic); Dabigatran Etexilate; Deferasirox; Deoxycholic Acid; Desmopressin; Digoxin; Drospirenone; Edoxaban; Eplerenone; Haloperidol; Ibritumomab; Lithium; Methotrexate; Nonsteroidal Anti-Inflammatory Agents; NSAID (COX-2 Inhibitor); Obinutuzumab; Omacetaxine; PEMEtrexed; Porfimer; Potassium-Sparing Diuretics; PRALAtrexate; Quinolone Antibiotics; Rivaroxaban; Salicylates; Tacrolimus (Systemic); Tenofovir Products; Thrombolytic Agents; Tolperisone; Tositumomab and Iodine I 131 Tositumomab; Urokinase; Vancomycin; Verteporfin; Vitamin K Antagonists

The levels/effects of Fenoprofen may be increased by: ACE Inhibitors; Alcohol (Ethyl); Angiotensin II Receptor Blockers; Antidepressants (Tricyclic, Tertiary Amine); Corticosteroids (Systemic); CycloSPORINE (Systemic); Dasatinib; Dexketoprofen; Diclofenac (Systemic); Felbinac; Floctafenine; Glucosamine; Herbs (Anticoagulant/Antiplatelet Properties); Ibrutinib; Ketorolac (Nasal); Ketorolac (Systemic); Limaprost; Loop Diuretics; Morniflumate; Multivitamins/Fluoride (with ADE); Multivitamins/Minerals (with ADEK, Folate, Iron); Multivitamins/Minerals (with AE, No Iron); Naftazone; Omega-3 Fatty Acids; Pelubiprofen; Pentosan Polysulfate Sodium; Pentoxifylline; Phenylbutazone; Probenecid; Prostacyclin Analogues; Selective Serotonin Reuptake Inhibitors; Serotonin/Norepinephrine Reuptake Inhibitors; Sodium Phosphates; Talniflumate; Tenoxicam; Thiazide and Thiazide-Like Diuretics; Tipranavir; Tolperisone; Vitamin E (Systemic); Zaltoprofen

Decreased Effect

Fenoprofen may decrease the levels/effects of: ACE Inhibitors; Aliskiren; Angiotensin II Receptor Blockers; Beta-Blockers; Eplerenone; HydrALAZINE; Loop Diuretics; Potassium-Sparing Diuretics; Prostaglandins (Ophthalmic); Salicylates; Selective Serotonin Reuptake Inhibitors; Thiazide and Thiazide-Like Diuretics

The levels/effects of Fenoprofen may be decreased by: Bile Acid Sequestrants; Salicylates

Food Interactions Fenoprofen peak serum levels may be decreased if taken with food; total amount absorbed is not affected. Management: Administer with food to minimize stomach upset.

Dietary Considerations May be taken with food or milk.

Pharmacodynamics/Kinetics

Onset of Action A few days; full benefit: up to 2 to 3 weeks

Half-life Elimination ~3 hours

Time to Peak Serum: ~2 hours

Pregnancy Considerations The use of an NSAID close to conception may be associated with an increased risk of miscarriage. Nonteratogenic effects, including prenatal constriction of the ductus arteriosus, persistent pulmonary hypertension of the newborn, oligohydramnios, necrotizing enterocolitis, renal dysfunction or failure, and intracranial hemorrhage have been observed in the fetus/neonate following in utero NSAID exposure. In addition, non-closure of the ductus arteriosus postnatally may occur and be resistant to medical management (Bermas 2014; Bloor 2013). Because they may cause premature closure of the ductus arteriosus, use of NSAIDs late in pregnancy should be avoided starting at 30 weeks gestation. The chronic use of NSAIDs in women of reproductive age may be associated with infertility that is reversible upon discontinuation of the medication.

Breastfeeding Considerations Fenoprofen is excreted in breast milk in concentrations ~1.6% of those in the maternal serum. According to the manufacturer, the decision to breastfeed during therapy should take into account the risk of exposure to the infant and the benefits of treatment to the mother.

Dosage Forms

Capsule, Oral:

Fenortho: 200 mg, 400 mg

Nalfon: 400 mg

Generic: 200 mg, 400 mg

Tablet, Oral:

Generic: 600 mg

FentaNYL (FEN ta nil)

Related Information

Management of the Chemically Dependent Patient *on page 1821*

Brand Names: US Abstral; Actiq; Duragesic; Fentora; Ionsys; Lazanda; Onsolis [DSC]; Sublimaze; Subsys

Brand Names: Canada Abstral; Apo-Fentanyl Matrix; Co-Fentanyl; Duragesic; Fentanyl Citrate Injection, USP; Fentora; Mylan-Fentanyl Matrix Patch; PMS-Fentanyl MTX; RAN-Fentanyl Matrix Patch; Sandoz Fentanyl Patch; Teva-Fentanyl

Generic Availability (US) Yes: Injection, lozenge, patch

Pharmacologic Category Analgesic, Opioid; Anilidopiperidine Opioid; General Anesthetic

Dental Use Adjunct in preoperative intravenous conscious sedation in patients undergoing dental surgery

Use

Injection:

Pain management: Relief of pain, preoperative medication.

Surgery: Adjunct to general or regional anesthesia.

Transdermal device (eg, Ionsys): **Postoperative pain, acute:** Short-term management of acute postoperative pain in adult patients requiring opioid analgesia in the hospital.

Limitations of use: Only for use in patients who are alert enough and have adequate cognitive ability to understand the directions for use. Not for home use. Transdermal device is for use only in patients in the hospital. Discontinue treatment with the device before patients leave the hospital. The device is for use after patients have been titrated to an acceptable level of analgesia using alternate opioid analgesics.

Transdermal patch (eg, Duragesic): **Chronic pain:** Management of pain in opioid-tolerant patients, severe enough to require daily, around-the-clock, long-term opioid treatment and for which alternative treatment options are inadequate.

Limitations of use: Because of the risks of addiction, abuse, and misuse with opioids, even at recommended doses, and because of the greater risks of overdose and death with extended-release opioid formulations, reserve fentanyl transdermal patch for use in patients for whom alternative treatment options (eg, nonopioid analgesics, immediate-release opioids) are ineffective, not tolerated, or would be otherwise inadequate to provide sufficient management of pain.

Transmucosal lozenge (eg, Actiq), buccal tablet (Fentora), buccal film (Onsolis), nasal spray (Lazanda), sublingual tablet (Abstral), sublingual spray (Subsys): **Cancer pain:** Management of breakthrough cancer pain in opioid-tolerant patients who are already receiving and who are tolerant to around-the-clock opioid therapy for their underlying persistent cancer pain.

Note: "Opioid-tolerant" patients are defined as patients who are taking at least:

Oral morphine 60 mg/day, **or**

Transdermal fentanyl 25 mcg/hour, **or**

Oral oxycodone 30 mg/day, **or**

Oral hydromorphone 8 mg/day, **or**

Oral oxymorphone 25 mg/day, **or**

Equianalgesic dose of another opioid for at least 1 week

Local Anesthetic/Vasoconstrictor Precautions No information available to require special precautions

Effects on Dental Treatment Key adverse event(s) related to dental treatment: Xerostomia, changes in salivation (normal salivary flow resumes upon discontinuation); Patients may experience orthostatic hypotension as they stand up after treatment; especially if lying in dental chair for extended periods of time. Use caution with sudden changes in position during and after dental treatment. Actiq may contribute to dental caries due to sugar content of oral lozenge; advise patients to maintain good oral hygiene. See Dental Comment.

Effects on Bleeding No information available to require special precautions

Adverse Reactions

>10%:

Central nervous system: Confusion, dizziness, drowsiness, fatigue, headache, sedation

Endocrine & metabolic: Dehydration

Gastrointestinal: Constipation, nausea, vomiting

Local: Application site erythema (transdermal device)

Neuromuscular & skeletal: Weakness

Respiratory: Dyspnea

1% to 10%:

Cardiovascular: Atrial fibrillation, bigeminy, cardiac arrhythmia, chest pain, deep vein thrombosis, edema, hypertension, hypotension, myocardial infarction, orthostatic hypotension, palpitations, peripheral edema, pulmonary embolism (nasal spray), sinus tachycardia, syncope, tachycardia, vasodilatation

Central nervous system: Abnormal dreams, abnormal gait, abnormality in thinking, agitation, altered sense of smell, amnesia, anxiety, ataxia, chills, depression, disorientation, dysphoria, euphoria, hallucination, hypertonia, hypoesthesia, hypothermia, insomnia, irritability, lack of concentration, lethargy, malaise, mental status changes, migraine, nervousness, neuropathy, paranoia, paresthesia, restlessness, speech disturbance, stupor, vertigo, withdrawal syndrome

Dermatologic: Alopecia, cellulitis, decubitus ulcer, diaphoresis, erythema, exfoliation of skin (application site, transdermal device), hyperhidrosis, local papules (application site, transdermal device), night sweats, pallor, papule, pruritus, pustules (application site, transdermal device), skin rash, vesicobullous rash (application site, transdermal device)

Endocrine & metabolic: Hot flash, hypercalcemia, hyperglycemia, hypoalbuminemia, hypocalcemia, hypokalemia, hypomagnesemia, hyponatremia, weight loss

Gastrointestinal: Abdominal distention, abdominal pain, anorexia, decreased appetite, diarrhea, dysgeusia, dyspepsia, dysphagia (buccal tablet/film/sublingual spray), flatulence, gastritis, gastroenteritis, gastroesophageal reflux disease, gastrointestinal hemorrhage, gastrointestinal ulcer (gingival, lip, mouth; transmucosal use/nasal spray), gingival pain (buccal tablet), gingivitis (lozenge), glossitis (lozenge), hematemesis, intestinal obstruction, periodontal abscess (lozenge/buccal tablet), rectal pain, stomatitis (lozenge/buccal tablet/sublingual tablet/ sublingual spray), tongue disease (sublingual tablet), xerostomia

Genitourinary: Urinary retention (3%), difficulty in micturition, dysuria, erectile dysfunction, mastalgia, urinary incontinence, urinary tract infection, urinary urgency, vaginal hemorrhage, vaginitis

Hematologic & oncologic: Anemia (3%), bruise, leukopenia, lymphadenopathy, neutropenia, thrombocytopenia

Hepatic: Ascites, increased serum alkaline phosphatase, increased serum AST, jaundice

Hypersensitivity: Hypersensitivity reaction

Infection: Abscess

Local: Application site burning (transdermal device), application site discharge (transdermal device), application site edema (transdermal device), application site irritation, application site itching (transdermal device), application site pain, application site rash (transdermal device), application site vesicles (transdermal device)

Neuromuscular & skeletal: Arthralgia, back pain, leg cramps, limb pain, myalgia, tremor

Ophthalmic: Blepharoptosis, blurred vision, diplopia, dry eye syndrome, strabismus, swelling of eye, visual disturbance

Renal: Renal failure

Respiratory: Apnea, asthma, atelectasis, bronchitis, cough, dyspnea (exertional), epistaxis, flu-like symptoms, hemoptysis, hyperventilation, hypoventilation, hypoxia, laryngitis, nasal congestion (nasal spray), nasal discomfort (nasal spray), nasopharyngitis, pharyngitis, pharyngolaryngeal pain, pneumonia, postnasal drip (nasal spray), rhinitis, rhinorrhea (nasal spray), sinusitis, upper respiratory tract infection, wheezing

Miscellaneous: Fever, wound healing impairment

<1%, postmarketing, and/or case reports: Allergic dermatitis, anaphylactoid reaction, anaphylaxis, angina pectoris, bradycardia, bronchoconstriction, candidiasis, chest wall rigidity, clonus, contact dermatitis, crusted skin, cyanosis, decreased libido, dental caries, dermatitis, drug dependence (physical and psychological; with prolonged use), eczema, emotional lability, eructation, esophageal stenosis, exfoliative dermatitis, falling, fecal impaction, flank pain, flushing, genitourinary tract spasm, gingival hemorrhage, gum line erosion, hematuria, hiccups, hostility, hyperesthesia, hypoglycemia, hypogonadism (Brennan 2013; Debono 2011), impaired consciousness, increased bronchial secretions, joint swelling, local hemorrhage, local hypersensitivity reaction, localized infection, local skin hyperpigmentation (lasted 2 to 3 weeks), local tissue necrosis, loss of consciousness, miosis, muscle rigidity (transient; observed in infants whose mothers were treated with IV fentanyl), muscle spasm, muscle twitching, myasthenia, nocturia, oliguria, pancytopenia, pleural effusion, polyuria, respiratory depression, respiratory distress, seizure, sexual disorder, skin erosion, Stevens-Johnson syndrome, swelling, swollen tongue, tonic-clonic seizures, tooth loss, upper abdominal pain, urticaria, voice disorder

Dental Usual Dosage Surgery: Adults:

Premedication: IM, slow IV: 25 to 100 mcg/dose 30 to 60 minutes prior to surgery

Adjunct to regional anesthesia: Slow IV: 25 to 100 mcg/dose over 1 to 2 minutes. **Note:** An IV should be in place with regional anesthesia so the IM route is rarely used but still maintained as an option in the package labeling.

Dosing

Adult Note: Ranges listed may not represent the maximum doses that may be required in some patients. Doses and dosage intervals should be titrated to pain relief/prevention. Monitor vital signs routinely. Single IM doses have duration of 1-2 hours, single IV doses last 0.5 to 1 hour.

Surgery:

Premedication: IM, slow IV: 50 to 100 mcg administered 30 to 60 minutes prior to surgery **or** slow IV: 25 to 50 mcg given shortly before induction (Barash, 2009)

Adjunct to general anesthesia: Slow IV:

Low dose: 1 to 2 mcg/**kg** depending on the indication (Miller, 2010); additional maintenance doses are generally not needed.

Moderate dose (fentanyl plus a sedative/hypnotic): Initial: 2 to 4 mcg/**kg**; Maintenance (bolus or infusion): 25 to 50 mcg every 15 to 30 minutes or 0.5 to 2 mcg/kg/**hour**. Discontinuing fentanyl infusion 30 to 60 minutes prior to the end of surgery will usually allow adequate ventilation upon emergence from anesthesia.

High dose (opioid anesthesia): 4 to 20 mcg/**kg** bolus then 2 to 10 mcg/kg/**hour** (Miller, 2010); **Note:** High-dose fentanyl (ie, 20 to 50 mcg/kg) is rarely used, but is still described in the manufacturer's label. The concept of fast-tracking and early extubation following cardiac surgery has essentially replaced high-dose fentanyl anesthesia.

Adjunct to regional anesthesia: 50 to 100 mcg IM or slow IV over 1 to 2 minutes. **Note:** An IV should be in place with regional anesthesia so the IM route is rarely used but still maintained as an option in the manufacturer's labeling.

Postoperative recovery: IM, slow IV: 50 to 100 mcg every 1 to 2 hours as needed.

Postoperative pain: Epidural (Canadian labeling; not in US labeling): Initial: 100 mcg (diluted in 8 mL of preservative free NS to final concentration of 10 mcg/mL); may repeat with additional 100 mcg boluses on demand or alternatively may administer by continuous infusion at a rate of 1 mcg/kg/hour.

Pain management:

Postoperative pain, acute: Transdermal device (Ionsys): Apply one device to chest or upper outer arm only. Only the patient may activate the device (40 mcg dose of fentanyl per activation; maximum 6 doses per hour). Only one device may be applied at a time for up to 24 hours or 80 doses, whichever comes first. May be used for a maximum of 72 hours, with each subsequent device applied to a different skin site. If inadequate analgesia is achieved with one device, either provide additional supplemental analgesic medication or replace with an alternate analgesic medication. Refer to manufacturer's labeling for activation instructions.

Note: For hospital use only by patients under medical supervision and direction and only after patients have been titrated to an acceptable level of analgesia using another opioid analgesic.

Severe pain:

Intermittent dosing: IM, IV (off-label dose): Slow IV: 25 to 35 mcg (based on ~70 kg patient) **or** 0.35 to 0.5 mcg/kg every 30 to 60 minutes as needed (SCCM [Barr, 2013]). **Note:** After the first dose, if severe pain persists and adverse effects are minimal at the time of expected peak effect (eg, ~5 minutes after IV administration), may repeat dose (APS, 2008). In addition, since the duration of activity with IV administration is 30 to 60 minutes, more frequent administration may be necessary when administered by this route.

Patient-controlled analgesia (PCA) (off-label use; American Pain Society, 2008; Miller, 2010): Opioid-naive: IV:

Usual concentration: 10 mcg/mL

Demand dose: Usual: 10 to 20 mcg

Lockout interval: 4 to 10 minutes

Usual basal rate: ≤50 mcg/hour. **Note:** Continuous basal infusions are not recommended for initial programming and should rarely be used; consider limiting infusion rate to 10 mcg/hour if used (Grass, 2005).

Critically-ill patients (off-label dose): Slow IV: 25 to 35 mcg (based on ~70 kg patient) **or** 0.35 to 0.5 mcg/kg every 30 to 60 minutes as needed (SCCM [Barr, 2013]). **Note:** More frequent dosing may be needed (eg, mechanically-ventilated patients).

Continuous infusion: 50 to 700 mcg/hour (based on ~70 kg patient) **or** 0.7 to 10 mcg/kg/**hour** (SCCM [Barr, 2013]).

Alternative continuous infusion dosing: 1 to 2 mcg/kg bolus followed by an initial rate of 1 to 2 mcg/**kg**/hour (Peng, 1999) **or** 25 to 100 mcg bolus followed by an initial rate of 25 to 200 mcg/**hour** (Liu, 2003). **Note:** When pain is not controlled, may administer an additional small bolus dose (eg, 25 to 50 mcg) prior to increasing the infusion rate (Loper 1990; Peng, 1999; Salomaki, 1991).

Intrathecal (off-label use; American Pain Society, 2008): **Must be preservative-free.** Doses must be adjusted for age, injection site, and patient's medical condition and degree of opioid tolerance.

Single dose: 5 to 25 mcg; may provide adequate relief for up to 6 hours

Continuous infusion: Not recommended in acute pain management due to risk of excessive accumulation. For chronic cancer pain, infusion of very small doses may be practical (American Pain Society, 2008).

Epidural (off-label use; American Pain Society, 2008): **Must be preservative-free.** Doses must be adjusted for age, injection site, and patient's medical condition and degree of opioid tolerance

Single dose: 25 to 100 mcg; may provide adequate relief for up to 8 hours

Continuous infusion: 25 to 100 mcg/hour (fentanyl alone). When combined with a local anesthetic (eg, bupivacaine or ropivacaine), fentanyl requirement are less (Manion, 2011).

Breakthrough cancer pain: Transmucosal: For patients who are tolerant to and currently receiving opioid therapy for persistent cancer pain; dosing should be individually titrated to provide adequate analgesia with minimal side effects. Dose titration should be done if patient requires more than 1 dose/breakthrough pain episode for several consecutive episodes. Patients experiencing >4 breakthrough pain episodes per day should have the dose of their long-term opioid re-evaluated. **Patients must remain on around-the-clock opioids during use.**

Lozenge (Actiq): **Note:** Do **not** convert patients from any other fentanyl product to Actiq on a mcg-per-mcg basis. Patients previously using another fentanyl product should be initiated at a dose of 200 mcg; individually titrate to provide adequate analgesia while minimizing adverse effects.

Initial dose: 200 mcg (consumed over 15 minutes) for all patients; if after 30 minutes from the start of the lozenge (ie, 15 minutes following the completion of the lozenge), the pain is unrelieved, a second 200 mcg dose may be given over 15 minutes. A maximum of 1 additional dose can be given per pain episode; **must wait at least 4 hours before treating another episode**. To limit the number of units in the home during titration, only prescribe an initial titration supply of six 200 mcg lozenges.

Dose titration: From the initial dose, closely follow patients and modify the dose until patient reaches a dose providing adequate analgesia using a single dosage unit per breakthrough cancer pain episode. If signs/symptoms of excessive opioid effects (eg, respiratory depression) occur, immediately remove the dosage unit from the patient's mouth, dispose of properly, and reduce subsequent doses. If adequate relief is not achieved 15 minutes after completion of the first dose (ie, 30 minutes after the start of the lozenge), only 1 additional lozenge of the same strength may be given for that episode; **must wait at least 4 hours before treating another episode.**

Maintenance dose: Once titrated to an effective dose, patients should generally use a single dosage unit per breakthrough pain episode. During any pain episode, if adequate relief is not achieved 15 minutes after completion of the first dose (ie, 30 minutes after the start of the lozenge), only 1 additional lozenge of the same strength may be given over 15 minutes for that episode; **must wait at least 4 hours before treating another episode**. Consumption should be limited to ≤4 units per day (once an effective breakthrough dose is found). If adequate analgesia is **not** provided after treating several episodes of breakthrough pain using the same dose, increase dose to next highest lozenge strength (initially dispense no more than 6 units of the new strength). Consider increasing the around-the-clock opioid therapy in patients experiencing >4 breakthrough pain episodes per day. If signs/symptoms of excessive opioid effects (eg, respiratory depression) occur, immediately remove the dosage unit from the patient's mouth, dispose of properly, and reduce subsequent doses.

Buccal film (Onsolis): **Note:** Do **not** convert patients from any other fentanyl product to Onsolis on a mcg-per-mcg basis. Patients previously using another fentanyl product should be initiated at a dose of 200 mcg; individually titrate to provide adequate analgesia while minimizing adverse effects.

Initial dose: 200 mcg for all patients; if after 30 minutes pain is unrelieved, the patient may use an alternative rescue medication as directed by their health care provider. Do **not** redose with Onsolis within an episode; buccal film should only be used once per breakthrough cancer pain episode. **Must wait at least 2 hours before treating another episode with buccal film.**

Dose titration: If titration required, increase dose in 200 mcg increments once per episode using multiples of the 200 mcg film (for doses up to 800 mcg); do not redose within a single episode of breakthrough pain and separate single doses by ≥2 hours. During titration, do not exceed 4 simultaneous applications of the 200 mcg films (800 mcg) (when using multiple films, do not place on top of each other; film may be placed on both sides of mouth); if >800 mcg required, treat next episode with one 1200 mcg film (maximum dose: 1200 mcg). Once maintenance dose is determined, all other unused films should be disposed of and that strength (using a single film) should be used. During any pain episode, if adequate relief is not achieved after 30 minutes following buccal film application, a rescue medication (as determined by health care provider) may be used.

Maintenance dose: Determined dose applied as a single film once per episode and separated by ≥2 hours (dose range: 200 to 1200 mcg); limit to 4 applications per day. Consider increasing the around-the-clock opioid therapy in patients experiencing >4 breakthrough pain episodes per day.

Buccal tablet (Fentora): **Note:** Do **not** convert patients from any other fentanyl product to Fentora on a mcg-per-mcg basis. Patients previously using another fentanyl product should be initiated at a dose of 100 mcg; individually titrate to provide adequate analgesia while minimizing adverse effects. For patients previously using the transmucosal lozenge (Actiq), the initial dose should be selected using the conversions listed; see *Conversion from lozenge (Actiq) to buccal tablet (Fentora)*.

Initial dose: 100 mcg for all patients unless patient already using Actiq; see *Conversion from lozenge (Actiq) to buccal tablet (Fentora)*; if after 30 minutes pain is unrelieved, the US labeling suggests that a second 100 mcg dose may be administered (maximum of 2 doses per breakthrough pain episode). The Canadian labeling recommends only a single dose per breakthrough pain episode; patients experiencing breakthrough pain after administration may take an alternative analgesic as rescue medication after 30 minutes. **Must wait at least 4 hours before treating another episode with Fentora buccal tablet.**

Dose titration: If titration required, 100 mcg dose may be increased to 200 mcg using two 100 mcg tablets (one on each side of mouth) with the next breakthrough pain episode. If 200 mcg dose is not successful, patient can use four 100 mcg tablets (two on each side of mouth) with the next breakthrough pain episode. If titration requires >400 mcg per dose, titrate using 200 mcg tablets; do not use more than 4 tablets simultaneously (maximum single dose: 800 mcg). During any pain episode, if adequate relief is not achieved after 30 minutes following buccal tablet application, a second dose of same strength per breakthrough pain episode may be used. The Canadian labeling recommends only a single dose per breakthrough pain episode; patients experiencing breakthrough pain after administration may take an alternative analgesic as rescue medication after 30 minutes. **Must wait at least 4 hours before treating another episode with Fentora buccal tablet.**

Maintenance dose: Following titration, the effective maintenance dose using 1 tablet of the appropriate strength should be administered once per episode; if after 30 minutes pain is unrelieved, may administer a second dose of the same strength; The Canadian labeling recommends only a single dose per breakthrough pain episode; patients experiencing breakthrough pain after administration may take an alternative analgesic as rescue medication after 30 minutes. **Must wait ≥4 hours before treating another episode with Fentora buccal tablet.** Limit to 4 applications per day. Consider increasing the around-the-clock opioid therapy in patients experiencing >4 breakthrough pain episodes per day. Once an effective maintenance dose has been established, the buccal tablet may be administered sublingually (alternate route). To prevent confusion, patient should only have one strength available at a time. Once maintenance dose is determined, all other unused tablets should be disposed of and that strength (using a single tablet) should be used. Using more than four buccal tablets at a time has not been studied.

Conversion from lozenge (Actiq) to buccal tablet (Fentora):

Lozenge dose 200 to 400 mcg: Initial buccal tablet dose is 100 mcg; may titrate using multiples of 100 mcg

Lozenge dose 600 to 800 mcg: Initial buccal tablet dose is 200 mcg; may titrate using multiples of 200 mcg

Lozenge dose 1200 to 1600 mcg: Initial buccal tablet dose is 400 mcg (using two 200 mcg tablets); may titrate using multiples of 200 mcg

Nasal spray (Lazanda): **Note:** Do **not** convert patients from any other fentanyl product to Lazanda on a mcg-per-mcg basis. Patients previously using another fentanyl product should be initiated at a dose of 100 mcg; individually titrate to provide adequate analgesia while minimizing adverse effects.

Initial dose: 100 mcg (one 100 mcg spray in one nostril) for all patients; if after 30 minutes pain is unrelieved, an alternative rescue medication may be used as directed by their health care provider. **Must wait at least 2 hours before treating another episode with Lazanda nasal spray.** However, for the next pain episode, increase to a higher dose using the recommended dose titration steps.

Dose titration: If titration required, increase to a higher dose for the next pain episode using these titration steps **(Note: Must wait at least 2 hours before treating another episode with Lazanda nasal spray)**: If no relief with 100 mcg dose, increase to 200 mcg dose per episode (one 100 mcg spray in each nostril); if no relief with 200 mcg dose, increase to 300 mcg dose per episode (alternating one 100 mcg spray in right nostril, one 100 mcg spray in left nostril, and one 100 mcg spray in the right nostril); if no relief with 300 mcg dose, increase to 400 mcg per episode (one 400 mcg spray in one nostril or alternating two 100 mcg sprays in each nostril); if no relief with 400 mcg dose, increase to 600 mcg dose per episode (one 300 mcg spray in each nostril); if no relief with 600 mcg dose, increase to 800 mcg dose per episode (one 400 mcg spray in each nostril). **Note:** Single doses >800 mcg have not been evaluated. There are no data supporting the use of a combination of dose strengths. Avoid use of a combination of dose strengths to treat an episode, as this may cause confusion and dosing errors.

Maintenance dose: Once maintenance dose for breakthrough pain episode has been determined, use that dose for subsequent episodes. For pain that is not relieved after 30 minutes of Lazanda administration or if a separate breakthrough pain episode occurs within the 2 hour window before the next Lazanda dose is permitted, a rescue medication may be used. Limit Lazanda use to ≤4 episodes of breakthrough pain per day. If patient is experiencing >4 breakthrough pain episodes per day, consider increasing the around-the-clock, long-acting opioid therapy; if long-acting opioid therapy dose is altered, re-evaluate and retitrate Lazanda dose as needed. If response to maintenance dose changes (increase in adverse reactions or alterations in pain relief), dose readjustment may be necessary.

Sublingual spray (Subsys): **Note:** Do **not** convert patients from any other fentanyl product to Subsys on a mcg-per-mcg basis. Patients previously using another fentanyl product should be initiated at a dose of 100 mcg; individually titrate to provide adequate analgesia while minimizing adverse effects. For patients previously using the transmucosal lozenge (Actiq), the initial dose should be selected using the conversions listed; see *Conversion from lozenge (Actiq) to sublingual spray (Subsys)*.

Initial dose: 100 mcg for all patients unless patient already using Actiq; see *Conversion from lozenge (Actiq) to sublingual spray (Subsys)*. If pain is unrelieved, 1 additional 100 mcg dose may be given 30 minutes after administration of the first dose. A maximum of 2 doses can be given per breakthrough pain episode. **Must wait at least 4 hours before treating another episode with sublingual spray.**

Dose titration: If titration required, titrate to a dose that provides adequate analgesia (with tolerable side effects) using the following titration steps: If no relief with 100 mcg dose, increase to 200 mcg dose (using one 200 mcg unit); if no relief with 200 mcg dose, increase to 400 mcg dose (using one 400 mcg unit); if no relief with 400 mcg dose, increase to 600 mcg dose (using one 600 mcg unit); if no relief with 600 mcg dose, increase to 800 mcg dose (using one 800 mcg unit); if no relief with 800 mcg dose, increase to 1200 mcg dose (using two 600 mcg units); if no relief with 1200 mcg dose, increase to 1600 mcg dose (using two 800 mcg units). During dose titration, if breakthrough pain unrelieved 30 minutes after Subsys administration, 1 additional dose using the same strength may be administered (maximum: 2 doses per breakthrough pain episode); **patient must wait 4 hours before treating another breakthrough pain episode with sublingual spray.**

Maintenance dose: Once maintenance dose for breakthrough pain episode has been determined, use that dose for subsequent episodes. If occasional episodes of unrelieved breakthrough pain occur following 30 minutes of Subsys administration, 1 additional dose using the same strength may be administered (maximum: 2 doses per breakthrough pain episode); **patient must wait 4 hours before treating another breakthrough pain episode with Subsys.** Once maintenance dose is determined, limit Subsys use to ≤4 episodes of breakthrough pain per day. If response to maintenance dose changes (increase in adverse reactions or alterations in pain relief), dose readjustment may be necessary. If patient is experiencing >4 breakthrough pain episodes per day, consider increasing the around-the-clock, long-acting opioid therapy.

Conversion from lozenge (Actiq) to sublingual spray (Subsys):

Lozenge dose 200 to 400 mcg: Initial sublingual spray dose is 100 mcg; may titrate using multiples of 100 mcg

Lozenge dose 600 to 800 mcg: Initial sublingual spray dose is 200 mcg; may titrate using multiples of 200 mcg

Lozenge dose 1,200 to 1,600 mcg: Initial sublingual spray dose is 400 mcg; may titrate using multiples of 400 mcg

Sublingual tablet (Abstral): **Note:** Do **not** convert patients from any other fentanyl product to Abstral on a mcg-per-mcg basis. Patients previously using another fentanyl product should be initiated at a dose of 100 mcg (except Actiq); individually titrate to provide adequate analgesia while minimizing adverse effects.

Initial dose:

US labeling: 100 mcg for all patients; if pain is unrelieved, a second 100 mcg dose may be given 30 minutes after administration of the first dose. A maximum of 2 doses can be given per breakthrough pain episode. **Must wait at least 2 hours before treating another episode with sublingual tablet.**

Canadian labeling: 100 mcg for all patients; if pain is unrelieved 30 minutes after administration of Abstral, an alternative rescue medication (other than Abstral) may be given. Administer only 1 dose of Abstral per breakthrough pain episode. **Must wait at least 2 hours before treating another episode with sublingual tablet.**

Dose titration: If titration required, increase in 100 mcg increments (up to 400 mcg) over consecutive breakthrough episodes. If titration requires >400 mcg per dose, increase in increments of 200 mcg, starting with 600 mcg dose and titrating up to 800 mcg. During titration, patients may use multiples of 100 mcg and/or 200 mcg tablets for any single dose; do not exceed 4 tablets at one time; safety and efficacy of doses >800 mcg have not been evaluated. During dose titration, if breakthrough pain unrelieved 30 minutes after sublingual tablet administration, the US labeling suggests that 1 additional dose using the same strength may be administered (maximum: 2 doses per breakthrough pain episode); the Canadian labeling recommends use of an alternative rescue medication and limits use of Abstral to 1 dose per breakthrough pain episode. **Patient must wait 2 hours before treating another breakthrough pain episode with sublingual tablet.**

Maintenance dose: Once maintenance dose for breakthrough pain episode has been determined, use only 1 tablet in the appropriate strength per episode; if pain is unrelieved with maintenance dose:

US labeling: A second dose may be given after 30 minutes; maximum of 2 doses/episode of breakthrough pain; separate treatment of subsequent episodes by ≥2 hours; limit treatment to ≤4 breakthrough episodes per day.

Canadian labeling: Administer alternative rescue medication after 30 minutes; maximum of 1 Abstral dose/episode of breakthrough pain; separate treatment of subsequent episodes by ≥2 hours; limit treatment to ≤4 breakthrough episodes per day.

Consider increasing the around-the-clock long-acting opioid therapy in patients experiencing >4 breakthrough pain episodes per day; if long-acting opioid therapy dose altered, re-evaluate and retitrate Abstral dose as needed.

Conversion from lozenge (Actiq) to sublingual tablet (Abstral):

Lozenge dose 200 mcg: Initial sublingual tablet dose is 100 mcg; may titrate using multiples of 100 mcg

Lozenge dose 400 to 1,200 mcg: Initial sublingual tablet dose is 200 mcg; may titrate using multiples of 200 mcg

Lozenge dose 1,600 mcg: Initial sublingual tablet dose is 400 mcg; may titrate using multiples of 400 mcg

Chronic pain management (opioid-tolerant patients only): Transdermal patch: Discontinue or taper all other around-the-clock or extended release opioids when initiating therapy with fentanyl transdermal patch.

Initial: To convert patients from oral or parenteral opioids to transdermal patch, a 24-hour analgesic requirement should be calculated (based on prior opioid use). Using the tables, the appropriate initial dose can be determined. The initial fentanyl dosage may be approximated from the 24-hour morphine dosage equivalent and titrated to minimize adverse effects and provide analgesia. Substantial interpatient variability exists in relative potency. Therefore, it is safer to underestimate a patient's daily fentanyl requirement and provide breakthrough pain relief with rescue medication (eg, immediate release opioid) than to overestimate requirements. With the initial application, the absorption of transdermal fentanyl requires several hours to reach plateau; therefore transdermal fentanyl is inappropriate for management of acute pain. Change patch every 72 hours.

Conversion from continuous infusion of fentanyl: In patients who have adequate pain relief with a fentanyl infusion, fentanyl may be converted to transdermal dosing at a rate equivalent to the intravenous rate. A two-step taper of the infusion to be completed over 12 hours has been recommended (Kornick, 2001) after the patch is applied. The infusion is decreased to 50% of the original rate six hours after the application of the first patch, and subsequently discontinued twelve hours after application.

Titration: Short-acting agents may be required until analgesic efficacy is established and/or as supplements for "breakthrough" pain. The amount of supplemental doses should be closely monitored. Appropriate dosage increases may be based on daily supplemental dosage using the ratio of 45 mg/24 hours of oral morphine to a 12.5 mcg/hour increase in fentanyl dosage (US labeling) or using the ratio of 45 to 59 mg/24 hours of oral morphine to a 12 mcg/hour increase in fentanyl dosage (Canadian labeling).

Frequency of adjustment: The dosage should not be titrated more frequently than every 3 days after the initial dose or every 6 days thereafter. Titrate dose based on the daily dose of supplemental opioids required by the patient on the second or third day of the initial application. **Note:** Upon discontinuation, ~17 hours are required for a 50% decrease in fentanyl levels.

Frequency of application: The majority of patients may be controlled on every 72-hour administration; however, a small number of adult patients require every 48-hour administration.

Discontinuation: When discontinuing transdermal fentanyl and not converting to another opioid, use a gradual downward titration, such as decreasing the dose by 50% every 6 days, to reduce the possibility of withdrawal symptoms.

Dose conversion guidelines for transdermal fentanyl (see tables).

Note: US and Canadian dose conversion guidelines differ; consult appropriate table. The conversion factors in these tables are only to be used for the conversion from current opioid therapy to Duragesic. Conversion factors in this table cannot be used to convert from Duragesic to another opioid (doing so may lead to fatal overdose due to overestimation of the new opioid). These are not tables of equianalgesic doses.

U.S. Labeling: Dose Conversion Guidelines: Recommended Initial Duragesic® Dose Based Upon Daily Oral Morphine Dose[1,2]

Oral 24-Hour Morphine (mg/day)	Duragesic Dose[3] (mcg/h)
60 to 134	25
135 to 224	50
225 to 314	75
315 to 404	100
405 to 494	125
495 to 584	150
585 to 674	175
675 to 764	200
765 to 854	225
855 to 944	250
945 to 1034	275
1035 to 1124	300

[1]The table should NOT be used to convert from transdermal fentanyl (Duragesic) to other opioid analgesics. Rather, following removal of the patch, titrate the dose of the new opioid until adequate analgesia is achieved.

[2]Recommendations are based on U.S. product labeling for Duragesic.

[3]Pediatric patients initiating therapy on a 25 mcg/hour Duragesic system should be opioid-tolerant and receiving at least 60 mg oral morphine equivalents per day.

U.S. Labeling: Dose Conversion Guidelines[1,2]

Current Analgesic	Daily Dosage (mg/day)			
Morphine (IM/IV)	10 to 22	23 to 37	38 to 52	53 to 67
Oxycodone (oral)	30 to 67	67.5 to 112	112.5 to 157	157.5 to 202
Codeine (oral)	150 to 447	-	-	-
Hydromorphone (oral)	8 to 17	17.1 to 28	28.1 to 39	39.1 to 51
Hydromorphone (IV)	1.5 to 3.4	3.5 to 5.6	5.7 to 7.9	8 to 10
Meperidine (IM)	75 to 165	166 to 278	279 to 390	391 to 503
Methadone (oral)	20 to 44	45 to 74	75 to 104	105 to 134
Fentanyl transdermal recommended dose (mcg/h)	**25 mcg/h**	**50 mcg/h**	**75 mcg/h**	**100 mcg/h**

[1]The table should NOT be used to convert from transdermal fentanyl (Duragesic) to other opioid analgesics. Rather, following removal of the patch, titrate the dose of the new opioid until adequate analgesia is achieved.

[2]Recommendations are based on U.S. product labeling for Duragesic.

Transdermal patch (Duragesic): Canadian labeling: Adults:

Canadian Labeling: Dose Conversion Guidelines (Adults): Recommended Initial Duragesic Dose Based Upon Daily Oral Morphine Dose[1,2]

Oral 24-Hour Morphine (Current Dose in mg/day)	Duragesic Dose (Initial Dose in mcg/h)
45 to 59	12
60 to 134	25
135 to 179	37
180 to 224	50
225 to 269	62
270 to 314	75
315 to 359	87
360 to 404	100
405 to 494	125
495 to 584	150
585 to 674	175
675 to 764	200
765 to 854	225
855 to 944	250
945 to 1034	275
1035 to 1124	300

[1]The table should NOT be used to convert from transdermal fentanyl (Duragesic) to other opioid analgesics. Rather, following removal of the patch, titrate the dose of the new opioid until adequate analgesia is achieved.

[2]Recommendations are based on Canadian product labeling for Duragesic.

Note: The 12 mcg/hour dose included in this table is to be used for incremental dose adjustment and is generally not recommended for initial dosing, except for patients in whom lower starting doses are deemed clinically appropriate

Canadian Labeling: Dosing Conversion Guidelines (Adults)[1,2]

Current Analgesic	Daily Dosage (mg/day)						
Morphine[3] (IM/IV)	20 to 44	45 to 60	61 to 75	76 to 90	n/a[4]	n/a[4]	n/a[1]
Oxycodone (oral)	30 to 66	67 to 90	91 to 112	113 to 134	135 to 157	158 to 179	180 to 202
Codeine (oral)	150 to 447	448 to 597	598 to 747	748 to 897	898 to 1047	1048 to 1197	1198 to 1347
Hydromorphone (oral)	8 to 10	17 to 22	23 to 28	29 to 33	34 to 39	40 to 45	46 to 51
Hydromorphone (IV)	4 to 8.4	8.5 to 11.4	11.5 to 14.4	14.5 to 16.5	16.6 to 19.5	19.6 to 22.5	22.6 to 25.5
Fentanyl transdermal recommended dose (mcg/h)	**25 mcg/h**	**37 mcg/h**	**50 mcg/h**	**62 mcg/h**	**75 mcg/h**	**87 mcg/h**	**100 mcg/h**

[1]The table should NOT be used to convert from transdermal fentanyl (Duragesic) to other opioid analgesics. Rather, following removal of the patch, titrate the dose of the new opioid until adequate analgesia is achieved.

[2]Recommendations are based on Canadian product labeling for Duragesic.

[3]Morphine dose conversion based upon I.M to oral dose ratio of 1:3.

[4]Insufficient data available to provide specific dosing recommendations. Use caution; adjust dose conservatively.

Geriatric Elderly have been found to be twice as sensitive as younger patients to the effects of fentanyl. A wide range of doses may be used. When choosing a dose, take into consideration the following patient factors: age, weight, physical status, underlying disease states, other drugs used, type of anesthesia used, and the surgical procedure to be performed.

Transmucosal lozenge (eg, Actiq): In clinical trials, patients who were >65 years of age were titrated to a mean dose that was 200 mcg less than that of younger patients.

Pediatric Note: Ranges listed may not represent the maximum doses that may be required in some patients. Doses and dosage intervals should be titrated to pain relief/prevention. Monitor vital signs routinely. Single IM doses have duration of 1 to 2 hours, single IV doses last 0.5 to 1 hour.

Surgery adjunct to anesthesia (induction and maintenance): Children ≥2 years and Adolescents: IV: 2 to 3 mcg/**kg**/dose every 1 to 2 hours as needed

Breakthrough cancer pain: Adolescents ≥16 years: Transmucosal lozenge (Actiq): Refer to adult dosing.

Chronic pain management: Children ≥2 years and Adolescents (opioid-tolerant patients): Transdermal patch (US labeling): Refer to adult dosing. **Note:** Canadian labeling does not approve of use in patients <18 years.

Pain management (off-label use): *Patient-controlled analgesia (PCA) (off-label use; American Pain Society, 2008):* Children <50 kg: IV: **Note:** Opioid-naive:

Usual concentration: 10 to 50 mcg/mL (varies by patient weight and institution)

Demand dose: 0.5 to 1 mcg/kg/dose

Lockout interval: 6 to 8 minutes

Usual basal rate (optional): ≤0.5 mcg/kg/**hour**. **Note:** Due to safety concerns, continuous basal infusions are not recommended for initial programming and should rarely be used (Grass, 2005).

Renal Impairment

Injection: No dosage adjustment provided in manufacturer's labeling, use with caution.

Transdermal (device): There are no dosage adjustments provided in the manufacturer's labeling (has not been studied); fentanyl pharmacokinetics may be altered in renal disease.

Transdermal (patch): Degree of impairment (ie, CrCl) not defined in manufacturer's labeling.

Mild-to-moderate impairment: Initial: Reduce dose by 50%.

Severe impairment: Use not recommended.

Transmucosal (buccal film/tablet, sublingual spray/tablet, lozenge) and nasal spray: Although fentanyl pharmacokinetics may be altered in renal disease, fentanyl can be used successfully in the management of breakthrough cancer pain. Doses should be titrated to reach clinical effect with careful monitoring of patients with severe renal disease.

Hepatic Impairment

Injection: No dosage adjustment provided in manufacturer's labeling; use with caution.

Transdermal (device): There are no dosage adjustments provided in the manufacturer's labeling (has not been studied); fentanyl pharmacokinetics may be altered in hepatic disease.

Transdermal (patch):

Mild-to-moderate impairment: Initial: Reduce dose by 50%.

Severe impairment: Use not recommended.

Transmucosal (buccal film/tablet, sublingual spray/tablet, lozenge) and nasal spray: Although fentanyl pharmacokinetics may be altered in hepatic disease, fentanyl can be used successfully in the management of breakthrough cancer pain. Doses should be titrated to reach clinical effect with careful monitoring of patients with severe hepatic disease.

Mechanism of Action Binds with stereospecific receptors at many sites within the CNS, increases pain threshold, alters pain reception, inhibits ascending pain pathways

Contraindications

Hypersensitivity to fentanyl or any component of the formulation

Additional contraindications for transdermal device (eg, Ionsys): Significant respiratory depression; acute or severe bronchial asthma; known or suspected paralytic ileus and GI obstruction; hypersensitivity to cetylpyridinium chloride (eg, Cepacol)

Additional contraindications for transdermal patches (eg, Duragesic): Severe respiratory disease or depression including acute asthma (unless patient is mechanically ventilated); paralytic ileus; patients requiring short-term therapy, management of acute or intermittent pain, postoperative or mild pain, and in patients who are **not** opioid tolerant

Additional contraindications for transmucosal buccal tablets (Fentora), buccal films (Onsolis), lozenges (eg, Actiq), sublingual tablets (Abstral), sublingual spray (Subsys), nasal spray (Lazanda): Contraindicated in the management of acute or postoperative pain (including headache, migraine, or dental pain), and in patients who are **not** opioid tolerant. Abstral and Onsolis also are contraindicated for acute pain management in the emergency room.

Canadian labeling: Additional contraindication (not in US labeling):

Injection: Septicemia; severe hemorrhage or shock; local infection at proposed injection site; disturbances in blood morphology and/or anticoagulant therapy or other concomitant drug therapy or medical conditions which could contraindicate the technique of epidural administration

Sublingual tablets (Abstral): Severe bronchial asthma, chronic obstructive airway, or status asthmaticus; acute respiratory depression; hypercapnia; cor pulmonale; known or suspected mechanical GI obstruction (eg, bowel obstruction or strictures) or any diseases/conditions that affect bowel transit (eg, ileus of any type); suspected surgical abdomen (eg, acute appendicitis or pancreatitis); mild pain that can be managed with other pain medications; acute alcoholism, delirium tremens, and convulsive disorders; severe CNS depression, increased cerebrospinal or intracranial pressure and head injury; concurrent use or use within 14 days of a monoamine oxidase (MAO) inhibitor; nursing women; during labor and delivery

Transdermal patch: Hypersensitivity to other opioids; suspected surgical abdomen (eg, acute appendicitis, pancreatitis); known or suspected mechanical GI obstruction (eg, bowel obstruction, strictures) or any diseases/conditions that affect bowel transit (eg, ileus of any type); acute alcoholism, delirium tremens, and convulsive disorders; severe CNS depression, increased cerebrospinal or intracranial pressure and head injury; concurrent use of MAO inhibitors or within 14 days of therapy; perioperative pain; women who are nursing, pregnant, or during labor and delivery

Transmucosal buccal tablets (Fentora): Hypersensitivity to other opioids; acute pain management in the emergency room; known or suspected mechanical GI obstruction (eg, bowel obstruction or strictures) or any diseases/conditions that affect bowel transit (eg, ileus of any type); suspected surgical abdomen (eg, acute appendicitis or pancreatitis); acute or severe bronchial asthma, chronic obstructive airway, status asthmaticus; acute respiratory depression; hypercapnia; cor pulmonale; acute alcoholism, delirium tremens, and convulsive disorders; severe CNS depression, increased cerebrospinal or intracranial pressure and head injury; concurrent use or use within 14 days of an MAO inhibitor

Documentation of allergenic cross-reactivity for opioid analgesics is limited. However, because of similarities in chemical structure and/or pharmacologic actions, the possibility of cross-sensitivity cannot be ruled out with certainty.

Warnings/Precautions An opioid-containing analgesic regimen should be tailored to each patient's needs and based upon the type of pain being treated (acute versus chronic), the route of administration, degree of tolerance for opioids (naive versus chronic user), age, weight, and medical condition. The optimal analgesic dose varies widely among patients. Doses should be titrated to pain relief/prevention. May cause CNS depression, which may impair physical or mental abilities; patients must be cautioned about performing tasks which require mental alertness (eg, operating machinery or driving). Effects may be potentiated when used with other sedative drugs or ethanol. Fentanyl shares the toxic potentials of opioid agonists, and precautions of opioid agonist therapy should be observed; use with caution in patients with bradycardia or bradyarrhythmias; rapid IV infusion may result in skeletal muscle and chest wall rigidity leading to respiratory distress and/or apnea, bronchoconstriction, laryngospasm; inject slowly over 3 to 5 minutes. Monitor for respiratory depression in patients with significant chronic obstructive pulmonary disease or cor pulmonale, and patients having a substantially decreased respiratory reserve, hypoxia, hypercarbia, or preexisting respiratory depression, particularly when initiating therapy and titrating with fentanyl; even therapeutic doses may decrease respiratory drive to the point of apnea. Consider the use of alternative nonopioid analgesics in these patients. **[US Boxed Warning]: Users are exposed to the risks of addiction, abuse, and misuse, potentially leading to overdose and death. Assess each patient's risk prior to prescribing; monitor all patients for development of these behaviors or conditions.** The risk for opioid abuse is increased in patients with a personal or family history of substance abuse (including drug or alcohol abuse or addiction). Other factors associated with increased risk include younger age and psychotropic medication use. Consider offering naloxone prescriptions in patients with factors associated with an increased risk for overdose, such as history of overdose or substance use disorder, higher opioid dosages (≥50 morphine milligram equivalents/day orally), and concomitant benzodiazepine use (Dowell [CDC 2016]). Use opioids with caution in chronic pain in patients with mental health conditions (eg, depression, anxiety disorders, post-traumatic stress disorder) due to increased risk for opioid use disorder and overdose; more frequent monitoring is recommended (Dowell [CDC 2016]). Use with caution in the elderly; may be more sensitive to adverse effects. Decrease initial dose. Use opioids for chronic pain with caution in this age group; monitor closely due to an increased potential for risks, including certain risks such as falls/fracture, cognitive impairment, and constipation. Clearance may also be reduced in older adults (with or without renal impairment) resulting in a narrow therapeutic window and increasing the risk for respiratory depression or overdose (Dowell [CDC 2016]). Use extreme caution in patients with COPD or other chronic respiratory conditions (some products may be contraindicated). Use caution with biliary tract impairment, pancreatitis, head injuries (some products may be contraindicated), morbid obesity, renal impairment, or hepatic dysfunction. **[US Boxed Warning]: Use with strong or moderate CYP3A4 inhibitors may result in increased effects and potentially fatal respiratory depression. In addition, discontinuation of a concomitant CYP 3A4 inducer may result in increased fentanyl concentrations. Monitor patients receiving any CYP 3A4 inhibitor or inducer.** Concurrent use of mixed agonist/antagonist analgesics (eg, pentazocine, nalbuphine, butorphanol) or partial agonist (eg, buprenorphine) analgesics may precipitate withdrawal symptoms and/or reduced analgesic efficacy in patients following prolonged therapy with mu opioid agonists. Abrupt discontinuation following prolonged use may also lead to withdrawal symptoms. May aggravate convulsions in patients with convulsive disorders, and may induce or aggravate seizures in some clinical settings. Monitor patients with a history of seizure disorders for worsened seizure control. Use opioids with caution for chronic pain and titrate dosage cautiously in patients with risk factors for sleep-disordered breathing, including HF and obesity. Avoid opioids in patients with moderate to severe sleep-disordered breathing (Dowell [CDC 2016]). May cause severe hypotension including orthostatic hypotension and syncope in ambulatory patients; risk is increased in patients whose ability to maintain blood pressure has already been compromised by a reduced blood volume; monitor these patients for signs of hypotension after initiating therapy. Potentially significant interactions may exist, requiring dose or frequency adjustment, additional monitoring, and/or selection of alternative therapy. Effects may be potentiated when used with other CNS depressants (eg, sedatives, anxiolytics, hypnotics, neuroleptics, other opioids). In the chronic pain setting, avoid prescribing opioids and benzodiazepines concurrently whenever possible; epidemiologic studies suggest there is an increased risk for potentially fatal overdose with concurrent use (Dowell [CDC 2016]).

Chronic pain: Opioids should not be used as first-line therapy for chronic pain management (pain >3-month duration or beyond time of normal tissue healing) due to limited short-term benefits, undetermined long-term benefits, and association with serious risks (eg, overdose, MI, auto accidents, risk of developing opioid use disorder). Preferred management includes nonpharmacologic therapy and nonopioid therapy (eg, NSAIDs, acetaminophen, certain anticonvulsants and antidepressants). If opioid therapy is initiated, it should be combined with nonpharmacologic and non-opioid therapy, as appropriate. Prior to initiation, known risks of opioid therapy should be discussed and realistic treatment goals for pain/function should be established, including consideration for discontinuation if benefits do not outweigh risks. Therapy should be continued only if clinically meaningful improvement in pain/function outweighs risks. Therapy should be initiated at the lowest effective dosage using immediate-release opioids (instead of extended-release/long-acting opioids). Risk associated with use increases with higher opioid dosages. Risks and benefits should be re-evaluated when increasing dosage to ≥50 morphine milligram equivalents (MME)/day orally; dosages ≥90 MME/day orally should be avoided unless carefully justified (Dowell [CDC 2016]).

Pediatric patients: **[US Boxed Warning]: Buccal film, buccal tablet, nasal spray, sublingual tablet, sublingual spray, and lozenge preparations contain an amount of medication that can be fatal to children. Keep all used and unused products out of the reach of children at all times and discard products properly.** Patients and caregivers should be counseled on the dangers to children including the risk of exposure to partially-consumed products.

[US Boxed Warning] Abstral, Actiq, Duragesic, Fentora, Ionsys, Lazanda, Onsolis, Subsys: May cause serious, life-threatening, or fatal respiratory depression, even when used as recommended. Monitor closely for respiratory depression, especially during initiation or dose escalation. Abstral, Actiq, Duragesic, Fentora, Lazanda, Onsolis, or Subsys should only be prescribed for opioid-tolerant patients. Risk of respiratory depression increased in elderly patients, debilitated patients, and patients with conditions associated with hypoxia or hypercapnia; usually occurs after administration of initial dose in nontolerant patients or when given with other drugs that depress respiratory function.

Transmucosal (buccal film/tablet, sublingual spray/tablet, lozenge) and nasal spray: **[US Boxed Warning]: Transmucosal and nasal fentanyl formulations are contraindicated in the management of acute or postoperative pain and in opioid nontolerant patients.** Should be used only for the care of opioid-tolerant cancer patients with breakthrough pain and is intended for use by specialists who are knowledgeable in treating cancer pain. **[US Boxed Warning]: Substantial differences exist in the pharmacokinetic profile of fentanyl products. Do not convert patients on a mcg-per-mcg basis from one fentanyl product to another fentanyl product; the substitution of one fentanyl product for another fentanyl product may result in a fatal overdose. [US Boxed Warning]: Available only through the TIRF REMS ACCESS program, a restricted distribution program with outpatients, prescribers who prescribe to outpatients, pharmacies (inpatient and outpatient), and distributor-required enrollment.** Avoid use of topical nasal decongestants (eg, oxymetazoline) during episodes of rhinitis when using fentanyl nasal spray; response to fentanyl may be delayed or reduced. Avoid use of sublingual spray in cancer patients with grade 2 or higher mucositis (fentanyl exposure increased); use with caution in patients with grade 1 mucositis, and closely monitor for respiratory and CNS depression.

Transdermal device: **[US Boxed Warning]: Available only through a restricted program under a Risk Evaluation and Mitigation Strategy (REMS) called the Ionsys REMS Program. [US Boxed Warning]: For use only in patients in the hospital. Discontinue treatment before patients leave the hospital. Only the patient should activate Ionsys dosing. Accidental exposure to an intact Ionsys device or to the hydrogel component, especially by children, through contact with skin or contact with mucous membranes, can result in a fatal overdose of fentanyl.** Following accidental contact with the device or its components, immediately rinse the affected area thoroughly with water. Do not use soap, alcohol, or other solvent because they may enhance the drug's ability to penetrate the skin; monitor for signs of respiratory or CNS depression. If the device is not handled correctly using gloves, healthcare professionals are at risk of accidental exposure to a fatal overdose of fentanyl. Ionsys device is considered magnetic resonance unsafe. The device contains metal parts and must be removed and properly disposed of before an MRI procedure to avoid injury to the patient and damage to device. It is unknown if exposure to an MRI procedure increases release of fentanyl from the device. Monitor any patients wearing the device with inadvertent exposure to an MRI for signs of CNS and respiratory depression. Use of Ionsys device during cardioversion, defibrillation, X-ray, CT, or diathermy can damage the device from the strong electromagnetic fields set up by these procedures. The device contains radio-opaque components and may interfere with an X-ray image or CT scan. Remove and properly dispose of the device prior to cardioversion, defibrillation, X-ray, CT, or diathermy. Avoid contact with synthetic materials (such as carpeted flooring) to reduce the possibility of electrostatic discharge and damage to the device. Avoid exposing the device to electronic security systems to reduce the possibility of damage. Use near communications equipment (eg, base stations for radio telephones and land mobile radios, amateur radio, AM and FM radio broadcast and TV broadcast Radio) and Radio Frequency Identification (RFID) transmitters can damage the device. Depending on the rated maximum output power and frequency of the transmitter, the recommended separation distance between the device and communications equipment or the RFID transmitter ranges between 0.12 and 23 meters. The low-level electrical current provided by the device does not result in electromagnetic interference with other electromechanical devices like pacemakers or electrical monitoring equipment. If exposure to the procedures listed above, electronic security systems, electrostatic discharge, communications equipment, or RFID transmitters occurs, and if the device does not appear to function normally, remove and replace with a new device. Topical skin reactions (erythema, sweating, vesicles, papules/pustules) may occur with use and are typically limited to the application site area. If a severe skin reaction is observed, remove device and discontinue further use. Ionsys is not for use in patients who are not alert and able to follow directions; avoid use in patients with impaired consciousness or coma. Avoid use in patients with circulatory shock; may cause vasodilation that can further reduce cardiac output and blood pressure.

Transdermal patch (Duragesic): **[US Boxed Warning]: Transdermal patch is contraindicated for use as an as-needed analgesic, in the management of acute or postoperative pain, or in patients who are opioid nontolerant. Monitor closely for respiratory depression during use, particularly during initiation of therapy or after dose increases.** Should only be prescribed by health care professionals who are knowledgeable in the use of potent opioids in the management of chronic pain. **[US Boxed Warning]: Exposure of application site and surrounding area to direct external heat sources (eg, heating pads, electric blankets, heat or tanning lamps, sunbathing, hot tubs) may increase fentanyl absorption and has resulted in fatalities. Patients who experience fever or increase in core body temperature should be monitored closely.** Serum fentanyl concentrations may increase by approximately one-third for patients with a body temperature of 40°C (104°F) secondary to a temperature-dependent increase in fentanyl release from the patch and increased skin permeability. **[US Boxed Warning]: Accidental exposure to fentanyl transdermal patch has resulted in fatal overdose in children and adults. Strict adherence to recommended handling and disposal instructions is necessary to prevent accidental exposures.** Avoid unclothed/unwashed application site exposure, inadvertent person-to-person patch transfer (eg, while hugging), incidental exposure (eg, sharing same bed, sitting on patch), intentional exposure (eg, chewing), or accidental exposure by caregivers when applying/removing patch. **[US Boxed Warning]: Prolonged maternal use of opioids during pregnancy can cause neonatal withdrawal syndrome in the newborn which may be life-threatening if not recognized and treated according to protocols developed by neonatology experts. If prolonged opioid therapy is required in a pregnant woman, patient should be warned of risk to the neonate and ensure treatment is available.** Should be applied only to intact skin. Use of a patch that has been cut, damaged, or altered in any way may result in overdosage. Patients who experience adverse reactions should be monitored for at least 24 hours after removal of the patch. Drug continues to be absorbed from the skin for 24 hours or more following removal of the patch. May contain conducting metal (eg, aluminum); remove patch prior to MRI.

Drug Interactions

Metabolism/Transport Effects Substrate of CYP3A4 (major); **Note:** Assignment of Major/Minor substrate status based on clinically relevant drug interaction potential

Avoid Concomitant Use

Avoid concomitant use of FentaNYL with any of the following: Azelastine (Nasal); Conivaptan; Crizotinib; Dapoxetine; Eluxadoline; Enzalutamide; Fusidic Acid (Systemic); Idelalisib; MAO Inhibitors; Methylene Blue; MiFEPRIStone; Mixed Agonist / Antagonist Opioids; Orphenadrine; Oxomemazine; Paraldehyde; Thalidomide

Increased Effect/Toxicity

FentaNYL may increase the levels/effects of: Alvimopan; Analgesics (Opioid); Azelastine (Nasal); Beta-Blockers; Blonanserin; Calcium Channel Blockers (Nondihydropyridine); Desmopressin; Diuretics; Eluxadoline; Flunitrazepam; HYDROcodone; MAO Inhibitors; Methotrimeprazine; Metoclopramide; MetyroSINE; Orphenadrine; OxyCODONE; Paraldehyde; Piribedil; Pramipexole; Ramosetron; ROPINIRole; Rotigotine; Selective Serotonin Reuptake Inhibitors; Serotonin Modulators; Suvorexant; Thalidomide; Zolpidem

The levels/effects of FentaNYL may be increased by: Amphetamines; Anticholinergic Agents; Antiemetics (5HT3 Antagonists); Brimonidine (Topical); Cannabis; Chlormethiazole; Chlorphenesin Carbamate; CNS Depressants; Conivaptan; Crizotinib; CYP3A4 Inhibitors (Moderate); CYP3A4 Inhibitors (Strong); Dapoxetine; Dasatinib; Dimethindene (Topical); Dronabinol; Droperidol; Fosaprepitant; Fusidic Acid (Systemic); Idelalisib; Ivacaftor; Kava Kava; Lofexidine; Magnesium Sulfate; Methotrimeprazine; Methylene Blue; Methylphenidate; MiFEPRIStone; Minocycline; Nabilone; Ombitasvir, Paritaprevir, Ritonavir, and Dasabuvir; Oxomemazine; Palbociclib; Perampanel;

Rufinamide; Simeprevir; Sodium Oxybate; Stiripentol; Succinylcholine; Tapentadol; Tetrahydrocannabinol

Decreased Effect

FentaNYL may decrease the levels/effects of: Diuretics; Gastrointestinal Agents (Prokinetic); Ioflupane I 123; Pegvisomant

The levels/effects of FentaNYL may be decreased by: Alpha-/Beta-Agonists (Indirect-Acting); Alpha1-Agonists; CYP3A4 Inducers (Moderate); CYP3A4 Inducers (Strong); Enzalutamide; Mixed Agonist / Antagonist Opioids; Nalmefene; Naltrexone; St John's Wort

Food Interactions Fentanyl concentrations may be increased by grapefruit juice. Management: Avoid concurrent intake of large quantities (>1 quart/day) of grapefruit juice.

Dietary Considerations Transmucosal lozenge contains 2 g sugar per unit.

Pharmacodynamics/Kinetics

Onset of Action

Children 3 to 12 years: Intranasal: 5 to 10 minutes (Borland 2002)

Adults: Analgesic: IM: 7 to 8 minutes; IV: Almost immediate (maximal analgesic and respiratory depressant effects may not be seen for several minutes); Transdermal patch (initial placement): 6 hours; Transmucosal: 5 to 15 minutes

Duration of Action IM: 1 to 2 hours; IV: 0.5 to 1 hour; Transdermal (removal of patch/no replacement): Related to blood level; some effects may last 72 to 96 hours due to extended half-life and absorption from the skin, fentanyl concentrations decrease by ~50% in 20 to 27 hours; Transmucosal: Related to blood level; respiratory depressant effect may last longer than analgesic effect

Half-life Elimination

IV:

Pediatric patients 5 months to 4.5 years: 2.4 hours

Pediatric patients 6 months to 14 years (after long term continuous infusion): ~21 hours (range: 11 to 36 hours)

Adults: 2 to 4 hours; when administered as a continuous infusion, the half-life prolongs with infusion duration due to the large volume of distribution (Sessler 2008)

Transdermal device: Terminal: ~16 hours

Transdermal patch: 20 to 27 hours (apparent half-life is influenced by continued fentanyl absorption from skin)

Transmucosal products: 3 to 14 hours (dose dependent)

Nasal spray: 15 to 25 hours (based on a multiple-dose pharmacokinetic study when doses are administered in the same nostril and separated by a 1-, 2-, or 4-hour time lapse)

Buccal film: ~14 hours

Buccal tablet: 100 to 200 mcg: 3 to 4 hours; 400 to 800 mcg: 11 to 12 hours

Time to Peak

Buccal film: 0.75 to 4 hours (median: 1 hour)

Buccal tablet: 20 to 240 minutes (median: 47 minutes)

Lozenge: 20 to 480 minutes (median: 20 to 40 minutes)

Nasal spray: Median: 15 to 21 minutes

Sublingual spray: 10 to 120 minutes (median: 90 minutes)

Sublingual tablet: 15 to 240 minutes (median: 30 to 60 minutes)

Transdermal patch: 20 to 72 hours; steady state serum concentrations are reached after two sequential 72-hour applications

Pregnancy Risk Factor C

Pregnancy Considerations Adverse events have been observed in some animal reproduction studies. Fentanyl crosses the placenta.

Fentanyl injection may be used for the management of pain during labor (ACOG 2002). When used for pain relief during labor, opioids may temporarily affect the heart rate of the fetus (ACOG 2002). Transient muscular rigidity has been observed in the neonate with fentanyl; symptoms of respiratory or neurological depression were not different than those observed in infants of untreated mothers.

[US Boxed Warning]: Prolonged maternal use of opioids during pregnancy can cause neonatal withdrawal syndrome in the newborn which may be life-threatening if not recognized and treated according to protocols developed by neonatology experts. If prolonged opioid therapy is required in a pregnant woman, ensure treatment is available and warn patient of risk to the neonate. If chronic opioid exposure occurs in pregnancy, adverse events in the newborn (including withdrawal) may occur; monitoring of the neonate is recommended. The minimum effective dose should be used if opioids are needed (Chou 2009). Symptoms characteristic of neonatal abstinence syndrome have been observed following chronic fentanyl use in pregnant women. Neonatal abstinence syndrome following opioid exposure may present with autonomic (eg, fever, temperature instability), gastrointestinal (eg, diarrhea, vomiting, poor feeding/weight gain), or neurologic (eg, high-pitched crying, increased muscle tone, irritability, seizure, tremor) symptoms (Dow 2012; Hudak 2012).

Long-term opioid use may cause secondary hypogonadism, which may lead to sexual dysfunction or infertility (Brennan 2013).

Transdermal patch, transdermal iontophoretic system (Ionsys), transmucosal lozenge, nasal spray (Lazanda), sublingual tablet, sublingual spray (Subsys), buccal tablet (Fentora), and buccal film (Onsolis) are not recommended for analgesia during labor and delivery.

Breastfeeding Considerations

Fentanyl is excreted in low concentrations in breast milk and breastfeeding is not recommended by the manufacturers.

Parenteral opioids used during labor have the potential to interfere with a newborn's natural reflex to nurse within the first few hours after birth. When needed, a short-acting opioid, such as fentanyl, is preferred for women who will be nursing (Montgomery, 2012)

breastfeeding is considered acceptable following single doses to the mother; however, limited information is available when used long-term (Spigset, 2000). Nursing infants exposed to large doses of opioids should be monitored for apnea and sedation (Montgomery, 2012).

Note: Transdermal patch, transmucosal lozenge, sublingual tablet, sublingual spray (Subsys), buccal tablet (Fentora), and buccal film (Onsolis) are not recommended in nursing women due to potential for sedation and/or respiratory depression.

Product Availability Onsolis: Reformulated product FDA approved August 2015; availability anticipated mid-2017. Consult prescribing information for additional information.

Controlled Substance C-II

Prescribing and Access Restrictions As a requirement of the REMS program, access is restricted.

Transmucosal immediate-release fentanyl products (eg, sublingual tablets and spray, oral lozenges, buccal tablets and soluble film, nasal spray) are only available through the Transmucosal Immediate-Release Fentanyl (TIRF) REMS ACCESS program. Enrollment in the program is required for outpatients, prescribers for outpatient use, pharmacies (inpatient and outpatient), and distributors. Enrollment is not required for inpatient administration (eg, hospitals, hospices, long-term care facilities), inpatients, and prescribers who prescribe to inpatients. Further information is available at 1-866-822-1483 or at www.TIRFREMSaccess.com

Note: Effective December, 2011, individual REMs programs for TIRF products were combined into a single access program (TIRF REMS Access). Prescribers and pharmacies that were enrolled in at least one individual REMS program for these products will automatically be transitioned to the single access program.

Dosage Forms

Injection, solution [preservative free]:

Sublimaze: 100 mcg/2 mL (2 mL); 250 mcg/5 mL (5 mL)

Generic: 100 mcg/2 mL (2 mL); 250 mcg/5 mL (5 mL); 500 mcg/10 mL (10 mL); 1000 mcg/ 20 mL (20 mL); 2500 mcg/50 mL (50 mL)

Liquid, sublingual, [spray]:

Subsys: 100 mcg (30s); 200 mcg (30s); 400 mcg (30s); 600 mcg (30s); 800 mcg (30s)

Lozenge, oral:

Actiq: 200 mcg (30s); 400 mcg (30s); 600 mcg (30s); 800 mcg (30s); 1200 mcg (30s); 1600 mcg (30s)

Generic: 200 mcg (30s); 400 mcg (30s); 600 mcg (30s); 800 mcg (30s); 1200 mcg (30s); 1600 mcg (30s)

Patch, transdermal:

Duragesic: 12 [delivers 12.5 mcg/hr] (5s); 25 [delivers 25 mcg/hr] (5s); 50 [delivers 50 mcg/hr] (5s); 75 [delivers 75 mcg/hr] (5s); 100 [delivers 100 mcg/hr] (5s)

Ionsys: 40 mcg/actuation (6s) [iontophoretic transdermal system]

Generic: 12 [delivers 12.5 mcg/hr] (5s); 25 [delivers 25 mcg/hr] (5s); 50 [delivers 50 mcg/hr] (5s); 75 [delivers 75 mcg/hr] (5s); 87.5 [delivers 87.5 mcg/hr] (5s); 100 [delivers 100 mcg/hr] (5s)

Powder, for prescription compounding: USP: 100% (1 g)

Solution, intranasal, as citrate [spray]:

Lazanda: 100 mcg/spray (5 mL); 300 mcg/spray (5 mL); 400 mcg/spray (5 mL) [delivers 8 metered sprays]

Tablet, for buccal application:

Fentora: 100 mcg (28s); 200 mcg (28s); 400 mcg (28s); 600 mcg (28s); 800 mcg (28s)

Tablet, sublingual:

Abstral: 100 mcg (12s, 32s); 200 mcg (12s, 32s); 300 mcg (12s, 32s); 400 mcg (12s, 32s); 600 mcg (32s); 800 mcg (32s)

Dosage Forms: Canada

Patch, transdermal, as base: 12 mcg/hr (5s); 25 mcg/hr (5s); 50 mcg/hr (5s); 75 mcg/hr (5s); 100 mcg/hr (5s)

Duragesic: 12 mcg/hr (5s); 25 mcg/hr (5s); 50 mcg/hr (5s); 75 mcg/hr (5s); 100 mcg/hr (5s)

Dental Comment Transdermal fentanyl should not be used as a pain reliever in dentistry due to danger of hypoventilation

Actiq is a solid formulation of fentanyl with a high sugar content of 2 g hydrated dextrates per unit. Frequent use of Actiq could result in significant dental problems including risk of dental decay. Dry mouth caused by fentanyl could add to the risk of caries. Oral adverse reactions reported in clinical trials have included tooth caries, gum hemorrhage, mouth ulcerations, oral moniliasis, dry mouth, and cheilitis.

Sedation: There is a subsequent slow release from muscle and fat which results in a terminal half-life that is beyond that of morphine. Fentanyl does not induce the release of histamine; therefore, fentanyl is preferable in patients with a predisposition to bronchospasm. Fentanyl is a good choice for use in cardiac patients because it lacks direct myocardial depression. The incidence of nausea is less than that reported with morphine or meperidine. The clinician should wait 2 to 3 minutes between doses to allow time for observation of the clinical effects of each administered dose.

Ferric Pyrophosphate Citrate

(FER ik pye roe FOS fate SIT rate)

Brand Names: US Triferic

Pharmacologic Category Iron Salt

Use

Iron replacement therapy in hemodialysis-dependent patients: Replacement of iron to maintain hemoglobin in adult patients with hemodialysis-dependent chronic kidney disease (HDD-CKD)

Limitations of use: Not intended for use in patients receiving peritoneal dialysis; has not been studied in patients receiving home hemodialysis

Local Anesthetic/Vasoconstrictor Precautions

No information available to require special precautions

Effects on Dental Treatment No significant effects or complications reported

Effects on Bleeding No information available to require special precautions

Adverse Reactions Note: Frequency not always defined.

>10%: Cardiovascular: Procedural hypotension (22%)

1% to 10%:

Cardiovascular: Peripheral edema (7%), clotted AV fistula (3%), dialysis access hemorrhage (3%)

Central nervous system: Headache (9%), fatigue (4%), dizziness

Dermatologic: Pruritus

Gastrointestinal: Constipation, nausea

Genitourinary: Urinary tract infection (5%)

Neuromuscular & skeletal: Muscle spasm (10%), limb pain (7%), back pain (5%), weakness (4%)

Respiratory: Dyspnea (6%)

Miscellaneous: Fever (5%)

<1%, postmarketing, and/or case reports: Anaphylaxis, hypersensitivity

Mechanism of Action Iron in the form of ferric pyrophosphate citrate and added to hemodialysate solution is administered to patients by transfer across the dialyzer membrane. Iron delivered into the circulation binds to transferrin for transport to erythroid precursor cells to be incorporated into hemoglobin.

Pharmacodynamics/Kinetics

Half-life Elimination ~1.48 hours

Pregnancy Considerations Adverse events were observed in animal reproduction studies. Females of reproductive potential should use effective contraception during treatment and for at least 2 weeks following completion of therapy.

Ferrous Sulfate (FER us SUL fate)

Brand Names: US BProtected Pedia Iron [OTC]; Fer-In-Sol [OTC]; Fer-Iron [OTC]; FeroSul [OTC]; Ferro-Bob [OTC]; FerrouSul [OTC]; Iron Supplement Childrens [OTC]; Slow Fe [OTC]; Slow Iron [OTC]; Slow Release Iron [OTC] [DSC]

Brand Names: Canada Apo-Ferrous Sulfate; Fer-In-Sol; Ferodan

Pharmacologic Category Iron Salt

Use Prevention and treatment of iron-deficiency anemias

Local Anesthetic/Vasoconstrictor Precautions No information available to require special precautions

Effects on Dental Treatment Do not prescribe tetracyclines simultaneously with iron since GI tract absorption of both tetracycline and iron may be inhibited. Liquid preparations may temporarily stain the teeth.

Effects on Bleeding No information available to require special precautions

Adverse Reactions Frequency not defined.

>10%: Gastrointestinal: Constipation, darkening of stools, epigastric pain, gastrointestinal irritation, nausea, stomach cramps, vomiting

1% to 10%:

Gastrointestinal: Dental discoloration (temporary; liquid preparations), diarrhea, heartburn

Genitourinary: Urine discoloration

<1%, postmarketing, and/or case reports: Contact dermatitis

General Dosage Range Oral:

Infants, Children and Adolescents: 1 to 6 mg elemental iron/kg/day in 1 to 3 divided doses

Adults: 60 mg to 200 mg elemental iron/day in 1 to 3 divided doses

Mechanism of Action Replaces iron, found in hemoglobin, myoglobin, and other enzymes; allows the transportation of oxygen via hemoglobin

Pharmacodynamics/Kinetics

Onset of Action Hematologic response: Oral: ~3-10 days

Peak effect: Reticulocytosis: 5-10 days; hemoglobin increases within 2-4 weeks

Pregnancy Considerations Iron crosses the placenta and fetal stores are obtained from the mother (McArdle 2011). Iron requirements are increased in pregnant women compared to nonpregnant females (IOM 2001). All pregnant women should be tested for iron deficiency anemia and treated with supplemental iron if needed (ACOG 2008; CDC 1998). Untreated iron deficiency anemia during pregnancy may be associated with an increased risk of low birth weight, preterm delivery, and perinatal mortality, as well as postpartum depression in the mother and decreased mental functioning in the offspring (ACOG 2008; CDC 1998; IOM 2001). Treatment improves maternal hematologic status and neonatal birth weight (Haider 2013).

Ferumoxytol (fer ue MOX i tol)

Brand Names: US Feraheme

Brand Names: Canada Feraheme

Pharmacologic Category Iron Salt

Use Iron-deficiency anemia in chronic kidney disease: Treatment of iron-deficiency anemia in adults with chronic kidney disease

Local Anesthetic/Vasoconstrictor Precautions No information available to require special precautions

Effects on Dental Treatment No significant effects or complications reported

Effects on Bleeding No information available to require special precautions

Adverse Reactions

1% to 10%:

Cardiovascular: Hypotension (≤3%), edema (2%), peripheral edema (2%), chest pain (1%), hypertension (1%)

Central nervous system: Dizziness (3%), headache (2%)

Dermatologic: Pruritus (1%), skin rash (1%)

Gastrointestinal: Diarrhea (4%), nausea (3%), constipation (2%), vomiting (2%), abdominal pain (1%)

Hypersensitivity: Hypersensitivity reactions (≤4%; serious hypersensitivity: <1%)

Neuromuscular & skeletal: Back pain (1%), muscle spasm (1%)

Respiratory: Cough (1%), dyspnea (1%)

Miscellaneous: Fever (1%)

<1%, postmarketing, and/or case reports: Anaphylactoid reaction, anaphylaxis, angioedema, cardiac arrhythmia, cardiac failure, cyanosis, fatigue, hypotension (clinically significant), infusion site reaction (including bruise, infusion site burning, infusion site erythema, infusion site irritation, infusion site swelling, infusion site warmth, local pain), ischemic heart disease, loss of consciousness, pulselessness, syncope, tachycardia, unresponsive to stimuli, urticaria, wheezing

General Dosage Range IV: *Adults:* 510 mg as an IV infusion; repeat once 3 to 8 days later

Mechanism of Action Superparamagnetic iron oxide coated with a low molecular weight semisynthetic carbohydrate; iron-carbohydrate complex enters the reticuloendothelial system macrophages of the liver, spleen, and bone marrow where the iron is released from the complex. The released iron is either transported into storage pools or is transported via plasma transferrin for incorporation into hemoglobin.

Pharmacodynamics/Kinetics

Half-life Elimination ~15 hours; ferumoxytol is not removed by hemodialysis

Pregnancy Risk Factor C

Pregnancy Considerations Adverse events were observed in animal reproduction studies. The Canadian labeling recommends avoiding use in women of childbearing potential not using adequate contraception.

Fesoterodine (fes oh TER oh deen)

Brand Names: US Toviaz

Brand Names: Canada Toviaz

Pharmacologic Category Anticholinergic Agent

Use Treatment of patients with an overactive bladder with symptoms of urinary frequency, urgency, or urge incontinence.

Local Anesthetic/Vasoconstrictor Precautions No information available to require special precautions

Effects on Dental Treatment Key adverse event(s) related to dental treatment: Prolonged use will cause significant xerostomia (normal salivary flow resumes upon discontinuation).

Effects on Bleeding No information available to require special precautions

Adverse Reactions

>10%: Gastrointestinal: Xerostomia (19% to 35%; dose-related)

1% to 10%:

Cardiovascular: Peripheral edema (1%)

Central nervous system: Insomnia (1%)

Dermatological: Skin rash (1%)

Endocrine & metabolic: Increased gamma-glutamyl transferase (1%)

Gastrointestinal: Constipation (4% to 6%), dyspepsia (2%), nausea (1% to 2%), abdominal pain (1%)

Genitourinary: Urinary tract infection (3% to 4%), dysuria (1% to 2%), urinary retention (1%)

Hepatic: Increased serum ALT (1%)

Neuromuscular & skeletal: Back pain (1% to 2%)

Ophthalmic: Dry eye syndrome (1% to 4%)

Respiratory: Upper respiratory tract infection (2% to 3%), cough (1% to 2%), dry throat (1% to 2%)

<1%, postmarketing, and/or case reports: Angina pectoris, angioedema, blurred vision, chest pain, diverticulitis, dizziness, drowsiness, facial edema, gastroenteritis, headache, heat exhaustion, hypersensitivity reaction, increased heart rate (dose-related), irritable bowel syndrome, palpitations, prolonged Q-T interval on ECG, pruritus, urticaria

General Dosage Range Dosage adjustment recommended in patients with renal impairment or on concomitant therapy

Oral: *Adults:* 4-8 mg once daily

Mechanism of Action Fesoterodine acts as a prodrug and is converted to an active metabolite, 5-hydroxymethyl tolterodine (5-HMT); 5-HMT is responsible for fesoterodine's antimuscarinic activity and acts as a competitive antagonist of muscarinic receptors.

Urinary bladder contractions are mediated by muscarinic receptors; fesoterodine inhibits the receptors in the bladder preventing symptoms of urgency and frequency.

Pharmacodynamics/Kinetics

Half-life Elimination ~7 hours

Time to Peak Plasma: 5-HMT: ~5 hours; C_{max} higher in poor CYP2D6 metabolizers

Pregnancy Risk Factor C

Pregnancy Considerations Adverse effects have been observed in some animal reproduction studies.

Fexofenadine (feks oh FEN a deen)

Brand Names: US Allegra Allergy Childrens [OTC]; Allegra Allergy [OTC]; Allergy 24-HR [OTC]; Fexofenadine HCl Childrens [OTC]; Mucinex Allergy [OTC]

Brand Names: Canada Allegra 12 Hour (OTC); Allegra 24 Hour (OTC)

Generic Availability (US) May be product dependent

Pharmacologic Category Histamine H_1 Antagonist; Histamine H_1 Antagonist, Second Generation; Piperidine Derivative

Use

Upper respiratory allergies: Temporary relief of runny nose, sneezing, itching of the nose or throat, and/or itchy, watery eyes due to hay fever or other upper respiratory allergies.

Canadian labeling: Additional use (not in US labeling): Treatment of chronic idiopathic urticaria.

Local Anesthetic/Vasoconstrictor Precautions No information available to require special precautions

Effects on Dental Treatment No significant effects or complications reported

Effects on Bleeding No information available to require special precautions

Adverse Reactions

>10%:

Central nervous system: Headache (5% to 11%)

Gastrointestinal: Vomiting (children 6 months to 5 years: 4% to 12%)

1% to 10%:

Central nervous system: Drowsiness (1% to 3%), fatigue (1% to 3%), dizziness (2%), pain (2%)

Gastrointestinal: Diarrhea (3% to 4%), nausea (2%), dyspepsia (1% to 2%)

Genitourinary: Dysmenorrhea (2%)

Infection: Viral infection (3%)

Neuromuscular & skeletal: Myalgia (3%), back pain (2% to 3%), limb pain (2%)

Otic: Otitis media (2% to 4%)

Respiratory: Upper respiratory tract infection (3% to 4%), cough (2% to 4%), rhinorrhea (1% to 2%)

Miscellaneous: Fever (2%)

<1%, postmarketing, and/or case reports: Hypersensitivity reaction (including anaphylaxis, angioedema, chest tightness, dyspnea, flushing, pruritus, skin rash, urticaria), insomnia, nervousness, nightmares, sleep disorder

Dosing

Adult & Geriatric

Chronic idiopathic urticaria: *Canadian labeling:* Oral: 60 mg every 12 hours; maximum: 120 mg/day

Upper respiratory allergies (OTC labeling): Oral:

US labeling:

Twice daily formulations: 60 mg every 12 hours (maximum: 120 mg/day)

Once daily formulations: 180 mg once daily (maximum: 180 mg/day)

Canadian labeling:

Perennial allergic rhinitis: 60 mg every 12 hours; maximum: 120 mg/day

Seasonal allergic rhinitis: 60 mg every 12 hours **or** 120 mg once daily; maximum: 120 mg/day

Pediatric

Chronic idiopathic urticaria: *Canadian labeling:* Children ≥12 years and Adolescents: Oral: Refer to adult dosing.

Upper respiratory allergies (OTC labeling): Oral:

US labeling:

Suspension:

Children 2 to 11 years: 30 mg (5 mL) every 12 hours; maximum: 60 mg/day

Children ≥12 years and Adolescents: 60 mg (10 mL) every 12 hours; maximum: 120 mg/day

Tablets:

Children 6 to 11 years: 30 mg every 12 hours; maximum: 60 mg/day

Children ≥12 years and Adolescents: Refer to adult dosing.

Canadian labeling: Children ≥12 years and Adolescents: Seasonal and perennial allergic rhinitis: Refer to adult dosing.

Renal Impairment There are no dosage adjustment provided in manufacturer's labeling; however, the following adjustments have been recommended (Aronoff 2007):

Adults:

GFR >50 mL/minute: No dosage adjustment necessary for twice daily dosing (ie, 60 mg every 12 hours).

GFR 10 to 50 mL/minute: Recommended dose every 12 to 24 hours.

GFR <10 mL/minute: Recommended dose every 24 hours.

Intermittent hemodialysis or peritoneal dialysis: Recommended dose every 24 hours.

Continuous renal replacement therapy (CRRT): 60 mg every 24 hours.

Infants, Children, and Adolescents:

GFR >50 mL/minute/1.73 m^2: No dosage adjustment necessary.

GFR 10 to 50 mL/minute/1.73 m^2: 60 mg every 24 hours.

GFR <10 mL/minute/1.73 m^2: 30 mg every 24 hours.

Intermittent hemodialysis or peritoneal dialysis: 30 mg every 24 hours.

Canadian labeling:

CrCl ≤80 mL/minute: Initial: 60 mg once daily.

Hemodialysis: Not effectively removed by hemodialysis.

Hepatic Impairment There are no dosage adjustments provided in the manufacturer's labeling; however, dosage adjustment may not be necessary as moderate to severe impairment does not substantially affect fexofenadine pharmacokinetics.

Mechanism of Action Fexofenadine is an active metabolite of terfenadine and like terfenadine it competes with histamine for H_1-receptor sites on effector cells in the gastrointestinal tract, blood vessels and respiratory tract; it appears that fexofenadine does not cross the blood-brain barrier to any appreciable degree, resulting in a reduced potential for sedation

Contraindications

OTC labeling: When used for self-medication do not use if you ever had an allergic reaction to fexofenadine or any component of the formulation.

Documentation of allergenic cross-reactivity for drugs antihistamines is limited. However, because of similarities in chemical structure and/or pharmacologic actions, the possibility of cross-sensitivity can not be ruled out with certainty.

Warnings/Precautions Use with caution in patients with renal impairment; dosage adjustment may be recommended. Orally disintegrating tablet may contains phenylalanine. Do not exceed recommended dosage; or administer at the same time with aluminum or magnesium antacids or with fruit juices. Potentially significant interactions may exist, requiring dose or frequency adjustment, additional monitoring, and/or selection of alternative therapy.

Drug Interactions

Metabolism/Transport Effects Substrate of CYP3A4 (minor), P-glycoprotein, SLCO1B1; **Note:** Assignment of Major/Minor substrate status based on clinically relevant drug interaction potential

Avoid Concomitant Use

Avoid concomitant use of Fexofenadine with any of the following: Aclidinium; Azelastine (Nasal); Cimetropium; Eluxadoline; Glucagon; Glycopyrrolate (Oral Inhalation); Ipratropium (Oral Inhalation); Levosulpiride; Nitroglycerin; Orphenadrine; Oxatomide; Oxomemazine; Paraldehyde; Potassium Chloride; Thalidomide; Tiotropium; Umeclidinium

Increased Effect/Toxicity

Fexofenadine may increase the levels/effects of: AbobotulinumtoxinA; Alcohol (Ethyl); Analgesics (Opioid); Anticholinergic Agents; Azelastine (Nasal); Blonanserin; Buprenorphine; Cimetropium; CNS Depressants; Eluxadoline; Flunitrazepam; Glucagon; Glycopyrrolate (Oral Inhalation); HYDROcodone; Methotrimeprazine; MetyroSINE; Mirabegron; Mirtazapine; OnabotulinumtoxinA; Orphenadrine; OxyCODONE; Paraldehyde; Piribedil; Potassium Chloride; Pramipexole; Ramosetron; RimabotulinumtoxinB; ROPINIRole; Rotigotine; Selective Serotonin Reuptake Inhibitors; Suvorexant; Thalidomide; Thiazide and Thiazide-Like Diuretics; Tiotropium; Topiramate; Zolpidem

The levels/effects of Fexofenadine may be increased by: Aclidinium; Brimonidine (Topical); Cannabis; Chloral Betaine; Chlormethiazole; Chlorphenesin Carbamate; Dimethindene (Topical); Doxylamine; Dronabinol; Droperidol; Eltrombopag; Erythromycin (Systemic); Gemfibrozil; HydrOXYzine; Ipratropium (Oral Inhalation); Itraconazole; Kava Kava; Ketoconazole (Systemic); Lofexidine; Lumacaftor; Magnesium Sulfate; Methotrimeprazine; Mianserin; Minocycline; Nabilone; Oxatomide; Oxomemazine; Perampanel; P-glycoprotein/ABCB1 Inhibitors; Pramlintide; Ranolazine; RifAMPin; Rufinamide; Sodium Oxybate; Tapentadol; Teriflunomide; Tetrahydrocannabinol; Trimeprazine; Umeclidinium; Verapamil

Decreased Effect

Fexofenadine may decrease the levels/effects of: Acetylcholinesterase Inhibitors; Benzylpenicilloyl Polylysine; Betahistine; Gastrointestinal Agents (Prokinetic); Hyaluronidase; Itopride; Levosulpiride; Nitroglycerin; Secretin

The levels/effects of Fexofenadine may be decreased by: Acetylcholinesterase Inhibitors; Amphetamines; Antacids; Grapefruit Juice; Lumacaftor; P-glycoprotein/ABCB1 Inducers; RifAMPin

Food Interactions High-fat meals decrease the bioavailability of fexofenadine by ~50%. Fruit juice (apple, grapefruit, orange) may decrease bioavailability of fexofenadine by ~36%. Management: Administer with water only, avoid fruit juice.

Dietary Considerations Some products may contain phenylalanine and/or sodium. Take suspension and tablets with water only; do not administer with fruit juices.

Pharmacodynamics/Kinetics

Onset of Action 2 hours (Simons 2004)

Duration of Action 24 hours (Simons 2004)

Half-life Elimination 14.4 hours (59% longer in patients with mild to moderate renal impairment [CrCl 41 to 80 mL/minute]; 72% longer in patients with severe renal impairment [CrCl 11 to 40 mL/minute]) (Markham 1998; Simons 2004)

Time to Peak Serum: ODT: 2 hours (4 hours with high-fat meal); Tablet: ~2.6 hours (Simons 2004); Suspension: ~1 hour

Pregnancy Considerations Limited information is available related to the use of fexofenadine in pregnancy. When a second generation antihistamine is needed, other agents with more information available regarding their use in pregnancy are currently preferred (Murase 2014; Powell 2015; Scadding 2008; Wallace 2008; Zuberbier 2014).

Breastfeeding Considerations Information specific to fexofenadine and breastfeeding has not been located.

Fexofenadine was detected in breast milk following administration of its parent compound, terfenadine, to breastfeeding mothers (Lucas 1995).

Drowsiness and irritability have been reported in breastfed infants exposed to antihistamines; only irritability was reported in infants exposed to fexofenadine's parent compound, terfenadine (Ito 1993). In general, second generation antihistamines are less sedating as compared to their first generation counterparts. If a breastfed infant is exposed to a second generation antihistamine via breast milk, they should be monitored for irritability, jitteriness, or drowsiness (Butler 2014).

When treatment with an antihistamine is needed in breastfeeding women, other second generation antihistamines with more information available regarding their use in this patient population are preferred (Butler 2014; Powell 2015; Zuberier 2014).

Dosage Forms

Suspension, Oral:

Allegra Allergy Childrens [OTC]: 30 mg/5 mL (120 mL, 240 mL)

Fexofenadine HCl Childrens [OTC]: 30 mg/5 mL (118 mL)

Tablet, Oral:

Allegra Allergy [OTC]: 60 mg, 180 mg

Allergy 24-HR [OTC]: 180 mg

Mucinex Allergy [OTC]: 180 mg

Generic: 60 mg, 180 mg

Tablet Dispersible, Oral:

Allegra Allergy Childrens [OTC]: 30 mg

Dosage Forms: Canada

Tablet, Oral:

Allegra 12 Hour: 60 mg

Allegra 24 Hour: 120 mg

Fibrinogen Concentrate (Human)

(fi BRIN o gin KON suhn trate HYU man)

Brand Names: US RiaSTAP

Brand Names: Canada RiaSTAP

Pharmacologic Category Blood Product Derivative

Use Congenital fibrinogen deficiency: Treatment of acute bleeding episodes in patients with congenital fibrinogen deficiency, including afibrinogenemia and hypofibrinogenemia.

Local Anesthetic/Vasoconstrictor Precautions

No information available to require special precautions

Effects on Dental Treatment No significant effects or complications reported

Effects on Bleeding Serious thromboembolism and thrombosis have been reported.

Adverse Reactions

>1%: Central nervous system: Fever, headache

Postmarketing and/or case reports: Allergic reactions, anaphylaxis, arterial thrombosis, chills, DVT, dyspnea, MI, nausea, pulmonary embolism, rash, thromboembolism, vomiting

General Dosage Range IV: *Children, Adolescents, and Adults:* When baseline fibrinogen level is known: Dose (mg/kg) = [Target level (mg/dL) - measured level (mg/dL)] **divided by** 1.7 (mg/dL per mg/kg body weight) **or** when baseline fibrinogen level is not known: 70 mg/kg

Mechanism of Action Fibrinogen (coagulation factor I), a protein found in normal plasma, is required to clot blood. Fibrinogen concentrate made from pooled human plasma replaces this protein which is missing or reduced in patients with a congenital fibrinogen deficiency.

Pharmacodynamics/Kinetics

Half-life Elimination

Biological fibrinogen: 100 hours (Kamath 2003)

Pediatric patients <16 years: Initial data suggests decreasesd compared to adults (Manco-Johnson 2009): 69.9 ± 8.5 hours

Adults: 78.7 ± 18.13 hours (range: 56 to 117 hours)

Pregnancy Risk Factor C

Pregnancy Considerations Animal reproduction studies have not been conducted. Increased pregnancy loss is associated with untreated congenital fibrinogen disorders (Acharya 2008).

Fibrin Sealant (FI brin SEEL ent)

Related Information

Antiplatelet and Anticoagulation Considerations in Dentistry *on page 1764*

Brand Names: US Artiss; Evarrest; Evicel; Raplixa; TachoSil; Tisseel

Brand Names: Canada Artiss; Tisseel

Pharmacologic Category Blood Product Derivative; Hemostatic Agent

Use

Colonic anastomosis sealing (Tisseel only): As an adjunct to standard surgical techniques (such as suture and ligature) to prevent leakage from colonic anastomoses following the reversal of temporary colostomies.

Facial rhytidectomy (Artiss only): To adhere tissue flaps during facial rhytidectomy surgery (face lift).

Hemostasis, adjunct:

Evarrest, Evicel: As an adjunct to hemostasis for use in patients undergoing surgery when control of bleeding by conventional surgical techniques (such as suture, ligature, and cautery) is ineffective or impractical.

Raplixa: As an adjunct to hemostasis for mild to moderate bleeding in adults undergoing surgery when control of bleeding by standard surgical techniques (such as suture, ligature, and cautery) is ineffective or impractical.

TachoSil: As an adjunct to hemostasis for use in cardiovascular and hepatic surgery when control of bleeding by standard surgical techniques (such as suture, ligature, or cautery) is ineffective or impractical.

Tisseel: As an adjunct to hemostasis in adult and pediatric patients (≥1 month) undergoing surgery when control of bleeding by conventional surgical techniques, including suture, ligature, and cautery, is ineffective or impractical. Tisseel is effective in heparinized patients.

Skin graft adhesion (Artiss only): To adhere autologous skin grafts to surgically prepared wound beds resulting from burns in adults and pediatric patients ≥1 year.

Local Anesthetic/Vasoconstrictor Precautions

No information available to require special precautions

Effects on Dental Treatment No significant effects or complications reported

Effects on Bleeding No information available to require special precautions

Adverse Reactions Frequency may vary by product and patient age.

>10%:

Cardiovascular: Atrial fibrillation (29%), hypertension (pediatric: 17%)

Gastrointestinal: Nausea (30%), diarrhea (pediatric: 17%)

Hematologic & oncologic: Anemia (23%)

Hepatic: Increased serum transaminases (pediatric: 11%)
Immunologic: Antibody development (equine collagen: 26% human thrombin: 2%, human fibrinogen: 1%)
Respiratory: Pleural effusion (23%)
1% to 10%:
Cardiovascular: Bradycardia (≥5%), peripheral edema (≥5%), thromboembolism (≤3%), deep vein thrombosis (≤1%)
Dermatologic: Pruritus (1%)
Immunologic: Graft complications (skin graft failure in burn patients: 3%)
Infection: Localized infection (grafts: ≥5%)
Miscellaneous: Postoperative complication (bile leakage after hepatic surgery; 7%), fever (6% to 7%), procedural complications (seroma; ≤4%)
Frequency not defined:
Hematologic & oncologic: Decreased hemoglobin, hematoma
Infection: Abscess (abdomen), staphylococcal infection
Local: Incision site hemorrhage
<1%, postmarketing, and/or case reports: Abdominal distension, anaphylactic shock, anaphylactoid reaction, anaphylaxis, angioedema, ascites, bile leakage (postprocedural), bronchospasm, catheter complication, cerebral embolism, cerebral infarction, chest discomfort, chills, dyspnea, edema, eosinophilia, erythema, flushing, gastrointestinal hemorrhage, granuloma, hemorrhage (internal, postprocedural), hemothorax, hepatitis C, hypersensitivity, hypotension, inflammation, ischemic bowel disease, laryngeal edema, local hemorrhage (spleen), multiorgan failure, mydriasis, nerve compression, paralysis, parathyroid disease, paresthesia, procedural complications (thoracic cavity drainage), pulmonary embolism, renal artery thrombosis, renal failure, respiratory distress, tachycardia, thrombosis, urticaria, wheezing, wound healing impairment

General Dosage Range Topical: *Infants >1 month, Children, Adolescents, and Adults:* Dosage varies greatly depending on product

Mechanism of Action Formation of a biodegradable adhesive is done by duplicating the last step of the coagulation cascade, the formation of fibrin from fibrinogen. Fibrinogen is the main component of the sealant solution. The solution also contains thrombin, which transforms fibrinogen from the sealer protein solution into fibrin, and fibrinolysis inhibitor (aprotinin), which prevents the premature degradation of fibrin. When mixed as directed, a viscous solution forms that sets into an elastic coagulum. Patches contain fibrinogen and thrombin that, in contact with bleeding surfaces, hydrate, form active fibrin, then produce a fibrin clot.

Pharmacodynamics/Kinetics

Onset of Action Artiss: Full adherence achieved: ~2 hours

Time to hemostasis: Evarrest: 4 minutes; Evicel: 4 to 10 minutes; Raplixa: 5 minutes; TachoSil: 6 minutes; Tisseel: 5 minutes

Pregnancy Risk Factor C (manufacturer dependent)

Pregnancy Considerations Animal reproduction studies have not been conducted.

Fidaxomicin (fye DAX oh mye sin)

Brand Names: US Dificid

Brand Names: Canada Dificid™

Pharmacologic Category Antibiotic, Macrolide

Use Treatment of *Clostridium difficile*-associated diarrhea (CDAD)

Local Anesthetic/Vasoconstrictor Precautions No information available to require special precautions

Effects on Dental Treatment No significant effects or complications reported

Effects on Bleeding No information available to require special precautions

Adverse Reactions

>10%: Gastrointestinal: Nausea (11%)
2% to 10%:
Gastrointestinal: Gastrointestinal hemorrhage (4%), abdominal pain, vomiting
Hematologic & oncologic: Anemia (2%), neutropenia (2%)
<2%, postmarketing, and/or case reports: Abdominal distention, abdominal tenderness, angioedema, decreased platelet count, decreased serum bicarbonate, dyspepsia, dysphagia, dyspnea, fixed drug eruption, flatulence, hepatotoxicity (idiosyncratic) (Chalasani, 2014), hyperglycemia, hypersensitivity reaction, increased liver enzymes, increased serum alkaline phosphatase, intestinal obstruction, megacolon, metabolic acidosis, pruritus, skin rash

General Dosage Range

Oral: *Adults:* 200 mg twice daily

Mechanism of Action Inhibits RNA polymerase sigma subunit resulting in inhibition of protein synthesis and cell death in susceptible organisms including *C. difficile*; bactericidal

Pregnancy Risk Factor B

Pregnancy Considerations Adverse events were not observed in animal reproduction studies. Due to the limited systemic absorption of fidaxomicin, exposure to the fetus is expected to be low.

Filgrastim (fil GRA stim)

Brand Names: US Granix; Neupogen; Zarxio

Brand Names: Canada Grastofil; Neupogen

Pharmacologic Category Colony Stimulating Factor, Hematopoietic Agent

Use

Myelosuppressive chemotherapy recipients with nonmyeloid malignancies:

Neupogen (filgrastim), Zarxio (filgrastim-sndz [biosimilar]), Grastofil [Canadian product]: To decrease the incidence of infection (neutropenic fever) in patients with nonmyeloid malignancies receiving myelosuppressive chemotherapy associated with a significant incidence of severe neutropenia with fever.

Granix (tbo-filgrastim): To decrease the duration of severe neutropenia in patients with nonmyeloid malignancies receiving myelosuppressive chemotherapy associated with a clinically significant incidence of neutropenic fever.

Acute myeloid leukemia (AML) following induction or consolidation chemotherapy (Neupogen, Zarxio, Grastofil [Canadian product]**):** To reduce the time to neutrophil recovery and the duration of fever following induction or consolidation chemotherapy in adults with AML.

Bone marrow transplantation (Neupogen, Zarxio, Grastofil [Canadian product]**):** To reduce the duration of neutropenia and neutropenia-related events (eg, neutropenic fever) in patients with nonmyeloid malignancies receiving myeloablative chemotherapy followed by marrow transplantation.

Hematopoietic radiation injury syndrome, acute (Neupogen): To increase survival in patients acutely exposed to myelosuppressive doses of radiation.

Peripheral blood progenitor cell collection and therapy (Neupogen, Zarxio, Grastofil [Canadian product]**):** Mobilization of autologous hematopoietic progenitor cells into the peripheral blood for apheresis collection.

Severe chronic neutropenia (Neupogen, Zarxio, Grastofil [Canadian product]**):** Long-term administration to reduce the incidence and duration of neutropenic complications (eg, fever, infections, oropharyngeal ulcers) in symptomatic patients with congenital, cyclic, or idiopathic neutropenia.

Local Anesthetic/Vasoconstrictor Precautions No information available to require special precautions

Effects on Dental Treatment No significant effects or complications reported

Effects on Bleeding No information available to require special precautions. Medical consultation may be considered to confirm adequate platelet counts.

Adverse Reactions

>10%:

Cardiovascular: Chest pain (5% to 13%)

Central nervous system: Fatigue (20%), dizziness (14%), pain (12%)

Dermatologic: Skin rash (2% to 14%)

Gastrointestinal: Nausea (10% to 43%)

Hematologic & oncologic: Thrombocytopenia (5% to 38%), splenomegaly (≥5%; severe chronic neutropenia: 30%), petechia (17%)

Hepatic: Increased serum alkaline phosphatase (6% to 11%)

Neuromuscular & skeletal: Ostealgia (5% to 33%; dose and cycle related), back pain (2% to 15%)

Respiratory: Epistaxis (2% to 15%), cough (14%), dyspnea (13%)

Miscellaneous: Fever (12% to 48%; dose and cycle related)

1% to 10%:

Cardiovascular: Peripheral edema (≥5%), hypertension (≥4%), cardiac arrhythmia (≤3%), myocardial infarction (≤3%)

Central nervous system: Headache (7% to 10%), hypoesthesia (≥5%), insomnia (≥5%), malaise (≥5%), mouth pain (≥5%)

Dermatologic: Alopecia (≥5%), erythema (≥2%), maculopapular rash (≥2%)

Endocrine & metabolic: Increased lactate dehydrogenase (6%)

Gastrointestinal: Vomiting (5% to 7%), decreased appetite (≥5%), constipation (≥2%), diarrhea (≥2%)

Genitourinary: Urinary tract infection (≥5%)

Hematologic & oncologic: Anemia (≥5%), leukocytosis (≤2%)

Hypersensitivity: Transfusion reaction (2% to 10%), hypersensitivity reaction (≥5%)

Immunologic: Antibody development (3%; no evidence of neutralizing response)

Infection: Sepsis (≥5%)

Neuromuscular & skeletal: Arthralgia (5% to 9%), limb pain (2% to 7%), muscle spasm (≥5%), musculoskeletal pain (≥5%) weakness (≥5%)

Respiratory: Bronchitis (≥5%), upper respiratory tract infection (≥5%)

<1%, postmarketing, and/or case reports: Anaphylaxis, capillary leak syndrome, cerebral hemorrhage, decreased bone mineral density, decreased hemoglobin, euthymia nodosum, exacerbation of psoriasis, facial edema, glomerulonephritis, hematuria, hemoptysis, hepatomegaly, hypersensitivity angiitis, hypotension, injection site reaction, osteoporosis, proteinuria, pulmonary alveolar hemorrhage, pulmonary infiltrates, renal insufficiency, respiratory distress syndrome, severe sickle cell crisis, splenic rupture, Sweet syndrome, tachycardia, urticaria, wheezing

General Dosage Range

IV: *Children, Adolescents, and Adults:* 5 to 10 mcg/kg/day

SubQ: *Children, Adolescents, and Adults:* 1.2 to 10 mcg/kg/day

Mechanism of Action Filgrastim, filgrastim-sndz, and tbo-filgrastim are granulocyte colony stimulating factors (G-CSF) produced by recombinant DNA technology. G-CSFs stimulate the production, maturation, and activation of neutrophils to increase both their migration and cytotoxicity.

Pharmacodynamics/Kinetics

Onset of Action

Filgrastim: 1 to 2 days

Tbo-filgrastim: Time to maximum ANC: 3 to 5 days

Duration of Action

Filgrastim: Neutrophil counts generally return to baseline within 4 days

Tbo-filgrastim: ANC returned to baseline by 21 days after completion of chemotherapy

Half-life Elimination

Neonates: 4.4 ± 0.4 hours (Gillan 1994)

Adults: Filgrastim: ~3.5 hours; Tbo-filgrastim: 3 to 4 hours

Time to Peak Serum: Filgrastim: SubQ: 2 to 8 hours; Tbo-filgrastim: 4 to 6 hours

Pregnancy Risk Factor C

Pregnancy Considerations Adverse events were observed in animal reproduction studies. Filgrastim has been shown to cross the placenta in humans. Information related to the use of granulocyte-colony stimulating factor (G-CSF) in pregnant patients with congenital, cyclic, or idiopathic neutropenia (Boxer 2015; Zeidler 2014) and G-CSF-induced allogeneic peripheral blood stem cells donation is limited (Leitner 2001; Shibata 2003). One review suggests avoiding use during the first trimester until additional outcome information is available (Pessach 2013). Data collected from the Severe Chronic Neutropenia International Registry (SCNIR) note dosing for chronic conditions may need adjusted in pregnant women; the lowest effective dose to maintain the absolute neutrophil count is recommended (Zeidler 2014).

Finasteride (fi NAS teer ide)

Brand Names: US Propecia; Proscar

Brand Names: Canada ACH-Finasteride; ACT-Finasteride; Apo-Finasteride; Auro-Finasteride; Dom-Finasteride; JAMP-Finasteride; Mint-Finasteride; Mylan-Finasteride; Mylan-Finasteride HG; PMS-Finasteride; Propecia; Proscar; RAN-Finasteride; ratio-Finasteride; Sandoz-Finasteride; Sandoz-Finasteride A; Teva-Finasteride; VAN-finasteride

Pharmacologic Category 5 Alpha-Reductase Inhibitor

Use

Androgenetic alopecia (Propecia): Treatment of male pattern hair loss in **men only**.

Limitations of use: Efficacy in bitemporal recession has not been established; not indicated for use in women.

Benign prostatic hyperplasia (Proscar): Treatment (monotherapy) of symptomatic benign prostatic hyperplasia (BPH) to improve symptoms, reduce the risk of acute urinary retention, and to reduce the risk of need for BPH-related surgery); used in combination with an alpha-blocker (doxazosin) to reduce the risk of symptomatic progression.

Limitations of use: Not approved for the prevention of prostate cancer.

Local Anesthetic/Vasoconstrictor Precautions No information available to require special precautions

Effects on Dental Treatment No significant effects or complications reported

Effects on Bleeding No information available to require special precautions

Adverse Reactions Note: "Combination therapy" refers to finasteride and doxazosin.

>10%:

Cardiovascular: Orthostatic hypotension (combination therapy 18%; monotherapy 9%)

Central nervous system: Dizziness (combination therapy 23%; monotherapy 7%)

Endocrine & metabolic: Decreased libido (combination therapy 12%; monotherapy 2% to 10%)

Genitourinary: Impotence (combination therapy 23%; monotherapy 5% to 19%), ejaculatory disorder (combination therapy 14%; monotherapy <1% to 7%)

Neuromuscular & skeletal: Weakness (combination therapy 17%; monotherapy 5%)

1% to 10%:

Cardiovascular: Edema (combination therapy 3%; monotherapy 1%)

Central nervous system: Drowsiness (combination therapy 3%; monotherapy 2%)

Dermatologic: Skin rash (monotherapy 1%)

Endocrine & metabolic: Gynecomastia (monotherapy 1% to 2%)

Genitourinary: Decreased ejaculate volume (monotherapy 2% to 4%), breast tenderness (monotherapy ≤1%)

Respiratory: Dyspnea (combination therapy 2%; monotherapy 1%), rhinitis (combination therapy 2%; monotherapy 1%)

<1%, postmarketing, and/or case reports: Altered mental status, change in libido, decreased testicular size, depression, disturbed sleep, hypersensitivity (angioedema, facial swelling, pharyngeal edema, pruritus, skin rash, swelling of the lips, swollen tongue, urticaria), male infertility (temporary), malignant neoplasm of the male breast, prostate cancer - high grade, prostatitis, reduction in penile curvature, reduction in penile size, sexual disorder (may not be reversible with discontinuation), testicular pain

General Dosage Range Oral: *Adults:* 1 mg or 5 mg once daily

Mechanism of Action Finasteride competitively inhibits type II 5-alpha reductase, resulting in inhibition of the conversion of testosterone to dihydrotestosterone and markedly suppresses serum dihydrotestosterone levels

Pharmacodynamics/Kinetics

Duration of Action Dihydrotestosterone levels return to normal within 14 days of discontinuation of treatment; BPH: Prostate volume returns to baseline within ~3 months after discontinuation; Male pattern baldness: Reversal of increased hair count within 12 months

Half-life Elimination 5 to 6 hours (range: 3 to 16 hours); Elderly (≥70 years): 8 hours (range: 6 to 15 hours)

Time to Peak Serum: 1 to 2 hours

Pregnancy Risk Factor X

Pregnancy Considerations

Use is contraindicated in women of childbearing potential.

Abnormalities of external male genitalia were reported in animal reproduction studies. Use is not indicated in women. Pregnant women are advised to avoid contact with crushed or broken tablets and the semen from a male partner exposed to finasteride.

Fingolimod (fin GOL i mod)

Brand Names: US Gilenya

Brand Names: Canada Gilenya

Pharmacologic Category Sphingosine 1-Phosphate (S1P) Receptor Modulator

Use Multiple sclerosis: Treatment of relapsing forms of multiple sclerosis (MS) to reduce the frequency of clinical exacerbations and to delay the accumulation of physical disability.

Local Anesthetic/Vasoconstrictor Precautions No information available to require special precautions

Effects on Dental Treatment Key adverse event(s) related to dental treatment: Increased blood pressure may occur with fingolimod; assess and plan treatment according to patient's blood pressure. Fingolimod causes immune suppression; medical consult needed prior to dental surgery.

Effects on Bleeding No information available to require special precautions

Adverse Reactions

>10%:

Central nervous system: Headache (25%)

Endocrine & metabolic: Increased gamma-glutamyl transfer (5% to ≤15%)

Gastrointestinal: Nausea (13%), diarrhea (12% to 13%), abdominal pain (11%)

Hepatic: Increased serum ALT (14% to ≤15%), increased serum AST (14% to ≤15%)

Infection: Influenza (11% to 13%)

Neuromuscular & skeletal: Back pain (10% to 12%)

Respiratory: Cough (10% to 12%), sinusitis (7% to 11%)

1% to 10%:

Cardiovascular: Hypertension (6% to 8%), atrioventricular block (first degree: 5%; second degree: 4%; third degree: ≤1%), bradycardia (≤4%)

Central nervous system: Depression (8%), dizziness (7%), migraine (5% to 6%), paresthesia (5%)

Dermatologic: Alopecia (3% to 4%), tinea (2% to 4%), eczema (3%), pruritus (3%), actinic keratosis (2%)

Endocrine & metabolic: Weight loss (5%), increased serum triglycerides (3%)

Gastrointestinal: Gastroenteritis (5%)

Hematologic & oncologic: Lymphocytopenia (4% to 7%), cutaneous papilloma (3%), leukopenia (2% to 3%), basal cell carcinoma (2%)

Neuromuscular & skeletal: Leg pain (≤10%), upper extremity pain (≤10%), weakness (2% to 3%)

Ophthalmic: Blurred vision (4%), eye pain (3%)

Respiratory: Dyspnea (8% to 9%), bronchitis (8%)

Miscellaneous: Herpes virus infection (9%), herpes zoster (2%)

<1%, postmarketing, and/or case reports: Angioedema, asystole, cerebrovascular accident (ischemic and hemorrhagic), cholestatic hepatitis, hepatocellular hepatitis, macular edema, malignant lymphoma (including B-cell and T-cell), multiorgan failure, non-Hodgkin's lymphoma, peripheral arterial disease,

pneumonia, progressive multifocal leukoencephalopathy (FDA Safety Alert, Aug 4, 2015), prolonged Q-T interval on ECG, reversible posterior leukoencephalopathy syndrome, skin rash, syncope, urticaria

General Dosage Range Oral: *Adults:* 0.5 mg once daily

Mechanism of Action Fingolimod-phosphate, active metabolite of fingolimod, binds to sphingosine 1-phosphate receptors 1, 3, 4, and 5. Fingolimod-phosphate blocks the lymphocytes' ability to emerge from lymph nodes; therefore, the amount of lymphocytes available to the central nervous system is decreased, which reduces central inflammation.

Pharmacodynamics/Kinetics

Half-life Elimination 6 to 9 days; prolonged by approximately 50% in patients with moderate or severe hepatic impairment

Time to Peak Plasma: 12 to 16 hours

Pregnancy Risk Factor C

Pregnancy Considerations Adverse events have been observed in animal reproduction studies. Elimination of fingolimod takes approximately 2 months; to avoid potential fetal harm, women of childbearing potential should use effective contraception to avoid pregnancy during and for 2 months after discontinuing treatment. Health care providers are encouraged to enroll pregnant women, or pregnant women may enroll themselves, in the Gilenya Pregnancy Registry (1-877-598-7237 or https://www.gilenyapregnancyregistry.com).

FlavoxATE (fla VOKS ate)

Related Information

Dentin Hypersensitivity, Acid Erosion, High Caries Index, Management of Alveolar Osteitis, and Xerostomia *on page 1857*

Brand Names: Canada Apo-Flavoxate; Urispas

Pharmacologic Category Antispasmodic Agent, Urinary

Use Antispasmodic to provide symptomatic relief of dysuria, nocturia, suprapubic pain, urgency, and incontinence in patients with cystitis, urethritis, urethrocystitis, urethrotrigonitis, and prostatitis

Local Anesthetic/Vasoconstrictor Precautions No information available to require special precautions

Effects on Dental Treatment Key adverse event(s) related to dental treatment: Xerostomia and changes in salivation (normal salivary flow resumes upon discontinuation), and dry throat.

Effects on Bleeding No information available to require special precautions

Adverse Reactions Frequency not defined.

Cardiovascular: Palpitations, tachycardia

Central nervous system: Confusion (especially in the elderly), drowsiness, headache, hyperpyrexia, nervousness, vertigo

Dermatologic: Rash, urticaria

Gastrointestinal: Nausea, vomiting, xerostomia

Genitourinary: Dysuria

Hematologic: Eosinophilia, leukopenia

Ocular: Blurred vision, intraocular pressure increased, ocular accommodation disorder

General Dosage Range Oral: *Children >12 years and Adults:* 100-200 mg 3-4 times daily

Mechanism of Action Synthetic antispasmodic with similar actions to that of propantheline; it exerts a direct relaxant effect on smooth muscles via phosphodiesterase inhibition, providing relief to a variety of smooth muscle spasms; it is especially useful for the treatment of bladder spasticity, whereby it produces an increase in urinary capacity

Pharmacodynamics/Kinetics

Onset of Action 55 minutes

Pregnancy Risk Factor B

Pregnancy Considerations Adverse events have not been observed in animal reproduction studies.

Flecainide (fle KAY nide)

Related Information

Clinical Risk Related to Drugs Prolonging QT Interval *on page 1772*

Brand Names: US Tambocor [DSC]

Brand Names: Canada Apo-Flecainide; Tambocor

Pharmacologic Category Antiarrhythmic Agent, Class Ic

Use

Paroxysmal atrial fibrillation/flutter and paroxysmal supraventricular tachycardias (prevention): For the prevention of paroxysmal atrial fibrillation/flutter associated with disabling symptoms and paroxysmal supraventricular tachycardias (PSVT), including atrioventricular nodal reentrant tachycardia, atrioventricular reentrant tachycardia, and other supraventricular tachycardias of unspecified mechanism associated with disabling symptoms in patients without structural heart disease.

Guideline recommendations: Due to safety risks, flecainide should be reserved for symptomatic supraventricular tachycardias (SVTs) in patients without structural or ischemic heart disease who are not candidates for, or prefer not to undergo, catheter ablation and in whom other therapies have failed or are contraindicated (ACC/AHA/HRS [Page 2015]).

Ventricular arrhythmias (prevention): Prevention of documented life-threatening ventricular tachyarrhythmias (eg, sustained ventricular tachycardia) in patients without structural heart disease.

Limitations of use: Use of flecainide is not recommended in patients with less severe ventricular arrhythmias, even if symptomatic. Because of the proarrhythmic effects of flecainide, its use should be reserved for patients in whom the benefits of treatment outweigh the risks. Flecainide should not be used in patients with chronic atrial fibrillation (not adequately studied) or recent MI. No evidence from controlled trials have demonstrated favorable effects of flecainide on survival or the incidence of sudden death.

Local Anesthetic/Vasoconstrictor Precautions Flecainide is one of the drugs confirmed to prolong the QT interval and is accepted as having a risk of causing torsade de pointes. The risk of drug-induced torsade de pointes is extremely low when a single QT interval prolonging drug is prescribed. In terms of epinephrine, it is not known what effect vasoconstrictors in the local anesthetic regimen will have in patients with a known history of congenital prolonged QT interval or in patients taking any medication that prolongs the QT interval. Until more information is obtained, it is suggested that the clinician consult with the physician prior to the use of a vasoconstrictor in suspected patients, and that the vasoconstrictor (epinephrine, mepivacaine and levonordefrin [Carbocaine® 2% with Neo-Cobefrin®]) be used with caution.

Effects on Dental Treatment No significant effects or complications reported

Effects on Bleeding No information available to require special precautions

Adverse Reactions

>10%:

Central nervous system: Dizziness (19% to 30%)

Ocular: Visual disturbances (16%)

Respiratory: Dyspnea (~10%)

1% to 10%:

Cardiovascular: Palpitation (6%), chest pain (5%), edema (3.5%), tachycardia (1% to 3%), proarrhythmic (4% to 12%), sinus node dysfunction (1.2%), syncope

Central nervous system: Headache (4% to 10%), fatigue (8%), nervousness (5%) additional symptoms occurring at a frequency between 1% and 3%: fever, malaise, hypoesthesia, paresis, ataxia, vertigo, somnolence, tinnitus, anxiety, insomnia, depression

Dermatologic: Rash (1% to 3%)

Gastrointestinal: Nausea (9%), constipation (1%), abdominal pain (3%), anorexia (1% to 3%), diarrhea (0.7% to 3%)

Neuromuscular & skeletal: Tremor (5%), weakness (5%), paresthesia (1%)

Ocular: Diplopia (1% to 3%), blurred vision

<1% (Limited to important or life-threatening): Bradycardia, paradoxical increase in ventricular rate in atrial fibrillation/flutter, heart block, increased P-R, QRS duration, ventricular arrhythmia, CHF, flushing, AV block, angina, hyper-/hypotension, amnesia, confusion, decreased libido, depersonalization, euphoria, apathy, nervousness, twitching, neuropathy, weakness, taste disturbance, urticaria, exfoliative dermatitis, pruritus, alopecia, flatulence, xerostomia, blood dyscrasias, possible hepatic dysfunction, paresthesia, eye pain, photophobia, bronchospasm, pneumonitis, swollen lips/tongue/mouth, arthralgia, myalgia, polyuria, urinary retention, leukopenia, granulocytopenia, thrombocytopenia, metallic taste, alters pacing threshold

Postmarketing and/or case reports: Tardive dyskinesia, corneal deposits

General Dosage Range Dosage adjustment recommended in patients with renal impairment

Oral:

Children: Initial: 50 to 100 mg/m²/day in 3 divided doses (maximum: 200 mg/m²/day)

Adults: Initial: 50 to 100 mg every 12 hours (maximum: 300 to 400 mg/day)

Mechanism of Action Class Ic antiarrhythmic; slows conduction in cardiac tissue by altering transport of ions across cell membranes; causes slight prolongation of refractory periods; decreases the rate of rise of the action potential without affecting its duration; increases electrical stimulation threshold of ventricle, His-Purkinje system; possesses local anesthetic and moderate negative inotropic effects

Pharmacodynamics/Kinetics

Half-life Elimination

Newborns: Up to ≤29 hours; 3 months: 11 to 12 hours; 12 months: 6 hours

Children: ~8 hours

Adolescents 12 to 15 years: ~11 to 12 hours

Adults: ~20 hours (range: 12 to 27 hours); increased in patients with heart failure (NYHA Class III) or renal dysfunction

Time to Peak Serum: ~3 hours (range: 1 to 6 hours)

Pregnancy Risk Factor C

Pregnancy Considerations Adverse events have been observed in some animal reproduction studies. Flecainide is recommended in the treatment of fetal tachycardia determined to be SVT. Flecainide may be also used for the ongoing management of SVT in highly symptomatic pregnant patients. The lowest effective dose is recommended; avoid use during the first trimester if possible (Page [ACC/AHA/HRS 2015]). Additional guidelines are available for management of cardiovascular diseases during pregnancy (ESG [Regitz-Zagrosek 2011]).

Dental Comment See Local Anesthetic/Vasoconstrictor Precautions

Flibanserin (flib AN ser in)

Brand Names: US Addyi

Pharmacologic Category Mixed 5-HT_{1A} Agonist/ 5-HT_{2A} Antagonist

Use

Hypoactive sexual desire disorder: Treatment of premenopausal women with acquired, generalized hypoactive sexual desire disorder (HSDD), as characterized by low sexual desire that causes marked distress or interpersonal difficulty and **not** due to a coexisting medical or psychiatric condition, problems within the relationship, or the effects of a medication or other drug substance.

Limitations of use: Flibanserin is not indicated for the treatment of HSDD in postmenopausal women or in men, or to enhance sexual performance.

Local Anesthetic/Vasoconstrictor Precautions No information available to require special precautions

Effects on Dental Treatment No significant effects or complications reported

Effects on Bleeding No information available to require special precautions

Adverse Reactions

>10%: Central nervous system: Dizziness (11%), drowsiness (11%)

1% to 10%:

Central nervous system: Fatigue (9%), insomnia (5%), anxiety (2%), sedation (1%), vertigo (1%)

Gastrointestinal: Nausea (10%), abdominal pain (2%), constipation (2%), xerostomia (2%)

<1%, postmarketing, and/or case reports: Appendicitis

General Dosage Range Oral: *Adults: Females (premenopausal):* 100 mg once daily

Mechanism of Action The mechanism of action in the treatment of premenopausal women with hypoactive sexual desire disorder is not known. Flibanserin exhibits agonist activity at 5-HT_{1A} and antagonist activity at 5-HT_{2A}; moderate antagonist activity is seen at the 5-HT_{2B}, 5-HT_{2C}, and dopamine D_4 receptors.

Pharmacodynamics/Kinetics

Half-life Elimination Terminal: ~11 hours; mild hepatic impairment: increased to 26 hours; CYP2C19 poor metabolizers: increased to 13.5 hours compared to CYP2C19 extensive metabolizers

Time to Peak 0.75 hours (range: 0.75 to 4 hours)

Pregnancy Considerations Adverse events were observed in some animal reproduction studies.

Prescribing and Access Restrictions As a requirement of the REMS program, access to the medication is restricted. Prescribers and pharmacies must be certified with the ADDYI REMS program; certified pharmacies may only dispense to patients pursuant to a prescription from a certified prescriber. More information, including a list of certified pharmacies, is available at www.-AddyiREMS.com or 844-746-5745.

Floctafenine (flok ta FEN een)

Related Information

Rheumatoid Arthritis, Osteoarthritis, and Osteoporosis *on page 1792*

Pharmacologic Category Analgesic, Nonopioid; Nonsteroidal Anti-inflammatory Drug (NSAID), Oral

Use Note: Not approved in the US

Pain: Short-term management of acute, mild-to-moderate pain

Local Anesthetic/Vasoconstrictor Precautions No information available to require special precautions

Effects on Dental Treatment Key adverse event(s) related to dental treatment: Xerostomia and changes in salivation (normal salivary flow resumes upon discontinuation), bitter taste. See Effects on Bleeding.

Effects on Bleeding Nonselective NSAIDs are known to reversibly decrease platelet aggregation via mechanisms different than observed with aspirin. Platelet function is restored as the drug is eliminated from the body. Dental professionals should be aware that recommendations differ between dental and general medical surgery. NSAIDs should be avoided (if possible) in general medical surgery patients for 3 to 5 half-lives of the drug (usually 1 to 3 days) prior to surgery to reduce the risk of excessive bleeding. However, there is no scientific evidence to warrant discontinuance of NSAIDs prior to dental surgery. In medically complicated patients or extensive oral surgery, the decision to interrupt therapy must be based on the risk to benefit in an individual patient and a medical consult is suggested. Routine interruption of NSAID therapy for most dental procedures is not warranted. If therapy is continued without interruption, the clinician should anticipate the potential for slower clotting times.

Adverse Reactions Frequency not defined.

Cardiovascular: Edema, flushing, tachycardia

Central nervous system: Bitter taste, depression, dizziness, drowsiness, fatigue, headache, insomnia, irritability, malaise, nervousness, vertigo

Dermatologic: Diaphoresis, pruritus, skin rash, urticaria

Endocrine & metabolic: Fluid retention, hyperkalemia, increased thirst

Gastrointestinal: Abdominal pain, constipation, diarrhea, dyspepsia, flatulence, gastrointestinal hemorrhage, gastrointestinal perforation (with gross bleeding), gastrointestinal ulcer, heartburn, nausea, vomiting, xerostomia

Genitourinary: Burning sensation on urination, cystitis, dysuria, hematuria

Hematologic & oncologic: Agranulocytosis, aplastic anemia, hemorrhage, leukopenia, neutropenia, thrombocytopenia

Hepatic: Hepatotoxicity, increased liver enzymes

Hypersensitivity: Anaphylaxis, angioedema

Ophthalmic: Blurred vision, vision loss

Otic: Tinnitus

Renal: Interstitial nephritis, polyuria, renal insufficiency (acute, reversible; with or without oliguria or anuria), urethritis, urine abnormality (strong smell)

Respiratory: Dyspnea (asthmatic-type)

General Dosage Range

Oral: *Adults:* 200 to 400 mg every 6 to 8 hours as needed (maximum: 1,200 mg/day)

Mechanism of Action Reversibly inhibits cyclooxygenase-1 and 2 (COX-1 and 2) enzymes, which results in decreased formation of prostaglandin precursors; has antipyretic, analgesic, and anti-inflammatory properties

Other proposed mechanisms not fully elucidated (and possibly contributing to the anti-inflammatory effect to varying degrees), include inhibiting chemotaxis, altering lymphocyte activity, inhibiting neutrophil aggregation/activation, and decreasing proinflammatory cytokine levels.

Pharmacodynamics/Kinetics

Duration of Action 6 to 8 hours

Half-life Elimination Initial phase (distribution): 1 hour; second phase (elimination): 8 hours

Time to Peak Plasma: Floctafenic acid: 1 to 2 hours

Pregnancy Considerations Floctafenic acid, the active metabolite of floctafenine crosses the placenta. In late pregnancy, NSAIDs may cause premature closure of the ductus arteriosus.

Product Availability Not available in the US

Floxuridine (floks YOOR i deen)

Brand Names: Canada FUDR®

Pharmacologic Category Antineoplastic Agent, Antimetabolite; Antineoplastic Agent, Antimetabolite (Pyrimidine Analog)

Use Colorectal cancer, hepatic metastases: Palliative management of hepatic metastases of colorectal cancer (administered by continuous regional intra-arterial infusion) in select patients considered incurable by surgical resection or other means.

Local Anesthetic/Vasoconstrictor Precautions No information available to require special precautions

Effects on Dental Treatment Key adverse event(s) related to dental treatment: Stomatitis.

Effects on Bleeding Thrombocytopenia and anemia can occur.

Adverse Reactions

>10%:

Gastrointestinal: Diarrhea (may be dose limiting), stomatitis

Hematologic & oncologic: Anemia, bone marrow depression (nadir: 7-10 days; may be dose limiting), leukopenia, thrombocytopenia

1% to 10%:

Dermatologic: Alopecia, dermatitis, localized erythema, skin hyperpigmentation, skin photosensitivity

Gastrointestinal: Anorexia, biliary sclerosis, cholecystitis

Hepatic: Jaundice

<1%, postmarketing, and/or case reports: Abdominal cramps, abdominal pain, BSP abnormality, change in prothrombin time, decreased erythrocyte sedimentation rate, decreased serum total protein, duodenal ulcer, duodenitis, enteritis, fever, gastritis, gastroenteritis, gastrointestinal hemorrhage, gastrointestinal ulcer, glossitis, hemorrhage, hepatic abscess, increased erythrocyte sedimentation rate, increased lactate dehydrogenase, increased serum alkaline phosphatase, increased serum bilirubin, increased serum total protein, increased serum transaminases, infusion related reaction (arterial aneurysm; arterial ischemia; arterial thrombosis; embolism; fibromyositis; thrombophlebitis; hepatic necrosis; abscesses; infection at catheter site; bleeding at catheter site; catheter blocked, displaced, or leaking), ischemic heart disease, lethargy, malaise, nausea, pharyngitis, skin rash, vomiting, weakness

General Dosage Range Dosage adjustment recommended in patients with hepatic impairment or who develop toxicities

Intra-arterial: *Adults:* 0.1-0.6 mg/kg/day

Mechanism of Action Floxuridine is catabolized to fluorouracil after intra-arterial administration, resulting in activity similar to fluorouracil; inhibits thymidylate synthetase and disrupts DNA and RNA synthesis.

Pregnancy Risk Factor D

Pregnancy Considerations Teratogenic effects have been observed in animal reproduction studies. Medications that inhibit DNA synthesis are known to be teratogenic in humans. Women of childbearing potential should avoid pregnancy.

Fluconazole (floo KOE na zole)

Related Information

Clinical Risk Related to Drugs Prolonging QT Interval *on page 1772*

Fungal Infections *on page 1847*

Related Sample Prescriptions

Fungal Infections - Sample Prescriptions *on page 35*

Brand Names: US Diflucan

Brand Names: Canada ACT Fluconazole; Apo-Fluconazole; CanesOral; CO Fluconazole; Diflucan; Diflucan injection; Diflucan One; Diflucan PWS; Dom-Fluconazole; Fluconazole Injection; Fluconazole Injection SDZ; Fluconazole Omega; Monicure; Mylan-Fluconazole; Novo-Fluconazole; PHL-Fluconazole; PMS-Fluconazole; PRO-Fluconazole; Riva-Fluconazole; Taro-Fluconazole

Generic Availability (US) Yes

Pharmacologic Category Antifungal Agent, Oral; Antifungal Agent, Parenteral

Dental Use Treatment of susceptible fungal infections in the oral cavity including candidiasis, oral thrush, and chronic mucocutaneous candidiasis treatment of esophageal and oropharyngeal candidiasis caused by *Candida* species; treatment of severe, chronic mucocutaneous candidiasis caused by *Candida* species

Use Treatment of candidiasis (esophageal, oropharyngeal, peritoneal, urinary tract, vaginal); systemic candida infections (eg, candidemia, disseminated candidiasis, and pneumonia); cryptococcal meningitis; antifungal prophylaxis in allogeneic bone marrow transplant recipients

Local Anesthetic/Vasoconstrictor Precautions Fluconazole is one of the drugs confirmed to prolong the QT interval and is accepted as having a risk of causing torsade de pointes. The risk of drug-induced torsade de pointes is extremely low when a single QT interval prolonging drug is prescribed. In terms of epinephrine, it is not known what effect vasoconstrictors in the local anesthetic regimen will have in patients with a known history of congenital prolonged QT interval or in patients taking any medication that prolongs the QT interval. Until more information is obtained, it is suggested that the clinician consult with the physician prior to the use of a vasoconstrictor in suspected patients, and that the vasoconstrictor (epinephrine, mepivacaine and levonordefrin [Carbocaine® 2% with Neo-Cobefrin®]) be used with caution.

Effects on Dental Treatment Key adverse event(s) related to dental treatment: Abnormal taste.

Effects on Bleeding No information available to require special precautions

Adverse Reactions Frequency not always defined.

Central nervous system: Headache (2% to 13%), dizziness (1%)

Dermatologic: Skin rash (2%)

Gastrointestinal: Nausea (2% to 7%), abdominal pain (2% to 6%), vomiting (2% to 5%), diarrhea (2% to 3%), dysgeusia (1%), dyspepsia (1%)

Hepatic: Hepatitis, increased serum alkaline phosphatase, increased serum ALT, increased serum AST, jaundice

<1%, postmarketing, and/or case reports: Acute generalized exanthematous pustulosis, agranulocytosis, alopecia, anaphylaxis, angioedema, cholestasis, diaphoresis, drowsiness, drug eruption, fatigue, fever, hepatic failure, hypercholesterolemia, hypertriglyceridemia, hypokalemia, insomnia, leukopenia, malaise, myalgia, neutropenia, paresthesia, prolonged Q-T interval on ECG, seizure, Stevens-Johnson syndrome, thrombocytopenia, torsades de pointes, toxic epidermal necrolysis, tremor, vertigo, weakness, xerostomia

Dental Usual Dosage Candidiasis: Adults:

Usual dosage range: 200 to 400 mg/day; duration and dosage depends on severity of infection

Oropharyngeal (long-term suppression): 200 mg/day; chronic therapy is recommended in immunocompromised patients with history of oropharyngeal candidiasis (OPC)

Dosing

Adult & Geriatric The daily dose of fluconazole is the same for both oral and IV administration

Usual dosage range: Oral, IV: 150 mg once **or** Loading dose: 200 to 800 mg; maintenance: 200 to 800 mg once daily; duration and dosage depend on location and severity of infection

Indication-specific dosing:

Blastomycosis (off-label use): Oral: *CNS disease:* Consolidation: 800 mg daily for ≥12 months and until resolution of CSF abnormalities (Chapman 2008)

Candidiasis:

Candidemia (neutropenic and non-neutropenic patients) (off-label dose) (IDSA [Pappas 2016]): Oral, IV:

Initial therapy (ie, first-line): Loading dose: 800 mg (12 mg/kg) on day 1, then 400 mg daily (6 mg/kg/day) for 14 days after first negative blood culture and resolution of signs/symptoms. **Note:** Not recommended as first-line therapy in patients with previous azole exposure, critical illness, or if at high risk of *C. glabrata* infection (elderly, diabetic, malignancy)

Step down therapy (ie, after patient has responded to initial therapy): Oral:

Isolates other than *C. glabrata*: 400 mg daily

Isolates of *C. glabrata* (fluconazole-susceptible): 800 mg daily

Duration: Continue for 14 days after first negative blood culture and resolution of signs/symptoms; step-down therapy to fluconazole (usually after 5 to 7 days in non-neutropenic patients) is recommended only in clinically stable patients with negative repeat cultures and fluconazole-susceptible isolates

Chronic, disseminated (hepatosplenic) (fluconazole-susceptible isolates): Oral: 400 mg daily (6 mg/kg/day) following several weeks of initial therapy with an amphotericin B lipid formulation or an echinocandin. Continue fluconazole until lesion resolution (usually several months) (IDSA [Pappas 2016])

CNS candidiasis: Oral, IV: 400 to 800 mg daily (6 to 12 mg/kg/day) as step-down therapy following initial therapy with liposomal amphotericin B (with or without flucytosine); continue fluconazole until signs/symptoms and CSF/radiological abnormalities have resolved (IDSA [Pappas 2016])

Empiric therapy, suspected invasive candidiasis (non-neutropenic patients in the ICU) (alternative therapy) (off-label use): Oral, IV: Loading dose: 800 mg (12 mg/kg) on day 1, then 400 mg daily (6 mg/kg/day); treatment should continue for 14 days in patients with clinical improvement. Consider discontinuing after 4 to 5 days in patients with no clinical response. **Note:** Not recommended for patients with previous azole exposure or those colonized with azole-resistant *Candida* spp. (Pappas [IDSA 2016])

Endophthalmitis (with or without vitritis): Oral, IV: Loading dose: 800 mg (12 mg/kg) on day 1, then 400 to 800 mg daily (6 to 12 mg/kg/day) for at least 4 to 6 weeks until examination indicates resolution; for patients with vitritis or with macular involvement (with or without vitritis), an intravitreal injection with voriconazole or amphotericin B deoxycholate is also recommended (IDSA [Pappas 2016])

Esophageal: Oral, IV:

Manufacturer's labeling: Loading dose: 200 mg on day 1, then maintenance dose of 100 to 400 mg daily for 21 days and for at least 2 weeks following resolution of symptoms

Alternate recommendations: 200 to 400 mg daily for 14 to 21 days; chronic suppressive therapy of 100 to 200 mg 3 times weekly may be used for recurrent infections (IDSA [Pappas 2016])

Intertrigo (off-label use): Oral, IV: 50 mg daily or 150 mg once weekly (Coldiron 1991; Nozickova 1998; Stengel 1994)

Intra-abdominal infections: Oral, IV: Loading dose: 800 mg (12 mg/kg) on day 1, then 400 mg daily (6 mg/kg/day); duration of therapy determined by clinical response and source control (IDSA [Pappas 2016])

Intravascular infections (IDSA [Pappas 2016]): Oral, IV:

Endocarditis, native or prosthetic valve: 400 to 800 mg daily (6 to 12 mg/kg/day) for at least 6 weeks after valve replacement surgery (longer durations recommended in patients with perivalvular abscesses or other complications); fluconazole should only be used as step-down therapy in clinically stable, culture-negative patients following initial therapy with an amphotericin B lipid formulation (with or without flucytosine) or an echinocandin; long-term or chronic suppressive therapy with fluconazole in absence of valve replacement surgery or in patients with a prosthetic valve endocarditis: 400 to 800 mg daily

Implantable cardiac devices (eg, pacemaker, ICD, VAD) infection: 400 to 800 mg daily (6 to 12 mg/kg/day) for 4 to 6 weeks after device removal (4 weeks for infections limited to generator pockets and at least 6 weeks for infections involving the wires); fluconazole should only be used as step-down in clinically stable, culture-negative patients following initial therapy with an amphotericin B lipid formulation (with or without flucytosine) or an echinocandin; chronic suppressive therapy with fluconazole (following initial antifungal therapy) when VAD cannot be removed and as long as device remains in place: 400 to 800 mg daily

Thrombophlebitis, suppurative: 400 to 800 mg daily (6 to 12 mg/kg/day) for at least 2 weeks after candidemia has cleared; fluconazole may be used as initial therapy or as step-down therapy following initial therapy with an amphotericin B lipid formulation or an echinocandin in clinically stable patients with fluconazole-susceptible isolates.

Oropharyngeal: Oral, IV:

Manufacturer's labeling: Loading dose: 200 mg on day 1; maintenance dose 100 mg daily for ≥2 weeks. **Note:** Therapy with 100 mg daily is associated with resistance development (Rex 1995).

Alternate recommendations: 100 to 200 mg daily for 7 to 14 days for moderate-to-severe disease; in patients with recurrent infection, chronic therapy of 100 mg 3 times weekly is recommended, if required (IDSA [Pappas 2016])

Osteoarticular (osteomyelitis or septic arthritis): Oral, IV: 400 mg daily (6 mg/kg/day) for 6 to 12 months (osteomyelitis) or 6 weeks (septic arthritis); alternatively, fluconazole 400 mg daily for 6 to 12 months (osteomyelitis) or at least 4 weeks (septic arthritis) may also be used following 2 weeks of initial treatment with an echinocandin or an amphotericin B lipid formulation. In patients with fluconazole-susceptible isolates and septic arthritis involving a prosthetic device which cannot be removed, chronic suppressive therapy with fluconazole 400 mg daily is recommended (IDSA [Pappas 2016])

Peritonitis: Oral, IV: 50-200 mg/day. **Note:** Some clinicians do not recommend using <200 mg daily (Chen 2004).

Prophylaxis: Oral, IV:

Bone marrow transplant: 400 mg once daily. Patients anticipated to have severe granulocytopenia should start therapy several days prior to the anticipated onset of neutropenia and continue for 7 days after the neutrophil count is >1000 mm^3.

High-risk ICU patients in units with high incidence of invasive candidiasis (off-label use): Loading dose: 800 mg (12 mg/kg) on day 1, then 400 mg once daily (6 mg/kg/day) (IDSA [Pappas 2016])

Peritoneal dialysis associated infection (concurrently treated with antibiotics), prevention of secondary fungal infection: 200 mg every 48 hours (Restrepo 2010)

Solid organ transplant: 200 to 400 mg once daily for at least 7 to 14 days (Pappas 2009)

Surgical (perioperative) prophylaxis in high-risk patients undergoing liver, pancreas, kidney, or pancreas-kidney transplantation (off-label use): IV: 400 mg given in the perioperative period and continued in the postoperative period for ≤28 days. Time of initiation and duration varies with transplant type and operative protocol (Bratzler 2013).

Urinary tract infections:

Manufacturer's labeling: UTI: Oral, IV: 50 to 200 mg once daily

Alternate recommendations (IDSA [Pappas 2016]):

Candiduria (asymptomatic), patients undergoing a urologic procedure: Oral: 400 mg once daily (6 mg/kg/day) several days before and after the procedure.

Cystitis (symptomatic): Oral: 200 mg once daily (3 mg/kg/day) for 2 weeks
Fungus balls: Oral: 200 to 400 mg once daily (3 to 6 mg/kg/day); concomitant irrigation of amphotericin B deoxycholate via nephrostomy tubes, if present, is also recommended
Pyelonephritis: Oral: 200 to 400 mg once daily for 2 weeks

Vaginal/Vulvovaginal: Oral:
Uncomplicated: Manufacturer's labeling: 150 mg as a single dose
Complicated or severe: 150 mg every 72 hours for 2 or 3 doses (Pappas [IDSA 2016]) **or** 150 mg every 72 hours for 2 doses (CDC [Workowski 2015])
Recurrent: 150 mg once daily for 10 to 14 days, followed by 150 mg once weekly for 6 months (Pappas 2009) **or** fluconazole 100 mg, 150 mg, or 200 mg every 72 hours (day 1, 4, and 7) for a total of 3 doses, then 100 mg, 150 mg, or 200 mg once weekly for 6 months (CDC [Workowski 2015])

Coccidioidomycosis, treatment (off-label use):
HIV-infected (HHS [OI adult 2015]):
Meningeal infections (consultation with specialist is advised): IV, Oral: 400 to 800 mg once daily; patients who complete initial therapy should be considered for lifelong suppressive therapy using fluconazole 400 mg once daily if CD4 counts remain <250 cells/mm^3.
Mild infections (eg, focal pneumonia): Oral: 400 mg once daily; patients who complete initial therapy should be considered for lifelong suppressive therapy using fluconazole 400 mg once daily if CD4 counts remain <250 cells/mm^3.
Non-HIV infected:
Extrapulmonary, bone and/or joint infection: Oral: A minimum dose of 800 mg once daily for 3 years to lifetime, depending on severity and host immunocompetence. **Note:** Amphotericin B may be used initially for severe disease and then switched to fluconazole (IDSA [Galgiani 2016])
Extrapulmonary, soft tissue infection (not associated with bone infection): Oral: 400 mg once daily (some experts use up to 800 mg once daily) for a minimum of 6 to 12 months (IDSA [Galgiani 2016])
HSCT (allogenic or autologous) or solid organ transplant clinically stable patients with active pulmonary infections (acute or chronic): Oral: 400 mg once daily, continued indefinitely or until discontinuation of antirejection therapy (IDSA [Galgiani 2016])
Meningitis: Oral: Initial: 400 to 1200 mg once daily with a lifelong duration (IDSA [Galgiani 2016])
Pneumonia, uncomplicated: Oral: 400 mg once daily (some experts use 800 mg once daily) for 3 to 6 months or longer, depending on response. **Note:** Antifungal treatment is recommended only for patients with severely debilitating illness or with extensive pulmonary involvement, concurrent diabetes, or frailty due to age or comorbidities (IDSA [Galgiani 2016])
Pneumonia, symptomatic chronic cavitary: Oral: 400 mg once daily for 12 months (Galgiani 2000; IDSA [Galgiani 2016])

Coccidioidomycosis, prophylaxis (off-label use): Oral:
HIV-infected patients (HHS [OI adult 2015]):
Primary prophylaxis in patients with a new positive IgM or IgG serologic test who live in disease-endemic areas and have CD4 counts <250 cells/mm^3: 400 mg once daily
Chronic suppressive therapy (secondary prophylaxis): 400 mg once daily
Non-HIV-infected patients:
Solid organ transplant patients: **Note:** The suggested regimens are for patients without active coccidioiomycosis who are undergoing organ transplantation in an endemic area.
Seronegative patients: 200 mg once daily for 6 to 12 months (IDSA [Galgiani 2016]
Seropositive patients: 400 mg once daily for 6 to 12 months (IDSA [Galgiani 2016]

Cryptococcosis:
Meningitis:
Manufacturer's labeling: Oral, IV: 400 mg for 1 dose, then 200 to 400 mg once daily for 10 to 12 weeks following negative CSF culture
Alternate dosing: HIV-infected:
Induction (alternative to preferred therapy): Oral, IV: 800 to 1,200 mg once daily with concomitant flucytosine for 6 weeks (Perfect 2010) **or** 400 to 800 mg once daily with concomitant flucytosine for at least 2 weeks (HHS [OI adult 2015]) **or** 1,200 mg once daily as monotherapy for at least 2 weeks (HHS [OI adult 2015])
Consolidation (preferred therapy): Oral, IV: 400 mg once daily for at least 8 weeks (HHS [OI adult 2015])
Maintenance (suppression) (preferred therapy): Oral: 200 mg once daily for at least 12 months; maintenance therapy may be stopped if the following criteria are fulfilled: induction, consolidation, and at least 12 months of maintenance therapy has been completed, patient remains asymptomatic from cryptococcal infection, and CD4 count ≥100 cells/mm^3 for ≥3 months and HIV RNA suppressed in response to effective ART (HHS [OI adult 2015])
Pulmonary (immunocompetent) (off-label use): 400 mg once daily for 6 to 12 months (Perfect 2010)

Pediatric The daily dose of fluconazole is the same for oral and IV administration
Usual dosage range: Oral, IV: Loading dose: 6 to 12 mg/kg/dose; maintenance: 3 to 12 mg/kg/dose once daily; duration and dosage depend on location and severity of infection

Indication-specific dosing:
Candidiasis: Oral, IV:
Esophageal:
Manufacturer's recommendation: Loading dose: 6 mg/kg/dose; maintenance: 3-12 mg/kg/dose once daily for 21 days and for at least 2 weeks following resolution of symptoms (maximum: 600 mg/day)
HIV-exposed/-infected: Loading dose: 6 mg/kg/dose once on day 1; maintenance: 3 to 6 mg/kg/dose once daily for 4 to 21 days (maximum: 400 mg/day) (CDC 2009)
Relapse suppression (HIV-exposed/-infected): 3 to 6 mg/kg/dose once daily (maximum: 200 mg/day) (CDC 2009)

Invasive disease (alternative therapy): 5 to 6 mg/kg/dose every 12 hours for ≥28 days (maximum: 600 mg/day) (CDC 2009)

Oropharyngeal:

Manufacturer's recommendation: Loading dose: 6 mg/kg/dose; maintenance: 3 mg/kg/dose once daily for ≥2 weeks (maximum: 600 mg/day)

HIV-exposed/-infected: 3 to 6 mg/kg/dose once daily for 7 to 14 days (maximum: 400 mg/day) (CDC 2009)

Surgical (perioperative) prophylaxis in high-risk patients undergoing liver, pancreas, kidney, or pancreas-kidney transplantation (off-label use): IV: 6 mg/kg given in the perioperative period and continued in the postoperative period for ≤28 days (maximum dose 400 mg). Time of initiation and duration varies with transplant type and operative protocol (Bratzler 2013).

Coccidioidomycosis: Oral, IV:

Children: *Meningeal infection, or in a stable patient with diffuse pulmonary or disseminated disease* (HIV-exposed/-infected):

Treatment: 5 to 6 mg/kg/dose twice daily (maximum daily dose: 800 mg/**day**) (CDC 2009) followed by chronic suppressive therapy (see below)

Relapse suppression: 6 mg/kg/dose once daily (maximum daily dose: 400 mg/**day**) (CDC 2009)

Adolescents: Treatment, primary prophylaxis, or chronic suppressive therapy (secondary prophylaxis): Refer to adult dosing.

Cryptococcosis: Oral, IV:

Meningitis: Manufacturer's labeling: 12 mg/kg/dose for 1 dose, then 6 to 12 mg/kg/day for 10-12 weeks following negative CSF culture

HIV-exposed/-infected:

CNS disease (alternative therapy in patients intolerant of amphotericin B):

Children:

Induction: 12 mg/kg/dose for 1 dose, then 6 to 12 mg/kg/day (maximum: 800 mg/day) for ≥2 weeks (in combination with flucytosine) (CDC 2009)

Consolidation: 10 to 12 mg/kg/day for 8 weeks (Perfect 2010) **or** 12 mg/kg/dose for 1 dose, then 6 to 12 mg/kg/day (maximum: 800 mg/day) for 8 weeks (CDC 2009)

Maintenance (suppression): 6 mg/kg/day (maximum: 200 mg/day) (CDC 2009; Perfect 2010)

Adolescents: Refer to adult dosing.

Non-CNS disease, disseminated (including severe pulmonary disease) (alternative therapy; off-label use): Induction: 12 mg/kg/dose for 1 dose, then 6 to 12 mg/kg/day (maximum: 600 mg/day) (CDC 2009)

Non-CNS disease, localized (including isolated pulmonary disease) (off-label use): 12 mg/kg/dose for 1 dose, then 6 to 12 mg/kg/day (maximum: 600 mg/day). **Note:** Duration depends upon infection site and severity (CDC 2009). For patients with pulmonary disease (not delineated by severity), the IDSA recommends a duration of 6 to 12 months (Perfect 2010).

Primary antifungal prophylaxis in pediatric oncology patients (guideline recommendations; Science 2014): Oral, IV:

Allogeneic hematopoietic stem cell transplant (HSCT): Infants ≥1 month, Children, and Adolescents <19 years: 6 to 12 mg/kg/day (maximum: 400 mg/day), begin at the start of conditioning; continue until engraftment

Allogeneic HSCT with grades 2 to 4 acute graft-versus-host-disease (GVHD) or chronic extensive GVHD: Begin with GVHD diagnosis, continue until GVHD resolves:

Infants ≥1 month and Children <13 years: 6 to 12 mg/kg/day (maximum: 400 mg/day)

Adolescents ≥13 years (where posaconazole is contraindicated): 6 to 12 mg/kg/day (maximum: 400 mg/day)

Autologous HSCT with neutropenia anticipated >7 days: Infants ≥1 month, Children, and Adolescents <19 years: 6 to 12 mg/kg/day (maximum: 400 mg/day), begin at the start of conditioning; continue until engraftment

Acute myeloid leukemia (AML) or myelodysplastic syndromes (MDS): Infants ≥1 month, Children, and Adolescents <19 years: 6 to 12 mg/kg/day (maximum: 400 mg/day) during chemotherapy associated neutropenia; alternative antifungals may be suggested for children ≥13 years in centers with a high local incidence of mold infections or if fluconazole is not available

Renal Impairment

Manufacturer's labeling: **Note:** Renal function estimated using the Cockcroft-Gault formula

No adjustment for vaginal candidiasis single-dose therapy

For multiple dosing in adults, administer loading dose of 50 to 400 mg, then adjust daily doses as follows (dosage reduction in children should parallel adult recommendations):

CrCl >50 mL/minute: No dosage adjustment necessary

CrCl ≤50 mL/minute (no dialysis): Reduce dose by 50%

End-stage renal disease on intermittent hemodialysis (IHD):

Manufacturer's labeling: 100% of daily dose (according to indication) after each dialysis session; on nondialysis days, patient should receive a reduced dose according to their CrCl.

Alternate recommendations: Doses of 200 to 400 mg every 48 to 72 hours **or** 100 to 200 mg every 24 hours have been recommended. **Note:** Dosing dependent on the assumption of 3 times/week, complete IHD sessions (Heintz 2009).

Continuous renal replacement therapy (CRRT) (Heintz 2009; Trotman 2005): Drug clearance is highly dependent on the method of renal replacement, filter type, and flow rate. Appropriate dosing requires close monitoring of pharmacologic response, signs of adverse reactions due to drug accumulation, as well as drug concentrations in relation to target trough (if appropriate). The following are general recommendations only (based on dialysate flow/ultrafiltration rates of 1 to 2 L/hour and minimal residual renal function) and should not supersede clinical judgment:

CVVH: Loading dose of 400 to 800 mg followed by 200 to 400 mg every 24 hours

CVVHD/CVVHDF: Loading dose of 400 to 800 mg followed by 400 to 800 mg every 24 hours (CVVHD or CVVHDF) **or** 800 mg every 24 hours (CVVHDF)

Note: Higher maintenance doses of 400 mg every 24 hours (CVVH), 800 mg every 24 hours (CVVHD), and 500 to 600 mg every 12 hours (CVVHDF) may be considered when treating resistant organisms and/or when employing combined ultrafiltration and dialysis flow rates of ≥2 L/hour for CVVHD/CVVHDF (Heintz 2009; Trotman 2005).

Hepatic Impairment There are no dosage adjustments provided in the manufacturer's labeling; use with caution.

Mechanism of Action Interferes with fungal cytochrome P450 activity (lanosterol 14-α-demethylase), decreasing ergosterol synthesis (principal sterol in fungal cell membrane) and inhibiting cell membrane formation

Contraindications Hypersensitivity to fluconazole or any component of the formulation (cross-reaction with other azole antifungal agents may occur, but has not been established; use caution); coadministration of terfenadine in adult patients receiving multiple doses of 400 mg or higher or with CYP3A4 substrates which may lead to QTc prolongation (eg, astemizole, cisapride, erythromycin, pimozide, or quinidine)

Warnings/Precautions Serious (and sometimes fatal) hepatic toxicity (eg, hepatitis, cholestasis, fulminant hepatic failure) has been observed. Use with caution in patients with renal and hepatic dysfunction or previous hepatotoxicity from other azole derivatives. Patients who develop abnormal liver function tests during fluconazole therapy should be monitored closely and discontinued if symptoms consistent with liver disease develop. Rare exfoliative skin disorders have been observed; fatal outcomes have been reported in patients with serious concomitant diseases. Monitor patients with deep seated fungal infections closely for rash development and discontinue if lesions progress. In patients with superficial fungal infections who develop a rash attributable to fluconazole, treatment should also be discontinued. Cases of QTc prolongation and torsade de pointes associated with fluconazole use have been reported (usually high dose or in combination with agents known to prolong the QT interval); use caution in patients with concomitant medications or conditions which are arrhythmogenic. Anaphylaxis has been reported rarely; use with caution in patients with hypersensitivity to other azoles. Potentially significant drug-drug interactions may exist, requiring dose or frequency adjustment, additional monitoring, and/or selection of alternative therapy. May occasionally cause dizziness or seizures; use caution driving or operating machines.

Powder for oral suspension contains sucrose; use caution with fructose intolerance, sucrose-isomaltase deficiency, or glucose-galactose malabsorption.

Benzyl alcohol and derivatives: Some dosage forms may contain sodium benzoate/benzoic acid; benzoic acid (benzoate) is a metabolite of benzyl alcohol; large amounts of benzyl alcohol (≥99 mg/kg/day) have been associated with a potentially fatal toxicity ("gasping syndrome") in neonates; the "gasping syndrome" consists of metabolic acidosis, respiratory distress, gasping respirations, CNS dysfunction (including convulsions, intracranial hemorrhage), hypotension, and cardiovascular collapse (AAP 1997; CDC 1982); some data suggests that benzoate displaces bilirubin from protein binding sites (Ahlfors 2001); avoid or use dosage forms containing benzyl alcohol derivative with caution in neonates. See manufacturer's labeling.

Drug Interactions

Metabolism/Transport Effects **Inhibits** CYP1A2 (weak), CYP2C19 (strong), CYP2C9 (moderate), CYP3A4 (moderate)

Avoid Concomitant Use

Avoid concomitant use of Fluconazole with any of the following: Aprepitant; Asunaprevir; Bosutinib; Budesonide (Systemic); Cisapride; Citalopram; Cobimetinib; Domperidone; Erythromycin (Systemic); Flibanserin; Ibrutinib; Ivabradine; Lomitapide; Naloxegol; Olaparib; Ospemifene; Pimozide; QuiNIDine; Saccharomyces boulardii; Simeprevir; Tolvaptan; Trabectedin; Ulipristal; Voriconazole

Increased Effect/Toxicity

Fluconazole may increase the levels/effects of: Alfentanil; Amitriptyline; AmLODIPine; Apixaban; Aprepitant; ARIPiprazole; Asunaprevir; AtorvaSTATin; Avanafil; Blonanserin; Bosentan; Bosutinib; Brexpiprazole; Bromocriptine; Budesonide (Systemic); Budesonide (Topical); BusPIRone; Busulfan; Calcium Channel Blockers; Cannabis; CarBAMazepine; Carvedilol; Cilostazol; Cisapride; Citalopram; CloZAPine; Cobimetinib; Colchicine; CycloSPORINE (Systemic); CYP2C19 Substrates; CYP2C9 Substrates; CYP3A4 Substrates; Dapoxetine; Deflazacort; Domperidone; DOXOrubicin (Conventional); Dronabinol; Eletriptan; Eliglustat; Eplerenone; Erythromycin (Systemic); Etravirine; Everolimus; FentaNYL; Flibanserin; Fluvastatin; Fosphenytoin; GuanFACINE; Halofantrine; Highest Risk QTc-Prolonging Agents; HYDROcodone; HydrOXYzine; Ibrutinib; Imatinib; Ivabradine; Ivacaftor; Lomitapide; Lovastatin; Lurasidone; Manidipine; Methadone; Mirodenafil; Moderate Risk QTc-Prolonging Agents; Naldemedine; Nalmefene; Naloxegol; Nateglinide; Nevirapine; NiMODipine; Olaparib; Ospemifene; OxyCODONE; Parecoxib; Phenytoin; Pimecrolimus; Pimozide; PredniSONE; Propafenone; Proton Pump Inhibitors; QuiNIDine; Ramelteon; Ranolazine; Red Yeast Rice; Rifamycin Derivatives; Rupatadine; Ruxolitinib; Salmeterol; SAXagliptin; Sildenafil; Simeprevir; Simvastatin; Sirolimus; Solifenacin; Sonidegib; Sulfonylureas; SUNItinib; Suvorexant; Tacrolimus (Systemic); Tadalafil; Telithromycin; Temsirolimus; Tetrahydrocannabinol; Ticagrelor; Tipranavir; TiZANidine; Tofacitinib; Tolvaptan; Trabectedin; Udenafil; Ulipristal; Vardenafil; Venetoclax; Vilazodone; Vindesine; Vitamin K Antagonists; Voriconazole; Zidovudine; Zopiclone

The levels/effects of Fluconazole may be increased by: Amitriptyline; Etravirine; MiFEPRIStone

Decreased Effect

Fluconazole may decrease the levels/effects of: Amphotericin B; Clopidogrel; Ifosfamide; Losartan; Saccharomyces boulardii

The levels/effects of Fluconazole may be decreased by: Didanosine; Etravirine; Rifamycin Derivatives

Pharmacodynamics/Kinetics

Half-life Elimination Normal renal function: ~30 hours (range: 20 to 50 hours); Elderly: 46.2 hours; Neonates (gestational age 26 to 29 weeks): 73.6 to 46.6 hours (decreases with increasing postnatal age); Pediatric patients 9 months to 15 years: 19.5 to 25 hours

Time to Peak Oral: 1 to 2 hours

Pregnancy Risk Factor C (single dose for vaginal candidiasis)/D (all other indications)

Pregnancy Considerations Adverse events have been observed in some animal reproduction studies. When used in high doses, fluconazole is teratogenic in animal studies. Following exposure during the first trimester, case reports have noted similar malformations in humans when used in higher doses (400 mg/day) over extended periods of time (Aleck 1997). Abnormalities reported include abnormal facies, abnormal calvarial development, arthrogryposis, brachycephaly, cleft palate, congenital heart disease, femoral bowing, thin ribs and long bones. Use of lower doses (150 mg as a single dose) does not suggest an increase risk to the fetus. Most azole antifungals, including fluconazole, are recommended to be avoided during pregnancy (IDSA [Pappas 2016]).

Breastfeeding Considerations Fluconazole is excreted into breast milk at concentrations similar to maternal plasma concentrations (Force 1995; Schilling 1993).

The relative infant dose (RID) of fluconazole is 5% to 21% when calculated using the highest breast milk concentration located and compared to an infant therapeutic dose of 3 to 12 mg/kg/day. In general, breastfeeding is considered acceptable when the RID is <10%; when an RID is >25% breastfeeding should generally be avoided (Anderson 2016; Ito 2000). Using the highest milk concentration (4.1 mcg/mL), the estimated daily infant dose via breast milk would be 0.62 mg/kg/day. This milk concentration was obtained following maternal administration of oral fluconazole 200 mg daily for 18 days; the apparent elimination half-life of fluconazole in breast milk was 26.9 hours (Schilling 1993).

Serious adverse events in nursing infants have not been reported following maternal use of fluconazole for nipple or breast candidiasis (Bodley 1997; Chetwynd 2002; Moorhead 2011); flushed cheeks, GI upset, loose stools, or mucous feces, and somnolence have been reported in breastfed infants (Moorhead 2011).

Although the manufacturer recommends that caution be exercised when administering fluconazole to breastfeeding women, existing recommendations state that fluconazole is considered compatible with breastfeeding when used in usual recommended doses (WHO 2002). Treatment of breastfeeding women with nipple or breast candidiasis with oral fluconazole is common, especially in persistent or recurring infections (Brent 2001). Untreated candida nipple or breast infections may be painful for the mother and can contribute to premature weaning (Brent 2001). The amount of fluconazole contained in the breast milk is not sufficient to treat mucocutaneous candidiasis in the infant (Force 1995; Schilling 1993); concurrent treatment of both the nursing infant and mother may be required (Chetwynd 2002).

Dosage Forms

Solution, Intravenous:

Generic: 100 mg (50 mL); 200 mg (100 mL); 400 mg (200 mL)

Solution, Intravenous [preservative free]:

Generic: 200 mg (100 mL); 400 mg (200 mL)

Suspension Reconstituted, Oral:

Diflucan: 10 mg/mL (35 mL); 40 mg/mL (35 mL)

Generic: 10 mg/mL (35 mL); 40 mg/mL (35 mL)

Tablet, Oral:

Diflucan: 50 mg, 100 mg, 150 mg, 200 mg

Generic: 50 mg, 100 mg, 150 mg, 200 mg

Dental Comment See Local Anesthetic/Vasoconstrictor Precautions

Flucytosine (floo SYE toe seen)

Brand Names: US Ancobon

Pharmacologic Category Antifungal Agent, Oral

Use Adjunctive treatment of systemic fungal infections (eg, septicemia, endocarditis, UTI, meningitis, or pulmonary) caused by susceptible strains of *Candida* or *Cryptococcus*

Local Anesthetic/Vasoconstrictor Precautions No information available to require special precautions

Effects on Dental Treatment No significant effects or complications reported

Effects on Bleeding No information available to require special precautions

Adverse Reactions Frequency not defined.

Cardiovascular: Cardiotoxicity, chest pain, ventricular dysfunction

Central nervous system: Ataxia, confusion, fatigue, hallucination, headache, paresthesia, parkinsonian-like syndrome, peripheral neuropathy, psychosis, sedation, seizure, vertigo

Dermatologic: Pruritus, skin photosensitivity, skin rash, toxic epidermal necrolysis, urticaria

Endocrine & metabolic: Hypoglycemia, hypokalemia

Gastrointestinal: Abdominal pain, anorexia, diarrhea, duodenal ulcer, enterocolitis, gastrointestinal hemorrhage, nausea, ulcerative colitis, vomiting, xerostomia

Genitourinary: Azotemia, crystalluria

Hematologic & oncologic: Agranulocytosis, anemia, aplastic anemia, bone marrow aplasia, eosinophilia, leukopenia, pancytopenia, thrombocytopenia

Hepatic: Hepatic injury (acute), hepatic insufficiency, hepatic necrosis, increased liver enzymes, increased serum bilirubin, jaundice

Hypersensitivity: Hypersensitivity reaction

Neuromuscular & skeletal: Weakness

Otic: Hearing loss

Renal: Increased blood urea nitrogen, increased serum creatinine, renal failure

Respiratory: Dyspnea

Miscellaneous: Fever

General Dosage Range Dosage adjustment recommended in patients with renal impairment

Oral: *Adults:* 50 to 150 mg/kg daily in 3 or 4 divided doses

Mechanism of Action Penetrates fungal cells and is converted to fluorouracil which competes with uracil interfering with fungal RNA and protein synthesis

Pharmacodynamics/Kinetics

Half-life Elimination Neonates: 4 to 34 hours (Baley, 1990); Infants: 7.4 hours; Adults: 2 to 5 hours; Anuria: 85 hours (range: 30 to 250); End-stage renal disease (ESRD): 75 to 200 hours

Time to Peak Serum: Neonates: 2.5 ± 1.3 hours; Adults: ~1 to 2 hours

Pregnancy Risk Factor C

Pregnancy Considerations Adverse events have been observed in some animal reproduction studies. Flucytosine is metabolized to fluorouracil which may cause adverse events if administered during pregnancy; refer to the Fluorouracil (Systemic) monograph for additional information.

Fludarabine (floo DARE a been)

Brand Names: US Fludara [DSC]

Brand Names: Canada Fludara; Fludarabine Phosphate for Injection; Fludarabine Phosphate for Injection, USP; Fludarabine Phosphate Injection, PPC STD.

Pharmacologic Category Antineoplastic Agent, Antimetabolite; Antineoplastic Agent, Antimetabolite (Purine Analog)

Use

Chronic lymphocytic leukemia (refractory or progressive): Treatment of B-cell chronic lymphocytic leukemia (CLL) in adults who have not responded to or have progressed during treatment with at least one standard regimen containing an alkylating agent.

Canadian labeling: Second-line treatment of chronic lymphocytic leukemia (Oral and IV); second-line treatment of low-grade, refractory non-Hodgkin lymphoma (IV only)

Local Anesthetic/Vasoconstrictor Precautions
No Information available to require special precautions

Effects on Dental Treatment Key adverse event(s) related to dental treatment: Stomatitis.

Effects on Bleeding Thrombocytopenia (nadir: 16 days) and anemia reported in the majority of patients.

Adverse Reactions

Frequency not always defined.

>10%:

Cardiovascular: Edema (8% to 19%)

Central nervous system: Fatigue (10% to 38%), neurological signs and symptoms (doses >96 mg/m^2/day for 5 to 7 days: 36%; doses <125 mg/m^2/cycle: <1%; characterized by cortical blindness, coma, and paralysis; symptom onset may be delayed for 3 to 4 weeks), pain (20% to 22%), chills (11% to 19%), paresthesia (4% to 12%)

Dermatologic: Skin rash (15%), diaphoresis (1% to 13%)

Gastrointestinal: Nausea and vomiting (31% to 36%), anorexia (7% to 34%), diarrhea (13% to 15%), gastrointestinal hemorrhage (3% to 13%)

Genitourinary: Urinary tract infection (2% to 15%)

Hematologic & oncologic: Anemia (60%), neutropenia (grade 4: 59%; nadir: ~13 days), thrombocytopenia (55%; nadir: ~16 days), bone marrow depression (nadir: 10 to 14 days; recovery: 5 to 7 weeks; dose-limiting toxicity)

Infection: Infection (33% to 44%)

Neuromuscular & skeletal: Weakness (9% to 65%), myalgia (4% to 16%)

Ophthalmic: Visual disturbance (3% to 15%)

Respiratory: Cough (10% to 44%), pneumonia (16% to 22%), dyspnea (9% to 22%), upper respiratory tract infection (2% to 16%)

Miscellaneous: Fever (60% to 69%)

1% to 10%:

Cardiovascular: Angina pectoris (≤6%), cardiac arrhythmia (≤3%), cardiac failure (≤3%), cerebrovascular accident (≤3%), myocardial infarction (≤3%), supraventricular tachycardia (≤3%), deep vein thrombosis (1% to 3%), phlebitis (1% to 3%), aneurysm (≤1%), transient ischemic attacks (≤1%)

Central nervous system: Malaise (6% to 8%), headache (≤3%), sleep disorder (1% to 3%), cerebellar syndrome (≤1%), depression (≤1%), difficulty thinking (≤1%)

Dermatologic: Alopecia (≤3%), pruritus (1% to 3%), seborrhea (≤1%)

Endocrine & metabolic: Hyperglycemia (1% to 6%), dehydration (≤1%)

Gastrointestinal: Stomatitis (≤9%), cholelithiasis (≤3%), esophagitis (≤3%), constipation (1% to 3%), mucositis (≤2%), dysphagia (≤1%)

Genitourinary: Dysuria (3% to 4%), urinary hesitancy (≤3%), hematuria (2% to 3%), proteinuria (≤1%)

Hematologic & oncologic: Hemorrhage (≤1%), tumor lysis syndrome (≤1%)

Hepatic: Abnormal hepatic function tests (1% to 3%), hepatic failure (≤1%)

Hypersensitivity: Anaphylaxis (≤1%)

Neuromuscular & skeletal: Osteoporosis (≤2%), arthralgia (≤1%)

Otic: Hearing loss (2% to 6%)

Renal: Renal failure (≤1%), renal function test abnormality (≤1%)

Respiratory: Pharyngitis (≤9%), hypersensitivity pneumonitis (≤6%), hemoptysis (1% to 6%), sinusitis (≤5%), bronchitis (≤1%), epistaxis (≤1%), hypoxia (≤1%)

<1%, postmarketing, and/or case reports: Acquired blood coagulation disorder, acute myelocytic leukemia (usually associated with prior or concurrent treatment with other anticancer agents), adult respiratory distress syndrome, agitation, autoimmune hemolytic anemia, autoimmune thrombocytopenia, blindness, bone marrow aplasia (trilineage), bone marrow depression (trilineage), cerebral hemorrhage, coma, confusion, Epstein-Barr-associated lymphoproliferative disorder, erythema multiforme, Evan's syndrome, flank pain, hemorrhagic cystitis, hyperkalemia, hyperphosphatemia, hyperuricemia, hypocalcemia, immune thrombocytopenia (autoimmune), increased liver enzymes, interstitial pulmonary infiltrate, malignant neoplasm of skin (new-onset or exacerbation), metabolic acidosis, myelodysplastic syndrome (usually associated with prior or concurrent treatment with other anticancer agents), myelofibrosis, opportunistic infection, optic neuritis, optic neuropathy, pancreatic disease (pancreatic enzymes abnormal), pancytopenia, pemphigus, pericardial effusion, peripheral neuropathy, pneumonitis, progressive multifocal leukoencephalopathy (PML), pulmonary fibrosis, pulmonary hemorrhage, reactivation of latent Epstein-Barr virus, reactivation of latent herpes zoster, respiratory distress, respiratory failure, seizure, Stevens-Johnson syndrome, toxic epidermal necrolysis, urate crystalluria, wrist-drop

General Dosage Range Dosage adjustment recommended in patients with renal impairment or who develop toxicities.

IV: *Adults:* 25 mg/m^2/day for 5 days every 28 days

Mechanism of Action Fludarabine inhibits DNA synthesis by inhibition of DNA polymerase and ribonucleotide reductase; also inhibits DNA primase and DNA ligase I

Pharmacodynamics/Kinetics

Half-life Elimination 2-fluoro-ara-A: Adults: ~20 hours

Time to Peak Oral: 1 to 2 hours

Pregnancy Risk Factor D

Pregnancy Considerations Adverse events were observed in animal reproduction studies. Based on the mechanism of action, fludarabine may cause fetal harm if administered during pregnancy. Effective contraception should be used to avoid pregnancy during and after treatment for women and men with female partners of reproductive potential.

Fludrocortisone (floo droe KOR ti sone)

Brand Names: Canada Florinef

Generic Availability (US) Yes

Pharmacologic Category Corticosteroid, Systemic

Use

Addison disease: Partial replacement therapy for primary and secondary adrenocortical insufficiency in Addison disease

Salt-losing adrenogenital syndrome: Treatment of salt-losing adrenogenital syndrome (congenital adrenal hyperplasia)

Local Anesthetic/Vasoconstrictor Precautions
No information available to require special precautions

Effects on Dental Treatment No significant effects or complications reported

Effects on Bleeding No information available to require special precautions

Adverse Reactions Frequency not defined.

Cardiovascular: Cardiac failure, cardiomegaly, edema, hypertension

Central nervous system: Delirium, depression, emotional lability, euphoria, hallucination, headache, increased intracranial pressure, insomnia, malaise, nervousness, personality changes, pseudotumor cerebri, psychiatric disturbance, psychosis, seizure, vertigo

Dermatologic: Acne vulgaris, atrophic striae, diaphoresis, erythema, hyperpigmentation, maculopapular rash, skin atrophy, skin rash, suppression of skin test reaction, urticaria

Endocrine & metabolic: Cushing's syndrome, diabetes mellitus, glycosuria, growth suppression, hirsutism, HPA-axis suppression, hyperglycemia, hypokalemia, hypokalemic alkalosis, impaired glucose tolerance, menstrual disease, negative nitrogen balance, subcutaneous fat atrophy

Gastrointestinal: Abdominal distention, esophageal ulcer, pancreatitis, peptic ulcer

Hematologic & oncologic: Bruise, petechia, purpura

Hypersensitivity: Anaphylaxis (generalized)

Neuromuscular & skeletal: Amyotrophy, bone fracture, myasthenia, myopathy, osteonecrosis (femoral and humeral heads), osteoporosis, vertebral compression fracture

Ophthalmic: Cataract, exophthalmos, glaucoma, increased intraocular pressure

Miscellaneous: Wound healing impairment

Dosing

Adult & Geriatric

Addison disease: Oral:

Manufacturer's labeling: Primary or secondary insufficiency: 0.1 mg daily; if transient hypertension develops, reduce dose to 0.05 mg daily; maintenance dosage range: 0.1 mg 3 times weekly to 0.2 mg daily. Preferred administration with cortisone or hydrocortisone.

Alternate recommendations: Primary adrenal insufficiency: Initial: 0.05 to 0.1 mg once daily in the morning (in combination with hydrocortisone or cortisone). Usual maintenance dose: 0.05 to 0.2 mg once daily. If hypertension develops, dose reduction is suggested; an antihypertensive may be necessary if hypertension remains uncontrolled (ES [Bornstein 2016]).

Salt-losing adrenogenital syndrome (or congenital adrenal hyperplasia): Oral: 0.1 to 0.2 mg daily

The Endocrine Society recommends a maintenance dose range of 0.05 to 0.2 mg once daily (in combination with hydrocortisone) for patients with congenital adrenal hyperplasia due to 21-hydroxylase deficiency (Speiser 2010).

Orthostatic hypotension (off-label use; Kearney 2009; Lahrmann 2006; Lanier 2011): Oral: Initial: 0.1 mg daily in conjunction with a high-salt diet and adequate fluid intake; may be increased in increments of 0.1 mg per week; maximum dose: 1 mg daily. **Note:** Doses exceeding 0.3 mg daily may not be beneficial and predispose patient to unwanted side effects (eg, hypertension, hypokalemia).

Pediatric

Adrenal insufficiency, autoimmune (aldosterone deficiency component Addison disease); replacement therapy (off-label dosing): Limited data available: Oral: 0.05 to 0.2 mg daily (Betterle 2002; Kliegman 2011)

Congenital adrenal hyperplasia (salt losers) (eg, 21-hydroxylase deficiency) (off-label dosing): Limited data available: **Note:** Use in combination with glucocorticoid therapy (eg, hydrocortisone); concurrent sodium replacement therapy may be required, particularly in young infants. Oral:

Infants, Children, and Adolescents (actively growing): Usual range: 0.05 to 0.2 mg daily in 1 or 2 divided doses; doses as high as 0.3 mg/day may be necessary (AAP 2000; AAP 2010; Speiser 2010)

Adolescents (fully grown): 0.05 to 0.2 mg once daily (AAP 2010; Speiser 2010)

Renal Impairment There are no dosage adjustments provided in the manufacturer's labeling; use with caution.

Hepatic Impairment There are no dosage adjustments provided in the manufacturer's labeling; use with caution.

Mechanism of Action Very potent mineralocorticoid with high glucocorticoid activity; used primarily for its mineralocorticoid effects. Promotes increased reabsorption of sodium and loss of potassium from renal distal tubules.

Contraindications

Hypersensitivity to fludrocortisone or any component of the formulation; systemic fungal infections

Documentation of allergenic cross-reactivity for corticosteroids is limited. However, because of similarities in chemical structure and/or pharmacologic actions, the possibility of cross-sensitivity cannot be ruled out with certainty.

Warnings/Precautions May cause hypercorticism or suppression of hypothalamic-pituitary-adrenal (HPA) axis, particularly in younger children or in patients receiving high doses for prolonged periods. HPA axis suppression may lead to adrenal crisis. Withdrawal and discontinuation of a corticosteroid should be done slowly and carefully. Rare cases of anaphylactoid reactions have been observed in patients receiving corticosteroids.

Prolonged use may increase risk of infection, mask acute infection (including fungal infections), prolong or exacerbate viral infections, or limit response to killed or inactivated vaccines. Exposure to chickenpox or measles should be avoided. Corticosteroids should not be used for cerebral malaria or viral hepatitis. Close observation is required in patients with latent tuberculosis (TB) and/or TB reactivity. Restrict use in active TB (only fulminating or disseminated TB in conjunction with antituberculosis treatment). Amebiasis should be ruled out in any patient with recent travel to tropic climates or unexplained diarrhea prior to initiation of corticosteroids. Use with extreme caution in patients with Strongyloides infections; hyperinfection, dissemination and fatalities have occurred.

Prolonged treatment with corticosteroids has been associated with the development of Kaposi sarcoma (case reports); if noted, discontinuation of therapy should be considered (Goedert 2002). Acute myopathy has been reported with high-dose corticosteroids, usually in patients with neuromuscular transmission disorders; may involve ocular and/or respiratory muscles; monitor creatine kinase; recovery may be delayed. Corticosteroid use may cause psychiatric disturbances, including euphoria, insomnia, mood swings, personality changes, severe depression to psychotic manifestation.

Preexisting psychiatric conditions may be exacerbated by corticosteroid use.

Use with caution in patients with GI diseases (diverticulitis, fresh intestinal anastomoses, active or latent peptic ulcer, ulcerative colitis, abscess or other pyogenic infection) due to perforation risk. Use with caution in patients with a history of ocular herpes simplex; corneal perforation has occurred; do not use in active ocular herpes simplex. Use with caution in patients with renal impairment; hepatic impairment; history of seizure disorder; myasthenia gravis; osteoporosis; diabetes mellitus; thyroid disease; HF and/or hypertension; in patients with cataracts and/or glaucoma; and the elderly. Use with caution following acute MI; corticosteroids have been associated with myocardial rupture. Potentially significant interactions may exist, requiring dose or frequency adjustment, additional monitoring, and/or selection of alternative therapy. When discontinuing therapy, withdraw therapy with gradual tapering of dose. Patients may require higher doses when subject to stress (ie, trauma, surgery, severe illness).

Drug Interactions

Metabolism/Transport Effects None known.

Avoid Concomitant Use

Avoid concomitant use of Fludrocortisone with any of the following: Aldesleukin; BCG (Intravesical); Desmopressin; Indium 111 Capromab Pendetide; MiFEPRIStone; Natalizumab; Pimecrolimus; Tacrolimus (Topical); Tofacitinib

Increased Effect/Toxicity

Fludrocortisone may increase the levels/effects of: Acetylcholinesterase Inhibitors; Amphotericin B; Androgens; Ceritinib; Deferasirox; Desirudin; Desmopressin; Fingolimod; Leflunomide; Loop Diuretics; Natalizumab; Nicorandil; NSAID (COX-2 Inhibitor); NSAID (Nonselective); Quinolone Antibiotics; Thiazide and Thiazide-Like Diuretics; Tofacitinib; Vaccines (Live); Warfarin

The levels/effects of Fludrocortisone may be increased by: Aprepitant; CYP3A4 Inhibitors (Strong); Denosumab; DilTIAZem; Estrogen Derivatives; Fosaprepitant; Indacaterol; MiFEPRIStone; Neuromuscular-Blocking Agents (Nondepolarizing); Ocrelizumab; Pimecrolimus; Roflumilast; Salicylates; Tacrolimus (Topical); Telaprevir; Trastuzumab

Decreased Effect

Fludrocortisone may decrease the levels/effects of: Aldesleukin; Antidiabetic Agents; BCG (Intravesical); Calcitriol (Systemic); Coccidioides immitis Skin Test; Corticorelin; Hyaluronidase; Indium 111 Capromab Pendetide; Isoniazid; Nivolumab; Salicylates; Sipuleucel-T; Telaprevir; Tertomotide; Urea Cycle Disorder Agents; Vaccines (Inactivated); Vaccines (Live)

The levels/effects of Fludrocortisone may be decreased by: Antacids; Bile Acid Sequestrants; CYP3A4 Inducers (Strong); Echinacea; MiFEPRIStone; Mitotane

Dietary Considerations Systemic use of mineralocorticoids/corticosteroids may require a diet with increased potassium, vitamins A, B_6, C, D, folate, calcium, zinc, and phosphorus, and decreased sodium. With fludrocortisone, a decrease in dietary sodium is often not required as the increased retention of sodium is usually the desired therapeutic effect.

Pharmacodynamics/Kinetics

Half-life Elimination Plasma: ≥3.5 hours; Biological: 18 to 36 hours

Pregnancy Risk Factor C

Pregnancy Considerations Animal reproduction studies have not been conducted with fludrocortisone; adverse events have been observed with corticosteroids in animal reproduction studies. Some studies have shown an association between first trimester systemic corticosteroid use and oral clefts (Park-Wyllie 2000; Pradat 2003). Systemic corticosteroids may also influence fetal growth (decreased birth weight); however, information is conflicting (Lunghi 2010). Hypoadrenalism may occur in newborns following maternal use of corticosteroids in pregnancy; monitor.

When systemic corticosteroids are needed in pregnancy, it is generally recommended to use the lowest effective dose for the shortest duration of time, avoiding high doses during the first trimester (Leachman 2006; Lunghi 2010). Fludrocortisone may be used to treat women during pregnancy who require therapy for congenital adrenal hyperplasia or primary adrenal insufficiency (Bornstein 2016; Speiser 2010).

Breastfeeding Considerations It is not known if fludrocortisone is excreted in breast milk; corticosteroids are excreted in breast milk. The manufacturer recommends that caution be exercised when administering fludrocortisone to nursing women.

Dosage Forms

Tablet, Oral:

Generic: 0.1 mg

Flumazenil (FLOO may ze nil)

Brand Names: Canada Anexate; Flumazenil Injection; Flumazenil Injection, USP; Romazicon

Generic Availability (US) Yes

Pharmacologic Category Antidote

Use Benzodiazepine antagonist; reverses sedative effects of benzodiazepines used in conscious sedation and general anesthesia; treatment of benzodiazepine overdose

Local Anesthetic/Vasoconstrictor Precautions No information available to require special precautions

Effects on Dental Treatment Key adverse event(s) related to dental treatment: Xerostomia (normal salivary flow resumes upon discontinuation).

Effects on Bleeding No information available to require special precautions

Adverse Reactions

>10%: Gastrointestinal: Vomiting (11%)

1% to 10%:

Cardiovascular: Palpitation (3% to 9%), flushing (1% to 3%), thrombophlebitis (1% to 3%), vasodilatation (1% to 3%)

Central nervous system: Ataxia (10%), dizziness (10%), vertigo (10%), agitation (3% to 9%), anxiety (3% to 9%), insomnia (3% to 9%), nervousness (3% to 9%), depersonalization (1% to 3%), depression (1% to 3%), dysphoria (1% to 3%), emotional lability (1% to 3%; including crying), euphoria (1% to 3%), fatigue (1% to 3%), headache (1% to 3%), hypoesthesia (1% to 3%), malaise (1% to 3%), paranoia (1% to 3%), paresthesia (1% to 3%)

Dermatologic: Dermatological disease (skin abnormality: 1% to 3%), diaphoresis (1% to 3%), skin rash (1% to 3%)

Endocrine & metabolic: Hot flash (1% to 3%)

Gastrointestinal: Xerostomia (3% to 9%), nausea (1% to 3%)

Local: Pain at injection site (3% to 9%), injection site reaction (1% to 3%)

Neuromuscular & skeletal: Weakness (1% to 3%), tremor

Ophthalmic: Blurred vision (3% to 9%), lacrimation (1% to 3%), visual disturbance (1% to 3%)

Respiratory: Dyspnea (3% to 9%), hyperventilation (3% to 9%)

<1%, postmarketing, and/or case reports: Auditory disturbance, bradycardia, cardiac arrhythmia, chest pain, confusion, decreased blood pressure, delirium, drowsiness, fear, hiccups, hyperacusis, hypertension, increased blood pressure, lack of concentration, panic attack, paroxysmal atrial tachycardia, reversible hearing loss, rigors, seizure (including generalized), sensation of cold, shivering, stupor, tachycardia, tinnitus, tongue edema, ventricular tachycardia, voice disorder, withdrawal syndrome

Dosing

Adult

Reversal of conscious sedation and general anesthesia: IV:

Initial dose: 0.2 mg over 15 seconds

Repeat doses (maximum: 4 doses): If desired level of consciousness is not obtained, 0.2 mg may be repeated at 1-minute intervals.

Maximum total cumulative dose: 1 mg (usual total dose: 0.6-1 mg). In the event of resedation: Repeat doses may be given at 20-minute intervals as needed at 0.2 mg per minute to a maximum of 1 mg total dose and 3 mg in 1 hour.

Suspected benzodiazepine overdose: IV:

Initial dose: 0.2 mg over 30 seconds; if the desired level of consciousness is not obtained 30 seconds after the dose, 0.3 mg can be given over 30 seconds

Repeat doses: 0.5 mg over 30 seconds repeated at 1-minute intervals

Maximum total cumulative dose: 3 mg (usual total dose: 1-3 mg). Patients with a partial response at 3 mg may require (rare) additional titration up to a total dose of 5 mg (although doses >3 mg do not reliably produce additional effects). If a patient has not responded 5 minutes after cumulative dose of 5 mg, the major cause of sedation is not likely due to benzodiazepines. In the event of resedation, repeat doses may be given at 20-minute intervals if needed, at 0.5 mg per minute to a maximum of 1 mg total dose and 3 mg in 1 hour.

Geriatric Refer to adult dosing. No differences in safety or efficacy have been reported; however, increased sensitivity may occur in some elderly patients.

Pediatric Reversal of benzodiazepine when used in conscious sedation: Children ≥1 year: IV:

Initial dose: 0.01 mg/kg over 15 seconds (maximum: 0.2 mg)

Repeat doses (maximum: 4 doses): If desired level of consciousness is not obtained, 0.01 mg/kg (maximum: 0.2 mg) repeated at 1-minute intervals

Maximum total cumulative dose: 1 mg or 0.05 mg/kg (whichever is lower)

Mean total dose: 0.65 mg (range: 0.08-1 mg)

Renal Impairment No dosage adjustment provided in manufacturer's labeling; however, pharmacokinetics are not significantly affected by renal failure (CrCl <10 mL/minute) or hemodialysis.

Hepatic Impairment Initial reversal: No dosage adjustment necessary. Repeat doses: Reduce dose or frequency.

Mechanism of Action Competitively inhibits the activity at the benzodiazepine receptor site on the GABA/benzodiazepine receptor complex. Flumazenil does not antagonize the CNS effect of drugs affecting GABA-ergic neurons by means other than the benzodiazepine receptor (ethanol, barbiturates, general anesthetics) and does not reverse the effects of opioids

Contraindications Hypersensitivity to flumazenil, benzodiazepines, or any component of the formulation; patients given benzodiazepines for control of potentially life-threatening conditions (eg, control of intracranial pressure or status epilepticus); patients who are showing signs of serious cyclic-antidepressant overdosage

Warnings/Precautions [U.S. Boxed Warning]: Benzodiazepine reversal may result in seizures; seizures may occur more frequently in patients on benzodiazepines for long-term sedation or following tricyclic antidepressant overdose. Dose should be individualized and practitioners should be prepared to manage seizures. Seizures may also develop in patients with concurrent major sedative-hypnotic drug withdrawal, recent therapy with repeated doses of parenteral benzodiazepines, myoclonic jerking or seizure activity prior to flumazenil administration. Use with caution in patients relying on a benzodiazepine for seizure control. May cause CNS depression, which may impair physical or mental abilities; patients must be cautioned about performing tasks which require mental alertness (eg, operating machinery or driving) for 24 hours after discharge.

Flumazenil may not reliably reverse respiratory depression/hypoventilation. Flumazenil is not a substitute for evaluation of oxygenation; establishing an airway and assisting ventilation, as necessary, is always the initial step in overdose management. Resedation occurs more frequently in patients where a large single dose or cumulative dose of a benzodiazepine is administered along with a neuromuscular-blocking agent and multiple anesthetic agents. Flumazenil should be used with caution in the intensive care unit because of increased risk of unrecognized benzodiazepine dependence in such settings. Should not be used to diagnose benzodiazepine-induced sedation. Reverse neuromuscular blockade before considering use. Flumazenil does not antagonize the CNS effects of other GABA agonists (such as ethanol, barbiturates, or general anesthetics); nor does it reverse opioids. Flumazenil does not consistently reverse amnesia; patient may not recall verbal instructions after procedure.

Use with caution in patients with a history of panic disorder; may provoke panic attacks. Use caution in drug and ethanol-dependent patients; these patients may also be dependent on benzodiazepines. Not recommended for treatment of benzodiazepine dependence. Use with caution in patients with a head injury; may alter cerebral blood flow or precipitate convulsions in patients receiving benzodiazepines. Use caution in patients with mixed drug overdoses; toxic effects of other drugs taken may emerge once benzodiazepine effects are reversed. Use caution in hepatic dysfunction; repeated doses of the drug should be reduced in frequency or amount.

Drug Interactions

Metabolism/Transport Effects None known.

Avoid Concomitant Use There are no known interactions where it is recommended to avoid concomitant use.

Increased Effect/Toxicity There are no known significant interactions involving an increase in effect.

Decreased Effect

Flumazenil may decrease the levels/effects of: Hypnotics (Nonbenzodiazepine)

Dietary Considerations Avoid alcohol for the first 24 hours after administration or as long as the effects of benzodiazepines exist.

Pharmacodynamics/Kinetics

Onset of Action 1-2 minutes; 80% response within 3 minutes; Peak effect: 6-10 minutes

Duration of Action Resedation occurs after ~1 hour (range: 19-50 minutes); duration related to dose given and benzodiazepine plasma concentrations; reversal effects of flumazenil may wear off before effects of benzodiazepine

Half-life Elimination

Children: Terminal: 20-75 minutes (mean: 40 minutes)
Adults: Alpha: 4-11 minutes; Terminal: 40-80 minutes
Moderate hepatic dysfunction: 1.3 hours
Severe hepatic impairment: 2.4 hours

Pregnancy Risk Factor C

Pregnancy Considerations Teratogenic effects were not seen in animal reproduction studies. Embryocidal effects were seen at large doses. Use during labor and delivery is not recommended. In general, medications used as antidotes should take into consideration the health and prognosis of the mother; antidotes should be administered to pregnant women if there is a clear indication for use and should not be withheld because of fears of teratogenicity (Bailey 2003).

Breastfeeding Considerations It is not known if flumazenil is excreted in breast milk. The manufacturer recommends that caution be used if administering to breastfeeding women.

Dosage Forms

Solution, Intravenous:

Generic: 0.5 mg/5 mL (5 mL); 1 mg/10 mL (10 mL)

Dental Comment Sedation: Patients should be monitored for at least 1 hour following administration of flumazenil to ensure full recovery. Flumazenil should only be used in an emergency situation and not as a means of hastening recovery from conscious sedation. When used to hasten recovery, emergence can be sudden and unpleasant. Flumazenil should be used with caution in patients routinely taking benzodiazepines for other therapeutic uses, withdrawal symptoms will be induced.

Flunarizine (floo NAR i zeen)

Brand Names: Canada Novo-Flunarizine

Pharmacologic Category Calcium Channel Blocker

Use Note: Not approved in the US

Migraine: Prophylaxis of migraine (with and without aura) in patients with frequent and severe attacks, who have not responded satisfactorily to other treatments, and/or do not tolerate other therapy (due to unacceptable adverse effects).

Limitation of use: Not indicated for treatment of acute attacks.

Local Anesthetic/Vasoconstrictor Precautions No information available to require special precautions

Effects on Dental Treatment Key adverse event(s) related to dental treatment: Xerostomia and changes in salivation (normal salivary flow resumes upon discontinuation).

Effects on Bleeding No information available to require special precautions

Adverse Reactions Frequency not always defined.

Central nervous system: Drowsiness (20%), anxiety, depression, dizziness, extrapyramidal reaction, fatigue, insomnia, motor dysfunction, sedation, sleep disorder, vertigo
Dermatologic: Skin rash
Endocrine & metabolic: Weight gain (15%), galactorrhea, increased serum prolactin, menstrual disease
Gastrointestinal: Heartburn, increased appetite, nausea, stomach pain, vomiting, xerostomia
Neuromuscular & skeletal: Myalgia, weakness

General Dosage Range Oral: *Adults <65 years:* 10 mg once daily

Mechanism of Action Flunarizine is a selective calcium channel blocker that prevents cellular calcium overload by reducing excessive transmembrane calcium influx; also has antihistamine properties. Has greater effect on decreasing the frequency of migraine attacks than on decreasing the severity or duration of attacks.

Pharmacodynamics/Kinetics

Half-life Elimination Variable; Alpha: ~2.4 to 5.5 hours (single dose); Beta: ~4 days (single dose), ~19 days (multidose)

Time to Peak 2 to 4 hours

Pregnancy Considerations Adverse events have been observed in animal reproduction studies.

Product Availability Not available in the US

Flunisolide (Nasal) (floo NISS oh lide)

Brand Names: Canada Apo-Flunisolide®; Nasalide®; Rhinalar®

Pharmacologic Category Corticosteroid, Nasal

Use Rhinitis: Management of the nasal symptoms associated with seasonal or perennial rhinitis

Local Anesthetic/Vasoconstrictor Precautions No information available to require special precautions

Effects on Dental Treatment Key adverse event(s) related to dental treatment: *Candida* infections of the nose, atrophic rhinitis, sneezing, nasal congestion, nasal dryness and burning, increased susceptibility to infections, dry throat, epistaxis

Effects on Bleeding No information available to require special precautions

Adverse Reactions

Frequency not always defined.

>10%:

Dermatologic: Burning sensation of the nose (≤13%)
Respiratory: Nasal congestion (15%), stinging sensation of the nose (≤13%)

1% to 10%:

Central nervous system: Anosmia
Respiratory: Dry nose, nasal mucosa irritation, rhinitis, sneezing

<1%, postmarketing, and/or case reports: Nasal mucosa ulcer

General Dosage Range Intranasal:

Children and Adolescents 6 to 14 years: 1 to 2 sprays 2 to 3 times/day (maximum: 4 sprays/day in each nostril)
Adolescents ≥15 years and Adults: 2 sprays twice daily (maximum: 8 sprays/day in each nostril)

Mechanism of Action Decreases inflammation by suppression of migration of polymorphonuclear leukocytes and reversal of increased capillary permeability; does not depress hypothalamus

Pregnancy Risk Factor C

Pregnancy Considerations Adverse effects were observed in some animal reproduction studies. Intranasal corticosteroids are recommended for the treatment of rhinitis during pregnancy; the lowest effective dose should be used (NAEPP, 2005; Wallace, 2008).

Flunisolide (Oral Inhalation) (floo NISS oh lide)

Related Information

Respiratory Diseases *on page 1777*

Brand Names: US Aerospan

Pharmacologic Category Corticosteroid, Inhalant (Oral)

Use Maintenance treatment and prophylactic therapy for asthma; to reduce or eliminate the need for oral corticosteroids in steroid-dependent asthma patients

Guideline recommendations: A low-dose inhaled corticosteroid (*in addition to an as-needed short acting beta$_2$-agonist*) is the initial preferred long term control medication for children, adolescents, and adult patients with persistent asthma who are candidates for treatment according to a step-wise treatment approach (GINA 2016; NAEPP 2007).

Local Anesthetic/Vasoconstrictor Precautions

No information available to require special precautions

Effects on Dental Treatment Key adverse event(s) related to dental treatment: *Candida* infections of the pharynx, sore throat, bitter taste, palpitations, dizziness, headache, nervousness, GI irritation, sneezing, coughing, upper respiratory tract infection, bronchitis, increased susceptibility to infections, xerostomia (normal salivary flow resumes upon discontinuation), dry throat, loss of taste, and diaphoresis.

Effects on Bleeding No information available to require special precautions

Adverse Reactions Frequency not always defined.

>10%:

Central nervous system: Headache (9% to 14%)

Respiratory: Pharyngitis (17% to 18%), rhinitis (4% to 16%)

1% to 10%:

Cardiovascular: Chest pain (1% to 3%), edema (1% to 3%), capillary fragility (≥1%), chest tightness (≥1%), hypertension (≥1%), palpitations (≥1%), peripheral edema (≥1%), tachycardia (≥1%)

Central nervous system: Pain (2% to 5%), dizziness (1% to 3%), insomnia (1% to 3%), migraine (1% to 3%), voice disorder (1% to 3%), anosmia (≥1%), anxiety (≥1%), depression (≥1%), fatigue (≥1%), hyperactivity (≥1%), hypoactivity (≥1%), irritability (≥1%), malaise (≥1%), mood changes (≥1%), numbness (≥1%), shakiness (≥1%), vertigo (≥1%)

Dermatologic: Skin rash (2% to 4%), erythema multiforme (1% to 3%), acne vulgaris (≥1%), diaphoresis (≥1%), eczema (≥1%), pruritus (≥1%), urticaria (≥1%)

Endocrine & metabolic: Weight gain (≥1%), adrenal suppression, adrenocortical insufficiency, growth suppression (children and adolescents), hypercorticoidism

Gastrointestinal: Vomiting (≤5%), dyspepsia (2% to 4%), abdominal pain (1% to 3%), diarrhea (1% to 3%), dysgeusia (1% to 3%), gastroenteritis (1% to 3%), nausea (1% to 3%), oral candidiasis (1% to 3%), ageusia (≥1%), constipation (≥1%), decreased appetite (≥1%), epigastric fullness (≥1%), flatulence (≥1%), glossitis (≥1%), heartburn (≥1%), mouth irritation (≥1%), sore throat (≥1%), stomach discomfort (≥1%), oropharyngeal candidiasis

Genitourinary: Urinary tract infection (1% to 4%), dysmenorrhea (1% to 3%), vaginitis (1% to 3%)

Hematologic & oncologic: Lymphadenopathy (≥1%)

Hypersensitivity: Hypersensitivity reaction (4% to 5%)

Infection: Bacterial infection (4%), infection (1% to 3%), cold symptoms (≥1%), influenza (≥1%)

Neuromuscular & skeletal: Back pain (1% to 3%), myalgia (1% to 3%), neck pain (1% to 3%), weakness (≥1%), decreased bone mineral density

Ophthalmic: Conjunctivitis (1% to 3%), blurred vision (≥1%), eye discomfort (≥1%), eye infection (≥1%), cataract, glaucoma, increased intraocular pressure

Otic: Otalgia (1% to 3%), otitis (≥1%)

Respiratory: Cough (9%), sinusitis (7% to 9%), epistaxis (3%), bronchitis (1% to 3%), laryngitis (1% to 3%), bronchospasm (≥1%), chest congestion (≥1%), dry throat (≥1%), dyspnea (≥1%), hoarseness (≥1%), increased bronchial secretions (≥1%), nasal congestion (≥1%), nasal mucosa irritation (≥1%), pleurisy (≥1%), pneumonia (≥1%), rhinorrhea (≥1%), sinus congestion (≥1%), sinus discomfort (≥1%), sinus drainage (≥1%), sinus infection (≥1%), sneezing (≥1%), throat irritation (≥1%), upper respiratory tract infection (≥1%), wheezing (≥1%), exacerbation of asthma

Miscellaneous: Fever (1% to 7%)

General Dosage Range Oral inhalation:

Children 6-11 years: 80 mcg twice daily (maximum: 160 mcg twice daily)

Children ≥12 years, Adolescents, and Adults: 160 mcg twice daily (maximum: 320 mcg twice daily)

Mechanism of Action Decreases airway inflammation by suppression of endogenous inflammatory mediators (kinins, histamine, liposomal enzymes, prostaglandins). Inhibits inflammatory cell migration and reverses increased capillary permeability to decrease access of inflammatory cells to the site of inflammation; does not depress hypothalamus.

Pharmacodynamics/Kinetics

Half-life Elimination 1.3-1.7 hours

Time to Peak Within 5-10 minutes

Pregnancy Risk Factor C

Pregnancy Considerations Adverse events were observed in animal reproduction studies. Hypoadrenalism may occur in infants born to mothers receiving corticosteroids during pregnancy. Based on available data, an overall increased risk of congenital malformations or a decrease in fetal growth has not been associated with maternal use of inhaled corticosteroids during pregnancy (Bakhireva, 2005; NAEPP, 2005; Namazy, 2004). Uncontrolled asthma is associated with adverse events in pregnancy (increased risk of perinatal mortality, pre-eclampsia, preterm birth, low birth weight infants). Inhaled corticosteroids are recommended for the treatment of asthma during pregnancy (most information available using budesonide) (ACOG, 2008; NAEPP, 2005).

Fluocinolone (Topical) (floo oh SIN oh lone)

Brand Names: US Capex; Derma-Smoothe/FS Body; Derma-Smoothe/FS Scalp; Fluocinolone Acetonide Body; Fluocinolone Acetonide Scalp; Synalar; Synalar (Cream); Synalar (Ointment); Synalar TS; Xilapak

Brand Names: Canada Derma-Smoothe/FS; Fluoderm; Synalar

Generic Availability (US) May be product dependent

Pharmacologic Category Corticosteroid, Topical

Dental Use Relief of inflammatory and pruritic manifestations (low, medium, high potency topical corticosteroid)

Use

Body oil: Treatment of moderate to severe atopic dermatitis in pediatric patients ≥3 months; treatment of atopic dermatitis in adults

Cream, ointment, topical solution: Relief of inflammatory and pruritic manifestations of corticosteroid-responsive dermatoses

Scalp oil: Treatment of psoriasis of the scalp in adults

Shampoo: Treatment of seborrheic dermatitis of the scalp

Local Anesthetic/Vasoconstrictor Precautions No information available to require special precautions

Effects on Dental Treatment No significant effects or complications reported

Effects on Bleeding No information available to require special precautions

Adverse Reactions Frequency not defined.

Cardiovascular: Intracranial hypertension (rare)

Central nervous system: Telangiectasia

Dermatologic: Acneiform eruptions, allergic contact dermatitis, atopic dermatitis (secondary), burning, dryness, erythema, folliculitis, irritation, itching, hypertrichosis, hypopigmentation, keratosis pilaris, miliaria, papules, perioral dermatitis, pustules, shiny skin, skin atrophy, striae

Endocrine & metabolic: Cushing's syndrome, HPA axis suppression

Otic: Ear infection

Miscellaneous: Herpes simplex, secondary infection

Dental Usual Dosage Inflammatory and pruritic manifestations: Adults: Topical: Apply to oral lesion 4 times/day, after meals and at bedtime

Dosing

Adult & Geriatric Note: Dosage should be based on severity of disease and patient response; use smallest amount for shortest period of time. Therapy should be discontinued when control is achieved.

Atopic dermatitis: Topical: Body oil: Apply thin film to affected area 3 times daily

Corticosteroid-responsive dermatoses: Topical: Cream, ointment, solution: Apply a thin layer to affected area 2 to 4 times daily; may use occlusive dressings to manage psoriasis or recalcitrant conditions

Scalp psoriasis: Topical: Scalp oil: Massage thoroughly into wet or dampened hair/scalp; cover with shower cap. Leave on overnight (or for at least 4 hours). Remove by washing hair with shampoo and rinsing thoroughly.

Seborrheic dermatitis of the scalp: Topical: Shampoo: Apply no more than 1 ounce to scalp once daily; work into lather and allow to remain on scalp for ~5 minutes. Remove from hair and scalp by rinsing thoroughly with water.

Pediatric Note: Dosage should be based on severity of disease and patient response; use smallest amount for shortest period of time. Therapy should be discontinued when control is achieved.

Atopic dermatitis, moderate to severe: Topical: Body oil: Infants ≥3 months, Children, and Adolescents: Moisten skin; apply a thin film to affected area twice daily; do not use for longer than 4 weeks

Corticosteroid-responsive dermatoses: Topical: Cream, ointment, solution: Children and Adolescents: Refer to adult dosing.

Renal Impairment There are no dosage adjustments provided in the manufacturer's labeling.

Hepatic Impairment There are no dosage adjustments provided in the manufacturer's labeling.

Mechanism of Action Topical corticosteroids have anti-inflammatory, antipruritic, and vasoconstrictive properties. May depress the formation, release, and activity of endogenous chemical mediators of inflammation (kinins, histamine, liposomal enzymes, prostaglandins) through the induction of phospholipase A_2 inhibitory proteins (lipocortins) and sequential inhibition of the release of arachidonic acid. Fluocinolone has low to intermediate range potency (dosage-form dependent).

Contraindications

Hypersensitivity to fluocinolone or any component of the formulation

Documentation of allergenic cross-reactivity for corticosteroids is limited. However, because of similarities in chemical structure and/or pharmacologic actions, the possibility of cross-sensitivity cannot be ruled out with certainty.

Warnings/Precautions Topical corticosteroids may be absorbed percutaneously. Absorption of topical corticosteroids may cause manifestations of Cushing syndrome, hyperglycemia, or glycosuria. Absorption is increased by the use of occlusive dressings, application to denuded skin, or application to large surface areas. May cause hypercorticism or suppression of hypothalamic-pituitary-adrenal (HPA) axis, particularly in younger children or in patients receiving high doses for prolonged periods. HPA axis suppression may lead to adrenal crisis. HPA axis suppression, intracranial hypertension, and Cushing syndrome have been reported in children receiving topical corticosteroids. Prolonged use may affect growth velocity; growth should be routinely monitored in pediatric patients. Allergic contact dermatitis can occur, it is usually diagnosed by failure to heal rather than clinical exacerbation. Prolonged treatment with corticosteroids has been associated with the development of Kaposi sarcoma (case reports); if noted, discontinuation of therapy should be considered (Goedert 2002). Local adverse reactions may occur (eg, skin atrophy, striae, telangiectasias, burning, itching, irritation, dryness, folliculitis, acneiform eruptions, hypopigmentation, perioral dermatitis, allergic contact dermatitis, secondary infection miliaria); may be irreversible. Local adverse reactions are more likely to occur with occlusive and/or prolonged use. If irritation develops, discontinued use and institute appropriate therapy. Concomitant skin infections may be present or develop during therapy; discontinue if dermatological infection persists despite appropriate antimicrobial therapy. Not for oral, ophthalmic, or intravaginal use; do not apply to the face, axillae, groin, or diaper area unless directed by health care provider. Use the least amount needed to cover the affected area; discontinue when control is achieved. If improvement is not seen within 2 weeks, reassess.

Derma-Smoothe/FS products may contain peanut oil; use caution in peanut-sensitive individuals.

Shampoo: Has not been proven to be effective in corticosteroid responsive dermatoses other than seborrheic dermatitis of the scalp.

Drug Interactions

Metabolism/Transport Effects None known.

Avoid Concomitant Use

Avoid concomitant use of Fluocinolone (Topical) with any of the following: Aldesleukin

Increased Effect/Toxicity

Fluocinolone (Topical) may increase the levels/effects of: Ceritinib; Deferasirox

Decreased Effect
Fluocinolone (Topical) may decrease the levels/effects of: Aldesleukin; Corticorelin; Hyaluronidase

Pregnancy Risk Factor C

Pregnancy Considerations Adverse events have been observed with corticosteroids in animal reproduction studies. In general, the use of topical corticosteroids during pregnancy is not considered to have significant risk; however, intrauterine growth retardation in the infant has been reported (rare). The use of large amounts or for prolonged periods of time should be avoided (Reed 1997).

Breastfeeding Considerations Systemic corticosteroids are excreted in human milk. It is not known if sufficient quantities of fluocinolone are absorbed following topical administration to produce detectable amounts in breast milk. Hypertension in the breastfeeding infant has been reported following corticosteroid ointment applied to the nipples (Reed 1997). The manufacturer recommends that caution be exercised when administering fluocinolone to breastfeeding women.

Dosage Forms

Cream, External:
Synalar: 0.025% (120 g)
Generic: 0.01% (15 g, 60 g); 0.025% (15 g, 60 g)

Kit, External:
Synalar (Cream): 0.025%
Synalar (Ointment): 0.025%
Synalar TS: 0.01%
Xilapak: 0.01%

Oil, External:
Derma-Smoothe/FS Body: 0.01% (118.28 mL)
Derma-Smoothe/FS Scalp: 0.01% (118.28 mL)
Fluocinolone Acetonide Body: 0.01% (118.28 mL)
Fluocinolone Acetonide Scalp: 0.01% (118.28 mL)

Ointment, External:
Synalar: 0.025% (120 g)
Generic: 0.025% (15 g, 60 g)

Shampoo, External:
Capex: 0.01% (120 mL)

Solution, External:
Synalar: 0.01% (60 mL, 90 mL)
Generic: 0.01% (60 mL)

Fluocinonide (floo oh SIN oh nide)

Related Information
Ulcerative, Erosive, and Painful Oral Mucosal Disorders *on page 1853*

Related Sample Prescriptions
Ulcerative and Erosive Disorders - Sample Prescriptions *on page 43*

Brand Names: US Vanos

Brand Names: Canada Lidemol; Lidex; Lyderm; Tiamol; Topactin; Topsyn

Generic Availability (US) Yes

Pharmacologic Category Corticosteroid, Topical

Dental Use Relief of inflammatory and pruritic manifestations (high potency topical corticosteroid)

Use Inflammatory and pruritic dermatologic conditions: Relief of the inflammatory and pruritic manifestations of corticosteroid-responsive dermatoses.

Local Anesthetic/Vasoconstrictor Precautions No information available to require special precautions

Effects on Dental Treatment No significant effects or complications reported

Effects on Bleeding No information available to require special precautions

Adverse Reactions Frequency not defined.
Central nervous system: Intracranial hypertension, localized burning
Dermatologic: Acne vulgaris, allergic dermatitis, atrophic striae, contact dermatitis, folliculitis, hypertrichosis, hypopigmentation, maceration of the skin, miliaria, perioral dermatitis, pruritus, skin atrophy, telangiectasia, xeroderma
Endocrine & metabolic: Cushing's syndrome, glycosuria, growth suppression, HPA-axis suppression, hyperglycemia
Infection: Secondary infection
Local: Local irritation

Dental Usual Dosage Pruritus and inflammation: Children and Adults: Topical (0.05% cream): Apply thin layer to affected area 2-4 times/day depending on the severity of the condition. Therapy should be discontinued when control is achieved; if no improvement is seen, reassessment of diagnosis may be necessary.

Dosing

Adult & Geriatric

Atopic dermatitis: Topical:
Cream, gel, ointment, solution (0.05%): Apply thin layer to affected area 2 to 4 times daily.
Cream (0.1%): Apply thin layer to affected areas once daily. Not recommended for use >2 consecutive weeks or >60 g/week total exposure. Therapy should be discontinued when control is achieved; if no improvement is seen within 2 weeks, reassessment of diagnosis may be necessary.

Psoriasis: Topical:
Cream, gel, ointment, solution (0.05%): Apply thin layer to affected area 2 to 4 times daily.
Cream (0.1%): Apply a thin layer once or twice daily to affected areas. Not recommended for use >2 consecutive weeks or >60 g/week total exposure. Therapy should be discontinued when control is achieved; if no improvement is seen within 2 weeks, reassess diagnosis.

Other inflammatory and pruritic dermatologic conditions besides atopic dermatitis or psoriasis: Topical:
Cream, gel, ointment, solution (0.05%): Apply thin layer to affected area 2 to 4 times daily.
Cream (0.1%): Apply thin layer to affected area once or twice daily. Not recommended for use >2 consecutive weeks or >60 g/week total exposure. Therapy should be discontinued when control is achieved; if no improvement is seen within 2 weeks, reassess diagnosis.

Pediatric

Atopic dermatitis, psoriasis, and other inflammatory and pruritic dermatologic conditions:
Children and Adolescents: Topical: Cream, gel, ointment, solution (0.05%): Refer to adult dosing.
Children ≥12 years and Adolescents: Topical: Cream (0.1%): Refer to adult dosing.

Renal Impairment There are no dosage adjustments provided in the manufacturer's labeling.

Hepatic Impairment There are no dosage adjustments provided in the manufacturer's labeling.

Mechanism of Action Topical corticosteroids have anti-inflammatory, antipruritic, and vasoconstrictive properties. May depress the formation, release, and activity of endogenous chemical mediators of inflammation (kinins, histamine, liposomal enzymes, prostaglandins) through the induction of phospholipase A_2 inhibitory proteins (lipocortins) and sequential inhibition of the release of arachidonic acid. Fluocinonide is fluorinated corticosteroid considered to be of high potency.

Contraindications Hypersensitivity to fluocinonide or any component of the formulation

Warnings/Precautions May cause hypercorticism or suppression of hypothalamic-pituitary-adrenal (HPA) axis, particularly in younger children or in patients receiving high doses for prolonged periods. HPA axis suppression may lead to adrenal crisis. Absorption of topical corticosteroids may cause manifestations of Cushing syndrome, hyperglycemia, or glycosuria. Absorption is increased by the use of occlusive dressings, application to denuded skin, or application to large surface areas.

Allergic contact dermatitis can occur, it is usually diagnosed by failure to heal rather than clinical exacerbation. Local adverse reactions may occur (eg, skin atrophy, striae, telangiectasias, burning, itching, irritation, dryness, folliculitis, acneiform eruptions, hypopigmentation, perioral dermatitis, allergic contact dermatitis, secondary infection miliaria); may be irreversible. Local adverse reactions are more likely to occur with occlusive and/or prolonged use. If irritation develops, discontinued use and institute appropriate therapy. Concomitant skin infections may be present or develop during therapy; discontinue if dermatological infection persists despite appropriate antimicrobial therapy. Prolonged treatment with corticosteroids has been associated with the development of Kaposi sarcoma (case reports); if noted, discontinuation of therapy should be considered. Lower-strength formulations (0.05%) may be used cautiously on face or opposing skin surfaces that may rub or touch (eg, skin folds of the groin, axilla, and breasts); higher-strength (0.1%) should not be used on the face, groin, or axillae. Children may absorb proportionally larger amounts after topical application and may be more prone to systemic effects. HPA axis suppression, intracranial hypertension, and Cushing syndrome have been reported in children receiving topical corticosteroids. Prolonged use may affect growth velocity; growth should be routinely monitored in pediatric patients. Treatment beyond 2 consecutive weeks with the 0.1% cream is not recommended and the total dosage should not exceed 60 g per week; therapy should be discontinued when control of the disease is achieved; if no improvement is seen within 2 weeks, reassess diagnosis; do not use more than half of the 120 g tube per week; should not be used in the treatment of rosacea or perioral dermatitis.

Drug Interactions

Metabolism/Transport Effects None known.

Avoid Concomitant Use

Avoid concomitant use of Fluocinonide with any of the following: Aldesleukin

Increased Effect/Toxicity

Fluocinonide may increase the levels/effects of: Ceritinib; Deferasirox

Decreased Effect

Fluocinonide may decrease the levels/effects of: Aldesleukin; Corticorelin; Hyaluronidase

Pregnancy Risk Factor C

Pregnancy Considerations Adverse events have been observed with corticosteroids in animal reproduction studies. Topical corticosteroids are preferred over systemic for treating conditions, such as psoriasis or atopic dermatitis in pregnant women; high-potency corticosteroids are not recommended during the first trimester. Topical products are not recommended for extensive use, in large quantities, or for long periods of time in pregnant women (Bae 2011; Koutroulis 2011; Leachman 2006). Information specific to the use of fluocinonide during pregnancy is limited (Valkova 2006).

Breastfeeding Considerations Systemic corticosteroids are excreted in human milk. It is not known if sufficient quantities of fluocinonide are absorbed following topical administration to produce detectable amounts in breast milk. Do not apply topical corticosteroids to nipples; hypertension was noted in a breastfeeding infant exposed to a topical corticosteroid while breastfeeding (Leachman 2006).

The manufacturer recommends that caution be exercised when administering fluocinonide 0.05% to nursing women. Because maternal use of systemic corticosteroids have the potential to cause adverse events in a breastfeeding infant (eg, growth suppression, interfere with endogenous corticosteroid production), the manufacturer recommends that a decision be made whether to discontinue breastfeeding or to discontinue the drug, taking into account the importance of treatment to the mother when using the fluocinonide 0.1%.

Dosage Forms

Cream, External:

Vanos: 0.1% (30 g, 60 g, 120 g)

Generic: 0.05% (15 g, 30 g, 60 g, 120 g); 0.1% (30 g, 60 g, 120 g)

Gel, External:

Generic: 0.05% (15 g, 30 g, 60 g)

Ointment, External:

Generic: 0.05% (15 g, 30 g, 60 g)

Solution, External:

Generic: 0.05% (20 mL, 60 mL)

Fluoride (FLOR ide)

Related Information

Dentifrices Without Sodium Lauryl Sulfate (SLS)[a] *on page 1911*

Dentin Hypersensitivity, Acid Erosion, High Caries Index, Management of Alveolar Osteitis, and Xerostomia *on page 1857*

Brand Names: US Act Kids [OTC]; Act Restoring [OTC]; Act Total Care Dry Mouth [OTC]; Act Total Care Sensitive [OTC]; Act Total Care [OTC]; Act [OTC]; CaviRinse [DSC]; Clinpro 5000; ControlRx [DSC]; Denta 5000 Plus; DentaGel; Fluor-A-Day; Fluorabon; Fluoridex; Fluoridex Daily Renewal; Fluoridex Enhanced Whitening; Fluorinse; Fluoritab; Flura-Drops; Gel-Kam Rinse; Gel-Kam [OTC]; Just For Kids [OTC]; Lozi-Flur; NeutraCare; NeutraGard Advanced; Omni Gel [OTC]; OrthoWash; parodontax [OTC]; PerioMed; Phos-Flur; Phos-Flur Rinse [OTC]; PreviDent; PreviDent 5000 Booster; PreviDent 5000 Booster Plus; PreviDent 5000 Dry Mouth; PreviDent 5000 Plus; Sensodyne Repair & Protect [OTC]; StanGard Perio

Brand Names: Canada Fluor-A-Day

Generic Availability (US) Yes: Excludes lozenge

Pharmacologic Category Nutritional Supplement

Dental Use Prevention of dental caries

Use Prevention of dental caries

Local Anesthetic/Vasoconstrictor Precautions No information available to require special precautions

Effects on Dental Treatment Key adverse event(s) related to dental treatment: Products containing stannous fluoride may stain teeth. See Dental Comment.

Effects on Bleeding No information available to require special precautions

Adverse Reactions Frequency not defined.

Dermatologic: Skin rash
Gastrointestinal: Dental discoloration (with products containing stannous fluoride; temporary), nausea
Hypersensitivity: Hypersensitivity reaction

Dosing

Adult & Geriatric

Cream or paste:

Clinpro 5000 paste, Control Rx 1.1%, Denta 5000 Plus: Once daily, in place of conventional toothpaste, brush teeth with a thin ribbon or pea-sized amount of paste for at least 2 minutes. Brush teeth with cream or paste once daily regardless of fluoride content of drinking water

Prevident 5000 Sensitive: Twice daily, brush teeth with a 1 inch strip of toothpaste for at least 1 minute. After brushing, expectorate and rinse mouth thoroughly. Brush teeth twice daily regardless of fluoride content of drinking water

Dental rinse or gel:

ACT Restoring 0.02% rinse, ACT Total Care 0.02% rinse: Twice daily after brushing, rinse 10 mL around and between teeth for 1 minute, then spit. Do not eat, drink, or rinse mouth for at least 30 minutes after treatment; do not swallow

ACT 0.05% rinse, Phos-Flur Rinse: Once daily after brushing, rinse 10 mL around and between teeth for 1 minute, then spit. Do not eat, drink, or rinse mouth for at least 30 minutes after treatment; do not swallow

Cavirinse, PreviDent rinse: Once weekly, rinse 10 mL vigorously around and between teeth for 1 minute, then spit; this should be done preferably at bedtime, after thoroughly brushing teeth; do not swallow. For maximum benefit with PreviDent rinse, do not eat, drink, or rinse mouth for at least 30 minutes after treatment.

Gel-Kam rinse: After diluting solution as directed, rinse with 15 mL for 1 minute at least daily, then spit. Repeat with remaining solution.

Lozenge: Lozi-FlurOne lozenge daily regardless of fluoride content of drinking water

Pediatric Oral: Children 6 months to 16 years: Fluor-A-Day, Fluorabon, Fluoritab drops, Flura-drops, Loziflur:

The recommended daily dose of oral fluoride supplement (mg), based on fluoride ion content (ppm) in drinking water (2.2 mg of sodium fluoride is equivalent to 1 mg of fluoride ion): See table.

Fluoride Ion

Fluoride Content of Drinking Water	Daily Dose, Oral (mg)
<0.3 ppm	
Birth - 6 mo	None
6 mo - 3 y	0.25
3-6 y	0.5
6-16 y	1
0.3-0.6 ppm	
Birth - 6 mo	None
6 mo - 3 y	None
3-6 y	0.25
6-16 y	0.5

Table from: Recommended dosage schedule of The American Dental Association, The American Academy of Pediatric Dentistry, and The American Academy of Pediatrics

Mechanism of Action Promotes remineralization of decalcified enamel; inhibits the cariogenic microbial process in dental plaque; increases tooth resistance to acid dissolution

Contraindications

Fluor-A-Day: When fluoride content of drinking water exceeds 0.6 ppm; patients with arthralgia, GI ulceration, chronic renal insufficiency and failure, or osteomalacia

Fluorabon: When fluoride content of drinking water exceeds 0.6 ppm

Fluoritab: Patients with dental fluorosis

Flura-Drops, Loziflur: When fluoride content of drinking water is ≥0.3 ppm

Warnings/Precautions Prolonged ingestion with excessive doses may result in dental fluorosis and osseous changes; do **not** exceed recommended dosage. Some products contain tartrazine.

Benzyl alcohol and derivatives: Some dosage forms may contain sodium benzoate/benzoic acid; benzoic acid (benzoate) is a metabolite of benzyl alcohol; large amounts of benzyl alcohol (≥99 mg/kg/day) have been associated with a potentially fatal toxicity ("gasping syndrome") in neonates; the "gasping syndrome" consists of metabolic acidosis, respiratory distress, gasping respirations, CNS dysfunction (including convulsions, intracranial hemorrhage), hypotension, and cardiovascular collapse (AAP ["Inactive" 1997]; CDC, 1982); some data suggests that benzoate displaces bilirubin from protein binding sites (Ahlfors, 2001); avoid or use dosage forms containing benzyl alcohol derivative with caution in neonates. See manufacturer's labeling.

Polysorbate 80: Some dosage forms may contain polysorbate 80 (also known as Tweens). Hypersensitivity reactions, usually a delayed reaction, have been reported following exposure to pharmaceutical products containing polysorbate 80 in certain individuals (Isaksson, 2002; Lucente 2000; Shelley, 1995). Thrombocytopenia, ascites, pulmonary deterioration, and renal and hepatic failure have been reported in premature neonates after receiving parenteral products containing polysorbate 80 (Alade, 1986; CDC, 1984). See manufacturer's labeling.

Drug Interactions

Metabolism/Transport Effects None known.

Avoid Concomitant Use There are no known interactions where it is recommended to avoid concomitant use.

Increased Effect/Toxicity There are no known significant interactions involving an increase in effect.

Decreased Effect There are no known significant interactions involving a decrease in effect.

Dietary Considerations Do not administer with dairy products.

Pregnancy Risk Factor B

Pregnancy Considerations Fluoride crosses the placenta and can be found in the fetal circulation (IOM, 1997). Adverse events have not been observed in animal reproduction studies; epidemiological studies in areas with high levels of fluorinated water have not shown an increase in adverse effects. Heavy exposure *in utero* may be linked to skeletal fluorosis seen later in childhood.

Breastfeeding Considerations Low concentrations of fluoride can be found in breast milk and the amount is not significantly affected by supplementation or concentrations in drinking water (IOM, 1997). The manufacturer recommends that caution be exercised when administering fluoride to nursing women.

Dosage Forms

Cream, oral:

Denta 5000 Plus: 1.1% (51 g)

PreviDent 5000 Plus: 1.1% (51 g)

Gel, oral:

PreviDent 5000 Booster: 1.1% (100 mL, 106 mL)

PreviDent 5000 Booster Plus: 1.1% (100 mL)

PreviDent 5000 Dry Mouth: 1.1% (100 mL)

Gel, topical:

DentaGel: 1.1% (56 g)

Gel-Kam [OTC]: 0.4% (129 g)

Just For Kids [OTC]: 0.4% (122 g)

NeutraCare: 1.1% (60 g)

NeutraGard Advanced: 1.1% (60 g)

Omni Gel [OTC]: 0.4% (122 g); 0.4% (122 g)

Phos-Flur: 1.1% (51 g)

PreviDent: 1.1% (56 g)

Liquid, oral:

Fluoritab: 0.125 mg/drop

Lozenge, oral:

Lozi-Flur: 2.21 mg (90s)

Paste, oral:

Clinpro 5000: 1.1% (113 g)

Fluoridex: 1.1% (112 g)

Fluoridex Enhanced Whitening: 1.1% (112 g)

parodontax [OTC]: 0.454% (96.4 g)

Sensodyne Repair & Protect [OTC]: 0.454% (96.4 g)

Solution, oral:

Act [OTC]: 0.05% (532 mL)

Act Kids [OTC]: 0.05% (500 mL, 532 mL)

Act Restoring [OTC]: 0.02% (1000 mL); 0.05% (532 mL)

Act Total Care [OTC]: 0.05% (90 mL, 532 mL, 1000 mL)

Fluor-A-Day: 0.278 mg/drop (30 mL)

Fluorabon: 0.55 mg/0.6 mL (60 mL)

Fluoridex Daily Renewal: 0.63% (248 mL)

Fluorinse: 0.2% (480 mL)

Flura-Drops: 0.55 mg/drop (24 mL)

Gel-Kam Rinse: 0.63% (300 mL)

OrthoWash: 0.044% (480 mL)

PerioMed: 0.63% (284 mL)

Phos-Flur Rinse [OTC]: 0.044% (473 mL, 500 mL)

PreviDent: 0.2% (473 mL)

StanGard Perio: 0.63% (284 mL)

Tablet, chewable, oral:

Fluor-A-Day: 0.55 mg, 2.2 mg

Fluoritab: 1.1 mg, 2.2 mg

Generic: 0.55 mg, 1.1 mg, 2.2 mg

Dental Comment Neutral pH fluoride preparations are preferred in patients with oral mucositis to reduce tissue irritation; long-term use of acidulated fluorides has been associated with enamel demineralization and damage to porcelain crowns

Fluorometholone (flure oh METH oh lone)

Brand Names: US Flarex; FML; FML Forte; FML Liquifilm

Brand Names: Canada Flarex; FML; FML Forte; PMS-Fluorometholone; Sandoz-Fluorometholone

Pharmacologic Category Corticosteroid, Ophthalmic

Use Ocular inflammation: Treatment of steroid-responsive inflammatory conditions of the eye

Local Anesthetic/Vasoconstrictor Precautions No information available to require special precautions

Effects on Dental Treatment No significant effects or complications reported

Effects on Bleeding No information available to require special precautions

Adverse Reactions Frequency not defined.

Dermatologic: Skin rash

Endocrine & metabolic: Hypercorticoidism (rare)

Gastrointestinal: Dysgeusia

Hypersensitivity: Hypersensitivity reaction

Ophthalmic: Bacterial eye infection (secondary), blurred vision, burning sensation of eyes, cataract, decreased visual acuity, erythema of eyelid, eye discharge, eye irritation, eyelid edema, eye pain, eye pruritus, foreign body sensation of eye, fungal eye infection (secondary), glaucoma, increased intraocular pressure, increased lacrimation, optic nerve damage, stinging of eyes, swelling of eye, viral eye infection (secondary), visual field defect, wound healing impairment

General Dosage Range Ophthalmic:

Ointment: *Children ≥2 years, Adolescents, and Adults:* Apply small amount (~1/2" ribbon) every 4 hours (initial: 24 to 48 hours) **or** 1 to 3 times daily

Suspension:

Children ≥2 years, Adolescents, and Adults (FML, FML Forte): Instill 1 drop every 4 hours (initial: 24 to 48 hours) **or** 1 drop 2 to 4 times daily

Adults (Flarex): Instill 2 drops (initial: 24 to 48 hours) **or** 1 to 2 drops 2 to 4 times daily

Mechanism of Action Corticosteroids inhibit the inflammatory response including edema, capillary dilation, leukocyte migration, and scar formation. Fluorometholone penetrates cells readily to induce the production of lipocortins. These proteins modulate the activity of prostaglandins and leukotrienes.

Pregnancy Risk Factor C

Pregnancy Considerations Teratogenic effects were observed in animal reproduction studies following use of ophthalmic fluorometholone. The extent of systemic absorption following topical application of the ophthalmic drops is not known.

Fluorouracil (Systemic) (flure oh YOOR a sil)

Related Information

Capecitabine *on page 288*

Brand Names: US Adrucil

Brand Names: Canada Fluorouracil Injection

Pharmacologic Category Antineoplastic Agent, Antimetabolite; Antineoplastic Agent, Antimetabolite (Pyrimidine Analog)

Use

Breast cancer: Management of breast cancer

Colon cancer: Management of colon cancer

Gastric cancer: Management of stomach (gastric) cancer

Pancreatic cancer: Management of pancreatic cancer

Rectal cancer: Management of rectal cancer

Local Anesthetic/Vasoconstrictor Precautions No information available to require special precautions

Effects on Dental Treatment Key adverse event(s) related to dental treatment: Stomatitis.

Effects on Bleeding Thrombocytopenia and anemia can occur during systemic therapy.

Adverse Reactions Frequency not defined. Toxicity depends on duration of treatment and/or rate of administration.

Cardiovascular: Angina pectoris, cardiac arrhythmia, cardiac failure, cerebrovascular accident, ischemic heart disease, local thrombophlebitis, myocardial infarction, vasospasm, vein pigmentation, ventricular ectopy

Central nervous system: Cerebellar syndrome (acute), confusion, disorientation, euphoria, headache

Dermatologic: Alopecia, changes in nails (including nail loss), dermatitis, maculopapular rash (pruritic), palmar-plantar erythrodysesthesia, skin fissure, skin photosensitivity, Stevens-Johnson syndrome, toxic epidermal necrolysis, xeroderma

Gastrointestinal: Anorexia, diarrhea, esophagopharyngitis, gastrointestinal hemorrhage, gastrointestinal ulcer, mesenteric ischemia (acute), nausea, stomatitis, tissue sloughing (gastrointestinal), vomiting

Hematologic & oncologic: Agranulocytosis, anemia, leukopenia (nadir: days 9 to 14; recovery by day 30), pancytopenia, thrombocytopenia

Hypersensitivity: Anaphylaxis, hypersensitivity reaction (generalized)

Ophthalmic: Lacrimal stenosis, lacrimation, nystagmus, photophobia, visual disturbance

Respiratory: Epistaxis

<1%, postmarketing, and/or case reports: Dysgeusia (Syed 2016)

General Dosage Range Dosage adjustment recommended in patients with hepatic or renal impairment or who develop toxicities

IV: *Adults:* Dosage varies greatly depending on indication

Mechanism of Action A pyrimidine analog antimetabolite that interferes with DNA and RNA synthesis; after activation, F-UMP (an active metabolite) is incorporated into RNA to replace uracil and inhibit cell growth; the active metabolite F-dUMP, inhibits thymidylate synthetase, depleting thymidine triphosphate (a necessary component of DNA synthesis).

Pharmacodynamics/Kinetics

Half-life Elimination 16 minutes (range: 8 to 20 minutes); two metabolites, F-dUMP and F-UMP, have prolonged half-lives depending on the type of tissue

Pregnancy Risk Factor D

Pregnancy Considerations Adverse effects (increased resorptions, embryolethality, and teratogenicity) have been observed in animal reproduction studies. Based on the mechanism of action, fluorouracil may cause fetal harm if administered during pregnancy (according to the manufacturer's labeling).

Chemotherapy, if indicated, may be administered to pregnant women with breast cancer as part of a combination chemotherapy regimen (common regimens administered during pregnancy include doxorubicin [or epirubicin], cyclophosphamide, and fluorouracil); chemotherapy should not be administered during the first trimester, after 35 weeks' gestation, or within 3 weeks of planned delivery (Amant 2010; Loibl 2006). The European Society for Medical Oncology has published guidelines for diagnosis, treatment, and follow-up of cancer during pregnancy. The guidelines recommend referral to a facility with expertise in cancer during pregnancy and encourage a multidisciplinary team (obstetrician, neonatologist, oncology team). In general, if chemotherapy is indicated, it should be avoided during in the first trimester, there should be a 3-week time period between the last chemotherapy dose and anticipated delivery, and chemotherapy should not be administered beyond week 33 of gestation (Peccatori 2013).

FLUoxetine (floo OKS e teen)

Related Information

Clinical Risk Related to Drugs Prolonging QT Interval *on page 1772*

Management of the Patient With Anxiety or Depression *on page 1873*

Vasoconstrictor Interactions With Antidepressants *on page 1913*

Brand Names: US PROzac; PROzac Weekly [DSC]; Sarafem

Brand Names: Canada Apo-Fluoxetine; Ava-Fluoxetine; CO Fluoxetine; Dom-Fluoxetine; Fluoxetine Capsules BP; FXT 40; Gen-Fluoxetine; JAMP-Fluoxetine; Mint-Fluoxetine; Mylan-Fluoxetine; Novo-Fluoxetine; Nu-Fluoxetine; PHL-Fluoxetine; PMS-Fluoxetine; PRO-Fluoxetine; Prozac; Q-Fluoxetine; ratio-Fluoxetine; Riva-Fluoxetine; Sandoz-Fluoxetine; Teva-Fluoxetine; ZYM-Fluoxetine

Generic Availability (US) Yes

Pharmacologic Category Antidepressant, Selective Serotonin Reuptake Inhibitor

Use Treatment of major depressive disorder (MDD); treatment of binge-eating and vomiting in patients with moderate-to-severe bulimia nervosa; obsessive-compulsive disorder (OCD); premenstrual dysphoric disorder (PMDD); panic disorder with or without agoraphobia; in combination with olanzapine for treatment-resistant or bipolar I depression

Local Anesthetic/Vasoconstrictor Precautions Although caution should be used in patients taking tricyclic antidepressants, no interactions have been reported with vasoconstrictors and fluoxetine, a nontricyclic antidepressant which acts to increase serotonin; no precautions appear to be needed. Fluoxetine is one of the drugs confirmed to prolong the QT interval and is accepted as having a risk of causing torsade de pointes. The risk of drug-induced torsade de pointes is extremely low when a single QT interval prolonging drug is prescribed. In terms of epinephrine, it is not known what effect vasoconstrictors in the local anesthetic regimen will have in patients with a known history of congenital prolonged QT interval or in patients taking any medication that prolongs the QT interval. Until more information is obtained, it is suggested that the clinician consult with the physician prior to the use of a vasoconstrictor in suspected patients, and that the vasoconstrictor (epinephrine, mepivacaine and levonordefrin [Carbocaine 2% with Neo-Cobefrin]) be used with caution.

Effects on Dental Treatment Key adverse event(s) related to dental treatment: Xerostomia (normal salivary flow resumes upon discontinuation) and taste perversion. Problems with SSRI-induced bruxism have been reported and may preclude their use. Clinicians attempting to evaluate any patient with bruxism or involuntary muscle movement, who is simultaneously being treated with an SSRI drug, should be aware of this potential association (see Effects on Bleeding and Dental Comment)

Effects on Bleeding Selective serotonin reuptake inhibitors such as fluoxetine may impair platelet aggregation due to platelet serotonin depletion, possibly increasing the risk of a bleeding complication. The risk of a bleeding complication can be increased by coadministration of other antiplatelet agents such as NSAIDs and aspirin.

Adverse Reactions Percentages listed for adverse effects as reported in placebo-controlled trials and were generally similar in adults and children; actual frequency may be dependent upon diagnosis and in some cases the range presented may be lower than or equal to placebo for a particular disorder.

>10%:

- Central nervous system: Insomnia (10% to 33%), headache (21%), drowsiness (5% to 17%), anxiety (6% to 15%), nervousness (8% to 14%), yawning (≤11%)
- Endocrine & metabolic: Decreased libido (1% to 11%)
- Gastrointestinal: Nausea (12% to 29%), diarrhea (8% to 18%), anorexia (4% to 17%), xerostomia (4% to 12%)
- Neuromuscular & skeletal: Weakness (9% to 21%), tremor (3% to 13%)
- Respiratory: Pharyngitis (10% to 11%)

1% to 10%:

- Cardiovascular: Vasodilation (1% to 5%), chest pain, hypertension, palpitations
- Central nervous system: Dizziness (9%), abnormal dreams (1% to 5%), abnormality in thinking (2%), agitation, amnesia, chills, confusion, emotional lability, sleep disorder
- Dermatologic: Diaphoresis (2% to 8%), skin rash (2% to 6%), pruritus (3%)
- Endocrine & metabolic: Weight loss (2%), hypermenorrhea (≥2%), increased thirst (≥2%), weight gain
- Gastrointestinal: Dyspepsia (6% to 10%), constipation (5%), flatulence (3%), vomiting (3%), dysgeusia, increased appetite
- Genitourinary: Ejaculatory disorder (≤7%), impotence (≤7%), urinary frequency
- Neuromuscular & skeletal: Hyperkinesia (≥2%)
- Ophthalmic: Visual disturbance (2%)
- Otic: Otalgia, tinnitus
- Respiratory: Flu-like symptoms (3% to 10%), sinusitis (2% to 6%), epistaxis (≥2%)

<1%, postmarketing, and/or case reports: Abnormal hepatic function tests, acne vulgaris, acute abdominal condition, akathisia, albuminuria, alopecia, amenorrhea, anaphylactoid reaction, anemia, angina pectoris, angle-closure glaucoma, aphthous stomatitis, aplastic anemia, arthritis, asthma, ataxia, atrial fibrillation, bruise, bruxism, bursitis, cardiac arrest, cardiac arrhythmia, cataract, cerebrovascular accident, cholelithiasis, cholestatic jaundice, colitis, congestive heart failure, dehydration, delusions, depersonalization, dyskinesia, dysphagia, dysuria, ecchymoses, edema, eosinophilic pneumonitis, equilibrium disturbance, erythema multiforme, erythema nodosum, esophagitis, euphoria, exfoliative dermatitis, extrapyramidal reaction (rare), gastritis, gastroenteritis, gastrointestinal ulcer, glossitis, gout, gynecological bleeding, gynecomastia, hallucination, hemolytic anemia (immune-related), hepatic failure, hepatic necrosis, hepatitis, hiccups, hostility, hypercholesteremia, hyperprolactinemia, hypersensitivity reaction, hypertonia, hyperventilation, hypoglycemia, hypokalemia, hyponatremia (possibly in association with SIADH), hypotension, hypothyroidism, immune thrombocytopenia, laryngeal edema, laryngospasm, leg cramps, lupus-like syndrome, malaise, melena, memory impairment, migraine, mydriasis, myocardial infarction, myoclonus, neuroleptic malignant syndrome (Stevens 2008), optic neuritis, orthostatic hypotension, ostealgia, pancreatitis, pancytopenia, paranoia, petechia, priapism, prolonged Q-T interval on ECG, pulmonary embolism, pulmonary fibrosis, pulmonary hypertension, purpuric rash, renal failure, serotonin syndrome, sexual disorder (may persist after discontinuation), skin photosensitivity, Stevens-Johnson syndrome, suicidal ideation, syncope, tachycardia, thrombocytopenia, toxic epidermal necrolysis, vasculitis, ventricular tachycardia (including torsades de pointes), violent behavior

Dosing

Adult

Depression, obsessive-compulsive disorder: Oral: 20 mg/day in the morning; may increase after several weeks by 20 mg/day increments; maximum: 80 mg/day; doses >20 mg may be given once daily or divided twice daily. **Note:** Lower doses of 5 to 10 mg/day have been used for initial treatment.

Indication-specific dosing:

Borderline personality disorder (off-label use): 20 mg daily; adjust dose based on response and tolerability up to 80 mg/day (APA [Oldham 2001]; Markovitz 1991; Salzman 1995; Zanarini 2004). Additional data may be necessary to further define the role of fluoxetine in this condition.

Bulimia nervosa: Oral: 60 mg/day; may titrate dose to 60 mg over several days

Depression: Oral: Initial: 20 mg/day; may increase after several weeks if inadequate response (maximum: 80 mg/day). Patients maintained on Prozac 20 mg/day may be changed to Prozac Weekly 90 mg/week, starting dose 7 days after the last 20 mg/day dose

Depression associated with bipolar I disorder (in combination with olanzapine): Oral: Initial: 20 mg in the evening; adjust as tolerated to usual range of 20 to 50 mg/day. See **"Note"** below.

Fibromyalgia (off-label use): Oral: Initial: 20 mg daily; may adjust dose based on response and tolerability in 10 to 20 mg increments at 2 week intervals up to 80 mg/day. Mean dose in clinical trials was 45 mg (range: 20 to 80 mg/day) (Arnold 2002)

Obsessive-compulsive disorder: Oral: Initial: 20 mg/day; may increase after several weeks if inadequate response; recommended range: 20 to 60 mg/day (maximum: 80 mg/day)

Panic disorder: Oral: Initial: 10 mg/day; after 1 week, increase to 20 mg/day; may increase after several weeks; doses >60 mg/day have not been evaluated

Post-traumatic stress disorder (PTSD) (off-label use): Oral: 20 to 40 mg/day

Premenstrual dysphoric disorder (Sarafem): Oral: 20 mg/day continuously, **or** 20 mg/day starting 14 days prior to menstruation and through first full day of menses (repeat with each cycle)

Raynaud's phenomena (off-label use): Oral: 20 mg/day (Coleiro 2001)

Social anxiety disorder (off-label use): Oral: Initial: 10 mg/day for 7 days; continue to increase the dose based on response and tolerability in 10 mg increments at intervals of at least 7 days to a target dose of 40 mg/day; typical range in clinical trial was 30 to 60 mg/day (Davidson 2004)

Treatment-resistant depression (in combination with olanzapine): Oral: Initial: 20 mg in the evening; adjust as tolerated to usual range of 20 to 50 mg/day. See **"Note."**

Note: When using individual components of fluoxetine with olanzapine rather than fixed-dose combination product (Symbyax), approximate dosage correspondence is as follows:

Olanzapine 2.5 mg + fluoxetine 20 mg = Symbyax 3/25

Olanzapine 5 mg + fluoxetine 20 mg = Symbyax 6/25
Olanzapine 12.5 mg + fluoxetine 20 mg = Symbyax 12/25
Olanzapine 5 mg + fluoxetine 50 mg = Symbyax 6/50
Olanzapine 12.5 mg + fluoxetine 50 mg = Symbyax 12/50

Discontinuation of therapy: Upon discontinuation of antidepressant therapy, gradually taper the dose to minimize the incidence of withdrawal symptoms and allow for the detection of re-emerging symptoms. Evidence supporting ideal taper rates is limited. APA and NICE guidelines suggest tapering therapy over at least several weeks with consideration to the half-life of the antidepressant; antidepressants with a shorter half-life may need to be tapered more conservatively. In addition for long-term treated patients, WFSBP guidelines recommend tapering over 4 to 6 months. If intolerable withdrawal symptoms occur following a dose reduction, consider resuming the previously prescribed dose and/or decrease dose at a more gradual rate (APA 2010; Bauer 2002; Haddad 2001; NCCMH 2010; Schatzberg 2006; Shelton 2001; Warner 2006).

MAO inhibitor recommendations:

Switching to or from an MAO inhibitor intended to treat psychiatric disorders:

Allow 14 days to elapse between discontinuing an MAO inhibitor intended to treat psychiatric disorders and initiation of fluoxetine.

Allow 5 weeks to elapse between discontinuing fluoxetine and initiation of an MAO inhibitor intended to treat psychiatric disorders.

Use with other MAO inhibitors (linezolid or IV methylene blue):

Do not initiate fluoxetine in patients receiving linezolid or IV methylene blue; consider other interventions for psychiatric condition.

If urgent treatment with linezolid or IV methylene blue is required in a patient already receiving fluoxetine and potential benefits outweigh potential risks, discontinue fluoxetine promptly and administer linezolid or IV methylene blue. Monitor for serotonin syndrome for 5 weeks or until 24 hours after the last dose of linezolid or IV methylene blue, whichever comes first. May resume fluoxetine 24 hours after the last dose of linezolid or IV methylene blue.

Geriatric Depression: Oral: Some patients may require an initial dose of 10 mg/day with dosage increases of 10 mg and 20 mg every several weeks as tolerated; should not be taken at night unless patient experiences sedation. Refer to adult dosing.

Discontinuation of therapy: Refer to adult dosing.

MAO inhibitor recommendations: Refer to adult dosing.

Pediatric

Depression: Children ≥8 years and Adolescents: Oral: 10 to 20 mg/day; lower-weight children can be started at 10 mg/day, may increase to 20 mg/day after 1 week if needed

Depression associated with bipolar I disorder (in combination with olanzapine): Children ≥10 years and Adolescents: Oral: Initial: 20 mg in the evening; adjust dose, if needed, as tolerated; safety of fluoxetine doses >50 mg in combination with doses >12 mg of olanzapine has not been studied in pediatrics. See **"Note"** below.

Obsessive-compulsive disorder: Children ≥7 years and Adolescents: Oral: Initial: 10 mg/day; may increase after 2 weeks if inadequate clinical response to 20 mg/day; further increases may be considered after several weeks to recommended range of 20 to 30 mg/day (lower weight children) or 20 to 60 mg/day (adolescents and higher weight children)

Selective mutism (off-label use): Children ≥5 years and Adolescents: Oral: Initial: 5 mg once daily for 7 days, then increase to 10 mg once daily for 7 days, and 20 mg once daily thereafter; may further titrate in 20 mg/day increments if needed every 2 weeks; maximum daily dose: 60 mg/day (Dummit 1996). Weight-based dosing: 0.2 mg/kg/day for 1 week, then 0.4 mg/kg/day for 1 week, then 0.6 mg/kg/day for 10 weeks; mean final dose in clinical trials: 21.4 mg/day (Black,1994). To fully assess therapeutic response, a therapeutic trial of at least 9 to 12 weeks or longer has been suggested (Black 1994; Dummit 1996; Kaakeh 2008).

Note: When using individual components of fluoxetine with olanzapine rather than fixed-dose combination product (Symbyax), approximate dosage correspondence is as follows:

Olanzapine 2.5 mg + fluoxetine 20 mg = Symbyax 3/25
Olanzapine 5 mg + fluoxetine 20 mg = Symbyax 6/25
Olanzapine 12.5 mg + fluoxetine 20 mg = Symbyax 12/25
Olanzapine 5 mg + fluoxetine 50 mg = Symbyax 6/50
Olanzapine 12.5 mg + fluoxetine 50 mg = Symbyax 12/50

Discontinuation of therapy: Refer to adult dosing.

MAO inhibitor recommendations: Refer to adult dosing.

Renal Impairment

Single dose studies: Pharmacokinetics of fluoxetine and norfluoxetine were similar among subjects with all levels of impaired renal function, including anephric patients on chronic hemodialysis.

Chronic administration: Additional accumulation of fluoxetine or norfluoxetine may occur in patients with severely impaired renal function.

Not removed by hemodialysis; use of lower dose or less frequent dosing is not usually necessary.

Hepatic Impairment Elimination half-life of fluoxetine is prolonged in patients with hepatic impairment. A lower dose or less frequent dosing of fluoxetine should be used in these patients.

Cirrhosis patient: Administer a lower dose or less frequent dosing interval.

Compensated cirrhosis without ascites: Administer 50% of normal dose.

Mechanism of Action Inhibits CNS neuron serotonin reuptake; minimal or no effect on reuptake of norepinephrine or dopamine; does not significantly bind to alpha-adrenergic, histamine, or cholinergic receptors

Contraindications Hypersensitivity to fluoxetine or any component of the formulation; use of MAO inhibitors intended to treat psychiatric disorders (concurrently, within 5 weeks of discontinuing fluoxetine, or within 2 weeks of discontinuing the MAO inhibitor); initiation of fluoxetine in a patient receiving linezolid or intravenous methylene blue; use with pimozide or thioridazine (**Note:** Thioridazine should not be initiated until 5 weeks after the discontinuation of fluoxetine)

Warnings/Precautions [US Boxed Warning]: Antidepressants increase the risk of suicidal thinking and behavior in children, adolescents, and young adults (18 to 24 years of age) with major depressive disorder (MDD) and other psychiatric disorders; consider risk prior to prescribing. Short-term studies did not show an increased risk in patients >24 years of age and showed a decreased risk in patients ≥65 years. Closely monitor all patients for clinical worsening, suicidality, or unusual changes in behavior, particularly during the initial 1 to 2 months of therapy or during periods of dosage adjustments (increases or decreases); the patient's family or caregiver should be instructed to closely observe the patient and communicate condition with healthcare provider. A medication guide concerning the use of antidepressants should be dispensed with each prescription. **Fluoxetine is FDA approved for the treatment of OCD in children ≥7 years of age and MDD in children ≥8 years of age.**

The possibility of a suicide attempt is inherent in major depression and may persist until remission occurs. Use caution in high-risk patients. Worsening depression and severe abrupt suicidality that are not part of the presenting symptoms may require discontinuation or modification of drug therapy. Prescriptions should be written for the smallest quantity consistent with good patient care. The patient's family or caregiver should be alerted to monitor patients for the emergence of suicidality and associated behaviors (such as agitation, irritability, hostility, impulsivity, and hypomania) and call healthcare provider.

May worsen psychosis in some patients or precipitate a shift to mania or hypomania in patients with bipolar disorder. Patients presenting with depressive symptoms should be screened for bipolar disorder. Monotherapy in patients with bipolar disorder should be avoided. **Fluoxetine monotherapy is not FDA approved for the treatment of bipolar depression.** May cause insomnia, anxiety, nervousness, or anorexia. Use with caution in patients where weight loss is undesirable. May impair cognitive or motor performance; caution operating hazardous machinery or driving.

QT prolongation and ventricular arrhythmia including torsade de pointes has occurred. Use with caution in patients with risk factors for QT prolongation, under conditions that predispose to arrhythmias, or increased fluoxetine exposure. Consider discontinuation of fluoxetine if ventricular arrhythmia suspected and initiate cardiac evaluation. Avoid concurrent use with other medications that increase QT interval.

Potentially life-threatening serotonin syndrome (SS) has occurred with serotonergic agents (eg, SSRIs, SNRIs), particularly when used in combination with other serotonergic agents (eg, triptans, TCAs, fentanyl, lithium, tramadol, buspirone, St John's wort, tryptophan) or agents that impair metabolism of serotonin (eg, MAO inhibitors intended to treat psychiatric disorders, other MAO inhibitors [ie, linezolid and intravenous methylene blue]). Discontinue treatment (and any concomitant serotonergic agent) immediately if signs/symptoms arise. Fluoxetine use has been associated with occurrences of significant rash and allergic events, including vasculitis, lupus-like syndrome, laryngospasm, anaphylactoid reactions, and pulmonary inflammatory disease. Discontinue if underlying cause of rash cannot be identified.

Use caution in patients with a previous seizure disorder or condition predisposing to seizures such as brain damage or alcoholism. May also cause agitation, sleep disturbances, and excessive CNS stimulation in older adults. May cause hyponatremia/SIADH (elderly at increased risk); volume depletion (diuretics may increase risk). May increase the risks associated with electroconvulsive treatment. Use caution with history of MI or unstable heart disease; use in these patients is limited. May alter glycemic control in patients with diabetes. Due to the long half-life of fluoxetine and its metabolites, the effects and interactions noted may persist for prolonged periods following discontinuation. May cause or exacerbate sexual dysfunction. May cause mild pupillary dilation, which in susceptible individuals can lead to an episode of narrow-angle glaucoma. Consider evaluating patients who have not had an iridectomy for narrow-angle glaucoma risk factors. Bone fractures have been associated with antidepressant treatment. Consider the possibility of a fragility fracture if an antidepressant-treated patient presents with unexplained bone pain, point tenderness, swelling, or bruising (Rabenda 2013; Rizzoli 2012). Potentially significant drug-drug interactions may exist, requiring dose or frequency adjustment, additional monitoring, and/or selection of alternative therapy.

Abrupt discontinuation or interruption of antidepressant therapy has been associated with a discontinuation syndrome. Symptoms arising may vary with antidepressant however commonly include nausea, vomiting, diarrhea, headaches, light-headedness, dizziness, diminished appetite, sweating, chills, tremors, paresthesias, fatigue, somnolence, and sleep disturbances (eg, vivid dreams, insomnia). Greater risks for developing a discontinuation syndrome have been associated with antidepressants with shorter half-lives, longer durations of treatment, and abrupt discontinuation. For antidepressants of short or intermediate half-lives, symptoms may emerge within 2 to 5 days after treatment discontinuation and last 7 to 14 days (APA 2010; Fava 2006; Haddad 2001; Shelton 2001; Warner 2006).

Benzyl alcohol and derivatives: Some dosage forms may contain sodium benzoate/benzoic acid; benzoic acid (benzoate) is a metabolite of benzyl alcohol; large amounts of benzyl alcohol (≥99 mg/kg/day) have been associated with a potentially fatal toxicity ("gasping syndrome") in neonates; the "gasping syndrome" consists of metabolic acidosis, respiratory distress, gasping respirations, CNS dysfunction (including convulsions, intracranial hemorrhage), hypotension, and cardiovascular collapse (AAP ["Inactive" 1997]; CDC 1982); some data suggests that benzoate displaces bilirubin from protein binding sites (Ahlfors 2001); avoid or use dosage forms containing benzyl alcohol derivative with caution in neonates. See manufacturer's labeling.

Drug Interactions

Metabolism/Transport Effects Substrate of CYP1A2 (minor), CYP2B6 (minor), CYP2C19 (minor), CYP2C9 (major), CYP2D6 (major), CYP2E1 (minor), CYP3A4 (minor); **Note:** Assignment of Major/Minor substrate status based on clinically relevant drug interaction potential; **Inhibits** CYP1A2 (weak), CYP2C19 (moderate), CYP2C9 (weak), CYP2D6 (strong)

Avoid Concomitant Use

Avoid concomitant use of FLUoxetine with any of the following: Clarithromycin; Dapoxetine; Dosulepin; Haloperidol; Highest Risk QTc-Prolonging Agents; Hydroxychloroquine; Iobenguane I 123; Ivabradine; Linezolid; MAO Inhibitors; Mequitazine; Methylene Blue; MiFEPRIStone; Moderate Risk QTc-Prolonging

Agents; Pimozide; Probucol; Promazine; Propafenone; Tamoxifen; Thioridazine; Tryptophan; Urokinase; Vinflunine; Ziprasidone

Increased Effect/Toxicity

FLUoxetine may increase the levels/effects of: Agents with Antiplatelet Properties; Anticoagulants; Antidepressants (Serotonin Reuptake Inhibitor/Antagonist); Antipsychotic Agents; Apixaban; ARIPiprazole; ARIPiprazole Lauroxil; Aspirin; AtoMOXetine; Beta-Blockers; Blood Glucose Lowering Agents; Brexpiprazole; BusPIRone; CarBAMazepine; Cephalothin; Cilostazol; Collagenase (Systemic); CYP2C19 Substrates; CYP2D6 Substrates; Dabigatran Etexilate; Deoxycholic Acid; Desmopressin; Dextromethorphan; Dosulepin; DOXOrubicin (Conventional); DULoxetine; Edoxaban; Fesoterodine; Flibanserin; Fosphenytoin; Haloperidol; Highest Risk QTc-Prolonging Agents; Ibritumomab; Indoramin; Mequitazine; Methylene Blue; Metoprolol; Mexiletine; Nebivolol; Nicergoline; NIFEdipine; NiMODipine; NSAID (COX-2 Inhibitor); NSAID (Nonselective); Obinutuzumab; Perhexiline; Phenytoin; Pimozide; Propafenone; Rivaroxaban; Salicylates; Serotonin Modulators; Tamsulosin; Thiazide and Thiazide-Like Diuretics; Thioridazine; Thrombolytic Agents; Timolol (Ophthalmic); TiZANidine; Tositumomab and Iodine I 131 Tositumomab; TraMADol; Tricyclic Antidepressants; Urokinase; Vitamin K Antagonists; Vortioxetine; Ziprasidone

The levels/effects of FLUoxetine may be increased by: Abiraterone Acetate; Alcohol (Ethyl); Analgesics (Opioid); Antiemetics (5HT3 Antagonists); Antipsychotic Agents; ARIPiprazole; Asunaprevir; Bilastine; Buprenorphine; BuPROPion; BusPIRone; Cimetidine; Clarithromycin; CNS Depressants; Cobicistat; CYP2C9 Inhibitors (Moderate); CYP2C9 Inhibitors (Strong); CYP2D6 Inhibitors (Moderate); CYP2D6 Inhibitors (Strong); Dapoxetine; Darunavir; Fosphenytoin; Glucosamine; Herbs (Anticoagulant/Antiplatelet Properties); Hydroxychloroquine; Ibrutinib; Imatinib; Indapamide; Ivabradine; Limaprost; Linezolid; Lithium; Lumacaftor; MAO Inhibitors; Metaxalone; Methylene Blue; Methylphenidate; Metoclopramide; MetyroSINE; MiFEPRIStone; Moderate Risk QTc-Prolonging Agents; Multivitamins/Fluoride (with ADE); Multivitamins/Minerals (with ADEK, Folate, Iron); Multivitamins/Minerals (with AE, No Iron); Omega-3 Fatty Acids; Pentosan Polysulfate Sodium; Pentoxifylline; Probucol; Promazine; Propafenone; Prostacyclin Analogues; QTc-Prolonging Agents (Indeterminate Risk and Risk Modifying); Tedizolid; Teneligliptin; TraMADol; Tryptophan; Vinflunine; Vitamin E (Systemic); Ziprasidone

Decreased Effect

FLUoxetine may decrease the levels/effects of: Clopidogrel; Codeine; HYDROcodone; Iobenguane I 123; Ioflupane I 123; Nicergoline; Tamoxifen; Thyroid Products; TraMADol

The levels/effects of FLUoxetine may be decreased by: CYP2C9 Inducers (Strong); Cyproheptadine; Dabrafenib; Enzalutamide; Lumacaftor; NSAID (COX-2 Inhibitor); NSAID (Nonselective); Peginterferon Alfa-2b

Dietary Considerations May be taken without regard to meals.

Pharmacodynamics/Kinetics

Onset of Action Depression: The onset of action is within a week; however, individual response varies greatly and full response may not be seen until 8 to 12 weeks after initiation of treatment.

Half-life Elimination Adults: Parent drug: 1 to 3 days (acute), 4 to 6 days (chronic), 7.6 days (cirrhosis); Metabolite (norfluoxetine): 9.3 days (range: 4 to 16 days), 12 days (cirrhosis)

Time to Peak Serum: 6 to 8 hours

Pregnancy Risk Factor C

Pregnancy Considerations Adverse events have been observed in animal reproduction studies. Fluoxetine and its metabolite cross the human placenta. An increased risk of teratogenic effects, including cardiovascular defects, may be associated with maternal use of fluoxetine or other SSRIs; however, available information is conflicting. Nonteratogenic effects in the newborn following SSRI/SNRI exposure late in the third trimester include respiratory distress, cyanosis, apnea, seizures, temperature instability, feeding difficulty, vomiting, hypoglycemia, hypo- or hypertonia, hyper-reflexia, jitteriness, irritability, constant crying, and tremor. Symptoms may be due to the toxicity of the SSRIs/SNRIs or a discontinuation syndrome and may be consistent with serotonin syndrome associated with SSRI treatment. Persistent pulmonary hypertension of the newborn (PPHN) has also been reported with SSRI exposure. The long-term effects of in utero SSRI exposure on infant development and behavior are not known.

Due to pregnancy-induced physiologic changes, women who are pregnant may require dose adjustments of fluoxetine to achieve euthymia. The ACOG recommends that therapy with SSRIs or SNRIs during pregnancy be individualized; treatment of depression during pregnancy should incorporate the clinical expertise of the mental health clinician, obstetrician, primary health care provider, and pediatrician. According to the American Psychiatric Association (APA), the risks of medication treatment should be weighed against other treatment options and untreated depression. For women who discontinue antidepressant medications during pregnancy and who may be at high risk for postpartum depression, the medications can be restarted following delivery. Treatment algorithms have been developed by the ACOG and the APA for the management of depression in women prior to conception and during pregnancy.

Pregnant women exposed to antidepressants during pregnancy are encouraged to enroll in the National Pregnancy Registry for Antidepressants (NPRAD). Women 18 to 45 years of age or their health care providers may contact the registry by calling 844-405-6185. Enrollment should be done as early in pregnancy as possible.

Breastfeeding Considerations Fluoxetine and its metabolite are excreted into breast milk and can be detected in the serum of breastfeeding infants. Concentrations in breast milk are variable. In comparison to other SSRIs, fluoxetine concentrations in breast milk are higher and adverse events have been observed in nursing infants. Maternal use of an SSRI during pregnancy may cause delayed milk secretion. breastfeeding is not recommended by the manufacturer. Long-term effects on development and behavior have not been studied.

Dosage Forms

Capsule, Oral:

PROzac: 10 mg, 20 mg, 40 mg

Generic: 10 mg, 20 mg, 40 mg

Capsule Delayed Release, Oral:

Generic: 90 mg

Solution, Oral:

Generic: 20 mg/5 mL (5 mL, 120 mL)

Tablet, Oral:
Sarafem: 10 mg, 20 mg
Generic: 10 mg, 20 mg, 60 mg

Dosage Forms: Canada Note: Refer to Dosage Forms. Delayed release capsules and tablets are not available in Canada.

Dental Comment Problems with SSRI-induced bruxism have been reported and may preclude their use; clinicians attempting to evaluate any patient with bruxism or involuntary muscle movement, who is simultaneously being treated with an SSRI drug, should be aware of the potential association (see Local Anesthetic/Vasoconstrictor Precautions)

Fluoxymesterone (floo oks i MES te rone)

Brand Names: US Androxy

Pharmacologic Category Androgen

Use Replacement therapy in the treatment of delayed male puberty; male hypogonadism (primary or hypogonadotropic); inoperable metastatic female breast cancer

Local Anesthetic/Vasoconstrictor Precautions No information available to require special precautions

Effects on Dental Treatment No significant effects or complications reported

Effects on Bleeding No information available to require special precautions

Adverse Reactions Frequency not defined.

Cardiovascular: Edema

Central nervous system: Anxiety, depression, headache, paresthesia

Dermatologic: Acne vulgaris, androgenetic alopecia

Endocrine & metabolic: Change in libido (decreased libido or increased libido), electrolyte disturbance (calcium, chloride, inorganic phosphate, potassium, and sodium retention), fluid retention, gynecomastia (males), hirsutism, hypercholesterolemia, menstrual disease (females; including amenorrhea)

Gastrointestinal: Gastrointestinal irritation, nausea, vomiting

Genitourinary: Benign prostatic hypertrophy (males), oligospermia (males, at higher doses), priapism (males), testicular atrophy (males), virilization (females; including clitoromegaly, deepening of the voice in females)

Hematologic & oncologic: Clotting factors suppression, polycythemia, prostate carcinoma (males)

Hepatic: Abnormal hepatic function tests, cholestatic jaundice, hepatic insufficiency

Hypersensitivity: Anaphylactoid reaction (non-immunologic anaphylaxis), hypersensitivity reaction

<1%, postmarketing, and/or case reports: Hepatic coma, hepatocellular neoplasm, hepatotoxicity (idiosyncratic; Chalasani 2014), peliosis hepatitis

General Dosage Range Oral:

Adults (females): 10-40 mg daily in divided doses

Adults (males): 2.5-20 mg daily

Mechanism of Action Synthetic derivative of testosterone; responsible for the normal growth and development of male sex hormones, male sex organs, and maintenance of secondary sex characteristics; large doses suppress endogenous testosterone release

Pharmacodynamics/Kinetics

Half-life Elimination 10 hours (range: 10-100 minutes)

Pregnancy Risk Factor X

Pregnancy Considerations Use is contraindicated in women who are or may become pregnant. May cause androgenic effects to the female fetus; clitoral hypertrophy, labial fusion, urogenital sinus defect, vaginal atresia, and ambiguous genitalia have been reported.

Controlled Substance C-III

FluPHENAZine (floo FEN a zeen)

Brand Names: Canada Apo-Fluphenazine; Fluphenazine Omega; Modecate Concentrate; PMS-Fluphenazine; PMS-Fluphenazine Decanoate

Pharmacologic Category First Generation (Typical) Antipsychotic; Phenothiazine Derivative

Use

Psychotic disorders: For the management of manifestations of psychotic disorders; decanoate injection is intended for use in the management of patients requiring prolonged therapy.

Limitations of use: Fluphenazine has not been shown to be effective in the management of behavioral complications in patients with mental retardation.

Local Anesthetic/Vasoconstrictor Precautions No information available to require special precautions

Effects on Dental Treatment Key adverse event(s) related to dental treatment: Xerostomia and increased salivation (normal salivary flow resumes upon discontinuation); nasal congestion is possible; since the drug is a dopamine antagonist, extrapyramidal symptoms of the TMJ are a possibility. Patients may experience orthostatic hypotension as they stand up after treatment; especially if lying in dental chair for extended periods of time. Use caution with sudden changes in position during and after dental treatment.

Effects on Bleeding No information available to require special precautions

Adverse Reactions Frequency not defined.

Cardiovascular: Cardiac arrhythmia, edema, hypertension, hypotension, tachycardia, variable blood pressure

Central nervous system: Akathisia, bizarre dream, cerebral edema, depression, disruption of body temperature regulation, dizziness, drowsiness, dystonia, EEG pattern changes, excitement, headache, hyperreflexia, lethargy, neuroleptic malignant syndrome, Parkinsonian-like syndrome, restlessness, seizure, tardive dyskinesia

Dermatologic: Dermatitis, eczema, erythema, pruritus, seborrhea, skin photosensitivity, skin pigmentation, skin rash, urticaria

Endocrine & metabolic: Amenorrhea, change in libido, galactorrhea, gynecomastia, increased serum prolactin, menstrual disease, SIADH (syndrome of inappropriate antidiuretic hormone secretion), weight gain

Gastrointestinal: Anorexia, constipation, paralytic ileus, salivation, xerostomia

Genitourinary: Bladder paralysis, ejaculatory disorder, impotence, mastalgia, urinary incontinence

Hematologic & oncologic: Agranulocytosis, eosinophilia, leukopenia, nonthrombocytopenic purpura, pancytopenia, thrombocytopenia

Hepatic: Cholestatic jaundice, hepatotoxicity

Neuromuscular & skeletal: Hemifacial spasm, systemic lupus erythematosus, tremor (fingers)

Ophthalmic: Blurred vision, corneal changes, glaucoma, lens disease, retinitis pigmentosa

Renal: Polyuria

Respiratory: Asthma, laryngeal edema, nasal congestion

General Dosage Range

IM (hydrochloride): *Adults:* Initial: 1.25 mg as a single dose; Maintenance: 2.5 to 10 mg/day in divided doses every 6 to 8 hours

IM, SubQ (Depot): *Adults:* Initial: 12.5 to 25 mg every 3 to 4 weeks; maximum: 100 mg

Oral: *Adults:* 1 to 10 mg/day in 3 or 4 divided doses or up to 5 mg once daily (with maintenance therapy); maximum: 40 mg/day

Mechanism of Action Fluphenazine is a piperazine phenothiazine antipsychotic which blocks nonselectively postsynaptic mesolimbic dopaminergic D_2 receptors in the brain (Risch 1996); fluphenazine has limited activity on histaminergic, muscarinic and alpha receptors (Richelson 1999)

Pharmacodynamics/Kinetics

Onset of Action Decanoate: 24 to 72 hours; Peak effect: Decanoate: 48 to 96 hours

Duration of Action Decanoate: ~4 weeks

Half-life Elimination Derivative dependent: Hydrochloride: Oral: 14.4 to 16.4 hours (Dysken 1981; Koytchev 1996); Decanoate: ~14 days (Altamura 2003)

Time to Peak Serum: Hydrochloride: Oral: 2.8 hours (Koytchev 1996); Decanoate: 8 to 10 hours (Altamura 2003)

Pregnancy Considerations Antipsychotic use during the third trimester of pregnancy has a risk for abnormal muscle movements (extrapyramidal symptoms [EPS]) and withdrawal symptoms in newborns following delivery. Symptoms in the newborn may include agitation, feeding disorder, hypertonia, hypotonia, respiratory distress, somnolence, and tremor; these effects may be self-limiting or require hospitalization. The ACOG recommends that therapy during pregnancy be individualized; treatment with psychiatric medications during pregnancy should incorporate the clinical expertise of the mental health clinician, obstetrician, primary healthcare provider, and pediatrician (ACOG 2008).

Flurandrenolide (flure an DREN oh lide)

Brand Names: US Cordran

Pharmacologic Category Corticosteroid, Topical

Use Corticosteroid-responsive dermatoses: Relief of inflammatory and pruritic manifestations of corticosteroid-responsive dermatoses

Local Anesthetic/Vasoconstrictor Precautions No information available to require special precautions

Effects on Dental Treatment No significant effects or complications reported

Effects on Bleeding No information available to require special precautions

Adverse Reactions Frequency not defined.

Central nervous system: Burning sensation

Dermatologic: Acne vulgaris, acneiform eruptions, allergic contact dermatitis, atrophic striae, folliculitis, hypopigmentation, hypertrichosis, maceration of the skin, miliaria, perioral dermatitis, pruritus, skin atrophy, xeroderma

Local: Local irritation

Infection: Secondary infection

Postmarketing and/or case reports: Hypersensitivity, skin discoloration

General Dosage Range Topical: *Children, Adolescents, and Adults:* Cream, lotion, ointment: Apply thin film to affected area 2 to 3 times per day; Tape: Apply 1 to 2 times per day.

Mechanism of Action Topical corticosteroids have anti-inflammatory, antipruritic, and vasoconstrictive properties. May depress the formation, release, and activity of endogenous chemical mediators of inflammation (kinins, histamine, liposomal enzymes, prostaglandins) through the induction of phospholipase A_2 inhibitory proteins (lipocortins) and sequential inhibition of the release of arachidonic acid. Flurandrenolide has intermediate range potency.

Pregnancy Risk Factor C

Pregnancy Considerations Adverse events have been observed with corticosteroids in animal reproduction studies. When topical corticosteroids are needed during pregnancy, low- to mid-potency preparations are preferred; higher-potency preparations should be used for the shortest time possible and fetal growth should be monitored (Chi, 2011; Chi, 2013). Topical products are not recommended for extensive use, in large quantities, or for long periods of time in pregnant women (Leachman, 2006).

Flurazepam (flure AZ e pam)

Related Information

Dentin Hypersensitivity, Acid Erosion, High Caries Index, Management of Alveolar Osteitis, and Xerostomia *on page 1857*

Brand Names: Canada Apo-Flurazepam; Bio-Flurazepam; Dalmane; PMS-Flurazepam; Som Pam

Generic Availability (US) Yes

Pharmacologic Category Hypnotic, Benzodiazepine

Use Insomnia: For the treatment of insomnia characterized by difficulty in falling asleep, frequent nocturnal awakenings, and/or early-morning awakenings.

Local Anesthetic/Vasoconstrictor Precautions No information available to require special precautions

Effects on Dental Treatment Key adverse event(s) related to dental treatment: Xerostomia and changes in salivation (normal salivary flow resumes upon discontinuation), and bitter taste.

Effects on Bleeding No information available to require special precautions

Adverse Reactions Frequency not defined.

Cardiovascular: Chest pain, flushing, hypotension, palpitations, syncope

Central nervous system: Abnormal reflexes (slowing), apprehension, ataxia, bitter taste, body pain, confusion, depression, dizziness, drowsiness, drug dependence, dysarthria, euphoria, falling, hallucination, hangover effect, headache, irritability, memory impairment, nervousness, paradoxical reaction, restlessness, slurred speech, staggering, talkativeness

Dermatologic: Diaphoresis, pruritus, skin rash

Endocrine & metabolic: Weight gain, weight loss

Gastrointestinal: Constipation, decreased appetite, diarrhea, gastric distress, gastrointestinal pain, heartburn, increased appetite, nausea, sialorrhea, vomiting, xerostomia

Hematologic & oncologic: Granulocytopenia, leukopenia

Hepatic: Abnormal bilirubin levels (total bilirubin increased), cholestatic jaundice, increased serum alkaline phosphatase, increased serum ALT, increased serum AST

Neuromuscular & skeletal: Arthralgia, weakness

Ophthalmic: Accommodation disturbance, blurred vision, burning sensation of eyes

Respiratory: Apnea, dyspnea

<1%, postmarketing, and/or case reports: Anaphylaxis, angioedema, parasomnias (cooking while sleeping, making phone calls while sleeping, sleep driving, sleep eating)

Dosing

Adult Insomnia: Adults: Oral: Initial: 15 mg at bedtime for women, and 15 to 30 mg at bedtime for men; may increase dose to 30 mg at bedtime as needed based on response

Geriatric Oral: 15 mg at bedtime

Renal Impairment There are no dosage adjustments provided in the manufacturer's labeling; use with caution.

Hepatic Impairment There are no dosage adjustments provided in the manufacturer's labeling; use with caution.

Mechanism of Action Binds to stereospecific benzodiazepine receptors on the postsynaptic GABA neuron at several sites within the central nervous system, including the limbic system, reticular formation. Enhancement of the inhibitory effect of GABA on neuronal excitability results by increased neuronal membrane permeability to chloride ions. This shift in chloride ions results in hyperpolarization (a less excitable state) and stabilization. Benzodiazepine receptors and effects appear to be linked to the GABA-A receptors. Benzodiazepines do not bind to GABA-B receptors (Vinkers, 2012).

Contraindications

Hypersensitivity to flurazepam, other benzodiazepines, or any component of the formulation; pregnancy

Documentation of allergenic cross-reactivity for benzodiazepines is limited. However, because of similarities in chemical structure and/or pharmacologic actions, the possibility of cross-sensitivity cannot be ruled out with certainty.

Warnings/Precautions Use with caution in elderly or debilitated patients, patients with hepatic or renal impairment, and patients with respiratory disease.

Causes CNS depression (dose related); patients must be cautioned about performing tasks which require mental alertness (eg, operating machinery or driving). Use with caution in patients receiving other CNS depressants or psychoactive agents. Benzodiazepines have been associated with falls and traumatic injury and should be used with extreme caution in patients who are at risk of these events.

Use caution in patients with depression, particularly if suicidal risk may be present. Minimize risks of overdose by prescribing the least amount of drug that is feasible in suicidal patients. Worsening of depressive symptoms has also been reported with use of benzodiazepines. Abnormal thinking and behavior changes including symptoms of decreased inhibition (eg, excessive aggressiveness and extroversion), bizarre behavior, agitation, hallucinations, and depersonalization have been reported with the use of benzodiazepine hypnotics. Some evidence suggests symptoms may be dose related. Use with caution in patients with a history of drug abuse or acute alcoholism; potential for drug dependency exists. Tolerance, psychological and physical dependence may occur with prolonged use. Rebound or withdrawal symptoms may occur following abrupt discontinuation or large decreases in dose. Use caution when reducing dose or withdrawing therapy; decrease slowly and monitor for withdrawal symptoms. Flumazenil may cause withdrawal in patients receiving long-term benzodiazepine therapy.

As a hypnotic, should be used only after evaluation of potential causes of sleep disturbance. Failure of sleep disturbance to resolve after 7 to 10 days may indicate psychiatric or medical illness. A worsening of insomnia or the emergence of new abnormalities of thought or behavior may represent unrecognized psychiatric or medical illness and requires immediate and careful evaluation. Reports of hypersensitivity reactions, including anaphylaxis and angioedema, have been reported with flurazepam. Patients who develop angioedema should not be rechallenged with flurazepam. An increased risk for hazardous sleep-related activities such as sleep-driving, cooking and eating food, having sex, and making phone calls while asleep have also been noted. Concurrent use of alcohol and other CNS depressants as well as increases in dose may increase the risk of these behaviors.

Benzodiazepines have been associated with anterograde amnesia. Paradoxical reactions have been reported, particularly in adolescent/pediatric or psychiatric patients. Flurazepam is a long half-life benzodiazepine. Duration of action after a single dose is determined by redistribution rather than metabolism. Tolerance develops to the hypnotic effects (Vinkers, 2012). Chronic use of this agent may increase the perioperative benzodiazepine dose needed to achieve desired effect. Does not have analgesic, antidepressant, or antipsychotic properties. Potentially significant drug-drug interactions may exist, requiring dose or frequency adjustment, additional monitoring, and/or selection of alternative therapy.

Drug Interactions

Metabolism/Transport Effects Substrate of CYP3A4 (major); **Note:** Assignment of Major/Minor substrate status based on clinically relevant drug interaction potential; **Inhibits** CYP2E1 (weak)

Avoid Concomitant Use

Avoid concomitant use of Flurazepam with any of the following: Azelastine (Nasal); Conivaptan; Fusidic Acid (Systemic); Idelalisib; Methadone; OLANZapine; Orphenadrine; Oxomemazine; Paraldehyde; Sodium Oxybate; Thalidomide

Increased Effect/Toxicity

Flurazepam may increase the levels/effects of: Alcohol (Ethyl); Analgesics (Opioid); Azelastine (Nasal); Blonanserin; Buprenorphine; CloZAPine; CNS Depressants; Flunitrazepam; HYDROcodone; Methadone; Methotrimeprazine; MetyroSINE; Mirtazapine; Orphenadrine; OxyCODONE; Paraldehyde; Piribedil; Pramipexole; ROPINIRole; Rotigotine; Selective Serotonin Reuptake Inhibitors; Sodium Oxybate; Suvorexant; Thalidomide; Zolpidem

The levels/effects of Flurazepam may be increased by: Aprepitant; Brimonidine (Topical); Cannabis; Chlormethiazole; Chlorphenesin Carbamate; Conivaptan; CYP3A4 Inhibitors (Moderate); CYP3A4 Inhibitors (Strong); Dasatinib; Dimethindene (Topical); Doxylamine; Dronabinol; Droperidol; Fosamprenavir; Fosaprepitant; Fusidic Acid (Systemic); HydrOXYzine; Idelalisib; Ivacaftor; Kava Kava; Lofexidine; Magnesium Sulfate; Methotrimeprazine; MiFEPRIStone; Minocycline; Nabilone; Netupitant; OLANZapine; Oxomemazine; Palbociclib; Perampanel; Ritonavir; Rufinamide; Saquinavir; Simeprevir; Stiripentol; Tapentadol; Teduglutide; Tetrahydrocannabinol; Trimeprazine

Decreased Effect

The levels/effects of Flurazepam may be decreased by: Bosentan; CYP3A4 Inducers (Moderate); CYP3A4

Inducers (Strong); Dabrafenib; Deferasirox; Enzalutamide; Mitotane; Siltuximab; St John's Wort; Theophylline Derivatives; Tocilizumab; Yohimbine

Food Interactions Benzodiazepine serum concentrations may be increased by grapefruit juice. Management: Limit or avoid grapefruit juice (Bjornsson, 2003).

Pharmacodynamics/Kinetics

Half-life Elimination

Flurazepam: 2.3 hours

N-desalkylflurazepam:

Adults: Single dose: 74 to 90 hours; Multiple doses: 111 to 113 hours

Elderly (61 to 85 years): Single dose: 120 to 160 hours; Multiple doses: 126 to 158 hours

Time to Peak Flurazepam: 30 to 60 minutes; N-desalkylflurazepam: 10.6 hours (range: 7.6 to 13.6 hours); N-hydroxyethylflurazepam: ~1 hour (Greenblatt, 1989)

Pregnancy Risk Factor C

Pregnancy Considerations Adverse events have been observed in animal reproduction studies for benzodiazepines. All benzodiazepines are assumed to cross the placenta. Teratogenic effects have been observed with some benzodiazepines; however, additional studies are needed. The incidence of premature birth and low birth weights may be increased following maternal use of benzodiazepines; hypoglycemia and respiratory problems in the neonate may occur following exposure late in pregnancy. Neonatal withdrawal symptoms may occur within days to weeks after birth and "floppy infant syndrome" (which also includes withdrawal symptoms) has been reported with some benzodiazepines (Bergman, 1992; Iqbal, 2002; Wikner, 2007). Neonatal depression has been observed, specifically following exposure to flurazepam when used maternally for 10 consecutive days prior to delivery. Serum levels of N-desalkylflurazepam were measurable in the infant during the first 4 days of life. Use of flurazepam during pregnancy is contraindicated.

Patients exposed to flurazepam during pregnancy are encouraged to enroll themselves into the North American Antiepileptic Drug (NAAED) Pregnancy Registry by calling 1-888-233-2334. Additional information is available at http://www.aedpregnancyregistry.org.

Breastfeeding Considerations Although information specific to flurazepam has not been located, all benzodiazepines are expected to be excreted into breast milk. Drowsiness, lethargy, or weight loss in nursing infants have been observed in case reports following maternal use of some benzodiazepines (Iqbal, 2002).

Controlled Substance C-IV

Dosage Forms

Capsule, Oral:

Generic: 15 mg, 30 mg

Flurbiprofen (Systemic) (flure BI proe fen)

Related Information

Rheumatoid Arthritis, Osteoarthritis, and Osteoporosis *on page 1792*

Temporomandibular Dysfunction (TMD), Chronic Pain, and Fibromyalgia *on page 1868*

Brand Names: Canada APO-Flurbiprofen FC; Teva-Flurbiprofen

Generic Availability (US) Yes

Pharmacologic Category Analgesic, Nonopioid; Nonsteroidal Anti-inflammatory Drug (NSAID), Oral

Dental Use Management of postoperative pain (off-label use)

Use

Rheumatoid arthritis, osteoarthritis: Relief of the signs and symptoms of rheumatoid arthritis (RA) and osteoarthritis (OA)

Canadian labeling: Additional use (not in US labeling): Relief of signs and symptoms of ankylosing spondylitis; relief of pain associated with dysmenorrhea; relief of mild to moderate pain accompanied by inflammation (eg, bursitis, tendinitis, soft tissue trauma)

Local Anesthetic/Vasoconstrictor Precautions No information available to require special precautions

Effects on Dental Treatment The dentist should be aware of the potential of abnormal coagulation. Caution should also be exercised in the use of NSAIDs in patients already on anticoagulant therapy with drugs such as warfarin (Coumadin®). See Effects on Bleeding.

Effects on Bleeding Nonselective NSAIDs such as flurbiprofen inhibit platelet aggregation and prolong bleeding time in some patients. Unlike aspirin, the NSAID effect on platelet function is quantitatively less, of shorter duration, and reversible.

Adverse Reactions

Frequency not defined.

>1%:

Cardiovascular: Edema

Central nervous system: Amnesia, anxiety, depression, dizziness, drowsiness, headache, hyperreflexia, insomnia, malaise, nervousness, vertigo

Dermatologic: Skin rash

Endocrine & metabolic: Weight changes

Gastrointestinal: Abdominal pain, constipation, diarrhea, dyspepsia, flatulence, gastrointestinal bleeding, nausea, vomiting

Hepatic: Increased liver enzymes

Neuromuscular & skeletal: Tremor, weakness

Ophthalmic: Visual disturbance

Otic: Tinnitus

Respiratory: Rhinitis

<1%, postmarketing, and/or case reports: Altered sense of smell, anaphylaxis, anemia, angioedema, asthma, bruise, cardiac failure, cerebral ischemia, confusion, decreased hematocrit, decreased hemoglobin, eczema, eosinophilia, epistaxis, exfoliative dermatitis, fever, gastric ulcer, hematuria, hepatitis, hepatotoxicity (idiosyncratic; Chalasani 2014), hypertension, hyperuricemia, interstitial nephritis, jaundice, leukopenia, paresthesia, peptic ulcer, pruritus, purpura, renal failure, skin photosensitivity, stomatitis, thrombocytopenia, toxic epidermal necrolysis, urticaria, vasodilatation

Dental Usual Dosage Management of postoperative pain (off-label use): Adults: Oral: 100 mg every 12 hours

Dosing

Adult Note: Use the lowest effective dose for the shortest possible duration.

US labeling:

Rheumatoid arthritis and osteoarthritis: Oral: Initial: 200 to 300 mg/day in 2 to 4 divided doses; maximum single dose: 100 mg (in a multiple dose daily regimen)

Canadian labeling: **Note:** If a dose is missed, take as soon as remembered; if next dose is due within 2 hours, a single dose should be taken and the next dose skipped.

Ankylosing spondylitis, osteoarthritis, rheumatoid arthritis: Oral: 200 mg/day in divided doses; some patients may require up to 300 mg/day during symptom exacerbations (maximum: 300 mg/day)

Dysmenorrhea: Oral: 50 mg 4 times daily

Pain (mild to moderately severe): Oral: 50 mg every 4 to 6 hours as needed

Geriatric Refer to adult dosing. Use with caution; reduce the initial dose to the lower end of the dosing range.

Renal Impairment

US labeling:

Mild impairment: There are no dosage adjustments provided in the manufacturer's labeling; use with caution.

Moderate to severe impairment: There are no dosage adjustments provided in the manufacturer's labeling; however dosage adjustment may be necessary due to possible metabolite accumulation. Avoid use in patients with advanced renal disease unless benefits are expected to outweigh risk of worsening renal function.

Continuous ambulatory peritoneal dialysis: Not removed by dialysis.

Canadian labeling:

CrCl ≥30 mL/minute or 0.5 mL/second: There are no dosage adjustments provided in the manufacturer's labeling; use with extreme caution.

CrCl <30 mL/minute or 0.5 mL/second: Use is contraindicated in severe renal impairment (CrCl <30 mL/minute or 0.5 mL/second) or deteriorating renal disease.

Continuous ambulatory peritoneal dialysis: Not removed by dialysis.

KDIGO 2012 guidelines provide the following recommendations for NSAIDs:

eGFR 30 to <60 mL/minute/1.73 m^2: Temporarily discontinue in patients with intercurrent disease that increases risk of acute kidney injury.

eGFR <30 mL/minute/1.73 m^2: Avoid use.

Hepatic Impairment

US labeling: There are no dosage adjustments provided in the manufacturer's labeling; reduced doses may be required due to extensive hepatic metabolism.

Canadian labeling: Use is contraindicated in severe hepatic impairment or active hepatic disease.

Mechanism of Action Reversibly inhibits cyclooxygenase-1 and 2 (COX-1 and 2) enzymes, which results in decreased formation of prostaglandin precursors; has antipyretic, analgesic, and anti-inflammatory properties

Other proposed mechanisms not fully elucidated (and possibly contributing to the anti-inflammatory effect to varying degrees), include inhibiting chemotaxis, altering lymphocyte activity, inhibiting neutrophil aggregation/activation, and decreasing proinflammatory cytokine levels.

Contraindications

Hypersensitivity to flurbiprofen or any component of the formulation; history of asthma, urticaria, or allergic-type reactions after taking aspirin or other NSAIDs; use in the setting of coronary artery bypass (CABG) surgery

Canadian labeling: Additional contraindications (not in US labeling): Severe uncontrolled heart failure; active gastric/duodenal/peptic ulcer; active GI bleeding; history of recurrent ulceration or active inflammatory GI disease; inflammatory bowel disease; severe hepatic impairment; active hepatic disease; severe renal impairment (CrCl <30 mL/minute or 0.5 mL/second) or deteriorating renal disease; cerebrovascular bleeding or other bleeding disorders; known hyperkalemia; children and adolescents <18 years of age; breast-feeding; pregnancy (third trimester)

Warnings/Precautions [US Boxed Warning]: NSAIDs cause an increased risk of serious (and potentially fatal) adverse cardiovascular thrombotic events, including MI and stroke. Risk may occur early during treatment and may increase with duration of use. Relative risk appears to be similar in those with and without known cardiovascular disease or risk factors for cardiovascular disease; however, absolute incidence of serious cardiovascular thrombotic events (which may occur early during treatment) was higher in patients with known cardiovascular disease or risk factors. New-onset hypertension or exacerbation of hypertension may occur (NSAIDs may also impair response to ACE inhibitors, thiazide diuretics, or loop diuretics); may contribute to cardiovascular events; monitor blood pressure; use with caution in patients with hypertension. May cause sodium and fluid retention; use with caution in patients with edema. Avoid use in heart failure (ACCF/AHA [Yancy 2013]). Avoid use in patients with a recent MI unless benefits outweigh risk of cardiovascular thrombotic events. Use the lowest effective dose for the shortest duration of time, consistent with individual patient goals, to reduce risk of cardiovascular events; alternate therapies should be considered for patients at high risk.

[US Boxed Warning]: Use is contraindicated in the setting of coronary artery bypass graft (CABG) surgery. Risk of MI and stroke may be increased with use following CABG surgery.

Platelet adhesion and aggregation may be decreased; may prolong bleeding time; patients with coagulation disorders or who are receiving anticoagulants should be monitored closely. Anemia may occur; patients on long-term NSAID therapy should be monitored for anemia. Rarely, NSAID use has been associated with potentially severe blood dyscrasias (eg, agranulocytosis, thrombocytopenia, aplastic anemia). NSAID use may compromise existing renal function; dose-dependent decreases in prostaglandin synthesis may result from NSAID use, reducing renal blood flow which may cause renal decompensation (usually reversible). Patients with impaired renal function, dehydration, hypovolemia, heart failure, hepatic impairment, those taking diuretics, and ACE inhibitors, and the elderly are at greater risk of renal toxicity. Rehydrate patient before starting therapy; monitor renal function closely. Long-term NSAID use may result in renal papillary necrosis and other renal injury.

Not recommended for use in patients with advanced renal disease; monitor closely if therapy must be initiated. The Canadian labeling contraindicates use in patients with severe renal impairment (CrCl <30 mL/minute or 0.5 mL/second) or deteriorating renal disease.

[US Boxed Warning]: NSAIDs cause increased risk of serious gastrointestinal inflammation, ulceration, bleeding, and perforation (may be fatal); elderly patients and patients with history of peptic ulcer disease and/or GI bleeding are at greater risk for serious GI events. These events may occur at any time during therapy and without warning. Avoid use in patients with active GI bleeding. Use caution with a history of GI ulcers, concurrent therapy known to increase the risk of GI bleeding (eg, aspirin, anticoagulants and/or corticosteroids, selective serotonin reuptake inhibitors), advanced hepatic disease, coagulopathy, smoking, use of alcohol, or in the elderly, or debilitated patients. Use the lowest effective dose for the shortest duration of time, consistent with individual patient goals, to reduce risk of GI adverse events; alternate therapies should be considered for patients at high risk. When used concomitantly with aspirin, a substantial increase in the risk of gastrointestinal complications (eg, ulcer) occurs; concomitant gastroprotective therapy (eg, proton pump inhibitors) is recommended (Bhatt 2008).

Use the lowest effective dose for the shortest duration of time, consistent with individual patient goals, to reduce risk of cardiovascular or GI adverse events. Alternate therapies should be considered for patients at high risk.

NSAIDs may cause potentially fatal serious skin adverse events including exfoliative dermatitis, Stevens-Johnson syndrome (SJS), and toxic epidermal necrolysis (TEN); may occur without warning; discontinue use at first sign of skin rash (or any other hypersensitivity). Anaphylactoid reactions may occur, even in patients without prior exposure; patients with "aspirin triad" (bronchial asthma, aspirin intolerance, rhinitis) may be at increased risk. Contraindicated in patients who experience bronchospasm, asthma, rhinitis, or urticaria with NSAID or aspirin therapy. Severe, rarely fatal, anaphylactic-like reactions to NSAIDs have been reported. Use caution in other forms of asthma. NSAIDs may increase the risk of aseptic meningitis (rare), especially in patients with autoimmune disorder (eg, systemic lupus erythematosus (SLE) mixed connective tissue disorders). NSAIDs may be associated with persistent urinary symptoms (bladder pain, dysuria, urinary frequency), hematuria or cystitis. The onset of these symptoms may occur at any time after the initiation of therapy. Some cases have become severe on continued treatment; discontinue therapy to ascertain if symptoms disappear. May cause drowsiness, dizziness, blurred vision, and other neurologic effects which may impair physical or mental abilities; patients must be cautioned about performing tasks which require mental alertness (eg, operating machinery or driving). Transaminase elevations have been reported with use; closely monitor patients with any abnormal LFT. Rare (sometimes fatal) severe hepatic reactions (eg, fulminant hepatitis, liver necrosis, hepatic failure) have occurred with NSAID use; discontinue immediately if signs or symptoms of hepatic disease develop or if systemic manifestations occur. Use with caution in patients with hepatic impairment; patients with hepatic impairment may require reduced doses due to extensive hepatic metabolism. Patients with advanced hepatic disease are at an increased risk of GI bleeding with NSAIDs. The Canadian labeling contraindicates use in patients with severe hepatic impairment or active hepatic disease. Use with caution; dosage adjustment in patients with moderate or severe impairment may be necessary due to possible metabolite accumulation. Avoid use in patients with advanced renal disease unless benefits are expected to outweigh risk of worsening renal function; monitor closely if therapy must be initiated. The Canadian labeling contraindicates use in patients with severe renal impairment (CrCl <30 mL/minute or 0.5 mL/second) or deteriorating renal disease. NSAID use may increase the risk of hyperkalemia, particularly in the elderly, diabetics, renal disease, and with concomitant use of other agents capable of inducing hyperkalemia (eg, ACE inhibitors). Monitor potassium closely. The Canadian labeling contraindicates use in patients with known hyperkalemia. Blurred and/or diminished vision has been reported; discontinue use and refer for ophthalmologic evaluation if such symptoms occur.

Elderly patients are at greater risk for serious GI, cardiovascular, and/or renal adverse events. Use with caution; consider reducing the initial dose.

Withhold for at least 4 to 6 half-lives prior to surgical or dental procedures. Potentially significant interactions may exist, requiring dose or frequency adjustment, additional monitoring, and/or selection of alternative therapy.

Drug Interactions

Metabolism/Transport Effects **Substrate** of CYP2C9 (minor); **Note:** Assignment of Major/Minor substrate status based on clinically relevant drug interaction potential; **Inhibits** CYP2C9 (weak)

Avoid Concomitant Use

Avoid concomitant use of Flurbiprofen (Systemic) with any of the following: Dexketoprofen; Floctafenine; Ketorolac (Nasal); Ketorolac (Systemic); Morniflumate; NSAID (COX-2 Inhibitor); Omacetaxine; Pelubiprofen; Phenylbutazone; Talniflumate; Tenoxicam; Urokinase; Zaltoprofen

Increased Effect/Toxicity

Flurbiprofen (Systemic) may increase the levels/effects of: 5-ASA Derivatives; Agents with Antiplatelet Properties; Aliskiren; Aminoglycosides; Aminolevulinic Acid; Anticoagulants; Apixaban; Bisphosphonate Derivatives; Cephalothin; Collagenase (Systemic); CycloSPORINE (Systemic); Dabigatran Etexilate; Deferasirox; Deoxycholic Acid; Desmopressin; Digoxin; Drospirenone; Edoxaban; Eplerenone; Haloperidol; Ibritumomab; Lithium; Methotrexate; Nonsteroidal Anti-Inflammatory Agents; NSAID (COX-2 Inhibitor); Obinutuzumab; Omacetaxine; PEMEtrexed; Porfimer; Potassium-Sparing Diuretics; PRALAtrexate; Quinolone Antibiotics; Rivaroxaban; Salicylates; Tacrolimus (Systemic); Tenofovir Products; Thrombolytic Agents; Tolperisone; Tositumomab and Iodine I 131 Tositumomab; Urokinase; Vancomycin; Verteporfin; Vitamin K Antagonists

The levels/effects of Flurbiprofen (Systemic) may be increased by: ACE Inhibitors; Alcohol (Ethyl); Angiotensin II Receptor Blockers; Antidepressants (Tricyclic, Tertiary Amine); Corticosteroids (Systemic); CycloSPORINE (Systemic); Dasatinib; Dexketoprofen; Diclofenac (Systemic); Felbinac; Floctafenine; Glucosamine; Herbs (Anticoagulant/Antiplatelet Properties); Ibrutinib; Ketorolac (Nasal); Ketorolac (Systemic); Limaprost; Loop Diuretics; Morniflumate; Multivitamins/Fluoride (with ADE); Multivitamins/Minerals (with ADEK, Folate, Iron); Multivitamins/Minerals (with AE, No Iron); Naftazone; Omega-3 Fatty Acids; Pelubiprofen; Pentosan Polysulfate Sodium; Pentoxifylline; Phenylbutazone; Probenecid; Prostacyclin Analogues; Selective Serotonin Reuptake Inhibitors; Serotonin/Norepinephrine Reuptake Inhibitors; Sodium Phosphates; Talniflumate; Tenoxicam; Thiazide and Thiazide-Like Diuretics; Tipranavir; Tolperisone; Vitamin E (Systemic); Zaltoprofen

Decreased Effect

Flurbiprofen (Systemic) may decrease the levels/effects of: ACE Inhibitors; Aliskiren; Angiotensin II Receptor Blockers; Beta-Blockers; Eplerenone; HydrALAZINE; Loop Diuretics; Potassium-Sparing Diuretics; Prostaglandins (Ophthalmic); Salicylates;

Selective Serotonin Reuptake Inhibitors; Thiazide and Thiazide-Like Diuretics

The levels/effects of Flurbiprofen (Systemic) may be decreased by: Bile Acid Sequestrants; Salicylates

Food Interactions Food may decrease the rate but not the extent of absorption. Management: May administer with food, milk, or antacid to decrease GI effects.

Pharmacodynamics/Kinetics

Half-life Elimination 4.7 to 5.7 hours

Time to Peak

~2 hours

Pregnancy Risk Factor C

Pregnancy Considerations Adverse events have not been observed in animal reproduction studies. NSAID exposure during the first trimester is not strongly associated with congenital malformations; however, cardiovascular anomalies and cleft palate have been observed following NSAID exposure in some studies. The use of an NSAID close to conception may be associated with an increased risk of miscarriage. Nonteratogenic effects have been observed following NSAID administration during the third trimester including myocardial degenerative changes, prenatal constriction of the ductus arteriosus, fetal tricuspid regurgitation, failure of the ductus arteriosus to close postnatally; renal dysfunction or failure, oligohydramnios; gastrointestinal bleeding or perforation, increased risk of necrotizing enterocolitis; intracranial bleeding (including intraventricular hemorrhage), platelet dysfunction with resultant bleeding; pulmonary hypertension. Because they may cause premature closure of the ductus arteriosus, use of NSAIDs late in pregnancy should be avoided (use after 31 or 32 weeks gestation is not recommended by some clinicians). The chronic use of NSAIDs in women of reproductive age may be associated with infertility that is reversible upon discontinuation of the medication. The Canadian labeling contraindicates use during the third trimester of pregnancy.

Breastfeeding Considerations Low levels of flurbiprofen are found in breast milk. According to the manufacturer, the decision to breast-feed during therapy should take into account the risk of exposure to the infant and the benefits of treatment to the mother. The Canadian labeling contraindicates use in breastfeeding women.

Dosage Forms

Tablet, Oral:

Generic: 50 mg, 100 mg

Flutamide (FLOO ta mide)

Brand Names: Canada Apo-Flutamide; Euflex; PMS-Flutamide; Teva-Flutamide

Pharmacologic Category Antineoplastic Agent, Antiandrogen

Use Prostate cancer: Management of locally confined Stage B_2 to C and Stage D_2 metastatic prostate cancer (in combination with a luteinizing hormone-releasing hormone [LHRH] agonist). For Stage B_2 to C prostate cancer, flutamide treatment (and goserelin) should start 8 weeks prior to initiating radiation therapy and continue during radiation therapy. To achieve treatment benefit in Stage D_2 metastatic prostate cancer, initiate flutamide with the LHRH agonist and continue until disease progression.

Local Anesthetic/Vasoconstrictor Precautions No information available to require special precautions

Effects on Dental Treatment No significant effects or complications reported

Effects on Bleeding Hemolytic anemia has been reported.

Adverse Reactions

>10%:

Endocrine & metabolic: Hot flash (46% to 61%), galactorrhea (9% to 42%), decreased libido (36%), increased lactate dehydrogenase (transient; mild)

Gastrointestinal: Diarrhea (12% to 40%), vomiting (11% to 12%)

Genitourinary: Impotence (33%), cystitis (16%), breast tenderness

Hematologic & oncologic: Rectal hemorrhage (14%), tumor flare

Hepatic: Increased serum AST (transient; mild)

1% to 10%:

Cardiovascular: Edema (4%), hypertension (1%)

Central nervous system: Anxiety, confusion, depression, dizziness, drowsiness, headache, insomnia, nervousness

Dermatologic: Skin rash (3% to 8%), ecchymoses, pruritus

Endocrine & metabolic: Gynecomastia (9%)

Gastrointestinal: Nausea (9%), proctitis (8%), gastric distress (4% to 6%), anorexia (4%), constipation, dyspepsia, increased appetite

Genitourinary: Hematuria (7%)

Hematologic & oncologic: Anemia (6%), leukopenia (3%), thrombocytopenia (1%)

Infection: Herpes zoster

Neuromuscular & skeletal: Weakness (1%)

<1%, postmarketing, and case reports: Cholestatic jaundice, hemolytic anemia, hepatic encephalopathy, hepatic failure, hepatic necrosis, hepatitis, hypersensitivity pneumonitis, increased blood urea nitrogen, increased gamma-glutamyl transferase, increased serum ALT, increased serum bilirubin, increased serum creatinine, jaundice, macrocytic anemia, malignant neoplasm of breast (male), methemoglobinemia, myocardial infarction, oligospermia, pulmonary embolism, skin photosensitivity, sulfhemoglobinemia, thrombophlebitis, urine discoloration (amber, yellow-green)

General Dosage Range Oral: *Adults (males):* 250 mg 3 times daily

Mechanism of Action Nonsteroidal antiandrogen that inhibits androgen uptake and/or inhibits binding of androgen in target tissues.

Pharmacodynamics/Kinetics

Half-life Elimination ~6 hours (2-hydroxyflutamide)

Time to Peak ~2 hours (2-hydroxyflutamide)

Pregnancy Risk Factor D

Pregnancy Considerations

Adverse events have been observed in animal reproduction studies. May cause fetal harm if administered in pregnancy. Flutamide is not indicated for use in women.

Fluticasone (Nasal) (floo TIK a sone)

Brand Names: US Flonase Allergy Relief [OTC]; Flonase Sensimist [OTC]; Flonase [DSC]; GoodSense Nasoflow [OTC]; Ticaspray; Veramyst [DSC]

Brand Names: Canada Apo-Fluticasone; Avamys; Flonase; ratio-Fluticasone

Pharmacologic Category Corticosteroid, Nasal

Use

Rx products:

Allergic rhinitis (Veramyst, Avamys [Canadian product], Flonase [Canadian product]): Management of seasonal and perennial allergic rhinitis in adults and children ≥2 years of age (Veramyst, Avamys) and in patients 4 to 17 years of age (Flonase)

Nonallergic rhinitis (Flonase): Management of the nasal symptoms of perennial nonallergic rhinitis in adults and pediatric patients ≥4 years of age

OTC products:

Upper respiratory allergies: Relief of hay fever or other upper respiratory allergies (eg, itchy and watery eyes, nasal congestion, runny nose, sneezing, itchy nose) in adults and children ≥4 years of age (Clarispray, Flonase Allergy Relief, Good Sense Nasoflow) or children ≥2 years of age (Flonase Sensimist)

Local Anesthetic/Vasoconstrictor Precautions No information available to require special precautions

Effects on Dental Treatment No significant effects or complications reported

Effects on Bleeding No information available to require special precautions

Adverse Reactions

>10%: Central nervous system: Headache (7% to 16%)

1% to 10%:

Central nervous system: Dizziness (1% to 3%), generalized ache (1% to 3%)

Gastrointestinal: Nausea and vomiting (3% to 5%), abdominal pain (1% to 3%), diarrhea (1% to 3%)

Neuromuscular & skeletal: Back pain (1%)

Respiratory: Pharyngitis (6% to 8%), epistaxis (4% to 7%), asthma-like symptoms (3% to 7%), cough (3% to 4%), pharyngolaryngeal pain (2% to 4%), blood in nasal mucous (1% to 3%), bronchitis (1% to 3%), flu-like symptoms (1% to 3%), rhinorrhea (1% to 3%), nasal mucosa ulcer (1%)

Miscellaneous: Fever (1% to 5%)

<1%, postmarketing, and/or case reports: Altered sense of smell, anaphylactoid reaction, anaphylaxis, angioedema, blurred vision, bronchospasm, burning sensation of the nose, cataract, conjunctivitis, dry eye syndrome, dry nose, dry throat, dysgeusia, dyspnea, eye irritation, facial edema, glaucoma, hoarseness, hypersensitivity reaction, increased intraocular pressure, increased serum AST, local irritation (nose), nasal candidiasis, nasal septum perforation (rare), palpitations, pruritus, psychomotor agitation, second degree atrioventricular block, sinus congestion, skin rash, sore nose, sore throat, throat irritation, tongue edema, tremor, urticaria, voice disorder, vulvovaginal candidiasis, wheezing

General Dosage Range Intranasal:

Propionate

Flonase (Rx):

Children ≥4 years and Adolescents: Initial: 1 spray (50 mcg/spray) per nostril once daily (100 mcg/day); Maintenance: 1 to 2 sprays per nostril once daily (100 to 200 mcg/day) (maximum: 2 sprays in each nostril [200 mcg]/day)

Adults: Initial: 2 sprays (50 mcg/spray) per nostril once daily (200 mcg/day); Maintenance: 1 to 2 sprays per nostril once daily (100 to 200 mcg/day) (maximum: 2 sprays in each nostril [200 mcg]/day)

Flonase Allergy Relief and ClariSpray (OTC):

Children 4 years to 11 years: 1 spray (50 mcg/spray) per nostril once daily (100 mcg/day).

Children ≥12 years, Adolescents, and Adults: Initial: 2 sprays (50 mcg/spray) per nostril once daily (200 mcg/day); Maintenance: 1 or 2 sprays per nostril once daily (100 to 200 mcg/day).

Furoate

Veramyst (Rx):

Children 2 to 11 years: Initial: 1 spray (27.5 mcg/spray) per nostril once daily (55 mcg/day); Maintenance: 1 to 2 sprays per nostril once daily (55 to 110 mcg/day) (maximum: 2 sprays in each nostril [110 mcg]/day)

Children ≥12 years, Adolescents, and Adults: Initial: 2 sprays (27.5 mcg/spray) per nostril once (110 mcg/day); Maintenance: 1 to 2 sprays per nostril once daily (55 to 110 mcg/day)

Flonase Sensimist: (OTC):

Children 2 to 11 years: 1 spray (27.5 mcg/spray) per nostril once daily (55 mcg/day).

Children ≥12 years, Adolescents, and Adults: Initial: 2 sprays (27.5 mcg/spray) per nostril once daily (110 mcg/day); Maintenance: 1 or 2 sprays per nostril once daily (55 to 110 mcg/day).

Mechanism of Action Fluticasone belongs to a group of corticosteroids which utilizes a fluorocarbothioate ester linkage at the 17 carbon position; extremely potent vasoconstrictive and anti-inflammatory activity

Pharmacodynamics/Kinetics

Onset of Action Maximal benefit may take several days

Half-life Elimination

IV: Fluticasone propionate: ~8 hours; Fluticasone furoate: ~15 hours

Pregnancy Risk Factor C

Pregnancy Considerations Adverse events have been observed in some animal reproduction studies. Hypoadrenalism may occur in newborns following maternal use of corticosteroids in pregnancy; monitor. Intranasal corticosteroids are recommended for the treatment of rhinitis during pregnancy; the lowest effective dose should be used (NAEPP 2005; Wallace 2008).

Fluticasone (Oral Inhalation) (floo TIK a sone)

Related Information

Respiratory Diseases *on page 1777*

Brand Names: US Arnuity Ellipta; Flovent Diskus; Flovent HFA

Brand Names: Canada Arnuity Ellipta; Flovent Diskus; Flovent HFA

Generic Availability (US) No

Pharmacologic Category Corticosteroid, Inhalant (Oral)

Use

Asthma:

ArmonAir Respiclick and Arnuity Ellipta: Maintenance treatment of asthma as prophylactic therapy in patients 12 years and older

Flovent Diskus and Flovent HFA: Maintenance treatment of asthma as prophylactic therapy in patients 4 years and older; for patients requiring oral corticosteroid therapy for asthma to assist in total discontinuation or reduction of total oral dose

Limitations of use: Not indicated for relief of acute bronchospasm

Guideline recommendations: A low-dose inhaled corticosteroid (*in addition to an as-needed short acting beta$_2$-agonist*) is the initial preferred long-term control medication for children, adolescents, and adult patients with persistent asthma who are candidates for treatment according to a step-wise treatment approach (GINA 2016; NAEPP 2007).

Local Anesthetic/Vasoconstrictor Precautions No information available to require special precautions

Effects on Dental Treatment Localized infections with *Candida albicans* or *Aspergillus niger* have occurred frequently in the mouth and pharynx with repetitive use of oral inhaler of corticosteroids. These infections may require treatment with appropriate antifungal therapy or discontinuance of treatment with corticosteroid inhaler.

Effects on Bleeding No information available to require special precautions

Adverse Reactions

>10%:

Central nervous system: Fatigue (≤16%), malaise (≤16%), headache (2% to 14%)

Gastrointestinal: Oral candidiasis (≤31%)

Neuromuscular & skeletal: Arthralgia (≤17%), arthritis (≤17%), musculoskeletal pain (2% to 12%)

Respiratory: Sinus infection (≤33%), sinusitis (≤33%), upper respiratory tract infection (2% to 31%), throat irritation (<1% to 22%), nasal congestion (≥3% to 16%), nasopharyngitis (8% to 13%), rhinitis (<1% to 13%), bronchitis (≤12%)

1% to 10%:

Cardiovascular: Hypertension (≤1%), subarachnoid hemorrhage (≤1%)

Central nervous system: Pain (10%), voice disorder (≤9%), procedural pain (<1% to 3%)

Dermatologic: Skin rash (8%), pruritus (6%)

Gastrointestinal: Nausea and vomiting (1% to 9%), viral gastrointestinal infection (3% to 5%), gastrointestinal distress (≤4%), gastrointestinal pain (≤4%), oropharyngeal candidiasis (3%), toothache (3%), viral gastroenteritis (3%), abdominal pain (≤3%)

Hematologic & oncologic: Malignant neoplasm of breast (≤1%)

Infection: Influenza (4% to 7%), viral infection (≤5%), abscess (≤1%)

Neuromuscular & skeletal: Muscle injury (≤5%), back pain (3%), herniated disk (≤1%)

Respiratory: Viral respiratory infection (1% to 9%), cough (≤9%), hoarseness (≤9%), pharyngitis (3% to 6%), upper respiratory tract inflammation (≤5%), oropharyngeal pain (3% to 4%), allergic rhinitis (≥3%)

Miscellaneous: Fever (1% to 7%), accidental injury (≤5%), amputation (≤1%)

<1%, postmarketing, and/or case reports: Acne vulgaris, adrenocortical insufficiency, aggressive behavior, agitation, allergic skin reaction, anaphylaxis (rare; occurred in patients with severe milk protein allergy taking Flovent Diskus), anxiety, aphonia, bacterial infection, bacterial reproductive infection, behavioral changes (very rare; includes hyperactivity and irritability in children), blepharoconjunctivitis, bronchospasm (immediate and delayed), bruise, burn, cataract (long-term use), change in appetite, chest symptoms, chest tightness, cholecystitis, Churg-Strauss syndrome, conjunctivitis, cranial nerve palsy, Cushingoid appearance, decreased bone mineral density (long-term use), decreased linear skeletal growth rate (children/adolescents), dental caries, dental discoloration, dental discomfort (and pain), depression, dermatitis, dermatological disease, diarrhea, disturbance in fluid balance, dizziness, drug toxicity, dyspepsia, dyspnea, ecchymoses, eczema, edema, eosinophilia, epistaxis, esophageal candidiasis, exacerbation of asthma, facial edema, folliculitis, fungal infection, gastrointestinal disease, glaucoma (long-term use), hematoma, HPA-axis suppression, hypercorticoidism, hyperglycemia, hypersensitivity reaction (immediate and delayed; includes ear, nose, and throat allergic disorders, anaphylaxis, angioedema, bronchospasm, hypotension, skin rash, urticaria), increased intraocular pressure (long-term use), inflammation (musculoskeletal), keratitis, laceration, laryngitis, migraine, mobility disorder, mood disorder, mouth disease (and tongue disease), muscle cramps, muscle rigidity (stiffness, tightness), muscle spasm, oral discomfort (and pain), oral mucosa ulcer, oral rash (and erythema), oropharyngeal edema, osteonecrosis (especially with current or past use of systemic steroids), osteoporosis, palpitations, paradoxical bronchospasm, paranasal sinus disease, photodermatitis, pneumonia, polyp (ear, nose, throat), post nasal drip, pressure-induced disorder, reduced salivation, restlessness, rhinorrhea, sleep disorder, soft tissue injury, sore throat, urinary tract infection, vasculitis, viral skin infection, weight gain, wheezing, wound

Dosing

Adult & Geriatric Asthma: Inhalation, oral: **Note:** Titrate to the lowest effective dose once asthma stability is achieved.

ArmonAir Respiclick (fluticasone propionate): **Note:** May increase dose after 2 weeks of therapy in patients who are not adequately controlled.

Dry powder inhaler:

No prior treatment with inhaled corticosteroids: Initial: 55 mcg twice daily; maximum: 232 mcg twice daily.

Prior treatment with inhaled corticosteroid: 55 mcg to 232 mcg twice daily (base starting dosage on strength of previous inhaled corticosteroid and disease severity); maximum: 232 mcg twice daily.

Arnuity Ellipta (fluticasone furoate): Dosing based on previous asthma therapy: **Note:** May increase dose after 2 weeks of therapy in patients who are not adequately controlled.

Dry powder inhaler:

No prior treatment with inhaled corticosteroids: Initial: 100 mcg once daily; maximum: 200 mcg/day.

Prior treatment with inhaled corticosteroids: Initial: 100 to 200 mcg once daily; maximum: 200 mcg/day.

Flovent HFA (fluticasone propionate):

US labeling: Dosing based on previous asthma therapy: **Note:** May increase dose after 2 weeks of therapy in patients who are not adequately controlled.

Metered dose inhaler:

Bronchodilator alone: Initial: 88 mcg twice daily; maximum: 440 mcg twice daily.

Inhaled corticosteroids: Initial: 88 to 220 mcg twice daily (initial dose >88 mcg twice daily may be considered in patients previously requiring higher doses of inhaled corticosteroids); maximum: 440 mcg twice daily.

Oral corticosteroids (OCS): Initial: 440 mcg twice daily; maximum: 880 mcg twice daily.

Canadian labeling: **Note:** May increase dose after ~1 week of therapy in patients who are not adequately controlled.

Metered dose inhaler:

Mild asthma: 100 to 250 mcg twice daily

Moderate asthma: 250 to 500 mcg twice daily

Severe asthma: 500 mcg twice daily; may increase up to 1,000 mcg twice daily in very severe patients (eg, patients using oral corticosteroids [OCS]).

Asthma guidelines:

National Asthma Education and Prevention Program guidelines (NAEPP 2007): HFA inhaler (refers to Flovent HFA 44 mcg, 110 mcg, and 220 mcg strengths available in US): **Note:** Administer in divided doses twice daily.

"Low" dose: 88 to 264 mcg/day.

"Medium" dose: >264 to 440 mcg/day.

"High" dose: >440 mcg/day

Global Initiative for Asthma guidelines (GINA 2016): HFA inhaler (refers to Flovent HFA 50 mcg, 125 mcg, and 250 mcg strengths available in Canada):

"Low" dose: 100 to 250 mcg daily.

"Medium" dose: >250 to 500 mcg daily.

"High" dose: >500 mcg daily.

Flovent Diskus (fluticasone propionate):

US labeling: **Note:** May increase dose after 2 weeks of therapy in patients who are not adequately controlled.

Dry powder inhaler: Dosing based on previous asthma therapy:

Bronchodilator alone: Initial: 100 mcg twice daily; maximum: 500 mcg twice daily.

Inhaled corticosteroids: Initial: 100 to 250 mcg twice daily; maximum: 500 mcg twice daily; initial dose >100 mcg twice daily may be considered in patients with poorer asthma control or those previously requiring high ranges of inhaled corticosteroids.

Oral corticosteroids (OCS): Initial: 500 to 1,000 mcg twice daily; maximum: 1,000 mcg twice daily.

Canadian labeling: **Note:** May increase dose after ~1 week of therapy in patients who are not adequately controlled.

Dry powder inhaler:

Mild asthma: 100 to 250 mcg twice daily.

Moderate asthma: 250 to 500 mcg twice daily.

Severe asthma: 500 mcg twice daily; may increase up to 1,000 mcg twice daily in very severe patients (eg, patients using oral corticosteroids [OCS]).

Asthma guidelines:

National Asthma Education and Prevention Program guidelines (NAEPP 2007): Dry powder inhaler (refers to Flovent Diskus 50 mcg, 100 mcg, and 250 mcg strengths available in the US and Canada, and the 500 mcg strength available in Canada): **Note:** Administer in divided doses twice daily:

"Low" dose: 100 to 300 mcg/day.

"Medium" dose: >300 to 500 mcg/day.

"High" dose: >500 mcg/day.

Global Initiative for Asthma guidelines (GINA 2016): Dry powder inhaler (refers to Flovent Diskus 50 mcg, 100 mcg, and 250 mcg strengths available in the US and Canada, and the 500 mcg strength available in Canada).

"Low" dose: 100 to 250 mcg daily.

"Medium" dose: >250 to 500 mcg daily.

"High" dose: >500 mcg daily.

Conversion: Conversion from oral systemic corticosteroids to orally inhaled corticosteroids: When converting from oral corticosteroids (OCS) to orally inhaled corticosteroids, initiate oral inhalation therapy in patients whose asthma is previously stabilized on OCS. Gradual OCS dose reductions should begin ~7 days after starting inhaled therapy. Reduce prednisone dose no more rapidly than 2.5 to 5 mg/day (or equivalent of other OCS) weekly. If adrenal insufficiency occurs, resume OCS therapy; initiate a more gradual withdrawal. When transitioning from systemic to inhaled corticosteroids, supplemental systemic corticosteroid therapy may be necessary during periods of stress or during severe asthma attacks.

Chronic obstructive pulmonary disease (stable) (off-label use): Inhalation, oral: 50 to 500 mcg/day in combination with a long-acting bronchodilator (GOLD 2014).

Eosinophilic esophagitis (off-label use): Oral (off-label route): 440 to 880 mcg of aerosolized fluticasone swallowed (not inhaled) twice daily (880 to 1,760 mcg/day) (Alexander 2012; Butz 2014; Chuang 2015; Murali 2015).

Pediatric

Asthma: Inhalation, oral: **Note:** Titrate to lowest effective dose once asthma stability achieved.

ArmonAir Respiclick (fluticasone propionate): Children ≥12 years and Adolescents: Refer to adult dosing.

Arnuity Ellipta (fluticasone furoate): Children ≥12 years and Adolescents: Refer to adult dosing.

Flovent HFA (fluticasone propionate):

US labeling:

Metered dose inhaler:

Children 4 to 11 years: Initial: 88 mcg twice daily; maximum: 88 mcg twice daily.

Children ≥12 years and Adolescents: Refer to adult dosing.

Canadian labeling:

Metered dose inhaler:

Children 1 to <4 years: 100 mcg twice daily.

Children 4 to <16 years: 100 mcg twice daily. **Note:** Manufacturer labeling recommends Flovent HFA be administered as a minimum of 2 inhalations twice daily; therefore, patients requiring lower or higher dosages than 100 mcg twice daily should use Flovent Diskus.

Adolescents ≥16 years and Adults: Refer to adult dosing.

Asthma guidelines:

National Asthma Education and Prevention Program guidelines (NAEPP 2007): HFA inhaler (refers to Flovent HFA 44 mcg, 110 mcg, and 220 mcg strengths available in US) Note: Administer in divided doses twice daily.

"Low" dose:

0 to 4 years: 176 mcg/day.

5 to 11 years: 88 to 176 mcg/day.

≥12 years: 88 to 264 mcg/day.

"Medium" dose:

0 to 4 years: >176 to 352 mcg/day.

5 to 11 years: >176 to 352 mcg/day.

≥12 years: >264 to 440 mcg/day.

"High" dose:

0 to 4 years: >352 mcg/day.

5 to 11 years: >352 mcg/day.

≥12 years: >440 mcg/day.

Global Initiative for Asthma guidelines (GINA 2016): HFA inhaler (refers to Flovent HFA 50 mcg, 125 mcg, and 250 mcg strengths available in Canada):

Children ≤5 years: "Low" dose: 100 mcg daily.

Children 6 to 11 years:
"Low" dose: 100 to 200 mcg daily.
"Medium" dose: >200 to 500 mcg daily.
"High" dose: >500 mcg daily.
Children ≥12 years and Adolescents: Refer to adult dosing.

Flovent Diskus (fluticasone propionate):

US labeling:

Dry powder inhaler:

Children 4 to 11 years: Initial: 50 mcg twice daily; may increase to maximum dose of 100 mcg twice daily in patients not adequately controlled after 2 weeks of therapy. Initial dose >50 mcg twice daily may be considered in patients with poorer asthma control or those previously requiring high ranges of inhaled corticosteroids.

Adolescents: Refer to adult dosing.

Canadian labeling:

Dry powder inhaler:

Children 4 to <16 years: Initial: 50 to 100 mcg twice daily; may increase up to 200 mcg twice daily after ~1 week of therapy in patients not adequately controlled.

Adolescents ≥16 years: Refer to adult dosing.

Asthma guidelines:

National Asthma Education and Prevention Program guidelines (NAEPP 2007): (administer in divided doses twice daily): Dry powder inhaler (refers to Flovent Diskus 50 mcg, 100 mcg, and 250 mcg strengths available in the US and Canada, and the 500 mcg strength available in Canada).

"Low" dose:
5 to 11 years: 100 to 200 mcg/day.
≥12 years: 100 to 300 mcg/day.
"Medium" dose:
5 to 11 years: >200 to 400 mcg/day.
≥12 years: >300 to 500 mcg/day.
"High" dose:
5 to 11 years: >400 mcg/day.
≥12 years: >500 mcg/day.

Global Initiative for Asthma guidelines (GINA 2016): Dry powder inhaler (refers to Flovent Diskus 50 mcg, 100 mcg, and 250 mcg strengths available in US and Canada, and the 500 mcg strength available in Canada).

Children 6 to 11 years:
"Low" dose: 100 to 200 mcg daily.
"Medium" dose: >200 to 400 mcg daily.
"High" dose: >400 mcg daily.
Children ≥12 years and Adolescents: Refer to adult dosing.

Conversion: Conversion from oral systemic corticosteroids to orally inhaled corticosteroids: When converting from oral corticosteroids (OCS) to orally inhaled corticosteroids, initiate oral inhalation therapy in patients whose asthma is previously stabilized on OCS. Gradual OCS dose reductions should begin ~7 days after starting inhaled therapy. Reduce prednisone dose no more rapidly than 2.5 to 5 mg/day (or equivalent of other OCS) weekly in children ≥12 years. Manufacturer's labeling does not provide a recommendation for children <12 years, although a similar approach to OCS dose reduction would seem advisable. If adrenal insufficiency occurs, resume OCS therapy; initiate a more gradual withdrawal. When transitioning from systemic to inhaled corticosteroids, supplemental systemic corticosteroid therapy may be necessary during periods of stress or during severe asthma attacks.

Eosinophilic esophagitis (off-label use): Oral (off-label route):

Children ≥2 years and Adolescents: 176 to 880 mcg/day of aerosolized fluticasone swallowed (not inhaled). Dose may be divided into 2 doses (Konikoff 2006; Teitelbaum 2002). Doses as high as 880 mcg twice daily have been reported (Butz 2014). Alternatively, may dose according to age:

Children 2 to 4 years: 88 mcg of aerosolized fluticasone swallowed (not inhaled) twice daily (176 mcg/day) (Teitelbaum 2002).

Children 5 to 10 years: 220 mcg of aerosolized fluticasone swallowed (not inhaled) twice daily (440 mcg/day) (Teitelbaum 2002).

Children ≥11 years and Adolescents:440 mcg of aerosolized fluticasone swallowed (not inhaled) twice daily (880 mcg/day) (Teitelbaum 2002).

Renal Impairment

Arnuity Ellipta: No dosage adjustment necessary.

ArmonAir Respiclick, Flovent Diskus and Flovent HFA: There are no dosage adjustments provided in the manufacturer's labeling (has not been studied).

Hepatic Impairment There are no dosage adjustment provided in the manufacturer's labeling (has not been studied); however, fluticasone is primarily cleared in the liver and plasma levels may be increased in patients with hepatic impairment. Arnuity Ellipta product labeling indicates that systemic exposure is increased up to 3-fold. Use with caution and closely monitor.

Mechanism of Action Fluticasone belongs to a group of corticosteroids which utilizes a fluorocarbothioate ester linkage at the 17 carbon position; extremely potent vasoconstrictive and anti-inflammatory activity. The effectiveness of inhaled fluticasone is due to its direct local effect.

Contraindications

Hypersensitivity to fluticasone or any component of the formulation; severe hypersensitivity to milk proteins or lactose (ArmonAir Respiclick, Arnuity Ellipta, Flovent Diskus); primary treatment of status asthmaticus or other acute episodes of asthma requiring intensive measures

Documentation of allergenic cross-reactivity for corticosteroids in this class is limited. However, because of similarities in chemical structure and/or pharmacologic actions, the possibility of cross-sensitivity cannot be ruled out with certainty.

Canadian labeling: Additional contraindications (not in US labeling): Flovent HFA and Flovent Diskus: Untreated fungal, bacterial or tubercular infections of the respiratory tract

Warnings/Precautions May cause hypercorticism or suppression of hypothalamic-pituitary-adrenal (HPA) axis. HPA axis suppression may lead to adrenal crisis. Withdrawal and discontinuation of a corticosteroid should be done slowly and carefully. Particular care is required when patients are transferred from systemic corticosteroids to inhaled corticosteroids due to possible adrenal insufficiency or withdrawal from steroids, including an increase in allergic symptoms. Patients receiving ≥20 mg per day of prednisone (or equivalent) may be most susceptible. Fatalities have occurred due to adrenal insufficiency in asthmatic patients during and after transfer from systemic corticosteroids to aerosol steroids; aerosol steroids do **not** provide the systemic steroid needed to treat patients having trauma, surgery, or infections. Select surgical patients on long-term, high-dose, inhaled corticosteroid (ICS), should be given stress doses of hydrocortisone intravenously during the surgical period and the dose reduced rapidly within 24 hours after surgery (NAEPP 2007).

Bronchospasm may occur with wheezing after inhalation; if this occurs, stop steroid and treat with a fast-acting bronchodilator. Immediate hypersensitivity reactions (eg, angioedema, bronchospasm, hypotension, rash, urticaria), including anaphylaxis, may occur. Supplemental steroids (oral or parenteral) may be needed during stress or severe asthma attacks. Short-acting beta$_2$-agonist (eg, albuterol) should be used for acute symptoms and symptoms occurring between treatments. Corticosteroid use may cause psychiatric disturbances, including depression, euphoria, insomnia, mood swings, and personality changes. Preexisting psychiatric conditions may be exacerbated by corticosteroid use. Prolonged use of corticosteroids may also increase the incidence of secondary infection, mask acute infection (including fungal infections), prolong or exacerbate viral infections, or limit response to vaccines. Avoid use if possible in patients with ocular herpes; active or quiescent tuberculosis infections of the respiratory tract; or untreated viral, fungal, parasitic or bacterial systemic infections. Exposure to chickenpox and measles should be avoided; if the patient is exposed, prophylaxis with varicella zoster immune globulin or pooled intramuscular immunoglobulin, respectively, may be indicated; if chickenpox develops, treatment with antiviral agents may be considered. Rare cases of vasculitis (Churg-Strauss syndrome) or other systemic eosinophilic conditions can occur. Prolonged treatment with corticosteroids has been associated with the development of Kaposi's sarcoma (case reports); if noted, discontinuation of therapy should be considered.

Use with caution in patients with thyroid disease, hepatic impairment, renal impairment, cardiovascular disease, diabetes, glaucoma, cataracts, myasthenia gravis, patients at risk for osteoporosis, patients at risk for seizures, or GI diseases (diverticulitis, peptic ulcer, ulcerative colitis) due to perforation risk. Use caution following acute MI (corticosteroids have been associated with myocardial rupture). When transferring to oral inhaler, previously suppressed allergic conditions (arthritis, rhinitis, conjunctivitis, eczema, eosinophilic conditions) may be unmasked. Local oropharyngeal *Candida* infections have been reported; if this occurs, treat appropriately while continuing fluticasone therapy. Patients should be instructed to rinse mouth with water without swallowing after each use.

Orally inhaled corticosteroids may cause a reduction in growth velocity in pediatric patients (~1 centimeter per year [range: 0.3 to 1.8 cm per year] and related to dose and duration of exposure). To minimize the systemic effects of orally inhaled corticosteroids, each patient should be titrated to the lowest effective dose. Growth should be routinely monitored in pediatric patients.

Potentially significant drug-drug interactions may exist, requiring dose or frequency adjustment, additional monitoring, and/or selection of alternative therapy. Not to be used in status asthmaticus or for the relief of acute bronchospasm. Flovent Diskus, ArmonAir Respiclick, and Arnuity Ellipta may contain lactose; very rare anaphylactic reactions have been reported in patients with severe milk protein allergy. Withdraw systemic corticosteroid therapy with gradual tapering of dose; consider reducing the daily prednisone dose by 2.5 to 5 mg on a weekly basis beginning at least 1 week after inhalation therapy. Monitor lung function, beta-agonist use, asthma symptoms, and for signs and symptoms of adrenal insufficiency (fatigue, lassitude, weakness, nausea and vomiting, hypotension) during withdrawal. Local yeast infections (eg, oropharyngeal candidiasis) may occur.

Drug Interactions

Metabolism/Transport Effects **Substrate** of CYP3A4 (major); **Note:** Assignment of Major/Minor substrate status based on clinically relevant drug interaction potential

Avoid Concomitant Use

Avoid concomitant use of Fluticasone (Oral Inhalation) with any of the following: Aldesleukin; BCG (Intravesical); Cobicistat; Conivaptan; Desmopressin; Fusidic Acid (Systemic); Idelalisib; Loxapine; Natalizumab; Pimecrolimus; Tacrolimus (Topical); Tipranavir; Tofacitinib

Increased Effect/Toxicity

Fluticasone (Oral Inhalation) may increase the levels/effects of: Amphotericin B; Deferasirox; Desmopressin; Fingolimod; Leflunomide; Loop Diuretics; Loxapine; Natalizumab; Thiazide and Thiazide-Like Diuretics; Tofacitinib

The levels/effects of Fluticasone (Oral Inhalation) may be increased by: Aprepitant; Cobicistat; Conivaptan; CYP3A4 Inhibitors (Moderate); CYP3A4 Inhibitors (Strong); Dasatinib; Denosumab; Fosaprepitant; Fusidic Acid (Systemic); Idelalisib; Ivacaftor; MiFEPRIStone; Netupitant; Ocrelizumab; Palbociclib; Pimecrolimus; Simeprevir; Stiripentol; Tacrolimus (Topical); Tipranavir; Trastuzumab

Decreased Effect

Fluticasone (Oral Inhalation) may decrease the levels/effects of: Aldesleukin; BCG (Intravesical); Coccidioides immitis Skin Test; Corticorelin; Hyaluronidase; Nivolumab; Sipuleucel-T; Tertomotide; Vaccines (Inactivated)

The levels/effects of Fluticasone (Oral Inhalation) may be decreased by: Echinacea

Dietary Considerations ArmonAir Respiclick, Arnuity Ellipta and Flovent Diskus may contain lactose; very rare anaphylactic reactions have been reported in patients with severe milk protein allergy.

Pharmacodynamics/Kinetics

Onset of Action Maximal benefit may take 1 to 2 weeks or longer

Half-life Elimination IV: ~8 hours; Oral inhalation (plasma elimination phase following repeat dosing): 24 hours (ArmonAir Respiclick: ~11.2 hours)

Time to Peak 0.5 to 1 hour

Pregnancy Considerations Adverse events were observed in some animal reproduction studies. Hypoadrenalism may occur in infants born to mothers receiving corticosteroids during pregnancy. Based on available data, an overall increased risk of congenital malformations or a decrease in fetal growth has not been associated with maternal use of inhaled corticosteroids during pregnancy (Bakhireva, 2005; NAEPP, 2005; Namazy, 2004). Uncontrolled asthma is associated with adverse events in pregnancy (increased risk of perinatal mortality, pre-eclampsia, preterm birth, low birth weight infants). Inhaled corticosteroids are recommended for the treatment of asthma during pregnancy (most information available using budesonide) (ACOG, 2008; NAEPP, 2005).

Breastfeeding Considerations Systemic corticosteroids are excreted in human milk. It is not known if sufficient quantities of fluticasone are absorbed following inhalation to produce detectable amounts in breast milk. According to the manufacturer, the decision to continue or discontinue breastfeeding during therapy should take into account the risk of infant exposure, the benefits of breastfeeding to the infant, and benefits of treatment to the mother. The use of inhaled corticosteroids is not considered a contraindication to breastfeeding (NAEPP 2005).

Product Availability

ArmonAir RespiClick: FDA approved January 2017; availability anticipated later in 2017.

Dosage Forms Considerations

Flovent HFA 10.6 g and 12 g canisters contain 120 inhalations.

Dosage Forms

Aerosol, Inhalation:

Flovent HFA: 44 mcg/actuation (10.6 g); 110 mcg/actuation (12 g); 220 mcg/actuation (12 g)

Aerosol Powder Breath Activated, Inhalation:

Arnuity Ellipta: 100 mcg/actuation (14 ea, 30 ea); 200 mcg/actuation (14 ea, 30 ea)

Flovent Diskus: 50 mcg/blister (60 ea); 100 mcg/blister (28 ea, 60 ea); 250 mcg/blister (28 ea, 60 ea)

Dosage Forms: Canada

Aerosol, for oral inhalation:

Flovent HFA: 50 mcg/inhalation (120 actuations); 125 mcg/inhalation (60 or 120 actuations); 250 mcg/inhalation (60 or 120 actuations)

Powder, for oral inhalation

Flovent Diskus: 50 mcg (60s); 100 mcg (60s); 250 mcg (60s); 500 mcg (60s)

Fluticasone and Salmeterol

(floo TIK a sone & sal ME te role)

Related Information

Fluticasone (Oral Inhalation) *on page 750*

Salmeterol *on page 1461*

Brand Names: US Advair Diskus; Advair HFA

Brand Names: Canada Advair; Advair Diskus

Generic Availability (US) No

Pharmacologic Category Beta$_2$ Agonist; Beta$_2$-Adrenergic Agonist, Long-Acting; Corticosteroid, Inhalant (Oral)

Use

Asthma: Treatment of asthma in patients 4 years and older (Advair Diskus) and in patients 12 years and older (Advair HFA, AirDuo RespiClick).

Chronic obstructive pulmonary disease (Advair Diskus only): Twice-daily maintenance treatment of airflow obstruction in patients with chronic obstructive pulmonary disease (COPD), including chronic bronchitis and/or emphysema. Fluticasone 250 mcg/salmeterol 50 mcg Diskus is also indicated to reduce exacerbations of COPD in patients with a history of exacerbations.

Fluticasone 250 mcg/salmeterol 50 mcg Diskus twice daily is the only approved dosage for the treatment of COPD because an efficacy advantage of the higher strength fluticasone 500 mcg/salmeterol 50 mcg Diskus over fluticasone 250 mcg/salmeterol 50 mcg Diskus has not been demonstrated.

Limitations of use: Fluticasone/salmeterol is not indicated for the relief of acute bronchospasm.

Local Anesthetic/Vasoconstrictor Precautions No information available to require special precautions

Effects on Dental Treatment Localized infections with *Candida albicans* or *Aspergillus niger* have occurred frequently in the mouth and pharynx with repetitive use of oral inhaler of corticosteroids. These infections may require treatment with appropriate antifungal therapy or discontinuance of treatment with corticosteroid inhaler.

Effects on Bleeding No information available to require special precautions

Adverse Reactions

>10%:

Central nervous system: Headache (12% to 21%)

Respiratory: Upper respiratory tract infection (16% to 27%), pharyngitis (9% to 13%)

>3% to 10%:

Central nervous system: Dizziness (1% to 4%), pain (1% to 4%)

Gastrointestinal: Nausea (3% to 6%), vomiting (3% to 6%), gastrointestinal infection (≤4%; including viral), diarrhea (2% to 4%), oral candidiasis (1% to 4%)

Neuromuscular & skeletal: Musculoskeletal pain (2% to 7%), myalgia (≤4%)

Respiratory: Throat irritation (7% to 9%), bronchitis (2% to 8%), upper respiratory tract inflammation (4% to 7%), lower respiratory tract infection (1% to 7%; COPD diagnosis and age >65 years increase risk), cough (3% to 6%), sinusitis (4% to 5%), viral respiratory tract infection (3% to 5%), hoarseness (1% to 5%)

1% to 3%:

Cardiovascular: Cardiac arrhythmia, chest symptoms, edema, myocardial infarction, palpitations, syncope, tachycardia

Central nervous system: Migraine, mouth pain, sleep disorder

Dermatologic: Dermatitis, diaphoresis, eczema, exfoliation of skin, urticaria, viral skin infection

Endocrine & metabolic: Fluid retention, hypothyroidism, weight gain

Gastrointestinal: Constipation, dysgeusia, oral mucosa ulcer

Genitourinary: Urinary tract infection

Hematologic & oncologic: Hematoma

Hepatic: Abnormal hepatic function tests

Hypersensitivity: Hypersensitivity reaction

Infection: Candidiasis (≤3%), bacterial infection, viral infection

Neuromuscular & skeletal: Muscle injury (≤3%), arthralgia, bone disease, bone fracture, muscle cramps, muscle rigidity, muscle spasm, ostealgia, rheumatoid arthritis, tremor

Ophthalmic: Conjunctivitis, eye redness, keratitis, xerophthalmia

Respiratory: Chest congestion, ENT infection, epistaxis, laryngitis, lower respiratory signs and symptoms (hemorrhage), nasal signs and symptoms (irritation), rhinitis, rhinorrhea, sneezing

Miscellaneous: Burn, laceration, wound

<1%, postmarketing, and/or case reports: Abdominal pain, aggressive behavior, agitation, anaphylaxis (some in patients with severe milk allergy [Diskus]), angioedema, atrial fibrillation, bronchospasm, cataract, change in menstrual flow, chest tightness, choking sensation, Churg-Strauss syndrome, contact dermatitis, cushingoid appearance, Cushing's syndrome, decreased linear skeletal growth rate, depression, dysmenorrhea, dyspepsia, dyspnea, ear sign or symptom (earache), ecchymoses, edema (facial, oropharyngeal), eosinophilia, esophageal candidiasis, exacerbation of asthma (serious and some fatal), glaucoma, hyperactivity, hypercorticoidism, hyperglycemia, hypersensitivity reaction (immediate and

delayed), hypertension, hypokalemia, hypothyroidism, increased intraocular pressure, influenza, irritability, laryngospasm, lassitude, myositis, osteoporosis, pallor, paranasal sinus disease, paresthesia, pelvic inflammatory disease, photodermatitis, restlessness, skin rash, stridor, supraventricular tachycardia, syncope, tracheitis, vaginitis, vasculitis (rare cases), ventricular tachycardia, vulvovaginal candidiasis, vulvovaginitis, wheezing, xerostomia

Dosing

Adult & Geriatric Do not use to transfer patients from systemic corticosteroid therapy. Patients receiving fluticasone/salmeterol should not use additional salmeterol or other inhaled, long-acting beta$_2$-agonists (eg, formoterol, arformoterol) for any other reason.

COPD: Oral Inhalation: Advair Diskus: Dry powder inhaler: Fluticasone 250 mcg/salmeterol 50 mcg twice daily, 12 hours apart. **Note:** This is the maximum dose.

Asthma (maintenance): Oral inhalation: **Note:** Titrate to the lowest effective dose once asthma stability is achieved.

Advair Diskus: Dry powder inhaler: One inhalation twice daily, morning and evening, 12 hours apart

Maximum dose: Fluticasone 500 mcg/salmeterol 50 mcg per inhalation (2 inhalations/day)

Advair HFA: Metered dose inhaler: Two inhalations twice daily, morning and evening, 12 hours apart

Maximum dose: Fluticasone 230 mcg/salmeterol 21 mcg per inhalation (4 inhalations/day)

AirDuo RespiClick: Dry powder inhaler: **Note:** Initial dose should be based upon asthma severity. May increase dose after 2 weeks of therapy in patients who are not adequately controlled.

No prior treatment with inhaled corticosteroids: Initial: One inhalation (fluticasone 55 mcg/salmeterol 14 mcg) twice daily (12 hours apart); maximum: 1 inhalation (fluticasone 232 mcg/salmeterol 14 mcg) twice daily.

Prior treatment with inhaled corticosteroid: One inhalation (fluticasone 55 to 232 mcg/salmeterol 14 mcg) twice daily (12 hours apart); maximum: 1 inhalation (fluticasone 232 mcg/salmeterol 14 mcg) twice daily.

Advair 125 or Advair 250 [Canadian products]: Metered dose inhaler: Two inhalations twice daily, morning and evening, 12 hours apart

Note: Initial dose prescribed should be based upon asthma severity. Dose should be increased after 2 weeks if adequate response is not achieved.

Pediatric Patients receiving fluticasone/salmeterol should not use additional salmeterol or other inhaled, long-acting beta$_2$-agonists (eg, formoterol, arformoterol) for any other reason.

Asthma (maintenance): Oral inhalation: **Note:** Titrate to the lowest effective dose once asthma stability is achieved.

Advair Diskus: Dry powder inhaler:

Children 4 to 11 years: Fluticasone 100 mcg/salmeterol 50 mcg twice daily, 12 hours apart. **Note:** This is the maximum dose.

Children ≥12 years and Adolescents: Refer to adult dosing.

Advair HFA: Metered dose inhaler: Children ≥12 years and Adolescents: Refer to adult dosing.

AirDuo RespiClick: Dry powder inhaler: Children ≥12 years and Adolescents: Refer to adult dosing.

Renal Impairment There are no dosage adjustments provided in the manufacturer's labeling (has not been studied).

Hepatic Impairment There are no dosage adjustment provided in the manufacturer's labeling (has not been studied); however, fluticasone and salmeterol are primarily cleared in the liver and plasma levels may be increased in these patients; use with caution and monitor closely.

Mechanism of Action

Combination of fluticasone (corticosteroid) and salmeterol (long-acting beta$_2$-agonist) designed to improve pulmonary function and control over what is produced by either agent when used alone. Because fluticasone and salmeterol act locally in the lung, plasma levels do not predict therapeutic effect.

Fluticasone: The mechanism of action for all topical corticosteroids is believed to be a combination of three important properties: Anti-inflammatory activity, immunosuppressive properties, and antiproliferative actions. Fluticasone has extremely potent vasoconstrictive and anti-inflammatory activity.

Salmeterol: Relaxes bronchial smooth muscle by selective action on beta$_2$-receptors with little effect on heart rate

Contraindications

Hypersensitivity to fluticasone, salmeterol, or any component of the formulation; status asthmaticus; acute episodes of asthma or COPD; severe hypersensitivity to milk proteins (Advair Diskus, AirDuo RespiClick)

Documentation of allergenic cross-reactivity for corticosteroids and sympathomimetics are limited. However, because of similarities in chemical structure and/or pharmacologic actions, the possibility of cross-sensitivity cannot be ruled out with certainty.

Canadian labeling: Additional contraindications (not in US labeling): IgE mediated allergic reactions to lactose; cardiac tachyarrhythmias; untreated fungal, bacterial, or tuberculosis infections of the respiratory tract

Warnings/Precautions

See individual agents.

Drug Interactions

Metabolism/Transport Effects Refer to individual components.

Avoid Concomitant Use

Avoid concomitant use of Fluticasone and Salmeterol with any of the following: Aldesleukin; BCG (Intravesical); Beta-Blockers (Nonselective); Cobicistat; Conivaptan; CYP3A4 Inhibitors (Strong); Desmopressin; Fusidic Acid (Systemic); Idelalisib; Iobenguane I 123; Long-Acting Beta2-Agonists; Loxapine; Natalizumab; Pimecrolimus; Tacrolimus (Topical); Telaprevir; Tipranavir; Tofacitinib

Increased Effect/Toxicity

Fluticasone and Salmeterol may increase the levels/effects of: Amphotericin B; Atosiban; Deferasirox; Desmopressin; Doxofylline; Fingolimod; Highest Risk QTc-Prolonging Agents; Leflunomide; Long-Acting Beta2-Agonists; Loop Diuretics; Loxapine; Moderate Risk QTc-Prolonging Agents; Natalizumab; Sympathomimetics; Thiazide and Thiazide-Like Diuretics; Tofacitinib

The levels/effects of Fluticasone and Salmeterol may be increased by: Aprepitant; AtoMOXetine; Cannabinoid-Containing Products; Cobicistat; Cocaine; Conivaptan; CYP3A4 Inhibitors (Moderate); CYP3A4 Inhibitors (Strong); Dasatinib; Denosumab; Fosaprepitant; Fusidic Acid (Systemic); Idelalisib; Ivacaftor; Linezolid; MAO Inhibitors; Netupitant; Ocrelizumab; Palbociclib; Pimecrolimus; Simeprevir; Stiripentol; Tacrolimus (Topical); Tedizolid; Telaprevir; Tipranavir; Trastuzumab; Tricyclic Antidepressants

Decreased Effect

Fluticasone and Salmeterol may decrease the levels/effects of: Aldesleukin; BCG (Intravesical); Coccidioides immitis Skin Test; Corticorelin; Hyaluronidase; Iobenguane I 123; Nivolumab; Sipuleucel-T; Tertomotide; Vaccines (Inactivated)

The levels/effects of Fluticasone and Salmeterol may be decreased by: Beta-Blockers (Beta1 Selective); Beta-Blockers (Nonselective); Betahistine; Echinacea

Dietary Considerations Advair Diskus powder for oral inhalation contains lactose; very rare anaphylactic reactions have been reported in patients with severe milk protein allergy.

Pregnancy Risk Factor C

Pregnancy Considerations Adverse events were observed in animal reproduction studies using this combination. Refer to individual agents.

Breastfeeding Considerations It is not known if fluticasone or salmeterol are present in breast milk. According to the manufacturer, the decision to continue or discontinue breastfeeding during therapy should take into account the risk of infant exposure, the benefits of breastfeeding to the infant, and benefits of treatment to the mother. Refer to individual agents.

Product Availability AirDuo RespiClick: FDA approved January 2017; availability anticipated later in 2017.

Dosage Forms Considerations

Advair HFA 8 g canisters contain 60 inhalations, and the 12 g canisters contain 120 inhalations

Dosage Forms

Aerosol, for oral inhalation:

Advair HFA:

45/21: Fluticasone propionate 45 mcg and salmeterol 21 mcg (8 g, 12 g) [chlorofluorocarbon free]

115/21: Fluticasone propionate 115 mcg and salmeterol 21 mcg (8 g, 12 g) [chlorofluorocarbon free]

230/21: Fluticasone propionate 230 mcg and salmeterol 21 mcg (8 g, 12 g) [chlorofluorocarbon free]

Powder, for oral inhalation:

Advair Diskus:

100/50: Fluticasone propionate 100 mcg and salmeterol 50 mcg (14s, 60s)

250/50: Fluticasone propionate 250 mcg and salmeterol 50 mcg (14s, 60s)

500/50: Fluticasone propionate 500 mcg and salmeterol 50 mcg (14s, 60s)

Dosage Forms: Canada

Aerosol, for oral inhalation:

Advair: 125/25: Fluticasone propionate 125 mcg and salmeterol 25 mcg (12 g); 250/25: Fluticasone propionate 250 mcg and salmeterol 25 mcg (12 g)

Fluticasone and Vilanterol

(floo TIK a sone & VYE lan ter ol)

Brand Names: US Breo Ellipta

Brand Names: Canada Breo Ellipta

Pharmacologic Category Beta$_2$ Agonist; Beta$_2$-Adrenergic Agonist, Long-Acting; Corticosteroid, Inhalant (Oral)

Use

Asthma: Treatment of asthma in patients ≥18 years.

Chronic obstructive pulmonary disease: Maintenance treatment of airflow obstruction in patients with chronic obstructive pulmonary disease (COPD), including chronic bronchitis and/or emphysema; to reduce exacerbations of COPD in patients with a history of exacerbations

Fluticasone 100 mcg/vilanterol 25 mcg is the only strength indicated for the treatment of COPD.

Limitations of use: Not indicated for the relief of acute bronchospasm.

Local Anesthetic/Vasoconstrictor Precautions

No information available to require special precautions.

Effects on Dental Treatment Key adverse event(s) related to dental treatment: Infections with *Candida albicans* in the mouth and throat (thrush).

Effects on Bleeding No information available to require special precautions.

Adverse Reactions Also see fluticasone (oral inhalation) monograph.

1% to 10%:

Cardiovascular: Hypertension (≥3%), peripheral edema (≥3%), extrasystoles (≥2%), supraventricular extrasystole (≥2%), ventricular premature contractions (≥2%)

Central nervous system: Headache (5% to 8%)

Gastrointestinal: Oropharyngeal candidiasis (2% to 5%), diarrhea (≥3%), upper abdominal pain (≥2%)

Infection: Influenza (≥3%)

Neuromuscular & skeletal: Arthralgia (2% to ≥3%), back pain (2% to ≥3%), bone fracture (2%)

Respiratory: Nasopharyngitis (6% to 10%), upper respiratory tract infection (≥2% to 7%), pneumonia (2% to 7%), oropharyngeal pain (2% to ≥3%), pharyngitis (2% to ≥3%), chronic obstructive pulmonary disease (≥3%), cough (1% to ≥3%), sinusitis (1% to ≥3%), bronchitis (<1% to ≥3%), acute sinusitis (≥2%), allergic rhinitis (≥2%), rhinitis (≥2%), viral respiratory tract infection (≥2%), voice disorder (2%)

Miscellaneous: Fever (2% to ≥3%)

<1%, postmarketing, and/or case reports: Anaphylaxis, angioedema, cataract, glaucoma, hypersensitivity reaction, muscle spasm, nervousness, palpitations, paradoxical bronchospasm, skin rash, tachycardia, tremor, urticaria

General Dosage Range

Oral inhalation: *Adults:*

Asthma: One inhalation (fluticasone 100 mcg/vilanterol 25 mcg or fluticasone 200 mcg/vilanterol 25 mcg) once daily (maximum: 1 inhalation [fluticasone 200 mcg/vilanterol 25 mcg] once daily).

Chronic obstructive pulmonary disease (COPD): One inhalation (fluticasone 100 mcg/vilanterol 25 mcg) once daily (maximum: 1 inhalation [fluticasone 100 mcg/vilanterol 25 mcg] once daily)

Mechanism of Action

Fluticasone is a corticosteroid with anti-inflammatory activity, immunosuppressive properties, and antiproliferative actions.

Vilanterol, a long acting beta$_2$-agonist, relaxes bronchial smooth muscle by selective action on beta$_2$-receptors with little effect on heart rate.

Pregnancy Risk Factor C

Pregnancy Considerations Adverse events have not been observed in animal reproduction studies. Hypoadrenalism may occur in infants born to mothers receiving corticosteroids during pregnancy (refer to the fluticasone, oral inhalation monograph for additional details). Beta-agonists have the potential to affect uterine contractility if administered during labor.

Fluvastatin (FLOO va sta tin)

Related Information

Cardiovascular Diseases *on page 1752*

Brand Names: US Lescol XL; Lescol [DSC]

Brand Names: Canada Lescol; Lescol XL; Teva-Fluvastatin

Pharmacologic Category Antilipemic Agent, HMG-CoA Reductase Inhibitor

Use

Dyslipidemias:

Heterozygous familial and nonfamilial hypercholesterolemia and mixed dyslipidemia: Adjunct to diet to reduce elevated total cholesterol (total-C), low-density lipoprotein-cholesterol (LDL-C), triglyceride, and apolipoprotein B (apo-B) levels and to increase HDL-C in adults with primary hypercholesterolemia and mixed dyslipidemia (Fredrickson types IIa and IIb)

Heterozygous familial hypercholesterolemia: As an adjunct to diet to reduce total-C, LDL-C, and apo B levels in children ≥10 years and adolescents ≤16 years of age (female patients must be at least 1 year postmenarche) with heterozygous familial hypercholesterolemia and an LDL-C that remains ≥190 mg/dL or ≥160 mg/dL (with ≥2 cardiovascular risk factors or a positive family history of premature cardiovascular disease).

Prevention of cardiovascular disease (CVD):

Secondary prevention of CVD: To slow the progression of coronary atherosclerosis in patients with coronary heart disease; reduce risk of coronary revascularization procedures in patients with coronary heart disease

Guideline recommendations:Primary and secondary prevention of atherosclerotic cardiovascular disease (ASCVD) to reduce the risk of ASCVD in select adult patients (ACC/AHA [Stone 2013]; NLA [Jacobson 2015]). Refer to respective guideline for specific recommendations.

Limitations of use: Has not been studied in conditions where the major abnormality is elevation of chylomicrons, very low-density lipoprotein (VLDL), or intermediate density lipoprotein (IDL) (ie, hyperlipoproteinemia types I, III, IV, or V).

Local Anesthetic/Vasoconstrictor Precautions No information available to require special precautions

Effects on Dental Treatment Key adverse event(s) related to dental treatment: Assess unusual presentations of muscle weakness or myopathy resulting from lipid therapy such as patient having a difficult time brushing teeth or weakness with chewing. Refer patient back to their physician for evaluation and adjustment of lipid therapy.

Effects on Bleeding No information available to require special precautions

Adverse Reactions Frequency not always defined. The following adverse events were reported with fluvastatin capsules; in general, adverse reactions reported with fluvastatin extended release tablet were similar, but incidences were lower. <1%/Postmarketing adverse reactions include additional class-related events that were not necessarily reported with fluvastatin therapy.

1% to 10%:

Central nervous system: Headache (9%), fatigue (3%), insomnia (3%)

Gastrointestinal: Dyspepsia (8%), abdominal pain (5%), diarrhea (5%), nausea (3%)

Genitourinary: Urinary tract infection (2%), interstitial cystitis (Huang 2015)

Neuromuscular & skeletal: Myalgia (5%)

Respiratory: Sinusitis (3%), bronchitis (2%)

<1%, postmarketing, and/or case reports: Alopecia, amnesia (reversible), anaphylaxis, angioedema, anorexia, anxiety, arthralgia, arthritis, blurred vision, cataract, changes in nails, chills, cholestatic jaundice, cognitive dysfunction (reversible), decreased libido, depression, dermatomyositis, dizziness, dry mucous membranes, dysgeusia, dyspnea, elevated glycosylated hemoglobin (HbA_{1c}), eosinophilia, erectile dysfunction, erythema multiforme, facial paresis, fever, flushing, fulminant hepatic necrosis, gynecomastia, hemolytic anemia, hepatic cirrhosis, hepatic neoplasm, hepatitis, hyperbilirubinemia, hypersensitivity reaction, immune-mediated necrotizing myopathy (IMNM), impairment of extraocular movement, impotence, increased creatine phosphokinase (>10x normal), increased erythrocyte sedimentation rate, increased gamma-glutamyl transferase, increased serum alkaline phosphatase, increased serum glucose, increased serum transaminases, interstitial pulmonary disease, leukopenia, liver steatosis, lupus-like syndrome, malaise, memory impairment (reversible), muscle cramps, myopathy, nodule, ophthalmoplegia, pancreatitis, paresthesia, peripheral nerve palsy, peripheral neuropathy, polymyalgia rheumatica, positive ANA titer, pruritus, psychic disorder, purpura, reversible confusional state, rhabdomyolysis, skin discoloration, skin photosensitivity, skin rash, Stevens-Johnson syndrome, thrombocytopenia, thyroid dysfunction, toxic epidermal necrolysis, tremor, urticaria, vasculitis, vertigo, vomiting, xeroderma

General Dosage Range Oral:

Extended release: *Adolescents 10-16 years (females 1 year postmenarche) and Adults:* 80 mg once daily

Immediate release:

Adolescents 10-16 years (females 1 year postmenarche): Initial: 20 mg once daily; Maintenance: Up to 80 mg/day in 2 divided doses

Adults: Initial: 20-40 mg once daily; Maintenance: Up to 80 mg/day in 2 divided doses

Mechanism of Action Acts by competitively inhibiting 3-hydroxyl-3-methylglutaryl-coenzyme A (HMG-CoA) reductase, the enzyme that catalyzes the reduction of HMG-CoA to mevalonate; this is an early rate-limiting step in cholesterol biosynthesis. HDL is increased while total, LDL, and VLDL cholesterols; apolipoprotein B; and plasma triglycerides are decreased. In addition to the ability of HMG-CoA reductase inhibitors to decrease levels of high-sensitivity C-reactive protein (hsCRP), they also possess pleiotropic properties including improved endothelial function, reduced inflammation at the site of the coronary plaque, inhibition of platelet aggregation, and anticoagulant effects (de Denus 2002; Ray 2005).

Pharmacodynamics/Kinetics

Onset of Action Peak effect: Maximal LDL-C reductions achieved within 4 weeks

Half-life Elimination Immediate-release: ~3 hours; Extended-release: 7.3 to 10.5 hours (due to prolonged absorption time) (Barilla 2004)

Time to Peak

Immediate-release: <1 hour (delayed more than 2-fold when administered with food as compared to administering 4 hours after the evening meal)

Extended-release: ~3 hours (minimally affected by low-fat meals; however, with a high-fat meal, delayed by 2-fold)

Pregnancy Risk Factor X

Pregnancy Considerations Studies in pregnant women have shown evidence of fetal abnormalities and use is contraindicated in women who are or may become pregnant. There are reports of congenital anomalies following maternal use of HMG-CoA reductase inhibitors in pregnancy; however, maternal disease, differences in specific agents used, and the low rates of exposure limit the interpretation of the available data (Godfrey 2012; Lecarpentier 2012). Cholesterol biosynthesis may be important in fetal development; serum cholesterol and triglycerides increase normally during pregnancy. The discontinuation of lipid lowering medications temporarily during pregnancy is not expected to have significant impact on the long term outcomes of primary hypercholesterolemia treatment.

HMG-CoA reductase inhibitors should be discontinued prior to pregnancy (ADA 2013). If treatment of dyslipidemias is needed in pregnant women or in women of reproductive age, other agents are preferred (Berglund 2012; Stone 2013). The manufacturer recommends administration to women of childbearing potential only when conception is highly unlikely and patients have been informed of potential hazards.

FluvoxaMINE (floo VOKS a meen)

Related Information

Management of the Patient With Anxiety or Depression *on page 1873*

Vasoconstrictor Interactions With Antidepressants *on page 1913*

Brand Names: US Luvox CR [DSC]

Brand Names: Canada ACT-Fluvoxamine; Apo-Fluvoxamine; Ava-Fluvoxamine; Dom-Fluvoxamine; Luvox; Novo-Fluvoxamine; PHL-Fluvoxamine; PMS-Fluvoxamine; ratio-Fluvoxamine; Riva-Fluvox; Sandoz-Fluvoxamine

Generic Availability (US) Yes

Pharmacologic Category Antidepressant, Selective Serotonin Reuptake Inhibitor

Use

Obsessive-compulsive disorder: Treatment of obsessive-compulsive disorder (OCD) in pediatric patients 8 to 17 years of age and adults.

Canadian labeling: Additional use (not in US labeling): **Depression:** Treatment of depression in adults

Local Anesthetic/Vasoconstrictor Precautions Although caution should be used in patients taking tricyclic antidepressants, no interactions have been reported with vasoconstrictors and fluvoxamine, a nontricyclic antidepressant which acts to increase serotonin; no precautions appear to be needed

Effects on Dental Treatment Key adverse event(s) related to dental treatment: Xerostomia (normal salivary flow resumes upon discontinuation) and abnormal taste. Problems with SSRI-induced bruxism have been reported and may preclude their use; clinicians attempting to evaluate any patient with bruxism or involuntary muscle movement, who is simultaneously being treated with an SSRI drug, should be aware of the potential association. See Effects on Bleeding and Dental Comment.

Effects on Bleeding Selective serotonin reuptake inhibitors such as fluvoxamine may impair platelet aggregation due to platelet serotonin depletion, possibly increasing the risk of a bleeding complication. The risk of a bleeding complication can be increased by coadministration of other antiplatelet agents such as NSAIDs and aspirin.

Adverse Reactions Frequency varies by dosage form and indication. Adverse reactions reported as a composite of all indications.

>10%:

Central nervous system: Headache (22% to 35%), insomnia (21% to 35%), drowsiness (22% to 27%), dizziness (11% to 15%), nervousness (10% to 12%)

Gastrointestinal: Nausea (34% to 40%), diarrhea (11% to 18%), xerostomia (10% to 14%), anorexia (6% to 14%)

Genitourinary: Ejaculatory disorder (8% to 11%)

Neuromuscular & skeletal: Weakness (14% to 26%)

1% to 10%:

Cardiovascular: Chest pain (3%), palpitations (3%), vasodilation (2% to 3%), hypertension (1% to 2%), edema (≥1%), hypotension (≥1%), syncope (≥1%)

Central nervous system: Pain (10%), anxiety (5% to 8%), anorgasmia (2% to 5%), yawning (2% to 5%), abnormal dreams (3%), abnormality in thinking (3%), paresthesia (3%), agitation (2% to 3%), apathy (≥1% to 3%), central nervous system stimulation (2%), chills (2%), depression (2%), hypertonia (2%), psychoneurosis (2%), twitching (2%), amnesia (≥1%), manic reaction (≥1%), myoclonus (≥1%), psychotic reaction (≥1%), malaise (≤1%)

Dermatologic: Diaphoresis (6% to 7%), ecchymoses (4%), acne vulgaris (2%)

Endocrine & metabolic: Decreased libido (2% to 10%; incidence higher in males), hypermenorrhea (3%), weight loss (≥1% to 2%), weight gain (≥1%)

Gastrointestinal: Dyspepsia (8% to 10%), constipation (4% to 10%), vomiting (5% to 6%), abdominal pain (5%), flatulence (4%), dysgeusia (2% to 3%), dysphagia (2%), gingivitis (2%)

Genitourinary: Urinary frequency (3%), sexual disorder (2% to 3%), impotence (2%), urinary tract infection (2%), urinary retention (1%)

Hepatic: Abnormal hepatic function tests (2%)

Infection: Viral infection (2%)

Neuromuscular & skeletal: Tremor (5% to 8%), myalgia (5%), hyperkinesia (≥1%), hypokinesia (≥1%)

Ophthalmic: Amblyopia (2% to 3%)

Renal: Polyuria (2%)

Respiratory: Upper respiratory tract infection (9%), pharyngitis (6%), flu-like symptoms (3%), laryngitis (3%), bronchitis (2%), dyspnea (2%), epistaxis (2%), increased cough (≥1%), sinusitis (≥1%)

<1%, postmarketing, and/or case reports: Abnormal gait, activation syndrome, acute renal failure, aggressive behavior, agranulocytosis, akinesia, amenorrhea, anaphylaxis, anemia, angina pectoris, angioedema, angle-closure glaucoma, anuria, aplastic anemia, apnea, asthma, ataxia, blurred vision, bradycardia, bruxism, bullous skin disease, cardiac conduction delay, cardiomyopathy, cardiorespiratory arrest, cerebrovascular accident, cholecystitis, cholelithiasis, colitis, crying, decreased white blood cell count, delirium, dental caries, dental extraction, diplopia, drowsiness (neonatal), dysarthria, dyskinesia, dystonia, extrapyramidal reaction, fatigue, feeling drunk, fever, first degree atrioventricular block, gastroesophageal reflux disease, gastrointestinal hemorrhage, glossalgia, goiter, hallucination, hematemesis, hematuria, hemoptysis, hepatitis, homicidal ideation, hypercholesterolemia, hyperglycemia, hypersensitivity reaction, hypoglycemia, hypokalemia, hyponatremia, hypothyroidism, IgA vasculitis, impulsivity, interstitial pulmonary disease, intestinal obstruction, irritability, jaundice, jitteriness, laryngismus, lethargy, leukocytosis, leukopenia, loss of consciousness, lymphadenopathy, melena, myasthenia, myocardial infarction, myopathy, neuroleptic malignant syndrome (Stevens 2008), outbursts of anger, pancreatitis, paralysis,

Parkinsonian-like syndrome, pericarditis, porphyria, priapism, prolonged Q-T interval on ECG, purpura, Raynaud's phenomenon (Khouri 2016; Peiró 2007), renal insufficiency, rhabdomyolysis, seizure, serotonin syndrome, shock, SIADH, ST segment changes on ECG, Stevens-Johnson syndrome, suicidal tendencies, supraventricular extrasystole, tachycardia, tardive dyskinesia, thrombocytopenia, thromboembolism, tooth abscess, toothache, toxic epidermal necrolysis, vasculitis, ventricular arrhythmia, ventricular tachycardia (including torsades de pointes)

Dosing

Adult

Obsessive-compulsive disorder: Oral:

Immediate release: Initial: 50 mg once daily at bedtime; may be increased in 50 mg increments at 4- to 7-day intervals, as tolerated; usual dose range: 100 to 300 mg daily; maximum dose: 300 mg daily. **Note:** US labeling recommends that daily doses >100 mg be given in 2 divided doses, with the larger dose administered at bedtime. Canadian labeling recommends that daily doses >150 mg be given in 2 divided doses with the larger dose administered at bedtime (maximum bedtime dose: 150 mg); if no improvement within 10 weeks consider discontinuing fluvoxamine therapy.

Extended release: Initial: 100 mg once daily at bedtime; may be increased in 50 mg increments at intervals of at least 1 week; usual dosage range: 100 to 300 mg daily; maximum dose: 300 mg daily

Depression (Canadian labeling; not an approved use in US labeling): Oral: Immediate release: Initial: 50 mg once daily at bedtime then after a few days may increase to 100 mg daily as tolerated; titrate gradually based on response and tolerability in 50 mg increments; usual dosage range: 100 to 200 mg daily; maximum dose: 300 mg daily. Doses >150 mg daily should be divided with maximum dose of 150 mg given at bedtime.

Bulimia nervosa (off-label use): Oral: Immediate release: Initial: 50 mg daily; increase dose based on response and tolerability up to 300 mg/day given in 1 or 2 divided doses (Brambilla 1995; Fichter 1996; Fichter 1997; Milano 2005). Additional data may be necessary to further define the role of fluvoxamine in this condition.

Panic disorder (off-label use): Oral: Immediate release: Initial: 25 to 50 mg daily; titrate gradually based on response and tolerability; usual dosage range: 100 to 200 mg daily (APA, 2009; Asnis, 2001).

Post-traumatic stress disorder (PTSD) (off-label use): Oral: Immediate release: 75 mg twice daily (Spivak, 2006).

Social anxiety disorder (off-label use): Oral:

Immediate release: Initial: 50 mg once daily; may increase in 50 mg increments at intervals of at least 1 week; usual dosage range: 100 to 300 mg daily (Asakura, 2007).

Extended release: Initial: 100 mg once daily at bedtime; may be increased in 50 mg increments at intervals of at least 1 week; usual dosage range: 100 to 300 mg daily; maximum dose: 300 mg daily (Davidson, 2004; Stein, 2003; Westenberg, 2004)

Discontinuation of therapy: Upon discontinuation of antidepressant therapy, gradually taper the dose to minimize the incidence of withdrawal symptoms and allow for the detection of re-emerging symptoms. Evidence supporting ideal taper rates is limited. APA and NICE guidelines suggest tapering therapy over at least several weeks with consideration to the half-life of the antidepressant; antidepressants with a shorter half-life may need to be tapered more conservatively. In addition for long-term treated patients, WFSBP guidelines recommend tapering over 4 to 6 months. If intolerable withdrawal symptoms occur following a dose reduction, consider resuming the previously prescribed dose and/or decrease dose at a more gradual rate (APA, 2007; APA,2010; Bauer, 2002; Haddad, 2001; NCCMH, 2010; Schatzberg, 2006; Shelton, 2001; Warner, 2006).

MAO inhibitor recommendations:

Switching to or from an MAO inhibitor intended to treat psychiatric disorders:

Allow 14 days to elapse between discontinuing an MAO inhibitor intended to treat psychiatric disorders and initiation of fluvoxamine.

Allow 14 days to elapse between discontinuing fluvoxamine and initiation of an MAO inhibitor intended to treat psychiatric disorders.

Use with other MAO inhibitors (linezolid or IV methylene blue):

Do not initiate fluvoxamine in patients receiving linezolid or IV methylene blue; consider other interventions for psychiatric condition.

If urgent treatment with linezolid or IV methylene blue is required in a patient already receiving fluvoxamine and potential benefits outweigh potential risks, discontinue fluvoxamine promptly and administer linezolid or IV methylene blue. Monitor for serotonin syndrome for 2 weeks or until 24 hours after the last dose of linezolid or IV methylene blue, whichever comes first. May resume fluvoxamine 24 hours after the last dose of linezolid or IV methylene blue. Risk of administering methylene blue by non-intravenous routes or in IV doses <1 mg/kg concurrently with fluvoxamine is unclear.

Geriatric Refer to adult dosing. Consider a lower initial dose; titrate slowly.

Pediatric Obsessive-compulsive disorder: Oral: **Note:** Not approved for use in patients <18 years of age in Canadian labeling.

Children and Adolescents 8 to 17 years:

Immediate release: Initial: 25 mg once daily at bedtime; may be increased in 25 mg increments at 4- to 7-day intervals, as tolerated, to maximum therapeutic benefit; usual dose range: 50 to 200 mg daily. **Note:** When total daily dose of immediate release exceeds 50 mg, the dose should be given in 2 divided doses with larger portion administered at bedtime.

Maximum dose: Children: 8 to 11 years: 200 mg daily; Adolescents: 300 mg daily; lower doses may be effective in female versus male patients

Extended release: The extended release formulation has not been evaluated in pediatric patients; the lowest available dose of extended release capsules may not be appropriate for pediatric patients naïve to fluvoxamine.

Discontinuation of therapy: Refer to adult dosing.

MAO inhibitor recommendations: Refer to adult dosing.

Renal Impairment There are no dosage adjustments provided in manufacturer's labeling. Limited data suggest fluvoxamine does not accumulate in patients with renal impairment. Canadian labeling recommends initiating therapy at a reduced dosage with close monitoring.

Hepatic Impairment There are no dosage adjustments provided in manufacturer's labeling. Limited data suggest fluvoxamine clearance is reduced in patients with hepatic impairment. Reduced initial dose and slow titration may be required. Monitor closely.

Mechanism of Action Inhibits CNS neuron serotonin uptake; minimal or no effect on reuptake of norepinephrine or dopamine; does not significantly bind to alpha-adrenergic, histamine or cholinergic receptors

Contraindications

Concurrent use with alosetron, pimozide, ramelteon, thioridazine, or tizanidine; use of MAO inhibitors intended to treat psychiatric disorders (concurrently or within 14 days of discontinuing either fluvoxamine or the MAO inhibitor); initiation of fluvoxamine in a patient receiving linezolid or intravenous methylene blue.

Canadian labeling: Additional contraindications (not in US labeling): Hypersensitivity to fluvoxamine or any component of the formulation; concurrent use with astemizole, cisapride, mesoridazine, or terfenadine.

Warnings/Precautions [US Boxed Warning]: Antidepressants increase the risk of suicidal thinking and behavior in children, adolescents, and young adults (18 to 24 years of age) with major depressive disorder (MDD) and other psychiatric disorders; consider risk prior to prescribing. Short-term studies did not show an increased risk in patients >24 years of age and showed a decreased risk in patients ≥65 years. Closely monitor patients for clinical worsening, suicidality, or unusual changes in behavior, particularly during the initial 1 to 2 months of therapy or during periods of dosage adjustments (increases or decreases); the patient's family or caregiver should be instructed to closely observe the patient and communicate condition with healthcare provider. A medication guide concerning the use of antidepressants should be dispensed with each prescription. **Fluvoxamine is FDA approved for the treatment of OCD in children ≥8 years of age.**

The possibility of a suicide attempt is inherent in major depression and may persist until remission occurs. Use caution in high-risk patients. Worsening depression and severe abrupt suicidality that are not part of the presenting symptoms may require discontinuation or modification of drug therapy. The patient's family or caregiver should be alerted to monitor patients for the emergence of suicidality and associated behaviors (such as agitation, irritability, hostility, impulsivity, and hypomania) and call healthcare provider.

May worsen psychosis in some patients or precipitate a shift to mania or hypomania in patients with bipolar disorder. Patients presenting with depressive symptoms should be screened for bipolar disorder. Monotherapy in patients with bipolar disorder should be avoided. **Fluvoxamine is not FDA approved for the treatment of bipolar depression.**

Potentially life-threatening serotonin syndrome (SS) has occurred with serotonergic agents (eg, SSRIs, SNRIs), particularly when used in combination with other serotonergic agents (eg, triptans, TCAs, fentanyl, lithium, tramadol, buspirone, St John's wort, tryptophan) or agents that impair metabolism of serotonin (eg, MAO inhibitors intended to treat psychiatric disorders, other MAO inhibitors [ie, linezolid and intravenous methylene blue]). Discontinue treatment (and any concomitant serotonergic agent) immediately if signs/symptoms arise. Fluvoxamine has a low potential to impair cognitive or motor performance; caution operating hazardous machinery or driving. Use caution in patients with a previous seizure disorder rand avoid use with unstable seizure disorder. Discontinue use if seizures occur or if seizure frequency increases. Potentially significant drug-drug interactions may exist, requiring dose or frequency adjustment, additional monitoring, and/or selection of alternative therapy. Fluvoxamine levels may be lower in patients who smoke.

Benefit/risks of combined therapy with electroconvulsive therapy have not been established. Bone fractures have been associated with antidepressant treatment. Consider the possibility of a fragility fracture if an antidepressant-treated patient presents with unexplained bone pain, point tenderness, swelling, or bruising (Rabenda, 2013; Rizzoli, 2012). Use with caution in patients with hepatic dysfunction and in elderly patients. May cause hyponatremia/SIADH (elderly at increased risk); volume depletion (diuretics may increase risk). Use with caution in patients at risk of bleeding or receiving concurrent anticoagulant therapy, although not consistently noted, fluvoxamine may cause impairment in platelet function. May cause or exacerbate sexual dysfunction. May cause mild pupillary dilation which in susceptible individuals can lead to an episode of narrow-angle glaucoma. Consider evaluating patients who have not had an iridectomy for narrow-angle glaucoma risk factors. Impaired glucose control (eg, hyperglycemia, hypoglycemia) has been reported; monitor for signs/symptoms of loss of glucose control particularly in diabetic patients. Abrupt discontinuation or interruption of antidepressant therapy has been associated with a discontinuation syndrome. Symptoms arising may vary with antidepressant however commonly include nausea, vomiting, diarrhea, headaches, light-headedness, dizziness, diminished appetite, sweating, chills, tremors, paresthesias, fatigue, somnolence, and sleep disturbances (eg, vivid dreams, insomnia). Greater risks for developing a discontinuation syndrome have been associated with antidepressants with shorter half-lives, longer durations of treatment, and abrupt discontinuation. For antidepressants of short or intermediate half-lives, symptoms may emerge within 2 to 5 days after treatment discontinuation and last 7 to 14 days (APA, 2010; Fava, 2006; Haddad, 2001; Shelton, 2001; Warner, 2006).

Drug Interactions

Metabolism/Transport Effects Substrate of CYP1A2 (major), CYP2D6 (major); **Note:** Assignment of Major/Minor substrate status based on clinically relevant drug interaction potential; **Inhibits** CYP1A2 (strong), CYP2C19 (moderate), CYP2C9 (weak), CYP3A4 (weak)

Avoid Concomitant Use

Avoid concomitant use of FluvoxaMINE with any of the following: Agomelatine; Alosetron; Dapoxetine; Dosulepin; DULoxetine; Iobenguane I 123; Linezolid; MAO Inhibitors; Methylene Blue; Pimozide; Pomalidomide; Ramelteon; Tasimelteon; Thioridazine; TiZANidine; Tryptophan; Urokinase

Increased Effect/Toxicity

FluvoxaMINE may increase the levels/effects of: Agents with Antiplatelet Properties; Agomelatine; Alosetron; ALPRAZolam; Anticoagulants; Antidepressants (Serotonin Reuptake Inhibitor/Antagonist); Antipsychotic Agents; Apixaban; ARIPiprazole; Asenapine; Aspirin; Bendamustine; Blood Glucose Lowering Agents; Bromazepam; BusPIRone; CarBAMazepine; Cephalothin; Cilostazol; Citalopram; Clopidogrel; CloZAPine; Collagenase (Systemic);

CYP1A2 Substrates; CYP2C19 Substrates; Dabigatran Etexilate; Deoxycholic Acid; Desmopressin; Dofetilide; Dosulepin; DULoxetine; Edoxaban; Erlotinib; Etizolam; Flibanserin; Fosphenytoin; Haloperidol; HYDROcodone; Ibritumomab; Lomitapide; Melatonin; Methadone; Methylene Blue; Mexiletine; NiMODipine; NSAID (COX-2 Inhibitor); NSAID (Nonselective); Obinutuzumab; OLANZapine; Pentoxifylline; Perhexiline; Phenytoin; Pimozide; Pirfenidone; Pomalidomide; Propafenone; Propranolol; QuiNIDine; Ramelteon; Rivaroxaban; Roflumilast; Ropivacaine; Salicylates; Serotonin Modulators; Tasimelteon; Theophylline Derivatives; Thiazide and Thiazide-Like Diuretics; Thioridazine; Thrombolytic Agents; TiZANidine; Tositumomab and Iodine I 131 Tositumomab; TraMADol; Tricyclic Antidepressants; Urokinase; Vitamin K Antagonists; Zolpidem

The levels/effects of FluvoxaMINE may be increased by: Abiraterone Acetate; Ajmaline; Alcohol (Ethyl); Analgesics (Opioid); Antiemetics (5HT3 Antagonists); Antipsychotic Agents; Asunaprevir; BuPROPion; BusPIRone; Cimetidine; CNS Depressants; Cobicistat; CYP1A2 Inhibitors (Moderate); CYP1A2 Inhibitors (Strong); CYP2D6 Inhibitors (Moderate); CYP2D6 Inhibitors (Strong); Dapoxetine; Darunavir; Dasatinib; Deferasirox; Glucosamine; Grapefruit Juice; Herbs (Anticoagulant/Antiplatelet Properties); Ibrutinib; Imatinib; Limaprost; Linezolid; Lithium; Lumefantrine; MAO Inhibitors; Metaxalone; Methadone; Methylene Blue; Methylphenidate; Metoclopramide; MetyroSINE; Multivitamins/Fluoride (with ADE); Multivitamins/Minerals (with ADEK, Folate, Iron); Multivitamins/Minerals (with AE, No Iron); Obeticholic Acid; Omega-3 Fatty Acids; Panobinostat; Peginterferon Alfa-2b; Pentosan Polysulfate Sodium; Pentoxifylline; Perhexiline; Prostacyclin Analogues; QuiNIDine; QuiNINE; Tedizolid; TraMADol; Tryptophan; Vemurafenib; Vitamin E (Systemic)

Decreased Effect

FluvoxaMINE may decrease the levels/effects of: Clopidogrel; Iobenguane I 123; Ioflupane I 123; Thyroid Products

The levels/effects of FluvoxaMINE may be decreased by: Cannabis; CYP1A2 Inducers (Strong); Cyproheptadine; Cyproterone; NSAID (COX-2 Inhibitor); NSAID (Nonselective); Peginterferon Alfa-2b; Teriflunomide

Pharmacodynamics/Kinetics

Onset of Action Individual responses may vary; however, 8 to 12 weeks of treatment are needed for patients with obsessive-compulsive disorder and 4to 8 weeks of treatment are needed for patients with depression before determining if a patient is partially or nonresponsive (APA, 2010; APA 2007)

Half-life Elimination ~14 to 16 hours; ~17 to 26 hours in the elderly

Time to Peak Plasma: 3 to 8 hours

Pregnancy Risk Factor C

Pregnancy Considerations Adverse events have been observed in animal reproduction studies. Fluvoxamine crosses the human placenta. An increased risk of teratogenic effects, including cardiovascular defects, may be associated with maternal use of fluvoxamine or other SSRIs; however, available information is conflicting. Nonteratogenic effects in the newborn following SSRI/SNRI exposure late in the third trimester include respiratory distress, cyanosis, apnea, seizures, temperature instability, feeding difficulty, vomiting, hypoglycemia, hypo- or hypertonia, hyper-reflexia, jitteriness, irritability, constant crying, and tremor. Symptoms may be due to the toxicity of the SSRIs/SNRIs or a discontinuation syndrome and may be consistent with serotonin syndrome associated with SSRI treatment. Persistent pulmonary hypertension of the newborn (PPHN) has also been reported with SSRI exposure. The long-term effects of in utero SSRI exposure on infant development and behavior are not known.

The ACOG recommends that therapy with SSRIs or SNRIs during pregnancy be individualized; treatment of depression during pregnancy should incorporate the clinical expertise of the mental health clinician, obstetrician, primary health care provider, and pediatrician. According to the American Psychiatric Association (APA), the risks of medication treatment should be weighed against other treatment options and untreated depression. For women who discontinue antidepressant medications during pregnancy and who may be at high risk for postpartum depression, the medications can be restarted following delivery. Treatment algorithms have been developed by the ACOG and the APA for the management of depression in women prior to conception and during pregnancy.

Pregnant women exposed to antidepressants during pregnancy are encouraged to enroll in the National Pregnancy Registry for Antidepressants (NPRAD). Women 18 to 45 years of age or their health care providers may contact the registry by calling 844-405-6185. Enrollment should be done as early in pregnancy as possible.

Breastfeeding Considerations Fluvoxamine is excreted in breast milk. Based on case reports, the dose the infant receives is relatively small and adverse events have not been observed. Adverse events have been reported in nursing infants exposed to some SSRIs. According to the manufacturer, the decision to continue or discontinue breastfeeding during therapy should take into account the risk of exposure to the infant and the benefits of treatment to the mother.

The long-term effects on development and behavior have not been studied; therefore, fluvoxamine should be prescribed to a mother who is breastfeeding only when the benefits outweigh the potential risks. Maternal use of an SSRI during pregnancy may cause delayed milk secretion.

Dosage Forms

Capsule Extended Release 24 Hour, Oral:

Generic: 100 mg, 150 mg

Tablet, Oral:

Generic: 25 mg, 50 mg, 100 mg

Dosage Forms: Canada Note: Refer to Dosage Forms. Extended release capsules are not available in Canada.

Dental Comment Problems with SSRI-induced bruxism have been reported and may preclude their use. Clinicians attempting to evaluate any patient with bruxism or involuntary muscle movement, who is simultaneously being treated with an SSRI drug, should be aware of the potential association.

Folic Acid (FOE lik AS id)

Brand Names: US FA-8 [OTC]

Brand Names: Canada Apo-Folic

Generic Availability (US) Yes

Pharmacologic Category Vitamin, Water Soluble

Use Megaloblastic and macrocytic anemias due to folate deficiency: Treatment of megaloblastic and macrocytic anemias due to folate deficiency

Local Anesthetic/Vasoconstrictor Precautions No information available to require special precautions

Effects on Dental Treatment No significant effects or complications reported

Effects on Bleeding No information available to require special precautions

Adverse Reactions Frequency not defined.

Cardiovascular: Flushing (slight)
Central nervous system: Malaise (general)
Dermatologic: Erythema, pruritus, skin rash
Hypersensitivity: Hypersensitivity reaction
Respiratory: Bronchospasm

Dosing

Adult

Megaloblastic and macrocytic anemias due to folate deficiency:

Manufacturer's labeling: Oral, IM, IV, SubQ: Initial: 0.4 to 1 mg/day. Higher doses may be required in resistant cases.

Maintenance dose: 0.4 mg/day

Pregnant and lactating women: Maintenance dose: 0.8 mg/day

Alternate recommendations (off-label dose): Oral: 1 to 5 mg once daily (Cook 2014); doses up to 15 mg once daily have also been recommended (Hoffbrand 2015).

Recommended daily allowance (RDA) (IOM, 1998): Expressed as dietary folate equivalents: Oral: 400 mcg/day

Pregnancy: 600 mcg/day

Lactation: 500 mcg/day

Prevention of neural tube defects (off-label use): Oral:

Females of childbearing potential: 400 to 800 mcg/day (USPSTF 2017)

Females at high risk, who have had a previous pregnancy with a neural tube defect, or with family history of neural tube defects: 4 mg/day (ACOG 2003)

Geriatric Refer to adult dosing. Vitamin B_{12} deficiency must be ruled out before initiating folate therapy due to frequency of combined nutritional deficiencies: RDA requirements (1999): 400 mcg/day (0.4 mg) minimum.

Pediatric

Megaloblastic and macrocytic anemias due to folate deficiency: Oral, IM, IV, SubQ: Initial: 0.4 to 1 mg/day. Higher doses may be required in resistant cases.

Maintenance dose:

Infants: 0.1 mg/day

Children <4 years: Up to 0.3 mg/day

Children ≥4 years, Adolescents, and Adults: Refer to adult dosing.

Adequate intake (AI) (IOM 1998): Expressed as folate equivalents: Oral: Infants:

1 to 6 months: 65 mcg/day

7 to 12 months: 80 mcg/day

Recommended daily allowance (RDA) (IOM 1998): Expressed as dietary folate equivalents: Oral:

Children 1 to 3 years: 150 mcg/day

Children 4 to 8 years: 200 mcg/day

Children 9 to 13 years: 300 mcg/day

Adolescents ≥14 years: Refer to adult dosing.

Mechanism of Action Folic acid is necessary for formation of a number of coenzymes in many metabolic systems, particularly for purine and pyrimidine synthesis; required for nucleoprotein synthesis and maintenance in erythropoiesis; stimulates WBC and platelet production in folate deficiency anemia. Folic acid enhances the metabolism of formic acid, the toxic metabolite of methanol, to nontoxic metabolites (off-label use).

Contraindications Hypersensitivity to folic acid or any component of the formulation

Warnings/Precautions Not appropriate for monotherapy with pernicious, aplastic, or normocytic anemias when anemia is present with vitamin B_{12} deficiency. Doses >0.1 mg/day may obscure pernicious anemia with continuing irreversible nerve damage progression. Resistance to treatment may occur with depressed hematopoiesis, alcoholism, and deficiencies of other vitamins. Injection contains benzyl alcohol (1.5%) as preservative (use care in administration to neonates).

Aluminum: The parenteral product may contain aluminum; toxic aluminum concentrations may be seen with high doses, prolonged use, or renal dysfunction. Premature neonates are at higher risk due to immature renal function and aluminum intake from other parenteral sources. Parenteral aluminum exposure of >4 to 5 mcg/kg/day is associated with CNS and bone toxicity; tissue loading may occur at lower doses (Federal Register, 2002). See manufacturer's labeling.

Benzyl alcohol and derivatives: Some dosage forms may contain benzyl alcohol; large amounts of benzyl alcohol (≥99 mg/kg/day) have been associated with a potentially fatal toxicity ("gasping syndrome") in neonates; the "gasping syndrome" consists of metabolic acidosis, respiratory distress, gasping respirations, CNS dysfunction (including convulsions, intracranial hemorrhage), hypotension and cardiovascular collapse (AAP ["Inactive" 1997]; CDC, 1982); some data suggests that benzoate displaces bilirubin from protein binding sites (Ahlfors, 2001); avoid or use dosage forms containing benzyl alcohol with caution in neonates. See manufacturer's labeling.

Drug Interactions

Metabolism/Transport Effects None known.

Avoid Concomitant Use

Avoid concomitant use of Folic Acid with any of the following: Raltitrexed

Increased Effect/Toxicity There are no known significant interactions involving an increase in effect.

Decreased Effect

Folic Acid may decrease the levels/effects of: Fosphenytoin; PHENobarbital; Phenytoin; Primidone; Raltitrexed

The levels/effects of Folic Acid may be decreased by: Green Tea; SulfaSALAzine

Dietary Considerations As of January 1998, the FDA has required manufacturers of enriched flour, bread, corn meal, pasta, rice, and other grain products to add folic acid to their products. The intent is to help decrease the risk of neural tube defects by increasing folic acid intake. Other foods which contain folic acid include dark green leafy vegetables, citrus fruits and juices, and lentils.

Pharmacodynamics/Kinetics

Onset of Action Peak effect: Oral: 0.5-1 hour

Time to Peak Oral: 1 hour

Pregnancy Risk Factor A

Pregnancy Considerations Water soluble vitamins cross the placenta. Folate requirements increase during pregnancy. Folate supplementation during the periconceptual period decreases the risk of neural tube defects (ACOG 2003; USPSTF 2009). Folate supplementation (doses larger than the RDA) is recommended for women who may become pregnant (IOM 1998). Folic acid is also indicated for the treatment of anemias due to folate deficiency in pregnant women.

Breastfeeding Considerations Folate is excreted in breast milk; concentrations are not affected by dietary intake unless the mother has a severe deficiency. Folate requirements increase in breastfeeding women (IOM 1998).

Dosage Forms

Capsule, Oral [preservative free]:
FA-8 [OTC]: 0.8 mg
Generic: 5 mg, 20 mg

Solution, Injection:
Generic: 5 mg/mL (10 mL)

Tablet, Oral:
Generic: 400 mcg, 800 mcg, 1 mg

Tablet, Oral [preservative free]:
FA-8 [OTC]: 800 mcg
Generic: 400 mcg, 800 mcg

Folic Acid, Cyanocobalamin, and Pyridoxine

(FOE lik AS id, sye an oh koe BAL a min, & peer i DOKS een)

Related Information

Cyanocobalamin *on page 426*
Folic Acid *on page 762*
Pyridoxine *on page 1407*

Brand Names: US Airavite; Av-VITE FB; CenFol; FaBB; Folastin [DSC]; Folbee; Folbic; Folcaps [DSC]; Folgard Rx; Folplex 2.2; Foltabs 800 [OTC]; Homocysteine Formula [OTC]; Virt-Gard; Virt-Vite; Virt-Vite Forte; Vita-Respa [DSC]

Pharmacologic Category Vitamin

Use Nutritional supplement in end-stage renal failure, dialysis, hyperhomocysteinemia, homocystinuria, malabsorption syndromes, dietary deficiencies

Local Anesthetic/Vasoconstrictor Precautions No information available to require special precautions

Effects on Dental Treatment No significant effects or complications reported

Effects on Bleeding No information available to require special precautions

Adverse Reactions See individual agents.

General Dosage Range Oral: *Adults:* 1 tablet (folic acid 0.4-2.5 mg/cyanocobalamin 115-2000 mcg/pyridoxine 10-25 mg) daily

Pregnancy Considerations See individual agents.

Follitropin Alfa (foe li TRO pin AL fa)

Brand Names: US Gonal-f; Gonal-f RFF; Gonal-f RFF Pen [DSC]; Gonal-f RFF Redi-ject

Brand Names: Canada Gonal-f; Gonal-f Pen

Pharmacologic Category Gonadotropin; Ovulation Stimulator

Use

Multifollicular development during Assisted Reproductive Technology (ART): To stimulate the development of multiple follicles with ART

Ovulation induction: Induction of ovulation in oligo-anovulatory infertile patients in whom the cause of infertility is functional and not caused by primary ovarian failure

Spermatogenesis induction (Gonal-f only): Induction of spermatogenesis in men with primary and secondary hypogonadotropic hypogonadism in whom the cause of infertility is not due to primary testicular failure

Local Anesthetic/Vasoconstrictor Precautions No information available to require special precautions

Effects on Dental Treatment Key adverse event(s) related to dental treatment: Stomatitis and toothache.

Effects on Bleeding No information available to require special precautions

Adverse Reactions Percentage may vary by indication, product formulation

>10%:

Cardiovascular: Varicocele (15%)
Central nervous system: Headache (13% to 27%)
Dermatologic: Acne vulgaris (males 59%)
Endocrine & metabolic: Ovarian cyst (4% to 15%)
Gastrointestinal: Abdominal pain (9% to 23%), nausea (4% to 14%), enlargement of abdomen (1% to 14%)
Genitourinary: Mastalgia (males 14%)
Local: Injection site reaction (males 15%; females 1% to 4%)
Respiratory: Upper respiratory tract infection (4% to 12%)

1% to 10%:

Cardiovascular: Chest pain (1% to 2%), hypotension (1% to 2%), palpitations (1% to 2%)
Central nervous system: Fatigue (males 9%; females 1% to 2%), pain (2% to 6%), emotional lability (5%), migraine (1% to 4%), dizziness (1% to 3%), malaise (2%), anxiety (1% to 2%), drowsiness (1% to 2%), nervousness (1% to 2%), paresthesia (1% to 2%)
Dermatologic: Acne vulgaris (females 4%), pruritus (1% to 2%)
Endocrine & metabolic: Gynecomastia (9%), intermenstrual bleeding (4% to 9%), ovarian hyperstimulation syndrome (5% to 7%; severe: <1%), weight gain (4%), menstrual disease (3%), hot flash (2%), ovarian disease (2%), increased thirst (1% to 2%)
Gastrointestinal: Diarrhea (1% to 8%), flatulence (4% to 7%), toothache (1% to 4%), vomiting (1% to 3%), aphthous stomatitis (2%), constipation (2%), dyspepsia (2%), anorexia (1% to 2%)
Genitourinary: Pelvic pain (7%), mastalgia (females 4% to 6%), vaginal hemorrhage (1% to 6%), cervical lesion (3%), genital candidiasis (3%), dysmenorrhea (1% to 3%), cystitis (2%), gynecological pain (2%), urinary frequency (2%), urinary tract infection (2%), uterine hemorrhage (2%), leukorrhea (1% to 2%)
Infection: Viral infection (2%)
Local: Bruising at injection site (10%), pain at injection site (3% to 9%), inflammation at injection site (1% to 4%), swelling at injection site (3%)
Neuromuscular & skeletal: Back pain (4% to 5%), myalgia (1% to 2%)
Respiratory: Rhinitis (≤7%), pharyngitis (3% to 7%), sinusitis (5% to 6%), flu-like symptoms (4%), cough (2% to 3%), asthma (1% to 2%), dyspnea (1% to 2%)
Miscellaneous: Fever (2% to 4%)

Postmarketing and/or case reports: Anaphylactoid reaction, anaphylaxis, depression, Epstein-Barr infection, hemoperitoneum, hemoptysis, hypersensitivity reaction, ovarian torsion, ovarian neoplasm, ovary enlargement, pulmonary complications (including atelectasis, acute respiratory distress syndrome, exacerbation of asthma), thromboembolism, vascular disease

General Dosage Range SubQ:

Adults (females): Initial: 75-225 units daily; Maximum: Up to 300-450 units daily

Adults (males): Gonal-f: Initial: 150 units 3 times weekly; Maximum: Up to 300 units 3 times weekly

Mechanism of Action Follitropin alfa is a human FSH preparation of recombinant DNA origin. Follitropins stimulate ovarian follicular growth in women who do not have primary ovarian failure, and stimulate spermatogenesis in men with hypogonadotrophic hypogonadism. FSH is required for normal follicular growth, maturation, gonadal steroid production, and spermatogenesis.

Pharmacodynamics/Kinetics

Onset of Action Peak effect:

Spermatogenesis, median: 6.8-12.4 months (range: 2.7-18.1 months)

Follicle development: Within cycle

Half-life Elimination SubQ: 24-53 hours in healthy female volunteers; 32-41 hours in healthy male volunteers

Time to Peak In healthy volunteers:

Females: SubQ: 8-16 hours

Males: SubQ: 11-20 hours

Pregnancy Risk Factor X

Pregnancy Considerations Ectopic pregnancy, congenital abnormalities, spontaneous abortion, and multiple births have been reported. The incidence of congenital abnormality may be slightly higher after ART than with spontaneous conception; higher incidence may be related to parenteral characteristics (maternal age, sperm characteristics). Follitropin Alfa is used for the induction of ovulation; use is contraindicated in women who are already pregnant.

Follitropin Beta (foe li TRO pin BAY ta)

Brand Names: US Follistim AQ

Brand Names: Canada Puregon

Pharmacologic Category Gonadotropin; Ovulation Stimulator

Use

Females: Induction of ovulation and pregnancy in anovulatory infertile patients in whom the cause of infertility is functional and not caused by primary ovarian failure; induction of pregnancy in normal ovulatory women undergoing Assisted Reproductive Technology (ART) (eg, *in vitro* fertilization [IVF], intracytoplasmic sperm injection [ICSI])

Males: Induction of spermatogenesis in men with primary and secondary hypogonadotropic hypogonadism in whom the cause of infertility is not due to primary testicular failure.

Local Anesthetic/Vasoconstrictor Precautions No information available to require special precautions

Effects on Dental Treatment No significant effects or complications reported

Effects on Bleeding No information available to require special precautions

Adverse Reactions Frequency may vary based on indication.

1% to 10%:

Central nervous system: Headache (7%), fatigue (2%)

Dermatologic: Acne vulgaris (7%), skin rash (3%)

Endocrine & metabolic: Ovarian hyperstimulation (6% to 8%), gynecomastia (3%), ovarian cyst (3%)

Gastrointestinal: Nausea (4%), abdominal distress (≤3%), abdominal pain (≤3%)

Genitourinary: Pelvic symptoms (discomfort: 8%), pelvic pain (6%)

Local: Injection site reaction (7%), pain at injection site (7%)

<1%, postmarketing, and/or case reports: Abdominal distention, breast tenderness, constipation, diarrhea, ovarian neoplasm, ovarian torsion, ovary enlargement, spontaneous abortion, thromboembolism, uterine hemorrhage, vaginal hemorrhage

General Dosage Range

IM, SubQ: *Adults (females):* Initial: 75-225 units/day; Maintenance: Up to 175-600 units/day

SubQ: *Adults (males):* 450 units/week

Mechanism of Action Follitropin beta is a human FSH preparation of recombinant DNA origin. Follitropins stimulate ovarian follicular growth in women who do not have primary ovarian failure and stimulate spermatogenesis in men with hypogonadotrophic hypogonadism. FSH is required for normal follicular growth, maturation, gonadal steroid production, and spermatogenesis.

Pharmacodynamics/Kinetics

Onset of Action Peak effect: Females: Follicle development: Within cycle

Half-life Elimination Females: IM: 44 hours (single dose), 27-30 hours (multiple doses); SubQ: 33 hours (single dose)

Time to Peak Females: SubQ: 13 hours

Pregnancy Risk Factor X

Pregnancy Considerations Ectopic pregnancies, congenital abnormalities, and multiple births have been reported. The incidence of congenital abnormality may be slightly higher after ART than with spontaneous conception; higher incidence may be related to parenteral characteristics (maternal age, sperm characteristics). Follitropin Beta is used for the induction of ovulation; use is contraindicated in women who are already pregnant.

Fomepizole (foe ME pi zole)

Brand Names: US Antizol

Brand Names: Canada Antizol

Pharmacologic Category Antidote

Use

Ethylene glycol or methanol poisoning: Treatment of methanol or ethylene glycol poisoning alone or in combination with hemodialysis

Note: Fomepizole is the preferred antidote for known or suspected ethylene glycol poisoning or methanol poisoning. If fomepizole is unavailable or if the patient is intolerant to fomepizole, ethanol therapy may be considered. Ethanol as an antidote is effective in the management of methanol and ethylene glycol poisoning (Thanacoody 2016; Zakharov 2015); however, ethanol is associated with a higher incidence of adverse events and medication errors (Bestic 2009; Lepik 2009; Lepik 2011).

Local Anesthetic/Vasoconstrictor Precautions No information available to require special precautions

Effects on Dental Treatment Key adverse event(s) related to dental treatment: Bad/metallic taste.

Effects on Bleeding No information available to require special precautions

Adverse Reactions

>10%:

Central nervous system: Headache (14%)

Gastrointestinal: Nausea (11%)

1% to 10% (≤3% unless otherwise noted):

Cardiovascular: Bradycardia, facial flushing, hypotension, phlebitis, shock, tachycardia

Central nervous system: Dizziness (6%), drowsiness (6%), metallic taste (≤6%), agitation, altered sense of smell, anxiety, seizure, speech disturbance, vertigo

Dermatologic: Skin rash

Gastrointestinal: Unpleasant taste (≤6%), abdominal pain, decreased appetite, diarrhea, heartburn, hiccups, vomiting

Genitourinary: Anuria
Hematologic & oncologic: Anemia, disseminated intravascular coagulation (DIC), eosinophilia, lymphangitis
Hepatic: Increased liver enzymes
Local: Application site reaction, inflammation at injection site, pain at injection site
Neuromuscular & skeletal: Back pain
Ophthalmic: Nystagmus, transient blurred vision, visual disturbance
Respiratory: Pharyngitis
Miscellaneous: Fever, multi-organ failure
<1%, postmarketing and/or case reports: Hypersensitivity reaction (mild; mild rash, eosinophilia)

General Dosage Range Dosage adjustment recommended in patients with renal impairment

IV: *Adults:* Loading dose of 15 mg/kg, followed by 10 mg/kg every 12 hours for 4 doses, then 15 mg/kg every 12 hours

Mechanism of Action Fomepizole competitively inhibits alcohol dehydrogenase, an enzyme which catalyzes the metabolism of ethanol, ethylene glycol, and methanol to their toxic metabolites. Ethylene glycol is metabolized to glycoaldehyde, then oxidized to glycolate, glyoxylate, and oxalate. Glycolate and oxalate are responsible for metabolic acidosis and renal damage. Methanol is metabolized to formaldehyde, then oxidized to formic acid. Formic acid is responsible for metabolic acidosis and visual disturbances.

Pharmacodynamics/Kinetics

Onset of Action Peak effect: Maximum: 1.5-2 hours

Half-life Elimination Has not been calculated; varies with dose

Pregnancy Risk Factor C

Pregnancy Considerations Animal reproduction studies have not been conducted. In general, medications used as antidotes should take into consideration the health and prognosis of the mother; antidotes should be administered to pregnant women if there is a clear indication for use and should not be withheld because of fears of teratogenicity (Bailey, 2003).

Fondaparinux (fon da PARE i nuks)

Brand Names: US Arixtra

Brand Names: Canada Arixtra

Pharmacologic Category Anticoagulant; Anticoagulant, Factor Xa Inhibitor

Use

Acute deep vein thrombosis: Treatment of acute deep vein thrombosis (DVT) in conjunction with warfarin.

Acute pulmonary embolism: Treatment of acute pulmonary embolism (PE) in conjunction with warfarin.

Deep vein thrombosis prophylaxis: Prophylaxis of DVT in patients undergoing surgery for hip replacement, knee replacement, hip fracture (including extended prophylaxis following hip fracture surgery), or abdominal surgery (in patients at risk for thromboembolic complications).

Canadian labeling: Additional uses; not approved in the US: Management of unstable angina or non-ST segment elevation myocardial infarction (UA/NSTEMI) for the prevention of death and subsequent MI; management of ST segment elevation MI (STEMI) for the prevention of death and myocardial reinfarction

Local Anesthetic/Vasoconstrictor Precautions No information available to require special precautions

Effects on Dental Treatment Key adverse event(s) related to dental treatment: Hemorrhage may occur at any site. See Effects on Bleeding.

Effects on Bleeding Dose related bleeding is the most common adverse event. Bleeding from the gums is reported (3%). Moderate thrombocytopenia occurs in 3% of patients and severe thrombocytopenia in 0.2%. Medical consult recommended.

Adverse Reactions As with all anticoagulants, bleeding is the major adverse effect. Hemorrhage may occur at any site. Risk appears increased by a number of factors including renal dysfunction, age (>75 years), and weight (<50 kg).

>10%: Hematologic & oncologic: Anemia (2% to 20%)

1% to 10%:
Cardiovascular: Hypotension (≤4%)
Central nervous system: Insomnia (≤5%), dizziness (≤4%), confusion (1% to 3%)
Dermatologic: Increased wound secretion (≤5%), skin blister (≤3%)
Endocrine & metabolic: Hypokalemia (≤4%)
Hematologic & oncologic: Purpura (≤4%), thrombocytopenia (50,000 to 100,000/mm^3: 3%), hematoma (2% to 3%), minor hemorrhage (2% to 3%), major hemorrhage (1% to 3%; risk of major hemorrhage increased as high as 5% in patients receiving initial dose <6 hours following surgery), postoperative hemorrhage (≤2%)
Hepatic: Increased serum ALT (>3 × ULN: 1% to 3%), increased serum AST (>3 × ULN: <1% to ≤2%)
Infection: postoperative wound infection (abdominal surgery: 5%)
Respiratory: Epistaxis (VTE: 1%)

<1%, postmarketing, and/or case reports: Anaphylactoid reaction, anaphylaxis, angioedema, catheter site thrombosis (during PCI; without heparin), elevated aPTT associated with bleeding, epidural hematoma, hemorrhagic death, injection site reaction (bleeding at injection site, skin rash, pruritus), intracranial hemorrhage, reoperation due to bleeding, severe thrombocytopenia (<50,000/mm^3), spinal hematoma, thrombocytopenia (with thrombosis)

General Dosage Range SubQ:
Adults <50 kg: Treatment: 5 mg once daily
Adults 50 to 100 kg: Prophylaxis: 2.5 mg once daily; Treatment: 7.5 mg once daily
Adults >100 kg: Prophylaxis: 2.5 mg once daily; Treatment: 10 mg once daily

Mechanism of Action Fondaparinux is a synthetic pentasaccharide that causes an antithrombin III-mediated selective inhibition of factor Xa. Neutralization of factor Xa interrupts the blood coagulation cascade and inhibits thrombin formation and thrombus development.

Pharmacodynamics/Kinetics

Half-life Elimination 17 to 21 hours; prolonged with renal impairment and in the elderly

Time to Peak SubQ: ~2 to 3 hours

Pregnancy Risk Factor B

Pregnancy Considerations Adverse events have not been observed in animal reproduction studies. Based on case reports, small amounts of fondaparinux have been detected in the umbilical cord following multiple doses during pregnancy (Dempfle 2004). Use of fondaparinux in pregnancy should be limited to those women who have severe allergic reactions to heparin, including heparin-induced thrombocytopenia, and who cannot receive danaparoid (Guyatt 2012).

Formoterol (for MOH te rol)

Related Information

Respiratory Diseases *on page 1777*

Brand Names: US Foradil Aerolizer [DSC]; Perforomist

Brand Names: Canada Foradil; Oxeze Turbuhaler

Pharmacologic Category $Beta_2$ Agonist; $Beta_2$-Adrenergic Agonist, Long-Acting

Use

US labeling:

Asthma: Treatment of asthma (only as concomitant therapy with an inhaled corticosteroid) in patients with reversible obstructive airway disease, including patients with symptoms of nocturnal asthma (Foradil Aerolizer).

Chronic obstructive pulmonary disease (COPD): Maintenance treatment of bronchoconstriction in patients with COPD (Foradil Aerolizer, Perforomist).

Exercise-induced bronchospasm: Prevention of exercise-induced bronchospasm when administered on an as-needed basis (monotherapy may be indicated in patients without persistent asthma) (Foradil Aerolizer).

Canadian labeling:

Asthma: Treatment of asthma (only as concomitant therapy with an inhaled corticosteroid) in patients with reversible obstructive airway disease, including patients with symptoms of nocturnal asthma (Foradil, Oxeze Turbuhaler).

COPD: Maintenance treatment of COPD (Foradil).

Exercise-induced bronchospasm: Prevention of exercise-induced bronchospasm when administered on an as-needed basis (monotherapy may be indicated in patients without persistent asthma) (Oxeze Turbuhaler).

Local Anesthetic/Vasoconstrictor Precautions No information available to require special precautions

Effects on Dental Treatment Key adverse event(s) related to dental treatment: Xerostomia (normal salivary flow resumes upon discontinuation).

Effects on Bleeding No information available to require special precautions

Adverse Reactions

1% to 10%:

Cardiovascular: Chest pain (2% to 3%)

Central nervous system: Anxiety (2%), dizziness (2%), insomnia (2%), voice disorder (1%), headache

Dermatologic: Pruritus (2%), skin rash (1%)

Gastrointestinal: Diarrhea (5%), nausea (5%), xerostomia (1% to 3%), vomiting (2%), abdominal pain, dyspepsia, gastroenteritis

Neuromuscular & skeletal: Muscle cramps (2%), tremor

Respiratory: Respiratory tract infection (3% to 7%), exacerbation of asthma (ages 5 to 12 years: 5% to 6%; age >12 years: <4%; acute deterioration: <1%), bronchitis (5%), pharyngitis (3% to 4%), sinusitis (3%), dyspnea (2%), tonsillitis (1%)

Miscellaneous: Fever (2%)

<1%, postmarketing, and/or case reports: Agitation, anaphylaxis (including severe hypotension/angioedema), angina pectoris, atrial fibrillation, behavioral changes, cardiac arrhythmia, cough, decreased glucose tolerance, dermatitis, disturbed sleep, dysgeusia, fatigue, hyperglycemia, hypertension, hypokalemia, malaise, metabolic acidosis, muscle spasm, nervousness, palpitations, paradoxical bronchospasm, prolonged Q-T interval on ECG, restlessness, tachycardia, urticaria, variable blood pressure, ventricular premature contractions

General Dosage Range Inhalation:

Powder for inhalation: *Children ≥5 years, Adolescents, and Adults:* 12 mcg every 12 hours (maximum: 24 mcg daily) **or** 12 mcg inhaled prior to exercise

Solution for nebulization: *Adults:* 20 mcg twice daily (maximum: 40 mcg daily)

Mechanism of Action Relaxes bronchial smooth muscle by selective action on $beta_2$ receptors with little effect on heart rate. Formoterol has a long-acting effect.

Pharmacodynamics/Kinetics

Onset of Action Powder for inhalation: Within 3 minutes

Peak effect: Powder for inhalation: 80% of peak effect within 15 minutes; Solution for nebulization: 2 hours

Duration of Action Improvement in FEV_1 observed for 12 hours in most patients

Half-life Elimination Powder: ~10-14 hours; Nebulized solution: ~7 hours

Time to Peak Maximum improvement in FEV_1 in 1-3 hours

Pregnancy Risk Factor C

Pregnancy Considerations Adverse events were observed in some animal reproduction studies. Formoterol has the potential to affect uterine contractility if administered during labor.

Uncontrolled asthma is associated with adverse events on pregnancy (increased risk of perinatal mortality, preeclampsia, preterm birth, low birth weight infants). Although data related to its use in pregnancy is limited, formoterol may be used as an alternative agent when a long-acting beta agonist is needed to treat moderate persistent or severe persistent asthma in pregnant women (NAEPP, 2005).

Product Availability Foradil Aerolizer is no longer available in the US.

Fosamprenavir (FOS am pren a veer)

Related Information

HIV Infection and AIDS *on page 1785*

Brand Names: US Lexiva

Brand Names: Canada Telzir

Pharmacologic Category Antiretroviral, Protease Inhibitor (Anti-HIV)

Use HIV-1 Infection: Treatment of HIV-1 infection, in combination with other antiretroviral agents

Local Anesthetic/Vasoconstrictor Precautions No information available to require special precautions

Effects on Dental Treatment No significant effects or complications reported

Effects on Bleeding No information available to require special precautions

Adverse Reactions

>10%:

Dermatologic: Skin rash (≤19%; onset: ~11 days; duration: ~13 days)

Endocrine & metabolic: Hypertriglyceridemia (>750 mg/dL: ≤11%)

Gastrointestinal: Diarrhea (5% to 13%; moderate-to-severe)

1% to 10%:

Central nervous system: Fatigue (2% to 4%; moderate-to-severe), headache (2% to 4%; moderate-to-severe)

Dermatologic: Pruritus (7% to 8%)

Endocrine & metabolic: Hyperglycemia (>251 mg/dL: ≤2%)

Gastrointestinal: Increased serum lipase (>2x ULN: 5% to 8%), nausea (3% to 7%; moderate-to-severe), vomiting (2% to 6%; moderate-to-severe), abdominal pain (≤2%; moderate-to-severe)

Hematologic & oncologic: Neutropenia (<750 cells/mm^3: 3%)

Hepatic: Increased serum transaminases (>5x ULN: 4% to 8%)

<1%, postmarketing, and/or case reports: Angioedema, cerebrovascular accident, hypercholesterolemia, myocardial infarction, nephrolithiasis, oral paresthesia, Stevens-Johnson syndrome

General Dosage Range Dosage adjustment recommended in patients with hepatic impairment or on concomitant therapy

Oral:

Infants ≥4 weeks, Children, and Adolescents (PI-naive patients) or Infants ≥6 months, Children, and Adolescents (PI-experienced patients): Ritonavir-boosted regimen:

<11 kg: 45 mg/kg/dose twice daily (plus ritonavir); maximum: 700 mg/dose

11 to <15 kg: 30 mg/kg/dose twice daily (plus ritonavir); maximum: 700 mg/dose

15 to <20 kg: 23 mg/kg/dose twice daily (plus ritonavir); maximum: 700 mg/dose

≥20 kg: 18 mg/kg/dose twice daily (plus ritonavir); maximum: 700 mg/dose

Children ≥2 years and Adolescents (PI-naive patients): Unboosted regimen:

<47 kg: 30 mg/kg/dose twice daily; maximum: 1,400 mg/dose

≥47 kg: 1,400 mg twice daily

Adults:

Ritonavir-boosted regimen: 700 mg twice daily **or** 1,400 mg once daily

Unboosted regimen: 1,400 mg twice daily

Mechanism of Action Fosamprenavir is rapidly and almost completely converted to amprenavir by cellular phosphatases *in vivo*. Amprenavir binds to the site of HIV-1 protease activity and inhibits cleavage of viral Gag-Pol polyprotein precursors into individual functional proteins required for infectious HIV. This results in the formation of immature, noninfectious viral particles.

Pharmacodynamics/Kinetics

Half-life Elimination ~7.7 hours (amprenavir)

Time to Peak 1.5 to 4 hours (median: 2.5 hours)

Pregnancy Risk Factor C

Pregnancy Considerations Adverse events were observed in some animal reproduction studies; data collected by the antiretroviral pregnancy registry are insufficient to evaluate human teratogenic risk. Fosamprenavir has a low level of transfer across the human placenta. A small increased risk of preterm birth has been associated with maternal use of protease inhibitor-based combination antiretroviral therapy during pregnancy; however, the benefits of use generally outweigh this risk and protease inhibitors (PIs) should not be withheld if otherwise recommended. Information related to stillbirth, low birth weight, and small for gestational age infants is limited. Long-term follow-up is recommended for all infants exposed to antiretroviral medications; children who develop significant organ system abnormalities of unknown etiology (particularly of the CNS or heart) should be evaluated for potential mitochondrial dysfunction. Hyperglycemia, new onset of diabetes mellitus, or diabetic ketoacidosis have been reported with PIs; it is not clear if pregnancy increases this risk.

Combination antiretroviral therapy (cART) therapy is recommended for all HIV-infected pregnant women to keep the viral load below the limit of detection and reduce the risk of perinatal transmission. When HIV is diagnosed during pregnancy in a woman who has never received antiretroviral therapy, cART should begin as soon as possible after diagnosis. The Health and Human Services (HHS) Perinatal HIV Guidelines note there are insufficient data to recommend use as initial therapy in antiretroviral-naive pregnant women. However, if used in pregnant women, fosamprenavir may be given with ritonavir-boosted twice-daily dosing. Unboosted fosamprenavir and once-daily dosing with ritonavir are not recommended. In general, women who become pregnant on a stable cART regimen may continue that regimen if viral suppression is effective, appropriate drug exposure can be achieved, contraindications for use in pregnancy are not present, and the regimen is well tolerated. Monitoring during pregnancy is more frequent than in non-pregnant adults; cART should be continued postpartum.

For HIV-infected couples planning a pregnancy, maximum viral suppression with cART is recommended prior to conception for the HIV-infected partner(s) and expert consultation is recommended; modification of therapy (if needed) and optimization of the woman's health should be done prior to conception. HIV-infected women not planning a pregnancy may use any available type of contraception, considering possible drug interactions and contraindications of the specific method. In addition, consistent use of condoms is also recommended (even during pregnancy) to prevent transmission of HIV or other sexually transmitted diseases.

Health care providers are encouraged to enroll pregnant women exposed to antiretroviral medications as early in pregnancy as possible in the Antiretroviral Pregnancy Registry (1-800-258-4263 or www.APRegistry.com). Health care providers caring for HIV-infected women and their infants may contact the National Perinatal HIV Hotline (888-448-8765) for clinical consultation (HHS [perinatal] 2016).

Fosaprepitant (fos a PRE pi tant)

Brand Names: US Emend

Brand Names: Canada Emend IV

Pharmacologic Category Antiemetic; Substance P/Neurokinin 1 Receptor Antagonist

Use

Prevention of chemotherapy-induced nausea and vomiting:

Prevention of acute and delayed nausea and vomiting associated with highly emetogenic chemotherapy, including high-dose cisplatin (initial and repeat courses; in combination with other antiemetics)

Prevention of delayed nausea and vomiting associated with moderately emetogenic chemotherapy (initial and repeat courses; in combination with other antiemetics)

Limitations of use: Fosaprepitant has not been studied for the management of existing nausea and vomiting.

Local Anesthetic/Vasoconstrictor Precautions No information available to require special precautions

Effects on Dental Treatment Key adverse event(s) related to dental treatment: Stomatitis, taste disturbances, xerostomia (normal salivary flow resumes upon discontinuation).

Effects on Bleeding No information available to require special precautions

Adverse Reactions Adverse reactions reported with aprepitant and fosaprepitant (as part of a combination chemotherapy regimen) occurring at a higher frequency than standard antiemetic therapy:

>10%:

Central nervous system: Fatigue (1% to 15%)

Gastrointestinal: Diarrhea (13%)

1% to 10%:

Central nervous system: Peripheral neuropathy (3%), headache (2%)

Gastrointestinal: Hiccups (5%), anorexia (2%), constipation (2%), dyspepsia (2%), eructation (1%)

Genitourinary: Urinary tract infection (2%)

Hematologic & oncologic: Neutropenia (8%), anemia (3%), leukopenia (2%)

Hepatic: Increased serum ALT (1% to 3%), increased serum AST (1%)

Local: Infusion-site reaction (2%; includes induration at injection site, infusion-site pain, local pruritus, local thrombophlebitis, or localized erythema)

Neuromuscular & skeletal: Weakness (4%), limb pain (2%)

<1%, postmarketing, and/or case reports: Abdominal distention, abdominal pain, abnormal dreams, abnormal gait, acne vulgaris, anaphylaxis, anemia, angioedema, anxiety, bradycardia, candidiasis, cardiovascular signs and symptoms, chest discomfort, chills, cognitive dysfunction, colitis (neutropenic), conjunctivitis, cough, decreased visual acuity, diaphoresis, disorientation, dizziness, drowsiness, dysarthria, dysgeusia, dyspnea, dysuria, edema, epigastric distress, erythema, euphoria, febrile neutropenia, fecal impaction, flatulence, flushing, gastroesophageal reflux, gastroesophageal reflux disease, hallucination, hematuria (microscopic), hot flash, hyperglycemia, hypersensitivity reaction, hypertension, hypoesthesia, hyponatremia, impaired consciousness, increased serum alkaline phosphatase, insomnia, intestinal obstruction, lethargy, loss of consciousness, malaise, miosis, muscle cramps, myalgia, myasthenia, nausea, obstipation, oily skin, palpitations, paresthesia, perforated duodenal ulcer, pharyngitis, pollakiuria, polydipsia, polyuria, post nasal drip, pruritus, seizure, sensory disturbance, SIADH (syndrome of inappropriate antidiuretic hormone secretion), skin lesion, skin photosensitivity, skin rash, sneezing, staphylococcal infection, Stevens-Johnson syndrome, stomatitis, throat irritation, tinnitus, toxic epidermal necrolysis, urticaria, vomiting, weight changes (gain/loss), wheezing, xerostomia

General Dosage Range IV: *Adults:* 150 mg as a single dose

Mechanism of Action Fosaprepitant is a prodrug of aprepitant, a substance P/neurokinin 1 (NK1) receptor antagonist. Fosaprepitant is rapidly converted to aprepitant, which prevents acute and delayed vomiting by inhibiting the substance P/neurokinin 1 (NK1) receptor; also augments the antiemetic activity of the 5-HT_3 receptor antagonist and corticosteroid activity and inhibits chemotherapy-induced emesis.

Pharmacodynamics/Kinetics

Half-life Elimination Aprepitant: ~9 to 13 hours

Time to Peak Fosaprepitant is converted to aprepitant within 30 minutes after the end of infusion

Pregnancy Considerations Adverse events were not observed in animal reproduction studies for aprepitant. Efficacy of hormonal contraceptive may be reduced; alternative or additional methods of contraception should be used both during treatment with fosaprepitant or aprepitant and for at least 1 month following the last fosaprepitant/aprepitant dose.

Foscarnet (fos KAR net)

Related Information

Systemic Viral Diseases *on page 1806*

Brand Names: US Foscavir

Brand Names: Canada Foscavir

Pharmacologic Category Antiviral Agent

Use

Cytomegalovirus retinitis: Treatment of cytomegalovirus (CMV) retinitis in persons with AIDS

Herpes simplex virus: Treatment of acyclovir-resistant mucocutaneous herpes simplex virus (HSV) infections in immunocompromised persons (eg, with advanced AIDS)

Local Anesthetic/Vasoconstrictor Precautions Foscarnet is one of the drugs confirmed to prolong the QT interval and is accepted as having a risk of causing torsade de pointes. In terms of epinephrine, it is not known what effect vasoconstrictors in the local anesthetic regimen will have in patients with a known history of congenital prolonged QT interval or in patients taking any medication that prolongs the QT interval. Until more information is obtained, it is suggested that the clinician consult with the physician prior to the use of a vasoconstrictor in suspected patients, and that the vasoconstrictor (epinephrine, mepivacaine and levonordefrin [Carbocaine® 2% with Neo-Cobefrin®]) be used with caution. See Dental Comment.

Effects on Dental Treatment Key adverse event(s) related to dental treatment: Xerostomia (normal salivary flow resumes upon discontinuation), taste perversion, and ulcerative stomatitis.

Effects on Bleeding No information available to require special precautions

Adverse Reactions

>10%:

Central nervous system: Headache (26%)

Endocrine & metabolic: Hypokalemia (16% to 48%), hypocalcemia (15% to 30%), hypomagnesemia (15% to 30%), hypophosphatemia (8% to 26%)

Gastrointestinal: Nausea (47%), diarrhea (30%), vomiting (26%)

Hematologic & oncologic: Anemia (33%), granulocytopenia (17%)

Renal: Renal insufficiency (27%)

Miscellaneous: Fever (65%)

1% to 10%:

Cardiovascular: Chest pain (1% to 5%; including transient chest pain as part of infusion reactions), edema (1% to 5%), facial edema (1% to 5%), first degree atrioventricular block (1% to 5%), flushing (1% to 5%), hypertension (1% to 5%), hypotension (1% to 5%), palpitations (1% to 5%), sinus tachycardia (1% to 5%), ST segment changes on ECG (1% to 5%), thrombosis (1% to 5%)

Central nervous system: Seizure (10%), anxiety (≥5%), confusion (≥5%), depression (≥5%), dizziness (≥5%), fatigue (≥5%), hypoesthesia (≥5%), malaise (≥5%), neuropathy (≥5%), pain (≥5%), paresthesia (≥5%), rigors (≥5%), abnormal electroencephalogram (1% to 5%), aggressive behavior (1% to 5%), agitation (1% to 5%), amnesia (1% to 5%), aphasia (1% to 5%), ataxia (1% to 5%), cerebrovascular disease (1% to 5%), dementia (1% to 5%), hallucination (1% to 5%), insomnia (1% to 5%), meningitis (1% to 5%), nervousness (1% to 5%), sensory disturbance (1% to 5%), somnolence (1% to 5%), stupor (1% to 5%)

Dermatologic: Diaphoresis (≥5%), skin rash (≥5%), dermal ulcer (1% to 5%), erythematous rash (1% to 5%), maculopapular rash (1% to 5%), pruritus (1% to 5%), seborrhea (1% to 5%), skin discoloration (1% to 5%)

Endocrine & metabolic: Hyperphosphatemia (6%), electrolyte disturbance (≥5%), abnormal albumin-Globulin ratio (1% to 5%), acidosis (1% to 5%), albuminuria (1% to 5%), cachexia (1% to 5%), hyponatremia (1% to 5%), increased lactate dehydrogenase (1% to 5%), increased thirst (1% to 5%), weight loss (1% to 5%)

Gastrointestinal: Abdominal pain (≥5%), anorexia (≥5%), aphthous stomatitis (1% to 5%), cachexia (1% to 5%), constipation (1% to 5%), dysgeusia (1% to 5%), dyspepsia (1% to 5%), dysphagia (1% to 5%), flatulence (1% to 5%), melena (1% to 5%), pancreatitis (1% to 5%), xerostomia (1% to 5%)

Genitourinary: Nephrotoxicity (8%), dysuria (1% to 5%), nocturia (1% to 5%), urinary retention (1% to 5%), urinary tract infection (1% to 5%)

Hematologic & oncologic: Bone marrow suppression (10%), leukopenia (≥5%), mineral abnormalities (≥5%), neutropenia (≥5%), abnormal white cell differential (1% to 5%), altered platelet function (1% to 5%), lymphadenopathy (1% to 5%), pseudolymphoma (1% to 5%), rectal hemorrhage (1% to 5%), sarcoma (1% to 5%), thrombocytopenia (1% to 5%)

Hepatic: Abnormal hepatic function tests (1% to 5%), increased lactate dehydrogenase (1% to 5%), increased serum alkaline phosphatase (1% to 5%), increased serum ALT (1% to 5%), increased serum AST (1% to 5%)

Infection: Infection (≥5%), sepsis (≥5%), abscess, bacterial infection (1% to 5%), fungal infection (1% to 5%)

Local: Inflammation at injection site (1% to 5%), pain at injection site (1% to 5%)

Neuromuscular & skeletal: Muscle spasm (≥5%), neuropathy (peripheral; ≥5%), weakness (≥5%), arthralgia (1% to 5%), back pain (1% to 5%), leg cramps (1% to 5%), myalgia (1% to 5%), tremor (1% to 5%)

Ophthalmic: Visual disturbance (≥5%), conjunctivitis (1% to 5%), eye pain (1% to 5%)

Renal: Decreased creatinine clearance (≥5%), increased serum creatinine (≥5%), acute renal failure (1% to 5%), increased blood urea nitrogen (1% to 5%), polyuria (1% to 5%)

Respiratory: Cough (≥5%), dyspnea (≥5%), bronchospasm (1% to 5%), flu-like symptoms (1% to 5%), hemoptysis (1% to 5%), pharyngitis (1% to 5%), pneumonia (1% to 5%), pneumothorax (1% to 5%), pulmonary infiltrates (1% to 5%), respiratory failure (1% to 5%), respiratory insufficiency (1% to 5%), rhinitis (1% to 5%), sinusitis (1% to 5%), stridor (1% to 5%)

<1%, postmarketing, and/or case reports: Coma, dehydration, diabetes insipidus (usually nephrogenic), erythema multiforme, esophageal ulcer, extravasation, Fanconi syndrome, gastrointestinal hemorrhage, glomerulonephritis, hematuria, hypercalcemia, hypersensitivity reaction (including anaphylactic shock, angioedema, urticaria), hypoproteinemia, increased amylase, increased creatine phosphokinase, increased gamma-glutamyl transferase, increased serum lipase, local irritation (genitals), localized edema, myasthenia, myopathy, myositis, nephrolithiasis, nephrotic syndrome, pancytopenia, penile ulceration, prolonged Q-T interval on ECG, proteinuria, renal disease (crystal-induced), renal tubular acidosis, renal tubular necrosis, rhabdomyolysis, SIADH, status epilepticus, Stevens-Johnson syndrome, torsades de pointes, toxic epidermal necrolysis, vaginal ulcer, ventricular arrhythmia

General Dosage Range Dosage adjustment recommended in patients with renal impairment

IV: *Adults:* Induction: CMV: 180 mg/kg/day in 2 to 3 evenly divided doses; HSV: 40 mg/kg/dose every 8 to 12 hours; Maintenance: CMV: 90 to 120 mg/kg once daily

Mechanism of Action Pyrophosphate analogue which acts as a noncompetitive inhibitor of many viral RNA and DNA polymerases as well as HIV reverse transcriptase. Similar to ganciclovir, foscarnet is a virostatic agent. Foscarnet does not require activation by thymidine kinase.

Pharmacodynamics/Kinetics

Half-life Elimination Elimination: ~3 to 4 hours; terminal: ~88 hours (due to bone deposition)

Pregnancy Risk Factor C

Pregnancy Considerations Adverse events have been observed in animal reproductions studies. A single case report of use during the third trimester with normal infant outcome was observed. Monitoring of amniotic fluid volumes by ultrasound is recommended weekly after 20 weeks of gestation to detect oligohydramnios (DHHS [adult] 2014).

Dental Comment See Local Anesthetic/Vasoconstrictor Precautions

Fosfomycin (fos foe MYE sin)

Brand Names: US Monurol

Brand Names: Canada Monurol

Pharmacologic Category Antibiotic, Miscellaneous

Use

Uncomplicated urinary tract infections: Treatment of uncomplicated urinary tract infections (acute cystitis) in women due to susceptible strains of *Escherichia coli* and *Enterococcus faecalis*.

Limitations of use: Not indicated for the treatment of pyelonephritis or perinephric abscess. If persistence or reappearance of bacteriuria occurs after treatment with fosfomycin, other therapeutic agents should be selected.

Local Anesthetic/Vasoconstrictor Precautions No information available to require special precautions

Effects on Dental Treatment No significant effects or complications reported

Effects on Bleeding No information available to require special precautions

Adverse Reactions

1% to 10%:

Central nervous system: Headache (4% to 10%), pain (2%), dizziness (1% to 2%)

Dermatologic: Skin rash (1%)

Gastrointestinal: Diarrhea (9% to 10%), nausea (4% to 5%), abdominal pain (2%), dyspepsia (1% to 2%)

Genitourinary: Vaginitis (6% to 8%), dysmenorrhea (3%)

Neuromuscular & skeletal: Back pain (3%), weakness (1% to 2%)

Respiratory: Rhinitis (5%), pharyngitis (3%)

<1%, postmarketing, and/or case reports: Abnormal stools, anaphylaxis, angioedema, anorexia, aplastic anemia, cholestatic jaundice, constipation, dermatological disease, drowsiness, dysuria, ear disease, exacerbation of asthma, fatigue, fever, flatulence, flu-like symptoms, hearing loss, hematuria, hepatic necrosis, increased serum ALT, insomnia, lymphadenopathy, menstrual disease, migraine, myalgia, nervousness, optic neuritis, paresthesia, pruritus, toxic megacolon, vomiting, xerostomia

General Dosage Range Oral: *Adults (females):* 3 g as a single dose

Mechanism of Action As a phosphoric acid derivative, fosfomycin inhibits bacterial wall synthesis (bactericidal) by inactivating the enzyme, pyruvyl transferase, which is critical in the synthesis of cell walls by bacteria

Pharmacodynamics/Kinetics

Half-life Elimination 3 to 8 hours; CrCl <54 mL/minute: 50 hours

Time to Peak Serum: 2 hours; within 4 hours with high-fat meal

Pregnancy Risk Factor B

Pregnancy Considerations Adverse events have not been observed in animal reproduction studies. Fosfomycin crosses the placenta. Several studies have used a single dose therapy with fosfomycin for the treatment of asymptomatic bacteriuria in pregnant women (Reeves, 1992). However, when treatment is needed in pregnant women, an appropriate antibiotic with a 3 to 7 day regimen is currently recommended (Nicolle, 2005).

Fosinopril (foe SIN oh pril)

Related Information

Cardiovascular Diseases *on page 1752*

Brand Names: Canada Apo-Fosinopril; Ava-Fosinopril; Jamp-Fosinopril; Mylan-Fosinopril; PMS-Fosinopril; RAN-Fosinopril; Riva-Fosinopril; Teva-Fosinopril

Generic Availability (US) Yes

Pharmacologic Category Angiotensin-Converting Enzyme (ACE) Inhibitor; Antihypertensive

Use

Hypertension: Treatment of hypertension, either alone or in combination with other antihypertensive agents

The 2014 guideline for the management of high blood pressure in adults (Eighth Joint National Committee [JNC 8]) recommends initiation of pharmacologic treatment to lower blood pressure for the following patients:

- Patients ≥60 years of age with systolic blood pressure (SBP) ≥150 mm Hg or diastolic blood pressure (DBP) ≥90 mm Hg. Goal of therapy is SBP <150 mm Hg and DBP <90 mm Hg.
- Patients <60 years of age with SBP ≥140 mm Hg or DBP is ≥90 mm Hg. Goal of therapy is SBP <140 mm Hg and DBP <90 mm Hg.
- Patients ≥18 years of age with diabetes and SBP ≥140 mm Hg or DBP ≥90 mm Hg. Goal of therapy is SBP <140 mm Hg and DBP <90 mm Hg.
- Patients ≥18 years of age with chronic kidney disease (CKD) and SBP ≥140 mm Hg or DBP ≥90 mm Hg. Goal of therapy is SBP <140 mm Hg and DBP <90 mm Hg.

In patients with CKD, regardless of race or diabetes status, the use of an ACE inhibitor (ACEI) or angiotensin receptor blocker (ARB) as initial therapy is recommended to improve kidney outcomes. In the general nonblack population (without CKD) including those with diabetes, initial antihypertensive treatment should consist of a thiazide-type diuretic, calcium channel blocker, ACEI, or ARB. In the general black population (without CKD) including those with diabetes, initial antihypertensive treatment should consist of a thiazide-type diuretic or a calcium channel blocker **instead of** an ACEI or ARB.

Heart failure: Adjunctive treatment of heart failure (HF)

The ACCF/AHA 2013 heart failure guidelines recommend the use of ACE inhibitors, along with other guideline directed medical therapies, to prevent heart failure in patients with a reduced ejection fraction who have a history of MI (Stage B HF), to prevent HF in any patient with a reduced ejection fraction (Stage B HF), or to treat those with HF and reduced ejection fraction (Stage C HFrEF) (ACCF/AHA [Yancy 2013]).

Local Anesthetic/Vasoconstrictor Precautions

No information available to require special precautions

Effects on Dental Treatment Key adverse event(s) related to dental treatment: Patients may experience orthostatic hypotension as they stand up after treatment; especially if lying in dental chair for extended periods of time. Use caution with sudden changes in position during and after dental treatment.

An angiotensin-converting enzyme (ACE) inhibitor cough is a dry, hacking, nonproductive cough that can potentially interfere with longer dental procedures if patient has this side effect.

Effects on Bleeding No information available to require special precautions

Adverse Reactions Frequency not always defined. Frequency ranges include data from hypertension and heart failure trials. Higher rates of adverse reactions have generally been noted in patients with CHF. However, the frequency of adverse effects associated with placebo is also increased in this population.

>10%: Central nervous system: Dizziness (1% to 2%; cardiac failure patients: ≤12%)

1% to 10%:

Cardiovascular: Orthostatic hypotension (1% to 2%), palpitations (1%)

Central nervous system: Headache (3%), noncardiac chest pain (≤2%), fatigue (1% to 2%)

Endocrine & metabolic: Hyperkalemia (3%)

Gastrointestinal: Diarrhea (2%), nausea and vomiting (1% to 2%)

Hepatic: Increased serum transaminases

Neuromuscular & skeletal: Musculoskeletal pain (≤3%), weakness (1%)

Renal: Increased serum creatinine, renal function decompensation (patients with bilateral renal artery stenosis or hypovolemia)

Respiratory: Cough (2% to 10%), upper respiratory infection (2%)

<1%, postmarketing, and/or case reports: Abdominal distention, anaphylactoid reaction, angina pectoris, angioedema, arthralgia, behavioral changes, bradycardia, bronchospasm, cerebral infarction, cerebrovascular accident, claudication, confusion, constipation, decreased libido, drowsiness, dysgeusia, dysphagia, edema, eosinophilia, epistaxis, eye irritation, flatulence, flushing, gout, heartburn, hepatitis, hepatomegaly, hyperhidrosis, hypertension, hypertensive crisis, hypotension, insomnia, laryngitis, lower extremity edema, lymphadenopathy, memory impairment, mood changes, myalgia, myocardial infarction, numbness, pancreatitis, paranasal sinus disease

(abnormality), paresthesia, pharyngitis, pleuritic chest pain, pruritus, renal insufficiency, shock, skin photosensitivity, skin rash, sleep disorder, syncope, tachycardia, tinnitus, tracheobronchitis, transient ischemic attacks, tremor, urinary frequency, urticaria, vertigo, visual disturbance, weight gain, xerostomia

Dosing

Adult & Geriatric

Heart failure: Oral: Per the manufacturer: Initial: 10 mg once daily (5 mg once daily if moderate to severe renal dysfunction is present or if aggressively diuresed); increase dose as needed and as tolerated over several weeks. Usual dosage range: 20 to 40 mg once daily (maximum dose: 40 mg once daily). If hypotension, orthostasis, or azotemia occurs during titration, consider decreasing concomitant diuretic dose, if any.

ACCF/AHA 2013 heart failure guidelines: Initial: 5 to 10 mg once daily. Target dose: 40 mg once daily (Yancy 2013).

Hypertension: Oral: Initial: 10 mg once daily; maximum dose: 80 mg once daily. May need to divide the dose into two if trough effect is inadequate. If patient is receiving a diuretic prior to initiation, consider discontinuation of the diuretic to reduce likelihood of hypotension, if possible 2 to 3 days before initiation of therapy. If blood pressure response is inadequate, resume diuretic therapy carefully. Usual dose range (ASH/ISH [Weber 2014]): 10 to 40 mg daily.

HIV-associated nephropathy (HIVAN) (off-label use): Oral: 10 mg once daily (Wei 2003).

Pediatric Hypertension: Children ≥6 years and Adolescents >50 kg: Oral: Initial: 5 to 10 mg once daily (maximum: 40 mg once daily)

Renal Impairment

Moderate-severe impairment: Initial dose reduction to 5 mg once daily recommended for heart failure patients. No other dose adjustments are required; hepatobiliary elimination partially compensates for diminished renal elimination.

Hemodialysis: Poorly dialyzed; supplemental dose not required (Gehr, 1993)

Peritoneal dialysis: Poorly dialyzed; supplemental dose not required (Gehr, 1991)

Hepatic Impairment There are no dosage adjustments provided in the manufacturer's labeling.

Mechanism of Action Competitive inhibitor of angiotensin-converting enzyme (ACE); prevents conversion of angiotensin I to angiotensin II, a potent vasoconstrictor; results in lower levels of angiotensin II which causes an increase in plasma renin activity and a reduction in aldosterone secretion; a CNS mechanism may also be involved in hypotensive effect as angiotensin II increases adrenergic outflow from CNS; vasoactive kallikreins may be decreased in conversion to active hormones by ACE inhibitors, thus reducing blood pressure

Contraindications Hypersensitivity to fosinopril, any other ACE inhibitor, or any component of the formulation; angioedema related to previous treatment with an ACE inhibitor; concomitant use with aliskiren in patients with diabetes mellitus

Warnings/Precautions Anaphylactic reactions may occur rarely with ACE inhibitors. At any time during treatment (especially following first dose), angioedema may occur rarely with ACE inhibitors; it may involve the head and neck (potentially compromising airway) or the intestine (presenting with abdominal pain). African-Americans may be at an increased risk and patients with idiopathic or hereditary angioedema may be at an increased risk. Risk may also be increased with concomitant use of mTOR inhibitor (eg, everolimus) therapy. Prolonged frequent monitoring may be required especially if tongue, glottis, or larynx are involved as they are associated with airway obstruction. Patients with a history of airway surgery may have a higher risk of airway obstruction. Aggressive early and appropriate management is critical. Use in patients with previous angioedema associated with ACE inhibitor therapy is contraindicated. Severe anaphylactoid reactions may be seen during hemodialysis (eg, CVVHD) with high-flux dialysis membranes (eg, AN69), and rarely, during low density lipoprotein apheresis with dextran sulfate cellulose. Rare cases of anaphylactoid reactions have been reported in patients undergoing sensitization treatment with hymenoptera (bee, wasp) venom while receiving ACE inhibitors.

Symptomatic hypotension with or without syncope can occur with ACE inhibitors (usually with the first several doses); effects are most often observed in volume-depleted patients; correct volume depletion prior to initiation; close monitoring of patient is required especially with initial dosing and dosing increases; blood pressure must be lowered at a rate appropriate for the patient's clinical condition. Initiation of therapy in patients with ischemic heart disease or cerebrovascular disease warrants close observation due to the potential consequences posed by falling blood pressure (eg, MI, stroke). Use with caution in hypertrophic cardiomyopathy with outflow tract obstruction and severe aortic stenosis. In patients on chronic ACE inhibitor therapy, intraoperative hypotension may occur with induction and maintenance of general anesthesia; use with caution before, during, or immediately after major surgery. Cardiopulmonary bypass, intraoperative blood loss, or vasodilating anesthesia increases endogenous renin release. Use of ACE inhibitors perioperatively will blunt angiotensin II formation and may result in hypotension. However, discontinuation of therapy prior to surgery is controversial. If continued preoperatively, avoidance of hypotensive agents during surgery is prudent (Hillis 2011). **[U.S. Boxed Warning]: Drugs that act on the renin-angiotensin system can cause injury and death to the developing fetus. Discontinue as soon as possible once pregnancy is detected.**

Hyperkalemia may occur with ACE inhibitors; risk factors include renal dysfunction, diabetes mellitus, concomitant use of potassium-sparing diuretics, potassium supplements, and/or potassium-containing salts. Use cautiously, if at all, with these agents and monitor potassium closely. Cough may occur with ACE inhibitors. Other causes of cough should be considered (eg, pulmonary congestion in patients with heart failure) and excluded prior to discontinuation. Use with caution in hepatic impairment; fosinopril undergoes hepatic and gut wall metabolism to its active form (fosinoprilat) and may accumulate in hepatic impairment. In patients with alcoholic or biliary cirrhosis, the rate of fosinoprilat formation was slowed, its total body clearance decreased and its AUC ~doubled.

May be associated with deterioration of renal function and/or increases in serum creatinine, particularly in patients with low renal blood flow (eg, renal artery stenosis, heart failure) whose glomerular filtration rate (GFR) is dependent on efferent arteriolar vasoconstriction by angiotensin II; deterioration may result in oliguria, acute renal failure, and progressive azotemia. Small increases in serum creatinine may occur following initiation; consider discontinuation only in patients with progressive and/or significant deterioration in renal function. Use with caution in patients with unstented unilateral/bilateral renal artery stenosis. When unstented bilateral renal artery stenosis is present, use is generally avoided due to the elevated risk of deterioration in renal function unless possible benefits outweigh risks. Potentially significant drug-drug interactions may exist, requiring dose or frequency adjustment, additional monitoring, and/or selection of alternative therapy.

Rare toxicities associated with ACE inhibitors include cholestatic jaundice (which may progress to fulminant hepatic necrosis), agranulocytosis, neutropenia or leukopenia with myeloid hypoplasia. Patients with collagen vascular diseases (especially with concomitant renal impairment) or renal impairment alone may be at increased risk for hematologic toxicity; periodically monitor CBC with differential in these patients.

Drug Interactions

Metabolism/Transport Effects None known.

Avoid Concomitant Use

Avoid concomitant use of Fosinopril with any of the following: Sacubitril

Increased Effect/Toxicity

Fosinopril may increase the levels/effects of: Allopurinol; Amifostine; Antipsychotic Agents (Second Generation [Atypical]); AzaTHIOprine; Ciprofloxacin (Systemic); Drospirenone; DULoxetine; Ferric Gluconate; Ferric Hydroxide Polymaltose Complex; Gold Sodium Thiomalate; Grass Pollen Allergen Extract (5 Grass Extract); Hypotension-Associated Agents; Iron Dextran Complex; Levodopa; Lithium; Nitroprusside; Nonsteroidal Anti-Inflammatory Agents; Pregabalin; Sacubitril; Sodium Phosphates

The levels/effects of Fosinopril may be increased by: Alfuzosin; Aliskiren; Angiotensin II Receptor Blockers; Barbiturates; Benperidol; Brimonidine (Topical); Canagliflozin; Dapoxetine; Diazoxide; DPP IV Inhibitors; Eplerenone; Everolimus; Heparin; Heparin (Low Molecular Weight); Herbs (Hypotensive Properties); Loop Diuretics; Lormetazepam; Molsidomine; Naftopidil; Nicergoline; Nicorandil; Obinutuzumab; Pentoxifylline; Phosphodiesterase 5 Inhibitors; Potassium Salts; Potassium-Sparing Diuretics; Prostacyclin Analogues; Quinagolide; Salicylates; Sirolimus; Temsirolimus; Thiazide and Thiazide-Like Diuretics; TiZANidine; Tolvaptan; Trimethoprim

Decreased Effect

The levels/effects of Fosinopril may be decreased by: Amphetamines; Antacids; Aprotinin; Herbs (Hypertensive Properties); Icatibant; Lanthanum; Methylphenidate; Nonsteroidal Anti-Inflammatory Agents; Salicylates; Yohimbine

Dietary Considerations Should not take a potassium salt supplement without the advice of healthcare provider.

Pharmacodynamics/Kinetics

Onset of Action 1 hour

Duration of Action 24 hours

Half-life Elimination Serum (fosinoprilat):

Children and Adolescents 6-16 years: 11-13 hours

Adults: 12 hours

Adults with CHF: 14 hours

Time to Peak Serum: ~3 hours

Pregnancy Risk Factor D

Pregnancy Considerations [US Boxed Warning]: Drugs that act on the renin-angiotensin system can cause injury and death to the developing fetus. Discontinue as soon as possible once pregnancy is detected. Fosinopril crosses the placenta. Drugs that act on the renin-angiotensin system are associated with oligohydramnios. Oligohydramnios, due to decreased fetal renal function, may lead to fetal lung hypoplasia and skeletal malformations. The use of these drugs in pregnancy is also associated with anuria, hypotension, renal failure, skull hypoplasia, and death in the fetus/neonate. Teratogenic effects may occur following maternal use of an ACE inhibitor during the first trimester, although this finding may be confounded by maternal disease. Because adverse fetal events are well documented with exposure later in pregnancy, ACE inhibitor use in pregnant women is not recommended (Seely 2014; Weber 2014). Infants exposed to an ACE inhibitor in utero should be monitored for hyperkalemia, hypotension, and oliguria. Oligohydramnios may not appear until after irreversible fetal injury has occurred. Exchange transfusions or dialysis may be required to reverse hypotension or improve renal function, although data related to the effectiveness in neonates is limited.

Chronic maternal hypertension itself is also associated with adverse events in the fetus/infant and mother. ACE inhibitors are not recommended for the treatment of uncomplicated hypertension in pregnancy (ACOG 2013) and they are specifically contraindicated for the treatment of hypertension and chronic heart failure during pregnancy by some guidelines (Regitz-Zagrosek 2011). In addition, ACE inhibitors should generally be avoided in women of reproductive age (ACOG 2013). If treatment for hypertension or chronic heart failure in pregnancy is needed, other agents should be used (ACOG 2013; Regitz-Zagrosek 2011).

Breastfeeding Considerations Fosinoprilat is excreted in breast milk. breastfeeding is not recommended by the manufacturer.

Dosage Forms

Tablet, Oral:

Generic: 10 mg, 20 mg, 40 mg

Fosinopril and Hydrochlorothiazide

(foe SIN oh pril & hye droe klor oh THYE a zide)

Related Information

Fosinopril *on page 771*

HydroCHLOROthiazide *on page 820*

Brand Names: Canada Monopril-HCT

Pharmacologic Category Angiotensin-Converting Enzyme (ACE) Inhibitor; Antihypertensive; Diuretic, Thiazide

Use Treatment of hypertension; not indicated for first-line treatment

Local Anesthetic/Vasoconstrictor Precautions No information available to require special precautions

Effects on Dental Treatment No significant effects or complications reported

Effects on Bleeding No information available to require special precautions

Adverse Reactions Reactions reported with combination product. Also see individual agents.

2% to 10%:

Cardiovascular: Orthostatic hypotension (2%)

Central nervous system: Fatigue (4%), dizziness (3%)

Neuromuscular & skeletal: Musculoskeletal pain (2%)

Respiratory: Cough (6%)

<2%, postmarketing, and/or case reports: Abdominal pain, angioedema, cardiac arrhythmia, change in libido, chest pain, depression, diarrhea, drowsiness, dyspepsia, dysuria, edema, eosinophilia, esophagitis,

fever, flushing, gastritis, gout, heartburn, hepatic necrosis, increased blood urea nitrogen (similar to placebo), increased liver enzymes (increased lactate dehydrogenase, increased serum alkaline phosphatase, increased serum bilirubin, increased serum transaminases), increased serum creatinine (similar to placebo), leukopenia, lump in breast, muscle cramps, myalgia, nausea, neutropenia, numbness, paresthesia, pharyngitis, pruritus, rhinitis, sexual disorder, sinus congestion, skin rash, syncope, tinnitus, urinary frequency, urinary tract infection, viral infection, vomiting, weakness

General Dosage Range Oral: *Adults:* Fosinopril 10-80 mg and hydrochlorothiazide 12.5-50 mg once daily

Mechanism of Action Fosinopril is a competitive inhibitor of angiotensin-converting enzyme (ACE); prevents conversion of angiotensin I to angiotensin II, a potent vasoconstrictor; results in lower levels of angiotensin II which causes an increase in plasma renin activity and a reduction in aldosterone secretion; a CNS mechanism may also be involved in hypotensive effect as angiotensin II increases adrenergic outflow from CNS; vasoactive kallikreins may be decreased in conversion to active hormones by ACE inhibitors, thus reducing blood pressure. Hydrochlorothiazide inhibits sodium reabsorption in the distal tubules causing increased excretion of sodium and water as well as potassium and hydrogen ions.

Pregnancy Risk Factor D

Pregnancy Considerations [U.S. Boxed Warning]: Drugs that act on the renin-angiotensin system can cause injury and death to the developing fetus. Discontinue as soon as possible once pregnancy is detected. See individual agents.

Fosphenytoin (FOS fen i toyn)

Related Information

Phenytoin *on page 1332*

Brand Names: US Cerebyx

Brand Names: Canada Cerebyx

Pharmacologic Category Anticonvulsant, Hydantoin

Use

Seizures: Control of generalized tonic-clonic status epilepticus and the prevention and treatment of seizures occurring during neurosurgery; short-term parenteral administration when oral phenytoin is not possible

Guideline recommendations: Status epilepticus: A benzodiazepine (eg, lorazepam, diazepam, midazolam) is the preferred initial treatment of status epilepticus according to clinical practice guidelines; fosphenytoin is an option in patients failing first-line treatment (AES [Glauser 2016]; NCS [Glauser 2016]).

Local Anesthetic/Vasoconstrictor Precautions No information available to require special precautions

Effects on Dental Treatment Key adverse event(s) related to dental treatment: Tongue disorder and dry mouth.

Effects on Bleeding No information available to require special precautions

Adverse Reactions Also refer to the phenytoin monograph for additional adverse reactions.

>10%:

Central nervous system: Dizziness (IV: 31%; IM: 5%), drowsiness (IV: 20%; IM: 7%), ataxia (IV: 4% to 11%; IM: 8%)

Dermatologic: Pruritus (IV: 49%; IM: 3%; generally transient; often reported in groin area)

Ophthalmic: Nystagmus (IV: 44%; IM: 15%)

1% to 10%:

Cardiovascular: Hypotension (IV: 8%), vasodilatation (IV: 6%), tachycardia (IV: 2%), facial edema (>1%), hypertension (>1%), atrial flutter (≤1%), bundle branch block (≤1%), cardiac failure (≤1%), cardiomegaly (≤1%), cerebral infarction (≤1%), edema (≤1%), orthostatic hypotension (≤1%), palpitations (≤1%), prolonged Q-T interval on ECG (≤1%), pulmonary embolism (≤1%), shock (≤1%), sinus bradycardia (≤1%), subdural hematoma (≤1%), syncope (≤1%), thrombophlebitis (≤1%), ventricular premature contractions (≤1%)

Central nervous system: Headache (IM: 9%; IV: 2%), stupor (IV: 8%), paresthesia (4%; generally transient; often reported in groin area; may be more common with IV), extrapyramidal reaction (≤4%; more common with IV), agitation (IV: 3%), hyporeflexia (IM: 3%), vertigo (IV: 2%), cerebral edema (≤2%; more common with IV), dysarthria (≤2%), hypoesthesia (≤2%; more common with IV), abnormality in thinking (>1%), chills (>1%), hyperreflexia (>1%), intracranial hypertension (>1%), myasthenia (>1%), nervousness (>1%), speech disturbance (>1%), akathisia (≤1%), altered sense of smell (≤1%), amnesia (≤1%), aphasia (≤1%), brain disease (≤1%), central nervous system depression (≤1%), cerebral hemorrhage (≤1%), coma (≤1%), confusion (≤1%), delirium (≤1%), depersonalization (≤1%), depression (≤1%), emotional lability (≤1%), encephalitis (≤1%), hemiplegia (≤1%), hostility (≤1%), hyperacusis (≤1%), hyperesthesia (≤1%), hypotonia (≤1%), insomnia (≤1%), malaise (≤1%), meningitis (≤1%), migraine (≤1%), myoclonus (≤1%), paralysis (≤1%), personality disorder (≤1%), positive Babinski sign (≤1%), psychoneurosis (≤1%), psychosis (≤1%), seizures (≤1%), twitching (≤1%)

Dermatologic: Ecchymoses (IM: 7%), skin rash (>1%), contact dermatitis (≤1%), cutaneous nodule (≤1%), diaphoresis (≤1%), maculopapular rash (≤1%), pustular rash (≤1%), skin discoloration (≤1%), skin photosensitivity (≤1%), urticaria (≤1%)

Endocrine & metabolic: Hypokalemia (>1%), acidosis (≤1%), albuminuria (≤1%), alkalosis (≤1%), cachexia (≤1%), dehydration (≤1%), diabetes insipidus (≤1%), hyperglycemia (≤1%), hyperkalemia (≤1%), hypophosphatemia (≤1%), ketosis (≤1%)

Gastrointestinal: Nausea (IV: 9%; IM: 5%), tongue disease (IV: 4%), xerostomia (IV: 4%), dysgeusia (3%), vomiting (IM: 3%; IV: 2%), constipation (>1%), ageusia (≤1%), anorexia (≤1%), diarrhea (≤1%), dyspepsia (≤1%), dysphagia (≤1%), flatulence (≤1%), gastritis (≤1%), gastrointestinal hemorrhage (≤1%), intestinal obstruction (≤1%), oral paresthesia (≤1%), sialorrhea (≤1%), tenesmus (≤1%)

Genitourinary: Pelvic pain (IV: 4%), dysuria (≤1%), genital edema (≤1%), oliguria (≤1%), urethral pain (≤1%), urinary incontinence (≤1%), urinary retention (≤1%), vaginitis (≤1%), vulvovaginal candidiasis (≤1%)

Hematologic & oncologic: Anemia (≤1%), hypochromic anemia (≤1%), leukocytosis (≤1%), leukopenia (≤1%), lymphadenopathy (≤1%), petechia (≤1%), thrombocytopenia (≤1%)

Hepatic: Abnormal hepatic function tests (≤1%)

Hypersensitivity: Tongue edema (≤1%)

Infection: Infection (>1%), cryptococcosis (≤1%), influenza (≤1%), sepsis (≤1%)
Local: Injection site reaction (>1%), pain at injection site (>1%), bleeding at injection site (≤1%), inflammation at injection site (≤1%), swelling at injection site (≤1%)
Neuromuscular & skeletal: Tremor (IM: 10%; IV: 3%), weakness (IM: 4%; IV: 2%), back pain (IV: 2%), arthralgia (≤1%), hyperkinesia (≤1%), hypokinesia (≤1%), leg cramps (≤1%), myalgia (≤1%), myopathy (≤1%)
Ophthalmic: Diplopia (IV: 3%), amblyopia (IV: 2%), conjunctivitis (≤1%), eye pain (≤1%), mydriasis (≤1%), photophobia (≤1%), visual field defect (≤1%)
Otic: Tinnitus (IV: 9%), deafness (≤2%; more common with IV), otalgia (≤1%)
Renal: Polyuria (≤1%), renal failure (≤1%)
Respiratory: Pneumonia (>1%), apnea (≤1%), aspiration pneumonia (≤1%), asthma (≤1%), atelectasis (≤1%), bronchitis (≤1%), cyanosis (≤1%), dyspnea (≤1%), epistaxis (≤1%), hemoptysis (≤1%), hyperventilation (≤1%), hypoxia (≤1%), increased bronchial secretions (≤1%), increased cough (≤1%), pharyngitis (≤1%), pneumothorax (≤1%), rhinitis (≤1%), sinusitis (≤1%)
Miscellaneous: Accidental injury (IM: 3%), fever (>1%)

Rare but important or life-threatening: DRESS syndrome, signs and symptoms of injection site ("purple glove syndrome"; edema, discoloration, and pain distal to injection site)

General Dosage Range

IM: *Adults:* Loading dose: 10 to 20 mg PE/kg; Maintenance: 4 to 6 mg PE/kg/day

IV:

Neonates, Infants, Children, and Adolescents: Loading dose: 10 to 20 mg PE/kg; Maintenance: 4 to 8 mg PE/kg/day

Adults: Loading dose: 10 to 20 mg PE/kg; Maintenance: 4 to 6 mg PE/kg/day

Mechanism of Action Diphosphate ester salt of phenytoin that acts as a water soluble prodrug of phenytoin; after administration, plasma esterases convert fosphenytoin to phosphate, formaldehyde (not expected to be clinically consequential [Fierro 1996]), and phenytoin as the active moiety. Phenytoin works by stabilizing neuronal membranes and decreasing seizure activity by increasing efflux or decreasing influx of sodium ions across cell membranes in the motor cortex during generation of nerve impulses

Pharmacodynamics/Kinetics

Half-life Elimination

Pediatric patients (ages: 1 day to 16.7 years): 8.3 minutes (range: 2.5 to 18.5 minutes) (Fischer 2003)

Adults:

Fosphenytoin: IV: ~15 minutes, IM: ~30 minutes.

Phenytoin: Variable (mean: 12 to 29 hours); pharmacokinetics of phenytoin are saturable

Time to Peak Conversion to phenytoin:

IV: Adults: Following IV administration (maximum rate of administration): ~15 minutes

IM:

Neonates and Infants ≤6 months: 1-3 hours was reported in a case series (n=3; PNA: 15 to 47 days) (Fischer 2003)

Pediatric patients >7 months: Therapeutic concentrations within 30 minutes; time to maximum serum concentration not reported (Fischer 2003)

Adults: ~3 hours; Therapeutic phenytoin concentrations may be achieved as early as 5 to 20 minutes following IM (gluteal) administration (Pryor 2001)

Pregnancy Considerations

Fosphenytoin is the prodrug of phenytoin. An increased risk of congenital malformations and adverse outcomes may occur following in utero phenytoin exposure. Reported malformations include orofacial clefts, cardiac defects, dysmorphic facial features, nail/digit hypoplasia, growth abnormalities including microcephaly, and mental deficiency. Isolated cases of malignancies (including neuroblastoma) and coagulation defects in the neonate (may be life threatening) following delivery have also been reported. Potentially life-threatening bleeding disorders in the newborn may also occur due to decreased concentrations of vitamin K-dependent clotting factors following phenytoin exposure in utero; vitamin K administration to the mother prior to delivery and the newborn after birth is recommended.

Also refer to the Phenytoin monograph for additional information.

Patients exposed to fosphenytoin during pregnancy are encouraged to enroll themselves into the North American Antiepileptic Drug (NAAED) Pregnancy Registry by calling 1-888-233-2334. Additional information is available at http://www.aedpregnancyregistry.org/.

Framycetin (fra mye CEE tin)

Brand Names: Canada Soframycin Eye Drops

Pharmacologic Category Antibiotic, Ophthalmic

Use Note: Not approved in the United States

Ophthalmic infection/conditions: Treatment of ophthalmic infections caused by susceptible bacteria (eg, *S. aureus*, *Proteus* spp., *P. aeruginosa*, coliforms); treatment of corneal ulcers, abrasions, and burns; prophylaxis following removal of foreign bodies

Local Anesthetic/Vasoconstrictor Precautions
No information available to require special precautions

Effects on Dental Treatment No significant effects or complications reported

Effects on Bleeding No information available to require special precautions

Adverse Reactions Frequency not defined.

Cardiovascular (with high doses): Cardiac arrhythmia, increased blood pressure, palpitations, tachycardia
Central nervous system (with high doses): Central nervous system depression, dizziness, drowsiness, headache, insomnia, nervousness
Gastrointestinal: Dry mucous membranes
Miscellaneous: Burn
Ophthalmic: Blurred vision
Respiratory: Rhinorrhea, sneezing, stinging sensation of the nose

General Dosage Range Ophthalmic: *Adults:* 1 to 2 drops in affected eye(s) 3 or 4 times daily; for acute conditions 1 to 2 drops in affected eye(s) every 1 to 2 hours (generally for the first 2 to 3 days)

Mechanism of Action Broad spectrum aminoglycoside antibiotic that is usually bactericidal; appears to inhibit protein synthesis in susceptible bacteria by binding ribosomal subunits. Active against many aerobic gram-negative organisms and some aerobic gram-positive bacteria.

Product Availability Not available in the US

Framycetin, Gramicidin, and Dexamethasone

(fra mye CEE tin, gram i SYE din, & deks a METH a sone)

Brand Names: Canada Sofracort

Pharmacologic Category Anti-inflammatory Agent, Ophthalmic; Antibiotic, Ophthalmic; Antibiotic, Otic; Corticosteroid, Ophthalmic; Corticosteroid, Otic

Use

Ophthalmic infections/inflammation: Treatment of the following conditions: blepharitis and infected eczema of the eyelid; allergic, infective and rosacea conjunctivitis; rosacea keratitis; scleritis and episcleritis; iridocyclitis; other inflammatory conditions of the anterior segment of the eye

Otic infections/inflammation: Treatment of otitis externa (acute and chronic) and other inflammatory and sebhorrheic conditions of the external ear

Local Anesthetic/Vasoconstrictor Precautions No information available to require special precautions

Effects on Dental Treatment No significant effects or complications reported

Effects on Bleeding No information available to require special precautions

Adverse Reactions

Frequency not defined. See individual agents for additional adverse reactions.

Hypersensitivity: Hypersensitivity

Ophthalmic: Burning sensation of eyes, corneal perforation, increased intraocular pressure, stinging of eyes

General Dosage Range

Ophthalmic: *Adults:*

Drops: 1 or 2 drops in affected eye(s) every 1 to 2 hours usually for 2 or 3 days, then follow with 1 or 2 drops 3 to 4 times daily.

Ointment: Apply to affected eye(s) 2 or 3 times daily or as a single dose at bedtime if drops have been used during the day.

Otic: *Adults:*

Drops: 2 or 3 drops in affected ear(s) 3 or 4 times daily.

Ointment: Apply to outer portion of and inside the ear canal and adjacent infected areas 2 or 3 times daily and at bedtime.

Mechanism of Action

Framycetin is a broad spectrum aminoglycoside antibiotic that is usually bactericidal; appears to inhibit protein synthesis in susceptible bacteria by binding ribosomal subunits. Active against many aerobic gram-negative organisms and some aerobic gram-positive organisms.

Gramicidin is a cyclic polypeptide antibiotic that alters the cation content of the bacterial cell wall; primarily effective against gram-positive organisms.

Dexamethasone decreases inflammation by suppression of neutrophil migration, decreased production of inflammatory mediators, and reversal of increased capillary permeability; suppresses normal immune response.

Pregnancy Considerations Refer to Dexamethasone (Ophthalmic) monograph.

Product Availability Not available in the US

Frovatriptan (froe va TRIP tan)

Related Information

Temporomandibular Dysfunction (TMD), Chronic Pain, and Fibromyalgia *on page 1868*

Brand Names: US Frova

Brand Names: Canada Frova

Pharmacologic Category Antimigraine Agent; Serotonin 5-$HT_{1B,\ 1D}$ Receptor Agonist

Use Migraines: Acute treatment of migraine with or without aura in adults.

Local Anesthetic/Vasoconstrictor Precautions No information available to require special precautions

Effects on Dental Treatment No significant effects or complications reported

Effects on Bleeding No information available to require special precautions

Adverse Reactions

1% to 10%:

Cardiovascular: Flushing (4%), hot or cold flashes (3%), chest pain (2%), palpitations (1%)

Central nervous system: Dizziness (8%), fatigue (5%), headache (4%), paresthesia (4%), drowsiness (≥2%), anxiety (1%), dysesthesia (1%), hypoesthesia (1%), insomnia (1%), pain (1%)

Dermatologic: Diaphoresis (1%)

Gastrointestinal: Xerostomia (3%), nausea (≥2%), dyspepsia (2%), abdominal pain (1%), diarrhea (1%), vomiting (1%)

Neuromuscular & skeletal: Musculoskeletal pain (3%)

Ophthalmic: Visual disturbance (1%)

Otic: Tinnitus (1%)

Respiratory: Rhinitis (1%), sinusitis (1%)

<1%, postmarketing, and/or case reports: Abnormal dreams, abnormal gait, abnormal lacrimation, abnormal reflexes, agitation, amnesia, anaphylactoid reaction, anaphylaxis, anorexia, arthralgia, ataxia, back pain, bradycardia, bullous rash, change in bowel habits, cheilitis, chest tightness, confusion, conjunctivitis, constipation, dehydration, depersonalization, depression, dysgeusia, dysphagia, dyspnea, ECG changes, emotional lability, epistaxis, eructation, esophageal spasm, euphoria, eye pain, fever, flatulence, gastroesophageal reflux disease, hiccups, hyperacusis, hyperesthesia, hypersensitivity reaction (including angioedema), hypertonia, hyperventilation, hypocalcemia, hypoglycemia, hypotonia, increased thirst, involuntary muscle movements, jaw tightness, lack of concentration, laryngitis, leg pain, malaise, mouth edema, myalgia, myasthenia, myocardial infarction, nervousness, nocturia, osteoarthritis, otalgia, peptic ulcer, personality disorder, pharyngitis, polyuria, pruritus, purpura, renal pain, rigors, salivary gland pain, seizure, sialorrhea, significant cardiovascular event, speech disturbance, stomatitis, syncope, tachycardia, tightness in chest and throat, tongue paralysis, toothache, tremor, urinary frequency, urine abnormality, vertigo, weakness

General Dosage Range Oral: *Adults:* 2.5 mg as a single dose, may repeat after 2 hours (maximum: 7.5 mg daily)

Mechanism of Action Selective agonist for serotonin (5-HT_{1B} and 5-HT_{1D} receptors) in cranial arteries; causes vasoconstriction and reduces sterile inflammation associated with antidromic neuronal transmission correlating with relief of migraine.

Pharmacodynamics/Kinetics

Half-life Elimination ~26 hours

Time to Peak 2-4 hours

Pregnancy Risk Factor C

Pregnancy Considerations Adverse events were observed in animal reproduction studies. Information related to the use of frovatriptan in pregnancy has not been located. Until additional information is available, other agents are preferred for the initial treatment of migraine in pregnancy (Da Silva, 2012; MacGregor, 2012; Williams, 2012).

Fructose, Dextrose, and Phosphoric Acid (FRUK tose, DEKS trose, & foss FOR ik AS id)

Brand Names: US Emetrol® [OTC]; Formula EM [OTC]; Kalmz [OTC]; Nausea Relief [OTC]; Nausetrol® [OTC]

Pharmacologic Category Antiemetic

Use Relief of nausea associated with upset stomach that occurs with intestinal or stomach flu, and food indiscretions

Local Anesthetic/Vasoconstrictor Precautions No information available to require special precautions

Effects on Dental Treatment No significant effects or complications reported

Effects on Bleeding No information available to require special precautions

General Dosage Range Oral:

Children ≥2-12 years: 5-10 mL every 15 minutes as needed; do not take for more than 1 hour (5 doses)

Children ≥12 years and Adults: 15-30 mL every 15 minutes as needed; do not take for more than 1 hour (5 doses)

Fulvestrant (fool VES trant)

Brand Names: US Faslodex

Brand Names: Canada Faslodex

Pharmacologic Category Antineoplastic Agent, Estrogen Receptor Antagonist

Use

Breast cancer, metastatic: Treatment of hormone-receptor (HR)-positive metastatic breast cancer (as monotherapy) in postmenopausal women with disease progression following antiestrogen therapy

Breast cancer, advanced or metastatic (second-line endocrine-based combination therapy): Treatment of HR-positive, human epidermal growth factor receptor 2 (HER2)-negative advanced or metastatic breast cancer (in combination with palbociclib) in women with disease progression following endocrine therapy

Local Anesthetic/Vasoconstrictor Precautions No information available to require special precautions

Effects on Dental Treatment No significant effects or complications reported

Effects on Bleeding No information available to require special precautions

Adverse Reactions Adverse reactions reported with 500 mg dose.

>10%:

Central nervous system: Fatigue (8% to 29%), headache (8% to 20%)

Gastrointestinal: Nausea (10% to 28%), diarrhea (19%), constipation (5% to 16%), stomatitis (13%)

Hematologic & oncologic: Anemia (13% to 40%; grade 3: 2%)

Hepatic: Increased liver enzymes (>15%; grades 3/4: 1% to 2%)

Infection: Infection (31%; including nasopharyngitis, upper respiratory infection, urinary tract infection, influenza, bronchitis, rhinitis, conjunctivitis, pneumonia, sinusitis, cystitis, oral herpes, respiratory tract infection)

Local: Pain at injection site (12%; including neuralgia, peripheral neuropathy, sciatica)

1% to 10%:

Dermatologic: Alopecia (6%), skin rash (6%), xeroderma (1%)

Endocrine & metabolic: Hot flash (7%)

Gastrointestinal: Decreased appetite (8%), anorexia (6%), vomiting (6%), dysgeusia (3%)

Hematologic & oncologic: Decreased platelet count (10%), leukopenia (5%; grade 3: 1%; grade 4: 1%), neutropenia (4%; grade 3: 1%), febrile neutropenia (1%; grade 4: 1%)

Neuromuscular & skeletal: Ostealgia (9%), arthralgia (8%), back pain (8%), limb pain (7%), musculoskeletal pain (6%), weakness (5% to 6%)

Ophthalmic: Blurred vision (2%), dry eye syndrome (2%), increased lacrimation (1%)

Respiratory: Cough (5%), dyspnea (4%), epistaxis (2%)

<1%, postmarketing, and/or case reports (reported with 250 or 500 mg dose): Angioedema, hepatic failure, hepatitis, hypersensitivity reaction, increased gamma-glutamyl transferase, increased serum bilirubin, myalgia, thrombosis, urticaria, vaginal hemorrhage, vertigo

General Dosage Range Dosage adjustment recommended in patients with hepatic impairment

IM: *Adults (postmenopausal women):* Initial: 500 mg on days 1, 15, and 29; Maintenance: 500 mg once monthly

Mechanism of Action Estrogen receptor antagonist; competitively binds to estrogen receptors on tumors and other tissue targets, producing a nuclear complex that causes a dose-related down-regulation of estrogen receptors and inhibits tumor growth.

Pharmacodynamics/Kinetics

Duration of Action IM: Steady state concentrations reached within first month, when administered with additional dose given 2 weeks following the initial dose; plasma levels maintained for at least 1 month

Half-life Elimination

Children 1 to 10 years: 70.4 ± 8.1 days

Adults 250 mg: ~40 days

Pregnancy Considerations Adverse events were observed in animal reproduction studies. Based on the mechanism of action, fulvestrant may cause fetal harm if administered during pregnancy. For females of reproductive potential, pregnancy testing is recommended within 7 days prior to initiation of fulvestrant and effective contraception should be used during treatment and for 1 year after the last fulvestrant dose. Animal data suggest that fulvestrant may affect female and male fertility (although not approved for use in men).

Furosemide (fyoor OH se mide)

Related Information

Cardiovascular Diseases *on page* 1752

Brand Names: US Lasix

Brand Names: Canada Apo-Furosemide; Bio-Furosemide; Furosemide Injection Sandoz Standard; Furosemide Injection, USP; Furosemide Special; Furosemide Special Injection; Lasix; Lasix Special; PMS-Furosemide; Teva-Furosemide

Generic Availability (US) Yes

Pharmacologic Category Antihypertensive; Diuretic, Loop

Use

Management of edema associated with heart failure and hepatic or renal disease; acute pulmonary edema; treatment of hypertension (alone or in combination with other antihypertensives)

Note: According to the Eighth Joint National Committee (JNC 8) guidelines, loop diuretics are **not** recommended for the initial treatment of hypertension

(James 2013). In patients with chronic kidney disease (ie, eGFR <30 mL/minute/1.73 m^2), the American Society of Hypertension/International Society of Hypertension (ASH/ISH) suggests that the use of a loop diuretic may be necessary (Weber 2014).

Local Anesthetic/Vasoconstrictor Precautions No information available to require special precautions

Effects on Dental Treatment No significant effects or complications reported

Effects on Bleeding No information available to require special precautions

Adverse Reactions Frequency not defined.

Cardiovascular: Acute hypotension, chronic aortitis, necrotizing angiitis, orthostatic hypotension, vasculitis

Central nervous system: Dizziness, fever, headache, hepatic encephalopathy, lightheadedness, restlessness, vertigo

Dermatologic: Bullous pemphigoid, cutaneous vasculitis, drug rash with eosinophilia and systemic symptoms (DRESS), erythema multiforme, exanthematous pustulosis (generalized), exfoliative dermatitis, photosensitivity, pruritus, purpura, rash, Stevens-Johnson syndrome, toxic epidermal necrolysis, urticaria

Endocrine & metabolic: Cholesterol and triglycerides increased, glucose tolerance test altered, gout, hyperglycemia, hyperuricemia, hypocalcemia, hypochloremia, hypokalemia, hypomagnesemia, hyponatremia, metabolic alkalosis

Gastrointestinal: Anorexia, constipation, cramping, diarrhea, nausea, oral and gastric irritation, pancreatitis, vomiting

Genitourinary: Urinary bladder spasm, urinary frequency

Hematologic: Agranulocytosis (rare), anemia, aplastic anemia (rare), eosinophilia, hemolytic anemia, leukopenia, thrombocytopenia

Hepatic: Intrahepatic cholestatic jaundice, ischemic hepatitis, liver enzymes increased

Local: Injection site pain (following IM injection), thrombophlebitis

Neuromuscular & skeletal: Muscle spasm, paresthesia, weakness

Ocular: Blurred vision, xanthopsia

Otic: Hearing impairment (reversible or permanent with rapid IV or IM administration), tinnitus

Renal: Allergic interstitial nephritis, fall in glomerular filtration rate and renal blood flow (due to overdiuresis), glycosuria, transient rise in BUN

Miscellaneous: Anaphylaxis (rare), exacerbate or activate systemic lupus erythematosus

Dosing

Adult

Note: Dose equivalency for patients with normal renal function (approximate): Furosemide 40 mg = bumetanide 1 mg = torsemide 20 mg = ethacrynic acid 50 mg

Acute pulmonary edema: IV: 40 mg over 1 to 2 minutes. If response not adequate within 1 hour, may increase dose to 80 mg. **Note:** Minimal additional response is gained by single doses over 160 to 200 mg; maximum dose: 200 mg (Brater 1998).

Edema, heart failure:

Oral: Initial: 20 to 80 mg/dose; if response is not adequate, may repeat the same dose or increase dose in increments of 20 to 40 mg/dose at intervals of 6 to 8 hours; may be titrated up to 600 mg daily with severe edematous states; usual maintenance dose interval is once or twice daily. ACCF/AHA 2013 heart failure guidelines recommend initial dosing of 20 to 40 mg once or twice daily and a maximum total daily dose of 600 mg (Yancy 2013). **Note:** Dosing frequency may be adjusted based on patient-specific diuretic needs.

IM, IV: Initial: 20 to 40 mg/dose; if response is not adequate, may repeat the same dose or increase dose in increments of 20 mg/dose and administer 1 to 2 hours after previous dose (maximum dose: 200 mg/dose). A higher initial dose may be considered for those receiving chronic oral diuretic therapy. Individually determined dose should then be given once or twice daily although some patients may initially require dosing as frequent as every 6 hours.

Continuous IV infusion (ACCF/AHA [Yancy 2013]); Brater 1998; Howard 2001): Initial: IV bolus dose 40 to 100 mg over 1 to 2 minutes, followed by continuous IV infusion rate of 10 to 40 mg/hour; repeat loading dose before increasing infusion rate. **Note:** With lower baseline CrCl (eg, CrCl <25 mL/minute), the upper end of the initial infusion dosage range should be considered. If urine output is <1 mL/kg/hour, double as necessary to a maximum of 80 to 160 mg/hour (Howard 2001; Schuller 1997). The risk associated with higher infusion rates (80 to 160 mg/hour) must be weighed against alternative strategies.

Hypertension: *Oral:* Initial: 40 mg twice daily; individualize according to patient response and use minimal dose necessary to maintain therapeutic response. If response inadequate, may add another antihypertensive. Usual dosage (ASH/ISH [Weber 2014]): 40 mg twice daily.

Ascites, due to cirrhosis (off-label dose): Oral: Initial: 40 mg once daily; titrate every 3 to 5 days as clinically indicated (usual maximum: 160 mg once daily); a furosemide to spironolactone dosing ratio of 40 mg (furosemide) to 100 mg (spironolactone) should be maintained (AASLD [Runyon 2012]).

Geriatric Oral, IM, IV: Initial: 20 mg/day; increase slowly to desired response.

Pediatric

Note: Dose equivalency for patients with normal renal function (approximate): Furosemide 40 mg = bumetanide 1 mg = torsemide 20 mg = ethacrynic acid 50 mg

Edema, heart failure: Infants and Children:

Oral: Initial: 2 mg/kg/dose increased in increments of 1-2 mg/kg/dose with each succeeding dose at intervals of 6-8 hours until a satisfactory response is achieved; maximum dose: 6 mg/kg/dose

IM, IV: Initial: 1 mg/kg/dose; if response not adequate, may increase dose in increments of 1 mg/kg/dose and administer not sooner than 2 hours after previous dose, until a satisfactory response is achieved; may administer maintenance dose at intervals of every 6-12 hours; maximum dose: 6 mg/kg/dose

Hypertension, resistant (off-label; AAP, 2004): Children 1-17 years: *Oral:* Initial: 0.5-2 mg/kg/dose once or twice daily; maximum dose: 6 mg/kg/dose

Renal Impairment

Acute renal failure: Doses up to 1-3 g daily may be necessary to initiate desired response; avoid use in oliguric states.

Not removed by hemo- or peritoneal dialysis; supplemental dose is not necessary.

Hepatic Impairment Diminished natriuretic effect with increased sensitivity to hypokalemia and volume depletion in cirrhosis. Monitor effects, particularly with high doses.

Mechanism of Action Inhibits reabsorption of sodium and chloride in the ascending loop of Henle and proximal and distal renal tubules, interfering with the chloride-binding cotransport system, thus causing increased excretion of water, sodium, chloride, magnesium, and calcium

Contraindications Hypersensitivity to furosemide or any component of the formulation; anuria

Canadian labeling: Additional contraindications (not in US labeling): Hypersensitivity to sulfonamide-derived drugs; complete renal shutdown; hepatic coma and precoma; uncorrected states of electrolyte depletion, hypovolemia, dehydration, or hypotension; jaundiced newborn infants or infants with disease(s) capable of causing hyperbilirubinemia and possibly kernicterus; breastfeeding. **Note:** Manufacturer labeling for Lasix Special and Furosemide Special Injection also includes: GFR <5 mL/minute or GFR >20 mL/minute; hepatic cirrhosis; renal failure accompanied by hepatic coma and precoma; renal failure due to poisoning with nephrotoxic or hepatotoxic substances.

Note: Although the approved product labeling states this medication is contraindicated with other sulfonamide-containing drug classes, the scientific basis of this statement has been challenged. See "Warnings/Precautions" for more detail.

Warnings/Precautions [US Boxed Warning]: If given in excessive amounts, furosemide, similar to other loop diuretics, can lead to profound diuresis, resulting in fluid and electrolyte depletion; close medical supervision and dose evaluation are required. Watch for and correct electrolyte disturbances; adjust dose to avoid dehydration. When electrolyte depletion is present, therapy should not be initiated unless serum electrolytes, especially potassium, are normalized. In cirrhosis, avoid electrolyte and acid/base imbalances that might lead to hepatic encephalopathy; correct electrolyte and acid/base imbalances prior to initiation when hepatic coma is present. Supplemental potassium or an aldosterone antagonist, when appropriate, may reduce risk of hypokalemia and metabolic alkalosis. Close monitoring warranted, especially with initiation of therapy. In contrast to thiazide diuretics, a loop diuretic can also lower serum calcium concentrations. Electrolyte disturbances can predispose a patient to serious cardiac arrhythmias. Potentially significant drug-drug interactions may exist, requiring dose or frequency adjustment, additional monitoring, and/or selection of alternative therapy.

Monitor fluid status and renal function in an attempt to prevent oliguria, azotemia, and reversible increases in BUN and creatinine; close medical supervision of aggressive diuresis is required. May increase risk of contrast-induced nephropathy. Diuretic resistance may occur in some patients, despite higher doses of loop diuretic treatment. Diuretic resistance can usually be overcome by intravenous administration, the use of two diuretics together (eg, furosemide and chlorothiazide), or the use of a diuretic with a positive inotropic agent. Rapid IV administration, severe renal impairment, excessive doses, hypoproteinemia, and concurrent use of other ototoxins is associated with ototoxicity. Asymptomatic hyperuricemia has been reported with use; rarely, gout may precipitate. Photosensitization may occur. Doses >80 mg may result in transient increase in free thyroid hormones, followed by an overall decrease in total thyroid hormone levels.

Use with caution in patients with prediabetes or diabetes mellitus; may see a change in glucose control. Use with caution in patients with systemic lupus erythematosus (SLE); may cause SLE exacerbation or activation. Avoid use of diuretics for treatment of elevated blood pressure in patients with primary adrenal insufficiency (Addison disease). Adjustment of glucocorticoid/mineralocorticoid therapy and/or use of other antihypertensive agents is preferred to treat hypertension (Bornstein 2016; Inder 2015). Use with caution in patients with prostatic hyperplasia/urinary stricture; may cause urinary retention. May lead to nephrocalcinosis or nephrolithiasis in premature infants or in children <4 years of age with chronic use. May prevent closure of patent ductus arteriosus in premature infants. Some dosage forms may contain propylene glycol; large amounts are potentially toxic and have been associated hyperosmolality, lactic acidosis, seizures, and respiratory depression; use caution. If given the morning of surgery, furosemide may render the patient volume depleted and blood pressure may be labile during general anesthesia.

Sulfonamide ("sulfa") allergy: The approved product labeling for many medications containing a sulfonamide chemical group includes a broad contraindication in patients with a prior allergic reaction to sulfonamides. There is a potential for cross-reactivity between members of a specific class (eg, two antibiotic sulfonamides). However, concerns for cross-reactivity have previously extended to all compounds containing the sulfonamide structure (SO_2NH_2). An expanded understanding of allergic mechanisms indicates cross-reactivity between antibiotic sulfonamides and nonantibiotic sulfonamides may not occur or at the very least this potential is extremely low (Brackett 2004; Johnson 2005; Slatore 2004; Tornero 2004). In particular, mechanisms of cross-reaction due to antibody production (anaphylaxis) are unlikely to occur with nonantibiotic sulfonamides. T-cell-mediated (type IV) reactions (eg, maculopapular rash) are less well understood and it is not possible to completely exclude this potential based on current insights. In cases where prior reactions were severe (Stevens-Johnson syndrome/TEN), some clinicians choose to avoid exposure to these classes.

Drug Interactions

Metabolism/Transport Effects Substrate of OAT3; **Inhibits** MRP2

Avoid Concomitant Use

Avoid concomitant use of Furosemide with any of the following: Chloral Hydrate; Desmopressin; Ethacrynic Acid; Levosulpiride; Mecamylamine; Promazine

Increased Effect/Toxicity

Furosemide may increase the levels/effects of: ACE Inhibitors; Ajmaline; Allopurinol; Amifostine; Aminoglycosides; Antipsychotic Agents (Second Generation [Atypical]); Bilastine; Cabozantinib; Cardiac Glycosides; Cefotiam; Ceftizoxime; Cephalothin; Chloral Betaine; Chloral Hydrate; CISplatin; Desmopressin; Dofetilide; DULoxetine; Ethacrynic Acid; Foscarnet; Hypotension-Associated Agents; Ivabradine; Levodopa; Levosulpiride; Lithium; Mecamylamine; Methotrexate; Neuromuscular-Blocking Agents; Nitroprusside; Nonsteroidal Anti-Inflammatory Agents; Promazine; RisperiDONE; Salicylates; Sodium Phosphates; Tobramycin (Oral Inhalation); Topiramate

The levels/effects of Furosemide may be increased by: Acebrophylline; Alfuzosin; Analgesics (Opioid); Barbiturates; Benperidol; Beta2-Agonists; Brimonidine (Topical); Canagliflozin; Cefazedone; Cephradine; Corticosteroids (Orally Inhaled); Corticosteroids (Systemic); CycloSPORINE (Systemic); Diacerein;

Diazoxide; Empagliflozin; Herbs (Hypotensive Properties); Ipragliflozin; Licorice; Lormetazepam; Methotrexate; Molsidomine; Naftopidil; Nicergoline; Nicorandil; Obinutuzumab; Pentoxifylline; Phosphodiesterase 5 Inhibitors; Probenecid; Prostacyclin Analogues; Quinagolide; Reboxetine; Teriflunomide

Decreased Effect

Furosemide may decrease the levels/effects of: Antidiabetic Agents; Lithium; Neuromuscular-Blocking Agents

The levels/effects of Furosemide may be decreased by: Aliskiren; Amphetamines; Analgesics (Opioid); Bile Acid Sequestrants; Fosphenytoin; Herbs (Hypertensive Properties); Methotrexate; Methylphenidate; Nonsteroidal Anti-Inflammatory Agents; Phenytoin; Probenecid; Salicylates; Sucralfate; Yohimbine

Food Interactions Furosemide serum levels may be decreased if taken with food. Management: Administer on an empty stomach.

Dietary Considerations May cause potassium loss; potassium supplement or dietary changes may be required.

Pharmacodynamics/Kinetics

Onset of Action Diuresis: Oral, S.L.: 30-60 minutes; IM: 30 minutes; IV: ~5 minutes

Symptomatic improvement with acute pulmonary edema: Within 15-20 minutes; occurs prior to diuretic effect

Peak effect: Oral: 1-2 hours

Duration of Action Oral, S.L.: 6-8 hours; IV: 2 hours

Half-life Elimination Normal renal function: 0.5-2 hours; End-stage renal disease: 9 hours

Pregnancy Risk Factor C

Pregnancy Considerations Adverse events have been observed in animal reproduction studies. Furosemide crosses the placenta (Riva 1978). Furosemide has been used to treat heart failure in pregnant women (ESC 2011; Johnson-Coyle 2012). Monitor fetal growth if used during pregnancy; may increase birth weight.

Breastfeeding Considerations Furosemide is excreted into breast milk; maternal use may suppress lactation. The manufacturer recommends that caution be used if administered to a nursing woman.

Dosage Forms

Solution, Injection:

Generic: 10 mg/mL (2 mL, 4 mL, 10 mL)

Solution, Injection [preservative free]:

Generic: 10 mg/mL (2 mL, 4 mL, 10 mL)

Solution, Oral:

Generic: 8 mg/mL (5 mL, 500 mL); 10 mg/mL (60 mL, 120 mL)

Tablet, Oral:

Lasix: 20 mg, 40 mg, 80 mg

Generic: 20 mg, 40 mg, 80 mg

Dosage Forms: Canada

Injection, solution [preservative free]:

Furosemide Special Injection: 10 mg/mL (25 mL)

Tablet, oral:

Lasix Special: 500 mg [scored]

Gabapentin (GA ba pen tin)

Related Information

Temporomandibular Dysfunction (TMD), Chronic Pain, and Fibromyalgia *on page 1868*

Brand Names: US Fanatrex FusePaq; Gralise; Gralise Starter; Neurontin

Brand Names: Canada ACT Gabapentin; Apo-Gabapentin; Auro-Gabapentin; Dom-Gabapentin; GD-Gabapentin; JAMP-Gabapentin; JAMP-Gabapentin Tablets; Mar-Gabapentin; Mylan-Gabapentin; Neurontin; PHL-Gabapentin; PMS-Gabapentin; PRO-Gabapentin; RAN-Gabapentin; Riva-Gabapentin; Teva-Gabapentin; Van-Gabapentin

Generic Availability (US) May be product dependent

Pharmacologic Category Anticonvulsant, Miscellaneous; GABA Analog

Dental Use Neuropathic pain (consult with physician)

Use

Postherpetic neuralgia: Management of postherpetic neuralgia (PHN) in adults.

Seizures, partial onset (excluding Gralise): As adjunctive therapy in the treatment of partial seizures with and without secondary generalization in adults and pediatric patients 3 years and older with epilepsy.

Local Anesthetic/Vasoconstrictor Precautions No information available to require special precautions

Effects on Dental Treatment Key adverse event(s) related to dental treatment: Xerostomia (normal salivary flow resumes upon discontinuation), dry throat, and dental abnormalities.

Effects on Bleeding No information available to require special precautions

Adverse Reactions As reported for immediate release (IR) formulations in patients >12 years of age, unless otherwise noted in children (3-12 years) or with use of Gralise

>10%:

Central nervous system: Dizziness (IR: 17% to 28%; children 3%; Gralise: 11%), drowsiness (IR: 19% to 21%; children 8%; Gralise: 5%), ataxia (1% to 13%), fatigue (11%; children 3%)

Infection: Viral infection (children 11%)

1% to 10%:

Cardiovascular: Peripheral edema (IR: 2% to 8%; Gralise: 4%), vasodilatation (1%)

Central nervous system: Hostility (children 5% to 8%), tremor (7%), emotional lability (children 4% to 6%), hyperkinesia (children 3% to 5%), headache (children and adolescents 3%), abnormality in thinking (2% to 3%; children 2%), abnormal gait (2%), amnesia (2%), depression (2%), nervousness (2%), pain (Gralise: 1% to 2%), hyperesthesia (1%), lethargy (Gralise: 1%), twitching (1%), vertigo (Gralise: 1%)

Dermatologic: Pruritus (1%), skin rash (1%)

Endocrine & metabolic: Weight gain (IR: Adults and children 2% to 3%; Gralise: 2%), hyperglycemia (1%)

Gastrointestinal: Diarrhea (IR: 6%), nausea and vomiting (3% to 4%; children 8%), xerostomia (IR: 2% to 5%; Gralise: 3%), constipation (IR: 1% to 4%; Gralise: 1%), abdominal pain (3%), dyspepsia (IR: 2%; Gralise: 1%), dry throat (2%), dental disease (2%), flatulence (2%), increased appetite (1%)

Genitourinary: Impotence (2%), urinary tract infection (Gralise: 2%)

Hematologic & oncologic: Decreased white blood cell count (1%), leukopenia (1%)

Infection: Infection (5%)

Neuromuscular & skeletal: Weakness (6%), back pain (IR: 2%; Gralise: 2%), dysarthria (2%), limb pain (Gralise: 2%), myalgia (2%), bone fracture (1%)

Ophthalmic: Nystagmus (8%), diplopia (1% to 6%), amblyopia (4%), blurred vision (3% to 4%), conjunctivitis (1%)

Otic: Otitis media (1%)

Respiratory: Rhinitis (4%), bronchitis (children 3%), nasopharyngitis (Gralise: 3%), respiratory tract infection (children 3%), pharyngitis (1% to 3%), cough (2%)

Miscellaneous: Fever (children 10%)

Postmarketing and case reports: Abnormal hepatic function, acute renal failure, altered serum glucose, anaphylaxis, anemia, angina pectoris, angioedema, aphasia, aspiration pneumonia, blindness, blood coagulation disorder, bradycardia, brain disease, breast hypertrophy, bronchospasm, cardiac arrhythmia (various), cerebrovascular accident, change in libido, cholestatic hepatitis, CNS neoplasm, colitis, confusion, Cushingoid appearance, DRESS syndrome, drug abuse, drug dependence, dyspnea, ejaculatory disorder, erythema multiforme, facial paralysis, falling, fecal incontinence, fulminant hepatitis, gastroenteritis, glaucoma, glycosuria, gynecomastia, hearing loss, heart block, hematemesis, hematuria, hemiplegia, hemorrhage, hepatitis, hepatomegaly, herpes zoster, hyperlipidemia, hypersensitivity reaction, hypertension, hyperthyroidism, hyperventilation, hypoglycemia, hyponatremia, hypotension, hypothyroidism, hypoventilation, increased creatine phosphokinase, increased liver enzymes, increased serum creatinine, jaundice, joint swelling, leukocytosis, loss of consciousness, lymphadenopathy, lymphocytosis, memory impairment, meningism, migraine, movement disorder, myocardial infarction, myoclonus (local), nephrolithiasis, nephrosis, nerve palsy, non-Hodgkin lymphoma, ovarian failure, palpitations, pancreatitis, paresthesia, peptic ulcer, pericardial effusion, pericardial rub, pericarditis, peripheral vascular disease, pneumonia, psychosis, pulmonary edema, pulmonary thromboembolism, purpura, retinopathy, rhabdomyolysis, seasonal allergy, sexual disorder, skin necrosis, status epilepticus, Stevens-Johnson syndrome, subdural hematoma, suicidal ideation, suicidal tendencies, syncope, tachycardia, thrombocytopenia, thrombophlebitis, tumor growth, withdrawal syndrome

Dental Usual Dosage

Pain (off-label use): Children >12 years and Adults: Oral: 300-1800 mg/day given in 3 divided doses has been the most common dosage range

Postherpetic neuralgia or neuropathic pain: Adults: Oral: Day 1: 300 mg, Day 2: 300 mg twice daily, Day 3: 300 mg 3 times/day; dose may be titrated as needed for pain relief (range: 1800-3600 mg/day, daily doses >1800 mg do not generally show greater benefit)

Dosing

Adult & Geriatric

Postherpetic neuralgia: Oral:

Day 1: 300 mg, Day 2: 300 mg twice daily, Day 3: 300 mg 3 times daily; dose may be titrated as needed for pain relief (range: 1,800 to 3,600 mg/day in divided doses, daily doses >1,800 mg do not generally show greater benefit)

Gralise only: Day 1: 300 mg, Day 2: 600 mg, Days 3 to 6: 900 mg once daily, Days 7 to 10: 1,200 mg once daily, Days 11 to 14: 1,500 mg once daily, Days ≥15: 1,800 mg once daily

Seizures, partial onset: Oral (excluding Gralise):

Initial: 300 mg 3 times daily; increase dosage based on response and tolerability; usual dosage: 900 to 1,800 mg/day administered in 3 divided doses; doses of up to 2,400 mg/day have been tolerated in long-term clinical studies; up to 3,600 mg/day has been tolerated in short-term studies

Note: If gabapentin is discontinued or if another anticonvulsant is added to therapy, it should be done slowly over a minimum of 1 week.

Alcohol dependence (off-label use): Oral: Immediate release: 300 mg once daily on day 1, followed by dosage escalation, based on response and tolerability, in increments of 300 mg/day up to a target dose of 1,800 mg/day in 3 divided doses (Brower 2008; Mason 2014; VA/DoD 2015).

Alcohol withdrawal (off-label use): Oral: Immediate release: 300 to 400 mg 3 times daily on days 1 through 3, then 300 to 400 mg twice daily on day 4, then discontinue. For breakthrough symptoms during days 1 through 4, consider providing single doses of 100 mg administered up to 3 times daily and a 300 mg dose reserved for the evening (Myrick 2009).

Brachioradial pruritus (off-label use): Oral: Immediate release: Initial: 100 mg 3 times daily; increase dose based on response and tolerability up to 1,800 mg/day (Bueller 1999; Kanitakis 2006; Winhoven 2004; Yilmaz 2010). Additional data may be necessary to further define the role of gabapentin in this condition.

Cough, chronic (refractory) (off-label use): Oral: Immediate release: 300 mg once daily on day 1, followed by dosage escalation in increments of 300 mg/day until cough symptoms cease, side effects are intolerable, or a maximum tolerated dose of 1,800 mg/day given in 2 divided doses is reached (ACCP [Gibson 2016]; Ryan 2012). Additional data may be necessary to further define the role of gabapentin in this condition.

Diabetic neuropathy (off-label use): Oral: Immediate release: 900 to 3,600 mg/day (Bril 2011)

Fibromyalgia syndrome (off-label use): Oral: Immediate release: Initial: 300 mg once daily at bedtime, increase in increments of 300 to 600 mg/day every 1 to 2 weeks based on response and tolerability up to 2,400 mg/day in divided doses. Median dosage in clinical trial was 1,800 mg/day with a range of 1,200 to 2,400 mg/day (Arnold 2007).

Hot flashes (off-label use): Oral: Immediate release: 300 mg once daily at bedtime on day 1, then 300 mg twice daily on day 2, then 300 mg 3 times daily (Butt 2008).

Neuropathic pain (off-label use): Oral: Immediate release: 1,200 to 3,600 mg/day in 3 divided doses (IASP [Finnerup 2015]).

Critically ill patients: Oral: Immediate release: Initial: 100 mg 3 times daily in combination with IV opioids; maintenance: 300 to 1,200 mg 3 times daily; maximum dose: 3,600 mg daily (SCCM [Barr 2013])

Postoperative pain (adjunct) (off-label use): Oral: Immediate release: 300 to 1,200 mg given the night before, 1 to 2 hours prior to surgery or immediately following surgery (Doleman 2015; Peng 2007; Yu 2013)

Restless legs syndrome (RLS) (off-label use): Oral: Immediate release: Initial: 300 mg once daily 2 hours before bedtime. Doses ≥600 mg/day have been given in 2 divided doses (late afternoon and 2 hours before bedtime). Dose may be titrated every 2 weeks until symptom relief achieved (range: 300 to 1,800 mg/day). Suggested maintenance dosing schedule: One-third of total daily dose given at 12 pm, remaining two-thirds total daily dose given at 8 pm. (Garcia-Borreguero 2002; Happe 2003; Saletu 2010; Vignatelli 2006)

Social anxiety disorder (off-label use): Oral: Immediate release: Initial: 300 mg twice daily; increase dose based on response and tolerability in increments of no more than 300 mg/day up to a maximum of 3,600 mg/day given in 3 divided doses. Doses for responders ranged from 900 to 3,600 mg/day in the clinical trial (Pande 1999). Additional data may be necessary to further define the role of gabapentin in this condition.

Uremic pruritus (off-label use): Oral: Immediate release: Initial: 100 mg after dialysis on hemodialysis days; may increase dose based on response and tolerability up to 400 mg after dialysis on hemodialysis days (Gunal 2004; Naini 2007; Nofal 2016; Razeghi 2009).

Pediatric

Seizures, partial onset:

Children 3 to 4 years: Oral (excluding Gralise) Initial: 10 to 15 mg/kg/day in 3 divided doses; titrate to effective dose over ~3 days; increase dosage based on response and tolerability; usual dosage: 40 mg/kg/day in 3 divided doses; dosages of up to 50 mg/kg/day have been tolerated in clinical studies:

Children 5 to 11 years: Oral (excluding Gralise): Initial: 10 to 15 mg/kg/day in 3 divided doses; titrate to effective dose over ~3 days; increase dosage based on response and tolerability; usual dosage: 25 to 35 mg/kg/day in 3 divided doses; dosages of up to 50 mg/kg/day have been tolerated in clinical studies

Children ≥12 years: Refer to adult dosing.

Note: If gabapentin is discontinued or if another anticonvulsant is added to therapy, it should be done slowly over a minimum of 1 week

Renal Impairment Children ≥12 years and Adults:

All products, excluding Gralise:

CrCl ≥60 mL/minute: 300 to 1,200 mg 3 times daily

CrCl >30 to 59 mL/minute: 200 to 700 mg twice daily

CrCl >15 to 29 mL/minute: 200 to 700 mg once daily

CrCl 15 mL/minute: 100 to 300 mg once daily

CrCl <15 mL/minute: Reduce daily dose in proportion to creatinine clearance based on dose for creatinine clearance of 15 mL/minute (eg, reduce dose by one-half [range: 50 to 150 mg/day] for CrCl 7.5 mL/minute)

ESRD requiring hemodialysis: Dose based on CrCl plus a single supplemental dose of 125 to 350 mg (given after each 4 hours of hemodialysis)

Gralise only: **Note:** Follow initial dose titration schedule if treatment-naive.

CrCl ≥60 mL/minute: 1,800 mg once daily

CrCl >30 to 59 mL/minute: 600 to 1,800 mg once daily; dependent on tolerability and clinical response

CrCl <30 mL/minute: Use is not recommended.

ESRD requiring hemodialysis: Use is not recommended.

Hepatic Impairment There are no dosage adjustments provided in the manufacturer's labeling; however, gabapentin is not hepatically metabolized.

Mechanism of Action Gabapentin is structurally related to GABA. However, it does not bind to $GABA_A$ or $GABA_B$ receptors, and it does not appear to influence synthesis or uptake of GABA. High affinity gabapentin binding sites have been located throughout the brain; these sites correspond to the presence of voltage-gated calcium channels specifically possessing the alpha-2-delta-1 subunit. This channel appears to be located presynaptically, and may modulate the release of excitatory neurotransmitters which participate in epileptogenesis and nociception.

Contraindications Hypersensitivity to gabapentin or any component of the formulation

Warnings/Precautions Antiepileptics are associated with an increased risk of suicidal behavior/thoughts with use (regardless of indication); patients should be monitored for signs/symptoms of depression, suicidal tendencies, and other unusual behavior changes during therapy and instructed to inform their healthcare provider immediately if symptoms occur. Avoid abrupt withdrawal, may precipitate seizures; Gralise should be withdrawn over ≥1 week. Use cautiously in patients with severe renal dysfunction; male rat studies demonstrated an association with pancreatic adenocarcinoma (clinical implication unknown). May cause CNS depression including somnolence and dizziness, which may impair physical or mental abilities. Patients must be cautioned about performing tasks which require mental alertness (eg, operating machinery or driving). Pediatric patients have shown increased incidence of CNS-related adverse effects, including emotional lability, hostility, changes in behavior and thinking, and hyperkinesia. Gabapentin immediate release and Gralise products are not interchangeable with each other **or** with gabapentin enacarbil (Horizant). The safety and efficacy of Gralise has not been studied in patients with epilepsy. Potentially serious, sometimes fatal multiorgan hypersensitivity (also known as drug reaction with eosinophilia and systemic symptoms [DRESS]) has been reported with some antiepileptic drugs, including gabapentin; may affect lymphatic, hepatic, renal, cardiac, and/or hematologic systems; fever, rash, and eosinophilia may also be present. Discontinue immediately if suspected. Anaphylaxis and/or angioedema may occur after the first dose or at any time during treatment; discontinue therapy and seek immediate medical care if signs or symptoms of anaphylaxis or angioedema occur. Potentially significant interactions may exist, requiring dose or frequency adjustment, additional monitoring, and/or selection of alternative therapy.

Drug Interactions

Metabolism/Transport Effects None known.

Avoid Concomitant Use

Avoid concomitant use of Gabapentin with any of the following: Azelastine (Nasal); Orphenadrine; Oxomemazine; Paraldehyde; Thalidomide

Increased Effect/Toxicity

Gabapentin may increase the levels/effects of: Alcohol (Ethyl); Analgesics (Opioid); Azelastine (Nasal); Blonanserin; Buprenorphine; CNS Depressants; Flunitrazepam; HYDROcodone; Methotrimeprazine; MetyroSINE; Mirtazapine; Morphine (Systemic); Orphenadrine; OxyCODONE; Paraldehyde; Piribedil; Pramipexole; ROPINIRole; Rotigotine; Selective Serotonin Reuptake Inhibitors; Suvorexant; Thalidomide; Zolpidem

The levels/effects of Gabapentin may be increased by: Brimonidine (Topical); Cannabis; Chlormethiazole; Chlorphenesin Carbamate; Dimethindene (Topical); Doxylamine; Dronabinol; Droperidol; HydrOXYzine; Kava Kava; Lofexidine; Magnesium Salts; Methotrimeprazine; Minocycline; Morphine (Systemic); Nabilone; Oxomemazine; Perampanel; Rufinamide; Sodium Oxybate; Tapentadol; Tetrahydrocannabinol; Trimeprazine

Decreased Effect

The levels/effects of Gabapentin may be decreased by: Antacids; Magnesium Salts; Mefloquine; Mianserin; Orlistat

Food Interactions Tablet, solution (immediate release): No significant effect on rate or extent of absorption; tablet (Gralise): Increases rate and extent of absorption. Management: Administer immediate release products without regard to food. Administer Gralise with food.

Dietary Considerations Gralise should be taken with food.

Pharmacodynamics/Kinetics

Half-life Elimination

Infants 1 month to Children 12 years: 4.7 hours

Adults, normal: 5 to 7 hours; increased half-life with decreased renal function; anuric adult patients: 132 hours; adults during hemodialysis: 3.8 hours

Time to Peak Immediate release: Infants 1 month to Children 12 years: 2 to 3 hours; Adults: 2 to 4 hours; Gralise: 8 hours

Pregnancy Risk Factor C

Pregnancy Considerations Adverse events have been observed in animal reproduction studies. Gabapentin crosses the placenta. In a small study (n=6), the umbilical/maternal plasma concentration ratio was ~1.74. Neonatal concentrations declined quickly after delivery and at 24 hours of life were ~27% of the cord blood concentrations at birth (gabapentin neonatal half-life ~14 hours) (Ohman 2005). Outcome data following maternal use of gabapentin during pregnancy is limited (Holmes 2012).

Patients exposed to gabapentin during pregnancy are encouraged to enroll in the North American Antiepileptic Drug (NAAED) Pregnancy Registry by calling 1 888-233-2334. Additional information is available at www.aedpregnancyregistry.org.

Breastfeeding Considerations Gabapentin is excreted in human breast milk. Per the manufacturer, a nursed infant could be exposed to ~1 mg/kg/day of gabapentin; the effect on the child is not known. Use in breastfeeding women only if the benefits to the mother outweigh the potential risk to the infant.

In a small study of breastfeeding women (n=6), the estimated exposure of gabapentin to the nursing infants was ~1% to 4% of the weight-adjusted maternal dose (sampling occurred from 12-97 days after delivery and maternal doses ranged from 600-2100 mg daily). Gabapentin was detected in the serum of 2 nursing infants 2-3 weeks after delivery and in 1 infant after 3 months of breastfeeding. Serum concentrations were <12% of the maternal plasma concentrations and <5% of those measured in the umbilical cord. Adverse events were not reported in the breast-fed infants (Ohman 2005).

Dosage Forms Considerations

Fanatrex FusePaq is a compounding kit for the preparation of an oral suspension. Refer to manufacturer's labeling for compounding instructions.

Dosage Forms

Capsule, Oral:

Neurontin: 100 mg, 300 mg, 400 mg

Generic: 100 mg, 300 mg, 400 mg

Miscellaneous, Oral:

Gralise Starter: 300 & 600 mg (78 ea)

Solution, Oral:

Neurontin: 250 mg/5 mL (470 mL)

Generic: 250 mg/5 mL (5 mL, 470 mL, 473 mL); 300 mg/6 mL (6 mL)

Suspension, Oral:

Fanatrex FusePaq: 25 mg/mL (420 mL)

Tablet, Oral:

Gralise: 300 mg, 600 mg

Neurontin: 600 mg, 800 mg

Generic: 600 mg, 800 mg

Gabapentin Enacarbil (gab a PEN tin en a KAR bil)

Brand Names: US Horizant

Pharmacologic Category Anticonvulsant, Miscellaneous

Use Treatment of moderate-to-severe restless leg syndrome (RLS); management of postherpetic neuralgia (PHN)

Local Anesthetic/Vasoconstrictor Precautions No information available to require special precautions

Effects on Dental Treatment Key adverse event(s) related to dental treatment: Xerostomia (normal salivary flow resumes upon discontinuation).

Effects on Bleeding No information available to require special precautions

Adverse Reactions Percentages reported are for restless leg syndrome (RLS) 600 mg daily and postherpetic neuralgia (PHN) 1200 mg daily.

>10%: Central nervous system: Drowsiness (RLS: ≤20%; PHN: ≤10%), sedation (RLS: ≤20%; PHN: ≤10%), dizziness (13% to 17%), headache (10% to 12%)

1% to 10%:

Cardiovascular: Peripheral edema (PHN: 6%; RLS: <1%)

Central nervous system: Fatigue (6%), irritability (≤4%), insomnia (PHN: 3%), equilibrium disturbance (<2%), depression (<2%), disorientation (<2%), intoxicated feeling (<2%), lethargy (<2%), vertigo (<2%)

Endocrine & metabolic: Weight gain (2% to 3%)

Gastrointestinal: Nausea (6% to 8%), flatulence (≤3%), xerostomia (≤3%), increased appetite (≤2%)

Ophthalmic: Blurred vision (≤2%)

<1%, postmarketing, and/or case reports: Breast hypertrophy (gabapentin), decreased libido, feeling abnormal, gynecomastia (gabapentin), increased creatine phosphokinase (gabapentin)

General Dosage Range Dosage adjustment recommended in patients with renal impairment.

Oral: *Adults:* 600 mg once daily (RLS) **or** 600 mg once daily for 3 days, then 600 mg twice daily (PHN)

Mechanism of Action Gabapentin enacarbil is a prodrug of gabapentin. Gabapentin is structurally related to GABA. However, it does not bind to $GABA_A$ or $GABA_B$ receptors, and it does not appear to influence synthesis or uptake of GABA. High affinity gabapentin binding sites have been located throughout the brain; these sites correspond to the presence of voltage-gated calcium channels specifically possessing the alpha-2-delta-1 subunit. This channel appears to be located presynaptically, and may modulate the release of excitatory neurotransmitters. These effects on RLS are unknown.

Pharmacodynamics/Kinetics

Half-life Elimination Prodrug hydrolyzed primarily in the intestines to gabapentin (active metabolite)

Time to Peak 5-6 hours

Pregnancy Risk Factor C

Pregnancy Considerations Adverse events were observed in animal reproduction studies. Gabapentin enacarbil is the prodrug of gabapentin; bioavailability following gabapentin enacarbil is increased in comparison to gabapentin (Backonja, 2011). Refer to Gabapentin monograph for information related to gabapentin exposure during pregnancy.

Gadoteridol (gad oh TER i dol)

Brand Names: US Prohance

Brand Names: Canada ProHance

Pharmacologic Category Diagnostic Agent; Gadolinium-Containing Contrast Agent; Radiological/Contrast Media, Nonionic (Low Osmolality); Radiological/Contrast Media, Paramagnetic Agent

Use

CNS imaging: For use in MRI in adults and children >2 years of age to visualize lesions with abnormal vascularity in the brain (intracranial lesions), spine, and associated tissues.

Extracranial/Extraspinal tissues imaging: For use in MRI in adults to visualize lesions in the head and neck.

Local Anesthetic/Vasoconstrictor Precautions No information available to require special precautions

Effects on Dental Treatment No significant effects or complications reported

Effects on Bleeding No information available to require special precautions

Adverse Reactions

1% to 10%: Gastrointestinal: Nausea (1%), dysgeusia (1%)

<1%, postmarketing, and/or case reports: Abdominal cramps, altered mental status, anaphylactoid reaction, anxiety, apnea, ataxia, atrioventricular junctional rhythm, bradycardia, chest pain, cough, cyanosis, deafness (transient), diaphoresis, diarrhea, dizziness, dysphagia, dyspnea, edema, facial edema, fever, flushing, gingivitis, headache, hypertension, hypotension, increased heart rate, injection site reaction, laryngeal edema, laryngismus, loss of consciousness, maculopapular rash, malaise, neck stiffness, nephrogenic systemic fibrosis (NSF/NFD), pain, pain at injection site, paresthesia, prolongation P-R interval on ECG, pruritus, rhinitis, seizure, sialorrhea, skin rash, stare, stupor, syncope, tingling sensation, tinnitus, tongue edema, tongue pruritus, tremor, urinary incontinence, urticaria, vasodepressor syncope, voice disorder, vomiting, watery eyes, wheezing, xerostomia

General Dosage Range IV:

Children ≥2 years and Adolescents: 0.1 mmol/kg (0.2 mL/kg)

Adults: 0.1 mmol/kg (0.2 mL/kg); may repeat 0.2 mmol/kg (0.4 mL/kg) once if needed [CNS imaging]

Mechanism of Action Gadoteridol is a gadolinium-containing paramagnetic agent. Exposure to an external magnetic field induces a large local magnetic field in exposed tissues. This local magnetism disrupts water protons in the vicinity, resulting in a change in proton density and spin characteristics, which can be detected by the imaging device.

Pharmacodynamics/Kinetics

Half-life Elimination 1.57 ± 0.08 hours

Pregnancy Risk Factor C

Pregnancy Considerations Adverse events were observed in animal reproduction studies. Gadolinium-based contrast agents cross the placenta; in general, their use in pregnant women is controversial (ACOG 2016). Use should be avoided unless critical for the care of the mother or fetus and it is not prudent to wait until after pregnancy. Agents with a low risk for development of nephrogenic systemic fibrosis should be used at the lowest effective dose (ACR 2015).

Galantamine (ga LAN ta meen)

Brand Names: US Razadyne; Razadyne ER

Brand Names: Canada Auro-Galantamine ER; Galantamine ER; Mylan-Galantamine ER; PAT-Galantamine ER; PMS-Galantamine ER; Reminyl ER; Teva-Galantamine ER

Pharmacologic Category Acetylcholinesterase Inhibitor (Central)

Use Treatment of mild-to-moderate dementia of Alzheimer's disease

Local Anesthetic/Vasoconstrictor Precautions No information available to require special precautions

Effects on Dental Treatment No significant effects or complications reported

Effects on Bleeding No information available to require special precautions

Adverse Reactions

>10%: Gastrointestinal: Nausea (21%), vomiting (11%)

1% to 10%:

Cardiovascular: Bradycardia (1%), syncope (1%)

Central nervous system: Dizziness (8%), headache (7%), depression (4%), falling (4%), fatigue (4%), drowsiness (2%), lethargy (1%), malaise (1%)

Endocrine & metabolic: Weight loss (5%)

Gastrointestinal: Decreased appetite (7%), diarrhea (7%), abdominal pain (4%), abdominal distress (2%), dyspepsia (2%)

Neuromuscular & skeletal: Tremor (2%), muscle spasm (1%)

Miscellaneous: Laceration (1%)

Frequency not defined:

Gastrointestinal: Anorexia

<1%, postmarketing, and/or case reports: Acute generalized exanthematous pustulosis, atrioventricular block, blurred vision, cerebrovascular accident, complete atrioventricular block, dehydration (includes rare, severe cases leading to renal insufficiency and renal failure), dysgeusia, erythema multiforme, first degree atrioventricular block, flushing, hallucination, hepatitis, hyperhidrosis, hypersensitivity reaction, hypersomnia, hypertension, hypotension, increased liver enzymes, myasthenia, myocardial infarction, palpitations, paresthesia, retching, seizure, sinus bradycardia, skin rash, Stevens-Johnson syndrome, supraventricular extrasystole, tinnitus

General Dosage Range Dosage adjustment recommended in patients with hepatic or renal impairment

Oral:

Extended-release: *Adults:* Initial: 8 mg once daily; Maintenance: 16 to 24 mg once daily

Immediate release: *Adults:* Initial: 4 mg twice daily; Maintenance: 16 to 24 mg daily in 2 divided doses

Mechanism of Action Centrally-acting cholinesterase inhibitor (competitive and reversible). It elevates acetylcholine in cerebral cortex by slowing the degradation of acetylcholine. Modulates nicotinic acetylcholine receptor to increase acetylcholine from surviving presynaptic nerve terminals. May increase glutamate and serotonin levels.

Pharmacodynamics/Kinetics

Half-life Elimination ~7 hours

Time to Peak Immediate release: 1 hour (2.5 hours with food); extended release: 4.5-5 hours

Pregnancy Risk Factor C

Pregnancy Considerations Adverse events have been observed in animal reproduction studies.

Galsulfase (gal SUL fase)

Brand Names: US Naglazyme

Pharmacologic Category Enzyme

Use Mucopolysaccharidosis VI: Replacement therapy in patients with mucopolysaccharidosis VI (MPS VI; Maroteaux-Lamy syndrome) to improve walking and stair-climbing capacity.

Local Anesthetic/Vasoconstrictor Precautions No information available to require special precautions

Effects on Dental Treatment No significant effects or complications reported

Effects on Bleeding No information available to require special precautions

Adverse Reactions

Note: Percentages reported are from a placebo-controlled study (39 patients, 19 on galsulfase); also included are adverse effects noted during other clinical studies.

Cardiovascular: Chest pain (16%), hypertension (11%)

Central nervous system: Pain (32%), chills (21%), absent reflexes (11%), malaise (11%), headache

Dermatologic: Skin rash (21%), pruritus, urticaria

Gastrointestinal: Abdominal pain (47%), gastroenteritis (11%), nausea, vomiting

Hypersensitivity: Angioedema

Neuromuscular & skeletal: Arthralgia (42%)

Ophthalmic: Conjunctivitis (21%), corneal opacity (increased, 11%)

Otic: Otalgia (42%), auditory impairment (11%)

Respiratory: Dyspnea (21%), pharyngitis (11%), nasal congestion (11%), apnea, laryngeal edema, respiratory distress

Miscellaneous: Antibody development (98%), infusion related reaction (56%), umbilical hernia (11%), fever

<1%, postmarketing, and/or case reports: Anaphylaxis, bradycardia, bronchospasm, cyanosis, erythema, hypotension, hypoxia, pallor, paresthesia, renal disease (membranous), respiratory failure, shock, spinal cord compression, tachycardia, tachypnea, thrombocytopenia

General Dosage Range IV: *Infants, Children, Adolescents, and Adults:* 1 mg/kg once weekly

Mechanism of Action Galsulfase is a recombinant form of N-acetylgalactosamine 4-sulfatase, produced in Chinese hamster cells. A deficiency of this enzyme leads to accumulation of the glycosaminoglycan dermatan sulfate in various tissues, causing progressive disease which includes decreased growth, skeletal deformities, upper airway obstruction, clouding of the cornea, heart disease, and coarse facial features. Exogenous replacement of this enzyme has been shown to improve mobility and physical function (measured by walking and stair-climbing).

Pharmacodynamics/Kinetics

Half-life Elimination Week 1: Median 9 minutes (range: 6 to 21 minutes); Week 24: Median 26 minutes (range: 8 to 40 minutes)

Pregnancy Risk Factor B

Pregnancy Considerations Adverse events have not been observed in animal reproduction studies. A pregnancy registry is available for women who may be exposed to galsulfase for the treatment of MPS VI during pregnancy (1-800-983-4587).

Ganciclovir (Systemic) (gan SYE kloe veer)

Related Information

Systemic Viral Diseases *on page 1806*

ValGANciclovir *on page 1625*

Brand Names: US Cytovene

Brand Names: Canada Cytovene; Ganciclovir for Injection

Generic Availability (US) Yes

Pharmacologic Category Antiviral Agent

Use

Cytomegalovirus disease prophylaxis in transplant patients: Prevention of cytomegalovirus (CMV) disease in transplant recipients at risk for CMV disease

Cytomegalovirus retinitis (immunocompromised patients): Treatment of CMV retinitis in immunocompromised patients, including patients with acquired immunodeficiency syndrome (AIDS)

Local Anesthetic/Vasoconstrictor Precautions No information available to require special precautions

Effects on Dental Treatment No significant effects or complications reported

Effects on Bleeding Anemia (15% to 25%), thrombocytopenia (57% in bone marrow transplant patients; less common in other populations [8%]), and unusual bleeding are frequently reported.

Adverse Reactions

>10%:

Dermatologic: Diaphoresis (12%)

Gastrointestinal: Diarrhea (44%), anorexia (14%), vomiting (13%)

Hematologic & oncologic: Thrombocytopenia (57%), leukopenia (41%), anemia (16% to 26%), neutropenia (ANC <500/mm^3: 12% to 14%)

Infection: Sepsis (15%)

Ophthalmic: Retinal detachment (11%; relationship to ganciclovir not established)

Renal: Increased serum creatinine (2% to 14%)

Miscellaneous: Fever (48%)

1% to 10%:

Central nervous system: Chills (10%), neuropathy (9%)

Dermatologic: Pruritus (5%)

<1%, postmarketing, and/or case reports: Alopecia, brain disease, bronchospasm, cardiac arrhythmia, cataract, cholestasis, coma, dyspnea, edema, eosinophilia, exfoliative dermatitis, extrapyramidal reaction, hemorrhage, hepatic failure, hepatitis, hypersensitivity reaction (including anaphylaxis), pancreatitis, pancytopenia, psychosis, pulmonary fibrosis, renal failure, rhabdomyolysis, seizure, SIADH (syndrome of inappropriate antidiuretic hormone secretion), Stevens-Johnson syndrome, torsades de pointes, urticaria, vision loss

Dosing

Adult & Geriatric

CMV retinitis (immunocompromised patients):

Manufacturer's labeling:

Induction therapy: IV: 5 mg/kg/dose every 12 hours for 14 to 21 days followed by maintenance therapy

Maintenance therapy: IV: 5 mg/kg/day as a single daily dose for 7 days/week or 6 mg/kg/day for 5 days/week

Alternate dosing (HHS [OI adult 2015]):

Peripheral lesions (alternative to preferred therapy): IV: Induction: 5 mg/kg/dose every 12 hours for 14 to 21 days followed by chronic maintenance (secondary prophylaxis)

Immediate sight-threatening lesions (adjacent to the optic nerve or fovea): Intravitreal injection (off-label route): Induction therapy: 2 mg of an extemporaneously prepared solution administered as intravitreal injections for 1 to 4 doses over a period of 7 to 10 days; administer with a concomitant systemically administered agent (oral valganciclovir preferred).

CMV disease prophylaxis in transplant patients: IV:

Manufacturer's labeling:

Induction therapy: 5 mg/kg/dose every 12 hours for 7 to 14 days

Maintenance therapy: 5 mg/kg/day as a single daily dose for 7 days/week or 6 mg/kg/day for 5 days/week; duration is dependent on clinical condition and degree of immunosuppression

Alternate dosing:

Hematopoietic cell transplant recipients (allogeneic): 5 mg/kg/dose every 12 hours for 5 to 7 days, then 5 mg/kg/dose every 24 hours until day 100 post-transplant (Tomblyn 2009).

Solid organ transplant recipients: 5 mg/kg/dose every 24 hours; duration of prophylaxis is dependent on type of transplant, as well as donor and recipient CMV serostatus (Kotton 2013).

CMV disease, chronic maintenance (secondary prophylaxis) in HIV-infected patients (off-label use; alternative to preferred therapy): IV: 5 mg/kg/dose 5 to 7 times weekly; continue until sustained CD4 count >100 cells/mm^3 in response to ART for 3 to 6 months; discontinue only after consultation with an ophthalmologist) (HHS [OI adult 2015]).

CMV disease, preemptive therapy (hematopoietic cell transplant recipients) (off-label use) (Tomblyn 2009): IV:

<100 days post-transplant: 5 mg/kg/dose every 12 hours for 7 days (autologous transplant) or 7 to 14 days (allogenic transplant), then 5 mg/kg/dose every 24 hours for 1 to 2 weeks or until the indicator test is negative (minimum total induction and maintenance treatment is 2 weeks when 14 days of twice daily is used and 3 weeks when a 7-day induction course is used).

>100 days post-transplant: 5 mg/kg/dose every 12 hours for 7 to 14 days, then 5 mg/kg/dose every 24 hours for 1 to 2 weeks or until the indicator test is negative.

CMV disease, treatment (solid organ transplant recipients) (off-label use): IV: 5 mg/kg/dose every 12 hours until 1 or 2 consecutive undetectable CMV viral load samples are obtained (minimum treatment course: 2 weeks) (Kotton 2013).

UL97 mutation for <5x ganciclovir EC50: 10 mg/kg/dose every 12 hours (Kotton 2013).

Ganciclovir-resistant strains: 5 mg/kg/dose every 24 hours in combination with daily foscarnet and monthly CMV hyperimmunoglobulin (Mylonakis 2002).

CMV esophagitis or colitis in HIV-infected patients (off-label use): IV: 5 mg/kg/dose every 12 hours, then change to oral valganciclovir therapy once oral therapy is tolerated; total duration of therapy: 21 to 42 days or until symptom resolution (HHS [OI adult 2015]).

CMV neurological disease in HIV-infected patients (off-label use): IV: 5 mg/kg/dose every 12 hours plus foscarnet until symptoms improve (HHS [OI adult 2015]).

Varicella-zoster: Acute retinal necrosis (ARN) in HIV-infected patients (off-label use): Intravitreal injection (off-label route): 2 mg of an extemporaneously prepared solution administered as an intravitreal injection twice weekly for 1 to 2 doses in combination with IV acyclovir for 10 to 14 days, followed by valacyclovir for 6 weeks (HHS [OI adult 2015]).

Varicella-zoster: Progressive outer retinal necrosis in HIV-infected patients (off-label use): IV: 5 mg/kg/dose every 12 hours (with or without IV foscarnet) **plus** intravitreal ganciclovir and/or intravitreal foscarnet (HHS [OI adult 2015]).

Pediatric

CMV retinitis:

Children: IV:

Induction therapy: 5 mg/kg/dose every 12 hours for 14 to 21 days followed by maintenance therapy

Maintenance therapy: 5 mg/kg/day as a single daily dose for 7 days/week or 6 mg/kg/day for 5 days/week

Adolescents: Refer to adult dosing.

CMV disease, chronic maintenance (secondary prophylaxis) in HIV-exposed/-infected patients (off-label use):

Infants and Children: IV: 5 mg/kg/dose daily (CDC 2009)

Adolescents (alternative to preferred therapy): Refer to adult dosing.

CMV disease, prophylaxis (secondary) in transplant patients: Children: IV: Refer to adult dosing.

CMV esophagitis or colitis in HIV-infected patients (off-label use): Adolescents: Refer to adult dosing.

CMV neurological disease in HIV-exposed/-infected patients (off-label use): Infants, Children, and Adolescents: IV: Refer to adult dosing.

Varicella-zoster: Acute retinal necrosis (ARN) in HIV-infected patients (off-label use): Adolescents: Refer to adult dosing.

Varicella-zoster: Progressive outer retinal necrosis in HIV-exposed/-infected patients (off-label use):

Infants and Children: IV: 5 mg/kg/dose every 12 hours plus systemic foscarnet and intravitreal ganciclovir or intravitreal foscarnet (CDC 2009)

Adolescents: Refer to adult dosing.

Renal Impairment Note: Renally adjusted dose recommendations are based on an induction dose of 5 mg/kg/dose every 12 hours and a maintenance dose of 5 mg/kg/dose every 24 hours.

IV (Induction):

CrCl ≥70 mL/minute: No dosage adjustment necessary.

CrCl 50 to 69 mL/minute: Administer 2.5 mg/kg/dose every 12 hours

CrCl 25 to 49 mL/minute: Administer 2.5 mg/kg/dose every 24 hours

CrCl 10 to 24 mL/minute: Administer 1.25 mg/kg/dose every 24 hours

CrCl <10 mL/minute: Administer 1.25 mg/kg/dose 3 times/week following hemodialysis.

IV (Maintenance):

CrCl ≥70 mL/minute: No dosage adjustment necessary.

CrCl 50 to 69 mL/minute: Administer 2.5 mg/kg/dose every 24 hours

CrCl 25 to 49 mL/minute: Administer 1.25 mg/kg/dose every 24 hours

CrCl 10 to 24 mL/minute: Administer 0.625 mg/kg/dose every 24 hours

CrCl <10 mL/minute: Administer 0.625 mg/kg/dose 3 times/week following hemodialysis.

Intermittent hemodialysis (IHD) (administer after hemodialysis on dialysis days): Dialyzable (50%): CMV Infection: IV: Induction: 1.25 mg/kg every 48 to 72 hours; Maintenance: 0.625 mg/kg every 48 to 72 hours. **Note:** Dosing dependent on the assumption of 3 times/week, complete IHD sessions (Heintz 2009).

Peritoneal dialysis (PD): Dose as for CrCl <10 mL/minute (Aronoff 2007).

Continuous renal replacement therapy (CRRT) (Heintz 2009; Trotman 2005): Drug clearance is highly dependent on the method of renal replacement, filter type, and flow rate. Appropriate dosing requires close monitoring of pharmacologic response, signs of adverse reactions due to drug accumulation, as well as drug concentrations in relation to target trough (if appropriate). The following are general recommendations only (based on dialysate flow/ultrafiltration rates of 1 to 2 L/hour and minimal residual renal function) and should not supersede clinical judgment: CMV Infection:

CVVH: IV: Induction: 2.5 mg/kg every 24 hours; Maintenance: 1.25 mg/kg every 24 hours

CVVHD/CVVHDF: IV: Induction: 2.5 mg/kg every 12 hours; Maintenance: 2.5 mg/kg every 24 hours

Hepatic Impairment There are no dosage adjustments provided in the manufacturer's labeling.

Mechanism of Action Ganciclovir is phosphorylated to a substrate which competitively inhibits the binding of deoxyguanosine triphosphate to DNA polymerase resulting in inhibition of viral DNA synthesis

Contraindications Hypersensitivity to ganciclovir, acyclovir, or any component of the formulation

Warnings/Precautions

[US Boxed Warning]: Granulocytopenia (neutropenia), anemia, and thrombocytopenia may occur. Neutropenia usually occurs during the first 1 to 2 weeks of treatment, but may occur at any time; counts generally recover within 3 to 7 days of treatment discontinuation. Use with caution in patients with preexisting hematologic abnormalities or with a history of hematologic abnormalities caused by other drugs, chemicals, or irradiation. Dosage adjustment or interruption of ganciclovir therapy may be necessary; do not administer to patients with an ANC <500 cells/mm^3 or platelet count <25,000 cells/mm^3. Use with caution in patients with renal impairment; dosage adjustment may be necessary. **[US Boxed Warning]: Animal studies have demonstrated carcinogenic and teratogenic effects, and inhibition of spermatogenesis.** Female patients should use effective contraception during therapy; male patients should use a barrier contraceptive during and for at least 90 days after therapy. Ensure patients are adequately hydrated. Avoid rapid infusion. Phlebitis and/or pain may occur at injection site despite adequate dilution; infuse solution into veins with adequate blood flow. **[US Boxed Warning]: Indicated only for treatment of CMV retinitis in the immunocompromised patient and CMV prevention in transplant patients at risk for CMV disease.** Potentially significant drug-drug interactions may exist, requiring dose or frequency adjustment, additional monitoring, and/or selection of alternative therapy.

Drug Interactions

Metabolism/Transport Effects None known.

Avoid Concomitant Use There are no known interactions where it is recommended to avoid concomitant use.

Increased Effect/Toxicity

Ganciclovir (Systemic) may increase the levels/effects of: Didanosine; Imipenem; Mycophenolate; Tenofovir Products; Zidovudine

The levels/effects of Ganciclovir (Systemic) may be increased by: Mycophenolate; Probenecid; Tenofovir Products

Decreased Effect There are no known significant interactions involving a decrease in effect.

Dietary Considerations Some products may contain sodium.

Pharmacodynamics/Kinetics

Half-life Elimination

Neonates 2 to 49 days of age: 2.4 hours

Children 9 months to 12 years: 2.4 ± 0.7 hours

Adults: Mean: IV: 3.5 ± 0.9 hours; Oral: 4.8 ± 0.9 hours; End-stage renal disease (ESRD): 10.7 ± 5.7 hours

Pregnancy Risk Factor C

Pregnancy Considerations [US Boxed Warning]: Animal studies have demonstrated carcinogenic and teratogenic effects, and inhibition of spermatogenesis. Female patients should use effective contraception during therapy; male patients should use a barrier contraceptive during and for at least 90 days after therapy.

Breastfeeding Considerations It is not known if ganciclovir is excreted in breast milk. Due to the potential for serious adverse reactions in the nursing infant, breastfeeding is not recommended by the manufacturer. In addition, in the United States, complete avoidance of breastfeeding by women who are also HIV-infected is recommended to decrease potential transmission of HIV (HHS [perinatal] 2016).

Dosage Forms

Solution Reconstituted, Intravenous:

Cytovene: 500 mg (1 ea)

Generic: 500 mg (1 ea)

Solution Reconstituted, Intravenous [preservative free]:

Generic: 500 mg (1 ea)

Ganirelix (ga ni REL ix)

Brand Names: Canada Orgalutran

Pharmacologic Category Gonadotropin Releasing Hormone Antagonist

Use Adjunct to controlled ovarian hyperstimulation: Inhibits premature luteinizing hormone (LH) surges in women undergoing controlled ovarian hyperstimulation.

Local Anesthetic/Vasoconstrictor Precautions No information available to require special precautions

Effects on Dental Treatment No significant effects or complications reported

Effects on Bleeding No information available to require special precautions

Adverse Reactions

1% to 10%:

Central nervous system: Headache (3%)

Endocrine & metabolic: Ovarian hyperstimulation syndrome (2%)

Gastrointestinal: Abdominal pain (1%), nausea (1%)

Genitourinary: Pelvic pain (5%), vaginal hemorrhage (2%)

Local: Injection site reaction (1%)

<1%, postmarketing, and/or case reports: Anaphylactoid reaction, hypersensitivity reaction

General Dosage Range SubQ: *Adults:* 250 mcg once daily

Mechanism of Action Competitively blocks the gonadotropin-release hormone receptors on the pituitary gonadotroph and transduction pathway. This suppresses gonadotropin secretion and luteinizing hormone secretion preventing ovulation until the follicles are of adequate size.

Pharmacodynamics/Kinetics

Duration of Action <48 hours

Half-life Elimination Single dose: 12.8 hours; Multiple dosing: 16.2 hours

Time to Peak 1.1 hours

Pregnancy Considerations Studies in animals have shown evidence of fetal abnormalities, including fetal resorption, and use is contraindicated in women who are pregnant. Fetal resorption is a result of hormonal alterations and could result in fetal loss in humans. Ganirelix is used to treat infertility; pregnancy should be ruled out prior to therapy.

Gatifloxacin (gat i FLOKS a sin)

Related Information

Bacterial Infections *on page 1835*

Brand Names: US Zymaxid

Brand Names: Canada Zymar

Generic Availability (US) Yes

Pharmacologic Category Antibiotic, Fluoroquinolone; Antibiotic, Ophthalmic

Use Conjunctivitis: Treatment of bacterial conjunctivitis caused by *Staphylococcus aureus*, *Staphylococcus epidermidis*, *Streptococcus mitis* group, *Streptococcus oralis*, *Streptococcus pneumoniae*, and *Haemophilus influenzae*.

Local Anesthetic/Vasoconstrictor Precautions No information available to require special precautions

Effects on Dental Treatment Key adverse event(s) related to dental treatment: Taste disturbance.

Effects on Bleeding No information available to require special precautions

Adverse Reactions

1% to 10%:

Central nervous system: Headache

Endocrine & metabolic: Chemosis

Gastrointestinal: Dysgeusia

Ophthalmic: Conjunctival hemorrhage, conjunctival irritation, conjunctivitis (worsening), decreased visual acuity, dry eye syndrome, eye discharge, eye irritation, eye pain, eye redness, eyelid edema, increased lacrimation, keratitis, papillary conjunctivitis

<1%, postmarketing, and/or case reports: Anaphylaxis, angioedema (including facial edema, oral edema, pharyngeal edema), blepharitis, blurred vision, dyspnea, eye pruritus, hypersensitivity reaction (including allergic dermatitis, eye allergy), nausea, pruritus (including skin rash), Stevens-Johnson syndrome, swelling of eye (including corneal edema, conjunctival edema), urticaria

Dosing

Adult & Geriatric

Bacterial conjunctivitis: Ophthalmic:

Zymar [Canadian product]:

Days 1 and 2: Instill 1 drop into affected eye(s) every 2 hours while awake (maximum: 8 times/day).

Days 3 to 7: Instill 1 drop into affected eye(s) 4 times/day while awake.

Zymaxid:

Day 1: Instill 1 drop into affected eye(s) every 2 hours while awake (maximum: 8 times/day).

Days 2 to 7: Instill 1 drop into affected eye(s) 2 to 4 times/day while awake.

Bacterial keratitis (off-label use): Ophthalmic: Instill 1 drop into affected eye(s) every 1 hour around the clock until healing begins (usually 48 to 72 hours); dosing frequency is then gradually reduced until the ulcer is completely healed, at which point, treatment can be discontinued (Parmar 2006; Shah 2010). One suggested tapering regimen is as follows: Days 3 to 6: Instill 1 drop into affected eye(s) every 2 hours around the clock; Days 7 to 9: Instill 1 drop into affected eye(s) every 2 hours while awake; Day 9 and on: Instill 1 drop into affected eye(s) every 6 hours and continue at this frequency until complete healing of ulcer (Shah 2010). **Note:** For central or severe keratitis, a loading dose of instillation every 5 to 15 minutes for the first 30 to 60 minutes may be considered (AAO 2013).

Pediatric Bacterial conjunctivitis: Children ≥1 year and Adolescents: Ophthalmic: Refer to adult dosing.

Renal Impairment There are no dosage adjustments provided in the manufacturer's labeling. However, dosage adjustment unlikely due to low systemic absorption.

Hepatic Impairment There are no dosage adjustments provided in the manufacturer's labeling. However, dosage adjustment unlikely due to low systemic absorption.

Mechanism of Action Gatifloxacin is a DNA gyrase inhibitor, and also inhibits topoisomerase IV. DNA gyrase (topoisomerase II) is an essential bacterial enzyme that maintains the superhelical structure of DNA. DNA gyrase is required for DNA replication and transcription, DNA repair, recombination, and transposition; inhibition is bactericidal.

Contraindications Hypersensitivity to gatifloxacin, other quinolones, or any component of the formulation

Warnings/Precautions Hypersensitivity reactions, including anaphylactic reactions, angioedema (including pharyngeal, laryngeal, or facial edema), dyspnea, urticaria, and itching, have been reported (even following a single dose) with topical ophthalmic gatifloxacin. Rare cases of Stevens-Johnson syndrome were also reported. If an allergic reaction occurs, discontinue use. Prolonged use may result in fungal or bacterial superinfection. If superinfection is suspected, institute appropriate alternative therapy. For topical ophthalmic use only. Do not inject ophthalmic solution subconjunctivally or introduce directly into the anterior chamber of the eye (may cause corneal endothelial cell injury). Contact lenses should not be worn during treatment of ophthalmic infections.

Drug Interactions

Metabolism/Transport Effects None known.

Avoid Concomitant Use There are no known interactions where it is recommended to avoid concomitant use.

Increased Effect/Toxicity There are no known significant interactions involving an increase in effect.

Decreased Effect There are no known significant interactions involving a decrease in effect.

Pregnancy Considerations Systemic concentrations of gatifloxacin following ophthalmic administration are below the limit of quantification. If ophthalmic agents are needed during pregnancy, the minimum effective dose should be used in combination with punctual occlusion for 3 to 5 minutes after application to decrease potential exposure to the fetus (Samples 1988).

Breastfeeding Considerations It is not known if gatifloxacin is excreted in breast milk. According to the manufacturer, the decision to continue or discontinue breastfeeding during therapy should take into account the risk of infant exposure, the benefits of breastfeeding to the infant, and benefits of treatment to the mother.

Dosage Forms

Solution, Ophthalmic:

Zymaxid: 0.5% (2.5 mL)

Generic: 0.5% (2.5 mL)

Dosage Forms: Canada

Solution, ophthalmic [drops]:

Zymar: 0.3% (1 mL, 2.5 mL, 5 mL)

Gefitinib (ge FI tye nib)

Brand Names: US Iressa

Brand Names: Canada IRESSA

Pharmacologic Category Antineoplastic Agent, Epidermal Growth Factor Receptor (EGFR) Inhibitor; Antineoplastic Agent, Tyrosine Kinase Inhibitor

Use

Non-small cell lung cancer:

US labeling: First-line treatment of metastatic non-small cell lung cancer (NSCLC) in tumors with epidermal growth factor receptor (EGFR) exon 19 deletions or exon 21 (L858R) substitution mutations as detected by an approved test.

Limitation of use: Safety and efficacy have not been established in patients with metastatic NSCLC whose tumors have EGFR mutations other than exon 19 deletions or exon 21 (L858R) substitution mutations

Canadian labeling: First-line treatment of locally advanced (nonresponsive to curative therapy) or metastatic NSCLC with activating mutations of the epidermal growth factor receptor tyrosine kinase (EGFR-TK).

Local Anesthetic/Vasoconstrictor Precautions No information available to require special precautions

Effects on Dental Treatment Key adverse event(s) related to dental treatment: Mouth ulceration.

Effects on Bleeding Bleeding has been reported in <1% of patients, but can be serious.

Adverse Reactions

>10%:

Central nervous system: Insomnia (15%), fatigue (14%)

Dermatologic: Dermatological reaction (47% to 58%), skin rash (52%), xeroderma (24%), pruritus (18%), paronychia (14%), acne vulgaris (11%), alopecia (5% to 11%)

Gastrointestinal: Diarrhea (29% to 47%; grades 3/4: 3%), anorexia (19% to 20%), nausea (17% to 18%), decreased appetite (17%), vomiting (13% to 14%), stomatitis (7% to 13%), constipation (12%)

Genitourinary: Proteinuria (8% to 35%)

Hepatic: Increased serum AST (8% to 40%; grades 3/4: 2% to 3%), increased serum ALT (11% to 38%; grades 3/4: 2% to 5%)

Neuromuscular & skeletal: Weakness (18%)

1% to 10%:

Central nervous system: Hypoesthesia (4%), peripheral sensory neuropathy (4%), peripheral neuropathy (2%)

Dermatologic: Nail disease (5% to 8%), acneiform eruption (6%)

Endocrine & metabolic: Dehydration (2%; secondary to diarrhea, nausea, vomiting, or anorexia)

Gastrointestinal: Xerostomia (2%)

Genitourinary: Cystitis (1%)

Hematologic & oncologic: Anemia (7%), pulmonary hemorrhage (4% to 5%), hemorrhage (4%; including epistaxis, hematuria), neutropenia (3%), leukopenia (2%), thrombocytopenia (1%)

Hepatic: Increased serum bilirubin (3%; grades 3/4: <1%)

Neuromuscular & skeletal: Myalgia (8%), arthralgia (6%)

Ophthalmic: Eye disease (6% to 7%; grades 3/4: <1%; including conjunctivitis, blepharitis, and dry eye)

Renal: Increased serum creatinine (2%)

Respiratory: Cough (9%), interstitial pulmonary disease (1%; grades 3/4: 3%)

Miscellaneous: Fever (9%)

<1%, postmarketing, and/or case reports: Angioedema, bullous skin disease, corneal erosion (reversible; may be associated with aberrant eyelash growth), decreased white blood cell count, erythema multiforme, fulminant hepatitis, gastrointestinal perforation, hemorrhagic cystitis, hepatic failure, hepatitis, hypersensitivity angiitis, hypersensitivity reaction, keratitis, keratoconjunctivitis sicca, pancreatitis, renal failure, skin fissure, Stevens-Johnson syndrome, toxic epidermal necrolysis, urticaria

General Dosage Range Dosage adjustment recommended for patients who develop toxicities or are on concomitant therapy.

Oral: *Adults:* 250 mg once daily.

Mechanism of Action Gefitinib is a tyrosine kinase inhibitor (TKI) which reversibly inhibits kinase activity of wild-type and select activation mutations of epidermal growth factor receptor (EGFR). EGFR is expressed on cell surfaces of normal and cancer cells and has a role in cell growth and proliferation. Gefitinib prevents autophosphorylation of tyrosine residues associated with the EGFR receptor, which blocks downstream signaling and EGFR-dependent proliferation. Gefitinib has a higher binding affinity for EGFR exon 19 deletion and exon 21 (L858R) substitution mutation than for wild-type EGFR.

Pharmacodynamics/Kinetics

Half-life Elimination Oral: 41 hours

Time to Peak Plasma: Oral: 3 to 7 hours

Pregnancy Considerations Adverse events have been observed in animal reproduction studies. Gefitinib may cause fetal harm when administered to a pregnant woman. Women of reproductive potential should use effective contraception during and for at least 2 weeks following gefitinib treatment.

Gelatin (Absorbable) (JEL a tin, ab SORB a ble)

Related Information

Antiplatelet and Anticoagulation Considerations in Dentistry *on page 1764*

Brand Names: US Gelfilm; Gelfoam; Gelfoam Compressed Size 100; Gelfoam Dental Pack Size 4; Gelfoam Sponge; Gelfoam Sponge Size 100; Gelfoam Sponge Size 200; Gelfoam Sponge Size 50

Generic Availability (US) No

Pharmacologic Category Hemostatic Agent

Dental Use Adjunct to provide hemostasis in oral and dental surgery

Use Adjunct to provide hemostasis in surgical procedures; adjunct in neuro, thoracic, or ocular surgeries to promote tissue repair and/or prevent adhesions (Gelfilm®)

Local Anesthetic/Vasoconstrictor Precautions No information available to require special precautions

Effects on Dental Treatment Key adverse event(s) related to dental treatment: Local infection and abscess formation.

Effects on Bleeding Used as adjunct to enhance hemostasis.

Adverse Reactions Cardiopulmonary bypass surgery (Gelfoam):

>10%: Cardiovascular: Atrial fibrillation (13%)

1% to 10%:

Cardiovascular: Cardiac failure (4%), atrial flutter (2%), peripheral vascular disease (2%), ventricular tachycardia (2%), heart block (1%)

Infection: Wound infection (6%)

Respiratory: Pneumothorax (2%), respiratory failure (2%)

Miscellaneous: Fever (1%)

Frequency not defined (Gelfoam was used in cited surgical procedures):

Central nervous system: Arachnoiditis (laminectomy operations), brain compression (brain implant surgery), cauda equina syndrome (laminectomy operations), giant cell granuloma in the brain (brain implant surgery), headache (laminectomy operations), meningitis (laminectomy operations), pain (laminectomy operations), paresthesia (laminectomy operations), spinal cord compression (brain implant surgery)

Gastrointestinal: Intestinal disease (laminectomy operations)

Genitourinary: Bladder dysfunction (laminectomy operations), impotence (laminectomy operations)

Hematologic & oncologic: Hematoma

Infection: Abscess, localized infection, toxic shock syndrome (nasal surgery)

Local: Localized edema (encapsulation of fluid)

Neuromuscular & skeletal: Prolonged fixation of tendon (tendon repair), spinal stenosis (laminectomy operations)

Otic: Hearing loss (tympanoplasty)

Miscellaneous: Fever, fibrosis (tendon repair), foreign body reaction, treatment failure (tympanoplasty; failure of absorption)

Dosing

Adult & Geriatric

Hemostasis (Gelfoam®): Note: Use minimum amount of product necessary to produce hemostasis; once hemostasis attained, excess product should be removed.

Dental sponge: Insert rolled sponge (dry or wet) into cavity or socket; apply light finger pressure for 1-2 minutes

Sponge: Apply appropriate size (dry or wet) with moderate pressure directly to bleeding site until bleeding stops; if first application does not stop bleeding, additional applications may be used with a new sponge

Powder: Apply paste to bleeding surface; remove excess paste when bleeding has stopped. Consult manufacturer's labeling for additional information.

Neurosurgery, thoracic, or ocular surgery (Gelfilm®): Use as directed per manufacturer's labeling.

Pediatric Refer to adult dosing.

Mechanism of Action Arrests bleeding by forming artificial clot and producing mechanical matrix which facilitates clotting

Contraindications

Gelfilm®: There are no contraindications listed in the manufacturer's labeling.

Gelfoam®: Hypersensitivity to porcine collagen; intravascular placement (embolus risk); closure of skin incisions (interferes with healing)

Warnings/Precautions Do not sterilize by heat; do not use in the presence of infection

Drug Interactions

Metabolism/Transport Effects None known.

Avoid Concomitant Use There are no known interactions where it is recommended to avoid concomitant use.

Increased Effect/Toxicity There are no known significant interactions involving an increase in effect.

Decreased Effect There are no known significant interactions involving a decrease in effect.

Pregnancy Considerations When administered topically, gelatin is completely absorbed; however, the amount of gelatin available systemically following topical application is unknown.

Dosage Forms

Film, External:

Gelfilm: (1 ea)

Film, Ophthalmic:

Gelfilm: (6 ea)

Miscellaneous, External:

Gelfoam Compressed Size 100: (6 ea)

Gelfoam Dental Pack Size 4: (2 ea)

Gelfoam Sponge: 12-7 MM (12 ea)

Gelfoam Sponge Size 50: (4 ea)

Gelfoam Sponge Size 100: (6 ea)

Gelfoam Sponge Size 200: (6 ea)

Powder, Mouth/Throat:

Gelfoam: (1 g)

Gemcitabine (jem SITE a been)

Brand Names: US Gemzar

Brand Names: Canada Gemcitabine For Injection; Gemcitabine For Injection Concentrate; Gemcitabine For Injection, USP; Gemcitabine Hydrochloride For Injection; Gemcitabine Injection; Gemcitabine Sun For Injection; Gemzar

Pharmacologic Category Antineoplastic Agent, Antimetabolite; Antineoplastic Agent, Antimetabolite (Pyrimidine Analog)

Use

Breast cancer: First-line treatment of metastatic breast cancer (in combination with paclitaxel) after failure of adjuvant chemotherapy which contained an anthracycline (unless contraindicated)

Non-small cell lung cancer (NSCLC): First-line treatment of inoperable, locally-advanced (stage IIIA or IIIB) or metastatic (stage IV) NSCLC (in combination with cisplatin)

Ovarian cancer: Treatment of advanced ovarian cancer (in combination with carboplatin) that has relapsed at least 6 months following completion of platinum-based chemotherapy

Pancreatic cancer: First-line treatment of locally-advanced (nonresectable stage II or III) or metastatic (stage IV) pancreatic adenocarcinoma

Local Anesthetic/Vasoconstrictor Precautions No information available to require special precautions

Effects on Dental Treatment Key adverse event(s) related to dental treatment: Stomatitis.

Effects on Bleeding Bleeding occurs in 2% to 17% of patients. Anemia (68% to 73%) and thrombocytopenia

(24% to 36%) frequently occur. Medical consult is recommended.

Adverse Reactions Frequency of adverse reactions reported for single-agent use of gemcitabine only; bone marrow depression is the dose-limiting toxicity.

>10%:

Cardiovascular: Peripheral edema (20%), edema (13%)

Central nervous system: Drowsiness (11%)

Dermatologic: Skin rash (30%), alopecia (15%)

Gastrointestinal: Nausea and vomiting (69%), diarrhea (19%), stomatitis (11%)

Genitourinary: Proteinuria (45%), hematuria (35%)

Hematologic & oncologic: Anemia (68%; grade 3: 7%; grade 4: 1%), neutropenia (63%; grade 3: 19%; grade 4: 6%), thrombocytopenia (24%; grade 3: 4%; grade 4: 1%), hemorrhage (17%; grade 3: <1%; grade 4: <1%)

Hepatic: Increased serum ALT (68%; grade 3: 8%, grade 4: 2%), increased serum AST (67%; grade 3: 6%; grade 4: 2%), increased serum alkaline phosphatase (55%; grade 3: 7%; grade 4: 2%), increased serum bilirubin (13%; grade 3: 2%, grade 4: <1%)

Infection: Infection (16%)

Renal: Increased blood urea nitrogen (16%)

Respiratory: Dyspnea (23%; grade 3: 3%; grade 4: <1%), flu-like symptoms (19%)

Miscellaneous: Fever (41%)

1% to 10%:

Central nervous system: Paresthesia (10%; grade 3: <1%)

Local: Injection site reaction (4%)

Renal: Increased serum creatinine (8%)

Respiratory: Bronchospasm (<2%)

<1%, postmarketing, and/or case reports (reported with single-agent use or with combination therapy): Adult respiratory distress syndrome, anaphylactoid reaction, anorexia, arthralgia, bullous skin disease, capillary leak syndrome, cardiac arrhythmia, cardiac failure, cellulitis, cerebrovascular accident (Kuenen 2002), constipation, desquamation, digital vasculitis, gangrene of skin or other tissue, hemolytic-uremic syndrome, hepatic failure, hepatic veno-occlusive disease, hepatotoxicity (rare), hyperglycemia, hypertension, hypocalcemia, hypotension, increased gamma-glutamyl transferase, interstitial pneumonitis, myocardial infarction, neuropathy, petechiae (Nishijima 2013; Zupancic 2007), pruritus (Curtis 2014), pulmonary edema, pulmonary fibrosis, radiation recall phenomenon, renal failure, respiratory failure, reversible posterior leukoencephalopathy syndrome, sepsis, supraventricular cardiac arrhythmia, thrombotic thrombocytopenic purpura (Nishijima 2013; Zupancic 2007)

General Dosage Range Dosage adjustment recommended in patients with hepatic impairment or who develop toxicities

IV: *Adults:* Dosage varies greatly depending on indication

Mechanism of Action A pyrimidine antimetabolite that inhibits DNA synthesis by inhibition of DNA polymerase and ribonucleotide reductase, cell cycle-specific for the S-phase of the cycle (also blocks cellular progression at G1/S-phase). Gemcitabine is phosphorylated intracellularly by deoxycytidine kinase to gemcitabine monophosphate, which is further phosphorylated to active metabolites gemcitabine diphosphate and gemcitabine triphosphate. Gemcitabine diphosphate inhibits DNA synthesis by inhibiting ribonucleotide reductase; gemcitabine triphosphate incorporates into DNA and inhibits DNA polymerase.

Pharmacodynamics/Kinetics

Half-life Elimination

Gemcitabine: Infusion time ≤70 minutes: 42 to 94 minutes; infusion time 3 to 4 hours: 4 to 10.5 hours (affected by age and gender)

Metabolite (gemcitabine triphosphate), terminal phase: 1.7 to 19.4 hours

Time to Peak 30 minutes after completion of infusion

Pregnancy Risk Factor D

Pregnancy Considerations Adverse events were observed in animal reproduction studies. May cause fetal harm if administered during pregnancy; adverse effects in reproduction are anticipated based on the mechanism of action.

Gemfibrozil (jem FI broe zil)

Related Information

Cardiovascular Diseases *on page 1752*

Brand Names: US Lopid

Brand Names: Canada Apo-Gemfibrozil; Dom-Gemfibrozil; Mylan-Gemfibrozil; Novo-Gemfibrozil; PHL-Gemfibrozil; PMS-Gemfibrozil; Teva-Gemfibrozil

Pharmacologic Category Antilipemic Agent, Fibric Acid

Use Treatment of hypertriglyceridemia in Fredrickson types IV and V hyperlipidemia for patients who are at greater risk for pancreatitis and who have not responded to dietary intervention; to reduce the risk of CHD development in Fredrickson type IIb patients without a history or symptoms of existing CHD who have not responded to dietary and other interventions (including pharmacologic treatment) and who have decreased HDL, increased LDL, and increased triglycerides

Local Anesthetic/Vasoconstrictor Precautions No information available to require special precautions

Effects on Dental Treatment No significant effects or complications reported

Effects on Bleeding Anemia has been reported in <1% of patients.

Adverse Reactions

>10%: Gastrointestinal: Dyspepsia (20%)

1% to 10%:

Cardiovascular: Atrial fibrillation (1%)

Central nervous system: Fatigue (4%), vertigo (2%)

Dermatologic: Eczema (2%), skin rash (2%)

Gastrointestinal: Abdominal pain (10%), nausea and vomiting (3%)

<1%, postmarketing and/or case reports (probable causation): Anemia, angioedema, arthralgia, blurred vision, bone marrow depression, cholecystitis, cholelithiasis, cholestatic jaundice, decreased libido, depression, dermatitis, dermatomyositis, dizziness, drowsiness, dysgeusia, eosinophilia, exfoliative dermatitis, headache, hypoesthesia, hypokalemia, impotence, increased creatine phosphokinase, increased serum alkaline phosphatase, increased serum bilirubin, increased serum transaminases, laryngeal edema, leukopenia, limb pain, myalgia, myasthenia, myopathy, nephrotoxicity, paresthesia, peripheral neuritis, polymyositis, pruritus, Raynaud phenomenon, rhabdomyolysis, synovitis, urticaria

Reports where causal relationship has not been established: Alopecia, anaphylaxis, cataract, colitis, confusion, extrasystoles, hepatic neoplasm, intracranial hemorrhage, lupus-like syndrome, pancreatitis, peripheral vascular disease, positive ANA titer, reduced fertility (male), renal insufficiency, retinal edema, seizure, skin photosensitivity, syncope, thrombocytopenia, vasculitis, weight loss

General Dosage Range Oral: *Adults:* 600 mg twice daily

Mechanism of Action The exact mechanism of action of gemfibrozil is unknown, however, several theories exist regarding the VLDL effect; it can inhibit lipolysis and decrease subsequent hepatic fatty acid uptake as well as inhibit hepatic secretion of VLDL; together these actions decrease serum VLDL levels; increases HDL-cholesterol; the mechanism behind HDL elevation is currently unknown

Pharmacodynamics/Kinetics

Onset of Action May require several days

Half-life Elimination 1.5 hours

Time to Peak Serum: 1 to 2 hours

Pregnancy Risk Factor C

Pregnancy Considerations Adverse events have been observed in animal reproduction studies. The Canadian product labeling specifically contraindicates use during pregnancy and recommends gemfibrozil be discontinued several months prior to conception.

Gemifloxacin (je mi FLOKS a sin)

Related Information

Bacterial Infections *on page 1835*

Clinical Risk Related to Drugs Prolonging QT Interval *on page 1772*

Brand Names: US Factive

Brand Names: Canada Factive

Generic Availability (US) No

Pharmacologic Category Antibiotic, Fluoroquinolone; Antibiotic, Respiratory Fluoroquinolone

Use Treatment of acute exacerbation of chronic bronchitis (in patients who have no other treatment options); treatment of community-acquired pneumonia (CAP), including pneumonia caused by multidrug-resistant strains of *S. pneumoniae* (MDRSP)

Local Anesthetic/Vasoconstrictor Precautions Gemifloxacin is one of the drugs confirmed to prolong the QT interval and is accepted as having a risk of causing torsade de pointes. The risk of drug-induced torsade de pointes is extremely low when a single QT interval prolonging drug is prescribed. In terms of epinephrine, it is not known what effect vasoconstrictors in the local anesthetic regimen will have in patients with a known history of congenital prolonged QT interval or in patients taking any medication that prolongs the QT interval. Until more information is obtained, it is suggested that the clinician consult with the physician prior to the use of a vasoconstrictor in suspected patients, and that the vasoconstrictor (epinephrine, mepivacaine and levonordefrin [Carbocaine® 2% with Neo-Cobefrin®]) be used with caution.

Effects on Dental Treatment No significant effects or complications reported

Effects on Bleeding No information available to require special precautions

Adverse Reactions

1% to 10%:

Central nervous system: Headache (4%), dizziness (2%)

Dermatologic: Skin rash (<1% to 5%)

Gastrointestinal: Diarrhea (5%), nausea (4%), abdominal pain (2%), vomiting (2%)

Hematologic: Change in neutrophil count (neutropenia/neutrophilia; 1%), increased platelets (1%), thrombocythemia (1%)

Hepatic: Increased serum transaminases (1% to 4%), increased gamma-glutamyl transferase (1%)

Neuromuscular & skeletal: Increased CPK (1%)

<1%, postmarketing and/or case reports: Acute renal failure, anaphylaxis, anemia, anorexia, antibiotic-associated colitis, arthralgia, back pain, candidiasis, constipation, decreased hematocrit, decreased hemoglobin, dermatitis, drowsiness, dysgeusia, dyspepsia, dyspnea, eczema, eosinophilia, erythema multiforme, exacerbation of myasthenia gravis, exfoliation of skin, facial edema, fatigue, flatulence, flushing, fungal infection, gastritis, gastroenteritis, genital candidiasis, granulocytopenia, hemorrhage, hepatotoxicity (idiosyncratic) (Chalasani, 2014), hot flash, hypercalcemia, hyperglycemia, hyperkalemia, hypernatremia, hypoalbuminemia, hypocalcemia, hypokalemia, hyponatremia, increased blood urea nitrogen, increased hematocrit, increased hemoglobin, increased INR, increased intracranial pressure, increased serum alkaline phosphatase, increased serum bilirubin, increased serum creatinine, insomnia, leukopenia, muscle cramps (leg), myalgia, nervousness, pain, peripheral edema, peripheral neuropathy, pharyngitis, pneumonia, prolonged Q-T interval on ECG, pruritus, pseudomembranous colitis, pseudotumor cerebri, retinal hemorrhage, rupture of tendon, skin photosensitivity, supraventricular tachycardia, syncope, tendonitis, thrombocytopenia, transient ischemic attacks, tremor, urticaria, uveitis, vaginitis, vertigo, visual disturbance, weakness, xerostomia

Dosing

Adult & Geriatric

Susceptible infections: Oral: 320 mg once daily

Acute exacerbations of chronic bronchitis: Oral: 320 mg once daily for 5 days

Community-acquired pneumonia (mild-to-moderate): Oral: 320 mg once daily for 5 or 7 days (decision to use 5- or 7-day regimen should be guided by initial sputum culture; 7 days are recommended for MDRSP, *Klebsiella*, or *M. catarrhalis* infection)

Gonococcal, uncomplicated urogenital infections (alternative therapy in patients with cephalosporin allergy, off-label use): Oral: 320 mg as a single dose in combination with oral azithromycin (CDC [Workowski 2015]; Kirkcaldy 2014)

Renal Impairment

CrCl >40 mL/minute: No dosage adjustment necessary.

CrCl ≤40 mL/minute (or patients on hemodialysis/CAPD): 160 mg once daily (administer dose following hemodialysis).

Hepatic Impairment No dosage adjustment necessary.

Mechanism of Action Gemifloxacin is a DNA gyrase inhibitor and also inhibits topoisomerase IV. DNA gyrase (topoisomerase IV) is an essential bacterial enzyme that maintains the superhelical structure of DNA. DNA gyrase is required for DNA replication and transcription, DNA repair, recombination, and transposition; bactericidal

Contraindications Hypersensitivity to gemifloxacin, other fluoroquinolones, or any component of the formulation

Warnings/Precautions [US Boxed Warning]: Fluoroquinolones are associated with disabling and potentially irreversible serious adverse reactions

that may occur together, including tendinitis and tendon rupture, peripheral neuropathy, and CNS effects. Discontinue gemifloxacin immediately and avoid use of fluoroquinolones in patients who experience any of these serious adverse reactions. Patients of any age or without pre-existing risk factors have experienced these reactions; may occur within hours to weeks after initiation. Fluoroquinolones have been associated with an increased risk of f tendonitis and tendon rupture in all ages; risk may be increased with concurrent corticosteroids, solid organ transplant recipients, and in patients >60 years of age, but has also occurred in patients without these risk factors. Rupture of the Achilles tendon has been reported most frequently; but other tendon sites (eg, rotator cuff, biceps, hand) have also been reported. Inflammation and rupture may occur bilaterally. Cases have been reported within hours or days of initiation, and up to several months after discontinuation of therapy. Strenuous physical activity, renal failure, and previous tendon disorders may be independent risk factor for tendon rupture. Discontinue at first sign of tendon pain, swelling, inflammation or rupture. Avoid use in patients with a history of tendon disorders or who have experienced tendinitis or tendon rupture. Use with caution in patients with rheumatoid arthritis; may increase risk of tendon rupture. Fluoroquinolones have been associated with an increased risk of CNS effects including seizures, increased intracranial pressure (including pseudotumor cerebri), and toxic psychosis; may also cause nervousness, agitation, insomnia, anxiety, nightmares, paranoia, dizziness, confusion, tremors, hallucinations, depression, and suicidal thoughts or actions. May occur following the first dose; discontinue immediately and avoid further use of fluoroquinolones in patients who experience these reactions. Use with caution in patients with known or suspected CNS disorder, or risk factors that may predispose to seizures or lower the seizure threshold. Fluoroquinolones have been associated with an increased risk of peripheral neuropathy; may occur soon after initiation of therapy and may be irreversible; discontinue if symptoms of sensory or sensorimotor neuropathy occur.

Avoid use in patients who have previously experienced peripheral neuropathy. **[US Boxed Warning]: Reserve use of gemifloxacin for treatment of acute bacterial exacerbation of chronic bronchitis for patients who have no alternative treatment options because of the risk of disabling and potentially serious adverse reactions (eg, tendinitis and tendon rupture, peripheral neuropathy, CNS effects).**

Fluoroquinolones may prolong QTc interval; avoid use of gemifloxacin in patients with a history of QTc prolongation, uncorrected hypokalemia, hypomagnesemia, or concurrent administration of other medications known to prolong the QT interval (including Class Ia and Class III antiarrhythmics, cisapride, erythromycin, antipsychotics, and tricyclic antidepressants). Use with caution in patients with significant bradycardia or acute myocardial ischemia. Use caution in renal dysfunction; dosage adjustment required for CrCl ≤40 mL/minute. Use with caution in elderly patients; adverse effects (eg, tendon rupture, QT changes) may be increased.

Fluoroquinolones have been associated with the development of serious, and sometimes fatal, hypoglycemia, most often in elderly diabetics, but also in patients without diabetes. Prompt identification and treatment of hypoglycemia is essential. Individual quinolones may differ in their potential to cause this effect. It was most evident with gatifloxacin (no longer marketed as s systemic formulation). Hyperglycemia has also been associated with the use of fluoroquinolones. Patients should be monitored closely for signs/symptoms of disordered glucose regulation.

Severe hypersensitivity reactions, including anaphylaxis, have occurred with quinolone therapy. Reactions may present as typical allergic symptoms after a single dose, or may manifest as severe idiosyncratic dermatologic, vascular, pulmonary, renal, hepatic, and/or hematologic events, usually after multiple doses. May cause maculopapular rash, usually 8 to 10 days after treatment initiation; risk factors may include age <40 years, female gender (including postmenopausal women on HRT), and treatment duration >7 days. Prompt discontinuation of drug should occur if skin rash or other symptoms arise. **[US Boxed Warning]: Quinolones may exacerbate myasthenia gravis; avoid use in patients with a known history of myasthenia gravis.** Cases of severe exacerbations, including the need for ventilatory support and deaths have been reported. Avoid excessive sunlight and take precautions to limit exposure (eg, loose fitting clothing, sunscreen); may cause moderate-to-severe phototoxicity reactions. Discontinue use if photosensitivity occurs. Prolonged use may result in fungal or bacterial superinfection, including *C. difficile*-associated diarrhea (CDAD) and pseudomembranous colitis; CDAD has been observed >2 months postantibiotic treatment. Hemolytic reactions may (rarely) occur with quinolone use in patients with latent or actual G6PD deficiency. Potentially significant drug-drug interactions may exist, requiring dose or frequency adjustment, additional monitoring, and/or selection of alternative therapy.

Drug Interactions

Metabolism/Transport Effects None known.

Avoid Concomitant Use

Avoid concomitant use of Gemifloxacin with any of the following: BCG (Intravesical); Cholera Vaccine; Highest Risk QTc-Prolonging Agents; Hydroxychloroquine; Ivabradine; MiFEPRIStone; Nadifloxacin; Probucol; Promazine; Strontium Ranelate; Vinflunine

Increased Effect/Toxicity

Gemifloxacin may increase the levels/effects of: Aminolevulinic Acid; Blood Glucose Lowering Agents; Delamanid; Heroin; Highest Risk QTc-Prolonging Agents; Moderate Risk QTc-Prolonging Agents; Porfimer; Varenicline; Verteporfin; Vitamin K Antagonists

The levels/effects of Gemifloxacin may be increased by: Corticosteroids (Systemic); Hydroxychloroquine; Ivabradine; MiFEPRIStone; Nadifloxacin; Nonsteroidal Anti-Inflammatory Agents; Probenecid; Probucol; Promazine; QTc-Prolonging Agents (Indeterminate Risk and Risk Modifying); Vinflunine

Decreased Effect

Gemifloxacin may decrease the levels/effects of: BCG (Intravesical); BCG Vaccine (Immunization); Blood Glucose Lowering Agents; Cholera Vaccine; Didanosine; Lactobacillus and Estriol; Mycophenolate; Sodium Picosulfate; Typhoid Vaccine

The levels/effects of Gemifloxacin may be decreased by: Antacids; Calcium Salts; Didanosine; Iron Salts; Magnesium Salts; Multivitamins/Minerals (with ADEK, Folate, Iron); Multivitamins/Minerals (with AE, No Iron); Quinapril; Sevelamer; Strontium Ranelate; Sucralfate; Zinc Salts

Dietary Considerations May take tablets with or without food, milk, or calcium supplements. Do not administer supplements (including multivitamins) containing iron, zinc, or magnesium within 3 hours before or 2 hours after gemifloxacin.

Pharmacodynamics/Kinetics

Half-life Elimination 7 hours (range 4-12 hours)

Time to Peak Plasma: 0.5-2 hours

Pregnancy Risk Factor C

Pregnancy Considerations Adverse events have been observed in some animal reproduction studies. Information specific to gemifloxacin use in pregnancy has not been located.

Breastfeeding Considerations It is not known if gemifloxacin is excreted in breast milk. breastfeeding is not recommended by the manufacturer.

Dosage Forms

Tablet, Oral:

Factive: 320 mg

Dental Comment See Local Anesthetic/Vasoconstrictor Precautions

Gemtuzumab Ozogamicin

(gem TOO zoo mab oh zog a MY sin)

Pharmacologic Category Antineoplastic Agent, Anti-CD33; Antineoplastic Agent, Antibody Drug Conjugate; Antineoplastic Agent, Monoclonal Antibody

Use Acute myeloid leukemia: Due to safety concerns, as well as lack of clinical benefit demonstrated in a post-approval clinical trial, gemtuzumab was withdrawn from the US commercial market in 2010.

Local Anesthetic/Vasoconstrictor Precautions No information available to require special precautions

Effects on Dental Treatment Key adverse event(s) related to dental treatment: Mucositis and stomatitis have been reported

Effects on Bleeding Bleeding reported in 13% of patients with gum hemorrhage reported in 9%. Bone marrow suppression with anemia and thrombocytopenia are common. Recovery of platelets may be delayed. Medical consult recommended.

Adverse Reactions Frequency not defined.

Cardiovascular: Hepatic veno-occlusive disease (sinusoidal obstruction syndrome [SOS]; higher frequency in patients with prior history of or subsequent hematopoietic stem cell transplant), hypertension, hypotension, peripheral edema, tachycardia

Central nervous system: Anxiety, cerebral hemorrhage, chills, depression, dizziness, headache, insomnia, intracranial hemorrhage, pain

Dermatologic: Pruritus, skin rash

Endocrine & metabolic: Hyperglycemia, hypocalcemia, hypokalemia, hypomagnesemia, hypophosphatemia, increased lactate dehydrogenase

Gastrointestinal: Abdominal pain, anorexia, diarrhea, dyspepsia, gingival hemorrhage, melena, mucositis, nausea, stomatitis, vomiting

Genitourinary: Hematuria, vaginal hemorrhage

Hematologic & oncologic: Anemia, bruise, disseminated intravascular coagulation (DIC), febrile neutropenia, hemorrhage, leukopenia, lymphocytopenia, neutropenia (median recovery: 40 to 51 days), petechia, prolonged partial thromboplastin time, prolonged prothrombin time, thrombocytopenia (median recovery: 36 to 51 days)

Hepatic: Ascites, hyperbilirubinemia, increased serum alkaline phosphatase, increased serum ALT, increased serum AST

Infection: Herpes simplex infection, infection, sepsis

Local: Injection site reaction

Neuromuscular & skeletal: Arthralgia, back pain, myalgia, weakness

Renal: Increased serum creatinine

Respiratory: Cough, dyspnea, epistaxis, hypoxia, pharyngitis, pneumonia, rhinitis

Miscellaneous: Fever, infusion-related reaction

<1%, postmarketing, and/or case reports: Acute respiratory distress, anaphylaxis, bradycardia, Budd-Chiari syndrome, gastrointestinal hemorrhage, hepatic failure, hepatosplenomegaly, hypersensitivity reaction, jaundice, neutropenic sepsis, non-cardiogenic pulmonary edema, portal vein thrombosis, pulmonary hemorrhage, renal insufficiency, renal failure (including renal failure secondary to tumor lysis syndrome)

Mechanism of Action Gemtuzumab ozogamicin is an antibody to CD33 antigen, which is expressed on leukemic blasts in 80% of AML patients. Binds to the CD33 antigen, resulting in internalization of the antibody-antigen complex. Following internalization, the calicheamicin derivative is released inside the myeloid cell. The calicheamicin derivative binds to DNA resulting in double strand breaks and cell death. Pluripotent stem cells and nonhematopoietic cells are not affected.

Pharmacodynamics/Kinetics

Half-life Elimination Total calicheamicin: Based on a 9 mg/m^2 dose: Initial dose: 41 hours, Repeat dose: 64 hours; Unconjugated: Initial dose: 143 hours

Pregnancy Considerations Teratogenic effects have been observed in animal reproduction studies. May cause fetal harm when administered to a pregnant woman. Women of childbearing potential should avoid becoming pregnant while receiving treatment.

Product Availability No longer commercially available in the US market for new patients. Available in Canada through a special access program.

Prescribing and Access Restrictions As of June 2010, gemtuzumab has been withdrawn from the US market and is no longer commercially available to new patients; gemtuzumab is only available in the US under an Investigational New Drug (IND) protocol.

In Canada, gemtuzumab is available through a special access program (access information is available from Health Canada).

Gentamicin (Systemic)

(jen ta MYE sin)

Brand Names: Canada Gentamicin Injection, USP

Pharmacologic Category Antibiotic, Aminoglycoside

Use Serious infections: Treatment of serious infections (eg, sepsis, meningitis, urinary tract infections, respiratory tract infections, peritonitis, bone infections, skin and soft tissue infections) caused by susceptible strains of the following microorganisms: *P. aeruginosa*, *Proteus* species (indole-positive and indole-negative), *Escherichia coli*, *Klebsiella* species, *Enterobacter* species, *Serratia* species, *Citrobacter* species, and *Staphylococcus* species (coagulase-positive and coagulase-negative); treatment of infective endocarditis caused by enterococci, in combination with other antibiotics.

Local Anesthetic/Vasoconstrictor Precautions No information available to require special precautions

Effects on Dental Treatment No significant effects or complications reported

Effects on Bleeding No information available to require special precautions

Adverse Reactions Frequency not defined.

Cardiovascular: Edema, hypertension, hypotension, phlebitis, thrombophlebitis

Central nervous system: Abnormal gait, ataxia, brain disease, confusion, depression, dizziness, drowsiness, headache, lethargy, myasthenia, numbness, paresthesia, peripheral neuropathy, pseudomotor cerebri, seizure, vertigo
Dermatologic: Alopecia, erythema, pruritus, skin rash, urticaria
Endocrine & metabolic: Hypocalcemia, hypokalemia, hypomagnesemia, hyponatremia, weight loss
Gastrointestinal: Anorexia, *Clostridium difficile*-associated diarrhea, decreased appetite, enterocolitis, nausea, sialorrhea, stomatitis, vomiting
Genitourinary: Casts in urine (hyaline, granular), changes in distal tubules (dysfunction), Fanconi-like syndrome (infants and adults; high dose, prolonged course), oliguria, proteinuria
Hematologic & oncologic: Agranulocytosis, anemia, eosinophilia, granulocytopenia, leukopenia, purpura, reticulocytopenia, reticulocytosis, splenomegaly, thrombocytopenia
Hepatic: Hepatomegaly, increased liver enzymes
Hypersensitivity: Anaphylaxis, anaphylactoid reaction, hypersensitivity reaction
Local: Injection site reaction, pain at injection site
Neuromuscular & skeletal: Arthralgia, muscle cramps, muscle fatigue (myasthenia gravis-like syndrome), muscle twitching, tremor, weakness
Ophthalmic: Visual disturbance
Otic: Auditory impairment, hearing loss (associated with persistently increased serum concentrations; early toxicity usually affects high-pitched sound), tinnitus
Renal: Decreased creatinine clearance, decreased urine specific gravity, increased blood urea nitrogen, increased serum creatinine, polyuria, renal failure (high trough serum concentrations), renal tubular necrosis
Respiratory: Dyspnea, laryngeal edema, pulmonary fibrosis, respiratory depression
Miscellaneous: Fever

General Dosage Range Dosage adjustment recommended in patients with renal impairment

IM, IV:

Infants: 2.5 mg/kg/dose every 8 hours
Children and Adolescents: 2 to 2.5 mg/kg/dose every 8 hours
Adults: 1 to 1.7 mg/kg/dose every 8 hours

Mechanism of Action Interferes with bacterial protein synthesis by binding to 30S and 50S ribosomal subunits resulting in a defective bacterial cell membrane

Pharmacodynamics/Kinetics

Half-life Elimination

Neonates: <1 week: 3 to 11.5 hours; 1 week to 1 month: 3 to 6 hours
Infants: 4 ± 1 hour
Children: 2 ± 1 hour
Adolescents: 1.5 ± 1 hour
Adults: ~2 hours (Regamey 1973); Renal failure: mean: 41 ± 24 hours; Range: 6 to 127 hours (Dager 2006)

Time to Peak Serum: IM: 30 to 90 minutes; IV: 30 minutes after 30-minute infusion (MacDougall 2011); **Note:** Distribution may be prolonged after larger doses. One study reported a 1.7-hour distribution period after a 60-minute, high-dose aminoglycoside infusion (Demczar 1997).

Pregnancy Risk Factor D

Pregnancy Considerations [US Boxed Warning]: Aminoglycosides may cause fetal harm if administered to a pregnant woman. Gentamicin crosses the placenta. There are several reports of total irreversible bilateral congenital deafness in children whose mothers received another aminoglycoside (streptomycin) during pregnancy. Although serious side effects to the fetus/infant have not been reported following maternal use of all aminoglycosides, a potential for harm exists.

Due to pregnancy-induced physiologic changes, some pharmacokinetic parameters of gentamicin may be altered (Popović 2007). Gentamicin use has been evaluated for various infections in pregnant women including the treatment of acute pyelonephritis (Jolley 2010) and as an alternative antibiotic for prophylactic use prior to cesarean delivery (Bratzler 2013).

Glatiramer Acetate (gla TIR a mer AS e tate)

Brand Names: US Copaxone; Glatopa
Brand Names: Canada Copaxone
Pharmacologic Category Biological, Miscellaneous
Use Multiple sclerosis: Treatment of patients with relapsing forms of multiple sclerosis (MS)

Local Anesthetic/Vasoconstrictor Precautions No information available to require special precautions

Effects on Dental Treatment Key adverse event(s) related to dental treatment: Ulcerative stomatitis, salivary gland enlargement, and oral *Candida* infection.

Effects on Bleeding No information available to require special precautions

Adverse Reactions

>10%:

Cardiovascular: Vasodilatation (3% to 20%), chest pain (2% to 13%)
Central nervous system: Pain (20%), anxiety (13%)
Dermatologic: Skin rash (2% to 19%), diaphoresis (15%)
Gastrointestinal: Nausea (2% to 15%)
Hypersensitivity: Immediate hypersensitivity (2% to 16%; postinjection, including flushing, chest pain, palpitations, anxiety, dyspnea, throat constriction, and/or urticaria)
Immunologic: Development of IgG antibodies (3 months: ≥3 x baseline: 80%; 12 months: 90%; ≥3 x baseline: 30%)
Infection: Infection (30%)
Local: Inflammation at injection site (2% to 49%), erythema at injection site (22% to 43%), pain at injection site (10% to 40%), itching at injection site (6% to 27%), residual mass at injection site (6% to 27%), swelling (1% to 19%)
Neuromuscular & skeletal: Weakness (22%), back pain (12%)
Respiratory: Dyspnea (3% to 14%), flu-like symptoms (3% to 14%), nasopharyngitis (11%)

1% to 10%:

Cardiovascular: Palpitations (7% to 9%), edema (8%), tachycardia (5%), facial edema (3%), peripheral edema (3%), syncope (3%), hypertension (1%)
Central nervous system: Migraine (4%), chills (2% to 3%), nervousness (2%), speech disturbance (2%), abnormal dreams (1%), emotional lability (1%), stupor (1%)
Dermatologic: Hyperhidrosis (7%), pruritus (5%), erythema (2% to 4%), urticaria (3%), skin atrophy (≥1%), warts (≥1%), eczema (1%), pustular rash (1%)
Endocrine & metabolic: Weight gain (3%), amenorrhea (1%), hypermenorrhea (1%)
Gastrointestinal: Vomiting (7%), gastroenteritis (6%), dysphagia (2%), aphthous stomatitis (≥1%), bowel

urgency (≥1%), dental caries (≥1%), enlargement of salivary glands (≥1%), oral candidiasis (≥1%)
Genitourinary: Urinary urgency (5%), vulvovaginal candidiasis (4%), abnormal Pap smear (≥1%), hematuria (≥1%), vaginal hemorrhage (≥1%), impotence (1%)
Hematologic & oncologic: Bruise (8%), lymphadenopathy (7%), benign skin neoplasm (2%)
Hypersensitivity: Hypersensitivity (3%)
Infection: Abscess (≥1%), herpes zoster (≥1%)
Local: Bleeding at injection site (5%), hypersensitivity reaction at injection site (4%), fibrosis at injection site (2%), lipoatrophy at injection site (≤2%), abscess at injection site (1%)
Neuromuscular & skeletal: Neck pain (8%), tremor (4%), laryngospasm (2%)
Ophthalmic: Diplopia (3%), visual field defect (1%)
Respiratory: Rhinitis (7%), bronchitis (6%), cough (6%), laryngismus (5%), viral respiratory tract infection (3%), hyperventilation (1%)
Miscellaneous: Fever (3% to 6%)

<1%, postmarketing, and/or case reports (Limited to important or life-threatening): Amyotrophy, anaphylactoid reaction, anemia, angina pectoris, angioedema, aphasia, arthritis, asthma, ataxia, atrial fibrillation, blepharoptosis, blindness, bradycardia, bursitis, carcinoma (breast, bladder, lung, ovarian), cardiac arrhythmia, cardiac failure, cardiomegaly, cardiomyopathy, cataract, cerebral edema, cerebrovascular accident, cholecystitis, cholelithiasis, CNS neoplasm, colitis, coma, corneal ulcer, coronary occlusion, Cushing's syndrome, cyanosis, decreased libido, deep vein thrombophlebitis, depersonalization, dermatitis, dry eye syndrome, duodenal ulcer, eosinophilia, erythema nodosum, esophageal ulcer, esophagitis, facial paralysis, fibrocystic breast disease, fourth heart sound, fungal dermatitis, furunculosis, gastrointestinal carcinoma, gastrointestinal hemorrhage, gastrointestinal ulcer, genitourinary neoplasm, glaucoma, gout, hallucination, hematemesis, hepatic cirrhosis, hepatitis, hepatomegaly, hernia, hydrocephalus, hypercholesterolemia, hyperthyroidism, hypokinesia, hypotension, hypothyroidism, hypoventilation, increased appetite, leukemia, leukopenia, lupus erythematosus, lymphedema, maculopapular rash, malignant neoplasm of cervix, malignant neoplasm of skin, mania, memory impairment, meningitis, mitral valve prolapse syndrome, moon face, muscle spasm, mydriasis, myelitis, myocardial infarction, myoclonus, nephrolithiasis, nephrosis, neuralgia, optic neuritis, oral mucosa ulcer, orthostatic hypotension, osteomyelitis, otitis externa, ovarian cyst, pancreatitis, pancytopenia, paraplegia, pericardial effusion, peripheral vascular disease, photophobia, pneumonia, priapism, pseudolymphoma, psoriasis, psychotic depression, pulmonary embolism, pyelonephritis, rectal hemorrhage, renal failure, seizures, sepsis, serum sickness, skin hypertrophy, skin photosensitivity, skin pigmentation, splenomegaly, stomatitis, suicidal tendencies, systemic lupus erythematosus, systolic heart murmur, tenosynovitis, thrombocytopenia, thrombophlebitis, thrombosis, tissue necrosis at injection site, urethritis, vesicobullous rash, weight loss, xeroderma

General Dosage Range SubQ: *Adults:* 20 mg once daily or 40 mg 3 times weekly

Mechanism of Action Glatiramer is a mixture of random polymers of four amino acids; L-alanine, L-glutamic acid, L-lysine, and L-tyrosine, the resulting mixture is antigenically similar to myelin basic protein, which is an important component of the myelin sheath of nerves; glatiramer is thought to induce and activate T-lymphocyte suppressor cells specific for a myelin antigen, it is also proposed that glatiramer interferes with the antigen-presenting function of certain immune cells opposing pathogenic T-cell function

Pregnancy Risk Factor B

Pregnancy Considerations Adverse events were not observed in animal reproduction studies. Limited information is available related to the use of glatiramer acetate in pregnancy (Amato 2015; Fragoso 2014; Ghezzi 2013; Giannini 2012). Until additional information is available, consideration should be given to discontinuing treatment if a woman becomes pregnant, or 1 month prior to becoming pregnant in women with mild disease (Coyle, 2012; Ghezzi 2013; Houtchens, 2013; Lu, 2013).

Gliclazide (GLYE kla zide)

Brand Names: Canada ACT Gliclazide MR; Apo-Gliclazide; Apo-Gliclazide MR; Diamicron; Diamicron MR; Gliclazide-80; Mint-Gliclazide MR; Mylan-Gliclazide; Mylan-Gliclazide MR; PMS-Gliclazide; Teva-Gliclazide

Pharmacologic Category Antidiabetic Agent, Sulfonylurea

Use Note: Not approved in the US

Diabetes mellitus, type 2: Management of type 2 diabetes mellitus (noninsulin dependent, NIDDM)

Local Anesthetic/Vasoconstrictor Precautions No information available to require special precautions

Effects on Dental Treatment Key adverse event(s) related to dental treatment: Patients with diabetes should be questioned by the dental professional at each dental visit to assess their risk for stress-induced hypoglycemia. The dental professional should inquire about the patient's routine (ie, work, sleep schedule, eating patterns), history of hypoglycemia, time of last medication dose, last meal, and most recent blood sugar assessment. Keep a supply of glucose tablets and other carbohydrates in the office to prepare for a hypoglycemic event. Seek medical attention when necessary (American Diabetes Association 2014).

Effects on Bleeding No information available to require special precautions

Adverse Reactions

>10%: Endocrine & metabolic: Hypoglycemia (11% to 12%)

1% to 10%:
Cardiovascular: Hypertension (3% to 4%), angina pectoris (2%), peripheral edema (1%)
Central nervous system: Headache (4% to 5%), dizziness (2%), depression (1% to 2%), insomnia (1% to 2%), neuralgia (≤1%)
Dermatologic: Dermatological disease (2%), dermatitis (1% to 2%), skin rash (1%; includes maculopapular rash, morbilliform rash), pruritus (≤1%)
Endocrine & metabolic: Hyperglycemia (2%), hyperlipidemia (≤1%), lipid metabolism disorder (≤1%)
Gastrointestinal: Diarrhea (2% to 3%), constipation (1% to 2%), gastroenteritis (1% to 2%), abdominal pain (1%), gastritis (1%), nausea (≤1%)
Genitourinary: Urinary tract infection (3%)
Infection: Viral infection (6% to 8%)
Neuromuscular & skeletal: Back pain (4% to 5%), arthralgia (3% to 4%), weakness (2% to 3%), arthropathy (2%), myalgia (2%), arthritis (1% to 2%), tendonitis (1%)
Ophthalmic: Conjunctivitis (1%)

Otic: Otitis media (≤1%)
Respiratory: Bronchitis (4% to 5%), rhinitis (4% to 5%), pharyngitis (4%), upper respiratory tract infection (3% to 4%), cough (2%), pneumonia (1% to 2%), sinusitis (1% to 2%)

Frequency not defined:
Endocrine & metabolic: Increased lactate dehydrogenase
Renal: Increased serum creatinine

<1%, postmarketing, and/or case reports: Abnormal lacrimation, acute pancreatitis, agranulocytosis, albuminuria, anal fissure, anemia, angioedema, anxiety, arteritis, asthma, auditory impairment, balanitis, bone disease (spine malformation), breast neoplasm (female; benign), bullous rash, bursitis, cardiac failure, carpal tunnel syndrome, cataract, cerebrovascular disease, chest pain, cholestatic jaundice, colitis, confusion, conjunctival hemorrhage, coronary artery disease, cystitis, dermal ulcer, diplopia, disulfiram-like reaction, DRESS syndrome, duodenal ulcer, dyspepsia, dyspnea, eczema, epigastric fullness, epistaxis, erythema, erythrocytopenia, esophagitis, fecal incontinence, fever, flatulence, fungal dermatitis, fungal infection, gastroesophageal reflux disease, gastrointestinal neoplasm (benign), glaucoma, glycosuria, gout, hemolytic anemia, hemorrhoids, hepatitis, hepatomegaly, hernia (congenital), hypercholesterolemia, hyperkeratosis, hypersensitivity angiitis, hypersensitivity reaction, hypertriglyceridemia, hypoglycemic coma, hyponatremia, hypotension, hypothyroidism, impotence, increased appetite, increased serum alkaline phosphatase, increased serum ALT, increased serum AST, increased serum transaminases, increased thirst, infection, leg pain, leukopenia, malaise, mastitis, melena, menstrual disease, myocardial infarction, nail disease, nephrolithiasis, nervousness, neuropathy, nocturia, onychomycosis, pain, palpitations, pancytopenia, polyuria, prostatic disease, renal cyst, retinopathy, sialorrhea, skeletal pain, Stevens-Johnson syndrome, tachycardia, thrombocytopenia, thrombophlebitis, tinnitus, toothache, toxic epidermal necrolysis, tracheitis, urticaria, vaginitis, vascular disease (vein disorder), visual disturbance, vitreous disorder, vomiting, weight gain, xeroderma, xerophthalmia, xerostomia

General Dosage Range Oral:
Immediate release: *Adults:* Initial: 80 mg twice daily; Maintenance: 80 to 320 mg/day (maximum: 320 mg/day)
Modified release: *Adults:* 30 to 120 mg once daily (maximum: 120 mg/day)

Mechanism of Action Stimulates insulin release from the pancreatic beta cells; reduces insulin uptake and glucose output by the liver; insulin sensitivity is increased at peripheral target sites. Reduces microthrombosis by decreasing platelet aggregation and adhesion, and by restoring fibrinolysis with an increase in tissue plasminogen activator (t-PA) activity. Antioxidant effects include a decrease in plasma levels of peroxidized lipids and increased erythrocyte superoxide dismutase activity.

Pharmacodynamics/Kinetics
Duration of Action Modified-release tablet: 24 hours
Half-life Elimination Immediate-release tablet: 10.4 hours; Modified-release tablet: 16 hours (range: 12 to 20 hours)
Time to Peak Immediate-release tablet: 4 to 6 hours; Modified-release tablet: ~6 hours

Pregnancy Considerations Use during pregnancy is contraindicated. Maternal hyperglycemia can be associated with adverse effects in the fetus, including macrosomia, neonatal hyperglycemia, and hyperbilirubinemia; the risk of congenital malformations is increased when the Hb A_{1c} is above the normal range. Diabetes can also be associated with adverse effects in the mother. Poorly-treated diabetes may cause end-organ damage that may in turn negatively affect obstetric outcomes. Physiologic glucose levels should be maintained prior to and during pregnancy to decrease the risk of adverse events in the mother and the fetus. Insulin is the drug of choice for the control of diabetes mellitus during pregnancy.

Product Availability Not available in the US

Glimepiride (GLYE me pye ride)

Related Information
Endocrine Disorders and Pregnancy *on page 1781*

Brand Names: US Amaryl

Brand Names: Canada Amaryl; Apo-Glimepiride; Novo-Glimepiride; PMS-Glimepiride; ratio-Glimepiride; Sandoz-Glimepiride

Pharmacologic Category Antidiabetic Agent, Sulfonylurea

Use Diabetes mellitus, type 2: As an adjunct to diet and exercise to improve glycemic control in adults with type 2 diabetes mellitus

Local Anesthetic/Vasoconstrictor Precautions No information available to require special precautions

Effects on Dental Treatment Key adverse event(s) related to dental treatment: Patients with diabetes should be questioned by the dental professional at each dental visit to assess their risk for stress-induced hypoglycemia. The dental professional should inquire about the patient's routine (ie, work, sleep schedule, eating patterns), history of hypoglycemia, time of last medication dose, last meal, and most recent blood sugar assessment. Keep a supply of glucose tablets and other carbohydrates in the office to prepare for a hypoglycemic event. Seek medical attention when necessary (American Diabetes Association, 2014).

Effects on Bleeding No information available to require special precautions

Adverse Reactions
>10%: Endocrine & metabolic: Hypoglycemia (4% to 20%)

1% to 10%:
Central nervous system: Dizziness (2%), headache
Gastrointestinal: Nausea (5%)
Hepatic: Increased serum ALT (2%)
Respiratory: Flu-like symptoms (5%)
Miscellaneous: Accidental injury (6%)

<1%, postmarketing, and/or case reports: Abnormal hepatic function tests, accommodation disturbance (early treatment), agranulocytosis, anaphylaxis, angioedema, anorexia, aplastic anemia, cholestatic jaundice, diarrhea, disulfiram-like reaction, dyspnea, epigastric fullness, erythema, gastrointestinal pain, hemolytic anemia, hepatic failure, hepatic insufficiency, hepatic porphyria, hepatitis, hypersensitivity, hypersensitivity angiitis, hyponatremia, hypotension, immune thrombocytopenia, leukopenia, maculopapular rash, morbilliform rash, pancytopenia, porphyria cutanea tarda, pruritus, shock, SIADH, skin photosensitivity, Stevens-Johnson syndrome, thrombocytopenia, urticaria, vomiting, weight gain

General Dosage Range Dosage adjustment recommended in patients with renal impairment

Oral:

Adults: Initial: 1 to 2 mg once daily; (maximum: 8 mg daily)

Elderly: Initial: 1 mg once daily

Mechanism of Action Stimulates insulin release from the pancreatic beta cells; reduces glucose output from the liver; insulin sensitivity is increased at peripheral target sites

Pharmacodynamics/Kinetics

Onset of Action Peak effect: Blood glucose reductions: 2 to 3 hours

Duration of Action 24 hours

Half-life Elimination 5 to 9 hours

Time to Peak 2 to 3 hours

Pregnancy Risk Factor C

Pregnancy Considerations Adverse events have been observed in some animal reproduction studies. Severe hypoglycemia lasting 4 to 10 days has been noted in infants born to mothers taking a sulfonylurea at the time of delivery. Information related to the use of glimepiride during pregnancy is limited (Balaguer Santamaria 2000; Kalyoncu 2005).

In women with diabetes, maternal hyperglycemia can be associated with congenital malformations as well as adverse effects in the fetus, neonate, and the mother (ACOG 2005; ADA 2016c; Kitzmiller 2008; Metzger 2007). To prevent adverse outcomes, prior to conception and throughout pregnancy maternal blood glucose and HbA_{1c} should be kept as close to target goals as possible but without causing significant hypoglycemia (ACOG 2013; ADA 2016c; Blumer 2013; Kitzmiller 2008). Agents other than glimepiride are currently recommended to treat diabetes in pregnant women (ACOG 2013; Blumer 2013).

GlipiZIDE (GLIP i zide)

Related Information

Endocrine Disorders and Pregnancy *on page 1781*

Brand Names: US GlipiZIDE XL; Glucotrol; Glucotrol XL

Pharmacologic Category Antidiabetic Agent, Sulfonylurea

Use Diabetes mellitus, type 2: Adjunct to diet and exercise to improve glycemic control in adults with type 2 diabetes mellitus (noninsulin dependent, NIDDM).

Local Anesthetic/Vasoconstrictor Precautions No information available to require special precautions

Effects on Dental Treatment Key adverse event(s) related to dental treatment: Patients with diabetes should be questioned by the dental professional at each dental visit to assess their risk for stress-induced hypoglycemia. The dental professional should inquire about the patient's routine (ie, work, sleep schedule, eating patterns), history of hypoglycemia, time of last medication dose, last meal, and most recent blood sugar assessment. Keep a supply of glucose tablets and other carbohydrates in the office to prepare for a hypoglycemic event. Seek medical attention when necessary (American Diabetes Association, 2014).

Effects on Bleeding No information available to require special precautions

Adverse Reactions Frequency not always defined.

Cardiovascular: Syncope (<3%)

Central nervous system: Dizziness (2% to 7%), nervousness (4%), anxiety (<3%), depression (<3%), hypoesthesia (<3%), insomnia (<3%), pain (<3%), paresthesia (<3%), drowsiness (2%), headache (2%)

Dermatologic: Diaphoresis (<3%), pruritus (1% to <3%), eczema (1%), erythema (1%), maculopapular rash (1%), morbilliform rash (1%), skin rash (1%), urticaria (1%)

Endocrine & metabolic: Hypoglycemia (<3%), increased lactate dehydrogenase

Gastrointestinal: Diarrhea (1% to 5%), flatulence (3%), dyspepsia (<3%), vomiting (<3%), constipation (1% to <3%), nausea (1% to <3%), abdominal pain (1%)

Hepatic: Increased serum alkaline phosphatase, increased serum AST

Neuromuscular & skeletal: Tremor (4%), arthralgia (<3%), leg cramps (<3%), myalgia (<3%)

Ophthalmic: Blurred vision (<3%)

Renal: Increased blood urea nitrogen, increased serum creatinine

Respiratory: Rhinitis (<3%)

1%, postmarketing, and/or case reports: Agranulocytosis, anorexia, aplastic anemia, bloody stools, cardiac arrhythmia, chills, cholestatic jaundice, confusion, conjunctivitis, decreased libido, disulfiram-like reaction, dyspnea, dysuria, edema, eye pain, flushing, hemolytic anemia, hepatic injury, hypertension, hypertonia, hyponatremia, jaundice, leukopenia, migraine, pancytopenia, pharyngitis, porphyria, retinal hemorrhage, SIADH (syndrome of inappropriate antidiuretic hormone secretion), skin photosensitivity, thrombocytopenia, unsteady gait, vertigo

General Dosage Range Dosage adjustment recommended in patients with hepatic impairment

Oral:

Immediate release:

Adults: Initial: 5 mg once daily; maximum: Maintenance: Up to 40 mg/day

Elderly: Initial: 2.5 mg once daily

Extended release:

Adults: Initial: 5 mg once daily; maximum: 20 mg/day

Elderly: Initial: 2.5 mg once daily.

Mechanism of Action Stimulates insulin release from the pancreatic beta cells; reduces glucose output from the liver; insulin sensitivity is increased at peripheral target sites

Pharmacodynamics/Kinetics

Duration of Action 12-24 hours

Half-life Elimination 2-5 hours

Time to Peak 1-3 hours; extended release tablets: 6-12 hours

Pregnancy Considerations Adverse events have been observed in some animal reproduction studies. Glipizide was found to cross the placenta in vitro (Elliott 1994). Severe hypoglycemia lasting 4 to 10 days has been noted in infants born to mothers taking a sulfonylurea at the time of delivery.

In women with diabetes, maternal hyperglycemia can be associated with congenital malformations as well as adverse effects in the fetus, neonate, and the mother (ACOG 2005; ADA 2016c; Kitzmiller 2008; Metzger 2007). To prevent adverse outcomes, prior to conception and throughout pregnancy, maternal blood glucose and HbA_{1c} should be kept as close to target goals as possible but without causing significant hypoglycemia (ACOG 2013; ADA 2016c; Blumer 2013; Kitzmiller 2008). Agents other than glipizide are currently recommended to treat diabetes in pregnant women (ACOG 2013; Blumer 2013).

The manufacturer recommends if glipizide is used during pregnancy, it should be discontinued at least 1 month before the expected delivery date.

Glucagon (GLOO ka gon)

Brand Names: US GlucaGen Diagnostic; GlucaGen HypoKit; Glucagon Emergency

Brand Names: Canada GlucaGen; GlucaGen HypoKit

Pharmacologic Category Antidote; Antidote, Hypoglycemia; Diagnostic Agent

Use

Diagnostic aid: As a diagnostic aid during radiologic examinations to temporarily inhibit movement of the GI tract in adults.

Hypoglycemia: Treatment of severe hypoglycemia in pediatric and adult patients. **Note:** The American Diabetes Association (ADA) recommends that glucagon be prescribed for all diabetic patients at significant risk of severe hypoglycemia; caregivers or family members of these patients should be trained on how to administer glucagon (ADA 2016).

Limitations of use: Products not packaged with a syringe and diluent necessary for rapid preparation and administration during an emergency outside of a health care facility are not indicated for the emergency treatment of hypoglycemia.

Local Anesthetic/Vasoconstrictor Precautions No information available to require special precautions

Effects on Dental Treatment No significant effects or complications reported

Effects on Bleeding No information available to require special precautions

Adverse Reactions Frequency not defined.

Cardiovascular: Hypertension, hypotension (up to 2 hours after GI procedures), increased blood pressure, increased pulse, tachycardia

Gastrointestinal: Nausea, vomiting (high incidence with rapid administration of high doses)

Miscellaneous: Anaphylaxis, hypersensitivity reaction

<1%, postmarketing, and/or case reports: Abdominal pain, hypoglycemia, hypoglycemic coma, respiratory distress, urticaria

General Dosage Range

IM, SubQ:

Infants and Children <20 kg (Glucagon Emergency Kit): 0.5 mg **or** 0.02-0.03 mg/kg/dose, may repeat

Infants and Children <25 kg or <6 years (GlucaGen): 0.5 mg, may repeat

Children and Adolescents ≥20 kg (Glucagon Emergency Kit) or ≥25 kg or ≥6 years (GlucaGen): 1 mg, may repeat

Adults (Glucagon Emergency Kit or GlucaGen): 1 mg, may repeat **or** 1 to 2 mg prior to gastrointestinal procedure

IV:

Infants and Children <20 kg (Glucagon Emergency Kit): 0.5 mg **or** 0.02 to 0.03 mg/kg/dose, may repeat

Infants and Children <25 kg **or** *<6 years (GlucaGen):* 0.5 mg, may repeat

Children ≥20 kg (Glucagon Emergency Kit) or ≥25 kg or ≥6 years (GlucaGen): 1 mg, may repeat

Adults (Glucagon Emergency Kit or GlucaGen): 1 mg, may repeat **or** 0.2 to 0.75 mg prior to gastrointestinal procedure

Mechanism of Action Stimulates adenylate cyclase to produce increased cyclic AMP, which promotes hepatic glycogenolysis and gluconeogenesis, causing a raise in blood glucose levels; antihypoglycemic effect requires preexisting hepatic glycogen stores. Extra hepatic effects of glucagon include relaxation of the smooth muscle of the stomach, duodenum, small bowel, and colon.

Pharmacodynamics/Kinetics

Onset of Action

Blood glucose levels: Peak effect: IV: 5 to 20 minutes; IM: 30 minutes; SubQ: 30 to 45 minutes

GI relaxation: IV: 45 seconds; IM: 4 to 10 minutes

Duration of Action

Glucose elevation: IV, IM, SubQ: 60 to 90 minutes

GI relaxation: IV: 9 to 25 minutes; IM: 12 to 32 minutes

Half-life Elimination Plasma: IV: 8 to 18 minutes; IM (apparent): 26 to 45 minutes

Time to Peak IM: ~10 to 12.5 minutes; SubQ: 20 minutes

Pregnancy Risk Factor B

Pregnancy Considerations Adverse events have not been observed in animal reproduction studies.

Glucose Polymers (GLOO kose POL i merz)

Brand Names: US Polycose® [OTC]

Pharmacologic Category Nutritional Supplement

Use Supplies calories for those persons not able to meet the caloric requirement with usual dietary intake

Local Anesthetic/Vasoconstrictor Precautions No information available to require special precautions

Effects on Dental Treatment No significant effects or complications reported

Effects on Bleeding No information available to require special precautions

General Dosage Range Oral: *Adults:* Add to foods, beverages, or water as needed

Glutamine (GLOO ta meen)

Brand Names: US GlutaMent [OTC]; Glutasolve [OTC]; GlutImmune [OTC]; NutreStore; Sympt-X [OTC]

Pharmacologic Category Amino Acid; Gastrointestinal Agent, Miscellaneous

Use

Nutritional supplementation: Medical food used to promote GI tract healing and nutritional supplementation with GI disorders, HIV/AIDS, cancer, and other critical illnesses

Short bowel syndrome (NutreStore only): For the treatment of short bowel syndrome in patients receiving specialized nutritional support when used in conjunction with a recombinant growth hormone that is approved for this indication

Note: A medical food is formulated to be administered enterally under the supervision of a physician and is intended for the specific dietary management of a disease or condition for which distinctive nutritional requirements are established by medical evaluation. Medical foods are not drugs and, therefore, are not subject to any FDA regulatory requirements that specifically apply to drugs (eg, requirement for written/oral prescription prior to dispensing, premarket review or approval, proof of safety and efficacy).

Local Anesthetic/Vasoconstrictor Precautions No information available to require special precautions

Effects on Dental Treatment No significant effects or complications reported

Effects on Bleeding No information available to require special precautions

Adverse Reactions Frequency not defined.

Cardiovascular: Facial edema, peripheral edema

Central nervous system: Dizziness, headache, hypoesthesia, pain

Dermatologic: Pruritus, skin rash

Gastrointestinal: Abdominal pain, flatulence, nausea, pancreatitis, tenesmus, vomiting
Infection: Infection, sepsis
Neuromuscular & skeletal: Arthralgia, back pain
Otic: Auditory disturbance, ear sign or symptom
Respiratory: Flu-like symptoms, rhinitis
Miscellaneous: Fever

General Dosage Range
Oral:
Children: 0.25 to 0.5 mg/kg/day given in 3 divided doses
Adults: 0.5 to 30 g/day in 3 divided doses **or** 5 g 6 times/day

Mechanism of Action Glutamine regulates gastrointestinal cell growth, function, and regeneration. Considered a "conditionally essential" amino acid during metabolic stress and injury.

Pharmacodynamics/Kinetics
Half-life Elimination Adults (healthy): IV: 1 hour
Time to Peak Adults (healthy): 30 minutes

Pregnancy Risk Factor C

Pregnancy Considerations Animal reproduction studies have not been conducted. Endogenous glutamine can be detected in cord blood and concentrations are decreased in low birth-weight infants (Ivorra 2012).

Product Availability Sympt-X is available in US in 300 g jars, 500 g jars and packets (10 g L-glutamine + 5 g maltodextrin)

GlyBURIDE (GLYE byoor ide)

Related Information
Endocrine Disorders and Pregnancy *on page* 1781

Brand Names: US Diabeta [DSC]; Glynase

Brand Names: Canada Apo-Glyburide; Ava-Glyburide; DiaBeta; Dom-Glyburide; Euglucon; Mylan-Glybe; PMS-Glyburide; PRO-Glyburide; ratio-Glyburide; Riva-Glyburide; Sandoz-Glyburide; Teva-Glyburide

Pharmacologic Category Antidiabetic Agent, Sulfonylurea

Use Type 2 diabetes mellitus: Adjunct to diet and exercise to improve glycemic control in adults with type 2 diabetes mellitus (noninsulin dependent, NIDDM)

Local Anesthetic/Vasoconstrictor Precautions No information available to require special precautions

Effects on Dental Treatment Key adverse event(s) related to dental treatment: Patients with diabetes should be questioned by the dental professional at each dental visit to assess their risk for stress-induced hypoglycemia. The dental professional should inquire about the patient's routine (ie, work, sleep schedule, eating patterns), history of hypoglycemia, time of last medication dose, last meal, and most recent blood sugar assessment. Keep a supply of glucose tablets and other carbohydrates in the office to prepare for a hypoglycemic event. Seek medical attention when necessary (American Diabetes Association, 2014).

Effects on Bleeding No information available to require special precautions

Adverse Reactions
1% to 10%:
Gastrointestinal: Epigastric fullness (≤2%), heartburn (≤2%), nausea (≤2%)
Hypersensitivity: Hypersensitivity reaction (2%; including erythema, maculopapular rash, morbilliform rash, pruritus, urticaria)
Frequency not defined:
Central nervous system: Disulfiram-like reaction
Endocrine & metabolic: Hypoglycemia, hyponatremia, weight gain
Genitourinary: Diuresis (minor)
Hematologic & oncologic: Hemolytic anemia
Hepatic: Cholestatic jaundice, hepatic failure, hepatitis
<1%, postmarketing, and/or case reports: Accommodation disturbance, angioedema, arthralgia, bullous rash, erythema multiforme, exfoliative dermatitis, increased serum transaminases, myalgia, vasculitis

General Dosage Range Oral:
Conventional tablets (Diaβeta): *Adults:* Initial: 1.25-5 mg once daily; Maintenance: 1.25-20 mg daily as single or divided doses (maximum: 20 mg daily)
Micronized tablets (Glynase PresTab): *Adults:* Initial: 0.75-3 mg once daily; Maintenance: 0.75-12 mg daily as single or divided doses (maximum: 12 mg daily)

Mechanism of Action Stimulates insulin release from the pancreatic beta cells; reduces glucose output from the liver; insulin sensitivity is increased at peripheral target sites

Pharmacodynamics/Kinetics
Onset of Action Serum insulin levels begin to increase 15-60 minutes after a single dose
Duration of Action ≤24 hours
Half-life Elimination Diaβeta: 10 hours; Glynase PresTab: ~4 hours; may be prolonged with renal or hepatic impairment
Time to Peak Serum: Adults: 2-4 hours

Pregnancy Risk Factor C

Pregnancy Considerations Outcomes of animal reproduction studies differ by manufacturer labeling. Glyburide crosses the placenta. Some pharmacokinetic properties of glyburide may change during pregnancy (Hebert 2009).

Severe hypoglycemia lasting 4 to 10 days has been noted in infants born to mothers taking a sulfonylurea at the time of delivery. Additional adverse maternal and fetal events have been noted in some studies and may be influenced by maternal glycemic control and/or differences in study design (Bertini 2005; Ekpebegh 2007; Joy 2012; Langer 2000; Langer 2005).

In women with diabetes, maternal hyperglycemia can be associated with congenital malformations as well as adverse effects in the fetus, neonate, and the mother (ACOG 2005; ADA 2016c; Kitzmiller 2008; Metzger 2007). To prevent adverse outcomes, prior to conception and throughout pregnancy, maternal blood glucose and HbA_{1c} should be kept as close to target goals as possible but without causing significant hypoglycemia (ACOG 2013; ADA 2016c; Blumer 2013; Kitzmiller 2008).

If an oral agent is needed for the treatment of GDM in pregnancy, agents other than glyburide are preferred (ADA 2016c). According to the manufacturer, if glyburide is used during pregnancy, it should be discontinued at least 2 weeks before the expected delivery date.

Glyburide and Metformin
(GLYE byoor ide & met FOR min)

Related Information
GlyBURIDE *on page* 800
MetFORMIN *on page* 1069

Brand Names: US Glucovance

Pharmacologic Category Antidiabetic Agent, Biguanide; Antidiabetic Agent, Sulfonylurea

Use Type 2 diabetes mellitus: As an adjunct to diet and exercise, to improve glycemic control in adults with type 2 diabetes (noninsulin dependent, NIDDM)

Local Anesthetic/Vasoconstrictor Precautions No information available to require special precautions

Effects on Dental Treatment Key adverse event(s) related to dental treatment: Patients with diabetes should be questioned by the dental professional at each dental visit to assess their risk for stress-induced hypoglycemia. The dental professional should inquire about the patient's routine (ie, work, sleep schedule, eating patterns), history of hypoglycemia, time of last medication dose, last meal, and most recent blood sugar assessment. Keep a supply of glucose tablets and other carbohydrates in the office to prepare for a hypoglycemic event. Seek medical attention when necessary (American Diabetes Association, 2014).

Effects on Bleeding No information available to require special precautions

Adverse Reactions Also see individual agents.

>10%:

Endocrine & metabolic: Hypoglycemia (11% to 38%, effects higher when increased doses were used as initial therapy)

Gastrointestinal: Gastrointestinal symptoms (38%; combined GI effects increased to 38% in patients taking high doses as initial therapy), diarrhea (17%)

Respiratory: Upper respiratory infection (17%)

1% to 10%:

Central nervous system: Headache (9%), dizziness (6%)

Gastrointestinal: Nausea (8%), vomiting (8%), abdominal pain (7%)

<1%, postmarketing, and/or case reports: Cholestatic jaundice, hepatitis

General Dosage Range Oral: *Adults:* Initial: Glyburide 1.25-5 mg and metformin 250-500 mg once or twice daily; Maintenance: Up to glyburide 20 mg/day and metformin 2000 mg/day

Mechanism of Action The combination of glyburide and metformin is used to improve glycemic control in patients with type 2 diabetes mellitus by using two different, but complementary, mechanisms of action:

Glyburide: Stimulates insulin release from the pancreatic beta cells; reduces glucose output from the liver; insulin sensitivity is increased at peripheral target sites

Metformin: Decreases hepatic glucose production, decreasing intestinal absorption of glucose and improves insulin sensitivity (increases peripheral glucose uptake and utilization)

Pharmacodynamics/Kinetics

Time to Peak Glucovance: 2.75 hours when taken with food

Pregnancy Risk Factor B

Pregnancy Considerations Animal reproduction studies were not conducted with this combination. Refer to individual agents.

Glycerin (GLIS er in)

Related Information

Dentifrices Without Sodium Lauryl Sulfate (SLS)[a] *on page 1911*

Brand Names: US Fleet Liquid Glycerin Supp [OTC]; Glycerin (Adult) [OTC]; Glycerin (Infants & Children) [OTC]; Glycerin (Pediatric) [OTC] [DSC]; Pedia-Lax [OTC]; Sani-Supp Adult [OTC]; Sani-Supp Pediatric [OTC]

Pharmacologic Category Laxative, Osmotic

Use

Constipation: Relief of occasional constipation.

Mouth/throat irritation: Temporary relief of minor discomfort and protection of irritated areas in sore mouth and sore throat.

Local Anesthetic/Vasoconstrictor Precautions No information available to require special precautions

Effects on Dental Treatment No significant effects or complications reported

Effects on Bleeding No information available to require special precautions

Adverse Reactions Frequency not defined.

Gastrointestinal: Abdominal cramps, rectal irritation, tenesmus

General Dosage Range

Oral: *Children ≥2 years, Adolescents, and Adults:* Apply a one-inch strip directly to tongue and oral cavity as needed

Rectal:

Children 2 to <6 years: One pediatric suppository once daily as needed **or** as directed

Children ≥6 years, Adolescents, and Adults: One adult suppository once daily as needed **or** as directed

Mechanism of Action Osmotic dehydrating agent which increases osmotic pressure; draws fluid into colon and thus stimulates evacuation

Pharmacodynamics/Kinetics

Onset of Action Constipation: Suppository: 15 to 30 minutes

Pregnancy Considerations Glycerin suppositories are generally considered safe to use during pregnancy (Cullen, 2007; Wald, 2003).

Glycerol Phenylbutyrate
(GLI ser ole fen il BYOO ti rate)

Brand Names: US Ravicti

Brand Names: Canada Ravicti

Pharmacologic Category Urea Cycle Disorder (UCD) Treatment Agent

Use Urea cycle disorders: Chronic management of urea cycle disorders (UCDs) in patients ≥2 years that cannot be managed by dietary protein restriction and/or amino acid supplementation alone

Local Anesthetic/Vasoconstrictor Precautions No information available to require special precautions

Effects on Dental Treatment No significant effects or complications reported

Effects on Bleeding No information available to require special precautions

Adverse Reactions

>10%:

Central nervous system: Headache (14%; children & adolescents: ≥10%)

Dermatologic: Skin rash (children & adolescents)

Endocrine & metabolic: Hyperammonemia (children & adolescents: ≥10%; adults: 5%)

Gastrointestinal: Diarrhea (16%), flatulence (14%), decreased appetite (children & adolescents: ≥10%; adults: 7%), vomiting (children & adolescents: ≥10%; adults: 7%), nausea (children & adolescents: ≥10%; adults: 2%), upper abdominal pain (children & adolescents)

1% to 10%:

Central nervous system: Fatigue (7%)

Gastrointestinal: Abdominal pain (7%), dyspepsia (5%)

Frequency not defined:

Central nervous system: Dizziness, peripheral neuropathy, seizure

Neuromuscular & skeletal: Tremor

<1%, postmarketing, and/or case reports: Body odor (including from hair, skin, urine), burning sensation of mouth, dysgeusia, gag reflex, retching

General Dosage Range Oral: *Children ≥2 years, Adolescents, and Adults:* 4.5 to 11.2 mL/m^2 (5 to 12.4 g/m^2) daily; dosage may vary if being switched from sodium phenylbutyrate; maximum: 17.5 mL/day (19 g/day).

Mechanism of Action Glycerol phenylbutyrate is a prodrug of phenylbutyrate (PBA) which is converted to phenylacetate (PAA) by β-oxidation. Phenylacetate conjugates glutamine to form phenylacetylglutamine (PAGN); PAGN serves as a substitute for urea and clears nitrogenous waste from the body when excreted in the urine.

Pharmacodynamics/Kinetics

Time to Peak

Time to peak, plasma: Phenylbutyrate: 2 hours; Phenylacetate: 4 hours; Phenylacetylglutamine: 4 hours

Time to steady state, plasma: Phenylbutyrate: 8 hours; Phenylacetate: 12 hours; Phenylacetylglutamine: 10 hours

Pregnancy Considerations

Adverse events have been observed in animal reproduction studies with doses also causing maternal toxicity.

Health care providers are encouraged to report any prenatal exposure to the manufacturer (www.ucdregistry.com or 1-855-823-2595).

Prescribing and Access Restrictions Ravicti is only available via select specialty pharmacies. Contact Hyperion UCD Support Services (855-823-7878 or http://www.ucdsupport.com/) for additional information.

Glycopyrrolate (Systemic)

(glye koe PYE roe late)

Brand Names: US Cuvposa; Glycate [DSC]; Robinul; Robinul-Forte

Brand Names: Canada Glycopyrrolate Injection, USP

Pharmacologic Category Anticholinergic Agent

Use

Chronic drooling (Cuvposa only): To reduce chronic, severe drooling in pediatric patients 3 to 16 years with neurologic conditions (eg, cerebral palsy) associated with problem drooling

Reduction of secretions (Robinul injection only): To reduce salivary, tracheobronchial, and pharyngeal secretions preoperatively; to reduce the volume and free acidity of gastric secretions

Reversal of bradycardia, vagal reflexes (Robinul injection only): To block cardiac vagal inhibitory reflexes during induction of anesthesia and intubation; intraoperatively to counteract surgically or drug-induced or vagal reflexes associated arrhythmias

Reversal of muscarinic effects of cholinergic agents (Robinul injection only): Protects against the peripheral muscarinic effects (eg, bradycardia and excessive secretions) of cholinergic agents such as neostigmine and pyridostigmine given to reverse the neuromuscular blockade due to non-depolarizing muscle relaxants

Local Anesthetic/Vasoconstrictor Precautions No information available to require special precautions

Effects on Dental Treatment Key adverse event(s) related to dental treatment: Significant xerostomia (normal salivary flow resumes upon discontinuation).

Effects on Bleeding No information available to require special precautions

Adverse Reactions Frequency not always defined.

Cardiovascular: Flushing (30%), pallor (≤2%), cardiac arrhythmias, heart block, hypertension, hypotension, palpitation, tachycardia

Central nervous system: Headache (15%), aggressiveness (≤2%), agitation (≤2%), crying (abnormal; ≤2%), irritability (≤2%), mood changes (≤2%), pain (≤2%), restlessness (≤2%), confusion, dizziness, drowsiness, excitement (higher incidence in older adults), insomnia, nervousness

Dermatologic: Dry skin (≤2%), pruritus (≤2%), rash (≤2%), hypohidrosis, urticaria

Endocrine & metabolic: Dehydration (≤2%)

Gastrointestinal: Vomiting (40%), xerostomia (40%), constipation (35%), abdominal distention (≤2%), abdominal pain (≤2%), flatulence (≤2%), retching (≤2%), intestinal obstruction, loss of taste, nausea, pseudo-obstruction

Genitourinary: Urinary retention (15%), urinary tract infection (≤2%), decreased lactation, impotence, urinary hesitancy

Neuromuscular & skeletal: Weakness

Ophthalmic: Nystagmus (≤2%), blurred vision, cycloplegia, increased intraocular pressure, mydriasis

Respiratory: Nasal congestion (30%), sinusitis (15%), upper respiratory tract infection (15%), bronchial secretion (thickening; ≤2%), nasal dryness (≤2%), pneumonia (≤2%)

<1%, postmarketing, and/or case reports: Arrhythmias, hypertension, hypotension, malignant hyperthermia, seizure

General Dosage Range Dosage varies greatly depending on indication.

Mechanism of Action Blocks the action of acetylcholine at parasympathetic sites in smooth muscle, secretory glands, and the CNS; indirectly reduces the rate of salivation by preventing the stimulation of acetylcholine receptors

Pharmacodynamics/Kinetics

Onset of Action IM: 15 to 30 minutes; IV: Within 1 minute; Peak effect: IM: Within ~30 to 45 minutes

Duration of Action Vagal effect: 2 to 3 hours; Inhibition of salivation: Up to 7 hours; Parenteral: 7 hours

Half-life Elimination Infants: 21.6 to 130 minutes; Children 19.2 to 99.2 minutes; IM: Adults: 0.55 to 1.25 hours; IV: 0.83 ± 0.13 hour; Oral solution: Adults: 3 hours

Time to Peak 3.1 hours

Pregnancy Risk Factor B (injection)

Pregnancy Considerations Adverse effects have not been observed in animal reproduction studies. Small amounts of glycopyrrolate cross the human placenta. Glycopyrrolate in doses of 0.004 mg/kg has not been found to affect fetal heart rate.

Glycopyrrolate (Oral Inhalation)

(glye koe PYE roe late)

Brand Names: US Seebri Neohaler

Brand Names: Canada Seebri Breezhaler

Pharmacologic Category Anticholinergic Agent; Anticholinergic Agent, Long-Acting

Use

Chronic obstructive pulmonary disease: Maintenance treatment of airflow obstruction in patients with chronic obstructive pulmonary disease (COPD), including chronic bronchitis and/or emphysema.

Limitations of use: Not indicated for the relief of an acute deterioration of COPD.

Local Anesthetic/Vasoconstrictor Precautions No information available to require special precautions

Effects on Dental Treatment Key adverse event(s) related to dental treatment: Significant xerostomia (normal salivary flow resumes upon discontinuation).

Effects on Bleeding No information available to require special precautions

Adverse Reactions

1% to 10%:

Central nervous system: Fatigue (≥2%)

Gastrointestinal: Diarrhea (≥2%), nausea (≥2%), upper abdominal pain (≥2%)

Neuromuscular & skeletal: Arthralgia (≥2%), back pain (≥2%)

Respiratory: Upper respiratory tract infection (2% to 3%), bronchitis (≥2%), dyspnea (≥2%), nasopharyngitis (≥2%), pneumonia (≥2%), rhinitis (≥2%), wheezing (≥2%), oropharyngeal pain (2%), sinusitis (1%)

<1% postmarketing, and/or case reports: Angioedema, atrial fibrillation, cough, diabetes mellitus, dysuria, gastroenteritis, hypersensitivity reaction, insomnia, paradoxical bronchospasm, peripheral pain, productive cough, pruritus, skin rash, vomiting

General Dosage Range

Oral inhalation: *Adults:* One capsule (15.6 mcg) inhaled twice daily (maximum: 31.2 mcg/day)

Mechanism of Action Competitively and reversibly inhibits the action of acetylcholine at muscarinic receptor subtypes 1 to 3 (greater affinity for subtypes 1 and 3) in bronchial smooth muscle thereby causing bronchodilation

Pharmacodynamics/Kinetics

Half-life Elimination 33 to 53 hours

Time to Peak Plasma: 5 minutes

Pregnancy Considerations Adverse events have been observed in some animal reproduction studies. Small amounts of glycopyrrolate cross the human placenta following IM injection.

Product Availability Seebri Neohaler: FDA approved October 2015; anticipated availability in first quarter of 2016.

Glycopyrrolate and Formoterol

(glye koe PYE roe late & for MOH te rol)

Brand Names: US Bevespi Aerosphere

Pharmacologic Category Anticholinergic Agent; Anticholinergic Agent, Long-Acting; Beta2 Agonist; $Beta_2$-Adrenergic Agonist, Long-Acting

Use

Chronic obstructive pulmonary disease: Maintenance treatment of airflow obstruction in patients with chronic obstructive pulmonary disease (COPD), including chronic bronchitis and/or emphysema

Limitations of use: Not indicated for the relief of acute bronchospasm or for the treatment of asthma

Local Anesthetic/Vasoconstrictor Precautions No information available to require special precautions

Effects on Dental Treatment No significant effects or complications reported

Effects on Bleeding No information available to require special precautions

Adverse Reactions See individual agents.

1% to 10%:

Genitourinary: Urinary tract infection (3%)

Respiratory: Cough (4%)

Frequency not defined:

Cardiovascular: Depression of ST segment on ECG, ECG changes (prolongation of the QTc interval), flattened T wave on ECG

Dermatologic: Skin rash, urticaria

Endocrine & metabolic: Exacerbation of diabetes mellitus, hypokalemia, ketoacidosis (exacerbation)

Genitourinary: Urinary retention (exacerbation)

Hypersensitivity: Angioedema, immediate hypersensitivity

Ophthalmic: Exacerbation of angle-closure glaucoma (narrow angle)

Respiratory: Paradoxical bronchospasm

General Dosage Range

Oral inhalation: *Adults:* 2 inhalations (glycopyrrolate 9 mcg/formoterol 4.8 mcg per inhalation) twice daily; (maximum: 2 inhalations twice daily).

Mechanism of Action

Glycopyrrolate: In COPD, competitively and reversibly inhibits the action of acetylcholine at muscarinic receptor subtypes 1-3 (greater affinity for subtypes 1 and 3) in bronchial smooth muscle thereby causing bronchodilation.

Formoterol: Relaxes bronchial smooth muscle by selective action on $beta_2$ receptors with little effect on heart rate. Formoterol has a long-acting effect.

Pregnancy Risk Factor C

Pregnancy Considerations Animal reproduction studies have not been conducted with this combination. Refer to individual monographs.

Gold Sodium Thiomalate

(gold SOW dee um thye oh MAL ate)

Brand Names: US Myochrysine [DSC]

Brand Names: Canada Myochrysine®

Pharmacologic Category Gold Compound

Use Adjunctive treatment of active rheumatoid arthritis

Local Anesthetic/Vasoconstrictor Precautions No information available to require special precautions

Effects on Dental Treatment Key adverse event(s) related to dental treatment: Stomatitis, gingivitis, and glossitis.

Effects on Bleeding No information available to require special precautions

Adverse Reactions Frequency not defined.

Cardiovascular: Bradycardia, syncope, vasomotor symptoms (nitritoid reaction)

Central nervous system: Confusion, Guillain Barre syndrome, hallucination, metallic taste, peripheral neuropathy, seizure

Dermatologic: Alopecia, dermatitis, onycholysis, pruritus, skin rash, urticaria

Gastrointestinal: Anorexia, abdominal cramps, cholestasis, diarrhea, dysphagia, gingivitis, glossitis, nausea, stomatitis, ulcerative enterocolitis, vomiting

Genitourinary: Glomerulitis, hematuria, nephrotic syndrome, proteinuria

Hematologic & oncologic: Agranulocytosis, aplastic anemia, eosinophilia, leukopenia, purpura, thrombocytopenia

Hepatic: Hepatitis, hepatotoxicity, jaundice

Hypersensitivity: Anaphylactoid reaction, anaphylaxis, angioedema, tongue edema
Neuromuscular & skeletal: Arthralgia
Ophthalmic: Conjunctivitis, corneal ulcer, gold deposits in ocular tissue, iritis
Respiratory: Bronchitis (gold bronchitis), dyspnea, interstitial pneumonitis, pulmonary fibrosis
Miscellaneous: Fever

General Dosage Range Dosage adjustment recommended in patients with renal impairment or who develop toxicities

IM:

Children: Test dose (recommended): 10 mg first week; Initial dosing: 1 mg/kg/week (maximum: 50 mg/injection); Maintenance: 1 mg/kg/dose (maximum: 50 mg/injection)

Adults: Test dose: 10 mg first week; Initial dosing: 25 mg second week, then 25-50 mg/week until 1 g cumulative dose has been given; Maintenance: 25-50 mg every other week for 2-20 weeks, then every 3-4 weeks

Mechanism of Action Unknown, may decrease prostaglandin synthesis or may alter cellular mechanisms by inhibiting sulfhydryl systems

Pharmacodynamics/Kinetics

Onset of Action Delayed; may require up to 3 months

Half-life Elimination 5 days; may be prolonged with multiple doses

Time to Peak Serum: 4-6 hours

Pregnancy Risk Factor C

Pregnancy Considerations Adverse events were observed in animal reproduction studies

Golimumab (goe LIM ue mab)

Related Information

Rheumatoid Arthritis, Osteoarthritis, and Osteoporosis *on page 1792*

Brand Names: US Simponi; Simponi Aria

Brand Names: Canada Simponi; Simponi I.V.

Pharmacologic Category Antipsoriatic Agent; Antirheumatic, Disease Modifying; Monoclonal Antibody; Tumor Necrosis Factor (TNF) Blocking Agent

Use

Ankylosing spondylitis (Simponi): Treatment of adults with active ankylosing spondylitis

Psoriatic arthritis (Simponi): Treatment of adults with active psoriatic arthritis (alone or in combination with methotrexate)

Rheumatoid arthritis (Simponi, Simponi Aria): Treatment of adults with moderately-to-severely active rheumatoid arthritis (in combination with methotrexate)

Ulcerative colitis (Simponi): Treatment of adults with moderately-to-severely active ulcerative colitis in patients with corticosteroid dependence or who are refractory or intolerant to oral aminosalicylates, oral corticosteroids, azathioprine, or 6-mercaptopurine (to induce and maintain clinical response, improve mucosal appearance during induction, induce clinical remission, and achieve and sustain remission in induction responders)

Local Anesthetic/Vasoconstrictor Precautions No information available to require special precautions

Effects on Dental Treatment No significant effects or complications reported

Effects on Bleeding No information available to require special precautions

Adverse Reactions

>10%:

Hematologic & oncologic: Positive ANA titer (≥1:160 titer, newly positive; 17% intravenous, 4% subcutaneous)
Infection: Infection (27% to 28%)
Respiratory: Upper respiratory tract infection (includes laryngitis, nasopharyngitis, pharyngitis, and rhinitis; 13% to 16%)

1% to 10%:

Cardiovascular: Hypertension (3%)
Central nervous system: Dizziness (<1% to 2%), paresthesia (<1% to 2%)
Dermatologic: Skin rash (3%)
Gastrointestinal: Constipation (≤1%)
Hematologic & oncologic: Leukopenia (≤1%)
Hepatic: Increased serum ALT (subcutaneous 4%; ≥3 x ULN: 2%; ≥5 x ULN: <1%), increased serum AST (<1% to 3%)
Immunologic: Antibody development (3% to 7%)
Infection: Viral infection (4% to 5%; includes herpes and influenza), fungal infection (superficial; <1% to 2%), bacterial infection (intravenous 1%), serious infection (≤1%)
Local: Injection site reaction (subcutaneous 3% to 6%)
Respiratory: Bronchitis (2% to 3%)
Miscellaneous: Fever (2%), infusion related reaction (intravenous 1%)

<1%, postmarketing, and/or case reports: Abscess, anaphylaxis, antibody development (anti-dsDNA), aspergillosis, atypical mycobacterial infection (subcutaneous), blastomycosis, bullous skin disease, candidiasis, cardiac failure (worsening or new onset), cellulitis, coccidioidomycosis, congestive heart failure, demyelinating disease of the central nervous system, cellulitis, coccidioidomycosis, decreased neutrophils (intravenous), exfoliation of skin, hepatotoxicity (idiosyncratic) (Chalasani 2014), histoplasmosis, Hodgkin lymphoma (initiation of therapy ≤18 years old), hypersensitivity angiitis (subcutaneous), hypersensitivity reaction, infective bursitis (subcutaneous), interstitial pulmonary disease (subcutaneous), leukemia, lupus-like syndrome, malignant lymphoma, malignant melanoma, malignant neoplasm (other than nonmelanoma skin cancer), Merkel cell carcinoma, multiple sclerosis, non-Hodgkin lymphoma (initiation of therapy ≤18 years old), neutropenia, optic neuritis, pancytopenia, peripheral demyelinating polyneuropathy, pneumocystosis, pneumonia, psoriasis (subcutaneous) including new onset, palmoplantar, pustular, or exacerbation), pyelonephritis, reactivation of HBV, sarcoidosis, sepsis, septic arthritis (subcutaneous), septic shock (subcutaneous), sinusitis, thrombocytopenia, tuberculosis (including reactivation of latent and new infection), vasculitis (subcutaneous)

General Dosage Range

IV: *Adults:* 2 mg/kg at weeks 0 and 4 and then every 8 weeks thereafter

SubQ: *Adults:* Induction: 200 mg at week 0, then 100 mg at week 2; maintenance: 100 mg every 4 weeks (ulcerative colitis) **or** 50 mg once per month

Mechanism of Action Human monoclonal antibody that binds to human tumor necrosis factor alpha (TNFα), thereby interfering with endogenous TNFα activity. Biological activities of TNFα include the induction of proinflammatory cytokines (interleukin [IL]-6, IL-8, Granulocyte-colony stimulating factor, granulocyte-macrophage colony stimulating factor), expression of adhesion molecules (E-selectin, vascular cell adhesion molecule [VCAM]-1, intercellular adhesion molecule

[ICAM]-1) necessary for leukocyte infiltration, activation of neutrophils and eosinophils.

Pharmacodynamics/Kinetics

Half-life Elimination ~2 weeks

Time to Peak SubQ: 2-6 days

Pregnancy Risk Factor B

Pregnancy Considerations Adverse events have not been observed in animal reproduction studies. Golimumab crosses the placenta. Based on data from other TNF-blockers, antibodies may be present in the newborn serum for up to 6 months and infants exposed to golimumab *in utero* may be at risk of increased infection. Administration of live vaccines to newborns is not recommended until 6 months after the last maternal dose. The Canadian labeling recommends that women of childbearing potential use reliable contraception during and for at least 6 months after discontinuation of golimumab therapy.

Gonadorelin (goe nad oh RELL in)

Brand Names: Canada Lutrepulse

Pharmacologic Category Gonadotropin

Use Note: Not approved in the US

Induction of ovulation in females with hypothalamic amenorrhea

Local Anesthetic/Vasoconstrictor Precautions No information available to require special precautions

Effects on Dental Treatment No significant effects or complications reported

Effects on Bleeding No information available to require special precautions

Adverse Reactions Frequency not defined.

Cardiovascular: Superficial thrombophlebitis

Local: Injection site irritation

<1%, postmarketing, and/or case reports: Abdominal pain, anaphylactic shock, anaphylaxis, antibody development (with long-term therapy, resulting in therapy failure), erythema at injection site, fever, headache, hypermenorrhea, inflammation at injection site (mild and severe), nausea, ovarian hyperstimulation syndrome (moderate)

General Dosage Range IV, SubQ: *Adults:* 1-20 mcg every 90 minutes

Mechanism of Action Stimulates the release of luteinizing hormone (LH) from the anterior pituitary gland

Pharmacodynamics/Kinetics

Onset of Action Response to therapy usually observed within 2-3 weeks

Half-life Elimination Terminal: ~10-40 minutes; increased in patients with renal impairment

Pregnancy Considerations The risk of fetal harm appears remote if gonadorelin is used during pregnancy. Clinical studies of pregnant women have not demonstrated an increased risk of fetal abnormalities during the first trimester. Follow-up reports of infants born to exposed mothers revealed no adverse effects or complications attributed to gonadorelin therapy. Based on its indicated use, gonadorelin treatment is continued for 2 weeks following ovulation to maintain the corpus luteum; initiation of treatment is not appropriate if pregnancy has been established.

Product Availability Not available in the US

Goserelin (GOE se rel in)

Brand Names: US Zoladex

Brand Names: Canada Zoladex; Zoladex LA

Pharmacologic Category Antineoplastic Agent, Gonadotropin-Releasing Hormone Agonist; Gonadotropin Releasing Hormone Agonist

Use

US labeling:

Breast cancer, advanced (3.6 mg only): Palliative treatment of advanced breast cancer in pre- and perimenopausal women (estrogen and progesterone receptor values may help to predict if goserelin is likely to be beneficial).

Endometrial thinning (3.6 mg only): Endometrial-thinning agent prior to endometrial ablation for dysfunctional uterine bleeding.

Endometriosis (3.6 mg only): Management of endometriosis, including pain relief and reduction of endometriotic lesions for the duration of therapy (goserelin experience for endometriosis has been limited to women 18 years and older treated for 6 months).

Prostate cancer, advanced (3.6 mg or 10.8 mg): Palliative treatment of advanced carcinoma of the prostate.

Prostate cancer, stage B2 to C (3.6 mg or 10.8 mg): Management of locally confined stage T2b to T4 (stage B2 to C) prostate cancer (in combination with an antiandrogen [eg, flutamide]); begin goserelin and antiandrogen therapy 8 weeks prior to initiating radiation therapy and continue during radiation therapy.

Canadian labeling:

Breast cancer, advanced (3.6 mg only): Palliative treatment of advanced breast cancer in pre- and perimenopausal women (with estrogen and/or progesterone receptor-positive tumors).

Breast cancer, early (3.6 mg only): Alternative to standard adjuvant chemotherapy in pre- and perimenopausal women with early breast cancer (with estrogen and/or progesterone receptor-positive tumors) who are unsuitable for, intolerant to, or decline chemotherapy.

Endometrial thinning (3.6 mg only): Endometrial-thinning agent prior to endometrial ablation.

Endometriosis (3.6 mg or 10.8 mg): Hormonal management of endometriosis, including pain relief and reduction of endometriotic lesions (goserelin experience for endometriosis has been limited to women 18 years and older treated for 6 months).

Prostate cancer, advanced (3.6 mg or 10.8 mg): Palliative treatment of hormone-dependent advanced carcinoma of the prostate (stage M1 or D2).

Prostate cancer, locally advanced (3.6 mg or 10.8 mg): Management of locally advanced (T3 or T4) or bulky stage T2b to T2c prostate cancer (in combination with a nonsteroidal antiandrogen and radiation therapy); begin goserelin and antiandrogen therapy 8 weeks prior to initiating radiation therapy and continue until completion of radiation therapy.

Prostate cancer, locally advanced (3.6 mg or 10.8 mg): Adjuvant hormone therapy to external beam irradiation in locally advanced prostate cancer (stage T3 to T4).

Local Anesthetic/Vasoconstrictor Precautions No information available to require special precautions

Effects on Dental Treatment Key adverse event(s) related to dental treatment: Xerostomia (normal salivary flow resumes upon discontinuation) and taste disturbances.

Effects on Bleeding No information available to require special precautions

Adverse Reactions Some frequencies not defined. Percentages reported with the 1-month implant:

>10%:

Cardiovascular: Vasodilatation (females 57%), peripheral edema (females 21%)

Central nervous system: Headache (females 32% to 75%; males 1% to 5%), emotional lability (females 60%), depression (females 54%; males 1% to 5%), pain (8% to 17%), dyspareunia (females 14%), insomnia (5% to 11%)

Dermatologic: Diaphoresis (females 16% to 45%; males 6%), acne vulgaris (females 42%; usually within 1 month after starting treatment), seborrhea (females 26%)

Endocrine & metabolic: Hot flash (females 57% to 96%; males 64%), decreased libido (females 48% to 61%), increased libido (females 12%)

Gastrointestinal: Abdominal pain (females 7% to 11%), nausea (5% to 11%)

Genitourinary: Vaginitis (75%), breast atrophy (females 33%), sexual disorder (males 21%), breast hypertrophy (females 18%), decrease in erectile frequency (18%), pelvic symptoms (females 18%), genitourinary signs and symptoms (lower; males 13%)

Hematologic & oncologic: Tumor flare (females 23%; males: Incidence not reported)

Infection: Infection (females 13%; males: Incidence not reported)

Neuromuscular & skeletal: Decreased bone mineral density (females 23%; ~4% decrease from baseline in 6 months; male: Incidence not reported), weakness (females 11%)

1% to 10%:

Cardiovascular: Edema (females 5%; male 7%), hypertension (1% to 6%), cardiac failure (males 5%), cardiac arrhythmia (males >1% to <5%), cerebrovascular accident (males >1% to <5%), peripheral vascular disease (males >1% to <5%), varicose veins (males >1% to <5%), chest pain (1% to <5%), myocardial infarction (males <1% to <5%), palpitations, tachycardia (females)

Central nervous system: Lethargy (females ≤8%), migraine (females 1% to 7%), dizziness (females 6%; male 5%), malaise (females ≤5%), chills (males >1% to <5%), anxiety (1% to <5%), nervousness (females 3% to 5%), voice disorder (females 3%), abnormality in thinking, drowsiness, paresthesia

Dermatologic: Skin rash (males 6% to 8%; female frequency not reported), hair disease (females 4%), pruritus (females 2%), alopecia, skin discoloration, xeroderma

Endocrine & metabolic: Gynecomastia (males 8%), hirsutism (7%), gout (males >1% to <5%), hyperglycemia (males >1% to <5%), weight gain (>1% to <5%)

Gastrointestinal: Anorexia (1% to 5%), gastric ulcer (males >1% to <5%), constipation (1% to <5%), diarrhea (1% to <5%), vomiting (1% to <5%), increased appetite (females 2%), dyspepsia, flatulence, xerostomia

Genitourinary: Pelvic pain (females 9%; males 6%), mastalgia (>1% to 7%), uterine hemorrhage (6%), vulvovaginitis (5%), breast swelling (males >1% to <5%), urinary tract obstruction (males: >1% to <5%), urinary tract infection (1% to <5%), urinary frequency, vaginal hemorrhage

Hematologic & oncologic: Anemia (males >1% to <5%), bruise, hemorrhage

Hypersensitivity: Hypersensitivity reaction

Infection: Sepsis (males >1% to <5%)

Local: Application site reaction (females 6%)

Neuromuscular & skeletal: Myalgia (females 3%, males frequency not reported), leg cramps (females 2%, males frequency not reported), hypertonia (females 1%; male frequency not reported), arthralgia, arthropathy

Ophthalmic: Amblyopia, dry eye syndrome

Renal: Renal insufficiency (<1% to >5%)

Respiratory: Upper respiratory tract infection (males 7%), chronic obstructive pulmonary disease (males 5%), flu-like symptoms (females 5%, male frequency not reported), pharyngitis (females 5%), sinusitis (females ≥1%; male frequency not reported), bronchitis, cough, epistaxis, rhinitis

Miscellaneous: Fever

<1%, postmarketing, and/or case reports (with monthly or 3-month implant): Anaphylaxis, bone fracture, convulsions, decreased glucose tolerance, decreased HDL cholesterol, deep vein thrombosis, diabetes mellitus, hypercalcemia, hypercholesterolemia, hyperlipidemia, hypotension, increased HDL cholesterol, increased LDL cholesterol, increased serum ALT, increased serum AST, increased serum triglycerides, injection site reaction (including vascular injury, pain, hematoma, hemorrhage, hemorrhagic shock), osteoporosis, ovarian cyst, ovarian hyperstimulation syndrome, pituitary apoplexy, pituitary neoplasm (including adenoma), pulmonary embolism, psychotic reaction, transient ischemic attacks

General Dosage Range SubQ: *Adults:* 3.6 mg every 28 days **or** 10.8 mg every 12 weeks

Mechanism of Action Goserelin (a gonadotropin-releasing hormone [GnRH] analog) causes an initial increase in luteinizing hormone (LH) and follicle stimulating hormone (FSH), chronic administration of goserelin results in a sustained suppression of pituitary gonadotropins. Serum testosterone falls to levels comparable to surgical castration. The exact mechanism of this effect is unknown, but may be related to changes in the control of LH or down-regulation of LH receptors.

Pharmacodynamics/Kinetics

Onset of Action

Females: Estradiol suppression reaches postmenopausal levels within 3 weeks and FSH and LH are suppressed to follicular phase levels within 4 weeks of initiation.

Males: Testosterone suppression reaches castrate levels within 2 to 4 weeks after initiation.

Duration of Action

Females: Estradiol, LH and FSH generally return to baseline levels within 12 weeks following the last monthly implant.

Males: Testosterone levels maintained at castrate levels throughout the duration of therapy.

Time to Peak SubQ: Male: 12 to 15 days, Female: 8 to 22 days

Pregnancy Risk Factor X (endometriosis, endometrial thinning); D (advanced breast cancer)

Pregnancy Considerations Adverse events were observed in animal reproduction studies. Goserelin induces hormonal changes which increase the risk for fetal loss and use is contraindicated in pregnancy unless being used for palliative treatment of advanced breast cancer.

Breast cancer: If used for the palliative treatment of breast cancer during pregnancy, the potential for increased fetal loss should be discussed with the patient.

Endometriosis, endometrial thinning: Use is contraindicated during pregnancy. Women of childbearing potential should not receive therapy until pregnancy has been excluded. Nonhormonal contraception is recommended for premenopausal women during therapy and for 12 weeks after therapy is discontinued. Although ovulation is usually inhibited and menstruation may stop, pregnancy prevention is not ensured during goserelin therapy. Changes in reproductive function may occur following chronic administration.

Granisetron (gra NI se tron)

Related Information

Clinical Risk Related to Drugs Prolonging QT Interval *on page 1772*

Brand Names: US Granisol [DSC]; Sancuso; Sustol

Brand Names: Canada Granisetron Hydrochloride Injection; Granisetron Hydrochloride Injection SDZ; Nat-Granisetron

Pharmacologic Category Antiemetic; Selective 5-HT_3 Receptor Antagonist

Use

Chemotherapy-associated nausea and vomiting: Prevention of nausea and vomiting associated with initial and repeat courses of emetogenic chemotherapy, including high-dose cisplatin (injection and tablets); prevention of nausea and vomiting associated with anthracycline/cyclophosphamide chemotherapy regimens; prevention of nausea and vomiting associated with moderately and/or highly emetogenic chemotherapy regimens of up to 5 consecutive days of duration (transdermal).

Radiation-associated nausea and vomiting: Prevention of nausea and vomiting associated with radiation therapy, including total body radiation and fractionated abdominal radiation (tablets).

Local Anesthetic/Vasoconstrictor Precautions Granisetron is one of the drugs confirmed to prolong the QT interval and is accepted as having a risk of causing torsade de pointes. The risk of drug-induced torsade de pointes is extremely low when a single QT interval prolonging drug is prescribed. In terms of epinephrine, it is not known what effect vasoconstrictors in the local anesthetic regimen will have in patients with a known history of congenital prolonged QT interval or in patients taking any medication that prolongs the QT interval. Until more information is obtained, it is suggested that the clinician consult with the physician prior to the use of a vasoconstrictor in suspected patients, and that the vasoconstrictor (epinephrine, mepivacaine and levonordefrin [Carbocaine® 2% with Neo-Cobefrin®]) be used with caution.

Effects on Dental Treatment No significant effects or complications reported

Effects on Bleeding No information available to require special precautions

Adverse Reactions

>10%:

Central nervous system: Headache (oral and IV: 3% to 21%; transdermal: <1%)

Gastrointestinal: Nausea (20%), constipation (oral and IV: 3% to 18%; transdermal: 5%), vomiting (12%)

Neuromuscular & skeletal: Weakness (oral: 14% to 18%; IV: 5%)

1% to 10%:

Cardiovascular: Prolonged Q-T interval on ECG (1% to 3%; >450 milliseconds, not associated with any arrhythmias), hypertension (oral and IV: 1% to 2%)

Central nervous system: Dizziness (5%), insomnia (oral and IV: ≤5%), drowsiness (1% to 4%), anxiety (oral and IV: ≤2%), agitation (IV: <2%), central nervous system stimulation (IV: <2%)

Dermatologic: Alopecia (3%), skin rash (IV: 1%)

Gastrointestinal: Diarrhea (oral and IV: 4% to 9%), decreased appetite (6%), dyspepsia (oral: 6%), abdominal pain (4% to 6%), dysgeusia (IV: 2%)

Hematologic & oncologic: Leukopenia (9%), anemia (4%), thrombocytopenia (2%)

Hepatic: Increased serum ALT (>2 x ULN: 3% to 6%), increased serum AST (>2 x ULN: 3% to 5%)

Miscellaneous: Fever (3% to 9%)

<1%, postmarketing, and/or case reports (all routes): Angina pectoris, application site reaction (including allergic rash, burn, discoloration, erythema, erythematous rash, irritation, macular rash, pain, papular rash, pruritus, urticaria, vesicles), atrial fibrillation, atrioventricular block, bradycardia, cardiac arrhythmia, chest pain, ECG abnormality, extrapyramidal reaction, hypersensitivity reaction (includes anaphylaxis, dyspnea, hypotension, urticaria), hypotension, palpitations, serotonin syndrome, sick sinus syndrome, sinus bradycardia, syncope, ventricular ectopy (includes nonsustained tachycardia)

General Dosage Range

Dosage adjustment may be recommended in patients with renal impairment.

IV:

Children ≥2 years: 10 mcg/kg/dose as a single dose or every 12 hours

Adults: 10 mcg/kg/dose as a single dose or every 12 hours

Oral: *Adults:* 2 mg/day in 1 to 2 divided dose

SubQ: *Adults:* 10 mg on day 1; do not administer more frequently than once every 7 days.

Transdermal: *Adults:* 1 patch prior to chemotherapy; Maximum duration: Patch may be worn up to 7 days

Mechanism of Action Selective 5-HT_3-receptor antagonist, blocking serotonin, both peripherally on vagal nerve terminals and centrally in the chemoreceptor trigger zone

Pharmacodynamics/Kinetics

Onset of Action IV: 1 to 3 minutes

Duration of Action Oral, IV: Generally up to 24 hours; SubQ (extended-release): Remains detectable in the plasma for 7 days

Half-life Elimination Oral: 6 hours; IV: Mean range: 5 to 9 hours; SubQ (extended-release): ~24 hours

Time to Peak Transdermal patch: Maximum systemic concentrations: ~48 hours after application (range: 24 to 168 hours); SubQ (extended-release): ~24 hours

Pregnancy Risk Factor B

Pregnancy Considerations Adverse events have not been observed in animal reproduction studies. In an ex vivo placental perfusion study, granisetron was shown to cross the placenta in a concentration (dose) dependent manner (Julius 2014). Initial studies note the pharmacokinetics of the transdermal system may be different in pregnant women. A relationship between granisetron plasma concentrations and relief of symptoms of nausea and vomiting of pregnancy was also observed (Cartis 2016). Some dosage forms (injection) may contain benzyl alcohol.

Product Availability Granisol oral solution has been discontinued in the US for more than 1 year.

Dental Comment See Local Anesthetic/Vasoconstrictor Precautions

Griseofulvin (gri see oh FUL vin)

Brand Names: US Grifulvin V [DSC]; Gris-PEG

Pharmacologic Category Antifungal Agent, Oral

Use

Dermatophyte infections: Treatment of the following dermatophyte infections of the skin, hair, and nails not adequately treated by topical therapy: Tinea corporis, tinea pedis, tinea cruris, tinea barbae, tinea capitis, tinea unguium (onychomycosis) when caused by one or more of the following species of fungi: *Trichophyton rubrum, Trichophyton tonsurans, Trichophyton mentagrophytes, Trichophyton interdigitalis, Trichophyton verrucosum, Trichophyton megnini, Trichophyton gallinae, Trichophyton crateriform, Trichophyton sulphureum, Trichophyton schoenleini, Microsporum audouini, Microsporum canis, Microsporum gypseum,* and *Epidermophyton floccosum.*

Limitations of use: Use for the prophylaxis of fungal infections has not been established; not effective for the treatment of tinea versicolor.

Local Anesthetic/Vasoconstrictor Precautions No information available to require special precautions

Effects on Dental Treatment Key adverse event(s) related to dental treatment: May cause soreness or irritation of mouth or tongue. May cause oral thrush.

Effects on Bleeding No information available to require special precautions

Adverse Reactions Frequency not defined.

Central nervous system: Confusion, dizziness, fatigue, headache, insomnia

Dermatologic: Dermatological reaction (erythema multiforme-like drug reaction), skin photosensitivity, skin rash (most common), urticaria (most common)

Gastrointestinal: Diarrhea, epigastric distress, gastrointestinal hemorrhage, nausea, oral candidiasis, vomiting

Genitourinary: Nephrosis

Hematologic & oncologic: Granulocytopenia

Hepatic: Hepatotoxicity

<1%, postmarketing, and/or case reports: Angioedema, increased serum bilirubin, increased serum transaminases, leukopenia, lupus-like syndrome, paresthesia, proteinuria, Stevens-Johnson syndrome, toxic epidermal necrolysis

General Dosage Range Oral:

Microsize:

Children >2 years and Adolescents: 10 mg/kg/day in single or divided doses (maximum: 500 mg daily)

Adults: 500 to 1,000 mg daily in single or divided doses

Ultramicrosize:

Children >2 years and Adolescents: 125 to 375 mg/day in single dose or 2 divided doses (maximum: 500 mg daily)

Adults: 375 mg daily in single or divided doses or up to 750 mg daily in divided doses

Mechanism of Action Inhibits fungal cell mitosis at metaphase; binds to human keratin making it resistant to fungal invasion

Pharmacodynamics/Kinetics

Half-life Elimination 9 to 24 hours

Time to Peak Serum: 4 hours

Pregnancy Risk Factor X

Pregnancy Considerations Teratogenic effects have been observed in animal reproduction studies. Griseofulvin crosses the placenta (Pacifici, 2006). Because adverse events have also been observed in humans (two cases of conjoined twins), use during pregnancy is contraindicated. Effective contraception should be used during therapy and for 1 month after therapy is discontinued in women of reproductive potential. Men should avoid fathering a child for at least 6 months after therapy.

GuaiFENesin (gwye FEN e sin)

Brand Names: US Altarussin [OTC]; Bidex [OTC]; Buckleys Chest Congestion [OTC]; Diabetic Siltussin DAS-Na [OTC]; Diabetic Tussin Mucus Relief [OTC] [DSC]; Diabetic Tussin [OTC]; Fenesin IR [OTC]; Geri-Tussin [OTC]; GoodSense Mucus Relief [OTC]; Iophen-NR [OTC] [DSC]; Liquibid [OTC]; Liquituss GG [OTC] [DSC]; Mucinex Chest Congestion Child [OTC]; Mucinex For Kids [OTC]; Mucinex Maximum Strength [OTC]; Mucinex [OTC]; Mucosa [OTC]; Mucus Relief Childrens [OTC]; Mucus Relief [OTC]; Mucus-ER [OTC] [DSC]; Organ-I NR [OTC]; Q-Tussin [OTC] [DSC]; Refenesen 400 [OTC]; Refenesen [OTC]; Robafen [OTC]; Robitussin Chest Congestion [OTC] [DSC]; Robitussin Mucus+Chest Congest [OTC]; Scot-Tussin Expectorant [OTC]; Siltussin DAS [OTC]; Siltussin SA [OTC]; Tussin Mucus & Chest Congest [OTC]; Tussin [OTC]; Xpect [OTC]

Brand Names: Canada Balminil Expectorant; Benylin Chest Congestion Extra Strength; Robitussin Mucus & Phlegm; Vicks DayQuil Mucus Control

Pharmacologic Category Expectorant

Use Cough (expectorant): Help loosen phlegm (mucus) and thin bronchial secretions to make coughs more productive

Local Anesthetic/Vasoconstrictor Precautions No information available to require special precautions

Effects on Dental Treatment No significant effects or complications reported

Effects on Bleeding No information available to require special precautions

Adverse Reactions Frequency not defined.

Central nervous system: Dizziness, drowsiness, headache

Dermatologic: Skin rash

Endocrine & metabolic: Hypouricemia

Gastrointestinal: Nausea, stomach pain, vomiting

<1%, postmarketing, and/or case reports: Nephrolithiasis (with consumption of large quantities)

General Dosage Range Oral:

Granules:

Children 4 years to <6 years: 100 mg every 4 hours as needed; maximum: 600 mg/24 hours

Children 6 years to <12 years: 100 to 200 mg every 4 hours as needed; maximum: 1,200 mg/24 hours

Children ≥12 years, Adolescents, and Adults: 200 to 400 mg every 4 hours as needed; maximum: 2,400 mg/24 hours

Extended-release tablet: Children ≥12 years, Adolescents, and Adults: 600 mg to 1,200 mg every 12 hours as needed; maximum: 2,400 mg/24 hours

Immediate-release tablet: Children ≥12 years, Adolescents, and Adults: 200 to 400 mg every 4 hours as needed; maximum: 2,400 mg/24 hours

Liquid:

Children 2 years to <4 years: Limited data available: 50 to 100 mg every 4 hours as needed; maximum: 600 mg/24 hours (Kliegman, 2007)

Children 4 years to <6 years: 50 to 100 mg every 4 hours as needed; maximum: 600 mg/24 hours

Children 6 years to <12 years: 100 to 200 mg every 4 hours as needed; maximum: 1,200 mg/24 hours

Children ≥12 years, Adolescents, and Adults: 200 to 400 mg every 4 hours as needed; maximum: 2,400 mg/24 hours

Mechanism of Action Thought to act as expectorant by increasing the effective hydration of the respiratory tract, maintains the sol layer needed for ciliary clearance and reduces the viscosity of respiratory mucus, thereby further facilitating its removal by natural clearance processes.

Guaifenesin inhibits cough reflex sensitivity in subjects with upper respiratory tract infections whose cough receptors are transiently hypersensitive, but not in healthy volunteers. Possible mechanisms include a central antitussive effect, or a peripheral effect by increased sputum volume serving as a barrier shielding cough receptors within the respiratory epithelium from the tussive stimulus (Dicpinigaitis 2003).

Pregnancy Considerations Based on the limited available data, an increased risk of adverse birth outcomes has not been observed following maternal use of guaifenesin in pregnancy (Aselton 1985; Heinonen 1977; Jick 1981; Lind 2013; Shaw 1998). Alcohol may be present in some liquid formulations of guaifenesin. If consumed in sufficient quantities during pregnancy, fetal alcohol syndrome may result (Chasnoff 1981).

Guaifenesin and Codeine

(gwye FEN e sin & KOE deen)

Related Information

Codeine *on page 410*

GuaiFENesin *on page 808*

Brand Names: US Allfen CD; Allfen CDX; Cheratussin AC; Codar GF [DSC]; Coditussin AC; Dex-Tuss; G Tussin AC; Guaiatussin AC; Guaifenesin AC Liquid; Iophen C-NR [DSC]; M-Clear; M-Clear WC; Mar-Cof CG; Ninjacof-XG; Robafen AC; Virtussin A/C

Pharmacologic Category Antitussive; Expectorant

Use Temporary control of cough due to minor throat and bronchial irritation

Local Anesthetic/Vasoconstrictor Precautions No information available to require special precautions

Effects on Dental Treatment Key adverse event(s) related to dental treatment: Xerostomia (normal salivary flow resumes upon discontinuation).

Effects on Bleeding No information available to require special precautions

Adverse Reactions Frequency not defined; also see individual agents.

Cardiovascular: Bradycardia, circulatory depression, flushing, orthostatic hypotension, palpitations, syncope, tachycardia

Central nervous system: Central nervous system depression, convulsions, disorientation, dizziness, dysphoria, euphoria, hallucination (transient), headache, sedation

Dermatologic: Diaphoresis, pruritus, urticaria

Gastrointestinal: Biliary tract spasm, constipation, gastrointestinal hypermotility (colonic motility increase with chronic ulcerative colitis), nausea, stomach pain, toxic megacolon (with acute ulcerative colitis), vomiting

Genitourinary: Oliguria, urinary retention

Hypersensitivity: Anaphylaxis, angioedema

Neuromuscular & skeletal: Weakness

Ophthalmic: Visual disturbance

Respiratory: Laryngeal edema, respiratory depression

General Dosage Range Oral: *Children ≥6 years and Adults:* Dosage varies greatly depending on product

Mechanism of Action

Guaifenesin may act as an expectorant by irritating the gastric mucosa and stimulating respiratory tract secretions, thereby increasing respiratory fluid volumes and decreasing phlegm viscosity

Codeine is an antitussive that controls cough by depressing the medullary cough center

Pregnancy Considerations See individual agents.

Controlled Substance Capsule: C-V; Liquid products: C-V; Tablet: C-III

Guaifenesin and Dextromethorphan

(gwye FEN e sin & deks troe meth OR fan)

Related Information

Dextromethorphan *on page 488*

GuaiFENesin *on page 808*

Brand Names: US Cheracol D [OTC]; Cheracol Plus [OTC]; Coricidin HBP Chest Congestion and Cough [OTC]; Delsym Cough + Chest Congestion DM [OTC]; Diabetic Siltussin-DM DAS-Na Maximum Strength [OTC]; Diabetic Siltussin-DM DAS-Na [OTC]; Diabetic Tussin DM Maximum Strength [OTC]; Diabetic Tussin DM [OTC]; Double Tussin DM [OTC]; Fenesin DM IR [OTC]; Guaicon DMS [OTC]; Iophen DM-NR [OTC] [DSC]; Kolephrin GG/DM [OTC]; Mucinex DM Maximum Strength [OTC]; Mucinex DM [OTC]; Mucinex Fast-Max DM Max [OTC]; Mucinex Kid's Cough Mini-Melts [OTC]; Mucinex Kid's Cough [OTC]; Q-Tussin DM [OTC]; Refenesen DM [OTC]; Robafen DM [OTC]; Robitussin Maximum Strength Cough + Congestion DM [OTC]; Robitussin Peak Cold Cough + Chest Congestion DM [OTC]; Robitussin Peak Cold Maximum Strength Cough + Chest Congestion DM [OTC]; Robitussin Peak Cold Sugar-Free Cough + Chest Congestion DM [OTC]; Safe Tussin DM [OTC]; Scot-Tussin Senior [OTC]; Silexin [OTC]; Siltussin DM DAS [OTC]; Siltussin DM [OTC]; Triaminic Cough & Congestion [OTC]; Vicks 44E [OTC]; Vicks DayQuil Mucus Control DM [OTC]; Vicks Nature Fusion Cough & Chest Congestion [OTC] [DSC]; Vicks Pediatric Formula 44E [OTC]; Zyncof [OTC]

Brand Names: Canada Balminil DM E; Benylin DM-E

Pharmacologic Category Antitussive; Expectorant

Use Temporary control of cough due to minor throat and bronchial irritation

Local Anesthetic/Vasoconstrictor Precautions No information available to require special precautions

Effects on Dental Treatment No significant effects or complications reported

Effects on Bleeding No information available to require special precautions

Adverse Reactions See individual agents.

General Dosage Range Oral:

Children 2-6 years: Guaifenesin 50-100 mg and dextromethorphan 2.5-5 mg every 4 hours (maximum: Guaifenesin 600 mg/day; Dextromethorphan 30 mg/day)

Children 6-12 years: Guaifenesin 100-200 mg and dextromethorphan 5-10 mg every 4 hours (maximum: Guaifenesin 1200 mg/day; Dextromethorphan 60 mg/day)

Children ≥12 years and Adults: Guaifenesin 200-400 mg and dextromethorphan 10-20 mg every 4 hours (maximum: Guaifenesin 2400 mg/day; Dextromethorphan 120 mg/day)

Mechanism of Action
Guaifenesin is thought to act as an expectorant by irritating the gastric mucosa and stimulating respiratory tract secretions, thereby increasing respiratory fluid volumes and decreasing phlegm viscosity
Dextromethorphan is a chemical relative of morphine lacking opioid properties except in overdose; controls cough by depressing the medullary cough center
Pregnancy Considerations See individual agents.

Guaifenesin, Dextromethorphan, and Phenylephrine
(gwye FEN e sin, deks troe meth OR fan, & fen il EF rin)

Related Information
Dextromethorphan *on page 488*
GuaiFENesin *on page 808*
Phenylephrine (Systemic) *on page 1330*
Brand Names: US Aquanaz [OTC]; Deconex DMX [OTC]; Duravent DM [OTC]; Endacon [OTC] [DSC]; Maxiphen DM [DSC]; Mucinex Children's Congestion & Cough [OTC]; Mucinex Children's Multi-Symptom Cold [OTC]; Mucinex Fast-Max Severe Congestion & Cough [OTC]; NeoTuss-D [OTC]; Nivanex DMX [OTC]; Relhist DMX [OTC]; Robafen CF Cough & Cold [OTC] [DSC]; Robitussin Children's Cough & Cold CF [OTC]; Robitussin Peak Cold Maximum Strength Multi-Symptom Cold [OTC]; Robitussin Peak Cold Multi-Symptom Cold [OTC]; Tusicof [OTC]; Tussin CF Cough & Cold [OTC]
Pharmacologic Category Antitussive; Decongestant
Use Symptomatic relief of dry nonproductive coughs and upper respiratory symptoms associated with hay fever, colds, or the flu
Local Anesthetic/Vasoconstrictor Precautions Use with caution since phenylephrine is a sympathomimetic amine which could interact with epinephrine to cause a pressor response
Effects on Dental Treatment Key adverse event(s) related to dental treatment:
Dextromethorphan: No significant effects or complications reported
Guaifenesin: No significant effects or complications reported
Phenylephrine: Up to 10% of patients could experience tachycardia, palpitations, and xerostomia (normal salivary flow resumes upon discontinuation); use vasoconstrictor with caution
Effects on Bleeding No information available to require special precautions
Adverse Reactions Frequency not defined. The following adverse events have been reported with the combination product. Also see individual agents.
Cardiovascular: Circulatory shock, palpitations, tachycardia
Central nervous system: Anxiety, central nervous system depression, convulsions, dizziness, drowsiness, excitability, fear, hallucination, headache, insomnia, irritability, nervousness
Gastrointestinal: Nausea, vomiting
Neuromuscular & skeletal: Tremor, weakness
Respiratory: Dyspnea
General Dosage Range Oral: *Children >4 years and Adults:* Dosage varies greatly depending on product
Mechanism of Action See individual agents.
Pregnancy Considerations See individual agents.

Guaifenesin, Pseudoephedrine, and Codeine
(gwye FEN e sin, soo doe e FED rin, & KOE deen)

Related Information
Codeine *on page 410*
GuaiFENesin *on page 808*
Pseudoephedrine *on page 1404*
Brand Names: US Cheratussin DAC [DSC]; Coditussin DAC; Guaifenesin DAC; Lortuss EX; Mytussin DAC [DSC]; Tricode GF [DSC]; Virtussin DAC
Brand Names: Canada Balminil Codeine + Decongestant + Expectorant; Benylin 2 Cold and Flu with Codeine; Calmylin PSE with Codeine
Pharmacologic Category Antitussive/Decongestant/Expectorant
Use Cough/nasal congestion: Temporarily relieves cough and nasal congestion associated with the common cold, allergic rhinitis, or other upper respiratory allergies
Local Anesthetic/Vasoconstrictor Precautions Use with caution since pseudoephedrine is a sympathomimetic amine which could interact with epinephrine to cause a pressor response
Effects on Dental Treatment Key adverse event(s) related to dental treatment:
Codeine: Xerostomia (normal salivary flow resumes upon discontinuation).
Guaifenesin: No significant effects or complications reported
Pseudoephedrine: Xerostomia (normal salivary flow resumes upon discontinuation).
Effects on Bleeding No information available to require special precautions
Adverse Reactions See individual agents.
General Dosage Range Oral:
Children 6 to <12 years: Codeine 10 mg/guaifenesin 100 mg/pseudoephedrine 30 mg (5 mL) every 4 hours (maximum: codeine 40 mg/guaifenesin 400 mg/pseudoephedrine 120 mg [20 mL] per 24 hours)
Children≥12 years, Adolescents, and Adults: Codeine 20 mg/guaifenesin 200 mg/pseudoephedrine 60 mg (10 mL) every 4 hours (maximum: codeine 80 mg/guaifenesin 800 mg/pseudoephedrine 240 mg [40 mL] per 24 hours)
Mechanism of Action
Codeine: Causes cough suppression by direct central action in the medulla; produces generalized CNS depression.
Guaifenesin: Thought to act as an expectorant by irritating the gastric mucosa and stimulating respiratory tract secretions, thereby increasing respiratory fluid volumes and decreasing mucous viscosity.
Pseudoephedrine: Directly stimulates alpha-adrenergic receptors of respiratory mucosa causing vasoconstriction; directly stimulates beta-adrenergic receptors causing bronchial relaxation, increased heart rate and contractility.
Pregnancy Considerations See individual agents.
Controlled Substance C-V

GuanFACINE (GWAHN fa seen)

Related Information
Cardiovascular Diseases *on page 1752*
Dentin Hypersensitivity, Acid Erosion, High Caries Index, Management of Alveolar Osteitis, and Xerostomia *on page 1857*
Brand Names: US Intuniv; Tenex [DSC]

Brand Names: Canada Intuniv XR

Pharmacologic Category $Alpha_2$-Adrenergic Agonist; Antihypertensive

Use

Attention-deficit/hyperactivity disorder (extended release only): Treatment of attention-deficit/hyperactivity disorder (ADHD) as monotherapy and as adjunctive therapy to stimulant medications.

Hypertension (immediate release only): Management of hypertension.

Local Anesthetic/Vasoconstrictor Precautions No information available to require special precautions

Effects on Dental Treatment Key adverse event(s) related to dental treatment: Xerostomia and changes in salivation (normal salivary flow resumes upon discontinuation).

Effects on Bleeding No information available to require special precautions

Adverse Reactions

>10%:

Central nervous system: Drowsiness (10% to 57%; dose-related), headache (4% to 28%), fatigue (5% to 22%), dizziness (4% to 16%; dose-related), insomnia (2% to 13%),

Gastrointestinal: Xerostomia (3% to 54%; dose-related), abdominal pain (≤8% to 19%; dose-related), decreased appetite (5% to 15%), constipation (2% to 15%; dose-related)

1% to 10%:

Cardiovascular: Hypotension (≤1% to 9%; dose-related; includes orthostatic), bradycardia (2% to 5%), atrioventricular block (≥2%), sinus arrhythmia (≥2%), syncope (1% to ≥2%)

Central nervous system: Irritability (5% to 8%), lethargy (3% to 8%), anxiety (2% to 5%), nightmares (3% to 4%), emotional lability (children and adolescents 6 to 17 years: 2% to 3%), agitation (≥2%), depression (≥2%)

Dermatologic: Skin rash (2% to 3%), pruritus (2%)

Endocrine & metabolic: Weight gain (≤2% to 3%)

Gastrointestinal: Nausea (≤5% to 7%), vomiting (2% to 7%), diarrhea (2% to 6%), dyspepsia (≥2%), stomach pain (≥2%)

Genitourinary: Impotence (≤3% to 7%), urinary incontinence (2% to 5%)

Neuromuscular & skeletal: Weakness (≤2% to 7%)

Respiratory: Asthma (≥2%)

Miscellaneous: Fever (8%; Biederman 2008)

Frequency not defined:

Cardiovascular: Chest pain, hypertension

Central nervous system: Convulsions

Dermatologic: Pallor

Genitourinary: Urinary frequency

Hepatic: Increased serum ALT

Hypersensitivity: Hypersensitivity reaction

<1%, postmarketing, and/or case reports: Abnormal hepatic function tests, aggressive behavior (immediate release; children), alopecia, amnesia, arthralgia, blurred vision, cardiac fibrillation, cerebrovascular accident, confusion, conjunctivitis, decreased libido, dermatitis, diaphoresis, dysgeusia, dysphagia, dyspnea, edema, exacerbation of cardiac disease (sinus node dysfunction, atrioventricular block), exfoliative dermatitis, hallucination, hypertensive encephalopathy (with abrupt discontinuation), hypokinesia, iritis, leg cramps, leg pain, malaise, mania (immediate release; children), myalgia, myocardial infarction, nervousness, nocturia, palpitations, paresis, paresthesia, purpura, Raynaud phenomenon, rebound hypertension, renal failure, rhinitis, tachycardia, tinnitus, tremor, vertigo, visual disturbance

General Dosage Range Oral:

Immediate release: *Children ≥12 years, Adolescents, and Adults:* 0.5 to 2 mg once daily

Extended release: *Children ≥6 years and Adolescents ≤17 years:* 1 to 7 mg once daily (weight-based dosing 0.05 to 0.12 mg/kg/day).

Mechanism of Action Guanfacine is a selective $alpha_{2A}$-adrenoreceptor agonist that reduces sympathetic nerve impulses, resulting in reduced sympathetic outflow and a subsequent decrease in vasomotor tone and heart rate. In addition, guanfacine preferentially binds postsynaptic $alpha_{2A}$-adrenoreceptors in the prefrontal cortex and has been theorized to improve delay-related firing of prefrontal cortex neurons. As a result, underlying working memory and behavioral inhibition are affected; thereby improving symptoms associated with ADHD. Guanfacine is not a CNS stimulant.

Pharmacodynamics/Kinetics

Duration of Action Antihypertensive effect: 24 hours following single dose

Half-life Elimination

Immediate release: ~17 hours (range: 10 to 30 hours)

Extended release: Children ≥6 years: 14.4 hours; Adolescents: 18 hours (Boellner 2007); Adults: 16 hours

Time to Peak Serum:

Immediate release: 2.6 hours (range: 1 to 4 hours)

Extended release: Children ≥6 years and Adolescents: 5 hours (Boellner 2007); Adults: 4 to 8 hours

Pregnancy Risk Factor B

Pregnancy Considerations Adverse events have not been observed in animal reproduction studies except in doses that also caused maternal toxicity. Information related to guanfacine use during pregnancy is limited (Philipp 1980). Untreated chronic maternal hypertension is associated with adverse events in the fetus, infant, and mother. If treatment for hypertension during pregnancy is needed, other agents are preferred (ACOG 2012).

Haloperidol (ha loe PER i dole)

Related Information

Clinical Risk Related to Drugs Prolonging QT Interval *on page 1772*

Brand Names: US Haldol; Haldol Decanoate

Brand Names: Canada Apo-Haloperidol; Haloperidol Injection, USP; Haloperidol-LA; Haloperidol-LA Omega; Novo-Peridol; PMS-Haloperidol; PMS-Haloperidol LA

Pharmacologic Category First Generation (Typical) Antipsychotic

Use

Behavioral disorders (tablet, concentrate): Treatment of severe behavioral problems in children with combative, explosive hyperexcitability that cannot be accounted for by immediate provocation. Reserve for use in these children only after failure to respond to psychotherapy or medications other than antipsychotics.

Hyperactivity (tablet, concentrate): Short-term treatment of hyperactive children who show excessive motor activity with accompanying conduct disorders consisting of some or all of the following symptoms: impulsivity, difficulty sustaining attention, aggression, mood lability, or poor frustration tolerance. Reserve for use in these children only after failure to respond to psychotherapy or medications other than antipsychotics.

Psychotic disorders (tablet, concentrate): Management of manifestations of psychotic disorders.

Schizophrenia:

IM, lactate: Treatment of schizophrenia.

IM, decanoate: Treatment of patients with schizophrenia who require prolonged parenteral antipsychotic therapy.

Tourette disorder (tablet, concentrate, IM lactate): Control of tics and vocal utterances in Tourette syndrome in adults and children.

Local Anesthetic/Vasoconstrictor Precautions Manufacturer's information states that haloperidol may block vasopressor activity of epinephrine. This has not been observed during use of epinephrine as a vasoconstrictor in local anesthesia. Haloperidol is one of the drugs confirmed to prolong the QT interval and is accepted as having a risk of causing torsade de pointes. The risk of drug-induced torsade de pointes is extremely low when a single QT interval prolonging drug is prescribed. In terms of epinephrine, it is not known what effect vasoconstrictors in the local anesthetic regimen will have in patients with a known history of congenital prolonged QT interval or in patients taking any medication that prolongs the QT interval. Until more information is obtained, it is suggested that the clinician consult with the physician prior to the use of a vasoconstrictor in suspected patients, and that the vasoconstrictor (epinephrine, mepivacaine and levonordefrin [Carbocaine® 2% with Neo-Cobefrin®]) be used with caution.

Effects on Dental Treatment Key adverse event(s) related to dental treatment: Xerostomia (normal salivary flow resumes upon discontinuation); nasal congestion is possible; since the drug is a dopamine antagonist, extrapyramidal symptoms of the TMJ are a possibility. Patients may experience orthostatic hypotension as they stand up after treatment; especially if lying in dental chair for extended periods of time. Use caution with sudden changes in position during and after dental treatment.

Effects on Bleeding No information available to require special precautions

Adverse Reactions Frequency not defined.

Cardiovascular: Abnormal T waves on ECG (with prolonged ventricular repolarization), cardiac arrhythmia, hypertension, hypotension, prolonged Q-T interval on ECG, tachycardia, torsades de pointes, ventricular arrhythmia

Central nervous system: Agitation, akathisia, anxiety, confusion, depression, drowsiness, dystonic reaction, euphoria, exacerbation of psychosis, extrapyramidal reaction, headache, heatstroke, hyperpyrexia, insomnia, lethargy, neuroleptic malignant syndrome, parkinsonian-like syndrome, restlessness, seizure, tardive dyskinesia, tardive dystonia, vertigo

Dermatologic: Acneiform eruption, alopecia, diaphoresis, maculopapular rash, skin photosensitivity (rare)

Endocrine & metabolic: Amenorrhea, galactorrhea, gynecomastia, hyperammonemia, hyperglycemia, hypoglycemia, hyponatremia, increased libido, menstrual disease

Gastrointestinal: Anorexia, constipation, diarrhea, dyspepsia, nausea, sialorrhea, vomiting, xerostomia

Genitourinary: Breast engorgement, lactation, mastalgia, priapism, sexual disorder, urinary retention

Hematologic & oncologic: Agranulocytosis (rare), anemia, decreased red blood cells, leukocytosis, leukopenia, lymphocytosis with monocytosis, neutropenia

Hepatic: Hepatic insufficiency, jaundice

Neuromuscular & skeletal: Laryngospasm, rhabdomyolysis

Ophthalmic: Blurred vision, cataract, retinopathy, visual disturbance

Respiratory: Bronchospasm, increased depth of respiration

General Dosage Range

IM:

Decanoate: *Adults:* Initial: 10 to 20 times the daily oral dose; Maintenance: 10 to 15 times the previous daily oral dose; administer at 4-week intervals

Lactate: *Adults:* 2 to 5 mg; subsequent doses may be administered as often as every 60 minutes, although 4- to 8-hour intervals may be satisfactory

Oral:

Children 3 to 12 years (15 to 40 kg): Initial: 0.5 mg daily in 2 to 3 divided doses; Maintenance: 0.05 to 0.15 mg/kg/day in 2 to 3 divided doses

Adults: Initial: 0.5 to 5 mg 2 to 3 times daily

Mechanism of Action Haloperidol is a butyrophenone antipsychotic that nonselectively blocks postsynaptic dopaminergic D_2 receptors in the brain (Richelson 1999; Risch 1996).

Pharmacodynamics/Kinetics

Half-life Elimination

Decanoate: 21 days

Lactate:

IM: 20 hours (Kudo 1999)

IV: 14 to 26 hours (Kudo 1999)

Oral: 14 to 37 hours (Kudo 1999)

Time to Peak

Decanoate: 6 days

Lactate:

IM: 20 minutes (Kudo 1999)

Oral: 2 to 6 hours (Kudo 1999)

Pregnancy Risk Factor C

Pregnancy Considerations Adverse events were observed in animal reproduction studies. Haloperidol crosses the placenta in humans (Newport 2007). Although haloperidol has not been found to be a major human teratogen, an association with limb malformations following first trimester exposure in humans cannot be ruled out (ACOG 2008; Diav-Citrin 2005). Antipsychotic use during the third trimester of pregnancy has a risk for abnormal muscle movements (extrapyramidal symptoms [EPS]) and withdrawal symptoms in newborns following delivery. Symptoms in the newborn may include agitation, feeding disorder, hypertonia, hypotonia, respiratory distress, somnolence, and tremor; these effects may be self-limiting or require hospitalization. If needed, the minimum effective maternal dose should be used in order to decrease the risk of EPS (ACOG 2008).

Dental Comment See Local Anesthetic/Vasoconstrictor Precautions

Heparin (HEP a rin)

Related Information

Cardiovascular Diseases *on page* 1752

Brand Names: US Hep Flush-10 [DSC]

Brand Names: Canada Heparin Leo; Heparin Lock Flush; Heparin Sodium Injection, USP

Pharmacologic Category Anticoagulant; Anticoagulant, Heparin

Use

Anticoagulation: Prophylaxis and treatment of thromboembolic disorders (eg, venous thromboembolism, pulmonary embolism) and thromboembolic complications associated with atrial fibrillation; prevention of clotting in arterial and cardiac surgery; as an anticoagulant for extracorporeal circulation and dialysis procedures

Note: Heparin lock flush solution is intended only to maintain patency of IV devices and is **not** to be used for systemic anticoagulant therapy.

Local Anesthetic/Vasoconstrictor Precautions No information available to require special precautions

Effects on Dental Treatment Key adverse event(s) related to dental treatment: Bleeding from the gums. See Effects on Bleeding.

Effects on Bleeding The most serious adverse effect is bleeding, including bleeding from the gums. Medical consult is recommended.

Adverse Reactions **Note**: Frequency not defined. Thrombocytopenia has been reported to occur at an incidence between 0% and 30%. It is often of no clinical significance. However, immunologically mediated heparin-induced thrombocytopenia (HIT) has been estimated to occur in 1% to 2% of patients, and is marked by a progressive fall in platelet counts and, in some cases, thromboembolic complications (skin necrosis, pulmonary embolism, gangrene of the extremities, cerebrovascular accident, or myocardial infarction).

Cardiovascular: Chest pain, hemorrhagic shock, shock, thrombosis, vasospasm (allergic; possibly related to thrombosis)

Central nervous system: Chills, headache, local dysesthesia (feet), peripheral neuropathy

Dermatologic: Dermal ulcer (rarely reported with deep subcutaneous injections; intramuscular injection [not recommended] is associated with a higher incidence of this effect), eczema, erythematous plaques (case reports), localized erythema (rarely reported with deep subcutaneous injections; intramuscular injection [not recommended] is associated with a higher incidence of this effect), skin necrosis, transient alopecia (delayed), urticaria

Endocrine & metabolic: Adrenal hemorrhage, hyperkalemia (suppression of aldosterone synthesis), hyperlipidemia (rebound; on discontinuation), ovarian hemorrhage

Gastrointestinal: Constipation, hematemesis, melena, nausea, vomiting

Genitourinary: Erectile dysfunction (frequent or persistent erection), hematuria

Hematologic & oncologic: Bruise (unexplained), gingival hemorrhage, hematoma (rarely reported with deep subcutaneous injections; intramuscular injection [not recommended] is associated with a higher incidence of this effect), hemorrhage, pulmonary hemorrhage, purpura, retroperitoneal hemorrhage, thrombocytopenia (see note)

Hepatic: Increased liver enzymes

Hypersensitivity: Anaphylactoid reaction, hypersensitivity reaction

Local: Local irritation, local pain (rarely reported with deep subcutaneous injections; intramuscular injection [not recommended] is associated with a high incidence of these effects)

Neuromuscular & skeletal: Osteoporosis (chronic therapy effect)

Ophthalmic: Allergic conjunctivitis, lacrimation

Respiratory: Asthma, bronchospasm (case reports), epistaxis, hemoptysis, rhinitis

Miscellaneous: Fever, heparin resistance

General Dosage Range

IV:

Infants, Children, and Adolescents: Initial loading dose: 75 units/kg over 10 minutes; then initial continuous maintenance infusion at: 28 units/kg/hour (infants) or 20 units/kg/hour (children and adolescents).

Adults: Dosage varies greatly depending on indication.

SubQ: *Adults:* Thromboprophylaxis: 5,000 units every 8 to 12 hours; Treatment: 17,500 units every 12 hours

Mechanism of Action Potentiates the action of antithrombin III and thereby inactivates thrombin (as well as activated coagulation factors IX, X, XI, XII, and plasmin) and prevents the conversion of fibrinogen to fibrin; heparin also stimulates release of lipoprotein lipase (lipoprotein lipase hydrolyzes triglycerides to glycerol and free fatty acids)

Pharmacodynamics/Kinetics

Onset of Action Anticoagulation: IV: Immediate; SubQ: ~20 to 30 minutes

Half-life Elimination

Age-related: Shorter half-life reported in premature neonates compared to adult patients

Premature neonates GA 25 to 36 weeks (data based on single dose of 100 units/kg within 4 hours of birth): Mean range: 35.5 to 41.6 minutes (McDonald 1981)

Dose-dependent: IV bolus: 25 units/kg: 30 minutes (Bjornsson 1982); 100 units/kg: 60 minutes (de Swart 1982); 400 units/kg: 150 minutes (Olsson 1963)

Mean: 1.5 hours; Range: 1 to 2 hours; affected by obesity, renal function, malignancy, presence of pulmonary embolism, and infections

Note: At therapeutic doses, elimination occurs rapidly via nonrenal mechanisms. With very high doses, renal elimination may play more of a role; however, dosage adjustment remains unnecessary for patients with renal impairment (Kandrotas 1992).

Pregnancy Risk Factor C

Pregnancy Considerations Increased resorptions were observed in some animal reproduction studies. Heparin does not cross the placenta. Heparin may be used for the prevention and treatment of thromboembolism in pregnant women; however the use of low molecular weight heparin (LMWH) is preferred. Twice-daily heparin should be discontinued prior to induction of labor or a planned cesarean delivery. In pregnant women with mechanical heart valves, adjusted-dose LMWH or adjusted-dose heparin may be used throughout pregnancy or until week 13 of gestation when therapy can be changed to warfarin. LMWH or heparin should be resumed close to delivery. In women who are at a very high risk for thromboembolism (older generation prosthesis in mitral position or history of thromboembolism), warfarin can be used throughout pregnancy and replaced with LMWH or heparin near term; the use of low-dose aspirin is also recommended. When choosing therapy, fetal outcomes (ie, pregnancy loss, malformations), maternal outcomes (ie, VTE, hemorrhage), burden of therapy, and maternal preference should be considered (Guyatt, 2012).

Some products contain benzyl alcohol as a preservative; their use in pregnant women is contraindicated by some manufacturers; use of a preservative free formulation is recommended.

Hepatitis A and Hepatitis B Recombinant Vaccine

(hep a TYE tis aye & hep a TYE tis bee ree KOM be nant vak SEEN)

Related Information

Systemic Viral Diseases *on page 1806*

Brand Names: US Twinrix

Brand Names: Canada Twinrix; Twinrix Junior

Pharmacologic Category Vaccine; Vaccine, Inactivated (Viral)

Use

Hepatitis A and B diseases prevention:

Twinrix: Active immunization of persons 18 years and older (US labeling) or 19 years and older (Canadian labeling) against disease caused by hepatitis A virus and hepatitis B virus (all known subtypes)

Canadian labeling: Additional uses (not in US labeling): Approved for active immunization of children and adolescents ages 1 to 15 years.

Twinrix Junior [Canadian product]: Active immunization of children and adolescents ages 1 to 18 years against disease caused by hepatitis A virus and hepatitis B virus (all known subtypes).

Limitations of use: Hepatitis A/hepatitis B vaccine cannot be used for postexposure prophylaxis.

Local Anesthetic/Vasoconstrictor Precautions No information available to require special precautions

Effects on Dental Treatment Key adverse event(s) related to dental treatment: Flu-like syndrome and upper respiratory tract infection.

Effects on Bleeding No information available to require special precautions

Adverse Reactions Incidence of adverse effects of the combination product were similar to those occurring after administration of hepatitis A vaccine and hepatitis B vaccine alone. (Incidence reported is not versus placebo.) Also see individual agents.

>10%:

Central nervous system: Headache (13% to 22%), fatigue (11% to 14%)

Local: Local soreness/soreness at injection site (35% to 41%), erythema at injection site (8% to 11%)

1% to 10%:

Dermatologic: Skin sclerosis (at injection site)

Gastrointestinal: Diarrhea (4% to 6%), nausea (2% to 4%), vomiting (≤1%)

Local: Local swelling (at injection site: 4% to 6%)

Respiratory: Upper respiratory tract infection

Miscellaneous: Fever (2% to 4%)

<1%, postmarketing, and/or case reports: Abdominal pain, abnormal hepatic function tests, agitation, alopecia, anaphylactoid reaction, anaphylaxis, angioedema, anorexia, arthralgia, arthritis, back pain, Bell's palsy, brain disease, bronchospasm, bruise, bruising at injection site, chills, conjunctivitis, diaphoresis, dizziness, drowsiness, dyspepsia, dyspnea (including asthma-like symptoms), eczema, encephalitis, erythema, erythema multiforme, erythema nodosum, flu-like symptoms, flushing, Guillain-Barre syndrome, hepatitis, herpes zoster, hyperhidrosis, hypersensitivity reaction, hypoesthesia, immune thrombocytopenia, injection site pruritus, injection site reaction (burning sensation at injection site, pain at injection site), insomnia, irritability, jaundice, lichen planus, malaise, meningitis, migraine, multiple sclerosis, myalgia, myasthenia, myelitis, neuropathy, neuritis, optic neuritis, otalgia, palpitations, paralysis, paresis, paresthesia, petechiae, respiratory tract disease, seizure, serum sickness-like reaction (days to weeks after vaccination), skin rash, syncope, tachycardia, thrombocytopenia, tinnitus, transverse myelitis, urticaria, vasculitis, vertigo, visual disturbance, weakness

General Dosage Range IM: *Adults:* 1 mL given on a 0-, 1-, and 6-month schedule for a total of 3 doses

Mechanism of Action

Hepatitis A vaccine, an inactivated virus vaccine, offers active immunization against hepatitis A virus infection at an effective immune response rate in up to 99% of subjects.

Recombinant hepatitis B vaccine is a noninfectious subunit viral vaccine. The vaccine is derived from hepatitis B surface antigen (HBsAg) produced through recombinant DNA techniques from yeast cells. The portion of the hepatitis B gene which codes for HBsAg is cloned into yeast which is then cultured to produce hepatitis B vaccine.

In immunocompetent people, Twinrix provides active immunization against hepatitis A virus infection (at an effective immune response rate >99% of subjects) and against hepatitis B virus infection (at an effective immune response rate of 93% to 97%) 30 days after completion of the 3-dose series. This is comparable to using hepatitis A vaccine and hepatitis B vaccine concomitantly.

Pharmacodynamics/Kinetics

Onset of Action Seroconversion for antibodies against HAV and HBV were detected 1 month after completion of the 3-dose series.

Duration of Action HAV and HBV seropositivity have been observed for 15 years in adults and for 10 years in children (Diaz-Mitoma 2008, Van Herck 2007).

Pregnancy Risk Factor C

Pregnancy Considerations Animal reproduction studies have not been conducted with this combination. Inactivated vaccines have not been shown to cause increased risks to the fetus (NCIRD/ACIP 2011).

Hepatitis A Vaccine (hep a TYE tis aye vak SEEN)

Related Information

Systemic Viral Diseases *on page 1806*

Brand Names: US Havrix; VAQTA

Brand Names: Canada Avaxim; Avaxim-Pediatric; HAVRIX; VAQTA

Pharmacologic Category Vaccine; Vaccine, Inactivated (Viral)

Use Hepatitis A virus disease prevention:

For active immunization of persons 12 months and older against disease caused by hepatitis A virus (HAV).

The Advisory Committee on Immunization Practices (ACIP) recommends routine vaccination for:

- All children ≥12 months of age (CDC/ACIP [Fiore 2006])
- All unvaccinated adults requesting protection from HAV infection (CDC/ACIP [Fiore 2006])
- Unvaccinated persons with any of the following conditions: Men who have sex with men; injection and non-injection illicit drug users; persons who work with HAV-infected primates or with HAV in a research laboratory setting; persons with chronic liver disease; patients who receive clotting-factor concentrates; persons traveling to or working in countries with high or intermediate levels of endemic HAV infection (CDC/ACIP [Fiore 2006])
- Unvaccinated persons who anticipate close personal contact with international adoptee from a country of intermediate to high endemicity of HAV, during their

first 60 days of arrival into the United States (eg, household contacts, babysitters) (CDC/ACIP 58 [36] 2009)
- Vaccination can be a component of hepatitis A outbreak response or as postexposure prophylaxis, as determined by local public health authorities (CDC/ACIP 56[41] 2007; CDC/ACIP [Fiore 2006])

Local Anesthetic/Vasoconstrictor Precautions No information available to require special precautions

Effects on Dental Treatment No significant effects or complications reported

Effects on Bleeding No information available to require special precautions

Adverse Reactions All serious adverse reactions must be reported to the U.S. Department of Health and Human Services (DHHS) Vaccine Adverse Event Reporting System (VAERS) at 1-800-822-7967 or online at https://vaers.hhs.gov/esub/index. In Canada, adverse reactions may be reported to local provincial/territorial health agencies or to the Vaccine Safety Section at Public Health Agency of Canada (1-866-844-0018).

Frequency dependent upon age, product used, and concomitant vaccine administration. In general, headache and injection site reactions were less common in younger children.

>10%:

Central nervous system: Drowsiness, headache, irritability

Gastrointestinal: Decreased appetite

Local: Erythema at injection site, injection site reaction (soreness, warmth), pain at injection site, swelling at injection site, tenderness at injection site

Neuromuscular & skeletal: Weakness

Miscellaneous: Fever (≥100.4°F [1-5 days postvaccination], >98.6°F [1-14 days postvaccination])

1% to 10%:

Central nervous system: Chills, fatigue, insomnia, malaise

Dermatologic: Skin rash

Endocrine & metabolic: Menstrual disease

Gastrointestinal: Abdominal pain, anorexia, constipation, diarrhea, gastroenteritis, nausea, vomiting

Local: Bruising at injection site, induration at injection site

Neuromuscular & skeletal: Arm pain, back pain, myalgia, stiffness

Ophthalmic: Conjunctivitis

Otic: Otitis media

Respiratory: Asthma, cough, nasal congestion, nasopharyngitis, pharyngitis, rhinitis, rhinorrhea, upper respiratory tract infection

Miscellaneous: Excessive crying, fever ≥102°F (1-5 days postvaccination)

<1%, postmarketing, and/or case reports: Anaphylaxis, angioedema, arthralgia, ataxia (cerebellar), bronchiolitis, bronchoconstriction, croup, dehydration, dermatitis, dizziness, dysgeusia, dyspnea, encephalitis, erythema multiforme, eye irritation, flu-like symptoms, Guillain-Barre syndrome, hematoma at injection site, hepatitis, hyperhidrosis, hypersensitivity reaction, hypertonia, hypoesthesia, increased creatine kinase, increased serum transaminases (transient), injection site reaction (nodule), insomnia, jaundice, lymphadenopathy, multiple sclerosis, myelitis, neuropathy, otitis, paresthesia, photophobia, pneumonia, pruritus, rash at injection site, respiratory congestion, seizure, serum sickness-like reaction, syncope, thrombocytopenia, urticaria, vasculitis, vertigo, viral exanthem, wheezing

General Dosage Range IM:

Children ≥12 years and Adolescents: 0.5 mL

Adults: 1 mL

Mechanism of Action As an inactivated virus vaccine, hepatitis A vaccine induces active immunity against hepatitis A virus infection

Pharmacodynamics/Kinetics

Onset of Action Protective antibodies develop in 95% of adults after the first dose and in 100% of adults after the second dose of the vaccine; ≥97% of children and adolescents will be seropositive within 1 month of the first dose and 100% will develop protective antibodies after receiving two doses. The efficacy of preventing hepatitis A disease in children living in highly infected areas is 94% to 100% (CDC 2012).

Duration of Action Protective antibodies induced by the vaccine may persist for ≥20 years (CDC 2012).

Pregnancy Risk Factor C

Pregnancy Considerations Animal reproduction studies have not been conducted. The safety of vaccination during pregnancy has not been determined, however, the theoretical risk to the infant is expected to be low. Inactivated vaccines have not been shown to cause increased risks to the fetus (NCIRD/ACIP 2011).

Hepatitis B Immune Globulin (Human)

(hep a TYE tis bee i MYUN GLOB yoo lin YU man)

Related Information

Systemic Viral Diseases *on page 1806*

Brand Names: US HepaGam B; HyperHEP B S/D; Nabi-HB

Brand Names: Canada HepaGam B; HyperHEP B S/D

Pharmacologic Category Blood Product Derivative; Immune Globulin

Use

Passive prophylactic immunity to hepatitis B following: Acute exposure to blood containing hepatitis B surface antigen (HBsAg); perinatal exposure of infants born to HBsAg-positive mothers; sexual exposure to HBsAg-positive persons; household exposure to persons with acute HBV infection

Prevention of hepatitis B virus recurrence after liver transplantation in HBsAg-positive transplant patients

Note: Hepatitis B immune globulin is not indicated for treatment of active hepatitis B infection and is ineffective in the treatment of chronic active hepatitis B infection.

Local Anesthetic/Vasoconstrictor Precautions No information available to require special precautions

Effects on Dental Treatment No significant effects or complications reported

Effects on Bleeding No information available to require special precautions

Adverse Reactions Reported with postexposure prophylaxis. Adverse events reported in liver transplant patients included tremor and hypotension, were associated with a single infusion during the first week of treatment, and did not recur with additional infusions.

>10%:

Central nervous system: Headache (14%)

Dermatologic: Erythema (12%)

1% to 10%:

Cardiovascular: Hypotension (2%)

Central nervous system: Malaise (6%)

Dermatologic: Ecchymoses (2%)

Gastrointestinal: Nausea (2% to 4%), vomiting (2%)

Hematologic & oncologic: Change in WBC count (2%)

Hepatic: Increased serum alkaline phosphatase (4%), increased liver enzymes (2%)

Local: Pain at injection site (4%)

Neuromuscular & skeletal: Myalgia (10%), joint stiffness (2%)

Renal: Increased serum creatinine (2%)

<1%, postmarketing, and/or case reports: Abdominal pain, anaphylactic reaction (rare), angioedema, back pain, chills, diaphoresis, dizziness, dyspnea, fever, flu-like symptoms, hypersensitivity, increased serum lipase, increased serum transaminases, sinus tachycardia, tenderness at injection site, urticaria

General Dosage Range

IM:

Newborns and Infants <12 months: 0.5 mL/dose

Children ≥12 months and Adults: 0.06 mL/kg/dose

IV: *Adults:* 20,000 units/dose daily for 8 days, then every 2 weeks for 6 doses, then once monthly

Mechanism of Action Hepatitis B immune globulin (HBIG) is a nonpyrogenic sterile solution containing immunoglobulin G (IgG) specific to hepatitis B surface antigen (HBsAg). HBIG differs from immune globulin in the amount of anti-HBs. Immune globulin is prepared from plasma that is not preselected for anti-HBs content. HBIG is prepared from plasma preselected for high titer anti-HBs. In the U.S., HBIG has an anti-HBs high titer >1:100,000 by IRA.

Pharmacodynamics/Kinetics

Duration of Action Postexposure prophylaxis: 3-6 months

Half-life Elimination 17-25 days

Time to Peak Serum: IM: 2-10 days

Pregnancy Risk Factor C

Pregnancy Considerations Animal reproduction studies have not been conducted. Use of HBIG is not contraindicated in pregnant women and may be used for postexposure prophylaxis when indicated (CDC, 2001). In addition, use of HBIG has been evaluated to reduce maternal to fetal transmission of hepatis B virus during pregnancy (ACOG, 2007)

Hepatitis B Vaccine (Recombinant)

(hep a TYE tis bee vak SEEN ree KOM be nant)

Related Information

Systemic Viral Diseases *on page 1806*

Brand Names: US Engerix-B; Recombivax HB

Brand Names: Canada Engerix-B; Recombivax HB

Pharmacologic Category Vaccine; Vaccine, Inactivated (Viral)

Use Hepatitis B disease prevention: Active immunization against infection caused by all known subtypes of hepatitis B virus (HBV)

The Advisory Committee on Immunization Practices (ACIP) recommends routine vaccination for the following:

- All neonates before hospital discharge (CDC/ACIP [Mast 2005])
- All unvaccinated infants and children (CDC/ACIP [Mast 2005])
- All unvaccinated adults requesting protection from HBV infection (CDC/ACIP [Mast 2006])
- All unvaccinated adults at risk for HBV infection such as those with:

  Behavioral risks: Sexually-active persons with >1 partner in a 6-month period; persons seeking evaluation or treatment for a sexually-transmitted disease; men who have sex with men; injection drug users (CDC/ACIP [Mast 2006])

  Occupational risks: Healthcare personnel (HCP) and public safety workers with reasonably anticipated risk for exposure to blood or blood contaminated body fluids (CDC/ACIP [Mast 2006])

  Medical risks: Persons with end-stage renal disease (including predialysis, hemodialysis, peritoneal dialysis, and home dialysis); persons with HIV infection; persons with chronic liver disease (CDC/ACIP [Mast 2006]). Adults (19 through 59 years of age) with diabetes mellitus type 1 or type 2 should be vaccinated as soon as possible following diagnosis. Adults ≥60 years with diabetes mellitus may also be vaccinated at the discretion of their treating clinician based on the likelihood of acquiring HBV infection (CDC/ACIP 60[50] 2011).

  Other risks: Household contacts and sex partners of persons with chronic HBV infection; residents and staff of facilities for developmentally disabled persons; international travelers to regions with high or intermediate levels of endemic HBV infection (CDC/ACIP [Mast 2006])

In addition, the ACIP recommends vaccination for any persons who are wounded in bombings or similar mass casualty events who have penetrating injuries or nonintact skin exposure, or who have contact with mucous membranes (exception - superficial contact with intact skin), and who cannot confirm receipt of a hepatitis B vaccination (CDC [Chapman 2008]).

Local Anesthetic/Vasoconstrictor Precautions No information available to require special precautions

Effects on Dental Treatment No significant effects or complications reported

Effects on Bleeding No information available to require special precautions

Adverse Reactions All serious adverse reactions must be reported to the U.S. Department of Health and Human Services (DHHS) Vaccine Adverse Event Reporting System (VAERS) at 1-800-822-7967 or online at https://vaers.hhs.gov/esub/index.

Frequency not defined. The most common adverse effects reported with both products included injection site reactions (>10%).

Cardiovascular: Flushing, hypotension

Central nervous system: Body pain, chills, dizziness, drowsiness, fatigue, headache, insomnia, irritability, malaise, paresthesia, tingling sensation, vertigo

Dermatologic: Diaphoresis, pruritus, skin rash, urticaria

Gastrointestinal: Abdominal pain, anorexia, decreased appetite, diarrhea, dyspepsia, nausea, stomach cramps, vomiting

Genitourinary: Dysuria

Hematologic & oncologic: Lymphadenopathy

Hypersensitivity: Angioedema

Infection: Influenza

Local: Bruising at injection site, erythema at injection site, induration at injection site, injection site nodule, itching at injection site, local soreness/soreness at injection site, pain at injection site, swelling at injection site, tenderness at injection site, warm sensation at injection site

Neuromuscular & skeletal: Arthralgia, back pain, myalgia, neck pain, neck stiffness, shoulder pain, weakness

Otic: Otalgia

Respiratory: Cough, pharyngitis, rhinitis, upper respiratory tract infection

Miscellaneous: Fever (≥37.5°C/100°F)

Postmarketing and/or case reports: Abnormal hepatic function tests, acute exacerbations of multiple sclerosis, agitation, alopecia, anaphylactoid reaction, anaphylaxis, apnea, arthritis, Bell's palsy, brain disease, bronchospasm, conjunctivitis, constipation, convulsions, eczema, encephalitis, erythema nodosum, erythema multiforme, febrile seizures, Guillain-Barre syndrome, herpes zoster, hypersensitivity reaction, hypoesthesia, increased erythrocyte sedimentation rate, increased liver enzymes, keratitis, lichen planus, limb pain, lupus-like syndrome, meningitis, migraine, multiple sclerosis, myasthenia, myelitis, neuritis, neuropathy, optic neuritis, palpitations, paralysis, paresis, periarteritis nodosa, peripheral neuropathy, petechia, purpura, radiculopathy, seizure, serum sickness-like reaction (may be delayed days to weeks), Stevens-Johnson syndrome, syncope, systemic lupus erythematosus, tachycardia, thrombocytopenia, tinnitus, transverse myelitis, uveitis, vasculitis, visual disturbance

General Dosage Range Dosage adjustment recommended in patients with renal impairment.

IM: Note: Various dosing regimens available

Birth to 19 years: 0.5 mL

Adults ≥20 years: 1 mL

Mechanism of Action Recombinant hepatitis B vaccine is a noninfectious subunit viral vaccine, which confers active immunity via formation of antihepatitis B antibodies. The vaccine is derived from hepatitis B surface antigen (HBsAg) produced through recombinant DNA techniques from yeast cells. The portion of the hepatitis B gene which codes for HBsAg is cloned into yeast, which is then cultured to produce hepatitis B vaccine.

Pharmacodynamics/Kinetics

Duration of Action Following a 3-dose series in children, up to 50% of patients will have low or undetectable anti-HB antibody 5 to 15 years postvaccination. However, anamnestic increases in anti-HB have been shown up to 23 years later suggesting a lifelong immune memory response (CDC/ACIP [Mast 2005]; CDC/ACIP [Mast 2006]).

Pregnancy Risk Factor C

Pregnancy Considerations Animal reproduction studies have not been conducted. The ACIP recommends HBsAg testing for all pregnant women. Based on limited data, there is no apparent risk to the fetus when the hepatitis B vaccine is administered during pregnancy. Pregnancy itself is not a contraindication to vaccination; vaccination should be considered if otherwise indicated (CDC/ACIP [Mast 2006]).

Dental Comment Immunization is recommended for dentists, oral surgeons, dental hygienists, dental nurses, and dental students

Hexylresorcinol (heks il re ZOR si nole)

Brand Names: US Sucrets® Original [OTC]

Pharmacologic Category Antiseptic, Topical; Local Anesthetic

Use Minor antiseptic and local anesthetic for sore throat; topical antiseptic for minor cuts or abrasions

Local Anesthetic/Vasoconstrictor Precautions No information available to require special precautions

Effects on Dental Treatment No significant effects or complications reported

Effects on Bleeding No information available to require special precautions

General Dosage Range Oral: *Children ≥6 years and Adults:* Up to 10 lozenges/day

Histrelin (his TREL in)

Brand Names: US Supprelin LA; Vantas

Brand Names: Canada Vantas

Pharmacologic Category Antineoplastic Agent, Gonadotropin-Releasing Hormone Agonist; Gonadotropin Releasing Hormone Agonist

Use

Central precocious puberty: Treatment of central precocious puberty (CPP) in children

Prostate cancer, advanced: Palliative treatment of advanced prostate cancer

Local Anesthetic/Vasoconstrictor Precautions No information available to require special precautions

Effects on Dental Treatment No significant effects or complications reported

Effects on Bleeding Anemia reported in <2% of patients

Adverse Reactions

CPP:

>10%: Dermatologic: Dermatological reaction (51%; insertion site reaction includes bruise, discomfort, pain, protrusion of implant area, pruritus, soreness, swelling, tingling)

>2% to 10%:

Dermatologic: Scarring (6%)

Genitourinary: Uterine hemorrhage (4%)

Local: Application site pain (4%)

Neuromuscular & skeletal: Keloid-like scar (6%)

Miscellaneous: Procedural complications (6%; suture-related), postoperative pain (4%)

≤2%, postmarketing, and/or case reports: Amblyopia, breast tenderness, dysmenorrhea, emotional lability, epistaxis, erythema, flu-like symptoms, gynecomastia, headache, hypermenorrhea, localized infection (implant site), migraine, pituitary apoplexy, pituitary neoplasm, precocious puberty (progression of central precocious puberty), pruritus, seizure, sensation of cold, weight gain

Prostate cancer:

>10%:

Dermatologic: Dermatological reaction (66%; implant site reaction includes bruise, erythema, pain, soreness, swelling, tenderness)

Endocrine & metabolic: Hot flash (66%)

2% to 10%:

Central nervous system: Fatigue (10%), headache (3%), insomnia (3%)

Endocrine & metabolic: Gynecomastia (4%), decreased libido (2%), weight gain (2%)

Gastrointestinal: Constipation (4%)

Genitourinary: Testicular atrophy (5%; expected pharmacological consequence of testosterone suppression), sexual disorder (4%)

Renal: Renal insufficiency (5%)

<2%, postmarketing, and/or case reports: Abdominal distress, alopecia, anemia, arthralgia, back pain, breast tenderness, bruise, decreased bone mineral density, depression, diaphoresis, dizziness, dyspnea on exertion, dysuria, fluid retention, flushing, food craving, genital pruritus, hematoma, hematuria, hepatic disease, hepatic injury (severe), hypercalcemia, hypercholesterolemia, hyperglycemia, increased appetite, increased lactate dehydrogenase, increased prostatic acid phosphatase, increased serum AST, increased serum creatinine, increased testosterone

level, irritability, lethargy, limb pain, malaise, mastalgia, muscle twitching, myalgia, nausea, neck pain, nephrolithiasis, night sweats, ostealgia, pain, palpitations, peripheral edema, pruritus, pituitary apoplexy, renal failure, sensation of cold, stent occlusion, tremor, urinary frequency, urinary retention, ventricular premature contractions, weakness, weight loss

General Dosage Range SubQ: *Children ≥2 years and Adults:* 50 mg implant, inserted every 12 months

Mechanism of Action Potent inhibitor of gonadotropin secretion; continuous administration results in, after an initiation phase, the suppression of luteinizing hormone (LH), follicle-stimulating hormone (FSH), and a subsequent decrease in testosterone and dihydrotestosterone (males) and estrone and estradiol (premenopausal females). Testosterone levels are reduced to castrate levels in males (treated for prostate cancer) within 2 to 4 weeks. Additionally, in patients with CPP, linear growth velocity is slowed (improves chance of attaining predicted adult height).

Pharmacodynamics/Kinetics

Onset of Action Prostate cancer: Chemical castration: Within 2 to 4 weeks; CPP: Progression of sexual development stops and growth is decreased within 1 month

Duration of Action 12 months (plus a few additional weeks of histrelin release)

Half-life Elimination Adults: Terminal: ~4 hours

Time to Peak Adults: 12 hours

Pregnancy Risk Factor X

Pregnancy Considerations Adverse events were observed in animal reproduction studies. May cause fetal harm or spontaneous abortion if administered during pregnancy. Histrelin is contraindicated for use during pregnancy or in women who may become pregnant.

Hyaluronate and Derivatives

(hye al yoor ON ate & dah RIV ah tives)

Brand Names: US Amvisc; Amvisc Plus; Bionect; Euflexxa; Gel-One; Gelsyn-3; GenVisc 850; Hyalgan; HyGel [DSC]; Hylase Wound [DSC]; Hymovis; Juvederm Ultra; Juvederm Ultra Plus; Juvederm Ultra Plus XC; Juvederm Ultra XC; Juvederm Voluma XC; Monovisc; Orthovisc; Perlane; Perlane-L [DSC]; Provisc; Restylane; Restylane Lyft; Restylane Silk; Restylane-L; Supartz FX; Supartz [DSC]; Synvisc; Synvisc-One

Brand Names: Canada Cystistat; Durolane; Ortho-Visc; Suplasyn

Pharmacologic Category Antirheumatic Miscellaneous; Cosmetic Agent, Implant; Ophthalmic Agent, Viscoelastic; Skin and Mucous Membrane Agent, Miscellaneous

Use

Intra-articular injection: Treatment of pain in osteoarthritis of the knee in patients who have failed nonpharmacologic treatment or simple analgesics (Euflexxa, Gel-One, Gelsyn-3, GenVisc 850, Hyalgan, Hymovis, Monovisc, OrthoVisc, Supartz, Supartz FX, Synvisc, Synvisc-One) or nonsteroidal anti-inflammatory drugs (NSAIDS) (Gel-One)

Intradermal:

Juvederm (all formulations except Volbella XC and Voluma XC), Perlane, Restylane, Restylane Defyne, Restylane Lyft, Restylane-L, Restylane Refyne: Correction of moderate to severe facial wrinkles or folds

Juvederm Volbella XC and Restylane Silk: Correction of perioral rhytids in adults >21 years.

Subcutaneous/supraperiosteal: Juvederm Voluma XC, Restylane Lyft: Correction of age-related volume deficit (deep [subcutaneous and/or supraperiosteal] injection) for cheek augmentation in the mid-face in adults >21 years

Ophthalmic: Surgical aid in cataract extraction (Amvisc, Amvisc Plus, Provisc); intraocular lens implantation (Amvisc, Amvisc Plus, Provisc); corneal transplant (Amvisc, Amvisc Plus); glaucoma filtration (Amvisc, Amvisc Plus); and retinal attachment surgery (Amvisc, Amvisc Plus)

Submucosal: Lip augmentation in adults >21 years (Restylane, Restylane-L, Restylane Silk, Juvederm Ultra XC, Juvederm Volbella XC)

Topical cream, gel: Management of skin ulcers and wounds (Bionect, Hylase Wound)

Local Anesthetic/Vasoconstrictor Precautions No information available to require special precautions

Effects on Dental Treatment No significant effects or complications reported

Effects on Bleeding No information available to require special precautions

Adverse Reactions Frequency not always defined and type of local reactions may vary by formulation and site of application/injection.

>10%:

Dermatologic: Skin discoloration at injection site (intradermal, subcutaneous, submucosal 4% to 78%)

Hematologic & oncologic: Bruise (intradermal 14% to 28%; more common in older patients; intra-articular <1%)

Local: Injection site (intradermal, subcutaneous, submucosal): Swelling (8% to 98%), tenderness (17% to 95%), erythema (11% to 93%), bruising (3% to 93%), induration (6% to 92%), pain (3% to 92%; most reports were mild and did not exceed 3 days post-injection), residual mass (3% to 90%), itching (10% to 47%)

Neuromuscular & skeletal: Arthralgia (intra-articular 9% to 25%), joint swelling (knee; intra-articular ≤14%), joint effusion (intra-articular ≤11%)

Miscellaneous: Swelling (intradermal 18% to 28%; more common in younger patients)

1% to 10%:

Cardiovascular: Presyncope (subcutaneous ≤5%), increased blood pressure (4%)

Central nervous system: Headache (submucosal, subcutaneous, intramuscular, intra-articular ≤7%), dizziness (subcutaneous ≤5%), hyperesthesia (injection site; subcutaneous ≤5%), hypoesthesia (injection site; subcutaneous ≤5%), malaise (subcutaneous ≤5%), tingling in the lips (subcutaneous ≤5%), falling (1% to ≤4%), fatigue (1%), paresthesia (intra-articular 1%)

Dermatologic: Hyperpigmentation (intradermal 9%; postinflammatory; in patients of African-American heritage and Fitzpatrick Skin Types IV, V, and VI), exfoliation of skin (submucosal 2% to 8%), cheilosis (subcutaneous ≤5%), fine wrinkling (subcutaneous ≤5%), local acneiform eruptions (subcutaneous ≤5%), local dryness (subcutaneous ≤5%), papule (injection site; subcutaneous ≤5%), rash at injection site (subcutaneous ≤5%), skin tightness (subcutaneous ≤5%)

Gastrointestinal: Oral herpes (subcutaneous ≤5%), toothache (intra-articular 4%), abdominal pain (1% to ≤4%), diarrhea (≤4%), dyspepsia (1% to ≤4%), nausea (≤4%)

Genitourinary: Urinary tract infection (1% to ≤4%)

Infection: Influenza (intra-articular 2%), infection (intra-articular 1%)

Local: Injection site reaction (1% to 6%), injection site nodule (subcutaneous ≤5%), injection site numbness (subcutaneous ≤5%), local skin exfoliation (subcutaneous ≤5%), pain at injection site (intra-articular ≤2% to 5%), swelling at injection site (intra-articular 2% to 3%), infection (intradermal, subcutaneous, submucosal 1%; including abscess/necrosis)

Neuromuscular & skeletal: Limb pain (intra-articular 5% to ≤8%), back pain (intra-articular ≤10%), puffiness of cheeks (upon waking up; subcutaneous ≤5%), leg pain (including discomfort 1% to ≤4%), connective tissue disease (intra-articular ≤4%), musculoskeletal disease (intra-articular 3% to ≤4%; including pain), tendonitis (intra-articular 2%), localized osteoarthritis (intra-articular ≤2%), arthropathy (intra-articular 1%), joint stiffness (intra-articular ≤1%)

Ophthalmic: Corneal edema, increased intraocular pressure (postoperative; transient), ophthalmic inflammation (postoperative; iritis, hypopyon)

Respiratory: Upper respiratory tract infection (intra-articular 1% to 6%), nasopharyngitis (intra-articular 10%; submucosal 5%), bronchitis (1% to ≤4%), flu-like symptoms (1% to ≤4%), rhinitis (1% to ≤4%), sinusitis (1% to ≤4%), oropharyngeal pain (intra-articular 2%), respiratory tract infection (intra-articular 2%)

Miscellaneous: Laceration (injection site; subcutaneous ≤5%), soft tissue injury (lips; subcutaneous ≤5%), wound (subcutaneous ≤5%), accidental injury (1% to ≤4%), fever (intra-articular 3%)

<1%, postmarketing, and/or case reports: Abnormal gait, abscess, acne vulgaris, anaphylactic shock, anaphylactoid reaction, anaphylaxis, angioedema, anxiety, bacterial infection, burning sensation, bursitis, capillary fragility, central nervous system disease, cystitis, drainage, dyspnea, edema, erythema, eyelid edema, facial swelling, feeling of heaviness, gouty arthritis, granuloma, hematoma, herpetic lesion, hypersensitivity reaction, hypertension, hypoesthesia, hypotension, injection site infection (abscess/necrosis), increased serum ALT, inflammation, injection site ischemia, injection site numbness, injection site pain, injection site scarring, keloids, leukocytosis, metallic taste, migration of implant, mouth edema, muscle spasm (knee), neck pain, peripheral edema, popliteal cyst, pruritic rash, pruritus, red face, respiratory difficulty, rhinorrhea, sensation of cold (knee), sensory disturbance, skin rash, sore throat, subcutaneous nodule, swelling of extremities, syncope, synovitis (knee), telangiectasia, thrombocytopenia (rare), tissue necrosis, urticaria, vasodepressor syncope, vertebral disk disease (protrusion), viral infection, visual disturbance, vomiting, xeroderma

General Dosage Range

Intra-articular: *Adults:* 16 to 30 mg once weekly for 2 to 5 doses (total injections: 2 to 5) **or** 30 to 88 mg once

Intradermal/subcutaneous/supraperiosteal: *Adults:* Inject as required for cosmetic effect (maximum: 20 mL/60 kg/year [Juvederm all formulations] or maximum: 6 mL/treatment [Perlane, Restylane, Restylane Lyft, Restylane-L] or maximum: 1 mL per correction per treatment session [Restylane Silk])

Ophthalmic: *Adults:* Depends upon procedure (slowly introduce a sufficient quantity into eye)

Submucosal: *Adults ≥21 years:* 2.2 mL for lips and perioral area (Juvederm Ultra XC) or 2.6 mL (Juvederm Volbella XC) initially then 1.5 mL (Juverderm Ultra XC) or 1.6 mL (Juvederm Volbella XC) for repeat treatment; maximum: 20 mL/60 kg/year (Juvederm Ultra XC/Juvederm Volbella XC) or maximum 1.5 mL per lip (upper or lower) per treatment session (Restylane, Restylane-L, Restylane Silk)

Topical: *Adults:* Apply to affected area 1 to 3 times daily

Mechanism of Action Sodium hyaluronate is a biological polysaccharide which is distributed widely in the extracellular matrix of connective tissue in man (vitreous and aqueous humor of the eye, synovial fluid, skin, and umbilical cord). Sodium hyaluronate and its derivatives form a viscoelastic solution in water (at physiological pH and ionic strength) which makes it suitable for aqueous and vitreous humor in ophthalmic surgery, and functions as a tissue and/or joint lubricant which plays an important role in modulating the interactions between adjacent tissues. Intradermal injection may decrease the depth of facial wrinkles. Transcutaneous injection for lip augmentation may correct perioral rhytids. Subcutaneous and/or supraperiosteal injection for cheek augmentation may correct age-related volume deficit. In the topical management of wounds and ulcers, sodium hyaluronate protects the skin against friction and abrasion.

Pregnancy Considerations Adverse events were not observed in animal reproduction studies. Safety for use in pregnant women has not been established.

Hyaluronidase (hye al yoor ON i dase)

Brand Names: US Amphadase; Hylenex; Vitrase

Pharmacologic Category Antidote, Extravasation; Enzyme

Use

Absorption and dispersion of injected drugs: As an adjuvant to increase the absorption and dispersion of other injected drugs.

Subcutaneous fluid administration: As an adjuvant in subcutaneous fluid administration (hypodermoclysis) for achieving hydration.

Subcutaneous urography: As an adjunct in subcutaneous urography for improving resorption of radiopaque agents.

Local Anesthetic/Vasoconstrictor Precautions No information available to require special precautions

Effects on Dental Treatment No significant effects or complications reported

Effects on Bleeding No information available to require special precautions

Adverse Reactions Frequency not defined.

Cardiovascular: Edema

Local: Injection site reaction

<1%, postmarketing, and/or case reports: Anaphylactic-like reactions (retrobulbar block or IV injections), anaphylaxis, angioedema, hypersensitivity reaction, urticaria

General Dosage Range

Intradermal: *Children, Adolescents, and Adults:* 0.02 mL (Amphadase 3 units, Hylenex 3 units, or Vitrase 4 units) of a 150 units/mL or 200 units/mL solution

SubQ:

Premature Infants: 150 or 200 units prior to fluid replacement

Children <3 years: 75 units over each scapula followed by injection of contrast medium at the same site **or** 150 or 200 units prior to fluid replacement

Children ≥3 years: 75 units over each scapula followed by injection of contrast medium at the same site **or** 150 or 200 units prior to fluid replacement **or** 50-300 units (usual dose: 150 units) prior to medication administration

Adolescents and Adults: 150 or 200 units prior to fluid replacement **or** 50-300 units (usual dose: 150 units) prior to medication administration

Mechanism of Action Enzymatically modifies the permeability of connective tissue through hydrolysis of hyaluronic acid, one of the chief components of tissue cement which offers resistance to diffusion of liquids through tissues; hyaluronidase increases the distribution/dispersion and absorption of locally injected or extravasated substances.

Pharmacodynamics/Kinetics

Onset of Action SubQ: Immediate; when used for extravasation, there is usually a reduction in swelling within 15-30 minutes after administration (Zenk, 1981b)

Duration of Action 24-48 hours (variable)

Pregnancy Risk Factor C

Pregnancy Considerations Adverse events have not been observed in animal reproduction studies (not conducted with all products). Administration during labor did not cause any increase in blood loss or differences in cervical trauma. It is not known whether it affects the fetus if used during labor. Hyaluronidase has been evaluated for use prior to intracytoplasmic sperm injection (ICSI) to increase male fertility (DeVos, 2008; Evison, 2009).

HydrALAZINE (hye DRAL a zeen)

Related Information

Cardiovascular Diseases *on page 1752*

Brand Names: Canada Apresoline

Pharmacologic Category Antihypertensive; Vasodilator

Use

Hypertension: Management of moderate to severe hypertension

Note: According to the Eighth Joint National Committee (JNC 8) guidelines, hydralazine is **not** recommended for the initial treatment of hypertension (James, 2013).

Local Anesthetic/Vasoconstrictor Precautions No information available to require special precautions

Effects on Dental Treatment No significant effects or complications reported

Effects on Bleeding No information available to require special precautions

Adverse Reactions Frequency not defined.

Cardiovascular: Angina pectoris, circulatory shock, flushing, orthostatic hypotension, palpitations, paradoxical pressor response, peripheral edema, tachycardia

Central nervous system: Anxiety, chills, depression, disorientation, dizziness, headache, increased intracranial pressure (IV; in patient with pre-existing increased intracranial pressure), peripheral neuritis, psychotic reaction

Dermatologic: Diaphoresis, pruritus, skin rash, urticaria

Gastrointestinal: Anorexia, constipation, diarrhea, nausea, paralytic ileus, vomiting

Genitourinary: Dysuria, impotence

Hematologic & oncologic: Agranulocytosis, decreased hemoglobin, decreased red blood cells, eosinophilia, hemolytic anemia, leukopenia

Neuromuscular & skeletal: Lupus-like syndrome (dose related; fever, arthralgia, splenomegaly, lymphadenopathy, asthenia, myalgia, malaise, pleuritic chest pain, edema, positive ANA, positive LE cells, maculopapular facial rash, positive direct Coombs' test, pericarditis, pericardial tamponade), muscle cramps, rheumatoid arthritis, tremor, weakness

Ophthalmic: Conjunctivitis, lacrimation

Respiratory: Dyspnea, nasal congestion

Miscellaneous: Fever

<1%, postmarketing, and/or case reports: Thrombocytopenia (IV)

General Dosage Range Dosage adjustment recommended in patients with renal impairment

IM, IV:

Children and Adolescents: Initial: 1.7 to 3.5 mg/kg/day divided in 4 to 6 doses

Adults: Initial: 10 to 20 mg/dose every 4 to 6 hours as needed

Oral:

Children and Adolescents: Initial: 0.75 mg/kg/day in 2 to 4 divided doses (maximum: 200 mg/day)

Adults: Initial: 10 mg 4 times daily; Maintenance: Up to 50 mg 4 times daily (up to 300 mg/day may be required in resistant patients)

Mechanism of Action Direct vasodilation of arterioles (with little effect on veins) with decreased systemic resistance

Pharmacodynamics/Kinetics

Onset of Action IV: 10 to 80 minutes

Duration of Action IM, IV: Up to 12 hours (Marik 2007); **Note:** Duration may vary depending on acetylator status of patient. Hypotension due to hydralazine may last longer even though the circulating half-life is much shorter (Marik, 2007; O'Malley, 1975).

Half-life Elimination 3 to 7 hours

Time to Peak Plasma: Oral: 1 to 2 hours

Pregnancy Risk Factor C

Pregnancy Considerations Adverse events have been observed in some animal reproduction studies. Hydralazine crosses the placenta (Liedholm, 1982). Intravenous hydralazine is recommended for use in the management of acute onset, severe hypertension (systolic BP ≥160 mm Hg or diastolic BP ≥110 mm Hg) with preeclampsia or eclampsia in pregnant and postpartum women. Untreated chronic maternal hypertension is associated with adverse events in the fetus, infant, and mother. If treatment for chronic hypertension in pregnancy is needed, other oral agents are preferred as initial therapy (ACOG, 2013; Magee, 2014).

HydroCHLOROthiazide
(hye droe klor oh THYE a zide)

Related Information

Cardiovascular Diseases *on page 1752*

Brand Names: US Microzide

Brand Names: Canada Apo-Hydro; Ava-Hydrochlorothiazide; Bio-Hydrochlorothiazide; PMS-Hydrochlorothiazide; Teva-Hydrochlorothiazide; Urozide

Generic Availability (US) Yes

Pharmacologic Category Antihypertensive; Diuretic, Thiazide

Use

Edema: Treatment of edema due to heart failure, hepatic cirrhosis (see "**Note**"), various forms of renal dysfunction (eg, nephrotic syndrome, acute glomerulosclerosis, chronic renal failure) (see "**Note**"), corticosteroid and estrogen therapy

Note: The use of hydrochlorothiazide in the treatment of edema for hepatic cirrhosis has largely been replaced by spironolactone. The use of hydrochlorothiazide in the management of edema in patients with renal dysfunction has largely been replaced by the use of loop diuretics (eg, furosemide).

Hypertension: Management of mild-to-moderate hypertension

Guideline recommendations:

Hypertension: The 2014 guideline for the management of high blood pressure in adults (Eighth Joint National Committee [JNC 8]) recommends initiation of pharmacologic treatment to lower blood pressure for the following patients:

- Patients ≥60 years of age with systolic blood pressure (SBP) ≥150 mm Hg or diastolic blood pressure (DBP) ≥90 mm Hg. Goal of therapy is SBP <150 mm Hg and DBP <90 mm Hg.
- Patients <60 years of age with SBP ≥140 mm Hg or DBP is ≥90 mm Hg. Goal of therapy is SBP <140 mm Hg and DBP <90 mm Hg.
- Patients ≥18 years of age with diabetes and SBP ≥140 mm Hg or DBP ≥90 mm Hg. Goal of therapy is SBP <140 mm Hg and DBP <90 mm Hg.
- Patients ≥18 years of age with chronic kidney disease (CKD) and SBP ≥140 mm Hg or DBP ≥90 mm Hg. Goal of therapy is SBP <140 mm Hg and DBP <90 mm Hg.

Chronic kidney disease (CKD) and hypertension: Regardless of race or diabetes status, the use of an ACE inhibitor (ACEI) or angiotensin receptor blocker (ARB) as initial therapy is recommended to improve kidney outcomes. In the general nonblack population (without CKD) including those with diabetes, initial antihypertensive treatment should consist of a thiazide-type diuretic, calcium channel blocker, ACEI, or ARB. In the general black population (without CKD), including those with diabetes, initial antihypertensive treatment should consist of a thiazide-type diuretic or a calcium channel blocker **instead of** an ACEI or ARB.

Coronary artery disease (CAD) and hypertension: The American Heart Association, American College of Cardiology and American Society of Hypertension (AHA/ACC/ASH) 2015 scientific statement for the treatment of hypertension in patients with coronary artery disease (CAD) recommends the use of a thiazide (or thiazide-like diuretic) as part of a regimen in patients with hypertension and chronic stable angina. A BP target of <140/90 mm Hg is reasonable for the secondary prevention of cardiovascular events. A lower target BP (<130/80 mm Hg) may be appropriate in some individuals with CAD, previous MI, stroke or transient ischemic attack, or CAD risk equivalents (AHA/ACC/ASH [Rosendorff 2015]).

Canadian labeling: Additional uses (not in US labeling):

Premenstrual tension with edema: Management of premenstrual tension with edema

Toxemia of pregnancy: Management of toxemia of pregnancy (including eclampsia). **Note:** Guidelines recommend alternative agents (Magee 2008)

Local Anesthetic/Vasoconstrictor Precautions No information available to require special precautions

Effects on Dental Treatment Key adverse event(s) related to dental treatment: Hypotension; Patients may experience orthostatic hypotension as they stand up after treatment; especially if lying in dental chair for extended periods of time. Use caution with sudden changes in position during and after dental treatment.

Effects on Bleeding No information available to require special precautions

Adverse Reactions Frequency not defined; the occurrence of adverse events are dose related, with the majority occurring with doses ≥25 mg.

Cardiovascular: Hypotension, necrotizing angiitis, orthostatic hypotension

Central nervous system: Dizziness, headache, paresthesia, restlessness, vertigo

Dermatologic: Alopecia, erythema multiforme, exfoliative dermatitis, skin photosensitivity, skin rash, Stevens-Johnson syndrome, toxic epidermal necrolysis, urticaria

Endocrine & metabolic: Glycosuria, hypercalcemia, hyperglycemia, hyperuricemia, hypochloremic alkalosis, hypokalemia, hypomagnesemia, hyponatremia

Gastrointestinal: Abdominal cramps, anorexia, constipation, diarrhea, gastric irritation, nausea, pancreatitis, sialadenitis, vomiting

Genitourinary: Impotence

Hematologic & oncologic: Agranulocytosis, aplastic anemia, hemolytic anemia, leukopenia, purpura, thrombocytopenia

Hepatic: Jaundice

Hypersensitivity: Anaphylaxis

Neuromuscular & skeletal: Muscle spasm, weakness

Ophthalmic: Transient blurred vision, xanthopsia

Renal: Interstitial nephritis, renal failure, renal insufficiency

Respiratory: Respiratory distress, pneumonitis, pulmonary edema

Miscellaneous: Fever

<1%, postmarketing, and/or case reports: Allergic myocarditis, eosinophilic pneumonitis, hepatic insufficiency, malignant neoplasm of lip (Friedman 2012), systemic lupus erythematosus

Dosing

Adult

Manufacturer's labeling:

Edema: Oral: 25 to 100 mg daily in 1 to 2 divided doses; may administer intermittently on alternate days or on 3 to 5 days each week.

Hypertension: Oral:

US labeling: Initial: 12.5 to 25 mg once daily; may increase up to 50 mg daily in 1 to 2 divided doses; minimal increase in response and more electrolyte disturbances are seen with doses >50 mg daily; may administer with other antihypertensives.

Canadian labeling: Initial: 12.5 to 100 mg daily as a single dose or in divided doses; titrate for effect. Up to 200 mg daily (in divided doses) may be necessary. If used concomitantly with other antihypertensive agents, reduce the dose of the concomitant antihypertensive by 50%.

Premenstrual tension with edema: Canadian labeling (not in US labeling): Oral: 25 to 50 mg daily once or twice daily (initiate at onset of symptoms and continue through the start of menses).

Toxemia of pregnancy: Canadian labeling (not in US labeling): Oral: 100 mg daily; may temporarily increase to 200 mg daily in divided doses for severe cases. May administer daily or intermittently once every 4 days. **Note:** Guidelines recommend use of alternative agents (Magee 2008).

Alternate recommendations:

Fluid retention (mild) in heart failure: Oral: Initial: 25 mg once or twice daily; maximum daily dose: 200 mg (ACCF/AHA [Yancy 2013])

Hypertension: Oral: Initial: 12.5 to 25 mg once daily; may increase dose to a target dose range of 25 to 50 mg once daily in 1 to 2 divided doses (JNC 8 [James 2014]); usual dosage range (ASH/ISH [Weber 2013]): 12.5 to 50 mg daily

Off-label use:

Calcium nephrolithiasis: 50 mg daily in 1 or 2 divided doses (AUA Guidelines [Pearle 2014])

Geriatric Oral: 12.5 to 25 mg once daily; titrate as necessary in increments of 12.5 mg. Minimal increase in response and more electrolyte disturbances are seen with doses >50 mg daily.

Pediatric Edema, hypertension: Note: In pediatric patients, chlorothiazide may be preferred over hydrochlorothiazide as there are more dosage formulations (eg, suspension) available: Oral (effect of drug may be decreased when used every day):

Manufacturer's labeling: Infants and Children: Usual dose:

<6 months: 1 to 3 mg/kg/day in 2 divided doses; maximum: 37.5 mg/day

6 months to 2 years: 1 to 2 mg/kg/day in 1 to 2 divided doses; maximum: 37.5 mg/day

2 to 12 years: 1 to 2 mg/kg/day in 1 to 2 divided doses; maximum: 100 mg daily

Alternate recommendations: Children and Adolescents: Initial: 1 mg/kg once daily; maximum 3 mg/kg/day not to exceed 50 mg/day (NHBPEP 2004; NHLBI, 2011)

Renal Impairment There are no dosage adjustments provided in the manufacturer's labeling (use is contraindicated with anuria). The following adjustments have been recommended (Aronoff 2007):

Adults:

CrCl ≥10 mL/minute: No dosage adjustment necessary. Usually ineffective with CrCl <30 mL/minute unless in combination with a loop diuretic.

CrCl <10 mL/minute: Use not recommended.

Pediatrics:

CrCl ≥30 mL/minute: No dosage adjustment necessary.

CrCl <30 mL/minute: Use not recommended.

Hepatic Impairment There are no dosage adjustments provided in the manufacturer's labeling. However, use with caution and monitor for precipitation of hepatic coma.

Mechanism of Action Inhibits sodium reabsorption in the distal tubules causing increased excretion of sodium and water as well as potassium and hydrogen ions

Contraindications

Hypersensitivity to hydrochlorothiazide, any component of the formulation, or sulfonamide-derived drugs; anuria

Note: Although some product labeling states this medication is contraindicated with other sulfonamide-containing drug classes, the scientific basis of this statement has been challenged. See "Warnings/Precautions" for more detail.

Canadian labeling: Additional contraindications (not in US labeling): Increasing azotemia and oliguria during treatment of severe progressive renal disease; breastfeeding

Documentation of allergenic cross-reactivity for thiazide-related diuretics is limited. However, because of similarities in chemical structure and/or pharmacologic actions, the possibility of cross-sensitivity cannot be ruled out with certainty.

Warnings/Precautions Hypersensitivity reactions may occur with hydrochlorothiazide. Risk is increased in patients with a history of allergy or bronchial asthma. Avoid in severe renal disease (ineffective as a diuretic). Electrolyte disturbances (hypokalemia, hypochloremic alkalosis, hypomagnesemia, hyponatremia) may occur. Development of electrolyte disturbances can be minimized when used in combination with other electrolyte sparing antihypertensives (eg, ACE inhibitors or angiotensin receptor blockers). (Sica 2011) Use with caution in severe hepatic dysfunction; hepatic encephalopathy can be caused by electrolyte disturbances. Use with extreme caution or avoid hydrochlorothiazide in the management of ascites due to cirrhosis; may lead to rapid development of hyponatremia when used in combination with spironolactone and furosemide (AASLD [Runyon 2012]). Avoid use of diuretics for treatment of elevated blood pressure in patients with primary adrenal insufficiency (Addison disease). Adjustment of glucocorticoid/mineralocorticoid therapy and/or use of other antihypertensive agents is preferred to treat hypertension (Bornstein 2016; Inder 2015). Gout may be precipitated in certain patients with a history of gout, a familial predisposition to gout, or chronic renal failure. Thiazide diuretics reduce calcium excretion; pathologic changes in the parathyroid glands with hypercalcemia and hypophosphatemia have been observed with prolonged use. Should be discontinued prior to testing for parathyroid function. Use with caution in patients with prediabetes and diabetes; may alter glucose control. May cause SLE exacerbation or activation. Use with caution in patients with moderate or high cholesterol concentrations; increased cholesterol and triglyceride levels have been reported. Photosensitization may occur. Correct hypokalemia before initiating therapy. Thiazide diuretics may decrease renal calcium excretion; consider avoiding use in patients with hypercalcemia. May cause acute transient myopia and acute angle-closure glaucoma, typically occurring within hours to weeks following initiation; discontinue therapy immediately in patients with acute decreases in visual acuity or ocular pain. Risk factors may include a history of sulfonamide or penicillin allergy. Cumulative effects may develop, including azotemia, in patients with impaired renal function. If given the morning of surgery, hydrochlorothiazide may render the patient volume depleted and blood pressure may be labile during general anesthesia. Potentially significant interactions may exist, requiring dose or frequency adjustment, additional monitoring, and/or selection of alternative therapy.

Sulfonamide ("sulfa") allergy: The FDA-approved product labeling for many medications containing a sulfonamide chemical group includes a broad contraindication in patients with a prior allergic reaction to sulfonamides. There is a potential for cross-reactivity between members of a specific class (eg, two antibiotic sulfonamides). However, concerns for cross-reactivity have previously extended to all compounds containing the sulfonamide structure (SO_2NH_2). An expanded understanding of allergic mechanisms indicates cross-reactivity between antibiotic sulfonamides and nonantibiotic sulfonamides may not occur or at the very least this potential is extremely low (Brackett 2004; Johnson 2005; Slatore 2004; Tornero 2004). In particular, mechanisms of cross-reaction due to antibody production (anaphylaxis) are unlikely to occur with nonantibiotic sulfonamides. T-cell-mediated (type IV) reactions (eg, maculopapular rash) are less well understood and it is not possible to completely exclude this potential based on current insights. In cases where prior reactions were severe (Stevens-Johnson syndrome/TEN), some clinicians choose to avoid exposure to these classes.

Some dosage forms may contain propylene glycol; large amounts are potentially toxic and have been associated with hyperosmolality, lactic acidosis, seizures and respiratory depression; use caution (AAP 1997; Zar 2007). See manufacturer's labeling.

Drug Interactions

Metabolism/Transport Effects None known.

Avoid Concomitant Use

Avoid concomitant use of HydroCHLOROthiazide with any of the following: Dofetilide; Levosulpiride; Mecamylamine; Promazine

Increased Effect/Toxicity

HydroCHLOROthiazide may increase the levels/effects of: ACE Inhibitors; Ajmaline; Allopurinol; Amifostine; Aminolevulinic Acid; Antipsychotic Agents (Second Generation [Atypical]); Benazepril; Calcium Salts; CarBAMazepine; Cardiac Glycosides; Cyclophosphamide; Diazoxide; Dofetilide; DULoxetine; Hypotension-Associated Agents; Ivabradine; Levodopa; Levosulpiride; Lithium; Mecamylamine; Multivitamins/Minerals (with ADEK, Folate, Iron); Multivitamins/Minerals (with AE, No Iron); Nitroprusside; Nonsteroidal Anti-Inflammatory Agents; OXcarbazepine; Porfimer; Promazine; Sodium Phosphates; Topiramate; Toremifene; Valsartan; Verteporfin; Vitamin D Analogs

The levels/effects of HydroCHLOROthiazide may be increased by: Alcohol (Ethyl); Alfuzosin; Analgesics (Opioid); Anticholinergic Agents; Barbiturates; Benperidol; Beta2-Agonists; Brimonidine (Topical); Corticosteroids (Orally Inhaled); Corticosteroids (Systemic); Dexketoprofen; Diacerein; Diazoxide; Herbs (Hypotensive Properties); Ipragliflozin; Licorice; Lormetazepam; Molsidomine; Multivitamins/Fluoride (with ADE); Naftopidil; Nicergoline; Nicorandil; Obinutuzumab; Pentoxifylline; Phosphodiesterase 5 Inhibitors; Prostacyclin Analogues; Quinagolide; Reboxetine; Selective Serotonin Reuptake Inhibitors; Valsartan

Decreased Effect

HydroCHLOROthiazide may decrease the levels/effects of: Antidiabetic Agents

The levels/effects of HydroCHLOROthiazide may be decreased by: Amphetamines; Analgesics (Opioid); Benazepril; Bile Acid Sequestrants; Herbs (Hypertensive Properties); Methylphenidate; Nonsteroidal Anti-Inflammatory Agents; Yohimbine

Pharmacodynamics/Kinetics

Onset of Action Diuresis: Infants: 2 to 6 hours (Chemtob 1989); Adults: ~2 hours; Peak effect: 4 to 6 hours

Duration of Action Infants: 8 hours (Chemtob 1989); Adults: 6 to 12 hours

Half-life Elimination ~6 to 15 hours

Time to Peak ~1 to 5 hours

Pregnancy Risk Factor B

Pregnancy Considerations Adverse events have not been observed in animal reproduction studies. Thiazide diuretics cross the placenta and are found in cord blood. Maternal use may cause may cause fetal or neonatal jaundice, thrombocytopenia, or other adverse events observed in adults. Use of thiazide diuretics to treat edema during normal pregnancies is not appropriate; use may be considered when edema is due to pathologic causes (as in the nonpregnant patient); monitor. Untreated chronic maternal hypertension is associated with adverse events in the fetus, infant, and mother (ACOG 2013). Women who required thiazide diuretics for the treatment of hypertension prior to pregnancy may continue their use (ACOG 2013).

Breastfeeding Considerations Thiazide diuretics are excreted in breast milk. Following a single oral maternal dose of hydrochlorothiazide 50 mg, the mean breast milk concentration was 80 ng/mL (samples collected over 24 hours) and hydrochlorothiazide was not detected in the blood of the breastfeeding infant (limit of detection 20 ng/mL) (Miller 1982). Peak plasma concentrations reported in adults following hydrochlorothiazide 12.5-100 mg are 70-490 ng/mL. Due to the potential for serious adverse reactions in the nursing infant, the manufacturer recommends a decision be made whether to discontinue nursing or to discontinue the drug, taking into account the importance of treatment to the mother (Canadian labeling contraindicates use in nursing women). Diuretics have the potential to decrease milk volume and suppress lactation.

Dosage Forms

Capsule, Oral:

Microzide: 12.5 mg

Generic: 12.5 mg

Tablet, Oral:

Generic: 12.5 mg, 25 mg, 50 mg

Hydrochlorothiazide and Triamterene

(hye droe klor oh THYE a zide & trye AM ter een)

Related Information

HydroCHLOROthiazide *on page 820*

Triamterene *on page 1606*

Brand Names: US Dyazide; Maxzide; Maxzide-25

Brand Names: Canada Apo-Triazide; Pro-Triazide; Teva-Triamterene HCTZ

Generic Availability (US) Yes

Pharmacologic Category Antihypertensive; Diuretic, Potassium-Sparing; Diuretic, Thiazide

Use Hypertension, edema: Treatment of hypertension or edema (not recommended for initial treatment) when hypokalemia has developed on hydrochlorothiazide alone or when the development of hypokalemia must be avoided.

Local Anesthetic/Vasoconstrictor Precautions No information available to require special precautions

Effects on Dental Treatment No significant effects or complications reported

Effects on Bleeding No information available to require special precautions

Adverse Reactions Also see individual agents. Frequency not defined.

Cardiovascular: Angina pectoris, cardiac arrhythmia, necrotizing angiitis, orthostatic hypotension, tachycardia

Central nervous system: Anxiety, depression, dizziness, fatigue, glossopyrosis, headache, insomnia, paresthesia, restlessness, vertigo

Dermatologic: Skin photosensitivity, skin rash, urticaria

Endocrine & metabolic: Acidosis, diabetes mellitus, glycosuria, hypercalcemia, hyperglycemia, hyperkalemia, hyperuricemia, hypochloremia, hypokalemia, hypomagnesemia, hyponatremia

Gastrointestinal: Abdominal pain, anorexia, constipation, diarrhea, dysgeusia, gastric distress, nausea, pancreatitis, sialadenitis, stomach cramps, tongue discoloration (bright orange), vomiting, xerostomia

Genitourinary: Impotence, urine discoloration, urine sedimentation abnormality

Hematologic & oncologic: Agranulocytosis, aplastic anemia, hemolytic anemia, leukopenia, megaloblastic anemia, purpura, thrombocytopenia
Hepatic: Abnormal liver function tests, jaundice
Hypersensitivity: Anaphylaxis
Neuromuscular & skeletal: Exacerbation of systemic lupus erythematosus, lupus-like syndrome (subacute, cutaneous), muscle cramps, weakness
Ophthalmic: Transient blurred vision, xanthopsia
Renal: Acute renal failure, increased blood urea nitrogen, increased serum creatinine, interstitial nephritis, nephrolithiasis
Respiratory: Dyspnea, hypersensitivity pneumonitis, pulmonary edema, respiratory distress
Miscellaneous: Fever
<1%, postmarketing, and/or case reports: Malignant neoplasm of lip (Friedman 2012)

Dosing

Adult & Geriatric

Hypertension, edema: Oral:

Hydrochlorothiazide 25 mg/triamterene 37.5 mg: 1 to 2 tablets/capsules once daily

Hydrochlorothiazide 25 mg/triamterene 50 mg: 1 to 2 capsules once daily

Hydrochlorothiazide 50 mg/triamterene 75 mg: 1 tablet daily

Renal Impairment There are no dosage adjustments provided in the manufacturer's labeling. Contraindicated in patients with anuria, acute and chronic renal insufficiency, or significant renal impairment.

Hepatic Impairment There are no dosage adjustments provided in the manufacturer's labeling; use with caution and monitor for precipitation of hepatic coma.

Mechanism of Action

Hydrochlorothiazide: Inhibits sodium reabsorption in the distal tubules causing increased excretion of sodium and water as well as potassium and hydrogen ions.

Triamterene: Blocks epithelial sodium channels in the late distal convoluted tubule (DCT) and collecting duct which inhibits sodium reabsorption from the lumen. This effectively reduces intracellular sodium, decreasing the function of Na+/K+ ATPase, leading to potassium retention and decreased calcium, magnesium, and hydrogen excretion. As sodium uptake capacity in the DCT/collecting duct is limited, the natriuretic, diuretic, and antihypertensive effects are generally considered weak.

Contraindications

Hypersensitivity to hydrochlorothiazide, triamterene, sulfonamide-derived drugs, or any component of the formulation; anuria; acute and chronic renal insufficiency or significant renal impairment; patients receiving other potassium-sparing diuretics, potassium-containing salt substitutes, or potassium supplements (except in severe cases of hypokalemia); preexisting hyperkalemia

Note: Although the FDA approved product labeling states this medication is contraindicated with other sulfonamide-containing drug classes, the scientific basis of this statement has been challenged. See "Warnings/Precautions" for more detail.

Warnings/Precautions See individual agents.

Drug Interactions

Metabolism/Transport Effects None known.

Avoid Concomitant Use

Avoid concomitant use of Hydrochlorothiazide and Triamterene with any of the following: CycloSPORINE (Systemic); Dofetilide; Levosulpiride; Mecamylamine; Promazine; Spironolactone; Tacrolimus (Systemic)

Increased Effect/Toxicity

Hydrochlorothiazide and Triamterene may increase the levels/effects of: ACE Inhibitors; Ajmaline; Allopurinol; Amifostine; Aminolevulinic Acid; Ammonium Chloride; Antipsychotic Agents (Second Generation [Atypical]); Benazepril; Calcium Salts; CarBAMazepine; Cardiac Glycosides; Cyclophosphamide; CycloSPORINE (Systemic); Diazoxide; Dofetilide; DULoxetine; Hypotension-Associated Agents; Ivabradine; Levodopa; Levosulpiride; Lithium; Mecamylamine; Multivitamins/Minerals (with ADEK, Folate, Iron); Multivitamins/Minerals (with AE, No Iron); Nitroprusside; Nonsteroidal Anti-Inflammatory Agents; OXcarbazepine; Porfimer; Promazine; Sodium Phosphates; Spironolactone; Tacrolimus (Systemic); Topiramate; Toremifene; Valsartan; Verteporfin; Vitamin D Analogs

The levels/effects of Hydrochlorothiazide and Triamterene may be increased by: Alcohol (Ethyl); Alfuzosin; Analgesics (Opioid); Angiotensin II Receptor Blockers; Anticholinergic Agents; Barbiturates; Benperidol; Beta2-Agonists; Brimonidine (Topical); Canagliflozin; Corticosteroids (Orally Inhaled); Corticosteroids (Systemic); Dexketoprofen; Diacerein; Diazoxide; Drospirenone; Eplerenone; Heparin; Heparin (Low Molecular Weight); Herbs (Hypotensive Properties); Indomethacin; Ipragliflozin; Licorice; Lormetazepam; Molsidomine; Multivitamins/Fluoride (with ADE); Naftopidil; Nicergoline; Nicorandil; Nonsteroidal Anti-Inflammatory Agents; Obinutuzumab; Pentoxifylline; Phosphodiesterase 5 Inhibitors; Potassium Salts; Prostacyclin Analogues; Quinagolide; Reboxetine; Selective Serotonin Reuptake Inhibitors; Tolvaptan; Valsartan

Decreased Effect

Hydrochlorothiazide and Triamterene may decrease the levels/effects of: Antidiabetic Agents; Cardiac Glycosides; QuiNIDine

The levels/effects of Hydrochlorothiazide and Triamterene may be decreased by: Amphetamines; Analgesics (Opioid); Benazepril; Bile Acid Sequestrants; Herbs (Hypertensive Properties); Methylphenidate; Nonsteroidal Anti-Inflammatory Agents; Yohimbine

Food Interactions See individual agents.

Pregnancy Risk Factor C

Pregnancy Considerations Animal reproduction studies have not been conducted with this combination product. See individual agents.

Breastfeeding Considerations Thiazide diuretics are found in breast milk; excretion of triamterene is not known. breastfeeding is not recommended by the manufacturer. See individual agents.

Dosage Forms

Capsule: Hydrochlorothiazide 25 mg and triamterene 37.5 mg; hydrochlorothiazide 25 mg and triamterene 50 mg

Dyazide: Hydrochlorothiazide 25 mg and triamterene 37.5 mg

Tablet: Hydrochlorothiazide 25 mg and triamterene 37.5 mg; hydrochlorothiazide 50 mg and triamterene 75 mg

Maxzide: Hydrochlorothiazide 50 mg and triamterene 75 mg [scored]

Maxzide-25: Hydrochlorothiazide 25 mg and triamterene 37.5 mg [scored]

Hydrocodone and Acetaminophen

(hye droe KOE done & a seet a MIN oh fen)

Related Information

Acetaminophen *on page 56*

Oral Pain *on page 1830*

Related Sample Prescriptions

Oral Pain - Sample Prescriptions *on page 28*

Brand Names: US hycet; Lorcet; Lorcet 10/650 [DSC]; Lorcet HD; Lorcet Plus; Lortab; Maxidone [DSC]; Norco; Stagesic [DSC]; Verdrocet; Vicodin; Vicodin ES; Vicodin HP; Xodol 10/300; Xodol 5/300; Xodol 7.5/300; Zamicet; Zolvit [DSC]; Zydone [DSC]

Generic Availability (US) Yes: Oral solution, tablet

Pharmacologic Category Analgesic Combination (Opioid); Analgesic, Opioid

Dental Use Treatment of postoperative pain

Use

Pain management: Management of pain severe enough to require an opioid analgesic and for which alternative treatments are inadequate.

Limitations of use: Reserve hydrocodone/acetaminophen for use in patients for whom alternative treatment options (eg, nonopioid analgesics) are ineffective, not tolerated, or would be otherwise inadequate to provide sufficient management of pain.

Local Anesthetic/Vasoconstrictor Precautions No information available to require special precautions

Effects on Dental Treatment No significant effects or complications reported (see Dental Comment)

Effects on Bleeding As a single agent, acetaminophen does not appear to affect bleeding or platelet aggregation. Acetaminophen may prolong the INR and increase bleeding in patients taking warfarin (Coumadin). For patients taking warfarin, single acetaminophen doses or acetaminophen therapy of short duration should be safe, but if large (>1.3 g/day) doses are administered for longer than 10-14 days, then the INR should be monitored (see Dental Comment).

Adverse Reactions Frequency not defined.

Cardiovascular: Bradycardia, cardiac arrest, circulatory shock, hypotension

Central nervous system: Anxiety, clouding of consciousness, coma, dizziness, drowsiness, drug dependence, dysphoria, euphoria, fear, lethargy, malaise, mental deficiency, mood changes, sedation, stupor

Dermatologic: Cold and clammy skin, diaphoresis, pruritus, skin rash

Endocrine & metabolic: Hypoglycemic coma

Gastrointestinal: Abdominal pain, constipation, gastric distress, heartburn, nausea, occult blood in stools, peptic ulcer, vomiting

Genitourinary: Nephrotoxicity, ureteral spasm, urinary retention

Hematologic & oncologic: Agranulocytosis, hemolytic anemia, iron deficiency anemia, prolonged bleeding time, thrombocytopenia

Hepatic: Hepatic necrosis, hepatitis

Hypersensitivity: Hypersensitivity reaction

Neuromuscular & skeletal: Vesicle sphincter spasm

Otic: Hearing loss (chronic overdose)

Renal: Renal tubular necrosis

Respiratory: Airway obstruction, apnea, dyspnea, respiratory depression (dose related)

Postmarketing and/or case reports: Hypogonadism (Brennan, 2013; Debono, 2011)

Dental Usual Dosage Postoperative pain: Oral:

Children and Adults ≥50 kg: Average starting dose in opioid naive patients: Hydrocodone 5 to 10 mg 4 times/day; the dosage of acetaminophen should be limited to ≤4 g/day (and possibly less in patients with hepatic impairment or ethanol use).

Dosage ranges (based on specific product labeling): Hydrocodone 2.5 to 10 mg every 4 to 6 hours; maximum: 60 mg hydrocodone/day (maximum dose of hydrocodone may be limited by the acetaminophen content of specific product)

Elderly: Doses should be titrated to appropriate analgesic effect; 2.5 to 5 mg of the hydrocodone component every 4 to 6 hours. Do not exceed 4 g/day of acetaminophen.

Dosing

Adult

Pain management: Oral:

Dosage ranges (based on specific product labeling): Hydrocodone 2.5 to 10 mg every 4 to 6 hours (maximum dose of hydrocodone may be limited by the acetaminophen content of specific product; refer to manufacturer's labeling); the dosage of acetaminophen should be limited to ≤4 g/day. Titrate to appropriate analgesic effect.

Discontinuation of therapy: Decrease dose by 25% to 50% every 2 to 4 days; monitor carefully for signs/symptoms of withdrawal. If patient displays withdrawal symptoms, increase dose to the previous level and then reduce dose more slowly by increasing interval between dose reductions, decreasing amount of daily dose reduction, or both.

Geriatric Refer to adult dosing. Initiate dosing at the lower end of the dosage range. Monitor closely.

Pediatric

Analgesic, opioid-naive: Oral: **Note:** Doses based on hydrocodone; titrate to appropriate analgesic effect. Maximum daily dose of acetaminophen should be limited to ≤75 mg/kg/**day** in ≤5 divided doses and not to exceed 4 g/**day**.

Infants and Children <2 **years** <50 kg (off-label): Initial: Hydrocodone 0.1 to 0.2 mg/kg/dose every 4 to 6 hours (American Pain Society 2008); in infants, reduced doses and close monitoring should be considered due to possible increased sensitivity to respiratory depressant effects; use with caution in infants.

Children ≥2 years and Adolescents <50 kg: Initial: Hydrocodone 0.1 to 0.2 mg/kg/dose every 4 to 6 hours (American Pain Society 2008)

Children ≥2 years and Adolescents ≥50 kg: Initial: Hydrocodone 5 to 10 mg every 4 to 6 hours (American Pain Society 2008)

Renal Impairment There are no specific dosage adjustments provided in the manufacturer's labeling; use with caution. Initiate therapy with a low dose and monitor closely.

Hepatic Impairment There are no specific dosage adjustments provided in the manufacturer's labeling; use with caution. Initiate therapy with a low dose and monitor closely.

Mechanism of Action

Hydrocodone: Binds to opiate receptors in the CNS, altering the perception of and response to pain; suppresses cough in medullary center; produces generalized CNS depression.

Acetaminophen: Inhibits the synthesis of prostaglandins in the CNS and peripherally blocks pain impulse generation; produces antipyresis from inhibition of hypothalamic heat-regulating center.

Contraindications

Hypersensitivity (eg, anaphylaxis) to hydrocodone, acetaminophen, or any component of the formulation;

significant respiratory depression; acute or severe bronchial asthma in an unmonitored setting or in the absence of resuscitative equipment; gastrointestinal obstruction, including paralytic ileus (known or suspected).

Documentation of allergenic cross-reactivity for opioids is limited. However, because of similarities in chemical structure and/or pharmacologic actions, the possibility of cross-sensitivity cannot be ruled out with certainty.

Warnings/Precautions [US Boxed Warning]: Serious, life-threatening, or fatal respiratory depression may occur. Monitor closely for respiratory depression, especially during initiation or dose escalation. Carbon dioxide retention from opioid-induced respiratory depression can exacerbate the sedating effects of opioids. Use opioids with caution and monitor for respiratory depression in patients with significant chronic obstructive pulmonary disease or cor pulmonale, and those having a substantially decreased respiratory reserve, hypoxia, hypercarbia, or preexisting respiratory depression, particularly when initiating therapy and titrating therapy; critical respiratory depression may occur, even at therapeutic dosages. Consider the use of alternative nonopioid analgesics in these patients. Avoid use in patients with impaired consciousness or coma as these patients are susceptible to intracranial effects of CO_2 retention. May cause severe hypotension (including orthostatic hypotension and syncope); use with caution in patients with hypovolemia, cardiovascular disease (including acute MI), or drugs which may exaggerate hypotensive effects (including phenothiazines or general anesthetics). Monitor for symptoms of hypotension following initiation or dose titration. Avoid use in patients with circulatory shock. May cause CNS depression, which may impair physical or mental abilities; patients must be cautioned about performing tasks which require mental alertness (eg, operating machinery or driving).

[US Boxed Warning]: Prolonged use of opioids during pregnancy can cause neonatal withdrawal syndrome, which may be life-threatening if not recognized and treated according to protocols developed by neonatology experts. If opioid use is required for a prolonged period in a pregnant woman, advise the patient of the risk of neonatal opioid withdrawal syndrome and ensure that appropriate treatment will be available. Signs and symptoms include irritability, hyperactivity and abnormal sleep pattern, high-pitched cry, tremor, vomiting, diarrhea, and failure to gain weight. Onset, duration, and severity depend on the drug used, duration of use, maternal dose, and rate of drug elimination by the newborn.

Use with caution in patients with hypersensitivity reactions to other phenanthrene derivative opioid agonists (morphine, hydromorphone, levorphanol, oxycodone, oxymorphone). Concurrent use of agonist/antagonist analgesics may precipitate withdrawal symptoms and/or reduced analgesic efficacy in patients following prolonged therapy with mu opioid agonists. Abrupt discontinuation following prolonged use may also lead to withdrawal symptoms. **[US Boxed Warning]: Use exposes patients and other users to the risks of addiction, abuse, and misuse, potentially leading to overdose and death. Assess each patient's risk prior to prescribing; monitor all patients regularly for development of these behaviors or conditions.** Use opioids for chronic pain with caution in patients at increased risk for misuse; factors associated with increased risk include previous substance use disorder, younger age, concomitant depression (major), and psychotropic medication use. Consider offering naloxone prescriptions in patients with factors associated with an increased risk for overdose, such as history of overdose or substance use disorder, higher opioid dosages (≥50 morphine milligram equivalents/day orally), and concomitant benzodiazepine use (Dowell [CDC 2016]). **[US Boxed Warning]: Accidental ingestion, especially in children, can result in a fatal overdose of hydrocodone.** Use opioids with caution for chronic pain in patients with mental health conditions (eg, depression, anxiety disorders, post-traumatic stress disorder) due to increased risk for opioid use disorder and overdose; more frequent monitoring is recommended (Dowell [CDC 2016]).

Use opioids with caution for chronic pain and titrate dosage cautiously in patients with risk factors for sleep-disordered breathing, including HF and obesity. Avoid opioids in patients with moderate to severe sleep-disordered breathing (Dowell [CDC 2016]). Use caution in patients with adrenal insufficiency (including Addison disease), biliary tract impairment, acute pancreatitis, delirium tremens, history of seizure disorders, alcoholic liver disease, toxic psychosis, thyroid dysfunction, prostatic hyperplasia and/or urinary stricture, hepatic and/or renal disease, and in cachectic or debilitated patients. Hydrocodone may cause constipation which may be problematic in patients with unstable angina and patients post-myocardial infarction. Use with extreme caution in patients with head injury, intracranial lesions, or elevated intracranial pressure; exaggerated elevation of ICP may occur. Use with caution in patients who are morbidly obese. May obscure diagnosis or clinical course of patients with acute abdominal conditions. Use with caution in the elderly; may be more sensitive to adverse effects; use opioids for chronic pain with caution in this age group; monitor closely due to an increased potential for risks, including certain risks such as falls/fracture, cognitive impairment, and constipation. Clearance may also be reduced in older adults (with or without renal impairment) resulting in a narrow therapeutic window and increasing the risk for respiratory depression or overdose (Dowell [CDC 2016]).

[US Boxed Warning]: Concomitant use of opioids with benzodiazepines or other CNS depressants, including alcohol, may result in profound sedation, respiratory depression, coma, and death. Reserve concomitant prescribing of hydrocodone/acetaminophen and benzodiazepines or other CNS depressants for use in patients for whom alternative treatment options are inadequate. Limit dosage and durations to the minimum required and follow patients for signs and symptoms of respiratory depression and sedation. [US Boxed Warning]: Use with all CYP3A4 inhibitors may result in an increase in hydrocodone plasma concentrations, which could increase or prolong adverse drug effects and may cause potentially fatal respiratory depression. In addition, discontinuation of a concomitant CYP 3A4 inducer may result in increased hydrocodone concentrations. Monitor patients receiving hydrocodone/acetaminophen and any CYP3A4 inhibitor or inducer. Potentially significant interactions may exist, requiring dose or frequency adjustment, additional monitoring, and/or selection of alternative therapy.

Rarely, acetaminophen may cause serious and potentially fatal skin reactions such as acute generalized exanthematous pustulosis, Stevens-Johnson syndrome (SJS), and toxic epidermal necrolysis (TEN). Discontinue treatment if severe skin reactions develop.

Due to the role of CYP2D6 in the metabolism of hydrocodone to hydromorphone (an active metabolite with higher binding affinity to mu-opioid receptors compared to hydrocodone), patients with genetic variations of CYP2D6, including "poor metabolizers" or "extensive metabolizers," may have decreased or increased hydromorphone formation, respectively. Variable effects in positive and negative opioid effects have been reported in these patients; however, limited data exists to determine if clinically significant differences of analgesia and toxicity can be predicted based on CYP2D6 phenotype (Hutchinson 2004; Otton 1993; Zhou 2009).

[US Boxed Warning]: Acetaminophen has been associated with cases of acute liver failure, at times resulting in liver transplant and death. Most of the cases of liver injury are associated with the use of acetaminophen at doses that exceed >4 g/day; and often involve more than 1 acetaminophen-containing product. Risk is increased with alcohol use, preexisting liver disease, and intake of more than one source of acetaminophen-containing medications. Chronic daily dosing in adults has also resulted in liver damage in some patients. Hypersensitivity and anaphylactic reactions have been reported with acetaminophen use; discontinue immediately if symptoms of allergic or hypersensitivity reactions occur. Use acetaminophen caution in patients with known G6PD deficiency. Limit acetaminophen dose from all sources (prescription and OTC) to <4 g/day.

An opioid-containing analgesic regimen should be tailored to each patient's needs and based upon the type of pain being treated (acute versus chronic), the route of administration, degree of tolerance for opioids (naive versus chronic user), age, weight, and medical condition. The optimal analgesic dose varies widely among patients; doses should be titrated to pain relief/prevention. Opioids decrease bowel motility; monitor for decreased bowel motility in postop patients receiving opioids. Use with caution in the perioperative setting; individualize treatment when transitioning from parenteral to oral analgesics. Some dosage forms may contain propylene glycol; large amounts are potentially toxic and have been associated hyperosmolality, lactic acidosis, seizures and respiratory depression; use caution (AAP 1997; Zar 2007).

Chronic pain: Opioids should not be used as first-line therapy for chronic pain management (pain >3-month duration or beyond time of normal tissue healing) due to limited short-term benefits, undetermined long-term benefits, and association with serious risks (eg, overdose, MI, auto accidents, risk of developing opioid use disorder). Preferred management includes nonpharmacologic therapy and nonopioid therapy (eg, NSAIDs, acetaminophen, certain anticonvulsants and antidepressants). If opioid therapy is initiated, it should be combined with nonpharmacologic and nonopioid therapy, as appropriate. Prior to initiation, known risks of opioid therapy should be discussed and realistic treatment goals for pain/function should be established, including consideration for discontinuation if benefits do not outweigh risks. Therapy should be continued only if clinically meaningful improvement in pain/function outweighs risks. Therapy should be initiated at the lowest effective dosage using immediate-release opioids (instead of extended-release/long-acting opioids). Risk associated with use increases with higher opioid dosages. Risks and benefits should be re-evaluated when increasing dosage to ≥50 morphine milligram equivalents (MME)/day; dosages ≥90 MME/day should be avoided unless carefully justified (Dowell [CDC 2016]).

Drug Interactions

Metabolism/Transport Effects Refer to individual components.

Avoid Concomitant Use

Avoid concomitant use of Hydrocodone and Acetaminophen with any of the following: Alcohol (Ethyl); Azelastine (Nasal); Conivaptan; Eluxadoline; Fusidic Acid (Systemic); Idelalisib; Mixed Agonist / Antagonist Opioids; Orphenadrine; Oxomemazine; Paraldehyde; Thalidomide

Increased Effect/Toxicity

Hydrocodone and Acetaminophen may increase the levels/effects of: Alvimopan; Azelastine (Nasal); Blonanserin; Busulfan; Dasatinib; Desmopressin; Diuretics; Eluxadoline; Flunitrazepam; Imatinib; Methotrimeprazine; MetyroSINE; Mipomersen; Orphenadrine; OxyCODONE; Paraldehyde; Phenylephrine (Systemic); Piribedil; Pramipexole; Prilocaine; Ramosetron; ROPINIRole; Rotigotine; Selective Serotonin Reuptake Inhibitors; Serotonin Modulators; Sodium Nitrite; SORAfenib; Suvorexant; Thalidomide; Vitamin K Antagonists; Zolpidem

The levels/effects of Hydrocodone and Acetaminophen may be increased by: Alcohol (Ethyl); Amphetamines; Anticholinergic Agents; Aprepitant; Brimonidine (Topical); Cannabis; Ceritinib; Chlormethiazole; Chlorphenesin Carbamate; CNS Depressants; Conivaptan; CYP3A4 Inhibitors (Moderate); CYP3A4 Inhibitors (Strong); CYP3A4 Inhibitors (Weak); Dapsone (Topical); Dasatinib; Dimethindene (Topical); Dronabinol; Droperidol; Fosaprepitant; Fusidic Acid (Systemic); Idelalisib; Isoniazid; Ivacaftor; Kava Kava; Lofexidine; Magnesium Sulfate; MAO Inhibitors; Methotrimeprazine; MetyraPONE; MiFEPRIStone; Minocycline; Nabilone; Netupitant; Nitric Oxide; Ombitasvir, Paritaprevir, and Ritonavir; Ombitasvir, Paritaprevir, Ritonavir, and Dasabuvir; Oxomemazine; Palbociclib; Perampanel; Probenecid; Rufinamide; Simeprevir; Sodium Oxybate; SORAfenib; Stiripentol; Succinylcholine; Tapentadol; Tetracaine (Topical); Tetrahydrocannabinol

Decreased Effect

Hydrocodone and Acetaminophen may decrease the levels/effects of: Diuretics; Gastrointestinal Agents (Prokinetic); Pegvisomant

The levels/effects of Hydrocodone and Acetaminophen may be decreased by: Bosentan; Cholestyramine Resin; CYP2D6 Inhibitors (Strong); CYP3A4 Inducers (Moderate); CYP3A4 Inducers (Strong); CYP3A4 Inducers (Weak); Dabrafenib; Deferasirox; Enzalutamide; Mitotane; Mixed Agonist / Antagonist Opioids; Nalmefene; Naltrexone; QuiNIDine; Siltuximab; St John's Wort; Tocilizumab

Pharmacodynamics/Kinetics

Onset of Action Hydrocodone: Opioid analgesic: 10 to 20 minutes

Duration of Action Hydrocodone: 4 to 8 hours

Half-life Elimination Hydrocodone: 3.3 to 4.4 hours

Pregnancy Risk Factor C

Pregnancy Considerations Animal reproduction studies have not been conducted with this combination. **[US Boxed Warning]: Prolonged use of opioids during pregnancy can cause neonatal withdrawal**

syndrome, which may be life-threatening if not recognized and treated according to protocols developed by neonatology experts. If opioid use is required for a prolonged period in a pregnant woman, advise the patient of the risk of neonatal opioid withdrawal syndrome and ensure treatment that appropriate treatment will be available. See individual agents.

Breastfeeding Considerations Acetaminophen and hydrocodone are excreted in breast milk. According to the manufacturer, the decision to continue or discontinue breastfeeding during therapy should take into account the risk of infant exposure, the benefits of breastfeeding to the infant, and benefits of treatment to the mother. See individual agents.

Controlled Substance C-II

Dosage Forms

Solution, oral:

hycet: Hydrocodone 7.5 mg and acetaminophen 325 mg per 15 mL

Zamicet: Hydrocodone 10 mg and acetaminophen 325 mg per 15 mL

Generic: Hydrocodone 7.5 mg and acetaminophen 325 mg per 15 mL

Tablet, oral:

Brands:

Lorcet: Hydrocodone 5 mg and acetaminophen 325 mg

Lorcet HD: Hydrocodone 10 mg and acetaminophen 325 mg

Lorcet Plus: Hydrocodone 7.5 mg and acetaminophen 325 mg

Norco: Hydrocodone 5 mg and acetaminophen 325 mg; hydrocodone 7.5 mg and acetaminophen 325 mg; hydrocodone 10 mg and acetaminophen 325 mg

Verdrocet: Hydrocodone 2.5 mg and acetaminophen 325 mg

Vicodin: Hydrocodone 5 mg and acetaminophen 300 mg

Vicodin ES: Hydrocodone 7.5 mg and acetaminophen 300 mg

Vicodin HP: Hydrocodone 10 mg and acetaminophen 300 mg

Xodol: 5/300: Hydrocodone 5 mg and acetaminophen 300 mg; 7.5/300: Hydrocodone 7.5 mg and acetaminophen 300 mg; 10/300: Hydrocodone 10 mg and acetaminophen 300 mg

Generics:

Hydrocodone 2.5 mg and acetaminophen 325 mg
Hydrocodone 5 mg and acetaminophen 300 mg
Hydrocodone 5 mg and acetaminophen 325 mg
Hydrocodone 7.5 mg and acetaminophen 300 mg
Hydrocodone 7.5 mg and acetaminophen 325 mg
Hydrocodone 10 mg and acetaminophen 300 mg
Hydrocodone 10 mg and acetaminophen 325 mg

Dental Comment Although the ***OTC product labeling*** for acetaminophen products state to limit the maximum dose to 3,000 mg daily (for extra strength) or 3,250 mg (for regular strength) (see this site for details: http://www.tylenolprofessional.com/extra-strength-tylenol-dosage-faq.html), it is still appropriate for patients to take up to 4,000 mg daily "under the direction of a healthcare provider" (http://www.tylenolprofessional.com/assets/v4/faqs-new-dosing.pdf).

Neither hydrocodone nor acetaminophen elicit anti-inflammatory effects. Because of addiction liability of opioid analgesics, the use of hydrocodone should be limited to 2-3 days postoperatively for treatment of dental pain. Nausea is the most common adverse effect seen after use in dental patients; sedation and constipation are second. Nausea elicited by opioid analgesics is centrally mediated and the presence or absence of food will not affect the degree nor incidence of nausea.

The acetaminophen component requires use with caution in patients who use alcohol, with preexisting liver disease, and those receiving more than one source of acetaminophen-containing medication.

Hepatotoxicity caused by acetaminophen is potentiated by chronic alcohol consumption. People who are taking acetaminophen, even at therapeutic doses, and consume alcohol are at risk of developing hepatotoxicity.

Acetaminophen may increase the levels and enhance the anticoagulant effects of vitamin K antagonists acenocoumarol and warfarin (Coumadin®). Studies have reported that acetaminophen has increased the INR in warfarin treated patients with daily acetaminophen doses as low as 2 g, particularly when taking acetaminophen for >1 week (Antlitz, 1968; Boeijinga, 1982; Gebauer, 2003; Hylek, 1998; Rubin, 1984). In addition, case reports of bleeding as a result of increased INR have been published (Bagheri, 1999; Bartle, 1991). There is no known mechanism of the interaction; furthermore, some studies have failed to demonstrate this interaction (Gadisseur, 2003; Kwan, 1995; van den Bemt, 2002). In terms of risk, the data suggest that acetaminophen and warfarin could interact in some clinically significant manner but that the benefits of concomitant use of acetaminophen for pain control in dental patients taking warfarin usually outweigh the risks. An appropriate monitoring plan should be in place to identify potential negative effects and dosage adjustments may be necessary in a minority of patients. The interaction may be more likely to occur with daily acetaminophen doses of >1.3 g for >1 week.

There are no reports of acetaminophen interacting with antiplatelet drugs such as aspirin, clopidogrel (Plavix®), or prasugrel (Effient™). Also, there are no reports of acetaminophen in combination with hydrocodone, codeine, or oxycodone interacting with warfarin (Coumadin®).

Hydrocodone and Ibuprofen

(hye droe KOE done & eye byoo PROE fen)

Related Information

Ibuprofen *on page 851*
Oral Pain *on page 1830*

Related Sample Prescriptions

Oral Pain - Sample Prescriptions *on page 28*

Brand Names: US Ibudone; Reprexain; Vicoprofen; Xylon

Brand Names: Canada Vicoprofen

Generic Availability (US) Yes

Pharmacologic Category Analgesic Combination (Opioid); Nonsteroidal Anti-inflammatory Drug (NSAID), Oral

Dental Use Short-term management (generally <10 days) of moderate-to-severe acute postoperative dental pain where an anti-inflammatory effect is desired

Use

Pain management: Short-term (generally <10 days) management of acute pain severe enough to require an opioid analgesic and for which alternative treatments are inadequate.

Limitations of use: Do not use hydrocodone/ibuprofen for the treatment of conditions such as osteoarthritis or rheumatoid arthritis. Reserve hydrocodone/ibuprofen for use in patients for whom alternative treatment options (eg, nonopioid analgesics) are ineffective, not tolerated, or would be otherwise inadequate to provide sufficient management of pain.

Local Anesthetic/Vasoconstrictor Precautions No information available to require special precautions

Effects on Dental Treatment Key adverse event(s) related to dental treatment: Xerostomia (normal salivary flow resumes upon discontinuation). See Effects on Bleeding.

Effects on Bleeding Nonselective NSAIDs such as ibuprofen inhibit platelet aggregation and prolong bleeding time in some patients. Unlike aspirin, the NSAID effect on platelet function is quantitatively less, of shorter duration, and reversible.

Adverse Reactions

>10%:

Central nervous system: Headache (27%), drowsiness (22%), dizziness (14%)

Gastrointestinal: Constipation (22%), nausea (21%), dyspepsia (12%)

1% to 10%:

Cardiovascular: Edema (3% to 9%), palpitations (<3%), vasodilatation (<3%)

Central nervous system: Anxiety (3% to 9%), insomnia (3% to 9%), nervousness (3% to 9%), abnormality in thinking (<3%), confusion (<3%), hypertonia (<3%), pain (<3%), paresthesia (<3%)

Dermatologic: Diaphoresis (3% to 9%), pruritus (3% to 9%)

Endocrine & metabolic: Increased thirst (<3%)

Gastrointestinal: Abdominal pain (3% to 9%), diarrhea (3% to 9%), flatulence (3% to 9%), hiccups (3% to 9%), vomiting (3% to 9%), xerostomia (3% to 9%), anorexia (<3%), gastritis (<3%), melena (<3%), oral mucosa ulcer (<3%)

Infection: Infection (3% to 9%)

Neuromuscular & skeletal: Weakness (3% to 9%)

Otic: Tinnitus (<3%)

Renal: Polyuria (<3%)

Respiratory: Flu-like symptoms (3% to 9%), dyspnea (<3%), pharyngitis (<3%), rhinitis (<3%)

Miscellaneous: Fever (<3%)

<1%, postmarketing, and/or case reports: Abnormal dreams, agitation, arthralgia, asthma, bronchitis, cardiac arrhythmia, chalky stools, cough, cystitis, decreased libido, depression, drug dependence (with prolonged use), dry eye syndrome, dysphagia, esophageal spasm, esophagitis, euphoria, exfoliative dermatitis, gastroenteritis, gastrointestinal hemorrhage, gastrointestinal perforation, GI inflammation, glossitis, glycosuria, hepatotoxicity (idiosyncratic) (Chalasani, 2014), hoarseness, hypersensitivity reaction, hypertension, hypogonadism (Brennan, 2013; Debono, 2011), hypotension, impotence, increased liver enzymes, mood changes, myalgia, neuralgia, pneumonia, pulmonary congestion, respiratory depression, sinusitis, skin rash, slurred speech, Stevens-Johnson syndrome, tachycardia, teeth clenching, toxic epidermal necrolysis, tremor, ulcer, unpleasant taste, urinary incontinence, urinary retention, urticaria, vertigo, visual disturbance, weight loss

Dental Usual Dosage Moderate-to-severe acute postoperative dental pain: Adults: Oral: 1-2 tablets every 4-6 hours as needed for pain; maximum: 5 tablets/day

Dosing

Adult

Pain management: Oral: One tablet (hydrocodone 2.5 mg to 10 mg/ibuprofen 200 mg) every 4 to 6 hours as needed; (maximum: 5 tablets [hydrocodone 12.5 to 50 mg/ibuprofen 1,000 mg] per 24 hours). **Note:** Short-term use is recommended (<10 days total therapy).

Discontinuation of therapy: Decrease dose by 25% to 50% every 2 to 4 days; monitor carefully for signs/symptoms of withdrawal. If patient displays withdrawal symptoms, increase dose to the previous level and then reduce dose more slowly by increasing interval between dose reductions, decreasing amount of daily dose reduction, or both.

Geriatric Refer to adult dosing. Initiate dosing at the lower end of the dosage range. Monitor closely.

Pediatric

Pain management: Oral: Adolescents ≥16 years: Refer to adult dosing.

Renal Impairment There are no dosage adjustments provided in the manufacturer's labeling. Initiate therapy with a low dose and monitor closely. Avoid use in advanced renal disease.

Hepatic Impairment There are no dosage adjustments provided in the manufacturer's labeling; use with caution; initiate therapy with a low dose and monitor closely in severe impairment.

Mechanism of Action

Hydrocodone: Binds to opiate receptors in the CNS, altering the perception of and response to pain; suppresses cough in medullary center; produces generalized CNS depression

Ibuprofen: Reversibly inhibits cyclooxygenase-1 and 2 (COX-1 and 2) enzymes, which result in decreased formation of prostaglandin precursors; has antipyretic, analgesic, and anti-inflammatory properties

Contraindications

Hypersensitivity (eg, anaphylactic reactions, serious skin reactions) to hydrocodone, ibuprofen, or any component of the formulation; significant respiratory depression; acute or severe bronchial asthma in an unmonitored setting or in the absence of resuscitative equipment; GI obstruction, including paralytic ileus (known or suspected); history of asthma, urticaria, or allergic-type reactions to aspirin or other NSAIDs; in the setting of coronary artery bypass graft (CABG) surgery.

Documentation of allergenic cross-reactivity for opioids is limited. However, because of similarities in chemical structure and/or pharmacologic actions, the possibility of cross-sensitivity cannot be ruled out with certainty.

Warnings/Precautions [US Boxed Warning]: Serious, life-threatening, or fatal respiratory depression may occur. Monitor closely for respiratory depression, especially during initiation or dose escalation. Carbon dioxide retention from opioid-induced respiratory depression can exacerbate the sedating effects of opioids. Use with caution and monitor for respiratory depression in patients with significant chronic obstructive pulmonary disease or cor pulmonale, and those having a substantially decreased respiratory reserve, hypoxia, hypercarbia, or preexisting respiratory depression, particularly when initiating therapy and titrating therapy; critical respiratory depression may occur, even at therapeutic dosages. Consider the use of alternative nonopioid analgesics in these patients. Avoid use in patients with impaired consciousness or coma as these patients are susceptible to intracranial effects of carbon dioxide retention. **[US Boxed Warning]: Concomitant**

use of opioids with benzodiazepines or other CNS depressants, including alcohol, may result in profound sedation, respiratory depression, coma, and death. Reserve concomitant prescribing of hydrocodone/ibuprofen and benzodiazepines or other CNS depressants for use in patients for whom alternative treatment options are inadequate. Limit dosage and durations to the minimum required and follow patients for signs and symptoms of respiratory depression and sedation. [US Boxed Warning]: Use with all CYP3A4 inhibitors may result in an increase in hydrocodone plasma concentrations, which could increase or prolong adverse drug effects and may cause potentially fatal respiratory depression. In addition, discontinuation of a concomitant CYP3A4 inducer may result in increased hydrocodone concentrations. Monitor patients receiving hydrocodone/ibuprofen and any CYP3A4 inhibitor or inducer. Potentially significant interactions may exist, requiring dose or frequency adjustment, additional monitoring, and/or selection of alternative therapy. **[US Boxed Warning]: Use exposes patients and other users to the risks of addiction, abuse, and misuse, potentially leading to overdose and death. Assess each patient's risk prior to prescribing; monitor all patients regularly for development of these behaviors or conditions.** Use with caution in patients with a history of drug abuse or acute alcoholism; potential for drug dependency exists. Other factors associated with increased risk include younger age, concomitant depression (major), and psychotropic medication use. **[US Boxed Warning]: Accidental ingestion of even one dose, especially in children, can result in a fatal overdose of hydrocodone.**

Even in patients without prior exposure anaphylactoid reactions may occur; patients with "aspirin triad" (bronchial asthma, aspirin intolerance, rhinitis) may be at increased risk. Contraindicated in patients who experience bronchospasm, asthma, rhinitis, or urticaria with NSAID or aspirin therapy. **[US Boxed Warning]: NSAIDs cause an increased risk of serious (and potentially fatal) adverse cardiovascular thrombotic events, including fatal MI and stroke. Risk may occur early during treatment and may increase with duration of use.** Relative risk appears to be similar in those with and without known cardiovascular disease or risk factors for cardiovascular disease; however, absolute incidence of cardiovascular events (which may occur early during treatment) was higher in patients with known cardiovascular disease or risk factors. New-onset hypertension or exacerbation of hypertension may occur (NSAIDS may also impair response to ACE inhibitors, thiazide diuretics, or loop diuretics); may contribute to cardiovascular events; monitor blood pressure; use with caution in patients with hypertension. May cause sodium and fluid retention; use with caution in patients with edema. Avoid use in heart failure (ACCF/AHA [Yancy 2013]). Avoid use in patients with a recent MI unless benefits outweigh risk of cardiovascular thrombotic events. Use the lowest effective dose for the shortest duration of time, consistent with individual patient goals, to reduce risk of cardiovascular events; alternate therapies should be considered for patients at high risk. **[US Boxed Warning]: NSAIDs cause an increased risk of serious gastrointestinal inflammation, ulceration, bleeding, and perforation (may be fatal); elderly patients and patients with history of peptic ulcer disease and/or GI bleeding are at greater risk for serious GI events. These events may occur at any time during therapy and without warning.** Avoid use in patients with active GI bleeding. Use caution with a history of GI ulcers, concurrent therapy known to increase the risk of GI bleeding (eg, aspirin, anticoagulants and/or corticosteroids, selective serotonin reuptake inhibitors), advanced hepatic disease, coagulopathy, smoking, use of alcohol, or in elderly or debilitated patients. Use the lowest effective dose for the shortest duration of time, consistent with individual patient goals, to reduce risk of GI adverse events; alternate therapies should be considered for patients at high risk. When used concomitantly with aspirin, a substantial increase in the risk of gastrointestinal complications (eg, ulcer) occurs; concomitant gastroprotective therapy (eg, proton pump inhibitors) is recommended (Bhatt 2008). Platelet adhesion and aggregation may be decreased; may prolong bleeding time; patients with coagulation disorders or who are receiving anticoagulants should be monitored closely. Anemia may occur; patients on long-term NSAID therapy should be monitored for anemia. Rarely, NSAID use has been associated with potentially severe blood dyscrasias (eg, agranulocytosis, thrombocytopenia, aplastic anemia). Transaminase elevations have been reported with use; closely monitor patients with any abnormal LFT. Rare (sometimes fatal) severe hepatic reactions (eg, fulminant hepatitis, liver necrosis, hepatic failure) have occurred with NSAID use; discontinue immediately if signs or symptoms of hepatic disease develop or if systemic manifestations occur. NSAID use may increase the risk of hyperkalemia, particularly in the elderly, diabetics, renal disease, and with concomitant use of other agents capable of inducing hyperkalemia (eg, ACE-inhibitors). Monitor potassium closely. Blurred/diminished vision, scotomata, and changes in color vision have been reported with ibuprofen. Discontinue therapy and refer for ophthalmologic evaluation if symptoms occur. NSAID use may compromise existing renal function; dose-dependent decreases in prostaglandin synthesis may result from NSAID use, reducing renal blood flow which may cause renal decompensation (usually reversible). Patients with impaired renal function, dehydration, hypovolemia, heart failure, hepatic impairment, those taking diuretics and ACE inhibitors, and the elderly are at greater risk of renal toxicity. Rehydrate patient before starting therapy; monitor renal function closely. Long-term NSAID use may result in renal papillary necrosis and other renal injury. **[US Boxed Warning]: Use is contraindicated in the setting of coronary artery bypass graft (CABG) surgery.** Risk of MI and stroke may be increased with use following CABG surgery. NSAIDs may cause serious skin adverse events including exfoliative dermatitis, Stevens-Johnson syndrome (SJS), and toxic epidermal necrolysis (TEN), which can be fatal and may occur without warning; discontinue use at first sign of skin rash (or any other hypersensitivity). NSAIDs may increase the risk of aseptic meningitis, especially in patients with systemic lupus erythematosus (SLE) and mixed connective tissue disorders. NSAID use may compromise existing renal function. Avoid use in patients with advanced renal disease.

May cause CNS depression, which may impair physical or mental abilities; patients must be cautioned about performing tasks which require mental alertness (eg, operating machinery or driving). May cause severe hypotension (including orthostatic hypotension and syncope); use with caution in patients with hypovolemia, cardiovascular disease (including acute MI), or drugs which may exaggerate hypotensive effects (including phenothiazines or general anesthetics). Monitor for symptoms of hypotension following initiation or dose titration. Avoid use in patients with circulatory shock. Use with caution in patients with hypersensitivity reactions to other phenanthrene derivative opioid agonists (codeine, hydromorphone, levorphanol, oxycodone, oxymorphone). May obscure diagnosis or clinical course of patients with acute abdominal conditions. Use with caution in patients who are morbidly obese (APS 2008). Use with caution in patients with adrenocortical insufficiency (including Addison disease), asthma, biliary tract dysfunction or including acute pancreatitis, delirium tremens, head injury, intracranial lesions, or elevated intracranial pressure (ICP); hepatic impairment; prostatic hyperplasia and/or urinary stricture; toxic psychosis; history of seizure disorder; and/or thyroid dysfunction. Use with caution in cachectic or debilitated patients and in the elderly; consider the use of alternative nonopioid analgesics in these patients. Opioid clearance may be reduced in older adults (with or without renal impairment) resulting in a narrow therapeutic window and increasing the risk for respiratory depression or overdose (Dowell [CDC 2016]).

Due to the role of CYP2D6 in the metabolism of hydrocodone to hydromorphone (an active metabolite with higher binding affinity to mu-opioid receptors compared to hydrocodone), patients with genetic variations of CYP2D6, including "poor metabolizers" or "extensive metabolizers," may have decreased or increased hydromorphone formation, respectively. Variable effects in positive and negative opioid effects have been reported in these patients; however, limited data exists to determine if clinically significant differences of analgesia and toxicity can be predicted based on CYP2D6 phenotype (Hutchinson 2004; Otton 1993; Zhou 2009).

[US Boxed Warning]: Prolonged use of opioids during pregnancy can cause neonatal withdrawal syndrome, which may be life-threatening if not recognized and treated according to protocols developed by neonatology experts. If opioid use is required for a prolonged period in a pregnant woman, advise the patient of the risk of neonatal opioid withdrawal syndrome and ensure that appropriate treatment will be available. Signs and symptoms include irritability, hyperactivity and abnormal sleep pattern, high-pitched cry, tremor, vomiting, diarrhea, and failure to gain weight. Onset, duration, and severity depend on the drug used, duration of use, maternal dose, and rate of drug elimination by the newborn.

An opioid-containing analgesic regimen should be tailored to each patient's needs and based upon the type of pain being treated (acute versus chronic), the route of administration, degree of tolerance for opioids (naive versus chronic user), age, weight, and medical condition. The optimal analgesic dose varies widely among patients; doses should be titrated to pain relief/prevention. Withhold for at least 4 to 6 half-lives prior to surgical or dental procedures (Douketis 2008). Opioids decrease bowel motility; monitor for decrease bowel motility in postop patients receiving opioids. Use with caution in the perioperative setting; individualize treatment when transitioning from parenteral to oral analgesics. Concurrent use of agonist/antagonist analgesics may precipitate withdrawal symptoms and/or reduced analgesic efficacy in patients following prolonged therapy with mu opioid agonists. Abrupt discontinuation following prolonged use may also lead to withdrawal symptoms.

Drug Interactions

Metabolism/Transport Effects Refer to individual components.

Avoid Concomitant Use

Avoid concomitant use of Hydrocodone and Ibuprofen with any of the following: Alcohol (Ethyl); Azelastine (Nasal); Conivaptan; Dexketoprofen; Eluxadoline; Floctafenine; Fusidic Acid (Systemic); Idelalisib; Ketorolac (Nasal); Ketorolac (Systemic); Mixed Agonist / Antagonist Opioids; Morniflumate; NSAID (COX-2 Inhibitor); Omacetaxine; Orphenadrine; Oxomemazine; Paraldehyde; Pelubiprofen; Phenylbutazone; Talniflumate; Tenoxicam; Thalidomide; Urokinase; Zaltoprofen

Increased Effect/Toxicity

Hydrocodone and Ibuprofen may increase the levels/effects of: 5-ASA Derivatives; Agents with Antiplatelet Properties; Aliskiren; Alvimopan; Aminoglycosides; Aminolevulinic Acid; Anticoagulants; Apixaban; Azelastine (Nasal); Bisphosphonate Derivatives; Blonanserin; Cephalothin; Collagenase (Systemic); CycloSPORINE (Systemic); Dabigatran Etexilate; Deferasirox; Deoxycholic Acid; Desmopressin; Digoxin; Diuretics; Drospirenone; Edoxaban; Eluxadoline; Eplerenone; Flunitrazepam; Ibritumomab; Lithium; Methotrexate; Methotrimeprazine; MetyroSINE; Nonsteroidal Anti-Inflammatory Agents; NSAID (COX-2 Inhibitor); Obinutuzumab; Omacetaxine; Orphenadrine; OxyCODONE; Paraldehyde; PEMEtrexed; Piribedil; Porfimer; Potassium-Sparing Diuretics; PRALAtrexate; Pramipexole; Quinolone Antibiotics; Ramosetron; Rivaroxaban; ROPINIRole; Rotigotine; Salicylates; Serotonin Modulators; Suvorexant; Tacrolimus (Systemic); Tenofovir Products; Thalidomide; Thrombolytic Agents; Tolperisone; Tositumomab and Iodine I 131 Tositumomab; Urokinase; Vancomycin; Verteporfin; Vitamin K Antagonists; Zolpidem

The levels/effects of Hydrocodone and Ibuprofen may be increased by: ACE Inhibitors; Alcohol (Ethyl); Amphetamines; Angiotensin II Receptor Blockers; Anticholinergic Agents; Aprepitant; Brimonidine (Topical); Cannabis; Ceritinib; Chlormethiazole; Chlorphenesin Carbamate; CNS Depressants; Conivaptan; Corticosteroids (Systemic); CycloSPORINE (Systemic); CYP3A4 Inhibitors (Moderate); CYP3A4 Inhibitors (Strong); CYP3A4 Inhibitors (Weak); Dasatinib; Dexketoprofen; Diclofenac (Systemic); Dimethindene (Topical); Dronabinol; Droperidol; Felbinac; Floctafenine; Fosaprepitant; Fusidic Acid (Systemic); Glucosamine; Herbs (Anticoagulant/Antiplatelet Properties); Ibrutinib; Idelalisib; Ivacaftor; Kava Kava; Ketorolac (Nasal); Ketorolac (Systemic); Limaprost; Lofexidine; Loop Diuretics; Magnesium Sulfate; MAO Inhibitors; Methotrimeprazine; MiFEPRIStone; Minocycline; Morniflumate; Multivitamins/Fluoride (with ADE); Multivitamins/Minerals (with ADEK, Folate, Iron); Multivitamins/Minerals (with AE, No Iron); Nabilone; Naftazone; Netupitant; Ombitasvir, Paritaprevir, and Ritonavir; Ombitasvir, Paritaprevir, Ritonavir, and Dasabuvir; Omega-3 Fatty Acids; Oxomemazine; Palbociclib; Pelubiprofen; Pentosan Polysulfate Sodium; Pentoxifylline; Perampanel; Phenylbutazone; Probenecid; Prostacyclin Analogues; Rufinamide; Selective Serotonin Reuptake Inhibitors; Serotonin/Norepinephrine Reuptake Inhibitors; Simeprevir; Sodium Oxybate; Sodium Phosphates; Stiripentol; Succinylcholine; Talniflumate; Tapentadol; Tenoxicam; Tetrahydrocannabinol; Thiazide and Thiazide-Like

Diuretics; Tipranavir; Tolperisone; Vitamin E (Systemic); Voriconazole; Zaltoprofen

Decreased Effect

Hydrocodone and Ibuprofen may decrease the levels/effects of: ACE Inhibitors; Aliskiren; Angiotensin II Receptor Blockers; Beta-Blockers; Diuretics; Eplerenone; Gastrointestinal Agents (Prokinetic); HydrALAZINE; Imatinib; Loop Diuretics; Pegvisomant; Potassium-Sparing Diuretics; Prostaglandins (Ophthalmic); Salicylates; Selective Serotonin Reuptake Inhibitors; Thiazide and Thiazide-Like Diuretics

The levels/effects of Hydrocodone and Ibuprofen may be decreased by: Bile Acid Sequestrants; Bosentan; CYP2D6 Inhibitors (Strong); CYP3A4 Inducers (Moderate); CYP3A4 Inducers (Strong); CYP3A4 Inducers (Weak); Dabrafenib; Deferasirox; Enzalutamide; Mitotane; Mixed Agonist / Antagonist Opioids; Nalmefene; Naltrexone; QuiNIDine; Salicylates; Siltuximab; St John's Wort; Tocilizumab

Food Interactions See individual agents.

Pharmacodynamics/Kinetics

Onset of Action Hydrocodone: Opioid analgesic: 10 to 20 minutes

Duration of Action Hydrocodone: 4 to 8 hours

Half-life Elimination Hydrocodone: 4.5 hours

Time to Peak Hydrocodone: 1.7 hours

Pregnancy Considerations Adverse events have been observed in some animal reproduction with this combination. **[US Boxed Warning]: Prolonged use of opioids during pregnancy can cause neonatal withdrawal syndrome, which may be life-threatening if not recognized and treated according to protocols developed by neonatology experts. If opioid use is required for a prolonged period in a pregnant woman, advise the patient of the risk of neonatal opioid withdrawal syndrome and ensure treatment that appropriate treatment will be available.** Refer to individual agents.

Breastfeeding Considerations Hydrocodone and ibuprofen are excreted in breast milk. According to the manufacturer, the decision to continue or discontinue breastfeeding during therapy should take into account the risk of infant exposure, the benefits of breastfeeding to the infant, and benefits of treatment to the mother. See individual agents.

Controlled Substance C-II

Dosage Forms

Tablet, oral:

Ibudone: 5/200: Hydrocodone 5 mg and ibuprofen 200 mg; 10/200: Hydrocodone 10 mg and ibuprofen 200 mg

Reprexain: 5/200: Hydrocodone 5 mg and ibuprofen 200 mg; 10/200: Hydrocodone 10 mg and ibuprofen 200 mg

Vicoprofen: 7.5/200: Hydrocodone 7.5 mg and ibuprofen 200 mg

Xylon: 10/200: Hydrocodone 10 mg and ibuprofen 200 mg

Generic: Hydrocodone 5 mg and ibuprofen 200 mg; Hydrocodone 7.5 mg and ibuprofen 200 mg; Hydrocodone 10 mg and ibuprofen 200 mg

Hydrocodone and Phenyltoloxamine

(hye droe KOE done & fen il to LOKS a meen)

Brand Names: Canada Tussionex®

Pharmacologic Category Alkylamine Derivative; Analgesic, Opioid; Antitussive; Histamine H_1 Antagonist; Histamine H_1 Antagonist, First Generation

Use Symptomatic relief of cough and upper respiratory symptoms associated with cold and allergy that does not respond to nonopioid antitussives

Local Anesthetic/Vasoconstrictor Precautions No information available to require special precautions

Effects on Dental Treatment No significant effects or complications reported

Effects on Bleeding No information available to require special precautions

Adverse Reactions Frequency not defined.

Cardiovascular: Tachycardia

Central nervous system: Drowsiness, drug dependence, hallucination, seizure

Dermatologic: Facial pruritus

Gastrointestinal: Constipation, nausea

Hypersensitivity: Hypersensitivity reaction

Respiratory: Dyspnea, respiratory depression

Postmarketing and/or case reports: Hypogonadism (Brennan 2013; Debono 2011)

General Dosage Range Oral:

Children ≥6 years: Hydrocodone 5 mg/phenyltoloxamine 10 mg (5 mL) every 12 hours (maximum dose: hydrocodone 10 mg/phenyltoloxamine 20 mg [10 mL] every 24 hours)

Adults: Hydrocodone 5 mg/phenyltoloxamine 10 mg (5 mL suspension or 1 tablet) every 8-12 hours (maximum dose: hydrocodone 10 mg/phenyltoloxamine 20 mg [10 mL suspension or 2 tablets] every 24 hours)

Mechanism of Action

Hydrocodone binds to opiate receptors in the CNS, altering the perception of and response to pain; suppresses cough in medullary center; produces generalized CNS depression.

Phenyltoloxamine competes with histamine for H_1-receptor sites on effector cells. May potentiate the antitussive effects of hydrocodone; sedative effects are also seen.

Pharmacodynamics/Kinetics

Duration of Action Antitussive effects: ≥8 hours

Half-life Elimination Hydrocodone: ~4 hours (Tussionex® Pennkinetic® U.S. prescribing information, 2008).

Product Availability Tussionex represents a different product in Canada than it does in the US. In Canada, Tussionex contains hydrocodone and phenyltoloxamine while in the US Tussionex (Pennkinetic) contains hydrocodone and chlorpheniramine.

Controlled Substance CDSA I

Hydrocortisone (Systemic)

(hye droe KOR ti sone)

Brand Names: US A-Hydrocort [DSC]; Cortef; Solu-CORTEF

Brand Names: Canada Cortef; Solu-Cortef

Generic Availability (US) May be product dependent

Pharmacologic Category Corticosteroid, Systemic

Dental Use Treatment of a variety of oral diseases of allergic, inflammatory, or autoimmune origin

Use

Allergic states: Control of severe or incapacitating allergic conditions intractable to adequate trials of conventional treatment in drug hypersensitivity reactions, perennial or seasonal allergic rhinitis, serum sickness, transfusion reactions, or acute noninfectious laryngeal edema (epinephrine is the drug of first choice).

Dermatologic diseases: Atopic dermatitis; bullous dermatitis herpetiformis; contact dermatitis; exfoliative dermatitis; exfoliative erythroderma; pemphigus; severe erythema multiforme (Stevens-Johnson syndrome); severe psoriasis; severe seborrheic dermatitis; mycosis fungoides.

Edematous states: To induce diuresis or remission of proteinuria in the nephrotic syndrome, without uremia, of the idiopathic type or that due to lupus erythematosus.

Endocrine disorders: Acute adrenocortical insufficiency; congenital adrenal hyperplasia; hypercalcemia associated with cancer; nonsuppurative thyroiditis; primary or secondary adrenocortical insufficiency; preoperatively and in the event of serious trauma or illness, in patients with known adrenal insufficiency or when adrenocortical reserve is doubtful; shock unresponsive to conventional therapy if adrenocortical insufficiency exists or is suspected.

GI diseases: To tide the patient over a critical period of the disease in ulcerative colitis and regional enteritis.

Hematologic disorders: Acquired (autoimmune) hemolytic anemia; congenital (erythroid) hypoplastic anemia (Diamond Blackfan anemia); erythroblastopenia (RBC anemia); idiopathic thrombocytopenic purpura in adults; pure red cell aplasia; select cases of secondary thrombocytopenia.

Neoplastic diseases: Palliative management of leukemias and lymphomas (adults); acute leukemia of childhood.

Nervous system: Acute exacerbations of multiple sclerosis; cerebral edema associated with primary or metastatic brain tumor, or craniotomy. **Note**: Treatment guidelines recommend the use of high-dose IV or oral methylprednisolone for acute exacerbations of multiple sclerosis (AAN [Scott 2011]; NICE 2014).

Ophthalmic diseases: Severe acute and chronic allergic and inflammatory processes involving the eye, such as allergic conjunctivitis; allergic corneal marginal ulcers; anterior segment inflammation; chorioretinitis; diffuse posterior uveitis and choroiditis; herpes zoster ophthalmicus; iritis and iridocyclitis; keratitis; optic neuritis; sympathetic ophthalmia; other ocular inflammatory conditions unresponsive to topical corticosteroids.

Respiratory diseases: Aspiration pneumonitis; bronchial asthma; berylliosis; fulminating or disseminated pulmonary tuberculosis when used concurrently with appropriate antituberculous chemotherapy; idiopathic eosinophilic pneumonias; Loeffler syndrome (not manageable by other means); symptomatic sarcoidosis.

Rheumatic disorders: As adjunctive therapy for short-term administration in acute and subacute bursitis, acute gouty arthritis, acute nonspecific tenosynovitis, ankylosing spondylitis, epicondylitis, posttraumatic osteoarthritis, psoriatic arthritis, rheumatoid arthritis, including juvenile rheumatoid arthritis, synovitis of osteoarthritis; during an exacerbation or as maintenance therapy in acute rheumatic carditis, dermatomyositis (polymyositis), temporal arteritis, and systemic lupus erythematosus.

Miscellaneous: Trichinosis with neurologic or myocardial involvement; tuberculous meningitis with subarachnoid block or impending block when used concurrently with appropriate antituberculous chemotherapy.

Local Anesthetic/Vasoconstrictor Precautions No information available to require special precautions

Effects on Dental Treatment No significant effects or complications reported

Effects on Bleeding No information available to require special precautions

Adverse Reactions Frequency not defined.

Cardiovascular: Atheromatous embolism, bradycardia, cardiac arrhythmia, cardiac failure, cardiomegaly, circulatory shock, edema, hypertension, hypertrophic cardiomyopathy (premature infants), myocardial rupture (post-myocardial infarction), syncope, tachycardia, thromboembolism, thrombophlebitis, vasculitis

Central nervous system: Delirium, depression, emotional lability, euphoria, hallucination, headache, increased intracranial pressure, insomnia, malaise, myasthenia, nervousness, neuritis, neuropathy, personality changes, pseudotumor cerebri, psychic disorder, psychosis, seizure, tingling of skin, vertigo

Dermatologic: Acne vulgaris, allergic dermatitis, alopecia, atrophic striae, burning sensation of skin, diaphoresis, erythema, exfoliation of skin, hyperpigmentation, hypopigmentation, skin atrophy, skin rash, sterile abscess, suppression of skin test reaction, urticaria, xeroderma

Endocrine & metabolic: Abnormalities in sperm motility (decreased/increased motility), adrenal suppression, alkalosis, amenorrhea, Cushing's syndrome, diabetes mellitus, fluid retention, growth suppression, hirsutism, HPA-axis suppression, hyperglycemia, hyperlipidemia, hypokalemia, hypokalemic alkalosis, impaired glucose tolerance, menstrual disease, negative nitrogen balance, protein catabolism, sodium retention, spermatozoa disorder (spermatogenesis decreased/increased), weight gain

Gastrointestinal: Abdominal distention, carbohydrate intolerance, dyspepsia, gastrointestinal perforation, hiccups, increased appetite, intestinal disease (intrathecal administration), nausea, pancreatitis, peptic ulcer, ulcerative esophagitis, vomiting

Genitourinary: Bladder dysfunction (intrathecal administration)

Hematologic & oncologic: Bruise, leukocytosis (transient), metastases, petechia

Hepatic: Hepatomegaly, increased serum transaminases

Hypersensitivity: Anaphylaxis, hypersensitivity reaction

Infection: Infection

Local: Atrophy at injection site, post-injection flare (intra-articular use), skin edema

Neuromuscular & skeletal: Abnormal fat deposits, amyotrophy, arthralgia, bone fracture, Charcot-like arthropathy, myopathy, osteonecrosis (femoral and humoral heads), osteoporosis, rupture of tendon, vertebral compression fracture

Ophthalmic: Cataract, exophthalmos, glaucoma, increased intraocular pressure

Miscellaneous: Tissue necrosis (avascular), wound healing impairment

Dosing

Adult & Geriatric Note: Adjust dose depending upon condition being treated and response of patient. The lowest possible dose should be used to control the condition; when dose reduction is possible, the dose should be reduced gradually. In life-threatening situations, parenteral doses larger than the oral dose may be needed.

Anti-inflammatory or immunosuppressive:

IM, IV: Initial: 100 to 500 mg/dose at intervals of 2, 4, or 6 hours.

Oral: Initial: 20 to 240 mg/day.

Multiple sclerosis, acute exacerbations:

Note: Treatment guidelines recommend the use of high-dose IV or oral methylprednisolone for acute exacerbations of multiple sclerosis (AAN [Scott 2011]; NICE 2014).

IM, IV: 800 mg/day for 1 week, followed by 320 mg every other day for 1 month.

Oral: 200 mg/day for 1 week, followed by 80 mg every other day for 1 month.

Adrenal insufficiency:

Acute adrenal insufficiency (adrenal crisis) (off-label dose): 100 mg IV bolus, immediately followed by 200 mg over 24 hours as a continuous IV infusion or in divided doses (IM or IV) every 6 hours, then 100 mg over 24 hours the following day (Allolio 2015; ES [Bornstein 2016]). Alternatively, may administer 100 mg IV bolus, then 50 to 75 mg IV every 6 hours for 24 hours, followed by a slow taper over the next 72 hours (administering doses every 4 to 6 hours during taper) (Gardner 2011). **Note:** Appropriate fluid resuscitation is also required (ES [Bornstein 2016]; Gardner 2011).

Chronic primary adrenal insufficiency (physiologic replacement) (off-label dose): Oral: 15 to 25 mg daily in 2 to 3 divided doses. Administer the largest dose in the morning upon awakening, followed by next dose 2 hours after lunch (two-dose regimen) or next dose at lunch, followed by smallest dose in the afternoon no later than 4 to 6 hours before bedtime (three-dose regimen) (ES [Bornstein 2016]).

Temporary adrenal insufficiency (temporary), physiologic replacement following resection of an ACTH-producing tumor or unilateral adrenalectomy (off-label dose): Oral: 10 to 12 mg/m2/day in 2 to 3 divided doses, with the first dose taken as soon as possible after waking; continue hydrocortisone until HPA axis recovers, generally 6 to 12 months following resection of ACTH-producing tumors or 18 months following unilateral adrenalectomy (ES [Neiman 2015]).

Congenital adrenal hyperplasia (off-label dose): Oral: 15 to 25 mg/day in 2 to 3 divided doses (Speiser 2010).

Stress dosing in patients known to be adrenally-suppressed (ie, prevention of adrenal crisis in glucocorticoid-treated patients) (off-label dose):

Sickness:

Illness with fever: Oral: Double the routine oral hydrocortisone dose until recovery for fever >38°C [100.4°F] or triple the routine oral hydrocortisone dose until recovery for fever >39°C [102.2°F]); return to standard dose within 1 to 2 days (Allolio 2015)

Gastroenteritis with vomiting and/or diarrhea: IM, SubQ: 100 mg dose given early in course of illness; repeat after 6 to 12 hours (Allolio 2015)

Severe infection (eg, pneumonia/with altered cognition): IM, SubQ: 100 mg dose given early in course of illness; repeat after 6 to 12 hours until recovery (Allolio 2015)

Surgery:

Minor stress (ie, inguinal herniorrhaphy): IV: 25 mg/day for 1 day (Coursin 2002; Salem 1994)

Moderate stress (ie, joint replacement, cholecystectomy): IV: 50 to 75 mg/day (25 mg every 8 to 12 hours) for 1 to 2 days (Coursin 2002; Salem 1994)

Major stress (pancreatoduodenectomy, esophagogastrectomy, cardiac surgery): IV: 100 to 150 mg/day (50 mg every 8 to 12 hours) for 2 to 3 days (Coursin 2002; Salem 1994)

Septic shock (off-label use): IV: 50 mg every 6 hours (Annane 2002; Sprung 2008). Practice guidelines suggest administering 200 mg daily as a continuous infusion over 24 hours to prevent adverse effects (eg, hyperglycemia) (Dellinger 2013; Weber-Carstens 2007); however, the impact of continuous infusion on patient outcomes has not been formally evaluated. Taper slowly (over several days) when vasopressors are no longer required; do not stop abruptly. **Note:** Hydrocortisone should be used alone (ie, without fludrocortisone) (Dellinger 2013).

Thyroid storm (off-label use): IV: 100 mg every 8 hours (JTA/JES [Satoh 2016]); an initial loading dose of 300 mg has also been recommended (ATA/AACE [Bahn 2011])

Pediatric Note: Adjust dose depending upon condition being treated and response of patient. The lowest possible dose should be used to control the condition; when dose reduction is possible, the dose should be reduced gradually. In life-threatening situations, parenteral doses larger than the oral dose may be needed.

Anti-inflammatory or immunosuppressive:

Infants and Children:

Oral: 2.5 to 10 mg/kg/day **or** 75 to 300 mg/m^2/day in divided doses every 6 to 8 hours (Kliegman 2007).

IM, IV:

Manufacturer labeling: Initial: 0.56 to 8 mg/kg/day or 20 to 240 mg/m^2/day in 3 or 4 divided doses.

Alternate dosing: 1 to 5 mg/kg/day **or** 30 to 150 mg/m^2/day divided every 12 to 24 hours (Kliegman 2007).

Adolescents: Oral, IM, IV, SubQ: 15 to 240 mg every 12 hours (Kliegman 2007).

Congenital adrenal hyperplasia (off-label dose): Oral: (tablets): Infants, Children, and Adolescents: **Note:** Administer morning dose as early as possible. Tablets may result in more reliable serum concentrations than oral liquid formulation; use of oral suspension is not recommended. Doses must be individualized by monitoring growth, bone age, and hormonal levels; mineralocorticoid (eg, fludrocortisone) and sodium supplement may be required in salt losers (AAP 2000; AAP 2010; Endocrine Society 2010).

Initial: 10 to 15 mg/m^2/day in 3 divided doses; higher initial doses (20 mg/m^2/day) may be required to achieve initial target hormone serum concentrations (AAP 2010; Endocrine Society 2010).

Maintenance dose: Usual requirement:

Infants: 2.5 to 5 mg/**dose** 3 times daily.

Children: 5 to 10 mg/**dose** 3 times daily.

Adolescents: Refer to adult dosing.

Physiologic replacement (off-label dose): Infants and Children: Oral: 8 to 10 mg/m^2/day divided every 8 hours; up to 12 mg/m^2/day in some patients; to replicate diurnal variation, the highest doses are typically administered in the morning and mid-day dose with the lower dose in the evening (Ahmet 2011; Elder 2015; Gupta 2008; Maguire 2007; Shulman 2007).

Septic shock (off-label use): Infants, Children, and Adolescents: IV: 50 to 100 mg/m^2/day (Dellinger 2013; Marx 2014; Shulman 2007); in some cases, doses may be titrated up to 50 mg/**kg**/day for shock reversal; however, efficacy data variable with the higher doses (Brierley 2009; Menon 2012). **Note:** Use recommended only in fluid refractory, catecholamine-resistant shock, and suspected or proven absolute (classic) adrenal insufficiency.

Renal Impairment There are no dosage adjustments provided in the manufacturer's labeling; use with caution.

Hepatic Impairment There are no dosage adjustments provided in the manufacturer's labeling; use with caution.

Mechanism of Action Short-acting corticosteroid with minimal sodium-retaining potential; decreases inflammation by suppression of migration of polymorphonuclear leukocytes and reversal of increased capillary permeability

Contraindications

Hypersensitivity to hydrocortisone or any component of the formulation; systemic fungal infections; use in premature infants (formulations containing benzyl alcohol only); idiopathic thrombocytopenia purpura (IM administration only); intrathecal administration; live or live, attenuated virus vaccines (with immunosuppressive doses of corticosteroids).

Documentation of allergenic cross-reactivity for corticosteroids is limited. However, because of similarities in chemical structure and/or pharmacologic actions, the possibility of cross-sensitivity cannot be ruled out with certainty.

Warnings/Precautions Corticosteroids are not approved for epidural injection. Serious neurologic events (eg, spinal cord infarction, paraplegia, quadriplegia, cortical blindness, stroke), some resulting in death, have been reported with epidural injection of corticosteroids, with and without use of fluoroscopy. Avoid injection or leakage into the dermis; dermal and/or subdermal skin depression may occur at the site of injection. Avoid deltoid muscle injection; subcutaneous atrophy may occur.

Use with caution in patients with thyroid disease, hepatic impairment, renal impairment, heart failure, hypertension, diabetes, glaucoma, cataracts, myasthenia gravis, osteoporosis, seizures, or GI diseases (diverticulitis, fresh intestinal anastomoses, active or latent peptic ulcer, ulcerative colitis, abscess or other pyogenic infection). Use caution following acute MI (corticosteroids have been associated with myocardial rupture). Use with caution in the elderly with the smallest possible effective dose for the shortest duration. May affect growth velocity; growth should be routinely monitored in pediatric patients. Withdraw therapy with gradual tapering of dose. Patients may require higher doses when subject to stress (ie, trauma, surgery, severe infection). Pheochromocytoma crisis has been reported with corticosteroids (may be fatal); consider the risk in patients with suspected pheochromocytoma.

May cause hypercorticism or suppression of hypothalamic-pituitary-adrenal (HPA) axis, particularly in younger children or in patients receiving high doses for prolonged periods. HPA axis suppression may lead to adrenal crisis. Withdrawal and discontinuation of a corticosteroid should be done slowly and carefully. Particular care is required when patients are transferred from systemic corticosteroids to inhaled products due to possible adrenal insufficiency or withdrawal from steroids, including an increase in allergic symptoms. Patients receiving >20 mg per day of prednisone (or equivalent) may be most susceptible. Fatalities have occurred due to adrenal insufficiency in asthmatic patients during and after transfer from systemic corticosteroids to aerosol steroids; aerosol steroids do not provide the systemic steroid needed to treat patients having trauma, surgery, or infections.

Acute myopathy has been reported with high dose corticosteroids, usually in patients with neuromuscular transmission disorders; may involve ocular and/or respiratory muscles; monitor creatine kinase; recovery may be delayed. Corticosteroid use may cause psychiatric disturbances, including euphoria, insomnia, mood swings, personality changes, severe depression, or psychotic manifestations. Preexisting psychiatric conditions may be exacerbated by corticosteroid use. Prolonged use of corticosteroids may increase the incidence of secondary infection, mask acute infection (including fungal infections), prolong or exacerbate viral infections, or limit response to killed or inactivated vaccines. Exposure to chickenpox or measles should be avoided; corticosteroids should not be used to treat ocular herpes simplex. Corticosteroids should not be used for cerebral malaria, fungal infections, or viral hepatitis. Close observation is required in patients with latent tuberculosis and/or TB reactivity; restrict use in active TB (only fulminating or disseminated TB in conjunction with antituberculosis treatment). Latent or active amebiasis should be ruled out in any patient with recent travel to tropical climates or unexplained diarrhea prior to corticosteroid initiation. Use with extreme caution in patients with *Strongyloides* infections; hyperinfection, dissemination and fatalities have occurred. Prolonged treatment with corticosteroids has been associated with the development of Kaposi sarcoma (case reports); if noted, discontinuation of therapy should be considered (Goedert 2002). High-dose corticosteroids should not be used to manage acute head injury. Rare cases of anaphylactoid reactions have been observed in patients receiving corticosteroids. Potentially significant drug-drug interactions may exist, requiring dose or frequency adjustment, additional monitoring, and/or selection of alternative therapy.

Benzyl alcohol and derivatives: Diluent for injection may contain benzyl alcohol and some dosage forms may contain sodium benzoate/benzoic acid; benzoic acid (benzoate) is a metabolite of benzyl alcohol; large amounts of benzyl alcohol (≥99 mg/kg/day) have been associated with a potentially fatal toxicity ("gasping syndrome") in neonates; the "gasping syndrome" consists of metabolic acidosis, respiratory distress, gasping respirations, CNS dysfunction (including convulsions, intracranial hemorrhage), hypotension and cardiovascular collapse (AAP ["Inactive" 1997]; CDC 1982); some data suggests that benzoate displaces bilirubin from protein binding sites (Ahlfors 2001); avoid or use dosage forms containing benzyl alcohol and/or benzyl alcohol derivative with caution in neonates. See manufacturer's labeling.

Drug Interactions

Metabolism/Transport Effects **Substrate** of CYP3A4 (minor), P-glycoprotein; **Note:** Assignment of Major/Minor substrate status based on clinically relevant drug interaction potential

Avoid Concomitant Use

Avoid concomitant use of Hydrocortisone (Systemic) with any of the following: Aldesleukin; BCG (Intravesical); Desmopressin; Indium 111 Capromab Pendetide; MiFEPRIStone; Natalizumab; Pimecrolimus; Tacrolimus (Topical); Tofacitinib

Increased Effect/Toxicity

Hydrocortisone (Systemic) may increase the levels/effects of: Acetylcholinesterase Inhibitors; Amphotericin B; Androgens; Ceritinib; Deferasirox; Desirudin; Desmopressin; Fingolimod; Leflunomide; Loop Diuretics; Natalizumab; Nicorandil; NSAID (COX-2 Inhibitor); NSAID (Nonselective); Quinolone Antibiotics; Thiazide and Thiazide-Like Diuretics; Tofacitinib; Vaccines (Live); Warfarin

The levels/effects of Hydrocortisone (Systemic) may be increased by: Aprepitant; CYP3A4 Inhibitors (Strong); Denosumab; DilTIAZem; Estrogen Derivatives; Fosaprepitant; Indacaterol; Lumacaftor; MiFEPRIStone; Neuromuscular-Blocking Agents (Nondepolarizing); Ocrelizumab; P-glycoprotein/ABCB1 Inhibitors; Pimecrolimus; Ranolazine; Roflumilast; Salicylates; Tacrolimus (Topical); Telaprevir; Trastuzumab

Decreased Effect

Hydrocortisone (Systemic) may decrease the levels/effects of: Aldesleukin; Antidiabetic Agents; BCG (Intravesical); Calcitriol (Systemic); Coccidioides immitis Skin Test; Corticorelin; Hyaluronidase; Indium 111 Capromab Pendetide; Isoniazid; Nivolumab; Salicylates; Sipuleucel-T; Telaprevir; Tertomotide; Urea Cycle Disorder Agents; Vaccines (Inactivated); Vaccines (Live)

The levels/effects of Hydrocortisone (Systemic) may be decreased by: Antacids; Bile Acid Sequestrants; CYP3A4 Inducers (Strong); Echinacea; Lumacaftor; MiFEPRIStone; Mitotane; P-glycoprotein/ABCB1 Inducers

Dietary Considerations Systemic use of corticosteroids may require a diet with increased potassium, vitamins A, B_6, C, D, folate, calcium, zinc, phosphorus, and decreased sodium. Some products may contain sodium.

Pharmacodynamics/Kinetics

Onset of Action IV: 1 hour

Half-life Elimination IV: 2 ± 0.3 hours; Oral: 1.8 ± 0.5 hours (Czock 2005)

Time to Peak

Plasma: Oral: 1.2 ± 0.4 hours (Czock 2005)

Pregnancy Risk Factor C

Pregnancy Considerations Adverse events have been observed with corticosteroids in animal reproduction studies. Some studies have shown an association between first trimester systemic corticosteroid use and oral clefts (Park-Wyllie 2000; Pradat 2003). Systemic corticosteroids may also influence fetal growth (decreased birth weight); however, information is conflicting (Lunghi 2010). Hypoadrenalism may occur in newborns following maternal use of corticosteroids in pregnancy (monitor). In general, when systemic corticosteroids are needed in pregnancy, it is recommended to use the lowest effective dose for the shortest duration of time, avoiding high doses during the first trimester (Leachman 2006; Lunghi 2010; Makol 2011; Østensen 2009). When treating women with Primary Adrenal Insufficiency (PAI) during pregnancy, hydrocortisone is the preferred corticosteroid. Doses may need adjusted as pregnancy progresses and stress doses may be required during active labor. Pregnant women with PAI should be monitored at least once each trimester (Bornstein 2016).

Breastfeeding Considerations Corticosteroids are excreted in breast milk. The manufacturer notes that when used systemically, maternal use of corticosteroids have the potential to cause adverse events in a nursing infant (eg, growth suppression, interfere with endogenous corticosteroid production). If there is concern about exposure to the infant, some guidelines recommend waiting 4 hours after the maternal dose of an oral systemic corticosteroid before breastfeeding in order to decrease potential exposure to the nursing infant (based on a study using prednisolone) (Bae 2011; Leachman 2006; Makol 2011; Ost 1985).

Dosage Forms

Solution Reconstituted, Injection [preservative free]:

Solu-CORTEF: 100 mg (1 ea); 100 mg (1 ea); 250 mg (1 ea); 500 mg (1 ea); 1000 mg (1 ea)

Tablet, Oral:

Cortef: 5 mg, 10 mg, 20 mg

Generic: 5 mg, 10 mg, 20 mg

Hydrocortisone (Topical) (hye droe KOR ti sone)

Brand Names: US Advanced Allergy Collection; Ala Scalp; Ala-Cort; Anti-Itch Maximum Strength [OTC]; Anucort-HC; Anusol-HC; Aquanil HC [OTC]; Beta HC [OTC]; Colocort; Cortaid Maximum Strength [OTC]; CortAlo [DSC]; Cortenema; Corticool [OTC]; Cortifoam; Dermasorb HC; First-Hydrocortisone; GRx HiCort 25 [DSC]; Hemmorex-HC; Hemril-30 [DSC]; Hydro Skin Maximum Strength [OTC]; Hydrocortisone in Absorbase; Hydrocortisone Max St [OTC]; Hydrocortisone Max St/12 Moist [OTC]; HydroSKIN [OTC]; Instacort 5 [OTC]; Locoid; Locoid Lipocream; Med-Derm Hydrocortisone [OTC]; Medi-First Hydrocortisone [OTC]; MiCort-HC; NuCort; NuZon [DSC]; Pandel; Pediaderm HC [DSC]; Preparation H Hydrocortisone [OTC]; Procto-Med HC; Procto-Pak; Proctocort; Proctocream HC [DSC]; Proctosol HC; Proctozone-HC; Recort Plus [OTC]; Rectacort-HC [DSC]; Rederm [OTC]; Sarnol-HC [OTC]; Scalacort; Scalacort DK; Scalpicin Maximum Strength [OTC]; Texacort; TheraCort [OTC] [DSC]; Westcort

Brand Names: Canada Aquacort; Cortamed; Cortenema; Cortifoam; Emo-Cort; Hycort; Hyderm; HydroVal; Locoid; Prevex HC; Sarna HC; Westcort

Generic Availability (US) May be product dependent

Pharmacologic Category Antihemorrhoidal Agent; Corticosteroid, Rectal; Corticosteroid, Topical

Use

Anal and genital itching (external): Use in postirradiation (factitial) proctitis, cryptitis, other inflammatory conditions of the anorectum; external genital, feminine, and anal itching.

Dermatoses: Relief of the inflammatory and pruritic manifestations of corticosteroid-responsive dermatoses (eg, eczema; psoriasis; poison ivy, oak, or sumac; insect bites; minor skin irritation; atopic dermatitis [mild to moderate]; seborrheic dermatitis).

Hemorrhoids: Use in inflamed hemorrhoids.

Ulcerative colitis (adjunctive therapy): Adjunctive treatment of ulcerative colitis, especially distal forms including ulcerative proctitis, ulcerative proctosigmoiditis, left-sided ulcerative colitis, and in some cases involving the transverse and ascending colons.

Local Anesthetic/Vasoconstrictor Precautions No information available to require special precautions

Effects on Dental Treatment No significant effects or complications reported

Effects on Bleeding No information available to require special precautions

Adverse Reactions Frequency not defined. Local adverse events presented. Adverse events similar to those observed with systemic absorption are also observed, especially following rectal use. Refer to the Hydrocortisone (Systemic) monograph for details.

Cream, ointment: Dermatologic: Acneiform eruption, atrophic striae, burning sensation of skin, folliculitis, hypertrichosis, hypopigmentation, maceration of the skin, miliaria, perioral dermatitis, pruritus, secondary skin infection, skin atrophy, skin irritation, xeroderma

Enema:
Central nervous system: Localized burning
Hematologic & oncologic: Rectal hemorrhage
Local: Local pain

Suppositories:
Central nervous system: Localized burning
Dermatologic: Allergic contact dermatitis, folliculitis, hypopigmentation, pruritus, xeroderma
Infection: Secondary infection

Dental Usual Dosage Treatment of a variety of oral diseases of allergic, inflammatory, or autoimmune origin: Children >2 years and Adults: Topical: Apply to affected area 2 to 4 times/day

Dosing

Adult & Geriatric

Dermatosis: Topical: Note: Discontinue when control achieved; if improvement not seen within 2 weeks, reassessment of diagnosis may be necessary.

Rx: Apply thin film to affected area 2 to 4 times daily.

Hydrocortisone butyrate (Locoid cream, Lipocream, ointment, solution): Apply thin film to affected area 2 to 3 times daily.

Hydrocortisone probutate (Pandel): Topical: Apply thin film to affected area 1 to 2 times daily.

Hydrocortisone valerate (Westcort): Topical: Apply thin film to affected area 2 to 3 times daily.

OTC: Apply thin film to the affected area up to 3 to 4 times daily.

Anal and genital itching, external: Topical: OTC labeling: Apply to affected area up to 3 to 4 times daily.

Hemorrhoids: Rectal: One suppository (25 or 30 mg) twice daily for 2 weeks. For severe cases of proctitis, 1 suppository 3 times daily or 2 suppositories twice daily may be needed. For factitial proctitis, duration of treatment may be up to 6 to 8 weeks.

Ulcerative colitis: Rectal:

Foam: One applicatorful (90 mg) 1 to 2 times daily for 2 to 3 weeks, and then every other day thereafter; use lowest dose to maintain clinical response; taper dose to discontinue long-term therapy

Suspension: One enema (100 mg) every night for 21 days or until remission (clinical improvement may precede improvement of mucosal integrity); 2 to 3 months of therapy may be required; to discontinue long-term therapy, gradually reduce administration to every other night for 2 or 3 weeks.

Pediatric

Atopic dermatitis: Topical: Infants ≥3 months, Children, and Adolescents: Hydrocortisone butyrate (Locoid Lipocream, Locoid lotion): Apply thin film to affected area twice daily.

Dermatosis: Topical: Note: Discontinue when control achieved; if improvement not seen within 2 weeks, reassessment of diagnosis may be necessary.

Rx: Apply thin film to affected area 2 to 4 times daily.

Hydrocortisone butyrate (Locoid cream, Lipocream, ointment, solution): Apply thin film to affected area 2 to 3 times daily.

OTC: Apply thin film to the affected area up to 3 to 4 times daily. Products labeled for OTC use (self-medication) should not be used in children <2 year.

Anal and genital itching, external: Topical: Children ≥12 years and Adolescents: OTC labeling: Refer to adult dosing.

Renal Impairment There are no dosage adjustments provided in the manufacturer's labeling.

Hepatic Impairment There are no dosage adjustments provided in the manufacturer's labeling.

Mechanism of Action Topical corticosteroids have anti-inflammatory, antipruritic, and vasoconstrictive properties. May depress the formation, release, and activity of endogenous chemical mediators of inflammation (kinins, histamine, liposomal enzymes, prostaglandins) through the induction of phospholipase A_2 inhibitory proteins (lipocortins) and sequential inhibition of the release of arachidonic acid. Hydrocortisone has low to intermediate range potency (dosage-form dependent).

Contraindications

Hypersensitivity to hydrocortisone or any component of the formulation; systemic fungal infections and ileocolostomy during the immediate or early postoperative period (rectal suspension); obstruction, abscess, perforation, peritonitis, fresh intestinal anastomoses, extensive fistulas, and sinus tracts (rectal foam).

OTC labeling: When used for self-medication, do not use for the treatment of diaper dermatitis.

Documentation of allergenic cross-reactivity for corticosteroids is limited. However, because of similarities in chemical structure and/or pharmacologic actions, the possibility of cross-sensitivity cannot be ruled out with certainty.

Warnings/Precautions May cause hypercorticism or suppression of hypothalamic-pituitary-adrenal (HPA) axis, particularly in younger children or in patients receiving high doses for prolonged periods. HPA axis suppression may lead to adrenal crisis. Withdrawal and discontinuation of a corticosteroid should be done slowly and carefully. Children may absorb proportionally larger amounts after topical application and may be more prone to systemic effects. HPA axis suppression, intracranial hypertension, and Cushing syndrome have been reported in children receiving topical corticosteroids. Prolonged use may affect growth velocity; growth should be routinely monitored in pediatric patients. Rare cases of anaphylactoid reactions have been observed in patients receiving corticosteroids. May require higher doses when subject to stress (ie, trauma, surgery, severe infection).

Prolonged use of corticosteroids may increase the incidence of secondary infection, mask acute infection (including fungal infections), prolong or exacerbate viral infections, or limit response to vaccines. Exposure to chickenpox or measles should be avoided; corticosteroids should not be used to treat ocular herpes simplex. Corticosteroids should not be used for cerebral malaria, fungal infections, or viral hepatitis. Close observation is required in patients with latent tuberculosis and/or tuberculosis reactivity; restrict use in active tuberculosis (only fulminating or disseminated tuberculosis in conjunction with antituberculosis treatment). Amebiasis should be ruled out in any patient with recent travel to tropical climates or unexplained diarrhea prior to initiation of corticosteroids.

Prolonged treatment with corticosteroids has been also associated with the development of Kaposi sarcoma (case reports); if noted, discontinuation of therapy should be considered. Acute myopathy has been reported with high-dose corticosteroids, usually in patients with neuromuscular transmission disorders; may involve ocular and/or respiratory muscles; monitor creatine kinase; recovery may be delayed. Corticosteroid use may cause psychiatric disturbances, including depression, euphoria, insomnia, mood swings, and personality changes. Preexisting psychiatric conditions may be exacerbated by corticosteroid use. Allergic contact dermatitis can occur and is usually diagnosed by failure to heal rather than clinical exacerbation; discontinue use if irritation occurs and treat appropriately.

Use with caution in patients with heart failure and/or hypertension, diabetes mellitus, GI diseases (diverticulitis, intestinal anastomoses peptic ulcer, nonspecific ulcerative colitis), hepatic impairment (including cirrhosis), osteoporosis, myasthenia gravis, osteoporosis, renal impairment, or thyroid disease. In patients with severe ulcerative colitis, it may be hazardous to delay surgery while waiting for response to treatment. Use with caution following acute myocardial infarction; corticosteroids have been associated with myocardial rupture. Use with caution in patients with cataracts and/or glaucoma; increased intraocular pressure, glaucoma, and cataracts have occurred with prolonged use.

Topical corticosteroids may be absorbed percutaneously. Absorption is increased by the use of occlusive dressings, application to denuded skin, prolonged use, or application to large surface areas. Avoid use of topical preparations with occlusive dressings or on weeping or exudative lesions. Topical use has been associated with local sensitization (redness, irritation); discontinue if sensitization is noted. Because of the risk of adverse effects associated with systemic absorption, topical corticosteroids should be used cautiously in elderly patients in the smallest possible effective dose for the shortest duration. After long-term use, withdraw therapy with gradual tapering of dose.

Benzyl alcohol: Some dosage forms may contain benzyl alcohol and/or sodium benzoate/benzoic acid; benzoic acid (benzoate) is a metabolite of benzyl alcohol; large amounts of benzyl alcohol (≥99 mg/kg/day) have been associated with a potentially fatal toxicity ("gasping syndrome") in neonates; the "gasping syndrome" consists of metabolic acidosis, respiratory distress, gasping respirations, CNS dysfunction (including convulsions, intracranial hemorrhage), hypotension and cardiovascular collapse (AAP ["Inactive" 1997]; CDC 1982); some data suggests that benzoate displaces bilirubin from protein binding sites (Ahlfors 2001); avoid or use dosage forms containing benzyl alcohol and/or benzyl alcohol derivative with caution in neonates. See manufacturer's labeling.

Rectal enema: Damage to the rectal wall may occur from improper or careless insertion of the enema tip. Use with caution when there is a probability of impending perforation, abscess, or other pyogenic infection; obstruction; or extensive fistulas and sinus tracts.

Rectal foam: Do not insert any part of the aerosol container directly into the anus. Contents are under pressure; do not burn or puncture the container; do not store at temperatures above 48.9°C (120°F). If there is not evidence of clinical or proctologic improvement within 2 or 3 weeks after initiation of therapy, or if the condition worsens, discontinue use. Contraindicated in obstruction, abscess, perforation, peritonitis, fresh intestinal anastomoses, extensive fistulas, and sinus tracts.

Self-medication (OTC use): Contact health care provider if condition worsens, symptoms persist for >7 days, or rectal bleeding occurs.

Drug Interactions

Metabolism/Transport Effects **Substrate** of CYP3A4 (minor); **Note:** Assignment of Major/Minor substrate status based on clinically relevant drug interaction potential

Avoid Concomitant Use

Avoid concomitant use of Hydrocortisone (Topical) with any of the following: Aldesleukin

Increased Effect/Toxicity

Hydrocortisone (Topical) may increase the levels/effects of: Ceritinib; Deferasirox

Decreased Effect

Hydrocortisone (Topical) may decrease the levels/effects of: Aldesleukin; Corticorelin; Hyaluronidase

Pregnancy Risk Factor C

Pregnancy Considerations Adverse events have been observed in animal reproduction studies. When topical corticosteroids are needed during pregnancy, low to mid potency preparations are preferred; higher potency preparations should be used for the shortest time possible and fetal growth should be monitored (Chi 2011; Chi 2013). Topical products are not recommended for extensive use, in large quantities, or for long periods of time in pregnant women (Leachman 2006).

Breastfeeding Considerations Systemic corticosteroids are excreted in human milk; it is not known if systemic absorption following topical administration of hydrocortisone results in detectable quantities in human milk. When used systemically, maternal use of corticosteroids has the potential to cause adverse events in a breastfeeding infant (eg, growth suppression, interfere with endogenous corticosteroid production). According to the manufacturer, the decision to continue or discontinue breastfeeding during therapy should take into account the risk of infant exposure, the benefits of breastfeeding to the infant, and benefits of treatment to the mother. Do not apply topical corticosteroids to nipples; hypertension was noted in a breastfeeding infant exposed to a topical corticosteroid while breastfeeding (Leachman 2006).

Dosage Forms Considerations

First-Hydrocortisone 10% gel is a compounding kit. Refer to manufacturer's labeling for compounding instructions.

Dosage Forms

Cream, External:

Ala-Cort: 1% (28.4 g, 85.2 g); 2.5% (30 g)
Anti-Itch Maximum Strength [OTC]: 1% (28 g)
Cortaid Maximum Strength [OTC]: 1% (28 g)
Hydrocortisone Max St [OTC]: 1% (28.4 g)
Hydrocortisone Max St/12 Moist [OTC]: 1% (28.4 g)
HydroSKIN [OTC]: 1% (28 g)
Instacort 5 [OTC]: 0.5% (28.4 g)
Locoid: 0.1% (15 g, 45 g)
Locoid Lipocream: 0.1% (45 g, 60 g)
Med-Derm Hydrocortisone [OTC]: 0.5% (30 g); 1% (30 g)
Medi-First Hydrocortisone [OTC]: 1% (1 ea)
MiCort-HC: 2.5% (4 g, 28.4 g)
Pandel: 0.1% (45 g, 80 g)
Preparation H Hydrocortisone [OTC]: 1% (26 g)
Recort Plus [OTC]: 1% (30 g)
Generic: 0.1% (15 g, 45 g, 60 g); 0.2% (15 g, 45 g, 60 g); 0.5% (15 g, 28.35 g, 28.4 g, 30 g); 1% (1 g, 1.5 g, 14.2 g, 20 g, 28 g, 28.35 g, 28.4 g, 30 g, 120 g, 453.6 g, 454 g); 2.5% (20 g, 28 g, 28.35 g, 30 g, 453.6 g)

Cream, Rectal:

Anusol-HC: 2.5% (30 g)
Procto-Med HC: 2.5% (30 g)
Procto-Pak: 1% (28.4 g)
Proctocort: 1% (28.35 g)

Proctosol HC: 2.5% (28.35 g)
Proctozone-HC: 2.5% (30 g)
Generic: 1% (28.4 g); 2.5% (30 g)

Enema, Rectal:
Colocort: 100 mg/60 mL (60 mL)
Cortenema: 100 mg/60 mL (60 mL)
Generic: 100 mg/60 mL (60 mL)

Foam, Rectal:
Cortifoam: 10% [90 mg/applicatorful] (15 g)

Gel, External:
Corticool [OTC]: 1% (42.53 g)
First-Hydrocortisone: 10% (60 g)

Kit, External:
Advanced Allergy Collection: 2.5%
Dermasorb HC: 2%
Scalacort DK: Hydrocortisone lotion 2% and Sal Acid 2% and sulfur 2%

Lotion, External:
Ala Scalp: 2% (29.6 mL)
Aquanil HC [OTC]: 1% (120 mL)
Beta HC [OTC]: 1% (60 mL)
Hydro Skin Maximum Strength [OTC]: 1% (118 mL)
HydroSKIN [OTC]: 1% (118 mL)
Locoid: 0.1% (59 mL, 118 mL)
NuCort: 2% (60 g)
Rederm [OTC]: 1% (120 mL)
Sarnol-HC [OTC]: 1% (59 mL)
Scalacort: 2% (29.6 mL)
Generic: 1% (114 g); 2.5% (59 mL, 118 mL)

Ointment, External:
Hydrocortisone in Absorbase: 1% (110 g)
Locoid: 0.1% (15 g, 45 g)
Westcort: 0.2% (15 g, 45 g, 60 g)
Generic: 0.1% (15 g, 45 g); 0.2% (15 g, 45 g, 60 g); 0.5% (28.35 g, 30 g); 2.5% (20 g, 28.35 g, 453.6 g, 454 g); 1% (25 g, 28 g, 28.35 g, 28.4 g, 30 g, 110 g, 430 g, 453.6 g)

Solution, External:
Locoid: 0.1% (60 mL)
Scalpicin Maximum Strength [OTC]: 1% (44 mL)
Texacort: 2.5% (30 mL)
Generic: 0.1% (20 mL, 60 mL)

Suppository, Rectal:
Anucort-HC: 25 mg (1 ea, 12 ea, 24 ea, 100 ea)
Anusol-HC: 25 mg (12 ea, 24 ea)
Hemmorex-HC: 25 mg (12 ea, 24 ea); 30 mg (12 ea)
Proctocort: 30 mg (12 ea)
Generic: 25 mg (12 ea, 24 ea); 30 mg (12 ea)

HYDROmorphone (hye droe MOR fone)

Related Information
Oral Pain *on page 1830*
OxyMORphone *on page 1274*

Brand Names: US Dilaudid; Dilaudid-HP [DSC]; Exalgo

Brand Names: Canada Apo-Hydromorphone; Dilaudid; Dilaudid-HP; Hydromorph Contin; Hydromorphone HP; Hydromorphone HP Forte Injection; Hydromorphone Hydrochloride Injection USP HP 10; Hydromorphone Hydrochloride Injection, USP; Jurnista; PMS-Hydromorphone; Teva-Hydromorphone

Pharmacologic Category Analgesic, Opioid

Use

Pain management:

Immediate release:

Tablet, oral solution, injection: Management of pain severe enough to require an opioid analgesic and for which alternate treatments are inadequate.

HP injection: Management of pain severe enough to require an opioid analgesic in opioid-tolerant patients who require higher doses of opioids and for which alternate treatments are inadequate.

Extended release: Management of pain in opioid-tolerant patients severe enough to require daily, around-the-clock, long-term opioid treatment and for which alternative treatment options are inadequate.

Limitations of use: Reserve for use in patients for whom alternative treatment options (eg, nonopioid analgesics, opioid combination products) are ineffective, not tolerated, or would be otherwise inadequate to provide sufficient management of pain. Hydromorphone ER is not indicated as an as-needed analgesic.

Moderate to severe pain: Suppository: Relief of moderate to severe pain such as that caused by biliary colic, burns, cancer, myocardial infarction, renal colic, surgery, and trauma (soft tissue and bone).

Local Anesthetic/Vasoconstrictor Precautions No information available to require special precautions

Effects on Dental Treatment Key adverse event(s) related to dental treatment: Xerostomia (normal salivary flow resumes upon discontinuation).

Effects on Bleeding No information available to require special precautions

Adverse Reactions Frequency not defined.

Cardiovascular: Bradycardia, extrasystoles, flushing (facial), hypertension, hypotension, palpitations, peripheral edema, peripheral vasodilation, syncope, tachycardia

Central nervous system: Abnormal dreams, abnormal gait, abnormality in thinking, aggressive behavior, agitation, apprehension, ataxia, brain disease, burning sensation of skin (Exalgo), central nervous system depression, chills, cognitive dysfunction, confusion, decreased body temperature (Exalgo), depression, disruption of body temperature regulation (Exalgo), dizziness, drowsiness, drug dependence, dysarthria, dysphoria, equilibrium disturbance, euphoria, fatigue, hallucination, headache, hyperesthesia, hyperreflexia, hypoesthesia, hypothermia, increased intracranial pressure, insomnia, lack of concentration, lethargy, malaise, memory impairment, mood changes, myoclonus, nervousness, painful defecation, panic attack, paranoia, paresthesia, psychomotor agitation, restlessness, sedation, seizure, sleep disorder (Exalgo), suicidal ideation, uncontrolled crying, vertigo

Dermatologic: Diaphoresis, erythema (Exalgo), hyperhidrosis, pruritus, skin rash, urticaria

Endocrine & metabolic: Antidiuretic effect, decreased amylase, decreased libido, decreased plasma testosterone, dehydration, fluid retention, hyperuricemia, hypokalemia, weight loss

Gastrointestinal: Abdominal distention, anal fissure, anorexia, bezoar formation (Exalgo), biliary tract spasm, constipation, decreased appetite, decreased gastrointestinal motility (Exalgo), delayed gastric emptying, diarrhea, diverticulitis, diverticulosis, duodenitis, dysgeusia, dysphagia, eructation, flatulence, gastroenteritis, gastroesophageal reflux disease (aggravated; Exalgo), hematochezia, increased appetite, intestinal perforation (large intestine; Exalgo), nausea, paralytic ileus, stomach cramps, vomiting, xerostomia

Genitourinary: Bladder spasm, decreased urine output, difficulty in micturition, dysuria, erectile dysfunction, hypogonadism, sexual disorder, ureteral spasm, urinary frequency, urinary hesitancy, urinary retention

Hematologic & oncologic: Oxygen desaturation

Hepatic: Increased liver enzymes
Hypersensitivity: Histamine release
Local: Pain at injection site, post-injection flare
Neuromuscular & skeletal: Arthralgia, dyskinesia, laryngospasm, muscle rigidity, muscle spasm, myalgia, tremor, weakness
Ophthalmic: Blurred vision, diplopia, dry eye syndrome, miosis, nystagmus
Otic: Tinnitus
Respiratory: Apnea, bronchospasm, dyspnea, flu-like symptoms (Exalgo), hyperventilation, hypoxia, respiratory depression, respiratory distress, rhinorrhea
Postmarketing and/or case reports: Angioedema, hypersensitivity, increased serum prolactin (Molitch 2008; Vuong 2010)

General Dosage Range Dosage adjustment recommended in patients with hepatic or renal impairment

IM, SubQ: *Adults:* 1 to 2 mg every 2 to 3 hours as needed

IV: *Adults:* 0.2 to 1 mg every 2 to 3 hours as needed

Oral:

Adults: Immediate release: 2 to 4 mg every 4 to 6 hours as needed (tablets) or 2.5 to 10 mg every 3 to 6 hours as needed (liquid); Extended release: Dose is individualized based on prior opioid use/dose

Elderly: Initiation at the low end of dosage range is recommended

Rectal: *Adults:* 3 mg every 6 to 8 hours as needed

Mechanism of Action Binds to opioid receptors in the CNS, causing inhibition of ascending pain pathways, altering the perception of and response to pain; causes cough suppression by direct central action in the medulla; produces generalized CNS depression

Pharmacodynamics/Kinetics

Onset of Action Analgesic:

Immediate release formulations:

Oral: 15 to 30 minutes; Peak effect: 30 to 60 minutes

IV: 5 minutes; Peak effect: 10 to 20 minutes

Extended release tablet: 6 hours; Peak effect: ~9 hours (Angst 2001)

Duration of Action

Immediate release formulations: Oral, IV: 3 to 4 hours; suppository may provide longer duration of effect

Extended release tablet: ~13 hours (Angst 2001)

Half-life Elimination

Immediate-release formulations: 2 to 3 hours

Extended-release tablets: Apparent half-life: ~11 hours (range: 8 to 15 hours)

Time to Peak Plasma:

Immediate-release tablet: ≤1 hour

Extended-release tablet: 12 to 16 hours

Extended-release capsule [Canadian product]: ~5 hours

Pregnancy Considerations Adverse events have been observed in some animal reproduction studies. Hydromorphone crosses the placenta. Some dosage forms are specifically contraindicated for use in obstetrical analgesia.

When used for pain relief during labor, opioids may temporarily affect the heart rate of the fetus (ACOG 2002). Monitor the neonate for respiratory depression if hydromorphone is used during labor.

[US Boxed Warning]: Prolonged use of opioids during pregnancy can cause neonatal withdrawal syndrome, which may be life-threatening if not recognized and treated according to protocols developed by neonatology experts. If opioid use is required for a prolonged period in a pregnant woman, advise the patient of the risk of neonatal opioid withdrawal syndrome and ensure that appropriate treatment will be available. If chronic opioid exposure occurs in pregnancy, adverse events in the newborn (including withdrawal) may occur; monitoring of the neonate is recommended. The minimum effective dose should be used if opioids are needed (Chou 2009). Neonatal abstinence syndrome following opioid exposure may present with autonomic (eg, fever, temperature instability), GI (eg, diarrhea, vomiting, poor feeding/weight gain), or neurologic (eg, high-pitched crying, increased muscle tone, irritability, seizure, tremor) symptoms (Dow 2012; Hudak 2012).

Long-term opioid use may cause secondary hypogonadism, which may lead to sexual dysfunction or infertility (Brennan 2013).

Controlled Substance C-II

Prescribing and Access Restrictions Exalgo: As a requirement of the REMS program, healthcare providers who prescribe Exalgo need to receive training on the proper use and potential risks of Exalgo. For training, please refer to http://www.exalgorems.com. Prescribers will need retraining every 2 years or following any significant changes to the Exalgo REMS program.

Hydroxocobalamin (hye droks oh koe BAL a min)

Brand Names: US Cyanokit

Brand Names: Canada Cyanokit

Pharmacologic Category Antidote; Vitamin, Water Soluble

Use

IM injection: Treatment of pernicious anemia; treatment of vitamin B_{12} deficiency due to dietary deficiencies or malabsorption diseases, inadequate secretion of intrinsic factor, competition for vitamin B_{12} by intestinal parasites/bacteria, or inadequate utilization of B_{12} (eg, during neoplastic treatment)

IV infusion (Cyanokit®): Treatment of cyanide poisoning (known or suspected)

Local Anesthetic/Vasoconstrictor Precautions No information available to require special precautions

Effects on Dental Treatment No significant effects or complications reported

Effects on Bleeding No information available to require special precautions

Adverse Reactions

IM injection: Frequency not defined:
Dermatologic: Pruritus, skin rash (transient)
Gastrointestinal: Diarrhea (mild, transient)
Hypersensitivity: Anaphylaxis
Local: Pain at injection site
Miscellaneous: Swelling (feeling of swelling of the entire body)

IV infusion (Cyanokit):
>10%:
Cardiovascular: Increased blood pressure (18% to 28%)
Central nervous system: Headache (6% to 33%)
Dermatologic: Erythema (94% to 100%; may last up to 2 weeks), skin rash (20% to 44%; predominantly acneiform eruption; can appear 7 to 28 days after administration and usually resolves within a few weeks)
Gastrointestinal: Nausea (6% to 11%)
Genitourinary: Urine discoloration (100%; may last up to 5 weeks after administration)

Hematologic & oncologic: Lymphocytopenia (8% to 17%)

Local: Infusion site reaction (6% to 39%)

Frequency not defined:

Cardiovascular: Chest discomfort, peripheral edema

Central nervous system: Dizziness, memory impairment, restlessness

Dermatologic: Pruritus, urticaria

Endocrine & Metabolic: Hot flash

Gastrointestinal: Abdominal distress, diarrhea, dyspepsia, dysphagia, hematochezia, vomiting

Hypersensitivity: Allergic reaction (including anaphylaxis)

Ophthalmic: Eye irritation, eye redness, swelling of eye

Respiratory: Dry throat, dyspnea, pharyngeal edema

<1%, postmarketing, and/or case reports: Angioedema

General Dosage Range

IM:

Children: Initial: 100 mcg once daily for ≥2 weeks (total dose: 1-5 **mg**); maintenance: 30-50 mcg once per month

Adults: Initial: 30 mcg once daily for 5-10 days; maintenance: 100-200 mcg once per month **or** 1000 mcg once

IV: *Adults:* 5 **g** as a single infusion; may repeat if needed (maximum: 10 **g** cumulative dose)

Mechanism of Action Hydroxocobalamin (vitamin B_{12a}) is a precursor to cyanocobalamin (vitamin B_{12}). Cyanocobalamin acts as a coenzyme for various metabolic functions, including fat and carbohydrate metabolism and protein synthesis, used in cell replication and hematopoiesis. In the presence of cyanide, each hydroxocobalamin molecule can bind one cyanide ion by displacing it for the hydroxo ligand linked to the trivalent cobalt ion, forming cyanocobalamin, which is then excreted in the urine.

Pharmacodynamics/Kinetics

Half-life Elimination 26-31 hours

Pregnancy Risk Factor C

Pregnancy Considerations Animal studies are insufficient to determine the effect, if any, on pregnancy or fetal development. There are no adequate and well-controlled studies in pregnant women. Data on the use of hydroxocobalamin in pregnancy for the treatment of cyanide poisoning and cobalamin defects are limited. In general, medications used as antidotes should take into consideration the health and prognosis of the mother; antidotes should be administered to pregnant women if there is a clear indication for use and should not be withheld because of fears of teratogenicity (Bailey, 2003).

Hydroxychloroquine (hye droks ee KLOR oh kwin)

Related Information

Rheumatoid Arthritis, Osteoarthritis, and Osteoporosis *on page 1792*

Brand Names: US Plaquenil

Brand Names: Canada Apo-Hydroxyquine; Gen-Hydroxychloroquine; Mylan-Hydroxychloroquine; Plaquenil; PRO-Hydroxyquine

Pharmacologic Category Aminoquinoline (Antimalarial); Antimalarial Agent

Use

Lupus erythematosus: Treatment of chronic discoid erythematosus and systemic lupus erythematosus (SLE) in adults.

Malaria: Treatment of uncomplicated malaria caused by susceptible strains of *Plasmodium vivax*, *P. malariae*, *P. ovale*, and *P. falciparum*; prophylaxis of malaria in geographic areas where chloroquine resistance is not reported.

Limitations of use: Hydroxychloroquine is not effective against chloroquine or hydroxychloroquine-resistant malaria strains of *Plasmodium* species; not recommended for the treatment of complicated malaria, for malaria prophylaxis in regions with chloroquine resistance, or for treatment when the *Plasmodium* species has not been identified; hydroxychloroquine does not prevent relapses of *P. vivax* and *P. ovale* infections because it is not effective against the hypnozoite forms of these parasites.

Rheumatoid arthritis: Treatment of acute and chronic rheumatoid arthritis (RA) in adults.

Local Anesthetic/Vasoconstrictor Precautions No information available to require special precautions

Effects on Dental Treatment No significant effects or complications reported

Effects on Bleeding Hematologic adverse effects such as anemia, aplastic anemia, and thrombocytopenia are rare.

Adverse Reactions Frequency not defined.

Cardiovascular: Cardiomyopathy (rare, relationship to hydroxychloroquine unclear)

Central nervous system: Ataxia, dizziness, emotional disturbance, headache, irritability, lassitude, nerve deafness, nervousness, nightmares, psychosis, seizure, suicidal tendencies (children may be more susceptible), vertigo

Dermatologic: Alopecia, bleaching of hair, bullous rash (including erythema multiforme, Stevens-Johnson syndrome, toxic epidermal necrolysis, photosensitivity, exfoliative dermatitis), dyschromia (skin and mucosal; black-blue color), exacerbation of psoriasis (nonlight sensitive), pruritus, urticaria

Endocrine & metabolic: Exacerbation of porphyria, weight loss

Gastrointestinal: Anorexia, diarrhea, nausea, stomach cramps, vomiting

Hematologic & oncologic: Agranulocytosis, anemia, aplastic anemia, hemolysis (in patients with glucose-6-phosphate deficiency), leukopenia, thrombocytopenia

Hepatic: Hepatic insufficiency (hepatic failure; isolated cases)

Hypersensitivity: Angioedema

Neuromuscular & skeletal: Myopathy (including palsy or neuromyopathy, leading to progressive weakness and atrophy of proximal muscle groups; may be associated with mild sensory changes, loss of deep tendon reflexes, and abnormal nerve conduction)

Ophthalmic: Accommodation disturbance, corneal changes (transient edema, punctate to lineal opacities, decreased sensitivity, deposits, visual disturbances, blurred vision, photophobia [reversible on discontinuation]), decreased visual acuity, epithelial keratopathy, macular degeneration, macular edema, maculopathy, nystagmus, optic disk disorder (pallor/atrophy), retinal pigment changes, retinal vascular disease (attenuation of arterioles), retinitis pigmentosa, retinopathy (early changes reversible [may progress despite discontinuation if advanced]), scotoma, vision color changes, visual field defect

Otic: Tinnitus

Respiratory: Bronchospasm, respiratory failure (myopathy-related)

Postmarketing and/or case reports: Hypoglycemia (Cansu, 2008; Unübol, 2011), keratopathy (Dosso, 2007)

General Dosage Range Oral:

Infants, Children, and Adolescents: 13 mg/kg for 1 to 2 doses, followed by 6.5 mg/kg for 3 doses or once weekly

Adults: Initial: 400 to 800 mg daily divided 1 to 2 times daily; Maintenance: 200 to 400 mg daily **or** 800 mg for 1 to 2 doses, followed by 400 mg for 3 doses or once weekly

Mechanism of Action Interferes with digestive vacuole function within sensitive malarial parasites by increasing the pH and interfering with lysosomal degradation of hemoglobin; inhibits locomotion of neutrophils and chemotaxis of eosinophils; impairs complement-dependent antigen-antibody reactions

Pharmacodynamics/Kinetics

Onset of Action Rheumatic disease: May require several weeks to respond

Half-life Elimination ~40 days (Tett 1993)

Pregnancy Considerations Hydroxychloroquine can be detected in the cord blood at delivery in concentrations similar to those in the maternal serum (Costedoat-Chalumeau 2002). In animal reproduction studies with chloroquine, accumulation in fetal ocular tissues was observed and remained for several months following drug elimination from the rest of the body. Based on available human data, an increased risk of fetal ocular toxicity has not been observed following maternal use of hydroxychloroquine, but additional studies are needed to confirm (Osadchy 2011).

Maternal lupus is associated with adverse maternal and fetal events; however, pregnancy outcomes may be improved if conception does not occur until the disease has been inactive for ≥6 months. Hydroxychloroquine is one of the medications recommended for the management of lupus and lupus nephritis in pregnant women. If pregnancy is detected during therapy, it should not be stopped (could precipitate a flare in maternal disease and exposure to the fetus will still continue for 6 to 8 weeks due to tissue binding) (Baer 2011; Bertsias 2012; Hahn 2012; Levy 2001). Maternal use of hydroxychloroquine may also decrease the incidence of cardiac malformations associated with neonatal lupus (Izmirly 2012).

Malaria infection in pregnant women may be more severe than in nonpregnant women and has a high risk of maternal and perinatal morbidity and mortality. Therefore, pregnant women and women who are likely to become pregnant are advised to avoid travel to malaria-risk areas. Hydroxychloroquine is recommended as an alternative treatment of pregnant women for uncomplicated malaria in chloroquine-sensitive regions (refer to current guidelines) (CDC 2011).

Women exposed to hydroxychloroquine for the treatment of rheumatoid arthritis or systemic lupus erythematosus during pregnancy may be enrolled in the Organization of Teratology Information Specialists (OTIS) Autoimmune Diseases Study pregnancy registry (877-311-8972).

HYDROXYprogesterone Caproate

(hye droks ee proe JES te rone CAP ro ate)

Brand Names: US Makena

Pharmacologic Category Progestin

Use

Preterm birth: To reduce the risk of preterm birth in women with a singleton pregnancy who have a history of singleton spontaneous preterm birth.

Limitation of use: Safety and efficacy have been demonstrated only in women with a prior spontaneous singleton preterm birth. Use is not intended for women with multiple gestations or other risk factors for preterm birth.

Local Anesthetic/Vasoconstrictor Precautions No information available to require special precautions

Effects on Dental Treatment No significant effects or complications reported

Effects on Bleeding No information available to require special precautions

Adverse Reactions

>10%:

- Dermatologic: Urticaria (12%)
- Genitourinary: Preterm labor (admission: 16%)
- Local: Pain at injection site (35%), swelling at injection site (17%)

1% to 10%:

- Cardiovascular: Preeclampsia (9%)
- Dermatologic: Pruritus (8%)
- Endocrine & metabolic: Gestational diabetes (6%)
- Gastrointestinal: Nausea (6%), diarrhea (2%)
- Genitourinary: Oligohydramnios (4%), stillborn infant (2%), spontaneous abortion (≤2%; <20 weeks gestation)
- Local: Local pruritus (6%)
- Miscellaneous: Nodule (5%)

<1%, postmarketing, and/or case reports: Angioedema, cellulitis at injection site, cervical dilation, cervical shortening, chest discomfort, decreased glucose tolerance, depression, dizziness, dyspnea, fatigue, fever, fluid retention, headache, hypersensitivity reaction, hypertension, hot flash, injection site reaction, jaundice, premature rupture of membranes, pulmonary embolism, skin rash, thromboembolic complications, urinary tract infection, vomiting

General Dosage Range IM: *Pregnant females:* 250 mg every 7 days

Mechanism of Action Hydroxyprogesterone is a synthetic progestin. The mechanism by which hydroxyprogesterone reduces the risk of recurrent preterm birth is not known.

Pharmacodynamics/Kinetics

Half-life Elimination Nonpregnant females: ~8 days; Pregnant females (singleton pregnancies): 16 days (range: 11-21 days) (Caritis 2012)

Time to Peak Serum: IM: Nonpregnant females: 3-7 days; Pregnant females (singleton pregnancies): 1-4 days (Caritis 2012)

Pregnancy Risk Factor B

Pregnancy Considerations Adverse events observed in some animal reproduction studies. Adverse events were not observed in human studies following second or third trimester exposure; use not studied during first trimester.

Maternal serum concentrations of hydroxyprogesterone caproate are widely variable and may be decreased in women with increased body mass index (BMI). Hydroxyprogesterone is metabolized by the placenta and reaches the fetal circulation. In one study, the cord: maternal concentration ratio averaged 0.2. Hydroxyprogesterone caproate was detected in cord blood when delivery occurred ≥44 days after the last injection (Cartitis 2012; Hemaue 2008).

Prescribing and Access Restrictions The Makena Care Connection™ is a comprehensive program for patients and healthcare providers which provides administrative support (including insurance benefit investigation and prescription fulfillment); financial and co-pay assistance for eligible patients; and treatment support (including educational information, home health care service and scheduled treatment reminders). The Makena Care Connection™ is available by calling 1-800-847-3418, Monday-Friday, 8 AM to 9 PM EST.

Hydroxyurea (hye droks ee yoor EE a)

Brand Names: US Droxia; Hydrea

Brand Names: Canada Apo-Hydroxyurea; Hydrea; Mylan-Hydroxyurea

Pharmacologic Category Antineoplastic Agent, Miscellaneous

Use

Chronic myeloid leukemia (Hydrea): Treatment of refractory chronic myeloid leukemia (CML)

Head and neck cancer (Hydrea): Management (with concomitant radiation therapy) of locally advanced squamous cell head and neck cancer (excluding lip cancer)

Sickle cell anemia (Droxia): Management of sickle cell anemia (to reduce the frequency of painful crises and to reduce the need for blood transfusions in patients with recurrent moderate to severe painful crises)

Local Anesthetic/Vasoconstrictor Precautions No information available to require special precautions

Effects on Dental Treatment No significant effects or complications reported

Effects on Bleeding Can cause life-threatening anemia and thrombocytopenia. Usually resolves within 14 days of discontinuation. Used to treat thrombocytosis. Medical consult recommended.

Adverse Reactions Frequency not always defined.

Cardiovascular: Edema, hypersensitivity angiitis

Central nervous system: Chills, disorientation, dizziness, drowsiness (dose-related), hallucination, head ache, malaise, peripheral neuropathy (HIV-infected patients), seizure, vasculitic ulcerations

Dermatologic: Eczema (infants and children 9 to 18 months: 13% [Thornburg 2012]), leg ulcer (7% [Hernández-Boluda 2011]), dermal ulcer (3% [Antonioli 2012]), nail discoloration (2% [Randi 2005]), alopecia (infrequent, [Hernández-Boluda 2011]), changes in nails (infrequent, [Hernández-Boluda 2011]), hyperpigmentation (infrequent, [Hernández-Boluda 2011]), atrophy of nail, dermatomyositis-like skin changes, desquamation, erythema (peripheral), facial erythema, gangrene of skin or other tissue, maculopapular rash, papule (violet), skin atrophy, skin carcinoma

Endocrine & metabolic: Increased uric acid

Gastrointestinal: Acute mucocutaneous toxicity (5% [Hernández-Boluda 2011]), diarrhea (infrequent, [Antonioli 2012]), gastric distress (infrequent, [Antonioli 2012]), nausea (infrequent, [Antonioli 2012]), oral mucosa ulcer (infrequent, [Hernández-Boluda 2011]), anorexia, BSP abnormality (retention), constipation, gastrointestinal irritation (potentiated with radiation therapy), mucositis (potentiated with radiation therapy), pancreatitis (HIV-infected patients), stomatitis, vomiting

Genitourinary: Dysuria

Hematologic & oncologic: Leukemia (4% [Hernández-Boluda 2011]; secondary; long-term use), leukopenia (2% [Hernández-Boluda 2011]), bone marrow depression (neutropenia [common], thrombocytopenia; hematologic recovery: within 2 weeks); abnormal erythropoiesis (megaloblastic; self-limiting), macrocytosis (MCV >97: 42% [Randi 2005]), reticulocytopenia (infants and children 9 to 18 months [Wang 2011])

Hepatic: Hepatic failure (HIV-infected patients), hepatotoxicity, increased liver enzymes

Neuromuscular & skeletal: Panniculitis (Antonioli 2012), weakness

Renal: Increased blood urea nitrogen, increased serum creatinine, renal tubular disease

Respiratory: Asthma (infants and children 9 to 18 months: 9% [Thornburg 2012]), dyspnea, pulmonary fibrosis (rare), pulmonary infiltrates (diffuse, rare)

<1%, postmarketing, and/or case reports: Actinic keratosis (Antonioli 2012), azoospermia, basal cell carcinoma (Antonioli 2012), cholestasis, hepatitis, hyperkeratosis (Antonioli 2012), lesion (dyschromic [Antonioli 2012]), malignant neoplasm (Wong 2014), mucous membrane lesion (Antonioli 2012), oligospermia, pneumonitis (Antonioli 2012), squamous cell carcinoma (Antonioli 2012), tumor lysis syndrome

General Dosage Range Dosage adjustment recommended in patients with renal impairment or who develop toxicities.

Oral: *Adults:* 15 to 35 mg/kg/day

Mechanism of Action Antimetabolite which selectively inhibits ribonucleoside diphosphate reductase, preventing the conversion of ribonucleotides to deoxyribonucleotides, halting the cell cycle at the G1/S phase and therefore has radiation sensitizing activity by maintaining cells in the G_1 phase and interfering with DNA repair. In sickle cell anemia, hydroxyurea increases red blood cell (RBC) hemoglobin F levels, RBC water content, deformability of sickled cells, and alters adhesion of RBCs to endothelium.

Pharmacodynamics/Kinetics

Onset of Action Sickle cell anemia: Fetal hemoglobin increase: 4 to 12 weeks

Half-life Elimination 1.9 to 3.9 hours (Gwilt 1998); Children: Sickle cell anemia: 1.7 hours (range: 0.7 to 3 hours) (Ware 2011)

Time to Peak

Children: "Fast" phenotype: 15 to 30 minutes; "Slow" phenotype: 60 to 120 minutes (Ware 2011)

Adults: 1 to 4 hours

Pregnancy Considerations Adverse effects have been observed in animal reproduction studies. Based on its mechanism of action, hydroxyurea may cause fetal harm if administered during pregnancy. Women of reproductive potential should be advised to avoid becoming pregnant during treatment (verify pregnancy status prior to starting hydroxyurea therapy) and should use effective contraception during and for at least 6 months after completion of therapy. Hydroxyurea use may damage spermatozoa and testicular tissue; males with female partners of reproductive potential should use effective contraception during and for at least 1 year after therapy. Azoospermia or oligospermia (sometimes reversible) has been observed in male patients; counsel males of reproductive potential about sperm banking prior to therapy initiation.

HydrOXYzine (hye DROKS i zeen)

Related Information

Management of the Patient With Anxiety or Depression *on page 1873*

Related Sample Prescriptions

Sedation (Prior to Dental Treatment) - Sample Prescriptions *on page 42*

Brand Names: US Vistaril

Brand Names: Canada Apo-Hydroxyzine; Atarax; Hydroxyzine Hydrochloride Injection, USP; Novo-Hydroxyzin; PMS-Hydroxyzine

Generic Availability (US) Yes

Pharmacologic Category Antiemetic; Histamine H_1 Antagonist; Histamine H_1 Antagonist, First Generation; Piperazine Derivative

Dental Use Treatment of anxiety, as a preoperative sedative in pediatric dentistry

Use

Oral:

Anxiety: Symptomatic relief of anxiety and tension associated with psychoneurosis; adjunct in organic disease states in which anxiety is manifested.

Perioperative adjunct: As a sedative when used as premedication and following general anesthesia

Pruritus: Management of pruritus due to allergic conditions (eg, chronic urticaria, atopic and contact dermatoses) and in histamine-mediated pruritus.

Intramuscular:

Allergic conditions: Adjunctive therapy in allergic conditions with strong emotional overlay (eg, asthma, chronic urticaria, pruritus).

Antiemetic: Control of nausea and vomiting.

Anxiety: Management of anxiety, tension, and psychomotor agitation in conditions of emotional stress, in preparation for dental procedures, and as adjunctive therapy in alcoholism; management of anxiety associated with organic disturbances. **Note:** Should not be used as the sole treatment of psychosis or of clearly demonstrated cases of depression.

Perioperative adjunct: As pre- and postoperative adjunctive medication to permit reduction in narcotic dosage, allay anxiety, and control emesis.

Peripartum adjunct: As pre- and postpartum adjunctive medication to permit reduction in narcotic dosage, allay anxiety, and control emesis.

Local Anesthetic/Vasoconstrictor Precautions No information available to require special precautions

Effects on Dental Treatment Key adverse event(s) related to dental treatment: Xerostomia (normal salivary flow resumes upon discontinuation) (see Dental Comment)

Effects on Bleeding No information available to require special precautions

Adverse Reactions Frequency not defined:

Central nervous system: Drowsiness (transient)

Gastrointestinal: Xerostomia

Respiratory: Respiratory depression (high doses)

<1%, postmarketing, and/or case reports: Acute generalized exanthematous pustulosis, fixed drug eruption, hallucination, headache, hypersensitivity reaction, involuntary movements, prolonged Q-T interval on ECG, pruritus, seizure (high doses), skin rash, torsades de pointes, tremor (high doses), urticaria

Dental Usual Dosage

Anxiety: Adults: Oral: 50-100 mg 4 times/day

Preoperative sedation:

Children:

Oral: 0.6 mg/kg/dose

IM: 0.5-1 mg/kg/dose

Adults:

Oral: 50-100 mg

IM: 25-100 mg

Dosing

Adult

Antiemetic: IM: 25 to 100 mg/dose

Anxiety:

Oral:

Manufacturer's labeling: 50 to 100 mg 4 times daily

Alternative recommendations (off-label dosing): 37.5 to 75 mg daily in divided doses (WFSBP [Bandelow 2008]; WFSBP [Bandelow 2012])

IM: Initial: 50 to 100 mg, then every 4 to 6 hours as needed

Peripartum adjunct: IM: 25 to 100 mg

Perioperative adjunct:

Oral: 50 to 100 mg

IM: 25 to 100 mg

Pruritus: Oral: 25 mg 3 to 4 times daily

Geriatric Initiate dosing using the lower end of the recommended dosage range. Refer to adult dosing.

Pediatric

Antiemetic: IM: 1.1 mg/kg/dose

Anxiety: Oral:

Children <6 years: 50 mg/day in divided doses

Children ≥6 years and Adolescents: 50 to 100 mg/day in divided doses

Perioperative adjunct:

Manufacturer's labeling: Children and Adolescents:

Oral: 0.6 mg/kg/dose

IM: 1.1 mg/kg/dose

Alternate dosing: Oral: Children 2 to 5 years: 1 mg/kg/dose as a single dose 30 to 45 minutes prior to procedure in combination with other sedatives (eg, midazolam, chloral hydrate) has been used in preschool children prior to dental procedures or echocardiograms (Chowdhury 2005; Roach 2010)

Pruritus: Oral:

Manufacturer's labeling:

Children <6 years: 50 mg/day in divided doses

Children ≥6 years and Adolescents: 50 to 100 mg/day in divided doses

Alternate dosing:

Patient weighing ≤40 kg: 2 mg/kg/day in divided doses (Simons 1994)

Patient weighing >40 kg: 25 to 50 mg once daily at bedtime or twice daily (Simons 1994)

Renal Impairment There are no dosage adjustments provided in the manufacturer's labeling; however, the following guidelines have been used by some clinicians (Aronoff, 2007):

Adults:

GFR >50 mL/minute: No adjustment recommended.

GFR ≤50 mL/minute: Administer 50% of normal dose.

Continuous renal replacement therapy (CRRT): Administer 50% of the normal dose.

Intermittent hemodialysis: Administer 50% of the normal dose.

Peritoneal dialysis: Administer 50% of the normal dose.

Hepatic Impairment There are no dosage adjustments provided in the manufacturer's labeling. In adults with primary biliary cirrhosis, change dosing interval to every 24 hours (Simons F 1989)

Mechanism of Action Competes with histamine for H_1-receptor sites on effector cells in the gastrointestinal tract, blood vessels, and respiratory tract (Simons

1994). Possesses skeletal muscle relaxing, bronchodilator, antihistamine, antiemetic, and analgesic properties.

Contraindications

Hypersensitivity to hydroxyzine or any component of the formulation; early pregnancy; prolonged QT interval

Additional contraindications:

Oral: Hypersensitivity to cetirizine or levocetirizine

Injection: SubQ, intra-arterial, or IV administration

Canadian labeling: Additional contraindications (not in US labeling): Oral: Hypersensitivity to other piperazine derivatives, aminophylline or ethylenediamine; history of history of cardiac arrhythmias; significant electrolyte imbalance (eg, hypokalemia, hypomagnesemia); significant bradycardia; family history of sudden cardiac death; concomitant use with other QT interval prolonging drugs or with CYP3A4/5 inhibitors; asthmatics who have previously experienced a serious anti-histamine induced adverse bronchopulmonary effect; porphyria.

Warnings/Precautions May rarely cause acute generalized exanthematous pustulosis (AGEP), a serious skin reaction involving fever, pustules and large areas of edematous erythema. Discontinue at first sign of skin rash, worsening of pre-existing skin reactions or any other sign of hypersensitivity; if signs or symptoms suggest AGEP, do not resume therapy. QT prolongation/torsades de pointes has been reported, with the majority occurring in patients with other risk factors for QT prolongation/torsades de pointes (eg, preexisting cardiac disease, electrolyte imbalances, concomitant arrhythmogenic use). Use with caution in patients with risk factors for QT prolongation, congenital long QT syndrome, a family history of long QT syndrome, other conditions that predispose to QT prolongation and ventricular arrhythmia, as well as recent myocardial infarction, uncompensated heart failure, and bradyarrhythmias. Oral hydroxyzine is contraindicated in patients with prolonged QT interval. May cause CNS depression, which may impair physical or mental abilities; patients must be cautioned about performing tasks that require mental alertness (eg, operating machinery, driving). Use with caution with narrow-angle glaucoma, prostatic hyperplasia, urinary stricture, asthma, or COPD. The effectiveness of hydroxyzine for long-term use (>4 months) has not been assessed; periodically reassess use. Potentially significant drug-drug interactions may exist, requiring dose or frequency adjustment, additional monitoring, and/or selection of alternative therapy.

For IM use only. Severe injection-site reactions have been reported with IM administration (eg, extensive tissue damage, necrosis, gangrene) requiring surgical intervention (including debridement, skin grafting, and amputation). SubQ, IV, and intra-arterial routes of administration are contraindicated. Intravascular hemolysis, thrombosis, and digital gangrene have been reported with IV or intra-arterial administration (Baumgartner 1979); SubQ administration may result in significant tissue damage. If **inadvertent** IV administration results in extravasation, stop infusion immediately and disconnect (leave cannula/needle in place); gently aspirate extravasated solution (do **NOT** flush the line); remove needle/cannula; elevate extremity.

Benzyl alcohol and derivatives: Some dosage forms may contain benzyl alcohol and/or sodium benzoate/benzoic acid; benzoic acid (benzoate) is a metabolite of benzyl alcohol; large amounts of benzyl alcohol (≥99 mg/kg/day) have been associated with a potentially fatal toxicity ("gasping syndrome") in neonates; the "gasping syndrome" consists of metabolic acidosis, respiratory distress, gasping respirations, CNS dysfunction (including convulsions, intracranial hemorrhage), hypotension, and cardiovascular collapse (AAP ["Inactive" 1997]; CDC 1982); some data suggest that benzoate displaces bilirubin from protein binding sites (Ahlfors 2001); avoid or use dosage forms containing benzyl alcohol and/or benzyl alcohol derivative with caution in neonates. See manufacturer's labeling.

Propylene glycol: Some dosage forms may contain propylene glycol; large amounts are potentially toxic and have been associated with hyperosmolality, lactic acidosis, seizures, and respiratory depression; use caution (AAP 1997; Zar 2007). See manufacturer's labeling.

Drug Interactions

Metabolism/Transport Effects None known.

Avoid Concomitant Use

Avoid concomitant use of HydrOXYzine with any of the following: Aclidinium; Azelastine (Nasal); Cimetropium; Eluxadoline; Glucagon; Glycopyrrolate (Oral Inhalation); Ipratropium (Oral Inhalation); Levosulpiride; Nitroglycerin; Orphenadrine; Oxatomide; Oxomemazine; Paraldehyde; Potassium Chloride; Thalidomide; Tiotropium; Umeclidinium

Increased Effect/Toxicity

HydrOXYzine may increase the levels/effects of: AbobotulinumtoxinA; Alcohol (Ethyl); Analgesics (Opioid); Anticholinergic Agents; Azelastine (Nasal); Barbiturates; Blonanserin; Buprenorphine; Cimetropium; CNS Depressants; Eluxadoline; Flunitrazepam; Glucagon; Glycopyrrolate (Oral Inhalation); Highest Risk QTc-Prolonging Agents; HYDROcodone; Meperidine; Methotrimeprazine; MetyroSINE; Mirabegron; Mirtazapine; Moderate Risk QTc-Prolonging Agents; OnabotulinumtoxinA; Orphenadrine; OxyCODONE; Paraldehyde; Piribedil; Potassium Chloride; Pramipexole; Ramosetron; RimabotulinumtoxinB; ROPINIRole; Rotigotine; Selective Serotonin Reuptake Inhibitors; Suvorexant; Thalidomide; Thiazide and Thiazide-Like Diuretics; Tiotropium; Topiramate; Zolpidem

The levels/effects of HydrOXYzine may be increased by: Aclidinium; Brimonidine (Topical); Cannabis; Chloral Betaine; Chlormethiazole; Chlorphenesin Carbamate; CYP3A4 Inhibitors (Moderate); CYP3A4 Inhibitors (Strong); Dimethindene (Topical); Doxylamine; Dronabinol; Droperidol; Ipratropium (Oral Inhalation); Kava Kava; Lofexidine; Magnesium Sulfate; Methotrimeprazine; Mianserin; MiFEPRIStone; Minocycline; Nabilone; Oxatomide; Oxomemazine; Perampanel; Pramlintide; Rufinamide; Sodium Oxybate; Tapentadol; Tetrahydrocannabinol; Trimeprazine; Umeclidinium

Decreased Effect

HydrOXYzine may decrease the levels/effects of: Acetylcholinesterase Inhibitors; Benzylpenicilloyl Polylysine; Betahistine; Gastrointestinal Agents (Prokinetic); Hyaluronidase; Itopride; Levosulpiride; Nitroglycerin; Secretin

The levels/effects of HydrOXYzine may be decreased by: Acetylcholinesterase Inhibitors; Amphetamines

Pharmacodynamics/Kinetics

Onset of Action Oral: 15 to 30 minutes; IM: Rapid

Duration of Action Decreased histamine-induced wheal and flare areas: 2 to ≥36 hours; Suppression of pruritus: 1 to 12 hours (Simon F 1984)

Half-life Elimination

Children and Adolescents 1 to 14 years (mean age: 6.1 ± 4.6 years): 7.1 ± 2.3 hours; **Note:** Half-life increased with increasing age and was 4 hours in patients 1-year old and 11 hours in a 14-year old patient (Simons F 1984a)

Adults: ~20 hours (Simons 1984); Elderly: ~29 hours (Simons K 1989); Hepatic dysfunction: ~37 hours (Simons F 1989)

Time to Peak Oral administration: Serum: ~2 hours; Peak suppression of antihistamine-induced wheal and flare: 4 to 12 hours (Simons F 1984)

Pregnancy Considerations Use of hydroxyzine early in pregnancy is contraindicated.

Adverse events were observed in animal reproduction studies. Hydroxyzine crosses the placenta. Possible withdrawal symptoms have been observed in neonates following chronic maternal use of hydroxyzine during pregnancy (Prenner 1977; Serreau 2005).

Hydroxyzine is approved for pre- and postpartum adjunctive therapy to reduce opioid dosage, treat anxiety, and control emesis. Hydroxyzine may be used as an antipruritic if systemic therapy is needed in pregnant women (use caution late in pregnancy) (Murase 2014); although other agents may be preferred (Powell 2015; Zuberbier 2014). Antihistamines are not recommended for treatment of pruritus associated with intrahepatic cholestasis in pregnancy (Ambros-Rudolph 2011; Kremer 2014).

Breastfeeding Considerations It is not known if hydroxyzine is present in breast milk.

Sedation has been reported in breastfed infants exposed to hydroxyzine (Soussan 2014). Breastfeeding is not recommended by the manufacturer. In general, if a breastfed infant is exposed to a first generation antihistamine via breast milk, they should be monitored for irritability or drowsiness.

When treatment with an antihistamine is needed in breastfeeding women, second generation antihistamines are preferred (Butler 2014; Powell 2015; Zuberier 2014).

Antihistamines may decrease maternal serum prolactin concentrations when administered prior to the establishment of lactation (Messinis 1985).

Dosage Forms

Capsule, Oral:

Vistaril: 25 mg, 50 mg

Generic: 25 mg, 50 mg, 100 mg

Syrup, Oral:

Generic: 10 mg/5 mL (25 mL, 118 mL, 473 mL)

Tablet, Oral:

Generic: 10 mg, 25 mg, 50 mg

Dental Comment An adult companion should accompany the patient to and from dental office.

Ibandronate (eye BAN droh nate)

Related Information

Osteonecrosis of the Jaw *on page 1796*

Rheumatoid Arthritis, Osteoarthritis, and Osteoporosis *on page 1792*

Brand Names: US Boniva

Generic Availability (US) Yes

Pharmacologic Category Bisphosphonate Derivative

Use

Postmenopausal osteoporosis: Treatment and prevention of osteoporosis in postmenopausal females.

Limitations of use: The optimal duration has not been determined. Safety and efficacy for osteoporosis treatment are based on clinical data of 3-years duration (oral) and 1-year duration (IV). All patients on bisphosphonate therapy should be re-evaluated periodically for the need to continue therapy. Consider discontinuing after 3 to 5 years in patients at low-risk for fracture. Re-evaluate fracture risk periodically in patients who discontinue therapy.

Local Anesthetic/Vasoconstrictor Precautions No information available to require special precautions

Effects on Dental Treatment Key adverse event(s) related to dental treatment: Osteonecrosis of the jaw (ONJ), generally associated with local infection and/or tooth extraction and often with delayed healing, has been reported in patients taking bisphosphonates. Symptoms included nonhealing extraction socket or an exposed jawbone. Most reported cases of bisphosphonate-associated osteonecrosis have been in cancer patients treated with intravenous bisphosphonates. However, some have occurred in patients with postmenopausal osteoporosis taking oral bisphosphonates. Dental surgery, particularly tooth extraction, may increase the risk for ONJ. Patients who develop ONJ while on bisphosphonate therapy should receive care by an oral surgeon. See Dental Comment.

Effects on Bleeding No information available to require special precautions

Adverse Reactions Percentages vary based on frequency of administration (daily vs monthly). Unless specified, percentages are reported with oral use.

>10%:

Gastrointestinal: Dyspepsia (4% to 12%)

Neuromuscular & skeletal: Back pain (4% to 14%)

Respiratory: Upper respiratory tract infection (2% to 34%)

1% to 10%:

Cardiovascular: Hypertension (6% to 7%)

Central nervous system: Headache (3% to 7%), dizziness (1% to 4%), fatigue (3%), insomnia (1% to 2%), depression (2%)

Dermatologic: Skin rash (1% to 2%)

Gastrointestinal: Abdominal pain (5% to 8%), diarrhea (2% to 7%), nausea (4% to 5%), dental disease (4%), constipation (3% to 4%), vomiting (3%), gastritis (2%), gastroenteritis (3%)

Genitourinary: Urinary tract infection (2% to 6%), cystitis (3%)

Hypersensitivity: Acute phase reaction-like symptoms (IV: 10%; oral: 3% to 9%), hypersensitivity reaction (3%)

Infection: Influenza (4% to 8%)

Local: Injection site reaction (<2%)

Neuromuscular & skeletal: Limb pain (1% to 8%), arthralgia (4% to 9%), myalgia (1% to 6%), arthropathy (4%), weakness (4%), localized osteoarthritis (1% to 3%), muscle cramps (2%)

Respiratory: Bronchitis (3% to 10%), pneumonia (6%), nasopharyngitis (3% to 4%), flu-like symptoms (1% to 3%), pharyngitis (3%)

Postmarketing and/or case reports: Acute renal failure, anaphylactic shock, anaphylaxis, angioedema, bronchospasm, bullous dermatitis, erythema multiforme, exacerbation of asthma, femur fracture (diaphyseal or subtrochanteric), hypocalcemia, iritis, musculoskeletal pain (bone, joint, or muscle; incapacitating), ophthalmic inflammation, osteonecrosis of the jaw, prolonged Q-T interval on ECG (Bonilla 2014), scleritis, Stevens-Johnson syndrome, uveitis

Dosing

Adult & Geriatric

Postmenopausal osteoporosis (treatment): Note: Consider discontinuing after 3 to 5 years of use for osteoporosis in patients at low-risk for fracture. Patients should receive supplemental calcium and vitamin D if dietary intake is inadequate.

Oral: 150 mg once monthly

IV: 3 mg every 3 months

Postmenopausal osteoporosis (prevention): Oral: 150 mg once monthly. **Note:** Patients should receive supplemental calcium and vitamin D if dietary intake is inadequate.

Hypercalcemia of malignancy (off-label use): IV: 2 to 6 mg over 1-2 hours (Pecherstorfer 2003; Ralston 1997)

Metastatic bone disease due to breast cancer (off-label use): IV: 6 mg every 3 to 4 weeks (Diel 2004)

Missed doses:

Oral: If once-monthly oral dose is missed, it should be given the next morning after remembered if the next month's scheduled dose is >7 days away. If the next month's scheduled dose is within 7 days, wait until the next month's scheduled dose. May then return to the original monthly schedule (original scheduled day of the month). Do not give >150 mg within 7 days.

IV: If an IV dose is missed, it should be administered as soon as it can be rescheduled. Thereafter, it should be given every 3 months from the date of the last injection.

Renal Impairment

Osteoporosis: Oral, IV:

CrCl ≥30 mL/minute: No dosage adjustment necessary.

CrCl <30 mL/minute: Use not recommended.

Oncologic uses (off-label): IV: CrCl <30 mL/minute: 2 mg every 3 to 4 weeks (von Moos 2005)

Hepatic Impairment There are no dosage adjustments provided in the manufacturer's labeling (has not been studied); however, ibandronate does not undergo hepatic metabolism.

Mechanism of Action A bisphosphonate which inhibits bone resorption via actions on osteoclasts or on osteoclast precursors; decreases the rate of bone resorption, leading to an indirect increase in bone mineral density.

Contraindications

Known hypersensitivity to ibandronate or any component of the formulation; hypocalcemia; oral tablets are also contraindicated in patients unable to stand or sit upright for at least 60 minutes and in patients with abnormalities of the esophagus which delay esophageal emptying, such as stricture or achalasia

Documentation of allergenic cross-reactivity for bisphosphonates is limited. However, because of similarities in chemical structure and/or pharmacologic actions, the possibility of cross-sensitivity cannot be ruled out with certainty.

Warnings/Precautions Hypocalcemia must be corrected before therapy initiation. Ensure adequate calcium and vitamin D intake.

Atypical femur fractures have been reported in patients receiving bisphosphonates for treatment/prevention of osteoporosis. The fractures include subtrochanteric femur (bone just below the hip joint) and diaphyseal femur (long segment of the thigh bone). Some patients experience prodromal pain weeks or months before the fracture occurs. It is unclear if bisphosphonate therapy is the cause for these fractures, although the majority of cases have been reported in patients taking bisphosphonates. Patients receiving long-term (>3-5 years) therapy may be at an increased risk. Discontinue bisphosphonate therapy in patients who develop a femoral shaft fracture.

Infrequently, severe (and occasionally debilitating) bone, joint, and/or muscle pain have been reported during bisphosphonate treatment. The onset of pain ranged from a single day to several months. Discontinue intravenous ibandronate therapy in patients who experience severe symptoms; symptoms usually resolve upon discontinuation. Some patients experienced recurrence when rechallenged with same drug or another bisphosphonate; avoid use in patients with a history of these symptoms in association with bisphosphonate therapy.

Oral bisphosphonates may cause dysphagia, esophagitis, esophageal or gastric ulcer; risk may increase in patients unable to comply with dosing instructions; discontinue use if new or worsening symptoms develop. Intravenous bisphosphonates may cause transient decreases in serum calcium and have also been associated with renal toxicity.

Osteonecrosis of the jaw (ONJ), also referred to as medication-related osteonecrosis of the jaw (MRONJ), has been reported in patients receiving bisphosphonates. Known risk factors for MRONJ include invasive dental procedures (eg, tooth extraction, dental implants, boney surgery), cancer diagnosis, concomitant therapy (eg, chemotherapy, corticosteroids, angiogenesis inhibitors), poor oral hygiene, ill-fitting dentures, and comorbid disorders (anemia, coagulopathy, infection, preexisting dental or periodontal disease). Risk may increase with increased duration of bisphosphonate use. According to a position paper by the American Association of Maxillofacial Surgeons (AAOMS), MRONJ has been associated with bisphosphonates and other antiresorptive agents (denosumab), and antiangiogenic agents (eg, bevacizumab, sunitinib) used for the treatment of osteoporosis or malignancy; risk is significantly higher in cancer patients receiving antiresorptive therapy compared to patients receiving osteoporosis treatment (regardless of medication used or dosing schedule). MRONJ risk is also increased with monthly IV antiresorptive therapy compared to the minimal risk associated with oral bisphosphonate use, although risk appears to increase with oral bisphosphonates when duration of therapy exceeds 4 years (AAOMS [Ruggiero 2014]). The manufacturer's labeling states that discontinuing bisphosphonates in patients requiring invasive dental procedures may reduce the risk of ONJ and clinical judgment by physician and/or oral surgeon should be used. However, the AAOMS suggests there is currently no evidence that interrupting oral bisphosphonate therapy alters the risk of ONJ following tooth extraction, and that no alternations or delay in any procedure common to oral/maxillofacial surgeons, periodontists, and other dental providers is necessary in patients receiving oral bisphosphonates for <4 years who have no clinical risk factors (special considerations apply to patients receiving dental implants). Conversely, in patients receiving oral bisphosphonates for >4 years **or** in patients receiving oral bisphosphonates for <4 years who have also taken corticosteroids or antiangiogenic medications concomitantly, the AAOMS recommends considering a 2-month drug free period prior to invasive dental procedures based on a theoretical benefit. Patients developing ONJ during therapy should receive care by an oral surgeon (AAOMS [Ruggiero 2014]). According to the manufacturer, discontinuation of oral bisphosphonate therapy should be considered (based on risk/benefit evaluation) in patients who develop ONJ.

Allergic reactions, including anaphylactic reaction/shock (some fatal), angioedema, bronchospasm, exacerbation of asthma, rash, Stevens-Johnson syndrome, erythema multiforme, and dermatitis bullous have been reported; discontinue immediately if anaphylactic or other severe hypersensitivity/allergic reactions occur. Use not recommended with severe renal impairment (CrCl <30 mL/minute). In the management of osteoporosis, re-evaluate the need for continued therapy periodically; the optimal duration of treatment has not yet been determined. Consider discontinuing after 3-5 years of use in patients at low-risk for fracture; following discontinuation, re-evaluate fracture risk periodically. Potentially significant drug-drug interactions may exist, requiring dose or frequency adjustment, additional monitoring, and/or selection of alternative therapy.

Drug Interactions

Metabolism/Transport Effects None known.

Avoid Concomitant Use There are no known interactions where it is recommended to avoid concomitant use.

Increased Effect/Toxicity

Ibandronate may increase the levels/effects of: Deferasirox; Highest Risk QTc-Prolonging Agents; Moderate Risk QTc-Prolonging Agents

The levels/effects of Ibandronate may be increased by: Aminoglycosides; MiFEPRIStone; Nonsteroidal Anti-Inflammatory Agents; Systemic Angiogenesis Inhibitors

Decreased Effect

The levels/effects of Ibandronate may be decreased by: Antacids; Calcium Salts; Iron Salts; Magnesium Salts; Multivitamins/Minerals (with ADEK, Folate, Iron); Multivitamins/Minerals (with AE, No Iron); Proton Pump Inhibitors

Food Interactions Food may reduce absorption; mean oral bioavailability is decreased up to 90% when given with food. Management: Take with a full glass (6-8 oz) of plain water, at least 60 minutes prior to any food, beverages, or medications. Mineral water with a high calcium content should be avoided. Wait at least 60 minutes after taking ibandronate before taking anything else.

Dietary Considerations

Ensure adequate calcium and vitamin D intake; if dietary intake is inadequate, dietary supplementation is recommended. Women and men should consume:

Calcium: 1,000 mg/day (men: 50 to 70 years) **or** 1,200 mg/day (women ≥51 years and men ≥71 years) (IOM 2011; NOF [Cosman 2014])

Vitamin D: 800 to 1,000 int. units daily (men and women ≥50 years) (NOF [Cosman 2014]). Recommended Dietary Allowance (RDA): 600 int. units daily (men and women ≤70 years) **or** 800 int. units daily (men and women ≥71 years) (IOM 2011).

Ibandronate tablet should be taken with a full glass (6 to 8 oz) of plain water, at least 60 minutes prior to any food, beverages, or medications. Mineral water with a high calcium content should be avoided.

Pharmacodynamics/Kinetics

Half-life Elimination

Oral: 150 mg dose: Terminal: 37 to 157 hours

IV: Terminal: ~5 to 25 hours

Time to Peak Oral: 0.5 to 2 hours

Pregnancy Considerations Adverse effects were observed in animal reproduction studies. It is not known if bisphosphonates cross the placenta, but fetal exposure is expected (Djokanovic, 2008; Stathopoulos, 2011). Bisphosphonates are incorporated into the bone matrix and gradually released over time. The amount available in the systemic circulation varies by dose and duration of therapy. Theoretically, there may be a risk of fetal harm when pregnancy follows the completion of therapy; however, available data have not shown that exposure to bisphosphonates during pregnancy significantly increases the risk of adverse fetal events (Djokanovic, 2008; Levy, 2009; Stathopoulos, 2011). Until additional data is available, most sources recommend discontinuing bisphosphonate therapy in women of reproductive potential as early as possible prior to a planned pregnancy; use in premenopausal women should be reserved for special circumstances when rapid bone loss is occurring (Bhalla, 2010; Pereira, 2012; Stathopoulos, 2011). Because hypocalcemia has been described following in utero bisphosphonate exposure, exposed infants should be monitored for hypocalcemia after birth (Djokanovic, 2008; Stathopoulos, 2011).

Breastfeeding Considerations It is not known if ibandronate is excreted into breast milk.

Dosage Forms

Solution, Intravenous:

Boniva: 3 mg/3 mL (3 mL)

Generic: 3 mg/3 mL (3 mL)

Solution, Intravenous [preservative free]:

Generic: 3 mg/3 mL (3 mL)

Tablet, Oral:

Boniva: 150 mg

Generic: 150 mg

Dental Comment A review of 2,408 published cases of bisphosphonate-associated osteonecrosis of the jaw bone (BP-associated ONJ) was done by Filleul 2010. BP therapy was associated with 89% of the cases to treat malignancies and 11% of the cases to treat non-malignant conditions. Information on the specific bisphosphonate used was available for 1,694 of the patients. Intravenous therapy (primarily zoledronic acid) was received by 88% of the patients and 12% received oral treatment (primarily alendronate). Of all the cases of BP-associated ONJ, 67% were preceded by tooth extraction and for 26% of patients, there was no predisposing factor identified.

A 2010 retrospective case review reported the prevalence of BP-associated ONJ in patients using alendronate-type drugs was one out of 952 patients or ~0.1% (Lo 2010). Of the 8,572 respondents, nine cases of ONJ were identified; five had developed ONJ spontaneously and four developed ONJ after tooth extraction. When extrapolated to patient-years of bisphosphonate exposure, this prevalence rate of 0.1% equates to a frequency of 28 cases per 100,000 person-years of oral bisphosphonate treatment. An Australian group (Mavrokokki 2007), identified the frequency of BP-associated ONJ in osteoporotic patients, mainly taking weekly oral alendronate, was 1 in 8,470 to 1 in 2,260 (0.01% to 0.04%) patients. If extractions were carried out, the calculated frequency was 1 in 1,130 to 1 in 296 (0.09% to 0.34%) patients. The median time to onset of ONJ in alendronate patients was 24 months.

According to the 2011 report by the American Dental Association (ADA), the incidence of BP-associated ONJ remains low and the benefits of using oral bisphosphonates significantly outweighs the risk of developing BP-associated ONJ for treatment and prevention of osteoporosis and cancer treatment (Hellstein 2011). The full 47-page report can be accessed at http://www.ada.org/~/media/ADA/Member%20Center/FIles/topics_ARONJ_report.ashx.

The ADA review of 2011 stated the incidence of oral BP-associated ONJ was one case for every 1,000 individuals exposed to oral bisphosphonates (0.1%) (Hellstein 2011).

The most comprehensive review to date on osteonecrosis of the jaw bone (ONJ) has been published in the *Journal of Bone and Mineral Research* (Khan 2015), and written by an International Task Force of authors, totaling 34, from academe; industry; clinical medical and dental practice; oral and maxillofacial surgery; bone and mineral research; epidemiology; medical and dental oncology; orthopedic surgery; osteoporosis research; muscle and bone research; endocrinology and diagnostic sciences. The work provides a systematic review of the literature and international consensus on the classification, incidence, pathophysiology, diagnosis, and management of ONJ in both oncology and osteoporosis patient populations. This review of the literature from January 2003 to April 2014, with 299 references, offers recommendations for management of ONJ based on multidisciplinary international consensus.

Prevalence and incidence of ONJ in osteoporosis patients from the Task Force report:

Prevalence – the percent of osteoporotic population affected with ONJ

After reviewing all literature reports on this subject, the Task Force concluded that the prevalence of ONJ in patients prescribed oral BPs for the treatment of osteoporosis ranges from 0% to 0.04% with the majority being below 0.001%. However, the Task Force does cite the study of (Lo et al) that evaluated the Kaiser Permanente database and found the prevalence of ONJ in those receiving BPs for more than 2 years to range from 0.05% to 0.21% and appeared to be related to duration of exposure. As mentioned above, the American Dental Association has previously reported that the prevalence of ONJ in osteoporosis patients using oral BPs to be 1 out of 1,000 or 0.1% (Hellstein 2011).

Incidence - the rate at which ONJ occurs or the number of times it happens

From currently available data, the incidence of ONJ in the osteoporosis patient population appears to be low ranging from 0.15% to less than 0.001% person-years drug exposure. In terms of the osteoporosis patient population taking oral BPs, the incidence ranges from 1.04 to 69 per 100,000 patient years of drug exposure.

Ibritumomab (ib ri TYOO mo mab)

Brand Names: US Zevalin Y-90

Brand Names: Canada Zevalin

Pharmacologic Category Antineoplastic Agent, Anti-CD20; Antineoplastic Agent, Monoclonal Antibody; Radiopharmaceutical

Use Non-Hodgkin lymphoma: Treatment of relapsed or refractory, low-grade or follicular B-cell non-Hodgkin lymphoma (NHL); treatment of previously untreated follicular NHL in patients who achieve a partial or complete response to first-line chemotherapy

Local Anesthetic/Vasoconstrictor Precautions No information available to require special precautions

Effects on Dental Treatment Key adverse event(s) related to dental treatment: Hypotension, cough, throat irritation, rhinitis.

Effects on Bleeding Chemotherapy may result in significant myelosuppression, potentially including significant reduction in platelet counts and altered hemostasis. In patients who are under active treatment with these agents, medical consult is suggested.

Adverse Reactions

>10%:

Central nervous system: Fatigue (33%)

Gastrointestinal: Nausea (18%), abdominal pain (17%), diarrhea (11%)

Hematologic & oncologic: Thrombocytopenia (62% to 95%; grades 3/4: 51% to 63%; nadir: 49-53 days; median duration: 24 days; median time to recovery: 13 days), neutropenia (45% to 77%; grades 3/4: 41% to 60%; nadir: 61-62 days; median duration: 22 days; median time to recovery: 12 days), anemia (22% to 61%; grades 3/4: 5% to 17%; nadir: 68-69 days), leukopenia (43%; grades 3/4: 36%), lymphocytopenia (26%; grades 3/4: 18%), metastases (1% to 13%; includes acute myelogenous leukemia and myelodysplastic syndrome)

Infection: Infection (within first 3 months: 29%; serious: 1% to 3%, 3 months to 4 years after treatment: 6%)

Neuromuscular & skeletal: Weakness (15%)

Respiratory: Nasopharyngitis (19%), cough (11%)

1% to 10%:

Cardiovascular: Hypertension (7%)

Central nervous system: Dizziness (7%)

Dermatologic: Night sweats (8%), pruritus (7%), skin rash (7%)

Gastrointestinal: Anorexia (8%)

Genitourinary: Urinary tract infection (7%)

Hematologic & oncologic: Petechia (8%), bruise (7%), severe cytopenia (prolonged: 5%)

Immunologic: Antibody development (HAMA/HACA: 1% to 3%)

Neuromuscular & skeletal: Myalgia (9%)

Respiratory: Bronchitis (8%), flu-like symptoms (8%), rhinitis (8%), pharyngolaryngeal pain (7%), sinusitis (7%), epistaxis (5%)

Miscellaneous: Fever (10%), biodistribution altered (1%)

<1%, postmarketing, and/or case reports: Adult respiratory distress syndrome, angioedema, bullous dermatitis, cardiogenic shock, chills, dyspnea, erythema multiforme, exfoliative dermatitis, febrile neutropenia, headache, hypoxia, infusion-related reaction, injection site reaction (erythema/ulceration following extravasation), myocardial infarction, pain, pulmonary infiltrates, radiation injury (delayed [~1 month]; in tissues in or near areas of lymphomatous involvement), sepsis, Stevens-Johnson syndrome, tissue necrosis (following Yttrium-90-ibritumomab extravasation), toxic epidermal necrolysis, ventricular fibrillation, vomiting

General Dosage Range IV: *Adults:* Day 7, 8, or 9: 0.3-0.4 mCi/kg (11.1-14.8 MBq/kg) actual body weight (maximum: 32 mCi [1184 MBq])

Mechanism of Action Ibritumomab is a monoclonal antibody directed against the CD20 antigen found on pre-B and mature B lymphocytes (normal and malignant). Ibritumomab binding induces apoptosis in B lymphocytes *in vitro*. It is combined with the chelator tiuxetan, which acts as a specific chelation site for Yttrium-90 (Y-90). The monoclonal antibody acts as a delivery system to direct the radioactive isotope to the targeted cells, however, binding has been observed in lymphoid cells throughout the body and in lymphoid nodules in organs such as the large and small intestines. Beta-emission induces cellular damage through the formation of free radicals (in both target cells and surrounding cells).

Pharmacodynamics/Kinetics

Duration of Action B cell recovery begins in ~12 weeks; generally in normal range within 9 months

Half-life Elimination Y-90 ibritumomab: 30 hours; Yttrium-90 decays with a physical half-life of 64 hours

Pregnancy Risk Factor D

Pregnancy Considerations Animal reproduction studies have not been conducted. Based on the radioactivity, Y-90 ibritumomab may cause fetal harm if administered during pregnancy. IgG molecules are known to cross the placenta. Women of childbearing potential should avoid becoming pregnant during treatment with ibritumomab. Both males and females should use effective contraception for at least 12 months following treatment. The effect on future fertility is unknown.

Ibrutinib (eye BROO ti nib)

Brand Names: US Imbruvica

Brand Names: Canada Imbruvica

Pharmacologic Category Antineoplastic Agent; Antineoplastic Agent, Bruton Tyrosine Kinase Inhibitor; Antineoplastic Agent, Tyrosine Kinase Inhibitor

Use

Chronic lymphocytic leukemia/small lymphocytic lymphoma: Treatment of chronic lymphocytic leukemia/small lymphocytic lymphoma (CLL/SLL); treatment of CLL/SLL in patients with 17p deletion.

Mantle cell lymphoma, previously treated: Treatment of mantle cell lymphoma (MCL) in patients who have received at least 1 prior therapy

Marginal zone lymphoma, relapsed/refractory: Treatment of marginal zone lymphoma (MZL) in patients who require systemic therapy and have received at least one prior anti-CD20-based therapy.

Waldenström macroglobulinemia: Treatment of Waldenström macroglobulinemia

Local Anesthetic/Vasoconstrictor Precautions No information available to require special precautions

Effects on Dental Treatment Key adverse event(s) related to dental treatment: Stomatitis has been reported

Effects on Bleeding Bleeding has been reported in up to 48% of patients, including gastrointestinal bleeding; decreased platelet count (57%; grades 3/4: 17%), decreased hemoglobin (41%; grades 3/4: 9%), bruise (30%), neutropenia (47%; grades 3/4: 29%), petechia (11%). Medical consult is recommended.

Adverse Reactions

>10%:

Cardiovascular: Peripheral edema (19% to 35%), hypertension (6% to 17%)

Central nervous system: Fatigue (21% to 44%), dizziness (11% to 20%), headache (12% to 18%), anxiety (16%), chills (12%)

Dermatologic: Skin rash (21% to 29%), skin infection (14% to 16%), pruritus (11% to 14%)

Endocrine & metabolic: Hyperuricemia (15% to 16%), hypoalbuminemia (14%), hypokalemia (13%), dehydration (12%)

Gastrointestinal: Diarrhea (37% to 59%), nausea (20% to 31%), constipation (14% to 25%), abdominal pain (14% to 24%), vomiting (11% to 23%), decreased appetite (16% to 21%), stomatitis (14% to 20%), dyspepsia (11% to 19%), gastroesophageal reflux disease (13%), upper abdominal pain (13%)

Genitourinary: Urinary tract infection (10% to 14%)

Hematologic & oncologic: Thrombocytopenia (43% to 69%; grades 3/4: 5% to 17%), neutropenia (22% to 53%; grades 3/4: 13% to 29%), bruise (12% to 51%; grades 3/4: ≤2%), decreased hemoglobin (13% to 43%; grades 3/4: ≤13%), hemorrhage (30%; grades ≥3: ≤6%; ≥grade 3 bleeding events include gastrointestinal bleeding, hematuria, postprocedural hemorrhage, intracranial hemorrhage, subdural hematoma), petechia (11% to 16%), malignant neoplasm (secondary; 3% to 16%; non-melanoma skin cancer was most frequently reported; also includes carcinoma and one case of histiocytic sarcoma)

Infection: Infection

Neuromuscular & skeletal: Musculoskeletal pain (25% to 40%), arthralgia (11% to 24%), muscle spasm (11% to 21%), weakness (14%), arthropathy (13%)

Ophthalmic: Dry eye syndrome (17%), increased lacrimation (13%), blurred vision (10% to 13%), decreased visual acuity (11%)

Respiratory: Upper respiratory tract infection (16% to 47%), dyspnea (12% to 27%), cough (13% to 22%), sinusitis (11% to 22%), epistaxis (11% to 19%), pneumonia (11% to 15%), oropharyngeal pain (14%), bronchitis (11%)

Miscellaneous: Fever (17% to 25%)

1% to 10%:

Cardiovascular: Atrial fibrillation (≤9%), atrial flutter (≤9%)

Renal: Increased serum creatinine (1.5 to 3 x ULN: 9)

<1%, postmarketing, and/or case reports: Abnormal platelet aggregation (Kamel 2015), hepatic failure, hypersensitivity (includes anaphylactic shock, angioedema, urticaria), interstitial pulmonary disease, onychoclasis, pneumonia due to *Pneumocystis carinii*, pneumonitis (Mato 2016), progressive multifocal leukoencephalopathy, renal failure, Stevens-Johnson syndrome, tumor lysis syndrome

General Dosage Range Dosage adjustment recommended in patients with hepatic impairment, on concomitant therapy, or who develop toxicities.

Oral: *Adults:* 420 to 560 mg once daily

Mechanism of Action Ibrutinib is a potent and irreversible inhibitor of Bruton's tyrosine kinase (BTK), an integral component of the B-cell receptor (BCR) and cytokine receptor pathways. Constitutive activation of B-cell receptor signaling is important for survival of malignant B-cells; BTK inhibition results in decreased malignant B-cell proliferation and survival.

Pharmacodynamics/Kinetics

Half-life Elimination 4 to 6 hours

Time to Peak 1 to 2 hours (4 hours under fed conditions [de Jong 2015])

Pregnancy Considerations Based on animal reproduction studies, ibrutinib may cause fetal harm if administered during pregnancy. For women of childbearing potential, verify pregnancy status prior to treatment initiation. Women of reproductive potential should avoid pregnancy during therapy and for 1 month after treatment cessation; males should avoid fathering a child during treatment and for 1 month after the last dose.

Ibuprofen (eye byoo PROE fen)

Related Information

Antiplatelet and Anticoagulation Considerations in Dentistry *on page 1764*

Oral Pain *on page 1830*

Rheumatoid Arthritis, Osteoarthritis, and Osteoporosis *on page 1792*

Temporomandibular Dysfunction (TMD), Chronic Pain, and Fibromyalgia *on page 1868*

Related Sample Prescriptions

Oral Pain - Sample Prescriptions *on page 28*

Brand Names: US Addaprin [OTC]; Advil Junior Strength [OTC]; Advil Migraine [OTC]; Advil [OTC]; Caldolor; Childrens Advil [OTC]; Childrens Motrin Jr Strength [OTC] [DSC]; Childrens Motrin [OTC]; Dyspel [OTC]; EnovaRX-Ibuprofen; Genpril [OTC]; GoodSense Ibuprofen Childrens [OTC]; I-Prin [OTC]; IBU-200 [OTC]; Ibuprofen Comfort Pac; Infants Advil [OTC]; KS Ibuprofen [OTC]; Motrin IB [OTC]; Motrin Infants Drops [OTC]; Motrin Junior Strength [OTC] [DSC]; Motrin [OTC] [DSC]; NeoProfen; Provil [OTC]

Brand Names: Canada Advil; Advil Pediatric Drops; Apo-Ibuprofen; Caldolor; Children's Advil; Children's Europrofen; Ibuprofen Muscle and Joint; Jamp-Ibuprofen; Motrin; Motrin (Children's); Motrin IB; Novo-Profen; Pamprin Ibuprofen Formula; PMS-Ibuprofen; Super Strength Motrin IB Liquid Gel Capsules

Generic Availability (US) May be product dependent

Pharmacologic Category Analgesic, Nonopioid; Nonsteroidal Anti-inflammatory Drug (NSAID), Oral; Nonsteroidal Anti-inflammatory Drug (NSAID), Parenteral

Dental Use Management of pain and swelling

Use

Oral: Inflammatory diseases and rheumatoid disorders, mild to moderate pain, fever, dysmenorrhea, osteoarthritis

Ibuprofen injection (Caldolor): Management of mild to moderate pain and management of moderate to severe pain as an adjunct to opioid analgesics in adults and children 6 months and older; reduction of fever in adults and children 6 months and older.

Ibuprofen lysine injection (NeoProfen): Patent ductus arteriosus (PDA): To close a clinically significant PDA in premature infants weighing between 500-1500 g who are no more than 32 weeks of gestational age when usual medical management (eg, diuretics, fluid restriction, respiratory support) is ineffective.

OTC labeling: Reduction of fever; management of pain due to headache, sore throat, arthritis, physical or athletic overexertion (eg, sprains/strains), menstrual pain, dental pain, minor muscle/bone/joint pain, backache, pain due to the common cold and flu

Local Anesthetic/Vasoconstrictor Precautions No information available to require special precautions

Effects on Dental Treatment The FDA notified consumers and healthcare professionals that the administration of ibuprofen for pain relief to patients taking aspirin for cardioprotection may interfere with aspirin's cardiovascular benefits. The FDA states that ibuprofen can interfere with the antiplatelet effect of low-dose aspirin (81 mg/day). This could result in diminished effectiveness of aspirin as used for cardioprotection and stroke prevention. The FDA adds that although ibuprofen and aspirin can be taken together, it is recommended that consumers talk with their healthcare providers for additional information. For more information, including how to advise aspirin patients requiring ibuprofen for pain relief, see Effects on Bleeding and Dental Comment. (http://www.fda.gov/Drugs/DrugSafety/PostmarketDrugSafetyInformationforPatientsandProviders/ucm110510.htm)

Effects on Bleeding Nonselective NSAIDs such as ibuprofen inhibit platelet aggregation and prolong bleeding time in some patients. Unlike aspirin, the NSAID effect on platelet function is quantitatively less, of shorter duration, and reversible.

Adverse Reactions

Oral:

1% to 10%:

Cardiovascular: Edema (1% to 3%)

Central nervous system: Dizziness (3% to 9%), headache (1% to 3%), nervousness (1% to 3%)

Dermatologic: Skin rash (3% to 9%), pruritus (1% to 3%)

Endocrine & metabolic: Fluid retention (1% to 3%)

Gastrointestinal: Epigastric pain (3% to 9%), heartburn (3% to 9%), nausea (3% to 9%), abdominal pain (1% to 3%), constipation (1% to 3%), decreased appetite (1% to 3%), diarrhea (1% to 3%), dyspepsia (1% to 3%), flatulence (1% to 3%), vomiting (1% to 3%)

Otic: Tinnitus (3% to 9%)

<1%, postmarketing, and/or case reports: Abnormal hepatic function tests, acute renal failure, agranulocytosis, allergic rhinitis, alopecia, amblyopia, anaphylaxis, aplastic anemia, aseptic meningitis, azotemia, blurred vision, bone marrow depression, bronchospasm, cardiac arrhythmia, cardiac failure, confusion, conjunctivitis, cystitis, decreased creatinine clearance, decreased hematocrit, decreased hemoglobin, decreased platelet aggregation, depression, drowsiness, dry eye syndrome, duodenal ulcer, emotional lability, eosinophilia, epistaxis, erythema multiforme, gastric ulcer, gastritis, gastrointestinal hemorrhage, gastrointestinal ulcer, hallucination, hearing loss, hematuria, hemolytic anemia, hepatitis, hepatotoxicity (idiosyncratic) (Chalasani 2014), hypertension, insomnia, jaundice, leukopenia, melena, neutropenia, palpitations, pancreatitis, peripheral neuropathy, polydipsia, polyuria, skin photosensitivity, Stevens-Johnson syndrome, tachycardia, thrombocytopenia, toxic amblyopia, toxic epidermal necrolysis, urticaria, vesiculobullous dermatitis, vision changes

Injection: Ibuprofen (Caldolor): Frequency not defined.

Cardiovascular: Edema, hypertension (10%; including exacerbation), myocardial infarction, peripheral edema (≤3%)

Central nervous system: Headache (12%), dizziness (4% to 6%)

Dermatologic: Exfoliative dermatitis, pruritus, skin rash, Stevens-Johnson syndrome, toxic epidermal necrolysis

Endocrine & metabolic: Hypokalemia (4% to 19%), hypoalbuminemia (10%), hypernatremia (7% to 10%), changes in LDH (7%)

Gastrointestinal: vomiting (22%), flatulence (16%), diarrhea (10%), dyspepsia (1% to 4%), abdominal discomfort (≤3%), abdominal pain, nausea

Genitourinary: Urinary retention (5%), renal toxicity

Hematologic & oncologic: Anemia (4% to 36%), eosinophilia (26%), hypoproteinemia (10% to 13%), neutropenia (13%), hemorrhage (10%), thrombocythemia (3% to 10%), wound hemorrhage (3%), decreased hemoglobin (2% to 3%)

Hepatic: Increased serum ALT (≤15%), increased serum AST (≤15%)

Hypersensitivity: Hypersensitivity reaction

Renal: Increased blood urea nitrogen (7% to 10%)

Respiratory: Bacterial pneumonia (3% to 10%), cough (3%)

<1%, postmarketing, and/or case reports: Hepatotoxicity (idiosyncratic) (Chalasani 2014)

Injection: Ibuprofen lysine (NeoProfen): Frequency not always defined.

Cardiovascular: Hypotension (7% to 10%), edema (4%), cardiac failure, hypotension, tachycardia

Central nervous system: Intraventricular hemorrhage (29%), convulsions, eating disorder, seizure

Dermatologic: Skin irritation (16%), skin lesion (≤16%)

Endocrine & metabolic: Hypocalcemia (12%), hypoglycemia (12%), adrenocortical insufficiency (7%), hypernatremia (7%), hyperglycemia

Gastrointestinal: Enterocolitis (22%), gastrointestinal disease (non NEC; 22%), abdominal distension, cholestasis, gastritis, gastroesophageal reflux disease, inguinal hernia, intestinal obstruction

Genitourinary: Urinary tract infection (9%), uremia (7%), decreased urine output (3%; small decrease reported on days 2 to 6 with compensatory increase in output on day 9)

Hematologic & oncologic: Anemia (32%), neutropenia, thrombocytopenia

Hepatic: Jaundice

Infection: Sepsis (43%), infection

Local: Injection site reaction

Renal: Increased blood urea nitrogen (7%), renal insufficiency (6%), increased serum creatinine (3%), renal failure (1%)

Respiratory: Apnea (28%), respiratory tract infection (19%), respiratory failure (10%), atelectasis (4%)

Miscellaneous: Reduced intake of food/fluids

<1%, postmarketing, and/or case reports: Gastrointestinal perforation, hepatotoxicity (idiosyncratic) (Chalasani 2014), necrotizing enterocolitis, pulmonary hypertension

Dental Usual Dosage

Analgesic/pain/fever/dysmenorrhea: Oral:

Children: 4-10 mg/kg/dose every 6-8 hours

Adults: 200-400 mg/dose every 4-6 hours (maximum daily dose: 1.2 g, unless directed by physician; under physician supervision daily doses ≤2.4 g may be used)

OTC labeling (analgesic, antipyretic): **Note:** Treatment for >10 days is not recommended unless directed by healthcare provider. Oral:

Children 6 months to 11 years: Use of weight to select dose is preferred; doses may be repeated every 6-8 hours (maximum: 4 doses/day)

Children ≥12 years and Adults: 200 mg every 4-6 hours as needed (maximum: 1200 mg/24 hours)

Dosing

Adult

Analgesia/pain/dysmenorrhea: Oral: 400 mg every 4 to 6 hours as needed

Analgesic: IV (Caldolor): 400 to 800 mg every 6 hours as needed (maximum: 3,200 mg/day). **Note:** Patients should be well hydrated prior to administration.

Antipyretic: IV (Caldolor): **Note**: Patients should be well hydrated prior to administration. Initial: 400 mg, then every 4 to 6 hours or 100 to 200 mg every 4 hours as needed (maximum: 3,200 mg/day).

Osteoarthritis, rheumatoid arthritis: Oral: 400 to 800 mg 3 to 4 times daily (maximum: 3,200 mg/day).

OTC labeling:

Analgesic, antipyretic: Oral: 200 mg every 4 to 6 hours as needed; if no relief may increase to 400 mg every 4 to 6 hours as needed (maximum: 1,200 mg/day); Duration: treatment for >10 days as an analgesic or >3 days as an antipyretic is not recommended unless directed by health care provider.

Migraine: Oral: 400 mg at onset of symptoms (maximum: 400 mg/24 hours unless directed by health care provider).

Pericarditis (off-label use): Oral: **Note:** Administer in combination with colchicine therapy. Concurrent gastroduodenal prophylaxis with a proton pump inhibitor has been used and is recommended (ESC [Adler 2015]; Imazio 2013; Imazio 2005). With pericarditis postmyocardial infarction, the ACCF/AHA prefers the use of aspirin (ACCF/AHA [O'Gara 2013]).

Acute pericarditis: 600 mg every 8 hours for 7 to 14 days followed by a gradual tapering of the dose by 200 to 400 mg every 1 to 2 weeks (ESC [Adler 2015]).

Recurrent pericarditis: 600 mg every 8 hours (range: 1,200 to 2,400 mg) for weeks to months until complete symptom resolution followed by a gradual tapering of the dose by 200 to 400 mg every 1 to 2 weeks (ESC [Adler 2015]).

Geriatric Refer to adult dosing. Use with caution; consider reduced initial dosage.

Pediatric

Analgesic:

IV (Caldolor): **Note:** Patients should be well hydrated prior to administration.

Infants ≥6 months and Children <12 years: 10 mg/kg (maximum dose: 400 mg) every 4 to 6 hours as needed; maximum daily dose: 40 mg/kg/day or 2,400 mg/day, whichever is less.

Children and Adolescents 12 to 17 years: 400 mg every 4 to 6 hours as needed; maximum daily dose: 2,400 mg/day.

Oral: Infants and Children <50 kg: Limited data available in infants <6 months: 4 to 10 mg/kg/dose every 6 to 8 hours; maximum single dose: 400 mg; maximum daily dose: 40 mg/kg/day (American Pain Society 2008; Berde 1990; Berde 2002; Kliegman 2011)

Antipyretic:

IV (Caldolor): **Note:** Patients should be well hydrated prior to administration.

Infants ≥6 months and Children <12 years: 10 mg/kg (maximum dose: 400 mg) every 4 to 6 hours as needed; maximum daily dose: 40 mg/kg/day or 2,400 mg/day, whichever is less.

Children and Adolescents 12 to 17 years: 400 mg every 4 to 6 hours as needed (maximum daily dose: 2,400 mg/day)

Oral: Infants ≥6 months, Children, and Adolescents: 5 to 10 mg/kg/dose every 6 to 8 hours; maximum single dose: 400 mg; maximum daily dose: 40 mg/kg/day up to 1,200 mg, unless directed by physician (under physician supervision, not to exceed maximum of 2,400 mg daily) (Litalien 2001; Sullivan 2011).

Juvenile idiopathic arthritis (JIA) (off-label use): Oral: Children and Adolescents: 30 to 40 mg/kg/**day** in 3 to 4 divided doses; start at lower end of dosing range and titrate; patients with milder disease may be treated with 20 mg/kg/day; patients with more severe disease may require up to 50 mg/kg/day; maximum single dose: 800 mg; maximum daily dose: 2,400 mg (Giannini 1990; Kliegman 2011; Litalien 2001).

Patent ductus arteriosus: IV (ibuprofen lysine [NeoProfen]): Infants weighing between 500 to 1,500 g and ≤32 weeks' GA: Initial dose: Ibuprofen 10 mg/kg, followed by two doses of 5 mg/kg at 24 and 48 hours. Dose should be based on birth weight.

OTC labeling (analgesic, antipyretic): Oral: **Note:** Discontinue use and consult health care provider if no improvement within 24 hours after initiating therapy or if symptoms persist >3 days or worsen.

Infants and Children 6 months to 11 years: See table; use of weight to select dose is preferred; doses may be repeated every 6 to 8 hours (maximum: 4 doses/day)

Children ≥12 years and Adolescents: Refer to adult dosing.

Ibuprofen Dosing (Infants and Children 6 months to 11 years)

Weight (Preferred)[a]		Age	Dosage (mg)
kg	lb		
5.4 to 8.1	12 to 17	6 to 11 mo	50
8.2 to 10.8	18 to 23	12 to 23 mo	75
10.9 to 16.3	24 to 35	2 to 3 y	100
16.4 to 21.7	36 to 47	4 to 5 y	150
21.8 to 27.2	48 to 59	6 to 8 y	200
27.3 to 32.6	60 to 71	9 to 10 y	250
32.7 to 43.2	72 to 95	11 y	300

[a]Manufacturer's recommendations are based on weight in pounds (OTC labeling); weight in kg listed here is derived from pounds and rounded; kg weight listed also is adjusted to allow for continuous weight ranges in kg.

Renal Impairment There are no dosage adjustments provided in the manufacturer's labeling; use with caution; avoid use in advanced renal disease.

KDIGO 2012 guidelines provide the following recommendations for NSAIDs:

eGFR 30 to <60 mL/minute/1.73 m^2: Avoid use in patients with intercurrent disease that increases risk of acute kidney injury

eGFR <30 mL/minute/1.73 m^2: Avoid use.

Neoprofen: If anuria or marked oliguria (urinary output <0.6 mL/kg/hour) evident at the scheduled time of the second or third dose, hold dose until renal function returns to normal. Use is contraindicated in preterm infants with significant renal impairment.

Hepatic Impairment There are no dosage adjustments provided in the manufacturer's labeling; use caution and discontinue if hepatic function worsens.

Mechanism of Action Reversibly inhibits cyclooxygenase-1 and 2 (COX-1 and 2) enzymes, which results in decreased formation of prostaglandin precursors; has antipyretic, analgesic, and anti-inflammatory properties

Other proposed mechanisms not fully elucidated (and possibly contributing to the anti-inflammatory effect to varying degrees), include inhibiting chemotaxis, altering lymphocyte activity, inhibiting neutrophil aggregation/activation, and decreasing proinflammatory cytokine levels.

Contraindications

Hypersensitivity to ibuprofen (eg, anaphylactic reactions, serious skin reactions) or any component of the formulation; history of asthma, urticaria, or allergic-type reaction to aspirin or other NSAIDs; aspirin triad (eg, bronchial asthma, aspirin intolerance, rhinitis); use in the setting of coronary artery bypass graft (CABG) surgery

Ibuprofen lysine (NeoProfen): Preterm neonates: With proven or suspected infection that is untreated; congenital heart disease in whom patency of the PDA is necessary for satisfactory pulmonary or systemic blood flow (eg, pulmonary atresia, severe coarctation of the aorta, severe tetralogy of Fallot); bleeding (especially those with active intracranial hemorrhage or GI bleeding); thrombocytopenia; coagulation defects; proven or suspected necrotizing enterocolitis; or significant renal function impairment.

Canadian labeling: Additional contraindications (not in US labeling): Cerebrovascular bleeding or other bleeding disorders; active gastric/duodenal/peptic ulcer, active GI bleeding; inflammatory bowel disease; uncontrolled heart failure; moderate [IV formulation only] to severe renal impairment (creatinine clearance [CrCl] <30 mL/minute); deteriorating renal disease; moderate [IV formulation only] to severe hepatic impairment; active hepatic disease; hyperkalemia; third trimester of pregnancy; breastfeeding; patients <18 years of age [IV formulation only]; patients <12 years of age [oral formulation only]; systemic lupus erythematosus [oral formulation only]; children suffering from dehydration as a result of acute diarrhea, vomiting, or lack of fluid intake

OTC labeling: When used for self-medication, do not use if previous allergic reaction to any other pain reliever/fever reducer; prior to or following cardiac surgery.

Warnings/Precautions [US Boxed Warning]: Use is contraindicated in the setting of coronary artery bypass graft (CABG) surgery. Risk of MI and stroke may be increased with use following CABG surgery. **[US Boxed Warning]: NSAIDs cause an increased risk of serious (and potentially fatal) adverse cardiovascular thrombotic events, including fatal MI and stroke. Risk may occur early during treatment and may increase with duration of use.** Relative risk appears to be similar in those with and without known cardiovascular disease or risk factors for cardiovascular disease; however, absolute incidence of cardiovascular events (which may occur early during treatment) was higher in patients with known cardiovascular disease or risk factors. New-onset hypertension or exacerbation of hypertension may occur (NSAIDS may also impair response to ACE inhibitors, thiazide diuretics, or loop diuretics); may contribute to cardiovascular events; monitor blood pressure; use with caution in patients with hypertension. May cause sodium and fluid retention; use with caution in patients with edema. Avoid use in heart failure (ACCF/AHA [Yancy 2013]). Avoid use in patients with a recent MI unless benefits outweigh risk of cardiovascular thrombotic events. Use the lowest effective dose for the shortest duration of time, consistent with individual patient goals, to reduce risk of cardiovascular events; alternate therapies should be considered for patients at high risk.

May increase the risk of aseptic meningitis, especially in patients with systemic lupus erythematosus (SLE) and mixed connective tissue disorders. Platelet adhesion and aggregation may be decreased; may prolong bleeding time; patients with coagulation disorders or who are receiving anticoagulants should be monitored closely. Anemia may occur; patients on long-term NSAID therapy should be monitored for anemia. Rarely, NSAID use may cause severe blood dyscrasias (eg, agranulocytosis, aplastic anemia, thrombocytopenia).

NSAID use may compromise existing renal function; dose-dependent decreases in prostaglandin synthesis may result from NSAID use, reducing renal blood flow, which may cause renal decompensation (usually reversible). NSAID use may increase the risk for hyperkalemia. Patients with impaired renal function, dehydration, hypovolemia, heart failure, hepatic impairment, those taking diuretics and ACE inhibitors, and the elderly are at greater risk of renal toxicity and hyperkalemia. Rehydrate patient before starting therapy; monitor renal function closely. Avoid use in patients with advanced renal disease; discontinue use with persistent or worsening abnormal renal function tests. Use of ibuprofen lysine (NeoProfen) is contraindicated in preterm infants with significant renal impairment. Long-term NSAID use may result in renal papillary necrosis and other renal injury.

[US Boxed Warning]: NSAIDs cause an increased risk of serious gastrointestinal inflammation, ulceration, bleeding, and perforation (may be fatal); elderly patients and patients with history of peptic ulcer disease and/or GI bleeding are at greater risk for serious GI events. These events may occur at any time during therapy and without warning. Avoid use in patients with active GI bleeding. Use caution with a history of GI ulcers, concurrent therapy known to increase the risk of GI bleeding (eg, aspirin, anticoagulants and/or corticosteroids, selective serotonin reuptake inhibitors), advanced hepatic disease, coagulopathy, smoking, use of alcohol, or in elderly or debilitated patients. Use the lowest effective dose for the shortest duration of time, consistent with individual patient goals, to reduce risk of GI adverse events; alternate therapies should be considered for patients at high risk. When used concomitantly with aspirin, a substantial increase in the risk of gastrointestinal complications (eg, ulcer) occurs; concomitant gastroprotective therapy (eg, proton pump inhibitors) is recommended (Bhatt 2008).

NSAIDs may cause potentially fatal serious skin adverse events including exfoliative dermatitis, Stevens-Johnson Syndrome (SJS) and toxic epidermal necrolysis (TEN); discontinue use at first sign of skin rash (or other hypersensitivity). Anaphylactoid reactions may occur, even without prior exposure; patients with "aspirin triad" (bronchial asthma, aspirin intolerance, rhinitis) may be at increased risk. Contraindicated in patients who experience bronchospasm, asthma, rhinitis, or urticaria with NSAID or aspirin therapy. Use caution in other forms of asthma.

May cause drowsiness, dizziness, blurred vision and other neurologic effects which may impair physical or mental abilities; patients must be cautioned about performing tasks which require mental alertness (eg, operating machinery or driving). Monitor vision with long-term therapy. Blurred/diminished vision, scotomata, and changes in color vision have been reported. Discontinue use with altered vision and perform ophthalmologic exam.

Use with caution in patients with hepatic impairment. Transaminase elevations have been reported with use; closely monitor patients with any abnormal LFT. Rare (sometimes fatal) severe hepatic reactions (eg, fulminant hepatitis, liver necrosis, hepatic failure) have occurred with NSAID use; discontinue immediately if signs or symptoms of hepatic disease develop or if systemic manifestations occur.

Some products may contain phenylalanine. Potentially significant drug interactions may exist, requiring dose or frequency adjustment, additional monitoring, and/or selection of alternative therapy. Withhold for at least 4 to 6 half-lives prior to surgical or dental procedures.

Ibuprofen injection (Caldolor) must be diluted prior to administration; hemolysis can occur if not diluted.

Ibuprofen lysine injection (NeoProfen): Hold second or third doses if urinary output is <0.6 mL/kg/hour. May alter signs of infection. May inhibit platelet aggregation; monitor for signs of bleeding. May displace bilirubin; use caution when total bilirubin is elevated. Long-term evaluations of neurodevelopment, growth, or diseases associated with prematurity following treatment have not been conducted. A second course of treatment, alternative pharmacologic therapy or surgery may be needed if the ductus arteriosus fails to close or reopens following the initial course of therapy.

Some dosage forms may contain sodium benzoate/benzoic acid; benzoic acid (benzoate) is a metabolite of benzyl alcohol; large amounts of benzyl alcohol (≥99 mg/kg/day) have been associated with a potentially fatal toxicity ("gasping syndrome") in neonates; the "gasping syndrome" consists of metabolic acidosis, respiratory distress, gasping respirations, CNS dysfunction (including convulsions, intracranial hemorrhage), hypotension, and cardiovascular collapse (AAP ["Inactive" 1997]; CDC 1982); some data suggests that benzoate displaces bilirubin from protein binding sites (Ahlfors 2001); avoid or use dosage forms containing benzyl alcohol derivative with caution in neonates. See manufacturer's labeling.

Some dosage forms may contain propylene glycol; large amounts are potentially toxic and have been associated hyperosmolality, lactic acidosis, seizures and respiratory depression; use caution (AAP ["Inactive" 1997]; Zar 2007).

Some dosage forms may contain polysorbate 80 (also known as Tweens). Hypersensitivity reactions, usually a delayed reaction, have been reported following exposure to pharmaceutical products containing polysorbate 80 in certain individuals (Isaksson 2002; Lucente 2000; Shelley 1995). Thrombocytopenia, ascites, pulmonary deterioration, and renal and hepatic failure have been reported in premature neonates after receiving parenteral products containing polysorbate 80 (Alade 1986; CDC 1984). See manufacturer's labeling.

Self medication (OTC use): Prior to self-medication, patients should contact health care provider if they have had recurring stomach pain or upset, ulcers, bleeding problems, high blood pressure, heart or kidney disease, other serious medical problems, are currently taking a diuretic, aspirin, anticoagulant, or are ≥60 years of age. If patients are using for migraines, they should also contact health care provider if they have not had a migraine diagnosis by healthcare provider, a headache that is different from usual migraine, worst headache of life, fever and neck stiffness, headache from head injury or coughing, first headache at ≥50 years of age, daily headache, or migraine requiring bed rest. Recommended dosages should not be exceeded, due to an increased risk of GI bleeding. Stop use and consult a health care provider if symptoms do not improve within first 24 hours of use (children), get worse, newly appear, fever lasts for >3 days or pain lasts >3 days (children) and >10 days (adults). Do not give for >10 days unless instructed by health care provider. Consuming ≥3 alcoholic beverages/day or taking longer than recommended may increase the risk of GI bleeding.

Drug Interactions

Metabolism/Transport Effects **Substrate** of CYP2C19 (minor), CYP2C9 (minor); **Note:** Assignment of Major/Minor substrate status based on clinically relevant drug interaction potential; **Inhibits** CYP2C9 (weak)

Avoid Concomitant Use

Avoid concomitant use of Ibuprofen with any of the following: Dexketoprofen; Floctafenine; Ketorolac (Nasal); Ketorolac (Systemic); Morniflumate; NSAID (COX-2 Inhibitor); Omacetaxine; Pelubiprofen; Phenylbutazone; Talniflumate; Tenoxicam; Urokinase; Zaltoprofen

Increased Effect/Toxicity

Ibuprofen may increase the levels/effects of: 5-ASA Derivatives; Agents with Antiplatelet Properties; Aliskiren; Aminoglycosides; Aminolevulinic Acid; Anticoagulants; Apixaban; Bisphosphonate Derivatives; Cephalothin; Collagenase (Systemic); CycloSPORINE (Systemic); Dabigatran Etexilate; Deferasirox; Deoxycholic Acid; Desmopressin; Digoxin; Drospirenone; Edoxaban; Eplerenone; Haloperidol; Ibritumomab; Lithium; Methotrexate; Nonsteroidal Anti-Inflammatory Agents; NSAID (COX-2 Inhibitor); Obinutuzumab; Omacetaxine; PEMEtrexed; Porfimer; Potassium-Sparing Diuretics; PRALAtrexate; Quinolone Antibiotics; Rivaroxaban; Salicylates; Tacrolimus (Systemic); Tenofovir Products; Thrombolytic Agents; Tolperisone; Tositumomab and Iodine I 131 Tositumomab; Urokinase; Vancomycin; Verteporfin; Vitamin K Antagonists

The levels/effects of Ibuprofen may be increased by: ACE Inhibitors; Alcohol (Ethyl); Angiotensin II Receptor Blockers; Antidepressants (Tricyclic, Tertiary Amine); Corticosteroids (Systemic); CycloSPORINE (Systemic); Dasatinib; Dexketoprofen; Diclofenac (Systemic); Felbinac; Floctafenine; Glucosamine; Herbs (Anticoagulant/Antiplatelet Properties); Ibrutinib; Ketorolac (Nasal); Ketorolac (Systemic); Limaprost; Loop Diuretics; Morniflumate; Multivitamins/Fluoride (with ADE); Multivitamins/Minerals (with ADEK, Folate, Iron); Multivitamins/Minerals (with AE, No Iron); Naftazone; Omega-3 Fatty Acids; Pelubiprofen; Pentosan Polysulfate Sodium; Pentoxifylline; Phenylbutazone; Probenecid; Prostacyclin Analogues; Selective Serotonin Reuptake Inhibitors; Serotonin/Norepinephrine Reuptake Inhibitors; Sodium Phosphates; Talniflumate; Tenoxicam; Thiazide and Thiazide-Like Diuretics; Tipranavir; Tolperisone; Vitamin E (Systemic); Voriconazole; Zaltoprofen

Decreased Effect

Ibuprofen may decrease the levels/effects of: ACE Inhibitors; Aliskiren; Angiotensin II Receptor Blockers; Beta-Blockers; Eplerenone; HydrALAZINE; Imatinib; Loop Diuretics; Potassium-Sparing Diuretics; Prostaglandins (Ophthalmic); Salicylates; Selective Serotonin Reuptake Inhibitors; Thiazide and Thiazide-Like Diuretics

The levels/effects of Ibuprofen may be decreased by: Bile Acid Sequestrants; Salicylates

Food Interactions Ibuprofen peak serum levels may be decreased if taken with food. Management: Administer with food.

Dietary Considerations Some products may contain phenylalanine and/or potassium.

Pharmacodynamics/Kinetics

Onset of Action

Onset of Action: Oral: Analgesic: Within 30 to 60 minutes (Davies 1998; Mehlisch 2013); Antipyretic: Single oral dose 8 mg/kg (Kauffman 1992): Infants ≤1 year: 69 ± 22 minutes; Children ≥6 years: Single oral dose 8 mg/kg (Kauffman 1992): 109 ± 64 minutes; Adults: <1 hour (Sullivan 2011)

Maximum effect: Antipyretic: 2-4 hours

Duration of Action Oral: Antipyretic: 6 to 8 hours (Sullivan 2011)

Half-life Elimination

IV:

Ibuprofen (Caldor):

- Pediatric patients: 6 months to <2 years: 1.8 hours; 2 to 16 years: ~1.5 hours
- Adults: 2.22 to 2.44 hours

Ibuprofen lysine (Neoprofen):

- Premature neonates, GA <32 weeks: Reported data highly variable
- R-enantiomer: 10 hours; S-enantiomer: 25.5 hours (Gregoire 2004)
  - Age-based observations:
    - PNA <1 day: 30.5 ± 4.2 hours (Aranda 1997)
    - PNA 3 days: 43.1 ± 26.1 hours (Van Overmeire 2001)
    - PNA 5 days: 26.8 ± 23.6 hours (Van Overmeire 2001)

Oral:

- Children 3 months to 10 years: Oral suspension: 1.6 ± 0.7 hours (Kauffman 1992)
- Adults: ~2 hours; End-stage renal disease: Unchanged (Aronoff 2007)

Time to Peak

Tablets: 1 to 2 hours; suspension: 1 hour

Children with cystic fibrosis (Scott 1999):

- Suspension (n=22): 0.74 ± 0.43 hours (median: 30 minutes)
- Chewable tablet (n=4): 1.5 ± 0.58 hours (median: 1.5 hours)
- Tablet (n=12): 1.33 ± 0.95 hours (median: 1 hour)

Pregnancy Considerations The chronic use of NSAIDs in women of reproductive age may be associated with infertility that is reversible upon discontinuation of the medication. Nonteratogenic effects, including prenatal constriction of the ductus arteriosus, persistent pulmonary hypertension of the newborn, oligohydramnios, necrotizing enterocolitis, renal dysfunction or failure, and intracranial hemorrhage have been observed in the fetus/neonate following in utero NSAID exposure. In addition, non-closure of the ductus arteriosus postnatally may occur and be resistant to medical management (Bermas 2014; Bloor 2013). Because they may cause premature closure of the ductus arteriosus, the use of NSAIDs late in pregnancy should be avoided. Product labeling for Caldolor specifically states use should be avoided starting at 30 weeks gestation.

Breastfeeding Considerations Ibuprofen is excreted in breast milk.

The relative infant dose (RID) of ibuprofen is 0.6% to 0.9% when calculated using the highest breast milk concentration located and compared to an infant therapeutic dose of 10 to 15 mg/kg/day. In general, breastfeeding is considered acceptable when the RID is <10% (Anderson 2016; Ito 2000). Using the highest milk concentration (0.59 mcg/mL), the estimated daily infant dose via breast milk is 0.089 mg/kg/day. This milk concentration was obtained following maternal administration of oral ibuprofen ≥ 600 mg/day (Rigourd 2014).

Based on the available data, adverse events have not been reported in nursing infants and milk production is not affected.

In general, NSAIDs may be used in postpartum women who wish to breast-feed and if needed for postpartum pain, ibuprofen is the preferred agent (Montgomery 2012). Ibuprofen is considered compatible with breastfeeding when used in usual recommended doses (WHO 2002). Use should be avoided in women nursing infants with platelet dysfunction or thrombocytopenia (Bloor 2013; Sammaritano 2014). The manufacturer recommends that the decision to breast-feed during therapy consider the risk of infant exposure, the benefits of breastfeeding to the infant, and benefits of treatment to the mother.

Dosage Forms Considerations

EnovaRX-Ibuprofen cream is compounded from a kit. Refer to manufacturer's labeling for compounding instructions.

Dosage Forms

Capsule, Oral:
- Advil [OTC]: 200 mg
- Advil Migraine [OTC]: 200 mg
- KS Ibuprofen [OTC]: 200 mg
- Generic: 200 mg

Cream, External:
- EnovaRX-Ibuprofen: 10% (60 g, 120 g)

Kit, Combination:
- Ibuprofen Comfort Pac: 800 mg

Solution, Intravenous:
- Caldolor: 800 mg/8 mL (8 mL)

Solution, Intravenous [preservative free]:
- NeoProfen: 10 mg/mL (2 mL)
- Generic: 10 mg/mL (2 mL)

Suspension, Oral:
- Childrens Advil [OTC]: 100 mg/5 mL (30 mL, 120 mL)
- Childrens Motrin [OTC]: 100 mg/5 mL (120 mL)
- GoodSense Ibuprofen Childrens [OTC]: 100 mg/5 mL (120 mL)
- Infants Advil [OTC]: 50 mg/1.25 mL (15 mL, 30 mL)
- Motrin Infants Drops [OTC]: 50 mg/1.25 mL (15 mL, 30 mL)
- Generic: 100 mg/5 mL (5 mL, 118 mL, 120 mL, 473 mL)

Tablet, Oral:
- Addaprin [OTC]: 200 mg
- Advil [OTC]: 200 mg
- Advil Junior Strength [OTC]: 100 mg
- Dyspel [OTC]: 200 mg
- Genpril [OTC]: 200 mg
- I-Prin [OTC]: 200 mg
- IBU-200 [OTC]: 200 mg
- Motrin IB [OTC]: 200 mg
- Provil [OTC]: 200 mg
- Generic: 200 mg, 400 mg, 600 mg, 800 mg

Tablet Chewable, Oral:
- Advil Junior Strength [OTC]: 100 mg

Dental Comment Preoperative use of ibuprofen at a dose of 400-600 mg every 6 hours 24 hours before the appointment decreases postoperative edema and hastens healing time.

New information from the FDA states that ibuprofen can interfere with the antiplatelet effect of low-dose aspirin (81 mg/day), potentially rendering aspirin less effective when used for cardioprotection and stroke protection. In situations where these drugs could be used concomitantly, the FDA has provided the following information.

Patients who use immediate release aspirin (not enteric-coated aspirin) and take a single dose or chronic doses of ibuprofen 400 mg, should dose the ibuprofen at least **30 minutes or longer after aspirin ingestion or more than 8 hours before aspirin ingestion** to avoid attenuation of aspirin's effect.

At this time, recommendations about the timing of ibuprofen 400 mg in patients taking enteric-coated low-dose aspirin cannot be made based on available data. One study however, showed that the antiplatelet effect of enteric-coated low-dose aspirin was attenuated when ibuprofen 400 mg was dosed 2, 7, and 12 hours after aspirin (Catella-Lawson 2001).

With occasional use of ibuprofen, there is likely to be minimal risk from any attenuation of the antiplatelet effect of low-dose aspirin, because of a long-lasting effect of aspirin on platelets.

Other over-the-counter (OTC) NSAIDs (ie, naproxen sodium and ketoprofen) should be viewed as having the potential to interfere with the antiplatelet effect of low-dose aspirin until proven otherwise. However, the FDA is unaware of any studies that have looked at the same type of interference by ketoprofen with low-dose aspirin. One study of naproxen and low-dose aspirin has suggested that naproxen may interfere with aspirin's antiplatelet activity when they are coadministered (Steinhubl 2005). However, naproxen 500 mg administered 2 hours before or after aspirin 100 mg, did not interfere with aspirin's antiplatelet effect. The FDA stated that there is no data looking at doses of naproxen <500 mg. Naproxen OTC strength is 220 mg tablets.

Ibuprofen, prescription dose of 800 mg 3 times daily, significantly diminishes the antiplatelet effects of low-dose aspirin (baby) in healthy volunteers. Diclofenac (Systemic), 50 mg 3 times daily, did not interfere with the antiplatelet effects of low-dose aspirin (baby) in healthy volunteers. Ibuprofen, and possibly other nonselective NSAIDs, may reduce the cardioprotective effects of aspirin. It seems prudent to avoid regular, frequent use of ibuprofen in patients receiving aspirin for its cardioprotective effects. Alternative analgesics (eg, acetaminophen) or prescription diclofenac in place of prescription ibuprofen may be a safer choice.

Ibuprofen and Famotidine

(eye byoo PROE fen & fa MOE ti deen)

Related Information

Famotidine *on page 688*
Ibuprofen *on page 851*

Brand Names: US Duexis

Pharmacologic Category Analgesic, Nonopioid; Histamine H_2 Antagonist; Nonsteroidal Anti-inflammatory Drug (NSAID), Oral

Use Osteoarthritis, rheumatoid arthritis: Relief of signs and symptoms of osteoarthritis and rheumatoid arthritis (RA) and to decrease the risk of developing upper GI ulcers

Local Anesthetic/Vasoconstrictor Precautions No information available to require special precautions

Effects on Dental Treatment See individual agents

Effects on Bleeding See individual agents

Adverse Reactions Percentages as reported for combination product. Also see individual agents.

1% to 10%:

Cardiovascular: Hypertension (3%), peripheral edema (2%)

Central nervous system: Headache (3%)
Gastrointestinal: Nausea (6%), diarrhea (5%), dyspepsia (5%), constipation (4%), abdominal distress (≤3%), abdominal pain (≤3%), gastroesophageal reflux disease (2%), vomiting (2%)
Genitourinary: Urinary tract infection (2%)
Hematologic & oncologic: Anemia (2%)
Infection: Influenza (2%)
Neuromuscular & skeletal: Back pain (2%), arthralgia (1%)
Respiratory: Upper respiratory tract infection (4%), bronchitis (2%), cough (2%), nasopharyngitis (2%), pharyngolaryngeal pain (2%), sinusitis (2%)
<1%, postmarketing, and/or case reports: Hepatotoxicity (idiosyncratic) (Chalasani 2014)

General Dosage Range Oral: *Adults:* One tablet (ibuprofen 800 mg/famotidine 26.6 mg) 3 times daily.

Mechanism of Action

Ibuprofen: Reversibly inhibits cyclooxygenase-1 and 2 (COX-1 and 2) enzymes, which results in in decreased formation of prostaglandin precursors; has antipyretic, analgesic, and anti-inflammatory properties

Famotidine: Competitive inhibition of histamine at H_2 receptors of the gastric parietal cells, which inhibits gastric acid secretion

Pregnancy Considerations Animal reproduction studies have not been conducted with this combination. Avoid use of ibuprofen/famotidine in pregnant women starting at 30 weeks of gestation (third trimester) due to the risk of premature closure of the fetal ductus arteriosus. Refer to individual agents.

Dental Comment See Individual agents

Ibutilide (i BYOO ti lide)

Related Information

Clinical Risk Related to Drugs Prolonging QT Interval *on page 1772*

Brand Names: US Corvert

Brand Names: Canada Corvert

Pharmacologic Category Antiarrhythmic Agent, Class III

Use

Atrial fibrillation/flutter: Rapid conversion of atrial fibrillation or atrial flutter of recent onset to sinus rhythm (effectiveness has not been determined in patients with arrhythmias >90 days in duration).

Note: According to the American Heart Association/ American College of Cardiology/Heart Rhythm Society guidelines for the management of atrial fibrillation, in patients with pre-excited atrial fibrillation and rapid ventricular response who are not hemodynamically compromised, the use of ibutilide to restore sinus rhythm or slow the ventricular rate is recommended (AHA/ACC/HRS [January, 2014]).

Local Anesthetic/Vasoconstrictor Precautions Ibutilide is one of the drugs confirmed to prolong the QT interval and is accepted as having a risk of causing torsade de pointes. The risk of drug-induced torsade de pointes is extremely low when a single QT interval prolonging drug is prescribed. In terms of epinephrine, it is not known what effect vasoconstrictors in the local anesthetic regimen will have in patients with a known history of congenital prolonged QT interval or in patients taking any medication that prolongs the QT interval. Until more information is obtained, it is suggested that the clinician consult with the physician prior to the use of a vasoconstrictor in suspected patients, and that the vasoconstrictor (epinephrine, mepivacaine and levonordefrin [Carbocaine® 2% with Neo-Cobefrin®]) be used with caution.

Effects on Dental Treatment No significant effects or complications reported

Effects on Bleeding No information available to require special precautions

Adverse Reactions

1% to 10%:

Cardiovascular: Nonsustained monomorphic ventricular tachycardia (5%), ventricular premature contractions (5), unsustained polymorphic ventricular tachycardia (3%), supraventricular tachycardia (≤3%), tachycardia (≤3%), atrioventricular block (2%), bundle branch block (2%), hypotension (2%), sustained polymorphic ventricular tachycardia (2%; eg, torsade de pointes; often requiring cardioversion), bradycardia (1%), hypertension (1%), palpitations (1%), prolonged Q-T interval on ECG (1%)
Central nervous system: Headache (4%)
Gastrointestinal: Nausea (>1%)

<1%, postmarketing, and/or case reports: Bullous rash (erythematous), cardiac failure, idioventricular rhythm, nodal arrhythmia, renal failure, supraventricular extrasystole, sustained monomorphic ventricular tachycardia

General Dosage Range IV:

Adults <60 kg: 0.01 mg/kg; may repeat once after 10 minutes

Adults ≥60 kg: 1 mg; may repeat once after 10 minutes

Mechanism of Action Exact mechanism of action is unknown; prolongs the action potential in cardiac tissue

Pharmacodynamics/Kinetics

Onset of Action Conversion to sinus rhythm: ≤90 minutes after start of infusion

Half-life Elimination ~6 hours (range: 2 to 12 hours)

Pregnancy Considerations Use in pregnancy may be considered (ESG [Regitz-Zagrosek 2011]); however, information related to the use of ibutilide in pregnancy is limited (Burkart 2007; Kockova 2007).

Dental Comment See Local Anesthetic/Vasoconstrictor Precautions

Icatibant (eye KAT i bant)

Brand Names: US Firazyr

Brand Names: Canada Firazyr

Pharmacologic Category Selective Bradykinin B2 Receptor Antagonist

Use Hereditary angioedema: Treatment of acute attacks of hereditary angioedema (HAE)

Local Anesthetic/Vasoconstrictor Precautions No information available to require special precautions

Effects on Dental Treatment No significant effects or complications reported

Effects on Bleeding No information available to require special precautions

Adverse Reactions

>10%: Local: Injection site reaction (97%)

1% to 10%:

Central nervous system: Dizziness (3%)
Hepatic: Increased serum transaminase (4%)
Miscellaneous: Fever (4%)

<1%: Antibody development (anti-icatibant, no association with efficacy observed), chest pain, headache, myocardial infarction, nausea, skin rash

General Dosage Range SubQ: *Adults:* 30 mg; may repeat every 6 hours as needed (maximum daily dose: 90 mg)

Mechanism of Action Icatibant is a selective competitive antagonist for the bradykinin B_2 receptor. Patients with HAE have an absence or dysfunction of C1-esterase-inhibitor which leads to the production of bradykinin. The presence of bradykinin may cause symptoms of localized swelling, inflammation, and pain. Icatibant inhibits bradykinin from binding at the B_2 receptor, thereby treating the symptoms associated with acute attack.

Pharmacodynamics/Kinetics

Onset of Action Median time to 50% decrease of symptoms: ~2 hours

Duration of Action Inhibits symptoms caused by bradykinin for ~6 hours

Half-life Elimination 1 to 1.8 hours

Time to Peak 0.75 hours

Pregnancy Risk Factor C

Pregnancy Considerations Adverse events were observed in animal reproduction studies with doses close to or less than the recommended human dose. Has not been adequately studied in pregnant women.

IDArubicin (eye da ROO bi sin)

Brand Names: US Idamycin PFS

Brand Names: Canada Idamycin PFS; Idarubicin Hydrochloride Injection

Pharmacologic Category Antineoplastic Agent, Anthracycline; Antineoplastic Agent, Topoisomerase II Inhibitor

Use Acute myeloid leukemia: Treatment of acute myeloid leukemia (AML) in adults (in combination with other approved chemotherapy agents).

Local Anesthetic/Vasoconstrictor Precautions No information available to require special precautions

Effects on Dental Treatment Key adverse event(s) related to dental treatment: Stomatitis.

Effects on Bleeding Platelet counts reach a nadir by day 10-15 and recover by day 21-28. Bleeding during periods of thrombocytopenia may occur.

Adverse Reactions The relative cardiotoxicity of idarubicin compared to doxorubicin is unclear. Some investigators report no increase in cardiac toxicity for adults at cumulative oral idarubicin doses up to 540 mg/m^2; other reports suggest a maximum cumulative intravenous dose of 150 mg/m^2.

>10%:

Cardiovascular: Cardiac failure (dose-related), ECG abnormalities (transient; includes atrial premature contractions, S-T wave changes, supraventricular tachycardia, ventricular premature contractions; generally asymptomatic and self-limiting)

Central nervous system: Headache

Dermatologic: Alopecia (25% to 30%), skin rash (11%), urticaria

Gastrointestinal: Vomiting (30% to 60%), gastrointestinal hemorrhage (30%), diarrhea (9% to 22%), stomatitis (11%), nausea

Genitourinary: Urine discoloration (darker yellow)

Hematologic & oncologic: Anemia (effects are generally less severe with oral dosing), bone marrow suppression (nadir: 10 to 15 days; recovery: 21 to 28 days; primarily leukopenia; effects are generally less severe with oral dosing), thrombocytopenia (effects are generally less severe with oral dosing)

Hepatic: Increased serum bilirubin (≤44%), increased serum transaminases (≤44%)

Miscellaneous: Radiation recall phenomenon

1% to 10%:

Central nervous system: Peripheral neuropathy, seizure

<1%, postmarketing, and/or case reports: Cardiomyopathy, hyperuricemia, myocarditis, typhlitis (neutropenic)

General Dosage Range Dosage adjustment recommended in patients with hepatic or renal impairment

IV: *Adults:* Induction: 12 mg/m^2/day for 3 days

Mechanism of Action Similar to daunorubicin, idarubicin inhibits DNA and RNA synthesis by intercalation between DNA base pairs and by steric obstruction. Although the exact mechanism is unclear, it appears that direct binding to DNA (intercalation) and inhibition of DNA repair (topoisomerase II inhibition) result in blockade of DNA and RNA synthesis and fragmentation of DNA.

Pharmacodynamics/Kinetics

Half-life Elimination

Children: Children ≥1 year and adolescents: 17.6 ± 6.8 hours (range: 8.3 to 29.6 hours) (Reid 1990)

Adults: 22 hours (range: 4 to 48 hours); >45 hours (idarubicinol)

Pregnancy Risk Factor D

Pregnancy Considerations Adverse events were observed in animal reproduction studies. Fetal fatality was noted in a case report following second trimester exposure in a pregnant woman. The manufacturer recommends that women of childbearing potential avoid pregnancy.

IdaruCIZUmab (eye da roo SIZ uh mab)

Brand Names: US Praxbind

Brand Names: Canada Praxbind

Pharmacologic Category Antidote; Monoclonal Antibody

Use Reversal of dabigatran: Reversal of the anticoagulant effects of dabigatran for emergency surgery/urgent procedures or in life-threatening or uncontrolled bleeding

Local Anesthetic/Vasoconstrictor Precautions No information available to require special precautions

Effects on Dental Treatment No significant effects or complications reported

Effects on Bleeding No information available to require special precautions

Adverse Reactions Frequency not always defined.

Central nervous system: Delirium (7%), headache (5%)

Endocrine & metabolic: Hypokalemia (7%)

Gastrointestinal: Constipation (7%)

Hypersensitivity: Hypersensitivity (including bronchospasm, hyperventilation, rash, and pruritus)

Respiratory: Pneumonia (6%)

Miscellaneous: Fever (6%)

<1%, postmarketing, and/or case reports (Pollack 2015): Acute ischemic stroke, cardiac arrest, circulatory shock, deep vein thrombosis, intracardiac thrombus (left atrium), multiorgan failure, myocardial infarction (NSTEMI), pulmonary edema, pulmonary embolism, respiratory failure, right heart failure

General Dosage Range IV: *Adults:* 5 g

Mechanism of Action Idarucizumab, a specific reversal agent for dabigatran, is a humanized monoclonal antibody fragment (Fab) that binds specifically to dabigatran and its acylglucuronide metabolites with an affinity for dabigatran that is ~350 times greater than that of thrombin, and neutralizes the anticoagulant effect within minutes (Das 2015; Schiele 2013).

Pharmacodynamics/Kinetics

Onset of Action Uncontrolled bleeding: Effects observed within minutes and hemostasis is restored at a median of 11.4 hours (Pollack 2015)

Duration of Action Usually at least 24 hours

Half-life Elimination 47 minutes (initial); 10.3 hours (terminal)

Pregnancy Considerations Animal reproduction studies have not been conducted.

Idelalisib (eye del a LIS ib)

Brand Names: US Zydelig

Brand Names: Canada Zydelig

Pharmacologic Category Antineoplastic Agent, Phosphatidylinositol 3-Kinase Inhibitor

Use

Chronic lymphocytic leukemia: Treatment of relapsed chronic lymphocytic leukemia (CLL) (in combination with rituximab) when rituximab alone is appropriate therapy due to other comorbidities

Follicular B-cell non-Hodgkin lymphoma: Treatment of relapsed follicular B-cell non-Hodgkin lymphoma after at least 2 prior systemic therapies

Small lymphocytic lymphoma: Treatment of relapsed small lymphocytic lymphoma (SLL) after at least 2 prior systemic therapies

Limitations of use: Idelalisib is not indicated or recommended for first-line treatment of CLL, follicular B-cell non-Hodgkin lymphoma, or SLL.

Local Anesthetic/Vasoconstrictor Precautions No information available to require special precautions

Effects on Dental Treatment No significant effects or complications reported

Effects on Bleeding Chemotherapy may result in significant myelosuppression, potentially including significant reduction in platelet counts and altered hemostasis. In patients who are under active treatment with these agents, medical consult is suggested.

Adverse Reactions As reported with monotherapy.

>10%:

Central nervous system: Fatigue (30%), insomnia (12%), headache (11%)

Dermatologic: Skin rash (21%), night sweats (12%)

Gastrointestinal: Diarrhea (47%), nausea (29%), abdominal pain (26%), decreased appetite (16%), vomiting (15%)

Hematologic & oncologic: Decreased neutrophils (53%; grade 3: 14%; grade 4: 11%), decreased hemoglobin (28%; grade 3: 2%), decreased platelet count (26%; grade 3: 3%; grade 4: 3%)

Hepatic: Increased serum ALT (50%), increased serum AST (41%), severe hepatotoxicity (18%)

Infection: Severe infection (21%; including sepsis, febrile neutropenia)

Neuromuscular & skeletal: Weakness (12%)

Respiratory: Cough (29%), pneumonia (15% to 25%), dyspnea (17%), upper respiratory tract infection (12%)

Miscellaneous: Fever (28%)

1% to 10%:

Cardiovascular: Peripheral edema (10%)

Respiratory: Pneumonitis (4%)

<1%, postmarketing, and/or case reports: Anaphylaxis, cytomegalovirus disease, erythematous rash, exfoliative dermatitis, hypersensitivity reaction, intestinal perforation, macular eruption, maculopapular rash, papular rash, pneumonia due to pneumocystic carinii, pruritic rash, Stevens-Johnson syndrome, toxic epidermal necrolysis

General Dosage Range Dosage adjustment recommended in patients with hepatic impairment or who develop toxicities.

Oral: *Adults:* 150 mg twice daily

Mechanism of Action Potent small molecule inhibitor of the delta isoform of phosphatidylinositol 3-kinase (PI3Kδ), which is highly expressed in malignant lymphoid B-cells. PI3Kδ inhibition results in apoptosis of malignant tumor cells. In addition, idelalisib inhibits several signaling pathways, including B-cell receptor, CXCR4 and CXCR5 signaling which may play important roles in CLL pathophysiology (Furman, 2014).

Pharmacodynamics/Kinetics

Half-life Elimination ~8 hours

Time to Peak Median: 1.5 hours

Pregnancy Risk Factor D

Pregnancy Considerations Adverse events were observed in animal reproduction studies. Women of reproductive potential should use effective contraception during therapy and for at least 1 month after treatment discontinuation.

Prescribing and Access Restrictions Available through specialty pharmacies. Further information may be obtained at http://www.zydeligaccessconnect.com/.

Idursulfase (eye dur SUL fase)

Brand Names: US Elaprase

Brand Names: Canada Elaprase

Pharmacologic Category Enzyme

Use Hunter syndrome: Replacement therapy in Hunter syndrome (mucopolysaccharidosis II; MPS II) for improvement of walking capacity

Local Anesthetic/Vasoconstrictor Precautions No information available to require special precautions

Effects on Dental Treatment No significant effects or complications reported

Effects on Bleeding No information available to require special precautions

Adverse Reactions

>10%:

Cardiovascular: Hypertension (25%), flushing (7% to 16%)

Central nervous system: Headache (28% to 59%), malaise (22%), anxiety (13%), fatigue (13%), irritability (13%)

Dermatologic: Pruritus (25% to 28%), skin rash (19% to 32%), urticaria (16%), dermatologic disease (13%), infusion site swelling (13%), pruritic rash (13%)

Gastrointestinal: Vomiting (5% to 14%), dyspepsia (13%)

Hypersensitivity: Hypersensitivity reaction (10% to 69%)

Immunologic: Antibody development (51%; neutralizing: 41% to 79%), development of IgG antibodies (51% to 68%)

Infection: Abscess (16%)

Neuromuscular & skeletal: Arthralgia (31%), limb pain (28%), musculoskeletal disease (16%), musculoskeletal pain (13% to 16%; includes chest wall musculoskeletal pain)

Ophthalmic: Visual disturbance (22%)

Otic: Otitis (children 16 months to 4 years: 11%)

Respiratory: Wheezing (19%), pneumonia (children 16 months to 4 years: 18%)

Miscellaneous: Fever (9% to 63%), infusion-related reaction (15%), accidental injury (13%; superficial)

1% to 10%:

Cardiovascular: Tachycardia (9%)

Central nervous system: Chills (9%), dizziness (5%)

Dermatologic: Erythema (7%)

Gastrointestinal: Diarrhea (9%), nausea (5%)

Hypersensitivity: Anaphylaxis (10%)

Respiratory: Cough (9%)

<1%, postmarketing, and/or case reports: Angioedema, cardiac arrhythmia, cardiac failure, cyanosis, hypotension, infection, loss of consciousness, pulmonary embolism, respiratory distress, respiratory failure, seizure

General Dosage Range IV: *Children ≥5 years, Adolescents, and Adults:* 0.5 mg/kg once weekly

Mechanism of Action Idursulfase is a recombinant form of iduronate-2-sulfatase, an enzyme needed to hydrolyze the mucopolysaccharides dermatan sulfate and heparan sulfate in various cells. Accumulation of these polysaccharides can lead to various manifestations of disease, including physical changes, CNS involvement, cardiac, respiratory, and mobility dysfunction. Replacement of this enzyme has been shown to improve walking capacity in patients with a deficiency.

Pharmacodynamics/Kinetics

Half-life Elimination Varies dependent upon age and presence of antibodies (particularly patients <7.5 years)

Children 16 months to <7.5 years: Week 1: 160 ± 69 minutes; Week 27: Antibody negative: 134 ± 19 minutes; antibody positive: 84 ±46 minutes

Children ≥7.5 years, Adolescents, and Adults <27 years: Mean range: 44 to 48 minutes

Pregnancy Risk Factor C

Pregnancy Considerations Animal reproduction studies have not been conducted.

Ifosfamide (eye FOSS fa mide)

Brand Names: US Ifex

Brand Names: Canada Ifex; Ifosfamide for Injection

Pharmacologic Category Antineoplastic Agent, Alkylating Agent; Antineoplastic Agent, Alkylating Agent (Nitrogen Mustard)

Use Testicular cancer: Treatment (third-line) of germ cell testicular cancer (in combination with other chemotherapy drugs and with concurrent mesna for prophylaxis of hemorrhagic cystitis)

Local Anesthetic/Vasoconstrictor Precautions No information available to require special precautions

Effects on Dental Treatment No significant effects or complications reported

Effects on Bleeding Thrombocytopenia occurs in ~20% of patients (grade 3/4: 8%). Medical consult recommended.

Adverse Reactions

>10%:

Central nervous system: Brain disease (≤15%), central nervous system toxicity (≤15%)

Dermatologic: Alopecia (83% to 90%; combination therapy: 100%)

Endocrine & metabolic: Metabolic acidosis (31%)

Gastrointestinal: Nausea (≤58%), vomiting (≤58%)

Hematologic & oncologic: Leukopenia (≤100%; grade 4: ≤50%; nadir: 8 to 14 days), anemia (38%), thrombocytopenia (20%; grades 3/4: ≤8%)

Renal: Hematuria (6% to 92%, reduced with mesna; grade 2 [gross hematuria]: 8% to 12%)

1% to 10%:

Cardiovascular: Localized phlebitis (2% to 3%)

Gastrointestinal: Anorexia (1%)

Hematologic & oncologic: Febrile neutropenia (1%)

Hepatic: Hepatic insufficiency (2% to 3%), increased serum bilirubin (2% to 3%), increased serum transaminases (2% to 3%)

Infection: Infection (8% to 10%)

Renal: Renal insufficiency (6%)

Miscellaneous: Fever (1%)

<1%, postmarketing, and/or case reports: Abdominal pain, abnormal gait, acute renal failure, agranulocytosis, altered hormone level (increased gonadotropin), amenorrhea, amnesia, anaphylaxis, angina pectoris, angioedema, anovulation, anuria, arthralgia, asterixis, atrial premature contractions, atrial fibrillation, atrial flutter, atrial premature contractions, azoospermia, blood coagulation disorder, blurred vision, bone marrow failure, bradycardia, bradyphrenia, bronchospasm, bundle branch block, capillary leak syndrome, cardiac arrhythmia, cardiac failure, cardiogenic shock, cardiomyopathy, cardiotoxicity, casts in urine, catatonia, chest pain, chills, cholestasis, chronic renal failure, colitis, conjunctivitis, constipation, cough, increased serum creatinine, decreased creatinine clearance, decreased plasma estrogen concentration, deep vein thrombosis, delirium, delusions, dermatitis, diarrhea, disseminated intravascular coagulation, dysarthria, dysesthesia, dyspnea, dysuria, ECG abnormality (QRS complex abnormal), edema, enterocolitis, erythema, extrapyramidal reaction, facial swelling, Fanconi's syndrome, fatigue, fecal incontinence, flushing, fulminant hepatitis, gastrointestinal hemorrhage, glycosuria, granulocytopenia, growth suppression (children), hearing loss, hemolytic anemia, hemolytic-uremic syndrome, hemorrhage (including myocardial), hemorrhagic cystitis, hepatic failure, hepatic veno-occlusive disease, hepatitis (cytolytic), hepatorenal syndrome, herpes zoster, hyperglycemia, hyperhidrosis, hypertension, hyperpigmentation, hypersensitivity pneumonitis, hypersensitivity reaction, hypocalcemia, hypoesthesia, hypokalemia, hyponatremia, hypophosphatemia, hypotension, hypoxia, intestinal obstruction, immunosuppression, increased blood urea nitrogen, increased creatinine clearance, increased gamma-glutamyl transferase, increased lactate dehydrogenase, increased serum alkaline phosphatase, infertility, infusion site reaction (erythema, inflammation, pain, pruritus, swelling, tenderness), inhibition of spermatogenesis, interstitial nephritis, interstitial pneumonitis, interstitial pulmonary disease, inversion T wave on ECG, irritable bladder, jaundice, left ventricular dysfunction (failure), leukoencephalopathy, limb pain, lymphocytopenia, malaise, mania, menopause (premature), mental status changes, metastases (including ALL, AML, APL, lymphoma, MDS, RCC, sarcomas, thyroid cancer), methemoglobinemia, mucosal inflammation, mucous membrane ulceration, multi-organ failure, muscle twitching, mutism, myalgia, myocardial infarction, myocarditis, nail disease, nephrogenic diabetes insipidus, neuralgia, neutropenia, oligospermia, oliguria, osteomalacia (adults), ovarian failure, pain, palmar-plantar erythrodysesthesia, pancreatitis, pancytopenia, panic attack, paranoia, parenchymal damage (renal), paresthesia, pericardial effusion, pericarditis, peripheral neuropathy, petechia, phosphaturia, physical health deterioration, pleural effusion, pneumonia (including *Pneumocystis jiroveci*), pneumonitis, pollakiuria, polydipsia, polyneuropathy, polyuria, portal vein

thrombosis, progressive multifocal leukoencephalopathy, proteinuria, pruritus, pulmonary edema, pulmonary embolism, pulmonary fibrosis, pulmonary hypertension, reduced ejection fraction, renal tubular acidosis, renal tubular necrosis, respiratory distress syndrome (acute), respiratory failure, reversible posterior leukoencephalopathy syndrome, rhabdomyolysis, rickets, salivation, seizure, sepsis, septic shock, SIADH, skin abnormalities related to radiation recall, skin necrosis, skin rash (including macular and papular), status epilepticus, sterility, Stevens-Johnson syndrome, stomatitis, ST segment changes on ECG, supraventricular extrasystole, tachycardia, talkativeness (logorrhea), tinnitus, toxic epidermal necrolysis, tumor lysis syndrome, typhlitis, uremia, urinary incontinence, urine abnormality (aminoaciduria and enzymuria), urticaria, vasculitis, ventricular fibrillation, ventricular premature contractions, ventricular tachycardia, vertigo, viral hepatitis, visual impairment, wound healing impairment

General Dosage Range Dosage adjustment recommended in patients with hepatic or renal impairment or who develop toxicities.

IV: *Adults:* 1200 mg/m^2/day for 5 days every 21 days

Mechanism of Action Causes cross-linking of strands of DNA by binding with nucleic acids and other intracellular structures, resulting in cell death; inhibits protein synthesis and DNA synthesis

Pharmacodynamics/Kinetics

Half-life Elimination

Increased in the elderly

High dose (3,800 to 5,000 mg/m^2): ~15 hours

Lower dose (1,600 to 2,400 mg/m^2): ~7 hours

Pregnancy Risk Factor D

Pregnancy Considerations Adverse effects have been observed in animal reproduction studies. Fetal growth retardation and neonatal anemia have been reported with exposure to ifosfamide-containing regimens during human pregnancy. Male and female fertility may be affected (dose and duration dependent). Ifosfamide interferes with oogenesis and spermatogenesis; amenorrhea, azoospermia, and sterility have been reported and may be irreversible. Avoid pregnancy during treatment; male patients should not father a child during and for at least 6 months after completion of therapy.

Iloperidone (eye loe PER i done)

Related Information

Clinical Risk Related to Drugs Prolonging QT Interval *on page 1772*

Brand Names: US Fanapt; Fanapt Titration Pack

Pharmacologic Category Second Generation (Atypical) Antipsychotic

Use Schizophrenia: Treatment of adults with schizophrenia

Local Anesthetic/Vasoconstrictor Precautions Iloperidone is one of the drugs confirmed to prolong the QT interval and is accepted as having a risk of causing torsade de pointes. The risk of drug-induced torsade de pointes is extremely low when a single QT interval prolonging drug is prescribed. In terms of epinephrine, it is not known what effect vasoconstrictors in the local anesthetic regimen will have in patients with a known history of congenital prolonged QT interval or in patients taking any medication that prolongs the QT interval. Until more information is obtained, it is suggested that the clinician consult with the physician prior to the use of a vasoconstrictor in suspected patients, and that the vasoconstrictor (epinephrine, mepivacaine and levonordefrin [Carbocaine 2% with Neo-Cobefrin]) be used with caution.

Effects on Dental Treatment Key adverse event(s) related to dental treatment: Xerostomia and changes in salivation (normal salivary flow resumes upon discontinuation); Patients may experience orthostatic hypotension as they stand up after treatment; especially if lying in dental chair for extended periods of time. Use caution with sudden changes in position during and after dental treatment.

Effects on Bleeding No information available to require special precautions

Adverse Reactions

>10%:

Cardiovascular: Tachycardia (3% to 12%; dose-related)

Central nervous system: Dizziness (10% to 20%; dose-related), drowsiness (9% to 15%)

Endocrine & metabolic: Increased serum prolactin (26%), weight gain (9% to 18%; dose-related)

1% to 10%:

Cardiovascular: Orthostatic hypotension (3% to 5%), hypotension (3%; dose-related), palpitations (≥1%)

Central nervous system: Fatigue (4% to 6%), extrapyramidal reaction (4% to 5%), lethargy (3%), aggressive behavior (≥1%), delusions (≥1%), restlessness (≥1%), dystonia (≤1%)

Dermatologic: Skin rash (3%)

Endocrine & metabolic: Increased serum triglycerides (10%), increased serum cholesterol (4%), weight loss (≥1%)

Gastrointestinal: Nausea (10%), xerostomia (8% to 10%), diarrhea (5% to 7%), abdominal distress (3%; dose-related)

Genitourinary: Ejaculation failure (2%), erectile dysfunction (≥1%), urinary incontinence (≥1%)

Hematologic & oncologic: Decreased hematocrit (≤1%)

Neuromuscular & skeletal: Arthralgia (3%), muscle rigidity (3%; dose-related), tremor (3%), muscle spasm (≥1%), myalgia (≥1%)

Ophthalmic: Blurred vision (3%), conjunctivitis (≥1%; including allergic)

Respiratory: Nasal congestion (5% to 8%), nasopharyngitis (≤4%), upper respiratory tract infection (2% to 3%), dyspnea (2%)

Frequency not defined: Genitourinary: Priapism

<1%, postmarketing, and/or case reports: Abnormal gait, acute renal failure, amenorrhea, amnesia, anemia, anorgasmia, aphthous stomatitis, asthma, blepharitis, bradykinesia, bulimia nervosa, cardiac arrhythmia, cataract, catatonia, cholelithiasis, confusion, decreased hemoglobin, decreased libido, dehydration, delirium, dry nose, duodenal ulcer, dyspnea on exertion, dysuria, edema, emotional lability, epistaxis, eyelid edema, fecal incontinence, first degree atrioventricular block, fluid retention, gastritis, gastroesophageal reflux disease, gynecomastia, hiatal hernia, hostility, hyperacidity, hyperemia (including conjunctival), hyperglycemia, hypermenorrhea, hypersensitivity reaction (including anaphylaxis; angioedema; throat tightness; oropharyngeal swelling; swelling of the face, lips, mouth, and tongue; urticaria; pruritus), hyperthermia, hypokalemia, hypothyroidism, impulse control disorder, increased appetite, increased neutrophils, increased thirst, iron deficiency anemia, leukopenia, major depressive disorder, mania, mastalgia, menstrual disease, nephrolithiasis,

neuroleptic malignant syndrome, nystagmus, obsessive compulsive disorder, oral mucosa ulcer, panic attack, paranoia, paresthesia, Parkinson's disease, pollakiuria, polydipsia (psychogenic), postmenopausal bleeding, prolonged Q-T interval on ECG, prostatitis, psychomotor agitation, restless leg syndrome, retrograde ejaculation, rhinorrhea, salivation, sinus congestion, sleep apnea, stomatitis, swelling of eye, syncope, testicular pain, tinnitus, torticollis, urinary retention, uterine hemorrhage, vertigo, xerophthalmia

General Dosage Range Oral: *Adults:* Initial: 1 mg twice daily; Dosage range: 6 to 12 mg twice daily (maximum: 24 mg/day)

Mechanism of Action Iloperidone is a piperidinyl-benzisoxazole atypical antipsychotic with mixed D_2/ 5-HT_2 antagonist activity. It exhibits high affinity for 5-HT_{2A}, $NE_{\alpha1}$, D_2, and D_3 receptors, low to moderate affinity for D_1, D_4, H_1, 5-HT_{1A}, 5-HT_6, and 5-HT_7 receptors, and no affinity for muscarinic receptors. The addition of serotonin antagonism to dopamine antagonism (classic neuroleptic mechanism) is thought to improve negative symptoms of psychoses and reduce the incidence of extrapyramidal side effects (Huttunen 1995). Iloperidone's low affinity for histamine H_1 receptors may decrease the risk for weight gain and somnolence while its affinity for $NE_{\alpha1/\alpha2C}$ may improve cognitive function but increase the risk for orthostasis (Arif 2011, Huttunen 1995, Nasrallah 2008).

Pharmacodynamics/Kinetics

Half-life Elimination

Extensive metabolizers: Iloperidone: 18 hours; P88: 26 hours; P95: 23 hours

Poor metabolizers: Iloperidone: 33 hours; P88: 37 hours; P95: 31 hours

Time to Peak Plasma: 2 to 4 hours

Pregnancy Considerations Adverse events have been observed in animal reproduction studies. Antipsychotic use during the third trimester of pregnancy has a risk for abnormal muscle movements (extrapyramidal symptoms [EPS]) and/or withdrawal symptoms in newborns following delivery. Symptoms in the newborn may include agitation, feeding disorder, hypertonia, hypotonia, respiratory distress, somnolence, and tremor; these effects may be self-limiting or require hospitalization. Iloperidone may cause hyperprolactinemia, which may decrease reproductive function in both males and females.

The ACOG recommends that therapy during pregnancy be individualized; treatment with psychiatric medications during pregnancy should incorporate the clinical expertise of the mental health clinician, obstetrician, primary healthcare provider, and pediatrician. Safety data related to atypical antipsychotics during pregnancy is limited and routine use is not recommended. However, if a woman is inadvertently exposed to an atypical antipsychotic while pregnant, continuing therapy may be preferable to switching to a typical antipsychotic that the fetus has not yet been exposed to; consider risk: benefit (ACOG, 2008).

Healthcare providers are encouraged to enroll women 18 to 45 years of age exposed to iloperidone during pregnancy in the Atypical Antipsychotics Pregnancy Registry (1-866-961-2388 or http://www.-womensmentalhealth.org/pregnancyregistry).

Dental Comment See Local Anesthetic/Vasoconstrictor Precautions

Iloprost (EYE loe prost)

Brand Names: US Ventavis

Pharmacologic Category Prostacyclin; Prostaglandin; Vasodilator

Use Pulmonary arterial hypertension: Treatment of pulmonary arterial hypertension (World Health Organization [WHO] group I) in patients with New York Heart Association (NYHA) class III or IV symptoms to improve exercise tolerance, symptoms, and diminish clinical deterioration.

Local Anesthetic/Vasoconstrictor Precautions No information available to require special precautions

Effects on Dental Treatment Key adverse event(s) related to dental treatment: Jaw pain (reported in >10% of patients).

Effects on Bleeding No information available to require special precautions

Adverse Reactions

>10%:

Cardiovascular: Flushing (27%), hypotension (11%)

Central nervous system: Headache (30%), trismus (12%)

Gastrointestinal: Nausea (13%)

Neuromuscular & skeletal: Jaw pain (12%)

Respiratory: Cough (39%), flu-like symptoms (14%)

1% to 10%:

Cardiovascular: Syncope (8%), palpitations (7%)

Central nervous system: Insomnia (8%)

Endocrine & metabolic: Increased gamma-glutamyl transferase (6%)

Gastrointestinal: Vomiting (7%), glossalgia (4%)

Hepatic: Increased serum alkaline phosphatase (6%)

Neuromuscular & skeletal: Back pain (7%), muscle cramps (6%)

Respiratory: Hemoptysis (5%), pneumonia (4%)

<1%, postmarketing, and/or case reports: Bronchospasm, cardiac failure, chest pain, dizziness, dyspnea, dysgeusia, epistaxis, hypersensitivity reaction, mouth irritation, paradoxical reaction (increased post-void residual urine volume), renal failure, skin rash, supraventricular tachycardia, thrombocytopenia, tongue irritation, wheezing

General Dosage Range Dosage adjustment recommended in patients with hepatic impairment.

Inhalation: *Adults:* Initial: 2.5 mcg/dose; Maintenance: 2.5-5 mcg/dose 6-9 times/day (maximum: 45 mcg/day)

Mechanism of Action Acutely, iloprost dilates systemic and pulmonary arterial vascular beds. With longer-term use, alters pulmonary vascular resistance and suppresses vascular smooth muscle proliferation. In addition, it is a mild endogenous inhibitor of platelet aggregation when aerosolized (Beghetti, 2002).

Pharmacodynamics/Kinetics

Duration of Action 30-60 minutes

Half-life Elimination 20-30 minutes (effect), 7-9 minutes (elimination)

Time to Peak Serum: Within 5 minutes after inhalation

Pregnancy Risk Factor C

Pregnancy Considerations Adverse events were observed in some animal reproduction studies. Information related to the use of iloprost in pregnancy is limited (Horng 2016). Women with pulmonary arterial hypertension (PAH) are encouraged to avoid pregnancy (McLaughlin 2009; Taichman 2014).

Imatinib (eye MAT eh nib)

Brand Names: US Gleevec

Brand Names: Canada ACT-Imatinib; Apo-Imatinib; Gleevec; Teva-Imatinib

Pharmacologic Category Antineoplastic Agent, BCR-ABL Tyrosine Kinase Inhibitor; Antineoplastic Agent, Tyrosine Kinase Inhibitor

Use

Acute lymphoblastic leukemia: Treatment of relapsed or refractory Philadelphia chromosome–positive (Ph+) acute lymphoblastic leukemia (ALL) in adults

Treatment of newly diagnosed Ph+ ALL in children (in combination with chemotherapy)

Aggressive systemic mastocytosis: Treatment of aggressive systemic mastocytosis without D816V c-Kit mutation as determined by an approved test (or c-Kit mutational status unknown) in adults

Chronic myeloid leukemia: Treatment of Ph+ chronic myeloid leukemia (CML) in chronic phase (newly diagnosed) in adults and children

Treatment of Ph+ CML in blast crisis, accelerated phase, or chronic phase after failure of interferon-alfa therapy

Dermatofibrosarcoma protuberans: Treatment of unresectable, recurrent, and/or metastatic dermatofibrosarcoma protuberans (DFSP) in adults

Gastrointestinal stromal tumors: Treatment of Kit (CD117)-positive unresectable and/or metastatic malignant gastrointestinal stromal tumors (GIST)

Adjuvant treatment of Kit (CD117)–positive GIST following complete gross resection

Hypereosinophilic syndrome and/or chronic eosinophilic leukemia: Treatment of hypereosinophilic syndrome (HES) and/or chronic eosinophilic leukemia (CEL) in adult patients who have the FIP1L1–platelet-derived growth factor (PDGF) receptor alpha fusion kinase (mutational analysis or fluorescent in situ hybridization [FISH] demonstration of CHIC2 allele deletion) and for patients with HES and/or CEL who are FIP1L1-PDGF receptor alpha fusion kinase negative or unknown

Myelodysplastic/Myeloproliferative diseases: Treatment of myelodysplastic syndrome/myeloproliferative diseases (MDS/MPD) associated with PDGF receptor gene rearrangements as determined by an approved test in adults

Local Anesthetic/Vasoconstrictor Precautions No information available to require special precautions

Effects on Dental Treatment Key adverse event(s) related to dental treatment: Mouth ulceration and taste disturbance.

Effects on Bleeding Bleeding was reported in 12% to 53% of patients. Cytopenias including thrombocytopenia (grade 4 severe: <33%) and anemia (25% to 80%; grade 4: <11%) have been reported. Medical consult is recommended.

Adverse Reactions Adverse reactions listed as a composite of data across many trials, except where noted for a specific indication.

>10%:

Cardiovascular: Edema (11% to 86%; includes aggravated edema, anasarca, ascites, pericardial effusion, peripheral edema, pulmonary edema, and superficial edema), facial edema (≤17%), chest pain (7% to 11%), hypotension (Ph+ ALL [pediatric])

Central nervous system: Fatigue (20% to 75%), pain (≤47%), headache (8% to 37%), dizziness (5% to 19%), insomnia (9% to 15%), depression (3% to 15%), taste disorder (≤13%), rigors (10% to 12%), anxiety (8% to 12%), paresthesia (≤12%), chills (≤11%)

Dermatologic: Skin rash (9% to 50%), dermatitis (GIST: ≤39%), pruritus (7% to 26%), night sweats (CML: 13% to 17%), alopecia (7% to 15%), diaphoresis (GIST: ≤13%)

Endocrine & metabolic: Increased lactate dehydrogenase (≤60%), weight gain (5% to 32%), decreased serum albumin (≤21%), hypokalemia (6% to 13%)

Gastrointestinal: Nausea (41% to 73%), diarrhea (25% to 59%), vomiting (11% to 58%), abdominal pain (3% to 57%), anorexia (≤36%), dyspepsia (11% to 27%), flatulence (≤25%), abdominal distension (≤19%), constipation (8% to 16%), stomatitis (≤16%)

Hematologic & oncologic: Hemorrhage (3% to 53%; grades 3/4: ≤19%), leukopenia (GIST: 5% to 47%; grades 3/4: 2%), hypoproteinemia (≤32%), anemia, neutropenia, thrombocytopenia

Hepatic: Increased serum AST (≤38%), increased serum ALT (≤34%), increased alkaline phosphatase (≤17%), increased serum bilirubin (≤13%), increased serum transaminases (Ph+ ALL [pediatric])

Infection: Influenza (Ph+ CML: ≤14%), infection (Ph+ ALL [pediatric])

Neuromuscular & skeletal: Muscle cramps (16% to 62%), musculoskeletal pain (adults: 38% to 49%; children: 21%), arthralgia (11% to 40%), myalgia (9% to 32%), weakness (≤21%), back pain (≤17%), limb pain (≤16%), ostealgia (≤11%)

Ophthalmic: Periorbital edema (15% to 74%), increased lacrimation (DFSP: 25%; GIST: ≤18%), eyelid edema (Ph+ CML: 19%), blurred vision (≤11%)

Renal: Increased serum creatinine (≤44%)

Respiratory: Nasopharyngitis (1% to 31%), cough (11% to 27%), upper respiratory tract infection (3% to 21%), dyspnea (≤21%), pharyngolaryngeal pain (≤18%), rhinitis (DFSP: 17%), pharyngitis (CML: 10% to 15%), flu-like symptoms (1% to 14%), pneumonia (CML: 4% to 13%), sinusitis (4% to 11%)

Miscellaneous: Fever (6% to 41%)

1% to 10%:

Cardiovascular: Palpitations (≤5%), hypertension (≤4%), cardiac failure (Ph+ CML: 1%), flushing, pleural effusion (Ph+ ALL [pediatric])

Central nervous system: Cerebral hemorrhage (≤9%), hypoesthesia, peripheral neuropathy

Dermatologic: Skin photosensitivity (4% to 7%), xeroderma (≤7%), erythema, nail disease

Endocrine & metabolic: Hypophosphatemia (10%), hyperglycemia (≤10%), weight loss (≤10%), hypocalcemia (GIST: ≤6%), fluid retention (Ph+ CML: 3%; pleural effusion, pericardial effusion, ascites, or pulmonary edema: 2%), hyperkalemia (1%)

Gastrointestinal: Decreased appetite (10%), gastroenteritis (≤10%), gastrointestinal hemorrhage (1% to 8%), gastritis, gastroesophageal reflux, increased serum lipase, xerostomia

Hematologic & oncologic: Lymphocytopenia (≤10%; grades 3/4: 1% to 2%), eosinophilia, febrile neutropenia, pancytopenia, purpura

Neuromuscular & skeletal: Joint swelling

Ophthalmic: Conjunctivitis (5% to 8%), conjunctival hemorrhage, dry eyes

Respiratory: Hypoxia (9%), oropharyngeal pain (Ph+ CML: ≤6%), epistaxis, pneumonitis (Ph+ ALL [pediatric])

<1%, postmarketing, and/or case reports: Actinic keratosis, acute generalized exanthematous pustulosis, anaphylactic shock, angina pectoris, angioedema, aplastic anemia, arthritis, ascites, atrial fibrillation, avascular necrosis of bones, blepharitis, bullous rash, cardiac arrhythmia, cardiac tamponade, cardiogenic shock, cataract, cellulitis, cerebral edema, cheilitis, cold extremities, colitis, confusion, decreased libido, decreased linear skeletal growth rate (children), dehydration, diverticulitis, DRESS syndrome, drowsiness, dyschromia, dysphagia, embolism, eructation, erythema multiforme, esophagitis, exfoliative dermatitis, folliculitis, fungal infection, gastric ulcer, gastrointestinal obstruction, gastrointestinal perforation, glaucoma, gout, gynecomastia, hearing loss, hematemesis, hematoma, hematuria, hemolytic anemia, hepatic failure, hepatic necrosis, hepatitis, hepatotoxicity, herpes simplex infection, herpes zoster, hypercalcemia, hypermenorrhea, hypersensitivity angiitis, hyperuricemia, hypomagnesemia, hyponatremia, hypothyroidism, IgA vasculitis, increased creatine phosphokinase, increased intracranial pressure, inflammatory bowel disease, interstitial pneumonitis, interstitial pulmonary disease, intestinal obstruction, jaundice, left ventricular dysfunction, lichen planus, lower respiratory tract infection, lymphadenopathy, macular edema, melena, memory impairment, menstrual disease, migraine, myocardial infarction, myopathy, onychoclasis, optic neuritis, oral mucosa ulcer, osteonecrosis (hip), ovarian cyst (hemorrhagic), palmar-plantar erythrodysesthesia, pancreatitis, papilledema, pericarditis, petechia, pleuritic chest pain, polyuria, psoriasis, pulmonary fibrosis, pulmonary hemorrhage, pulmonary hypertension, Raynaud phenomenon, reactivation of HBV, renal failure, respiratory failure, restless leg syndrome, retinal hemorrhage, rhabdomyolysis, ruptured corpus luteal cyst, sciatica, scrotal edema, seizure, sepsis, sexual disorder, Stevens-Johnson syndrome, subconjunctival hemorrhage, subdural hematoma, Sweet syndrome, syncope, tachycardia, telangiectasia (gastric antral), thrombocythemia, thrombosis, tinnitus, toxic epidermal necrolysis, tremor, tumor hemorrhage (GIST), tumor lysis syndrome, urinary tract infection, urticaria, vertigo, vesicular eruption, vitreous hemorrhage

General Dosage Range Dosage adjustment recommended in patients with hepatic or renal impairment, on concomitant therapy, and/or who develop toxicities

Oral:

Children ≥1 year and Adolescents: 340 mg/m^2/day in 1 to 2 divided doses (maximum: 600 mg daily)

Adults: 100 to 800 mg daily in 1 to 2 divided doses

Mechanism of Action Inhibits Bcr-Abl tyrosine kinase, the constitutive abnormal gene product of the Philadelphia chromosome in chronic myeloid leukemia (CML). Inhibition of this enzyme blocks proliferation and induces apoptosis in Bcr-Abl positive cell lines as well as in fresh leukemic cells in Philadelphia chromosome positive CML. Also inhibits tyrosine kinase for platelet-derived growth factor (PDGF), stem cell factor (SCF), c-Kit, and cellular events mediated by PDGF and SCF.

Pharmacodynamics/Kinetics

Half-life Elimination Adults: Parent drug: ~18 hours; N-desmethyl metabolite: ~40 hours; Children: Parent drug: ~15 hours

Time to Peak 2 to 4 hours

Pregnancy Considerations Adverse events have been observed in animal reproduction studies. Women of childbearing potential are advised not to become pregnant (female patients and female partners of male patients); highly effective contraception should be used during treatment and for 2 weeks after the last imatinib dose. Case reports of pregnancies while on therapy (both males and females) include reports of spontaneous abortion, minor abnormalities (hypospadias, pyloric stenosis, and small intestine rotation) at or shortly after birth, and other congenital abnormalities including skeletal malformations, hypoplastic lungs, exomphalos, kidney abnormalities, hydrocephalus, cerebellar hypoplasia, and cardiac defects.

Retrospective case reports of women with CML in complete hematologic response (CHR) with cytogenic response (partial or complete) who interrupted imatinib therapy due to pregnancy, demonstrated a loss of response in some patients while off treatment. At 18 months after treatment reinitiation following delivery, CHR was again achieved in all patients and cytogenic response was achieved in some patients. Cytogenetic response rates may not be at as high as compared to patients with 18 months of uninterrupted therapy (Ault 2006; Pye 2008).

Imiglucerase (i mi GLOO ser ace)

Brand Names: US Cerezyme

Brand Names: Canada Cerezyme

Pharmacologic Category Enzyme

Use

Gaucher disease:

U.S. labeling: Long-term enzyme replacement therapy for patients with type 1 Gaucher disease that results in at least one of the following: anemia, bone disease, hepatomegaly or splenomegaly, and thrombocytopenia

Canadian labeling: Long-term enzyme replacement therapy for patients with type 1 Gaucher disease or patients with type 3 Gaucher disease who display non-neurological manifestations (anemia, bone disease, hepatomegaly or splenomegaly, and thrombocytopenia) of the disease.

Local Anesthetic/Vasoconstrictor Precautions No information available to require special precautions

Effects on Dental Treatment No significant effects or complications reported

Effects on Bleeding No information available to require special precautions

Adverse Reactions

1% to 10%:

Cardiovascular: Tachycardia (<2%)

Central nervous system: Chills (<2%), dizziness (<2%), fatigue (<2%), headache (<2%)

Dermatologic: Pruritus (<2%), skin rash (<2%)

Gastrointestinal: Abdominal distress (<2%), diarrhea (<2%), nausea (<2%), vomiting (<2%)

Hypersensitivity: Hypersensitivity reaction (7%; symptoms may include angioedema, chest discomfort, cough, cyanosis, dyspnea, flushing, hypotension, paresthesia, pruritus, urticaria)

Neuromuscular & skeletal: Back pain (<2%)

Miscellaneous: Fever (<2%)

<1%, postmarketing, and/or case reports: Anaphylactoid reaction; burning sensation at injection site, cyanosis, peripheral edema, pneumonia, pulmonary hypertension, rigors, sterile abscess at injection site, swelling at injection site

General Dosage Range IV:

Children and Adolescents: Initial: 30 to 60 units/kg/dose every 2 weeks (Andersson 2005; Baldellou 2004; Charrow 2004)

Adults: Initial range: 2.5 units/kg 3 times weekly to 60 units/kg every 2 weeks

Mechanism of Action Imiglucerase is an analogue of glucocerebrosidase; it is produced by recombinant DNA technology using mammalian cell culture. Glucocerebrosidase is an enzyme deficient in Gaucher's disease. It is needed to catalyze the hydrolysis of glucocerebroside to glucose and ceramide.

Pharmacodynamics/Kinetics

Onset of Action Significant improvement in symptoms: Hepatosplenomegaly and hematologic abnormalities: Within 6 months; Improvement in bone mineralization: Noted at 80 to 104 weeks of therapy

Half-life Elimination 3.6 to 10.4 minutes

Pregnancy Risk Factor C

Pregnancy Considerations Animal reproduction studies have not been conducted; however, imiglucerase has been used safely during pregnancy based on available data (Sherer, 2003; Zimran, 2009). Doses of imiglucerase should be based on prepregnancy weight and adjusted as clinically indicated (Granovsky-Grisaru, 2011).

Imipenem and Cilastatin

(i mi PEN em & sye la STAT in)

Brand Names: US Primaxin I.V.

Brand Names: Canada Imipenem and Cilastatin for Injection; Imipenem and Cilastatin for Injection, USP; Primaxin; RAN-Imipenem-Cilastatin

Pharmacologic Category Antibiotic, Carbapenem

Use

Bacterial septicemia: Treatment of septicemia caused by *Enterococcus faecalis, Staphylococcus aureus* (penicillinase-producing), *Escherichia coli, Klebsiella* species, *Pseudomonas aeruginosa, Serratia* species, *Enterobacter* species, *Bacteroides* species (including *Bacteroides fragilis*).

Bone and joint infections: Treatment of bone and joint infections caused by *E. faecalis, S. aureus* (penicillinase-producing), *Staphylococcus epidermidis, Enterobacter* species, *P. aeruginosa*.

Endocarditis: Treatment of endocarditis caused by *S. aureus* (penicillinase-producing).

Gynecologic infections: Treatment of gynecologic infections caused by *E. faecalis; S. aureus* (penicillinase-producing), *S. epidermidis, Streptococcus agalactiae* (group B streptococci), *E. coli, Klebsiella* species, *Proteus* species, *Enterobacter* species, *Bifidobacterium* species, *Bacteroides* species (including *B. fragilis), Gardnerella vaginalis*; *Peptococcus* species, *Peptostreptococcus* species, *Propionibacterium* species.

Intra-abdominal infections: Treatment of intra-abdominal infections caused by *E. faecalis, S. aureus* (penicillinase-producing), *S. epidermidis, E. coli, Klebsiella* species, *Enterobacter* species, *Proteus* species, *Morganella morganii, P. aeruginosa, Citrobacter* species, *Clostridium* species, *Bacteroides* species (including *B. fragilis*), *Fusobacterium* species, *Peptococcus* species, *Peptostreptococcus* species, *Eubacterium* species, *Propionibacterium* species, *Bifidobacterium* species.

Lower respiratory tract infections: Treatment of lower respiratory tract infections caused by *S. aureus* (penicillinase-producing), *E. coli, Klebsiella* species, *Enterobacter* species, *Haemophilus influenzae, Haemophilus parainfluenzae, Acinetobacter* species, *Serratia marcescens*.

Skin and skin structure infections: Treatment of skin and skin structure infections caused by *E. faecalis, S. aureus* (penicillinase-producing), S. *epidermidis, E. coli, Klebsiella* species, *Enterobacter species, Proteus vulgaris, Providencia rettgeri, M. morganii, P. aeruginosa, Serratia* species, *Citrobacter* species, *Acinetobacter* species, *Bacteroides* species (including *B. fragilis*), *Fusobacterium* species, *Peptococcus* species, *Peptostreptococcus* species.

Urinary tract infections (complicated and uncomplicated): Treatment of uncomplicated and complicated urinary tract infections caused by *E. faecalis, S. aureus* (penicillinase-producing), *E. coli, Klebsiella* species, *Enterobacter* species, *P. vulgaris, Providencia rettgeri, M. morganii, P. aeruginosa.*

Limitations of use: Not indicated in patients with meningitis because safety and efficacy have not been established; not recommend in pediatric patients with CNS infections because of the risk of seizures.

Local Anesthetic/Vasoconstrictor Precautions No information available to require special precautions

Effects on Dental Treatment No significant effects or complications reported

Effects on Bleeding No information available to require special precautions

Adverse Reactions

>10%

Hematologic & oncologic: Decreased hematocrit (infants and children 3 months to 12 years: 10%; neonates and infants <3 months: 2%), decreased hemoglobin (infants and children 3 months to 12 years: 15%), eosinophilia (neonates, infants, and children to 12 years: 9% to 13%), thrombocythemia (infants and children 3 months to 12 years: 13%; neonates and infants <3 months: 4%)

Hepatic: Increased serum AST (infants and children 3 months to 12 years: 18%; neonates and infants <3 months: 6%), increased serum ALT (infants and children 3 months to 12 years: 11%; neonates and infants <3 months: 3%)

1% to 10%:

Cardiovascular: Phlebitis (2% to 3%), tachycardia (neonates and infants ≤3 months: 2%; adults <1%)

Central nervous system: Seizure (neonates and infants ≤3 months: 6%; adults <1%)

Dermatologic: Skin rash (≤2%)

Gastrointestinal: Diarrhea (neonates, infants, and children to 12 years: 3% to 4%; adults 2%), nausea (2%), oral candidiasis (neonates and infants ≤3 months: 2%), vomiting (≤1% to 2%), gastroenteritis (≤1%)

Genitourinary: Proteinuria (infants and children 3 months to 12 years: 8%), urine discoloration (≤1%), oliguria (neonates and infants ≤3 months: 2%; adults <1%)

Hematologic & oncologic: Neutropenia (infants and children 3 months to 12 years: 3%; adults <1%), decreased platelet count (neonates and infants <3 months: 2%), increased hematocrit (neonates and infants <3 months: 1%)

Hepatic: Increased serum alkaline phosphatase (neonates and infants <3 months: 3%), increased serum bilirubin (neonates and infants <3 months: 3%), decreased serum bilirubin (neonates and infants <3 months: 1%)

Local: Irritation at injection site (infants, children, and adolescents 3 months to 16 years: 1%)

Renal: Increased serum creatinine (neonates and infants <3 months: 5%)

<1%, postmarketing and/or case reports: Abdominal pain, acute renal failure, agitation, agranulocytosis, anaphylaxis, angioedema, back pain (thoracic spinal), basophilia, bilirubinuria, bone marrow depression, brain disease, candidiasis, casts in urine, change in prothrombin time, chest discomfort, *Clostridium difficile* associated diarrhea, confusion, cyanosis, decreased serum sodium, dental discoloration, dizziness, drowsiness, drug fever, dysgeusia, dyskinesia, dyspnea, erythema at injection site, erythema multiforme, fever, flushing, glossitis, hallucination, headache, hearing loss, heartburn, hematuria, hemolytic anemia, hemorrhagic colitis, hepatic failure, hepatitis (including fulminant onset), hyperchloremia, hyperhidrosis, hypersensitivity, hyperventilation, hypotension, increased blood urea nitrogen, increased lactate dehydrogenase, increased monocytes, increased serum potassium, increased urinary urobilinogen, induration at injection site, injection site infection, jaundice, leukocytosis, leukocyturia, leukopenia, lymphocytosis, myoclonus, neutropenia, pain at injection site, palpitations, pancytopenia, paresthesia, polyarthralgia, polyuria, positive direct Coombs' test, pruritus, pruritus vulvae, pseudomembranous colitis, pseudomonas infection (resistant *P. aeruginosa*), psychiatric disturbances, sialorrhea, skin changes (texture), sore throat, Stevens-Johnson syndrome, thrombocytopenia, tinnitus, tongue changes (papillar hypertrophy), tongue discoloration, toxic epidermal necrolysis, tremor, urticaria, vertigo, weakness

General Dosage Range Dosage adjustment recommended in patients with renal impairment.

IV:

Infants ≥3 months, Children, and Adolescents: 15 to 25 mg/kg every 6 hours (maximum dose: 4 g/day)

Adults: 500 to 1,000 mg every 6 hours or 1,000 mg every 8 hours (maximum dose: 4 g/day)

Mechanism of Action Inhibits bacterial cell wall synthesis by binding to one or more of the penicillin-binding proteins (PBPs); which in turn inhibits the final transpeptidation step of peptidoglycan synthesis in bacterial cell walls, thus inhibiting cell wall biosynthesis. Bacteria eventually lyse due to ongoing activity of cell wall autolytic enzymes (autolysins and murein hydrolases) while cell wall assembly is arrested. Cilastatin prevents renal metabolism of imipenem by competitive inhibition of dehydropeptidase along the brush border of the renal tubules.

Pharmacodynamics/Kinetics

Half-life Elimination IV: Both drugs: Prolonged with renal impairment:

Neonates: Imipenem: 1.7 to 2.4 hours; Cilastatin: 3.9 to 6.3 hours (Freij 1985)

Infants and Children: Imipenem: 1.2 hours (Blumer 1996)

Adults: ~60 minutes

Pregnancy Risk Factor C

Pregnancy Considerations Adverse events have not been observed in animal reproduction studies. Due to pregnancy induced physiologic changes, some pharmacokinetic parameters of imipenem/cilastatin may be altered. Pregnant women have a larger volume of distribution resulting in lower serum peak levels than for the same dose in nonpregnant women. Clearance is also increased.

Imipramine (im IP ra meen)

Related Information

Vasoconstrictor Interactions With Antidepressants *on page 1913*

Brand Names: US Tofranil; Tofranil-PM [DSC]

Brand Names: Canada Impril; Novo-Pramine; PMS Imipramine

Pharmacologic Category Antidepressant, Tricyclic (Tertiary Amine)

Use

Childhood enuresis: As temporary adjunctive therapy in reducing enuresis in children ≥6 years of age, after possible organic causes have been excluded by appropriate tests

Depression: Treatment of depression

Local Anesthetic/Vasoconstrictor Precautions Use with caution; epinephrine and levonordefrin have been shown to have an increased pressor response in combination with TCAs. Imipramine is one of the drugs confirmed to prolong the QT interval and is accepted as having a risk of causing torsade de pointes. The risk of drug-induced torsade de pointes is extremely low when a single QT interval prolonging drug is prescribed. In terms of epinephrine, it is not known what effect vasoconstrictors in the local anesthetic regimen will have in patients with a known history of congenital prolonged QT interval or in patients taking any medication that prolongs the QT interval. Until more information is obtained, it is suggested that the clinician consult with the physician prior to the use of a vasoconstrictor in suspected patients, and that the vasoconstrictor (epinephrine, mepivacaine and levonordefrin [Carbocaine® 2% with Neo-Cobefrin®]) be used with caution.

Effects on Dental Treatment Key adverse event(s) related to dental treatment: Xerostomia and changes in salivation (normal salivary flow resumes upon discontinuation). Long-term treatment with TCAs, such as imipramine, increases the risk of caries by reducing salivation and salivary buffer capacity. In a study by Rundergren, et al, pathological alterations were observed in the oral mucosa of 72% of 58 patients; 55% had new carious lesions after taking TCAs for a median of 5 1/2 years. Current research is investigating the use of the salivary stimulant pilocarpine to overcome the xerostomia from imipramine.

Effects on Bleeding No information available to require special precautions

Adverse Reactions Reported for tricyclic antidepressants in general. Frequency not defined.

Cardiovascular: Cardiac arrhythmia, cardiac failure, cerebrovascular accident, ECG changes, heart block, hypertension, myocardial infarction, orthostatic hypotension, palpitations, tachycardia

Central nervous system: Agitation, anxiety, ataxia, confusion, delusions, disorientation, dizziness, drowsiness, EEG pattern changes, extrapyramidal reaction, falling, fatigue, hallucination, headache, hypomania, insomnia, nightmares, numbness, paresthesia, peripheral neuropathy, psychosis, restlessness, seizure, taste disorder, tingling sensation

Dermatologic: Alopecia, diaphoresis, pruritus, skin photosensitivity, skin rash, urticaria

Endocrine & metabolic: Decreased libido, decreased serum glucose, galactorrhea, gynecomastia, increased libido, increased serum glucose, SIADH, weight gain, weight loss

Gastrointestinal: Abdominal cramps, anorexia, constipation, diarrhea, epigastric distress, intestinal obstruction, melanoglossia, nausea, stomatitis, sublingual adenitis, vomiting, xerostomia

Genitourinary: Breast hypertrophy, impotence, testicular swelling, urinary hesitancy, urinary retention, urinary tract dilation

Hematologic & oncologic: Agranulocytosis, eosinophilia, petechia, purpura, thrombocytopenia

Hepatic: Cholestatic jaundice, increased serum transaminases

Hypersensitivity: Hypersensitivity (eg, drug fever, edema)

Neuromuscular & skeletal: Tremor, weakness

Ophthalmic: Accommodation disturbance, angle-closure glaucoma, blurred vision, mydriasis

Otic: Tinnitus

General Dosage Range Oral:

Children ≥6-12 years: Initial: 25 mg at bedtime, may increase to 50 mg at bedtime if no response (maximum: 2.5 mg/kg/day; 50 mg daily)

Children >12 years: Initial: 25 mg at bedtime, may increase to 75 mg at bedtime if not response (maximum: 75 mg daily) **or** 30-40 mg daily, increase gradually, to a maximum of 100 mg daily in single or divided doses

Adults: Initial: 75-150 mg daily, increase gradually to a maximum of 200 mg daily (outpatients) or 300 mg daily (inpatients) in divided doses or a single dose at bedtime

Elderly: Initial: 25-50 mg at bedtime (maximum: 100 mg daily)

Mechanism of Action Traditionally believed to increase the synaptic concentration of serotonin and/or norepinephrine in the central nervous system by inhibition of their reuptake by the presynaptic neuronal membrane. However, additional receptor effects have been found including desensitization of adenyl cyclase, down regulation of beta-adrenergic receptors, and down regulation of serotonin receptors.

Pharmacodynamics/Kinetics

Onset of Action Depression: Individual responses vary, however 4-8 weeks of treatment is needed before determining if a patient is partially or nonresponsive (APA 2010).

Half-life Elimination 8-21 hours (Salle 1990); Mean: Children: 11 hours; Adults: 16-17 hours; Desipramine (active metabolite): 22-28 hours

Time to Peak Serum: 2-6 hours (Sallee 1990)

Pregnancy Considerations Animal reproduction studies are inconclusive. Congenital abnormalities have been reported in humans; however, a causal relationship has not been established. Tricyclic antidepressants may be associated with irritability, jitteriness, and convulsions (rare) in the neonate (Yonkers 2009). Due to pregnancy-induced physiologic changes, women who are pregnant may require dose adjustments late in pregnancy to achieve euthymia (Altshuler 1996).

The ACOG recommends that therapy for depression during pregnancy be individualized; treatment should incorporate the clinical expertise of the mental health clinician, obstetrician, primary health care provider, and pediatrician (ACOG 2008). According to the American Psychiatric Association (APA), the risks of medication treatment should be weighed against other treatment options and untreated depression. For women who discontinue antidepressant medications during pregnancy and who may be at high risk for postpartum depression, the medications can be restarted following delivery (APA 2010). Treatment algorithms have been developed by the ACOG and the APA for the management of depression in women prior to conception and during pregnancy (Yonkers 2009).

Pregnant women exposed to antidepressants during pregnancy are encouraged to enroll in the National Pregnancy Registry for Antidepressants (NPRAD). Women 18 to 45 years of age or their health care providers may contact the registry by calling 844-405-6185. Enrollment should be done as early in pregnancy as possible.

Dental Comment See Local Anesthetic/Vasoconstrictor Precautions

Imiquimod (i mi KWI mod)

Related Information

Systemic Viral Diseases *on page 1806*

Viral Infections *on page 1849*

Brand Names: US Aldara; Zyclara; Zyclara Pump

Brand Names: Canada Aldara P; Apo-Imiquimod; Vyloma; Zyclara

Generic Availability (US) Yes

Pharmacologic Category Skin and Mucous Membrane Agent; Topical Skin Product

Use

Aldara: Treatment of external genital and perianal warts/condyloma acuminata; nonhyperkeratotic, nonhypertrophic actinic keratosis on face or scalp; superficial basal cell carcinoma (sBCC) with a maximum tumor diameter of 2 cm located on the trunk (excluding anogenital skin), neck, or extremities (excluding hands or feet)

Vyloma (Canadian availability; not available in the US): Treatment of external genital and perianal warts/condyloma acuminata

Zyclara:

US labeling: Treatment of external genital and perianal warts/condyloma acuminata (3.75% formulation), treatment of clinically typical visible or palpable, actinic keratoses on face or scalp (2.5% or 3.75% formulation)

Canadian labeling: Treatment of clinically typical visible or palpable, actinic keratoses on face or scalp

Local Anesthetic/Vasoconstrictor Precautions No information available to require special precautions

Effects on Dental Treatment No significant effects or complications reported

Effects on Bleeding No information available to require special precautions

Adverse Reactions Note: Frequency of reactions vary and are related to the degree of inflammation associated with the treated disease, number of weekly applications, product formulation, and individual sensitivity.

>10%:

Dermatologic: Localized erythema (58% to 100%; remote: 2%), xeroderma (local; including flaking, scaling; 18% to 93%; remote: 1%), crusted skin (local; 4% to 93%), skin sclerosis (local; 5% to 84%), dermal ulcer (local; 4% to 62%; remote: 2%), localized vesiculation (2% to 31%), excoriation (local; remote: 1%)

Infection: Fungal infection (2% to 11%)

Local: Localized edema (12% to 78%; remote: 1%), application site discharge (22% to 51%), local pruritus (3% to 32%), localized burning (9% to 26%)

Respiratory: Upper respiratory tract infection (15% to 33%)

1% to 10%:

Cardiovascular: Chest pain, localized blanching

Central nervous system: Headache (2% to 6%), fatigue (1% to 4%), dizziness (<1% to 3%), local discomfort (soreness; ≤3%), rigors (1%), anxiety, pain, tingling of skin (local)
Dermatologic: Skin pain (local; 1% to 8%), skin hypertrophy (local; 3%), skin infection (local; 1% to 3%), eczema (2%), cheilitis (≤2%), alopecia (1%), dermal hemorrhage (local), localized rash, papule (local), seborrhoeic keratosis, skin tenderness (local), stinging of the skin (local), tinea (cruris)
Endocrine & metabolic: Increased serum glucose
Gastrointestinal: Nausea (1% to 4%), diarrhea (1% to 3%), anorexia (≤3%), vomiting (1%), dyspepsia
Genitourinary: Bacterial vaginosis (3%), urinary tract infection (1%)
Hematologic & oncologic: Squamous cell carcinoma (4%), lymphadenopathy (2% to 3%)
Infection: Herpes simplex (≤3%)
Local: Local irritation (3% to 6%)
Neuromuscular & skeletal: Arthralgia (1% to 3%), myalgia (≥1%), back pain
Respiratory: Sinusitis (7%), flu-like symptoms (<1% to 4%), cough, pharyngitis, rhinitis
Miscellaneous: Fever (≤3%)

Postmarketing and/or case reports: Abdominal pain, acute exacerbations of multiple sclerosis, agitation, anemia, angioedema, atrial fibrillation, capillary leak syndrome, cardiac failure, cardiomyopathy, cellulitis (local), cerebrovascular accident, chills, depression, dermatitis, dyspnea, dysuria, erythema multiforme, erythema (scrotal), exacerbation of psoriasis, exacerbation of ulcerative colitis, exfoliative dermatitis, febrile seizures, Henoch-Schönlein purpura (IgA vasculitis), hepatic insufficiency, herpes zoster, hyperpigmentation, immune thrombocytopenia (ITP), insomnia, ischemia, lethargy, leukopenia, malignant lymphoma, myocardial infarction, pain (scrotal), palpitations, pancytopenia, paresis, proteinuria, psoriasis, pulmonary edema, scrotal edema, seizure, squamous cell carcinoma, supraventricular tachycardia, syncope, tachycardia, thrombocytopenia, thyroiditis, ulcerative colitis, ulcer (scrotal), urinary retention, urticaria, vertebral disk disease (spondylitis onset or exacerbated)

Dosing

Adult & Geriatric Note: Imiquimod treatment should not be prolonged beyond recommended period due to missed doses or rest periods.

U.S. labeling:

Perianal warts/condyloma acuminata: Topical:

Aldara: Apply a thin layer 3 times/week on alternative days prior to bedtime and leave on skin for 6-10 hours. Remove by washing with mild soap and water. Continue imiquimod treatment until there is total clearance of the genital/perianal warts or a maximum duration of therapy of 16 weeks.

Zyclara 3.75%: Apply a thin layer using up to 1 packet or 1 full actuation of pump once daily prior to bedtime and leave on skin for ~8 hours. Remove with mild soap and water. Continue treatment until there is total clearance of the warts or a maximum duration of therapy of 8 weeks. Patient should not receive more than 56 packets or 2 x 7.5 g pumps or 1 x 15 g pump per course of treatment.

Actinic keratosis: Topical: **Note:** Prescribed course of therapy should be completed even if all lesions appear to be gone. Safety and efficacy of repeated use in a previously treated area has not been established.

Aldara: Treatment should be limited to areas ≤25 cm^2; apply 2 times/week for 16 weeks to a treatment area on face or scalp (but not both concurrently); no more than 1 packet should be applied at each application and no more than 36 packets applied per 16 weeks; apply prior to bedtime and leave on skin for ~8 hours. Remove with mild soap and water.

Zyclara 2.5%, 3.75%: Treatment consists of 2 cycles (14 days each) separated by 1 rest period (14 days) with no treatment. Apply up to 2 packets or 2 full actuations of pump once daily at bedtime to affected area on either face or balding scalp (but not both concurrently); leave on skin for ~8 hours. Remove with mild soap and water. Patient should not receive more than 56 packets or 2 x 7.5 g pumps or 1 x 15 g pump per 2 cycles of treatment.

Superficial basal cell carcinoma: Topical: Aldara: Apply once daily prior to bedtime, 5 days/week for 6 weeks. No more than 36 packets should be used during the 6-week treatment period. Tumor treatment area should not exceed 3 cm (maximum of 2 cm tumor diameter plus a 1 cm margin of skin around the tumor). The diameter of cream droplet applied should range from 4 mm to 7 mm for tumor areas of 0.5 cm to 2 cm, respectively. Leave on skin for ~8 hours. Remove with mild soap and water. Safety and efficacy of repeated use in a previously treated area have not been established.

Canadian labeling:

Actinic keratosis: Topical: **Note:** Prescribed course of therapy should be completed even if all lesions appear to be gone; safety and efficacy of repeated use in a previously treated area have not been established.

Aldara: Treatment should be limited to areas ≤25 cm^2; apply 2 times/week for 16 weeks to a treatment area on face or scalp (but not both concurrently); no more than 1 packet should be applied at each application; apply prior to bedtime and leave on skin for ~8 hours. Remove with mild soap and water.

Zyclara: Treatment should be limited to an area <200 cm^2 on the face or scalp and consists of 2 cycles (14 days each) separated by 1 rest period (14 days) with no treatment. Apply up to 2 packets or 2 full actuations of pump once daily at bedtime to affected area on either face or balding scalp (but not both concurrently). Leave on skin for ~8 hours. Remove with mild soap and water. Patient should not receive more than 56 packets or 2 x 7.5 g pumps or 1 x 15 g pump per 2 cycles of treatment.

External genital and/or perianal warts/condyloma acuminata: Topical:

Aldara: Apply a thin layer 3 times/week prior to bedtime and leave on skin for 6-10 hours. Remove with mild soap and water. Examples of 3 times/week application schedules are: Monday, Wednesday, Friday; or Tuesday, Thursday, Saturday. Continue treatment until there is total clearance of the warts or a maximum duration of therapy of 16 weeks.

Vyloma: Apply a thin layer once daily prior to bedtime and leave on skin for ~8 hours. Remove with mild soap and water. Continue treatment until there is total clearance of the warts or maximum duration of therapy of 8 weeks.

Superficial basal cell carcinoma: Topical: Aldara: Apply once daily prior to bedtime, 5 days/week for 6 weeks. Tumor treatment area should not exceed 3 cm (maximum of 2 cm tumor diameter plus a 1 cm margin of skin around the tumor). The diameter of cream droplet applied should range from 4 mm to 7 mm for tumor areas of 0.5 cm to 2 cm, respectively. Leave on skin for ~8 hours. Remove with mild soap and water. Safety and efficacy of repeated use in a previously treated area have not been established.

Common warts (off-label use): Topical (5% cream): Apply once daily prior to bedtime for 5 days/week for up to 16 weeks (Hengge, 2000) or apply twice daily for up to 24 weeks (Grussendorf-Conen, 2002)

Herpes simplex virus (HSV) infection, acyclovir-resistant (off-label use): Apply to lesions once daily for 5 consecutive days (CDC [Workowski 2015])

Pediatric External genital and perianal warts/condyloma acuminata: Topical: Aldara: Children ≥12 years: Refer to adult dosing.

Renal Impairment There are no dosage adjustments provided in the manufacturer's labeling.

Hepatic Impairment There are no dosage adjustments provided in the manufacturer's labeling.

Adjustment for Toxicity

Local skin reactions (eg, erythema, edema, scabbing, etc): Temporarily interrupt treatment for up to several days for severe or intolerable reactions; may consider resuming therapy once reaction subsides.

Systemic/flu-like reactions (eg, malaise, fever, rigors, etc): Consider temporary interruption of therapy.

Vulvar swelling: Interrupt or discontinue therapy for severe vulvar swelling.

Mechanism of Action Precise mechanism of action is unknown; Toll-like receptor 7 agonist that induces cytokines, including interferon-alpha and others

Contraindications

U.S. labeling: There are no contraindications listed within the approved manufacturer's labeling.

Canadian labeling: Hypersensitivity to imiquimod or any component of the formulation

Warnings/Precautions Imiquimod is not intended for oral, nasal, intravaginal, or ophthalmic use. Topical imiquimod administration is not recommended until tissue is healed from any previous drug or surgical treatment. Treatment should not be prolonged beyond recommended period due to missed doses or rest periods. Imiquimod has the potential to exacerbate inflammatory conditions of the skin (including chronic graft-versus-host disease). Intense inflammatory reactions may occur, and may be accompanied by systemic symptoms (fever, malaise, myalgia); interruption of therapy should be considered. Severe inflammation of female external genitalia following topical application may lead to severe vulvar swelling and urinary retention; interruption or discontinuation of therapy may be necessary.

May increase sunburn susceptibility; in an animal study, topical imiquimod administration and concurrent ultraviolet radiation decreased the median time to skin tumor formation. Patients should protect themselves from the sun and artificial forms of sunlight. Safety and efficacy have not been established for immunosuppressed patients, or for basal cell nevus syndrome or xeroderma pigmentosum. Following 2 randomized, double-blind, placebo-controlled trials, efficacy of imiquimod was not established for molluscum contagiosum in children 2-12 years of age. Use with caution in patients with preexisting autoimmune disorders (onset or exacerbation of disease has been reported rarely with imiquimod).

Basal cell carcinoma: Use in basal cell carcinoma should be limited to superficial carcinomas with a maximum diameter of 2 cm. Safety and efficacy in treatment of sBCC lesions of the face, head, and anogenital area, or other subtypes of basal cell carcinoma (including nodular and morpheaform), have not been established.

Actinic keratosis: Safety and efficacy of repeated use of Aldara or Zyclara in a previously treated area have not been established. Prescribed course of therapy should be completed even if all lesions appear to be gone.

Genital warts: Safety and efficacy of Zyclara 2.75% in the treatment of external genital warts have not been established. Imiquimod has not been evaluated for the treatment of urethral, intravaginal, cervical, rectal, or intra-anal human papilloma viral disease and is not recommended for these conditions.

Drug Interactions

Metabolism/Transport Effects Substrate of CYP1A2 (minor), CYP3A4 (minor); **Note:** Assignment of Major/Minor substrate status based on clinically relevant drug interaction potential

Avoid Concomitant Use

Avoid concomitant use of Imiquimod with any of the following: BCG (Intravesical); Natalizumab; Pimecrolimus; Tacrolimus (Topical); Tofacitinib; Vaccines (Live)

Increased Effect/Toxicity

Imiquimod may increase the levels/effects of: Fingolimod; Leflunomide; Natalizumab; Tofacitinib; Vaccines (Live)

The levels/effects of Imiquimod may be increased by: Denosumab; Ocrelizumab; Pimecrolimus; Roflumilast; Tacrolimus (Topical); Trastuzumab

Decreased Effect

Imiquimod may decrease the levels/effects of: BCG (Intravesical); Coccidioides immitis Skin Test; Nivolumab; Sipuleucel-T; Tertomotide; Vaccines (Inactivated); Vaccines (Live)

The levels/effects of Imiquimod may be decreased by: Echinacea

Pharmacodynamics/Kinetics

Time to Peak 9-12 hours

Pregnancy Risk Factor C

Pregnancy Considerations Adverse events were observed in some animal reproduction studies following oral administration. Imiquimod may weaken condoms and vaginal diaphragms. Imiquimod appears to pose a low risk, but use in pregnant women should be avoided until additional data are available (CDC [Workowski 2015]).

Breastfeeding Considerations It is not known if imiquimod is excreted in breast milk. The manufacturer recommends that caution be exercised when administering imiquimod to nursing women.

Dosage Forms

Cream, External:

Aldara: 5% (12 ea)
Zyclara: 3.75% (28 ea)
Zyclara Pump: 2.5% (7.5 g); 3.75% (7.5 g)
Generic: 5% (1 ea, 12 ea, 24 ea)

Dosage Forms: Canada

Cream, topical:

Vyloma: 3.75% (28s)

Dental Comment Imiquimod cream 5% has been used for actinic cheilitis or keratosis. Imiquimod 2.5% and

3.75% cream is FDA approved to treat actinic keratosis. Adverse events of erosion/ulcerations have been reported with topical use. Imiquimod use in the treatment of oral papilloma virus remains inadequately studied.

Immune Globulin (i MYUN GLOB yoo lin)

Related Information

Systemic Viral Diseases *on page 1806*

Brand Names: US Bivigam; Carimune NF; Cuvitru; Flebogamma DIF; GamaSTAN S/D; Gammagard; Gammagard S/D Less IgA; Gammagard S/D [DSC]; Gammaked; Gammaplex; Gamunex-C; Hizentra; Hyqvia; Octagam; Privigen

Brand Names: Canada Gamastan S/D; Gammagard Liquid; Gammagard S/D; Gamunex; Hizentra; IGIVnex; Octagam 10%; Panzyga; Privigen

Generic Availability (US) No

Pharmacologic Category Blood Product Derivative; Immune Globulin

Use

Chronic inflammatory demyelinating polyneuropathy: Treatment of chronic inflammatory demyelinating polyneuropathy (CIDP) (Gammaked, Gamunex-C)

Chronic lymphocytic leukemia: Prevention of bacterial infection in patients with hypogammaglobulinemia and/or recurrent bacterial infections with B-cell chronic lymphocytic leukemia (CLL) (Gammagard S/D)

Immune thrombocytopenia:

Treatment of acute immune thrombocytopenia (ITP) (Carimune NF, Gammagard S/D, Gammaked, Gamunex-C).

Treatment of chronic ITP (Carimune NF, Flebogamma DIF 10%, Gammagard S/D, Gammaked, Gammaplex, Gamunex-C, Octagam 10%, Panzyga [Canadian product]), Privigen

Immunodeficiency syndromes: Treatment of primary humoral immunodeficiency syndromes (congenital agammaglobulinemia, severe combined immunodeficiency syndromes [SCIDS], common variable immunodeficiency, X-linked agammaglobulinemia, Wiskott-Aldrich syndrome) (Bivigam, Carimune NF, Cuvitru, Flebogamma DIF, HyQvia, Gammagard Liquid, Gammagard S/D, Gammaked, Gammaplex, Gamunex-C, Hizentra, Octagam 5%, Panzyga [Canadian product], Privigen); Treatment of secondary immunodeficiency (Panzyga [Canadian product])

Kawasaki syndrome: Prevention of coronary artery aneurysms associated with Kawasaki syndrome (in combination with aspirin) (Gammagard S/D)

Multifocal motor neuropathy: Treatment of multifocal motor neuropathy (MMN) (Gammagard Liquid)

Passive immunity: Provision of passive immunity in the following susceptible individuals (GamaSTAN S/D):

Hepatitis A: Pre-exposure prophylaxis; postexposure: within 14 days and/or prior to manifestation of disease

Measles: For use within 6 days of exposure in an unvaccinated person, who has not previously had measles

Rubella: Postexposure prophylaxis to reduce the risk of infection and fetal damage in exposed pregnant women who will not consider therapeutic abortion

Varicella: For immunosuppressed patients when varicella zoster immune globulin is not available

Local Anesthetic/Vasoconstrictor Precautions No information available to require special precautions

Effects on Dental Treatment No significant effects or complications reported

Effects on Bleeding No information available to require special precautions

Adverse Reactions Adverse effects are reported as class effects rather than for specific products. Adverse effects occur with intravenous administration unless otherwise specified. Some clinical trials were extremely small and skewed the incidence upward ("≤" indicates this trend).

>10%

Cardiovascular: Hypotension (≤14%; children and adolescents: 25%), tachycardia (5%; children and adolescents: 25%), decreased diastolic blood pressure (5%; children and adolescents: 21%), decreased heart rate (16%)

Central nervous system: Headache (2% to 75%; children and adolescents: 42%; subcutaneous: 13% to 21%), fatigue (6% to 29%; subcutaneous: 11%), chills (5% to 19%), pain (5% to 15%), rigors (7% to 13%), dizziness (≤13%)

Dermatologic: Injection site pruritus (2% to 45%), ecchymosis (≤40%)

Gastrointestinal: Sore throat (11% to 35%), abdominal pain (6% to ≤33%; children and adolescents: 8%), diarrhea (5% to 28%; children and adolescents: 8%), vomiting (≤26%; children and adolescents: 8%; subcutaneous: 7%), nausea (5% to 22%; children and adolescents: 8%; subcutaneous: 7%), upper abdominal pain (6% to 20%; children and adolescents: ≤15%)

Hematologic & oncologic: Positive direct Coombs test (≤47%), purpura (≤40%), hemorrhage (29%), petechiae (21%), thrombocytopenia (15%), anemia (6% to 11%)

Hepatic: Increased serum ALT (all elevations were transient and generally mild: ≤18%, children and adolescents, >2.5 x ULN: ≤7%; subcutaneous: ≤3%), increased serum alkaline phosphatase (subcutaneous: ≤13%; mild and transient), hyperbilirubinemia (unconjugated: 11%; conjugated: 9%; total: 5%)

Immunologic: Antibody development (subcutaneous: 18%; non-neutralizing antibodies to recombinant human hyaluronidase)

Local: Pain at injection site (injection/infusion site: ≤21%), erythema at injection site (3% to 21%), infusion site reaction (6% to 13%; subcutaneous: 75%)

Neuromuscular and skeletal: Arthralgia (<5% to 20%; subcutaneous: 6%), limb pain (intravenous/subcutaneous: 6% to 15%), muscle cramps (≤14%), back pain (5% to 11%)

Otic: Otalgia (9% to 18%; subcutaneous: 6%)

Renal: Nephrolithiasis (≤16%)

Respiratory: Cough (6% to 54%), nasal congestion (≤52%), rhinitis (5% to 51%), sinusitis (≤50%), pharyngitis (5% to 41%), asthma (9% to 29%; including exacerbation), upper respiratory tract infection (8% to 25%), epistaxis (7% to 23%), bronchitis (5% to 22%), nasopharyngitis (17%), rhinorrhea (7% to 17%), sinus congestion (15%), nasal mucosa swelling (≤13%), wheezing (9% to 11%)

Miscellaneous: Fever (10% to 33%; subcutaneous: 6% to 7%), accidental injury (13%)

1% to 10%

Cardiovascular: Chest pain (≤9%), hypertension (≤9%), peripheral edema (8%), cardiac arrest (≤8%; Octagam: 5%), heart murmur (7%), chest discomfort (≤7%), flushing (6%), thrombosis (≤2%)

Central nervous system: Insomnia (9%), migraine (5% to 7%), lethargy (≤6%), fibromyalgia syndrome (exacerbation: 5%), malaise (≤5%), vertigo (≤5%)
Dermatologic: Skin rash (5% to 10%), urticaria (5% to 8%; may be transient), cellulitis (≤8%), hyperhidrosis (6%), eczema (≤5%; may be transient), xeroderma (≤5%)
Endocrine & metabolic: Ketonuria (≤8%; Octagam: 5%), dehydration (≤6%), increased lactate dehydrogenase (5%)
Gastrointestinal: Dyspepsia (6% to 9%), gastroenteritis (≤8%), pseudomembranous colitis (≤8%), gastritis (6%), stomach discomfort (6%)
Genitourinary: Vulvovaginal candidiasis (9%), urinary tract infection (≤9%), cystitis (≤5%), dysuria (≤5%)
Hematologic & oncologic: Decreased hematocrit (5%)
Hepatic: Increased serum AST (intravenous/subcutaneous: ≤9%), decreased serum alkaline phosphatase (subcutaneous: ≤3%)
Infection: Fungal infection (7% to 9%), influenza (5%), coxsackievirus (≤2%)
Local: Local swelling (at injection/infusion site: ≤8%), local inflammation (at infusion site: 7%)
Neuromuscular & skeletal: Weakness (≤10%), myalgia (≤8%), muscle spasm (7%), myasthenia (7%), neck pain (6%), joint effusion (≤6%), joint swelling (≤6%)
Ophthalmic: Conjunctivitis (9%), eye discharge (7%), eye irritation (7%)
Otic: Otitis media (7% to 8%)
Renal: Increased serum creatinine (9%)
Respiratory: Exacerbation of asthma (7% to 9%), tonsil disease (children: 8%), dyspnea (7% to 8%), pharyngolaryngeal pain (5% to 8%), pneumonia (≤8%), oropharyngeal pain (6% to 7%), post nasal drip (7%), throat irritation (7%), flu-like symptoms (6%)
Miscellaneous: Positive culture (≤8%)

Frequency not defined:
Cardiovascular: Facial flushing
Central nervous system: Drowsiness
Hematologic & oncologic: Hematoma
Local: Localized tenderness (intramuscular), local pain (intramuscular/subcutaneous)
Neuromuscular & skeletal: Leg cramps
Ophthalmic: Blurred vision
Renal: Increased blood urea nitrogen

<1%, postmarketing, and/or case reports: Acute renal disease, acute renal failure, acute respiratory distress, agitation, allergic dermatitis, alopecia, altered blood pressure, anaphylactic shock, anaphylactoid reaction, anaphylaxis, angioedema, anorexia, anxiety, apnea, arterial thrombosis, aseptic meningitis, bradycardia, bronchospasm, bullous dermatitis, burning sensation, cerebrovascular accident, chest tightness, circulatory shock, coma, cyanosis, deep vein thrombosis, dermatitis, disseminated intravascular coagulation (intravenous, subcutaneous, intramuscular; FDA Safety Communication, November 13, 2012), edema, epidermolysis, erythema (may be transient), erythema multiforme, erythematous rash, exacerbation of autoimmune pure red cell aplasia, eye pain, facial edema, hematuria, hemoglobinuria, hemolysis (may be mild), hemolytic anemia (may be delayed), hepatic insufficiency, hepatitis (non-infectious), hypersensitivity reaction, hyperventilation, hypervolemia, hypoxemia, jaundice, laryngospasm, leukopenia, loss of consciousness, lymphadenopathy, muscle rigidity, musculoskeletal pain, myocardial infarction, osmotic nephrosis, oxygen saturation decreased, pallor, palpitations, pancytopenia, paresthesia, peripheral vascular insufficiency, pharyngeal edema, phlebitis, photophobia, proximal tubular nephropathy, pulmonary edema, pulmonary embolism, renal failure, renal insufficiency, renal tubular necrosis, respiratory distress, respiratory failure, restlessness, retinal thrombosis, seizure, Stevens-Johnson syndrome, syncope, thromboembolism, thrombophlebitis, transfusion-related acute lung injury, transient ischemic attacks, tremor, urine discoloration, vena cava thrombosis, visual impairment

Dosing

Adult Note: Some clinicians may administer IGIV formulations FDA approved only for intravenous administration as a subcutaneous infusion based on clinical judgment and patient tolerability.

B-cell chronic lymphocytic leukemia (CLL) with hypogammaglobulinemia, prevention of bacterial infections (Gammagard S/D): IV: 400 mg/kg every 3 to 4 weeks

Chronic inflammatory demyelinating polyneuropathy (CIDP) (Gammaked, Gamunex-C): IV: Loading dose: 2,000 mg/kg (in divided doses over 2 to 4 consecutive days); Maintenance: 1,000 mg/kg administered over 1 day every 3 weeks. Alternatively, administer 500 mg/kg/day for 2 consecutive days every 3 weeks.

Hepatitis A (GamaSTAN S/D): IM:

Preexposure prophylaxis upon travel into endemic areas (hepatitis A vaccine preferred):
0.02 **mL**/kg for anticipated risk of exposure <3 months
0.06 **mL**/kg for anticipated risk of exposure ≥3 months; repeat every 4 to 6 months

Postexposure prophylaxis: 0.02 **mL**/kg given within 14 days of exposure and/or prior to manifestation of disease; not needed if at least 1 dose of hepatitis A vaccine was given at ≥1 month before exposure (CDC 2006)

Immune thrombocytopenia (ITP):

Carimune NF: IV: Initial: 400 mg/kg/day for 2 to 5 consecutive days (6% solution recommended); Maintenance: 400 mg/kg (no more frequent than daily) as needed to maintain platelet count ≥30,000/mm^3 and/or to control significant bleeding; may increase dose if needed (range: 800 to 1,000 mg/kg).

Flebogamma DIF 10%: IV: 1,000 mg/kg once daily for 2 consecutive days

Gammagard S/D: IV: 1,000 mg/kg; up to 3 total doses may be given on alternate days based on patient response and/or platelet count.

Gammaked, Gamunex-C: IV: 1,000 mg/kg/day for 2 consecutive days (second dose may be withheld if adequate platelet response in 24 hours) **or** 400 mg/kg once daily for 5 consecutive days

Gammaplex, Octagam 10%, Privigen: IV: 1,000 mg/kg/day for 2 consecutive days

Panzyga [Canadian product]: IV: 1,000 mg/kg/day for 2 consecutive days; may repeat treatment in patients who relapse

American Society of Hematology Guidelines: Newly diagnosed ITP with platelets <30,000/mm^3: First line treatment: IV: 1,000 mg/kg as a single dose, may repeat if necessary (Neunert 2011)

Measles:

GamaSTAN S/D: IM:
Immunocompetent: 0.25 **mL**/kg given within 6 days of exposure

Immunocompromised children: 0.5 **mL**/kg (maximum dose: 15 **mL**) immediately following exposure

Postexposure prophylaxis, any nonimmune person (off-label population): Patients ≤30 kg: 0.5 **mL**/kg (maximum dose: 15 **mL**) within 6 days of exposure. If patient >30 kg, patient will have lower titers than what is recommended due to the maximum volume that can be administered (CDC 2013)

Gammaked, Gamunex-C, Octagam 5%: IV:

Preexposure prophylaxis in patients with primary humoral immunodeficiency (**ONLY** if routine dose is <400 mg/kg): ≥400 mg/kg immediately before expected exposure followed by resumption of prior dosing in 3 to 4 weeks.

Postexposure prophylaxis in patients with primary humoral immunodeficiency: 400 mg/kg administered as soon as possible after exposure followed by resumption of prior dosing in 3 to 4 weeks.

Postexposure prophylaxis, any nonimmune person (off-label population): 400 mg/kg within 6 days of exposure (CDC 2013)

Hizentra: SubQ infusion:

Preexposure prophylaxis in patients with primary humoral immunodeficiency at risk of measles exposure (eg, during an outbreak; travel to endemic area):

Patients receiving weekly or more frequent dosing: Ensure total weekly dose of ≥200 mg/kg for 2 consecutive weeks followed by resumption of prior dosing schedule

Patients receiving biweekly dosing: Administer ≥400 mg/kg once followed by resumption of prior dosing schedule.

Postexposure prophylaxis in patients with primary humoral immunodeficiency regardless of prior dosing schedule (daily, weekly, or biweekly): 400 mg/kg administered as soon as possible after exposure followed by resumption of prior dosing schedule.

ACIP recommendations: The Advisory Committee on Immunization Practices (ACIP) recommends postexposure prophylaxis with immune globulin (IG) to any nonimmune person exposed to measles. The following patient groups are at risk for severe measles complications and should receive IG therapy: Infants <12 months of age, pregnant women without evidence of immunity; severely compromised persons (eg, persons with severe primary immunodeficiency; some bone marrow transplant patients; some ALL patients; and some patients with AIDS or HIV infection [refer to guidelines for additional details]). IGIM is recommended for infants <12 months of age. IGIV is recommended for pregnant women and immunocompromised persons. Although prophylaxis may be given to any nonimmune person, priority should be given to those at greatest risk for measles complications and also to persons exposed in settings with intense, prolonged, close contact (eg, households, daycare centers, classrooms). Following IG administration, any nonimmune person should then receive the measles mumps and rubella (MMR) vaccine if the person is ≥12 months of age at the time of vaccine administration and the vaccine is not otherwise contraindicated. MMR should not be given until 6 months following IGIM or 8 months following IGIV administration. If a person is already receiving IGIV therapy, a dose of 400 mg/kg IV within 3 weeks prior to exposure (or 200 mg/kg SubQ for 2 consecutive weeks prior to exposure if previously on SubQ therapy) should be sufficient to prevent measles infection. IG therapy is not indicated for any person who already received one dose of a measles-containing vaccine at ≥12 months of age unless they are severely immunocompromised (CDC 2013).

Multifocal motor neuropathy (MMN) (Gammagard Liquid): IV: 500 to 2400 mg/kg/**month** based upon response

Primary humoral immunodeficiency disorders:

IV infusion dosing:

Bivigam, Gammaplex: IV: 300 to 800 mg/kg every 3 to 4 weeks; dose adjusted based on monitored trough serum IgG concentrations and clinical response

Carimune NF: IV: 400 to 800 mg/kg every 3 to 4 weeks. **Note:** In previously untreated agammaglobulinemic or hypogammaglobulinemic patients use a 3% solution; may administer subsequent infusions with a higher concentration if patient tolerates lower concentration.

Flebogamma DIF 5%, Flebogamma DIF 10%, Gammagard Liquid, Gammagard S/D, Gammaked, Gamunex-C, Octagam 5%: IV: 300 to 600 mg/kg every 3 to 4 weeks; dose adjusted based on monitored trough serum IgG concentrations and clinical response

Privigen, Panzyga [Canadian product]: IV: 200 to 800 mg/kg every 3 to 4 weeks; dose adjusted based on monitored trough serum IgG concentrations and clinical response

Switching to weekly subcutaneous infusion dosing:

Gammagard Liquid, Gammaked, Gamunex-C: SubQ infusion: Begin 1 week after last IV dose. Use the following equation to calculate initial dose:

Initial weekly dose (grams) = [1.37 x IGIV dose (grams)] divided by [IV dose interval (weeks)]

Note: For subsequent dose adjustments, refer to product labeling.

Hizentra: SubQ infusion: For weekly or frequent (up to daily) dosing, begin 1 week after last IV infusion or SubQ infusion. For biweekly (every 2 week) dosing, begin 1 or 2 weeks after last IV infusion or 1 week after the last SubQ weekly infusion. **Note:** Patient should have received an IV immune globulin routinely for at least 3 months before switching to SubQ. Use the following equation to calculate initial weekly dose:

Initial weekly dose (grams) = [Previous IGIV dose (grams)] divided by [IV dose interval (eg, 3 or 4 weeks)] then multiply by 1.37. For patients switching to Hizentra from a different SubQ formulation, the previous weekly SubQ dose should be used initially. To convert the dose (in grams) to mL, multiply the calculated dose (in g) by 5.

Note: Provided the total weekly dose is maintained, any dosing interval from daily up to biweekly (every 2 weeks) may be used. For patients switching to Hizentra from a different SubQ formulation, the previous weekly SubQ dose should be used initially. Use the following calculations to calculate frequent or biweekly dosing:

Biweekly dosing (grams) = multiply the calculated or previous weekly dose by 2.

Frequent (2 to 7 times per week) dosing (grams) = divide the calculated or previous weekly dose by the desired number of times per week (eg, for 3 times per week dosing, divide weekly dose by 3)

Note: For subsequent dose adjustments, refer to product labeling.

SubQ infusion dosing:

Cuvitru: SubQ:

Patients switching from another IG SubQ product: SubQ infusion:

Weekly dosing (grams): Weekly dose is the same as the prior immune globulin subcutaneous weekly dose

Biweekly dosing (grams): Multiply the calculated weekly dose by 2

Frequent (2 to 7 times per week) dosing (grams): Divide the calculated weekly dose by the desired number of administration times per week

Note: For subsequent dose adjustments, refer to product labeling.

Patients switching from IGIV therapy or Hyqvia: SubQ infusion: Begin treatment one week after patient's last immune globulin IV or Hyqvia infusion

Initial weekly dosing (grams): Divide the previous immune globulin IV or Hyqvia dose (grams) by the number of weeks between IV doses, then multiply this dose by 1.3 (dose adjustment factor)

Biweekly dosing (grams): Multiply the calculated weekly dose by 2

Frequent (2 to 7 times per week) dosing (grams): Divide the calculated weekly dose by the desired number of times per week

Note: For subsequent dose adjustments, refer to product labeling.

HyQvia: SubQ: See manufacturer's labeling for initial ramp-up schedule (initiating treatment with a full monthly dose has not been evaluated); dose adjusted based on monitored trough serum IgG concentrations and clinical response after initial ramp-up. **Note:** For patients previously on another IgG treatment, administer the first dose ~1 week after the last infusion of previous treatment.

Patients naive to IgG therapy or switching from IG SubQ therapy: SubQ infusion: 300 to 600 mg/kg every 3 to 4 weeks, after the initial dose ramp-up

Patients switching from IGIV therapy: SubQ infusion: Administer the same dose and frequency as the previous IGIV therapy after the initial dose ramp-up. For subsequent dose adjustments, refer to product labeling.

Rubella (GamaSTAN S/D): IM: Postexposure prophylaxis during pregnancy: 0.55 **mL**/kg

Secondary immunodeficiency: Panzyga [Canadian product]: IV: 200 to 800 mg/kg every 3 to 4 weeks; dose adjusted based on monitored trough serum IgG concentrations and clinical response

Varicella (GamaSTAN S/D): IM: Prophylaxis: 0.6 to 1.2 **mL**/kg (varicella zoster immune globulin preferred) within 72 hours of exposure (Gershon 1978). **Note:** For patients at risk of thrombosis, administer at the lower end of the recommended dosage range.

Off-label uses: IV:

Acquired hypogammaglobulinemia secondary to malignancy (off-label use): 400 mg/kg/dose every 3 weeks; reevaluate every 4 to 6 months (Anderson 2007)

Antibody-mediated rejection in cardiac transplantation, treatment (off-label use): Dose/frequency/duration of treatment varies greatly: 100 to 2,000 mg/kg (dose may be divided into 2 or 4 doses) 1 to 3 times per week, often given after each plasmapheresis; may be re-dosed monthly, if re-dose necessary and based on response (AHA [Colvin 2015]; ISHLT [Costanzo 2010]).

Dermatomyositis/polymyositis (refractory) (use in combination with other agents in patients with dermatomyositis) (off-label use): 2,000 mg/kg per treatment course administered in divided doses over 2 to 5 consecutive days (eg, 400 mg/kg/day for 5 days); maximum (per treatment course): 2,000 mg/kg (Feasby 2007).

Guillain-Barré syndrome (off-label use): A total dose of 2 g/kg per treatment course, given in divided doses over 2 to 5 consecutive days (eg, 400 mg/kg/day for 5 days) (Feasby 2007; Hughes 2014). European Federation of Neurological Societies (EFNS) guidelines recommend the 5-day treatment regimen (Elovaara, 2008).

Hematopoietic cell transplantation (HCT) with hypogammaglobulinemia (IgG <400 mg/dL), prevention of bacterial infection (off-label use): **Note:** Increase dose or frequency to maintain IgG concentration >400 mg/dL.

≤100 days post-HCT: 500 mg/kg/dose once weekly (Tomblyn 2009)

>100 days post-HCT: 500 mg/kg/dose every 3 to 4 weeks (Tomblyn 2009)

HIV-associated thrombocytopenia (off-label use): 1,000 mg/kg/day for 2 days (Anderson 2007)

Lambert-Eaton myasthenic syndrome (LEMS) (off-label use): 1,000 mg/kg/day for 2 days (Bain 1996; Patwa 2012)

Myasthenia gravis (acute exacerbation) (off-label use): Adjunctive therapy: 2 g/kg per treatment course, administered in divided doses over 2 to 5 consecutive days (eg, 400 mg/kg/day for 5 days) (Barth 2011; Feasby 2007; Zinman 2007). **Note:** A single dose of 1 g/kg may have similar efficacy to 1 g/kg given on 2 consecutive days (Gajdos 2005)

Relapsing-remitting multiple sclerosis (off-label use): 1,000 mg/kg per month, with or without an induction of 400 mg/kg/day for 5 days (Feasby 2007). Optimal dosing has not been established.

Geriatric Refer to adult dosing. Use with caution; administer the minimum dose and infusion rate practicable.

Pediatric Note: HyQvia and Octagam 10% are **not** FDA-approved for use in children.

Children and Adolescents:

Hepatitis A: Refer to adult dosing.

Immune thrombocytopenia (ITP):

Carimune NF: IV: Initial: 400 mg/kg/day for 2 to 5 consecutive days (6% solution recommended); Maintenance: 400 mg/kg (no more frequent than daily) as needed to maintain platelet count ≥30,000/mm^3 and/or to control significant bleeding; may increase dose if needed (range: 800 to 1,000 mg/kg). For acute ITP, may discontinue after day 2 if platelet response is adequate (30,000 to 50,000/mm^3) after the first 2 doses.

Flebogamma DIF 10%: Children ≥2 years and Adolescents: IV: 1,000 mg/kg once daily for 2 consecutive days

Gammaked, Gamunex-C: IV: 1,000 mg/kg/day for 2 consecutive days (second dose may be withheld if adequate platelet response in 24 hours) **or** 400 mg/kg once daily for 5 consecutive days.

Privigen: IV: 1,000 mg/kg/day for 2 consecutive days (not approved for use in pediatric patients <15 years of age).

American Society of Hematology Guidelines: Newly diagnosed ITP: Initial pharmacologic management: Children and Adolescents: IV: 800 to 1,000 mg/kg as a single dose (Neunert 2011).

Kawasaki syndrome: IV:

Gammagard S/D: 1,000 mg/kg as a single dose **or** 400 mg/kg/day for 4 consecutive days. Begin within 7 days of onset of fever.

AHA guidelines (2004): 2,000 mg/kg as a single dose within 10 days of disease onset

Note: Must be used in combination with aspirin: 80 to 100 mg/kg/day orally, divided every 6 hours for up to 14 days (until fever resolves for at least 48 hours); then decrease dose to 3 to 5 mg/kg/day once daily. In patients without coronary artery abnormalities, give lower dose for 6 to 8 weeks. In patients with coronary artery abnormalities, low-dose aspirin should be continued indefinitely.

Measles: Refer to adult dosing.

Primary humoral immunodeficiency disorders:

IV infusion dosing:

Bivigam: IV: Children ≥6 years and Adolescents: 300 to 800 mg/kg every 3 to 4 weeks; dose adjusted based on monitored trough serum IgG concentrations and clinical response

Carimune NF: IV: Children and Adolescents: 400 to 800 mg/kg every 3 to 4 weeks. **Note:** In previously untreated agammaglobulinemic or hypogammaglobulinemic patients use a 3% solution; may administer subsequent infusions with a higher concentration if patient tolerates lower concentration.

Flebogamma DIF 5%: IV: Children ≥2 years, and Adolescents: 300 to 600 mg/kg every 3 to 4 weeks; dose adjusted based on monitored trough serum IgG concentrations and clinical response

Gammagard Liquid, Gammagard S/D: IV: Children ≥2 years and Adolescents: 300 to 600 mg/kg every 3 to 4 weeks; dose adjusted based on monitored trough serum IgG concentrations and clinical response.

Gammaked, Gamunex-C: IV: Children ≥2 years and Adolescents: 300 to 600 mg/kg every 3 to 4 weeks; dose adjusted based on monitored trough serum IgG concentrations and clinical response.

Gammaplex: IV: Children ≥2 years, and Adolescents: 300 to 800 mg/kg every 3 to 4 weeks; dose adjusted based on monitored trough serum IgG concentrations and clinical response.

Octagam 5%: IV: Children and Adolescents: 300 to 600 mg/kg every 3 to 4 weeks; dose adjusted based on monitored trough serum IgG concentrations and clinical response.

Panzyga [Canadian product]: IV: Children ≥2 years and Adolescents: 200 to 800 mg/kg every 3 to 4 weeks; dose adjusted based on monitored trough serum IgG concentrations and clinical response.

Privigen: IV: Children ≥3 years and Adolescents: 200 to 800 mg/kg every 3 to 4 weeks; dose adjusted based on monitored trough serum IgG concentrations and clinical response

Switching to weekly subcutaneous infusion dosing:

Gammagard Liquid, Gammaked, Gamunex-C: Children ≥2 years and Adolescents:

SubQ infusion: Begin 1 week after last IV dose. Use the following equation to calculate initial dose:

Initial weekly dose (grams) = [1.37 x IGIV dose (grams)] divided by [IV dose interval (weeks)]

Note: For subsequent dose adjustments, refer to product labeling.

Hizentra: SubQ infusion: Children ≥2 years and Adolescents: For weekly or frequent (up to daily) dosing, begin 1 week after last IV infusion or SubQ infusion. For biweekly (every 2 week) dosing, begin 1 or 2 weeks after last IV infusion or 1 week after the last SubQ weekly infusion. **Note:** Patient should have received an IV immune globulin routinely for at least 3 months before switching to SubQ. Use the following equation to calculate initial weekly dose:

Initial weekly dose (grams) = [Previous IGIV dose (grams)] divided by [IV dose interval (eg, 3 or 4 weeks)] then multiply by 1.37. If switching from a different SubQ formulation to Hizentra, maintain previous weekly SubQ dose initially. To convert the dose (in grams) to mL, multiply the calculated dose (in grams) by 5.

Note: Provided the total weekly dose is maintained, any dosing interval from daily up to biweekly (every 2 weeks) may be used. Use the following calculations to calculate frequent or biweekly dosing:

Biweekly dosing (grams) = multiply the calculated or previous weekly dose by 2.

Frequent (2 to 7 times per week) dosing (grams) = divide the calculated or previous weekly dose by the desired number of times per week (eg, for 3 times per week dosing, divide weekly dose by 3).

Note: For subsequent dose adjustments, refer to product labeling.

SubQ infusion dosing:

Cuvitru: SubQ infusion: Children ≥2 years and Adolescents: Refer to adult dosing.

Secondary immunodeficiency: Panzyga [Canadian product]: IV: Children ≥2 years and Adolescents: 200 to 800 mg/kg every 3 to 4 weeks; dose adjusted based on monitored trough serum IgG concentrations and clinical response.

Varicella: Refer to adult dosing.

Dermatomyositis/polymyositis (refractory) (use in combination with other agents in patients with dermatomyositis) (off-label use): IV: 2,000 mg/kg per treatment course administered in divided doses over 2 consecutive days (eg, 1,000 mg/kg/day for 2 days); maximum (per treatment course): 2,000 mg/kg (Feasby 2007)

Guillain-Barré syndrome (off-label use): Children and Adolescents: IV: 1,000 mg/kg/day for 2 days (Feasby 2007; Korinthenberg 2005) **or** 400 mg/kg/day for 5 days (El-Bayoumi 2011; Korinthenberg 2005).Two-day regimens have been associated with a higher incidence of early relapse (Korinthenberg 2005). American Academy of Neurology guidelines state optimal dosing has not been established (Patwa 2012).

Hematopoietic cell transplantation (HCT) with hypogammaglobulinemia (IgG <400 mg/dL), prevention of bacterial infection (off-label use)

(Tomblyn 2009): IV: **Note:** Increase dose or frequency to maintain IgG concentration >400 mg/dL.

≤100 days post-HCT:

Infants and Children (Allogeneic HCT recipients): IV: 400 mg/kg/dose once monthly

Adolescents: IV: 500 mg/kg/dose once weekly

>100 days post-HCT: Infants, Children, and Adolescents: IV: 500 mg/kg/dose every 3 to 4 weeks

HIV infection [prophylaxis of bacterial infection in patients with hypogammaglobulinemia (IgG <400 mg/dL)] (off-label use): Infants and Children: IV:

Primary prophylaxis for serious bacterial infections: 400 mg/kg/dose every 2 to 4 weeks (DHHS [pediatric] 2013)

Secondary prophylaxis for invasive bacterial infections: Should only be used if subsequent infections are frequent severe infections (>2 infections during a 1-year period): 400 mg/kg/dose every 2 to 4 weeks (DHHS [pediatric] 2013)

Myasthenia gravis (acute exacerbation) (off-label use): Adolescents: Refer to adult dosing.

Renal Impairment

IV: Use with caution due to risk of immune globulin-induced renal dysfunction; the rate of infusion and concentration of solution should be minimized. Discontinue if renal function deteriorates during treatment.

IM: There are no dosage adjustments provided in the manufacturer's labeling.

SubQ infusion: There are no dosage adjustments provided in the manufacturer's labeling; consider lower, more frequent dosing.

Hepatic Impairment IM, IV, SubQ infusion: There are no dosage adjustments provided in the manufacturer's labeling.

Obesity Some clinicians dose IGIV on ideal body weight or an adjusted ideal body weight in morbidly obese patients (Siegel 2010).

Mechanism of Action Replacement therapy for primary and secondary immunodeficiencies, and IgG antibodies against bacteria, viral, parasitic and mycoplasma antigens; interference with F_c receptors on the cells of the reticuloendothelial system for autoimmune cytopenias and ITP; provides passive immunity by increasing the antibody titer and antigen-antibody reaction potential

Contraindications Hypersensitivity to immune globulin or any component of the formulation; IgA deficiency (with anti-IgA antibodies and history of hypersensitivity); hyperprolinemia (Hizentra, Privigen); isolated IgA deficiency (GamaSTAN S/D); severe thrombocytopenia or coagulation disorders where IM injections are contraindicated (GamaSTAN S/D); hypersensitivity to corn (Octagam); hereditary intolerance to fructose (excluding Flebogamma); infants/neonates for whom sucrose or fructose tolerance has not been established (Gammaplex); hypersensitivity to hyaluronidase or recombinant human hyaluronidase (HyQvia)

Warnings/Precautions [US Boxed Warning]: IV administration only: Acute renal dysfunction (increased serum creatinine, oliguria, acute renal failure, osmotic nephrosis) can rarely occur and has been associated with fatalities; usually within 7 days of use (more likely with products stabilized with sucrose). Use with caution in the elderly, patients with renal disease, diabetes mellitus, overweight, hypovolemia, volume depletion, sepsis, paraproteinemia, and nephrotoxic medications due to risk of renal dysfunction. In patients at risk of renal dysfunction, ensure adequate hydration prior to administration; the dose, rate of infusion and concentration of solution should be minimized. Assess renal function prior to treatment and periodically thereafter. Discontinue if renal function deteriorates.

[US Boxed Warning]: Thrombosis may occur with immune globulin products even in the absence of risk factors for thrombosis. For patients at risk of thrombosis (eg, advanced age, history of atherosclerosis, impaired cardiac output, prolonged immobilization, hypercoagulable conditions, history of venous or arterial thrombosis, use of estrogens, indwelling central vascular catheters, hyperviscosity, and cardiovascular risk factors), administer at the minimum dose and infusion rate practicable. Ensure adequate hydration before administration. Monitor for signs and symptoms of thrombosis and assess blood viscosity in patients at risk for hyperviscosity such as those with cryoglobulins, fasting chylomicronemia/severe hypertriglyceridemia, or monoclonal gammopathies.

High-dose regimens (1 g/kg for 1 to 2 days) are not recommended for individuals with fluid overload or where fluid volume may be of concern. Hypersensitivity and anaphylactic reactions can occur (some severe); patients with anti-IgA antibodies are at greater risk; a severe fall in blood pressure may rarely occur with anaphylactic reaction, discontinue therapy and institute immediate treatment (including epinephrine 1 mg/mL) should be available. Product of human plasma; may potentially contain infectious agents which could transmit disease, including unknown or emerging viruses and other pathogens. Screening of donors, as well as testing and/or inactivation or removal of certain viruses, reduces the risk. Infections thought to be transmitted by this product should be reported to the manufacturer. Aseptic meningitis may occur with high doses (≥1 g/kg) and/or rapid infusion; syndrome usually appears within several hours to 2 days following treatment; usually resolves within several days after product is discontinued; female patients or patients with a migraine history may be at higher risk for AMS. Increased risk of hypersensitivity, especially in patients with anti-IgA antibodies; use is contraindicated in patients with IgA deficiency (with antibodies against IgA and history of hypersensitivity) or isolated IgA deficiency (GamaSTAN S/D). Increased risk of hematoma formation when administered subcutaneously for the treatment of ITP.

Intravenous immune globulin has been associated with antiglobulin hemolysis (acute or delayed). Cases of hemolysis-related renal impairment/failure or disseminated intravascular coagulation (DIC) have been reported. Risk factors associated with hemolysis include high doses (≥2 g/kg) given either as a single administration or divided over several days, underlying associated inflammatory conditions, and non-O blood type (FDA 2012). An underlying inflammatory state (eg, elevated C-reactive protein or erythrocyte sedimentation rate) may also increase the risk. Closely monitor patients for signs of hemolytic anemia, particularly in patients with pre-existing anemia and/or cardiovascular or pulmonary compromise. In chronic ITP, assess risk versus benefit of high-dose regimen in patients with increased risk of thrombosis, hemolysis, acute kidney injury, or volume overload.

Patients should be adequately hydrated prior to initiation of therapy. Do not infuse into or around an infected area due to the risk of spreading a localized infection. Hyperproteinemia, increased serum viscosity and hyponatremia may occur; distinguish hyponatremia from pseudohyponatremia to prevent volume depletion, a further increase in serum viscosity, and a higher risk of thrombotic events. Patients should be monitored for adverse events during and after the infusion. Stop administration with signs of infusion reaction (fever, chills, nausea, vomiting, and rarely shock). Risk may be increased with initial treatment, when switching brands of immune globulin, and with treatment interruptions of >8 weeks. Monitor for transfusion-related acute lung injury (TRALI); noncardiogenic pulmonary edema has been reported with immune globulin use. TRALI is characterized by severe respiratory distress, pulmonary edema, normal left ventricular function, hypoxemia, and fever (in the presence of normal left ventricular function) and usually occurs within 1 to 6 hours after infusion. Response to live vaccinations may be impaired. Some clinicians may administer intravenous immune globulin products as a subcutaneous infusion based on patient tolerability and clinical judgment. SubQ infusion should begin 1 week after the last IV dose; dose should be individualized based on clinical response and serum IgG trough concentrations; consider premedicating with acetaminophen and diphenhydramine.

Use with caution in the elderly; may be at increased risk for renal dysfunction/failure and thromboembolic events. Some products may contain maltose, which may result in falsely elevated blood glucose readings; maltose-containing products may be contraindicated in patients with an allergy to corn. Some products may contain sodium and/or sucrose. Some dosage forms may contain polysorbate 80 (also known as Tweens). Hypersensitivity reactions, usually a delayed reaction, have been reported following exposure to pharmaceutical products containing polysorbate 80 in certain individuals (Isaksson, 2002; Lucente 2000; Shelley, 1995). Thrombocytopenia, ascites, pulmonary deterioration, and renal and hepatic failure have been reported in premature neonates after receiving parenteral products containing polysorbate 80 (Alade, 1986; CDC, 1984). See manufacturer's labeling. Some products may contain sorbitol; do not use immune globulin in patients with fructose intolerance. Hizentra and Privigen contain the stabilizer L-proline and are contraindicated in patients with hyperprolinemia. Packaging of some products may contain natural latex/natural rubber; skin testing should not be performed with GamaSTAN S/D as local irritation can occur and be misinterpreted as a positive reaction. Potentially significant interactions may exist, requiring dose or frequency adjustment, additional monitoring, and/or selection of alternative therapy.

Drug Interactions

Metabolism/Transport Effects None known.

Avoid Concomitant Use There are no known interactions where it is recommended to avoid concomitant use.

Increased Effect/Toxicity

The levels/effects of Immune Globulin may be increased by: Estrogen Derivatives

Decreased Effect

Immune Globulin may decrease the levels/effects of: Vaccines (Live)

Dietary Considerations Some products may contain sodium.

Pharmacodynamics/Kinetics

Onset of Action IV: Provides immediate antibody levels

Immune thrombocytopenia: Initial response: 1 to 3 days; Peak response: 2 to 7 days (Neunert 2011)

Duration of Action IM, IV: Immune effects: 3 to 4 weeks (variable)

Half-life Elimination IM: ~23 days; SubQ: ~59 days (HyQvia): IV: IgG (variable among patients): Healthy subjects: 14 to 24 days; Patients with congenital humoral immunodeficiencies: 26 to 40 days; hypermetabolism associated with fever and infection have coincided with a shortened half-life

Time to Peak

Plasma: SubQ: Cuvitru: ~4.4 days; Gammagard Liquid: 2.9 days; Hizentra: 2.9 days; HyQvia: ~5 days

Serum: IM: ~48 hours

Pregnancy Risk Factor C

Pregnancy Considerations Animal reproduction studies have not been conducted. Immune globulins cross the placenta in increased amounts after 30 weeks gestation. Intravenous immune globulin has been recommended for use in fetal-neonatal alloimmune thrombocytopenia and pregnancy-associated ITP (Anderson, 2007). Intravenous immune globulin is recommended to prevent measles in nonimmune women exposed during pregnancy (CDC, 2013). May also be used in postexposure prophylaxis for rubella to reduce the risk of infection and fetal damage in exposed pregnant women who will not consider therapeutic abortion (per GamaSTAN S/D product labeling; use for postexposure rubella prophylaxis is not currently recommended [CDC, 2013]).

HyQvia: Women who become pregnant during treatment are encouraged to enroll in the HyQvia Pregnancy Registry (1-866-424-6724).

Breastfeeding Considerations It is not known if immune globulin from these preparations is excreted in breast milk. According to the manufacturer, the decision to continue or discontinue breastfeeding during therapy should take into account the risk of infant exposure, the benefits of breastfeeding to the infant, and benefits of treatment to the mother. The manufacturer of HyQvia recommends administration to nursing women only if clearly indicated.

Dosage Forms Considerations

Carimune NF may contain a significant amount of sodium and also contains sucrose.

Gammagard S/D may contain a significant amount of sodium and also contains glucose.

Octagam contains maltose.

Hyqvia Kit is supplied with a Hyaluronidase (Human Recombinant) component intended for injection prior to Immune Globulin administration to improve dispersion and absorption of the Immune Globulin.

Dosage Forms

Injectable, Intramuscular [preservative free]:

GamaSTAN S/D: 15% to 18% [150 to 180 mg/mL] (2 mL, 10 mL)

Kit, Subcutaneous:

Hyqvia: 2.5 g/25 mL, 5 g/50 mL, 10 g/100 mL, 20 g/200 mL, 30 g/300 mL

Solution, Injection [preservative free]:

Gammagard: 1 g/10 mL (10 mL); 2.5 g/25 mL (25 mL); 5 g/50 mL (50 mL); 10 g/100 mL (100 mL); 20 g/200 mL (200 mL); 30 g/300 mL (300 mL)

Gammaked: 1 g/10 mL (10 mL); 2.5 g/25 mL (25 mL); 5 g/50 mL (50 mL); 10 g/100 mL (100 mL); 20 g/200 mL (200 mL)

Gamunex-C: 1 g/10 mL (10 mL); 2.5 g/25 mL (25 mL); 5 g/50 mL (50 mL); 10 g/100 mL (100 mL); 20 g/200 mL (200 mL); 40 g/400 mL (400 mL)

Solution, Intravenous [preservative free]:

Bivigam: 5 g/50 mL (50 mL); 10 g/100 mL (100 mL)

Flebogamma DIF: 0.5 g/10 mL (10 mL); 5 g/50 mL (50 mL); 5 g/100 mL (100 mL); 10 g/100 mL (100 mL); 20 g/200 mL (200 mL); 20 g/400 mL (400 mL); 10 g/200 mL (200 mL); 2.5 g/50 mL (50 mL)

Gammaplex: 5 g/50 mL (50 mL); 5 g/100 mL (100 mL); 10 g/100 mL (100 mL); 20 g/200 mL (200 mL); 20 g/400 mL (400 mL); 10 g/200 mL (200 mL)

Octagam: 1 g/20 mL (20 mL); 2 g/20 mL (20 mL); 5 g/50 mL (50 mL); 5 g/100 mL (100 mL); 10 g/100 mL (100 mL); 20 g/200 mL (200 mL); 25 g/500 mL (500 mL); 10 g/200 mL (200 mL); 2.5 g/50 mL (50 mL)

Privigen: 5 g/50 mL (50 mL); 10 g/100 mL (100 mL); 20 g/200 mL (200 mL); 40 g/400 mL (400 mL)

Solution, Subcutaneous [preservative free]:

Cuvitru: 1 g/5 mL (5 mL); 2 g/10 mL (10 mL); 4 g/20 mL (20 mL); 8 g/40 mL (40 mL)

Hizentra: 1 g/5 mL (5 mL); 2 g/10 mL (10 mL); 4 g/20 mL (20 mL); 10 g/50 mL (50 mL)

Solution Reconstituted, Intravenous [preservative free]:

Carimune NF: 6 g (1 ea); 12 g (1 ea)

Gammagard S/D Less IgA: 5 g (1 ea); 10 g (1 ea)

IncobotulinumtoxinA

(in kuh BOT yoo lin num TOKS in aye)

Related Information

Dentin Hypersensitivity, Acid Erosion, High Caries Index, Management of Alveolar Osteitis, and Xerostomia *on page 1857*

Brand Names: US Xeomin

Brand Names: Canada Xeomin; Xeomin Cosmetic

Generic Availability (US) No

Pharmacologic Category Neuromuscular Blocker Agent, Toxin; Ophthalmic Agent, Toxin

Use

US labeling:

Blepharospasm: Treatment of adults with blepharospasm in patients previously treated with onabotulinumtoxinA (Botox).

Cervical dystonia: Treatment of adults with cervical dystonia in both botulinum toxin-naïve and previously treated patients.

Glabellar lines: Temporary improvement in the appearance of moderate to severe glabellar lines associated with corrugator and/or procerus muscle activity in adult patients.

Upper limb spasticity: Treatment of upper limb spasticity in adult patients.

Canadian labeling:

Xeomin:

Cervical dystonia: Treatment of cervical dystonia (spasmodic torticollis) in adults.

Hypertonicity disorders: Treatment of hypertonicity disorders of the seventh nerve (eg, blepharospasm, hemifacial spasm) in adults.

Upper limb spasticity: Treatment of poststroke spasticity of upper limb(s) in adults.

Xeomin Cosmetic: **Glabellar lines:** Temporary improvement in the appearance of moderate to severe glabellar lines in adults.

Local Anesthetic/Vasoconstrictor Precautions No information available to require special precautions

Effects on Dental Treatment Key adverse event(s) related to dental treatment: Xerostomia (normal salivary flow resumes upon discontinuation).

Effects on Bleeding No information available to require special precautions

Adverse Reactions

Upper limb spasticity and cervical dystonia:

>10%:

Central nervous system: Myasthenia (cervical dystonia: 7% to 11%)

Gastrointestinal: Dysphagia (cervical dystonia: 13% to 18%)

Neuromuscular & skeletal: Neck pain (cervical dystonia: 7% to 15%)

1% to 10%:

Central nervous system: Seizure (upper limb spasticity: 3%)

Gastrointestinal: Xerostomia (upper limb spasticity: 2%)

Local: Pain at injection site (cervical dystonia: 9%)

Neuromuscular & skeletal: Musculoskeletal pain (cervical dystonia: 4% to 7%)

Respiratory: Nasopharyngitis (upper limb spasticity: 2%), upper respiratory tract infection (upper limb spasticity: 2%)

Blepharospasm and glabellar lines:

>10%:

Gastrointestinal: Xerostomia (blepharospasm: 16%)

Ophthalmic: Blepharoptosis (blepharospasm: 19%; reduction of glabellar lines: <1%), dry eye syndrome (blepharospasm: 16%), visual disturbance (blepharospasm: 12%)

1% to 10%:

Central nervous system: Headache (blepharospasm: 7%; reduction of glabellar lines: 5%)

Gastrointestinal: Diarrhea (blepharospasm: 8%)

Respiratory: Dyspnea (blepharospasm: 5%), nasopharyngitis (blepharospasm: 5%), respiratory tract infection (blepharospasm: 5%)

<1%, postmarketing and/or case reports: Any indication: Abdominal distention, abnormal dreams, allergic dermatitis, alopecia, anaphylaxis, antibody development, asthma, blepharospasm, blurred vision, cardiac insufficiency, circulatory shock, corneal perforation, cough, diplopia, drug eruption, dysarthria, edema, erythema, eye disease, eyelid edema, facial pain, facial paresis, fatigue, flu-like symptoms, hematoma at injection site, herpes zoster, hypersensitivity reaction, inflammation at injection site, injection site reaction, lymphadenopathy, madarosis, muscle spasm, myalgia, nausea, pruritus, reduced blinking (leading to corneal ulceration), serum sickness, skin rash, swelling of eye, trismus, urinary incontinence, urticaria, vascular insufficiency, voice disorder, weakness

Dosing

Adult

Blepharospasm: IM:

US labeling: Initial: Total dose should be the same as previously administered onabotulinumtoxinA dose. If prior onabotulinumtoxinA dose is not known: 1.25 to 2.5 units/injection site (maximum initial dose: 35 units/eye or 70 units/both eyes). Number and location of injection sites based on disease severity and previous dose/response to onabotulinumtoxinA (in clinical trials, a mean number of 6 injections per eye were administered). Cumulative dose should not exceed 35 units/eye or 70 units/both eyes administered no more frequently than every 3 months.

Canadian labeling: Initial: 1.25 to 2.5 units/injection site (maximum initial dose: 25 units/eye for treatment-naïve patients; 35 units/eye for patients previously receiving unknown dose). Titrate dose and interval for maximum patient benefit. Total dose should not exceed 100 units per treatment session. Administer no more frequently than every 3 months.

Cervical dystonia: IM:

US labeling: Initial total dose: 120 units (in clinical trials, similar efficacy was noted with initial total doses of 120 and 240 units and between treatment experienced and treatment naïve patients). Dose and number of injection sites should be individualized based on prior treatment, response, duration of effect, adverse events, number/location of muscle(s) to be treated and disease severity. In clinical trials most patients received a total of 2 to 10 injections into treated muscles. Administer no more frequently than every 3 months. Maximum cumulative dose per treatment session: 400 units.

Canadian labeling: Usual total dose does not exceed 200 units (maximum: 300 units; maximum dose per injection site: 50 units); administer no more frequently than every 3 months

Reduction of glabellar lines: IM: Inject 4 units into each of the 5 sites (2 injections in each corrugator muscle and 1 injection in the procerus muscle) for a total dose of 20 units per treatment session. Administer no more frequently than every 3 months.

Upper limb spasticity: IM:

US labeling: Initiate dosing at the low end of the dosing range and titrate as clinically indicated. Base dosage, frequency and number of injection sites on size, number and location of muscles to be treated, severity of spasticity, presence of local muscle weakness, patient's response to previous treatment and adverse event history. Administer no more frequently than every 3 months. Maximum cumulative dose per treatment session: 400 units.

Clenched fist: Flexor digitorum superficialis or flexor digitorum profundus: 25 to 100 units divided into 2 injection sites

Flexed wrist:

Flexor carpi radialis: 25 to 100 units divided into 1 to 2 injection sites

Flexor carpi ulnaris: 20 to 100 units divided into 1 to 2 injection sites

Flexed elbow:

Brachioradialis: 25 to 100 units divided into 1 to 3 injection sites

Biceps: 50 to 200 units divided into 1 to 4 injection sites

Brachialis: 25 to 100 units divided into 1 to 2 injection sites

Pronated forearm:

Pronator quadratus: 10 to 50 units in 1 injection

Pronator teres: 25 to 75 units divided into 1 to 2 injections

Thumb-in-palm:

Flexor pollicis longus: 10 to 50 units in 1 injection

Adductor pollicis: 5 to 30 units in 1 injection

Flexor pollicis brevis/opponens pollicis: 5 to 30 units in 1 injection

Canadian labeling: Initiate dosing at the low end of the dosing range and titrate as clinically indicated. Administer no more frequently than every 3 months. Total dose should not exceed 400 units in a treatment session.

Flexed wrist: Total initial dose 90 units

Flexor carpi radialis: Initial dose 50 units; subsequent dose range 25 to 100 units divided into 1 to 2 injection sites

Flexor carpi ulnaris: Initial dose 40 units; subsequent dose range 20 to 100 units divided into 1 to 2 injection sites

Clenched fist: Total initial dose 80 units

Flexor digitorum superficialis: Initial dose 40 units; subsequent dose range 40 to 100 units divided into 2 injection sites

Flexor digitorum profundus: Initial dose 40 units; subsequent dose range 40 to 100 units divided into 2 injection sites

Flexed elbow: Total initial dose 130 to 190 units

Brachioradialis: Initial dose 60 units; subsequent dose range 25 to 100 units divided into 1 to 3 injection sites

Biceps: Initial dose 80 units; subsequent dose range 75 to 200 units divided into 1 to 4 injection sites

Brachialis: Initial dose 50 units; subsequent dose range 25 to 100 units divided into 1 to 2 injection sites

Pronated forearm: Total initial dose 25 to 65 units

Pronator quadratus: Initial dose 25 units; subsequent dose range 10 to 50 units in 1 injection

Pronator teres: Initial dose 40 units; subsequent dose range 25 to 75 units divided into 1 to 2 injections

Thumb-in-palm: Total initial dose 10 to 40 units

Flexor pollicis longus: Initial dose 20 units; subsequent dose range 10 to 50 units in 1 injection

Adductor pollicis: Initial dose 10 units; subsequent dose range 5 to 30 units in 1 injection

Flexor pollicis brevis/opponens pollicis: Initial dose 10 units; subsequent dose range 5 to 30 units in 1 injection

Geriatric Refer to adult dosing. Initiate therapy at lowest recommended dose.

Renal Impairment There are no dosage adjustments provided in manufacturer's labeling.

Hepatic Impairment There are no dosage adjustments provided in manufacturer's labeling.

Mechanism of Action IncobotulinumtoxinA is a neurotoxin produced from *Clostridium botulinum* that inhibits acetylcholine release from peripheral cholinergic nerve endings. Inhibition occurs sequentially via binding and internalization of the neurotoxin into presynaptic cholinergic nerve terminals, translocation to the nerve terminal cytosol, and enzymatic cleavage of SNAP25, a protein necessary for acetylcholine release. Inhibition of acetylcholine release at the neuromuscular junction produces a state of denervation. Muscle inactivation persists until new fibrils grow from the nerve and form junction plates on new areas of the muscle-cell walls.

Contraindications

Hypersensitivity to botulinum toxin or any component of the formulation; infection at the proposed injection site(s)

Canadian labeling: Additional contraindications (not in US labeling): Generalized disorders of muscle activity (eg, myasthenia gravis, Lambert-Eaton syndrome)

Warnings/Precautions [US Boxed Warning]: Distant spread of botulinum toxin beyond the site of injection has been reported; dysphagia and breathing difficulties have occurred and may be life threatening; other symptoms reported include blurred vision, diplopia, dysarthria, dysphonia, generalized muscle weakness, ptosis, and urinary incontinence which may develop within hours or weeks following

injection. The risk is likely greatest in children treated for the unapproved use of spasticity. Systemic effects have occurred following use in approved and unapproved uses, including low doses. Use caution in patients with underlying conditions which may predispose them to these symptoms. Immediate medical attention required if respiratory, speech, or swallowing difficulties appear. Hypersensitivity and anaphylactic reactions may occur; discontinue therapy immediately with signs/symptoms of hypersensitivity. Immediate medical treatment should be available. Higher doses, more frequent administration, or young age at disease onset may result in neutralizing antibody formation and loss of efficacy. Use caution in patients with bleeding disorders and/or receiving anticoagulation therapy. May impair ability to drive and/or operate machinery; if loss of strength, muscle weakness, or impaired vision occurs, patients should avoid driving or engaging in other hazardous activities.

Product contains albumin and may carry a remote risk of virus transmission. Use caution if there is excessive weakness or atrophy at the proposed injection site(s); use is contraindicated if infection is present at injection site. Use with caution in patients with neuromuscular diseases (such as myasthenia gravis or Lambert-Eaton syndrome [contraindicated in Canadian labeling]), neuropathic disorders (such as amyotrophic lateral sclerosis), and patients with pre-existing cardiovascular disease (rare reports of arrhythmia and MI). Long-term effects of chronic therapy are unknown. Botulinum products (abobotulinumtoxinA, incobotulinumtoxinA, onabotulinumtoxinA, rimabotulinumtoxinB) are not interchangeable; potency units are specific to each preparation and cannot be compared or converted to any other botulinum product.

Cervical dystonia: Dysphagia is common and may occur within hours to weeks and persist for several months after administration. If severe, alternative feeding methods may be required. Risk factors include smaller neck muscle mass or bilateral injections into the sternocleidomastoid muscle. Use extreme caution in patients with pre-existing respiratory disease; may weaken accessory muscles that are necessary for these patients to maintain adequate ventilation. Incidence of dysphagia may be reduced by limiting dose administered into sternocleidomastoid muscle. Risk of aspiration resulting from severe dysphagia is increased in patients with decreased respiratory function.

Reduced blinking from injection of the orbicularis muscle can lead to corneal exposure and ulceration. Careful testing of corneal sensation, avoidance of lower lid injections to prevent ectropion, and treatment of epithelial defects are necessary. Soft contact lenses, application of protective drops or ointment, or covering the affected eye may help. Gentle pressure at injection site may limit bruising of eyelid. Use caution in patients with angle-closure glaucoma. Potentially significant drug-drug interactions may exist, requiring dose or frequency adjustment, additional monitoring, and/or selection of alternative therapy.

Pharmacodynamics/Kinetics

Onset of Action Improvement: ~4 to 7 days

Duration of Action ~3 to 4 months

Pregnancy Risk Factor C

Pregnancy Considerations Adverse events were observed in some animal reproduction studies. Canadian labeling does not recommend use for temporary improvement in appearance of moderate to severe glabellar lines during pregnancy.

Breastfeeding Considerations It is not known if incobotulinumtoxinA is excreted in breast milk. The US labeling recommends that caution be exercised when administering incobotulinumtoxinA to nursing women. The Canadian labeling does not recommend use in nursing women.

Dosage Forms

Solution Reconstituted, Intramuscular [preservative free]:

Xeomin: 50 units (1 ea); 100 units (1 ea); 200 units (1 ea)

Dosage Forms: Canada

Injection, powder for reconstitution:

Xeomin Cosmetic: 100 units

Indacaterol (in da KA ter ol)

Related Information

Respiratory Diseases *on page 1777*

Brand Names: US Arcapta Neohaler

Brand Names: Canada Onbrez Breezhaler

Pharmacologic Category $Beta_2$ Agonist; $Beta_2$-Adrenergic Agonist, Long-Acting

Use

Chronic obstructive pulmonary disease (maintenance): Long-term maintenance treatment of airflow obstruction in chronic obstructive pulmonary disease (COPD) including chronic bronchitis and/or emphysema

Limitations of use: Not indicated for treatment of acute deterioration of COPD or for treatment of asthma.

Local Anesthetic/Vasoconstrictor Precautions No information available to require special precautions

Effects on Dental Treatment Key adverse event(s) related to dental treatment: oropharyngeal pain has been reported

Effects on Bleeding No information available to require special precautions

Adverse Reactions

>10%: Respiratory: Cough (post-inhalation 7% to 24%)

1% to 10%:

Central nervous system: Headache (5%)

Gastrointestinal: Nausea (2%)

Respiratory: Nasopharyngitis (5%), oropharyngeal pain (2%)

<1%, postmarketing, and/or case reports: Dizziness, hypersensitivity reaction, palpitations, paradoxical bronchospasm, pruritus, skin rash, tachycardia

General Dosage Range Inhalation: *Adults:* Contents of 1 capsule (75 mcg) inhaled once daily using Neohaler inhaler.

Mechanism of Action Relaxes bronchial smooth muscle by selective action on $beta_2$-receptors with little effect on heart rate; acts locally in the lung.

Pharmacodynamics/Kinetics

Onset of Action 5 minutes; Peak effect: 1-4 hours

Duration of Action 24 hours

Half-life Elimination 40-56 hours

Time to Peak Serum: ~15 minutes

Pregnancy Risk Factor C

Pregnancy Considerations Adverse events were not observed in animal reproduction studies. Beta agonists may interfere with uterine contractility if administered during labor.

Indapamide (in DAP a mide)

Related Information

Cardiovascular Diseases *on page 1752*

Brand Names: Canada Apo-Indapamide; Dom-Indapamide; JAMP-Indapamide; Lozide; Mylan-Indapamide; PHL-Indapamide; PMS-Indapamide; PRO-Indapamide; Riva-Indapamide; Teva-Indapamide

Pharmacologic Category Antihypertensive; Diuretic, Thiazide-Related

Use

Heart failure: Treatment of edema in heart failure

Hypertension: Management of mild-to-moderate hypertension

Guideline recommendations:

Hypertension: The 2014 guideline for the management of high blood pressure in adults (Eighth Joint National Committee [JNC 8]) recommends initiation of pharmacologic treatment to lower blood pressure for the following patients:

- Patients ≥60 years of age with systolic blood pressure (SBP) ≥150 mm Hg or diastolic blood pressure (DBP) ≥90 mm Hg. Goal of therapy is SBP <150 mm Hg and DBP <90 mm Hg.
- Patients <60 years of age with SBP ≥140 mm Hg or DBP is ≥90 mm Hg. Goal of therapy is SBP <140 mm Hg and DBP <90 mm Hg.
- Patients ≥18 years of age with diabetes and SBP ≥140 mm Hg or DBP ≥90 mm Hg. Goal of therapy is SBP <140 mm Hg and DBP <90 mm Hg.
- Patients ≥18 years of age with chronic kidney disease (CKD) and SBP ≥140 mm Hg or DBP ≥90 mm Hg. Goal of therapy is SBP <140 mm Hg and DBP <90 mm Hg.

Chronic kidney disease (CKD) and hypertension: Regardless of race or diabetes status, the use of an ACE inhibitor (ACEI) or angiotensin receptor blocker (ARB) as initial therapy is recommended to improve kidney outcomes. In the general nonblack population (without CKD) including those with diabetes, initial antihypertensive treatment should consist of a thiazide-type diuretic, calcium channel blocker, ACEI, or ARB. In the general black population (without CKD), including those with diabetes, initial antihypertensive treatment should consist of a thiazide-type diuretic or a calcium channel blocker **instead of** an ACEI or ARB.

Coronary artery disease (CAD) and hypertension: The American Heart Association, American College of Cardiology and American Society of Hypertension (AHA/ACC/ASH) 2015 scientific statement for the treatment of hypertension in patients with coronary artery disease (CAD) recommends the use of a thiazide (or thiazide-like diuretic) as part of a regimen in patients with hypertension and chronic stable angina. A BP target of <140/90 mm Hg is reasonable for the secondary prevention of cardiovascular events. A lower target BP (<130/80 mm Hg) may be appropriate in some individuals with CAD, previous MI, stroke or transient ischemic attack, or CAD risk equivalents (AHA/ACC/ASH [Rosendorff 2015]).

Local Anesthetic/Vasoconstrictor Precautions Indapamide is one of the drugs confirmed to prolong the QT interval and is accepted as having a risk of causing torsade de pointes. The risk of drug-induced torsade de pointes is extremely low when a single QT interval prolonging drug is prescribed. In terms of epinephrine, it is not known what effect vasoconstrictors in the local anesthetic regimen will have in patients with a known history of congenital prolonged QT interval or in patients taking any medication that prolongs the QT interval. Until more information is obtained, it is suggested that the clinician consult with the physician prior to the use of a vasoconstrictor in suspected patients, and that the vasoconstrictor (epinephrine, mepivacaine and levonordefrin [Carbocaine® 2% with Neo-Cobefrin®]) be used with caution.

Effects on Dental Treatment Key adverse event(s) related to dental treatment: Palpitations, flushing, xerostomia (normal salivary flow resumes upon discontinuation), and rhinorrhea; Patients may experience orthostatic hypotension as they stand up after treatment; especially if lying in dental chair for extended periods of time. Use caution with sudden changes in position during and after dental treatment.

Effects on Bleeding No information available to require special precautions

Adverse Reactions

≥5%:

Central nervous system: Agitation, anxiety, dizziness, fatigue, headache, irritability, lethargy, malaise, nervousness (dose-dependent), pain, paresthesia, tension

Endocrine & metabolic: Hypokalemia (<3.5 mEq/L: 20% to 72%, dose-dependent)

Infection: Infection

Neuromuscular & skeletal: Back pain, muscle cramps, muscle spasm, weakness

Respiratory: Rhinitis

≥1% to <5%:

Cardiovascular: Cardiac arrhythmia, chest pain, flushing, orthostatic hypotension, palpitations, peripheral edema, vasculitis, ventricular premature contractions

Central nervous system: Depression, drowsiness, hypertonia, insomnia, vertigo

Dermatologic: Pruritus, skin rash, urticaria

Endocrine & metabolic: Decreased libido, glycosuria, hyperglycemia, hyperuricemia, hypochloremia, hyponatremia, weight loss

Gastrointestinal: Abdominal cramps, abdominal pain, anorexia, constipation, diarrhea, dyspepsia, gastric irritation, nausea, vomiting, xerostomia

Genitourinary: Nocturia

Ophthalmic: Blurred vision, conjunctivitis

Renal: Increased blood urea nitrogen, increased serum creatinine, polyuria

Respiratory: Cough, flu-like symptoms, pharyngitis, rhinorrhea, sinusitis

<1%, postmarketing, and/or case reports: Abnormal hepatic function tests, agranulocytosis, anaphylaxis, aplastic anemia, bullous rash, cholestatic jaundice, erythema multiforme, fever, hepatitis, hypercalcemia, leukopenia, pancreatitis, pneumonitis, purpura, skin photosensitivity, Stevens-Johnson syndrome, thrombocytopenia, torsades de pointes

General Dosage Range Oral: *Adults:* 1.25-5 mg once daily

Mechanism of Action Diuretic effect is localized at the proximal segment of the distal tubule of the nephron; it does not appear to have significant effect on glomerular filtration rate nor renal blood flow; like other diuretics, it enhances sodium, chloride, and water excretion by interfering with the transport of sodium ions across the renal tubular epithelium

Pharmacodynamics/Kinetics

Half-life Elimination Biphasic: 14 and 25 hours

Time to Peak 2 hours

Pregnancy Risk Factor B

Pregnancy Considerations Adverse events were not observed in animal reproduction studies. Diuretics cross the placenta and are found in cord blood. Maternal use may cause may cause fetal or neonatal jaundice, thrombocytopenia, or other adverse events observed in adults. Use of diuretics during normal pregnancies is not appropriate; use may be considered when edema is due to pathologic causes (as in the nonpregnant patient); monitor.

Dental Comment See Local Anesthetic/Vasoconstrictor Precautions

Indinavir (in DIN a veer)

Related Information

HIV Infection and AIDS *on page 1785*

Brand Names: US Crixivan

Brand Names: Canada Crixivan

Pharmacologic Category Antiretroviral, Protease Inhibitor (Anti-HIV)

Use HIV-1 infection: Treatment of HIV infection in combination with other antiretroviral agents

Local Anesthetic/Vasoconstrictor Precautions No information available to require special precautions

Effects on Dental Treatment Key adverse event(s) related to dental treatment: Abnormal taste.

Effects on Bleeding Spontaneous bleeding has been reported in patients with hemophilia and concurrent HIV infection. Medical consult recommended.

Adverse Reactions

>10%:

Gastrointestinal: Abdominal pain (17%), nausea (12%)

Hepatic: Hyperbilirubinemia (12% to 14%; dose dependent)

Renal: Nephrolithiasis (including flank pain with/without hematuria; ≤29% pediatric patients; ≤12% adult patients; dose dependent), urolithiasis (including flank pain with/without hematuria; ≤29% pediatric patients; ≤12% adult patients; dose dependent)

1% to 10%:

Central nervous system: Headache (5%), dizziness (3%), drowsiness (2%), malaise (2%), fatigue (≤2%)

Dermatologic: Pruritus (4%), skin rash (1%)

Gastrointestinal: Vomiting (8%), anorexia (3%), diarrhea (3%), dysgeusia (3%), gastroesophageal reflux disease (3%), dyspepsia (2%), increased appetite (2%), increased serum amylase (2%)

Genitourinary: Dysuria (2%)

Hematologic & oncologic: Neutropenia (2%), anemia (1%)

Hepatic: Increased serum transaminases (4% to 5%), jaundice (2%)

Neuromuscular & skeletal: Back pain (8%), weakness (≤2%)

Renal: Hydronephrosis (3%)

Respiratory: Cough (2%)

Miscellaneous: Fever (2%)

<1%, postmarketing, and/or case reports: Abdominal distention, acute renal failure, alopecia, anaphylactoid reaction, angina pectoris, arthralgia, cerebrovascular disease, crystalluria, decreased hemoglobin, depression, diabetes mellitus, erythema multiforme, hemolytic anemia, hemorrhage (spontaneous in patients with hemophilia A or B), hepatic failure, hepatitis, hyperglycemia, hyperpigmentation, immune reconstitution syndrome, increased serum cholesterol, increased serum triglycerides, interstitial nephritis (with medullary calcification and cortical atrophy), leukocyturia (severe and asymptomatic), myocardial infarction, oral paresthesia, pancreatitis, paronychia, periarthritis, pharyngitis, prolonged Q-T interval on ECG, pyelonephritis, redistribution of body fat, renal failure, renal insufficiency, Stevens-Johnson syndrome, thrombocytopenia, torsades de pointes, upper respiratory tract infection, urticaria, vasculitis, xeroderma

General Dosage Range Dosage adjustment recommended in patients with hepatic impairment or on concomitant therapy

Oral: *Adults:* 800 mg every 8 hours

Mechanism of Action Binds to the site of HIV-1 protease activity and inhibits cleavage of viral Gag-Pol polyprotein precursors into individual functional proteins required for infectious HIV. This results in the formation of immature, noninfectious viral particles.

Pharmacodynamics/Kinetics

Half-life Elimination Children 4 to 17 years (n=18): 1.1 hours; Adults: 1.8 ± 0.4 hours; Adults with hepatic insufficiency: 2.8 ± 0.5 hours

Time to Peak 0.8 ± 0.3 hours

Pregnancy Risk Factor C

Pregnancy Considerations Adverse events were observed in some animal reproduction studies. Placental passage in humans with unboosted dosing is minimal. No increased risk of overall birth defects has been observed according to data collected by the antiretroviral pregnancy registry. A small increased risk of preterm birth has been associated with maternal use of protease inhibitor-based combination antiretroviral therapy during pregnancy; however, the benefits of use generally outweigh this risk and protease inhibitors (PIs) should not be withheld if otherwise recommended. Information related to stillbirth, low birth weight, and small for gestational age infants is limited. Long-term follow-up is recommended for all infants exposed to antiretroviral medications; children who develop significant organ system abnormalities of unknown etiology (particularly of the CNS or heart) should be evaluated for potential mitochondrial dysfunction. Hyperbilirubinemia may occur in neonates following in utero exposure to indinavir. Hyperglycemia, new onset of diabetes mellitus, or diabetic ketoacidosis have been reported with PIs; it is not clear if pregnancy increases this risk.

Combination antiretroviral therapy (cART) therapy is recommended for all HIV-infected pregnant women to keep the viral load below the limit of detection and reduce the risk of perinatal transmission. When HIV is diagnosed during pregnancy in a woman who has never received antiretroviral therapy, cART should begin as soon as possible after diagnosis. The Health and Humans Services (HHS) Perinatal HIV Guidelines do not recommend indinavir for initial therapy in antiretroviral-naive pregnant women due to concerns regarding maternal kidney stones or maternal hyperbilirubinemia; if used, must be given in combination with low-dose ritonavir boosting during pregnancy although the optimal dose has not yet been established. Plasma concentrations of unboosted indinavir are decreased during pregnancy. In general, women who become pregnant on a stable cART regimen may continue that regimen if viral suppression is effective, appropriate drug exposure can be achieved, contraindications for use in pregnancy are not present, and the regimen is well tolerated. Monitoring during pregnancy is more frequent than in non-pregnant adults; cART should be continued postpartum.

For HIV-infected couples planning a pregnancy, maximum viral suppression with cART is recommended prior to conception for the HIV-infected partner(s) and expert consultation is recommended; modification of therapy (if needed) and optimization of the woman's health should be done prior to conception. HIV-infected women not planning a pregnancy may use any available type of contraception, considering possible drug interactions and contraindications of the specific method. In addition, consistent use of condoms is also recommended (even during pregnancy) to prevent transmission of HIV or other sexually transmitted diseases.

Health care providers are encouraged to enroll pregnant women exposed to antiretroviral medications as early in pregnancy as possible in the Antiretroviral Pregnancy Registry (1-800-258-4263 or www.-APRegistry.com). Health care providers caring for HIV-infected women and their infants may contact the National Perinatal HIV Hotline (888-448-8765) for clinical consultation (HHS [perinatal] 2016).

Indomethacin (in doe METH a sin)

Related Information

Rheumatoid Arthritis, Osteoarthritis, and Osteoporosis *on page 1792*

Temporomandibular Dysfunction (TMD), Chronic Pain, and Fibromyalgia *on page 1868*

Brand Names: US Indocin; Tivorbex

Brand Names: Canada Novo-Methacin; Pro-Indo; ratio-Indomethacin; Sandoz-Indomethacin

Generic Availability (US) May be product dependent

Pharmacologic Category Analgesic, Nonopioid; Nonsteroidal Anti-inflammatory Drug (NSAID), Oral; Nonsteroidal Anti-inflammatory Drug (NSAID), Parenteral

Use

Acute pain, mild to moderate (Tivorbex only): Treatment of mild to moderate acute pain in adults.

Arthritis (excluding Tivorbex): Treatment of moderate to severe rheumatoid arthritis (RA), including acute flares of chronic disease; moderate to severe osteoarthritis (OA); acute gouty arthritis (except extended-release [ER] capsules).

Inflammatory conditions (excluding Tivorbex): Treatment of moderate to severe ankylosing spondylitis; acute painful bursitis and/or tendinitis of the shoulder (excluding Canadian products).

Patent ductus arteriosus (IV only): To close a hemodynamically significant patent ductus arteriosus in premature infants weighing between 500 and 1,750 g when 48 hours usual medical management (eg, fluid restriction, diuretics, digitalis, respiratory support) is ineffective.

Local Anesthetic/Vasoconstrictor Precautions No information available to require special precautions

Effects on Dental Treatment The dentist should be aware of the potential of abnormal coagulation. Caution should also be exercised in the use of NSAIDs in patients already on anticoagulant therapy with drugs such as warfarin (Coumadin®). See Effects on Bleeding.

Effects on Bleeding Nonselective NSAIDs such as indomethacin inhibit platelet aggregation and prolong bleeding time in some patients. Unlike aspirin, the NSAID effect on platelet function is quantitatively less, of shorter duration, and reversible.

Adverse Reactions

>10%:

Central nervous system: Headache (12% to 16%)

Gastrointestinal: Vomiting (≤12%)

Hematologic & oncologic: Postoperative hemorrhage (≤11%)

1% to 10%:

Cardiovascular: Presyncope (≤3%), syncope (≤2%)

Central nervous system: Dizziness (3% to 9%), depression (<3%), drowsiness (<3%), fatigue (<3%), malaise (<3%), vertigo (<3%)

Dermatologic: Pruritus (1% to 4%), hyperhidrosis (2%), skin rash (1% to 2%)

Endocrine & metabolic: Hot flash (2%)

Gastrointestinal: Epigastric pain (3% to 9%), heartburn (3% to 9%), nausea (3% to 9%), dyspepsia (2% to 9%), constipation (≤6%), diarrhea (≤3%), abdominal pain (<3%), decreased appetite (≥2%), rectal irritation (suppository), tenesmus (suppository)

Otic: Tinnitus (<3%)

Miscellaneous: Swelling (3%; postprocedural)

<1%, postmarketing, and/or case reports: Acute respiratory distress, agranulocytosis, alopecia, allergic rhinitis, anaphylaxis, anemia, angioedema, anorexia, anxiety, aphthous stomatitis, aplastic anemia, aseptic meningitis, asthma, bloating, blurred vision, bone marrow depression, breast hypertrophy, breast tenderness, bronchospasm, cardiac arrhythmia, cardiac failure, cerebrovascular accident, chest pain, cholestatic jaundice, coma, confusion, conjunctivitis, convulsions, corneal deposits, cystitis, deafness, depersonalization, depression, diaphoresis, diplopia, disseminated intravascular coagulation, dry eye syndrome, dysarthria, dyspnea, ecchymoses, edema, epistaxis, erythema multiforme, erythema nodosum, exacerbation of epilepsy, exacerbation of Parkinson's disease, exfoliative dermatitis, fatigue, fever, flatulence, fluid retention, flushing, gastritis, gastroenteritis, gastrointestinal hemorrhage, gastrointestinal perforation (rare), gastrointestinal ulcer, GI inflammation, glycosuria, gynecomastia, hearing loss, hematuria, hemodynamic deterioration (patients with severe heart failure and hyponatremia), hemolytic anemia, hepatic failure, hepatic necrosis, hepatitis (including fatal cases), hepatotoxicity (idiosyncratic) (Chalasani, 2014), hyperglycemia, hyperkalemia, hypersensitivity reaction, hypertension, hypotension, immune thrombocytopenia, increased blood urea nitrogen, increased liver enzymes, insomnia, intestinal obstruction, interstitial nephritis, intestinal stenosis, involuntary muscle movements, jaundice, leukopenia, maculopathy, myocardial infarction, necrotizing fasciitis, nephrotic syndrome, nervousness, oliguria, palpitations, paresthesia, peptic ulcer, peripheral neuropathy, petechiae, polydipsia, polyuria, proctitis, proteinuria, psychic disturbance, psychosis, pulmonary edema, purpura, rectal hemorrhage, regional ileitis, renal failure, renal insufficiency, retinal disturbance, shock, significant cardiovascular event, Stevens-Johnson syndrome, stomatitis, syncope, tachycardia, thrombocytopenia, thrombophlebitis, toxic amblyopia, toxic epidermal necrolysis, ulcerative colitis, urinary frequency, urticaria, vaginal hemorrhage, vasculitis, weakness, weight gain

Dosing

Adult

Inflammatory/rheumatoid disorders: Note: Use lowest effective dose for the shortest duration possible.

Oral (immediate-release [excluding Tivorbex)]), rectal: 25 mg 2 to 3 times daily; if well tolerated, increase daily dosage by 25 or 50 mg at weekly intervals until satisfactory response or a total daily dose of 150 to 200 mg/day (maximum dose: 200 mg/day) is reached. In patients with arthritis and persistent night pain and/or morning stiffness may give the larger portion (up to maximum of 100 mg) of the total daily dose at bedtime.

Oral (extended-release capsules): Initial: 75 mg once daily, may increase to 75 mg twice daily (maximum dose: 150 mg/day).

Bursitis/tendonitis of the shoulder: Oral (excluding Tivorbex and Canadian products), rectal (excluding Canadian products): Initial dose: 75 to 150 mg/day in 3 to 4 divided doses **or** 1 to 2 divided doses for extended release; usual treatment is 7 to 14 days; discontinue after signs/symptoms of inflammation have been controlled for several days.

Acute gouty arthritis: Oral (excluding extended-release capsules and Tivorbex), rectal: 50 mg 3 times daily until pain is tolerable then rapidly reduce dose to complete cessation of drug.

Acute pain (mild to moderate): Oral (Tivorbex only): 20 mg 3 times daily or 40 mg 2 or 3 times daily

Prevention of pancreatitis post-endoscopic retrograde cholangiopancreatography (ERCP) (off-label use): Rectal: 100 mg immediately after ERCP (Elmunzer, 2012)

Geriatric Refer to adult dosing. Use lowest recommended dose and frequency in elderly to initiate therapy for indications listed in adult dosing.

Pediatric

Patent ductus arteriosus:

Neonates weighing between 500 to 1,750 g: IV: Initial: 0.2 mg/kg, followed by 2 doses depending on postnatal age (PNA):

PNA at time of FIRST dose <48 hours: 0.1 mg/kg at 12- to 24-hour intervals

PNA at time of FIRST dose 2 to 7 days: 0.2 mg/kg at 12- to 24-hour intervals

PNA at time of FIRST dose >7 days: 0.25 mg/kg at 12- to 24-hour intervals

Note: In general, may use 12-hour dosing interval if urine output >1 mL/kg/hour after prior dose; use 24-hour dosing interval if urine output is <1 mL/kg/hour but >0.6 mL/kg/hour. Doses should be withheld if patient has oliguria (urine output <0.6 mL/kg/hour) or anuria at the scheduled time of the second or third dose; do not give additional doses until renal function has returned to normal. If the ductus arteriosus closes or is significantly reduced in size after 48 hours or more from completion of first course, no further doses are necessary. If the ductus arteriosus reopens, a second course of 1 to 3 doses may be given; if unresponsive after 2 doses, surgery may be necessary.

Inflammatory/rheumatoid disorders: Note: Use lowest effective dose for the shortest duration possible. Canadian labeling contraindicates use in children and adolescents <14 years.

Children ≥2 years (limited data available): Oral (excluding extended release capsules and Tivorbex): 1 to 2 mg/kg/day in 2 to 4 divided doses; maximum daily dose: 4 mg/kg/day or 200 mg/day, whichever is less

Adolescents >14 years:

Oral (immediate release [excluding Tivorbex]), rectal: Refer to adult dosing.

Oral (extended release capsules): Refer to adult dosing.

Renal Impairment

US labeling:

Oral/rectal: There are no dosage adjustments provided in the manufacturer's labeling; not recommended in patients with advanced renal disease.

Injection: If anuria or marked oliguria (urinary output <0.6 mL/kg/hour) evident at the scheduled time of the second or third dose, hold dose until renal function returns to normal. Use is contraindicated in neonates with significant renal impairment.

Canadian labeling:

Mild to moderate impairment: There are no dosage adjustments provided in the manufacturer's labeling; use with caution and consider lower doses.

Severe impairment (CrCl <30 mL/minute) or deteriorating renal function: Use is contraindicated.

KDIGO 2012 guidelines provide the following recommendations for NSAIDs:

eGFR 30 to <60 mL/minute/1.73 m^2: Temporarily discontinue in patients with intercurrent disease that increases risk of acute kidney injury.

eGFR <30 mL/minute/1.73 m^2: Avoid use.

Hepatic Impairment

US labeling: There are no dosage adjustments provided in the manufacturer's labeling; use with caution.

Canadian labeling: There are no dosage adjustments provided in the manufacturer's labeling. Use is contraindicated in severe liver impairment or active liver disease.

Mechanism of Action Reversibly inhibits cyclooxygenase-1 and 2 (COX-1 and 2) enzymes, which results in decreased formation of prostaglandin precursors; has antipyretic, analgesic, and anti-inflammatory properties

Other proposed mechanisms not fully elucidated (and possibly contributing to the anti-inflammatory effect to varying degrees), include inhibiting chemotaxis, altering lymphocyte activity, inhibiting neutrophil aggregation/activation, and decreasing proinflammatory cytokine levels.

Contraindications

Hypersensitivity (eg, anaphylactic reactions, serious skin reactions) to indomethacin or any component of the formulation; use in the setting of coronary artery bypass graft (CABG) surgery; history of asthma, urticaria, or allergic-type reactions after taking aspirin or other NSAID agents; patients with a history of proctitis or recent rectal bleeding (suppositories).

Neonates (IV only): Necrotizing enterocolitis (proven or suspected); significant renal impairment; active bleeding (including intracranial hemorrhage and gastrointestinal bleeding), thrombocytopenia, coagulation defects; untreated infection (proven or suspected); congenital heart disease where patency of the ductus arteriosus is necessary for adequate pulmonary or systemic blood flow (eg, pulmonary atresia, severe tetralogy of Fallot, severe coarctation of the aorta)

Canadian labeling: Additional contraindications (not in US labeling): Severe uncontrolled heart failure; known hyperkalemia; active gastric/duodenal/peptic ulcer; active GI bleed; history of recurrent GI ulceration; active GI inflammatory disease; cerebrovascular bleeding or other bleeding disorders; severe hepatic impairment or active liver disease; severe renal impairment (CrCl <30 mL/minute) or deteriorating renal function; concurrent use with other NSAIDs; complete or partial syndrome of nasal polyps; children and adolescents <14 years of age; breastfeeding; pregnancy (third trimester)

Warnings/Precautions [US Boxed Warning]: NSAIDs cause an increased risk of serious (and potentially fatal) adverse cardiovascular thrombotic events, including MI and stroke. Risk may occur early during treatment and may increase with duration of use. Relative risk appears to be similar in those with and without known cardiovascular disease or risk factors for cardiovascular disease; however, absolute incidence of serious cardiovascular thrombotic events (which may occur early during treatment) was higher in patients with known cardiovascular disease or risk factors and in those receiving higher doses. New-onset hypertension or exacerbation of hypertension may occur (NSAIDs may also impair response to ACE inhibitors, thiazide diuretics, or loop diuretics); may contribute to cardiovascular events; monitor blood pressure; use with caution in patients with hypertension. May cause sodium and fluid retention, use with caution in patients with edema. Avoid use in heart failure (ACCF/AHA [Yancy 2013]). Avoid use in patients with recent MI unless benefits outweigh risk of cardiovascular thrombotic events. Use the lowest effective dose for the shortest duration of time, consistent with individual patient goals, to reduce risk of cardiovascular events; alternate therapies should be considered for patients at high risk. **[US Boxed Warning]: Use is contraindicated in the setting of coronary artery bypass graft (CABG) surgery.** Risk of MI and stroke may be increased with use following CABG surgery.

Even in patients without prior exposure anaphylactoid reactions may occur; patients with "aspirin triad" (bronchial asthma, aspirin intolerance, rhinitis) may be at increased risk. Contraindicated in patients with aspirin-sensitive asthma; severe and potentially fatal bronchospasm may occur. Use caution in patients with other forms of asthma. May cause drowsiness, dizziness, blurred vision, and other neurologic effects which may impair physical or mental abilities; patients must be cautioned about performing tasks which require mental alertness (eg, operating machinery or driving). Headache may occur; cessation of therapy required if headache persists after dosage reduction.

[US Boxed Warning]: NSAIDs cause increased risk of serious gastrointestinal inflammation, ulceration, bleeding, and perforation (may be fatal); elderly patients and patients with history of peptic ulcer disease and/or GI bleeding are at greater risk for serious GI events. These events may occur at any time during therapy and without warning. Avoid use in patients with active GI bleeding. Use caution with a history of GI ulcers, concurrent therapy known to increase the risk of GI bleeding (eg, aspirin, anticoagulants and/or corticosteroids, selective serotonin reuptake inhibitors), advanced hepatic disease, coagulopathy, smoking, use of alcohol, or in the elderly or debilitated patients. Use the lowest effective dose for the shortest duration of time, consistent with individual patient goals, to reduce risk of GI adverse events; alternate therapies should be considered for patients at high risk. When used concomitantly with aspirin, a substantial increase in the risk of gastrointestinal complications (eg, ulcer) occurs; concomitant gastroprotective therapy (eg, proton pump inhibitors) is recommended (Bhatt 2008).

Platelet adhesion and aggregation may be decreased; may prolong bleeding time; patients with coagulation disorders or who are receiving anticoagulants should be monitored closely. Anemia may occur; patients on long-term NSAID therapy should be monitored for anemia. Rarely, NSAID use has been associated with potentially severe blood dyscrasias (eg, agranulocytosis, thrombocytopenia, aplastic anemia). Transaminase elevations have been reported with use; closely monitor patients with any abnormal LFT. Rare, sometimes fatal severe hepatic reactions (eg, fulminant hepatitis, hepatic necrosis, hepatic failure) have occurred with NSAID use; discontinue immediately if clinical signs or symptoms of liver disease develop or if systemic manifestations occur. Use with caution in patients with hepatic impairment; patients with advanced hepatic disease are at an increased risk of GI bleeding with NSAIDs. Canadian labeling contraindicates use in severe hepatic impairment or active liver disease.

NSAID use may increase the risk of hyperkalemia, particularly in the elderly, diabetics, renal disease, and with concomitant use of other agents capable of inducing hyperkalemia (eg, ACE-inhibitors). Monitor potassium closely. Prolonged therapy may cause corneal deposits and retinal disturbances, including those of the macula. Discontinue use with blurred or diminished vision and perform ophthalmologic exam. Periodically evaluate vision in all patients receiving long-term therapy.

NSAID use may compromise existing renal function; dose-dependent decreases in prostaglandin synthesis may result from NSAID use, reducing renal blood flow which may cause renal decompensation (usually reversible). Patients with impaired renal function, dehydration, hypovolemia, heart failure, hepatic impairment, those taking diuretics, and ACE inhibitors, and the elderly are at greater risk of renal toxicity. Rehydrate patient before starting therapy; monitor renal function closely. Long-term NSAID use may result in renal papillary necrosis and other renal injury. Avoid use in patients with advanced renal disease; discontinue use with persistent or worsening abnormal renal function tests. The injection formulation is contraindicated in neonates with significant renal impairment. Canadian labeling contraindicates use in severe renal impairment (CrCl <30 mL/minute) or deteriorating renal function.

NSAIDs may cause potentially fatal serious skin adverse events including exfoliative dermatitis, Stevens-Johnson syndrome (SJS), and toxic epidermal necrolysis (TEN); may occur without warning; discontinue use at first sign of skin rash (or any other hypersensitivity). May increase the risk of aseptic meningitis, especially in patients with systemic lupus erythematosus (SLE) and mixed connective tissue disorders. Use caution with depression, epilepsy, or Parkinson disease. Potentially significant interactions may exist, requiring dose or frequency adjustment, additional monitoring, and/or selection of alternative therapy.

Elderly patients are at greater risk for serious GI, cardiovascular, and/or renal adverse events; use with caution. Indomethacin may cause confusion or, rarely, psychosis; remain alert to the possibility of such adverse reactions in elderly patients.

Oral: There have been cases of hepatotoxicity reported in pediatric patients with juvenile rheumatoid arthritis, including fatalities. Closely monitor if needed in pediatric patients ≥2 years and periodically assess liver function.

Tivorbex is not indicated for long-term use. Withhold for at least 4 to 6 half-lives prior to surgical or dental procedures.

Drug Interactions

Metabolism/Transport Effects **Substrate** of CYP2C19 (minor), CYP2C9 (minor); **Note:** Assignment of Major/Minor substrate status based on clinically relevant drug interaction potential; **Inhibits** CYP2C9 (weak)

Avoid Concomitant Use

Avoid concomitant use of Indomethacin with any of the following: Dexketoprofen; Floctafenine; Ketorolac (Nasal); Ketorolac (Systemic); Morniflumate; NSAID (COX-2 Inhibitor); Omacetaxine; Pelubiprofen; Phenylbutazone; Talniflumate; Tenoxicam; Urokinase; Zaltoprofen

Increased Effect/Toxicity

Indomethacin may increase the levels/effects of: 5-ASA Derivatives; Agents with Antiplatelet Properties; Aliskiren; Aminoglycosides; Aminolevulinic Acid; Anticoagulants; Apixaban; Bisphosphonate Derivatives; Cephalothin; Collagenase (Systemic); CycloSPORINE (Systemic); Dabigatran Etexilate; Deferasirox; Deoxycholic Acid; Desmopressin; Digoxin; Drospirenone; Edoxaban; Eplerenone; Haloperidol; Ibritumomab; Lithium; Methotrexate; Nonsteroidal Anti-Inflammatory Agents; NSAID (COX-2 Inhibitor); Obinutuzumab; Omacetaxine; PEMEtrexed; Porfimer; Potassium-Sparing Diuretics; PRALAtrexate; Quinolone Antibiotics; Rivaroxaban; Salicylates; Tacrolimus (Systemic); Tenofovir Products; Thrombolytic Agents; Tiludronate; Tolperisone; Tositumomab and Iodine I 131 Tositumomab; Triamterene; Urokinase; Vancomycin; Verteporfin; Vitamin K Antagonists

The levels/effects of Indomethacin may be increased by: ACE Inhibitors; Alcohol (Ethyl); Angiotensin II Receptor Blockers; Antidepressants (Tricyclic, Tertiary Amine); Corticosteroids (Systemic); CycloSPORINE (Systemic); Dasatinib; Dexketoprofen; Diclofenac (Systemic); Felbinac; Floctafenine; Glucosamine; Herbs (Anticoagulant/Antiplatelet Properties); Ibrutinib; Ketorolac (Nasal); Ketorolac (Systemic); Limaprost; Loop Diuretics; Morniflumate; Multivitamins/Fluoride (with ADE); Multivitamins/Minerals (with ADEK, Folate, Iron); Multivitamins/Minerals (with AE, No Iron); Naftazone; Omega-3 Fatty Acids; Pelubiprofen; Pentosan Polysulfate Sodium; Pentoxifylline; Phenylbutazone; Probenecid; Prostacyclin Analogues; Selective Serotonin Reuptake Inhibitors; Serotonin/Norepinephrine Reuptake Inhibitors; Sodium Phosphates; Talniflumate; Tenoxicam; Thiazide and Thiazide-Like Diuretics; Tipranavir; Tolperisone; Vitamin E (Systemic); Zaltoprofen

Decreased Effect

Indomethacin may decrease the levels/effects of: ACE Inhibitors; Aliskiren; Angiotensin II Receptor Blockers; Beta-Blockers; Eplerenone; Glucagon; HydrALAZINE; Loop Diuretics; Potassium-Sparing Diuretics; Prostaglandins (Ophthalmic); Salicylates; Selective Serotonin Reuptake Inhibitors; Thiazide and Thiazide-Like Diuretics

The levels/effects of Indomethacin may be decreased by: Bile Acid Sequestrants; Salicylates

Food Interactions Food may decrease the rate but not the extent of absorption. Indomethacin peak serum levels may be delayed if taken with food. Management: Administer with food or milk to minimize GI upset.

Dietary Considerations May cause GI upset; take with food or milk to minimize

Pharmacodynamics/Kinetics

Onset of Action ~30 minutes

Duration of Action 4 to 6 hours

Half-life Elimination

Neonates: Postnatal age (PNA) <2 weeks: ~20 hours; PNA >2 weeks: ~11 hours; Adults: 2.6-11.2 hours; 7.6 hours (Tivorbex)

Time to Peak Oral: Immediate release: 2 hours; Tivorbex capsules: 1.67 hours

Pregnancy Risk Factor C (<30 weeks gestation); C/D (≥30 weeks gestation [manufacturer specific])

Pregnancy Considerations Adverse events have been observed in animal reproduction studies; studies in pregnant women have demonstrated risk to the fetus if administered at ≥30 weeks gestation. Indomethacin crosses the placenta and can be detected in fetal plasma and amniotic fluid. Indomethacin exposure during the first trimester is not strongly associated with congenital malformations; however, cardiovascular anomalies and cleft palate have been observed following NSAID exposure in some studies. The use of an NSAID close to conception may be associated with an increased risk of miscarriage. Nonteratogenic effects have been observed following NSAID administration during the third trimester, including myocardial degenerative changes, prenatal constriction of the ductus arteriosus, failure of the ductus arteriosus to close postnatally, and fetal tricuspid regurgitation; renal dysfunction or failure, oligohydramnios; gastrointestinal bleeding or perforation, increased risk of necrotizing enterocolitis; intracranial bleeding (including intraventricular hemorrhage), platelet dysfunction with resultant bleeding; and pulmonary hypertension. The risk of fetal ductal constriction following maternal use of indomethacin is increased with gestational age and duration of therapy. Because they may cause premature closure of the ductus arteriosus, use of NSAIDs late in pregnancy should be avoided (use after 31 or 32 weeks gestation is not recommended by some clinicians). Indomethacin has been used for a short duration (eg, ≤48 hours) in the management of preterm labor. Indomethacin should be used with caution in pregnant women with hypertension. The chronic use of NSAIDs in women of reproductive age may be associated with infertility that is reversible upon discontinuation of the medication. Use during pregnancy (third trimester) is contraindicated in the Canadian labeling.

Breastfeeding Considerations Indomethacin is excreted into breast milk and low amounts have been measured in the plasma of nursing infants. Seizures in a nursing infant were observed in one case report, although adverse events have not been noted in other cases. breastfeeding is not recommended by most manufacturers (use is contraindicated in the Canadian labeling); Tivorbex may be used with caution during breastfeeding. (The therapeutic use of indomethacin is contraindicated in neonates with significant renal failure.) Hypertensive crisis and psychiatric side effects have been noted in case reports following use of indomethacin for analgesia in postpartum women. Use with caution in nursing women with hypertensive disorders of pregnancy or preexisting renal disease.

Dosage Forms

Capsule, Oral:

Tivorbex: 20 mg, 40 mg

Generic: 25 mg, 50 mg

Capsule Extended Release, Oral:

Generic: 75 mg

Solution Reconstituted, Intravenous:

Generic: 1 mg (1 ea)

Solution Reconstituted, Intravenous [preservative free]:
Generic: 1 mg (1 ea)
Suppository, Rectal:
Indocin: 50 mg (30 ea)
Suspension, Oral:
Indocin: 25 mg/5 mL (237 mL)

Dosage Forms: Canada Note: Refer also to Dosage Forms. Extended release capsule, intravenous solution, and oral suspension are not available in Canada.
Suppository, Rectal: 100 mg

InFLIXimab (in FLIKS e mab)

Related Information
Rheumatoid Arthritis, Osteoarthritis, and Osteoporosis *on page 1792*

Brand Names: US Inflectra; Remicade

Brand Names: Canada Inflectra; Remicade; Remsima

Pharmacologic Category Antirheumatic, Disease Modifying; Gastrointestinal Agent, Miscellaneous; Immunosuppressant Agent; Monoclonal Antibody; Tumor Necrosis Factor (TNF) Blocking Agent

Use
Ankylosing spondylitis: Treatment of adults with active ankylosing spondylitis (to reduce signs/symptoms)
Crohn disease: Treatment of adults and pediatric patients ≥6 years with moderately to severely active Crohn disease who have had inadequate responses to conventional therapy (to reduce signs/symptoms and induce and maintain clinical remission) or to reduce the number of draining enterocutaneous and rectovaginal fistulas and maintain fistula closure in adults
Plaque psoriasis: Treatment of adults with chronic, severe (extensive and/or disabling) plaque psoriasis as an alternative to other systemic therapy
Psoriatic arthritis: Treatment of adults with psoriatic arthritis (to reduce signs/symptoms of active arthritis and inhibit progression of structural damage and improve physical function)
Rheumatoid arthritis: Treatment of adults with moderately to severely active rheumatoid arthritis (with methotrexate) (to reduce signs/symptoms of active arthritis and inhibit progression of structural damage and improve physical function)
Ulcerative colitis: Treatment of adults and pediatric patients ≥6 years with moderately to severely active ulcerative colitis with inadequate response to conventional therapy (to reduce signs/symptoms and induce and maintain clinical remission, mucosal healing and eliminate corticosteroid use)

Note: Inflectra and Remsima [Canadian product] are biosimilar agents; approved uses may vary (see product labeling).

Local Anesthetic/Vasoconstrictor Precautions
No information available to require special precautions

Effects on Dental Treatment No significant effects or complications reported

Effects on Bleeding Has been associated with thrombocytopenia, anemia, and hemolytic anemia, but incidence may vary with indication.

Adverse Reactions
>10%:
Central nervous system: Headache (18%)
Gastrointestinal: Abdominal pain (Crohn disease: 26%; other indications: 12%), nausea (21%)
Hepatic: Increased serum ALT (<3x ULN: 17% to 51%; ≥3x ULN: 2% to 10%; ≥5x ULN: 1% to 4%)
Immunologic: Increased ANA titer (~50%), antibody development (double-stranded DNA, 20%), antibody development (anti-infliximab; variable; ~10% to 15% [range: 6% to 61%]; Mayer 2006)
Infection: Infection (Crohn disease: 50% to 59%; other indications: 27% to 36%), abscess (Crohn disease patients with fistulizing disease: 6% to 15%)
Respiratory: Upper respiratory tract infection (32%), sinusitis (14%), cough (12%), pharyngitis (12%)
Miscellaneous: Infusion related reaction (18%; severe: <1%)

1% to 10%:
Cardiovascular: Flushing (Crohn disease: 9%), hypertension (7%), chest pain (≤1%), bradycardia (≥0.2%), edema (≥0.2%), hypotension (≥0.2%), thrombophlebitis (deep) (≥0.2%)
Central nervous system: Fatigue (9%), pain (8%), chills (≤3%), dizziness (≥0.2%)
Dermatologic: Skin rash (1% to 10%), pruritus (≤7%), cellulitis (≥0.2%), diaphoresis (≥0.2%)
Endocrine & metabolic: Dehydration (≥0.2%)
Gastrointestinal: Dyspepsia (10%), GI moniliasis (5%), constipation (≥0.2%), intestinal obstruction (≥0.2%)
Genitourinary: Urinary tract infection (8%)
Hematologic & oncologic: Anemia (children with Crohn disease: 11%; adults: ≥0.2%), hemolytic anemia (≥0.2%), leukopenia (Crohn disease: 9%; other indications: ≥0.2%), lymphadenopathy (≥0.2%), malignant lymphoma (≥0.2%), neutropenia (Crohn disease: 7%), pancytopenia (≥0.2%), sarcoidosis (≥0.2%), thrombocytopenia (≥0.2%)
Hepatic: Hepatitis (≥0.2%)
Hypersensitivity: Hypersensitivity reaction (Crohn disease: 6%; other indications: ≥0.2%), delayed hypersensitivity (plaque psoriasis: 1%), serum sickness (≥0.2%)
Infection: Viral infection (Crohn disease: 8%), bacterial infection (Crohn disease: 6%), serious infection (1% to 5%), sepsis (≥0.2%)
Neuromuscular & skeletal: Arthralgia (1% to 8%), bone fracture (Crohn disease: 7%), myalgia (1%)
Respiratory: Bronchitis (10%), dyspnea (≤1%), lower respiratory tract infection (≥0.2%), pleurisy (≥0.2%), pulmonary edema (≥0.2%)
Miscellaneous: Fever (≤3% to 7%)

<1%, postmarketing, and/or case reports: Acute hepatic failure, agranulocytosis, anaphylactic shock, anaphylaxis, angina pectoris, antibody development, autoimmune hepatitis, bronchospasm, cardiac failure (worsening), cholecystitis, cholestasis, chronic inflammatory demyelinating polyneuropathy, confusion, convulsions, demyelinating disease of the central nervous system (eg, multiple sclerosis, optic neuritis), demyelinating disease (peripheral; eg, Guillain-Barré syndrome, chronic inflammatory demyelinating polyneuropathy, multifocal motor neuropathy), dysgeusia, erythema multiforme, erythematous rash, exacerbation of psoriasis, gastrointestinal hemorrhage, hepatic carcinoma, hepatic failure, hepatic injury, hepatitis B (reactivation), hepatotoxicity (idiosyncratic) (Chalasani 2014), hepatosplenic T-cell lymphomas (mainly young adult or adolescent males), Hodgkin lymphoma, immune thrombocytopenia, interstitial fibrosis, interstitial pneumonitis, intestinal stenosis, jaundice, laryngeal edema, leukemia, liver function tests increased (transient), lupus-like syndrome (drug-induced), malignant melanoma, malignant neoplasm (leiomyosarcoma), meningitis, Merkel

cell carcinoma, myocardial infarction, nephrolithiasis, neuritis, neuropathy, numbness, opportunistic infection, pancreatitis, pericardial effusion, peripheral neuropathy, pharyngeal edema, pleural effusion, pneumonia, psoriasis (including new onset, palmoplantar, pustular, or exacerbation), pulmonary disease, pulmonary fibrosis, reactivated tuberculosis, renal cell carcinoma, renal failure, seizure, Stevens-Johnson syndrome, syncope, tachycardia, tendon disease, thrombotic thrombocytopenia purpura, tingling sensation, toxic epidermal necrolysis, transverse myelitis, tuberculosis, ulcer, urticaria, vasculitis (systemic and cutaneous), vision loss (transient)

General Dosage Range Dosage adjustment is required in heart failure patients.

IV:

Children ≥6 years and Adolescents: Initial: 5 mg/kg at 0, 2, and 6 weeks; Maintenance: 5 mg/kg every 8 weeks

Adults: Initial: 3 to 10 mg/kg at 0, 2, and 6 weeks; Maintenance: 3 to 10 mg/kg every 8 weeks **or** 5 mg/kg every 6 weeks

Mechanism of Action Infliximab is a chimeric monoclonal antibody that binds to human tumor necrosis factor alpha (TNFα), thereby interfering with endogenous TNFα activity. Elevated TNFα levels have been found in involved tissues/fluids of patients with rheumatoid arthritis, ankylosing spondylitis, psoriatic arthritis, plaque psoriasis, Crohn disease and ulcerative colitis. Biological activities of TNFα include the induction of proinflammatory cytokines (interleukins), enhancement of leukocyte migration, activation of neutrophils and eosinophils, and the induction of acute phase reactants and tissue degrading enzymes. Animal models have shown TNFα expression causes polyarthritis, and infliximab can prevent disease as well as allow diseased joints to heal.

Pharmacodynamics/Kinetics

Onset of Action Crohn disease: 1 to 2 weeks; Rheumatoid arthritis: 3 to 7 days

Duration of Action Crohn disease: 8 to 48 weeks; Rheumatoid arthritis: 6 to 12 weeks

Half-life Elimination 7 to 12 days (Klotz 2007)

Pregnancy Risk Factor B

Pregnancy Considerations Animal reproduction studies have not been conducted. Infliximab crosses the placenta and can be detected in the serum of infants for up to 6 months following in utero exposure. A fatal outcome has been reported in an infant who received a live vaccine (BCG) after in utero exposure to infliximab; it is recommended to wait ≥6 months following birth before administering any live vaccine to infants exposed to infliximab in utero. If a biologic agent such as infliximab is needed to treat inflammatory bowel disease during pregnancy, it is recommended to hold therapy after 30 weeks gestation (Habal, 2012).

Healthcare providers are also encouraged to enroll women exposed to infliximab during pregnancy in the MotherToBaby Autoimmune Diseases Study by contacting the Organization of Teratology Information Specialists (OTIS) (877-311-8972).

Influenza A Virus Vaccine (H5N1)

(in floo EN za aye VYE rus vak SEEN H5N1)

Pharmacologic Category Vaccine, Inactivated (Viral)

Use Influenza A (H5N1) immunization:

GlaxoSmithKline product (adjuvanted): For active immunization of persons ≥18 years of age at increased risk of exposure to the influenza A (H5N1) virus subtype contained in the vaccine

Sanofi Pasteur product: For active immunization of persons 18-64 years of age at increased risk of exposure to the influenza A (H5N1) virus subtype contained in the vaccine

Local Anesthetic/Vasoconstrictor Precautions No information available to require special precautions

Effects on Dental Treatment No significant effects or complications reported

Effects on Bleeding No information available to require special precautions

Adverse Reactions All serious adverse reactions must be reported to the U.S. Department of Health and Human Services (DHHS) Vaccine Adverse Event Reporting System (VAERS) 1-800-822-7967 or online at https://vaers.hhs.gov/esub/index.

>10%:

Central nervous system: Headache (3% to 35%), fatigue (34%), shivering (17%)

Dermatologic: Diaphoresis (11%)

Local: Pain at injection site (74% to 83%), tenderness at injection site (70%), erythema at injection site (9% to 20%), swelling at injection site (10% to 15%)

Neuromuscular & skeletal: Myalgia (45%), arthralgia (25%)

1% to 10%:

Gastrointestinal: Nausea (10%), diarrhea (6%)

Local: Itching at injection site (2%), burning sensation at injection site (1%)

Respiratory: Nasal congestion (1%)

Miscellaneous: Fever (5%)

<1%: Celiac disease, cerebrovascular accident, convulsions, cranial nerve palsy (IV), Crohn's disease, erythema nodosum, facial paralysis, giant-cell arteritis, hepatitis, injection site reaction, malignant neoplasm of thyroid, organ transplant rejection (corneal), polymyalgia rheumatica, psoriasis, pulmonary embolism, radiculopathy, rheumatoid arthritis, rheumatoid lung, skin rash

General Dosage Range IM:

Adults ≥18 years: GlaxoSmithKline product (adjuvanted): 0.5 mL, followed by a second 0.5 mL dose given 21 days later

Adults 18-64 years: Sanofi Pasteur product: 1 mL, followed by second 1 mL dose given 28 days later

Mechanism of Action

The GlaxoSmithKline product is an adjuvanted monovalent split virus (inactivated) preparation of the type A, subtype H5N1 avian strain of influenza virus (A/Indonesia/05/2005)

The Sanofi Pasteur product is a monovalent, split virus (inactivated) preparation of the type A, subtype H5N1 avian strain of influenza virus (A/Vietnam/1203/2004)

Both promote active immunity to influenza A H5N1 (avian).

Pharmacodynamics/Kinetics

Onset of Action

GlaxoSmithKline product (adjuvanted): Fourfold increase in antibody titers (measured by hemagglutination inhibition [HI]) occurred in up to 90% of patients 18-64 years of age and 74% of patients ≥65 years of age 21 days after the second dose

Sanofi Pasteur product: Fourfold increase in antibody titers (measured by HI) occurred in up to 58% of patients 28 days after the second dose (Treanor, 2006).

Pregnancy Risk Factor B/C (product specific)

Pregnancy Considerations Adverse events were not observed in animal reproduction studies using the

H5N1 vaccine GlaxoSmithKline adjuvanted product; animal reproduction studies have not been conducted with the Sanofi Pasteur product. Inactivated viral vaccines have not been shown to cause increased risks to the fetus (CDC, 2011).

Product Availability Products will not be commercially available; distribution will be limited as part of the US Strategic National Stockpile.

GlaxoSmithKline product (adjuvanted) product, (also referred to as Q-Pan H5N1 influenza vaccine): FDA approved November 2013.

Prescribing and Access Restrictions Commercial distribution is not planned. The vaccine will be included as part of the U.S. Strategic National Stockpile. It will be distributed by public health officials if needed.

Influenza Virus Vaccine (Inactivated)

(in floo EN za VYE rus vak SEEN, in ak ti VAY ted)

Brand Names: US Afluria; Afluria Quadrivalent; Fluad; Fluarix Quadrivalent; Flucelvax Quadrivalent; Flucelvax [DSC]; FluLaval Quadrivalent; Fluvirin; Fluzone High-Dose; Fluzone Intradermal Quadrivalent; Fluzone Quadrivalent; Fluzone [DSC]

Brand Names: Canada Agriflu; Fluad; Fluad Pediatric; Flulaval Tetra; Fluviral; Fluzone High-Dose; Fluzone Quadrivalent; Influvac

Pharmacologic Category Vaccine; Vaccine, Inactivated (Viral)

Use Influenza disease prevention: Active immunization against influenza disease caused by influenza virus subtypes A and type B contained in the vaccine in the following persons:

US labeling:

- 6 months and older (FluLaval Quadrivalent, Fluzone Quadrivalent)
- 3 years and older (Fluarix Quadrivalent)
- 4 years and older (Flucelvax Quadrivalent, Fluvirin)
- 5 years and older (Afluria)
- 18 years and older (Afluria Quadrivalent)
- 18 through 64 years of age (Fluzone Intradermal Quadrivalent)
- 65 years and older (Fluad, Fluzone High-Dose)

Canadian labeling:

- 6 months to <2 years (Fluad Pediatric)
- 6 months and older (Agriflu, FluLaval Tetra, Fluviral, Fluzone Quadrivalent)
- 18 years and older (Influvac)
- 65 years and older (Fluad, Fluzone High-Dose)

The Advisory Committee on Immunization Practices (ACIP) recommends routine annual vaccination with the seasonal influenza vaccine for all persons ≥6 months of age who do not otherwise have contraindications to the vaccine (ACIP [Grohskopf 2016]).

The ACIP recommends use of any age and risk factor appropriate product and does not have a preferential recommendation for use of the trivalent inactivated influenza vaccine (IIV_3) or the quadrivalent inactivated influenza vaccine (IIV_4). In addition to the IIV products, other alternative products are available for certain patient populations: Persons 18 years and older may receive vaccination with the recombinant influenza vaccine (RIV). Although live attenuated influenza vaccine ($LAIV_4$) is FDA approved for healthy nonpregnant persons aged 2 to 49 years, the ACIP has made the interim recommendation that $LAIV_4$ should not be used for any population for the 2016-17 season due to concerns regarding low effectiveness during the 2013-14 and 2015-16 seasons (ACIP [Grohskopf 2016]).

The Canadian National Advisory Committee on Immunization (NACI) recommends annual vaccination with seasonal influenza vaccine for all persons ≥6 months who do not otherwise have contraindications to the vaccine. Healthy, nonpregnant persons aged 2 to 59 years may receive vaccination with the seasonal live, attenuated influenza vaccine (LAIV) (nasal spray). When readily available and no contraindications exist, NACI prefers use of LAIV (nasal spray) in healthy persons 2 to 17 years of age. LAIV is not recommended in patients with severe asthma or wheezing requiring medical attention in the 7 days prior to vaccination, adults with chronic health conditions, and children and adults who are immunocompromised. Where LAIV is not recommended, use of quadrivalent inactivated influenza vaccine (QIV) or trivalent inactivated influenza vaccine (TIV) if QIV is not available, is recommended (NACI 2016).

When vaccine supply is limited, target groups for vaccination (those at higher risk of complications from influenza infection and their close contacts) include the following (CDC/ACIP [Grohskopf 2016]):

- Infants and children 6 to 59 months of age
- Persons ≥50 years of age
- Infants, children, and adolescents (6 months to 18 years of age) who are receiving long-term aspirin therapy, and therefore, may be at risk for developing Reye's syndrome after influenza
- Women who are or will be pregnant during the influenza season
- Patients with chronic pulmonary disorders (including asthma) or cardiovascular systems disorders (except hypertension), renal, hepatic, neurologic, hematologic, or metabolic disorders (including diabetes mellitus)
- Persons who have immunosuppression (including immunosuppression caused by medications or HIV)
- Residents of nursing homes and other long-term care facilities
- American Indians/Alaska Natives
- Morbidly obese (BMI ≥40)
- Healthcare personnel
- Household contacts (including children) and caregivers of neonates, infants, and children <5 years (particularly children <6 months) and adults ≥50 years
- Household contacts (including children) and caregivers of persons with medical conditions which put them at high risk of complications from influenza infection

Local Anesthetic/Vasoconstrictor Precautions No information available to require special precautions

Effects on Dental Treatment No significant effects or complications reported

Effects on Bleeding No information available to require special precautions

Adverse Reactions Frequency not defined. Adverse reactions in adults ≥65 years of age may be greater using the high-dose vaccine, but are typically mild and transient.

Cardiovascular: Chest tightness, hypertension

Central nervous system: Chills, drowsiness, fatigue, headache, irritability, malaise, migraine, shivering

Dermatologic: Diaphoresis, ecchymoses

Gastrointestinal: Decreased appetite, diarrhea, gastroenteritis, nausea, sore throat, upper abdominal pain, vomiting

Infection: Infection, varicella

Local: Injection site reactions (including bruising, erythema, hematoma at injection site, induration, inflammation, itching at injection site, pain, soreness, swelling at injection site, tenderness at injection site)

Neuromuscular & skeletal: Arthralgia, back pain, myalgia (may start within 6 to 12 hours and last 1 to 2 days; incidence generally equal to placebo in adults; occurs more frequently than placebo in children)

Ophthalmic: Eye redness

Respiratory: Bronchitis, cough, dyspnea, nasal congestion, nasopharyngitis, oropharyngeal pain, pharyngitis, pharyngolaryngeal pain, respiratory congestion (upper), rhinitis, rhinorrhea, upper respiratory tract infection, wheezing

Miscellaneous: Crying (infants and children 6 to 35 months), fever

Postmarketing and/or case reports: Abdominal pain, abnormal gait, anaphylactic shock, anaphylaxis, angioedema, arthritis, asthma, Bell's palsy, brachial plexopathy, brain disease, bronchospasm, cellulitis, chest pain, confusion, conjunctivitis, constriction of the pharynx, dizziness, dysphagia, erythema multiforme, eye irritation, eye pain, facial edema, facial paralysis, febrile seizures, feeling hot, flu-like symptoms, flushing, Guillain-Barre syndrome, hot flash, hypersensitivity reaction (including oculorespiratory syndrome, an acute, self-limited reaction with ocular and respiratory symptoms) (CDC/ACIP [Grohskopf 2013]), hypoesthesia, hypokinesia, IgA vasculitis, injection site reactions (cellulitis, mass, sterile abscess, warmth), insomnia, laryngitis, limb pain, lymphadenopathy, maculopapular rash, microscopic polyangiitis (vasculitis), musculoskeletal pain, myasthenia, myelitis (including encephalomyelitis), neck pain, neuralgia, neuritis (including brachial), neuropathy, ocular hyperemia, optic neuritis, optic neuropathy, pallor, paralysis (including limb), paresthesia, pharyngeal edema, photophobia, presyncope, pruritus, respiratory distress, seizure, serum sickness, skin rash, Stevens-Johnson syndrome, stridor, swelling of eye (including eyelid), swelling of injected limb (lasting >1 week), swelling of mouth, swollen tongue, syncope, tachycardia, thrombocytopenia, tonsillitis, transverse myelitis, tremor, urticaria, vasculitis (including transient renal involvement), vasodilatation, vertigo, vesicobullous rash, voice disorder, weakness

General Dosage Range

IM:

Children 6 to 35 months: 0.25 to 0.5 mL/dose (product dependent; 1 or 2 doses per season)

Children 3 to 9 years: 0.5 mL/dose (1 or 2 doses per season)

Children ≥9 years, Adolescents, and Adults: 0.5 mL/dose (1 dose per season)

Intradermal: *Adults:* 18 to 64 years: 0.1 mL/dose (1 dose per season)

Mechanism of Action Promotes immunity to seasonal influenza virus by inducing specific antibody production. Each year the formulation is standardized according to the US Public Health Service. Preparations from previous seasons must not be used.

Pharmacodynamics/Kinetics

Onset of Action Most adults have antibody protection within 2 weeks of vaccination (CDC/ACIP [Grohskopf 2016])

Duration of Action ≥6 to 8 months when vaccine is antigenically similar to circulating virus (CDC/ACIP [Grohskopf 2016]); response may be diminished in persons ≥65 years and limited evidence suggests titers may decline significantly 6 months following vaccination in this population (CDC/ACIP [Grohskopf 2016]).

Pregnancy Risk Factor B/C (manufacturer specific)

Pregnancy Considerations Adverse events were not observed in animal reproduction studies. Inactivated influenza vaccine has not been shown to cause fetal harm when given to pregnant women, although information related to use in the first trimester is limited. Maternal influenza infection may be associated with adverse fetal events. Following maternal immunization with the inactivated influenza virus vaccine, vaccine specific antibodies are observed in the newborn (CDC/ACIP [Grohskopf 2016]).

Pregnant women are at an increased risk of complications from influenza infection. The inactivated influenza vaccine provides protective concentrations of antibodies in pregnant women and does not increase the risk for adverse maternal outcomes (CDC/ACIP [Grohskopf 2016]). Influenza vaccination with the inactivated influenza vaccine (IIV) is recommended for all women who are or will become pregnant during the influenza season and who do not otherwise have contraindications to the vaccine (CDC/ACIP [Grohskopf 2016]). Pregnant women should observe the same precautions as non-pregnant women to reduce the risk of exposure to influenza and other respiratory infections (CDC/HHS 2016). When vaccine supply is limited, focus on delivering the vaccine should be given to women who are pregnant or will be pregnant during the flu season, as well as mothers of newborns and contacts or caregivers of children <5 years of age (CDC/ACIP [Grohskopf 2016]). Vaccination may be done at any time during pregnancy (ACOG 2014).

Health care providers are encouraged to refer women exposed to the influenza vaccine during pregnancy to the Vaccines and Medications in Pregnancy Surveillance System (VAMPSS) by contacting The Organization of Teratology Information Specialists (OTIS) at (877) 311-8972.

Women exposed to FluLaval Quadrivalent, or Fluarix Quadrivalent vaccine during pregnancy or their health care provider may also contact the GlaxoSmithKline registry at 888-452-9622.

Health care providers may enroll women exposed to Fluzone Intradermal Quadrivalent or Fluzone Quadrivalent during pregnancy in the Sanofi Pasteur vaccination registry at 800-822-2463.

Influenza Virus Vaccine (Live/Attenuated)

(in floo EN za VYE rus vak SEEN live ah TEN yoo aye ted)

Brand Names: US FluMist Quadrivalent; FluMist [DSC]

Brand Names: Canada FluMist Quadrivalent

Pharmacologic Category Vaccine; Vaccine, Live (Viral)

Use Influenza disease prevention:

US labeling: Active immunization of individuals 2 to 49 years of age against influenza disease caused by influenza virus subtypes A and type B contained in the vaccine.

The Advisory Committee on Immunization Practices (ACIP) recommends routine annual vaccination with seasonal influenza vaccine for all persons ≥6 months who do not otherwise have contraindications to vaccination. Although live attenuated influenza vaccine

(LAIV4) is FDA approved for healthy nonpregnant persons aged 2 to 49 years, the ACIP has made the interim recommendation that LAIV4 should not be used for any population for the 2016-17 season due to concerns regarding low effectiveness during the 2013-14 and 2015-16 seasons. Alternative products are available for certain patient populations: Persons ≥6 months may receive the trivalent inactivated influenza vaccine (IIV_3) or the quadrivalent inactivated influenza vaccine (IIV_4) and persons 18 years and older may receive vaccination with the recombinant influenza vaccine (RIV) (CDC/ACIP [Grohskopf 2016]).

Canadian labeling: Active immunization of individuals 2 to 59 years of age against influenza disease caused by influenza virus subtypes A and type B contained in the vaccine.

The Canadian National Advisory Committee on Immunization (NACI) recommends annual vaccination with seasonal influenza vaccine for all persons ≥6 months who do not otherwise have contraindications to the vaccine. Healthy, nonpregnant persons aged 2 to 59 years may receive vaccination with the seasonal live, attenuated influenza vaccine (LAIV) (nasal spray). When readily available and no contraindications exist, NACI prefers use of LAIV (nasal spray) in healthy persons 2 to 17 years of age. LAIV is not recommended in patients with severe asthma or wheezing requiring medical attention in the 7 days prior to vaccination, adults with chronic health conditions, and children and adults who are immunocompromised. Where LAIV is not recommended, use of quadrivalent inactivated influenza vaccine (QIV), or trivalent inactivated influenza vaccine (TIV) if QIV is not available, is recommended (NACI 2016).

Local Anesthetic/Vasoconstrictor Precautions No information available to require special precautions

Effects on Dental Treatment No significant effects or complications reported

Effects on Bleeding No information available to require special precautions

Adverse Reactions

Frequency of events reported within 10 days.

>10%:

Central nervous system: Headache (adults: 40%; children: 3% to 9%), irritability (children: 12% to 21%), lethargy (children: 7% to 14%)

Gastrointestinal: Sore throat (adults: 28%; children: 5% to 11%), decreased appetite (children: 13% to 21%), abdominal pain (children: 2% to 12%)

Neuromuscular & skeletal: Fatigue (adults: ≤26%), weakness (adults: ≤26%), myalgia (adults: 17%; children: 2% to 6%)

Respiratory: Nasal congestion (children: ≤58%; adults: ≤44%), rhinorrhea (children: ≤58%; adults: ≤44%), cough (adults: 14%)

1% to 10%:

Central nervous system: Chills (adults: 9%; children: 2% to 4%)

Otic: Otitis media (children: 3%)

Respiratory: Wheezing (children: 6 to 23 months: 6%; 24 to 59 months: 2%), sinusitis (adults: 4%), sneezing (children: 2%)

Miscellaneous: Fever (children: 100°F to 101°F: 6% to 9%; >101°F: 1% to 4%)

<1%, postmarketing, and/or case reports: Anaphylaxis, Bell's palsy, diarrhea, encephalitis (vaccine-associated), epistaxis, exacerbation of asthma, facial edema, Guillain-Barre syndrome, hypersensitivity reaction, meningitis (including eosinophilic meningitis), nausea, pericarditis, skin rash, subacute necrotizing encephalomyelopathy (Leigh syndrome exacerbation), urticaria, vomiting

General Dosage Range Intranasal:

Children 2 to 8 years: 0.2 mL/dose (1 or 2 doses per season)

Children ≥9 years, Adolescents, and Adults ≤49 years: 0.2 mL/dose (1 dose per season)

Mechanism of Action The vaccine contains live attenuated viruses which infect and replicate within the cells lining the nasopharynx. Promotes immunity to seasonal influenza virus by inducing specific antibody production. Each year the formulation is standardized according to the US Public Health Service. Preparations from previous seasons must not be used.

Pharmacodynamics/Kinetics

Onset of Action Most adults have antibody protection within 2 weeks of vaccination (CDC/ACIP [Grohskopf 2016])

Duration of Action ≥6 to 8 months when vaccine is antigenically similar to circulating virus (CDC/ACIP [Grohskopf 2016]); response may be diminished in persons ≥65 years and limited evidence suggests titers may decline significantly 6 months following vaccination in this population (CDC/ACIP [Grohskopf 2016])

Pregnancy Risk Factor B

Pregnancy Considerations Adverse events were not observed in animal reproduction studies. LAIV is not recommended for use during pregnancy. Influenza vaccination with the inactivated influenza vaccine (IIV) is recommended for all women who are or will become pregnant during the influenza season and who do not otherwise have contraindications to the vaccine (CDC/ACIP [Grohskopf 2016]).

The nasal vaccine contains the same strains of influenza A and B found in the injection. Information specific to the use of LAIV in pregnancy is limited.

Health care providers are encouraged to refer women exposed to the influenza vaccine during pregnancy to the Vaccines and Medications in Pregnancy Surveillance System (VAMPSS) by contacting The Organization of Teratology Information Specialists (OTIS) at (877) 311-8972.

Influenza Virus Vaccine (Recombinant)

(in floo EN za VYE rus vak SEEN ree KOM be nant)

Brand Names: US Flublok

Pharmacologic Category Vaccine; Vaccine, Recombinant

Use Influenza disease prevention: Active immunization against influenza disease caused by influenza virus subtypes A and type B contained in the vaccine in persons 18 years of age and older

The Advisory Committee on Immunization Practices (ACIP) recommends routine annual vaccination with seasonal influenza vaccine for all persons ≥6 months who do not otherwise have contraindications to the vaccine. ACIP recommends use of any age and risk factor appropriate product. Persons 18 years of age and older may receive vaccination with the recombinant influenza vaccine (RIV). In addition to RIV, other products are available for certain patient populations: Persons ≥6 months of age may receive the trivalent inactivated influenza vaccine (IIV_3) or the quadrivalent inactivated influenza vaccine (IIV_4). Although live attenuated influenza vaccine (LAIV4) is FDA approved for healthy nonpregnant persons aged 2 to 49 years, the ACIP has made the interim recommendation that LAIV4 should not be used for any population for the 2016-17 season due to concerns regarding low effectiveness during the 2013-14 and 2015-16 seasons (CDC/ACIP [Grohskopf 2016]).

When vaccine supply is limited, target groups for vaccination (those at higher risk of complications from influenza infection and their close contacts) include the following (CDC/ACIP [Grohskopf 2016]):

- Infants and children 6 to 59 months of age
- Persons ≥50 years of age
- Residents of nursing homes and other long-term care facilities
- Patients with chronic pulmonary disorders (including asthma) or cardiovascular systems disorders (except hypertension), renal, hepatic, neurologic, hematologic, or metabolic disorders (including diabetes mellitus)
- Persons who have immunosuppression (including immunosuppression caused by medications or HIV)
- Infants, children, and adolescents (6 months to 18 years of age) who are receiving long-term aspirin therapy, and therefore, may be at risk for developing Reye syndrome after influenza
- Women who are or will be pregnant during the influenza season
- Healthcare personnel
- Household contacts (including children) and caregivers of neonates, infants, and children <5 years (particularly children <6 months) and adults ≥50 years
- Household contacts (including children) and caregivers of persons with medical conditions which put them at high risk of complications from influenza infection
- American Indians/Alaska Natives
- Morbidly obese (BMI ≥40)

Local Anesthetic/Vasoconstrictor Precautions No information available to require special precautions

Effects on Dental Treatment No significant effects or complications reported

Effects on Bleeding No information available to require special precautions

Adverse Reactions All serious adverse reactions must be reported to the US Department of Health and Human Services (DHHS) Vaccine Adverse Event Reporting System (VAERS) 1-800-822-7967 or online at https://vaers.hhs.gov/esub/index. In Canada, adverse reactions may be reported to local provincial/territorial health agencies or to the Vaccine Safety Section at Public Health Agency of Canada (1-866-844-0018).

Note: Older adults refers to adults ≥50 years of age

>10%:

Central nervous system: Headache (older adults 10% to 17%), fatigue (13% to 15%)

Local: Pain at injection site (37%, older adults 19% to 32%)

Neuromuscular & skeletal: Myalgia (8% to 11%)

1% to 10%:

Central nervous system: Chills (older adults 5%)

Gastrointestinal: Nausea (4% to 6%)

Local: Injection site reactions (3% to 7%; includes redness, swelling and firmness)

Neuromuscular & skeletal: Arthralgia (older adults 6% to 8%)

Respiratory: Cough (1% to 2%), nasal congestion (1% to 2%), nasopharyngitis (1% to 2%), pharyngolaryngeal pain (1% to 2%), rhinorrhea (1% to 2%), upper respiratory tract infection (1% to 2%)

<1%, postmarketing and/or case reports: Anaphylactoid reaction, anaphylaxis, hypersensitivity, hypersensitivity reaction, pleuropericarditis

General Dosage Range

IM: *Adults ≥18 years:* 0.5 mL/dose (1 per season)

Mechanism of Action Promotes immunity to seasonal influenza virus by inducing specific antibody production. Each year the formulation is standardized according to the US Public Health Service. Preparations from previous seasons must not be used.

Pharmacodynamics/Kinetics

Onset of Action Most adults have antibody protection within 2 weeks of vaccination (CDC/ACIP [Grohskopf 2016]).

Duration of Action When vaccine is antigenically similar to circulating virus ≥6 to 8 months (CDC/ACIP [Grohskopf 2016]); response may be diminished in persons ≥65 years and limited evidence suggests titers may decline significantly 6 months following vaccination in this population (CDC/ACIP [Grohskopf 2016]).

Pregnancy Considerations Adverse events were not observed in animal reproduction studies. Information specific to the use of RIV in pregnancy has not been located.

Pregnant women are at an increased risk of complications from influenza infection (Rasmussen 2008). Influenza vaccination with the inactivated influenza vaccine (IIV) is recommended for all women who are or will become pregnant during the influenza season and who do not otherwise have contraindications to the vaccine (CDC/ACIP [Grohskopf 2016]).

Pregnant women should observe the same precautions as nonpregnant women to reduce the risk of exposure to influenza and other respiratory infections (CDC/HHS 2016). When vaccine supply is limited, focus on delivering the vaccine should be given to women who are pregnant or will be pregnant during the flu season, as well as mothers of newborns and contacts or caregivers of children <5 years of age (CDC/ACIP [Grohskopf 2016]).

Health care providers are encouraged to refer women exposed to the influenza vaccine during pregnancy to the *Vaccines and Medications in Pregnancy Surveillance System* (VAMPSS) by contacting The Organization of Teratology Information Specialists (OTIS) at (877) 311-8972. Women exposed to this vaccine during pregnancy may also contact the Flublok pregnancy registry at 888-855-7871.

Product Availability Flublok Quadrivalent: FDA approved October 2016; availability anticipated for the 2017-2018 flu season. Consult the prescribing information for additional information.

Ingenol Mebutate (IN je nol MEB u tate)

Brand Names: US Picato

Brand Names: Canada Picato

Pharmacologic Category Topical Skin Product

Use Actinic keratosis: Topical treatment of actinic keratosis

Local Anesthetic/Vasoconstrictor Precautions No information available to require special precautions

Effects on Dental Treatment No significant effects or complications reported

Effects on Bleeding No information available to require special precautions

Adverse Reactions Percentages represent face/scalp and trunk/extremities incidences unless otherwise specified.

>10%:

Dermatologic: Erythema (92% to 94%), desquamation (≤90%), exfoliation of skin (≤90%), crusted skin (74% to 80%), swelling of skin (face/scalp: 79%; trunk/extremities: 64%), localized vesiculation (face/scalp: ≤56%; trunk/extremities: ≤44%), pustules (face/scalp: ≤56%; trunk/extremities: ≤44%), dermal ulcer (≤32%), skin erosion (≤32%), application site pain (face/scalp: 15%, trunk/extremities: 2%)

1% to 10%:

Central nervous system: Headache (face/scalp: 2%)

Dermatologic: Application site pruritus (8%), application site irritation (trunk/extremities: 4%), skin infection (face/scalp: 3%; at application site)

Ophthalmic: Periorbital edema (face/scalp: 3%)

Respiratory: Nasopharyngitis (trunk/extremities: 2%)

Frequency not defined:

Ophthalmic: Conjunctivitis, eyelid edema, eye pain

<1%, postmarketing, and/or case reports: Anaphylaxis, conjunctivitis (chemical-induced), corneal injury (burn), eye injury (FDA Safety Alert, August 21, 2015), herpes zoster, pigmentation alteration (application site), scarring (application site), severe hypersensitivity (includes allergic contact dermatitis)

General Dosage Range Topical: *Adults:* Apply once daily for 2 days (0.05%) or 3 days (0.015%)

Mechanism of Action Ingenol mebutate appears to induce primary necrosis of actinic keratosis with a subsequent neutrophil-mediated inflammatory response with antibody-dependent cytotoxicity of residual disease cells; killing residual disease cells may prevent future relapse (Ramsay 2011; Siller 2010).

Pregnancy Risk Factor C

Pregnancy Considerations Adverse events were observed in some animal reproduction studies following IV administration of ingenol mebutate. Absorption is limited in humans following topical application.

Inosine Pranobex (EYE no seen PRA no becks)

Brand Names: Canada Imunovir®

Pharmacologic Category Antiviral Agent; Immunomodulator, Systemic

Use Note: Not approved in the US

Treatment of slowly progressive subacute sclerosing panencephalitis (SSPE); may delay neurologic deterioration and prolong life expectancy

Local Anesthetic/Vasoconstrictor Precautions No information available to require special precautions

Effects on Dental Treatment No significant effects or complications reported

Effects on Bleeding No information available to require special precautions

Adverse Reactions Frequency not defined.

Central nervous system: Dizziness, fatigue, headache, insomnia, nervousness

Dermatologic: Pruritus, skin rash

Endocrine & metabolic: Hyperuricemia

Gastrointestinal: Constipation, diarrhea, gastric distress

Genitourinary: Increased urine output

Neuromuscular & skeletal: Arthralgia

General Dosage Range Oral: *Children, Adolescents, and Adults:* Subacute sclerosing panencephalitis: 50 mg/kg/day in 3 or 4 equally divided doses (maximum: 3 g daily)

Mechanism of Action Exact mechanism has not been fully elucidated; may possess antiviral and immunomodulating effects by potentiating T-lymphocyte and macrophage cell function and by influencing cytokine production (Milano, 1991; Petrova, 2010; Wybran, 1978).

Pharmacodynamics/Kinetics

Half-life Elimination ~50 minutes (Campoli-Richards, 1986)

Time to Peak 1 hour (Campoli-Richards, 1986)

Pregnancy Considerations Adverse effects to the fetus were not observed in animal reproduction studies. Due to the altered immune status of pregnant women, SSPE may be exacerbated during pregnancy and may progress rapidly. Because this condition is rare, use of inosine pranobex in pregnant women is limited to case reports (Cole, 2007)

Product Availability Not available in the US

Insulin Aspart (IN soo lin AS part)

Related Information

Endocrine Disorders and Pregnancy *on page 1781*

Insulin Regular *on page 903*

Brand Names: US NovoLOG; NovoLOG FlexPen; NovoLOG PenFill

Brand Names: Canada NovoRapid

Pharmacologic Category Insulin, Rapid-Acting

Use Treatment of type 1 diabetes mellitus (insulin dependent, IDDM) and type 2 diabetes mellitus (noninsulin dependent, NIDDM) to improve glycemic control

Local Anesthetic/Vasoconstrictor Precautions No information available to require special precautions

Effects on Dental Treatment Key adverse event(s) related to dental treatment: Patients with diabetes should be questioned by the dental professional at each dental visit to assess their risk for stress-induced hypoglycemia. The dental professional should inquire about the patient's routine (ie, work, sleep schedule, eating patterns), history of hypoglycemia, time of last medication dose, last meal, and most recent blood sugar assessment. Keep a supply of glucose tablets and other carbohydrates in the office to prepare for a hypoglycemic event. Seek medical attention when necessary (American Diabetes Association, 2014).

Effects on Bleeding No information available to require special precautions

Adverse Reactions Rates of adverse reactions were defined during combination therapy with NPH insulin.

>10%:

Endocrine & metabolic: Hypoglycemia (Type 1 combination regimens: 75%; Type 2 combination regimens: 27%), severe hypoglycemia (Type 1 combination regimens: adults administration: 17%, children & adolescents administration: 6%; Type 1 combination regimens: children & adolescents insulin pump administration: 10%; adults insulin pump administration: 2%; Type 2 combination regimens: 10%)

Central nervous system: Headache (5% to 12%), hyporeflexia (11%)

Miscellaneous: Accidental injury (11%)

1% to 10%:

Cardiovascular: Chest pain (5%)

Central nervous system: Sensory disturbance (9%)

Dermatologic: Onychomycosis (10%), skin changes (5%)
Gastrointestinal: Nausea (7%), abdominal pain (5%), diarrhea (5%)
Genitourinary: Urinary tract infection (8%)
Respiratory: Sinusitis (5%)
>1%, postmarketing, and/or case reports: Anaphylaxis, local hypersensitivity reaction (secondary to excipient metacresol), myalgia (secondary to excipient metacresol)

General Dosage Range SubQ: *Children ≥2 years, Adolescents, and Adults:* Daily doses are expressed as the **total units/kg/day of all insulin formulations combined.** Diabetes mellitus, type 1: Initial: 0.2 to 0.6 units/kg/day in divided doses; usual maintenance: 0.5 to 1 units/kg/day in divided doses.

Mechanism of Action Insulin acts via specific membrane-bound receptors on target tissues to regulate metabolism of carbohydrate, protein, and fats. Target organs for insulin include the liver, skeletal muscle, and adipose tissue.

Within the liver, insulin stimulates hepatic glycogen synthesis. Insulin promotes hepatic synthesis of fatty acids, which are released into the circulation as lipoproteins. Skeletal muscle effects of insulin include increased protein synthesis and increased glycogen synthesis. Within adipose tissue, insulin stimulates the processing of circulating lipoproteins to provide free fatty acids, facilitating triglyceride synthesis and storage by adipocytes; it also directly inhibits the hydrolysis of triglycerides. In addition, insulin stimulates the cellular uptake of amino acids and increases cellular permeability to several ions, including potassium, magnesium, and phosphate. By activating sodium-potassium ATPases, insulin promotes the intracellular movement of potassium.

Normally secreted by the pancreas, insulin products are manufactured for pharmacologic use through recombinant DNA technology using either *E. coli* or *Saccharomyces cerevisiae*. Insulin aspart differs from human insulin by containing aspartic acid at position B28 in comparison to the proline found in human insulin. Insulins are categorized based on the onset, peak, and duration of effect (eg, rapid-, short-, intermediate-, and long-acting insulin). Insulin aspart is a rapid-acting insulin analog.

Pharmacodynamics/Kinetics

Onset of Action 0.2 to 0.3 hours; Peak effect: 1 to 3 hours

Duration of Action 3 to 5 hours

Half-life Elimination SubQ: 81 minutes

Time to Peak Plasma: 40 to 50 minutes

Pregnancy Risk Factor B

Pregnancy Considerations Dose-related adverse effects were observed in animal reproduction studies. Insulin aspart can be detected in cord blood (Pettitt 2007).

In women with diabetes, maternal hyperglycemia can be associated with congenital malformations as well as adverse effects in the fetus, neonate, and the mother (ACOG 2005; ADA 2016d; Kitzmiller 2008; Metzger 2007). To prevent adverse outcomes, prior to conception and throughout pregnancy maternal blood glucose and HbA_{1c} should be kept as close to target goals as possible but without causing significant hypoglycemia (ACOG 2013; ADA 2016d; Blumer 2013; Kitzmiller 2008; Lambert 2013). Prior to pregnancy, effective contraception should be used until glycemic control is achieved (ADA 2016d; Kitzmiller 2008).

Insulin requirements tend to fall during the first trimester of pregnancy and increase in the later trimesters, peaking at 28 to 32 weeks of gestation. Following delivery, insulin requirements decrease rapidly (ACOG 2005). Insulin aspart may be used to treat diabetes in pregnant women (ACOG 2013; Blumer 2013; Kitzmiller 2008; Lambert 2013).

Insulin Aspart Protamine and Insulin Aspart (IN soo lin AS part PROE ta meen & IN soo lin AS part)

Related Information

Insulin Regular *on page 903*

Brand Names: US NovoLOG® Mix 70/30; NovoLOG® Mix 70/30 FlexPen®

Brand Names: Canada NovoMix® 30

Pharmacologic Category Insulin, Combination

Use Diabetes mellitus: Treatment of type 1 diabetes mellitus (insulin dependent, IDDM) and type 2 diabetes mellitus (noninsulin dependent, NIDDM) to improve glycemic control

Local Anesthetic/Vasoconstrictor Precautions No information available to require special precautions

Effects on Dental Treatment Key adverse event(s) related to dental treatment: Patients with diabetes should be questioned by the dental professional at each dental visit to assess their risk for stress-induced hypoglycemia. The dental professional should inquire about the patient's routine (ie, work, sleep schedule, eating patterns), history of hypoglycemia, time of last medication dose, last meal, and most recent blood sugar assessment. Keep a supply of glucose tablets and other carbohydrates in the office to prepare for a hypoglycemic event. Seek medical attention when necessary (American Diabetes Association, 2014).

Effects on Bleeding No information available to require special precautions

Adverse Reactions Frequency not defined.
Cardiovascular: Palpitations, peripheral edema, tachycardia
Central nervous system: Confusion, fatigue, headache, hypothermia, loss of consciousness, myasthenia, paresthesia
Dermatologic: Diaphoresis, erythema, pallor, pruritus, skin rash, urticaria
Endocrine & metabolic: Hypoglycemia, hypokalemia, lipodystrophy, weight gain
Gastrointestinal: Hunger, nausea, oral paresthesia
Hypersensitivity: Anaphylaxis, hypersensitivity reaction (systemic symptoms), local insulin hypersensitivity reaction
Immunologic: Antibody development (no change in efficacy)
Local: Injection site reaction (including itching at injection site, pain at injection site, stinging at injection site, or warm sensation at injection site)
Neuromuscular & skeletal: Lipoatrophy, tremor
Ophthalmic: Blurred vision, presbyopia (transient)

General Dosage Range SubQ: *Adults:* Diabetes mellitus, type 1 or 2: **Not** intended for initial therapy; basal insulin requirements should be established **first** to direct dosing of combination insulin products.

Mechanism of Action Insulin acts via specific membrane-bound receptors on target tissues to regulate metabolism of carbohydrate, protein, and fats. Target organs for insulin include the liver, skeletal muscle, and adipose tissue.

Within the liver, insulin stimulates hepatic glycogen synthesis. Insulin promotes hepatic synthesis of fatty acids, which are released into the circulation as lipoproteins. Skeletal muscle effects of insulin include increased protein synthesis and increased glycogen synthesis. Within adipose tissue, insulin stimulates the processing of circulating lipoproteins to provide free fatty acids, facilitating triglyceride synthesis and storage by adipocytes; also directly inhibits the hydrolysis of triglycerides. In addition, insulin stimulates the cellular uptake of amino acids and increases cellular permeability to several ions, including potassium, magnesium, and phosphate. By activating sodium-potassium ATPases, insulin promotes the intracellular movement of potassium.

Normally secreted by the pancreas, insulin products are manufactured for pharmacologic use through recombinant DNA technology using either *E. coli* or *Saccharomyces cerevisiae*. Insulin aspart differs from human insulin by containing aspartic acid at position B28 in comparison to the proline found in human insulin. Insulins are categorized based on the onset, peak, and duration of effect (eg, rapid-, short-, intermediate-, and long-acting insulin). Insulin aspart protamine and insulin aspart is an intermediate-acting combination product with a more rapid onset and similar duration of action as compared to that of insulin NPH and insulin regular combination products.

Pharmacodynamics/Kinetics

Onset of Action 10-20 minutes; Peak effect: 1-4 hours

Duration of Action 18-24 hours

Half-life Elimination ~8-9 hours

Time to Peak 1-1.5 hours

Pregnancy Risk Factor B

Pregnancy Considerations Animal reproduction studies have not been conducted. Biphasic insulin aspart (insulin aspart protamine suspension 70% [intermediate acting] and insulin aspart solution 30% [rapid acting]) was found to be comparable to biphasic human insulin (Insulin NPH suspension 70% [intermediate acting] and insulin regular solution 30% [short acting]) in initial studies of women with gestational diabetes mellitus (Balaji 2010; Balaji 2012).

In women with diabetes, maternal hyperglycemia can be associated with congenital malformations as well as adverse effects in the fetus, neonate, and the mother (ACOG 2005; ADA 2016d; Kitzmiller 2008; Metzger 2007). To prevent adverse outcomes, prior to conception and throughout pregnancy maternal blood glucose and HbA_{1c} should be kept as close to target goals as possible but without causing significant hypoglycemia (ACOG 2013; ADA 2016d; Blumer 2013; Kitzmiller 2008; Lambert 2013). Prior to pregnancy, effective contraception should be used until glycemic control is achieved (ADA 2016d; Kitzmiller 2008).

Insulin requirements tend to fall during the first trimester of pregnancy and increase in the later trimesters, peaking at 28 to 32 weeks of gestation. Following delivery, insulin requirements decrease rapidly (ACOG 2005).

Insulin Degludec (IN su lin de GLOO dek)

Brand Names: US Tresiba FlexTouch

Pharmacologic Category Insulin, Long-Acting

Use Diabetes mellitus: To improve glycemic control in patients 1 year of age and older with type 1 or type 2 diabetes mellitus

Local Anesthetic/Vasoconstrictor Precautions No information available to require special precautions

Effects on Dental Treatment Key adverse event(s) related to dental treatment: Patients with diabetes should be questioned by the dental professional at each dental visit to assess their risk for stress-induced hypoglycemia. The dental professional should inquire about the patient's routine (ie, work, sleep schedule, eating patterns), history of hypoglycemia, time of last medication dose, last meal, and most recent blood sugar assessment. Keep a supply of glucose tablets and other carbohydrates in the office to prepare for a hypoglycemic event. Seek medical attention when necessary (American Diabetes Association, 2014).

Effects on Bleeding No information available to require special precautions

Adverse Reactions Frequency not always defined.

Cardiovascular: Peripheral edema (1% to 3%)

Central nervous system: Headache (9% to 12%)

Endocrine & metabolic: Severe hypoglycemia (10% to 13%, type 1 diabetics on combination therapy; ≤5%, type 2 diabetics on combination therapy), antibody development, hypoglycemia, hypokalemia, weight gain

Gastrointestinal: Diarrhea (6%, type 2 diabetes), gastroenteritis (5%, type 1 diabetes)

Local: Injection site reaction (4%; including hematoma, pain, hemorrhage, erythema, warmth, swelling, mass, nodules, and discoloration), hypertrophy at injection site, lipoatrophy at injection site

Respiratory: Nasopharyngitis (13% to 24%), upper respiratory tract infection (8% to 12%), sinusitis (5%, type 1 diabetes)

<1%, postmarketing and/or case reports: Hypersensitivity reaction

General Dosage Range

SubQ:

Children ≥1 year and Adolescents (requiring at least 5 units of insulin degludec):

Diabetes mellitus (type 1): *Insulin-naive patients:* One-third to one-half the total daily insulin requirement administered as insulin degludec once daily (general rule for initial total daily insulin dose, 0.2 to 0.4 units/kg)

Diabetes mellitus (type 1 or type 2): *Insulin-experienced patients:* Initiate insulin degludec at 80% of the total daily long or intermediate-acting insulin unit dose from which the patient is being converted.

Adults:

Diabetes mellitus, type 1:

Insulin-naive: Initial: One-third to one-half the total daily insulin dose administered as insulin degludec once daily (general rule for initial total daily insulin dose, 0.2 to 0.4 units/kg)

Insulin-experienced: Initiate with same unit dose as the total daily long or intermediate-acting insulin unit dose from which the patient is being converted.

Diabetes mellitus, type 2:

Insulin-naive: Initial: 10 units once daily

Insulin-experienced: Initiate with same unit dose as the total daily long or intermediate-acting insulin unit dose

Mechanism of Action Insulin acts via specific membrane-bound receptors on target tissues to regulate metabolism of carbohydrate, protein, and fats. Target organs for insulin include the liver, skeletal muscle, and adipose tissue.

Within the liver, insulin stimulates hepatic glycogen synthesis. Insulin promotes hepatic synthesis of fatty acids, which are released into the circulation as lipoproteins. Skeletal muscle effects of insulin include increased protein synthesis and increased glycogen synthesis. Within adipose tissue, insulin stimulates the processing of circulating lipoproteins to provide free fatty acids, facilitating triglyceride synthesis and storage by adipocytes; also directly inhibits the hydrolysis of triglycerides. In addition, insulin stimulates the cellular uptake of amino acids and increases cellular permeability to several ions, including potassium, magnesium, and phosphate. By activating sodium-potassium ATPases, insulin promotes the intracellular movement of potassium.

Normally secreted by the pancreas, insulin products are manufactured for pharmacologic use through recombinant DNA technology using either *E. coli* or *Saccharomyces cerevisiae*. Insulin degludec differs from human insulin by the omission of the amino acid threonine in position B-30 of the B-chain, and the subsequent addition of a side chain composed of glutamic acid and a C16 fatty acid. Insulins are categorized based on the onset, peak, and duration of effect (eg, rapid-, short-, intermediate-, and long-acting insulin). Insulin degludec is a long-acting, human insulin analog.

Pharmacodynamics/Kinetics

Onset of Action ~1 hour

Half-life Elimination ~25 hours (independent of dose)

Time to Peak 9 hours

Pregnancy Risk Factor C

Pregnancy Considerations Adverse events were observed in animal reproduction studies secondary to maternal hypoglycemia. Information specific to insulin degludec use in pregnant women has not been located.

In women with diabetes, maternal hyperglycemia can be associated with congenital malformations as well as adverse effects in the fetus, neonate, and the mother (ACOG 2005; ADA 2016d; Kitzmiller 2008; Metzger 2007). To prevent adverse outcomes, prior to conception and throughout pregnancy maternal blood glucose and HbA_{1c} should be kept as close to target goals as possible but without causing significant hypoglycemia (ACOG 2013; ADA 2016d; Blumer 2013; Kitzmiller 2008; Lambert 2013). Prior to pregnancy, effective contraception should be used until glycemic control is achieved (ADA 2016d; Kitzmiller 2008).

Insulin requirements tend to fall during the first trimester of pregnancy and increase in the later trimesters, peaking at 28 to 32 weeks of gestation. Following delivery, insulin requirements decrease rapidly (ACOG 2005).

Insulin Degludec and Insulin Aspart

(IN su lin de GLOO dek & IN soo lin AS part)

Pharmacologic Category Insulin, Combination

Use Diabetes mellitus: To improve glycemic control in patients ≥1 year of age with diabetes mellitus

Local Anesthetic/Vasoconstrictor Precautions No information available to require special precautions

Effects on Dental Treatment Key adverse event(s) related to dental treatment: Patients with diabetes should be questioned by the dental professional at each dental visit to assess their risk for stress-induced hypoglycemia. The dental professional should inquire about the patient's routine (ie, work, sleep schedule, eating patterns), history of hypoglycemia, time of last medication dose, last meal, and most recent blood sugar assessment. Keep a supply of glucose tablets and other carbohydrates in the office to prepare for a hypoglycemic event. Seek medical attention when necessary (American Diabetes Association, 2014).

Effects on Bleeding No information available to require special precautions

Adverse Reactions Frequency not always defined.

Cardiovascular: Peripheral edema (2%)

Central nervous system: Headache (6% to 10%)

Endocrine & metabolic: Severe hypoglycemia (13%, type 1 diabetics using combination insulin regimen; ≤3%, type 2 diabetes), hypoglycemia, weight gain

Immunologic: Antibody development

Infection: Influenza (7%, type 1 diabetes)

Local: Injection site reaction (2%; including hematoma, pain, hemorrhage, erythema, swelling, warmth, nodules, mass, discoloration, and pruritus), hypertrophy at injection site, lipoatrophy at injection site

Respiratory: Nasopharyngitis (11% to 25%), upper respiratory tract infection (6% to 9%)

<1%, postmarketing and/or case reports: Hypersensitivity, urticaria

General Dosage Range SubQ:

Children ≥1 year and Adolescents:

Insulin naive (type 1 diabetes mellitus): Initial: One-third to one-half the total daily insulin dose

Insulin-experienced (type 1 or type 2 diabetes mellitus): Initiate insulin degludec/insulin aspart 70/30 at 80% of the total daily mixed insulin dose or at 80% of the long- or intermediate-acting insulin component of the daily regimen once daily. Patients receiving mealtime short- or rapid-acting insulins should continue those insulins at the same dose for meals **NOT** covered by insulin degludec/insulin aspart 70/30

Adults:

Type 1 diabetes mellitus: Insulin-naive: Initial: One-third to one-half the total daily insulin dose

Type 2 diabetes mellitus: Insulin-naive: Initial: 10 units once daily

Mechanism of Action

Insulin acts via specific membrane-bound receptors on target tissues to regulate metabolism of carbohydrate, protein, and fats. Target organs for insulin include the liver, skeletal muscle, and adipose tissue.

Within the liver, insulin stimulates hepatic glycogen synthesis. Insulin promotes hepatic synthesis of fatty acids, which are released into the circulation as lipoproteins. Skeletal muscle effects of insulin include increased protein synthesis and increased glycogen synthesis. Within adipose tissue, insulin stimulates the processing of circulating lipoproteins to provide free fatty acids, facilitating triglyceride synthesis and storage by adipocytes; also directly inhibits the hydrolysis of triglycerides. In addition, insulin stimulates the cellular uptake of amino acids and increases cellular permeability to several ions, including potassium, magnesium, and phosphate. By activating sodium-potassium ATPases, insulin promotes the intracellular movement of potassium.

Normally secreted by the pancreas, insulin products are manufactured for pharmacologic use through recombinant DNA technology using either *E. coli* or *Saccharomyces cerevisiae*. Insulins are categorized based on the onset, peak, and duration of effect (eg, rapid-, short-, intermediate-, and long-acting insulin). Insulin degludec is a long-acting insulin analog and insulin aspart is a rapid-acting insulin analog.

Pharmacodynamics/Kinetics

Onset of Action Insulin aspart: 14 minutes

Duration of Action Insulin degludec: >24 hours

Half-life Elimination Insulin degludec: ~25 hours

Time to Peak Insulin aspart: 72 minutes

Pregnancy Considerations Refer to individual monographs.

Product Availability Ryzodeg 70/30: FDA approved September 2015; anticipated availability is currently undetermined.

Insulin Detemir (IN soo lin DE te mir)

Related Information

Endocrine Disorders and Pregnancy *on page 1781*

Insulin Regular *on page 903*

Brand Names: US Levemir; Levemir FlexPen [DSC]; Levemir FlexTouch

Brand Names: Canada Levemir

Pharmacologic Category Insulin, Long-Acting

Use Treatment of type 1 diabetes mellitus (insulin dependent, IDDM) and type 2 diabetes mellitus (noninsulin dependent, NIDDM) to improve glycemic control

Local Anesthetic/Vasoconstrictor Precautions No information available to require special precautions

Effects on Dental Treatment Key adverse event(s) related to dental treatment: Patients with diabetes should be questioned by the dental professional at each dental visit to assess their risk for stress-induced hypoglycemia. The dental professional should inquire about the patient's routine (ie, work, sleep schedule, eating patterns), history of hypoglycemia, time of last medication dose, last meal, and most recent blood sugar assessment. Keep a supply of glucose tablets and other carbohydrates in the office to prepare for a hypoglycemic event. Seek medical attention when necessary (American Diabetes Association, 2014).

Effects on Bleeding No information available to require special precautions

Adverse Reactions

>10%:

Central nervous system: Headache (adults: 7% to 23%, children: 31%)

Endocrine & metabolic: Hypoglycemia (Type 1 combination regimens: children & adolescents: 93% to 95%, adults: 82% to 88%; Type 2 combination regimens: adults: 9% to 41%), severe hypoglycemia (Type 1 combination regimens: children & adolescents: 2% to 16%; adults 5% to 9%; Type 2 combination regimens: adults: ≤2%)

Gastrointestinal: Gastroenteritis (children & adolescents: 17%), abdominal pain (6%; children & adolescents: 13%)

Respiratory: Upper respiratory tract infection (13% to 26%; children & adolescents: 36%), pharyngitis (10%; children & adolescents: 17%), flu-like symptoms (8%; children & adolescents: 14%)

1% to 10%:

Gastrointestinal: Nausea (children & adolescents: 7%), vomiting (children & adolescents: 7%)

Infection: Viral infection (children & adolescents: 7%)

Respiratory: Cough (children & adolescents: 8%), rhinitis (children & adolescents: 7%)

Miscellaneous: Fever (children & adolescents: 10%)

<1%, postmarketing, and/or case reports: Pain at injection site

General Dosage Range SubQ:

Children ≥2 years, Adolescents, and Adults: Diabetes mellitus, type 1: Initial dose: Approximately one-third of the total daily insulin requirement administered in 1 to 2 divided doses.

Adults: Diabetes mellitus, type 2: Initial: 10 units **or** 0.1 to 0.2 units/kg in 1 to 2 divided doses

Mechanism of Action Insulin acts via specific membrane-bound receptors on target tissues to regulate metabolism of carbohydrate, protein, and fats. Target organs for insulin include the liver, skeletal muscle, and adipose tissue.

Within the liver, insulin stimulates hepatic glycogen synthesis. Insulin promotes hepatic synthesis of fatty acids, which are released into the circulation as lipoproteins. Skeletal muscle effects of insulin include increased protein synthesis and increased glycogen synthesis. Within adipose tissue, insulin stimulates the processing of circulating lipoproteins to provide free fatty acids, facilitating triglyceride synthesis and storage by adipocytes; also directly inhibits the hydrolysis of triglycerides. In addition, insulin stimulates the cellular uptake of amino acids and increases cellular permeability to several ions, including potassium, magnesium, and phosphate. By activating sodium-potassium ATPases, insulin promotes the intracellular movement of potassium.

Normally secreted by the pancreas, insulin products are manufactured for pharmacologic use through recombinant DNA technology using either *E. coli* or *Saccharomyces cerevisiae*. Insulin detemir differs from human insulin by the omission of threonine in position B30 and the addition of a C14 fatty acid chain to the amino acid located at position B29. Insulins are categorized based on the onset, peak, and duration of effect (eg, rapid-, short-, intermediate-, and long-acting insulin).

Pharmacodynamics/Kinetics

Onset of Action 3 to 4 hours; Peak effect: 3 to 9 hours (Plank 2005)

Duration of Action Dose dependent: 6 to 23 hours; **Note:** Duration is dose-dependent. At lower dosages (0.1 to 0.2 units/kg), mean duration is variable (5.7 to 12.1 hours). At 0.4 units/kg, the mean duration was 19.9 hours. At high dosages (≥0.8 units/kg) the duration is longer and less variable (mean of 22 to 23 hours) (Plank 2005).

Half-life Elimination 5 to 7 hours (dose-dependent)

Time to Peak Plasma: 6 to 8 hours

Pregnancy Risk Factor B

Pregnancy Considerations Dose-related adverse events were observed in animal reproduction studies. Insulin detemir has been detected in cord blood. An increased risk of fetal abnormalities has not been observed following the use of insulin detemir in pregnancy; pregnancy outcomes are similar following maternal use of insulin detemir and NPH insulin.

In women with diabetes, maternal hyperglycemia can be associated with congenital malformations as well as adverse effects in the fetus, neonate, and the mother (ACOG 2005; ADA 2016d; Kitzmiller 2008; Metzger 2007). To prevent adverse outcomes, prior to conception and throughout pregnancy maternal blood glucose and HbA_{1c} should be kept as close to target goals as possible but without causing significant hypoglycemia (ACOG 2013; ADA 2016d; Blumer 2013; Kitzmiller 2008; Lambert 2013). Prior to pregnancy, effective contraception should be used until glycemic control is achieved (ADA 2016d; Kitzmiller 2008).

Insulin requirements tend to fall during the first trimester of pregnancy and increase in the later trimesters, peaking at 28 to 32 weeks of gestation. Following delivery, insulin requirements decrease rapidly (ACOG 2005). Women who are stable on insulin detemir prior to conception may continue it during pregnancy. Pregnant women may also be switched to insulin detemir during pregnancy when therapy with NPH insulin is not adequate (Blumer 2013).

Insulin Glargine (IN soo lin GLAR jeen)

Related Information

Endocrine Disorders and Pregnancy *on page 1781*
Insulin Regular *on page 903*

Brand Names: US Basaglar KwikPen; Lantus; Lantus SoloStar; Toujeo SoloStar

Brand Names: Canada Lantus; Toujeo SoloStar

Pharmacologic Category Insulin, Long-Acting

Use

Diabetes mellitus: To improve glycemic control in adults with type 1 diabetes mellitus (insulin dependent, IDDM) and type 2 diabetes mellitus (noninsulin, NIDDM); to improve glycemic control in children ≥6 years with type 1 diabetes mellitus (Lantus and Basaglar only)

Limitations of use: Not recommended for the treatment of diabetic ketoacidosis.

Local Anesthetic/Vasoconstrictor Precautions No information available to require special precautions

Effects on Dental Treatment Key adverse event(s) related to dental treatment: Patients with diabetes should be questioned by the dental professional at each dental visit to assess their risk for stress-induced hypoglycemia. The dental professional should inquire about the patient's routine (ie, work, sleep schedule, eating patterns), history of hypoglycemia, time of last medication dose, last meal, and most recent blood sugar assessment. Keep a supply of glucose tablets and other carbohydrates in the office to prepare for a hypoglycemic event. Seek medical attention when necessary (American Diabetes Association 2014).

Effects on Bleeding No information available to require special precautions

Adverse Reactions Primarily symptoms of hypoglycemia.

>10%

Cardiovascular: Hypertension (20%), peripheral edema (20%)

Central nervous system: Depression (11%)

Endocrine & metabolic: Hypoglycemia (Type I on combination regimens: ≤69%; Type II on combination regimens: ≤8%; monotherapy in adults ≥50 years old: 6% [ORIGIN trial])

Gastrointestinal: Diarrhea (11%)

Genitourinary: Urinary tract infection (11%)

Immunologic: Antibody development (20% to 44%; effect on therapy not reported)

Infection: Influenza (19%), infection (9% to 14%)

Neuromuscular & skeletal: Arthralgia (14%), back pain (13%), limb pain (13%)

Ophthalmic: Cataract (18%), retinopathy (14%)

Respiratory: Upper respiratory tract infection (adults: 6% to 29%; children & adolescents: 14%), sinusitis (19%), bronchitis (15%), nasopharyngitis (7% to 13%), cough (12%)

1% to 10%:

Cardiovascular: Retinal vascular disease (6%)

Central nervous system: Headache (6% to 10%)

Local: Pain at injection site (3%)

Respiratory: Pharyngitis (children & adolescents: 8%), rhinitis (children & adolescents: 5%)

Miscellaneous: Accidental injury (6%)

Frequency not defined:

Endocrine & metabolic: Sodium retention

Local: Erythema at injection site, itching at injection site, localized edema, swelling at injection site

<1%, postmarketing, and/or case reports: Anaphylaxis, angioedema, bronchospasm, hyperglycemia, hypersensitivity reaction, hypertrophy at injection site, hypokalemia, hypotension, injection site reaction (including urticaria and inflammation), lipoatrophy at injection site, lipoatrophy at injection site, shock, skin rash, weight gain

General Dosage Range SubQ:

*Children ≥6 years and Adolescents:*Diabetes mellitus, type 1: Lantus, Basaglar: Initial dose: Approximately one-third of the total daily insulin requirement administered once daily

Adults:

Diabetes mellitus, type 1: Lantus, Basaglar, Toujeo: Initial dose: Approximately one-third to one-half of the total daily insulin requirement administered once daily

Diabetes mellitus, type 2: Initial: 0.2 units/kg once daily; for Lantus or Basaglar, up to 10 units/day initially is recommended.

Mechanism of Action Insulin acts via specific membrane-bound receptors on target tissues to regulate metabolism of carbohydrate, protein, and fats. Target organs for insulin include the liver, skeletal muscle, and adipose tissue.

Within the liver, insulin stimulates hepatic glycogen synthesis. Insulin promotes hepatic synthesis of fatty acids, which are released into the circulation as lipoproteins. Skeletal muscle effects of insulin include increased protein synthesis and increased glycogen synthesis. Within adipose tissue, insulin stimulates the processing of circulating lipoproteins to provide free fatty acids, facilitating triglyceride synthesis and storage by adipocytes; also directly inhibits the hydrolysis of triglycerides. In addition, insulin stimulates the cellular uptake of amino acids and increases cellular permeability to several ions, including potassium, magnesium, and phosphate. By activating sodium-potassium ATPases, insulin promotes the intracellular movement of potassium.

Normally secreted by the pancreas, insulin products are manufactured for pharmacologic use through recombinant DNA technology using either *E. coli* or *Saccharomyces cerevisiae*. Insulin glargine differs from human insulin by adding two arginines to the C-terminus of the B-chain in addition to containing glycine at position A21 in comparison to the asparagine found in human insulin. Insulins are categorized based on the onset, peak, and duration of effect (eg, rapid-, short-, intermediate-, and long-acting insulin). Insulin glargine is a long-acting insulin analog.

Pharmacodynamics/Kinetics

Onset of Action

Basaglar: Peak effect: No pronounced peak

Lantus: 3 to 4 hours; Peak effect: No pronounced peak

Toujeo: 6 hours

Duration of Action Lantus, Basaglar: Generally 24 hours or longer; reported range (Lantus): 10.8 to >24 hours (up to ~30 hours documented in some studies) (Heinemann 2000)

Time to Peak Plasma: Lantus: No pronounced peak; Basaglar: ~12 hours

Pregnancy Considerations In animal reproduction studies, outcomes were similar to those observed with regular insulin. In women with diabetes, maternal hyperglycemia can be associated with congenital malformations as well as adverse effects in the fetus, neonate, and the mother (ACOG 2005; ADA 2016d; Kitzmiller 2008; Metzger 2007). To prevent adverse outcomes, prior to conception and throughout pregnancy maternal blood glucose and HbA_{1c} should be kept as close to target goals as possible but without causing significant hypoglycemia (ACOG 2013; ADA 2016d; Blumer 2013; Kitzmiller 2008; Lambert 2013). Prior to pregnancy, effective contraception should be used until glycemic control is achieved (ADA 2016; Kitzmiller 2008).

Insulin requirements tend to fall during the first trimester of pregnancy and increase in the later trimesters, peaking at 28 to 32 weeks of gestation. Following delivery, insulin requirements decrease rapidly (ACOG 2005).

Because insulin glargine has an increased affinity to the insulin-like growth factor (IGF-I) receptor, there are theoretical concerns that it may contribute to adverse events when used during pregnancy (Jovanovic 2007; Lambert 2013), although this has not been observed in available studies (Lambert 2013; Lepercq 2012; Pollex 2011). Women who are stable on insulin glargine prior to conception may continue it during pregnancy. Theoretical concerns of insulin glargine should be discussed prior to conception (Blumer 2013).

Insulin Glargine and Lixisenatide

(IN soo lin GLAR jeen & lix i SEN a tide)

Brand Names: US Soliqua

Pharmacologic Category Antidiabetic Agent, Glucagon-Like Peptide-1 (GLP-1) Receptor Agonist; Insulin, Long-Acting

Use Diabetes mellitus, type 2: As an adjunct to diet and exercise to improve glycemic control in adults with type 2 diabetes mellitus inadequately controlled on basal insulin (<60 units daily) or lixisenatide

Local Anesthetic/Vasoconstrictor Precautions No information available to require special precautions

Effects on Dental Treatment Key adverse event(s) related to dental treatment: Patients with diabetes should be questioned by the dental professional at each dental visit to assess their risk for stress-induced hypoglycemia. The dental professional should inquire about the patient's routine (ie, work, sleep schedule, eating patterns), history of hypoglycemia, time of last medication dose, last meal, and most recent blood sugar assessment. Keep a supply of glucose tablets and other carbohydrates in the office to prepare for a hypoglycemic event. Seek medical attention when necessary (American Diabetes Association 2014).

Effects on Bleeding No information available to require special precautions

Adverse Reactions Also see individual agents.

>10%:

Endocrine & metabolic: Hypoglycemia (26% to 40%)
Immunologic: Antibody development (21% to 26%)

1% to 10%:

Central nervous system: Headache (5%)
Endocrine & metabolic: Severe hypoglycemia (≤1%)
Gastrointestinal: Nausea (10%), diarrhea (7%)
Local: Injection site reaction (2%)
Respiratory: Nasopharyngitis (7%), upper respiratory tract infection (6%)

Frequency not defined: Local: Hypertrophy at injection site, lipoatrophy at injection site

<1%, postmarketing, and/or case reports: Abdominal distention, abdominal pain, constipation, decreased appetite, dyspepsia, flatulence, gastritis, gastroesophageal reflux disease, vomiting

General Dosage Range SubQ: *Adults*: 15 units (insulin glargine 15 units/lixisenatide 5 mcg) to 60 units (insulin glargine 60 units/lixisenatide 20 mcg) once daily; maximum dose: 60 units (insulin glargine 60 units/lixisenatide 20 mcg)/day

Mechanism of Action Refer to individual agents.

Pregnancy Considerations Adverse events were observed in some animal reproduction studies. Refer to individual monographs.

Insulin Glulisine (IN soo lin gloo LIS een)

Related Information

Endocrine Disorders and Pregnancy *on page 1781*
Insulin Regular *on page 903*

Brand Names: US Apidra; Apidra SoloStar

Brand Names: Canada Apidra

Pharmacologic Category Insulin, Rapid-Acting

Use Treatment of type 1 diabetes mellitus (insulin dependent, IDDM) and type 2 diabetes mellitus (noninsulin dependent, NIDDM) to improve glycemic control

Local Anesthetic/Vasoconstrictor Precautions No information available to require special precautions

Effects on Dental Treatment Key adverse event(s) related to dental treatment: Patients with diabetes should be questioned by the dental professional at each dental visit to assess their risk for stress-induced hypoglycemia. The dental professional should inquire about the patient's routine (ie, work, sleep schedule, eating patterns), history of hypoglycemia, time of last medication dose, last meal, and most recent blood sugar assessment. Keep a supply of glucose tablets and other carbohydrates in the office to prepare for a hypoglycemic event. Seek medical attention when necessary (American Diabetes Association, 2014).

Effects on Bleeding No information available to require special precautions

Adverse Reactions

>10%

Endocrine & metabolic: Severe hypoglycemia (1% to 8%; children and adolescents, type 1 diabetes: 16%)
Respiratory: Nasopharyngitis (8% to 11%), upper respiratory tract infection (7% to 11%)

1% to 10%

Cardiovascular: Peripheral edema (8%; adults, type 2 diabetes), hypertension (4%; adults, type 2 diabetes)
Central nervous system: Headache (7%; children and adolescents, type 1 diabetes), hypoglycemic seizure (6%; children and adolescents, type 1 diabetes)
Endocrine & metabolic: Hypoglycemia (7%; adults, type 1 diabetes)
Hypersensitivity: Hypersensitivity reaction (4%)
Infection: Influenza (4% to 6%)
Local: Infusion site reaction (10%)
Neuromuscular & skeletal: Arthralgia (6%; adults, type 2 diabetes)

Frequency not defined:

Dermatologic: Pruritus, skin rash
Endocrine & metabolic: Hypokalemia, weight gain
Hypersensitivity: Anaphylaxis
Immunologic: Antibody development (no effect on drug efficacy)
Local: Hypertrophy at injection site, lipoatrophy at injection site

<1%, postmarketing, and/or case reports: Catheter complication

General Dosage Range SubQ: *Children ≥4 years, Adolescents and Adults:* Diabetes mellitus, type 1: **Note:** Multiple daily doses or continuous subcutaneous infusions guided by blood glucose monitoring are the standard of diabetes care. Combinations of insulin formulations are commonly used. The daily doses presented below are expressed as the **total units/kg/day of all insulin formulations combined.**

Initial: 0.2-0.6 units/kg/day in divided doses; usual maintenance: 0.5-1 units/kg/day in divided doses.

Mechanism of Action Insulin acts via specific membrane-bound receptors on target tissues to regulate metabolism of carbohydrate, protein, and fats. Target organs for insulin include the liver, skeletal muscle, and adipose tissue.

Within the liver, insulin stimulates hepatic glycogen synthesis. Insulin promotes hepatic synthesis of fatty acids, which are released into the circulation as lipoproteins. Skeletal muscle effects of insulin include increased protein synthesis and increased glycogen synthesis. Within adipose tissue, insulin stimulates the processing of circulating lipoproteins to provide free fatty acids, facilitating triglyceride synthesis and storage by adipocytes; also directly inhibits the hydrolysis of triglycerides. In addition, insulin stimulates the cellular uptake of amino acids and increases cellular permeability to several ions, including potassium, magnesium, and phosphate. By activating sodium-potassium ATPases, insulin promotes the intracellular movement of potassium.

Normally secreted by the pancreas, insulin products are manufactured for pharmacologic use through recombinant DNA technology using either *E. coli* or *Saccharomyces cerevisiae*. Insulin glulisine differs from human insulin by containing a lysine and glutamic acid at positions B3 and B29, respectively, in comparison to the asparagine and lysine found at B3 and B29 in human insulin. Insulins are categorized based on the onset, peak, and duration of effect (eg, rapid-, short-, intermediate-, and long-acting insulin). Insulin glulisine is a rapid-acting insulin analog.

Pharmacodynamics/Kinetics

Onset of Action 0.2-0.5 hours; Peak effect: 1.6-2.8 hours

Duration of Action 3-4 hours

Half-life Elimination

IV: 13 minutes

SubQ: 42 minutes

Time to Peak Plasma: 60 minutes (range: 40-120 minutes)

Pregnancy Risk Factor C

Pregnancy Considerations In animal reproduction studies, outcomes were similar to those observed with regular insulin.

In women with diabetes, maternal hyperglycemia can be associated with congenital malformations as well as adverse effects in the fetus, neonate, and the mother (ACOG 2005; ADA 2016d; Kitzmiller 2008; Metzger 2007). To prevent adverse outcomes, prior to conception and throughout pregnancy maternal blood glucose and HbA_{1c} should be kept as close to target goals as possible but without causing significant hypoglycemia (ACOG 2013; ADA 2016d; Blumer 2013; Kitzmiller 2008; Lambert 2013). Prior to pregnancy, effective contraception should be used until glycemic control is achieved (ADA 2016d; Kitzmiller 2008).

Insulin requirements tend to fall during the first trimester of pregnancy and increase in the later trimesters, peaking at 28 to 32 weeks of gestation. Following delivery, insulin requirements decrease rapidly (ACOG 2005).

Due to lack of clinical data, insulin glulisine is not currently recommended for use in pregnant women (Blumer 2013).

Insulin Lispro (IN soo lin LYE sproe)

Related Information

Endocrine Disorders and Pregnancy *on page 1781*

Insulin Regular *on page 903*

Brand Names: US HumaLOG; HumaLOG KwikPen

Brand Names: Canada Humalog; HumaLOG KwikPen

Pharmacologic Category Insulin, Rapid-Acting

Use

Diabetes mellitus: Treatment of type 1 diabetes mellitus (insulin dependent, IDDM) and type 2 diabetes mellitus (noninsulin dependent, NIDDM) to improve glycemic control

According to the manufacturer's labeling, only the U 100 (eg, 100 units/mL) strength is approved for use in children ≥3 years by continuous subcutaneous insulin infusion (CSII) pumps.

Local Anesthetic/Vasoconstrictor Precautions No information available to require special precautions

Effects on Dental Treatment Key adverse event(s) related to dental treatment: Patients with diabetes should be questioned by the dental professional at each dental visit to assess their risk for stress-induced hypoglycemia. The dental professional should inquire about the patient's routine (ie, work, sleep schedule, eating patterns), history of hypoglycemia, time of last medication dose, last meal, and most recent blood sugar assessment. Keep a supply of glucose tablets and other carbohydrates in the office to prepare for a hypoglycemic event. Seek medical attention when necessary (American Diabetes Association, 2014).

Effects on Bleeding No information available to require special precautions

Adverse Reactions Frequency not always defined.

Cardiovascular: Peripheral edema

Central nervous system: Headache (type 1 diabetes: 30%; type 2 diabetes: 12%), pain (11% to 20%)

Endocrine & metabolic: Hypoglycemia, hypokalemia, weight gain

Gastrointestinal: Diarrhea (type 1 diabetes: 9%), nausea (type 1 diabetes: 6%)

Genitourinary: Urinary tract infection (type 1 diabetes: 6%)

Hypersensitivity: Hypersensitivity reaction

Immunologic: Antibody development

Infection: Infection (10% to 14%)

Local: Hypertrophy at injection site, injection site reaction, lipoatrophy at injection site

Neuromuscular & skeletal: Myalgia (type 1 diabetes: 7%; most likely secondary to excipient metacresol)

Respiratory: Flu-like symptoms (type 1 diabetes: 35%; type 2 diabetes: 6%), pharyngitis (type 1 diabetes: 33%; type 2 diabetes: 7%), rhinitis (type 1 diabetes: 25%; type 2 diabetes: 8%)

General Dosage Range SubQ: *Children ≥3 years, Adolescents and Adults:* Daily doses are expressed as the **total units/kg/day of all insulin formulations combined.** Diabetes mellitus, type 1: Initial: 0.2-0.6 units/kg/day in divided doses; usual maintenance: 0.5-1 units/kg/day in divided doses.

Mechanism of Action Insulin acts via specific membrane-bound receptors on target tissues to regulate metabolism of carbohydrate, protein, and fats. Target organs for insulin include the liver, skeletal muscle, and adipose tissue.

Within the liver, insulin stimulates hepatic glycogen synthesis. Insulin promotes hepatic synthesis of fatty acids, which are released into the circulation as lipoproteins. Skeletal muscle effects of insulin include increased protein synthesis and increased glycogen synthesis. Within adipose tissue, insulin stimulates the processing of circulating lipoproteins to provide free fatty acids, facilitating triglyceride synthesis and storage by adipocytes; also directly inhibits the hydrolysis of triglycerides. In addition, insulin stimulates the cellular uptake of amino acids and increases cellular permeability to several ions, including potassium, magnesium, and phosphate. By activating sodium-potassium ATPases, insulin promotes the intracellular movement of potassium.

Normally secreted by the pancreas, insulin products are manufactured for pharmacologic use through recombinant DNA technology using either *E. coli* or *Saccharomyces cerevisiae*. Insulin lispro differs from human insulin by containing a lysine and proline at positions B28 and B29, respectively, in comparison to the proline and lysine found at B28 and B29 in human insulin. Insulins are categorized based on the onset, peak, and duration of effect (eg, rapid-, short-, intermediate-, and long-acting insulin). Insulin lispro is a rapid-acting insulin analog.

Pharmacodynamics/Kinetics

Onset of Action SubQ: 0.25-0.5 hours; Peak effect: SubQ: 0.5-2.5 hours

Duration of Action SubQ: ≤5 hours

Half-life Elimination ~1 hour

Time to Peak Plasma: SubQ: 0.5-1.5 hours

Pregnancy Risk Factor B

Pregnancy Considerations Adverse events have not been observed in animal reproduction studies. Insulin lispro has not been shown to cross the placenta at standard clinical doses (Boskovic 2003; Holcberg 2004; Jovanovic 1999).

In women with diabetes, maternal hyperglycemia can be associated with congenital malformations as well as adverse effects in the fetus, neonate, and the mother (ACOG 2005; ADA 2016d; Kitzmiller 2008; Metzger 2007). To prevent adverse outcomes, prior to conception and throughout pregnancy maternal blood glucose and HbA_{1c} should be kept as close to target goals as possible but without causing significant hypoglycemia (ACOG 2013; ADA 2016d; Blumer 2013; Kitzmiller 2008; Lambert 2013). Prior to pregnancy, effective contraception should be used until glycemic control is achieved (ADA 2016d; Kitzmiller 2008).

Insulin requirements tend to fall during the first trimester of pregnancy and increase in the later trimesters, peaking at 28 to 32 weeks of gestation. Following delivery, insulin requirements decrease rapidly (ACOG 2005). Insulin lispro may be used to treat diabetes in pregnant women (ACOG 2013; Blumer 2013; Kitzmiller 2008; Lambert 2013)

Insulin Lispro Protamine and Insulin Lispro

(IN soo lin LYE sproe PROE ta meen & IN soo lin LYE sproe)

Related Information

Insulin Regular *on page 903*

Brand Names: US HumaLOG Mix; HumaLOG Mix 50/50; HumaLOG Mix 50/50 KwikPen; HumaLOG Mix 75/25; HumaLOG Mix 75/25 KwikPen

Brand Names: Canada Humalog Mix 25; Humalog Mix 50

Pharmacologic Category Insulin, Combination

Use Treatment of type 1 diabetes mellitus (insulin dependent, IDDM) and type 2 diabetes mellitus (noninsulin dependent, NIDDM) to improve glycemic control

Local Anesthetic/Vasoconstrictor Precautions No information available to require special precautions

Effects on Dental Treatment Key adverse event(s) related to dental treatment: Patients with diabetes should be questioned by the dental professional at each dental visit to assess their risk for stress-induced hypoglycemia. The dental professional should inquire about the patient's routine (ie, work, sleep schedule, eating patterns), history of hypoglycemia, time of last medication dose, last meal, and most recent blood sugar assessment. Keep a supply of glucose tablets and other carbohydrates in the office to prepare for a hypoglycemic event. Seek medical attention when necessary (American Diabetes Association, 2014).

Effects on Bleeding No information available to require special precautions

Adverse Reactions Also see insulin lispro for additional reactions.

Dermatologic: Pruritus, skin rash
Endocrine & metabolic: Hypoglycemia, lipodystrophy
Hypersensitivity: Hypersensitivity reaction
Local: Injection site reaction, lipotrophy at injection site

General Dosage Range SubQ: *Adults:* Diabetes mellitus, type 1 or 2: **Not** intended for initial therapy; basal insulin requirements should be established **first** to direct dosing of combination insulin products.

Mechanism of Action Insulin acts via specific membrane-bound receptors on target tissues to regulate metabolism of carbohydrate, protein, and fats. Target organs for insulin include the liver, skeletal muscle, and adipose tissue.

Within the liver, insulin stimulates hepatic glycogen synthesis. Insulin promotes hepatic synthesis of fatty acids, which are released into the circulation as lipoproteins. Skeletal muscle effects of insulin include increased protein synthesis and increased glycogen synthesis. Within adipose tissue, insulin stimulates the processing of circulating lipoproteins to provide free fatty acids, facilitating triglyceride synthesis and storage by adipocytes; also directly inhibits the hydrolysis of triglycerides. In addition, insulin stimulates the cellular uptake of amino acids and increases cellular permeability to several ions, including potassium, magnesium, and phosphate. By activating sodium-potassium ATPases, insulin promotes the intracellular movement of potassium.

Normally secreted by the pancreas, insulin products are manufactured for pharmacologic use through recombinant DNA technology using either *E. coli* or *Saccharomyces cerevisiae*. Insulin lispro differs from human insulin by containing a lysine and proline at positions B28 and B29, respectively, in comparison to the proline and lysine found at B28 and B29 in human insulin.

Insulins are categorized based on the onset, peak, and duration of effect (eg, rapid-, short-, intermediate-, and long-acting insulin). Insulin lispro protamine and insulin lispro is an intermediate-acting combination product with a more rapid onset and similar duration of action as compared to that of insulin NPH and insulin regular combination products.

Pharmacodynamics/Kinetics

Onset of Action 0.25-0.5 hours; Peak effect: Humalog Mix 50/50: 0.8-4.8 hours; Humalog Mix 75/25: 1-6.5 hours

Duration of Action 14-24 hours

Time to Peak Plasma: Humalog Mix 50/50: 0.75-13.5 hours; Humalog Mix 75/25: 0.5-4 hours

Pregnancy Risk Factor B

Pregnancy Considerations Adverse events have not been observed in animal reproduction studies. Insulin lispro has not been shown to cross the placenta at standard clinical doses (Boskovic 2003; Holcberg 2004; Jovanovic 1999).

In women with diabetes, maternal hyperglycemia can be associated with congenital malformations as well as adverse effects in the fetus, neonate, and the mother (ACOG 2005; ADA 2016d; Kitzmiller 2008; Metzger 2007). To prevent adverse outcomes, prior to conception and throughout pregnancy maternal blood glucose and HbA_{1c} should be kept as close to target goals as possible but without causing significant hypoglycemia (ACOG 2013; ADA 2016d; Blumer 2013; Kitzmiller 2008; Lambert 2013). Prior to pregnancy, effective contraception should be used until glycemic control is achieved (ADA 2016d; Kitzmiller 2008).

Insulin requirements tend to fall during the first trimester of pregnancy and increase in the later trimesters, peaking at 28 to 32 weeks of gestation. Following delivery, insulin requirements decrease rapidly (ACOG 2005).

Prior to pregnancy, women with diabetes who are trying to conceive should be treated with multiple daily doses of insulin or continuous subcutaneous insulin infusion (CSII) as opposed to split-dose, premixed insulin therapy. This is to allow for better glucose control and flexibility during pregnancy (Blumer 2013).

Insulin NPH (IN soo lin N P H)

Related Information

Endocrine Disorders and Pregnancy *on page 1781*
Insulin Regular *on page 903*

Brand Names: US HumuLIN N KwikPen [OTC]; HumuLIN N Pen [OTC] [DSC]; HumuLIN N [OTC]; NovoLIN N ReliOn [OTC]; NovoLIN N [OTC]

Brand Names: Canada Humulin N; Novolin ge NPH

Pharmacologic Category Insulin, Intermediate-Acting

Use Treatment of type 1 diabetes mellitus (insulin dependent, IDDM) and type 2 diabetes mellitus (noninsulin dependent, NIDDM) to improve glycemic control

Local Anesthetic/Vasoconstrictor Precautions No information available to require special precautions

Effects on Dental Treatment Key adverse event(s) related to dental treatment: Patients with diabetes should be questioned by the dental professional at each dental visit to assess their risk for stress-induced hypoglycemia. The dental professional should inquire about the patient's routine (ie, work, sleep schedule, eating patterns), history of hypoglycemia, time of last medication dose, last meal, and most recent blood sugar assessment. Keep a supply of glucose tablets and other carbohydrates in the office to prepare for a hypoglycemic event. Seek medical attention when necessary (American Diabetes Association, 2014).

Effects on Bleeding No information available to require special precautions

Adverse Reactions Frequency not defined.

Cardiovascular: Peripheral edema

Endocrine & metabolic: Hypoglycemia, hypokalemia, weight gain

Hypersensitivity: Hypersensitivity reaction

Immunologic: Immunogenicity

Local: Atrophy at injection site, hypertrophy at injection site, injection site reaction (including redness, swelling, and itching)

Neuromuscular & skeletal: Swelling of extremities

Ophthalmic: Visual disturbance

General Dosage Range SubQ:

Children ≥2 years, Adolescents, and Adults: Daily doses are expressed as the **total units/kg/day of all insulin formulations combined.** Diabetes mellitus, type 1: Initial: 0.2-0.6 units/kg/day in divided doses; usual maintenance: 0.5-1 units/kg/day in divided doses.

Adults: Diabetes mellitus, type 2: Initial: 0.2 units/kg/day or 10 units/day in divided doses before meals.

Mechanism of Action Insulin acts via specific membrane-bound receptors on target tissues to regulate metabolism of carbohydrate, protein, and fats. Target organs for insulin include the liver, skeletal muscle, and adipose tissue.

Within the liver, insulin stimulates hepatic glycogen synthesis. Insulin promotes hepatic synthesis of fatty acids, which are released into the circulation as lipoproteins. Skeletal muscle effects of insulin include increased protein synthesis and increased glycogen synthesis. Within adipose tissue, insulin stimulates the processing of circulating lipoproteins to provide free fatty acids, facilitating triglyceride synthesis and storage by adipocytes; also directly inhibits the hydrolysis of triglycerides. In addition, insulin stimulates the cellular uptake of amino acids and increases cellular permeability to several ions, including potassium, magnesium, and phosphate. By activating sodium-potassium ATPases, insulin promotes the intracellular movement of potassium.

Normally secreted by the pancreas, insulin products are manufactured for pharmacologic use through recombinant DNA technology using either *E. coli* or *Saccharomyces cerevisiae*. Insulins are categorized based on the onset, peak, and duration of effect (eg, rapid-, short-, intermediate-, and long-acting insulin). Insulin NPH, an isophane suspension of human insulin, is an intermediate-acting insulin.

Pharmacodynamics/Kinetics

Onset of Action 1-2 hours; Peak effect: 4-12 hours

Duration of Action 14-24 hours

Time to Peak Plasma: 6-10 hours

Pregnancy Risk Factor B

Pregnancy Considerations Animal reproduction studies have not been conducted; however, use provides maternal and fetal benefits.

In women with diabetes, maternal hyperglycemia can be associated with congenital malformations as well as adverse effects in the fetus, neonate, and the mother (ACOG 2005; ADA 2016d; Kitzmiller 2008; Metzger 2007). To prevent adverse outcomes, prior to conception and throughout pregnancy maternal blood glucose and HbA_{1c} should be kept as close to target goals as possible but without causing significant hypoglycemia

(ACOG 2013; ADA 2016d; Blumer 2013; Kitzmiller 2008; Lambert 2013). Prior to pregnancy, effective contraception should be used until glycemic control is achieved (ADA 2016d; Kitzmiller 2008).

Insulin requirements tend to fall during the first trimester of pregnancy and increase in the later trimesters, peaking at 28 to 32 weeks of gestation. Following delivery, insulin requirements decrease rapidly (ACOG 2005). NPH insulin may be used to treat diabetes in pregnant women (Blumer 2013; Kitzmiller 2008; Lambert 2013).

Insulin NPH and Insulin Regular

(IN soo lin N P H & IN soo lin REG yoo ler)

Related Information

Insulin Regular *on page 903*

Brand Names: US HumuLIN 70/30; HumuLIN 70/30 KwikPen; NovoLIN 70/30

Brand Names: Canada Humulin 20/80; Humulin 70/30; Novolin ge 30/70; Novolin ge 40/60; Novolin ge 50/50

Pharmacologic Category Insulin, Combination

Use Treatment of type 1 diabetes mellitus (insulin dependent, IDDM) and type 2 diabetes mellitus (noninsulin dependent, NIDDM) to improve glycemic control

Local Anesthetic/Vasoconstrictor Precautions No information available to require special precautions

Effects on Dental Treatment Key adverse event(s) related to dental treatment: Patients with diabetes should be questioned by the dental professional at each dental visit to assess their risk for stress-induced hypoglycemia. The dental professional should inquire about the patient's routine (ie, work, sleep schedule, eating patterns), history of hypoglycemia, time of last medication dose, last meal, and most recent blood sugar assessment. Keep a supply of glucose tablets and other carbohydrates in the office to prepare for a hypoglycemic event. Seek medical attention when necessary (American Diabetes Association, 2014).

Effects on Bleeding No information available to require special precautions

Adverse Reactions See individual agents. Frequency not defined.

Cardiovascular: Peripheral edema

Dermatologic: Pruritus

Endocrine & metabolic: Hypoglycemia, hypokalemia, weight gain

Hypersensitivity: Hypersensitivity reaction

Immunologic: Immunogenicity

Local: Hypertrophy at injection site, lipoatrophy at injection site

General Dosage Range SubQ:

Children, Adolescents, and Adults: Daily doses are expressed as the **total units/kg/day of all insulin formulations combined.** Diabetes mellitus, type 1: Initial: 0.2-0.6 units/kg/day in divided doses; usual maintenance: 0.5-1 units/kg/day in divided doses.

Adults: Diabetes mellitus, type 2: **Not** intended for initial therapy; basal insulin requirements should be established **first** to direct dosing of combination insulin products.

Mechanism of Action Insulin acts via specific membrane-bound receptors on target tissues to regulate metabolism of carbohydrate, protein, and fats. Target organs for insulin include the liver, skeletal muscle, and adipose tissue.

Within the liver, insulin stimulates hepatic glycogen synthesis. Insulin promotes hepatic synthesis of fatty acids, which are released into the circulation as lipoproteins. Skeletal muscle effects of insulin include increased protein synthesis and increased glycogen synthesis. Within adipose tissue, insulin stimulates the processing of circulating lipoproteins to provide free fatty acids, facilitating triglyceride synthesis and storage by adipocytes; also directly inhibits the hydrolysis of triglycerides. In addition, insulin stimulates the cellular uptake of amino acids and increases cellular permeability to several ions, including potassium, magnesium, and phosphate. By activating sodium-potassium ATPases, insulin promotes the intracellular movement of potassium.

Normally secreted by the pancreas, insulin products are manufactured for pharmacologic use through recombinant DNA technology using either *E. coli* or *Saccharomyces cerevisiae*. Insulins are categorized based on the onset, peak, and duration of effect (eg, rapid-, short-, intermediate-, and long-acting insulin). Insulin NPH (an isophane suspension of human insulin) and insulin regular is an intermediate-acting combination insulin product with a more rapid onset than that of insulin NPH alone.

Pharmacodynamics/Kinetics

Onset of Action 0.5 hours; Peak effect: 2-12 hours

Duration of Action 18-24 hours

Time to Peak Based on individual components:

Insulin regular: 0.8-2 hours

Insulin NPH: 6-10 hours

Pregnancy Risk Factor B

Pregnancy Considerations Animal reproduction studies have not been conducted, however use provides maternal and fetal benefits.

In women with diabetes, maternal hyperglycemia can be associated with congenital malformations as well as adverse effects in the fetus, neonate, and the mother (ACOG 2005; ADA 2016; Kitzmiller 2008; Metzger 2007). To prevent adverse outcomes, prior to conception and throughout pregnancy maternal blood glucose and HbA_{1c} should be kept as close to target goals as possible but without causing significant hypoglycemia (ACOG 2013; ADA 2016; Blumer 2013; Kitzmiller 2008; Lambert 2013). Prior to pregnancy, effective contraception should be used until glycemic control is achieved (ADA 2016; Kitzmiller 2008).

Insulin requirements tend to fall during the first trimester of pregnancy and increase in the later trimesters, peaking at 28 to 32 weeks of gestation. Following delivery, insulin requirements decrease rapidly (ACOG 2005).

Prior to pregnancy, women with diabetes who are trying to conceive should be treated with multiple daily doses of insulin or continuous subcutaneous insulin infusion (CSII) as opposed to split-dose, premixed insulin therapy. This is to allow for better glucose control and flexibility during pregnancy (Blumer 2013).

Insulin (Oral Inhalation) (IN soo lin)

Brand Names: US Afrezza

Pharmacologic Category Insulin, Rapid-Acting

Use Diabetes mellitus, type 1 or type 2: Treatment of diabetes mellitus (type 1 or type 2) to improve glycemic control

Local Anesthetic/Vasoconstrictor Precautions No information available to require special precautions

Effects on Dental Treatment Key adverse event(s) related to dental treatment: Patients with diabetes should be questioned by the dental professional at each dental visit to assess their risk for stress-induced hypoglycemia. The dental professional should inquire about the patient's routine (ie, work, sleep schedule, eating patterns), history of hypoglycemia, time of last medication dose, last meal, and most recent blood sugar assessment. Keep a supply of glucose tablets and other carbohydrates in the office to prepare for a hypoglycemic event. Seek medical attention when necessary (American Diabetes Association 2014).

Effects on Bleeding No information available to require special precautions

Adverse Reactions

>10%:

Endocrine & metabolic: Hypoglycemia (67%)

Respiratory: Acute bronchospasm (patients with asthma: 29%), cough (26% to 29%)

1% to 10%:

Central nervous system: Headache (5%), fatigue (2%)

Endocrine & metabolic: Severe hypoglycemia (5%)

Gastrointestinal: Sore throat (≤6%), diarrhea (3%), nausea (2%)

Genitourinary: Urinary tract infection (2%)

Respiratory: Reduced forced expiratory volume (6%; ≥15% decline), throat irritation (≤6%), bronchitis (3%), decreased lung function (3%), productive cough (2%)

<1%, postmarketing, and/or case reports: Antibody development (drug efficacy not affected), diabetic ketoacidosis (diabetes mellitus, type 1), hypersensitivity reaction, hypokalemia

General Dosage Range Inhalation: *Adults:* Diabetes mellitus, type 1 or type 2: 4 to 24 units at each meal (eg, 3 times daily).

Mechanism of Action

Insulin acts via specific membrane-bound receptors on target tissues to regulate metabolism of carbohydrate, protein, and fats. Target organs for insulin include the liver, skeletal muscle, and adipose tissue.

Within the liver, insulin stimulates hepatic glycogen synthesis. Insulin promotes hepatic synthesis of fatty acids, which are released into the circulation as lipoproteins. Skeletal muscle effects of insulin include increased protein synthesis and increased glycogen synthesis. Within adipose tissue, insulin stimulates the processing of circulating lipoproteins to provide free fatty acids, facilitating triglyceride synthesis and storage by adipocytes; also directly inhibits the hydrolysis of triglycerides. In addition, insulin stimulates the cellular uptake of amino acids and increases cellular permeability to several ions, including potassium, magnesium, and phosphate. By activating sodium-potassium ATPases, insulin promotes the intracellular movement of potassium.

Normally secreted by the pancreas, insulin products are manufactured for pharmacologic use through recombinant DNA technology using either *E. coli* or *Saccharomyces cerevisiae*. Inhaled human insulin has an identical structure to that of native human insulin and is adsorbed onto carrier particles which dissolve within the lungs after inhalation leading to rapid absorption of insulin in the systemic circulation. Insulins are categorized based on the onset, peak, and duration of effect (eg, rapid-, short-, intermediate-, and long-acting insulin). Inhaled insulin is an ultra-rapid acting insulin.

Pharmacodynamics/Kinetics

Onset of Action Peak effect: ~53 minutes

Duration of Action ~160 to 180 minutes

Half-life Elimination 28 to 39 minutes

Time to Peak 12 to 15 minutes

Pregnancy Risk Factor C

Pregnancy Considerations Adverse events were observed in some animal reproduction studies conducted using the carrier particles (vehicle) used to deliver regular insulin for inhalation.

In women with diabetes, maternal hyperglycemia can be associated with congenital malformations as well as adverse effects in the fetus, neonate, and the mother (ACOG 2005; ADA 2016c; Kitzmiller 2008; Metzger 2007). To prevent adverse outcomes, prior to conception and throughout pregnancy maternal blood glucose and HbA_{1c} should be kept as close to target goals as possible but without causing significant hypoglycemia (ACOG 2013; ADA 2016c; Blumer 2013; Kitzmiller 2008; Lambert 2013). Prior to pregnancy, effective contraception should be used until glycemic control is achieved (ADA 2016c; Kitzmiller 2008).

Insulin requirements tend to fall during the first trimester of pregnancy and increase in the later trimesters, peaking at 28 to 32 weeks of gestation. Following delivery, insulin requirements decrease rapidly (ACOG 2005).

Rapid acting insulins, such as insulin aspart or insulin lispro may be preferred over regular human insulin in women trying to conceive (Blumer 2013). Information specific to the use of inhaled insulin during pregnancy is limited (Makam 2009). Refer to the Insulin Regular monograph for additional information related to the use of insulin in pregnancy.

Insulin Regular (IN soo lin REG yoo ler)

Related Information

Endocrine Disorders and Pregnancy *on page 1781*

Insulin Aspart *on page 892*

Insulin Aspart Protamine and Insulin Aspart *on page 893*

Insulin Detemir *on page 896*

Insulin Glargine *on page 897*

Insulin Glulisine *on page 898*

Insulin Lispro *on page 899*

Insulin Lispro Protamine and Insulin Lispro *on page 900*

Insulin NPH *on page 901*

Insulin NPH and Insulin Regular *on page 902*

Brand Names: US HumuLIN R U-500 (CONCENTRATED); HumuLIN R U-500 KwikPen; HumuLIN R [OTC]; NovoLIN R ReliOn [OTC]; NovoLIN R [OTC]

Brand Names: Canada Humulin R; Novolin ge Toronto

Pharmacologic Category Insulin, Short-Acting

Use Diabetes mellitus: To improve glycemic control in adult and pediatric patients with diabetes mellitus requiring daily doses of more than 200 units of insulin per day

Local Anesthetic/Vasoconstrictor Precautions No information available to require special precautions

Effects on Dental Treatment Key adverse event(s) related to dental treatment: Patients with diabetes should be questioned by the dental professional at each dental visit to assess their risk for stress-induced hypoglycemia. The dental professional should inquire about the patient's routine (ie, work, sleep schedule, eating patterns), history of hypoglycemia, time of last medication dose, last meal, and most recent blood sugar assessment. Keep a supply of glucose tablets and other carbohydrates in the office to prepare for a ▶

hypoglycemic event. Seek medical attention when necessary (American Diabetes Association 2014).

Effects on Bleeding No information available to require special precautions

Adverse Reactions Frequency not always defined.

Cardiovascular: Peripheral edema

Dermatologic: Erythema at injection site, injection site pruritus

Endocrine & metabolic: Hypoglycemia, hypokalemia, weight gain

Hypersensitivity: Anaphylaxis, hypersensitivity, hypersensitivity reaction

Local: Hypertrophy at injection site, lipoatrophy at injection site

General Dosage Range Dosage adjustment recommended in patients with renal impairment

IV, SubQ: *Children, Adolescents, and Adults:* Daily doses are expressed as the **total units/kg/day of all insulin formulations combined**. Diabetes mellitus, type 1: Initial: 0.2 to 0.6 units/kg/day in divided doses; usual maintenance: 0.5 to 1 units/kg/day in divided doses.

Mechanism of Action Insulin acts via specific membrane-bound receptors on target tissues to regulate metabolism of carbohydrate, protein, and fats. Target organs for insulin include the liver, skeletal muscle, and adipose tissue.

Within the liver, insulin stimulates hepatic glycogen synthesis. Insulin promotes hepatic synthesis of fatty acids, which are released into the circulation as lipoproteins. Skeletal muscle effects of insulin include increased protein synthesis and increased glycogen synthesis. Within adipose tissue, insulin stimulates the processing of circulating lipoproteins to provide free fatty acids, facilitating triglyceride synthesis and storage by adipocytes; also directly inhibits the hydrolysis of triglycerides. In addition, insulin stimulates the cellular uptake of amino acids and increases cellular permeability to several ions, including potassium, magnesium, and phosphate. By activating sodium-potassium ATPases, insulin promotes the intracellular movement of potassium.

Normally secreted by the pancreas, insulin products are manufactured for pharmacologic use through recombinant DNA technology using either *E. coli* or *Saccharomyces cerevisiae*. Regular insulin has an identical structure to that of native human insulin. Insulins are categorized based on the onset, peak, and duration of effect (eg, rapid-, short-, intermediate-, and long-acting insulin). Insulin regular is a short-acting insulin analog.

Pharmacodynamics/Kinetics

Onset of Action SubQ: 0.25 to 0.5 hours; Peak effect: SubQ: U-100: 2.5 to 5 hours; U-500: 4 to 8 hours

Duration of Action

IV: U-100: 2 to 6 hours

SubQ: U-100: 4 to 12 hours (may increase with dose); U-500: 13 to 24 hours

Half-life Elimination IV: ~0.5 to 1 hour (dose-dependent); SubQ: 1.5 hours

Time to Peak Plasma: SubQ: 0.8 to 2 hours

Pregnancy Risk Factor B

Pregnancy Considerations Animal reproduction studies have not been conducted. Exogenous insulin bound to anti-insulin antibodies can be detected in cord blood (Menon 1990)

In women with diabetes, maternal hyperglycemia can be associated with congenital malformations as well as adverse effects in the fetus, neonate, and the mother (ACOG 2005; ADA 2016a; Kitzmiller 2008; Metzger 2007). To prevent adverse outcomes, prior to conception and throughout pregnancy, maternal blood glucose and HbA_{1c} should be kept as close to target goals as possible but without causing significant hypoglycemia (ACOG 2013; ADA 2016a; Blumer 2013; Kitzmiller 2008; Lambert 2013). Prior to pregnancy, effective contraception should be used until glycemic control is achieved (ADA 2016a; Kitzmiller 2008).

Insulin requirements tend to fall during the first trimester of pregnancy and increase in the later trimesters, peaking at 28 to 32 weeks of gestation. Following delivery, insulin requirements decrease rapidly (ACOG 2005).

Rapid-acting insulins, such as insulin aspart or insulin lispro may be preferred over regular human insulin in women trying to conceive (Blumer 2013); however, there is no need to switch a pregnant woman who is well-controlled on injectable human insulin to a short acting analogue (Lambert 2013). Regular insulin is used intravenously for glycemic control during labor.

Interferon Alfa-2b (in ter FEER on AL fa too bee)

Related Information

Dentin Hypersensitivity, Acid Erosion, High Caries Index, Management of Alveolar Osteitis, and Xerostomia *on page 1857*

Systemic Viral Diseases *on page 1806*

Brand Names: US Intron A

Brand Names: Canada Intron A

Generic Availability (US) No

Pharmacologic Category Antineoplastic Agent, Biological Response Modulator; Biological Response Modulator; Immunomodulator, Systemic; Interferon

Use

AIDS-related Kaposi sarcoma: Treatment of patients 18 years and older with AIDS-related Kaposi sarcoma

Chronic hepatitis B: Treatment of chronic hepatitis B in patients 1 year and older with compensated liver disease

Chronic hepatitis C: Treatment of chronic hepatitis C in patients 18 years and older with compensated liver disease who have a history of blood or blood-product exposure and/or are hepatitis C virus (HCV) antibody-positive; in combination with ribavirin for treatment of chronic hepatitis C in patients 3 years and older with compensated liver disease previously untreated with alpha interferon therapy and in patients 18 years and older who have relapsed following alpha interferon therapy

Condylomata acuminata: Treatment of patients 18 years and older with condylomata acuminata involving external surfaces of the genital and perianal areas

Follicular lymphoma: Initial treatment of clinically aggressive follicular non-Hodgkin lymphoma in conjunction with anthracycline-containing combination chemotherapy in patients 18 years and older

Hairy cell leukemia: Treatment of patients 18 years and older with hairy cell leukemia

Malignant melanoma: Adjuvant to surgical treatment in patients 18 years and older with malignant melanoma who are free of disease but at high risk for systemic recurrence, within 56 days of surgery

Local Anesthetic/Vasoconstrictor Precautions No information available to require special precautions

Effects on Dental Treatment Key adverse event(s) related to dental treatment: Xerostomia (normal salivary flow resumes upon discontinuation), metallic taste, taste alteration, and gingivitis.

Effects on Bleeding Hematologic toxicity associated with dose and disease being treated. Thrombocytopenia may be as high as 15%. Medical consult recommended.

Adverse Reactions Note: In a majority of patients, a flu-like symptom (fever, chills, tachycardia, malaise, myalgia, headache), occurs within 1-2 hours of administration; may last up to 24 hours and may be dose limiting.

>10%:

- Cardiovascular: Chest pain (≤28%)
- Central nervous system: Fatigue (8% to 96%), headache (21% to 62%), chills (≤54%), rigors (≤42%), depression (3% to 40%; grades 3/4: 2%), drowsiness (≤33%), dizziness (≤24%), irritability (≤22%), paresthesia (1% to 21%), pain (≤18%), right upper quadrant pain (≤15%), amnesia (≤14%), lack of concentration (≤14%), malaise (≤14%), confusion (≤12%), insomnia (≤12%)
- Dermatologic: Alopecia (≤38%), skin rash (≤25%), diaphoresis (1% to 21%), pruritus (≤11%)
- Endocrine & metabolic: Weight loss (<1% to 13%), amenorrhea (≤12%)
- Gastrointestinal: Anorexia (1% to 69%), nausea, (17% to 66%), diarrhea (2% to 45%), vomiting (children 27%; adults 2% to 32%), xerostomia (≤28%), dysgeusia (≤24%), abdominal pain (1% to 23%), constipation (≤14%), gingivitis (≤14%)
- Hematologic & oncologic: Neutropenia (≤92%; grade 4: 1% to 4%), leukopenia (≤68%), anemia (≤32%), thrombocytopenia (≤15%)
- Hepatic: Increased serum AST (≤63%; grades 3/4: 14%), increased serum ALT (≤15%), increased serum alkaline phosphatase (≤13%)
- Infection: Candidiasis (≤17%)
- Local: Injection site reaction (≤20%)
- Neuromuscular & skeletal: Myalgia (28% to 75%), weakness (≤63%), skeletal pain (≤21%), arthralgia (≤19%), back pain (≤19%)
- Renal: Increased blood urea nitrogen (≤12%)
- Respiratory: Flu-like symptoms (≤79%), dyspnea (≤34%), cough (≤31%), pharyngitis (≤31%), sinusitis (≤21%)
- Miscellaneous: Fever (34% to 94%; more common in children)

5% to 10%:

- Cardiovascular: Edema (≤10%), hypertension (≤9%)
- Central nervous system: Hypoesthesia (≤10%), anxiety (≤9%), vertigo (≤8%), agitation (≤7%)
- Dermatologic: Xeroderma (≤10%), dermatitis (≤8%)
- Endocrine & metabolic: Decreased libido (≤5%)
- Gastrointestinal: Loose stools (≤10%), dyspepsia (≤8%)
- Genitourinary: Urinary tract infection (≤5%)
- Hematologic & oncologic: Purpura (≤5%)
- Infection: Infection (≤7%), herpes virus infection (≤5%)
- Renal: Polyuria (≤10%), increased serum creatinine (≤6%)
- Respiratory: Bronchitis (≤10%), nasal congestion (≤10%), epistaxis (≤7%)

<5%, postmarketing, and/or case reports:

- Cardiovascular: Angina pectoris, arteritis, atrial fibrillation, bradycardia, cardiac arrhythmia, cardiac failure, cardiomegaly, cardiomyopathy, cerebrovascular accident, coronary artery disease, extrasystoles, flushing, heart valve disease, hypotension, myocardial infarction, palpitations, peripheral ischemia, periarteritis nodosa, pulmonary embolism, Raynaud's phenomenon, reduced ejection fraction, retinal vein occlusion, syncope, tachycardia, thrombosis, vasculitis
- Central nervous system: Nervousness (≤3%), aggressive behavior, aphasia, ataxia, Bell's palsy, carpal tunnel syndrome, coma, dysphasia, extrapyramidal reaction, hallucination, homicidal ideation, hyporeflexia, hypothermia, mania, migraine, neuralgia, neuropathy, paranoia, peripheral neuropathy, psychoneurosis, psychosis, suicidal ideation, seizure
- Dermatologic: Cellulitis, eczema, epidermal cyst, erythema, erythema multiforme, erythematous rash, exacerbation of psoriasis, folliculitis, lichenoid dermatitis, lipoma, maculopapular rash, psoriasis, skin photosensitivity, Stevens-Johnson syndrome, toxic epidermal necrolysis, urticaria
- Endocrine & metabolic: Increased lactate dehydrogenase (≤1%), albuminuria, dehydration, diabetes mellitus, goiter, hirsutism, hot flash, hypercalcemia, hyperglycemia, hyperthyroidism, hypertriglyceridemia, hypothyroidism, pituitary insufficiency, menorrhagia
- Gastrointestinal: Aphthous stomatitis, biliary colic, colitis, esophagitis, gastritis, gastrointestinal hemorrhage, mucositis, pancreatitis, stomatitis
- Genitourinary: Cystitis, dysuria, hematuria, impotence, leukorrhea, mastitis, nephrotic syndrome, nocturia, pelvic pain, proteinuria, sexual disorder, urinary incontinence, uterine hemorrhage
- Hematologic & oncologic: Aplastic anemia (rarely), exacerbation of sarcoidosis, granulocytopenia, hemolytic anemia, hypochromic anemia, immune thrombocytopenia, lipoma, lymphadenitis, lymphadenopathy, lymphocytopenia, lymphocytosis, pancytopenia, pure red cell aplasia, rectal hemorrhage, sarcoidosis, thrombotic thrombocytopenic purpura
- Hepatic: Abnormal hepatic function tests, ascites, hepatic encephalopathy, hepatic failure, hepatitis, hepatotoxicity, hyperbilirubinemia, jaundice
- Hypersensitivity: Anaphylaxis, angioedema, hypersensitivity reaction (acute)
- Infection: Abscess, fungal infection, sepsis
- Local: Tissue necrosis at injection site
- Neuromuscular & skeletal: Amyotrophy, arthritis, leg cramps, myositis, rhabdomyolysis, rheumatoid arthritis, spondylitis, systemic lupus erythematosus, tendonitis, tremor
- Ophthalmic: Blurred vision, conjunctivitis, macular edema, nystagmus, optic neuritis, papilledema, photophobia, retinal cotton-wool spot, retinal detachment (serous), retinal thrombosis, Vogt-Koyanagi-Harada syndrome
- Otic: Auditory impairment, hearing loss
- Renal: Renal failure, renal insufficiency
- Respiratory: Asthma, bronchiolitis obliterans, bronchoconstriction, bronchospasm, cyanosis, hemoptysis, hypoventilation, interstitial pneumonitis, pleural effusion, pneumonia, pneumothorax, pulmonary fibrosis, pulmonary hypertension, pulmonary infiltrates, respiratory insufficiency, upper respiratory tract infection, wheezing
- Miscellaneous: Abscess, alcohol intolerance

Dosing

Adult & Geriatric Consider premedication with acetaminophen prior to administration to reduce the incidence of some adverse reactions. Not all dosage forms and strengths are appropriate for all indications; refer to product labeling for details. Interferon alfa-2b at doses ≥10 million units/m^2 is associated with a moderate emetic potential; antiemetics may be recommended to prevent nausea and vomiting.

Hairy cell leukemia: IM, SubQ: 2 million units/m^2 3 times weekly for up to 6 months (may continue treatment with sustained treatment response); discontinue for disease progression or failure to respond after 6 months

Lymphoma (follicular): SubQ: 5 million units 3 times weekly for up to 18 months

Malignant melanoma: Induction: 20 million units/m^2 IV for 5 consecutive days per week for 4 weeks, followed by maintenance dosing of 10 million units/m^2 SubQ 3 times weekly for 48 weeks

AIDS-related Kaposi sarcoma: IM, SubQ: 30 million units/m^2 3 times weekly; continue until disease progression or until maximal response has been achieved after 16 weeks

Chronic hepatitis B: IM, SubQ: 5 million units/ daily or 10 million units 3 times weekly for 16 weeks

Chronic hepatitis C: IM, SubQ: 3 million units 3 times weekly. In patients with normalization of ALT at 16 weeks, continue treatment (if tolerated) for 18-24 months; consider discontinuation if normalization does not occur at 16 weeks. **Note:** May be used in combination therapy with ribavirin in previously untreated patients or in patients who relapse following alpha interferon therapy.

Condyloma acuminata: Intralesionally: 1 million units/lesion (maximum: 5 lesions per treatment) 3 times weekly (on alternate days) for 3 weeks. May administer a second course at 12-16 weeks.

Pediatric Consider premedication with acetaminophen prior to administration to reduce the incidence of some adverse reactions. Not all dosage forms and strengths are appropriate for all indications; refer to product labeling for details.

Note: The following dosing may also be used in **infants** in the setting of HIV-exposure/-infection (CDC 2009).

Chronic hepatitis B (including HIV coinfection): SubQ: Children and Adolescents 1 to 17 years: 3 million units/m^2 3 times weekly for 1 week, followed by 6 million units/m^2 3 times weekly (maximum: 10 million units per dose); total duration of therapy 16 to 24 weeks (treat for 24 weeks in HIV-exposure/-infection)

Chronic hepatitis C with HIV coinfection: IM, SubQ: Children and Adolescents 1 to 17 years: 3 to 5 million units/m^2 3 times weekly (maximum: 3 million units per dose) with ribavirin for 48 weeks, regardless of HCV genotype (CDC 2009)

Renal Impairment

Renal impairment at treatment initiation: Combination therapy with ribavirin (hepatitis C) is contraindicated in patients with CrCl <50 mL/minute; use combination therapy with ribavirin (hepatitis C) with caution in patients with impaired renal function and CrCl ≥50 mL/minute.

Renal toxicity during treatment: *Indication-specific adjustments:* Lymphoma (follicular): Serum creatinine >2 mg/dL: Permanently discontinue.

Hepatic Impairment

Hepatic impairment at treatment initiation: There are no dosage adjustments provided in the manufacturer's labeling. Contraindicated in patients with decompensated liver disease or autoimmune hepatitis.

Hepatotoxicity during treatment: Permanently discontinue for severe (grade 3) hepatic injury or hepatic decompensation (Child-Pugh class B and C [score >6]).

Indication-specific adjustments:

Lymphoma (follicular): AST >5 times ULN: Permanently discontinue.

Malignant melanoma (induction and maintenance):

ALT/AST >5 to 10 times ULN: Temporarily withhold; resume with a 50% dose reduction when adverse reaction abates

ALT/AST >10 times ULN: Permanently discontinue.

Adjustment for Toxicity

Hematologic toxicity (also refer to indication specified adjustments below): ANC <500/mm^3 or platelets <25,000/mm^3: Discontinue treatment.

Hypersensitivity reaction (acute, serious), ophthalmic disorders (new or worsening), thyroid abnormality development (which cannot be normalized with medication), signs or symptoms of liver failure: Discontinue treatment.

Liver function abnormality, pulmonary infiltrate development, evidence of pulmonary function impairment, or autoimmune disorder development, triglycerides >1,000 mg/dL: Monitor closely and discontinue if appropriate. Permanently discontinue for severe (grade 3) hepatic injury or hepatic decompensation (Child-Pugh class B and C [score >6]).

Neuropsychiatric disorders (during treatment):

Clinical depression or other psychiatric problem: Monitor closely during and for 6 months after treatment.

Severe depression or other psychiatric disorder: Discontinue treatment.

Persistent or worsening psychiatric symptoms, suicidal ideation, aggression towards others: Discontinue treatment and follow with appropriate psychiatric intervention.

Manufacturer-recommended adjustments, listed according to indication:

Lymphoma (follicular):

Neutrophils >1000/mm^3 to <1,500/mm^3: Reduce dose by 50%; may re-escalate to starting dose when neutrophils return to >1,500/mm^3

Severe toxicity (neutrophils <1000/mm^3 or platelets <50,000/mm^3): Temporarily withhold.

AST >5 times ULN or serum creatinine >2 mg/dL: Permanently discontinue.

Hairy cell leukemia:

Platelet count <50,000/mm^3: Do not administer intramuscularly (administer SubQ instead).

Severe toxicity: Reduce dose by 50% or temporarily withhold and resume with 50% dose reduction; permanently discontinue if persistent or recurrent severe toxicity is noted.

Chronic hepatitis B:

WBC <1,500/mm^3, granulocytes <750/mm^3, or platelet count <50,000/mm^3, or other laboratory abnormality or severe adverse reaction: Reduce dose by 50%; may re-escalate to starting dose upon resolution of hematologic toxicity. Discontinue for persistent intolerance.

WBC <1,000/mm^3, granulocytes <500/mm^3, or platelet count <25,000/mm^3: Permanently discontinue

Chronic hepatitis C: Severe toxicity: Reduce dose by 50% or temporarily withhold until subsides; permanently discontinue for persistent toxicities after dosage reduction.

AIDS-related Kaposi sarcoma: Severe toxicity: Reduce dose by 50% or temporarily withhold; may resume at reduced dose with toxicity resolution; permanently discontinue for persistent/recurrent toxicities.

Malignant melanoma (induction and maintenance):

Severe toxicity including neutrophils >250/mm^3 to <500/mm^3 or ALT/AST >5 to 10 times ULN: Temporarily withhold; resume with a 50% dose reduction when adverse reaction abates.

Neutrophils <250/mm^3, ALT/AST >10 times ULN, or severe/persistent adverse reactions: Permanently discontinue.

Mechanism of Action Binds to a specific receptor on the cell wall to initiate intracellular activity; multiple effects can be detected including induction of gene transcription. Inhibits cellular growth, alters the state of cellular differentiation, interferes with oncogene expression, alters cell surface antigen expression, increases phagocytic activity of macrophages, and augments cytotoxicity of lymphocytes for target cells

Contraindications

Hypersensitivity to interferon alfa or any component of the formulation; decompensated liver disease; autoimmune hepatitis

Combination therapy with interferon alfa-2b and ribavirin is also contraindicated in women who are pregnant, in males with pregnant partners; in patients with hemoglobinopathies (eg, thalassemia major, sickle-cell anemia); creatinine clearance <50 mL/minute; or hypersensitivity to ribavirin or any component of the formulation

Documentation of allergenic cross-reactivity for interferons is limited. However, because of similarities in chemical structure and/or pharmacologic actions, the possibility of cross-sensitivity cannot be ruled out with certainty.

Warnings/Precautions [US Boxed Warning]: May cause or aggravate fatal or life-threatening autoimmune disorders, neuropsychiatric symptoms (including depression and/or suicidal thoughts/behaviors), ischemic, and/or infectious disorders; monitor closely with clinical and laboratory evaluations (periodic); discontinue treatment for severe persistent or worsening symptoms; some cases may resolve with discontinuation.

Neuropsychiatric disorders: May cause neuropsychiatric events, including depression, psychosis, mania, suicidal behavior/ideation, attempts and completed suicides and homicidal ideation; may occur in patients with or without previous psychiatric symptoms. Effects are usually rapidly reversible upon therapy discontinuation, but have persisted up to three weeks. If psychiatric symptoms persist or worsen, or suicidal or homicidal ideation or aggressive behavior towards others is identified, discontinue treatment, and follow the patient closely. Careful neuropsychiatric monitoring is recommended during and for 6 months after treatment in patients who develop psychiatric disorders (including clinical depression). New or exacerbated neuropsychiatric or substance abuse disorders are best managed with early intervention. Use with caution in patients with a history of psychiatric disorders. Drug screening and periodic health evaluation (including monitoring of psychiatric symptoms) is recommended if initiating treatment in patients with coexisting psychiatric condition or substance abuse disorders. Suicidal ideation or attempts may occur more frequently in pediatric patients (eg, adolescents) when compared to adults. Higher doses, usually in elderly patients, may result in increased CNS toxicity (eg, obtundation and coma).

Hepatic disease: May cause hepatotoxicity; monitor closely if abnormal liver function tests develop. A transient increase in ALT (≥2 times baseline) may occur in patients treated with interferon alfa-2b for chronic hepatitis B. Therapy generally may continue; monitor. Worsening and potentially fatal liver disease, including jaundice, hepatic encephalopathy, and hepatic failure have been reported in patients receiving interferon alfa for chronic hepatitis B and C with decompensated liver disease, autoimmune hepatitis, history of autoimmune disease, and immunosuppressed transplant recipients; avoid use in these patients; use is contraindicated in decompensated liver disease. Patients with cirrhosis are at increased risk of hepatic decompensation. Therapy should be discontinued for any patient developing signs and symptoms of liver failure. Permanently discontinue for severe (grade 3) hepatic injury or hepatic decompensation (Child-Pugh class B and C [score >6]). Chronic hepatitis B or C patients with a history of autoimmune disease or who are immunosuppressed transplant recipients should not receive interferon alfa-2b.

Bone marrow suppression: Causes bone marrow suppression, including potentially severe cytopenias, and very rarely, aplastic anemia. Discontinue treatment for severe neutropenia (ANC <500/mm^3) or thrombocytopenia (platelets <25,000/mm^3). Hemolytic anemia (hemoglobin <10 g/dL) was observed when combined with ribavirin; anemia occurred within 1 to 2 weeks of initiation of therapy. Use caution in patients with preexisting myelosuppression and in patients with concomitant medications which cause myelosuppression.

Autoimmune disorders: Avoid use in patients with history of autoimmune disorders; development of autoimmune disorders (thrombocytopenia, vasculitis, Raynaud's disease, rheumatoid arthritis, lupus erythematosus and rhabdomyolysis) has been associated with use. Monitor closely; consider discontinuing. Worsening of psoriasis and sarcoidosis (and the development of new sarcoidosis) have been reported; use extreme caution.

Cardiovascular disease/coagulation disorders: Use caution and monitor closely in patients with cardiovascular disease (ischemic or thromboembolic), arrhythmias, hypertension, and in patients with a history of MI or prior therapy with cardiotoxic drugs. Patients with preexisting cardiac disease and/or advanced cancer should have baseline and periodic ECGs. May cause hypotension (during administration or delayed up to 2 days), arrhythmia, tachycardia (≥150 bpm), cardiomyopathy (~2% in AIDS-related Kaposi Sarcoma patients), and/or MI. Some experiencing cardiovascular adverse effects had no prior history of cardiac disease. Supraventricular arrhythmias occur rarely, and are associated with preexisting cardiac disease or prior therapy with cardiotoxic agents. Dose modification, discontinuation, and/or additional therapies may be necessary. In a scientific statement from the American Heart Association, interferon has been determined to be an agent that may either cause reversible direct myocardial toxicity or exacerbate underlying myocardial dysfunction (magnitude: moderate/major) (AHA [Page 2016]). Hemorrhagic cerebrovascular events have been observed with therapy. Use caution in patients with coagulation disorders.

Endocrine disorders: Thyroid disorders (possibly reversible) have been reported; use caution in patients with preexisting thyroid disease. TSH levels should be within normal limits prior to initiating interferon. Treatment should not be initiated in patients with preexisting thyroid disease who cannot be maintained in normal ranges by medication. Discontinue interferon use in patients who develop thyroid abnormalities during treatment and in patients with thyroid disease who subsequently cannot maintain normal ranges with thyroid medication. Discontinuation of interferon therapy may or may not reverse thyroid dysfunction. Diabetes mellitus has been reported; discontinue if cannot effectively manage with medication. Use with caution in patients with a history of diabetes mellitus, particularly if prone to DKA. Hypertriglyceridemia has been reported; discontinue if persistent and severe, and/or combined with symptoms of pancreatitis.

Pulmonary disease: Dyspnea, pulmonary infiltrates, pulmonary hypertension, interstitial pneumonitis, pneumonia, bronchiolitis obliterans, and sarcoidosis may be induced or aggravated by treatment, sometimes resulting in respiratory failure or fatality. Has been reported more in patients being treated for chronic hepatitis C, although has also occurred with use for oncology indications. Patients with fever, cough, dyspnea or other respiratory symptoms should be evaluated with a chest x-ray; monitor closely and consider discontinuing treatment with evidence of impaired pulmonary function. Use with caution in patients with a history of pulmonary disease.

Ophthalmic disorders: Decreased or loss of vision, macular edema, optic neuritis, retinal hemorrhages, cotton wool spots, papilledema, retinal detachment (serous), and retinal artery or vein thrombosis have occurred (or been aggravated) in patients receiving alpha interferons. Use caution in patients with preexisting eye disorders; monitor closely; a complete eye exam should be done promptly in patients who develop ocular symptoms; discontinue with new or worsening ophthalmic disorders.

Dental and periodontic disorders: In patients receiving combination interferon and ribavirin therapy, dental and periodontal disorders have been reported; additionally, dry mouth can damage teeth and mouth mucous membranes during chronic therapy.

Commonly associated with fever and flu-like symptoms; rule out other causes/infection with persistent fever; use with caution in patients with debilitating conditions. Acute hypersensitivity reactions (eg, urticaria, angioedema, bronchoconstriction, anaphylaxis) have been reported (rarely) with alfa interferons. If an acute reaction develops, discontinue therapy immediately; transient rashes have occurred in some patients following injection, but have not necessitated treatment interruption. Do not treat patients with visceral AIDS-related Kaposi sarcoma associated with rapidly-progressing or life-threatening disease. Some formulations contain albumin, which may carry a remote risk of viral transmission. Due to differences in dosage, patients should not change brands of interferons without the concurrence of their healthcare provider. Combination therapy with ribavirin is associated with birth defects and/or fetal mortality and hemolytic anemia. Do not use combination therapy with ribavirin in patients with CrCl <50 mL/minute. Interferon alfa-2b at doses ≥10 million units/m^2 is associated with a moderate emetic potential; antiemetics may be recommended to prevent nausea and vomiting. Potentially significant drug-drug interactions may exist, requiring dose or frequency adjustment, additional monitoring, and/or selection of alternative therapy.

Some dosage forms may contain polysorbate 80 (also known as Tweens). Hypersensitivity reactions, usually a delayed reaction, have been reported following exposure to pharmaceutical products containing polysorbate 80 in certain individuals (Isaksson 2002; Lucente 2000; Shelley 1995). Thrombocytopenia, ascites, pulmonary deterioration, and renal and hepatic failure have been reported in premature neonates after receiving parenteral products containing polysorbate 80 (Alade 1986; CDC 1984). See manufacturer's labeling.

Drug Interactions

Metabolism/Transport Effects Inhibits CYP1A2 (weak)

Avoid Concomitant Use

Avoid concomitant use of Interferon Alfa-2b with any of the following: BCG (Intravesical); Deferiprone; Dipyrone; Telbivudine

Increased Effect/Toxicity

Interferon Alfa-2b may increase the levels/effects of: Aldesleukin; CloZAPine; Deferiprone; Methadone; Ribavirin (Oral Inhalation); Ribavirin (Systemic); Telbivudine; Theophylline Derivatives; TiZANidine; Zidovudine

The levels/effects of Interferon Alfa-2b may be increased by: Dipyrone; Promazine

Decreased Effect

Interferon Alfa-2b may decrease the levels/effects of: BCG (Intravesical)

Pharmacodynamics/Kinetics

Half-life Elimination IV: ~2 hours; IM, SubQ: ~2-3 hours

Time to Peak Serum: IM, SubQ: ~3-12 hours; IV: By the end of a 30-minute infusion

Pregnancy Risk Factor C / X in combination with ribavirin

Pregnancy Considerations Animal reproduction studies have demonstrated abortifacient effects. Disruption of the normal menstrual cycle was also observed in animal studies; therefore, the manufacturer recommends that reliable contraception is used in women of childbearing potential. Alfa interferon is endogenous to normal amniotic fluid. In vitro administration studies have reported that when administered to the mother, it does not cross the placenta. Case reports of use in pregnant women are limited. The Perinatal HIV Guidelines Working Group does not recommend that interferon-alfa be used during pregnancy. Interferon alfa-2b monotherapy should only be used in pregnancy when the potential benefit to the mother justifies the possible risk to the fetus. Combination therapy with ribavirin is contraindicated in pregnancy (refer to Ribavirin (Systemic) monograph); two forms of contraception should be used during combination therapy and patients should have monthly pregnancy tests. A pregnancy registry has been established for women inadvertently exposed to ribavirin while pregnant (800-593-2214).

Breastfeeding Considerations Breast milk samples obtained from a lactating mother prior to and after administration of interferon alfa-2b showed that interferon alfa is present in breast milk and administration of the medication did not significantly affect endogenous levels. breastfeeding is not linked to the spread of hepatitis C virus; however, if nipples are cracked or bleeding, breastfeeding is not recommended. Mothers coinfected with HIV are discouraged from breastfeeding to decrease potential transmission of HIV.

Dosage Forms

Solution, Injection:

Intron A: 6,000,000 units/mL (3.8 mL); 10,000,000 units/mL (3.2 mL)

Solution Reconstituted, Injection [preservative free]:

Intron A: 10,000,000 units (1 ea); 18,000,000 units (1 ea); 50,000,000 units (1 ea)

Interferon Alfa-n3 (in ter FEER on AL fa en three)

Related Information

Dentin Hypersensitivity, Acid Erosion, High Caries Index, Management of Alveolar Osteitis, and Xerostomia *on page 1857*

Systemic Viral Diseases *on page 1806*

Brand Names: US Alferon N

Brand Names: Canada Alferon N

Pharmacologic Category Interferon

Use Condylomata acuminata: Intralesional treatment of refractory or recurring external condylomata acuminata (venereal or genital warts) in patients 18 years of age or older.

Local Anesthetic/Vasoconstrictor Precautions No information available to require special precautions

Effects on Dental Treatment Key adverse event(s) related to dental treatment: Xerostomia (normal salivary flow resumes upon discontinuation), metallic taste, tongue hyperesthesia, abnormal taste, thirst, rhinitis, pharyngitis, nosebleed, increased diaphoresis, taste disturbance, and gingivitis.

Effects on Bleeding No information available to require special precautions

Adverse Reactions Adverse reaction incidence noted below is specific to intralesional administration in patients with condylomata acuminata.

>10%:

Central nervous system: Headache (31%), chills (14%), fatigue (14%)

Hematologic & oncologic: Decreased white blood cell count (11%)

Neuromuscular & skeletal: Myalgia (45%)

Respiratory: Flu-like symptoms (30%; includes headache, fever, and/or myalgia; abated with repeated dosing)

Miscellaneous: Fever (40%)

1% to 10%:

Central nervous system: Malaise (9%), dizziness (9%), depression (2%), insomnia (2%), vasodepressor syncope (2%), hyperesthesia (tongue: 1%), paresthesia (1%)

Dermatologic: Diaphoresis (2%), pruritus (2%)

Endocrine & metabolic: Increased thirst (1%)

Gastrointestinal: Nausea (4%), vomiting (3%), dyspepsia (3%), diarrhea (2%), dysgeusia (1%)

Hematologic & oncologic: Adenopathy (groin: 1%)

Neuromuscular & skeletal: Arthralgia (5%), back pain (4%), muscle cramps (1%)

Ophthalmic: Visual disturbance (1%)

Respiratory: Rhinitis (2%), epistaxis (1%), pharyngitis (1%)

<1%, postmarketing, and/or case reports: Dysuria, hepatotoxicity (idiosyncratic; Chalasani 2014), hot flash, lack of concentration, nervousness, skin photosensitivity

General Dosage Range Intralesional: *Adults:* 250,000 units (0.05 mL) per wart twice weekly (maximum: 8 weeks) (maximum dose per treatment session: 2.5 million units [0.5 mL])

Mechanism of Action Interferons interact with cells through high affinity cell surface receptors. Following activation, multiple effects can be detected including induction of gene transcription. Inhibits cellular growth, alters the state of cellular differentiation, interferes with oncogene expression, alters cell surface antigen expression, increases phagocytic activity of macrophages, and augments cytotoxicity of lymphocytes for target cells

Pregnancy Risk Factor C

Pregnancy Considerations Animal reproduction studies have not been conducted. Menstrual irregularities have been reported; effective contraception is recommended during treatment.

Interferon Beta-1a (in ter FEER on BAY ta won aye)

Brand Names: US Avonex; Avonex Pen; Rebif; Rebif Rebidose; Rebif Rebidose Titration Pack; Rebif Titration Pack

Brand Names: Canada Avonex; Rebif

Pharmacologic Category Interferon

Use

US labeling: Treatment of relapsing forms of multiple sclerosis (MS) to decrease the frequency of clinical exacerbations and delay the accumulation of physical disability

Canadian labeling:

Treatment of relapsing forms of multiple sclerosis (MS) to decrease the frequency of clinical exacerbations, delay the accumulation of physical disability, reduce the requirement for steroids, reduce the number of hospitalizations, and reduce disease burden

To decrease the number and volume of active brain lesions, decrease overall disease burden, and delay onset of clinically definite MS in patients who have experienced a single demyelinating event.

Local Anesthetic/Vasoconstrictor Precautions No information available to require special precautions

Effects on Dental Treatment Key adverse event(s) related to dental treatment: Xerostomia and changes in salivation (normal salivary flow resumes upon discontinuation), and toothache.

Effects on Bleeding Thrombocytopenia has been reported in 2% to 8% of patients. Medical consult recommended.

Adverse Reactions Adverse reactions reported as a composite of both commercially-available products. Spectrum and incidence of reactions is generally similar between products, but consult individual product labels for specific incidence.

>10%:

Central nervous system: Headache (58% to 70%), fatigue (33% to 41%), depression (18% to 25%), pain (23%), chills (19%), dizziness (14%)

Gastrointestinal: Nausea (23%), abdominal pain (8% to 22%)

Genitourinary: Urinary tract infection (17%)

Hematologic & oncologic: Leukopenia (28% to 36%), lymphadenopathy (11% to 12%)

Hepatic: Increased serum ALT (20% to 27%), increased serum AST (10% to 17%)

Immunologic: Antibody development (neutralizing; significance not known; Rebif: 24% to 31%; Avonex: 5%)

Local: Injection site reaction (3% to 92%)

Neuromuscular & skeletal: Myalgia (25% to 29%), back pain (23% to 25%), weakness (24%), skeletal pain (10% to 15%), rigors (6% to 13%)
Ophthalmic: Visual disturbance (7% to 13%)
Respiratory: Flu-like symptoms (49% to 59%), sinusitis (14%), upper respiratory tract infection (14%)
Miscellaneous: Fever (20% to 28%)

1% to 10%:
Cardiovascular: Chest pain (5% to 8%), vasodilation (2%)
Central nervous system: Hypertonia (6% to 7%), migraine (5%), ataxia (4% to 5%), drowsiness (4% to 5%), malaise (4% to 5%), seizure (1% to 5%), suicidal tendencies (4%)
Dermatologic: Erythematous rash (5% to 7%), maculopapular rash (4% to 5%), alopecia (4%), hyperhidrosis (4%), urticaria
Endocrine & metabolic: Thyroid disease (4% to 6%)
Gastrointestinal: Xerostomia (1% to 5%), toothache (3%)
Genitourinary: Urinary frequency (2% to 7%), urinary incontinence (2% to 4%), urine abnormality (3%)
Hematologic & oncologic: Thrombocytopenia (2% to 8%), anemia (3% to 5%)
Hepatic: Hyperbilirubinemia (2% to 3%)
Infection: Infection (7%)
Local: Pain at injection site (8%), bruising at injection site (6%), inflammation at injection site (6%), tissue necrosis at injection site (1% to 3%)
Neuromuscular & skeletal: Arthralgia (9%)
Ophthalmic: Eye disease (4%), xerophthalmia (1% to 3%)
Respiratory: Bronchitis (8%)

<1%, postmarketing, and/or case reports: Abnormal gait, abnormal healing, abnormal hepatic function tests, abscess, abscess at injection site, amnesia, anaphylaxis, angioedema, anxiety, arteritis, arthritis, ascites, autoimmune hepatitis, basal cell carcinoma, Bell's palsy, bloody stools, breast fibroadenosis, cardiac arrhythmia, cardiac failure, cardiomyopathy, cellulitis, cellulitis at injection site, clumsiness, cold and clammy skin, colitis, confusion, conjunctivitis, constipation, contact dermatitis, dehydration, depersonalization, dermal ulcer, diaphoresis, diverticulitis, drug dependence, dyspnea, dysuria, ecchymoses, emotional lability, emphysema, epididymitis, erythema, erythema multiforme, eye pain, facial edema, facial paralysis, fibrocystic breast changes, fibrosis at injection site, furunculosis, gallbladder disease, gastritis, gastrointestinal hemorrhage, genital pruritus, gingival hemorrhage, gingivitis, gynecomastia, hematuria, hemolytic-uremic syndrome, hemoptysis, hemorrhage, hepatic failure, hepatic injury, hepatic neoplasm, hepatitis, hepatomegaly, hepatotoxicity (idiosyncratic) (Chalasani 2014), hernia, hiccups, hyperesthesia, hypermenorrhea, hypersensitivity reaction at injection site, hyperthyroidism, hyperventilation, hypoglycemia, hypokalemia, hypomagnesemia, hypotension, hypothyroidism, immune thrombocytopenia, increased appetite, increased coagulation time, increased libido, increased thirst, intestinal obstruction, intestinal perforation, labyrinthitis, laryngitis, leukorrhea, lipoma, lump in breast, lupus erythematosus, menopause, myasthenia, neoplasm, nephrolithiasis, neurological signs and symptoms (transient; may mimic multiple sclerosis exacerbations), nevus, nocturia, orolingual edema, orthostatic hypotension, osteonecrosis, otalgia, palpitations, pancytopenia, paresthesia, pelvic inflammatory disease, penile disease, pericarditis, periodontal abscess, periodontitis, peripheral ischemia, peripheral vascular disease, petechia, Peyronie disease, pharyngeal edema, pneumonia, polyuria, postmenopausal bleeding, proctitis, prostatic disease, pruritus, psychiatric disturbance (new or worsening; including suicidal ideation), psychoneurosis, pulmonary embolism, pulmonary hypertension (Govern 2015; Health Canada Nov. 2, 2016), pyelonephritis, renal pain, retinal vascular disease, seborrhea, sepsis, severe weakness (transient), skin blister, skin discoloration, skin photosensitivity, skin rash, spider telangiectasia, Stevens-Johnson syndrome, synovitis, tachycardia, telangiectasia, testicular disease, thromboembolism, thrombotic thrombocytopenic purpura, tongue disease, urethral pain, urinary retention, urinary urgency, uterine fibroids, uterine hemorrhage, vaginal hemorrhage, vascular disease, vesicular eruption, vitreous opacity, vomiting

General Dosage Range Dosage adjustment recommended in patients who develop toxicities

IM: *Adults:* Initial: 30 mcg once weekly **or** 7.5 mcg (week 1) then titrate in increments of 7.5 mcg once weekly (weeks 2 to 4) to 30 mcg once weekly

SubQ: *Adults:* Initial: 4.4 or 8.8 mcg 3 times weekly for 2 weeks; Titration: 11 or 22 mcg 3 times weekly for 2 weeks; Target dose: 22 or 44 mcg 3 times weekly

Mechanism of Action Interferon beta differs from naturally occurring human protein by a single amino acid substitution and the lack of carbohydrate side chains; alters the expression and response to surface antigens and can enhance immune cell activities. Properties of interferon beta that modify biologic responses are mediated by cell surface receptor interactions; mechanism in the treatment of MS is unknown.

Pharmacodynamics/Kinetics

Onset of Action Avonex: 12 hours (based on biological response markers)

Duration of Action Avonex: 4 days (based on biological response markers)

Half-life Elimination Avonex: ~19 hours (range: 8-54 hours); Rebif: 69 hours

Time to Peak Serum: Avonex (IM): ~15 hours (range: 6-36 hours); Rebif (SubQ): 16 hours

Pregnancy Risk Factor C

Pregnancy Considerations Adverse events have not been observed in animal reproduction studies; however, the possibility of adverse effects cannot be ruled out. Preliminary data from the Avonex pregnancy registry (published in abstract) do not show an increased risk of adverse fetal events when exposure occurs during pregnancy (Richman, 2012; Tomczyk, 2013); however, other studies have reported conflicting results. Until additional information is available, consideration should be given to discontinuing treatment if a woman becomes pregnant, or 1 month prior to becoming pregnant in women with mild disease (Coyle, 2012; Houtchens, 2013; Lu, 2013). Rebif Canadian product monograph contraindicates use in pregnant women.

Interferon Beta-1b (in ter FEER on BAY ta won bee)

Brand Names: US Betaseron; Extavia

Brand Names: Canada Betaseron; Extavia

Pharmacologic Category Interferon

Use

Multiple sclerosis: Treatment of relapsing forms of multiple sclerosis (MS) to reduce the frequency of clinical exacerbations.

Canadian labeling: Additional use (not in US labeling): Treatment of secondary progressive MS

Local Anesthetic/Vasoconstrictor Precautions No information available to require special precautions

Effects on Dental Treatment No significant effects or complications reported

Effects on Bleeding Thrombocytopenia has been reported. Medical consult recommended.

Adverse Reactions

>10%:

Cardiovascular: Peripheral edema (12% to 15%), chest pain (9% to 11%)

Central nervous system: Headache (50% to 57%), pain (42% to 51%), hypertonia (40% to 50%), myasthenia (46%), chills (21% to 25%), dizziness (24%), insomnia (21% to 24%), ataxia (17% to 21%)

Dermatologic: Skin rash (21% to 24%), dermatological disease (10% to 12%)

Gastrointestinal: Nausea (27%), constipation (20%), diarrhea (19%), abdominal pain (16% to 19%), dyspepsia (14%)

Genitourinary: Urinary urgency (11% to 13%), uterine hemorrhage (9% to 11%)

Hematologic & oncologic: Lymphocytopenia (86% to 88%), leukopenia (13% to 18%), neutropenia (13% to 14%)

Immunologic: Antibody development (≤45%; neutralizing; significance not known)

Local: Injection site reaction (78% to 85%; including inflammation [53%], pain [18%], tissue necrosis [4% to 5%], hypersensitivity reaction [4%], swelling [2% to 3%], residual mass [2%])

Neuromuscular & skeletal: Weakness (53% to 61%), arthralgia (31%), myalgia (23% to 27%)

Respiratory: Flu-like symptoms (decreases over treatment course; 57% to 60%)

Miscellaneous: Fever (31% to 36%)

1% to 10%:

Cardiovascular: Vasodilatation (8%), hypertension (6% to 7%), peripheral vascular disease (6%), palpitations (4%), tachycardia (4%)

Central nervous system: Anxiety (10%), malaise (6% to 8%), nervousness (7%)

Dermatologic: Diaphoresis (8%), alopecia (4%)

Endocrine & metabolic: Hypermenorrhea (8%), dysmenorrhea (7%), weight gain (7%)

Genitourinary: Impotence (8% to 9%), cystitis (8%), urinary frequency (7%), pelvic pain (6%), prostatic disease (3%)

Hematologic & oncologic: Lymphadenopathy (6% to 8%)

Hepatic: Increased serum ALT (>5 x baseline: 10% to 12%), increased serum AST (>5 x baseline: 3% to 4%)

Hypersensitivity: Hypersensitivity (3%)

Neuromuscular & skeletal: Leg cramps (4%)

Respiratory: Dyspnea (6% to 7%)

<1%, postmarketing, and/or case reports: Anaphylactoid reaction, anaphylaxis, anemia, anorexia, apnea, asthma, ataxia, autoimmune hepatitis, blindness, bronchospasm, capillary leak syndrome (in patients with preexisting monoclonal gammopathy), cardiac arrhythmia, cardiomegaly, cardiomyopathy, cerebral hemorrhage, cholecystitis, coma, confusion, convulsion, deep vein thrombosis, delirium, depersonalization, depression, diabetes mellitus, diabetes insipidus, emotional lability, erythema nodosum, esophagitis, ethanol sensitization, exfoliative dermatitis, gastrointestinal hemorrhage, hallucinations, hematemesis, hemolytic-uremic syndrome, hepatic failure, hepatic injury, hepatitis, hepatomegaly, hepatotoxicity (idiosyncratic) (Chalasani 2014), hypercalcemia, hyperglycemia, hyperthyroidism, hyperuricemia, hypocalcemia, hypoglycemia, hypothermia, hypothyroidism, increased gamma-glutamyl transferase, increased serum bilirubin, increased serum triglycerides, lupus erythematosus, maculopapular rash, manic behavior, myocardial infarction, nephrolithiasis, pancreatitis, paresthesia, pericardial effusion, pneumonia, pruritus, psoriasis, psychosis, pulmonary embolism, pulmonary hypertension (Govern 2015; Health Canada Nov. 2, 2016), renal disease (nephritic syndrome), sepsis, shock, skin discoloration, skin photosensitivity, suicidal ideation, syncope, SIADH, thrombocytopenia, thrombotic thrombocytopenic purpura, thyroid dysfunction, tongue edema, tremor, urinary tract infection, urosepsis, urticaria, vaginal hemorrhage, vasculitis, vesiculobullous dermatitis, vomiting, weight loss

General Dosage Range SubQ: *Adults:* 0.0625-0.25 mg every other day

Mechanism of Action Interferon beta-1b differs from naturally occurring human protein by a single amino acid substitution and the lack of carbohydrate side chains; mechanism in the treatment of MS is unknown; however, immunomodulatory effects attributed to interferon beta-1b include enhancement of suppressor T cell activity, reduction of proinflammatory cytokines, down-regulation of antigen presentation, and reduced trafficking of lymphocytes into the central nervous system. Improves MRI lesions, decreases relapse rate, and disease severity in patients with secondary progressive MS.

Pharmacodynamics/Kinetics

Half-life Elimination 8 minutes to 4.3 hours

Time to Peak 1-8 hours

Pregnancy Risk Factor C

Pregnancy Considerations Adverse events have been observed in animal reproduction studies. Spontaneous abortions were reported in 4 women during a clinical trial. Women with multiple sclerosis are generally recommended to discontinue therapy prior to conception (Lu, 2012). The Canadian labeling contraindicates use in pregnant women.

Interferon Gamma-1b

(in ter FEER on GAM ah won bee)

Brand Names: US Actimmune

Pharmacologic Category Interferon

Use

Chronic granulomatous disease: Reduction in the frequency and severity of serious infections associated with chronic granulomatous disease

Malignant osteopetrosis (severe): To delay time to disease progression in patients with severe, malignant osteopetrosis

Local Anesthetic/Vasoconstrictor Precautions No information available to require special precautions

Effects on Dental Treatment No significant effects or complications reported

Effects on Bleeding Dose related (>100 mcg/m^2 administered 3 times weekly) thrombocytopenia has been reported. Medical consult recommended.

Adverse Reactions Based on 50 mcg/m^2 dose administered 3 times weekly for chronic granulomatous disease

>10%:
Central nervous system: Fever (52%), headache (33%), chills (14%), fatigue (14%)
Dermatologic: Rash (17%)
Gastrointestinal: Diarrhea (14%), vomiting (13%)
Local: Injection site erythema or tenderness (14%)

1% to 10%:
Central nervous system: Depression (3%)
Gastrointestinal: Nausea (10%), abdominal pain (8%)
Neuromuscular & skeletal: Myalgia (6%), arthralgia (2%), back pain (2%)

Postmarketing and/or case reports: Alkaline phosphatase elevated, atopic dermatitis, granulomatous colitis, hepatomegaly, hypersensitivity reactions, hypokalemia, neutropenia, Stevens-Johnson syndrome

Additional adverse reactions noted at doses >100 mcg/m^2 administered 3 times weekly: ALT increased, AST increased, autoantibodies increased, bronchospasm, chest discomfort, confusion, dermatomyositis exacerbation, disorientation, DVT, gait disturbance, GI bleeding, hallucinations, heart block, heart failure, hepatic insufficiency, hyperglycemia, hypertriglyceridemia, hyponatremia, hypotension, interstitial pneumonitis, lupus-like syndrome, MI, neutropenia, pancreatitis (may be fatal), Parkinsonian symptoms, PE, proteinuria, renal insufficiency (reversible), seizure, syncope, tachyarrhythmia, tachypnea, thrombocytopenia, TIA

General Dosage Range Dosage adjustment recommended in patients who develop toxicities

SubQ: *Infants, Children, Adolescents, and Adults:*
BSA ≤0.5 m^2: 1.5 mcg/kg/dose 3 times weekly; maximum dose: 50 mcg/m^2
BSA >0.5 m^2: 50 mcg/m^2 (1 million units/m^2) 3 times weekly; maximum dose: 50 mcg/m^2

Mechanism of Action Interferon gamma participates in immunoregulation by enhancing the oxidative metabolism of macrophages; it also enhances antibody dependent cellular cytotoxicity, activates natural killer cells and has a role in the expression of Fc receptors and major histocompatibility antigens.

Pharmacodynamics/Kinetics
Half-life Elimination IM: ~3 hours, SubQ: ~6 hours
Time to Peak Plasma: IM: ~4 hours (1.5 ng/mL); SubQ: ~7 hours (0.6 ng/mL)

Pregnancy Considerations Adverse events have been observed in animal reproduction studies.

Iodine (EYE oh dyne)

Pharmacologic Category Antiseptic, Topical

Use Used topically as an antiseptic in the management of minor, superficial skin wounds and has been used to disinfect the skin preoperatively

Local Anesthetic/Vasoconstrictor Precautions No information available to require special precautions

Effects on Dental Treatment No significant effects or complications reported

Effects on Bleeding No information available to require special precautions

Adverse Reactions Topical: Frequency not defined.
Dermatologic: Eczema, localized erythema
Endocrine & metabolic: Increased thyroid stimulating hormone level
Hypersensitivity: Hypersensitivity reaction
Local: Local irritation, local pain, localized edema

Reactions reported more likely observed following large doses or chronic iodine intoxication; frequency not defined.
Central nervous system: Headache, metallic taste
Dermatologic: Acne vulgaris, skin rash (including ioderma), urticaria
Endocrine & metabolic: Hypothyroidism
Gastrointestinal: Diarrhea
Hematologic & oncologic: Adenopathy, eosinophilia, mucous membrane bleeding
Hypersensitivity: Angioedema
Neuromuscular & skeletal: Arthralgia
Ophthalmic: Eyelid edema
Respiratory: Pulmonary edema
Miscellaneous: Fever

General Dosage Range Topical: *Adults:* Antiseptic: Apply to affected area 1-3 times/day; Ulcer/wound cleansing: Apply to clean wound 3 times/week (maximum: 50 g/application; 150 g/week)

Mechanism of Action Iodine is required for thyroid hormone synthesis. Iodine is also known to be a powerful broad spectrum germicidal agent effective against a wide range of bacteria, viruses, fungi, protozoa, and spores. Iodosorb® and Iodoflex™ contain iodine in hydrophilic beads of cadexomer which allows a slow release of iodine into the wound and absorption of fluid, bacteria, and other substances from the wound

Pregnancy Considerations An adequate amount of iodine intake is essential for thyroid function. Iodine crosses the placenta and requirements are increased during pregnancy. Iodine deficiency in pregnancy can lead to neurologic damage in the newborn; an extreme form, cretinism, is characterized by gross mental retardation, short stature, deaf mutism, and spasticity. Large amounts of iodine during pregnancy can cause fetal goiter or hyperthyroidism. Transient hypothyroidism in the newborn has also been reported following topical or vaginal use prior to delivery.

Iodine I-125 Human Serum Albumin

(EYE oh dyne eye one TWEN tee five HYU man SEER um al BYOO min)

Brand Names: US Jeanatope

Pharmacologic Category Radiopharmaceutical

Use Radiopharmaceutical imaging agent used to detect total blood and plasma volume

Local Anesthetic/Vasoconstrictor Precautions No information available to require special precautions

Effects on Dental Treatment No significant effects or complications reported

Effects on Bleeding No information available to require special precautions

Adverse Reactions Frequency not defined.
Central nervous system: Aseptic meningitis (chemical), hyperpyrexia
Hypersensitivity: Hypersensitivity reaction

Pharmacodynamics/Kinetics
Half-life Elimination Biologic half-life: ~14 days; Physical half-life: ~60 days
Time to Peak Intravascular: 10 minutes; Extravascular: 2-4 days

Pregnancy Considerations Radiopharmaceuticals have the potential to cause fetal harm. Use during pregnancy only if clearly needed. In patients of childbearing age, the manufacturer recommends performing elective tests within 10 days of the onset of menses.

Iodipamide Meglumine

(eye oh DI pa mide MEG loo meen)

Brand Names: US Cholografin Meglumine [DSC]

Pharmacologic Category Iodinated Contrast Media; Radiological/Contrast Media, Ionic (High Osmolality)

Use Radiopaque contrast agent: Intravenous (IV) cholangiography and cholecystography for visualization of: the gallbladder and biliary ducts in the differential diagnosis of acute abdominal conditions; biliary ducts, especially in patients with symptoms after cholecystectomy; and gallbladder in patients unable to take oral contrast media or to absorb contrast media from the gastrointestinal tract.

Local Anesthetic/Vasoconstrictor Precautions No information available to require special precautions

Effects on Dental Treatment No significant effects or complications reported

Effects on Bleeding No information available to require special precautions

Adverse Reactions Frequency not defined.

Endocrine & metabolic: Altered thyroid hormone levels (transient suppression; premature infants and infants with underlying medical conditions may be more vulnerable), hypothyroidism

Hypersensitivity: Hypersensitivity reaction

Renal: Renal failure, renal function test abnormality

Miscellaneous: Infusion-related reactions (generally mild and transient; associated with rapid infusion rates; includes chills, diaphoresis, dizziness, fever, flushing, headache, nausea, pallor, restlessness, sensation of warmth, sialorrhea, sneezing, tremor, upper abdominal pressure, vomiting)

<1%, postmarketing, and/or case reports: Anaphylactoid reaction, cardiac abnormality, cyanosis, dyspnea, eyelid edema, hypotension, laryngospasm

General Dosage Range IV:

Infants and Children: 0.3-0.6 mL/kg (maximum: 20 mL)

Adults: 20 mL

Pregnancy Considerations In general, iodinated contrast media agents may cross the placenta; use should be avoided unless absolutely required to obtain diagnostic information that will influence the care of the mother or fetus during pregnancy (ACOG 2016; ACR 2015).

Iodixanol (EYE oh dix an ole)

Brand Names: US Visipaque

Brand Names: Canada Visipaque

Pharmacologic Category Iodinated Contrast Media; Radiological/Contrast Media, Nonionic (Iso-Osmolality)

Use

Intra-arterial:

Iodixanol injection (270 mgI/mL) is indicated for intra-arterial digital subtraction angiography.

Iodixanol injection (320 mgI/mL) is indicated for angiocardiography (left ventriculography and selective coronary arteriography), peripheral arteriography, visceral arteriography, and cerebral arteriography.

Intravenous:

Iodixanol injection (270 mgI/mL) is indicated for contrast enhanced computed tomography (CECT) imaging of the head and body, excretory urograph, and peripheral venography.

Iodixanol injection (320 mgI/mL) is indicated for CECT imaging of the head and body, and excretory urography.

Local Anesthetic/Vasoconstrictor Precautions No information available to require special precautions

Effects on Dental Treatment Key adverse event(s) related to dental treatment: Taste perversion.

Effects on Bleeding No information available to require special precautions

Adverse Reactions

>10%:

Local: Discomfort at injection site (≤30%), pain at injection site (≤30%), warm sensation at injection site (≤30%)

1% to 10%:

Cardiovascular: Angina pectoris (≤2%), chest pain (≤2%)

Central nervous system: Headache (≤3%), migraine (≤3%), vertigo (2%), altered sense of smell (1%), paresthesia (1%)

Dermatologic: Pruritus (2%), erythema (≤2%), skin rash (≤2%; nonurticarial)

Gastrointestinal: Dysgeusia (4%), nausea (3%)

Frequency not defined:

Endocrine & metabolic: Decreased thyroid hormones (transient; premature infants and infants with underlying medical conditions may be more vulnerable), hypothyroidism

<1%, postmarketing, and/or case reports: Acute renal failure, agitation, amnesia, anaphylactoid reaction, anaphylaxis, anxiety, apnea (children), asthma, atrioventricular block (children), back pain, bronchitis, bundle branch block (children), cardiac arrhythmia (children), cardiac failure (children), cerebrovascular disease, confusion, cortical blindness, diaphoresis, diarrhea, disseminated intravascular coagulation (children), dizziness, dyskinesia, dyspepsia, dyspnea, edema, fatigue, fever (children), flushing, hematoma, hematuria, hemorrhage, hypersensitivity reaction, hypertension, hypoesthesia, hypoglycemia, insomnia, malaise, nervousness, orthostatic hypotension, peripheral ischemia, pharyngeal edema, polymyalgia rheumatica, pulmonary edema, pulmonary embolism, renal function abnormality, respiratory depression, rhinitis, scotoma, seizure, sensory disturbance, shock, stupor, syncope, tinnitus, urticaria, visual disturbance, vomiting

General Dosage Range

IV:

Children >1-12 years: Iodixanol 270 mg iodine/mL: 1-2 mL/kg (maximum: 2 mL/kg)

Children >12 years and Adults: Iodixanol 270 mg and 320 mg iodine/mL: Concentration and dose vary based on study type; refer to product labeling (maximum total dose: 80 g iodine)

Intra-arterial:

Children >1-12 years: Iodixanol 320 mg iodine/mL: 1-2 mL/kg (maximum: 4 mL/kg)

Children >12 years and Adults: Iodixanol 320 mg iodine/mL: Dose individualized based on injection site and study type; refer to product labeling (maximum total dose: 80 g iodine)

Mechanism of Action Opacifies vessels in the path of flow permitting radiographic imaging of internal structures.

Pharmacodynamics/Kinetics

Onset of Action Kidney:

Visualization: Renal parenchyma: 30 to 60 seconds; calyces and pelves (normal renal function): 1 to 3 minutes

Optimum contrast: 5 to 15 minutes

Half-life Elimination

Pediatric patients (Johnson 2001):

Newborns to Infants <2 months: 4.1 ± 1.4 hours

Infants 2 to 6 months: 2.8 ± 0.6 hours

Infants 6 to 12 months: 2.4 ± 0.4 hours

Children 1 to <3 years: 2.2 ± 0.5 hours

Children 3 to <12 years: 2.3 ± 0.5 hours
Adults: 2.1 ± 0.1 hours; increased to 23 hours in renal impairment (mean CrCl: 13.61 ± 4.67 mL/minute)

Time to Peak

Children: IV: 0.75 to 1.25 hours
Adults: Immediate; peak enhancement at 15 to 120 seconds; optimum renal contrast at 5 to 15 minutes; brain contrast at up to 1 hour

Pregnancy Risk Factor B

Pregnancy Considerations Adverse events have not been observed in animal reproduction studies. In general, iodinated contrast media agents may cross the placenta; use should be avoided unless absolutely required to obtain diagnostic information that will influence the care of the mother or fetus during pregnancy (ACOG 2016; ACR 2015).

Iodoquinol (eye oh doe KWIN ole)

Brand Names: US Aloquin; Yodoxin [DSC]

Brand Names: Canada Diodoquin

Pharmacologic Category Amebicide

Use Treatment of intestinal amebiasis due to trophozoite and cyst forms of *Entamoeba histolytica*

Local Anesthetic/Vasoconstrictor Precautions No information available to require special precautions

Effects on Dental Treatment No significant effects or complications reported

Effects on Bleeding No information available to require special precautions

Adverse Reactions Frequency not defined.

Central nervous system: Chills, headache, peripheral neuropathy, vertigo
Dermatologic: Pruritus, skin rash, urticaria
Endocrine & metabolic: Goiter
Gastrointestinal: Abdominal cramps, diarrhea, nausea, pruritus ani, vomiting
Ophthalmic: Optic atrophy, optic neuritis
Miscellaneous: Fever

General Dosage Range Oral:

Children: 30-40 mg/kg daily in 3 divided doses (maximum: 1.95 g daily)
Adults: 650 mg 3 times daily (maximum: 1.95 g daily)

Mechanism of Action Contact amebicide that works in the lumen of the intestine by an unknown mechanism

Pregnancy Considerations There is very limited data on the use of iodoquinol during pregnancy and safety has not been established.

Iodoquinol and Hydrocortisone
(eye oh doe KWIN ole & hye droe KOR ti sone)

Related Information

Hydrocortisone (Topical) *on page 836*
Iodoquinol *on page 914*

Related Sample Prescriptions

Fungal Infections - Sample Prescriptions *on page 35*

Brand Names: US Alcortin A; Dermazene; Vytone

Generic Availability (US) Yes: Cream

Pharmacologic Category Antifungal Agent, Topical; Corticosteroid, Topical

Dental Use Reported to be useful in the treatment of angular cheilitis

Use Dermatoses: Treatment of eczema (including impetiginized, nuchal, and nummular); acne urticata; anogenital pruritus (vulvae, scroti, ani), atopic and contact dermatitis, endogenous chronic infectious dermatitis; chronic eczematoid otitis externa; folliculitis, intertrigo; lichen simplex chronicus; moniliasis; dermatoses (mycotic or bacterial); neurodermatitis (localized or systemic); pyoderma, stasis dermatitis

Local Anesthetic/Vasoconstrictor Precautions No information available to require special precautions

Effects on Dental Treatment No significant effects or complications reported

Effects on Bleeding No information available to require special precautions

Adverse Reactions See individual agents.

Dental Usual Dosage Angular cheilitis: Adults: Topical: Apply 3-4 times daily

Dosing

Adult & Geriatric Dermatoses: Topical: Apply 3-4 times daily to affected area(s)

Pediatric Dermatoses: Children ≥12 years and Adolescents: Topical: Refer to adult dosing.

Renal Impairment

There are no dosage adjustments provided in the manufacturer's labeling.

Hepatic Impairment

There are no dosage adjustments provided in the manufacturer's labeling.

Mechanism of Action See individual agents.

Contraindications Hypersensitivity to iodoquinol, hydrocortisone, or any component of the formulation

Warnings/Precautions

Based on **iodoquinol** component: Optic neuritis, optic atrophy, and peripheral neuropathy have occurred following prolonged use; avoid long-term therapy

Based on **hydrocortisone** component:

Use with caution in patients with hyperthyroidism, cirrhosis, nonspecific ulcerative colitis, hypertension, osteoporosis, thromboembolic tendencies, CHF, convulsive disorders, myasthenia gravis, thrombophlebitis, peptic ulcer, diabetes

Acute adrenal insufficiency may occur with abrupt withdrawal (depending on degree of systemic absorption) after long-term therapy or with stress; young pediatric patients may be more susceptible to adrenal axis suppression from topical therapy

Drug Interactions

Metabolism/Transport Effects Refer to individual components.

Avoid Concomitant Use

Avoid concomitant use of Iodoquinol and Hydrocortisone with any of the following: Aldesleukin

Increased Effect/Toxicity

Iodoquinol and Hydrocortisone may increase the levels/effects of: Ceritinib; Deferasirox

Decreased Effect

Iodoquinol and Hydrocortisone may decrease the levels/effects of: Aldesleukin; Corticorelin; Hyaluronidase

Pregnancy Risk Factor C

Pregnancy Considerations Animal reproduction studies have not been conducted with this combination. Refer to individual monographs.

Breastfeeding Considerations It is not known if iodoquinol or hydrocortisone are excreted in breast milk following use of this preparation. The manufacturer recommends that caution be used if administered to nursing women. Also refer to individual monographs.

Dosage Forms

Cream, topical:

Dermazene: Iodoquinol 1% and hydrocortisone 1% (30 g)
Vytone: Iodoquinol 1% and hydrocortisone 1.9% per 2 g packet (30s)

Generic: Iodoquinol 1% and hydrocortisone acetate 1% (30 g); Iodoquinol 1% and hydrocortisone 1.9% per 2 g packet (30s)

Gel, topical:

Alcortin A: Iodoquinol 1% and hydrocortisone 2% (2 g, 48 g)

Iohexol (eye oh HEX ole)

Brand Names: US Omnipaque

Brand Names: Canada Omnipaque

Pharmacologic Category Contrast Agent; Iodinated Contrast Media; Radiological/Contrast Media, Nonionic (High Osmolality); Radiological/Contrast Media, Nonionic (Low Osmolality)

Use

Imaging: Adults:

Intrathecal: Iohexol 180, 240, and 300: Myelography (lumbar, thoracic, cervical, and total columnar), and contrast enhancement for computerized tomography (CT) (myelography, cisternography, ventriculography)

Intravascular:

Iohexol 140: Intra-arterial digital subtraction angiography of head, neck, abdominal, renal, and peripheral vessels

Iohexol 240: Contrast enhancement for CT head imaging and peripheral venography (phlebography)

Iohexol 300: Aortography (including studies of aortic arch, abdominal aorta [and branches], contrast enhancement for CT head and body imaging, cerebral arteriography, peripheral venography (phlebography), and excretory urography

Iohexol 350: Angiocardiography (ventriculography, selective coronary arteriography), aortography (including studies of aortic root, aortic arch, ascending aorta, abdominal aorta [and branches]), contrast enhancement for CT head and body imaging, intravenous digital subtraction angiography of head, neck, abdominal renal and peripheral vessels, peripheral arteriography, and excretory urography

Oral/body cavity:

Iohexol (diluted) and Iohexol 300: Contrast enhanced abdomen CT

Iohexol 240: Arthrography, endoscopic retrograde pancreatography and cholangiopancreatography, herniography, and hysterosalpingography

Iohexol 300: Arthrography, hysterosalpingography

Iohexol 350: Arthrography and oral pass-through gastrointestinal examination

Iohexol (Oraltag): Contrast enhancement for CT abdomen and pelvis imaging

Imaging: Pediatrics:

Intrathecal: Iohexol 180: Myelography (lumbar, thoracic, cervical, and total columnar), and contrast enhancement for CT (myelography, cisternography)

Intravascular:

Iohexol 240: Contrast enhancement for CT head imaging

Iohexol 300: Angiocardiography (ventriculography), contrast enhancement for CT head imaging, and excretory urography

Iohexol 350: Angiocardiography (ventriculography, pulmonary arteriography, and venography; studies of collateral arteries and aortography, including aortic root, aortic arch, ascending and descending aorta)

Oral/body cavity:

Iohexol (diluted): Voiding cystourethrography

Iohexol 180, 240, and 300: Gastrointestinal tract examination

Iohexol (diluted) and Iohexol 240 or 300: Contrast enhanced abdomen CT

Iohexol (Oraltag): Contrast enhancement for CT abdomen and pelvis imaging

Local Anesthetic/Vasoconstrictor Precautions No information available to require special precautions

Effects on Dental Treatment No significant effects or complications reported

Effects on Bleeding No information available to require special precautions

Adverse Reactions Children generally have a lower frequency of reactions than adults.

>10%:

Cardiovascular: Cardiac arrhythmia (digital arteriography: 7% to 16%; other intravascular uses: 2%; transient PVC and PACs most reported)

Central nervous system: Pain (≤49%, procedurally dependent), sensation of pressure (joint injection: 42%), headache (myelography: 9% to 18%; cerebral arteriography: 6%; all other uses: ≤3%), localized warm feeling (≤13%)

Gastrointestinal: Diarrhea (oral pass-thru: 36% to 42%; all other uses: ≤3%), nausea (≤15%), vomiting (≤11%)

Neuromuscular & skeletal: Leg pain (phlebography: 21%, transient and mild)

Ophthalmic: Vision disturbance (cerebral arteriography: 15%, all other uses: ≤2%; photomas of ≤1 second), blurred vision (≤2%)

Miscellaneous: Swelling (22%; mostly reported with arthrography and likely to be procedurally related)

1% to 10%:

Cardiovascular: Angina pectoris (angiocardiography: 8%; intravascular: ≤1%), hypotension (≤3%), transient ischemic attacks (intravascular: ≤2%), abdominal distress (oral/body cavity: ≤1%), bradycardia (intravascular and angiocardiography: ≤1%), chest pain (intravascular: ≤1%), hypertension (≤1%), syncope (≤1%), tachycardia (intravascular and angiocardiography: ≤1%)

Central nervous system: Drowsiness (≤3%), dizziness (≤2%; usually transient), malaise (≤1%), myasthenia (oral/body cavity; joint injection: ≤1%), vertigo (≤1%)

Dermatologic: Urticaria (intravascular; oral/body cavity: ≤2%)

Gastrointestinal: Flatulence (herniography: 10%; oral/body cavity; oral pass-thru: ≤2%), abdominal pain (oral, adults: 7%; oral, children: 2%), dysgeusia (≤1%)

Local: Hematoma at injection site (≤1%)

Neuromuscular & skeletal: Back pain (intrathecal, adults: ≤8%; intrathecal, children: 1%), neck pain (≤8%), stiffness (≤8%), tremor (≤1%)

Ophthalmic: Blurred vision (≤2%)

Miscellaneous: Fever (≤5%; incidence higher in children receiving iohexol orally), sialadenitis

Frequency not defined:

Central nervous system: Seizure

Hypersensitivity: Anaphylactoid reaction, anaphylaxis, hypersensitivity reaction

Respiratory: Bronchospasm

Miscellaneous: Sialadenitis

<1%, postmarketing, and/or case reports: Abscess, anemia, anorexia, anxiety, apnea, asystole, cerebral infarction, cough, diaphoresis, difficulty in micturition, dyspepsia, dyspnea, feeling of heaviness, heart block,

hemiparesis, hypertonia, hypoglycemia, laryngitis, motor dysfunction, muscle cramps, neuralgia, nystagmus, paresthesia, photophobia, pruritus, purpura, respiratory congestion, rhinitis, shivering, skin rash, speech disturbance, stomach pain, thrombophlebitis, tinnitus, vasodepressor syncope, ventricular tachycardia, visual hallucination, xerostomia

Mechanism of Action Opacification of vessels and anatomical structures in the path of flow of the contrast media which allows for radiographic visualization

Pharmacodynamics/Kinetics

Duration of Action

CNS: ~30 minutes following intrathecal administration, 60 minutes following intravenous administration

Serum: 15 to 120 seconds

Pregnancy Risk Factor B

Pregnancy Considerations Adverse effects were not observed in animal reproduction studies. Use for hysterosalpingography is contraindicated during pregnancy. In general, iodinated contrast media agents may cross the placenta; use should be avoided unless absolutely required to obtain diagnostic information that will influence the care of the mother or fetus during pregnancy (ACOG 2016; ACR 2015).

Iopamidol (eye oh PA mi dole)

Brand Names: US Isovue-200; Isovue-250; Isovue-300; Isovue-370; Isovue-M 200; Isovue-M 300

Pharmacologic Category Contrast Agent; Iodinated Contrast Media; Radiological/Contrast Media, Nonionic (Low Osmolality)

Use

Angiography: *Isovue*: Diagnostic agent for angiography throughout the cardiovascular system, including cerebral and peripheral arteriography, coronary arteriography and ventriculography, pediatric angiocardiography, selective visceral arteriography and aortography, peripheral venography (phlebography)

Computed tomography:

Isovue: Diagnostic agent for adult and pediatric contrast enhancement of computed tomographic (CECT) head and body imaging

Isovue-M: Diagnostic agent for CECT cisternography and ventriculography in adults

Myelography: *Isovue-M:* Diagnostic agent for myelography (lumbar, thoracic, cervical, total columnar) in adults; diagnostic agent for myelography (lumbar, thoracic) in children >2 years

Urography: *Isovue:* Diagnostic agent for adult and pediatric excretory urography

Local Anesthetic/Vasoconstrictor Precautions No information available to require special precautions

Effects on Dental Treatment No significant effects or complications reported

Effects on Bleeding No information available to require special precautions

Adverse Reactions Frequency not always defined.

Cardiovascular: Angina pectoris (3%), flushing (2%)

Central nervous system: Headache (≤16%), pain (3%)

Endocrine & metabolic: Hot flash (2% to 3%), altered thyroid hormone levels (transient suppression; premature infants and infants with underlying medical conditions may be more vulnerable), hypothyroidism

Gastrointestinal: Nausea (1% to 7%), vomiting (≤4%)

Neuromuscular & skeletal: Back pain (2%)

≤1%, postmarketing, and/or case reports: Abdominal cramps, abnormal aspartate transaminase, abnormal blood platelet aggregation, abnormal serum calcium, abnormal uric acid levels, albuminuria, amnesia (temporary), anaphylactoid reaction, anorexia, apnea, arterial spasm, asthma, ataxia, atrioventricular block, back spasm, bacterial meningitis, bigeminy, bradycardia, burning sensation, cardiac arrhythmia, cardiorespiratory arrest, change in creatinine, change in RBC count, change in WBC count, chest pain, chest tightness, chills, circulatory shock, cold extremities, coma, confusion, conjunctivitis, constriction of the pharynx, cortical blindness (temporary), cough, decreased partial thromboplastin time, decreased prothrombin time, decreased serum fibrinogen, depression of ST segment on ECG, diaphoresis, diarrhea, dizziness, dysgeusia, dyspnea, ECG changes (prolonged Q-T interval, prolonged R-R interval, T-wave amplitude), EEG pattern changes (usually slow wave activity), erythrocyte agglutination, exacerbation of decreased peripheral perfusion, extrasystoles, eye pruritus, facial edema, facial grimace, fatigue, fever, flushing sensation, genitourinary pain, hallucination, hearing loss (transitory), heartburn, hematuria, hypersensitivity reaction, hypertension, hypotension, increased left ventricular end-diastolic pressure, involuntary muscle movements, irritability, ischemic heart disease, lacrimation, laryngeal edema, leg cramps, leg pain, localized burning, localized irritation (cervicobrachial, meningeal, lumbosacral radicular), malaise, muscle spasm, musculoskeletal pain, myasthenia, myocardial infarction, nasal congestion, neck pain, neurological signs and symptoms, numbness, pain at injection site (usually due to extravasation and/or erythematous swelling), pallor, paralysis, paresthesia, periorbital edema, peripheral neuropathy, pruritus, pulmonary edema, renal disease (contrast-associated), renal infarction, renal tubular necrosis (with oliguria and anuria), retching (severe), rhinitis, sciatica, seizure (focal and motor), signs and symptoms of aseptic meningitis, skin rash, sneezing, stress, syncope, systolic hypotension, tachycardia, thrombophlebitis, tingling of the arms, tinnitus, transient ischemic attacks, tremor, trigeminal neuralgia, urinary retention, urticaria, vasodepressor syncope, vasodilatation, ventricular fibrillation, visual disturbance, watery eyes, weakness, worsening of cyanosis

General Dosage Range Dosing is based on numerous variables including: type of examination, route of administration, patient age/weight, and product. Consult specific product information for detailed dosing.

Mechanism of Action Opacification of vessels and anatomical structures in the path of flow of the contrast media which allows for radiographic visualization.

Pharmacodynamics/Kinetics

Half-life Elimination ~2 hours; prolonged in renal impairment

Pregnancy Risk Factor B

Pregnancy Considerations Adverse events have not been observed in animal reproduction studies. Iopamidol crosses the placenta and can be detected in the newborn gut at birth (Fitzpatrick 2011; Huang 2014). Thyroid dysfunction in the neonate has not been reported (ACR 2015; Atwell 2011). In general, use of iodinated contrast media should be avoided unless absolutely required to obtain diagnostic information that will influence the care of the mother or fetus during pregnancy (ACOG 2016; ACR 2015).

Iopromide (eye oh PROE mide)

Brand Names: US Ultravist

Brand Names: Canada Ultravist

Pharmacologic Category Iodinated Contrast Media; Radiological/Contrast Media, Nonionic (Low Osmolality)

Use

Intra-arterial: Enhance imaging in digital subtraction angiography, cerebral arteriography and peripheral arteriography, coronary arteriography and left ventriculography, visceral angiography and aortography.

Intravenous: Enhance imaging in peripheral venography, excretory urography, and contrast-enhanced computed tomographic imaging of the head and body (intrathoracic, intra-abdominal, and retroperitoneal regions) for the evaluation of neoplastic and nonneoplastic lesions.

Local Anesthetic/Vasoconstrictor Precautions No information available to require special precautions

Effects on Dental Treatment Key adverse event(s) related to dental treatment: Abnormal taste.

Effects on Bleeding No information available to require special precautions

Adverse Reactions

1% to 10%:

Cardiovascular: Vasodilatation (4%), chest pain (3%), hypertension (1%)

Central nervous system: Headache (6%), pain (2%), dizziness (1%)

Gastrointestinal: Nausea (4%), vomiting (2%), dysgeusia (1%)

Genitourinary: Urinary urgency (3%)

Local: Hematoma at injection site (3%), pain at injection site (1%)

Neuromuscular & skeletal: Back pain (3%)

Ophthalmic: Visual disturbance (2%)

<1%, postmarketing and/or case reports: Abdominal pain, abnormal lacrimation, agitation, amnesia, anaphylaxis, angioedema (children), anxiety, aphasia, apnea, arthralgia, asthma, ataxia, bradycardia, bullous rash (delayed), cardiac failure, cerebral edema (children), chills, complete atrioventricular block, confusion, conjunctivitis (children), constipation, coronary thrombosis, cough, depression, diabetes insipidus (children), diaphoresis, diarrhea, drowsiness, dysmenorrhea, dyspepsia, dyspnea, dysuria, emotional lability, epistaxis (children), erythema (delayed), facial edema, fever, fixed drug eruption (children), hematuria, hemopericardium, hypersensitivity reaction, hypertonia, hypoesthesia, hypotension, hypotonia, hypovolemic shock, hypoxemia, hypoxia, injection site reaction (edema, erythema, skin rash, warm feeling), insomnia, joint effusion (children), laryngeal edema, malaise, migraine (children), mucous membrane disease (swelling; children), muscle cramps (children), myasthenia, mydriasis, neck pain, neuropathy, papular rash (delayed), paresthesia, pharyngitis, polydipsia, pruritus, pulmonary hypertension, renal disease, renal failure, renal pain, salivation, seizure, skin discoloration, skin rash (delayed), sneezing (delayed), sore throat, speech disturbance, syncope, tachycardia, tenesmus, thrombosis, thyroid dysfunction (underactive; premature infants and infants with underlying medical conditions are more vulnerable; FDA Safety Alert 2015), tongue paralysis, tremor, urinary retention, urticaria (may be delayed), vascular disease, ventricular fibrillation, ventricular premature contractions, vertigo (children), visual field defect, weakness, xerostomia

Mechanism of Action Iopromide opacifies vessels in its path of flow, permitting radiographic visualization of internal structures.

Pharmacodynamics/Kinetics

Half-life Elimination Main elimination phase: 2 hours; Terminal phase: 6.2 hours

Time to Peak

Intravascular: Contrast enhancement: 15 to 120 seconds after bolus injection

Intravenous: Contrast enhancement: Kidneys: 5 to 15 minutes

Pregnancy Risk Factor B

Pregnancy Considerations Adverse events have not been observed in animal reproduction studies. Iopromide crosses the placenta and was detected in a newborn gut and urine at birth (Vanhaesebrouck 2005). Thyroid dysfunction in the neonate has not been reported (ACR 2015; Kochi 2012). In general, use of iodinated contrast media should be avoided unless absolutely required to obtain diagnostic information that will influence the care of the mother or fetus during pregnancy (ACOG 2015; ACR 2015).

Iothalamate Meglumine

(eye oh thal A mate MEG loo meen)

Brand Names: US Conray; Conray 30; Conray 43; Cysto-Conray II

Brand Names: Canada Conray 30; Conray 43; Conray 60; Cysto-Conray II

Pharmacologic Category Iodinated Contrast Media; Radiological/Contrast Media, Ionic (High Osmolality)

Use Imaging:

Conray: Excretory urography, cerebral angiography, peripheral arteriography, venography, arthrography, direct cholangiography, endoscopic retrograde cholangiopancreatography, contrast enhancement of CT brain images, cranial computerized angiotomography, IV digital subtraction angiography and arterial digital subtraction angiography; enhancement of CT scans performed for detection and evaluation of lesions in the liver, pancreas, kidneys, abdominal aorta, mediastinum, abdominal cavity and retroperitoneal space.

Conray 30: IV infusion urography, contrast enhancement of computed tomographic (CT) brain images and arterial digital subtraction angiography.

Conray 43: Lower extremity venography, IV infusion urography, contrast enhancement of CT brain images and arterial digital subtraction angiography; enhancement of CT scans performed for detection and evaluation of lesions in the liver, pancreas, kidneys, abdominal aorta, mediastinum, abdominal cavity and retroperitoneal space; retrograde cystography, cystourethrography and retrograde pyelography.

Cysto-Conray II: Retrograde cystography and cystourethrography.

Local Anesthetic/Vasoconstrictor Precautions No information available to require special precautions

Effects on Dental Treatment No significant effects or complications reported

Effects on Bleeding No information available to require special precautions

Adverse Reactions Frequency not defined. Adverse reactions that are specific to certain procedures are listed with the procedure.

Cardiovascular: Bradycardia (cerebral angiography), cardiac arrest (rare), cardiac arrhythmia (rare), cardiac fibrillation (rare), cerebrovascular accident (cerebral angiography), chest tightness, coronary insufficiency (rare), decreased blood pressure (cerebral angiography; transient), duodenal wall intravasation (endoscopic retrograde cholangiopancreatography), facial edema, facial flushing, flushing, hypotensive shock (rare), peripheral edema, syncope, tachycardia (direct cholangiography), thrombophlebitis (rare), thrombosis, vasoconstriction, vasodilatation, venospasm

Central nervous system: Amnesia (cerebral angiography), aphasia, chills (without fever), choking sensation, coma, convulsions, dizziness, flushing sensation, headache, localized burning (face and neck; cerebral angiography), paresthesia (due to injection rate)

Dermatologic: Diaphoresis, ecchymoses, erythema, gangrene (very rare; venography), maculopapular rash, pruritus, urticaria

Endocrine & metabolic: Altered thyroid hormone levels (transient suppression; premature infants and infants with underlying medical conditions may be more vulnerable; FDA Safety Alert 2015), hypothyroidism

Gastrointestinal: Nausea, pancholangitis (direct cholangiography), pancreatitis (direct cholangiography, endoscopic retrograde cholangiopancreatography), severe abdominal pain (endoscopic retrograde cholangiopancreatography), vomiting, xerostomia

Hematologic & oncologic: Abnormal erythropoiesis, disseminated intravascular coagulation (extremely rare), erythrocyte agglutination, hematoma, hemorrhage (peripheral arteriography and venography), interference in clot formation

Hepatic: Hepatic abscess (direct cholangiography)

Hypersensitivity: Anaphylaxis (rare; with loss of consciousness and coma), angioedema

Infection: Septicemia (direct cholangiography, endoscopic retrograde cholangiopancreatography)

Local: Extravasation (with burning pain)

Neuromuscular & skeletal: Arthralgia (arthrography), brachial plexus injury (peripheral arteriography and venography), laryngospasm, muscle spasm, tremor

Ophthalmic: Conjunctival abnormalities

Renal: Renal disease, renal failure (temporary)

Respiratory: Apnea, bronchospasm (with or without edema), cough, cyanosis, dyspnea, exacerbation of asthma, nasal congestion, pulmonary edema, sneezing, wheezing

Miscellaneous: Fever (direct cholangiography, endoscopic retrograde cholangiopancreatography), tissue necrosis

General Dosage Range
Dosage varies greatly depending on indication.

Mechanism of Action Radiopaque contrast agent; opacifies vessels in the path of the flow of the contrast medium, permitting radiographic visualization of the internal structures of the body.

Pharmacodynamics/Kinetics

Half-life Elimination 90 minutes

Pregnancy Risk Factor B/C (product dependent)

Pregnancy Considerations Adverse events were not observed in animal reproduction studies. In general, iodinated contrast media agents may cross the placenta; use should be avoided unless absolutely required to obtain diagnostic information that will influence the care of the mother or fetus during pregnancy (ACOG 2016; ACR 2015).

Ipilimumab (ip i LIM u mab)

Brand Names: US Yervoy

Brand Names: Canada Yervoy

Pharmacologic Category Antineoplastic Agent, Monoclonal Antibody

Use

Melanoma, unresectable or metastatic: Treatment of unresectable or metastatic melanoma

Melanoma, adjuvant treatment: Adjuvant treatment of cutaneous melanoma in patients with pathologic involvement of regional lymph nodes of more than 1 mm who have undergone complete resection, including total lymphadenectomy

Local Anesthetic/Vasoconstrictor Precautions
No information available to require special precautions

Effects on Dental Treatment No significant effects or complications reported

Effects on Bleeding No information available to require special precautions

Adverse Reactions

>10%:

Central nervous system: Fatigue (41% to 46%), headache (15% to 33% [Hodi 2010])

Dermatologic: Pruritus (24% to 45% [Hodi 2010]), skin rash (19% to 50% [Hodi 2010]), dermatitis (grade 2: 12% to 21%; grades 3/4: 2% to 4% [includes Stevens-Johnson syndrome, toxic epidermal necrolysis, dermal ulceration, necrotic, bullous or hemorrhagic dermatitis])

Endocrine & metabolic: Weight loss (32%), pituitary insufficiency (4%; grade 2: ≤2% to 16%; grades 3/4: 2% to 7%)

Gastrointestinal: Diarrhea (32% to 49%), nausea (25% to 35% [Hodi 2010]), decreased appetite (14% to 27% [Hodi 2010]), increased serum lipase (26%), vomiting (13% to 24% [Hodi 2010]), constipation (21% [Hodi 2010]), colitis (8% to 16%), enterocolitis (grade 2: 5% to 14%; grades 3 to 5: 7% to 16%), increased serum amylase (17%), abdominal pain (15% [Hodi 2010])

Hematologic & oncologic: Decreased hemoglobin (25%), anemia (12% [Hodi 2010])

Hepatic: Increased serum ALT (≤2% to 46% [Hodi 2010]), increased serum AST (≤38% [Hodi 2010]), increased serum alkaline phosphatase (17%), increased serum bilirubin (11%), hepatitis (grade 2: 5%; grades 3/4: 11%)

Respiratory: Cough (16% [Hodi 2010]), dyspnea (15% [Hodi 2010])

Miscellaneous: Fever (12% to 18% [Hodi 2010])

1% to 10%:

Central nervous system: Insomnia (10%), neuropathy (grade 2: <1%; grades 3 to 5: 2%)

Dermatologic: Urticaria (2%), vitiligo (2% [Hodi 2010])

Endocrine & metabolic: Hypophysitis (2% [Hodi 2010]), adrenal insufficiency (≤2% [Hodi 2010]), hypothyroidism (≤2% [Hodi 2010])

Gastrointestinal: Intestinal perforation (1% to 2%), pancreatitis (1%)

Hematologic & oncologic: Eosinophilia (1% to 2%)

Hepatic: Hepatotoxicity (grade 2: 3%)

Immunologic: Antibody development (1%)

Renal: Increased serum creatinine (10%), nephritis (≤1%)

<1%, postmarketing, and/or case reports: Acute respiratory distress, adrenocortical insufficiency (Hodi 2010), arthritis, blepharitis, bronchiolitis obliterans organizing pneumonia (Barjaktarevic 2013), capillary leak syndrome (Hodi 2010), conjunctivitis, Cushing syndrome, DRESS syndrome, encephalitis, episcleritis, erythema multiforme, esophagitis, gastrointestinal ulcer, giant-cell arteritis, Graves' ophthalmopathy, Guillain-Barré syndrome, hemolytic anemia, hepatic failure, hepatitis (immune-mediated), hypersensitivity angiitis, hyperthyroidism, hypoacusis (neurosensory), hypogonadism, increased thyroid stimulating hormone level, infusion related reaction, iritis, meningitis, myasthenia gravis, myelofibrosis, myocarditis, myositis,

myositis (ocular), pericarditis, peripheral motor neuropathy, peritonitis, pneumonitis, polymyalgia rheumatica, polymyositis, psoriasis, renal failure, sarcoidosis, scleritis, sepsis, thyroiditis (autoimmune), uveitis, vascular disease, vasculitis

General Dosage Range Dosage adjustment recommended in patients who develop toxicities.

IV: *Adults:* 3 mg/kg every 3 weeks for 4 doses or 10 mg/kg every 3 weeks for 4 doses followed by 10 mg/kg every 12 weeks

Mechanism of Action Ipilimumab is a recombinant human IgG1 immunoglobulin monoclonal antibody which binds to the cytotoxic T-lymphocyte associated antigen 4 (CTLA-4). CTLA-4 is a down-regulator of T-cell activation pathways. Blocking CTLA-4 allows for enhanced T-cell activation and proliferation. In melanoma, ipilimumab may indirectly mediate T-cell immune responses against tumors.

Pharmacodynamics/Kinetics

Half-life Elimination Terminal: 15.4 days

Pregnancy Considerations

Adverse effects were observed in animal reproduction studies. Ipilimumab is an IgG1 immunoglobulin and human IgG1 is known to cross the placenta, therefore, ipilimumab may be expected to reach the fetus. Ipilimumab may cause fetal harm if administered during pregnancy (based on the mechanism of action). Women of reproductive potential should use effective contraception during treatment and for 3 months following the last ipilimumab dose.

A pregnancy registry has been established to collect information about women exposed to ipilimumab during pregnancy.Advise pregnant women to enroll in the Pregnancy Safety Surveillance Study by calling 1-844-593-7869.

Ipratropium (Nasal) (i pra TROE pee um)

Brand Names: US Atrovent [DSC]

Brand Names: Canada Alti-Ipratropium; Apo-Ipravent; Atrovent; Mylan-Ipratropium Solution

Pharmacologic Category Anticholinergic Agent

Use

Allergic/nonallergic perennial rhinitis (0.03% solution): Symptomatic relief of rhinorrhea associated with allergic and nonallergic perennial rhinitis in adults and children ≥6 years.

Colds (0.06% solution): Symptomatic relief of rhinorrhea associated with the common cold in adults and children ≥5 years.

Seasonal allergic rhinitis (0.06% solution): Symptomatic relief of rhinorrhea associated with seasonal allergic rhinitis in adults and children ≥5 years.

Local Anesthetic/Vasoconstrictor Precautions

No information available to require special precautions

Effects on Dental Treatment No significant effects or complications reported

Effects on Bleeding No information available to require special precautions

Adverse Reactions

1% to 10%:

Central nervous system: Headache (4% to 10%)

Gastrointestinal: Dysgeusia (≤4%), xerostomia (1% to 4%), diarrhea (2%), nausea (2%)

Respiratory: Upper respiratory tract infection (5% to 10%), epistaxis (6% to 9%), pharyngitis (≤8%), dry nose (≤5%), nasal mucosa irritation (2%), nasal congestion (1%)

<2%, postmarketing, and/or case reports: Anaphylaxis, angioedema, blurred vision, burning sensation of the nose, conjunctivitis, cough, dizziness, eye irritation, hoarseness, increased thirst, laryngospasm, palpitations, skin rash, tachycardia, tinnitus, urticaria

General Dosage Range Intranasal:

0.03% solution: *Children ≥6 years, Adolescents, and Adults:* Two sprays in each nostril 2 to 3 times/day

0.06% solution: *Children ≥5 years, Adolescents, and Adults:* Two sprays in each nostril 3 to 4 times/day

Mechanism of Action Local application to nasal mucosa inhibits serous and seromucous gland secretions.

Pharmacodynamics/Kinetics

Onset of Action 15 minutes

Pregnancy Risk Factor B

Pregnancy Considerations Adverse events have not been observed in animal reproduction studies.

Ipratropium (Oral Inhalation)

(i pra TROE pee um)

Related Information

Dentin Hypersensitivity, Acid Erosion, High Caries Index, Management of Alveolar Osteitis, and Xerostomia *on page 1857*

Respiratory Diseases *on page 1777*

Brand Names: US Atrovent HFA

Brand Names: Canada Apo Ipravent Solution; Apo-Ipravent Sterules; Atrovent HFA; Dom-Ipratropium; Gen Ipratropium; Mylan-Ipratropium; PHL-Ipratropium; PMS-Ipratropium; ratio-Ipratropium UDV; Teva-Ipratropium Sterinebs

Pharmacologic Category Anticholinergic Agent

Use Chronic obstructive pulmonary disease: Maintenance treatment of bronchospasm associated with chronic obstructive pulmonary disease (COPD), including chronic bronchitis and emphysema

Local Anesthetic/Vasoconstrictor Precautions

No information available to require special precautions

Effects on Dental Treatment Key adverse event(s) related to dental treatment: Xerostomia and changes in salivation (normal salivary flow resumes upon discontinuation), and dry mucous membranes.

Effects on Bleeding No information available to require special precautions

Adverse Reactions

>10%: Respiratory: Bronchitis (10% to 23%), exacerbation of chronic obstructive pulmonary disease (8% to 23%), sinusitis (1% to 11%)

1% to 10%:

Central nervous system: Headache (6% to 7%), dizziness (3%)

Gastrointestinal: Dyspepsia (1% to 5%), nausea (4%), xerostomia (2% to 4%), dysgeusia (1%)

Genitourinary: Urinary tract infection (2% to 10%)

Neuromuscular & skeletal: Back pain (2% to 7%)

Respiratory: Dyspnea (7% to 8%), flu-like symptoms (4% to 8%), cough (>3%), rhinitis (>3%), upper respiratory tract infection (>3%)

<1%, postmarketing, and/or case reports: Accommodation disturbance, acute eye pain, anaphylaxis, angioedema, blurred vision, bronchospasm, conjunctival hyperemia, constipation, corneal edema, decreased gastrointestinal motility, diarrhea, dry throat, glaucoma, hypersensitivity reaction, hypotension, increased intraocular pressure, laryngospasm, mouth edema, mydriasis, nausea, palpitations, pharyngeal edema, pruritus, skin rash, stomatitis, tachycardia,

throat irritation, urinary retention, urticaria, visual halos around lights, vomiting

General Dosage Range

Metered-dose inhaler: *Adults:* 2 inhalations 4 times daily (maximum: 12 inhalations in 24 hours)

Nebulization: *Children >12 years and Adults:* 500 mcg every 6 to 8 hours

Mechanism of Action Blocks the action of acetylcholine at parasympathetic sites in bronchial smooth muscle causing bronchodilation; local application to nasal mucosa inhibits serous and seromucous gland secretions.

Pharmacodynamics/Kinetics

Onset of Action Bronchodilation: Within 15 minutes; Peak effect: 1-2 hours

Duration of Action Oral inhalation: 2-4 hours; Nebulization: 4-5 hours, up to 7-8 hours in some patients

Half-life Elimination 2 hours

Pregnancy Risk Factor B

Pregnancy Considerations Teratogenic effects were not observed in animal studies. Inhaled ipratropium is recommended for use as additional therapy for pregnant women with severe asthma exacerbations.

Ipratropium and Albuterol

(i pra TROE pee um & al BYOO ter ole)

Related Information

Albuterol *on page 85*

Ipratropium (Oral Inhalation) *on page 919*

Brand Names: US Combivent Respimat; DuoNeb [DSC]

Brand Names: Canada Apo-Salvent-Ipravent Sterules; Combivent Respimat; Combivent UDV; ratio-Ipra Sal UDV; Teva-Combo Sterinebs

Pharmacologic Category Anticholinergic Agent; $Beta_2$-Adrenergic Agonist

Use Chronic obstructive pulmonary disease: Treatment of chronic obstructive pulmonary disease (COPD) in those patients who are currently on a regular bronchodilator who continue to have bronchospasms and require a second bronchodilator

Local Anesthetic/Vasoconstrictor Precautions No information available to require special precautions

Effects on Dental Treatment Key adverse event(s) related to dental treatment: Xerostomia (normal salivary flow resumes upon discontinuation), dry mucous membrane, and unusual taste.

Effects on Bleeding No information available to require special precautions

Adverse Reactions

Percentages reported with combination product (not versus placebo). Also see individual agents.

>10%: Respiratory: Bronchitis (2% to 12%), upper respiratory tract infection (3% to 11%)

1% to 10%:

Cardiovascular: Chest pain (≤3%), angina (<2%), arrhythmia (<2%), edema (<2%), hypertension (<2%), palpitation (<2%), tachycardia (<2%)

Central nervous system: Headache (3% to 6%), pain (1% to 3%), dizziness (<2%), fatigue (<2%), insomnia (<2%), nervousness (<2%)

Dermatologic: Pruritus (<2%), rash (<2%)

Endocrine & metabolic: Hypokalemia (<2%)

Gastrointestinal: Diarrhea (≤2%), dyspepsia (≤2%), nausea (1% to 2%), constipation (<2%), dry throat (<2%), sputum increased (<2%), taste perversion (<2%), vomiting (<2%), xerostomia (<2%)

Genitourinary: Urinary tract infection (≤2%), dysuria (<2%)

Neuromuscular & skeletal: Arthralgia (<2%), muscle spasms (<2%), myalgia (<2%), paresthesia (<2%), tremor (<2%), weakness (<2%), leg cramps (1%)

Ocular: Eye pain (<2%)

Respiratory: Lung disease (6%), dyspnea (2% to 5%), cough (3% to 7%), pharyngitis (2% to 4%), bronchospasm (<2%), pharyngolaryngeal pain (<2%), wheezing (<2%), respiratory disorder (3%), sinusitis (2%), pneumonia (1%), rhinitis (1%)

Miscellaneous: Dysphonia (<2%), flu-like syndrome (1%)

<1%, postmarketing, and/or case reports: Accommodation abnormal, allergic reactions (angioedema of tongue, lips or face; laryngospasm, pruritus, rash, urticaria); alopecia, anaphylactic reaction, angioedema, blurred vision, CNS stimulation, conjunctival hyperemia, coordination difficulty, COPD exacerbation, corneal edema, drowsiness, flushing, gastrointestinal motility disorder, glaucoma, halo vision, hoarseness, heartburn, hyperhidrosis, hypersensitivity reactions, hypotension, intraocular pressure increased, mental disorder, metabolic acidosis, mucosal ulcers, muscle weakness, myocardial ischemia, mydriasis, narrow-angle glaucoma precipitation, nasal congestion, ocular irritation, pharyngeal edema, stomatitis, throat irritation, urinary retention

General Dosage Range

Solution for inhalation: *Adults:* 1 inhalation 4 times daily (maximum: 6 inhalations/24 hours)

Nebulization: *Adults:* 3 mL every 6 hours (maximum: 3 mL every 4 hours)

Mechanism of Action See individual agents.

Pregnancy Risk Factor C

Pregnancy Considerations Animal reproduction studies have not been conducted with this combination. See individual agents.

Ipratropium and Fenoterol

(i pra TROE pee um & fen oh TER ole)

Related Information

Ipratropium (Oral Inhalation) *on page 919*

Brand Names: Canada Duovent UDV

Pharmacologic Category Anticholinergic Agent; $Beta_2$-Adrenergic Agonist

Use Note: Not approved in the US

Bronchospasm: Treatment of bronchospasm associated with acute severe exacerbation of COPD or bronchial asthma in patients ≥12 years of age

Local Anesthetic/Vasoconstrictor Precautions No information available to require special precautions

Effects on Dental Treatment Key adverse event(s) related to dental treatment: Xerostomia (normal salivary flow resumes upon discontinuation).

Effects on Bleeding No information available to require special precautions

Adverse Reactions Frequency not defined.

Cardiovascular: Atrial fibrillation, cardiac arrhythmia, hypertension, hypotension, ischemic heart disease, palpitations, prolonged QT interval on ECG, supraventricular tachycardia, tachycardia

Central nervous system: Dizziness, headache, nervousness, psychological disorder

Dermatologic: Diaphoresis

Endocrine & metabolic: Hyperglycemia, hypokalemia

Gastrointestinal: Constipation, diarrhea, nausea, vomiting, xerostomia

Genitourinary: Urinary retention

Hypersensitivity: Hypersensitivity reaction (anaphylaxis, angioedema, bronchospasm, laryngospasm, oropharyngeal edema, skin rash, urticaria)

Neuromuscular & skeletal: Muscle cramps, myalgia, tremor, weakness

Ophthalmic: Accommodation disturbance, acute angle-closure glaucoma, eye pain, increased intraocular pressure, mydriasis

Respiratory: Bronchospasm (inhalation-induced), cough, pharyngitis, throat irritation

General Dosage Range Nebulization: *Children ≥12 years, Adolescents, and Adults:* Usual dose: 4 mL

Mechanism of Action

Ipratropium: Blocks the action of acetylcholine at parasympathetic sites in bronchial smooth muscle causing bronchodilation

Fenoterol: Relaxes bronchial smooth muscle by action on $beta_2$-receptors

Pharmacodynamics/Kinetics

Onset of Action

Ipratropium: Bronchodilation: Within 15 minutes; Peak effect: 1 to 2 hours

Fenoterol: Bronchodilation: 5 minutes; Peak effect: 30 to 60 minutes

Duration of Action

Ipratropium: 4 to 8 hours

Fenoterol: 6 to 8 hours

Half-life Elimination

Ipratropium: 1.6 hours

Fenoterol: ~3 hours

Pregnancy Considerations Adverse events were not observed in animal reproduction studies using this combination via inhalation. Adverse events were observed in animal reproduction studies using oral formulations of each component.

Product Availability Not available in the US

Irbesartan (ir be SAR tan)

Related Information

Cardiovascular Diseases *on page 1752*

Brand Names: US Avapro

Brand Names: Canada ACT-Irbesartan; Apo-Irbesartan; Auro-Irbesartan; Ava-Irbesartan; Avapro; Dom-Irbesartan; JAMP Irbesartan; Mylan-Irbesartan; PMS-Irbesartan; RAN-Irbesartan; ratio-Irbesartan; Sandoz-Irbesartan; Teva-Irbesartan

Pharmacologic Category Angiotensin II Receptor Blocker; Antihypertensive

Use

Diabetic nephropathy: Treatment of diabetic nephropathy with an elevated serum creatinine and proteinuria (>300 mg/day) in patients with type 2 diabetes and hypertension.

Hypertension: Management of hypertension (alone or in combination with other antihypertensives).

Guideline recommendations:

Hypertension: The 2014 guideline for the management of high blood pressure in adults (Eighth Joint National Committee [JNC 8; James, 2013]) recommends initiation of pharmacologic treatment to lower blood pressure for the following patients:

- Patients ≥60 years of age with systolic blood pressure (SBP) ≥150 mm Hg or diastolic blood pressure (DBP) ≥90 mm Hg. Goal of therapy is SBP <150 mm Hg and DBP <90 mm Hg.
- Patients <60 years of age with SBP ≥140 mm Hg or DBP ≥90 mm Hg. Goal of therapy is SBP <140 mm Hg and DBP <90 mm Hg.
- Patients ≥18 years of age with diabetes and SBP ≥140 mm Hg or DBP ≥90 mm Hg. Goal of therapy is SBP <140 mm Hg and DBP <90 mm Hg.
- Patients ≥18 years of age with chronic kidney disease (CKD) and SBP ≥140 mm Hg or DBP ≥90 mm Hg. Goal of therapy is SBP <140 mm Hg and DBP <90 mm Hg.

Chronic kidney disease (CKD) and hypertension: Regardless of race or diabetes status, the use of an ACE inhibitor (ACEI) or angiotensin receptor blocker (ARB) as initial therapy is recommended to improve kidney outcomes. In the general non-black population (without CKD), including those with diabetes, initial antihypertensive treatment should consist of a thiazide-type diuretic, calcium channel blocker, ACEI, or ARB. In the general black population (without CKD), including those with diabetes, initial antihypertensive treatment should consist of a thiazide-type diuretic or a calcium channel blocker instead of an ACEI or ARB.

Coronary artery disease and hypertension: The American Heart Association, American College of Cardiology and American Society of Hypertension (AHA/ACC/ASH) 2015 scientific statement for the treatment of hypertension in patients with coronary artery disease (CAD) recommends the use of an ARB (or ACE inhibitor) as part of a regimen in patients with hypertension and chronic stable angina if there is prior MI, LV systolic dysfunction, diabetes mellitus, or CKD. A BP target of <140/90 mm Hg is reasonable for the secondary prevention of cardiovascular events. A lower target BP (<130/80 mm Hg) may be appropriate in some individuals with CAD, previous MI, stroke or transient ischemic attack, or CAD risk equivalents (AHA/ACC/ASH [Rosendorff 2015]).

Local Anesthetic/Vasoconstrictor Precautions No information available to require special precautions

Effects on Dental Treatment Key adverse event(s) related to dental treatment: Patients may experience orthostatic hypotension as they stand up after treatment; especially if lying in dental chair for extended periods of time. Use caution with sudden changes in position during and after dental treatment.

Effects on Bleeding No information available to require special precautions

Adverse Reactions Unless otherwise indicated, percentage of incidence is reported for patients with hypertension.

>10%: Endocrine & metabolic: Hyperkalemia (diabetic nephropathy: 19%; rarely seen in hypertension)

1% to 10%:

Cardiovascular: Orthostatic hypotension (diabetic nephropathy: 5%: hypertension: <1%)

Central nervous system: Dizziness (diabetic nephropathy: 10%), fatigue (4%)

Gastrointestinal: Diarrhea (3%), dyspepsia (2%)

Respiratory: Upper respiratory tract infection (9%)

<1%, postmarketing, and/or case reports: Abdominal distention, anemia (case report; Simonetti 2007), angina pectoris, angioedema, arthritis, auditory disturbance, bronchitis, bursitis, cardiac arrhythmia, cardiac failure, cerebrovascular accident, chills, conjunctivitis, constipation, decreased libido, depression, dermatitis, drowsiness, dyspnea, ecchymoses, epistaxis, erythema, facial edema, fever, flatulence, flushing, gastroenteritis, gout, hepatitis, hypertension,

hypertensive crisis, hypotension, increased liver enzymes, increased serum transaminases, jaundice, muscle cramps, myalgia, myasthenia, myocardial infarction, nasal congestion, noncardiac chest pain, numbness, otalgia, otic infection, paresthesia, prostatic disease, pruritus, pulmonary congestion, renal failure, renal insufficiency, sexual disorder, sleep disorder, thrombocytopenia, transient ischemic attacks, tremor, upper extremity edema, urination disorder, urticaria, visual disturbance, wheezing

General Dosage Range Oral: *Adults:* Initial: 75 to 150 mg once daily; Maintenance: 75 to 300 mg once daily

Mechanism of Action Irbesartan is an angiotensin receptor antagonist. Angiotensin II acts as a vasoconstrictor. In addition to causing direct vasoconstriction, angiotensin II also stimulates the release of aldosterone. Once aldosterone is released, sodium as well as water are reabsorbed. The end result is an elevation in blood pressure. Irbesartan binds to the AT1 angiotensin II receptor. This binding prevents angiotensin II from binding to the receptor thereby blocking the vasoconstriction and the aldosterone secreting effects of angiotensin II.

Pharmacodynamics/Kinetics

Onset of Action

Peak levels in 1 to 2 hours

Maximum effect: 3-6 hours postdose; with chronic dosing maximum effect: ~2 weeks

Duration of Action >24 hours

Half-life Elimination Terminal: 11 to 15 hours

Time to Peak Serum: 1.5 to 2 hours

Pregnancy Risk Factor D

Pregnancy Considerations [US Boxed Warning]: Drugs that act on the renin-angiotensin system can cause injury and death to the developing fetus. Discontinue as soon as possible once pregnancy is detected. The use of drugs which act on the renin-angiotensin system are associated with oligohydramnios. Oligohydramnios, due to decreased fetal renal function, may lead to fetal lung hypoplasia and skeletal malformations. Use is also associated with anuria, hypotension, renal failure, skull hypoplasia, and death in the fetus/neonate. The exposed fetus should be monitored for fetal growth, amniotic fluid volume, and organ formation. Infants exposed *in utero* should be monitored for hyperkalemia, hypotension, and oliguria (exchange transfusions or dialysis may be needed). These adverse events are generally associated with maternal use in the second and third trimesters.

Untreated chronic maternal hypertension is also associated with adverse events in the fetus, infant, and mother. The use of angiotensin II receptor blockers is not recommended to treat chronic uncomplicated hypertension in pregnant women and should generally be avoided in women of reproductive potential (ACOG, 2013).

Irinotecan (Conventional)

(eye rye no TEE kan con VEN sha nal)

Brand Names: US Camptosar

Brand Names: Canada Camptosar; Irinotecan For Injection; Irinotecan Hydrochloride Injection; Irinotecan Hydrochloride Trihydrate For Injection; Irinotecan Hydrochloride Trihydrate Injection

Pharmacologic Category Antineoplastic Agent, Camptothecin; Antineoplastic Agent, Topoisomerase I Inhibitor

Use Colorectal cancer, metastatic: Treatment of metastatic carcinoma of the colon or rectum

Local Anesthetic/Vasoconstrictor Precautions No information available to require special precautions

Effects on Dental Treatment Key adverse event(s) related to dental treatment: Increased salivation, mucositis, and stomatitis.

Effects on Bleeding Hematologic adverse effects include anemia (60% to 97%) and thrombocytopenia (96%; grades 3/4: 1% to 4%). Bleeding and hemorrhage have been noted in 1% to 5% of patients. Medical consult recommended.

Adverse Reactions Frequency of adverse reactions reported for single-agent use of irinotecan only. In limited pediatric experience, dehydration (often associated with severe hypokalemia and hyponatremia) was among the most significant grade 3/4 adverse events, with a frequency up to 29%. In addition, grade 3/4 infection was reported in 24%.

>10%:

Cardiovascular: Vasodilatation (9% to 11%)

Central nervous system: Cholinergic syndrome (47%; includes diaphoresis, flushing, increased peristalsis, lacrimation, miosis, rhinitis, sialorrhea), pain (23% to 24%), dizziness (15% to 21%), insomnia (19%), headache (17%), chills (14%)

Dermatologic: Alopecia (46% to 72%), diaphoresis (16%), skin rash (13% to 14%)

Endocrine & metabolic: Weight loss (30%), dehydration (15%)

Gastrointestinal: Diarrhea (late: 83% to 88%, grades 3/4: 14% to 31%; early: 43% to 51%, grades 3/4: 7% to 22%), nausea (70% to 86%), abdominal pain (57% to 68%), vomiting (62% to 67%), abdominal cramps (57%), anorexia (44% to 55%), constipation (30% to 32%), mucositis (30%), flatulence (12%), stomatitis (12%)

Hematologic & oncologic: Anemia (60% to 97%; grades 3/4: 5% to 7%), leukopenia (63% to 96%, grades 3/4: 14% to 28%), thrombocytopenia (96%, grades 3/4: 1% to 4%), neutropenia (30% to 96%; grades 3/4: 14% to 31%)

Hepatic: Increased serum bilirubin (84%), increased serum alkaline phosphatase (13%)

Infection: Infection (14%)

Neuromuscular & skeletal: Weakness (69% to 76%), back pain (14%)

Respiratory: Dyspnea (22%), cough (17% to 20%), rhinitis (16%)

Miscellaneous: Fever (44% to 45%)

1% to 10%:

Cardiovascular: Edema (10%), hypotension (6%), thromboembolism (5%)

Central nervous system: Drowsiness (9%), confusion (3%)

Gastrointestinal: Abdominal fullness (10%), dyspepsia (10%)

Hematologic & oncologic: Febrile neutropenia (grades 3/4: 2% to 6%), hemorrhage (grades 3/4: 1% to 5%), neutropenic infection (grades 3/4: 1% to 2%)

Hepatic: Increased serum AST (10%), ascites (grades 3/4: ≤9%), jaundice (grades 3/4: ≤9%)

Respiratory: Pneumonia (4%)

<1%, postmarketing, and/or case reports: Acute renal failure, anaphylactoid reaction, anaphylaxis, angina pectoris, arterial thrombosis, bradycardia, cardiac arrhythmia, cerebral infarction, cerebrovascular accident, circulatory shock, colitis, deep vein thrombophlebitis, dysarthria, embolism, gastrointestinal hemorrhage, gastrointestinal obstruction,

hepatomegaly, hiccups, hyperglycemia, hypersensitivity reaction, hyponatremia, immune thrombocytopenia, increased amylase, increased serum ALT, increased serum lipase, interstitial pulmonary disease, intestinal obstruction, intestinal perforation, ischemic colitis, ischemic heart disease, lymphocytopenia, megacolon, muscle cramps, myocardial infarction, pancreatitis, paresthesia, peripheral vascular disease, pulmonary embolism; pulmonary toxicity (includes dyspnea, fever, reticulonodular infiltrates on chest x-ray), renal insufficiency, syncope, thrombophlebitis, thrombosis, typhlitis (including neutropenic typhlitis), ulcer, ulcerative colitis, vertigo

General Dosage Range Dosage adjustment recommended in patients with hepatic impairment or who develop toxicities

IV: *Adults:* Dosage varies greatly depending on indication

Mechanism of Action Irinotecan and its active metabolite (SN-38) bind reversibly to topoisomerase I-DNA complex preventing religation of the cleaved DNA strand. This results in the accumulation of cleavable complexes and double-strand DNA breaks. As mammalian cells cannot efficiently repair these breaks, cell death consistent with S-phase cell cycle specificity occurs, leading to termination of cellular replication.

Pharmacodynamics/Kinetics

Half-life Elimination

Children and Adolescents (Ma, 2000): Irinotecan: 2.66 hours (range: 1.82-4.47 hours); SN-38 (active metabolite): 1.58 hours (range: 0.29-8.28 hours)

Adults: Irinotecan: 6 to 12 hours; SN-38: ~10 to 20 hours

Time to Peak

Irinotecan: Oral: Children and Adolescents: 3 hours (Wagner 2010a)

SN-38: Following 90-minute infusion: ~1 hour

Pregnancy Risk Factor D

Pregnancy Considerations Adverse events were observed in animal reproduction studies. Information related to the use of irinotecan (conventional) during pregnancy is limited (Cirillo 2012; Taylor 2009). May cause fetal harm if administered during pregnancy. Women of childbearing potential should avoid becoming pregnant while receiving treatment.

Irinotecan (Liposomal)

(eye rye no TEE kan lye po SO mal)

Brand Names: US Onivyde

Pharmacologic Category Antineoplastic Agent, Camptothecin; Antineoplastic Agent, Topoisomerase I Inhibitor

Use

Pancreatic adenocarcinoma, metastatic: Treatment of metastatic adenocarcinoma of the pancreas (in combination with fluorouracil and leucovorin) disease progression following gemcitabine-based therapy.

Limitations of use: Irinotecan (liposomal) is not indicated as a single agent for the treatment of metastatic adenocarcinoma of the pancreas.

Local Anesthetic/Vasoconstrictor Precautions No information available to require special precautions

Effects on Dental Treatment Key adverse event(s) related to dental treatment: Stomatitis has been reported

Effects on Bleeding Hematologic adverse effects include anemia (97%), neutropenia (52%) and thrombocytopenia (41%)

Adverse Reactions Frequency not always defined. Percentages reported as part of combination chemotherapy regimens.

Cardiovascular: Septic shock (≥2%)

Central nervous system: Fatigue (≤56%)

Dermatologic: Alopecia (14%)

Endocrine & metabolic: Hypoalbuminemia (43%), hypomagnesemia (35%), hypocalcemia (32%), hypokalemia (32%), hypophosphatemia (29%), hyponatremia (27%), weight loss (17%), dehydration (8%)

Gastrointestinal: Diarrhea (59%, grade 3/4: 13%; early onset 30%, grade 3/4: 3%; late onset 43%, grade 3/4: 9%), vomiting (52%), nausea (51%), decreased appetite (44%), stomatitis (32%), gastroenteritis (3%)

Hematologic & oncologic: Anemia (97%, grades 3/4: 6%), lymphocytopenia (81%, grades 3/4: 27%), neutropenia (52%, grades 3/4: 20%; incidence of neutropenia was higher among Asian patients), thrombocytopenia (41%, grades 3/4: 2%), febrile neutropenia (≤3%, grades 3/4: ≤3%)

Hepatic: Increased serum ALT (51%)

Hypersensitivity: Severe hypersensitivity

Infection: Sepsis (4%, grades 3/4: 3%), neutropenic sepsis (≤3%, grades 3/4: ≤3%)

Local: Catheter infection (3%)

Neuromuscular & skeletal: Weakness (≤56%)

Renal: Increased creatinine clearance (18%), acute renal failure (≥2%)

Respiratory: Pneumonia (>2%), interstitial pulmonary disease

Miscellaneous: Fever (23%)

General Dosage Range Dosage adjustment recommended in patients who develop toxicities.

IV: *Adults:* 70 mg/m^2 every 2 weeks (in combination with fluorouracil and leucovorin); reduce initial starting dose to 50 mg/m^2 in patients known to be homozygous for the UGT1A1*28 allele

Mechanism of Action Irinotecan (liposomal) is a topoisomerase 1 inhibitor encapsulated in a lipid bilayer (liposome). Irinotecan and its active metabolite (SN-38) bind reversibly to topoisomerase I-DNA complex preventing re-ligation of the cleaved DNA strand. This results in the accumulation of cleavable complexes and double-strand DNA breaks. As mammalian cells cannot efficiently repair these breaks, cell death consistent with S-phase cell cycle specificity occurs, leading to termination of cellular replication.

Pharmacodynamics/Kinetics

Half-life Elimination Total irinotecan: ~26 hours; SN-38: ~68 hours

Pregnancy Considerations Animal reproduction studies have not been conducted with the liposomal formulation. Based on the mechanism of action as well as animal data using irinotecan (conventional), irinotecan (liposomal) may cause fetal harm if administered during pregnancy. Women of childbearing potential should use effective contraception while receiving treatment and avoid pregnancy for one month following the last dose. Males with female partners of reproductive potential should use condoms during therapy and for four months following the last dose.

Isavuconazonium Sulfate

(eye sa vue koe na ZOE nee um sul FATE)

Brand Names: US Cresemba

Pharmacologic Category Antifungal Agent, Azole Derivative; Antifungal Agent, Oral; Antifungal Agent, Parenteral

Use

Aspergillosis: Treatment of invasive aspergillosis in adults

Mucormycosis: Treatment of invasive mucormycosis in adults

Local Anesthetic/Vasoconstrictor Precautions No information available to require special precautions

Effects on Dental Treatment No significant effects or complications reported

Effects on Bleeding No information available to require special precautions

Adverse Reactions Frequency not always defined.

>10%:

Cardiovascular: Peripheral edema (11% to 15%)

Central nervous system: Headache (17%), fatigue (11%), insomnia (11%)

Endocrine & metabolic: Hypokalemia (14% to 19%)

Gastrointestinal: Nausea (26% to 28%), vomiting (25%), diarrhea (22% to 24%), abdominal pain (17%), constipation (13% to 14%)

Hepatic: Increased liver enzymes (16% to 17%)

Respiratory: Dyspnea (12% to 17%), cough (12%)

1% to 10%:

Cardiovascular: Chest pain (9%), hypotension (8%), atrial fibrillation (<5%), atrial flutter (<5%), bradycardia (<5%), cardiac arrest (<5%), catheter site thrombosis (<5%), extrasystoles (<5%), palpitations (<5%), shortened QT interval (<5%), supraventricular extrasystole (<5%), supraventricular tachycardia (<5%), syncope (<5%), thrombophlebitis (<5%), ventricular premature contractions (<5%)

Central nervous system: Delirium (9%), anxiety (8%), brain disease (<5%), chills (<5%), confusion (<5%), convulsions (<5%), depression (<5%), drowsiness (<5%), falling (<5%), hallucination (<5%), hypoesthesia (<5%), malaise (<5%), migraine (<5%), peripheral neuropathy (<5%), stupor (<5%), vertigo (<5%), dizziness, hypoesthesia, paresthesia

Dermatologic: Skin rash (9%), pruritus (8%), alopecia (<5%), dermatitis (<5%), erythema (<5%), exfoliative dermatitis (<5%), urticaria (<5%)

Endocrine & metabolic: Hypomagnesemia (5%), hypoalbuminemia (<5%), hypoglycemia (<5%), hyponatremia (<5%)

Gastrointestinal: Decreased appetite (9%), dyspepsia (6%), abdominal distention (<5%), cholecystitis (<5%), cholelithiasis (<5%), cholestasis (<5%), dysgeusia (<5%), gastritis (<5%), gingivitis (<5%), stomatitis (<5%)

Genitourinary: Hematuria (<5%), proteinuria (<5%)

Hematologic & oncologic: Agranulocytosis (<5%), leukopenia (<5%), pancytopenia (<5%), petechia (<5%)

Hepatic: Hepatitis (<5%), hepatomegaly (<5%), increased serum ALT (>3x ULN ≤4%; >10x ULN ≤1%), increased serum AST (>3x ULN ≤4%; >10x ULN ≤1%), hepatic failure, increased serum transaminases

Hypersensitivity: Hypersensitivity (<5%)

Local: Injection site reaction (6%)

Neuromuscular & Skeletal: Back pain (10%), myositis (<5%), neck pain (<5%), ostealgia (<5%), tremor (<5%)

Ophthalmic: Optic neuropathy (<5%)

Otic: Tinnitus (<5%)

Respiratory: Acute respiratory tract failure (7%), bronchospasm (<5%), tachypnea (<5%)

General Dosage Range Note: Dosage expressed as milligrams of isavuconazonium sulfate

IV, Oral: *Adults:* 372 mg (isavuconazole 200 mg) every 8 hours for 6 doses, then 372 mg once daily

Mechanism of Action Isavuconazonium sulfate is a prodrug that is rapidly hydrolyzed in the blood to active isavuconazole. Isavuconazole inhibits the synthesis of ergosterol, a key component of the fungal cell membrane, through the inhibition of cytochrome P-450 dependent enzyme lanosterol 14-alpha-demethylase. This enzyme is responsible for the conversion of lanosterol to ergosterol. An accumulation of methylated sterol precursors and a depletion of ergosterol within the fungal cell membrane weakens the membrane structure and function.

Pharmacodynamics/Kinetics

Half-life Elimination IV: 130 hours

Time to Peak Oral: 2 to 3 hours

Pregnancy Risk Factor C

Pregnancy Considerations Adverse events were observed in animal reproduction studies. Based on animal data, isavuconazonium sulfate may have the potential to increase the risk of adverse developmental events if used in pregnant women.

Isocarboxazid (eye soe kar BOKS a zid)

Related Information

Vasoconstrictor Interactions With Antidepressants *on page 1913*

Brand Names: US Marplan

Pharmacologic Category Antidepressant, Monoamine Oxidase Inhibitor

Use Treatment of depression

Local Anesthetic/Vasoconstrictor Precautions Attempts should be made to avoid use of vasoconstrictor due to possibility of hypertensive episodes with monoamine oxidase inhibitors

Effects on Dental Treatment Key adverse event(s) related to dental treatment: Xerostomia (normal salivary flow resumes upon discontinuation); Patients may experience orthostatic hypotension as they stand up after treatment; especially if lying in dental chair for extended periods of time. Use caution with sudden changes in position during and after dental treatment.

Effects on Bleeding No information available to require special precautions

Adverse Reactions

>10%: Central nervous system: Dizziness (29%), headache (15%)

1% to 10%:

Cardiovascular: Orthostatic hypotension (4%), palpitations (2%), syncope (2%)

Central nervous system: Disturbed sleep (5%), drowsiness (4%), anxiety (2%), chills (2%), feeling of heaviness (2%), forgetfulness (2%), hyperactivity (2%), lethargy (2%), myoclonus (2%), paresthesia (2%), sedation (2%)

Dermatologic: Diaphoresis (2%)

Gastrointestinal: Xerostomia (9%), constipation (7%), nausea (6%), diarrhea (2%)

Genitourinary: Urinary frequency (2%), impotence (2%), urinary hesitancy (1%)

Neuromuscular & skeletal: Tremor (4%)

<1%, postmarketing, and/or case reports: Akathisia, ataxia, coma, dysuria, euphoria, hallucination, hematologic abnormality, melanoglossia, neuritis, sexual disorder, SIADH (syndrome of inappropriate antidiuretic hormone secretion), skin photosensitivity, spider telangiectasia, toxic amblyopia, urinary incontinence, urinary retention

General Dosage Range Oral: *Adults:* Initial: 10 mg 2 times/day; may increase to a maximum of 60 mg/day divided in 2-4 doses

Mechanism of Action Thought to act by increasing endogenous concentrations of epinephrine, norepinephrine, dopamine, and serotonin through inhibition of the enzyme (monoamine oxidase) responsible for the breakdown of these neurotransmitters

Pregnancy Risk Factor C

Pregnancy Considerations Animal reproduction studies have not been conducted.

Pregnant women exposed to antidepressants during pregnancy are encouraged to enroll in the National Pregnancy Registry for Antidepressants (NPRAD). Women 18 to 45 years of age or their health care providers may contact the registry by calling 844-405-6185. Enrollment should be done as early in pregnancy as possible.

Isoniazid (eye soe NYE a zid)

Brand Names: Canada Dom-Isoniazid; Isotamine; PDP-Isoniazid

Pharmacologic Category Antitubercular Agent

Use

Active tuberculosis infections: Treatment of susceptible active tuberculosis (eg, *Mycobacterium tuberculosis*) infections.

Latent tuberculosis infection (LTBI): Treatment of LTBI caused by *Mycobacterium tuberculosis* (also referred to as prophylaxis or preventive therapy). **Note:** To identify candidates for LTBI treatment, refer to CDC guidelines (http://www.cdc.gov/tb/publications/ltbi/pdf/TargetedLTBI.pdf) for current recommendations.

Local Anesthetic/Vasoconstrictor Precautions No information available to require special precautions

Effects on Dental Treatment Key adverse event(s) related to dental treatment: Xerostomia (normal salivary flow resumes upon discontinuation).

Effects on Bleeding Anemia and thrombocytopenia have been reported.

Adverse Reactions

>10%: Hepatic: Increased serum transaminases (mild and transient 10% to 20%)

Frequency not defined.

Cardiovascular: Vasculitis

Central nervous system: Brain disease, memory impairment, paresthesia, peripheral neuropathy, psychosis, seizure

Dermatologic: Skin rash (morbilliform, maculopapular, pruritic, or exfoliative), toxic epidermal necrolysis

Endocrine & metabolic: Gynecomastia, hyperglycemia, metabolic acidosis, pellagra, pyridoxine deficiency

Gastrointestinal: Epigastric distress, nausea, pancreatitis, vomiting

Genitourinary: Bilirubinuria

Hematologic & oncologic: Agranulocytosis, anemia (sideroblastic, hemolytic, or aplastic), eosinophilia, lymphadenopathy, thrombocytopenia

Hepatic: Hepatitis (risk increases with age; 2% in patients ≥50 years), hyperbilirubinemia, jaundice

Immunologic: DRESS syndrome

Neuromuscular & skeletal: Lupus-like syndrome, rheumatic disease

Ophthalmic: Optic atrophy, optic neuritis

Miscellaneous: Fever

Postmarketing and/or case reports: Hepatotoxicity (idiosyncratic) (Chalasani 2014)

General Dosage Range Oral, IM: Dosage varies greatly depending on indication

Mechanism of Action Isoniazid inhibits the synthesis of mycoloic acids, an essential component of the bacterial cell wall. At therapeutic levels isoniazid is bacteriocidal against actively growing intracellular and extracellular *Mycobacterium tuberculosis* organisms.

Pharmacodynamics/Kinetics

Half-life Elimination May be prolonged in patients with impaired hepatic function or severe renal impairment

Fast acetylators: 30 to 100 minutes; Slow acetylators: 2 to 5 hours

Time to Peak Serum: 1 to 2 hours

Pregnancy Risk Factor C

Pregnancy Considerations Adverse events were observed in some animal reproduction studies. Isoniazid crosses the human placenta. Due to the risk of tuberculosis to the fetus, treatment is recommended when the probability of maternal disease is moderate to high. Drug-susceptible TB guidelines recommend isoniazid as part of the initial treatment regimen. Isoniazid is also recommended for the treatment of TB in pregnant women with HIV-coinfection. Pyridoxine supplementation is recommended (Nahid 2016). Due to biologic changes during pregnancy and early postpartum, pregnant women may have increased susceptibility to tuberculosis infection or reactivation of latent disease (Mathad 2012).

Isoproterenol (eye soe proe TER e nole)

Related Information

Dentin Hypersensitivity, Acid Erosion, High Caries Index, Management of Alveolar Osteitis, and Xerostomia *on page 1857*

Brand Names: US Isuprel

Pharmacologic Category $Beta_1$- & $Beta_2$-Adrenergic Agonist Agent

Use Manufacturer's labeled indications (see **"Note"**): Mild or transient episodes of heart block that do not require electric shock or pacemaker therapy; serious episodes of heart block and Adams-Stokes attacks (except when caused by ventricular tachycardia or fibrillation); cardiac arrest until electric shock or pacemaker therapy is available; bronchospasm during anesthesia; adjunct to fluid and electrolyte replacement therapy and other drugs and procedures in the treatment of hypovolemic or septic shock and low cardiac output states (eg, decompensated heart failure, cardiogenic shock)

Note: The use of isoproterenol in advanced cardiac life support (ACLS) has largely been supplanted by the use of other adrenergic agents (eg, epinephrine and dopamine). The use of isoproterenol for bronchospasm during anesthesia and cardiogenic, hypovolemic, or septic shock is no longer recommended. See *Off-label Use* for more appropriate, yet unlabeled, uses.

Local Anesthetic/Vasoconstrictor Precautions No information available to require special precautions

Effects on Dental Treatment Key adverse event(s) related to dental treatment: Xerostomia and changes in salivation (normal salivary flow resumes upon discontinuation).

Effects on Bleeding No information available to require special precautions

Adverse Reactions Frequency not defined.

Cardiovascular: Adams-Stokes syndrome, angina pectoris, flushing, hypertension, hypotension, pallor, palpitations, paradoxical bradycardia (with tilt table testing), tachyarrhythmia, ventricular arrhythmia, ventricular premature contractions
Central nervous system: Dizziness, headache, nervousness, restlessness, seizure (Adams-Stokes)
Dermatologic: Diaphoresis
Endocrine & metabolic: Hypokalemia, increased serum glucose
Gastrointestinal: Nausea, vomiting
Neuromuscular & skeletal: Tremor, weakness
Ophthalmic: Blurred vision
Respiratory: Dyspnea, pulmonary edema

General Dosage Range Continuous IV infusion:
Children: 0.05-2 mcg/**kg**/minute; titrate to patient response
Adults: 2-10 mcg/minute; titrate to patient response

Mechanism of Action Stimulates $beta_1$- and $beta_2$-receptors resulting in relaxation of bronchial, GI, and uterine smooth muscle, increased heart rate and contractility, vasodilation of peripheral vasculature

Pharmacodynamics/Kinetics
Onset of Action IV: Immediate
Duration of Action IV: 10-15 minutes
Half-life Elimination 2.5-5 minutes

Pregnancy Risk Factor C

Pregnancy Considerations Animal reproduction studies have not been conducted by the manufacturer. Use of isoproterenol may interfere with uterine contractions at term (Mahon, 1967).

Isosorbide Dinitrate
(eye soe SOR bide dye NYE trate)

Related Information
Cardiovascular Diseases *on page 1752*
Isosorbide Mononitrate *on page 926*

Brand Names: US Dilatrate-SR; IsoDitrate ER; Isordil Titradose

Brand Names: Canada ISDN; PMS-Isosorbide

Pharmacologic Category Antianginal Agent; Vasodilator

Use
Angina pectoris, prevention: Prevention of angina pectoris due to coronary artery disease.
Note: Due to slower onset of action, isosorbide dinitrate is not the drug of choice to abort an acute anginal episode.

Local Anesthetic/Vasoconstrictor Precautions No information available to require special precautions

Effects on Dental Treatment Key adverse event(s) related to dental treatment: Xerostomia and changes in salivation (normal salivary flow resumes upon discontinuation).

Effects on Bleeding No information available to require special precautions

Adverse Reactions Frequency not defined.
Cardiovascular: Hypotension, orthostatic hypotension, rebound hypertension (uncommon), syncope (uncommon), unstable angina pectoris (uncommon)
Central nervous system: Dizziness (related to blood pressure changes), headache (most common)
Hematologic & oncologic: Methemoglobinemia (rare; overdose)

General Dosage Range
Oral:
Immediate release: *Adults:* 5 to 40 mg 2 to 3 times daily
Sustained release: *Adults:* 40 to 160 mg daily in divided doses

Mechanism of Action Isosorbide dinitrate and other nitrates form free radical nitric oxide. In smooth muscle, nitric oxide activates guanylate cyclase which increases guanosine 3'5' monophosphate (cGMP) leading to dephosphorylation of myosin light chains and smooth muscle relaxation. Produces a vasodilator effect on the peripheral veins and arteries with more prominent effects on the veins. Primarily reduces cardiac oxygen demand by decreasing preload (left ventricular end-diastolic pressure); may modestly reduce afterload. Additionally, coronary artery dilation improves collateral flow to ischemic regions.

Pharmacodynamics/Kinetics
Onset of Action Sublingual tablet: ~2 to 5 minutes; Oral tablet and capsule (includes extended-release formulations): ~1 hour
Duration of Action Sublingual tablet: 1 to 2 hours; Oral tablet and capsule (includes extended-release formulations): Up to 8 hours
Half-life Elimination Parent drug: ~1 hour; Metabolites (5-mononitrate: 5 hours; 2-mononitrate: 2 hours)

Pregnancy Risk Factor C

Pregnancy Considerations Adverse events have been observed in some animal reproduction studies. Nitric oxide donors, such as isosorbide, have been evaluated for pre-eclampsia and cervical ripening; isosorbide dinitrate use in these conditions is not currently recommended (Kalidindi 2012; Ramirez 2011).

Product Availability Sublingual tablets have been discontinued in the US for more than 1 year.

Isosorbide Mononitrate
(eye soe SOR bide mon oh NYE trate)

Related Information
Cardiovascular Diseases *on page 1752*
Isosorbide Dinitrate *on page 926*

Brand Names: US Imdur [DSC]

Brand Names: Canada Apo-ISMN; Imdur; PMS-ISMN; PRO-ISMN

Pharmacologic Category Antianginal Agent; Vasodilator

Use Angina pectoris: Treatment (immediate-release only) and prevention of angina pectoris caused by coronary artery disease. **Note:** The onset of action of oral isosorbide mononitrate is not sufficiently rapid for this product to be useful in aborting an acute anginal episode.

Local Anesthetic/Vasoconstrictor Precautions No information available to require special precautions

Effects on Dental Treatment No significant effects or complications reported

Effects on Bleeding No information available to require special precautions

Adverse Reactions
>10%: Central nervous system: Headache (13% to 35%)
1% to 10%:
Cardiovascular: Angina pectoris (≤2%), flushing (≤2%)
Central nervous system: Dizziness (≤4%), fatigue (≤4%), pain (≤4%), emotional lability (≤2%)
Dermatologic: Pruritus (≤2%), skin rash (≤2%)
Gastrointestinal: Nausea (≤3%), abdominal pain (≤2%), diarrhea (≤2%)
Hypersensitivity: Hypersensitivity reaction (≤2%)
Respiratory: Upper respiratory infection (≤4%), increased cough (≤2%)

<1%, postmarketing, and/or case reports: Amblyopia, anorexia, anxiety, asthma, back pain, bradycardia, cardiac arrhythmia, cerebrovascular accident, depression, diaphoresis, dysgeusia, dyspepsia, dyspnea, edema, hypertension, hypotension, increased thirst, insomnia, lack of concentration, methemoglobinemia (rare; overdose), muscle cramps, myocardial infarction, neck pain, nervousness, nightmares, orthostatic hypotension, pallor, palpitations, paresthesia, prostatic disease, restlessness, sinusitis, susurrus aurium, tachycardia, tremor, vertigo, vomiting, xerostomia

General Dosage Range Oral:

Extended release: *Adults:* Initial: 30 to 60 mg once daily; Maintenance: 30 to 240 mg once daily

Immediate release: *Adults:* 5 to 20 mg twice daily

Mechanism of Action Nitroglycerin and other nitrates form free radical nitric oxide. In smooth muscle, nitric oxide activates guanylate cyclase which increases guanosine 3'5' monophosphate (cGMP) leading to dephosphorylation of myosin light chains and smooth muscle relaxation. Produces a vasodilator effect on the peripheral veins and arteries with more prominent effects on the veins. Primarily reduces cardiac oxygen demand by decreasing preload (left ventricular end-diastolic pressure); may modestly reduce afterload; dilates coronary arteries and improves collateral flow to ischemic regions.

Pharmacodynamics/Kinetics

Onset of Action 30 to 45 minutes (Thadani 1987)

Duration of Action Immediate release: ≥6 hours (Thadani 1987); Extended release: ≥12 to 24 hours (Anderson 2007)

Half-life Elimination ~5 to 6 hours (Thadani 1987)

Time to Peak Plasma: 30 to 60 minutes

Pregnancy Risk Factor B

Pregnancy Considerations Adverse events have been observed in some animal reproduction studies. Nitric oxide donors, such as isosorbide, have been evaluated for pre-eclampsia and cervical ripening; isosorbide mononitrate use in these conditions is not currently recommended (Kalidindi 2012; Ramirez 2011).

ISOtretinoin (eye soe TRET i noyn)

Related Information

Dentin Hypersensitivity, Acid Erosion, High Caries Index, Management of Alveolar Osteitis, and Xerostomia *on page 1857*

Brand Names: US Absorica; Amnesteem [DSC]; Claravis; Myorisan; Zenatane

Brand Names: Canada Accutane; Clarus; Epuris

Pharmacologic Category Acne Products; Antineoplastic Agent, Retinoic Acid Derivative; Retinoic Acid Derivative

Use Acne, severe recalcitrant nodular: Treatment of severe recalcitrant nodular acne unresponsive to conventional therapy (including systemic antibiotics)

Local Anesthetic/Vasoconstrictor Precautions No information available to require special precautions

Effects on Dental Treatment Key adverse event(s) related to dental treatment: Xerostomia and changes in salivation (normal salivary flow resumes upon discontinuation).

Effects on Bleeding No information available to require special precautions

Adverse Reactions

>10%:

Endocrine & metabolic: Increased serum triglycerides (25%)

Neuromuscular & skeletal: Back pain (children: 29%)

1% to 10%:

Ophthalmic: Conjunctivitis (4%), blepharitis (1%), chalazion (1%), hordeolum (1%)

Frequency not defined:

Cardiovascular: Cerebrovascular accident, chest pain, edema, flushing, palpitations, syncope, tachycardia, thrombosis

Central nervous system: Aggressive behavior, attempted suicide, depression, dizziness, drowsiness, emotional lability, fatigue, headache, insomnia, lethargy, malaise, nervousness, paresthesia, pseudotumor cerebri, psychosis, seizure, suicidal ideation, violent behavior

Dermatologic: Acne fulminans, allergic skin reaction, alopecia, cheilitis, diaphoresis, eczema, eruptive xanthoma, facial erythema, hair disease, hirsutism, hyperpigmentation, hypopigmentation, nail disease, paronychia, pruritus, pyogenic granuloma, scaling of skin of feet, skin atrophy, skin photosensitivity, skin rash, sunburn (increased susceptibility), superficial peeling of palms, xeroderma

Endocrine & metabolic: Decreased HDL cholesterol, increased gamma-glutamyl transferase, increased lactate dehydrogenase, increased serum cholesterol, increased serum glucose, hyperuricemia, menstrual disease, weight loss

Gastrointestinal: Colitis, esophagitis, esophageal ulcer, gastrointestinal symptoms (nonspecific), gingival hemorrhage, gingivitis, inflammatory bowel disease, nausea, pancreatitis, xerostomia

Genitourinary: Genitourinary disease (nonspecific findings), hematuria, proteinuria, pyuria, renal vasculitis

Hematologic & oncologic: Anemia, bruise, lymphadenopathy, neutropenia, purpura, thrombocytopenia

Hepatic: Increased serum alkaline phosphatase, increased serum ALT, increased serum AST, hepatitis

Hypersensitivity: Anaphylaxis, hypersensitivity reaction

Infection: Herpes simplex infection (disseminated), infection

Neuromuscular & skeletal: Arthralgia, arthritis, bone disease, calcification of ligament, calcification of tendon, decreased bone mineral density, increased creatine phosphokinase, myalgia, premature epiphyseal closure, skeletal hyperostosis, tendonitis, weakness

Ophthalmic: Cataract, corneal opacity, keratitis, nocturnal amblyopia, optic neuritis, photophobia, vision color changes, visual disturbance

Otic: Auditory impairment, tinnitus

Renal: Glomerulonephritis

Respiratory: Bronchospasm, dry nose, epistaxis, respiratory tract infection, voice disorder, Wegener's granulomatosis

Miscellaneous: Wound healing impairment

<1%, postmarketing, and/or case reports: Agranulocytosis, contact lens intolerance, decreased visual acuity, dry eye syndrome, erythema multiforme, eye pain, increased osmolarity (tears), meibomian gland disease (atrophy and abnormal gland secretion), myopia, rhabdomyolysis, Stevens-Johnson syndrome, toxic epidermal necrolysis

General Dosage Range Oral:
Children ≥12 years to Adolescents ≤17 years: 0.5 to 1 mg/kg/day in 2 divided doses
Adults: 0.5 to 2 mg/kg/day in 2 divided doses

Mechanism of Action Reduces sebaceous gland size and reduces sebum production in acne treatment; in neuroblastoma, decreases cell proliferation and induces differentiation

Pharmacodynamics/Kinetics

Half-life Elimination Terminal: Parent drug: 21 hours; Metabolite: 21 to 24 hours

Time to Peak Serum: 3 to 5 hours

Pregnancy Risk Factor X

Pregnancy Considerations Isotretinoin and its metabolites can be detected in fetal tissue following maternal use during pregnancy (Benifla 1995; Kraft 1989). **[US Boxed Warnings]: Use of isotretinoin is contraindicated in females who are or may become pregnant. Birth defects (facial, eye, ear, skull, central nervous system, cardiovascular, thymus and parathyroid gland abnormalities) have been noted following isotretinoin exposure during pregnancy and the risk for severe birth defects is high, with any dose or even with short treatment duration. Low IQ scores have also been reported. The risk for spontaneous abortion and premature births is increased. Because of the high likelihood of teratogenic effects, all patients (male and female), prescribers, wholesalers, and dispensing pharmacists must register and be active in the iPLEDGE™ risk evaluation and mitigation strategy (REMS) program; do not prescribe isotretinoin for women who are or who are likely to become pregnant while using the drug. If pregnancy occurs during therapy, isotretinoin should be discontinued immediately and the patient referred to an obstetrician-gynecologist specializing in reproductive toxicity.** This medication is contraindicated in females of childbearing potential unless they are able to comply with the guidelines of the iPLEDGE™ pregnancy prevention program. Females of childbearing potential must have two negative pregnancy tests with a sensitivity of at least 25 milliunits/mL prior to beginning therapy and testing should continue monthly during therapy. Females of childbearing potential should not become pregnant during therapy or for 1 month following discontinuation of isotretinoin. Upon discontinuation of treatment, females of childbearing potential should have a pregnancy test after their last dose and again one month after their last dose. Two forms of contraception should be continued during this time. Any pregnancies should be reported to the iPLEDGE™ program (www.ipledgeprogram.com or 866-495-0654) and the FDA through MedWatch (800-FDA-1088).

Prescribing and Access Restrictions As a requirement of the REMS program, access to this medication is restricted. All patients (male and female), prescribers, wholesalers, and dispensing pharmacists must register and be active in the iPLEDGE™ risk management program, designed to eliminate fetal exposures to isotretinoin. This program covers all isotretinoin products (brand and generic). The iPLEDGE™ program requires that all patients meet qualification criteria and monthly program requirements (eg, pregnancy testing). Healthcare providers can only prescribe a maximum 30-day supply at each monthly visit and must counsel patients on the iPLEDGE™ program requirements and confirm counseling via the iPLEDGE™ automated system. Registration, activation, and additional information are provided at www.ipledgeprogram.com or by calling 866-495-0654.

Isoxsuprine (eye SOKS syoo preen)

Pharmacologic Category Vasodilator

Use

Cerebrovascular insufficiency: Relief of symptoms associated with cerebrovascular insufficiency.

Peripheral vascular diseases: Treatment of peripheral vascular diseases, such as arteriosclerosis obliterans, thromboangiitis obliterans (Buerger disease), and Raynaud disease.

Note: More appropriate therapies (medical or surgical) should be considered; efficacy of isoxsuprine in the treatment of these conditions has not been well established.

Local Anesthetic/Vasoconstrictor Precautions No information available to require special precautions

Effects on Dental Treatment May enhance effects of other vasodilators.

Effects on Bleeding No information available to require special precautions

Adverse Reactions Frequency not defined.
Cardiovascular: Chest pain, hypotension, tachycardia
Central nervous system: Dizziness
Dermatologic: Skin rash
Gastrointestinal: Abdominal distress, nausea, vomiting

General Dosage Range
Oral: *Adults:* 10 to 20 mg 3 or 4 times daily

Mechanism of Action Isoxsuprine increases muscle blood flow, but skin blood flow is usually unaffected. Rather than increasing muscle blood flow by beta-receptor stimulation, isoxsuprine probably has a direct action on vascular smooth muscle. The generally accepted mechanism of action of isoxsuprine on the uterus is beta-adrenergic stimulation (Kaindl 1959; Samuels 1959).

Pharmacodynamics/Kinetics

Time to Peak Time to peak, serum: ~1 hour; serum concentrations maintained for at least 3 hours (Kaindl 1959)

Pregnancy Considerations Isoxsuprine crosses the placenta. Adverse effects (eg, hypocalcemia, hypoglycemia, hypotension, and ileus) requiring treatment have been observed in infants born to mothers who received isoxsuprine during pregnancy. Maternal and fetal tachycardia have occurred with use and pulmonary edema has been reported with maternal use of beta stimulants (Brazy 1979; Brazy 1981). Although isoxsuprine has been evaluated for the treatment of preterm labor, use for this indication is not currently recommended (ACOG 171 2016).

Isradipine (iz RA di peen)

Related Information

Calcium Channel Blockers and Gingival Hyperplasia *on page 1908*
Cardiovascular Diseases *on page 1752*

Pharmacologic Category Antihypertensive; Calcium Channel Blocker; Calcium Channel Blocker, Dihydropyridine

Use Hypertension: Management of hypertension (may be used alone or concurrently with thiazide-type diuretics).

The 2014 guideline for the management of high blood pressure in adults (JNC 8) recommends initiation of pharmacologic treatment to lower blood pressure for the following patients (JNC8 [James, 2013]):

- Patients ≥60 years of age, with systolic blood pressure (SBP) ≥150 mm Hg or diastolic blood pressure (DBP) ≥90 mm Hg. Goal of therapy is SBP <150 mm Hg and DBP <90 mm Hg.
- Patients <60 years of age, with SBP ≥140 mm Hg or DBP ≥90 mm Hg. Goal of therapy is SBP <140 mm Hg and DBP <90 mm Hg.
- Patients ≥18 years of age with diabetes, with SBP ≥140 mm Hg or DBP ≥90 mm Hg. Goal of therapy is SBP <140 mm Hg and DBP <90 mm Hg.
- Patients ≥18 years of age with chronic kidney disease (CKD), with SBP ≥140 mm Hg or DBP ≥90 mm Hg. Goal of therapy is SBP <140 mm Hg and DBP <90 mm Hg.

In patients with chronic kidney disease (CKD), regardless of race or diabetes status, the use of an ACE inhibitor (ACEI) or angiotensin receptor blocker (ARB) as initial therapy is recommended to improve kidney outcomes. In the general nonblack population (without CKD) including those with diabetes, initial antihypertensive treatment should consist of a thiazide-type diuretic, calcium channel blocker, ACEI, or ARB. In the general black population (without CKD) including those with diabetes, initial antihypertensive treatment should consist of a thiazide-type diuretic or a calcium channel blocker **instead of** an ACEI or ARB.

Local Anesthetic/Vasoconstrictor Precautions Isradipine is one of the drugs confirmed to prolong the QT interval and is accepted as having a risk of causing torsade de pointes. The risk of drug-induced torsade de pointes is extremely low when a single QT interval prolonging drug is prescribed. In terms of epinephrine, it is not known what effect vasoconstrictors in the local anesthetic regimen will have in patients with a known history of congenital prolonged QT interval or in patients taking any medication that prolongs the QT interval. Until more information is obtained, it is suggested that the clinician consult with the physician prior to the use of a vasoconstrictor in suspected patients, and that the vasoconstrictor (epinephrine, mepivacaine and levonordefrin [Carbocaine® 2% with Neo-Cobefrin®]) be used with caution.

Effects on Dental Treatment Unlike other calcium channel blockers, information is sparse as to whether isradipine causes gingival hyperplasia. Consultation with physician is suggested if hyperplasia is observed in patients taking isradipine.

Effects on Bleeding No information available to require special precautions

Adverse Reactions

>10%: Central nervous system: Headache (dose related 2% to 22%)

1% to 10%:

Cardiovascular: Edema (dose related 1% to 9%), flushing (dose related 1% to 5%), palpitations (dose related 1% to 5%), chest pain (3%), tachycardia (1% to 3%)

Central nervous system: Fatigue (dose related ≤9%), dizziness (2% to 8%)

Dermatologic: Skin rash (2%)

Gastrointestinal: Nausea (3% to 5%), abdominal distress (≤3%), diarrhea (≤3%), vomiting (≤1%)

Neuromuscular & skeletal: Weakness (≤1%)

Renal: Urinary frequency (1% to 3%)

Respiratory: Dyspnea (3%)

<1%, postmarketing, and/or case reports: Atrial fibrillation, cardiac failure, cerebrovascular accident, constipation, cough, decreased libido, depression, drowsiness, foot cramps, hyperhidrosis, hypotension, impotence, increased liver enzymes, insomnia, leg cramps, lethargy, leukopenia, myocardial infarction, nervousness, nocturia, numbness, paresthesia, pruritus, sore throat, syncope, transient ischemic attacks, urticaria, ventricular fibrillation, visual disturbance, xerostomia

General Dosage Range Dosage adjustment recommended in patients with hepatic or renal impairment

Oral: *Adults:* Initial: 2.5 mg twice daily; Usual range: 2.5-10 mg daily

Mechanism of Action Inhibits calcium ion from entering the "slow channels" or select voltage-sensitive areas of vascular smooth muscle and myocardium during depolarization, producing relaxation of vascular smooth muscle, resulting in coronary vasodilation and reduced blood pressure; increases myocardial oxygen delivery in patients with vasospastic angina

Pharmacodynamics/Kinetics

Onset of Action 2-3 hours; **Note:** Full hypotensive effect may not occur for 2-4 weeks

Duration of Action >12 hours

Half-life Elimination Alpha half-life: 1.5-2 hours; Terminal half-life: 8 hours

Time to Peak Serum: 1-1.5 hours

Pregnancy Risk Factor C

Pregnancy Considerations Adverse events were not observed in animal reproduction studies when using doses that were not maternally toxic. Isradipine crosses the human placenta (Lunell, 1993). Untreated chronic maternal hypertension is associated with adverse events in the fetus, infant, and mother. If treatment for hypertension during pregnancy is needed, other agents are preferred (ACOG, 2013).

Dental Comment See Local Anesthetic/Vasoconstrictor Precautions

Itraconazole (i tra KOE na zole)

Brand Names: US Onmel; Sporanox; Sporanox Pulsepak

Brand Names: Canada Sporanox

Generic Availability (US) May be product dependent

Pharmacologic Category Antifungal Agent, Oral

Dental Use Treatment of susceptible fungal infections in immunocompromised and immunocompetent patients including blastomycosis and histoplasmosis; has activity against *Aspergillus, Candida, Coccidioides, Cryptococcus, Sporothrix,* and chromomycosis. Useful in superficial mycoses including dermatophytoses (eg, tinea capitis), pityriasis versicolor, sebopsoriasis, vaginal and chronic mucocutaneous candidiases; systemic mycoses including candidiasis, meningeal and disseminated cryptococcal infections, paracoccidioidomycosis, coccidioidomycoses; miscellaneous mycoses such as sporotrichosis, chromomycosis, leishmaniasis, fungal keratitis, alternariosis, zygomycosis.

Use

Aspergillosis (capsules): Treatment of pulmonary and extrapulmonary aspergillosis in immunocompromised and nonimmunocompromised patients who are intolerant of or refractory to amphotericin B therapy. **Note:** IDSA Aspergillosis guidelines recommend amphotericin B formulations for invasive aspergillosis (initial or salvage) only when voriconazole is contraindicated or not tolerated (IDSA [Patterson 2016]).

Blastomycosis (capsules): Treatment of pulmonary and extrapulmonary blastomycosis in immunocompromised and nonimmunocompromised patients.

Histoplasmosis (capsules): Treatment of histoplasmosis, including chronic cavitary pulmonary disease and disseminated, nonmeningeal histoplasmosis in immunocompromised and nonimmunocompromised patients.

Onychomycosis:

Capsules: Treatment of onychomycosis of the toenail, with or without fingernail involvement, and onychomycosis of the fingernail caused by dermatophytes (tinea unguium) in nonimmunocompromised patients

Tablets: Treatment of onychomycosis of the toenail caused by *Trichophyton rubrum* or *Trichophyton mentagrophytes* in nonimmunocompromised patients

Oropharyngeal/Esophageal candidiasis (oral solution): Treatment of oropharyngeal and esophageal candidiasis

***Canadian labeling:* Oral capsules: Additional indications (not in US labeling):**

Candidiasis, oral and/or esophageal: Treatment of oral and/or esophageal candidiasis in immunocompromised and immunocompetent patients

Chromomycosis: Treatment of chromomycosis in immunocompromised and immunocompetent patients

Dermatomycoses: Treatment of dermatomycoses due to tinea pedis, tinea cruris, tinea corporis, and of pityriasis versicolor in patients for whom oral therapy is appropriate

Onychomycosis: Treatment of onychomycosis in immunocompromised and immunocompetent patients

Paracoccidioidomycosis: Treatment of paracoccidioidomycosis in immunocompromised and immunocompetent patients

Sporotrichosis: Treatment of cutaneous and lymphatic sporotrichosis in immunocompromised and immunocompetent patients

Local Anesthetic/Vasoconstrictor Precautions No information available to require special precautions

Effects on Dental Treatment No significant effects or complications reported

Effects on Bleeding No information available to require special precautions

Adverse Reactions

>10%: Gastrointestinal: Diarrhea (2% to 11%), nausea (2% to 11%)

1% to 10%:

Cardiovascular: Edema (4%), chest pain (3%), hypertension (2% to 3%),

Central nervous system: Headache (1% to 10%), dizziness (1% to 4%), anxiety (3%), depression (2% to 3%), fatigue (2% to 3%), pain (2% to 3%), malaise (1% to 3%), abnormal dreams (2%)

Dermatologic: Skin rash (3% to 9%), pruritus (≤5%), diaphoresis (3%)

Endocrine & metabolic: Hypertriglyceridemia (≤3%), hypokalemia (2%)

Gastrointestinal: Vomiting (5% to 7%), abdominal pain (2% to 6%), dyspepsia (≤4%), flatulence (≤4%), gastrointestinal disease (≤4%), gingivitis (3%), aphthous stomatitis (≤3%), constipation (2% to 3%), gastritis (2%), gastroenteritis (2%), increased appetite (2%)

Genitourinary: Cystitis (3%), urinary tract infection (1% to 3%)

Hepatic: Abnormal hepatic function tests (≤4%), increased liver enzymes (3% to 4%)

Infection: Herpes zoster (2%)

Neuromuscular & skeletal: Bursitis (3%), myalgia (≤3%), tremor (2%), weakness (≤2%)

Respiratory: Rhinitis (5% to 9%), upper respiratory tract infection (6% to 8%), sinusitis (2% to 7%), cough (1% to 4%), dyspnea (2%), increased bronchial secretions (2%), pneumonia (2%), pharyngitis (≤2%)

Miscellaneous: Fever (2% to 7%)

<2%, postmarketing, and/or case reports: Abnormal urinalysis, acute generalized exanthematous pustulosis, adrenocortical insufficiency, albuminuria, alopecia, anaphylactoid reaction, anaphylaxis, angioedema, anorexia, arthralgia, blurred vision, cardiac arrhythmia, cardiac failure, chills, confusion, congestive heart failure, decreased libido, dehydration, diplopia, drowsiness, dysgeusia, dysphagia, erectile dysfunction, erythema multiforme, erythematous rash, exfoliative dermatitis, facial edema, gynecomastia, hearing loss, hematuria, hepatic failure, hepatitis, hepatotoxicity, hot flash, hyperbilirubinemia, hyperglycemia, hyperhidrosis, hyperkalemia, hypersensitivity angiitis, hypersensitivity reaction, hypoesthesia, hypomagnesemia, hypotension, impotence, increased blood urea nitrogen, increased creatine phosphokinase, increased gamma-glutamyl transferase, increased lactate dehydrogenase, increased serum alkaline phosphatase, increased serum ALT, increased serum AST, insomnia, jaundice, left heart failure, leukopenia, menstrual disease, mucosal inflammation, neutropenia, orthostatic hypotension, pancreatitis, paresthesia, peripheral edema, peripheral neuropathy, pharyngolaryngeal pain, pollakiuria, pulmonary edema, renal insufficiency, rigors, serum sickness, sinus bradycardia, skin photosensitivity, Stevens-Johnson syndrome, tachycardia, thrombocytopenia, tinnitus, toxic epidermal necrolysis, urinary incontinence, urticaria, vasculitis, vertigo, voice disorder

Dental Usual Dosage Oropharyngeal candidiasis: Adults: Oral solution: 200 mg once daily for 1-2 weeks; in patients unresponsive or refractory to fluconazole: 100 mg twice daily (clinical response expected in 1-2 weeks)

Dosing

Adult & Geriatric Note: Capsule and oral solution formulations are not bioequivalent (oral solution has higher bioavailability) and thus are not interchangeable. Generally, oral solution is the preferred formulation because of improved absorption (IDSA [Kauffman 2007]; HHS [OI adult 2016]).

Aspergillosis, invasive (salvage therapy):

Manufacturer's labeling: Oral capsule: 200 to 400 mg daily. For life-threatening infections, administer a loading dose of 200 mg 3 times daily (total: 600 mg daily) for the first 3 days of therapy. Continue treatment for at least 3 months and until clinical and laboratory evidence suggest that infection has resolved.

Alternate recommendations: Oral solution: 200 mg twice daily; duration of therapy is a minimum of 6 to 12 weeks, although duration is highly dependent on degree/duration of immunosuppression, disease site, and evidence of disease improvement (IDSA [Patterson 2016])

Blastomycosis: *Manufacturer labeling:* Oral capsule: Initial: 200 mg once daily; if no clinical improvement or evidence of progressive infection, may increase dose in increments of 100 mg up to maximum of

400 mg daily. Doses >200 mg daily should be administered in 2 divided doses. **Note:** For life-threatening infections, the US labeling recommends administering a loading dose of 200 mg 3 times daily (total: 600 mg daily) for the first 3 days of therapy. Continue treatment for at least 3 months and until clinical and laboratory evidence suggest that infection has resolved.

Alternative dosing: 200 mg 3 times daily for 3 days, then 200 mg twice daily for 6 to 12 months; in moderately severe to severe infection, therapy should be initiated with ~2 weeks of amphotericin B (Chapman 2008).

Candidiasis: Oral:

Esophageal:

US labeling: Oral solution: 100 to 200 mg once daily for a minimum of 3 weeks; continue dosing for 2 weeks after resolution of symptoms

Alternate dosing: Oral solution: Fluconazole-refractory disease: 200 mg once daily for 14 to 21 days (IDSA [Pappas 2016])

Canadian labeling:

Oral solution: 100 to 200 mg once daily for a minimum of 3 weeks; continue dosing for 2 weeks after resolution of symptoms

Oral capsules: 100 mg once daily for 4 weeks; increase dose to 200 mg once daily in patients with AIDS and neutropenic patients

Alternate dosing: HIV-infected patients: Oral solution: 200 mg once daily for 14 to 21 days (HHS [OI adult 2016])

Oropharyngeal:

US labeling: Oral solution: 200 mg once daily for 1 to 2 weeks; in patients unresponsive or refractory to fluconazole: 100 mg twice daily (clinical response expected in 2 to 4 weeks)

Alternate dosing: Oral solution: Fluconazole-refractory disease: 200 mg once daily for up to 28 days (IDSA [Pappas 2016])

Canadian labeling:

Oral solution: 200 mg once daily or in divided doses daily for 1 to 2 weeks

Oral capsules: 100 mg once daily for 2 weeks; increase dose to 200 mg once daily in patients with AIDS and neutropenic patients

Alternate dosing: HIV-infected patients (alternative to preferred therapy): Oral solution: 200 mg once daily for 7 to 14 days (HHS [OI adult 2016])

Vulvo-vaginal (uncomplicated) in HIV-infected patients (alternative to preferred therapy) (off-label use): Oral solution: 200 mg once daily for 3 to 7 days (HHS [OI adult 2016])

Chromomycosis: Canadian labeling (not in US labeling): Oral: 200 mg once daily for 6 months (when due to *Fonsecaea pedrosoi*) or 100 mg once daily for 3 months (when due to *Cladosporium carrioni*)

Coccidioidomycosis (nonprogressive, nondisseminated disease): 200 mg twice daily or 3 times daily (Galgiani 2005)

Coccidioidal pneumonia: Oral:

Mild to moderate: 200 mg twice daily (Galgiani 2005)

HIV-infected patients (focal pneumonia): 200 mg twice daily (HHS [OI adult 2016])

Coccidioidal meningitis: Oral: 400 to 600 mg daily (Galgiani 2005)

Coccidioidal meningitis in HIV-infected patients (off-label use) (HHS [OI adult 2016]) (alternative to preferred therapy): Oral:

Treatment: 200 mg 3 times daily for 3 days, then 200 mg twice daily, followed by chronic suppressive therapy

Chronic suppressive therapy: 200 mg twice daily continued indefinitely, even with increase in CD4 count on ART

Cryptococcosis in HIV-infected patients (off-label use) (alternative to preferred therapy): Oral: *Treatment, consolidation therapy:* 200 mg twice daily for ≥8 weeks (HHS [OI adult 2016])

Histoplasmosis:

Treatment:

Manufacturer's labeling: Oral capsule: Initial: 200 mg once daily; if no clinical improvement or evidence of progressive infection, may increase dose in increments of 100 mg up to maximum of 400 mg daily. Doses >200 mg daily should be administered in 2 divided doses. **Note:** For life-threatening infections, the US labeling recommends administering a loading dose of 200 mg 3 times daily (total: 600 mg daily) for the first 3 days of therapy. Continue treatment for at least 3 months and until clinical and laboratory evidence suggest that infection has resolved.

Alternate dosing: 200 mg 3 times daily for 3 days, then 200 mg twice daily (or once daily in mild-moderate disease) for 6 to 12 weeks in mild-moderate disease or ≥12 months in progressive disseminated or chronic cavitary pulmonary histoplasmosis; in moderately severe to severe infection, therapy should be initiated with ~2 weeks of a lipid formation of amphotericin B (Wheat, 2007). Duration of twice daily maintenance therapy should be at least 12 months in HIV-infected patients (HHS [OI adult 2016])

Prophylaxis (off-label use):

Primary prophylaxis in HIV-infected patients: 200 mg once daily; primary prophylaxis is indicated when CD4 count <150 cells/mm^3 and at increased risk of exposure (HHS [OI adult 2016])

Long-term suppression therapy (secondary prophylaxis) in HIV-infected patients: 200 mg once daily; long-term suppressive therapy is indicated in patients who relapse despite appropriate therapy or in patients with CNS or severe disseminated infection (HHS [OI adult 2016])

Microsporidiosis, disseminated (caused by *Trachipleistophora* or *Anncaliia*) in HIV-infected patients (off-label use): Oral: 400 mg once daily in combination with albendazole (HHS [OI adult 2016])

Onychomycosis (fingernail involvement only): Oral capsule: 200 mg twice daily for 1 week; repeat 1-week course after 3-week off-time

Onychomycosis (toenails due to *Trichophyton rubrum* or *T. mentagrophytes*): Oral tablet: 200 mg once daily for 12 consecutive weeks.

Onychomycosis (toenails with or without fingernail involvement): Oral capsule: 200 mg once daily for 12 consecutive weeks

Canadian labeling (not in US labeling): "Pulse-dosing": 200 mg twice daily for 1 week; repeat 1-week course twice with 3-week off-time between each course

Paracoccidioidomycosis: Canadian labeling (not in US labeling): Oral capsule: 100 mg once daily for 6 months

Penicilliosis in HIV-infected patients (off-label use) (HHS [OI adult 2016]): Oral:

Primary prophylaxis: 200 mg once daily for patients with a CD4 count <100 cells/mm^3 who spend extensive time in northern Thailand, Vietnam, and Southern China, especially rural areas

Treatment: 200 mg twice daily for 8 weeks (mild disease) or 10 weeks (severe infections), then continue with maintenance therapy. In severely-ill patients, initiate therapy with 2 weeks of liposomal amphotericin B.

Chronic maintenance (secondary prophylaxis): 200 mg once daily until CD4 count >100 cells/mm^3 for ≥6 months in response to ART

Pityriasis versicolor: Canadian labeling (not in US labeling): Oral: 200 mg once daily for 7 days

Sporotrichosis: Oral:

Lymphocutaneous: 200 mg daily for 3 to 6 months (Kauffman, 2007)

Canadian labeling (not in US labeling): 100 mg once daily for 3 months

Osteoarticular and pulmonary: 200 mg twice daily for ≥1 years (may use amphotericin B initially for stabilization) (Kauffman, 2007)

Tinea corporis or tinea cruris: Canadian labeling (not in US labeling): Oral capsule: 100 mg once daily for 14 consecutive days or 200 mg once daily for 7 consecutive days. **Note:** Equivalency between regimens not established.

Tinea pedis: Canadian labeling (not in US labeling): Oral capsule: 100 mg once daily for 28 consecutive days or 200 mg twice daily for 7 consecutive days. **Note:** Equivalency between regimens not established. Patients with chronic resistant infection may benefit from lower dose and extended treatment time (100 mg once daily for 28 days).

Pediatric Note: Capsule and oral solution formulations are not bioequivalent (oral solution has higher bioavailability) and thus are not interchangeable. Generally, oral solution is the preferred formulation because of improved absorption (HHS [OI pediatric 2013]).

Usual dosage range: Limited data available: Infants, Children, and Adolescents: Oral capsule or solution: 2.5 to 5 mg/kg/dose every 12 hours for treatment; for relapse prevention, once daily dose may be considered; usual maximum daily dose: 200 mg/day (Bradley 2015; *Red Book* [AAP 2015]); some infections may require up to 400 mg/day.

Indication-specific dosing:

Blastomycosis (off-label population) (Chapman 2008; *Red Book* [AAP 2015]): Limited data available: Infants, Children, and Adolescents: Oral capsule or solution:

Mild to moderate pulmonary and extrapulmonary disease: 5 mg/kg/dose twice daily for 6 to 12 months; maximum dose: 200 mg/dose.

Severe or CNS infection (step down therapy after amphotericin B response): 5 mg/kg/dose twice daily; total therapy duration: At least 12 months; maximum dose: 200 mg/dose.

Candidiasis (HIV-exposed/-positive) (HHS [OI adult 2016]; HHS [OI pediatric 2013]): Oral solution: Limited data available:

Oropharyngeal, treatment (off-label population):

Infants and Children: If fluconazole-refractory: 2.5 mg/kg/dose twice daily for 7 to 14 days; maximum daily dose range: 200 to 400 mg/**day**

Adolescents: 200 mg once daily for 7 to 14 days

Esophageal, treatment (off-label population):

Infants and Children: 2.5 mg/kg/dose twice daily for at least 21 days and at least 2 weeks following resolution of symptoms

Adolescents: 200 mg once daily for 14 to 21 days

Vulvovaginal, uncomplicated (off-label use): Adolescents: 200 mg once daily for 3 to 7 days

Secondary prophylaxis (off-label use):

Infants and Children: 2.5 mg/kg/dose twice daily, maximum daily dose: 200 mg/**day**

Adolescents: Oropharyngeal candidiasis (suppressive): 200 mg once daily

Candidiasis, invasive (off-label use): Oral solution: Limited data available:

Primary prophylaxis (ESCMID [Hope 2012]): Children ≥2 years and Adolescents:

AML and recurrent leukemia: 2.5 mg/kg every 12 hours after last dose of chemotherapy; continue until neutrophil recovery.

HSCT, allogeneic: 2.5 mg/kg every 12 hours after completion of the conditioning regimen; continue until at least day +100.

HSCT, autologous: 2.5 mg/kg every 12 hours after last dose of chemotherapy; continue until neutrophil recovery.

Coccidioidomycosis, (HIV-exposed/-positive) (off-label use) (HHS [OI adult 2016]; HHS [OI pediatric 2013]):

Treatment:

Mild to moderate infection, non-CNS (eg, focal pneumonitis):

Infants and Children: Oral solution: 2 to 5 mg/kg/dose 3 times daily for 3 days followed by 2 to 5 mg/kg/dose twice daily; maximum dose: 200 mg/dose. Duration of treatment determined by rate of clinical response. For skeletal infection, 5 mg/kg/dose twice daily for 12 months (Bradley 2015).

Adolescents: Oral: 200 mg twice daily.

Severe infection, non-CNS (with amphotericin B or as step down therapy after amphotericin B response):

Infants and Children: Oral: 5 mg/kg/dose twice daily; total therapy duration: at least 12 months; maximum dose: 200 mg/dose. Product formulation not specified.

Adolescents: Oral: 200 mg twice daily.

CNS disease/meningitis:

Infants and Children: Not recommended; drug of choice for this age group is fluconazole.

Adolescents: Oral: 200 mg 3 times daily for 3 days, then 200 mg twice daily; product formulation not specified.

Relapse prevention:

Infants and Children: Oral: 2 to 5 mg/kg/dose twice daily; maximum dose: 200 mg/dose

Adolescents: Oral: 200 mg twice daily

Cryptococcus (HIV-exposed/-positive) (off-label use) (HHS [OI pediatric 2013]): Infants and Children: Oral solution: Limited data available:

Treatment, consolidation therapy: Oral solution (preferred): Initial: 2.5 to 5 mg/kg/dose 3 times daily (maximum daily dose: 600 mg daily) for 3 days (9 doses) followed by 5 to 10 mg/kg/day divided once or twice daily (maximum daily dose: 400 mg daily) for a minimum of 8 weeks

Relapse prevention: 5 mg/kg/dose once daily (maximum daily dose: 200 mg/day).

Histoplasmosis (off-label population) (HHS [OI adult 2016]; HHS [OI pediatric 2013]; IDSA [Wheat 2007]; *Red Book* [AAP 2015]): Oral solution (preferred): Limited data available:

Primary prophylaxis in HIV-infected patients: Adolescents: Refer to adult dosing.

Treatment, acute primary pulmonary disease: Infants and Children: 2 to 5 mg/kg/dose 3 times daily for 3 days (9 doses) followed by 2 to 5 mg/kg/dose twice daily; maximum dose: 200 mg/dose. Duration of therapy for HIV-exposed/-positive patients is 12 months or for HIV-exposed/-positive children with functional cellular immunity (CD4 percentage >20% or >300 cells/mm^3 if age ≥6 years) 12 weeks of treatment may be adequate if clinically improved and urine antigen concentrations decreased. For non-HIV-exposed/-positive patients, a duration of 6 to 12 weeks is recommended depending on severity.

Treatment, mild disseminated disease:

Infants and Children: 2 to 5 mg/kg/dose 3 times daily for 3 days (9 doses) followed by 2 to 5 mg/kg/dose twice daily; maximum dose: 200 mg/dose. Duration for HIV-exposed/-positive patients: At least 12 months. Duration for non-HIV-exposed/-positive: 3 months.

Adolescents: 200 mg 3 times daily for 3 days, then 200 mg twice daily. Duration for HIV-exposed/-positive patients: At least 12 months. Duration for non-HIV-exposed/-positive: 3 months.

Consolidation treatment for moderate-severe to severe disseminated disease, including CNS infection (following appropriate induction therapy):

Infants and Children: 2 to 5 mg/kg/dose 3 times daily for 3 days (9 doses) followed by 2 to 5 mg/kg/dose twice daily; maximum dose: 200 mg/dose. Duration for HIV-exposed/-positive patients: 12 months for non-CNS disseminated disease or for ≥12 months for CNS infection as determined by clinical response. Duration for non-HIV-exposed/-positive: At least 3 months.

Adolescents: 200 mg 3 times daily for 3 days (disseminated disease) or until resolution of abnormal CSF findings (CNS infection), then 200 mg twice daily. Duration for HIV-exposed/-positive patients: 12 months for non-CNS disseminated disease or for ≥12 months for CNS infection as determined by clinical response. Duration for non-HIV-exposed/-positive: At least 3 months.

Long-term suppression therapy (secondary prophylaxis):

Infants and Children: 5 to 10 mg/kg/dose once daily; maximum dose: 200 mg/dose

Adolescents: Refer to adult dosing.

Microsporidiosis, disseminated (caused by *Trachipleistophora* or *Anncaliia*) in HIV-infected patients (off-label use): Adolescents: Refer to adult dosing.

Penicilliosis in HIV-infected patients (off-label use): Adolescents: Refer to adult dosing.

Sporotrichosis (off-label population) (Kauffman 2007; *Red Book* [AAP 2015]): Limited data available: Infants, Children, and Adolescents: Oral solution (preferred):

Lymphocutaneous or localized cutaneous: 3 to 5 mg/kg/dose twice daily; continue until 2 to 4 weeks after all lesions have resolved, usual total duration: 3 to 6 months; maximum dose: 200 mg/dose.

Visceral or disseminated (step down therapy after amphotericin B response): 3 to 5 mg/kg/dose twice daily; continue until total therapy duration: at least 12 months; maximum dose: 200 mg/dose.

Renal Impairment

The manufacturer's labeling states to use with caution in patients with renal impairment; dosage adjustment may be needed. Limited data suggest that no dosage adjustments are required in renal impairment; wide variations observed in plasma concentrations versus time profiles in patients with uremia, or receiving hemodialysis or continuous ambulatory peritoneal dialysis (Boelaert, 1988).

Hemodialysis: Nondialyzable

Hepatic Impairment There are no dosage adjustments provided in the manufacturer's labeling; however, use caution and monitor closely for signs/symptoms of toxicity.

Mechanism of Action Interferes with cytochrome P450 activity, decreasing ergosterol synthesis (principal sterol in fungal cell membrane) and inhibiting cell membrane formation

Contraindications

Hypersensitivity to itraconazole or any component of the formulation; concurrent administration with cisapride, disopyramide, dofetilide, dronedarone, eplerenone, ergot derivatives, felodipine, irinotecan, ivabradine, lovastatin, lurasidone, methadone, midazolam (oral), nisoldipine, pimozide, quinidine, ranolazine, simvastatin, ticagrelor, or triazolam; concurrent administration with colchicine, fesoterodine, telithromycin, and solifenacin in patients with varying degrees of renal or hepatic impairment; treatment of onychomycosis (or other non-life-threatening indications) in patients with evidence of ventricular dysfunction, such as congestive heart failure (CHF) or a history of CHF; treatment of onychomycosis in women who are pregnant or contemplating pregnancy

Canadian labeling: Additional contraindications (not in US labeling): Concurrent administration with domperidone, eletriptan, fesoterodine in patients with moderate to severe renal or hepatic impairment, or solifenacin in patients with severe renal impairment or moderate to severe hepatic impairment (capsule, oral solution); Concurrent administration with the following drugs (none of which are available in Canada): Astemizole, bepridil, halofantrine, ivabradine, lercanidipine, levacetylmethadol, mizolastine, telithromycin (in patients with severe renal or hepatic impairment), sertindole, terfenadine (capsule, oral solution); treatment of dermatomycosis (tinea pedis, tinea cruris, tinea corporis, pityriasis versicolor) in women who are pregnant or intend to become pregnant (capsule)

Warnings/Precautions [US Boxed Warning]: Negative inotropic effects have been observed following intravenous administration. Discontinue or reassess use if signs or symptoms of HF (heart failure) occur during treatment. [US Boxed Warning]: Use is contraindicated for treatment of onychomycosis in patients with ventricular dysfunction such as heart failure (HF) or a history of HF. Cases of HF, peripheral edema, and pulmonary edema have occurred in patients treated for onychomycosis. HF has been reported, particularly in patients receiving a total daily oral dose of 400 mg. Use with caution in patients with risk factors for HF (COPD, renal failure, edematous disorders, ischemic or valvular disease). Discontinue if signs or symptoms of HF or neuropathy occur during treatment. In a scientific statement from the American Heart Association, itraconazole has been determined to be an agent that may exacerbate underlying myocardial dysfunction (magnitude: major); may consider use when treating life-threatening fungal infections (AHA [Page 2016]). Due to potential toxicity, the manufacturer recommends confirmation of diagnosis testing of nail specimens prior to treatment of onychomycosis. The Canadian labeling contraindicates use in the treatment of dermatomycoses (tinea corporis, tinea cruris, tinea pedis, pityriasis versicolor) in patients with evidence of ventricular dysfunction or a history of HF.

[US Boxed Warning]: Coadministration with itraconazole can cause elevated plasma concentrations of certain drugs and can lead to QT prolongation and ventricular tachyarrhythmias, including torsades de pointes. Coadministration with methadone, disopyramide, dofetilide, dronedarone, quinidine, ergot alkaloids, irinotecan, lurasidone, oral midazolam, pimozide, triazolam, felodipine, nisoldipine, ranolazine, eplerenone, cisapride, lovastatin, simvastatin, ticagrelor and, in subjects with varying degrees of renal or hepatic impairment, colchicine, fesoterodine, telithromycin, and solifenacin is contraindicated. Life-threatening or cardiac dysrhythmias and/or sudden death have occurred in patients taking CYP 3A inhibitors such as cisapride, pimozide, methadone or quinidine. Additional potentially significant interactions may exist, requiring dose or frequency adjustment, additional monitoring, and/or selection of alternative therapy.

May cause CNS depression, which may impair physical or mental abilities; patients must be cautioned about performing tasks that require mental alertness (eg, operating machinery, driving). Use with caution in patients with renal impairment; dosage adjustment may be needed. Use caution in patients with a history of hypersensitivity to other azoles. Rare cases of serious hepatotoxicity (including liver failure and death) have been reported (including some cases occurring within the first week of therapy); hepatotoxicity was reported in some patients without pre-existing liver disease or risk factors. Use with caution in patients with pre-existing hepatic impairment; monitor liver function closely. Not recommended for use in patients with active liver disease, elevated liver enzymes, or prior hepatotoxic reactions to other drugs unless the expected benefit exceeds the risk of hepatotoxicity. Discontinue treatment if signs or symptoms of hepatotoxicity develop. Transient or permanent hearing loss has been reported. Quinidine (a contraindicated drug) was used concurrently in several of these cases. Hearing loss usually resolves after discontinuation, but may persist in some patients.

Large differences in itraconazole pharmacokinetic parameters have been observed in cystic fibrosis patients receiving the solution; if a patient with cystic fibrosis does not respond to therapy, alternate therapies should be considered. Due to differences in bioavailability, oral capsules and oral solution cannot be used interchangeably. Only the oral solution has proven efficacy for oral and esophageal candidiasis. Initiation of treatment with oral solution is not recommended in patients at immediate risk for systemic candidiasis (eg, patients with severe neutropenia). Absorption of itraconazole capsules is reduced when gastric acidity is reduced; administer capsules or tablets with an acidic beverage (eg, cola) in patients with reduced gastric acidity and separate administration from acid suppressive therapy. Some dosage forms may contain propylene glycol; large amounts are potentially toxic and have been associated hyperosmolality, lactic acidosis, seizures and respiratory depression; use caution (AAP, 1997; Zar, 2007). The Canadian labeling contraindicates use in the treatment of dermatomycoses (tinea corporis, tinea cruris, tinea pedis, pityriasis versicolor) in women who are pregnant or intend to become pregnant.

Drug Interactions

Metabolism/Transport Effects Substrate of CYP3A4 (major); **Note:** Assignment of Major/Minor substrate status based on clinically relevant drug interaction potential; **Inhibits** CYP3A4 (strong), P-glycoprotein

Avoid Concomitant Use

Avoid concomitant use of Itraconazole with any of the following: Ado-Trastuzumab Emtansine; Alfuzosin; Aliskiren; ALPRAZolam; Aprepitant; Astemizole; Asunaprevir; Avanafil; Axitinib; Barnidipine; Blonanserin; Bosutinib; Bromocriptine; Budesonide (Systemic); Ceritinib; Cisapride; Clobetasone; Cobimetinib; Conivaptan; Crizotinib; CYP3A4 Inducers (Strong); Dabrafenib; Dapoxetine; Dihydroergotamine; Disopyramide; Dofetilide; Domperidone; Dronedarone; Efavirenz; Eletriptan; Eplerenone; Ergoloid Mesylates; Ergonovine; Ergotamine; Estazolam; Everolimus; Felodipine; Flibanserin; Fusidic Acid (Systemic); Halofantrine; Ibrutinib; Idelalisib; Irinotecan Products; Isavuconazonium Sulfate; Ivabradine; Lapatinib; Lercanidipine; Lomitapide; Lovastatin; Lumacaftor; Lurasidone; Macitentan; Methadone; Methylergonovine; Midazolam; Naloxegol; Nevirapine; Nilotinib; NiMODipine; Nisoldipine; Olaparib; Palbociclib; PAZOPanib; Pimozide; QuiNIDine; Radotinib; Ranolazine; Red Yeast Rice; Regorafenib; Rivaroxaban; Rupatadine; Saccharomyces boulardii; Salmeterol; Silodosin; Simeprevir; Simvastatin; Sonidegib; Suvorexant; Tamsulosin; Telithromycin; Terfenadine; Ticagrelor; Tolvaptan; Topotecan; Toremifene; Trabectedin; Triazolam; Udenafil; Ulipristal; Vemurafenib; VinCRIStine (Liposomal); Vinflunine; Vorapaxar

Increased Effect/Toxicity

Itraconazole may increase the levels/effects of: Ado-Trastuzumab Emtansine; Afatinib; Alfuzosin; Aliskiren; Alitretinoin (Systemic); Almotriptan; Alosetron; ALPRAZolam; Apixaban; Aprepitant; ARIPiprazole; ARIPiprazole Lauroxil; Astemizole; Asunaprevir; AtorvaSTATin; Avanafil; Axitinib; Barnidipine; Bedaquiline; Benperidol; Bilastine; Blonanserin; Boceprevir; Bortezomib; Bosentan; Bosutinib; Brentuximab Vedotin; Brexpiprazole; Brinzolamide; Bromocriptine; Budesonide (Nasal); Budesonide (Oral Inhalation); Budesonide (Systemic); Budesonide (Topical); Buprenorphine; BusPIRone; Busulfan; Cabazitaxel; Cabozantinib; Calcifediol; Calcium Channel Blockers; Cannabidiol; Cannabis; Cardiac Glycosides; Cariprazine; Ceritinib; Cilostazol; Cisapride; Clobetasone; CloZAPine; Cobicistat; Cobimetinib; Colchicine; Conivaptan; Corticosteroids (Orally Inhaled); Corticosteroids (Systemic); Crizotinib; CycloSPORINE (Systemic); CYP3A4 Substrates; Dabigatran Etexilate; Dabrafenib; Daclatasvir; Dapoxetine; Darunavir; Dasatinib; Deflazacort; Delamanid; Dienogest; Dihydroergotamine; Disopyramide; DOCEtaxel; Dofetilide; Domperidone; DOXOrubicin (Conventional); Dronabinol; Dronedarone; Drospirenone; Dutasteride; Edoxaban; Eletriptan; Eliglustat; Elvitegravir; Eplerenone; Ergoloid Mesylates; Ergonovine; Ergotamine; Erlotinib; Estazolam; Eszopiclone; Etizolam; Etravirine;

Everolimus; Felodipine; FentaNYL; Fesoterodine; Fexofenadine; Flibanserin; Fluticasone (Nasal); Fluticasone (Oral Inhalation); Fosamprenavir; Gefitinib; GuanFACINE; Halofantrine; Highest Risk QTc-Prolonging Agents; HYDROcodone; HydrOXYzine; Ibrutinib; Iloperidone; Imatinib; Imidafenacin; Indinavir; Irinotecan Products; Isavuconazonium Sulfate; Ivabradine; Ivacaftor; Ixabepilone; Lacosamide; Lapatinib; Lercanidipine; Levobupivacaine; Levomilnacipran; Lomitapide; Losartan; Lovastatin; Lurasidone; Macitentan; Manidipine; Maraviroc; MedroxyPROGESTERone; Methadone; Methylergonovine; MethylPREDNISolone; Midazolam; MiFEPRIStone; Mirodenafil; Moderate Risk QTc-Prolonging Agents; Naldemedine; Naloxegol; Nilotinib; NiMODipine; Nintedanib; Nisoldipine; Olaparib; Ospemifene; Oxybutynin; OxyCODONE; Palbociclib; Paliperidone; Panobinostat; Parecoxib; Paricalcitol; PAZOPanib; P-glycoprotein/ABCB1 Substrates; Pimavanserin; Pimecrolimus; Pimozide; PONATinib; Pranlukast; Pravastatin; Praziquantel; PrednisoLONE (Systemic); PredniSONE; Propafenone; Prucalopride; QUEtiapine; QuiNIDine; Radotinib; Ramelteon; Ranolazine; Reboxetine; Red Yeast Rice; Regorafenib; Repaglinide; Retapamulin; Ribociclib; RifAXIMin; Rilpivirine; Riociguat; Rivaroxaban; RomiDEPsin; Rosuvastatin; Rupatadine; Ruxolitinib; Salmeterol; Saquinavir; SAXagliptin; Sildenafil; Silodosin; Simeprevir; Simvastatin; Sirolimus; Solifenacin; Sonidegib; SORAfenib; SUNItinib; Suvorexant; Tacrolimus (Systemic); Tacrolimus (Topical); Tadalafil; Tamsulosin; Tasimelteon; Telaprevir; Telithromycin; Temsirolimus; Terfenadine; Tetrahydrocannabinol; Ticagrelor; Tofacitinib; Tolterodine; Tolvaptan; Topotecan; Toremifene; Trabectedin; TraMADol; Triazolam; Udenafil; Ulipristal; Vardenafil; Vemurafenib; Venetoclax; Vilazodone; VinBLAStine; VinCRIStine; VinCRIStine (Liposomal); Vindesine; Vinflunine; Vinorelbine; Vitamin K Antagonists; Vorapaxar; Zolpidem; Zopiclone; Zuclopenthixol

The levels/effects of Itraconazole may be increased by: Boceprevir; Cobicistat; Conivaptan; CYP3A4 Inhibitors (Moderate); CYP3A4 Inhibitors (Strong); Darunavir; Etravirine; Fosamprenavir; Fusidic Acid (Systemic); Grapefruit Juice; Idelalisib; Indinavir; Lopinavir; MiFEPRIStone; Netupitant; Ritonavir; Saquinavir; Stiripentol; Telaprevir; Telithromycin; Tipranavir

Decreased Effect

Itraconazole may decrease the levels/effects of: Amphotericin B; Doxercalciferol; Ifosfamide; Meloxicam; Prasugrel; Saccharomyces boulardii; Ticagrelor

The levels/effects of Itraconazole may be decreased by: Antacids; Bosentan; CYP3A4 Inducers (Moderate); CYP3A4 Inducers (Strong); Deferasirox; Didanosine; Efavirenz; Etravirine; Grapefruit Juice; H2-Antagonists; Isoniazid; Lumacaftor; Nevirapine; Proton Pump Inhibitors; Siltuximab; St John's Wort; Tocilizumab

Food Interactions

Capsules: Absorption enhanced by food and possibly by gastric acidity. Cola drinks have been shown to increase the absorption of the capsules in patients with achlorhydria or those taking H_2-receptor antagonists or other gastric acid suppressors. Grapefruit/grapefruit juice may increase serum levels. Management: Take capsules immediately after meals. Avoid grapefruit juice.

Solution: Food decreases the bioavailability and increases the time to peak concentration. Management: Take solution on an empty stomach 1 hour before or 2 hours after meals.

Dietary Considerations

Capsule, tablet: Take with food.

Solution: Take without food, if possible.

Pharmacodynamics/Kinetics

Half-life Elimination

Children (6 months to 12 years): Oral solution: ~36 hours; Metabolite hydroxy-itraconazole: ~18 hours

Adults: Oral: Single dose: 16 to 28 hours, Multiple doses: 42 to 49 hours; Cirrhosis (single dose): 37 hours (range: 20 to 54 hours)

Time to Peak Plasma: Capsules/tablets: 2 to 5 hours; Oral solution: 2.5 hours

Pregnancy Risk Factor C

Pregnancy Considerations Dose-related adverse events were observed in animal reproduction studies at maternally toxic doses. Itraconazole exposure during the first trimester of pregnancy has not been associated with congenital malformations; however, an increase in the rate of early fetal loss has been reported (Bar-Oz 2000; DeSantis 2009; Molgaard-Nielsen 2013). Congenital abnormalities (eg, skeletal, genitourinary tract, cardiovascular and ophthalmic malformations, chromosomal abnormalities, and multiple malformations) have been reported during postmarketing surveillance; however, a causal relationship has not been established.

Itraconazole is approved for the treatment of various fungal infections; however, when treatment of a systemic fungal infection is needed in pregnant women, itraconazole should be avoided, especially during the first trimester (Chapman 2008; Galgiani 2005; HHS [OI adult 2015]; Pappas 2016; Perfect 2010; Wheat 2007).

Due to the potential risk of congenital malformations, the manufacturer recommends that when used for the treatment of onychomycosis in women of reproductive potential, effective contraception should be used during treatment and for 2 months following treatment. Therapy should begin on the second or third day following menses.

Breastfeeding Considerations Itraconazole is excreted into breast milk. According to the manufacturer, the decision to continue or discontinue breastfeeding during therapy should take into account the risk of infant exposure, the benefits of breastfeeding to the infant, and benefits of treatment to the mother (Sporanox prescribing information 2015).

In the United States, where formula is accessible, affordable, safe, and sustainable, and the risk of infant mortality due to diarrhea and respiratory infections is low, complete avoidance of breastfeeding is recommended in women who are coinfected with HIV to decrease potential transmission of HIV (HHS [perinatal] 2016).

Dosage Forms

Capsule, Oral:

Sporanox: 100 mg

Sporanox Pulsepak: 100 mg

Generic: 100 mg

Solution, Oral:

Sporanox: 10 mg/mL (150 mL)

Tablet, Oral:

Onmel: 200 mg

Ivabradine (eye VAB ra deen)

Brand Names: US Corlanor

Pharmacologic Category Cardiovascular Agent, Miscellaneous

Use Heart failure: To reduce the risk of hospitalization for worsening heart failure in patients with stable, symptomatic (NYHA class II to III according to the ACC/AHA/HFSA heart failure guidelines [Yancy 2016]) chronic heart failure with left ventricular ejection fraction ≤35%, who are in sinus rhythm with resting heart rate ≥70 beats per minute (bpm) and either are on maximally tolerated doses of beta blockers or have a contraindication to beta-blocker use.

Local Anesthetic/Vasoconstrictor Precautions No information available to require special precautions

Effects on Dental Treatment No significant effects or complications reported

Effects on Bleeding No information available to require special precautions

Adverse Reactions

1% to 10%:

Cardiovascular: Bradycardia (6% to 10%), hypertension (9%), atrial fibrillation (5% to 8%)

Central nervous system: Phosphene (3%)

Frequency not defined: Cardiovascular: Heart block, sinoatrial arrest

<1%, postmarketing, and/or case reports: Angioedema, diplopia, erythema, hypotension, pruritus, skin rash, syncope, torsades de pointes, urticaria, ventricular fibrillation, ventricular tachycardia, vertigo, visual impairment

Mechanism of Action Selective and specific inhibition of the hyperpolarization-activated cyclic nucleotide-gated (HCN) channels (f-channels) within the sinoatrial (SA) node of cardiac tissue resulting in disruption of If ion current flow prolonging diastolic depolarization, slowing firing in the SA node, and ultimately reducing heart rate. Has not demonstrated effects on myocardial contractility or relaxation, ventricular repolarization, or conduction apart from the sinus node effects. Partial inhibition of the retinal I_h current (similar to the cardiac I_f current) may explain visual disturbances (eg, phosphenes) (Nawarskas 2015).

Pharmacodynamics/Kinetics

Half-life Elimination Distribution half-life: 2 hours; Effective half-life: ~6 hours

Time to Peak Plasma: ~1 hour (fasting); ~2 hours (with food)

Pregnancy Considerations Adverse events have been observed in animal reproduction studies, and fetal harm may occur if ivabradine is administered to pregnant women. Effective contraception is recommended in women of reproductive potential. If treatment is needed during pregnancy, closely monitor for destabilization of heart failure that could potentially result from heart rate slowing caused by ivabradine, especially during the first trimester. Pregnant women with chronic heart failure should also be monitored for preterm birth.

Ivacaftor (eye va KAF tor)

Brand Names: US Kalydeco

Brand Names: Canada Kalydeco

Pharmacologic Category Cystic Fibrosis Transmembrane Conductance Regulator Potentiator

Use

Cystic fibrosis:

US labeling: For the treatment of cystic fibrosis (CF) in patients ≥2 years of age who have one of the following mutations in the cystic fibrosis transmembrane conductance regulator (CFTR) gene: G551D, G1244E, G1349D, G178R, G551S, R117H, S1251N, S1255P, S549N, or S549R.

If the patient's genotype is unknown, a US Food and Drug Administration-cleared cystic fibrosis mutation test should be used to detect the presence of a CFTR mutation followed by verification with bidirectional sequencing when recommended by the mutation test instructions for use.

Canadian labeling: For the treatment of cystic fibrosis (CF) in patients ≥6 years of age who have one of the following mutations in the cystic fibrosis transmembrane conductance regulator (CFTR) gene: G551D, G1244E, G1349D, G178R, G551S, S1251N, S1255P, S549N, S549R, or G970R; patients ≥18 years with an R117H mutation in the CFTR gene

Limitations of use: According to the manufacturer labeling, ivacaftor is not effective in patients with CF who are homozygous for the F508del mutation in the CTFR gene.

Local Anesthetic/Vasoconstrictor Precautions No information available to require special precautions

Effects on Dental Treatment Key adverse event(s) related to dental treatment: Oropharyngeal pain has been reported

Effects on Bleeding No information available to require special precautions

Adverse Reactions Frequency not always defined.

>10%:

Central nervous system: Headache (24%)

Dermatologic: Skin rash (13%)

Gastrointestinal: Abdominal pain (16%), diarrhea (13%), nausea (12%)

Respiratory: Oropharyngeal pain (22%), upper respiratory tract infection (22%), nasal congestion (20%), nasopharyngitis (15%)

1% to 10%:

Central nervous system: Dizziness (9%)

Dermatologic: Acne vulgaris (4% to 7%)

Endocrine & metabolic: Increased serum glucose (4% to 7%), hypoglycemia

Hepatic: Increased liver enzymes (4% to 7%), increased serum ALT (4% to 7%)

Neuromuscular & skeletal: Arthralgia (4% to 7%), musculoskeletal chest pain (4% to 7%), myalgia (4% to 7%)

Ophthalmic: Cataract (children ≤12)

Respiratory: Change in bronchial secretions (4% to 7%; bacteria present), pharyngeal erythema (4% to 7%), pleuritic chest pain (4% to 7%), rhinitis (4% to 7%), sinus congestion (4% to 7%), sinus headache (4% to 7%), wheezing (4% to 7%)

Miscellaneous: Bacteria in sputum (4% to 7%)

General Dosage Range Dosage adjustment recommended in patients with hepatic impairment or on concomitant therapy.

Oral granules: *Children 2 to <6 years:*

<14 kg: 50 mg packet every 12 hours

≥14 kg: 75 mg packet every 12 hours

Oral tablet: *Children ≥6 years, Adolescents, and Adults:* 150 mg every 12 hours

Mechanism of Action Potentiates epithelial cell chloride ion transport of defective (G551D mutant) cell-surface CFTR protein thereby improving the regulation of salt and water absorption and secretion in various tissues (eg, lung, gastrointestinal tract).

Pharmacodynamics/Kinetics

Onset of Action FEV_1 increased, sweat chloride decreased within ~2 weeks

Half-life Elimination ~12 hours

Time to Peak ~4 hours

Pregnancy Considerations Information related to ivacaftor use in pregnancy is limited (Kaminski 2016; Ladores 2017; Marco 2015).

Ivermectin (Systemic) (eye ver MEK tin)

Brand Names: US Stromectol

Pharmacologic Category Anthelmintic

Use

Onchocerciasis: Treatment of onchocerciasis due to the immature form of *Onchocerca volvulus*.

Limitations of use: Ivermectin has **no** activity against **adult** *Onchocerca volvulus* parasites. The adult parasites reside in subcutaneous nodules which are infrequently palpable. Surgical excision may be considered as removal of these nodules will eliminate the microfilariae-producing adult parasites.

Strongyloidiasis, intestinal: Treatment of intestinal (eg, nondisseminated) strongyloidiasis due to *Strongyloides stercoralis*.

Local Anesthetic/Vasoconstrictor Precautions No information available to require special precautions

Effects on Dental Treatment No significant effects or complications reported

Effects on Bleeding No information available to require special precautions

Adverse Reactions

>10%:

Dermatologic: Pruritus (3%; Mazzotti reaction, associated with onchocerciasis: 28%), dermatological reaction (Mazzotti reaction, associated with onchocerciasis: 23%; includes edema, urticarial rash)

Hematologic & oncologic: Lymphadenitis (Mazzotti reaction, associated with onchocerciasis: 1% to 14%)

Neuromuscular & skeletal: Arthralgia (Mazzotti reaction, associated with onchocerciasis: ≤9%), synovitis (Mazzotti reaction, associated with onchocerciasis: ≤9%)

Miscellaneous: Fever (Mazzotti reaction, associated with onchocerciasis: 23%)

1% to 10%:

Cardiovascular: Tachycardia (4%), peripheral edema (3%), facial edema (1%), orthostatic hypotension (1%)

Central nervous system: Dizziness (3%)

Gastrointestinal: Diarrhea (2%), nausea (2%)

Hematologic & oncologic: Eosinophilia (3%), decreased white blood cell count (3%), increased hemoglobin (1%)

Hepatic: Increased serum ALT (2%), increased serum AST (2%)

<1%, postmarketing, and/or case reports: Abdominal distention, abdominal pain, abnormal gait, abnormal sensation in eyes, anemia, anorexia, anterior uveitis, ataxia, back pain, brain disease (rare; associated with loiasis), chest discomfort, chorioretinitis, coma, confusion, conjunctival hemorrhage (associated with onchocerciasis), conjunctivitis, constipation, drowsiness, dyspnea, exacerbation of asthma, eye redness, eyelid edema, fatigue, fecal incontinence, headache, hepatitis, hypotension, increased serum bilirubin, keratitis, lethargy, leukopenia, mental status changes, myalgia, neck pain, posterior uveitis, seizure, skin rash, Stevens-Johnson syndrome, stupor, temporary vision loss, toxic epidermal necrolysis, tremor, urinary incontinence, urticaria, vertigo, vomiting, weakness

General Dosage Range Oral: *Children ≥15 kg, Adolescents, and Adults:* 150-200 mcg/kg as a single dose

Mechanism of Action Ivermectin is a semisynthetic anthelminthic agent; it binds selectively and with strong affinity to glutamate-gated chloride ion channels which occur in invertebrate nerve and muscle cells. This leads to increased permeability of cell membranes to chloride ions then hyperpolarization of the nerve or muscle cell, and death of the parasite.

Pharmacodynamics/Kinetics

Half-life Elimination 18 hours

Time to Peak ~4 hours

Pregnancy Risk Factor C

Pregnancy Considerations Adverse events have been observed in animal reproduction studies. Although use in pregnancy is likely low risk, other agents are currently recommended for the treatment of pediculosis pubis or scabies in pregnant women (CDC [Workowski 2015]).

Ivermectin (Topical) (eye ver MEK tin)

Brand Names: US Sklice; Soolantra

Pharmacologic Category Antiparasitic Agent, Topical; Pediculocide

Use

Head lice (Pediculus capitis) (Sklice lotion): Treatment of head lice infestations in patients 6 months and older.

Rosacea (Soolantra cream): Treatment of inflammatory lesions of rosacea in adult patients.

Local Anesthetic/Vasoconstrictor Precautions No information available to require special precautions

Effects on Dental Treatment No significant effects or complications reported

Effects on Bleeding No information available to require special precautions

Adverse Reactions

1% to 10%:

Central nervous system: Localized burning (≤1%)

Dermatologic: Skin irritation (≤1%)

<1%, postmarketing, and/or case reports: Conjunctivitis, eye irritation, ocular hyperemia, seborrheic dermatitis of scalp, xeroderma

General Dosage Range

Topical cream: *Adults:* Apply to each affected area (eg, forehead, chin, nose, each cheek) once daily.

Topical lotion: *Children ≥6 months, Adolescents, and Adults:* Apply sufficient amount (up to 1 tube) to completely cover dry scalp and hair; for single-dose use only

Mechanism of Action

In pediculosis capitus treatment, ivermectin is a semisynthetic anthelminthic agent; it binds selectively and with strong affinity to glutamate-gated chloride ion channels which occur in invertebrate nerve and muscle cells. This leads to increased permeability of cell membranes to chloride ions then hyperpolarization of the nerve or muscle cell, and death of the parasite.

In rosacea treatment, the mechanism of action is unknown.

Pharmacodynamics/Kinetics

Half-life Elimination Cream: ~6.5 days

Time to Peak Cream: ~10 hours post application

Pregnancy Risk Factor C

Pregnancy Considerations Adverse events have been observed in animal reproduction studies following oral administration. Although use in pregnancy is likely low risk, other agents are currently recommended for the treatment of pediculosis pubis or scabies in pregnant women (CDC [Workowski 2015]).

Ixabepilone (ix ab EP i lone)

Brand Names: US Ixempra Kit

Pharmacologic Category Antineoplastic Agent, Antimicrotubular; Antineoplastic Agent, Epothilone B Analog

Use Breast cancer: Treatment of metastatic or locally-advanced breast cancer resistant to treatment with an anthracycline and a taxane, or if taxane-resistant and further anthracycline therapy is contraindicated (in combination with capecitabine) or as monotherapy in tumors are resistant or refractory to anthracyclines, taxanes, and capecitabine.

Anthracycline resistance is defined as progression during treatment or within 3 months in the metastatic setting (within 6 months in the adjuvant setting). Taxane resistance is defined as progression during treatment within 4 months in the metastatic setting (within 12 months in the adjuvant setting).

Local Anesthetic/Vasoconstrictor Precautions No information available to require special precautions

Effects on Dental Treatment Key adverse event(s) related to dental treatment: Stomatitis, mucositis, and taste perversion.

Effects on Bleeding Anemia and thrombocytopenia (grades 3/4: 2% to 5%) are dose-limiting toxicities. Medical consult recommended.

Adverse Reactions

Percentages reported with monotherapy.

>10%:

Central nervous system: Peripheral neuropathy (63%; grades 3/4: 14%; grade 3/4 median onset: cycle 4), peripheral sensory neuropathy (62%; grades 3/4: 14%), headache (11%)

Dermatologic: Alopecia (48%)

Gastrointestinal: Nausea (42%), vomiting (29%), mucositis (≤29%), stomatitis (≤29%), diarrhea (22%), anorexia (19%), constipation (16%), abdominal pain (13%)

Hematologic & oncologic: Leukopenia (grade 3: 36%; grade 4: 13%), neutropenia (grade 3: 31%; grade 4: 23%)

Neuromuscular & skeletal: Weakness (56%), arthralgia (≤49%), myalgia (≤49%), musculoskeletal pain (20%)

1% to 10%:

Cardiovascular: Edema (9%), chest pain (5%)

Central nervous system: Peripheral motor neuropathy (10%; grade 3: 1%), pain (8%), dizziness (7%), insomnia (5%)

Dermatologic: Nail disease (9%), skin rash (9%), palmar-plantar erythrodysesthesia (8%), pruritus (6%), desquamation (2%), hyperpigmentation (2%)

Endocrine & metabolic: Hot flash (6%), weight loss (6%), dehydration (2%)

Gastrointestinal: Dysgeusia (6%), gastroesophageal reflux (6%)

Hematologic & oncologic: Anemia (grade 3: 6%; grade 4: 2%), febrile neutropenia (3%; grade 3: 3%), thrombocytopenia (grade 3: 5%; grade 4: 2%)

Hypersensitivity: Hypersensitivity (5%; grade 3: 1%)

Infection: Infection (5%)

Ophthalmic: Increased lacrimation (4%)

Respiratory: Dyspnea (9%), upper respiratory tract infection (6%), cough (2%)

Miscellaneous: Fever (8%)

Mono- and combination therapy: <1%, postmarketing, and/or case reports: Acute hepatic failure, acute pulmonary edema, angina pectoris, atrial flutter, autonomic neuropathy, blood coagulation disorder, cardiomyopathy, cerebral hemorrhage, colitis, delayed gastric emptying, dysphagia, embolism, enterocolitis, erythema multiforme, gastrointestinal hemorrhage, hemorrhage, hypokalemia, hyponatremia, hypotension, hypovolemia, hypovolemic shock, hypoxia, increased gamma-glutamyl transferase, increased serum alkaline phosphatase, increased serum transaminases, interstitial pneumonitis, intestinal obstruction, jaundice, left ventricular dysfunction, metabolic acidosis, myocardial infarction, nephrolithiasis, neutropenic infection, orthostatic hypotension, pneumonia, pneumonitis, radiation recall phenomenon, renal failure, respiratory failure, sepsis, septic shock, supraventricular cardiac arrhythmia, syncope, thrombosis, trismus, urinary tract infection, vasculitis, voice disorder

General Dosage Range Dosage adjustment recommended in patients with hepatic impairment or who develop toxicities

IV: *Adults:* 40 mg/m^2 every 3 weeks (maximum dose: 88 mg)

Mechanism of Action Epothilone B analog; binds to the beta-tubulin subunit of the microtubule, stabilizing microtubular promoting tubulin polymerization and stabilizing microtubular function, thus arresting the cell cycle (at the G2/M phase) and inducing apoptosis. Activity in taxane-resistant cells has been demonstrated.

Pharmacodynamics/Kinetics

Half-life Elimination ~52 hours

Time to Peak At the end of infusion (3 hours)

Pregnancy Risk Factor D

Pregnancy Considerations Adverse events were observed in animal reproduction studies. Women of childbearing potential should be advised to use effective contraception during treatment.

Ixazomib (ix AZ oh mib)

Brand Names: US Ninlaro

Pharmacologic Category Antineoplastic Agent, Proteasome Inhibitor

Use Multiple myeloma: Treatment of multiple myeloma (in combination with lenalidomide and dexamethasone) in patients who have received at least one prior therapy

Local Anesthetic/Vasoconstrictor Precautions No information available to require special precautions

Effects on Dental Treatment No significant effects or complications reported

Effects on Bleeding Cytopenias including thrombocytopenia (grades 3/4, 26%) has been reported. Medical consult is recommended.

Adverse Reactions Adverse reaction percentages reported as part of a combination regimen with lenalidomide and dexamethasone.

>10%

Cardiovascular: Peripheral edema (25%)

Central nervous system: Peripheral neuropathy (28%; grade 3: 2%), peripheral sensory neuropathy (19%)

Dermatologic: Skin rash (19%)

Gastrointestinal: Diarrhea (42%), constipation (34%), nausea (26%), vomiting (22%)

Hematologic & oncologic: Thrombocytopenia (78%; grades 3/4: 26%), neutropenia (67%; grades 3/4: 26%)

Neuromuscular & skeletal: Back pain (21%)
Ophthalmic: Eye disease (26%)
Respiratory: Upper respiratory tract infection (19%)

1% to 10%:

Hepatic: Hepatic insufficiency (6%)
Infection: Herpes zoster (4%; <1% with antiviral prophylaxis)
Ophthalmic: Blurred vision (6%), conjunctivitis (6%), xerophthalmia (5%)

<1%, postmarketing, and/or case reports: Cholestatic hepatitis, hepatocellular hepatitis, hepatotoxicity, liver steatosis, peripheral motor neuropathy, reversible posterior leukoencephalopathy syndrome, Stevens-Johnson syndrome, Sweet's syndrome, thrombotic thrombocytopenic purpura, transverse myelitis, tumor lysis syndrome

General Dosage Range

Dosage adjustment recommended in patients with renal or hepatic impairment, or who develop toxicities.

Oral: *Adults:* 4 mg once weekly on days 1, 8, and 15 of a 28-day treatment cycle

Mechanism of Action Ixazomib reversibly inhibits proteasomes, enzyme complexes which regulate protein homeostasis within the cell. Specifically, it reversibly inhibits chymotrypsin-like activity of the beta 5 subunit of the 20S proteasome, leading to activation of signaling cascades, cell-cycle arrest, and apoptosis.

Pharmacodynamics/Kinetics

Half-life Elimination Terminal: 9.5 days

Time to Peak Median: 1 hour

Pregnancy Considerations Based on animal data and the mechanism of action, ixazomib is expected to cause fetal harm if used during pregnancy. Males and females of reproductive potential should use effective contraception during therapy and for 90 days after the last dose.

When used for the treatment of multiple myeloma, ixazomib is indicated to be used with lenalidomide and dexamethasone. Lenalidomide is contraindicated for use during pregnancy (refer to lenalidomide monograph for details). Dexamethasone is a weak to moderate CYP3A4 inducer, and may decrease the efficacy of hormonal contraceptives. Women using hormonal contraception should also use a barrier method.

Prescribing and Access Restrictions Available through specialty pharmacies and distributors. Further information may be obtained from the manufacturer, Takeda Oncology, at 1-800-390-5663 or at http://www.-ninlarohcp.com.

Ixekizumab (ix ee KIZ ue mab)

Brand Names: US Taltz

Brand Names: Canada Taltz

Pharmacologic Category Antipsoriatic Agent; Interleukin-17A Receptor Antagonist; Monoclonal Antibody

Use Plaque psoriasis: Treatment of moderate to severe plaque psoriasis in adult patients who are candidates for systemic therapy or phototherapy.

Local Anesthetic/Vasoconstrictor Precautions No information available to require special precautions

Effects on Dental Treatment No significant effects or complications reported

Effects on Bleeding No information available to require special precautions

Adverse Reactions

>10%:

Hematologic & oncologic: Neutropenia (11%)
Immunologic: Antibody development (9% to 22%; neutralizing antibodies associated with decreased drug concentration and loss of efficacy: 2%)
Infection: Infection (26% to 38%; maintenance period: 57%)
Local: Injection site reaction (17%; most frequently, erythema and pain)
Respiratory: Upper respiratory tract infection (14%)

1% to 10%:

Dermatologic: Tinea (2%)
Gastrointestinal: Nausea (2%)
Hematologic & oncologic: Thrombocytopenia (3%)

<1%, postmarketing, and/or case reports: Anaphylaxis, angioedema, conjunctivitis, Crohn disease, influenza, oral candidiasis, rhinitis, serious infection (maintenance period), ulcerative colitis, urticaria

General Dosage Range SubQ: *Adults:* 160 mg once, followed by 80 mg at weeks 2, 4, 6, 8, 10 and 12, and then 80 mg every 4 weeks.

Mechanism of Action Ixekizumab is a humanized IgG4 monoclonal antibody that selectively binds with the interleukin 17A (IL-17A) cytokine and inhibits its interaction with the IL-17 receptor. IL-17A is a naturally occurring cytokine that is involved in normal inflammatory and immune responses. Ixekizumab inhibits the release of proinflammatory cytokines and chemokines.

Pharmacodynamics/Kinetics

Half-life Elimination 13 days

Time to Peak ~4 days

Pregnancy Considerations Adverse events were not observed in animal reproduction study, however an increase in neonatal deaths was observed when dosing continued throughout pregnancy. Human IgG is known to cross the placenta.

In general, maternal use of monoclonal antibodies during pregnancy may increase the risk of infection to the exposed infant or interfere with vaccine administration in the newborn (Mervic 2014). Other agents are currently preferred for the treatment of plaque psoriasis in pregnant women (Hsu 2012).

Ketamine (KEET a meen)

Brand Names: US Ketalar

Brand Names: Canada Ketalar; Ketamine Hydrochloride Injection, USP

Pharmacologic Category General Anesthetic

Use Anesthesia: Induction and maintenance of general anesthesia

Local Anesthetic/Vasoconstrictor Precautions No information available to require special precautions

Effects on Dental Treatment Key adverse event(s) related to dental treatment: Increased salivation.

Effects on Bleeding No information available to require special precautions

Adverse Reactions

>10%: Central nervous system: Prolonged emergence from anesthesia (12%; includes confusion, delirium, dreamlike state, excitement, hallucinations, irrational behavior, vivid imagery)

Frequency not defined:

Cardiovascular: Bradycardia, cardiac arrhythmia, hypotension, increased blood pressure, increased pulse
Central nervous system: Drug dependence, hypertonia (tonic-clonic movements sometimes resembling seizures), increased cerebrospinal fluid pressure

Dermatologic: Erythema (transient), morbilliform rash (transient), rash at injection site
Endocrine & metabolic: Central diabetes insipidus (Hatab 2014)
Gastrointestinal: Anorexia, nausea, sialorrhea (Hatab 2014), vomiting
Genitourinary (reactions can be severe in patients with a history of chronic ketamine use/abuse): Bladder dysfunction (reduced capacity), cystitis (including cystitis noninfective, cystitis interstitial, cystitis ulcerative, cystitis erosive, cystitis hemorrhagic), dysuria, hematuria, urinary frequency, urinary incontinence, urinary urgency
Hypersensitivity: Anaphylaxis
Local: Pain at injection site
Neuromuscular & skeletal: Laryngospasm
Ophthalmic: Diplopia, increased intraocular pressure, nystagmus
Renal: Hydronephrosis
Respiratory: Airway obstruction, apnea, respiratory depression

General Dosage Range
IM: *Adolescents ≥16 years and Adults:* 6.5 to 13 mg/kg
IV:
Adolescents ≥16 years: 1 to 4.5 mg/kg
Adults: 1 to 4.5 mg/kg **or** 0.1 to 0.5 mg/minute as a continuous infusion

Mechanism of Action Produces a cataleptic-like state in which the patient is dissociated from the surrounding environment by direct action on the cortex and limbic system. Ketamine is a noncompetitive NMDA receptor antagonist that blocks glutamate. Low (subanesthetic) doses produce analgesia, and modulate central sensitization, hyperalgesia and opioid tolerance. Reduces polysynaptic spinal reflexes.

Pharmacodynamics/Kinetics

Onset of Action
IV: Anesthetic effect: Within 30 seconds
IM: Anesthetic effect: 3 to 4 minutes; Analgesia: Within 10 to 15 minutes
Intranasal: Analgesic effect: Within 10 minutes (Carr 2004); Sedation: Children 2 to 6 years: 5 to 8 minutes (Bahetwar 2011)
Oral: Analgesia: Within 30 minutes; Sedation: Children 2 to 8 years (Turhanoglu 2003):
4 mg/kg/dose: 12.9 ± 1.9 minutes
6 mg/kg/dose: 10.4 ± 2.9 minutes
8 mg/kg/dose: 9.5 ± 1.9 minutes

Duration of Action
IV: Anesthetic effect: 5 to 10 minutes; Recovery: 1 to 2 hours
IM: Anesthetic effect: 12 to 25 minutes; Analgesia: 15 to 30 minutes; Recovery: 3 to 4 hours
Intranasal: Analgesic effect: Up to 60 minutes (Carr 2004); Recovery: Children 2 to 6 years: 34 to 46 minutes (Bahetwar 2011)

Half-life Elimination Alpha: 10 to 15 minutes; Beta: 2.5 hours

Time to Peak
Plasma:
IM: 5 to 30 minutes (Clements 1982)
Intranasal: 10 to 14 minutes (Huge 2010); Children 2 to 9 years: ~20 minutes (Malinovsky 1996)
Oral: ~30 minutes (Soto 2012)
Rectal: Children 2 to 9 years: ~45 minutes (Malinovsky 1996)

Pregnancy Considerations Adverse events have not been observed in animal reproduction studies. Ketamine crosses the placenta and can be detected in fetal tissue. Ketamine produces dose dependent increases in uterine contractions; effects may vary by trimester. The plasma clearance of ketamine is reduced during pregnancy. Dose related neonatal depression and decreased APGAR scores have been reported with large doses administered at delivery (Ghoneim 1977; Little 1972; White 1982). Although ketamine has been used during vaginal delivery and cesarean section, use in pregnancy, including obstetrics (either vaginal or abdominal delivery) is not recommended by the manufacturer (Akamatsu 1974; Little 1972; Mercier 1998).

Controlled Substance C-III

Ketoconazole (Systemic) (kee toe KOE na zole)

Related Information
Fungal Infections *on page 1847*

Related Sample Prescriptions
Fungal Infections - Sample Prescriptions *on page 35*

Brand Names: Canada Apo-Ketoconazole; Teva-Ketoconazole

Generic Availability (US) Yes

Pharmacologic Category Antifungal Agent, Imidazole Derivative; Antifungal Agent, Oral

Dental Use Treatment of susceptible fungal infections in the oral cavity including candidiasis, oral thrush, and chronic mucocutaneous candidiasis

Use Fungal infections (systemic):
US labeling: Treatment of susceptible systemic fungal infections, including blastomycosis, histoplasmosis, paracoccidioidomycosis, coccidioidomycosis, and chromomycosis in patients who have failed or who are intolerant to other antifungal therapies
Limitations of use: Ketoconazole should only be used when other effective antifungal therapy is not available or tolerated **and** the potential benefits outweigh the potential risks.
Canadian labeling: Treatment of serious or life-threatening systemic fungal infections (eg, systemic candidiasis, chronic mucocutaneous candidiasis, coccidioidomycosis, paracoccidioidomycosis, histoplasmosis, and chromomycosis) where alternate therapy is inappropriate or ineffective; may be considered for severe dermatophytoses unresponsive to other therapy

Local Anesthetic/Vasoconstrictor Precautions No information available to require special precautions

Effects on Dental Treatment No significant effects or complications reported

Effects on Bleeding No information available to require special precautions

Adverse Reactions Frequency not always defined.
Cardiovascular: Orthostatic hypotension, peripheral edema
Central nervous system: Fatigue, insomnia, malaise, nervousness, paresthesia
Dermatologic: Pruritus (2%), alopecia, dermatitis, erythema, erythema multiforme, skin rash, urticaria, xeroderma
Endocrine & metabolic: Hot flash, hyperlipidemia, menstrual disease
Gastrointestinal: Nausea (3%), vomiting (3%), abdominal pain (1%), anorexia, constipation, dysgeusia, dyspepsia, flatulence, increased appetite, tongue discoloration, upper abdominal pain, xerostomia
Hematologic & oncologic: Decreased platelet count
Hepatic: Jaundice
Hypersensitivity: Anaphylactoid reaction
Neuromuscular & skeletal: Myalgia, weakness
Respiratory: Epistaxis

Miscellaneous: Alcohol intolerance

<1%, postmarketing, and/or case reports: Acute generalized exanthematous pustulosis, adrenocortical insufficiency (≥400 mg/day), anaphylactic shock, anaphylaxis, angioedema, arthralgia, azoospermia, bulging fontanel (infants), chills, cholestatic hepatitis, cirrhosis, decreased plasma testosterone (impaired at 800 mg/day), depression, diarrhea, dizziness, drowsiness, erectile dysfunction (doses >200-400 mg/day), fever, gynecomastia, headache, hemolytic anemia, hepatic failure, hepatic necrosis, hepatitis, hepatotoxicity, hypertriglyceridemia, hypersensitivity reaction, impotence, increased intracranial pressure (reversible), leukopenia, myopathy, papilledema, photophobia, prolonged Q-T interval on ECG, skin photosensitivity, suicidal tendencies, thrombocytopenia

Dental Usual Dosage Oral fungal infections: Oral:

Children ≥2 years: 3.3-6.6 mg/kg/day as a single dose for 1-2 weeks for candidiasis, for at least 4 weeks in recalcitrant dermatophyte infections, and for up to 6 months for other systemic mycoses

Adults: 200-400 mg/day as a single daily dose for durations as stated above

Dosing

Adult & Geriatric

Fungal infections (systemic): Oral: 200 mg once daily; may increase to 400 mg once daily if response is insufficient. Continue until active fungal infection is resolved; some infections may require a treatment duration of up to 6 months.

Prostate cancer, advanced (off-label use): Oral: 400 mg 3 times daily (in combination with oral hydrocortisone) until disease progression (Ryan 2007; Small 2004)

Cushing syndrome (off-label use): Oral: Initial: 400 to 600 mg daily in 2 or 3 divided doses; may increase dose by 200 mg daily every 7 to 28 days up to a maximum of 1,200 mg daily in 2 or 3 divided doses; dosage range: 200 to 1,200 mg daily; mean effective dose in most studies: 600 to 800 mg daily in 2 divided doses (Castinotti 2014; ES [Nieman 2015]; Miller 1993)

Pediatric Fungal infections (systemic): Children >2 years: Oral: 3.3 to 6.6 mg/kg once daily. Continue until active fungal infection is resolved; some infections may require a treatment duration of up to 6 months.

Renal Impairment There are no dosage adjustments provided in the manufacturer's labeling. However, some resources suggest that no dosage adjustment is necessary in mild-to-severe impairment (Aronoff 2007).

End-stage renal disease (ESRD) on intermittent hemodialysis: Supplemental dose is not necessary (Aronoff 2007). Not dialyzable.

Hepatic Impairment Use is contraindicated in acute or chronic liver disease.

Hepatotoxicity during treatment:

US labeling: If ALT >ULN or 30% above baseline (or if patient is symptomatic), interrupt therapy and obtain full hepatic function panel. Upon normalization of liver function, may consider resuming therapy if benefit outweighs risk (hepatotoxicity has been reported on rechallenge).

Canadian labeling: Discontinue therapy for liver function tests >3 times ULN or if abnormalities persist, worsen, or are associated with hepatotoxicity symptoms.

Mechanism of Action Alters the permeability of the cell wall by blocking fungal cytochrome P450; inhibits biosynthesis of triglycerides and phospholipids by fungi; inhibits several fungal enzymes that results in a build-up of toxic concentrations of hydrogen peroxide; for management of prostate cancer, ketoconazole inhibits androgen synthesis

Contraindications

Hypersensitivity to ketoconazole or any component of the formulation; acute or chronic liver disease; coadministration with alprazolam, cisapride, colchicine, disopyramide, dofetilide, dronedarone, eplerenone, ergot alkaloids (eg, dihydroergotamine, ergometrine, ergotamine, methylergometrine), felodipine, HMG-CoA reductase inhibitors (eg, lovastatin, simvastatin), irinotecan, lurasidone, methadone, oral midazolam, nisoldipine, pimozide, quinidine, ranolazine, tolvaptan, triazolam

Canadian labeling: Additional contraindications (not in U.S. labeling): Women of childbearing potential unless effective forms of contraception are used; coadministration with astemizole or terfenadine

Warnings/Precautions [US Boxed Warning]: Use only when other effective antifungal therapy is unavailable or not tolerated and the benefits of ketoconazole treatment are considered to outweigh the risks. Ketoconazole oral tablets are approved to treat systemic fungal infections and should not be prescribed to treat skin and nail fungal infections; the risks of serious liver damage, adrenal gland problems and drug-drug interactions outweigh any potential benefit. Ketoconazole has poor penetration into cerebral-spinal fluid and should not be used to treat fungal meningitis.

[US Boxed Warning]: Ketoconazole has been associated with hepatotoxicity, including fatal cases and cases requiring liver transplantation; some patients had no apparent risk factors for hepatic disease. Patients should be advised of the hepatotoxicity risks and monitored closely. Toxicity was observed after a median duration of therapy of ~4 weeks but has also been noted after as little as 3 days; may occur when patients receive high doses for short durations or low doses for long durations. Most cases have been observed in the treatment of onychomycosis. Use with caution in patients with preexisting hepatic impairment, those on prolonged therapy and/or taking other hepatotoxic drugs concurrently. Hepatic dysfunction is typically (but not always) reversible upon discontinuation. Obtain liver function tests at baseline and frequently throughout therapy; serum ALT should be monitored weekly throughout therapy. Discontinue therapy for elevated hepatic enzymes that persist or worsen or if accompanied by signs/symptoms (eg, jaundice, nausea/vomiting, dark urine) of hepatic injury.

High doses of ketoconazole may depress adrenocortical function; returns to baseline upon discontinuation of therapy. Recommended maximum dosing should not be exceeded. Monitor adrenal function as clinically necessary, particularly in patients with adrenal insufficiency and in patients under prolonged stress (eg, intensive care, major surgery). In European clinical trials of men with metastatic prostate cancer, fatalities were reported in a small number of study participants within 14 days of initiating high-dose ketoconazole (1,200 mg daily); a causal effect has not been established. In animal studies, increased long bone fragility with cases of fracture has been observed with high-dose ketoconazole. Careful dose selection may be advisable for patients susceptible to bone fragility (eg, postmenopausal women, elderly). Cases of hypersensitivity reactions (including rare cases of anaphylaxis) have been reported; some reactions occurred after the initial dose.

[US Boxed Warning]: Concomitant use with cisapride, disopyramide, dofetilide, dronedarone, methadone, pimozide, quinidine, and ranolazine is contraindicated due to the possible occurrence of life-threatening ventricular arrhythmias such as torsade de pointes. Concomitant use with HMG-CoA reductase inhibitors (eg, lovastatin, simvastatin) or with oral midazolam, triazolam, and alprazolam is contraindicated. Absorption is reduced in patients with achlorhydria; administer with acidic liquids (eg, soda pop). Avoid concomitant use of drugs that decrease gastric acidity (eg, proton pump inhibitors, antacids, H_2-blockers). Other potentially significant interactions may exist, requiring dose or frequency adjustment, additional monitoring, and/or selection of alternative therapy.

Drug Interactions

Metabolism/Transport Effects

Substrate of CYP3A4 (major); **Note:** Assignment of Major/Minor substrate status based on clinically relevant drug interaction potential; **Inhibits** CYP1A2 (weak), CYP2A6 (moderate), CYP2C19 (weak), CYP2C8 (weak), CYP2C9 (moderate), CYP3A4 (strong), P-glycoprotein, UGT1A1

Avoid Concomitant Use

Avoid concomitant use of Ketoconazole (Systemic) with any of the following: Ado-Trastuzumab Emtansine; Alfuzosin; ALPRAZolam; Amodiaquine; Aprepitant; Artesunate; Astemizole; Asunaprevir; Avanafil; Axitinib; Barnidipine; Blonanserin; Bosutinib; Bromocriptine; Budesonide (Systemic); Ceritinib; Cisapride; Cobimetinib; Conivaptan; Crizotinib; Dabrafenib; Dapoxetine; Dihydroergotamine; Disopyramide; Dofetilide; Domperidone; Dronedarone; Efavirenz; Elbasvir; Eletriptan; Eplerenone; Ergoloid Mesylates; Ergonovine; Ergotamine; Estazolam; Everolimus; Felodipine; Flibanserin; Grazoprevir; Halofantrine; Ibrutinib; Indium 111 Capromab Pendetide; Irinotecan Products; Isavuconazonium Sulfate; Ivabradine; Lapatinib; Lercanidipine; Lobeglitazone; Lomitapide; Lovastatin; Lumacaftor; Lurasidone; Macitentan; Methadone; Methylergonovine; Midazolam; Naloxegol; Nevirapine; Nilotinib; NiMODipine; Nisoldipine; Olaparib; Palbociclib; PAZOPanib; Pimozide; QuiNIDine; Radotinib; Ranolazine; Red Yeast Rice; Regorafenib; Rivaroxaban; Rupatadine; Saccharomyces boulardii; Salmeterol; Silodosin; Simeprevir; Simvastatin; Sonidegib; Suvorexant; Tamsulosin; Tegafur; Telithromycin; Terfenadine; Ticagrelor; Tolvaptan; Topotecan; Toremifene; Trabectedin; Triazolam; Udenafil; Ulipristal; Vemurafenib; VinCRIStine (Liposomal); Vinflunine; Vorapaxar

Increased Effect/Toxicity

Ketoconazole (Systemic) may increase the levels/effects of: Ado-Trastuzumab Emtansine; Afatinib; Alcohol (Ethyl); Alfuzosin; Aliskiren; Alitretinoin (Systemic); Almotriptan; Alosetron; ALPRAZolam; Amodiaquine; Antihepaciviral Combination Products; Apixaban; Aprepitant; ARIPiprazole; ARIPiprazole Lauroxil; Artesunate; Astemizole; Asunaprevir; AtorvaSTATin; Avanafil; Axitinib; Barnidipine; Bedaquiline; Benperidol; Bilastine; Blonanserin; Boceprevir; Bortezomib; Bosentan; Bosutinib; Brentuximab Vedotin; Brexpiprazole; Brinzolamide; Bromocriptine; Budesonide (Nasal); Budesonide (Oral Inhalation); Budesonide (Systemic); Budesonide (Topical); Buprenorphine; BusPIRone; Busulfan; Cabazitaxel; Cabozantinib; Calcifediol; Calcium Channel Blockers; Cannabidiol; Cannabis; Carbocisteine; Cariprazine; Carvedilol; Ceritinib; Cilostazol; Cisapride; CloZAPine; Cobicistat; Cobimetinib; Colchicine; Conivaptan; Corticosteroids (Orally Inhaled); Corticosteroids (Systemic); Crizotinib; CycloSPORINE (Systemic); CYP2A6 Substrates; CYP2C9 Substrates; CYP3A4 Substrates; Dabigatran Etexilate; Dabrafenib; Daclatasvir; Dapoxetine; Darunavir; Dasatinib; Deflazacort; Delamanid; Dienogest; Dihydroergotamine; Disopyramide; DOCEtaxel; Dofetilide; Domperidone; DOXOrubicin (Conventional); Dronabinol; Dronedarone; Drospirenone; Dutasteride; Edoxaban; Elbasvir; Eletriptan; Eliglustat; Elvitegravir; Eplerenone; Ergoloid Mesylates; Ergonovine; Ergotamine; Erlotinib; Estazolam; Eszopiclone; Etizolam; Etravirine; Everolimus; Felodipine; FentaNYL; Fesoterodine; Fexofenadine; Fimasartan; Fingolimod; Flibanserin; Fluticasone (Nasal); Fluticasone (Oral Inhalation); Fosamprenavir; Fosphenytoin; Gefitinib; Grazoprevir; GuanFACINE; Halofantrine; Highest Risk QTc-Prolonging Agents; HYDROcodone; HydrOXYzine; Ibrutinib; Idelalisib; Iloperidone; Imatinib; Imidafenacin; Indinavir; Irinotecan Products; Isavuconazonium Sulfate; Ivabradine; Ivacaftor; Ixabepilone; Lacosamide; Lapatinib; Lercanidipine; Levobupivacaine; Levomilnacipran; Lobeglitazone; Lomitapide; Lopinavir; Losartan; Lovastatin; Lurasidone; Macitentan; Manidipine; Maraviroc; MedroxyPROGESTERone; Methadone; Methylergonovine; MethylPREDNISolone; Midazolam; MiFEPRIStone; Mirabegron; Mirodenafil; Moderate Risk QTc-Prolonging Agents; Naldemedine; Naloxegol; Nilotinib; NiMODipine; Nintedanib; Nisoldipine; Olaparib; Ospemifene; Oxybutynin; OxyCODONE; Palbociclib; Panobinostat; Parecoxib; Paricalcitol; PAZOPanib; P-glycoprotein/ABCB1 Substrates; Phenytoin; Pimavanserin; Pimecrolimus; Pimozide; PONATinib; Pranlukast; Praziquantel; PrednisoLONE (Systemic); PredniSONE; Propafenone; Proton Pump Inhibitors; Prucalopride; QUEtiapine; QuiNIDine; Radotinib; Ramelteon; Ranolazine; Reboxetine; Red Yeast Rice; Regorafenib; Repaglinide; Retapamulin; Ribociclib; Rifamycin Derivatives; RifAXIMin; Rilpivirine; Riociguat; Rivaroxaban; RomiDEPsin; Rupatadine; Ruxolitinib; Salmeterol; Saquinavir; SAXagliptin; Sildenafil; Silodosin; Simeprevir; Simvastatin; Sirolimus; Solifenacin; Sonidegib; SORAfenib; SUNItinib; Suvorexant; Tacrolimus (Systemic); Tacrolimus (Topical); Tadalafil; Tamsulosin; Tasimelteon; Telaprevir; Telithromycin; Temsirolimus; Teneligliptin; Terfenadine; Tetrahydrocannabinol; Ticagrelor; TiZANidine; Tofacitinib; Tolterodine; Tolvaptan; Topotecan; Toremifene; Trabectedin; TraMADol; Triazolam; Udenafil; Ulipristal; Vardenafil; Vemurafenib; Venetoclax; Vilazodone; VinCRIStine (Liposomal); Vindesine; Vinflunine; Vinorelbine; Vitamin K Antagonists; Vorapaxar; Zolpidem; Zopiclone; Zuclopenthixol

The levels/effects of Ketoconazole (Systemic) may be increased by: Antihepaciviral Combination Products; AtorvaSTATin; Boceprevir; Cobicistat; Darunavir; Etravirine; Fosamprenavir; Indinavir; Lopinavir; MiFEPRIStone; Ritonavir; Saquinavir; Telaprevir; Telithromycin; Tipranavir

Decreased Effect

Ketoconazole (Systemic) may decrease the levels/effects of: Amphotericin B; Artesunate; Choline C 11; Doxercalciferol; Ifosfamide; Indium 111 Capromab Pendetide; Prasugrel; Saccharomyces boulardii; Tegafur; Ticagrelor

The levels/effects of Ketoconazole (Systemic) may be decreased by: Antacids; Bosentan; CYP3A4 Inducers (Moderate); CYP3A4 Inducers (Strong); Deferasirox; Didanosine; Efavirenz; Enzalutamide; Etravirine; Fosphenytoin; H2-Antagonists; Isoniazid; Lumacaftor; Mitotane; Nevirapine; Phenytoin; Proton Pump Inhibitors; Rifamycin Derivatives; Rilpivirine; Siltuximab; St John's Wort; Sucralfate; Tocilizumab

Food Interactions Ketoconazole peak serum levels may be prolonged if taken with food. Management: May administer with food or milk to decrease GI adverse effects.

Dietary Considerations May be taken with food or milk to decrease GI adverse effects.

Pharmacodynamics/Kinetics

Half-life Elimination Biphasic: Initial: 2 hours; Terminal: 8 hours

Time to Peak Serum: 1-2 hours

Pregnancy Risk Factor C

Pregnancy Considerations Adverse events have been observed in animal reproduction studies.

Based on limited data, an increased risk of adverse events in pregnancy has not been observed (Amado 1990; Berwaerts 1999; Boronat 2011; Carter 2008; Costenaro 2015; Kazy 2005; Molgaard-Nielsen 2013; Prebtani 2000). However, because ketonconazole exhibits antiandrogenic effects, there is a theoretical risk for the impairment of sex organ differentiation following exposure to ketonconazole during critical times of organogenesis (Pilmis 2015).

Ketoconazole is approved for the treatment of blastomycosis, coccidioidomycosis, histoplasmosis, chromomycosis, and paracoccidioidomycosis in patients who have failed or who are intolerant to other antifungal therapies. When treatment of systemic fungal infections is needed in pregnant women, alternative antifungal agents should be used (Chapman 2008; Galgiani 2005).

Ketoconazole is an effective and recommended agent for the medical treatment of Cushing syndrome (Nieman 2015). Cushing syndrome during pregnancy is associated with neonatal and maternal morbidity and mortality (Aron 1990; Lindsay 2005). In pregnant women with Cushing syndrome, the treatment of choice is surgical intervention or, in patients not eligible for surgical intervention, medical therapy with metyrapone (Nieman 2015). Some experts recommend reserving ketoconazole for the treatment of pregnant women with Cushing syndrome who require emergent medical therapy but cannot tolerate the preferred treatment (Lindsay 2005).

Breastfeeding Considerations Ketoconazole is excreted into breast milk. breastfeeding is not recommended by the manufacturer. Milk concentrations following an oral ketoconazole dose of 200 mg daily for 10 days were ≤0.22 mcg/mL in a case report. Using the reported peak milk concentration of 0.22 mcg/mL in this patient, the estimated exposure to the breastfeeding infant would be 0.033 mg/kg/day (relative infant dose 1.4% based on the weight-adjusted maternal dose of 200 mg/day) (Moretti 1995).

Dosage Forms

Tablet, Oral:

Generic: 200 mg

Ketoconazole (Topical) (kee toe KOE na zole)

Related Information

Fungal Infections *on page 1847*

Related Sample Prescriptions

Fungal Infections - Sample Prescriptions *on page 35*

Brand Names: US Extina; Ketodan; Nizoral; Nizoral A-D [OTC]; Xolegel

Brand Names: Canada Ketoderm; Nizoral

Generic Availability (US) May be product dependent

Pharmacologic Category Antifungal Agent, Imidazole Derivative; Antifungal Agent, Topical

Use

Cream: Treatment of tinea corporis (ringworm), tinea cruris (jock itch), and tinea pedis (athlete's foot) caused by *Trichophyton rubrum*, *Trichophyton mentagrophytes*, and *Epidermophyton floccosum*; treatment of tinea (pityriasis) versicolor caused by *Pityrosporum orbiculare* (also known as *Malassezia furfur*); treatment of cutaneous candidiasis caused by *Candida* sp; treatment of seborrheic dermatitis

Foam, gel: Treatment of seborrheic dermatitis in immunocompetent adults and children 12 years and older

Limitations of use: Safety and efficacy for the treatment of fungal infections have not been established.

Shampoo:

US labeling: Treatment of tinea versicolor caused by or presumed to be caused by *P. orbiculare* (*M. furfur* or *Malassezia orbiculare*)

Canadian labeling: Treatment and prophylaxis of conditions caused by *Pityrosporum* (eg, pityriasis capitis [dandruff]); treatment of seborrheic dermatitis

OTC labeling: Controls flaking, scaling, and itching associated with dandruff

Local Anesthetic/Vasoconstrictor Precautions No information available to require special precautions

Effects on Dental Treatment No significant effects or complications reported

Effects on Bleeding No information available to require special precautions

Adverse Reactions

Topical cream/gel:

1% to 10%:

Central nervous system: Localized burning (4%)

Dermatologic: Stinging of the skin (5%)

Frequency not defined:

Central nervous system: Dizziness, headache, pain, paresthesia

Dermatologic: Acne vulgaris, erythema, facial swelling, impetigo, nail discoloration, pruritus, pustules, pyogenic granuloma, xeroderma

Hypersensitivity: Hypersensitivity reaction, contact dermatitis (possibly related to sulfites or propylene glycol)

Local: Application site discharge, local irritation (severe)

Ophthalmic: Eye irritation, keratoconjunctivitis sicca, swelling of eye

Topical foam:

1% to 10%: Local: Application site burning (10%), application site reaction (6%)

Frequency not defined: Dermatologic: Contact dermatitis, erythema, pruritus, skin rash, xeroderma

Shampoo:

1% to 10%:

Dermatologic: Pruritus (≤3%), xeroderma (≤3%), abnormal hair texture (<1%), loss of scalp hair (<1%), scalp pustules (<1%)

Local: Application site reaction (≤3%), local irritation (<1%)

Frequency not defined:

Central nervous system: Burning sensation

Dermatologic: Alopecia, dry hair, hair discoloration, oily hair, skin rash, urticaria

Hypersensitivity: Anaphylaxis, angioedema, hypersensitivity reaction

Dosing

Adult & Geriatric

Cutaneous candidiasis: Topical: Cream: Apply once daily to cover the affected and immediate surrounding area for 2 weeks. **Note:** Canadian labeling recommends a duration of 2 to 3 weeks.

Dandruff: Topical:

Shampoo 1% (OTC labeling): Apply to wet hair, lather, and rinse thoroughly; repeat. Use every 3 to 4 days for up to 8 weeks; then apply only as needed to control dandruff.

Shampoo 2% (Canadian product only): Apply 5 to 10 mL to wet scalp, lather, leave on 3 to 5 minutes, and rinse; apply once every 1 to 2 weeks (prophylaxis) or twice weekly for 2 to 4 weeks (treatment).

Seborrheic dermatitis: Topical:

Cream: Apply to the affected area twice daily for 4 weeks or until clinical response is noted

Foam: Apply to affected area twice daily for 4 weeks

Gel: Apply to the affected area once daily for 2 weeks

Shampoo 2% (Canadian product only; OTC labeling): Apply 5 to 10 mL to wet scalp, lather, leave on 3 to 5 minutes, and rinse; apply twice weekly for 2 to 4 weeks.

Tinea corporis, tinea cruris, tinea pedis: Topical:

Cream: Apply to the affected and immediate surrounding area once daily.

Duration of treatment:

US labeling: Tinea corporis, cruris: 2 weeks; tinea pedis: 6 weeks.

Canadian labeling: Tinea corporis: 3 to 4 weeks; tinea cruris: 2 to 4 weeks; tinea pedis: 4 to 6 weeks.

Tinea versicolor: Topical:

Cream: Apply once daily to cover the affected and immediate surrounding area for 2 weeks. **Note:** Canadian labeling recommends a duration of 2 to 3 weeks.

Shampoo 2%: Apply to affected area of damp skin, lather, leave on 5 minutes, and rinse (one application is usually sufficient)

Susceptible fungal infections in the oral cavity (candidiasis, oral thrush, and chronic mucocutaneous candidiasis) (off-label use): Topical: Cream: Apply locally as directed with a thin coat to inner surface of denture and affected areas after meals

Pediatric

Dandruff: Topical:

Shampoo 1% (OTC labeling): Children ≥12 years and Adolescents: Refer to adult dosing.

Shampoo 2% (Canadian product only): Children >12 years and Adolescents: Refer to adult dosing.

Seborrheic dermatitis: Topical:

Foam, gel: Children ≥12 years and Adolescents: Refer to adult dosing.

Shampoo 2% (Canadian product only): Children >12 years and Adolescents: Refer to adult dosing.

Renal Impairment There are no dosage adjustments provided in the manufacturer's labeling. However, dosage adjustment unlikely due to low systemic absorption.

Hepatic Impairment There are no dosage adjustments provided in the manufacturer's labeling. However, dosage adjustment unlikely due to low systemic absorption.

Mechanism of Action

Alters the permeability of the cell wall by blocking fungal cytochrome P450; inhibits biosynthesis of triglycerides and phospholipids by fungi; inhibits several fungal enzymes that results in a build-up of toxic concentrations of hydrogen peroxide; also inhibits androgen synthesis

Contraindications

Hypersensitivity to ketoconazole or any component of the formulation.

OTC labeling: When used for self-medication, do not use on scalp that is broken or inflamed.

Documentation of allergenic cross-reactivity for azole antifungals is limited. However, because of similarities in chemical structure and/or pharmacologic actions, the possibility of cross-sensitivity cannot be ruled out with certainty.

Warnings/Precautions

Severe hypersensitivity reactions (including contact sensitization, photoallergenicity, and anaphylaxis [rare]) have been reported; discontinue use if hypersensitivity occurs. May cause irritation at the site of application; discontinue use if irritation occurs. Avoid contact with the eyes and other mucous membranes. Not for ophthalmic, oral, or intravaginal use. If condition worsens or does not improve after the treatment period, discontinue use and contact health care provider. Some dosage forms contain sulfites which may cause allergic-type reactions (including anaphylaxis) as well as life-threatening or less severe asthmatic episodes in certain individuals. Avoid exposure of gel to fire, flames, or smoking during or immediately after application. Foam formulation contains alcohol and propane/butane; do not expose to open flame and/or smoking during or immediately after application; do not puncture and/or incinerate container. Use of shampoo may remove curl from permanently wavy hair, cause hair discoloration, and changes in hair texture.

Drug Interactions

Metabolism/Transport Effects None known.

Avoid Concomitant Use There are no known interactions where it is recommended to avoid concomitant use.

Increased Effect/Toxicity There are no known significant interactions involving an increase in effect.

Decreased Effect There are no known significant interactions involving a decrease in effect.

Pregnancy Risk Factor C

Pregnancy Considerations Adverse events have been observed in animal reproduction studies with oral ketoconazole. Ketoconazole is not detectable in the plasma following chronic use of the shampoo.

Breastfeeding Considerations Ketoconazole has been detected in breast milk following oral dosing. Although it is not detected in the plasma following chronic use of the shampoo, and concentrations in the plasma following application of the gel are <250 times those observed with oral dosing, the manufacturers recommend that caution be used when administering ketoconazole to nursing women.

Dosage Forms

Cream, External:

Generic: 2% (15 g, 30 g, 60 g)

Foam, External:

Extina: 2% (50 g, 100 g)

Ketodan: 2% (100 g)

Generic: 2% (50 g, 100 g)

Gel, External:
Xolegel: 2% (45 g)
Kit, External:
Ketodan: 2%
Shampoo, External:
Nizoral: 2% (120 mL)
Nizoral A-D [OTC]: 1% (125 mL, 200 mL)
Generic: 2% (120 mL)

Ketoprofen (kee toe PROE fen)

Related Information

Oral Pain *on page 1830*

Rheumatoid Arthritis, Osteoarthritis, and Osteoporosis *on page 1792*

Temporomandibular Dysfunction (TMD), Chronic Pain, and Fibromyalgia *on page 1868*

Brand Names: US Active-Ketoprofen; Ketophene Rapidpaq

Brand Names: Canada Ketoprofen SR; Ketoprofen-E; PMS-Ketoprofen; PMS-Ketoprofen-E

Generic Availability (US) Yes

Pharmacologic Category Analgesic, Nonopioid; Nonsteroidal Anti-inflammatory Drug (NSAID), Oral

Dental Use Management of pain and swelling

Use

Osteoarthritis: Management of the signs and symptoms of osteoarthritis

Pain (immediate release only). Management of pain

Primary dysmenorrhea (immediate release only): Treatment of primary dysmenorrhea

Rheumatoid arthritis: Management of the signs and symptoms of rheumatoid arthritis

Canadian labeling: Additional use (not in US labeling): Treatment of ankylosing spondylitis

Local Anesthetic/Vasoconstrictor Precautions No information available to require special precautions

Effects on Dental Treatment Key adverse event(s) related to dental treatment: Stomatitis.

According to the FDA, the over-the-counter NSAID ketoprofen should be viewed as having the potential to interfere with the antiplatelet effect of low-dose aspirin until proven otherwise. This statement was provided in the same warning from the FDA that ibuprofen can interfere with the antiplatelet effect of low-dose aspirin (81 mg/day), potentially rendering aspirin less effective when used for cardioprotection and stroke protection. In situations where these drugs could be used concomitantly, the FDA has provided the following information: Patients who use immediate release aspirin (not enteric-coated aspirin) and take single doses of ibuprofen 400 mg, should dose the ibuprofen at least 30 minutes or longer after aspirin ingestion or more than 8 hours before aspirin ingestion to avoid attenuation of aspirin's effect. Similar recommendations may hold for concomitant ketoprofen and aspirin use. See Effects on Bleeding.

At this time, recommendations about the timing of ibuprofen 400 mg or other NSAIDs (such as ketoprofen) in patients taking enteric-coated low-dose aspirin cannot be made based on available data.

Effects on Bleeding Nonselective NSAIDs such as ketoprofen inhibit platelet aggregation and prolong bleeding time in some patients. Unlike aspirin, the NSAID effect on platelet function is quantitatively less, of shorter duration, and reversible.

Adverse Reactions

>10%:

Gastrointestinal: Dyspepsia (11%)

Hepatic: Abnormal hepatic function tests (≤15%)

1% to 10%:

Cardiovascular: Peripheral edema (2%)

Central nervous system: Headache (3% to 9%), dizziness (>1%), abnormal dreams, depression, drowsiness, insomnia, malaise, nervousness

Dermatologic: Skin rash (>1%)

Gastrointestinal: Abdominal pain (3% to 9%), constipation (3% to 9%), diarrhea (3% to 9%), flatulence (3% to 9%), nausea (3% to 9%), gastrointestinal hemorrhage (>2%), peptic ulcer (>2%), anorexia (>1%), stomatitis (>1%), vomiting (>1%)

Genitourinary: Urinary tract irritation (>1%)

Ophthalmic: Visual disturbance (>1%)

Otic: Tinnitus (>1%)

Renal: Renal insufficiency (3% to 9%)

<1%, postmarketing, and/or case reports: Acute renal tubular disease, agranulocytosis, allergic rhinitis, alopecia, anaphylaxis, anemia, angioedema, aseptic meningitis, auditory impairment, blurred vision, bone marrow depression, bronchospasm, buccal necrosis, bullous rash, cardiac arrhythmia, cardiac failure, change in libido, chills, cholestatic hepatitis, confusion, conjunctivitis, cystitis, dysphoria, dyspnea, eczema, edema, epistaxis, erythema multiforme, exacerbation of diabetes mellitus, exfoliative dermatitis, facial edema, fluid retention, gastritis, gastrointestinal perforation, gastrointestinal ulcer, gynecomastia, hallucination, hematemesis, hematuria, hemolytic anemia, hemoptysis, hepatic insufficiency, hepatitis, hepatotoxicity (idiosyncratic; Chalasani 2014), hot flash, hypersensitivity reaction, hypertension, hyponatremia, impotence, infection, interstitial nephritis, jaundice, laryngeal edema, leukopenia, melena, microvesicular steatosis, migraine, myocardial infarction, nephrotic syndrome, occult blood in stools, onycholysis, palpitations, pancreatitis, peripheral neuropathy, peripheral vascular disease, polydipsia, polyuria, pruritus, purpura, purpuric rash, renal failure, renal papillary necrosis, retinal hemorrhage, septicemia, shock, skin photosensitivity, Stevens-Johnson syndrome, tachycardia, thrombocytopenia, toxic amblyopia, toxic epidermal necrolysis, ulcerative bowel lesion, ulcerative colitis, urticaria, vasodilatation, xerostomia

Dental Usual Dosage Mild-to-moderate pain: Children ≥16 years and Adults: Oral: Capsule: 25 to 50 mg every 6 to 8 hours up to a maximum of 300 mg/day

Dosing

Adult Note: The enteric coated tablet and extended release formulations are not recommended for the treatment of acute pain. Lower doses should be considered in small or debilitated patients.

Oral:

Rheumatoid arthritis or osteoarthritis:

Immediate release: US labeling: 50 mg 4 times daily **or** 75 mg 3 times daily; up to a maximum of 300 mg/day

Immediate release or enteric coated: Canadian labeling: 50 mg 3 or 4 times daily; up to 200 mg daily; twice daily regimen (eg, 100 mg twice daily) may be considered after maintenance dose is established although some patients respond more favorably to more frequent dosing. For severe rheumatic activity or an inadequate response to lower dosages, may consider dose increase up to a maximum 300 mg daily.

Extended release: 200 mg once daily

Dysmenorrhea, pain: Immediate release: 25 to 50 mg every 6 to 8 hours up to a maximum of 300 mg/day

Rectal suppository [Canadian product]: **Ankylosing spondylitis, osteoarthritis, or rheumatoid arthritis:** Insert one suppository rectally in the morning and evening (twice daily) or at bedtime (once daily). May supplement with divided oral dosing up to a combined rectal/oral maximum of 200 mg daily; for severe rheumatic activity or an inadequate response to lower dosages, a combined rectal/oral dose up to 300 mg daily may be considered. Patients should be maintained at the lowest effective dose.

Geriatric

U.S. labeling: Oral: Manufacturer labeling recommends that the initial dose should be decreased in patients >75 years but does not provide specific dosing recommendations; use caution when dosage changes are made.

Canadian labeling: Oral: Reduce initial dose by 33% to 50%; Rectal: Manufacturer labeling recommends that the initial dose should be decreased but does not provide specific dosing recommendation.

Renal Impairment In general, NSAIDs are not recommended for use in patients with advanced renal disease, but the manufacturer of ketoprofen does provide some guidelines for adjustment in renal dysfunction:

US labeling:

Mild impairment: Maximum dose: 150 mg/day

Severe impairment: GFR <25 mL/minute/1.73 m^2: Maximum dose: 100 mg/day

Canadian labeling: Reduce initial dose by 33% to 50%.

Hepatic Impairment Hepatic impairment and serum albumin <3.5 g/dL: Maximum initial dose: 100 mg/day

Mechanism of Action Reversibly inhibits cyclooxygenase-1 and 2 (COX-1 and 2) enzymes, which results in decreased formation of prostaglandin precursors; has antipyretic, analgesic, and anti-inflammatory properties

Other proposed mechanisms not fully elucidated (and possibly contributing to the anti-inflammatory effect to varying degrees), include inhibiting chemotaxis, altering lymphocyte activity, inhibiting neutrophil aggregation/activation, and decreasing proinflammatory cytokine levels.

Contraindications

Hypersensitivity to ketoprofen or any component of the formulation; history of asthma, urticaria, or allergic-type reactions after taking aspirin or other NSAIDs; use in the setting of CABG surgery

Canadian labeling: Additional contraindications (not in US labeling): Active peptic ulcer or active inflammatory disease of the GI tract; inflammatory lesions or recent bleeding of the rectum or anus (suppository only)

Warnings/Precautions [US Boxed Warning]: NSAIDs cause an increased risk of serious (and potentially fatal) adverse cardiovascular thrombotic events, including MI and stroke. Risk may occur early during treatment and may increase with duration of use. Relative risk appears to be similar in those with and without known cardiovascular disease or risk factors for cardiovascular disease; however, absolute incidence of serious cardiovascular thrombotic events (which may occur early during treatment) was higher in patients with known cardiovascular disease or risk factors and in those receiving higher doses. New onset hypertension or exacerbation of hypertension may occur (NSAIDs may also impair response to ACE inhibitors, thiazide diuretics, or loop diuretics); may contribute to cardiovascular events; monitor blood pressure; use with caution in patients with hypertension. May cause sodium and fluid retention, use with caution in patients with edema. Avoid use in heart failure (ACCF/AHA [Yancy 2013]). Avoid use in patients with a recent MI unless benefits outweigh risk of cardiovascular thrombotic events Use the lowest effective dose for the shortest duration of time, consistent with individual patient goals, to reduce risk of cardiovascular events; alternate therapies should be considered for patients at high risk. **[US Boxed Warning]: Use is contraindicated in the setting of coronary artery bypass graft (CABG) surgery.** Risk of MI and stroke may be increased with use following CABG surgery.

NSAID use may compromise existing renal function; dose-dependent decreases in prostaglandin synthesis may result from NSAID use, reducing renal blood flow which may cause renal decompensation (usually reversible). Patients with impaired renal function, dehydration, hypovolemia, heart failure, hepatic impairment, those taking diuretics, and ACE inhibitors, and the elderly are at greater risk of renal toxicity. Rehydrate patient before starting therapy; monitor renal function closely. Long-term NSAID use may result in renal papillary necrosis and other renal injury. Rehydrate patient before starting therapy; monitor renal function closely. Avoid use in patients with advanced renal disease; discontinue use with persistent or worsening abnormal renal function tests. Long-term NSAID use may result in renal papillary necrosis.

[US Boxed Warning]: NSAIDs cause increased risk of serious gastrointestinal inflammation, ulceration, bleeding, and perforation (may be fatal); elderly patients and patients with history of peptic ulcer disease and/or GI bleeding are at greater risk of serious GI events. These events may occur at any time during therapy and without warning. Avoid use in patients with active GI bleeding. Use caution with a history of GI ulcers, concurrent therapy known to increase the risk of GI bleeding (eg, aspirin, anticoagulants and/or corticosteroids, selective serotonin reuptake inhibitors), advanced hepatic disease, coagulopathy, smoking, use of alcohol, or in elderly or debilitated patients. Use the lowest effective dose for the shortest duration of time, consistent with individual patient goals, to reduce risk of GI adverse events; alternate therapies should be considered for patients at high risk. When used concomitantly with aspirin, a substantial increase in the risk of gastrointestinal complications (eg, ulcer) occurs; concomitant gastroprotective therapy (eg, proton pump inhibitors) is recommended (Bhatt 2008). Platelet adhesion and aggregation may be decreased; may prolong bleeding time; patients with coagulation disorders or who are receiving anticoagulants should be monitored closely. Anemia may occur; patients on long-term NSAID therapy should be monitored for anemia. Rarely, NSAID use may cause severe blood dyscrasias (eg, agranulocytosis, aplastic anemia, thrombocytopenia).

May cause drowsiness, dizziness, blurred vision and other neurologic effects which may impair physical or mental abilities; patients must be cautioned about performing tasks which require mental alertness (eg, operating machinery or driving). Discontinue use with blurred or diminished vision and perform ophthalmologic exam. Monitor vision with long-term therapy.

NSAIDs may cause potentially fatal serious skin adverse events including exfoliative dermatitis, Stevens-Johnson syndrome (SJS), and toxic epidermal necrolysis (TEN); may occur without warning; discontinue use at first sign of skin rash (or any other hypersensitivity). Anaphylactoid reactions may occur, even without prior exposure; patients with "aspirin triad" (bronchial asthma, aspirin intolerance, rhinitis) may be at increased risk. Contraindicated in patients who experience bronchospasm, asthma, rhinitis, or urticaria with NSAID or aspirin therapy. Use caution in other forms of asthma.

Elderly patients are at greater risk for serious GI, cardiovascular, and/or renal adverse events; use with caution. Use with caution in patients with hepatic impairment; patients with advanced hepatic disease are at an increased risk of GI bleeding with NSAIDs. Systemic exposure may be increased in patients with chronic disease and/or hypoalbuminemia. Closely monitor patients with any abnormal liver function test (LFT). Transaminase elevations have been reported with use; closely monitor patients with any abnormal LFT. Rare (sometimes fatal) severe hepatic reactions (eg, fulminant hepatitis, hepatic necrosis, hepatic failure) have occurred with NSAID use; discontinue immediately if signs or symptoms of hepatic disease develop or if systemic manifestations occur. NSAID use may increase the risk of hyperkalemia, particularly in the elderly, diabetics, renal disease, and with concomitant use of other agents capable of inducing hyperkalemia (eg, ACE-inhibitors). Monitor potassium closely.

May increase the risk of aseptic meningitis, especially in patients with systemic lupus erythematosus (SLE) and mixed connective tissue disorders. Withhold for at least 4 to 6 half-lives prior to surgical or dental procedures. Potentially significant interactions may exist, requiring dose or frequency adjustment, additional monitoring, and/or selection of alternative therapy. Consult drug interactions database for more detailed information.

Drug Interactions

Metabolism/Transport Effects **Substrate** of OAT3; **Inhibits** CYP2C9 (weak)

Avoid Concomitant Use

Avoid concomitant use of Ketoprofen with any of the following: Dexketoprofen; Floctafenine; Ketorolac (Nasal); Ketorolac (Systemic); Morniflumate; NSAID (COX-2 Inhibitor); Omacetaxine; Pelubiprofen; Phenylbutazone; Talniflumate; Tenoxicam; Urokinase; Zaltoprofen

Increased Effect/Toxicity

Ketoprofen may increase the levels/effects of: 5-ASA Derivatives; Agents with Antiplatelet Properties; Aliskiren; Aminoglycosides; Aminolevulinic Acid; Anticoagulants; Apixaban; Bisphosphonate Derivatives; Cephalothin; Collagenase (Systemic); CycloSPORINE (Systemic); Dabigatran Etexilate; Deferasirox; Deoxycholic Acid; Desmopressin; Digoxin; Drospirenone; Edoxaban; Eplerenone; Haloperidol; Ibritumomab; Lithium; Methotrexate; Nonsteroidal Anti-Inflammatory Agents; NSAID (COX-2 Inhibitor); Obinutuzumab; Omacetaxine; PEMEtrexed; Porfimer; Potassium-Sparing Diuretics; PRALAtrexate; Quinolone Antibiotics; Rivaroxaban; Salicylates; Tacrolimus (Systemic); Tenofovir Products; Thrombolytic Agents; Tolperisone; Tositumomab and Iodine I 131 Tositumomab; Urokinase; Vancomycin; Verteporfin; Vitamin K Antagonists

The levels/effects of Ketoprofen may be increased by: ACE Inhibitors; Alcohol (Ethyl); Angiotensin II Receptor Blockers; Antidepressants (Tricyclic, Tertiary Amine); Corticosteroids (Systemic); CycloSPORINE (Systemic); Dasatinib; Dexketoprofen; Diclofenac (Systemic); Felbinac; Floctafenine; Glucosamine; Herbs (Anticoagulant/Antiplatelet Properties); Ibrutinib; Ketorolac (Nasal); Ketorolac (Systemic); Limaprost; Loop Diuretics; Morniflumate; Multivitamins/Fluoride (with ADE); Multivitamins/Minerals (with ADEK, Folate, Iron); Multivitamins/Minerals (with AE, No Iron); Naftazone; Omega-3 Fatty Acids; Pelubiprofen; Pentosan Polysulfate Sodium; Pentoxifylline; Phenylbutazone; Probenecid; Prostacyclin Analogues; Selective Serotonin Reuptake Inhibitors; Serotonin/Norepinephrine Reuptake Inhibitors; Sodium Phosphates; Talniflumate; Tenoxicam; Teriflunomide; Thiazide and Thiazide-Like Diuretics; Tipranavir; Tolperisone; Vitamin E (Systemic); Zaltoprofen

Decreased Effect

Ketoprofen may decrease the levels/effects of: ACE Inhibitors; Aliskiren; Angiotensin II Receptor Blockers; Beta-Blockers; Eplerenone; HydrALAZINE; Loop Diuretics; Potassium-Sparing Diuretics; Prostaglandins (Ophthalmic); Salicylates; Selective Serotonin Reuptake Inhibitors; Thiazide and Thiazide-Like Diuretics

The levels/effects of Ketoprofen may be decreased by: Bile Acid Sequestrants; Salicylates

Dietary Considerations To minimize gastrointestinal effects, administer with food or milk.

Pharmacodynamics/Kinetics

Onset of Action Regular release: <30 minutes

Duration of Action Regular release: Up to 6 hours

Half-life Elimination

Regular release: 2 to 4 hours; Renal impairment: Mild: 3 hours; moderate to severe: 5 to 9 hours

Enteric coated tablet [Canadian product]: 2 hours

Extended release: ~3 to 7.5 hours

Rectal suppository [Canadian product]: ~2 to 2.5 hours

Time to Peak Regular release: 0.5 to 2 hours; Extended release capsule: 6 to 7 hours; Extended release tablet [Canadian product]: 5 to 6 hours; Enteric coated tablet [Canadian product]: 1 to 2 hours; Rectal suppository [Canadian product]: ~1 hour

Pregnancy Risk Factor C

Pregnancy Considerations Adverse events have not been observed in the initial animal reproduction studies. Ketoprofen crosses the placenta. NSAID exposure during the first trimester is not strongly associated with congenital malformations; however, cardiovascular anomalies and cleft palate have been observed following NSAID exposure in some studies. The use of an NSAID close to conception may be associated with an increased risk of miscarriage. Nonteratogenic effects have been observed following NSAID administration during the third trimester including myocardial degenerative changes, prenatal constriction of the ductus arteriosus, fetal tricuspid regurgitation, failure of the ductus arteriosus to close postnatally; renal dysfunction or failure, oligohydramnios; gastrointestinal bleeding or perforation, increased risk of necrotizing enterocolitis; intracranial bleeding (including intraventricular hemorrhage), platelet dysfunction with resultant bleeding; pulmonary hypertension. Because they may cause premature closure of the ductus arteriosus, use of NSAIDs late in pregnancy should be avoided (use after 31 or 32 weeks gestation is not recommended by some clinicians). The chronic use of NSAIDs in women of reproductive age may be associated with infertility that is reversible upon discontinuation of the medication.

Breastfeeding Considerations Small amounts of ketoprofen are found in breast milk (Jacqz-Aigrain,

2007). breastfeeding is not recommended by the manufacturer.

Dosage Forms Considerations Active-Ketoprofen and Ketophene Rapidpaq creams are compounded from a kit. Refer to manufacturer's labeling for compounding instructions.

Dosage Forms

Capsule, Oral:

Generic: 50 mg, 75 mg

Capsule Extended Release 24 Hour, Oral:

Generic: 200 mg

Cream, External:

Active-Ketoprofen: 5% (120 g)

Ketophene Rapidpaq: 20% (100 g)

Dosage Forms: Canada

Note: Refer also to Dosage Forms. Extended release capsule and external cream are not available in Canada.

Enteric coated tablet, Oral: 50 mg, 100 mg

Extended release tablet, Oral: 200 mg

Suppository, Rectal: 50 mg, 100 mg

Ketorolac (Systemic) (KEE toe role ak)

Related Information

Oral Pain *on page 1830*

Rheumatoid Arthritis, Osteoarthritis, and Osteoporosis *on page 1792*

Temporomandibular Dysfunction (TMD), Chronic Pain, and Fibromyalgia *on page 1868*

Brand Names: US ReadySharp Ketorolac

Brand Names: Canada Apo-Ketorolac Injectable; Ketorolac Tromethamine Injection, USP; Toradol; Toradol IM

Generic Availability (US) May be product dependent

Pharmacologic Category Analgesic, Nonopioid; Nonsteroidal Anti-inflammatory Drug (NSAID), Oral; Nonsteroidal Anti-inflammatory Drug (NSAID), Parenteral

Dental Use Short-term (≤5 days) management of moderate-to-severe acute pain requiring analgesia at the opioid level

Use Pain management:

US labeling: Short-term (≤5 days) management of moderate to severe acute pain requiring analgesia at the opioid level

Canadian labeling:

Oral: Short-term (≤5 days) management of moderate to moderately severe acute pain following surgery (eg, dental, general, or orthopaedic surgery); short-term (≤7 days) management of moderate to moderately severe acute musculoskeletal pain (eg, pain associated with trauma, post-partum uterine cramping)

Injection: Short-term (≤2 days) management of moderate to severe acute pain following major surgery (eg, major abdominal, orthopaedic, or gynecologic procedures)

Local Anesthetic/Vasoconstrictor Precautions No information available to require special precautions

Effects on Dental Treatment Key adverse event(s) related to dental treatment: Xerostomia (normal salivary flow resumes upon discontinuation) and stomatitis.

NSAID formulations are known to reversibly decrease platelet aggregation via mechanisms different than observed with aspirin. The dentist should be aware of the potential of abnormal coagulation. Caution should also be exercised in the use of NSAIDs in patients already on anticoagulant therapy with drugs such as warfarin (Coumadin®). See Dental Comment.

Effects on Bleeding Nonselective NSAIDs such as ketorolac inhibit platelet aggregation and prolong bleeding time in some patients. Unlike aspirin, the NSAID effect on platelet function is quantitatively less, of shorter duration, and reversible.

Adverse Reactions Frequencies noted for parenteral administration:

>10%:

Central nervous system: Headache (17%)

Gastrointestinal: Gastrointestinal pain (13%), dyspepsia (12%), nausea (12%)

>1% to 10%:

Cardiovascular: Edema (4%), hypertension

Central nervous system: Dizziness (7%), drowsiness (6%)

Dermatologic: Diaphoresis, pruritus, skin rash

Gastrointestinal: Diarrhea (7%), constipation, flatulence, gastrointestinal fullness, gastrointestinal hemorrhage, gastrointestinal perforation, gastrointestinal ulcer, heartburn, stomatitis, vomiting

Hematologic & oncologic: Anemia, prolonged bleeding time, purpura

Hepatic: Increased liver enzymes

Local: Pain at injection site (2%)

Otic: Tinnitus

Renal: Renal function abnormality

<1%, postmarketing, and/or case reports: Abnormality in thinking, acute pancreatitis, acute renal failure, agranulocytosis, alopecia, anaphylactoid reaction, anaphylaxis, angioedema, anxiety, aplastic anemia, aseptic meningitis, asthma, azotemia, blurred vision, bradycardia, bronchospasm, bruise, cardiac arrhythmia, chest pain, cholestatic jaundice, coma, confusion, congestive heart failure, conjunctivitis, cough, cystitis, depression, dyspnea, dysuria, eosinophilia, epistaxis, eructation, erythema multiforme, esophagitis, euphoria, exacerbation of urinary frequency, exfoliative dermatitis, extrapyramidal reaction, fever, flank pain, flushing, gastritis, glossitis, hallucination, hearing loss, hematemesis, hematuria, hemolytic anemia, hemolytic-uremic syndrome, hepatic failure, hepatitis, hepatotoxicity (idiosyncratic) (Chalasani, 2014), hyperglycemia, hyperkalemia, hyperkinesis, hypersensitivity reaction, hyponatremia, hypotension, increased susceptibility to infection, increased thirst, infertility, inflammatory bowel disease, insomnia, interstitial nephritis, jaundice, lack of concentration, laryngeal edema, leukopenia, lymphadenopathy, maculopapular rash, melena, myocardial infarction, nephritis, nervousness, oliguria, pallor, palpitations, pancytopenia, paresthesia, pneumonia, polyuria, proteinuria, psychosis, pulmonary edema, rectal hemorrhage, renal failure, respiratory depression, rhinitis, seizure, sepsis, skin photosensitivity, Stevens-Johnson syndrome, stomatitis (ulcerative), stupor, syncope, tachycardia, thrombocytopenia, tongue edema, toxic epidermal necrolysis, tremor, urinary retention, urticaria, vasculitis, vertigo, weakness, weight gain, wound hemorrhage (postoperative), xerostomia

Dental Usual Dosage

Short-term (≤5 days) management of moderate-to-severe acute pain requiring analgesia at the opioid level (**Note:** The maximum combined duration of treatment (for parenteral and oral) is 5 days; do not increase dose or frequency; supplement with low-dose opioids if needed for breakthrough pain). For patients <50 kg and/or ≥65 years, see Geriatric dosing.

Adults:

IM: 60 mg as a single dose or 30 mg every 6 hours (maximum daily dose: 120 mg)

IV: 30 mg as a single dose or 30 mg every 6 hours (maximum daily dose: 120 mg)

Oral: 20 mg, followed by 10 mg every 4-6 hours; do not exceed 40 mg/day; oral dosing is intended to be a continuation of IM or IV therapy only

Dosage adjustments in elderly (≥65 years), renal insufficiency, or low body weight (<50 kg): Note: These groups have an increased incidence of GI bleeding, ulceration, and perforation. The maximum combined duration of treatment (for parenteral and oral) is 5 days.

IM: 30 mg as a single dose or 15 mg every 6 hours (maximum daily dose: 60 mg)

IV: 15 mg as a single dose or 15 mg every 6 hours (maximum daily dose: 60 mg)

Oral: 10 mg, followed by 10 mg every 4-6 hours; do not exceed 40 mg/day; oral dosing is intended to be a continuation of IM or IV therapy only

Dosing

Adult

Pain management (acute; moderately severe) in patients ≥50 kg: Note: The maximum combined duration of treatment (for parenteral and oral) is 5 days; do not increase dose or frequency; supplement with low-dose opioids if needed for breakthrough pain. Oral formulation should not be given as an initial dose.

US labeling:

IM: 60 mg as a single dose or 30 mg every 6 hours (maximum: 120 mg/day)

IV: 30 mg as a single dose or 30 mg every 6 hours (maximum: 120 mg/day)

IM, IV: Critically-ill patients (off-label dose): 30 mg once, followed by 15 to 30 mg every 6 hours for up to 5 days (maximum: 120 mg/day) (Barr 2013)

Oral: 20 mg, followed by 10 mg every 4 to 6 hours as needed; maximum: 40 mg/day; oral dosing is intended to be a continuation of IM or IV therapy only

Canadian labeling:

IM: Initial: 10 mg to 30 mg as a single dose and then every 4 to 6 hours as needed (maximum: 120 mg/day) for up to 2 days; lowest effective dose should be utilized

Oral: 10 mg every 4 to 6 hours as needed (maximum: 40 mg/day); therapy should not exceed 5 days for postoperative pain and 7 days for musculoskeletal pain

Conversion from IM to oral: Total combined dose (IM and oral) should not exceed 120 mg/day on the day of conversion; oral dose should not exceed 40 mg/day on subsequent days. When used as a continuation of IM therapy, total duration of therapy (IM and oral) should not exceed 5 days.

Dosage adjustment for low body weight (<50 kg): Refer to geriatric dosing.

Geriatric

Pain management (acute; moderately severe): Adults ≥65 years: **Note:** May have an increased incidence of GI bleeding, ulceration, and perforation. The maximum combined duration of treatment (for parenteral and oral) is 5 days. Oral formulation should not be given as an initial dose.

US labeling:

IM: 30 mg as a single dose or 15 mg every 6 hours (maximum: 60 mg/day)

IV: 15 mg as a single dose or 15 mg every 6 hours (maximum: 60 mg/day)

Oral: 10 mg, followed by 10 mg every 4 to 6 hours as needed; maximum: 40 mg/day; oral dosing is intended to be a continuation of IM or IV therapy only

Canadian labeling:

IM: Initial: 10 mg as a single dose and then the lowest effective dose every 4 to 6 hours as needed; maximum: 60 mg/day

Oral: Refer to adult dosing; lowest effective dose is recommended

Pediatric Pain management (acute; moderately severe): Adolescents ≥17 years: Refer to adult dosing.

Renal Impairment

US labeling:

Mild to moderate impairment:

IM: 30 mg as a single dose or 15 mg every 6 hours (maximum: 60 mg/day)

IV: 15 mg as a single dose or 15 mg every 6 hours (maximum: 60 mg/day)

Oral: 10 mg, followed by 10 mg every 4 to 6 hours as needed; maximum: 40 mg/day; oral dosing is intended to be a continuation of IM or IV therapy only

Note: The maximum combined duration of treatment (for parenteral and oral) is 5 days.

Advanced impairment or patients at risk for renal failure due to volume depletion: Use is contraindicated.

Dialysis: Not readily dialyzable due to high protein binding

Canadian labeling:

Serum creatinine: 1.9 mg/dL to 5 mg/dL (170 micromol/L to 442 micromol/L): IM: Reduce dose by 50%; maximum: 60 mg/day. Use with caution and monitor closely.

Serum creatinine: >5 mg/dL (>442 micromol/L): Use is contraindicated.

Note: The maximum combined duration of treatment (for parenteral and oral) is 5 days.

Hepatic Impairment

US labeling: There are no dosage adjustments provided in the manufacturer's labeling. Use with caution, may cause elevation of liver enzymes; discontinue if clinical signs and symptoms of liver disease develop.

Canadian labeling:

Mild or moderate impairment: No dosage adjustment necessary; use with caution

Severe impairment or active hepatic disease: Use is contraindicated

Mechanism of Action Reversibly inhibits cyclooxygenase-1 and 2 (COX-1 and 2) enzymes, which results in decreased formation of prostaglandin precursors; has antipyretic, analgesic, and anti-inflammatory properties

Other proposed mechanisms not fully elucidated (and possibly contributing to the anti-inflammatory effect to varying degrees), include inhibiting chemotaxis, altering lymphocyte activity, inhibiting neutrophil aggregation/activation, and decreasing proinflammatory cytokine levels.

Contraindications

Hypersensitivity to ketorolac, aspirin, other NSAIDs, or any component of the formulation; active or history of peptic ulcer disease; recent or history of GI bleeding or perforation; history of asthma, urticaria, or allergic-type reactions after taking aspirin or other NSAIDs; advanced renal disease or risk of renal failure (due to volume depletion); prophylactic analgesic before any major surgery; suspected or confirmed cerebrovascular bleeding, hemorrhagic diathesis, incomplete hemostasis, or high risk of bleeding; concurrent use with aspirin, other NSAIDs, probenecid, or pentoxifylline; epidural or intrathecal administration (injection only); use in the setting of coronary artery bypass graft (CABG) surgery; labor and delivery.

Canadian labeling: Additional contraindications (not in US labeling): Intraoperative use; coagulation disorders; active GI bleeding; postoperative patients with high-bleeding risk; severe uncontrolled heart failure; inflammatory bowel disease; severe hepatic impairment or active hepatic disease; moderate to severe renal impairment (serum creatinine >442 micromol/L and/or creatinine clearance <30 mL/minute) or deteriorating renal; known hyperkalemia; third trimester of pregnancy; breastfeeding; use in children and adolescents <18 years of age

Warnings/Precautions [US Boxed Warning]: Inhibits platelet function; contraindicated in patients with cerebrovascular bleeding (suspected or confirmed), hemorrhagic diathesis, incomplete hemostasis and patients at high risk for bleeding. Platelet adhesion and aggregation may be decreased; may prolong bleeding time; patients with coagulation disorders or who are receiving anticoagulants should be monitored closely. Anemia may occur; patients on long-term NSAID therapy should be monitored for anemia. Rarely, NSAID use has been associated with potentially severe blood dyscrasias (eg, agranulocytosis, thrombocytopenia, aplastic anemia). **[US Boxed Warning]: NSAIDs cause an increased risk of serious (and potentially fatal) adverse cardiovascular thrombotic events, including MI and stroke. Risk may occur early during treatment and may increase with duration of use.** Relative risk appears to be similar in those with and without known cardiovascular disease or risk factors for cardiovascular disease; however, absolute incidence of serious cardiovascular thrombotic events (which may occur early during treatment) was higher in patients with known cardiovascular disease or risk factors and in those receiving higher doses. New onset hypertension or exacerbation of hypertension may occur (NSAIDs may also impair response to ACE inhibitors, thiazide diuretics, or loop diuretics); may contribute to cardiovascular events; monitor blood pressure; use with caution in patients with hypertension. May cause sodium and fluid retention, use with caution in patients with edema. Avoid use in heart failure (ACCF/AHA [Yancy 2013]). Avoid use in patients with a recent MI unless benefits outweigh risk of cardiovascular thrombotic events. Use the lowest effective dose for the shortest duration of time, consistent with individual patient goals, to reduce risk of cardiovascular events; alternate therapies should be considered for patients at high risk. **[US Boxed Warning]: Use is contraindicated as prophylactic analgesic before any major surgery and is contraindicated in the setting of coronary artery bypass graft (CABG) surgery.** Risk of MI and stroke may be increased with use following CABG surgery. Wound bleeding and postoperative hematomas have been associated with ketorolac use in the perioperative setting.

[US Boxed Warning]: Ketorolac is contraindicated in patients with advanced renal impairment and in patients at risk for renal failure due to volume depletion. NSAID use may compromise existing renal function; dose-dependent decreases in prostaglandin synthesis may result from NSAID use, reducing renal blood flow, which may cause renal decompensation (usually reversible). Patients with impaired renal function, dehydration, hypovolemia, heart failure, hepatic impairment, those taking diuretics and ACE inhibitors, and the elderly are at greater risk of renal toxicity. Rehydrate patient before starting therapy; monitor renal function closely. Acute renal failure, interstitial nephritis, and nephrotic syndrome have been reported with ketorolac use; papillary necrosis and renal injury have been reported with long-term use of NSAIDs. Use with caution in patients with renal impairment or history of kidney disease. Dosage adjustment is required in patients with moderate elevation in serum creatinine.

[US Boxed Warning]: NSAIDs cause increased risk of serious gastrointestinal inflammation, ulceration, bleeding, and perforation (may be fatal); elderly patients and patients with history of peptic ulcer disease and/or GI bleeding are at greater risk of serious GI events. These events may occur at any time during therapy and without warning. Avoid use in patients with active GI bleeding. Use caution with a history of GI ulcers, inflammatory bowel disease, concurrent therapy known to increase the risk of GI bleeding (eg, aspirin, anticoagulants and/or corticosteroids, selective serotonin reuptake inhibitors), advanced hepatic disease, coagulopathy, smoking, use of alcohol, or in the elderly or debilitated patients. Use the lowest effective dose for the shortest duration of time, consistent with individual patient goals, to reduce risk of GI adverse events; alternate therapies should be considered for patients at high risk. When used concomitantly with aspirin, a substantial increase in the risk of gastrointestinal complications (eg, ulcer) occurs; concomitant gastroprotective therapy (eg, proton pump inhibitors) is recommended (Bhatt 2008). **[US Boxed Warning]: Ketorolac injection is contraindicated in patients with prior hypersensitivity reaction to aspirin or NSAIDs.** NSAIDs may cause potentially fatal serious skin adverse events including exfoliative dermatitis, Stevens-Johnson syndrome (SJS), and toxic epidermal necrolysis (TEN); may occur without warning; discontinue use at first sign of skin rash (or any other hypersensitivity). Hypersensitivity or anaphylactoid reactions may occur, even without prior exposure; patients with "aspirin triad" (bronchial asthma, aspirin intolerance, rhinitis) may be at increased risk. Contraindicated in patients who experience bronchospasm, asthma, rhinitis, or urticaria with NSAID or aspirin therapy. Use caution in other forms of asthma.

Use with caution in patients with hepatic impairment or a history of hepatic disease; patients with advanced hepatic disease are at an increased risk of GI bleeding with NSAIDs. Transaminase elevations have been reported with use; closely monitor patients with any abnormal LFT. Rare (sometimes fatal) severe hepatic reactions (eg, jaundice, fulminant hepatitis, hepatic necrosis, hepatic failure) have occurred with NSAID use; discontinue immediately if signs or symptoms of hepatic disease develop or if systemic manifestations occur. NSAID use may increase the risk of hyperkalemia, particularly in the elderly, diabetics, renal disease, and with concomitant use of other agents capable of inducing hyperkalemia (eg, ACE-inhibitors). Monitor potassium closely.

[US Boxed Warning]: Dosage adjustment is required for patients ≥65 years of age. Elderly patients are at greater risk for serious GI, cardiovascular, and/or renal adverse events; use with caution. **[US Boxed Warning]: Dosage adjustment is required for patients weighing <50 kg (<110 pounds). [US Boxed Warning]: Ketorolac is contraindicated during labor**

and delivery (may inhibit uterine contractions and adversely affect fetal circulation). [US Boxed Warning]: Concurrent use of ketorolac with aspirin or other NSAIDs is contraindicated due to the increased risk of adverse reactions.

[US Boxed Warning]: Contraindicated for epidural or intrathecal administration (formulation contains alcohol). [US Boxed Warning]: Systemic ketorolac is indicated for short term (≤5 days) use in adults for treatment of moderately severe acute pain requiring opioid-level analgesia. [US Boxed Warning]: Oral therapy is only indicated for use as continuation treatment, following parenteral ketorolac and is not indicated for minor or chronic painful conditions. Do not exceed maximum daily recommended doses; does not improve efficacy but may increase the risk of serious adverse effects. The combined therapy duration (oral and parenteral) should not exceed 5 days. **[US Boxed Warning]: Ketorolac is not indicated for use in pediatric patients.**

Potentially significant drug-drug interactions may exist, requiring dose or frequency adjustment, additional monitoring, and/or selection of alternative therapy.

NSAIDs may increase the risk of aseptic meningitis, especially in patients with systemic lupus erythematosus (SLE) and mixed connective tissue disorders. May cause drowsiness, dizziness, blurred vision and other neurologic effects which may impair physical or mental abilities; patients must be cautioned about performing tasks which require mental alertness (eg, operating machinery or driving). Withhold for at least 4 to 6 half-lives prior to surgical or dental procedures.

Drug Interactions

Metabolism/Transport Effects None known.

Avoid Concomitant Use

Avoid concomitant use of Ketorolac (Systemic) with any of the following: Aspirin; Dexketoprofen; Floctafenine; Ketorolac (Nasal); Morniflumate; Nonsteroidal Anti-Inflammatory Agents; Omacetaxine; Pelubiprofen; Pentoxifylline; Phenylbutazone; Probenecid; Talniflumate; Tenoxicam; Urokinase; Zaltoprofen

Increased Effect/Toxicity

Ketorolac (Systemic) may increase the levels/effects of: 5-ASA Derivatives; Agents with Antiplatelet Properties; Aliskiren; Aminoglycosides; Aminolevulinic Acid; Anticoagulants; Apixaban; Aspirin; Bisphosphonate Derivatives; Cephalothin; Collagenase (Systemic); CycloSPORINE (Systemic); Dabigatran Etexilate; Deferasirox; Deoxycholic Acid; Desmopressin; Digoxin; Drospirenone; Edoxaban; Eplerenone; Haloperidol; Ibritumomab; Lithium; Methotrexate; Neuromuscular-Blocking Agents (Nondepolarizing); Nonsteroidal Anti-Inflammatory Agents; Obinutuzumab; Omacetaxine; PEMEtrexed; Pentoxifylline; Porfimer; Potassium-Sparing Diuretics; PRALAtrexate; Quinolone Antibiotics; Rivaroxaban; Salicylates; Tacrolimus (Systemic); Tenofovir Products; Thrombolytic Agents; Tolperisone; Tositumomab and Iodine I 131 Tositumomab; Urokinase; Vancomycin; Verteporfin; Vitamin K Antagonists

The levels/effects of Ketorolac (Systemic) may be increased by: ACE Inhibitors; Alcohol (Ethyl); Angiotensin II Receptor Blockers; Antidepressants (Tricyclic, Tertiary Amine); Corticosteroids (Systemic); CycloSPORINE (Systemic); Dasatinib; Dexketoprofen; Felbinac; Floctafenine; Glucosamine; Herbs (Anticoagulant/Antiplatelet Properties); Ibrutinib; Ketorolac (Nasal); Limaprost; Loop Diuretics; Morniflumate; Multivitamins/Fluoride (with ADE); Multivitamins/Minerals (with ADEK, Folate, Iron); Multivitamins/Minerals (with AE, No Iron); Naftazone; Omega-3 Fatty Acids; Pelubiprofen; Pentosan Polysulfate Sodium; Phenylbutazone; Probenecid; Prostacyclin Analogues; Selective Serotonin Reuptake Inhibitors; Serotonin/Norepinephrine Reuptake Inhibitors; Sodium Phosphates; Talniflumate; Tenoxicam; Thiazide and Thiazide-Like Diuretics; Tipranavir; Tolperisone; Vitamin E (Systemic); Zaltoprofen

Decreased Effect

Ketorolac (Systemic) may decrease the levels/effects of: ACE Inhibitors; Aliskiren; Angiotensin II Receptor Blockers; Aspirin; Beta-Blockers; Eplerenone; HydrALAZINE; Loop Diuretics; Potassium-Sparing Diuretics; Prostaglandins (Ophthalmic); Salicylates; Selective Serotonin Reuptake Inhibitors; Thiazide and Thiazide-Like Diuretics

The levels/effects of Ketorolac (Systemic) may be decreased by: Bile Acid Sequestrants; Salicylates

Food Interactions High-fat meals may delay time to peak (by ~1 hour) and decrease peak concentrations. Management: Administer tablet with food or milk to decrease gastrointestinal distress.

Dietary Considerations Administer tablet with food or milk to decrease gastrointestinal distress.

Pharmacodynamics/Kinetics

Onset of Action Analgesic: Oral: 30-60 minutes; IM, IV: ~30 minutes; Peak effect: Analgesic: Oral: 2 to 3 hours; IM, IV: ≤2-3 hours

Duration of Action Analgesic: 4-6 hours

Half-life Elimination

Infants 6-18 months of age (n=25): S-enantiomer: 0.83 ± 0.7 hours; R-enantiomer: 4 ± 0.8 hours (Lynn 2007)

Children:

- 1-16 years (n=36): Mean: 3 ± 1.1 hours (Dsida 2002)
- 3-18 years (n=24): Mean: 3.8 ± 2.6 hours
- 4-8 years (n=10): Mean: ~6 hours; Range: 3.5-10 hours

Adults:

- Mean: ~5 hours; Range: 2-9 hours [S-enantiomer ~2.5 hours (biologically active); R-enantiomer ~5 hours]
- With renal impairment: S_{cr} 1.9-5 mg/dL: Mean: ~11 hours; Range: 4-19 hours
- Renal dialysis patients: Mean: ~14 hours; Range: 0-40 hours

Time to Peak Serum: Oral: ~45 minutes; IM: 30-60 minutes; IV: 1-3 minutes

Pregnancy Risk Factor C

Pregnancy Considerations Adverse events were observed in some animal reproduction studies. Ketorolac crosses the placenta (Walker 1988). NSAID exposure during the first trimester is not strongly associated with congenital malformations; however, cardiovascular anomalies and cleft palate have been observed following NSAID exposure in some studies (Ericson 2001). The use of an NSAID close to conception may be associated with an increased risk of miscarriage (Li 2003; Nielsen 2001). Nonteratogenic effects have been observed following NSAID administration during the third trimester, including myocardial degenerative changes, prenatal constriction of the ductus arteriosus, fetal tricuspid regurgitation, failure of the ductus arteriosus to close postnatally; renal dysfunction or failure, oligohydramnios; gastrointestinal bleeding or perforation, increased risk of necrotizing enterocolitis; intracranial bleeding (including intraventricular hemorrhage), platelet dysfunction with resultant bleeding; pulmonary hypertension (Van den Veyver 1993). Because they may cause premature closure of the ductus arteriosus, use of NSAIDs late in pregnancy should be avoided (use after 31 or 32 weeks gestation is not recommended by some clinicians) (Moise 1993). **[US Boxed Warning]: Ketorolac is contraindicated during labor and delivery (may inhibit uterine contractions and adversely affect fetal circulation).** The chronic use of NSAIDs in women of reproductive age may be associated with infertility that is reversible upon discontinuation of the medication.

Breastfeeding Considerations Ketorolac is present in breast milk (Wischnik 1989).

The relative infant dose (RID) of ketorolac is 0.21% when calculated using the highest breast milk concentration located and compared to a weight-adjusted maternal dose of 40 mg/day. In general, breastfeeding is considered acceptable when the RID is <10%; when an RID is >25% breastfeeding should generally be avoided (Anderson 2016; Ito 2000). Using the highest milk concentration (7.9 ng/mL), the estimated daily infant dose via breast milk is 1.185 mcg/kg/day. This milk concentration was obtained following maternal administration of oral ketorolac 10 mg four times a day for 2 days in women 2 to 6 days postpartum (Wischnik 1989).

In general, NSAIDs may be used in postpartum women who wish to breastfeed; however, agents other than ketorolac are preferred (Montgomery 2012) and use should be avoided in women breastfeeding infants with platelet dysfunction or thrombocytopenia (Bloor 2013; Sammaritano 2014). The manufacturer recommends that caution be used if administered to breastfeeding women.

Dosage Forms

Kit, Injection:
ReadySharp Ketorolac: 15 mg/mL

Solution, Injection:
Generic: 15 mg/mL (1 mL); 30 mg/mL (1 mL); 60 mg/2 mL (2 mL)

Solution, Injection [preservative free]:
Generic: 15 mg/mL (1 mL); 30 mg/mL (1 mL)

Solution, Intramuscular:
Generic: 60 mg/2 mL (2 mL)

Solution, Intramuscular [preservative free]:
Generic: 60 mg/2 mL (2 mL)

Tablet, Oral:
Generic: 10 mg

Dental Comment According to the manufacturer, ketorolac has been used inappropriately by physicians in the past. The drug had been prescribed to NSAID-sensitive patients, patients with GI bleeding, and for long-term use; a warning has been issued regarding increased incidence and severity of GI complications with increasing doses and duration of use. Labeling now includes the statement that ketorolac inhibits platelet function and is indicated for up to 5 days use only.

Ketotifen (Systemic) (kee toe TYE fen)

Related Information

Respiratory Diseases *on page 1777*

Brand Names: Canada APO-Ketotifen; Novo-Ketotifen; Zaditen

Pharmacologic Category Histamine H_1 Antagonist; Histamine H_1 Antagonist, Second Generation; Mast Cell Stabilizer; Piperidine Derivative

Use Note: Not approved in the US

Atopic asthma: Adjunctive therapy in the chronic treatment of mild, atopic asthma in children

Limitations of use: Not indicated for acute prevention or treatment of acute asthma attacks.

Local Anesthetic/Vasoconstrictor Precautions No information available to require special precautions

Effects on Dental Treatment No significant effects or complications reported

Effects on Bleeding No information available to require special precautions

Adverse Reactions

1% to 10%:

Central nervous system: Disturbed sleep (1%), headache (1%)

Dermatologic: Skin rash (4%), urticaria (1%)

Endocrine & metabolic: Weight gain (5%)

Gastrointestinal: Abdominal pain (1%), increased appetite (1%)

Infection: Influenza (3%)

Ophthalmic: Eyelid edema (1%)

Respiratory: Respiratory tract infection (4%), epistaxis (1%)

<1%, postmarketing, and/or case reports: Cystitis, dizziness, erythema multiforme, excitement, hepatitis, increased serum transaminases, insomnia, irritability, nervousness, Stevens-Johnson syndrome, thrombocytopenia, xerostomia

General Dosage Range Oral:

Infants and Children 6 months to 3 years: Initial: 0.05 mg/kg once daily or in 2 divided doses for 5 days; Maintenance: 0.05 mg/kg/dose twice daily (maximum dose: 1 mg twice daily)

Children >3 years and Adolescents: Initial: 1 mg once daily or in 2 divided doses for 5 days; Maintenance: 1 mg twice daily

Mechanism of Action Exhibits noncompetitive H_1-receptor antagonist and mast cell stabilizer properties. Efficacy in asthma likely results from a combination of anti-inflammatory and antihistaminergic actions including interference with chemokine-induced migration of eosinophils into inflamed airways, inhibition of airway hyper-reactivity due to platelet activating factor (PAF), antagonism of leukotriene-induced bronchoconstriction.

Pharmacodynamics/Kinetics

Half-life Elimination Biphasic: Distribution: 3 to 5 hours; Elimination: 21 hours

Time to Peak Plasma: 2 to 4 hours

Pregnancy Considerations Adverse events have been observed in some animal studies.

Product Availability Not available in the US

Ketotifen (Ophthalmic) (kee toe TYE fen)

Brand Names: US Alaway Childrens Allergy [OTC]; Alaway [OTC]; Claritin Eye [OTC]; Eye Itch Relief [OTC]; TheraTears Allergy [OTC]; Zaditor [OTC]; ZyrTEC Itchy Eye [OTC] [DSC]

Brand Names: Canada Zaditor

Pharmacologic Category Histamine H_1 Antagonist; Histamine H_1 Antagonist, Second Generation; Mast Cell Stabilizer; Piperidine Derivative

Use Allergic conjunctivitis: Temporary relief of eye itching due to allergic conjunctivitis

Local Anesthetic/Vasoconstrictor Precautions No information available to require special precautions

Effects on Dental Treatment Key adverse event(s) related to dental treatment: Pharyngitis.

Effects on Bleeding No information available to require special precautions

Adverse Reactions Reactions are generally mild, transient, and local as systemic exposure following topical ocular administration is minimal.

>10%:

Central nervous system: Headache (≤10% to ≤25%)

Ophthalmic: Conjunctival injection (≤10% to ≤25%)

Respiratory: Rhinitis (≤10% to ≤25%)

1% to 10%:

Hypersensitivity: Hypersensitivity reaction (ophthalmic; <5%)

Ophthalmic: Circumocular rash (<5%), conjunctivitis (<5%), disease of the lacrimal apparatus (<5%), eye pain (<5%), keratitis (<5%), mydriasis (<5%), photophobia (<5%), burning sensation of eyes (<3%), eye discharge (<3%), eyelid disease (<3%), eye pruritus (<3%), stinging of eyes (<3%), xerophthalmia (<3%)

Respiratory: Flu-like symptoms (<5%), pharyngitis (<5%)

General Dosage Range Ophthalmic: *Children ≥3 years, Adolescents, and Adults:* Instill 1 drop into the affected eye(s) twice daily, every 8 to 12 hours

Mechanism of Action Exhibits noncompetitive H_1-receptor antagonist and mast cell stabilizer properties. Efficacy in conjunctivitis likely results from a combination of anti-inflammatory and antihistaminergic actions including interference with chemokine-induced migration of eosinophils into inflamed conjunctiva.

Pharmacodynamics/Kinetics

Onset of Action Within minutes (Zaditor Canadian product monograph, 2012)

Duration of Action Up to 12 hours (Zaditor Canadian product monograph, 2012)

Pregnancy Considerations Topical ocular administration has not been studied.

Labetalol (la BET a lole)

Related Information

Cardiovascular Diseases *on page 1752*

Brand Names: US Trandate [DSC]

Brand Names: Canada Apo-Labetalol; Labetalol Hydrochloride Injection, USP; Trandate

Pharmacologic Category Antihypertensive; Beta-Blocker With Alpha-Blocking Activity

Use Hypertension: Management of hypertension (IV indicated for severe hypertension only [eg, hypertensive emergencies])

The 2014 guideline for the management of high blood pressure in adults (Eighth Joint National Committee [JNC 8]) recommends initiation of pharmacologic treatment to lower blood pressure for the following patients (JNC8 [James, 2013]):

- Patients ≥60 years of age, with systolic blood pressure (SBP) ≥150 mm Hg or diastolic blood pressure (DBP) ≥90 mm Hg. Goal of therapy is SBP <150 mm Hg and DBP <90 mm Hg.
- Patients <60 years of age, with SBP ≥140 mm Hg or DBP ≥90 mm Hg. Goal of therapy is SBP <140 mm Hg and DBP <90 mm Hg.
- Patients ≥18 years of age with diabetes, with SBP ≥140 mm Hg or DBP ≥90 mm Hg. Goal of therapy is SBP <140 mm Hg and DBP <90 mm Hg.
- Patients ≥18 years of age with chronic kidney disease (CKD), with SBP ≥140 mm Hg or DBP ≥90 mm Hg. Goal of therapy is SBP <140 mm Hg and DBP <90 mm Hg.

In patients with CKD, regardless of race or diabetes status, the use of an ACE inhibitor (ACEI) or angiotensin receptor blocker (ARB) as initial therapy is recommended to improve kidney outcomes. In the general nonblack population (without CKD) including those with diabetes, initial antihypertensive treatment should consist of a thiazide-type diuretic, calcium channel blocker, ACEI, or ARB. In the general black population (without CKD) including those with diabetes, initial antihypertensive treatment should consist of a thiazide-type diuretic or a calcium channel blocker **instead of** an ACEI or ARB.

Local Anesthetic/Vasoconstrictor Precautions Use with caution; epinephrine has interacted with nonselective beta-blockers to result in initial hypertensive episode followed by bradycardia

Effects on Dental Treatment Key adverse event(s) related to dental treatment: Taste disorder.

Many nonsteroidal anti-inflammatory drugs, such as ibuprofen and indomethacin, can reduce the hypotensive effect of beta-blockers after 3 or more weeks of therapy with the NSAID. Short-term NSAID use (ie, 3 days) requires no special precautions in patients taking beta-blockers.

Effects on Bleeding No information available to require special precautions

Adverse Reactions

>10%:

Cardiovascular: Orthostatic hypotension (intravenous: ≤58%)

Central nervous system: Dizziness (1% to 20%), fatigue (1% to 11%)

Gastrointestinal: Nausea (≤19%)

1% to 10%:

Cardiovascular: Hypotension (1% to 5%), edema (≤2%), flushing (1%), ventricular arrhythmia (intravenous: 1%)

Central nervous system: Paresthesia (≤5%), drowsiness (3%), headache (2%), vertigo (1% to 2%)

Dermatologic: Tingling of the scalp (≤7%), diaphoresis (≤4%), pruritus (1%), skin rash (1%)

Gastrointestinal: Dyspepsia (≤4%), vomiting (≤3%), dysgeusia (1%)

Genitourinary: Ejaculatory failure (<5%), impotence (1% to 4%)

Hepatic: Increased serum transaminases (4%)

Neuromuscular & skeletal: Weakness (1%)

Ophthalmic: Visual disturbance (1%)

Renal: Increased blood urea nitrogen (≤8%)

Respiratory: Nasal congestion (1% to 6%), dyspnea (2%)

<1%, postmarketing, and/or case reports: Anaphylactoid reaction, angioedema, bradycardia, bronchospasm, cardiac failure, cholestatic jaundice, diabetes insipidus, heart block, hepatic necrosis, hepatitis, hypersensitivity reaction, Peyronie's disease, positive ANA titer, psoriasiform eruption, Raynaud's phenomenon, syncope, systemic lupus erythematosus, toxic myopathy, transient alopecia, urinary retention, urticaria

General Dosage Range

IV: *Adults:* Bolus: 20 mg IV push over 2 minutes; may administer 40 or 80 mg at 10-minute intervals, up to 300 mg total cumulative dose; Infusion: 2 mg/minute; usual total dose required: 50 to 200 mg (maximum: 300 mg total cumulative dose)

Oral: *Adults:* Initial: 100 mg twice daily; may increase every 2 to 3 days by 100 mg twice daily (titration increments not to exceed 200 mg twice daily) until desired response is obtained; some patients may require up to 2,400 mg daily.

Mechanism of Action Blocks alpha-, $beta_1$-, and $beta_2$-adrenergic receptor sites; elevated renins are reduced. The ratios of alpha- to beta-blockade differ depending on the route of administration: 1:3 (oral) and 1:7 (IV).

Pharmacodynamics/Kinetics

Onset of Action Oral: 20 minutes to 2 hours (McNeil 1984); IV: Within 5 minutes (Goa 1989); Peak effect: Oral: 2 to 4 hours; IV: 5 to 15 minutes (Goa 1989)

Duration of Action Blood pressure response:

Oral: 8 to 12 hours (dose dependent)

IV: Average: 16 to 18 hours (dose dependent)

Half-life Elimination Oral: 6 to 8 hours; IV: ~5.5 hours

Time to Peak Plasma: Oral: 1 to 2 hours

Pregnancy Risk Factor C

Pregnancy Considerations Adverse events have been observed in some animal reproduction studies. Labetalol crosses the placenta and can be detected in cord blood and infant serum after delivery (Haraldsson 1989; Rogers 1990). Fetal/neonatal bradycardia, hypoglycemia, hypotension, and/or respiratory depression have been observed following in utero exposure to labetalol. Reduced birth weight has also been observed following in utero exposure to beta-blockers as a class; adequate facilities for monitoring infants at birth is generally recommended.

Untreated chronic maternal hypertension and preeclampsia are also associated with adverse events in the fetus, infant, and mother. Oral labetalol is considered an appropriate agent for the treatment of chronic hypertension in pregnancy (ACOG 2013; Magee 2014). Intravenous labetalol is recommended for use in the management of acute onset, severe hypertension (systolic BP ≥160 mm Hg or diastolic BP ≥110 mm Hg) with preeclampsia or eclampsia in pregnant and postpartum women. In general, avoid use of labetalol in women with asthma or heart failure (ACOG 2015; Magee 2014).

Lacosamide (la KOE sa mide)

Brand Names: US Vimpat

Brand Names: Canada Vimpat

Pharmacologic Category Anticonvulsant, Miscellaneous

Use Partial-onset seizures:

US labeling: Monotherapy or adjunctive therapy in the treatment of partial-onset seizures in patients ≥17 years.

Canadian labeling: Adjunctive therapy in the treatment of partial-onset seizures in adults who are not satisfactorily controlled with conventional therapy.

Local Anesthetic/Vasoconstrictor Precautions Lacosamide may prolong PR interval resulting in cardiac conduction problems; it is not known what effect vasoconstrictors will have in patients taking medications that could prolong PR interval. It is suggested that the clinician consult with the physician prior to use of vasoconstrictor in suspected patients; use vasoconstrictor with caution.

Effects on Dental Treatment No significant effects or complications reported

Effects on Bleeding No information available to require special precautions

Adverse Reactions The majority of adverse events are dose-dependent.

>10%:

Central nervous system: Dizziness (16% to 53%), fatigue (7% to 15%), ataxia (4% to 15%), headache (11% to 14%)

Gastrointestinal: Nausea (7% to 17%), vomiting (6% to 16%)

Neuromuscular & skeletal: Tremor (4% to 12%)

Ophthalmic: Diplopia (6% to 16%), blurred vision (2% to 16%)

1% to 10%:

Cardiovascular: Syncope (adults 1%; dose-related: >400 mg/day)

Central nervous system: Drowsiness (5% to 8%), memory impairment (2% to 6%), equilibrium disturbance (1% to 6%), vertigo (3% to 5%), abnormal gait (2% to 4%), depression (2%)

Dermatologic: Pruritus (2% to 3%)

Gastrointestinal: Diarrhea (3% to 5%)

Hematologic & oncologic: Bruise (2% to 4%)

Hepatic: Increased serum ALT (1%)

Local: Pain at injection site (3%), local irritation (1%)

Neuromuscular & skeletal: Weakness (2% to 4%)

Ophthalmic: Nystagmus (2% to 10%)

Miscellaneous: Laceration (2% to 3%)

<1%, postmarketing, and/or case reports: Abnormal hepatic function tests, acute psychosis, aggressive behavior, agitation, agranulocytosis, anemia, angioedema, atrial fibrillation, atrial flutter, atrioventricular block, bradycardia, cerebellar syndrome, cognitive dysfunction, confusion, constipation, disturbance in attention, DRESS syndrome, dysarthria, dyspepsia, erythema at injection site, euphoria, falling, fever, hallucination, hepatitis, hypoaesthesia (oral), insomnia, intoxicated feeling, irritability, mood changes, muscle spasm, nephritis, neutropenia, palpitations, paresthesia, skin rash, Stevens-Johnson syndrome, tinnitus, toxic epidermal necrolysis, urticaria, xerostomia

General Dosage Range Dosage adjustment recommended in patients with hepatic or renal impairment

IV, Oral: *Adolescents ≥17 years and Adults:* Initial: 50 to 100 mg twice daily; Maintenance dose: 100 to 200 mg twice daily (maximum: 400 mg daily)

Mechanism of Action *In vitro* studies have shown that lacosamide stabilizes hyperexcitable neuronal membranes and inhibits repetitive neuronal firing by enhancing the slow inactivation of sodium channels (with no effects on fast inactivation of sodium channels).

Pharmacodynamics/Kinetics

Half-life Elimination ~13 hours

Time to Peak Oral: 1-4 hours

Pregnancy Risk Factor C

Pregnancy Considerations Adverse events were observed in animal reproduction studies. Information related to pregnancy outcomes following maternal use of lacosamide is limited (Hoeltzenbein 2011). In general, maternal polytherapy with antiepileptic drugs may increase the risk of congenital malformations; monotherapy with the lowest effective dose is recommended. Newborns of women taking antiepileptic medications may be at an increased risk of adverse events (Harden and Meader 2009).

Patients exposed to lacosamide during pregnancy are encouraged to enroll themselves into the NAAED Pregnancy Registry by calling 1-888-233-2334. Additional information is available at http://www.-aedpregnancyregistry.org.

Controlled Substance C-V

Lactobacillus (lak toe ba SIL us)

Related Information

Ulcerative, Erosive, and Painful Oral Mucosal Disorders *on page 1853*

Brand Names: US Advanced Probiotic [OTC]; Bacid [OTC]; Culturelle [OTC]; Dialyvite Probiotic [OTC]; Dofus [OTC]; Flora-Q [OTC]; Floranex [OTC]; Kala [OTC]; Lactinex [OTC]; Lacto-Bifidus [OTC]; Lacto-Key [OTC]; Lacto-Pectin [OTC]; Lacto-TriBlend [OTC]; Megadophilus [OTC]; MoreDophilus [OTC]; Pedia-Lax Probiotic Yums [OTC]; ReZyst IM; Risa-Bid [OTC]; RisaQuad [OTC]; RisaQuad-2 [OTC]; Superdophilus [OTC]; Visbiome [OTC]; VSL #3 [OTC]; VSL #3-DS

Brand Names: Canada Bacid; Bio-K+; Fermalac

Generic Availability (US) Yes

Pharmacologic Category Dietary Supplement; Probiotic

Dental Use Treatment of uncomplicated diarrhea, particularly that caused by antibiotic therapy; re-establish normal physiologic and bacterial flora of the intestinal tract

Use

Dietary supplement: Probiotic to promote normal bacterial flora of the intestinal tract; probiotic supplement for breastfed or partially breastfed infants experiencing excessive crying, colic, and fussiness (Gerber Soothe Colic only).

Medical food:

Visbiome: Dietary management of pouchitis, ulcerative colitis, and irritable bowel syndrome.

VSL#3: Dietary management of an ileal pouch or ulcerative colitis.

Local Anesthetic/Vasoconstrictor Precautions No information available to require special precautions

Effects on Dental Treatment No significant effects or complications reported

Effects on Bleeding No information available to require special precautions

Adverse Reactions Frequency not defined.

Gastrointestinal: Bloating (intestinal), flatulence

Dental Usual Dosage Dietary supplement: Oral: Dosing varies by manufacturer; consult product labeling

Children (Culturelle): 1 capsule daily

Adults:

Bacid: 2 caplets/day

Culturelle: 1 capsule daily; may increase to twice daily

Flora-Q: 1 capsule/day

Lacto-Key 100 or 600: 1-2 capsules/day

Lactinex: 1 packet or 4 tablets 3-4 times/day

VSL #3: 1-8 sachets or 2-32 capsules/day

VSL #3-DS: 1-4 packets/day

Dosing

Adult & Geriatric

Dietary supplement/medical food: Oral: Dosing varies by manufacturer; consult product labeling.

Acidophilus products: 2 capsules 2 to 4 times daily or 1 to 2 wafers 2 to 4 times daily

Culturelle Digestive Health capsule and chewable tablet: 1 capsule or chewable tablet once daily; may increase chewable tablet to twice daily to alleviate digestive distress or during travel

Floranex: 4 tablets 3 to 4 times daily

Flora-Q: 1 capsule once daily

Lactinex: 1 packet or 4 tablets 3 to 4 times daily

Visbiome:

Irritable bowel syndrome: 2 to 4 capsules or ½ to 1 packet per day

Pouchitis: 2 to 4 packets/day

Ulcerative colitis (active): 4 to 8 packets/day

Ulcerative colitis (maintenance): 4 to 8 capsules or 1 to 2 packets per day

VSL #3: 1 to 8 packets or 2 to 8 capsules/day

VSL #3-DS: 1 to 4 packets/day

Pediatric

Dietary supplement/medical food: Oral: Dosing varies by manufacturer; consult product labeling

Infants: Gerber Soothe: 5 drops once daily

Infants, Children, and Adolescents:

Visbiome:

<2 years: **Note:** Do not use in premature infants in the NICU.

Irritable bowel syndrome or ulcerative colitis (maintenance): 1 capsule or 1/4 packet per day

Ulcerative colitis (active): 1 to 2 capsules or 1/4 to 1/2 packet per day

2 to 5 years:

Irritable bowel syndrome or ulcerative colitis (maintenance): 2 capsules or 1/2 packet per day

Ulcerative colitis (active): 2 to 4 capsules or 1/2 to 1 packet per day

6 to 11 years:

Irritable bowel syndrome: 2 capsules or 1/2 packet per day

Ulcerative colitis (active): 4 to 8 capsules or 1 to 2 packets per day

Ulcerative colitis (maintenance): 2 to 4 capsules or 1/2 to 1 packet per day

12 to 17 years:

Irritable bowel syndrome: 2 to 4 capsules or 1/2 to 1 packet per day

Ulcerative colitis (active): 8 to 16 capsules or 2 to 4 packets per day

Ulcerative colitis (maintenance): 4 to 8 capsules or 1 to 2 packets per day

Children ≥1 year and Adolescents:

Culturelle Digestive capsule: 1 capsule once daily

Culturelle Digestive Health and Culturelle Kids chewable tablet: Children ≥3 years: 1 chewable tablet once daily; may increase to twice daily to alleviate digestive distress or during travel

Culturelle Kids packet: 1 packet once daily; may increase to twice daily to alleviate digestive distress

VSL #3: 1 to 4 packets or 1 to 8 capsules/day

VSL #3 Junior: 1 to 4 packets/day

VSL #3-DS: 1 to 2 packets/day

Renal Impairment There are no dosage adjustments provided in the manufacturer's labeling.

Hepatic Impairment There are no dosage adjustments provided in the manufacturer's labeling.

Mechanism of Action Helps re-establish normal intestinal flora; suppresses the growth of potentially pathogenic microorganisms by producing lactic acid which favors the establishment of an aciduric flora.

Contraindications OTC labeling: When used for self-medication, do not use if sensitive to milk protein (product specific).

Warnings/Precautions Probiotics are classified as dietary supplements; therefore, there are no safety reviews or approved therapeutic indications by the FDA. Use dietary supplements containing live bacteria or yeast with caution in immunocompromised patients. A fatal case of GI mucormycosis caused by the mold *Rhizopus oryzae* has been previously reported in a premature infant administered a dietary supplement containing 3 species of live bacteria (FDA Safety Information 2014). There is no conclusive evidence to ▶

support widespread use in the treatment of diarrhea. Significant differences may exist from one preparation compared to another with respect to biologic activity and composition. Some products may contain lactose; use with caution in patients with lactose intolerance.

Drug Interactions

Metabolism/Transport Effects None known.

Avoid Concomitant Use There are no known interactions where it is recommended to avoid concomitant use.

Increased Effect/Toxicity There are no known significant interactions involving an increase in effect.

Decreased Effect There are no known significant interactions involving a decrease in effect.

Dietary Considerations Some products may contain lactose, potassium, and/or sodium.

Dosage Forms

Capsule:

Advanced Probiotic [OTC]: *L. acidophilus, L. casei, L. delbrueckii,* and *L. rhamnosus* GG 10 billion live cultures

Culturelle [OTC]: *L. rhamnosus* GG 10 billion colony-forming units

Dofus [OTC]: *L. acidophilus* and *L. bifidus* 10:1 ratio

Flora-Q [OTC]: *L. acidophilus* and *L. paracasei* ≥8 billion colony-forming units

Lacto-Key [OTC]:

100: *L. acidophilus* 1 billion colony-forming units

600: *L. acidophilus* 6 billion colony-forming units

Lacto-Bifidus [OTC]:

100: *L. bifidus* 1 billion colony-forming units

600: *L. bifidus* 6 billion colony-forming units

Lacto-Pectin [OTC]: *L. acidophilus, L. casei, L. plantarum, L. rhamnosus, Bifidobacterium breve, and B. longum* 20 billion colony-forming units

Lacto-TriBlend [OTC]:

100: *L. acidophilus, L. bifidus,* and *L. bulgaricus* 1 billion colony-forming units

600: *L. acidophilus, L. bifidus,* and *L. bulgaricus* 6 billion colony-forming units

Megadophilus [OTC], Superdophilus [OTC]: *L. acidophilus* 2 billion units

RisaQuad [OTC]: *L. acidophilus* and *L. paracasei* 8 billion colony-forming units

RisaQuad-2 [OTC]: *L. acidophilus* and *L. paracasei* 16 billion colony-forming units

Visbiome [OTC]: *L. acidophilus, L. plantarum, L. paracasei, L. bulgaricus, Bifidobacterium breve, B. longum, B. infantis, and Streptococcus thermophilus* 112 billion live cells

VSL #3 [OTC]: *L. acidophilus, L. plantarum, L. paracasei, L. bulgaricus, Bifidobacterium breve, B. longum, B. infantis, and Streptococcus thermophilus* 112 billion live cells

Caplet:

Bacid [OTC]: *L. acidophilus* and *L. bulgaricus* [also contains *Bifidobacterium bifidum* and *Streptococcus thermophilus*]

Risa-Bid [OTC]: *L. acidophilus* and *L. bulgaricus* [also contains *Bifidobacterium bifidum* and *Streptococcus thermophilus*]

Granules:

Floranex [OTC], Lactinex [OTC]: *L. acidophilus* and *L. bulgaricus* 100 million live cells per 1 g packet (12s)

Powder:

Lacto-TriBlend [OTC]: *L. acidophilus, L. bifidus,* and *L. bulgaricus* 10 billion colony-forming units per ¼ teaspoon

Megadophilus [OTC], Superdophilus [OTC]: *L. acidophilus* 2 billion units per half-teaspoon

MoreDophilus [OTC]: *L. acidophilus* 12.4 billion units per teaspoon

VSL #3 [OTC]: *L. acidophilus, L. plantarum, L. paracasei, L. bulgaricus* 450 billion live cells

VSL #3-DS: *L. acidophilus, L. plantarum, L. paracasei, L. bulgaricus* 900 billion live cells

Tablet: *L. acidophilus* 35 million and *L. sporogenes* 25 million

Floranex [OTC]: *L. acidophilus* and *L. bulgaricus* 1 million colony-forming units

Kala [OTC]: *L. acidophilus* 200 million units

Tablet, chewable: *L. reuteri* 100 million organisms

Dialyvite Probiotic: *L. acidophilus* and *Bifidobacterium lactis* 10 billion cells

Lactinex [OTC]: *L. acidophilus* and *L. bulgaricus* 1 million live cells

Pedia-Lax Probiotic Yums [OTC]: *L. reuteri* 100 million organisms

ReZyst IM: *L. acidophilus* and *Bifidobacterium* 150 mg [3 billion lives cells]

Wafer: *L. acidophilus* 90 mg and *L. bifidus* 25 mg (100s)

LamiVUDine (la MI vyoo deen)

Related Information

HIV Infection and AIDS *on page 1785*

Systemic Viral Diseases *on page 1806*

Brand Names: US Epivir; Epivir HBV

Brand Names: Canada 3TC; Apo-Lamivudine; Apo-Lamivudine HBV; Auro-Lamivudine; Heptovir

Pharmacologic Category Antihepadnaviral, Reverse Transcriptase Inhibitor, Nucleoside (Anti-HBV); Antiretroviral, Reverse Transcriptase Inhibitor, Nucleoside (Anti-HIV)

Use

Chronic hepatitis B (Epivir HBV): Treatment of chronic hepatitis B associated with evidence of hepatitis B viral replication and active liver inflammation.

Limitations of use: Use only when an alternative antiviral agent with a higher genetic barrier to resistance is not available or appropriate; has not been evaluated in patients with HBV-HIV-1 coinfection, hepatitis C virus or hepatitis delta virus; has also not been evaluated in patients with chronic HBV infection with decompensated liver disease or in liver transplant recipients.

HIV-1 infection (Epivir): Treatment of HIV-1 in combination with other antiretroviral agents

Local Anesthetic/Vasoconstrictor Precautions No information available to require special precautions

Effects on Dental Treatment No significant effects or complications reported

Effects on Bleeding No information available to require special precautions relative to hemostasis.

Adverse Reactions Incidence data include patients on combination therapy with other antiretroviral agents.

>10%:

Central nervous system: Headache (21% to 35%), fatigue (24% to 27%), neuropathy (12%), insomnia (11%)

Gastrointestinal: Nausea (15% to 33%), diarrhea (14% to 18%), pancreatitis (≤18%; higher percentage in pediatric patients), abdominal pain (9% to 16%), vomiting (13% to 15%), sore throat (13%)

Hematologic & oncologic: Neutropenia (7% to 15%)

Hepatic: Increased serum transaminases (2% to 11%)

Infection: Infection (25%; includes ear, nose, and throat)

Neuromuscular & skeletal: Myalgia (8% to 14%), musculoskeletal pain (12%)
Respiratory: Nasal signs and symptoms (20%), cough (18%)

1% to 10%:

Central nervous system: Dizziness (10%), depression (9%), chills (7% to 10%)
Dermatologic: Skin rash (5% to 9%)
Gastrointestinal: Anorexia (10%), increased serum lipase (10%), abdominal cramps (6%), dyspepsia (5%), increased amylase (≤4%), heartburn
Hematologic & oncologic: Thrombocytopenia (1% to 4%), hemoglobinemia (2% to 3%)
Neuromuscular & skeletal: Increased creatine phosphokinase (9%), arthralgia (5% to 7%)
Miscellaneous: Fever (7% to 10%)

<1%, postmarketing, and/or case reports: Alopecia, anaphylaxis, anemia, exacerbation of hepatitis B, hepatomegaly, hyperbilirubinemia, hyperglycemia, immune reconstitution syndrome, lactic acidosis, liver steatosis, lymphadenopathy, myasthenia, paresthesia, peripheral neuropathy, pruritus, pure red cell aplasia, redistribution of body fat, rhabdomyolysis, splenomegaly, stomatitis, urticaria, weakness, wheezing

General Dosage Range Dosage adjustment recommended in patients with renal impairment

Oral:

HIV-1 infection:

Infants ≥3 months, Children, and Adolescents:

Oral solution: 8 mg/kg/day in 1 to 2 divided doses (maximum: 300 mg/day)

Oral tablets:

14 to <20 kg: 75 mg twice daily **or** 150 mg once daily
≥20 to <25 kg: 75 mg in the morning, 150 mg in the evening **or** 225 mg once daily
≥25 kg: 150 mg twice daily **or** 300 mg once daily

Adults: 150 mg twice daily or 300 mg once daily

Hepatitis B infection:

Children 2 to 17 years: 3 mg/kg/dose once daily (maximum: 100 mg/day);
Adults: 100 mg once daily

Mechanism of Action Lamivudine is a cytosine analog. *In vitro*, lamivudine is triphosphorylated, the principle mode of action is inhibition of HIV reverse transcription via viral DNA chain termination; inhibits RNA- and DNA-dependent DNA polymerase activities of reverse transcriptase. In hepatitis B, the monophosphate form of lamivudine is incorporated into the viral DNA by hepatitis B virus polymerase, resulting in DNA chain termination.

Pharmacodynamics/Kinetics

Half-life Elimination

Intracellular: 10 to 15 hours
Elimination:
Children 4 months to 14 years: 2 ± 0.6 hours
Adults: 5 to 7 hours; increased with renal impairment

Time to Peak

Pediatric patients 0.5 to 17 years: Median: 1.5 hours (range: 0.5 to 4 hours) (Lewis 1996)
Adolescents 13 to 17 years: 0.5 to 1 hour
Adults: Fed: 3.2 hours; Fasted: 0.9 hours

Pregnancy Risk Factor C

Pregnancy Considerations Adverse events were observed in some animal reproduction studies. Lamivudine has a high level of transfer across the human placenta. No increased risk of overall birth defects has been observed following first trimester exposure according to data collected by the antiretroviral pregnancy registry. Maternal antiretroviral therapy may increase the risk of preterm delivery, although, available information is conflicting possibly due to variability of maternal factors (disease severity; initiation of therapy); however, maternal antiretroviral medication should not be withheld due to concerns of preterm birth. Based on data collected by the antiretroviral pregnancy registry, the risk of spontaneous abortions, induced abortions, and preterm birth is less in lamivudine-containing regimens compared with regimens without lamivudine. Information related to stillbirth, low birth weight, and small for gestational age infants is limited. Long-term follow-up is recommended for all infants exposed to antiretroviral medications; children who develop significant organ system abnormalities of unknown etiology (particularly of the CNS or heart) should be evaluated for potential mitochondrial dysfunction. Cases of lactic acidosis and hepatic steatosis related to mitochondrial toxicity have been reported with use of nucleoside reverse transcriptase inhibitors (NRTIs). These adverse events are similar to other rare but life-threatening syndromes that occur during pregnancy (eg, HELLP syndrome). In general, NRTIs are well tolerated and the benefits of use generally outweigh potential risk.

Combination antiretroviral therapy (cART) therapy is recommended for all HIV-infected pregnant women to keep the viral load below the limit of detection and reduce the risk of perinatal transmission. When HIV is diagnosed during pregnancy in a woman who has never received antiretroviral therapy, cART should begin as soon as possible after diagnosis. The Health and Human Services (HHS) Perinatal HIV Guidelines consider lamivudine in combination with either abacavir or tenofovir disoproxil fumarate to be a preferred NRTI backbone for initial therapy in antiretroviral-naive pregnant women. The lamivudine/abacavir backbone is not recommended with atazanavir/ritonavir or efavirenz if pretreatment HIV RNA is >100,000 copies/mL. The guidelines consider lamivudine with zidovudine to be an alternative NRTI backbone for initial therapy in antiretroviral-naive pregnant women. The guidelines also consider lamivudine plus tenofovir disoproxil fumarate a recommended dual NRTI backbone in regimens for HIV/HBV-coinfected pregnant women. Use caution with hepatitis B coinfection; hepatitis B flare may occur if lamivudine is discontinued. The pharmacokinetics of lamivudine during pregnancy are not significantly altered and dosage adjustment is not required. In general, women who become pregnant on a stable cART regimen may continue that regimen if viral suppression is effective, appropriate drug exposure can be achieved, contraindications for use in pregnancy are not present, and the regimen is well tolerated. Monitoring during pregnancy is more frequent than in non-pregnant adults; cART should be continued postpartum.

For HIV-infected couples planning a pregnancy, maximum viral suppression with cART is recommended prior to conception for the HIV-infected partner(s) and expert consultation is recommended; modification of therapy (if needed) and optimization of the woman's health should be done prior to conception. HIV-infected women not planning a pregnancy may use any available type of contraception, considering possible drug interactions and contraindications of the specific method. In addition, consistent use of condoms is also recommended (even during pregnancy) to prevent transmission of HIV or other sexually transmitted diseases.

Health care providers are encouraged to enroll pregnant women exposed to antiretroviral medications as early in pregnancy as possible in the Antiretroviral Pregnancy Registry (1-800-258-4263 or www.APRegistry.com). Health care providers caring for HIV-infected women and their infants may contact the National Perinatal HIV Hotline (888-448-8765) for clinical consultation (HHS [perinatal] 2016).

Lamivudine and Zidovudine

(la MI vyoo deen & zye DOE vyoo deen)

Related Information

HIV Infection and AIDS *on page* 1785

LamiVUDine *on page* 956

Zidovudine *on page* 1672

Brand Names: US Combivir

Brand Names: Canada Apo-Lamivudine-Zidovudine; Combivir; Teva-Lamivudine/Zidovudine

Pharmacologic Category Antiretroviral, Reverse Transcriptase Inhibitor, Nucleoside (Anti-HIV)

Use HIV-1 infection: Treatment of HIV-1 infection in combination with other antiretrovirals.

Local Anesthetic/Vasoconstrictor Precautions No information available to require special precautions

Effects on Dental Treatment No significant effects or complications reported

Effects on Bleeding No information available to require special precautions relative to hemostasis.

Adverse Reactions See individual agents.

General Dosage Range Oral: *Children and Adolescents weighing ≥30 kg, and Adults:* One tablet (lamivudine 150 mg/zidovudine 300 mg) twice daily

Mechanism of Action The combination of zidovudine and lamivudine is believed to act synergistically to inhibit reverse transcriptase via DNA chain termination after incorporation of the nucleoside analogue as well as to delay the emergence of mutations conferring resistance

Pregnancy Considerations In general, women who become pregnant on a stable combination antiretroviral therapy (cART) regimen may continue that regimen if viral suppression is effective, appropriate drug exposure can be achieved, contraindications for use in pregnancy are not present, and the regimen is well tolerated. The Health and Human Services (HHS) Perinatal HIV Guidelines consider lamivudine in combination with zidovudine as an alternative NRTI backbone for initial therapy in antiretroviral-naive pregnant women. Although use of this combination has the most experience for in pregnant women, it has an increased potential for hematologic toxicity and requires twice-daily dosing (HHS [perinatal] 2016).

See individual agents.

LamoTRIgine

(la MOE tri jeen)

Brand Names: US LaMICtal; LaMICtal ODT; LaMICtal Starter; LaMICtal XR

Brand Names: Canada Apo-Lamotrigine; Auro-Lamotrigine; Lamictal; Mylan-Lamotrigine; PMS-Lamotrigine; ratio-Lamotrigine; Teva-Lamotrigine

Pharmacologic Category Anticonvulsant, Miscellaneous

Use

Bipolar I disorder (immediate release only): Maintenance treatment of bipolar I disorder to delay the time to occurrence of mood episodes (depression, mania, hypomania, mixed episodes) in patients treated for acute mood episodes with standard therapy.

Epilepsy:

Adjunctive therapy:

Immediate release: Adjunctive therapy for partial-onset seizures, generalized seizures of Lennox-Gastaut syndrome, and primary generalized tonic-clonic seizures in adults and children 2 years and older.

Extended release: Adjunctive therapy for primary generalized tonic-clonic seizures and partial-onset seizures with or without secondary generalization in patients 13 years and older.

Monotherapy:

Immediate release: Conversion to monotherapy in adults (16 years and older) with partial-onset seizures who are receiving treatment with carbamazepine, phenytoin, phenobarbital, primidone, or valproate as the single antiepileptic drug (AED).

Extended release: Conversion to monotherapy in patients 13 years and older with partial-onset seizures who are receiving treatment with a single AED.

Local Anesthetic/Vasoconstrictor Precautions No information available to require special precautions

Effects on Dental Treatment Key adverse event(s) related to dental treatment: Xerostomia (normal salivary flow resumes upon discontinuation).

Effects on Bleeding Thrombocytopenia and anemia have been reported in <1% of patients.

Adverse Reactions Percentages reported in adults on monotherapy for epilepsy or bipolar disorder.

>10%: Gastrointestinal: Nausea (7% to 14%)

1% to 10%:

Cardiovascular: Chest pain (5%), peripheral edema (2% to 5%), edema (1% to 5%)

Central nervous system: Insomnia (5% to 10%), drowsiness (9%), fatigue (8%), dizziness (7%), ataxia (2% to 7%), anxiety (5%), pain (5%), irritability (2% to 5%), suicidal ideation (2% to 5%), abnormal dreams (1% to 5%), abnormality in thinking (1% to 5%), agitation (1% to 5%), amnesia (1% to 5%), depression (1% to 5%), dyspraxia (1% to 5%), emotional lability (1% to 5%), hypoesthesia (1% to 5%), migraine (1% to 5%), hyperreflexia (>2% to <5%), hyporeflexia (>2% to <5%), confusion (1%), paresthesia (≥1%)

Dermatologic: Skin rash (nonserious 7%; requiring hospitalization ≤1%), dermatitis (2% to 5%), diaphoresis (2% to 5%), xeroderma (2% to 5%)

Endocrine & metabolic: Dysmenorrhea (5% to 7%), weight loss (5%), weight gain (1% to 5%)

Gastrointestinal: Vomiting (5% to 9%), dyspepsia (7%), abdominal pain (6%), xerostomia (2% to 6%), constipation (5%), anorexia (2% to 5%), peptic ulcer (2% to 5%), flatulence (1% to 5%),

Genitourinary: Increased libido (2% to 5%), urinary frequency (1% to 5%)

Hematologic & oncologic: Rectal hemorrhage (2% to 5%)

Infection: Infection (5%)

Neuromuscular & skeletal: Back pain (8%), weakness (2% to 5%), arthralgia (1% to 5%), myalgia (1% to 5%), neck pain (1% to 5%)

Ophthalmic: Nystagmus (2% to 5%), visual disturbance (2% to 5%), amblyopia (≥1%)

Respiratory: Rhinitis (7%), cough (5%), pharyngitis (5%), bronchitis (2% to 5%), dyspnea (2% to 5%), epistaxis (2% to 5%), sinusitis (1% to 5%), nasopharyngitis (≥3%), upper respiratory tract infection (≥3%)

Miscellaneous: Fever (1% to 5%)

<1%, postmarketing and/or case reports (any indication): Abnormal hepatic function tests, abnormal lacrimation, accommodation disturbance, acne vulgaris, acute renal failure, ageusia, agranulocytosis, akathisia, alcohol intolerance, alopecia, altered sense of smell, amyotrophy, anemia, angioedema, anorgasmia, apathy, aphasia, aplastic anemia, apnea, arthritis, aseptic meningitis, blepharoptosis, breast abscess, breast neoplasm, bruise, bursitis, central nervous system depression, cerebellar syndrome, chills, choreoathetosis, conjunctivitis, cystitis, deafness, decreased fibrin, decreased libido, decreased serum fibrinogen, deep vein thrombophlebitis, delirium, delusions, depersonalization, depression, dermatitis (exfoliative, fungal), disseminated intravascular coagulation, DRESS syndrome, dry eye syndrome, dysarthria, dysphagia, dysphoria, dystonia, dysuria, ecchymosis, ejaculatory disorder, eosinophilia, epididymitis, eructation, erythema multiforme, esophagitis, euphoria, exacerbation of Parkinson disease, extrapyramidal reaction, flushing, gastritis, gastrointestinal hemorrhage, gingival hemorrhage, gingival hyperplasia, gingivitis, glossitis, goiter, hallucination, hematemesis, hematuria, hemiplegia, hemolytic anemia, hemorrhage, hepatitis, hepatotoxicity (idiosyncratic) (Chalasani, 2014), herpes zoster, hiccups, hirsutism, hostility, hot flash, hyperalgesia, hyperbilirubinemia, hyperesthesia, hyperglycemia, hyperkinesia, hypermenorrhagia, hypersensitivity reaction, hypertension, hypertonia, hyperventilation, hypokinesia, hypothyroidism, hypotonia, immunosuppression (progressive), impotence, increased appetite, increased gamma glutamyl transpeptidase, increased serum alkaline phosphatase, increased serum ALT, increased serum AST, increased serum creatinine, iron deficiency anemia, lactation, leg cramps, leukocytosis, leukoderma, leukopenia, lupus-like syndrome, lymphadenopathy, lymphocytosis, macrocytic anemia, maculopapular rash, malaise, manic depressive reaction, melena, memory impairment, movement disorder, multiorgan failure, muscle spasm, myasthenia, myoclonus, neuralgia, neutropenia, nightmares, nocturia, oral mucosa ulcer, orthostatic hypotension, oscillopsia, otalgia, palpitations, pancreatitis, pancytopenia, panic attack, paralysis, paranoid reaction, pathological fracture, peripheral neuritis, personality disorder, petechia, petechial rash, photophobia, polyuria, pruritus, psychoneurosis, psychosis, pure red cell aplasia, pustular rash, racing mind, renal pain, rhabdomyolysis, sialorrhea, skin discoloration, sleep disorder, status epilepticus, Stevens-Johnson syndrome, strabismus, suicidal tendencies, syncope, tachycardia, tendinous contracture, thrombocytopenia, tics, tinnitus, tongue edema, tonic-clonic seizures (exacerbation), toxic epidermal necrolysis, twitching, urinary incontinence, urinary retention, urinary urgency, urticaria, uveitis, vasculitis, vasodilation, vesiculobullous dermatitis, visual field defect, withdrawal seizures, yawning

General Dosage Range Dosage adjustment recommended in patients with hepatic or renal impairment or on concomitant therapy

Oral:

Immediate release formulation:

Children 2 to 12 years: Dosage varies greatly depending on indication

Children >12 years, Adolescents, and Adults: Dosage varies greatly depending on indication

Extended release formulation: *Adolescents ≥13 years and Adults:* Dosage varies greatly depending on indication

Mechanism of Action A triazine derivative which inhibits release of glutamate (an excitatory amino acid) and inhibits voltage-sensitive sodium channels, which stabilizes neuronal membranes. Lamotrigine has weak inhibitory effect on the 5-HT_3 receptor; *in vitro* inhibits dihydrofolate reductase.

Pharmacodynamics/Kinetics

Half-life Elimination

Pediatric patients:

No concomitant enzyme-inducing AED (ie, phenytoin, phenobarbital, carbamazepine, primidone): Infants and Children 10 months to 5 years: 19 hours (range: 13 to 27 hours)

Concomitant valproate derivative therapy:

Infants and Children 10 months to 5 years: 45 hours (range: 30 to 52 hours)

Children 5 to 11 years: 66 hours (50 to 74 hours)

Concomitant enzyme-inducing AEDs (ie, phenytoin, phenobarbital, carbamazepine, primidone):

Infants and Children 10 months to 5 years: 7.7 hours (range: 6 to 11 hours)

Children 5 to 11 years: 7 hours (range: 4 to 10 hours)

Concomitant enzyme-inducing AEDs plus valproate derivative therapy: Children 5 to 11 years: 19 hours (range: 7 to 31 hours)

Adults:

Immediate release: 25 to 33 hours, Elderly: 25 to 43 hours; Extended release: Similar to immediate release

Concomitant valproic acid therapy: 48 to 70 hours

Concomitant phenytoin, phenobarbital, primidone, or carbamazepine therapy: 13 to 14 hours

Concomitant phenytoin, phenobarbital, primidone, or carbamazepine plus valproate therapy: 27 hours

Chronic renal failure: 43 hours

Hemodialysis: 13 hours during dialysis; 57 hours between dialysis (~20% of a dose is eliminated in a 4-hour dialysis session)

Hepatic impairment:

Mild: 46 ± 20 hours

Moderate: 72 ± 44 hours

Severe without ascites: 67 ± 11 hours

Severe with ascites: 100 ± 48 hours

Time to Peak Plasma: Immediate release: 1 to 5 hours (dependent on adjunct therapy); Extended release: 4 to 11 hours (dependent on adjunct therapy)

Pregnancy Risk Factor C

Pregnancy Considerations Adverse events have been observed in animal reproduction studies. Lamotrigine crosses the human placenta and can be measured in the plasma of exposed newborns (Harden and Pennell, 2009; Ohman, 2000). An overall increase in major congenital malformations has not been observed in available studies; however, an increased risk for cleft lip or cleft palate has not been ruled out (Cunnington, 2011; Hernández-Díaz, 2012; Holmes, 2012). An increased risk of malformations following maternal lamotrigine use may be associated with larger doses (Cunnington, 2007; Tomson, 2011). Polytherapy may increase the risk of congenital malformations; monotherapy with the lowest effective dose is recommended (Harden and Meader, 2009).

Due to pregnancy-induced physiologic changes, women who are pregnant may require dose adjustments of lamotrigine in order to maintain clinical response; monitoring during pregnancy should be considered (Harden and Pennell, 2009). For women with epilepsy who are planning a pregnancy in advance, baseline serum concentrations should be measured once or twice prior to pregnancy during a period when seizure control is optimal. Monitoring can then be continued up to once a month during pregnancy and every second day during the first week postpartum (Patsalos, 2008). In women taking lamotrigine who are trying to avoid pregnancy, potentially significant interactions may exist with hormone-containing contraceptives; consult drug interactions database for more detailed information.

Pregnancy registries are available for women who have been exposed to lamotrigine. Patients may enroll themselves in the North American Antiepileptic Drug (NAAED) Pregnancy Registry by calling (888) 233-2334. Additional information is available at www.-aedpregnancyregistry.org.

Lanolin (LAN oh lin)

Brand Names: US HPA Lanolin; Lan-O-Soothe

Pharmacologic Category Topical Skin Product

Use Skin protectant/conditioner for sore or cracked nipples due to breastfeeding

Local Anesthetic/Vasoconstrictor Precautions No information available to require special precautions

Effects on Dental Treatment No significant effects or complications reported

Effects on Bleeding No information available to require special precautions

Adverse Reactions There are no adverse reactions listed in the manufacturer's labeling.

General Dosage Range Topical: Adults: Apply to affected area as needed

Lanreotide (lan REE oh tide)

Brand Names: US Somatuline Depot

Brand Names: Canada Somatuline Autogel

Pharmacologic Category Somatostatin Analog

Use

US labeling:

Acromegaly: Long-term treatment of acromegalic patients who have had an inadequate response to surgery and/or radiotherapy, or for whom surgery and/or radiotherapy is not an option.

Gastroenteropancreatic neuroendocrine tumors: Treatment (to improve progression-free survival) of unresectable, well- or moderately-differentiated, locally advanced or metastatic gastroenteropancreatic neuroendocrine tumors (GEP-NETs).

Canadian labeling:

Acromegaly: Long-term treatment of patients with acromegaly due to pituitary tumors who have had an inadequate response to surgery and/or radiotherapy, or for whom surgery and/or radiotherapy is not an option; relief of symptoms associated with acromegaly.

Enteropancreatic neuroendocrine tumors: Treatment (to delay progression) of enteropancreatic neuroendocrine tumors in patients with grade 1 or a subset of grade 2 (equivalent to Ki67 <10%) unresectable, locally advanced, or metastatic disease.

Local Anesthetic/Vasoconstrictor Precautions No information available to require special precautions

Effects on Dental Treatment No significant effects or complications reported

Effects on Bleeding No information available to require special precautions

Adverse Reactions

>10%:

Cardiovascular: Bradycardia (3% to 18%), hypertension (5% to 14%)

Central nervous system: Headache (5% to 16%)

Endocrine & metabolic: Weight loss (5% to 11%), dysglycemia (≤7%; includes diabetes, hyperglycemia, and hypoglycemia)

Gastrointestinal: Diarrhea (26% to 65%; dose related), abdominal pain (7% to 34%; dose related), vomiting (5% to 19%), flatulence (≤14%; dose related), nausea (9% to 11%)

Hematologic: Anemia (3% to 14%)

Hepatic: Cholelithiasis (2% to 27%), gallbladder sludge (20%)

Local: Injection site reaction (6% to 22%; induration 5%; pain 4%; mass 2%)

Neuromuscular & skeletal: Musculoskeletal pain (19%)

1% to 10%:

Cardiovascular: Sinus bradycardia (3% to 7%)

Central nervous system: Dizziness (9%), depression (7%)

Gastrointestinal: Loose stools (6% to 9%), constipation (5% to 8%)

Immunologic: Antibody development (<1% to 4%)

Neuromuscular & skeletal: Arthralgia (7% to 10%)

<1%, postmarketing, and/or case reports: Anaphylaxis, angioedema, cholecystitis, decreased heart rate, dysautonomia, hypersensitivity, hypothyroidism, induration at injection site (persistent), injection site pruritus, malaise, pancreatitis, steatorrhea, valvular regurgitation (aortic, mitral)

General Dosage Range Dosage adjustment recommended in patients with hepatic or renal impairment.

SubQ: *Adults:*

Acromegaly: Initial: 90 mg once every 4 weeks for 3 months; Maintenance: 60 to 120 mg once every 4 weeks **or** 120 mg once every 6 or 8 weeks

Gastroenteropancreatic neuroendocrine tumors: 120 mg once every 4 weeks

Mechanism of Action Synthetic octapeptide analogue of somatostatin which is a peptide inhibitor of multiple endocrine, neuroendocrine, and exocrine mechanisms. Displays a greater affinity for somatostatin type 2 (SSTR2) and type 5 (SSTR5) receptors found in pituitary gland, pancreas, and growth hormone (GH) secreting neoplasms of pituitary gland and a lesser affinity for somatostatin receptors 1, 3, and 4. Reduces GH secretion and also reduces the levels of insulin-like growth factor 1.

Pharmacodynamics/Kinetics

Half-life Elimination *Depot*: 23 to 30 days

Time to Peak Mean: 7 to 12 hours (Somatuline Canadian labeling 2015)

Pregnancy Risk Factor C

Pregnancy Considerations Adverse events were observed in animal reproduction studies. Information related to the use of lanreotide in pregnancy is limited (deMenis, 1999) and it is recommended to discontinue therapy during pregnancy (Chandraharan 2003; Melmed 2012).

Lansoprazole (lan SOE pra zole)

Related Information

Gastrointestinal Disorders *on page 1775*

Brand Names: US First-Lansoprazole; GoodSense Lansoprazole [OTC]; Heartburn Relief 24 Hour [OTC] [DSC]; Heartburn Treatment 24 Hour [OTC]; Prevacid; Prevacid 24HR [OTC]; Prevacid SoluTab

Brand Names: Canada Apo-Lansoprazole; Mylan-Lansoprazole; PMS-Lansoprazole; Prevacid; Prevacid FasTab; Q-Lansoprazole; RAN-Lansoprazole; Riva-Lansoprazole; Sandoz-Lansoprazole; Teva-Lansoprazole

Generic Availability (US) May be product dependent

Pharmacologic Category Proton Pump Inhibitor; Substituted Benzimidazole

Use

Gastroesophageal reflux disease (GERD): Short-term (up to 8 weeks) treatment of symptomatic GERD; short-term (up to 8 weeks) treatment for all grades of erosive esophagitis; to maintain healing of erosive esophagitis.

Hypersecretory conditions: Long-term treatment of pathological hypersecretory conditions, including Zollinger-Ellison syndrome.

Peptic ulcer disease: Short-term (4 weeks) treatment of active duodenal ulcers; maintenance treatment of healed duodenal ulcers; as part of a multidrug regimen for H. pylori eradication to reduce the risk of duodenal ulcer recurrence; short-term (up to 8 weeks) treatment of active benign gastric ulcer; treatment of NSAID-associated gastric ulcer; to reduce the risk of NSAID-associated gastric ulcer in patients with a history of gastric ulcer who require an NSAID.

OTC labeling: Relief of frequent heartburn (≥2 days/week)

Local Anesthetic/Vasoconstrictor Precautions No information available to require special precautions

Effects on Dental Treatment No significant effects or complications reported

Effects on Bleeding No information available to require special precautions

Adverse Reactions

1% to 10%:

Central nervous system: Headache (children 1 to 11 years 3%, 12 to 17 years 7%), dizziness (children 12 to 17 years 3%; adults <1%)

Gastrointestinal: Diarrhea (1% to 5%; 60 mg/day: 7%), abdominal pain (children 12 to 17 years 5%; adults 2%), constipation (children 1 to 11 years 5%; adults 1%), nausea (children 12 to 17 years 3%; adults 1%)

<1%, postmarketing, and/or case reports (limited to important or life-threatening): Abdomen enlarged, abnormal dreams, abnormal menses, abnormal stools, abnormal vision, agitation, agranulocytosis, albuminuria, allergic reaction, alkaline phosphatase increased, ALT increased, alopecia, amblyopia, amnesia, anaphylactoid reaction, anemia, angina, anorexia, anxiety, aplastic anemia, appetite increased, arrhythmia, AST increased, arthralgia, arthritis, asthma, avitaminosis, bezoar, bilirubinemia, blepharitis, blurred vision, bradycardia, breast enlargement, breast pain, breast tenderness, bronchitis, candidiasis, carcinoma, cardiospasm, cataract, cerebrovascular accident, cerebral infarction, chest pain, chills, cholelithiasis, cholesterol increased/decreased, chronic renal disease (Lazarus 2016), *Clostridium difficile*-associated diarrhea (CDAD), colitis, confusion, conjunctivitis, cough increased, creatinine increased, deafness, dehydration, dementia, depersonalization, depression, diabetes mellitus, diaphoresis, diplopia, dry eyes, dry skin, dyspepsia, dysphagia, dyspnea, dysmenorrhea, dysuria, edema, electrolyte imbalance, emotional lability, enteritis, eosinophilia, epistaxis, eructation, erythema multiforme, esophageal stenosis, esophageal ulcer, esophagitis, fecal discoloration, fever, fixed eruption, flatulence, flu-like syndrome, fracture, fundic gland polyps, gastric nodules, gastrin levels increased, gastritis, gastroenteritis, gastrointestinal anomaly, gastrointestinal hemorrhage, GGTP increased/decreased, glaucoma, glucocorticoid levels increased, glossitis, glycosuria, goiter, gout, gum hemorrhage, gynecomastia, halitosis, hallucinations, hematemesis, hematuria, hemiplegia, hemolysis, hemolytic anemia, hemoptysis, hepatotoxicity, hostility aggravated, hyper-/hypoglycemia, hyperkinesia, hyperlipemia, hypertonia, hypoesthesia, hyper-/hypotension, hypomagnesemia, hypothyroidism, impotence, infection, insomnia, interstitial nephritis, kidney calculus, laryngeal neoplasia, LDH increased, leg cramps, leukopenia, leukorrhea, libido decreased/increased, liver function test abnormal, lung fibrosis, lymphadenopathy, maculopapular rash, malaise, melena, menorrhagia, migraine, moniliasis (oral), mouth ulceration, musculoskeletal pain, myalgia, myasthenia, myositis, MI, nervousness, neurosis, neutropenia, pain, palpitation, pancreatitis, pancytopenia, paresthesia, parosmia, pelvic pain, peripheral edema, pharyngitis, photophobia, platelet abnormalities, pneumonia, polyuria, pruritus, ptosis, rash, rectal hemorrhage, retinal degeneration, rhinitis, salivation increased, seizure, shock, sinusitis, skin carcinoma, sleep disorder, somnolence, speech disorder, Stevens-Johnson syndrome, stomatitis, stridor, syncope, synovitis, tachycardia, taste loss, taste perversion, tenesmus, thirst, thrombocytopenia, thrombotic thrombocytopenic purpura, tinnitus, tremor, tongue disorder, toxic epidermal necrolysis, ulcerative colitis, ulcerative stomatitis, upper respiratory inflammation, upper respiratory infection, urethral pain, urinary frequency/urgency, urination impaired, urinary retention, urinary tract infection, urticaria, vaginitis, vasodilation, vertigo, visual field defect, vomiting, weakness, WBC abnormal, weight gain/loss, xerostomia

Dosing

Adult & Geriatric

Symptomatic GERD: Oral: Short-term treatment: 15 mg once daily for up to 8 weeks

Erosive esophagitis: Oral: Short-term treatment: 30 mg once daily for up to 8 weeks; continued treatment for an additional 8 weeks may be considered for recurrence or for patients who do not heal after the first 8 weeks of therapy. Maintenance therapy: 15 mg once daily; controlled studies did not extend past 12 months of therapy

Hypersecretory conditions: Oral: Initial: 60 mg once daily; adjust dose based upon patient response and to reduce acid secretion to <10 mEq/hour (5 mEq/hour in patients with prior gastric surgery); doses of 90 mg twice daily have been used; administer doses >120 mg/day in divided doses

Peptic ulcer disease:

Duodenal ulcer: Oral: Short-term treatment: 15 mg once daily for 4 weeks; maintenance therapy: 15 mg once daily

Gastric ulcer: Oral: Short-term treatment: 30 mg once daily for up to 8 weeks. Some clinical trial data suggests a dose of 15 mg once daily for up to 8 weeks may also be effective.

***Helicobacter pylori* eradication:** 30 mg 3 times daily administered with amoxicillin 1,000 mg 3 times daily for 14 days **or** 30 mg twice daily administered with amoxicillin 1,000 mg *and* clarithromycin 500 mg twice daily for 10 to 14 days

American College of Gastroenterology guidelines (Chey 2007):

Nonpenicillin allergy: 30 mg twice daily administered with amoxicillin 1,000 mg *and* clarithromycin 500 mg twice daily for 10 to 14 days

Penicillin allergy: 30 mg twice daily administered with clarithromycin 500 mg *and* metronidazole 500 mg twice daily for 10 to 14 days **or** 30 mg once or twice daily administered with bismuth subsalicylate 525 mg *and* metronidazole 250 mg *plus* tetracycline 500 mg 4 times daily for 10 to 14 days

NSAID-associated gastric ulcer (healing): Oral: 30 mg once daily for 8 weeks; controlled studies did not extend past 8 weeks

NSAID-associated gastric ulcer (to reduce risk): Oral: 15 mg once daily for up to 12 weeks; controlled studies did not extend past 12 weeks

Heartburn (OTC labeling): Oral: 15 mg once daily for 14 days; may repeat 14 days of therapy every 4 months. Do not take for >14 days or more often than every 4 months, unless instructed by health care provider.

Stress ulcer prophylaxis, ICU patients (off-label use): Oral: 30 mg once daily (Brophy 2010; Olsen 2008). **Note:** Intended for patients with associated risk factors (eg, coagulopathy, mechanical ventilation for ≥48 hours, severe sepsis); discontinue use once risk factors have resolved (Dellinger 2013).

Pediatric

GERD, erosive esophagitis: Children 1 to 11 years: Oral:

≤30 kg: 15 mg once daily for up to 12 weeks

>30 kg: 30 mg once daily for up to 12 weeks

Note: Doses were increased in some pediatric patients if still symptomatic after 2 or more weeks of treatment (maximum dose: 30 mg twice daily)

GERD:

Erosive esophagitis: Children 12 to 17 years: Oral: 30 mg once daily for up to 8 weeks

Nonerosive GERD: Children 12 to 17 years: Oral: 15 mg once daily for up to 8 weeks

Renal Impairment No dosage adjustment necessary.

Hepatic Impairment

Mild or moderate impairment: No dosage adjustment necessary.

Severe impairment: There are no dosage adjustments provided in the manufacturer's labeling; however, bioavailability is increased in hepatic impairment. Consider dose reduction.

Mechanism of Action Decreases acid secretion in gastric parietal cells through inhibition of (H+, K+)-ATPase enzyme system, blocking the final step in gastric acid production.

Contraindications Hypersensitivity (eg, anaphylaxis, angioedema, anaphylactic shock, angioedema, bronchospasm, acute interstitial nephritis, urticaria) to lansoprazole or any component of the formulation

Warnings/Precautions Use of proton pump inhibitors (PPIs) may increase the risk of gastrointestinal infections (eg, *Salmonella, Campylobacter*). Relief of symptoms does not preclude the presence of a gastric malignancy. No reports of enterochromaffin-like (ECL) cell carcinoids, dysplasia, or neoplasia have occurred. Use of proton pump inhibitors (PPIs) may increase risk of CDAD, especially in hospitalized patients; consider CDAD diagnosis in patients with persistent diarrhea that does not improve. Use the lowest dose and shortest duration of PPI therapy appropriate for the condition being treated. Severe liver dysfunction may require dosage reductions. Decreased *H. pylori* eradication rates have been observed with short-term (≤7 days) combination therapy. The American College of Gastroenterology recommends 10 to 14 days of therapy (triple or quadruple) for eradication of *H. pylori* (Chey 2007).

PPIs may diminish the therapeutic effect of clopidogrel thought to be due to reduced formation of the active metabolite of clopidogrel. The manufacturer of clopidogrel recommends either avoidance of both omeprazole (even when scheduled 12 hours apart) and esomeprazole or use of a PPI with comparatively less effect on the active metabolite of clopidogrel (eg, pantoprazole). Although lansoprazole exhibits the most potent CYP2C19 inhibition *in vitro* (Li 2004; Ogilvie 2011), an *in vivo* study of extensive CYP2C19 metabolizers showed less reduction of the active metabolite of clopidogrel by lansoprazole/dexlansoprazole compared to esomeprazole/omeprazole (Frelinger 2012). The manufacturer of lansoprazole states that no dosage adjustment is necessary for clopidogrel when used concurrently. In contrast to these warnings, others have recommended the continued use of PPIs, regardless of the degree of inhibition, in patients with a history of GI bleeding or multiple risk factors for GI bleeding who are also receiving clopidogrel since no evidence has established clinically meaningful differences in outcome; however, a clinically-significant interaction cannot be excluded in those who are poor metabolizers of clopidogrel (Abraham 2010; Levine 2011). Potentially significant interactions may exist, requiring dose or frequency adjustment, additional monitoring, and/or selection of alternative therapy.

Increased incidence of osteoporosis-related bone fractures of the hip, spine, or wrist may occur with PPI therapy. Patients on high-dose or long-term therapy should be monitored. Use the lowest effective dose for the shortest duration of time, use vitamin D and calcium supplementation, and follow appropriate guidelines to reduce risk of fractures in patients at risk. Acute interstitial nephritis has been observed in patients taking PPIs; may occur at any time during therapy and is generally due to an idiopathic hypersensitivity reaction. Discontinue if acute interstitial nephritis develops. Lansoprazole has been shown to be ineffective for the treatment of symptomatic GERD in children 1 month to <1 year.

Cutaneous and systemic lupus erythematosus: Has been reported as new onset or exacerbation of existing autoimmune disease; most cases were cutaneous lupus erythematosus (CLE), most commonly, subacute CLE (occurring within weeks to years after continuous therapy). Systemic lupus erythematosus (SLE) is less common (typically occurs within days to years after initiating treatment) and occurred primarily in young adults up to elderly patients. Discontinue therapy if signs or symptoms of CLE or SLE occur and refer to a specialist for evaluation; most patients improve 4 to 12 weeks after discontinuation of lansoprazole.

Hypomagnesemia, reported rarely, usually with prolonged PPI use of ≥3 months (most cases >1 year of therapy); may be symptomatic or asymptomatic; severe cases may cause tetany, seizures, and cardiac arrhythmias. Consider obtaining serum magnesium concentrations prior to beginning long-term therapy, especially if taking concomitant digoxin, diuretics, or other drugs known to cause hypomagnesemia; and periodically thereafter. Hypomagnesemia may be corrected by magnesium supplementation, although discontinuation of lansoprazole may be necessary; magnesium levels typically return to normal within 1 week of stopping.

Prolonged treatment (≥2 years) may lead to vitamin B_{12} malabsorption and subsequent vitamin B_{12} deficiency. The magnitude of the deficiency is dose-related and the association is stronger in females and those younger in age (<30 years); prevalence is decreased after discontinuation of therapy (Lam 2013).

Benzyl alcohol and derivatives: Some dosage forms may contain benzyl alcohol; large amounts of benzyl alcohol (≥99 mg/kg/day) have been associated with a potentially fatal toxicity ("gasping syndrome") in neonates; the "gasping syndrome" consists of metabolic acidosis, respiratory distress, gasping respirations, CNS dysfunction (including convulsions, intracranial hemorrhage), hypotension, and cardiovascular collapse (AAP ["Inactive" 1997]; CDC 1982); some data suggests that benzoate displaces bilirubin from protein binding sites (Ahlfors 2001); avoid or use dosage forms containing benzyl alcohol with caution in neonates. See manufacturer's labeling. Prevacid SoluTab and Prevacid FasTab [Canadian product] contain phenylalanine.

When used for self-medication, patients should be instructed not to use if they have difficulty swallowing, are vomiting blood, or have bloody or black stools. Prior to use, patients should contact healthcare provider if they have liver disease, heartburn for >3 months, heartburn with dizziness, lightheadedness, or sweating, MI symptoms, frequent chest pain, frequent wheezing (especially with heartburn), unexplained weight loss, nausea/vomiting, stomach pain, or are taking antifungals, atazanavir, digoxin, tacrolimus, theophylline, or warfarin. Patients should stop use and consult a healthcare provider if heartburn continues or worsens, or if they need to take for >14 days or more often than every 4 months. Patients should be informed that it may take 1 to 4 days for full effect to be seen; should not be used for immediate relief.

Drug Interactions

Metabolism/Transport Effects **Substrate** of CYP2C19 (major), CYP2C9 (minor), CYP3A4 (major); **Note:** Assignment of Major/Minor substrate status based on clinically relevant drug interaction potential; **Inhibits** CYP2C9 (weak); **Induces** CYP1A2 (weak/moderate)

Avoid Concomitant Use

Avoid concomitant use of Lansoprazole with any of the following: Dasatinib; Delavirdine; Erlotinib; Nelfinavir; PAZOPanib; Rilpivirine; Risedronate; Velpatasvir

Increased Effect/Toxicity

Lansoprazole may increase the levels/effects of: Amphetamine; Dexmethylphenidate; Dextroamphetamine; Imatinib; Methotrexate; Methylphenidate; Raltegravir; Risedronate; Saquinavir; Tacrolimus (Systemic); Vitamin K Antagonists; Voriconazole

The levels/effects of Lansoprazole may be increased by: Fluconazole; Ketoconazole (Systemic); Voriconazole

Decreased Effect

Lansoprazole may decrease the levels/effects of: Atazanavir; Bisphosphonate Derivatives; Bosutinib; Capecitabine; Cefditoren; Clopidogrel; Cysteamine (Systemic); Dabigatran Etexilate; Dabrafenib; Dasatinib; Delavirdine; Erlotinib; Gefitinib; Indinavir; Iron Salts; Itraconazole; Ketoconazole (Systemic); Ledipasvir; Mesalamine; Multivitamins/Minerals (with ADEK, Folate, Iron); Mycophenolate; Nelfinavir; Nilotinib; PAZOPanib; Posaconazole; Rilpivirine; Riociguat; Risedronate; Velpatasvir

The levels/effects of Lansoprazole may be decreased by: Bosentan; CYP2C19 Inducers (Strong); CYP3A4 Inducers (Moderate); CYP3A4 Inducers (Strong); Dabrafenib; Deferasirox; Enzalutamide; Mitotane; Siltuximab; St John's Wort; Tipranavir; Tocilizumab

Food Interactions Prolonged treatment (≥2 years) may lead to malabsorption of dietary vitamin B_{12} and subsequent vitamin B_{12} deficiency (Lam 2013).

Dietary Considerations Should be taken before eating; best if taken before breakfast. Some products may contain phenylalanine.

Pharmacodynamics/Kinetics

Onset of Action Gastric acid suppression: Oral: 1 to 3 hours

Duration of Action Gastric acid suppression: Oral: >1 day

Half-life Elimination Children: 1.2 to 1.5 hours; Adults: 1.5 ± 1 hour; Elderly: 2 to 3 hours; Hepatic impairment: 3 to 7 hours

Time to Peak Plasma: 1.7 hours

Pregnancy Risk Factor B

Pregnancy Considerations Adverse events have not been observed in animal reproduction studies. An increased risk of hypospadias was reported following maternal use of proton pump inhibitors (PPIs) during pregnancy (Anderka 2012), but this was based on a small number of exposures and the same association was not found in another study (Erichsen 2012). Most available studies have not shown an increased risk of major birth defects following maternal use of PPIs during pregnancy (Diav-Citrin 2005; Matok 2012; Pasternak 2010). When treating GERD in pregnancy, PPIs may be used when clinically indicated (Katz 2013).

Breastfeeding Considerations It is not known if lansoprazole is excreted in breast milk. Due to the potential for serious adverse reactions in the nursing infant, the manufacturer recommends a decision be made whether to discontinue nursing or to discontinue the drug, taking into account the importance of treatment to the mother.

Dosage Forms Considerations

First-Lansoprazole suspension is a compounding kit. Refer to manufacturer's labeling for compounding instructions.

Dosage Forms

Capsule Delayed Release, Oral:

GoodSense Lansoprazole [OTC]: 15 mg

Heartburn Treatment 24 Hour [OTC]: 15 mg

Prevacid: 15 mg, 30 mg

Prevacid 24HR [OTC]: 15 mg

Generic: 15 mg, 30 mg

Suspension, Oral:

First-Lansoprazole: 3 mg/mL (90 mL, 150 mL, 300 mL)

Tablet Dispersible, Oral:

Prevacid SoluTab: 15 mg, 30 mg

Dosage Forms: Canada

Tablet Dispersible, Oral:

Prevacid SoluTab: 15 mg, 30 mg [contains aspartame]

Lansoprazole, Amoxicillin, and Clarithromycin

(lan SOE pra zole, a moks i SIL in, & kla RITH roe mye sin)

Related Information

Amoxicillin *on page 121*
Clarithromycin *on page 377*
Gastrointestinal Disorders *on page 1775*
Lansoprazole *on page 961*

Brand Names: US Prevpac

Brand Names: Canada Hp-PAC

Pharmacologic Category Antibiotic, Macrolide Combination; Antibiotic, Penicillin; Gastrointestinal Agent, Miscellaneous; Proton Pump Inhibitor; Substituted Benzimidazole

Use ***Helicobacter pylori*** **eradication:** Eradication of *H. pylori* infection to reduce the risk of recurrent duodenal ulcer in patients with active or 1-year history of duodenal ulcer

Local Anesthetic/Vasoconstrictor Precautions No information available to require special precautions

Effects on Dental Treatment Key adverse event(s) related to dental treatment: Taste perversion.

Effects on Bleeding No information available to require special precautions

Adverse Reactions Also see individual agents.

3% to 10%:

Central nervous system: Headache (6%), confusion (<3%), dizziness (<3%)
Dermatologic: Dermatological reaction (<3%)
Endocrine & metabolic: Increased thirst (<3%)
Gastrointestinal: Diarrhea (7%), dysgeusia (5%), abdominal pain (<3%), anorectal pruritus (<3%), darkening of stools (<3%), glossitis (<3%), nausea (<3%), oral candidiasis (<3%), stomatitis (<3%), tongue discoloration (<3%), tongue disease (<3%), vomiting (<3%), xerostomia (<3%)
Genitourinary: Vaginitis (<3%), vulvovaginal candidiasis (<3%)
Neuromuscular & skeletal: Myalgia (<3%)

<3%, postmarketing, and/or case reports: Hepatotoxicity (idiosyncratic) (Chalasani 2014)

General Dosage Range Oral: *Adults:* Lansoprazole 30 mg, amoxicillin 1 g, and clarithromycin 500 mg taken together twice daily

Mechanism of Action

Lansoprazole: Suppresses gastric acid secretion by blocking the acid (proton) pump within gastric parietal cells.
Amoxicillin: Inhibits bacterial cell wall mucopeptide synthesis.
Clarithromycin: Inhibits microbial protein synthesis.

Pregnancy Risk Factor C

Pregnancy Considerations Adverse events have been observed in some animal reproduction studies. Refer to individual agents.

Lapatinib (la PA ti nib)

Related Information

Clinical Risk Related to Drugs Prolonging QT Interval *on page 1772*

Brand Names: US Tykerb

Brand Names: Canada Tykerb

Pharmacologic Category Antineoplastic Agent, Anti-HER2; Antineoplastic Agent, Epidermal Growth Factor Receptor (EGFR) Inhibitor; Antineoplastic Agent, Tyrosine Kinase Inhibitor

Use

Breast cancer: Treatment of human epidermal growth receptor type 2 (HER2) overexpressing advanced or metastatic breast cancer (in combination with capecitabine) in patients who have received prior therapy (with an anthracycline, a taxane, and trastuzumab); HER2 overexpressing hormone receptor–positive metastatic breast cancer in postmenopausal women where hormone therapy is indicated (in combination with letrozole)

Limitations of use: Patients should have disease progression on trastuzumab prior to initiation of treatment with lapatinib in combination with capecitabine.

Local Anesthetic/Vasoconstrictor Precautions Lapatinib is one of the drugs confirmed to prolong the QT interval and is accepted as having a risk of causing torsade de pointes. The risk of drug-induced torsade de pointes is extremely low when a single QT interval prolonging drug is prescribed. In terms of epinephrine, it is not known what effect vasoconstrictors in the local anesthetic regimen will have in patients with a known history of congenital prolonged QT interval or in patients taking any medication that prolongs the QT interval. Until more information is obtained, it is suggested that the clinician consult with the physician prior to the use of a vasoconstrictor in suspected patients, and that the vasoconstrictor (epinephrine, mepivacaine and levonordefrin [Carbocaine® 2% with Neo-Cobefrin®]) be used with caution.

Effects on Dental Treatment Key adverse event(s) related to dental treatment: Stomatitis.

Effects on Bleeding Anemia and thrombocytopenia have been reported. Medical consult recommended.

Adverse Reactions Percentages reported for combination therapy.

>10%:

Central nervous system: Fatigue (≤20%), headache (14%)
Dermatologic: Palmar-plantar erythrodysesthesia (with capecitabine: 53%; grade 3: 12%), skin rash (28% to 44%), alopecia (13%), xeroderma (10% to 13%), pruritus (12%), nail disease (11%)
Gastrointestinal: Diarrhea (64% to 65%; grade 3: 9% to 13%; grade 4: ≤1%), nausea (31% to 44%), vomiting (17% to 26%), mucositis (15%), abdominal pain (≤15%), stomatitis (14%), anorexia (11%), dyspepsia (11%)
Hematologic: Decreased hemoglobin (with capecitabine: 56%; grade 3: <1%), decreased neutrophils (with capecitabine: 22%; grade 3: 3%; grade 4: <1%), decreased platelet count (with capecitabine: 18%; grade 3: <1%)
Hepatic: Increased serum AST (49% to 53%; grade 3: 2% to 6%; grade 4: <1%), increased serum ALT (37% to 46%; grade 3: 2% to 5%; grade 4: <1%), increased serum bilirubin (22% to 45%; grade 3: ≤4%; grade 4: <1%)
Neuromuscular & skeletal: Limb pain (12%), weakness (12%), back pain (11%)
Respiratory: Dyspnea (12%), epistaxis (11%)

1% to 10%: Central nervous system: Insomnia (10%)

<1%, postmarketing, and/or case reports: Anaphylaxis, hepatotoxicity, hypersensitivity, interstitial pulmonary disease, left ventricular ejection fraction, paronychia, pneumonitis, prolonged Q-T interval on ECG, severe dermatological reaction

General Dosage Range Dosage adjustment recommended in patients with hepatic impairment, on concomitant therapy, or who develop toxicities

Oral: *Adults:* 1250 to 1500 mg once daily

Mechanism of Action Tyrosine kinase (dual kinase) inhibitor; inhibits EGFR (ErbB1) and HER2 (ErbB2) by reversibly binding to tyrosine kinase, blocking phosphorylation and activation of downstream second messengers (Erk1/2 and Akt), regulating cellular proliferation and survival in ErbB- and ErbB2-expressing tumors. Combination therapy with lapatinib and endocrine therapy may overcome endocrine resistance occurring in HER2+ and hormone receptor positive disease.

Pharmacodynamics/Kinetics

Half-life Elimination ~24 hours

Time to Peak ~4 hours (Burris 2009)

Pregnancy Risk Factor D

Pregnancy Considerations Adverse events were demonstrated in animal reproduction studies. Lapatinib may cause fetal harm if administered during pregnancy. Women of childbearing potential should be advised to avoid pregnancy during treatment.

European Society for Medical Oncology (ESMO) guidelines for cancer during pregnancy recommend delaying treatment with HER-2 targeted agents until after delivery in pregnant patients with HER-2 positive disease (Peccatori 2013).

Prescribing and Access Restrictions Lapatinib is available through specialty pharmacies only. Information is available at www.gskcta.com or 1-866-265-6491.

Dental Comment See Local Anesthetic/Vasoconstrictor Precautions

Laronidase (lair OH ni days)

Brand Names: US Aldurazyme

Brand Names: Canada Aldurazyme®

Pharmacologic Category Enzyme

Use Treatment of Hurler and Hurler-Scheie forms of mucopolysaccharidosis I (MPS I); treatment of Scheie form of MPS I in patients with moderate-to-severe symptoms

Local Anesthetic/Vasoconstrictor Precautions No information available to require special precautions

Effects on Dental Treatment No significant effects or complications reported

Effects on Bleeding Thrombocytopenia has been reported.

Adverse Reactions Unless otherwise noted, adverse reactions were reported in patients ≥6 years of age.

>10%:

Cardiovascular: Flushing (11% to 23%), venous irritation (poor venous access: 14%)

Central nervous system: Chills (infants and children 6 months to 5 years: 20%), hyperreflexia (14%), paresthesia (14%)

Dermatologic: Skin rash (13% to 36%; infants and children 6 months to 5 years: ≥5%)

Immunologic: Antibody development (93% to 97%; infants and children 6 months to 5 years: 100%)

Local: Injection site reaction (18%)

Otic: Otitis media (infants and children 6 months to 5 years: 20%)

Respiratory: Upper respiratory tract infection (32%)

Miscellaneous: Infusion-related reaction (32% to 49%; may be severe; infants and children 6 months to 5 years: 35%), fever (11%; infants and children 6 months to 5 years: 30%)

1% to 10%:

Cardiovascular: Hypertension (infants and children 6 months to 5 years: 10%), oxygen saturation decreased (infants and children 6 months to 5 years: 10%), tachycardia (infants and children 6 months to 5 years: 10%), chest pain (9%), edema (9%), facial edema (9%), hypotension (9%), hot and cold flashes (7%)

Central nervous system: Headache (9%)

Dermatologic: Pallor (infants and children 6 months to 5 years: ≥5%), pruritus (4%), urticaria (4%), hyperhidrosis

Gastrointestinal: Abdominal pain (≤9%), abdominal distress (≤9%), diarrhea (7%), vomiting (4%)

Hematologic & oncologic: Thrombocytopenia (9%)

Hepatic: Hyperbilirubinemia (9%)

Hypersensitivity: Severe hypersensitivity (1%)

Local: Abscess at injection site (9%), pain at injection site (9%)

Neuromuscular & skeletal: Tremor (infants and children 6 months to 5 years: ≥5%), arthralgia (4%), back pain, musculoskeletal pain

Ophthalmic: Corneal opacity (9%)

Respiratory: Rales (infants and children 6 months to 5 years: ≥5%), respiratory distress (infants and children 6 months to 5 years: ≥5%), wheezing (infants and children 6 months to 5 years: ≥5%), bronchospasm, cough, dyspnea

<1%, postmarketing, and/or case reports: Anaphylaxis, angioedema, cardiac failure, cyanosis, erythema, fatigue, laryngeal edema, peripheral edema, pneumonia, respiratory failure

General Dosage Range IV: *Children ≥6 months and Adults:* 0.58 mg/kg once weekly

Mechanism of Action Laronidase is a recombinant (replacement) form of α-L-iduronidase derived from Chinese hamster cells. α-L-iduronidase is an enzyme needed to break down endogenous glycosaminoglycans (GAGs) within lysosomes. A deficiency of α-L-iduronidase leads to an accumulation of GAGs, causing cellular, tissue, and organ dysfunction as seen in MPS I. Improved pulmonary function and walking capacity have been demonstrated with the administration of laronidase to patients with Hurler, Hurler-Scheie, or Scheie (with moderate-to-severe symptoms) forms of MPS.

Pharmacodynamics/Kinetics

Half-life Elimination

Infants and Children 6 months to 5 years: 0.3-1.9 hours

Children ≥6 years and Adults: 1.5-3.6 hours

Pregnancy Risk Factor B

Pregnancy Considerations Teratogenic effects were not observed in animal reproduction studies. Patients are encouraged to enroll in the MPS I registry (800-745-4447 or www.MPSIregistry.com).

Latanoprost (la TA noe prost)

Brand Names: US Xalatan

Brand Names: Canada ACT Latanoprost; Apo-Latanoprost; GD-Latanoprost; Med-Latanoprost; Monoprost; PMS-Latanoprost; Riva-Latanoprost; Sandoz-Latanoprost; Xalatan

Pharmacologic Category Ophthalmic Agent, Antiglaucoma; Prostaglandin, Ophthalmic

Use Elevated intraocular pressure: Reduction of elevated intraocular pressure (IOP) in patients with open-angle glaucoma and ocular hypertension.

Local Anesthetic/Vasoconstrictor Precautions No information available to require special precautions

Effects on Dental Treatment No significant effects or complications reported

Effects on Bleeding No information available to require special precautions

Adverse Reactions

>5% to 15%:

Central nervous system: Foreign body sensation of eye (13%)

Ophthalmic: Epithelial keratopathy (punctate; 10%), stinging of eyes (9%), blurred vision (8%), conjunctival hyperemia (8%), eye pruritus (8%), burning sensation of eyes (7%), iris hyperpigmentation (7%)

1% to 5%:

Cardiovascular: Angina pectoris (≥1% to ≤2%), chest pain (≥1% to ≤2%)

Dermatologic: Erythema of eyelid (3%), allergic skin reaction (≤1%), skin rash (≤1%)

Infection: Common cold (≤3%), influenza (≤3%)

Neuromuscular & skeletal: Arthralgia (≤1%), back pain (≤1%), myalgia (≤1%)

Ophthalmic: Eyelid pain (4%), lacrimation (4%), crusting of eyelid (3%), dry eye syndrome (3%), eye pain (3%), photophobia (2%), eyelid edema (1%)

Respiratory: Upper respiratory tract infection (≤3%)

<1%, postmarketing, and/or case reports: Asthma, conjunctivitis, corneal edema, corneal erosion, diplopia, dizziness, dyspnea, embolism (retinal artery), eye discharge, eye disease (periorbital and lid changes resulting in deepening of the eyelid sulcus), headache, herpes simplex keratitis, hyperpigmentation of eyelashes, hyperpigmentation of eyelids, increased eyelash length, increased eyelash thickness, increased growth in number of eyelashes, iritis, keratitis, macular edema, retinal detachment, toxic epidermal necrolysis, uveitis, vitreous hemorrhage (from diabetic retinopathy)

General Dosage Range Ophthalmic: *Adults:* One drop in the affected eye(s) once daily in the evening

Mechanism of Action Latanoprost is a prostaglandin F_2-alpha analog believed to reduce intraocular pressure by increasing the outflow of the aqueous humor

Pharmacodynamics/Kinetics

Onset of Action 3 to 4 hours; Peak effect: Maximum: 8 to 12 hours

Half-life Elimination 17 minutes

Pregnancy Risk Factor C

Pregnancy Considerations Adverse events were observed in animal reproduction studies at maternally toxic doses.

Leflunomide (le FLOO noh mide)

Related Information

Rheumatoid Arthritis, Osteoarthritis, and Osteoporosis *on page 1792*

Brand Names: US Arava

Brand Names: Canada Apo-Leflunomide; Arava; Mylan-Leflunomide; PHL-Leflunomide; PMS-Leflunomide; Sandoz-Leflunomide; Teva-Leflunomide

Pharmacologic Category Antirheumatic, Disease Modifying

Use Rheumatoid arthritis: Treatment of adults with active rheumatoid arthritis (RA).

Local Anesthetic/Vasoconstrictor Precautions No information available to require special precautions

Effects on Dental Treatment Key adverse event(s) related to dental treatment: Xerostomia (normal salivary flow resumes upon discontinuation), stomatitis, oral candidiasis, abnormal taste, enlarged salivary gland, esophagitis, and gingivitis.

Effects on Bleeding There have been rare reports of thrombocytopenia.

Adverse Reactions

>10%:

Central nervous system: Headache (7% to 13%)

Dermatologic: Alopecia (9% to 17%), skin rash (10% to 12%)

Gastrointestinal: Diarrhea (17% to 27%), nausea (9% to 13%)

1% to 10%:

Cardiovascular: Hypertension (9% to 10%)

Central nervous system: Dizziness (4% to 7%)

Dermatologic: Pruritus (4% to 6%)

Gastrointestinal: Gastrointestinal pain (5% to 8%), abdominal pain (5% to 6%), oral mucosa ulcer (3% to 5%), vomiting (3% to 5%)

Hepatic: Abnormal hepatic function tests (5% to 10%), increased serum ALT (>3 x ULN: 2% to 4%; reversible)

Hypersensitivity: Hypersensitivity reaction (1% to 5%)

Neuromuscular & skeletal: Back pain (5% to 8%), weakness (3% to 6%), tenosynovitis (2% to 5%)

Respiratory: Bronchitis (5% to 8%), rhinitis (2% to 5%)

Frequency not defined:

Cardiovascular: Chest pain, increased blood pressure, leg thrombophlebitis, palpitations, varicose veins

Central nervous system: Drowsiness, malaise

Endocrine & metabolic: Increased gamma-glutamyl transferase

Gastrointestinal: Anorexia, enlargement of salivary glands, flatulence, sore throat, xerostomia

Genitourinary: Vulvovaginal candidiasis

Hematologic & oncologic: Leukocytosis, thrombocytopenia

Hepatic: Hyperbilirubinemia, increased serum alkaline phosphatase, increased serum AST

Hypersensitivity: Anaphylaxis

Infection: Abscess

Ophthalmic: Blurred vision, eye disease, papilledema, retinal hemorrhage, retinopathy

Respiratory: Dyspnea, flu-like symptoms

<1%, postmarketing and/or case reports: Agranulocytosis, angioedema, cholestasis, colitis (including microscopic colitis), cutaneous lupus erythematosus, DRESS syndrome, erythema multiforme, exacerbation of psoriasis, hepatitis, hepatotoxicity (rare, including hepatic necrosis and hepatic failure), interstitial pneumonitis, interstitial pulmonary disease, jaundice, leukopenia, necrotizing angiitis (cutaneous), neutropenia, opportunistic infection, pancreatitis, pancytopenia, peripheral neuropathy, pulmonary fibrosis, pulmonary hypertension, pustular psoriasis, sepsis (including *Pneumocystis jiroveci* pneumonia and aspergillosis), severe infection, Stevens-Johnson syndrome, toxic epidermal necrolysis, vasculitis

General Dosage Range Dosage adjustment recommended in patients who develop toxicities

Oral: *Adults:* Loading dose: 100 mg once daily for 3 days; Maintenance range: 10 to 20 mg once daily

Mechanism of Action Leflunomide is an immunomodulatory agent that inhibits pyrimidine synthesis, resulting in antiproliferative and anti-inflammatory effects. Leflunomide is a prodrug; the active metabolite is responsible for activity. For CMV, may interfere with virion assembly.

Pharmacodynamics/Kinetics

Half-life Elimination Teriflunomide: Mean: 18 to 19 days; enterohepatic recycling appears to contribute to the long half-life of this agent, since activated charcoal and cholestyramine substantially reduce plasma half-life

Time to Peak Teriflunomide: 6 to 12 hours

Pregnancy Considerations [US Boxed Warning]: Leflunomide is contraindicated in pregnant women because of the potential for fetal harm. Adverse events were observed in animal reproduction studies with doses lower than the expected human exposure. Exclude pregnancy before the start of treatment in females of reproductive potential. Advise females of reproductive potential to use effective contraception during treatment and during an accelerated elimination procedure after treatment is discontinued. Discontinue therapy and use an accelerated elimination procedure if pregnancy occurs during treatment. Women of reproductive potential should not receive therapy until pregnancy has been excluded, they have been counseled concerning fetal risk, and reliable contraceptive measures have been confirmed. Following treatment, pregnancy should be avoided until undetectable serum concentrations (<0.02 mg/L) are verified. This may be accomplished by the use of an enhanced drug elimination procedure using cholestyramine. Serum concentrations <0.02 mg/L should be verified by 2 separate tests performed at least 14 days apart. If serum concentrations are >0.02 mg/L, additional cholestyramine treatment should be considered. As an alternative to cholestyramine, the Canadian labeling recommends that activated charcoal may be used to enhance drug elimination.

It is not known if males taking leflunomide may contribute to fetal toxicity. Males taking leflunomide who wish to father a child should consider discontinuing therapy and using the cholestyramine procedure to eliminate the medication. The Canadian labeling recommends avoiding use in males capable of fathering a child and who are not using reliable contraception during and for a total of 2 years after treatment unless an elimination procedure is used; for men receiving treatment and desiring to father a child, serum concentrations of the active metabolite should be verified by 2 separate tests performed at least 14 days apart. If levels <0.02 mg/L are confirmed with the second test, an additional waiting period of 3 months is recommended.

Health care providers are encouraged to enroll women exposed to leflunomide during pregnancy in the Pregnancy Registry (877-311-8972 or http://www.pregnancystudies.org/participate-ina-study/).

Lenalidomide (le na LID oh mide)

Brand Names: US Revlimid

Brand Names: Canada Revlimid

Pharmacologic Category Angiogenesis Inhibitor; Antineoplastic Agent; Immunomodulator, Systemic

Use

Mantle cell lymphoma: Treatment of patients with mantle cell lymphoma that has relapsed or progressed after 2 prior therapies (one of which included bortezomib).

Multiple myeloma: Treatment of multiple myeloma (in combination with dexamethasone) and as maintenance therapy following autologous hematopoietic stem cell transplantation.

Myelodysplastic syndromes: Treatment of patients with transfusion-dependent anemia due to low- or intermediate-1-risk myelodysplastic syndromes (MDS) associated with a deletion 5q (del 5q) cytogenetic abnormality with or without additional cytogenetic abnormalities

Limitations of use: Lenalidomide is not indicated and is not recommended for the treatment of chronic lymphocytic leukemia (CLL) outside of controlled clinical trials.

Local Anesthetic/Vasoconstrictor Precautions No information available to require special precautions

Effects on Dental Treatment Key adverse event(s) related to dental treatment: Xerostomia (normal salivary flow resumes upon discontinuation), taste perversion.

Effects on Bleeding Associated with significant thrombocytopenia and anemia. Medical consult recommended.

Adverse Reactions Frequency not always defined; may vary based on indication and/or concomitant therapy.

Cardiovascular: Peripheral edema (8% to 26%), edema (10%), deep vein thrombosis (4% to 10%; grades 3/4: ≤8%), hypotension (7% to 10%), hypertension (6% to 8%), chest pain (5% to 8%), atrial fibrillation (3% to 7%; grades 3/4: ≤4%), palpitations (5%), myocardial infarction (1% to <5%), pulmonary embolism (2% to 4%; grades 3/4: 1% to 4%), syncope (grades 3/4: 1% to 3%), tachycardia (grades 3/4: 2%), cerebrovascular accident (≤2%), angina pectoris (≥1%), bradycardia (≥1%), cerebral ischemia (≥1%), cardiac failure (1%), cardiac arrest, cardiogenic shock, cardiomyopathy, cardiorespiratory arrest, cerebral infarction, increased cardiac enzymes (troponin I), ischemia, ischemic heart disease, septic shock, subarachnoid hemorrhage, supraventricular cardiac arrhythmia, tachyarrhythmia, thrombophlebitis, thrombosis, transient ischemic attacks, ventricular dysfunction

Central nervous system: Fatigue (29% to 44%), insomnia (10% to 28%), dizziness (20% to 23%), headache (10% to 20%), depression (5% to 11%), chills (5% to 10%), falling (5% to 8%), hypoesthesia (7%), lethargy (7%), pain (7%), neuropathy (including peripheral, 5% to 7%), rigors (6%), noncardiac chest pain (3% to 6%), emotional lability (≥1%), glossalgia (≥1%), hallucination (≥1%), malaise (≥1%), abnormal gait, aphasia, cerebellar infarction, confusion, dysarthria, impaired consciousness, migraine, spinal cord compression, vertigo

Dermatologic: Pruritus (4% to 42%), skin rash (19% to 36%), xeroderma (9% to 14%), diaphoresis (7% to 10%), night sweats (8%), ecchymoses (5%), erythema (5%), cellulitis (≤5%), hyperpigmentation (≥1%), Sweet's syndrome

Endocrine & metabolic: Weight loss (9% to 20%), hypokalemia (7% to 17%), hyperglycemia (4% to 12%), hypocalcemia (3% to 11%), hypothyroidism (7%), hypomagnesemia (6% to 7%), dehydration (3% to 7%), diabetes mellitus (<5%), gout (<5%), hypophosphatemia (<5%, grades 3/4: ≤3%), hyponatremia (2% to <5%), hirsutism (≥1%), loss of libido (≥1%), Graves' disease, hypernatremia, hypoglycemia

Gastrointestinal: Diarrhea (17% to 49%), constipation (16% to 41%), nausea (24% to 30%), decreased appetite (7% to 23%), abdominal pain (8% to 21%), anorexia (10% to 16%), dysgeusia (4% to 15%), vomiting (10% to 12%), dyspepsia (5% to 11%), xerostomia (7%), loose stools (6%), gastroenteritis (2% to 6%), gastrointestinal hemorrhage (≥1%), biliary obstruction, cholecystitis, colonic polyps, diverticulitis, dysphagia, gastritis, gastroesophageal reflux disease, infection of mouth, inguinal hernia (obstructive), intestinal obstruction, intestinal perforation, irritable bowel syndrome, ischemic colitis, melena

Genitourinary: Urinary tract infection (4% to 14%), dysuria (7%), erectile dysfunction (≥1%), azotemia, hematuria, pelvic pain, perirectal obsess, urolithiasis, urosepsis

Hematologic & oncologic: Thrombocytopenia (19% to 62%; grades 3/4: 8% to 50%; MDS: Onset: 28 days [range: 8 to 290 days]; recovery: 22 days [range: 5 to 224 days]), neutropenia (33% to 61%; grades 3/4: 27% to 53%; MDS: Onset: 42 days [range: 14 to 411 days]; recovery: 17 days [range: 2 to 170 days]), anemia (12% to 44%; grades 3/4: 6% to 19%), leukopenia (8% to 15%; grades 3/4: 4% to 7%), tumor flare (10%), lymphocytopenia (5% to 7%; grades 3/4: 3% to 4%), bruise (3% to 6%), febrile neutropenia (1% to 6%; grades 3/4: 1% to 6%), second primary malignant neoplasms (≤5%, including AML, lymphomas, solid tumors), squamous cell carcinoma of skin (3% to <5%; grades 3/4: ≤3%), pancytopenia (<5%; grades 3/4: ≤2%), basal cell carcinoma (<5%; grades 3/4: <1%), granulocytopenia (grades 3/4: 2%), autoimmune hemolytic anemia (≥1%), acute leukemia, blood coagulation disorder, bone marrow depression, bronchogenic carcinoma, decreased hemoglobin, hemolysis, hemolytic anemia (including warm type), lung carcinoma, malignant lymphoma, myelocytic leukemia, neutropenic infection, pancreatitis, postoperative hemorrhage, prostate carcinoma, rectal hemorrhage, splenic infarction

Hepatic: Increased serum ALT (8%), abnormal hepatic function tests (≥1%), hepatic failure, hyperbilirubinemia

Hypersensitivity: Hypersensitivity reaction, transfusion reaction

Infection: Influenza (3% to 6%), sepsis (including *Enterobacter*, 3% to 6%; grades 3/4: 2% to 5%), bacteremia (1%), bacterial infection, clostridium infection, fungal infection, herpes virus infection, kidney infection, Klebsiella infection, localized infection, pseudomonas infection, staphylococcal infection

Local: Catheter infection

Neuromuscular & skeletal: Muscle cramps (18% to 33%), back pain (13% to 32%), weakness (14% to 28%), arthralgia (8% to 22%), tremor (21%), muscle spasm (11% to 21%), ostealgia (1% to 16%), limb pain (5% to 15%), musculoskeletal pain (7% to 13%), musculoskeletal chest pain (7% to 11%), myalgia (9%), myasthenia (5% to 8%), neck pain (2% to 8%), arthritis, bone fracture (femur, femoral neck, pelvis, hip, rib, spinal compression), calcium pyrophosphate deposition disease

Ophthalmic: Blurred vision (17%), cataract (≤14%; grades 3/4: ≤6%), subcapsular posterior cataract (<5%), blindness (≥1%), ocular hypertension (≥1%)

Otic: Otic infection

Renal: Renal failure (4% to 10%), increased serum creatinine

Respiratory: Cough (13% to 28%), upper respiratory tract infection (6% to 25%), dyspnea (17% to 24%), nasopharyngitis (6% to 23%), pneumonia (9% to 18%), bronchitis (6% to 17%), pharyngitis (14% to 16%), epistaxis (3% to 15%), oropharyngeal pain (3% to 10%), sinusitis (7% to 8%), pleural effusion (7%; grades 3/4: 1%), dyspnea on exertion (≤7%), respiratory tract infection (4% to 7%), rhinitis (3% to 7%), lower respiratory tract infection (2% to 6%), hypoxia (2%; grades 3/4: 1%), hoarseness (≥1%), pneumonitis (grades 3/4: 1%), pulmonary hypertension (grades 3/4: 1%), respiratory distress (1%; grades 3/4: 1% to 2%), chronic obstructive pulmonary disease, interstitial pulmonary disease, pulmonary edema, pulmonary infiltrates, respiratory failure, wheezing

Miscellaneous: Fever (14% to 28%), physical health deterioration (2%), multiorgan failure (grades 3/4: 1%), mass (renal), nodule

<1%, postmarketing, and/or case reports: Angioedema, atrial flutter, catheter infection, circulatory shock, desquamation, drug overdose, erythema multiforme, Fanconi's syndrome, hematologic disease (impaired stem cell mobilization), hemorrhage, hemorrhagic diathesis, hepatitis, intracranial hemorrhage, leukoencephalopathy, myopathy, nephrolithiasis, orthostatic hypotension, peripheral ischemia, pseudomembranous colitis, pseudomonas infection, pulmonary edema, pulmonary infiltrates, rectal hemorrhage, renal tubular necrosis, Stevens-Johnson syndrome, stomatitis, toxic epidermal necrolysis, tumor lysis syndrome, urinary retention, urticaria, viral infection

General Dosage Range Dosage adjustment recommended in patients with renal impairment or who develop toxicities

Oral: *Adults:* 10 once daily **or** 25 mg once daily for 21 of 28 days

Mechanism of Action Lenalidomide has immunomodulatory, antiangiogenic, and antineoplastic characteristics via multiple mechanisms. It selectively inhibits secretion of proinflammatory cytokines (potent inhibitor of tumor necrosis factor-alpha secretion); enhances cell-mediated immunity by stimulating proliferation of anti-CD3 stimulated T cells (resulting in increased IL-2 and interferon gamma secretion); inhibits trophic signals to angiogenic factors in cells. Inhibits the growth of myeloma cells by inducing cell cycle arrest and cell death.

Pharmacodynamics/Kinetics

Half-life Elimination 3 to 5 hours

Time to Peak MDS or myeloma patients: 0.5 to 6 hours

Pregnancy Considerations [US Boxed Warning]: Do not use lenalidomide in pregnant women. Lenalidomide is an analogue of thalidomide (a human teratogen) and could potentially cause severe birth defects or embryo-fetal death; use is contraindicated during pregnancy and pregnancy must be avoided while taking lenalidomide. Obtain 2 negative pregnancy tests prior to initiation of treatment; 2 forms of contraception (or abstain from heterosexual intercourse) must be used at least 4 weeks prior to, during, and for 4 weeks after lenalidomide treatment (and during treatment interruptions). In order to decrease the risk of embryo-fetal exposure, lenalidomide is available only through a restricted distribution program (Revlimid REMS).

Women of childbearing potential should be treated only if they are able to comply with the conditions of the Revlimid REMS program. Women of reproductive potential must avoid pregnancy beginning 4 weeks prior to therapy, during therapy, during therapy interruptions, and for ≥4 weeks after therapy is discontinued. Two forms of effective/reliable contraception (eg, tubal ligation, IUD, hormonal birth control methods, male latex or synthetic condom, diaphragm, or cervical cap) or total abstinence from heterosexual intercourse must be used by females who are not infertile or who have not had a hysterectomy. A negative pregnancy test (sensitivity of at least 50 milliunits/mL) 10 to 14 days prior to therapy, within 24 hours prior to beginning therapy, weekly during the first 4 weeks, and every 4 weeks (every 2 weeks for women with irregular menstrual cycles) thereafter is required for women of childbearing potential. Lenalidomide must be immediately discontinued for a missed period, abnormal pregnancy test or abnormal menstrual bleeding; refer patient to a reproductive toxicity specialist if pregnancy occurs during treatment.

Lenalidomide is also present in the semen of males. Males (including those vasectomized) should use a latex or synthetic condom during any sexual contact with women of childbearing age during treatment, during treatment interruptions, and for 4 weeks after discontinuation. Male patients should not donate sperm during, and for 4 weeks after treatment, and during therapy interruptions.

A pregnancy exposure registry has been created to monitor outcomes in females exposed to lenalidomide during pregnancy and female partners of male patients and to understand the root cause for the pregnancy. The pregnancy exposure registry may be contacted at 1-888-423-5436. The parent or legal guardian for patients between 12 and 18 years of age must agree to ensure compliance with the required guidelines. Any suspected fetal exposure should be reported to the FDA via the MedWatch program (1-800-FDA-1088) and to Celgene Corporation (1-888-423-5436).

Prescribing and Access Restrictions As a requirement of the REMS program, access to this medication is restricted. Lenalidomide is approved for marketing in the US only under a Food and Drug Administration (FDA) approved, restricted distribution program called Revlimid REMS (https://www.celgeneriskmanagement.com or 1-888-423-5436). Prescribers and pharmacies must be certified with the program to prescribe or dispense lenalidomide; patients must comply with the program requirements. No more than a 4-week supply should be dispensed. Prescriptions must be filled within 7 days (for females of reproductive potential) or within 30 days (for all other patients) after authorization number obtained. Subsequent prescriptions may be filled only if fewer than 7 days of therapy remain on the previous prescription. A new prescription is required for further dispensing (a telephone prescription may not be accepted). Pregnancy testing is required for females of childbearing potential. In Canada, distribution is restricted through RevAid (www.RevAid.ca or 1-888-738-2431).

Lenvatinib (len VA ti nib)

Brand Names: US Lenvima 10 MG Daily Dose; Lenvima 14 MG Daily Dose; Lenvima 18 MG Daily Dose; Lenvima 20 MG Daily Dose; Lenvima 24 MG Daily Dose; Lenvima 8 MG Daily Dose

Brand Names: Canada Lenvima

Pharmacologic Category Antineoplastic Agent, Tyrosine Kinase Inhibitor; Antineoplastic Agent, Vascular Endothelial Growth Factor (VEGF) Inhibitor

Use

Renal cell carcinoma, advanced: Treatment of advanced renal cell carcinoma (in combination with everolimus) following one prior anti-angiogenic therapy.

Thyroid cancer, differentiated: Treatment of locally recurrent or metastatic, progressive, radioactive iodine-refractory differentiated thyroid cancer (DTC)

Local Anesthetic/Vasoconstrictor Precautions Hypertension can occur in significant numbers of patients; monitor for hypertension prior to using local anesthetic with vasoconstrictor; medical consult if necessary.

Lenvatinib is one of the drugs confirmed to prolong the QT interval and is accepted as having a risk of causing torsade de pointes. The risk of drug-induced torsade de pointes is extremely low when a single QT interval prolonging drug is prescribed. In terms of epinephrine, it is not known what effect vasoconstrictors in the local anesthetic regimen will have in patients with a known history of congenital prolonged QT interval or in patients taking any medication that prolongs the QT interval. Until more information is obtained, it is suggested that the clinician consult with the physician prior to the use of a vasoconstrictor in suspected patients, and that the vasoconstrictor (epinephrine, mepivacaine, and levonordefrin [Carbocaine 2% with Neo-Cobefrin]) be used with caution.

Effects on Dental Treatment Key adverse event(s) related to dental treatment: Xerostomia (normal salivary flow resumes after discontinuation). Mouth pain, stomatitis, infection of the mouth have been reported.

Effects on Bleeding Chemotherapy may result in significant myelosuppression, potentially including reduction in platelet counts (grades 3/4: 2%); Bleeding has been reported in 35% of patients. In patients who are under active treatment with these agents, medical consult is suggested.

Adverse Reactions

>10%:

Cardiovascular: Hypertension (73%; grades 3/4: ≤44%), peripheral edema (21%; grades 3/4: <1%)

Central nervous system: Fatigue (67%; grades 3/4: 11%), headache (38%; grades 3/4: 3%), voice disorder (31%; grades 3/4: 1%), mouth pain (25%; grades 3/4: 1%), dizziness (15%; grades 3/4: <1%), insomnia (12%)

Dermatologic: Palmar-plantar erythrodysesthesia (32%; grades 3/4: 3%), skin rash (21%; grades 3/4: <1%), alopecia (12%)

Endocrine & metabolic: Increased thyroid stimulating hormone level (57%), weight loss (51%; grades 3/4: 13%)

Gastrointestinal: Diarrhea (67%; grades 3/4: 9%), decreased appetite (54%; grades 3/4: 7%), nausea (47%; grades 3/4: 2%), stomatitis (41%; grades 3/4: 5%), vomiting (36%; grades 3/4: 2%), abdominal pain (31%; grades 3/4: 2%), constipation (29%), dysgeusia (18%), xerostomia (17%; grades 3/4: <1%), dyspepsia (13%, grades 3/4: <1%), infection of mouth (10%; grades 3/4: 1%)

Genitourinary: Proteinuria (34%; grade 3: 11%), urinary tract infection (11%; grades 3/4: 1%)

Hematologic & oncologic: Hemorrhage (35%; grades ≥3: 2%)

Neuromuscular & skeletal: Arthralgia (≤62%; grades 3/4: ≤5%), myalgia (≤62%, grades 3/4: ≤5%)

Renal: Renal insufficiency (14%; grade 3 or higher: 3%)

Respiratory: Cough (24%), epistaxis (12%)

1% to 10%:

Cardiovascular: Hypotension (9%; grades 3/4: 2%), prolonged Q-T interval on ECG (9%; grades 3/4: 2%), thromboembolic complications (5%; grade 3 or higher: 3%; arterial events), pulmonary embolism (3%), reduced ejection fraction (2%; ejection fraction reduced by >20%)

Dermatologic: Hyperkeratosis (7%)

Endocrine & metabolic: Dehydration (9%; grades 3/4: 2%), hypocalcemia (grades 3/4: 9%), hypokalemia (grades 3/4: 6%), hypercalcemia (>5%), hypercholesterolemia (>5%), hyperkalemia (>5%), hypoalbuminemia (>5%), hypoglycemia (>5%), hypomagnesemia (>5%)

Gastrointestinal: Increased serum amylase (>5%), increased serum lipase (grades 3/4: 4%), gastrointestinal fistula (2%)

Hematologic & oncologic: Decreased platelet count (grades 3/4: 2%)

Hepatic: Hyperbilirubinemia (>5%), increased serum alkaline phosphatase (>5%), increased serum AST (grades 3 or higher: 5%), increased serum ALT (grades 3 or higher: 4%)

Renal: Increased serum creatinine (grades 3/4: 3%)

Respiratory: Pulmonary edema (7%; grade 3 or higher: 2%)

<1%, postmarketing, and/or case reports: Reversible posterior leukoencephalopathy syndrome, tumor hemorrhage

General Dosage Range Dosage adjustment recommended in patients with renal or hepatic impairment or who develop toxicities.

Oral: *Adults:* 18 or 24 mg once daily

Mechanism of Action Lenvatinib is a multitargeted tyrosine kinase inhibitor of vascular endothelial growth factor (VEGF) receptors VEGFR1 (FLT1), VEGFR2 (KDR), VEGFR3 (FLT4), fibroblast growth factor (FGF) receptors FGFR1, 2, 3, and 4, platelet derived growth factor receptor alpha (PDGFRα), KIT, and RET. Inhibition of these receptor tyrosine kinases leads to decreased tumor growth and slowing of cancer progression. Combining lenvatinib with everolimus has demonstrated increased antiangiogenic and antitumor activity by decreasing human endothelial cell proliferation, tube formation, and VEGF signaling (in vitro) compared to either drug alone.

Pharmacodynamics/Kinetics

Half-life Elimination ~28 hours

Time to Peak 1 to 4 hours

Pregnancy Considerations Adverse events were observed in animal reproduction studies. Based on the mechanism of action, lenvatinib may cause fetal harm if administered in pregnancy. Females of reproductive potential should use effective contraception during lenvatinib treatment and for at least 2 weeks after completion of therapy.

Prescribing and Access Restrictions Lenvatinib is available only through specialty pharmacies. For further information on patient assistance, product availability, and prescribing instructions, please refer to the following website: http://www.lenvima.com/hcp/pharmacy-financial-options

Lesinurad (le SIN ure ad)

Brand Names: US Zurampic

Pharmacologic Category Antigout Agent; Uric Acid Transporter 1 (URAT1) Inhibitor

Use

Hyperuricemia associated with gout: Treatment of hyperuricemia associated with gout (in combination with a xanthine oxidase inhibitor) in patients who have not achieved target serum uric acid levels with a xanthine oxidase inhibitor alone.

Limitations of use: Lesinurad is not recommended for the treatment of asymptomatic hyperuricemia. Lesinurad should not be used as monotherapy.

Local Anesthetic/Vasoconstrictor Precautions No information available to require special precautions

Effects on Dental Treatment No significant effects or complications reported

Effects on Bleeding No information available to require special precautions

Adverse Reactions Incidence reported in combination with a xanthine oxidase inhibitor.

1% to 10%:

Central nervous system: Headache (5%)

Gastrointestinal: Gastroesophageal reflux disease (3%)

Infection: Influenza (5%)

Renal: Increased serum creatinine (≤6%; 1.5 x to <2.0 x baseline: 4%; ≥2.0 x baseline: 2%; most elevations were transient and resolved without therapy interruption), renal failure (2%)

Frequency not defined:

Cardiovascular: Cerebrovascular accident, myocardial infarction

Renal: Acute renal failure

<1%, postmarketing, and/or case reports: Nephrolithiasis

General Dosage Range Oral: *Adults:* 200 mg once daily (maximum dose: 200 mg/day).

Mechanism of Action Lesinurad inhibits the function of transporter proteins involved in renal uric acid reabsorption (uric acid transporter 1 [URAT1] and organic anion transporter 4 [OAT4]), and lowers serum uric acid levels and increases renal clearance and fractional excretion of uric acid in patients with gout.

Pharmacodynamics/Kinetics

Half-life Elimination ~5 hours

Time to Peak Within 1 to 4 hours

Pregnancy Considerations

Adverse events were not observed in animal reproduction studies.

All forms of hormonal contraceptives (eg, oral, injectable, topical) may be less effective during therapy with lesinurad. Additional methods of contraception are recommended during therapy.

Letrozole (LET roe zole)

Brand Names: US Femara

Brand Names: Canada ACH-Letrozole; Apo-Letrozole; Auro-Letrozole; Bio-Letrozole; Femara; JAMP-Letrozole; Mar-Letrozole; MED-Letrozole; Nat-Letrozole; PMS-Letrozole; RAN-Letrozole; Riva-Letrozole; Sandoz-Letrozole; Teva-Letrozole; Van-Letrozole; Zinda-Letrozole

Pharmacologic Category Antineoplastic Agent, Aromatase Inhibitor

Use Breast cancer in postmenopausal women: Adjuvant treatment of hormone receptor-positive early breast cancer, extended adjuvant treatment of early breast cancer after 5 years of tamoxifen; treatment of advanced breast cancer with disease progression following antiestrogen therapy; first-line treatment of hormone receptor–positive or hormone receptor-unknown, locally-advanced, or metastatic breast cancer

Local Anesthetic/Vasoconstrictor Precautions No information available to require special precautions

Effects on Dental Treatment No significant effects or complications reported

Effects on Bleeding Thrombocytopenia has been reported but relationship to letrozole is unclear.

Adverse Reactions

>10%:

Cardiovascular: Edema (7% to 18%)

Central nervous system: Headache (4% to 20%), dizziness (3% to 14%), fatigue (8% to 13%)
Dermatologic: Diaphoresis (≤24%), night sweats (15%)
Endocrine & metabolic: Hypercholesterolemia (3% to 52%), hot flash (6% to 50%), weight gain (2% to 13%)
Gastrointestinal: Nausea (9% to 17%), constipation (2% to 11%)
Neuromuscular & skeletal: Weakness (4% to 34%), arthralgia (8% to 25%), arthritis (7% to 25%), ostealgia (5% to 22%), back pain (5% to 18%), decreased bone mineral density (≤5% to 15%), osteoporosis (≤5% to 15%), bone fracture (10% to 14%)
Respiratory: Dyspnea (6% to 18%), cough (6% to 13%)

1% to 10%:
Cardiovascular: Chest pain (6% to 8%), hypertension (5% to 8%), chest wall pain (6%), peripheral edema (5%), cerebrovascular accident (2% to 3%; including hemorrhagic stroke, thrombotic stroke), thromboembolism (2% to 3%; including portal vein thrombosis, pulmonary embolism, thrombophlebitis, venous thrombosis), angina pectoris (1% to 2%), myocardial infarction (1% to 2%), transient ischemic attacks
Central nervous system: Insomnia (6% to 7%), pain (5%), anxiety (<5%), depression (<5%), vertigo (<5%), drowsiness (3%)
Dermatologic: Skin rash (5%), alopecia (3% to 5%), pruritus (1%)
Endocrine & metabolic: Weight loss (6% to 7%), hypercalcemia (<5%)
Gastrointestinal: Diarrhea (5% to 8%), vomiting (3% to 7%), abdominal pain (6%), anorexia (1% to 5%), dyspepsia (3%)
Genitourinary: Mastalgia (2% to 7%), urinary tract infection (6%), vaginal dryness (5%), vaginal hemorrhage (5%), vaginal irritation (5%)
Hematologic & oncologic: Metastases (2% to 4%)
Infection: Infection (7%), influenza (6%), viral infection (6%)
Neuromuscular & skeletal: Limb pain (4% to 10%), myalgia (7% to 9%)
Ophthalmic: Cataract (2%)
Renal: Renal disease (5%)
Respiratory: Pleural effusion (<5%)

<1%, postmarketing, and/or case reports: Anaphylaxis, angioedema, arterial thrombosis, blurred vision, cardiac failure, carpal tunnel syndrome, dysesthesia, dysgeusia, endometrial carcinoma, endometrial hyperplasia, erythema multiforme, eye irritation, fever, hepatitis, hypoesthesia, increased appetite, increased liver enzymes, increased thirst, irritability, leukopenia, memory impairment, nervousness, palpitations, paresthesia, stomatitis, tachycardia, thrombocytopenia, toxic epidermal necrolysis, trigger finger, urinary frequency, urticaria, vaginal discharge, xeroderma, xerostomia

General Dosage Range Dosage adjustment recommended in patients with hepatic impairment

Oral: *Adults (postmenopausal females):* 2.5 mg once daily

Mechanism of Action Nonsteroidal competitive inhibitor of the aromatase enzyme system which binds to the heme group of aromatase, a cytochrome P450 enzyme which catalyzes conversion of androgens to estrogens (specifically, androstenedione to estrone and testosterone to estradiol). This leads to inhibition of the enzyme and a significant reduction in plasma estrogen (estrone, estradiol and estrone sulfate) levels. Does not affect synthesis of adrenal or thyroid hormones, aldosterone, or androgens.

Pharmacodynamics/Kinetics

Half-life Elimination Terminal: ~2 days

Time to Peak Steady state, plasma: 2 to 6 weeks; steady state serum concentrations are 1.5 to 2 times higher than single-dose values. In girls 3 to 9 years, steady state concentrations were 25% to 67% that of the mean adult values (Feuillan 2007)

Pregnancy Risk Factor X

Pregnancy Considerations Adverse events were observed in animal reproduction studies. Letrozole is approved for use in postmenopausal women only (no clinical benefit for breast cancer has been demonstrated in premenopausal women). Use in women who are or who may become pregnant is contraindicated. Women who are perimenopausal or recently postmenopausal should use adequate contraception until postmenopausal status is fully established.

Leucovorin Calcium (loo koe VOR in KAL see um)

Brand Names: Canada Lederle Leucovorin; Leucovorin Calcium Injection; Leucovorin Calcium Injection USP

Pharmacologic Category Antidote; Chemotherapy Modulating Agent; Rescue Agent (Chemotherapy); Vitamin, Water Soluble

Use

Colorectal cancer, advanced: Injection: Palliative treatment of advanced colorectal cancer to prolong survival (in combination with 5-fluorouracil).

Methotrexate toxicity:

Injection: Rescue agent after high-dose methotrexate treatment in osteosarcoma and to diminish the toxicity and counteract the effects of impaired methotrexate elimination and of inadvertent overdosage of folic acid antagonists.

Oral: Rescue agent to diminish toxicity and counteract effects of impaired methotrexate elimination and inadvertent overdoses of folic acid antagonists.

Megaloblastic anemia: Injection: Treatment of megaloblastic anemias due to folic acid deficiency (when oral therapy is not feasible).

Local Anesthetic/Vasoconstrictor Precautions No information available to require special precautions

Effects on Dental Treatment No significant effects or complications reported

Effects on Bleeding No information available to require special precautions

Adverse Reactions Frequency not defined. Toxicities (especially gastrointestinal toxicity) of fluorouracil are enhanced when used in combination with leucovorin.
Dermatologic: Erythema, pruritus, skin rash, urticaria
Hematologic & oncologic: Thrombocythemia
Hypersensitivity: Anaphylactoid reaction, hypersensitivity reaction
Respiratory: Wheezing

General Dosage Range

IM, IV, Oral: *Children and Adults:* Dosage varies greatly depending on indication.

Mechanism of Action A reduced form of folic acid, leucovorin supplies the necessary cofactor blocked by methotrexate. Leucovorin actively competes with methotrexate for transport sites, displaces methotrexate from intracellular binding sites, and restores active folate stores required for DNA/RNA synthesis. Stabilizes the binding of 5-dUMP and thymidylate synthetase, enhancing the activity of fluorouracil. When administered with pyrimethamine for the treatment of opportunistic infections, leucovorin reduces the risk for hematologic toxicity (HHS [OI adult 2015]).

Methanol toxicity treatment: Formic acid (methanol's toxic metabolite) is normally metabolized to carbon dioxide and water by 10-formyltetrahydrofolate dehydrogenase after being bound to tetrahydrofolate. Administering a source of tetrahydrofolate may aid the body in eliminating formic acid (Barceloux, 2002).

Pharmacodynamics/Kinetics

Half-life Elimination ~4 to 8 hours

Time to Peak Oral: ~2 hours; IV: Total folates: 10 minutes; 5MTHF: ~1 hour; IM: Total folates: 52 minutes; 5MTHF: 2.8 hours

Pregnancy Risk Factor C

Pregnancy Considerations Animal reproduction studies have not been conducted. Leucovorin is a biologically active form of folic acid. Adequate amounts of folic acid are recommended during pregnancy. Refer to Folic Acid monograph.

Leuprolide (loo PROE lide)

Brand Names: US Eligard; Lupron Depot (1-Month); Lupron Depot (3-Month); Lupron Depot (4-Month); Lupron Depot (6-Month); Lupron Depot-Ped (1-Month); Lupron Depot-Ped (3-Month)

Brand Names: Canada Eligard; Lupron; Lupron Depot

Pharmacologic Category Antineoplastic Agent, Gonadotropin-Releasing Hormone Agonist; Gonadotropin Releasing Hormone Agonist

Use

Central precocious puberty: Treatment of children with central precocious puberty (CPP). CPP is defined as early onset of secondary sexual characteristics (usually <8 years of age in girls and <9 years of age in boys) associated with pubertal pituitary gonadotropin activation; may have a significantly advanced bone age resulting in diminished adult height.

Limitations of use: Prior to treatment initiation, confirm clinical diagnosis of CPP with blood concentrations of luteinizing hormone (LH) (basal or stimulated with a gonadotropin-releasing hormone [GnRH] analog), sex steroids, and bone age assessment (versus chronological age). Baseline evaluations should include height and weight measurements, diagnostic brain imaging (to rule out intracranial tumor), pelvic/testicular/adrenal ultrasound (to rule out steroid-secreting tumors), human chorionic gonadotropin levels (to rule out a chorionic gonadotropin-secreting tumor), and adrenal steroid measurements (to exclude congenital adrenal hyperplasia).

Endometriosis: Management of endometriosis, including pain relief and reduction of endometriotic lesions. Initial management of endometriosis and symptom recurrence (in combination with norethindrone acetate).

Limitations of use: Experience with leuprolide depot in females has been limited to women ≥18 years; treatment should be limited to 6 months.

Prostate cancer, advanced: Palliative treatment of advanced prostate cancer

Uterine leiomyomata (fibroids): Treatment (preoperative) of anemia caused by uterine leiomyomata (fibroids).

Limitations of use: Experience with leuprolide depot in females has been limited to women ≥18 years.

Local Anesthetic/Vasoconstrictor Precautions No information available to require special precautions

Effects on Dental Treatment Key adverse event(s) related to dental treatment: Gum hemorrhage, gingivitis, dry mucous membranes, and dysphagia.

Effects on Bleeding Decreased and increased platelet count has been reported.

Adverse Reactions

Children (percentages based on 1-month and 3-month pediatric formulations combined):

>10%: Local: Pain at injection site (≤20%)

2% to 10%:

Cardiovascular: Vasodilatation (2%)

Central nervous system: Emotional lability (5%), mood changes (5%), headache (3% to 5%), pain (3%)

Dermatologic: Acne vulgaris (3%), seborrhea (3%), skin rash (3% including erythema multiforme)

Endocrine & metabolic: Weight gain (≤7%)

Genitourinary: Vaginal discharge (3%), vaginal hemorrhage (3%), vaginitis (3%)

Local: Injection site reaction (≤9%)

<2%: Abnormal gait, alopecia, arthralgia, asthma, body odor, bradycardia, cervix disease, constipation, cough, decreased appetite, decreased visual acuity, depression, dizziness, drowsiness, dysmenorrhea, dyspepsia, dysphagia, epistaxis, excessive crying, feminization, fever, flu-like symptoms, gingivitis, goiter, growth suppression, gynecomastia, hirsutism, hyperhidrosis, hyperkinesia, hypersensitivity reaction, hypertension, increased appetite, infection, lacrimation, leukoderma, limb pain, musculoskeletal pain, myalgia, myopathy, nausea, nervousness, obesity, pallor, peripheral edema, personality disorder, pharyngitis, precocious puberty, purpura, rhinitis, sinusitis, skin striae, syncope, urinary incontinence, vomiting, weakness

Adults: Note: For prostate cancer treatment, an initial rise in serum testosterone concentrations may cause "tumor flare" or worsening of symptoms, including bone pain, neuropathy, hematuria, or ureteral or bladder outlet obstruction during the first 2 weeks. Similarly, an initial increase in estradiol levels, with a temporary worsening of symptoms, may occur in women treated with leuprolide.

Delayed release formulations:

>10%:

Cardiovascular: Edema (≤14%)

Central nervous system: Headache (≤65%), pain (<2% to 33%), depression (≤31%), insomnia (≤31%), fatigue (≤17%), dizziness (≤16%)

Dermatologic: Allergic skin reaction (≤12%)

Endocrine & metabolic: Hot flash (25% to 98%), weight changes (≤13%), hyperlipidemia (≤12%), decreased libido (≤11%)

Gastrointestinal: Nausea and vomiting (≤25%), gastrointestinal disease (14%), change in bowel habits (≤14%)

Genitourinary: Vaginitis (11% to 28%), testicular atrophy (≤20%), genitourinary complaint (13% to 15%)

Local: Burning sensation at injection site burning (transient: ≤35%)

Neuromuscular & skeletal: Weakness (≤18%), arthropathy (≤12%)

Respiratory: Flu-like symptoms (≤12%), respiratory tract disease (11%)

1% to 10% (limited to important or life-threatening):

Cardiovascular: Angina pectoris (<5%), atrial fibrillation (<5%), bradycardia (<5%), cardiac arrhythmia

(<5%), cardiac failure (<5%), deep thrombophlebitis (<5%), hyper-/hypotension (<5%), palpitations (<5%), syncope (<5%), tachycardia (<5%)

Central nervous system: Nervousness (≤8%), paresthesia (≤8%), anxiety (≤6%), agitation (<5%), confusion (<5%), delusions (<5%), dementia (<5%), neuropathy (<5%), paralysis (<5%), seizure (<5%), ostealgia (<2%)

Dermatologic: Acne vulgaris (≤10%), alopecia (≤5%), diaphoresis (≤5%), cellulitis (<5%), hair disease (<5%), pruritus (≤3%), skin rash (≤2%)

Endocrine & metabolic: Dehydration (≤8%), gynecomastia (≤7%), decreased serum bicarbonate (≥5%), hypercholesterolemia (≥5%), hyperglycemia (≥5%), hyperphosphatemia (≥5%), hyperuricemia (≥5%), hypoalbuminemia (≥5%), hypocholesterolemia (≥5%), hypoproteinemia (≥5%), increased lactate dehydrogenase (≥5%), increased prostatic acid phosphatase (≥5%), menstrual disorder (≤2%), hirsutism (<2%)

Gastrointestinal: Anorexia (<5%), dysphagia (<5%), eructation (<5%), gastric ulcer (<5%), gastrointestinal hemorrhage (<5%), intestinal obstruction (<5%), peptic ulcer (<5%), constipation (≤3%), gastroenteritis (≤3%), diarrhea (≤2%)

Genitourinary: Mastalgia (≤6%), impotence (≤5%), balanitis (<5%), breast hypertrophy (<5%), lactation (<5%), penile disease (<5%), testicular disease (<5%), urinary incontinence (<5%), urinary tract infection (<5%), nocturia (≤4%), testicular pain (≤4%), dysuria (≤2%), bladder spasm (<2%), erectile dysfunction (<2%), hematuria (<2%), urinary retention (<2%), urinary urgency (<2%)

Hematologic & oncologic: Change in platelet count (increased; ≥5%), decreased prostatic acid phosphatase (≥5%), eosinophilia (≥5%), leukopenia (≥5%), bruise (≤5%), ecchymoses (<5%), lymphadenopathy (<5%), neoplasm (<5%), anemia, decreased hematocrit, decreased hemoglobin

Hepatic: Abnormal hepatic function tests (≥5%), increased serum AST (≥5%), prolonged partial thromboplastin time (≥5%), prolonged prothrombin time (≥5%), hepatomegaly (<5%)

Hypersensitivity: Hypersensitivity reaction (<5%)

Infection: Infection (5%)

Local: Pain at injection site (2% to 5%), injection site reaction (<5%), erythema at injection site (1% to 3%)

Neuromuscular & skeletal: Myalgia (≤8%), neuromuscular disease (<5%), pathological fracture (<5%), arthralgia (≤1%)

Renal: Decreased urine specific gravity (≥5%), increased blood urea nitrogen (≥5%), increased serum creatinine (≥5%), increased urine specific gravity (≥5%), polyuria (2% to 4%)

Respiratory: Emphysema (<5%), epistaxis (<5%), hemoptysis (<5%), increased bronchial secretions (<5%), pleural effusion (<5%), pulmonary edema (<5%), dyspnea (≤2%), cough (≤1%)

Miscellaneous: Fever (<5%)

Immediate release formulation:

>10%:

Cardiovascular: ECG changes (19%), peripheral edema (12%)

Central nervous system: Pain (13%)

Endocrine & metabolic: Hot flash (55%)

1% to 10% (limited to important or life-threatening):

Cardiovascular: Hypertension (8%), heart murmur (3%), thrombophlebitis (2%), cardiac failure (1%), angina pectoris, cardiac arrhythmia, myocardial infarction, pulmonary embolism, syncope

Central nervous system: Headache (7%), insomnia (7%), dizziness (5%), ostealgia (5%), anxiety, depression, fatigue, fever, nervousness, peripheral neuropathy

Dermatologic: Dermatitis (5%), alopecia, hyperpigmentation, pruritus, skin lesion

Endocrine & metabolic: Decreased libido, diabetes mellitus, goiter, gynecomastia, hypercalcemia, hypoglycemia

Gastrointestinal: Constipation (7%), anorexia (6%), nausea and vomiting (5%), diarrhea, dysphagia, gastrointestinal hemorrhage, peptic ulcer, rectal polyps

Genitourinary: Decreased testicular size (7%), hematuria (6%), urinary frequency (6%), impotence (4%), urinary tract infection (3%), bladder spasm, dysuria, incontinence, mastalgia, testicular pain, urinary tract obstruction

Hematologic & oncologic: Anemia (5%), bruise

Infection: Infection

Local: Injection site reaction

Neuromuscular & skeletal: Weakness (10%)

Ophthalmic: Blurred vision

Renal: Increased blood urea nitrogen, increased serum creatinine

Respiratory: Dyspnea (2%), cough, pneumonia, pulmonary fibrosis

Miscellaneous: Fever, inflammation

Children and Adults: *Any formulations:* Postmarketing and/or case reports: Abdominal pain, abscess at injection site, anaphylaxis, anaphylactoid reaction, asthma, bone fracture (spine), cerebrovascular accident, convulsions, coronary artery disease, decreased white blood cell count, diabetes mellitus, fibromyalgia syndrome (arthralgia/myalgia, headaches, GI distress), flushing, hemoptysis, hepatic injury, hepatic insufficiency, hepatotoxicity, hyperuricemia, hypokalemia, hypoproteinemia, induration at injection site, interstitial pulmonary disease, leukocytosis, myocardial infarction, osteopenia, paralysis, penile swelling, peripheral neuropathy, pituitary apoplexy (cardiovascular collapse, mental status altered, ophthalmoplegia, sudden headache, visual changes, vomiting), prolonged QT interval on ECG, prostate pain, pulmonary embolism, pulmonary infiltrates, retroperitoneal fibrosis (pelvic), seizure, skin photosensitivity, suicidal ideation (rare), tenosynovitis (symptoms), thrombocytopenia, transient ischemic attacks, urticaria

General Dosage Range IM, SubQ: *Children and Adults:* Dosage varies greatly depending on indication

Mechanism of Action Leuprolide, is an agonist of gonadotropin releasing hormone (GnRH). Acting as a potent inhibitor of gonadotropin secretion; continuous administration results in suppression of ovarian and testicular steroidogenesis due to decreased levels of LH and FSH with subsequent decrease in testosterone (male) and estrogen (female) levels. In males, testosterone levels are reduced to below castrate levels. Leuprolide may also have a direct inhibitory effect on the testes, and act by a different mechanism not directly related to reduction in serum testosterone.

Pharmacodynamics/Kinetics

Onset of Action

Onset of action: Following transient increase, testosterone suppression occurs in ~2 to 4 weeks of continued therapy

Onset of therapeutic suppression for precocious puberty: Leuprolide: 2 to 4 weeks; Leuprolide depot: 1 month

Half-life Elimination
~3 hours

Pregnancy Risk Factor X

Pregnancy Considerations Adverse events were observed in animal reproduction studies. Pregnancy must be excluded prior to the start of treatment. Although leuprolide usually inhibits ovulation and stops menstruation, contraception is not ensured and a non-hormonal contraceptive should be used. Use is contraindicated in pregnant women.

Levalbuterol (leve al BYOO ter ole)

Related Information
Respiratory Diseases *on page 1777*

Brand Names: US Xopenex; Xopenex Concentrate; Xopenex HFA

Pharmacologic Category $Beta_2$ Agonist

Use Bronchospasm: Treatment or prevention of bronchospasm in patients with reversible obstructive airway disease

Local Anesthetic/Vasoconstrictor Precautions No information available to require special precautions

Effects on Dental Treatment No significant effects or complications reported

Effects on Bleeding No information available to require special precautions

Adverse Reactions
>10%:
Central nervous system: Headache (children: 12%)
Gastrointestinal: Vomiting (children: 11%)
Infection: Viral infection (≤12%)
Respiratory: Rhinitis (6% to 11%)
>2% to 10%:
Cardiovascular: Tachycardia (adolescents and adults: 3%)
Central nervous system: Nervousness (adolescents and adults: 3% to 10%), dizziness (adolescents and adults: 3%), migraine (adolescents and adults: 3%), anxiety (adolescents and adults: ≤3%), pain (adolescents and adults: ≤3%)
Dermatologic: Skin rash (children: 8%), urticaria (children: 3%)
Gastrointestinal: Diarrhea (children: 2% to 6%; adolescents and adults: <2%), dyspepsia (adolescents and adults: ≤3%)
Hematologic & oncologic: Lymphadenopathy (≤3%)
Neuromuscular & skeletal: Tremor (adolescents and adults: ≤7%), leg cramps (adolescents and adults: ≤3%), weakness (children: 3%), myalgia (≤2%)
Respiratory: Pharyngitis (7% to 10%), asthma (9%), cough (adolescents and adults: 4%), sinusitis (adolescents and adults: 4%), flu-like symptoms (adolescents and adults: ≤4%), bronchitis (children: 3%), nasal mucosa swelling (1% to 3%)
Miscellaneous: Fever (children: 9%), accidental injury (children 5% to 9%; adolescents and adults: 3%)
Frequency not defined:
Endocrine & metabolic: Decreased serum potassium, increased heart rate, increased serum glucose, paradoxical bronchospasm
Hypersensitivity: Hypersensitivity reaction (including bronchospasm, oropharyngeal edema)
<2%, postmarketing, and/or case reports: Acne vulgaris, anaphylaxis, angina pectoris, angioedema, atrial fibrillation, cardiac arrhythmia, chest pain, chills, constipation, conjunctivitis, dry throat, dysmenorrhea, dyspnea, ECG abnormality, epistaxis, extrasystoles, eye pruritus, gastroenteritis, gastroesophageal reflux disease, hematuria, hyperesthesia (hand), hypertension, hypokalemia, hypotension, insomnia, metabolic acidosis, nausea, otalgia, paresthesia, pulmonary disease, supraventricular cardiac arrhythmia, syncope, vertigo, voice disorder, vulvovaginal candidiasis, xerostomia

General Dosage Range
Metered-dose inhaler: *Children ≥4 years, Adolescents, and Adults:* 1 to 2 inhalations (45 to 90 mcg) every 4 to 6 hours
Nebulization solution:
Children 6 to 11 years: 0.31 mg 3 times daily (maximum: 0.63 mg 3 times daily)
Children ≥12 years, Adolescents, and Adults: 0.63 to 1.25 mg every 8 hours as needed (maximum: 1.25 mg 3 times daily)
Elderly: Initial: 0.63 mg

Mechanism of Action Relaxes bronchial smooth muscle by action on $beta_2$-receptors with little effect on heart rate

Pharmacodynamics/Kinetics
Onset of Action Measured as a 15% increase in FEV_1:
Metered-dose inhaler: 5.5 to 10.2 minutes; Peak effect: 76 to 78 minutes
Nebulization solution: 10 to 17 minutes; Peak effect: 1.5 hours
Duration of Action Measured as a 15% increase in FEV_1:
Metered-dose inhaler: 3 to 4 hours (up to 6 hours in some patients)
Nebulization solution: 5 to 6 hours (up to 8 hours in some patients)
Half-life Elimination 3.3 to 4 hours
Time to Peak Nebulization solution: Children: 0.3 to 0.6 hours, Adults: 0.2 hours

Pregnancy Risk Factor C

Pregnancy Considerations Adverse events were not observed in animal reproduction studies. Congenital anomalies (cleft palate, limb defects) have rarely been reported following maternal use of racemic albuterol during pregnancy. Multiple medications were used in most cases, no specific pattern of defects has been reported, and no relationship to racemic albuterol has been established. Beta-agonists may interfere with uterine contractility if administered during labor.

Pregnant women with poorly controlled asthma or asthma exacerbations may have a greater fetal/maternal risk than what is associated with appropriately used medications. Uncontrolled asthma is associated with an increased risk of perinatal mortality, pre-eclampsia, preterm birth, and low birth weight infants. Acute asthma exacerbations should be treated aggressively with short-acting beta-2 agonists (SABA) to prevent fetal hypoxia (GINA 2016; Namazy 2016). If high doses of SABA are needed during the last 48 hours of labor and delivery, monitor blood glucose in the newborn for 24 hours after birth (GINA 2016). If initiating treatment during pregnancy, use of an agent with more data in pregnant women may be preferred (Namazy 2016).

LevETIRAcetam (lee va tye RA se tam)

Brand Names: US Keppra; Keppra XR; Roweepra; Spritam

Brand Names: Canada Abbott-Levetiracetam; ACT Levetiracetam; Apo-Levetiracetam; Auro-Levetiracetam; Dom-Levetiracetam; JAMP-Levetiracetam;

Keppra; PHL-Levetiracetam; PMS-Levetiracetam; PRO-Levetiracetam; RAN-Levetiracetam

Pharmacologic Category Anticonvulsant, Miscellaneous

Use

Myoclonic seizures:

Immediate-release tablets/oral solution/tablets for oral suspension: Adjunctive therapy in the treatment of myoclonic seizures in adults and adolescents 12 years and older with juvenile myoclonic epilepsy.

IV: Adjunctive therapy in the treatment of myoclonic seizures in adults and adolescents 12 years and older with juvenile myoclonic epilepsy.

Partial-onset seizures:

Immediate-release tablets/oral solution/tablets for oral suspension: Adjunctive therapy in the treatment of partial-onset seizures in adults and children 1 month and older (Keppra) or 4 years and older and more than 20 kg (Spritam) with epilepsy.

Extended-release tablets: Adjunctive therapy in the treatment of partial-onset seizures in adults and adolescents 12 years and older with epilepsy.

IV: Adjunctive therapy in the treatment of partial-onset seizures in adults and children 1 month and older with epilepsy.

Primary generalized tonic-clonic seizures:

Immediate-release tablets/oral solution/tablets for oral suspension: Adjunctive therapy in the treatment of primary generalized tonic-clonic seizures in adults and children 6 years and older with idiopathic generalized epilepsy.

IV: Adjunctive therapy in the treatment of primary generalized tonic-clonic seizures in adults and children 6 years and older with idiopathic generalized epilepsy.

Local Anesthetic/Vasoconstrictor Precautions No information available to require special precautions

Effects on Dental Treatment No significant effects or complications reported

Effects on Bleeding No information available to require special precautions

Adverse Reactions

Incidences are for all indications and populations (adults and children) unless otherwise specified.

>10%:

Cardiovascular: Increased blood pressure (diastolic; infants and children: 17%)

Central nervous system: Behavioral problems (includes aggression, agitation, anger, anxiety, apathy, depersonalization, emotional lability, irritability, neurosis: children and adolescents: 7% to 38%; adults: 7% to 13%), headache (14% to 19%), drowsiness (8% to 15%); immediate release 4,000 mg/day, no titration: 45%; serious [patients hospitalized]: <1%), psychotic symptoms (infants and children: 17%; adults: 1%), irritability (infants, children, and adolescents: 6% to 12%), fatigue (10% to 11%)

Gastrointestinal: Vomiting (children and adolescents: 15%)

Infection: Infection (13%)

Neuromuscular & skeletal: Weakness (15%)

Respiratory: Nasopharyngitis (7% to 15%)

1% to 10%:

Central nervous system: Aggressive behavior (children and adolescents: 10%; adults: 1%), dizziness (5% to 9%), pain (7%), lethargy (children and adolescents: 6%), insomnia (children and adolescents: 5%), depression (3% to 5%), vertigo (3% to 5%), emotional lability (2% to 5%), agitation (children and adolescents: 4%), nervousness (4%), ataxia (partial-onset seizures: 3%; includes abnormal gait, incoordination), falling (children and adolescents: 3%), mood changes (children and adolescents: 3%), confusion (2% to 3%), amnesia (2%), anxiety (2%), hostility (2%), paranoia (children and adolescents: 2%), paresthesia (2%), sedation (children and adolescents: 2%)

Gastrointestinal: Upper abdominal pain (children and adolescents: 9%), decreased appetite (children and adolescents: 8%), diarrhea (6% to 8%), nausea (5%), anorexia (3% to 4%), constipation (children and adolescents: 3%), gastroenteritis (children and adolescents: 2%)

Hematologic & oncologic: Eosinophilia (children and adolescents: 9%), bruise (children and adolescents: 3%), decreased white blood cell count (3%), decreased neutrophils (2%)

Infection: Influenza (3% to 8%)

Neuromuscular & skeletal: Neck pain (2% to 8%), arthralgia (children and adolescents: 2%), joint sprain (children and adolescents: 2%)

Ophthalmic: Conjunctivitis (children and adolescents: 2%), diplopia (2%)

Otic: Otalgia (children and adolescents: 2%)

Respiratory: Nasal congestion (children and adolescents: 9%), cough (2% to 9%), pharyngolaryngeal pain (children and adolescents: 7%), pharyngitis (6% to 7%), rhinitis (2% to 4%), sinusitis (2%)

Miscellaneous: Head trauma (children and adolescents: 4%)

<1%, postmarketing and/or case reports: Abnormal hepatic function tests, acute renal failure, agranulocytosis, alopecia, blurred vision, choreoathetosis, decreased hematocrit, decreased hemoglobin, decreased red blood cells, disturbance in attention, DRESS syndrome, dyskinesia, eczema, equilibrium disturbance, erythema multiforme, hepatic failure, hepatitis, hyperkinesia, hyponatremia, leukopenia, memory impairment, myalgia, myasthenia, neutropenia, pancreatitis, pancytopenia (with bone marrow suppression in some cases), panic attack, personality disorder, pruritus, psychosis, skin rash, Stevens-Johnson syndrome, suicidal ideation, suicidal tendencies, thrombocytopenia, toxic epidermal necrolysis, weight loss

General Dosage Range Dosage adjustment recommended in patients with renal impairment

Oral:

Immediate release (tablets, oral solution):

Infants 1 to <6 months: Initial: 7 mg/kg twice daily; Maintenance: 7 to 21 mg/kg/dose twice daily (maximum: 42 mg/kg/day)

Infants and Children 6 months to <4 years: Initial: 10 mg/kg twice daily; Maintenance: 10 to 25 mg/kg twice daily (maximum: 50 mg/kg/day)

Children and Adolescents 4 to <16 years: Initial: 10 mg/kg twice daily; Maintenance: 10 to 30 mg/kg twice daily (maximum: 60 mg/kg/day or 3,000 mg/day)

Children and Adolescents ≥12 years: Initial: 500 mg twice daily; Maintenance: 500 to 1,500 mg twice daily (maximum: 3,000 mg/day)

Adults: Initial: 500 mg twice daily; Maintenance: 500 to 1,500 mg twice daily (maximum: 3,000 mg/day)

Immediate release (tablets for oral suspension):

Children ≥4 years and weighing 20 kg to 40 kg: Initial: 250 mg twice daily; Maintenance: 750 mg twice daily (maximum: 1,500 mg/day)

Children ≥4 years (weighing >40 kg), Adolescents, and Adults: Initial: 500 mg twice daily; Maintenance: 1,500 mg twice daily (maximum: 3,000 mg/day)

Extended release: *Children ≥12 years, Adolescents, and Adults:* Initial: 1,000 mg once daily; Maintenance: 1,000 to 3,000 mg once daily (maximum: 3,000 mg/day)

IV:

Infants 1 to <6 months: Initial: 7 mg/kg twice daily; Maintenance: 7 to 21 mg/kg/dose twice daily

Infants and Children 6 months to <4 years: Initial: 10 mg/kg twice daily; Maintenance: 10 to 25 mg/kg twice daily

Children and Adolescents 4 to <16 years: Initial: 10 mg/kg twice daily; Maintenance: 10 to 30 mg/kg twice daily (maximum: 60 mg/kg/day or 3,000 mg/day)

Children ≥12 years, Adolescents and Adults: Initial: 500 mg twice daily; Maintenance: 500 to 1,500 mg twice daily (maximum: 3,000 mg/day)

Mechanism of Action The precise mechanism by which levetiracetam exerts its antiepileptic effect is unknown. However, several studies have suggested the mechanism may involve one or more of the following central pharmacologic effects: inhibition of voltage-dependent N-type calcium channels; facilitation of GABA-ergic inhibitory transmission through displacement of negative modulators; reduction of delayed rectifier potassium current; and/or binding to synaptic proteins which modulate neurotransmitter release.

Pharmacodynamics/Kinetics

Onset of Action Peak effect: Oral: 1 hour

Half-life Elimination Increased in patients with renal impairment

Infants and Children <4 years: 5.3 ± 1.3 hours (Glauser 2007)

Children 4 to 12 years: 6 ± 1.1 hours (Pellock 2001)

Adults: ~6 to 8 hours; extended release tablet: ~7 hours

Time to Peak

Oral solution: Fasting infants and children <4 years: 1.4 ± 0.9 hours

Oral: Immediate release: Fasting adults and children: ~1 hour

Oral: Extended release: ~4 hours; median time to peak is 2 hours longer in the fed state

Pregnancy Risk Factor C

Pregnancy Considerations Adverse effects were observed in animal reproduction studies. Levetiracetam crosses the placenta and can be detected in the newborn following delivery (Johannessen 2005; Lopez-Fraile 2009; Tomson 2007). An increase in the overall rate of major congenital malformations has not been observed following maternal use of levetiracetam. Available studies have not been large enough to determine if there is an increased risk of specific birth defects (Hernandez-Diaz 2012; Mawhinney 2013; Mølgaard-Nielsen 2011; Vajda 2012). In general, maternal polytherapy with antiepileptic drugs may increase the risk of congenital malformations; monotherapy with the lowest effective dose is recommended. Newborns of women taking antiepileptic medications may be at an increased risk of SGA and a 1 minute APGAR score <7 (Harden and Meader 2009). Plasma concentrations of levetiracetam gradually decrease during pregnancy, especially during the third trimester, due to physiologic changes which occur; patients should be monitored during pregnancy and postpartum.

A registry is available for women exposed to levetiracetam during pregnancy: Pregnant women may enroll themselves into the North American Antiepileptic Drug (AED) Pregnancy Registry (888-233-2334 or http://www.aedpregnancyregistry.org/).

Levobunolol (lee voe BYOO noe lole)

Brand Names: US Betagan

Brand Names: Canada Apo-Levobunolol®; Betagan®; Novo-Levobunolol; PMS-Levobunolol; Ratio-Levobunolol; Sandoz-Levobunolol

Pharmacologic Category Beta-Adrenergic Blocker, Nonselective; Ophthalmic Agent, Antiglaucoma

Use To lower intraocular pressure in chronic open-angle glaucoma or ocular hypertension

Local Anesthetic/Vasoconstrictor Precautions No information available to require special precautions

Effects on Dental Treatment Key adverse event(s) related to dental treatment: Levobunolol is a nonselective beta-blocker and may enhance the pressor response to epinephrine, resulting in hypertension and bradycardia. Many nonsteroidal anti-inflammatory drugs, such as ibuprofen and indomethacin, can reduce the hypotensive effect of beta-blockers after 3 or more weeks of therapy with the NSAID. Short-term NSAID use (ie, 3 days) requires no special precautions in patients taking beta-blockers.

Effects on Bleeding No information available to require special precautions

Adverse Reactions

>10%: Ophthalmic: Burning sensation of eyes (≤33%), stinging of eyes (≤33%)

1% to 10%: Ophthalmic: Blepharoconjunctivitis (5%)

Frequency not defined:

Cardiovascular: Bradycardia, cardiac arrhythmia, cardiac failure, cerebral ischemia, cerebrovascular accident, chest pain, heart block, hypotension, palpitations, syncope

Central nervous system: Ataxia (transient), confusion, depression, dizziness, exacerbation of myasthenia gravis, headache, lethargy, paresthesia

Dermatologic: Alopecia, erythema, pruritus, skin rash, Stevens-Johnson syndrome, urticaria

Endocrine & metabolic: Hypoglycemia (masked)

Gastrointestinal: Diarrhea, nausea

Genitourinary: Impotence

Hypersensitivity: Hypersensitivity reaction

Neuromuscular & skeletal: Weakness

Ophthalmic: Blepharoptosis, conjunctivitis, decreased corneal sensitivity, diplopia, iridocyclitis, keratitis, visual disturbance

Respiratory: Bronchospasm, dyspnea, nasal congestion, respiratory failure

General Dosage Range Ophthalmic: *Adults:* Instill 1 drop in the affected eye(s) 1-2 times daily

Mechanism of Action A nonselective beta-adrenergic blocking agent that lowers intraocular pressure by reducing aqueous humor production and possibly increases the outflow of aqueous humor

Pharmacodynamics/Kinetics

Onset of Action Within 1 hour; Peak effect: 2-6 hours

Duration of Action Up to 24 hours

Pregnancy Risk Factor C

Pregnancy Considerations Adverse events have been observed in some animal reproduction studies. The same adverse effects observed with systemic administration of beta-blockers may occur following ophthalmic use of levobunolol. If ophthalmic agents are needed for the treatment of glaucoma during pregnancy, the minimum effective dose should be used in combination with punctual occlusion to decrease potential exposure to the fetus (Johnson 2001; Salim 2014; Samples 1988).

Levocabastine (Nasal) (LEE voe kab as teen)

Brand Names: Canada Livostin

Pharmacologic Category Histamine H_1 Antagonist; Histamine H_1 Antagonist, Second Generation; Piperidine Derivative

Use Note: Not approved in the US

Allergic rhinitis: Symptomatic treatment of allergic rhinitis in patients 12 years and older.

Local Anesthetic/Vasoconstrictor Precautions No information available to require special precautions

Effects on Dental Treatment Key adverse event(s) related to dental treatment: Xerostomia (normal salivary flow resumes upon discontinuation)

Effects on Bleeding No information available to require special precautions

Adverse Reactions Most adverse reactions are transient. Frequency not always defined.

1% to 10%:

Central nervous system: Fatigue (1%)

Local: Application site burning, application site irritation, application site pain, application site reaction (dryness, discomfort)

Ophthalmic: Eye irritation (3%; mostly with concomitant levocabastine eye drop administration)

Respiratory: Epistaxis (1%), pharyngolaryngeal pain, sinusitis

<1%, postmarketing, and/or case reports: Abdominal pain, anaphylaxis, application site reactions (nasal edema), bronchospasm, cough, dry nose, dysgeusia, dyspnea, eyelid edema, facial edema, hearing loss, hypersensitivity, increased appetite, malaise, nasal congestion, nasal obstruction (aggravated), nausea, palpitations, pruritus of ear (external), pruritus of nose, respiratory tract disease, rhinorrhea, skin rash, tachycardia, throat irritation, weight gain

General Dosage Range Intranasal: *Children ≥12 years, Adolescents, and Adults ≤65 years:* 2 sprays in each nostril 2 to 4 times/day

Mechanism of Action Potent, selective histamine H_1-receptor antagonist

Pharmacodynamics/Kinetics

Onset of Action 10 minutes

Half-life Elimination 35 to 40 hours

Time to Peak 3 hours

Pregnancy Considerations Adverse events were observed in some animal reproduction studies when using oral doses much larger than the equivalent maximum human nasal dose.

Product Availability Not available in the US

LevOCARNitine (lee voe KAR ni teen)

Brand Names: US Carnitor; Carnitor SF; G-LevoCarnitine S/F [OTC]; McCarnitine [OTC]

Brand Names: Canada Carnitor

Pharmacologic Category Dietary Supplement

Use

Carnitine deficiency in patients with end-stage renal disease requiring hemodialysis (injection only): Prevention and treatment of carnitine deficiency in patients with end-stage renal disease (ESRD) who are undergoing dialysis.

Dietary supplement (OTC only): As a levocarnitine dietary supplement.

Primary systemic carnitine deficiency (oral [Rx] only): Treatment of primary systemic carnitine deficiency.

Secondary carnitine deficiency (oral [Rx] and injection): Acute and chronic treatment of patients with an inborn error of metabolism which results in a secondary carnitine deficiency.

Local Anesthetic/Vasoconstrictor Precautions No information available to require special precautions

Effects on Dental Treatment Key adverse event(s) related to dental treatment: Taste perversion.

Effects on Bleeding No information available to require special precautions

Adverse Reactions

Frequencies noted with hemodialysis patients.

>10%:

Cardiovascular: Hypertension (intravenous: 18% to 21%), chest pain (intravenous: 15%)

Central nervous system: Headache (intravenous: 37%), dizziness (intravenous: 15% to 18%), paresthesia (intravenous: 12%)

Endocrine & metabolic: Hypercalcemia (intravenous: 6% to 15%)

Gastrointestinal: Diarrhea (intravenous: 35%), abdominal pain (intravenous: 21%), vomiting (intravenous: 21%), nausea (intravenous: 12%)

Hematologic & oncologic: Anemia (intravenous: 5% to 12%)

Infection: Infection (intravenous: 24%)

Neuromuscular & skeletal: Weakness (intravenous: 9% to 12%)

Respiratory: Cough (intravenous: 18%), rhinitis (intravenous: 11%)

Miscellaneous: Accidental injury (intravenous: 12%), fever (intravenous: 6% to 12%)

1% to 10%:

Cardiovascular: Tachycardia (intravenous: 6% to 9%), palpitations (intravenous: 3% to 8%), vascular disease (intravenous: 6%), peripheral edema (intravenous: 5% to 6%), ECG abnormality (intravenous: 3% to 6%), atrial fibrillation (intravenous: 2% to 6%)

Central nervous system: Drug dependence (intravenous: 6%), vertigo (intravenous: 6%), depression (intravenous: 5% to 6%)

Dermatologic: Skin rash (intravenous: 5%)

Endocrine & metabolic: Weight loss (intravenous: 8%), parathyroid disorder (intravenous: 6%), weight gain (intravenous: 3% to 6%)

Gastrointestinal: Dysgeusia (intravenous: 2% to 9%), melena (intravenous: 6%), anorexia (intravenous: 5% to 6%), gastrointestinal disorder (intravenous: 3% to 6%)

Hematologic & oncologic: Hemorrhage (intravenous: 9%)

Hypersensitivity: Hypersensitivity reaction (intravenous: 6%)

Ophthalmic: Amblyopia (intravenous: 6%), eye disease (intravenous: 3% to 6%)

Renal: Renal failure (intravenous: 6%)

Respiratory: Bronchitis (intravenous: 3% to 5%)

Frequency not defined:

Gastrointestinal: Gastritis (intravenous)

Miscellaneous: Body odor

<1%, postmarketing, and/or case reports: Abdominal cramps, change in prothrombin time, hypoglycemia, myasthenia (uremic patients), rhabdomyolysis, seizure, vitamin K deficiency

General Dosage Range
IV:
Infants, Children, and Adolescents: 50 mg/kg/day in divided doses (maximum reported dose: 300 mg/kg/day) **or** 10 to 20 mg/kg after each hemodialysis session
Adults: 50 mg/kg/day in divided doses (maximum reported dose: 300 mg/kg/day) **or** 10 to 20 mg/kg after each hemodialysis session
Oral:
Infants, Children, and Adolescents: Initial: 50 mg/kg/day in divided doses; Maintenance: 50 to 100 mg/kg/day in divided doses (maximum dose: 3,000 mg/day)
Adults: 990 mg (tablet) 2 to 3 times a day **or** 1,000 to 3,000 mg/day (oral solution) in divided doses

Mechanism of Action Carnitine is a naturally occurring metabolic compound which functions as a carrier molecule for long-chain fatty acids within the mitochondria, facilitating energy production. Carnitine deficiency is associated with accumulation of excess acyl CoA esters and disruption of intermediary metabolism.

Pharmacodynamics/Kinetics
Half-life Elimination 17.4 hours
Time to Peak Oral: 3.3 hours

Pregnancy Risk Factor B

Pregnancy Considerations Teratogenic effects were not observed in animal studies. Carnitine is a naturally occurring substance in mammalian metabolism.

Levocetirizine (LEE vo se TI ra zeen)

Brand Names: US Xyzal

Pharmacologic Category Histamine H_1 Antagonist; Histamine H_1 Antagonist, Second Generation; Piperazine Derivative

Use
Chronic idiopathic urticaria: Treatment of uncomplicated skin manifestations of chronic idiopathic urticaria in adults and pediatric patients 6 months and older
Perennial allergic rhinitis: Relief of symptoms associated with perennial allergic rhinitis in adults and pediatric patients 6 months to 2 years
Allergic rhinitis (OTC only): Temporary relief of symptoms due to hay fever or other respiratory allergies (including rhinitis, sneezing, itchy/watery eyes, or itching of the throat/nose) in adults and pediatric patients 2 years and older

Local Anesthetic/Vasoconstrictor Precautions No information available to require special precautions

Effects on Dental Treatment Key adverse event(s) related to dental treatment: Xerostomia and changes in salivation (normal salivary flow resumes upon discontinuation).

Effects on Bleeding No information available to require special precautions

Adverse Reactions
>10%: Gastrointestinal: Diarrhea (infants: 13%; children: 4%)
1% to 10%:
Central nervous system: Drowsiness (3% to 6%), fatigue (adolescents and adults: 1% to 4%)
Gastrointestinal: Constipation (infants: 7%), vomiting (children: 4%), xerostomia (adolescents and adults: 2% to 3%)
Otic: Otitis media (children: 3%)
Respiratory: Nasopharyngitis (adolescents and adults: 4% to 6%), cough (children: 3%), epistaxis (children: 2%), pharyngitis (adolescents and adults: 1% to 2%)
Miscellaneous: Fever (children: 4%)
Frequency not defined: Neuromuscular & skeletal: Weakness
<1%, postmarketing, and/or case reports: Aggressive behavior, agitation, anaphylaxis, angioedema, arthralgia, blurred vision, depression, dizziness, dysgeusia, dyspnea, dysuria, edema, fixed drug eruption, hallucination, hepatitis, hypersensitivity reaction, increased appetite, increased serum bilirubin, increased serum transaminases, insomnia, movement disorder (including dystonia and oculogyric crisis), myalgia, nausea, palpitations, paresthesia, pruritus, seizure, skin rash, suicidal ideation, syncope, tachycardia, tremor, urinary retention, urticaria, vertigo, visual disturbances, weight gain

General Dosage Range Dosage adjustment recommended in patients with renal impairment
Oral:
Children 6 months to 5 years: 1.25 mg once daily; maximum dose: 1.25 mg/day
Children 6 to 11 years: 2.5 mg once daily; maximum dose: 2.5 mg/day
Children ≥12 years, Adolescents, and Adults: 2.5 to 5 mg once daily; maximum dose (allergic rhinitis): 5 mg/day

Mechanism of Action Levocetirizine is an antihistamine which selectively competes with histamine for H_1-receptor sites on effector cells in the gastrointestinal tract, blood vessels, and respiratory tract. Levocetirizine, the active enantiomer of cetirizine, has twice the binding affinity at the H_1-receptor compared to cetirizine.

Pharmacodynamics/Kinetics
Onset of Action 1 hour (Devillier 2008)
Duration of Action 24 hours (Devillier 2008)
Half-life Elimination Children 1 to 2 years: Oral solution: 4.09 ± 0.67 hours (Cranswick 2005); Children 6 to 11 years: Oral tablet: 5.7 ± 0.2 hours (Simons 2005); Adults: ~8 to 9 hours
Time to Peak Children 1 to 2 years: Oral solution: Median: 1 hour (range: 1 to 6 hours) (Cranswick 2005); Children 6 to 11 years: Oral tablet: 1.2 ± 0.2 hours (Simons 2005); Adults: Oral solution: 0.5 hours; Tablet: 0.9 hours

Pregnancy Risk Factor B

Pregnancy Considerations Adverse events have not been observed in animal reproduction studies; therefore, the manufacturer classifies levocetirizine as pregnancy category B. The use of antihistamines for the treatment of rhinitis during pregnancy is generally considered to be safe at recommended doses. Information related to the use of levocetirizine during pregnancy is limited; therefore, other agents are preferred. Levocetirizine is the active enantiomer of cetirizine; refer to the Cetirizine monograph for additional information.

Levodopa, Carbidopa, and Entacapone
(lee voe DOE pa, kar bi DOE pa, & en TA ka pone)

Related Information
Carbidopa *on page* 298
Entacapone *on page* 577

Brand Names: US Stalevo

Brand Names: Canada Stalevo

Pharmacologic Category Anti-Parkinson Agent, COMT Inhibitor; Anti-Parkinson Agent, Decarboxylase Inhibitor; Anti-Parkinson Agent, Dopamine Precursor

Use Parkinson disease: Treatment of Parkinson disease.

Local Anesthetic/Vasoconstrictor Precautions No information available to require special precautions

Effects on Dental Treatment No significant effects or complications reported

Effects on Bleeding No information available to require special precautions

Adverse Reactions See individual agents.

General Dosage Range Oral: *Adults:* 1 tablet (50 to 200 mg levodopa per 12.5 to 50 mg carbidopa per 200 mg entacapone) at each dosing interval (maximum: entacapone 1600 mg/day, carbidopa 300 mg/day, levodopa 1200 mg/day)

Mechanism of Action

Levodopa: The metabolic precursor of dopamine, a chemical depleted in Parkinson's disease. Levodopa is able to circulate in the plasma and cross the blood-brain-barrier (BBB), where it is converted by striatal enzymes to dopamine.

Carbidopa: Inhibits the peripheral plasma breakdown of levodopa by inhibiting its decarboxylation; increases available levodopa at the BBB

Entacapone: A reversible and selective inhibitor of catechol-O-methyltransferase (COMT). Alters the pharmacokinetics of levodopa, resulting in more sustained levodopa serum levels and increased concentrations available for absorption across the BBB.

Pharmacodynamics/Kinetics

Half-life Elimination Levodopa: 1.7 hours (range: 1.1 to 3.2 hours); Carbidopa: 1.6 to 2 hours (range ~1 to 4 hours); Entacapone: ~1 hour (range: 0.3 to 4.5 hours)

Time to Peak Levodopa: ~1 to 2 hours; Carbidopa: 2.5 to 3.4 hours; Entacapone: ~1 hour

Pregnancy Risk Factor C

Pregnancy Considerations Adverse effects were observed with carbidopa/levodopa, and entacapone in some animal reproduction studies. Refer to the entacapone and the carbidopa/levodopa monographs for additional information.

LevoFLOXacin (Systemic)

(lee voe FLOKS a sin)

Related Information

Clinical Risk Related to Drugs Prolonging QT Interval *on page 1772*

Gastrointestinal Disorders *on page 1775*

Related Sample Prescriptions

Bacterial Infections and Periodontal Diseases - Sample Prescriptions *on page 32*

Brand Names: US Levaquin

Brand Names: Canada ACT Levofloxacin; APO-Levofloxacin; Levaquin; Levaquin in 5% Dextrose Injection; Mylan-Levofloxacin; PMS-Levofloxacin; Sandoz-Levofloxacin; Teva-Levofloxacin

Generic Availability (US) Yes

Pharmacologic Category Antibiotic, Fluoroquinolone; Antibiotic, Respiratory Fluoroquinolone

Use

Treatment of community-acquired pneumonia, including multidrug resistant strains of *S. pneumoniae* (MDRSP); nosocomial pneumonia; acute bacterial exacerbation of chronic bronchitis; acute bacterial rhinosinusitis (ABRS); prostatitis (chronic bacterial), urinary tract infection (uncomplicated or complicated); acute pyelonephritis; skin or skin structure infections (uncomplicated or complicated); reduce incidence or disease progression of inhalational anthrax (postexposure); prophylaxis and treatment of plague (pneumonic and septicemic) due to *Y. pestis*

Limitations of use: Because fluoroquinolones have been associated with disabling and potentially irreversible serious adverse reactions (eg, tendinitis and tendon rupture, peripheral neuropathy, CNS effects), reserve levofloxacin for use in patients who have no alternative treatment options for acute exacerbation of chronic bronchitis, acute bacterial sinusitis, and uncomplicated urinary tract infections.

Local Anesthetic/Vasoconstrictor Precautions Levofloxacin is one of the drugs confirmed to prolong the QT interval and is accepted as having a risk of causing torsade de pointes. The risk of drug-induced torsade de pointes is extremely low when a single QT interval prolonging drug is prescribed. In terms of epinephrine, it is not known what effect vasoconstrictors in the local anesthetic regimen will have in patients with a known history of congenital prolonged QT interval or in patients taking any medication that prolongs the QT interval. Until more information is obtained, it is suggested that the clinician consult with the physician prior to the use of a vasoconstrictor in suspected patients, and that the vasoconstrictor (epinephrine, mepivacaine and levonordefrin [Carbocaine® 2% with Neo-Cobefrin®]) be used with caution.

Effects on Dental Treatment No significant effects or complications reported

Effects on Bleeding No information available to require special precautions

Adverse Reactions

1% to 10%:

Cardiovascular: Chest pain (1%), edema (1%)

Central nervous system: Headache (6%), insomnia (4%), dizziness (3%)

Dermatologic: Skin rash (2%), pruritus (1%)

Gastrointestinal: Nausea (7%), diarrhea (5%), constipation (3%), abdominal pain (2%), dyspepsia (2%), vomiting (2%)

Genitourinary: Vaginitis (1%)

Infection: Candidiasis (1%)

Local: Injection site reaction (1%)

Respiratory: Dyspnea (1%)

<1%, postmarketing, and/or case reports: Abnormal electroencephalogram, abnormal gait, acute generalized exanthematous pustolosis, acute renal failure, ageusia, agitation, agranulocytosis, altered sense of smell, anaphylactoid reaction, anemia (including aplastic and hemolytic), anorexia, anosmia, anxiety, arthralgia, blurred vision, brain disease (rare), bronchospasm, cardiac arrest, cardiac arrhythmia (including ventricular tachycardia/fibrillation and torsade de pointes), casts in urine, *Clostridium difficile*-associated diarrhea, confusion, convulsions, crystalluria, decreased visual acuity, depression, dermatological disease, drowsiness, dysgeusia, elevation in serum levels of skeletal-muscle enzymes, eosinophilia, epistaxis, erythema multiforme, esophagitis, exacerbation of myasthenia gravis, fever, gastritis (including gastroenteritis), glossitis, granulocytopenia, hallucination, hepatic failure (some fatal), hepatic insufficiency, hepatitis, hepatotoxicity (idiosyncratic) (Chalasani 2014), hyperglycemia, hyperkalemia, hyperkinesia, hypersensitivity pneumonitis, hypersensitivity reaction (including anaphylaxis, angioedema, rash, pneumonitis, and serum sickness), hypertension, hypertonia, hypoacusis, hypoglycemia, hypotension, increased INR, increased intracranial pressure, increased serum alkaline phosphatase, increased serum transaminases, interstitial nephritis, intestinal obstruction, jaundice, leukocytosis, leukopenia, leukorrhea, lymphadenopathy, multiorgan failure, muscle injury,

muscle spasm, myalgia, palpitations, pancreatitis, pancytopenia, paralysis, paranoia, paresthesia, peripheral neuropathy (may be irreversible), phlebitis, phototoxicity, prolonged prothrombin time, prolonged Q-T interval on ECG, pseudotumor cerebri, psychosis, renal function abnormality, restlessness, rhabdomyolysis, rupture of tendon, scotoma, seizure, skeletal pain, skin photosensitivity, sleep disorder (including abnormal dreams and nightmares), Stevens-Johnson syndrome, stomatitis, suicidal ideation, syncope, tachycardia, tendonitis, tinnitus, toxic epidermal necrolysis, toxic psychosis, thrombocytopenia (including thrombotic thrombocytopenic purpura), tremor, urticaria, uveitis, vasculitis (leukocytoclastic), vasodilatation, vertigo, visual disturbance (including diplopia), voice disorder

Dosing

Adult & Geriatric Note: Sequential therapy (intravenous to oral) may be instituted based on prescriber's discretion.

Acute bacterial rhinosinusitis: Oral, IV:
- Manufacturer's labeling: 750 mg every 24 hours for 5 days or 500 mg every 24 hours for 10 to 14 days
- Alternate recommendations: 500 mg every 24 hours for 5 to 7 days (Chow 2012)

Anthrax (inhalational): Oral, IV: 500 mg every 24 hours for 60 days, beginning as soon as possible after exposure

Bite wounds (animal/human) (off-label use): Oral, IV: **Note:** Recommended as an alternative therapy for human bite wound in patients hypersensitive to beta-lactams: 750 mg once daily; in combination with metronidazole or clindamycin (IDSA [Stevens 2014])

***Chlamydia trachomatis* urogenital infection (alternative to preferred therapy) (off-label use):** Oral: 500 mg once daily for 7 days (CDC [Workowski 2015])

Chronic bronchitis (acute bacterial exacerbation): Oral: 500 mg every 24 hours for 7 days; Canadian labeling (not in US labeling) also includes a dosage regimen of 750 mg every 24 hours for 5 days

Diabetic foot infections, moderate to severe (off-label use): Oral, IV: **Note:** Initial treatment should begin with an IV regimen for severe infections; moderate infections may initially be treated with IV or oral regimen (IDSA [Lipsky 2012]): 750 mg once daily (Graham 2002); use in combination with clindamycin (limited evidence supporting clindamycin for severe *S. aureus* infections) (IDSA [Lipsky 2012])

Diverticulitis, peritonitis (off-label use) (Solomkin, [IDSA] 2010): Oral, IV: 750 mg every 24 hours for 7 to 10 days; use adjunctive metronidazole therapy

Epididymitis (off-label use; CDC [Workowski 2015]): Oral:
- *Likely caused by enteric organisms:* 500 mg once daily for 10 days
- *Likely caused by sexually-transmitted chlamydia and gonorrhea and enteric organisms in men who practice insertive anal sex:* 500 mg once daily for 10 days in combination with ceftriaxone

Intra-abdominal infection, complicated, community-acquired (in combination with metronidazole) (off-label use) (Solomkin, [IDSA] 2010): IV: 750 mg once daily for 4 to 7 days (provided source controlled). **Note:** Avoid using in settings where *E. coli* susceptibility to fluoroquinolones is <90%.

Neutropenia (chemotherapy-induced), antibacterial prophylaxis (off-label use): Oral: 500 mg once daily (Bucaneve 2005; Cullen 2005)

Pelvic inflammatory disease (in patients allergic to cephalosporins; off-label use): Oral: 500 mg once daily for 14 days with concomitant metronidazole; **Note:** The CDC recommends use as an alternative therapy only if standard parenteral cephalosporin therapy is not feasible, community prevalence, and individual risk of quinolone-resistant gonococcal organisms is low. Culture sensitivity must be confirmed (CDC [Workowski 2015]).

Plague (prophylaxis and treatment): Oral, IV: 500 mg every 24 hours for 10 to 14 days, beginning as soon as possible after exposure. **Note:** Dose of 750 mg once daily may be considered if clinically warranted.

Pneumonia:
- *Community-acquired (CAP):* Oral, IV: 500 mg every 24 hours for 7 to 14 days or 750 mg every 24 hours for 5 days; **Note:** CAP guidelines recommend the 750 mg dose (IDSA/ATS [Mandell 2007])
- *Hospital-acquired or ventilator- associated pneumonia:* IV: 750 mg every 24 hours for 7 days; may consider shorter or longer duration depending on rate of clinical improvement. When used as empiric therapy, use in combination with an agent active against MRSA (unless coverage of MSSA only is appropriate) with or without an additional antipseudomonal agent (dependent on patient and institution-specific risk factors) (Kalil 2016).

Prostatitis (chronic bacterial): Oral, IV: 500 mg every 24 hours for 28 days

Skin and skin structure infections: Oral, IV:
- *Uncomplicated:* 500 mg every 24 hours for 7 to 10 days
- *Complicated:* 750 mg every 24 hours for 7 to 14 days

Surgical (preoperative) prophylaxis (off-label use): IV: 500 mg within 120 minutes prior to surgical incision (Bratzler 2013)

Surgical site infections (intestinal or genitourinary tract; perineum or axilla) (off-label use): IV: 750 mg every 24 hours, in combination with metronidazole (IDSA [Stevens 2014])

Traveler's diarrhea (off-label use): Oral: 500 mg once daily for 1 to 3 days (IDSA [Hill 2006])

Tuberculosis, drug-resistant tuberculosis, or intolerance to first-line agents (off-label use): Oral: 500 to 1,000 mg every 24 hours (CDC 2003)

Urethritis, nongonococcal (off-label use): Oral: 500 mg every 24 hours for 7 days (CDC [Workowski 2015])

Urinary tract infections: Oral, IV:
- *Uncomplicated:* 250 mg once daily for 3 days
- *Complicated, including pyelonephritis:* 250 mg once daily for 10 days **or** 750 mg once daily for 5 days

Pediatric

Acute bacterial rhinosinusitis (off-label use): Oral, IV: 10 to 20 mg/kg/day divided every 12 to 24 hours for 10 to 14 days (maximum: 500 mg daily). **Note:** Recommended in patients with a type I penicillin allergy, after failure of initial therapy or in patients at risk for antibiotic resistance (eg, daycare attendance, age <2 years, recent hospitalization, antibiotic use within the past month) (Chow 2012).

Anthrax (inhalational, postexposure): Oral, IV
- Infants ≥6 months and Children ≤50 kg: 8 mg/kg every 12 hours for 60 days (do not exceed 250 mg/dose), beginning as soon as possible after exposure
- Children >50 kg: 500 mg every 24 hours for 60 days, beginning as soon as possible after exposure

***Chlamydia trachomatis* urogenital infection (alternative to preferred therapy) (off-label use):** Adolescents: Refer to adult dosing.

Community-acquired pneumonia (CAP) (IDSA/PIDS 2011): Note: May consider addition of vancomycin or clindamycin to empiric therapy if community-acquired MRSA suspected; alternative to ceftriaxone or cefotaxime in patients not fully immunized for *H. influenzae* type b and *S. pneumoniae*, or significant local resistance to penicillin in invasive pneumococcal strains.

Infants ≥6 months and Children ≤4 years:

S. pneumoniae (MICs to penicillin ≤2.0 mcg/mL), mild infection or step-down therapy (alternative to amoxicillin): Oral: 8 to 10 mg/kg/dose every 12 hours (maximum: 750 mg daily)

S. pneumoniae (MICs to penicillin ≥4.0 mcg/mL):

Moderate-to-severe infection (alternative to ceftriaxone): IV: 8 to 10 mg/kg/dose every 12 hours (maximum: 750 mg daily)

Mild infection, step-down therapy (preferred): Oral: 8 to 10 mg/kg/dose every 12 hours (maximum: 750 mg daily)

H. influenzae, moderate-to-severe infection (alternative to ampicillin, ceftriaxone, or cefotaxime): IV: 8 to 10 mg/kg/dose every 12 hours (maximum: 750 mg daily)

Atypical pathogens, moderate-to-severe infection (alternative to azithromycin) or empiric treatment (alternative to azithromycin +/ beta-lactam; should be limited to macrolide allergic/intolerant patients): Oral, IV: 8 to 10 mg/kg/dose every 12 hours (maximum: 750 mg daily)

Children 5 to 16 years:

S. pneumoniae (MICs to penicillin ≤2.0 mcg/mL), mild infection or step-down therapy (alternative to amoxicillin): Oral: 8 to 10 mg/kg/dose once daily (maximum: 750 mg daily)

S. pneumoniae (MICs to penicillin ≥4.0 mcg/mL):

Moderate-to-severe infection (alternative to ceftriaxone): IV: 8 to 10 mg/kg/dose once daily (maximum: 750 mg daily)

Mild infection, step-down therapy (preferred): Oral: 8 to 10 mg/kg/dose once daily (maximum: 750 mg daily)

H. influenzae, moderate-to-severe infection (alternative to ampicillin, ceftriaxone, or cefotaxime): IV: 8 to 10 mg/kg/dose once daily (maximum: 750 mg daily)

Atypical pathogens:

Moderate-to-severe infection (alternative to azithromycin): Oral, IV: 8 to 10 mg/kg/dose once daily (maximum: 750 mg daily)

Mild infection, step-down therapy (alternative to azithromycin in adolescents with skeletal maturity): Oral: 500 mg once daily

Plague (prophylaxis and treatment): Infants ≥6 months and Children: Oral, IV:

≤50 kg: 8 mg/kg every 12 hours for 10 to 14 days (do not exceed 250 mg/dose), beginning as soon as possible after exposure

>50 kg: 500 mg every 24 hours for 10 to 14 days, beginning as soon as possible after exposure. **Note:** Dose of 750 mg once daily may be considered if clinically warranted.

Surgical (preoperative) prophylaxis (off-label use): Children ≥1 year: IV: 10 mg/kg within 120 minutes prior to surgical incision (maximum: 500 mg) (Bratzler 2013)

Renal Impairment IV, Oral:

Normal renal function dosing of 250 mg daily:

CrCl 20 to 49 mL/minute: No dosage adjustment required.

CrCl 10 to 19 mL/minute: Administer 250 mg every 48 hours (except in uncomplicated UTI, where no dosage adjustment is required).

Hemodialysis/chronic ambulatory peritoneal dialysis (CAPD): No information available.

Normal renal function dosing of 500 mg daily:

CrCl 20 to 49 mL/minute: Administer 500 mg initial dose, followed by 250 mg every 24 hours.

CrCl 10 to 19 mL/minute: Administer 500 mg initial dose, followed by 250 mg every 48 hours.

Hemodialysis/chronic ambulatory peritoneal dialysis (CAPD): Administer 500 mg initial dose, followed by 250 mg every 48 hours; supplemental doses are not required following either hemodialysis or CAPD

Normal renal function dosing of 750 mg daily:

CrCl 20 to 49 mL/minute: Administer 750 mg every 48 hours.

CrCl 10 to 19 mL/minute: Administer 750 mg initial dose, followed by 500 mg every 48 hours.

Hemodialysis/chronic ambulatory peritoneal dialysis (CAPD): Administer 750 mg initial dose, followed by 500 mg every 48 hours; supplemental doses are not required following either hemodialysis or CAPD.

Normal renal function dosing of 750 or 1,000 mg daily (treatment of tuberculosis **only**) (CDC 2003): CrCl <30 mL/minute: Administer 750 or 1,000 mg 3 times per week (in hemodialysis patients administer after dialysis on dialysis days).

Continuous renal replacement therapy (CRRT) (Heintz 2009; Trotman 2005): Drug clearance is highly dependent on the method of renal replacement, filter type, and flow rate. Appropriate dosing requires close monitoring of pharmacologic response, signs of adverse reactions due to drug accumulation, as well as drug concentrations in relation to target trough (if appropriate). The following are general recommendations only (based on dialysate flow/ultrafiltration rates of 1 to 2 L/hour and minimal residual renal function) and should not supersede clinical judgment:

CVVH: Loading dose of 500 to 750 mg followed by 250 mg every 24 hours.

CVVHD: Loading dose of 500 to 750 mg followed by 250 to 500 mg every 24 hours.

CVVHDF: Loading dose of 500 to 750 mg followed by 250 to 750 mg every 24 hours.

Hepatic Impairment IV, Oral: No dosage adjustment provided in manufacturer's labeling (has not been studied). However, dosage adjustment unlikely due to limited hepatic metabolism.

Mechanism of Action As the S(-) enantiomer of the fluoroquinolone, ofloxacin, levofloxacin, inhibits DNA-gyrase in susceptible organisms thereby inhibits relaxation of supercoiled DNA and promotes breakage of DNA strands. DNA gyrase (topoisomerase II), is an essential bacterial enzyme that maintains the superhelical structure of DNA and is required for DNA replication and transcription, DNA repair, recombination, and transposition.

Contraindications Hypersensitivity to levofloxacin, any component of the formulation, or other quinolones

Canadian labeling: Additional contraindications (not in U.S. labeling): History of tendonitis or tendon rupture associated with use of any quinolone antimicrobial agent

Warnings/Precautions [US Boxed Warning]: Fluoroquinolones are associated with disabling and

potentially irreversible serious adverse reactions that may occur together, including tendinitis and tendon rupture, peripheral neuropathy, and CNS effects. Discontinue levofloxacin immediately and avoid use of fluoroquinolones in patients who experience any of these serious adverse reactions. Patients of any age or without preexisting risk factors have experienced these reactions; may occur within hours to weeks after initiation. **[U.S. Boxed Warning]: Reserve use of levofloxacin for treatment of acute bacterial sinusitis, acute bacterial exacerbation of chronic bronchitis, or uncomplicated urinary tract infection for patients who have no alternative treatment options because of the risk of disabling and potentially serious adverse reactions (eg, tendinitis and tendon rupture, peripheral neuropathy, CNS effects).** Use with caution in patients with rheumatoid arthritis; may increase risk of tendon rupture. Fluoroquinolones have been associated with an increased risk of CNS effects, including seizures, increased intracranial pressure (including pseudotumor cerebri), and toxic psychosis; may also cause nervousness, agitation, insomnia, anxiety, nightmares, paranoia, dizziness, confusion, tremors, hallucinations, depression, and suicidal thoughts or actions. May occur following the first dose; discontinue immediately and avoid further use of fluoroquinolones in patients who experience these reactions. Use with caution in patients with known or suspected CNS disorder, or risk factors that may predispose to seizures or lower the seizure threshold. Fluoroquinolones have been associated with an increased risk of peripheral neuropathy; may occur soon after initiation of therapy and may be irreversible; discontinue if symptoms of sensory or sensorimotor neuropathy occur. Avoid use in patients who have previously experienced peripheral neuropathy.

Use with caution in patients with renal impairment; dosage adjustment required. Use with caution in elderly patients; adverse effects (eg, hepatotoxicity, tendon rupture, QT changes) may be increased. Safety of use in pediatric patients for >14 days of therapy has not been studied; increased incidence of musculoskeletal disorders (eg, arthralgia, tendon rupture) has been observed in children. Avoid excessive sunlight and take precautions to limit exposure (eg, loose fitting clothing, sunscreen); may cause moderate to severe phototoxicity reactions. Discontinue use if photosensitivity occurs. Fluoroquinolones may prolong QT_c interval; avoid use in patients with a history of QT_c prolongation, uncorrected hypokalemia, hypomagnesemia, or concurrent administration of other medications known to prolong the QT interval (including Class Ia and Class III antiarrhythmics, cisapride, erythromycin, antipsychotics, and tricyclic antidepressants). Fluoroquinolones have been associated with the development of serious, and sometimes fatal, hypoglycemia. These events have occurred most often in elderly patients with diabetes, but have also been reported in patients without a prior history of diabetes. Prompt identification and treatment of hypoglycemia is essential. Individual quinolones may differ in their potential to cause this effect. It was most evident with gatifloxacin (no longer marketed as systemic formulation). Hyperglycemia has also been associated with the use of fluoroquinolones. Patients should be monitored closely for signs/symptoms of disordered glucose regulation.

Severe hypersensitivity reactions, including anaphylaxis, have occurred with quinolone therapy. Reactions may present as typical allergic symptoms after a single dose, or may manifest as severe idiosyncratic dermatologic, vascular, pulmonary, renal, hepatic, and/or hematologic events, usually after multiple doses. Prompt discontinuation of drug should occur if skin rash or other symptoms arise. Prolonged use may result in fungal or bacterial superinfection, including *C. difficile*-associated diarrhea (CDAD) and pseudomembranous colitis; CDAD has been observed >2 months postantibiotic treatment. **[U.S. Boxed Warning]: Quinolones may exacerbate myasthenia gravis; avoid use in patients with known history of myasthenia gravis.** Cases of severe exacerbations, including the need for ventilatory support and deaths, have been reported. Unrelated to hypersensitivity, severe hepatotoxicity (including acute hepatitis and fatalities) has been reported. Elderly patients may be at greater risk. Discontinue therapy immediately if signs and symptoms of hepatitis occur. Hemolytic reactions may (rarely) occur with quinolone use in patients with latent or actual G6PD deficiency. Potentially significant drug-drug interactions may exist, requiring dose or frequency adjustment, additional monitoring, and/or selection of alternative therapy.

Some dosage forms may contain benzyl alcohol; large amounts of benzyl alcohol (≥99 mg/kg/day) have been associated with a potentially fatal toxicity ("gasping syndrome") in neonates; the "gasping syndrome" consists of metabolic acidosis, respiratory distress, gasping respirations, CNS dysfunction (including convulsions, intracranial hemorrhage), hypotension, and cardiovascular collapse (AAP ["Inactive" 1997]; CDC 1982); some data suggests that benzoate displaces bilirubin from protein binding sites (Ahlfors 2001); avoid or use dosage forms containing benzyl alcohol with caution in neonates. See manufacturer's labeling.

Drug Interactions

Metabolism/Transport Effects None known.

Avoid Concomitant Use

Avoid concomitant use of LevoFLOXacin (Systemic) with any of the following: BCG (Intravesical); Cholera Vaccine; Highest Risk QTc-Prolonging Agents; Hydroxychloroquine; Ivabradine; MiFEPRIStone; Nadifloxacin; Probucol; Promazine; Strontium Ranelate; Vinflunine

Increased Effect/Toxicity

LevoFLOXacin (Systemic) may increase the levels/effects of: Aminolevulinic Acid; Blood Glucose Lowering Agents; Delamanid; Heroin; Highest Risk QTc-Prolonging Agents; Moderate Risk QTc-Prolonging Agents; Porfimer; Tacrolimus (Systemic); Varenicline; Verteporfin; Vitamin K Antagonists

The levels/effects of LevoFLOXacin (Systemic) may be increased by: Corticosteroids (Systemic); Hydroxychloroquine; Ivabradine; MiFEPRIStone; Nadifloxacin; Nonsteroidal Anti-Inflammatory Agents; Probenecid; Probucol; Promazine; QTc-Prolonging Agents (Indeterminate Risk and Risk Modifying); Vinflunine

Decreased Effect

LevoFLOXacin (Systemic) may decrease the levels/effects of: BCG (Intravesical); BCG Vaccine (Immunization); Blood Glucose Lowering Agents; Cholera Vaccine; Didanosine; Lactobacillus and Estriol; Mycophenolate; Sodium Picosulfate; Typhoid Vaccine

The levels/effects of LevoFLOXacin (Systemic) may be decreased by: Antacids; Calcium Salts; Didanosine; Iron Salts; Lanthanum; Magnesium Salts; Multivitamins/Minerals (with ADEK, Folate, Iron); Multivitamins/Minerals (with AE, No Iron); Quinapril; Sevelamer; Strontium Ranelate; Sucralfate; Zinc Salts

Dietary Considerations Tablets may be taken without regard to meals. Oral solution should be administered on an empty stomach (1 hour before or 2 hours after a meal). Take 2 hours before or 2 hours after multiple vitamins, antacids, or other products containing magnesium, aluminum, iron, or zinc.

Pharmacodynamics/Kinetics

Half-life Elimination

Infants ≥6 months and Children ≤5 years: ~4 hours (Chien 2005)

Children 5 to 10 years: 4.8 hours (Chien 2005)

Children 10 to 12 years: 5.4 hours (Chien 2005)

Children 12 to 16 years: 6 hours (Chien 2005)

Adults: ~6 to 8 hours

Adults, renal impairment: 27 ± 10 hours (CrCl 20 to 49 mL/minute); 35 ± 5 hours (CrCl <20 mL/minute)

Time to Peak 1 to 2 hours

Pregnancy Risk Factor C

Pregnancy Considerations Adverse events have been observed in some animal reproduction studies. Levofloxacin crosses the placenta and can be detected in the amniotic fluid and cord blood (Ozyüncü and Beksac 2010; Ozyüncü and Nemutl, 2010). Information specific to levofloxacin use during pregnancy is limited (Padberg 2014).

Breastfeeding Considerations Levofloxacin is excreted in breast milk.

The relative infant dose (RID) of levofloxacin is 6% when calculated using the highest breast milk concentration located and compared to a therapeutic infant dose of 20 mg/kg/day. In general, breastfeeding is considered acceptable when the relative infant dose is <10% (Anderson 2016; Ito 2000). Using the highest milk concentration (8.2 mcg/mL), the estimated daily infant dose via breast milk is 1.23 mg/kg/day. This milk concentration was obtained following a maternal dose of IV levofloxacin 500 mg/day on day 10 of therapy; the half-life in the breast milk was approximately 7 hours (Cahill 2005).

In general, antibiotics that are present in breast milk may cause nondose-related modification of bowel flora. Monitor infants for GI disturbances (WHO 2002). The manufacturer does not recommend use of levofloxacin in nursing women due to concerns of serious adverse reactions. The risk of articular damage in nursing infants exposed to other quinolones (ie, ciprofloxacin) is considered low even in children receiving high therapeutic doses. Therefore, some sources do not consider maternal use of these agents to be a reason to discontinue nursing as long as the infant is monitored for gastrointestinal symptoms (eg, diarrhea) which could occur following antibiotic exposure (Kaplan 2015). Other sources recommend avoiding quinolone antibiotics if alternative agents are available (WHO 2002).

Dosage Forms

Solution, Intravenous:

Generic: 250 mg/50 mL (50 mL); 500 mg/100 mL (100 mL); 750 mg/150 mL (150 mL)

Solution, Intravenous [preservative free]:

Generic: 250 mg/50 mL (50 mL); 500 mg/100 mL (100 mL); 750 mg/150 mL (150 mL); 25 mg/mL (20 mL, 30 mL)

Solution, Oral:

Generic: 25 mg/mL (10 mL, 20 mL, 100 mL, 200 mL, 480 mL)

Tablet, Oral:

Levaquin: 250 mg, 500 mg, 750 mg

Generic: 250 mg, 500 mg, 750 mg

Dental Comment See Local Anesthetic/Vasoconstrictor Precautions

LEVOleucovorin (lee voe loo koe VOR in)

Brand Names: US Fusilev

Pharmacologic Category Antidote; Chemotherapy Modulating Agent; Rescue Agent (Chemotherapy)

Use

Colorectal cancer, metastatic: Palliative treatment of advanced, metastatic colorectal cancer (in combination with fluorouracil).

Folic acid antagonist overdose: Antidote to diminish toxicity in inadvertent overdosage of folic acid antagonists.

High-dose methotrexate rescue: Rescue agent after high-dose methotrexate therapy in osteosarcoma treatment.

Impaired methotrexate elimination: Antidote to diminish toxicity and counteract effects of impaired methotrexate elimination.

Limitations of use: Levoleucovorin is not indicated for the treatment of pernicious anemia or megaloblastic anemias secondary to the lack of vitamin B_{12} (improper use may result in hematologic remission with progressive neurologic manifestations).

Local Anesthetic/Vasoconstrictor Precautions No information available to require special precautions

Effects on Dental Treatment Key adverse event(s) related to dental treatment: Stomatitis and taste perversion.

Effects on Bleeding No information available to require special precautions

Adverse Reactions Adverse reactions reported with levoleucovorin either as a part of combination chemotherapy or following chemotherapy.

>10%:

Central nervous system: Fatigue (≤29%), malaise (≤29%)

Dermatologic: Dermatitis (6% to 29%), alopecia (≤26%)

Gastrointestinal: Stomatitis (38% to 72%; grades 3/4: 6% to 12%), diarrhea (6% to 70%; grades 3/4: ≤19%), nausea (19% to 62%), vomiting (38% to 40%), anorexia (≤24%), decreased appetite (≤24%), abdominal pain (≤14%)

Neuromuscular & skeletal: Weakness (≤29%)

1% to 10%:

Central nervous system: Confusion (6%), neuropathy (6%)

Gastrointestinal: Dysgeusia (6%), dyspepsia (6%), typhlitis (6%)

Renal: Renal insufficiency (6%)

Respiratory: Dyspnea (6%)

<1%, postmarketing, and/or case reports: Hypersensitivity reaction, pruritus, rigors, skin rash, temperature change

General Dosage Range IV: *Children, Adolescents, and Adults:* Dosing varies greatly depending on indication

Mechanism of Action Levoleucovorin counteracts the toxic (and therapeutic) effects of folic acid antagonists (eg, methotrexate) which act by inhibiting dihydrofolate reductase. Levoleucovorin is the levo isomeric and pharmacologic active form of leucovorin (levoleucovorin does not require reduction by dihydrofolate reductase). A reduced derivative of folic acid, leucovorin supplies the necessary cofactor blocked by methotrexate.

Leucovorin enhances the activity (and toxicity) of fluorouracil by stabilizing the binding of 5-fluoro-2'-deoxyuridine-5'-monophosphate (FdUMP; a fluorouracil metabolite) to thymidylate synthetase resulting in inhibition of this enzyme.

Pharmacodynamics/Kinetics

Half-life Elimination

Total-tetrahydrofolate: 5.1 hours; (6)-5-methyl-5,6,7,8-tetrahydrofolate: 6.8 hours

Time to Peak Serum: IV (healthy volunteers; 15 mg dose): 0.9 hours

Pregnancy Risk Factor C

Pregnancy Considerations Animal reproduction studies have not been conducted. Levoleucovorin is the levo isomeric form of racemic leucovorin, a biologically active form of folic acid. Adequate amounts of folic acid are recommended during pregnancy. Refer to Folic Acid monograph.

Levomilnacipran (lee voe mil NA si pran)

Brand Names: US Fetzima; Fetzima Titration

Brand Names: Canada Fetzima

Pharmacologic Category Antidepressant, Serotonin/Norepinephrine Reuptake Inhibitor

Use Major depressive disorder: Treatment of major depressive disorder (MDD)

Local Anesthetic/Vasoconstrictor Precautions Although levomilnacipran is not a tricyclic antidepressant, it blocks norepinephrine reuptake within the CNS synapses as part of the mechanism of action. It has been suggested that vasoconstrictors be administered with caution and vital signs monitored in dental patients taking antidepressants that affect norepinephrine in this way.

Effects on Dental Treatment Key adverse events(s) related to dental treatment: Bruxism (<2%) has been reported; Patients may experience orthostatic hypotension (6% to 12%) as they stand up after treatment; especially if lying in dental chair for extended periods of time. Use caution with sudden changes in position during and after dental treatment.

Effects on Bleeding Serotonin/norepinephrine reuptake inhibitors (SNRIs) may impair platelet aggregation resulting in increased risk of bleeding events, particularly if used concomitantly with aspirin or NSAIDs.

Adverse Reactions

>10%:

Cardiovascular: Orthostatic hypotension (6% to 12%; dose related)

Gastrointestinal: Nausea (17%)

1% to 10%:

Cardiovascular: Increased heart rate (6%), tachycardia (6%), palpitations (5%), hypertension (3%), hypotension (3%), increased blood pressure (3%), angina pectoris (<2%), chest pain (<2%), supraventricular extrasystole (<2%), syncope (<2%), ventricular premature contractions (<2%)

Central nervous system: Aggressive behavior (<2%), agitation (<2%), extrapyramidal reaction (<2%), migraine (<2%), outbursts of anger (<2%), panic attack (<2%), paresthesia (<2%), tension (<2%), yawning (<2%)

Dermatologic: Hyperhidrosis (9%), skin rash (2%), pruritus (<2%), urticaria (<2%), xeroderma (<2%)

Endocrine & metabolic: Hot flash (3%), hypercholesterolemia (<2%), increased thirst (<2%)

Gastrointestinal: Constipation (9%), vomiting (5%), decreased appetite (3%), abdominal pain (<2%), bruxism (<2%), flatulence (<2%)

Genitourinary: Erectile dysfunction (6% to 10%; dose related), urinary hesitancy (4% to 6%; dose related), ejaculatory disorder (5%), testicular pain (4%), hematuria (<2%), pollakiuria (<2%), proteinuria (<2%)

Hepatic: Abnormal hepatic function tests (<2%)

Ophthalmic: Blurred vision (<2%), conjunctival hemorrhage (<2%), dry eye syndrome (<2%)

<1%, postmarketing, and/or case reports: Angle-closure glaucoma, hemorrhagic diathesis, mydriasis, seizure

General Dosage Range Dosage adjustment recommended in patients with renal impairment.

Oral: *Adults:* Initial: 20 mg once daily; Maintenance: 40-120 mg once daily; Maximum: 120 mg daily

Mechanism of Action Levomilnacipran, the more active enantiomer of milnacipran, is a potent inhibitor of norepinephrine and serotonin reuptake (Montgomery, 2013).

Pharmacodynamics/Kinetics

Half-life Elimination 12 hours

Time to Peak 6 to 8 hours

Pregnancy Risk Factor C

Pregnancy Considerations Adverse events were observed in some animal reproduction studies. Nonteratogenic effects in the newborn following SSRI/SNRI exposure late in the third trimester include respiratory distress, cyanosis, apnea, seizures, temperature instability, feeding difficulty, vomiting, hypoglycemia, hypo- or hypertonia, hyper-reflexia, jitteriness, irritability, constant crying, and tremor. Symptoms may be due to the toxicity of the SSRIs/SNRIs or a discontinuation syndrome and may be consistent with serotonin syndrome associated with SSRI treatment.

Women treated for major depression and who are euthymic prior to pregnancy are more likely to experience a relapse when medication is discontinued as compared to pregnant women who continue taking antidepressant medications (Cohen 2006). The ACOG recommends that therapy with SSRIs or SNRIs during pregnancy be individualized; treatment of depression during pregnancy should incorporate the clinical expertise of the mental health clinician, obstetrician, primary health care provider, and pediatrician. According to the American Psychiatric Association (APA), the risks of medication treatment should be weighed against other treatment options and untreated depression. For women who discontinue antidepressant medications during pregnancy and who may be at high risk for postpartum depression, the medications can be restarted following delivery. Treatment algorithms have been developed by the ACOG and the APA for the management of depression in women prior to conception and during pregnancy (ACOG 2008; APA 2010; Yonkers 2009).

Pregnant women exposed to antidepressants during pregnancy are encouraged to enroll in the National Pregnancy Registry for Antidepressants (NPRAD). Women 18 to 45 years of age or their health care providers may contact the registry by calling 844-405-6185. Enrollment should be done as early in pregnancy as possible.

Levothyroxine (lee voe thye ROKS een)

Related Information

Endocrine Disorders and Pregnancy *on page 1781*

Brand Names: US Levothroid [DSC]; Levoxyl; Synthroid; Tirosint; Unithroid; Unithroid Direct

Brand Names: Canada Eltroxin; Levothyroxine Sodium; Levothyroxine Sodium for Injection; Synthroid

Generic Availability (US) May be product dependent

Pharmacologic Category Thyroid Product

Use

Oral:

Hypothyroidism: Replacement or supplemental therapy in congenital or acquired hypothyroidism of any etiology, except transient hypothyroidism during the recovery phase of subacute thyroiditis. Specific indications include primary (thyroidal), secondary (pituitary), and tertiary (hypothalamic) hypothyroidism and subclinical hypothyroidism. Primary hypothyroidism may result from functional deficiency, primary atrophy, partial or total congenital absence of the thyroid gland, or from the effects of surgery, radiation, or drugs, with or without the presence of goiter. **Note:** ATA/AACE guidelines recommend levothyroxine monotherapy as the preferred thyroid preparation for the treatment of hypothyroidism (ATA/AACE [Garber 2012]).

Pituitary thyrotropin-stimulating hormone suppression: Prevention or treatment of various types of euthyroid goiters, including thyroid nodules, subacute or chronic lymphocytic thyroiditis (Hashimoto thyroiditis), multinodular goiter and as an adjunct to surgery and radioiodine therapy in the management of thyrotropin-dependent well-differentiated thyroid cancer.

Injectable:

US labeling: Treatment of myxedema coma

Canadian labeling: Refer to oral indications; IV may be substituted for oral when rapid repletion is required; IV or IM may be used when oral administration is not possible.

Local Anesthetic/Vasoconstrictor Precautions No precautions with vasoconstrictor are necessary if patient is well controlled with levothyroxine

Effects on Dental Treatment No significant effects or complications reported

Effects on Bleeding No information available to require special precautions

Adverse Reactions Frequency not defined.

Cardiovascular: Angina pectoris, cardiac arrest, cardiac arrhythmia, congestive heart failure, flushing, hypertension, increased pulse, myocardial infarction, palpitations, tachycardia

Central nervous system: Anxiety, choking sensation (Levoxyl), emotional lability, fatigue, headache, heat intolerance, hyperactivity, insomnia, irritability, myasthenia, nervousness, pseudotumor cerebri (children), seizure (rare)

Dermatologic: Alopecia, diaphoresis

Endocrine & metabolic: Menstrual disease, weight loss

Gastrointestinal: Abdominal cramps, diarrhea, dysphagia (Levoxyl), gag reflex (Levoxyl), increased appetite, vomiting

Genitourinary: Infertility

Hepatic: Increased liver enzymes

Hypersensitivity: Hypersensitivity (to inactive ingredients; symptoms include urticaria, pruritus, rash, flushing, angioedema, GI symptoms, fever, arthralgia, serum sickness, wheezing)

Neuromuscular & skeletal: Decreased bone mineral density, slipped capital femoral epiphysis (children), tremor

Respiratory: Dyspnea

Miscellaneous: Fever

<1%, postmarketing, and/or case reports: Dysgeusia (Syed 2016)

Dosing

Adult Doses should be adjusted based on clinical response and laboratory parameters.

Hypothyroidism: Oral:

Adults, healthy adults <50 years of age, children in whom growth and puberty are complete, and older adults who have been recently treated for hyperthyroidism or who have been hypothyroid for only a few months:

~1.7 mcg/kg/day; usual doses are ≤200 mcg daily (range: 100 to 125 mcg daily [70 kg adult]); doses ≥300 mcg daily are rare (consider poor compliance, malabsorption, and/or drug interactions). Titrate dose every 6 weeks. The Canadian labeling includes detailed dosage titration information. Refer to manufacturer labeling for specific recommendations.

Alternate recommendations (off-label dose): Adults (healthy adults <50 years of age): ~1.6 mcg/kg/day. Full replacement doses should be considered when initiating therapy in young healthy adults with overt hypothyroidism and after planned (eg, in preparation for thyroid cancer imaging and therapy) or short-term inadvertent lapses in therapy. Patients presenting with subclinical hypothyroidism do not require full replacement doses (ATA/AACE [Garber 2012]).

Adults <50 years with cardiac disease: Initial: 25 to 50 mcg daily; adjust dose by 12.5 to 25 mcg increments at 6- to 8-week intervals as needed

Adults >50 years: Refer to geriatric dosing.

IM, IV: (Canadian labeling; off-label route [IM] and off-label use in US): 50% of the oral dose; alternatively, some clinicians administer up to 80% of the oral dose. **Note:** Bioavailability of the oral formulation is highly variable, but absorption has been measured to be ~80%, when the oral tablet formulation was administered in the recommended fasting state (Dickerson 2010; Fish 1987).

Severe hypothyroidism: Oral: Initial: 12.5 to 25 mcg daily; adjust dose by 25 mcg daily every 2 to 4 weeks as appropriate

Subclinical hypothyroidism (if treated): Oral: Manufacturer's labeling: 1 mcg/kg/day. Alternate recommendations (off-label dose): 25 to 75 mcg daily, with higher doses usually required for those presenting with higher TSH values (ATA/AACE [Garber 2012])

TSH suppression: Oral:

Well-differentiated thyroid cancer (papillary and follicular): Highly individualized; Doses >2 mcg/kg/day may be needed to suppress TSH to <0.1 milliunits/L in intermediate- to high-risk tumors. Low-risk tumors may be maintained at or slightly below the lower limit of normal (0.1 to 0.5 milliunits/L) (Cooper 2009).

Benign nodules and nontoxic multinodular goiter: Routine use of T_4 for TSH suppression is not recommended in patients with benign thyroid nodules. In patients deemed appropriate candidates, treatment should never be fully suppressive (TSH <0.1 milliunits/L) (Cooper 2009; Gharib 2010). The Canadian labeling recommends an initial dose of

1.7 to 2 mcg/kg/day (target TSH: 0.1 to 0.3 milliunits/L). Avoid use if TSH is already suppressed.

Myxedema coma or stupor: IV: 300 to 500 mcg initially, followed by 50 to 100 mcg once daily until patient is able to tolerate oral administration; smaller doses should be considered in patients with cardiovascular disease

Alternate recommendations (off-label dose): Initial loading dose: 200 to 400 mcg; followed by a daily replacement dose of 1.2 mcg/kg/day (which is 75% of the 1.6 mcg/kg oral daily replacement dose reduced for IV administration); smaller doses should be considered for smaller or older patients and those with a history of coronary disease or arrhythmia; institute oral therapy after the patient improves clinically (ATA [Jonklaas 2014])

Cadaveric organ recovery (hormonal resuscitation) (off-label use): IV: Initial: 20 mcg bolus followed by a continuous infusion of 10 mcg/hour administered to the brain-dead donor who is hemodynamically unstable requiring significant vasopressor support; give concomitantly with methylprednisolone, dextrose, and regular insulin (Salim 2007).

Geriatric Doses should be adjusted based on clinical response and laboratory parameters.

Hypothyroidism:

Adults >50 years without cardiac disease: Initial: 25 to 50 mcg daily; adjust dose by 12.5 to 25 mcg increments at 6- to 8-week intervals as needed

Adults >50 years with cardiac disease: Initial: 12.5 to 25 mcg daily; adjust dose by 12.5 to 25 mcg increments at 4- to 6-week intervals (many clinicians prefer to adjust at 6- to 8-week intervals)

Elderly patients may require <1 mcg/kg/day. Elderly patients often require 20% to 25% less per kilogram than younger patients due to decreased body mass (ATA/AACE [Garber 2012]): Refer to adult dosing.

Myxedema coma: Refer to adult dosing; lower doses may be needed.

Pediatric Hypothyroidism: Infants and Children: Doses should be adjusted based on clinical response and laboratory parameters.

Oral: Daily dosage based on body weight and age as listed below:

1 to 3 months: 10 to 15 mcg/kg/day; if the infant is at risk for development of cardiac failure, use a lower starting dose of 25 mcg daily; if the initial serum T_4 is very low (<5 mcg/dL) begin treatment at a higher dosage of approximately 50 mcg daily (12 to 17 mcg/kg/day) (AAP 2006; Selva 2002)

3 to 6 months: 8 to 10 mcg/kg/day

6 to 12 months: 6 to 8 mcg/kg/day

1 to 5 years: 5 to 6 mcg/kg/day

6 to 12 years: 4 to 5 mcg/kg/day

>12 years: 2 to 3 mcg/kg/day

Growth and puberty complete: 1.7 mcg/kg/day; refer to adult dosing (US labeling) or 1.6 to 1.7 mcg/kg/day (Canadian labeling).

Note: Hyperactivity in older children may be minimized by starting at 1/4 of the recommended dose and increasing each week by that amount until the full dose is achieved (4 weeks).

Children with severe or chronic hypothyroidism should be started at 25 mcg daily; adjust dose by 25 mcg every 2 to 4 weeks.

IM (off-label route in US), IV: Refer to adult dosing.

Renal Impairment There are no dosage adjustments provided in the manufacturer's labeling.

Hepatic Impairment There are no dosage adjustments provided in the manufacturer's labeling.

Adjustment for Toxicity

Cardiac symptoms (onset or worsening): Manufacturer labeling recommends reducing dosage or withholding therapy for 7 days and then resuming therapy at reduced dosage. Specific dosing recommendations are not provided.

Mechanism of Action Levothyroxine (T_4) is a synthetic form of thyroxine, an endogenous hormone secreted by the thyroid gland. T_4 is converted to its active metabolite, L-triiodothyronine (T_3). Thyroid hormones (T_4 and T_3) then bind to thyroid receptor proteins in the cell nucleus and exert metabolic effects through control of DNA transcription and protein synthesis; involved in normal metabolism, growth, and development; promotes gluconeogenesis, increases utilization and mobilization of glycogen stores, and stimulates protein synthesis, increases basal metabolic rate

Contraindications

Hypersensitivity to levothyroxine sodium or any component of the formulation; acute MI; untreated subclinical (suppressed serum TSH level with normal T3 and T4 levels) or overt thyrotoxicosis of any etiology; uncorrected adrenal insufficiency.

Capsule: Additional contraindication: Inability to swallow capsules (eg, infants, small children)

Injection:

US labeling: There are no contraindications listed in the manufacturer's labeling when used for labeled indication (treatment of myxedema coma); consider contraindications for oral therapy if using as a temporary substitute for oral treatment (off-label use) in patients with chronic hypothyroidism.

Canadian labeling: Hypersensitivity to levothyroxine sodium or any component of the formulation; acute MI; thyrotoxicosis of any etiology; uncorrected adrenal insufficiency.

Warnings/Precautions [US Boxed Warning]: Thyroid supplements are ineffective and potentially toxic when used for the treatment of obesity or for weight reduction, especially in euthyroid patients. High doses may produce serious or even life-threatening toxic effects particularly when used with some anorectic drugs (eg, sympathomimetic amines). Levothyroxine, either alone or with other concomitant therapeutic agents, should not be used for the treatment of obesity or for weight loss. Routine use of T_4 for TSH suppression is not recommended in patients with benign thyroid nodules. In patients deemed appropriate candidates, treatment should never be fully suppressive (TSH <0.1 milliunits/L). Use with caution and reduce dosage in patients with cardiovascular disease, including heart failure; patients with developing or worsening cardiac symptoms should have their dose reduced or therapy withheld for 7 days then resumed at a reduced dose. Use cautiously in the elderly; suppressed TSH levels may increase risk of atrial fibrillation and mortality secondary to cardiovascular disease (Gharib 2010; Parle 2001). Increase dose slowly in the elderly and monitor for signs/symptoms of angina (ATA/AACE [Garber 2012]). Patients with adrenal insufficiency, myxedema, diabetes mellitus and insipidus may have symptoms exaggerated or aggravated. Use is contraindicated in patients with uncorrected adrenal insufficiency. Treatment with glucocorticoids should precede levothyroxine therapy in patients with adrenal insufficiency (ATA/AACE [Garber 2012]). Chronic hypothyroidism predisposes patients to coronary artery disease. Long-term therapy can decrease bone mineral density. Levoxyl may rapidly swell and disintegrate causing choking or gagging (should be administered with a full glass of water); use caution in patients with dysphagia or other swallowing disorders. Potentially significant drug-drug interactions may exist, requiring dose or frequency adjustment, additional monitoring, and/or selection of alternative therapy.

Drug Interactions

Metabolism/Transport Effects None known.

Avoid Concomitant Use

Avoid concomitant use of Levothyroxine with any of the following: Sodium Iodide I131; Sucroferric Oxyhydroxide

Increased Effect/Toxicity

Levothyroxine may increase the levels/effects of: Tricyclic Antidepressants; Vitamin K Antagonists

The levels/effects of Levothyroxine may be increased by: Piracetam

Decreased Effect

Levothyroxine may decrease the levels/effects of: Sodium Iodide I131; Theophylline Derivatives

The levels/effects of Levothyroxine may be decreased by: Aluminum Hydroxide; Bile Acid Sequestrants; Calcium Polystyrene Sulfonate; Calcium Salts; CarBAMazepine; Ciprofloxacin (Systemic); Estrogen Derivatives; Fosphenytoin; Iron Salts; Lanthanum; Magnesium Salts; Multivitamins/Minerals (with ADEK, Folate, Iron); Orlistat; Patiromer; Phenytoin; Polaprezinc; Raloxifene; RifAMPin; Selective Serotonin Reuptake Inhibitors; Sevelamer; Sodium Polystyrene Sulfonate; Sucralfate; Sucroferric Oxyhydroxide

Food Interactions Taking levothyroxine with enteral nutrition may cause reduced bioavailability and may lower serum thyroxine levels leading to signs or symptoms of hypothyroidism. Soybean flour (infant formula), soy, grapefruit juice, espresso coffee, cottonseed meal, walnuts, and dietary fiber may interfere with absorption of levothyroxine from the GI tract. Management: Take in the morning on an empty stomach at least 30 minutes before food. Consider an increase in dose if taken with enteral tube feed.

Pharmacodynamics/Kinetics

Onset of Action Oral: 3 to 5 days; IV: Within 6 to 8 hours

Half-life Elimination Euthyroid: 6 to 8 days; Hypothyroid: 9 to 10 days; Hyperthyroid: 3 to 4 days

Time to Peak Serum: 2 to 4 hours

Pregnancy Risk Factor A

Pregnancy Considerations Endogenous thyroid hormones minimally cross the placenta; the fetal thyroid becomes active around the end of the first trimester. Levothyroxine has not been shown to increase the risk of congenital abnormalities.

Uncontrolled maternal hypothyroidism may result in adverse neonatal outcomes (eg, premature birth, low birth weight, and respiratory distress) and adverse maternal outcomes (eg, spontaneous abortion, preeclampsia, stillbirth, and premature delivery). To prevent adverse events, normal maternal thyroid function should be maintained prior to conception and throughout pregnancy. TSH concentrations should be monitored every 4 weeks during the first half of pregnancy, at least once between weeks 26 and 32, and ~6 weeks postpartum. Levothyroxine is considered the treatment of choice for the control of hypothyroidism during pregnancy. Due to alterations of endogenous maternal thyroid hormones, the levothyroxine dose may need to be increased during pregnancy and the dose usually needs to be decreased after delivery (Stagnaro-Green 2011).

Breastfeeding Considerations Endogenous thyroid hormones are minimally found in breast milk. The manufacturer recommends that caution be used if administered to a nursing woman.

The amount of endogenous thyroxine found in breast milk does not influence infant plasma thyroid values (van Wassenaer 2002). Levothyroxine was not found to cause adverse events to the infant or mother during breastfeeding (Ito 1993). Adequate thyroid hormone concentrations are required to maintain normal lactation. Appropriate levothyroxine doses should be continued during breastfeeding.

Product Availability Tirosint-Sol (levothyroxine oral solution): FDA approved December 2016; anticipated availability is currently unknown. Information pertaining to this product within the monograph is pending revision.Consult the prescribing information for additional information.

Dosage Forms

Capsule, Oral:

Tirosint: 13 mcg, 25 mcg, 50 mcg, 75 mcg, 88 mcg, 100 mcg, 112 mcg, 125 mcg, 137 mcg, 150 mcg

Solution Reconstituted, Intravenous [preservative free]:

Generic: 100 mcg (1 ea); 200 mcg (1 ea); 500 mcg (1 ea)

Tablet, Oral:

Levoxyl: 25 mcg, 50 mcg, 75 mcg, 88 mcg, 100 mcg, 112 mcg, 125 mcg, 137 mcg, 150 mcg, 175 mcg, 200 mcg

Synthroid: 25 mcg, 50 mcg, 75 mcg, 88 mcg, 100 mcg, 112 mcg, 125 mcg, 137 mcg, 150 mcg, 175 mcg, 200 mcg, 300 mcg

Unithroid: 25 mcg, 50 mcg, 75 mcg, 88 mcg, 100 mcg, 112 mcg, 125 mcg, 137 mcg, 150 mcg, 175 mcg, 200 mcg, 300 mcg

Unithroid Direct: 25 mcg, 50 mcg, 75 mcg, 88 mcg, 100 mcg, 112 mcg, 125 mcg, 150 mcg, 175 mcg, 200 mcg, 300 mcg

Generic: 25 mcg, 50 mcg, 75 mcg, 88 mcg, 100 mcg, 112 mcg, 125 mcg, 137 mcg, 150 mcg, 175 mcg, 200 mcg, 300 mcg

Dosage Forms: Canada Refer also to Dosage Forms.

Note: Capsules are not available in Canada.

Tablet, Oral, as sodium:

Eltroxin: 50 mcg, 100 mcg, 150 mcg, 200 mcg, 300 mcg

Lidocaine (Systemic) (LYE doe kane)

Related Information

Oral Pain *on page 1830*

Brand Names: US ReadySharp Lidocaine; Xylocaine; Xylocaine (Cardiac); Xylocaine-MPF

Brand Names: Canada Xylocard

Generic Availability (US) May be product dependent

Pharmacologic Category Antiarrhythmic Agent, Class Ib; Local Anesthetic

Dental Use Amide-type injectable local anesthetic

Use Local and regional anesthesia by infiltration, nerve block, epidural, or spinal techniques; acute treatment of ventricular arrhythmias from myocardial infarction or cardiac manipulation (eg, cardiac surgery)

Note: The routine prophylactic use of lidocaine to prevent arrhythmia associated with fibrinolytic administration or to suppress isolated ventricular premature beats, couplets, runs of accelerated idioventricular rhythm, and nonsustained ventricular tachycardia (VT) is not recommended (ACCF/AHA [O'Gara, 2013]).

Local Anesthetic/Vasoconstrictor Precautions No information available to require special precautions

Effects on Dental Treatment Key adverse event(s) related to dental treatment: Metallic taste.

Effects on Bleeding No information available to require special precautions

Adverse Reactions Effects vary with route of administration. Many effects are dose-related.

1% to 10%:

Central nervous system: Headache (positional headache following spinal anesthesia: 3%), shivering (following spinal anesthesia: 2%), radiculopathy (≤2%; transient pain; subarachnoid administration)

Frequency not defined:

Cardiovascular: Bradycardia, arterial spasm, cardiac arrhythmia, circulatory shock, edema, flushing, heart block, hypotension (including following spinal anesthesia), local thrombophlebitis, sinus node depression, vascular insufficiency (periarticular injections)

Central nervous system: Agitation, anxiety, apprehension, cauda equina syndrome (following spinal anesthesia), coma, confusion, disorientation, dizziness, drowsiness, euphoria, hallucination, hyperesthesia, hypoesthesia, intolerance to temperature, lethargy, loss of consciousness, metallic taste, nervousness, paresthesia, peripheral neuropathy (following spinal anesthesia), psychosis, seizure, slurred speech, twitching

Gastrointestinal: Nausea (including following spinal anesthesia), vomiting

Hypersensitivity: Anaphylactoid reaction, anaphylaxis, hypersensitivity reaction

Neuromuscular & skeletal: Tremor, weakness

Otic: Tinnitus

Respiratory: Bronchospasm, dyspnea, respiratory depression, respiratory insufficiency (following spinal anesthesia)

<1%, postmarketing, and/or case reports: Asystole, dermatological reaction, diplopia (following spinal anesthesia), methemoglobinemia

Dental Usual Dosage Dosage varies with the anesthetic procedure, degree of anesthesia needed, vascularity of tissue, duration of anesthesia required, and physical condition of patient.

Anesthetic, local injectable: Children and Adults: Varies with procedure, degree of anesthesia needed, vascularity of tissue, duration of anesthesia required, and physical condition of patient; maximum: 4.5 mg/kg/dose not to exceed 300 mg; do not repeat within 2 hours.

Dosing

Adult & Geriatric

Antiarrhythmic (ACLS 2010; ACLS 2015):

VF or pulseless VT (after defibrillation attempts, CPR, and vasopressor administration), alternative to amiodarone: IV, intraosseous (IO): Initial: 1 to 1.5 mg/kg. If refractory VF or pulseless VT, repeat 0.5 to 0.75 mg/kg bolus every 5 to 10 minutes (maximum cumulative dose: 3 mg/kg). Follow with continuous infusion (1 to 4 mg/minute) after return of perfusion. Reappearance of arrhythmia during constant infusion: 0.5 mg/kg bolus and reassessment of infusion (Zipes 2000)

Endotracheal (loading dose only): 2 to 3.75 mg/kg (2 to 2.5 times the recommended IV dose); dilute in 5 to 10 mL NS or sterile water. **Note:** Absorption is greater with sterile water and results in less impairment of PaO_2.

Hemodynamically stable monomorphic VT: IV: 1 to 1.5 mg/kg; repeat with 0.5 to 0.75 mg/kg every 5 to 10 minutes as necessary (maximum cumulative dose: 3 mg/kg). Follow with continuous infusion of 1 to 4 mg/minute (or 14 to 57 mcg/kg/minute).

Note: Reduce maintenance infusion in patients with CHF, shock, or hepatic disease; initiate infusion at 10 mcg/kg/minute (maximum dose: 1.5 mg/minute or 20 mcg/kg/minute).

Anesthesia, local injectable: Varies with procedure, degree of anesthesia needed, vascularity of tissue, duration of anesthesia required, and physical condition of patient.

Cutaneous infiltration: Maximum: 4.5 mg/kg/dose not to exceed 300 mg; do not repeat within 2 hours.

Intraosseous line or infusion pain: Lidocaine 1% or 2% preservative-free solution: Intraosseous: Initial dose: 40 mg over 1 to 2 minutes; usual adult dose range and maximum: 20 to 50 mg/dose; after allowing lidocaine to dwell for up to 1 minute, follow with NS flush; immediately following the NS flush, some centers administer a second lower (50% dose reduction) lidocaine dose over 30 to 60 seconds (usual adult maximum repeat dose: 20 mg/dose); if discomfort reoccurs, may repeat doses at a maximum frequency of every 45 minutes during intraosseous access; maximum total dose not established (Philbeck 2010; Schalk 2011). **Note:** Intraosseous access devices have a minimum weight and age for a particular device in addition to specific instruction for insertion and validation; consult product specific information for more detail.

Interstitial cystitis (bladder pain syndrome) (off-label use): Intravesical:

Various dosage regimens of alkalinized lidocaine alone or with heparin (20,000 to 50,000 units) have been used. There is a risk of precipitation if proper alkalinization does not occur. Lidocaine stability and pH should be determined after the components have been mixed, prior to administration (Parsons 2012)

Single instillation: Single intravesical administration of lidocaine (200 mg)/heparin (50,000 units)/sodium bicarbonate (420 mg) in 15 mL of sterile water, instilled into the bladder via catheter and allowed to dwell for 30 minutes before drainage (Parsons 2012).

Weekly instillation: Weekly bladder instillations for 12 consecutive weeks with lidocaine 4% (5 mL)/heparin (20,000 units)/sodium bicarbonate 7% (25 mL), instilled into an empty bladder via catheter and allowed to dwell for 30 minutes before drainage (Nomiya 2013).

Daily instillation: Daily bladder instillations for 5 days with lidocaine (200 mg)/sodium bicarbonate 8.4% solution (final volume of 10 mL), instilled into an empty bladder and allowed to dwell for 1 hour before drainage (Nickel 2009).

Pediatric

Ventricular arrhythmias, shock-refractory VF or pulseless VT (PALS [de Caen 2015]; PALS [Kleinman 2010]): Infants, Children, and Adolescents:

IV, intraosseous (IO):

Loading dose: 1 mg/kg; follow with continuous infusion; may administer second bolus if delay between initial bolus and start of infusion is >15 minutes

Continuous infusion: 20 to 50 mcg/kg/minute. Per the manufacturer, do not exceed 20 mcg/kg/minute in patients with shock, hepatic disease, cardiac arrest, or CHF.

Endotracheal: Loading dose: 2 to 3 mg/kg; flush with 5 mL of NS and follow with 5 assisted manual ventilations

Anesthesia, local injectable: Dose varies with procedure, degree of anesthesia needed, vascularity of tissue, duration of anesthesia required, and physical condition of patient

Cutaneous infiltration: Children and Adolescents: Typically solutions with concentration <2% should be used (allow for larger volumes); maximum dose: 5 mg/kg/dose not to exceed the recommended adult maximum dose of 300 mg/dose; do not repeat within 2 hours (Kliegman 2016)

Intraosseous line or infusion pain: Infants, Children, and Adolescents: Lidocaine 1% or 2% preservative-free solution: Intraosseous: Initial dose: 0.5 mg/kg over 1 to 2 minutes; usual adult dose range and maximum: 20 to 50 mg/dose; follow with NS flush; immediately following the NS flush, some centers administer a second lower (50% dose reduction) lidocaine dose over 30 to 60 seconds (usual adult maximum repeat dose: 20 mg/dose); if discomfort reoccurs, may repeat doses at a maximum frequency of every 45 minutes during intraosseous access; maximum total dose not established, some centers suggest that dose should not exceed: 3 mg/kg/24 hours (Hartholt 2010; Nagler 2011; Philbeck 2010; Schalk 2011). **Note:** Intraosseous access devices have a minimum weight and age for a particular device in addition to specific instruction for insertion and validation; consult product specific information for more detail.

Renal Impairment No dosage adjustment provided in manufacturer's labeling. However, accumulation of metabolites may be increased in renal dysfunction. Not dialyzable (0% to 5%) by hemo- or peritoneal dialysis; supplemental dose is not necessary.

Hepatic Impairment Use with caution; reduce maintenance infusion. Initial: 0.75 mg/minute or 10 mcg/kg/minute; maximum dose: 1.5 mg/minute or 20 mcg/kg/minute. Monitor lidocaine concentrations closely and adjust infusion rate as necessary; consider alternative therapy.

Mechanism of Action Class Ib antiarrhythmic; suppresses automaticity of conduction tissue, by increasing electrical stimulation threshold of ventricle, His-Purkinje system, and spontaneous depolarization of the ventricles during diastole by a direct action on the tissues; blocks both the initiation and conduction of nerve impulses by decreasing the neuronal membrane's permeability to sodium ions, which results in inhibition of depolarization with resultant blockade of conduction

Contraindications Hypersensitivity to lidocaine or any component of the formulation; hypersensitivity to another local anesthetic of the amide type; Adam-Stokes syndrome; Wolff-Parkinson-White syndrome; severe degrees of SA, AV, or intraventricular heart block (except in patients with a functioning artificial pacemaker); premixed injection may contain corn-derived dextrose and its use is contraindicated in patients with allergy to corn or corn-related products

Warnings/Precautions Use caution in patients with severe hepatic dysfunction or pseudocholinesterase deficiency; may have increased risk of lidocaine toxicity.

Intravenous: Constant ECG monitoring is necessary during IV administration. Use cautiously in hepatic impairment, HF, marked hypoxia, severe respiratory depression, hypovolemia, history of malignant hyperthermia, or shock. Increased ventricular rate may be seen when administered to a patient with atrial fibrillation. Correct electrolyte disturbances, especially hypokalemia or hypomagnesemia, prior to use and throughout therapy. Use is contraindicated in patients with Wolff-Parkinson-White syndrome and severe degrees of SA, AV, or intraventricular heart block (except in patients with a functioning artificial pacemaker). Correct any underlying causes of ventricular arrhythmias. Monitor closely for signs and symptoms of CNS toxicity. The elderly may be prone to increased CNS and cardiovascular side effects. Reduce dose in hepatic dysfunction and CHF.

Benzyl alcohol and derivatives: Some dosage forms may contain benzyl alcohol; large amounts of benzyl alcohol (≥99 mg/kg/day) have been associated with a potentially fatal toxicity ("gasping syndrome") in neonates; the "gasping syndrome" consists of metabolic acidosis, respiratory distress, gasping respirations, CNS dysfunction (including convulsions, intracranial hemorrhage), hypotension, and cardiovascular collapse (AAP ["Inactive" 1997]; CDC, 1982); some data suggests that benzoate displaces bilirubin from protein binding sites (Ahlfors, 2001); avoid or use dosage forms containing benzyl alcohol with caution in neonates. See manufacturer's labeling.

Injectable anesthetic: Follow appropriate administration techniques so as not to administer any intravascularly. Continuous intra-articular infusion of local anesthetics after arthroscopic or other surgical procedures is **not** an approved use; chondrolysis (primarily in the shoulder joint) has occurred following infusion, with some cases requiring arthroplasty or shoulder replacement. Solutions containing antimicrobial preservatives should not be used for epidural or spinal anesthesia. Some solutions contain a bisulfite; avoid in patients who are allergic to bisulfite. Resuscitative equipment, medicine and oxygen should be available in case of emergency. Use products containing epinephrine cautiously in patients with significant vascular disease, compromised blood flow, or during or following general anesthesia (increased risk of arrhythmias). Adjust the dose for the elderly, pediatric, acutely ill, and debilitated patients.

Drug Interactions

Metabolism/Transport Effects Substrate of CYP1A2 (major), CYP2A6 (minor), CYP2B6 (minor), CYP2C9 (minor), CYP3A4 (major); **Note:** Assignment of Major/Minor substrate status based on clinically relevant drug interaction potential; **Inhibits** CYP1A2 (weak)

Avoid Concomitant Use

Avoid concomitant use of Lidocaine (Systemic) with any of the following: Conivaptan; Fusidic Acid (Systemic); Idelalisib; Saquinavir

Increased Effect/Toxicity

Lidocaine (Systemic) may increase the levels/effects of: Bupivacaine (Liposomal); CloZAPine; Neuromuscular-Blocking Agents; Prilocaine; Sodium Nitrite; TiZANidine

The levels/effects of Lidocaine (Systemic) may be increased by: Abiraterone Acetate; Amiodarone; Aprepitant; Beta-Blockers; Conivaptan; CYP1A2 Inhibitors (Moderate); CYP1A2 Inhibitors (Strong); CYP3A4 Inhibitors (Moderate); CYP3A4 Inhibitors (Strong); Dapsone (Topical); Dasatinib; Deferasirox;

Disopyramide; Fosaprepitant; Fusidic Acid (Systemic); Hyaluronidase; Idelalisib; Ivacaftor; MiFEPRIStone; Netupitant; Nitric Oxide; Obeticholic Acid; Palbociclib; Peginterferon Alfa-2b; Saquinavir; Simeprevir; Stiripentol; Telaprevir; Tetracaine (Topical); Vemurafenib

Decreased Effect

Lidocaine (Systemic) may decrease the levels/effects of: Technetium Tc 99m Tilmanocept

The levels/effects of Lidocaine (Systemic) may be decreased by: Bosentan; Cannabis; CYP1A2 Inducers (Strong); CYP3A4 Inducers (Moderate); CYP3A4 Inducers (Strong); Cyproterone; Dabrafenib; Deferasirox; Enzalutamide; Etravirine; Mitotane; Siltuximab; St John's Wort; Teriflunomide; Tocilizumab

Dietary Considerations Premixed injection may contain corn-derived dextrose and its use is contraindicated in patients with allergy to corn-related products.

Pharmacodynamics/Kinetics

Onset of Action Single bolus dose: 45 to 90 seconds

Duration of Action 10 to 20 minutes

Half-life Elimination Biphasic: Prolonged with congestive heart failure, liver disease, shock, severe renal disease; Initial: 7 to 30 minutes; Terminal: Infants, premature: 3.2 hours, Adults: 1.5 to 2 hours

Pregnancy Risk Factor B

Pregnancy Considerations Adverse events were not observed in animal reproduction studies. Lidocaine and its metabolites cross the placenta and can be detected in the fetal circulation following injection (Cavalli 2004; Mitani 1987). Adverse reactions in the fetus/neonate may affect the CNS, heart, or peripheral vascular tone. Fetal heart monitoring is recommended. Lidocaine injection is approved for obstetric analgesia. Lidocaine administered by local infiltration is used to provide analgesia prior to episiotomy and during repair of obstetric lacerations (ACOG 2002). Administration by the perineal route may result in greater absorption than administration by the epidural route (Cavalli 2004). Cumulative exposure from all routes of administration should be considered. Medications used for the treatment of cardiac arrest in pregnancy are the same as in the non-pregnant woman. Doses and indications should follow current Advanced Cardiovascular Life Support guidelines. Appropriate medications should not be withheld due to concerns of fetal teratogenicity (Jeejeebhoy [AHA] 2015).

Breastfeeding Considerations Lidocaine is excreted into breast milk. The manufacturer recommends that caution be used when administered to a nursing woman. When administered by injection for dental or obstetric analgesia, small amounts are detected in breast milk; oral bioavailability to the nursing infant is expected to be low and the amount of lidocaine available to the nursing infant would not be expected to cause adverse events (Lebedevs, 1993; Ortega, 1999). Cumulative exposure from all routes of administration should be considered.

Dosage Forms

Kit, Injection:

ReadySharp Lidocaine: 1%

Solution, Injection:

Xylocaine: 0.5% (50 mL); 1% (20 mL, 50 mL); 2% (10 mL, 20 mL, 50 mL)

Generic: 0.5% (50 mL); 1% (2 mL, 10 mL, 20 mL, 50 mL); 2% (2 mL, 20 mL, 50 mL)

Solution, Injection [preservative free]:

Xylocaine-MPF: 0.5% (50 mL); 1% (2 mL, 5 mL, 10 mL, 30 mL); 1.5% (10 mL, 20 mL); 2% (5 mL, 10 mL); 4% (5 mL)

Generic: 0.5% (50 mL); 1% (2 mL, 5 mL, 30 mL); 1.5% (20 mL); 2% (2 mL, 5 mL, 10 mL); 4% (5 mL)

Solution, Intravenous:

Xylocaine (Cardiac): 2% [20 mg/mL] (5 mL)

Generic: 0.4% [4 mg/mL] (250 mL, 500 mL); 0.8% [8 mg/mL] (250 mL); 1% [10 mg/mL] (5 mL); 2% [20 mg/mL] (5 mL); 5% [50 mg/mL] (2 mL)

Solution, Intravenous [preservative free]:

Generic: 1% [10 mg/mL] (5 mL); 2% [20 mg/mL] (5 mL)

Lidocaine (Topical) (LYE doe kane)

Related Information

Perioral Premalignant Lesions and Management of Patients Undergoing Cancer Therapy *on page 1875*

Viral Infections *on page 1849*

Brand Names: US Alocane Emergency Burn Max Str [OTC]; Anastia; AneCream [OTC]; AneCream5 [OTC]; Astero; CidalEaze; Eha; EnovaRX-Lidocaine HCl; Glydo; LC-4 Lidocaine [OTC]; LC-5 Lidocaine [OTC]; LDO Plus; Lido-K; Lidocaine PAK; Lidocin [DSC]; Lidoderm; Lidopac; Lidopin; LidoRx; Lidotral; Lidotrans 5 Pak; Lidovex; Lidovin; Lidozol; LMX 4 Plus [OTC]; LMX 4 [OTC]; LMX 5 [OTC]; LTA 360 Kit [DSC]; Numbonex; Predator [OTC]; Premium Lidocaine; Prozena [DSC]; Prozena [OTC] [DSC]; RectaSmoothe [OTC]; Recti-Care [OTC]; Topicaine 5 [OTC]; Topicaine [OTC] [DSC]; Venipuncture Px1 Phlebotomy; Xolido XP [OTC]; Xolido [OTC]; Xryliderm; Xylocaine; Zeyocaine; Zingo

Brand Names: Canada Betacaine; Lidodan; Lidoderm; Maxilene; Xylocaine

Generic Availability (US) May be product dependent

Pharmacologic Category Analgesic, Topical; Local Anesthetic

Dental Use Topical local anesthetic

Patch: Production of mild topical anesthesia of accessible mucous membranes of the mouth prior to superficial dental procedures

Oral topical solution (viscous): Reduce gagging during dental impressions and x-rays

Use

Intradermal injection (Zingo): Topical local analgesia prior to venipuncture or peripheral intravenous (IV) cannulation in children ≥3 years; topical local analgesia prior to venipuncture in adults.

Jelly: Prevention and control of pain in procedures involving the male and female urethra; for topical treatment of painful urethritis

Oral topical solution (2% viscous): Topical anesthesia of irritated or inflamed oral mucous membranes and pharyngeal tissue; reducing gagging during the taking of x-ray. **Note:** Not approved for relief of teething pain and discomfort in infants and children; serious adverse (toxic) effects have been reported (AAP 2011; AAPD 2012; ISMP 2014).

Oral topical solution (4%): Topical anesthesia of accessible mucous membranes of the oral and nasal cavities and proximal portions of the digestive tract. **Note:** Not approved for relief of teething pain and discomfort in infants and children; serious adverse (toxic) effects have been reported (AAP 2011; AAPD 2012; ISMP 2014).

Oral topical solution (metered-dose spray) [Canadian product]: Topical anesthesia of accessible mucous membranes of the oral and nasal cavities and proximal portions of the digestive tract.

Patch (Lidoderm): Relief of pain associated with postherpetic neuralgia

Patch (LidoPatch): Temporary relief of localized pain

Rectal: Temporary relief of pain and itching due to anorectal disorders

Topical: Local anesthetic for mucous membrane of the oropharynx; lubricant for intubation; use in laser/cosmetic surgeries; pruritus, pruritic eczemas, insect bites, pain, soreness, minor burns (including sunburns), cuts, and abrasions of the skin; discomfort due to pruritus ani, pruritus vulvae, hemorrhoids, anal fissures, and similar conditions of the skin and mucous membranes.

Local Anesthetic/Vasoconstrictor Precautions No information available to require special precautions

Effects on Dental Treatment Key adverse event(s) related to dental treatment: Metallic taste.

Effects on Bleeding No information available to require special precautions

Adverse Reactions Frequency not always defined. **Note:** Adverse effects vary with formulation and extent of systemic absorption; children may be at increased risk.

Cardiovascular: Edema (intradermal powder: 4% to 8%), bradycardia

Central nervous system: Apprehension, confusion, dizziness, drowsiness, paresthesia

Dermatologic: Erythema (adults, intradermal powder: 67%; children 3 to 18 years, intradermal powder: 53%), petechia (intradermal powder: 44% to 46%), pruritus (intradermal powder: 9%), dermatitis, exacerbation of pain (topical patch), skin depigmentation (topical patch), skin edema (topical patch), skin rash, urticaria

Gastrointestinal: Nausea (intradermal powder: 2%), vomiting (intradermal powder: 1%)

Hematologic and oncologic: Bruise (topical patch), methemoglobinemia

Hypersensitivity: Anaphylactoid reaction, angioedema, hypersensitivity reaction

Local: Local irritation (topical patch)

Neuromuscular & skeletal: Weakness

Dental Usual Dosage Anesthesia, topical:

Oral topical solution (viscous): **Note:** Not approved for relief of teething pain and discomfort in infants and children; serious adverse (toxic) effects have been reported; AAP, AAPD, and ISMP strongly discourage use (AAP 2011; AAPD 2012; ISMP 2014).

Infants and Children <3 years: ≤1.2 mL applied to area with a cotton-tipped applicator no more frequently than every 3 hours (maximum: 4 doses per 12-hour period); use only if the underlying condition requires treatment with product volume of ≤1.2 mL)

Children ≥3 years and Adolescents: Should not exceed 4.5mg/kg/dose (or 300mg/dose); swished in the mouth and spit out no more frequently than every 3 hours (maximum: 4 doses per 12-hour period)

Adults: Anesthesia of the mouth: 15 mL swished in the mouth and spit out no more frequently than every 3 hours (maximum: 8 doses per 24-hour period)

Postherpetic neuralgia: Adults: Patch: Apply patch to most painful area. Up to 3 patches may be applied in a single application. Patch may remain in place for up to 12 hours in any 24-hour period.

Dosing

Adult Anesthesia, topical:

Cream:

LidaMantle, Lidovex: Skin irritation: Apply a thin film to affected area 2 to 3 times daily as needed

LMX 4: Skin irritation: Apply up to 3 to 4 times daily to intact skin

LMX 5: Relief of anorectal pain and itching: Apply to affected area up to 6 times daily

Gel: Apply to affected area ≤4 times daily as needed (maximum dose: 4.5 mg/kg, not to exceed 300 mg)

Intradermal injection: Apply one intradermal lidocaine (0.5 mg) device to the site planned for venipuncture, 1 to 3 minutes prior to needle insertion.

Topical solution: Apply 1 to 5 mL (40 to 200 mg) to affected area

Jelly: Maximum dose: 30 mL (600 mg) in any 12-hour period:

Anesthesia of male urethra: 5 to 30 mL (100 to 600 mg)

Anesthesia of female urethra: 3 to 5 mL (60 to 100 mg)

Lotion: Apply a thin film to affected area 2 or 3 times daily.

Ointment: Apply as a single application not exceeding 5 g of ointment (equivalent to lidocaine base 250 mg); maximum: 20 g of ointment/day (equivalent to lidocaine base 1,000 mg/day).

Oral topical solution (2% viscous):

Anesthesia of the mouth: 15 mL swished in the mouth and spit out no more frequently than every 3 hours (maximum: 4.5 mg/kg [or 300 mg per dose]; 8 doses per 24-hour period)

Anesthesia of the pharynx: 15 mL gargled no more frequently than every 3 hours (maximum: 4.5 mg/kg [or 300 mg per dose]; 8 doses per 24-hour period); may be swallowed

Oral topical solution (4%): **Note:** For use in mucous membranes of oral and nasal cavities and proximal GI tract. Apply 1 to 5 mL (40 to 200 mg) to affected area (maximum dose: 4.5 mg/kg, not to exceed 300 mg per dose)

Oral topical endotracheal solution, metered-dose spray (10 mg/actuation) [Canadian product]:

Nasal: 20 to 60 mg (maximum dose: 500 mg for procedure <1 minute or 600 mg for procedure >5 minutes)

Oropharyngeal: 20 to 200 mg (maximum dose: 500 mg for procedure <1 minute or 600 mg for procedure >5 minutes)

Respiratory tract: 50 to 400 mg (maximum dose: 400 mg for procedure <1 minute or 600 mg for procedure >5 minutes)

Trachea, larynx, bronchi: 50 to 200 mg (maximum dose: 200 mg for procedure <1 minute or 400 mg for procedure >5 minutes)

Patch:

Lidoderm: Postherpetic neuralgia: Apply patch to most painful area. Up to 3 patches may be applied in a single application. Patch(es) may remain in place for up to 12 hours in any 24-hour period.

LidoPatch: Pain (localized): Apply patch to painful area. Patch may remain in place for up to 12 hours in any 24-hour period. No more than 1 patch should be used in a 24-hour period.

Geriatric Refer to adult dosing. Administer reduced doses commensurate with age and physical status.

Pediatric Anesthesia, topical: Note: Smaller areas of treatment recommended in younger or smaller patients (<12 months or <10 kg) or those with impaired elimination (Fein 2012); use lowest effective dose

Cream:

LidaMantle, Lidovex: Skin irritation: Children and Adolescents: Refer to adult dosing.

LMX 4 (liposomal lidocaine 4%):

Skin irritation: Children ≥2 years and Adolescents: Refer to adult dosing.

Minor dermal procedures (eg, IV access, venipuncture, lumbar puncture, abscess drainage, joint aspiration); anesthetic (off-label):

Infants and Children <4 years: 1 g applied to site (6.25 cm^2 of skin) 30 minutes prior to procedure (Fein 2012; Taddio 2004)

Children ≥4 years and Adolescents ≤17 years: 1 g to 2.5 g applied to site (6.25 cm^2 of skin) 30 minutes prior to procedure (Eichenfield 2002; Fein 2012; Koh 2004; Luhman 2004; Taddio 2004)

LMX 5: Relief of anorectal pain and itching: Children ≥12 years and Adolescents: Refer to adult dosing.

Jelly: Children and Adolescents: Dose varies with age and weight (maximum dose: 4.5 mg/kg)

Intradermal injection: Children ≥3 years and Adolescents: Apply one intradermal lidocaine (0.5 mg) device to the site planned for venipuncture or IV cannulation, 1 to 3 minutes prior to needle insertion.

Lotion: Children and Adolescents: Refer to adult dosing.

Ointment: Children and Adolescents: Dose varies with age and weight, apply single application not exceeding 5 g of ointment (equivalent to lidocaine base 250 mg); maximum dose: lidocaine base 4.5 mg/kg.

Oral topical solution (2% viscous): **Note:** Not approved for relief of teething pain and discomfort in infants and children; serious adverse (toxic) effects have been reported; AAP, AAPD, and ISMP strongly discourage use (AAP 2011; AAPD 2012; ISMP 2014).

Infants and Children <3 years: ≤1.2 mL applied to area with a cotton-tipped applicator no more frequently than every 3 hours (maximum: 4 doses per 12-hour period; use only if the underlying condition requires treatment with product volume of ≤1.2 mL)

Children ≥3 years and Adolescents: Do not exceed 4.5 mg/kg/dose (or 300 mg per dose); swished in the mouth and spit out no more frequently than every 3 hours (maximum: 4 doses per 12-hour period)

Oral topical solution (4%): **Note:** For use in mucous membranes of oral and nasal cavities and proximal GI tract. Children and Adolescents: Dose varies with age and weight (maximum dose: 4.5 mg/kg)

Oral topical endotracheal solution, metered-dose spray (10 mg/actuation) [Canadian product]: Children ≥2 years and Adolescents: Dose varies with age and weight (maximum dose [children ≥2 to <12 years]: Laryngotracheal: 3 mg/kg; nasal/oropharyngeal: 4 to 5 mg/kg)

Renal Impairment There are no dosage adjustments provided in the manufacturer's labeling.

Hepatic Impairment There are no dosage adjustments provided in the manufacturer's labeling; use caution in patients with severe hepatic disease.

Mechanism of Action Blocks both the initiation and conduction of nerve impulses by decreasing the neuronal membrane's permeability to sodium ions, which results in inhibition of depolarization with resultant blockade of conduction

Contraindications Hypersensitivity to lidocaine or any component of the formulation; hypersensitivity to another local anesthetic of the amide type; traumatized mucosa, bacterial infection at the site of application (lotion and Lidovex only).

Warnings/Precautions Use with caution in patients with known drug sensitivities. Allergic reactions (cutaneous lesions, urticaria, edema, or anaphylactoid reactions) may be a result of sensitivity to lidocaine (rare) or preservatives used in formulations. Patients allergic to para-aminobenzoic acid (PABA) derivatives (eg, procaine, tetracaine, benzocaine) have not shown cross sensitivity to lidocaine. Potentially life-threatening side effects (eg, irregular heart beat, seizures, coma, respiratory depression, death) have occurred when used prior to cosmetic procedures. Excessive dosing for any indication (eg, application to large areas, use above recommended dose, application to denuded or inflamed skin, or wearing of device for longer than recommended), smaller patients, and/or impaired elimination may lead to increased absorption and systemic toxicity; patient should adhere strictly to recommended dosage and administration guidelines; serious adverse effects may require the use of supportive care and resuscitative equipment. Use caution in patients with severe hepatic disease and/or pseudocholinesterase deficiency due to diminished ability to metabolize systemically-absorbed lidocaine. Use with caution in patients with severe shock or heart block. Use with extreme caution in the presence of sepsis/or severely traumatized mucosa due to an increased risk of rapid systemic absorption at application site. Elderly, debilitated patients, children, and acutely ill patients should be given reduced doses commensurate with their age and physical status. Use intradermal injection with caution in patients with bleeding tendencies/platelet disorders; may have a higher risk of superficial dermal bleeding. May potentially trigger malignant hyperthermia; follow standard protocol for identification and treatment.

When topical anesthetics are used prior to cosmetic or medical procedures, the lowest amount of anesthetic necessary for pain relief should be applied. High systemic levels and toxic effects (eg, methemoglobinemia, irregular heart beats, respiratory depression, seizures, death) have been reported in patients who (without supervision of a trained professional) have applied topical anesthetics in large amounts (or to large areas of the skin), left these products on for prolonged periods of time, or have used wraps/dressings to cover the skin following application. Irritation, sensitivity and/or infection may occur at the site of application; discontinue use and institute appropriate therapy if local effects occur. Potentially significant interactions may exist, requiring dose or frequency adjustment, additional monitoring, and/or selection of alternative therapy.

Topical cream, liquid, lotion, gel, and ointment: Do not leave on large body areas for >2 hours. Not for ophthalmic use. Some products are not recommended for use on mucous membranes; consult specific product labeling.

Intradermal injection: Only use on skin locations where an adequate seal can be maintained. Do not use on body orifices, mucous membranes, around the eyes, or on areas with a compromised skin barrier.

Topical oral solution/viscous: **[US Boxed Warning]: Life-threatening and fatal events in infants and young children:** Postmarketing cases of seizures, cardiopulmonary arrest, and death in patients <3 years have been reported with use of lidocaine 2% viscous solution when it was not administered in strict adherence to the dosing and administration recommendations. Lidocaine 2% viscous solution should generally not be used for teething pain. For other conditions, the use of lidocaine 2% viscous solution in patients <3 years should be limited to those situations where safer alternatives are not available or have been tried but failed. To decrease the risk of serious adverse events, instruct caregivers to strictly adhere to the prescribed dose and frequency of administration, and store the prescription bottle safely out of reach of children. Multiple cases of seizures (including fatalities) have occurred in pediatric patients using viscous lidocaine for oral discomfort, including teething pain and stomatitis (Curtis 2009; Giard 1983; Gonzalez del Ray 1994; Hess 1988; Mofenson 1983; Puczynski 1985; Rothstein 1982; Smith 1992). The FDA recommends against using topical OTC medications for teething pain as some products may cause harm. The American Academy of Pediatrics (AAP) recommends managing teething pain with a chilled (not frozen) teething ring or gently rubbing/massaging with the caregiver's finger.

When used in mouth or throat, topical anesthesia may impair swallowing and increase aspiration risk. Avoid food for ≥60 minutes following oral or throat application. This is especially important in the pediatric population. Numbness may increase the danger of tongue/buccal biting trauma; ingesting food or chewing gum should be avoided while mouth or throat is anesthetized. Excessive doses or frequent application may result in high plasma levels and serious adverse effects; strictly adhere to dosing instructions. Use measuring devices to measure the correct volume, if applicable, to ensure accuracy of dose.

Use of topical anesthetics for teething is discouraged by the AAP, the American Academy of Pediatric Dentistry, and the ISMP (AAP 2012; AAPD 2012; ISMP 2014).

Topical patch: Apply only on intact skin. Do not use around or in the eyes. To avoid accidental ingestion by children, store and dispose of products out of the reach of children. Avoid exposing application site to external heat sources (eg, heating pad, electric blanket, heat lamp, hot tub).

Benzyl alcohol and derivatives: Some dosage forms may contain benzyl alcohol; large amounts of benzyl alcohol (≥99 mg/kg/day) have been associated with a potentially fatal toxicity ("gasping syndrome") in neonates; the "gasping syndrome" consists of metabolic acidosis, respiratory distress, gasping respirations, CNS dysfunction (including convulsions, intracranial hemorrhage), hypotension, and cardiovascular collapse (AAP ["Inactive" 1997]; CDC 1982); some data suggests that benzoate displaces bilirubin from protein binding sites (Ahlfors 2001); avoid or use dosage forms containing benzyl alcohol with caution in neonates.

Some dosage forms may contain polysorbate 80 (also known as Tweens). Hypersensitivity reactions, usually a delayed reaction, have been reported following exposure to pharmaceutical products containing polysorbate 80 in certain individuals (Isaksson 2002; Lucente 2000; Shelley 1995). Thrombocytopenia, ascites, pulmonary deterioration, and renal and hepatic failure have been reported in premature neonates after receiving parenteral products containing polysorbate 80 (Alade 1986; CDC 1984). See manufacturer's labeling.

Drug Interactions

Metabolism/Transport Effects **Substrate** of CYP1A2 (major), CYP2A6 (minor), CYP2B6 (minor), CYP2C9 (minor), CYP3A4 (major); **Note:** Assignment of Major/Minor substrate status based on clinically relevant drug interaction potential; **Inhibits** CYP1A2 (weak)

Avoid Concomitant Use

Avoid concomitant use of Lidocaine (Topical) with any of the following: Conivaptan; Fusidic Acid (Systemic); Idelalisib

Increased Effect/Toxicity

Lidocaine (Topical) may increase the levels/effects of: Antiarrhythmic Agents (Class III); CloZAPine; Prilocaine; Sodium Nitrite; TiZANidine

The levels/effects of Lidocaine (Topical) may be increased by: Abiraterone Acetate; Antiarrhythmic Agents (Class III); Aprepitant; Beta-Blockers; Conivaptan; CYP1A2 Inhibitors (Moderate); CYP1A2 Inhibitors (Strong); CYP3A4 Inhibitors (Moderate); CYP3A4 Inhibitors (Strong); Dapsone (Topical); Dasatinib; Deferasirox; Disopyramide; Fosaprepitant; Fusidic Acid (Systemic); Idelalisib; Ivacaftor; MiFEPRIStone; Netupitant; Nitric Oxide; Obeticholic Acid; Palbociclib; Peginterferon Alfa-2b; Simeprevir; Stiripentol; Tetracaine (Topical); Vemurafenib

Decreased Effect There are no known significant interactions involving a decrease in effect.

Pharmacodynamics/Kinetics

Onset of Action Intradermal injection: 1 to 3 minutes; Topical: 3 to 5 minutes; Transdermal: ~4 hours (Davies 2004)

Duration of Action Intradermal injection: 10 minutes

Half-life Elimination

IV: 1.5 to 2 hours; prolonged 2-fold or more in hepatic impairment

Time to Peak Transdermal (5%): 11 hours (following application of 3 patches)

Pregnancy Risk Factor B

Pregnancy Considerations Adverse events were not observed in animal reproduction studies using the systemic injection. Lidocaine and its metabolites cross the placenta and can be detected in the fetal circulation following injection (Cavalli 2004; Mitani 1987). The amount of lidocaine absorbed topically (and therefore available systemically to potentially reach the fetus) varies by dose administered, duration of exposure, and site of application. Cumulative exposure from all routes of administration should be considered.

Breastfeeding Considerations Lidocaine is excreted into breast milk. The manufacturer recommends caution be used when administering lidocaine to nursing women. When administered by injection for dental or obstetric analgesia, small amounts are detected in breast milk; oral bioavailability to the nursing infant is expected to be low. The amount of lidocaine available to the nursing infant would not be expected to cause adverse events (Lebedevs 1993; Ortega 1999). Cumulative exposure from all routes of administration should be considered.

Dosage Forms Considerations

EnovaRX-Lidocaine cream is compounded from a kit. Refer to manufacturer's package insert for compounding instructions.

Dosage Forms

Cream, External:

AneCream [OTC]: 4% (5 g, 15 g, 30 g)
AneCream5 [OTC]: 5% (15 g)
CidalEaze: 3% (453.6 g)
EnovaRX-Lidocaine HCl: 5% (60 g, 120 g); 10% (60 g, 120 g)
LC-4 Lidocaine [OTC]: 4% (45 g)
LC-5 Lidocaine [OTC]: 5% (45 g)
Lidopin: 3% (28 g, 85 g); 3.25% (28 g, 85 g)
Lidotral: 3.88% (85 g)
Lidovex: 3.75% (60 g)
Lidovin: 3.95% (60 g)
Lidozol: 3.75% (60 g)
LMX 4 [OTC]: 4% (5 g, 15 g, 30 g)
LMX 5 [OTC]: 5% (15 g, 30 g)
Predator [OTC]: 4% (63 g)
RectaSmoothe [OTC]: 5% (30 g)
RectiCare [OTC]: 5% (15 g, 30 g)
Xolido [OTC]: 2% (118 mL)
Xolido XP [OTC]: 4% (118 mL)
Generic: 3% (28.3 g, 28.35 g, 85 g); 4% (5 g, 15 g, 30 g, 120 g); 5% (15 g, 30 g)

Gel, External:

Alocane Emergency Burn Max Str [OTC]: 4% (75 mL)
Astero: 4% (30 mL)
LDO Plus: 4% (30 mL)
LidoRx: 3% (10 mL, 30 mL, 90 mL)
Topicaine 5 [OTC]: 5% (10 g, 30 g, 113 g)
Generic: 2% (5 mL, 20 mL, 30 mL)

Gel, External [preservative free]:

Glydo: 2% (6 mL, 11 mL)
Generic: 2% (5 mL, 10 mL)

Jet-injector, Intradermal:

Zingo: 0.5 mg (1 ea)

Kit, External:

AneCream [OTC]: 4%
Lidopac: 5%
Lidotrans 5 Pak: 5%
LMX 4 Plus [OTC]: 4%
Venipuncture Px1 Phlebotomy: 2%
Xryliderm: 5%
Zeyocaine: 5%
Generic: 4%

Lotion, External:

Anastia: 2.75% (15 g)
Eha: 4% (88 mL)
Lido-K: 3% (177 mL)
Numbonex: 2.75% (30 g)
Generic: 3% (118 mL, 177 mL)

Ointment, External:

Lidocaine PAK: 5% (30 g)
Premium Lidocaine: 5% (50 g)
Generic: 5% (30 g, 35.44 g, 50 g, 2500 g)

Patch, External:

Lidoderm: 5% (1 ea, 30 ea)
Generic: 5% (1 ea, 15 ea, 30 ea)

Solution, External:

Xylocaine: 4% (50 mL)
Generic: 4% (50 mL)

Solution, Mouth/Throat:

Generic: 2% (15 mL, 100 mL)

Solution, Mouth/Throat [preservative free]:

Generic: 4% (4 mL)

Dosage Forms: Canada

Solution, Mouth/Throat:

Xylocaine Endotracheal: 10 mg/actuation (50 mL)

Lidocaine and Epinephrine

(LYE doe kane & ep i NEF rin)

Related Information

EPINEPHrine (Systemic) *on page 580*
Lidocaine (Systemic) *on page 987*
Oral Pain *on page 1830*

Brand Names: US Lignospan Forte; Lignospan Standard; Xylocaine MPF With Epinephrine; Xylocaine With Epinephrine

Brand Names: Canada Xylocaine With Epinephrine

Generic Availability (US) Yes

Pharmacologic Category Local Anesthetic

Dental Use Amide-type anesthetic used for local infiltration anesthesia injection near nerve trunks to produce nerve block

Use Anesthesia, local: Production of local anesthesia by nerve block or infiltration for dental procedures.

Local Anesthetic/Vasoconstrictor Precautions No information available to require special precautions

Effects on Dental Treatment It is common to misinterpret psychogenic responses to local anesthetic injection as an allergic reaction. Intraoral injections are perceived by many patients as a stressful procedure in dentistry. Common symptoms to this stress are diaphoresis, palpitations, hyperventilation. Patients may exhibit hypersensitivity to bisulfites contained in local anesthetic solution to prevent oxidation of epinephrine. In general, patients reacting to bisulfites have a history of asthma and their airways are hyper-reactive to asthmatic syndrome.

Degree of adverse effects in the CNS and cardiovascular system is directly related to the blood levels of lidocaine: Bradycardia, hypersensitivity reactions (rare; may be manifest as dermatologic reactions and edema at injection site), asthmatic syndromes

High blood levels: Anxiety, restlessness, disorientation, confusion, dizziness, tremors, seizures, CNS depression (resulting in somnolence, unconsciousness and possible respiratory arrest), nausea, and vomiting.

Effects on Bleeding No information available to require special precautions

Adverse Reactions Degree of adverse effects in the central nervous system and cardiovascular system are directly related to the blood levels of lidocaine. The effects below are more likely to occur after systemic administration rather than infiltration.

Cardiovascular: Cardiac conduction delay (decreased electrical excitability, decreased myocardial conduction rate; results in bradycardia and low cardiac output), depression of myocardial contractility
Central nervous system: Acute stress reaction, anxiety, central nervous system depression (results in drowsiness, loss of consciousness, respiratory arrest), confusion, disorientation, dizziness, restlessness, seizure
Gastrointestinal: Nausea, vomiting
Neuromuscular & skeletal: Tremor
<1%, postmarketing, and/or case reports: Asthma, hypersensitivity reaction (includes allergic skin reaction, swelling at injection site)

Dental Usual Dosage Dosage varies with the anesthetic procedure, degree of anesthesia needed, vascularity of tissue, duration of anesthesia required, and physical condition of patient.

Dental anesthesia, infiltration, or conduction block:
Children <12 years: 20-30 mg (1-1.5 mL) of lidocaine hydrochloride as a 2% solution with epinephrine

1:100,000; maximum: 4.5 mg of lidocaine hydrochloride/kg of body weight or 100-150 mg as a single dose

Children ≥12 years and Adults: Do not exceed 7 mg/kg body weight or 300 mg of lidocaine hydrochloride and 3 mcg (0.003 mg) of epinephrine/kg of body weight or 0.2 mg epinephrine per dental appointment. The effective anesthetic dose varies with procedure, intensity of anesthesia needed, duration of anesthesia required, and physical condition of the patient. Always use the lowest effective dose along with careful aspiration.

The following numbers of dental carpules (1.7 mL or 1.8 mL) provide the indicated amounts of lidocaine hydrochloride 2% and epinephrine 1:100,000 (see table):

# of Cartridges (1.7 mL or 1.8 mL)	Lidocaine HCl (2%) (mg)		Epinephrine 1:100,000 (mg)	
	(1.7 mL cartridge)	(1.8 mL cartridge)	(1.7 mL cartridge)	(1.8 mL cartridge)
1	34	36	0.017	0.018
2	68	72	0.034	0.036
3	102	108	0.051	0.054
4	136	144	0.068	0.072
5	170	180	0.085	0.090
6	204	216	0.102	0.108
7	238	252	0.119	0.126
8	272	288	0.136	0.144
9	306	324	0.153	0.162
10	340	360	0.170	0.180

For most routine dental procedures, lidocaine hydrochloride 2% with epinephrine 1:100,000 is preferred. When a more pronounced hemostasis is required, a 1:50,000 epinephrine concentration should be used. The following numbers of dental cartridges (1.7 mL or 1.8 mL) provide the indicated amounts of lidocaine hydrochloride 2% and epinephrine 1:50,000.

# of Cartridges (1.7 mL or 1.8 mL)	Lidocaine HCl (2%) (mg)		Epinephrine 1:50,000 (mg)	
	(1.7 mL cartridge)	(1.8 mL cartridge)	(1.7 mL cartridge)	(1.8 mL cartridge)
1	34	36	0.034	0.036
2	68	72	0.068	0.072
3	102	108	0.102	0.108
4	136	144	0.136	0.144
5	170	180	0.170	0.180
6	204	216	0.204	0.216

Dosing

Adult

Anesthesia:

Dental: Oral infiltration/mandibular block: Initial: 1 to 5 mL (lidocaine 20 mg to 100 mg). **Note:** For most routine dental procedures, lidocaine 2% with epinephrine 1:100,000 is preferred. When a more pronounced hemostasis is required, use a 1:50,000 epinephrine concentration. Do not exceed 7 mg/kg body weight, up to a maximum range of 300 mg (usual dental practice) to 500 mg (approved product labeling) of lidocaine and 3 mcg (0.003 mg) of epinephrine/kg of body weight or 0.2 mg epinephrine per dental appointment.

Epidural: Administer a test dose (eg, 2 to 3 mL of lidocaine 1.5%) at least 5 minutes prior to injecting the total volume required for a lumbar or caudal block. Dosage varies with the number of dermatomes to be anesthetized (generally 2 to 3 mL of lidocaine 1%, 1.5%, or 2% with epinephrine [1:200,000] per dermatome). For continuous epidural or caudal anesthesia, the maximum dose should not be administered at intervals of <90 minutes. Maximum total dose for paracervical block: 200 mg/90 minutes (50% of the total dose to each side, with 5 minutes between sides).

Local: Infiltration: Dosage varies with procedure, degree of anesthesia needed, vascularity of tissue, duration of anesthesia required, and physical condition of patient. Maximum dose of lidocaine: 7 mg/kg (up to 500 mg). Use lidocaine 1%, 1.5%, or 2% with epinephrine (1:200,000) as single dose units.

Geriatric Refer to adult dosing; use with caution and at reduced dosages.

Pediatric Dosage varies with procedure, degree of anesthesia needed, vascularity of tissue, duration of anesthesia required, and physical condition of patient. Maximum lidocaine dose: 7 mg/kg (up to 500 mg).

Dental anesthesia: Note: For most routine dental procedures, lidocaine 2% with epinephrine 1:100,000 is preferred. When a more pronounced hemostasis is required, a 1:50,000 epinephrine concentration should be used.

Children <10 years: Oral infiltration/mandibular block: It is rarely necessary to administer >0.9 to 1 mL (lidocaine 18 mg to 20 mg) per procedure involving a single tooth, maxillary infiltration for 2 to 3 teeth, or mandibular block of an entire quadrant.

Children ≥10 years and Adolescents: Refer to adult dosing.

Renal Impairment

There are no dosage adjustments provided in the manufacturer's labeling. However, accumulation of metabolites may be increased in renal impairment.

Dialysis: Not dialyzable (0% to 5%) by hemo- or peritoneal dialysis; supplemental dose is not necessary (Aronoff 2007).

Hepatic Impairment There are no dosage adjustments provided in the manufacturer's labeling; use with caution (hepatically metabolized); patients with severe hepatic impairment are at greater risk of lidocaine toxicity.

Mechanism of Action

Lidocaine: Blocks both the initiation and conduction of nerve impulses by decreasing the neuronal membrane's permeability to sodium ions, which results in inhibition of depolarization with resultant blockade of conduction.

Epinephrine: Increases the duration of action of lidocaine by causing vasoconstriction (via alpha effects) which slows the vascular absorption of lidocaine.

Contraindications

Hypersensitivity to lidocaine, other local anesthetics of the amide type, epinephrine, or any component of the formulation.

Canadian labeling: Additional contraindications (not in US labeling): Hypersensitivity to para amino benzoic acid (PABA).

Warnings/Precautions Lidocaine can cause cardiac depression (eg, bradycardia, hypotension); patients with hypovolemia may be at increased risk. Careful and constant monitoring of the patient's state of consciousness should be done following each local anesthetic injection; at such times, restlessness, anxiety, tinnitus, dizziness, blurred vision, tremors, depression, drowsiness, may be early warning signs of CNS toxicity. Treatment is primarily symptomatic and supportive. Use with caution in patients with bradycardia, severe shock, heart block, or impaired cardiovascular function; use with caution in areas of the body supplied by end arteries or having otherwise compromised blood supply. Patients with peripheral vascular disease or hypertensive vascular disease may exhibit exaggerated vasoconstrictor response. Ischemic injury (eg, exfoliating, ulcerating lesions) or necrosis may result.

Anaphylactic reactions may occur following administration. Continuous intra-articular infusion of local anesthetics after arthroscopic or other surgical procedures is not an approved use; chondrolysis (primarily in the shoulder joint) has occurred following infusion, with some cases requiring arthroplasty or shoulder replacement. Local anesthetics may cause methemoglobinemia and have been associated with occurrences of respiratory arrest. Use with caution in patients with severe renal impairment, hepatic impairment, diabetes and in patients with poorly controlled hyperthyroidism. Use with caution in children, the elderly and in acutely ill or debilitated patients; reduce dose consistent with age and physical status. Potentially significant interactions may exist, requiring dose or frequency adjustment, additional monitoring, and/or selection of alternative therapy.

Avoid intravascular injections. Aspirate the syringe prior to administration; the needle must be repositioned until no return of blood can be elicited by aspiration; however, absence of blood in the syringe does not guarantee that intravascular injection has been avoided. Use with caution when there is inflammation and/or sepsis in the region of the proposed injection. Do not use injections containing preservatives (eg, methylparaben) for epidural or spinal anesthesia, or for any route of administration that would introduce solution into the cerebrospinal fluid. Use lumbar and caudal epidural anesthesia with extreme caution in patients with existing neurological disease, spinal deformities, septicemia, and impaired cardiovascular function (eg, severe hypertension). Repeat doses of lidocaine may cause significant increases in blood levels with each repeated dose due to slow accumulation of the drug or its metabolites. Tolerance to elevated blood levels varies with the status of the patient. Dental practitioners and/or clinicians using local anesthetic agents should be well trained in diagnosis and management of emergencies that may arise from the use of these agents. Resuscitative equipment, oxygen, and other resuscitative drugs should be available for immediate use.

Some dosage forms may contain benzyl alcohol; large amounts of benzyl alcohol (≥99 mg/kg/day) have been associated with a potentially fatal toxicity ("gasping syndrome") in neonates; the "gasping syndrome" consists of metabolic acidosis, respiratory distress, gasping respirations, CNS dysfunction (including convulsions, intracranial hemorrhage), hypotension and cardiovascular collapse (AAP 1997; CDC 1982); some data suggests that benzoate displaces bilirubin from protein binding sites (Ahlfors 2001); avoid or use dosage forms containing benzyl alcohol with caution in neonates See manufacturer's labeling. May contain sodium metabisulfite; use caution in patients with a sulfite allergy.

Drug Interactions

Metabolism/Transport Effects Refer to individual components.

Avoid Concomitant Use

Avoid concomitant use of Lidocaine and Epinephrine with any of the following: Blonanserin; Ergot Derivatives; Iobenguane I 123; Lurasidone

Increased Effect/Toxicity

Lidocaine and Epinephrine may increase the levels/effects of: Doxofylline; Lurasidone; Sympathomimetics

The levels/effects of Lidocaine and Epinephrine may be increased by: AtoMOXetine; Beta-Blockers; Cannabinoid-Containing Products; Cocaine; COMT Inhibitors; Ergot Derivatives; Hyaluronidase; Inhalational Anesthetics; Linezolid; MAO Inhibitors; Serotonin/Norepinephrine Reuptake Inhibitors; Tedizolid; Tricyclic Antidepressants

Decreased Effect

Lidocaine and Epinephrine may decrease the levels/effects of: Antidiabetic Agents; Benzylpenicilloyl Polylysine; Iobenguane I 123

The levels/effects of Lidocaine and Epinephrine may be decreased by: Alpha1-Blockers; Benperidol; Blonanserin; CloZAPine; Promethazine; Spironolactone

Pharmacodynamics/Kinetics

Onset of Action Dental: ≤2 to 4 minutes

Duration of Action Dental: ~2.5 hours (infiltration); 3 to 3.5 hours (nerve block); dose and anesthetic procedure dependent

Pregnancy Risk Factor B

Pregnancy Considerations Adverse events have not been observed in animal reproduction studies. See individual agents.

Breastfeeding Considerations It is not known if lidocaine/epinephrine is excreted in breast milk. The manufacturer recommends that caution be exercised when administering lidocaine/epinephrine to nursing women. See individual agents.

Dosage Forms

Injection, solution:

Xylocaine with Epinephrine:

0.5% / 1:200,000: Lidocaine hydrochloride 0.5% [5 mg/mL] and epinephrine 1:200,000 (50 mL)

1% / 1:100,000: Lidocaine hydrochloride 1% [10 mg/mL] and epinephrine 1:100,000 (10 mL, 20 mL, 50 mL)

2% / 1:100,000: Lidocaine hydrochloride 2% [20 mg/mL] and epinephrine 1:100,000 (10 mL, 20 mL, 50 mL)

Generic:

0.5% / 1:200,000: Lidocaine hydrochloride 0.5% [5 mg/mL] and epinephrine 1:200,000 (50 mL)

1% / 1:100,000: Lidocaine hydrochloride 1% [10 mg/mL] and epinephrine 1:100,000 (20 mL, 30 mL, 50 mL)

2% / 1:100,000: Lidocaine hydrochloride 2% [20 mg/mL] and epinephrine 1:100,000 (30 mL, 50 mL)

Injection, solution [preservative free]:

Xylocaine-MPF with Epinephrine:

1% / 1:200,000: Lidocaine hydrochloride 1% [10 mg/mL] and epinephrine 1:200,000 (5 mL, 10 mL, 30 mL)

1.5% / 1:200,000: Lidocaine hydrochloride 1.5% [15 mg/mL] and epinephrine 1:200,000 (5 mL, 10 mL, 30 mL)

2% / 1:200,000: Lidocaine hydrochloride 2% [20 mg/mL] and epinephrine 1:200,000 (5 mL, 10 mL, 20 mL)

Generic:
1.5% / 1:200,000: Lidocaine hydrochloride 1.5% [15 mg/mL] and epinephrine 1:200,000 (5 mL, 30 mL)
2% / 1:200,000: Lidocaine hydrochloride 2% [20 mg/mL] and epinephrine 1:200,000 (20 mL)

Injection, solution [for dental use]:
Lignospan Forte: 2% / 1:50,000: Lidocaine hydrochloride 2% [20 mg/mL] and epinephrine 1:50,000 (1.7 mL)
Lignospan Standard: 2% / 1:100,000: Lidocaine hydrochloride 2% [20 mg/mL] and epinephrine 1:100,000 (1.7 mL)
Xylocaine Dental with Epinephrine:
2% / 1:50,000: Lidocaine hydrochloride 2% [20 mg/mL] and epinephrine 1:50,000 (1.7 mL)
2% / 1:100,000: Lidocaine hydrochloride 2% [20 mg/mL] and epinephrine 1:100,000 (1.7 mL)
Generic:
2% / 1:50,000: Lidocaine hydrochloride 2% [20 mg/mL] and epinephrine 1:50,000 (1.7 mL, 1.8 mL)
2% / 1:100,000: Lidocaine hydrochloride 2% [20 mg/mL] and epinephrine 1:100,000 (1.7 mL, 1.8 mL)

Dental Comment Oral paresthesia: The occurrence of oral paresthesia associated with 4% solutions of prilocaine or articaine, although rare, continue to be slightly more frequent than other local anesthetics. From 1999-2008, there were 182 cases of nonsurgical paresthesia (Gaffen, 2009). Of the cases, 172 involved mandibular block injection only. Another eight cases involved mandibular block combined with at least one other type of anesthetic injection. A single case involved infiltration around tooth number 35 (European numbering system; tooth number 20 for Universal numbering system) and the final case involved infiltration and intraligamentary injection in the maxillary anterior region.

A 2010 report, reviewed adverse events submitted voluntarily over a 10-year period involving the dental local anesthetics articaine, bupivacaine, lidocaine, mepivacaine, and prilocaine in the United States. Lidocaine reported incidence: One case per 181,076,673 cartridges sold. The reported incidence of paresthesia was one case for 13,800,970 cartridges of all local anesthetics sold in the U.S. (Garisto, 2010).

Lidocaine and Prilocaine

(LYE doe kane & PRIL oh kane)

Related Information
Lidocaine (Topical) *on page 990*
Prilocaine *on page 1385*

Brand Names: US AgonEaze; Anodyne LPT; DermacinRx Empricaine; DermacinRx Prizopak; EMLA [DSC]; Leva Set; Lidopril; Lidopril XR; LiProZonePak; Livixil Pak; LP Lite Pak; Medolor Pak; Oraqix; Prilolid; Relador Pak; Venipuncture CPI

Brand Names: Canada EMLA; Oraqix

Generic Availability (US) Yes: Cream

Pharmacologic Category Local Anesthetic

Dental Use
Periodontal gel (Oraqix®): Use in adults who require localized anesthesia in periodontal pockets during scaling and/or root planing.
Topical: Amide-type topical anesthetic for use on normal intact skin to provide local analgesia for minor procedures such as IV cannulation or venipuncture

Use
US labeling:
Cream: Topical anesthetic for use on normal intact skin to provide local analgesia; for use on genital mucous membranes for superficial minor surgery; and as pretreatment for infiltration anesthesia.
Periodontal gel: Topical anesthetic for use in periodontal pockets during scaling and/or root planing procedures

Canadian labeling:
Cream: Topical anesthetic for use on intact skin in connection with: IV cannulation or venipuncture; superficial surgical procedures (eg, split skin grafting, electrolysis, removal of molluscum contagiosum); laser treatment for superficial skin surgery (eg, telangiectasia, port wine stains, warts, moles, skin nodules, scar tissue); surgical procedures of genital mucosa (≤10 minutes) on small superficial localized lesions (eg, removal of condylomata by laser or cautery, biopsies); local infiltration anesthesia in genital mucous membranes; mechanical cleansing/debridement of leg ulcers; vaccination with measles-mumps-rubella (MMR), diphtheria-pertussis-tetanus-poliovirus (DPTP), *Haemophilus influenzae* b, and hepatitis B.
Patch: Topical anesthetic for use on intact skin in connection with IV cannulation or venipuncture; vaccination with measles-mumps-rubella (MMR), diphtheria-pertussis-tetanus-poliovirus (DPTP), *Haemophilus influenzae* b, and hepatitis B.
Periodontal gel: Topical anesthetic for use in periodontal pockets during scaling and/or root planing procedures

Local Anesthetic/Vasoconstrictor Precautions
No information available to require special precautions

Effects on Dental Treatment Key adverse event(s) related to dental treatment: Application site reactions in the oral cavity in 52/391 patients (13%) included pain, soreness, irritation, numbness, ulcerations, vesicles, edema, abscess and/or redness in the treated area. The 13% represented adverse effects occurring in more than one patient. Each patient was counted only once per adverse event. Taste perversion also reported (2%) including complaints of bad or bitter taste for up to 4 hours after administration.

Effects on Bleeding No information available to require special precautions

Adverse Reactions
Cream/patch:
>10%:
Dermatologic: Pallor (local: 37%)
Local: Application site erythema (21% to 30%), application site burning (17%)
1% to 10%:
Central nervous system: Local alterations in temperature sensations (7%)
Local: Application site edema (6% to 10%), application site pruritus (2%)
Frequency not defined:
Dermatologic: Hyperpigmentation, stinging of the skin (local), urticaria
Hematologic & oncologic: Local purpuric or petechial reaction
<1%, postmarketing, and/or case reports: Anaphylactic shock, angioedema, application site rash, blistering of foreskin, bronchospasm, central nervous system depression, central nervous system stimulation, central nervous system toxicity (high dose), circulatory

shock (high dose), hypotension, local hypersensitivity reaction, methemoglobinemia (high dose)

Periodontal gel:

>10%: Local: Application site reaction (13%, includes abscess, edema, irritation, numbness, pain, ulceration, vesicles)

1% to 10%:

Central nervous system: Bitter taste (2%), fatigue (1%)

Gastrointestinal: Nausea (1%)

Hypersensitivity: Local hypersensitivity reaction

Respiratory: Flu-like symptoms (1%), respiratory tract infection (1%)

Dental Usual Dosage Oraqix: Gel: Apply on gingival margin around selected teeth using the blunt-tipped applicator included in package. Wait 30 seconds, then fill the periodontal pockets using the blunt-tipped applicator until gel becomes visible at the gingival margin. Wait another 30 seconds before starting treatment. Maximum recommended dose: One treatment session: 5 cartridges (8.5 g)

Dosing

Adult Anesthetic: Topical:

Cream (intact skin): **Note:** Apply a thick layer to intact skin and cover with an occlusive dressing. Dermal analgesia can be expected to increase for up to 3 hours under occlusive dressing and persist for 1 to 2 hours after removal of the cream.

US labeling:

Minor dermal procedures (eg, IV cannulation or venipuncture): Apply 2.5 g (1/2 of the 5 g tube) over 20 to 25 cm^2 of skin surface area) for at least 1 hour

Major dermal procedures (eg, more painful dermatological procedures involving a larger skin area such as split thickness skin graft harvesting): Apply 2 g per 10 cm^2 of skin and allow to remain in contact with the skin for at least 2 hours.

Adult male genital skin (eg, pretreatment prior to local anesthetic infiltration): Apply 1 g per 10 cm^2 to the skin surface for 15 minutes. Local anesthetic infiltration should be performed immediately after removal of cream.

Adult female genital mucous membranes: Minor procedures (eg, removal of condylomata acuminata, pretreatment for local anesthetic infiltration): Apply 5 to 10 g for 5 to 10 minutes. The local anesthetic infiltration or procedure should be performed immediately after removal of cream.

Canadian labeling:

Minor dermal procedures (eg, IV cannulation, venipuncture, surgical or laser treatment): Apply 2 g (~1/2 of the 5 g tube) over ~13.5 cm^2 for at least 1 hour but no longer than 5 hours

Major dermal procedures (eg, split-skin grafting): 1.5 to 2 g per 10 cm^2 (maximum: 60 g per 400 cm^2) for at least 2 hours but no longer than 5 hours

Genital mucosa (eg, surgical procedures ≤10 minutes such as localized wart removal, and prior to local anesthetic infiltration): Apply 2 g (~1/2 of 5 g tube) per lesion (maximum: 10 g) for 5 to 10 minutes. Initiate procedure immediately after removing cream.

Leg ulcers (eg, mechanical cleansing/surgical debridement): Apply ~1 to 2 g per 10 cm^2 (maximum: 10 g) for at least 30 minutes and up to 60 minutes for necrotic tissue that is more difficult to penetrate. Initiate procedure immediately after removing cream.

Periodontal gel (Oraqix): Apply on gingival margin around selected teeth using the blunt-tipped applicator included in package. Wait 30 seconds, then fill the periodontal pockets using the blunt-tipped applicator until gel becomes visible at the gingival margin. Wait another 30 seconds before starting treatment. May reapply; maximum recommended dose: One treatment session: 5 cartridges (8.5 g)

Transdermal patch [Canadian product]: Minor procedures (eg, needle insertion): Apply 1 or more patches to intact skin surface area <10 cm^2 for at least 1 hour (maximum application time: 5 hours)

Geriatric Smaller areas of treatment may be necessary depending on status of patient (eg, debilitated, impaired hepatic function). Refer to adult dosing.

Pediatric Although the incidence of systemic adverse effects is very low, caution should be exercised, particularly when applying over large areas and leaving on for >2 hours

Local anesthetic (procedures): Infants and Children (intact skin): Topical: **Note:** If a patient >3 months of age does not meet the minimum weight requirement, the maximum total dose should be restricted to the corresponding maximum based on patient weight.

Cream: Should **not** be used in neonates with a gestation age <37 weeks nor in infants <12 months of age who are receiving treatment with methemoglobin-inducing agents

Dosing is based on child's age and weight:

Age 0 to 3 months or <5 kg: Apply a maximum of 1 g over no more than 10 cm^2 of skin; leave on for no longer than 1 hour

Age 3 months to 12 months and >5 kg: Apply no more than a maximum 2 g total over no more than 20 cm^2 of skin; leave on for no longer than 4 hours

Age 1 to 6 years and >10 kg: Apply no more than a maximum of 10 g total over no more than 100 cm^2 of skin. US labeling recommends leaving on for no longer than 4 hours. Canadian labeling recommends leaving on for no longer than 5 hours.

Age 7 to 12 years and >20 kg: Apply no more than a maximum 20 g total over no more than 200 cm^2 of skin. US labeling recommends leaving on for no longer than 4 hours. Canadian labeling recommends leaving on for no longer than 5 hours.

Transdermal patch [Canadian product]: **Note:** Should not be used in neonates with a gestation age <37 weeks nor in infants <12 months of age who are receiving treatment with methemoglobin-inducing agents

Dosing is based on child's age and weight: Apply patch(es) to skin area(s) <10 cm^2:

Age 0 to 3 months or <5 kg: Apply 1 patch and leave on for ~1 hour (do not exceed 1-hour application time); do not apply more than 1 patch at same time; safety of repeated dosing not established

Age 3 months to 12 months and >5 kg: Apply 1 to 2 patches for ~1 hour (maximum application time: 4 hours); do not apply more than 2 patches at the same time

Age 1 to 6 years and >10 kg: Apply 1 or more patches for minimum of 1 hour (maximum application time: 5 hours); maximum dose: 10 patches

Age 7 to 12 years and >20 kg: Apply 1 or more patches for a minimum of 1 hour (maximum application time: 5 hours); maximum dose: 20 patches

Renal Impairment There are no dosage adjustments provided in the manufacturer labeling. Lidocaine and prilocaine primarily undergo hepatic metabolism and their pharmacokinetics are not expected to be changed significantly in renal impairment.

Hepatic Impairment Smaller areas of treatment are recommended for patients with severe hepatic impairment.

Mechanism of Action Local anesthetic action occurs by stabilization of neuronal membranes and inhibiting the ionic fluxes required for the initiation and conduction of impulses

Contraindications

Hypersensitivity to local anesthetics of the amide type or any component of the formulation

Canadian labeling: Additional contraindications (not in US labeling): Congenital or idiopathic methemoglobinemia.

Cream and patch only: Infants ≤12 months of age who require treatment with methemoglobin-inducing agents; preterm infants (gestational age <37 weeks); procedures requiring large amounts over a large body area that are not conducted in a facility with health care professionals trained in the diagnosis and management of dose-related toxicity and other acute emergencies, and with appropriate resuscitative treatments and equipment.

Warnings/Precautions Methemoglobinemia has been reported in infants and children; associated with large doses, larger-than-recommended areas of application, neonates and infants <3 months of age, and concomitant use of methemoglobinemia-inducing agents (eg, acetaminophen, benzocaine, chloroquine, dapsone, nitrofurantoin, nitroglycerin, nitroprusside, phenobarbital, phenytoin, quinine, sulfonamides). Neonates and infants up to 3 months of age should be monitored for methemoglobinemia. Do not use in preterm neonates (gestational age <37 weeks), infants <12 months of age requiring treatment with methemoglobinemia-inducing agents, or in patients with congenital or idiopathic methemoglobinemia. Patients with glucose-6-phosphate dehydrogenase (G6PD) deficiency may be more susceptible to drug-induced methemoglobinemia. Allergic and anaphylactic reactions may occur. Patients allergic to paraaminobenzoic acid derivatives (eg, procaine, tetracaine, benzocaine) have not shown cross sensitivity to lidocaine and/or prilocaine; use with caution in patients with a history of drug sensitivities.

Although the incidence of systemic adverse reactions with use of the cream is very low, caution should be exercised, particularly when applying over large areas and leaving on for longer than 2 hours. When used prior to cosmetic or medical procedures, the smallest amount of cream necessary for pain relief should be applied. High systemic levels and toxic effects (eg, methemoglobinemia, irregular heartbeats, respiratory depression, seizures, death) have been reported in patients who (without supervision of a trained professional) have applied topical anesthetics in large amounts (or to large areas of the skin), left these products on for a prolonged time, or have used wraps/dressings to cover the skin following application. Do not apply to broken or inflamed skin, open wounds or near the eyes. Avoid use in situations where penetration or migration past the tympanic membrane into the middle ear is possible; ototoxicity has been observed in animal studies. Avoid inadvertent trauma to the treated area (eg, scratching, rubbing, exposure to extreme hot or cold temperatures) until complete sensation has returned.

Use with caution in patients with severe hepatic impairment; smaller treatment area may be required due to risk of increased systemic exposure. Use with caution in patients with severe impairment of impulse initiation and conduction in the heart (eg, grade II and III AV block, pronounced bradycardia). Use with caution in patients with atopic dermatitis; rapid and greater absorption through the skin is observed in these patients; a shorter application time should be used. Use with caution in the debilitated or acutely ill patients and elderly patients; smaller treatment area may be required. Potentially significant drug-drug interactions may exist, requiring dose or frequency adjustment, additional monitoring, and/or selection of alternative therapy.

Do not use periodontal gel with standard dental syringes; only use with the supplied blunt-tipped applicator.

Drug Interactions

Metabolism/Transport Effects Refer to individual components.

Avoid Concomitant Use

Avoid concomitant use of Lidocaine and Prilocaine with any of the following: Bupivacaine (Liposomal); Conivaptan; Fusidic Acid (Systemic); Idelalisib

Increased Effect/Toxicity

Lidocaine and Prilocaine may increase the levels/effects of: Antiarrhythmic Agents (Class III); Bupivacaine (Liposomal); CloZAPine; Neuromuscular-Blocking Agents; Prilocaine; Sodium Nitrite; TiZANidine

The levels/effects of Lidocaine and Prilocaine may be increased by: Abiraterone Acetate; Antiarrhythmic Agents (Class III); Aprepitant; Beta-Blockers; Conivaptan; CYP1A2 Inhibitors (Moderate); CYP1A2 Inhibitors (Strong); CYP3A4 Inhibitors (Moderate); CYP3A4 Inhibitors (Strong); Dapsone (Topical); Dasatinib; Deferasirox; Disopyramide; Fosaprepitant; Fusidic Acid (Systemic); Hyaluronidase; Idelalisib; Ivacaftor; Methemoglobinemia Associated Agents; MiFEPRIStone; Netupitant; Nitric Oxide; Obeticholic Acid; Palbociclib; Peginterferon Alfa-2b; Simeprevir; Stiripentol; Tetracaine (Topical); Vemurafenib

Decreased Effect

Lidocaine and Prilocaine may decrease the levels/effects of: Technetium Tc 99m Tilmanocept

Pharmacodynamics/Kinetics

Onset of Action

EMLA: 1 hour (more rapid in genital mucosa: 5 to 10 minutes); Peak effect: 2 to 3 hours

Oraqix: ≤30 seconds

Duration of Action

EMLA: 1 to 2 hours after removal; Genital mucosa: 15 to 20 minutes after application (range: 5 to 45 minutes)

Oraqix: ~20 minutes

Pregnancy Risk Factor B

Pregnancy Considerations Animal reproduction studies have not been conducted with this combination. Lidocaine and prilocaine cross the placenta. Their use is not contraindicated during labor and delivery. Refer to individual agents.

Breastfeeding Considerations Lidocaine is excreted in breast milk; excretion of prilocaine in breast milk unknown; however, systemic absorption following topical application is expected to be low. The manufacturer recommends that caution be exercised when administering to nursing women. Refer to individual agents.

Dosage Forms

Cream, topical:

AgonEaze: Lidocaine 2.5% and prilocaine 2.5% (2 x 30 g)

Anodyne LPT: Lidocaine 2.5% and prilocaine 2.5% (3 x 30 g)
DermacinRx Empricaine: Lidocaine 2.5% and prilocaine 2.5% (1 x 30 g)
DermacinRx Prizopak: Lidocaine 2.5% and prilocaine 2.5% (3 x 30 g)
Leva Set: Lidocaine 2.5% and prilocaine 2.5% (3 x 30 g)
Lidopril: Lidocaine 2.5% and prilocaine 2.5% (3 x 30 g)
Lidopril XR: Lidocaine 2.5% and prilocaine 2.5% (2 x 30 g)
LiProZonePak: Lidocaine 2.5% and prilocaine 2.5% (3 x 30 g)
Livixil Pak: Lidocaine 2.5% and prilocaine 2.5% (3 x 30 g)
LP Lite Pak: Lidocaine 2.5% and prilocaine 2.5% (2 x 30 g)
Medolor Pak: Lidocaine 2.5% and prilocaine 2.5% (3 x 30 g)
Prilolid: Lidocaine 2.5% and prilocaine 2.5% (1 x 30 g)
Relador Pak: Lidocaine 2.5% and prilocaine 2.5% (3 x 30 g)
Venipuncture CPI: Lidocaine 2.5% and prilocaine 2.5% (5 g)
Generic: Lidocaine 2.5% and prilocaine 2.5% (5 g, 30 g, 5800 g, 18,000 g)

Gel, periodontal:
Oraqix: Lidocaine 2.5% and prilocaine 2.5% (1.7 g)

Dosage Forms: Canada

Patch, transdermal:
EMLA Patch: Lidocaine 2.5% and prilocaine 2.5% per patch (2s, 20s)

Lidocaine and Tetracaine

(LYE doe kane & TET ra kane)

Related Information

Lidocaine (Topical) *on page 990*
Tetracaine (Topical) *on page 1548*

Brand Names: US Pliaglis; Synera

Generic Availability (US) Yes: cream

Pharmacologic Category Analgesic, Topical; Local Anesthetic

Use

Cream: For use on intact skin in adults to provide topical local analgesia for superficial dermatological procedures.

Patch: For use on intact skin in patients ≥ 3 years to provide local analgesia for superficial venous access and superficial dermatological procedures.

Local Anesthetic/Vasoconstrictor Precautions No information available to require special precautions

Effects on Dental Treatment No significant effects or complications reported

Effects on Bleeding No information available to require special precautions

Adverse Reactions Also see individual agents.

>10%: Dermatologic: Erythema (47% to 71%), localized blanching (12% to 16%), skin edema (12% to 14%)

1% to 10%:

Central nervous system: Dizziness (≤1%), drowsiness (≤1%), headache (≤1%)

Dermatologic: Application site dermatitis (<4%), application site rash (<4%), local discoloration (<4%), acne vulgaris (≤1%), ecchymosis (≤1%), maculopapular rash (≤1%), xeroderma (≤1%)

Gastrointestinal: Nausea (≤1%), vomiting (≤1%)

Hematologic & oncologic: Petechial rash (≤1%)

<1%, postmarketing, and/or case reports: Anaphylactoid reaction, angioedema, apprehension, blepharitis, bronchospasm, burning sensation of skin, confusion, convulsions, dehydration, diaphoresis, fever, hypersensitivity reaction, hyperventilation, infection, pain, pallor, paresthesia, pharyngitis, pruritus, respiratory depression, skin blister, stupor, syncope, tremor, urticaria, vesiculobullous dermatitis

Dosing

Adult & Geriatric

Anesthesia, topical:

Cream: Superficial dermatological procedures: Prior to procedure, apply to intact skin for 20 to 60 minutes. Amount of cream varies depending on size of the surface area to be treated; see manufacturer's labeling for detailed information.

Patch:

Venipuncture or intravenous cannulation: Prior to procedure, apply to intact skin for 20 to 30 minutes; **Note:** May use another patch at a new location to facilitate venous access after a failed attempt; remove previous patch.

Superficial dermatological procedures: Prior to procedure, apply to intact skin for 30 minutes

Pediatric

Anesthesia, topical: Children ≥3 years and Adolescents: Patch: Refer to adult dosing.

Renal Impairment There are no dosage adjustments provided in the manufacturer's labeling. Lidocaine primarily undergoes hepatic metabolism and its pharmacokinetics are not expected to be changed significantly following topical administration of recommended doses in renal impairment.

Hepatic Impairment There are no dosage adjustments provided in the manufacturer's labeling (has not been studied). Use caution in patients with severe hepatic dysfunction.

Mechanism of Action Local anesthetic action occurs by stabilization of neuronal membranes and inhibiting the sodium ion fluxes required for the initiation and conduction of impulses.

Contraindications Hypersensitivity to lidocaine, tetracaine, amide or ester-type anesthetic agents, para-aminobenzoic acid (PABA), or any other component of the formulation

Warnings/Precautions Hypersensitivity or anaphylactic reactions may occur. Use with caution in patients who may be sensitive to systemic effects (eg, acutely ill, debilitated, elderly). If being used with other products containing local anesthetic, consider potential for additive effects. Avoid contact with eye; loss of protective reflexes may predispose to corneal irritation and/or abrasion. Application to broken or inflamed skin or mucous membranes may lead to increased systemic absorption. Use caution in patients with severe hepatic disease or pseudocholinesterase deficiency. Not for use at home. Methemoglobinemia has been reported with local anesthetics including tetracaine. Use caution in patients with congenital or idiopathic methemoglobinemia, children <12 months of age, concurrent use with methemoglobin-inducing medications, or in those patients with glucose-6-phosphate dehydrogenase deficiencies.

Application of patch for longer duration than recommended, or simultaneous or sequential application of multiple patches is not recommended because of the risk for increased drug absorption and possible adverse reactions. May contain conducting metal (eg, iron); remove patch prior to MRI. Proper storage and disposal of used patches are essential to prevent accidental exposures, especially in children; accidental exposure may result in serious adverse effects.

Application of cream for longer duration than recommended, or application over larger surface areas is not recommended because of the risk for increased drug absorption and possible adverse reactions.

Drug Interactions

Metabolism/Transport Effects Refer to individual components.

Avoid Concomitant Use

Avoid concomitant use of Lidocaine and Tetracaine with any of the following: Conivaptan; Fusidic Acid (Systemic); Idelalisib

Increased Effect/Toxicity

Lidocaine and Tetracaine may increase the levels/effects of: Antiarrhythmic Agents (Class III); CloZAPine; Methemoglobinemia Associated Agents; Prilocaine; Sodium Nitrite; TiZANidine

The levels/effects of Lidocaine and Tetracaine may be increased by: Abiraterone Acetate; Antiarrhythmic Agents (Class III); Aprepitant; Beta-Blockers; Conivaptan; CYP1A2 Inhibitors (Moderate); CYP1A2 Inhibitors (Strong); CYP3A4 Inhibitors (Moderate); CYP3A4 Inhibitors (Strong); Dapsone (Topical); Dasatinib; Deferasirox; Disopyramide; Fosaprepitant; Fusidic Acid (Systemic); Idelalisib; Ivacaftor; MiFEPRIStone; Netupitant; Nitric Oxide; Obeticholic Acid; Palbociclib; Peginterferon Alfa-2b; Simeprevir; Stiripentol; Tetracaine (Topical); Vemurafenib

Decreased Effect There are no known significant interactions involving a decrease in effect.

Pharmacodynamics/Kinetics

Onset of Action Within 20 to 30 minutes

Duration of Action Cream: 11 hours

Half-life Elimination Lidocaine: Adults: 1.8 hours

Pregnancy Risk Factor B

Pregnancy Considerations Adverse effects have not been observed in animal reproduction studies with this combination. Systemic absorption following topical application is expected to be low. Systemic absorption would be required in order for lidocaine and tetracaine to cross the placenta and reach the fetus. Refer to Lidocaine (Systemic), Lidocaine (Topical), and Tetracaine (Systemic) monographs.

Breastfeeding Considerations Lidocaine is excreted in breast milk; it is not known if tetracaine is excreted in breast milk. Systemic absorption following topical application is expected to be low; according to the manufacturer, the small amount ingested by a nursing infant would not be expected to cause adverse events. The manufacturer recommends that caution be exercised if administered to nursing women. Refer to Lidocaine (Systemic), Lidocaine (Topical), and Tetracaine (Systemic) monographs.

Dosage Forms

Cream, external:

Pliaglis: Lidocaine 7% and tetracaine 7% (30 g, 100 g)

Patch, transdermal:

Synera: Lidocaine 70 mg and tetracaine 70 mg (10s)

Lifitegrast (lif i TEG rast)

Brand Names: US Xiidra

Pharmacologic Category Lymphocyte Function-Associated Antigen 1 (LFA-1) Antagonist

Use Dry eye disease: Treatment of the signs and symptoms of dry eye disease (DED).

Local Anesthetic/Vasoconstrictor Precautions No information available to require special precautions

Effects on Dental Treatment No significant effects or complications reported

Effects on Bleeding No information available to require special precautions

Adverse Reactions

5% to 25%:

Gastrointestinal: Dysgeusia

Local: Application site irritation

Ophthalmic: Decreased visual acuity

1% to 5%:

Central nervous system: Headache

Ophthalmic: Blurred vision, conjunctival hyperemia, eye discharge, eye discomfort, eye irritation, eye pruritus, increased lacrimation

Respiratory: Sinusitis

General Dosage Range Ophthalmic: *Adults:* Instill 1 drop into each eye every 12 hours.

Mechanism of Action Lifitegrast binds to the integrin lymphocyte function-associated antigen-1 (LFA-1) and blocks the interaction of LFA-1 with its cognate ligand intercellular adhesion molecule-1 (ICAM-1).

Pregnancy Considerations Adverse events were observed in some animal reproduction studies following intravenous administration. Systemic exposure following ophthalmic administration is low. In general, if ophthalmic agents are needed during pregnancy, the minimum effective dose should be used in combination with punctual occlusion to decrease potential exposure to the fetus (Samples 1988)

Linaclotide (lin AK loe tide)

Brand Names: US Linzess

Brand Names: Canada Constella

Pharmacologic Category Gastrointestinal Agent, Miscellaneous; Guanylate Cyclase-C (GC-C) Agonist

Use

Chronic idiopathic constipation: Treatment of chronic idiopathic constipation (CIC) in adults

Irritable bowel syndrome with constipation: Treatment of irritable bowel syndrome with constipation (IBS-C) in adults

Local Anesthetic/Vasoconstrictor Precautions No information available to require special precautions

Effects on Dental Treatment Key adverse event(s) related to dental treatment: Upper respiratory tract infection and sinusitis

Effects on Bleeding No information available to require special precautions

Adverse Reactions Adverse reactions reported with use in IBS-C and CIC.

>10%: Gastrointestinal: Diarrhea (16% to 20%; severe diarrhea: 2%)

1% to 10%:

Central nervous system: Headache (4%), fatigue (<2%)

Endocrine & metabolic: Dehydration (≤1%)

Gastrointestinal: Abdominal pain (7%), flatulence (4% to 6%), abdominal distension (2% to 3%), viral gastroenteritis (≤3%), dyspepsia (<2%), fecal incontinence (<2%), gastroesophageal reflux disease (<2%), vomiting (<2%)

Respiratory: Upper respiratory tract infection (5%), sinusitis (3%)

<1%, postmarketing, and/or case reports: Hematochezia, hypersensitivity reaction, melena, rectal hemorrhage, urticaria

General Dosage Range
Oral: *Adults:* 72 mcg, 145 mcg, or 290 mcg once daily

Mechanism of Action Linaclotide and its active metabolite bind and agonize guanylate cyclase-C on the luminal surface of intestinal epithelium. Intracellular and extracellular cyclic guanosine monophosphate (cGMP) concentrations are subsequently increased resulting in chloride and bicarbonate secretion into the intestinal lumen. Intestinal fluid increases and GI transit time is decreased. Increased extracellular cGMP may decrease visceral pain by reducing pain-sensing nerve activity.

Pregnancy Considerations Linaclotide and its metabolite are not measurable in plasma when used at recommended doses. Maternal use is not expected to result in fetal exposure.

Linagliptin (lin a GLIP tin)

Related Information
Endocrine Disorders and Pregnancy *on page 1781*

Brand Names: US Tradjenta

Brand Names: Canada Trajenta

Pharmacologic Category Antidiabetic Agent, Dipeptidyl Peptidase 4 (DPP-4) Inhibitor

Use Diabetes mellitus, type 2: As an adjunct to diet and exercise to improve glycemic control in adults with type 2 diabetes (noninsulin dependent, NIDDM) as monotherapy or in combination with other antidiabetic agents

Local Anesthetic/Vasoconstrictor Precautions No information available to require special precautions

Effects on Dental Treatment Linagliptin-dependent patients with diabetes should be appointed for dental treatment in the morning in order to minimize chance of stress-induced hypoglycemia.

Effects on Bleeding No information available to require special precautions

Adverse Reactions
Incidences may include use in combination therapy regimens.
1% to 10%:
Endocrine & metabolic: Hypoglycemia (7%), increased uric acid (3%)
Respiratory: Nasopharyngitis (7%), cough (2%)
Frequency not defined:
Dermatologic: Urticaria
Neuromuscular & skeletal: Myalgia
Respiratory: Asthma
<1%, postmarketing, and/or case reports: Acute pancreatitis, anaphylaxis, angioedema, bullous pemphigoid, exfoliation of skin, oral mucosa ulcer, severe arthralgia, severe hypersensitivity, skin rash, stomatitis

General Dosage Range Oral: *Adults:* 5 mg once daily
Concomitant use with insulin and/or insulin secretagogues (eg, sulfonylureas): Reduced dose of insulin and/or insulin secretagogues may be needed.

Mechanism of Action Linagliptin inhibits dipeptidyl peptidase IV (DPP-IV) enzyme resulting in prolonged active incretin levels. Incretin hormones (eg, glucagon-like peptide-1 [GLP-1] and glucose-dependent insulinotropic polypeptide [GIP]) regulate glucose homeostasis by increasing insulin synthesis and release from pancreatic beta cells and decreasing glucagon secretion from pancreatic alpha cells. Decreased glucagon secretion results in decreased hepatic glucose production. Under normal physiologic circumstances, incretin hormones are released by the intestine throughout the day and levels are increased in response to a meal; incretin hormones are rapidly inactivated by the DPP-IV enzyme.

Pharmacodynamics/Kinetics
Half-life Elimination Effective (therapeutic): ~12 hours; Terminal (DPP-IV saturable binding): >100 hours
Time to Peak 1.5 hours

Pregnancy Risk Factor B

Pregnancy Considerations Adverse events were not observed in animal reproduction studies, except with doses that were also maternally toxic.

In women with diabetes, maternal hyperglycemia can be associated with congenital malformations as well as adverse effects in the fetus, neonate, and the mother (ACOG 2005; ADA 2016c; Kitzmiller 2008; Metzger 2007). To prevent adverse outcomes, prior to conception and throughout pregnancy, maternal blood glucose and HbA_{1c} should be kept as close to target goals as possible but without causing significant hypoglycemia (ACOG 2013; ADA 2016c; Blumer 2013; Kitzmiller 2008). Agents other than linagliptin are currently recommended to treat diabetes in pregnant women (ACOG 2013; Blumer 2013).

Linagliptin and Metformin
(lin a GLIP tin & met FOR min)

Related Information
Linagliptin *on page 1002*
MetFORMIN *on page 1069*

Brand Names: US Jentadueto; Jentadueto XR

Brand Names: Canada Jentadueto

Pharmacologic Category Antidiabetic Agent, Biguanide; Antidiabetic Agent, Dipeptidyl Peptidase 4 (DPP-4) Inhibitor

Use Diabetes mellitus type 2: As an adjunct to diet and exercise to improve glycemic control in adults with type 2 diabetes mellitus (noninsulin dependent, NIDDM) when treatment with both linagliptin and metformin is appropriate.

Local Anesthetic/Vasoconstrictor Precautions No information available to require special precautions

Effects on Dental Treatment
Linagliptin-dependent patients with diabetes should be appointed for dental treatment in the morning in order to minimize chance of stress-induced hypoglycemia.
Metformin-dependent patients with diabetes (noninsulin dependent, Type 2) should be appointed for dental treatment in the morning in order to minimize chance of stress-induced hypoglycemia.

Effects on Bleeding No information available to require special precautions

Adverse Reactions Reactions/percentages reported with combination product; also see individual agents. Frequency not always defined.
Dermatologic: Pruritus
Gastrointestinal: Diarrhea (6%), decreased appetite, nausea, pancreatitis, vomiting
Hypersensitivity: Hypersensitivity reaction
Respiratory: Nasopharyngitis (6%), cough
<1%, postmarketing, and/or case reports: Severe arthralgia (FDA Safety Alert, Aug 28, 2015)

General Dosage Range Oral: *Adults:* Linagliptin 2.5 mg and metformin 500 to 1,000 mg twice daily or linagliptin 5 mg and metformin 1,000 to 2,000 mg once daily (maximum: linagliptin 5 mg/metformin 2,000 mg per day)

Mechanism of Action

Linagliptin inhibits dipeptidyl peptidase IV (DPP-IV) enzymes resulting in prolonged active incretin levels. Incretin hormones [eg, glucagon-like peptide-1 (GLP-1) and glucose-dependent insulinotropic polypeptide (GIP)] regulate glucose homeostasis by increasing insulin synthesis and release from pancreatic beta cells and decreasing glucagon secretion from pancreatic alpha cells. Decreased glucagon secretion results in decreased hepatic glucose production. Under normal physiologic circumstances, incretin hormones are released by the intestine throughout the day and levels are increased in response to a meal; incretin hormones are rapidly inactivated by DPP-IV enzymes.

Metformin decreases hepatic glucose production, decreasing intestinal absorption of glucose, and improves insulin sensitivity (increases peripheral glucose uptake and utilization).

Pregnancy Risk Factor B

Pregnancy Considerations Adverse events were not observed in animal reproduction studies using this combination, except with doses that were maternally toxic. Metformin crosses the placenta. Refer to individual agents.

Lincomycin (lin koe MYE sin)

Brand Names: US Lincocin

Brand Names: Canada Lincocin

Pharmacologic Category Antibiotic, Lincosamide

Use Bacterial infections (serious): Treatment of serious infections caused by susceptible strains of streptococci, pneumococci, and staphylococci. Use should be reserved for penicillin-allergic patients or other patients for whom, in the judgment of the health care provider, a penicillin is inappropriate.

Local Anesthetic/Vasoconstrictor Precautions No information available to require special precautions

Effects on Dental Treatment Key adverse event(s) related to dental treatment: Glossitis and stomatitis.

Effects on Bleeding No information available to require special precautions

Adverse Reactions Frequency not defined: Gastrointestinal: Colitis, severe colitis

<1%, postmarketing, and/or case reports: Abdominal distress, abdominal pain, abnormal hepatic function tests, abscess at injection site, agranulocytosis, anaphylaxis, angioedema, aplastic anemia, azotemia, bullous dermatitis, *Clostridium difficile* associated diarrhea, diarrhea, drowsiness, erythema multiforme, exfoliative dermatitis, glossitis, headache, hypersensitivity reaction, hypotension, immune thrombocytopenia, increased serum transaminases, induration at injection site, irritation at injection site, jaundice, leukopenia, nausea, neutropenia, oliguria, pain at injection site, pancytopenia, proteinuria, pruritus, pruritus ani, pseudomembranous colitis, renal insufficiency, serum sickness, skin rash, Stevens-Johnson syndrome, stomatitis, thrombophlebitis, tinnitus, urticaria, vaginal infection, vertigo, vomiting

General Dosage Range Dosage adjustment recommended in patients with renal impairment

IM:

Infants >1 month, Children, and Adolescents: 10 mg/kg every 12 to 24 hours

Adults: 600 mg every 12 to 24 hours

IV:

Infants >1 month, Children, and Adolescents: 10 to 20 mg/kg/day divided every 8 to 12 hours (maximum: 8 g daily)

Adults: 600 mg to 1 g every 8 to 12 hours (maximum: 8 g daily)

Ophthalmic: Subconjunctival injection: *Adults:* 75 mg as single dose

Mechanism of Action Lincosamide antibiotic isolated from a strain of *Streptomyces lincolnensis*; lincomycin, like clindamycin, inhibits bacterial protein synthesis by specifically binding on the 50S subunit and affecting the process of peptide chain initiation. Since only one molecule of antibiotic can bind to a single ribosome, the concomitant use of erythromycin and lincomycin is not recommended.

Pharmacodynamics/Kinetics

Half-life Elimination Serum: ~5 hours; prolonged with renal or hepatic impairment

Time to Peak Serum: IM: 1 hour

Pregnancy Risk Factor C

Pregnancy Considerations Adverse events were not observed in animal reproduction studies. Lincomycin crosses the placenta at term and can be detected in cord blood and the amniotic fluid (Medina 1963). Lincomycin injection may also contain benzyl alcohol, which may cross the placenta.

Linezolid (li NE zoh lid)

Brand Names: US Zyvox

Brand Names: Canada Apo-Linezolid; Linezolid Injection; Sandoz-Linezolid; Zyvoxam

Pharmacologic Category Antibiotic, Oxazolidinone

Use

Enterococcal infections (vancomycin-resistant): Treatment of vancomycin-resistant (VRE) *Enterococcus faecium* infections, including cases with concurrent bacteremia. **Note:** Not a preferred agent in resistant *E. faecalis* infections which are usually susceptible to beta-lactams (O'Driscoll 2015).

Pneumonia:

Community-acquired: Treatment of community-acquired pneumonia (CAP) caused by *Streptococcus pneumoniae*, including cases with concurrent bacteremia, or *Staphylococcus aureus* (methicillin-susceptible isolates only). **Note:** Not a preferred agent for CAP; may be used as an alternate choice in multi-drug resistant *S. pneumoniae* and MRSA pneumonia. For methicillin-susceptible *S. aureus*, the use of beta-lactams is preferred (IDSA/ATS [Mandell 2007]).

Hospital-acquired or healthcare-associated: Treatment of hospital-acquired or healthcare-associated pneumonia caused by *S. aureus* (methicillin-susceptible and -resistant isolates), or *S. pneumoniae*. **Note:** For methicillin-susceptible *S. aureus*, the use of beta-lactams is preferred (IDSA/ATS [Kalil 2016]).

Skin and skin structure infections:

Complicated: Treatment of complicated skin and skin structure infections, including diabetic foot infections, without concomitant osteomyelitis, caused by *S. aureus* (methicillin-susceptible and -resistant isolates), *Streptococcus pyogenes*, or *Streptococcus agalactiae*.

Uncomplicated: Treatment of uncomplicated skin and skin structure infections caused by *S. aureus* (methicillin-susceptible isolates) or *S. pyogenes*.

Note: Generally reserved as alternate for skin and skin structure infections due to MRSA (IDSA [Liu 2011]; IDSA [Stevens 2014]).

Limitations of use: Linezolid has not been studied in the treatment of decubitus ulcers. Linezolid is not indicated for treatment of gram-negative infections; if a concomitant gram-negative pathogen is documented or suspected, initiate specific therapy immediately.

Local Anesthetic/Vasoconstrictor Precautions Linezolid has mild monoamine oxidase inhibitor properties. The clinician is reminded that vasoconstrictors have the potential to interact with MAO-Is to result in elevation of blood pressure. Caution is suggested.

Effects on Dental Treatment Key adverse event(s) related to dental treatment: Oral *Candida* infection, taste alteration, and tongue discoloration.

Effects on Bleeding No information available to require special precautions

Adverse Reactions Percentages as reported in adults; frequency similar in pediatric patients unless otherwise noted.

>10%:

Central nervous system: Headache (<1% to 11%)

Gastrointestinal: Diarrhea (3% to 11%)

Hematologic & oncologic: Decreased hemoglobin (1% to 16%), thrombocytopenia (<1% to 13%), leukopenia (children 1% to 12%; adults <1% to 2%)

1% to 10%:

Central nervous system: Insomnia (3%), dizziness (≤3%), vertigo (children 1%)

Dermatologic: Skin rash (1% to 2%), pruritus (children 1%)

Endocrine & metabolic: Increased amylase (<1% to 2%), increased lactate dehydrogenase (<1% to 2%)

Gastrointestinal: Nausea (1% to 10%), vomiting (1% to 9%), increased serum lipase (3% to 4%), constipation (2%), dysgeusia (1% to 2%), loose stools (children 1% to 2%), oral candidiasis (1% to 2%), abdominal pain (≤2%), tongue discoloration (≤1%), pancreatitis

Genitourinary: Vulvovaginal candidiasis (1% to 2%)

Hematologic & oncologic: Neutropenia (children 1% to 6%; adults ≤1%), anemia (children ≤6%; adults ≤2%), eosinophilia (children ≤2%)

Hepatic: Increased serum ALT (≤10%), increased serum bilirubin (children ≤6%; adults ≤1%), increased serum AST (adults 2% to 5%), increased serum alkaline phosphatase (<1% to 4%), abnormal hepatic function tests (≤2%)

Infection: Fungal infection (≤1% to 2%)

Renal: Increased blood urea nitrogen (≤2%), increased serum creatinine (<1% to 2%)

Miscellaneous: Fever (2%)

<1%, postmarketing, and/or case reports: Anaphylaxis, angioedema, blurred vision, bullous skin disease, *Clostridium difficile*-associated diarrhea, convulsions, dental discoloration, dyspepsia, hypertension, hypoglycemia, lactic acidosis, optic neuropathy, pancytopenia, peripheral neuropathy, rhabdomyolysis, seizures, serotonin syndrome (with concurrent use of other serotonergic agents), Stevens-Johnson syndrome, vision loss

General Dosage Range

IV:

Children ≤11 years: 10 mg/kg every 8 hours (maximum dose: 600 mg)

Children ≥12 years, Adolescents, and Adults: 600 mg every 12 hours

Oral:

Children <5 years: 10 mg/kg every 8 hours (maximum: 600 mg/dose)

Children 5 to 11 years: 10 mg/kg every 8 to 12 hours (maximum: 600 mg/dose)

Children ≥12 years, Adolescents, and Adults: 400 to 600 mg every 12 hours

Mechanism of Action Inhibits bacterial protein synthesis by binding to bacterial 23S ribosomal RNA of the 50S subunit. This prevents the formation of a functional 70S initiation complex that is essential for the bacterial translation process. Linezolid is bacteriostatic against enterococci and staphylococci and bactericidal against most strains of streptococci.

Pharmacodynamics/Kinetics

Half-life Elimination

Preterm neonates <1 week: 5.6 hours

Full-term neonates <1 week: 3 hours

Full-term neonates ≥1 week to ≤28 days: 1.5 hours

Infants >28 days to <3 months: 1.8 hours

Infants and Children 3 months to 11 years: 2.9 hours

Adolescents: 4.1 hours

Adults: 4.9 hours

Time to Peak Adults: Oral: 1 to 2 hours

Pregnancy Risk Factor C

Pregnancy Considerations Adverse effects were observed in some animal reproduction studies at doses that were also maternally toxic. Information related to linezolid use during pregnancy is limited.

Liothyronine (lye oh THYE roe neen)

Related Information

Endocrine Disorders and Pregnancy *on page 1781*

Brand Names: US Cytomel; Triostat

Brand Names: Canada Cytomel

Pharmacologic Category Thyroid Product

Use

Thyroid disorders: Oral: Replacement or supplemental therapy in hypothyroidism of any etiology, except transient hypothyroidism during the recovery phase of subacute thyroiditis; as a pituitary thyroid-stimulating hormone (TSH) suppressant in the management or prevention of nontoxic goiter, thyroid nodules, subacute or chronic autoimmune thyroiditis (Hashimoto's), and multinodular goiter; a diagnostic agent in suppression tests to differentiate suspected mild hyperthyroidism or thyroid gland autonomy

Myxedema coma/precoma: IV: Treatment of myxedema coma/precoma

Note: May be used in patients allergic to desiccated thyroid or thyroid extract derived from pork or beef.

Local Anesthetic/Vasoconstrictor Precautions No precautions with vasoconstrictor are necessary if patient is well controlled with liothyronine

Effects on Dental Treatment No significant effects or complications reported

Effects on Bleeding No information available to require special precautions

Adverse Reactions

1% to 10%: Cardiovascular: Cardiac arrhythmia (6%), tachycardia (3%), hypotension (2%), myocardial infarction (2%)

<1%, postmarketing, and/or case reports: Allergic skin reaction, angina pectoris, cardiac failure, fever, hypertension, phlebitis, twitching

General Dosage Range

IV: *Adults:* 10 to 50 mcg/dose

Oral:

Infants: Initial: 5 mcg/day; Usual maintenance dose: 20 mcg/day

Children 1 to 3 years: Initial: 5 mcg/day; Usual maintenance dose: 50 mcg/day

Children >3 years: Initial: 5 mcg/day; Maintenance: Up to 100 mcg/day

Adults: Initial 5 to 25 mcg/day; Maintenance range 5 to 100 mcg/day

Elderly: Initial: 5 mcg/day

Mechanism of Action Exact mechanism of action is unknown; however, it is believed the thyroid hormone exerts its many metabolic effects through control of DNA transcription and protein synthesis; involved in normal metabolism, growth, and development; promotes gluconeogenesis, increases utilization and mobilization of glycogen stores, and stimulates protein synthesis, increases basal metabolic rate

Pharmacodynamics/Kinetics

Onset of Action ~3 hours

Half-life Elimination 0.75 days (Brent 2011)

Pregnancy Risk Factor A

Pregnancy Considerations Endogenous thyroid hormones minimally cross the placenta; the fetal thyroid becomes active around the end of the first trimester. Liothyronine has not been found to increase the risk of teratogenic or adverse effects following maternal use during pregnancy.

Uncontrolled maternal hypothyroidism may result in adverse neonatal and maternal outcomes. To prevent adverse events, normal maternal thyroid function should be maintained prior to conception and throughout pregnancy. Levothyroxine is considered the treatment of choice for the control of hypothyroidism during pregnancy.

Liotrix (LYE oh triks)

Related Information

Endocrine Disorders and Pregnancy *on page 1781*

Brand Names: US Thyrolar

Brand Names: Canada Thyrolar

Pharmacologic Category Thyroid Product

Use

Replacement or supplemental therapy in hypothyroidism (uniform mixture of T_4:T_3 in 4:1 ratio by weight)

Thyroid-stimulating hormone (TSH) suppressant therapy used in the management of thyroid cancer (levothyroxine is generally recommended for this indication); prevention or treatment of euthyroid goiters (eg, thyroid nodules, subacute or chronic lymphocytic thyroiditis [Hashimoto's], multinodular goiters)

Diagnostic agent in suppression tests to diagnose suspected mild hyperthyroidism or to demonstrate thyroid gland autonomy

Local Anesthetic/Vasoconstrictor Precautions No precautions with vasoconstrictor are necessary if patient is well controlled with liotrix

Effects on Dental Treatment No significant effects or complications reported

Effects on Bleeding No information available to require special precautions

Adverse Reactions Frequency not defined.

Cardiovascular: Cardiac arrhythmia, chest pain, increased blood pressure, palpitations, tachycardia

Central nervous system: Anxiety, ataxia, headache, insomnia, nervousness

Dermatologic: Alopecia, diaphoresis, pruritus, urticaria

Endocrine & metabolic: Menstrual disease, weight loss

Gastrointestinal: Abdominal cramps, constipation, diarrhea, increased appetite, nausea, vomiting

Neuromuscular & skeletal: Myalgia, tremor, tremor of hands

Respiratory: Dyspnea

Miscellaneous: Fever

<1%, postmarketing, and/or case reports: Allergic skin reaction

General Dosage Range Oral:

Children 0-6 months: Levothyroxine 12.5-25 mcg/Liothyronine 3.1-6.25 mcg once daily

Children 6-12 months: Levothyroxine 25-37.5 mcg/Liothyronine 6.25-9.35 mcg once daily

Children 1-5 years: Levothyroxine 37.5-50 mcg/Liothyronine 9.35-12.5 mcg once daily

Children 6-12 years: Levothyroxine 50-75 mcg/Liothyronine 12.5-18.75 mcg once daily

Children >12 years: Levothyroxine 75 mcg/Liothyronine 18.75 mcg once daily

Adults: Initial: Levothyroxine 25 mcg/Liothyronine 6.25 mcg once daily; Usual maintenance: Levothyroxine 50-100 mcg/Liothyronine 12.5-25 mcg once daily

Elderly: Initial: Levothyroxine 12.5-25 mcg/Liothyronine 3.1-6.25 mcg once daily

Mechanism of Action The primary active compound is T_3 (triiodothyronine), which may be converted from T_4 (thyroxine) and then circulates throughout the body to influence growth and maturation of various tissues. Liotrix is uniform mixture of synthetic T_4 and T_3 in 4:1 ratio; exact mechanism of action is unknown; however, it is believed the thyroid hormone exerts its many metabolic effects through control of DNA transcription and protein synthesis; involved in normal metabolism, growth, and development; promotes gluconeogenesis, increases utilization and mobilization of glycogen stores and stimulates protein synthesis, increases basal metabolic rate

Pharmacodynamics/Kinetics

Onset of Action Liothyronine (T_3): ~3 hours

Half-life Elimination

T_4: Euthyroid: 6-7 days; Hyperthyroid: 3-4 days; Hypothyroid: 9-10 days

T_3: 2.5 days

Time to Peak Serum: T_4: 2-4 hours; T_3: 2-3 days

Pregnancy Risk Factor A

Pregnancy Considerations Endogenous thyroid hormones minimally cross the placenta; the fetal thyroid becomes active around the end of the first trimester. Liotrix has not been found to increase the risk of adverse effects following maternal use during pregnancy.

Uncontrolled maternal hypothyroidism may result in adverse neonatal and maternal outcomes. To prevent adverse events, normal maternal thyroid function should be maintained prior to conception and throughout pregnancy. Levothyroxine is considered the treatment of choice for the control of hypothyroidism during pregnancy.

Liraglutide (lir a GLOO tide)

Related Information

Endocrine Disorders and Pregnancy *on page 1781*

Brand Names: US Saxenda; Victoza

Brand Names: Canada Victoza

Pharmacologic Category Antidiabetic Agent, Glucagon-Like Peptide-1 (GLP-1) Receptor Agonist

Use

Chronic weight management (Saxenda): As an adjunct to a reduced-calorie diet and increased physical activity for chronic weight management in adult patients with an initial body mass index of 30 kg/m² or greater (obese) or 27 kg/m² or greater (overweight) in the presence of at least one weight-related comorbid condition (eg, hypertension, type 2 diabetes mellitus, dyslipidemia)

Diabetes mellitus, type 2 (Victoza): As an adjunct to diet and exercise to improve glycemic control in adults with type 2 diabetes mellitus.

Local Anesthetic/Vasoconstrictor Precautions No information available to require special precautions

Effects on Dental Treatment Key adverse event(s) related to dental treatment: Schedule type 1 and type 2 diabetic patients for dental treatment in the morning in order to minimize chance of stress-induced hypoglycemia.

Effects on Bleeding No information available to require special precautions

Adverse Reactions

Obesity:

>10%:

Cardiovascular: Increased heart rate (>10 bpm from baseline: 34%; >20 bpm from baseline: 5%)

Central nervous system: Headache (14%)

Endocrine & metabolic: Hypoglycemia (Type 2 diabetics: Combination therapy with sulfonylurea: 44%; monotherapy: 16%; nondiabetic patients: 2% to 3%)

Gastrointestinal: Nausea (39%), diarrhea (21%), constipation (19%), vomiting (16%)

1% to 10%:

Cardiovascular: Tachycardia (6%; one resting heart rate >100 bpm)

Central nervous system: Fatigue (8%), dizziness (7%)

Gastrointestinal: Decreased appetite (10%), dyspepsia (10%), abdominal distension (5%), abdominal pain (5%), eructation (5%), gastroenteritis (5%), gastroesophageal reflux disease (5%), increased serum lipase (5%; >3 x ULN: 2%), upper abdominal pain (5%), flatulence (4%), viral gastroenteritis (3%), cholelithiasis (2%), xerostomia (2%)

Genitourinary: Urinary tract infection (4%)

Immunologic: Antibody development (3%; neutralizing: 1%)

Local: Injection site reactions (3% to 14%; including erythema [1% to 3%], itching [1% to 3%], rash [1% to 3%])

Neuromuscular & skeletal: Weakness (2%)

Type 2 diabetes mellitus: Incidence reported in monotherapy trials unless otherwise specified.

>10%:

Central nervous system: Headache (10% to 11%)

Endocrine & metabolic: Increased amylase (in patients with renal impairment: 15%)

Gastrointestinal: Gastrointestinal disease (43%), nausea (18% to 20%), diarrhea (10% to 12%), increased serum lipase (in patients with renal impairment: 33%)

Infection: Infection (patients with antibodies: 40%)

Respiratory: Upper respiratory tract infection (7%; patients with antibodies: 11%)

1% to 10%:

Gastrointestinal: Decreased appetite (9% to 10%), dyspepsia (combination trials: 9%, monotherapy: 4% to 7%), vomiting (6% to 9%), constipation (5%)

Hepatic: Hyperbilirubinemia (monotherapy and combination trials: 4%)

Immunologic: Antibody development: Low titers (concentrations not requiring dilution of serum), monotherapy and combination trials: 9%, neutralizing antibodies: 2%, antibodies did not reduce efficacy; cross-reacting antiliraglutide antibodies to native GLP-1 (monotherapy: 7%; combination trials: 5%)

Local: Injection site reactions (monotherapy and combination trials: 2% [includes rash, erythema])

Neuromuscular & skeletal: Back pain (4% to 5%)

Respiratory: Nasopharyngitis (9% to 10%)

<1%, postmarketing, and/or case reports (any indication): Acute renal failure, anaphylaxis, angioedema, asthma, benign gastrointestinal neoplasm (colorectal), bronchospasm, carcinoma (papillary thyroid), cholecystitis, cholestasis, chronic renal failure (exacerbation), dehydration, dysgeusia, facial edema, first degree atrioventricular block, hepatitis, hypersensitivity reaction, increased liver enzymes, increased serum calcitonin, increased serum creatinine, increased susceptibility to infection, left bundle branch block, malaise, malignant neoplasm (including colorectal carcinoma), malignant neoplasm of breast, medullary thyroid carcinoma, oropharyngeal edema, pancreatitis (including acute, chronic, hemorrhagic, and necrotizing), papillary thyroid carcinoma, pharyngeal edema, pruritus, right bundle branch block, skin rash, suicidal ideation, systolic hypotension, thyroid disease (C-cell hyperplasia), urticaria

General Dosage Range SubQ: *Adults:* Initial: 0.6 mg once daily; maintenance: 1.2 to 1.8 mg once daily (diabetes mellitus type 2); 3 mg once daily (chronic weight management)

Mechanism of Action Liraglutide is a long acting analog of human glucagon-like peptide-1 (GLP-1) (an incretin hormone) which increases glucose-dependent insulin secretion, decreases inappropriate glucagon secretion, increases B-cell growth/replication, slows gastric emptying, and decreases food intake. Liraglutide administration results in decreases in hemoglobin A_{1c} by approximately 1%.

Pharmacodynamics/Kinetics

Half-life Elimination ~13 hours

Time to Peak Plasma: to 12 hours

Pregnancy Risk Factor X (Saxenda)/C (Victoza)

Pregnancy Considerations Use of liraglutide for chronic weight management is contraindicated in pregnant women (lack of potential benefit and possible fetal harm). An increased risk of adverse maternal and fetal outcomes is associated with obesity; however, medications for weight loss therapy are not recommended at conception or during pregnancy (ACOG 156 2015).

In women with diabetes, maternal hyperglycemia can be associated with congenital malformations as well as adverse effects in the fetus, neonate, and the mother (ACOG 2005; ADA 2016c; Kitzmiller 2008; Metzger 2007). To prevent adverse outcomes, prior to conception and throughout pregnancy maternal blood glucose and HbA1c should be kept as close to target goals as possible but without causing significant hypoglycemia (ACOG 137 2013; ADA 2016c; Blumer 2013; Kitzmiller 2008). Agents other than liraglutide are currently recommended to treat diabetes in pregnant women (ACOG 137 2013; Blumer 2013).

Lisdexamfetamine (lis dex am FET a meen)

Brand Names: US Vyvanse

Brand Names: Canada Vyvanse

Pharmacologic Category Central Nervous System Stimulant

Use

Attention-deficit/hyperactivity disorder: Treatment of attention-deficit/hyperactivity disorder (ADHD).

Binge eating disorder: Treatment of moderate to severe binge eating disorder in adults.

Local Anesthetic/Vasoconstrictor Precautions Use vasoconstrictor with caution in patients taking lisdexamfetamine. Amphetamines enhance the sympathomimetic response of epinephrine or mepivacaine and levonordefrin (Carbocaine® 2% with Neo-Cobefrin®) leading to potential hypertension and cardiotoxicity.

Effects on Dental Treatment Key adverse event(s) related to dental treatment: Lisdexamfetamine causes tachycardia, increases in blood pressure, and palpitations. Consider monitoring blood pressure prior to using local anesthetic with a vasoconstrictor. Symptoms associated with bruxism have been observed in some patients.

Effects on Bleeding No information available to require special precautions

Adverse Reactions

>10%:

Central nervous system: Insomnia (13% to 27%)

Gastrointestinal: Decreased appetite (children and adolescents: 34% to 39%; adults: 8% to 27%), xerostomia (adults: 26% to 36%; children and adolescents: 4% to 5%), upper abdominal pain (children: 12%; adults: 2%)

1% to 10%:

Cardiovascular: Increased heart rate (adults: 2% to 7%), increased blood pressure (adults: 3%)

Central nervous system: Irritability (children: 10%), anxiety (adults: 5% to 6%), jitteriness (adults: 4% to 6%), dizziness (children: 5%), agitation (adults: 3%), emotional lability (children: 3%), restlessness (adults: 2% to 3%), drowsiness (children: 2%), increased energy (adults: 2%), nightmares (adults: 2%), paresthesia (adults: 2%), tics (children: 2%)

Dermatologic: Hyperhidrosis (adults: 3% to 4%), skin rash (children: 3%), pruritus (adults: 2%)

Endocrine & metabolic: Weight loss (children and adolescents: 9%; adults: 3% to 4%), decreased libido (adults: <2%)

Gastrointestinal: Vomiting (children: 9%; adults: 2%), diarrhea (adults: 7%), nausea (6% to 7%), constipation (adults: 6%), anorexia (adults: 5%), gastroenteritis (adults: 2%)

Genitourinary: Erectile dysfunction (adults: 3%)

Neuromuscular & skeletal: Tremor (adults: 2%)

Respiratory: Dyspnea (adults: 2%), oropharyngeal pain (2%)

Miscellaneous: Fever (children: 2%)

<1%, postmarketing, and/or case reports: Accommodation disturbance, aggressive behavior, anaphylaxis, angioedema, blurred vision, bruxism, cardiomyopathy, decreased linear skeletal growth rate, depression, dermatillomania, diplopia, dysgeusia, dyskinesia, excoriation, frequent erections, hallucination, headache, hepatitis (eosinophilic), hypersensitivity, mania, mydriasis, palpitations, peripheral vascular insufficiency, prolonged erection, psychotic reaction, Raynaud phenomenon, seizure, Stevens-Johnson syndrome, urticaria

General Dosage Range

Dosage adjustment recommended in patients with renal impairment.

Oral: *Children ≥6 years, Adolescents, and Adults:* Initial: 30 mg once daily (maximum: 70 mg/day)

Mechanism of Action The exact mechanism of lisdexamfetamine in ADHD and binge eating disorder is not known. Lisdexamfetamine dimesylate is a prodrug that is converted to the active component dextroamphetamine (a noncatecholamine, sympathomimetic amine). Amphetamines are noncatecholamine, sympathomimetic amines that cause release of catecholamines (primarily dopamine and norepinephrine) from their storage sites in the presynaptic nerve terminals. A less significant mechanism may include their ability to block the reuptake of catecholamines by competitive inhibition.

Pharmacodynamics/Kinetics

Half-life Elimination Lisdexamfetamine: <1 hour; Dextroamphetamine: 10 to 13 hours

Time to Peak T_{max}: Lisdexamfetamine: Children 6 to 12 years: 1 hour (fasting); Adults: ~1 hour; Dextroamphetamine: Children 6 to 12 years: 3.5 hours (fasting); Adults: 3.8 hours (fasting), 4.7 hours (after a high-fat meal)

Pregnancy Considerations Lisdexamfetamine is converted to dextroamphetamine. The majority of human data is based on illicit amphetamine/methamphetamine exposure and not from therapeutic maternal use (Golub 2005). Use of amphetamines during pregnancy may lead to an increased risk of premature birth and low birth weight; newborns may experience symptoms of withdrawal. Behavioral problems may also occur later in childhood (LaGasse 2012).

Product Availability Vyvanse chewable tablets: FDA approved January 2017; availability anticipated in March 2017. Information pertaining to this product within the monograph is pending revision. Consult the prescribing information for additional information.

Controlled Substance C-II

Lisinopril (lyse IN oh pril)

Related Information

Cardiovascular Diseases *on page 1752*

Brand Names: US Prinivil; Qbrelis; Zestril

Brand Names: Canada ACT Lisinopril; Apo-Lisinopril; Auro-Lisinopril; Dom-Lisinopril; JAMP-Lisinopril; Mylan-Lisinopril; PMS-Lisinopril; Prinivil; PRO-Lisinopril; RAN-Lisinopril; Riva-Lisinopril; Sandoz-Lisinopril; Teva-Lisinopril (Type P); Teva-Lisinopril (Type Z); Zestril

Generic Availability (US) May be product dependent

Pharmacologic Category Angiotensin-Converting Enzyme (ACE) Inhibitor; Antihypertensive

Use

Acute myocardial infarction: Treatment of acute myocardial infarction (MI) within 24 hours in hemodynamically-stable patients to improve survival.

Heart failure: Adjunctive therapy in treatment systolic of heart failure (HF).

Hypertension: Management of hypertension in adult and pediatric patients 6 years and older (monotherapy or in combination with other antihypertensives).

Guideline recommendations:

Heart failure: The ACCF/AHA 2013 heart failure guidelines recommend the use of ACE inhibitors, along with other guideline directed medical therapies, to prevent HF in patients with a reduced ejection fraction who have a history of MI (stage B HF), to prevent HF in any patient with a reduced ejection fraction (stage B HF), or to treat those with HF and reduced ejection fraction (stage C HFrEF) (Yancy, 2013).

Hypertension: The 2014 guideline for the management of high blood pressure in adults (Eighth Joint National Committee [JNC 8]) recommends initiation of pharmacologic treatment to lower blood pressure for the following patients:

- Patients ≥60 years of age with systolic blood pressure (SBP) ≥150 mm Hg or diastolic blood pressure (DBP) ≥90 mm Hg. Goal of therapy is SBP <150 mm Hg and DBP <90 mm Hg.
- Patients <60 years of age with SBP ≥140 mm Hg or DBP is ≥90 mm Hg. Goal of therapy is SBP <140 mm Hg and DBP <90 mm Hg.
- Patients ≥18 years of age with diabetes and SBP ≥140 mm Hg or DBP ≥90 mm Hg. Goal of therapy is SBP <140 mm Hg and DBP <90 mm Hg.
- Patients ≥18 years of age with chronic kidney disease (CKD) and SBP ≥140 mm Hg or DBP ≥90 mm Hg. Goal of therapy is SBP <140 mm Hg and DBP <90 mm Hg.

Chronic kidney disease (CKD) and hypertension: Regardless of race or diabetes status, the use of an ACE inhibitor (ACEI) or angiotensin receptor blocker (ARB) as initial therapy is recommended to improve kidney outcomes. In the general nonblack population (without CKD) including those with diabetes, initial antihypertensive treatment should consist of a thiazide-type diuretic, calcium channel blocker, ACEI, or ARB. In the general black population (without CKD) including those with diabetes, initial antihypertensive treatment should consist of a thiazide-type diuretic or a calcium channel blocker **instead of** an ACEI or ARB.

Coronary artery disease (CAD) and hypertension: The American Heart Association, American College of Cardiology and American Society of Hypertension (AHA/ACC/ASH) 2015 scientific statement for the treatment of hypertension in patients with CAD recommends the use of an ACE inhibitor (or an ARB) as part of a regimen in patients with hypertension and chronic stable angina if there is prior MI, LV systolic dysfunction, diabetes mellitus, or CKD. A BP target of <140/90 mm Hg is reasonable for the secondary prevention of cardiovascular events. A lower target BP (<130/80 mm Hg) may be appropriate in some individuals with CAD, previous MI, stroke or transient ischemic attack, or CAD risk equivalents (AHA/ACC/ASH [Rosendorff 2015]).

STEMI: The 2013 American College of Cardiology Foundation/American Heart Association (ACCF/AHA) guidelines for the management of patients with ST-elevation myocardial infarction (STEMI) states that an ACE inhibitor should be initiated within the first 24 hours after STEMI in patients with anterior MI, heart failure, or left ventricular ejection fraction (LVEF) of 0.4 or less. It is also reasonable to initiate an ACE inhibitor in all patients with STEMI (O'Gara, 2013).

Local Anesthetic/Vasoconstrictor Precautions No information available to require special precautions

Effects on Dental Treatment Key adverse event(s) related to dental treatment: Patients may experience orthostatic hypotension as they stand up after treatment; especially if lying in dental chair for extended periods of time. Use caution with sudden changes in position during and after dental treatment.

An angiotensin-converting enzyme (ACE) Inhibitor cough is a dry, hacking, nonproductive cough that can potentially interfere with longer dental procedures if patient has this side effect.

Effects on Bleeding No information available to require special precautions

Adverse Reactions

>10%:

Cardiovascular: Hypotension (4% to 11%)

Central nervous system: Dizziness (4% to 19%)

Renal: Increased serum creatinine (≤10%; transient), increased blood urea nitrogen (≤2%; transient)

1% to 10%:

Cardiovascular: Syncope (5% to 7%), chest pain (2% to 3%), flushing (≥1%), orthostatic effect (≥1%), vasculitis (≥1%)

Central nervous system: Headache (4% to 6%), altered sense of smell (≥1%), fatigue (≥1%), paresthesia (≥1%), vertigo (≥1%)

Dermatologic: Skin rash (≥1% to 2%), alopecia (≥1%), diaphoresis (≥1%), erythema (≥1%), pruritus (≥1%), skin photosensitivity (≥1%), Stevens-Johnson syndrome (≥1%), toxic epidermal necrolysis (≥1%), urticaria (≥1%)

Endocrine & metabolic: Hyperkalemia (2% to 6%), diabetes mellitus (≥1%), gout (≥1%), SIADH (≥1%)

Gastrointestinal: Diarrhea (≥1% to 4%), constipation (≥1%), dysgeusia (≥1%), flatulence (≥1%), pancreatitis (≥1%), xerostomia (≥1%)

Genitourinary: Impotence (≥1%)

Hematologic & oncologic: Bone marrow depression (≥1%), eosinophilia (≥1%), hemolytic anemia (≥1%), increased erythrocyte sedimentation rate (≥1%), leukocytosis (≥1%), leukopenia (≥1%), neutropenia (≥1%), positive ANA titer (≥1%), thrombocytopenia (≥1%; mean decrease of 0.4 mg/dL)

Neuromuscular & skeletal: Arthralgia (≥1%), arthritis (≥1%), myalgia (≥1%), weakness (≥1%)

Ophthalmic: Blurred vision (≥1%), diplopia (≥1%), photophobia (≥1%), vision loss (≥1%)

Otic: Tinnitus (≥1%)

Renal: Renal insufficiency (in patients with acute myocardial infarction: 1% to 2%)

Respiratory: Cough (3% to 4%)

Frequency not defined:

Hematologic & oncologic: Decreased hematocrit, decreased hemoglobin (mean decrease of 1.3%)

Hepatic: Increased liver enzymes, increased serum bilirubin

<1%, postmarketing, and/or case reports: Acute renal failure, angioedema, confusion, cutaneous pseudolymphoma, dehydration, fever, hallucination, hypoglycemia (diabetic patients on oral antidiabetic agents or insulin), hyponatremia, mood changes (including depressive symptoms), psoriasis, visual hallucination

Dosing

Adult

Acute myocardial infarction (within 24 hours in hemodynamically stable patients): Oral: 5 mg immediately, then 5 mg at 24 hours, 10 mg at 48 hours, and then 10 mg once daily for ≥6 weeks. Patients should continue to receive standard treatments such as thrombolytics, aspirin, and beta-blockers.

According to the 2013 ACCF/AHA guidelines for STEMI: Initial: 2.5 to 5 mg once daily; titrate to 10 mg daily or higher as tolerated (O'Gara 2013).

Note: For patients with SBP >100 to 120 mm Hg following infarct, initiate therapy with 2.5 mg once daily for 3 days; if SBP falls to ≤100 mm Hg give maintenance dose of 5 mg once daily (may temporarily reduce to 2.5 mg once daily if necessary). Discontinue if SBP <90 mm Hg for >1 hour.

Heart failure: Oral: Initial: 2.5 to 5 mg once daily; increase by no more than 10 mg increments at intervals no less than 2 weeks to the highest tolerated dose (maximum: 40 mg/day). Usual maintenance: 5 to 40 mg once daily. Target dose: 20 to 40 mg once daily (ACCF/AHA [Yancy 2013])

Note: If patient has hyponatremia (serum sodium <130 mEq/L), then initial dose should be 2.5 mg once daily.

Hypertension: Oral: Initial: 10 mg once daily (not maintained on a diuretic) or 5 mg once daily (maintained on a diuretic); adjust dose according to blood pressure response. Target dose (JNC 8 [James 2013]): 40 mg once daily; usual dosage range (ASH/ISH [Weber 2014]): 10 to 40 mg daily

Note: Antihypertensive effect may diminish toward the end of the dosing interval especially with doses of 10 mg daily. An increased dose may aid in extending the duration of antihypertensive effect. Doses up to 80 mg daily have been used, but do not appear to give greater effect. If possible, consider discontinuing diuretics 2 to 3 days prior to initiating lisinopril; restart diuretic, if needed, after blood pressure is stable.

Geriatric Refer to adult dosing. In the management of hypertension, consider lower initial doses (eg, 2.5 to 5 mg once daily) and titrate to response (Aronow, 2011).

Pediatric

Hypertension: Note: Compounded and commercially available oral solutions available in multiple concentrations; precautions should be taken to verify and avoid confusion between the different concentrations; dose should be clearly presented as mg.

Children <6 years (off-label population): Limited data available: Oral: Initial: 0.07 to 0.1 mg/kg once daily (maximum initial dose: 5 mg/day); increase dose at 1- to 2-week intervals; maximum: 0.6 mg/kg/day or 40 mg/day (NHBPEP 2004; NHLBI 2011; Raes 2007).

Children ≥6 years and Adolescents: Oral: Initial: 0.07 to 0.1 mg/kg once daily (maximum initial dose: 5 mg/day); increase dose at 1- to 2-week intervals; maximum: 0.6 mg/kg/day or 40 mg/day (NHBPEP 2004; NHLBI 2011; Raes 2007).

Renal Impairment

Adults:

Acute myocardial infarction (within 24 hours in hemodynamically stable patients):

CrCl >30 mL/minute: No dosage adjustment necessary.

CrCl 10 to 30 mL/minute: Initial: 2.5 mg once daily (maximum: 40 mg/day).

CrCl <10 mL/minute: Initial: 2.5 mg once daily (maximum: 40 mg/day).

Hemodialysis: Initial: 2.5 mg once daily (dialyzable) (maximum: 40 mg/day).

Heart failure:

CrCl >30 mL/minute: No dosage adjustment necessary.

CrCl 10 to 30 mL/minute: Initial: 2.5 mg once daily (maximum: 40 mg/day)

CrCl <10 mL/minute: Initial: 2.5 mg once daily (maximum: 40 mg/day)

Hemodialysis: Initial: 2.5 mg once daily (dialyzable) (maximum: 40 mg/day)

Hypertension:

CrCl >30 mL/minute: No dosage adjustment necessary.

CrCl 10 to 30 mL/minute: Initial: 5 mg once daily (maximum: 40 mg/day)

CrCl <10 mL/minute: Initial: 2.5 mg once daily (maximum: 40 mg/day)

Hemodialysis: Initial: 2.5 mg once daily (dialyzable) (maximum: 40 mg/day)

In addition, the following dosage adjustments have been recommended (Aronoff 2007):

GFR >50 mL/minute: No dosage adjustment necessary.

GFR 10 to 50 mL/minute: Administer 50% to 75% of usual dose.

GFR <10 mL/minute: Administer 25% to 50% of usual dose.

Intermittent hemodialysis: Dose after dialysis.

Continuous renal replacement therapy (CRRT): Administer 50% to 75% of usual dose.

Children ≥ 6 years and Adolescents:

Manufacturer's labeling:

GFR >30 mL/minute/1.73 m^2: No dosage adjustment necessary.

GFR <30 mL/minute/1.73 m^2: Use is not recommended.

In addition, the following dosage adjustments have been recommended (Aronoff 2007):

GFR >50 mL/minute/1.73 m^2: No dosage adjustment necessary.

GFR 10 to 50 mL/minute/1.73 m^2: Administer 50% of usual dose.

GFR <10 mL/minute/1.73 m^2: Administer 25% of usual dose.

Intermittent hemodialysis: Administer 25% of usual dose.

Peritoneal dialysis (PD): Administer 25% of usual dose.

Continuous renal replacement therapy (CRRT): Administer 50% of usual dose.

Hepatic Impairment There are no dosage adjustments provided in the manufacturer's labeling; use with caution.

Mechanism of Action Competitive inhibitor of angiotensin-converting enzyme (ACE); prevents conversion of angiotensin I to angiotensin II, a potent vasoconstrictor; results in lower levels of angiotensin II which causes an increase in plasma renin activity and a reduction in aldosterone secretion; a CNS mechanism may also be involved in hypotensive effect as angiotensin II increases adrenergic outflow from CNS; vasoactive kallikreins may be decreased in conversion to active hormones by ACE inhibitors, thus reducing blood pressure

Contraindications

Hypersensitivity to lisinopril, other ACE inhibitors, or any component of the formulation; angioedema related to previous treatment with an ACE inhibitor; idiopathic or hereditary angioedema; concomitant use with aliskiren in patients with diabetes mellitus.

Documentation of allergenic cross-reactivity for ACE inhibitors is limited. However, because of similarities in chemical structure and/or pharmacologic actions, the possibility of cross-sensitivity cannot be ruled out with certainty.

Canadian labeling: Additional contraindications (not in US labeling): Concomitant use with aliskiren-containing drugs in patients with moderate-to-severe renal impairment (GFR <60 mL/minute/1.73 m^2).

Warnings/Precautions Anaphylactic reactions may occur rarely with ACE inhibitors. At any time during treatment (especially following first dose), angioedema may occur rarely with ACE inhibitors; it may involve the head and neck (potentially compromising airway) or the intestine (presenting with abdominal pain). African-Americans may be at an increased risk. Risk may also be increased with concomitant use of mTOR inhibitor (eg, everolimus) therapy. Prolonged frequent monitoring may be required especially if tongue, glottis, or larynx are involved as they are associated with airway obstruction. Patients with a history of airway surgery may have a higher risk of airway obstruction. Aggressive early and appropriate management is critical. Use in patients with idiopathic or hereditary angioedema or previous angioedema associated with ACE inhibitor therapy is contraindicated. Severe anaphylactoid reactions may be seen during hemodialysis (eg, CVVHD) with high-flux dialysis membranes (eg, AN69), and rarely, during low density lipoprotein apheresis with dextran sulfate cellulose. Rare cases of anaphylactoid reactions have been reported in patients undergoing sensitization treatment with hymenoptera (bee, wasp) venom while receiving ACE inhibitors.

Symptomatic hypotension with or without syncope can occur with ACE inhibitors (usually with the first several doses). Effects are most often observed in volume depleted patients; correct volume depletion prior to initiation. Close monitoring of patient is required especially within the first few weeks of initial dosing and with dosing increases; blood pressure must be lowered at a rate appropriate for the patient's clinical condition. Initiation of therapy in patients with ischemic heart disease or cerebrovascular disease warrants close observation due to the potential consequences posed by falling blood pressure (eg, MI, stroke). Avoid use in hemodynamically unstable patients after acute MI. Use with caution in hypertrophic cardiomyopathy with outflow tract obstruction and severe aortic stenosis. In patients on chronic ACE inhibitor therapy, intraoperative hypotension may occur with induction and maintenance of general anesthesia; use with caution before, during, or immediately after major surgery. Cardiopulmonary bypass, intraoperative blood loss, or vasodilating anesthesia increases endogenous renin release. Use of ACE inhibitors perioperatively will blunt angiotensin II formation and may result in hypotension. However, discontinuation of therapy prior to surgery is controversial. If continued preoperatively, avoidance of hypotensive agents during surgery is prudent (Hillis 2011). **[US Boxed Warning]: Drugs that act on the renin-angiotensin system can cause injury and death to the developing fetus. Discontinue as soon as possible once pregnancy is detected.**

Hyperkalemia may occur with ACE inhibitors; risk factors include renal impairment, diabetes mellitus, concomitant use of potassium-sparing diuretics, potassium supplements, and/or potassium-containing salts. Use cautiously, if at all, with these agents and monitor potassium closely. Cough may occur with ACE inhibitors. Other causes of cough should be considered (eg, pulmonary congestion in patients with heart failure) and excluded prior to discontinuation. ACE inhibitors effectiveness is less in black patients than in non-black patients. In addition, ACE inhibitors cause a higher rate of angioedema in black than in non-black patients.

Use with caution in preexisting renal insufficiency; avoid rapid dosage escalation which may lead to further renal impairment. May be associated with deterioration of renal function and/or increases in BUN and serum creatinine, particularly in patients with low renal blood flow (eg, renal artery stenosis, heart failure) whose glomerular filtration rate (GFR) is dependent on efferent arteriolar vasoconstriction by angiotensin II; deterioration may result in oliguria, acute renal failure, and progressive azotemia. Small (benign) increases in serum creatinine may occur following initiation; consider discontinuation only in patients with progressive and/or significant deterioration in renal function (Bakris 2000). Use with caution in patients with unstented unilateral/bilateral renal artery stenosis. When unstented bilateral renal artery stenosis is present, use is generally avoided due to the elevated risk of deterioration in renal function unless possible benefits outweigh risks. In a retrospective cohort study of elderly patients (≥65 years) with MI and impaired left ventricular function, administration of an ACE inhibitor was associated with a survival benefit, including patients with serum creatinine concentrations >3 mg/dL (265 micromol/L) (Frances 2000).

Potentially significant drug-drug interactions may exist, requiring dose or frequency adjustment, additional monitoring, and/or selection of alternative therapy. Use with caution in patients with hepatic impairment; consider baseline hepatic function tests prior to initiating therapy. Rare toxicities associated with ACE inhibitors include cholestatic jaundice or hepatitis (which may progress to fulminant hepatic necrosis), anemia, neutropenia with myeloid hypoplasia, agranulocytosis, or thrombocytopenia. Patients with collagen vascular diseases (especially with concomitant renal impairment) or renal impairment alone may be at increased risk for hematologic toxicity; periodically monitor CBC with differential in these patients.

Some dosage forms may contain sodium benzoate/benzoic acid; benzoic acid (benzoate) is a metabolite of benzyl alcohol; large amounts of benzyl alcohol (≥99 mg/kg/day) have been associated with a potentially fatal toxicity ("gasping syndrome") in neonates; the "gasping syndrome" consists of metabolic acidosis, respiratory distress, gasping respirations, CNS dysfunction (including convulsions, intracranial hemorrhage), hypotension, and cardiovascular collapse (AAP ["Inactive" 1997]; CDC 1982). Some data suggest that benzoate displaces bilirubin from protein-binding sites (Ahlfors 2001); avoid or use dosage forms containing benzyl alcohol derivative with caution in neonates. See manufacturer's labeling.

Drug Interactions

Metabolism/Transport Effects None known.

Avoid Concomitant Use

Avoid concomitant use of Lisinopril with any of the following: Sacubitril

Increased Effect/Toxicity

Lisinopril may increase the levels/effects of: Allopurinol; Amifostine; Antipsychotic Agents (Second Generation [Atypical]); AzaTHIOprine; Ciprofloxacin (Systemic); Drospirenone; DULoxetine; Ferric Gluconate; Ferric Hydroxide Polymaltose Complex; Gold Sodium Thiomalate; Grass Pollen Allergen Extract (5 Grass Extract); Hypotension-Associated Agents; Iron Dextran Complex; Levodopa; Lithium; Nitroprusside;

Nonsteroidal Anti-Inflammatory Agents; Pregabalin; Sacubitril; Sodium Phosphates

The levels/effects of Lisinopril may be increased by: Alfuzosin; Aliskiren; Angiotensin II Receptor Blockers; Barbiturates; Benperidol; Brimonidine (Topical); Canagliflozin; Dapoxetine; Diazoxide; DPP-IV Inhibitors; Eplerenone; Everolimus; Heparin; Heparin (Low Molecular Weight); Herbs (Hypotensive Properties); Loop Diuretics; Lormetazepam; Molsidomine; Naftopidil; Nicergoline; Nicorandil; Obinutuzumab; Pentoxifylline; Phosphodiesterase 5 Inhibitors; Potassium Salts; Potassium-Sparing Diuretics; Prostacyclin Analogues; Quinagolide; Salicylates; Sirolimus; Temsirolimus; Thiazide and Thiazide-Like Diuretics; TiZANidine; Tolvaptan; Trimethoprim

Decreased Effect

The levels/effects of Lisinopril may be decreased by: Amphetamines; Aprotinin; Herbs (Hypertensive Properties); Icatibant; Lanthanum; Methylphenidate; Nonsteroidal Anti-Inflammatory Agents; Salicylates; Yohimbine

Dietary Considerations Use potassium-containing salt substitutes cautiously in patients with diabetes, patients with renal impairment, or those maintained on potassium supplements or potassium-sparing diuretics.

Pharmacodynamics/Kinetics

Onset of Action 1 hour; Peak effect: Hypotensive: Oral: ~6 hours

Duration of Action 24 hours

Half-life Elimination 12 hours

Time to Peak

Pediatric patients 6 months to 15 years: Median (range): 5 to 6 hours (Hogg 2007)

Adults: ~7 hours

Pregnancy Considerations [US Boxed Warning]: Drugs that act on the renin-angiotensin system can cause injury and death to the developing fetus. Discontinue as soon as possible once pregnancy is detected. Lisinopril crosses the placenta (Bhatt-Mehta 1993; Filler 2003).

Drugs that act on the renin-angiotensin system are associated with oligohydramnios. Oligohydramnios, due to decreased fetal renal function, may lead to fetal lung hypoplasia and skeletal malformations. The use of these drugs in pregnancy is also associated with anuria, hypotension, renal failure, skull hypoplasia, and death in the fetus/neonate. Teratogenic effects may occur following maternal use of an ACE inhibitor during the first trimester, although this finding may be confounded by maternal disease. Because adverse fetal events are well documented with exposure later in pregnancy, ACE inhibitor use in pregnant women is not recommended (Seely 2014; Weber 2014). Infants exposed to an ACE inhibitor in utero should be monitored for hyperkalemia, hypotension, and oliguria. Oligohydramnios may not appear until after irreversible fetal injury has occurred. Exchange transfusions or dialysis may be required to reverse hypotension or improve renal function, although data related to the effectiveness in neonates is limited.

Chronic maternal hypertension itself is also associated with adverse events in the fetus/infant and mother. ACE inhibitors are not recommended for the treatment of uncomplicated hypertension in pregnancy (ACOG 2013) and they are specifically contraindicated for the treatment of hypertension and chronic heart failure during pregnancy by some guidelines (Regitz-Zagrosek 2011). In addition, ACE inhibitors should generally be avoided in women of reproductive age (ACOG 2013). If treatment for hypertension or chronic heart failure in pregnancy is needed, other agents should be used (ACOG 2013; Regitz-Zagrosek 2011).

Breastfeeding Considerations It is not known if lisinopril is present in breast milk.

Due to the potential for serious adverse reactions in the breastfed infant, breastfeeding is not recommended by the manufacturer.

Peripartum cardiomyopathy (PPCM) that is diagnosed postpartum may be treated with ACE inhibitors; however, lisinopril is not the preferred ACE inhibitor (Regitz-Zagrosek 2011). In addition, breastfeeding is not recommended for women with PPCM due to the high metabolic demands of lactation and breastfeeding (Regitz-Zagrosek 2011; Sliwa 2010).

Dosage Forms

Solution, Oral:

Qbrelis: 1 mg/mL (150 mL)

Tablet, Oral:

Prinivil: 5 mg, 10 mg, 20 mg

Zestril: 2.5 mg, 5 mg, 10 mg, 20 mg, 30 mg, 40 mg

Generic: 2.5 mg, 5 mg, 10 mg, 20 mg, 30 mg, 40 mg

Lithium (LITH ee um)

Brand Names: US Lithobid

Brand Names: Canada Apo-Lithium Carbonate; Carbolith; Lithane; Lithmax; PMS-Lithium Carbonate; PMS-Lithium Citrate

Generic Availability (US) Yes

Pharmacologic Category Antimanic Agent

Use Bipolar disorder: Acute treatment of manic episodes and maintenance therapy for patients with a diagnosis of bipolar disorder.

Local Anesthetic/Vasoconstrictor Precautions No information available to require special precautions

Effects on Dental Treatment Key adverse event(s) related to dental treatment: Xerostomia and changes in salivation (normal salivary flow resumes upon discontinuation), salivary gland swelling, and metallic taste. Avoid NSAIDs if analgesics are required since lithium toxicity has been reported with concomitant administration; acetaminophen products (ie, singly or with opioids) are recommended.

Effects on Bleeding No information available to require special precautions

Adverse Reactions Frequency not always defined.

Cardiovascular: Abnormal T waves on ECG, bradycardia, cardiac arrhythmia, chest tightness, circulatory shock, cold extremities, edema, hypotension, myxedema, sinus node dysfunction, startled response, syncope

Central nervous system: Ataxia, blackout spells, cogwheel rigidity, coma, confusion, dizziness, drowsiness, dystonia, EEG pattern changes, extrapyramidal reaction, fatigue, hallucination, headache, hyperactive deep tendon reflex, hypertonia, involuntary choreoathetoid movements, lethargy, local anesthesia, memory impairment, loss of consciousness, metallic taste, myasthenia gravis (rare), pseudotumor cerebri, psychomotor retardation, reduced intellectual ability, restlessness, salty taste, sedation, seizure, slowed intellectual functioning, slurred speech, stupor, tics, vertigo, worsening of organic brain syndromes

Dermatologic: Acne vulgaris, alopecia, blue-gray skin pigmentation, dermal ulcer, dry or thinning of hair, exacerbation of psoriasis, folliculitis, pruritus, psoriasis, skin rash, xerosis

Endocrine & metabolic: Hypothyroidism (females 14%; males 5% [Johnston 1999]; children and adolescents: <1% (Findling 2015), albuminuria, dehydration, diabetes insipidus, euthyroid goiter, glycosuria, hypercalcemia (secondary to hyperparathyroidism [McKnight 2012]), hyperglycemia, hyperparathyroidism, hyperthyroidism, increased radioactive iodine uptake, increased thirst, polydipsia, weight gain, weight loss

Gastrointestinal: Abdominal pain, anorexia, dental caries, diarrhea, dysgeusia, dyspepsia, excessive salivation, flatulence, gastritis, nausea, vomiting, sialadenitis, sialorrhea, swelling of lips, xerostomia

Genitourinary: Impotence, incontinence, oliguria

Hematologic & oncologic: Leukocytosis

Hypersensitivity: Angioedema

Neuromuscular & skeletal: Joint swelling, muscle hyperirritability, neuromuscular excitability, polyarthralgia, tremor

Ophthalmic: Blurred vision, exophthalmos, nystagmus, transient scotoma

Otic: Tinnitus

Renal: Decreased creatinine clearance, polyuria

Miscellaneous: Fever

Dosing

Adult Note: Monitor serum concentrations and clinical response (efficacy and toxicity) to determine proper dose. Each 5 mL of lithium citrate oral solution contains 8 mEq of lithium ion, equivalent to the amount of lithium in 300 mg of lithium carbonate immediate release capsules/tablets.

Bipolar disorder (acute mania, acute depression [off-label use], and maintenance): Oral:

Immediate release: Initial: Initiate at low dose (eg, 300 mg 3 times daily or less); increase gradually based on response and tolerability (APA 2002); usual dosage: 900 to 1,800 mg/day in 3 to 4 divided doses

Extended release: Initiate at low dose (eg, 450 mg 2 times daily or less); increase gradually based on response and tolerability (APA 2002); usual dosage: 900 to 1,800 mg/day in 2 divided doses

Depression, augmentation of antidepressant (off-label use): Oral: Initial: Initiate at a low dose (eg, 300 mg once daily or 300 mg twice daily); increase gradually based on response and tolerability; usual dosage: 600 to 1200 mg daily in divided doses (Bauer 2003a; Bauer 2003b; Nelson 2014)

Geriatric Bipolar disorder (acute mania, acute depression [off-label use], and maintenance): Initiate therapy with lower doses; refer to adult dosing.

Pediatric Note: Monitor serum concentrations and clinical response (efficacy and toxicity) to determine proper dose. Each 5 mL of lithium citrate oral solution contains 8 mEq of lithium ion, equivalent to the amount of lithium in 300 mg of lithium carbonate immediate release capsules/tablets.

Bipolar disorder:

Immediate release: Oral: Children ≥6 years and Adolescents (off-label dose): Limited data available in ages <12 years. **Note:** Dosing in patients 6 years of age extrapolated from clinical experience (Kliegman 2007).

Patient weight <30 kg: Initial: 300 mg twice daily; increase dose at weekly intervals based on response and tolerability (including serum lithium concentration ≤1.4 mEq/L) in 300 mg/day increments up to a weight-dependent maximum daily dose. Patients <23 kg: 900 mg/day; patients ≥23 kg: 40 mg/kg/day. For maintenance therapy (long-term), doses were titrated to maintain the target serum trough concentration of 0.8 to 1.2 mEq/L as tolerated (Findling 2011; Findling 2013; Findling 2015).

Patient weight ≥30 kg: Initial: 300 mg 3 times daily; during first week of therapy (midweek), may increase dose by 300 mg/day; then continue to increase dose at weekly intervals in 300 mg/day increments to clinical response and as tolerated (including serum lithium concentration ≤1.4 mEq/L) not to exceed a maximum daily dose of 40 mg/kg/day. For maintenance therapy (long-term), doses were titrated to maintain the target serum trough concentration of 0.8 to 1.2 mEq/L as tolerated (Findling 2011; Findling 2013; Findling 2015).

Extended release: Oral: Children ≥12 years and Adolescents (off-label dose):

Fixed dosing: <22 kg: 600 mg/day; 22 to 41 kg: 900 mg/day; >41 kg: 1,200 mg/day administered in 2 divided doses (Kliegman 2016).

Weight-based dosing: Initial: 15 mg/kg/dose twice daily; maximum initial dose: 600 mg/dose; increase dose at weekly intervals as tolerated to target serum lithium concentration of 1 to 1.2 mEq/L (Patel 2006).

Renal Impairment

CrCl 10 to 50 mL/minute: Administer 50% to 75% of normal dose (Aronoff 2007).

CrCl <10 mL/minute: Administer 25% to 50% of normal dose (Aronoff 2007).

End-stage renal disease (ESRD) with hemodialysis: Dose after dialysis (Aronoff 2007).

Continuous renal replacement therapy (CRRT): Administer 50% to 75% of normal dose (Aronoff 2007).

Hepatic Impairment There are no dosage adjustments provided in manufacturer's labeling.

Mechanism of Action

The precise mechanism of action in mood disorders is unknown. Traditionally thought to alter cation transport across cell membranes in nerve and muscle cells, influence the reuptake of serotonin and/or norepinephrine, and inhibit second messenger systems involving the phosphatidylinositol cycle (Ward, 1994). May also provide neuroprotective effects by increasing glutamate clearance, inhibiting apoptotic glycogen synthase kinase activity, increasing the levels of antiapoptotic protein Bcl-2 and, enhancing the expression of neurotropic factors, including brain-derived neurotrophic factor (Sanacora 2008).

Contraindications

Hypersensitivity to lithium or any component of the formulation

Immediate-release capsule, solution and tablet: Severe cardiovascular or renal disease, severe debilitation, dehydration, sodium depletion, concurrent use with diuretics

Warnings/Precautions

[US Boxed Warning]: Lithium toxicity is closely related to serum concentrations and can occur at doses close to therapeutic levels. Facilities for prompt and accurate serum lithium determinations should be available before initiating therapy. Normal fluid and salt intake must be maintained during therapy. Lithium should generally not be given to patients with significant renal or cardiovascular disease, severe debilitation or dehydration, or sodium depletion due to risk of lithium toxicity; if use is unavoidable, lithium may be undertaken with extreme caution, including frequent serum lithium determinations and possibly hospitalization. Discontinue therapy if such clinical signs of lithium toxicity occur (eg, diarrhea, vomiting, tremor, mild ataxia, drowsiness, or muscular weakness). Higher serum concentrations may be required and tolerated during an acute manic phase; however, the tolerance decreases when symptoms subside. Use with caution in patients at risk of suicide (suicidal thoughts or behavior) by drug overdose; lithium has a narrow therapeutic index (APA 2002). In a scientific statement from the American Heart Association, lithium has been determined to be an agent that may cause direct myocardial toxicity that is reversible upon discontinuation (magnitude: major) (AHA [Page 2016]).

Hypercalcemia with or without hyperparathyroidism has been reported. Risks are greater in women and possibly in older patients; symptom onset does not appear to be related to therapy duration (Lehmann 2013). Serum calcium levels typically range from slightly above normal to over 15 mg/dL and PTH levels may range from high normal to several times the upper limit of normal (Lehmann 2013); magnesium levels are often elevated; serum phosphate levels may be either normal or low (Grandjean 2009). Monitor calcium and PTH levels as clinically indicated. Consider discontinuation if clinical manifestations of hypercalcemia are present (fatigue, weakness, abdominal pain, constipation, nephrolithiasis, bone pain) or if calcium levels are >11.4 mg/dL. Following discontinuation, check serum calcium levels weekly for one month for return to baseline. Changes are usually reversible if lithium is discontinued; however, sustained hypercalcemia and parathyroid gland enlargement has been reported (Lehmann 2013).

Chronic therapy results in diminished renal concentrating ability (nephrogenic diabetes insipidus); this is usually reversible when lithium is discontinued. Monitor for changes in renal function and avoid dehydration; re-evaluation of treatment may be necessary. Morphologic changes with glomerular and interstitial fibrosis and nephron atrophy have been reported in patients on chronic lithium therapy; morphologic changes have also been reported in patients with bipolar disorder never exposed to lithium. The relationship between morphologic changes and renal function, and the association with lithium therapy, have not been established. If polyuria develops during lithium therapy, consolidating to once daily dosing may decrease urine output (APA 2002; Carter 2013).

Generally avoid use in patients with significant renal disease, cardiovascular disease, fluid loss, or sodium depletion and in severely debilitated patients due to an increased risk of lithium toxicity. If use is unavoidable, use extreme caution and monitor serum lithium levels closely. Decreased tolerance to lithium has been reported with sweating or diarrhea and, if such occur, supplemental fluid and salt should be administered under careful medical supervision and lithium intake reduced or suspended until the condition is resolved. In addition, concomitant infection with elevated temperatures may also necessitate a temporary reduction or cessation of therapy. Lithium may unmask Brugada syndrome; avoid use in patients with or suspected of having Brugada syndrome. Consult with a cardiologist if a patient is suspected of having Brugada syndrome or has risk factors for Brugada syndrome (eg, unexplained syncope, a family history of Brugada syndrome, a family history of sudden death before the age of 45 years), or if unexplained syncope or palpitations develop after starting therapy. Use with caution in patients with thyroid disease. May cause hypothyroidism, generally within 6 to 18 months of initiating treatment. Women may be at an increased risk. If hypothyroidism develops and symptoms of bipolar disorder are well-controlled, consider continuing lithium and treating hypothyroidism (APA 2002). Use with caution in the elderly patients due to an increased risk of lithium toxicity. May cause CNS depression, which may impair physical or mental abilities; patients must be cautioned about performing tasks which require mental alertness (eg, operating machinery or driving). Potentially significant interactions may exist, requiring dose or frequency adjustment, additional monitoring, and/or selection of alternative therapy.

Some dosage forms may contain benzyl alcohol; large amounts of benzyl alcohol (≥99 mg/kg/day) have been associated with a potentially fatal toxicity ("gasping syndrome") in neonates; the "gasping syndrome" consists of metabolic acidosis, respiratory distress, gasping respirations, CNS dysfunction (including convulsions, intracranial hemorrhage), hypotension, and cardiovascular collapse (AAP ["Inactive" 1997]; CDC 1982); some data suggest that benzoate displaces bilirubin from protein binding sites (Ahlfors 2001); avoid or use dosage forms containing benzyl alcohol with caution in neonates. See manufacturer's labeling. Some dosage forms may contain propylene glycol; large amounts are potentially toxic and have been associated with hyperosmolality, lactic acidosis, seizures and respiratory depression; use caution (AAP 1997; Zar 2007). See manufacturer's labeling.

Drug Interactions

Metabolism/Transport Effects None known.

Avoid Concomitant Use

Avoid concomitant use of Lithium with any of the following: Dapoxetine; Methylene Blue

Increased Effect/Toxicity

Lithium may increase the levels/effects of: Antipsychotic Agents; Highest Risk QTc-Prolonging Agents; Metoclopramide; Moderate Risk QTc-Prolonging Agents; Neuromuscular-Blocking Agents; Potassium Iodate; Selective Serotonin Reuptake Inhibitors; Serotonin Modulators; TraMADol; Tricyclic Antidepressants

The levels/effects of Lithium may be increased by: ACE Inhibitors; Analgesics (Opioid); Angiotensin II Receptor Blockers; Antiemetics (5HT3 Antagonists); Calcium Channel Blockers (Nondihydropyridine); CarBAMazepine; Dapoxetine; Desmopressin; Eplerenone; Fosphenytoin; Linezolid; Loop Diuretics; MAO Inhibitors; Metaxalone; Methyldopa; Methylene Blue; Methylphenidate; MiFEPRIStone; Nonsteroidal Anti-Inflammatory Agents; Phenytoin; Potassium Iodide; Thiazide and Thiazide-Like Diuretics; Topiramate; TraMADol

Decreased Effect

Lithium may decrease the levels/effects of: Amphetamines; Antipsychotic Agents; Desmopressin

The levels/effects of Lithium may be decreased by: Caffeine and Caffeine Containing Products; Calcitonin; Calcium Polystyrene Sulfonate; Carbonic Anhydrase Inhibitors; Loop Diuretics; Sodium Bicarbonate; Sodium Chloride; Sodium Polystyrene Sulfonate; Theophylline Derivatives

Dietary Considerations May be taken with meals to avoid GI upset; maintain adequate salt and fluid intake.

Pharmacodynamics/Kinetics

Half-life Elimination

Pediatric patients 7 to 17 years: $t_{1/2\ (beta)}$: 27 hours (Findling 2010)

Adults: 18 to 36 hours; prolonged in elderly patients (28.5 hours) (Ward 1994)

Time to Peak Serum: Nonsustained release: ~0.5 to 3 hours; Extended release: 2 to 6 hours; Solution: 15 to 60 minutes (Ward 1994)

Pregnancy Risk Factor D

Pregnancy Considerations Adverse events have been observed in animal reproduction studies. Lithium crosses the placenta in concentrations similar to those in the maternal plasma (Newport 2005). Cardiac malformations in the infant, including Ebstein anomaly, are associated with use of lithium during the first trimester of pregnancy. Other adverse events including polyhydramnios, fetal/neonatal cardiac arrhythmias, hypoglycemia, diabetes insipidus, changes in thyroid function, premature delivery, floppy infant syndrome, or neonatal lithium toxicity are associated with lithium exposure when used later in pregnancy (ACOG 2008). The incidence of adverse events may be associated with higher maternal doses (Newport 2005).

Due to pregnancy-induced physiologic changes, women who are pregnant may require dose adjustments of lithium to achieve euthymia and avoid toxicity (ACOG 2008; Grandjean 2009; Yonkers 2011).

For planned pregnancies, use of lithium during the first trimester should be avoided if possible (Grandjean 2009). If lithium is needed during pregnancy, the minimum effective dose should be used, maternal serum concentrations should be monitored, and consideration should be given to start therapy after the period of organogenesis; lithium should be suspended 24 to 48 hours prior to delivery or at the onset of labor when delivery is spontaneous, then restarted when the patient is medically stable after delivery (ACOG 2008; Grandjean 2009; Newport 2005). Fetal echocardiography should be considered if first trimester exposure occurs (ACOG 2008).

Breastfeeding Considerations Lithium is excreted in breast milk and serum concentrations of nursing infants may be 10% to 50% of the maternal serum concentration (Grandjean 2009). Hypotonia, hypothermia, cyanosis, electrocardiogram changes, and lethargy have been reported in nursing infants (ACOG 2008). It is generally recommended that breastfeeding be avoided during maternal use of lithium; however, treatment may be continued in appropriately selected patients (Grandjean 2009; Sharma 2009; Viguera 2007). The hydration status of the nursing infant and maternal serum concentrations of lithium should be monitored (ACOG 2008). In addition, monitor the infant for lethargy, growth, and feeding problems; obtain infant serum concentrations only if clinical concerns arise (Bogen 2012; Yonkers 2011). Long-term effects on development and behavior have not been studied (ACOG 2008; Grandjean 2009).

Dosage Forms

Capsule, Oral:

Generic: 150 mg, 300 mg, 600 mg

Solution, Oral:

Generic: 8 mEq/5 mL (5 mL, 500 mL)

Tablet, Oral:

Generic: 300 mg

Tablet Extended Release, Oral:

Lithobid: 300 mg

Generic: 300 mg, 450 mg

Lixisenatide (lix i SEN a tide)

Brand Names: US Adlyxin; Adlyxin Starter Pack

Pharmacologic Category Antidiabetic Agent, Glucagon-Like Peptide-1 (GLP-1) Receptor Agonist

Use Diabetes mellitus, type 2: Treatment of type 2 diabetes mellitus (noninsulin dependent, NIDDM) to improve glycemic control in adult patients as an adjunct to diet and exercise

Local Anesthetic/Vasoconstrictor Precautions No information available to require special precautions

Effects on Dental Treatment No significant effects or complications reported

Effects on Bleeding No information available to require special precautions

Adverse Reactions

>10%:

Gastrointestinal: Gastrointestinal symptoms (40%; most were mild to moderate and within the first 3 weeks of starting treatment), nausea (25%)

Immunologic: Antibody development (70%: 2% had high antibody concentrations [>100 nmol/L] and experienced an attenuated glycemic response)

1% to 10%:

Central nervous system: Headache (9%), dizziness (7%)

Gastrointestinal: Vomiting (10%), diarrhea (8%), constipation (3%), dyspepsia (3%), abdominal distension (2%), upper abdominal pain (2%)

Local: Injection site reaction (4%; including pain, pruritus, and erythema)

<1%, postmarketing, and/or case reports: Acute renal injury, hypersensitivity reaction, pancreatitis (acute, chronic, and edematous), renal insufficiency

General Dosage Range SubQ: *Adults:* Initial: 10 mcg once daily; maintenance: 20 mcg once daily.

Mechanism of Action Lixisenatide is a selective glucagon-like peptide-1 (GLP-1) receptor agonist. Acting on the same receptor as the endogenous hormone incretin, lixisenatide increases glucose-dependent insulin secretion, decreases inappropriate glucagon secretion, and slows gastric emptying.

Pharmacodynamics/Kinetics

Half-life Elimination ~3 hours

Time to Peak 1 to 3.5 hours

Pregnancy Considerations

Adverse events were observed in some animal reproduction studies.

In women with diabetes, maternal hyperglycemia can be associated with congenital malformations as well as adverse effects in the fetus, neonate, and the mother (ACOG 60 2005; ADA 2016a; Kitzmiller 2008; Metzger 2007). To prevent adverse outcomes, prior to conception and throughout pregnancy maternal blood glucose and HbA_{1c} should be kept as close to target goals as possible but without causing significant hypoglycemia (ACOG 137 2013; ADA 2016a; Blumer 2013; Kitzmiller 2008). Prior to pregnancy, effective contraception should be used until glycemic control is achieved (ADA 2016a; Kitzmiller 2008). Other agents are currently recommended to treat diabetes in pregnant women (ACOG 137 2013; Blumer 2013).

L-Lysine (el LYE seen)

Related Information

Viral Infections *on page 1849*

Brand Names: US Lysine4000 [OTC]

Generic Availability (US) Yes

Pharmacologic Category Nutritional Supplement

Dental Use Prevention of recurrent herpes simplex infection

Use Improves utilization of vegetable proteins; prevention of recurrent herpes simplex infection

Local Anesthetic/Vasoconstrictor Precautions No information available to require special precautions

Effects on Dental Treatment No significant effects or complications reported

Effects on Bleeding No information available to require special precautions

Dental Usual Dosage Recurrent herpes simplex infection: Adults: Oral: 500-3000 mg/day; begin treatment during early stage of recurrence.

Dosing

Adult & Geriatric Oral:

Supplement: 334-1500 mg/day

Prevention of recurrent herpes simplex infection: 500-3000 mg/day; begin treatment during early stage of recurrence

Pregnancy Considerations L-lysine crosses the placenta in humans (Ronzoni, 1999; Schneider, 1979). Lysine is an essential amino acid. The RDA for lysine is increased in pregnant women (IOM, 2005).

Breastfeeding Considerations Lysine is an essential amino acid and is found in breast milk. The RDA for lysine is increased in breastfeeding women (IOM, 2005).

Dosage Forms

Capsule, Oral:

Generic: 500 mg

Packet, Oral:

Lysine4000 [OTC]: 4000 mg (30 ea)

Tablet, Oral:

Generic: 500 mg, 1000 mg

Lodoxamide (loe DOKS a mide)

Brand Names: US Alomide

Brand Names: Canada Alomide

Pharmacologic Category Mast Cell Stabilizer

Use Ocular disorders: Treatment of the ocular disorders referred to by the terms vernal keratoconjunctivitis, vernal conjunctivitis, and vernal keratitis

Local Anesthetic/Vasoconstrictor Precautions No information available to require special precautions

Effects on Dental Treatment No significant effects or complications reported

Effects on Bleeding No information available to require special precautions

Adverse Reactions

>10%: Ophthalmic: Burning sensation of eyes (transient), eye discomfort (transient), stinging of eyes (transient)

1% to 10%:

Central nervous system: Foreign body sensation of eye, headache

Ophthalmic: Blurred vision, crystalline eye deposits, eye pruritus, lacrimation, ocular hyperemia, ocular edema, xerophthalmia

1%, postmarketing, and/or case reports: Asthenopia, blepharitis, chemosis, corneal abrasion, corneal erosion, corneal ulcer, dizziness, drowsiness, dry nose, epitheliopathy, eye pain, keratitis, nausea, ocular warming sensation, skin rash, sneezing, stomach discomfort, swelling of eye

General Dosage Range Ophthalmic: *Children ≥2 years, Adolescents, and Adults:* Instill 1 to 2 drops in each affected eye 4 times daily

Mechanism of Action Mast cell stabilizer that inhibits the *in vivo* type I immediate hypersensitivity reaction to increase cutaneous vascular permeability associated with IgE and antigen-mediated reactions

Pharmacodynamics/Kinetics

Half-life Elimination 8.5 hours

Pregnancy Risk Factor B

Pregnancy Considerations Adverse events have not been observed in animal reproduction studies following oral administration. The amount of lodoxamide available systemically following ophthalmic administration is below the level of detection.

Lomitapide (loe MI ta pide)

Related Information

Cardiovascular Diseases *on page 1752*

Brand Names: US Juxtapid

Brand Names: Canada Juxtapid

Pharmacologic Category Antilipemic Agent, Microsomal Triglyceride Transfer Protein (MTP) Inhibitor

Use Homozygous familial hypercholesterolemia: Adjunct to a low-fat diet and other lipid-lowering treatments, including low-density lipoprotein (LDL) apheresis where available, to reduce low-density lipoprotein cholesterol (LDL-C), total cholesterol, apolipoprotein B (apo B), and non-high-density lipoprotein cholesterol (non-HDL-C) in patients with homozygous familial hypercholesterolemia (HoFH).

Local Anesthetic/Vasoconstrictor Precautions No information available to require special precautions

Effects on Dental Treatment

Key adverse event(s) related to dental treatment: Nasal congestion, nasopharyngitis, and pharyngolaryngeal pain

Effects on Bleeding No information available to require special precautions

Adverse Reactions

>10%:

Cardiovascular: Chest pain (24%)

Central nervous system: Fatigue (17%)

Gastrointestinal: Diarrhea (79%; severe: 14%), nausea (65%), dyspepsia (38%), vomiting (34%; severe: 10%), abdominal pain (34%; severe: 7%), weight loss (24%), abdominal discomfort (21%; severe: 7%), abdominal distension (21%; severe: 7%), constipation (21%), flatulence (21%), gastroenteritis (14%)

Hepatic: Liver steatosis (increase in hepatic fat >5%: 78%; >20% fat increase: 13%), increased serum transaminases ≥3 times upper limit of normal (34%), increased serum transaminases (17%; severe: 10%)

Neuromuscular & skeletal: Back pain (14%)

Respiratory: Nasopharyngitis (17%), pharyngolaryngeal pain (14%)

Miscellaneous: Influenza (21%)

1% to 10%:

Cardiovascular: Angina pectoris (10%), palpitation (10%)

Central nervous system: Dizziness (10%), fever (10%), headache (10%)

Gastrointestinal: Frequent bowel movement (10%), gastroesophageal reflux disease (10%), rectal tenesmus (10%)

Hepatic: Hepatotoxicity (severe: 10%)

Respiratory: Nasal congestion (10%)

<1%, postmarketing, and/or case reports: Abnormal pulmonary function test, anemia, anxiety, arthralgia, asthenia, chills, cough, decreased appetite, dehydration, early satiety, eructation, eye swelling, gait disturbance, gastroenteritis, hematemesis, hematuria, hepatomegaly, hyperhidrosis, hypersensitivity, increase neutrophil, increased appetite, increased gamma-glutamyl transferase, increased serum bilirubin, increased white blood cell count, joint swelling, lower gastrointestinal hemorrhage, malaise, muscle twitching, myalgia, myocardial infarction, pain in extremity, paresthesia, pharyngeal lesion, prolonged prothrombin time, proteinuria, pruritus, pyrexia, reflux, esophagitis, sinusitis, skin rash, somnolence, transient ischemic attack, vertigo, xeroderma, xerostomia

General Dosage Range Dosage adjustment recommended in patients on concomitant therapy, with renal or hepatic impairment, or who develop toxicities.

Oral: *Adults:* 5 to 60 mg once daily

Mechanism of Action Lomitapide directly binds to and inhibits microsomal triglyceride transfer protein (MTP) which is located in the lumen of the endoplasmic reticulum. MTP inhibition prevents the assembly of apo-B containing lipoproteins in enterocytes and hepatocytes resulting in reduced production of chylomicrons and VLDL and subsequently reduces plasma LDL-C concentrations.

Pharmacodynamics/Kinetics

Half-life Elimination 39.7 hours

Time to Peak ~6 hours

Pregnancy Risk Factor X

Pregnancy Considerations Adverse effects have been observed in animal reproduction studies using doses lower than equivalent human doses. Use is contraindicated in pregnant women. Discontinue immediately if pregnancy occurs during treatment. Women of reproductive potential should have a negative pregnancy test prior to therapy and effective contraception must be used during treatment. Dose adjustment may be required for women using oral contraceptives.

Health care providers are encouraged to enroll women exposed to lomitapide during pregnancy in the Global Lomitapide Pregnancy Exposure Registry by calling 1-877-902-4099.

Prescribing and Access Restrictions As a requirement of the REMS program, access to this medication is restricted. Prescribers must enroll in the Juxtapid REMS program and complete the Prescriber Training Module and complete, sign, and submit the Prescriber Enrollment Form to the Juxtapid REMS program. Pharmacies must educate all pharmacy staff involved in the dispensing of Juxtapid on the REMS program requirements, put processes in place to verify (prior to dispensing Juxtapid) that the prescriber is certified and the Prescription Authorization Form is received with each new prescription. Pharmacies must also agree to be audited to ensure that all processes and procedures in place are being followed in accordance with the program and be able to provide prescription data to the REMS program. Additional information is available at www.JUXTAPIDREMSProgram.com or at 1-855-898-2743.

Lomustine (loe MUS teen)

Brand Names: US Gleostine

Brand Names: Canada CeeNU

Pharmacologic Category Antineoplastic Agent, Alkylating Agent; Antineoplastic Agent, Alkylating Agent (Nitrosourea)

Use

Brain tumors: Treatment of primary and metastatic brain tumors (after appropriate surgical and/or radiotherapeutic procedures).

Hodgkin lymphoma: Treatment (in combination with other chemotherapy agents) of Hodgkin lymphoma which has progressed following initial chemotherapy; however, the use of lomustine in the management of Hodgkin lymphoma is limited due to efficacy of other chemotherapy agents/regimens.

Local Anesthetic/Vasoconstrictor Precautions No information available to require special precautions

Effects on Dental Treatment No significant effects or complications reported

Effects on Bleeding Delayed and cumulative myelosuppression is the major adverse effect and includes thrombocytopenia and anemia. Medical consult recommended.

Adverse Reactions

>10%:

Gastrointestinal: Nausea and vomiting, (onset: 3 to 6 hours after oral administration; duration: <24 hours)

Hematologic & oncologic: Leukopenia (65%; nadir: 5 to 6 weeks; recovery 6 to 8 weeks), bone marrow depression (dose-limiting, delayed, cumulative), thrombocytopenia (nadir: 4 weeks; recovery 5 to 6 weeks)

Frequency not defined:

Central nervous system: Ataxia, disorientation, dysarthria, lethargy

Dermatologic: Alopecia

Gastrointestinal: Stomatitis

Genitourinary: Azotemia (progressive), drug-induced nephrotoxicity, nephron atrophy

Hematologic & oncologic: Acute leukemia, anemia, bone marrow dysplasia

Hepatic: Hepatotoxicity, increased serum alkaline phosphatase, increased serum bilirubin, increased serum transaminases

Ophthalmic: Blindness, optic atrophy, visual disturbance

Renal: Renal failure

Respiratory: Pulmonary fibrosis, pulmonary infiltrates

General Dosage Range Dosage adjustment recommended in patients with renal impairment or who develop toxicities

Oral: *Children and Adults:* 100 to 130 mg/m^2 as a single dose once every 6 weeks

Mechanism of Action Inhibits DNA, RNA, and protein synthesis via alkylation and carbamylation of DNA and RNA; lomustine is cell cycle non-specific (Perry 2012)

Pharmacodynamics/Kinetics

Half-life Elimination Metabolites: 16 to 48 hours

Time to Peak Serum: ~3 hours (Perry 2012)

Pregnancy Considerations Adverse effects have been observed in animal reproduction studies. Based on the mechanism of action, lomustine may cause fetal harm when administered to a pregnant woman. Women of reproductive potential should use effective contraception during treatment and for 2 weeks after the final lomustine dose. Males with female partners of reproductive potential should use effective contraception during treatment and for 3.5 months (US labeling) or 6 months (Canadian labeling) after the final lomustine dose.

Loperamide (loe PER a mide)

Brand Names: US Anti-Diarrheal [OTC]; Diamode [OTC]; Imodium A-D [OTC]; Loperamide A-D [OTC]

Brand Names: Canada Apo-Loperamide; Diarr-Eze; Dom-Loperamide; Imodium; Loperacap; Novo-Loperamide; PMS-Loperamine; Rho-Loperamine; Rhoxal-loperamide; Riva-Loperamide; Sandoz-Loperamide

Pharmacologic Category Antidiarrheal

Use

Diarrhea:

Rx labeling: Control and symptomatic relief of chronic diarrhea associated with inflammatory bowel disease in adults; acute nonspecific diarrhea in patients ≥2 years; to reduce volume of ileostomy discharge

OTC labeling: Control of symptoms of diarrhea, including Traveler's diarrhea

Local Anesthetic/Vasoconstrictor Precautions No information available to require special precautions

Effects on Dental Treatment No significant effects or complications reported

Effects on Bleeding No information available to require special precautions

Adverse Reactions 1% to 10%:

Central nervous system: Dizziness (1%)

Gastrointestinal: Constipation (2% to 5%), abdominal cramps (≤3%), nausea (≤3%)

<1%, postmarketing, and/or case reports: Abdominal discomfort, abdominal distention, abdominal pain, anaphylactic shock, anaphylactoid reaction, angioedema, bullous rash (rare), drowsiness, dyspepsia, erythema multiforme (rare), fatigue, flatulence, hypersensitivity reaction, megacolon, paralytic ileus, pruritus, skin rash, Stevens-Johnson syndrome (rare), toxic epidermal necrolysis (rare), toxic megacolon, urinary retention, urticaria, vomiting, xerostomia

General Dosage Range Oral:

Children 2 to 5 years (13 to 20 kg): Initial: 1 mg 3 times daily for first 24 hours; Maintenance: 0.1 mg/kg after each loose stool (maximum: 3 mg/day)

Children 6 to 8 years (20 to 30 kg): Initial: 2 mg twice daily for first 24 hours; Maintenance: 0.1 mg/kg after each loose stool **or** 2 mg after first loose stool, followed by 1 mg after each subsequent stool (maximum: 4 mg/day)

Children 8 to 12 years (>30 kg): Initial: 2 mg 3 times daily for first 24 hours; Maintenance: 0.1 mg/kg after each loose stool (maximum: 6 mg/day)

Children 9 to 11 years: 2 mg after first loose stool, followed by 1 mg after each subsequent stool (maximum: 6 mg/day)

Children ≥12 years and Adolescents: Initial: 4 mg after first loose stool, followed by 2 mg after each subsequent stool (maximum: 8 mg/day)

Adults: Initial: 4 mg followed by 2 mg after each loose stool (maximum: 8 to 16 mg/day) **or** 4 to 8 mg/day in divided doses

Mechanism of Action Acts directly on circular and longitudinal intestinal muscles, through the opioid receptor, to inhibit peristalsis and prolong transit time; reduces fecal volume, increases viscosity, and diminishes fluid and electrolyte loss; demonstrates antisecretory activity. Loperamide increases tone on the anal sphincter

Pharmacodynamics/Kinetics

Half-life Elimination 9.4 to 14.4 hours

Time to Peak Liquid: 2.5 hours; Capsule: ~5 hours

Pregnancy Risk Factor C

Pregnancy Considerations Adverse effects have not been observed in animal reproduction studies. Information related to loperamide use in pregnancy is limited and data is conflicting (Einarson 2000; Källén 2008). For acute diarrhea in pregnant women, some clinicians recommend oral rehydration and dietary changes; loperamide in small amounts may be used only if symptoms are disabling (Wald 2003).

Lopinavir and Ritonavir

(loe PIN a veer & ri TOE na vir)

Related Information

HIV Infection and AIDS *on page 1785*

Ritonavir *on page 1443*

Brand Names: US Kaletra

Brand Names: Canada Kaletra

Pharmacologic Category Antiretroviral, Protease Inhibitor (Anti-HIV)

Use HIV-1 infection: Treatment of HIV-1 infection in adults and pediatric patients 14 days and older in combination with other antiretroviral agents

Local Anesthetic/Vasoconstrictor Precautions No information available to require special precautions

Effects on Dental Treatment Key adverse event(s) related to dental treatment: Dysphagia.

Effects on Bleeding Increased bleeding has been reported in HIV-infected patients with hemophilia (types A and B). Pediatric patients (4%) reported thrombocytopenia and less than 2% of adults reported anemia.

Adverse Reactions Data presented for short- and long-term combination antiretroviral therapy in both protease inhibitor experienced and naïve patients.

>10%:

Dermatologic: Skin rash (children 12%; adults ≤5%)

Endocrine & metabolic: Hypercholesterolemia (3% to 39%), increased serum triglycerides (3% to 36%), increased gamma-glutamyl transferase (10% to 29%)

Gastrointestinal: Diarrhea (7% to 28%; greater with once-daily dosing), dysgeusia (children 22%; adults <2%), vomiting (children 21%; adults 2% to 7%), nausea (5% to 16%), abdominal pain (1% to 11%)

Hepatic: Increased serum ALT (grade 3/4: 1% to 11%)

Respiratory: Upper respiratory tract infection (14%)

>2% to 10%:

Cardiovascular: Vasodilation (≤3%)

Central nervous system: Fatigue (8%, including weakness), headache (2% to 6%), anxiety (4%), insomnia (≤4%)

Dermatologic: Skin infection (3%, including cellulitis, folliculitis, furuncle)

Endocrine & metabolic: Hypertriglyceridemia (6%), hyperglycemia (≤5%), hyperuricemia (≤5%), alteration in sodium (children 3%), weight loss (≤3%)

Gastrointestinal: Increased serum amylase (3% to 8%), dyspepsia (≤6%), increased serum lipase (3% to 5%), flatulence (1% to 4%), gastroenteritis (3%)

Hematologic & oncologic: Thrombocytopenia (grade 3/4: 4% children), neutropenia (grade 3/4: 1% to 5%)

Hepatic: Increased serum AST (grade 3/4: 2% to 10%), hepatitis (4%, including increased AST, ALT, and gamma-glutamyl transferase), increased serum bilirubin (children 3%; adults 1%)

Hypersensitivity: Hypersensitivity (3%, including urticaria and angioedema)

Neuromuscular & skeletal: Weakness (≤9%), musculoskeletal pain (6%)

Respiratory: Lower respiratory tract infection (8%)

≤2%: Abdominal distension, abnormal dreams, abnormality in thinking, acne vulgaris, ageusia, agitation, alopecia, amenorrhea, amnesia, anemia, anorexia, apathy, arthralgia, asthma, ataxia, atherosclerotic disease, atrial fibrillation, atrioventricular block (second and third degree), atrophic striae, back pain, bacterial infection, benign neoplasm, bradycardia, brain disease, breast hypertrophy, bronchitis, cerebral infarction, cerebrovascular accident, change in appetite, chest pain, chills, cholangitis, cholecystitis, confusion, constipation, cough, Cushing's syndrome, cyst, decreased creatinine clearance, decreased glucose tolerance, decreased libido, deep vein thrombosis, dehydration, depression, dermal ulcer, diabetes mellitus, dizziness, drowsiness, duodenitis, dyskinesia, dysphagia, dyspnea, eczema, edema, ejaculatory disorder, emotional lability, enteritis, enterocolitis, erectile dysfunction, eructation, erythema multiforme, esophagitis, exfoliative dermatitis, extrapyramidal reaction, facial edema, facial paralysis, fecal incontinence, fever, first degree atrioventricular block, flu-like symptoms, gastritis, gastroesophageal reflux disease, gastrointestinal hemorrhage, gastrointestinal ulcer, gynecomastia, hematuria, hemorrhagic colitis, hemorrhoids, hepatic insufficiency, hepatomegaly, hyperacusis, hyperhidrosis, hypermenorrhea, hypersensitivity reaction, hypertension, hypertonia, hypogonadism (males), hypophosphatemia, hypothyroidism, immune reconstitution syndrome, impotence, jaundice, lactic acidosis, leukopenia, lipoma, liver steatosis, liver tenderness, lymphadenopathy, maculopapular rash, malaise, migraine, myalgia, myocardial infarction, neoplasm, nephritis, nervousness, neuropathy, night sweats, obesity, oral mucosa ulcer, orthostatic hypotension, osteonecrosis, otitis media, palpitations, pancreatitis, paresthesia, periodontitis, peripheral edema, peripheral neuropathy, pharyngitis, prolonged Q-T interval on ECG, propylene glycol toxicity (preterm neonates [includes cardiomyopathy, lactic acidosis, acute renal failure, respiratory complications]), pruritus, pulmonary edema, rectal hemorrhage, redistribution of body fat (including facial wasting), renal failure, rhabdomyolysis, rhinitis, seborrhea, seizure, sialadenitis, sinusitis, skin discoloration, splenomegaly, Stevens-Johnson syndrome, stomatitis, thrombophlebitis, tinnitus, torsades de pointes, tremor, tricuspid regurgitation, vasculitis, vertigo, viral infection, visual disturbance, vitamin deficiency, weight gain, xeroderma, xerostomia

General Dosage Range Dosage adjustment recommended in patients on concomitant therapy

Oral:

Infants 14 days to 6 months: Oral solution: Lopinavir 16 mg/kg or 300 mg/m^2 twice daily

Infants, Children, and Adolescents >6 months to <18 years:

Oral solution:

- <15 kg: Lopinavir 12 mg /kg twice daily (maximum dose: Lopinavir 400 mg/ritonavir 100 mg)
- 15 to 40 kg: Lopinavir 10 mg /kg twice daily (maximum dose: Lopinavir 400 mg/ritonavir 100 mg)
- >40 kg: Lopinavir 400 mg/ritonavir 100 mg twice daily

Tablets:

- 15 to 25 kg: Lopinavir 200 mg/ritonavir 50 mg twice daily
- >25 to 35 kg: Lopinavir 300 mg/ritonavir 75 mg twice daily
- >35 kg: Lopinavir 400 mg/ritonavir 100 mg twice daily

Adults: Lopinavir 400 mg/ritonavir 100 mg twice daily **or** lopinavir 800 mg/ritonavir 200 mg once daily

Mechanism of Action A coformulation of lopinavir and ritonavir. The lopinavir component binds to the site of HIV-1 protease activity and inhibits the cleavage of viral Gag-Pol polyprotein precursors into individual functional proteins required for infectious HIV. This results in the formation of immature, noninfectious viral particles. The ritonavir component inhibits the CYP3A metabolism of lopinavir, allowing increased plasma levels of lopinavir.

Pharmacodynamics/Kinetics

Half-life Elimination Lopinavir: 5 to 6 hours

Time to Peak Lopinavir: ~4 hours

Pregnancy Considerations Lopinavir/ritonavir has a low level of transfer across the human placenta. Based on information collected by the Antiretroviral Pregnancy Registry, an increased risk of teratogenic effects has not been observed in humans. A small increased risk of preterm birth has been associated with maternal use of protease inhibitor-based combination antiretroviral therapy during pregnancy; however, the benefits of use generally outweigh this risk and protease inhibitors (PIs) should not be withheld if otherwise recommended. Information related to stillbirth, low birth weight, and small for gestational age infants is limited. Long-term follow-up is recommended for all infants exposed to antiretroviral medications; children who develop significant organ system abnormalities of unknown etiology (particularly of the CNS or heart) should be evaluated for potential mitochondrial dysfunction. Hyperglycemia, new onset of diabetes mellitus, or diabetic ketoacidosis have been reported with PIs; it is not clear if pregnancy increases this risk.

Combination antiretroviral therapy (cART) therapy is recommended for all HIV-infected pregnant women to keep the viral load below the limit of detection and reduce the risk of perinatal transmission. When HIV is diagnosed during pregnancy in a woman who has never received antiretroviral therapy, cART should begin as soon as possible after diagnosis. Although there are an abundance of data related to the use of lopinavir/ritonavir during pregnancy, the Health and Human Services (HHS) Perinatal HIV Guidelines consider lopinavir/ritonavir to be an alternative protease inhibitor for initial therapy in antiretroviral-naive pregnant women due to the need for twice daily dosing and increased incidence of nausea. Lopinavir/ritonavir is not recommended for use in pregnant women with lopinavir-resistance-associated amino acid substitutions. In addition, once-daily dosing is not recommended during pregnancy and use of the oral solution should be avoided (due to alcohol and propylene glycol content). Pharmacokinetic studies suggest that standard dosing during pregnancy may provide decreased plasma concentrations; dose adjustments are required in women during the second and third trimesters of pregnancy. In general, women who become pregnant on a stable cART regimen may continue that regimen if viral suppression is effective, appropriate drug exposure can be achieved, contraindications for use in pregnancy are not present, and the regimen is well tolerated. Monitoring during pregnancy is more frequent than in non-pregnant adults; cART should be continued postpartum.

For HIV-infected couples planning a pregnancy, maximum viral suppression with cART is recommended prior to conception for the HIV-infected partner(s) and expert consultation is recommended; modification of therapy (if needed) and optimization of the woman's health should be done prior to conception. HIV-infected women not planning a pregnancy may use any available type of contraception, considering possible drug interactions and contraindications of the specific method. In addition, consistent use of condoms is also recommended (even during pregnancy) to prevent transmission of HIV or other sexually transmitted diseases

Health care providers are encouraged to enroll pregnant women exposed to antiretroviral medications as early in pregnancy as possible in the Antiretroviral Pregnancy Registry (1-800-258-4263 or www.-APRegistry.com). Health care providers caring for HIV-infected women and their infants may contact the National Perinatal HIV Hotline (888-448-8765) for clinical consultation (HHS [perinatal] 2016).

Loratadine (lor AT a deen)

Related Information

Dentin Hypersensitivity, Acid Erosion, High Caries Index, Management of Alveolar Osteitis, and Xerostomia *on page 1857*

Brand Names: US Alavert [OTC]; Allergy Relief For Kids [OTC]; Allergy Relief [OTC]; Allergy [OTC]; Childrens Loratadine [OTC]; Claritin Childrens [OTC]; Claritin Reditabs [OTC]; Claritin [OTC]; Loradamed [OTC]; Loratadine Childrens [OTC]; Loratadine Hives Relief [OTC]; QlearQuil 24 Hour Relief [OTC] [DSC]; Triaminic Allerchews [OTC]

Brand Names: Canada Apo-Loratadine; Claritin®; Claritin® Kids

Pharmacologic Category Histamine H_1 Antagonist; Histamine H_1 Antagonist, Second Generation; Piperidine Derivative

Use

Allergic rhinitis: Relief of nasal and non-nasal symptoms of seasonal allergic rhinitis

Urticaria: Treatment of itching due to hives (urticarial)

Local Anesthetic/Vasoconstrictor Precautions No information available to require special precautions

Effects on Dental Treatment Key adverse event(s) related to dental treatment: Xerostomia (normal salivary flow resumes upon discontinuation) and stomatitis in children (2-5 years).

Effects on Bleeding No information available to require special precautions

Adverse Reactions

>10%: Central nervous system: Headache (adults: 12%)

1% to 10%:

Central nervous system: Drowsiness (adults: 8%), nervousness (children 6 to 12 years: 4%), fatigue (adults: 4%; children 6 to 12 years: 3%; children 2 to 5 years: 2% to 3%), malaise (children 6 to 12 years: 2%), voice disorder (children 6 to 12 years: 2%)

Dermatologic: Skin rash (children 2 to 5 years: 2% to 3%)

Gastrointestinal: Xerostomia (adults: 3%), stomatitis (children 2 to 5 years: 2% to 3%), abdominal pain (children 6 to 12 years: 2%)

Infection: Viral infection (children 2 to 5 years: 2% to 3%)

Neuromuscular & skeletal: Hyperkinesia (children 6 to 12 years: 3%)

Ophthalmic: Conjunctivitis (children 6 to 12 years: 2%)

Respiratory: Wheezing (children 6 to 12 years: 4%), epistaxis (children 2 to 5 years: 2% to 3%), flu-like symptoms (children 2 to 5 years: 2% to 3%), pharyngitis (children 2 to 5 years: 2% to 3%), upper respiratory tract infection (children 6 to 12 years: 2%)

<2%, postmarketing, and/or case reports: Abnormal lacrimation, agitation, alopecia, altered micturition, altered salivation, amnesia, anaphylaxis, angioedema, anorexia, anxiety, arthralgia, back pain, blepharospasm, blurred vision, breast hypertrophy, bronchitis, bronchospasm, chest pain, confusion, constipation, cough, decreased libido, depression, dermatitis, diaphoresis, diarrhea, dizziness, dry hair, dry nose, dysgeusia, dysmenorrhea, dyspepsia, dyspnea, erythema multiforme, eye pain, flatulence, flushing, gastritis, hemoptysis, hepatic insufficiency, hepatic necrosis, hepatitis, hiccups, hypermenorrhea, hypertension, hypertonia, hypoesthesia, hypotension, impotence, increased appetite, increased thirst, insomnia, irritability, jaundice, lack of concentration, laryngitis, leg cramps, loose stools, mastalgia, migraine, myalgia, nausea, nightmares, otalgia, palpitations, paresthesia, peripheral edema, pruritus, purpura, rigors, seizure, sinusitis, skin photosensitivity, sneezing, supraventricular tachycardia, syncope, tachycardia, thrombocytopenia, tinnitus, tremor, urinary incontinence, urinary retention, urine discoloration, urticaria, vaginitis, vertigo, vomiting, weakness, weight gain, xeroderma

General Dosage Range

Oral:

Children 2-5 years: 5 mg once daily

Children ≥6 years and Adults: 10 mg once daily

Mechanism of Action Long-acting tricyclic antihistamine with selective peripheral histamine H_1-receptor antagonistic properties

Pharmacodynamics/Kinetics

Onset of Action 1-3 hours; Peak effect: 8-12 hours

Duration of Action >24 hours

Half-life Elimination 8.4 hours (range: 3 to 20 hours) (loratadine), 28 hours (range: 8.8 to 92 hours) (metabolite) (Claritin prescribing information 2000); hepatic impairment: 24 hours (loratadine), 37 hours (metabolite) (Claritin prescribing information 2000)

Time to Peak Loratadine: 1.3 hours (loratadine), 2.3 hours (metabolite) (Claritin prescribing information 2000)

Pregnancy Considerations Maternal use of loratadine has not been associated with an increased risk of major malformations. Loratadine may be used for the treatment of allergic rhinitis and urticaria during pregnancy (NAEPP 2005; Wallace 2008; Zuberbier 2014).

Loratadine and Pseudoephedrine

(lor AT a deen & soo doe e FED rin)

Related Information

Bacterial Infections *on page 1835*

Loratadine *on page 1019*

Pseudoephedrine *on page 1404*

Brand Names: US Alavert Allergy and Sinus [OTC]; Claritin-D 12 Hour Allergy & Congestion [OTC]; Claritin-D 24 Hour Allergy & Congestion [OTC]; Loratadine-D 12 Hour [OTC]

Brand Names: Canada Chlor-Tripolon ND; Claritin Extra; Claritin Liberator

Pharmacologic Category Alpha/Beta Agonist; Decongestant; Histamine H_1 Antagonist; Histamine H_1 Antagonist, Second Generation; Piperidine Derivative

Use Cold, allergy symptoms: Temporary relief of sinus and nasal congestion, runny nose, sneezing, itching of nose or throat and itchy, watery eyes due to common cold, hay fever (allergic rhinitis), or other upper respiratory allergies or sinusitis

Local Anesthetic/Vasoconstrictor Precautions Use with caution since pseudoephedrine is a sympathomimetic amine which could interact with epinephrine to cause a pressor response

Effects on Dental Treatment Key adverse event(s) related to dental treatment: Pseudoephedrine: Xerostomia (normal salivary flow resumes upon discontinuation).

Effects on Bleeding No information available to require special precautions

Adverse Reactions See individual agents.

General Dosage Range Oral: *Children ≥12 years, Adolescents, and Adults:*

Loratadine 5 mg/pseudoephedrine 120 mg: One tablet every 12 hours (maximum: 2 tablets/day)

Loratadine 10 mg/pseudoephedrine 240 mg: One tablet daily (maximum: 1 tablet/day)

Pregnancy Considerations See individual agents.

LORazepam (lor A ze pam)

Related Information

Dentin Hypersensitivity, Acid Erosion, High Caries Index, Management of Alveolar Osteitis, and Xerostomia *on page 1857*

Management of the Patient With Anxiety or Depression *on page 1873*

Temporomandibular Dysfunction (TMD), Chronic Pain, and Fibromyalgia *on page 1868*

Related Sample Prescriptions

Sedation (Prior to Dental Treatment) - Sample Prescriptions *on page 42*

Brand Names: US Ativan; LORazepam Intensol

Brand Names: Canada Apo-Lorazepam; Ativan; Dom-Lorazepam; Lorazepam Injection, USP; PHL-Lorazepam; PMS-Lorazepam; PRO-Lorazepam; Teva-Lorazepam

Generic Availability (US) Yes

Pharmacologic Category Anticonvulsant, Benzodiazepine; Benzodiazepine

Dental Use Short-term relief of anxiety prior to dental appointment

Use

Anxiety (oral): Management of anxiety disorders, short-term (≤4 months) relief of anxiety symptoms, or anxiety associated with depressive symptoms, or anxiety/stress-associated insomnia

Anesthesia premedication (parenteral): Anesthesia premedication to relieve anxiety or to produce amnesia (diminish recall) or sedation

Anesthesia premedication (sublingual): *Canadian labeling:* Anesthesia premedication to relieve anxiety prior to surgical procedures

Status epilepticus (parenteral): Treatment of status epilepticus (adults).

Local Anesthetic/Vasoconstrictor Precautions No information available to require special precautions

Effects on Dental Treatment Key adverse event(s) related to dental treatment: Xerostomia (normal salivary flow resumes upon discontinuation) (see Dental Comment)

Effects on Bleeding No information available to require special precautions

Adverse Reactions Frequency not always defined.

Cardiovascular: Hypotension (≤2%)

Central nervous system: Sedation (≤16%), dizziness (≤7%), drowsiness (2% to 4%), unsteadiness (3%), headache (1%), coma (≤1%), stupor (≤1%), aggressive behavior, agitation, akathisia, amnesia, anxiety, central nervous system stimulation, disinhibition, disorientation, dysarthria, euphoria, excitement, extrapyramidal reaction, fatigue, hostility, hypothermia, irritability, mania, memory impairment, outbursts of anger, psychosis, seizures, sleep apnea (exacerbation), sleep disturbances, slurred speech, suicidal behavior, suicidal ideation, vertigo

Dermatologic: Alopecia, skin rash

Gastrointestinal: Changes in appetite, constipation

Endocrine & metabolic: Change in libido, hyponatremia, SIADH

Genitourinary: Impotence, orgasm disturbance

Hematologic & oncologic: Agranulocytosis, pancytopenia, thrombocytopenia

Hepatic: Increased serum alkaline phosphatase, increased serum bilirubin, increased serum transaminases, jaundice

Hypersensitivity: Anaphylaxis, anaphylactoid reaction, hypersensitivity reaction

Local: Pain at injection site (IM: 1% to 17%; IV: ≤2%), erythema at injection site (≤2%)

Neuromuscular & skeletal: Weakness (≤4%)

Ophthalmic: Visual disturbances (including diplopia and blurred vision)

Respiratory: Respiratory failure (1% to 2%), apnea (1%), hypoventilation (≤1%), exacerbation of obstructive pulmonary disease, nasal congestion, respiratory depression, worsening of sleep apnea

<1%, postmarketing, and/or case reports: Abnormal gait, abnormal hepatic function tests, abnormality in thinking, acidosis, cardiac arrhythmia, ataxia, blood coagulation disorder, bradycardia, cardiac arrest, cardiac failure, cerebral edema, chills, confusion, convulsions, cystitis, decreased mental acuity, delirium, depression, drug dependence (with prolonged use), drug toxicity (polyethylene glycol or propylene glycol poisoning [prolonged IV infusion]), excessive crying, gastrointestinal hemorrhage, hallucinations, hearing loss, heart block, hematologic abnormality, hepatotoxicity, hypertension, hyperventilation, hyporeflexia, infection, injection site reaction, myoclonus, nausea, nervousness, neuroleptic malignant syndrome, paralysis, pericardial effusion, pheochromocytoma (aggravation), pneumothorax, pulmonary edema, pulmonary hemorrhage, pulmonary hypertension, restlessness, seizure, sialorrhea, tachycardia, tremor, urinary incontinence, ventricular arrhythmia, vomiting, withdrawal syndrome

Dental Usual Dosage

Anxiety and sedation: Adults: Oral: 1 to 10 mg/day in 2 to 3 divided doses; usual dose: 2 to 6 mg/day in divided doses

Preoperative: Adults:

IM: 0.05 mg/kg administered 2 hours before surgery (maximum: 4 mg/dose)

IV: 0.044 mg/kg 15 to 20 minutes before surgery (usual maximum: 2 mg/dose)

Preprocedural anxiety: Adults: Oral: 1 to 2 mg 1 hour before procedure

Dosing

Adult

Anxiety disorder: Oral: Initial: 2 to 3 mg daily in 2 to 3 divided doses; usual dose: 2 to 6 mg daily in divided doses; however, daily dose may vary from 1 to 10 mg/day

Insomnia due to anxiety or stress: Oral:

<65 years: 0.5 to 2 mg at bedtime (Winkelman 2015)

≥65 years: 0.5 to 1 mg at bedtime (Winkelman, 2015)

Note: The manufacturer recommends higher dosing (ie, 2 to 4 mg at bedtime); however, generally, it is a safer approach to employ the above recommended doses.

Premedication for anesthesia:

IM: 0.05 mg/kg administered 2 hours before surgery (maximum dose: 4 mg)

IV: 0.044 mg/kg administered 15 to 20 minutes before surgery (usual dose: 2 mg; maximum dose: 4 mg). **Note:** Doses >2 mg should generally not be exceeded in patients >50 years.

Sublingual tablet [Canadian product]: 0.05 mg/kg 1 to 2 hours before surgery (maximum dose: 4 mg)

Status epilepticus: IV:

American Epilepsy Society and Neurocritical Care Society recommendations: 0.1 mg/kg (maximum dose: 4 mg) given at a maximum rate of 2 mg/minute; may repeat in 5 to 10 minutes (AES [Glauser 2016]; NCS [Brophy 2012]). **Note:** Dilute dose 1:1 with saline.

Manufacturer's labeling: 4 mg given slowly (2 mg/minute); may repeat in 10 to 15 minutes. May be given IM, but IV preferred.

Agitation in the ICU patient (off-label use): IV: Loading dose: 0.02 to 0.04 mg/kg (maximum single dose: 2 mg); Maintenance: 0.02 to 0.06 mg/kg every 2 to 6 hours as needed **or** 0.01 to 0.1 mg/kg/hour; maximum dose: ≤10 mg/hour (Barr 2013)

Alcohol withdrawal delirium (off-label use) (Mayo-Smith 2004):

IV: 1 to 4 mg every 5 to 15 minutes until calm, then every hour as needed to maintain light somnolence

IM: 1 to 4 mg every 30 to 60 minutes until calm, then every hour as needed to maintain light somnolence

Alcohol withdrawal syndrome (off-label use) (Mayo-Smith, 1997):

Oral, IM, IV (fixed-dose regimen): 2 mg every 6 hours for 4 doses, then 1 mg every 6 hours for 8 additional doses

Oral, IM, IV (symptom-triggered regimen): 2 to 4 mg every 1 hour as needed; dose determined by a validated severity assessment scale

Chemotherapy-associated nausea and vomiting (off-label use): Breakthrough nausea/vomiting or as adjunct to standard antiemetics: Oral, IV, Sublingual (off-label route): 0.5 to 2 mg every 6 hours as needed (Lohr 2008)

Partial complex seizures, refractory (off-label use): Oral: 1 mg twice daily; increase biweekly in increments of 1 mg twice daily until seizures stop or side effects occur (Walker, 1984); however, additional data may be necessary to further define the role of lorazepam in this condition

Psychogenic catatonia (off-label use):

IM, Sublingual (off-label route): 1 to 2 mg; repeat dose in 3 hours then again in another 3 hours if initial and subsequent doses, respectively, are ineffective (Rosebush, 1990; Rosebush 2010); however, additional data may be necessary to further define the role of lorazepam in this condition

or

Oral, IM, IV: Initial: 1 mg; may repeat in 5 minutes if necessary. If initial challenge is unsuccessful, may increase dose up to 4 to 8 mg per day; may continue treatment for up to 5 days (Bush, 1996); however, additional data may be necessary to further define the role of lorazepam in this condition

Rapid tranquilization of the agitated patient (off-label use): Oral, IM, IV: 1 to 3 mg administered every 30 to 60 minutes; may be administered with an antipsychotic (eg, haloperidol) (Allen 2005; Battaglia 2005; De Fruyt 2004; Wilson 2012). **Note:** When administering IM, may consider a lower initial dose (eg, 0.5 mg) (Allen 2005).

Dosage adjustment for lorazepam with concomitant medications: *Probenecid or valproic acid:* Reduce lorazepam dose by 50%

Geriatric Refer also to adult dosing. Dose selection should generally be on the low end of the dosage range (initial dose not to exceed 2 mg).

Anxiety disorder: Oral:

US labeling: Initial: 1 to 2 mg daily in divided doses

Canadian labeling: Initial: 0.5 mg daily; titrate cautiously as tolerated

Premedication for anesthesia: IM, IV: *Canadian labeling:* Reduce the initial dose by approximately 50% and adjust as needed and tolerated; IV dose should generally not exceed 2 mg in patients >50 years.

Pediatric

Chemotherapy-associated nausea and vomiting (off-label use):

Anticipatory nausea/vomiting (prevention and treatment): Infants ≥1 month, Children, and Adolescents: Oral: 0.04 to 0.08 mg/kg/dose (maximum dose: 2 mg) once at bedtime the evening prior to chemotherapy and once the next day before chemotherapy (Dupuis 2014)

Breakthrough nausea/vomiting: Children ≥2 years and Adolescents: IV: 0.025 to 0.05 mg/kg/dose (maximum dose: 2 mg) every 6 hours as needed (Dupuis 2003); however, additional data may be necessary to further define the role of lorazepam in children for chemotherapy-associated nausea and vomiting

Status epilepticus: Infants, Children, and Adolescents (off-label use):

American Epilepsy Society and Neurocritical Care Society recommendations: IV: 0.1 mg/kg (maximum dose: 4 mg) given at a maximum rate of 2 mg/minute; may repeat in 5 to 10 minutes (AES [Glauser 2016]; NCS [Brophy 2012]). **Note:** Dilute dose 1:1 with saline.

American Academy of Pediatrics recommendation: IV, IM: 0.05 to 0.1 mg/kg (maximum dose: 4 mg); may repeat dose every 10 to 15 minutes if seizure continues (AAP [Hegenbarth 2008])

Dosage adjustment for lorazepam with concomitant medications: *Probenecid or valproic acid:* Reduce lorazepam dose by 50%

Renal Impairment

Oral: No dosage adjustment necessary (Aronoff 2007).

IM, IV: Risk of propylene glycol toxicity. Monitor closely if using for prolonged periods of time or at high doses.

Mild-to-moderate disease: Use with caution.

Severe disease or failure: Use is not recommended.

Hepatic Impairment

Oral:

Mild-to-moderate disease: No dose adjustment necessary.

Severe insufficiency and/or encephalopathy: Use with caution; may require lower doses.

IM, IV:

Mild-to-moderate disease: Use with caution.

Severe disease or failure: Use is not recommended.

Mechanism of Action Binds to stereospecific benzodiazepine receptors on the postsynaptic GABA neuron at several sites within the central nervous system, including the limbic system, reticular formation. Enhancement of the inhibitory effect of GABA on neuronal excitability results by increased neuronal membrane permeability to chloride ions. This shift in chloride ions results in hyperpolarization (a less excitable state) and stabilization. Benzodiazepine receptors and effects appear to be linked to the GABA-A receptors. Benzodiazepines do not bind to GABA-B receptors.

Contraindications

Hypersensitivity to lorazepam, any component of the formulation, or other benzodiazepines (cross-sensitivity with other benzodiazepines may exist); acute narrow-angle glaucoma; sleep apnea (parenteral); intra-arterial injection of parenteral formulation; severe respiratory insufficiency (except during mechanical ventilation)

Canadian labeling: Additional contraindications (not in the US labeling): Myasthenia gravis

Warnings/Precautions [US Boxed Warning]: Concomitant use of benzodiazepines and opioids may result in profound sedation, respiratory depression, coma, and death. Reserve concomitant prescribing of these drugs for use in patients for whom alternative treatment options are inadequate. Limit dosages and durations to the minimum required. Follow patients for signs and symptoms of respiratory depression and sedation. In patients already receiving an opioid analgesic, prescribe a lower initial dose of lorazepam than indicated in the absence of an opioid and titrate based on clinical response. If an opioid is initiated in a patient already taking lorazepam, prescribe a lower initial dose of the opioid and titrate based upon clinical response.

Use with caution in elderly or debilitated patients, patients with hepatic disease (including alcoholics) or renal impairment. Use with caution in patients with respiratory disease (COPD or sleep apnea) or limited pulmonary reserve, or impaired gag reflex. Initial doses in elderly or debilitated patients should be at the lower end of the dosing range. May worsen hepatic encephalopathy.

Causes CNS depression (dose-related) resulting in sedation, dizziness, confusion, or ataxia which may impair physical and mental capabilities. Patients must be cautioned about performing tasks which require mental alertness (eg, operating machinery or driving). Effects may be potentiated when used with other sedative drugs or ethanol. Potentially significant drug-drug interactions may exist, requiring dose or frequency adjustment, additional monitoring, and/or selection of alternative therapy. Benzodiazepines have been associated with falls and traumatic injury and should be used with extreme caution in patients who are at risk of these events.

Lorazepam may cause anterograde amnesia. Paradoxical reactions, including hyperactive or aggressive behavior have been reported with benzodiazepines, particularly in adolescent/pediatric or psychiatric patients. Does not have analgesic, antidepressant, or antipsychotic properties.

Preexisting depression may worsen or emerge during therapy. Not recommended for use in primary depressive or psychotic disorders. Should not be used in patients at risk for suicide without adequate antidepressant treatment. Risk of dependence increases in patients with a history of alcohol or drug abuse and those with significant personality disorders; use with caution in these patients. Tolerance, psychological and physical dependence may also occur with higher dosages and prolonged use. The risk of dependence is decreased with short-term treatment (2 to 4 weeks); evaluate the need for continued treatment prior to extending therapy duration. Benzodiazepines have been associated with dependence and acute withdrawal symptoms on discontinuation or reduction in dose. Acute withdrawal, including seizures, may be precipitated after administration of flumazenil to patients receiving long-term benzodiazepine therapy. Lorazepam is a short half-life benzodiazepine. Tolerance develops to the sedative, hypnotic, and anticonvulsant effects. It does not develop to the anxiolytic effects (Vinkers 2012). Chronic use of this agent may increase the perioperative benzodiazepine dose needed to achieve desired effect.

As a hypnotic agent, should be used only after evaluation of potential causes of sleep disturbance. Failure of sleep disturbance to resolve after 7 to 10 days may indicate psychiatric or medical illness. A worsening of insomnia or the emergence of new abnormalities of thought or behavior may represent unrecognized psychiatric or medical illness and requires immediate and careful evaluation.

Status epilepticus should not be treated with injectable benzodiazepines alone; requires close observation and management and possibly ventilatory support. When used as a component of preanesthesia, monitor for heavy sedation and airway obstruction; equipment necessary to maintain airway and ventilatory support should be available. Parenteral formulation of lorazepam contains polyethylene glycol which has resulted in toxicity during high-dose and/or longer-term infusions. Parenteral formulation also contains propylene glycol (PG); may be associated with dose-related toxicity and can occur ≥48 hours after initiation of lorazepam. Limited data suggest increased risk of PG accumulation at doses of ≥6 mg/hour for 48 hours or more (Nelson 2008). Monitor for signs of toxicity which may include acute renal failure, lactic acidosis, and/or osmol gap. May consider using enteral delivery of lorazepam tablets to decrease the risk of PG toxicity (Lugo 1999).

Benzyl alcohol and derivatives: Some dosage forms may contain benzyl alcohol; large amounts of benzyl alcohol (≥99 mg/kg/day) have been associated with a potentially fatal toxicity ("gasping syndrome") in neonates; the "gasping syndrome" consists of metabolic acidosis, respiratory distress, gasping respirations, CNS dysfunction (including convulsions, intracranial hemorrhage), hypotension, and cardiovascular collapse (AAP ["Inactive" 1997]; CDC 1982); some data suggests that benzoate displaces bilirubin from protein binding sites (Ahlfors 2001); avoid or use dosage forms containing benzyl alcohol with caution in neonates. See manufacturer's labeling.

Drug Interactions

Metabolism/Transport Effects None known.

Avoid Concomitant Use

Avoid concomitant use of LORazepam with any of the following: Azelastine (Nasal); Methadone; OLANZapine; Orphenadrine; Oxomemazine; Paraldehyde; Sodium Oxybate; Thalidomide

Increased Effect/Toxicity

LORazepam may increase the levels/effects of: Alcohol (Ethyl); Analgesics (Opioid); Azelastine (Nasal);

Blonanserin; Buprenorphine; CloZAPine; CNS Depressants; Flunitrazepam; Fosphenytoin; HYDROcodone; Methadone; Methotrimeprazine; MetyroSINE; Mirtazapine; Orphenadrine; OxyCODONE; Paraldehyde; Phenytoin; Piribedil; Pramipexole; ROPINIRole; Rotigotine; Selective Serotonin Reuptake Inhibitors; Sodium Oxybate; Suvorexant; Thalidomide; Zolpidem

The levels/effects of LORazepam may be increased by: Brimonidine (Topical); Cannabis; Chlormethiazole; Chlorphenesin Carbamate; Dimethindene (Topical); Doxylamine; Dronabinol; Droperidol; HydrOXYzine; Kava Kava; Lofexidine; Loxapine; Magnesium Sulfate; Methotrimeprazine; Minocycline; Nabilone; OLANZapine; Oxomemazine; Perampanel; Probenecid; Rufinamide; Tapentadol; Teduglutide; Tetrahydrocannabinol; Trimeprazine; Valproate Products

Decreased Effect

The levels/effects of LORazepam may be decreased by: Theophylline Derivatives; Yohimbine

Pharmacodynamics/Kinetics

Onset of Action

Anticonvulsant: IV: Within 10 minutes
Hypnosis: IM: 20 to 30 minutes
Sedation: IV: Within 2 to 3 minutes (Greenblatt 1983)

Duration of Action Anesthesia premedication: Adults: IM, IV: ~6 to 8 hours

Half-life Elimination

Full-term neonates: IV: 40.2 ± 16.5 hours; range: 18 to 73 hours (McDermott 1992)
Pediatric patients (Chamberlain 2012): IV:
- 5 months to <3 years: 15.8 hours (range: 5.9 to 28.4 hours)
- 3 to <13 years: 16.9 hours (range: 7.5 to 40.6 hours)
- 13 to <18 years: 17.8 hours (range: 8.2 to 42 hours)

Adults: Oral: ~12 hours; IV: ~14 hours; IM: ~13 to 18 hours (Greenblatt 1981), End-stage renal disease (ESRD): ~18 hours

Time to Peak IM: ≤3 hours; Oral: ~2 hours; Sublingual tablet [Canadian product]: 1 hour

Pregnancy Considerations Lorazepam and its metabolite cross the human placenta. Teratogenic effects in humans have been observed with some benzodiazepines (including lorazepam); however, additional studies are needed. The incidence of premature birth and low birth weights may be increased following maternal use of benzodiazepines; hypoglycemia and respiratory problems in the neonate may occur following exposure late in pregnancy. Neonatal withdrawal symptoms may occur within days to weeks after birth and "floppy infant syndrome" (which also includes withdrawal symptoms) have been reported with some benzodiazepines (including lorazepam). Elimination of lorazepam in the newborn infant is slow; following in utero exposure, term infants may excrete lorazepam for up to 8 days (Bergman 1992; Iqbal 2002; Wikner 2007).

Breastfeeding Considerations Lorazepam is present in breast milk.

The relative infant dose (RID) of lorazepam is 2.4% to 4.7% when calculated using the highest breast milk concentration located following benzodiazepine monotherapy with lorazepam and compared to an infant therapeutic dose of 0.15 to 0.3 mg/kg/day (0.05 mg/kg/dose every 4 to 8 hours). In general, breastfeeding is considered acceptable when the RID is <10% (Anderson 2016; Ito 2000); however, some sources note breastfeeding should only be considered if the RID is <5% for psychotropic agents (Larsen 2015). Using the highest total milk concentration (12 mcg/L free lorazepam plus 35 mcg/L conjugated lorazepam), the estimated the daily infant dose via breast milk is 7.05 mcg/kg/day. These milk concentrations were obtained following maternal administration of oral lorazepam 2.5 mg twice daily for the first five days postpartum; the mother had begun treatment with lorazepam prior to delivery (route, dose, and duration not specified) (Whitelaw 1981). Higher milk concentrations were observed in one mother who received both oral lorazepam and lormetazepam, which is partially metabolized to lorazepam (Lemmer 2007).

In general, sedation, lethargy, irritability, poor weight gain, and apnea have been reported in breastfed infants exposed to benzodiazepines; however, these adverse effects were not observed in breastfed infants exposed to lorazepam (Kelly 2012). The manufacturer warns of the potential for sedation, irritability, and impaired suckling in the infant. Monitor breastfed infants for drowsiness (WHO 2002).

Although the manufacturer recommends that lorazepam should not be administered to breastfeeding women unless the expected benefit to the woman outweighs the potential risk to the infant, short-acting benzodiazepines, including lorazepam, are considered compatible with breastfeeding (WHO 2002; Kelly 2012). When possible, limit exposure to single doses (WHO 2002).

Controlled Substance C-IV

Dosage Forms

Concentrate, Oral:
LORazepam Intensol: 2 mg/mL (30 mL)
Generic: 2 mg/mL (30 mL)

Solution, Injection:
Ativan: 2 mg/mL (1 mL, 10 mL); 4 mg/mL (1 mL, 10 mL)
Generic: 2 mg/mL (1 mL, 10 mL); 4 mg/mL (1 mL, 10 mL)

Tablet, Oral:
Ativan: 0.5 mg, 1 mg, 2 mg
Generic: 0.5 mg, 1 mg, 2 mg

Dosage Forms: Canada

Tablet, Sublingual: 0.5 mg, 1 mg, 2 mg

Dental Comment An adult companion should accompany the patient to and from dental office.

Lorcaserin (lor KA ser in)

Brand Names: US Belviq; Belviq XR

Pharmacologic Category Anorexiant; Serotonin 5-HT_{2C} Receptor Agonist

Use Weight management: Chronic weight management, as an adjunct to a reduced-calorie diet and increased physical activity, in adults with either an initial body mass index (BMI) of ≥30 kg/m^2 **or** an initial BMI of ≥27 kg/m^2 and at least one weight-related comorbid condition (eg, hypertension, dyslipidemia, type 2 diabetes).

Local Anesthetic/Vasoconstrictor Precautions No information available to require special precautions

Effects on Dental Treatment No significant effects or complications reported

Effects on Bleeding No information available to require special precautions

Adverse Reactions

>10%:
Central nervous system: Headache (15% to 17%)
Endocrine & metabolic: Hypoglycemia (diabetic patients 29%; symptomatic 7%; severe: 2%)

Hematologic: Abnormal lymphocytes (below lower limit of normal after ≥1 year, 12%)
Neuromuscular & skeletal: Back pain (6% to 12%)
Respiratory: Upper respiratory tract infection (14%), nasopharyngitis (11% to 13%)

1% to 10%:

Cardiovascular: Hypertension (5%), peripheral edema (5%), decreased heart rate (less than 50 bpm: 4% to 5%), acquired valvular heart disease (3%)
Central nervous system: Dizziness (7% to 9%), fatigue (7%), anxiety (4%), insomnia (4%), depression (3%), stress (3%), cognitive dysfunction (2%), psychiatric disturbance (2%)
Endocrine & metabolic: Increased serum prolactin (7%; 2 x ULN: 2%; 5 x ULN: <1%), exacerbation of diabetes mellitus (3%)
Gastrointestinal: Nausea (8% to 9%), diarrhea (7%), constipation (6%), xerostomia (5%), vomiting (4%), gastroenteritis (3%), toothache (3%), decreased appetite (2%)
Genitourinary: Urinary tract infection (7% to 9%)
Hematologic: Decreased hemoglobin (10%), decreased neutrophils (6%)
Hypersensitivity: Seasonal allergy (3%)
Neuromuscular & skeletal: Muscle spasm (5%), musculoskeletal pain (2%)
Ocular: Eye disease (5% to 6%)
Respiratory: Cough (4% to 8%), oropharyngeal pain (4%), sinus congestion (3%)

<1%, postmarketing, and/or case reports: Hypersensitivity reaction, serotonin syndrome

General Dosage Range Oral: *Adults:* 10 mg twice daily (maximum: 10 mg twice daily)

Mechanism of Action Lorcaserin is believed to activate serotonin 5-HT_{2C} receptors, which stimulate proopiomelanocortin (POMC) neurons in the arcuate nucleus of the hypothalamus, leading to increased alpha-melanocortin stimulating hormone release at melanocortin-4 receptors and resulting in satiety and decreased food intake. At recommended doses, lorcaserin has greater affinity for 5-HT_{2C} receptors compared to other 5-HT receptor subtypes (including 5-HT_{2A} and 5-HT_{2B}), the 5-HT receptor transporter, and 5-HT reuptake sites (Hurren, 2011).

Pharmacodynamics/Kinetics

Half-life Elimination ~11 hours (immediate-release); ~12 hours (extended-release)

Time to Peak 1.5 to 2 hours (immediate release); 10 hours (extended release)

Pregnancy Risk Factor X

Pregnancy Considerations Adverse events have been observed in some animal reproduction studies. Due to the fact that weight loss during pregnancy offers no clinical benefit, lorcaserin is contraindicated in pregnancy. Obese and overweight women should be encouraged to participate in weight reduction programs prior to attempting pregnancy; weight gain during pregnancy should be determined by their prepregnancy BMI and current guidelines (ADA 2009; IOM 2009).

Controlled Substance C-IV

Losartan (loe SAR tan)

Related Information

Cardiovascular Diseases *on page 1752*

Brand Names: US Cozaar

Brand Names: Canada ACT Losartan; Apo-Losartan; Auro-Losartan; Cozaar; JAMP-Losartan; Mint-Losartan; Mylan-Losartan; PMS-Losartan; RAN-Losartan; Sandoz Losartan; Septa Losartan; Teva-Losartan

Pharmacologic Category Angiotensin II Receptor Blocker; Antihypertensive

Use

Diabetic nephropathy: Treatment of diabetic nephropathy with an elevated serum creatinine and proteinuria (urinary albumin to creatinine ratio ≥300 mg/g) in patients with type 2 diabetes and a history of hypertension.

Hypertension: Management of hypertension in adults and children ≥6 years.

Hypertension with left ventricular hypertrophy: To reduce the risk of stroke in patients with hypertension and left ventricular hypertrophy (LVH). Evidence suggests that this benefit does not apply to black patients.

Guideline recommendations:

Hypertension: The 2014 guideline for the management of high blood pressure in adults (Eighth Joint National Committee [JNC 8]) recommends initiation of pharmacologic treatment to lower blood pressure for the following patients:

- Patients ≥60 years of age with systolic blood pressure (SBP) ≥150 mm Hg or diastolic blood pressure (DBP) ≥90 mm Hg. Goal of therapy is SBP <150 mm Hg and DBP <90 mm Hg.
- Patients <60 years of age with SBP ≥140 mm Hg or DBP is ≥90 mm Hg. Goal of therapy is SBP <140 mm Hg and DBP <90 mm Hg.
- Patients ≥18 years of age with diabetes and SBP ≥140 mm Hg or DBP ≥90 mm Hg. Goal of therapy is SBP <140 mm Hg and DBP <90 mm Hg.
- Patients ≥18 years of age with chronic kidney disease (CKD) and SBP ≥140 mm Hg or DBP ≥90 mm Hg. Goal of therapy is SBP <140 mm Hg and DBP <90 mm Hg.

Chronic kidney disease (CKD) and hypertension: Regardless of race or diabetes status, the use of an ACE inhibitor (ACEI) or angiotensin receptor blocker (ARB) as initial therapy is recommended to improve kidney outcomes. In the general nonblack population (without CKD) including those with diabetes, initial antihypertensive treatment should consist of a thiazide-type diuretic, calcium channel blocker, ACEI, or ARB. In the general black population (without CKD) including those with diabetes, initial antihypertensive treatment should consist of a thiazide-type diuretic or a calcium channel blocker instead of an ACEI or ARB.

Coronary artery disease and hypertension: The American Heart Association, American College of Cardiology and American Society of Hypertension (AHA/ACC/ASH) 2015 scientific statement for the treatment of hypertension in patients with coronary artery disease (CAD) recommends the use of an ARB (or ACE inhibitor) as part of a regimen in patients with hypertension and chronic stable angina if there is prior MI, LV systolic dysfunction, diabetes mellitus, or CKD. A BP target of <140/90 mm Hg is reasonable for the secondary prevention of cardiovascular events. A lower target BP (<130/80 mm Hg) may be appropriate in some individuals with CAD, previous MI, stroke or transient ischemic attack, or CAD risk equivalents (AHA/ACC/ASH [Rosendorff 2015]).

Local Anesthetic/Vasoconstrictor Precautions No information available to require special precautions

Effects on Dental Treatment Key adverse event(s) related to dental treatment: Patients may experience

orthostatic hypotension as they stand up after treatment; especially if lying in dental chair for extended periods of time. Use caution with sudden changes in position during and after dental treatment.

Effects on Bleeding No information available to require special precautions

Adverse Reactions The incidence of some adverse reactions varied based on the underlying disease state. Notations are made, where applicable, for data derived from trials conducted in type 2 diabetic nephropathy and hypertensive patients, respectively. Frequency not always defined.

Cardiovascular: Chest pain (type 2 diabetic nephropathy: ≥4%), hypotension (type 2 diabetic nephropathy: ≥4%), orthostatic hypotension (type 2 diabetic nephropathy: ≥4%)

Central nervous system: Myasthenia (type 2 diabetic nephropathy: ≥4%), dizziness (hypertension: 3%), fatigue (type 2 diabetic nephropathy)

Endocrine & metabolic: Hyperkalemia (type 2 diabetic nephropathy: ≥4%), hypoglycemia (type 2 diabetic nephropathy: ≥4%)

Gastrointestinal: Diarrhea (type 2 diabetic nephropathy: ≥4%)

Genitourinary: Urinary tract infection (type 2 diabetic nephropathy: ≥4%)

Hematologic & oncologic: Anemia (type 2 diabetic nephropathy: ≥4%)

Neuromuscular & skeletal: Back pain (2% to ≥4%), weakness (type 2 diabetic nephropathy)

Respiratory: Cough (hypertension: 17%; incidence higher in patients with previous cough related to ACE inhibitor therapy), upper respiratory tract infection (hypertension: 8%), nasal congestion (hypertension: 2%)

<2%, postmarketing, and/or case reports: Abdominal pain, abnormal hepatic function tests, anaphylaxis, anemia, angioedema, arthralgia, atrial fibrillation, cerebrovascular accident, constipation, depression, drowsiness, dysgeusia, dyspnea, edema, erectile dysfunction, erythroderma, headache, hepatitis, hyponatremia, IgA vasculitis, impotence, malaise, migraine, myalgia, myositis, nausea, palpitations, paresthesia, pruritus, rhabdomyolysis, skin photosensitivity, skin rash, sleep disorder, syncope, taste disorder, thrombocytopenia, tinnitus, urticaria, vasculitis, vertigo, vomiting

General Dosage Range Dosage adjustment recommended in patients with hepatic impairment

Oral:

Children ≥6 years and Adolescents ≤16 years: Initial: 0.7 mg/kg once daily (maximum: 50 mg/day); Maintenance: Doses >1.4 mg/kg (>100 mg) once daily have not been studied

Adults: Initial: 25 to 50 mg once daily; Maintenance: 25 to 100 mg daily in 1 to 2 divided doses (maximum: 100 mg/day)

Mechanism of Action As a selective and competitive, nonpeptide angiotensin II receptor antagonist, losartan blocks the vasoconstrictor and aldosterone-secreting effects of angiotensin II; losartan interacts reversibly at the AT1 and AT2 receptors of many tissues and has slow dissociation kinetics; its affinity for the AT1 receptor is 1000 times greater than the AT2 receptor. Angiotensin II receptor antagonists may induce a more complete inhibition of the renin-angiotensin system than ACE inhibitors, they do not affect the response to bradykinin, and are less likely to be associated with nonrenin-angiotensin effects (eg, cough and angioedema). Losartan increases urinary flow rate and in addition to being natriuretic and kaliuretic, increases excretion of chloride, magnesium, uric acid, calcium, and phosphate.

Pharmacodynamics/Kinetics

Onset of Action ~6 hours

Half-life Elimination

Losartan: Children 6 to 16 years: 2.3 ± 0.8 hours; Adults: 2.1 ± 0.7 hours

E-3174 (active metabolite): Children 6 to 16 years: 5.6 ± 1.2 hours; Adults: 7.4 ± 2.4 hours

Time to Peak Serum: Losartan: Children: 2 hours, Adults: 1 hour; E-3174 (active metabolite): Children: 4.1 hours, Adults: 3.5 hours

Pregnancy Risk Factor D

Pregnancy Considerations [US Boxed Warning]: Drugs that act on the renin-angiotensin system can cause injury and death to the developing fetus. Discontinue as soon as possible once pregnancy is detected. The use of drugs which act on the renin-angiotensin system are associated with oligohydramnios. Oligohydramnios, due to decreased fetal renal function, may lead to fetal lung hypoplasia and skeletal malformations. Use is also associated with anuria, hypotension, renal failure, skull hypoplasia, and death in the fetus/neonate. The exposed fetus should be monitored for fetal growth, amniotic fluid volume, and organ formation. Infants exposed *in utero* should be monitored for hyperkalemia, hypotension, and oliguria (exchange transfusions or dialysis may be needed). These adverse events are generally associated with maternal use in the second and third trimesters.

Untreated chronic maternal hypertension is also associated with adverse events in the fetus, infant, and mother. The use of angiotensin II receptor blockers is not recommended to treat chronic uncomplicated hypertension in pregnant women and should generally be avoided in women of reproductive potential (ACOG, 2013).

Losartan and Hydrochlorothiazide

(loe SAR tan & hye droe klor oh THYE a zide)

Related Information

HydroCHLOROthiazide *on page 820*

Losartan *on page 1024*

Brand Names: US Hyzaar

Brand Names: Canada ACT Losartan/HCT; Apo-Losartan/HCTZ; Auro-Losartan HCT; Hyzaar; Hyzaar DS; JAMP-Losartan HCTZ; Losartan-HCT; Losartan-HCTZ; Mint-Losartan/HCTZ; Mint-Losartan/HCTZ DS; Mylan-Losartan/HCTZ; PMS-Losartan/HCTZ; Sandoz-Losartan HCT; Sandoz-Losartan HCT DS; Teva-Losartan/HCTZ

Pharmacologic Category Angiotensin II Receptor Blocker; Antihypertensive; Diuretic, Thiazide

Use

Hypertension: Management of hypertension.

Hypertension with left ventricular hypertrophy: To reduce the risk of stroke in patients with hypertension and left ventricular hypertrophy (LVH). Evidence suggests that this benefit does not apply to black patients.

Local Anesthetic/Vasoconstrictor Precautions No information available to require special precautions

Effects on Dental Treatment Key adverse event(s) related to dental treatment: Patients may experience orthostatic hypotension as they stand up after treatment; especially if lying in dental chair for extended periods of time. Use caution with sudden changes in position during and after dental treatment.

Effects on Bleeding No information available to require special precautions

Adverse Reactions Based on clinical trials of the combination product in patients with primary hypertension. Also see individual agents.

1% to 10%:

Central nervous system: Dizziness (6%)

Neuromuscular & skeletal: Back pain (2%)

Respiratory: Upper respiratory tract infection (6%)

<2%, postmarketing, case reports, or frequency not defined (some reactions attributed to single component): Abdominal pain, adult respiratory distress syndrome, agranulocytosis, anaphylaxis, anemia, anorexia, aplastic anemia, arthralgia, blurred vision (transient), chest pain, constipation, cutaneous lupus erythematous, diarrhea, dysgeusia, dyspepsia, edema, electrolyte disturbance, erectile dysfunction, erythroderma, fever, gastric irritation, glycosuria, headache, hemolytic anemia, hepatic insufficiency, hepatitis, hyperglycemia, hyperuricemia, hypokalemia, hyponatremia, impotence, insomnia, interstitial nephritis, jaundice (intrahepatic cholestatic jaundice), leukopenia, malaise, migraine, muscle cramps, muscle spasm, myalgia, nasal congestion, nausea, necrotizing angiitis (vasculitis, cutaneous vasculitis), orthostatic effect (dose-related), palpitations, pancreatitis, paranasal sinus disease, paresthesia, pharyngitis, pruritus, purpura, renal failure, renal insufficiency, respiratory distress (including pneumonitis and pulmonary edema), restlessness, rhabdomyolysis, sialadenitis, skin photosensitivity, skin rash, swelling, tachycardia, thrombocytopenia, toxic epidermal necrolysis, urticaria, vomiting, weakness, xanthopsia

General Dosage Range Oral: *Adults:* Losartan 50 to 100 mg/hydrochlorothiazide 12.5 to 25 mg once daily (maximum dose: losartan 100 mg/hydrochlorothiazide 25 mg per day).

Mechanism of Action

Losartan: As a selective and competitive, nonpeptide angiotensin II receptor antagonist, losartan blocks the vasoconstrictor and aldosterone-secreting effects of angiotensin II; losartan interacts reversibly at the AT1 and AT2 receptors of many tissues and has slow dissociation kinetics; its affinity for the AT1 receptor is 1000 times greater than the AT2 receptor. Angiotensin II receptor antagonists may induce a more complete inhibition of the renin-angiotensin system than ACE inhibitors, they do not affect the response to bradykinin, and are less likely to be associated with nonrenin-angiotensin effects (eg, cough and angioedema). Losartan increases urinary flow rate and in addition to being natriuretic and kaliuretic, increases excretion of chloride, magnesium, uric acid, calcium, and phosphate.

Hydrochlorothiazide: Inhibits sodium reabsorption in the distal tubules causing increased excretion of sodium and water as well as potassium and hydrogen ions.

Pregnancy Risk Factor D

Pregnancy Considerations [US Boxed Warning]: Drugs that act on the renin-angiotensin system can cause injury and death to the developing fetus. Discontinue as soon as possible once pregnancy is detected. See individual agents.

Loteprednol (loe te PRED nol)

Brand Names: US Alrex; Lotemax

Brand Names: Canada Alrex; Lotemax

Pharmacologic Category Corticosteroid, Ophthalmic

Use

Seasonal allergic conjunctivitis (0.2% suspension): Temporary relief of signs and symptoms of seasonal allergic conjunctivitis

Postoperative inflammation/pain (0.5% suspension/ointment/gel): Treatment of postoperative inflammation and pain following ocular surgery

Ophthalmic inflammatory conditions (0.5% suspension): Treatment of steroid-responsive inflammatory conditions of the palpebral and bulbar conjunctiva, cornea, and anterior segment of the globe (eg, allergic conjunctivitis, acne rosacea, superficial punctate keratitis, herpes zoster keratitis, iritis, cyclitis, selected infective conjunctivitis, when the inherent hazard of steroid use is accepted to obtain an advisable diminution in edema and inflammation)

Local Anesthetic/Vasoconstrictor Precautions No information available to require special precautions

Effects on Dental Treatment No significant effects or complications reported

Effects on Bleeding No information available to require special precautions

Adverse Reactions

>10%:

Central nervous system: Foreign body sensation (2% to 15%), headache (2% to <15%)

Dermatologic: Pruritus (5% to 15%)

Endocrine & metabolic: Chemosis (5% to 15%)

Local: Application site burning (5% to 15%)

Ophthalmic: Anterior chamber inflammation (5% to 25%), blurred vision (5% to 15%), epiphora (5% to 15%), eye discharge (5% to 15%), photophobia (5% to 15%), visual disturbance (5% to 15%), xerophthalmia (5% to 15%)

Respiratory: Pharyngitis (<15%), rhinitis (<15%)

1% to 10%:

Ophthalmic: Conjunctival hyperemia (4% to 5%), corneal edema (4% to 5%), eye pain (2% to 5%), blepharitis (<5%), conjunctivitis (<5%), corneal changes (<5%), eye irritation (<5%), keratoconjunctivitis (<5%), uveitis (<5%), increased intraocular pressure (2%)

Miscellaneous: Papilla (<5%)

General Dosage Range Ophthalmic: *Adults:* Ointment: Apply ~1/2 inch ribbon into affected eye(s) 4 times daily; Gel: Instill 1 to 2 drops into affected eye(s) 4 times daily; Suspension: Instill 1 to 2 drops into affected eye(s) 4 times daily

Mechanism of Action Corticosteroids inhibit the inflammatory response including edema, capillary dilation, leukocyte migration, and scar formation. Loteprednol is highly lipid soluble and penetrates cells readily to induce the production of lipocortins. These proteins modulate the activity of prostaglandins and leukotrienes.

Pharmacodynamics/Kinetics

Onset of Action Seasonal allergic conjunctivitis: Reduction of symptoms seen within 2 hours of instillation

Pregnancy Risk Factor C

Pregnancy Considerations Adverse events have been observed in animal reproduction studies following oral administration. The amount of loteprednol absorbed systemically following ophthalmic administration is not known but expected to be <1 ng/mL.

Lovastatin (LOE va sta tin)

Related Information

Cardiovascular Diseases *on page 1752*

Brand Names: US Altoprev; Mevacor

Brand Names: Canada ACT Lovastatin; Apo-Lovastatin; CO Lovastatin; Dom-Lovastatin; Mylan-Lovastatin; PHL-Lovastatin; PMS-Lovastatin; PRO-Lovastatin; Riva-Lovastatin; Sandoz-Lovastatin; Teva-Lovastatin

Generic Availability (US) May be product dependent

Pharmacologic Category Antilipemic Agent, HMG-CoA Reductase Inhibitor

Use

Adjunct to dietary therapy to decrease elevated serum total and LDL-cholesterol concentrations in primary hypercholesterolemia

Primary prevention of coronary artery disease (patients without symptomatic disease with average to moderately elevated total and LDL-cholesterol and below average HDL-cholesterol); slow progression of coronary atherosclerosis in patients with coronary heart disease and reduce the risk of myocardial infarction, unstable angina, and coronary revascularization procedures.

Adjunct to dietary therapy in adolescent patients (10-17 years of age, females >1 year postmenarche) with heterozygous familial hypercholesterolemia having LDL >189 mg/dL, **or** LDL >160 mg/dL with positive family history of premature cardiovascular disease (CVD), **or** LDL >160 mg/dL with the presence of at least two other CVD risk factors

Guideline recommendations: Primary and secondary prevention of atherosclerotic cardiovascular disease (ASCVD) to reduce the risk of ASCVD in select adult patients (ACC/AHA [Stone 2013]; NLA [Jacobson 2015]). Refer to respective guideline for specific recommendations.

Local Anesthetic/Vasoconstrictor Precautions No information available to require special precautions

Effects on Dental Treatment Key adverse event(s) related to dental treatment: Assess unusual presentations of muscle weakness or myopathy resulting from lipid therapy such as patient having a difficult time brushing teeth or weakness with chewing. Refer patient back to their physician for evaluation and adjustment of lipid therapy.

Effects on Bleeding No information available to require special precautions

Adverse Reactions Percentages as reported with immediate-release tablets; similar adverse reactions seen with extended-release tablets.

>10%: Neuromuscular & skeletal: Increased creatine phosphokinase (>2x normal) (11%)

1% to 10%:

Central nervous system: Headache (2% to 3%), dizziness (≤1%)

Dermatologic: Skin rash (≤1%)

Gastrointestinal: Flatulence (4% to 5%), constipation (2% to 4%), abdominal pain (2% to 3%), diarrhea (2% to 3%), nausea (2% to 3%), dyspepsia (1% to 2%)

Neuromuscular & skeletal: Myalgia (2% to 3%), weakness (1% to 2%), muscle cramps (≤1%)

Ophthalmic: Blurred vision (≤1%)

Frequency not defined: Genitourinary: Cystitis (interstitial; Huang 2015)

<1%, postmarketing, and/or case reports: Acid regurgitation, alopecia, amnesia (reversible), arthralgia, chest pain, cognitive dysfunction (reversible), dermatomyositis, diabetes mellitus (new-onset), elevated glycosylated hemoglobin (HbA_{1c}), eye irritation, increased blood glucose, insomnia, leg pain, memory impairment (reversible), paresthesia, pruritus, reversible confusional state, vomiting, xerostomia

Dosing

Adult

Dyslipidemia and primary prevention of CAD: Oral:

Immediate release: Initial: 20 mg once daily with evening meal, then adjust at 4-week intervals; maximum dose: 80 mg daily

Extended release: Initial: 20, 40, or 60 mg once daily at bedtime, then adjust at 4-week intervals; maximum dose: 60 mg daily

Note: Doses should be individualized according to the baseline LDL-cholesterol levels, the recommended goal of therapy, and patient response. For patients requiring smaller reductions in cholesterol, the use of the extended release tablet is not recommended; consider use of immediate release formulation.

Prevention of cardiovascular disease/reduce the risk of ASCVD:

ACC/AHA Blood Cholesterol Guideline recommendations (ACC/AHA [Stone 2013]): Adults ≥21 years:

Primary prevention:

LDL-C ≥190 mg/dL: High intensity therapy necessary; use alternate statin therapy (eg, atorvastatin or rosuvastatin)

Type 1 or 2 diabetes and age 40-75 years: Moderate intensity therapy: Immediate release: 40 mg once daily

Type 1 or 2 diabetes, age 40-75 years, and an estimated 10-year ASCVD risk ≥7.5%: High intensity therapy necessary; use alternate statin therapy (eg, atorvastatin or rosuvastatin)

Age 40-75 years and an estimated 10-year ASCVD risk ≥7.5%: Moderate to high intensity therapy: Immediate release: 40 mg once daily or consider using high intensity statin therapy (eg, atorvastatin or rosuvastatin)

Secondary prevention:

Patient has clinical ASCVD (eg, coronary heart disease, stroke/TIA, or peripheral arterial disease presumed to be of atherosclerotic origin) or is post-CABG (AHA [Kulik 2015]) **and:**

Age ≤75 years: High intensity therapy necessary; use alternate statin therapy (eg, atorvastatin or rosuvastatin)

Age >75 years or not a candidate for high intensity therapy: Moderate intensity therapy: Immediate release: 40 mg once daily

NLA Dyslipidemia Guideline recommendations (NLA [Jacobson 2015]): Adults ≥20 years:

Primary or secondary prevention: Note: Treatment initiation using either moderate- or high-intensity statin therapy is recommended in qualifying patients based on ASCVD risk assessment criteria and baseline non-HDL-C and LDL-C values. Dosage should be individualized based on patient characteristics, tolerance to therapy and with consideration for non-HDL-C and LDL-C treatment goals.

Moderate-intensity therapy (30 to 50% reduction of LDL-C generally): Immediate release: 40 mg once daily

High-intensity therapy (≥50% reduction of LDL-C generally): Use alternate statin therapy (eg, atorvastatin, rosuvastatin)

Dosage adjustment for lovastatin with concomitant medications:

Amiodarone: Maximum recommended lovastatin dose (extended release and immediate release): 40 mg daily

Danazol, diltiazem, dronedarone, or verapamil: Initial lovastatin (immediate release) dose: 10 mg daily; Maximum recommended lovastatin (extended release and immediate release) dose: 20 mg daily

Lomitapide: Consider lovastatin dose reduction (per lomitapide manufacturer).

Geriatric Immediate release: Refer to adult dosing; Extended release: Initial: 20 mg once daily at bedtime

Pediatric

Heterozygous familial hypercholesterolemia: Oral (immediate release tablet): Adolescents 10-17 years:

LDL reduction <20%: Initial: 10 mg daily with evening meal

LDL reduction ≥20%: Initial: 20 mg daily with evening meal

Usual range: 10-40 mg once daily with evening meal, then adjust dose at 4-week intervals; maximum dose per manufacturer: 40 mg daily

Dosage adjustment for lovastatin with concomitant medications (amiodarone, danazol, diltiazem, dronedarone, lomitapide, or verapamil): Refer to adult dosing.

Renal Impairment CrCl <30 mL/minute: Use with caution and carefully consider doses >20 mg/day.

Hepatic Impairment No dosage adjustment provided in manufacturer's labeling (has not been studied).

Adjustment for Toxicity

Severe muscle symptoms or fatigue: Promptly discontinue use; evaluate CPK, creatinine, and urinalysis for myoglobinuria (Stone 2013).

Mild to moderate muscle symptoms: Discontinue use until symptoms can be evaluated; evaluate patient for conditions that may increase the risk for muscle symptoms (eg, hypothyroidism, reduced renal or hepatic function, rheumatologic disorders such as polymyalgia rheumatica, steroid myopathy, vitamin D deficiency, or primary muscle diseases). Upon resolution, resume the original or lower dose of lovastatin. If muscle symptoms recur, discontinue lovastatin use. After muscle symptom resolution, may then use a low dose of a different statin; gradually increase if tolerated. In the absence of continued statin use, if muscle symptoms or elevated CPK continues after 2 months, consider other causes of muscle symptoms. If determined to be due to another condition aside from statin use, may resume statin therapy at the original dose (Stone 2013).

Mechanism of Action Lovastatin acts by competitively inhibiting 3-hydroxyl-3-methylglutaryl-coenzyme A (HMG-CoA) reductase, the enzyme that catalyzes the rate-limiting step in cholesterol biosynthesis. In addition to the ability of HMG-CoA reductase inhibitors to decrease levels of high-sensitivity C-reactive protein (hsCRP), they also possess pleiotropic properties including improved endothelial function, reduced inflammation at the site of the coronary plaque, inhibition of platelet aggregation, and anticoagulant effects (de Denus 2002; Ray 2005).

Contraindications

Hypersensitivity to lovastatin or any component of the formulation; active liver disease; unexplained persistent elevations of serum transaminases; concomitant use of strong CYP3A4 inhibitors (eg, clarithromycin, erythromycin, itraconazole, ketoconazole, nefazodone, posaconazole, voriconazole, protease inhibitors [including boceprevir and telaprevir], telithromycin, cobicistat-containing products); pregnancy; breast-feeding

Canadian labeling: Additional contraindications (not in US labeling): Concomitant use of cyclosporine

Warnings/Precautions Secondary causes of hyperlipidemia should be ruled out prior to therapy. Liver enzyme tests should be obtained at baseline and as clinically indicated; routine periodic monitoring of liver enzymes is not necessary. Use with caution in patients who consume large amounts of ethanol or have a history of liver disease; use is contraindicated with active liver disease and with unexplained transaminase elevations. Rhabdomyolysis with or without acute renal failure has occurred. Risk of rhabdomyolysis is dose-related and increased with concurrent use of lipid-lowering agents which may also cause rhabdomyolysis (fibric acid derivatives or niacin at doses ≥1 g/day) or during concurrent use with potent CYP3A4 inhibitors. Use is contraindicated in patients taking strong CYP3A4 inhibitors. Concomitant use of lovastatin with some drugs may require cautious use, may not be recommended, may require dosage adjustments, or may be contraindicated. Increases in HbA_{1c} and fasting blood glucose have been reported with HMG-CoA reductase inhibitors; however, the benefits of statin therapy far outweigh the risk of dysglycemia. Monitor closely if used with other drugs associated with myopathy (eg, colchicine). Patients should be instructed to report unexplained muscle pain or weakness; lovastatin should be discontinued if myopathy is suspected/confirmed. Immune-mediated necrotizing myopathy (IMNM), an autoimmune-mediated myopathy, has been reported (rarely) with HMG-CoA reductase inhibitor therapy. IMNM presents as proximal muscle weakness with elevated CPK levels, which persists despite discontinuation of HMG-CoA reductase inhibitor therapy; additionally, muscle biopsy may show necrotizing myopathy with limited inflammation; immunosuppressive therapy (eg, corticosteroids, azathioprine) may be used for treatment. The manufacturer recommends temporary discontinuation for elective major surgery, acute medical or surgical conditions, or in any patient experiencing an acute or serious condition predisposing to renal failure (eg, sepsis, hypotension, trauma, uncontrolled seizures). Based on current research and clinical guidelines (Fleisher 2009), HMG-CoA reductase inhibitors should be continued in the perioperative period. Use with caution in patients with advanced age; these patients are predisposed to myopathy.

Drug Interactions

Metabolism/Transport Effects Substrate of CYP3A4 (major), P-glycoprotein; **Note:** Assignment of Major/Minor substrate status based on clinically relevant drug interaction potential; **Inhibits** CYP2C9 (weak)

Avoid Concomitant Use

Avoid concomitant use of Lovastatin with any of the following: Boceprevir; Clarithromycin; Conivaptan; CycloSPORINE (Systemic); CYP3A4 Inhibitors (Strong); Erythromycin (Systemic); Fusidic Acid (Systemic); Gemfibrozil; Idelalisib; MiFEPRIStone;

Protease Inhibitors; Red Yeast Rice; Telaprevir; Telithromycin

Increased Effect/Toxicity

Lovastatin may increase the levels/effects of: Dabigatran Etexilate; DAPTOmycin; DilTIAZem; PAZOPanib; Repaglinide; Trabectedin; Vitamin K Antagonists

The levels/effects of Lovastatin may be increased by: Acipimox; Amiodarone; Aprepitant; Asunaprevir; Azithromycin (Systemic); Bezafibrate; Boceprevir; Ciprofibrate; Clarithromycin; Colchicine; Conivaptan; CycloSPORINE (Systemic); CYP3A4 Inhibitors (Moderate); CYP3A4 Inhibitors (Strong); Cyproterone; Daclatasvir; Danazol; Dasatinib; DilTIAZem; Dronedarone; Elbasvir; Erythromycin (Systemic); Fenofibrate and Derivatives; Fluconazole; Fosaprepitant; Fusidic Acid (Systemic); Gemfibrozil; Grapefruit Juice; Grazoprevir; Idelalisib; Ivacaftor; Lomitapide; MiFEPRIStone; Netupitant; Niacin; Niacinamide; Palbociclib; P-glycoprotein/ABCB1 Inhibitors; Protease Inhibitors; QuiNINE; Raltegravir; Ranolazine; Red Yeast Rice; Rupatadine; Simeprevir; Stiripentol; Telaprevir; Telithromycin; Ticagrelor; Verapamil

Decreased Effect

Lovastatin may decrease the levels/effects of: Lanthanum

The levels/effects of Lovastatin may be decreased by: Antacids; Bosentan; CYP3A4 Inducers (Moderate); CYP3A4 Inducers (Strong); Dabrafenib; Deferasirox; Efavirenz; Enzalutamide; Etravirine; Fosphenytoin; Mitotane; Phenytoin; Rifamycin Derivatives; Siltuximab; St John's Wort; Tocilizumab

Food Interactions Food decreases the bioavailability of lovastatin extended release tablets and increases the bioavailability of lovastatin immediate release tablets. Lovastatin serum concentrations may be increased if taken with grapefruit juice. Management: Avoid combination.

Dietary Considerations Before initiation of therapy, patients should be placed on a standard cholesterol-lowering diet for 6 weeks and the diet should be continued during drug therapy. Avoid intake of grapefruit juice; may increase toxicity. Immediate release tablet should be taken with the evening meal.

Red yeast rice contains variable amounts of several compounds that are structurally similar to HMG-CoA reductase inhibitors, primarily monacolin K (or mevinolin) which is structurally identical to lovastatin; concurrent use of red yeast rice with HMG-CoA reductase inhibitors may increase the incidence of adverse and toxic effects (Lapi 2008; Smith 2003).

Pharmacodynamics/Kinetics

Onset of Action LDL cholesterol reductions: 3 days

Half-life Elimination 1.1-1.7 hours

Time to Peak Serum: Immediate release: 2-4 hours; extended release: 12-14 hours

Pregnancy Risk Factor X

Pregnancy Considerations Adverse events were observed in animal reproduction studies. There are reports of congenital anomalies following maternal use of HMG-CoA reductase inhibitors in pregnancy; however, maternal disease, differences in specific agents used, and the low rates of exposure limit the interpretation of the available data (Godfrey 2012; Lecarpentier 2012). Cholesterol biosynthesis may be important in fetal development; serum cholesterol and triglycerides increase normally during pregnancy. The discontinuation of lipid lowering medications temporarily during pregnancy is not expected to have significant impact on the long term outcomes of primary hypercholesterolemia treatment.

Use of lovastatin is contraindicated in pregnancy. HMG-CoA reductase inhibitors should be discontinued prior to pregnancy (ADA 2013). If treatment of dyslipidemias is needed in pregnant women or in women of reproductive age, other agents are preferred (Berglund 2012; Stone 2013). The manufacturer recommends administration to women of childbearing potential only when conception is highly unlikely and patients have been informed of potential hazards.

Breastfeeding Considerations It is not known if lovastatin is excreted into breast milk. Due to the potential for serious adverse reactions in a nursing infant, use while breastfeeding is contraindicated by the manufacturer.

Dosage Forms

Tablet, Oral:

Mevacor: 20 mg, 40 mg

Generic: 10 mg, 20 mg, 40 mg

Tablet Extended Release 24 Hour, Oral:

Altoprev: 20 mg, 40 mg, 60 mg

Dosage Forms: Canada

Refer to Dosage Forms. **Note:** Extended release tablet is not available in Canada.

Loxapine (LOKS a peen)

Related Information

Dentin Hypersensitivity, Acid Erosion, High Caries Index, Management of Alveolar Osteitis, and Xerostomia *on page 1857*

Brand Names: US Adasuve; Loxitane [DSC]

Brand Names: Canada Apo-Loxapine; Dom-Loxapine; Loxapac; PHL-Loxapine; Xylac

Pharmacologic Category First Generation (Typical) Antipsychotic

Use

Schizophrenia: IM, Oral: Treatment of schizophrenia.

Agitation associated with schizophrenia or bipolar I disorder: Inhalation: Acute treatment of agitation associated with schizophrenia or bipolar I disorder in adults. **Note**: As part of the Adasuve REMS program to mitigate the risk of bronchospasm, loxapine inhalation must be administered only in an enrolled health care facility.

Local Anesthetic/Vasoconstrictor Precautions Loxapine is one of the drugs confirmed to prolong the QT interval and is accepted as having a risk of causing torsade de pointes. The risk of drug-induced torsade de pointes is extremely low when a single QT interval prolonging drug is prescribed. In terms of epinephrine, it is not known what effect vasoconstrictors in the local anesthetic regimen will have in patients with a known history of congenital prolonged QT interval or in patients taking any medication that prolongs the QT interval. Until more information is obtained, it is suggested that the clinician consult with the physician prior to the use of a vasoconstrictor in suspected patients, and that the vasoconstrictor (epinephrine, mepivacaine and levonordefrin [Carbocaine® 2% with Neo-Cobefrin®]) be used with caution.

Effects on Dental Treatment Key adverse event(s) related to dental treatment:

Xerostomia and changes in salivation (normal salivary flow resumes upon discontinuation).

Significant hypotension may occur, especially when the drug is administered parenterally; Patients may experience orthostatic hypotension as they stand up after treatment; especially if lying in dental chair for extended periods of time. Use caution with sudden changes in position during and after dental treatment. Orthostatic hypotension is due to alpha-receptor blockade, the elderly are at greater risk for orthostatic hypotension.

Tardive dyskinesia: Prevalence rate may be 40% in elderly; development of the syndrome and the irreversible nature are proportional to duration and total cumulative dose over time. Extrapyramidal reactions are more common in elderly with up to 50% developing these reactions after 60 years of age. Drug-induced Parkinson's syndrome occurs often; akathisia is the most common extrapyramidal reaction in elderly.

Increased confusion, memory loss, psychotic behavior, and agitation frequently occur as a consequence of anticholinergic effects. Antipsychotic associated sedation in nonpsychotic patients is extremely unpleasant due to feelings of depersonalization, derealization, and dysphoria.

Effects on Bleeding No information available to require special precautions

Adverse Reactions

Inhalation: Frequency not always defined.

Cardiovascular: Hypotension (3%), syncope (2%)

Central nervous system: Sedation (12%)

Gastrointestinal: Dysgeusia (14%)

Hypersensitivity: Hypersensitivity

Respiratory: Respiratory distress (includes bronchospasm, chest pain, cough, dyspnea, pharyngeal edema, wheezing; asthma patients: 54%; COPD patients: 19%), throat irritation (3%)

<1%: Extrapyramidal reaction

Oral: Frequency not defined.

Cardiovascular: ECG changes, edema, flushing (facial), hypertension, hypotension, orthostatic hypotension, syncope, tachycardia

Central nervous system: Agitation, confusion, disruption of body temperature regulation, dizziness, drowsiness, extrapyramidal reaction (akathisia, akinesia, dystonia, drug-induced parkinson's disease, tardive dyskinesia), headache, hyperpyrexia, insomnia, neuroleptic malignant syndrome (NMS), numbness, paresthesia, sedation, seizure, slurred speech, tension, unsteady gait

Dermatologic: Alopecia, dermatitis, pruritus, seborrhea, skin photosensitivity, skin rash

Endocrine & metabolic: Amenorrhea, galactorrhea, gynecomastia, hyperprolactinemia, menstrual disease, polydipsia, weight gain, weight loss

Gastrointestinal: Constipation, nausea, paralytic ileus, vomiting, xerostomia

Genitourinary: Impotence, priapism (rare), urinary retention

Hematologic & oncologic: Agranulocytosis, leukopenia, thrombocytopenia

Hepatic: Hepatitis, increased serum ALT, increased serum AST, jaundice

Neuromuscular & skeletal: Muscle twitching, weakness

Ophthalmic: Blepharoptosis, blurred vision

Respiratory: Dyspnea, nasal congestion

General Dosage Range

Oral: *Adults:* Initial: 10 mg twice daily (up to 50 mg daily); Usual maintenance: 20 to 100 mg daily in 2 to 4 divided doses (maximum: 250 mg/day)

Inhalation: *Adults:* 10 mg once daily; maximum dose: 10 mg per 24 hour period

Mechanism of Action Loxapine is a dibenzoxazepine antipsychotic that blocks postsynaptic mesolimbic D_1 and D_2 receptors in the brain, and also possesses serotonin 5-HT_2-blocking activity.

Pharmacodynamics/Kinetics

Onset of Action

Oral, IM: Within 30 minutes; Peak effect: 1.5 to 3 hours

Inhalation: 2 minutes

Duration of Action Oral, IM: ~12 hours

Half-life Elimination Biphasic: Oral: Initial: 5 hours; Terminal: 19 hours; Inhalation: 6 to 8 hours

Pregnancy Risk Factor C

Pregnancy Considerations Adverse events have been observed in animal reproduction studies. Antipsychotic use during the third trimester of pregnancy has a risk for abnormal muscle movements (extrapyramidal symptoms [EPS]) and withdrawal symptoms in newborns following delivery. Symptoms in the newborn may include agitation, feeding disorder, hypertonia, hypotonia, respiratory distress, somnolence, and tremor; these effects may be self-limiting or require hospitalization.

Prescribing and Access Restrictions Adasuve is only available through a restricted program called Adasuve REMS. In order to distribute, dispense and administer Adasuve, health care facilities must be enrolled and comply with REMS requirements (including on-site access to supplies and personnel trained to manage acute bronchospasm and ready access to emergency response services. Facilities must have a short-acting bronchodilator (eg, albuterol), including a nebulizer and inhalation solution, for the immediate treatment of bronchospasm. Information is available at www.adasuverems.com or 855-755-0492.

Dental Comment See Local Anesthetic/Vasoconstrictor Precautions

---

Lubiprostone (loo bi PROS tone)

Brand Names: US Amitiza

Pharmacologic Category Chloride Channel Activator; Gastrointestinal Agent, Miscellaneous

Use

Chronic idiopathic constipation: Treatment of chronic idiopathic constipation in adults

Irritable bowel syndrome with constipation: Treatment of irritable bowel syndrome (IBS) with constipation in women ≥18 years

Opioid-induced constipation: Treatment of opioid-induced constipation in adults with chronic noncancer pain

Local Anesthetic/Vasoconstrictor Precautions No information available to require special precautions

Effects on Dental Treatment Key adverse event(s) related to dental treatment: Xerostomia (normal salivary flow resumes upon discontinuation).

Effects on Bleeding No information available to require special precautions

Adverse Reactions

>10%:

Central nervous system: Headache (2% to 11%)

Gastrointestinal: Nausea (8% to 29%; dose related; males: 8%; older adults: 19%), diarrhea (7% to 12%)

1% to 10%:

Cardiovascular: Edema (≤3%), chest discomfort (≤2%), chest pain (≤2%), peripheral edema (1%)

Central nervous system: Dizziness (3%), fatigue (≤2%)

Gastrointestinal: Abdominal pain (4% to 8%), flatulence (4% to 6%), abdominal distention (3% to 6%), abdominal distress (3%), loose stools (≤3%), vomiting (≤3%), dyspepsia (≤2%), xerostomia (≤1%)
Respiratory: Dyspnea (≤3%)
<1%, postmarketing, and/or case reports: Anorexia, anxiety, bowel urgency, constipation, cough, decreased appetite, decreased serum potassium, depression, diaphoresis, dysgeusia, eructation, erythema, fecal impaction, fecal incontinence, fibromyalgia syndrome, frequent bowel movements, gastritis, gastroesophageal reflux disease, gastrointestinal disease, hyperhidrosis, hypersensitivity reaction (including skin rash, swelling, throat tightness), hypotension, increased serum ALT, increased serum AST, influenza, ischemic colitis, joint swelling, lethargy, malaise, muscle cramps, muscle spasm, myalgia, pain, palpitations, pharyngolaryngeal pain, pollakiuria, rectal hemorrhage, syncope, tachycardia, tremor, urinary tract infection, weakness, weight gain

General Dosage Range Dosage adjustment recommended in hepatic impairment.

Oral:

Adults (females): 8 mcg twice daily **or** 24 mcg twice daily

Adults (males): 24 mcg twice daily

Mechanism of Action A chloride channel activator that acts locally on the apical membrane of the gastrointestinal tract to increase intestinal fluid secretion and improve fecal transit. This action bypasses the antisecretory effects of opiates, which suppress secretomotor neuron excitability.

Pharmacodynamics/Kinetics

Half-life Elimination M3: 0.9 to 1.4 hours

Time to Peak Plasma: M3: ~1.1 hour

Pregnancy Risk Factor C

Pregnancy Considerations Adverse events have been observed in animal reproduction studies.

Luliconazole (loo li KON a zole)

Brand Names: US Luzu

Pharmacologic Category Antifungal Agent, Topical

Use Fungal infections: Topical treatment of interdigital tinea pedis, tinea cruris, and tinea corporis caused by *Trichophyton rubrum* and *Epidermophyton floccosum*, in patients 18 years and older

Local Anesthetic/Vasoconstrictor Precautions No information available to require special precautions

Effects on Dental Treatment No significant effects or complications reported

Effects on Bleeding No information available to require special precautions

Adverse Reactions <1%, postmarketing, and/or case reports: Application site reaction, cellulitis, contact dermatitis

General Dosage Range Topical: *Adults:* Apply once daily.

Mechanism of Action Azole antifungal that appears to inhibit ergosterol synthesis by inhibiting the enzyme lanosterol demethylase, resulting in decreased amounts of ergosterol and a corresponding accumulation of lanosterol.

Pregnancy Considerations Adverse events were observed in some animal reproduction studies. Small amounts of luliconazole are absorbed systemically.

Lumacaftor and Ivacaftor

(loo ma KAF tor & eye va KAF tor)

Brand Names: US Orkambi

Brand Names: Canada Orkambi

Pharmacologic Category Cystic Fibrosis Transmembrane Conductance Regulator Potentiator

Use

Cystic fibrosis: Treatment of cystic fibrosis (CF) in patients age 6 years and older who are homozygous for the F508del mutation in the CFTR gene. If the patient's genotype is unknown, an FDA-cleared CF mutation test should be used to detect the presence of the F508del mutation on both alleles of the CFTR gene.

Limitations of use: Efficacy and safety have not been established in patients with CF other than those homozygous for the F508del mutation.

Local Anesthetic/Vasoconstrictor Precautions No information available to require special precautions

Effects on Dental Treatment No significant effects or complications reported

Effects on Bleeding No information available to require special precautions

Adverse Reactions Incidences listed are for adolescents and adults unless otherwise specified.

>10%:
Cardiovascular: Chest discomfort (≤22%, children: ≤3%)
Gastrointestinal: Nausea (13%), diarrhea (12%)
Hepatic: Increased serum ALT (children: >5x to >8x ULN: ≤5% to ≤9%; >3X ULN: ≤19%), Increased serum AST (children: >5x to >8x ULN: ≤5% to ≤9%; >3X ULN: ≤19%)
Respiratory: Dyspnea (13% to ≤22%, children: ≤3%), changes in respiration (9% to ≤22%; children: ≤3%), nasopharyngitis (13%)

1% to 10%:
Cardiovascular: Increased systolic blood pressure (>140 mmHg: ≤4%), increased diastolic blood pressure (>90 mmHg: ≤2%)
Central nervous system: Fatigue (9%)
Dermatologic: Skin rash (7%)
Endocrine & metabolic: Menstrual disease (10%; including amenorrhea, dysmenorrhea, menorrhagia, menstrual irregular; more common in patients using hormonal contraceptives)
Gastrointestinal: Flatulence (7%)
Infection: Influenza (5%)
Neuromuscular & skeletal: Increased creatine phosphokinase (≤7%)
Respiratory: Upper respiratory tract infection (10%), rhinorrhea (6%)

<1%, postmarketing, and/or case reports: Hepatic encephalopathy, increased serum bilirubin, increased serum transaminases

General Dosage Range Dosage adjustment recommended in patients with hepatic impairment, patients on concomitant therapy, and in patients who develop toxicities.

Oral:

Children 6 to 11 years: Lumacaftor 100 mg/ivacaftor 125 mg: 2 tablets (lumacaftor 200 mg/ivacaftor 250 mg) every 12 hours.

Children ≥12 years, Adolescents, and Adults: Lumacaftor 200 mg/ivacaftor 125 mg: 2 tablets (lumacaftor 400 mg/ivacaftor 250 mg) every 12 hours

Mechanism of Action Lumacaftor improves the conformational stability of F508del-CFTR, resulting in increased processing and trafficking of mature protein to the cell surface. Ivacaftor is a CFTR potentiator that facilitates increased chloride transport by potentiating the channel-open probability (or gating) of the CFTR protein at the cell surface.

Pharmacodynamics/Kinetics

Half-life Elimination

Ivacaftor: ~9 hours (when administered with lumacaftor in healthy subjects)

Lumacaftor: ~26 hours (in patients with CF)

Time to Peak

Ivacaftor: ~4 hours (fed state)

Lumacaftor: ~4 hours (fed state)

Pregnancy Considerations Adverse events have not been observed in animal reproduction studies when testing the individual agents.

Lurasidone (loo RAS i done)

Brand Names: US Latuda

Brand Names: Canada Latuda

Pharmacologic Category Second Generation (Atypical) Antipsychotic

Use

Bipolar depression: Treatment of adults with depressive episodes associated with bipolar I disorder, both as monotherapy and as an adjunct to lithium or divalproex

Schizophrenia: Treatment of adults and adolescents with schizophrenia

Local Anesthetic/Vasoconstrictor Precautions No information available to require special precautions

Effects on Dental Treatment Key adverse event(s) related to dental treatment: Salivary hypersecretion has been reported (normal salivary flow resumes upon discontinuation)

Effects on Bleeding No information available to require special precautions

Adverse Reactions Frequencies reported for schizophrenia unless otherwise noted.

10%:

Central nervous system: Drowsiness (dose-related: 8% to 27%; depressive episodes, monotherapy: 11%), extrapyramidal reaction (dose-related: 14% to 26%; depressive episodes, monotherapy: 7%), akathisia (dose-related: 6% to 22%; depressive episodes, monotherapy: 8% to 11%), parkinsonian-like syndrome (6% to 17%; depressive episodes, monotherapy: 8%)

Endocrine & metabolic: Increased serum triglycerides (10% to 14%), increased serum glucose (fasting, 10% to 14%), increased serum cholesterol (6% to 14%)

Gastrointestinal: Nausea (dose-related; 10%; depressive episodes, monotherapy: 14%)

1% to 10%:

Cardiovascular: Orthostatic hypotension (1% to 2%), tachycardia

Central nervous system: Insomnia (10%), agitation (5%), anxiety (5%; depressive episodes, monotherapy: 4%), dizziness (4%), dystonia (≤7%; depressive episodes, monotherapy: ≤2%), restlessness (1% to 3%)

Dermatologic: Pruritus, skin rash

Endocrine & metabolic: Increased serum prolactin (≥5 x ULN: females: 8%; males: ≤2%), weight gain (≥7% increase in baseline body weight: 2% to 6%)

Gastrointestinal: Vomiting (8%; depressive episodes, monotherapy: 4%), dyspepsia (6%), xerostomia (depressive episodes, monotherapy: 5%), diarrhea (≥1%; depressive episodes, monotherapy: 4%), sialorrhea (2%), abdominal pain, decreased appetite

Genitourinary: Urinary tract infection (depressive episodes, monotherapy: 2%)

Infection: Influenza (depressive episodes, monotherapy: 2%)

Neuromuscular & skeletal: Back pain (3%; depressive episodes, monotherapy: 2%), increased creatine phosphokinase

Ophthalmic: Blurred vision

Renal: Increased serum creatinine (3% to 7%; depressive episodes, monotherapy: 2% to 4%)

Respiratory: Nasopharyngitis (depressive episodes, monotherapy: 4%)

<1%: Abnormal dreams, amenorrhea, anemia, angina pectoris, angioedema, atrioventricular block, bradycardia, breast hypertrophy, cerebrovascular accident, dysarthria, gastritis, dysphagia, dysmenorrhea, dysuria, erectile dysfunction, galactorrhea, hypertension, hypomania, leukopenia, mania, mastalgia, neuroleptic malignant syndrome, panic attack, renal failure, rhabdomyolysis, seizure, sleep disorder, suicidal ideation, syncope, tardive dyskinesia, venous thromboembolism, vertigo

General Dosage Range Dosage adjustment recommended in patients with hepatic or renal impairment or on concomitant therapy.

Oral:

Adolescents ≤17 years: Initial 40 mg once daily (maximum: 80 mg/day)

Adults: Initial: 20 to 40 mg once daily (maximum: 120 to 160 mg/day)

Mechanism of Action Lurasidone is a benzoisothiazol-derivative atypical antipsychotic with mixed serotonin-dopamine antagonist activity. It exhibits high affinity for D_2, 5-HT_{2A}, and 5-HT_7 receptors; moderate affinity for alpha$_{2C}$-adrenergic receptors; and is a partial agonist for 5-HT_{1A} receptors. Lurasidone has no significant affinity for muscarinic M_1 and histamine H_1 receptors. The addition of serotonin antagonism to dopamine antagonism (classic neuroleptic mechanism) is thought to improve negative symptoms of psychoses and reduce the incidence of extrapyramidal side effects as compared to typical antipsychotics (Huttunen 1995).

Pharmacodynamics/Kinetics

Half-life Elimination 18 to 40 hours; Main active metabolite, ID-14283 (exo-hydroxy metabolite), exhibits a half-life of 7.5 to 10 hours (Citrome 2011)

Time to Peak 1 to 3 hours; steady state concentrations achieved within 7 days

Pregnancy Considerations Antipsychotic use during the third trimester of pregnancy has a risk for abnormal muscle movements (extrapyramidal symptoms [EPS]) and/or withdrawal symptoms in newborns following delivery. Symptoms in the newborn may include agitation, feeding disorder, hypertonia, hypotonia, respiratory distress, somnolence, and tremor; these effects may be self-limiting or require hospitalization. Lurasidone may cause hyperprolactinemia, which may decrease reproductive function in both males and females.

The ACOG recommends that therapy during pregnancy be individualized; treatment with psychiatric medications during pregnancy should incorporate the clinical expertise of the mental health clinician, obstetrician, primary healthcare provider, and pediatrician. Safety data related to atypical antipsychotics during pregnancy is limited and routine use is not recommended. However, if a woman is inadvertently exposed to an atypical antipsychotic while pregnant, continuing therapy may be preferable to switching to a typical antipsychotic that the fetus has not yet been exposed to; consider risk: benefit (ACOG 2008).

Healthcare providers are encouraged to enroll women 18-45 years of age exposed to lurasidone during pregnancy in the Atypical Antipsychotics Pregnancy Registry (866-961-2388 or http://www.womensmentalhealth.org/pregnancyregistry).

Lutropin Alfa (LOO troe pin AL fa)

Brand Names: Canada Luveris

Pharmacologic Category Gonadotropin; Ovulation Stimulator

Use Note: Not approved in the US

Infertility: Stimulation of follicular development in infertile hypogonadotropic hypogonadal (HH) women with profound luteinizing hormone (LH) deficiency (<1.2 units/L); to be used in combination with follitropin alfa

Local Anesthetic/Vasoconstrictor Precautions No information available to require special precautions

Effects on Dental Treatment No significant effects or complications reported

Effects on Bleeding No information available to require special precautions

Adverse Reactions

>10%:

Central nervous system: Headache (3% to 19%), pain (≤13%)

Endocrine & metabolic: Ovarian cyst (3% to 27%)

Gastrointestinal: Flatulence (≤16%), abdominal pain (7% to 15%)

Genitourinary: Dysmenorrhea (18%), mastalgia (7% to 18%)

1% to 10%:

Central nervous system: Fatigue (3% to 9%)

Endocrine & metabolic: Ovarian hyperstimulation (≤9%), ovarian disease (3% to 6%), increased serum cholesterol (4%)

Gastrointestinal: Nausea (3% to 9%), constipation (4% to 7%), diarrhea (≤6%)

Hepatic: Increased serum ALT (4%), increased serum AST (4%)

Local: Injection site reaction (≤7%)

Respiratory: Upper respiratory tract infection (≤3%)

<1%, postmarketing, and/or case reports: Accidental injury, acne vulgaris, anaphylaxis, anxiety, back pain, breast hypertrophy, conjunctivitis, cough, dental caries, depression, dizziness, drowsiness, dyspnea, dysuria, ectopic pregnancy, edema, endometrium disease, enlargement of abdomen, fever, flu-like symptoms, genital edema, hemorrhage (in pregnancy), herpes simplex infection, hyperkinesia, hypersensitivity reaction, infection, insomnia, Klebsiella species, leg cramps, leg pain, leukorrhea, malaise, nail disease, nervousness, ovarian hyperstimulation syndrome, ovary enlargement, pelvic congestion syndrome, pelvic pain, pharyngitis, porphyria, premenstrual syndrome, rhinitis, shock, skeletal pain, skin rash, spontaneous abortion, thromboembolism, urination disorder (change in frequency), uterine disease, uterine spasm, vaginal hemorrhage, vaginitis, vasodilatation, vomiting, vulvovaginal candidiasis, weakness, xeroderma

General Dosage Range SubQ: *Adults (females ≥16 years to ≤60 years):* 75 units daily

Mechanism of Action Lutropin alfa is a recombinant luteinizing hormone prepared using Chinese hamster cell ovaries. Administration leads to increased follicular estradiol secretion needed for follicle stimulating hormone induced follicular development.

Pharmacodynamics/Kinetics

Half-life Elimination Terminal: 21 hours

Time to Peak Serum: 9 hours

Pregnancy Considerations Adverse events have been observed in animal reproduction studies. Ectopic pregnancy, miscarriage, spontaneous abortion, and multiple births have been reported. The incidence of congenital abnormality may be slightly higher after assisted reproductive techniques than with spontaneous conception; higher incidence may be related to parenteral characteristics (maternal age, sperm characteristics). Lutropin alfa is used to stimulate follicular development; use is contraindicated in women who are already pregnant.

Product Availability Not available in the US

Macitentan (ma si TEN tan)

Brand Names: US Opsumit

Brand Names: Canada Opsumit

Pharmacologic Category Endothelin Receptor Antagonist; Vasodilator

Use Pulmonary arterial hypertension: Treatment of pulmonary arterial hypertension (PAH) (WHO Group I) to delay disease progression.

Local Anesthetic/Vasoconstrictor Precautions No information available to require special precautions

Effects on Dental Treatment No significant effects or complications reported

Effects on Bleeding No information available to require special precautions

Adverse Reactions

>10%:

Central nervous system: Headache (14%)

Hematologic & oncologic: Anemia (13%)

Respiratory: Nasopharyngitis (≤20%), pharyngitis (≤20%), bronchitis (12%)

1% to 10%:

Genitourinary: Urinary tract infection (9%)

Hematologic & oncologic: Decreased hemoglobin (9%)

Hepatic: Increased liver enzymes (>8 x ULN: 2%)

Infection: Influenza (6%)

<1%, postmarketing, and/or case reports: Angioedema, edema, fluid retention, hepatic insufficiency, hepatotoxicity, hypersensitivity reaction, increased serum ALT, increased serum AST, nasal congestion, pruritus, rash, symptomatic hypotension

General Dosage Range Oral: *Adults:* 10 mg once daily (maximum: 10 mg daily)

Mechanism of Action Blocks endothelin (ET)-1 from binding to endothelin receptor subtypes ET_A and ET_B on vascular endothelium and smooth muscle. Stimulation of these receptors is associated with vasoconstriction, fibrosis, proliferation, hypertrophy, and inflammation.

Pharmacodynamics/Kinetics

Half-life Elimination ~16 hours (active metabolite: ~48 hours)

Time to Peak Plasma: 8 hours

Pregnancy Risk Factor X

Pregnancy Considerations Use is contraindicated in pregnant women. **[US Boxed Warnings]: Macitentan may cause fetal harm if given to pregnant women; do not administer to women who are pregnant. Macitentan is available to females only through the restricted OPSUMIT Risk Evaluation and**

Mitigation Strategy (REMS) Program. All females of reproductive potential should have a negative pregnancy test prior to beginning therapy and testing should continue monthly during treatment and one month after discontinuing therapy. Females of childbearing potential should not become pregnant during therapy or for 1 month following discontinuation of macitentan by using acceptable methods of contraception. All females regardless of their reproductive potential must be enrolled in the REMS program; prescribers and pharmacies must also be enrolled in the program. Females of reproductive potential must be able to comply with pregnancy testing and contraception requirements of the program. Women may use one highly effective form of contraception (intrauterine device, contraceptive implant, or tubal sterilization) or a combination of methods (hormonal contraceptive with a barrier method or two barrier methods). A hormonal contraceptive or barrier method must be used in addition to a partner's vasectomy, if that method is chosen. Females should be counseled on pregnancy prevention and planning and instructed to notify their prescriber immediately if a pregnancy should occur. Women with pulmonary arterial hypertension (PAH) are encouraged to avoid pregnancy (McLaughlin 2009; Taichman 2014). Fertility may be affected in males.

Mafenide (MA fe nide)

Brand Names: US Sulfamylon

Pharmacologic Category Antibiotic, Topical

Use Burn treatment: For adjunctive therapy of patients with second- and third-degree burns (cream); for use as an adjunctive topical antimicrobial agent to control bacterial infection when used under moist dressings over meshed autografts on excised burn wounds (powder for solution)

Local Anesthetic/Vasoconstrictor Precautions No information available to require special precautions

Effects on Dental Treatment No significant effects or complications reported

Effects on Bleeding No information available to require special precautions

Adverse Reactions Frequency not defined.

Cardiovascular: Edema, facial edema

Dermatologic: Erythema, maceration, pruritus, rash, urticaria

Endocrine & metabolic: Hyperchloremia, metabolic acidosis

Gastrointestinal: Diarrhea (following accidental ingestion)

Hematologic: Bleeding, bone marrow suppression, DIC, eosinophilia, hemolytic anemia, porphyria

Local: Blisters, burning sensation, excoriation, pain

Respiratory: Dyspnea, hyperventilation, pCO_2 decreased, tachypnea

Miscellaneous: Hypersensitivity

General Dosage Range Topical:

Children, Adolescents, and Adults: Cream: Apply to a thickness of approximately 1/16 inch once or twice daily.

Infants ≥3 months, Children, Adolescents, and Adults: Powder for solution: Wet an 8-ply burn dressing with solution and cover graft area. Keep dressing wet every 4 to 8 hours; dressing may be left in place for ≤5 days.

Mechanism of Action As a sulfonamide, mafenide interferes with bacterial folic acid synthesis through competitive inhibition of para-aminobenzoic acid. Spectrum of activity encompasses both gram positive and negative organisms, including *Pseudomonas* and some anaerobes.

Pharmacodynamics/Kinetics

Time to Peak Serum: Cream 11%: 2 to 4 hours; Burn tissue: Cream 11%: 2 hours, Solution 5%: 4 hours

Pregnancy Risk Factor C

Pregnancy Considerations Adverse events were not observed in animal reproduction studies using an oral preparation. The manufacturer does not recommended use in women of childbearing potential unless the burn area covers >20% of the total body surface or when benefits of treatment outweigh possible risks to the fetus.

Magnesium Carbonate, Calcium Carbonate, and Folic Acid

(mag NEE zhum KAR bun ate, KAL see um KAR bun ate, & FOE lik AS id)

Related Information

Calcium Carbonate *on page 280*

Folic Acid *on page 762*

Brand Names: US MagneBind 400

Pharmacologic Category Calcium Salt; Electrolyte Supplement, Oral; Magnesium Salt; Vitamin; Vitamin, Water Soluble

Use Prevention or treatment of nutritional deficiencies

Local Anesthetic/Vasoconstrictor Precautions No information available to require special precautions

Effects on Dental Treatment No significant effects or complications reported

Effects on Bleeding No information available to require special precautions

General Dosage Range Oral: *Adults:* 1-3 tablets 3 times/day

Pregnancy Considerations See individual agents.

Magnesium Citrate (mag NEE zhum SIT rate)

Brand Names: US Citroma [OTC]; GoodSense Magnesium Citrate [OTC]

Brand Names: Canada Citro-Mag

Pharmacologic Category Laxative, Saline; Magnesium Salt

Use Occasional constipation: Treatment of occasional constipation

Local Anesthetic/Vasoconstrictor Precautions No information available to require special precautions

Effects on Dental Treatment Key adverse event(s) related to dental treatment: Magnesium products may prevent GI absorption of tetracyclines by forming a large ionized chelated molecule with the tetracyclines in the stomach. Tetracyclines should be given at least 1 hour before magnesium.

Effects on Bleeding No information available to require special precautions

Adverse Reactions Frequency not defined: Gastrointestinal: Abdominal pain, diarrhea, flatulence, nausea, vomiting

General Dosage Range Oral solution:

Children 2-6 years: 60-90 mL given once or in divided doses (maximum: 90 mL/24 hours)

Children 6-12 years: 90-210 mL given once or in divided doses

Children >12 years, Adolescents, and Adults: 195-300 mL given once or in divided doses

Mechanism of Action Promotes bowel evacuation by causing osmotic retention of fluid which distends the colon with increased peristaltic activity

Pharmacodynamics/Kinetics

Onset of Action Laxative effect: Oral solution: 0.5 to 6 hours

Pregnancy Considerations Magnesium crosses the placenta; serum concentrations in the fetus are similar to those in the mother (Idama, 1998; Osada, 2002). The American Gastroenterological Association considers the use of magnesium citrate as a laxative to be low risk in pregnancy, but long term use should be avoided (not the preferred treatment of chronic constipation) (Mahadevan, 2006).

Magnesium Hydroxide

(mag NEE zhum hye DROKS ide)

Brand Names: US Dulcolax Milk of Magnesia [OTC]; Milk of Magnesia Concentrate [OTC]; Milk of Magnesia [OTC]; Pedia-Lax [OTC]; Phillips [OTC] [DSC]

Pharmacologic Category Antacid; Laxative; Magnesium Salt

Use

Antacid: For the temporary relief of heartburn, upset stomach, sour stomach, or acid indigestion.

Laxative (occasional constipation): For relief of occasional constipation. This product generally produces bowel movement in 30 minutes to 6 hours.

Local Anesthetic/Vasoconstrictor Precautions No information available to require special precautions

Effects on Dental Treatment Key adverse event(s) related to dental treatment: Magnesium products may prevent GI absorption of tetracyclines by forming a large ionized chelated molecule with the tetracyclines in the stomach. Tetracyclines should be given at least 1 hour before magnesium.

Effects on Bleeding No information available to require special precautions

General Dosage Range Oral:

Liquid:

Children 2 to 5 years: OTC laxative: Magnesium hydroxide 400 mg/5 mL: 5 to 15 mL/day

Children 6 to 11 years: OTC laxative:

Magnesium hydroxide 400 mg/5 mL: 15 to 30 mL/day

Magnesium hydroxide 1,200 mg/5 mL: 5 to 10 mL/day

Children ≥12 years, Adolescents, and Adults:

OTC laxative:

Magnesium hydroxide 400 mg/5 mL: 30 to 60 mL/day

Magnesium hydroxide 800 mg/5mL: 15 to 30 mL/day

Magnesium hydroxide 1,200 mg/5mL: 10 to 20 mL/day

OTC antacid: Magnesium hydroxide 400 mg/5 mL: 5 to 15 mL up to 4 times/day (maximum: 60 mL/day)

Chewable tablet:

Magnesium hydroxide 311 mg/tablet:

Children 3 to 5 years: OTC laxative: 2 tablets/day

Children 6 to 11 years: OTC laxative: 4 tablets/day

Children ≥12 years, Adolescents, and Adults:

OTC laxative: Magnesium hydroxide 311 mg/tablet: 8 tablets/day

OTC antacid: Magnesium hydroxide 311 mg/tablet: 2 to 4 tablets up to 4 times/day (maximum: 4 doses/day)

Magnesium hydroxide 400 mg/tablet:

Children 2 to 5 years: OTC laxative: 1 to 3 tablets/day (maximum daily dose: 3 tablets)

Children 6 to 11 years: OTC laxative: 3 to 6 tablets/day (maximum daily dose: 6 tablets)

Mechanism of Action Promotes bowel evacuation by causing osmotic retention of fluid which distends the colon with increased peristaltic activity; reacts with hydrochloric acid in stomach to form magnesium chloride

Pharmacodynamics/Kinetics

Onset of Action Laxative: 30 minutes to 6 hours

Pregnancy Considerations Magnesium crosses the placenta; serum concentrations in the fetus are similar to those in the mother (Idama 1998; Osada 2002). The American Gastroenterological Association considers the use of magnesium containing antacids to be low risk in pregnancy (Mahadevan 2006).

Magnesium L-aspartate Hydrochloride

(mag NEE zhum el as PAR tate hye droe KLOR ide)

Brand Names: US Maginex™ DS [OTC]; Maginex™ [OTC]

Pharmacologic Category Electrolyte Supplement, Oral; Magnesium Salt

Use Dietary supplement

Local Anesthetic/Vasoconstrictor Precautions No information available to require special precautions

Effects on Dental Treatment Key adverse event(s) related to dental treatment: Magnesium ions prevent GI absorption of tetracycline by forming a large, ionized, chelated molecule with the magnesium ion and tetracyclines in the stomach. Magnesium supplement should not be taken within 2-4 hours of oral tetracycline or other members of the tetracycline family.

Effects on Bleeding No information available to require special precautions

Adverse Reactions

Frequency not defined: Gastrointestinal: Abdominal cramps, diarrhea (excessive oral doses), flatulence

General Dosage Range Oral:

RDA (in terms of elemental magnesium):

Children 1-13 years: 80-240 mg daily

Children ≥14 years and Adults: 310-420 mg daily

Dietary supplement: OTC labeling (dosage in terms of magnesium-L-aspartate hydrochloride salt): *Adults:* One packet or 2 tablets (1230 mg) up to 3 times daily

Mechanism of Action Magnesium is important as a cofactor in many enzymatic reactions in the body involving protein synthesis and carbohydrate metabolism (at least 300 enzymatic reactions require magnesium). Actions on lipoprotein lipase have been found to be important in reducing serum cholesterol and on sodium/potassium ATPase in promoting polarization (eg, neuromuscular functioning).

Pregnancy Considerations Magnesium crosses the placenta; serum concentrations in the fetus are similar to those in the mother (Idama, 1998; Osada, 2002).

Magnesium Salicylate

(mag NEE zhum sa LIS i late)

Related Information

Temporomandibular Dysfunction (TMD), Chronic Pain, and Fibromyalgia *on page 1868*

Brand Names: US Doans Extra Strength [OTC]; Doans Pills [OTC]

Pharmacologic Category Salicylate

Use Mild-to-moderate pain, fever, various inflammatory conditions; relief of pain and inflammation of rheumatoid arthritis and osteoarthritis

Local Anesthetic/Vasoconstrictor Precautions No information available to require special precautions

Effects on Dental Treatment The dentist should be aware of the potential of abnormal coagulation. Caution should also be exercised in the use of NSAIDs in patients already on anticoagulant therapy with drugs such as warfarin (Coumadin®). See Effects on Bleeding.

Effects on Bleeding No information available to require special precautions

Adverse Reactions Refer to Aspirin monograph.

General Dosage Range Oral: *Children ≥12 years and Adults:*

Doan's® Extra Strength, Momentum®: 2 caplets every 6 hours as needed (maximum: 8 caplets/day)

Keygesic: 1 tablet every 4 hours as needed (maximum: 4 tablets/day)

Pharmacodynamics/Kinetics

Half-life Elimination 2 hours; increased with repeated dosing

Time to Peak 1.5 hours

Pregnancy Considerations Refer to Aspirin monograph for additional information.

Maltodextrin (mal toe DEK strin)

Brand Names: US Multidex [OTC]

Pharmacologic Category Anti-inflammatory, Locally Applied

Use Treatment of infected or noninfected wounds

Local Anesthetic/Vasoconstrictor Precautions No information available to require special precautions

Effects on Dental Treatment No significant effects or complications reported (see Dental Comment)

Effects on Bleeding No information available to require special precautions

General Dosage Range

Topical: *Adults:* Apply to wounds with dressing changes

Mechanism of Action Forms a protective barrier over wound providing an environment which promotes tissue growth.

Maprotiline (ma PROE ti leen)

Related Information

Dentin Hypersensitivity, Acid Erosion, High Caries Index, Management of Alveolar Osteitis, and Xerostomia *on page 1857*

Vasoconstrictor Interactions With Antidepressants *on page 1913*

Brand Names: Canada Teva-Maprotiline

Pharmacologic Category Antidepressant, Tetracyclic

Use

Anxiety: Relief of anxiety associated with depression

Depression: Treatment of major depressive disorder (MDD)

Local Anesthetic/Vasoconstrictor Precautions Although maprotiline is not a tricyclic antidepressant, it does block norepinephrine reuptake within CNS synapses as part of its mechanisms. It has been suggested that vasoconstrictor be administered with caution and to monitor vital signs in dental patients taking antidepressants that affect norepinephrine in this way, including maprotiline. Epinephrine and levonordefrin have been shown to have an increased pressor response in combination with TCAs. Maprotiline is one of the drugs confirmed to prolong the QT interval and is accepted as having a risk of causing torsade de pointes. The risk of drug-induced torsade de pointes is extremely low when a single QT interval prolonging drug is prescribed. In terms of epinephrine, it is not known what effect vasoconstrictors in the local anesthetic regimen will have in patients with a known history of congenital prolonged QT interval or in patients taking any medication that prolongs the QT interval. Until more information is obtained, it is suggested that the clinician consult with the physician prior to the use of a vasoconstrictor in suspected patients, and that the vasoconstrictor (epinephrine, mepivacaine and levonordefrin [Carbocaine® 2% with Neo-Cobefrin®]) be used with caution.

Effects on Dental Treatment Key adverse event(s) related to dental treatment: Xerostomia and changes in salivation (normal salivary flow resumes upon discontinuation).

Effects on Bleeding No information available to require special precautions

Adverse Reactions

>10%:

Central nervous system: Drowsiness (16%)

Gastrointestinal: Xerostomia (22%)

1% to 10%:

Central nervous system: Dizziness (8%), nervousness (6%), fatigue (4%), headache (4%), anxiety (3%), agitation (2%), insomnia (2%)

Gastrointestinal: Constipation (6%), nausea (2%)

Neuromuscular & skeletal: Weakness (4%), tremor (3%)

Ophthalmic: Blurred vision (4%)

<1%, postmarketing, and/or case reports: Abdominal cramps, abnormal liver function tests, accommodation disturbance, agranulocytosis, akathisia, alopecia, angle-closure glaucoma, ataxia, bitter taste, breast hypertrophy (female), cardiac arrhythmia, cerebrovascular accident, confusion, decreased libido, delusions, diaphoresis (excessive), diarrhea, disorientation, dysarthria, dysphagia, edema, EEG pattern changes, eosinophilia, epigastric distress, extrapyramidal reaction, feeling abnormal, fever, flushing, galactorrhea, gynecomastia (male), hallucination, heart block, hyperactivity, hyperglycemia, hypertension, hypoglycemia, hypomania, hypotension, impotence, increased libido, interstitial pneumonitis, jaundice, mania, melanoglossia, memory impairment, mydriasis, myocardial infarction, nasal congestion, nightmares, numbness, palpitations, paralytic ileus, peripheral neuropathy, petechia, pruritus, psychosis exacerbation, purpura, restlessness, sialorrhea, skin photosensitivity, skin rash, seizure, Stevens-Johnson syndrome, stomatitis, sublingual adenitis, syncope, tachycardia, testicle swelling, thrombocytopenia, tingling sensation, tinnitus, toxic epidermal necrolysis, urinary frequency, urinary hesitancy, urinary retention, vomiting, weight gain, weight loss

General Dosage Range Oral:

Adults: Initial: 25 to 75 mg once daily or in divided doses; Usual dosage: 150 to 225 mg once daily or in divided doses (maximum: 225 mg daily)

Elderly: Initial: 25 mg once daily; Usual dosage: 50 to 75 mg once daily or in divided doses

Mechanism of Action Increases the synaptic concentration of norepinephrine in the central nervous system by inhibition of its reuptake by the presynaptic neuronal membrane.

Pharmacodynamics/Kinetics

Onset of Action Individual responses may vary; however, 4-8 weeks of treatment are needed before determining if a patient with depression is partially or non-responsive (APA, 2010)

Half-life Elimination Serum: ~28 to 105 hours (Alkalay, 1980)

Time to Peak Serum: 8 to 24 hours (Alkalay, 1980; Pinder 1977)

Pregnancy Risk Factor B

Pregnancy Considerations Adverse events have not been observed in animal reproduction studies.

The ACOG recommends that therapy for depression during pregnancy be individualized; treatment should incorporate the clinical expertise of the mental health clinician, obstetrician, primary health care provider, and pediatrician (ACOG 2008). According to the American Psychiatric Association (APA), the risks of medication treatment should be weighed against other treatment options and untreated depression. For women who discontinue antidepressant medications during pregnancy and who may be at high risk for postpartum depression, the medications can be restarted following delivery (APA 2010). Treatment algorithms have been developed by the ACOG and the APA for the management of depression in women prior to conception and during pregnancy (Yonkers 2009).

Pregnant women exposed to antidepressants during pregnancy are encouraged to enroll in the National Pregnancy Registry for Antidepressants (NPRAD). Women 18 to 45 years of age or their health care providers may contact the registry by calling 844-405-6185. Enrollment should be done as early in pregnancy as possible.

Dental Comment See Local Anesthetic/Vasoconstrictor Precautions

Maraviroc (mah RAV er rock)

Related Information

HIV Infection and AIDS *on page 1785*

Brand Names: US Selzentry

Brand Names: Canada Celsentri

Pharmacologic Category Antiretroviral, CCR5 Antagonist (Anti-HIV)

Use HIV-1 infection: Treatment of only CCR5-tropic HIV-1 infection in patients 2 years and older and weighing ≥10 kg, in combination with other antiretroviral agents

Local Anesthetic/Vasoconstrictor Precautions No information available to require special precautions

Effects on Dental Treatment Key adverse event(s) related to dental treatment: Stomatitis has been observed.

Effects on Bleeding No information available to require special precautions relative to hemostasis.

Adverse Reactions Includes data from both treatment-naive and treatment-experienced patients. Unless otherwise noted, frequency of adverse events is as reported in adults receiving combination antiretroviral therapy.

>10%:

Dermatologic: Skin rash (11%)

Gastrointestinal: Vomiting (children and adolescents: 12%; may be more common with oral solution)

Infection: Infection (55%)

Respiratory: Upper respiratory tract infection (23% to 32%), cough (14%)

Miscellaneous: Fever (13%)

1% to 10%:

Cardiovascular: Hypertension (3%), cardiac failure (<2%), cerebrovascular accident (<2%), coronary artery disease (<2%), coronary occlusion (<2%), endocarditis (<2%), myocardial infarction (<2%), portal vein thrombosis (<2%), septic shock (<2%), unstable angina pectoris (<2%)

Central nervous system: Dizziness (9%; children and adolescents: 3%; including postural dizziness), insomnia (8%), paresthesia (≤5%), dysesthesia (≤5%), anxiety (4%), impaired consciousness (4%), depression (4%), peripheral neuropathy (4%), malaise (≤4%), pain (≤4%), sensory disturbance (3% to 4%; includes body temperature perception disorder), memory impairment (3%), epilepsy (<2%), loss of consciousness (<2%), meningitis (<2%; includes viral), facial paralysis (<2%), seizure (<2%)

Dermatologic: Nail disease (6%; nail and nail bed disorder [excluding infection and infestation]), sweat gland disease (5%; apocrine and eccrine gland disorders), folliculitis (4%), pruritus (4%), tinea (4%), acne vulgaris (3%), alopecia (2%), erythema (2%), condyloma acuminatum (2%)

Endocrine & metabolic: Lipodystrophy (3% to 4%)

Gastrointestinal: Abdominal distension (≤10%), bloating (≤10%), flatulence (≤10%), decreased gastrointestinal motility (9%), change in appetite (8%), constipation (6%; may be more common with oral solution), abdominal pain (children and adolescents: 4%; may be more common with oral solution), diarrhea (children and adolescents: 4%; may be more common with oral solution), nausea (children and adolescents: 4%; may be more common with oral solution), carcinoma in situ of esophagus (<2%), colitis (*Clostridium difficile*-associated: <2%)

Genitourinary: Genitourinary complaint (urinary tract/bladder symptoms, 3% to 5%), ejaculatory disorder (≤3%), erectile dysfunction (≤3%)

Hematologic & oncologic: Anemia (8%), neutropenia (4% to 6%), benign skin neoplasm (3%), basal cell carcinoma (<2%), bone marrow depression (<2%), Bowen disease (<2%), carcinoma (nasopharyngeal: <2%), hypoplastic anemia (<2%), liver metastases (<2%), malignant lymphoma (including diffuse large B-cell and anaplastic large cell lymphomas T- and null-cell types), malignant neoplasm (anal: <2%), malignant neoplasm of bile duct (cholangiocarcinoma; <2%), malignant neoplasm of tongue (<2%; malignant stage unspecified), neoplasm (<2%; includes abdominal and unspecified malignant endocrine neoplasm), squamous cell carcinoma (<2%), squamous cell carcinoma of skin (<2%)

Hepatic: Increased serum AST (>5 x ULN: 5%), cholestatic jaundice (<2%), hepatic cirrhosis (<2%), hepatic failure (<2%), jaundice (<2%)

Infection: Herpes virus infection (7% to 8%), bacterial infection (6%), herpes zoster (≤5%), varicella zoster infection (≤5%), meningococcal infection (3%) viral infection (3%), influenza (2%), bacterial infection (treponema <2%)

Neuromuscular & skeletal: Arthropathy (6% to 7%), myalgia (3%), increased creatine phosphokinase (<2%), myositis (<2%; may be infective), osteonecrosis (<2%), rhabdomyolysis (<2%), tremor (<2%; excluding congenital)

Ophthalmic: Conjunctivitis (2%), eye disease (2%; includes infection and inflammation), hemianopia (<2%), visual field defect (<2%)

Otic: Otitis media (2%)

Respiratory: Bronchitis (7% to 13%), upper respiratory complaint (6% to 9%), sinusitis (7%), irregular breathing (4%), nasal congestion (≤4%), rhinitis (≤4%), lower respiratory tract infection (≤3%), pulmonary infection (≤3%), paranasal sinus disease (3%), pneumonia (<2%)

Frequency not defined:

Hepatic: Hepatitis, hepatotoxicity

Immunologic: Immune reconstitution syndrome

<1%, postmarketing, and/or case reports: DRESS syndrome, ischemic heart disease, Stevens-Johnson syndrome, toxic epidermal necrolysis

General Dosage Range Dosage adjustment recommended in patients with renal impairment or on concomitant therapy

Oral:

Children ≥2 years and ≥10 kg and Adolescents: Dosage varies greatly depending on weight and concomitant therapy

Adults: 150 to 600 mg twice daily

Mechanism of Action Maraviroc, a CCR5 antagonist, selectively and reversibly binds to the chemokine (C-C motif receptor 5 [CCR5]) coreceptors located on human CD4 cells. CCR5 antagonism prevents interaction between the human CCR5 coreceptor and the gp120 subunit of the viral envelope glycoprotein, thereby inhibiting gp120 conformational change required for CCR5-tropic HIV-1 fusion with the CD4 cell and subsequent cell entry.

Pharmacodynamics/Kinetics

Half-life Elimination 14 to 18 hours

Time to Peak Plasma: 0.5 to 4 hours

Pregnancy Considerations Maraviroc has moderate transfer across the human placenta. Data collected by the antiretroviral pregnancy registry are insufficient to evaluate human teratogenic risk. Maternal antiretroviral therapy may increase the risk of preterm delivery, although available information is conflicting possibly due to variability of maternal factors (disease severity; initiation of therapy); however, maternal antiretroviral medication should not be withheld due to concerns of preterm birth. Information related to stillbirth, low birth weight, and small for gestational age infants is limited. Long-term follow-up is recommended for all infants exposed to antiretroviral medications; children who develop significant organ system abnormalities of unknown etiology (particularly of the CNS or heart) should be evaluated for potential mitochondrial dysfunction.

Combination antiretroviral therapy (cART) therapy is recommended for all HIV-infected pregnant women to keep the viral load below the limit of detection and reduce the risk of perinatal transmission. When HIV is diagnosed during pregnancy in a woman who has never received antiretroviral therapy, cART should begin as soon as possible after diagnosis. The Health and Human Services (HHS) Perinatal HIV Guidelines note there are insufficient data to recommend use of maraviroc as initial therapy in antiretroviral-naive pregnant women. Dose adjustments are not needed in pregnancy. In general, women who become pregnant on a stable cART regimen may continue that regimen if viral suppression is effective, appropriate drug exposure can be achieved, contraindications for use in pregnancy are not present, and the regimen is well tolerated. Monitoring during pregnancy is more frequent than in nonpregnant adults; cART should be continued postpartum.

For HIV-infected couples planning a pregnancy, maximum viral suppression with cART is recommended prior to conception for the HIV-infected partner(s) and expert consultation is recommended; modification of therapy (if needed) and optimization of the woman's health should be done prior to conception. HIV-infected women not planning a pregnancy may use any available type of contraception, considering possible drug interactions and contraindications of the specific method. In addition, consistent use of condoms is also recommended (even during pregnancy) to prevent transmission of HIV or other sexually transmitted diseases.

Health care providers are encouraged to enroll pregnant women exposed to antiretroviral medications as early in pregnancy as possible in the Antiretroviral Pregnancy Registry (1-800-258-4263 or www.APRegistry.com). Health care providers caring for HIV-infected women and their infants may contact the National Perinatal HIV Hotline (888-448-8765) for clinical consultation (HHS [perinatal] 2016).

Product Availability Selzentry 20 mg/mL oral solution: FDA approved November 2016; availability anticipated end of first quarter or beginning of second quarter 2017. Consult the prescribing information for additional information.

Measles, Mumps, and Rubella Virus Vaccine (MEE zels, mumpz & roo BEL a VYE rus vak SEEN)

Brand Names: US M-M-R II

Brand Names: Canada M-M-R II; Priorix

Pharmacologic Category Vaccine; Vaccine, Live (Viral)

Use Measles, mumps, and rubella prophylaxis: Active immunization for simultaneous vaccination against measles, mumps, and rubella in patients ≥12 months of age

The Advisory Committee on Immunization Practices (ACIP) recommends routine vaccination for the following (CDC/ACIP [McLean 2013]):

- All children (first dose given at 12 to 15 months of age)
- Adults born in 1957 or later (without evidence of immunity or documentation of vaccination). Vaccine may be given to adults born prior to 1957 if they do not have contraindications to the MMR vaccine.
- Adults at higher risk for exposure to and transmission of measles mumps and rubella should receive special consideration for vaccination, unless an acceptable evidence of immunity exists. This includes international travelers, persons attending colleges and other post high school education, persons working in healthcare facilities.

Local Anesthetic/Vasoconstrictor Precautions No information available to require special precautions

Effects on Dental Treatment No significant effects or complications reported

Effects on Bleeding No information available to require special precautions

Adverse Reactions All serious adverse reactions must be reported to the US Department of Health and Human Services (DHHS) Vaccine Adverse Event Reporting System (VAERS) 1-800-822-7967 or online at https://vaers.hhs.gov/esub/index. In Canada, adverse reactions may be reported to local provincial/territorial health agencies or to the Vaccine Safety Section at Public Health Agency of Canada (1-866-844-0018).

Frequency not always defined:

Cardiovascular: Syncope, vasculitis

Central nervous system: Acute disseminated encephalomyelitis, ataxia, dizziness, Guillain-Barré syndrome, headache, irritability, malaise, nerve deafness, paresthesia, polyneuropathy, retrobulbar neuritis, seizure, subacute sclerosing panencephalitis, transverse myelitis

Dermatologic: Erythema multiforme, morbilliform rash, pruritus, rash, Stevens-Johnson syndrome, urticaria

Endocrine & metabolic: Diabetes mellitus

Gastrointestinal: Diarrhea, nausea, pancreatitis, parotitis, sore throat, vomiting

Genitourinary: Epididymitis, orchitis

Hematologic & oncologic: Leukocytosis, lymphadenopathy (regional), purpura, thrombocytopenia

Hypersensitivity: Anaphylactoid reaction, anaphylaxis, angioedema

Infection: Atypical measles

Local: Injection site reaction (including burning, induration, redness, stinging, swelling, tenderness, vesiculation, wheal and flare)

Neuromuscular & skeletal: Arthropathy (arthralgia/arthritis: Women 12% to 26%; children ≤3%), myalgia, panniculitis

Ophthalmic: Conjunctivitis, oculomotor nerve paralysis, optic neuritis, optic papillitis, retinitis

Otic: Otitis media

Respiratory: Bronchospasm, cough, pneumonia, rhinitis

Miscellaneous: Febrile seizures, fever

<1%, postmarketing, and/or case reports: Aseptic meningitis (associated with Urabe strain of mumps vaccine), brain disease, encephalitis

General Dosage Range SubQ:

Children ≥12 months: 0.5 mL per dose for 2 doses

Adults: 0.5 mL per dose for 1 or 2 doses

Mechanism of Action As a live, attenuated vaccine, MMR vaccine offers active immunity to disease caused by the measles, mumps, and rubella viruses.

Pharmacodynamics/Kinetics

Onset of Action The median seroconversion after 1 vaccine dose is 96% (measles), 99% (rubella), mumps (94%) (CDC/ACIP [McLean 2013]).

Duration of Action The median duration of immunity after 2 doses is ≥15 years for all components of the vaccine (CDC/ACIP [McLean 2013]).

Pregnancy Risk Factor C

Pregnancy Considerations Animal reproduction studies have not been conducted. It is not known whether this vaccine can cause fetal harm or affect reproduction capacity. Based on information collected following inadvertent administration during pregnancy, adverse events have not been observed following use of rubella vaccine. However, theoretical risks cannot be ruled out; use of this vaccine is contraindicated in pregnant females and should not be administered to women trying to conceive. The manufacturer recommends that pregnancy be avoided for 3 months after vaccine administration. The Advisory Committee on Immunization Practices (ACIP) recommends that pregnancy should be avoided for 28 days following vaccination. The risk of congenital rubella syndrome following vaccination is significantly less than the risk associated following infection; therefore, inadvertent administration of MMR during pregnancy is not considered an indication to terminate pregnancy.

Adverse consequences of natural infection in unvaccinated pregnant women have been reported. Measles infection during pregnancy may increase the risk of premature labor, preterm delivery, spontaneous abortion and low birth weights. Rubella infection during the first trimester may lead to miscarriages, stillbirths, and congenital rubella syndrome (includes auditory, ophthalmic, cardiac and neurologic defects; intrauterine and postnatal growth retardation); fetal rubella infection can occur during any trimester of pregnancy. Maternal mumps infection during the first trimester may increase the risk of spontaneous abortion or intrauterine fetal death. Sterility in males and infertility in prepubescent females may also occur with natural mumps infection.

Prenatal screening is recommended for all pregnant women who lack evidence of rubella immunity. Women of childbearing age without documentation of rubella vaccination or serologic evidence of immunity should be vaccinated (for women of childbearing potential, birth prior to 1957 is not acceptable evidence of immunity to rubella). Women who are pregnant should be vaccinated upon completion or termination of pregnancy, prior to discharge. Household contacts of pregnant women may be vaccinated (CDC/ACIP [McLean, 2013]).

Measles, Mumps, Rubella, and Varicella Virus Vaccine

(MEE zels, mumpz, roo BEL a, & var i SEL a VYE rus vak SEEN)

Brand Names: US ProQuad

Brand Names: Canada Priorix-Tetra; ProQuad

Pharmacologic Category Vaccine; Vaccine, Live (Viral)

Use

Measles, mumps, rubella, and varicella vaccination: To provide active immunization for the prevention of measles, mumps, rubella, and varicella in children 12 months to 12 years of age.

The Advisory Committee on Immunization Practices (ACIP) recommends routine vaccination against measles, mumps, rubella, and varicella in healthy children; the first dose should be given at 12 to 15 months of age and the second dose at 4 to 6 years of age. For children receiving their first dose at 12 to 47 months of age, either the MMRV combination vaccine or separate MMR and varicella vaccines can be used. The ACIP prefers administration of separate MMR and varicella vaccines as the first dose in this age group unless the parent or caregiver expresses preference for the MMRV combination. For children receiving the first dose at ≥48 months or their second dose at any age, use of MMRV is preferred. For children with a personal or family history of seizures, the ACIP recommends vaccination with separate MMR and varicella vaccines, as opposed to the MMRV combination vaccine (CDC/ACIP [Marin 2010]).

Canadian labeling (not in US labeling): MMRV combination vaccine is approved for use in healthy children (Priorix-Tetra: 9 months to 6 years; ProQuad: 12 months to 6 years); may consider use in healthy children ≤12 years of age based upon prior experience with the separate component (live-attenuated MMR or live-attenuated varicella [OKA-strain]) vaccines.

Local Anesthetic/Vasoconstrictor Precautions No information available to require special precautions

Effects on Dental Treatment No significant effects or complications reported

Effects on Bleeding No information available to require special precautions

Adverse Reactions All serious adverse reactions must be reported to the US Department of Health and Human Services (DHHS) Vaccine Adverse Event Reporting System (VAERS) 1-800-822-7967 or online at https://vaers.hhs.gov/esub/index. In Canada, adverse reactions may be reported to local provincial/territorial health agencies or to the Vaccine Safety Section at Public Health Agency of Canada (1-866-844-0018).

Also refer to Measles, Mumps, and Rubella Vaccine (M-M-R II) and Varicella Virus Vaccine (Varivax) monographs for additional adverse reactions reported with those agents.

>10%:

Local: Pain at injection site (16% to 41%; pain, tenderness, soreness), erythema at injection site (11% to 24%), swelling at injection site (8% to 16%)

Miscellaneous: Fever (8% to 22%; ≥38.9°C [≥102°F])

1% to 10%:

Central nervous system: Irritability (2% to 7%), drowsiness (1%)

Dermatologic: Morbilliform rash (≤6%), rubella-like rash (≤4%), varicella-like rash (≤3%), rash at injection site (2%), skin rash (≤2%), vesicular eruption (≤2%), eczema (1%), pruritus (1%), viral exanthem (1%)

Gastrointestinal: Vomiting (1%), diarrhea (≤1%)

Local: Bleeding at injection site (1% to 2%), bruising at injection site (≤2%)

Respiratory: Upper respiratory tract infection (1% to 2%), rhinorrhea (1%), nasopharyngitis (≤1%)

<1%, postmarketing, and/or case reports: Abdominal pain, abnormal dreams, acute disseminated encephalomyelitis, agitation, anaphylactoid reaction, anaphylaxis, angioneurotic edema, apathy, aplastic anemia, arthralgia, arthritis, aseptic meningitis, ataxia, atypical measles, Bell's palsy, brain disease, bronchitis, bronchospasm, candidiasis, cellulitis, cerebrovascular accident, convulsions (including afebrile events), dizziness, encephalitis, epididymitis, epistaxis, erythema multiforme, extravasation, eyelid edema (in immunocompromised individuals), facial edema, febrile seizures, flatulence, Guillain-Barré syndrome, headache, hematochezia, herpes simplex infection, herpes zoster, hypersomnia, IgA vasculitis, impetigo, infection, inflammation, influenza, injection site reaction (burning and/or stinging of short duration, discoloration, eczema, edema/swelling, hematoma, hive-like rash, induration, lump, vesicles, wheal and flare), lip disease, lymphadenitis, lymphadenopathy (regional), musculoskeletal pain, myalgia, necrotizing retinitis, nerve deafness, nervousness, oculomotor nerve paralysis, optic neuritis, optic papillitis, oral mucosa ulcer, orchitis, otalgia, pain (hip, leg, neck), panniculitis, paresthesia, parotitis, parotitis (disseminated), peripheral edema, pneumonia, polyneuropathy, pulmonary congestion, pulmonary infection, purpura, retinitis, retrobulbar neuritis, rhinitis, rough skin, sinusitis, skin infection, skin sclerosis, sneezing, sore throat, Stevens-Johnson syndrome, subacute sclerosing panencephalitis, sunburn, swelling, syncope, thrombocytopenia, transverse myelitis, trauma, tremor, varicella (vaccine strain), venipuncture site hemorrhage, viral infection (rubella vaccine), warm sensation at injection site, wheezing, xeroderma

General Dosage Range SubQ: *Children 12 months to 12 years:* 1 or 2 doses (0.5 mL)

Mechanism of Action A live, attenuated virus vaccine that induces active immunity to disease caused by the measles, mumps, rubella, and varicella-zoster viruses.

Pharmacodynamics/Kinetics

Onset of Action At 6 weeks postvaccination of a single dose, the antibody response rate in healthy children 12 to 23 months of age was ~91% to 99%. Following a second dose to children <3 years of age, the observed antibody response rate was ~98% to 99%.

Duration of Action Antibody levels persist 10 years or longer in most healthy recipients. Refer to the Varicella Virus Vaccine monograph and the Measles, Mumps, and Rubella Virus Vaccine monograph for details.

Pregnancy Considerations Animal reproduction studies have not been conducted. Use is contraindicated in pregnant females and pregnancy should be avoided for 3 months (per manufacturer labeling) following vaccination. The ACIP and manufacturer of Priorix-Tetra (Canadian product) recommends that pregnancy should be avoided for 1 month following vaccination with any of the individual components of this vaccine.

Any exposures to the vaccine during pregnancy or within 3 months prior to pregnancy should be reported to the manufacturer (Merck & Co, 877-888-4231) or to VAERS (800-822-7967) as suspected adverse reactions.

Refer to the Varicella Virus Vaccine monograph and the Measles, Mumps, and Rubella Virus Vaccine monograph for additional information.

Mebendazole (me BEN da zole)

Brand Names: US Emverm

Brand Names: Canada Vermox

Pharmacologic Category Anthelmintic

Use Intestinal nematode infection: Treatment of *Ancylostoma duodenale* or *Necator americanus* (hookworms), *Ascaris lumbricoides* (roundworms), *Enterobius vermicularis* (pinworms), and *Trichuris trichiura* (whipworms) in single or mixed infections.

Local Anesthetic/Vasoconstrictor Precautions No information available to require special precautions

Effects on Dental Treatment No significant effects or complications reported

Effects on Bleeding No information available to require special precautions

Adverse Reactions Frequency not defined.

Gastrointestinal: Abdominal pain, anorexia, diarrhea, flatulence, nausea, vomiting

Hepatic: Hepatitis

<1%, postmarketing, and/or case reports: Abnormal hepatic function tests, agranulocytosis, alopecia, anaphylaxis, angioedema, decreased ejaculate volume (Parasitic Infections 2013), dizziness, glomerulonephritis, hepatitis, hypersensitivity reaction, leukopenia (Parasitic Infections 2013), neutropenia, seizure, skin rash, Stevens-Johnson syndrome, toxic epidermal necrolysis, urticaria

General Dosage Range Oral: *Children ≥2 years; Adolescents, and Adults:* 100 mg as a single dose **or** twice daily

Mechanism of Action Inhibits the formation of helminth microtubules; selectively and irreversibly blocks glucose uptake and other nutrients in susceptible adult intestine-dwelling helminths

Pharmacodynamics/Kinetics

Half-life Elimination 3 to 6 hours

Time to Peak Serum: Variable (0.5 to 6 hours)

Pregnancy Risk Factor C

Pregnancy Considerations Adverse events have been observed in animal reproduction studies. Based on available data, adverse pregnancy outcomes have not been observed following use in pregnancy (Diav-Citrin 2003; Gyorkos 2006). Treatment of pinworm in pregnancy may be considered; however, the CDC suggests postponing therapy until the third trimester when possible (CDC 2016).

Prescribing and Access Restrictions Vermox 500 mg chewable tablets are only available through Johnson & Johnson's Vermox Donation Program to help reduce the burden of soil-transmitted helminths in endemic countries. There are currently no plans to make Vermox 500 mg chewable tablets commercially available.

Mecamylamine (mek a MIL a meen)

Brand Names: US Vecamyl

Pharmacologic Category Ganglionic Blocking Agent

Use Hypertension: Management of moderately severe to severe essential hypertension and in uncomplicated malignant hypertension.

Local Anesthetic/Vasoconstrictor Precautions No information available to require special precautions

Effects on Dental Treatment Key adverse event(s) related to dental treatment: Xerostomia (normal salivary flow resumes upon discontinuation). Patients may experience orthostatic (postural) hypotension as they stand up after treatment, especially if lying in dental chair for extended periods of time. Use caution with sudden changes in position during and after dental treatment.

Effects on Bleeding No information available to require special precautions

Adverse Reactions Frequency not defined.

Cardiovascular: Orthostatic hypotension, syncope

Central nervous system: Altered mental status, choreiform movements, convulsions, fatigue, orthostatic dizziness, paresthesia, sedation

Endocrine & metabolic: Decreased libido

Gastrointestinal: Anorexia, constipation (sometimes preceded by small, frequent stools), glossitis, intestinal obstruction, nausea, vomiting, xerostomia

Genitourinary: Impotence, urinary retention

Neuromuscular & skeletal: Tremor, weakness

Ophthalmic: Blurred vision, mydriasis

Respiratory: Pulmonary edema, pulmonary fibrosis

General Dosage Range Oral: *Adults:* Initial: 2.5 mg twice daily; average dose: 25 mg/day (usually in 3 divided doses)

Mechanism of Action Mecamylamine inhibits acetylcholine at the autonomic ganglia, causing a decrease in blood pressure. The blood pressure lowering effect is predominantly orthostatic; the supine blood pressure is also significantly decreased.

Pharmacodynamics/Kinetics

Onset of Action 0.5 to 2 hours

Duration of Action 6 to ≥12 hours

Pregnancy Risk Factor C

Pregnancy Considerations Animal reproduction studies have not been conducted. Mecamylamine crosses the placenta.

Mecasermin (mek a SER min)

Brand Names: US Increlex

Pharmacologic Category Growth Hormone

Use Primary insulin-like growth factor-1 deficiency: Treatment of growth failure in children with severe primary insulin-like growth factor 1 (IGF-1) deficiency or with growth hormone (GH) gene deletion who have developed neutralizing antibodies to GH.

Local Anesthetic/Vasoconstrictor Precautions No information available to require special precautions

Effects on Dental Treatment No significant effects or complications reported

Effects on Bleeding No information available to require special precautions

Adverse Reactions

≥5%:

Cardiovascular: Heart murmur

Central nervous system: Dizziness, headache, seizure

Endocrine & metabolic: Hypoglycemia (42%), lipohypertrophy (injection site), thymus hypertrophy

Gastrointestinal: Vomiting

Local: Bruising at injection site

Neuromuscular & skeletal: Arthralgia, limb pain

Otic: Abnormal tympanometry, fluid in ear (middle ear), hypoacusis, otalgia, otitis media, serous otitis media

Respiratory: Tonsillar hypertrophy (15%), snoring

<5%, postmarketing, and/or case reports: Abnormal hair texture, alopecia, anaphylaxis, angioedema, antibody development, cardiomegaly, dyspnea, heart valve disease, hypercholesterolemia, hypersensitivity, hypertriglyceridemia, hypoglycemic seizure, increased lactate dehydrogenase, increased serum ALT, increased serum AST, injection site reaction (eg, erythema, pain, hematoma, hemorrhage, induration, rash, swelling), intracranial hypertension, itching at injection site, loss of consciousness (secondary to hypoglycemia), obstructive sleep apnea syndrome, osteonecrosis (occasionally associated with slipped capital femoral epiphysis), thickening of the soft tissues of the face, urticaria, urticaria at injection site

General Dosage Range SubQ: *Children ≥2 years and Adolescents:* Initial: 0.04-0.08 mg/kg twice daily; Maintenance: 0.04-0.12 mg/kg twice daily

Mechanism of Action Mecasermin is an insulin-like growth factor (IGF-1) produced using recombinant DNA technology to replace endogenous IGF-1. Endogenous IGF-1 circulates predominately bound to insulin-like growth factor-binding protein-3 (IGFBP-3) and a growth hormone-dependent acid-labile subunit (ALS). Acting at receptors in the liver and other tissues, endogenous growth hormone (GH) stimulates the synthesis and secretion of IGF-1. In patients with primary severe IGF-1 deficiency, growth hormone receptors in the liver are unresponsive to GH, leading to reduced endogenous IGF-I concentrations and decreased growth (skeletal, cell, and organ). Endogenous IGF-1 also suppresses liver glucose production, stimulates peripheral glucose utilization, and has an inhibitory effect on insulin secretion.

Pharmacodynamics/Kinetics

Half-life Elimination Severe primary IGFD: ~5.8 hours

Time to Peak Serum: 2 hours

Pregnancy Risk Factor C

Pregnancy Considerations Teratogenic effects were not observed in animal studies

Meclizine (MEK li zeen)

Brand Names: US Dramamine Less Drowsy [OTC]; Medi-Meclizine [OTC] [DSC]; Motion-Time [OTC]; Travel Sickness [OTC]; Vertin-32 [OTC] [DSC]

Pharmacologic Category Antiemetic; Histamine H_1 Antagonist; Histamine H_1 Antagonist, First Generation; Piperazine Derivative

Use

Motion sickness: Prevention and treatment of nausea, vomiting, or dizziness associated with motion sickness.

Vertigo: Possibly effective for management of vertigo associated with diseases affecting vestibular system.

Local Anesthetic/Vasoconstrictor Precautions No information available to require special precautions

Effects on Dental Treatment Key adverse event(s) related to dental treatment: Slight to moderate drowsiness, thickening of bronchial secretions, significant xerostomia (normal salivary flow resumes upon discontinuation).

Effects on Bleeding No information available to require special precautions

Adverse Reactions Frequency not defined.

Central nervous system: Drowsiness, fatigue, headache
Gastrointestinal: Vomiting, xerostomia
Hypersensitivity: Anaphylactoid reaction
Ophthalmic: Blurred vision

General Dosage Range Oral: *Children ≥12 years, Adolescents, and Adults:* 25 to 50 mg 1 hour before travel, may repeat every 24 hours if needed **or** 25 to 100 mg/day in divided doses

Mechanism of Action Antihistamine that suppresses vestibular end-organ receptors and inhibits activation of central cholinergic pathways (Oosterveld 1985)

Pharmacodynamics/Kinetics

Onset of Action ~1 hour (Wang 2012)

Duration of Action ~24 hours (Wang 2012)

Half-life Elimination 5.2 ± 0.8 hours (Wang 2011, Wang 2012)

Time to Peak Plasma: 3.1 ± 1.4 hours (Wang 2011, Wang 2012)

Pregnancy Risk Factor B

Pregnancy Considerations Adverse events have been observed in animal reproduction studies. Based on epidemiologic studies, maternal meclizine use has generally not resulted in an increased risk of fetal abnormalities.

Meclofenamate (me kloe fen AM ate)

Related Information

Rheumatoid Arthritis, Osteoarthritis, and Osteoporosis *on page 1792*

Temporomandibular Dysfunction (TMD), Chronic Pain, and Fibromyalgia *on page 1868*

Pharmacologic Category Analgesic, Nonopioid; Nonsteroidal Anti-inflammatory Drug (NSAID), Oral

Use

Acute gouty arthritis: Acute and long-term use in the relief of signs and symptoms of acute gouty arthritis.

Ankylosing spondylitis: Acute and long-term use in the relief of signs and symptoms of ankylosing spondylitis.

Arthritis: Relief of signs and symptoms of juvenile arthritis, osteoarthritis, and rheumatoid arthritis.

Bursitis/tendinitis of the shoulder: Acute and long-term use in the relief of signs and symptoms of acute painful shoulder (acute subacromial bursitis/supraspinatus tendinitis).

Fever: Reduction of fever in adults.

Pain, mild to moderate: Relief of mild to moderate pain in adults.

Primary dysmenorrhea/excessive menstrual blood loss: Treatment of primary dysmenorrhea and idiopathic heavy menstrual blood loss.

Local Anesthetic/Vasoconstrictor Precautions No information available to require special precautions

Effects on Dental Treatment The dentist should be aware of the potential of abnormal coagulation. Caution should also be exercised in the use of NSAIDs in patients already on anticoagulant therapy with drugs such as warfarin (Coumadin®). Recovery of platelet function usually occurs 1-2 days after discontinuation of NSAIDs. See Effects on Bleeding.

Effects on Bleeding Nonselective NSAIDs such as meclofenamate inhibit platelet aggregation and prolong bleeding time in some patients. Unlike aspirin, the NSAID effect on platelet function is quantitatively less, of shorter duration, and reversible.

Adverse Reactions

>10%:

Central nervous system: Dizziness
Dermatologic: Skin rash
Gastrointestinal: Abdominal cramps, dyspepsia, heartburn, nausea

1% to 10%:

Central nervous system: Headache, nervousness
Dermatologic: Pruritus
Endocrine & metabolic: Fluid retention
Gastrointestinal: Vomiting
Otic: Tinnitus

<1%, postmarketing, and/or case reports: Acute renal failure, agranulocytosis, allergic rhinitis, anemia, angioedema, aseptic meningitis, auditory impairment, blurred vision, bone marrow depression, cardiac arrhythmia, cardiac failure, confusion, conjunctivitis, cystitis, depression, drowsiness, dyspnea, epistaxis, erythema multiforme, gastritis, gastrointestinal ulcer, hallucination, hemolytic anemia, hepatitis, hepatotoxicity (idiosyncratic; Chalasani 2014), hot flash, hypertension, insomnia, leukopenia, peripheral neuropathy, polydipsia, polyuria, Stevens-Johnson syndrome, tachycardia, thrombocytopenia, toxic amblyopia, toxic epidermal necrolysis, urticaria, xerophthalmia

General Dosage Range Oral: *Adolescents ≥14 years and Adults:* 50 to 100 mg every 4 to 6 hours (maximum: 400 mg/day)

Mechanism of Action Reversibly inhibits cyclooxygenase-1 and 2 (COX-1 and 2) enzymes, which results in decreased formation of prostaglandin precursors; has antipyretic, analgesic, and anti-inflammatory properties.

Other proposed mechanisms not fully elucidated (and possibly contributing to the anti-inflammatory effect to varying degrees) include inhibiting chemotaxis, altering lymphocyte activity, inhibiting neutrophil aggregation/activation, and decreasing proinflammatory cytokine levels.

Pharmacodynamics/Kinetics

Duration of Action 2 to 4 hours

Half-life Elimination Meclofenamate sodium: 0.8 to 2.1 hours; Metabolite I: ~15 hours

Time to Peak Serum: Meclofenamate sodium: 0.5 to 2 hours; Metabolite I: 0.5 to 4 hours

Pregnancy Risk Factor C

Pregnancy Considerations Adverse events have not been observed in animal reproduction studies. NSAID exposure during the first trimester is not strongly associated with congenital malformations; however, cardiovascular anomalies and cleft palate have been observed following NSAID exposure in some studies. The use of an NSAID close to conception may be associated with an increased risk of miscarriage. Nonteratogenic effects have been observed following NSAID administration during the third trimester including myocardial degenerative changes, prenatal constriction of the ductus arteriosus, fetal tricuspid regurgitation, failure of the ductus arteriosus to close postnatally; renal dysfunction or failure, oligohydramnios; gastrointestinal bleeding or perforation, increased risk of necrotizing enterocolitis; intracranial bleeding (including intraventricular hemorrhage), platelet dysfunction with resultant bleeding; pulmonary hypertension. Because they may cause premature closure of the ductus arteriosus, use of NSAIDs late in pregnancy should be avoided (use after 31 or 32 weeks gestation is not recommended by some clinicians). The chronic use of NSAIDs in women of reproductive age may be associated with infertility that is reversible upon discontinuation of the medication.

Medium Chain Triglycerides

(mee DEE um chane trye GLIS er ides)

Brand Names: US Betaquik [OTC]; Liquigen [OTC]; MCT Oil [OTC]

Brand Names: Canada MCT Oil

Pharmacologic Category Nutritional Supplement

Use Dietary supplement: A medical food for use in the nutritional management of patients who cannot efficiently digest and absorb conventional long chain food fats

Local Anesthetic/Vasoconstrictor Precautions No information available to require special precautions

Effects on Dental Treatment No significant effects or complications reported

Effects on Bleeding No information available to require special precautions

Adverse Reactions Frequency not defined.

Endocrine & metabolic: Decreased HDL cholesterol (>6 months daily use), increased serum triglycerides (>6 months daily use)

Gastrointestinal: Abdominal cramps, abdominal pain, bloating, diarrhea, nausea

General Dosage Range Oral: *Adults:* MCT Oil: 15 to 20 mL per dose (maximum daily dose: 100 mL).

Mechanism of Action MCTs are saturated fatty acids in chains of 6-12 carbon atoms. They are water soluble and can pass directly through intestinal cell membranes into portal venous blood. Unlike long chain fats, MCTs do not require the presence of bile acids and pancreatic lipase for absorption. MCTs provide a source of calories while reducing the amount of malabsorbed fat remaining in stool (Gracey, 1970; Ruppin, 1980).

Pharmacodynamics/Kinetics

Onset of Action Octanoic acid appeared in each subject by 30 minutes following ingestion; effect on seizures in children: Within 6 weeks

MedroxyPROGESTERone

(me DROKS ee proe JES te rone)

Related Information

Endocrine Disorders and Pregnancy *on page 1781*

Brand Names: US Depo-Provera; Depo-SubQ Provera 104; Provera

Brand Names: Canada Alti-MPA; Apo-Medroxy; Depo-Prevera; Depo-Provera; Dom-Medroxyprogesterone; Gen-Medroxy; Medroxy; Medroxyprogesterone Acetate Injectable Suspension USP; Novo-Medrone; PMS-Medroxyprogesterone; Provera; Provera-Pak; Teva-Medroxyprogesterone

Pharmacologic Category Contraceptive; Progestin

Use

Abnormal uterine bleeding (tablet): Treatment of abnormal uterine bleeding due to hormonal imbalance in the absence of organic pathology, such as fibroids or uterine cancer.

Amenorrhea, secondary (tablet): Treatment of secondary amenorrhea due to hormonal imbalance in the absence of organic pathology, such as fibroids or uterine cancer.

Contraception (104 mg/0.65 mL and 150 mg/mL injection): Prevention of pregnancy in women of childbearing potential.

Endometrial hyperplasia (tablet): Prevention of endometrial hyperplasia in nonhysterectomized postmenopausal women receiving daily oral conjugated estrogens 0.625 mg.

Endometrial carcinoma (400 mg/mL injection) (100 mg tablet [Canadian product]): Adjunctive therapy and/or palliative treatment of inoperable, recurrent, and/or metastatic endometrial carcinoma.

Endometriosis (104 mg/0.65 mL injection): Management of endometriosis-associated pain.

Local Anesthetic/Vasoconstrictor Precautions No information available to require special precautions

Effects on Dental Treatment Progestins may predispose the patient to gingival bleeding.

Effects on Bleeding No information available to require special precautions

Adverse Reactions Adverse effects as reported with any dosage form.

>10%:

Central nervous system: Headache (9% to 17%), nervousness (11%)

Endocrine & metabolic: Amenorrhea (IM: 55% at 12 months; 68% at 24 months; SubQ: 6%), weight gain (IM: >10 lbs at 24 months: 38%; SubQ: 6%), menstrual disease (IM: 57% at 12 months; 32% at 24 months; SubQ: 1% to 7%)

Gastrointestinal: Abdominal pain (1% to 11%)

1% to 10%:

Cardiovascular: Edema (2%)

Central nervous system: Dizziness (1% to 6%), anxiety (1% to <5%), depression (1% to <5%), insomnia (1% to <5%), irritability (1% to <5%), fatigue (<5%)

Dermatologic: Acne vulgaris (1% to <5%), alopecia (1%), skin rash (1%)

Endocrine & metabolic: Decreased libido (1% to 6%), change in menstrual flow (menometrorrhagia; 1% to <5%), hypermenorrhea (1% to <5%), hot flash (1% to <5%)

Gastrointestinal: Abdominal distension (1% to <5%), diarrhea (1% to <5%), nausea (1% to <5%), bloating (2%)

Genitourinary: Abnormal Pap smear (1% to <5%), bacterial vaginosis (1% to <5%), breast tenderness

(1% to <5%), dysmenorrhea (1% to <5%), mastalgia (1% to <5%), urinary tract infection (1% to <5%), uterine hemorrhage (1% to <5%), vaginal hemorrhage (1% to <5%), vaginitis (1% to <5%), vulvovaginal candidiasis (1% to <5%), leukorrhea (3%)

Infection: Influenza (1% to <5%)

Local: Pain at injection site (1% to <5%), atrophy at injection site (≤1%), induration at injection site (≤1%)

Neuromuscular & skeletal: Arthralgia (1% to <5%), back pain (1% to <5%), limb pain (1% to <5%), leg cramps (4%), weakness (≤4%)

Respiratory: Bronchitis (1% to <5%), nasopharyngitis (1% to <5%), pharyngitis (1% to <5%), sinusitis (1% to <5%), upper respiratory tract infection (1% to <5%)

Frequency not defined:

Central nervous system: Euphoria, malaise

Endocrine & metabolic: Cushing syndrome, hypercalcemia, lipodystrophy

Genitourinary: Breakthrough bleeding, spotting

Local: Injection site nodule, tenderness at injection site

<1%, postmarketing, and/or case reports: Anaphylaxis, anaphylactoid reaction, anemia, angioedema, anxiety, asthma, axillary swelling, Bell palsy, body odor, breast changes, cervical cancer, change in appetite, change in cervical erosion, change in cervical secretions, chest pain, chills, chloasma, cholestatic jaundice, decreased bone mineral density, decreased glucose tolerance, decreased lactation, deep vein thrombosis, delayed return to fertility, diaphoresis, drowsiness, dyspareunia, dyspnea, fever, galactorrhea, genitourinary infection, hematologic abnormality, hirsutism, hoarseness, hypersensitivity reaction, increased libido, increased thirst, jaundice, lump in breast, malignant neoplasm of breast, nipple bleeding, nipple discharge, oligomenorrhea, optic neuritis, osteoporosis, paralysis, paresthesia, pathological fracture due to osteoporosis, pruritus, pulmonary embolism, rectal hemorrhage, residual mass at injection site, retinal thrombosis, scleroderma, seizure, skin discoloration (melasma), skin discoloration at injection site, sterile abscess at injection site, syncope, tachycardia, thrombophlebitis, urticaria, uterine hyperplasia, vaginal cyst, varicose veins, weight loss, xeroderma

General Dosage Range

IM:

Adolescents and Adults: Contraception: 150 mg every 3 months (every 13 weeks)

Adults: Endometrial cancer: 400 to 1000 mg/week

Oral: *Adolescents and Adults:* 5 to 10 mg once daily

SubQ: *Adolescents and Adults:* 104 mg every 3 months (every 12 to 14 weeks)

Mechanism of Action Medroxyprogesterone acetate (MPA) transforms a proliferative endometrium into a secretory endometrium. When administered with conjugated estrogens, MPA reduces the incidence of endometrial hyperplasia and risk of adenocarcinoma. When used as an injection for contraception (doses of 150 mg IM or 104 mg SubQ), MPA inhibits secretion of pituitary gonadotropins, which prevents follicular maturation and ovulation and causes endometrial thinning. Progestogens, such as medroxyprogesterone when used for endometriosis, lead to atrophy of the endometrial tissue. They may also suppress new growth and implantation. Pain associated with endometriosis is decreased (ASRM, 2014).

Pharmacodynamics/Kinetics

Onset of Action Time to ovulation (after last injection): 10 months (range: 6 to 12 months)

Half-life Elimination Oral: 12 to 17 hours; IM (Depo-Provera Contraceptive): ~50 days; SubQ: ~43 days

Time to Peak Oral: 2 to 4 hours; IM (Depo-Provera Contraceptive): ~3 weeks; SubQ: ~1 week

Pregnancy Risk Factor X (tablet)

Pregnancy Considerations Most products are contraindicated in women who are pregnant, suspected to be pregnant or as a diagnostic test for pregnancy. In general, there is not an increased risk of birth defects following inadvertent use of the injectable medroxyprogesterone acetate (MPA) contraceptives early in pregnancy. Hypospadias has been reported in male babies and clitoral enlargement and labial fusion have been reported in female babies exposed to MPA during the first trimester of pregnancy. High doses impair fertility. Ectopic pregnancies have been reported with use of the MPA contraceptive injection. Median time to conception/return to ovulation following discontinuation of MPA contraceptive injection is 10 months following the last injection and is unrelated to the duration of use.

Mefenamic Acid (me fe NAM ik AS id)

Related Information

Rheumatoid Arthritis, Osteoarthritis, and Osteoporosis *on page 1792*

Temporomandibular Dysfunction (TMD), Chronic Pain, and Fibromyalgia *on page 1868*

Brand Names: US Ponstel

Brand Names: Canada Dom-Mefenamic Acid; Mefenamic; PMS-Mefenamic Acid; Ponstan

Pharmacologic Category Analgesic, Nonopioid; Nonsteroidal Anti-inflammatory Drug (NSAID), Oral

Use

Pain, mild to moderate: Relief of mild to moderate pain in patients ≥14 years, when therapy will not exceed 1 week.

Primary dysmenorrhea: Treatment of primary dysmenorrhea.

Local Anesthetic/Vasoconstrictor Precautions No information available to require special precautions

Effects on Dental Treatment The dentist should be aware of the potential of abnormal coagulation. Caution should also be exercised in the use of NSAIDs in patients already on anticoagulant therapy with drugs such as warfarin (Coumadin®). Recovery of platelet function usually occurs 1-2 days after discontinuation of NSAIDs. See Effects on Bleeding.

Effects on Bleeding Nonselective NSAIDs such as mefenamic acid inhibit platelet aggregation and prolong bleeding time in some patients. Unlike aspirin, the NSAID effect on platelet function is quantitatively less, of shorter duration, and reversible.

Adverse Reactions

1% to 10%:

Central nervous system: Dizziness (3% to 9%), headache, nervousness

Dermatologic: Pruritus, skin rash

Endocrine & metabolic: Fluid retention

Gastrointestinal: Abdominal cramps, abdominal distress, abdominal pain, constipation, diarrhea, duodenal ulcer (with bleeding or perforation), dyspepsia, flatulence, gastric ulcer (with bleeding or perforation), gastritis, heartburn, nausea, vomiting

Hematologic & oncologic: Hemorrhage

Hepatic: Increased liver enzymes

Otic: Tinnitus

<1%, postmarketing, and/or case reports: Acute renal failure, agranulocytosis, allergic rhinitis, anemia,

angioedema, aseptic meningitis, auditory impairment, blurred vision, bone marrow depression, cardiac arrhythmia, cardiac failure, confusion, conjunctivitis, cystitis, depression, drowsiness, dyspnea, epistaxis, erythema multiforme, gastrointestinal ulcer, hallucination, hemolytic anemia, hepatitis, hepatotoxicity (idiosyncratic; Chalasani 2014), hot flash, hypertension, insomnia, leukopenia, peripheral neuropathy, polydipsia, polyuria, Stevens-Johnson syndrome, stomatitis, tachycardia, thrombocytopenia, toxic amblyopia, toxic epidermal necrolysis, urticaria, xerophthalmia

General Dosage Range Oral: *Adolescents ≥14 years and Adults:* Initial: 500 mg, then 250 mg every 6 hours as needed

Mechanism of Action Reversibly inhibits cyclooxygenase-1 and 2 (COX-1 and 2) enzymes, which results in decreased formation of prostaglandin precursors; has antipyretic, analgesic, and anti-inflammatory properties.

Other proposed mechanisms not fully elucidated (and possibly contributing to the anti-inflammatory effect to varying degrees) include inhibiting chemotaxis, altering lymphocyte activity, inhibiting neutrophil aggregation/activation, and decreasing proinflammatory cytokine levels.

Pharmacodynamics/Kinetics

Half-life Elimination ~2 hours

Time to Peak 2 to 4 hours

Pregnancy Considerations Adverse events have not been observed in animal reproduction studies. NSAID exposure during the first trimester is not strongly associated with congenital malformations; however, cardiovascular anomalies and cleft palate have been observed following NSAID exposure in some studies. The use of an NSAID close to conception may be associated with an increased risk of miscarriage. Nonteratogenic effects have been observed following NSAID administration during the third trimester including myocardial degenerative changes, prenatal constriction of the ductus arteriosus, fetal tricuspid regurgitation, failure of the ductus arteriosus to close postnatally; renal dysfunction or failure, oligohydramnios; gastrointestinal bleeding or perforation, increased risk of necrotizing enterocolitis; intracranial bleeding (including intraventricular hemorrhage), platelet dysfunction with resultant bleeding; pulmonary hypertension. Because they may cause premature closure of the ductus arteriosus, use of NSAIDs late in pregnancy should be avoided (use after 31 or 32 weeks gestation is not recommended by some clinicians). The chronic use of NSAIDs in women of reproductive age may be associated with infertility that is reversible upon discontinuation of the medication.

Mefloquine (ME floe kwin)

Pharmacologic Category Antimalarial Agent

Use Treatment of mild-to-moderate acute malarial infections and prevention of malaria caused by *Plasmodium falciparum* (including chloroquine-resistant strains) or *P. vivax*

Note: Due to geographical resistance and cross-resistance, consult current CDC guidelines.

Local Anesthetic/Vasoconstrictor Precautions No information available to require special precautions

Effects on Dental Treatment No significant effects or complications reported

Effects on Bleeding No information available to require special precautions

Adverse Reactions

1% to 10%:

Central nervous system: Chills, dizziness, fatigue, headache

Dermatologic: Skin rash

Gastrointestinal: Vomiting (3%), abdominal pain, decreased appetite, diarrhea, nausea

Neuromuscular & skeletal: Myalgia

Otic: Tinnitus

Miscellaneous: Fever

<1%, postmarketing, and/or case reports: Abnormal dreams, abnormal T waves on ECG, aggressive behavior, agitation, alopecia, anxiety, arthralgia, ataxia, atrioventricular block, auditory impairment, bradycardia, brain disease, cardiac arrhythmia, cardiac conduction disturbance (transient), chest pain, confusion, decreased hematocrit, depression, diaphoresis, drowsiness, dyspepsia, dyspnea, edema, emotional lability, erythema, erythema multiforme, extrasystoles, flushing, forgetfulness, hallucination, hypersensitivity pneumonitis, hypertension, hypotension, increased liver enzymes, insomnia, irregular pulse, leukocytosis, leukopenia, loss of balance, malaise, mood changes, muscle cramps, myasthenia, palpitations, panic attack, paranoia, paresthesia, prolonged Q-T interval on ECG, pruritus, psychosis, restlessness, seizure, Stevens-Johnson syndrome, suicidal ideation (causal relationship not established), suicidal tendencies (causal relationship not established), syncope, tachycardia, thrombocytopenia, tremor, urticaria, vertigo, visual disturbance, weakness

General Dosage Range Oral:

Children ≥6 months: Prophylaxis: 5 mg/kg/once weekly (maximum: 250 mg/dose); Treatment: 20-25 mg/kg/day in 2 divided doses (maximum: 1250 mg)

Adults: Prophylaxis: 250 mg once weekly; Treatment: 1250 mg (5 tablets) as a single dose

Mechanism of Action Mefloquine is a quinoline-methanol compound structurally similar to quinine; mefloquine's effectiveness in the treatment and prophylaxis of malaria is due to the destruction of the asexual blood forms of the malarial pathogens that affect humans, *Plasmodium falciparum*, *P. vivax*

Pharmacodynamics/Kinetics

Half-life Elimination Children 4 to 10 years: Mean range: 11.6 to 13.6 days (range: 6.5 to 33 days) (Price 1999); Adults: ~3 weeks (range: 2 to 4 weeks); may be decreased during infection (2 weeks) (WHO 2010)

Time to Peak Plasma: ~17 hours (range: 6 to 24 hours)

Pregnancy Risk Factor B

Pregnancy Considerations Adverse events have been observed in animal reproduction studies. Mefloquine crosses the placenta; however, clinical experience with mefloquine has not shown adverse effects in pregnant women. Use with caution during pregnancy if travel to endemic areas cannot be postponed. Malaria infection in pregnant women may be more severe than in nonpregnant women and may increase the risk of adverse pregnancy outcomes. Nonpregnant women of childbearing potential are advised to use contraception and avoid pregnancy during malaria prophylaxis and for 3 months thereafter. In case of an unplanned pregnancy, treatment with mefloquine is not considered a reason for pregnancy termination. CDC treatment guidelines are available for the use of mefloquine in the treatment of malaria during pregnancy (CDC, 2013b).

Megestrol (me JES trole)

Brand Names: US Megace ES; Megace Oral
Brand Names: Canada Megace OS; Megestrol
Pharmacologic Category Antineoplastic Agent, Hormone; Appetite Stimulant; Progestin
Use
Anorexia or cachexia: *Suspension:* Treatment of anorexia, cachexia, or unexplained significant weight loss in patients with AIDS
Limitations of use: Treatment of AIDS-related weight loss should only be initiated after addressing the treatable causes (eg, malignancy, infection, malabsorption, endocrine disease, renal disease, psychiatric disorder) for weight loss. Megestrol is not intended to prevent weight loss.
Breast cancer: *Tablet:* Treatment (palliative) of advanced breast cancer
Endometrial cancer: *Tablet:* Treatment (palliative) of advanced endometrial carcinoma
Additional Canadian use (not an approved use in the U.S.): *Tablet:* Treatment of anorexia, cachexia, or weight loss secondary to metastatic cancer
Local Anesthetic/Vasoconstrictor Precautions No information available to require special precautions
Effects on Dental Treatment No significant effects or complications reported
Effects on Bleeding Thromboembolic events have been reported.
Adverse Reactions
Frequency not always defined.
Cardiovascular: Hypertension (4% to 8%), cardiomyopathy (1% to 3%), chest pain (1% to 3%), edema (1% to 3%), palpitations (1% to 3%), peripheral edema (1% to 3%), cardiac failure
Central nervous system: Headache (3% to 10%), pain (4% to 6%, similar to placebo), insomnia (1% to 6%), abnormality in thinking (1% to 3%), confusion (1% to 3%), convulsions (1% to 3%), depression (1% to 3%), hypoesthesia (1% to 3%), neuropathy (1% to 3%), paresthesia (1% to 3%), carpal tunnel syndrome, lethargy, malaise, mood changes
Dermatologic: Skin rash (6% to 12%), alopecia (1% to 3%), dermatological disease (1% to 3%), diaphoresis (1% to 3%), pruritus (1% to 3%), vesicobullous dermatitis (1% to 3%)
Endocrine & metabolic: Hyperglycemia (6%), decreased libido (1% to 5%), albuminuria (1% to 3%), gynecomastia (1% to 3%), increased lactate dehydrogenase (1% to 3%), adrenocortical insufficiency, amenorrhea, Cushing's syndrome, diabetes mellitus, hot flash, HPA-axis suppression, hypercalcemia, weight gain (not attributed to edema or fluid retention)
Gastrointestinal: Diarrhea (10%, similar to placebo), flatulence (6% to 10%), vomiting (4% to 6%), nausea (4% to 5%), dyspepsia (2% to 3%), abdominal pain (1% to 3%), constipation (1% to 3%), oral moniliasis (1% to 3%), sialorrhea (1% to 3%), xerostomia (1% to 3%)
Genitourinary: Impotence (4% to 14%), urinary incontinence (1% to 3%), urinary tract infection (1% to 3%), urinary frequency (1% to 2%), breakthrough bleeding
Hematologic & oncologic: Leukopenia (1% to 3%), sarcoma (1% to 3%), tumor flare
Hepatic: Hepatomegaly (1% to 3%)
Infection: Candidiasis (1% to 3%), herpes virus infection (1% to 3%), infection (1% to 3%)
Neuromuscular & skeletal: Weakness (5% to 6%)
Ophthalmic: Amblyopia (1% to 3%)
Respiratory: Cough (1% to 3%), dyspnea (1% to 3%), pharyngitis (1% to 3%), pulmonary disorder (1% to 3%), pneumonia (1%), hyperventilation
Miscellaneous: Fever (1% to 6%)
Postmarketing and/or case reports: Decreased glucose tolerance, thromboembolic phenomena (including deep vein thrombosis, pulmonary embolism, thrombophlebitis)
General Dosage Range Oral: *Adults:* Suspension: 400 to 800 mg daily; Tablet: 40 to 320 mg daily
Mechanism of Action A synthetic progestin with antiestrogenic properties which disrupt the estrogen receptor cycle. Megestrol interferes with the normal estrogen cycle and results in a lower LH titer. May also have a direct effect on the endometrium. Megestrol is an antineoplastic progestin thought to act through an antileutenizing effect mediated via the pituitary. May stimulate appetite by antagonizing the metabolic effects of catabolic cytokines.
Pharmacodynamics/Kinetics
Onset of Action Antineoplastic: 2 months of continuous therapy; Weight gain: 2 to 4 weeks
Half-life Elimination Suspension: 20 to 50 hours; Tablet: 13 to 105 hours
Time to Peak Serum: Tablet: 2 to 3 hours; Suspension: 3 to 5 hours
Pregnancy Risk Factor D (tablet) / X (suspension)
Pregnancy Considerations Adverse events were demonstrated in animal reproduction studies. May cause fetal harm if administered to a pregnant woman. Use during pregnancy is contraindicated (suspension) and appropriate contraception is recommended in women who may become pregnant. In clinical studies, megestrol was shown to cause breakthrough vaginal bleeding in women.

Meloxicam (mel OKS i kam)

Related Information
Rheumatoid Arthritis, Osteoarthritis, and Osteoporosis *on page 1792*
Brand Names: US Meloxicam Comfort Pac; Mobic; Vivlodex
Brand Names: Canada ACT Meloxicam; Apo-Meloxicam; Auro-Meloxicam; Dom-Meloxicam; Mobicox; Mylan-Meloxicam; PHL-Meloxicam; PMS-Meloxicam; Teva-Meloxicam
Generic Availability (US) May be product dependent
Pharmacologic Category Analgesic, Nonopioid; Nonsteroidal Anti-inflammatory Drug (NSAID), Oral
Use
Osteoarthritis: Relief of the signs and symptoms of osteoarthritis (OA); management of OA pain.
Rheumatoid arthritis (tablet and suspension only): Relief of signs and symptoms of rheumatoid arthritis (RA); relief of the signs and symptoms of pauciarticular or polyarticular course juvenile RA in patients ≥2 years (suspension) and in patients weighing ≥60 kg (tablet).
Local Anesthetic/Vasoconstrictor Precautions No information available to require special precautions
Effects on Dental Treatment Key adverse event(s) related to dental treatment: Taste perversion, ulcerative stomatitis, and xerostomia (normal salivary flow resumes upon discontinuation). The dentist should be aware of the potential of abnormal coagulation. Caution should also be exercised in the use of NSAIDs in patients already on anticoagulant therapy with drugs

such as warfarin (Coumadin®). See Effects on Bleeding.

Effects on Bleeding Nonselective NSAIDs such as meloxicam inhibit platelet aggregation and prolong bleeding time in some patients. Unlike aspirin, the NSAID effect on platelet function is quantitatively less, of shorter duration, and reversible.

Adverse Reactions Percentages reported in adult patients. Reactions similar in pediatric patients; abdominal pain, diarrhea, fever, headache, pyrexia, and vomiting were reported more commonly than in adult patients.

1% to 10%:

Cardiovascular: Edema (≤5%), angina pectoris (<2%), cardiac arrhythmia (<2%), cardiac failure (<2%), facial edema (<2%), hypertension (<2%), hypotension (<2%), myocardial infarction (<2%), palpitations (<2%), paresthesia (<2%), syncope (<2%), tachycardia (<2%), vasculitis (<2%)

Central nervous system: Pain (≤5%), headache (2% to 4%), dizziness (1% to 4%), insomnia (≤4%), falling (1% to 3%), abnormal dreams (<2%), anxiety (<2%), confusion (<2%), convulsions (<2%), depression (<2%), drowsiness (<2%), fatigue (<2%), malaise (<2%), nervousness (<2%), vertigo (<2%)

Dermatologic: Skin rash (≤3%), pruritus (≤2%), bullous rash (<2%), diaphoresis (<2%), skin photosensitivity (<2%), urticaria (<2%)

Endocrine & metabolic: Albuminuria (<2%), dehydration (<2%), hot flash (<2%), increased gamma-glutamyl transferase (<2%), weight gain (<2%), weight loss (<2%)

Gastrointestinal: Dyspepsia (4% to 10%), diarrhea (2% to 8%), nausea (2% to 7%), abdominal pain (2% to 5%), constipation (≤3%), flatulence (≤3%), vomiting (≤3%), aphthous stomatitis (<2%), colitis (<2%), duodenal ulcer (<2%), dysgeusia (<2%), eructation (<2%), esophagitis (<2%), gastrointestinal perforation (<2%; including duodenal, gastric), gastric ulcer (<2%), gastritis (<2%), gastroesophageal reflux disease (<2%), gastrointestinal hemorrhage (<2%), hematemesis (<2%), increased appetite (<2%), intestinal perforation (<2%), melena (<2%), pancreatitis (<2%), xerostomia (<2%)

Genitourinary: Urinary tract infection (≤7%), urinary frequency (≤2%), hematuria (<2%)

Hematologic & oncologic: Anemia (≤4%), leukopenia (<2%), purpura (<2%), thrombocytopenia (<2%)

Hepatic: Hepatitis (<2%), hyperbilirubinemia (<2%), increased serum ALT (<2%), increased serum AST (<2%)

Hypersensitivity: Angioedema (<2%), hypersensitivity reaction (<2%)

Neuromuscular & skeletal: Arthralgia (≤5%), back pain (≤3%), tremor (<2%)

Ophthalmic: Conjunctivitis (<2%), visual disturbance (<2%)

Otic: Tinnitus (<2%)

Renal: Increased blood urea nitrogen (<2%), increased serum creatinine (<2%), renal failure (<2%)

Respiratory: Upper respiratory tract infection (≤8%), flu-like symptoms (3% to 6%), pharyngitis (3%), cough (≤2%), asthma (<2%)

Miscellaneous: Fever (<2%)

<1%, postmarketing, and/or case reports: Acute urinary retention, agranulocytosis, alopecia, anaphylactoid reaction, anaphylaxis, bronchospasm, dyspnea, erythema multiforme, exfoliative dermatitis, hepatic failure, hepatotoxicity (idiosyncratic) (Chalasani 2014), interstitial nephritis, jaundice, mood changes, renal insufficiency, renal papillary necrosis, shock, Stevens-Johnson syndrome, toxic epidermal necrolysis

Dosing

Adult Note: Capsules are not interchangeable with other formulations of oral meloxicam even if the total milligram strength is the same. Do not substitute similar dose strengths of other meloxicam products.

Osteoarthritis: Capsule: Oral: Initial: 5 mg once daily; some patients may receive additional benefit from increasing dose to 10 mg once daily; maximum dose: 10 mg/day

Osteoarthritis, rheumatoid arthritis: Tablet/Suspension: Oral: Initial: 7.5 mg once daily; some patients may receive additional benefit from increasing dose to 15 mg once daily; maximum dose: 15 mg/day

Geriatric Refer to adult dosing. Use with caution; initiate dose at lower end of the dosing range.

Pediatric

Juvenile rheumatoid arthritis: Oral:

Note: Capsules are not interchangeable with other formulations of oral meloxicam even if the total milligram strength is the same. Do not substitute similar dose strengths of other meloxicam products.

Suspension: Children ≥2 years and Adolescents: 0.125 mg/kg once daily; maximum dose: 7.5 mg/day.

Tablet: Children and Adolescents weighing ≥60 kg: 7.5 mg once daily.

Renal Impairment

US labeling:

CrCl ≥20 mL/minute: No dosage adjustment necessary.

CrCl <20 mL/minute: There are no dosage adjustments provided in the manufacturer's labeling (has not been studied); use is not recommended.

Hemodialysis (not dialyzable): Use with caution and monitor closely. Maximum dose: 7.5 mg/day (tablet/suspension); 5 mg/day (capsule). **Note:** Additional dose not necessary after hemodialysis.

Canadian labeling:

CrCl ≥30 mL/minute: No dosage adjustment necessary.

CrCl <30 mL/minute or deteriorating renal function: Use is contraindicated.

Hemodialysis (not dialyzable): Maximum dose: 7.5 mg/day. **Note:** Additional dose not necessary after hemodialysis

KDIGO 2012 guidelines provide the following recommendations for NSAIDs:

eGFR 30 to <60 mL/minute/1.73 m^2: Temporarily discontinue in patients with intercurrent disease that increases risk of acute kidney injury.

eGFR <30 mL/minute/1.73 m^2: Avoid use.

Hepatic Impairment

US labeling:

Mild to moderate impairment (Child-Pugh class A or B): No dosage adjustment necessary.

Severe impairment (Child-Pugh class C): There are no dosage adjustments provided in the manufacturer's labeling (has not been studied); use with caution.

Canadian labeling:

Mild to moderate impairment: No dosage adjustment necessary.

Severe impairment or active liver disease: Use is contraindicated.

Mechanism of Action Reversibly inhibits cyclooxygenase-1 and 2 (COX-1 and 2) enzymes, which results in decreased formation of prostaglandin precursors; has antipyretic, analgesic, and anti-inflammatory properties

Other proposed mechanisms not fully elucidated (and possibly contributing to the anti-inflammatory effect to varying degrees), include inhibiting chemotaxis, altering lymphocyte activity, inhibiting neutrophil aggregation/activation, and decreasing proinflammatory cytokine levels.

Contraindications

Hypersensitivity to meloxicam or any component of the formulation; history of asthma, urticaria, or other allergic-type reactions after taking aspirin or other NSAIDs; use in the setting of coronary artery bypass graft (CABG) surgery.

Canadian labeling: Additional contraindications (not in US labeling): Pregnancy (third trimester); breastfeeding; severe uncontrolled heart failure; active or recent GI/gastric/duodenal/peptic ulceration/perforation; active GI bleeding; cerebrovascular bleeding or other bleeding disorders; inflammatory bowel disease (Crohn disease or ulcerative colitis); severe liver impairment or active liver disease; severe renal impairment (creatinine clearance [CrCl] <30 mL/minute or 0.5 mL/second) or deteriorating renal disease; known hyperkalemia; pediatric patients <18 years; rare hereditary conditions that may be incompatible with an excipient of the product.

Warnings/Precautions [US Boxed Warning]: NSAIDs cause an increased risk of serious (and potentially fatal) adverse cardiovascular thrombotic events, including MI and stroke. Risk may occur early during treatment and may increase with duration of use. Relative risk appears to be similar in those with and without known cardiovascular disease or risk factors for cardiovascular disease; however, absolute incidence of serious cardiovascular thrombotic events (which may occur early during treatment) was higher in patients with known cardiovascular disease or risk factors. New onset hypertension or exacerbation of hypertension may occur (NSAIDs may also impair response to ACE inhibitors, thiazide diuretics, or loop diuretics); may contribute to cardiovascular events; monitor blood pressure; use with caution in patients with hypertension. May cause sodium and fluid retention, use with caution in patients with edema. Avoid use in patients with heart failure (ACCF/AHA [Yancy 2013]). Avoid use in patients with recent MI unless benefits outweigh risk of cardiovascular thrombotic events. Use the lowest effective dose for the shortest duration of time, consistent with individual patient goals, to reduce risk of cardiovascular events; alternate therapies should be considered for patients at high risk.

[US Boxed Warning]: Use is contraindicated in the setting of coronary artery bypass graft (CABG) surgery. Risk of MI and stroke may be increased with use within the first 10 to 14 days following CABG surgery.

Platelet adhesion and aggregation may be decreased; may prolong bleeding time; patients with coagulation disorders or who are receiving anticoagulants should be monitored closely. Anemia may occur; patients on long-term NSAID therapy should be monitored for anemia. Rarely, NSAID use may cause severe blood dyscrasias (eg, agranulocytosis, aplastic anemia, thrombocytopenia).

NSAID use may compromise existing renal function. Dose-dependent decreases in prostaglandin synthesis may result from NSAID use, causing a reduction in renal blood flow which may cause renal decompensation (usually reversible). Patients with impaired renal function, dehydration, hypovolemia, heart failure, hepatic impairment, those taking diuretics, ACE inhibitors, angiotensin II receptor blockers, and the elderly are at greater risk for renal toxicity. Rehydrate patient before starting therapy; monitor renal function closely. Avoid use in patients with advanced renal disease unless benefits are expected to outweigh risk of worsening renal function; monitor closely if therapy must be initiated. Long-term NSAID use may result in renal papillary necrosis. NSAID use may increase the risk of hyperkalemia, particularly in the elderly, diabetics, renal disease, and with concomitant use of other agents capable of inducing hyperkalemia (eg, angiotensin-converting enzyme [ACE] inhibitors). Monitor potassium closely.

[US Boxed Warning]: NSAIDs cause an increased risk of serious gastrointestinal inflammation, ulceration, bleeding, and perforation (may be fatal); elderly patients and patients with history of peptic ulcer disease and/or GI bleeding are at greater risk for serious GI events. These events may occur at any time during therapy and without warning. Avoid use in patients with active GI bleeding. Use caution with a history of GI ulcers, concurrent therapy known to increase the risk of GI bleeding (eg, aspirin, anticoagulants and/or corticosteroids, selective serotonin reuptake inhibitors), advanced hepatic disease, coagulopathy, smoking, use of alcohol, or in elderly or debilitated patients. Use the lowest effective dose for the shortest duration of time, consistent with individual patient goals, to reduce risk of GI adverse events; alternate therapies should be considered for patients at high risk. When used concomitantly with aspirin, a substantial increase in the risk of gastrointestinal complications (eg, ulcer) occurs; concomitant gastroprotective therapy (eg, proton pump inhibitors) is recommended (Bhatt 2008).

NSAIDs may cause potentially fatal serious skin adverse events including exfoliative dermatitis, Stevens-Johnson syndrome (SJS) and toxic epidermal necrolysis (TEN); may occur without warning; discontinue use at first appearance of skin rash (or any other sign of hypersensitivity). Anaphylactoid reactions may occur, even without prior exposure; patients with "aspirin triad" (bronchial asthma, aspirin intolerance, rhinitis) may be at increased risk. Contraindicated in patients who experience bronchospasm, asthma, rhinitis, or urticaria with NSAID or aspirin therapy. Use caution in other forms of asthma. Use with caution in patients with hepatic impairment; patients with hepatic impairment may require reduced doses due to extensive hepatic metabolism. Patients with advanced hepatic disease are at an increased risk of GI bleeding with NSAIDs. Transaminase elevations have been reported with use; closely monitor patients with any abnormal LFT. Rare (sometimes fatal) severe hepatic reactions (eg, fulminant hepatitis, liver necrosis, hepatic failure) have occurred with NSAID use; discontinue immediately if signs or symptoms of hepatic disease develop or if systemic manifestations occur.

NSAIDs may cause drowsiness, dizziness, blurred vision, and other neurologic effects which may impair physical or mental abilities; patients must be cautioned about performing tasks that require mental alertness (eg, operating machinery or driving). Potentially significant interactions may exist, requiring dose or frequency adjustment, additional monitoring, and/or selection of alternative therapy. Blurred and/or diminished vision has been reported; discontinue use and refer for ophthalmologic evaluation if such symptoms occur. Elderly patients are at greater risk for serious GI, cardiovascular, and/or renal adverse events. Use with caution; initiate dose at the lower end of the dosing range.

Oral suspension formulation may contain sorbitol. Concomitant use with sodium polystyrene sulfonate (Kayexalate) may cause intestinal necrosis (including fatal cases); combined use should be avoided. Withhold for at least 4 to 6 half-lives prior to surgical or dental procedures.

Drug Interactions

Metabolism/Transport Effects **Substrate** of CYP2C9 (major), CYP3A4 (minor); **Note:** Assignment of Major/Minor substrate status based on clinically relevant drug interaction potential

Avoid Concomitant Use

Avoid concomitant use of Meloxicam with any of the following: Calcium Polystyrene Sulfonate; Dexketoprofen; Floctafenine; Ketorolac (Nasal); Ketorolac (Systemic); Morniflumate; NSAID (COX-2 Inhibitor); Omacetaxine; Pelubiprofen; Phenylbutazone; Sodium Polystyrene Sulfonate; Talniflumate; Tenoxicam; Urokinase; Zaltoprofen

Increased Effect/Toxicity

Meloxicam may increase the levels/effects of: 5-ASA Derivatives; Agents with Antiplatelet Properties; Aliskiren; Aminoglycosides; Aminolevulinic Acid; Anticoagulants; Apixaban; Bisphosphonate Derivatives; Calcium Polystyrene Sulfonate; Cephalothin; Collagenase (Systemic); CycloSPORINE (Systemic); Dabigatran Etexilate; Deferasirox; Deoxycholic Acid; Desmopressin; Digoxin; Drospirenone; Edoxaban; Eplerenone; Haloperidol; Ibritumomab; Lithium; Methotrexate; Nonsteroidal Anti-Inflammatory Agents; NSAID (COX-2 Inhibitor); Obinutuzumab; Omacetaxine; PEMEtrexed; Porfimer; Potassium-Sparing Diuretics; PRALAtrexate; Quinolone Antibiotics; Rivaroxaban; Salicylates; Sodium Polystyrene Sulfonate; Tacrolimus (Systemic); Tenofovir Products; Thrombolytic Agents; Tolperisone; Tositumomab and Iodine I 131 Tositumomab; Urokinase; Vancomycin; Verteporfin; Vitamin K Antagonists

The levels/effects of Meloxicam may be increased by: ACE Inhibitors; Alcohol (Ethyl); Angiotensin II Receptor Blockers; Antidepressants (Tricyclic, Tertiary Amine); Ceritinib; Corticosteroids (Systemic); CycloSPORINE (Systemic); CYP2C9 Inhibitors (Moderate); CYP2C9 Inhibitors (Strong); Dasatinib; Dexketoprofen; Diclofenac (Systemic); Felbinac; Floctafenine; Glucosamine; Herbs (Anticoagulant/Antiplatelet Properties); Ibrutinib; Ketorolac (Nasal); Ketorolac (Systemic); Limaprost; Loop Diuretics; Lumacaftor; MiFEPRIStone; Morniflumate; Multivitamins/Fluoride (with ADE); Multivitamins/Minerals (with ADEK, Folate, Iron); Multivitamins/Minerals (with AE, No Iron); Naftazone; Omega-3 Fatty Acids; Pelubiprofen; Pentosan Polysulfate Sodium; Pentoxifylline; Phenylbutazone; Probenecid; Prostacyclin Analogues; Selective Serotonin Reuptake Inhibitors; Serotonin/Norepinephrine Reuptake Inhibitors; Sodium Phosphates; Talniflumate; Tenoxicam; Thiazide and Thiazide-Like Diuretics; Tipranavir; Tolperisone; Vitamin E (Systemic); Voriconazole; Zaltoprofen

Decreased Effect

Meloxicam may decrease the levels/effects of: ACE Inhibitors; Aliskiren; Angiotensin II Receptor Blockers; Beta-Blockers; Eplerenone; HydrALAZINE; Loop Diuretics; Potassium-Sparing Diuretics; Prostaglandins (Ophthalmic); Salicylates; Selective Serotonin Reuptake Inhibitors; Thiazide and Thiazide-Like Diuretics

The levels/effects of Meloxicam may be decreased by: Bile Acid Sequestrants; CYP2C9 Inducers (Strong); Dabrafenib; Enzalutamide; Itraconazole; Lumacaftor; Salicylates

Dietary Considerations May be taken with food or milk to minimize gastrointestinal irritation.

Pharmacodynamics/Kinetics

Half-life Elimination

Children 2 to 6 years (n=7): 13.4 hours (Burgos-Vargas 2004)

Children and Adolescents 7 to 16 years (n=11): 12.7 hours (Burgos-Vargas 2004)

Adults: ~15 to 22 hours

Time to Peak

Children and Adolescents 2 to 16 years (n=18): Suspension: Initial: 1 to 3 hours; secondary: 6 to 12 hours (Burgos-Vargas 2004)

Adults: Initial: Within 2 hours (capsule); 4 to 5 hours (tablet); Secondary: ~8 hours (capsule); 12 to 14 hours (tablet)

Pregnancy Considerations Adverse events have been observed in the initial animal reproduction studies. Meloxicam crosses the placenta. NSAID exposure during the first trimester is not strongly associated with congenital malformations; however, cardiovascular anomalies and cleft palate have been observed following NSAID exposure in some studies. The use of an NSAID close to conception may be associated with an increased risk of miscarriage. Nonteratogenic effects have been observed following NSAID administration during the third trimester including myocardial degenerative changes, prenatal constriction of the ductus arteriosus, fetal tricuspid regurgitation, failure of the ductus arteriosus to close postnatally; renal dysfunction or failure, oligohydramnios; GI bleeding or perforation, increased risk of necrotizing enterocolitis; intracranial bleeding (including intraventricular hemorrhage), platelet dysfunction with resultant bleeding; pulmonary hypertension. Because they may cause premature closure of the ductus arteriosus, use of NSAIDs late in pregnancy should be avoided (use after 31 or 32 weeks gestation is not recommended by some clinicians). Product labeling for meloxicam specifically notes that use at ≥30 weeks' gestation should be avoided. The chronic use of NSAIDs in women of reproductive age may be associated with infertility that is reversible upon discontinuation of the medication.

Breastfeeding Considerations It is not known if meloxicam is excreted in breast milk. According to the manufacturer, the decision to breast-feed during therapy should take into account the risk of exposure to the infant and the benefits of treatment to the mother.

Dosage Forms Considerations

Meloxicam Comfort Pac is a kit containing meloxicam oral tablets 15 mg, and Duraflex topical gel.

Dosage Forms

Capsule, Oral:

Vivlodex: 5 mg, 10 mg

Kit, Combination:

Meloxicam Comfort Pac: 15 mg

Tablet, Oral:

Mobic: 7.5 mg, 15 mg

Generic: 7.5 mg, 15 mg, 15 mg

Dosage Forms: Canada **Note:** Refer also to Dosage Forms. Combination kit and oral suspension are not available in Canada.

Tablet, Oral:
Mobicox: 7.5 mg, 15 mg

Melphalan (MEL fa lan)

Brand Names: US Alkeran; Evomela

Brand Names: Canada Alkeran

Pharmacologic Category Antineoplastic Agent, Alkylating Agent; Antineoplastic Agent, Alkylating Agent (Nitrogen Mustard)

Use

Multiple myeloma: Palliative treatment of multiple myeloma (injection [Alkeran and Evomela] and tablets); high-dose conditioning treatment prior to hematopoietic stem cell transplantation (HSCT) (Evomela only).

Ovarian cancer: Palliative treatment of nonresectable epithelial ovarian carcinoma (tablets)

Local Anesthetic/Vasoconstrictor Precautions No information available to require special precautions

Effects on Dental Treatment Key adverse event(s) related to dental treatment: Stomatitis.

Effects on Bleeding Severe myelosuppression including anemia and thrombocytopenia occurs which may result in bleeding. Medical consult recommended.

Adverse Reactions

>10%:

Cardiovascular: Peripheral edema (conditioning: 33%)

Central nervous system: Fatigue (≥50%; conditioning: 77%), dizziness (conditioning: 38%)

Endocrine & metabolic: Hypokalemia (≥50% conditioning: 74%), hypophosphatemia (conditioning: 49%)

Gastrointestinal: Diarrhea (≥50%; conditioning: 93%), nausea (≥50%; conditioning: 90%), vomiting (≥50%; conditioning: 64%), decreased appetite (conditioning: 49%), constipation (conditioning: 48%), mucositis (conditioning: 38%), abdominal pain (conditioning: 28%), dysgeusia (conditioning: 28%), stomatitis (conditioning: 28%), dyspepsia (conditioning: 26%)

Hematologic & oncologic: Anemia (≥50%), decreased absolute lymphocyte count (≥50%), decreased neutrophils (≥50%), decreased platelet count (≥50%; nadir: 14 to 21 days; recovery: 28 to 35 days), decreased white blood cell count (≥50%; nadir: 14 to 21 days; recovery: 28 to 35 days), febrile neutropenia (conditioning: 41%; grades 3/4: 28%)

Miscellaneous: Fever (conditioning: 48%)

1% to 10%:

Gastrointestinal: Hematochezia

Genitourinary: Amenorrhea (9%)

Hypersensitivity: Hypersensitivity reaction (IV: 2%; less common in oral formula; includes bronchospasm, dyspnea, edema, hypotension, pruritus, skin rash, tachycardia, urticaria), anaphylaxis (≤2%)

Renal: Renal failure

Frequency not defined:

Cardiovascular: Hepatic veno-occlusive disease (hepatic sinusoidal obstruction syndrome; SOS), vasculitis

Central nervous system: Flushing sensation, tingling sensation

Endocrine & metabolic: SIADH (dose related; Greenbaum-Lefkoe 1985)

Genitourinary: Infertility, inhibition of testicular function

Hematologic & oncologic: Bone marrow depression

Hepatic: Hepatitis, increased serum transaminases, jaundice

Renal: Increased blood urea nitrogen

Miscellaneous: Chromosomal abnormality

<1%, postmarketing, and/or case reports: Alopecia, bone marrow failure (irreversible), hemolytic anemia, interstitial pneumonitis, maculopapular rash, pulmonary fibrosis, skin ulceration at injection site, tissue necrosis at injection site (rarely requiring skin grafting)

General Dosage Range Dosage adjustment recommended in patients with renal impairment or who develop toxicities

IV: *Adults:* 16 mg/m^2 administered at 2-week intervals for 4 doses, then repeat at 4-week intervals (palliative treatment) **or** 100 mg/m^2 daily for 2 days on day -3 and day -2 prior to autologous stem cell transplantation on day 0.

Oral: *Adults:* Dosage varies greatly depending on indication

Mechanism of Action Alkylating agent which is a derivative of mechlorethamine that inhibits DNA and RNA synthesis via formation of carbonium ions; cross-links strands of DNA; acts on both resting and rapidly dividing tumor cells.

Pharmacodynamics/Kinetics

Half-life Elimination Terminal: IV: ~75 minutes; Oral: 1.5 ± 0.83 hours

Time to Peak Serum: Oral: ~1 to 2 hours

Pregnancy Risk Factor D

Pregnancy Considerations Adverse effects have been observed in animal reproduction studies. May cause fetal harm if administered during pregnancy. Women of reproductive potential should be advised to avoid pregnancy while on and after melphalan therapy. Males with female partners of reproductive potential should use effective contraception during and after melphalan treatment. Therapy may suppress ovarian function leading to amenorrhea. Reversible and irreversible testicular suppression has been reported in male patients after melphalan administration.

Memantine (me MAN teen)

Brand Names: US Namenda; Namenda Titration Pak; Namenda XR; Namenda XR Titration Pack

Brand Names: Canada ACT Memantine; Apo-Memantine; Ebixa; Med-Memantine; Mylan-Memantine; PMS-Memantine; RAN-Memantine; ratio-Memantine; Riva-Memantine; Sandoz-Memantine

Pharmacologic Category N-Methyl-D-Aspartate Receptor Antagonist

Use Alzheimer disease: Treatment of moderate to severe dementia of the Alzheimer type.

Local Anesthetic/Vasoconstrictor Precautions No information available to require special precautions

Effects on Dental Treatment No significant effects or complications reported

Effects on Bleeding No information available to require special precautions

Adverse Reactions Adverse reactions similar in immediate and extended release formulations except as noted.

1% to 10%:

Cardiovascular: Hypertension (4%), hypotension (extended release: 2%)

Central nervous system: Dizziness (5% to 7%), confusion (6%), headache (6%), anxiety (extended release: 4%), depression (extended release: 3%), drowsiness (3%), hallucination (3%), pain (3%), aggressive behavior (2%), fatigue (2%)

Endocrine & metabolic: Weight gain (extended release: 3%)

Gastrointestinal: Diarrhea (5%), constipation (3% to 5%), vomiting (2% to 3%), abdominal pain (2%)
Genitourinary: Urinary incontinence (2%)
Infection: Influenza (4%)
Neuromuscular & skeletal: Back pain (3%)
Respiratory: Cough (4%), dyspnea (2%)

<1%, postmarketing, and/or case reports: Abnormal gait, abnormal hepatic function tests, acne vulgaris, agitation, agranulocytosis, anorexia, arthralgia, aspiration pneumonia, atrioventricular block, bone fracture, bradycardia, brain disease, bronchitis, cardiac failure, carpal tunnel syndrome, cerebral infarction, cerebrovascular accident, chest pain, cholelithiasis, claudication, colitis, coma, complete atrioventricular block, convulsions, decreased appetite, deep vein thrombosis, dehydration, delusions, dementia (Alzheimer type), disorientation, drug-induced Parkinson disease, dyskinesia, falling, fecal incontinence, fever, gastritis, gastroesophageal reflux disease, hepatic failure, hepatitis (including cytolytic and cholestatic), hyperglycemia, hyperlipidemia, hypoglycemia, impaired consciousness, impotence, increased INR, increased serum alkaline phosphatase, increased serum creatinine, insomnia, intracranial hemorrhage, irritability, lethargy, leukopenia, limb pain, loss of consciousness, malaise, myoclonus, nasopharyngitis, nausea, neuroleptic malignant syndrome, neutropenia, otitis media, pancreatitis, pancytopenia, peripheral edema, prolonged Q-T interval on ECG, psychotic reaction, renal failure, renal function test abnormality, renal insufficiency, restlessness, second degree atrioventricular block, sepsis, SIADH, Stevens-Johnson syndrome, suicidal ideation, suicidal tendencies, supraventricular tachycardia, tardive dyskinesia, thrombocytopenia, thrombotic thrombocytopenic purpura, tonic-clonic seizures, torsades de pointes, tremor, upper respiratory tract infection, urinary tract infection, weakness

General Dosage Range Dosage adjustment recommended in patients with renal impairment

Oral: *Adults:* Immediate release: Initial: 5 mg once daily; Target: 20 mg daily in 2 divided doses; Extended release: Initial: 7 mg once daily; Target: 28 mg once daily

Mechanism of Action Glutamate, the primary excitatory amino acid in the CNS, may contribute to the pathogenesis of Alzheimer's disease (AD) by overstimulating various glutamate receptors leading to excitotoxicity and neuronal cell death. Memantine is an uncompetitive antagonist of the N-methyl-D-aspartate (NMDA) type of glutamate receptors, located ubiquitously throughout the brain. Under normal physiologic conditions, the (unstimulated) NMDA receptor ion channel is blocked by magnesium ions, which are displaced after agonist-induced depolarization. Pathologic or excessive receptor activation, as postulated to occur during AD, prevents magnesium from reentering and blocking the channel pore resulting in a chronically open state and excessive calcium influx. Memantine binds to the intra-pore magnesium site, but with longer dwell time, and thus functions as an effective receptor blocker only under conditions of excessive stimulation; memantine does not affect normal neurotransmission.

Pharmacodynamics/Kinetics

Half-life Elimination Terminal: ~60 to 80 hours

Time to Peak Time to peak, serum: Immediate release: 3 to 7 hours; Extended release: 9 to 12 hours

Pregnancy Risk Factor B

Pregnancy Considerations Adverse events have been observed in animal reproduction studies.

Meningococcal Group B Vaccine

(me NIN joe kok al groop bee vak SEEN)

Brand Names: US Bexsero; Trumenba

Brand Names: Canada Bexsero

Pharmacologic Category Vaccine; Vaccine, Inactivated (Bacterial)

Use Meningococcal disease prevention:

US labeling: Active immunization of children, adolescents, and adults aged 10 to 25 years against invasive meningococcal disease caused by *N. meningitidis* serogroup B.

The Advisory Committee on Immunization Practices (ACIP) recommends routine vaccination of certain groups of persons ≥10 years of age (ACIP [Folaranmi 2015]):

- Persons with persistent complement component deficiencies (including patients who are taking eculizumab [Solaris])
- Persons with anatomic or functional asplenia (including sickle cell disease)
- Microbiologists routinely exposed to isolates of *Neisseria meningitidis*
- Persons identified to be at increased risk due to a serogroup B meningococcal disease outbreak

The ACIP states that a meningococcal group B vaccination series may be administered to adolescents and young adults aged 16 to 23 years to provide short term protection against most strains of serogroup B meningococcal disease. The preferred age for vaccination is 16 to 18 years (ACIP [MacNeil 2015]).

Canadian labeling: Additional ages (not in US labeling): Bexsero: Indicated for infants ≥2 months, children, and adolescents through 17 years

Local Anesthetic/Vasoconstrictor Precautions No information available to require special precautions

Effects on Dental Treatment No significant effects or complications reported

Effects on Bleeding No information available to require special precautions

Adverse Reactions All serious adverse reactions must be reported to the US Department of Health and Human Services (DHHS) Vaccine Adverse Event Reporting System (VAERS) 1-800-822-7967 or online at https://vaers.hhs.gov/esub/index. In Canada, adverse reactions may be reported to local provincial/territorial health agencies or to the Vaccine Safety Section at Public Health Agency of Canada (1-866-844-0018). Frequencies reported may include concomitant administration with routine pediatric vaccines or other vaccines.

>10%:

Central nervous system: Irritability (infants and children ≤10 years: 43% to 79%), drowsiness (infants and children <2 years: 53% to 72%; children 2 to 10 years: 30% to 51%), excessive crying (infants and children <2 years: 56% to 69%; children 2 to 10 years: 27% to 33%), fatigue (children ≥10 years, adolescents, and adults: 35% to 62%), headache (10 to 25 years: 33% to 55%; children 2 to 10 years: 10% to 20%; adults >14%), malaise (children and adolescents 11 to 17 years: 50% to 56%; adults: 14%), chills (children and adolescents 11 to 17 years: 16% to 29%)

Gastrointestinal: Change in appetite (infants and children ≤10 years: 21% to 51%), diarrhea (children 2 to 10 years: 2% to 37%; infants and children <2 years: 18% to 24%; children and adolescents 11 to 17: years 9% to 15%), nausea (children ≥10 years, adolescents, and adults: 16% to 19%), vomiting (infants, children, and adolescents: ≤13%)

Local: Pain at injection site (children ≥2 years, adolescents, and adults: 82% to 98%), erythema at injection site (children 2 to 10 years: 60% to 98%; infants and children <2 years: 60% to 64%; children ≥10 years, adolescents, and adults 45% to 54%), tenderness at injection site (children 2 to 10 years: 81% to 89%; infants and children <2 years: 65% to 66%), swelling at injection site (children 2 to 10 years: 26% to 63%; children and adolescents 11 to 17 years: 18% to 39%; infants and children <2 years: 26% to 31%), induration at injection site (infants and children ≤10 years: 33% to 56%; children ≥10 years, adolescents, and adults: 28% to 40%)

Neuromuscular & skeletal: Myalgia (children ≥10 years, adolescents, and adults: 31% to 57%), arthralgia (children ≥2 years, adolescents, and adults: 13% to 33%)

Miscellaneous: Fever (infants and children <2 years: 69% to 79%, ≥40°C [104°F] ≤1%; children 2 to 10 years: 10% to 28%, ≥40°C [104°F] ≤3%; children 10 years, adolescents, and adults: 1% to 8%)

1% to 10%:

Dermatologic: Skin rash (children 2 to 10 years: ≤9%), urticaria (infants and children <2 years: 5% to 6%)

Respiratory: Upper respiratory tract infection (infants ≤7 months: 10%; mostly considered unrelated to vaccination), nasopharyngitis (children ≥10 years, adolescents, and adults: ≥2%)

<1% (postmarketing, and/or case reports): Eczema (infants and children <2 years), febrile seizures (infants and children <2 years), hypersensitivity reaction (includes anaphylaxis), injection site blister formation, Kawasaki syndrome (infants and children <2 years), pallor (infants and children <2 years), seizure (infants and children <2 years), swelling of eye, syncope, vasodepressor syncope

Mechanism of Action

Bexsero: Induces immunity against meningococcal disease caused by serogroup B *Neisseria meningitidis* (MenB) via the formation of antibodies directed toward the recombinant protein antigens combined together with outer membrane vesicles (OMV) from a group B strain.

Trumenba: Protection against invasive meningococcal disease is conferred mainly by complement-mediated antibody-dependent killing of *N. meningitidis*.

Efficacy:

Bexsero: Composite hSBA titer response one month after the second dose: 63% to 88%

Trumenba: 84% of adolescents had a ≥4-fold rise in hSBA titer and composite response after the third dose.

Pregnancy Risk Factor B

Pregnancy Considerations Adverse events were not observed in animal reproduction studies. Inactivated vaccines have not been shown to cause increased risks to the fetus (NCIRD/ACIP 2011).

Health care providers are encouraged to enroll women exposed to Bexsero during pregnancy in the Bexsero Pregnancy Registry (1-877- 413-4759); women may also enroll themselves.

Meningococcal (Groups A / C / Y and W-135) Diphtheria Conjugate Vaccine

(me NIN joe kok al groops aye, see, why & dubl yoo won thur tee fyve dif THEER ee a KON joo gate vak SEEN)

Brand Names: US Menactra; Menveo

Brand Names: Canada Menactra; Menveo

Pharmacologic Category Vaccine; Vaccine, Inactivated (Bacterial)

Use

Meningococcal disease prevention: Provide active immunization against invasive meningococcal disease caused by *N. meningitidis* serogroups A, C, Y, and W-135.

The Advisory Committee on Immunization Practices (ACIP) (CDC/ACIP [Cohn 2013]; CDC/ACIP [MacNeil 2014]; CDC/ACIP [MacNeil 2016]):

ACIP recommends routine vaccination of the following:

- Children and adolescents 11 to 18 years of age
- Persons ≥2 months of age who are at increased risk of meningococcal disease
- Persons (in all recommended age groups) at increased risk who are part of outbreaks caused by vaccine preventable serogroups

Those at increased risk of meningococcal disease include the following:

- Persons ≥2 months with medical conditions such as anatomic or functional asplenia (including sickle cell disease), HIV, or persistent compliment component deficiencies (eg, C_5-C_9, properdin, factor H, or factor D)
- Persons ≥2 months of age that travel to or reside in countries where meningococcal disease is hyperendemic or epidemic, especially if contact with the local population will be prolonged
- Unvaccinated or incompletely vaccinated first year college students living in residence halls
- Military recruits
- Microbiologists with occupational exposure

The Canadian National Advisory Committee on Immunization (NACI): NACI recommends a routine vaccination at ~12 years of age but no booster unless at a continued high risk of exposure. Either quadrivalent vaccine may be used; NACI does not have a preference. NACI recommends use of Menveo (off-label use) for high risk persons 2 months to 2 years of age if vaccination with a quadrivalent vaccine is needed; may also be considered for use in persons ≥56 years of age (NACI, 39[1] 2013). Additional recommendations may be found at www.phac-aspc.gc.ca/publicat/ccdr-rmtc/13vol39/acs-dcc-1/index-eng.-php

Local Anesthetic/Vasoconstrictor Precautions No information available to require special precautions

Effects on Dental Treatment No significant effects or complications reported

Effects on Bleeding No information available to require special precautions

Adverse Reactions Actual percentages may vary by product and age group:

>10%:

Central nervous system: Drowsiness, excessive crying, fatigue, headache, irritability, malaise

Gastrointestinal: Anorexia, change in appetite, diarrhea, nausea, vomiting

Local: Erythema at injection site, induration at injection site, pain at injection site, swelling at injection site, tenderness at injection site

Neuromuscular & skeletal: Arthralgia, myalgia
Miscellaneous: Fever

1% to 10%:
Central nervous system: Chills
Dermatologic: Skin rash

<1%, postmarketing, and/or case reports: Acute disseminated encephalomyelitis, anaphylactoid reaction, anaphylaxis, apnea (premature infants), appendicitis, auditory impairment, Bell's palsy, blepharoptosis, convulsions (including tonic), Cushing's syndrome, dehydration, depression, dizziness, dyspnea, equilibrium disturbance, exfoliation of skin, facial paresis, falling, febrile seizures, gastroenteritis, Guillain-Barre syndrome, hypersensitivity, hypotension, increased serum ALT, inflammation at injection site, injection site cellulitis, Kawasaki syndrome, laryngitis, oropharyngeal pain, ostealgia, otalgia, paresthesia, pelvic inflammatory disease, pneumonia, pruritus, pruritus at injection site, seizure, simple partial seizures, staphylococcal infection, suicidal tendencies, syncope (including vasovagal), transverse myelitis, upper airway swelling, urticaria, varicella, vertebral disc disease, vertigo, vestibular disturbance, viral hepatitis, wheezing

General Dosage Range IM:

Menactra:

Infants ≥9 months and Children <2 years: 0.5 mL/dose given as a 2-dose series, 3 months apart

Children ≥2 years, Adolescents, and Adults ≤55 years: 0.5 mL as a single dose

Menveo: Age at initial vaccination:

Infants ≥2 months to <7 months: 0.5 mL/dose given as a 4-dose series at 2, 4, 6, and 12 months of age

Infants ≥7 months and Children <2 years: 0.5 mL/dose given as a 2-dose series, with the second dose given during the second year of life and at least 3 months after the first dose

Children ≥2 to <6 years: 0.5 mL/dose given as a single dose; for children at continued high risk of meningococcal disease, give an additional dose given 2 months after the first dose

Children ≥6 years, Adolescents, and Adults ≤55 years: 0.5 mL/dose given as a single dose

Mechanism of Action Induces immunity against meningococcal disease via the formation of bactericidal antibodies directed toward the polysaccharide capsular components of *Neisseria meningitidis* serogroups A, C, Y and W-135.

Pregnancy Risk Factor B

Pregnancy Considerations Adverse events were not observed in animal reproduction studies conducted with Menactra. Limited information is available following inadvertent use of Menactra during pregnancy (Zheteyeva 2013). Patients should contact the Sanofi Pasteur Inc vaccine registry at 1-800-822-2463 if they are pregnant or become aware they were pregnant at the time of Menactra vaccination.

Adverse events were not observed in animal reproduction studies conducted with Menveo. Limited information is available following inadvertent use of Menveo during pregnancy. Patients should contact the Novartis Vaccines and Diagnostics Inc. pregnancy registry at 1-877-413-4759 if they are pregnant or become aware they were pregnant at the time of Menveo vaccination.

Inactivated bacterial vaccines have not been shown to cause increased risks to the fetus (NCIRD/ACIP 2011). Pregnancy should not preclude vaccination if indicated (CDC/ACIP [Cohn 2013]).

Meningococcal Polysaccharide (Groups C and Y) and *Haemophilus* b Tetanus Toxoid Conjugate Vaccine

(me NIN joe kok al pol i SAK a ride groops see & why & he MOF i lus bee TET a nus TOKS oyd KON joo gate vak SEEN)

Brand Names: US Menhibrix

Pharmacologic Category Vaccine; Vaccine, Inactivated (Bacterial)

Use Meningococcal and *Haemophilus influenza* type b disease prevention: To provide active immunity to prevent invasive disease caused by meningococcal serogroups C and Y and *Haemophilus influenzae* type b

The Advisory Committee on Immunization Practices (ACIP) (CDC/ACIP [Cohn 2013]) recommends vaccination only for infants 2-18 months of age who are at increased risk for meningococcal disease, including:

- Infants with persistent complement pathway deficiencies
- Infants with anatomic or functional asplenia, including sickle cell disease
- Infants in communities with serogroups C and Y meningococcal disease outbreaks

The ACIP does not recommend routine vaccination for infants not at increased risk for meningococcal disease. In addition, infants traveling to certain areas (eg, meningitis belt of sub-Saharan Africa) will require a meningococcal vaccine with serogroups A and W_{135}; vaccination with Hib-MenCY-TT will not be adequate (CDC/ACIP [Cohn 2013])

Local Anesthetic/Vasoconstrictor Precautions No information available to require special precautions

Effects on Dental Treatment No significant effects or complications reported

Effects on Bleeding No information available to require special precautions

Adverse Reactions

>10%:
Central nervous system: Irritability (62% to 71%), drowsiness (49% to 63%)
Gastrointestinal: Decreased appetite (30% to 34%)
Local: Pain at injection site (41% to 46%), erythema at injection site (21% to 36%), swelling at injection site (15% to 25%)
Miscellaneous: Fever ≥100.4°F/38°C (11% to 26%)

<1%, postmarketing, and/or case reports: Anaphylactoid reaction, anaphylaxis, angioedema, apnea, hypersensitivity reaction, hypotonic/hyporesponsive episode, induration at injection site, seizure (with or without fever), skin rash, swelling of injected limb (extensive), syncope, urticaria, vasodepressor syncope

General Dosage Range

IM: *Infants ≥6 weeks and Children ≤18 months:* 0.5 mL/dose given as a four-dose series at 2, 4, 6, and 12-15 months of age

Mechanism of Action Provides active immunity against meningococcal disease via the formation of bactericidal antibodies directed toward the polysaccharide capsular components of *Neisseria meningitidis* serogroups C and Y; stimulates production of anticapsular antibodies and to *Haemophilus influenzae* type b

Pharmacodynamics/Kinetics

Onset of Action Antibody response to the components of the vaccine occurs in ≥95% of children following the third dose and ≥98% following the fourth dose.

Pregnancy Risk Factor C

Pregnancy Considerations Animal reproduction studies have not been conducted.

Meningococcal Polysaccharide Vaccine (Groups A, C, Y, and W-135)

(me NIN joe kok al pol i SAK a ride vak SEEN groops aye, see, why & dubl yoo won thur tee fyve)

Brand Names: US Menomune-A/C/Y/W-135

Brand Names: Canada Menomune-A/C/Y/W-135

Pharmacologic Category Vaccine; Vaccine, Inactivated (Bacterial)

Use

Meningococcal disease prevention: Active immunization of patients 2 years and older to prevent invasive meningococcal disease caused by *Neisseria meningitidis* serogroups A, C, Y, and W-135.

The Advisory Committee on Immunization Practices (ACIP) recommends routine vaccination for persons at increased risk for meningococcal disease. Meningococcal quadrivalent conjugate vaccine (MenACWY; Menactra, Menveo) is preferred; meningococcal polysaccharide vaccine (MPSV4; Menomune) is preferred in meningococcal vaccine-naive adults ≥56 years of age requiring only a single vaccination (CDC/ACIP [Cohn 2013]).

Those at increased risk of meningococcal disease include the following:

- Persons ≥2 months of age with medical conditions such as anatomical or functional asplenia or persistent compliment component deficiencies (eg, C_5-C_9, properdin, factor H, or factor D)
- Persons ≥9 months of age that travel to or reside in countries where meningococcal disease is hyperendemic or epidemic, especially if contact with the local population will be prolonged
- Unvaccinated or incompletely vaccinated first year college students living in residence halls
- Military recruits
- Microbiologists with occupational exposure
- Persons (in all recommended age groups) at risk who are part of outbreaks caused by vaccine preventable serogroups

Local Anesthetic/Vasoconstrictor Precautions No information available to require special precautions

Effects on Dental Treatment No significant effects or complications reported

Effects on Bleeding No information available to require special precautions

Adverse Reactions

>10%:

Central nervous system: Headache (29% to 42%), fatigue (children ≥11 years, adolescents, and adults: 25% to 32%), malaise (children ≥11 years, adolescents, and adults: 17% to 22%), irritability (children 2 to 10 years: 12%), drowsiness (children 2 to 10 years: 11%)

Gastrointestinal: Diarrhea (10% to 14%)

Local: Pain at injection site (adults: 48%; children and adolescents 2 to 18 years: 26% to 29%), erythema at injection site (adults: 16%; children and adolescents 2 to 18 years: 6% to 8%), induration at injection site (4% to 11%)

Neuromuscular & skeletal: Arthralgia (adults: 16%; children and adolescents 2 to 18 years: 5% to 10%)

1% to 10%:

Central nervous system: Chills (children ≥11 years, adolescents, and adults: 4% to 6%)

Dermatologic: Skin rash (children and adolescents 2 to 18 years: 1% to 3%; adults: <1%)

Gastrointestinal: Anorexia (8% to 10%), vomiting (1% to 3%)

Local: Swelling at injection site (3% to 8%)

Miscellaneous: Fever (children and adolescents 2 to 18 years: 3% to 5%; adults: <1%)

Postmarketing and/or case reports: Dizziness, Guillain-Barré syndrome, hypersensitivity (angioedema, dyspnea, pruritus, rash, urticaria), myalgia, nausea, paresthesia, vasodepressor syncope, weakness

General Dosage Range SubQ: *Children ≥2 years, Adolescents, and Adults:* 0.5 mL as a single dose

Mechanism of Action Induces the formation of bactericidal antibodies to meningococcal antigens; the presence of these antibodies is strongly correlated with immunity to meningococcal disease caused by *Neisseria meningitidis* groups A, C, Y and W-135.

Pharmacodynamics/Kinetics

Onset of Action Antibody levels: 7-10 days

Duration of Action Antibodies against group A and C polysaccharides decline markedly (to prevaccination levels) over the first 3 years following a single dose of vaccine, especially in children <4 years of age

Pregnancy Risk Factor C

Pregnancy Considerations Animal reproduction studies have not been conducted. Inactivated bacterial vaccines have not been shown to cause increased risks to the fetus (NCIRD/ACIP 2011). Pregnancy should not preclude vaccination if indicated (CDC/ACIP [Cohn 2013]).

Menotropins

(men oh TROE pins)

Brand Names: US Menopur; Repronex [DSC]

Brand Names: Canada Menopur; Repronex

Pharmacologic Category Gonadotropin; Ovulation Stimulator

Use

Menopur: For multiple follicle development and pregnancy in ovulatory women as part of an assisted reproductive technology (ART) cycle

Repronex: In conjunction with hCG to for multiple follicular development (controlled ovarian stimulation) and ovulation induction in women who have previously received GnRH agonist or antagonist for pituitary suppression

Limitations of use: Prior to therapy, preform a complete gynecologic exam and endocrinologic evaluation to diagnose the cause of infertility; exclude the possibility of pregnancy; evaluate the fertility status of the male partner; exclude a diagnosis of primary ovarian failure.

Local Anesthetic/Vasoconstrictor Precautions No information available to require special precautions

Effects on Dental Treatment No significant effects or complications reported

Effects on Bleeding Has been associated with thrombotic events; however, no information available to require special precautions in dental procedures.

Adverse Reactions Adverse effects may vary according to specific product, route, and/or dosage.

>10%:

Central nervous system: Headache (≤34%)

Gastrointestinal: Abdominal pain (≤18%), nausea (≤12%)

Endocrine & metabolic: Ovarian hyperstimulation syndrome (≤13%; dose related)

Local: Injection site reaction (4% to 12%)

1% to 10%:
- Cardiovascular: Flushing
- Central nervous system: Dizziness, malaise, migraine
- Endocrine & metabolic: Hot flash, menstrual disease, ovarian disease
- Gastrointestinal: Abdominal cramps, constipation, diarrhea, enlargement of abdomen, gastrointestinal fullness, vomiting
- Genitourinary: Breast tenderness, ectopic pregnancy, vaginal hemorrhage
- Infection: Infection
- Local: Pain at injection site, swelling at injection site
- Neuromuscular & skeletal: Back pain
- Respiratory: Cough, flu-like symptoms, respiratory tract disease

Frequency not defined:
- Cardiovascular: Cerebrovascular accident, embolism, tachycardia, thrombosis (arterial or venous)
- Dermatologic: Skin rash, urticaria
- Endocrine & metabolic: Ovary enlargement
- Hematologic & oncologic: Hemoperitoneum
- Hypersensitivity: Anaphylaxis, angioedema, hypersensitivity reaction
- Local: Local tissue necrosis (limb necrosis)
- Respiratory: Acute respiratory distress, atelectasis, dyspnea, laryngeal edema, tachypnea
- Miscellaneous: Organ infarction (lung), ovarian torsion

General Dosage Range

IM: *Adults (females):* Repronex: Initial; 150 units daily for 5 days **or** 225 units daily; Maintenance: up to 450 units daily (maximum: 12 days of therapy)

SubQ: *Adults (females):* Menopur: Initial: 225 units daily for 5 days; Maintenance: up to 450 units daily (maximum: 20 days of therapy); Repronex: Initial: 150 units daily for 5 days **or** 225 units daily; Maintenance: up to 450 units daily (maximum: 12 days of therapy)

Mechanism of Action Menotropins is a purified combination of follicle stimulating hormone (FSH) and luteinizing hormone (LH) extracted from the urine of postmenopausal women. Treatment provides ovarian follicular growth and maturation in females who do not have primary ovarian failure. Also stimulates spermatogenesis in males (off-label use)

Pharmacodynamics/Kinetics

Half-life Elimination

Menopur: FSH 11-13 hours (following multiple doses)

Repronex: FSH ~54-59 hours (following a single dose)

Time to Peak FSH (following a single dose): Menopur: 18 hours (SubQ); Repronex: 12 hours (SubQ), 18 hours (IM)

Pregnancy Risk Factor X

Pregnancy Considerations Ectopic pregnancy, congenital abnormalities, spontaneous abortion, and multifetal gestations/births have been reported. The incidence of congenital abnormality may be slightly higher after ART than with spontaneous conception; higher incidence may be related to parenteral characteristics (maternal age, genetics, sperm characteristics). Menotropins are used for the induction of ovulation and with ART; use is contraindicated in women who are already pregnant.

Mepenzolate (me PEN zoe late)

Brand Names: US Cantil [DSC]

Brand Names: Canada Cantil®

Pharmacologic Category Anticholinergic Agent; Antispasmodic Agent, Gastrointestinal

Use Adjunctive treatment of peptic ulcer disease; has not been shown to be effective in contributing to the healing of peptic ulcer, preventing complications, or decreasing the rate of recurrence

Local Anesthetic/Vasoconstrictor Precautions No information available to require special precautions

Effects on Dental Treatment Key adverse event(s) related to dental treatment: Xerostomia (normal salivary flow resumes upon discontinuation), dry throat, dysphagia, and loss of taste.

Effects on Bleeding No information available to require special precautions

Adverse Reactions Frequency not defined.
- Cardiovascular: Palpitations, tachycardia
- Central nervous system: Confusion, dizziness, drowsiness, headache, insomnia, nervousness
- Dermatologic: Hypohidrosis, urticaria
- Gastrointestinal: Ageusia, bloating, constipation, delayed gastric emptying, nausea, vomiting, xerostomia
- Genitourinary: Decreased lactation, impotence, urinary hesitancy, urinary retention
- Hypersensitivity: Anaphylaxis
- Neuromuscular & skeletal: Weakness
- Ophthalmic: Blurred vision, cycloplegia, increased intraocular pressure, mydriasis

General Dosage Range Oral: *Adults:* 25-50 mg 4 times/day

Mechanism of Action Mepenzolate is a postganglionic parasympathetic inhibitor. It decreases gastric acid and pepsin secretion and suppresses spontaneous contractions of the colon.

Pregnancy Risk Factor B

Pregnancy Considerations Adverse events were not observed in animal reproduction studies.

Meperidine (me PER i deen)

Related Information

Management of the Patient With Anxiety or Depression *on page 1873*

Brand Names: US Demerol

Brand Names: Canada Demerol

Generic Availability (US) Yes

Pharmacologic Category Analgesic, Opioid

Dental Use Adjunct in preoperative intravenous conscious sedation in patients undergoing dental surgery; alternate oral opioid in patients allergic to codeine to treat moderate to moderate-severe pain

Use

Pain management: Management of acute pain severe enough to require an opioid analgesic and for which alternative treatments are inadequate; obstetrical analgesia; preoperative medication

Limitations of use: Reserve meperidine for use in patients for whom alternative treatment options (eg, non-opioid analgesics, opioid combination products) are ineffective, not tolerated, or would be otherwise inadequate to provide sufficient management of pain. Do not use for treatment of chronic pain. Prolonged use may increase the risk of toxicity (eg, seizures) from the accumulation of the meperidine metabolite, normeperidine.

Local Anesthetic/Vasoconstrictor Precautions No information available to require special precautions

Effects on Dental Treatment Key adverse event(s) related to dental treatment: Xerostomia (normal salivary flow resumes upon discontinuation). See Dental Comment.

Effects on Bleeding No information available to require special precautions

Adverse Reactions Frequency not defined.

Cardiovascular: Bradycardia, cardiac arrest, circulatory depression, flushing, hypotension, palpitations, shock, syncope, tachycardia

Central nervous system: Agitation, confusion, delirium, disorientation, dizziness, drug dependence (physical dependence), habituation, hallucination, headache, increased intracranial pressure, involuntary muscle movements (including muscle twitching, myoclonus), mood changes (including euphoria, dysphoria), sedation, seizure (associated with metabolite accumulation), serotonin syndrome

Dermatologic: Diaphoresis, pruritus, skin rash, urticaria

Gastrointestinal: Biliary colic, constipation, nausea, spasm of sphincter of Oddi, vomiting, xerostomia

Genitourinary: Urinary retention

Hypersensitivity: Anaphylaxis, histamine release, hypersensitivity reaction

Local: Injection site reaction (including pain, wheal, and flare)

Neuromuscular & skeletal: Tremor, weakness

Ophthalmic: Visual disturbance

Respiratory: Dyspnea, respiratory arrest, respiratory depression

<1%, postmarketing, and/or case reports: Hypogonadism (Brennan 2013; Debono 2011)

Dental Usual Dosage Note: The American Pain Society (2008) and ISMP (2007) do not recommend meperidine's use as an analgesic. If use in acute pain (in patients without renal or CNS disease) cannot be avoided, treatment should be limited to ≤48 hours and doses should not exceed 600 mg/24 hours. Oral route is not recommended for treatment of acute or chronic pain. If IV route is required, consider a reduced dose. Patients with prior opioid exposure may require higher initial doses.

Pain (analgesic): Adults: Oral: Initial: Opioid-naive: 50 mg every 3 to 4 hours as needed; usual dosage range: 50 to 150 mg every 3 to 4 hours as needed (manufacturer's recommendation; oral route is not recommended for acute pain)

Dosing

Adult Note: The American Pain Society (2008) and ISMP (2007) do not recommend meperidine's use as an analgesic. If use in acute pain (in patients without renal or CNS disease) cannot be avoided, treatment should be limited to ≤48 hours and doses should not exceed 600 mg/24 hours. Oral route is not recommended for treatment of acute or chronic pain. If IV route is required, consider a reduced dose. Patients with prior opioid exposure may require higher initial doses.

Pain management:

Acute pain: Oral, IM, SubQ: 50 to 150 mg every 3 to 4 hours as needed.

Discontinuation of therapy: For patients on long term opioid therapy, decrease dose by 25% to 50% every 2 to 4 days; monitor for signs/symptoms of withdrawal. If patient displays withdrawal symptoms, increase dose to previous dose and then reduce dose more slowly by increasing interval between dose reductions, decreasing amount of daily dose reduction, or both.

Obstetrical analgesia: IM, SubQ: 50 to 100 mg when pain becomes regular; may repeat at 1- to 3-hour intervals.

Preoperatively: IM, SubQ: 50 to 100 mg administered 30 to 90 minutes before the beginning of anesthesia.

Dosage adjustment for concomitant therapy: Concomitant phenothiazines/tranquilizers: Reduce meperidine dose by 25% to 50% when administered concomitantly with phenothiazines and other tranquilizers.

Postoperative shivering (off-label use): IV: 25 to 50 mg once (Crowley 2008; Kranke 2002; Mercandante 1994; Wang 1999)

Geriatric Avoid use (American Pain Society 2008; ISMP 2007).

Pediatric Note: The American Pain Society (2008) and ISMP (2007) do not recommend meperidine's use as an analgesic. If use in acute pain (in patients without renal or CNS disease) cannot be avoided, treatment should be limited to ≤48 hours and doses should not exceed 600 mg/24 hours. Oral route is not recommended for treatment of acute or chronic pain. If IV route is required, consider a reduced dose. Patients with prior opioid exposure may require higher initial doses.

Pain management:

Acute pain: Oral, IM, SubQ: 1.1 to 1.8 mg/kg/dose every 3 to 4 hours as needed (maximum: 50 to 150 mg/dose)

Discontinuation of therapy: Refer to adult dosing.

Preoperatively: Children and Adolescents: IM, SubQ: 1.1 to 2.2 mg/kg administered 30 to 90 minutes before the beginning of anesthesia (maximum: 50 to 100 mg/dose).

Dosage adjustment for concomitant therapy: Refer to adult dosing.

Renal Impairment Avoid use in renal impairment (American Pain Society 2008; ISMP 2007).

Hepatic Impairment There are no dosage adjustments provided in the manufacturer's labeling; use with caution and titrate slowly; monitor closely for signs of CNS and respiratory depression

Mechanism of Action Binds to opioid receptors in the CNS, causing inhibition of ascending pain pathways, altering the perception of and response to pain; produces generalized CNS depression

Contraindications

Hypersensitivity to meperidine or any component of the formulation; use with or within 14 days of MAO inhibitors; significant respiratory depression; acute or severe bronchial asthma in an unmonitored setting or in the absence of resuscitative equipment; GI obstruction, including paralytic ileus (known or suspected).

Documentation of allergenic cross-reactivity for opioids is limited. However, because of similarities in chemical structure and/or pharmacologic actions, the possibility of cross-sensitivity cannot be ruled out with certainty.

Warnings/Precautions **[US Boxed Warning]: Serious, life-threatening, or fatal respiratory depression may occur. Monitor closely for respiratory depression, especially during initiation or dose escalation.** Carbon dioxide retention from opioid-induced respiratory depression can exacerbate the sedating effects of opioids. Use with caution and monitor for respiratory depression in patients with significant chronic obstructive pulmonary disease or cor pulmonale, and those with a substantially decreased respiratory reserve, hypoxia, hypercapnia, or preexisting respiratory depression, particularly when initiating and titrating therapy; critical respiratory depression may occur, even at therapeutic dosages. Consider the use of alternative nonopioid analgesics in these patients.

[US Boxed Warning]: Concomitant use of opioids with benzodiazepines or other CNS depressants, including alcohol, may result in profound sedation, respiratory depression, coma, and death. Reserve concomitant prescribing of meperidine and benzodiazepines or other CNS depressants for use in patients for whom alternative treatment options are inadequate. Limit dosage and durations to the minimum required and follow patients for signs and symptoms of respiratory depression and sedation. [US Boxed Warning]: Use with all CYP3A4 inhibitors may result in an increase in meperidine plasma concentrations, which could increase or prolong adverse drug effects and may cause potentially fatal respiratory depression. In addition, discontinuation of a concomitant CYP3A4 inducer may result in increased meperidine concentrations. Monitor patients receiving meperidine and any CYP3A4 inhibitor or inducer. [US Boxed Warning]: Concomitant use of meperidine with MAOIs can result in coma, severe respiratory depression, cyanosis, and hypotension. Use of meperidine with MAOIs within last 14 days is contraindicated. Potentially significant drug interactions may exist, requiring dose or frequency adjustment, additional monitoring, and/or selection of alternative therapy.

Meperidine offers no advantage over other opioids as an analgesic and has unique neurotoxicity. The use of meperidine in acute pain and/or cancer pain management should be avoided (American Pain Society [APS] 2008; ISMP 2007). Use is not recommended for the management of chronic pain. Normeperidine (an active metabolite and CNS stimulant) may accumulate and precipitate anxiety, tremors, or seizures; risk increases with CNS or renal dysfunction, prolonged use (>48 hours), and cumulative dose (>600 mg/24 hours in adults); oral meperidine should not be used since first-pass metabolism decreases efficacy while increasing normeperidine concentrations (American Pain Society [APS] 2008). Avoid in the elderly and in patients with renal impairment (APS 2008; ISMP 2007).

May cause CNS depression, which may impair physical or mental abilities; patients must be cautioned about performing tasks which require mental alertness (eg, operating machinery or driving). Use with extreme caution in patients with head injury, intracranial lesions, elevated intracranial pressure. Avoid use in patients with impaired consciousness or coma as these patients are susceptible to intracranial effects of carbon dioxide retention. Use with caution in patients with hepatic disorders, supraventricular tachycardias (including atrial flutter), biliary tract dysfunction (including acute pancreatitis), delirium tremens, toxic psychosis, thyroid dysfunction, morbid obesity, adrenal insufficiency, Addison disease, seizure disorders, prostatic hyperplasia, urethral stricture, pheochromocytoma, and in cachectic or debilitated patients. May obscure diagnosis or clinical course of patients with acute abdominal conditions. May cause severe hypotension (including orthostatic hypotension and syncope); use with caution in patients with hypovolemia, cardiovascular disease (including acute MI), or drugs which may exaggerate hypotensive effects (including phenothiazines or general anesthetics). Monitor for symptoms of hypotension following initiation or dose titration. Use caution. Avoid use in patients with circulatory shock.

May cause constipation which may be problematic in patients with unstable angina and patients post-myocardial infarction. Consider preventive measures (eg, stool softener, increased fiber) to reduce the potential for constipation. Serotonin syndrome may occur with concomitant use of serotonergic agents (eg, SSRIs, SNRIs, triptans, TCAs), lithium, St. John's wort, agents that impair metabolism of serotonin (eg, MAO inhibitors), or agents that impair metabolism of tramadol (eg, CYP2D6 and 3A4 inhibitors). An opioid-containing analgesic regimen should be tailored to each patient's needs and based upon the route of administration, degree of tolerance for opioids (naive versus chronic user), age, weight, and medical condition. The optimal analgesic dose varies widely among patients; doses should be titrated to pain relief/prevention. Opioids decrease bowel motility; monitor for decrease bowel motility in postop patients receiving opioids. Use with caution in the perioperative setting; individualize treatment when transitioning from parenteral to oral analgesics. Concurrent use of mixed agonist/antagonist analgesics (eg, pentazocine, nalbuphine, butorphanol) or partial agonist (eg, buprenorphine) analgesics may precipitate withdrawal symptoms and/or reduced analgesic efficacy in patients following prolonged therapy with mu opioid agonists. Taper dose gradually when discontinuing.

In patients with sickle cell anemia, use with caution and decrease initial dose, normeperidine (active metabolite) may accumulate and induce seizures in these patients; **Note:** Meperidine recommended for use in sickle cell patients by the American Pain Society (APS 2008) and should only be used in sickle cell patients with a vaso-occlusive crisis (VOC) if it is the only effective opioid for an individual patient (NHLBI 2014).

Some preparations contain may sulfites which may cause allergic reaction. **[US Boxed Warning]: Meperidine exposes patients and other users to the risks of addiction, abuse, and misuse, potentially leading to overdose and death. Assess each patient's risk prior to prescribing; monitor all patients regularly for development of these behaviors or conditions.** Use with caution in patients with a history of drug abuse or acute alcoholism; potential for drug dependency exists. Other factors associated with increased risk for misuse include younger age, concomitant depression (major), and psychotropic medication use. **[US Boxed Warning]: Accidental ingestion of even one dose, especially in children, can result in a fatal overdose of meperidine.**

[US Boxed Warning]: Prolonged use of opioids during pregnancy can cause neonatal withdrawal syndrome, which may be life-threatening if not recognized and treated according to protocols developed by neonatology experts. If opioid use is required for a prolonged period in a pregnant woman, advise the patient of the risk of neonatal opioid withdrawal syndrome and ensure that appropriate treatment will be available. Signs and symptoms include irritability, hyperactivity and abnormal sleep pattern, high pitched cry, tremor, vomiting, diarrhea and failure to gain weight. Onset, duration and severity depend on the drug used, duration of use, maternal dose, and rate of drug elimination by the newborn.

Parenteral: Administer IV injections very slowly, preferably in the form of a diluted solution. Do not administer IV unless a narcotic antagonist and the facilities for assisted or controlled respiration are immediately available. When meperidine is given parenterally, especially IV, the patient should be lying down.

Some dosage forms may contain sodium benzoate/ benzoic acid; benzoic acid (benzoate) is a metabolite of benzyl alcohol; large amounts of benzyl alcohol (≥99 mg/kg/day) have been associated with a potentially fatal toxicity ("gasping syndrome") in neonates; the "gasping syndrome" consists of metabolic acidosis, respiratory distress, gasping respirations, CNS dysfunction (including convulsions, intracranial hemorrhage), hypotension, and cardiovascular collapse (AAP ["Inactive" 1997]; CDC 1982); some data suggests that benzoate displaces bilirubin from protein binding sites (Ahlfors 2001); avoid or use dosage forms containing benzyl alcohol derivative with caution in neonates. See manufacturer's labeling.

Drug Interactions

Metabolism/Transport Effects None known.

Avoid Concomitant Use

Avoid concomitant use of Meperidine with any of the following: Azelastine (Nasal); Dapoxetine; Eluxadoline; MAO Inhibitors; Methylene Blue; Mixed Agonist / Antagonist Opioids; Orphenadrine; Oxomemazine; Paraldehyde; Thalidomide

Increased Effect/Toxicity

Meperidine may increase the levels/effects of: Alvimopan; Analgesics (Opioid); Azelastine (Nasal); Blonanserin; Desmopressin; Diuretics; Eluxadoline; Flunitrazepam; HYDROcodone; Iohexol; Iomeprol; Iopamidol; Methotrimeprazine; Metoclopramide; MetyroSINE; Orphenadrine; OxyCODONE; Paraldehyde; Piribedil; Pramipexole; Ramosetron; ROPINIRole; Rotigotine; Selective Serotonin Reuptake Inhibitors; Serotonin Modulators; Suvorexant; Thalidomide; Zolpidem

The levels/effects of Meperidine may be increased by: Amphetamines; Anticholinergic Agents; Antiemetics (5HT3 Antagonists); Brimonidine (Topical); Cannabis; Chlormethiazole; Chlorphenesin Carbamate; Cimetidine; CNS Depressants; Dapoxetine; Dimethindene (Topical); Dronabinol; Droperidol; HydrOXYzine; Kava Kava; Lofexidine; Magnesium Sulfate; MAO Inhibitors; Methotrimeprazine; Methylene Blue; Methylphenidate; Minocycline; Nabilone; Oxomemazine; Perampanel; Protease Inhibitors; Rufinamide; Sodium Oxybate; Succinylcholine; Tapentadol; Tetrahydrocannabinol

Decreased Effect

Meperidine may decrease the levels/effects of: Diuretics; Gastrointestinal Agents (Prokinetic); Pegvisomant

The levels/effects of Meperidine may be decreased by: Fosphenytoin; Mixed Agonist / Antagonist Opioids; Nalmefene; Naltrexone; Phenytoin; Protease Inhibitors

Pharmacodynamics/Kinetics

Onset of Action Analgesic: Oral, IM, SubQ: 10 to 15 minutes; IV: ~5 minutes. Peak effect: IV: 5 to 7 minutes; IM, SubQ.: ~1 hour; Oral: 2 hours

Duration of Action Oral, IM, SubQ.: 2 to 4 hours; IV: 2 to 3 hours

Half-life Elimination

Parent drug: Terminal phase:

Preterm infants 3.6 to 65 days of age: 11.9 hours (range: 3.3 to 59.4 hours)

Term infants: 0.3 to 4 days of age: 10.7 hours (range: 4.9 to 16.8 hours); 26 to 73 days of age: 8.2 hours (range: 5.7 to 31.7 hours)

Neonates: 23 hours (range: 12 to 39 hours)

Infants 3 to 18 months: 2.3 hours

Children 5 to 8 years: 3 hours

Adults: 2.5 to 4 hours, Liver disease: 7 to 11 hours

Normeperidine (active metabolite): Neonates: 30 to 85 hours; Adults: 8 to 16 hours; normeperidine half-life is dependent on renal function and can accumulate with high doses or in patients with decreased renal function; normeperidine may precipitate tremors or seizures

Pregnancy Considerations Animal reproduction studies have not been conducted. Meperidine crosses the placenta; meperidine and its active metabolite accumulate in the fetus. Respiratory or CNS depression should be expected to occur in the newborn if maternal IM administration occurs within a few hours of delivery (Mattingly 2003). When used for pain relief during labor, opioids may temporarily affect the heart rate of the fetus. Due to the prolonged half-life of the active metabolite, dose-dependent sedation in the neonate may be observed for 2-3 days following delivery. Meperidine has been used for the management of pain during labor; however, due to adverse maternal and fetal effects, other opioids may be preferred. Meperidine should also be avoided following delivery when postoperative analgesia is needed (ACOG 2002).

[US Boxed Warning]: Prolonged use of opioids during pregnancy can cause neonatal withdrawal syndrome, which may be life-threatening if not recognized and treated according to protocols developed by neonatology experts. If opioid use is required for a prolonged period in a pregnant woman, advise the patient of the risk of neonatal opioid withdrawal syndrome and ensure that appropriate treatment will be available. If chronic opioid exposure occurs in pregnancy, adverse events in the newborn (including withdrawal) may occur; monitoring of the neonate is recommended. The minimum effective dose should be used if opioids are needed (Chou 2009). Neonatal abstinence syndrome following opioid exposure may present with autonomic (eg, fever, temperature instability), gastrointestinal (eg, diarrhea, vomiting, poor feeding/weight gain), or neurologic (eg, high-pitched crying, increased muscle tone, irritability, seizure, tremor) symptoms (Dow 2012; Hudak 2012).

Long-term opioid use may cause secondary hypogonadism, which may lead to sexual dysfunction or infertility (Brennan 2013).

Breastfeeding Considerations Meperidine is excreted in breast milk and may cause CNS and/or respiratory depression in the breastfeeding infant. According to the manufacturer, the decision to continue or discontinue breastfeeding during therapy should take into account the risk of infant exposure, the benefits of breastfeeding to the infant, and benefits of treatment to the mother.

Small concentrations of meperidine are excreted into breast milk following single doses. With multiple doses, concentrations of meperidine and the active metabolite may increase and both are slowly eliminated by a breastfeeding infant (Spigset 2000). Parenteral opioids used during labor have the potential to interfere with a newborns natural reflex to nurse within the first few hours after birth. Breastfeeding infants exposed to large doses of opioids should be monitored for apnea and sedation. If treatment for pain in breastfeeding women is needed, other agents are preferred (Montgomery 2012)

Controlled Substance C-II

Dosage Forms

Solution, Injection:

Demerol: 25 mg/mL (1 mL); 25 mg/0.5 mL (0.5 mL); 50 mg/mL (1 mL, 30 mL); 75 mg/1.5 mL (1.5 mL); 100 mg/2 mL (2 mL); 75 mg/mL (1 mL); 100 mg/mL (1 mL, 20 mL)

Generic: 10 mg/mL (30 mL); 25 mg/mL (1 mL); 50 mg/mL (1 mL); 100 mg/mL (1 mL)

Solution, Oral:

Generic: 50 mg/5 mL (500 mL)

Tablet, Oral:

Demerol: 100 mg

Generic: 50 mg, 100 mg

Dental Comment Meperidine is not to be used as the opioid drug of first choice. It is recommended only to be used in codeine-allergic patients when an opioid analgesic is indicated. Meperidine is not an anti-inflammatory agent. Meperidine, as with other opioid analgesics, is recommended only for limited acute dosing (ie, 3 days or less); common adverse effects in the dental patient are nausea, sedation, and constipation. Meperidine has a significant addiction liability, especially when given long-term.

Meperidine and Promethazine

(me PER i deen & proe METH a zeen)

Generic Availability (US) Yes

Pharmacologic Category Analgesic Combination (Opioid)

Use Pain: Possibly effective as analgesia for moderate to moderately severe pain.

Local Anesthetic/Vasoconstrictor Precautions No information available to require special precautions

Effects on Dental Treatment Key adverse event(s) related to dental treatment: Xerostomia (normal salivary flow resumes upon discontinuation).

Effects on Bleeding No information available to require special precautions

Adverse Reactions See individual agents.

Dosing

Adult & Geriatric Pain: Oral: One meperidine 50 mg/promethazine 25 mg capsule every 4 to 6 hours as needed.

Renal Impairment There are no dosage adjustments provided in the manufacturer's labeling. Use of meperidine should be avoided in renal impairment (ISMP, 2007).

Hepatic Impairment There are no dosage adjustments provided in the manufacturer's labeling; use with caution.

Mechanism of Action Meperidine is a opioid analgesic; promethazine is a phenothiazine derivative with sedative and anti-emetic activity. Also see individual agents.

Contraindications

Hypersensitivity to meperidine or promethazine or any component of the formulation; use with or within 14 days of MAO inhibitors; in comatose states; children <2 years of age.

Documentation of allergenic cross-reactivity for opioid analgesics is limited. However, because of similarities in chemical structure and/or pharmacologic actions, the possibility of cross-sensitivity cannot be ruled out with certainty.

Warnings/Precautions See individual agents.

Drug Interactions

Metabolism/Transport Effects Refer to individual components.

Avoid Concomitant Use

Avoid concomitant use of Meperidine and Promethazine with any of the following: Aclidinium; Azelastine (Nasal); Cimetropium; Dapoxetine; Eluxadoline; Glucagon; Glycopyrrolate (Oral Inhalation); Ipratropium (Oral Inhalation); Levosulpiride; MAO Inhibitors; Methylene Blue; Metoclopramide; Mixed Agonist / Antagonist Opioids; Nitroglycerin; Orphenadrine; Oxatomide; Oxomemazine; Paraldehyde; Potassium Chloride; Thalidomide; Tiotropium; Umeclidinium

Increased Effect/Toxicity

Meperidine and Promethazine may increase the levels/effects of: AbobotulinumtoxinA; Alvimopan; Analgesics (Opioid); Anticholinergic Agents; Azelastine (Nasal); Blonanserin; Cimetropium; Desmopressin; Diuretics; Eluxadoline; Flunitrazepam; Glucagon; Glycopyrrolate (Oral Inhalation); Highest Risk QTc-Prolonging Agents; HYDROcodone; Iohexol; Iomeprol; Iopamidol; Methotrimeprazine; Mirabegron; Moderate Risk QTc-Prolonging Agents; OnabotulinumtoxinA; Orphenadrine; OxyCODONE; Paraldehyde; Perhexiline; Piribedil; Potassium Chloride; Pramipexole; Ramosetron; RimabotulinumtoxinB; ROPINIRole; Rotigotine; Selective Serotonin Reuptake Inhibitors; Serotonin Modulators; Suvorexant; Thalidomide; Thiazide and Thiazide-Like Diuretics; Tiotropium; Zolpidem

The levels/effects of Meperidine and Promethazine may be increased by: Abiraterone Acetate; Aclidinium; Amphetamines; Anticholinergic Agents; Antiemetics (5HT3 Antagonists); Asunaprevir; Brimonidine (Topical); Cannabis; Chlormethiazole; Chlorphenesin Carbamate; Cimetidine; CNS Depressants; Cobicistat; CYP2D6 Inhibitors (Moderate); CYP2D6 Inhibitors (Strong); Dapoxetine; Dimethindene (Topical); Dronabinol; Droperidol; HydrOXYzine; Imatinib; Ipratropium (Oral Inhalation); Kava Kava; Lofexidine; Magnesium Sulfate; MAO Inhibitors; Methotrimeprazine; Methylene Blue; Methylphenidate; Metoclopramide; MetyroSINE; MiFEPRIStone; Minocycline; Nabilone; Oxatomide; Oxomemazine; Panobinostat; Peginterferon Alfa-2b; Perampanel; Perhexiline; Pramlintide; Protease Inhibitors; Rufinamide; Sodium Oxybate; Succinylcholine; Tapentadol; Tetrahydrocannabinol; Thiotepa; Umeclidinium

Decreased Effect

Meperidine and Promethazine may decrease the levels/effects of: Acetylcholinesterase Inhibitors; Diuretics; EPINEPHrine (Nasal); EPINEPHrine (Oral Inhalation); Epinephrine (Racemic); EPINEPHrine (Systemic); Gastrointestinal Agents (Prokinetic); Itopride; Levosulpiride; Nitroglycerin; Pegvisomant; Secretin

The levels/effects of Meperidine and Promethazine may be decreased by: Acetylcholinesterase Inhibitors; CYP2B6 Inducers (Moderate); Dabrafenib; Fosphenytoin; Lumacaftor; Mixed Agonist / Antagonist Opioids; Nalmefene; Naltrexone; Peginterferon Alfa-2b; Phenytoin; Protease Inhibitors

Food Interactions

Ethanol: Avoid ethanol (may increase CNS depression).

Herb/Nutraceutical: Avoid valerian, St John's wort, kava kava, gotu kola (may increase CNS depression).

Pregnancy Considerations Animal reproduction studies have not been conducted with this combination. Meperidine crosses the placenta and may cause respiratory depression in the newborn. Promethazine may inhibit platelet aggregation in the newborn if used within 2 weeks of delivery. The manufacturer does not recommend use of this combination product prior to labor. Refer to individual monographs.

Breastfeeding Considerations Meperidine is excreted into breast-milk (Spigset, 2000); excretion of promethazine is not known. Due to the potential for serious adverse reactions in the nursing infant, the manufacturer recommends a decision be made whether to discontinue nursing or to discontinue the drug, taking into account the importance of treatment to the mother. Refer to individual monographs.

Controlled Substance C-II

Dosage Forms Capsule, Oral: Meperidine hydrochloride 50 mg and promethazine hydrochloride 25 mg

Mepivacaine (me PIV a kane)

Related Information

Oral Pain *on page 1830*

Brand Names: US Carbocaine; Carbocaine Preservative-Free; Polocaine; Polocaine Dental; Polocaine-MPF; Scandonest 3% Plain

Brand Names: Canada Carbocaine; Polocaine

Generic Availability (US) Yes

Pharmacologic Category Local Anesthetic

Dental Use Amide-type anesthetic used for local infiltration anesthesia; injection near nerve trunks to produce nerve block

Use Local or regional analgesia; anesthesia by local infiltration, peripheral and central neural techniques (epidural and caudal); **not** for use in spinal anesthesia

Local Anesthetic/Vasoconstrictor Precautions No information available to require special precautions

Effects on Dental Treatment Key adverse event(s) related to dental treatment: Degree of adverse effects in the CNS and cardiovascular system is directly related to blood levels of mepivacaine (frequency not defined; more likely to occur after systemic administration rather than infiltration): Bradycardia, cardiovascular collapse, hypotension, myocardial depression, ventricular arrhythmias, nausea, vomiting, respiratory arrest, anaphylactoid reactions, blurred vision, heart block, transient stinging or burning at injection site

High blood levels: Anxiety, restlessness, disorientation, confusion, dizziness, and seizures, followed by CNS depression resulting in somnolence, unconsciousness, and possible respiratory arrest.

In some cases, symptoms of CNS stimulation may be absent and the primary CNS effects are somnolence and unconsciousness.

It is common to misinterpret psychogenic responses to local anesthetic injection as an allergic reaction. Intraoral injections are perceived by many patients as a stressful procedure in dentistry. Common symptoms to this stress are diaphoresis, palpitations, hyperventilation, generalized pallor, and a fainting feeling.

Effects on Bleeding No information available to require special precautions

Adverse Reactions Frequency not defined. Degree of adverse effects in the CNS and cardiovascular system is directly related to the blood levels of mepivacaine, route of administration, and physical status of the patient. The effects below are more likely to occur after systemic administration rather than infiltration.

Cardiovascular: Bradycardia, cardiac insufficiency, cardiovascular depression, cardiovascular stimulation, heart block, hypertension, hypotension, low cardiac output, syncope, tachycardia, ventricular arrhythmia

Central nervous system: Anxiety, chills, confusion, convulsions, depression, dizziness, drowsiness, excitement, loss of consciousness, increased body temperature, nervousness, paralysis, persistent anesthesia, restlessness

Dermatologic: Diaphoresis, erythema, pruritus, urticaria

Gastrointestinal: Fecal incontinence, nausea, oral paresthesia (persistent; involving lips, tongue, and oral tissues), vomiting

Genitourinary: Urinary incontinence, urinary retention

Hematologic & oncologic: Methemoglobinemia

Hypersensitivity: Anaphylactoid reaction, angioedema, hypersensitivity reaction

Neuromuscular & skeletal: Chondrolysis (continuous intra-articular administration), tremor, weakness

Ophthalmic: Blurred vision, miosis

Otic: Tinnitus

Respiratory: Apnea, respiratory depression, sneezing

Dental Usual Dosage

Injectable local anesthetic: Dose varies with procedure, degree of anesthesia needed, vascularity of tissue, duration of anesthesia required, and physical condition of patient. The smallest dose and concentration required to produce the desired effect should be used.

Children: Injection: According to the manufacturer, a mepivacaine dose up to 6.6 mg/kg or 400 mg (whichever is less) may be administered during any single dental sitting. For most procedures, doses >180 mg are unnecessary. The American Academy of Pediatric Dentistry (AAPD) recommends a maximum mepivacaine dose of 4.4 mg/kg or a maximum total dose of 300 mg in any single dental sitting (AAPD 2015).

Adults: Maximum single or total dose given for one procedure: 400 mg; 500 mg if epinephrine has been added (Barash, 2009)

Cervical, brachial, intercostal, pudendal nerve block: 5-40 mL of a 1% solution (maximum: 400 mg) **or** 5-20 mL of a 2% solution (maximum: 400 mg). For pudendal block, inject one-half the total dose each side.

Transvaginal block (paracervical plus pudendal): Up to 30 mL (total for both sides) of a 1% solution (maximum: 300 mg). Inject one-half the total dose each side.

Paracervical block: Up to 20 mL (total for both sides) of a 1% solution (maximum: 200 mg). Inject one-half the total dose to each side. This is the maximum recommended dose per 90-minute procedure; inject slowly with 5 minutes between sides.

Caudal and epidural block (preservative free solutions only): 15-30 mL of a 1% solution (maximum: 300 mg) **or** 10-25 mL of a 1.5% solution (maximum: 375 mg) **or** 10-20 mL of a 2% solution (maximum: 400 mg)

Infiltration: Up to 40 mL of a 1% solution (maximum: 400 mg); up to 50 mL if epinephrine has been added (maximum: 500 mg) (Barash, 2009); an equivalent amount of a 0.5% solution (prepared by diluting the 1% solution with NS) may be used for large areas

Peripheral nerve block to provide a surgical level of anesthesia (Miller, 2010):

Major nerve block (blockade of two or more distinct nerves, a nerve plexus, or very large nerves at more proximal sites: 30-50 mL of a 1% or 1.5% solution (maximum: 500 mg)

Minor nerve block (blockade of a single nerve [eg, ulnar or radial]): 5-20 mL of a 1% solution (maximum: 200 mg)

Therapeutic block: 1-5 mL of 1% solution (maximum: 50 mg) **or** 1-5 mL of 2% solution (maximum: 100 mg)

Elderly: Decreased doses suggested by manufacturer's labeling; however, no dosing adjustments provided. Refer to adult dosing.

Dosage adjustment in renal impairment: No dosage adjustment provided in manufacturer's labeling; use with caution.

Dosage adjustment in hepatic impairment: No dosage adjustment provided in manufacturer's labeling; use with caution.

Dosing

Adult Note: Dose varies with procedure, degree of anesthesia needed, vascularity of tissue, duration of anesthesia required, and physical condition of patient. The smallest dose and concentration required to produce the desired effect should be used.

Local or regional anesthesia (eg, epidural, caudal, or peripheral nerve blocks):

Maximum single or total dose given for one procedure: 400 mg; 500 mg if epinephrine has been added (Barash 2009)

Cervical, brachial, intercostal, pudendal nerve block: 5 to 40 mL of a 1% solution (maximum: 400 mg) **or** 5 to 20 mL of a 2% solution (maximum: 400 mg). For pudendal block, inject one-half the total dose each side.

Transvaginal block (paracervical plus pudendal): Up to 30 mL (total for both sides) of a 1% solution (maximum: 300 mg). Inject one-half the total dose each side.

Paracervical block: Up to 20 mL (total for both sides) of a 1% solution (maximum: 200 mg). Inject one-half the total dose to each side. This is the maximum recommended dose per 90-minute procedure; inject slowly with 5 minutes between sides.

Caudal and epidural block (preservative free solutions only): 15 to 30 mL of a 1% solution (maximum: 300 mg) **or** 10 to 25 mL of a 1.5% solution (maximum: 375 mg) **or** 10 to 20 mL of a 2% solution (maximum: 400 mg)

Infiltration: Up to 40 mL of a 1% solution (maximum: 400 mg); up to 50 mL if epinephrine has been added (maximum: 500 mg) (Barash 2009); an equivalent amount of a 0.5% solution (prepared by diluting the 1% solution with NS) may be used for large areas

Peripheral nerve block to provide a surgical level of anesthesia (Miller 2010):

Major nerve block (blockade of two or more distinct nerves, a nerve plexus, or very large nerves at more proximal sites: 30 to 50 mL of a 1% or 1.5% solution (maximum: 500 mg)

Minor nerve block (blockade of a single nerve [eg, ulnar or radial]): 5 to 20 mL of a 1% solution (maximum: 200 mg)

Therapeutic block: 1 to 5 mL of 1% solution (maximum: 50 mg) **or** 1 to 5 mL of 2% solution (maximum: 100 mg)

Dental anesthesia: Note:

Single site in upper or lower jaw: 51 mg as a 3% solution

Infiltration and nerve block of entire oral cavity: 270 mg as a 3% solution; up to a maximum of 6.6 mg/kg of body weight but not to exceed 300 mg per appointment. Manufacturer's maximum recommended dose is not more than 400 mg to normal healthy adults.

The following number of dental cartridges (1.7 mL) provide the indicated amounts of mepivacaine dental anesthetic 3%. See table.

# of Cartridges (1.7 mL)	Mepivacaine mg (3%)
1	51
2	102
3	153
4	204
5	255
6	306
7	357
8	408

Geriatric Decreased doses suggested by manufacturer's labeling; however, no dosing adjustments provided. Refer to adult dosing.

Pediatric Note: Dose varies with procedure, degree of anesthesia needed, vascularity of tissue, duration of anesthesia required, and physical condition of patient. The smallest dose and concentration required to produce the desired effect should be used.

Local or regional anesthesia (eg, epidural, caudal, or peripheral nerve blocks): Maximum single or total dose given for one procedure: 5 to 6 mg/kg (maximum adult dose per manufacturer 400 mg); only concentrations <2% should be used in children <3 years or <14 kg (30 lbs)

Dental anesthesia:

Children <10 years: Up to 5 to 6 mg/kg of body weight; maximum pediatric dosage must be carefully calculated on the basis of patient's weight but must not exceed 270 mg of the 3% solution (manufacturer labeling). The American Academy of Pediatric Dentistry (AAPD) recommends a maximum mepivacaine dose of 4.4 mg/kg or a maximum total dose of 300 mg in any single dental sitting (AAPD 2015).

Children >10 years: Dental anesthesia: Refer to adult dosing.

Renal Impairment There are no dosage adjustments provided in the manufacturer's labeling; use with caution.

Hepatic Impairment There are no dosage adjustments provided in the manufacturer's labeling; use with caution.

Mechanism of Action Mepivacaine is an amide local anesthetic similar to lidocaine. Local anesthetics bind selectively to the intracellular surface of sodium channels to block influx of sodium into the axon. As a result, depolarization necessary for action potential propagation and subsequent nerve function is prevented. The block at the sodium channel is reversible. When drug diffuses away from the axon, sodium channel function is restored and nerve propagation returns.

Contraindications Hypersensitivity to mepivacaine, other amide-type local anesthetics, or any component of the formulation

Warnings/Precautions Careful and constant monitoring of the patient's state of consciousness should be done following each local anesthetic injection; at such times, restlessness, anxiety, tinnitus, dizziness, blurred vision, tremors, depression, or drowsiness may be early warning signs of CNS toxicity; treatment is primarily symptomatic and supportive. Continuous intra-articular infusion of local anesthetics after arthroscopic or other surgical procedures is **not** an approved use;

chondrolysis (primarily in the shoulder joint) has occurred following infusion, with some cases requiring arthroplasty or shoulder replacement. Use with caution in patients with cardiac disease, hepatic or renal disease, or hyperthyroidism. Local anesthetics have been associated with rare occurrences of sudden respiratory arrest; convulsions due to systemic toxicity leading to cardiac arrest have been reported presumably due to intravascular injection. A test dose is recommended prior to epidural administration and all reinforcing doses with continuous catheter technique. Do not use solutions containing preservatives for caudal or epidural block. Use caution in debilitated, elderly, or acutely-ill patients; dose reduction may be required. Resuscitative equipment, oxygen, and other resuscitative drugs should be available for immediate use.

Drug Interactions

Metabolism/Transport Effects None known.

Avoid Concomitant Use

Avoid concomitant use of Mepivacaine with any of the following: Bupivacaine (Liposomal)

Increased Effect/Toxicity

Mepivacaine may increase the levels/effects of: Bupivacaine (Liposomal); Neuromuscular-Blocking Agents

The levels/effects of Mepivacaine may be increased by: Beta-Blockers; Hyaluronidase

Decreased Effect

Mepivacaine may decrease the levels/effects of: Technetium Tc 99m Tilmanocept

Pharmacodynamics/Kinetics

Onset of Action Route and dose dependent: Range: 3 to 20 minutes; Dental: Upper jaw: 30 to 120 seconds; Lower jaw: 1 to 4 minutes

Duration of Action Route and dose dependent: 2 to 2.5 hours; Dental: Upper jaw: 20 minutes; Lower jaw: 40 minutes

Half-life Elimination Neonates: 8.7-9 hours; Adults: 1.9-3 hours

Pregnancy Risk Factor C

Pregnancy Considerations Animal reproduction studies have not been conducted. Mepivacaine has been used in obstetrical analgesia.

Breastfeeding Considerations It is not known if mepivacaine is excreted in breast milk. The manufacturer recommends that caution be exercised when administering mepivacaine to breastfeeding women. Usual infiltration doses of mepivacaine dental anesthetic given to breastfeeding mothers has not been shown to affect the health of the breastfeeding infant.

Dosage Forms

Solution, Injection:

Carbocaine: 1% (50 mL); 2% (50 mL)

Polocaine: 1% (50 mL); 2% (50 mL)

Solution, Injection [preservative free]:

Carbocaine Preservative-Free: 1% (30 mL); 1.5% (30 mL); 2% (20 mL)

Polocaine-MPF: 1% (30 mL); 1.5% (30 mL); 2% (20 mL)

Solution, Injection [dental use]:

Carbocaine: 3% (1.7 mL)

Polocaine Dental: 3% (1.7 mL)

Scandonest 3% Plain: 3% (1.7 mL)

Dental Comment Oral paresthesia: The occurrence of oral paresthesia associated with 4% solutions of prilocaine or articaine, although rare, continue to be slightly more frequent than other local anesthetics. From 1999 to 2008, there were 182 cases of nonsurgical paresthesia (Gaffen 2009). Of the cases, 172 involved mandibular block injection only.

A 2010 report, reviewed adverse events submitted voluntarily over a 10-year period involving the dental local anesthetics articaine, bupivacaine, lidocaine, mepivacaine, and prilocaine in the United States. Mepivacaine reported incidence: One case per 623,112,900 cartridges sold. The reported incidence of paresthesia was one case for 13,800,970 cartridges of all local anesthetics sold in the US (Garisto 2010).

Mepivacaine and Levonordefrin

(me PIV a kane & lee voe nor DEF rin)

Related Information

Mepivacaine *on page 1060*

Oral Pain *on page 1830*

Brand Names: US Carbocaine® 2% with Neo-Cobefrin®; Scandonest® 2% L

Brand Names: Canada Carbocaine® 2% with Neo-Cobefrin®; Scandonest 2%® with Levonordefrin

Generic Availability (US) No

Pharmacologic Category Local Anesthetic

Dental Use Amide-type anesthetic used for local infiltration anesthesia; injection near nerve trunks to produce nerve block

Use Amide-type anesthetic used for local infiltration anesthesia; injection near nerve trunks to produce nerve block

Local Anesthetic/Vasoconstrictor Precautions No information available to require special precautions

Effects on Dental Treatment It is common to misinterpret psychogenic responses to local anesthetic injection as an allergic reaction. Intraoral injections are perceived by many patients as a stressful procedure in dentistry. Common symptoms to this stress are diaphoresis, palpitations, hyperventilation, generalized pallor and a fainting feeling. Patients may exhibit hypersensitivity to bisulfites contained in local anesthetic solution to prevent oxidation of levonordefrin. In general, patients reacting to bisulfites have a history of asthma and their airways are hyper-reactive to asthmatic syndrome.

Degree of adverse effects in the CNS and cardiovascular system is directly related to the blood levels of mepivacaine (frequency not defined; more likely to occur after systemic administration rather than infiltration): Bradycardia and reduction in cardiac output, nausea, vomiting, tremors, hypersensitivity reactions (extremely rare; may be manifest as dermatologic reactions and edema at injection site), asthmatic syndromes

High blood levels: Anxiety, restlessness, disorientation, confusion, dizziness, and seizures, followed by CNS depression resulting in somnolence, unconsciousness and possible respiratory arrest.

In some cases, symptoms of CNS stimulation may be absent and the primary CNS effects are somnolence and unconsciousness.

See Dental Comment.

Effects on Bleeding No information available to require special precautions

Adverse Reactions Frequency not defined. Degree of adverse effects in the CNS and cardiovascular system is directly related to the blood levels of mepivacaine. The effects below are more likely to occur after systemic administration rather than infiltration.

Central nervous system: Disorientation, dizziness, drowsiness, excitement, loss of consciousness, nervousness, seizure

Hypersensitivity: Hypersensitivity reaction

Neuromuscular & skeletal: Tremor
Ophthalmic: Blurred vision
<1%, postmarketing, and/or case reports: Anaphylactoid reaction, oral paresthesia (lips, oral tissues, and tongue; usually due to nerve blocks of the trigeminal nerve)

Dental Usual Dosage Note: Dosage varies with the anesthetic procedure, degree of anesthesia needed, vascularity of tissue, duration of anesthesia required, and physical condition of patient. Always use the lowest effective dose along with careful aspiration.

Children: Calculate the weight-specific maximum mepivacaine dose; regardless of the patient's weight, the maximum pediatric **mepivacaine** dose is 5 to 6 mg/kg or 180 mg (whichever is less) during any single dental sitting (manufacturer labeling). Pediatric Weight-Specific Maximum Mepivacaine Dose (mg) = [Weight (lbs)/150] x 180 (manufacturer labeling). The American Academy of Pediatric Dentistry (AAPD) recommends a maximum dose of 4.4 mg/kg or a maximum total dose of 300 mg in any single dental sitting (AAPD, 2009).

Adults: Injection: Usual dose: Mepivacaine 34 mg (1.7 mL) per site or mepivacaine 180 mg (9 mL) for entire oral cavity; maximum cumulative **mepivacaine** dose: 6.6 mg/kg or 400 mg (whichever is less) during any single dental sitting

The following numbers of dental carpules (1.7 mL) provide the indicated amounts of mepivacaine hydrochloride 2% and levonordefrin 1:20,000. See table.

# of Cartridges (1.7 mL)	Mepivacaine (mg) (2%)	Vasoconstrictor (mg) (Levonordefrin 1:20,000)
1	34	0.085
2	68	0.170
3	102	0.255
4	136	0.340
5	170	0.425
6	204	0.510
7	238	0.595
8	272	0.680
9	306	0.765
10	340	0.850

Dosing

Adult & Geriatric Note: Dosage varies with the anesthetic procedure, degree of anesthesia needed, vascularity of tissue, duration of anesthesia required, and physical condition of patient. Always use the lowest effective dose along with careful aspiration.

Dental anesthesia, infiltration, or conduction block: Usual dose: Mepivacaine 34 mg (1.7 mL) per site or mepivacaine 180 mg (9 mL) for entire oral cavity; maximum cumulative **mepivacaine** dose: 6.6 mg/kg or 400 mg (whichever is less) during any single dental sitting

Pediatric Note: Dosage varies with the anesthetic procedure, degree of anesthesia needed, vascularity of tissue, duration of anesthesia required, and physical condition of patient. Always use the lowest effective dose along with careful aspiration.

Dental anesthesia, infiltration, or conduction block: Calculate the weight-specific maximum **mepivacaine** dose; regardless of the patient's weight, the maximum pediatric **mepivacaine** dose is 6.6 mg/kg or 180 mg (whichever is less) during any single dental sitting

Renal Impairment No dosage adjustment provided in manufacturer's labeling; use with caution.

Hepatic Impairment No dosage adjustment provided in manufacturer's labeling; use with caution.

Mechanism of Action Local anesthetics bind selectively to the intracellular surface of sodium channels to block influx of sodium into the axon. As a result, depolarization necessary for action potential propagation and subsequent nerve function is prevented. The block at the sodium channel is reversible. When drug diffuses away from the axon, sodium channel function is restored and nerve propagation returns.

Levonordefrin prolongs the duration of the anesthetic actions of mepivacaine by causing vasoconstriction (alpha-adrenergic receptor agonist) of the vasculature surrounding the nerve axons. This prevents the diffusion of mepivacaine away from the nerves resulting in a longer retention in the axon.

Contraindications Hypersensitivity to local anesthetics of the amide-type or any component of the formulation

Warnings/Precautions Local anesthetics have been associated with rare occurrences of sudden respiratory arrest. Careful and constant monitoring of the patient's state of consciousness should be done following each local anesthetic injection; at such times, restlessness, anxiety, tinnitus, dizziness, blurred vision, tremors, depression, or drowsiness may be early warning signs of CNS toxicity. Treatment is primarily symptomatic and supportive. Convulsions due to systemic toxicity leading to cardiac arrest have also been reported, presumably following unintentional intravascular injection. Methemoglobinemia has been reported with local anesthetics including mepivacaine; clinically significant methemoglobinemia requires immediate treatment with oxygen and/or methylene blue.

Use with caution in patients with arteriosclerotic heart disease, cerebral vascular insufficiency, heart block, hypertension, and ischemic heart disease; minimal amounts of vasoconstrictor should be used in this patient population. Use with caution in patients with diabetes, hepatic or renal impairment, and hyperthyroidism. Use with caution in pediatric or elderly patients or in patients who are acutely ill or debilitated; reduce dose consistent with age and physical status. Use caution in patients with asthma; products may contains potassium metabisulfite which may cause severe hypersensitivity reactions (anaphylaxis) in some individuals. Use with caution and reduce dosage when administering to patients receiving other CNS depressants; effects with other sedative drugs may be potentiated.

Intravascular injections should be avoided; aspiration should be performed prior to administration; the needle must be repositioned until no return of blood can be elicited by aspiration; however, absence of blood in the syringe does not guarantee that intravascular injection has been avoided. To avoid serious adverse effects and high plasma levels, the lowest dosage resulting in effective anesthesia should be administered. Repeated doses may cause significant increases in blood levels with each repeated dose due to the possibility of accumulation of the drug or its metabolites. Tolerance to elevated blood levels varies with patient status. Dental practitioners using local anesthetic agents should be well trained in diagnosis and management of emergencies that may arise from the use of these agents.

Resuscitative equipment, oxygen, and other resuscitative drugs should be available for immediate use.

Drug Interactions

Metabolism/Transport Effects None known.

Avoid Concomitant Use

Avoid concomitant use of Mepivacaine and Levonordefrin with any of the following: Bupivacaine (Liposomal); Ergot Derivatives; Iobenguane I 123; MAO Inhibitors

Increased Effect/Toxicity

Mepivacaine and Levonordefrin may increase the levels/effects of: Bupivacaine (Liposomal); Doxofylline; Neuromuscular-Blocking Agents; Sympathomimetics

The levels/effects of Mepivacaine and Levonordefrin may be increased by: AtoMOXetine; Beta-Blockers; Cannabinoid-Containing Products; Cocaine; Ergot Derivatives; Hyaluronidase; MAO Inhibitors; Serotonin/Norepinephrine Reuptake Inhibitors; Tricyclic Antidepressants

Decreased Effect

Mepivacaine and Levonordefrin may decrease the levels/effects of: Benzylpenicilloyl Polylysine; Iobenguane I 123; Technetium Tc 99m Tilmanocept

The levels/effects of Mepivacaine and Levonordefrin may be decreased by: Alpha1-Blockers; Spironolactone

Pharmacodynamics/Kinetics

Onset of Action Upper jaw: 30-120 seconds; Lower jaw: 1-4 minutes

Duration of Action

Upper jaw: 1-2.5 hours; Lower jaw: 2.5-5.5 hours
Infiltration: 50 minutes
Inferior alveolar block: 75 minutes

Pregnancy Risk Factor C

Pregnancy Considerations Animal reproduction studies have not been conducted with this combination.

Breastfeeding Considerations Usual infiltration doses of mepivacaine with levonordefrin given to nursing mothers has not been shown to affect the health of the nursing infant.

Dosage Forms

Injection, solution [for dental use]:

Carbocaine® 2% with Neo-Cobefrin®: Mepivacaine 2% and levonordefrin 1:20,000 (1.7 mL)

Scandonest® 2% L: Mepivacaine 2% and levonordefrin 1:20,000 (1.7 mL)

Dental Comment Oral paresthesia: The occurrence of oral paresthesia associated with 4% solutions of prilocaine or articaine, although rare, continue to be slightly more frequent than other local anesthetics. From 1999-2008, there were 182 cases of nonsurgical paresthesia (Gaffen, 2009). Of the cases, 172 involved mandibular block injection only. A 2010 report, reviewed adverse events submitted voluntarily over a 10-year period involving the dental local anesthetics articaine, bupivacaine, lidocaine, mepivacaine, and prilocaine in the United States. Mepivacaine reported incidence: One case per 623,112,900 cartridges sold. The reported incidence of paresthesia was one case for 13,800,970 cartridges of all local anesthetics sold in the U.S. (Garisto, 2010). Levonordefrin may interact with medications such as beta-blockers, monoamine oxidase inhibitors, ergot derivatives, and tricyclic antidepressants to enhance vasopressor effects. Consult interaction analysis for full review.

Mepolizumab (me poe LIZ ue mab)

Brand Names: US Nucala

Brand Names: Canada Nucala

Pharmacologic Category Interleukin-5 Receptor Antagonist; Monoclonal Antibody, Anti-Asthmatic

Use

Asthma: Add-on maintenance treatment of severe asthma in adults and children 12 years and older (US labeling) or adults (Canadian labeling) with an eosinophilic phenotype

Limitations of use: Not indicated for the relief of acute bronchospasm or status asthmaticus

Local Anesthetic/Vasoconstrictor Precautions No information available to require special precautions

Effects on Dental Treatment No significant effects or complications reported

Effects on Bleeding No information available to require special precautions

Adverse Reactions

>10%:

Central nervous system: Headache (19%)

1% to 10%:

Central nervous system: Fatigue (5%)
Dermatologic: Eczema (3%), pruritus (3%)
Gastrointestinal: Upper abdominal pain (3%)
Genitourinary: Urinary tract infection (3%)
Immunologic: Immunogenicity (6%; neutralizing: <1%)
Infection: Influenza (3%)
Local: Injection site reaction (8%; includes burning sensation, erythema, pain, pruritus, swelling)
Neuromuscular & skeletal: Back pain (5%), muscle spasm (3%)

Frequency not defined:

Hypersensitivity: Delayed hypersensitivity
Infection: Herpes zoster

<1%, postmarketing, and/or case reports: Hypersensitivity reaction (including anaphylaxis, angioedema, bronchospasm, hypotension, skin rash, urticaria)

General Dosage Range SubQ: Children ≥12 years, Adolescents, and Adults: 100 mg once every 4 weeks

Mechanism of Action Mepolizumab is an interleukin-5 antagonist (IgG1 kappa). IL-5 is the major cytokine responsible for the growth and differentiation, recruitment, activation, and survival of eosinophils (a cell type associated with inflammation and an important component of the pathogenesis of asthma). Mepolizumab, by inhibiting IL-5 signaling, reduces the production and survival of eosinophils; however, the mechanism of mepolizumab action in asthma has not been definitively established.

Pharmacodynamics/Kinetics

Half-life Elimination Terminal: 16 to 22 days

Pregnancy Considerations

Adverse events were not observed in animal reproduction studies. Mepolizumab is expected to cross the placenta; potential effects to the fetus may be greater in the second and third trimesters. Uncontrolled asthma is associated with adverse events on pregnancy (increased risk of preeclampsia, preterm birth, low birth weight infants). Asthma should be closely monitored in pregnant women.

Patients or health care providers are encouraged to enroll women exposed to mepolizumab during pregnancy in an asthma pregnancy registry (1-877-311-8972 or http://www.mothertobaby.org/asthma). The Canadian labeling advises that women who become pregnant during therapy or up to 4 months after discontinuation of therapy notify their healthcare provider.

Meprobamate (me proe BA mate)

Pharmacologic Category Antianxiety Agent, Miscellaneous

Use

Anxiety: Management of anxiety disorders

Limitations of use: Meprobamate is not a preferred treatment option for anxiety disorders per the American Psychiatric Association, World Federation of Societies of Biological Psychiatry, and British Association for Psychopharmacology guidelines (APA [Stein 2009]; BAP [Baldwin 2014]; WFSBP [Bandelow 2012]).

Local Anesthetic/Vasoconstrictor Precautions No information available to require special precautions

Effects on Dental Treatment No significant effects or complications reported

Effects on Bleeding No information available to require special precautions

Adverse Reactions Frequency not defined.

Cardiovascular: Abnormal electroencephalogram, cardiac arrhythmia, peripheral edema, palpitations, severe hypotension, syncope, tachycardia

Central nervous system: Ataxia, chills, dizziness, drowsiness, euphoria, headache, overstimulation, paradoxical excitation, paresthesia, slurred speech, vertigo

Dermatologic: Dermatitis, erythema multiforme, skin rash, Stevens-Johnson syndrome

Endocrine & metabolic: Exacerbation of porphyria

Gastrointestinal: Diarrhea, nausea, proctitis, stomatitis, vomiting

Genitourinary: Anuria, oliguria

Hematologic & oncologic: Agranulocytosis, aplastic anemia, bruise, eosinophilia, immune thrombocytopenia, leukopenia, petechia, purpura

Hypersensitivity: Anaphylaxis, angioedema, hypersensitivity reaction

Neuromuscular & skeletal: Weakness

Ophthalmic: Accommodation disturbance

Respiratory: Bronchospasm

Miscellaneous: Fever

General Dosage Range

Oral:

Children ≥6 years: 200 to 600 mg/day in 2 to 3 divided doses

Adolescents and Adults: 1,200 to 1,600 mg/day in 3 to 4 divided doses, up to 2,400 mg/day

Mechanism of Action Affects the thalamus and limbic system; also appears to inhibit multineuronal spinal reflexes

Pharmacodynamics/Kinetics

Onset of Action Sedation: ~1 hour

Half-life Elimination 10 hours

Pregnancy Considerations Meprobamate crosses the placenta and is found in cord blood in concentrations similar to those in the maternal plasma. Maternal use may be associated with congenital malformations; avoid use during pregnancy.

Controlled Substance C-IV

Mercaptopurine (mer kap toe PURE een)

Brand Names: US Purinethol [DSC]; Purixan

Brand Names: Canada Purinethol

Pharmacologic Category Antineoplastic Agent, Antimetabolite; Antineoplastic Agent, Antimetabolite (Purine Analog); Immunosuppressant Agent

Use Acute lymphoblastic leukemia: Treatment of acute lymphoblastic leukemia (ALL), as part of a combination chemotherapy regimen

Local Anesthetic/Vasoconstrictor Precautions No information available to require special precautions

Effects on Dental Treatment Key adverse event(s) related to dental treatment: Stomatitis and mucositis.

Effects on Bleeding Significant bleeding has been associated with drug-induced thrombocytopenia and altered hemostasis. Medical consult recommended.

Adverse Reactions Frequency not always defined.

Central nervous system: Malaise (5% to 20%), drug fever

Dermatologic: Skin rash (5% to 20%), hyperpigmentation (<5%), urticaria (<5%), alopecia

Endocrine & metabolic: Hyperuricemia (<5%)

Gastrointestinal: Anorexia (5% to 20%), diarrhea (5% to 20%), nausea (5% to 20%; minimal), vomiting (5% to 20%; minimal), oral lesion (<5%), pancreatitis (<5%), cholestasis, mucositis, sprue-like symptoms, stomach pain, ulcerative bowel lesion

Genitourinary: Oligospermia, renal toxicity, uricosuria

Hematologic & oncologic: Bone marrow depression (>20%; onset 7-10 days; nadir 14 days; recovery: 21 days), anemia, granulocytopenia, hemorrhage, hepatosplenic T-cell lymphomas, leukopenia, lymphocytopenia, metastases, neutropenia, thrombocytopenia

Hepatic: Hyperbilirubinemia (<5%), increased serum transaminases (<5%), ascites, hepatic encephalopathy, hepatic fibrosis, hepatic injury, hepatic necrosis, hepatomegaly, hepatotoxicity, intrahepatic cholestasis, jaundice, toxic hepatitis

Immunologic: Immunosuppression

Infection: Infection

Respiratory: Pulmonary fibrosis

General Dosage Range Dosage adjustment recommended in patients with hepatic or renal impairment or on concomitant therapy

Oral: *Children and Adults:* Maintenance: 1.5 to 2.5 mg/kg once daily or 50 to 75 mg/m^2 once daily

Mechanism of Action Mercaptopurine is a purine antagonist which inhibits DNA and RNA synthesis; acts as false metabolite and is incorporated into DNA and RNA, eventually inhibiting their synthesis; specific for the S phase of the cell cycle

Pharmacodynamics/Kinetics

Half-life Elimination Children: 21 minutes; Adults: 47 minutes

Time to Peak Serum: Within 2 hours

Pregnancy Risk Factor D

Pregnancy Considerations May cause fetal harm if administered during pregnancy. Case reports of fetal loss have been noted with mercaptopurine administration during the first trimester; adverse effects have also been noted with second and third trimester use. Women of child bearing potential should avoid becoming pregnant during treatment.

Prescribing and Access Restrictions For specialty or local pharmacy distribution and availability contact AnovoRx at http://www.purixan-us.com/find-purixan/ or call 888-470-0904.

Meropenem (mer oh PEN em)

Brand Names: US Merrem

Brand Names: Canada Meropenem For Injection; Merrem

Pharmacologic Category Antibiotic, Carbapenem

Use

Bacterial meningitis: Treatment of bacterial meningitis in pediatric patients 3 months and older caused by *Haemophilus influenzae*, *Neisseria meningitidis*, and penicillin-susceptible isolates of *Streptococcus pneumoniae*.

Skin and skin structure infections, complicated: Treatment of complicated skin and skin structure infections in adults and pediatric patients 3 months and older caused by *Staphylococcus aureus* (methicillin-susceptible isolates only), *Streptococcus pyogenes*, *Streptococcus agalactiae*, viridans group streptococci, *Enterococcus faecalis* (vancomycin-susceptible isolates only), *Pseudomonas aeruginosa*, *Escherichia coli*, *Proteus mirabilis*, *Bacteroides fragilis*, and *Peptostreptococcus* species.

Intra-abdominal infections: Treatment of complicated appendicitis and peritonitis in adult and pediatric patients caused by viridans group streptococci, *E. coli*, *Klebsiella pneumoniae*, *P. aeruginosa*, *B. fragilis*, *B. thetaiotaomicron*, and *Peptostreptococcus* species.

Local Anesthetic/Vasoconstrictor Precautions No information available to require special precautions

Effects on Dental Treatment Key adverse event(s) related to dental treatment: Oral *Candida* infection (pediatric patients) and glossitis.

Effects on Bleeding No information available to require special precautions

Adverse Reactions

1% to 10%:

Cardiovascular: Peripheral vascular disease (>1%), shock (1%), bradycardia (≤1%), cardiac arrest (≤1%), cardiac failure (≤1%), chest pain (≤1%), hypertension (≤1%), hypotension (≤1%), myocardial infarction (≤1%), peripheral edema (≤1%), pulmonary embolism (≤1%), syncope (≤1%), tachycardia (≤1%)

Central nervous system: Headache (2% to 8%), convulsions (neonates and infants <3 months: 5%), pain (≤5%), agitation (≤1%), anxiety (≤1%), chills (≤1%), confusion (≤1%), delirium (≤1%), depression (≤1%), dizziness (≤1%), drowsiness (≤1%), hallucination (≤1%), insomnia (≤1%), nervousness (≤1%), paresthesia (≤1%), seizure (≤1%)

Dermatologic: Skin rash (2% to 3%, includes diaper-area moniliasis in infants), pruritus (1%), dermal ulcer (≤1%), diaphoresis (≤1%), urticaria (≤1%)

Endocrine & metabolic: Hypoglycemia (>1%), hypervolemia (≤1%)

Gastrointestinal: Nausea (≤8%), diarrhea (4% to 7%), constipation (1% to 7%), vomiting (≤4%), oral candidiasis (≤2%), gastrointestinal disease (>1%), glossitis (1%), abdominal pain (≤1%), anorexia (≤1%), dyspepsia (≤1%), enlargement of abdomen (≤1%), flatulence (≤1%), intestinal obstruction (≤1%)

Genitourinary: Dysuria (≤1%), pelvic pain (≤1%), urinary incontinence (≤1%), vulvovaginal candidiasis (≤1%)

Hematologic & oncologic: Anemia (≤6%), hypochromic anemia (≤1%)

Hepatic: Hyperbilirubinemia (conjugated; neonates and infants <3 months: 5%), cholestatic jaundice (≤1%), hepatic failure (≤1%), jaundice (≤1%)

Infection: Sepsis (2%)

Local: Inflammation at injection site (2%)

Neuromuscular & skeletal: Back pain (≤1%), weakness (≤1%)

Renal: Renal failure (≤1%)

Respiratory: Pharyngitis (>1%), pneumonia (>1%), apnea (1%), asthma (≤1%), cough (≤1%), dyspnea (≤1%), hypoxia (≤1%), pleural effusion (≤1%), pulmonary edema (≤1%), respiratory tract disease (≤1%)

Miscellaneous: Accidental injury (>1%), fever (≤1%)

<1%, postmarketing, and/or case reports: Agranulocytosis, angioedema, anorexia, asthma, bradycardia, change in platelet count, cholestatic jaundice, *Clostridium difficile* associated diarrhea, confusion, decreased hematocrit, decreased hemoglobin, decreased partial thromboplastin time, decreased prothrombin time, decreased white blood cell count, delirium, depression, dermal ulcer, DRESS syndrome, eosinophilia, erythema multiforme, gastrointestinal hemorrhage, hallucination, hematuria, hemolytic anemia, hemoperitoneum, hepatic failure, hypertension, hypervolemia, hypochromic anemia, hypokalemia, hypotension, hypoxia, increased blood urea nitrogen, increased lactate dehydrogenase, increased serum alkaline phosphatase, increased serum ALT, increased serum AST, increased serum bilirubin, increased serum creatinine, ileus, intestinal obstruction, jaundice, leukocytosis, leukopenia, myocardial infarction, neutropenia, peripheral edema, pleural effusion, positive direct Coombs test, positive indirect Coombs test, pulmonary edema, pulmonary embolism, renal failure, seizure, Stevens-Johnson syndrome, tachycardia, toxic epidermal necrolysis, urinary incontinence, vulvovaginal candidiasis

General Dosage Range Dosage adjustment recommended in patients with renal impairment

IV:

Infants <3 months:

Gestational age <32 weeks:

Postnatal age <14 days: 20 mg/kg/dose every 12 hours

Postnatal age ≥14 days: 20 mg/kg/dose every 8 hours

Gestational age ≥32 weeks:

Postnatal age <14 days: 20 mg/kg/dose every 8 hours

Postnatal age ≥14 days: 30 mg/kg/dose every 8 hours

Infants ≥3 months, Children, and Adolescents (≤50 kg): 10 to 40 mg/kg every 8 hours (maximum: 2 **g** every 8 hours)

Children and Adolescents ≥50 kg and Adults: 500 mg to 2 **g** every 8 hours

Mechanism of Action Inhibits bacterial cell wall synthesis by binding to several of the penicillin-binding proteins, which in turn inhibit the final transpeptidation step of peptidoglycan synthesis in bacterial cell walls, thus inhibiting cell wall biosynthesis; bacteria eventually lyse due to ongoing activity of cell wall autolytic enzymes (autolysins and murein hydrolases) while cell wall assembly is arrested

Pharmacodynamics/Kinetics

Half-life Elimination

Neonates and Infants ≤3 months: Median: 2.7 hours; range: 1.6- 3.8 hours (Smith 2011)

Infants and Children 3 months to 2 years: 1.5 hours

Children 2-12 years and Adults: 1 hour

Time to Peak Tissue: ~1 hour following infusion except in bile, lung, and muscle; CSF: 2 to 3 hours with inflamed meninges

Pregnancy Risk Factor B

Pregnancy Considerations Adverse events were not observed in animal reproduction studies. Incomplete transplacental transfer of meropenem was found using an *ex vivo* human perfusion model.

Mesalamine (me SAL a meen)

Brand Names: US Apriso; Asacol HD; Canasa; Delzicol; Lialda; Pentasa; Rowasa; SfRowasa

Brand Names: Canada Asacol; Asacol 800; Mesasal; Mezavant; Pentasa; Salofalk; Teva-5 ASA

Pharmacologic Category 5-Aminosalicylic Acid Derivative

Use

US labeling:

Oral:

Apriso: Maintenance of remission of ulcerative colitis in patients ≥18 years

Asacol HD: Treatment of moderately active ulcerative colitis in adults

Delzicol: Treatment of mildly to moderately active ulcerative colitis in patients ≥5 years; maintenance of remission of ulcerative colitis in adults

Lialda, Pentasa: Treatment and maintenance of remission of mildly to moderately active ulcerative colitis

Rectal: Treatment of active mild to moderate distal ulcerative colitis (suspension only), proctosigmoiditis (suspension only), or proctitis (suspension and suppository)

Canadian labeling:

Oral:

Asacol, Mezavant: Treatment and maintenance of remission of mildly- to moderately-active ulcerative colitis

Asacol 800: Treatment of moderately active ulcerative colitis

Mesasal: Treatment and maintenance of remission of ulcerative colitis

Pentasa: Treatment and maintenance of remission of mildly to moderately active ulcerative colitis; treatment and maintenance of remission of mild to moderate Crohn disease

Rectal: Treatment and maintenance of remission of distal ulcerative colitis (extending to splenic flexure) and as adjunctive therapy in more extensive disease (suspension only); treatment and maintenance of ulcerative proctitis (suppository only)

Local Anesthetic/Vasoconstrictor Precautions No information available to require special precautions

Effects on Dental Treatment Key adverse event(s) related to dental treatment: Pharyngitis.

Effects on Bleeding No information available to require special precautions

Adverse Reactions Adverse effects vary depending upon dosage form; frequency similar in adult and pediatric patients unless otherwise noted. Incidence usually on lower end with enema and suppository dosage forms.

>10%:

Central nervous system: Headache (adults: 2% to 14%; children and adolescents: 10%), pain (≤14%)

Gastrointestinal: Eructation (≤26%), abdominal pain (2% to 21%), exacerbation of ulcerative colitis (children and adolescents: 12%; adults: 2% to 3%), constipation (≤11%)

Respiratory: Nasopharyngitis (children and adolescents: 15%; adults: 1% to 4%), pharyngitis (11%)

1% to 10%:

Cardiovascular: Chest pain (3%), peripheral edema (3%), vasodilation (≥2%), syncope (children and adolescents: 2%), hypertension (1%)

Central nervous system: Dizziness (≤9%), hypertonia (5%), chills (3%), fatigue (<3%), vertigo (<3%), anxiety (≥2%), migraine (≥2%), nervousness (≥2%), paresthesia (≥2%), insomnia (≤2%), malaise (≤2%)

Dermatologic: Skin rash (1% to 6%), diaphoresis (≤3%), pruritus (≤3%), alopecia (<3%), acne vulgaris (≤2%)

Endocrine & metabolic: Increased serum triglycerides (<3%), weight loss (children and adolescents: 2%)

Gastrointestinal: Diarrhea (2% to 8%), flatulence (≤6%), vomiting (≤5%), dyspepsia (≤4%), nausea (≤4%), abnormal stools (≥2%), gastroenteritis (≥2%), gastrointestinal hemorrhage (<1% to ≥2%), tenesmus (≥2%), hemorrhoids (≥2%), bloody diarrhea (children and adolescents: 2%), pancreatitis (children and adolescents: 2%), rectal pain (2%), sclerosing cholangitis (children and adolescents: 2%), abdominal distention (≥1%), anorectal pain (1%; on insertion of enema tip), nausea and vomiting (1%)

Genitourinary: Hematuria (<3%), urinary frequency (<1% to ≥2%)

Hematologic & oncologic: Decreased hemoglobin (<3%), decreased hematocrit (<3%), rectal hemorrhage (<1% to ≥2%), anemia (children and adolescents: 2%)

Hepatic: Cholestatic hepatitis (<3%), increased serum transaminases (<3%), abnormal hepatic function tests (2%), increased serum ALT (1%)

Hypersensitivity: Anaphylaxis (2%)

Infection: Infection (≥2%), viral infection (children and adolescents: 2%; adenovirus)

Neuromuscular & skeletal: Back pain (6%), arthralgia (≤5%), myalgia (≤3%), weakness (<1% to ≥2%), arthritis (2%), musculoskeletal pain (2%; leg/joint)

Ophthalmic: Visual disturbance (≥2%), conjunctivitis (≤2%)

Otic: Tinnitus (<3%), otalgia (≥2%)

Renal: Decreased creatinine clearance (<3%), polyuria (≥2%)

Respiratory: Rhinitis (8%), sinusitis (children and adolescents: 7%; adults: ≥2%), flu-like symptoms (1% to ≥5%), cough (≤5%), dyspnea (<3%), bronchitis (≥2%)

Miscellaneous: Fever (≤1% to ≥5%), intolerance syndrome (3%)

<1%, postmarketing, and/or case reports: Abdominal cramps, abdominal distention, abnormal T waves on ECG, abnormal uterine bleeding, agranulocytosis, albuminuria, alopecia, amenorrhea, angioedema, anorectal pain, anorexia, aplastic anemia, blurred vision, cholecystitis, cholestatic jaundice, colitis, confusion, decreased libido, depression, disorientation, DRESS syndrome, drowsiness, drug fever, duodenal ulcer, dysgeusia, dysmenorrhea, dysphagia, dysuria, ecchymoses, eczema, edema, emotional lability, eosinophilia, eosinophilic pneumonitis, epididymitis, erythema, erythema nodosum, esophageal ulcer, Eustachian tube congestion, exacerbation of asthma, eye pain, facial edema, fatigue, fecal discoloration, fecal incontinence, frequent bowel movements, gastritis, gout, granulocytopenia, Guillain-Barré syndrome, hepatic cirrhosis, hepatic failure, hepatic injury, hepatic necrosis, hepatitis, hepatotoxicity, hyperesthesia, hypermenorrhea, hypersensitivity pneumonitis, hypersensitivity reaction, hypomenorrhea, hypotension, idiopathic nephrotic syndrome, increased appetite, increased blood urea nitrogen, increased gamma-glutamyl transferase, increased lactate dehydrogenase, increased serum alkaline

phosphatase, increased serum amylase, increased serum AST, increased serum bilirubin, increased serum creatinine, increased serum lipase, increased thirst, infertility, interstitial nephritis, interstitial pneumonitis, jaundice, Kawasaki-like syndrome, leg cramps, leukopenia, lichen planus, lupus-like syndrome, lymphadenopathy, mastalgia, mucus stools, myocarditis, nail disease, neck pain, nephrotoxicity, neutropenia, oligospermia, oral candidiasis, oral mucosa ulcer, painful defecation, palpitations, pancytopenia, perforated peptic ulcer, perianal skin irritation, pericardial effusion, pericarditis, peripheral neuropathy, pharyngolaryngeal pain, pleurisy, pneumonitis, prurigo, pruritus, psoriasis, pulmonary infiltrates, pulmonary interstitial fibrosis, pyoderma gangrenosum, rectal discharge, rectal pain, rectal polyp, rectal tenesmus, renal disease (including minimal change nephropathy), renal failure, rheumatoid arthritis, skin photosensitivity, Stevens-Johnson syndrome, stomatitis, systemic lupus erythematosus, tachycardia, thrombocythemia, thrombocytopenia, transverse myelitis, tremor, urinary urgency, urticaria, xeroderma, xerostomia

General Dosage Range

Oral:

Children ≥5 years and Adolescents: Delzicol:

17 to 32 kg: 800 mg in the morning and 400 mg in the evening; maximum dose: 1,200 mg/day

33 to 53 kg: 1,200 mg in the morning and 800 mg in the evening; maximum dose: 2,000 mg/day

54 to 90 kg: 1,200 mg in the morning and 1,200 mg in the evening; maximum dose: 2,400 mg/day

Adults:

Capsule: Apriso: 1.5 g once daily; Delzicol: 1.6 g in 2 to 4 divided doses or 2.4 g in 3 divided doses; Pentasa: 1 g 4 times daily

Tablet: Asacol HD: 1.6 g 3 times daily; Lialda: 2.4 or 4.8 g once daily

Rectal: *Adults:* Retention enema: 60 mL (4 g) at bedtime, retained overnight (~8 hours); Suppository: 1,000 mg (1 suppository) at bedtime

Mechanism of Action Mesalamine (5-aminosalicylic acid) is the active component of sulfasalazine; the specific mechanism of action is unknown; however, it is thought that mesalamine modulates local chemical mediators of the inflammatory response, especially leukotrienes, and is also postulated to be a free radical scavenger or an inhibitor of tumor necrosis factor (TNF); action appears topical rather than systemic

Pharmacodynamics/Kinetics

Half-life Elimination 5-ASA and N-acetyl-5-ASA: Variable; ~25 hours (range: 2 to 296 hours)

Time to Peak

Capsule: Apriso: ~4 hours; Delzicol: ~10 hours; Pentasa: 3 hours

Rectal: Pentasa, Salofalk [Canadian products]: 2 to 6 hours

Tablet: Asacol HD (formulated with dibutyl phthalate [DBP]): 10 to 16 hours; Asacol HD (formulated without DBP): ~24 hours (mean); Lialda: 9 to 12 hours

Canadian products: Asacol: 7 hours; Asacol 800: 10 hours; Mesasal: ~7 hours; Mezavant [Canadian product]: 8 hours (range: 4 to 34 hours)

Pregnancy Risk Factor B

Pregnancy Considerations Adverse events have not been observed in animal reproduction studies. Mesalamine is known to cross the placenta. An increased rate of congenital malformations has not been observed in human studies. Preterm birth, still birth and decreased birth weight have been observed; however, these events may also be due to maternal disease.

Dibutyl phthalate (DBP) may be an inactive ingredient in the enteric coating of some products (eg,Asacol, Asacol HD); adverse effects in male rats were noted at doses greater than the recommended human dose. Refer to product labeling for current formulation.

When treatment for inflammatory bowel disease is needed during pregnancy, mesalamine may be used, although products with DBP should be avoided (Habal 2012; Mottet 2009).

Product Availability Asacol HD: A new formulation (without dibutyl phthalate [DBP]) has been approved in the United States. Anticipated availability is late 2016.

Metaproterenol (met a proe TER e nol)

Related Information

Respiratory Diseases *on page 1777*

Brand Names: Canada Apo-Orciprenaline®; ratio-Orciprenaline®; Tanta-Orciprenaline®

Pharmacologic Category Beta$_2$ Agonist

Use Bronchodilator in reversible airway obstruction due to asthma or COPD

Local Anesthetic/Vasoconstrictor Precautions No information available to require special precautions

Effects on Dental Treatment Key adverse event(s) related to dental treatment: Bad taste and xerostomia (normal salivary flow resumes upon discontinuation).

Effects on Bleeding No information available to require special precautions

Adverse Reactions

>10%:

Cardiovascular: Tachycardia (6% to 17%)

Central nervous system: Nervousness (5% to 20%)

Neuromuscular & skeletal: Tremor (2% to 17%)

1% to 10%:

Cardiovascular: Palpitations (4%)

Central nervous system: Headache (1% to 7%), dizziness (2%), insomnia (2%), fatigue (1%)

Gastrointestinal: Nausea (1% to 4%), diarrhea (1%)

Respiratory: Exacerbation of asthma (2%)

<1%, postmarketing, and/or case reports: Blurred vision, change in appetite, chest pain, chills, clonus, cough, diaphoresis, drowsiness, edema, facial edema, fever, flu-like symptoms, hypertension, laryngeal disease, muscle spasm, pain, pruritus, sensory disturbance, swelling of fingers, syncope, unpleasant taste, urticaria, vomiting, weakness, xerostomia

General Dosage Range Oral:

Children <6 years: 1.3-2.6 mg/kg/day divided every 6-8 hours

Children 6-9 years (or <27 kg): 10 mg/dose 3-4 times/day

Children >9 years (or ≥27 kg) and Adults: 20 mg 3-4 times/day

Mechanism of Action Stimulates beta$_2$-receptors which increases the conversion of adenosine triphosphate (ATP) to 3'-5'-cyclic adenosine monophosphate (cAMP), resulting in bronchial smooth muscle relaxation

Pharmacodynamics/Kinetics

Onset of Action Bronchodilation: Oral: ~30 minutes; Peak effect: Oral: ~1 hour

Duration of Action ~2 to 6 hours, regardless of route administered

Pregnancy Risk Factor C

Pregnancy Considerations Adverse events were observed in some animal reproduction studies. Beta agonists, including metaproterenol, may interfere with uterine contractility if administered during labor; maternal and fetal tachycardia have been observed (Baillie, 1970; Tyack, 1971).

Uncontrolled asthma is associated with adverse events on pregnancy (increased risk of perinatal mortality, preeclampsia, preterm birth, low birth weight infants). Oral beta$_2$-receptor agonists are not recommended to treat asthma during pregnancy (NAEPP, 2005).

Metaxalone (me TAKS a lone)

Brand Names: US Metaxall; Skelaxin

Brand Names: Canada Skelaxin

Generic Availability (US) Yes

Pharmacologic Category Skeletal Muscle Relaxant

Use ***Musculoskeletal conditions:*** Relief of discomforts associated with acute, painful musculoskeletal conditions.

Local Anesthetic/Vasoconstrictor Precautions No information available to require special precautions

Effects on Dental Treatment No significant effects or complications reported

Effects on Bleeding No information available to require special precautions

Adverse Reactions Frequency not defined.

Central nervous system: Dizziness, drowsiness, headache, irritability, nervousness

Dermatologic: Skin rash (with or without pruritus)

Gastrointestinal: Gastrointestinal upset, nausea, vomiting

Hematologic & oncologic: Hemolytic anemia, leukopenia

Hepatic: Jaundice

Hypersensitivity: Anaphylactoid reaction (rare), hypersensitivity reaction

Dosing

Adult & Geriatric Musculoskeletal conditions: Oral: 800 mg 3 to 4 times daily

Pediatric Musculoskeletal conditions: Adolescents ≥13 years: Refer to adult dosing.

Renal Impairment There are no dosage adjustments provided in the manufacturer's labeling; use with caution; contraindicated with significant renal impairment.

Hepatic Impairment There are no dosage adjustments provided in the manufacturer's labeling; use with caution; contraindicated with significant hepatic impairment.

Mechanism of Action Precise mechanism has not been established; however, its clinical effect may be associated with general depression of the nervous system; has no direct effect on the contractile mechanism of striated muscle, the nerve fiber or the motor end plate.

Contraindications Hypersensitivity to metaxalone or any component of the formulation; significantly impaired hepatic or renal function, tendency to drug-induced, hemolytic, or other anemias

Warnings/Precautions May cause CNS depression. CNS depressant effects may be augmented when used in conjunction with other depressants (eg, barbiturates, ethanol), when taken with food, or in the elderly. May impair mental and/or physical ability to perform hazardous tasks such as operating machinery or driving a motor vehicle. Use with caution in patients with impaired renal or hepatic function (contraindicated if significant impairment); routine monitoring of transaminases is recommended. Potentially life-threatening serotonin syndrome has been reported; generally occurs when used concomitantly with serotonergic drugs (eg, tramadol, SSRIs), or when exceeding recommended doses. Potentially significant interactions may exist, requiring dose or frequency adjustment, additional monitoring, and/or selection of alternative therapy.

Drug Interactions

Metabolism/Transport Effects Substrate of CYP1A2 (minor), CYP2C19 (minor), CYP2C8 (minor), CYP2C9 (minor), CYP2D6 (minor), CYP2E1 (minor), CYP3A4 (minor); **Note:** Assignment of Major/Minor substrate status based on clinically relevant drug interaction potential

Avoid Concomitant Use

Avoid concomitant use of Metaxalone with any of the following: Azelastine (Nasal); Orphenadrine; Oxomemazine; Paraldehyde; Thalidomide

Increased Effect/Toxicity

Metaxalone may increase the levels/effects of: Alcohol (Ethyl); Analgesics (Opioid); Azelastine (Nasal); Blonanserin; Buprenorphine; CNS Depressants; Flunitrazepam; HYDROcodone; Methotrimeprazine; MetyroSINE; Mirtazapine; Orphenadrine; OxyCODONE; Paraldehyde; Piribedil; Pramipexole; ROPINIRole; Rotigotine; Serotonin Modulators; Suvorexant; Thalidomide; Zolpidem

The levels/effects of Metaxalone may be increased by: Brimonidine (Topical); Cannabis; Chlormethiazole; Chlorphenesin Carbamate; Dimethindene (Topical); Doxylamine; Dronabinol; Droperidol; HydrOXYzine; Kava Kava; Lofexidine; Magnesium Sulfate; Methotrimeprazine; Minocycline; Nabilone; Oxomemazine; Perampanel; Rufinamide; Sodium Oxybate; Tapentadol; Tetrahydrocannabinol; Tolperisone; Trimeprazine

Decreased Effect There are no known significant interactions involving a decrease in effect.

Food Interactions Bioavailability may be increased with food (may increase CNS depression). Management: Administer without regard to food. Monitor patients.

Dietary Considerations Administration with food may increase serum concentrations.

Pharmacodynamics/Kinetics

Half-life Elimination 9 ± 4.8 hours

Time to Peak ~3 hours

Pregnancy Considerations Adverse events have not been observed in animal reproduction studies. Use during pregnancy (especially first trimester) only if benefits outweigh risks.

Breastfeeding Considerations It is not known if metaxalone is excreted in breast milk. breastfeeding is not recommended by the manufacturer.

Dosage Forms

Tablet, Oral:

Metaxall: 800 mg

Skelaxin: 800 mg

Generic: 400 mg, 800 mg

MetFORMIN (met FOR min)

Related Information

Endocrine Disorders and Pregnancy *on page* 1781

Brand Names: US D-Care DM2; Fortamet; Glucophage; Glucophage XR; Glumetza; Riomet

Brand Names: Canada ACT-Metformin; Apo-Metformin; Auro-Metformin; Dom-Metformin; ECL-Metformin; Glucophage; Glumetza; Glycon; JAMP-Metformin; JAMP-Metformin Blackberry; Mar-Metformin; Metformin

FC; Mint-Metformin; Mylan-Metformin; PHL-Metformin; PMS-Metformin; PRO-Metformin; RAN-Metformin; ratio-Metformin; Riva-Metformin; Sandoz-Metformin FC; Septa-Metformin; Teva-Metformin

Generic Availability (US) May be product dependent

Pharmacologic Category Antidiabetic Agent, Biguanide

Use

Diabetes mellitus, type 2: Management of type 2 diabetes mellitus (noninsulin dependent, NIDDM) when hyperglycemia cannot be managed with diet and exercise alone.

Note: If not contraindicated and if tolerated, metformin is the preferred initial pharmacologic agent for type 2 diabetes management (ADA 2016a).

Local Anesthetic/Vasoconstrictor Precautions No information available to require special precautions

Effects on Dental Treatment Key adverse event(s) related to dental treatment: Taste disorder.

Metformin-dependent patients with diabetes (noninsulin dependent, Type 2) should be appointed for dental treatment in morning in order to minimize chance of stress-induced hypoglycemia.

Effects on Bleeding No information available to require special precautions

Adverse Reactions

>10%: Gastrointestinal: Diarrhea (IR tablet: 53%; ER tablet: 10%), nausea and vomiting (IR tablet: 26%; ER tablet: 7%), flatulence (12%)

1% to 10%:

Cardiovascular: Chest discomfort (1% to 5%), flushing (1% to 5%), palpitations (1% to 5%)

Central nervous system: Headache (6%), chills (1% to 5%), dizziness (1% to 5%), taste disorder (1% to 5%)

Dermatologic: Diaphoresis (1% to 5%), nail disease (1% to 5%), skin rash (1% to 5%)

Endocrine & metabolic: Decreased vitamin B_{12} serum concentrate (7%), hypoglycemia (1% to 5%)

Gastrointestinal: Dyspepsia (≤1% to 7%), abdominal distress (6%), abdominal distention (1% to 5%), abdominal pain (1% to 5%), abnormal stools (1% to 5%), constipation (1% to 5%), heartburn (≤1% to 5%)

Neuromuscular & skeletal: Weakness (9%), myalgia (1% to 5%)

Respiratory: Dyspnea (1% to 5%), flu-like symptoms (1% to 5%), upper respiratory tract infection (1% to 5%)

<1%, postmarketing and/or case reports: Lactic acidosis, megaloblastic anemia

Dosing

Adult

Diabetes mellitus, type 2: Oral: **Note:** Allow 1 to 2 weeks between dose titrations: Clinically significant responses may not be seen at doses <1,500 mg daily; however, a lower recommended starting dose and gradual increased dosage is recommended to minimize gastrointestinal symptoms.

Immediate-release tablet or solution: Adults ≥17 years: Initial: 500 mg twice daily **or** 850 mg once daily; titrate in increments of 500 mg weekly or 850 mg every other week; may also titrate from 500 mg twice a day to 850 mg twice a day after 2 weeks

If a dose >2,000 mg/day is required, it may be better tolerated in 3 divided doses. Maximum recommended dose: 2,550 mg/day.

Extended-release tablet: **Note:** If glycemic control is not achieved at maximum dose, may divide dose and administer twice daily.

Initial: 500 to 1000 mg once daily; dosage may be increased by 500 mg weekly up to a maximum of 2,000 mg/day (Glucophage XR, Glumetza) or 2,500 mg/day (Fortamet)

Conversion from immediate-release to extended-release tablets: Patients receiving metformin immediate release may be switched to metformin ER once daily at the same total daily dose, up to 2,000 mg once daily (2,500 mg for Fortamet)

Transfer from other antidiabetic agents: No transition period is generally necessary except when transferring from chlorpropamide. When transferring from chlorpropamide, care should be exercised during the first 2 weeks because of the prolonged retention of chlorpropamide in the body, leading to overlapping drug effects and possible hypoglycemia.

Concomitant use with insulin or insulin secretagogues: Reduced dose of insulin or insulin secretagogues (eg, sulfonylureas) may be needed.

Diabetes mellitus, type 2, prevention (off-label use): *Immediate-release tablet or solution:* Oral: Initial: 850 mg once daily; Target: 850 mg twice daily (Knowler 2002)

Polycystic ovary syndrome with anovulatory infertility (off-label use): Females: Oral:

Immediate release: 1,500 to 2,000 mg/day in 2 or 3 divided doses (Johnson 2010; Moll 2006; Morin-Papunen 2012)

Extended release: 1,000 mg twice daily (Legro 2007)

Note: Metformin should be initiated at lower doses (500 mg daily) and increased gradually over 1 to 2 weeks to the target dose to minimize adverse effects (eg, GI intolerance) (Johnson 2010; Legro 2007; Moll 2006; Morin-Papunen 2012)

Polycystic ovary syndrome with menstrual irregularities (off-label use): Females: Oral: *Immediate release:* 500 mg 2 or 3 times daily, up to 1,000 mg twice daily (Costello 2007; Morin-Papunen 2003; Meyer 2007; Moghetti 2000). The dose of metformin should be increased gradually to minimize GI adverse effects (Meyer 2007)

Note: When metformin is used, cyclic progestin therapy may be added for the first 6 months of metformin treatment, until regular cycles are established.

Prevention of ovarian hyperstimulation syndrome with polycystic ovary syndrome (off-label use): Females: Oral: *Immediate release:* 1,000 mg to 2,550 mg per day as 500 mg 2 or 3 times per day **or** 850 mg 2 or 3 times per day (Palomba 2013; Palomba 2011; Tang 2006; Tso 2014). The dose of metformin should be increased gradually to minimize GI adverse effects.

Note: Pretreatment with metformin may be started as early as 16 weeks prior (but typically 4 to 5 weeks prior) to as late as the first day of gonadotropin-releasing hormone (GnRH) agonist administration; some studies continued metformin therapy during gonadotropin ovarian stimulation (Tso 2014).

Geriatric Refer to adult dosing. The initial and maintenance dosing should be conservative, due to the potential for decreased renal function (monitor).

Pediatric Diabetes mellitus, type 2: Oral: **Note:** Allow 1 to 2 weeks between dose titrations: Clinically significant responses may not be seen at doses <1,500 mg daily; however, a lower recommended starting dose and gradual increased dosage is recommended to minimize gastrointestinal symptoms.

Immediate-release tablet or solution:

Children ≥10 years and Adolescents ≤16 years: Initial: 500 mg twice daily; increases in daily dosage should be made in increments of 500 mg at weekly intervals, given in divided doses, up to a maximum of 2,000 mg daily

Adolescents ≥17 years: Refer to adult dosing.

Extended-release tablet: Adolescents ≥17 years: Fortamet, Glucophage XR: Refer to adult dosing.

Renal Impairment

eGFR >45 mL/minute/1.73 m^2: No dosage adjustment necessary; monitor renal function at least annually. More frequent monitoring (every 3 to 6 months) has been recommended for patients with eGFR >45 to <60 mL/minute/1.73 m^2 (Lipska 2011).

eGFR 30 to 45 mL/minute/1.73 m^2: Use is not recommended for initiation of therapy; if eGFR falls to <45 mL/minute/1.73 m^2 during therapy, consider benefits/risks of continuing therapy. Alternatively, may consider dosage reduction (eg, 50% reduction or 50% of maximal dose), monitor renal function every 3 months (Lipska 2011).

eGFR <30 mL/minute/1.73 m^2: Use is contraindicated.

Hepatic Impairment The manufacturer recommends avoiding metformin since liver disease is considered a risk factor for the development of lactic acidosis during metformin therapy. However, continued use of metformin in diabetics with liver dysfunction, including cirrhosis, has been used successfully and may be associated with a survival benefit in carefully selected patients; use cautiously in patients at risk for lactic acidosis (eg, renal impairment, alcohol use) (Brackett 2010; Zhang 2014).

Mechanism of Action Decreases hepatic glucose production, decreasing intestinal absorption of glucose and improves insulin sensitivity (increases peripheral glucose uptake and utilization)

Contraindications

US labeling: Hypersensitivity to metformin or any component of the formulation; severe renal dysfunction (eGFR <30 mL/minute/1.73 m^2); acute or chronic metabolic acidosis with or without coma (including diabetic ketoacidosis).

Canadian labeling: Hypersensitivity to metformin or any component of the formulation; renal function unknown, renal impairment, and serum creatinine levels above the upper limit of normal range; renal disease or renal dysfunction (serum creatinine ≥136 micromol/L in males or ≥124 micromol/L in females or abnormal creatinine clearance <60 mL/minute) which may result from conditions such as cardiovascular collapse (shock), acute myocardial infarction, and septicemia; unstable and/or insulin-dependent (type I) diabetes mellitus; acute or chronic metabolic acidosis, including diabetic ketoacidosis, with or without coma, history of ketoacidosis with or without coma; history of lactic acidosis (regardless of precipitating factors); excessive alcohol intake (acute or chronic); severe hepatic dysfunction or clinical or laboratory evidence of hepatic disease; cardiovascular collapse and disease states associated with hypoxemia including cardiorespiratory insufficiency, which are often associated with hyperlactacidemia; stress conditions (eg, severe infection, trauma, surgery and postoperative recovery phase); severe dehydration; pregnancy; breastfeeding

Warnings/Precautions [US Boxed Warning]: Postmarketing cases of metformin-associated lactic acidosis have resulted in death, hypothermia, hypotension, and resistant bradyarrhythmias. The onset is often subtle, accompanied by nonspecific symptoms (eg, malaise, myalgias, respiratory distress, somnolence, abdominal pain); elevated blood lactate levels (>5 mmol/L); anion gap acidosis (without evidence of ketonuria or ketonemia); increased lactate:pyruvate ratio; metformin plasma levels generally >5 mcg/mL. Risk factors for lactic acidosis include patients with renal impairment, concomitant use of certain drugs (eg, carbonic anhydrase inhibitors such as topiramate), ≥65 years, having a radiologic study with contrast, surgery and other procedures, hypoxic states (eg, acute heart failure), excessive alcohol intake, and hepatic impairment. Discontinue immediately if lactic acidosis is suspected; prompt hemodialysis is recommended. Lactic acidosis should be suspected in any patient with diabetes receiving metformin with evidence of acidosis but without evidence of ketoacidosis. Discontinue use in patients with conditions associated with dehydration, hypoperfusion, sepsis, or hypoxemia. Temporarily discontinue therapy in patients with restricted food and fluid intake. The risk of accumulation and lactic acidosis increases with the degree of impairment of renal function. In a scientific statement from the American Heart Association, metformin has been determined to be an agent that may exacerbate underlying myocardial dysfunction (magnitude: major) (AHA [Page 2016]).

Metformin is substantially excreted by the kidney; assess renal function prior to initiation of therapy using estimated glomerular filtration rate (eGFR). Initiation of therapy is not recommended if eGFR is between 30 to 45 mL/minute/1.73 m^2 and is contraindicated if eGFR <30 mL/minute/1.73 m^2. Assess benefits/risks of continuing therapy in patients with whose eGFR falls below 45 mL/minute/1.73 m^2 during therapy. Metformin should be withheld in patients with prerenal azotemia. Use with caution in the elderly, risk of metformin associated lactic acidosis increases with age. Use of concomitant medications that may affect renal function (ie, affect tubular secretion) may also affect metformin disposition. Therapy should be suspended for any surgical procedures, excluding minor procedures not associated with restricted food and fluid intake. Restart only after normal oral intake resumed and normal renal function is verified. Temporarily discontinue metformin at the time of or before iodinated contrast imaging procedures in patients with an eGFR 30 to 60 mL/minute/1.73 m^2; or with a history of hepatic disease, alcoholism, or heart failure; or in patients who will receive intra-arterial iodinated contrast. Reevaluate eGFR 48 hours after imaging procedure; restart if renal function is stable. Alternatively, the American College of Radiology (ACR) guidelines recommend that metformin may be used prior to or following administration of iodinated contrast media in patients with no evidence of acute kidney injury (AKI) and with an eGFR ≥30 mL/minute/1.73 m^2; ACR guidelines recommend temporary discontinuation of metformin in patients with known AKI or severe chronic kidney disease (stage IV or V [ie, eGFR <30 mL/minute/1.73 m^2]) or who are undergoing arterial catheter studies (ACR 2015).

Use with caution in patients with impaired liver function. Patient must be instructed to avoid excessive acute or chronic ethanol use; ethanol may potentiate metformin's effect on lactate metabolism. May impair vitamin B_{12} absorption, particularly in those with inadequate vitamin B_{12} or calcium intake/absorption; very rarely associated with anemia. Rapid reversal of vitamin B_{12} deficiency may be observed with discontinuation of therapy or supplementation. Monitor vitamin B_{12} serum concentrations periodically with long-term therapy. Administration of oral antidiabetic drugs has been reported to be associated with increased cardiovascular mortality; metformin does not appear to share this risk. Potentially significant interactions may exist, requiring dose or frequency adjustment, additional monitoring, and/or selection of alternative therapy. Insoluble tablet shell of Glumetza 1,000 mg extended release tablet may remain intact and be visible in the stool. Other extended released tablets (Fortamet, Glucophage XR, Glumetza 500 mg) may appear in the stool as a soft mass resembling the tablet. Diabetes self-management education (DSME) is essential to maximize the effectiveness of therapy. Not indicated for use in patients with insulin-dependent diabetes mellitus (IDDM) (type 1) or for the treatment of diabetic ketoacidosis.

Drug Interactions

Metabolism/Transport Effects Substrate of OCT2

Avoid Concomitant Use

Avoid concomitant use of MetFORMIN with any of the following: Alcohol (Ethyl)

Increased Effect/Toxicity

MetFORMIN may increase the levels/effects of: Dalfampridine; Dofetilide; Hypoglycemia-Associated Agents

The levels/effects of MetFORMIN may be increased by: Alcohol (Ethyl); Alpha-Lipoic Acid; Androgens; BuPROPion; Carbonic Anhydrase Inhibitors; Cephalexin; Cimetidine; Dalfampridine; Dolutegravir; Glycopyrrolate (Systemic); Iodinated Contrast Agents; Isavuconazonium Sulfate; LamoTRIgine; MAO Inhibitors; Ombitasvir, Paritaprevir, and Ritonavir; Ombitasvir, Paritaprevir, Ritonavir, and Dasabuvir; Ondansetron; Pegvisomant; Prothionamide; Quinolone Antibiotics; Ranolazine; Salicylates; Selective Serotonin Reuptake Inhibitors; Topiramate; Trimethoprim; Vandetanib

Decreased Effect

MetFORMIN may decrease the levels/effects of: Trospium

The levels/effects of MetFORMIN may be decreased by: Hyperglycemia-Associated Agents; Patiromer; Quinolone Antibiotics; Thiazide and Thiazide-Like Diuretics; Verapamil

Food Interactions Food decreases the extent and slightly delays the absorption. Management: Administer with a meal.

Dietary Considerations Drug may cause GI upset; take with food (to decrease GI upset). Take at the same time(s) each day. Dietary modification based on ADA recommendations is a part of therapy. Monitor for signs and symptoms of vitamin B_{12} and/or folic acid deficiency; supplementation may be required.

Pharmacodynamics/Kinetics

Onset of Action Within days; maximum effects up to 2 weeks

Half-life Elimination Plasma: 4 to 9 hours; Blood ~17.6 hours

Time to Peak Immediate release: 2 to 3 hours; Extended release: 7 hours (range: 4 to 8 hours)

Pregnancy Risk Factor B

Pregnancy Considerations Adverse events have not been observed in animal reproduction studies. Metformin has been found to cross the placenta in concentrations which may be comparable to those found in the maternal plasma. Pharmacokinetic studies suggest that clearance of metformin may increase during pregnancy and dosing may need adjusted in some women when used during the third trimester (Charles 2006; de Oliveira Baraldi 2011; Eyal 2010; Gardiner 2003; Hughes 2006; Vanky 2005).

An increased risk of birth defects or adverse fetal/neonatal outcomes has not been observed following maternal use of metformin for GDM or type 2 diabetes when glycemic control is maintained (Balani 2009; Coetzee 1979; Coetzee 1984; Ekpebegh 2007; Niromanesh 2012; Rowan 2008; Rowan 2010; Tertti 2008).

In women with diabetes, maternal hyperglycemia can be associated with congenital malformations as well as adverse effects in the fetus, neonate, and the mother (ACOG 2005; ADA 2016e; Kitzmiller 2008; Metzger 2007). To prevent adverse outcomes, prior to conception and throughout pregnancy maternal blood glucose and HbA_{1c} should be kept as close to target goals as possible but without causing significant hypoglycemia (ACOG 2013; ADA 2016e; Blumer 2013; Kitzmiller 2008).

Metformin may be used to treat GDM when non-pharmacologic therapy is not effective in maintaining glucose control (ADA 2016e).

Breastfeeding Considerations Metformin is present in breast milk.

The relative infant dose (RID) of metformin is 1.08% when calculated using the highest average breast milk concentration located and compared to a weight-adjusted maternal dose of 6.55 mg/kg/day. In general, breastfeeding is considered acceptable when the RID is <10%; when an RID is >25% breastfeeding should generally be avoided (Anderson 2016; Ito 2000). Using the highest average milk concentration (0.47 mcg/mL), the estimated daily infant dose via breast milk is 0.07 mg/kg/day. This milk concentration was obtained following maternal administration of metformin 500 mg twice daily and the RID was calculated using the actual weight of the woman in the study (Briggs 2005).

Small amounts of metformin have been detected in the serum of breastfeeding infants. Because breast milk concentrations of metformin stay relatively constant, avoiding breastfeeding around peak plasma concentrations in the mother would not be helpful in reducing metformin exposure to the infant (Briggs 2005; Eyal 2010; Gardiner 2003; Hale 2002).

According to the manufacturer, due to the potential for hypoglycemia in the breastfeeding infant, a decision should be made whether to discontinue breastfeeding or to discontinue the drug, taking into account the importance of treatment to the mother. However, breastfeeding is encouraged for all women, including those with diabetes (ACOG 2005; ADA 2016e; Blumer 2013; Metzger 2007). Metformin may be used in breastfeeding women (Blumer 2013).

Dosage Forms Considerations

Extended release tablets utilize differing release mechanisms: Glucophage XR uses dual hydrophilic polymer matrix systems, Fortamet uses single-composition osmotic technology, and Glumetza uses gastric retention technology.

Dosage Forms

Kit, Combination:

D-Care DM2: Extended release tablet, as hydrochloride: 500 mg

Solution, Oral:

Riomet: 500 mg/5 mL (118 mL, 473 mL)

Tablet, Oral:

Glucophage: 500 mg, 850 mg, 1000 mg

Generic: 500 mg, 850 mg, 1000 mg

Tablet Extended Release 24 Hour, Oral:

Fortamet: 500 mg, 1000 mg

Glucophage XR: 500 mg, 750 mg

Glumetza: 500 mg, 1000 mg

Generic: 500 mg, 750 mg, 1000 mg

Dosage Forms: Canada

Tablet, oral:

Glycon: 500 mg, 850 mg

Methadone (METH a done)

Related Information

Clinical Risk Related to Drugs Prolonging QT Interval *on page 1772*

Brand Names: US Dolophine; Methadone HCl Intensol; Methadose; Methadose Sugar-Free

Brand Names: Canada Metadol; Metadol-D; Methadose

Pharmacologic Category Analgesic, Opioid

Use

Detoxification: Detoxification and maintenance treatment of opioid addiction (heroin or other morphine-like drugs), in conjunction with appropriate social and medical services; injection is only for temporary treatment in patients unable to take oral medication.

Limitations of use: Injection: Not approved for outpatient treatment of opioid dependence; only use in patients unable to take oral medication (eg, hospitalized patients).

Pain management:

Injection: Management of pain severe enough to require an opioid analgesic and for which alternative treatment options are inadequate.

Oral (Dolophine only): Management of pain severe enough to require daily, around-the-clock, long-term opioid treatment and for which alternative treatment options are inadequate.

Limitations of use: Reserve for use in patients for whom alternative treatment options (eg, nonopioid analgesics, opioid combination products) are ineffective, not tolerated, or would be otherwise inadequate to provide sufficient management of pain. Dolophine is not indicated for use as an as-needed analgesic.

Local Anesthetic/Vasoconstrictor Precautions Methadone is one of the drugs confirmed to prolong the QT interval and is accepted as having a risk of causing torsade de pointes. The risk of drug-induced torsade de pointes is extremely low when a single QT interval prolonging drug is prescribed. In terms of epinephrine, it is not known what effect vasoconstrictors in the local anesthetic regimen will have in patients with a known history of congenital prolonged QT interval or in patients taking any medication that prolongs the QT interval. Until more information is obtained, it is suggested that the clinician consult with the physician prior to the use of a vasoconstrictor in suspected patients, and that the vasoconstrictor (epinephrine, levonordefrin [Neo-Cobefrin®]) be used with caution.

Effects on Dental Treatment Key adverse event(s) related to dental treatment: Significant xerostomia (normal salivary flow resumes upon discontinuation) and glossitis.

Effects on Bleeding No information available to require special precautions

Adverse Reactions Frequency not defined. During prolonged administration, adverse effects may decrease over several weeks; however, constipation and sweating may persist.

Cardiovascular: Bigeminy, bradycardia, cardiac arrest, cardiac arrhythmia, cardiac failure, cardiomyopathy, ECG changes, edema, extrasystoles, flushing, hypotension, inversion T wave on ECG, orthostatic hypotension, palpitations, peripheral vasodilation, phlebitis, prolonged Q-T interval on ECG, shock, syncope, tachycardia, torsades de pointes, ventricular fibrillation, ventricular tachycardia

Central nervous system: Agitation, confusion, disorientation, dizziness, drowsiness, drug dependence (physical dependence), dysphoria, euphoria, habituation, hallucination, headache, insomnia, sedation, seizure

Dermatologic: Diaphoresis, hemorrhagic urticaria (can occur locally with intravenous administration [rare]), localized erythema (intravenous/subcutaneous), pruritus, rash at injection site (intravenous), skin rash, urticaria, urticaria at injection site (intravenous)

Endocrine & metabolic: Amenorrhea, antidiuretic effect, decreased libido, hypokalemia, hypomagnesemia, weight gain

Gastrointestinal: Abdominal pain, anorexia, biliary tract spasm, constipation, glossitis, nausea, stomach cramps, vomiting, xerostomia

Genitourinary: Impotence, urinary hesitancy, urinary retention

Hematologic: Thrombocytopenia (reversible, reported in patients with chronic hepatitis)

Local: Local pruritus (intravenous), local pain (intravenous/subcutaneous), local swelling (intravenous/subcutaneous)

Neuromuscular & skeletal: Weakness

Ophthalmic: Miosis, visual disturbance

Respiratory: Pulmonary edema, respiratory arrest, respiratory depression

<1%, postmarketing, and/or case reports: Hypogonadism (Brennan 2013; Debono 2011), increased serum prolactin (transient increase with chronic use; Molltch 2008)

General Dosage Range

IM, IV, SubQ: *Adults:* Initial: 2.5 to 10 mg every 8 to 12 hours

Oral: *Adults:* Detoxification: Initial: Up to 40 mg/day; Maintenance: 80 to 120 mg/day; Pain management: 2.5 mg every 8 to 12 hours as needed

Mechanism of Action Binds to opiate receptors in the CNS, causing inhibition of ascending pain pathways, altering the perception of and response to pain; produces generalized CNS depression. Methadone has also been shown to have N-methyl-D-aspartate (NMDA) receptor antagonism.

Pharmacodynamics/Kinetics

Onset of Action Oral: Analgesic: 0.5 to 1 hour; Parenteral: 10 to 20 minutes; Peak effect: Parenteral: 1 to 2 hours; Oral: Continuous dosing: 3 to 5 days

Duration of Action Analgesia: Oral: 4 to 8 hours (single-dose studies), increases to 22 to 48 hours with repeated doses; slow release from the liver and other tissues may prolong duration of action

Half-life Elimination Terminal: Children: 19 ± 14 hours (range: 4 to 62 hours); Adults: 8 to 59 hours; may be prolonged with alkaline pH

Time to Peak 1 to 7.5 hours

Pregnancy Risk Factor C

Pregnancy Considerations Adverse events have been observed in animal reproduction studies. Methadone crosses the placenta and can be detected in cord blood, amniotic fluid, and newborn urine.

Methadone is considered the standard of care when treating opioid addiction in pregnant women. Women receiving methadone for the treatment of addiction should be maintained on their daily dose of methadone in addition to receiving the same pain management options during labor and delivery as opioid-naive women; maintenance doses of methadone will not provide adequate pain relief. Opioid agonist-antagonists should be avoided for the treatment of labor pain in women maintained on methadone due to the risk of precipitating acute withdrawal (ACOG 2012; Dow 2012).

Data is available related to fetal/neonatal outcomes following maternal use of methadone during pregnancy. Information collected by the Teratogen Information System is complicated by maternal use of illicit drugs, nutrition, infection, and psychosocial circumstances. However, pregnant women in methadone treatment programs are reported to have improved fetal outcomes compared to pregnant women using illicit drugs. Fetal growth, birth weight, length, and/or head circumference may be decreased in infants born to opioid-addicted mothers treated with methadone during pregnancy. Growth deficits do not appear to persist; however, decreased performance on psychometric and behavioral tests has been found to continue into childhood. Abnormal fetal nonstress tests have also been reported.

[US Boxed Warning]: Prolonged use of opioids during pregnancy can cause neonatal withdrawal syndrome, which may be life-threatening if not recognized and treated according to protocols developed by neonatology experts. If opioid use is required for a prolonged period in a pregnant woman, advise the patient of the risk of neonatal opioid withdrawal syndrome and ensure that appropriate treatment will be available. Withdrawal symptoms in the neonate may be observed up to 2 to 4 weeks after delivery and should be expected (ACOG 2012). Neonatal abstinence syndrome following opioid exposure may present with autonomic (eg, fever, temperature instability), gastrointestinal (eg, diarrhea, vomiting, poor feeding/weight gain), or neurologic (eg, high-pitched crying, increased muscle tone, irritability, seizure, tremor) symptoms (Dow 2012; Hudak 2012). Monitoring is recommended for neonates born to mothers receiving methadone for neonatal abstinence syndrome (Chou 2014).

Methadone clearance in pregnant women is increased and half-life is decreased during the 2nd and 3rd trimesters of pregnancy; the dosage of methadone may need increased or dosing interval decreased during pregnancy to avoid withdrawal symptoms in the mother. Dosage may need decreased following delivery (ACOG 2012).

Long-term opioid use may cause secondary hypogonadism, which may lead to sexual dysfunction or infertility (Brennan 2013). Amenorrhea may also develop secondary to substance abuse; pregnancy may occur following the initiation of buprenorphine or methadone maintenance treatment. Contraception counseling is recommended to prevent unplanned pregnancies (Dow 2012).

Controlled Substance C-II

Prescribing and Access Restrictions When used for treatment of opioid addiction: May only be dispensed in accordance to guidelines established by the Substance Abuse and Mental Health Services Administration's (SAMHSA) Center for Substance Abuse Treatment (CSAT). Regulations regarding methadone use may vary by state and/or country. Obtain advice from appropriate regulatory agencies and/or consult with pain management/palliative care specialists.

Note: Regulatory Exceptions to the General Requirement to Provide Opioid Agonist Treatment (per manufacturer's labeling):

1. During inpatient care, when the patient was admitted for any condition other than concurrent opioid addiction, to facilitate the treatment of the primary admitting diagnosis.
2. During an emergency period of no longer than 3 days while definitive care for the addiction is being sought in an appropriately licensed facility.

Dental Comment See Local Anesthetic/Vasoconstrictor Precautions

Methamphetamine (meth am FET a meen)

Related Information

Management of the Chemically Dependent Patient *on page 1821*

Brand Names: US Desoxyn

Brand Names: Canada Desoxyn

Pharmacologic Category Anorexiant; Central Nervous System Stimulant; Sympathomimetic

Use

Attention-deficit/hyperactivity disorder (ADHD): For a stabilizing effect in children >6 years with a behavioral syndrome characterized by the following group of developmentally inappropriate symptoms: Moderate to severe distractibility, short attention span, hyperactivity, emotional lability, and impulsivity

Exogenous obesity: Short-term (ie, a few weeks) adjunct in a regimen of weight reduction based on caloric restriction, for patients in whom obesity is refractory to alternative therapy (eg, repeated diets, group programs, other drugs)

Local Anesthetic/Vasoconstrictor Precautions Use vasoconstrictor with caution in patients taking methamphetamine. Amphetamines enhance the sympathomimetic response of epinephrine and norepinephrine leading to potential hypertension and cardiotoxicity.

Effects on Dental Treatment Key adverse event(s) related to dental treatment: Methamphetamine causes tachycardia, increases in blood pressure, and palpitations. Consider monitoring blood pressure prior to using local anesthetic with a vasoconstrictor. Symptoms associated with bruxism have been observed in some patients.

Effects on Bleeding No information available to require special precautions

Adverse Reactions Frequency not defined.

Cardiovascular: Hypertension, increased blood pressure, palpitations, tachycardia

Central nervous system: Dizziness, drug dependence (prolonged use), dysphoria, euphoria, exacerbation of tics (motor, phonic, and Tourette's syndrome), headache, insomnia, overstimulation, psychotic symptoms, restlessness

Dermatologic: Urticaria

Endocrine & metabolic: Change in libido, growth suppression (children)

Gastrointestinal: Constipation, diarrhea, gastrointestinal distress, unpleasant taste, xerostomia

Genitourinary: Frequent erections, impotence, prolonged erection

Neuromuscular & skeletal: Rhabdomyolysis, tremor

General Dosage Range Oral:

Children ≥6 years and Adolescents: ADHD: Initial: 5 mg once or twice daily; usual maintenance dose: 20 to 25 mg daily in 1 or 2 divided doses

Children ≥12 years, Adolescents, and Adults: Exogenous obesity: 5 mg before each meal

Mechanism of Action A sympathomimetic amine related to ephedrine and amphetamine with CNS stimulant activity; causes release of catecholamines (primarily dopamine and other catecholamines) from their storage sites in the presynaptic nerve terminals. Inhibits reuptake and metabolism of catecholamines through inhibition of monoamine transporters and oxidase.

Pharmacodynamics/Kinetics

Half-life Elimination 4 to 5 hours

Pregnancy Risk Factor C

Pregnancy Considerations Adverse events have been observed in animal reproduction studies. Methamphetamine and amphetamine were detected in newborn tissues following intermittent maternal use of Desoxyn during pregnancy (Garriott 1973). The majority of human data is based on illicit amphetamine/methamphetamine exposure and not from therapeutic maternal use (Golub 2005). Use of amphetamines during pregnancy may lead to an increased risk of premature birth and low birth weight; newborns may experience symptoms of withdrawal. Behavioral problems may also occur later in childhood (LaGasse 2012).

Controlled Substance C II

MethazolAMIDE (meth a ZOE la mide)

Brand Names: US Neptazane

Brand Names: Canada Apo-Methazolamide®

Pharmacologic Category Carbonic Anhydrase Inhibitor; Diuretic, Carbonic Anhydrase Inhibitor; Ophthalmic Agent, Antiglaucoma

Use Treatment of chronic open-angle or secondary glaucoma; short-term therapy of acute angle-closure glaucoma prior to surgery

Local Anesthetic/Vasoconstrictor Precautions No information available to require special precautions

Effects on Dental Treatment Key adverse event(s) related to dental treatment: Xerostomia (normal salivary flow resumes upon discontinuation) and metallic taste.

Effects on Bleeding No information available to require special precautions

Adverse Reactions Frequency not defined.

Central nervous system: Confusion, drowsiness, fatigue, flaccid paralysis, malaise, paresthesia, seizure

Dermatologic: Erythema multiforme, skin photosensitivity, skin rash, Stevens-Johnson syndrome, toxic epidermal necrolysis, urticaria

Endocrine & metabolic: Electrolyte disturbance, glycosuria, metabolic acidosis

Gastrointestinal: Decreased appetite, diarrhea, dysgeusia, melena, nausea, vomiting

Genitourinary: Crystalluria, hematuria

Hematologic & oncologic: Agranulocytosis, aplastic anemia, bone marrow depression, hemolytic anemia, immune thrombocytopenia, leukopenia, pancytopenia

Hepatic: Fulminant hepatic necrosis, hepatic insufficiency

Hypersensitivity: Anaphylaxis, hypersensitivity reaction

Ophthalmic: Myopia

Otic: Auditory disturbance, tinnitus

Renal: Nephrolithiasis, polyuria

Miscellaneous: Fever

General Dosage Range Oral: *Adults:* 50-100 mg 2-3 times/day

Mechanism of Action Noncompetitive inhibition of the enzyme carbonic anhydrase; thought that carbonic anhydrase is located at the luminal border of cells of the proximal tubule. When the enzyme is inhibited, there is an increase in urine volume and a change to an alkaline pH with a subsequent decrease in the excretion of titratable acid and ammonia.

Pharmacodynamics/Kinetics

Onset of Action Slow in comparison with acetazolamide (2-4 hours); Peak effect: 6-8 hours

Duration of Action 10-18 hours

Half-life Elimination ~14 hours

Pregnancy Risk Factor C

Pregnancy Considerations Adverse events were observed in animal reproduction studies.

Methenamine (meth EN a meen)

Brand Names: US Hiprex

Brand Names: Canada Mandelamine

Pharmacologic Category Antibiotic, Miscellaneous

Use Urinary tract infection, prophylaxis/suppression: Prophylaxis or suppression of recurrent urinary tract infections when long-term therapy is indicated and infection has been eradicated by appropriate antimicrobial treatment

Local Anesthetic/Vasoconstrictor Precautions No information available to require special precautions

Effects on Dental Treatment No significant effects or complications reported

Effects on Bleeding No information available to require special precautions

Adverse Reactions Large doses (higher than recommended) have resulted in bladder irritation, frequent/painful micturition, albuminuria, and hematuria.

<4%:

Dermatologic: Pruritus, skin rash

Gastrointestinal: Dyspepsia, nausea, vomiting

<1%, postmarketing, and/or case reports: Increased serum ALT (reversible), increased serum AST (reversible)

General Dosage Range Oral:

Hippurate:

Children 6 to 12 years: 500 to 1,000 mg twice daily

Adolescents and Adults: 1,000 mg twice daily

Mandelate:

Children <6 years: 250 mg per 14 kg body weight 4 times daily

Children 6 to 12 years: 500 mg 4 times daily

Adolescents and Adults: 1,000 mg 4 times daily

Mechanism of Action Methenamine is hydrolyzed to formaldehyde and ammonia in acidic urine; formaldehyde has nonspecific bactericidal action. Other components, hippuric acid or mandelic acid, aid in maintaining urine acidity and may aid in suppressing bacteria.

Pharmacodynamics/Kinetics

Half-life Elimination ~4 hours (Allgén 1979)

Time to Peak 1 to 2 hours (Allgén 1979)

Pregnancy Risk Factor C (methenamine mandelate)

Pregnancy Considerations Adverse events have not been observed in animal reproduction studies with methenamine hippurate; animal reproduction studies have not been conducted with methenamine mandelate. Methenamine crosses the placenta and distributes to amniotic fluid (Allgén, 1979). An increased risk of adverse fetal effects has not been observed in available studies (Furness, 1975; Gordon, 1972; Heinonen,

1977). Methenamine use has been shown to interfere with urine estriol concentrations if measured via acid hydrolysis. Use of enzyme hydrolysis prevents this lab interference.

Methenamine, Phenyl Salicylate, Methylene Blue, Benzoic Acid, and Hyoscyamine

(meth EN a meen, fen nil sa LIS i late, METH i leen bloo, ben ZOE ik AS id & hye oh SYE a meen)

Related Information

Methenamine *on page 1075*

Brand Names: US Hyophen; Prosed/DS [DSC]; Urophen MB

Pharmacologic Category Antibiotic, Miscellaneous

Use Urinary tract discomfort secondary to hypermotility resulting from infection or diagnostic procedures

Local Anesthetic/Vasoconstrictor Precautions No information available to require special precautions

Effects on Dental Treatment Key adverse event(s) related to dental treatment: Xerostomia (normal salivary flow resumes upon discontinuation).

Effects on Bleeding No information available to require special precautions

Adverse Reactions Frequency not defined.

Cardiovascular: Flushing, tachycardia

Central nervous system: Dizziness

Gastrointestinal: Fecal discoloration (blue), nausea, vomiting, xerostomia

Genitourinary: Difficulty in micturition, urinary retention (acute), urine discoloration (blue)

Ophthalmic: Blurred vision

Respiratory: Dyspnea

General Dosage Range Oral: *Adults:* 1 tablet 4 times/day

Pregnancy Risk Factor C

Pregnancy Considerations Reproduction studies have not been conducted with this combination. Methenamine and hyoscyamine cross the placenta.

Methenamine, Sodium Phosphate Monobasic, Phenyl Salicylate, Methylene Blue, and Hyoscyamine

(meth EN a meen, SOW dee um FOS fate mon oh BAY sik, fen nil sa LIS i late, METH i leen bloo, & hye oh SYE a meen)

Related Information

Methenamine *on page 1075*

Brand Names: US Azuphen MB; Hyolev MB; Phosphasal; Ur N-C; Uramit MB; Urelle; Uretron D/S; Uribel; Urimar-T; Urin DS; Uro-458; Uro-L [DSC]; Uro-MP; UroAv-81; UroAv-B; Ustell; Uticap; Utira-C; Utrona-C

Pharmacologic Category Antibiotic, Miscellaneous

Use Treatment of symptoms of irritative voiding; relief of local symptoms associated with urinary tract infections; relief of urinary tract symptoms caused by diagnostic procedures

Local Anesthetic/Vasoconstrictor Precautions No information available to require special precautions

Effects on Dental Treatment Key adverse event(s) related to dental treatment: Xerostomia (normal salivary flow resumes upon discontinuation).

Effects on Bleeding No information available to require special precautions

Adverse Reactions Frequency not defined.

Cardiovascular: Flushing, tachycardia

Central nervous system: Dizziness

Gastrointestinal: Nausea, vomiting, xerostomia

Genitourinary: Acute urinary retention, difficulty in micturition, urine discoloration (blue)

Ophthalmic: Blurred vision

Respiratory: Dyspnea

General Dosage Range Oral: *Adults:* 1 tablet 4 times/day

Pregnancy Risk Factor C

Pregnancy Considerations Reproduction studies have not been conducted with this combination. Methenamine and hyoscyamine cross the placenta.

MethIMAzole (meth IM a zole)

Related Information

Endocrine Disorders and Pregnancy *on page 1781*

Brand Names: US Tapazole

Brand Names: Canada Dom-Methimazole; PHL-Methimazole; Tapazole

Pharmacologic Category Antithyroid Agent; Thioamide

Use Hyperthyroidism: Treatment of hyperthyroidism in patients with Graves' disease or toxic multinodular goiter (surgery or radioactive iodine therapy is not appropriate); amelioration of hyperthyroid symptoms in preparation for thyroidectomy or radioactive iodine therapy.

Local Anesthetic/Vasoconstrictor Precautions No information available to require special precautions

Effects on Dental Treatment Key adverse event(s) related to dental treatment: Abnormal taste and salivary gland swelling.

Effects on Bleeding No information available to require special precautions

Adverse Reactions Frequency not defined.

Cardiovascular: Antineutrophil cytoplasmic antibody-positive vasculitis, edema, hypersensitivity angiitis, periarteritis

Central nervous system: Drowsiness, headache, neuritis, paresthesia, vertigo

Dermatologic: Alopecia, exfoliative dermatitis, pruritus, skin pigmentation, skin rash, urticaria

Endocrine & metabolic: Goiter, hypoglycemic coma, insulin autoimmune syndrome, weight gain

Gastrointestinal: Ageusia, constipation, enlargement of salivary glands, epigastric distress, nausea, vomiting

Hematologic & oncologic: Agranulocytosis, aplastic anemia, granulocytopenia, hypoprothrombinemia, leukopenia, lymphadenopathy, thrombocytopenia

Hepatic: Hepatic necrosis, hepatitis, jaundice

Neuromuscular & skeletal: Arthralgia, lupus-like syndrome, myalgia

Renal: Nephritis

Miscellaneous: Fever

General Dosage Range Oral:

Children and Adolescents: Initial: 0.4 mg/kg/day in 3 divided doses; Maintenance: 0.2 mg/kg/day in 3 divided doses

Adults: Initial: 15 to 60 mg daily in 3 divided doses; Maintenance: 5 to 15 mg daily in 3 divided doses

Mechanism of Action Inhibits the synthesis of thyroid hormones by blocking the oxidation of iodine in the thyroid gland; blocks synthesis of thyroxine and triiodothyronine (T_3); does not inactivate circulating T_4 and T_3

Pharmacodynamics/Kinetics

Onset of Action Antithyroid: 12 to 18 hours (Clark 2006)

Duration of Action 36 to 72 hours (Clark 2006)

Half-life Elimination 4 to 6 hours (Clark 2006)

Time to Peak Serum: 1 to 2 hours (Clark 2006)

Pregnancy Risk Factor D

Pregnancy Considerations Methimazole has been found to readily cross the placenta. Congenital anomalies, including esophageal atresia, choanal atresia, aplasia cutis, and dysmorphic facies, have been observed in neonates born to mothers taking methimazole during pregnancy (Stangaro-Green 2011). Nonteratogenic adverse events, including fetal and neonatal hypothyroidism, have been observed following maternal methimazole use. The transfer of thyroid-stimulating immunoglobulins can stimulate the fetal thyroid in utero and transiently after delivery and may increase the risk of fetal or neonatal hyperthyroidism (De Groot 2012; Stangaro-Green 2011).

Uncontrolled maternal hyperthyroidism may result in adverse neonatal outcomes (eg, prematurity, low birth weight, infants born small for gestational age) and adverse maternal outcomes (eg, pre-eclampsia, congestive heart failure) (ACOG 2002; Stangaro-Green 2011). To prevent adverse fetal and maternal events, normal maternal thyroid function should be maintained prior to conception and throughout pregnancy. Antithyroid treatment is recommended for the control of hyperthyroidism during pregnancy. Due to an increased risk of congenital anomalies with methimazole, propylthiouracil is preferred during the first trimester of pregnancy and methimazole is preferred during the second and third trimesters of pregnancy (ACOG 2002; De Groot 2012; Stangaro-Green 2011). If drug therapy is changed, maternal thyroid function should be monitored after 2 weeks and then every 2 to 4 weeks (De Groot 2012).

The severity of hyperthyroidism may fluctuate throughout pregnancy and may result in decreased dose requirements or discontinuation of methimazole 2 to 3 weeks prior to delivery.

Methocarbamol (meth oh KAR ba mole)

Related Information

Temporomandibular Dysfunction (TMD), Chronic Pain, and Fibromyalgia *on page 1868*

Brand Names: US Robaxin; Robaxin-750

Brand Names: Canada Robaxin

Generic Availability (US) Yes

Pharmacologic Category Skeletal Muscle Relaxant

Dental Use Treatment of muscle spasm associated with acute temporomandibular joint pain (TMJ)

Use Adjunctive treatment of muscle spasm associated with acute painful musculoskeletal conditions

Local Anesthetic/Vasoconstrictor Precautions No information available to require special precautions

Effects on Dental Treatment Key adverse event(s) related to dental treatment: Metallic taste.

Effects on Bleeding No information available to require special precautions

Adverse Reactions Frequency not defined.

Cardiovascular: Bradycardia, flushing, hypotension, syncope, thrombophlebitis

Central nervous system: Amnesia, ataxia (mild), confusion, dizziness, drowsiness, headache, insomnia, metallic taste, sedation, seizure, vertigo

Dermatologic: Pruritus, skin rash, urticaria

Gastrointestinal: Dyspepsia, nausea, vomiting

Hematologic & oncologic: Leukopenia

Hepatic: Jaundice

Hypersensitivity: Angioedema, hypersensitivity reaction (including anaphylaxis)

Local: Pain at injection site

Ophthalmic: Blurred vision, conjunctivitis, diplopia, nystagmus

Respiratory: Nasal congestion

Miscellaneous: Fever

Dental Usual Dosage Muscle spasm associated with acute TMJ pain: Children ≥16 years and Adults: Oral: 1.5 g 4 times/day for 2-3 days (up to 8 g/day may be given in severe conditions), then decrease to 4-4.5 g/day in 3-6 divided doses

Dosing

Adult

Muscle spasm:

Oral: 1.5 g 4 times/day for 2-3 days (up to 8 g/day may be given in severe conditions), then decrease to 4-4.5 g/day in 3-6 divided doses

IM, IV: Initial: 1 g; may repeat every 8 hours if oral administration not possible; maximum dose: 3 g/day for no more than 3 consecutive days. If condition persists, may repeat course of therapy after a drug-free interval of 48 hours.

Tetanus: IV: Initial dose: 1-2 g by direct IV injection, which may be followed by an additional 1-2 g by infusion (maximum initial dose: 3 g total); may repeat initial dose every 6 hours until NG tube or oral therapy possible; total oral daily dose of up to 24 g may be needed; injection should not be used for more than 3 consecutive days

Pediatric

Tetanus (recommended **only** for use in tetanus): IV: 15 mg/kg/dose or 500 mg/m²/dose, may repeat every 6 hours if needed; maximum dose: 1.8 g/m²/day for 3 days only

Muscle spasm: Oral: Children ≥16 years: Refer to adult dosing.

Renal Impairment No dosage adjustment provided in manufacturer's labeling. However, administration of the parenteral formulation is contraindicated in patients with renal dysfunction due to the presence of polyethylene glycol.

Hepatic Impairment No dosage adjustment provided in manufacturer's labeling. However, elimination may be reduced in patients with cirrhosis.

Mechanism of Action Causes skeletal muscle relaxation by general CNS depression

Contraindications Hypersensitivity to methocarbamol or any component of the formulation; renal impairment (injection formulation)

Warnings/Precautions May cause CNS depression, which may impair physical or mental abilities; patients must be cautioned about performing tasks which require mental alertness (eg, operating machinery or driving). Effects may be potentiated when used with other sedative drugs or ethanol. Plasma protein binding and clearance are decreased and the half-life is increased in patients with hepatic impairment.

Injection: Contraindicated in renal impairment. Contains polyethylene glycol. Rate of injection should not exceed 3 mL/minute; solution is hypertonic; avoid extravasation. Use with caution in patients with a history of seizures. Use caution with hepatic impairment. Vial stopper contains latex. Recommended only for the treatment of tetanus in pediatric patients.

Drug Interactions

Metabolism/Transport Effects None known.

Avoid Concomitant Use

Avoid concomitant use of Methocarbamol with any of the following: Azelastine (Nasal); Orphenadrine; Oxomemazine; Paraldehyde; Thalidomide

Increased Effect/Toxicity

Methocarbamol may increase the levels/effects of: Alcohol (Ethyl); Analgesics (Opioid); Azelastine (Nasal); Blonanserin; Buprenorphine; CNS Depressants; Flunitrazepam; HYDROcodone; Methotrimeprazine; MetyroSINE; Mirtazapine; Orphenadrine; OxyCODONE; Paraldehyde; Piribedil; Pramipexole; ROPINIRole; Rotigotine; Selective Serotonin Reuptake Inhibitors; Suvorexant; Thalidomide; Zolpidem

The levels/effects of Methocarbamol may be increased by: Brimonidine (Topical); Cannabis; Chlormethiazole; Chlorphenesin Carbamate; Dimethindene (Topical); Doxylamine; Dronabinol; Droperidol; Eperisone; HydrOXYzine; Kava Kava; Lofexidine; Magnesium Sulfate; Methotrimeprazine; Minocycline; Nabilone; Oxomemazine; Perampanel; Rufinamide; Sodium Oxybate; Tapentadol; Tetrahydrocannabinol; Tolperisone; Trimeprazine

Decreased Effect

Methocarbamol may decrease the levels/effects of: Pyridostigmine

Pharmacodynamics/Kinetics

Onset of Action Muscle relaxation: Oral: ~30 minutes

Half-life Elimination 1 to 2 hours

Time to Peak Serum: Oral: 1 to 2 hours

Pregnancy Risk Factor C

Pregnancy Considerations Animal reproduction studies have not been conducted. The manufacturer notes that fetal and congenital abnormalities have been rarely reported following *in utero* exposure. Use during pregnancy only if clearly needed.

Breastfeeding Considerations It is not known if methocarbamol is excreted in breast milk. The manufacturer recommends that caution be exercised when administering methocarbamol to nursing women.

Dosage Forms

Solution, Injection:

Robaxin: 1000 mg/10 mL (10 mL)

Generic: 1000 mg/10 mL (10 mL)

Solution, Injection [preservative free]:

Generic: 1000 mg/10 mL (10 mL)

Tablet, Oral:

Robaxin: 500 mg

Robaxin-750: 750 mg

Generic: 500 mg, 750 mg

Methohexital (meth oh HEKS i tal)

Brand Names: US Brevital Sodium

Brand Names: Canada Brevital

Generic Availability (US) May be product dependent

Pharmacologic Category Barbiturate; General Anesthetic

Dental Use Induction and maintenance of general anesthesia for short procedures

Use

Induction of anesthesia: Induction of anesthesia prior to the use of other general anesthetic agents; to supplement other anesthetic agents for longer surgical procedures. **Note:** Use to maintain anesthesia using either the manufacturer recommended continuous infusion or intermittent dosing has fallen out of favor.

Procedural sedation: Short surgical, diagnostic, or therapeutic procedures associated with minimal painful stimuli.

Local Anesthetic/Vasoconstrictor Precautions No information available to require special precautions

Effects on Dental Treatment No significant effects or complications reported

Effects on Bleeding No information available to require special precautions

Adverse Reactions Frequency not defined.

Cardiovascular: Circulatory depression, circulatory shock, hypotension, local thrombophlebitis, tachycardia

Central nervous system: Anxiety, delirium (emergence), headache, involuntary muscle movements, neuropathy (adjacent to injection site), radial nerve palsy, restlessness, seizure, twitching

Dermatologic: Erythema, pruritus, urticaria

Gastrointestinal: Abdominal pain, hiccups, nausea, salivation, vomiting

Hepatic: Increased serum transaminases

Local: Pain at injection site

Neuromuscular & skeletal: Laryngospasm, muscle rigidity, tremor

Respiratory: Apnea, bronchospasm, cough, dyspnea, respiratory depression, rhinitis

<1%, postmarketing, and/or case reports: Anaphylaxis

Dental Usual Dosage Induction and maintenance of general anesthesia for short procedures: Doses must be titrated to effect: Adults: IV: Induction: 50-120 mg to start; 20-40 mg every 4-7 minutes

Dosing

Adult

Anesthesia: IV: Induction: 1 to 1.5 mg/kg of a 1% solution; doses must be titrated to effect. **Note:** Use to maintain anesthesia using either the manufacturer recommended continuous infusion or intermittent dosing has fallen out of favor.

Procedural sedation (off-label dose): IV: 0.75 to 1 mg/kg; can redose 0.5 mg/kg every 2 to 5 minutes as needed (Bahn 2005)

Wada test (off-label use): Intracarotid (off-label route): 3 to 4 mg over 3 seconds; following signs of recovery, administer a second dose of 2 mg over 2 seconds (Buchtel 2002)

Geriatric Refer to adult dosing. Reduce dose or administer at the low end of the dosage range.

Pediatric

Anesthesia: Doses must be titrated to effect.

Manufacturer recommendations: **Induction:**

Infants ≥1 month, Children, and Adolescents:

IM: 6.6 to 10 mg/kg of a 5% solution

Rectal: 25 mg/kg of a 1% solution

Alternative recommendations (off-label dosing):

Induction: Children and Adolescents:

IM: 5 to 10 mg/kg/dose of a 5% solution

IV: 1 to 2 mg/kg/dose of a 1% solution (Bjorkman 1987)

Procedural sedation: Children and Adolescents: IV: Initial: 0.5 mg/kg of a 1% solution given immediately prior to procedure; titrate dose to achieve level of sedation as needed, in increments of 0.5 mg/kg to a maximum dose of 2 mg/kg; **Note**: In the prospective phase of a study, 20 children (mean age: 26 months) undergoing emergency CT scans required a mean dose of 1 ± 0.5 mg/kg/dose with a mean total dose of 14 ± 7.5 mg/kg (Sedik 2001)

Preoperative, anesthesia induction, or preprocedural: Children and Adolescents: Rectal: Usual: 25 mg/kg/dose; range: 20 to 35 mg/kg/dose; maximum dose: 500 mg/dose; give as 10% (100 mg/mL) aqueous solution 5 to15 minutes prior to procedure (Bjorkman 1987; Pomeranz 2000)

Renal Impairment There are no dosage adjustments provided in the manufacturer's labeling; use with caution.

Hepatic Impairment There are no dosage adjustments provided in the manufacturer's labeling. However, adjustment may be necessary due to hepatic metabolism. Use with caution.

Mechanism of Action Methohexital is an ultra short-acting IV barbiturate anesthetic. Barbiturates depress the sensory cortex, decrease motor activity, and alter cerebellar function producing drowsiness, sedation, and hypnosis.

Contraindications Hypersensitivity to methohexital or any component of the formulation; porphyria (latent or manifest); patients in whom general anesthesia is contraindicated

Warnings/Precautions Use with caution in patients with liver impairment, renal impairment, severe anemia, extreme obesity, or seizure disorder, debilitated patients, the elderly and children. Use with caution in patients with cardiovascular disease including heart failure; consider monitoring cardiac function. Methohexital may enhance preexisting circulatory depression, severe cardiovascular instability, or a shock-like condition; consider using another induction agent in these patients. May cause temporary hypotension and tachycardia; use with caution in hemodynamically unstable patients (hypotension or shock) or severe hypertension. May cause respiratory depression; use with caution in patients with pulmonary disease. Use with caution in patients with asthma and chronic obstructive pulmonary disease. Use with extreme caution in patients with ongoing status asthmaticus; hiccups, coughing, laryngospasm, and muscle twitching have occurred impairing ventilation. May cause CNS depression, which may impair physical or mental abilities; patients must be cautioned about performing tasks that require mental alertness (eg, operating machinery or driving); however, the duration of action is ≤10 minutes when used for procedural sedation (Bahn 2005).

Postmarketing studies have indicated that the use of hypnotic/sedative agents for sleep has been associated with hypersensitivity reactions including anaphylaxis as well as angioedema. Potentially significant interactions may exist, requiring dose or frequency adjustment, additional monitoring, and/or selection of alternative therapy. Repeated dosing or continuous infusions may cause cumulative effects. Ensure patient has intravenous access; extravasation or intra-arterial injection causes necrosis. **[US Boxed Warning]: Should only be administered in hospitals or ambulatory care settings with continuous monitoring of respiratory (eg, pulse oximetry) and cardiac function. Immediate availability of resuscitative drugs and age- and size-appropriate intubation equipment and trained personnel experienced in handling their use should be immediately available and personnel trained in their use and skilled in airway management should be assured. For deeply sedated patients, a designated individual other than the healthcare provider performing the procedure should be present to continuously monitor the patient.** Maintenance of a patent airway and adequacy of ventilation must be ensured during use. Laryngospasm is common during induction with all barbiturates.

Drug Interactions

Metabolism/Transport Effects None known.

Avoid Concomitant Use

Avoid concomitant use of Methohexital with any of the following: Azelastine (Nasal); Hemin; Methoxyflurane; Mianserin; Orphenadrine; Oxomemazine; Paraldehyde; Somatostatin Acetate; Thalidomide; Ulipristal

Increased Effect/Toxicity

Methohexital may increase the levels/effects of: Alcohol (Ethyl); Analgesics (Opioid); Azelastine (Nasal); Blonanserin; Blood Pressure Lowering Agents; Buprenorphine; CNS Depressants; Flunitrazepam; HYDROcodone; Methotrimeprazine; Methoxyflurane; MetyroSINE; Mirtazapine; Orphenadrine; OxyCODONE; Paraldehyde; Piribedil; Pramipexole; ROPINIRole; Rotigotine; Selective Serotonin Reuptake Inhibitors; Suvorexant; Thalidomide; Thiazide and Thiazide-Like Diuretics; Zolpidem

The levels/effects of Methohexital may be increased by: Brimonidine (Topical); Cannabis; Chloramphenicol; Chlormethiazole; Chlorphenesin Carbamate; Dimethindene (Topical); Doxylamine; Dronabinol; Droperidol; Felbamate; HydrOXYzine; Kava Kava; Lofexidine; Magnesium Sulfate; Methotrimeprazine; Mianserin; Minocycline; Nabilone; Oxomemazine; Perampanel; Primidone; Rufinamide; Sodium Oxybate; Somatostatin Acetate; Tapentadol; Tetrahydrocannabinol; Trimeprazine; Valproate Products

Decreased Effect

Methohexital may decrease the levels/effects of: Beta-Blockers; Calcium Channel Blockers; Chloramphenicol; Contraceptives (Estrogens); Contraceptives (Progestins); CycloSPORINE (Systemic); Doxycycline; Felbamate; Hemin; LamoTRIgine; Methoxyflurane; Mianserin; Propacetamol; Teniposide; Theophylline Derivatives; Tricyclic Antidepressants; Ulipristal; Valproate Products; Vitamin K Antagonists

The levels/effects of Methohexital may be decreased by: Mianserin; Multivitamins/Minerals (with ADEK, Folate, Iron); Pyridoxine; Rifamycin Derivatives

Pharmacodynamics/Kinetics

Onset of Action IV: Immediate; IM (pediatrics): 2 to 10 minutes; Rectal (pediatrics): 5 to 15 minutes

Duration of Action Single dose:

IM: 1 to 1.5 hours

IV: Time to clinical recovery (ie, awake time, sitting and standing steadily, duration of amnesia): 5 to 15 minutes (psychomotor impairment may continue for up to 8 hours) (Barash 2009; Fredman 1994; Korttila 1975)

Rectal (pediatrics): 45 to 60 minutes (Cote 1994)

Half-life Elimination 1.6 to 3.9 hours (Ghoneim 1985)

Pregnancy Risk Factor B

Pregnancy Considerations Adverse events have not been observed in animal reproduction studies. Methohexital crosses the placenta.

Breastfeeding Considerations Methohexital is minimally excreted in breast milk and levels decline rapidly after administration. Interruption of breastfeeding is unnecessary (Borgatta 1997). The manufacturer recommends that caution be exercised when administering methohexital to nursing women.

Controlled Substance C-IV

Dosage Forms

Solution Prefilled Syringe, Intravenous:

Generic: 100 mg/10 mL (10 mL)

Solution Reconstituted, Injection:

Brevital Sodium: 500 mg (1 ea); 2.5 g (1 ea)

Methotrexate (meth oh TREKS ate)

Related Information

Rheumatoid Arthritis, Osteoarthritis, and Osteoporosis *on page 1792*

Brand Names: US Otrexup; Rasuvo; Rheumatrex [DSC]; Trexall

Brand Names: Canada Apo-Methotrexate; JAMP-Methotrexate; Methotrexate Injection USP; Methotrexate Injection, BP; Methotrexate Sodium Injection; Metoject; ratio-Methotrexate Sodium

Generic Availability (US) May be product dependent

Pharmacologic Category Antineoplastic Agent, Antimetabolite (Antifolate); Antirheumatic, Disease Modifying; Immunosuppressant Agent

Use

Oncology uses: Acute lymphoblastic leukemia (ALL) maintenance treatment, ALL meningeal leukemia (preservative-free only; prophylaxis and treatment); treatment of trophoblastic neoplasms (gestational choriocarcinoma, chorioadenoma destruens and hydatidiform mole), breast cancer, head and neck cancer (epidermoid), cutaneous T-Cell lymphoma (advanced mycosis fungoides), lung cancer (squamous cell and small cell), advanced non-Hodgkin lymphomas (NHL), osteosarcoma (preservative-free only).

Nononcology uses: Treatment of psoriasis (severe, recalcitrant, disabling) that is unresponsive to other therapies; severe, active rheumatoid arthritis (RA) that is unresponsive to or intolerant of first-line therapy including full dose nonsteroidal anti-inflammatory agents (NSAIDs); active polyarticular-course juvenile idiopathic arthritis (pJIA) that is unresponsive to or intolerant of first-line therapy including full dose nonsteroidal anti-inflammatory agents (NSAIDs).

Limitations of use: Otrexup and Rasuvo are not indicated for the treatment of neoplastic diseases.

Guideline recommendations: Rheumatoid arthritis: Treatment initiation with a disease-modifying antirheumatic drug (DMARD) is recommended in DMARD-naïve patients with either early rheumatoid arthritis (RA) (disease duration <6 months) or established RA (disease duration ≥6 months). Methotrexate is the preferred initial DMARD for most early or established RA patients (Singh [ACR 2016]).

Local Anesthetic/Vasoconstrictor Precautions No information available to require special precautions

Effects on Dental Treatment Key adverse event(s) related to dental treatment: Ulcerative stomatitis, gingivitis, glossitis, and mucositis (dose dependent; appears 3-7 days post-therapy and resolves within 2 weeks). Dental professionals should note before prescribing NSAIDS that concurrent administration with methotrexate may cause severe bone marrow suppression, aplastic anemia, and GI toxicity (see Warnings). Although the risk is lower at the methotrexate dosages used for rheumatoid conditions/psoriasis, the addition of an NSAID or salicylate may still lead to unexpected toxicities; caution is warranted.

Effects on Bleeding Suppression of hematopoiesis may cause myelosuppression including thrombocytopenia. Medical consult recommended.

Adverse Reactions Note: Adverse reactions vary by route and dosage. Frequency not always defined.

Cardiovascular: Arterial thrombosis, cerebral thrombosis, chest pain, deep vein thrombosis, hypotension, pericardial effusion, pericarditis, plaque erosion (psoriasis), pulmonary embolism, retinal thrombosis, thrombophlebitis, vasculitis

Central nervous system: Dizziness (≤3%), headache (pJIA 1%), abnormal cranial sensation, brain disease, chemical arachnoiditis (intrathecal; acute), chills, cognitive dysfunction (has been reported at low dosage), drowsiness, fatigue, leukoencephalopathy (intravenous administration after craniospinal irradiation or repeated high-dose therapy; may be chronic), malaise, mood changes (has been reported at low dosage), neurological signs and symptoms (at high dosages; including confusion, hemiparesis, transient blindness, seizures, and coma), severe neurotoxicity (reported with unexpectedly increased frequency among pediatric patients with acute lymphoblastic leukemia who were treated with intermediate-dose intravenous methotrexate), speech disturbance

Dermatologic: Alopecia (≤10%), burning sensation of skin (psoriasis 3% to 10%), skin photosensitivity (3% to 10%), skin rash (≤3%), dermatitis (rheumatoid arthritis 1% to 3%), pruritus (rheumatoid arthritis 1% to 3%), acne vulgaris, dermal ulcer, diaphoresis, ecchymoses, erythema multiforme, erythematous rash, exfoliative dermatitis, furunculosis, hyperpigmentation, hypopigmentation, skin abnormalities related to radiation recall, skin necrosis, Stevens-Johnson syndrome, telangiectasia, toxic epidermal necrolysis, urticaria

Endocrine & metabolic: Decreased libido, decreased serum albumin, diabetes mellitus, gynecomastia, menstrual disease

Gastrointestinal: Diarrhea (≤11%), nausea and vomiting (≤11%), stomatitis (2% to 10%), abdominal distress, anorexia, aphthous stomatitis, enteritis, gastrointestinal hemorrhage, gingivitis, hematemesis, intestinal perforation, melena

Genitourinary: Azotemia, cystitis, defective oogenesis, defective spermatogenesis, dysuria, hematuria, impotence, infertility, oligospermia, pancreatitis, proteinuria, severe renal disease, vaginal discharge

Hematologic & oncologic: Thrombocytopenia (rheumatoid arthritis 3% to 10%; platelet count <100,000/mm^3), leukopenia (1% to 3%; WBC <3000/mm^3), pancytopenia (rheumatoid arthritis 1% to 3%), agranulocytosis, anemia, aplastic anemia, bone marrow depression (nadir: 7-10 days), decreased hematocrit, eosinophilia, gastric ulcer, hypogammaglobulinemia, lymphadenopathy, lymphoma, lymphoproliferative disorder, neutropenia, non-Hodgkin's lymphoma (in patients receiving low-dose oral methotrexate), tumor lysis syndrome

Hepatic: Increased liver enzymes (14% to 15%), cirrhosis (chronic therapy), hepatic failure, hepatic fibrosis (chronic therapy), hepatitis (acute), hepatotoxicity

Hypersensitivity: Anaphylactoid reaction

Infection: Cryptococcosis, cytomegalovirus disease (including cytomegaloviral pneumonia, sepsis, nocardiosis), herpes simplex infection, herpes zoster, histoplasmosis, infection, pneumonia due to *pneumocystis jiroveci*, vaccinia (disseminated; following smallpox immunization)

Neuromuscular & skeletal: Arthralgia, myalgia, myelopathy (subacute), osteonecrosis (with radiotherapy), osteoporosis, stress fracture

Ophthalmic: Blurred vision, conjunctivitis, eye pain, visual disturbance
Otic: Tinnitus
Renal: Renal failure
Respiratory: Interstitial pneumonitis (rheumatoid arthritis 1%), chronic obstructive pulmonary disease, cough, epistaxis, pharyngitis, pneumonia, pulmonary alveolitis, pulmonary disease, pulmonary fibrosis, respiratory failure, upper respiratory tract infection
Miscellaneous: Fever, nodule, tissue necrosis

Dosing

Adult Note: Methotrexate doses between 100 to 500 mg/m² **may require** leucovorin calcium rescue. Doses >500 mg/m² **require** leucovorin calcium rescue (refer to Dosing – Adjustment for Toxicity for leucovorin calcium dosing). Doses ≥250 mg/m² (IV) are associated with moderate emetic potential. Antiemetics may be recommended to prevent nausea and vomiting.

Acute lymphoblastic leukemia (ALL):

Meningeal leukemia prophylaxis or treatment: Intrathecal: Manufacturer's labeling: 12 mg (maximum 15 mg/dose) every 2 to 7 days; continue for 1 dose beyond CSF cell count normalization. **Note:** Optimal intrathecal chemotherapy dosing should be based on age rather than on body surface area (BSA); CSF volume correlates with age and not to BSA (Bleyer 1983; Kerr 2001).

CALGB 8811 regimen (Larson, 1995; combination therapy):

Early intensification: Intrathecal: 15 mg day 1 of early intensification phase, repeat in 4 weeks

CNS prophylaxis/interim maintenance phase:
Intrathecal: 15 mg day 1, 8, 15, 22, and 29
Oral: 20 mg/m² days 36, 43, 50, 57, and 64

Prolonged maintenance: Oral: 20 mg/m² days 1, 8, 15, and 22 every 4 weeks for 24 months from diagnosis

Dose-intensive regimen (Kantarjian, 2000; combination therapy):

IV: 200 mg/m² over 2 hours, followed by 800 mg/m² over 24 hours beginning day 1, (followed by leucovorin rescue) of even numbered cycles (in combination with cytarabine; alternates with Hyper-CVAD)

CNS prophylaxis: Intrathecal: 12 mg on day 2 of each cycle; duration depends on risk

Maintenance: IV: 10 mg/m²/day for 5 days every month for 2 years (in combination with prednisone, vincristine, and mercaptopurine)

Breast cancer: IV: CMF regimen: 40 mg/m² days 1 and 8 every 4 weeks (in combination with cyclophosphamide and fluorouracil) for 6 to 12 cycles (Bonadonna 1995; Levine 1998)

Choriocarcinoma, chorioadenoma, gestational trophoblastic diseases: 15 to 30 mg oral or IM daily for a 5 day course; may repeat for 3 to 5 courses (manufacturer's labeling) **or** 100 mg/m² IV over 30 minutes followed by 200 mg/m² IV over 12 hours (with leucovorin 24 hours after the start of methotrexate), administer a second course if hCG levels plateau for 3 consecutive weeks (Garrett 2002) **or** 100 mg/m² IV push followed by 200 mg/m² IV over 12 hours on day 1 (with leucovorin 24 hours after the start of methotrexate; in combination with dactinomycin, etoposide, vincristine, and cyclophosphamide) every 14 days and continuing for at least 2 cycles after hCG level is normal (Escobar 2003; Lurain 2006)

Head and neck cancer, advanced: IV: 40 mg/m² once weekly until disease progression or unacceptable toxicity (Forastiere 1992; Guardiola 2004; Stewart 2009)

Lymphoma, non-Hodgkin: IV:

CODOX-M/IVAC regimen (Mead, 2008): Cycles 1 and 3 of CODOX-M (CODOX-M alternates with IVAC)

Adults ≤65 years: IV: 300 mg/m² over 1 hour (on day 10) followed by 2700 mg/m² over 23 hours (with leucovorin rescue)

Adults >65 years: IV: 100 mg/m² over 1 hour (on day 10) followed by 900 mg/m² over 23 hours (with leucovorin rescue)

Hyper-CVAD alternating with high-dose methotrexate/cytarabine regimen: IV: 1000 mg/m² over 24 hours on day 1 during even courses (2, 4, 6, and 8) of 21-day treatment cycles (Thomas 2006) **or** 200 mg/m² bolus day 1 followed by 800 mg/m² over 24 hours during even courses (2, 4, 6, and 8) of 21-day treatment cycles (Khouri 1998) with leucovorin rescue

Mycosis fungoides (cutaneous T-cell lymphoma): 5 to 50 mg once weekly or 15 to 37.5 mg twice weekly orally or IM for early stages (manufacturer's labeling) **or** 25 mg orally once weekly, may increase to 50 mg once weekly (Zackheim 2003)

Osteosarcoma: Adults ≤30 years: IV: MAP regimen: 12 g/m² (maximum: 20 g/dose) over 4 hours (followed by leucovorin rescue) for 4 doses during induction (before surgery) at weeks 4, 5, 9, and 10, and for 8 doses during maintenance (after surgery) at weeks 15, 16, 20, 21, 24, 25, 28, and 29 (in combination with doxorubicin and cisplatin) (Bielack 2015; Whelan 2015); other combinations, intervals, age ranges, and doses (8 to 14 g/m²/dose) have been described (with leucovorin rescue), refer to specific reference for details (Bacci 2000; Bacci 2003; Goorin 2003; Le Deley 2007; Meyers 1992; Meyers 2005; Weiner 1986; Winkler 1988)

Psoriasis: Note: Some experts recommend concomitant folic acid 1 to 5 mg daily (except the day of methotrexate) to reduce hematologic, gastrointestinal, and hepatic adverse events related to methotrexate.

Oral: Initial: 2.5 to 5 mg/dose every 12 hours for 3 doses per week **or**

Oral, IM, IV, SubQ: Initial: 10 to 25 mg given once weekly; adjust dose gradually to optimal response (doses above 20 mg once weekly are associated with an increased incidence of toxicity); doses >30 mg per week should not be exceeded.

Note: An initial test dose of 2.5 to 5 mg is recommended in patients with risk factors for hematologic toxicity or renal impairment. (Kalb, 2009).

Rheumatoid arthritis: Note: Some experts recommend concomitant folic acid at a dose of least 5 mg per week (except the day of methotrexate) to reduce hematologic, gastrointestinal, and hepatic adverse events related to methotrexate.

Oral (manufacturer labeling): Initial: 7.5 mg once weekly or 2.5 mg every 12 hours for 3 doses per week; adjust dose gradually to optimal response (dosage exceeding 20 mg once weekly are associated with an increased incidence of toxicity; *alternatively*, 10 to 15 mg once weekly, increased by 5 mg every 2 to 4 weeks to a maximum of 20 to 30 mg once weekly has been recommended by some experts. Consider parenteral therapy with inadequate response or intolerance to oral therapy (Visser 2009).

SubQ: Initial: 7.5 mg once weekly; adjust dose gradually to optimal response (doses above 20 mg once weekly are associated with an increased incidence of toxicity)

IM: 7.5 mg once weekly; adjust dose gradually to optimal response (doses above 20 mg once weekly are associated with an increased incidence of toxicity)

Off-label uses:

Acute promyelocytic leukemia (APL) maintenance phase:

Oral: 15 mg/m^2 once weekly for 2 years (Ades 2008) or 20 mg/m^2 once weekly for 1 year (Powell 2010)

IM: 15 mg/m^2 once weekly for 2 years (Sanz 2004)

Bladder cancer (off-label use): IV:

Dose-dense MVAC regimen: 30 mg/m^2 day 1 every 2 weeks (in combination with vinblastine, doxorubicin, and cisplatin) (Sternberg 2001)

CMV regimen: 30 mg/m^2 days 1 and 8 every 3 weeks for 3 cycles (in combination with cisplatin, vinblastine and leucovorin rescue) (Griffiths 2011)

CNS lymphoma (off-label use): IV: 8000 mg/m^2 over 4 hours (followed by leucovorin rescue) every 14 days until complete response or a maximum of 8 cycles; if complete response, follow with 2 consolidation cycles at the same dose every 14 days (with leucovorin rescue), followed by 11 maintenance cycles of 8000 mg/m^2 every 28 days with leucovorin rescue (Batchelor 2003) **or** 2500 mg/m^2 over 2 to 3 hours every 14 days for 5 doses (in combination with vincristine, procarbazine, intrathecal methotrexate, leucovorin, dexamethasone, and cytarabine) (De Angelis 2002) **or** 3500 mg/m^2 over 2 hours on day 2 every 2 weeks (in combination with rituximab, vincristine, procarbazine, and leucovorin [with intraomaya methotrexate 12 mg between days 5 and 12 of each cycle if positive CSF cytology]) for 5 to 7 induction cycles (Shah 2007)

Crohn disease, moderate/severe, corticosteroid-dependent or refractory (off-label use):

Remission induction or reduction of steroid use: IM, SubQ: 25 mg once weekly (Lichtenstein 2009)

Remission maintenance: IM: 15 mg once weekly (Feagan 2000; Lichtenstein 2009)

Dermatomyositis/polymyositis (off-label uses):

Oral: Initial: 7.5 to 15 mg per week, often adjunctively with high-dose corticosteroid therapy; may increase in weekly 2.5 mg increments to target dose of 10 to 25 mg per week (**Note:** Administration of folate 5 to 7 mg per week has been used to reduce side effects) (Briemberg 2003; Newman 1995; Wiendl 2008).

IV, IM: Doses of 20 to 60 mg/week have been employed if failure with oral therapy (doses >50 mg/week may require leucovorin calcium rescue) (Briemberg 2003)

Ectopic pregnancy (off-label use): IM:

Single-dose regimen: Methotrexate 50 mg/m^2 on day 1; Measure serum hCG levels on days 4 and 7; if needed, repeat dose on day 7 (ACOG 2008; ASRM 2006; Barnhart 2009)

Two-dose regimen: Methotrexate 50 mg/m^2 on day 1; Measure serum hCG levels on day 4 and administer a second dose of methotrexate 50 mg/m^2; Measure serum hCG levels on day 7 and if needed, administer a third dose of 50 mg/m^2 (ACOG 2008; Barnhart 2009)

Multidose regimen: Methotrexate 1 mg/kg on day 1; leucovorin calcium 0.1 mg/kg IM on day 2; measure serum hCG on day 2; methotrexate 1 mg/kg on day 3; leucovorin calcium 0.1 mg/kg on day 4; measure serum hCG on day 4; continue up to a total of 4 courses based on hCG concentrations (ACOG 2008; ASRM 2006; Barnhart 2009)

Graft-versus-host disease, acute (aGVHD), prophylaxis: IV: 15 mg/m^2/dose on day 1 and 10 mg/m^2/dose on days 3 and 6 after allogeneic transplant (in combination with cyclosporine and prednisone) (Chao 1993; Chao 2000; Ross 1999) **or** 15 mg/m^2/dose on day 1 and 10 mg/m^2/dose on days 3, 6, and 11 after allogeneic transplant (in combination with cyclosporine) (Chao 2000) **or** 15 mg/m^2/dose on day 1 and 10 mg/m^2/dose on days 3, 6, and 11 after allogeneic transplant (in combination with cyclosporine, followed by leucovorin); may omit day 11 methotrexate for grade 2 or higher toxicity (Ruutu 2013)

Multiple sclerosis (off-label use): Oral: 7.5 or 20 mg once weekly either alone or as add-on therapy to interferon beta-1a (Calabresi 2002; Goodkin 1996; Lugaresi 2001)

Nonleukemic meningeal cancer (off-label uses): Intrathecal: 12 mg/dose twice weekly for 4 weeks, then weekly for 4 doses, then monthly for 4 doses (Glantz 1998) **or** 10 mg twice weekly for 4 weeks, then weekly for 1 month, then every 2 weeks for 2 months (Glantz 1999) **or** 10 to 15 mg twice weekly for 4 weeks, then once weekly for 4 weeks, then a maintenance regimen of once a month (Chamberlain, 2010)

Soft tissue sarcoma (desmoid tumors, aggressive fibromatosis), advanced (off-label use): IV: 30 mg/m^2 every 7 to 10 days (dose usually rounded to 50 mg) in combination with vinblastine for 1 year (Azzarelli, 2001)

Systemic lupus erythematosus, moderate-to-severe (off-label use): Oral: Initial: 7.5 mg once weekly; may increase by 2.5 mg increments weekly (maximum: 20 mg once weekly), in combination with prednisone (Fortin, 2008)

Takayasu arteritis, refractory or relapsing disease (off-label use): Oral: Initial dose: 0.3 mg/kg/week (maximum: 15 mg per week), titrated by 2.5 mg increments every 1 to 2 weeks until reaching a maximum tolerated weekly dose of 25 mg (use in combination with a corticosteroid; Hoffman 1994)

Uveitis (off-label use): Oral: 7.5 to 20 mg once weekly either alone or in conjunction with other corticosteroids/immunosuppressants (Diaz-Llopis 2009; Galor 2008; Kaplan-Messas 2003; Munoz-Fernandez 2009)

Geriatric Refer to adult dosing; adjust for renal impairment.

Breast cancer: Patients >60 years: IV: CMF regimen: 30 mg/m^2 days 1 and 8 every 4 weeks (in combination with cyclophosphamide and fluorouracil) for up to 12 cycles (Bonadonna, 1995)

Meningeal leukemia: Intrathecal: Consider a dose reduction (CSF volume and turnover may decrease with age)

Non-Hodgkin lymphoma: CODOX-M/IVAC regimen (Mead, 2008): Cycles 1 and 3 of CODOX-M (CODOX-M alternates with IVAC): IV: 100 mg over 1 hour (on day 10) followed by 900 mg over 23 hours (with leucovorin rescue)

Rheumatoid arthritis/psoriasis: Oral: Initial: 5 to 7.5 mg per week, not to exceed 20 mg per week

Pediatric Note: Methotrexate doses between 100 to 500 mg/m² **may require** leucovorin calcium rescue. Doses >500 mg/m² **require** leucovorin calcium rescue (refer to Dosing – Adjustment for Toxicity for leucovorin calcium dosing). In children, doses ≥12 g/m² (IV) are associated with a high emetic potential; doses ≥250 mg/m² (IV) are associated with moderate emetic potential (Dupuis 2011). Antiemetics may be recommended to prevent nausea and vomiting.

Polyarticular juvenile idiopathic arthritis (pJIA): Oral, IM, SubQ: Initial: 10 mg/m² once weekly, adjust gradually to optimum response; doses up to 20 to 30 mg/m² once weekly have been used (doses above 20 mg/m² once weekly may be associated with an increased risk of toxicity)

Acute lymphoblastic leukemia (ALL; intrathecal therapy is also administered [refer to specific reference]):

Consolidation/intensification phases (as part of a combination regimen): 1,000 mg/m² IV over 24 hours in week 1 of intensification and 20 mg/m² IM (use 50% dose reduction if on same day as intrathecal methotrexate) on day 1 of week 2 of intensification phase; Intensification repeats every 2 weeks for a total of 12 courses (Mahoney 2000) **or** 5000 mg/m² IV over 24 hours days 0, 22, 36, and 50 of consolidation phase (Schrappe 2000) with leucovorin rescue

Interim maintenance (as part of a combination regimen): 15 mg/m² orally days 0, 7, 14, 21, 28, and 35 of interim maintenance phase (Seibel 2008) **or** 100 mg/m² (escalate dose by 50 mg/m² each dose) IV days 0, 10, 20, 30, and 40 of increased intensity interim maintenance phase (Seibel 2008)

Maintenance (as part of a combination regimen): 20 mg/m² IM weekly on day 1 of weeks 25 to 130 (Mahoney 2000) **or** 20 mg/m² orally days 7, 14, 21, 28, 35, 42, 49, 56, 63, 70, and 77 (Seibel, 2008)

T-cell acute lymphoblastic leukemia (Asselin 2011; triple intrathecal therapy is also administered [refer to specific reference]):

Induction (weeks 1 to 6; as part of a combination regimen): IV:

Low dose: 40 mg/m² day 2

High dose: 500 mg/m² over 30 minutes followed by 4500 mg/m² over 23.5 hours (with leucovorin rescue) day 22

Consolidation (weeks 7 to 33; combination chemotherapy): IV: High dose: 500 mg/m² over 30 minutes followed by 4500 mg/m² over 23.5 hours (with leucovorin rescue) in weeks 7, 10, and 13 with leucovorin rescue

Continuation (weeks 34 to 108; combination chemotherapy): IV, IM: 30 mg/m² weekly until 2 years after documented complete remission

ALL, CNS prophylaxis triple intrathecal therapy (off-label dosing): Intrathecal: Age-based dosing (in combination with cytarabine and hydrocortisone): Days of administration vary based on risk status and protocol; refer to institutional protocols or reference for details (Matloub 2006):

<2 years: 8 mg

2 to <3 years: 10 mg

3 to ≤8 years: 12 mg

>8 years: 15 mg

Meningeal leukemia, prophylaxis or treatment: Intrathecal: 6 to 12 mg/dose (based on age) every 2 to 7 days; continue for 1 dose beyond CSF cell count normalization. **Note:** Optimal intrathecal chemotherapy dosing should be based on age rather than on body surface area (BSA); CSF volume correlates with age and not to BSA (Bleyer 1983; Kerr 2001):

<1 year: 6 mg/dose

1 year: 8 mg/dose

2 years: 10 mg/dose

≥3 years: 12 mg/dose

Osteosarcoma: IV: MAP regimen: 12 g/m² (maximum: 20 g/dose) over 4 hours (followed by leucovorin rescue) for 4 doses during induction (before surgery) at weeks 4, 5, 9, and 10, and for 8 doses during maintenance (after surgery) at weeks 15, 16, 20, 21, 24, 25, 28, and 29 (in combination with doxorubicin and cisplatin) (Bielack 2015; Whelan 2015); other combinations, intervals, and doses (8 to 14 g/m²/dose) have been described (with leucovorin rescue), refer to specific reference for details (Bacci 2000; Bacci 2003; Goorin 2003; Le Deley 2007; Meyers 1992; Meyers 2005; Weiner 1986; Winkler 1988)

Crohn disease, induction and maintenance (off-label use): SubQ: 15 mg/m² once weekly; maximum dose: 25 mg (Rufo 2012)

Dermatomyositis (off-label use): Oral, SubQ (preferred): The lesser of 15 mg/m² or 1 mg/kg once weekly (maximum dose: 40 mg/week) in combination with corticosteroids (Huber 2010) **or** 15 mg/m² once weekly (range: 10 to 20 mg/m² once weekly; maximum dose: 25 mg/week) in combination with prednisone (Ramanan 2005)

Graft-versus-host disease, acute (aGVHD) prophylaxis (off-label use): IV: Refer to adult dosing.

Renal Impairment There are no dosage adjustments provided in the manufacturer's labeling. The following adjustments have been recommended:

Aronoff, 2007:

Adults:

CrCl 10 to 50 mL/minute: Administer 50% of dose

CrCl <10 mL/minute: Avoid use

Intermittent hemodialysis: Administer 50% of dose (post dialysis)

Continuous renal replacement therapy (CRRT): Administer 50% of dose

Children:

CrCl 10 to 50 mL/minute/1.73 m²: Administer 50% of dose

CrCl <10 mL/minute/1.73 m²: Administer 30% of dose

Intermittent hemodialysis: Administer 30% of dose (post dialysis)

Continuous ambulatory peritoneal dialysis (CAPD): Administer 30% of dose

Continuous renal replacement therapy (CRRT): Administer 50% of dose

Kintzel, 1995:

CrCl 46 to 60 mL/minute: Administer 65% of normal dose

CrCl 31 to 45 mL/minute: Administer 50% of normal dose

CrCl <30 mL/minute: Avoid use

Hemodialysis patients with cancer (Janus, 2010): Administer 25% of dose after hemodialysis; monitor closely for toxicity

High-dose methotrexate, dose-intensive regimen for ALL (200 mg/m^2 over 2 hours, followed by 800 mg/m^2 over 24 hours with leucovorin rescue [Kantarjian, 2000]):

Serum creatinine <1.5 mg/dL: No dosage adjustment necessary

Serum creatinine 1.5 to 2 mg/dL: Administer 75% of dose

Serum creatinine >2 mg/dL: Administer 50% of dose

Hepatic Impairment There are no dosage adjustments provided in the manufacturer's labeling; use with caution in patients with impaired hepatic function or preexisting hepatic damage. The following adjustments have been recommended (Floyd, 2006):

Bilirubin 3.1 to 5 mg/dL **or** transaminases >3 times ULN: Administer 75% of dose

Bilirubin >5 mg/dL: Avoid use

Obesity *ASCO Guidelines for appropriate chemotherapy dosing in obese adults with cancer (excludes leukemias):* Utilize patient's actual body weight (full weight) for calculation of body surface area- or weight-based dosing, particularly when the intent of therapy is curative; manage regimen-related toxicities in the same manner as for nonobese patients; if a dose reduction is utilized due to toxicity, consider resumption of full weight-based dosing with subsequent cycles, especially if cause of toxicity (eg, hepatic or renal impairment) is resolved (Griggs, 2012).

Adjustment for Toxicity

Methotrexate toxicities:

Nonhematologic toxicity: Diarrhea, stomatitis, or vomiting which may lead to dehydration: Discontinue until recovery

Hematologic toxicity:

Psoriasis, rheumatoid arthritis: Significant blood count decrease: Discontinue immediately.

Oncologic uses: Profound granulocytopenia and fever: Evaluate immediately; consider broad-spectrum parenteral antimicrobial coverage

Leucovorin calcium dosing (from methotrexate injection prescribing information; other leucovorin dosing/schedules may be specific to chemotherapy protocols):

Normal methotrexate elimination (serum methotrexate level ~10 micromolar at 24 hours after administration, 1 micromolar at 48 hours, and <0.2 micromolar at 72 hours): Leucovorin calcium 15 mg (oral, IM, or IV) every 6 hours for 60 hours (10 doses) beginning 24 hours after the start of methotrexate infusion

Delayed late methotrexate elimination (serum methotrexate level remaining >0.2 micromolar at 72 hours and >0.05 micromolar at 96 hours after administration): Continue leucovorin calcium 15 mg (oral, IM or IV) every 6 hours until methotrexate level is <0.05 micromolar

Delayed early methotrexate elimination and/or acute renal injury (serum methotrexate level ≥50 micromolar at 24 hours, or ≥5 micromolar at 48 hours, or a doubling of serum creatinine level at 24 hours after methotrexate administration): Leucovorin calcium 150 mg IV every 3 hours until methotrexate level is <1 micromolar, then 15 mg IV every 3 hours until methotrexate level <0.05 micromolar

Leucovorin nomogram dosing for high-dose methotrexate overexposure (**generalized dosing** derived from reference nomogram figures, refer to each reference [Bleyer, 1978; Bleyer, 1981; Widemann, 2006] or institution-specific nomogram for details):

At 24 hours:

For methotrexate levels of ≥100 micromolar at ~24 hours, leucovorin is initially dosed at 1000 mg/m^2 every 6 hours

For methotrexate levels of ≥10 to <100 micromolar at 24 hours, leucovorin is initially dosed at 100 mg/m^2 every 3 or 6 hours

For methotrexate levels of ~1 to 10 micromolar at 24 hours, leucovorin is initially dosed at 10 mg/m^2 every 3 or 6 hours

At 48 hours:

For methotrexate levels of ≥100 micromolar at 48 hours, leucovorin is dosed at 1000 mg/m^2 every 6 hours

For methotrexate levels of ≥10 to <100 micromolar at 48 hours, leucovorin is dosed at 100 mg/m^2 every 3 hours

For methotrexate levels of ~1 to 10 micromolar at 48 hours, leucovorin is dosed at 100 mg/m^2 every 6 hours **or** 10 to 100 mg/m^2 every 3 hours

At 72 hours:

For methotrexate levels of ≥10 micromolar at 72 hours, leucovorin is dosed at 100 to 1000 mg/m^2 every 3 to 6 hours

For methotrexate levels of ~1 to 10 micromolar at 72 hours, leucovorin is dosed at 10 to 100 mg/m^2 every 3 hours

For methotrexate levels of ~0.1 to 1 micromolar at 72 hours, leucovorin is dosed at 10 mg/m^2 every 3 to 6 hours

If serum creatinine is increased more than 50% above baseline, increase the standard leucovorin dose to 100 mg/m^2 every 3 hours, then adjust according to methotrexate levels above.

Follow methotrexate levels daily, leucovorin may be discontinued when methotrexate level is <0.1 micromolar

Mechanism of Action Methotrexate is a folate antimetabolite that inhibits DNA synthesis, repair, and cellular replication. Methotrexate irreversibly binds to and inhibits dihydrofolate reductase, inhibiting the formation of reduced folates, and thymidylate synthetase, resulting in inhibition of purine and thymidylic acid synthesis, thus interfering with DNA synthesis, repair, and cellular replication. Methotrexate is cell cycle specific for the S phase of the cycle. Actively proliferative tissues are more susceptible to the effects of methotrexate.

The MOA in the treatment of rheumatoid arthritis is unknown, but may affect immune function. In psoriasis, methotrexate is thought to target rapidly proliferating epithelial cells in the skin.

In Crohn disease, it may have immune modulator and anti-inflammatory activity.

Contraindications

Known hypersensitivity to methotrexate or any component of the formulation; breastfeeding

Additional contraindications for patients with psoriasis or rheumatoid arthritis: Pregnancy, alcoholism, alcoholic liver disease or other chronic liver disease, immunodeficiency syndromes (overt or laboratory evidence); preexisting blood dyscrasias (eg, bone marrow hypoplasia, leukopenia, thrombocytopenia, significant anemia)

Warnings/Precautions

[US Boxed Warning]: Methotrexate causes hepatotoxicity, fibrosis, and cirrhosis, but generally only after prolonged use. Acutely, liver enzyme elevations are frequently seen. These are usually transient and asymptomatic, and also do not appear predictive of subsequent hepatic disease. Liver biopsy after sustained use often shows histologic changes, and fibrosis and cirrhosis have been reported; these latter lesions often are not preceded by symptoms or abnormal liver function tests in the psoriasis population. For this reason, periodic liver biopsies are usually recommended for psoriatic patients who are under long-term treatment. Persistent abnormalities in liver function tests may precede appearance of fibrosis or cirrhosis in the rheumatoid arthritis population. Risk is related to cumulative dose (≥1.5 g) and prolonged exposure. Monitor closely (with liver function tests, including serum albumin) for liver toxicities. Liver enzyme elevations may be noted, but may not be predictive of hepatic disease in long term treatment for psoriasis (but generally is predictive in rheumatoid arthritis [RA] treatment). Discontinue methotrexate with moderate to severe change in liver biopsy. Risk factors for hepatotoxicity include history of above moderate ethanol consumption, persistent abnormal liver chemistries, history of chronic liver disease (including hepatitis B or C), family history of inheritable liver disease, diabetes, obesity, hyperlipidemia, lack of folate supplementation during methotrexate therapy, cumulative methotrexate dose exceeding 1.5 g, continuous daily methotrexate dosing and history of significant exposure to hepatotoxic drugs. Use caution with preexisting liver impairment; may require dosage reduction. Use caution when used with other hepatotoxic agents (azathioprine, retinoids, sulfasalazine). **[US Boxed Warning]: Methotrexate elimination is reduced in patients with ascites and pleural effusions;** resulting in prolonged half-life and toxicity; may require dose reduction or discontinuation. Monitor closely for toxicity.

May cause renal damage leading to acute renal failure, especially with high-dose methotrexate; monitor renal function and methotrexate levels closely, maintain adequate hydration and urinary alkalinization. Use caution in osteosarcoma patients treated with high-dose methotrexate in combination with nephrotoxic chemotherapy (eg, cisplatin). **[US Boxed Warning]: Methotrexate elimination is reduced in patients with renal impairment; monitor closely for toxicity; may require dose reduction or, in some cases, discontinuation of methotrexate administration. [US Boxed Warning]: Tumor lysis syndrome may occur in patients with high tumor burden; appropriate supportive and pharmacologic measures may prevent or alleviate tumor lysis syndrome.**

[US Boxed Warning]: Methotrexate-induced lung disease, including acute or chronic interstitial pneumonitis, is a potentially dangerous lesion, which may occur acutely at any time during therapy and has been reported at low doses. It is not always fully reversible and fatalities have been reported. Pulmonary symptoms (especially a dry, nonproductive cough) may require interruption of treatment and careful investigation. Pulmonary symptoms may occur at any time during therapy and at any dosage; monitor closely for pulmonary symptoms, particularly dry, nonproductive cough. Other potential symptoms include fever, dyspnea, hypoxemia, or pulmonary infiltrate. **[US Boxed Warning]: Methotrexate elimination is reduced in patients with pleural effusions;** may require dose reduction or discontinuation. Monitor closely for toxicity.

[US Boxed Warning]: Unexpectedly severe (sometimes fatal) bone marrow suppression and aplastic anemia have been reported with concomitant administration of methotrexate (usually in high dosage) along with some nonsteroidal anti-inflammatory drugs (NSAIDs); anemia, pancytopenia, leukopenia, neutropenia, and/or thrombocytopenia may occur. Use caution in patients with preexisting bone marrow suppression. Discontinue treatment (immediately) in RA or psoriasis if a significant decrease in hematologic components is noted. **[US Boxed Warning]: Malignant lymphomas, which may regress following withdrawal of methotrexate, may occur in patients receiving low-dose methotrexate and, thus, may not require cytotoxic treatment. Discontinue methotrexate first and, if the lymphoma does not regress, appropriate treatment should be instituted.** Discontinue methotrexate if lymphoma does not regress. Other secondary tumors have been reported.

[US Boxed Warning]: Gastrointestinal toxicity may occur (may be unexpectedly severe, usually occurs with high doses along with concomitant use of some NSAIDs); diarrhea and ulcerative stomatitis may require treatment interruption; otherwise hemorrhagic enteritis and death from intestinal perforation may occur. Use with caution in patients with peptic ulcer disease, ulcerative colitis. In children, doses ≥12 g/m^2 (IV) are associated with a high emetic potential; doses ≥250 mg/m^2 (IV) in adults and children are associated with moderate emetic potential (Dupuis 2011). Antiemetics may be recommended to prevent nausea and vomiting.

May cause neurotoxicity. Leukoencephalopathy has been reported (case reports), usually in patients who have received cranial irradiation and IV methotrexate. Chronic leukoencephalopathy has been reported with high-dose methotrexate (with leucovorin rescue and even without cranial irradiation) and with intrathecal methotrexate; discontinuing methotrexate does not always result in complete recovery; may be progressive and fatal. Serious neurotoxicity, including generalized and focal seizures has occurred (usually in pediatric ALL patients receiving intermediate-dose (1 g/m^2 IV methotrexate); leukoencephalopathy and/or microangiopathic calcifications were noted on diagnostic imaging studies in symptomatic patients. A transient acute stroke-like encephalopathy has been observed, usually with high-dose regimens; manifestations may include confusion, hemiparesis, transient blindness, seizure, and coma. Chemical arachnoiditis (headache, back pain, nuchal rigidity, fever) and myelopathy may result from intrathecal administration. May cause dizziness and fatigue; may affect the ability to drive or operate heavy machinery.

[US Boxed Warning]: Severe, occasionally fatal skin reactions have been reported following single or multiple doses of methotrexate. Reactions have occurred within days of oral, intramuscular, intravenous, or intrathecal methotrexate administration. Recovery has been reported with discontinuation of therapy. Dermatologic reactions have included toxic epidermal necrolysis, Stevens-Johnson syndrome, exfoliative dermatitis, skin necrosis, and erythema multiforme. Radiation dermatitis and sunburn may be precipitated by methotrexate administration. Psoriatic lesions may be worsened by concomitant exposure to ultraviolet radiation.

Potentially significant drug-drug interactions may exist, requiring dose or frequency adjustment, additional monitoring, and/or selection of alternative therapy. Do not administer NSAIDs prior to or during high-dose methotrexate therapy; may increase and prolong serum methotrexate levels. Doses used for psoriasis may still lead to unexpected toxicities; use caution when administering NSAIDs or salicylates with lower doses of methotrexate for RA. Methotrexate may increase the levels and effects of mercaptopurine; may require dosage adjustments. Vitamins containing folate may decrease response to systemic methotrexate; folate deficiency may increase methotrexate toxicity. Concomitant use of proton pump inhibitors with methotrexate (primarily high-dose methotrexate) may elevate and prolong serum methotrexate and metabolite (hydroxymethotrexate) levels; may lead to toxicities; use with caution. Immunization may be ineffective during methotrexate treatment. Immunization with live vaccines is not recommended; cases of disseminated vaccinia infections due to live vaccines have been reported. **[US Boxed Warning]: Concomitant methotrexate administration with radiotherapy may increase the risk of soft tissue necrosis and osteonecrosis.**

[US Boxed Warnings]: Because of the possibility of serious toxic reactions (which can be fatal), methotrexate should be used only in life threatening neoplastic diseases or in patients with psoriasis or rheumatoid arthritis with severe, recalcitrant, disabling disease which is not adequately responsive to other forms of therapy. Deaths have been reported with the use of methotrexate in the treatment of malignancy, psoriasis, and rheumatoid arthritis. Patients should be closely monitored for bone marrow, liver, lung, skin, and kidney toxicities. Patients should be informed by their physician of the risks involved and be under a physician's care throughout therapy. The use of methotrexate high-dose regimens recommended for osteosarcoma requires meticulous care. High-dose regimens of methotrexate injection for other neoplastic diseases are investigational, and a therapeutic advantage has not been established. Should be administered under the supervision of a physician experienced in the use of antimetabolite therapy. Immune suppression may lead to potentially fatal opportunistic infections, including *Pneumocystis jirovecii* pneumonia (PCP). Use methotrexate with extreme caution in patients with an active infection (contraindicated in patients with immunodeficiency syndrome). **[US Boxed Warnings]: Use only preservative-free methotrexate formulations and diluents for intrathecal and high-dose therapy. Do NOT use formulations or diluents containing preservatives for intrathecal and high-dose therapy because they contain benzyl alcohol. Methotrexate has been reported to cause fetal death and/or congenital abnormalities. Methotrexate is not recommended for women of childbearing potential unless there is clear medical evidence that the benefits can be expected to outweigh the considered risks. Pregnant women with psoriasis or rheumatoid arthritis should not receive methotrexate. Some products are contraindicated in pregnant women.** May cause impairment of fertility, oligospermia, and menstrual dysfunction. Toxicity from methotrexate or any immunosuppressive is increased in the elderly. Methotrexate injection may contain benzyl alcohol and should not be used in neonates. Errors have occurred (some resulting in death) when methotrexate was administered as a "daily" dose instead of a "weekly" dose intended for some indications. The ISMP Targeted Medication Safety Best Practices for Hospitals recommends hospitals use a weekly dosage regimen default for oral methotrexate orders, with a hard stop override requiring verification of appropriate oncology indication; manual systems should require verification of an oncology indication prior to dispensing oral methotrexate for daily administration. Pharmacists should provide patient education for patients discharged on weekly oral methotrexate; education should include written leaflets that contain clear instructions about the weekly dosing schedule and explain the danger of taking extra doses (ISMP 2014).

When used for intrathecal administration, should not be prepared during the preparation of any other agents; after preparation, store intrathecal medications in an isolated location or container clearly marked with a label identifying as "intrathecal" use only; delivery of intrathecal medications to the patient should only be with other medications intended for administration into the central nervous system (Jacobson 2009).

Benzyl alcohol and derivatives: Some dosage forms may contain benzyl alcohol; large amounts of benzyl alcohol (≥99 mg/kg/day) have been associated with a potentially fatal toxicity ("gasping syndrome") in neonates; the "gasping syndrome" consists of metabolic acidosis, respiratory distress, gasping respirations, CNS dysfunction (including convulsions, intracranial hemorrhage), hypotension, and cardiovascular collapse (AAP ["Inactive" 1997]; CDC 1982); some data suggests that benzoate displaces bilirubin from protein binding sites (Ahlfors 2001); avoid or use dosage forms containing benzyl alcohol with caution in neonates. See manufacturer's labeling.

Glucarpidase is an enzyme that rapidly hydrolyzes extracellular methotrexate into inactive metabolites, allowing for a rapid reduction of methotrexate concentrations. Glucarpidase may be used for methotrexate overexposure; it is approved for the treatment of toxic plasma methotrexate concentrations (>1 micromole/L) in patients with delayed clearance due to renal impairment.

Drug Interactions

Metabolism/Transport Effects Substrate of BCRP, OAT3, P-glycoprotein, SLCO1B1

Avoid Concomitant Use

Avoid concomitant use of Methotrexate with any of the following: Acitretin; BCG (Intravesical); Deferiprone; Dipyrone; Foscarnet; Natalizumab; Pimecrolimus; Tacrolimus (Topical)

Increased Effect/Toxicity

Methotrexate may increase the levels/effects of: CloZAPine; CycloSPORINE (Systemic); Deferiprone; Dipyrone; Fingolimod; Leflunomide; Loop Diuretics; Natalizumab; Tegafur; Theophylline Derivatives; Tofacitinib; Vaccines (Live)

The levels/effects of Methotrexate may be increased by: Acitretin; Alitretinoin (Systemic); Ciprofloxacin (Systemic); CycloSPORINE (Systemic); Denosumab; Dexketoprofen; Diethylamine Salicylate; Dipyrone; Eltrombopag; Foscarnet; Fosphenytoin-Phenytoin; Gemfibrozil; Ibrutinib; LevETIRAcetam; Loop

Diuretics; Lumacaftor; Mipomersen; Nonsteroidal Anti-Inflammatory Agents; Ocrelizumab; Palifermin; Penicillins; P-glycoprotein/ABCB1 Inhibitors; Pimecrolimus; Probenecid; Promazine; Proton Pump Inhibitors; Ranolazine; Roflumilast; Salicylates; SulfaSALAzine; Sulfonamide Derivatives; Tacrolimus (Topical); Teriflunomide; Trastuzumab; Trimethoprim

Decreased Effect

Methotrexate may decrease the levels/effects of: BCG (Intravesical); Coccidioides immitis Skin Test; Fosphenytoin-Phenytoin; Lenograstim; Loop Diuretics; Nivolumab; Sapropterin; Sipuleucel-T; Tertomotide; Vaccines (Inactivated); Vaccines (Live)

The levels/effects of Methotrexate may be decreased by: Bile Acid Sequestrants; Cephalothin; Echinacea; Lumacaftor; P-glycoprotein/ABCB1 Inducers

Food Interactions Methotrexate peak serum levels may be decreased if taken with food. Milk-rich foods may decrease methotrexate absorption. Management: Administer without regard to food.

Dietary Considerations Some products may contain sodium.

Pharmacodynamics/Kinetics

Onset of Action Antirheumatic: 3 to 6 weeks; additional improvement may continue longer than 12 weeks

Half-life Elimination

Children: ALL: 0.7 to 5.8 hours (dose range: 6.3 to 30 mg/m^2); JIA: 0.9 to 2.3 hours (dose range: 3.75 to 26.2 mg/m^2)

Adults: Low dose: 3 to 10 hours; High dose: 8 to 15 hours

Time to Peak Serum: Oral: Children: 0.67 to 4 hours (reported for a 15 mg/m2 dose); Adults: 1 to 2 hours; Children and Adults: IM: 30 to 60 minutes

Pregnancy Risk Factor X (psoriasis, rheumatoid arthritis)

Pregnancy Considerations [US Boxed Warning]: Methotrexate has been reported to cause fetal death and/or congenital abnormalities. Methotrexate is not recommended for women of childbearing potential unless there is clear medical evidence that the benefits can be expected to outweigh the considered risks. Pregnant women with psoriasis or rheumatoid arthritis should not receive methotrexate. Some products are contraindicated in pregnant women. Studies in animals and pregnant women have shown evidence of fetal abnormalities; therefore, the manufacturer classifies methotrexate as pregnancy category X (for psoriasis or RA). A pattern of congenital malformations associated with maternal methotrexate use is referred to as the aminopterin/methotrexate syndrome. Features of the syndrome include CNS, skeletal, and cardiac abnormalities. Low birth weight and developmental delay have also been reported. The use of methotrexate may impair fertility and cause menstrual irregularities or oligospermia during treatment and following therapy. Methotrexate is approved for the treatment of trophoblastic neoplasms (gestational choriocarcinoma, chorioadenoma destruens, and hydatidiform mole) and has been used for the medical management of ectopic pregnancy and the medical management of abortion. Pregnancy should be excluded prior to therapy in women of childbearing potential. Use for the treatment of neoplastic diseases only when the potential benefit to the mother outweighs the possible risk to the fetus. Pregnancy should be avoided for ≥3 months following treatment in male patients and ≥1 ovulatory cycle in female patients. A registry is available for pregnant women exposed to autoimmune medications including methotrexate. For additional information contact the Organization of Teratology Information Specialists, OTIS Autoimmune Diseases Study, at 877-311-8972.

Breastfeeding Considerations Low amounts of methotrexate are excreted into breast milk. Due to the potential for serious adverse reactions in a breastfeeding infant, use is contraindicated in nursing mothers.

Dosage Forms

Solution, Injection:

Generic: 250 mg/10 mL (10 mL); 50 mg/2 mL (2 mL)

Solution, Injection [preservative free]:

Generic: 1 g/40 mL (40 mL); 100 mg/4 mL (4 mL); 200 mg/8 mL (8 mL); 250 mg/10 mL (10 mL); 50 mg/2 mL (2 mL)

Solution Auto-injector, Subcutaneous [preservative free]:

Otrexup: 7.5 mg/0.4 mL (0.4 mL); 10 mg/0.4 mL (0.4 mL); 12.5 mg/0.4 mL (0.4 mL); 15 mg/0.4 mL (0.4 mL); 17.5 mg/0.4 mL (0.4 mL); 20 mg/0.4 mL (0.4 mL); 22.5 mg/0.4 mL (0.4 mL); 25 mg/0.4mL (0.4 mL)

Rasuvo: 7.5 mg/0.15 mL (0.15 mL); 10 mg/0.2 mL (0.2 mL); 12.5 mg/0.25 mL (0.25 mL); 15 mg/0.3 mL (0.3 mL); 17.5 mg/0.35 mL (0.35 mL); 20 mg/0.4 mL (0.4 mL); 22.5 mg/0.45 mL (0.45 mL); 25 mg/0.5 mL (0.5 mL); 27.5 mg/0.55 mL (0.55 mL); 30 mg/0.6 mL (0.6 mL)

Solution Reconstituted, Injection [preservative free]:

Generic: 1 g (1 ea)

Tablet, Oral:

Trexall: 5 mg, 7.5 mg, 10 mg, 15 mg

Generic: 2.5 mg

Methotrimeprazine (meth oh trye MEP ra zeen)

Brand Names: Canada Methoprazine; Novo-Meprazine; Nozinan; PMS-Methotrimeprazine

Pharmacologic Category Analgesic, Nonopioid; Antimanic Agent; First Generation (Typical) Antipsychotic

Use Note: Not approved in the US

Anxiety/tension: Treatment of conditions associated with anxiety and tension (eg, autonomic disturbances personality disturbances, emotional disorders secondary to physical conditions)

Insomnia: Management of insomnia, sedation

Nausea/vomiting: Management of nausea and vomiting

Pain: Management of pain, including pain caused by neuralgia or cancer and as adjunct to general anesthesia (pre- and postoperatively)

Psychiatric disorders: Treatment of schizophrenia, senile psychosis, and manic-depressive syndromes

Local Anesthetic/Vasoconstrictor Precautions Methotrimeprazine is one of the drugs confirmed to prolong the QT interval and is accepted as having a risk of causing torsade de pointes. The risk of drug-induced torsade de pointes is extremely low when a single QT interval prolonging drug is prescribed. In terms of epinephrine, it is not known what effect vasoconstrictors in the local anesthetic regimen will have in patients with a known history of congenital prolonged QT interval or in patients taking any medication that prolongs the QT interval. Until more information is obtained, it is suggested that the clinician consult with the physician prior to the use of a vasoconstrictor in suspected patients, and that the vasoconstrictor (epinephrine, mepivacaine and levonordefrin [Carbocaine® 2% with Neo-Cobefrin®]) be used with caution. See Dental Comment.

Effects on Dental Treatment Key adverse event(s) related to dental treatment: Anticholinergic side effects can cause a reduction of saliva production or secretion, contributing to discomfort and dental disease (ie, caries, oral candidiasis, and periodontal disease). Phenothiazines can cause extrapyramidal reactions which may appear as muscle twitching or increased motor activity of the face, neck, or head.

Effects on Bleeding No information available to require special precautions

Adverse Reactions Frequencies not defined; some reactions listed are based on reports for other agents in this same pharmacologic class, and may not be specifically reported for methotrimeprazine.

Cardiovascular: Orthostatic hypotension, pulmonary embolism, tachycardia, venous thromboembolism

Central nervous system: Disruption of body temperature regulation, dizziness, drowsiness; drug-induced extrapyramidal reaction (including akathisia, dystonia, Parkinsonian-like syndrome, tardive dyskinesia); headache, neuroleptic malignant syndrome (NMS), seizure

Dermatologic: Diaphoresis, skin rash

Endocrine & metabolic: Change in libido, decreased glucose tolerance, gynecomastia, hyperglycemia, menstrual disease, weight gain

Gastrointestinal: Constipation, intestinal obstruction, nausea, necrotizing enterocolitis, vomiting, xerostomia

Genitourinary: Ejaculatory disorder, priapism, urinary incontinence, urinary retention

Hematologic & oncologic: Eosinophilia, hemolytic anemia, immune thrombocytopenia, leukopenia, pancytopenia

Hepatic: Cholestatic jaundice, hepatotoxicity

Renal: Polyuria

<1%, postmarketing, and/or case reports: Agranulocytosis, prolonged Q-T interval on ECG, skin photosensitivity

General Dosage Range

IM:

Children and Adolescents: 0.0625 to 0.125 mg/kg/day as a single dose or in several divided doses

Adults: 10 to 25 mg every 8 hours **or** 75 to 100 mg/day in 3 to 4 divided doses

IV: *Children and Adolescents:* 0.0625 mg/kg in 250 mL D_5W infused at a rate of 20 to 40 drops/minute

Oral:

Children and Adolescents: 0.25 mg/kg/day in 2 to 3 divided doses (maximum: 40 mg/day [children <12 years])

Adults: 6 to 75 mg/day in 2 to 3 divided doses (maximum: doses ≥1,000 mg/day have been used) **or** 10 to 25 mg at bedtime

Mechanism of Action Aliphatic phenothiazine that antagonizes D1 and D2 dopamine receptor subtypes; also binds alpha-1, alpha-2, serotonin (5-HT_1 and 5-HT_2), and muscarinic (M_1 and M_2) receptors (Lal 1993)

Pharmacodynamics/Kinetics

Onset of Action Injection: 1 hour (Nozinan datasheet, Sanofi Aventis New Zealand limited 2010)

Duration of Action 2 to 4 hours (Nozinan datasheet, Sanofi Aventis New Zealand limited 2010)

Half-life Elimination 15 to 30 hours (Dahl 1976)

Time to Peak Serum: IM: 0.5 to 1.5 hours; Oral: 1 to 3 hours (Nozinan datasheet, Sanofi Aventis New Zealand limited 2010)

Pregnancy Considerations Antipsychotic use during the third trimester of pregnancy has a risk for abnormal muscle movements (extrapyramidal symptoms [EPS]) and withdrawal symptoms in newborns following delivery. Symptoms in the newborn may include agitation, feeding disorder, hypertonia, hypotonia, respiratory distress, somnolence, and tremor; these effects may be self-limiting or require hospitalization. Hyperprolactinemia associated with methotrimeprazine may lead to impaired fertility in women. Limited data suggest that methotrimeprazine may also be associated with impaired fertility in men.

Product Availability Not available in the US

Dental Comment This drug is known to prolong the QT interval. The QT interval is measured as the time and distance between the Q point of the QRS complex and the end of the T wave in the ECG tracing. After adjustment for heart rate, the QT interval is defined as prolonged if it is more than 450 msec in men and 460 msec in women. A long QT syndrome was first described in the 1950s and 60s as a congenital syndrome involving QT interval prolongation and syncope and sudden death. Some of the congenital long QT syndromes were characterized by a peculiar electrocardiographic appearance of the QRS complex involving a premature atria beat followed by a pause, then a subsequent sinus beat showing marked QT prolongation and deformity. This type of cardiac arrhythmia was originally termed "torsade de pointes" (translated from the French as "twisting of the points").

Prolongation of the QT interval is thought to result from delayed ventricular repolarization. The repolarization process within the myocardial cell is due to the efflux of intracellular potassium. The channels associated with this current can be blocked by many drugs and predispose the electrical propagation cycle to torsade de pointes.

Methotrimeprazine is one of the drugs confirmed to prolong the QT interval and is accepted as having a risk of causing torsade de pointes. The risk of drug-induced torsade de pointes is extremely low when a single QT interval prolonging drug is prescribed. In terms of epinephrine, it is not known what effect vasoconstrictors in the local anesthetic regimen will have in patients with a known history of congenital prolonged QT interval or in patients taking any medication that prolongs the QT interval. Until more information is obtained, it is suggested that the clinician consult with the physician prior to the use of a vasoconstrictor in suspected patients, and that the vasoconstrictor (epinephrine, levonordefrin [Neo-Cobefrin®]) be used with caution.

Methoxy Polyethylene Glycol-Epoetin Beta (meth OX ee pol i ETH i leen GLY kol e POE e tin BAY ta)

Brand Names: US Mircera

Pharmacologic Category Colony Stimulating Factor; Erythropoiesis-Stimulating Agent (ESA); Hematopoietic Agent

Use

Anemia: Treatment of anemia associated with chronic kidney disease (CKD) in adult patients on dialysis and patients not on dialysis.

Limitations of use: Not indicated and is not recommended in the treatment of anemia due to cancer chemotherapy or as a substitute for red blood cell (RBC) transfusions in patients who require immediate correction of anemia; has not been shown to improve symptoms, physical functioning or health-related quality of life.

Local Anesthetic/Vasoconstrictor Precautions No information available to require special precautions

Effects on Dental Treatment No significant effects or complications reported

Effects on Bleeding Although erythropoiesis-stimulating agents have been associated with thromboembolic events, there is no information available to require special precautions for dental procedures.

Adverse Reactions

>10%:

Cardiovascular: Exacerbation of hypertension (27%), hypertension (13%)

Gastrointestinal: Diarrhea (11%)

Respiratory: Nasopharyngitis (11%)

1% to 10%:

Cardiovascular: Procedural hypotension (8%), arteriovenous fistula site complication (5%), hypotension (5%), thrombosis (5%; arteriovenous fistula)

Central nervous system: Headache (9%)

Endocrine & metabolic: Hypervolemia (7%)

Gastrointestinal: Vomiting (6%), constipation (5%), gastrointestinal hemorrhage (1%)

Genitourinary: Urinary tract infection (5%)

Hematologic & oncologic: Hemorrhage (5%)

Neuromuscular & skeletal: Muscle spasm (8%), back pain (6%), limb pain (5%)

Respiratory: Upper respiratory tract infection (9%), cough (6%)

<1%, postmarketing, and/or case reports: Anaphylaxis, angioedema, bronchospasm, hypertensive encephalopathy, pruritus, pure red cell aplasia, seizure, severe anemia, skin rash, Stevens-Johnson syndrome, tachycardia, toxic epidermal necrolysis, urticaria

Mechanism of Action Methoxy polyethylene glycol-epoetin beta is an erythropoietin receptor activator; erythropoietin is a primary growth factor for erythroid development and is produced in the kidney and released into the bloodstream in response to hypoxia. In response to hypoxia, erythropoietin interacts with erythroid progenitor cells to increase red blood cell production.

Pharmacodynamics/Kinetics

Onset of Action Hemoglobin increase (following a single initial dose): 7 to 15 days

Half-life Elimination

IV: 134 ± 65 hours

SubQ: 139 ± 67 hours

Time to Peak SubQ: 72 hours

Pregnancy Risk Factor C

Pregnancy Considerations Adverse events were observed in some animal reproduction studies.

Prescribing and Access Restrictions Distribution is restricted to certain dialysis centers.

Methscopolamine (meth skoe POL a meen)

Related Information

Dentin Hypersensitivity, Acid Erosion, High Caries Index, Management of Alveolar Osteitis, and Xerostomia *on page 1857*

Brand Names: US Pamine; Pamine Forte

Brand Names: Canada Pamine

Pharmacologic Category Anticholinergic Agent

Use

Peptic ulcer (adjunctive): Adjunctive therapy for the treatment of peptic ulcer

Limitations of use: Has not been shown to be effective in contributing to the healing of peptic ulcer, decreasing the rate of recurrence, or preventing complications

Local Anesthetic/Vasoconstrictor Precautions No information available to require special precautions

Effects on Dental Treatment Key adverse event(s) related to dental treatment: Xerostomia and changes in salivation (normal salivary flow resumes upon discontinuation), and dry throat and nose. Anticholinergic side effects can cause a reduction of saliva production or secretion, contributing to discomfort and dental disease (ie, caries, oral candidiasis and periodontal disease).

Effects on Bleeding No information available to require special precautions

Adverse Reactions Frequency not defined.

Cardiovascular: Palpitation, tachycardia

Central nervous system: Headache, insomnia, flushing, nervousness, drowsiness, dizziness, confusion, fever, CNS stimulation may be produced with large doses

Dermatologic: Dry skin, urticaria

Endocrine & metabolic: Lactation suppressed

Gastrointestinal: Constipation, xerostomia, dry throat, dysphagia, nausea, vomiting, loss of taste

Genitourinary: Impotence, urinary hesitancy, urinary retention

Neuromuscular & skeletal: Weakness

Ocular: Blurred vision, cycloplegia, ocular tension increased, pupil dilation

Respiratory: Dry nose

Miscellaneous: Allergic reaction, diaphoresis decreased, hypersensitivity reactions, anaphylaxis

General Dosage Range Oral: *Adults:* Initial: 2.5 mg 30 minutes before meals and 2.5 to 5 mg at bedtime; for severe symptoms, may initiate with 5 mg 30 minutes before meals and 5 mg at bedtime.

Mechanism of Action Methscopolamine is a quaternary ammonium derivative of scopolamine that exerts anticholinergic effects, which include reducing the volume and total acid content of gastric secretion, inhibiting gastrointestinal motility and salivary secretion, dilation of the pupil, and inhibition of accommodation that results in blurring of vision.

Pharmacodynamics/Kinetics

Onset of Action ~1 hour

Duration of Action 4 to 6 hours

Pregnancy Risk Factor C

Pregnancy Considerations Animal reproduction studies have not been conducted. Methscopolamine is a derivative of scopolamine. Scopolamine is reported to cross the placenta; fetal toxicity noted in case reports.

Methsuximide (meth SUKS i mide)

Brand Names: US Celontin

Brand Names: Canada Celontin®

Pharmacologic Category Anticonvulsant, Succinimide

Use Absence (petit mal) seizures, refractory: Control of absence (petit mal) seizures that are refractory to other drugs

Local Anesthetic/Vasoconstrictor Precautions No information available to require special precautions

Effects on Dental Treatment No significant effects or complications reported

Effects on Bleeding No information available to require special precautions

Adverse Reactions Frequency not defined.

Cardiovascular: Hyperemia

Central nervous system: Aggressiveness, ataxia, confusion, depression, dizziness, drowsiness, hallucinations (auditory), headache, hypochondriacal behavior, insomnia, irritability, mental instability, mental slowness, nervousness, psychosis, suicidal behavior

Dermatologic: Pruritus, rash, Stevens-Johnson syndrome, urticaria

Gastrointestinal: Abdominal pain, anorexia, constipation, diarrhea, epigastric pain, nausea, vomiting, weight loss

Genitourinary: Hematuria (microscopic), proteinuria

Hematologic: Eosinophilia, leukopenia, monocytosis, pancytopenia

Ocular: Blurred vision, periorbital edema, photophobia

Miscellaneous: Hiccups, systemic lupus erythematosus

General Dosage Range Oral: *Adults:* Initial: 300 mg/day for 1 week; Maintenance: Up to 1.2 g/day in 2-4 divided doses

Mechanism of Action Increases the seizure threshold and suppresses paroxysmal spike-and-wave pattern in absence seizures; depresses nerve transmission in the motor cortex

Pharmacodynamics/Kinetics

Half-life Elimination

2 to 4 hours

N-desmethylmethsuximide: Children: 26 hours; Adults: 28 to 80 hours

Time to Peak Serum: 1 to 3 hours

Pregnancy Considerations Epilepsy itself, the number of medications, genetic factors, or a combination of these may influence the teratogenicity of anticonvulsant therapy. In general, polytherapy may increase the risk of congenital malformations; monotherapy with the lowest effective dose is recommended (Harden 2009). For women with epilepsy who are planning a pregnancy in advance, baseline serum concentrations should be measured once or twice prior to pregnancy during a period when seizure control is optimal. Monitoring can then be continued up to once a month during pregnancy in women with stable seizure control (Patsalos 2008).

Patients exposed to methsuximide during pregnancy are encouraged to enroll themselves into the NAAED Pregnancy Registry by calling 1-888-233-2334. Additional information is available at www.-aedpregnancyregistry.org.

Methyldopa (meth il DOE pa)

Related Information

Cardiovascular Diseases *on page 1752*

Brand Names: Canada Methyldopa

Pharmacologic Category $Alpha_2$-Adrenergic Agonist; Antihypertensive

Use

Hypertension: Management of hypertension

Note: According to the Eighth Joint National Committee (JNC 8) guidelines, methyldopa is **not** recommended for the initial treatment of hypertension (James 2013).

Local Anesthetic/Vasoconstrictor Precautions No information available to require special precautions

Effects on Dental Treatment Key adverse event(s) related to dental treatment: Xerostomia (normal salivary flow resumes upon discontinuation). Anticholinergic side effects can cause a reduction of saliva production or secretion, contributing to discomfort and dental disease (ie, caries, oral candidiasis, and periodontal disease).

Effects on Bleeding No information available to require special precautions

Adverse Reactions

Frequency not defined.

Cardiovascular: Bradycardia, cardiac failure, exacerbation of angina pectoris, myocarditis, orthostatic hypotension, paradoxical pressor response (intravenous use), pericarditis, peripheral edema, prolonged carotid sinus syncope, vasculitis

Central nervous system: Bell's palsy, cerebrovascular insufficiency (symptoms), choreoathetosis, decreased mental acuity, depression, dizziness, drug fever, headache, nightmares, paresthesia, Parkinson's disease, sedation

Dermatologic: Skin rash, toxic epidermal necrolysis

Endocrine & metabolic: Amenorrhea, decreased libido, gynecomastia, hyperprolactinemia, weight gain

Gastrointestinal: Abdominal distention, colitis, constipation, diarrhea, flatulence, glossalgia, melanoglossia, nausea, pancreatitis, sialadenitis, vomiting, xerostomia

Genitourinary: Breast hypertrophy, impotence, lactation

Hematologic & oncologic: Bone marrow depression, eosinophilia, granulocytopenia, hemolytic anemia, leukopenia, positive ANA titer, positive direct Coombs test, thrombocytopenia

Hepatic: Abnormal hepatic function tests, hepatic disease (hepatitis), jaundice

Neuromuscular & skeletal: Arthralgia, lupus-like syndrome, myalgia, positive rheumatoid factor, weakness

Renal: Increased blood urea nitrogen

Respiratory: Nasal congestion

Miscellaneous: Positive LE cell preparation

General Dosage Range Dosage adjustment recommended in patients with renal impairment

IV:

Children and Adolescents: 5 to 10 mg/kg/dose every 6 to 8 hours (maximum: 65 mg/kg/day or 3,000 mg/day)

Adults: 250 to 500 mg every 6 to 8 hours (maximum: 1,000 mg every 6 hours)

Oral:

Children and Adolescents: Initial: 10 mg/kg/day in 2 to 4 divided doses (maximum: 65 mg/kg/day or 3,000 mg/day)

Adults: Initial: 250 mg 2 to 3 times daily (maximum: 3,000 mg/day)

Mechanism of Action Stimulation of central alpha-adrenergic receptors by a false neurotransmitter (alpha-methylnorepinephrine) that results in a decreased sympathetic outflow to the heart, kidneys, and peripheral vasculature

Pharmacodynamics/Kinetics

Onset of Action Peak effect: Hypotensive: Oral, IV: Single-dose: Within 3 to 6 hours; Multiple-dose: 48 to 72 hours

Duration of Action Oral: Single-dose: 12 to 24 hours, Multiple-dose: 24 to 48 hours; IV: 10 to 16 hours

Half-life Elimination Neonates: 10 to 20 hours; Adults:1.5 to 2 hours; End-stage renal disease: Prolonged (Myhre 1982)

Time to Peak Plasma: Oral: 2 to 4 hours (Myhre 1982)

Pregnancy Risk Factor B/C (injectable)

Pregnancy Considerations Adverse events have not been observed in animal reproduction studies. Methyldopa crosses the placenta and appears in cord blood. Available data show use during pregnancy does not cause fetal harm and improves fetal outcomes.

Untreated chronic maternal hypertension is associated with adverse events in the fetus, infant, and mother. If treatment for chronic hypertension during pregnancy is needed, methyldopa is one of the preferred agents. If an injectable agent is needed for the urgent control of acute hypertension in pregnancy, other agents are preferred (ACOG, 2013).

Methylergonovine (meth il er goe NOE veen)

Brand Names: US Methergine

Brand Names: Canada Methergine®

Pharmacologic Category Ergot Derivative

Use Management of uterine atony, hemorrhage and subinvolution of the uterus following delivery of the placenta; control of uterine hemorrhage following delivery of the anterior shoulder in the second stage of labor

Local Anesthetic/Vasoconstrictor Precautions Use vasoconstrictor with caution in patients taking methylergonovine; this ergot alkaloid derivative causes constriction of peripheral blood vessels

Effects on Dental Treatment No significant effects or complications reported

Effects on Bleeding Thrombosis has been reported; however, there are no special precautions associated with bleeding related to dental procedures.

Adverse Reactions Frequency not defined.

Cardiovascular: Angina pectoris, arterial spasm, atrioventricular block, bradycardia, cerebrovascular accident, chest pain, hypertension, hypotension, local thrombophlebitis, myocardial infarction, palpitations, paresthesia, tachycardia, vasospasm, ventricular fibrillation

Central nervous system: Dizziness, hallucination, headache, seizure

Dermatologic: Diaphoresis, skin rash

Endocrine & metabolic: Water intoxication

Gastrointestinal: Abdominal pain, diarrhea, nausea, unpleasant taste, vomiting

Genitourinary: Hematuria

Hypersensitivity: Anaphylaxis

Neuromuscular & skeletal: Leg cramps

Otic: Tinnitus

Respiratory: Dyspnea, nasal congestion

General Dosage Range

IM, IV: *Adults:* 0.2 mg after delivery; may repeat every 2-4 hours

Oral: *Adults:* 0.2 mg 3-4 times daily in the puerperium

Mechanism of Action Increases the tone, rate and amplitude of contractions on the smooth muscles of the uterus, producing sustained contractions which shortens the third stage of labor and reduces blood loss.

Pharmacodynamics/Kinetics

Onset of Action Oxytocic: Oral: 5-10 minutes; IM: 2-5 minutes; IV: Immediately

Duration of Action Oral: ~3 hours; IM: ~3 hours; IV: 45 minutes

Half-life Elimination ~3 hours (range: 1.5-12.7 hours)

Time to Peak Serum: Oral: 0.3-2 hours; IM: 0.2-0.6 hours

Pregnancy Risk Factor C

Pregnancy Considerations Animal reproduction studies have not been conducted. Methylergonovine is intended for use after delivery of the infant; use is contraindicated during pregnancy.

Methylfolate (meth il FO late)

Brand Names: US Deplin 15; Deplin 7.5; Deplin [DSC]; Elfolate; L-Methylfolate Formula 15; L-Methylfolate Formula 7.5; L-Methylfolate Forte

Generic Availability (US) Yes

Pharmacologic Category Medical Food

Use Medical food for the nutritional requirements of patients with suboptimal L-methylfolate and have major depressive disorder or who have or are at risk for hyperhomocysteinemia and have schizophrenia

Note: A medical food is formulated to be administered enterally under the supervision of a physician and is intended for the specific dietary management of a disease or condition for which distinctive nutritional requirements are established by medical evaluation. Medical foods are not drugs and, therefore, are not subject to any FDA regulatory requirements that specifically apply to drugs (eg, requirement for written/oral prescription prior to dispensing, premarket review or approval, proof of safety and efficacy).

Local Anesthetic/Vasoconstrictor Precautions No information available to require special precautions

Effects on Dental Treatment No significant effects or complications reported

Effects on Bleeding No information available to require special precautions

Dosing

Adult & Geriatric Medicinal food: Oral: 7.5-15 mg daily

Mechanism of Action Methylfolate, or L-methylfolate, is the active form of folate in the body, which can be transported into peripheral tissues and across the blood-brain barrier. Folate is necessary for formation of numerous coenzymes in many metabolic systems, particularly for purine, pyrimidine, and nucleoprotein synthesis, and maintenance in erythropoiesis; stimulates WBC and platelet production in folate deficiency anemia.

Contraindications Hypersensitivity to any component of the formulation

Warnings/Precautions Folate administration is not appropriate for monotherapy with pernicious or other megaloblastic anemias when anemia is present with vitamin B_{12} deficiency. Doses >0.1 mg/day may obscure pernicious anemia with continuing irreversible nerve damage progression. Product is a medicinal food for use only under the supervision of a healthcare provider.

Drug Interactions

Metabolism/Transport Effects None known.

Avoid Concomitant Use

Avoid concomitant use of Methylfolate with any of the following: Raltitrexed

Increased Effect/Toxicity There are no known significant interactions involving an increase in effect.

Decreased Effect

Methylfolate may decrease the levels/effects of: CarBAMazepine; Fosphenytoin; PHENobarbital; Phenytoin; Primidone; Pyrimethamine; Raltitrexed; Valproate Products

The levels/effects of Methylfolate may be decreased by: Cholestyramine Resin; Colestipol; SulfaSALAzine

Dosage Forms

Capsule, Oral:

Deplin 15: L-methylfolate 15 mg and Schizochytrium algae

Deplin 7.5: L-methylfolate 7.5 mg and Schizochytrium algae
L-Methylfolate Formula 15: L-methylfolate 15 mg and Schizochytrium algae
L-Methylfolate Formula 7.5: L-methylfolate 7.5 mg and Schizochytrium algae
L-Methylfolate Forte: L-methylfolate 15 mg and Schizochytrium algae, L-methylfolate 7.5 mg and Schizochytrium algae

Tablet, Oral:
Elfolate: 7.5 mg, 15 mg
Generic: 7.5 mg, 15 mg

Methylnaltrexone (meth il nal TREKS one)

Brand Names: US Relistor
Brand Names: Canada Relistor
Pharmacologic Category Gastrointestinal Agent, Miscellaneous; Opioid Antagonist, Peripherally-Acting
Use
Opioid-induced constipation with advanced illness (injection only): Treatment of opioid-induced constipation in adults with advanced illness (receiving palliative care) who have an inadequate response to conventional laxative regimens.
Opioid-induced constipation with chronic non-cancer pain (tablets and injection): Treatment of opioid-induced constipation in adults with chronic non-cancer pain.
Local Anesthetic/Vasoconstrictor Precautions No information available to require special precautions
Effects on Dental Treatment No significant effects or complications reported
Effects on Bleeding No information available to require special precautions
Adverse Reactions
>10%: Gastrointestinal: Abdominal pain (14% to 29%), flatulence (13%), nausea (9% to 12%)
1% to 10%:
Central nervous system: Dizziness (7%), headache (4%), anxiety (2%), chills (1%)
Dermatologic: Hyperhidrosis (3% to 6%)
Endocrine & metabolic: Hot flash (3%)
Gastrointestinal: Diarrhea (5% to 6%), abdominal distention (4%), vomiting (2%)
Neuromuscular & skeletal: Muscle spasm (2%), tremor (1%)
Respiratory: Rhinorrhea (2%)
<1%, postmarketing, and/or case reports: Abdominal cramps, diaphoresis, flushing, gastrointestinal perforation, increased body temperature (Thomas 2008), malaise, opioid withdrawal syndrome, pain, syncope (Portenoy 2008)
General Dosage Range Dosage adjustment recommended in patients hepatic and renal impairment.
Oral: Opioid-induced constipation with chronic non-cancer pain: Adults: 450 mg once daily
SubQ:
Opioid-induced constipation with chronic non-cancer pain: Adults: 12 mg once daily
Opioid-induced constipation with advanced illness:
Adults <38 kg and >114 kg: 0.15 mg/kg (round dose up to nearest 0.1 mL of volume) every other day as needed (maximum: 1 dose/24 hours)
Adults 38 to <62 kg: 8 mg every other day as needed (maximum: 1 dose/24 hours)
Adults 62 to 114 kg: 12 mg every other day as needed (maximum: 1 dose/24 hours)

Mechanism of Action An opioid receptor antagonist which blocks opioid binding at the mu receptor, methylnaltrexone is a quaternary derivative of naltrexone with restricted ability to cross the blood-brain barrier. It therefore functions as a peripheral acting opioid antagonist, including actions on the gastrointestinal tract to inhibit opioid-induced decreased gastrointestinal motility and delay in gastrointestinal transit time, thereby decreasing opioid-induced constipation. Does not affect opioid analgesic effects.
Pharmacodynamics/Kinetics
Half-life Elimination Terminal: ~15 hours (oral)
Time to Peak SubQ: 30 minutes; Oral: ~1.5 hours (delayed by 2 hours with high fat meal)
Pregnancy Considerations Adverse events have not been observed in animal reproduction studies. Maternal use of methylnaltrexone during pregnancy may precipitate opioid withdrawal effects in newborn.

Methylphenidate (meth il FEN i date)

Brand Names: US Aptensio XR; Concerta; Daytrana; Metadate CD; Metadate ER; Methylin; QuilliChew ER; Quillivant XR; Ritalin; Ritalin LA; Ritalin SR [DSC]
Brand Names: Canada Apo-Methylphenidate; Apo-Methylphenidate SR; Biphentin; Concerta; PHL-Methylphenidate; PMS-Methylphenidate; ratio-Methylphenidate; Ritalin; Ritalin SR; Sandoz-Methylphenidate SR; Teva-Methylphenidate ER-C
Generic Availability (US) May be product dependent
Pharmacologic Category Central Nervous System Stimulant
Use
Attention-deficit/hyperactivity disorder: Treatment of attention-deficit/hyperactivity disorder (ADHD).
Narcolepsy: Symptomatic management of narcolepsy (except Aptensio XR, Concerta, Daytrana, Metadate CD, Ritalin LA, QuilliChew ER, Quillivant XR, and Biphentin [Canadian product]).
Local Anesthetic/Vasoconstrictor Precautions No information available to require special precautions
Effects on Dental Treatment Key adverse event(s) related to dental treatment: Methylphenidate causes tachycardia, increases in blood pressure, and palpitations. Consider monitoring blood pressure prior to using local anesthetic with a vasoconstrictor. Symptoms associated with bruxism have been observed in some patients.
Effects on Bleeding No information available to require special precautions
Adverse Reactions
>10%:
Central nervous system: Headache (2% to 22%), insomnia (including initial insomnia; 2% to 13%), irritability (6% to 11%)
Gastrointestinal: Decreased appetite (2% to 26%), xerostomia (oral: 14%), nausea (2% to 13%)
1% to 10%:
Cardiovascular: Tachycardia (oral: 5%; transdermal: ≤1%), palpitations (oral: 3%; transdermal: <1%)
Central nervous system: Emotional lability (1% to 9%), anxiety (oral: 8%), tics (transdermal: 7%; oral: 2%), dizziness (2% to 7%), depressed mood (oral: 4%; transdermal: <1%), nervousness (oral: 3%; transdermal: <1%), restlessness (oral: 3%), aggressive behavior (oral: 2%), agitation (oral: 2%), depression (oral: 2%), hypertonia (oral: 2%), lack of emotion (oral: 2%), vertigo (oral: 2%), confusion (oral: 1%),

sedation (oral: 1%), tension (oral: 1%), tension headache (oral: 1%), paresthesia (≤1%)
Dermatologic: Hyperhidrosis (oral: 5%), excoriation (oral: 4%), skin rash (oral: 2%)
Endocrine & metabolic: Weight loss (2% to 9%), decreased libido (oral: 2%)
Gastrointestinal: Vomiting (transdermal: 10%; oral: 2% to 3%), abdominal pain (transdermal: 5% to 7%), upper abdominal pain (oral: 6%), anorexia (2% to 5%), bruxism (oral: 2%), dyspepsia (oral: 2%), motion sickness (oral: 2%), constipation (oral: 1%)
Neuromuscular & skeletal: Tremor (oral: 3%)
Ophthalmic: Blurred vision (oral: 2%; transdermal: <1%), eye pain (oral: 2%)
Respiratory: Nasopharyngitis (oral: 3%), cough (oral: 2%), upper respiratory tract infection (oral: 2%), oropharyngeal pain (oral: 1% to 2%)
Miscellaneous: Fever (oral: 2%)

Frequency not defined:
Cardiovascular: Cardiac arrhythmia, decreased blood pressure, decreased pulse, heart murmur, hypertension, increased pulse
Central nervous system: Gilles de la Tourette's syndrome (rare), hypervigilance, jitteriness, mood changes, outbursts of anger, panic attack, psychomotor agitation, sleep disorder, toxic psychosis
Dermatologic: Macular eruption
Endocrine & metabolic: Growth suppression, hot flash, increased thirst
Gastrointestinal: Abdominal distress, diarrhea
Genitourinary: Erectile dysfunction
Hematologic & oncologic: Anemia, leukopenia
Hepatic: Increased serum ALT
Neuromuscular & skeletal: Muscle spasm, weakness
Ophthalmic: Dry eye syndrome
Respiratory: Dyspnea, sinusitis

<1%, postmarketing, and/or case reports: Accommodation disturbance, allergic contact dermatitis, allergic contact sensitivity, alopecia, angina pectoris, application site reaction (including bleeding, bruising, burn, burning, dermatitis, discharge, discoloration, discomfort, dryness, eczema, edema, erosion, erythema, excoriation, exfoliation, fissure, hyperpigmentation, hypopigmentation, induration, infection, inflammation, irritation, pain, papules, paresthesia, pruritus, scab, skin rash, swelling, ulcer, urticaria, vesicles, warmth), arthralgia, auditory hallucination, bradycardia, cerebral arteritis, cerebrovascular occlusion, change in libido, change in WBC count, chest discomfort, chest pain, decreased platelet count, decreased therapeutic response, diplopia, disorientation, drowsiness, dyskinesia, erythema, extrasystoles, fatigue, hallucination, hepatic failure (acute), hepatic injury (severe), hyperpyrexia, hypersensitivity reaction (including angioedema, anaphylaxis, auricular swelling, bullous conditions, exfoliative dermatitis, erythema multiforme with histopathological findings of necrotizing vasculitis, pruritus), immune thrombocytopenia, increased blood pressure, increased heart rate, increased liver enzymes, increased serum alkaline phosphatase, increased serum bilirubin, lethargy, leukoderma (chemical; FDA Safety Alert 2015), loss of scalp hair, mania, muscle twitching, myalgia, mydriasis, neuroleptic malignant syndrome, pancytopenia, peripheral vascular insufficiency, priapism, Raynaud's phenomenon, rhabdomyolysis, seizure, supraventricular tachycardia, talkativeness, thrombocytopenia, tonic-clonic seizures, urticaria, ventricular premature contractions, visual disturbance, visual hallucination

Dosing

Adult

ADHD: Oral:

Immediate release (IR) products (tablets, chewable tablets, and solution): Initial: 5 mg twice daily, before breakfast and lunch; increase by 5 to 10 mg daily at weekly intervals; maximum dose: 60 mg/day (in 2 to 3 divided doses).

Extended release (ER), sustained release (SR) products (capsules, tablets, chewable tablets, and oral suspension):

Concerta: (Adults <65 years):
Patients not currently taking methylphenidate: Initial: 18 to 36 mg once every morning
Patients currently taking immediate release (IR) methylphenidate: Initial: **Note:** Dosing based on current regimen and clinical judgment; suggested dosing listed below:
- Patients taking IR methylphenidate 5 mg 2 to 3 times daily **or** (Canadian labeling; not in US labeling) methylphenidate SR 20 mg daily: 18 mg once every morning
- Patients taking IR methylphenidate 10 mg 2 to 3 times daily **or** (Canadian labeling; not in US labeling) methylphenidate SR 40 mg daily: 36 mg once every morning
- Patients taking IR methylphenidate 15 mg 2 to 3 times daily **or** (Canadian labeling; not in US labeling) methylphenidate SR 60 mg daily: 54 mg once every morning
- Patients taking IR methylphenidate 20 mg 2 to 3 times daily: 72 mg once every morning

Dose adjustment: May increase dose in increments of 18 mg at weekly intervals. A dosage strength of 27 mg is available for situations in which a dosage between 18 to 36 mg is desired. Maximum dose: 72 mg/day.

Aptensio XR: Initial: 10 mg once daily; may be titrated in 10 mg increments at weekly intervals; maximum: 60 mg/day

Biphentin [Canadian product]: Patients not currently taking methylphenidate: Initial: 10 to 20 mg once daily; may be adjusted in 10 mg increments at weekly intervals to a maximum dose of 80 mg/day.
Conversion from immediate release methylphenidate formulations to Biphentin: Use equivalent total daily dose administered once daily.

Metadate ER, Ritalin-SR: May be given in place of immediate release products (duration of action ~8 hours), once the immediate release formulation daily dose is titrated and the titrated 8-hour dosage corresponds to sustained or extended release tablet size; maximum: 60 mg/day

Metadate CD, Quillivant XR: Initial: 20 mg once daily; may be adjusted in 10 to 20 mg increments at weekly intervals; maximum: 60 mg/day

QuilliChew E R: Initial: 20 mg once daily in the morning; may be adjusted by 10, 15 or 20 mg at weekly intervals (tablets are scored and may be broken in half to achieve the 10 mg and 15 mg doses); maximum: 60 mg/day
Conversion from other methylphenidate formulations to QuilliChew ER: Discontinue previous formulation and titrate using above schedule; do not substitute on a milligram-per-milligram basis

Ritalin LA: Initial: 20 mg once daily (10 mg once daily may be considered for some patients); may be adjusted in 10 mg increments at weekly intervals; maximum: 60 mg/day

Conversion from immediate release or sustained release methylphenidate formulation to Ritalin LA: Use equivalent total daily dose administered once daily.

Narcolepsy: Oral:

Immediate release tablets and solution *(Methylin, Ritalin):* Initial: 5 mg twice daily before breakfast and lunch; increase by 5 to 10 mg daily at weekly intervals; maximum dose: 60 mg/day (in 2 to 3 divided doses).

Extended and sustained release tablets *(Metadate ER, Ritalin-SR):* May be given in place of immediate release products (duration of action ~8 hours), once the immediate release formulation daily dose is titrated and the titrated 8-hour dosage corresponds to sustained or extended release tablet size; maximum: 60 mg/day.

Depression in medically-ill older adults or adult patients with terminal illness and/or receiving palliative care (off-label use): Oral: Initial: ***Immediate release:*** 2.5 to 5 mg once daily before breakfast or twice daily before breakfast and lunch; increase by 2.5 to 5 mg daily every 1 to 3 days in divided doses before breakfast and lunch as tolerated; maximum dose: 20 to 40 mg/day (Hardy, 2009; Kerr 2012). *Do **not** use sustained release product.*

Fatigue, cancer-related (off-label use): Oral: Immediate release: Initial: 5 mg twice daily (at 8 am and 1 pm); increase based on tolerability in increments of 10 mg/day every 3 days up to a maximum of 40 mg/day (Kerr 2012).

Geriatric

ADHD/Narcolepsy: Refer to adult dosing.

Major depressive disorder (antidepressant augmentation; off-label use): Oral: Initial: ***Immediate release:*** 2.5 mg twice daily (given at 9 am and 3 pm); increase dosage based on response and tolerability in increments of 2.5 mg twice daily every 3 to 4 days up to 40 mg/day. Average dose in clinical trials was ~15 to 16 mg/day (Lavrestky 2015; Lavrestky 2006).

Pediatric

ADHD:

Oral, immediate release (IR) products (tablets, chewable tablets, and solution): Children ≥6 years and Adolescents: Initial: 5 mg twice daily, before breakfast and lunch; increase by 5 to 10 mg daily at weekly intervals; maximum dose: 60 mg/day (in 2 to 3 divided doses).

Oral, extended release (ER), sustained release (SR) products (capsules, tablets, chewable tablets, and oral suspension):

Children ≥6 years and Adolescents <18 years:

Concerta: **Note:** For adolescents ≥18 years, refer to adult dosing.

Patients not currently taking methylphenidate: Initial: 18 mg once daily in the morning

Patients currently taking immediate release (IR) methylphenidate: Initial: **Note:** Dosing based on current regimen and clinical judgment; suggested dosing listed below:

- Patients taking IR methylphenidate 5 mg 2 to 3 times daily **or** (Canadian labeling; not in US labeling) methylphenidate SR 20 mg daily: 18 mg once every morning
- Patients taking IR methylphenidate 10 mg 2 to 3 times daily **or** (Canadian labeling; not in US labeling) methylphenidate SR 40 mg daily: 36 mg once every morning
- Patients taking IR methylphenidate 15 mg 2 to 3 times daily **or** (Canadian labeling; not in US labeling) methylphenidate SR 60 mg daily: 54 mg once every morning
- Patients taking IR methylphenidate 20 mg 2 to 3 times daily: 72 mg once every morning

Dose adjustment: May increase dose in increments of 18 mg at weekly intervals. A dosage strength of 27 mg is available for situations in which a dosage between 18 to 36 mg is desired.

Maximum dose: 54 mg/day in children 6 to 12 years **or** 2 mg/kg/day (up to 72 mg/day) in adolescents <18 years

Children ≥6 years and Adolescents:

Aptensio XR: Initial: 10 mg once daily; may be titrated in 10 mg increments at weekly intervals; maximum: 60 mg/day

Biphentin [Canadian product]: Patients not currently taking methylphenidate: Initial: 10 to 20 mg once daily; may be adjusted in 10 mg increments at weekly intervals. Maximum: 60 mg/day. **Note:** In some children >60 kg, a maximum dose of 1 mg/kg/day (not to exceed 80 mg/day) may be necessary; however, close monitoring for adverse events is required. Reduce dose or discontinue if adverse events arise.

Conversion from immediate release methylphenidate formulations to Biphentin: Use equivalent total daily dose administered once daily.

Metadate ER, Ritalin-SR: May be given in place of immediate release products (duration of action ~8 hours), once the immediate release formulation daily dose is titrated and the titrated 8-hour dosage corresponds to sustained or extended release tablet size; maximum: 60 mg/day

Metadate CD, Quillivant XR: Initial: 20 mg once daily; may be adjusted in 10 to 20 mg increments at weekly intervals; maximum: 60 mg/day

QuilliChew ER: Initial: 20 mg once daily in the morning; may be adjusted by 10, 15 or 20 mg at weekly intervals (tablets are scored and may be broken in half to achieve the 10 mg and 15 mg doses); maximum: 60 mg/day

Conversion from other methylphenidate formulations to QuilliChew ER: Discontinue previous formulation and titrate using above schedule; do not substitute on a milligram-per-milligram basis

Ritalin LA: Initial: 20 mg once daily (10 mg once daily may be considered for some patients); may be adjusted in 10 mg increments at weekly intervals; maximum: 60 mg/day

Conversion from immediate release or sustained release methylphenidate formulation to Ritalin LA: Use equivalent total daily dose administered once daily.

Transdermal: (Daytrana): Children ≥6 years and Adolescents <18 years: Initial: 10 mg patch once daily; remove up to 9 hours after application. Titrate based on response and tolerability; may increase to next transdermal dose no more frequently than every week. **Note:** Application should occur 2 hours prior to desired effect. Drug absorption may continue for a period of time after patch removal. The prescribing information recommends patients converting from another formulation of methylphenidate should be initiated at 10 mg regardless of their previous dose and titrated as needed due to the differences in bioavailability of the transdermal formulation. However, some clinicians have supported higher starting patch doses for patients converting from oral methylphenidate doses of >20 mg daily; for example, the 15 mg (18.75 cm^2) patch has been investigated to have the same effect as 22.5 mg daily of the immediate release preparation, 27 mg/day of the osmotic release preparation, or 20 mg daily of the encapsulated bead preparation (Arnold, 2007).

Narcolepsy: Oral: Children ≥6 years and Adolescents: Refer to adult dosing.

Renal Impairment

Oral: There are no dosage adjustments provided in the manufacturer's labeling (has not been studied); undergoes extensive metabolism to a renally eliminated metabolite with little or no pharmacologic activity.

Transdermal: There are no dosage adjustments provided in the manufacturer's labeling (has not been studied).

Hepatic Impairment

Oral: There are no dosage adjustments provided in the manufacturer's labeling (has not been studied).

Transdermal: There are no dosage adjustments provided in the manufacturer's labeling (has not been studied).

Mechanism of Action Mild CNS stimulant; blocks the reuptake of norepinephrine and dopamine into presynaptic neurons; appears to stimulate the cerebral cortex and subcortical structures similar to amphetamines

Contraindications

US labeling: Hypersensitivity to methylphenidate or any component of the formulation; use during or within 14 days following MAO inhibitor therapy; marked anxiety, tension, and agitation (excluding Aptensio XR, QuilliChew ER, and Quillivant XR); glaucoma (excluding Aptensio XR, QuilliChew ER, and Quillivant XR); family history or diagnosis of Tourette syndrome or tics (excluding Aptensio XR, QuilliChew ER, and Quillivant XR)

Additional contraindications: Metadate CD: Severe hypertension, heart failure, arrhythmia, hyperthyroidism or thyrotoxicosis, recent MI or angina; concomitant use of halogenated anesthetics; patients with rare hereditary problems of fructose intolerance, glucose-galactose malabsorption, or sucrose-isomaltase insufficiency

Canadian labeling: Hypersensitivity to methylphenidate or any component of the formulation; marked anxiety, tension, and agitation; glaucoma; use during or within 14 days following MAO inhibitor therapy; family history or diagnosis of Tourette syndrome or tics (excluding Concerta), thyrotoxicosis, advanced arteriosclerosis, symptomatic cardiovascular disease, or moderate to severe hypertension

Additional contraindications: Ritalin and Ritalin SR: Pheochromocytoma

Warnings/Precautions CNS stimulant use has been associated with serious cardiovascular events (eg, sudden death, arrhythmia, and myocardial infarction (MI) in children and adolescents; sudden death, stroke, and MI in adults) in patients with and without preexisting structural cardiac abnormalities or other serious heart problems (Shin 2016). These products should be avoided in patients with known serious structural cardiac abnormalities, cardiomyopathy, serious heart rhythm abnormalities, or other serious cardiac problems that could further increase their risk of sudden death. Patients should be carefully evaluated for cardiac disease prior to initiation of therapy. Use of stimulants can cause an increase in blood pressure and heart rate, although some patients may have larger than average increases. Use caution with hypertension, hyperthyroidism, or other cardiovascular conditions that might be exacerbated by increases in blood pressure or heart rate. Some products are contraindicated in patients with heart failure, arrhythmias, severe hypertension, hyperthyroidism, angina, or recent MI. Stimulants are associated with peripheral vasculopathy, including Raynaud phenomenon; signs/symptoms are usually mild and intermittent, and generally improve with dose reduction or discontinuation. Digital ulceration and/or soft tissue breakdown have been observed rarely; monitor for digital changes during therapy and seek further evaluation (eg, rheumatology) if necessary. Prolonged and painful erections (priapism), sometimes requiring surgical intervention, have been reported (rarely) with methylphenidate and atomoxetine use in pediatric and adult patients. Priapism has been reported to develop after some time on the drug, often subsequent to an increase in dose but also during a period of drug withdrawal (drug holidays or discontinuation). Patients with certain hematological dyscrasias (eg, sickle cell disease), malignancies, perineal trauma, or concomitant use of alcohol, illicit drugs, or other medications associated with priapism may be at increased risk. Patients who develop abnormally sustained or frequent and painful erections should discontinue therapy and seek immediate medical attention. An emergent urological consultation should be obtained in severe cases. Priapism has been associated with different dosage forms and products; it is not known if rechallenge with a different formulation will risk recurrence. Avoidance of stimulants and atomoxetine may be preferred in patients with severe cases that were slow to resolve and/or required detumescence (Eiland 2014).

Has demonstrated value as part of a comprehensive treatment program for ADHD. Use with caution in patients with bipolar disorder (may induce mixed/manic episode). May exacerbate symptoms of behavior and thought disorder in psychotic patients; new-onset psychosis or mania may occur with stimulant use. Patients should be screened for bipolar disorder prior to treatment; consider discontinuation if such symptoms (eg, delusional thinking, hallucinations, mania) occur. May be associated with aggressive behavior or hostility (causal relationship not established); monitor for development or worsening of these behaviors. Suicidal ideation, attempts and very rarely, completed suicide have been reported. Monitor for suicide-related behavior. Use caution with seizure disorders (may reduce seizure threshold). Use with caution in patients with Tourette syndrome or other tic disorders. Stimulants may exacerbate tics (motor and phonic) and Tourette syndrome; however, evidence demonstrating increased tics is limited. Evaluate for tics and Tourette syndrome prior to therapy initiation; use is contraindicated with some products (AACAP [Murphy 2013; Pliszka 2007]). Use caution in patients with history of ethanol or drug abuse. May exacerbate symptoms of behavior and thought disorder in psychotic patients. **[US Boxed Warning]: Potential for drug dependency exists - avoid abrupt discontinuation in patients who have received for prolonged periods.** Visual disturbances have been reported (rare). Hypersensitivity reactions, such as angioedema and anaphylactic reactions have been reported. May cause CNS depression, which may impair physical or mental abilities; patients must be cautioned about performing tasks that require mental alertness (eg, operating machinery or driving). Appetite suppression may occur, particularly in children. Use of stimulants has been associated with weight loss and slowing of growth rate; monitor growth rate and weight during treatment; treatment interruption may be necessary in patients who are not increasing in height or gaining weight as expected.

Concerta should not be used in patients with esophageal motility disorders or preexisting severe gastrointestinal narrowing (small bowel disease, short gut syndrome, history of peritonitis, cystic fibrosis, chronic intestinal pseudo-obstruction, Meckel diverticulum). Concomitant use of Metadate CD with halogenated anesthetics is contraindicated; may cause sudden elevations in blood pressure; if surgery is planned, do not administer Metadate CD on the day of surgery. Transdermal system may cause allergic contact sensitization, characterized by intense local reactions (edema, papules) that may spread beyond the patch site; sensitization may subsequently manifest systemically with other routes of methylphenidate administration; monitor closely. Avoid exposure of application site to any direct external heat sources (eg, hair dryers, heating pads, electric blankets); may increase the rate and extent of absorption and risk of overdose. Efficacy of transdermal methylphenidate therapy for >7 weeks has not been established. Transdermal system may cause a persistent loss of skin pigmentation at and around the application site, as well as at distant sites from the application site; loss of skin pigmentation may continue after discontinuation of transdermal system. May resemble vitiligo especially if loss of skin pigmentation occurs at areas distant from application site; use with caution in patients with a history and/or family history of vitiligo. Monitor for signs of skin depigmentation; immediately discontinue use if patient experiences chemical leukoderma. Potentially significant drug-drug interactions may exist, requiring dose or frequency adjustment, additional monitoring, and/or selection of alternative therapy. Biphentin [Canadian product] controlled release capsules are not interchangeable with other controlled release formulations. Some dosage forms may contain lactose or sucrose; use with caution in patients intolerant to either component (some manufacturer labels recommend avoiding use in such patients).

Some dosage forms may contain sodium benzoate/benzoic acid; benzoic acid (benzoate) is a metabolite of benzyl alcohol; large amounts of benzyl alcohol (≥99 mg/kg/day) have been associated with a potentially fatal toxicity ("gasping syndrome") in neonates; the "gasping syndrome" consists of metabolic acidosis, respiratory distress, gasping respirations, CNS dysfunction (including convulsions, intracranial hemorrhage), hypotension, and cardiovascular collapse (AAP ["Inactive" 1997]; CDC, 1982); some data suggests that benzoate displaces bilirubin from protein binding sites (Ahlfors, 2001); avoid or use dosage forms containing benzyl alcohol derivative with caution in neonates. See manufacturer's labeling. Some dosage forms contain phenylalanine, which can be harmful to patients with phenylketonuria (PKU). Before prescribing, consider the combined daily amount of phenylalanine from all sources.

Drug Interactions

Metabolism/Transport Effects None known.

Avoid Concomitant Use

Avoid concomitant use of Methylphenidate with any of the following: Acebrophylline; Alcohol (Ethyl); Inhalational Anesthetics; Iobenguane I 123; MAO Inhibitors

Increased Effect/Toxicity

Methylphenidate may increase the levels/effects of: Anti-Parkinson Agents (Dopamine Agonist); Antipsychotic Agents; CloNIDine; Doxofylline; Fosphenytoin; Inhalational Anesthetics; Iohexol; Iomeprol; Iopamidol; PHENobarbital; Phenytoin; Primidone; Serotonin Modulators; Sympathomimetics; Tricyclic Antidepressants; Vitamin K Antagonists

The levels/effects of Methylphenidate may be increased by: Acebrophylline; Alcohol (Ethyl); Antacids; Antipsychotic Agents; AtoMOXetine; Cannabinoid-Containing Products; Cocaine; H2-Antagonists; MAO Inhibitors; Proton Pump Inhibitors

Decreased Effect

Methylphenidate may decrease the levels/effects of: Antihypertensive Agents; Iobenguane I 123; Ioflupane I 123

Food Interactions

Ethanol: Alcohol consumption increases the rate of methylphenidate release from Metadate CD (extended-release capsules), Ritalin LA (extended-release capsules), and QuilliChew ER (extended-release chewable tablet), but not from Concerta (extended-release tablet); an *in vitro* study involving Metadate CD and Ritalin LA showed that an alcohol concentration of 40% resulted in 84% and 98% of the methylphenidate being released in the first hour, respectively; a study involving Quillichew ER showed that an alcohol concentration of 40% resulted in 90% of the methylphenidate being released in the first hour. Management: Avoid consuming alcohol during therapy.

Food: Food may increase oral absorption of immediate-release tablet/solution/chewable tablet. Management: Administer 30 to 45 minutes before meals.

Dietary Considerations Administer immediate release (IR) tablet (Ritalin), IR solution (Methylin), IR chewable tablet (Methylin), and sustained released tablet (Ritalin-SR) 30-45 minutes before meals. Some products may contain phenylalanine.

Pharmacodynamics/Kinetics

Onset of Action

Onset of action (AAP 2011): Children:

Oral:

Immediate release formulations [chewable tablet, oral solution, tablet (Methylin, Ritalin)]: 20 to 60 minutes

Extended release formulations [Capsule (Metadate CD, Ritalin LA), tablets (Concerta)]: 20 to 60 minutes

Sustained release tablet (Ritalin-SR): 60 to 180 minutes

Transdermal (Daytrana): 60 minutes

Maximum effect: Oral: Immediate release tablet: Within 2 hours; Sustained release tablet: Within 4 to 7 hours

Duration of Action

Oral (AAP 2011): Children:

Immediate release formulations [Chewable tablet, oral solution, immediate release tablet (Methylin, Ritalin)]: 3 to 5 hours

Extended release capsule (Metadate CD, Ritalin LA): 6 to 8 hours

Extended release tablet (Concerta): 12 hours
Sustained release tablet (Ritalin-SR): 2 to 6 hours
Transdermal (Daytrana): Children: 11 to 12 hours (AAP 2011)

Half-life Elimination

Immediate release chewable tablet: Methylin: Adults: 3 hours
Controlled release capsule: Biphentin [Canadian product]: Children: 2.4 hours; Adults: 2.1 hours
Extended release capsule:
Aptensio XR: Adults: ~5 hours
Metadate CD: Adults: 6.8 hours
Ritalin LA: Children: ~2.45 hours (range: 1.5 to 4 hours); Adults: ~3.3 hours (range: 3 to 4.2 hours)
Extended release chewable tablets: ~5.2 hours
Extended release suspension: Quillivant XR: Children ≥9 years, Adolescents, and Adults: ~5 hours
Extended release tablet: Concerta: Adolescents and Adults: ~3.5 hours
Immediate release solution: Methylin: Adults: 2.7 hours
Immediate release tablet: Children: 2.5 hours (range: 1.8 to 5.3 hours); Adults: 3.5 hours (range: 1.3 to 7.7 hours)
Sustained release tablet: Adults: 3.4 hours
Transdermal: Children and Adolescents 6 to 17 years: *d*-methylphenidate ~4 to 5 hours, *l*-methylphenidate 1.4 to 2.9 hours

Time to Peak

Immediate release chewable tablet: Methylin: ~1 to 2 hours
Extended release chewable tablet: QuilliChew ER: 5 hours (median)
Controlled release capsule: Biphentin [Canadian product]: Children: Initial: ~2.5 hours; Adults: Initial: ~2 hours
Extended release capsule:
Aptensio XR: Adults: Initial: ~2 hours; Second peak: ~8 hours
Metadate CD: Children: Initial: ~1.5 hours; Second peak: ~4.5 hours
Ritalin LA:
Children: Initial: 1 to 3 hours; Second peak: 5 to 11 hours
Adults: Initial: 1.3 to 4 hours; Second peak: 4.3 to 6.5 hours
Extended release suspension: Quillivant XR: Children (9 to 12 years): 4.05 hours (range: 3.98 to 6 hours); Adolescents (13 to 15 years): 2 hours (range: 1.98 to 4 hours); Adults: 4 hours (range: 1.3 to 7.3 hours)
Extended release tablet: Concerta: Initial: ~1 hours, followed by gradually ascending concentrations over 5 to 9 hours; Mean peak: 6 to 10 hours
Immediate release solution: Methylin: 1 to 2 hours
Immediate release tablet: Children: 1.9 hours (range: 0.3 to 4.4 hours)
Sustained release tablet: Children: 4.7 hours (range: 1.3 to 8.2 hours)
Transdermal: ~8 to 10 hours

Pregnancy Risk Factor C

Pregnancy Considerations Adverse events have been observed in animal reproduction studies. Information related to the use of methylphenidate in pregnant women with attention-deficit/hyperactivity disorder (Bolea-Akmanac, 2013; Dideriksen, 2013) or narcolepsy (Maurovich-Horvat, 2013; Thorpy, 2013) is limited.

Breastfeeding Considerations Methylphenidate is excreted in breast milk, resulting in relative infant doses of 0.16% to 0.7% of the weight adjusted maternal dose. Adverse events were not noted in two case reports; however, both were older (6 months of age and 11 months of age) and exposure was limited (Hackett, 2006; Spigset, 2007). According to the manufacturer, the decision to continue or discontinue breastfeeding during therapy should take into account the risk of exposure to the infant and the benefits of treatment to the mother. Monitor breastfeeding infants for adverse reactions, such as agitation, anorexia, insomnia, and reduced weight gain.

Controlled Substance C-II

Dosage Forms

Capsule Extended Release, Oral:
Metadate CD: 10 mg, 20 mg, 30 mg, 40 mg, 50 mg, 60 mg
Generic: 10 mg, 20 mg, 30 mg, 40 mg, 50 mg, 60 mg

Capsule Extended Release 24 Hour, Oral:
Aptensio XR: 10 mg, 15 mg, 20 mg, 30 mg, 40 mg, 50 mg, 60 mg
Ritalin LA: 10 mg, 20 mg, 30 mg, 40 mg
Generic: 20 mg, 30 mg, 40 mg, 60 mg

Patch, Transdermal:
Daytrana: 10 mg/9 hr (30 ea); 15 mg/9 hr (30 ea); 20 mg/9 hr (30 ea); 30 mg/9 hr (30 ea)

Solution, Oral:
Methylin: 5 mg/5 mL (500 mL); 10 mg/5 mL (500 mL)
Generic: 5 mg/5 mL (500 mL); 10 mg/5 mL (500 mL)

Suspension Reconstituted, Oral:
Quillivant XR: 25 mg/5 mL (60 mL, 120 mL, 150 mL, 180 mL)

Tablet, Oral:
Ritalin: 5 mg, 10 mg, 20 mg
Generic: 5 mg, 10 mg, 20 mg

Tablet Chewable, Oral:
Methylin: 2.5 mg, 5 mg, 10 mg
Generic: 2.5 mg, 5 mg, 10 mg

Tablet Chewable Extended Release, Oral:
QuilliChew ER: 20 mg, 30 mg, 40 mg

Tablet Extended Release, Oral:
Concerta: 18 mg, 27 mg, 36 mg, 54 mg
Metadate ER: 20 mg
Generic: 10 mg, 18 mg, 20 mg, 27 mg, 36 mg, 54 mg

Tablet Extended Release 24 Hour, Oral:
Generic: 18 mg, 27 mg, 36 mg, 54 mg

Dosage Forms: Canada

Capsule, controlled release, oral:
Biphentin: 10 mg, 15 mg, 20 mg, 30 mg, 40 mg, 50 mg, 60 mg, 80 mg

---

MethylPREDNISolone (meth il pred NIS oh lone)

Related Information

Respiratory Diseases *on page 1777*

Related Sample Prescriptions

Ulcerative and Erosive Disorders - Sample Prescriptions *on page 43*

Brand Names: US A-Methapred; DEPO-Medrol; Medrol; ReadySharp Methylprednisolone; SOLU-medrol

Brand Names: Canada Depo-Medrol; Medrol; Methylprednisolone Acetate; Methylprednisolone Sodium Succinate For Injection; Methylprednisolone Sodium Succinate For Injection USP; Solu-Medrol

Generic Availability (US) May be product dependent

Pharmacologic Category Corticosteroid, Systemic

Dental Use Treatment of a variety of oral diseases of allergic, inflammatory, or autoimmune origin

Use

Oral, IM, and IV administration:

Allergic: Control of severe or incapacitating allergic conditions intractable to adequate trials of conventional treatment in atopic dermatitis, drug hypersensitivity reactions, seasonal or perennial allergic rhinitis, serum sickness, and/or transfusion reactions.

Dermatologic: Bullous dermatitis herpetiformis; contact dermatitis; exfoliative dermatitis; exfoliative erythroderma; mycosis fungoides; pemphigus; erythema multiforme (Stevens-Johnson syndrome); severe psoriasis; severe seborrheic dermatitis.

Endocrine: Congenital adrenal hyperplasia; hypercalcemia associated with cancer; nonsuppurative thyroiditis; primary or secondary adrenocortical insufficiency (hydrocortisone or cortisone is the first choice; synthetic analogs may be used in conjunction with mineralocorticoids where applicable).

GI: To tide the patient over a critical period of the disease in Crohn disease or ulcerative colitis.

Hematologic: Acquired (autoimmune) hemolytic anemia; congenital (erythroid) hypoplastic anemia (Diamond Blackfan anemia); erythroblastopenia (RBC anemia; oral only); idiopathic thrombocytopenic purpura (adults; oral and IV only); pure red cell aplasia (excluding oral); secondary thrombocytopenia.

Neoplastic: Palliative management of leukemias and lymphomas.

Nervous system: Acute exacerbations of multiple sclerosis; cerebral edema associated with primary or metastatic brain tumor, craniotomy, or head injury (excluding oral).

Ophthalmic:

Oral: Severe acute and chronic allergic and inflammatory processes involving the eye and its adnexa such as allergic conjunctivitis; allergic corneal marginal ulcers; anterior segment inflammation; chorioretinitis; diffuse posterior uveitis and choroiditis; herpes zoster ophthalmicus; iritis and iridocyclitis; keratitis; optic neuritis; sympathetic ophthalmia; uveitis.

Injection: Sympathetic ophthalmia; temporal arteritis, uveitis and other ocular inflammatory conditions unresponsive to topical corticosteroids.

Renal: To induce diuresis or remission of proteinuria in nephrotic syndrome, with or without uremia, of the idiopathic type or that due to lupus erythematosus.

Respiratory: Aspiration pneumonitis (oral only); asthma; berylliosis; fulminating or disseminated pulmonary tuberculosis when used concurrently with appropriate antituberculous chemotherapy; idiopathic eosinophilic pneumonias; symptomatic sarcoidosis.

Rheumatic: As adjunctive therapy for short-term administration in acute rheumatic carditis, acute gouty arthritis, ankylosing spondylitis, dermatomyositis, polymyositis, psoriatic arthritis, rheumatoid arthritis (including juvenile rheumatoid arthritis), systemic lupus erythematosus; as adjunctive therapy for short-term administration in acute and subacute bursitis, acute nonspecific tenosynovitis, epicondylitis, posttraumatic osteoarthritis, relapsing polychondritis, synovitis of osteoarthritis (oral only).

Miscellaneous: Trichinosis with neurologic or myocardial involvement; tuberculous meningitis with subarachnoid block or impending block when used concurrently with appropriate antituberculous chemotherapy.

Intra-articular or soft tissue administration (methylprednisolone acetate only): As adjunctive therapy for short-term administration in acute gouty arthritis, acute and subacute bursitis, acute nonspecific tenosynovitis, epicondylitis, rheumatoid arthritis, and/or synovitis of osteoarthritis.

Intralesional administration (methylprednisolone acetate only): Alopecia areata; discoid lupus erythematosus; keloids; localized hypertrophic; infiltrated, inflammatory lesions of granuloma annulare; lichen planus; lichen simplex chronicus (neurodermatitis); psoriatic plaques; necrobiosis lipoidica diabeticorum. May be useful in cystic tumor of an aponeurosis or tendon (ganglia).

Local Anesthetic/Vasoconstrictor Precautions No information available to require special precautions

Effects on Dental Treatment Key adverse event(s) related to dental treatment: Ulcerative esophagitis.

Effects on Bleeding No information available to require special precautions

Adverse Reactions Frequency not defined.

Cardiovascular: Arrhythmias, bradycardia, cardiac arrest, cardiomegaly, circulatory collapse, congestive heart failure, edema, fat embolism, hypertension, hypertrophic cardiomyopathy in premature infants, myocardial rupture (post MI), syncope, tachycardia, thromboembolism, vasculitis

Central nervous system: Delirium, depression, emotional instability, euphoria, hallucinations, headache, intracranial pressure increased, insomnia, malaise, mood swings, nervousness, neuritis, personality changes, psychic disorders, pseudotumor cerebri (usually following discontinuation), seizure, vertigo

Dermatologic: Acne, allergic dermatitis, alopecia, dry scaly skin, ecchymoses, edema, erythema, hirsutism, hyper-/hypopigmentation, hypertrichosis, impaired wound healing, petechiae, rash, skin atrophy, sterile abscess, skin test reaction impaired, striae, urticaria

Endocrine & metabolic: Adrenal suppression, amenorrhea, carbohydrate intolerance increased, Cushing's syndrome, diabetes mellitus, fluid retention, glucose intolerance, growth suppression (children), hyperglycemia, hyperlipidemia, hypokalemia, hypokalemic alkalosis, menstrual irregularities, negative nitrogen balance, pituitary-adrenal axis suppression, protein catabolism, sodium and water retention

Gastrointestinal: Abdominal distention, appetite increased, bowel/bladder dysfunction (after intrathecal administration), gastrointestinal hemorrhage, gastrointestinal perforation, nausea, pancreatitis, peptic ulcer, perforation of the small and large intestine, ulcerative esophagitis, vomiting, weight gain

Hematologic: Leukocytosis (transient)

Hepatic: Hepatomegaly, transaminases increased

Local: Postinjection flare (intra-articular use), thrombophlebitis

Neuromuscular & skeletal: Arthralgia, arthropathy, aseptic necrosis (femoral and humoral heads), fractures, muscle mass loss, muscle weakness, myopathy (particularly in conjunction with neuromuscular disease or neuromuscular-blocking agents), neuropathy, osteoporosis, parasthesia, tendon rupture, vertebral compression fractures, weakness

Ocular: Cataracts, exophthalmoses, glaucoma, intraocular pressure increased

Renal: Glycosuria

Respiratory: Pulmonary edema

Miscellaneous: Abnormal fat disposition, anaphylactoid reaction, anaphylaxis, angioedema, avascular necrosis, diaphoresis, hiccups, hypersensitivity reactions, infections, secondary malignancy

<1%, postmarketing, and/or case reports: Venous thrombosis (Johannesdottir 2013)

Dental Usual Dosage Anti-inflammatory or immunosuppressive: Adults: Oral: 2 to 60 mg/day in 1 to 4 divided doses to start, followed by gradual reduction in dosage to the lowest possible level consistent with maintaining an adequate clinical response.

Dosing

Adult & Geriatric The lowest possible dose should be used to control the condition; when dose reduction is possible, the dose should be reduced gradually. **Only sodium succinate salt may be given IV.**

Allergic conditions: Oral: Tapered-dosage schedule (eg, dose-pack containing 21 x 4 mg tablets):

Day 1: 24 mg on day 1 administered as 8 mg (2 tablets) before breakfast, 4 mg (1 tablet) after lunch, 4 mg (1 tablet) after supper, and 8 mg (2 tablets) at bedtime **OR** 24 mg (6 tablets) as a single dose or divided into 2 or 3 doses upon initiation (regardless of time of day)

Day 2: 20 mg on day 2 administered as 4 mg (1 tablet) before breakfast, 4 mg (1 tablet) after lunch, 4 mg (1 tablet) after supper, and 8 mg (2 tablets) at bedtime

Day 3: 16 mg on day 3 administered as 4 mg (1 tablet) before breakfast, 4 mg (1 tablet) after lunch, 4 mg (1 tablet) after supper, and 4 mg (1 tablet) at bedtime

Day 4: 12 mg on day 4 administered as 4 mg (1 tablet) before breakfast, 4 mg (1 tablet) after lunch, and 4 mg (1 tablet) at bedtime

Day 5: 8 mg on day 5 administered as 4 mg (1 tablet) before breakfast and 4 mg (1 tablet) at bedtime

Day 6: 4 mg on day 6 administered as 4 mg (1 tablet) before breakfast

Anti-inflammatory or immunosuppressive: Note: Initial dosage depends upon condition being treated; adjust subsequent doses based on patient response.

Oral: 4 to 48 mg/day in 1 to 4 divided doses initially, followed by gradual reduction in dosage to the lowest possible level consistent with maintaining an adequate clinical response.

IM (succinate): 10 to 40 mg/day initially

IM (acetate): 4 to 120 mg single dose; repeated injections may be necessary for recurrent or chronic conditions.

IV (succinate): 10 to 40 mg over a period of several minutes and repeated IV or IM at intervals depending on clinical response; when high dosages are needed, administer 30 mg/kg over a period ≥30 minutes and may be repeated every 4 to 6 hours for 48 hours.

Intralesional (acetate): 20 to 60 mg; for large lesions, it may be necessary to distribute doses ranging from 20 to 40 mg by repeated local injections; 1 to 4 injections are usually employed with intervals between injections varying with the type of lesion being treated and clinical response.

Soft tissue (acetate): 4 to 30 mg; repeated injections may be necessary for recurrent or chronic conditions.

Arthritis: Intra-articular (acetate): Administer every 1 to 5 weeks.

Large joints (eg, knee, ankle, shoulder): 20 to 80 mg

Medium joints (eg, elbow, wrist): 10 to 40 mg

Small joints (eg, metacarpophalangeal, interphalangeal, sternoclavicular, acromioclavicular): 4 to 10 mg

Asthma, exacerbations:

Acute, short-course "burst" (NAEPP 2007):

Oral: 40 to 60 mg/day in divided doses once or twice daily for 3 to 10 days; **Note:** Burst should be continued until symptoms resolve and peak expiratory flow is at least 80% of personal best; usually requires 3 to 10 days of treatment; longer treatment may be required.

IM (**acetate**): 240 mg as a one-time dose; **Note:** This may be given in place of short-course "burst" of oral steroids in patients who are vomiting or if compliance is a problem.

Hospital/emergency medical care doses: Oral, IV: 40 to 80 mg/day in divided doses once or twice daily until peak expiratory flow is 70% of predicted or personal best.

Asthma, long-term (maintenance) (NAEPP 2007): Oral: 7.5 to 60 mg once daily in the morning or every other day as needed for asthma control

Multiple sclerosis, acute exacerbation:

Note: Treatment guidelines recommend high-dose IV methylprednisolone succinate or oral methylprednisolone for acute exacerbations of multiple sclerosis (AAN [Scott 2011]); NICE 2014).

Manufacturer's labeling: Oral, IV (succinate only), IM (acetate or succinate): 160 mg daily for 1 week, followed by 64 mg every other day for 1 month.

Off-label dosing:

Oral: 500 mg daily for 5 days (NICE 2014).

IV (succinate only): 1,000 mg daily for 3 to 7 days (AAN [Scott 2011]; NICE 2014).

Bronchiolitis obliterans syndrome, prevention (off-label use): IV (sodium succinate): 1000 mg daily for 3 days. **Note:** Many centers use 10 to 15 mg/kg/day for smaller patients (Meyer 2014).

Cadaveric organ recovery (hormonal resuscitation) (off-label use): IV (sodium succinate): 15 mg/kg **or** 2,000 mg bolus administered to the brain-dead donor who is hemodynamically unstable requiring significant vasopressor support; give concomitantly with vasopressin, levothyroxine or liothyronine (preferred), dextrose (if bolus dose insulin used), and regular insulin (bolus dose or continuous infusion). If continuous infusion insulin is employed, maintain blood glucose 120 to 180 mg/dL (Rosendale 2003a; Rosendale 2003b; Rosengard 2002; Salim 2007; Zaroff 2002).

Cardiac transplant: Acute cellular rejection (treatment) or antibody-mediated rejection (treatment) (off-label use): IV (sodium succinate): 250 to 1,000 mg daily for 3 days (AHA [Colvin 2015]; ISHLT [Costanzo 2010]).

COPD exacerbation (off-label use): Note: Dose, frequency, and duration of therapy not established. GOLD guidelines recommend the use of oral prednisone; however, methylprednisolone may be used as an alternative (GOLD [Decramer 2014]). No comparative studies exist to examine safety and efficacy between low-, medium-, or high-dose regimens. While several clinical trials have examined the use of methylprednisolone in this setting, these trials included low numbers of patients, employed vastly different regimens, and/or examined different clinical outcomes (Albert 1980; Alía 2011; Niewoehner 1999; Sayiner 2001; Shortall 2002; Vrondracek 2006; Willaert 2002). Current dosing strategies are empiric and have not been established by clinical trials. Based on expert opinion, commonly used regimens ranging from 60 to 125 mg IV administered 1 to 4 times daily followed by oral therapy (eg, prednisone 40 mg once daily) for a total of 5 to 14 days of therapy may be employed; the shorter duration (ie, 5 days) may be preferred (Leuppi 2013); however, comparative prospective data does not exist. IV administration with a higher dose (eg, ≥60 mg) may be preferred for those patients with impending or actual acute respiratory failure; outcome trials not available for this approach.

Dermatomyositis/polymyositis (off-label dosing): IV (succinate): 1,000 mg daily for 3 to 5 days for severe muscle weakness, followed by conversion to oral prednisone (Drake 1996)

Gout, acute (off-label dosing): IV (succinate), IM: Initial: 0.5 to 2 mg/kg; may be repeated as clinically indicated (ACR guidelines [Khanna 2012])

Lupus nephritis (off-label dosing): High-dose "pulse" therapy: IV (succinate): 0.5 to 1 g/day for 3 days (Ponticelli 2010)

***Pneumocystis* pneumonia in AIDS patients (off-label use):** IV (succinate): 30 mg twice daily on days 1 to 5, then 30 mg once daily on days 6 to 10, then 15 mg once daily on days 11 to 21 (CDC 2009a).

Spinal cord injury, acute (off-label use): IV (succinate): 30 mg/kg over 15 minutes followed in 45 minutes by a continuous infusion of 5.4 mg/kg/hour for 23 hours; **Note:** Due to insufficient evidence of clinical efficacy (ie, preserving or improving spinal cord function), the routine use of methylprednisolone in the treatment of acute spinal cord injury is no longer recommended. If used in this setting, methylprednisolone should not be initiated >8 hours after the injury; not effective in penetrating trauma (eg, gunshot) (Consortium for Spinal Cord Medicine 2008).

Pediatric The lowest possible dose should be used to control the condition; when dose reduction is possible, the dose should be reduced gradually. **Only sodium succinate salt may be given IV.**

Anti-inflammatory or immunosuppressive: Note: Initial dosage depends upon condition being treated; adjust subsequent doses based on patient response.

Infants, Children, and Adolescents: Oral, IM (acetate or succinate), IV (succinate): Initial: 0.11 to 1.6 mg/kg/day or 3.2 to 48 mg/**m**²/day in 3 to 4 divided doses; usual range: 0.5 to 1.7 mg/kg/day (Kliegman 2015); for oral, IM (succinate), and IV (succinate) may also administer in divided doses every 6 to 12 hours (Kliegman 2015); for IM (acetate) administer as a single daily dose

"Pulse" therapy: IV (succinate): 30 mg/kg/dose once daily for 1 to 5 days; maximum: 1,000 mg/day (Kliegman 2015)

Long-acting: IM (acetate): 4 to 80 mg every 1 to 2 weeks

Asthma, exacerbations:

Acute, short-course "burst" (NAEPP 2007):

Infants and Children <12 years:

Oral: 1 to 2 mg/kg/day in divided doses once or twice daily for 3 to 10 days; maximum daily dose: 60 mg/**day**; **Note:** Burst should be continued until symptoms resolve or patient achieves peak expiratory flow 80% of personal best; usually requires 3 to 10 days of treatment (~5 days on average); longer treatment may be required

IM (**acetate**): **Note:** This may be given in place of short-course "burst" of oral steroids in patients who are vomiting or if compliance is a problem.

Children ≤4 years: 7.5 mg/kg as a one-time dose; maximum dose: 240 mg

Children 5 to 11 years: 240 mg as a one-time dose

Children ≥12 years and Adolescents: Oral, IM (acetate): Refer to adult dosing.

Hospital/emergency medical care doses:

Infants and Children <12 years: Oral, IV: 1 to 2 mg/kg/day in 2 divided doses; maximum daily dose: 60 mg/day; continue until peak expiratory flow is 70% of predicted or personal best

Children ≥12 years and Adolescents: Oral, IV: Refer to adult dosing

Status asthmaticus (previous NAEPP guidelines; still used by some clinicians): Children: IV: Loading dose: 2 mg/kg/dose, then 0.5 to 1 mg/kg/dose every 6 hours; **Note:** See NAEPP 2007 guidelines for asthma exacerbations (emergency medical care or hospital doses) listed above

Asthma, long-term treatment (maintenance) (NAEPP, 2007):

Infants and Children <12 years: Oral: 0.25 to 2 mg/kg/day once daily in the morning or every other day as needed for asthma control; maximum daily dose: 60 mg/day

Children ≥12 years and Adolescents: Oral: Refer to adult dosing

Lupus nephritis (off-label dosing): Children and Adolescents: IV (succinate): High-dose "pulse" therapy: 30 mg/kg/dose or 600 to 1,000 mg/**m**²/dose once daily for 3 days; maximum dose: 1,000 mg/day (Adams 2006; Marks 2010)

***Pneumocystis* pneumonia; moderate or severe infection (off-label use): Note:** Initiate therapy within 72 hours of diagnosis, if possible.

Infants and Children: IV (succinate): 1 mg/kg/dose every 6 hours on days 1 to 7, then 1 mg/kg/dose twice daily on days 8 and 9, then 0.5 mg/kg/dose twice daily on days 10 and 11, and then 1 mg/kg/dose once daily on days 12 to 16 (CDC 2009)

Adolescents: IV (succinate): Refer to adult dosing

Spinal cord injury, acute (off-label use): IV (succinate): 30 mg/kg over 15 minutes, followed in 45 minutes by a continuous infusion of 5.4 mg/kg/hour for 23 hours. **Note:** Due to insufficient evidence of clinical efficacy (ie, preserving or improving spinal cord function), the routine use of methylprednisolone in the treatment of acute spinal cord injury is no longer recommended. If used in this setting, methylprednisolone should not be initiated >8 hours after the injury; not effective in penetrating trauma (eg, gunshot) (Consortium for Spinal Cord Medicine 2008).

Renal Impairment There are no dosage adjustments provided in the manufacturer's labeling; use with caution.

Hepatic Impairment There are no dosage adjustments provided in the manufacturer's labeling; use with caution.

Mechanism of Action In a tissue-specific manner, corticosteroids regulate gene expression subsequent to binding specific intracellular receptors and translocation into the nucleus. Corticosteroids exert a wide array of physiologic effects including modulation of carbohydrate, protein, and lipid metabolism and maintenance of fluid and electrolyte homeostasis. Moreover cardiovascular, immunologic, musculoskeletal, endocrine, and neurologic physiology are influenced by corticosteroids. Decreases inflammation by suppression of migration of polymorphonuclear leukocytes and reversal of increased capillary permeability.

Contraindications

Hypersensitivity to methylprednisolone or any component of the formulation; systemic fungal infection (except intra-articular injection for localized joint conditions); intrathecal administration; live or attenuated virus vaccines (with immunosuppressive doses of corticosteroids); use in premature infants (formulations containing benzyl alcohol preservative only); idiopathic thrombocytopenic purpura (IM administration only)

Canadian labeling: Additional contraindications (not in US labeling):

Methylprednisolone tablets: Herpes simplex of the eye, vaccinia and varicella (except for short-term or emergency therapy)

Methylprednisolone acetate injection: Epidural or intravascular administration; intra-articular injections in unstable joints; herpes simplex of the eye, vaccinia and varicella (except for short-term or emergency therapy)

Methylprednisolone sodium succinate: Hypersensitivity to cow's milk or its components or other dairy products which may contain trace amounts of milk ingredients; epidural administration; herpes simplex of the eye, vaccinia and varicella, arrested tuberculosis, acute psychoses, Cushing syndrome, peptic ulcer, markedly elevated serum creatinine (except for short-term or emergency therapy)

Documentation of allergenic cross-reactivity for corticosteroids is limited. However, because of similarities in chemical structure and/or pharmacologic actions, the possibility of cross-sensitivity cannot be ruled out with certainty.

Warnings/Precautions Corticosteroids are not approved for epidural injection. Serious neurologic events (eg, spinal cord infarction, paraplegia, quadriplegia, cortical blindness, stroke), some resulting in death, have been reported with epidural injection of corticosteroids, with and without use of fluoroscopy.

High doses of methylprednisolone IV (usually doses of 1 g/day) may induce a toxic form of acute hepatitis (rare); serious hepatic injury may occur, resulting in acute liver failure and death. Time to onset can be several weeks or longer; resolution has been observed after discontinuation of therapy. Discontinue methylprednisolone if toxic hepatitis occurs. Avoid use of high doses in patients with a history of methylprednisone-induced toxic hepatitis.

Use with caution in patients with thyroid disease, hepatic impairment, renal impairment, cardiovascular disease, diabetes, glaucoma, cataracts, myasthenia gravis, osteoporosis, seizures, or GI diseases (diverticulitis, fresh intestinal anastomoses, active or latent peptic ulcer, ulcerative colitis, abscess or other pyogenic infection) due to perforation risk. Not recommended for the treatment of optic neuritis; may increase frequency of new episodes. Use with caution in patients with a history of ocular herpes simplex; corneal perforation has occurred; do not use in active ocular herpes simplex. Use caution following acute MI (corticosteroids have been associated with myocardial rupture).

Use with caution in the elderly with the smallest possible effective dose for the shortest duration. May affect growth velocity; growth should be routinely monitored in pediatric patients. Withdraw therapy with gradual tapering of dose. Patients may require higher doses when subject to stress (ie, trauma, surgery, severe infection). May cause hypercorticism or suppression of hypothalamic-pituitary-adrenal (HPA) axis, particularly in younger children or in patients receiving high doses for prolonged periods. HPA axis suppression may lead to adrenal crisis. Withdrawal and discontinuation of a corticosteroid should be done slowly and carefully. Particular care is required when patients are transferred from systemic corticosteroids to inhaled products due to possible adrenal insufficiency or withdrawal from steroids, including an increase in allergic symptoms. Patients receiving >20 mg per day of prednisone (or equivalent) may be most susceptible. Fatalities have occurred due to adrenal insufficiency in asthmatic patients during and after transfer from systemic corticosteroids to aerosol steroids; aerosol steroids do not provide the systemic steroid needed to treat patients having trauma, surgery, or infections. Use in septic shock or sepsis syndrome may increase mortality in some populations (eg, patients with elevated serum creatinine, patients who develop secondary infections after use).

Acute myopathy has been reported with high dose corticosteroids, usually in patients with neuromuscular transmission disorders; may involve ocular and/or respiratory muscles; monitor creatine kinase; recovery may be delayed. Corticosteroid use may cause psychiatric disturbances, including euphoria, insomnia, mood swings, personality changes, severe depression, or psychotic manifestations. Preexisting psychiatric conditions may be exacerbated by corticosteroid use. Prolonged use of corticosteroids may increase the incidence of secondary infection, cause activation of latent infections, mask acute infection (including fungal infections), prolong or exacerbate viral or parasitic infections, or limit response to killed or inactivated vaccines. Exposure to chickenpox or measles should be avoided; corticosteroids should not be used to treat ocular herpes simplex. Corticosteroids should not be used for cerebral malaria, fungal infections, or viral hepatitis. Close observation is required in patients with latent tuberculosis and/or TB reactivity; restrict use in active TB (only fulminating or disseminated TB in conjunction with antituberculosis treatment). Amebiasis should be ruled out in any patient with recent travel to tropic climates or unexplained diarrhea prior to initiation of corticosteroids. Use with extreme caution in patients with *Strongyloides* infections; hyperinfection, dissemination and fatalities have occurred. Prolonged treatment with corticosteroids has been associated with the development of Kaposi sarcoma (case reports); discontinuation may result in clinical improvement (Goedert 2002).

High-dose corticosteroids should not be used to manage acute head injury. Rare cases of anaphylactoid reactions have been observed in patients receiving corticosteroids. Avoid injection or leakage into the dermis; dermal and/or subdermal skin depression may occur at the site of injection. Avoid deltoid muscle injection; subcutaneous atrophy may occur. Septic arthritis may occur as a complication to parenteral therapy; institute appropriate antimicrobial therapy as required. Potentially significant drug-drug interactions may exist, requiring dose or frequency adjustment, additional monitoring, and/or selection of alternative therapy.

Methylprednisolone **acetate** IM injection (multiple-dose vial) and the diluent for methylprednisolone **sodium succinate** injection may contain benzyl alcohol; large amounts of benzyl alcohol (≥99 mg/kg/day) have been associated with a potentially fatal toxicity ("gasping syndrome") in neonates; the "gasping syndrome" consists of metabolic acidosis, respiratory distress, gasping respirations, CNS dysfunction (including convulsions, intracranial hemorrhage), hypotension, and cardiovascular collapse (AAP ["Inactive" 1997]; CDC 1982); some data suggests that benzoate displaces bilirubin from protein binding sites (Ahlfors 2001); avoid or use dosage forms containing benzyl alcohol with caution in neonates.

Some dosage forms may contain polysorbate 80 (also known as Tweens). Hypersensitivity reactions, usually a delayed reaction, have been reported following exposure to pharmaceutical products containing polysorbate 80 in certain individuals (Isaksson 2002; Lucente 2000; Shelley 1995). Thrombocytopenia, ascites, pulmonary deterioration, and renal and hepatic failure have been reported in premature neonates after receiving parenteral products containing polysorbate 80 (Alade 1986; CDC 1984). See manufacturer's labeling.

Drug Interactions

Metabolism/Transport Effects **Substrate** of CYP3A4 (minor); **Note:** Assignment of Major/Minor substrate status based on clinically relevant drug interaction potential; **Inhibits** CYP2C8 (weak)

Avoid Concomitant Use

Avoid concomitant use of MethylPREDNISolone with any of the following: Aldesleukin; Amodiaquine; BCG (Intravesical); Desmopressin; Indium 111 Capromab Pendetide; MiFEPRIStone; Natalizumab; Pimecrolimus; Tacrolimus (Topical); Tofacitinib

Increased Effect/Toxicity

MethylPREDNISolone may increase the levels/effects of: Acetylcholinesterase Inhibitors; Amodiaquine; Amphotericin B; Androgens; CycloSPORINE (Systemic); Deferasirox; Desirudin; Desmopressin; Fingolimod; Leflunomide; Loop Diuretics; Natalizumab; Nicorandil; NSAID (COX-2 Inhibitor); NSAID (Nonselective); Quinolone Antibiotics; Thiazide and Thiazide-Like Diuretics; Tofacitinib; Vaccines (Live); Warfarin

The levels/effects of MethylPREDNISolone may be increased by: Aprepitant; CycloSPORINE (Systemic); CYP3A4 Inhibitors (Strong); Denosumab; DilTIAZem; Estrogen Derivatives; Fosaprepitant; Indacaterol; MiFEPRIStone; Neuromuscular-Blocking Agents (Nondepolarizing); Ocrelizumab; Pimecrolimus; Roflumilast; Salicylates; Tacrolimus (Topical); Telaprevir; Trastuzumab

Decreased Effect

MethylPREDNISolone may decrease the levels/effects of: Aldesleukin; Antidiabetic Agents; BCG (Intravesical); Calcitriol (Systemic); Coccidioides immitis Skin Test; Corticorelin; CycloSPORINE (Systemic); Hyaluronidase; Indium 111 Capromab Pendetide; Isoniazid; Nivolumab; Salicylates; Sipuleucel-T; Telaprevir; Tertomotide; Urea Cycle Disorder Agents; Vaccines (Inactivated); Vaccines (Live)

The levels/effects of MethylPREDNISolone may be decreased by: Antacids; Bile Acid Sequestrants; CYP3A4 Inducers (Strong); Echinacea; MiFEPRIStone; Mitotane

Dietary Considerations Take tablets with meals to decrease GI upset; need diet rich in pyridoxine, vitamin C, vitamin D, folate, calcium, phosphorus, and protein.

Pharmacodynamics/Kinetics

Onset of Action IV (succinate): Within 1 hour; Intra-articular (IV acetate): 1 week

Duration of Action Intra-articular (IV acetate): 1 to 5 weeks

Half-life Elimination

Adolescents: IV: 1.9 ± 0.7 hours (age range: 12 to 20 years; Rouster-Stevens 2008)

Adults: Oral: 2.5 ± 1.2 hours (Czock 2005); IV (succinate): 0.25 ± 0.1 hour (Czock 2005)

Time to Peak

Oral: 2.1 ± 0.7 hours (Czock 2005)

IV (succinate): 0.8 hours (Czock 2005)

Pregnancy Risk Factor C

Pregnancy Considerations Adverse events have been observed with corticosteroids in animal reproduction studies. Methylprednisolone crosses the placenta (Anderson 1981). Some studies have shown an association between first trimester systemic corticosteroid use and oral clefts or decreased birth weight; however, information is conflicting and may be influenced by maternal dose/indication for use (Lunghi 2010; Park-Wyllie 2000; Pradat 2003). Hypoadrenalism may occur in newborns following maternal use of corticosteroids in pregnancy; monitor.

When systemic corticosteroids are needed in pregnancy for rheumatic disorders, it is generally recommended to use the lowest effective dose for the shortest duration of time, avoiding high doses during the first trimester (Götestam Skorpen 2016; Makol 2011; Østensen 2009).

For dermatologic disorders in pregnant women, systemic corticosteroids are generally not preferred for initial therapy; should be avoided during the first trimester; and used during the second or third trimester at the lowest effective dose (Bae 2012; Leachman 2006).

Pregnant women with poorly controlled asthma or asthma exacerbations may have a greater fetal/maternal risk than what is associated with appropriately used medications. Uncontrolled asthma is associated with an increased risk of perinatal mortality, preeclampsia, preterm birth, and low birth weight infants. Inhaled corticosteroids are recommended for the treatment of asthma during pregnancy; however, systemic corticosteroids should be used to control acute exacerbations or treat severe persistent asthma (ACOG 2008; GINA 2016; Namazy 2016).

The National Transplantation Pregnancy Registry (NTPR) is a registry which follows pregnancies which occur in maternal transplant recipients or those fathered by male transplant recipients. The NTPR encourages reporting of pregnancies following solid organ transplant by contacting them at 877-955-6877 or NTPR@giftoflifeinstitute.org.

Breastfeeding Considerations Methylprednisolone is present in breast milk (Cooper 2015; Strijbos 2015).

The relative infant dose (RID) of methylprednisolone is 2.8% to 5.6% when calculated using the highest breast milk concentration located and compared to a weight-adjusted infant dose of 15 to 30 mg/kg/day. In general, breastfeeding is considered acceptable when the RID is <10%; when an RID is >25% breastfeeding should generally be avoided (Anderson 2016; Ito 2000). Using the highest milk concentration (5.55 mcg/mL), the estimated daily infant dose via breast milk is 0.8325 mg/kg/day. This milk concentration was obtained following maternal administration of methylprednisolone 1,000 mg IV infused over 2 hours. The maximum milk concentration occurred 1 hour after the maternal dose and methylprednisolone was below the limits of quantification 12 hours after the dose (Cooper 2015).

The manufacturer notes that when used systemically, maternal use of corticosteroids have the potential to cause adverse events in a breastfeeding infant (eg, growth suppression, interfere with endogenous corticosteroid production) and therefore recommends a decision be made whether to discontinue breastfeeding or to discontinue the drug, taking into account the importance of treatment to the mother.

Corticosteroids are generally considered acceptable in breastfeeding women when used in usual doses (Götestam Skorpen 2016; WHO 2002); however, monitoring of the nursing infant is recommended (WHO 2002). If there is concern about exposure to the infant, some guidelines recommend waiting 4 hours after the maternal dose of an oral systemic corticosteroid before breastfeeding in order to decrease potential exposure to the breastfeeding infant (based on a study using prednisolone) (Bae 2012; Butler 2014; Götestam Skorpen 2016; Leachman 2006; Makol 2011; Ost 1985).

Dosage Forms

Kit, Injection:
ReadySharp Methylprednisolone: 80 mg/mL

Solution Reconstituted, Injection:
A-Methapred: 40 mg (1 ea)
SOLU-medrol: 500 mg (1 ea); 1000 mg (1 ea); 2 g (1 ea)
Generic: 40 mg (1 ea); 125 mg (1 ea); 1000 mg (1 ea)

Solution Reconstituted, Injection [preservative free]:
SOLU-medrol: 40 mg (1 ea); 125 mg (1 ea); 500 mg (1 ea); 1000 mg (1 ea)

Suspension, Injection:
DEPO Medrol: 20 mg/mL (5 mL); 40 mg/mL (1 mL, 5 mL, 10 mL); 80 mg/mL (1 mL, 5 mL)
Generic: 40 mg/mL (1 mL, 5 mL, 10 mL); 80 mg/mL (1 mL, 5 mL)

Tablet, Oral:
Medrol: 2 mg, 8 mg, 16 mg, 32 mg, 4 mg
Generic: 8 mg, 16 mg, 32 mg, 4 mg

Tablet Therapy Pack, Oral:
Medrol: 4 mg (21 ea)
Generic: 4 mg (21 ea)

MethylTESTOSTERone (meth il tes TOS te rone)

Brand Names: US Android; Methitest; Testred

Pharmacologic Category Androgen

Use

Males:

Delayed puberty: To stimulate puberty in carefully selected males with clearly delayed puberty.

Hypogonadotropic hypogonadism (congenital or acquired): Treatment of idiopathic gonadotropin or luteinizing hormone-releasing hormone (LHRH) deficiency, or pituitary hypothalamic injury from tumors, trauma, or radiation.

Primary hypogonadism (congenital or acquired): Treatment of testicular failure caused by cryptorchidism, bilateral torsion, orchitis, vanishing testis syndrome; or orchidectomy.

Females:

Breast cancer, metastatic: Secondarily in women with advancing inoperable metastatic (skeletal) mammary cancer who are 1 to 5 years postmenopausal; has also been used in premenopausal women with breast cancer who have benefited from oophorectomy and are considered to have a hormone-responsive tumor.

Local Anesthetic/Vasoconstrictor Precautions No information available to require special precautions

Effects on Dental Treatment No significant effects or complications reported

Effects on Bleeding No information available to require special precautions

Adverse Reactions Frequency not defined.

Cardiovascular: Edema

Central nervous system: Anxiety, depression, headache, paresthesia

Dermatologic: Acne vulgaris, androgenetic alopecia

Endocrine & metabolic: Change in libido, gynecomastia (males), hirsutism (females), hypercalcemia, hypercholesterolemia, menstrual disease (includes amenorrhea)

Gastrointestinal: Nausea, vomiting

Genitourinary: Benign prostatic hypertrophy (males), impotence (males), mastalgia (females), oligospermia (males; at high doses), priapism (males), testicular atrophy (males), virilization (males and females)

Hematologic & oncologic: Clotting factors suppression, polycythemia, prostate carcinoma (males)

Hepatic: Abnormal liver function tests, cholestatic hepatitis, hepatic insufficiency, hepatic necrosis, jaundice, peliosis hepatitis

<1%, postmarketing, and/or case reports: Anaphylactoid reaction, hepatocellular neoplasm, hepatotoxicity (idiosyncratic; Chalasani 2014)

General Dosage Range

Oral:

Adolescents (males) and Adults: 10 to 50 mg daily

Adults (females): 50 to 200 mg daily

Mechanism of Action Endogenous androgen stimulates receptors in organs and tissues to promote growth and development of male sex organs and maintains secondary sex characteristics in androgen-deficient males

Pharmacodynamics/Kinetics

Half-life Elimination Variable: 10 to 100 minutes

Pregnancy Risk Factor X

Pregnancy Considerations Use is contraindicated in women who are or may become pregnant. May cause virilization of the external genitalis of the female fetus, including clitoromegaly, abnormal vaginal development, and fusion of genital folds to form a scrotal-like structure. The degree of masculinization is dose related and most likely to occur when androgens are administered in the first trimester. If a patient becomes pregnant while taking androgens, she should be counseled on the potential hazard to the fetus.

Controlled Substance C-III

Metipranolol (met i PRAN oh lol)

Pharmacologic Category Beta-Blocker, Nonselective; Ophthalmic Agent, Antiglaucoma

Use Treatment of chronic open-angle glaucoma or ocular hypertension

Local Anesthetic/Vasoconstrictor Precautions No information available to require special precautions

Effects on Dental Treatment Metipranolol is a nonselective beta-blocker and may enhance the pressor response to epinephrine, resulting in hypertension and bradycardia. Many nonsteroidal anti-inflammatory drugs, such as ibuprofen and indomethacin, can reduce the hypotensive effect of beta-blockers after 3 or more weeks of therapy with the NSAID. Short-term NSAID use (ie, 3 days) requires no special precautions in patients taking beta-blockers.

Effects on Bleeding No information available to require special precautions

Adverse Reactions Frequency not defined.

Cardiovascular: Angina, atrial fibrillation, bradycardia, hypertension, MI, palpitation

Central nervous system: Anxiety, depression, dizziness, headache, nervousness, somnolence

Dermatologic: Rash

Gastrointestinal: Nausea

Neuromuscular & skeletal: Arthritis, myalgia, weakness

Ocular: Abnormal vision, blepharitis, blurred vision, browache, conjunctivitis, discomfort, edema, eyelid dermatitis, photophobia, tearing, uveitis

Respiratory: Bronchitis, cough, dyspnea, epistaxis, rhinitis

Miscellaneous: Allergic reaction

General Dosage Range Ophthalmic: *Adults:* Instill 1 drop into affected eye(s) twice daily

Mechanism of Action Beta-adrenoceptor-blocking agent; lacks intrinsic sympathomimetic activity and membrane-stabilizing effects and possesses only slight local anesthetic activity; mechanism of action of metipranolol in reducing intraocular pressure appears to be via reduced production of aqueous humor. This effect may be related to a reduction in blood flow to the iris root-ciliary body. It remains unclear if the reduction in intraocular pressure observed with beta-blockers is actually secondary to beta-adrenoceptor blockade.

Pharmacodynamics/Kinetics

Onset of Action ≤30 minutes; Peak effect: Maximum: ~2 hours

Duration of Action Intraocular pressure reduction: Up to 24 hours

Half-life Elimination ~3 hours

Pregnancy Risk Factor C

Pregnancy Considerations Adverse events were observed in some animal reproduction studies. The same adverse effects observed with systemic administration of beta-blockers may occur following ophthalmic use of metipranolol. If ophthalmic agents are needed for the treatment of glaucoma during pregnancy, the minimum effective dose should be used in combination with punctal occlusion to decrease potential exposure to the fetus (Johnson 2001; Salim 2014; Samples 1988).

Metoclopramide (met oh KLOE pra mide)

Brand Names: US Metozolv ODT [DSC]; Reglan

Brand Names: Canada Apo-Metoclop; Metoclopramide Hydrochloride Injection; Metoclopramide Omega; Metonia; Nu-Metoclopramide; PMS-Metoclopramide

Pharmacologic Category Antiemetic; Gastrointestinal Agent, Prokinetic

Use

US labeling:

Injection:

Diabetic gastroparesis (diabetic gastric stasis): Relief of symptoms associated with acute and recurrent diabetic gastric stasis.

Prevention of nausea and vomiting associated with emetogenic cancer chemotherapy: Prophylaxis of vomiting associated with emetogenic cancer chemotherapy.

Prevention of postoperative nausea and vomiting: Prophylaxis of postoperative nausea and vomiting in circumstances where nasogastric suction is undesirable.

Radiological examination: To stimulate gastric emptying and intestinal transit of barium when delayed emptying interferes with radiological examination of the stomach and/or small intestine.

Small bowel intubation: To facilitate small bowel intubation in adults and pediatrics in whom the tube does not pass the pylorus with conventional maneuvers.

Oral:

Diabetic gastroparesis (diabetic gastric stasis): Relief of symptoms associated with acute and recurrent diabetic gastroparesis (gastric stasis) in adults.

Gastroesophageal reflux: Short-term (4 to 12 weeks) therapy for adults with documented symptomatic gastroesophageal reflux disease (GERD) who fail to respond to conventional therapy.

Limitations of use: Oral metoclopramide is indicated for adults only. Treatment should not exceed 12-week duration.

Canadian labeling:

Injection:

Gastroparesis: Adjunctive therapy in the management of gastroparesis associated with subacute and chronic gastritis and sequelae of surgical procedures (eg, vagotomy, pyloroplasty).

Prevention of vomiting associated with cancer chemotherapy regimens that include cisplatin: Prophylaxis of vomiting associated with cancer chemotherapy regimens that include cisplatin.

Prevention of postoperative nausea and vomiting: Prophylaxis of postoperative nausea and vomiting.

Small bowel intubation: To facilitate small bowel intubation.

Oral:

Gastroparesis: Adjunctive therapy in the management of gastroparesis associated with subacute and chronic gastritis and sequelae of surgical procedures (eg, vagotomy, pyloroplasty).

Prevention of postoperative vomiting: Prophylaxis of postoperative vomiting induced by opioids.

Radiological examination: To stimulate gastric emptying and intestinal transit of barium when delayed emptying interferes with radiological examination of the stomach and/or small intestine.

Small bowel intubation: To facilitate small bowel intubation.

Limitations of use: Treatment should not exceed 12-week duration.

Local Anesthetic/Vasoconstrictor Precautions No information available to require special precautions

Effects on Dental Treatment Metoclopramide has relatively few adverse effects when used in low doses; however, extrapyramidal effects including akathisia (motor restlessness), acute dystonia (spasmodic contractures), pseudoparkinsonism, and tardive dyskinesia can occur. These effects are more likely in the elderly, patients taking other dopamine antagonists (including antipsychotic agents and some antiemetic agents), and patients with Parkinson's disease. Metoclopramide will increase gastric emptying which will aid in the absorption of orally administered anxiolytic or sedative agents used for minimal or moderate sedation as well as promote the emptying of the stomach following procedures during which blood may be swallowed causing GI upset.

Effects on Bleeding No information available to require special precautions

Adverse Reactions Frequency not always defined.

Cardiovascular: Atrioventricular block, bradycardia, congestive heart failure, flushing (following high IV doses), hypertension, hypotension, supraventricular tachycardia

Central nervous system: Drowsiness (~10% to 70%; dose related), dystonic reaction (<1% to 25%; dose and age related), lassitude (~10%), restlessness (~10%), fatigue (2% to 10%), headache (4% to 5%), dizziness (1% to 4%), somnolence (2% to 3%), akathisia, confusion, depression, drug-induced Parkinson's disease, hallucination (rare), insomnia, neuroleptic malignant syndrome (rare), seizure, suicidal ideation, tardive dyskinesia

Dermatologic: Skin rash, urticaria

Endocrine & metabolic: Amenorrhea, fluid retention, galactorrhea, gynecomastia, hyperprolactinemia, porphyria

Gastrointestinal: Nausea (4% to 6%), vomiting (1% to 2%), diarrhea

Genitourinary: Impotence, urinary frequency, urinary incontinence

Hematologic & oncologic: Agranulocytosis, leukopenia, methemoglobinemia, neutropenia, sulfhemoglobinemia

Hepatic: Hepatotoxicity (rare)

Hypersensitivity: Angioedema (rare), hypersensitivity reaction

Neuromuscular & skeletal: Laryngospasm (rare)

Ophthalmic: Visual disturbance

Respiratory: Bronchospasm, laryngeal edema (rare)

General Dosage Range Dosage adjustment recommended in patients with renal impairment

IM: *Adults:* 10 to 20 mg as a single dose **or** 10 mg before each meal and at bedtime

IV:

Children <6 years: 0.1 mg/kg as a single dose

Children 6 to 14 years: 2.5 to 5 mg as a single dose

Children >14 years: 10 mg as a single dose

Adults: 10 mg before each meal and at bedtime **or** 1 to 2 mg/kg every 2 to 3 hours **or** 10 mg as a single dose

Oral: *Adults:* 10 to 15 mg up to 4 times daily

Mechanism of Action Blocks dopamine receptors and (when given in higher doses) also blocks serotonin receptors in chemoreceptor trigger zone of the CNS; enhances the response to acetylcholine of tissue in upper GI tract causing enhanced motility and accelerated gastric emptying without stimulating gastric, biliary, or pancreatic secretions; increases lower esophageal sphincter tone

Pharmacodynamics/Kinetics

Onset of Action Oral: 30 to 60 minutes; IV: 1 to 3 minutes; IM: 10 to 15 minutes

Duration of Action Therapeutic: 1 to 2 hours, regardless of route

Half-life Elimination Normal renal function: Neonates, PMA 31 to 40 weeks: 5.4 hours (Kearns 1998); Infants: 4.15 hours (range: 2.23 to 10.3 hours) (Kearns, 1988); Children: ~4 hours (range: 2 to 12.5 hours); half-life and clearance may be dose-dependent; Adults: 5 to 6 hours (may be dose dependent)

Time to Peak Serum: Oral: Neonates, PMA 31 to 40 weeks: 2.45 hours (Kearns 1998); Infants: 2.2 hours; Adults: 1 to 2 hours

Pregnancy Risk Factor B

Pregnancy Considerations Adverse events were not observed in animal reproduction studies. Metoclopramide crosses the placenta and can be detected in cord blood and amniotic fluid (Arvela 1983; Bylsma-Howell 1983). Available evidence suggests safe use during pregnancy (ACOG 2015; Berkovitch 2002; Matok 2009; Sørensen 2000). Evidence related to the efficacy for the treatment of nausea and vomiting of pregnancy is limited (ACOG 2015; Arsenault 2002); metoclopramide may be used for prophylaxis of nausea and vomiting associated with cesarean delivery (ASA 2016; Smith 2011).

MetOLazone (me TOLE a zone)

Related Information

Cardiovascular Diseases *on page 1752*

Brand Names: US Zaroxolyn [DSC]

Brand Names: Canada Zaroxolyn

Pharmacologic Category Diuretic, Thiazide-Related

Use

Edema: Treatment of edema in congestive heart failure and edema accompanying renal diseases, including the nephrotic syndrome and states of diminished renal function.

Hypertension: Treatment of hypertension.

Guideline recommendations:

Coronary artery disease (CAD) and hypertension: The American Heart Association, American College of Cardiology and American Society of Hypertension (AHA/ACC/ASH) 2015 scientific statement for the treatment of hypertension in patients with coronary artery disease (CAD) recommends the use of a thiazide (or thiazide-like diuretic) as part of a regimen in patients with hypertension and chronic stable angina. A BP target of <140/90 mm Hg is reasonable for the secondary prevention of cardiovascular events. A lower target BP (<130/80 mm Hg) may be appropriate in some individuals with CAD, previous MI, stroke or transient ischemic attack, or CAD risk equivalents (AHA/ACC/ASH [Rosendorff 2015]).

Local Anesthetic/Vasoconstrictor Precautions No information available to require special precautions

Effects on Dental Treatment Key adverse event(s) related to dental treatment: Xerostomia (normal salivary flow resumes upon discontinuation); Patients may experience orthostatic hypotension as they stand up after treatment; especially if lying in dental chair for extended periods of time. Use caution with sudden changes in position during and after dental treatment.

Effects on Bleeding No information available to require special precautions

Adverse Reactions Frequency not defined.

Cardiovascular: Chest discomfort, chest pain, necrotizing angiitis, orthostatic hypotension, palpitations, syncope, venous thrombosis

Central nervous system: Chills, depression, dizziness, drowsiness, fatigue, headache, neuropathy, paresthesia, restlessness, vertigo

Dermatologic: Pruritus, skin necrosis, skin photosensitivity, skin rash, Stevens-Johnson syndrome, toxic epidermal necrolysis, urticaria

Endocrine & metabolic: Glycosuria, gout, hypercalcemia, hyperglycemia, hyperuricemia, hypochloremia, hypochloremic alkalosis, hypokalemia, hypomagnesemia, hyponatremia, hypophosphatemia, hypovolemia

Gastrointestinal: Abdominal pain, anorexia, bloating, constipation, diarrhea, epigastric distress, nausea, pancreatitis, vomiting, xerostomia

Genitourinary: Impotence

Hematologic & oncologic: Agranulocytosis, aplastic anemia, hemoconcentration, hypoplastic anemia, leukopenia, petechia, purpura, thrombocytopenia

Hepatic: Cholestatic jaundice, hepatitis

Neuromuscular & skeletal: Arthralgia, muscle cramps, muscle spasm, weakness

Ophthalmic: Transient blurred vision

Renal: Increased blood urea nitrogen

General Dosage Range Oral: *Adults:* 2.5-20 mg once daily

Mechanism of Action Inhibits sodium reabsorption in the distal tubules causing increased excretion of sodium and water, as well as, potassium and hydrogen ions

Pharmacodynamics/Kinetics

Onset of Action Diuresis: ~60 minutes

Duration of Action ≥24 hours

Half-life Elimination 6 to 20 hours

Time to Peak ~8 hours.

Pregnancy Risk Factor B

Pregnancy Considerations Adverse events have not been observed in animal reproduction studies. Metolazone crosses the placenta and appears in cord blood. Hypoglycemia, hypokalemia, hyponatremia, jaundice, and thrombocytopenia are reported as complications to the fetus or newborn following maternal use of thiazide diuretics.

Metoprolol (me toe PROE lole)

Related Information

Cardiovascular Diseases *on page 1752*

Brand Names: US Lopressor; Toprol XL

Brand Names: Canada Apo-Metoprolol; Apo-Metoprolol (Type L); Apo-Metoprolol SR; Betaloc; Dom-Metoprolol-B; Dom-Metoprolol-L; JAMP-Metoprolol-L; Lopresor; Lopresor SR; Metoprolol SR; Metoprolol Tartrate Injection, USP; Metoprolol-100; Metoprolol-25; Metoprolol-50; Metoprolol-L; Mylan-Metoprolol (Type L); PMS-Metoprolol-B; PMS-Metoprolol-L; Riva-Metoprolol-L; Sandoz-Metoprolol (Type L); Sandoz-Metoprolol SR; Teva-Metoprolol

Generic Availability (US) Yes

Pharmacologic Category Antianginal Agent; Antihypertensive; Beta-Blocker, Beta-1 Selective

Use

Angina (oral formulations): Long term treatment of angina pectoris.

Heart failure (extended-release oral formulation): Treatment of stable, symptomatic (NYHA Class II or III) heart failure of ischemic, hypertensive, or cardiomyopathic origin to reduce the rate of mortality plus hospitalization in patients already receiving ACE inhibitors, diuretics, and/or digoxin.

Hypertension (oral formulations): Management of hypertension.

Myocardial infarction (immediate-release oral formulation; injection): Treatment of hemodynamically stable acute myocardial infarction (MI) to reduce cardiovascular mortality (injection to be used in combination with metoprolol oral maintenance therapy).

Guideline recommendations:

Acute coronary syndromes (eg, myocardial infarction, non-ST-elevation ACS [NSTE-ACS]): According to the ACCF/AHA guidelines for the management of ST-elevation myocardial infarction (STEMI) and the AHA/ACC guidelines for the management of non-ST-elevation ACS (NSTE-ACS), oral beta-blockers should be initiated within the first 24 hours unless the patient has signs of heart failure, evidence of a low-output state, an increased risk for cardiogenic shock, or other contraindications (ACC/AHA [Amsterdam 2014]; ACCF/AHA [O'Gara 2013]). Use of sustained-release metoprolol is a recommended beta-blocker therapy in patients with concomitant NSTE-ACS, stabilized HF, and reduced systolic function (ACC/AHA [Amsterdam 2014]). Intravenous beta-blocker use should be reserved for patients post-STEMI who have refractory hypertension or ongoing ischemia (ACCF/AHA [O'Gara 2013]).

Heart failure: The ACCF/AHA 2013 heart failure guidelines recommend the use of 1 of 3 beta blockers (ie, bisoprolol, carvedilol, or extended-release metoprolol succinate) for all patients with recent or remote history of MI or ACS and reduced ejection fraction (rEF) to reduce mortality, for all patients with rEF to prevent symptomatic HF (even if no history of MI), and for all patients with current or prior symptoms of HF with reduced ejection fraction (HFrEF), unless contraindicated, to reduce morbidity and mortality (ACCF/AHA [Yancy 2013]).

Hypertension: The 2014 guideline for the management of high blood pressure in adults (Eighth Joint National Committee [JNC 8]) recommends initiation of pharmacologic treatment to lower blood pressure for the following patients (JNC8 [James 2013]):

- Patients ≥60 years of age, with systolic blood pressure (SBP) ≥150 mm Hg or diastolic blood pressure (DBP) ≥90 mm Hg. Goal of therapy is SBP <150 mm Hg and DBP <90 mm Hg.
- Patients <60 years of age, with SBP ≥140 mm Hg or DBP ≥90 mm Hg. Goal of therapy is SBP <140 mm Hg and DBP <90 mm Hg.
- Patients ≥18 years of age with diabetes, with SBP ≥140 mm Hg or DBP ≥90 mm Hg. Goal of therapy is SBP <140 mm Hg and DBP <90 mm Hg.
- Patients ≥18 years of age with chronic kidney disease (CKD), with SBP ≥140 mm Hg or DBP ≥90 mm Hg. Goal of therapy is SBP <140 mm Hg and DBP <90 mm Hg.

Chronic kidney disease (CKD) and hypertension: Regardless of race or diabetes status, the use of an ACE inhibitor (ACEI) or angiotensin receptor blocker (ARB) as initial therapy is recommended to improve kidney outcomes. In the general non-black population (without CKD) including those with diabetes, initial antihypertensive treatment should consist of a thiazide-type diuretic, calcium channel blocker, ACEI, or ARB. In the general black population (without CKD) including those with diabetes, initial antihypertensive treatment should consist of a thiazide-type diuretic or a calcium channel blocker **instead of** an ACEI or ARB.

Coronary artery disease (CAD) and hypertension: The American Heart Association, American College of Cardiology and American Society of Hypertension (AHA/ACC/ASH) 2015 scientific statement for the treatment of hypertension in patients with coronary artery disease (CAD) recommends the use of a beta blocker as part of a regimen in patients with hypertension and chronic stable angina with a history of prior MI. A BP target of <140/90 mm Hg is reasonable for the secondary prevention of cardiovascular events. A lower target BP (<130/80 mm Hg) may be appropriate in some individuals with CAD, previous MI, stroke or transient ischemic attack, or CAD risk equivalents (AHA/ACC/ASH [Rosendorff 2015]).

Local Anesthetic/Vasoconstrictor Precautions No information available to require special precautions

Effects on Dental Treatment Metoprolol is a cardioselective beta-blocker. Local anesthetic with vasoconstrictor can be safely used in patients medicated with metoprolol. Nonselective beta-blockers (ie, propranolol, nadolol) enhance the pressor response to epinephrine, resulting in hypertension and bradycardia; this has not been reported for metoprolol. Many nonsteroidal anti-inflammatory drugs, such as ibuprofen and indomethacin, can reduce the hypotensive effect of beta-blockers after 3 or more weeks of therapy with the NSAID. Short-term NSAID use (ie, 3 days) requires no special precautions in patients taking beta-blockers.

Effects on Bleeding No information available to require special precautions

Adverse Reactions Frequency not always defined.

Cardiovascular: Hypotension (1% to 27%), bradycardia (2% to 16%), first degree atrioventricular block (5%), arterial insufficiency (usually Raynaud type: 1%), cardiac failure (1%), cerebrovascular accident (1%), cold extremities (1%), palpitations (1%), peripheral edema (1%), claudication

Central nervous system: Dizziness (2% to 10%), fatigue (1% to 10%), depression (>2% to 5%), vertigo (≤2%), confusion, disturbed sleep, hallucination, headache, insomnia, nightmares, temporary amnesia

Dermatology: Pruritus (5%), rash (>2% to 5%), exacerbation of psoriasis, skin photosensitivity

Endocrine & metabolic: Decreased libido, unstable diabetes

Gastrointestinal: Diarrhea (>2% to 5%), constipation (1%), flatulence (1%), heartburn (1%), stomach pain (1%), xerostomia (1%), nausea (≤1%), vomiting

Neuromuscular & skeletal: Musculoskeletal pain

Ophthalmic: Blurred vision, visual disturbance

Otic: Tinnitus

Respiratory: Dyspnea (≤3%), bronchospasm (1%), wheezing (1%), rhinitis

Miscellaneous: Accidental injury (1%)

<1%, postmarketing and/or case reports: Abdominal pain, agranulocytosis, alopecia (reversible), anxiety, arthralgia, arthritis, chest pain, decreased HDL cholesterol, diaphoresis, drowsiness, dry eye syndrome, gangrene of skin or other tissue, hepatic insufficiency, hepatitis, impotence, increased lactate dehydrogenase, increased serum alkaline phosphatase, increased serum transaminases, increased serum triglycerides, jaundice, nervousness, paresthesia, Peyronie's disease, retroperitoneal fibrosis, syncope, taste disorder, weight gain

Dosing

Adult

Angina: Oral:

Immediate release (metoprolol tartrate): Initial: 50 mg twice daily; usual dosage range: 50 to 200 mg twice daily; may increase dose at weekly intervals to desired effect (maximum: 400 mg/day).

Extended release (metoprolol succinate): Initial: 100 mg once daily; may increase dose at weekly intervals to desired effect (maximum: 400 mg/day).

Atrial fibrillation/flutter (ventricular rate control) (acute treatment; off-label use) (AHA/ACC/HRS [January 2014]; AHA [Neumar 2010]): IV: 2.5 to 5 mg every 2 to 5 minutes (maximum total dose: 15 mg over a 10- to 15-minute period). **Note:** Initiate cautiously in patients with concomitant heart failure. Avoid in patients with decompensated heart failure; electrical cardioversion preferred.

Maintenance: Oral (immediate release [metoprolol tartrate]): 25 to 100 mg twice daily; Oral (extended release [metoprolol succinate]): 50 to 400 mg once daily

Heart failure: Note: Initiate only in stable patients or hospitalized patients after volume status has been optimized and IV diuretics, vasodilators, and inotropic agents have all been successfully discontinued. Caution should be used when initiating in patients who required inotropes during their hospital course. Increase dose gradually and monitor for congestive signs and symptoms of HF making every effort to achieve target dose shown to be effective (ACCF/AHA [Yancy 2013]; HFSA [Lindenfeld 2010]; MERIT-HF Study Group 1999).

Oral: *Extended release (metoprolol succinate):* Initial: 25 mg once daily (reduce to 12.5 mg once daily in NYHA class higher than class II); may double dosage every 2 weeks as tolerated up to target dose of 200 mg/day.

ACCF/AHA 2013 Heart Failure Guidelines: Oral (extended release [metoprolol succinate]): Initial: 12.5 to 25 mg once daily; maximum dose: 200 mg/day (Yancy 2013).

Hypertension: Oral:

Immediate release (metoprolol tartrate): Initial: 50 mg twice daily; effective dosage range: 100 to 450 mg daily in 2 to 3 divided doses; may increase dose at weekly (or longer) intervals to desired effect; maximum dose: 450 mg/day; usual dosage range (ASH/ISH [Weber 2014]): 50 to 100 mg twice daily; target dose (JNC 8 [James 2013]): 100 to 200 mg daily

Extended release (metoprolol succinate): Initial: 25 to 100 mg once daily; may increase dose at weekly (or longer) intervals to desired effect; maximum: 400 mg/day.

Hypertension/ventricular rate control: IV (in patients having nonfunctioning GI tract): Initial: 1.25 to 5 mg every 6 to 12 hours; titrate initial dose to response. Initially, low doses may be appropriate to establish response (Huckleberry 2003); however, although not routine, up to 15 mg administered as frequently as every 3 hours has been employed in patients with refractory tachycardia.

Myocardial infarction:

Early treatment: **Note:** The ACCF/AHA guidelines for the management of STEMI recommend the use of IV metoprolol at the time of presentation only in patients with STEMI who are hypertensive or have ongoing ischemia without contraindications. Oral metoprolol (immediate release) initiated within the first 24 hours is recommended in all other patients. Do not initiate metoprolol in those with signs of heart failure, a low output state, increased risk of cardiogenic shock, or other contraindications (eg, second- or third-degree heart block) (ACCF/AHA [O'Gara 2013]).

IV: 5 mg every 5 minutes as tolerated for up to 3 doses in the early treatment of ST elevation myocardial infarction; titrate to heart rate and blood pressure; then begin oral therapy (ACCF/AHA [O'Gara 2013]).

Oral: 25 to 50 mg (metoprolol tartrate [immediate release]) every 6 to 12 hours; transition over the next 2 to 3 days to twice daily dosing of metoprolol tartrate (immediate release) or to daily metoprolol succinate (extended release) and increase as tolerated to a maximum dose of 200 mg/day (ACCF/AHA [O'Gara 2013]).

Secondary prevention (off-label use): Oral: Immediate release (metoprolol tartrate): 25 to 100 mg twice daily; optimize dose based on heart rate and blood pressure; continue indefinitely (Olsson 1992).

Supraventricular tachycardia (off-label use):

Acute treatment: IV: Initial: 2.5 to 5 mg bolus over 2 minutes, may repeat with 2.5 to 5 mg bolus within a 10-minute period, up to 3 doses (ACC/AHA/HRS [Page 2015])

Ongoing management: Oral: Initial: 50 mg once daily (extended-release [metoprolol succinate]) **or** 25 mg twice daily (immediate-release [metoprolol tartrate]); maximum maintenance dose: 400 mg once daily (extended-release [metoprolol succinate]) **or** 200 mg twice daily (immediate-release [metoprolol tartrate]) (ACC/AHA/HRS [Page 2015])

Thyrotoxicosis (off-label use): Oral: Immediate release (metoprolol tartrate): 25 to 50 mg every 6 hours; may also consider administering extended-release formulation (metoprolol succinate) (Bahn 2011).

Note: Switching dosage forms:

When switching from immediate release (metoprolol tartrate) to extended release (metoprolol succinate), the same total daily dose of metoprolol should be used.

When switching between oral and intravenous dosage forms, in most cases, equivalent beta-blocking effect is achieved when doses in a 2.5:1 (Oral:IV) ratio is used. However, in one bioavailability study including healthy volunteers, a range of Oral:IV conversion ratios was found to be approximately 2:1 to 5:1 (Regardh 1974). Therefore, patient variability may exist and a specific ratio may not apply to all patients, especially if comorbid conditions are present. For example, based on a range of 2.5:1 to 5:1 ratios, if the patient is receiving a chronic oral dose of 25 mg twice daily (50 mg daily), this would translate to 2.5 to 5 mg IV every 6 hours. Recognizing that patients receiving larger chronic oral doses should not automatically be converted to a large IV dose, consideration should be given to further reducing the initial IV dose and basing subsequent doses on the clinical response (Huckleberry 2003).

Geriatric Refer to adult dosing. In the management of hypertension, consider lower initial doses and titrate to response (Aronow 2011).

Pediatric

Hypertension: Oral:

Immediate-release tablet (metoprolol tartrate): Children ≥1 year and Adolescents ≤17 years (off-label population): Initial: 0.5 to 1 mg/kg/dose (maximum initial dose: 25 mg/dose) twice daily. Adjust dose based on patient response; maximum daily dose: 6 mg/kg/day or 200 mg/day, whichever is less (NHLBI 2011; NHBPEP 2004).

Extended-release tablet (metoprolol succinate): Children ≥6 years and Adolescents: Initial: 1 mg/kg once daily (maximum initial dose: 50 mg/dose). Adjust dose based on patient response (maximum: 2 mg/kg/day or 200 mg/day, whichever is less)

Renal Impairment No dosage adjustment necessary.

Hepatic Impairment There are no specific dosage adjustments provided in the manufacturer's labeling. Consider initiating with reduced doses and gradual dosage titration due to extensive hepatic metabolism.

Mechanism of Action Selective inhibitor of beta$_1$-adrenergic receptors; competitively blocks beta$_1$-receptors, with little or no effect on beta$_2$-receptors at oral doses <100 mg (in adults); does not exhibit any membrane stabilizing or intrinsic sympathomimetic activity

Contraindications

Hypersensitivity to metoprolol, any component of the formulation, or other beta-blockers; second- or third-degree heart block.

Note: Additional contraindications are formulation and/or indication specific.

Immediate-release tablets/injectable formulation:

Hypertension and angina (oral only): Sinus bradycardia; cardiogenic shock; overt heart failure; sick sinus syndrome; severe peripheral arterial circulatory disorders

Myocardial infarction (oral and injection): Severe sinus bradycardia (heart rate <45 beats/minute); significant first-degree heart block (P-R interval ≥0.24 seconds); systolic blood pressure <100 mm Hg; moderate to severe cardiac failure

Extended-release tablet: Severe bradycardia, cardiogenic shock; decompensated heart failure; sick sinus syndrome (except in patients with a functioning artificial pacemaker)

Canadian labeling: Additional contraindications (not in US labeling): Cor pulmonale; untreated pheochromocytoma; asthma and other obstructive respiratory disease (injection only); concomitant use with anesthesia agents that cause myocardial depression

Warnings/Precautions [US Boxed Warning]: Beta-blocker therapy should not be withdrawn abruptly (particularly in patients with CAD), but gradually tapered over 1 to 2 weeks to avoid acute tachycardia, hypertension, and/or ischemia. Severe exacerbation of angina, ventricular arrhythmias, and myocardial infarction (MI) have been reported following abrupt withdrawal of beta-blocker therapy. Temporary but prompt resumption of beta-blocker therapy may be indicated with worsening of angina or acute coronary insufficiency. Consider preexisting conditions such as sick sinus syndrome before initiating. Metoprolol commonly produces mild first-degree heart block. May also produce severe first-, second-, or third-degree heart block. Patients with acute MI (especially right ventricular MI) have a high risk of developing heart block of varying degrees. If severe heart block occurs, metoprolol should be discontinued and measures to increase heart rate should be employed. Symptomatic hypotension may occur with use. May precipitate or aggravate symptoms of arterial insufficiency in patients with PVD and Raynaud disease; use with caution and monitor for progression of arterial obstruction. Beta-blockers without alpha1-adrenergic receptor blocking activity should be avoided in patients with Prinzmetal variant angina because unopposed alpha1-adrenergic receptors mediate coronary vasoconstriction and can worsen anginal symptoms (Mayer 1998). Bradycardia, including sinus pause, heart block, and cardiac arrest, may occur. Patients with first-degree AV block, sinus node dysfunction, or conduction disorders may be at increased risk. Monitor heart rate and rhythm; if severe bradycardia occurs, reduce dose or discontinue therapy. Potentially significant interactions may exist, requiring dose or frequency adjustment, additional monitoring, and/or selection of alternative therapy.

In general, beta-blockers should be avoided in patients with bronchospastic disease. Metoprolol, with B_1 selectivity, should be used cautiously in bronchospastic disease with close monitoring. Use cautiously in patients with diabetes; may mask prominent hypoglycemic symptoms and/or mask signs and symptoms. May mask signs of hyperthyroidism (eg, tachycardia); if hyperthyroidism is suspected, carefully manage and monitor; abrupt withdrawal may exacerbate symptoms of hyperthyroidism or precipitate thyroid storm. Alterations in thyroid function tests may be observed. Use caution with hepatic impairment. Use with caution in patients with myasthenia gravis or psychiatric disease (may cause or exacerbate CNS depression). Chronic beta-blocker therapy should not be routinely withdrawn prior to major surgery. Adequate alpha-blockade is required prior to use of any beta-blocker for patients with untreated pheochromocytoma. May induce or exacerbate psoriasis. Use caution with history of severe anaphylaxis to allergens; patients taking beta-blockers may become more sensitive to repeated allergen challenges. Treatment of anaphylaxis (eg, epinephrine) in patients taking beta-blockers may be ineffective or promote undesirable effects. Bradycardia may be observed more frequently in elderly patients (>65 years of age); dosage reductions may be necessary. May cause CNS depression, which may impair physical or mental abilities; patients must be cautioned about performing tasks that require mental alertness (eg, operating machinery, driving).

Extended release: Use with caution in patients with compensated heart failure; monitor for a worsening of heart failure. May need to increase diuretics and wait until clinically stable to advance dose to target.

Drug Interactions

Metabolism/Transport Effects **Substrate** of CYP2C19 (minor), CYP2D6 (major); **Note:** Assignment of Major/Minor substrate status based on clinically relevant drug interaction potential

Avoid Concomitant Use

Avoid concomitant use of Metoprolol with any of the following: Ceritinib; Floctafenine; Methacholine; Rivastigmine

Increased Effect/Toxicity

Metoprolol may increase the levels/effects of: Alpha-/Beta-Agonists (Direct-Acting); Alpha1-Blockers; Alpha2-Agonists; Amifostine; Antipsychotic Agents (Phenothiazines); Antipsychotic Agents (Second Generation [Atypical]); Bradycardia-Causing Agents; Bupivacaine; Cardiac Glycosides; Ceritinib; Cholinergic Agonists; Disopyramide; Ergot Derivatives; Fingolimod; Grass Pollen Allergen Extract (5 Grass Extract); Hypotension-Associated Agents; Insulin; Ivabradine; Lacosamide; Levodopa; Lidocaine (Systemic); Lidocaine (Topical); Mepivacaine; Methacholine; Midodrine; Nitroprusside; Sulfonylureas

The levels/effects of Metoprolol may be increased by: Abiraterone Acetate; Acetylcholinesterase Inhibitors; Ajmaline; Alfuzosin; Alpha2-Agonists; Aminoquinolines (Antimalarial); Amiodarone; Anilidopiperidine Opioids; Antipsychotic Agents (Phenothiazines); Asunaprevir; Barbiturates; Benperidol; Bretylium; Brimonidine (Topical); Calcium Channel Blockers (Nondihydropyridine); Cobicistat; CYP2D6 Inhibitors; Diazoxide; Dipyridamole; Disopyramide; Dronedarone; Floctafenine; Herbs (Hypotensive Properties); Imatinib; Lercanidipine; Lormetazepam; Lumefantrine; Methoxyflurane; Mirabegron; Molsidomine; Naftopidil; Nicergoline; Nicorandil; NIFEdipine; Obinutuzumab; Panobinostat; Peginterferon Alfa-2b; Pentoxifylline; Phosphodiesterase 5 Inhibitors; Propafenone; Prostacyclin Analogues; Quinagolide; QuiNINE; Regorafenib; Reserpine; Rivastigmine; Ruxolitinib; Selective Serotonin Reuptake Inhibitors; Tofacitinib

Decreased Effect

Metoprolol may decrease the levels/effects of: Beta2-Agonists; Lercanidipine; Theophylline Derivatives

The levels/effects of Metoprolol may be decreased by: Amphetamines; Barbiturates; Herbs (Hypertensive Properties); Methylphenidate; Mirabegron; Nonsteroidal Anti-Inflammatory Agents; Peginterferon Alfa-2b; Rifamycin Derivatives; Yohimbine

Food Interactions Food increases absorption. Metoprolol serum levels may be increased if taken with food. Management: Take immediate release tartrate tablets with food; succinate can be taken with or without food.

Dietary Considerations Immediate-release tablets should be taken with or immediately following food (Melander 1977).

Pharmacodynamics/Kinetics

Onset of Action Oral: Immediate release tablets: Within 1 hour; Peak effect: Oral: 1 to 2 hours (Regårdh 1980); IV: 20 minutes (when infused over 10 minutes)

Duration of Action Oral: Immediate release: Variable (dose-related; 50% reduction in maximum heart rate after single doses of 20, 50, and 100 mg occurred at 3.3, 5, and 6.4 hours, respectively), Extended release: ~24 hours

Half-life Elimination Neonates: 5 to 10 hours (Morselli 1989); Adults: 3 to 4 hours (7 to 9 hours in poor CYP2D6 metabolizers or hepatic impairment)

Pregnancy Risk Factor C

Pregnancy Considerations Adverse events have been observed in animal reproduction studies. Metoprolol and the metabolite alpha-hydroxymetoprolol cross the placenta and can be detected in cord blood (Lindeberg 1987; Ryu 2015).

Adverse events, such as fetal/neonatal bradycardia, hypoglycemia, and reduced birth weight, have been observed following in utero exposure to beta-blockers as a class. Adequate facilities for monitoring infants at birth is generally recommended. The pharmacokinetics of metoprolol may be changed during pregnancy; the degree of changes may be dependent upon maternal CYP2D6 genotype (Ryu 2015).

Untreated chronic maternal hypertension and preeclampsia are also associated with adverse events in the fetus, infant, and mother (ACOG 2015; Magee 2014). Recommendations for the treatment of hypertension in pregnancy vary by guideline, but use of metoprolol may be considered (ESC [Regitz-Zagrosek 2011]; Magee 2014). Heart failure, peripartum cardiomyopathy, and valvular heart disease may cause severe complications in pregnant women; metoprolol is recommended when use of a beta-blocker is indicated (AHA/ACC [Nishimura 2014]; ESC [Regitz-Zagrosek 2011]; Sliwa 2010). Use of metoprolol may be considered for some arrhythmias, including SVT, when a beta-blocker is needed (ACC/AHA/HRS [Page 2015]; ESC [Regitz-Zagrosek 2011]). Use of metoprolol may be considered if migraine prophylaxis is needed in a pregnant woman (Pringsheim 2012).

Breastfeeding Considerations Metoprolol is excreted in breast milk in small quantities. An infant consuming 1 L of breast milk daily would receive <1 mg of the drug. breastfeeding is not recommended for women with heart failure related to PPCM due to the high metabolic demands of lactation and breastfeeding (ESC [Regitz-Zagrosek 2011]; Sliwa 2010).

Dosage Forms

Solution, Intravenous:

Generic: 5 mg/5 mL (5 mL)

Solution, Intravenous [preservative free]:
Generic: 5 mg/5 mL (5 mL)
Solution Cartridge, Intravenous:
Generic: 5 mg/5 mL (5 mL)
Tablet, Oral:
Lopressor: 50 mg, 100 mg
Generic: 25 mg, 37.5 mg, 50 mg, 75 mg, 100 mg
Tablet Extended Release 24 Hour, Oral:
Toprol XL: 25 mg, 50 mg, 100 mg, 200 mg
Generic: 25 mg, 50 mg, 100 mg, 200 mg

Metreleptin (met re LEP tin)

Brand Names: US Myalept
Pharmacologic Category Leptin Analog
Use
Lipodystrophy: Replacement therapy to treat the complications of leptin deficiency, in addition to diet, in patients with congenital or acquired generalized lipodystrophy.
Limitations of use: Not indicated for use in patients with HIV-related lipodystrophy or for use in patients with metabolic disease (eg, diabetes mellitus, hypertriglyceridemia) without concurrent evidence of congenital or acquired generalized lipodystrophy.
Local Anesthetic/Vasoconstrictor Precautions No information available to require special precautions
Effects on Dental Treatment No significant effects or complications reported
Effects on Bleeding No information available to require special precautions
Adverse Reactions Frequency not always defined.
Central nervous system: Headache (13%), dizziness (8%), fatigue (8%), paresthesia (6%)
Dermatologic: Urticaria (≤4%)
Endocrine & metabolic: Hypoglycemia (13%), weight loss (13%), ovarian cyst (8%), decreased glucose tolerance (in patients with antibodies to metreleptin), diabetes mellitus (in patients with antibodies to metreleptin), increased serum triglycerides (in patients with antibodies to metreleptin), weight gain (in patients with antibodies to metreleptin)
Gastrointestinal: Abdominal pain (10%), nausea (8%), diarrhea (6%), pancreatitis (4%; in patients with a history of pancreatitis)
Genitourinary: Proteinuria (6%)
Hematologic & oncologic: Anemia (6%), elevated glycosylated hemoglobin (in patients with antibodies to metreleptin)
Immunologic: Immunogenicity (anti-metreleptin antibodies: 84%; anti-metreleptin antibodies with neutralizing activity associated with adverse events consistent with loss of endogenous leptin activity and/or loss of metreleptin efficacy: 6%)
Infection: Severe infection (in patients with antibodies to metreleptin)
Local: Erythema at injection site (≤4%)
Neuromuscular & skeletal: Arthralgia (8%), back pain (6%)
Otic: Otic infection (8%)
Respiratory: Upper respiratory tract infection (8%)
Miscellaneous: Fever (6%)
<1%, postmarketing, and/or case reports: Anaplastic large cell lymphoma, autoimmune hepatitis (progression), hypersensitivity (including anaphylaxis, skin rash, urticaria), membranoproliferative glomerulonephritis (progression), T-cell lymphoma
General Dosage Range SubQ:
Infants, Children, Adolescents, and Adults:
Baseline weight ≤40 kg: Initial dose: 0.06 mg/kg once daily; increase or decrease by 0.02 mg/kg daily based on response or adverse effects. Maximum dose: 0.13 mg/kg once daily.
Baseline weight >40 kg: Initial dose: 2.5 mg (males) or 5 mg (females) once daily; increase or decrease by 1.25-2.5 mg daily based on response or adverse effects. Maximum dose: 10 mg once daily.
Mechanism of Action Recombinant human leptin analog that binds to and activates the human leptin receptor (ObR) (which belongs to the class I cytokine family of receptors that signals through the JAK/STAT transduction pathway) to treat complications of leptin deficiency associated with generalized lipodystrophy.
Pharmacodynamics/Kinetics
Half-life Elimination 3.8-4.7 hours
Time to Peak 4 hours (range: 2-8 hours)
Pregnancy Risk Factor C
Pregnancy Considerations Adverse events were observed in animal reproduction studies. Because metreleptin can restore metabolic and endocrine function, normal menses may be restored in women with previous amenorrhea; fertility may be restored and pregnancies may occur. Reports of use of metreleptin during pregnancy are limited (Chou 2011; Chou 2013; Maguire 2013).

Adverse pregnancy outcomes are associated with lipodystrophy in pregnant women, including eclampsia, gestational diabetes, intrauterine growth retardation, intrauterine death, macrosomia, and miscarriage. Based on in vitro data, metreleptin may inhibit uterine contractility during labor. A monitoring program is available for pregnant women exposed to metreleptin during pregnancy. Pregnant women or their health care provider may enroll by calling 1-855-669-2537.
Prescribing and Access Restrictions As a requirement of the REMS program, access to this medication is restricted. Prescribers must be certified with the program by enrolling and completing training. Pharmacies must be certified with the program and only dispense metreleptin after the receipt of the prescription authorization form for each new prescription. Additional information is available at 1-855-669-2537 or www.-MYALEPTREMS.com.

MetroNIDAZOLE (Systemic)
(met roe NYE da zole)

Related Information
Bacterial Infections *on page 1835*
Gastrointestinal Disorders *on page 1775*
Periodontal Diseases *on page 1844*
Ulcerative, Erosive, and Painful Oral Mucosal Disorders *on page 1853*
Related Sample Prescriptions
Bacterial Infections and Periodontal Diseases - Sample Prescriptions *on page 32*
Brand Names: US First-Metronidazole 100; First-Metronidazole 50; Flagyl; Flagyl ER [DSC]; Metro
Brand Names: Canada Flagyl; Metronidazole Injection USP; Novo-Nidazol; PMS-Metronidazole
Generic Availability (US) May be product dependent
Pharmacologic Category Amebicide; Antibiotic, Miscellaneous; Antiprotozoal, Nitroimidazole
Dental Use Treatment of oral soft tissue infections due to anaerobic bacteria including all anaerobic cocci, anaerobic gram-negative bacilli (*Bacteroides*), and gram-positive spore-forming bacilli (*Clostridium*). Useful

as single agent or in combination with amoxicillin, amoxicillin/clavulanic acid, or ciprofloxacin in the treatment of periodontitis associated with presence of *Actinobacillus actinomycetemcomitans* (AA). In aggressive periodontitis, greatest benefit is seen after 3 months of therapy. No benefit was seen after 6 months of therapy (Varela, 2011).

Use

Amebiasis: Oral immediate-release tablet and capsule: Treatment of acute intestinal amebiasis (amebic dysentery) and amebic liver abscess

Limitations of use (oral immediate-release tablet, capsule and injection): When used for amebic liver abscess, may be used concurrently with percutaneous needle aspiration when it is clinically indicated.

Anaerobic bacterial infections (caused by *Bacteroides* spp., including the *B. fragilis* group): Oral immediate-release tablet, capsule, and injection:

Bacterial septicemia: Treatment of bacterial septicemia (also caused by *Clostridium* spp.)

Bone and joint infections: Treatment (adjunctive therapy) of bone and joint infections

CNS Infections: Treatment of CNS infections, including meningitis and brain abscess

Endocarditis: Treatment of endocarditis

Gynecologic infections: Treatment of gynecologic infections including endometritis, endomyometritis, tubo-ovarian abscess, or postsurgical vaginal cuff infection (also caused by *Clostridium* spp., *Peptococcus* spp., *Peptostreptococcus* spp., and *Fusobacterium* spp.)

Intra-abdominal infections: Treatment of intra-abdominal infections, including peritonitis, intra-abdominal abscess and liver abscess (also caused by *Clostridium* spp., *Eubacterium* spp., *Peptococcus* spp., and *Peptostreptococcus* spp.)

Lower respiratory tract infections: Treatment of lower respiratory tract infections, including pneumonia, empyema and lung abscess

Skin and skin structure infections: Treatment of skin and skin structure infections (also caused by *Clostridium* spp., *Peptococcus* spp., *Peptostreptococcus* spp., and *Fusobacterium* spp.)

Bacterial vaginosis: Oral extended-release tablet: Treatment of bacterial vaginosis in nonpregnant women

Surgical prophylaxis (colorectal surgery): Injection: Preoperative, intraoperative, and postoperative prophylaxis to reduce the incidence of postoperative infection in patients undergoing elective colorectal surgery classified as contaminated or potentially contaminated

Trichomoniasis: Oral immediate-release tablet, capsule, and injection. Treatment of infections caused by *Trichomonas vaginalis*, including treatment of asymptomatic sexual partners

Local Anesthetic/Vasoconstrictor Precautions No information available to require special precautions

Effects on Dental Treatment Key adverse event(s) related to dental treatment: Unusual/metallic taste, glossitis, stomatitis, xerostomia (normal salivary flow resumes upon discontinuation), and furry tongue.

Effects on Bleeding No information available to require special precautions

Adverse Reactions

>10%:

Central nervous system: Headache (18%)

Gastrointestinal: Nausea (10% to 12%)

Genitourinary: Vaginitis (15%)

1% to 10%:

Central nervous system: Metallic taste (9%), dizziness (4%)

Dermatologic: Genital pruritus (5%)

Gastrointestinal: Abdominal pain (4%), diarrhea (4%), xerostomia (2%)

Genitourinary: Dysmenorrhea (3%), urine abnormality (3%), urinary tract infection (2%)

Infection: Bacterial infection (7%), candidiasis (3%)

Respiratory: Flu-like symptoms (6%), upper respiratory tract infection (4%), pharyngitis (3%), sinusitis (3%)

Frequency not defined:

Cardiovascular: Flattened T-wave on ECG, flushing, syncope

Central nervous system: Aseptic meningitis, ataxia, brain disease, confusion, convulsions, depression, disulfiram-like reaction (with alcohol), dysarthria, insomnia, irritability, peripheral neuropathy, psychosis, seizure, sensation of pelvic pressure, vertigo

Dermatologic: Erythematous rash, pruritus, Stevens-Johnson syndrome, toxic epidermal necrolysis, urticaria

Endocrine & metabolic: Decreased libido

Gastrointestinal: Abdominal cramps, abdominal distress, anorexia, constipation, dyspareunia, epigastric distress, glossitis, hairy tongue, hiccups, pancreatitis (rare), proctitis, stomatitis, vomiting

Genitourinary: Cystitis, dark urine (rare), dysuria, urinary incontinence, vaginal dryness, vulvovaginal candidiasis

Hematologic & oncologic: Neutropenia (reversible), thrombocytopenia (reversible, rare)

Immunologic: Serum sickness-like reaction (joint pains)

Local: Inflammation at injection site (IV)

Neuromuscular & skeletal: Arthralgia, weakness

Ophthalmic: Optic neuropathy

Renal: Polyuria

Respiratory: Nasal congestion, rhinitis

Miscellaneous: Fever, lesion (central nervous system, reversible)

Dental Usual Dosage

Anaerobic infections/abscess: Adults: Oral, IV: 500 mg every 6-8 hours, not to exceed 4 g/day

Periodontitis treatment (monotherapy or combination) associated with the presence of *Actinobacillus actinomycetemcomitans* (AA): Adults: Oral: 250-500 mg every 8 hours for 8-10 days used in addition to scaling and root planing (Varela 2011)

Dosing

Adult & Geriatric

Amebiasis (acute dysentery): Oral: Immediate-release tablets and capsules: 750 mg every 8 hours for 5 to 10 days

Amebic liver abscess: Oral:

Immediate-release tablets: 500 to 750 mg every 8 hours for 5 to 10 days

Capsules: 750 mg every 8 hours for 5 to 10 days

Bacterial vaginosis or vaginitis due to *Gardnerella, Mobiluncus:* Oral: Tablet:

Immediate release (off-label use): 500 mg twice daily for 7 days (CDC [Workowski 2015])

Extended release: 750 mg once daily for 7 days

Intra-abdominal infection:

Manufacturer's labeling: Oral (immediate release), IV: 500 mg every 6 hours (maximum: 4 g/day); **Note:** Initial: 1 g IV loading dose may be administered

Alternate dosing:

Acute diverticulitis, outpatient treatment: Oral (immediate release): 500 mg every 6 to 8 hours; use in combination with a fluoroquinolone (eg, ciprofloxacin) or sulfamethoxazole and trimethoprim (Jacobs 2007)

Complicated, community-acquired, mild to moderate (in combination with cephalosporin or fluoroquinolone): IV: 500 mg every 8 to 12 hours **or** 1.5 g every 24 hours for 4 to 7 days (provided source controlled) (Solomkin 2010)

Pelvic inflammatory disease (off-label dose): Oral (immediate release):

Mild to moderately severe: 500 mg twice daily for 14 days (may be added to a combination of a third-generation parenteral cephalosporin and doxycycline) (CDC [Workowski 2015])

With tubo-ovarian abscess: 500 mg twice daily to complete at least 14 days of therapy (in combination with doxycycline following a parenteral therapy regimen)

Trichomoniasis (index case and sex partner): Oral:

Immediate-release tablets:

Manufacturer's labeling: 250 mg every 8 hours for 7 days **or** 1 g twice daily for 2 doses (on same day) **or** 2 g as a single dose

Alternate dosing: 2 g as a single dose (preferred regimen) **or** 500 mg twice daily for 7 days (off-label dose) (CDC [Workowski 2015])

Capsules: 375 mg twice daily for 7 days

Trichomoniasis in HIV-infected women (off-label dose): Oral (immediate release): 500 mg twice daily for 7 days (CDC [Workowski 2015])

Trichomoniasis, persistent or recurrent (ie, treatment failure of nitroimidazole [eg metronidazole] single-dose therapy) (index case; treatment of sex partner; off-label dose): Oral (immediate release): 500 mg twice daily for 7 days. If this regimen also fails, consider 2 g once daily for 7 days (CDC [Workowski 2015])

Balantidiasis (off-label use): IV, Oral (immediate release): 750 mg 3 times daily for ≥5 days (Anagyrou 2003; Schuster 2008)

Bite wounds (animal/human) (off-label use) (IDSA [Stevens 2014]): Note: Use in combination with a second- or third-generation cephalosporin, levofloxacin, or sulfamethoxazole/trimethoprim for animal bites, or in combination with ciprofloxacin or levofloxacin for human bites.

Oral: 250 to 500 mg 3 times daily

IV: 500 mg every 8 hours

***Clostridium difficile*-associated diarrhea (CDAD) (off-label use): Note:** Recent guideline recommends converting to oral vancomycin therapy if the patient does not show a clear clinical response after 5 to 7 days of metronidazole therapy (Surawicz 2013)

Mild to moderate infection: Oral (immediate release): 500 mg 3 times daily for 10 to 14 days (Cohen 2010; Surawicz 2013)

Severe complicated infection (no abdominal distention): IV: 500 mg 3 times daily with oral vancomycin for 10 to 14 days (Surawicz 2013)

Severe complicated infection (with ileus, toxic colitis, and/or abdominal distention): IV: 500 mg 3 times daily with oral and rectal vancomycin for 10 to 14 days (Surawicz 2013)

Crohn disease, mild to moderate (off-label use): Oral (immediate release): 10 to 20 mg/kg/day (Lichtenstein 2009) or 500 mg twice daily (in combination with ciprofloxacin) (Steinhart 2002).

***Dientamoeba fragilis* infections (off-label use):** Oral (immediate release): 500 to 750 mg 3 times daily for 10 days (CDC 2012)

Giardiasis (off-label use): Oral (immediate release): 250 to 500 mg 3 times daily for 5 to 10 days (Granados 2012)

***Helicobacter pylori* eradication (off-label use):** Oral (immediate release):

Triple therapy: Metronidazole 500 mg twice daily for 10 to 14 days, in combination with clarithromycin and a proton pump inhibitor (Chey 2007)

Quadruple therapy: Metronidazole 250 mg 4 times daily for 10 to 14 days, in combination with bismuth subsalicylate, a tetracycline, and either ranitidine or a proton pump inhibitor (Chey 2007)

Periodontitis (associated with aggressive disease; off-label use): Oral (immediate release): 250 mg every 8 hours in combination with amoxicillin for 10 days; used in addition to scaling, root planing and pocket irrigation (Silva-Senem 2013)

Pouchitis (post ileal pouch-anal anastomosis, acute treatment; off-label use): Oral (immediate release): 400 to 500 mg three times daily for 7 days (Holubar 2010; Wall 2011)

Prophylaxis against sexually-transmitted diseases following sexual assault (off-label use): Oral (immediate release): 2 g as a single dose in combination with ceftriaxone and azithromycin (CDC [Workowski 2015])

Skin and soft tissue necrotizing infections (off-label use): IV: 500 mg every 6 hours, in combination with cefotaxime or ceftriaxone for empiric therapy of polymicrobial infections. Continue until further debridement is not necessary, patient has clinically improved, and patient is afebrile for 48 to 72 hours (IDSA [Stevens 2014]).

Surgical prophylaxis:

Manufacturer's labeling: IV: 15 mg/kg 1 hour prior to surgical incision; followed by 7.5 mg/kg 6 and 12 hours after initial dose

Alternate dosing:

IV: 500 mg within 60 minutes prior to surgical incision in combination with other antibiotics (Bratzler 2013). **Note:** Considered a recommended agent for select procedures other than colorectal surgery (off-label use) (Bratzler 2013).

Oral (for colorectal surgical prophylaxis only; immediate release; off-label use): 1 g every 3 to 4 hours for 3 doses, starting after mechanical bowel preparation the afternoon and evening before the procedure with or without additional oral antibiotics and with an appropriate IV antibiotic prophylaxis regimen (Bratzler 2013).

Surgical site infections (intestinal or GU tract; axilla or perineum) (off-label use): IV: 500 mg every 8 hours; in combination with ceftriaxone, ciprofloxacin, or levofloxacin (IDSA [Stevens 2014]).

Tetanus (*Clostridium tetani* infection; off-label use): Oral (immediate release): 500 mg every 6 hours for 7 to 10 days in combination with supportive therapy (Ahmadsyah, 1985)

Urethritis, nongonococcal (recurrent or persistent urethritis in men who have sex with women and who live in regions where *T. vaginalis* is prevalent; off-label use): Oral (immediate release): 2 g as a single dose. **Note:** Compliance with initial regimen and lack of re-exposure to an untreated sex partner should be excluded prior to use (CDC [Workowski 2015])

Pediatric

Infants, Children, and Adolescents:

Amebiasis: Oral: 35 to 50 mg/kg/day in divided doses every 8 hours for 7 to 10 days (*Red Book* [AAP 2012])

Trichomoniasis: Oral: 15 mg/kg/day in divided doses every 8 hours for 7 days (*Red Book* [AAP 2012])

Anaerobic infections (off-label dosing):

Oral: 30 to 50 mg/kg/day in divided doses every 8 hours (maximum: 2,250 mg/day) (*Red Book* [AAP 2012])

IV: 22.5 to 40 mg/kg/day in divided doses every 8 hours (maximum: 1,500 mg/day) (*Red Book* [AAP 2012])

Balantidiasis (off-label use): Oral: 35 to 50 mg/kg/day in 3 divided doses for 5 days (*Red Book* [AAP 2012]; Schuster 2008)

***Clostridium difficile*-associated diarrhea (CDAD; off-label use):** Oral: 30 mg/kg/day divided every 6 hours for ≥10 days (maximum: 2 g/day) (*Red Book* [AAP 2012]; Schutze 2013). **Note:** Recommended agent for the initial treatment of mild to moderate disease and for first relapse (*Red Book* [AAP 2012]; Schutze 2013).

Giardiasis (off-label use): Oral: 15 mg/kg/day in divided doses every 8 hours for 5 to 10 days (Granados 2012; *Red Book* [AAP 2012])

***Helicobacter pylori* eradication (off-label use):** Oral: 20 mg/kg/day in 2 divided doses for 10 to 14 days in combination therapy with amoxicillin and either a proton pump inhibitor or bismuth subsalicylate daily or 20 mg/kg/day in 2 divided doses on days 6 through 10 in combination therapy with a proton pump inhibitor and clarithromycin (after treatment with amoxicillin and a proton pump inhibitor for days 1 through 5) (maximum: 1 g/day) (Koletzko 2011)

Skin and soft tissue necrotizing infections (off-label use): IV: 7.5 mg/kg every 6 hours, in combination with cefotaxime for empiric therapy of polymicrobial infections. Continue until further debridement is not necessary, patient has clinically improved, and patient is afebrile for 48 to 72 hours (IDSA [Stevens 2014]).

Surgical (preoperative) prophylaxis (off-label use):

Infants <1,200 g: IV: 7.5 mg/kg within 60 minutes prior to surgical incision in combination with other antibiotics (Bratzler 2013).

Infants ≥1,200 g and Children ≥1 year:

IV: 15 mg/kg within 60 minutes prior to surgical incision in combination with other antibiotics (maximum: 500 mg per dose) (Bratzler 2013).

Oral (for colorectal surgical prophylaxis only): 15 mg/kg (maximum: 1,000 mg) every 3 to 4 hours for 3 doses, starting after mechanical bowel preparation the afternoon and evening before the procedure, with or without additional oral antibiotics and with an appropriate IV antibiotic prophylaxis regimen (Bratzler 2013).

Tetanus (*Clostridium tetani* infection, off-label use): Oral, IV: 30 mg/kg per day in divided doses every 6 hours for 10 to 14 days in combination with tetanus immune globulin and supportive therapy (maximum: 4 g/day) (*Red Book* [AAP 2012])

Adolescents: Oral:

Pelvic inflammatory disease (off-label dosing): Refer to adult dosing

Prophylaxis against sexually-transmitted diseases following sexual assault (off-label use): Refer to adult dosing.

Vaginal infections:

Vaginitis (*Trichomonas vaginalis*; off-label use): 2 g as a single dose (*Red Book* [AAP 2012])

Vaginosis (bacterial; off-label use): 500 mg twice daily for 7 days (*Red Book* [AAP 2012])

Renal Impairment

Manufacturer's labeling:

Mild, moderate, or severe impairment: There are no dosage adjustments provided in the manufacturer's labeling; however, decreased renal function does not alter the single-dose pharmacokinetics

End-stage renal disease (ESRD) requiring dialysis: Metronidazole metabolites may accumulate; monitor for adverse events. Accumulated metabolites may be rapidly removed by dialysis:

Intermittent hemodialysis (IHD): If administration cannot be separated from hemodialysis, consider supplemental dose following hemodialysis.

Peritoneal dialysis (PD): No dosage adjustment necessary.

Alternate dosing:

Intermittent hemodialysis (IHD) (administer after hemodialysis on dialysis days): Dialyzable (50% to 100%): 500 mg every 8 to 12 hours. **Note:** Dosing regimen highly dependent on clinical indication (trichomoniasis vs *C. difficile* colitis) (Heintz 2009). **Note:** Dosing dependent on the assumption of thrice weekly, complete IHD sessions.

Continuous renal replacement therapy (CRRT) (Heintz 2009; Trotman 2005): Drug clearance is highly dependent on the method of renal replacement, filter type, and flow rate. Appropriate dosing requires close monitoring of pharmacologic response, signs of adverse reactions due to drug accumulation, as well as drug concentrations in relation to target trough (if appropriate). The following are general recommendations only (based on dialysate flow/ultrafiltration rates of 1 to 2 L/hour and minimal residual renal function) and should not supersede clinical judgment:

CVVH/CVVHD/CVVHDF: 500 mg every 6 to 12 hours (or per clinical indication; dosage reduction generally not necessary)

Hepatic Impairment

Manufacturer's labeling:

Mild or moderate impairment (Child-Pugh class A or B): No dosage adjustment necessary; use with caution and monitor for adverse events

Severe impairment (Child-Pugh class C):

Extended-release tablets: Use is not recommended.

Immediate-release capsules:

Amebiasis: 375 mg 3 times daily

Trichomoniasis: 375 mg once daily

Immediate-release tablets, injection: Reduce dose by 50%

Alternate dosing: The pharmacokinetics of a single oral 500 mg dose were not altered in patients with cirrhosis; initial dose reduction is therefore not necessary (Daneshmend, 1982). In one study of IV metronidazole, patients with alcoholic liver disease (with or without cirrhosis), demonstrated a prolonged elimination half-life (eg, ~18 hours). The authors recommended the dose be reduced accordingly (clearance was reduced by ~62%) and the frequency may be prolonged (eg, every 12 hours instead of every 6 hours) (Lau, 1987). In another single IV dose study using metronidazole metabolism to predict hepatic function, patients classified as Child-Pugh class C demonstrated a half-life of ~21.5 hours (Muscara, 1995).

Mechanism of Action After diffusing into the organism, interacts with DNA to cause a loss of helical DNA structure and strand breakage resulting in inhibition of protein synthesis and cell death in susceptible organisms

Contraindications Hypersensitivity to metronidazole, nitroimidazole derivatives, or any component of the formulation; pregnant patients (first trimester) with trichomoniasis; use of disulfiram within the past 2 weeks; use of alcohol or propylene glycol-containing products during therapy or within 3 days of therapy discontinuation

Warnings/Precautions [US Boxed Warning]: Possibly carcinogenic based on animal data. Reserve use for conditions described in Use; unnecessary use should be avoided. Use with caution in patients with severe liver impairment and ESRD due to potential accumulation; reduce dosage in patients with severe liver impairment and consider dosage reduction in patients with severe renal impairment (CrCl <10 mL/minute) who are receiving prolonged therapy. Dose should not specifically be reduced in anuric patients (accumulated metabolites may be rapidly removed by dialysis). Hemodialysis patients may need supplemental dosing. Use with caution in patients with blood dyscrasias (monitor CBC with differential at baseline, during and after treatment) or history of seizures.

Aseptic meningitis (symptoms may occur within hours of a dose); encephalopathy (cerebellar toxicity with ataxia, dizziness, dysarthria and/or CNS lesions); seizures; and peripheral and optic neuropathies have been reported especially with increased doses and chronic treatment; monitor and consider discontinuation of therapy if symptoms occur. Prolonged use may result in fungal or bacterial superinfection, including *C. difficile*-associated diarrhea (CDAD) and pseudomembranous colitis; CDAD has been observed >2 months postantibiotic treatment. Guidelines recommend the use of oral metronidazole for initial treatment of mild to moderate *C. difficile* infection and the use of oral vancomycin for initial treatment of severe *C. difficile* infection (with or without IV metronidazole depending on the presence of complications). May treat recurrent mild to moderate infection once with oral metronidazole; avoid use beyond first reoccurrence (Cohen 2010; Surawicz 2013). Candidiasis infection (known or unknown) maybe more prominent during metronidazole treatment, antifungal treatment required.

Abdominal cramps, nausea, vomiting, headaches, and flushing have been reported with oral and injectable metronidazole and concomitant alcohol consumption; avoid alcoholic beverages or products containing propylene glycol during oral and injectable therapy and for at least 3 days after oral therapy. Do not use extended-release tablets in patients with severe hepatic impairment (Child-Pugh class C) unless benefit outweighs risk. Use injection with caution in patients with heart failure, edema or other sodium retaining states, including corticosteroid treatment. In patients receiving continuous nasogastric secretion aspiration, sufficient metronidazole may be removed in the aspirate to cause a reduction in serum levels. Potentially significant drug-drug interactions may exist, requiring dose or frequency adjustment, additional monitoring, and/or selection of alternative therapy.

Drug Interactions

Metabolism/Transport Effects **Substrate** of CYP2A6 (minor); **Note:** Assignment of Major/Minor substrate status based on clinically relevant drug interaction potential; **Inhibits** CYP2C9 (weak)

Avoid Concomitant Use

Avoid concomitant use of MetroNIDAZOLE (Systemic) with any of the following: Alcohol (Ethyl); BCG (Intravesical); Carbocisteine; Cholera Vaccine; Disulfiram; Mebendazole; Ritonavir

Increased Effect/Toxicity

MetroNIDAZOLE (Systemic) may increase the levels/effects of: Alcohol (Ethyl); Busulfan; Capecitabine; Carbocisteine; Dronabinol; Fluorouracil (Systemic); Fosphenytoin; Highest Risk QTc-Prolonging Agents; Lopinavir; Moderate Risk QTc-Prolonging Agents; Phenytoin; Tegafur; Tipranavir; Vitamin K Antagonists

The levels/effects of MetroNIDAZOLE (Systemic) may be increased by: Disulfiram; Mebendazole; MiFEPRIStone; Ritonavir

Decreased Effect

MetroNIDAZOLE (Systemic) may decrease the levels/effects of: BCG (Intravesical); BCG Vaccine (Immunization); Cholera Vaccine; Lactobacillus and Estriol; Mycophenolate; Sodium Picosulfate; Typhoid Vaccine

The levels/effects of MetroNIDAZOLE (Systemic) may be decreased by: Fosphenytoin; PHENobarbital; Phenytoin; Primidone

Food Interactions Peak antibiotic serum concentration lowered and delayed, but total drug absorbed not affected.

Dietary Considerations

Immediate-release tablets and capsules may be administered with food to minimize stomach upset. Extended-release tablets should be taken on an empty stomach (1 hour before or 2 hours after meals).

Sodium: Injectable dosage form may contain sodium.

Ethanol: Use of ethanol is contraindicated during therapy and for 3 days after therapy discontinuation.

Pharmacodynamics/Kinetics

Half-life Elimination

Neonates <7 days (Jager-Roman 1982): Within first week of life, more prolonged than with lower GA:

GA 28 to 30 weeks: 75.3 ± 16.9 hours

GA 32 to 35 weeks: 35.4 ± 1.5 hours

GA 36 to 40 weeks: 24.8 ± 1.6 hours

Neonates ≥7 days: ~22.5 hours (Upadhyaya 1988)

Children and Adolescents: 6 to 10 hours (Lamp 1999)

Adults: ~8 hours

Time to Peak Serum: Oral: Immediate release: 1-2 hours; Extended release: ~5 hours

Pregnancy Risk Factor B

Pregnancy Considerations Use of metronidazole during the first trimester of pregnancy is contraindicated by the manufacturer for the treatment of trichomoniasis. Metronidazole crosses the placenta. Cleft lip with or without cleft palate has been reported following first trimester exposure to metronidazole; however, most studies have not shown an increased risk of congenital anomalies or other adverse events to the fetus following maternal use during pregnancy. Because metronidazole was carcinogenic in some animal species, concern has been raised whether metronidazole should be used during pregnancy. Available studies have not shown an increased risk of infant cancer following metronidazole exposure during pregnancy; however, the ability to detect a signal for this may have been limited.

Metronidazole pharmacokinetics are similar between pregnant and nonpregnant patients (Amon 1981; Visser 1984; Wang 2011). Bacterial vaginosis has been associated with adverse pregnancy outcomes; metronidazole is recommended for the treatment of symptomatic bacterial vaginosis in pregnant patients (CDC [Workowski 2015]). Vaginal trichomoniasis has been also associated with adverse pregnancy outcomes; use of metronidazole for this indication during the first trimester is contraindicated by the manufacturer; however, some guidelines note treatment can be given at any stage of pregnancy (CDC [Workowski 2015]). Metronidazole may also be used for the treatment of giardiasis in pregnant women (some sources recommend second and third trimester administration only) (Gardner 2001; HHS [OI adult 2015]) and symptomatic amebiasis during pregnancy (HHS [OI adult 2015]; Li 1996). Short courses may be used for the treatment of pouchitis or perianal disease in pregnant women with inflammatory bowel disease (avoid use in the first trimester) (van der Woude 2015).The use of other agents is preferred when treatment is needed during pregnancy for *Clostridium difficile* (Surawicz 2013) or *Helicobacter pylori* (Mahadevan 2006). Consult current guidelines for appropriate use in pregnant women.

Breastfeeding Considerations Metronidazole and its active hydroxyl metabolite are excreted in breast milk at concentrations similar to maternal plasma concentrations.

The relative infant dose (RID) of metronidazole is 13.7% to 22.9% when calculated using the highest average breast milk concentration reported and compared to an oral infant therapeutic dose of 30 to 50 mg/kg/day. In general, breastfeeding is considered acceptable when the RID is <10%; when an RID is >25% breastfeeding should generally be avoided (Anderson 2016; Ito 2000). Using the highest average milk concentration (45.8 mcg/mL), the estimated daily infant dose via breast milk is 6.87 mg/kg/day. This milk concentration was obtained following a single maternal dose of oral metronidazole 2,000 mg; the authors estimated the infant would have been exposed to metronidazole 21.8 mg over the first 24 hours after the dose (Erickson 1981).

The highest average milk concentration occurred 2 to 4 hours after a single oral maternal dose; the half-life in breast milk was ~9 to 10 hours (Erickson 1982). Metronidazole and its active metabolite can be detected in the serum of nursing infants (Gray 1961; Heisterberg 1983; Passmore 1988).

Loose stools, oral and perianal *Candida* growth, and oral thrush have been reported in breastfeeding infants exposed to metronidazole (Passmore 1988)

The manufacturer warns of the risk of carcinogenicity in patients exposed to metronidazole based on animal studies; theoretically, this risk is also present in breastfeeding infants exposed to metronidazole via breast milk. Therefore, the manufacturer recommends a decision be made whether to discontinue breastfeeding or to discontinue the drug, taking into account the importance of treatment to the mother. Some guidelines note if metronidazole is given, breastfeeding should be withheld for 12 to 24 hours after a single dose (CDC [Workowski 2015]; WHO 2002); alternatively, the mother may pump and discard breast milk for 24 hours after taking the last metronidazole dose. Breastfeeding should be avoided in women requiring treatment with metronidazole for inflammatory bowel disease (van der Woude 2015). Use of other agents is preferred when treating breastfeeding women for *Clostridium difficile* infection (Surawicz 2013).

Dosage Forms Considerations Parenteral solution contains 28 mEq of sodium/gram of metronidazole.

First-Metronidazole oral suspension is a compounding kit. Refer to manufacturer's labeling for compounding instructions.

Dosage Forms

Capsule, Oral:
Flagyl: 375 mg
Generic: 375 mg

Solution, Intravenous:
Metro: 500 mg (100 mL)
Generic: 500 mg (100 mL)

Suspension Reconstituted, Oral:
First-Metronidazole 50: 50 mg/mL (150 mL)
First-Metronidazole 100: 100 mg/mL (150 mL)

Tablet, Oral:
Flagyl: 250 mg, 500 mg
Generic: 250 mg, 500 mg

Mexiletine (meks IL e teen)

Brand Names: Canada Novo-Mexiletine

Pharmacologic Category Antiarrhythmic Agent, Class Ib

Use

Ventricular arrhythmias: Management of life-threatening ventricular arrhythmias

Note: The American College of Cardiology/American Heart Association/European Society of Cardiology (ACC/AHA/ESC) states that mexiletine may be considered for those with long QT syndrome who present with torsades de pointes (ACC/AHA/ESC [Zipes 2006])

Local Anesthetic/Vasoconstrictor Precautions No information available to require special precautions

Effects on Dental Treatment Key adverse event(s) related to dental treatment: Xerostomia (normal salivary flow resumes upon discontinuation).

Effects on Bleeding No information available to require special precautions

Adverse Reactions

>10%:

Cardiovascular: Exacerbation of cardiac arrhythmia (10% to 15%; patients with malignant arrhythmia)
Central nervous system: Dizziness (11% to 25%), ataxia (10% to 20%), nervousness (5% to 10%), unsteady gait
Gastrointestinal: Gastrointestinal distress (41%), nausea (≤40%), vomiting (≤40%)
Neuromuscular & skeletal: Tremor (13%)

1% to 10%:

Cardiovascular: Palpitations (4% to 8%), chest pain (3% to 8%), angina pectoris (2%), ventricular premature contractions (1% to 2%)
Central nervous system: Insomnia (5% to 7%), numbness (fingers or toes: 2% to 4%), depression (2%), paresthesia (2%), confusion, headache
Dermatologic: Skin rash (4%)
Gastrointestinal: Constipation (≤5%), diarrhea (≤5%), xerostomia (3%), abdominal pain (1%)
Neuromuscular & skeletal: Weakness (5%), arthralgia (1%)
Ophthalmic: Blurred vision (5% to 7%), nystagmus (6%)

Otic: Tinnitus (2% to 3%)
Respiratory: Dyspnea (3%)
<1%, postmarketing, and/or case reports: Agranulocytosis, alopecia, amnesia (short-term), atrioventricular block, cardiac conduction disturbance, cardiac failure (patients with pre-existing ventricular dysfunction), cardiogenic shock, decreased libido, diaphoresis, diplopia, dysphagia, edema, esophageal ulcer, exfoliative dermatitis, hallucination, hepatic necrosis, hepatitis, hot flash, hypertension, hypotension, impotence, increased liver enzymes, increased serum transaminases, leukopenia, lupus-like syndrome (drug-induced), malaise, myelofibrosis (patients with pre-existing myeloid abnormalities), pancreatitis (rare), peptic ulcer, pharyngitis, positive ANA titer, psychological disorder, psychosis, pulmonary fibrosis, salivary gland disease, seizure, sinoatrial arrest, Stevens-Johnson syndrome, syncope, thrombocytopenia, torsades de pointes, upper gastrointestinal hemorrhage, urinary hesitancy, urinary retention, urticaria

General Dosage Range Dosage adjustment recommended in patients with hepatic impairment

Oral: *Adults:* Initial: 200 mg every 8 hours; Maintenance: 200-300 mg every 8 hours (maximum: 1.2 g/day)

Mechanism of Action Class IB antiarrhythmic, structurally related to lidocaine, which inhibits inward sodium current, decreases rate of rise of phase 0, increases effective refractory period/action potential duration ratio

Pharmacodynamics/Kinetics

Onset of Action 30 to 120 minutes (with loading regimen)

Half-life Elimination ~10 to 12 hours; ~15 hours in severe renal impairment (CrCl <10 ml/min); ~25 hours in moderate to severe hepatic impairment

Time to Peak Serum: 2 to 3 hours

Pregnancy Risk Factor C

Pregnancy Considerations Adverse events have been observed in some animal reproduction studies. A few case reports have demonstrated safe use of mexiletine in pregnant women (Gregg 1988; Lownes 1987; Timmis 1980).

Micafungin (mi ka FUN gin)

Related Information

Fungal Infections *on page 1847*

Brand Names: US Mycamine

Brand Names: Canada Mycamine

Pharmacologic Category Antifungal Agent, Parenteral; Echinocandin

Use

Candidemia, acute disseminated candidiasis, *Candida* peritonitis and abscesses: Treatment of candidemia, acute disseminated candidiasis, *Candida* peritonitis and abscesses

Esophageal candidiasis: Treatment of esophageal candidiasis

Prophylaxis of *Candida* infections: Prophylaxis of *Candida* infections in patients undergoing hematopoietic stem cell transplantation (HSCT)

Local Anesthetic/Vasoconstrictor Precautions No information available to require special precautions

Effects on Dental Treatment No significant effects or complications reported

Effects on Bleeding May cause thrombocytopenia in ≤15% of patients.

Adverse Reactions Frequency of adverse events generally higher following prophylaxis of *Candida* infections in hematopoietic stem cell transplant recipients.

>10%:

Cardiovascular: Tachycardia (3% to 26%), localized phlebitis (with peripheral administration; 5% to 19%)
Central nervous system: Headache (2% to 44%), insomnia (4% to 37%), anxiety (≤23%), dizziness (13%)
Dermatologic: Pruritus (pediatric patients ages 3 days through 16 years: ≤33%; adults 6%), skin rash (2% to 30%), urticaria (pediatric patients ages 3 days through 16 years: ≤19%; adults <5%)
Endocrine & metabolic: Hypokalemia (14% to 18%), hypomagnesemia (6% to 13%)
Gastrointestinal: Diarrhea (7% to 77%), nausea (7% to 71%), vomiting (7% to 66%), abdominal pain (2% to 35%), abdominal distension (pediatric patients ages 3 days through 16 years: 2% to 19%), mucositis (14%), constipation (11%)
Genitourinary: Decreased urine output (pediatric patients ages 3 days through 16 years: ≤23%), hematuria (pediatric patients ages 3 days through 16 years: ≤23%)
Hematologic & oncologic: Neutropenia (5% to 75%), thrombocytopenia (4% to 75%), anemia (pediatric patients ages 3 days through 16 years: 13% to 51%; adults 3% to 10%), febrile neutropenia (≤16%)
Hepatic: Increased serum ALT (pediatric patients ages 3 days through 16 years: ≤16%; adults 5%), abnormal hepatic function tests (pediatric patients ages 3 days through 16 years: <15%; adults 4%), hyperbilirubinemia (pediatric patients ages 3 days through 16 years: <15%; adults <1%)
Renal: Renal failure (pediatric patients ages 3 days through 16 years: <15%)
Miscellaneous: Fever (pediatric patients ages 3 days through 16 years: 9% to 61%; adults 7% to 20%), infusion related reaction (pediatric patients ages 3 days through 16 years: ≤16%; adults <5%)

1% to 10%:

Cardiovascular: Hypotension (6% to 10%), peripheral edema (7%), edema (5%), atrial fibrillation (3% to 5%), bradycardia (3% to 5%), hypertension (3% to 5%), cardiac arrest (<5%), myocardial infarction (<5%), pericardial effusion (<5%)
Central nervous system: Rigors (9%), fatigue (6%), brain disease (<5%), convulsions (<5%), delirium (<5%), intracranial hemorrhage (<5%)
Endocrine & metabolic: Hypocalcemia (7%), hypoglycemia (6% to 7%), hyperglycemia (6%), hypernatremia (4% to 6%), hypervolemia (5%), hyperkalemia (4% to 5%)
Gastrointestinal: Anorexia (6%), dyspepsia (6%)
Hematologic & oncologic: Blood coagulation disorder (<5%), pancytopenia (<5%), thrombotic thrombocytopenic purpura (<5%)
Hepatic: Increased serum alkaline phosphatase (3% to 8%), increased serum AST (3% to 6%), hepatic failure (<5%), hepatic injury (<5%), hepatomegaly (<5%), jaundice (<5%)
Hypersensitivity: Anaphylaxis (<5%), hypersensivity reaction (<5%)
Infection: Bacteremia (5% to 9%), sepsis (5% to 6%)
Local: Venous thrombosis at injection site (<5%)
Neuromuscular & skeletal: Back pain (5%)
Respiratory: Epistaxis (≤9%), cough (8%), dyspnea (6%)

<1%, postmarketing and/or case reports, or frequency not defined: Acidosis, acute renal failure,

anaphylactoid reaction, anuria, apnea, arthralgia, cardiac arrhythmia, cyanosis, decreased white blood cell count, deep vein thrombosis, disseminated intravascular coagulation, erythema multiforme, facial edema, hemoglobinuria, hemolysis, hemolytic anemia, hepatic insufficiency, hepatitis, hiccups, hyponatremia, hypoxia, increased blood urea nitrogen, increased serum creatinine, infection, injection site reaction, oliguria, pneumonia, pulmonary embolism, renal insufficiency, renal tubular necrosis, seizure, shock, skin necrosis, Stevens-Johnson syndrome, thrombophlebitis, tissue necrosis at injection site, toxic epidermal necrolysis, vasodilatation

General Dosage Range IV:

Infants ≥4 months, Children, and Adolescents: Prophylaxis: 1 mg/kg once daily (maximum: 50 mg daily); Treatment: 2 to 3 mg/kg once daily (maximum: 100 to 150 mg daily)

Adults: Prophylaxis: 50 mg once daily; Treatment: 100 to 150 mg once daily

Mechanism of Action Concentration-dependent inhibition of 1,3-beta-D-glucan synthase resulting in reduced formation of 1,3-beta-D-glucan, an essential polysaccharide comprising 30% to 60% of *Candida* cell walls (absent in mammalian cells); decreased glucan content leads to osmotic instability and cellular lysis

Pharmacodynamics/Kinetics

Half-life Elimination

Preterm infants: PNA <1 week: 6.7 hours (Kawada 2009); PNA >3 weeks: Mean 8.3 hours (range: 5.6 to 11 hours) (Heresi 2006)

Children 4 months to 16 years: ≤30 kg: 12.5 ± 4.6 hours; >30 kg: 13.6 ± 8.8 hours

Healthy Adults: 11 to 21 hours

Adults receiving bone marrow or peripheral stem-cell transplantation: 10.7 to 13.5 hours (Carver 2004)

Pregnancy Risk Factor C

Pregnancy Considerations Adverse events have been observed in animal reproduction studies. There are no adequate and well-controlled studies in pregnant women. Use only if benefit outweighs risk.

Miconazole (Oral) (mi KON a zole)

Related Information

Fungal Infections *on page 1847*

Brand Names: US Oravig

Pharmacologic Category Antifungal Agent, Imidazole Derivative; Antifungal Agent, Oral Nonabsorbed

Use Treatment of oropharyngeal candidiasis

Local Anesthetic/Vasoconstrictor Precautions No information available to require special precautions

Effects on Dental Treatment Key adverse event(s) related to dental treatment: Application site reaction (including burning, discomfort, edema, glossodynia, pain, pruritus, toothache, ulceration), abnormal taste, oral discomfort, xerostomia and changes in salivation (normal salivary flow resumes upon discontinuation)

Effects on Bleeding No information available to require special precautions

Adverse Reactions

>10%: Local: Application site reaction (10% to 12%; including glossalgia, local discomfort, local pain, local pruritus, localized burning, localized edema, oral mucosa ulcer, toothache)

1% to 10%:

Central nervous system: Headache (5% to 8%), fatigue (3%), pain (1%)

Dermatologic: Pruritus (2%)

Endocrine & metabolic: Increased gamma-glutamyl transferase (1%)

Gastrointestinal: Diarrhea (6% to 9%), nausea (1% to 7%), dysgeusia (3% to 4%), vomiting (1% to 4%), oral discomfort (3%), xerostomia (3%), abdominal pain (1% to 3%), ageusia (2%), gastroenteritis (1%), sore throat (1%)

Hematologic & oncologic: Anemia (3%), lymphocytopenia (2%), neutropenia (1%)

Respiratory: Cough (3%), upper respiratory tract infection (2%)

General Dosage Range Buccal: *Children ≥16 years and Adults:* 50 mg (1 tablet) once daily

Mechanism of Action Inhibits biosynthesis of ergosterol, damaging the fungal cell wall membrane, which increases permeability causing leaking of nutrients

Pharmacodynamics/Kinetics

Duration of Action Buccal adhesion: 15 hours

Pregnancy Risk Factor C

Pregnancy Considerations Adverse events were observed in some animal reproduction studies. There is minimal systemic absorption following buccal application.

Miconazole (Topical) (mi KON a zole)

Related Information

Fungal Infections *on page 1847*

Brand Names: US Aloe Vesta Antifungal [OTC]; Aloe Vesta Clear Antifungal [OTC]; Antifungal [OTC]; Azolen Tincture [OTC]; Baza Antifungal [OTC]; Carrington Antifungal [OTC]; Critic-Aid Clear AF [OTC]; Cruex Prescription Strength [OTC]; DermaFungal [OTC]; Desenex Jock Itch [OTC]; Desenex Spray [OTC] [DSC]; Desenex [OTC]; Fungoid Tincture [OTC]; Lotrimin AF Deodorant Powder [OTC]; Lotrimin AF Jock Itch Powder [OTC]; Lotrimin AF Powder [OTC]; Lotrimin AF [OTC]; Micaderm [OTC]; Micatin [OTC]; Miconazole 3; Miconazole 3 Combo Pack [OTC]; Miconazole 7 [OTC]; Micro Guard [OTC]; Miranel AF [OTC]; Mitrazol [OTC] [DSC]; Podactin [OTC]; Remedy Antifungal Clear [OTC]; Remedy Antifungal [OTC]; Remedy Phytoplex Antifungal [OTC]; Secura Antifungal Extra Thick [OTC]; Secura Antifungal [OTC]; Soothe & Cool INZO Antifungal [OTC]; Triple Paste AF [OTC]; Vagistat-3 [OTC]; Zeasorb-AF [OTC]

Brand Names: Canada Dermazole; Micatin; Micozole; Monistat; Monistat 3

Pharmacologic Category Antifungal Agent, Imidazole Derivative; Antifungal Agent, Oral Nonabsorbed/Partially Absorbed; Antifungal Agent, Topical; Antifungal Agent, Vaginal

Use Treatment of vulvovaginal candidiasis and a variety of skin and mucous membrane fungal infections

Local Anesthetic/Vasoconstrictor Precautions No information available to require special precautions

Effects on Dental Treatment No significant effects or complications reported

Effects on Bleeding No information available to require special precautions

Adverse Reactions Frequency not defined.

Topical:

Dermatologic: Allergic contact dermatitis, burning sensation of skin, maceration of skin

Vaginal:

Gastrointestinal: Abdominal cramps

Genitourinary: Vulvovaginal burning, vulvovaginal irritation, vulvovaginal pruritus

General Dosage Range

Intravaginal: *Children ≥12 years and Adults:* Insert 1 applicatorful or suppository (100 mg or 200 mg) once daily at bedtime **or** insert 1 suppository (1200 mg) as a single dose.

Topical: *Children and Adults:* Apply twice daily **or** dissolve 1 effervescent tablet in ~1 gallon of water and soak feet for 15-30 minutes

Mechanism of Action Inhibits biosynthesis of ergosterol, damaging the fungal cell wall membrane, which increases permeability causing leaking of nutrients

Pharmacodynamics/Kinetics

Half-life Elimination Multiphasic degradation: Alpha: 40 minutes; Beta: 126 minutes; Terminal: 24 hours

Pregnancy Considerations Following vaginal administration, small amounts are absorbed systemically (Stevens 2002). Adverse fetal events have not been observed (Czeizel 2004). Vaginal topical azole products (7-day therapies only) are the preferred treatment of vulvovaginal candidiasis in pregnant women. This product may weaken latex condoms and diaphragms (CDC [Workowski 2015]).

Midazolam (MID aye zoe lam)

Brand Names: Canada Midazolam Injection

Generic Availability (US) Yes

Pharmacologic Category Anticonvulsant, Benzodiazepine; Benzodiazepine

Dental Use Sedation component in IV conscious sedation in oral surgery patients; syrup formulation is used for children to help alleviate anxiety before a dental procedure

Use

Anesthesia: IV: Induction of general anesthesia before administration of other anesthetic agents; maintenance of anesthesia as a component of balanced anesthesia.

Sedation/anxiolysis/amnesia (preoperative/procedural):

IM: Preoperative sedation, anxiolysis, and amnesia.

IV: Sedation, anxiolysis, and amnesia prior to or during diagnostic, therapeutic, or endoscopic procedures, or prior to surgery.

Oral: Sedation, anxiolysis, and amnesia in children prior to diagnostic, therapeutic or endoscopic procedures or before induction of anesthesia.

Sedation for mechanically-ventilated patients: IV: Sedation of intubated and mechanically-ventilated patients as a component of anesthesia or during treatment in a critical care setting by continuous IV infusion.

Local Anesthetic/Vasoconstrictor Precautions No information available to require special precautions

Effects on Dental Treatment No significant effects or complications reported (see Dental Comment)

Effects on Bleeding No information available to require special precautions

Adverse Reactions As reported in adults unless otherwise noted.

>10%: Respiratory: Bradypnea, decreased tidal volume

1% to 10%:

Cardiovascular: Hypotension (children: 3%)

Central nervous system: Drowsiness (1%), headache (1%), seizure-like activity (children: 1%), drug dependence (physical and psychological dependence with prolonged use), myoclonus (preterm infants), severe sedation

Gastrointestinal: Hiccups (adults: 4%; children: 1%), nausea (3%), vomiting (3%)

Local: Injection site reaction (IM: ≤4%, IV: ≤5%; severity less than diazepam), pain at injection site (IM: ≤4%, IV: ≤5%; severity less than diazepam)

Ophthalmic: Nystagmus (children: 1%)

Respiratory: Apnea (children: 3%), cough (1%)

Miscellaneous: Paradoxical reaction (children: 2%)

<1%, postmarketing, and/or case reports: Acidic taste, agitation, amnesia, bigeminy, bradycardia, bronchospasm, confusion, delirium (emergence), dyspnea, euphoria, hallucination, hyperventilation, laryngospasm, sialorrhea, skin rash, tachycardia, ventricular premature contractions, wheezing

Dental Usual Dosage Adults:

Preoperative sedation:

IM: 0.07 to 0.08 mg/kg 30 to 60 minutes prior to surgery/procedure; usual dose: 5 mg; **Note:** Reduce dose in patients with COPD, high-risk patients, patients ≥60 years of age, and patients receiving other opioids or CNS depressants

IV: 0.02 to 0.04 mg/kg; repeat every 5 minutes as needed to desired effect or up to 0.1 to 0.2 mg/kg

Intranasal (not an approved route): 0.2 mg/kg (up to 0.4 mg/kg in some studies); administer 30 to 45 minutes prior to surgery/procedure

Conscious sedation: IV: Initial: 0.5 to 2 mg slow IV over at least 2 minutes; slowly titrate to effect by repeating doses every 2 to 3 minutes if needed; usual total dose: 2.5 to 5 mg; use decreased doses in elderly.

Healthy Adults <60 years: Initial: Some patients respond to doses as low as 1 mg; no more than 2.5 mg should be administered over a period of 2 minutes. Additional doses of midazolam may be administered after a 2-minute waiting period and evaluation of sedation after each dose increment. A total dose >5 mg is generally not needed. If opioids or other CNS depressants are administered concomitantly, the midazolam dose should be reduced by 30%.

Dosing

Adult Note: The dose of midazolam needs to be individualized based on the patient's age, underlying diseases, and concurrent medications. Consider reducing dose by 20% to 50% in elderly, chronically ill, or debilitated patients and those receiving opioids or other CNS depressants (Miller 2010).

Anesthesia: IV:

Induction: Adults <55 years:

Unpremedicated patients: Initial: 0.3 to 0.35 mg/kg over 20 to 30 seconds; after 2 minutes, may repeat if necessary at ~25% of initial dose every 2 minutes, up to a total dose of 0.6 mg/kg in resistant cases.

Premedicated patients: Usual dosage range: 0.05 to 0.2 mg/kg (Barash 2009; Miller 2010). Use of 0.2 mg/kg administered over 5 to 10 seconds has been shown to safely produce anesthesia within 30 seconds (Samuelson 1981) and is recommended for ASA physical status P1 and P2 patients. When used with other anesthetic drugs (ie, co-induction), the dose is <0.1 mg/kg (Miller 2010).

ASA physical status >P3 or debilitation: Reduce dose by at least 20% (Miller 2010).

Maintenance: 0.05 mg/kg as needed (Miller 2010), or continuous infusion 0.015 to 0.06 mg/kg/**hour** (0.25 to 1 **mcg**/kg/minute) (Barash 2009; Miller 2010)

Sedation/anxiolysis/amnesia (preoperative/procedural):

Manufacturer's labeling:

Healthy adults <60 years:

IM: 0.07 to 0.08 mg/kg 30 to 60 minutes prior to surgery/procedure; usual dose: 5 mg

IV:

Initial: Some patients respond to doses as low as 1 mg; no more than 2.5 mg should be administered over a period of at least 2 minutes. Additional doses of midazolam may be administered after at least a 2-minute waiting period and evaluation of sedation after each dose increment. A total dose >5 mg is generally not needed.

Premedicated patients: Reduce initial dose by 30%

Maintenance: 25% of dose used to reach sedative effect

Adults ≥60 years, debilitated, or chronically ill: Refer to geriatric dosing.

Alternate recommendations:

Intranasal (off-label route): 0.1 mg/kg; administer 15 minutes prior to surgery/procedure (Uygur-Bayramiçli 2002). **Note:** Use 5 mg/mL injectable solution to deliver dose. Due to the low pH of the solution, burning upon administration is likely to occur (Bailey 2017; Bozkurt 2007).

IV (off-label dosing): Initial: 0.5 to 2 mg over at least 2 minutes; slowly titrate to effect by repeating doses every 2 to 3 minutes if needed; usual total dose: 2.5 to 5 mg (ASGE [Waring 2003])

Sedation in mechanically-ventilated patients: **Note**: Nonbenzodiazepine sedation may be preferred (SCCM [Barr 2013]). IV: Initial: 0.01 to 0.05 mg/kg (~0.5 to 4 mg); may repeat at 10- to 15-minute intervals until adequate sedation achieved; maintenance infusion: 0.02 to 0.1 mg/kg/**hour** (0.3 to 1.7 **mcg**/kg/minute). Titrate to reach desired level of sedation. Titration to maintain a light rather than a deep level of sedation is recommended unless clinically contraindicated (SCCM [Barr 2013]). May consider a trial of daily awakening; if agitated after discontinuation of drip, then restart at 50% of the previous dose (Kress 2000).

Palliative sedation (off-label use): Note: Use of midazolam in this setting should be done in close consult with or by an experienced palliative care provider. Ensure that flumazenil is readily available in the case of inadvertent overdose (ESMO [Cherney 2014]).

IV, SubQ: Continuous infusion: Initial: 0.5 to 1 mg/hour; may increase as needed. Usual dosage range: 1 to 20 mg/hour; may also intermittently administer 1 to 5 mg during infusion as needed (ESMO [Cherney 2014]). Some have recommended an initial bolus dose of 5 to 10 mg (size of dose depending on patient weight, age, and degree of debility) (Johanson 1993).

Status epilepticus (off-label use):

IM: 10 mg once (AES [Glauser 2016]) **or** 0.2 mg/kg once (maximum dose: 10 mg) (NCS [Brophy 2012]). **Note:** Midazolam IM is the preferred treatment in patients *without* IV access. Buccal and intranasal midazolam administration has also been used in patients without IV access, although these off-label routes are less well studied (AES [Glauser 2016]; Bailey 2017; deHaan 2010; NCS [Brophy 2012]; Scheepers 2000).

Prehospital status epilepticus: IM: 10 mg once; has been administered by paramedics when convulsions last >5 minutes **or** if convulsions are occurring after having intermittent seizures without regaining consciousness for >5 minutes (Silbergleit 2012).

Intranasal: Limited data available: 0.2 mg/kg (NCS [Brophy 2012]). **Note:** Use 5 mg/mL injectable concentrated solution to deliver dose. Due to the low pH of the solution, burning upon administration is likely to occur (Bailey 2017; Bozkurt 2007).

Buccal: Limited data available: 0.5 mg/kg (NCS [Brophy 2012])

Status epilepticus, refractory (off-label use): IV: **Note:** Mechanical ventilation and cardiovascular monitoring required; titrate dose to cessation of electrographic seizures or burst suppression (NCS [Brophy 2012]).

Neurocritical Care Society recommendations:

Loading dose: 0.2 mg/kg followed by a continuous infusion (NCS [Brophy 2012]).

Continuous infusion: 0.05 to 2 mg/kg/**hour** (0.83 to 33.2 **mcg**/kg/minute) titrated to cessation of electrographic seizures or burst suppression. If patient experiences breakthrough status epilepticus while on the continuous infusion, administer a bolus of 0.1 to 0.2 mg/kg and increase infusion rate by 0.05 to 0.1 mg/kg/**hour** (0.83 to 1.66 **mcg**/kg/minute) every 3 to 4 hours (NCS [Brophy 2012]). Doses up to 2.9 mg/kg/hour have been described in the literature (Fernandez 2014). **Note:** A period of at least 24 to 48 hours of electrographic control is recommended prior to withdrawing the continuous infusion; withdraw gradually to prevent recurrent status epilepticus.

Geriatric

Oral: Use is not recommended.

Parenteral: The dose of midazolam needs to be individualized based on the patient's age, underlying diseases, and concurrent medications. Consider reducing dose by 20% to 50% in elderly, chronically ill, or debilitated patients and those receiving opioids or other CNS depressants (Miller 2010).

Anesthesia: IV:

Induction: Adults ≥55 years:

Unpremedicated patients: Initial: 0.3 mg/kg

Premedicated patients: Reduce dose by at least 20% (Miller 2010).

Maintenance: Refer to adult dosing.

Sedation/Anxiolysis/Amnesia (preoperative/procedural):

Manufacturer's labeling:

IM: 2 to 3 mg (or 0.02 to 0.05 mg/kg) 30 to 60 minutes prior to surgery/procedure; some may only require 1 mg if anticipated intensity and duration of sedation is less critical.

IV:

Initial: Some patients respond to doses as low as 1 mg; no more than 1.5 mg should be administered over a period of at least 2 minutes. Additional doses of no more than 1 mg over at least 2 minutes may be administered after at least a 2-minute waiting period and evaluation of sedation after each dose increment. A total dose of >3.5 mg is generally not needed.

Premedicated patients: Reduce initial dose by 50%

Maintenance: 25% of dose used to reach sedative effect

Alternate recommendations (off-label dosing): IV: Initial: 0.5 to 2 mg administered over at least 2 minutes (smaller doses may be used in the elderly); slowly titrate to effect by repeating doses every 2 to 3 minutes if needed; usual total dose: 2.5 to 5 mg (ASGE [Waring 2003])

Pediatric Note: The dose of midazolam needs to be individualized based on the patient's age, underlying diseases, and concurrent medications. Decrease dose (by ~30%) if opioids or other CNS depressants are administered concomitantly. Children <6 years may require higher doses and closer monitoring than older children; in children with obesity, calculate dose based on ideal body weight.

Sedation/Anxiolysis/Amnesia (preoperative/procedural): Infants ≥6 months, Children, and Adolescents ≤16 years:

Oral: 0.25 to 0.5 mg/kg (maximum: 20 mg) as a single dose 20 to 30 minutes prior to procedure. Children <6 years or less cooperative patients may require as much as 1 mg/kg as a single dose; 0.25 mg/kg may suffice for children 6 to 16 years of age or for cooperative patients. Doses of 0.5 to 0.75 mg/kg administered 20 to 30 minutes prior to procedure have also been suggested; however, doses above 0.5 mg/kg typically do not improve the sedative and anxiolytic effects but increase side effects during recovery (Bozkurt 2007).

IM: 0.1 to 0.15 mg/kg 30 to 60 minutes before surgery or procedure; range: 0.05 to 0.15 mg/kg; doses up to 0.5 mg/kg have been used in more anxious patients; maximum total dose: 10 mg

Intranasal (off-label route): 0.2 to 0.5 mg/kg (maximum total dose: 10 mg or 5 mg per nare); may be administered 10 to 20 minutes prior to procedure (Bozkurt 2007; Chiaretti 2011). **Note:** Use 5 mg/mL injectable concentrated solution to deliver dose. Due to the low pH of the solution, burning upon administration is likely to occur.

IV:

Infants <6 months: Limited information is available in nonintubated infants; dosing recommendations not clear; infants <6 months are at higher risk for airway obstruction and hypoventilation; titrate dose in small increments to desired effect

Infants 6 months to Children 5 years: Initial: 0.05 to 0.1 mg/kg; total dose of 0.6 mg/kg may be required; maximum total dose: 6 mg

Children 6 to 12 years: Initial: 0.025 to 0.05 mg/kg; total doses of 0.4 mg/kg may be required; maximum total dose: 10 mg

Children 12 to 16 years: Refer to adult dosing; maximum total dose: 10 mg

Rectal (off-label route): 0.5 to 0.75 mg/kg (maximum: 20 mg) as a single dose 20 to 30 minutes prior to procedure (Bozkurt 2007).

Sedation in mechanically-ventilated patients (off-label dosing): Infants, Children, and Adolescents: IV: Loading dose: 0.05 to 0.2 mg/kg, followed by initial continuous infusion: 0.06 to 0.12 mg/kg/**hour** (1 to 2 **mcg**/kg/minute); range in clinical trials: 0.024 to 0.564 mg/kg/**hour** (0.4 to 9.4 **mcg**/kg/minute) (Hartman 2009)

Seizures (off-label use): Children and Adolescents: IM: 0.2 mg/kg (maximum dose: 6 mg); may repeat every 10 to 15 minutes (AAP [Hegenbarth 2008]; Chamberlain 1997)

Status epilepticus (off-label use): Children and Adolescents:

IM (AES [Glauser 2016]; NCS [Brophy 2012]):

<13 kg: Not evaluated

13 to 40 kg: 5 mg once

>40 kg: 10 mg once

Note: Midazolam IM is the preferred treatment in patients *without* IV access. Buccal and intranasal midazolam administration have also been used in patients without IV access, although those off-label routes are less well studied (NCS [Brophy 2012]; AES [Glauser 2016]). For prehospital status epilepticus, midazolam IM has been be administered by paramedics when convulsions last >5 minutes or if convulsions are occurring after having intermittent seizures without regaining consciousness for >5 minutes (Silbergleit 2012).

Intranasal: Limited data available: 0.2 mg/kg (NCS [Brophy 2012]). **Note:** Use 5 mg/mL injectable concentrated solution to deliver dose (Ljungman 2000). Due to the low pH of the solution, burning upon administration is likely to occur (Bozkurt 2007).

Buccal: Limited data available: 0.5 mg/kg (NCS [Brophy 2012])

Status epilepticus, refractory (off-label use): Infants, Children, and Adolescents: IV: **Note:** Mechanical ventilation and cardiovascular monitoring required; titrate dose to cessation of electrographic seizures or burst suppression (NCS [Brophy 2012])

Neurocritical Care Society recommendations (NCS [Brophy 2012]):

Loading dose: 0.2 mg/kg followed by a continuous infusion.

Continuous infusion: 0.05 to 2 mg/kg/**hour** (0.83 to 33.2 **mcg**/kg/minute) titrated to cessation of electrographic seizures or burst suppression. If patient experiences breakthrough status epilepticus while on the continuous infusion, administer a bolus of 0.1 to 0.2 mg/kg and increase infusion rate by 0.05 to 0.1 mg/kg/**hour** (0.83 to 1.66 **mcg**/kg/minute) every 3 to 4 hours. **Note:** A period of at least 24 to 48 hours of electrographic control is recommended prior to withdrawing the continuous infusion; withdraw gradually to prevent recurrent status epilepticus.

American Academy of Pediatrics recommendations (AAP [Hegenbarth 2008]):

Loading dose: 0.15 to 0.2 mg/kg followed by a continuous infusion.

Continuous infusion: 1 mcg/kg/minute titrated every 15 minutes by increments of 1 mcg/kg/minute until the cessation of seizures (maximum: 5 mcg/kg/minute)

Renal Impairment There are no dosage adjustments provided in the manufacturer's labeling; use with caution; half-life of midazolam and metabolites may be prolonged. Patients with renal failure receiving a continuous infusion cannot adequately eliminate the active hydroxylated metabolites (eg, 1-hydroxymidazolam) contributing to prolonged sedation sometimes for days after discontinuation (Spina 2007).

Intermittent hemodialysis: Supplemental dose is not necessary.

Continuous venovenous hemofiltration (CVVH): Unconjugated 1-hydroxymidazolam not effectively removed; 1-hydroxymidazolamglucuronide effectively removed; sieving coefficient = 0.45 (Swart 2005).

Peritoneal dialysis: Significant drug removal is unlikely based on physiochemical characteristics.

Hepatic Impairment

There are no dosage adjustments provided in the manufacturer's labeling; use with caution.

Single dose (eg, induction): No dosage adjustment recommended; patients with hepatic impairment may be more sensitive compared to patients without hepatic impairment; anticipate longer duration of action (MacGilchrist 1986; Trouvin 1988).

Multiple dosing or continuous infusion: Expect longer duration of action and accumulation; based on patient response, dosage reduction likely to be necessary (Trouvin 1988).

Mechanism of Action Binds to stereospecific benzodiazepine receptors on the postsynaptic GABA neuron at several sites within the central nervous system, including the limbic system, reticular formation. Enhancement of the inhibitory effect of GABA on neuronal excitability results by increased neuronal membrane permeability to chloride ions. This shift in chloride ions results in hyperpolarization (a less excitable state) and stabilization. Benzodiazepine receptors and effects appear to be linked to the GABA-A receptors. Benzodiazepines do not bind to GABA-B receptors (Brunton 2011).

Contraindications

Hypersensitivity to midazolam or any component of the formulation; intrathecal or epidural injection of parenteral forms containing preservatives (ie, benzyl alcohol); acute narrow-angle glaucoma.

Concurrent use of oral midazolam with protease inhibitors (amprenavir, atazanavir, atazanavir-cobicistat, darunavir, indinavir, lopinavir-ritonavir, nelfinavir, ritonavir, saquinavir, tipranavir); concurrent use of oral or injectable midazolam with fosamprenavir.

Documentation of allergenic cross-reactivity for benzodiazepines is limited. However, because of similarities in chemical structure and/or pharmacologic actions, the possibility of cross-sensitivity can not be ruled out with certainty.

Warnings/Precautions **[US Boxed Warning]: Has been associated with respiratory depression and respiratory arrest, especially when used for sedation in noncritical care settings; airway obstruction, desaturation, hypoxia, and apnea have also been reported, most often when used concomitantly with other CNS depressants (eg, opioids). In some cases, death or hypoxic encephalopathy resulted. Use only in hospital or ambulatory care settings that provide for continuous monitoring of respiratory and cardiac function (ie, pulse oximetry). Immediate availability of resuscitative drugs and age- and size-appropriate equipment for bag/valve/mask ventilation and intubation, and personnel trained in their use and skilled in airway management should be assured. For deeply sedated patients, a dedicated individual, other than the practitioner performing the procedure, should monitor the patient throughout the procedure.** Risk of cardiorespiratory adverse events is increased in patients with abnormal airway anatomy, cyanotic congenital heart disease, sepsis or severe pulmonary disease. **[US Boxed Warning]: Concomitant use of benzodiazepines and opioids may result in profound sedation, respiratory depression, coma, and death. Reserve concomitant prescribing of these drugs for use in patients for whom alternative treatment options are inadequate. Limit dosages and durations to the minimum required. Follow patients for signs and symptoms of respiratory depression and sedation.**

Benzodiazepines have been associated with anterograde amnesia (Nelson 1999). May cause CNS depression, which may impair physical or mental abilities; patients must be cautioned about performing tasks which require mental alertness (eg, operating machinery or driving). A minimum of 1 day should elapse after midazolam administration before attempting these tasks. Paradoxical reactions, including agitation, hyperactive or aggressive behavior, involuntary movements (including tonic/clonic movements and muscle tremor) and combativeness have been reported with benzodiazepines. Consideration should be given to the possibility of cerebral hypoxia or true paradoxical reactions. Should such reactions occur, the response to each dose of midazolam and all other drugs, including local anesthetics, should be evaluated before proceeding. May consider treatment with flumazenil (Massanari 1997). May cause hypotension; hemodynamic events are more common in pediatric patients or patients with hemodynamic instability. Use with caution in patients with glaucoma, heart failure, obesity, respiratory disease (eg, COPD) or renal impairment. Use benzodiazepines with caution in patients with an impaired gag reflex. Use with caution in debilitated patients; decreased dosages recommended. Use with caution in the elderly; decreased dosages recommended. Use of oral midazolam is not recommended in the elderly. Pediatric patients with cardiac or respiratory compromise may be sensitive to the respiratory depressant effect of midazolam. Pediatric patients undergoing procedures involving the upper airway (eg, upper endoscopy, dental care) are vulnerable to episodes of desaturation and hypoventilation. Use with extreme caution in patients who are at risk of falls; benzodiazepines have been associated with falls and traumatic injury (Nelson 1999).

Does not have analgesic, antidepressant, or antipsychotic properties. Does not protect against increases in intracranial pressure, heart rate, and/or blood pressure during intubation. Do not use in shock, coma, or acute alcohol intoxication with depression of vital signs. Avoid intra-arterial administration or extravasation of parenteral formulation. Use during upper airway procedures (ie, endoscopy, dental care) may increase risk of hypoventilation. Prolonged responses have been noted following extended administration by continuous infusion (possibly due to metabolite accumulation) or in the presence of drugs which inhibit midazolam metabolism. Oral midazolam is intended for use in monitored settings only and not for chronic or home use. Midazolam is a short half-life benzodiazepine and may be of benefit in patients where a rapidly and short-acting agent is desired (acute agitation). Duration of action after a single dose is determined by redistribution rather than metabolism. Tolerance develops to the sedative and anticonvulsant effects. It does not develop to the anxiolytic effects (Vinkers 2012). Withdrawal symptoms (convulsions, hallucinations, tremor, abdominal and muscle cramps, vomiting and sweating) may occur following abrupt discontinuation or large decreases in dose. Use caution when reducing dose or withdrawing therapy; decrease slowly and monitor for withdrawal symptoms. Potentially significant interactions may exist, requiring dose or frequency adjustment, additional monitoring, and/or selection of alternative therapy.

Injection: **[US Boxed Warning]: Do not administer by rapid IV injection in neonates; severe hypotension**

and seizures have been reported following rapid IV administration, particularly with concomitant fentanyl use. Neonates are also vulnerable to profound and/or prolonged respiratory effects of midazolam. **[US Boxed Warning]: The initial IV dose for sedation in adults may be as little as 1 mg, but should not exceed 2.5 mg in a healthy adult. Lower doses are necessary for older (over 60 years) or debilitated patients and in patients receiving concomitant narcotics or other CNS depressants. The initial dose and all subsequent doses should always be titrated slowly; administer over at least 2 minutes and allow an additional 2 or more minutes to fully evaluate the sedative effect. The use of the 1 mg/mL formulation or dilution of the 1 mg/mL or 5 mg/mL formulation is recommended to facilitate slower injection. Doses of sedative medications in pediatric patients must be calculated on a mg/kg basis, and initial doses and all subsequent doses should always be titrated slowly. The initial pediatric dose of midazolam for sedation/anxiolysis/amnesia is age, procedure, and route dependent.** Use IV midazolam with caution in patients with uncompensated acute illnesses, such as severe fluid or electrolyte disturbances. Avoid rapid IV administration in pediatric patients with cardiovascular instability.

Some dosage forms may contain benzyl alcohol; large amounts of benzyl alcohol (≥99 mg/kg/day) have been associated with a potentially fatal toxicity ("gasping syndrome") in neonates; the "gasping syndrome" consists of metabolic acidosis, respiratory distress, gasping respirations, CNS dysfunction (including convulsions, intracranial hemorrhage), hypotension, and cardiovascular collapse (AAP ["Inactive" 1997]; CDC 1982); some data suggests that benzoate displaces bilirubin from protein binding sites (Ahlfors 2001); avoid or use dosage forms containing benzyl alcohol with caution in neonates. See manufacturer's labeling.

Drug Interactions

Metabolism/Transport Effects **Substrate** of CYP2B6 (minor), CYP3A4 (major); **Note:** Assignment of Major/Minor substrate status based on clinically relevant drug interaction potential; **Inhibits** CYP2C8 (weak), CYP2C9 (weak)

Avoid Concomitant Use

Avoid concomitant use of Midazolam with any of the following: Amodiaquine; Antihepaciviral Combination Products; Azelastine (Nasal); Boceprevir; Cobicistat; Conivaptan; Fusidic Acid (Systemic); Idelalisib; Itraconazole; Ketoconazole (Systemic); Methadone; OLANZapine; Orphenadrine; Oxomemazine; Paraldehyde; Protease Inhibitors; Sodium Oxybate; Telaprevir; Thalidomide

Increased Effect/Toxicity

Midazolam may increase the levels/effects of: Alcohol (Ethyl); Amodiaquine; Analgesics (Opioid); Azelastine (Nasal); Blonanserin; Buprenorphine; CloZAPine; CNS Depressants; Flunitrazepam; HYDROcodone; Methadone; Methotrimeprazine; MetyroSINE; Mirtazapine; Orphenadrine; OxyCODONE; Paraldehyde; Piribedil; Pramipexole; Propofol; ROPINIRole; Rotigotine; Selective Serotonin Reuptake Inhibitors; Sodium Oxybate; Suvorexant; Thalidomide; Zolpidem

The levels/effects of Midazolam may be increased by: Antihepaciviral Combination Products; Aprepitant; AtorvaSTATin; Boceprevir; Brimonidine (Topical); Cannabis; Chlormethiazole; Chlorphenesin Carbamate; Cobicistat; Conivaptan; CYP3A4 Inhibitors (Moderate); CYP3A4 Inhibitors (Strong); Dasatinib; Dimethindene (Topical); Doxylamine; Dronabinol; Droperidol; Fosaprepitant; Fusidic Acid (Systemic); HydrOXYzine; Idelalisib; Itraconazole; Ivacaftor; Kava Kava; Ketoconazole (Systemic); Lofexidine; Macrolide Antibiotics; Magnesium Sulfate; Methotrimeprazine; MiFEPRIStone; Minocycline; Nabilone; Netupitant; OLANZapine; Oxomemazine; Palbociclib; Perampanel; Propofol; Protease Inhibitors; Roxithromycin; Rufinamide; Simeprevir; Stiripentol; Tapentadol; Teduglutide; Telaprevir; Tetrahydrocannabinol; Tofisopam; Trimeprazine

Decreased Effect

The levels/effects of Midazolam may be decreased by: Bosentan; CYP3A4 Inducers (Moderate); CYP3A4 Inducers (Strong); Dabrafenib; Deferasirox; Enzalutamide; Ginkgo Biloba; Mitotane; Siltuximab; St John's Wort; Theophylline Derivatives; Tocilizumab; Yohimbine

Food Interactions Grapefruit juice may increase serum concentrations of midazolam. Management: Avoid concurrent use of grapefruit juice with oral midazolam.

Dietary Considerations Avoid grapefruit juice with oral syrup.

Pharmacodynamics/Kinetics

Onset of Action

IM: Sedation: Children: Within 5 minutes; Adults: ~15 minutes; IV: 3 to 5 minutes; Oral: 10 to 20 minutes; Intranasal: Children: 5.55 ± 2.22 minutes (Lee-Kim 2004); Adults: Within 5 minutes

Peak effect: IM: Children: 15 to 30 minutes; Adults: 30 to 60 minutes; IV: 3 to 5 minutes; Intranasal: Children: 10 minutes (al-Rakaf 2001)

Duration of Action IM: Up to 6 hours; Mean: 2 hours; Intranasal: Children: 23.1 minutes (Chiaretti 2011); IV: Single dose: <2 hours (dose-dependent) (Fragen 1997)

Half-life Elimination

Prolonged in cirrhosis, congestive heart failure, obesity, renal failure, and elderly. **Note:** In patients with renal failure, reduced elimination of active hydroxylated metabolites leads to drug accumulation and prolonged sedation.

Preterm infants (n=24; GA: 26 to 34 weeks; PNA: 3 to 11 days): Median: 6.3 hours (range: 2.6 to 17.7 hours) (de Wildt 2001)

Neonates: 4 to 12 hours; seriously ill neonates: 6.5 to 12 hours

Children: IV: 2.9 to 4.5 hours; Syrup: 2.2 to 6.8 hours

Adults: 3 hours (range: 1.8 to 6.8 hours)

Time to Peak IM: 0.5 to 1 hour; Oral: 0.17 to 2.65 hours

Pregnancy Risk Factor D

Pregnancy Considerations Adverse events have not been observed in animal reproduction studies. Midazolam has been found to cross the human placenta and can be detected in the serum of the umbilical vein and artery, as well as the amniotic fluid. Teratogenic effects have been observed with some benzodiazepines; however, additional studies are needed. The incidence of premature birth and low birth weights may be increased following maternal use of benzodiazepines; hypoglycemia and respiratory problems in the neonate may occur following exposure late in pregnancy. Neonatal withdrawal symptoms may occur within days to weeks after birth and "floppy infant syndrome" (which also includes withdrawal symptoms) have been reported with some benzodiazepines (Bergman 1992; Iqbal 2002; Wikner 2007).

Breastfeeding Considerations Midazolam and hydroxymidazolam can be detected in breast milk. Based on information from two women, 2 to 3 months postpartum, the half-life of midazolam in breast milk is ~1 hour. Milk concentrations were below the limit of detection (<5 nmol/L) 4 hours after a single maternal dose of midazolam 15 mg. Drowsiness, lethargy, or weight loss in nursing infants have been observed in case reports following maternal use of some benzodiazepines (Iqbal 2002; Matheson 1990). The manufacturer recommends that caution be exercised when administering midazolam to nursing women.

Controlled Substance C-IV

Dosage Forms

Solution, Injection:

Generic: 2 mg/2 mL (2 mL); 5 mg/5 mL (5 mL); 10 mg/10 mL (10 mL); 5 mg/mL (1 mL); 10 mg/2 mL (2 mL); 25 mg/5 mL (5 mL); 50 mg/10 mL (10 mL)

Solution, Injection [preservative free]:

Generic: 2 mg/2 mL (2 mL); 5 mg/5 mL (5 mL); 5 mg/mL (1 mL); 10 mg/2 mL (2 mL)

Syrup, Oral:

Generic: 2 mg/mL (118 mL)

Dental Comment An adult companion should accompany the patient to and from dental office.

Compared to oral sedation, intranasal (IN) sedation resulted in greater irritability during the first 10-15 minutes after administration, but a faster onset and shorter duration of sedation with improved behavior following onset of sedation. (Johnson 2010; Lee-Kim 2004). Monitor oxygen saturation with midazolam. If desaturation occurs, reposition airway (head tilt, chin lift).

Midodrine (MI doe dreen)

Brand Names: Canada Amatine; Apo-Midodrine

Pharmacologic Category $Alpha_1$ Agonist

Use Orthostatic hypotension: Treatment of symptomatic orthostatic hypotension

Local Anesthetic/Vasoconstrictor Precautions No information available to require special precautions

Effects on Dental Treatment Key adverse event(s) related to dental treatment: Xerostomia (normal salivary flow resumes upon discontinuation).

Effects on Bleeding No information available to require special precautions

Adverse Reactions

>10%:

Cardiovascular: Supine hypertension (7% to 13%)

Central nervous system: Paresthesia (18%)

Dermatologic: Piloerection (13%), pruritus (12%)

Genitourinary: Dysuria (≤13%), urinary retention, urinary urgency

Renal: Polyuria

1% to 10%:

Central nervous system: Chills (5%), pain (5%)

Dermatologic: Skin rash (2%)

Gastrointestinal: Abdominal pain

<1%, postmarketing, and/or case reports: Anxiety, aphthous stomatitis, back pain, confusion, dizziness, drowsiness, erythema multiforme, facial flushing, flatulence, flushing, gastrointestinal distress, headache, heartburn, hyperesthesia, increased intracranial pressure, insomnia, leg cramps, nausea, visual field defect, weakness, xeroderma, xerostomia

General Dosage Range Dosage adjustment recommended in patients with renal impairment

Oral: *Adults:* 10 mg 3 times daily

Mechanism of Action Midodrine forms an active metabolite, desglymidodrine, which is an $alpha_1$-agonist. This agent increases arteriolar and venous tone resulting in a rise in standing, sitting, and supine systolic and diastolic blood pressure in patients with orthostatic hypotension.

Pharmacodynamics/Kinetics

Onset of Action ~1 hour

Duration of Action 2 to 3 hours

Half-life Elimination Desglymidodrine: ~3 to 4 hours; Midodrine: 25 minutes

Time to Peak Desglymidodrine: 1 to 2 hours; Midodrine: 30 minutes

Pregnancy Risk Factor C

Pregnancy Considerations Adverse events were observed in animal reproduction studies. Information related to the use of midodrine in pregnancy is limited (Glatter, 2005).

MiFEPRIStone (mi FE pris tone)

Related Information

Clinical Risk Related to Drugs Prolonging QT Interval *on page 1772*

Brand Names: US Korlym; Mifeprex

Pharmacologic Category Abortifacient; Antineoplastic Agent, Hormone Antagonist; Antiprogestin; Cortisol Receptor Blocker

Use

Korlym: To control hyperglycemia occurring secondary to hypercortisolism in patients with endogenous Cushing's syndrome who have type 2 diabetes mellitus or glucose intolerance and who failed surgery or who are not surgical candidates

Mifeprex: Medical termination of intrauterine pregnancy through 70 days gestation, in combination with misoprostol.

Local Anesthetic/Vasoconstrictor Precautions Mifepristone is one of the drugs confirmed to prolong the QT interval and is accepted as having a risk of causing torsade de pointes. The risk of drug-induced torsade de pointes is extremely low when a single QT interval prolonging drug is prescribed. In terms of epinephrine, it is not known what effect vasoconstrictors in the local anesthetic regimen will have in patients with a known history of congenital prolonged QT interval or in patients taking any medication that prolongs the QT interval. Until more information is obtained, it is suggested that the clinician consult with the physician prior to the use of a vasoconstrictor in suspected patients, and that the vasoconstrictor (epinephrine, mepivacaine and levonordefrin [Carbocaine® 2% with Neo-Cobefrin®]) be used with caution.

Effects on Dental Treatment No significant effects or complications reported

Effects on Bleeding No information available to require special precautions

Adverse Reactions

Adverse reactions occur with treatment of hyperglycemia in patients with Cushing syndrome unless otherwise specified.

>10%:

Cardiovascular: Peripheral edema (26%), hypertension (24%)

Central nervous system: Fatigue (hyperglycemia: 48%; pregnancy termination: 10%), headache (hyperglycemia: 44%; pregnancy termination: 2% to 31%), dizziness (hyperglycemia: 22%; pregnancy termination: 1% to 12%), pain (14%)

Endocrine & metabolic: Hypokalemia (34% to 44%), abnormal thyroid function test (18%)

Gastrointestinal: Abdominal cramps (pregnancy termination: 96%), nausea (pregnancy termination: 43% to 61%; hyperglycemia: 48%), vomiting (hyperglycemia and pregnancy termination: 18% to 26%), decreased appetite (20%), diarrhea (hyperglycemia and pregnancy termination: 12% to 20%), xerostomia (18%)

Genitourinary: Uterine cramps (pregnancy termination: 83%), endometrium disease (hypertrophy: 38%), vaginal hemorrhage (14%; when used for pregnancy termination, vaginal bleeding for 9 to 16 days is expected, with the first 2 days being the heaviest; 8% of these patients experience bleeding for ≥30 days)

Neuromuscular & skeletal: Arthralgia (30%), back pain (hyperglycemia and pregnancy termination: 9% to 16%), myalgia (14%), limb pain (12%)

Respiratory: Dyspnea (16%), sinusitis (hyperglycemia: 14%; pregnancy termination: 2%), nasopharyngitis (12%)

1% to 10%:

Cardiovascular: Edema (5% to 10%), pitting edema (5% to 10%), syncope (pregnancy termination: 1% to 2%)

Central nervous system: Anxiety (hyperglycemia: 10%; pregnancy termination: 2%), drowsiness (10%), flank pain (5% to 10%), malaise (5% to 10%), insomnia (pregnancy termination: 3%), rigors (pregnancy termination: 3%)

Dermatologic: Pruritus (4%), skin rash (4%)

Endocrine & metabolic: Hypoglycemia (5% to 10%), increased serum triglycerides (5% to 10%), increased thirst (5% to 10%), adrenocortical insufficiency (4%)

Gastrointestinal: Anorexia (10%), constipation (10%), abdominal pain (5% to 10%), gastroesophageal reflux disease (5% to 10%), dyspepsia (pregnancy termination: 3%)

Genitourinary: Uterine hemorrhage (pregnancy termination: 5%), vaginitis (pregnancy termination: 3%), leukorrhea (pregnancy termination: 2%), pelvic pain (pregnancy termination: 2%), endometriosis (pregnancy termination: ≤1%), salpingitis (pregnancy termination: ≤1%), pelvic inflammatory disease (pregnancy termination: ≤1%)

Hematologic & oncologic: Decreased hemoglobin (pregnancy termination: 6%; >2 g/dL), anemia (pregnancy termination: 2%)

Infection: Viral infection (pregnancy termination: 4%)

Neuromuscular & skeletal: Musculoskeletal chest pain (5% to 10%), weakness (pregnancy termination: 2%), leg pain (pregnancy termination: 2%)

Miscellaneous: Fever (pregnancy termination: 4%)

Frequency not defined: Endocrine & metabolic: Decreased HDL cholesterol

<1%, postmarketing, and/or case reports: Acute pancreatitis, adult respiratory distress syndrome, bacterial infection (including an ectopic bacteria such as *Clostridium sordellii*), disseminated intravascular coagulopathy, dyspnea, ectopic pregnancy (rupture), exacerbation of Crohn's disease, hypersensitivity reaction (including urticaria), hypotension, infection (post-abortion), loss of consciousness, myocardial infarction, pelvic infection, prolonged Q-T interval on ECG, sepsis, septic shock, sickle cell disease (sickle cell crisis; Gary 2006), tachycardia, toxic shock syndrome

General Dosage Range Dosage adjustment recommended in patients with hepatic or renal impairment or on concomitant therapy when treating hyperglycemia in patients with Cushing syndrome.

Oral: *Adults:* Hyperglycemia in patients with Cushing syndrome: 300 to 1,200 mg once daily (maximum: 1,200 mg once daily, not to exceed 20 mg/kg/day); Termination of pregnancy: Day 1: 200 mg as a single dose

Mechanism of Action Mifepristone is a synthetic steroid. At low doses, it competitively binds to the intracellular progesterone receptor, blocking the effects of progesterone. When used for the termination of pregnancy, this leads to contraction-inducing activity in the myometrium. In the absence of progesterone, mifepristone acts as a partial progesterone agonist. At high doses used for the treatment of hyperglycemia in patients with Cushing's syndrome, mifepristone blocks the effect of cortisol at the glucocorticoid receptor (antagonizes the effects of cortisol on glucose metabolism) while at the same time increasing circulating cortisol concentrations.

Pharmacodynamics/Kinetics

Half-life Elimination Single dose: Terminal: 18 hours following a slower phase where 50% eliminated between 12-72 hours; Multiple doses (600 mg/day): 85 hours

Time to Peak Oral: 90 minutes; Range: Single dose: 1-2 hours, Multiple doses: 1-4 hours

Pregnancy Risk Factor X (Cushing syndrome)

Pregnancy Considerations Mifepristone is contraindicated for use in pregnant women when used to control hyperglycemia in Cushing syndrome.

Korlym: **[US Boxed Warning]: Use of mifepristone will result in termination of pregnancy.** When used to control hyperglycemia in women with Cushing's syndrome, **pregnancy must be excluded prior to initiation of therapy. Nonhormonal contraception must be used during treatment and for 1 month after discontinuation of therapy unless the patient has had surgical sterilization. Pregnancy must be excluded if treatment is interrupted for ≥14 days.**

Mifeprex: This medication is used to terminate pregnancy; there are no approved treatment indications for its use during pregnancy. If treatment fails, there is a risk of fetal malformation. In sexually active women, pregnancy can occur prior to the first menstrual period following treatment. Appropriate contraception can be started as soon as termination of pregnancy is confirmed or before sexual intercourse is resumed.

Prescribing and Access Restrictions

Korlym is only available through a restricted access program. For prescriber registration and patient enrollment forms, please refer to http://www.korlym.com/hcp/how-to-prescribe-korlym.php or call 1-855-4Korlym (1-855-456-7596).

Mifeprex: As a requirement of the REMS program, prescriber's must be certified with the program by completing the prescriber agreement form. A medication guide and a copy of the patient agreement form, which must be signed by the patient and prescriber, must be given to the patient prior to receiving the medication. A signed copy of the patient agreement should be kept in the patient's medical record.

Mifeprex is only available direct from Danco Laboratories' distributor and is dispensed to patients only in clinics, medical offices, and hospitals by or under the supervision of a certified prescriber. To obtain the product, please refer to http://www.earlyoptionpill.com or call 1-877-432-7596.

Investigators wishing to obtain the agent for use in oncology patients must apply for a patient-specific IND from the FDA.

Dental Comment See Local Anesthetic/Vasoconstrictor Precautions

Miglitol (MIG li tol)

Related Information

Endocrine Disorders and Pregnancy *on page 1781*

Brand Names: US Glyset

Pharmacologic Category Antidiabetic Agent, Alpha-Glucosidase Inhibitor

Use Type 2 diabetes mellitus (noninsulin-dependent, NIDDM):

Monotherapy as an adjunct to diet to improve glycemic control in patients with type 2 diabetes mellitus (noninsulin-dependent, NIDDM) whose hyperglycemia cannot be managed with diet alone

Combination therapy with a sulfonylurea when diet plus either miglitol or a sulfonylurea alone do not result in adequate glycemic control. The effect of miglitol to enhance glycemic control is additive to that of sulfonylureas when used in combination.

Local Anesthetic/Vasoconstrictor Precautions No information available to require special precautions

Effects on Dental Treatment No significant effects or complications reported

Effects on Bleeding No information available to require special precautions

Adverse Reactions

>10%: Gastrointestinal: Flatulence (42%), diarrhea (29%), abdominal pain (12%)

1% to 10%: Dermatologic: Skin rash (4%)

<1%, postmarketing, and/or case reports: Abdominal distention, gastrointestinal pain, intestinal obstruction, nausea, paralytic ileus, pneumatosis cystoides intestinalis

General Dosage Range Oral: *Adults:* Initial: 25 mg 3 times daily; Maintenance: 25-100 mg 3 times daily (maximum: 300 mg daily)

Mechanism of Action In contrast to sulfonylureas, miglitol does not enhance insulin secretion; the antihyperglycemic action of miglitol results from a reversible inhibition of membrane-bound intestinal alpha-glucosidases which hydrolyze oligosaccharides and disaccharides to glucose and other monosaccharides in the brush border of the small intestine. In patients with diabetes, this enzyme inhibition results in delayed glucose absorption and lowering of postprandial hyperglycemia.

Pharmacodynamics/Kinetics

Half-life Elimination ~2 hours

Time to Peak 2-3 hours

Pregnancy Risk Factor B

Pregnancy Considerations Adverse events have not been reported in animal reproduction studies.

In women with diabetes, maternal hyperglycemia can be associated with congenital malformations as well as adverse effects in the fetus, neonate, and the mother (ACOG 2005; ADA 2016c; Kitzmiller 2008; Metzger 2007). To prevent adverse outcomes, prior to conception and throughout pregnancy maternal blood glucose and HbA_{1c} should be kept as close to target goals as possible but without causing significant hypoglycemia (ACOG 2013; ADA 2016c; Blumer 2013; Kitzmiller 2008).

Agents other than miglitol are not currently recommended for use in pregnant women for the management of gestational diabetes mellitus (GDM) or type 2 diabetes mellitus (ACOG 2013; Blumer 2013).

Miglustat (MIG loo stat)

Brand Names: US Zavesca

Brand Names: Canada Zavesca

Pharmacologic Category Enzyme Inhibitor; Glucosylceramide Synthase Inhibitor

Use Gaucher disease: Treatment of adult patients with mild-to-moderate type 1 Gaucher disease for whom enzyme replacement therapy is not a therapeutic option (eg, due to allergy, hypersensitivity, or poor venous access)

Local Anesthetic/Vasoconstrictor Precautions No information available to require special precautions

Effects on Dental Treatment No significant effects or complications reported

Effects on Bleeding No information available to require special precautions

Adverse Reactions Percentages reported from open-label, uncontrolled monotherapy trials.

>10%:

Central nervous system: Headache (21% to 22%), dizziness (≤11%)

Endocrine & metabolic: Weight loss (39% to 67%)

Gastrointestinal: Diarrhea (89% to 100%), abdominal pain (18% to 67%), flatulence (29% to 50%), nausea (8% to 22%), vomiting (4% to 11%)

Neuromuscular & skeletal: Tremor (11% to 30%), weakness (17%), leg cramps (4% to 11%)

Ophthalmic: Visual disturbance (≤17%)

1% to 10%:

Central nervous system: Memory impairment (8%), unsteady gait (8%), paresthesia (≤7%), migraine (≤6%)

Endocrine & metabolic: Menstrual disease (≤6%)

Gastrointestinal: Abdominal distension (8%), constipation (8%), xerostomia (8%), anorexia (≤7%), dyspepsia (≤7%), bloating (≤6%), epigastric pain (≤6%)

Hematologic & oncologic: Thrombocytopenia (6% to 7%)

Neuromuscular & skeletal: Back pain (8%)

General Dosage Range Dosage adjustment recommended in patients with renal impairment and in patients who develop toxicities

Oral: *Adults:* 100 mg 1 to 3 times daily

Mechanism of Action Miglustat competitively and reversibly inhibits the enzyme needed to produce glycosphingolipids and decreases the rate of glycosphingolipid glucosylceramide formation. Glucosylceramide accumulates in type 1 Gaucher disease, causing complications specific to this disease.

Pharmacodynamics/Kinetics

Half-life Elimination 6-7 hours

Time to Peak Plasma: 2-2.5 hours

Pregnancy Risk Factor C

Pregnancy Considerations Adverse events were observed in animal reproduction studies. In addition, adverse effects on spermatogenesis and reduced fertility were observed in male animal studies; however, no effect on sperm was observed in healthy male patients. Uncontrolled type 1 Gaucher disease is associated an increased risk of spontaneous abortion; maternal hepatosplenomegaly and thrombocytopenia may also occur and lead to adverse pregnancy outcomes.

Milnacipran (mil NAY ci pran)

Related Information

Vasoconstrictor Interactions With Antidepressants *on page 1913*

Brand Names: US Savella; Savella Titration Pack

Pharmacologic Category Antidepressant, Serotonin/Norepinephrine Reuptake Inhibitor

Use Management of fibromyalgia

Local Anesthetic/Vasoconstrictor Precautions Although milnacipran is not a tricyclic antidepressant, it blocks norepinephrine reuptake within the CNS synapses as part of the mechanism of action. It has been suggested that vasoconstrictors be administered with caution and vial signs monitored in dental patients taking antidepressants that affect norepinephrine in this way.

Effects on Dental Treatment Key adverse event(s) related to dental treatment: Xerostomia and changes in salivation (normal salivary flow resumes upon discontinuation) and taste perversion.

Effects on Bleeding Serotonin/norepinephrine reuptake inhibitors (SNRIs) may impair platelet aggregation resulting in increased risk of bleeding events, particularly if used concomitantly with aspirin or NSAIDs.

Adverse Reactions

>10%:

Central nervous system: Headache (18%), insomnia (12%)

Endocrine & metabolic: Hot flash (12%)

Gastrointestinal: Nausea (37%), constipation (16%)

1% to 10%:

Cardiovascular: Palpitations (7%), increased heart rate (6%), hypertension (5%), flushing (3%), increased blood pressure (3%), tachycardia (2%), peripheral edema (≥1%)

Central nervous system: Dizziness (10%), migraine (5%), chills (2%), depression (≥1%), drowsiness (≥1%), falling (≥1%), fatigue (≥1%), irritability (≥1%)

Dermatologic: Hyperhidrosis (9%), skin rash (3%), night sweats (≥1%)

Endocrine & metabolic: Decreased libido (≥2%), hypercholesterolemia (≥1%), weight changes (≥1%)

Gastrointestinal: Vomiting (7%), xerostomia (5%), abdominal pain (3%), decreased appetite (2%), abdominal distension (≥1%), diarrhea (≥1%), dysgeusia (≥1%), dyspepsia (≥1%), flatulence (≥1%), gastroesophageal reflux disease (≥1%)

Genitourinary: Decreased urine output (≥2%), dysuria (≥2%), ejaculation failure (≥2%), ejaculatory disorder (≥2%), erectile dysfunction (≥2%), prostatitis (≥2%), scrotal pain (≥2%), testicular pain (≥2%), testicular swelling (≥2%), urethral pain (≥2%), urinary hesitancy (≥2%), urinary retention (≥2%), cystitis (≥1%), urinary tract infection (≥1%)

Neuromuscular & skeletal: Tremor (2%)

Ophthalmic: Blurred vision (2%)

Respiratory: Dyspnea (2%)

Miscellaneous: Fever (≥1%)

<1%, postmarketing, and/or case reports: Accommodation disturbance, acute pancreatitis, acute renal failure, aggressive behavior, angle-closure glaucoma, anorexia, delirium, erythema multiforme, galactorrhea, hallucination, hepatitis, homicidal ideation, hyperprolactinemia, hypertensive crisis, hyponatremia, leukopenia, loss of consciousness, neuroleptic malignant syndrome (Stevens 2008), neutropenia, outbursts of anger, parkinsonian-like syndrome, Raynaud's phenomenon (Khouri 2016; Peiró 2007), rhabdomyolysis, seizure, serotonin syndrome, Stevens-Johnson syndrome, supraventricular tachycardia, thrombocytopenia

General Dosage Range Dosage adjustment recommended in patients with renal impairment

Oral: *Adults:* 50 mg twice daily

Mechanism of Action Potent inhibitor of norepinephrine and serotonin reuptake (3:1). Milnacipran has no significant activity for serotonergic, alpha- and beta-adrenergic, muscarinic, histaminergic, dopaminergic, opiate, benzodiazepine, and GABA receptors. It does not possess MAO-inhibitory activity.

Pharmacodynamics/Kinetics

Half-life Elimination 6-8 hours

Time to Peak Plasma: Oral: 2-4 hours

Pregnancy Risk Factor C

Pregnancy Considerations Adverse events were observed in some animal reproduction studies. Nonteratogenic effects in the newborn following SSRI/SNRI exposure late in the third trimester include respiratory distress, cyanosis, apnea, seizures, temperature instability, feeding difficulty, vomiting, hypoglycemia, hyper- or hypotonia, hyper-reflexia, jitteriness, irritability, constant crying, and tremor. Symptoms may be due to the toxicity of the SNRIs/SSRIs or a discontinuation syndrome and may be consistent with serotonin syndrome associated with SSRI treatment. The long-term effects of *in utero* SNRI/SSRI exposure on infant development and behavior are not known.

Women inadvertently exposed to milnacipran during pregnancy may be enrolled in the Savella Pregnancy Registry (877-643-3010 or http://www.savellapregnancyregistry.com).

Milrinone (MIL ri none)

Brand Names: Canada Milrinone Lactate Injection

Pharmacologic Category Inotrope; Phosphodiesterase-3 Enzyme Inhibitor

Use Inotropic support in heart failure: Short-term IV therapy of acutely-decompensated heart failure

American College of Cardiology/American Heart Association heart failure (HF) guideline recommendations (ACCF/AHA [Yancy 2013]): To maintain systemic perfusion and preserve end-organ performance in patients with cardiogenic shock; bridge therapy in stage D HF unresponsive to guideline-directed medical therapy and device therapy in patients awaiting heart transplant or mechanical circulatory support; short-term management of hospitalized patients with severe systolic dysfunction presenting with low blood pressure and significantly depressed cardiac output; long-term management (palliative therapy) in select patients with stage D HF unresponsive to guideline-directed medical therapy and device therapy who are not candidates for heart transplant or mechanical circulatory support.

Local Anesthetic/Vasoconstrictor Precautions No information available to require special precautions

Effects on Dental Treatment No significant effects or complications reported

Effects on Bleeding No information available to require special precautions

Adverse Reactions
>10%: Cardiovascular: Ventricular arrhythmia (ventricular ectopy: 9%, nonsustained ventricular tachycardia: 3%, ventricular tachycardia: 1%, ventricular fibrillation: <1%)
1% to 10%:
Cardiovascular: Supraventricular cardiac arrhythmia (4%), hypotension (3%), angina pectoris (≤1%), chest pain (≤1%)
Central nervous system: Headache (3%)
<1%, postmarketing, and/or case reports: Anaphylaxis, atrial fibrillation, bronchospasm, hepatic insufficiency, hypokalemia, injection site reaction, myocardial infarction, skin rash, thrombocytopenia, torsades de pointes, tremor

General Dosage Range Dosage adjustment recommended in patients with renal impairment
IV: *Adults:* Loading dose (optional): 50 mcg/kg; Maintenance: 0.125 to 0.75 mcg/kg/minute

Mechanism of Action A selective phosphodiesterase inhibitor in cardiac and vascular tissue, resulting in vasodilation and inotropic effects with little chronotropic activity.

Pharmacodynamics/Kinetics
Onset of Action IV: 5 to 15 minutes
Half-life Elimination
Infants (after cardiac surgery): 3.15 ± 2 hours (Ramamoorthy 1998)
Children (after cardiac surgery): 1.86 ± 2 hours (Ramamoorthy 1998)
Adults:
Heart failure: 2.3 to 2.4 hours; renal impairment prolongs half-life (Rocci 1987)
Severe heart failure undergoing continuous venovenous hemofiltration (CVVH): 20.1 ± 3.3 hours (Taniguchi 2000)

Pregnancy Risk Factor C

Pregnancy Considerations Adverse events have not been observed in animal reproduction studies; however, increased resorption was reported in some studies.

Minocycline (mi noe SYE kleen)

Related Information
Periodontal Diseases *on page 1844*

Related Sample Prescriptions
Bacterial Infections and Periodontal Diseases - Sample Prescriptions *on page 32*

Brand Names: US Dynacin [DSC]; Minocin; Solodyn

Brand Names: Canada Apo-Minocycline; Dom-Minocycline; Mylan-Minocycline; PHL-Minocycline; PMS-Minocycline; Sandoz-Minocycline; Teva-Minocycline

Generic Availability (US) May be product dependent

Pharmacologic Category Antibiotic, Tetracycline Derivative

Use
Acute intestinal amebiasis: Adjunctive therapy to amebicides in the treatment of acute intestinal amebiasis
Acne:
Oral (immediate release) and IV: Adjunctive therapy for the treatment of severe acne
Oral (extended-release): Treatment of only inflammatory lesions of non-nodular moderate to severe acne vulgaris in patients 12 years and older
Actinomycosis: Treatment of actinomycosis caused by *Actinomyces israelii* when penicillin is contraindicated
Anthrax: Treatment of anthrax caused by *Bacillus anthracis* when penicillin is contraindicated
Asymptomatic carriers of *Neisseria meningitidis:* *Oral (immediate-release):* To eliminate the meningococci from the nasopharynx of asymptomatic carriers of *N. meningitidis*
Campylobacter: Treatment of infections caused by *Campylobacter fetus*
Cholera: Treatment of cholera caused by *Vibrio cholerae*
Clostridium: Treatment of infections caused by *Clostridium* spp when penicillin is contraindicated
Gram-negative infections: Treatment of infections caused by susceptible *Acinetobacter* spp, *Escherichia coli*, *Enterobacter aerogenes*, *Shigella* spp
Listeriosis: Treatment of listeriosis due to *Listeria monocytogenes* when penicillin is contraindicated
Meningitis: Treatment of meningitis due to *Neisseria meningitidis*
Ophthalmic infections: Treatment of inclusion conjunctivitis or trachoma caused by *Chlamydia trachomatis*
Relapsing fever: Treatment of relapsing fever caused by *Borrelia recurrentis*
Respiratory tract infections: Treatment of respiratory tract infections caused by *Haemophilus influenzae*, *Klebsiella* spp, or *Mycoplasma pneumonia*. For the treatment of upper respiratory tract infections caused by *Streptococcus pneumoniae*.
Rickettsial infections: Treatment of Rocky Mountain spotted fever, typhus fever and the typhus group, Q fever, rickettsialpox, and tick fevers caused by *Rickettsiae*
Sexually transmitted infections: Treatment of lymphogranuloma venereum caused by *C. trachomatis*; nongonococcal urethritis, endocervical, or rectal infections in adults caused by *Ureaplasma urealyticum* or *C. trachomatis*; donovanosis (granuloma inguinale) caused by *Klebsiella granulomatis*; syphilis caused by *Treponema pallidum* subspecies *pallidum*, when penicillin is contraindicated
Skin and skin structure infections: Treatment of skin and skin structure infections caused by *Staphylococcus aureus*
Limitations of use: Not considered a first line agent for any staphylococcal infection
Urinary tract infections: Treatment of urinary tract infections caused by *Klebsiella* species
Vincent infection: Treatment of Vincent infection caused by *Fusobacterium fusiforme* when penicillin is contraindicated
Yaws: Treatment of yaws caused by *T. pallidum* subspecies pertenue when penicillin is contraindicated
Zoonotic infections: Treatment of psittacosis (ornithosis) due to *Chlamydia psittaci*; plague due to *Yersinia pestis*; tularemia due to *Francisella tularensis*; brucellosis due to *Brucella* spp (in conjunction with streptomycin); bartonellosis due to *Bartonella bacilliformis*

Local Anesthetic/Vasoconstrictor Precautions No information available to require special precautions

Effects on Dental Treatment Key adverse event(s) related to dental treatment: Discoloration of teeth (children). Opportunistic "superinfection" with *Candida albicans*; tetracyclines are not recommended for use during pregnancy or in children ≤8 years of age since they have been reported to cause enamel hypoplasia and permanent teeth discoloration. The use of tetracycline's should only be used in these patients if other agents are contraindicated or alternative antimicrobials will not ▶

eradicate the organism. Long-term use associated with oral candidiasis.

Effects on Bleeding No information available to require special precautions

Adverse Reactions

1% to 10%:

Central nervous system: Dizziness (9%), fatigue (9%), malaise (4%), drowsiness (2%)

Dermatologic: Pruritus (5%), urticaria (2%)

Neuromuscular & skeletal: Arthralgia (1%)

Otic: Tinnitus (2%)

Postmarketing and/or case reports: Acute renal failure (reversible), anaphylaxis, angioedema, autoimmune hepatitis, balanitis, bulging fontanel, *Clostridium difficile* associated diarrhea, DRESS syndrome, dysphagia, enterocolitis, eosinophilia, erythema multiforme, exacerbation of systemic lupus erythematosus, exfoliative dermatitis, fixed drug eruption, glossitis, hearing loss, hemolytic anemia, hepatic failure, hepatitis, hepatotoxicity (idiosyncratic) (Chalasani 2014), hypersensitivity, IgA vasculitis, lupus-like syndrome, malignant neoplasm of thyroid, microscopic thyroid discoloration (brown-black), mucous membrane pigmentation, myocarditis, pancreatitis, pericarditis, pneumonitis, polyarthralgia, pseudomembranous colitis, pseudotumor cerebri, pulmonary infiltrates (with eosinophilia), serum sickness, skin photosensitivity, skin pigmentation, Stevens-Johnson syndrome, thrombocytopenia, thyroid dysfunction, tooth discoloration, vasculitis

Dosing

Adult & Geriatric

Usual dosage range:

IV: Initial: 200 mg for 1 dose; Maintenance: 100 mg every 12 hours (maximum: 400 mg daily)

Oral: Initial: 200 mg for 1 dose; Maintenance: 100 mg every 12 hours; more frequent dosing intervals may be used (100 to 200 mg initially, followed by 50 mg 4 times daily)

Acne: Oral: Capsule or immediate-release tablet: 50 to 100 mg twice daily. **Note:** The shortest possible duration should be used to minimize development of bacterial resistance; re-evaluate at 3 at 4 months (AAD [Zaenglein 2016])

Acne (inflammatory, non-nodular, moderate to severe): Note: Therapy should be continued for 12 weeks. Safety of use beyond 12 weeks has not been established.

Extended-release capsule (Ximino): Oral: 1 mg/kg (rounded to the nearest capsule) once daily

Extended-release tablet (Solodyn): Oral:

45 to 49 kg: 45 mg once daily
50 to 59 kg: 55 mg once daily
60 to 71 kg: 65 mg once daily
72 to 84 kg: 80 mg once daily
85 to 96 kg: 90 mg once daily
97 to 110 kg: 105 mg once daily
111 to 125 kg: 115 mg once daily
126 to 136 kg: 135 mg once daily

Cellulitis (purulent) due to community-acquired MRSA (off-label use): Oral: Initial: 200 mg; Maintenance: 100 mg twice daily for 5-10 days (Liu 2011)

Chlamydial or *Ureaplasma urealyticum* infection, uncomplicated: Oral, IV: Urethral, endocervical, or rectal: 100 mg every 12 hours for at least 7 days

Gonococcal infection, uncomplicated (males): Oral, IV:

Without urethritis or anorectal infection: Initial: 200 mg for 1 dose; Maintenance: 100 mg every 12 hours for at least 4 days (cultures 2 to 3 days post-therapy)

Urethritis: 100 mg every 12 hours for 5 days

Meningococcal carrier state (manufacturer's labeling): Oral: 100 mg every 12 hours for 5 days. **Note:** CDC recommendations do not mention use of minocycline for eradicating nasopharyngeal carriage of meningococcal

Mycobacterium marinum: Oral: 100 mg every 12 hours for 6 to 8 weeks

Nocardiosis (off-label use): Oral: 100 to 200 mg every 12 hours, with or without other concomitant antimicrobials (Lerner 1996). Additional data may be necessary to further define the role of minocycline in this condition.

Prosthetic joint infection:

Staphylococci (oxacillin-sensitive or –resistant) oral phase treatment (after completion of pathogen-specific IV therapy) following 1-stage exchange:

Total ankle, elbow, hip, or shoulder arthroplasty: 100 mg twice daily for 3 months; **Note:** Must be used in combination with rifampin (Osmon 2013)

Total knee arthroplasty: 100 mg twice daily for 6 months; **Note:** Must be used in combination with rifampin (Osmon 2013)

Chronic oral antimicrobial suppression (off-label use): Oral:

Propionibacterium spp (alternative to penicillin or amoxicillin): 100 mg twice daily (Osmon 2013)

Staphylococci (oxacillin-resistant): 100 mg twice daily (Osmon 2013)

Rheumatoid arthritis (off-label use): Oral: 100 mg twice daily (Kloppenburg 1994; O'Dell 1997; O'Dell 2001; Stone 2003; Tilley 1995)

Syphilis: Oral, IV: Initial: 200 mg for 1 dose; Maintenance: 100 mg every 12 hours for 10 to 15 days

Pediatric

Usual dosage range: Children >8 years and Adolescents: Oral, IV: Initial: 4 mg/kg/dose for 1 dose; Maintenance: 2 mg/kg/dose every 12 hours (maximum: 400 mg daily)

Acne (inflammatory, non-nodular, moderate to severe): Children ≥12 years and Adolescents: Oral: Refer to adult dosing.

Cellulitis (purulent) due to community-acquired MRSA (off-label use): Oral: Children >8 years: Initial: 4 mg/kg (maximum: 200 mg); Maintenance: 2 mg/kg/dose (maximum: 100 mg) every 12 hours for 5 to 10 days (Liu 2011)

Renal Impairment Use with caution. Consider decreasing dose or increasing dosing interval (extended release).

CrCl ≥80 mL/minute: No dosage adjustment necessary

CrCl <80 mL/minute: Do not exceed 200 mg daily

Hepatic Impairment There are no dosage adjustments provided in the manufacturer's labeling; however, hepatotoxicity has been reported. Use with caution.

Mechanism of Action Inhibits bacterial protein synthesis by binding with the 30S and possibly the 50S ribosomal subunit(s) of susceptible bacteria; cell wall synthesis is not affected.

Contraindications

Hypersensitivity to minocycline, other tetracyclines, or any component of the formulation

Documentation of allergenic cross-reactivity for tetracyclines is limited. However, because of similarities in chemical structure and/or pharmacologic actions, the possibility of cross-sensitivity cannot be ruled out with certainty.

Warnings/Precautions Anaphylaxis has been reported; discontinue drug immediately and institute supportive measures. May be associated with increases in BUN secondary to antianabolic effects; use caution in patients with renal impairment as this may lead to azotemia, hyperphosphatemia, acidosis, and possibly to drug accumulation and potential hepatotoxicity. Serious liver injury, including irreversible drug induced hepatitis and fulminant hepatic failure (sometimes fatal) have been reported with use for acne treatment; use caution in patients with hepatic insufficiency or in conjunction with other hepatotoxic drugs. Autoimmune syndromes (including serum sickness [eg, fever, arthralgia and malaise]) have been reported; discontinue if symptoms occur and assess liver function tests, ANA, and CBC. CNS effects (lightheadedness, dizziness, vertigo) may occur; patients must be cautioned about performing tasks which require mental alertness (eg, operating machinery or driving); symptoms usually disappear with continued therapy and when the drug is discontinued. Benign intracranial hypertension (pseudotumor cerebri [PTC]) (including headache, blurred vision, diplopia, vision loss, and/or papilledema) has been associated with use. Women of childbearing age who are overweight or have a history of intracranial hypertension are at greater risk. Concomitant use of isotretinoin (known to cause PTC) and minocycline should be avoided. Benign intracranial hypertension typically resolves after discontinuation of treatment; however, permanent visual loss is possible. If visual symptoms develop during treatment, prompt ophthalmologic evaluation is warranted. Intracranial pressure can remain elevated for weeks after drug discontinuation; monitor patients until they stabilize.

May cause photosensitivity; discontinue if skin erythema occurs. Use skin protection and avoid prolonged exposure to sunlight; avoid use of use tanning equipment or UVA/B treatment. Hyperpigmentation may occur in nails, bone, skin (including scar and injury sites), eyes, sclerae, thyroid, oral cavity, visceral tissue, and heart valves; skin and oral hyperpigmentation are independent of dose or administration duration. Prolonged use may result in fungal or bacterial superinfection, including *C. difficile*-associated diarrhea (CDAD) and pseudomembranous colitis; CDAD has been observed >2 months postantibiotic treatment. May cause tooth enamel hypoplasia, or permanent tooth discoloration; more common with long-term use, but observed with repeated, short courses; use of tetracyclines should be avoided during tooth development (infancy and children <8 years of age) unless other drugs are not likely to be effective or are contraindicated. Do not use during pregnancy. In addition to affecting tooth development, tetracycline use has been associated with retardation of skeletal development and reduced bone growth. Erythema multiforme, Stevens Johnson syndrome, or rash, along with eosinophilia, fever, and organ failure (Drug Rash with Eosinophilia and Systemic Symptoms [DRESS] syndrome) has been reported; discontinue treatment immediately if DRESS syndrome is suspected. Parenteral (IV) formulation contains magnesium; monitor serum magnesium in patients with renal impairment and signs of magnesium intoxication (eg, flushing, sweating, hypotension, depressed reflexes, flaccid paralysis, hypothermia, circulatory collapse, cardiac and CNS depression leading to respiratory paralysis). Also use with caution and closely monitor patients with heart block or myocardial damage. Potentially significant drug-drug interactions may exist, requiring dose or frequency adjustment, additional monitoring, and/or selection of alternative therapy.

Appropriate use: Acne: The American Academy of Dermatology acne guidelines recommends minocycline be used as adjunctive treatment for moderate and severe acne and forms of inflammatory acne that are resistant to topical treatments. Concomitant topical therapy with benzoyl peroxide or a retinoid is recommended should be administered with systemic antibiotic therapy (eg, minocycline) and continued for maintenance after the antibiotic course is completed (AAD [Zaenglein 2016]).

Drug Interactions

Metabolism/Transport Effects None known.

Avoid Concomitant Use

Avoid concomitant use of Minocycline with any of the following: BCG (Intravesical); Cholera Vaccine; Mecamylamine; Methoxyflurane; Retinoic Acid Derivatives; Strontium Ranelate

Increased Effect/Toxicity

Minocycline may increase the levels/effects of: Aminolevulinic Acid; CNS Depressants; Mecamylamine; Methoxyflurane; Mipomersen; Neuromuscular-Blocking Agents; Porfimer; Retinoic Acid Derivatives; Verteporfin; Vitamin K Antagonists

Decreased Effect

Minocycline may decrease the levels/effects of: Atazanavir; BCG (Intravesical); BCG Vaccine (Immunization); Cholera Vaccine; Iron Salts; Lactobacillus and Estriol; Penicillins; Sodium Picosulfate; Typhoid Vaccine

The levels/effects of Minocycline may be decreased by: Antacids; Bile Acid Sequestrants; Bismuth Subcitrate; Bismuth Subsalicylate; Calcium Salts; Iron Salts; Lanthanum; Magnesium Salts; Multivitamins/Minerals (with ADEK, Folate, Iron); Multivitamins/Minerals (with AE, No Iron); Quinapril; Strontium Ranelate; Sucralfate; Sucroferric Oxyhydroxide; Zinc Salts

Food Interactions Minocycline serum concentrations are not significantly altered if taken with food or dairy products. Management: Administer without regard to food.

Pharmacodynamics/Kinetics

Half-life Elimination IV: 15 to 23 hours; 11 to 16 hours (hepatic impairment); 18 to 69 hours (renal impairment); Oral: 16 hours (range: 11 to 17 hours)

Time to Peak Capsule, pellet filled: 1 to 4 hours; Tablet: 1 to 3 hours; Extended release tablet: 3.5 to 4 hours

Pregnancy Risk Factor D

Pregnancy Considerations Minocycline crosses the placenta. Tetracycline-class antibiotics may cause fetal harm following maternal use in pregnancy. Rare spontaneous reports of congenital anomalies, including limb reduction, have been reported following maternal minocycline use. Due to limited information, a causal association cannot be established. Tetracyclines accumulate in developing teeth and long tubular bones (Mylonas 2011). Permanent discoloration of teeth (yellow, gray, brown) can occur following in utero exposure and is more likely to occur following long-term or repeated exposure.

As a class, tetracyclines are generally considered second-line antibiotics in pregnant women and their use should be avoided (Mylonas 2011). Minocycline is not recommended for the treatment of Rocky Mountain Spotted Fever (Biggs 2016), Q fever (Anderson 2013), or anthrax infection (Meaney-Delman 2014) in pregnant women. When systemic antibiotics are needed for dermatologic conditions in pregnant women, other agents are preferred (Kong 2013; Murase 2014).

Breastfeeding Considerations Minocycline is excreted in breast milk (Brogden 1975).

According to the manufacturer, the decision to continue or discontinue breastfeeding during therapy should take into account the risk of exposure to the infant and the benefits of treatment to the mother. Oral absorption is not affected by dairy products; therefore, oral absorption of minocycline by the breastfeeding infant would not be expected to be diminished by the calcium in the maternal milk. There have been case reports of black discoloration of breast milk in women taking minocycline (Basler 1985; Hunt 1996).

As a class, tetracyclines have generally been avoided in nursing women due to theoretical concerns that they may permanently stain the teeth of the breastfeeding infant (Chung 2002). Some sources note that breastfeeding can continue during tetracycline therapy (Chung 2002; WHO 2002) but recommend use of alternative medications when possible (WHO 2002). Other sources note that short-term exposure may be acceptable; however, long-term use of tetracyclines (eg, for the treatment of acne) should be avoided in breastfeeding women (Pugashetti 2013). In general, antibiotics that are present in breast milk may cause nondose-related modification of bowel flora. Monitor infants for GI disturbances (Chung 2002; WHO 2002).

Product Availability Ximino: FDA approved August 2015; availability anticipated in fourth quarter of 2015. Ximino is indicated to treat inflammatory lesions of nonnodular moderate to severe acne vulgaris in patients 12 years of age and older. Consult prescribing information for additional information.

Dosage Forms Considerations

Minocin Kit contains minocycline oral capsules packaged with T3 Calming Wipes

Minocin for injection contains magnesium 2.2 mEq per vial

Dosage Forms

Capsule, Oral:

Minocin: 50 mg, 75 mg, 100 mg

Generic: 50 mg, 75 mg, 100 mg

Solution Reconstituted, Intravenous:

Minocin: 100 mg (1 ea)

Tablet, Oral:

Generic: 50 mg, 75 mg, 100 mg

Tablet Extended Release 24 Hour, Oral:

Solodyn: 55 mg, 65 mg, 80 mg, 105 mg, 115 mg

Generic: 45 mg, 90 mg, 135 mg

Minoxidil (Systemic) (mi NOKS i dil)

Related Information

Cardiovascular Diseases *on page 1752*

Brand Names: Canada Loniten

Pharmacologic Category Antihypertensive; Vasodilator, Direct-Acting

Use

Hypertension: Treatment of hypertension that is symptomatic or associated with target organ damage, and is not manageable with maximum therapeutic doses of a diuretic plus 2 other antihypertensives. Use in milder degrees of hypertension is not recommended because the benefit-risk ratio in such patients has not been defined.

Note: According to the Eighth Joint National Committee (JNC 8) guidelines, minoxidil is **not** recommended for the initial treatment of hypertension (James, 2013).

Local Anesthetic/Vasoconstrictor Precautions No information available to require special precautions

Effects on Dental Treatment No significant effects or complications reported

Effects on Bleeding No information available to require special precautions

Adverse Reactions Frequency not always defined.

Cardiovascular: ECG changes (T-wave changes 60%), edema (reversible, 7% to 10%), pericardial effusion (occasionally with tamponade, 3%), angina pectoris, cardiac failure, pericarditis, tachycardia

Dermatologic: Hypertrichosis (80%), bullous rash (rare), skin rash, Stevens-Johnson syndrome (rare), toxic epidermal necrolysis

Endocrine & metabolic: Sodium retention, water retention, weight gain

Gastrointestinal: Nausea, vomiting

Hematologic & oncologic: Decreased hematocrit (transient, hemodilution), decreased red blood cells (transient, hemodilution), hemoglobin (transient, hemodilution), leukopenia (rare), thrombocytopenia (rare)

Hepatic: Ascites, increased serum alkaline phosphatase

Renal: Increased blood urea nitrogen (transient), increased serum creatinine (transient)

Respiratory: Pulmonary edema (Lee 2011)

<1%, postmarketing, and/or case reports: Breast tenderness (rare)

General Dosage Range Oral:

Children <12 years: Initial: 0.2 mg/kg once daily (maximum daily initial dose: 5 mg daily); Usual dosage: 0.25 to 1 mg/kg/day in 1 to 3 divided doses (maximum daily dose: 50 mg daily)

Children ≥12 years, Adolescents, and Adults: Initial: 5 mg once daily; Usual dosage range: 2.5 to 40 mg daily in 1 to 2 divided doses (maximum: 100 mg daily)

Elderly: Initial: 2.5 mg once daily

Mechanism of Action Produces vasodilation by directly relaxing arteriolar smooth muscle, with little effect on veins; effects may be mediated by cyclic AMP; stimulation of hair growth is secondary to vasodilation, increased cutaneous blood flow and stimulation of resting hair follicles

Pharmacodynamics/Kinetics

Onset of Action Hypotensive: ~30 minutes; Peak effect: 2 to 3 hours

Duration of Action Up to 2 to 5 days

Half-life Elimination 3.5 to 4.2 hours

Pregnancy Risk Factor C

Pregnancy Considerations Adverse events were observed in some animal studies. Neonatal hypertrichosis has been reported following exposure to minoxidil during pregnancy.

Mipomersen (mi poe MER sen)

Brand Names: US Kynamro

Pharmacologic Category Antihyperlipidemic Agent, Apolipoprotein B Antisense Oligonucleotide

Use Homozygous familial hypercholesterolemia: Adjunct to dietary therapy and other lipid-lowering treatments to reduce low-density lipoprotein cholesterol

(LDL-C), total cholesterol (TC), apolipoprotein B (apo B), and non-high-density lipoprotein cholesterol (non-HDL-C) in patients with homozygous familial hypercholesterolemia (HoFH)

Local Anesthetic/Vasoconstrictor Precautions No information available to require special precautions

Effects on Dental Treatment No significant effects or complications reported

Effects on Bleeding No information available to require special precautions

Adverse Reactions

>10%:

Central nervous system: Fatigue (15%), headache (12%)

Dermatologic: Skin discoloration at injection site (17%)

Gastrointestinal: Nausea (14%)

Hepatic: Increased serum ALT (≥3 x ULN to <5 x ULN: 12%; ≥5 x ULN to <10 x ULN: 3%; ≥10 x ULN: 1%)

Immunologic: Antibody development (38%)

Local: Injection site reaction (84%), erythema at injection site (59%), pain at injection site (56%), hematoma at injection site (32%), itching at injection site (29%), swelling at injection site (18%)

Respiratory: Flu-like symptoms (13% to 30%)

1% to 10%:

Cardiovascular: Hypertension (7%), peripheral edema (5%), angina pectoris (4%), palpitations (3%)

Central nervous system: Chills (6%), insomnia (3%)

Gastrointestinal: Vomiting (4%), abdominal pain (3%)

Genitourinary: Proteinuria (9%)

Hematologic & oncologic: Neoplasms (4%, benign and malignant)

Hepatic: Increased serum AST (≥3 x ULN to <5 x ULN: 7%; ≥5 x ULN to <10 x ULN: 3%), liver steatosis (7%), abnormal hepatic function tests (5%), increased liver enzymes (3%)

Hypersensitivity: Recall skin sensitization (8%, including local erythema, tenderness, and/or pruritus at previous injection sites)

Neuromuscular & skeletal: Limb pain (7%), musculoskeletal pain (4%)

Miscellaneous: Fever (8%)

<1%, postmarketing, and/or case reports: Angioedema, hypersensitivity reaction, immune thrombocytopenia, skin rash, urticaria

General Dosage Range

Dosage adjustment recommended in patients who develop toxicities.

SubQ: *Adults:* 200 mg once weekly

Mechanism of Action Mipomersen is an oligonucleotide inhibitor of apo B-100 synthesis. ApoB is the main component of LDL-C and very low density lipoprotein (VLDL), which is the precursor to LDL-C. Mipomersen binds to the messenger ribonucleic acid (mRNA) of apoB in a sequence-specific manner which results in degradation (RNase H-mediated) or disruption of the mRNA thereby reducing formation of apoB.

Pharmacodynamics/Kinetics

Half-life Elimination ~1 to 2 months

Time to Peak ~3 to 4 hours

Pregnancy Risk Factor B

Pregnancy Considerations Adverse events have not been observed in animal reproduction studies. Females of reproductive potential should use effective contraception during therapy.

Prescribing and Access Restrictions As a requirement of the REMS program, access to this medication is restricted. Prescribers must enroll in the Kynamro REMS program and complete the prescriber training and complete, sign, and submit the Prescriber Enrollment Form to the Kynamro REMS program. The prescriber must then complete the Prescriber Training before activation within the Kynamro REMS program. Pharmacies must educate all pharmacy staff involved in the dispensing of Kynamro on the REMS program requirements, put processes in place to verify (prior to dispensing Kynamro) that the prescriber is certified and the Prescription Authorization Form is received with each new prescription. Pharmacies must also agree to be audited to ensure that all processes and procedures in place are being followed in accordance with the program and be able to provide prescription data to the REMS program.

Mirabegron (mir a BEG ron)

Brand Names: US Myrbetriq

Brand Names: Canada Myrbetriq

Pharmacologic Category $Beta_3$ Agonist

Use Overactive bladder: Treatment of overactive bladder (OAB) with symptoms of urinary frequency, urgency, or urge urinary incontinence

Local Anesthetic/Vasoconstrictor Precautions No information available to require special precautions

Effects on Dental Treatment Key adverse event(s) related to dental treatment: Xerostomia (normal salivary flow resumes upon discontinuation)

Effects on Bleeding No information available to require special precautions

Adverse Reactions

>10%: Cardiovascular: Hypertension (9% to 11%)

1% to 10%:

Cardiovascular: Tachycardia (2%)

Central nervous system: Headache (4%), dizziness (3%)

Gastrointestinal: Constipation (2% to 3%), xerostomia (3%), diarrhea (2%), abdominal pain (1%)

Genitourinary: Urinary tract infection (3% to 6%), cystitis (2%)

Infection: Influenza (3%)

Neuromuscular & skeletal: Back pain (3%), arthralgia (2%)

Respiratory: Nasopharyngitis (4%), sinusitis (3%)

<1%, postmarketing, and/or case reports: Abdominal distension, angioedema (angioedema of the face, angioedema of the lips, angioedema of the throat, angioedema of the tongue with or without respiratory symptoms), atrial fibrillation, bladder pain, blurred vision, breast cancer, cerebrovascular accident, dry eye syndrome, dyspepsia, gastritis, elevated gamma-glutamyl transferase, glaucoma, increased lactate dehydrogenase, increased serum ALT, increased serum AST, leukocytoclastic vasculitis, lip edema, malignant neoplasm of lung, malignant neoplasm of prostate, nausea, nephrolithiasis, osteoarthritis, palpitations, pruritus, purpura, rhinitis, skin rash, Stevens-Johnson syndrome, urinary retention, urticaria, vaginal infection, vulvovaginal pruritus

General Dosage Range Dosage adjustment recommended in patients with renal and hepatic impairment

Oral: *Adults:* Initial: 25 mg once daily; Maintenance: 25 to 50 mg once daily

Mechanism of Action Mirabegron, a beta-3 adrenergic receptor agonist, activates beta-3 adrenergic receptors in the bladder resulting in relaxation of the detrusor smooth muscle during the urine storage phase, thus increasing bladder capacity. At usual doses, mirabegron is believed to display selectivity for the beta-3 adrenergic receptor subtype compared to its affinity for the beta-1 and -2 adrenoceptor subtypes. Data have shown that beta-adrenoceptors, predominately the beta-3 subtype, mediate detrusor smooth muscle tone and promote the storage function of the human bladder.

Pharmacodynamics/Kinetics

Onset of Action Efficacy is seen within 8 weeks; steady state achieved within 7 days

Half-life Elimination ~50 hours

Time to Peak ~3.5 hours

Pregnancy Risk Factor C

Pregnancy Considerations Adverse effects have been observed in some animal reproduction studies.

Mirtazapine (mir TAZ a peen)

Related Information

Vasoconstrictor Interactions With Antidepressants *on page 1913*

Brand Names: US Remeron; Remeron SolTab

Brand Names: Canada Apo-Mirtazapine; Auro-Mirtazapine; Auro-Mirtazapine OD; Ava-Mirtazapine; Dom-Mirtazapine; GD-Mirtazapine OD; Jamp-Mirtazapine; Mylan-Mirtazapine; PMS-Mirtazapine; PRO-Mirtazapine; ratio-Mirtazapine; Remeron; Remeron RD; Riva-Mirtazapine; Sandoz-Mirtazapine; Teva-Mirtazapine; Teva-Mirtazapine OD; ZYM-Mirtazapine

Pharmacologic Category Antidepressant, Alpha-2 Antagonist

Use Major depressive disorder: Treatment of major depressive disorder (MDD)

Local Anesthetic/Vasoconstrictor Precautions Although mirtazapine is not a tricyclic antidepressant, it results in increased norepinephrine release as part of its mechanisms. It has been suggested that vasoconstrictor be administered with caution and to monitor vital signs in dental patients taking antidepressants that affect norepinephrine in this way, including mirtazapine.

Effects on Dental Treatment Key adverse event(s) related to dental treatment: Significant xerostomia (normal salivary flow resumes upon discontinuation).

Effects on Bleeding No information available to require special precautions

Adverse Reactions Frequency not always defined.

>10%:

Central nervous system: Drowsiness (54%)

Endocrine & metabolic: Weight gain (12%; weight gain of >7% reported in 8% of adults, 49% of pediatric patients), increased serum cholesterol (15%)

Gastrointestinal: Xerostomia (25%), increased appetite (17%), constipation (13%)

1% to 10%:

Cardiovascular: Peripheral edema (2%), edema (1%), hypertension, vasodilatation

Central nervous system: Dizziness (7%), abnormal dreams (4%), abnormality in thinking (3%), confusion (2%), agitation, amnesia, anxiety, apathy, depression, hypoesthesia, malaise, myasthenia, paresthesia, twitching, vertigo

Dermatologic: Pruritus, skin rash

Endocrine & metabolic: Increased serum triglycerides (6%), increased thirst

Gastrointestinal: Abdominal pain, anorexia, vomiting

Genitourinary: Urinary frequency (2%), urinary tract infection

Hepatic: Increased serum ALT (≥3 times ULN: 2%)

Neuromuscular & skeletal: Weakness (8%), back pain (2%), myalgia (2%), tremor (2%), arthralgia, hyperkinesia, hypokinesia

Respiratory: Flu-like symptoms (5%), dyspnea (1%), increased cough, sinusitis

<1%, postmarketing, and/or case reports: Abnormal accommodation, abnormal healing, abnormal hepatic function tests, abnormal lacrimation, acne vulgaris, ageusia, akathisia, alopecia, altered sense of smell, amenorrhea, anemia, angina pectoris, angle-closure glaucoma, aphasia, aphthous stomatitis, arthritis, asphyxia, asthma, ataxia, atrial arrhythmia, bigeminy, blepharitis, bone fracture, bone marrow depression (granulocytopenia, agranulocytopenia, aplastic anemia), bradycardia, breast engorgement, breast hypertrophy, bronchitis, bullous dermatitis, bursitis, cardiac arrest, cardiomegaly, cellulitis, cerebral ischemia, chest pain, chills, cholecystitis, colitis, conjunctivitis, cystitis, deafness, dehydration, delirium, delusions, dementia, depersonalization, dermal ulcer, diabetes mellitus, diarrhea, diplopia, drug dependence, dysarthria, dyskinesia, dysmenorrhea, dystonia, dysuria, ejaculatory disorder, emotional lability, enlargement of abdomen, enlargement of salivary glands, eosinophilia, epistaxis, eructation, erythema multiforme, euphoria, exfoliative dermatitis, extrapyramidal reaction, eye pain, facial edema, fatigue, fever, gastritis, gastroenteritis, gingival hemorrhage, glaucoma, glossitis, goiter, gout, hallucination, headache, hematuria, hepatic cirrhosis, herpes simplex infection, herpes zoster, hiccups, hostility, hyperacusis, hyperreflexia, hypoesthesia (oral), hyponatremia, hypotension, hypothyroidism, hypotonia, impotence, increased acid phosphatase, increased creatine phosphokinase, increased libido, increased serum AST, insomnia, intestinal obstruction, keratoconjunctivitis, laryngitis, left heart failure, lethargy, leukopenia, leukorrhea, lymphadenopathy, lymphocytosis, manic reaction, mastalgia, menorrhagia, migraine, mouth edema, myocardial infarction, myoclonus, myositis, nausea, neck pain, neck stiffness, nephrolithiasis, nightmares, nystagmus, oral candidiasis, orthostatic hypotension, ostealgia, osteoarthritis, osteoporosis, otalgia, otitis media, pancreatitis, pancytopenia, paralysis, paranoia, petechia, phlebitis, pneumonia, pneumothorax, polyuria, prolonged Q-T interval on ECG, psychomotor agitation, psychoneurosis, psychotic depression, pulmonary embolism, restless leg syndrome, rhabdomyolysis, rupture of tendon, seborrhea, sedation, seizure, serotonin syndrome, sialorrhea, skin hypertrophy, skin photosensitivity, Stevens-Johnson syndrome, stomatitis, stupor, suicidal behavior, suicidal ideation, syncope, tenosynovitis, thrombocytopenia, tongue discoloration, tongue edema, tonic-clonic seizures, torsades de pointes (rare), toxic epidermal necrolysis, ulcer, urethritis, urinary incontinence, urinary retention, urinary urgency, urticaria, uterine hemorrhage, vaginitis, vascular headache, ventricular fibrillation, ventricular premature contractions, ventricular tachycardia, weight loss, withdrawal syndrome, xeroderma

General Dosage Range Oral: *Adults:* Initial: 15 mg nightly; Maintenance: 15 to 45 mg nightly; Maximum: 45 mg/day

Mechanism of Action Mirtazapine is a tetracyclic antidepressant that works by its central presynaptic alpha$_2$-adrenergic antagonist effects, which results in increased release of norepinephrine and serotonin. It is also a potent antagonist of 5-HT$_2$ and 5-HT$_3$ serotonin receptors and H$_1$ histamine receptors and a moderate peripheral alpha$_1$-adrenergic and muscarinic antagonist; it does not inhibit the reuptake of norepinephrine or serotonin.

Pharmacodynamics/Kinetics

Half-life Elimination 20 to 40 hours; increased with renal or hepatic impairment

Time to Peak Serum: ~2 hours

Pregnancy Risk Factor C

Pregnancy Considerations Adverse events were observed in some animal reproduction studies. A significant increase in major teratogenic effects has not been observed in humans following exposure to mirtazapine during pregnancy; however, some nonteratogenic adverse events (similar to those observed with SSRI agents) have been reported (Djulus 2006; Einarson 2009; Lennestål, 2007). Mirtazapine was found to cross the placenta following a maternal overdose (Hatzidaki 2008).

The ACOG recommends that therapy with antidepressants during pregnancy be individualized; treatment of depression during pregnancy should incorporate the clinical expertise of the mental health clinician, obstetrician, primary health care provider, and pediatrician. According to the American Psychiatric Association (APA), the risks of medication treatment should be weighed against other treatment options and untreated depression. Consideration should be given to using agents with safety data in pregnancy. For women who discontinue antidepressant medications during pregnancy and who may be at high risk for postpartum depression, the medications can be restarted following delivery. Treatment algorithms have been developed by the ACOG and the APA for the management of depression in women prior to conception and during pregnancy (ACOG 2008; APA 2010; Yonkers 2009).

Pregnant women exposed to antidepressants during pregnancy are encouraged to enroll in the National Pregnancy Registry for Antidepressants (NPRAD). Women 18 to 45 years of age or their health care providers may contact the registry by calling 844-405-6185. Enrollment should be done as early in pregnancy as possible.

MiSOPROStol (mye soe PROST ole)

Brand Names: US Cytotec

Brand Names: Canada Novo-Misoprostol; PMS-Misoprostol

Pharmacologic Category Prostaglandin

Use

NSAID-induced gastric ulcers, prevention: To reduce the risk of of NSAID-induced gastric ulcers in patients at high risk of complications

Termination of intrauterine pregnancy: Medical termination of intrauterine pregnancy through 70 days' gestation in combination with mifepristone (Mifeprex prescribing information March 2016)

Local Anesthetic/Vasoconstrictor Precautions No information available to require special precautions

Effects on Dental Treatment No significant effects or complications reported

Effects on Bleeding No information available to require special precautions

Adverse Reactions

>10%: Gastrointestinal: Diarrhea, abdominal pain

1% to 10%:

Central nervous system: Headache

Gastrointestinal: Constipation, dyspepsia, flatulence, nausea, vomiting

<1%, postmarketing, and/or case reports: Abnormal hepatobiliary function, alopecia, anaphylaxis, anemia, anxiety, arterial thrombosis, arthralgia, back pain, bronchitis, bronchospasm, cardiac arrhythmia, cerebrovascular accident, change in appetite, chest pain, chills, confusion, conjunctivitis, deafness, depression, dermatitis, diaphoresis, dizziness, drowsiness, dysgeusia, dysphagia, dyspnea, dysuria, edema, epistaxis, fatigue, fever, gastroesophageal reflux disease, gastrointestinal hemorrhage, GI inflammation, gingivitis, glycosuria, gout, gynecological disease (cramps, dysmenorrhea, hypermenorrhea, spotting, postmenopausal vaginal bleeding, and other menstrual disorders), hematuria, hypertension, hypotension, impotence, increased amylase, increased blood urea nitrogen, increased cardiac enzymes, increased erythrocyte sedimentation rate, increased serum alkaline phosphatase, increased thirst, loss of libido, mastalgia, muscle cramps, myalgia, myocardial infarction, neuropathy, otalgia, pallor, phlebitis, pneumonia, polyuria, psychoneurosis, pulmonary embolism, purpura, rigors, skin rash, stiffness, syncope, thrombocytopenia, tinnitus, upper respiratory tract infection, urinary tract infection, uterine rupture, visual disturbance, weakness, weight changes

General Dosage Range Oral: *Adults:* 100 to 200 mcg 4 times daily

Mechanism of Action Misoprostol is a synthetic prostaglandin E_1 analog that replaces the protective prostaglandins consumed with prostaglandin-inhibiting therapies (eg, NSAIDs); has been shown to induce uterine contractions

Pharmacodynamics/Kinetics

Onset of Action Inhibition of gastric acid secretion: 30 minutes

Duration of Action Inhibition of gastric acid secretion: 3 hours

Half-life Elimination Misoprostol acid: 20 to 40 minutes

Time to Peak Serum: Misoprostol acid: Fasting: 12 ± 3 minutes

Pregnancy Risk Factor X

Pregnancy Considerations Use for the prevention of NSAID-induced gastric ulcers is contraindicated in pregnant women.

[US Boxed Warning]: Use of misoprostol during pregnancy may cause birth defects, abortion, premature birth, or uterine rupture. Uterine rupture has been reported when misoprostol was administered in pregnant women to induce labor or to induce abortion. The risk of uterine rupture increases with advancing gestational ages and with prior uterine surgery, including cesarean delivery. Misoprostol is not to be used to reduce the risk of NSAID-induced ulcers in woman of childbearing potential unless she is at risk of complications from gastric ulcers associated with NSAID use, or is at high risk of developing gastric ulceration. In such patients, misoprostol may be prescribed if the patient has had a negative serum pregnancy test within 2 weeks prior to beginning therapy; is capable of complying with effective contraceptive measures; has received both oral and written warnings of the hazards of misoprostol, the risk of possible contraception failure, and the danger to other women of childbearing potential if the drug is taken by mistake; and will begin misoprostol only on the second or third day of the next normal menstrual period. Due to the abortifacient property of this medication, patients must be warned not to give this drug to others.

Congenital anomalies following first trimester exposure have been reported, including skull defects, cranial nerve palsies, facial malformations, and limb defects. Misoprostol may produce uterine contractions; fetal death, uterine perforation, and abortion may occur.

Misoprostol is FDA approved for the medical termination of pregnancy of ≤70 days in conjunction with mifepristone.

Because misoprostol may induce or augment uterine contractions, it has been used off-label as a cervical-ripening agent for induction of labor. Misoprostol should not be used for this purpose during the third trimester in women who have had a prior cesarean delivery or major uterine surgery because the risk of uterine rupture is increased (ACOG 107 2009; ACOG 115 2010). It has also been used for the treatment of incomplete or missed abortion (ACOG 427 2009), early pregnancy loss (ACOG 150 2015), or severe postpartum hemorrhage (ACOG 76 2006; FIGO 2012a; FIGO 2012b). Some guidelines recommend misoprostol for postpartum hemorrhage only secondary to oxytocin in situations where oxytocin is not available (Leduc 2000; FIGO 2012a; FIGO 2012b). Various routes of administration have been used for postpartum hemorrhage. Sublingual administration has the most rapid onset, the oral route produces the most pronounced initial increase in tonus, and rectal and vaginal routes exhibit longer durations of action as compared to oral and sublingual routes (Leduc 2009). Adverse events associated with off-label obstetric uses include uterine tachysystole (may impair placental blood flow), uterine rupture, amniotic fluid embolism, or adverse fetal heart changes.

MitoMYcin (Systemic) (mye toe MYE sin)

Brand Names: Canada Mitomycin For Injection; Mitomycin For Injection USP; Mutamycin

Pharmacologic Category Antineoplastic Agent, Antibiotic

Use

Gastric cancer: Treatment of disseminated adenocarcinoma of the stomach (in combination with other chemotherapy agents) and as palliative treatment when other modalities have failed.

Pancreatic cancer: Treatment of disseminated adenocarcinoma of the pancreas (in combination with other chemotherapy agents) and as palliative treatment when other modalities have failed.

Limitations of use: Not recommended for single-agent primary therapy or to replace appropriate surgery and/or radiotherapy in the treatment of these conditions.

Local Anesthetic/Vasoconstrictor Precautions No information available to require special precautions

Effects on Dental Treatment Key adverse event(s) related to dental treatment: Stomatitis.

Effects on Bleeding Bone marrow toxicity (pancytopenia) including thrombocytopenia, leukopenia, and anemia has been reported in 64% of patients. Medical consult recommended.

Adverse Reactions

>10%:

Gastrointestinal: Anorexia (14%), nausea (14%), vomiting (14%)

Hematologic & oncologic: Bone marrow depression (64%; onset: 4 weeks; recovery: 8 to 10 weeks), hemolytic-uremic syndrome (HUS; ≤15%), thrombotic thrombocytopenic purpura (TTP; ≤15%)

Miscellaneous: Fever (14%)

1% to 10%:

Dermatologic: Alopecia (4%)

Gastrointestinal: Mucous membrane disease (toxicity: 4%), stomatitis (4%)

Renal: Increased serum creatinine (2%)

<1%, postmarketing, and/or case reports: Adult respiratory distress syndrome (ARDS), bladder spasm (intravesical administration), cardiac failure, dyspnea, extravasation reactions, fibrosis (bladder; intravesical administration), hepatic veno-occlusive disease (SOS), interstitial fibrosis, malaise, nonproductive cough, pulmonary infiltrates, renal failure (irreversible), skin rash, weakness

General Dosage Range Dosage adjustment recommended in patients with renal impairment or who develop toxicities.

IV: *Adults:* 20 mg/m^2 every 6 to 8 weeks

Mechanism of Action Mitomycin alkylates DNA to produce DNA cross-linking (primarily with guanine and cytosine pairs) and inhibits DNA and RNA synthesis. Mitomycin is not cell cycle specific but has its maximum effect against cells in late G and early S phases (Perry 2012).

Pharmacodynamics/Kinetics

Half-life Elimination 17 minutes (30 mg dose)

Pregnancy Considerations Adverse events have been observed in animal reproduction studies.

Mitotane (MYE toe tane)

Brand Names: US Lysodren

Brand Names: Canada Lysodren

Pharmacologic Category Antineoplastic Agent, Miscellaneous

Use Adrenocortical carcinoma: Treatment of inoperable (functional or nonfunctional) adrenocortical carcinoma

Local Anesthetic/Vasoconstrictor Precautions No information available to require special precautions

Effects on Dental Treatment No significant effects or complications reported

Effects on Bleeding No information available to require special precautions

Adverse Reactions The majority of adverse events are dose-dependent.

>10%:

Central nervous system: Central nervous system depression (32%), lethargy/drowsiness (25%), dizziness/vertigo (15%)

Dermatologic: Skin rash (15%)

Gastrointestinal: Anorexia (24%), nausea (39%), vomiting (37%), diarrhea (13%)

Neuromuscular & skeletal: Weakness (12%)

1% to 10%:

Central nervous system: Headache (5%), confusion (3%)

Neuromuscular & skeletal: Tremor (3%)

<1%, postmarketing, and/or case reports: Abnormal thyroid function test, adrenocortical insufficiency, albuminuria, anemia, ataxia, autoimmune hepatitis, blurred vision, brain damage (may be reversible) cataract, decreased protein-bound iodine, diplopia, dysarthria, flushing, generalized aches, growth suppression, gynecomastia, hematuria, hemorrhagic cystitis, hepatitis, hypercholesterolemia, hyperpyrexia, hypertension, hypertriglyceridemia, hypogonadism (primary), hypouricemia, increased gamma-glutamyl transferase, increased liver enzymes, increased serum transaminases, increased serum triglycerides, increased

sex hormone binding globulin, leukopenia, macular edema, maculopathy, memory impairment, mental deficiency, mucositis, myalgia, neuropathy, neutropenia, orthostatic hypotension, prolonged bleeding time, psychological disturbances (neuro), retinopathy (toxic), thrombocytopenia

General Dosage Range Dosage adjustment recommended in patients who develop toxicities

Oral: *Adults:* Initial: 2 to 6 g daily in 3 to 4 divided doses; titrate to achieve target concentration (14 to 20 mcg/mL)

Mechanism of Action Adrenolytic agent that suppresses (directly) the adrenal cortex and alters the peripheral metabolism of steroids

Pharmacodynamics/Kinetics

Onset of Action Antitumor response: Achieved at serum concentrations ≥14 mcg/mL; Pediatric patients: In experience with treatment of adenocarcinoma reported 1.5 to 12.5 months to reach 10 mcg/mL with subsequent rapid escalation of serum concentration, clinical response may be observed earlier (Rodriguez-Galindo 2005; Zancanella 2006).

Duration of Action Measurable serum levels may persist for months after discontinuation (Veytsman 2009).

Half-life Elimination 18 to 159 days (median: 53 days)

Pregnancy Considerations Animal reproduction studies have not been conducted. May cause fetal harm if administered during pregnancy; adverse outcomes have been reported. Women of reproductive potential should use effective contraception during treatment and after treatment until plasma levels are no longer detected.

MitoXANTRONE (mye toe ZAN trone)

Brand Names: Canada Mitoxantrone Injection; Mitoxantrone Injection USP

Pharmacologic Category Antineoplastic Agent, Anthracenedione; Antineoplastic Agent, Topoisomerase II Inhibitor

Use Initial treatment of acute nonlymphocytic leukemias (ANLL [includes myelogenous, promyelocytic, monocytic and erythroid leukemias]); treatment of advanced hormone-refractory prostate cancer; secondary progressive or relapsing-remitting multiple sclerosis (MS)

Canadian labeling: Additional uses (not in U.S. labeling): Treatment of metastatic breast cancer, relapsed leukemia (adults), lymphoma, and hepatocellular carcinoma

Local Anesthetic/Vasoconstrictor Precautions No information available to require special precautions

Effects on Dental Treatment Key adverse event(s) related to dental treatment: Mucositis and stomatitis.

Effects on Bleeding Myelosuppression is an extension of the pharmacologic effects; therefore, thrombocytopenia (grades 3/4: 3% to 4%) is expected. Anemia may also occur. Medical consult recommended.

Adverse Reactions Includes events reported with any indication; incidence varies based on treatment, dose, and/or concomitant medications.

>10%:

Cardiovascular: Edema (10% to 30%), cardiac disease (≤18%), cardiac arrhythmia (3% to 18%), ECG changes (≤11%)

Central nervous system: Pain (8% to 41%), fatigue (≤39%), headache (6% to 13%)

Dermatologic: Alopecia (20% to 61%), nail bed changes (≤11%)

Endocrine & metabolic: Menstrual disease (26% to 61%), amenorrhea (28% to 53%), hyperglycemia (10% to 31%), weight gain (≤17%), weight loss (≤17%), increased gamma-glutamyl transferase (3% to 15%)

Gastrointestinal: Nausea (26% to 76%), vomiting (6% to 72%), diarrhea (14% to 47%), mucositis (10% to 29%; onset: ≤1 week), stomatitis (8% to 29%; onset: ≤1 week), anorexia (22% to 25%), constipation (10% to 16%), gastrointestinal hemorrhage (2% to 16%), abdominal pain (9% to 15%), dyspepsia (5% to 14%)

Genitourinary: Urinary tract infection (7% to 32%), hematuria (≤11%), urine abnormality (5% to 11%)

Hematologic & oncologic: Neutropenia (79% to 100%; onset: ≤3 weeks; grade 4: 23% to 54%), leukopenia (9% to 100%), lymphocytopenia (72% to 95%), anemia (≤75%), decreased hemoglobin (≤75%), thrombocytopenia (33% to 39%; grades 3/4: 3% to 4%), bruise (≤11%), febrile neutropenia (≤11%), petechia (≤11%)

Hepatic: Increased serum alkaline phosphatase (≤37%), increased serum transaminases (5% to 20%)

Infection: Infection (4% to 60%), sepsis (≤34%), fungal infection (9% to 15%)

Neuromuscular & skeletal: Weakness (≤24%)

Renal: Increased blood urea nitrogen (≤22%), increased serum creatinine (≤13%)

Respiratory: Upper respiratory tract infection (7% to 53%), pharyngitis (≤19%), dyspnea (6% to 18%), cough (5% to 13%)

Miscellaneous: Fever (6% to 78%)

1% to 10%:

Cardiovascular: Cardiac failure (≤5%), ischemia (≤5%), decreased left ventricular ejection fraction (≤5%), hypertension (≤4%)

Central nervous system: Chills (≤5%), anxiety (5%), depression (5%), seizure (2% to 4%)

Dermatologic: Diaphoresis (≤9%), skin infection (≤5%)

Endocrine & metabolic: Hypocalcemia (10%), hypokalemia (7% to 10%), hyponatremia (9%), hypermenorrhea (7%)

Gastrointestinal: Aphthous stomatitis (≤10%)

Genitourinary: Impotence (≤7%), proteinuria (≤6%), sterility (≤5%)

Hematologic & oncologic: Granulocytopenia (6%), hemorrhage (5% to 6%), acute leukemia (≤3%; secondary; includes AML, APL)

Hepatic: Jaundice (3% to 7%)

Infection: Fungal infection (cutaneous: ≤10%)

Neuromuscular & skeletal: Back pain (6% to 8%), arthralgia (≤5%), myalgia (≤5%)

Ophthalmic: Conjunctivitis (≤5%), blurred vision (≤3%)

Renal: Renal failure (≤8%)

Respiratory: Rhinitis (10%), pneumonia (≤9%), sinusitis (≤6%)

<1%, postmarketing, and/or case reports: Anaphylactoid reaction, anaphylaxis, chest pain, dehydration, hypersensitivity reaction, interstitial pneumonitis (with combination chemotherapy), hyperuricemia, hypotension, ocular discoloration (blue discoloration of sclera), phlebitis (at infusion site), skin rash, tachycardia, urine discoloration (blue-green), urticaria

General Dosage Range IV: *Adults:* 12 mg/m^2/day once daily for 2-3 days **or** 12-14 mg/m^2 every 3 weeks **or** 12 mg/m^2 every 3 months (multiple sclerosis; maximum lifetime cumulative dose: 140 mg/m^2)

Mechanism of Action Related to the anthracyclines, mitoxantrone intercalates into DNA resulting in cross-links and strand breaks; binds to nucleic acids and inhibits DNA and RNA synthesis by template disordering and steric obstruction; replication is decreased by binding to DNA topoisomerase II and seems to inhibit the incorporation of uridine into RNA and thymidine into DNA; active throughout entire cell cycle (cell-cycle non-specific)

Pharmacodynamics/Kinetics

Half-life Elimination Terminal: 23 to 215 hours (median: ~75 hours); may be prolonged with hepatic impairment

Pregnancy Risk Factor D

Pregnancy Considerations Adverse events have been observed in animal reproduction studies. Based on the mechanism of action, mitoxantrone may cause fetal harm if administered during pregnancy. Use of effective contraception during therapy is recommended. Information related to pregnancy outcomes following maternal use of mitoxantrone in pregnancy is limited (Amato 2015; Houtchens 2013; NTP 2013).

Infertility and amenorrhea have been reported in women with MS using mitoxantrone (Amato 2015; Houtchens 2013). Women with multiple sclerosis who are of reproductive potential should have a pregnancy test prior to each dose. Women who wish to become pregnant should discontinue therapy at least 2 to 3 months prior to conception (Houtchens 2013).

The European Society for Medical Oncology has published guidelines for diagnosis, treatment, and follow-up of cancer during pregnancy. The guidelines recommend referral to a facility with expertise in cancer during pregnancy and encourage a multidisciplinary team (obstetrician, neonatologist, oncology team). In general, if chemotherapy is indicated, it should be avoided in the first trimester, there should be a 3-week time period between the last chemotherapy dose and anticipated delivery, and chemotherapy should not be administered beyond week 33 of gestation (Peccatori 2013).

Modafinil (moe DAF i nil)

Brand Names: US Provigil

Brand Names: Canada Alertec; Apo-Modafinil; Auro-Modafinil; Bio-Modafinil; Mar-Modafinil; Teva-Modafinil

Pharmacologic Category Central Nervous System Stimulant

Use

Narcolepsy: To improve wakefulness in adult patients with excessive sleepiness associated with narcolepsy.

Obstructive sleep apnea: To improve wakefulness in adult patients with obstructive sleep apnea (OSA)

Shift work sleep disorder: To improve wakefulness in adult patients with shift work sleep disorder (SWSD)

Local Anesthetic/Vasoconstrictor Precautions Use vasoconstrictor with caution. Patients may experience heart palpitations and increased heart rate when taking modafinil.

Effects on Dental Treatment Key adverse event(s) related to dental treatment: Modafinil causes tachycardia, increases in blood pressure, and palpitations. Consider monitoring blood pressure prior to using local anesthetic with a vasoconstrictor. Symptoms associated with bruxism have been observed in some patients.

Effects on Bleeding No information available to require special precautions

Adverse Reactions

Frequency not always defined.

Cardiovascular: Chest pain (3%), hypertension (3%), palpitations (2%), tachycardia (2%), vasodilatation (2%), edema (1%)

Central nervous system: Headache (adults 34%; children 20% [Biederman 2005]; dose related), nervousness (7%), anxiety (5%; dose related), dizziness (5%), insomnia (5%), depression (2%), drowsiness (2%), paresthesia (2%), agitation (1%), chills (1%), confusion (1%), emotional lability (1%), hypertonia (1%), vertigo (1%)

Dermatologic: Diaphoresis (1%)

Endocrine & metabolic: Weight loss (children 5% [Greenhill 2006]), increased thirst (1%), increased gamma-glutamyl transferase

Gastrointestinal: Decreased appetite (children 16% [Biederman 2005]), abdominal pain (children 12% [Greenhill 2006]), nausea (11%), diarrhea (6%), dyspepsia (5%), xerostomia (4%), anorexia (4%), constipation (2%), dysgeusia (1%), flatulence (1%), oral mucosa ulcer (1%)

Genitourinary: Urine abnormality (1%)

Hematologic & oncologic: Eosinophilia (1%)

Hepatic: Abnormal hepatic function tests (2%), increased serum alkaline phosphatase

Neuromuscular & skeletal: Back pain (6%), dyskinesia (1%), hyperkinesia (1%), tremor (1%)

Ocular: Abnormal vision (1%)

Respiratory: Rhinitis (7%), pharyngitis (4%), asthma (1%), epistaxis (1%)

Postmarketing and/or case reports: Aggressive behavior, agranulocytosis, anaphylaxis, angioedema, delusions, DRESS syndrome, erythema multiforme (pediatric patients), hallucination, hypersensitivity, mania, multiorgan hypersensitivity, psychomotor agitation, psychosis, skin rash (includes some severe cases requiring hospitalization), Stevens-Johnson syndrome, suicidal ideation, toxic epidermal necrolysis

General Dosage Range Dosage adjustment recommended in patients with hepatic impairment.

Oral: *Adults:* 200 mg once daily

Mechanism of Action The exact mechanism of action is unclear, it does not appear to alter the release of dopamine or norepinephrine, it may exert its stimulant effects by decreasing GABA-mediated neurotransmission, although this theory has not yet been fully evaluated; several studies also suggest that an intact central alpha-adrenergic system is required for modafinil's activity; the drug increases high-frequency alpha waves while decreasing both delta and theta wave activity, and these effects are consistent with generalized increases in mental alertness

Pharmacodynamics/Kinetics

Half-life Elimination Effective half-life: 15 hours

Time to Peak Serum: 2 to 4 hours; may be delayed ~1 hour with food.

Pregnancy Risk Factor C

Pregnancy Considerations Adverse events have been observed in some animal reproduction studies. An increased risk of spontaneous abortion and intrauterine growth restriction has been reported with modafinil. Efficacy of steroidal contraceptives (including depot and implantable contraceptives) may be decreased; alternate means of contraception should be considered during therapy and for 1 month after modafinil is discontinued.

Health care providers are encouraged to register pregnant patients exposed to modafinil, or pregnant women may enroll themselves, by calling (866-404-4106).

Controlled Substance C-IV

Moexipril (mo EKS i pril)

Related Information

Cardiovascular Diseases *on page 1752*

Brand Names: US Univasc [DSC]

Pharmacologic Category Angiotensin-Converting Enzyme (ACE) Inhibitor; Antihypertensive

Use

Hypertension: Management of hypertension

Guideline recommendations:

Hypertension: The 2014 guideline for the management of high blood pressure in adults (Eighth Joint National Committee [JNC 8]) recommends initiation of pharmacologic treatment to lower blood pressure for the following patients:

- Patients ≥60 years of age with systolic blood pressure (SBP) ≥150 mm Hg or diastolic blood pressure (DBP) ≥90 mm Hg. Goal of therapy is SBP <150 mm Hg and DBP <90 mm Hg.
- Patients <60 years of age with SBP ≥140 mm Hg or DBP is ≥90 mm Hg. Goal of therapy is SBP <140 mm Hg and DBP <90 mm Hg.
- Patients ≥18 years of age with diabetes and SBP ≥140 mm Hg or DBP ≥90 mm Hg. Goal of therapy is SBP <140 mm Hg and DBP <90 mm Hg.
- Patients ≥18 years of age with chronic kidney disease (CKD) and SBP ≥140 mm Hg or DBP ≥90 mm Hg. Goal of therapy is SBP <140 mm Hg and DBP <90 mm Hg.

Chronic kidney disease (CKD) and hypertension: Regardless of race or diabetes status, the use of an ACE inhibitor (ACEI) or angiotensin receptor blocker (ARB) as initial therapy is recommended to improve kidney outcomes. In the general nonblack population (without CKD) including those with diabetes, initial antihypertensive treatment should consist of a thiazide-type diuretic, calcium channel blocker, ACEI, or ARB. In the general black population (without CKD) including those with diabetes, initial antihypertensive treatment should consist of a thiazide-type diuretic or a calcium channel blocker **instead of** an ACEI or ARB.

Coronary artery disease (CAD) and hypertension: The American Heart Association, American College of Cardiology and American Society of Hypertension (AHA/ACC/ASH) 2015 scientific statement for the treatment of hypertension in patients with CAD recommends the use of an ACE inhibitor (or an ARB) as part of a regimen in patients with hypertension and chronic stable angina if there is prior MI, LV systolic dysfunction, diabetes mellitus, or CKD. A BP target of <140/90 mm Hg is reasonable for the secondary prevention of cardiovascular events. A lower target BP (<130/80 mm Hg) may be appropriate in some individuals with CAD, previous MI, stroke or transient ischemic attack, or CAD risk equivalents (AHA/ACC/ASH [Rosendorff 2015]).

Local Anesthetic/Vasoconstrictor Precautions No information available to require special precautions

Effects on Dental Treatment Key adverse event(s) related to dental treatment: Patients may experience orthostatic hypotension as they stand up after treatment; especially if lying in dental chair for extended periods of time. Use caution with sudden changes in position during and after dental treatment.

An angiotensin-converting enzyme (ACE) Inhibitor cough is a dry, hacking, nonproductive cough that can potentially interfere with longer dental procedures if patient has this side effect.

Effects on Bleeding No information available to require special precautions

Adverse Reactions

1% to 10%:

Cardiovascular: Flushing, hypotension, peripheral edema

Central nervous system: Dizziness, fatigue, headache

Dermatologic: Alopecia, skin rash

Endocrine & metabolic: Hyperkalemia, hyponatremia

Gastrointestinal: Diarrhea, heartburn, nausea

Neuromuscular & skeletal: Myalgia

Renal: Increased blood urea nitrogen (reversible), increased serum creatinine (reversible), polyuria

Respiratory: Cough, pharyngitis, sinusitis, upper respiratory tract infection

<1%, postmarketing, and/or case reports: Anemia, angioedema, bronchospasm, cardiac arrhythmia, cerebrovascular accident, chest pain, dyspnea, eosinophilic pneumonitis, hepatitis, hypercholesterolemia, increased liver enzymes, myocardial infarction, oliguria, orthostatic hypotension, palpitations, proteinuria, syncope

General Dosage Range Dosage adjustment recommended in patients with renal impairment.

Oral: *Adults:* Initial: 3.75 to 7.5 mg once daily; maintenance: 7.5 to 30 mg/day in 1 or 2 divided doses

Mechanism of Action Competitive inhibitor of angiotensin-converting enzyme (ACE); prevents conversion of angiotensin I to angiotensin II, a potent vasoconstrictor; results in lower levels of angiotensin II which causes an increase in plasma renin activity and a reduction in aldosterone secretion

Pharmacodynamics/Kinetics

Onset of Action Within 2 hours; Peak effect: 3 to 6 hours

Duration of Action 24 hours

Half-life Elimination Moexipril: 1.3 hours; Moexiprilat: 2 to 9.8 hours

Time to Peak Moexiprilat: ~1.5 hours

Pregnancy Risk Factor D

Pregnancy Considerations [US Boxed Warning]: Drugs that act on the renin-angiotensin system can cause injury and death to the developing fetus. Discontinue as soon as possible once pregnancy is detected. Drugs that act on the renin-angiotensin system are associated with oligohydramnios. Oligohydramnios, due to decreased fetal renal function, may lead to fetal lung hypoplasia and skeletal malformations. The use of these drugs in pregnancy is also associated with anuria, hypotension, renal failure, skull hypoplasia, and death in the fetus/neonate. Teratogenic effects may occur following maternal use of an ACE inhibitor during the first trimester, although this finding may be confounded by maternal disease. Because adverse fetal events are well documented with exposure later in pregnancy, ACE inhibitor use in pregnant women is not recommended (Seely 2014; Weber 2014). Infants exposed to an ACE inhibitor in utero should be monitored for hyperkalemia, hypotension, and oliguria. Oligohydramnios may not appear until after irreversible fetal injury has occurred. Exchange transfusions or dialysis may be required to reverse hypotension or improve renal function, although data related to the effectiveness in neonates is limited.

Chronic maternal hypertension itself is also associated with adverse events in the fetus/infant and mother. ACE inhibitors are not recommended for the treatment of uncomplicated hypertension in pregnancy (ACOG 2013) and they are specifically contraindicated for the treatment of hypertension and chronic heart failure during pregnancy by some guidelines (Regitz-Zagrosek 2011). In addition, ACE inhibitors should generally be avoided in women of reproductive age (ACOG 2013). If treatment for hypertension in pregnancy is needed, other agents should be used (ACOG 2013; Regitz-Zagrosek 2011).

Mometasone (Oral Inhalation)

(moe MET a sone)

Related Information

Respiratory Diseases *on page 1777*

Brand Names: US Asmanex 120 Metered Doses; Asmanex 14 Metered Doses; Asmanex 30 Metered Doses; Asmanex 60 Metered Doses; Asmanex 7 Metered Doses; Asmanex HFA

Brand Names: Canada Asmanex Twisthaler

Generic Availability (US) No

Pharmacologic Category Corticosteroid, Inhalant (Oral)

Use

Asthma: Maintenance treatment of asthma as prophylactic therapy in patients 4 years and older (Asmanex Twisthaler) and 12 years and older (Asmanex HFA)

Limitations of use: Not indicated for the relief of acute bronchospasm.

Guideline recommendations: A low-dose inhaled corticosteroid (in addition to an as-needed short-acting beta-2 agonist) is the initial preferred long-term control medication for children, adolescents, and adult patients with persistent asthma who are candidates for treatment according to a step-wise treatment approach (GINA 2016; NAEPP 2007).

Local Anesthetic/Vasoconstrictor Precautions No information available to require special precautions

Effects on Dental Treatment Localized infections with *Candida albicans* or *Aspergillus niger* occur frequently in the mouth and pharynx with repetitive use of an oral inhaler; may require treatment with appropriate antifungal therapy or discontinuance of inhaler use.

Effects on Bleeding No information available to require special precautions

Adverse Reactions

>10%:

Central nervous system: Headache (3% to 22%), fatigue (1% to 13%), depression (11%)

Gastrointestinal: Oral candidiasis (≤22%)

Neuromuscular & skeletal: Musculoskeletal pain (8% to 22%), arthralgia (13%)

Respiratory: Sinusitis (3% to 22%), allergic rhinitis (adolescents & adults 14% to 20%; children 4%), upper respiratory tract infection (8% to 15%), pharyngitis (8% to 13%)

1% to 10%:

Central nervous system: Pain (1% to <3%)

Gastrointestinal: Abdominal pain (3% to 6%), dyspepsia (5%), nausea (3%), vomiting (1% to ≤3%), anorexia (1% to <3%), gastroenteritis (1% to <3%)

Genitourinary: Dysmenorrhea (9%), urinary tract infection (children 2%)

Hematologic & oncologic: Bruise (children 2%)

Infection: Influenza (4%), infection (1% to <3%)

Neuromuscular & skeletal: Back pain (6%), myalgia (3%)

Ophthalmic: Increased intraocular pressure (3%)

Otic: Otalgia (1% to <3%)

Respiratory: Sinus congestion (9%), nasopharyngitis (5% to 8%), bronchitis (3%), dry throat (1% to <3%), epistaxis (1% to <3%), flu-like symptoms (1% to <3%), nasal discomfort (1% to <3%), voice disorder (1% to <3%)

Miscellaneous: Fever (children 7%)

Postmarketing and/or case reports: Anaphylaxis, angioedema, bronchospasm, cataract, cough, dyspnea, exacerbation of asthma, glaucoma, growth suppression, hypersensitivity, pruritus, skin rash, wheezing

Dosing

Adult & Geriatric Asthma: Oral inhalation: **Note:** Dosage forms of Asmanex Twisthaler available in the United States (110 mcg and 220 mcg Twisthaler) deliver 100 and 200 mcg mometasone furoate per actuation respectively. Maximum effects may not be evident for 1 to 2 weeks or longer; higher doses may provide additional asthma control in patients who do not respond adequately after 2 weeks of therapy. Doses should be titrated to the lowest effective dose.

US labeling:

Previous therapy:

Bronchodilators: Asmanex Twisthaler: Initial: 220 mcg daily (maximum: 440 mcg/day); may be given in the evening or in divided doses twice daily

Inhaled corticosteroids:

Asmanex HFA: Maximum: 400 mcg twice daily (800 mcg/day)

Inhaled medium-dose corticosteroids: Asmanex HFA 100 mcg inhaler: 200 mcg twice daily

Inhaled high-dose corticosteroids: Asmanex HFA 200 mcg inhaler: 400 mcg twice daily

Asmanex Twisthaler: Initial: 220 mcg daily (maximum: 440 mcg/day); may be given in the evening or in divided doses twice daily

Oral corticosteroids: **Note:** Prednisone should be reduced slowly (ie, no faster than 2.5 mg daily on a weekly basis), beginning after at least 1 week of mometasone use

Asmanex HFA: Initial: 400 mcg twice daily (maximum: 800 mcg/day)

Asmanex Twisthaler: Initial: 440 mcg twice daily (maximum: 880 mcg/day)

Canadian labeling:

Usual dose: 200 to 400 mcg once daily in the evening or 200 mcg twice daily administered in the morning and evening. **Note:** Manufacturer suggests that there is a greater chance of achieving asthma control if once-daily dosing is administered in the evening. Some patients (eg, previously receiving high-dose inhaled corticosteroids) may respond more favorably to 400 mcg daily administered in 2 divided doses. Titrate to the lowest effective dose.

Severe asthma and requiring oral corticosteroids: Initial: 400 mcg twice daily administered in the morning and evening (maximum: 800 mcg daily). Taper off oral corticosteroid gradually by decreasing daily prednisone dose by 1 mg daily (or equivalent of other corticosteroid) no sooner than on a weekly basis, beginning after at least 1 week of mometasone use; upon successful taper off of oral steroids, titrate mometasone to lowest effective dose.

Asthma Guidelines: National Asthma Education and Prevention Program guidelines (NAEPP 2007): Dry powder inhaler (refers to Asmanex 200 mcg strength available in U.S.) **Note:** 220 mcg inhaler delivers 200 mcg mometasone furoate per actuation; NAEPP uses doses based on delivery, while manufacturer recommended doses are based on inhaler amount

"Low" dose: 200 mcg daily

"Medium" dose: 400 mcg daily

"High" dose: >400 mcg daily

Pediatric

Asthma: Oral inhalation: **Note:** Dosage forms of Asmanex Twisthaler available in the United States (110 mcg and 220 mcg Twisthaler) deliver 100 and 200 mcg mometasone furoate per actuation respectively. Maximum effects may not be evident for 1 to 2 weeks or longer; higher doses may provide additional asthma control in patients who do not respond adequately after 2 weeks of therapy. Doses should be titrated to the lowest effective dose.

Children 4 to 11 years: Asmanex Twisthaler: 110 mcg once daily in the evening (maximum: 110 mcg/day)

Children ≥12 years and Adolescents: Asmanex HFA and Asmanex Twisthaler: Refer to adult dosing.

Asthma Guidelines: National Asthma Education and Prevention Program guidelines (NAEPP 2007): Dry powder inhaler (refers to Asmanex 200 mcg strength available in United States) **Note:** 220 mcg inhaler delivers 200 mcg mometasone furoate per actuation; NAEPP uses doses based on delivery, while manufacturer recommended doses are based on inhaler amount.

Children ≥12 years and Adolescents: Refer to adult dosing.

Renal Impairment There are no dosage adjustments provided in the manufacturer's labeling (has not been studied).

Hepatic Impairment There are no dosage adjustments provided in the manufacturer's labeling (has not been studied). However, mometasone exposure may increase with severity of hepatic impairment.

Mechanism of Action May depress the formation, release, and activity of endogenous chemical mediators of inflammation (kinins, histamine, liposomal enzymes, prostaglandins). Leukocytes and macrophages may have to be present for the initiation of responses mediated by the above substances. Inhibits the margination and subsequent cell migration to the area of injury, and also reverses the dilatation and increased vessel permeability in the area resulting in decreased access of cells to the sites of injury.

Contraindications

Hypersensitivity to mometasone or any component of the formulation; hypersensitivity to milk proteins (Asmanex Twisthaler only); primary treatment of status asthmaticus or other acute episodes of asthma for which intensive measures are required

Documentation of allergenic cross-reactivity for corticosteroids is limited. However, because of similarities in chemical structure and/or pharmacologic actions, the possibility of cross-sensitivity cannot be ruled out with certainty.

Canadian labeling: Additional contraindications (not in US labeling): Untreated systemic fungal, bacterial, viral, or parasitic infections; active or quiet tuberculosis infection of the respiratory tract; ocular herpes simplex

Warnings/Precautions May cause hypercorticism or suppression of hypothalamic-pituitary-adrenal (HPA) axis, particularly in younger children or in patients receiving high doses for prolonged periods. HPA axis suppression may lead to adrenal crisis. Withdrawal and discontinuation of a corticosteroid should be done slowly and carefully. Particular care is required when patients are transferred from systemic corticosteroids to inhaled products due to possible adrenal insufficiency or withdrawal from steroids, including an increase in allergic symptoms. Adult patients receiving >20 mg per day of prednisone (or equivalent) may be most susceptible. Fatalities have occurred due to adrenal insufficiency in asthmatic patients during and after transfer from systemic corticosteroids to aerosol steroids; aerosol steroids do not provide the systemic steroid needed to treat patients having trauma, surgery, or infections. Select surgical patients on long-term, high-dose, inhaled corticosteroids should be given stress doses of hydrocortisone intravenously during the surgical period and the dose reduced rapidly within 24 hours after surgery (NAEPP 2007). When transferring to oral inhaler, previously suppressed allergic conditions (rhinitis, conjunctivitis, eczema) may be unmasked.

Paradoxical bronchospasm may occur with wheezing after inhalation; if this occurs, stop steroid and treat with a fast-acting bronchodilator. Supplemental steroids (oral or parenteral) may be needed during stress or severe asthma attacks. Not to be used in status asthmaticus or for the relief of acute bronchospasm. Corticosteroid use may cause psychiatric disturbances, including depression, euphoria, insomnia, mood swings, and personality changes. Preexisting psychiatric conditions may be exacerbated by corticosteroid use. Prolonged use of corticosteroids may increase the incidence of secondary infection, mask acute infection (including fungal infections), prolong or exacerbate viral infections, or limit response to vaccines. Avoid use if possible in patients with ocular herpes; active or quiescent tuberculosis infections of the respiratory tract; or untreated viral, fungal, or bacterial or parasitic systemic infections. Exposure to chickenpox or measles should be avoided; if the patient is exposed to chickenpox, prophylaxis with varicella zoster immune globulin or pooled intravenous immunoglobulin may be indicated; if chickenpox develops, treatment with antiviral agents may be considered. If exposure to measles, prophylaxis with pooled intramuscular immunoglobulin may be indicated.

Prolonged treatment with corticosteroids has been associated with the development of Kaposi sarcoma (case reports); if noted, discontinuation of therapy should be considered (Goedert 2002). Rare cases of vasculitis (Churg-Strauss syndrome) or other systemic eosinophilic conditions can occur; often associated with decrease and/or withdrawal of oral corticosteroid therapy following initiation of inhaled corticosteroid. Local oropharyngeal *Candida* infections have been reported; if occurs, treat appropriately while continuing mometasone therapy. Patients should be instructed to rinse mouth after each use.

Hypersensitivity reactions including allergic dermatitis, anaphylaxis, angioedema, bronchospasm, flushing, pruritus, rash, and urticaria have been reported; if these symptoms occur discontinue use. Use with caution in patients with thyroid disease, hepatic impairment, renal impairment, cardiovascular disease, diabetes, glaucoma, cataracts, myasthenia gravis, patients at risk for seizures, or GI diseases (diverticulitis, peptic ulcer, ulcerative colitis) due to perforation risk. Use caution following acute MI (corticosteroids have been associated with myocardial rupture). Use with caution in patients with major risk factors for decreased bone mineral count such as prolonged immobilization, family history of osteoporosis, or chronic use of drugs that can reduce bone mass (eg, anticonvulsants, oral corticosteroids); long-term use of inhaled corticosteroids have been associated with decreases in bone mineral density. Because of the risk of adverse effects, systemic corticosteroids should be used cautiously in the elderly in the smallest possible effective dose for the shortest duration.

Orally inhaled corticosteroids may cause a reduction in growth velocity in pediatric patients (~1 cm per year [range, 0.3 to 1.8 cm per year] and related to dose and duration of exposure). To minimize the systemic effects of orally inhaled corticosteroids, each patient should be titrated to the lowest effective dose. Growth should be routinely monitored in pediatric patients. Prior to use, the dose and duration of treatment should be based on the risk versus benefit for each individual patient. In general, use the smallest effective dose for the shortest duration of time to minimize adverse events. Short-acting beta-2 agonist (eg, albuterol) should be used for acute symptoms and symptoms occurring between treatments. Withdraw systemic corticosteroid therapy with gradual tapering of dose; consider reducing the daily prednisone dose by 2.5 mg on a weekly basis beginning after at least 1 week of inhalation therapy. Monitor lung function, beta-agonist use, asthma symptoms, and for signs and symptoms of adrenal insufficiency (fatigue, lassitude, weakness, nausea and vomiting, hypotension) during withdrawal. Asmanex Twisthaler may contain lactose; very rare anaphylactic reactions have been reported in patients with severe milk protein allergy. Potentially significant interactions may exist, requiring dose or frequency adjustment, additional monitoring, and/or selection of alternative therapy.

Drug Interactions

Metabolism/Transport Effects **Substrate** of CYP3A4 (minor); **Note:** Assignment of Major/Minor substrate status based on clinically relevant drug interaction potential

Avoid Concomitant Use

Avoid concomitant use of Mometasone (Oral Inhalation) with any of the following: Aldesleukin; Desmopressin; Loxapine

Increased Effect/Toxicity

Mometasone (Oral Inhalation) may increase the levels/effects of: Amphotericin B; Ceritinib; Deferasirox; Desmopressin; Loop Diuretics; Loxapine; Thiazide and Thiazide-Like Diuretics

The levels/effects of Mometasone (Oral Inhalation) may be increased by: CYP3A4 Inhibitors (Strong)

Decreased Effect

Mometasone (Oral Inhalation) may decrease the levels/effects of: Aldesleukin; Corticorelin; Hyaluronidase

Dietary Considerations Asmanex Twisthaler may contain lactose.

Pharmacodynamics/Kinetics

Onset of Action Maximum effects may not be evident for ≥1 to 2 weeks

Duration of Action Duration after discontinuation: Several days or more

Half-life Elimination Mean: 5 hours

Time to Peak Plasma: 0.5 to 2.5 hours

Pregnancy Risk Factor C

Pregnancy Considerations Adverse events have been observed in some animal reproduction studies. Hypoadrenalism may occur in infants born to mothers receiving corticosteroids during pregnancy. Based on available data, an overall increased risk of congenital malformations or a decrease in fetal growth has not been associated with maternal use of inhaled corticosteroids during pregnancy (Bakhireva 2005; NAEPP 2005; Namazy 2004). Uncontrolled asthma is associated with adverse events in pregnancy (increased risk of perinatal mortality, preeclampsia, preterm birth, low birth weight infants). Inhaled corticosteroids are recommended for the treatment of asthma during pregnancy (most information available using budesonide) (ACOG 2008; NAEPP 2005).

Breastfeeding Considerations Systemic corticosteroids are excreted in human milk. It is not known if sufficient quantities of mometasone are absorbed following oral inhalation to produce detectable amounts in breast milk; however, oral absorption is limited (<1%). According to the manufacturer, the decision to continue or discontinue breastfeeding during therapy should take into account the risk of infant exposure, the benefits of breastfeeding to the infant, and benefits of treatment to the mother. The use of inhaled corticosteroids is not considered a contraindication to breastfeeding (NAEPP 2005).

Dosage Forms Considerations

Asmanex HFA inhaler delivers 120 actuations.

Dosage Forms

Aerosol, Inhalation:

Asmanex HFA: 100 mcg/actuation (13 g); 200 mcg/actuation (13 g)

Aerosol Powder Breath Activated, Inhalation:

Asmanex 120 Metered Doses: 220 mcg/INH (1 ea)
Asmanex 14 Metered Doses: 220 mcg/INH (1 ea)
Asmanex 30 Metered Doses: 110 mcg/INH (1 ea); 220 mcg/INH (1 ea)
Asmanex 60 Metered Doses: 220 mcg/INH (1 ea)
Asmanex 7 Metered Doses: 110 mcg/INH (1 ea)

Dosage Forms: Canada

Powder, for oral inhalation:

Asmanex Twisthaler: 200 mcg (30 doses, 60 doses); 400 mcg (30 doses, 60 doses)

Mometasone (Nasal) (moe MET a sone)

Brand Names: US Nasonex; Propel Mini

Brand Names: Canada Apo-Mometasone; Mosa-spray; Nasonex

Pharmacologic Category Corticosteroid, Nasal

Use

Allergic rhinitis (seasonal and perennial): Treatment of nasal symptoms of seasonal allergic and perennial allergic rhinitis in adults and pediatric patients ≥2 years.

Nasal congestion associated with seasonal rhinitis: Relief of nasal congestion associated with seasonal allergic rhinitis in adults and pediatric patients ≥2 years.

Nasal polyps: Treatment of nasal polyps in adults.

Seasonal allergic rhinitis (prophylaxis): Prophylaxis of nasal symptoms of seasonal allergic rhinitis in adults and pediatric patients ≥12 years.

Local Anesthetic/Vasoconstrictor Precautions No information available to require special precautions

Effects on Dental Treatment No significant effects or complications reported

Effects on Bleeding Shown to cause localized epistaxis (nosebleed) with prolonged use. The localized epistaxis is reversible following discontinuation of the drug. Impacts relating to the systemic circulation do not warrant special precautions.

Adverse Reactions

>10%:

Central nervous system: Headache (17% to 26%)

Infection: Viral infection (nasal inhalation: 8% to 14%)

Respiratory: Pharyngitis (8% to 13%), cough (nasal inhalation: 7% to 13%), epistaxis (1% to 11%)

1% to 10%:

Gastrointestinal: Diarrhea, dyspepsia, vomiting

Genitourinary: Dysmenorrhea

Neuromuscular & skeletal: Musculoskeletal pain, myalgia

Ophthalmic: Conjunctivitis

Otic: Otitis media

Respiratory: Asthma, flu-like symptoms, nasal mucosa irritation, rhinitis, sinusitis, upper respiratory tract infection, wheezing

<1%, postmarketing, and/or case reports: Altered sense of smell (rare), anaphylaxis, angioedema, burning sensation of the nose, dysgeusia (rare), growth suppression, nasal candidiasis, nasal mucosa ulcer, nasal septum perforation, oral candidiasis (nasal inhalation)

General Dosage Range Intranasal:

Children 2 to 11 years: 1 spray (50 mcg) in each nostril once daily (total daily dose: 100 mcg)

Children ≥12 years, Adolescents, and Adults: 2 sprays (100 mcg) in each nostril once or twice daily

Mechanism of Action May depress the formation, release, and activity of endogenous chemical mediators of inflammation (kinins, histamine, liposomal enzymes, prostaglandins). Leukocytes and macrophages may have to be present for the initiation of responses mediated by the above substances. Inhibits the margination and subsequent cell migration to the area of injury, and also reverses the dilatation and increased vessel permeability in the area resulting in decreased access of cells to the sites of injury.

Pharmacodynamics/Kinetics

Onset of Action Improvement in allergic rhinitis symptoms may be seen within 11 hours; Maximum effect: Within 1 to 2 weeks after starting therapy

Half-life Elimination 6 hours (IV)

Pregnancy Risk Factor C

Pregnancy Considerations Adverse events have been observed in some animal reproduction studies. Hypoadrenalism may occur in newborns following maternal use of corticosteroids in pregnancy; monitor. Intranasal corticosteroids are recommended for the treatment of rhinitis during pregnancy; the lowest effective dose should be used (NAEPP 2005; Wallace 2008).

Mometasone and Formoterol

(moe MET a sone & for MOH te rol)

Related Information

Formoterol *on page 767*

Mometasone (Oral Inhalation) *on page 1138*

Brand Names: US Dulera

Brand Names: Canada Zenhale

Pharmacologic Category $Beta_2$ Agonist, Long-Acting; $Beta_2$-Adrenergic Agonist, Long-Acting; Corticosteroid, Inhalant (Oral)

Use Asthma: Treatment of asthma in patients 12 years and older.

Limitations of use: Mometasone/formoterol is not indicated for the relief of acute bronchospasm.

Local Anesthetic/Vasoconstrictor Precautions No information available to require special precautions

Effects on Dental Treatment Key adverse event(s) related to dental treatment: Formoterol: Xerostomia (normal salivary flow resumes upon discontinuation). Localized infections with *Candida albicans* or *Aspergillus niger* have occurred frequently in the mouth and pharynx with repetitive use of oral inhaler of corticosteroids. These infections may require treatment with appropriate antifungal therapy or discontinuance of treatment with corticosteroid inhaler.

Effects on Bleeding No information available to require special precautions

Adverse Reactions Also see individual agents.

1% to 10%:

Central nervous system: Headache (≤5%)

Respiratory: Nasopharyngitis (5%), voice disorder (4% to 5%), sinusitis (2% to 3%)

<1%, postmarketing, and/or case reports: Anaphylactoid reaction, anaphylaxis, angina pectoris, angioedema, atrial fibrillation, cardiac arrhythmia, exacerbation of asthma, hyperglycemia, hypertension, hypokalemia, hypotension (including severe), increased blood pressure, hypersensitivity reaction, oral candidiasis, prolonged Q-T interval on ECG, pruritus, skin rash, tachyarrhythmia, ventricular premature contractions

General Dosage Range Inhalation: *Children ≥12 years, Adolescents, and Adults:* 2 inhalations twice daily (maximum: Mometasone 800 mcg/formoterol 20 mcg per day)

Mechanism of Action Formoterol relaxes bronchial smooth muscle by selective action on $beta_2$ receptors with little effect on heart rate. Formoterol has a long-acting effect.

Mometasone is a corticosteroid which controls the rate of protein synthesis, depresses the migration of polymorphonuclear leukocytes/fibroblasts, and reverses capillary permeability and lysosomal stabilization at the cellular level to prevent or control inflammation.

Pregnancy Considerations Animal reproduction studies have not been conducted with this combination. See individual agents.

Montelukast (mon te LOO kast)

Related Information

Respiratory Diseases *on page 1777*

Brand Names: US Singulair

Brand Names: Canada ACH-Montelukast; Apo-Montelukast; Auro-Montelukast; Auro-Montelukast Chewable Tablets; Dom-Montelukast; Dom-Montelukast FC; Jamp-Montelukast; Mar-Montelukast; Mint-Montelukast; Montelukast Sodium Tablets; Mylan-Montelukast; PMS-Montelukast; PMS-Montelukast FC; RAN-Montelukast; Riva-Montelukast FC; Sandoz-Montelukast; Sandoz-Montelukast Granules; Singulair; Teva-Montelukast

Pharmacologic Category Leukotriene-Receptor Antagonist

Use

Prophylaxis and chronic treatment of asthma; relief of symptoms of seasonal allergic rhinitis and perennial allergic rhinitis; prevention of exercise-induced bronchoconstriction.

Note: American Academy of Otolaryngology, Head and Neck Surgery (AAO-HNS) guidelines recommend *against* montelukast use as first-line therapy for allergic rhinitis (except in patients with concurrent asthma) (Seidman, 2015 [AAO-HNS, 2015]).

Local Anesthetic/Vasoconstrictor Precautions No information available to require special precautions

Effects on Dental Treatment Key adverse event(s) related to dental treatment: Dental pain.

Effects on Bleeding Postmarket safety evaluation has identified increased bleeding tendency and thrombocytopenia.

Adverse Reactions

1% to 10%:

Central nervous system: Headache (children and adolescents: ≥2%), dizziness (adolescents and adults: 2%), fatigue (adolescents and adults: ≤2%)

Dermatologic: Atopic dermatitis (children: ≥2%), dermatitis (children: ≥2%), eczema (children: ≥2%), skin infection (children: ≥2%), urticaria (children: ≥2%), skin rash (2%)

Gastrointestinal: Abdominal pain (children: ≥2%), diarrhea (children and adolescents: ≥2%), nausea (children and adolescents: ≥2%), tooth infection (children: ≥2%), dyspepsia (2%), gastroenteritis (2%), toothache (adolescents and adults: 2%)

Genitourinary: Pyuria (adolescents and adults: 1%)

Hepatic: Increased serum AST (adolescents and adults: 2%), increased serum ALT (adolescents and adults: ≥1%)

Infection: Influenza (children and adolescents: ≥2%), varicella (children: ≥2%), viral infection (children and adolescents: ≥2%)

Neuromuscular & skeletal: Weakness (adolescents and adults: ≤2%)

Ophthalmic: Conjunctivitis (children: ≥2%), myopia (children: ≥2%)

Otic: Otalgia (children: ≥2%), otitis (children and adolescents: ≥2%), otitis media (children and adolescents: ≥2%)

Respiratory: Cough (3%), acute bronchitis (children: ≥2%), laryngitis (children and adolescents: ≥2%), pharyngitis (children: ≥2%), pneumonia (children: ≥2%), rhinitis (infective; children: ≥2%), rhinorrhea (children: ≥2%), nasal congestion (adolescents and adults: 2%), epistaxis (adolescents and adults: ≥1%), sinus headache (adolescents and adults: ≥1%), sinusitis (≥1%), upper respiratory tract infection (≥1%)

Miscellaneous: Fever (2%), trauma (adolescents and adults: 1%)

<1%, postmarketing and/or case reports: Abnormal dreams, aggressive behavior, agitation, anaphylaxis, angioedema, anxiety, arthralgia, behavioral changes, bruise, Churg-Strauss syndrome, depression, diarrhea, disorientation, drowsiness, edema, eosinophilia (systemic), eosinophilic pneumonitis, epistaxis, erythema multiforme, erythema nodosum, hallucination, hemorrhagic diathesis, hepatic eosinophilic infiltration, hepatitis (mixed pattern, hepatocellular, and cholestatic), hostility, hypersensitivity reaction, hypoesthesia, insomnia, irritability, lack of concentration, memory impairment, mood changes, muscle cramps, myalgia, nausea, palpitations, pancreatitis, paresthesia, pruritus, restlessness, seizure, somnambulism, Stevens-Johnson syndrome, suicidal ideation, suicidal tendencies, thrombocytopenia, tics, toxic epidermal necrolysis, tremor, urinary incontinence, urticaria, vasculitis, vomiting

General Dosage Range Oral:

Children 6 months to <6 years: 4 mg once daily

Children ≥6 years and Adolescents <15 years: 5 mg once daily **or** 5 mg 2 hours prior to exercise

Children ≥15 years and Adults: 10 mg once daily **or** 10 mg 2 hours prior to exercise

Mechanism of Action Selective leukotriene receptor antagonist that inhibits the cysteinyl leukotriene receptor. Cysteinyl leukotrienes and leukotriene receptor occupation have been correlated with the pathophysiology of asthma, including airway edema, smooth muscle contraction, and altered cellular activity associated with the inflammatory process, which contribute to the signs and symptoms of asthma. Cysteinyl leukotrienes are also released from the nasal mucosa following allergen exposure leading to symptoms associated with allergic rhinitis (Jarvis, 2000).

Pharmacodynamics/Kinetics

Duration of Action >24 hours

Half-life Elimination 2.7-5.5 hours; Mild-to-moderate hepatic impairment: 7.4 hours

Time to Peak Tablet: 10 mg: 3 to 4 hours (fasting); Chewable tablet: 4 mg (children 2 to 5 years): 2 hours (fasting); Chewable tablet 5 mg: 2 to 2.5 hours (fasting); Granules: 2.3 ± 1 hours (fasting) and 6.4 ± 2.9 hours (with high-fat meal)

Pregnancy Risk Factor B

Pregnancy Considerations Adverse events have not been observed in animal reproduction studies. Structural defects have been reported in neonates exposed to montelukast *in utero*; however, a specific pattern and relationship to montelukast has not been established. Based on available data, an increased risk of teratogenic effects has not been observed with montelukast use in pregnancy (Bakhireva 2007; Nelsen 2012; Sarkar 2009). Uncontrolled asthma is associated with adverse events on pregnancy (increased risk of perinatal mortality, pre-eclampsia, preterm birth, low birth weight infants). Montelukast may be considered for use in women who had a favorable response prior to becoming pregnant; however, initiating a leukotriene receptor antagonist during pregnancy is an alternative (but not preferred) treatment option for mild persistent asthma (NAEPP 2005).

Morphine (Systemic) (MOR feen)

Related Information

Management of the Chemically Dependent Patient *on page 1821*

OxyMORphone *on page 1274*

Brand Names: US Arymo ER; AVINza [DSC]; Duramorph; Infumorph 200; Infumorph 500; Kadian; MS Contin

Brand Names: Canada Doloral; Kadian; M-Eslon; M.O.S. 10; M.O.S. 20; M.O.S. 30; M.O.S.-SR; M.O.S.-Sulfate; Morphine Extra Forte Injection; Morphine Forte Injection; Morphine HP; Morphine LP Epidural; Morphine SR; Morphine-EPD; MS Contin; MS Contin SRT; MS-IR; Novo-Morphine SR; PMS-Morphine Sulfate SR; ratio-Morphine; ratio-Morphine SR; Sandoz-Morphine SR; Statex; Teva-Morphine SR

Generic Availability (US) May be product dependent

Pharmacologic Category Analgesic, Opioid

Use

Pain management:

Injection: Management of pain severe enough to require an opioid analgesic and for which alternative treatments are inadequate.

Preservative-free solutions only:

Duramorph: Epidural or intrathecal management of pain without attendant loss of motor, sensory, or sympathetic function. **Note:** Not for use in continuous microinfusion devices.

Infumorph: Used in continuous microinfusion devices for intrathecal or epidural administration in management of intractable chronic pain severe enough to require an opioid analgesic and for which less invasive means of controlling pain are inadequate. **Note:** Not for single-dose IV, IM, or subcutaneous administration or single-dose neuraxial injection.

Oral:

Extended-release: Management of pain severe enough to require daily, around-the-clock, long-term opioid treatment and for which alternative treatment options are inadequate.

Immediate-release: Management of acute and chronic pain severe enough to require an opioid analgesic and for which alternative treatments are inadequate. Oral solution 100 mg per 5 mL (20 mg/mL) is for opioid-tolerant patients.

Limitations of use: Reserve morphine for use in patients for whom alternative treatment options (eg, nonopioid analgesics, opioid combination products) are ineffective, not tolerated, or would be otherwise inadequate to provide sufficient management of pain. ER formulations are not indicated as as-needed analgesics.

Severe pain: Rectal: Relief of severe chronic and acute pain.

Local Anesthetic/Vasoconstrictor Precautions No information available to require special precautions

Effects on Dental Treatment Key adverse event(s) related to dental treatment: Xerostomia (normal salivary flow resumes upon discontinuation) and dysphagia. Anticholinergic side effects can cause a reduction of saliva production or secretion, contributing to discomfort and dental disease (ie, caries, oral candidiasis, and periodontal disease).

Effects on Bleeding No information available to require special precautions

Adverse Reactions Note: Individual patient differences are unpredictable and percentage may differ in acute pain (surgical) treatment. Reactions may be dose, formulation, and/or route dependent.

Frequency not always defined.

>10%

Cardiovascular: Oxygen saturation decreased

Central nervous system: Drowsiness (9% to >10%), headache (<2% to >10%)

Gastrointestinal: Constipation (9% to >10%), nausea (7% to >10%), vomiting (2% to >10%)

Genitourinary: Urinary retention (<2% to 16%; primarily in males; may be prolonged, up to 20 hours, following epidural or intrathecal use)

Hypersensitivity: Histamine release

Local: Pain at injection site

Neuromuscular & skeletal: Weakness

1% to 10%:

Cardiovascular: Peripheral edema (3% to 10%), chest pain (2% to <3%), atrial fibrillation (<2% to <3%), bradycardia (<2%), edema (<2%), facial flushing (<2%), flushing (<2%), hypertension (<2%), hypotension (<2%), palpitations (<2%), syncope (<2%), tachycardia (<2%), vasodilatation (<2%), circulatory depression, orthostatic hypotension, presyncope, shock

Central nervous system: Depression (5% to 10%), insomnia (<2% to 10%), paresthesia (<2% to 10%), dizziness (6%), anxiety (<2% to 6%), abnormality in thinking (<2% to <5%), confusion (<2% to <5%), convulsions (<5%), pain (3%), agitation (<2%), amnesia (<2%), apathy (<2%), ataxia (<2%), chills (<2%), decreased cough reflex (<2%), dream abnormalities (<2%), euphoria (<2%), hallucination (<2%), hypoesthesia (<2%), lack of concentration (<2%), lethargy (<2%), malaise (<2%), myoclonus (<2%), seizure (<2%), slurred speech (<2%), vertigo (<2%), voice disorder (<2%), withdrawal syndrome (<2%), abnormal gait, apprehension, coma, delirium, drug dependence, dysphoria, false sense of well-being, feeling abnormal, mood changes, nervousness, restlessness, rigors, sedation

Dermatologic: Diaphoresis (5% to 10%), skin rash (3% to 10%), decubitus ulcer (<2%), pallor (<2%), pruritus (<2%, may be dose related), urticaria, xeroderma

Endocrine & metabolic: Gynecomastia (<2% to <3%), amenorrhea (<2%), decreased libido (<2%), hyponatremia (<2%), antidiuretic effect, hypogonadism, hypokalemia, increased release of antidiuretic hormone, increased thirst, weight loss

Gastrointestinal: Abdominal pain (5% to 10%), diarrhea (5% to 10%), anorexia (3% to 10%), xerostomia (3% to 10%), biliary colic (<2%), delayed gastric emptying (<2%), dyspepsia (<2%), dysphagia (<2%), gastric atony (<2%), gastroesophageal reflux disease (<2%), hiccups (<2%), abdominal distension, dysgeusia, flatulence, gastroenteritis, GI irritation, paralytic ileus, rectal disease

Genitourinary: Urinary tract infection (5% to 10%), impotence (<2%), prolonged labor (<2%), urinary hesitancy (<2%), urine abnormality (<2%), abnormal ejaculation, bladder spasm, decreased urine output, dysuria, hypogonadism, oliguria

Hematologic & oncologic: Anemia (2% to <5%), thrombocytopenia (<2% to <5%), leukopenia (2%), hematocrit decreased

Hepatic: Increased liver function enzymes

Hypersensitivity: Hypersensitivity reaction

Infection: Infection

Local: Local irritation

Neuromuscular & skeletal: Back pain (<2% to 10%), asthenia (2%), tremor (2%), arthralgia (<2%), bone pain (<2%), foot-drop (<2%), decreased bone mineral density, muscle rigidity, muscle twitching

Ophthalmic: Amblyopia (<2%), blurred vision (<2%), conjunctivitis (<2%), diplopia (<2%), miosis (<2%), nystagmus (<2%), eye pain, visual disturbance

Respiratory: Dyspnea (3% to 10%), flu-like symptoms (<2% to 10%), hypoventilation (<5%), asthma (<2%), atelectasis (<2%), hypoxia (<2%), pulmonary edema (noncardiogenic, <2%), respiratory depression (<2%), respiratory insufficiency (<2%), rhinitis (<2%), hypercapnia

Miscellaneous: Accidental injury (2% to 10%), fever (2% to 10%)

<1%, postmarketing, and/or case reports: Anaphylaxis, apnea, biliary tract spasm, bronchospasm, decreased cough reflex, dehydration, disorientation, disruption of body temperature regulation, fatigue, genitourinary tract spasm, hemorrhagic urticaria, hyperalgesia, hypertonia, increased intracranial pressure, increased serum prolactin (Molitch 2008; Vuong 2010), intestinal obstruction, laryngospasm, menstrual irregularities, paradoxical central nervous system stimulation, sepsis, toxic psychosis

Dosing

Adult These are guidelines and do not represent the doses that may be required in all patients. Doses and dosage intervals should be titrated to pain relief/prevention.

Pain management:

IM, SubQ: **Note:** Repeated SubQ administration causes local tissue irritation, pain, and induration. The use of IM injections is no longer recommended especially for repeated administration due to painful administration, variable absorption and lag time to peak effect; other routes are more reliable and less painful (APS, 2008).

Initial: Opioid naive: 5 to 10 mg every 4 hours as needed; usual dosage range: 5 to 15 mg every 4 hours as needed. Patients with prior opioid exposure may require higher initial doses.

IV: Initial: Opioid naive: 2.5 to 5 mg every 3 to 4 hours; patients with prior opioid exposure may require higher initial doses. **Note:** Administration of 2 to 3 mg every 5 minutes until pain relief or if associated sedation, oxygen saturation <95%, or serious adverse event occurs may be appropriate in treating acute moderate to severe pain in settings such as the immediate postoperative period or the emergency department (Aubrun, 2012; Lvovschi, 2008); dose reduction in the immediate postoperative period (postanesthesia care unit) in the elderly is usually not necessary (Aubrun, 2002). A maximum cumulative dose (eg, 10 mg) prompting reevaluation of continued morphine use and/or dose should be included as part of any medication order intended for short-term use (eg, PACU orders). Refer to institution-specific protocols as appropriate.

Acute myocardial infarction, analgesia (off-label dose): Initial management: 4 to 8 mg (lower doses in elderly patients); subsequently may give 2 to 8 mg every 5 to 15 minutes as needed (O'Gara, 2012)

Critically ill patients, analgesia (off-label dose): 2 to 4 mg every 1 to 2 hours **or** 4 to 8 mg every 3 to 4 hours as needed (Barr, 2013)

IV, SubQ continuous infusion: Opioid tolerant: 0.8 to 10 mg/hour; usual range: 20 to 50 mg/hour (higher doses have been reported) (Citron 1984). **Note:** May administer a loading dose (amount administered should depend on severity of pain) prior to initiating the infusion. A continuous (basal) infusion is not recommended in an opioid-naive patient (ISMP 2009)

Continuous infusion for critically ill patients: Usual dosage range: 2 to 30 mg/hour (Barr, 2013)

Patient-controlled analgesia (PCA) (APS, 2008): **Note:** In opioid-naive patients, consider lower end of dosing range:

Usual concentration: 1 mg/mL

Demand dose: Usual: 1 mg; range: 0.5 to 2.5 mg

Lockout interval: 5 to 10 minutes

Epidural: **Note: Must be preservative free.** Administer with extreme caution and in reduced dosage to geriatric or debilitated patients. Vigilant monitoring is particularly important in these patients.

Single dose: **Lumbar region:** Astramorph/PF, Duramorph: 30 to 100 mcg/kg (optimal range: 2.5 to 3.75 mg; may depend upon patient comorbidities) (Bujedo 2012; Sultan 2011)

Continuous infusion (may be combined with bupivacaine): 0.2 to 0.4 mg/hour (Bujedo 2012). According to the manufacturer, Duramorph is not for use in continuous microinfusion devices.

Continuous microinfusion (Infumorph):

Opioid naive: Initial: 3.5 to 7.5 mg over 24 hours

Opioid tolerant: Initial: 4.5 to 10 mg over 24 hours, titrate to effect; usual maximum is ~30 mg per 24 hours

Intrathecal: **Note: Must be preservative free.** Administer with extreme caution and in reduced dosage to geriatric or debilitated patients. Intrathecal dose is usually 1/10 (one-tenth) that of epidural dosage.

Opioid naive:

Single dose: Lumbar region: Astramorph/PF, Duramorph:

Manufacturer's labeling: 0.2 to 1 mg may provide satisfactory pain relief for up to 24 hours. (Caution: This is only 0.4 to 2 mL of the 0.5 mg/mL potency or 0.2 to 1 mL of the 1 mg/mL potency.) Do not inject intrathecally more than 2 mL of the 0.5 mg/mL potency or 1 mL of the 1 mg/mL potency; repeat doses are not recommended.

Alternative recommendations: 0.1 to 0.3 mg (may provide adequate relief for up to 24 hours; APS, 2008); repeat doses are **not** recommended. If pain recurs within 24 hours of administration, use of an alternate route of administration is recommended. **Note:** Although product labeling recommends doses up to 1 mg, an analgesic ceiling exists with doses >0.3 mg and the risk of respiratory depression is higher with doses >0.3 mg (Rathmell 2005).

Continuous microinfusion (Infumorph): Lumbar region: After initial in-hospital evaluation of response to single-dose injections of Astramorph/PF or Duramorph, the initial dose of Infumorph is 0.2 to 1 mg over 24 hours.

Opioid tolerant: Continuous microinfusion (Infumorph): Lumbar region: Dosage range: 1 to 10 mg over 24 hours, titrate to effect; usual maximum is ~20 mg over 24 hours

Note: Limited experience with continuous intrathecal infusion of morphine has shown that the daily doses have to be increased over time. Employ doses >20 mg/day with caution.

Oral (immediate-release formulations): Opioid naive: Initial: **Note:** Usual dosage range: 10 to 30 mg every 4 hours as needed. Patients with prior opioid exposure may require higher initial doses.

Solution: 10 to 20 mg every 4 hours as needed.

Tablet: 15 to 30 mg every 4 hours as needed.

Oral (extended-release formulations): **Note:** Patients taking opioids chronically may become tolerant and require doses higher than the usual dosage range to maintain the desired effect. Tolerance can be managed by appropriate dose titration. There is no optimal or maximal dose for morphine in chronic pain. The appropriate dose is one that relieves pain throughout its dosing interval without causing unmanageable side effects. Consider total daily dose, potency, prior opioid use, degree of opioid experience and tolerance, conversion from previous opioid (including opioid formulation), patient's general condition, concurrent medications, and type and severity of pain during prescribing process. Opioid tolerance is defined as: Patients already taking at least 60 mg of oral morphine daily, 25 mcg transdermal fentanyl per hour, 30 mg of oral oxycodone daily, 8 mg oral hydromorphone daily, 25 mg of oral oxymorphone daily, 60 mg oral hydrocodone, or an equivalent dose of another opioid for at least 1 week.

A patient's morphine requirement should be established using immediate-release formulations. Conversion to long-acting products may be considered when chronic, continuous treatment is required. Higher dosages should be reserved for use only in opioid-tolerant patients.

Capsules, extended release (Avinza): Daily dose administered once daily (for best results, administer at same time each day). **Note:** Avinza 90 mg and 120 mg are only indicated for use in opioid-tolerant patents.

Use as the first opioid analgesic or use in patients who are **not** opioid tolerant: Initial: 30 mg once daily

Titration and maintenance: Adjust in increments ≤30 mg daily every 3 to 4 days. Maximum: 1600 mg daily due to fumaric acid content.

Capsules, extended release (Kadian): **Note:** Kadian 100 and 200 mg and a total daily dose >120 mg are only for use in opioid-tolerant patients.

Use as the first opioid analgesic: Has not been evaluated. Use an immediate-release morphine formulation and then convert patients to Kadian in the same fashion as initiating therapy in a nonopioid-tolerant patient.

Use in patients who are **not** opioid tolerant: Initial: 30 mg once daily.

Titration and maintenance: Dose adjustments may be done every 1 to 2 days.

Tablets, extended release (Arymo ER):

Use as the first opioid analgesic or in patients who are **not** opioid tolerant: Initial: 15 mg every 8 to 12 hours.

Titration and maintenance: Dose adjustments may be done every 1 to 2 days.

Tablets, extended release (MorphaBond ER):

Use as the first opioid analgesic or who are **not** opioid tolerant: Initial: 15 mg every 12 hours.

Titration and maintenance: Dose adjustments may be done every 1 to 2 days.

Tablets, extended release (MS Contin): **Note:** MS Contin 100 mg and 200 mg tablets are only for use in opioid-tolerant patients.

Use as the first opioid analgesic: Initial: 15 mg every 8 to 12 hours

Use in patients who are **not** opioid tolerant: Initial: 15 mg every 12 hours.

Titration and maintenance: Dose adjustments may be done every 1 to 2 days.

Rectal: 10 to 20 mg every 4 hours

Conversion from other oral morphine formulations to extended-release formulations:

Arymo ER, MS Contin: Total daily oral morphine dose may be administered either in 2 divided doses daily (every 12 hours) **or** in 3 divided doses (every 8 hours).

Avinza: Total daily morphine dose administered once daily. The first dose of Avinza may be taken with the last dose of the immediate-release morphine. Maximum: 1,600 mg daily due to fumaric acid content.

Kadian: Total daily oral morphine dose may be either administered once daily or in 2 divided doses daily (every 12 hours).

MorphaBond ER: Total daily oral morphine dose administered in 2 divided doses (every 12 hours).

Conversion from parenteral morphine or other opioids to extended-release formulations: Substantial interpatient variability exists in relative potency. Therefore, it is safer to underestimate a patient's daily oral morphine requirement and provide breakthrough pain relief with immediate-release morphine than to overestimate requirements. Consider the parenteral to oral morphine ratio or other oral or parenteral opioids to oral morphine conversions.

Parenteral to oral morphine ratio: Between 2 to 6 mg of oral morphine may be required for analgesia equivalent to 1 mg of parenteral morphine. An oral dose 3 times the daily parenteral dose may be sufficient in chronic pain settings.

Other parenteral or oral nonmorphine opioids to oral morphine: Specific recommendations are not available; refer to published relative potency data realizing that such ratios are only approximations. In general, it is safest to administer 50% of the estimated daily morphine requirement as the initial dose, and to manage inadequate analgesia by supplementation with immediate-release morphine.

Conversion from methadone to extended-release formulations: Close monitoring is required when converting methadone to another opioid. Ratio between methadone and other opioid agonists varies widely according to previous dose exposure. Methadone has a long half-life and can accumulate in the plasma.

Discontinuation of oral formulations: Decrease dose by 25% to 50% every 2 to 4 days; monitor carefully for signs/symptoms of withdrawal. If patient displays withdrawal symptoms, increase dose to previous dose and then reduce dose more slowly by increasing interval between dose reductions, decreasing amount of daily dose reduction, or both.

Geriatric Refer to adult dosing. Use with caution; may require reduced dosage.

Pediatric These are guidelines and do not represent the doses that may be required in all patients. Doses and dosage intervals should be titrated to pain relief/prevention.

Acute pain (moderate to severe): Note: The use of IM injections is no longer recommended, especially for repeated administration due to painful administration, variable absorption, and lag time to peak effect; other routes are more reliable and less painful (American Pain Society 2008).

Infants ≤6 months, nonventilated: **Note:** Infants <3 months of age are more susceptible to respiratory depression; lower doses are recommended (American Pain Society 2008):

Oral: Oral solution (2 mg/mL or 4 mg/mL): 0.08 to 0.1 mg/kg/dose every 3 to 4 hours (American Pain Society 2008; Berde 2002)

IV or SubQ: 0.025 to 0.03 mg/kg/dose every 2 to 4 hours as needed (American Pain Society 2008; Berde 2002).

Infants >6 months, Children, and Adolescents:

Oral: Immediate-release tablets, oral solution (2 mg/mL or 4 mg/mL):

Patient weight <50 kg: 0.2 to 0.5 mg/kg/dose every 3 to 4 hours as needed; some experts have recommended an initial dose of 0.3 mg/kg for severe pain; usual initial maximum dose: 15 to 20 mg (American Pain Society 2008; APA 2012; Berde 2002)

Patient weight ≥50 kg: 15 to 20 mg every 3 to 4 hours as needed (American Pain Society 2008; Berde 2002)

IM, IV, or SubQ; intermittent dosing:
Patient weight <50 kg: Initial: 0.05 mg/kg/dose; usual range: 0.1 to 0.2 mg/kg/dose every 2 to 4 hours as needed; usual maximum dose: Infants: 2 mg/dose; Children 1 to 6 years: 4 mg/dose; Children 7 to 12 years: 8 mg/dose; Adolescents: 10 mg/dose
Patient weight ≥50 kg: Initial: 2 to 5 mg every 2 to 4 hours as needed; higher doses have been recommended (5 to 8 mg every 2 to 4 hours as needed) and may be needed in tolerant patients (Berde 2002; Kliegman 2011)
Continuous IV infusion, SubQ continuous infusion:
Patient weight <50 kg: Initial: 0.01 mg/kg/hour (10 mcg/kg/hour); titrate carefully to effect; dosage range: 0.01 to 0.04 **mg**/kg/**hour** (10 to 40 mcg/kg/**hour**) (APA 2012; Friedrichsdorf 2007; Golianu 2000)
Patient weight ≥50 kg: 1.5 mg/**hour** (Berde 2002)
Conversion from intermittent IV morphine: Administer the patient's total daily IV morphine dose over 24 hours as a continuous infusion; titrate dose to appropriate effect

Analgesia for minor procedures/sedation: Infants, Children, and Adolescents: IV: 0.05 to 0.1 mg/kg/dose; administer 5 minutes before the procedure; maximum dose: 4 mg; may repeat dose in 5 minutes if necessary (Cramton 2012; Zeltzer 1990)

Patient-controlled analgesia (PCA), opioid-naive: **Note:** All patients should receive an initial loading dose of an analgesic (to attain adequate control of pain) before starting PCA for maintenance. Adjust doses, lockouts, and limits based on required loading dose, age, state of health, and presence of opioid tolerance. Use lower end of dosing range for opioid-naïve. Assess patient and pain control at regular intervals and adjust settings if needed (American Pain Society 2008): IV:
Children ≥5 years and Adolescents, weighing <50 kg: **Note:** PCA has been used in children as young as 5 years of age; however, clinicians need to assess children 5 to 8 years of age to determine if they are able to use the PCA device correctly (American Pain Society 2008).
Usual concentration: 1 mg/mL
Demand dose: Usual initial: 0.02 mg/kg/dose; usual range: 0.01 to 0.03 mg/kg/dose
Lockout: Usual initial: 5 doses/hour
Lockout interval: Range: 6 to 8 minutes
Usual basal rate: 0 to 0.03 mg/kg/hour
Children ≥5 years and Adolescents, weighing ≥50 kg:
Usual concentration: 1 mg/mL
Demand dose: Usual initial: 1 mg; usual range: 0.5 to 2.5 mg
Lockout interval: Usual initial: 6 minutes; usual range: 5 to 10 minutes

Renal Impairment According to the manufacturer's labeling, no specific dosage adjustments are provided (all formulations). In general, the manufacturers recommend starting cautiously with lower doses; titrating slowly while carefully monitoring for side effects. However, the choice of an alternate opioid may be prudent in patients with baseline renal impairment or rapidly changing renal function especially since other analgesics may be safer and reduced initial morphine dosing may result in suboptimal analgesia. Although clearance of morphine is similar to patients with normal renal function, glucuronide metabolites (M3G [inactive as an analgesic; may contribute to CNS stimulation] and M6G [active analgesic]) accumulate in renal impairment resulting in increased sensitivity; patients may experience severe and prolonged respiratory depression which may even be delayed (Lugo 2002; Niscola 2010).

Hepatic Impairment There are no dosage adjustment provided in the manufacturer's labeling. Pharmacokinetics unchanged in mild liver disease; substantial extrahepatic metabolism may occur. In cirrhosis, increases in half-life and AUC suggest dosage adjustment required.

Mechanism of Action Binds to opioid receptors in the CNS, causing inhibition of ascending pain pathways, altering the perception of and response to pain; produces generalized CNS depression

Contraindications

Hypersensitivity (eg, anaphylaxis) to morphine or any component of the formulation; significant respiratory depression; acute or severe bronchial asthma in an unmonitored setting or in the absence of resuscitative equipment; concurrent use of monoamine oxidase inhibitors (MAOIs) or use of MAOIs within the last 14 days; GI obstruction, including paralytic ileus (known or suspected).

Documentation of allergenic cross-reactivity for opioids is limited. However, because of similarities in chemical structure and/or pharmacologic actions, the possibility of cross-sensitivity cannot be ruled out with certainty.

Additional contraindications:
Epidural/intrathecal: Astramorph/PF, Duramorph, Infumorph: Infection at infusion site; concomitant anticoagulant therapy; uncontrolled bleeding diathesis; presence of any other concomitant therapy or medical condition that would render administration hazardous; upper airway obstruction (Astramorph/PF only).
Rectal: Severe CNS depression; cardiac arrhythmias, heart failure due to chronic lung disease; increased intracranial or cerebrospinal pressure, head injuries, brain tumor; acute alcoholism, delirium tremens; seizure disorder; use after biliary tract surgery, suspected surgical abdomen, surgical anastomosis

Warnings/Precautions An opioid-containing analgesic regimen should be tailored to each patient's needs and based upon the type of pain being treated (acute versus chronic), the route of administration, degree of tolerance for opioids (naive versus chronic user), age, weight, and medical condition. The optimal analgesic dose varies widely among patients.

[US Boxed Warning]: Serious, life-threatening, or fatal respiratory depression may occur. Monitor closely for respiratory depression, especially during initiation or dose escalation. Swallow ER morphine formulations whole (or may sprinkle the contents of the capsule on applesauce and swallow without chewing); crushing, chewing, or dissolving the ER formulations can cause rapid release and absorption of a potentially fatal dose of morphine. Carbon dioxide retention from opioid-induced respiratory depression can exacerbate the sedating effects of opioids. Use with caution and monitor for respiratory depression in patients with significant chronic obstructive pulmonary disease or cor pulmonale and patients having a substantially decreased respiratory reserve, hypoxia, hypercarbia, or preexisting respiratory depression, particularly when initiating therapy and titrating with morphine; consider the use of alternative nonopioid analgesics in these patients. Use opioids with caution for chronic pain and titrate dosage cautiously in patients with risk factors for sleep-disordered breathing, including HF and obesity. Avoid opioids in patients with moderate to severe sleep-disordered breathing (Dowell [CDC 2016]). Infants <3 months of age are more susceptible to respiratory depression, use with caution and generally in reduced doses in this age group (APS 2008).

Use caution in patients with hypersensitivity reactions to other phenanthrene derivative opioid agonists (codeine, hydrocodone, hydromorphone, levorphanol, oxycodone, oxymorphone). Avoid use in patients with impaired consciousness or coma. May obscure diagnosis or clinical course of patients with acute abdominal conditions. May cause constipation, which may be problematic in patients with unstable angina and patients post-myocardial infarction. Some preparations contain sulfites, which may cause allergic reactions.

May cause CNS depression, which may impair physical or mental abilities; patients must be cautioned about performing tasks that require mental alertness (eg, operating machinery or driving). **[US Boxed Warning]: Concomitant use of opioids with benzodiazepines or other CNS depressants, including alcohol, may result in profound sedation, respiratory depression, coma, and death. Reserve concomitant prescribing of morphine and benzodiazepines or other CNS depressants for use in patients for whom alternative treatment options are inadequate. Limit dosage and durations to the minimum required and follow patients for signs and symptoms of respiratory depression and sedation. [US Boxed Warning]: Patients should not consume alcoholic beverages or medication containing ethanol while taking ER capsules; ethanol may increase morphine plasma levels, resulting in a potentially fatal overdose.** Potentially significant interactions may exist, requiring dose or frequency adjustment, additional monitoring, and/or selection of alternative therapy.

[US Boxed Warning]: Morphine exposes patients and other users to the risks of addiction, abuse, and misuse, potentially leading to overdose and death. Assess each patient's risk prior to prescribing; monitor all patients regularly for development of these behaviors or conditions. Use with caution in patients with a history of drug abuse or acute alcoholism; potential for drug dependency exists. Other factors associated with increased risk include younger age, concomitant depression (major), and psychotropic medication use. Consider offering naloxone prescriptions in patients with factors associated with an increased risk for overdose, such as history of overdose or substance use disorder, higher opioid dosages (≥50 morphine milligram equivalents/day orally), and concomitant benzodiazepine use (Dowell [CDC 2016]).

May cause severe hypotension (including orthostatic hypotension and syncope); use with caution in patients with hypovolemia, cardiovascular disease (including acute MI), circulatory shock, or drugs that may exaggerate hypotensive effects (including phenothiazines or general anesthetics). Monitor for symptoms of hypotension following initiation or dose titration. Avoid use in patients with circulatory shock. Use with extreme caution in patients with adrenal insufficiency, including Addison disease; biliary tract dysfunction or acute pancreatitis; head injury, intracranial lesions, or elevated intracranial pressure; delirium tremens; prostatic hyperplasia and/or urinary stricture; renal and/or hepatic impairment; seizure disorders; thyroid dysfunction; or toxic psychosis. Use opioids for chronic pain with caution in patients with mental health conditions (eg, depression, anxiety disorders, post-traumatic stress disorder) due to increased risk for opioid use disorder and overdose; more frequent monitoring is recommended (Dowell [CDC 2016]). Concurrent use of mixed agonist/antagonist analgesics (eg, pentazocine, nalbuphine, butorphanol) or partial agonist (eg, buprenorphine) analgesics may precipitate withdrawal symptoms and/or reduced analgesic efficacy in patients following prolonged therapy with mu opioid agonists. Taper dose gradually when discontinuing.

Use with caution in patients who are morbidly obese. Use with caution in cachectic or debilitated patients; there is a greater potential for critical respiratory depression, even at therapeutic dosages. Consider the use of alternative nonopioid analgesics in these patients. Use with caution in elderly patients; may be more sensitive to adverse effects, including life-threatening respiratory depression. Decrease initial dose. In the setting of chronic pain, monitor closely due to an increased potential for risks, including certain risks such as falls/fracture, cognitive impairment, and constipation. Clearance may also be reduced in older adults (with or without renal impairment) resulting in a narrow therapeutic window and increasing the risk for respiratory depression or overdose (Dowell [CDC 2016]). Consider the use of alternative nonopioid analgesics in these patients. Opioids decrease bowel motility; monitor for decreased bowel motility in postop patients receiving opioids. Use with caution in the perioperative setting; individualize treatment when transitioning from parenteral to oral analgesics. Some dosage forms may be contraindicated after biliary tract surgery, suspected surgical abdomen, or surgical anastomosis.

Avinza capsules contain fumaric acid; dangerous quantities of fumaric acid may be ingested when >1,600 mg/day is used; serious renal toxicity may occur above the maximum dose. **[US Boxed Warning]: Prolonged maternal use of opioids during pregnancy can cause neonatal withdrawal syndrome in the newborn, which may be life-threatening if not recognized and treated according to protocols developed by neonatology experts. If prolonged opioid therapy is required in a pregnant woman, ensure treatment is available and warn patient of risk to the neonate.** Signs and symptoms include irritability, hyperactivity, abnormal sleep pattern, high-pitched cry, tremor, vomiting, diarrhea, and failure to gain weight. Onset, duration, and severity depend on the drug used, duration of use, maternal dose, and rate of drug elimination by the newborn. **[US Boxed Warning]: Accidental ingestion of even one dose, especially in children, can result in a fatal overdose of morphine.**

Oral solutions: **[US Boxed Warning]: Ensure accuracy when prescribing, dispensing, and administering morphine oral solution. Dosing errors due to confusion between mg and mL, and other morphine solutions of different concentrations, can result in accidental overdose and death.** The 100 mg per 5 mL (20 mg/mL) is for use in opioid-tolerant patients only.

Injections: **[US Boxed Warning]: Because of delay in maximum CNS effect with IV administration (30 minutes), rapid IV administration may result in overdosing. Observe patients in a fully equipped and staffed environment for at least 24 hours after each test dose of Infumorph and, as indicated, for the first several days after surgery.** Products are designed for administration by specific routes (ie, IV, intrathecal, epidural). Use caution when prescribing, dispensing, or administering to use formulations only by intended route(s). Rapid IV administration may result in chest wall rigidity. Use with caution when injecting IM into chilled areas or in patients with hypotension or shock (impaired perfusion may prevent complete absorption); if repeated injections are administered, an excessive amount may be suddenly absorbed if normal circulation is re-established.

Infumorph, Duramorph: Neuroaxial administration: **[US Boxed Warning]: Because of the risk of severe adverse effects when the epidural or intrathecal route of administration is employed, patients must be observed in a fully equipped and staffed environment for at least 24 hours after the initial dose. Single-dose Duramorph neuraxial administration may result in acute or delayed respiratory depression up to 24 hours. Monitor patients receiving Infumorph for the first several days after catheter implantation.** Naloxone injection should be immediately available. Thoracic epidural administration has been shown to dramatically increase the risk of early and late respiratory depression. High doses (>20 mg/day) of neuraxial morphine may produce myoclonic events. Patients with reduced circulating blood volume or impaired myocardial function, or on concomitant sympatholytic drugs should be monitored for orthostatic hypotension, a frequent complication in single-dose neuraxial morphine.

Infumorph: Should only be used in microinfusion devices; not for IV, IM, or SubQ administration or for single-dose administration. Administer intrathecal doses of 10 and 25 mg/mL to the lumbar area. Monitor closely, especially in the first 24 hours. Inflammatory masses (eg, granulomas), some resulting in severe neurologic impairment, have occurred when receiving Infumorph via indwelling intrathecal catheter; monitor carefully for new neurologic signs/symptoms. Improper or erroneous substitution of Infumorph for regular Duramorph is likely to result in serious overdosage, leading to seizures, respiratory depression, and possibly a fatal outcome.

ER formulations: Therapy should only be prescribed by health care providers familiar with the use of potent opioids for chronic pain. ER products are not interchangeable. When determining a generic equivalent or switching from one ER product to another, a thorough understanding of the pharmacokinetic properties is important in determining the proper generic equivalent or proper dose of the other extended-release product (review of the manufacturer's label may be necessary).

Arymo ER: Moistened tablets may become sticky, leading to difficulty in swallowing the tablets; choking, gagging, regurgitation, and tablets getting stuck in the throat may occur. Tablet stickiness and swelling may also predispose patients to intestinal obstruction and exacerbation of diverticulitis. Do not pre-soak, lick, or otherwise wet tablets prior to placing in the mouth; take one tablet at a time with enough water to ensure complete swallowing. Consider use of an alternative analgesic in patients who have difficulty swallowing and patients at risk for underlying GI disorders resulting in a small GI lumen (eg, esophageal cancer, colon cancer).

Chronic pain (outside of end-of-life or palliative care, active cancer treatment, sickle cell disease, or medication-assisted treatment for opioid use disorder) in outpatient setting in adults: Opioids should not be used as first-line therapy for chronic pain management (pain >3-month duration or beyond time of normal tissue healing) due to limited short-term benefits, undetermined long-term benefits, and association with serious risks (eg, overdose, MI, auto accidents, risk of developing opioid use disorder). Preferred management includes nonpharmacologic therapy and nonopioid therapy (eg, NSAIDS, acetaminophen, certain anticonvulsants and antidepressants). If opioid therapy is initiated, it should be combined with nonpharmacologic and nonopioid therapy, as appropriate. Prior to initiation, known risks of opioid therapy should be discussed and realistic treatment goals for pain/function should be established, including consideration for discontinuation if benefits do not outweigh risks. Therapy should be continued only if clinically meaningful improvement in pain/function outweighs risks. Therapy should be initiated at the lowest effective dosage using immediate-release opioids (instead of extended-release/long-acting opioids). Risk associated with use increases with higher opioid dosages. Risks and benefits should be re-evaluated when increasing dosage to ≥50 morphine milligram equivalents (MME)/day orally; dosages ≥90 MME/day orally should be avoided unless carefully justified (Dowell [CDC 2016]).

Some dosage forms may contain sodium benzoate/benzoic acid; benzoic acid (benzoate) is a metabolite of benzyl alcohol; large amounts of benzyl alcohol (≥99 mg/kg/day) have been associated with a potentially fatal toxicity ("gasping syndrome") in neonates; the "gasping syndrome" consists of metabolic acidosis, respiratory distress, gasping respirations, CNS dysfunction (including convulsions, intracranial hemorrhage), hypotension, and cardiovascular collapse (AAP ["Inactive" 1997]; CDC, 1982); some data suggests that benzoate displaces bilirubin from protein binding sites (Ahlfors, 2001); avoid or use dosage forms containing benzyl alcohol derivative with caution in neonates. See manufacturer's labeling.

Drug Interactions

Metabolism/Transport Effects Substrate of CYP2D6 (minor), P-glycoprotein, UGT1A1; **Note:** Assignment of Major/Minor substrate status based on clinically relevant drug interaction potential

Avoid Concomitant Use

Avoid concomitant use of Morphine (Systemic) with any of the following: Azelastine (Nasal); Eluxadoline; MAO Inhibitors; Mixed Agonist / Antagonist Opioids; Orphenadrine; Oxomemazine; Paraldehyde; Thalidomide

Increased Effect/Toxicity

Morphine (Systemic) may increase the levels/effects of: Alvimopan; Amifostine; Analgesics (Opioid); Azelastine (Nasal); Blonanserin; Desmopressin; Diuretics; DULoxetine; Eluxadoline; Esmolol; Flunitrazepam; Gabapentin; HYDROcodone; Hypotension-Associated Agents; Levodopa; Methotrimeprazine; MetyroSINE; Nitroprusside; Orphenadrine; OxyCODONE; Paraldehyde; Piribedil; Pramipexole; Ramosetron; ROPINIRole; Rotigotine; Selective Serotonin Reuptake Inhibitors; Serotonin Modulators; Suvorexant; Thalidomide; Zolpidem

The levels/effects of Morphine (Systemic) may be increased by: Alfuzosin; Amphetamines; Anticholinergic Agents; Blood Pressure Lowering Agents; Brimonidine (Topical); Cannabis; Chlormethiazole; Chlorphenesin Carbamate; CNS Depressants; Diazoxide; Dimethindene (Topical); Dronabinol; Droperidol; Gabapentin; Herbs (Hypotensive Properties); Kava

Kava; Lofexidine; Lumacaftor; Magnesium Sulfate; MAO Inhibitors; Methotrimeprazine; Minocycline; Molsidomine; Nabilone; Naftopidil; Nicergoline; Nicorandil; Obinutuzumab; Oxomemazine; Pentoxifylline; Perampanel; P-glycoprotein/ABCB1 Inhibitors; Phosphodiesterase 5 Inhibitors; Prostacyclin Analogues; Quinagolide; Ranolazine; Rufinamide; Sodium Oxybate; Succinylcholine; Tapentadol; Tetrahydrocannabinol

Decreased Effect

Morphine (Systemic) may decrease the levels/effects of: Antiplatelet Agents (P2Y12 Inhibitors); Diuretics; Gastrointestinal Agents (Prokinetic); Pegvisomant

The levels/effects of Morphine (Systemic) may be decreased by: Lumacaftor; Mixed Agonist / Antagonist Opioids; Nalmefene; Naltrexone; P-glycoprotein/ABCB1 Inducers; RifAMPin

Food Interactions

Ethanol: Alcoholic beverages or ethanol-containing products may disrupt extended release formulation resulting in rapid release of entire morphine dose. Management: Avoid alcohol. **Do not administer Avinza or Kadian with alcoholic beverages or ethanol-containing prescription or nonprescription products.**

Food: Administration of oral morphine solution with food may increase bioavailability (ie, a report of 34% increase in morphine AUC when morphine oral solution followed a high-fat meal). The bioavailability of Avinza, MorphaBond, MS Contin, or Kadian does not appear to be affected by food. Management: Take consistently with or without meals.

Dietary Considerations Morphine may cause GI upset; take with food if GI upset occurs. Be consistent when taking morphine with or without meals.

Pharmacodynamics/Kinetics

Onset of Action Patient dependent; dosing must be individualized: Oral (immediate release): ~30 minutes; IV: 5 to 10 minutes

Duration of Action Patient dependent; dosing must be individualized: Pain relief:

Immediate-release formulations (tablet, oral solution, injection): 3 to 5 hours

Extended-release capsule and tablet: 8 to 24 hours (formulation dependent)

Epidural or intrathecal: Single dose: Up to 24 hours (Bujedo 2012)

Suppository: 3 to 7 hours

Half-life Elimination

Preterm: 10 to 20 hours

Neonates: 7.6 hours (range: 4.5 to 13.3 hours)

Infants 1 to 3 months: Median: 6.2 hours (range: 5 to 10 hours) (McRorie 1992)

Infants 3 to 6 months: Median: 4.5 hours (range: 3.8 to 7.3 hours) (McRorie 1992)

Infants 6 months to Children 2.5 years: Median: 2.9 hours (range: 1.4 to 7.8 hours) (McRorie 1992)

Preschool Children: 1 to 2 hours

Children with sickle cell disease (age: 6 to 19 years): ~1.3 hours (Dampier 1995)

Adults: Immediate-release forms: 2 to 4 hours; Avinza: ~24 hours; Kadian: 11 to 13 hours

Time to Peak

Plasma:

Tablets, oral solution, epidural: 1 hour

Extended release tablets: 3 to 4 hours; Avinza: 30 minutes (maintained for 24 hours); Kadian: ~10 hours

Suppository: 20 to 60 minutes

SubQ: 50 to 90 minutes

IM: 30 to 60 minutes

IV: 20 minutes

Cerebrospinal fluid: After an oral dose of controlled release morphine concentrations peak at 8 hours for both normal and reduced renal function; morphine-6-glucuronide (active analgesic) and morphine-3-glucuronide distribution into the CNS may be delayed peaking at 12 hours in patients with normal renal function or up to 24 hours in patients with ESRD (peak level of morphine-6-glucuronide is ~15 times higher than patients with normal renal function) (D'Honneur 1994).

Pregnancy Considerations Adverse events have been observed in some animal reproduction studies. Morphine crosses the human placenta. The frequency of congenital malformations has not been reported to be greater than expected in children from mothers treated with morphine during pregnancy. However, following *in utero* exposure, infants may exhibit withdrawal, decreased brain volume (reversible), small size, decreased ventilatory response to CO_2, and increased risk of sudden infant death syndrome.

Morphine sulfate injection may be used for the management of pain during labor (ACOG, 2002); however, some manufacturers specifically contraindicate use of the injection during labor when a premature birth is anticipated. When used for pain relief during labor, opioids may temporarily affect the heart rate of the fetus. Morphine injection may also be used to treat pain following delivery (ACOG, 2002).

[US Boxed Warning]: Prolonged use of opioids during pregnancy can cause neonatal withdrawal syndrome, which may be life-threatening if not recognized and treated according to protocols developed by neonatology experts. If opioid use is required for a prolonged period in a pregnant woman, advise the patient of the risk of neonatal opioid withdrawal syndrome and ensure that appropriate treatment will be available. If chronic opioid exposure occurs in pregnancy, adverse events in the newborn (including withdrawal) may occur; monitoring of the neonate is recommended. The minimum effective dose should be used if opioids are needed (Chou 2009). Neonatal abstinence syndrome following opioid exposure may present with autonomic (eg, fever, temperature instability), gastrointestinal (eg, diarrhea, vomiting, poor feeding/weight gain), or neurologic (eg, high-pitched crying, increased muscle tone, irritability, seizure, tremor) symptoms (Dow 2012, Hudak 2012).

Long-term opioid use may cause secondary hypogonadism, which may lead to sexual dysfunction or infertility (Brennan, 2013).

Breastfeeding Considerations Morphine is excreted in breast milk. M6G, the active metabolite of morphine, can also be detected in breast milk (Baka 2002).

The actual amount received by a nursing infant varies greatly and is dependent upon route of maternal administration, maternal plasma concentration, volume of milk ingested by the infant, and the extent of metabolism. Morphine has been detected in the urine of a nursing infant following maternal epidural dosing after cesarean section (Zakowski 1993).

Excess sedation and respiratory depression may be observed in nursing infants; withdrawal may occur in infants when maternal morphine is stopped.

Current guidelines note that nonopioid analgesics are preferred for postpartum pain in breastfeeding women (Montgomery 2012); however, when a narcotic is needed to treat maternal pain, morphine is one of the preferred agents (Montgomery 2012; Sachs 2013). **Note:** Not all formulations are indicated for intermittent pain control. Analgesics delivered by PCA or administered by the epidural route help limit infant exposure (Sachs 2013). When intravenous or intramuscular opioids are needed, moderate to low doses of parenteral morphine may be preferred (Montgomery 2012). In general, a single, occasional dose of morphine may be compatible with breastfeeding. Mothers should closely monitor their nursing infants (WHO 2002).

Product Availability MorphaBond (morphine sulfate extended-release tablets): FDA approved October 2015; anticipated availability is currently unknown.

Controlled Substance C-II

Dosage Forms

Capsule Extended Release 24 Hour, Oral:

Kadian: 10 mg, 20 mg, 30 mg, 40 mg, 50 mg, 60 mg, 80 mg, 100 mg, 200 mg

Generic: 10 mg, 20 mg, 30 mg, 45 mg, 50 mg, 60 mg, 75 mg, 80 mg, 90 mg, 100 mg, 120 mg

Device, Intramuscular:

Generic: 10 mg/0.7 mL (0.7 mL)

Solution, Injection:

Generic: 2 mg/mL (1 mL); 4 mg/mL (1 mL); 5 mg/mL (1 mL); 8 mg/mL (1 mL); 10 mg/mL (1 mL, 10 mL); 15 mg/mL (1 mL, 20 mL)

Solution, Injection [preservative free]:

Duramorph: 0.5 mg/mL (10 mL); 1 mg/mL (10 mL)

Infumorph 200: 200 mg/20 mL (10 mg/mL) (20 mL)

Infumorph 500: 500 mg/20 mL (25 mg/mL) (20 mL)

Generic: 0.5 mg/mL (10 mL); 1 mg/mL (10 mL)

Solution, Intravenous:

Generic: 1 mg/mL (10 mL, 30 mL, 100 mL); 25 mg/mL (4 mL, 10 mL); 50 mg/mL (20 mL, 50 mL); 1000 mg/100 mL (100 mL)

Solution, Intravenous [preservative free]:

Generic: 1 mg/mL (30 mL); 2 mg/mL (1 mL); 4 mg/mL (1 mL); 150 mg/30 mL (30 mL); 8 mg/mL (1 mL); 10 mg/mL (1 mL); 15 mg/mL (1 mL); 25 mg/mL (10 mL)

Solution, Oral:

Generic: 10 mg/5 mL (5 mL, 15 mL, 100 mL, 500 mL); 20 mg/5 mL (5 mL, 100 mL, 500 mL); 20 mg/mL (15 mL, 30 mL, 120 mL, 240 mL); 100 mg/5 mL (15 mL, 30 mL, 120 mL, 240 mL)

Solution Prefilled Syringe, Intravenous:

Generic: 50 mg/50 mL (50 mL)

Suppository, Rectal:

Generic: 5 mg (12 ea); 10 mg (12 ea); 20 mg (12 ea); 30 mg (12 ea)

Tablet, Oral:

Generic: 15 mg, 30 mg

Tablet Extended Release, Oral:

MS Contin: 15 mg, 30 mg, 60 mg, 100 mg, 200 mg

Generic: 15 mg, 30 mg, 60 mg, 100 mg, 200 mg

Tablet Extended Release Abuse-Deterrent, Oral:

Arymo ER: 15 mg (100 ea); 30 mg (100 ea); 60 mg (100 ea)

Dosage Forms: Canada

Solution, oral:

Doloral: 1 mg/mL; 5 mg/mL [not available in US]

Mouthwash (Antiseptic) (MOUTH wosh)

Related Information

Bacterial Infections *on page 1835*

Dentin Hypersensitivity, Acid Erosion, High Caries Index, Management of Alveolar Osteitis, and Xerostomia *on page 1857*

Periodontal Diseases *on page 1844*

Ulcerative, Erosive, and Painful Oral Mucosal Disorders *on page 1853*

Related Sample Prescriptions

Antimicrobial Oral Rinse - Sample Prescriptions *on page 31*

Brand Names: US Crest Scope Outlast [OTC]; Crest Scope [OTC]; Listerine Antiseptic [OTC]; Listerine Naturals Antiseptic [OTC]; Listerine Ultraclean Antiseptic [OTC]; Oragesic [OTC] [DSC]

Generic Availability (US) Yes

Pharmacologic Category Antimicrobial Mouth Rinse; Antiplaque Agent; Mouthwash

Dental Use Aid in prevention and reduction of plaque and gingivitis; halitosis

Use Aid in prevention and reduction of plaque and gingivitis; halitosis

Local Anesthetic/Vasoconstrictor Precautions No information available to require special precautions

Effects on Dental Treatment No significant effects or complications reported (see Dental Comment)

Effects on Bleeding No information available to require special precautions

Adverse Reactions No data reported

Dental Usual Dosage Plaque/gingivitis prevention: Adults: Oral: Rinse full strength for 30 seconds with 20 mL morning and night

Dosing

Adult & Geriatric Plaque/gingivitis prevention: Oral: Rinse full strength for 30 seconds with 20 mL morning and night

Contraindications Hypersensitivity to any component of the formulation

Dental Comment Active ingredients:

Listerine® Antiseptic: Thymol 0.064%, eucalyptus 0.092%, methyl salicylate 0.060%, menthol 0.042%, alcohol 26.9%, water, benzoic acid, poloxamer 407, sodium benzoate, caramel

Fresh Burst Listerine® Antiseptic: Thymol 0.064%, eucalyptus 0.092%, methyl salicylate 0.060%, menthol 0.042%, alcohol 26.9%, water, benzoic acid, poloxamer 407, sodium benzoate, flavoring, sodium, saccharin, sodium citrate, citric acid, D&C yellow #10, FD&C green #3

Cool Mint Listerine® Antiseptic: Thymol 0.064%, eucalyptus 0.092%, methyl salicylate 0.060%, menthol 0.042%, alcohol 26.9%, water, benzoic acid, poloxamer 407, sodium benzoate, flavoring, sodium, saccharin, sodium citrate, citric acid, FD&C green #3

The following information is endorsed on the label of the Listerine® products by the Council on Scientific Affairs, American Dental Association: "Listerine® Antiseptic has been shown to help prevent and reduce supragingival plaque accumulation and gingivitis when used in a conscientiously applied program of oral hygiene and regular professional care. Its effect on periodontitis has not been determined."

Moxifloxacin (Systemic) (moxs i FLOKS a sin)

Related Information

Bacterial Infections *on page 1835*

Clinical Risk Related to Drugs Prolonging QT Interval *on page 1772*

Brand Names: US Avelox; Avelox ABC Pack [DSC]

Brand Names: Canada Auro-Moxifloxacin; Avelox; Avelox I.V.; Bio-Moxifloxacin; JAMP-Moxifloxacin; Mar-Moxifloxacin; Priva-Moxifloxacin; Teva-Moxifloxacin

Generic Availability (US) Yes

Pharmacologic Category Antibiotic, Fluoroquinolone; Antibiotic, Respiratory Fluoroquinolone

Use

Treatment of mild to moderate community-acquired pneumonia, including multidrug-resistant *Streptococcus pneumoniae* (MDRSP); acute bacterial exacerbation of chronic bronchitis; acute bacterial sinusitis; complicated and uncomplicated skin and skin structure infections; complicated intra-abdominal infections; prophylaxis and treatment of plague, including pneumonic and septicemic plague, due to *Yersinia pestis*.

Limitations of use: Because fluoroquinolones have been associated with disabling and potentially irreversible serious adverse reactions (eg, tendinitis and tendon rupture, peripheral neuropathy, CNS effects), reserve moxifloxacin for use in patients who have no alternative treatment options for acute exacerbation of chronic bronchitis or acute sinusitis.

Local Anesthetic/Vasoconstrictor Precautions Moxifloxacin is one of the drugs confirmed to prolong the QT interval and is accepted as having a risk of causing torsade de pointes. The risk of drug-induced torsade de pointes is extremely low when a single QT interval prolonging drug is prescribed. In terms of epinephrine, it is not known what effect vasoconstrictors in the local anesthetic regimen will have in patients with a known history of congenital prolonged QT interval or in patients taking any medication that prolongs the QT interval. Until more information is obtained, it is suggested that the clinician consult with the physician prior to the use of a vasoconstrictor in suspected patients, and that the vasoconstrictor (epinephrine, mepivacaine and levonordefrin [Carbocaine® 2% with Neo-Cobefrin®]) be used with caution.

Effects on Dental Treatment Key adverse event(s) related to dental treatment: Dry mouth, glossitis, stomatitis, and taste perversion.

Effects on Bleeding Anemia, prolonged prothrombin activation, prolonged activated partial thromboplastin time, increased platelet count, decreased hemoglobin, decreased hematocrit have been reported in a subset of all patients receiving systemic moxifloxacin at therapeutic concentrations. As a consequence, prothrombin time should be closely monitored during moxifloxacin therapy, especially if administered concomitantly with warfarin.

Adverse Reactions

2% to 10%:

Central nervous system: Headache (≤4%), dizziness (3%), insomnia (2%)

Endocrine & metabolic: Decreased serum glucose (≥2%), hyperchloremia (≥2%), increased serum albumin (≥2%)

Gastrointestinal: Nausea (7%), diarrhea (6%), decreased amylase (≥2%), constipation (2%), vomiting (2%), abdominal pain (1% to 2%)

Hematologic & oncologic: Decreased basophils (≥2%), decreased hemoglobin (≥2%), decreased neutrophils (≥2%), decreased prothrombin time (≥2%), decreased red blood cells (≥2%), eosinopenia (≥2%), increased MCH (≥2%), increased neutrophils (≥2%), leukocytosis (≥2%), prolonged prothrombin time (≥2%)

Hepatic: Decreased serum bilirubin (≥2%), increased serum bilirubin (≥2%)

Immunologic: Increased serum globulins (≥2%)

Renal: Increased ionized serum calcium (≥2%)

Respiratory: Hypoxia (≥2%)

0.1% to <2%:

Cardiovascular: Angina pectoris, atrial fibrillation, bradycardia, cardiac arrest, cardiac failure, chest discomfort, chest pain, edema, hypertension, hypotension, increased blood pressure, palpitations, peripheral edema, phlebitis, prolonged Q-T interval on ECG, syncope, tachycardia

Central nervous system: Agitation, anxiety, chills, confusion, depression, disorientation, drowsiness, facial pain, fatigue, hallucination, hypoesthesia, lethargy, malaise, nervousness, noncardiac chest pain, pain, paresthesia, restlessness, vertigo

Dermatologic: Allergic dermatitis, erythema, hyperhidrosis, night sweats, pruritus, skin rash, urticaria

Endocrine & metabolic: Hypokalemia (1%), dehydration, hyperglycemia, hyperlipidemia, increased gamma-glutamyl transferase, increased lactate dehydrogenase, increased serum glucose, increased serum triglycerides, increased uric acid

Gastrointestinal: Dyspepsia (1%), abdominal discomfort, abdominal distension, anorexia, decreased appetite, dysgeusia, flatulence, gastritis, gastroenteritis, gastroesophageal reflux disease, increased amylase, increased serum lipase, oral candidiasis, xerostomia

Genitourinary: Dysuria, fungal vaginosis, vaginal infection, vulvovaginal candidiasis, vulvovaginal pruritus

Hematologic & oncologic: Anemia (1%), decreased hematocrit, eosinophilia, leukopenia, prolonged partial thromboplastin time, thrombocythemia, thrombocytopenia

Hepatic: Increased serum ALT (1%), abnormal hepatic function tests, increased liver enzymes, increased serum alkaline phosphatase, increased serum AST, increased serum transaminases

Hypersensitivity: Hypersensitivity reaction

Infection: Candidiasis, fungal infection (including oral)

Local: Extravasation

Neuromuscular & skeletal: Arthralgia, back pain, limb pain, muscle spasms, musculoskeletal pain, myalgia, tremor, weakness

Ophthalmic: Blurred vision

Otic: Tinnitus

Renal: Increased blood urea nitrogen, increased serum creatinine, renal failure

Respiratory: Asthma, bronchospasm, dyspnea, wheezing

Miscellaneous: Fever (1%)

<0.1%, postmarketing, and/or case reports: Abnormal gait, agranulocytosis, anaphylactic shock, anaphylaxis, angioedema, aplastic anemia, ataxia, auditory impairment, cholestatic jaundice, *Clostridium difficile* associated diarrhea, deafness (reversible), decreased INR, ECG abnormality, exacerbation of myasthenia gravis, facial edema, hemolytic anemia, hepatic failure, hepatic necrosis, hepatitis (predominantly cholestatic), hepatotoxicity (idiosyncratic) (Chalasani 2014),

hypoglycemia, increased intracranial pressure, interstitial nephritis, jaundice, laryngeal edema, myasthenia, nightmares, pancytopenia, paranoia, peripheral neuropathy (may be irreversible), pharyngeal edema, phototoxicity, pneumonitis (allergic), polyneuropathy, pseudomembranous colitis, pseudotumor cerebri, psychotic reaction, renal insufficiency, rupture of tendon, seizure, serum sickness, skin photosensitivity, Stevens-Johnson syndrome, suicidal ideation, suicidal tendencies, tendonitis, thrombotic thrombocytopenic purpura, toxic epidermal necrolysis, ventricular tachyarrhythmias (including torsade de pointes and cardiac arrest [usually in patients with concurrent, severe proarrhythmic conditions]), vasculitis, vision loss (transient)

Dosing

Adult & Geriatric

Acute bacterial rhinosinusitis: Oral, IV: 400 mg every 24 hours for 10 days (manufacturer's labeling) or 5 to 7 days (Chow 2012). **Note:** Recommended in patients with beta-lactam allergy; may also be used if initial therapy fails, in areas with high endemic rates of penicillin nonsusceptible *S. pneumoniae*, those with severe infections, age >65 years, recent hospitalization, antibiotic use within the past month, or who are immunocompromised.

Anthrax (off-label use) (CDC [Hendricks 2014]):

Inhalational (postexposure prophylaxis): Oral: 400 mg every 24 hours for 60 days

Cutaneous (without systemic involvement): Oral: 400 mg every 24 hours for 7 to 10 days for naturally acquired infection; 60 days for bioterrorism-related cases

Systemic (including meningitis), treatment: IV: 400 mg every 24 hours; use in combination with a protein synthesis inhibitor (eg, clindamycin, linezolid); if meningitis is suspected or cannot be ruled out, use in combination with another bactericidal antimicrobial (eg, beta-lactam) and a protein synthesis inhibitor (eg, clindamycin, linezolid). Duration of therapy is 2 weeks or until clinically stable when meningitis has been excluded; ≥2 to 3 weeks for possible/confirmed meningitis. Patients exposed to aerosolized spores require prophylaxis to complete an antimicrobial course of 60 days from illness onset.

Bacterial meningitis (off-label use): IV: 400 mg every 24 hours for 10 to 14 days (IDSA [Tunkel 2004])

Bite wounds (animal/human) (off-label use): Oral, IV: **Note:** Recommended as an alternative therapy for human bite wound in patients hypersensitive to beta-lactams: 400 mg once daily (IDSA [Stevens 2014])

Chronic bronchitis, acute bacterial exacerbation: Oral, IV: 400 mg every 24 hours for 5 days

Community-acquired pneumonia (CAP) (including MDRSP): Oral, IV:

Manufacturer's labeling: 400 mg every 24 hours for 7 to 14 days

Alternate dosing: 400 mg every 24 hours for 5 days (IDSA [Mandell 2007])

Diabetic foot infection (off-label use): Oral, IV: 400 mg once daily (Vick-Fragoso 2009)

Intra-abdominal infections, complicated: Oral, IV: 400 mg every 24 hours for 5 to 14 days (initiate with IV); **Note:** 2010 IDSA guidelines recommend a treatment duration of 4 to 7 days (provided source controlled) for community-acquired, mild to moderate IAI

Mycoplasma genitalium (off-label use): Oral: 400 mg every 24 hours for 7, 10, or 14 days (Bissessor 2015; CDC [Workowski 2015])

Nocardiosis (off-label use): Oral, IV: 400 mg once daily; may be used in combination with other antimicrobials (Fihman 2006; Kandasamy 2008; Tripodi 2011). Additional data may be necessary to further define the role of moxifloxacin in this condition.

Pelvic inflammatory disease (in patients allergic to cephalosporins) (off-label use): Oral: 400 mg every 24 hours for 14 days. **Note:** The CDC recommends use as an alternative therapy only if standard parenteral cephalosporin therapy is not feasible and community prevalence of quinolone-resistant gonococcal organisms is low. Culture sensitivity must be confirmed (CDC [Workowski 2015])

Plague: Oral, IV: 400 mg every 24 hours for 10 to 14 days

Skin and skin structure infections: Oral, IV:

Complicated: 400 mg every 24 hours for 7 to 21 days

Uncomplicated: 400 mg every 24 hours for 7 days

Surgical (perioperative) prophylaxis (off-label use): IV: 400 mg within 120 minutes prior to surgical incision (Bratzler 2013).

Tuberculosis, drug-resistant tuberculosis, or intolerance to first-line agents (off-label use): Oral: 400 mg every 24 hours (CDC 2003)

Pediatric

Community-acquired pneumonia (CAP) due to atypical pathogens (*M. pneumoniae, Chlamydophila* [also known as *Chlamydia*] *pneumoniae, C. trachomatis*), mild infection or step-down therapy in adolescents with skeletal maturity, (alternative to azithromycin) (IDSA/PIDS 2011) (off-label use): Adolescents: Oral: 400 mg once daily

Surgical (perioperative) prophylaxis (off-label use): Children ≥1 year and Adolescents: IV: 10 mg/kg within 120 minutes prior to surgical incision (maximum dose: 400 mg) (Bratzler 2013)

Renal Impairment No dosage adjustment necessary. Poorly dialyzed; no supplemental dose or dosage adjustment necessary, including patients on intermittent hemodialysis, peritoneal dialysis, or continuous renal replacement therapy (eg, CVVHD).

Hepatic Impairment No dosage adjustment necessary; however, use with caution in this patient population secondary to the risk of QT prolongation.

Mechanism of Action Moxifloxacin is a DNA gyrase inhibitor, and also inhibits topoisomerase IV. DNA gyrase (topoisomerase II) is an essential bacterial enzyme that maintains the superhelical structure of DNA. DNA gyrase is required for DNA replication and transcription, DNA repair, recombination, and transposition; inhibition is bactericidal.

Contraindications Hypersensitivity to moxifloxacin, other quinolone antibiotics, or any component of the formulation

Warnings/Precautions

[US Boxed Warning]: Fluoroquinolones are associated with disabling and potentially irreversible serious adverse reactions that may occur together, including tendinitis and tendon rupture, peripheral neuropathy, and CNS effects. Discontinue moxifloxacin immediately and avoid use of fluoroquinolones in patients who experience any of these serious adverse reactions. Patients of any age or without pre-existing risk factors have experienced these reactions; may occur within hours to weeks after initiation. **[US Boxed Warning]: Reserve use of moxifloxacin for treatment of acute bacterial sinusitis or acute**

bacterial exacerbation of chronic bronchitis for patients who have no alternative treatment options because of the risk of disabling and potentially serious adverse reactions (eg, tendinitis and tendon rupture, peripheral neuropathy, CNS effects).

Fluoroquinolones have been associated with an increased risk of tendonitis and tendon rupture in all ages; risk may be increased with concurrent corticosteroids, solid organ transplant recipients, and in patients >60 years of age, but has also occurred in patients without these risk factors. Rupture of the Achilles tendon has been reported most frequently; but other tendon sites (eg, rotator cuff, biceps, hand) have also been reported. Inflammation and rupture may occur bilaterally. Cases have been reported within hours or days of initiation, and up to several months after discontinuation of therapy. Strenuous physical activity, renal failure, and previous tendon disorders may be independent risk factor for tendon rupture. Discontinue at first sign of tendon pain, swelling, inflammation or rupture. Avoid use in patients with a history of tendon disorders or who have experienced tendinitis or tendon rupture. Use with caution in patients with rheumatoid arthritis; may increase risk of tendon rupture. Fluoroquinolones have been associated with an increased risk of CNS effects including seizures, increased intracranial pressure (including pseudotumor cerebri), and toxic psychosis; may also cause nervousness, agitation, insomnia, anxiety, nightmares, paranoia, dizziness, confusion, tremors, hallucinations, depression, and suicidal thoughts or actions. May occur following the first dose; discontinue immediately and avoid further use of fluoroquinolones in patients who experience these reactions. Use with caution in patients with known or suspected CNS disorder, or risk factors that may predispose to seizures or lower the seizure threshold. Fluoroquinolones have been associated with an increased risk of peripheral neuropathy; may occur soon after initiation of therapy and may be irreversible; discontinue if symptoms of sensory or sensorimotor neuropathy occur. Avoid use in patients who have previously experienced peripheral neuropathy.

Fluoroquinolones may prolong QTc interval; avoid use in patients with known QTc prolongation, ventricular arrhythmias including torsades de pointes, proarrhythmic conditions (eg, clinically significant bradycardia, acute myocardial ischemia), uncorrected hypokalemia, hypomagnesemia, or concurrent administration of other medications known to prolong the QT interval (including Class Ia and Class III antiarrhythmics, cisapride, erythromycin, antipsychotics, and tricyclic antidepressants). Use with caution in patients with significant bradycardia or acute myocardial ischemia. Use with caution in patients with mild, moderate, or severe hepatic impairment or liver cirrhosis; may increase the risk of QT prolongation. Fulminant hepatitis potentially leading to liver failure (including fatalities) has been reported with use; advise patients to discontinue treatment and promptly report signs/ symptoms of hepatitis (eg, abdominal pain, jaundice, dark urine, pale stools). Use with caution in patients with renal failure (risk of tendon rupture increased).

Use with caution in diabetes; glucose regulation may be altered. Fluoroquinolones have been associated with the development of serious, and sometimes fatal, hypoglycemia, most often in elderly diabetics, but also in patients without diabetes. Prompt identification and treatment of hypoglycemia is essential. Individual quinolones may differ in their potential to cause this effect. It was most evident with gatifloxacin (no longer available systemically). Hyperglycemia has also been associated with the use of fluoroquinolones. Patients should be monitored closely for signs/symptoms of disordered glucose regulation.

Severe hypersensitivity reactions, including anaphylaxis, have occurred with quinolone therapy. Reactions may present as typical allergic symptoms after a single dose, or may manifest as severe idiosyncratic dermatologic, vascular, pulmonary, renal, hepatic, and/or hematologic events, usually after multiple doses. Prompt discontinuation of drug should occur if skin rash or other symptoms arise. Avoid excessive sunlight and take precautions to limit exposure (eg, loose fitting clothing, sunscreen); may cause moderate to severe phototoxicity reactions. Discontinue use if photosensitivity occurs. Prolonged use may result in fungal or bacterial superinfection, including *C. difficile*-associated diarrhea (CDAD) and pseudomembranous colitis; CDAD has been observed >2 months postantibiotic treatment.

[US Boxed Warning]: May exacerbate myasthenia gravis; avoid use in patients with a known history of myasthenia gravis. Cases of severe exacerbations, including the need for ventilatory support, and deaths have been reported. Hemolytic reactions may (rarely) occur with quinolone use in patients with latent or actual G6PD deficiency. Adverse effects (eg, tendon rupture, QT changes) may be increased in elderly patients. Efficacy of systemically administered moxifloxacin (oral, intravenous) in pediatric patients have not been established. Potentially significant interactions may exist, requiring dose or frequency adjustment, additional monitoring, and/or selection of alternative therapy.

Drug Interactions

Metabolism/Transport Effects

None known.

Avoid Concomitant Use

Avoid concomitant use of Moxifloxacin (Systemic) with any of the following: BCG (Intravesical); Cholera Vaccine; Delamanid; Highest Risk QTc-Prolonging Agents; Hydroxychloroquine; Ivabradine; Mequitazine; MiFEPRIStone; Nadifloxacin; Probucol; Promazine; Strontium Ranelate; Vinflunine

Increased Effect/Toxicity

Moxifloxacin (Systemic) may increase the levels/effects of: Aminolevulinic Acid; Blood Glucose Lowering Agents; Delamanid; Heroin; Highest Risk QTc-Prolonging Agents; Mequitazine; Moderate Risk QTc-Prolonging Agents; Porfimer; Varenicline; Verteporfin; Vitamin K Antagonists

The levels/effects of Moxifloxacin (Systemic) may be increased by: Corticosteroids (Systemic); Hydroxychloroquine; Ivabradine; MIFEPRIStone; Nadifloxacin; Nonsteroidal Anti-Inflammatory Agents; Probucol; Promazine; QTc-Prolonging Agents (Indeterminate Risk and Risk Modifying); Vinflunine

Decreased Effect

Moxifloxacin (Systemic) may decrease the levels/effects of: BCG (Intravesical); BCG Vaccine (Immunization); Blood Glucose Lowering Agents; Cholera Vaccine; Didanosine; Lactobacillus and Estriol; Mycophenolate; Sodium Picosulfate; Typhoid Vaccine

The levels/effects of Moxifloxacin (Systemic) may be decreased by: Antacids; Didanosine; Iron Salts; Lanthanum; Magnesium Salts; Multivitamins/Minerals (with ADEK, Folate, Iron); Multivitamins/Minerals (with AE, No Iron); Quinapril; Sevelamer; Strontium Ranelate; Sucralfate; Zinc Salts

Food Interactions Absorption is not affected by administration with a high-fat meal or yogurt.

Dietary Considerations

Take 4 hours before or 8 hours after multiple vitamins, antacids, or other products containing magnesium, aluminum, iron, or zinc.

Avelox IV infusion (premixed in sodium chloride 0.8%) contains sodium 34.2 mEq (~787 mg)/250 mL.

Pharmacodynamics/Kinetics

Half-life Elimination Single dose: Oral: 12-16 hours; IV: 8-15 hours

Pregnancy Considerations Adverse events have been observed in some animal reproduction studies. Moxifloxacin crosses the placenta and can be detected in the amniotic fluid and cord blood (Ozyüncü and Beksac 2010; Ozyüncü and Nemutlu, 2010). Information specific to moxifloxacin use in pregnant women is limited (Padberg, 2014).

Breastfeeding Considerations It is not known if moxifloxacin is excreted in breast milk. According to the manufacturer, the decision to continue or discontinue breastfeeding during therapy should take into account the risk of infant exposure, the benefits of breastfeeding to the infant, and benefits of treatment to the mother.

Dosage Forms

Solution, Intravenous:

Avelox: 400 mg/250 mL (250 mL)

Generic: 400 mg/250 mL (250 mL)

Tablet, Oral:

Avelox: 400 mg

Generic: 400 mg

Dental Comment See Local Anesthetic/Vasoconstrictor Precautions

Mucosal Coating Agent

(myoo KOH sul KOH ting AY gent)

Brand Names: US Episil; Gelclair; Mucotrol; MuGard; Orafate; ProThelial

Generic Availability (US) No

Pharmacologic Category Gastrointestinal Agent, Miscellaneous

Dental Use Management of oral mucosal pain and protection from further irritation caused by oral mucositis/stomatitis (resulting from chemotherapy or radiation therapy); irritation; lesions, periodontal and gingival inflammation, tooth extractions, and wounds due to oral surgery; chafing; minor lesions; traumatic ulcers, and abrasions caused by braces/ill-fitting dentures or disease; diffuse aphthous ulcers (canker sores).

Use Mucosal protection: Management of oral mucosal pain and protection from further irritation caused by oral mucositis/stomatitis (resulting from chemotherapy or radiation therapy); irritation; lesions, periodontal and gingival inflammation, tooth extractions, and wounds/ lesions due to oral surgery; chafing; minor lesions; traumatic ulcers, and abrasions caused by braces/ill-fitting dentures or disease; diffuse aphthous ulcers (canker sores).

Local Anesthetic/Vasoconstrictor Precautions No information available to require special precautions

Effects on Dental Treatment No significant effects or complications reported

Effects on Bleeding No information available to require special precautions

Adverse Reactions

<1%, postmarketing, and/or case reports: Burning sensation of mouth, mild stinging sensation (oral cavity), oral inflammation (mild)

Dental Usual Dosage Oral: Adults: Mucosal protection:

Episil: Apply 1 to 3 pumps to the oral cavity 2 to 3 times daily, or as needed.

Gelclair: Rinse, gargle, and spit 15 mL (1 single-use packet) mixed water 3 times daily, or as needed.

Mucotrol: Slowly dissolve 1 wafer by swishing around in the mouth, 3 times daily, or as needed.

MuGard: Rinse with 5 mL 4 to 6 times daily; may use up to 10 mL if needed to fully coat inside of mouth.

Orafate:

General dental use: Use 2 times daily for the first day or as directed and then for 1 to 4 weeks thereafter (maximum 40 mL daily).

Following dental cleaning (scaling/root planing): Brush 1.25 mL into gingival pocket twice daily for a week (maximum: 40 mL daily).

Following tooth extraction: Place 1.25 to 2.5 mL into wound 3 times daily, then twice daily or as instructed (maximum: 40 mL daily).

Following tonsillectomy or uvuloplasty: Place 2.5 to 5 mL into tongue and swish, gargle, then spit as instructed (maximum: 40 mL daily).

ProThelial: 2.5 to 5 mL every 8 hours on the first day; 2.5 to 5 mL every 12 hours thereafter (maximum: 40 mL daily).

Dosing

Adult & Geriatric Mucosal protection: Oral:

Episil: Apply 1 to 3 pumps to the oral cavity 2 to 3 times daily, or as needed; maximum duration for continuous use: 30 days

Gelclair: Rinse, gargle, and spit 15 mL (1 single-use packet) mixed in water 3 times daily, or as needed.

Mucotrol: Slowly dissolve 1 wafer by swishing around in the mouth, 3 times daily, or as needed

MuGard: Rinse with 5 mL 4 to 6 times daily (for oral mucositis/stomatitis) or 4 to 6 times daily or as needed (for other ulcerative conditions); may use up to 10 mL if needed to fully coat inside of mouth

Orafate:

Oral inflammation: Brush 1.25 to 2.5 mL across the front and back of gingiva 2 times daily for the first day then once daily at bedtime until healed (maximum: 10 mL per 24 hours)

Following dental cleaning (scaling/root planing): Brush 1.25 to 2.5 mL into gingival area daily for 4 weeks as directed (maximum: 10 mL per 24 hours)

Following tooth extraction or gingival (gum) surgery: Place 1.25 to 2.5 mL into wound 3 times daily the first day, then twice daily or as instructed until healed (maximum: 10 mL per 24 hours)

Following tonsillectomy or other oral soft tissue surgery: Place 2.5 to 5 mL into wound 3 times daily on the first day then twice daily or as directed (maximum: 10 mL per 24 hours)

ProThelial: Usual dosage: 2.5 to 5 mL every 8 hours on the first day; 2.5 to 5 mL every 12 hours thereafter (maximum: 40 mL daily)

Prevention of chemo-radiation mucositis (beginning the first day of cancer treatment):

Grade 1 or 2: 2.5 to 5 mL 3 times a day for 1 day, followed by 2.5 to 5 mL twice daily until 1 week after completion of chemo-radiation therapy

Grade 3 or 4: 10 mL 3 times a day, continue until 1 week after completion of chemo-radiation therapy

Treatment of chemo-radiation mucositis:

Grade 1 or 2: 2.5 to 5 mL 3 times a day for 1 day, followed by 2.5 to 5 mL twice daily until 1 week after completion of chemo-radiation therapy

Grade 3 or 4: 10 mL 3 times a day for 2 days, followed by 5 to 10 mL twice daily until 1 week after completion of chemo-radiation therapy

Pediatric Mucosal protection: Children ≥12 years and Adolescents: Oral: Orafate: Refer to adult Orafate dosing.

Mechanism of Action Adheres to the mucosal surface of mouth forming a protective film or coating over the irritated areas and lesions, protecting the lesion from further irritation and pain.

Contraindications

Hypersensitivity to any ingredient or component of the formulation

Additional product-specific contraindications: Episil: Hypersensitivity to peanuts, soya, or peppermint oil

Warnings/Precautions May decrease absorption of sublingually administered medications. Episil contains alcohol (may cause irritation when applied), propylene glycol (may cause skin irritation), soy, and peppermint oil (may cause allergic reaction). Avoid eating or drinking for at least 1 hour (Mucotrol, MuGard, Orafate, ProThelial) or 30 to 60 minutes (Gelclair) following use. Consult a health care provider if no improvement is seen after 7 days of use. Orafate and ProThelial are safe if swallowed; however, evaluate swallowing capability prior to use to minimize incidental ingestion. Orafate and ProThelial may cause constipation if swallowed.

Drug Interactions

Metabolism/Transport Effects None known.

Avoid Concomitant Use There are no known interactions where it is recommended to avoid concomitant use.

Increased Effect/Toxicity There are no known significant interactions involving an increase in effect.

Decreased Effect There are no known significant interactions involving a decrease in effect.

Dosage Forms Considerations Orafate and ProThelial each contain sucralfate (as a 10% paste).

Dosage Forms

Gel, Mouth/Throat:

Gelclair: 15 mL/packet (15 mL)

Liquid, Mouth/Throat:

Episil: (10 mL)

MuGard: (5 mL, 240 mL)

Paste, Mouth/Throat:

Orafate: 10% (30 mL)

ProThelial: 10% (125 mL, 250 mL, 500 mL)

Wafer, Mouth/Throat:

Mucotrol: (21 ea, 45 ea)

Mupirocin (myoo PEER oh sin)

Brand Names: US Bactroban; Bactroban Nasal; Centany; Centany AT

Brand Names: Canada Bactroban

Pharmacologic Category Antibiotic, Topical

Use Topical infection:

Intranasal: Eradication of nasal colonization with methicillin-resistant *S. aureus* (MRSA) in adult and pediatric patients ≥12 years of age and health care workers as part of a comprehensive infection control program to reduce the risk of infection among patients at high risk of MRSA infection during institutional outbreaks of infections with this microorganism

Limitations of use: Insufficient data for use as part of an intervention program to prevent autoinfection of high-risk patients from their own *S. aureus* nasal colonization or for general prophylaxis of any infection in any patient population.

Topical cream: Treatment of secondary infected traumatic skin lesions (up to 10 cm in length or 100 cm^2 in area) due to susceptible strains of *S. aureus* and *S. pyogenes*

Topical ointment: Treatment of impetigo due to *S. aureus* and *S. pyogenes*

Local Anesthetic/Vasoconstrictor Precautions No information available to require special precautions

Effects on Dental Treatment Key adverse event(s) related to dental treatment: Xerostomia (normal salivary flow resumes upon discontinuation) and taste perversion.

Effects on Bleeding No information available to require special precautions

Adverse Reactions

1% to 10%:

Central nervous system: Headache (2% to 9%), localized burning (<4%), stinging sensation (<2%)

Dermatologic: Pruritus (≤2%), skin rash (≤1%)

Gastrointestinal: Nausea (1% to 5%), dysgeusia (3%)

Local: Local pain (<2%)

Respiratory: Rhinitis (6%), respiratory congestion (5%), pharyngitis (4%), cough (2%)

<1%, postmarketing, and/or case reports: Abdominal pain, aphthous stomatitis, blepharitis, cellulitis, *Clostridium difficile* associated diarrhea, contact dermatitis, dermatitis, diarrhea, dizziness, epistaxis, erythema, hypersensitivity reaction, increased wound secretion, localized edema, localized tenderness, otalgia, urticaria, wound infection (secondary), xeroderma, xerostomia

General Dosage Range

Intranasal: *Children ≥12 years, Adolescents, and Adults:* Approximately one-half of the ointment from the single-use tube should be applied into one nostril and the other half into the other nostril twice daily

Topical: *Infants ≥2 months, Children, Adolescents, and Adults:* Apply to affected area 3 times daily

Mechanism of Action Binds to bacterial isoleucyl transfer-RNA synthetase resulting in the inhibition of protein synthesis

Pharmacodynamics/Kinetics

Half-life Elimination 17 to 36 minutes

Pregnancy Risk Factor B

Pregnancy Considerations Adverse events have not been observed in animal reproduction studies.

Mycophenolate (mye koe FEN oh late)

Brand Names: US CellCept; CellCept Intravenous; Myfortic

Brand Names: Canada Ach-Mycophenolate; Apo-Mycophenolate; CellCept; CellCept I.V.; CO Mycophenolate; JAMP-Mycophenolate; Myfortic; Mylan-Mycophenolate; Novo-Mycophenolate; Sandoz-Mycophenolate Mofetil; Vanc-Mycophenolate

Pharmacologic Category Immunosuppressant Agent

Use Organ transplantation: Prophylaxis of organ rejection concomitantly with cyclosporine and corticosteroids in patients receiving allogeneic renal (CellCept, Myfortic), cardiac (CellCept), or hepatic (CellCept) transplants

Local Anesthetic/Vasoconstrictor Precautions No information available to require special precautions

Effects on Dental Treatment Key adverse event(s) related to dental treatment: Mouth ulceration, gum hyperplasia, gingivitis, dry mouth, dysphagia, oral *Candida* infection, and stomatitis (see Dental Comment)

Effects on Bleeding May be associated with hematologic effects, potentially including significant reduction in platelet counts with altered hemostasis. In patients who are under active treatment, medical consult is suggested.

Adverse Reactions Data for incidence >20% as reported in adults following oral dosing of CellCept alone in renal, cardiac, and hepatic allograft rejection studies. Profile in 3% to <20% range reflects use in combination with cyclosporine and corticosteroids. In general, lower doses used in renal rejection patients had less adverse effects than higher doses. Rates of adverse effects were similar for each indication, except for those unique to the specific organ involved. The type of adverse effects observed in pediatric patients was similar to those seen in adults, with the exception of abdominal pain, anemia, diarrhea, fever, hypertension, infection, pharyngitis, respiratory tract infection, sepsis, and vomiting, which were more frequent in pediatric patients; lymphoproliferative disorder was the only type of malignancy observed. Percentages of adverse reactions were similar in studies comparing CellCept to Myfortic in patients following renal transplant.

>20%:

Cardiovascular: Hypertension (28% to 78%), hypotension (33%), peripheral edema (27% to 64%), edema (27% to 28%), chest pain (26%), tachycardia (20% to 22%)

Central nervous system: Pain (31% to 76%), headache (16% to 54%), insomnia (41% to 52%), dizziness (29%), anxiety (28%), paresthesia (21%)

Dermatologic: Skin rash (22%)

Endocrine & metabolic: Hyperglycemia (44% to 47%), hypercholesterolemia (41%), hypomagnesemia (39%), hypokalemia (32% to 37%), hypocalcemia (30%), increased lactate dehydrogenase (23%), hyperkalemia (22%)

Gastrointestinal: Abdominal pain (25% to 63%), nausea (20% to 55%), diarrhea (31% to 51%), constipation (19% to 41%), vomiting (33% to 34%), anorexia (25%), dyspepsia (22%)

Genitourinary: Urinary tract infection (37%)

Hematologic & oncologic: Leukopenia (23% to 46%), anemia (26% to 43%), leukocytosis (22% to 41%), thrombocytopenia (24% to 38%), hypochromic anemia (25%)

Hepatic: Abnormal hepatic function tests (25%), ascites (24%)

Infection: Sepsis (27%), infection (18% to 27%), candidiasis (17% to 22%), herpes simplex infection (10% to 21%)

Neuromuscular & skeletal: Back pain (35% to 47%), weakness (35% to 43%), tremor (24% to 34%)

Renal: Increased serum creatinine (39%), increased blood urea nitrogen (35%), renal function abnormality (22% to 26%)

Respiratory: Dyspnea (31% to 37%), respiratory tract infection (22% to 37%), pleural effusion (34%), cough (31%), pulmonary disease (22% to 30%), sinusitis (26%)

Miscellaneous: Fever (21% to 52%)

3% to <20%:

Cardiovascular: Angina pectoris, arterial thrombosis, atrial fibrillation, atrial flutter, bradycardia, cardiac arrhythmia, cardiac failure, extrasystoles, facial edema, increased venous pressure, orthostatic hypotension, palpitations, pericardial effusion, peripheral vascular disorder, supraventricular extrasystole, supraventricular tachycardia, syncope, thrombosis, vasodilatation, vasospasm, ventricular premature contractions, ventricular tachycardia

Central nervous system: Abnormality in thinking, agitation, confusion, delirium, depression, drowsiness, emotional lability, hallucination, hypertonia, hypoesthesia, malaise, myasthenia, nervousness, neuropathy, psychosis, seizure, vertigo, voice disorder

Dermatologic: Acne vulgaris, alopecia, cellulitis, dermal ulcer, diaphoresis, fungal dermatitis, pallor, pruritus, skin hypertrophy, vesiculobullous dermatitis

Endocrine & metabolic: Acidosis, albuminuria, alkalosis, Cushing's syndrome, dehydration, diabetes mellitus, gout, hirsutism, hypercalcemia, hyperphosphatemia, hyperlipidemia, hypervolemia, hypochloremia, hypoglycemia, hyponatremia, hypophosphatemia, hypoproteinemia, hypothyroidism, hypovolemia, increased gamma-glutamyl transferase, increased thirst, parathyroid disease, weight gain, weight loss

Gastrointestinal: Mucocutaneous candidiasis (16% to 18%), cholangitis, dysphagia, enlargement of abdomen, esophagitis, flatulence, gastric disease, gastric ulcer, gastritis, gastroenteritis, gastrointestinal hemorrhage, GI moniliasis, gingival hyperplasia, gingivitis, hernia, hiccups, intestinal obstruction, melena, oral candidiasis, oral mucosa ulcer, peritonitis, stomatitis, xerostomia

Genitourinary: Dysuria, hematuria, impotence, nocturia, oliguria, pelvic pain, prostatic disease, scrotal edema, urinary frequency, urinary incontinence, urinary retention, urinary tract abnormality

Hematologic & oncologic: Blood coagulation disorder, bruise, hemophthalmos, hemorrhage, neoplasm, neutropenia, pancytopenia, petechia, polycythemia, prolonged prothrombin time, prolonged partial thromboplastin time, skin carcinoma

Hepatic: Cholestatic jaundice, hepatic insuffiency, hepatitis, hyperbilirubinemia, increased serum alkaline phosphatase, increased serum transaminases, jaundice

Infection: Cytomegalovirus disease (viremia/syndrome: 12% to 14%; tissue invasive disease: 6% to 12%), herpes zoster (cutaneous disease: 4% to 10%), abscess (local), infection (of ileus)

Neuromuscular & skeletal: Arthralgia, arthropathy, leg cramps, myalgia, neck pain, osteoporosis

Ophthalmic: Abnormal lacrimation, amblyopia, cataract, conjunctivitis, visual disturbance

Otic: Deafness, ear disease, otalgia, tinnitus

Renal: Hydronephrosis, increased serum creatinine, pyelonephritis, renal failure, renal tubular necrosis

Respiratory: Apnea, asthma, atelectasis, bronchitis, epistaxis, flu-like symptoms, hemoptysis, hyperventilation, hypoxia, increased bronchial secretions, pharyngitis, pneumonia, pneumothorax, pulmonary edema, pulmonary hypertension, respiratory acidosis, respiratory tract infection (moniliasis), rhinitis

Miscellaneous: Abnormal healing, cyst, fever and chills

<1%, postmarketing and/or case reports: Atypical mycobacterial infection, bronchiectasis (Boddana 2011, Rook 2006), colitis, endocarditis (infectious), gastrointestinal perforation, hypogammaglobulinemia (Boddana 2011; Keven 2003; Robertson 2009), interstitial pulmonary disease, lymphoproliferative disorder, malabsorption (intestinal villous atrophy), malignant lymphoma, malignant neoplasm, meningitis,

pancreatitis, progressive multifocal leukoencephalopathy, pulmonary fibrosis, pure red cell aplasia, renal disease (BK virus-associated), tuberculosis

General Dosage Range Dosage adjustment recommended in patient with renal impairment and who develop toxicities

IV: CellCept: *Adults:* 1 to 1.5 g twice daily

Oral:

Cellcept:

Infants ≥3 months and Children (suspension): 600 mg/m²/dose twice daily (maximum: 1 g twice daily)

Children and Adolescents with BSA 1.25 to 1.5 m² (capsule): 750 mg twice daily

Children and Adolescents with BSA >1.5 m² (capsule or tablet): 1 g twice daily

Adults: 1 to 1.5 g twice daily

Myfortic:

Children ≥5 years and Adolescents with BSA 1.19 to 1.58 m²: 400 mg/m² twice daily **or** 540 mg twice daily (maximum: 1080 mg daily)

Children ≥5 years and Adolescents with BSA >1.58 m²: 400 mg/m² twice daily **or** 720 mg twice daily (maximum: 1440 mg daily)

Adults: 720 mg twice daily

Mechanism of Action MPA exhibits a cytostatic effect on T and B lymphocytes. It is an inhibitor of inosine monophosphate dehydrogenase (IMPDH) which inhibits *de novo* guanosine nucleotide synthesis. T and B lymphocytes are dependent on this pathway for proliferation.

Pharmacodynamics/Kinetics

Onset of Action Peak effect: Correlation of toxicity or efficacy is still being developed, however, one study indicated that 12-hour AUCs >40 mcg/mL/hour were correlated with efficacy and decreased episodes of rejection

Half-life Elimination

CellCept: MPA: Oral: 18 hours; IV: 17 hours

Myfortic: MPA: Oral: 8 to16 hours; MPAG: 13 to 17 hours

Time to Peak Plasma: Oral: MPA:

CellCept: 1 to 1.5 hours

Myfortic: 1.5 to 2.75 hours

Pregnancy Risk Factor D

Pregnancy Considerations [US Boxed Warning]: Mycophenolate is associated with an increased risk of congenital malformations and first trimester pregnancy loss when used by pregnant women. Females of reproductive potential must be counseled about pregnancy prevention and planning. Alternative agents should be considered for women planning a pregnancy. The following congenital malformations have been reported following exposure during pregnancy: external ear abnormalities, cleft lip and palate, anomalies of the distal limbs, heart, esophagus, kidney, and nervous system. Spontaneous abortions have also been noted. Females of reproductive potential (girls who have entered puberty, women with a uterus who have not passed through clinically confirmed menopause) should have a negative pregnancy test with a sensitivity of ≥25 milliunits/mL immediately before therapy and the test should be repeated 8 to 10 days later. Pregnancy tests should be repeated during routine follow-up visits. Acceptable forms of contraception should be used during treatment and for 6 weeks after therapy is discontinued. The effectiveness of hormonal contraceptive agents may be affected by mycophenolate. Mycophenolate is not recommended for the treatment of psoriasis in pregnant women (Menter 2009). For women with lupus nephritis taking mycophenolate and who are planning a pregnancy, mycophenolate should be discontinued at least 6 weeks prior to trying to conceive (Hahn 2012).

Health care providers should report female exposures to mycophenolate during pregnancy or within 6 weeks of discontinuing therapy to the Mycophenolate Pregnancy Registry (800-617-8191).

The National Transplantation Pregnancy Registry (NTPR) is a registry which follows pregnancies which occur in maternal transplant recipients or those fathered by male transplant recipients. The NTPR encourages reporting of pregnancies following solid organ transplant by contacting them at 877-955-6877 or NTPR@giftoflifeinstitute.org.

Dental Comment Consider a medical consultation prior to any invasive dental procedure in patients who have received an organ transplant; delayed wound healing due to the immunosuppressive effects and an increased potential for postoperative infection may be of concern.

Nabumetone (na BYOO me tone)

Related Information

Rheumatoid Arthritis, Osteoarthritis, and Osteoporosis *on page 1792*

Temporomandibular Dysfunction (TMD), Chronic Pain, and Fibromyalgia *on page 1868*

Brand Names: Canada Apo-Nabumetone; Mylan-Nabumetone; Teva-Nabumetone

Generic Availability (US) Yes

Pharmacologic Category Analgesic, Nonopioid; Nonsteroidal Anti-inflammatory Drug (NSAID), Oral

Use Arthritis: Relief of signs and symptoms of osteoarthritis and rheumatoid arthritis.

Local Anesthetic/Vasoconstrictor Precautions No information available to require special precautions

Effects on Dental Treatment Key adverse event(s) related to dental treatment: Xerostomia (normal salivary flow resumes upon discontinuation) and stomatitis. The dentist should be aware of the potential of abnormal coagulation. Caution should also be exercised in the use of NSAIDs in patients already on anticoagulant therapy with drugs such as warfarin (Coumadin®). See Effects on Bleeding.

Effects on Bleeding Nonselective NSAIDs, such as nabumetone, inhibit platelet aggregation and prolong bleeding time in some patients. Unlike aspirin, the NSAID effect on platelet function is quantitatively less, of shorter duration, and reversible. Normal platelet function should occur in ~5 elimination half-lives or in <10 hours after discontinuation of nabumetone. Concomitant use of other NSAIDs should be avoided.

Adverse Reactions

>10%: Gastrointestinal: Diarrhea (14%), dyspepsia (13%), abdominal pain (12%)

1% to 10%:

Cardiovascular: Edema (3% to 9%)

Central nervous system: Dizziness (3% to 9%), headache (3% to 9%), drowsiness (1% to 3%), fatigue (1% to 3%), insomnia (1% to 3%), nervousness (1% to 3%)

Dermatologic: Pruritus (3% to 9%), skin rash (3% to 9%), diaphoresis (1% to 3%)

Gastrointestinal: Constipation (3% to 9%), flatulence (3% to 9%), nausea (3% to 9%), occult blood in stools (3% to 9%), gastritis (1% to 3%), stomatitis

(1% to 3%), vomiting (1% to 3%), xerostomia (1% to 3%)

Otic: Tinnitus

<1%, postmarketing, and/or case reports: Acne vulgaris, agitation, albuminuria, alopecia, anaphylactoid reaction, anaphylaxis, anemia, angina pectoris, angioedema, anorexia, anxiety, asthma, azotemia, bullous rash, cardiac arrhythmia, cardiac failure, chills, cholelithiasis, confusion, cough, depression, duodenal ulcer, duodenitis, dysphagia, dyspnea, dysuria, eosinophilic pneumonitis, eructation, fever, erythema multiforme, gastric ulcer, gastroenteritis, gastrointestinal hemorrhage, gingivitis, glossitis, granulocytopenia, hematuria, hepatic failure, hepatic insufficiency, hepatotoxicity (idiosyncratic) (Chalasani, 2014), hyperbilirubinemia, hyperglycemia, hypersensitivity pneumonitis, hypertension, hyperuricemia, hypokalemia, impotence, interstitial nephritis, interstitial pneumonitis, jaundice, leukopenia, malaise, melena, myocardial infarction, nephrolithiasis, nephrotic syndrome, nightmares, palpitations, pancreatitis, paresthesia, pseudoporphyria (cutanea tarda), rectal hemorrhage, renal failure, skin photosensitivity, Stevens-Johnson syndrome, syncope, taste disorder, thrombocytopenia, thrombophlebitis, toxic epidermal necrolysis, tremor, urticaria, vasculitis, vertigo, visual disturbance, weakness, weight gain, weight loss

Dosing

Adult

Arthritis: Oral: Initial: 1,000 mg as a single dose; adjust dose based on patient response up to 2,000 mg/day in 1 to 2 divided doses; doses >2,000 mg/day have not been studied.

Note: Patients <50 kg are less likely to require doses >1,000 mg/day.

Geriatric Use with caution. Refer to adult dosing.

Renal Impairment

In general, NSAIDs are not recommended for use in patients with advanced renal disease, but the manufacturer of nabumetone does provide some guidelines for adjustment in renal impairment:

CrCl ≥50 mL/minute: No dosage adjustment necessary.

CrCl 30 to 49 mL/minute: Initial maximum dose: 750 mg once daily; maximum daily dose: 1,500 mg/day

CrCl <30 mL/minute: Initial maximum dose: 500 mg once daily; maximum daily dose: 1,000 mg/day

Hemodialysis: Nondialyzable

KDIGO 2012 guidelines provide the following recommendations for NSAIDs:

eGFR 30 to <60 mL/minute/1.73 m^2: Temporarily discontinue in patients with intercurrent disease that increases risk of acute kidney injury.

eGFR <30 mL/minute/1.73 m^2: Avoid use.

Hepatic Impairment There are no dosage adjustments provided in the manufacturer's labeling (data limited in severe impairment); use with caution. Prodrug activation and metabolism are hepatic function dependent and may be reduced in severe hepatic impairment.

Mechanism of Action Reversibly inhibits cyclooxygenase-1 and 2 (COX-1 and 2) enzymes, which results in decreased formation of prostaglandin precursors; has antipyretic, analgesic, and anti-inflammatory properties

Other proposed mechanisms not fully elucidated (and possibly contributing to the anti-inflammatory effect to varying degrees), include inhibiting chemotaxis, altering lymphocyte activity, inhibiting neutrophil aggregation/activation, and decreasing proinflammatory cytokine levels.

Contraindications

Hypersensitivity to nabumetone or any component of the formulation; history of asthma, urticaria, or allergic-type reactions after taking aspirin or other NSAIDs; use in the setting of coronary artery bypass graft (CABG) surgery

Canadian labeling: Additional contraindications (not in US labeling): Hypersensitivity to other NSAIDs, active peptic ulcer; history of recurrent ulceration or active GI inflammatory disease; severely impaired or deteriorating renal function; complete or partial syndrome of nasal polyps; significant hepatic impairment or active liver disease; concurrent use with other NSAIDs

Warnings/Precautions [US Boxed Warning]: NSAIDs cause an increased risk of serious (and potentially fatal) adverse cardiovascular thrombotic events, including MI and stroke. Risk may occur early during treatment and may increase with duration of use. Relative risk appears to be similar in those with and without known cardiovascular disease or risk factors for cardiovascular disease; however, absolute incidence of serious cardiovascular thrombotic events (which may occur early during treatment) was higher in patients with known cardiovascular disease or risk factors and in those receiving higher doses. New-onset hypertension or exacerbation of hypertension may occur (NSAIDs may also impair response to ACE inhibitors, thiazide diuretics, or loop diuretics); may contribute to cardiovascular events; monitor blood pressure; use with caution in patients with hypertension. May cause sodium and fluid retention; use with caution in patients with edema. Avoid use in heart failure (ACCF/AHA [Yancy 2013]). Avoid use in patients with a recent MI unless benefits outweigh risk of cardiovascular thrombotic events. Use the lowest effective dose for the shortest duration of time, consistent with individual patient goals, to reduce risk of cardiovascular events; alternate therapies should be considered for patients at high risk.

Platelet adhesion and aggregation may be decreased; may prolong bleeding time; patients with coagulation disorders or who are receiving anticoagulants should be monitored closely. Anemia may occur; patients on long-term NSAID therapy should be monitored for anemia. Rarely, NSAID use may cause severe blood dyscrasias (eg, agranulocytosis, aplastic anemia, thrombocytopenia).

NSAID use may compromise existing renal function; dose-dependent decreases in prostaglandin synthesis may result from NSAID use, reducing renal blood flow which may cause renal decompensation (usually reversible). Patients with impaired renal function, dehydration, heart failure, hypovolemia, liver dysfunction, those taking diuretics, and ACE inhibitors, and the elderly are at greater risk of renal toxicity. Rehydrate patient before starting therapy; monitor renal function closely. Long-term NSAID use may result in renal papillary necrosis and other renal injury. Not recommended for use in patients with advanced renal disease; monitor closely if therapy must be initiated.

[US Boxed Warning]: NSAIDs cause an increased risk of serious gastrointestinal inflammation, ulceration, bleeding, and perforation (may be fatal); elderly patients and patients with history of peptic ulcer disease and/or GI bleeding are at greater risk for serious GI events. These events may occur at any time during therapy and without warning. Avoid use in patients with active GI bleeding. Use caution with a history of GI ulcers, concurrent therapy known to increase the risk of GI bleeding (eg, aspirin, anticoagulants and/or corticosteroids, selective serotonin reuptake inhibitors), advanced hepatic disease, coagulopathy, smoking, use of alcohol, or in elderly or debilitated patients. Use the lowest effective dose for the shortest duration of time, consistent with individual patient goals, to reduce risk of GI adverse events; alternate therapies should be considered for patients at high risk. When used concomitantly with aspirin, a substantial increase in the risk of gastrointestinal complications (eg, ulcer) occurs; concomitant gastroprotective therapy (eg, proton pump inhibitors) is recommended (Bhatt 2008).

Use the lowest effective dose for the shortest duration of time, consistent with individual patient goals, to reduce risk of cardiovascular or GI adverse events. Alternate therapies should be considered for patients at high risk. Elderly patients are at greater risk for serious GI, cardiovascular, and/or renal adverse events; use with caution.

NSAIDs may cause potentially fatal serious skin adverse events including exfoliative dermatitis, Stevens-Johnson syndrome (SJS) and toxic epidermal necrolysis (TEN); may occur without warning; discontinue use at first sign of skin rash (or other hypersensitivity). Anaphylactoid reactions may occur, even without prior exposure; patients with "aspirin triad" (bronchial asthma, aspirin intolerance, rhinitis) may be at increased risk. Contraindicated in patients who experience bronchospasm, asthma, rhinitis, or urticaria with NSAID or aspirin therapy. Use caution in other forms of asthma.

Use with caution in patients with hepatic impairment; patients with advanced hepatic disease are at an increased risk of GI bleeding with NSAIDs. Closely monitor patients with any abnormal LFT. Transaminase elevations have been reported with use; closely monitor patients with any abnormal LFT. Rare (sometimes fatal) severe hepatic reactions (eg, fulminant hepatitis, liver necrosis, hepatic failure) have occurred with NSAID use; discontinue immediately if signs or symptoms of hepatic disease develop or if systemic manifestations occur.

NSAIDs may cause drowsiness, dizziness, blurred vision and other neurologic effects which may impair physical or mental abilities; patients must be cautioned about performing tasks which require mental alertness (eg, operating machinery or driving).

Withhold for at least 4 to 6 half-lives prior to surgical or dental procedures. May cause photosensitivity reactions. Potentially significant interactions may exist, requiring dose or frequency adjustment, additional monitoring, and/or selection of alternative therapy.

Drug Interactions

Metabolism/Transport Effects None known.

Avoid Concomitant Use

Avoid concomitant use of Nabumetone with any of the following: Dexketoprofen; Floctafenine; Ketorolac (Nasal); Ketorolac (Systemic); Morniflumate; NSAID (COX-2 Inhibitor); Omacetaxine; Pelubiprofen; Phenylbutazone; Talniflumate; Tenoxicam; Urokinase; Zaltoprofen

Increased Effect/Toxicity

Nabumetone may increase the levels/effects of: 5-ASA Derivatives; Agents with Antiplatelet Properties; Aliskiren; Aminoglycosides; Aminolevulinic Acid; Anticoagulants; Apixaban; Bisphosphonate Derivatives; Cephalothin; Collagenase (Systemic); CycloSPORINE (Systemic); Dabigatran Etexilate; Deferasirox; Deoxycholic Acid; Desmopressin; Digoxin; Drospirenone; Edoxaban; Eplerenone; Haloperidol; Ibritumomab; Lithium; Methotrexate; Nonsteroidal Anti-Inflammatory Agents; NSAID (COX-2 Inhibitor); Obinutuzumab; Omacetaxine; PEMEtrexed; Porfimer; Potassium-Sparing Diuretics; PRALAtrexate; Quinolone Antibiotics; Rivaroxaban; Salicylates; Tacrolimus (Systemic); Tenofovir Products; Thrombolytic Agents; Tolperisone; Tositumomab and Iodine I 131 Tositumomab; Urokinase; Vancomycin; Verteporfin; Vitamin K Antagonists

The levels/effects of Nabumetone may be increased by: ACE Inhibitors; Alcohol (Ethyl); Angiotensin II Receptor Blockers; Antidepressants (Tricyclic, Tertiary Amine); Corticosteroids (Systemic); CycloSPORINE (Systemic); Dasatinib; Dexketoprofen; Diclofenac (Systemic); Felbinac; Floctafenine; Glucosamine; Herbs (Anticoagulant/Antiplatelet Properties); Ibrutinib; Ketorolac (Nasal); Ketorolac (Systemic); Limaprost; Loop Diuretics; Morniflumate; Multivitamins/Fluoride (with ADE); Multivitamins/Minerals (with ADEK, Folate, Iron); Multivitamins/Minerals (with AE, No Iron); Naftazone; Omega-3 Fatty Acids; Pelubiprofen; Pentosan Polysulfate Sodium; Pentoxifylline; Phenylbutazone; Probenecid; Prostacyclin Analogues; Selective Serotonin Reuptake Inhibitors; Serotonin/Norepinephrine Reuptake Inhibitors; Sodium Phosphates; Talniflumate; Tenoxicam; Thiazide and Thiazide-Like Diuretics; Tipranavir; Tolperisone; Vitamin E (Systemic); Zaltoprofen

Decreased Effect

Nabumetone may decrease the levels/effects of: ACE Inhibitors; Aliskiren; Angiotensin II Receptor Blockers; Beta-Blockers; Eplerenone; HydrALAZINE; Loop Diuretics; Potassium-Sparing Diuretics; Prostaglandins (Ophthalmic); Salicylates; Selective Serotonin Reuptake Inhibitors; Thiazide and Thiazide-Like Diuretics

The levels/effects of Nabumetone may be decreased by: Bile Acid Sequestrants; Salicylates

Food Interactions Nabumetone peak serum concentrations may be increased if taken with food or dairy products. Management: Administer without regard to food.

Pharmacodynamics/Kinetics

Half-life Elimination 6MNA: ~24 hours; terminal half-life was increased ~50% in patients with CrCl 30 to 49 mL/minute

Time to Peak Serum: 6MNA: Oral: Adults: 2.5 to 3 hours; Elderly: 4 hours

Pregnancy Risk Factor C

Pregnancy Considerations Adverse events have not been observed in animal reproduction studies. NSAID exposure during the first trimester is not strongly associated with congenital malformations; however, cardiovascular anomalies and cleft palate have been observed following NSAID exposure in some studies. The use of an NSAID close to conception may be associated with an increased risk of miscarriage. Nonteratogenic effects have been observed following NSAID administration during the third trimester including myocardial degenerative changes, prenatal constriction of the ductus arteriosus, fetal tricuspid ▶

regurgitation, failure of the ductus arteriosus to close postnatally; renal dysfunction or failure, oligohydramnios; gastrointestinal bleeding or perforation, increased risk of necrotizing enterocolitis; intracranial bleeding (including intraventricular hemorrhage), platelet dysfunction with resultant bleeding; pulmonary hypertension. Because they may cause premature closure of the ductus arteriosus, use of NSAIDs late in pregnancy should be avoided (use after 31 or 32 weeks gestation is not recommended by some clinicians). The chronic use of NSAIDs in women of reproductive age may be associated with infertility that is reversible upon discontinuation of the medication. A registry is available for pregnant women exposed to autoimmune medications including nabumetone. For additional information contact the Organization of Teratology Information Specialists, OTIS Autoimmune Diseases Study, at 877-311-8972.

Breastfeeding Considerations It is not known if nabumetone or 6MNA are excreted in breast milk. Due to the potential for serious adverse reactions in the nursing infant, the manufacturer recommends a decision be made whether to discontinue nursing or to discontinue the drug, taking into account the importance of treatment to the mother.

Dosage Forms

Tablet, Oral:

Generic: 500 mg, 750 mg

Nadolol (NAY doe lol)

Related Information

Cardiovascular Diseases *on page* 1752

Brand Names: US Corgard

Brand Names: Canada Apo-Nadol; Teva-Nadolol

Pharmacologic Category Antianginal Agent; Antihypertensive; Beta-Blocker, Nonselective

Use Treatment of hypertension and angina pectoris

Guideline recommendations:

Hypertension: The 2014 guideline for the management of high blood pressure in adults (Eighth Joint National Committee [JNC 8]) recommends initiation of pharmacologic treatment to lower blood pressure for the following patients (JNC8 [James 2013]):

- Patients ≥60 years of age, with systolic blood pressure (SBP) ≥150 mm Hg or diastolic blood pressure (DBP) ≥90 mm Hg. Goal of therapy is SBP <150 mm Hg and DBP <90 mm Hg.
- Patients <60 years of age, with SBP ≥140 mm Hg or DBP ≥90 mm Hg. Goal of therapy is SBP <140 mm Hg and DBP <90 mm Hg.
- Patients ≥18 years of age with diabetes, with SBP ≥140 mm Hg or DBP ≥90 mm Hg. Goal of therapy is SBP <140 mm Hg and DBP <90 mm Hg.
- Patients ≥18 years of age with chronic kidney disease (CKD), with SBP ≥140 mm Hg or DBP ≥90 mm Hg. Goal of therapy is SBP <140 mm Hg and DBP <90 mm Hg.

Chronic kidney disease (CKD) and hypertension: Regardless of race or diabetes status, the use of an ACE inhibitor (ACEI) or angiotensin receptor blocker (ARB) as initial therapy is recommended to improve kidney outcomes. In the general nonblack population (without CKD) including those with diabetes, initial antihypertensive treatment should consist of a thiazide-type diuretic, calcium channel blocker, ACEI, or ARB. In the general black population (without CKD) including those with diabetes, initial antihypertensive treatment should consist of a thiazide-type diuretic or a calcium channel blocker **instead of** an ACEI or ARB.

Coronary artery disease (CAD) and hypertension: The American Heart Association, American College of Cardiology, and American Society of Hypertension (AHA/ACC/ASH) 2015 scientific statement for the treatment of hypertension in patients with CAD recommends the use of a beta blocker as part of a regimen in patients with hypertension and chronic stable angina with a history of prior MI. A BP target of <140/90 mm Hg is reasonable for the secondary prevention of cardiovascular events. A lower target BP (<130/80 mm Hg) may be appropriate in some individuals with CAD, previous MI, stroke or transient ischemic attack, or CAD risk equivalents (AHA/ACC/ASH [Rosendorff 2015]).

Local Anesthetic/Vasoconstrictor Precautions Use with caution; epinephrine has interacted with nonselective beta-blockers to result in initial hypertensive episode followed by bradycardia

Effects on Dental Treatment Nadolol is a nonselective beta-blocker and may enhance the pressor response to epinephrine, resulting in hypertension and bradycardia. Many nonsteroidal anti-inflammatory drugs, such as ibuprofen and indomethacin, can reduce the hypotensive effect of beta-blockers after 3 or more weeks of therapy with the NSAID. Short-term NSAID use (ie, 3 days) requires no special precautions in patients taking beta-blockers.

Effects on Bleeding No information available to require special precautions

Adverse Reactions

>10%: Central nervous system: Drowsiness, insomnia

1% to 10%:

Cardiovascular: Atrioventricular block, bradycardia, cardiac conduction disturbance, cardiac failure, cold extremities, edema, hypotension, palpitations, peripheral vascular insufficiency, Raynaud's phenomenon

Central nervous system: Depression, dizziness, fatigue, sedation

<1%, postmarketing, and/or case reports: Abdominal distress, anorexia, behavioral changes, bloating, blurred vision, bronchospasm, cardiac arrhythmia, chest pain, confusion (especially in the elderly), constipation, cough, decreased libido, diaphoresis, diarrhea, dyspepsia, dyspnea, facial edema, flatulence, hallucination, headache, impotence, nasal congestion, nausea, nervousness, paresthesia, pruritus, skin rash, slurred speech, thrombocytopenia, tinnitus, transient alopecia, vomiting, weight gain, xeroderma, xerophthalmia, xerostomia

General Dosage Range Dosage adjustment recommended in patients with renal impairment

Oral:

Adults: Initial: 40 mg once daily; Maintenance: 40 to 320 mg once daily

Elderly: Initial: 20 mg once daily; Maintenance: 20 to 240 mg once daily

Mechanism of Action Competitively blocks response to $beta_1$- and $beta_2$-adrenergic stimulation; does not exhibit any membrane stabilizing or intrinsic sympathomimetic activity. Nonselective beta-adrenergic blockers (propranolol, nadolol) reduce portal pressure by producing splanchnic vasoconstriction ($beta_2$ effect) thereby reducing portal blood flow.

Pharmacodynamics/Kinetics

Duration of Action 17 to 24 hours

Half-life Elimination

Infants 3 to 22 months (n=3): 3.2 to 4.3 hours (Mehta 1992)

Children 10 years (n=1): 15.7 hours (Mehta 1992)

Children ~15 years (n=1): 7.3 hours (Mehta 1992)

Adults: 20 to 24 hours; prolonged with renal impairment; (up to 45 hours in severe impairment) (Herrera 1979)

Time to Peak Serum: 3 to 4 hours

Pregnancy Risk Factor C

Pregnancy Considerations Adverse events were observed in some animal reproduction studies. Nadolol crosses the placenta and is measurable in infant serum after birth (Fox 1985). Bradycardia and hypoglycemia have been observed in neonates following maternal use of nadolol during pregnancy. Reduced birth weight has also been observed following in utero exposure to beta-blockers as a class. Adequate facilities for monitoring infants at birth is generally recommended.

Untreated chronic maternal hypertension and preeclampsia are also associated with adverse events in the fetus, infant, and mother (ACOG 2015; Magee 2014). Although beta-blockers may be used when treatment of hypertension in pregnancy is indicated, agents other than nadolol are preferred (ACOG 2013; Magee 2014).

Nadroparin (nad roe PA rin)

Related Information

Cardiovascular Diseases *on page 1752*

Brand Names: Canada Fraxiparine; Fraxiparine Forte

Pharmacologic Category Anticoagulant; Anticoagulant, Low Molecular Weight Heparin

Use

Fraxiparine:

Acute coronary syndromes: Treatment of unstable angina and non-ST-elevation myocardial infarction (NSTEMI) myocardial infarction (ie, non-Q wave MI)

Anticoagulation during hemodialysis: Prevention of clotting during hemodialysis

Deep vein thrombosis: Treatment of deep vein thrombosis (DVT)

Thromboprophylaxis: Prophylaxis of thromboembolic disorders (particularly DVT and pulmonary embolism [PE]) in general and orthopedic surgery

Fraxiparine Forte: Treatment of deep vein thrombosis (DVT)

Local Anesthetic/Vasoconstrictor Precautions No information available to require special precautions

Effects on Dental Treatment Key adverse event(s) related to dental treatment: Bleeding is the major adverse effect of nadroparin. See Effects on Bleeding.

Effects on Bleeding As with all anticoagulants, bleeding is the major adverse effect of nadroparin. Hemorrhage may occur at virtually any site; risk is dependent on multiple variables including the intensity of anticoagulation and patient susceptibility. At the recommended doses, LMWHS do not significantly influence platelet aggregation or affect global clotting time (ie, PT or aPTT). Medical consult is suggested.

Adverse Reactions Frequency not defined. As with all anticoagulants, bleeding is the major adverse effect of nadroparin. Hemorrhage may occur at virtually any site. Risk is dependent on multiple variables.

Cardiovascular: Arterial thrombosis, thromboembolism, venous thrombosis

Dermatologic: Skin rash

Endocrine & metabolic: Calcinosis, hypoaldosteronism (causing hyperkalemia and/or hyponatremia)

Hematological & oncologic: Hemorrhage, thrombocythemia, thrombocytopenia

Hepatic: Increased serum ALT, increased serum AST

Hypersensitivity: Hypersensitivity reaction

Local: Hematoma at injection site, pain at injection site

Neuromuscular & skeletal: Osteopenia

<1%, postmarketing, and/or case reports: Anaphylactoid reaction (very rare), angioedema (very rare), eosinophilia (very rare), erythema, priapism (very rare), pruritus, skin necrosis (rare), urticaria

General Dosage Range Dosage adjustment recommended in patients with renal impairment. Dosage varies greatly depending on indication.

Mechanism of Action Nadroparin has high anti-Xa activity, but low anti-IIa activity. The greater ratio of anti-Xa activity has the potential to provide equivalent antithrombic efficacy with reduced hemorrhagic complications.

Pharmacodynamics/Kinetics

Duration of Action Anti-Xa activity: 18 hours

Half-life Elimination 3.5 hours (prolonged in renal impairment)

Time to Peak Serum: SubQ: 3 to 6 hours

Pregnancy Considerations Adverse events were not observed in animal reproduction studies. Low molecular weight heparin (LMWH) does not cross the placenta; increased risks of fetal bleeding or teratogenic effects have not been reported. LMWH is recommended over unfractionated heparin for the treatment of acute venous thromboembolism (VTE) in pregnant women. LMWH is also recommended over unfractionated heparin for VTE prophylaxis in pregnant women with certain risk factors. LMWH should be discontinued prior to induction of labor or a planned cesarean delivery When choosing therapy, fetal outcomes (ie, pregnancy loss, malformations), maternal outcomes (ie, VTE, hemorrhage), burden of therapy, and maternal preference should be considered (Guyatt, 2012).

Product Availability Not available in the US

Nafarelin (naf a REL in)

Brand Names: US Synarel

Brand Names: Canada Synarel

Pharmacologic Category Gonadotropin Releasing Hormone Agonist

Use

Central precocious puberty: Treatment of central precocious puberty (CPP) (gonadotropin-dependent precocious puberty) in children of both sexes.

Endometriosis: Management of endometriosis, including pain relief and reduction of endometriotic lesions.

Local Anesthetic/Vasoconstrictor Precautions No information available to require special precautions

Effects on Dental Treatment No significant effects or complications reported

Effects on Bleeding No information available to require special precautions

Adverse Reactions Note: Adverse events may be more frequent in the first 6 weeks of treatment due to stimulation of the pituitary-gonadal axis.

CPP: 1% to 10%:

Central nervous system: Emotional lability (6%)

Dermatologic: Acne vulgaris (10%), hypertrichosis (transient, pubic region: 5%), body odor (4%), seborrhea (3%)
Endocrine & metabolic: Breast hypertrophy (8%; transient), vaginal hemorrhage (8%), hot flashes (3%; transient), vaginal discharge (3%)
Hypersensitivity: Hypersensitivity reaction (3%; including chest pain, pruritus, dyspnea, skin rash)
Respiratory: Rhinitis (5%)

Endometriosis:

>10%:

Central nervous system: Headache (18%), emotional lability (16%)
Dermatologic: Acne vulgaris (14%)
Endocrine & metabolic: Hot flash (90%), decreased libido (23%), hyperphosphatemia (10% to 15%), hypocalcemia (10% to 15%), hypertriglyceridemia (12%)
Genitourinary: Vaginal dryness (19%)
Hematologic & oncologic: Change in WBC count (10% to 15%; decreased), eosinophilia (10% to 15%)

1% to 10%:

Cardiovascular: Edema (8%)
Central nervous system: Insomnia (8%), depression (3%)
Dermatologic: Hirsutism (3%)
Endocrine & metabolic: Breast atrophy (10%), hypercholesterolemia (6%), increased libido (2%)
Gastrointestinal: Weight gain (8%), weight loss (2%)
Neuromuscular & skeletal: Myalgia (10%), decreased bone mineral density
Respiratory: Nasal mucosa irritation (10%)

<1%, postmarketing, and/or case reports (any indication): Arterial thromboembolism, arthralgia, breast engorgement, chloasma, convulsions, eye pain, hepatic injury, increased serum ALT, increased serum AST, lactation, maculopapular rash, palpitations, paresthesia, pituitary apoplexy, seizures, venous thromboembolism, weakness

General Dosage Range Nasal:

Children: Two sprays (400 mcg) into each nostril twice daily; may increase to 3 sprays (600 mcg) into alternating nostrils 3 times daily

Adults: One spray (200 mcg) into 1 to 2 nostrils twice daily

Mechanism of Action Potent synthetic decapeptide analogue of gonadotropin-releasing hormone (GnRH; LHRH) which is approximately 200 times more potent than GnRH in terms of pituitary release of luteinizing hormone (LH) and follicle-stimulating hormone (FSH). Effects on the pituitary gland and sex hormones are dependent upon its length of administration. After acute administration, an initial stimulation of the release of LH and FSH from the pituitary is observed; an increase in androgens and estrogens subsequently follows. Continued administration of nafarelin, however, suppresses gonadotrope responsiveness to endogenous GnRH resulting in reduced secretion of LH and FSH and, secondarily, decreased ovarian and testicular steroid production.

Pharmacodynamics/Kinetics

Half-life Elimination ~3 hours; Metabolites: ~86 hours

Time to Peak Serum: 10 to 45 minutes

Pregnancy Risk Factor X

Pregnancy Considerations Adverse events were observed in some animal reproduction studies. Use is contraindicated in pregnant women and pregnancy should be excluded prior to initiating treatment. Ovulation is inhibited and menstruation is stopped when used appropriately for the treatment of endometriosis, however contraception is not assured. Nonhormonal contraception is recommended. There is no evidence that pregnancy rates are enhanced or adversely affected by use.

Nafcillin (naf SIL in)

Pharmacologic Category Antibiotic, Penicillin

Use Staphylococcal infections: Treatment of infections caused by susceptible penicillinase-producing staphylococci; empiric therapy in suspected cases of resistant staphylococcal infections.

Local Anesthetic/Vasoconstrictor Precautions No information available to require special precautions

Effects on Dental Treatment Key adverse event(s) related to dental treatment: Prolonged use of penicillins may lead to the development of oral candidiasis.

Effects on Bleeding Abnormal clinical bleeding episodes with concurrent platelet aggregation dysfunction have been observed during therapeutic use. This occurrence is enhanced during coexposure with epinephrine. As a result, the clinician should be mindful for adverse bleeding episodes in nafcillin-treated individuals, especially displaying "fight or flight" sympathetic responses (eg, high blood pressure, tachycardia). This reaction may be more likely with penicillins combined with a beta-lactamase inhibitor and/or with agents that have greater activity against specific enteric bacterial species.

Adverse Reactions Frequency not always defined.

Central nervous system: Neurotoxicity (high doses)
Dermatologic: Skin necrosis (with sloughing; subcutaneous extravasation)
Gastrointestinal: *Clostridium difficile* associated diarrhea
Hematologic & oncologic: Agranulocytosis, bone marrow depression, neutropenia
Hypersensitivity: Anaphylaxis, hypersensitivity reaction (immediate and delayed; general incidence of 1% to 10% for penicillins), serum sickness
Local: Inflammation at injection site, injection site phlebitis, local skin exfoliation (at injection site), pain at injection site, swelling at injection site
<1%, postmarketing, and/or case reports: Cholestatic hepatitis, diarrhea, fever, hypokalemia, increased serum ALT, increased serum AST, increased serum bilirubin, interstitial nephritis, lupus erythematosus (drug-induced), nausea, pruritus, renal tubular disease, skin rash (including bullous skin eruptions), vomiting

General Dosage Range IM, IV: *Adults:* Dosage varies greatly depending on indication

Mechanism of Action Interferes with bacterial cell wall synthesis during active multiplication, causing cell wall destruction and resultant bactericidal activity against susceptible bacteria; resistant to inactivation by staphylococcal penicillinase

Pharmacodynamics/Kinetics

Half-life Elimination

Neonates <3 weeks: 2.2 to 5.5 hours; 4 to 9 weeks: 1.2 to 2.3 hours
Infants and Children 1 month to 14 years: 0.75 to 1.9 hours
Adults: Normal renal/hepatic function: 33 to 61 minutes

Time to Peak Serum: IM: 30-60 minutes

Pregnancy Risk Factor B

Pregnancy Considerations Adverse events have not been observed in animal reproduction studies. Information specific to nafcillin use in pregnancy is limited. Maternal use of penicillins has generally not resulted in an increased risk of birth defects.

Naftifine (NAF ti feen)

Brand Names: US Naftin

Pharmacologic Category Antifungal Agent, Topical

Use

Tinea infections: Cream 1% and 2%, Gel 1%: Topical treatment of tinea cruris (jock itch), tinea corporis (ringworm), and tinea pedis (athlete's foot).

Tinea pedis: Gel 2%: Topical treatment of tinea pedis (athlete's foot).

Local Anesthetic/Vasoconstrictor Precautions No information available to require special precautions

Effects on Dental Treatment No significant effects or complications reported

Effects on Bleeding No information available to require special precautions

Adverse Reactions

1% to 10%:

Dermatologic: Burning sensation of skin (5% to 6%), xeroderma (3%), skin irritation (2%), erythema (≤2%), pruritus (1% to 2%)

Local: Application site reaction (2%)

<1%, postmarketing, and/or case reports: Agranulocytosis, crusted skin, dizziness, headache, inflammation, leukopenia, maceration, pain, rash, serous drainage, skin blister, skin tenderness, swelling of skin

General Dosage Range Topical:

Children ≥2 years, Adolescents, and Adults: Cream 2%: Apply once daily

Children ≥12 years, Adolescents, and Adults: Cream 2% and gel 2%: Apply once daily

Adults: Cream 1% and gel 1%: Apply once daily (cream) or twice daily (gel)

Mechanism of Action Synthetic, broad-spectrum antifungal agent in the allylamine class; appears to have both fungistatic and fungicidal activity. Exhibits antifungal activity by selectively inhibiting the enzyme squalene epoxidase in a dose-dependent manner which results in a reduced synthesis of ergosterol, the primary sterol within the fungal membrane, and increased squalene in cells.

Pharmacodynamics/Kinetics

Half-life Elimination 2 to 3 days

Pregnancy Risk Factor B

Pregnancy Considerations Adverse events were not observed in animal reproduction studies following oral administration. Naftifine is absorbed systemically (4% to 6%) following topical administration.

Nalbuphine (NAL byoo feen)

Brand Names: Canada Nubain

Pharmacologic Category Analgesic, Opioid; Analgesic, Opioid Partial Agonist

Use

Pain management: Management of pain severe enough to require an opioid analgesic and for which alternative treatments are inadequate.

Limitations of use: Reserve nalbuphine for use in patients for whom alternative treatment options (eg, nonopioid analgesics) are ineffective, not tolerated, or would be otherwise inadequate to provide sufficient management of pain.

Surgical anesthesia supplement: Supplement to balanced anesthesia, for preoperative and postoperative analgesia, and for obstetrical analgesia during labor and delivery.

Local Anesthetic/Vasoconstrictor Precautions No information available to require special precautions

Effects on Dental Treatment Key adverse event(s) related to dental treatment: Xerostomia and changes in salivation (normal salivary flow resumes upon discontinuation). Anticholinergic side effects can cause a reduction of saliva production or secretion, contributing to discomfort and dental disease (ie, caries, oral candidiasis, and periodontal disease).

Effects on Bleeding No information available to require special precautions

Adverse Reactions

>10%: Central nervous system: Sedation (36%)

1% to 10%:

Central nervous system: Dizziness (5%), headache (3%)

Dermatologic: Cold and clammy skin (9%)

Gastrointestinal: Nausea and vomiting (6%), xerostomia (4%)

<1%, postmarketing, and/or case reports: Abdominal pain, abnormal dreams, agitation, anaphylactoid reaction, anaphylaxis, anxiety, asthma, bitter taste, blurred vision, bradycardia, burning sensation, cardiac arrest, confusion, crying, delusions, depersonalization, depression, derealization, diaphoresis, drowsiness, dyspepsia, dysphoria, euphoria, fever, floating feeling, flushing, hallucination, hostility, hypersensitivity reaction, hypertension, hypogonadism (Brennan 2013; Debono 2011), hypotension, injection site reaction (pain, swelling, redness, burning), intestinal cramps, laryngeal edema, loss of consciousness, nervousness, numbness, pruritus, pulmonary edema, respiratory depression, respiratory distress, restlessness, seizure, skin rash, speech disturbance, stridor, tachycardia, tingling sensation, tremor, urinary urgency, urticaria

General Dosage Range

IM, SubQ: *Adults:* Based on 70 kg individual: 10 mg every 3 to 6 hours as needed; maximum dose in nonopioid-dependent patient: 20 mg/dose; 160 mg/day

IV: *Adults:*

Pain management: Based on 70 kg individual: 10 mg every 3 to 6 hours as needed; maximum dose in nonopioid-tolerant patient: 20 mg/dose; 160 mg/day

Surgical anesthesia supplement: Induction: 0.3 to 3 mg/kg over 10 to 15 minutes; maintenance: 0.25 to 0.5 mg/kg as required

Mechanism of Action Agonist of kappa opiate receptors and partial antagonist of mu opiate receptors in the CNS, causing inhibition of ascending pain pathways, altering the perception of and response to pain; produces generalized CNS depression

Pharmacodynamics/Kinetics

Onset of Action Peak effect: SubQ, IM: <15 minutes; IV: 2 to 3 minutes

Duration of Action 3 to 6 hours

Half-life Elimination

Children: 0.9 to 3.5 hours; however, overall trend observed is longer half-life as age increases (Bressolle 2011; Jaillon 1989)

Adults: 5 hours

Pregnancy Considerations Adverse events have been observed in some animal reproduction studies. Nalbuphine crosses the placenta. Nalbuphine is approved for use in obstetrical analgesia during labor and delivery. When used for pain relief during labor, opioids may temporarily affect the heart rate of the fetus (ACOG 2002) and severe fetal bradycardia has been reported following use of nalbuphine in labor/delivery. Fetal bradycardia may occur when administered earlier in pregnancy (not documented). Use only if clearly needed, with monitoring to detect and manage possible adverse fetal effects. Naloxone has been reported to reverse bradycardia. Newborn should be monitored for respiratory depression or bradycardia following nalbuphine use in labor.

If chronic opioid exposure occurs in pregnancy, adverse events in the newborn (including withdrawal) may occur; monitoring of the neonate is recommended. The minimum effective dose should be used if opioids are needed (Chou 2009). Neonatal abstinence syndrome following opioid exposure may present with autonomic (eg, fever, temperature instability), gastrointestinal (eg, diarrhea, vomiting, poor feeding/weight gain), or neurologic (eg, high-pitched crying, increased muscle tone, irritability, seizure, tremor) symptoms (Dow 2012; Hudak 2012).

Naloxegol (nal OX ee gol)

Brand Names: US Movantik

Brand Names: Canada Movantik

Pharmacologic Category Gastrointestinal Agent, Miscellaneous; Opioid Antagonist, Peripherally-Acting

Use Opioid-induced constipation: Treatment of opioid-induced constipation (OIC) in adult patients with chronic noncancer pain.

Local Anesthetic/Vasoconstrictor Precautions No information available to require special precautions

Effects on Dental Treatment No significant effects or complications reported

Effects on Bleeding No information available to require special precautions

Adverse Reactions

>10%: Gastrointestinal: Abdominal pain (12% to 21%)

1% to 10%:

Central nervous system: Headache (4%)

Dermatologic: Hyperhidrosis (≤3%)

Gastrointestinal: Diarrhea (6% to 9%), nausea (7% to 8%), flatulence (3% to 6%), vomiting (5%)

<1%, postmarketing, and/or case reports: Anxiety, arthritis, back pain, chills, gastrointestinal perforation, irritability, joint pain, yawning

General Dosage Range Dosage adjustment recommended in patients with renal impairment or on concomitant therapy.

Oral: *Adults:* 25 mg once daily

Mechanism of Action Naloxegol is a mu-opioid receptor antagonist. It is composed of naloxone conjugated with a polyethylene glycol polymer, which limits its ability to cross the blood-brain barrier. When administered at the recommended dose, naloxegol functions peripherally in tissues such as the GI tract, thereby decreasing the constipation associated with opioids (Webster, 2013).

Pharmacodynamics/Kinetics

Half-life Elimination 6 to 11 hours

Time to Peak <2 hours; in majority of subjects, a secondary C_{max} occurs ~0.4 to 3 hours after the first C_{max}

Pregnancy Risk Factor C

Pregnancy Considerations Adverse events were not observed in animal reproduction studies. However, exposure during pregnancy may potentiate opioid withdrawal in the fetus.

Naloxone (nal OKS one)

Brand Names: US Evzio; Narcan

Brand Names: Canada Naloxone Hydrochloride Injection; Naloxone Hydrochloride Injection USP

Generic Availability (US) May be product dependent

Pharmacologic Category Antidote; Opioid Antagonist

Dental Use Reverse overdose effects of the two opioid agents, fentanyl and meperidine, used in the technique of IV conscious sedation

Use

Opioid overdose: For the complete or partial reversal of opioid depression (including respiratory depression) induced by natural and synthetic opioids (eg, propoxyphene, methadone, nalbuphine, butorphanol, pentazocine). Naloxone is also indicated for the diagnosis of suspected or known acute opioid overdosage.

Evzio (IM, SubQ) intranasal: For the emergency treatment of known or suspected opioid overdose as manifested by respiratory and/or CNS depression. Intended for immediate administration as emergency therapy in settings where opioids may be present. Not a substitute for emergency medical care.

Limitations of use: Restrict prescription of naloxone 2 mg nasal spray to opioid-dependent patients expected to be at risk for severe opioid withdrawal in situations where there is low risk for accidental or intentional opioid exposure by household contacts.

Local Anesthetic/Vasoconstrictor Precautions No information available to require special precautions

Effects on Dental Treatment No significant effects or complications reported

Effects on Bleeding No information available to require special precautions

Adverse Reactions

Cardiovascular: Flushing (parenteral), hypertension, hypotension, tachycardia, ventricular fibrillation, ventricular tachycardia

Central nervous system: Agitation, body pain, brain disease, coma, confusion (parenteral), disorientation (parenteral), dizziness (parenteral), excessive crying (neonates), hallucination (parenteral), headache (nasal), hyperreflexia (neonates), irritability, nervousness, outbursts of anger (parenteral), paresthesia (parenteral), restlessness, seizure (neonates), shivering, tonic-clonic seizures (parenteral), withdrawal syndrome, yawning

Dermatologic: Diaphoresis, piloerection, xeroderma (nasal)

Endocrine & metabolic: Hot flash (parenteral)

Gastrointestinal: Abdominal cramps, constipation (nasal), diarrhea, nausea, toothache (nasal), vomiting

Local: Erythema at injection site (parenteral), injection site reaction

Neuromuscular & skeletal: Muscle spasm (nasal), musculoskeletal pain (nasal), tremor, weakness

Respiratory: Dry nose (nasal), dyspnea, hypoxia (parenteral), nasal congestion (nasal), nasal discomfort (pain; nasal), nasal mucosa swelling (nasal), pulmonary edema, respiratory depression (parenteral), rhinitis (nasal), rhinorrhea, sneezing

Miscellaneous: Fever

Dental Usual Dosage Opioid overdose: Adults: IV: 0.4 to 2 mg every 2 to 3 minutes as needed; may need to repeat doses every 20 to 60 minutes, if no response is observed after 10 mg, question the diagnosis. **Note:** Use 0.1 to 0.2 mg increments in patients who are opioid dependent and in postoperative patients to avoid large cardiovascular changes.

Dosing

Adult & Geriatric Note: Available routes of administration include IV (preferred), IM, SubQ, and intranasal; other available routes (off-label) include inhalation via nebulization (adults only), and intraosseous (IO). Endotracheal administration is the least desirable and is supported by only anecdotal evidence (case report) (AHA [Neumar 2010]):

Opioid overdose:

Note: For the initial treatment of an opioid-associated life-threatening emergency, the American Heart Association recommends, after initiation of CPR, the use of intranasal or IM naloxone with a repeat dose as needed. If there is an initial patient response (ie, purposeful movement, regular breathing, moan or other response) but the patient then stops responding, begin CPR and repeat naloxone dose. If no initial response, continue CPR and use AED as appropriate (AHA [Lavonas 2015]).

IV, IM, SubQ: Initial: 0.4 to 2 mg; may need to repeat doses every 2 to 3 minutes. A lower initial dose (0.1 to 0.2 mg) should be considered for patients with opioid dependence to avoid acute withdrawal or if there are concerns regarding concurrent stimulant overdose (Mokhlesi 2003). After reversal, may need to readminister dose(s) at a later interval (ie, 20 to 60 minutes) depending on type/duration of opioid. If no response is observed after 10 mg total, consider other causes of respiratory depression. **Note:** May be given endotracheally (off-label route) as 2 to 2.5 times the initial IV dose (ie, 0.8 to 5 mg) (AHA [Neumar 2010]).

IM, SubQ: Evzio: 0.4 mg or 2 mg (contents of 1 auto-injector) as a single dose; may repeat every 2 to 3 minutes until emergency medical assistance becomes available.

Continuous infusion (off-label dosing): IV: **Note:** For use with exposures to long-acting opioids (eg, methadone), sustained release product, and symptomatic body packers after initial naloxone response. Calculate dosage/hour based on effective intermittent dose used and duration of adequate response seen (Tenenbein 1984) **or** use two-thirds (2/3) of the initial effective naloxone bolus on an hourly basis (typically 0.25 to 6.25 mg/hour); one-half (1/2) of the initial bolus dose should be readministered 15 minutes after initiation of the continuous infusion to prevent a drop in naloxone levels; adjust infusion rate as needed to assure adequate ventilation and prevent withdrawal symptoms (Goldfrank 1986).

Inhalation via nebulization (off-label route): 2 mg; may repeat. Switch to IV or IM administration when possible (Weber 2012). **Note:** This administration method is not included in the AHA recommendations for initial management of opioid-associated life-threatening emergency (AHA [Lavonas 2015]).

Intranasal: **Note:** Onset of action is slightly delayed compared to IM or IV routes (Kelly 2005; Robertson 2009):

2 or 4 mg (contents of 1 nasal spray) as a single dose in one nostril; may repeat every 2 to 3 minutes in alternating nostrils until medical assistance becomes available.

Off label dosing: 2 mg (1 mg per nostril) using generic injectable solution (with a mucosal atomization device); may repeat in 3 to 5 minutes if respiratory depression persists (AHA [Lavonas 2015]; AHA [Vanden Hoek 2010]; Kelly 2005; Robertson 2009; Walley 2013).

Reversal of respiratory depression with therapeutic opioid doses: IV: Initial: 0.02 to 0.2 mg; titrate to avoid profound withdrawal, seizures, arrhythmias, or severe pain (APS 2008; Doyon 2010; AHA [Lavonas 2015]). **Note:** May be given endotracheally (off-label route) as 2 to 2.5 times the initial recommended IV dose (ie, 0.04 to 0.5 mg) (AHA [Neumar 2010]).

Continuous infusion (off-label dosing): IV: **Note:** For use with exposures to long-acting opioids (eg, methadone) or sustained release products. Calculate dosage/hour based on effective intermittent dose used and duration of adequate response seen (Tenenbein 1984) **or** use two-thirds (2/3) of the initial effective naloxone bolus on an hourly basis (typically 0.2 to 0.6 mg/hour); one-half (1/2) of the initial bolus dose should be readministered 15 minutes after initiation of the continuous infusion to prevent a drop in naloxone levels; adjust infusion rate as needed to assure adequate ventilation and prevent withdrawal symptoms (Goldfrank 1986).

Opioid-dependent patients being treated for cancer pain (off-label dosing): IV: **Note:** May dilute 0.4 mg/mL (1 mL) ampule into 9 mL of normal saline for a total volume of 10 mL to achieve a 0.04 mg/mL (40 **mcg**/mL) concentration.

0.02 mg (20 **mcg**) IV push; administer every 2 minutes until improvement in symptoms (APS guidelines, v.6.2008) **or**

0.04 to 0.08 mg (40 to 80 **mcg**) slow IV push; administer every 30 to 60 seconds until improvement in symptoms; if no response is observed after total naloxone dose 1 mg, consider other causes of respiratory depression. If respiratory depression is due to long-acting opioids, may consider administering naloxone as a continuous infusion starting at 66% of the total bolus dose (or 0.2 mg per hour) to reverse the opioid toxicity (Howlett 2016).

Postoperative reversal: IV: 0.1 to 0.2 mg every 2 to 3 minutes until desired response (adequate ventilation and alertness without significant pain). **Note:** Repeat doses may be needed within 1 to 2 hour intervals depending on type, dose, and timing of the last dose of opioid administered.

Opioid-induced pruritus (off-label use): IV infusion: 0.25 **mcg/kg/hour** (Gan 1997). Doses up to ~3 **mcg/kg/hour** have been employed (Kendrick 1996). However, doses >2 **mcg/kg/hour** are more likely to lead to reversal of analgesia and are not recommended (Kjellberg 2001; Miller 2011). **Note:** Monitor pain control; verify that the naloxone is not reversing analgesia.

Pediatric

Opioid overdose:

PALS Guidelines *(off-label dosing)* (AHA [Kleinman 2010]):

IV (preferred), intraosseous (off-label route): **Note:** May be administered IM, SubQ, or endotracheal (off-label route), but onset of action may be delayed, especially if patient has poor perfusion; endotracheal preferred if IV/intraosseous route not available; doses may need to be repeated. **Note:** The use of naloxone is not recommended as part of initial resuscitative efforts in the delivery room for neonates with respiratory depression; support ventilation to improve oxygenation and heart rate (AHA [Kattwinkel 2010]):

Infants and Children <5 years or ≤20 kg (off-label dose): 0.1 mg/kg/dose (maximum dose: 2 mg); repeat every 2 to 3 minutes if needed

Children ≥5 years or >20 kg and Adolescents: 2 mg; if no response, repeat every 2 to 3 minutes

Endotracheal (off-label route): Infants, Children, and Adolescents: Optimal endotracheal dose unknown; current expert recommendations are 2 to 3 times the IV dose.

Manufacturer's labeling:

IV: Infants, Children and Adolescents: Initial: 0.01 mg/kg/dose; if no response, a subsequent dose of 0.1 mg/kg may be given

Continuous IV infusion (off-label dosing): Infants, Children and Adolescents: 24 to 40 mcg/kg/hour has been reported (Gourlay 1983; Lewis 1984; Tenenbein 1984). Doses as low as 2.5 mcg/kg/hour have been reported in adults and a dose of 160 mcg/kg/hour was reported in one neonate (Tenenbein 1984). If continuous infusion is required, calculate dosage/hour based on effective intermittent dose used and duration of adequate response seen (Tenenbein 1984) or use two-thirds of the initial effective naloxone bolus on an hourly basis; titrate dose. **Note:** The infusion should be discontinued by reducing the infusion in decrements of 25%; closely monitor the patient (eg, pulse oximetry and respiratory rate) after each adjustment and after discontinuation of the infusion for recurrence of opioid-induced respiratory depression (Perry 1996).

IM, SubQ: Infants, Children and Adolescents: Initial: 0.01 mg/kg/dose; if no response, a subsequent dose of 0.1 mg/kg may be given; **Note:** If using IM or SubQ route, dose should be given in divided doses.

Auto-injector: Evzio: Neonates, Infants, Children and Adolescents: 0.4 mg or 2 mg (contents of 1 auto-injector) as a single dose; may repeat every 2 to 3 minutes until emergency medical assistance becomes available.

Intranasal: Neonates, Infants, Children and Adolescents: 2 or 4 mg (contents of 1 nasal spray) as a single dose in one nostril; may repeat every 2 to 3 minutes in alternating nostrils until medical assistance becomes available. **Note:** Onset of action is slightly delayed compared to IM or IV routes (Kelly 2005; Robertson 2009). In neonates with known or suspected exposure to maternal opioid use, consider using another form of naloxone to allow dosing according to weight and titration to effect.

Reversal of respiratory depression with therapeutic opioid dosing:

PALS guidelines *(off-label dosing)* (AHA [Kleinman 2010]): Infants, Children, and Adolescents: IV: 0.001 to 0.005 mg/kg/dose; titrate to effect. **Note:** AAP recommends a wider dosage range of 0.001 to 0.015 mg/kg/dose (Hegenbarth 2008)

Manufacturer's labeling: Infants, Children, and Adolescents: IV: Initial: 0.005 to 0.01 mg; repeat every 2 to 3 minutes as needed based on response

Renal Impairment There are no dosage adjustments provided in the manufacturer's labeling.

Hepatic Impairment There are no dosage adjustments provided in the manufacturer's labeling.

Mechanism of Action Pure opioid antagonist that competes and displaces opioids at opioid receptor sites

Contraindications Hypersensitivity to naloxone or any component of the formulation

Warnings/Precautions Use with caution in patients with cardiovascular disease or in patients receiving medications with potential adverse cardiovascular effects (eg, hypotension, pulmonary edema, or arrhythmias); pulmonary edema and cardiovascular instability, including ventricular fibrillation, have been reported in association with abrupt reversal when using opioid antagonists. Administration of naloxone causes the release of catecholamines, which may precipitate acute withdrawal or unmask pain in those who regularly take opioids. Symptoms of acute withdrawal in opioid-dependent patients may include pain, tachycardia, hypertension, fever, sweating, abdominal cramps, diarrhea, nausea, vomiting, agitation, and irritability. In neonates born to mothers with opioid dependence, opioid withdrawal may be life-threatening and symptoms may include excessive crying, shrill cry, failure to feed, seizures, and hyperactive reflexes. In settings other than acute opioid overdose (eg, postoperative patients), carefully titrate the dose to reverse hypoventilation; do not fully awaken patient or reverse analgesic effect (postoperative patient). The 2 mg nasal spray is less likely to precipitate severe opioid withdrawal compared to the 4 mg dose; however, the 2 mg dose may not provide an adequate and timely reversal in patients who have been exposed to an overdose of a potent or very high dose of opioids. Excessive dosages should be avoided after use of opioids in surgery. Abrupt postoperative reversal may result in nausea, vomiting, sweating, tachycardia, hypertension, seizures, and other cardiovascular events (including pulmonary edema and arrhythmias). Reversal of partial opioid agonists or mixed opioid agonist/antagonists (eg, buprenorphine, pentazocine) may be incomplete and larger or repeat doses of naloxone may be required. Recurrence of respiratory and/or CNS depression is possible if the opioid involved is long-acting; continuously observe patients until there is no further risk of recurrent respiratory or CNS depression.

To prevent overdose deaths, there are initiatives to dispense naloxone for self- or buddy-administration to patients at risk of opioid overdose (eg, recipients of high-dose opioids, suspected or confirmed history of illicit opioid use) and individuals likely to be present in an overdose situation (eg, family members of illicit drug users) (Albert 2011; Bennett 2011). Clinical practice guidelines recommend patients being treated for opioid use disorder should be given prescriptions for naloxone. Patients and family members/significant others should be trained in the use of naloxone in overdose (Kampman [ASAM 2015]). Evzio is indicated for emergency treatment. Needleless administration via nebulization and the intranasal route by first responders and bystanders has also been described (Doe-Simkins 2009; Weber 2012). Needleless administration provides an alternative route of administration in patients with venous scarring due to illicit drug use (eg, heroin). There is a low incidence of death following naloxone reversal of opioid toxicity in patients who refuse transport to a healthcare facility (Wampler 2011). Nevertheless, patients who received naloxone in the out-of-hospital setting should seek immediate emergency medical assistance after the first dose due to the likelihood that respiratory and/or central nervous system depression will return.

When the auto-injector is administered to infants <1 year of age, monitor the injection site for residual needle parts and signs of infection.

Drug Interactions

Metabolism/Transport Effects None known.

Avoid Concomitant Use

Avoid concomitant use of Naloxone with any of the following: Methylnaltrexone; Naldemedine; Naloxegol

Increased Effect/Toxicity

Naloxone may increase the levels/effects of: Naldemedine; Naloxegol

The levels/effects of Naloxone may be increased by: Methylnaltrexone

Decreased Effect There are no known significant interactions involving a decrease in effect.

Pharmacodynamics/Kinetics

Onset of Action Endotracheal, IM, SubQ: 2 to 5 minutes; Inhalation via nebulization: ~5 minutes (Mycyk 2003); Intranasal: ~8 to 13 minutes (Kelley 2005; Robertson 2009); IV: ~2 minutes

Duration of Action Depending on route of administration, ~30 to 120 minutes; IV has a shorter duration of action than IM administration; since naloxone's action is shorter than that of most opioids, repeated doses are usually needed

Half-life Elimination Neonates: Mean 3.1 ± 0.5 hours; Adults: IM, IV, or SubQ: 0.5 to 1.5 hours; Intranasal: ~2 hours

Time to Peak IM, SubQ: 15 minutes; Intranasal: 19.8 to 30 minutes

Pregnancy Risk Factor C (product-specific)

Pregnancy Considerations Adverse events were not observed in animal reproduction studies. Naloxone crosses the placenta and may precipitate opioid withdrawal in the fetus. Naloxone is not recommended for use in pregnant women with opioid use disorder except in situations of life threatening overdose (Kampman [ASAM 2015]). Use to diagnose opioid dependence during pregnancy is contraindicated (ACOG 2012). In general, medications used as antidotes should take into consideration the health and prognosis of the mother; antidotes should be administered to pregnant women if there is a clear indication for use and should not be withheld because of fears of teratogenicity (Bailey 2003). Use caution in pregnant women with mild-to-moderate hypertension during labor; severe hypertension may occur.

Breastfeeding Considerations It is not known if naloxone is excreted into breast milk, however, systemic absorption following oral administration is low (Smith 2012) and any exposure of naloxone to a nursing infant would therefore be limited. Since naloxone is used for opioid reversal, the opioid concentrations in the milk of a breastfeeding mother and potential transfer of the opioid to the infant should be considered. According to the manufacturer, the decision to continue or discontinue breastfeeding during therapy should take into account the risk of infant exposure, the benefits of breastfeeding to the infant, and benefits of treatment to the mother.

Product Availability

Evzio 2 mg/0.4 mL auto-injector: FDA approved October 2016; anticipated availability in the first half of 2017.

Narcan 2 mg Nasal Spray: FDA approved January 2017; anticipated availability is currently unknown.

Dosage Forms

Liquid, Nasal:

Narcan: 4 mg/0.1 mL (1 ea)

Solution, Injection:

Generic: 0.4 mg/mL (1 mL); 4 mg/10 mL (10 mL)

Solution Auto-injector, Injection:

Evzio: 0.4 mg/0.4 mL (0.4 mL); 2 mg/0.4 mL (0.4 mL)

Solution Cartridge, Injection:

Generic: 0.4 mg/mL (1 mL)

Solution Prefilled Syringe, Injection [preservative free]:

Generic: 2 mg/2 mL (2 mL)

Naltrexone (nal TREKS one)

Brand Names: US ReVia [DSC]; Vivitrol

Brand Names: Canada ReVia

Pharmacologic Category Antidote; Opioid Antagonist

Use

Alcohol dependence: Treatment of alcohol dependence.

Opioid dependence: For the blockade of the effects of exogenously administered opioids.

Local Anesthetic/Vasoconstrictor Precautions No information available to require special precautions

Effects on Dental Treatment Key adverse event(s) related to dental treatment: Dry mouth.

Effects on Bleeding No information available to require special precautions

Adverse Reactions Combined reporting of adverse events from oral and injectable formulations.

>10%:

Cardiovascular: Syncope (13%)

Central nervous system: Headache (3% to 25%), insomnia (3% to 14%), dizziness (4% to 13%), anxiety (2% to 12%), decreased energy (>10%), nervousness (4% to >10%)

Gastrointestinal: Nausea (10% to 33%), vomiting (3% to 14%), decreased appetite (14%), diarrhea (13%), abdominal pain (11%), abdominal cramps

Hepatic: Increased serum ALT (13%)

Local: Injection site reaction (≤69%; includes bruise, induration, nodules, pain, pruritus, swelling, tenderness)

Neuromuscular & skeletal: Increased creatine phosphokinase (11% to 39%), arthralgia (12%), myalgia (>10%)

Respiratory: Pharyngitis (7% to 11%)

1% to 10%:

Cardiovascular: Hypertension (5%)

Central nervous system: Suicidal ideation (≤10%), delayed ejaculation (<10%), depression (8%), drowsiness (2% to 4%), fatigue (4%), chills, depressed mood, increased energy, irritability

Dermatologic: Skin rash (6% to 10%)

Endocrine & metabolic: Increased gamma-glutamyl transferase (7%), increased thirst, polydipsia

Gastrointestinal: Xerostomia (5%), toothache (4%), constipation
Genitourinary: Impotence (<10%)
Hepatic: Increased serum AST (2% to 10%)
Infection: Influenza (5%)
Neuromuscular & skeletal: Muscle cramps (8%), back pain (6%)

<1%, postmarketing, and/or case reports: Abnormality in thinking, acne vulgaris, acute ischemic stroke, agitation, alopecia, altered blood pressure, angina pectoris, anorexia, atrial fibrillation, blurred vision, burning sensation of eyes, cardiac failure, cerebral aneurysm, chest pain, chest tightness, cholecystitis, cholelithiasis, chronic obstructive pulmonary disease, cold extremities, colitis, confusion, cough, decreased libido, deep vein thrombosis, dehydration, delirium, diaphoresis, disorientation, dyspnea, dysuria, ECG changes, edema, eosinophilia (transient), eosinophilic pneumonitis, epistaxis, euphoria, eye pain, fever, flatulence, gastrointestinal hemorrhage, groin pain, hallucination, hemorrhoids, hepatic insufficiency, hepatitis, herpes labialis, hoarseness, hot flash, hypercholesterolemia, hyperkinesia, hypersensitivity reaction (includes anaphylaxis, angioedema, and urticaria), increased appetite, increased bronchial secretions, increased libido, knee pain, leg pain, leukocytosis, lymphadenopathy, malaise, myocardial infarction, nasal congestion, nightmares, oily skin, opioid withdrawal syndrome, otalgia, palpitations, pancreatitis, paralytic ileus, paranoia, perirectal abscess, photophobia, pneumonia, pulmonary embolism, restlessness, rhinorrhea, rigors, seizure, shoulder pain, sinusitis, sneezing, sore throat, swelling of eye, tachycardia, thrombocytopenia, tinea pedis, tinnitus, tremor, twitching, ulcer, urinary frequency, urinary tract infection, visual disturbance, weakness, weight gain, weight loss, yawning

General Dosage Range

IM: *Adults:* 380 mg once every 4 weeks

Oral: *Adults:* 25-50 mg once daily

Mechanism of Action Naltrexone (a pure opioid antagonist) is a cyclopropyl derivative of oxymorphone similar in structure to naloxone and nalorphine (a morphine derivative); it acts as a competitive antagonist at opioid receptor sites, showing the highest affinity for mu receptors.

Pharmacodynamics/Kinetics

Duration of Action Oral: 50 mg: 24 hours; 100 mg: 48 hours; 150 mg: 72 hours; IM: 4 weeks

Half-life Elimination Oral: 4 hours; 6-beta-naltrexol: 13 hours; IM: naltrexone and 6-beta-naltrexol: 5-10 days (dependent upon erosion of polymer)

Time to Peak Serum: Oral: ~60 minutes; IM: Biphasic: ~2 hours (first peak), ~2-3 days (second peak)

Pregnancy Risk Factor C

Pregnancy Considerations Adverse events were observed in animal reproduction studies. Information related to the use of naltrexone during pregnancy is limited (Farid 2008). Clinical practice guidelines recommend that if a women being treated with naltrexone for the treatment of opioid use disorder becomes pregnant, naltrexone should be discontinued if the patient and physician agree that the risk of relapse if low. If patient is concerned about relapse and wishes to continue naltrexone, the patient should be informed of the potential risks of continuing treatment and consent for ongoing treatment should be obtained. If naltrexone is discontinued and the patient subsequently relapses, consideration should be given for treatment with methadone or buprenorphine (Kampman [ASAM 2015]).

Naltrexone and Bupropion

(nal TREKS one & byoo PROE pee on)

Brand Names: US Contrave

Pharmacologic Category Anorexiant; Antidepressant, Dopamine/Norepinephrine-Reuptake Inhibitor; Opioid Antagonist

Use Weight management: Adjunct to a reduced-calorie diet and increased physical activity for chronic weight management in adults with an initial body mass index (BMI) of ≥30 kg/m^2 or ≥27 kg/m^2 in the presence of at least one weight-related comorbid condition (eg, hypertension, type 2 diabetes mellitus, and/or dyslipidemia)

Limitations of use: The effect of naltrexone/bupropion on cardiovascular morbidity and mortality has not been established. The safety and effectiveness of naltrexone/bupropion in combination with other products intended for weight loss, including prescription drugs, over-the-counter drugs, and herbal preparations, have not been established.

Local Anesthetic/Vasoconstrictor Precautions Part of the mechanism of buproprion is to block reuptake of norepinephrine along with dopamine. Because of the potential for norepinephrine elevation within CNS synapses, it is suggested that vasoconstrictor be administered with caution and to monitor vital signs in dental patients taking antidepressants that affect norepinephrine in this way.

Effects on Dental Treatment No significant effects or complications reported

Effects on Bleeding No information available to require special precautions

Adverse Reactions

>10%:

Central nervous system: Headache (18%), sleep disorder (14%)
Gastrointestinal: Nausea (33%), constipation (19%), vomiting (11%)

1% to 10%:

Cardiovascular: Hypertension (≤6%), increased blood pressure (≤6%), palpitations (2%), myocardial infarction (<2%), presyncope (<2%), tachycardia (<2%)
Central nervous system: Dizziness (10%), insomnia (9%; ≥65 years of age: 11%), depression (6%; ≥ 65 years of age: 7%), anxiety (4% to 6%), fatigue (4%), irritability (3%), disturbance in attention (<2% to 3%), abnormal dreams (<2%), agitation (<2%), altered mental status (<2%), amnesia (<2%), derealization (<2%), emotional lability (<2%), equilibrium disturbance (<2%), feeling abnormal (<2%), feeling hot (<2%), intention tremor (<2%), jitteriness (<2%), lethargy (<2%), memory impairment (<2%), nervousness (<2%), tension (<2%), vertigo (<2%)
Dermatologic: Hyperhidrosis (3%), alopecia (<2%)
Endocrine: Hot flash (4%), dehydration (<2%), increased thirst (<2%)
Gastrointestinal: Xerostomia (8%), diarrhea (7%), upper abdominal pain (4%), viral gastroenteritis (4%), abdominal pain (3%), dysgeusia (2%), cholecystitis (<2%), eructation (<2%), hematochezia (<2%), hernia (<2%), lower abdominal pain (<2%), motion sickness (<2%), swelling of lips (<2%)
Genitourinary: Urinary tract infection (3%), erectile dysfunction (<2%), irregular menses (<2%), urinary urgency (<2%), vaginal dryness (<2%), vaginal hemorrhage (<2%)
Hematologic & oncologic: Decreased hematocrit (<2%)
Hepatic: Increased liver enzymes (<2%)

Infection: Kidney infection (<2%), staphylococcal infection (<2%)

Neuromuscular & skeletal: Tremor (4%), strain (2%), herniated disk (<2%), jaw pain (<2%), weakness (<2%)

Otic: Tinnitus (3%)

Renal: Increased serum creatinine (<2%)

Respiratory: Pneumonia (<2%)

<1%, Postmarketing, and/or case reports: Hypoglycemia (concomitant use of antidiabetic medications), increased heart rate (resting), syncope

Mechanism of Action Naltrexone is a pure opioid antagonist, and bupropion is a relatively weak inhibitor of the neuronal reuptake of dopamine and norepinephrine. The exact neurochemical effects of naltrexone/bupropion leading to weight loss are not fully understood. Effects may result from action on areas of the brain involved in the regulation of food intake: the hypothalamus (appetite regulatory center) and the mesolimbic dopamine circuit (reward system).

Pregnancy Risk Factor X

Pregnancy Considerations Animal reproduction studies have not been conducted with this combination. Adverse fetal events following maternal use of bupropion during pregnancy have been reported in some studies. Weight-loss therapy is not recommended for pregnant women. Obese and overweight women should be encouraged to participate in weight reduction programs prior to attempting pregnancy; weight gain during pregnancy should be determined by their prepregnancy BMI and current guidelines (ADA, 2009; IOM, 2009). Use of this product is contraindicated in pregnant women.

Naphazoline and Pheniramine

(naf AZ oh leen & fen NIR a meen)

Brand Names: US Naphcon-A [OTC]; Opcon-A [OTC]; Visine-A [OTC]

Brand Names: Canada Naphcon-A; Visine Advanced Allergy

Pharmacologic Category Alkylamine Derivative; Alpha$_1$ Agonist; Histamine H_1 Antagonist; Histamine H_1 Antagonist, First Generation; Imidazoline Derivative; Ophthalmic Agent, Vasoconstrictor

Use Ocular itching/redness: Temporary relief of itching and redness of the eye(s) caused by grass, ragweed, pollen, animal dander and hair.

Local Anesthetic/Vasoconstrictor Precautions No information available to require special precautions

Effects on Dental Treatment No significant effects or complications reported

Effects on Bleeding No information available to require special precautions

Adverse Reactions Frequency not defined.

Central nervous system: Tingling sensation (eye)

Ophthalmic: Mydriasis

General Dosage Range Ophthalmic: *Children ≥6 years, Adolescents, and Adults:* Instill 1 to 2 drops into the affected eye(s) up to 4 times daily

Mechanism of Action

Naphazoline: Stimulates alpha-adrenergic receptors in the arterioles of the conjunctiva to produce vasoconstriction.

Pheniramine: Inhibits the effect of histamine on conjunctival epithelial cells by preventing its release from mast cells.

Naproxen (na PROKS en)

Related Information

Oral Pain *on page 1830*

Rheumatoid Arthritis, Osteoarthritis, and Osteoporosis *on page 1792*

Temporomandibular Dysfunction (TMD), Chronic Pain, and Fibromyalgia *on page 1868*

Related Sample Prescriptions

Oral Pain - Sample Prescriptions *on page 28*

Brand Names: US Aleve [OTC]; All Day Pain Relief [OTC]; All Day Relief [OTC]; Anaprox DS; Anaprox [DSC]; EC-Naprosyn; EnovaRX-Naproxen; Equipto-Naproxen; Flanax Pain Relief; Flanax Pain Relief [OTC]; GoodSense Naproxen Sodium [OTC]; Mediproxen [OTC]; Naprelan; Naproderm [DSC]; Naprosyn; Naproxen Comfort Pac; Naproxen DR; Naproxen Kit [DSC]

Brand Names: Canada Aleve; Anaprox; Anaprox DS; Apo-Napro-Na; Apo-Napro-Na DS; Apo-Naproxen; Apo-Naproxen EC; Apo-Naproxen SR; Ava-Naproxen EC; Maxidol; Mylan-Naproxen EC; Naprelan; Naprosyn; Naproxen EC; Naproxen Sodium DS; Naproxen-NA; Naproxen-NA DF; Pediapharm Naproxen Suspension; PMS-Naproxen; PMS-Naproxen EC; PRO-Naproxen EC; Teva-Naproxen; Teva-Naproxen EC; Teva-Naproxen Sodium; Teva-Naproxen Sodium DS; Teva-Naproxen SR

Generic Availability (US) May be product dependent

Pharmacologic Category Analgesic, Nonopioid; Nonsteroidal Anti-inflammatory Drug (NSAID), Oral

Dental Use Management of pain and swelling

Use

Acute gout/Ankylosing spondylitis/Bursitis/Juvenile arthritis/Juvenile rheumatoid arthritis/Osteoarthritis/Rheumatoid arthritis/Tendonitis (Rx products only): Relief of the signs and symptoms of acute gout, ankylosing spondylitis, bursitis, juvenile arthritis (excluding ER tablets), juvenile rheumatoid arthritis (oral suspension only), osteoarthritis, rheumatoid arthritis, and tendonitis. Delayed-release naproxen is not recommended for initial treatment of acute pain.

Pain/Primary dysmenorrhea (Rx and OTC products): Relief of mild to moderate pain and the treatment of primary dysmenorrhea. Delayed-release naproxen is not recommended for initial treatment of acute pain.

Local Anesthetic/Vasoconstrictor Precautions No information available to require special precautions

Effects on Dental Treatment Key adverse event(s) related to dental treatment: Stomatitis.

Naproxen and naproxen sodium have the potential to interfere with the antiplatelet effect of low-dose aspirin. One study of naproxen and low-dose aspirin has suggested that naproxen may interfere with aspirin's antiplatelet activity when they are coadministered (Steinhubl, 2005). However, naproxen 500 mg administered 2 hours before or after aspirin 100 mg did not interfere with aspirin's antiplatelet effect. The FDA stated that there is no data looking at doses of naproxen <500 mg. Naproxen over-the-counter strength is 220 mg tablets.

The FDA has warned that ibuprofen can interfere with the antiplatelet effect of low-dose aspirin (81 mg/day), potentially rendering aspirin less effective when used for cardioprotection and stroke protection. In situations where these drugs could be used concomitantly, the FDA has proved the following information: Patients who use immediate release aspirin (not enteric-coated aspirin) and take single doses of ibuprofen 400 mg, should dose the ibuprofen at least 30 minutes or longer after aspirin ingestion or more than 8 hours before aspirin ingestion to avoid attenuation of aspirin's effect. Similar recommendations may hold for concomitant may hold for concomitant naproxen and aspirin use. See Effects on Bleeding.

Effects on Bleeding Nonselective NSAIDs, such as naproxen, inhibit platelet aggregation and prolong bleeding time in some patients. Unlike aspirin, the NSAID effect on platelet function is quantitatively less, of shorter duration, and reversible. Normal platelet function should occur in ~5 elimination half-lives or in <10 hours after discontinuation of naproxen. Concomitant use of other NSAIDs should be avoided.

Adverse Reactions

1% to 10%:

Cardiovascular: Edema (3% to 9%), palpitations (<3%)

Central nervous system: Dizziness (≤9%), drowsiness (3% to 9%), headache (3% to 9%), vertigo (<3%)

Dermatologic: Pruritus (3% to 9%), skin rash (3% to 9%), ecchymoses (3% to 9%), diaphoresis (<3%)

Endocrine & metabolic: Fluid retention (3% to 9%), increased thirst (<3%)

Gastrointestinal: Abdominal pain (3% to 9%), constipation (3% to 9%), nausea (3% to 9%), heartburn (3% to 9%), diarrhea (<3%), dyspepsia (<3%), stomatitis (<3%), flatulence, gastrointestinal hemorrhage, gastrointestinal perforation, gastrointestinal ulcer, vomiting

Hematologic & oncologic: Hemolysis (3% to 9%), purpura (<3%), anemia, prolonged bleeding time

Hepatic: Increased liver enzymes

Ophthalmic: Visual disturbance (<3%)

Otic: Tinnitus (3% to 9%), auditory disturbance (<3%)

Renal: Renal function abnormality

Respiratory: Dyspnea (3% to 9%)

<1%, postmarketing, and/or case reports: Abnormal dreams, agranulocytosis, alopecia, anaphylactoid reaction, anaphylaxis, angioedema, aphthous stomatitis, aseptic meningitis, asthma, blurred vision, cardiac arrhythmia, cardiac failure, cognitive dysfunction, colitis, coma, confusion, conjunctivitis, cystitis, depression, dysuria, eosinophilia, eosinophilic pneumonitis, erythema multiforme, exfoliative dermatitis, fever, glossitis, granulocytopenia, hallucination, hematemesis, hepatic failure, hepatitis, hepatotoxicity (idiosyncratic) (Chalasani, 2014), hyperglycemia, hypertension, hypoglycemia, hypotension, infection, interstitial nephritis, melena, jaundice, leukopenia, lymphadenopathy, menstrual disease, malaise, myalgia, myasthenia, myocardial infarction, oliguria, pancreatitis, pancytopenia, paresthesia, pneumonia, polyuria, proteinuria, rectal hemorrhage, renal failure, renal papillary necrosis, respiratory depression, sepsis, skin photosensitivity, Stevens-Johnson syndrome, tachycardia, seizure, syncope, thrombocytopenia, toxic epidermal necrolysis, vasculitis

Dental Usual Dosage

Mild-to-moderate pain: Adults: Initial: 500 mg, then 250 mg every 6 to 8 hours; maximum: 1250 mg/day naproxen base

Pain/fever (OTC labeling): Children ≥12 years and Adults: 200 mg naproxen base every 8 to 12 hours; if needed, may take 400 mg naproxen base for the initial dose; maximum: 400 mg naproxen base in any 8- to 12-hour period or 600 mg naproxen base/24 hours

Dosing

Adult Note: Dosage expressed as naproxen base; 200 mg naproxen base is equivalent to 220 mg naproxen sodium. For relief of acute pain, naproxen sodium may be preferred due to more rapid absorption and onset; naproxen base may also be used however EC-Naprosyn is not recommended.

Ankylosing spondylitis, osteoarthritis, rheumatoid arthritis: Oral: 500 to 1,000 mg daily in 2 divided doses; in patients who require higher level of anti-inflammatory/analgesic activity and have tolerated lower doses, may increase to 1,500 mg/day for limited time period (<6 months)

Naproxen extended-release tablets: Initial: 750 to 1,000 mg once daily; in patients who require higher level of anti-inflammatory/analgesic activity and have tolerated lower doses, may temporarily increase to 1,500 mg once daily

Rectal suppository [Canadian product]: Insert one 500 mg suppository into the rectum once daily (**Note:** Suppository may be used to substitute for one oral dose in patients receiving 1,000 mg naproxen daily).

Gout, acute: Oral: Initial: 750 mg, followed by 250 mg every 8 hours until attack subsides

Naproxen extended-release tablets: Initial: 1,000 to 1,500 mg once daily followed by 1,000 mg once daily until attack subsides

Pain (mild to moderate), dysmenorrhea, acute tendonitis, bursitis: Oral: Initial: 500 mg, followed by 500 mg every 12 hours or 250 mg every 6 to 8 hours; maximum daily dose: Day 1: 1,250 mg; subsequent daily doses should not exceed 1,000 mg

Naproxen extended-release tablets: Oral: Initial: 1,000 mg once daily; may temporarily increase to 1,500 mg once daily if greater pain relief is needed. Dose should be subsequently reduced to a maximum of 1,000 mg daily.

Episodic migraine prevention (off-label use): Oral: 250 to 500 mg twice daily (EFNS [Evers 2009]). Continue treatment for 2 to 3 months to assess clinical benefit; consider tapering or discontinuing dose if headaches are well-controlled after 3 to 6 months (AAN [Silberstein 2000]).

Migraine, acute (off label use): Initial: 750 mg; an additional 250 to 500 mg may be given if needed (maximum: 1,250 mg in 24 hours) (Andersson, 1989; Nestvold, 1985).

OTC labeling: Pain, fever: 200 mg every 8 to 12 hours; if needed, may take 400 mg for the initial dose; maximum: 400 mg in any 8- to 12-hour period or 600 mg/24 hours

Geriatric Use with caution; consider using a reduced dose. Refer to adult dosing.

Pediatric Note: Dosage expressed as naproxen base; 200 mg naproxen base is equivalent to 220 mg naproxen sodium.

Juvenile idiopathic arthritis: Children >2 years and Adolescents: Oral: **Note:** Oral suspension is recommended: 10 mg/kg/day in 2 divided doses (up to 15 mg/kg/day has been tolerated). Do not exceed 15 mg/kg/day.

OTC labeling: Pain, fever: Children ≥12 years and Adolescents: Oral: Refer to adult dosing.

Ankylosing spondylitis, osteoarthritis, rheumatoid arthritis: Adolescents ≥16 years: Rectal suppository [Canadian product]: Refer to adult dosing.

Renal Impairment

CrCl ≥30 mL/minute: There are no specific dosage adjustments provided in the manufacturer's labeling; use with caution and consider using a reduced dose. Use is not recommended in patients with moderate renal impairment.

CrCl <30 mL/minute: Use is not recommended; avoid use in patients with advanced renal disease.

KDIGO 2012 guidelines provide the following recommendations for NSAIDs:

eGFR 30 to <60 mL/minute/1.73 m^2:Temporarily discontinue in patients with intercurrent disease that increases risk of acute kidney injury.

eGFR <30 mL/minute/1.73 m^2: Avoid use.

Hepatic Impairment There are no specific dosage adjustments provided in the manufacturer's labeling; use with caution and consider using a reduced dose.

Mechanism of Action Reversibly inhibits cyclooxygenase-1 and 2 (COX-1 and 2) enzymes, which results in decreased formation of prostaglandin precursors; has antipyretic, analgesic, and anti-inflammatory properties

Other proposed mechanisms not fully elucidated (and possibly contributing to the anti-inflammatory effect to varying degrees), include inhibiting chemotaxis, altering lymphocyte activity, inhibiting neutrophil aggregation/activation, and decreasing proinflammatory cytokine levels.

Contraindications

Hypersensitivity to naproxen (eg, anaphylactic reactions, serious skin reactions) or any component of the formulation; history of asthma, urticaria, or allergic-type reactions after taking aspirin or other NSAIDs; use in the setting of coronary artery bypass graft (CABG) surgery

Canadian labeling: Additional contraindications (not in US labeling): Active gastric, duodenal, or peptic ulcers; active GI bleeding; cerebrovascular bleeding or other bleeding disorders; active GI inflammatory disease; severe liver impairment or active liver disease; severe renal impairment (CrCl <30 mL/minute) or deteriorating renal disease; severe uncontrolled heart failure; known hyperkalemia; third trimester of pregnancy; breastfeeding; inflammatory lesions or recent bleeding of the rectum or anus (suppository only); use in patients <16 years of age (suppository only); use in patients <18 years of age (naproxen enteric coated and sustained release tablets and naproxen sodium tablets); use in children <2 years (naproxen tablets and suspension).

Warnings/Precautions [US Boxed Warning]: NSAIDs cause an increased risk of serious (and potentially fatal) adverse cardiovascular thrombotic events, including MI and stroke. Risk may occur early during treatment and may increase with duration of use. Relative risk appears to be similar in those with and without known cardiovascular disease or risk factors for cardiovascular disease; however, absolute incidence of serious cardiovascular thrombotic events (which may occur early during treatment) was higher in patients with known cardiovascular disease or risk factors and in those receiving higher doses. New-onset hypertension or exacerbation of hypertension may occur (NSAIDs may also impair response to ACE inhibitors, thiazide diuretics, or loop diuretics); may contribute to cardiovascular events; monitor blood pressure; use with caution in patients with hypertension. May cause sodium and fluid retention, use with caution in patients with edema. Avoid use in heart failure (ACCF/AHA [Yancy 2013]). Avoid use in patients with a recent MI unless benefits outweigh risk of cardiovascular thrombotic events. Use the lowest effective dose for the shortest duration of time, consistent with individual patient goals, to reduce risk of cardiovascular events; alternate therapies should be considered for patients at high risk. **[US Boxed Warning]: Use is contraindicated in the setting of coronary artery bypass graft (CABG) surgery.** Risk of MI and stroke may be increased with use following CABG surgery.

NSAIDs cause increased risk of serious gastrointestinal inflammation, ulceration, bleeding, and perforation (may be fatal); elderly patients and patients with history of peptic ulcer disease and/or GI bleeding are at greater risk of serious GI events. These events may occur at any time during therapy and without warning. Avoid use in patients with active GI bleeding. Use caution with a history of GI ulcers, concurrent therapy known to increase the risk of GI bleeding (eg, aspirin, anticoagulants and/or corticosteroids, selective serotonin reuptake inhibitors), advanced hepatic disease, coagulopathy, smoking, use of alcohol, or in elderly or debilitated patients. Use the lowest effective dose for the shortest duration of time, consistent with individual patient goals, to reduce risk of GI adverse events; alternate therapies should be considered for patients at high risk. When used concomitantly with aspirin, a substantial increase in the risk of gastrointestinal complications (eg, ulcer) occurs; concomitant gastroprotective therapy (eg, proton pump inhibitors) is recommended (Bhatt 2008).

May increase the risk of aseptic meningitis, especially in patients with systemic lupus erythematosus (SLE) and mixed connective tissue disorders. Platelet adhesion and aggregation may be decreased; may prolong bleeding time; patients with coagulation disorders or who are receiving anticoagulants should be monitored closely. Anemia may occur; patients on long-term NSAID therapy should be monitored for anemia. Rarely, NSAID use may cause severe blood dyscrasias (eg, agranulocytosis, aplastic anemia, thrombocytopenia).

NSAID use may compromise existing renal function; dose-dependent decreases in prostaglandin synthesis may result from NSAID use, reducing renal blood flow which may cause renal decompensation (usually reversible). Patients with impaired renal function, dehydration, hypovolemia, heart failure, hepatic impairment, those taking diuretics, and ACE inhibitors, and the elderly are at greater risk of renal toxicity. Rehydrate patient before starting therapy; monitor renal function closely. Long-term NSAID use may result in renal papillary necrosis and other renal injury. Avoid use in patients with advanced renal disease; discontinue use with persistent or worsening abnormal renal function tests.

NSAIDs may cause potentially fatal serious skin adverse events including exfoliative dermatitis, Stevens-Johnson Syndrome (SJS) and toxic epidermal necrolysis (TEN); may occur without warning; discontinue use at first sign of skin rash (or other hypersensitivity). Anaphylactoid reactions may occur, even without prior exposure; patients with "aspirin triad" (bronchial asthma, aspirin intolerance, rhinitis) may be at increased risk. Contraindicated in patients with aspirin-sensitive asthma; severe and potentially fatal bronchospasm may occur. Use caution in patients with other forms of asthma.

Transaminase elevations have been reported with use; closely monitor patients with any abnormal LFT. Rare (sometimes fatal) severe hepatic reactions (eg, fulminant hepatitis, hepatic necrosis, hepatic failure) have occurred with NSAID use; discontinue immediately if signs or symptoms of hepatic disease develop or if systemic manifestations occur. Use with caution in patients with hepatic impairment; patients with advanced hepatic disease are at an increased risk of GI bleeding with NSAIDs.

May cause drowsiness, dizziness, blurred vision and other neurologic effects which may impair physical or mental abilities; patients must be cautioned about performing tasks which require mental alertness (eg, operating machinery or driving). Discontinue use with blurred or diminished vision and perform ophthalmologic exam. Monitor vision with long-term therapy. Withhold for at least 4-6 half-lives prior to surgical or dental procedures.

Elderly patients are at greater risk for serious GI, cardiovascular, and/or renal adverse events; use with caution. Naproxen sodium contains about 1 mEq of sodium per 250 mg of naproxen; consider this in patients whose overall intake of sodium must be severely restricted. Potentially significant interactions may exist, requiring dose or frequency adjustment, additional monitoring, and/or selection of alternative therapy.

OTC labeling: Prior to self-medication, patients should contact healthcare provider if they have had recurring stomach pain or upset, ulcers, bleeding problems, asthma, high blood pressure, heart or kidney disease, other serious medical problems, are currently taking a diuretic, anticoagulant, other NSAIDs, or are ≥60 years of age. Recommended dosages and duration should not be exceeded, due to an increased risk of GI bleeding, MI, and stroke. Patients should stop use and consult a healthcare provider if symptoms get worse, newly appear, or continue; if an allergic reaction occurs; if feeling faint, vomit blood or have bloody/black stools; if having difficulty swallowing or heartburn, or if fever lasts for >3 days or pain >10 days. Consuming ≥3 alcoholic beverages/day or taking longer than recommended may increase the risk of GI bleeding. Not for self-medication (OTC use) in children <12 years of age.

Drug Interactions

Metabolism/Transport Effects Substrate of CYP1A2 (minor), CYP2C9 (minor); **Note:** Assignment of Major/Minor substrate status based on clinically relevant drug interaction potential

Avoid Concomitant Use

Avoid concomitant use of Naproxen with any of the following: Dexketoprofen; Floctafenine; Ketorolac (Nasal); Ketorolac (Systemic); Morniflumate; NSAID (COX-2 Inhibitor); Omacetaxine; Pelubiprofen; Phenylbutazone; Talniflumate; Tenoxicam; Urokinase; Zaltoprofen

Increased Effect/Toxicity

Naproxen may increase the levels/effects of: 5-ASA Derivatives; Agents with Antiplatelet Properties; Aliskiren; Aminoglycosides; Aminolevulinic Acid; Anticoagulants; Apixaban; Bisphosphonate Derivatives; Cephalothin; Collagenase (Systemic); CycloSPORINE (Systemic); Dabigatran Etexilate; Deferasirox; Deoxycholic Acid; Desmopressin; Digoxin; Drospirenone; Edoxaban; Eplerenone; Haloperidol; Ibritumomab; Lithium; Methotrexate; Nonsteroidal Anti-Inflammatory Agents; NSAID (COX-2 Inhibitor); Obinutuzumab; Omacetaxine; PEMEtrexed; Porfimer; Potassium-Sparing Diuretics; PRALAtrexate; Quinolone Antibiotics; Rivaroxaban; Salicylates; Tacrolimus (Systemic); Tenofovir Products; Thrombolytic Agents; Tolperisone; Tositumomab and Iodine I 131 Tositumomab; Urokinase; Vancomycin; Verteporfin; Vitamin K Antagonists

The levels/effects of Naproxen may be increased by: ACE Inhibitors; Alcohol (Ethyl); Angiotensin II Receptor Blockers; Antidepressants (Tricyclic, Tertiary Amine); Corticosteroids (Systemic); CycloSPORINE (Systemic); Dasatinib; Dexketoprofen; Diclofenac (Systemic); Felbinac; Floctafenine; Glucosamine; Herbs (Anticoagulant/Antiplatelet Properties); Ibrutinib; Ketorolac (Nasal); Ketorolac (Systemic); Limaprost; Loop Diuretics; Morniflumate; Multivitamins/Fluoride (with ADE); Multivitamins/Minerals (with ADEK, Folate, Iron); Multivitamins/Minerals (with AE, No Iron); Naftazone; Omega-3 Fatty Acids; Pelubiprofen; Pentosan Polysulfate Sodium; Pentoxifylline; Phenylbutazone; Probenecid; Prostacyclin Analogues; Selective Serotonin Reuptake Inhibitors; Serotonin/Norepinephrine Reuptake Inhibitors; Sodium Phosphates; Talniflumate; Tenoxicam; Thiazide and Thiazide-Like Diuretics; Tipranavir; Tolperisone; Vitamin E (Systemic); Zaltoprofen

Decreased Effect

Naproxen may decrease the levels/effects of: ACE Inhibitors; Aliskiren; Angiotensin II Receptor Blockers; Beta-Blockers; Eplerenone; HydrALAZINE; Loop Diuretics; Potassium-Sparing Diuretics; Prostaglandins (Ophthalmic); Salicylates; Selective Serotonin Reuptake Inhibitors; Thiazide and Thiazide-Like Diuretics

The levels/effects of Naproxen may be decreased by: Bile Acid Sequestrants; Salicylates

Food Interactions Naproxen absorption rate/levels may be decreased if taken with food. Management: Administer with food, milk, or antacids to decrease GI adverse effects.

Dietary Considerations Drug may cause GI upset, bleeding, ulceration, perforation; take with food or milk to minimize GI upset.

Pharmacodynamics/Kinetics

Onset of Action Analgesic: 30 to 60 minutes

Duration of Action Analgesic: <12 hours

Half-life Elimination

Children: Range: 8 to 17 hours

Children 8 to 14 years: 8 to 10 hours

Adults: Normal renal function: 12 to 17 hours; Moderate-to-severe renal impairment: ~15 to 21 hours (Anttila 1980)

Time to Peak Serum:

Tablets, naproxen: 2 to 4 hours

Tablets, naproxen sodium: 1 to 2 hours

Tablets, delayed-release (empty stomach): 4 to 6 hours; range: 2 to 12 hours

Tablets, delayed-release (with food): 12 hours; range: 4 to 24 hours

Suspension: 1 to 4 hours

Suppository [Canadian product]: 2 to 3 hours

Pregnancy Considerations Adverse events have been observed in some animal reproduction studies. Naproxen crosses the placenta and can be detected in fetal tissue and the serum of newborn infants following in utero exposure. NSAID exposure during the first trimester is not strongly associated with congenital malformations; however, cardiovascular anomalies and cleft palate have been observed following NSAID exposure in some studies. The use of a NSAID close to conception may be associated with an increased risk of miscarriage. Nonteratogenic effects have been observed following NSAID administration during the third trimester including: Myocardial degenerative changes, prenatal constriction of the ductus arteriosus, fetal tricuspid regurgitation, failure of the ductus arteriosus to close postnatally; renal dysfunction or failure, oligohydramnios; gastrointestinal bleeding or perforation, increased risk of necrotizing enterocolitis; intracranial bleeding (including intraventricular hemorrhage), platelet dysfunction with resultant bleeding; pulmonary hypertension. Because they may cause premature closure of the ductus arteriosus, use of NSAIDs late in pregnancy should be avoided (use after 31 or 32 weeks gestation is not recommended by some clinicians). The chronic use of NSAIDs in women of reproductive age may be associated with infertility that is reversible upon discontinuation of the medication. A registry is available for pregnant women exposed to autoimmune medications including naproxen. For additional information contact the Organization of Teratology Information Specialists, OTIS Autoimmune Diseases Study, at (877) 311-8972.

Breastfeeding Considerations Naproxen is present in breast milk.

The relative infant dose (RID) of naproxen is 3.3% when calculated using the highest breast milk concentration located and compared to a weight adjusted maternal dose of 750 mg/day. In general, breastfeeding is considered acceptable when the RID is <10%; when an RID is >25% breastfeeding should generally be avoided (Anderson 2016; Ito 2000). Using the highest milk concentration (2.37 mcg/mL), the estimated daily infant dose via breast milk is 0.36 mg/kg/day. This milk concentration was obtained following maternal administration of oral naproxen 375 mg twice daily. Naproxen was detected in the urine of the breastfeeding infant (Jamali 1982; Jamali 1983).

In a study which included 20 mother-infant pairs, there were two cases of drowsiness and one case of vomiting in the breastfed infants (Ito 1993).

In general, NSAIDs may be used in postpartum women who wish to breastfeed; however, agents other than naproxen may be preferred (Montgomery 2012) and use should be avoided in women nursing infants with platelet dysfunction or thrombocytopenia (Bloor 2013; Sammaritano 2014). When needed, naproxen may be considered for short-term use (<1 week) (Montgomery 2012). Other agents are preferred for treatment of migraine in a woman who is breastfeeding because the risk profile of naproxen is less certain (Amundsen 2015). Due to the potential effects of prostaglandin-inhibiting drugs on neonates, the manufacturer recommends that breastfeeding be avoided.

Dosage Forms Considerations

EnovaRX-Naproxen and Equipto-Naproxen creams are compounded from a kit. Refer to manufacturer's package insert for compounding instructions.

Naproxen Comfort Pac kit contains naproxen tablets and Duraflex Comfort Gel

Flanax Pain Relief kit contains naproxen tablets and Flanax Liniment

Dosage Forms

Capsule, Oral:
- Aleve [OTC]: 220 mg

Cream, External:
- EnovaRX-Naproxen: 10% (60 g, 120 g)
- Equipto-Naproxen: 10% (120 g)

Kit, Combination:
- Flanax Pain Relief: 500 mg
- Naproxen Comfort Pac: 500 mg

Suspension, Oral:
- Naprosyn: 125 mg/5 mL (473 mL, 480 mL)
- Generic: 125 mg/5 mL (473 mL, 500 mL)

Tablet, Oral:
- Aleve [OTC]: 220 mg
- All Day Pain Relief [OTC]: 220 mg
- All Day Relief [OTC]: 220 mg
- Anaprox DS: 550 mg
- Flanax Pain Relief [OTC]: 220 mg
- GoodSense Naproxen Sodium [OTC]: 220 mg
- Mediproxen [OTC]: 220 mg
- Naprosyn: 500 mg
- Generic: 220 mg, 250 mg, 275 mg, 375 mg, 500 mg, 550 mg

Tablet Delayed Release, Oral:
- EC-Naprosyn: 375 mg, 500 mg
- Naproxen DR: 375 mg, 500 mg

Tablet Extended Release 24 Hour, Oral:
- Naprelan: 375 mg, 500 mg, 750 mg
- Generic: 375 mg, 500 mg

Naproxen and Esomeprazole

(na PROKS en & es oh ME pray zol)

Related Information

Esomeprazole *on page 604*

Naproxen *on page 1160*

Rheumatoid Arthritis, Osteoarthritis, and Osteoporosis *on page 1792*

Brand Names: US Vimovo

Brand Names: Canada Vimovo

Pharmacologic Category Analgesic, Nonopioid; Nonsteroidal Anti-inflammatory Drug (NSAID), Oral; Proton Pump Inhibitor; Substituted Benzimidazole

Use

Osteoarthritis, rheumatoid arthritis, ankylosing spondylitis: Reduction of the risk of NSAID-associated gastric ulcers in patients at risk of developing gastric ulcers who require an NSAID for the relief of signs and symptoms of osteoarthritis, rheumatoid arthritis, and ankylosing spondylitis

Limitations of use: Not recommended for the initial treatment of pain; controlled studies do not extend beyond 6 months.

Local Anesthetic/Vasoconstrictor Precautions No information available to require special precautions

Effects on Dental Treatment Key adverse event(s) related to dental treatment: Esomeprazole: Xerostomia (normal salivary flow resumes upon discontinuation)

Effects on Bleeding Nonselective NSAIDs, such as naproxen and esomeprazole, inhibit platelet aggregation and prolong bleeding time in some patients. Unlike aspirin, the NSAID effect on platelet function is quantitatively less, of shorter duration, and reversible. Normal platelet function should occur in ~5 elimination half-lives or in <10 hours after discontinuation of naproxen and esomeprazole. Concomitant use of other NSAIDs should be avoided.

Adverse Reactions Also see individual agents.

>10%: Gastrointestinal: Gastritis (17%)

1% to 10%:
- Cardiovascular: Peripheral edema (3%)
- Central nervous system: Dizziness (3%), headache (3%)
- Gastrointestinal: Diarrhea (6%), constipation (4%), flatulence (4%), upper abdominal pain (4%), dysgeusia (2%)
- Genitourinary: Urinary tract infection (2%)
- Respiratory: Upper respiratory tract infection (5%)

<1%, postmarketing and/or case reports: Abdominal distention, abdominal pain, abnormal gait, acute interstitial nephritis, bruise, falling, gastroesophageal reflux disease, hematochezia, joint swelling, muscle spasm, renal tubular necrosis

General Dosage Range Oral: *Adults:* One tablet (naproxen 375 or 500 mg/esomeprazole 20 mg) twice daily

Mechanism of Action

Naproxen: Reversibly inhibits cyclooxygenase-1 and 2 (COX-1 and 2) enzymes, which result in decreased formation of prostaglandin precursors; has antipyretic, analgesic, and anti-inflammatory properties

Esomeprazole: Proton pump inhibitor which decreases acid secretion in gastric parietal cells

Pregnancy Considerations Animal reproduction studies have not been conducted with this combination. Because they may cause premature closure of the ductus arteriosus, use of NSAIDs late in pregnancy should be avoided. Refer to individual agents.

Naratriptan (NAR a trip tan)

Related Information

Temporomandibular Dysfunction (TMD), Chronic Pain, and Fibromyalgia *on page 1868*

Brand Names: US Amerge

Brand Names: Canada Amerge; Sandoz-Naratriptan; Teva-Naratriptan

Pharmacologic Category Antimigraine Agent; Serotonin 5-$HT_{1B,\ 1D}$ Receptor Agonist

Use Migraines: Acute treatment of migraine attacks with or without aura in adults.

Local Anesthetic/Vasoconstrictor Precautions No information available to require special precautions

Effects on Dental Treatment No significant effects or complications reported

Effects on Bleeding No information available to require special precautions

Adverse Reactions

1% to 10%:

Central nervous system: Pain (4%), fatigue (2%), dizziness (1% to 2%), drowsiness (1% to 2%), paresthesia (1% to 2%), hot and cold flashes (1%), sensation of pressure (1%; chest/neck/throat/jaw), vertigo (1%)

Gastrointestinal: Nausea (4% to 5%), vomiting (1%), xerostomia (1%)

Neuromuscular & skeletal: Neck pain (2%)

Ophthalmic: Photophobia (1%)

Respiratory: Constriction of the pharynx (2%), ENT infection (1%)

<1%, postmarketing, and/or case reports (limited to important or life-threatening): Abnormal bilirubin levels, abnormal hepatic function tests, anaphylactoid reaction, anaphylaxis, anemia, angina pectoris, angioedema, bradycardia, cerebral infarction, colonic ischemia, coronary artery vasospasm, depression, dyspnea, ECG changes (atrial fibrillation, atrial flutter, premature ventricular contractions, PR prolongation, or QT_c prolongation), glycosuria, hallucination, heart murmur, hypercholesterolemia, hyperglycemia, hyperlipidemia, hypersensitivity reaction (some cases severe, including circulatory collapse), hypertension, hypotension, hypothyroidism, ischemic heart disease, ketonuria, myocardial infarction, palpitations, panic, seizure, serotonin syndrome, skin rash, subarachnoid hemorrhage, subconjunctival hemorrhage, syncope, thrombocytopenia, transient ischemic attacks, ventricular fibrillation, ventricular tachycardia

General Dosage Range Dosage adjustment recommended in patients with hepatic or renal impairment

Oral: *Adults:* 1 to 2.5 mg, may repeat after 4 hours (maximum: 5 mg/day)

Mechanism of Action Selective agonist for serotonin (5-HT_{1B} and 5-HT_{1D} receptors) in cranial arteries; causes vasoconstriction and reduces sterile inflammation associated with antidromic neuronal transmission correlating with relief of migraine

Pharmacodynamics/Kinetics

Onset of Action ~1-2 hours (Bomhof, 1999; Tfelt-Hansen, 2000)

Half-life Elimination 6 hours; Increased in renal impairment (moderate impairment; mean: 11 hours; range: 7 to 20 hours); Increased in hepatic impairment (moderate impairment: 8 to 16 hours)

Time to Peak 2-3 hours

Pregnancy Considerations Pregnancy outcome information for naratriptan is available from a pregnancy registry sponsored by GlaxoSmithKline. As of September 2012, data were available for 57 infants/fetuses exposed to naratriptan, and seven exposed to both naratriptan and sumatriptan. Following naratriptan exposure, there was one infant born with a birth defect; this infant was also exposed to sumatriptan during the first trimester of pregnancy. The pregnancy registry was closed to enrollment in January 2012, and additional information may be obtained from the manufacturer. Additional information related to the use of naratriptan in pregnancy is limited (Källén 2011, Nezvalová-Henriksen 2010, Nezvalová-Henriksen 2012). Until additional information is available, other agents are preferred for the initial treatment of migraine in pregnancy (Da Silva 2012, MacGregor 2012, Williams 2012).

Natalizumab (na ta LIZ u mab)

Brand Names: US Tysabri

Brand Names: Canada Tysabri

Pharmacologic Category Gastrointestinal Agent, Miscellaneous; Monoclonal Antibody, Selective Adhesion-Molecule Inhibitor

Use

Crohn disease: For inducing and maintaining clinical response and remission in adult patients with moderately to severely active Crohn disease with evidence of inflammation who have had an inadequate response to, or are unable to tolerate, conventional Crohn disease therapies and inhibitors of tumor necrosis factor-alpha (TNF-alpha).

Multiple sclerosis: As monotherapy for the treatment of patients with relapsing forms of multiple sclerosis (MS). Natalizumab increases the risk of PML. When initiating and continuing treatment with natalizumab, consider whether the expected benefit of natalizumab is sufficient to offset this risk.

Canada labeling: Treatment of relapsing forms of multiple sclerosis in patients who have had an inadequate response to, or are unable to tolerate, other therapies for multiple sclerosis.

Local Anesthetic/Vasoconstrictor Precautions No information available to require special precautions

Effects on Dental Treatment No significant effects or complications reported

Effects on Bleeding No information available to require special precautions

Adverse Reactions

>10%:

Central nervous system: Headache (32% to 38%), fatigue (10% to 27%), depression (≤19%)

Dermatologic: Skin rash (6% to 12%)

Gastrointestinal: Nausea (≤17%), gastroenteritis (≤11%), abdominal distress (≤11%)

Genitourinary: Urinary tract infection (3% to 21%)

Infection: Influenza (≤12%)

Neuromuscular & skeletal: Arthralgia (8% to 19%), limb pain (16%), back pain (≤12%)

Respiratory: Upper respiratory tract infection (≤22%), lower respiratory tract infection (≤17%), flu-like symptoms (≤11%)

Miscellaneous: Infusion related reaction (11% to 24%)

1% to 10%:

Cardiovascular: Peripheral edema (5% to 6%), chest discomfort (≤5%), syncope (≤2%)

Central nervous system: Vertigo (≤6%), dysesthesia (3%), rigors (≤3%), drowsiness (≤2%)

Dermatologic: Dermatitis (≤7%), pruritus (≤4%), urticaria (≤2%), thermal injury (1%), night sweats (≤1%), xeroderma (≤1%)

Endocrine & metabolic: Menstrual disease (≤5%), amenorrhea (≤2%), ovarian cyst (≤2%), weight changes (≤2%)

Gastrointestinal: Diarrhea (10%), tooth infection (≤9%), dyspepsia (≤5%), abdominal pain (≤4%), constipation (≤4%), toothache (≤4%), flatulence (≤3%), aphthous stomatitis (≤2%), cholelithiasis (≤1%), gingival disease (infection: 1%)

Genitourinary: Vaginal infection (≤10%), vaginitis (≤10%), urinary frequency (≤9%), dysmenorrhea (2% to 6%), urinary incontinence (≤4%)

Hematologic & oncologic: Hematoma (1%)

Hepatic: Increased serum transaminases (≤5%)

Hypersensitivity: Hypersensitivity reaction (acute: 2% to 4%; serious acute: ≤1%; delayed: ≤5%)

Immunologic: Antibody development (9% to 10%)

Infection: Herpes virus infection (≤8%), viral infection (≤7%), serious infection (2% to 3%)

Local: Bleeding at injection site (≤3%)

Neuromuscular & skeletal: Muscle cramps (≤5%), tremor (1% to 3%), joint swelling (≤2%)

Respiratory: Sinusitis (≤8%), cough (≤7%), tonsillitis (≤7%), pharyngolaryngeal pain (≤6%), epistaxis (2%)

Miscellaneous: Limb injury (3%), laceration (2%)

<1%, postmarketing, and/or case reports: Acne vulgaris, agitation, anaphylactoid reaction, anaphylaxis, anemia, angina pectoris, appendicitis, aspergillosis (bronchopulmonary), decreased hemoglobin (mild, transient), dizziness, dyspnea, erythema, exacerbation of Crohn's disease, fever, flushing, gastroenteritis (cryptosporidial), hepatic failure, hepatitis (cytomegalovirus), hepatotoxicity, herpes simplex encephalitis, hypotension, immune reconstitution syndrome, increased serum bilirubin, infection (*Burkholderia cepacia*), joint stiffness, lethargy, leukocytosis, meningitis (herpes), nasopharyngitis, opportunistic infection (including bronchopulmonary infections, meningitis, and progressive multifocal leukoencephalopathy [PML]), muscle spasm, myasthenia, nail disease (onychorrhexis), paresis, pericarditis (case report), petechiae, pharyngitis, pneumonia (includes pneumonia caused by *Pneumocystis jirovecii* and varicella), psychomotor disturbance (hyperactivity), pulmonary infection (*Mycobacterium avium intracellulare*), suicidal ideation, tachycardia, thrombocytopenia, thrombophlebitis, vasodilatation

General Dosage Range IV: *Adults:* 300 mg every 4 weeks

Mechanism of Action Natalizumab is a monoclonal antibody against the alpha-4 subunit of integrin molecules. These molecules are important to adhesion and migration of cells from the vasculature into inflamed tissue. Natalizumab blocks integrin association with vascular receptors, limiting adhesion and transmigration of leukocytes. Efficacy in specific disorders may be related to reduction in specific inflammatory cell populations in target tissues. In multiple sclerosis, efficacy may be related to blockade of T-lymphocyte migration into the central nervous system; treatment results in a decreased frequency of relapse. In Crohn disease, natalizumab decreases inflammation by binding to alpha-4 integrin, blocking adhesion and migration of leukocytes in the gut.

Pharmacodynamics/Kinetics

Half-life Elimination Crohn disease: 3 to 17 days; Multiple sclerosis: 7 to 15 days

Pregnancy Risk Factor C

Pregnancy Considerations Adverse events have been observed in animal reproduction studies. Natalizumab crosses the placenta (Haghikia 2015). Hematological alterations such as anemia and thrombocytopenia have been noted following maternal use during pregnancy. The risk of spontaneous abortion may also be increased (Amato 2015; Ebrahimi 2015; Haghikia 2015).

Pregnant women exposed to natalizumab should be enrolled in the Tysabri Pregnancy Exposure Registry 1-800-456-2255.

Prescribing and Access Restrictions

US: Tysabri is deemed to have an approved REMS program. As a requirement of the REMS program, access to this medication is restricted. Patients must be enrolled in the Tysabri Outreach Unified Commitment to Health (TOUCH™) Prescribing Program (800-456-2255) to receive natalizumab (MS-TOUCH™ for multiple sclerosis or CD-TOUCH™ for Crohn disease). Healthcare providers must also register with the program in order to prescribe, dispense or administer natalizumab. Treatment must be reauthorized every 6 months. Natalizumab is available only through infusion centers registered with the TOUCH™ program; infusion center information is available at 1-800-456-2255.

Canada: Patients receiving natalizumab therapy for multiple sclerosis are to be enrolled in the Biogen Idec ONE Program™ (855-676 6300) This program is associated with the prescribing, administration, and monitoring of Canadian patients receiving natalizumab. Clinicians are educated on the appropriate use of natalizumab and are expected to discuss the benefits/risks of therapy. Clinicians should evaluate patients every 6 months during treatment.

Natamycin (na ta MYE sin)

Brand Names: US Natacyn

Pharmacologic Category Antifungal Agent, Ophthalmic

Use Ocular fungal infections: Treatment of fungal blepharitis, conjunctivitis, and keratitis caused by susceptible organisms, including *Fusarium solani* keratitis.

Local Anesthetic/Vasoconstrictor Precautions No information available to require special precautions

Effects on Dental Treatment No significant effects or complications reported

Effects on Bleeding No information available to require special precautions

Adverse Reactions Postmarketing and/or case reports: Allergic reaction, chest pain, corneal opacity, dyspnea, eye discomfort, edema, hyperemia, irritation and/or pain, foreign body sensation, parasthesia, tearing, vision changes

General Dosage Range Ophthalmic: *Adults:* Initial: Instill 1 drop in conjunctival sac every 1 to 2 hours for 3 to 4 days; Maintenance: 1 drop 4 to 8 times daily

Mechanism of Action Binds to sterol in fungal cell membrane and changes the cell wall permeability allowing for a reduction of cellular contents

Pregnancy Risk Factor C

Pregnancy Considerations Animal reproduction studies have not been conducted.

Nateglinide (na te GLYE nide)

Related Information

Endocrine Disorders and Pregnancy *on page 1781*

Brand Names: US Starlix

Brand Names: Canada Starlix

Pharmacologic Category Antidiabetic Agent, Meglitinide Analog

Use

Type 2 diabetes mellitus: Treatment of adults with type 2 diabetes mellitus as an adjunct to diet and exercise to improve glycemic control

Limitations of use: Should not be used in patients with type 1 diabetes mellitus or diabetic ketoacidosis.

Local Anesthetic/Vasoconstrictor Precautions No information available to require special precautions

Effects on Dental Treatment No significant effects or complications reported

Effects on Bleeding May increase overall bleeding times

Adverse Reactions As reported with nateglinide monotherapy:

>10%: Respiratory: Upper respiratory infection (11%)

1% to 10%:

Central nervous system: Dizziness (4%)

Endocrine & metabolic: Hypoglycemia (2%), increased uric acid, weight gain

Neuromuscular & skeletal: Arthropathy (3%)

Respiratory: Flu-like symptoms (4%)

Miscellaneous: Accidental injury (3%)

Postmarketing and/or case reports: Cholestatic hepatitis, hypersensitivity reaction (including pruritus, rash, urticaria), increased liver enzymes, jaundice

General Dosage Range Oral: *Adults:* 60-120 mg 3 times daily

Mechanism of Action Nonsulfonylurea hypoglycemic agent which blocks ATP-dependent potassium channels, depolarizing the membrane and facilitating calcium entry through calcium channels. Increased intracellular calcium stimulates insulin release from the pancreatic beta cells. Nateglinide-induced insulin release is glucose-dependent.

Pharmacodynamics/Kinetics

Onset of Action Insulin secretion: ~20 minutes; Peak effect: 1 hour

Duration of Action 4 hours

Half-life Elimination 1.5 hours

Time to Peak ≤1 hour

Pregnancy Risk Factor C

Pregnancy Considerations Adverse events have been observed in animal reproduction studies. Information describing the effects of nateglinide on pregnancy outcomes is limited (Twaites 2007).

In women with diabetes, maternal hyperglycemia can be associated with congenital malformations as well as adverse effects in the fetus, neonate, and the mother (ACOG 2005; ADA 2016c; Kitzmiller 2008; Metzger 2007). To prevent adverse outcomes, prior to conception and throughout pregnancy maternal blood glucose and HbA_{1c} should be kept as close to target goals as possible but without causing significant hypoglycemia (ACOG 2013; ADA 2016c; Blumer 2013; Kitzmiller 2008). Other agents are currently recommended to treat diabetes in pregnant women (ACOG 2013; Blumer 2013).

Nebivolol (ne BIV oh lole)

Related Information

Cardiovascular Diseases *on page 1752*

Brand Names: US Bystolic

Brand Names: Canada Bystolic

Pharmacologic Category Antihypertensive; Beta-Blocker, Beta-1 Selective

Use

Hypertension: Treatment of hypertension, alone or in combination with other agents

Guideline recommendations:

Hypertension: The 2014 guideline for the management of high blood pressure in adults (Eighth Joint National Committee [JNC 8]) recommends initiation of pharmacologic treatment to lower blood pressure for the following patients (JNC8 [James 2013]):

- Patients ≥60 years of age, with systolic blood pressure (SBP) ≥150 mm Hg or diastolic blood pressure (DBP) ≥90 mm Hg. Goal of therapy is SBP <150 mm Hg and DBP <90 mm Hg.
- Patients <60 years of age, with SBP ≥140 mm Hg or DBP ≥90 mm Hg. Goal of therapy is SBP <140 mm Hg and DBP <90 mm Hg.
- Patients ≥18 years of age with diabetes, with SBP ≥140 mm Hg or DBP ≥90 mm Hg. Goal of therapy is SBP <140 mm Hg and DBP <90 mm Hg.
- Patients ≥18 years of age with chronic kidney disease (CKD), with SBP ≥140 mm Hg or DBP ≥90 mm Hg. Goal of therapy is SBP <140 mm Hg and DBP <90 mm Hg.

Chronic kidney disease (CKD) and hypertension: Regardless of race or diabetes status, the use of an ACE inhibitor (ACEI) or angiotensin receptor blocker (ARB) as initial therapy is recommended to improve kidney outcomes. In the general nonblack population (without CKD) including those with diabetes, initial antihypertensive treatment should consist of a thiazide-type diuretic, calcium channel blocker, ACEI, or ARB. In the general black population (without CKD) including those with diabetes, initial antihypertensive treatment should consist of a thiazide-type diuretic or a calcium channel blocker **instead of** an ACEI or ARB.

Coronary artery disease (CAD) and hypertension: The American Heart Association, American College of Cardiology, and American Society of Hypertension (AHA/ACC/ASH) 2015 scientific statement for the treatment of hypertension in patients with CAD recommends the use of a beta blocker as part of a regimen in patients with hypertension and chronic stable angina with a history of prior MI. A BP target of

<140/90 mm Hg is reasonable for the secondary prevention of cardiovascular events. A lower target BP (<130/80 mm Hg) may be appropriate in some individuals with CAD, previous MI, stroke or transient ischemic attack, or CAD risk equivalents (AHA/ACC/ASH [Rosendorff 2015]).

Local Anesthetic/Vasoconstrictor Precautions No information available to require special precautions

Effects on Dental Treatment Nebivolol is a cardioselective beta-blocker. Local anesthetic with vasoconstrictor can be safely used in patients medicated with nebivolol. Nonselective beta-blockers (ie, propranolol, nadolol) enhance the pressor response to epinephrine, resulting in hypertension and bradycardia; this has not been reported for nebivolol. Many nonsteroidal anti-inflammatory drugs, such as ibuprofen and indomethacin, can reduce the hypotensive effect of beta-blockers after 3 or more weeks of therapy with the NSAID. Short-term NSAID use (ie, 3 days) requires no special precautions in patients taking beta-blockers.

Effects on Bleeding No information available to require special precautions

Adverse Reactions

1% to 10%:

Cardiovascular: Peripheral edema (1%), bradycardia (≤1%), chest pain (≤1%)

Central nervous system: Headache (6% to 9%), fatigue (dose-related; 2% to 5%), dizziness (2% to 4%), insomnia (1%), paresthesia

Dermatologic: Skin rash (≤1%)

Endocrine & metabolic: Decreased HDL cholesterol, hypercholesterolemia, increased serum triglycerides, increased uric acid

Gastrointestinal: Diarrhea (dose-related; 2% to 3%), nausea (1% to 3%), abdominal pain

Hematologic & oncologic: Decreased platelet count

Neuromuscular & skeletal: Weakness

Renal: Increased blood urea nitrogen

Respiratory: Dyspnea (≤1%)

<1%, postmarketing, and/or case reports: Acute pulmonary edema, acute renal failure, angioedema, atrioventricular block (second and third degree), bronchospasm, claudication, dermatological disease, drowsiness, erectile dysfunction, hepatic insufficiency, hypersensitivity angiitis, hypersensitivity reaction, increased serum ALT, increased serum AST, increased serum bilirubin, myocardial infarction, peripheral ischemia, pruritus, psoriasis, Raynaud's phenomenon, syncope, thrombocytopenia, urticaria, vertigo, vomiting

General Dosage Range Dosage adjustment recommended in patients with hepatic or renal impairment

Oral: *Adults:* Initial: 5 mg once daily; Maintenance: 5 to 40 mg once daily

Mechanism of Action Highly-selective inhibitor of $beta_1$-adrenergic receptors; at doses ≤10 mg nebivolol preferentially blocks $beta_1$-receptors. Nebivolol, unlike other beta-blockers, also produces an endothelium-derived nitric oxide-dependent vasodilation resulting in a reduction of systemic vascular resistance.

Pharmacodynamics/Kinetics

Half-life Elimination Terminal: 12 hours (extensive metabolizers) or 19 hours (poor metabolizers); up to 32 hours has been reported in poor metabolizers (Mangrella, 1998).

Time to Peak 1.5 to 4 hours

Pregnancy Risk Factor C

Pregnancy Considerations Adverse events have been observed in some animal reproduction studies. Adverse events, such as fetal/neonatal bradycardia, hypoglycemia, reduced birth weight, have been observed following in utero exposure to beta-blockers as a class. Adequate facilities for monitoring infants at birth is generally recommended.

Untreated chronic maternal hypertension and preeclampsia are also associated with adverse events in the fetus, infant, and mother (ACOG 2015; Magee 2014). Although beta-blockers may be used when treatment of hypertension in pregnancy is indicated, agents other than nebivolol are preferred (ACOG 2013; Magee 2014; Regitz-Zagrosek 2011).

Nebivolol and Valsartan

(ne BIV oh lole & val SAR tan)

Brand Names: US Byvalson

Pharmacologic Category Angiotensin II Receptor Blocker; Antihypertensive; Antihypertensive, Combination; Beta-Blocker, Beta-1 Selective

Use Hypertension: Management of hypertension (monotherapy or in combination with other antihypertensive agents).

Local Anesthetic/Vasoconstrictor Precautions No information available to require special precautions

Effects on Dental Treatment Key adverse events(s) related to dental treatment: Nebivolol component is a cardioselective beta-blocker. Local anesthetic with vasoconstrictor can be safely used in patients medicated with nebivolol. Nonselective beta-blockers (ie, propranolol, nadolol) enhance the pressor response to epinephrine, resulting in hypertension and bradycardia; this has not been reported for nebivolol. Many nonsteroidal anti-inflammatory drugs, such as ibuprofen and indomethacin, can reduce the hypotensive effect of beta-blockers after 3 or more weeks of therapy with the NSAID. Short-term NSAID use (ie, 3 days) requires no special precautions in patients taking beta-blockers.

Effects on Bleeding No information available to require special precautions

Adverse Reactions See individual agents for reactions.

Mechanism of Action

Nebivolol: Highly-selective inhibitor of $beta_1$-adrenergic receptors; at doses ≤10 mg nebivolol preferentially blocks $beta_1$-receptors. Nebivolol, unlike other beta-blockers, also produces an endothelium-derived nitric oxide-dependent vasodilation resulting in a reduction of systemic vascular resistance.

Valsartan: Produces direct antagonism of the angiotensin II (AT2) receptors, unlike the ACE inhibitors. It displaces angiotensin II from the AT1 receptor and produces its blood pressure-lowering effects by antagonizing AT1-induced vasoconstriction, aldosterone release, catecholamine release, arginine vasopressin release, water intake, and hypertrophic responses. This action results in more efficient blockade of the cardiovascular effects of angiotensin II and fewer side effects than the ACE inhibitors.

Pregnancy Considerations [US Boxed Warning]: Drugs that act on the renin-angiotensin system can cause injury and death to the developing fetus. Discontinue as soon as possible once pregnancy is detected. Refer to individual monographs.

Necitumumab (ne si TOOM oo mab)

Brand Names: US Portrazza

Pharmacologic Category Antineoplastic Agent, Epidermal Growth Factor Receptor (EGFR) Inhibitor; Antineoplastic Agent, Monoclonal Antibody

Use

Non-small cell lung cancer (squamous), metastatic: First-line treatment of metastatic squamous non-small cell lung cancer (NSCLC) in combination with gemcitabine and cisplatin

Limitations of use: Not indicated for treatment of nonsquamous non-small cell lung cancer.

Local Anesthetic/Vasoconstrictor Precautions No information available to require special precautions

Effects on Dental Treatment Key adverse event(s) related to dental treatment: Stomatitis (11%) has been reported

Effects on Bleeding No information available to require special precautions

Adverse Reactions Adverse reaction percentages reported as part of a combination regimen with gemcitabine and cisplatin.

>10%:

Central nervous system: Headache (11%)

Dermatologic: Skin toxicity (79%; grades 3/4: 8%), skin rash (44%; grades 3/4: 4%), acneiform eruption (15%; grades 3/4: 1%)

Endocrine & metabolic: Hypomagnesemia (43% to 83%; grades 3/4: 20%), hypocalcemia (45%; grades 3/4: 6%; with albumin corrected: 36%; grades 3/4: 4%), hypophosphatemia (31%; grades 3/4: 8%), hypokalemia (28%; grades 3/4: 5%), weight loss (13%)

Gastrointestinal: Vomiting (29%), diarrhea (16%), stomatitis (11%)

1% to 10%:

Cardiovascular: Venous thromboembolism (9%; grades 3/4: 5%), arterial thromboembolism (5%; grades 3/4: 4%), pulmonary embolism (5%), cardiorespiratory arrest (3%), deep vein thrombosis (2%), cerebrovascular accident (≤2%), ischemia (≤2%), myocardial infarction (1%)

Dermatologic: Acne vulgaris (9%), paronychia (7%), pruritus (7%), xeroderma (7%), skin fissure (5%)

Immunologic: Antibody development (4%; neutralizing: 1%)

Ophthalmic: Conjunctivitis (7%)

Respiratory: Hemoptysis (10%)

Miscellaneous: Infusion related reaction (2%; grade 3: <1%)

General Dosage Range Dosage adjustment recommend for patients who develop toxicities.

IV: *Adults:* 800 mg on days 1 and 8 of each 3-week treatment cycle

Mechanism of Action Necitumumab is a recombinant human IgG1 EGFR monoclonal antibody which binds (with a high affinity) to the ligand binding site of the EGFR receptor to prevent receptor activation and downstream signaling (Thatcher 2015).

Pharmacodynamics/Kinetics

Half-life Elimination ~14 days

Pregnancy Considerations Necitumumab is expected to cross the placenta. Based on animal data and the mechanism of action, necitumumab is expected to cause fetal harm if administered during pregnancy. Women of reproductive potential should use effective contraception during therapy and for 3 months after the last dose.

Nedocromil (ne doe KROE mil)

Brand Names: US Alocril

Brand Names: Canada Alocril®

Pharmacologic Category Mast Cell Stabilizer

Use Treatment of itching associated with allergic conjunctivitis

Local Anesthetic/Vasoconstrictor Precautions No information available to require special precautions

Effects on Dental Treatment Key adverse event(s) related to dental treatment: Unpleasant taste.

Effects on Bleeding No information available to require special precautions

Adverse Reactions

>10%:

Central nervous system: Headache (40%)

Gastrointestinal: Unpleasant taste

Ophthalmic: Burning sensation of eyes, eye irritation, stinging of eyes

Respiratory: Nasal congestion

1% to 10%:

Ophthalmic: Conjunctivitis, eye redness, photophobia

Respiratory: Asthma, rhinitis

General Dosage Range

Ophthalmic: *Children ≥3 years and Adults:* 1-2 drops in each eye twice daily

Mechanism of Action Inhibits the activation of and mediator release from a variety of inflammatory cell types associated with hypersensitivity reactions including eosinophils, neutrophils, macrophages, mast cells, monocytes, and platelets; it inhibits the release of histamine, leukotrienes, and slow-reacting substance of anaphylaxis.

Pregnancy Risk Factor B

Pregnancy Considerations There are no well-controlled studies in pregnant women. Animal studies show no evidence of teratogenicity or harm to fetus. Additionally, nedocromil has minimal systemic absorption.

Nefazodone (nef AY zoe done)

Related Information

Dentin Hypersensitivity, Acid Erosion, High Caries Index, Management of Alveolar Osteitis, and Xerostomia *on page 1857*

Vasoconstrictor Interactions With Antidepressants *on page 1913*

Pharmacologic Category Antidepressant, Serotonin Reuptake Inhibitor/Antagonist

Use Depression: Treatment of depression

Local Anesthetic/Vasoconstrictor Precautions Nefazodone inhibits reuptake of both serotonin and norepinephrine and also blocks some serotonin receptors. No precautions with vasoconstrictors appear to be necessary.

Effects on Dental Treatment Key adverse event(s) related to dental treatment: Significant xerostomia (normal salivary flow resumes upon discontinuation) and taste perversion.

Effects on Bleeding No information available to require special precautions

Adverse Reactions

>10%:

Central nervous system: Agitation, dizziness, drowsiness, headache, insomnia

Gastrointestinal: Constipation, nausea, xerostomia

Neuromuscular & skeletal: Weakness

1% to 10%:

Cardiovascular: Bradycardia, hypotension, orthostatic hypotension, peripheral edema, vasodilation

Central nervous system: Abnormal dreams, ataxia, chills, confusion, hypertonia, lack of concentration, memory impairment, paresthesia, psychomotor retardation

Dermatologic: Pruritus, skin rash

Endocrine & metabolic: Decreased libido, increased thirst

Gastrointestinal: Diarrhea, dysgeusia, dyspepsia, gastroenteritis, increased appetite, vomiting

Genitourinary: Impotence, mastalgia, urinary frequency, urinary retention

Hematologic & oncologic: Decreased hematocrit

Infection: Infection

Neuromuscular & skeletal: Arthralgia, neck stiffness, tremor

Ophthalmic: Blurred vision (9%), visual disturbance (7%), eye pain, visual field defect

Otic: Tinnitus

Respiratory: Bronchitis, cough, dyspnea, flu-like symptoms, pharyngitis

Miscellaneous: Fever

<1%, postmarketing, and/or case reports: Abnormal gait, abnormal hepatic function tests, abnormality in thinking, accommodation disturbance, acne vulgaris, ageusia, alopecia, amenorrhea, anemia, angina pectoris, angioedema, angle-closure glaucoma, anorgasmia, apathy, arthritis, asthma, atrioventricular block, attempted suicide, breast hypertrophy, bruise, bursitis, cardiac failure, cellulitis, cerebrovascular accident, colitis, conjunctivitis, convulsions, cystitis, deafness, dehydration, depersonalization, derealization, diplopia, disturbance in attention, dry eye syndrome, dysarthria, eczema, ejaculatory disorder, enlargement of abdomen, epistaxis, eructation, esophagitis, euphoria, facial edema, galactorrhea, gastritis, gingivitis, gout, gynecomastia, halitosis, hallucination, hangover effect, heavy eyelids, hematuria, hemorrhage, hepatic failure, hepatic necrosis, hepatitis, hernia, hiccups, hostility, hyperacusis, hypercholesterolemia, hyperesthesia, hyperkinesia, hypermenorrhea, hypersensitivity reaction, hypertension, hyperventilation, hypoglycemia, hyponatremia, hypotonia, increased lactic dehydrogenase, increased libido, increased serum ALT, increased serum AST, increased serum prolactin, keratoconjunctivitis, laryngitis, leukopenia, lymphadenopathy, maculopapular rash, malaise, metrorrhagia, muscle rigidity, mydriasis, myoclonus, nephrolithiasis, neuralgia, neuroleptic malignant syndrome (Stevens, 2008), nocturia, nocturnal amblyopia, oliguria, oral candidiasis, oral mucosa ulcer, otalgia, pallor, paranoia, pelvic pain, peptic ulcer, periodontal abscess, photophobia, pneumonia, polyuria, priapism, rectal hemorrhage, rhabdomyolysis (with lovastatin/simvastatin), serotonin syndrome, sialorrhea, skin photosensitivity, Stevens-Johnson syndrome, stomatitis, suicidal ideation, syncope, tachycardia, tendinous contracture, tendonitis, tenosynovitis, thrombocytopenia, tonic-clonic seizures, twitching, ulcerative colitis, urinary incontinence, urinary urgency, urticaria, uterine fibroid enlargement, uterine hemorrhage, vaginal hemorrhage, varicose veins, ventricular premature contractions, vertigo, vesiculobullous dermatitis, voice disorder, weight loss, xeroderma, yawning

General Dosage Range Oral:

Adults: Initial: 200 mg daily in 2 divided doses; Maintenance: Up to 600 mg daily in 2 divided doses

Elderly: Initial: 50 mg twice daily

Mechanism of Action Inhibits neuronal reuptake of serotonin and norepinephrine; also blocks 5-HT_2 and $alpha_1$ receptors; has no significant affinity for $alpha_2$, beta-adrenergic, 5-HT_{1A}, cholinergic, dopaminergic, or benzodiazepine receptors

Pharmacodynamics/Kinetics

Half-life Elimination Note: Active metabolites persist longer in all populations.

Children: 4.1 hours

Adolescents: 3.9 hours

Adults: Parent drug: 2 to 4 hours; active metabolites: 1.4 to 8 hours

Time to Peak Note: Prolonged in presence of food

Children and Adolescents: 0.5 to 1 hour

Adults: Serum: 1 hour

Pregnancy Risk Factor C

Pregnancy Considerations Adverse effects were observed in some animal reproduction studies. When nefazodone is taken during pregnancy, an increased risk of major malformations has not been observed in the limited number of pregnancies studied (Einarson 2003; Einarson 2009). The long-term effects of in utero exposure to nefazodone on infant development and behavior are not known.

The ACOG recommends that therapy with antidepressants during pregnancy be individualized; treatment of depression during pregnancy should incorporate the clinical expertise of the mental health clinician, obstetrician, primary health care provider, and pediatrician. According to the American Psychiatric Association (APA), the risks of medication treatment should be weighed against other treatment options and untreated depression. Consideration should be given to using agents with safety data in pregnancy. For women who discontinue antidepressant medications during pregnancy and who may be at high risk for postpartum depression, the medications can be restarted following delivery. Treatment algorithms have been developed by the ACOG and the APA for the management of depression in women prior to conception and during pregnancy (ACOG 2008; APA 2010; Yonkers 2009).

Pregnant women exposed to antidepressants during pregnancy are encouraged to enroll in the National Pregnancy Registry for Antidepressants (NPRAD). Women 18 to 45 years of age or their health care providers may contact the registry by calling 844-405-6185. Enrollment should be done as early in pregnancy as possible.

Nelarabine (nel AY re been)

Brand Names: US Arranon

Brand Names: Canada Atriance

Pharmacologic Category Antineoplastic Agent, Antimetabolite; Antineoplastic Agent, Antimetabolite (Purine Analog)

Use T-cell acute lymphoblastic leukemia/lymphoma: Treatment of relapsed or refractory T-cell acute lymphoblastic leukemia/lymphoma following at least 2 chemotherapy regimens.

Local Anesthetic/Vasoconstrictor Precautions No information available to require special precautions

Effects on Dental Treatment Key adverse event(s) related to dental treatment: Taste perversion and stomatitis.

Effects on Bleeding Chemotherapy may result in significant myelosuppression. Thrombocytopenia has been reported in 86% to 88% (grade 4: 22% to 32%).

Nosebleeds have occurred in 8% of patients. In patients who are under active treatment with these agents, medical consult is suggested.

Adverse Reactions Pediatric adverse reactions fell within a range similar to adults except where noted.

>10%:

Cardiovascular: Peripheral edema (15%), edema (11%)

Central nervous system: Fatigue (50%), drowsiness (7% to 23%), dizziness (21%), peripheral neuropathy (12% to 21%; grades 2/3: 11% to 14%; may be similar to Guillain-Barré syndrome), headache (15% to 17%), hypoesthesia (6% to 17%), paresthesia (4% to 15%), pain (1% to 11%; includes neuropathic pain)

Endocrine & metabolic: Hypokalemia (11%)

Gastrointestinal: Nausea (41%), diarrhea (22%), vomiting (10% to 22%), constipation (21%)

Hematologic & oncologic: Anemia (95% to 99%; grade 4: 10% to 14%), neutropenia (81% to 94%; grade 4: children 62%, adults 49%), thrombocytopenia (86% to 88%; grade 4: 22% to 32%), leukopenia (38%; grade 4: 7%), febrile neutropenia (12%; grade 4: 1%), petechia (12%)

Hepatic: Increased serum transaminases (12%)

Neuromuscular & skeletal: Weakness (6% to 17%), myalgia (13%)

Respiratory: Cough (25%), dyspnea (7% to 20%)

Miscellaneous: Fever (23%)

1% to 10%:

Cardiovascular: Hypotension (8%), sinus tachycardia (8%), chest pain (5%)

Central nervous system: Ataxia (1% to 9%), confusion (8%), myasthenia (8%), rigors (8%), insomnia (7%), abnormal gait (6%), depression (6%), impaired consciousness (6%), noncardiac chest pain (5%), motor dysfunction (4%), amnesia (3%), equilibrium disturbance (2%), sensory disturbance (1% to 2%), disturbance in attention (1%), dysarthria (1%), hydrocephalus (1%), hypertonia (1%), hyporeflexia (1%), lethargy (1%), mental status changes (1%), nerve palsy (1%), paralysis (1%; including nerve paralysis), sciatica (1%), speech disturbance (1%), aphasia, brain disease, cerebral hemorrhage, coma, hemiparesis, intracranial hemorrhage, leukoencephalopathy, loss of consciousness, seizure

Endocrine & metabolic: Decreased serum albumin (10%), hypocalcemia (8%), dehydration (7%), hyperglycemia (6%), hypoglycemia (6%), hypomagnesemia (6%)

Gastrointestinal: Abdominal pain (9%), anorexia (9%), stomatitis (8%), abdominal distention (6%), dysgeusia (3%)

Hepatic: Increased serum bilirubin (10%), increased serum AST (6%)

Infection: Infection (5% to 9%)

Neuromuscular & skeletal: Arthralgia (9%), back pain (8%), limb pain (7%), tremor (4% to 5%)

Ophthalmic: Blurred vision (4%), nystagmus (1%)

Renal: Increased serum creatinine (6%)

Respiratory: Pleural effusion (10%), epistaxis (8%), pneumonia (8%), sinusitis (7%), wheezing (5%), sinus headache (1%)

<1%, postmarketing, and/or case reports: Demyelinating disease (craniospinal demyelination), increased creatine phosphokinase, opportunistic infection, pneumothorax, progressive multifocal leukoencephalopathy, rhabdomyolysis, tumor lysis syndrome

General Dosage Range IV:

Children: 650 mg/m^2/dose on days 1 through 5; repeat every 21 days

Adults: 1,500 mg/m^2/dose on days 1, 3, and 5; repeat every 21 days

Mechanism of Action Nelarabine, a prodrug of ara-G, is demethylated by adenosine deaminase to ara-G and then converted to ara-GTP. Ara-GTP is incorporated into the DNA of the leukemic blasts, leading to inhibition of DNA synthesis and inducing apoptosis. Ara-GTP appears to accumulate at higher levels in T-cells, which correlates to clinical response.

Pharmacodynamics/Kinetics

Half-life Elimination Pediatric patients: Nelarabine: 13 minutes, Ara-G: 2 hours; Adults: Nelarabine: 18 minutes, Ara-G: 3 hours

Time to Peak Adults: 3 to 25 hours (of day 1)

Pregnancy Risk Factor D

Pregnancy Considerations Adverse effects were observed in animal reproduction studies and nelarabine may cause fetal harm if administered during pregnancy. Women of childbearing potential should be advised to use effective contraception and avoid becoming pregnant during therapy.

The European Society for Medical Oncology has published guidelines for diagnosis, treatment, and follow-up of cancer during pregnancy. The guidelines recommend referral to a facility with expertise in cancer during pregnancy and encourage a multidisciplinary team (obstetrician, neonatologist, oncology team). In general, if chemotherapy is indicated, it should be avoided during the first trimester, there should be a 3-week time period between the last chemotherapy dose and anticipated delivery, and chemotherapy should not be administered beyond week 33 of gestation. Specific use of nelarabine is not discussed (Peccatori 2013).

Nelfinavir (nel FIN a veer)

Related Information

HIV Infection and AIDS *on page 1785*

Viral Infections *on page 1849*

Brand Names: US Viracept

Brand Names: Canada Viracept

Generic Availability (US) No

Pharmacologic Category Antiretroviral, Protease Inhibitor (Anti-HIV)

Use HIV-1 infection: In combination with other antiretroviral therapy in the treatment of HIV infection

Local Anesthetic/Vasoconstrictor Precautions No information available to require special precautions

Effects on Dental Treatment Key adverse event(s) related to dental treatment: Mouth ulcers.

Effects on Bleeding Increased bleeding has been noted with protease inhibitors in patients with hemophilia A or B. No information available to require routine special precautions relative to hemostasis in other patients.

Adverse Reactions

>10%: Gastrointestinal: Diarrhea (adults: 14% to 20%; children: 39% to 47%)

1% to 10%:

Central nervous system: Anxiety (<2%), depression (<2%), dizziness (<2%), drowsiness (<2%), emotional lability (<2%), headache (<2%), insomnia (<2%), malaise (<2%), migraine (<2%), myasthenia (<2%), pain (<2%), paresthesia (<2%), seizure (<2%), sleep disorder (<2%), suicidal ideation (<2%)

Dermatologic: Skin rash (adults: 1% to 3%), dermatitis (<2%), diaphoresis (<2%), folliculitis (<2%), fungal dermatitis (<2%), maculopapular rash (<2%), pruritus (<2%), urticaria (<2%)

Endocrine & metabolic: Dehydration (<2%), hyperglycemia (<2%), hyperlipidemia (<2%), hyperuricemia (<2%), hypoglycemia (<2%), increased amylase (<2%), increased gamma-glutamyl transferase (<2%), increased lactate dehydrogenase (<2%), lipodystrophy (<2%), redistribution of body fat (<2%)

Gastrointestinal: Nausea (adults: 3% to 7%), flatulence (adults: 1% to 5%), abdominal pain (<2%), anorexia (<2%), dyspepsia (<2%), epigastric pain (<2%), gastrointestinal hemorrhage (<2%), oral mucosa ulcer (<2%), pancreatitis (<2%), vomiting (<2%)

Genitourinary: Sexual disorder (<2%), urine abnormality (<2%)

Hematologic & oncologic: Lymphocytopenia (adults: 1% to 6%), decreased neutrophils (adults: 1% to 5%), anemia (<2%), leukopenia (<2%), thrombocytopenia (<2%)

Hepatic: Abnormal hepatic function tests (<2%), hepatitis (<2%), increased serum alkaline phosphatase (<2%), increased serum transaminases (<2%)

Hypersensitivity: Hypersensitivity reaction (<2%; including bronchospasm, edema, and skin rash)

Neuromuscular & skeletal: Arthralgia (<2%), arthritis (<2%), back pain (<2%), hyperkinesia (<2%), increased creatine phosphokinase (<2%), lipoatrophy (<2%), lipotrophy (<2%), muscle cramps (<2%), myalgia (<2%), myopathy (<2%), weakness (<2%)

Ophthalmic: Acute iritis (<2%), eye disease (<2%)

Renal: Nephrolithiasis (<2%)

Respiratory: Dyspnea (<2%), pharyngitis (<2%), rhinitis (<2%), sinusitis (<2%)

Miscellaneous: Fever (<2%)

<1%, postmarketing, and/or case reports: Hyperbilirubinemia, immune reconstitution syndrome, jaundice, metabolic acidosis, prolonged Q-T interval on ECG, torsades de pointes

Dosing

Adult & Geriatric HIV-1 infection, treatment: Oral: 750 mg 3 times daily or 1250 mg twice daily with meals in combination with other antiretroviral therapies. **Note:** The HHS Perinatal HIV Guidelines do not recommend the 3-times-daily dosing in pregnant women (HHS [perinatal] 2018).

Pediatric

HIV-1 infection, treatment: Oral:

Children 2 to <13 years: **Note:** Pediatric guidelines recommend twice-daily dosing (HHS [pediatric] 2016).

Weight-directed dosing: 45 to 55 mg/kg twice daily (maximum dose: 1,250 mg/dose) **or** 25 to 35 mg/kg (maximum dose: 750 mg/dose) 3 times daily; daily doses >2,500 mg/day have not been studied in children.

Fixed dosing:

10 to <13 kg: 500 mg (2 tablets) twice daily **or** 250 mg (1 tablet) 3 times daily

13 to <19 kg: 750 mg (3 tablets) twice daily **or** 500 mg (2 tablets) 3 times daily

19 to <21 kg: 1000 mg (4 tablets) twice daily **or** 500 mg (2 tablets) 3 times daily

≥21 kg: 1000 to 1250 mg (4 to 5 tablets) twice daily **or** 750 mg (3 tablets) 3 times daily

Adolescents: Refer to adult dosing. **Note:** Some adolescent patients require doses higher than adults to achieve similar nelfinavir AUCs; consider the use of serum drug concentrations to guide optimal dosing (HHS [pediatric] 2016).

Renal Impairment There are no dosage adjustments provided in the manufacturer's labeling (has not been studied). However, since <2% excreted in urine a dosage reduction would not be expected. Guidelines suggest that no dosage adjustment is necessary (HHS [adult] 2015).

Hepatic Impairment

Mild impairment (Child-Pugh class A): No dosage adjustment necessary.

Moderate to severe impairment (Child-Pugh class B or C): Use not recommended.

Mechanism of Action

Binds to the site of HIV-1 protease activity and inhibits cleavage of viral Gag-Pol polyprotein precursors into individual functional proteins required for infectious HIV. This results in the formation of immature, noninfectious viral particles.

Contraindications

Coadministration with drugs that are highly dependent on CYP3A for clearance and for which elevated or reduced plasma concentrations are associated with serious and/or life-threatening events or lead to reduced efficacy of nelfinavir (eg, alfuzosin, amiodarone, cisapride, ergot derivatives [eg, dihydroergotamine, ergonovine, ergotamine, methylergonovine], lovastatin, lurasidone, oral midazolam, pimozide, quinidine, rifampin, sildenafil [when used for the treatment of pulmonary hypertension], simvastatin, St John's wort, triazolam).

Canadian labeling: Additional contraindications (not in US labeling): Clinically significant hypersensitivity to nelfinavir or any component of the formulation; coadministration with midazolam (regardless of dosage form)

Warnings/Precautions

Potentially significant drug-drug interactions may exist, requiring dose or frequency adjustment, additional monitoring, and/or selection of alternative therapy.

Use caution with hepatic impairment; use not recommended with moderate-to-severe impairment. Diarrhea occurs frequently with use, particularly in children; a secretory diarrhea mediated via a calcium-dependent process may also occur; calcium carbonate administered at the same time as nelfinavir has been used to treat this adverse effect in adults without affecting plasma concentrations of nelfinavir or its major metabolite. Warn patients that redistribution of body fat can occur. New-onset diabetes mellitus, exacerbation of diabetes, and hyperglycemia have been reported in HIV-infected patients receiving protease inhibitors. Use with caution in patients with hemophilia A or B; increased bleeding during protease inhibitor therapy has been reported. Patients may develop immune reconstitution syndrome resulting in the occurrence of an inflammatory response to an indolent or residual opportunistic infection during initial HIV treatment or activation of autoimmune disorders (eg, Graves disease, polymyositis, Guillain-Barré syndrome) later in therapy; further evaluation and treatment may be required.

Drug Interactions

Metabolism/Transport Effects Substrate of CYP2C19 (major), CYP2C9 (minor), CYP2D6 (minor), CYP3A4 (major), P-glycoprotein; **Note:** Assignment of Major/Minor substrate status based on clinically relevant drug interaction potential; **Inhibits** BCRP, CYP1A2 (weak), CYP2C9 (weak), CYP3A4 (strong); **Induces** CYP2B6 (weak)

Avoid Concomitant Use

Avoid concomitant use of Nelfinavir with any of the following: Ado-Trastuzumab Emtansine; Alfuzosin; Amiodarone; Aprepitant; Astemizole; Asunaprevir; Avanafil; Axitinib; Barnidipine; Blonanserin; Bosutinib; Bromocriptine; Budesonide (Systemic); Ceritinib; Cisapride; Cobimetinib; Conivaptan; Crizotinib; Dabrafenib; Dapoxetine; Domperidone; Dronedarone; Eletriptan; Eplerenone; Ergot Derivatives; Everolimus; Flibanserin; Halofantrine; Ibrutinib; Irinotecan Products; Isavuconazonium Sulfate; Ivabradine; Lapatinib; Lercanidipine; Lomitapide; Lovastatin; Lurasidone; Macitentan; Midazolam; Naloxegol; Nilotinib; NiMODipine; Nisoldipine; Olaparib; Palbociclib; Pimozide; Proton Pump Inhibitors; QuiNIDine; Radotinib; Ranolazine; Red Yeast Rice; Regorafenib; RifAMPin; Rupatadine; Salmeterol; Silodosin; Simeprevir; Simvastatin; Sonidegib; St John's Wort; Suvorexant; Tacrolimus (Systemic); Tamsulosin; Terfenadine; Ticagrelor; Tipranavir; Tolvaptan; Toremifene; Trabectedin; Triazolam; Udenafil; Ulipristal; Vemurafenib; VinCRIStine (Liposomal); Vinflunine; Vorapaxar

Increased Effect/Toxicity

Nelfinavir may increase the levels/effects of: Ado-Trastuzumab Emtansine; Afatinib; Alfuzosin; Alitretinoin (Systemic); Almotriptan; Alosetron; ALPRAZolam; Amiodarone; AmLODIPine; Apixaban; Aprepitant; ARIPiprazole; ARIPiprazole Lauroxil; Astemizole; Asunaprevir; AtorvaSTATin; Avanafil; Axitinib; Azithromycin (Systemic); Barnidipine; Bedaquiline; Benperidol; Blonanserin; Bortezomib; Bosentan; Bosutinib; Brentuximab Vedotin; Brexpiprazole; Brinzolamide; Bromocriptine; Budesonide (Nasal); Budesonide (Oral Inhalation); Budesonide (Systemic); Budesonide (Topical); Buprenorphine; Cabazitaxel; Cabozantinib; Calcifediol; Calcium Channel Blockers (Nondihydropyridine); Cannabidiol; Cannabis; CarBAMazepine; Cariprazine; Ceritinib; Cilostazol; Cisapride; Clarithromycin; CloZAPine; Cobimetinib; Colchicine; Conivaptan; Corticosteroids (Orally Inhaled); Corticosteroids (Systemic); Crizotinib; Cyclophosphamide; CycloSPORINE (Systemic); CYP3A4 Substrates; Dabrafenib; Daclatasvir; Dapoxetine; Dasatinib; Deflazacort; Delamanid; DOCEtaxel; Domperidone; DOXOrubicin (Conventional); Dronabinol; Dronedarone; Dutasteride; Eletriptan; Eliglustat; Enfuvirtide; Eplerenone; Ergot Derivatives; Erlotinib; Estazolam; Eszopiclone; Etizolam; Everolimus; FentaNYL; Fesoterodine; Flibanserin; Fluticasone (Nasal); Fluticasone (Oral Inhalation); Gefitinib; GuanFACINE; Halofantrine; Highest Risk QTc-Prolonging Agents; HYDROcodone; HydrOXYzine; Ibrutinib; Idelalisib; Iloperidone; Imatinib; Imidafenacin; Irinotecan Products; Isavuconazonium Sulfate; Ivabradine; Ivacaftor; Ixabepilone; Lacosamide; Lapatinib; Lercanidipine; Levobupivacaine; Levomilnacipran; Lomitapide; Lovastatin; Lurasidone; Macitentan; Manidipine; Maraviroc; Meperidine; MethylPREDNISolone; Midazolam; MiFEPRIStone; Mirodenafil; Moderate Risk QTc-Prolonging Agents; Naldemedine; Naloxegol; Nefazodone; Nilotinib; NiMODipine; Nisoldipine; Olaparib; Ospemifene; Oxybutynin; OxyCODONE; Palbociclib; Panobinostat; Parecoxib; Paricalcitol; PAZOPanib; Pimavanserin; Pimecrolimus; Pimozide; PONATinib; Pranlukast; Praziquantel; PrednisoLONE (Systemic); PredniSONE; Propafenone; Protease Inhibitors; QUEtiapine; QuiNIDine; Radotinib; Ramelteon; Ranolazine; Reboxetine; Red Yeast Rice; Regorafenib; Repaglinide; Retapamulin; Ribociclib; Rifabutin; Rilpivirine; Riociguat; RomiDEPsin; Rosuvastatin; Rupatadine; Ruxolitinib; Salmeterol; SAXagliptin; Sildenafil; Silodosin; Simeprevir; Simvastatin; Sirolimus; Sonidegib; SORAfenib; Suvorexant; Tacrolimus (Systemic); Tacrolimus (Topical); Tadalafil; Tamsulosin; Tasimelteon; Telithromycin; Temsirolimus; Terfenadine; Tetrahydrocannabinol; Ticagrelor; TiZANidine; Tofacitinib; Tolterodine; Tolvaptan; Toremifene; Trabectedin; TraMADol; TraZODone; Triazolam; Tricyclic Antidepressants; Udenafil; Ulipristal; Vardenafil; Vemurafenib; Venetoclax; Vilazodone; VinCRIStine (Liposomal); Vindesine; Vinflunine; Vinorelbine; Vorapaxar; Warfarin; Zolpidem; Zopiclone; Zuclopenthixol

The levels/effects of Nelfinavir may be increased by: Clarithromycin; CycloSPORINE (Systemic); Delavirdine; Enfuvirtide; Etravirine; Lopinavir; MiFEPRIStone; P-glycoprotein/ABCB1 Inhibitors; Simeprevir; Voriconazole

Decreased Effect

Nelfinavir may decrease the levels/effects of: Abacavir; Antidiabetic Agents; Boceprevir; Clarithromycin; Contraceptives (Estrogens); Contraceptives (Progestins); Delavirdine; Doxercalciferol; Estriol (Systemic); Estriol (Topical); Etravirine; Fosphenytoin; Ifosfamide; Lopinavir; Meperidine; Methadone; Phenytoin; Prasugrel; Pravastatin; Theophylline Derivatives; Ticagrelor; Valproate Products; Warfarin; Zidovudine

The levels/effects of Nelfinavir may be decreased by: Boceprevir; Bosentan; CarBAMazepine; CYP3A4 Inducers (Moderate); CYP3A4 Inducers (Strong); Deferasirox; Enzalutamide; Fosphenytoin; Garlic; H2-Antagonists; Mitotane; Nevirapine; Orlistat; Phenytoin; Proton Pump Inhibitors; Rifabutin; RifAMPin; Siltuximab; St John's Wort; Tipranavir; Tocilizumab

Food Interactions Nelfinavir taken with food increases plasma concentration time curve (AUC) by two- to threefold. Management: Administer with a meal. Do not administer with acidic food or juice (orange juice, apple juice, or applesauce) since the combination may have a bitter taste.

Dietary Considerations Should be taken as scheduled with a meal.

Pharmacodynamics/Kinetics

Half-life Elimination 3.5 to 5 hours

Time to Peak Serum: 2 to 4 hours

Pregnancy Risk Factor B

Pregnancy Considerations Adverse events were not observed in animal reproduction studies. Nelfinavir has a minimal to low level of transfer across the human placenta. No increased risk of overall birth defects has been observed following first trimester exposure according to data collected by the antiretroviral pregnancy registry. A small increased risk of preterm birth has been associated with maternal use of protease inhibitor-based combination antiretroviral therapy during pregnancy; however, the benefits of use generally outweigh this risk and protease inhibitors (PIs) should not be withheld if otherwise recommended. Information related to stillbirth, low birth weight, and small for gestational age infants is limited. Long-term follow-up is recommended for all infants exposed to antiretroviral medications; children who develop significant organ system abnormalities of unknown etiology (particularly of the CNS or heart) should be evaluated for potential mitochondrial dysfunction. Hyperglycemia, new onset of diabetes mellitus, or diabetic ketoacidosis have been reported with PIs; it is not clear if pregnancy increases this risk.

Combination antiretroviral therapy (cART) therapy is recommended for all HIV-infected pregnant women to keep the viral load below the limit of detection and reduce the risk of perinatal transmission. When HIV is diagnosed during pregnancy in a woman who has never received antiretroviral therapy, cART should begin as soon as possible after diagnosis. The Health and Humans Services (HHS) Perinatal HIV Guidelines do not recommended nelfinavir for initial therapy in antiretroviral-naive pregnant women due to lower viral suppression when compared to other regimens. A standard dose of 1,250 mg twice daily has been shown to provide adequate plasma concentrations although lower and variable levels may occur late in pregnancy; the standard 750 mg 3 times daily dosing is not recommended in pregnant women. In general, women who become pregnant on a stable cART regimen may continue that regimen if viral suppression is effective, appropriate drug exposure can be achieved, contraindications for use in pregnancy are not present, and the regimen is well tolerated. Monitoring during pregnancy is more frequent than in non-pregnant adults; cART should be continued postpartum.

For HIV-infected couples planning a pregnancy, maximum viral suppression with cART is recommended prior to conception for the HIV-infected partner(s) and expert consultation is recommended; modification of therapy (if needed) and optimization of the woman's health should be done prior to conception. HIV-infected women not planning a pregnancy may use any available type of contraception, considering possible drug interactions and contraindications of the specific method. In addition, consistent use of condoms is also recommended (even during pregnancy) to prevent transmission of HIV or other sexually transmitted diseases.

Health care providers are encouraged to enroll pregnant women exposed to antiretroviral medications as early in pregnancy as possible in the Antiretroviral Pregnancy Registry (1-800-258-4263 or www.-APRegistry.com). Health care providers caring for HIV-infected women and their infants may contact the National Perinatal HIV Hotline (888-448-8765) for clinical consultation (HHS [perinatal] 2016).

Breastfeeding Considerations Minimal amounts of nelfinavir are excreted into breast milk and plasma concentrations in the nursing infant were undetectable. Maternal or infant antiretroviral therapy does not completely eliminate the risk of postnatal HIV transmission. In addition, multiclass-resistant virus has been detected in breastfeeding infants despite maternal therapy. Therefore, in the United States, where formula is accessible, affordable, safe, and sustainable, and the risk of infant mortality due to diarrhea and respiratory infections is low, complete avoidance of breastfeeding by HIV-infected women is recommended to decrease potential transmission of HIV (HHS [perinatal] 2016).

Dosage Forms

Tablet, Oral:

Viracept: 250 mg, 625 mg

Neomycin (nee oh MYE sin)

Pharmacologic Category Ammonium Detoxicant; Antibiotic, Aminoglycoside

Use

Hepatic coma (portal-systemic encephalopathy): Adjunctive therapy in hepatic coma.

Surgical (perioperative) prophylaxis: Adjunctive therapy as part of a regimen for the suppression of the normal bacterial bowel flora (eg, preoperative bowel preparation), given concomitantly with enteric-coated erythromycin base.

Local Anesthetic/Vasoconstrictor Precautions No information available to require special precautions

Effects on Dental Treatment No significant effects or complications reported

Effects on Bleeding No information available to require special precautions

Adverse Reactions

>10%:

Central nervous system: Sore mouth

Gastrointestinal: Anorectal pain, diarrhea, mouth irritation, nausea, rectal irritation, vomiting

<1%, postmarketing, and/or case reports: Auditory ototoxicity, dyspnea, eosinophilia, nephrotoxicity, neurotoxicity, vestibular ototoxicity

General Dosage Range Oral: *Adults:* Encephalopathy/hepatic insufficiency: 4 to 12 g daily in divided doses every 4 to 6 hours; Preoperative GI preparation: 1 g for 3 doses

Mechanism of Action Interferes with bacterial protein synthesis by binding to 30S ribosomal subunits

Pharmacodynamics/Kinetics

Time to Peak

1 to 4 hours

Pregnancy Risk Factor D

Pregnancy Considerations Animal reproduction studies have not been conducted. Aminoglycosides cross the placenta. Aminoglycosides may cause fetal harm if administered to a pregnant woman. There are several reports of total irreversible bilateral congenital deafness in children whose mothers received another aminoglycoside (streptomycin) during pregnancy. Although serious side effects to the fetus/infant have not been reported following maternal use of all aminoglycosides, a potential for harm exists. Large oral doses may cause malabsorption of some nutrients in the mother.

Neomycin and Polymyxin B

(nee oh MYE sin & pol i MIKS in bee)

Related Information

Neomycin *on page 1183*

Polymyxin B *on page 1353*

Brand Names: US Neosporin G.U. Irrigant

Brand Names: Canada Neosporin Irrigating Solution

Pharmacologic Category Antibiotic, Topical; Genitourinary Irrigant

Use Urinary bladder irrigant: Continuous irrigant or rinse for short-term use (up to 10 days) in the urinary bladder of abacteriuric patients to help prevent bacteriuria and gram-negative rod septicemia associated with the use of indwelling catheters.

Local Anesthetic/Vasoconstrictor Precautions No information available to require special precautions

Effects on Dental Treatment No significant effects or complications reported

Effects on Bleeding No information available to require special precautions

Adverse Reactions Frequency not defined.

Central nervous system: Localized burning

Dermatologic: Contact dermatitis, erythema, skin rash, urticaria

Genitourinary: Bladder mucosa irritation, nephrotoxicity

Neuromuscular & skeletal: Neuromuscular blockade

Otic: Ototoxicity

General Dosage Range Urinary bladder irrigation: *Children, Adolescents, and Adults:* Add 1 mL irrigant to 1,000 mL isotonic saline solution per day as a continuous irrigation for up to 10 days.

Mechanism of Action

Neomycin: Interferes with bacterial protein synthesis by binding to 30S ribosomal subunits.

Polymyxin B: Binds to phospholipids, alters permeability, and damages the bacterial cytoplasmic membrane permitting leakage of intracellular constituents.

Pregnancy Considerations Animal reproduction studies have not been conducted with this combination; however, there are reports of total irreversible bilateral congenital deafness in children whose mothers received streptomycin during pregnancy. See individual agents.

Nepafenac (ne pa FEN ak)

Brand Names: US Ilevro; Nevanac

Brand Names: Canada Ilevro; Nevanac

Pharmacologic Category Nonsteroidal Anti-inflammatory Drug (NSAID), Ophthalmic

Use Treatment of pain and inflammation associated with cataract surgery

Local Anesthetic/Vasoconstrictor Precautions No information available to require special precautions

Effects on Dental Treatment The dentist should be aware of the potential of abnormal coagulation. Caution should also be exercised in the use of NSAIDs in patients already on anticoagulant therapy with drugs such as warfarin (Coumadin®). See Effects on Bleeding.

Effects on Bleeding Nonselective NSAIDs, such as nepafenac, inhibit platelet aggregation and prolong bleeding time in some patients. Unlike aspirin, the NSAID effect on platelet function is quantitatively less, of shorter duration, and reversible. Normal platelet function should occur in ~5 elimination half-lives or in <10 hours after discontinuation of nepafenac. Concomitant use of other NSAIDs should be avoided.

Adverse Reactions

1% to 10%:

Cardiovascular: Hypertension (1% to 4%)

Central nervous system: Foreign body sensation of eye (5% to 10%), headache (1% to 4%)

Gastrointestinal: Nausea (1% to 4%), vomiting (1% to 4%)

Ophthalmic: Capsular opacity (5% to 10%), decreased visual acuity (5% to 10%), increased intraocular pressure (5% to 10%), sticky sensation of eye (5% to 10%), conjunctival edema (1% to 5%), corneal edema (1% to 5%), crusting of eyelid (1% to 5%), eye discomfort (1% to 5%), eye pain (1% to 5%), eye pruritus (1% to 5%), lacrimation (1% to 5%), ocular hyperemia (1% to 5%), photophobia (1% to 5%), vitreous detachment (1% to 5%), xerophthalmia (1% to 5%)

Respiratory: Sinusitis (1% to 4%)

General Dosage Range Ophthalmic: *Children ≥10 years, Adolescents, and Adults:*

Ilevro™: Instill 1 drop into affected eye(s) once daily

Nevanac®: Instill 1 drop into affected eye(s) 3 times/day

Mechanism of Action Nepafenac is a prodrug which once converted to amfenac inhibits prostaglandin synthesis by decreasing the activity of the enzyme, cyclooxygenase, which results in decreased formation of prostaglandin precursors.

Pregnancy Risk Factor C

Pregnancy Considerations Teratogenic events were not observed in animal reproduction studies. Exposure to nonsteroidal anti-inflammatory drugs late in pregnancy may lead to premature closure of the ductus arteriosus.

Nesiritide (ni SIR i tide)

Brand Names: US Natrecor

Pharmacologic Category Natriuretic Peptide, B-Type, Human

Use Treatment of acutely decompensated heart failure (HF) with dyspnea at rest or with minimal activity

Local Anesthetic/Vasoconstrictor Precautions No information available to require special precautions

Effects on Dental Treatment No significant effects or complications reported

Effects on Bleeding No information available to require special precautions

Adverse Reactions Note: Incidences of adverse reactions include unapproved dosing regimens as well as combination therapy data.

>10%:

Cardiovascular: Hypotension (4% to 12%)

Renal: Increased serum creatinine (28% with >0.5 mg/dL above baseline; 5% with 50% greater serum creatinine levels than at baseline), renal insufficiency (>25% decrease in glomerular filtration rate: 31%)

1% to 10%:

Central nervous system: Headache (7%)

Endocrine & metabolic: Hypoglycemia (≥2%)

Gastrointestinal: Nausea (3%)

Neuromuscular & skeletal: Back pain (3%)

<1%, postmarketing and/or case reports: Extravasation, hypersensitivity reactions, pruritus, skin rash

General Dosage Range IV: *Adults:* Bolus: 2 mcg/kg; Infusion: Initial: 0.01 mcg/kg/minute (maximum: 0.03 mcg/kg/minute)

Mechanism of Action Binds to guanylate cyclase receptor on vascular smooth muscle and endothelial cells, increasing intracellular cyclic GMP, resulting in smooth muscle cell relaxation. Has been shown to produce dose-dependent reductions in pulmonary capillary wedge pressure (PCWP) and systemic arterial pressure.

Pharmacodynamics/Kinetics

Onset of Action PCWP reduction: 15 minutes (60% of 3-hour effect achieved within this time period); Peak effect: Within 1 hour

Duration of Action >60 minutes (up to several hours) for systolic blood pressure; hemodynamic effects persist longer than serum half-life would predict

Half-life Elimination Initial (distribution) ~2 minutes; Terminal: ~18 minutes

Pregnancy Risk Factor C

Pregnancy Considerations Adverse events were not observed in an animal reproduction study. Nesiritide is a recombinant B-type natriuretic peptide (rhBNP). BNP and NT-proBNP (which has been used as a marker of BNP), are endogenous peptides and NT-proBNP is measurable in the umbilical cord serum of normal pregnancies. Information related to the administration of nesiritide during pregnancy has not been located.

Netupitant and Palonosetron
(net UE pi tant & pal oh NOE se tron)

Brand Names: US Akynzeo

Pharmacologic Category Antiemetic; Selective 5-HT_3 Receptor Antagonist; Substance P/Neurokinin 1 Receptor Antagonist

Use Chemotherapy-induced nausea and vomiting: Prevention of acute and delayed nausea and vomiting associated with initial and repeat courses of cancer chemotherapy, including, but not limited to, highly emetogenic chemotherapy.

Local Anesthetic/Vasoconstrictor Precautions No information available to require special precautions

Effects on Dental Treatment No significant effects or complications reported

Effects on Bleeding No information available to require special precautions

Adverse Reactions 1% to 10%:

- Central nervous system: Headache (9%), fatigue (4% to 7%)
- Dermatologic: Erythema (3%)
- Gastrointestinal: Dyspepsia (4%), constipation (3%)
- Neuromuscular & skeletal: Weakness (8%)

General Dosage Range Oral: *Adults:* One capsule ~1 hour prior to initiation of chemotherapy on day 1.

Mechanism of Action Netupitant is a selective substance P/neurokinin (NK_1) receptor antagonist, which augments the antiemetic activity of 5-HT_3 receptor antagonists and corticosteroids to inhibit acute and delayed chemotherapy-induced emesis. Palonosetron is a selective 5-HT_3 receptor antagonist, which blocks serotonin, both on vagal nerve terminals in the periphery and centrally in the chemoreceptor trigger zone. Palonosetron inhibits the cross-talk between the 5-HT_3 and NK_1 receptors. The combination of palonosetron and netupitant works synergistically to inhibit substance P response to a greater extent than either agent alone (Aapro, 2014).

Pharmacodynamics/Kinetics

Half-life Elimination Netupitant: 80 ± 29 hours; Palonosetron: 48 ± 19 hours

Time to Peak Netupitant and palonosetron: ~5 hours

Pregnancy Considerations Adverse events were observed in some animal reproduction studies using the components of this combination product.

Nevirapine (ne VYE ra peen)

Related Information

HIV Infection and AIDS *on page 1785*

Brand Names: US Viramune; Viramune XR

Brand Names: Canada Apo-Nevirapine XR; Auro-Nevirapine; Mylan-Nevirapine; PMS-Nevirapine; Teva-Nevirapine; Viramune; Viramune XR

Pharmacologic Category Antiretroviral, Reverse Transcriptase Inhibitor, Non-nucleoside (Anti-HIV)

Use In combination therapy with other antiretroviral agents for the treatment of HIV-1

Local Anesthetic/Vasoconstrictor Precautions No information available to require special precautions

Effects on Dental Treatment Key adverse event(s) related to dental treatment: Ulcerative stomatitis and oral lesions.

Effects on Bleeding No information available to require special precautions relative to hemostasis.

Adverse Reactions Potentially life-threatening nevirapine-associated adverse effects may present with the following symptoms: Abrupt onset of flu-like symptoms, abdominal pain, jaundice, or fever with or without rash; may progress to hepatic failure with encephalopathy. Skin rash is present in approximately 50% of cases.

>10%:

- Dermatologic: Skin rash (1% to 7%; grades 1/2: 13%; grades 3/4: 2%)
- Endocrine & metabolic: Increased serum cholesterol (240 to 300 mg/dL: 18% to 19%; >300 mg/dL: 3% to 4%), increased LDL cholesterol (160 to 190 mg/dL: 15%; >190 mg/dL: 5%)
- Hematologic & oncologic: Neutropenia (4% to 13%; grades 3/4: 1% to 2%)
- Hepatic: Increased serum ALT (2.6 to 5 x ULN: 10% to 13%; ≥5.1 x ULN: 6% to 7%), hepatic disease (2% to 11%; symptomatic, including hepatitis and hepatic failure: risk higher in ARV-naïve women with CD4 counts >250 cells/mm^3 and ARV-naïve men with CD4 counts >400 cells/mm^3)

1% to 10%:

- Central nervous system: Fatigue (≤5%), headache (1% to 4%)
- Endocrine & metabolic: Increased amylase (1.6 to 5 x ULN: 7% to 8%; ≥5.1 x ULN: <1%)
- Gastrointestinal: Nausea (≤9%), abdominal pain (≤2%), diarrhea (≤2%)
- Hepatic: Increased serum AST (2.6 to 5 x ULN: 7% to 9%; ≥5.1 x ULN: 4% to 5%)
- Neuromuscular & skeletal: Arthralgia (2%)
- Miscellaneous: Fever (1% to 2%)

<1%, postmarketing, and/or case reports: Anaphylaxis, anemia, angioedema, aphthous stomatitis, bullous rash, cholestatic hepatitis, conjunctivitis, drowsiness, DRESS syndrome (drug reaction with eosinophilia and systemic symptoms), eosinophilia, facial edema, fulminant hepatitis, granulocytopenia, hepatic necrosis, hypersensitivity reaction, hypophosphatemia, immune reconstitution syndrome, jaundice, lipotrophy, lymphadenopathy, malaise, myalgia, oral lesion, paresthesia, redistribution of body fat, renal insufficiency, rhabdomyolysis, skin blister, Stevens-Johnson syndrome, toxic epidermal necrolysis, urticaria, vomiting

General Dosage Range Dosage adjustment recommended in patients who are receiving hemodialysis.

Oral, immediate release:

Infants and Children <8 years: Initial: 150-200 mg/m^2/dose once daily (maximum: 200 mg daily); Maintenance: 150-200 mg/m^2/dose twice daily (maximum: 400 mg daily).

Children ≥8 years: Initial: 120-150 mg/m^2/dose once daily (maximum: 200 mg daily); Maintenance: 120-150 mg/m^2/dose twice daily (maximum: 400 mg daily)

Adolescents and Adults: Initial: 200 mg once daily; Maintenance: 200 mg twice daily

Oral, extended release:

Children 6 to <18 years: Maintenance:

- 0.58 m^2 to 0.83 m^2: 200 mg once daily
- 0.84 m^2 to 1.16 m^2: 300 mg once daily
- ≥1.17 m^2: 400 mg once daily (do not exceed 400 mg daily)

Adults: Maintenance: 400 mg once daily

Mechanism of Action As a non-nucleoside reverse transcriptase inhibitor, nevirapine has activity against HIV-1 by binding to reverse transcriptase. It consequently blocks the RNA-dependent and DNA-dependent DNA polymerase activities including HIV-1 replication. It does not require intracellular phosphorylation for antiviral activity.

Pharmacodynamics/Kinetics

Half-life Elimination Decreases over 2- to 4-week time with chronic dosing due to autoinduction (ie, half-life = 45 hours initially [single dose] and decreases to 25 to 30 hours [multiple dosing])

Time to Peak Serum: Immediate release: 4 hours; Extended release:~24 hours

Pregnancy Risk Factor B

Pregnancy Considerations Teratogenic effects were not observed in animal reproduction studies. Nevirapine has a high level of transfer across the human placenta. No increased risk of overall birth defects following first trimester exposure according to data collected by the antiretroviral pregnancy registry. Maternal antiretroviral therapy may increase the risk of preterm delivery, although available information is conflicting possibly due to variability of maternal factors (disease severity; initiation of therapy); however, maternal antiretroviral medication should not be withheld due to concerns of preterm birth. Information related to stillbirth, low birth weight, and small for gestational age infants is limited. Long-term follow-up is recommended for all infants exposed to antiretroviral medications; children who develop significant organ system abnormalities of unknown etiology (particularly of the CNS or heart) should be evaluated for potential mitochondrial dysfunction. Hypersensitivity reactions (including severe life-threatening hepatic toxicity and rash) are more common in women than men, and the greatest risk is within the first 6 to 18 weeks of therapy (see Boxed Warning); pregnancy does not appear to increase this risk.

Combination antiretroviral therapy (cART) therapy is recommended for all HIV-infected pregnant women to keep the viral load below the limit of detection and reduce the risk of perinatal transmission. When HIV is diagnosed during pregnancy in a woman who has never received antiretroviral therapy, cART should begin as soon as possible after diagnosis. The Health and Human Services (HHS) Perinatal HIV Guidelines do not recommend nevirapine as an initial NNRTI for use in antiretroviral-naive pregnant patients because of the potential for adverse events, complex dosing, and low barrier to resistance. Pharmacokinetics may be altered during pregnancy; however, dose adjustment is not currently recommended. In general, women who become pregnant on a stable cART regimen may continue that regimen if viral suppression is effective, appropriate drug exposure can be achieved, contraindications for use in pregnancy are not present, and the regimen is well tolerated. Monitoring during pregnancy is more frequent than in non-pregnant adults; cART should be continued postpartum. Women who become pregnant while on nevirapine therapy and are tolerating it well may continue. Frequent monitoring is recommended.

For HIV-infected couples planning a pregnancy, maximum viral suppression with cART is recommended prior to conception for the HIV-infected partner(s) and expert consultation is recommended; modification of therapy (if needed) and optimization of the woman's health should be done prior to conception. HIV-infected women not planning a pregnancy may use any available type of contraception, considering possible drug interactions and contraindications of the specific method. In addition, consistent use of condoms is also recommended (even during pregnancy) to prevent transmission of HIV or other sexually transmitted diseases.

Health care providers are encouraged to enroll pregnant women exposed to antiretroviral medications as early in pregnancy as possible in the Antiretroviral Pregnancy Registry (1-800-258-4263 or www.APRegistry.com). Health care providers caring for HIV-infected women and their infants may contact the National Perinatal HIV Hotline (888-448-8765) for clinical consultation (HHS [perinatal] 2016).

Niacin (NYE a sin)

Related Information

Cardiovascular Diseases *on page 1752*

Brand Names: US Niacin-50 [OTC]; Niacor; Niaspan; Slo-Niacin [OTC]

Brand Names: Canada Niaspan; Niaspan FCT; Niodan

Generic Availability (US) Yes

Pharmacologic Category Antilipemic Agent, Miscellaneous; Vitamin, Water Soluble

Use Treatment of dyslipidemias (Fredrickson types IIa and IIb or primary hypercholesterolemia) as mono- or adjunctive therapy; to lower the risk of recurrent MI in patients with a history of MI and hyperlipidemia; to slow progression or promote regression of coronary artery disease; adjunctive therapy for severe hypertriglyceridemia in adult patients at risk of pancreatitis; dietary supplement

Local Anesthetic/Vasoconstrictor Precautions No information available to require special precautions

Effects on Dental Treatment No significant effects or complications reported

Effects on Bleeding Sustained-release niacin has been shown to prolong blood clotting times, as observed by significant clotting factor synthesis deficiency and coagulopathy defined by prothrombin times 1.5 times greater than control. Caution is advised in patients with bleeding disorders or those using other anticoagulant medications. Mild leukopenia and increased eosinophil levels have also been reported.

Adverse Reactions Frequency not defined.

Cardiovascular: Atrial fibrillation, cardiac arrhythmia, edema, flushing, hypotension, orthostatic hypotension, palpitations, tachycardia

Central nervous system: Chills, dizziness, headache, insomnia, migraine, myasthenia, nervousness, pain, paresthesia

Dermatologic: Acanthosis nigricans, burning sensation of skin, diaphoresis, hyperpigmentation, maculopapular rash, pruritus, skin discoloration, skin rash, urticaria, xeroderma

Endocrine & metabolic: Decreased glucose tolerance, decreased serum phosphate, gout, hyperuricemia, increased amylase, increased lactate dehydrogenase

Gastrointestinal: Abdominal pain, diarrhea, dyspepsia, eructation, flatulence, nausea, peptic ulcer, vomiting

Hematologic & oncologic: Decreased platelet count, prolonged prothrombin time

Hepatic: Hepatitis, increased serum bilirubin, increased serum transaminases (dose-related), jaundice,

Neuromuscular & skeletal: Increased creatine phosphokinase, leg cramps, myalgia, myopathy (with concurrent HMG-CoA reductase inhibitor), weakness

Ophthalmic: Blurred vision, cystoid macular edema, toxic amblyopia

Respiratory: Cough, dyspnea

<1%, postmarketing, and/or case reports: Hepatic necrosis, hypersensitivity reaction (includes anaphylaxis, angioedema, laryngismus, vesiculobullous rash), rhabdomyolysis (with concurrent HMG-CoA reductase inhibitor), syncope

Dosing

Adult & Geriatric Note: Formulations of niacin (regular release versus extended release) are not interchangeable.

Recommended daily allowances (National Academy of Sciences, 1998): Oral:

≥19 years: Females: 14 mg daily; Males: 16 mg daily

Pregnancy (all ages): 18 mg daily

Lactation (all ages): 17 mg daily

Dietary supplement (OTC labeling): Oral: 50 mg twice daily or 100 mg once daily. **Note:** Many over-the-counter formulations exist.

Hyperlipidemia: Oral:

Regular release formulation (Niacor): Initial: 250 mg once daily (with evening meal); increase frequency and/or dose every 4 to 7 days to desired response or first-level therapeutic dose (1.5 to 2 g daily in 2 to 3 divided doses); after 2 months, may increase at 2- to 4-week intervals to 3 g daily in 3 divided doses (maximum dose: 6 g daily in 3 divided doses). **Note:** Many over-the-counter formulations exist.

ACC/AHA Blood Cholesterol Guideline recommendations: Initial: 100 mg administered 3 times daily; increase dose gradually as tolerated to 3 g daily divided in 2 to 3 doses (Stone, 2013)

Sustained release (or controlled release) formulations: **Note:** Several over-the-counter formulations exist. Slo-Niacin: Usual dosage is 250 to 750 mg once daily, taken morning or evening, or as directed. Before using more than 500 mg daily, patient should consult health care provider.

Extended release formulation (Niaspan): Initial: 500 mg at bedtime for 4 weeks, then 1 g at bedtime for 4 weeks; adjust dose to response and tolerance; may increase daily dose every 4 weeks by not more than 500 mg daily to a maximum of 2 g daily. Recommended maintenance dose: 1,000 to 2,000 mg at bedtime.

ACC/AHA Blood Cholesterol Guideline recommendations: Initial: 500 mg once daily; increase dose gradually (ie, no sooner than at weekly intervals) over 4 to 8 weeks as tolerated to a maximum dose of 2 g once daily (Stone, 2013)

Pellagra (off-label use): Oral: 50 to 100 mg 3 to 4 times daily; maximum: 500 mg daily (Prousky 2003; Delgado-Sanchez 2008; DesGroseilliers 1976; Oldham 2012). Some experts prefer niacinamide for treatment due to more favorable side effect profile (Hegyi 2004; Jen 2010).

Pediatric Note: Formulations of niacin (regular release versus extended release) are not interchangeable.

Adequate intake (National Academy of Sciences, 1998): Oral:

0 to 5 months: 2 mg daily

6 to 11 months: 3 mg daily

Recommended daily allowances (National Academy of Sciences, 1998): Oral:

1 to 3 years: 6 mg daily

4 to 8 years: 8 mg daily

9 to 13 years: 12 mg daily

14 to 18 years: Females: 14 mg daily; Males: 16 mg daily

≥19 years: Refer to adult dosing.

Pellagra (off-label use) Oral: 50 to 100 mg 3 times daily. Some experts prefer niacinamide for treatment due to more favorable side effect profile (Hegyi 2004; Jen 2010).

Renal Impairment There are no dosage adjustments provided in the manufacturer's labeling (has not been studied); use with caution.

Hepatic Impairment There are no dosage adjustments provided in the manufacturer's labeling (has not been studied). Contraindicated in patients with significant or unexplained hepatic dysfunction, active liver disease or unexplained persistent transaminase elevations.

Adjustment for Toxicity Hepatic toxicity: Transaminases rise ≥3 times ULN, either persistent or if symptoms of nausea, fever, and/or malaise occur: Discontinue therapy.

Mechanism of Action Niacin (nicotinic acid) is bioconverted to nicotinamide which is further converted to nicotinamide adenine dinucleotide (NAD+) and the hydride equivalent (NADH) which are coenzymes necessary for tissue metabolism, lipid metabolism, and glycogenolysis (Belenky, 2006; Suave, 2008). The mechanism by which niacin (in lipid-lowering doses) affects plasma lipoproteins is not fully understood. It may involve several actions including partial inhibition of release of free fatty acids from adipose tissue, and increased lipoprotein lipase activity, which may increase the rate of chylomicron triglyceride removal from plasma. Ultimately, niacin reduces total cholesterol, apolipoprotein (apo) B, triglycerides, VLDL, LDL, lipoprotein (a), and increases HDL and other important components and subfractions (eg, LPA-I) (Kamanna, 2000)

Contraindications Hypersensitivity to niacin, niacinamide, or any component of the formulation; active hepatic disease or significant or unexplained persistent elevations in hepatic transaminases; active peptic ulcer; arterial hemorrhage

Warnings/Precautions Prior to initiation, secondary causes for hypercholesterolemia (eg, poorly controlled diabetes mellitus, hypothyroidism) should be excluded; management with diet and other nonpharmacologic measures (eg, exercise or weight reduction) should be attempted prior to initiation. Use has not been evaluated in Fredrickson type I or III dyslipidemias. Use with caution in patients with unstable angina or in the acute phase of an MI or renal disease. In patients with preexisting coronary artery disease, the incidence of atrial fibrillation was observed more frequently in those receiving immediate release (crystalline) niacin as compared to placebo (Coronary Drug Project Research Group, 1975). Niacin should not be used if patient experiences new-onset atrial fibrillation during therapy (Stone, 2013). Niacin may increase fasting blood glucose, although clinical data suggest increases are generally modest (<5%) (Guyton, 2007). Use niacin with caution in patients with diabetes. Monitor glucose; adjustment of diet and/or hypoglycemic therapy may be necessary. Niacin should not be used if patient experiences persistent hyperglycemia during therapy (Stone, 2013). Use with caution in patients predisposed to gout; niacin should not be used if patient experiences acute gout during therapy (Stone, 2013).

Use with caution in patients with a past history of hepatic impairment and/or who consume substantial amounts of ethanol; contraindicated with active liver disease or unexplained persistent transaminase elevation. Niacin should not be used if hepatic transaminase elevations >2 to 3 times upper limit of normal occur during therapy (Stone, 2013). Rare cases of rhabdomyolysis have occurred during concomitant use with HMG-CoA reductase inhibitors. With concurrent use or if symptoms suggestive of myopathy occur, monitor creatine phosphokinase (CPK) and potassium; use with caution in patients with renal impairment, inadequately treated hypothyroidism, patients with diabetes or the elderly; risk for myopathy and rhabdomyolysis may be increased. May cause gastrointestinal distress, vomiting, diarrhea, or aggravate peptic ulcer. Gastrointestinal distress may be attenuated with a gradual increase in dose and administration with food. Use is contraindicated in patients with active peptic ulcer disease; use with caution in patients with a past history of peptic ulcer. Niacin should not be used if patient experiences unexplained abdominal pain or gastrointestinal symptoms or unexplained weight loss during therapy (Stone, 2013). Dose-related reductions in platelet count and increases of prothrombin time may occur. Has been associated with small but statistically significant dose-related reductions in phosphorus levels. Monitor phosphorus levels periodically in patients at risk for hypophosphatemia.

Formulations of niacin (immediate release versus extended release) are not interchangeable (bioavailability varies); cases of severe hepatotoxicity, including fulminant hepatic necrosis, have occurred in patients who have substituted niacin products at equivalent doses. Patients should be initiated with low doses (eg, niacin extended release 500 mg at bedtime) with titration to achieve desired response. Flushing and pruritus, common adverse effects of niacin, may be attenuated with a gradual increase in dose, administering with food, avoidance of concurrent ingestion of ethanol or hot liquids, and/or by taking aspirin (adults: 325 mg) (Stone, 2013). May also use other NSAIDs according to the manufacturer. Flushing associated with extended release preparation is significantly reduced (Guyton, 2007). For immediate release preparations, may administer in 2 to 3 divided doses to reduce the frequency and severity. Niacin should not be used if patient experiences persistent severe cutaneous symptoms during therapy (Stone, 2013).

Potentially significant interactions may exist, requiring dose or frequency adjustment, additional monitoring, and/or selection of alternative therapy.

Drug Interactions

Metabolism/Transport Effects None known.

Avoid Concomitant Use There are no known interactions where it is recommended to avoid concomitant use.

Increased Effect/Toxicity

Niacin may increase the levels/effects of: HMG-CoA Reductase Inhibitors; Rosuvastatin; Simvastatin

The levels/effects of Niacin may be increased by: Alcohol (Ethyl)

Decreased Effect

Niacin may decrease the levels/effects of: Antidiabetic Agents

The levels/effects of Niacin may be decreased by: Bile Acid Sequestrants

Dietary Considerations Should be taken with meal; low-fat meal if treating hyperlipidemia. Avoid alcohol, hot drinks, and spicy foods around the time of niacin dose.

Pharmacodynamics/Kinetics

Half-life Elimination 25 to 48 minutes

Time to Peak Serum: Immediate release formulation: 30 to 60 minutes; extended release formulation: 4 to 5 hours

Pregnancy Risk Factor C

Pregnancy Considerations Animal reproduction studies have not been conducted. Water soluble vitamins cross the placenta. When used as a dietary supplement, niacin requirements may be increased in pregnant women compared to nonpregnant women (IOM, 1998). It is not known if niacin at lipid-lowering doses is harmful to the developing fetus. If a woman becomes pregnant while receiving niacin for primary hypercholesterolemia, niacin should be discontinued. If a woman becomes pregnant while receiving niacin for hypertriglyceridemia, the benefits and risks of continuing niacin should be assessed on an individual basis.

Breastfeeding Considerations Niacin is excreted in breast milk. When used as a dietary supplement, niacin requirements may be increased in breastfeeding women compared to non-breastfeeding women (IOM, 1998). Due to the potential for serious adverse reactions in the breastfeeding infant, the manufacturer recommends a decision be made whether to discontinue breastfeeding or to discontinue the drug, taking into account the importance of treatment to the mother.

Dosage Forms

Capsule Extended Release, Oral:
Generic: 250 mg, 500 mg

Capsule Extended Release, Oral [preservative free]:
Generic: 250 mg, 500 mg

Powder, Oral:
Generic: (100 g, 1000 g)

Tablet, Oral:
Niacin-50 [OTC]: 50 mg
Niacor: 500 mg
Generic: 50 mg, 100 mg, 250 mg, 500 mg

Tablet, Oral [preservative free]:
Generic: 100 mg, 500 mg

Tablet Extended Release, Oral:
Niaspan: 500 mg, 750 mg, 1000 mg
Slo-Niacin [OTC]: 250 mg, 500 mg, 750 mg
Generic: 500 mg, 750 mg, 1000 mg

Tablet Extended Release, Oral [preservative free]:
Generic: 250 mg, 500 mg, 1000 mg

Niacinamide (nye a SIN a mide)

Pharmacologic Category Vitamin, Water Soluble

Use Dietary supplement

Local Anesthetic/Vasoconstrictor Precautions No information available to require special precautions

Effects on Dental Treatment No significant effects or complications reported

Effects on Bleeding No information available to require special precautions

General Dosage Range Oral:

Children: 10-50 mg every 6 hours

Adults: Initial: 100 mg every 6 hours; Maintenance: 50 mg every 8-12 hours

Mechanism of Action Used by the body as a source of niacin; is a component of two coenzymes which is necessary for tissue respiration, lipid metabolism, and glycogenolysis; does not have hypolipidemia or vasodilating effects.

Pharmacodynamics/Kinetics

Half-life Elimination 45 minutes

Time to Peak Serum: 20-70 minutes

Pregnancy Considerations Water-soluble vitamins cross the placenta (IOM, 1998).

NiCARdipine (nye KAR de peen)

Related Information

Calcium Channel Blockers and Gingival Hyperplasia *on page 1908*

Cardiovascular Diseases *on page 1752*

Brand Names: US Cardene IV; Cardene SR [DSC]

Pharmacologic Category Antianginal Agent; Antihypertensive; Calcium Channel Blocker; Calcium Channel Blocker, Dihydropyridine

Use

Angina: Management of chronic stable angina (oral immediate-release product only)

Hypertension: Management of hypertension (oral immediate- and sustained-release products and IV); parenteral only for short-term use when oral treatment is not feasible or not desirable

The 2014 guideline for the management of high blood pressure in adults (JNC 8) recommends initiation of pharmacologic treatment to lower blood pressure for the following patients (JNC 8 [James 2013]):

- Patients ≥60 years of age with systolic blood pressure (SBP) ≥150 mm Hg or diastolic blood pressure (DBP) ≥90 mm Hg. Goal of therapy is SBP <150 mm Hg and DBP <90 mm Hg.
- Patients <60 years of age with SBP ≥140 mm Hg or DBP ≥90 mm Hg. Goal of therapy is SBP <140 mm Hg and DBP <90 mm Hg.
- Patients ≥18 years of age with diabetes with SBP ≥140 mm Hg or DBP ≥90 mm Hg. Goal of therapy is SBP <140 mm Hg and DBP <90 mm Hg.
- Patients ≥18 years of age with chronic kidney disease (CKD) with SBP ≥140 mm Hg or DBP ≥90 mm Hg. Goal of therapy is SBP <140 mm Hg and DBP <90 mm Hg.

In patients with chronic kidney disease (CKD), regardless of race or diabetes status, the use of an ACE inhibitor (ACEI) or angiotensin receptor blocker (ARB) as initial therapy is recommended to improve kidney outcomes. In the general nonblack population (without CKD) including those with diabetes, initial antihypertensive treatment should consist of a thiazide-type diuretic, calcium channel blocker, ACEI, or ARB. In the general black population (without CKD) including those with diabetes, initial antihypertensive treatment should consist of a thiazide-type diuretic or a calcium channel blocker instead of an ACEI or ARB.

Local Anesthetic/Vasoconstrictor Precautions No information available to require special precautions

Effects on Dental Treatment Key adverse event(s) related to dental treatment: Xerostomia (normal salivary flow resumes upon discontinuation). Other drugs of this class can cause gingival hyperplasia (ie, nifedipine). The first case of nicardipine-induced gingival hyperplasia has been reported in a child taking 40-50 mg daily for 20 months.

Effects on Bleeding No information available to require special precautions

Adverse Reactions

1% to 10%:

Cardiovascular: Flushing (6% to 10%), pedal edema (dose related; 7% to 8%), exacerbation of angina pectoris (dose related; 6%), hypotension (IV 6%), palpitations (3% to 4%), tachycardia (1% to 4%), chest pain (IV 1%), extrasystoles (IV 1%), hemopericardium (IV 1%), hypertension (IV 1%), supraventricular tachycardia (IV 1%), edema (≤1%)

Central nervous system: Headache (6% to 15%), dizziness (4% to 7%), hypoesthesia (1%), intracranial hemorrhage (1%), pain (1%), somnolence (1%)

Dermatologic: Diaphoresis (1%), skin rash (≤1%)

Endocrine & metabolic: Hypokalemia (IV 1%)

Gastrointestinal: Nausea and vomiting (IV 5%), nausea (2%), dyspepsia (≤2%), abdominal pain (IV 1%), xerostomia (≤1%)

Genitourinary: Hematuria (1%)

Local: Injection site reaction (IV 1%), pain at injection site (IV 1%)

Neuromuscular & skeletal: Weakness (4% to 6%), myalgia (1%), paresthesia (1%)

<1%, postmarketing, and/or case reports: Abnormal dreams, abnormal hepatic function tests, abnormal vision, angina pectoris, anxiety, arthralgia, atrial fibrillation (not distinguishable from natural history of atherosclerotic vascular disease), atrioventricular block, atypical chest pain, blurred vision, cerebral ischemia (not distinguishable from natural history of atherosclerotic vascular disease), confusion, conjunctivitis, constipation, deep vein thrombophlebitis, depression, depression of ST segment on ECG, dyspnea, ear disease, ECG abnormal, fever, gingival hyperplasia, heart block (not distinguishable from natural history of atherosclerotic vascular disease), hot flash, hyperkinesia, hypersensitivity reaction, hypertonia, hypophosphatemia, impotence, infection, insomnia, inversion T wave on ECG, malaise, myocardial infarction (chronic therapy; may be due to disease progression), neck pain, nervousness, nocturia, orthostatic hypotension, oxygen saturation decreased (possible pulmonary shunting), parotitis, pericarditis (not distinguishable from natural history of atherosclerotic vascular disease), peripheral vascular disease, respiratory tract disease, rhinitis, sinus node dysfunction (chronic therapy; may be due to disease progression), sinusitis, sore throat, sustained tachycardia, syncope, thrombocytopenia, tinnitus, tremor, urinary frequency, ventricular extrasystoles, ventricular tachycardia, vertigo, vomiting

General Dosage Range Dosage adjustment recommended in patients with hepatic impairment

IV: *Adults:* Initial: 5 mg/hour; Maintenance: 3 to 15 mg/hour

Oral:

Immediate release: *Adults:* Initial: 20 mg 3 times daily; Maintenance: 20 to 40 mg 3 times daily

Sustained release: *Adults:* Initial: 30 mg twice daily; Maintenance: 30 to 60 mg twice daily

Mechanism of Action Inhibits calcium ion from entering the "slow channels" or select voltage-sensitive areas of vascular smooth muscle and myocardium during depolarization, producing a relaxation of coronary vascular smooth muscle and coronary vasodilation; increases myocardial oxygen delivery in patients with vasospastic angina

Pharmacodynamics/Kinetics

Onset of Action

IV: Within minutes (constant infusion); Oral: 0.5 to 2 hours

Peak effect: Immediate capsules: 1 to 2 hours; Sustained release capsules (at steady state): Sustained from 2 to 6 hours postdose; IV continuous infusion: 50% of the maximum effect is seen by 45 minutes

Duration of Action

IV: ≤8 hours. Upon discontinuation of continuous infusion, a 50% decrease in effect is seen in ~30 minutes with gradual discontinuing antihypertensive effects for ~50 hours.

Oral: Immediate release: ≤8 hours, Sustained release: 8 to 12 hours.

Half-life Elimination

Follows dose-dependent (nonlinear) pharmacokinetics; "apparent" or calculated half-life is dependent upon serum concentrations.

Oral: Half-life over the first 8 hours after oral dosing is 2 to 4 hours; terminal half-life: 8.6 hours.

IV: After IV infusion, serum concentrations decrease tri-exponentially; alpha half-life: 3 minutes; beta half-life: 45 minutes; terminal half-life: 14 hours (**Note:** Terminal half-life can only be seen after long-term infusions).

Time to Peak Serum: Oral: Immediate release: 30 to 120 minutes (mean: 1 hour); Sustained release: 60 to 240 minutes

Pregnancy Risk Factor C

Pregnancy Considerations Adverse events have been observed in some animal reproduction studies. Nicardipine has been used for the treatment of severe hypertension in pregnancy and preterm labor. Nicardipine crosses the placenta; changes in fetal heart rate, neonatal hypotension and neonatal acidosis have been observed following maternal use (rare; based on limited data). Adverse effects reported in pregnant women are generally similar to those reported in nonpregnant patients; however, pulmonary edema has been observed (Nij 2010). Untreated chronic maternal hypertension is also associated with adverse events in the fetus, infant, and mother. If treatment for hypertension during pregnancy is needed, other agents are preferred (ACOG 2013).

Product Availability Cardene SR has been discontinued in the US for more than 1 year.

Nicotine (nik oh TEEN)

Related Information

Management of the Chemically Dependent Patient *on page 1821*

Brand Names: US Nicoderm CQ [OTC]; Nicorelief [OTC]; NICOrelief [OTC] [DSC]; Nicorette Mini [OTC]; Nicorette Starter Kit [OTC]; Nicorette [OTC]; Nicotine Step 1 [OTC]; Nicotine Step 2 [OTC]; Nicotine Step 3 [OTC]; Nicotrol; Nicotrol NS; Thrive [OTC]

Brand Names: Canada Habitrol; Nicoderm; Nicorette; Nicorette Plus; Nicotrol

Generic Availability (US) May be product dependent

Pharmacologic Category Smoking Cessation Aid

Dental Use Treatment to aid smoking cessation for the relief of nicotine withdrawal symptoms (including nicotine craving)

Use Smoking cessation: Treatment to aid smoking cessation for the relief of nicotine withdrawal symptoms (including nicotine craving)

Local Anesthetic/Vasoconstrictor Precautions No information available to require special precautions

Effects on Dental Treatment Key adverse event(s) related to dental treatment: Chewing gum: Excessive salivation, mouth/throat soreness, jaw muscle ache, hiccups, tachycardia, headache (mild), vomiting, belching, nausea, xerostomia (normal salivary flow resumes upon discontinuation), dizziness, nervousness, GI distress, hoarseness, and muscle pain.

Effects on Bleeding No information available to require special precautions

Adverse Reactions

Nasal spray/inhaler:

>10%:

Central nervous system: Headache (18% to 26%)

Gastrointestinal: Inhaler: Mouth irritation (≤66%), dyspepsia (18%)

Respiratory: Inhaler: Throat irritation (≤66%), cough (32%), rhinitis (23%)

1% to 10%:

Central nervous system: Withdrawal syndrome

Dermatologic: Acne vulgaris (3%), burning sensation of the nose (nasal spray)

Gastrointestinal: Flatulence (4%), gingival disease (4%), diarrhea, dysgeusia, hiccups, nausea, tooth enamel damage (abrasions)

Genitourinary: Dysmenorrhea (3%)

Neuromuscular & skeletal: Back pain (6%), arthralgia (5%), jaw pain, neck pain

Respiratory: Sinusitis

<1%, postmarketing, and/or case reports: Amnesia, aphasia, bronchitis, bronchospasm, edema, hypersensitivity reaction, increased bronchial secretions, migraine, numbness, pain, purpura, skin rash, visual disturbance, xerostomia

Adverse events reported for chewing gum, lozenge, and/or transdermal systems were reported in prescription labeling. Frequency not defined; may be product- or dose-specific:

Central nervous system: Depression, dizziness, headache, insomnia, lack of concentration, nervousness, pain, paresthesia

Dermatologic: Diaphoresis

Gastrointestinal: Aphthous stomatitis, constipation, diarrhea, dysgeusia, dyspepsia, flatulence, gingival hemorrhage, glossitis, hiccups, nausea, sialorrhea, stomatitis, tooth enamel damage (abrasions), xerostomia

Dermatologic: Skin rash

Hypersensitivity: Hypersensitivity reaction

Local: Application site reaction, localized edema, localized erythema

Neuromuscular & skeletal: Arthralgia, jaw pain, myalgia

Respiratory: Cough, sinusitis

Dental Usual Dosage

Tobacco cessation (patients should be advised to completely stop smoking upon initiation of therapy): Adults:

Gum: Chew 1 piece of gum when urge to smoke, up to 24 pieces/day. Patients who smoke <25 cigarettes/day should start with 2-mg strength; patients smoking ≥25 cigarettes/day should start with the 4-mg strength. Use according to the following 12-week dosing schedule:

Weeks 1-6: Chew 1 piece of gum every 1-2 hours; to increase chances of quitting, chew at least 9 pieces/day during the first 6 weeks

Weeks 7-9: Chew 1 piece of gum every 2-4 hours

Weeks 10-12: Chew 1 piece of gum every 4-8 hours

Inhaler: Oral: Usually 6 to 16 cartridges per day; best effect was achieved by frequent continuous puffing (20 minutes); recommended duration of treatment is 3 months, after which patients may be weaned from the inhaler by gradual reduction of the daily dose over 6-12 weeks

Lozenge: Oral: Patients who smoke their first cigarette within 30 minutes of waking should use the 4 mg strength; otherwise the 2 mg strength is recommended. Use according to the following 12-week dosing schedule:

Weeks 1-6: One lozenge every 1-2 hours

Weeks 7-9: One lozenge every 2-4 hours

Weeks 10-12: One lozenge every 4-8 hours

Note: Use at least 9 lozenges/day during first 6 weeks to improve chances of quitting; do not use more than one lozenge at a time (maximum: 5 lozenges every 6 hours, 20 lozenges/day)

Spray: Nasal: 1-2 sprays/hour; do not exceed more than 5 doses (10 sprays) per hour [maximum: 40 doses/day (80 sprays); each dose (2 sprays) contains 1 mg of nicotine]

Transdermal patch: Topical: **Note:** Adjustment may be required during initial treatment (move to higher dose if experiencing withdrawal symptoms; lower dose if side effects are experienced).

NicoDerm CQ®:

Patients smoking >10 cigarettes/day: Begin with step 1 (21 mg/day) for 6 weeks, **followed by** step 2 (14 mg/day) for 2 weeks; **finish with** step 3 (7 mg/day) for 2 weeks

Patients smoking ≤10 cigarettes/day: Begin with step 2 (14 mg/day) for 6 weeks, **followed by** step 3 (7 mg/day) for 2 weeks

Dosing

Adult & Geriatric

Tobacco cessation (patients should be advised to completely stop smoking upon initiation of therapy):

Gum: Chew 1 piece of gum when urge to smoke occurs. If strong or frequent cravings are present after 1 piece of gum, may use a second piece within the hour (do not continuously use one piece after the other). Patients who smoke their first cigarette within 30 minutes of waking should use the 4 mg strength; otherwise the 2 mg strength is recommended. Use according to the following 12-week dosing schedule:

Weeks 1 to 6: Chew 1 piece of gum every 1 to 2 hours (maximum: 24 pieces/day); to increase chances of quitting, chew at least 9 pieces/day during the first 6 weeks

Weeks 7 to 9: Chew 1 piece of gum every 2 to 4 hours (maximum: 24 pieces/day)

Weeks 10 to 12: Chew 1 piece of gum every 4 to 8 hours (maximum: 24 pieces/day)

Inhalation: Oral: Initial: Usually 6 to 16 cartridges per day; best effect was achieved by frequent continuous puffing (20 minutes); maximum: 16 cartridges/day; recommended duration of treatment is 3 months, after which patients may be weaned from the inhaler by gradual reduction of the daily dose over 6 to 12 weeks. Use beyond 6 months is not recommended (has not been studied).

Lozenge: Oral: 1 lozenge when urge to smoke occurs; do not use more than 1 lozenge at a time. Patients who smoke their first cigarette within 30 minutes of waking should use the 4 mg strength; otherwise the 2 mg strength is recommended. Use according to the following 12-week dosing schedule:

Weeks 1 to 6: 1 lozenge every 1 to 2 hours (maximum: 5 lozenges every 6 hours; 20 lozenges/day); to increase chances of quitting, use at least 9 lozenges/day during the first 6 weeks

Weeks 7 to 9: 1 lozenge every 2 to 4 hours (maximum: 5 lozenges every 6 hours; 20 lozenges/day)

Weeks 10 to 12: 1 lozenge every 4 to 8 hours (maximum: 5 lozenges every 6 hours; 20 lozenges/day)

Nasal: Spray: 1 to 2 doses/hour (each dose [2 sprays, one in each nostril] contains 1 mg of nicotine); do not exceed more than 5 doses (10 sprays) per hour [maximum: 40 mg/day (80 sprays)] or 3 months of treatment. **Note:** For best results, use at least the recommended minimum of 8 doses per day (less is unlikely to be effective).

Transdermal patch: Topical: **Note:** Adjustment may be required during initial treatment (move to higher dose if experiencing withdrawal symptoms; lower dose if side effects are experienced).

Patients smoking >10 cigarettes/day: Begin with step 1 (21 mg/day) for 6 weeks, **followed by** step 2 (14 mg/day) for 2 weeks; **finish with** step 3 (7 mg/day) for 2 weeks

Patients smoking ≤10 cigarettes/day: Begin with step 2 (14 mg/day) for 6 weeks, **followed by** step 3 (7 mg/day) for 2 weeks

Renal Impairment There are no dosage adjustments provided in the manufacturer's labeling (has not been studied). Only severe renal impairment should affect clearance of nicotine or its metabolites from circulation.

Hepatic Impairment There are no dosage adjustments provided in the manufacturer's labeling (has not been studied); because total system clearance of nicotine is dependent on hepatic blood flow, anticipate reduced clearance.

Mechanism of Action Nicotine, a naturally occurring alkaloid, binds stereo-selectively to nicotinic-cholinergic receptors at the autonomic ganglia, in the adrenal medulla, at neuromuscular junctions, and in the brain. Two types of CNS effects are believed to be the basis of nicotine's positively reinforcing properties; a stimulating effect is exerted mainly in the cortex via the locus ceruleus and a reward effect is exerted in the limbic system. At low doses the stimulant effects predominate while at high doses the reward effects predominate.

Contraindications

Hypersensitivity to nicotine or any component of the formulation.

OTC labeling: Nicorette lozenge: When used for self-medication, do not use if you are allergic to soya.

Warnings/Precautions Urge patients to stop smoking completely when initiating therapy. Nicotine can increase heart rate and blood pressure. The risk versus the benefits should be weighed in patients with cardiovascular or peripheral vascular diseases, specifically patients with a history of myocardial infarction and/or angina pectoris, serious cardiac arrhythmias, or vasospastic diseases (Buerger disease, Prinzmetal variant angina and Raynaud phenomena); use caution in patients with angina, hypertension, or recent MI. Discontinue use if irregular heartbeat or palpitations occur. Use caution in patients with accelerated hypertension due to the risk of malignant hypertension. Generally, avoid use during the immediate postmyocardial infarction period, in patients with serious arrhythmias, or with severe or worsening angina. Use with caution in patients with insulin-dependent diabetes, active peptic ulcer disease; severe hepatic impairment; hyperthyroidism; pheochromocytoma; severe renal impairment.

OTC labeling: When used for self-medication, discontinue use and contact a health care provider if symptoms of nicotine overdose (eg, nausea, vomiting, dizziness, diarrhea, weakness, rapid heartbeat) or an allergic reaction (eg, difficulty breathing, rash) occurs.

Chewing gum and lozenge: When used for self-medication, consult a health care provider before use in patients on a sodium-restricted diet and in patients with a history of seizures. Discontinue chewing gum and consult a health care provider if mouth, teeth or jaw problems occur. Discontinue lozenge and consult a health care provider if mouth problems, persistent indigestion, or severe sore throat occurs.

Inhaler: Use with caution in patients with bronchospastic disease (eg, asthma, chronic pulmonary disease); may cause bronchospasm due to potential airway irritation; other forms of nicotine replacement may be preferred in patients with severe bronchospastic airway disease. Sustained use (beyond 6 months) by patients who quit smoking is not recommended.

Nasal spray: Use of nasal product is not recommended with chronic nasal disorders (eg, allergy, rhinitis, nasal polyps, and sinusitis). Exacerbations of bronchospasm has been reported in patients with preexisting asthma; use in patients with severe reactive airway disease is not recommended. Nasal mucosa irritation may occur. Sustained use (beyond 6 months) by patients who quit smoking is not recommended.

Transdermal patch: May contain conducting metal (eg, aluminum); remove patch prior to MRI. When used for self-medication, consult a health care provider before use in patients who have an allergy to adhesive tape or who have skin problems. Discontinue use and contact a health care provider if skin redness caused by the patch does not resolve after 4 days or if inflammation or rash occurs. If vivid dreams or other sleep disturbances occur, remove the patch at bedtime and apply another patch in the morning.

Drug Interactions

Metabolism/Transport Effects **Substrate** of CYP1A2 (minor), CYP2A6 (minor), CYP2B6 (minor), CYP2C19 (minor), CYP2C9 (minor), CYP2D6 (minor), CYP2E1 (minor), CYP3A4 (minor); **Note:** Assignment of Major/Minor substrate status based on clinically relevant drug interaction potential; **Inhibits** CYP2A6 (weak), CYP2E1 (weak)

Avoid Concomitant Use There are no known interactions where it is recommended to avoid concomitant use.

Increased Effect/Toxicity

Nicotine may increase the levels/effects of: Adenosine

The levels/effects of Nicotine may be increased by: Cimetidine; Varenicline

Decreased Effect There are no known significant interactions involving a decrease in effect.

Food Interactions Lozenge: Acidic foods/beverages decrease absorption of nicotine.

Dietary Considerations Some products may contain phenylalanine and/or sodium.

Pharmacodynamics/Kinetics

Onset of Action Intranasal: More closely approximate the time course of plasma nicotine levels observed after cigarette smoking than other dosage forms (Svensson, 1987)

Half-life Elimination Transdermal: ~4 hours (Bannon, 1989); Nasal spray: 1 to 2 hours; Inhaler: 1 to 2 hours

Time to Peak Serum: Transdermal: ~2 to 8 hours (Bannon, 1989; DeVeaugh-Geiss, 2010); Intranasal: 4 to 15 minutes; Oral inhalation: ≤15 minutes; Gum: ~30 minutes (Svensson, 1987)

Pregnancy Risk Factor D (RX products)

Pregnancy Considerations Adverse events have been observed in animal reproduction studies. Nicotine crosses the placenta (HHS 2014). Maternal smoking is associated with birth defects (HHS 2014; Hachshaw 2011); the incidence of birth defects following nicotine replacement therapy may be similar (limited data) (Dhalwani 2015). Nicotine exposure via cigarette smoke may cause increased ectopic pregnancy, low birth weight, increased risk of spontaneous abortion, increased perinatal mortality; increased aortic blood flow, increased heart rate, decreased uterine blood flow, and decreased breathing have been reported in the fetus. Smoking during pregnancy is associated with sudden infant death syndrome (SIDS), an increased risk of asthma, infantile colic, and childhood obesity (ACOG 2010; HHS 2014). Women who are pregnant should be encouraged not to smoke. The use of nicotine replacement products to aid in smoking cessation has not been adequately studied in pregnant women (amount of nicotine exposure is varied). Nonpharmacologic treatments are recommended. If the benefits of nicotine replacement therapy outweigh the unknown risks, it should be done under close supervision (ACOG, 2010).

Breastfeeding Considerations Nicotine from cigarette smoke is found in breast milk and can be absorbed orally by the infant; hepatic clearance is likely lowest at birth. The amount of nicotine in breast milk from replacement products varies. Nicotine replacement therapy is considered to be compatible with breast feeding if the amount of nicotine is less than that received from smoking. Use of short acting products (gum, lozenges) is preferred (Sachs 2013). The manufacturer recommends caution be exercised when administering nicotine to breastfeeding women.

Dosage Forms Considerations

Nicotrol NS contains approximately 200 sprays.

Dosage Forms

Gum, Mouth/Throat:

Nicorelief [OTC]: 2 mg (50 ea, 110 ea); 4 mg (50 ea, 110 ea)

Nicorette [OTC]: 2 mg (20 ea, 100 ea, 110 ea, 160 ea, 170 ea, 190 ea, 200 ea); 4 mg (20 ea, 100 ea, 110 ea, 160 ea, 170 ea, 190 ea, 200 ea)

Nicorette Starter Kit [OTC]: 2 mg (100 ea, 110 ea); 4 mg (110 ea)

Thrive [OTC]: 2 mg (100 ea); 4 mg (100 ea, 110 ea)

Generic: 2 mg (20 ea, 40 ea, 50 ea, 100 ea, 110 ea); 4 mg (20 ea, 40 ea, 50 ea, 100 ea, 110 ea)

Inhaler, Inhalation:

Nicotrol: 10 mg (168 ea)

Kit, Transdermal:

Generic: 7 mg/24 hr (14s) & 14 mg/24 hr (14s) & 21 mg/24 hr (28s)

Lozenge, Mouth/Throat:

Nicorette [OTC]: 2 mg (24 ea, 27 ea, 72 ea, 108 ea, 168 ea); 4 mg (24 ea, 72 ea, 108 ea, 168 ea)

Nicorette Mini [OTC]: 2 mg (20 ea, 81 ea, 135 ea); 4 mg (20 ea, 81 ea, 135 ea)

Generic: 2 mg (24 ea, 27 ea, 72 ea); 4 mg (24 ea, 27 ea, 72 ea)

Patch 24 Hour, Transdermal:

Nicoderm CQ [OTC]: 7 mg/24 hr (14 ea); 14 mg/24 hr (14 ea, 21 ea); 21 mg/24 hr (7 ea, 14 ea, 21 ea)

Nicotine Step 3 [OTC]: 7 mg/24 hr (14 ea)

Nicotine Step 2 [OTC]: 14 mg/24 hr (14 ea)
Nicotine Step 1 [OTC]: 21 mg/24 hr (14 ea)
Generic: 7 mg/24 hr (1 ea, 7 ea, 14 ea); 14 mg/24 hr (1 ea, 7 ea, 14 ea); 21 mg/24 hr (1 ea, 7 ea, 14 ea, 28 ea)

Solution, Nasal:
Nicotrol NS: 10 mg/mL (10 mL)

NIFEdipine (nye FED i peen)

Related Information

Calcium Channel Blockers and Gingival Hyperplasia *on page 1908*
Cardiovascular Diseases *on page 1752*

Brand Names: US Adalat CC; Afeditab CR; Nifediac CC [DSC]; Nifedical XL [DSC]; Procardia; Procardia XL

Brand Names: Canada Adalat XL; Apo-Nifed PA; Mylan-Nifedipine Extended Release; Nifedipine ER; PMS-Nifedipine; PMS-Nifedipine ER

Generic Availability (US) Yes

Pharmacologic Category Antianginal Agent; Antihypertensive; Calcium Channel Blocker; Calcium Channel Blocker, Dihydropyridine

Use

Management of chronic stable or vasospastic angina; treatment of hypertension (sustained release products only)

The 2014 guideline for the management of high blood pressure in adults (JNC 8) recommends initiation of pharmacologic treatment to lower blood pressure for the following patients (JNC 8 [James, 2013]):

- Patients ≥60 years of age with systolic blood pressure (SBP) ≥150 mm Hg or diastolic blood pressure (DBP) ≥90 mm Hg. Goal of therapy is SBP <150 mm Hg and DBP <90 mm Hg.
- Patients <60 years of age with SBP ≥140 mm Hg or DBP ≥90 mm Hg. Goal of therapy is SBP <140 mm Hg and DBP <90 mm Hg.
- Patients ≥18 years of age with diabetes with SBP ≥140 mm Hg or DBP ≥90 mm Hg. Goal of therapy is SBP <140 mm Hg and DBP <90 mm Hg.
- Patients ≥18 years of age with chronic kidney disease (CKD) with SBP ≥140 mm Hg or DBP ≥90 mm Hg. Goal of therapy is SBP <140 mm Hg and DBP <90 mm Hg.

In patients with chronic kidney disease (CKD), regardless of race or diabetes status, the use of an ACE inhibitor (ACEI) or angiotensin receptor blocker (ARB) as initial therapy is recommended to improve kidney outcomes. In the general nonblack population (without CKD) including those with diabetes, initial antihypertensive treatment should consist of a thiazide-type diuretic, calcium channel blocker, ACEI, or ARB. In the general black population (without CKD) including those with diabetes, initial antihypertensive treatment should consist of a thiazide-type diuretic or a calcium channel blocker instead of an ACEI or ARB.

Local Anesthetic/Vasoconstrictor Precautions
No information available to require special precautions

Effects on Dental Treatment Nifedipine has been reported to cause 10% incidence of gingival hyperplasia; effects from 30-100 mg/day have appeared after 1-9 months. Discontinuance results in complete disappearance or marked regression of symptoms; symptoms will reappear upon remedication. Marked regression occurs after 1 week and complete disappearance of symptoms has occurred within 15 days. If a gingivectomy is performed and use of the drug is continued or resumed, hyperplasia usually will recur. The success of the gingivectomy usually requires that the medication be discontinued or that a switch to a noncalcium channel blocker be made. If for some reason nifedipine cannot be discontinued, hyperplasia has not recurred after gingivectomy when extensive plaque control was performed. If nifedipine is changed to another class of cardiovascular agent, the gingival hyperplasia will probably regress and resolve. Switching to another calcium channel blocker may result in continued hyperplasia.

Effects on Bleeding No information available to require special precautions

Adverse Reactions

>10%:

Cardiovascular: Flushing (10% to 25%; extended release: 3% to 4%), peripheral edema (7% to 30%)
Central nervous system: Dizziness (10% to 27%), headache (10% to 23%)
Gastrointestinal: Heartburn (≤11%), nausea (≤11%)

1% to 10%:

Cardiovascular: Palpitations (≤7%), transient hypotension (5%), cardiac failure (2%)
Central nervous system: Mood changes (≤7%), nervousness (≤7%), fatigue (6%), chills (≤2%), disturbed sleep (≤2%), equilibrium disturbance (≤2%), jitteriness (≤2%), shakiness (≤2%)
Dermatologic: Dermatitis (≤2%), diaphoresis (≤2%), pruritus (≤2%), urticaria (≤2%)
Gastrointestinal: Gingival hyperplasia (≤10%), sore throat (≤6%), abdominal cramps (≤2%), constipation (≤2%), diarrhea (≤2%), flatulence (≤2%)
Genitourinary: Sexual difficulty (≤2%)
Neuromuscular & skeletal: Muscle cramps (≤8%), tremor (≤8%), weakness (<3%), joint stiffness (≤2%)
Ophthalmic: Blurred vision (≤2%)
Respiratory: Cough (≤6%), nasal congestion (≤6%), wheezing (≤6%), chest congestion (≤2%), dyspnea (≤2%)
Miscellaneous: Fever (≤2%), inflammation (≤2%)

<1%, postmarketing, and/or case reports: Acute generalized exanthematous pustulosis, agranulocytosis, alopecia, altered sense of smell, anemia, aplastic anemia, angina pectoris, angioedema, arthritis (with positive ANA), bezoar formation, cardiac arrhythmia, cerebral ischemia, depression, dysgeusia, epistaxis, extrapyramidal reaction, erectile dysfunction, erythema multiforme, erythromelalgia, exfoliative dermatitis, facial edema, gastroesophageal reflux disease, gastrointestinal obstruction, gastrointestinal ulcer, gynecomastia, hematuria, hepatitis (allergic), ischemia, leukopenia, malignant neoplasm of lip (Friedman 2012), memory impairment, migraine, myalgia, myoclonus, nocturia, paranoia, parotitis, periorbital edema, polyuria, purpura, skin photosensitivity, Stevens-Johnson syndrome, syncope, tachycardia, thrombocytopenia, tinnitus, toxic epidermal necrolysis, transient blindness, ventricular arrhythmia

Dosing

Adult Dosage adjustments should occur at 7- to 14-day intervals to allow for adequate assessment of new dose; however, if clinically indicated, titration may be done more rapidly with appropriate monitoring; when switching from immediate-release to sustained-release formulations, use same total daily dose.

Chronic stable or vasospastic angina: Oral:
Immediate release: Initial: 10 mg 3 times daily; usual dose: 10 to 20 mg 3 times daily; coronary artery spasm may require up to 20 to 30 mg 3 to 4 times daily; single doses >30 mg and total daily doses >120 mg are rarely needed; maximum: 180 mg

daily; **Note:** Do not use for acute anginal episodes; may precipitate myocardial infarction

Extended release: Initial: 30 or 60 mg once daily; titrate as clinically indicated. Doses >90 mg daily should be used with caution and only if necessary (maximum: 120 mg daily)

Hypertension: Oral: Extended release: Initial: 30 or 60 mg once daily; usual dosage range (ASH/ISH [Weber 2014]): 30 to 90 mg daily; maximum: 90 to 120 mg daily

Hypertension emergency in pregnancy (systolic BP ≥160 mm Hg or diastolic BP ≥110 mm Hg) (off-label dose): Oral: Immediate release: 10 mg; may repeat with a 20 mg dose in 20 minutes if needed. Also refer to administration protocols developed by the American College of Obstetricians and Gynecologists (ACOG 2015).

High altitude pulmonary edema (off-label use; Luks 2010): Oral:

Prevention: Extended release: 30 mg every 12 hours starting the day before ascent and may be discontinued after staying at the same elevation for 5 days or if descent initiated

Treatment: Extended release: 30 mg every 12 hours

Pulmonary hypertension (off-label use): Oral: Extended release: Initial: 30 mg twice daily; may increase cautiously to 120 to 240 mg daily (ESC [Galie 2004])

Raynaud's phenomenon (off-label use): Oral:

Extended release: Dosage range: 30 to 120 mg once daily (Thompson 2005; Wigley 2002)

Immediate release: 10 to 30 mg 3 times daily (Thompson 2005; Wigley 2002)

Ureteral calculi (distal) (off-label use): Oral: 10 to 30 mg 3 times daily for up to 4 weeks or until expulsion of lower stones (Ye 2011; Zhang 2009)

Geriatric Refer to adult dosing. In the management of hypertension, consider lower initial doses and titrate to response (Aronow, 2011).

Pediatric

High altitude pulmonary edema (off-label use; Pollard, 2001): Oral: **Note:** Treatment with NIFEdipine is only necessary if response to oxygen and/or descent is unsatisfactory; extended release preparation is preferred, but with proper dose and frequency adjustment:

Immediate release: 0.5 mg/kg/dose (maximum: 20 mg/dose) every 8 hours

Hypertension (off-label use): Oral: Children 1 to 17 years: Extended release tablet: Initial: 0.2 to 0.5 mg/kg/day once daily or in 2 divided doses; maximum: 3 mg/kg/day up to 120 mg daily

Renal Impairment There are no dosage adjustments provided in manufacturer's labeling (has not been studied); the pharmacokinetics of nifedipine are not significantly influenced by the degree of renal impairment (only trace amounts of unchanged drug are found in urine).

Hemodialysis: Supplemental dose is not necessary.

Peritoneal dialysis effects: Supplemental dose is not necessary.

Hepatic Impairment There are no dosage adjustments provided in manufacturer's labeling (has not been studied); use with caution. Clearance of nifedipine is reduced in cirrhotic patients, which may lead to increased systemic exposure; monitor closely for adverse effects/toxicity and consider dose adjustments.

Mechanism of Action Inhibits calcium ion from entering the "slow channels" or select voltage-sensitive areas of vascular smooth muscle and myocardium during depolarization, producing a relaxation of coronary vascular smooth muscle and coronary vasodilation; increases myocardial oxygen delivery in patients with vasospastic angina; also reduces peripheral vascular resistance, producing a reduction in arterial blood pressure.

Contraindications

Hypersensitivity to nifedipine or any component of the formulation

Note: Considered contraindicated in patients with ST-elevation myocardial infarction (STEMI) (ACCF/AHA [O'Gara 2013]).

Canadian labeling: Additional contraindications (not in US labeling): Severe hypotension; cardiovascular shock; breastfeeding; pregnancy or women of child-bearing potential. **Note:** SOGC and ACOG guidelines recommend nifedipine as a preferred agent for maternal hypertension (ACOG 2013; SOGC [Magee 2014]). Extended release only: Hypersensitivity to other dihydropyridine calcium antagonists; Kock pouch (ileostomy after proctocolectomy); moderate or severe hepatic impairment; severe gastrointestinal obstructive disorders

Warnings/Precautions Symptomatic hypotension with or without syncope can rarely occur; blood pressure must be lowered at a rate appropriate for the patient's clinical condition. **The use of immediate release nifedipine (sublingually or orally) in hypertensive emergencies and urgencies is neither safe nor effective.** Serious adverse events (eg, death, cerebrovascular ischemia, syncope, stroke, acute myocardial infarction, and fetal distress) have been reported. **Immediate release nifedipine should not be used for acute blood pressure reduction.**

Blood pressure lowering should be done at a rate appropriate for the patient's condition. Rapid drops in blood pressure can lead to arterial insufficiency. Increased angina and/or MI have occurred with initiation or dosage titration of dihydropyridine calcium channel blockers; use with caution in patients with obstructive coronary disease especially in the absence of concurrent beta-blockade. In patients with unstable angina/non-STEMI, the use of immediate-release nifedipine is not recommended except with concomitant beta-blockade (ACCF/AHA [Anderson, 2013]). Use with caution before major surgery. Cardiopulmonary bypass, intraoperative blood loss or vasodilating anesthesia may result in severe hypotension and/or increased fluid requirements. Consider withdrawing nifedipine (>36 hours) before surgery if possible.

The most common side effect is peripheral edema; occurs within 2-3 weeks of starting therapy. Reflex tachycardia may occur with use. Use with caution in severe aortic stenosis (especially with concomitant beta-adrenergic blocker), severe left ventricular dysfunction, renal impairment, hypertrophic cardiomyopathy (especially obstructive), concomitant therapy with beta-blockers or digoxin, and edema. The ACCF/AHA heart failure guidelines recommend to avoid use in patients with heart failure due to lack of benefit and/or worse outcomes with calcium channel blockers in general (Yancy, 2013). Use caution in patients with severe hepatic impairment. Clearance of nifedipine is reduced in cirrhotic patients leading to increased systemic exposure; monitor closely for adverse effects/toxicity and consider dose adjustments. Mild and transient elevations in liver function enzymes may be apparent within 8 weeks of therapy initiation. Abrupt withdrawal may cause rebound angina in patients with CAD. Immediate release formulations should not be used to manage primary hypertension, adequate studies to evaluate outcomes have not been conducted. Avoid use of extended release tablets (Procardia XL) in patients with known stricture/narrowing of the GI tract. Adalat CC tablets contain lactose; do not use with galactose intolerance, Lapp lactase deficiency, or glucose-galactose malabsorption syndromes.

Potentially significant drug-drug interactions may exist, requiring dose or frequency adjustment, additional monitoring, and/or selection of alternative therapy.

Drug Interactions

Metabolism/Transport Effects Substrate of CYP2D6 (minor), CYP3A4 (major); **Note:** Assignment of Major/Minor substrate status based on clinically relevant drug interaction potential; **Inhibits** BCRP, CYP1A2 (weak), CYP2C9 (weak)

Avoid Concomitant Use

Avoid concomitant use of NIFEdipine with any of the following: Conivaptan; CYP3A4 Inducers (Strong); Fusidic Acid (Systemic); Grapefruit Juice; Idelalisib; Phenytoin; St John's Wort

Increased Effect/Toxicity

NIFEdipine may increase the levels/effects of: Amifostine; Antipsychotic Agents (Second Generation [Atypical]); Atosiban; Beta-Blockers; Calcium Channel Blockers (Nondihydropyridine); CloZAPine; CycloSPORINE (Systemic); Digoxin; DULoxetine; Hypotension-Associated Agents; Levodopa; Magnesium Salts; Neuromuscular-Blocking Agents (Nondepolarizing); Nitroprusside; Phenytoin; QuiNIDine; Tacrolimus (Systemic); TiZANidine; VinCRIStine; VinCRIStine (Liposomal)

The levels/effects of NIFEdipine may be increased by: Alcohol (Ethyl); Alfuzosin; Alpha1 Blockers; Antifungal Agents (Azole Derivatives, Systemic); Aprepitant; Barbiturates; Benperidol; Brimonidine (Topical); Calcium Channel Blockers (Nondihydropyridine); Cimetidine; Cisapride; Conivaptan; CycloSPORINE (Systemic); CYP3A4 Inhibitors (Moderate); CYP3A4 Inhibitors (Strong); Dapoxetine; Dasatinib; Diazoxide; Fluconazole; FLUoxetine; Fosaprepitant; Fusidic Acid (Systemic); Grapefruit Juice; Herbs (Hypotensive Properties); Idelalisib; Ivacaftor; Lormetazepam; Macrolide Antibiotics; Magnesium Salts; MiFEPRIStone; Molsidomine; Naftopidil; Netupitant; Nicergoline; Nicorandil; Obinutuzumab; Palbociclib; Pentoxifylline; Phosphodiesterase 5 Inhibitors; Prostacyclin Analogues; Quinagolide; QuiNIDine; Simeprevir; Stiripentol

Decreased Effect

NIFEdipine may decrease the levels/effects of: Clopidogrel; QuiNIDine

The levels/effects of NIFEdipine may be decreased by: Amphetamines; Barbiturates; Bosentan; Calcium Salts; CYP3A4 Inducers (Moderate); CYP3A4 Inducers (Strong); Dabrafenib; Deferasirox; Efavirenz; Herbs (Hypertensive Properties); Melatonin; Methylphenidate; Nafcillin; Phenytoin; Siltuximab; St John's Wort; Tocilizumab; Yohimbine

Food Interactions Nifedipine serum levels may be decreased if taken with food. Food may decrease the rate but not the extent of absorption of Procardia XL®. Increased nifedipine concentrations resulting in therapeutic and vasodilator side effects, including severe hypotension and myocardial ischemia, may occur if nifedipine is taken by patients ingesting grapefruit. Management: Avoid grapefruit/grapefruit juice.

Dietary Considerations Avoid grapefruit juice with all products.

Immediate release: Capsule is rapidly absorbed orally if it is administered without food, but may result in vasodilator side effects; if flushing is problematic, administration with low-fat meals may decrease. In general, can take with or without food.

Extended release: Adalat CC, Afeditab CR, Nifediac CC: Take on an empty stomach (manufacturer's labeling). Other extended release products may not have this recommendation; consult product labeling.

Pharmacodynamics/Kinetics

Onset of Action Immediate release: ~20 minutes

Half-life Elimination Adults: Healthy: 2 to 5 hours; Cirrhosis: 7 hours; Elderly: 7 hours (extended release tablet)

Pregnancy Risk Factor C

Pregnancy Considerations

Adverse events were observed in animal reproduction studies. Nifedipine crosses the placenta and small amounts can be detected in the urine of newborn infants (Manninen 1991; Silberschmidt 2008). An increase in perinatal asphyxia, cesarean delivery, prematurity, and intrauterine growth retardation have been reported following maternal use. Untreated chronic maternal hypertension is also associated with adverse events in the fetus, infant, and mother. If treatment for chronic hypertension during pregnancy is needed, nifedipine is one of the preferred agents (ACOG 2013; SOGC [Magee 2014]). Nifedipine is also recommended for the management of acute onset, severe hypertension (systolic BP ≥160 mm Hg or diastolic BP ≥110 mm Hg) with preeclampsia or eclampsia in pregnant and postpartum women (ACOG 2015; Magee 2014).

Nifedipine has also been evaluated for the treatment of preterm labor. Tocolytics may be used for the short-term (48 hour) prolongation of pregnancy to allow for the administration of antenatal steroids and should not be used prior to fetal viability or when the risks of use to the fetus or mother are greater than the risk of preterm birth (ACOG 171 2016). Nifedipine is ineffective for maintenance tocolytic therapy (ACOG 171 2016; Roos 2013).

Breastfeeding Considerations Nifedipine is excreted into breast milk.

The relative infant dose (RID) of nifedipine is 0.27% to 3.2% when calculated using the highest breast milk concentration located and compared to an infant therapeutic dose of 0.25 to 3 mg/kg/day. In general, breastfeeding is considered acceptable when the RID is <10%; when an RID is >25% breastfeeding should generally be avoided (Anderson 2016; Ito 2000). Using the highest milk concentration (53.35 ng/mL), the estimated daily infant dose via breast milk is 8 mcg/kg/day. This milk concentration was obtained following maternal administration of oral nifedipine 30 mg three times daily (Ehrenkrantz 1989).

Milk concentrations reached a peak within 1 hour of maternal administration of immediate release capsules (Ehrenkrantz 1989; Penny 1989). The half-life of nifedipine in breast milk has been reported to be ~3 hours (Ehrenkrantz 1989).

The use of nifedipine in breastfeeding women for the treatment of Raynaud phenomenon has been described in case reports and case series; no adverse events were noted in the infants exposed to nifedipine via breast milk (Anderson 2004; Barrett 2013; Garrison

2002; Page 2006; Wu 2012). According to the manufacturer, the decision to continue or discontinue breastfeeding during therapy should take into account the risk of infant exposure, the benefits of breastfeeding to the infant, and benefits of treatment to the mother.

The Academy of Breastfeeding Medicine recommends the use of nifedipine for the treatment of Raynaud phenomenon of the nipple in breastfeeding mothers (Berens 2016).

Dosage Forms

Capsule, Oral:
- Procardia: 10 mg
- Generic: 10 mg, 20 mg

Tablet Extended Release 24 Hour, Oral:
- Adalat CC: 30 mg, 60 mg, 90 mg
- Afeditab CR: 30 mg, 60 mg
- Procardia XL: 30 mg, 60 mg, 90 mg
- Generic: 30 mg, 60 mg, 90 mg

Nilotinib (nye LOE ti nib)

Related Information

Clinical Risk Related to Drugs Prolonging QT Interval *on page 1772*

Brand Names: US Tasigna

Brand Names: Canada Tasigna

Pharmacologic Category Antineoplastic Agent, BCR-ABL Tyrosine Kinase Inhibitor; Antineoplastic Agent, Tyrosine Kinase Inhibitor

Use Chronic myelogenous leukemia:

Treatment of adults with newly diagnosed Philadelphia chromosome-positive chronic myelogenous leukemia (CML) in chronic phase.

Treatment of chronic- and accelerated-phase Philadelphia chromosome-positive CML in adults resistant or intolerant to prior therapy that included imatinib.

Local Anesthetic/Vasoconstrictor Precautions Nilotinib is one of the drugs confirmed to prolong the QT interval and is accepted as having a risk of causing torsade de pointes. The risk of drug-induced torsade de pointes is extremely low when a single QT interval prolonging drug is prescribed. In terms of epinephrine, it is not known what effect vasoconstrictors in the local anesthetic regimen will have in patients with a known history of congenital prolonged QT interval or in patients taking any medication that prolongs the QT interval. Until more information is obtained, it is suggested that the clinician consult with the physician prior to the use of a vasoconstrictor in suspected patients, and that the vasoconstrictor (epinephrine, mepivacaine and levonordefrin [Carbocaine® 2% with Neo-Cobefrin®]) be used with caution.

Effects on Dental Treatment Key adverse event(s) related to dental treatment: Mouth ulcerations, stomatitis

Effects on Bleeding Chemotherapy may result in significant myelosuppression. Thrombocytopenia (grades 3/4) occurs in 10% to 37% of patients (median duration 22 days). In patients who are under active treatment with these agents, medical consult is suggested.

Adverse Reactions

>10%:

Cardiovascular: Peripheral edema (≤15%; grade 3/4: <1%), hypertension (10% to 11%)

Central nervous system: Headache (20% to 35%), fatigue (21% to 32%), insomnia (7% to 12%), dizziness (≤12%)

Dermatologic: Skin rash (≤38%; grades 3/4: ≤2%), pruritus (20% to 32%), night sweats (12% to 27%), alopecia (11% to 13%), xeroderma (>5% to 12%)

Endocrine & metabolic: Increased serum glucose (50%), hyperglycemia (≤50%; grades 3/4: 7% to 12%), increased serum cholesterol (28%), hypophosphatemia (≥10%; grades 3/4: 5% to 17%)

Gastrointestinal: Nausea (20% to 37%), vomiting (11% to 29%), diarrhea (14% to 28%), increased serum lipase (28%; grades 3/4: 9% to 18%), constipation (17% to 26%), upper abdominal pain (12% to 18%; grades 3/4: <1%), abdominal pain (15% to 16%), decreased appetite (including anorexia; 15%)

Hematologic & oncologic: Neutropenia (grades 3/4: 12% to 42%; median duration: 15 days), thrombocytopenia (grades 3/4: 10% to 42%; median duration: 22 days), anemia (grades 3/4: 4% to 27%)

Hepatic: Hepatic: Increased serum ALT (10% to 72%; grades 3/4: 4%), increased serum AST (10% to 47%; grades 3/4: 1% to 3%), hyperbilirubinemia (≥10%; grades 3/4: 4% to 9%), increased serum ALT (≥10%; grades 3/4: 4%), increased serum AST (≥10%; grades 3/4: 1% to 3%)

Infection: Influenza (≤13%)

Neuromuscular & skeletal: Arthralgia (16% to 26%), limb pain (11% to 20%), back pain (15% to 19%), myalgia (14% to 19%), weakness (11% to 16%), ostealgia (14% to 15%), muscle spasm (11% to 15%), musculoskeletal pain (11% to 12%)

Respiratory: Cough (14% to 27%), nasopharyngitis (≤27%), upper respiratory tract infection (≤17%), dyspnea (9% to 15%; exertional), oropharyngeal pain (≤12%), flu-like symptoms (11%)

Miscellaneous: Fever (11% to 28%)

1% to 10%:

Cardiovascular: Ischemic heart disease (5% to 9%), peripheral arterial disease (3% to 4%), cerebral ischemia (1% to 3%), pericardial effusion (≤2%; grades 3/4: ≤1%), angina pectoris, cardiac arrhythmia (including AV block, atrial fibrillation, bradycardia, cardiac flutter, extrasystoles, and tachycardia), chest discomfort, chest pain (including noncardiac), flushing, palpitations, prolonged Q-T interval on ECG

Central nervous system: Anxiety, depression, flank pain, hypoesthesia, malaise, myasthenia, pain, paresthesia, peripheral neuropathy, vertigo, voice disorder

Dermatologic: Acne vulgaris, dermatitis (including allergic and acneiform), eczema, erythema, folliculitis, hyperhidrosis, urticaria

Endocrine & metabolic: Hypokalemia (grades 3/4: ≤9%), hyponatremia (grades 3/4: ≤7%), hyperkalemia (grades 3/4: 2% to 6%), hypocalcemia (grades 3/4: ≤5%), decreased serum albumin (grades 3/4: ≤4%), fluid retention (grades 3/4: 3% to 4%), diabetes mellitus, hypercalcemia, hypercholesterolemia, hyperlipidemia, hyperphosphatemia, hypertriglyceridemia, hypomagnesemia, increased gamma-glutamyl transferase, increased HDL cholesterol, increased VLDL, weight gain, weight loss

Gastrointestinal: Dyspepsia (4% to 10%), gastrointestinal hemorrhage (≤5%), abdominal distension, abdominal distress, dysgeusia, flatulence, increased serum amylase, pancreatitis

Genitourinary: Pollakiuria

Hematologic & oncologic: Hemorrhage (grades 3/4: 1% to 2%), bruise, cutaneous papilloma, decreased hemoglobin, eosinophilia, febrile neutropenia, hemophthalmos, leukopenia, lymphocytopenia, pancytopenia

Hepatic: Ascites (≤2%; grades 3/4: ≤1%), increased serum alkaline phosphatase (grades 3/4: ≤1%), hepatic insufficiency
Immunologic: Change in serum protein (decreased globulins)
Neuromuscular & skeletal: Increased creatine phosphokinase, neck pain
Ophthalmic: Eyelid edema (1%), conjunctivitis, eye pruritus, periorbital edema, xerophthalmia
Respiratory: Pleural effusion (≤2%; grades 3/4: ≤1%), pulmonary edema (≤2%; grades 3/4: ≤1%), epistaxis

Frequency not defined:
Cardiovascular: Hypotension, occlusive arterial disease (basilar, peripheral), pericarditis, reduced ejection fraction, shock (hemorrhagic), thrombosis, ventricular dysfunction
Central nervous system: Amnesia, breast induration, cerebral edema, confusion, disorientation, dysesthesia, dysphoria, lethargy, restless leg syndrome
Dermatologic: Dermal ulcer, erythema multiforme, erythema nodosum, exfoliative dermatitis, furuncle, hyperkeratosis, palmar-plantar erythrodysesthesia, psoriasis, skin atrophy, skin blister, skin discoloration, skin hyperpigmentation, skin hypertrophy, skin photosensitivity, tinea pedis
Endocrine & metabolic: Altered hormone level (insulin C-peptide decreased), hypermenorrhea, hyperparathyroidism (secondary), hyperuricemia, hypoglycemia, thyroiditis
Gastrointestinal: Cholestasis, enterocolitis, gastric ulcer (perforation possible), gingivitis, hematemesis, hemorrhoids, hiatal hernia, intestinal obstruction, oral lesion (papilloma), rectal hemorrhage, ulcerative esophagitis
Genitourinary: Hematuria, urinary incontinence, urine discoloration
Hematologic & oncologic: Increased parathyroid hormone, leukocytosis, paraproteinemia, petechiae, retroperitoneal hemorrhage, thrombocythemia
Hepatic: Hepatomegaly
Hypersensitivity: Hypersensitivity
Infection: Abscess, reactivation of HBV, sepsis
Local: Local swelling (nipple), localized edema
Neuromuscular & Skeletal: Arthritis
Ophthalmic: Blepharitis, diplopia, eye pain, optic neuritis, papilledema, photophobia, retinopathy (central serous chorioretinopathy), swelling of eye
Otic: Auditory impairment, otalgia, tinnitus
Renal: Renal failure
Respiratory: Pulmonary hypertension, wheezing
Miscellaneous: Benign nodule (sebaceous hyperplasia), cyst (dermal), troponin increased

<1%, postmarketing, and/or case reports: Allergic skin reaction, arteriosclerosis, ascorbic acid deficiency (Oak 2016), blurred vision, bronchitis, candidiasis, cardiac failure, cardiomegaly, cerebral infarction, chills, conjunctival hemorrhage, coronary artery disease, cyanosis, decreased visual acuity, dehydration, dysuria, ecchymoses, erectile dysfunction, esophageal pain, eye irritation, facial edema, gastritis, gastroenteritis, gastroesophageal reflux disease, gout, gynecomastia, heart murmur, hematoma, hepatitis, hepatotoxicity, herpes simplex infection, hyperemia (scleral, conjunctival, ocular), hyperesthesia, hypertensive crisis, hyperthyroidism, hypothyroidism, increased appetite, increased blood urea nitrogen, increased lactate dehydrogenase, increased serum creatinine, interstitial pulmonary disease, intracranial hemorrhage, jaundice, joint swelling, lack of concentration, local alterations in temperature sensations, local discomfort (sensitive teeth), loss of consciousness, mastalgia, melena, mesenteric artery occlusion, migraine, myocardial infarction, nocturia, nonhemorrhagic stroke, occlusive arterial disease (coronary), oral mucosa ulcer, pharyngolaryngeal pain, photopsia, pleurisy, pleuritic chest pain, pneumonia, sinusitis, skin pain, stiffness, stomatitis, syncope, throat irritation, transient ischemic attacks, tremor, tumor lysis syndrome, urinary tract infection, urinary urgency, xerostomia

General Dosage Range Dosage adjustment recommended in patients with hepatic impairment, on concomitant therapy, or who develop toxicities

Oral: *Adults:* 300 to 400 mg twice daily

Mechanism of Action Selective tyrosine kinase inhibitor that targets BCR-ABL kinase, c-KIT and platelet derived growth factor receptor (PDGFR); does not have activity against the SRC family. Inhibits BCR-ABL mediated proliferation of leukemic cell lines by binding to the ATP-binding site of BCR-ABL and inhibiting tyrosine kinase activity. Nilotinib has activity in imatinib-resistant BCR-ABL kinase mutations.

Pharmacodynamics/Kinetics

Half-life Elimination ~15 to 17 hours

Time to Peak 3 hours

Pregnancy Risk Factor D

Pregnancy Considerations Adverse effects were observed in animal reproduction studies. May cause fetal harm if administered during pregnancy. Women of childbearing potential should be advised to use effective contraception during treatment.

Dental Comment See Local Anesthetic/Vasoconstrictor Precautions

Nilutamide (ni LOO ta mide)

Brand Names: US Nilandron

Brand Names: Canada Anandron

Pharmacologic Category Antineoplastic Agent, Antiandrogen

Use Prostate cancer, metastatic: Treatment of metastatic prostate cancer (in combination with surgical castration)

Local Anesthetic/Vasoconstrictor Precautions No information available to require special precautions

Effects on Dental Treatment Key adverse event(s) related to dental treatment: Xerostomia (normal salivary flow resumes upon discontinuation).

Effects on Bleeding Although significant myelosuppression with associated altered hemostasis has been reported for many chemotherapeutic agents, myelosuppression is not common with nilutamide and no specific precautions appear to necessary.

Adverse Reactions Reactions reported from monotherapy and combination therapy.

>10%:
Endocrine & metabolic: Hot flash (28%)
Ophthalmic: Nocturnal amblyopia (13% to 57%)

1% to 10%:
Cardiovascular: Hypertension (5%), cardiac failure (3%), angina pectoris (2%), edema (2%), syncope (2%)
Central nervous system: Dizziness (7%), paresthesia (3%), malaise (2%), nervousness (2%)
Dermatologic: Pruritus (2%)
Endocrine & metabolic: Hyperglycemia (4%), increased haptoglobin (2%), weight loss (2%)

Gastrointestinal: Nausea (10%), constipation (7%), diarrhea (2%), gastrointestinal hemorrhage (2%), melena (2%), xerostomia (2%)
Hematologic & oncologic: Leukopenia (3%)
Hepatic: Increased serum ALT (8%), increased serum AST (8%), increased serum alkaline phosphatase (3%)
Neuromuscular & skeletal: Arthritis (2%)
Ophthalmic: Visual disturbance (7%), cataract (2%), photophobia (2%)
Renal: Increased blood urea nitrogen (2%), increased serum creatinine (2%)
Respiratory: Dyspnea (6%), cough (2%), interstitial pneumonitis (2%), rhinitis (2%)
Miscellaneous: Alcohol intolerance (5%)

<1%, postmarketing, and/or case reports: Anxiety, aplastic anemia, cold extremities, gynecomastia, headache, hepatic injury, hepatitis, maculopapular rash, palpitations, prolonged Q-T interval on ECG, urticaria, vomiting, weight gain

General Dosage Range Oral: *Adults:* Initial: 300 mg once daily for 30 days; Maintenance: 150 mg once daily

Mechanism of Action Nilutamide is a nonsteroidal antiandrogen which blocks testosterone effects at the androgen receptor level, preventing androgen response.

Pharmacodynamics/Kinetics

Half-life Elimination Terminal: 38 to 59 hours; Metabolites: 59 to 126 hours

Pregnancy Considerations Animal reproduction studies have not been conducted. Nilutamide is not indicated for use in women.

NiMODipine (nye MOE di peen)

Related Information

Calcium Channel Blockers and Gingival Hyperplasia *on page 1908*

Brand Names: US Nymalize

Brand Names: Canada Nimotop

Pharmacologic Category Calcium Channel Blocker; Calcium Channel Blocker, Dihydropyridine

Use Subarachnoid hemorrhage: For the improvement of neurological outcome by reducing the incidence and severity of ischemic deficits in adult patients with subarachnoid hemorrhage (SAH) from ruptured intracranial berry aneurysms regardless of their postictus neurological condition (ie, Hunt and Hess grades I to V)

Local Anesthetic/Vasoconstrictor Precautions No information available to require special precautions

Effects on Dental Treatment Other drugs of this class can cause gingival hyperplasia (ie, nifedipine) but there have been no reports for nimodipine.

Effects on Bleeding No information available to require special precautions

Adverse Reactions

1% to 10%:
Cardiovascular: Decreased blood pressure (4% to 5%), bradycardia (1%)
Central nervous system: Headache (1%)
Gastrointestinal: Nausea (1%)

<1%, postmarketing, and/or case reports: Anemia, decreased platelet count, diaphoresis, disseminated intravascular coagulation, dizziness, edema, flushing, gastrointestinal hemorrhage, gastrointestinal pseudo-obstruction, hematoma, hepatitis, hypertension, increased lactate dehydrogenase, increased serum alkaline phosphatase, increased serum ALT, increased serum glucose, intestinal obstruction, jaundice, muscle cramps, palpitations, pruritus, rebound vasospasm, thrombocytopenia, vomiting, wheezing

General Dosage Range Dosage adjustment recommended in patients with hepatic impairment

Oral: *Adults:* 60 mg every 4 hours

Mechanism of Action Nimodipine shares the pharmacology of other calcium channel blockers; animal studies indicate that nimodipine has a greater effect on cerebral arterials than other arterials; this increased specificity may be due to the drug's increased lipophilicity and cerebral distribution as compared to nifedipine; inhibits calcium ion from entering the "slow channels" or select voltage sensitive areas of vascular smooth muscle and myocardium during depolarization

Pharmacodynamics/Kinetics

Half-life Elimination 1 to 2 hours; prolonged with renal impairment

Time to Peak Serum: ~1 hour

Pregnancy Risk Factor C

Pregnancy Considerations Adverse events have been observed in animal reproduction studies. Nimodipine crosses the placenta (Belfort, 1994). Nimodipine has been evaluated for the management of pre-eclampsia (Belfort, 1994; Belfort, 2003), but it is not one of the agents currently recommended for severe intrapartum or postpartum hypertension associated with preeclampsia or eclampsia (ACOG, 2015).

Nintedanib (nin TED a nib)

Brand Names: US Ofev

Brand Names: Canada Ofev

Pharmacologic Category Tyrosine Kinase Inhibitor

Use Idiopathic pulmonary fibrosis: Treatment of idiopathic pulmonary fibrosis (IPF).

Local Anesthetic/Vasoconstrictor Precautions Nintedanib may cause hypertension; monitor blood pressure prior to vasoconstrictor use

Effects on Dental Treatment No significant effects or complications reported

Effects on Bleeding Altered hemostasis resulting in increased risk of bleeding. Medical consult is suggested prior to any dental surgical procedures.

Adverse Reactions

>10%:
Gastrointestinal: Diarrhea (62%), nausea (24%), abdominal pain (15%; includes abdominal tenderness, gastrointestinal pain, lower abdominal pain, upper abdominal pain), vomiting (12%), decreased appetite (11%)
Hepatic: Increased liver enzymes (14%; includes abnormal alanine aminotransferase, abnormal aspartate aminotransferase, abnormal gamma-glutamyl transferase, abnormal hepatic function tests, hepatic insufficiency, increased serum ALT, increased serum AST, increased gamma-glutamyl transferase, increased serum alkaline phosphatase, increased serum transaminases)

1% to 10%:
Cardiovascular: Hypertension (5%; includes hypertensive cardiomyopathy, hypertensive crisis), arterial thrombosis (3%), myocardial infarction (2%)
Central nervous system: Headache (8%)
Endocrine & metabolic: Weight loss (10%), hypothyroidism (1%)
Hematologic and oncologic: Hemorrhage (10%)
Respiratory: Bronchitis (1%)

<1%, postmarketing, and/or case reports: Gastrointestinal perforation

General Dosage Range Dosage adjustment recommended in patients with hepatic impairment or who develop toxicity.

Oral: *Adults:* 150 mg every 12 hours (maximum: 300 mg/day)

Mechanism of Action Inhibits multiple receptor tyrosine kinases (RTKs) and nonreceptor tyrosine kinases (nRTKs), including platelet-derived growth factor (PDGFR alpha and PDGFR beta); fibroblast growth factor receptor (FGFR1, FGFR2, FGFR3); vascular endothelial growth factor (VEGFR1, VEGFR2, and VEGFR3); and Fms-like tyrosine kinase-3 (FLT3). Nintedanib binds competitively to the adenosine triphosphate (ATP) binding pocket of these receptors and blocks the intracellular signaling which is crucial for the proliferation, migration, and transformation of fibroblasts.

Pharmacodynamics/Kinetics

Half-life Elimination 9.5 hours

Time to Peak 2 hours (4 hours with food)

Pregnancy Considerations Based on the mechanism of action and adverse events observed in animal reproduction studies, nintedanib may be expected to cause fetal harm if used during pregnancy. Women of reproductive potential should use adequate contraception during therapy; pregnancy status should be obtained before treatment and pregnancy should be avoided; effective contraception should be used during therapy and for at least 3 months after the last dose. Based on animal studies, nintedanib may reduce female fertility.

Nisoldipine (nye SOL di peen)

Related Information

Calcium Channel Blockers and Gingival Hyperplasia *on page 1908*

Cardiovascular Diseases *on page 1752*

Brand Names: US Sular

Pharmacologic Category Antihypertensive; Calcium Channel Blocker; Calcium Channel Blocker, Dihydropyridine

Use

Hypertension: Management of hypertension, alone or in combination with other antihypertensive agents

The 2014 guideline for the management of high blood pressure in adults (JNC 8) recommends initiation of pharmacologic treatment to lower blood pressure for the following patients (JNC 8 [James, 2013]):

- Patients ≥60 years of age with systolic blood pressure (SBP) ≥150 mm Hg or diastolic blood pressure (DBP) ≥90 mm Hg. Goal of therapy is SBP <150 mm Hg and DBP <90 mm Hg.
- Patients <60 years of age with SBP ≥140 mm Hg or DBP ≥90 mm Hg. Goal of therapy is SBP <140 mm Hg and DBP <90 mm Hg.
- Patients ≥18 years of age with diabetes with SBP ≥140 mm Hg or DBP ≥90 mm Hg. Goal of therapy is SBP <140 mm Hg and DBP <90 mm Hg.
- Patients ≥18 years of age with chronic kidney disease (CKD) with SBP ≥140 mm Hg or DBP ≥90 mm Hg. Goal of therapy is SBP <140 mm Hg and DBP <90 mm Hg.

In patients with chronic kidney disease (CKD), regardless of race or diabetes status, the use of an ACE inhibitor (ACEI) or angiotensin receptor blocker (ARB) as initial therapy is recommended to improve kidney outcomes. In the general nonblack population (without CKD) including those with diabetes, initial antihypertensive treatment should consist of a thiazide-type diuretic, calcium channel blocker, ACEI, or ARB. In the general black population (without CKD) including those with diabetes, initial antihypertensive treatment should consist of a thiazide-type diuretic or a calcium channel blocker instead of an ACEI or ARB.

Local Anesthetic/Vasoconstrictor Precautions No information available to require special precautions

Effects on Dental Treatment Key adverse event(s) related to dental treatment: Xerostomia (normal salivary flow resumes upon discontinuation).

Unlike other calcium channel blockers, information is sparse as to whether nisoldipine causes gingival hyperplasia. Consultation with physician is suggested if hyperplasia is observed in patients taking nisoldipine.

Effects on Bleeding No information available to require special precautions

Adverse Reactions

>10%:

Cardiovascular: Peripheral edema (7% to 29%; dose-related)

Central nervous system: Headache (22%)

1% to 10%:

Cardiovascular: Vasodilatation (4%), palpitations (3%), exacerbation of angina pectoris (2%), chest pain (2%)

Central nervous system: Dizziness (3% to 10%)

Dermatologic: Skin rash (2%)

Gastrointestinal: Nausea (2%)

Respiratory: Pharyngitis (5%), sinusitis (3%)

<1%, postmarketing, and/or case reports: Abnormal dreams, abnormal hepatic function tests, abnormal T waves on ECG (flattening, inversion, non-specific changes), alopecia, amblyopia, amnesia, anemia, anorexia, anxiety, arthralgia, arthritis, asthma, ataxia, atrial fibrillation, blepharitis, bruise, cardiac failure (decompensated), cellulitis, cerebral ischemia, cerebrovascular accident, colitis, conjunctivitis, decreased libido, depression, dermal ulcer, diabetes mellitus, diaphoresis, diarrhea, drowsiness, dysgeusia, dyspepsia, dysphagia, dyspnea, dysuria, ejection murmur (systolic), epistaxis, exfoliative dermatitis, facial edema, fever, first degree atrioventricular block, flu-like symptoms, gastritis, gastrointestinal hemorrhage, gingival hyperplasia, glaucoma, glossitis, gout, gynecomastia, hematuria, hepatomegaly, herpes simplex infection, herpes zoster, hypersensitivity reaction (eg, angioedema, chest tightness, hypotension, shortness of breath, skin rash, tachycardia), hypertension, hypertonia, hypoesthesia, hypokalemia, hypotension, increased appetite, increased blood urea nitrogen, increased creatine phosphokinase, increased nonprotein nitrogen, increased serum creatinine, insomnia, jugular vein distention, keratoconjunctivitis, leukopenia, maculopapular rash, malaise, melena, migraine, myalgia, myasthenia, myocardial infarction, myositis, nocturia, oral mucosa ulcer, orthostatic hypotension, paresthesia, petechia, pleural effusion, pruritus, pustular rash, rales, retinal detachment, skin discoloration, skin photosensitivity, supraventricular tachycardia, syncope, tenosynovitis, thyroiditis, tremor, urinary frequency, urticaria, vaginal hemorrhage, venous insufficiency, ventricular premature contractions, vertigo, vision loss (temporary, unilateral), vitreous opacity, weight changes (gain/loss), wheezing (end inspiratory wheeze), xerostomia

General Dosage Range Dosage adjustment recommended in patients with hepatic impairment

Oral:

Adults:

Sular (Geomatrix delivery system): Initial: 17 mg once daily; Maintenance: 17-34 mg once daily (maximum: 34 mg/day)

Nisoldipine extended-release (original formulation): Initial: 20 mg once daily; Maintenance: 10-40 mg once daily (maximum: 60 mg/day)

Elderly: Sular (Geomatrix delivery system): Initial: 8.5 mg once daily; Nisoldipine extended-release (original formulation): Initial: 10 mg once daily

Mechanism of Action As a dihydropyridine calcium channel blocker, structurally similar to nifedipine, nisoldipine impedes the movement of calcium ions into vascular smooth muscle and cardiac muscle. Dihydropyridines are potent vasodilators and are not as likely to suppress cardiac contractility and slow cardiac conduction as other calcium antagonists such as verapamil and diltiazem; nisoldipine is 5-10 times as potent a vasodilator as nifedipine.

Pharmacodynamics/Kinetics

Duration of Action >24 hours

Half-life Elimination 9-18 hours

Time to Peak 4-14 hours

Pregnancy Risk Factor C

Pregnancy Considerations Adverse events were not observed in animal reproduction studies when using doses that were not maternally toxic. Untreated chronic maternal hypertension is associated with adverse events in the fetus, infant, and mother. If treatment for hypertension during pregnancy is needed, other agents are preferred (ACOG, 2013).

Nitazoxanide (nye ta ZOX a nide)

Brand Names: US Alinia

Pharmacologic Category Antiprotozoal

Use Diarrhea, infectious: Treatment of diarrhea caused by *Cryptosporidium parvum* or *Giardia lamblia*

Local Anesthetic/Vasoconstrictor Precautions No information available to require special precautions

Effects on Dental Treatment No significant effects or complications reported

Effects on Bleeding No information available to require special precautions

Adverse Reactions

1% to 10%:

Central nervous system: Headache (>2%)

Gastrointestinal: Abdominal pain (>2%), nausea (>2%)

Genitourinary: Urine discoloration (>2%)

<1%, postmarketing, and/or case reports: Diarrhea (exacerbation), dizziness, dyspnea, gastroesophageal reflux disease, skin rash, urticaria

General Dosage Range Oral:

Children 1 to 3 years: 100 mg every 12 hours (oral suspension)

Children 4 to 11 years: 200 mg every 12 hours (oral suspension)

Children ≥12 years, Adolescents, and Adults: 500 mg every 12 hours (oral suspension or tablets)

Mechanism of Action Nitazoxanide is rapidly metabolized to the active metabolite tizoxanide *in vivo*. Activity may be due to interference with the pyruvate:ferredoxin oxidoreductase (PFOR) enzyme-dependent electron transfer reaction which is essential to anaerobic metabolism. *In vitro*, nitazoxanide and tizoxanide inhibit the growth of sporozoites and oocysts of *Cryptosporidium parvum* and trophozoites of *Giardia lamblia*.

Pharmacodynamics/Kinetics

Half-life Elimination

Tizoxanide: 1 to 1.6 hours

Time to Peak Plasma: Tizoxanide and tizoxanide glucuronide: 1-4 hours

Pregnancy Considerations Adverse events have not been observed in animal reproduction studies. Human data is not available; however, nitazoxanide may be used during pregnancy after the first trimester in women with severe symptoms of cryptosporidiosis (HHS [opportunistic; adult] 2015).

Nitisinone (ni TIS i known)

Brand Names: US Orfadin

Pharmacologic Category 4-Hydroxyphenylpyruvate Dioxygenase Inhibitor

Use Hereditary tyrosinemia type 1: Treatment of hereditary tyrosinemia type 1 (HT-1) as an adjunct to dietary restriction of tyrosine and phenylalanine

Local Anesthetic/Vasoconstrictor Precautions No information available to require special precautions

Effects on Dental Treatment No significant effects or complications reported

Effects on Bleeding Thrombocytopenia occurs in about 3% of patients and may be due to underlying liver disease.

Adverse Reactions

>10%:

Endocrine & metabolic: Increased plasma tyrosine

1% to 10%:

Dermatologic: Alopecia (1%), exfoliative dermatitis (1%), maculopapular rash (1%), pruritus (1%), xeroderma (1%)

Endocrine & metabolic: Porphyria (1%)

Hematologic & oncologic: Leukopenia (3%), thrombocytopenia (3%), granulocytopenia (1%)

Hepatic: Hepatic failure (7%), hepatic neoplasm (malignant: 5%; benign: 3%)

Ophthalmic: Conjunctivitis (2%), corneal opacity (2%), keratitis (2%), photophobia (2%), blepharitis (1%), cataract (1%), eye pain (1%)

Respiratory: Epistaxis (1%)

<1%, postmarketing, and/or case reports: Abdominal pain, brain disease, brain neoplasm, bronchitis, corneal ulcer, cyanosis, diarrhea, enanthema, gastric distress, gastrointestinal hemorrhage, headache, hepatomegaly, hyperkinesia, hypoglycemia, increased liver enzymes, melena, seizure, septicemia

General Dosage Range Oral: *Infants, Children, Adolescents, and Adults:* Initial: 1 mg/kg once daily; maximum: 2 mg/kg once daily

Mechanism of Action In patients with HT-1, tyrosine metabolism is interrupted due to a lack of the enzyme (fumarylacetoacetate hydrolase) needed in the last step of tyrosine degradation. Toxic metabolites of tyrosine accumulate and cause liver and kidney toxicity. Nitisinone competitively inhibits 4-hydroxyphenyl-pyruvate dioxygenase, an enzyme present early in the tyrosine degradation pathway, thereby preventing the build-up of the toxic metabolites.

Pharmacodynamics/Kinetics

Half-life Elimination Healthy volunteers: Terminal half-life: 54 hours

Time to Peak Healthy volunteers: Capsule: ~3.5 hours (range, 0.75 to 8 hours); Suspension: 0.38 hours (range, 0.25 to 4 hours)

Pregnancy Considerations Adverse events have been observed in animal reproduction studies.

Product Availability Orfadin 4 mg/mL oral suspension: FDA approved April 2016; anticipated availability is currently unknown. Information pertaining to this product within the monograph is pending revision. Consult the prescribing information for additional information.

Prescribing and Access Restrictions Distributed by Orfadin4U comprehensive patient support program. Information regarding acquisition of product may be obtained by calling 877-473-3179. Additional information can be found at http://www.orfadin.com

Nitrazepam (nye TRA ze pam)

Brand Names: Canada Apo-Nitrazepam; Mogadon; Sandoz-Nitrazepam

Pharmacologic Category Benzodiazepine

Use Note: Not approved in the US

Insomnia: Short-term treatment and symptomatic relief of insomnia characterized by difficulty in falling asleep, frequent nocturnal awakenings, and/or early morning awakenings

Limitations of use: Restrict use to insomnia that impairs normal daytime functioning. Treatment should typically not exceed 7 to 10 consecutive days. Reevaluation of the patient is required if treatment continues for >2 to 3 consecutive weeks. Prescriptions should be written for short-term use (7 to 10 days) and limited to ≤1 month supply.

Seizures: Management of myoclonic seizures

Local Anesthetic/Vasoconstrictor Precautions No information available to require special precautions.

Effects on Dental Treatment Key adverse event(s) related to dental treatment. Excessive salivation has been reported. The mechanism of this effect is unknown, since many benzodiazepines cause xerostomia rather than salivation excess.

Effects on Bleeding No information available to require special precautions

Adverse Reactions Frequency not defined.

Cardiovascular: Hypotension, palpitations

Central nervous system: Aggressive behavior, agitation, amnesia, ataxia, confusion, delusions, depression, disorientation, dizziness, excitement, falling, fatigue, hallucination, hangover effect, headache, hyperactivity, irritability, lethargy, myasthenia, nervousness, nightmares, outbursts of anger, psychosis, restlessness, sedation, staggering, withdrawal syndrome (chronic use)

Dermatologic: Dermatological reaction

Endocrine & metabolic: Change in libido

Gastrointestinal: Constipation, diarrhea, heartburn, nausea, sialorrhea, vomiting

Hematologic & oncologic: Granulocytopenia, leukopenia

Hepatic: Abnormal hepatic function tests

Hypersensitivity: Anaphylaxis (or anaphylactoid reaction; angioedema, dyspnea, nausea, pharyngeal edema, vomiting)

Neuromuscular & skeletal: Muscle spasticity

Ophthalmic: Blurred vision

Respiratory: Aspiration, dyspnea, increased bronchial secretions

General Dosage Range Oral:

Infants and Children ≤30 kg: 0.3 to 1 mg/kg/day in 3 divided doses

Adults: 5 to 10 mg once daily

Elderly and debilitated patients: 2.5 to 5 mg once daily

Mechanism of Action Binds to stereospecific benzodiazepine receptors on the postsynaptic GABA neuron at several sites within the CNS, including the limbic system, reticular formation. Enhancement of the inhibitory effect of GABA on neuronal excitability results by increased neuronal membrane permeability to chloride ions. This shift in chloride ions results in hyperpolarization (a less excitable state) and stabilization. Benzodiazepine receptors and effects appear to be linked to the GABA-A receptors. Benzodiazepines do not bind to GABA-B receptors.

Pharmacodynamics/Kinetics

Onset of Action 20 to 50 minutes

Half-life Elimination 30 hours (range: 18 to 57 hours), Elderly/ill patients: 40 hours

Time to Peak ~3 hours

Pregnancy Considerations Use during pregnancy is not recommended. Nitrazepam crosses the human placenta. Teratogenic effects have been observed with some benzodiazepines; however, additional studies are needed. The incidence of premature birth and low birth weights may be increased following maternal use of benzodiazepines; hypoglycemia and respiratory problems in the neonate may occur following exposure late in pregnancy. Neonatal withdrawal symptoms may occur within days to weeks after birth and "floppy infant syndrome" (which also includes withdrawal symptoms) have been reported with some benzodiazepines (Bergman, 1992; Iqbal, 2002; Wikner, 2007).

Product Availability Not available in the US

Controlled Substance CDSA IV

Nitric Oxide (NYE trik OKS ide)

Brand Names: US INOmax

Brand Names: Canada INOmax; Noxivent

Pharmacologic Category Vasodilator, Pulmonary

Use Hypoxic respiratory failure associated with pulmonary hypertension in neonates: Treatment of term and near-term (>34 weeks gestational age) neonates with hypoxic respiratory failure associated with clinical or echocardiographic evidence of pulmonary hypertension to improve oxygenation and reduce the need for extracorporeal membrane oxygenation. Used in conjunction with ventilatory support and other agents.

Local Anesthetic/Vasoconstrictor Precautions No information available to require special precautions

Effects on Dental Treatment No significant effects or complications reported

Effects on Bleeding No information available to require special precautions

Adverse Reactions

>10%: Cardiovascular: Hypotension (14%)

Postmarketing and/or case reports: Hypoxemia, methemoglobinemia, pulmonary edema

Note: Occupational exposure (eg, hospital staff) may result in chest discomfort, dizziness, dry throat, dyspnea, and headache.

General Dosage Range Inhalation: *Neonates (>34 weeks gestational age):* 20 ppm

Mechanism of Action In neonates with persistent pulmonary hypertension, nitric oxide improves oxygenation. Nitric oxide relaxes vascular smooth muscle by binding to the heme moiety of cytosolic guanylate cyclase, activating guanylate cyclase and increasing intracellular levels of cyclic guanosine 3',5'-monophosphate, which leads to vasodilation. When inhaled, pulmonary vasodilation occurs and an increase in the partial pressure of arterial oxygen results. Dilation of pulmonary vessels in well ventilated lung areas redistributes blood flow away from lung areas where ventilation/perfusion ratios are poor.

Pregnancy Risk Factor C

Pregnancy Considerations Adverse events have been observed in animal reproduction studies. Nitric oxide is not indicated for use in adults.

Nitrofurantoin (nye troe fyoor AN toyn)

Brand Names: US Furadantin; Macrobid; Macrodantin

Brand Names: Canada Apo-Nitrofurantoin; Macrobid; Macrodantin; Novo-Furantoin; Teva-Nitrofurantoin

Pharmacologic Category Antibiotic, Miscellaneous

Use

Urinary tract infections: For the treatment of urinary tract infections (UTIs) when caused by susceptible strains of *Escherichia coli*, enterococci, *Staphylococcus aureus*, and certain susceptible strains of *Klebsiella* and *Enterobacter* species.

Acute cystitis: Nitrofurantoin monohydrate/macrocrystals: Indicated only for the treatment of acute uncomplicated UTIs (acute cystitis) caused by susceptible strains of *E. coli* or *Staphylococcus saprophyticus* in patients ≥12 years of age.

Local Anesthetic/Vasoconstrictor Precautions No information available to require special precautions

Effects on Dental Treatment No significant effects or complications reported

Effects on Bleeding No information available to require special precautions

Adverse Reactions Frequency not defined.

Cardiovascular: ECG changes (nonspecific ST/T wave changes, bundle branch block)

Central nervous system: Bulging fontanel (infants), chills, confusion, depression, dizziness, drowsiness, headache, malaise, numbness, paresthesia, peripheral neuropathy, pseudotumor cerebri, psychotic reaction, vertigo

Dermatologic: Alopecia, erythema multiforme, exfoliative dermatitis, pruritus, skin rash (eczematous, erythematous, maculopapular), Stevens-Johnson syndrome, urticaria

Endocrine & metabolic: Hyperphosphatemia

Gastrointestinal: Abdominal pain, anorexia, *Clostridium difficile* associated diarrhea, constipation, diarrhea, dyspepsia, flatulence, nausea, pancreatitis, pseudomembranous colitis, sialadenitis, vomiting

Genitourinary: Urine discoloration (brown)

Hematologic & oncologic: Agranulocytosis, aplastic anemia, eosinophilia, glucose-6-phosphate dehydrogenase deficiency anemia, granulocytopenia, hemoglobin decreased, hemolytic anemia, leukopenia, megaloblastic anemia, thrombocytopenia

Hepatic: Cholestatic jaundice, hepatitis, hepatic necrosis, increased serum transaminases

Hypersensitivity: Anaphylaxis, angioedema, hypersensitivity (including acute pulmonary hypersensitivity)

Infection: Superinfection (eg, *Pseudomonas* or *Candida*)

Neuromuscular & skeletal: Arthralgia, lupus-like syndrome, myalgia, weakness

Ophthalmic: Amblyopia, nystagmus, optic neuritis

Respiratory: Acute pulmonary reaction (symptoms include chills, chest pain, cough, dyspnea, fever, and eosinophilia), cough, cyanosis, dyspnea, pneumonitis, pulmonary fibrosis (with long-term use), pulmonary infiltration

Miscellaneous: Fever

Postmarketing and/or case reports: Hepatotoxicity (idiosyncratic) (Chalasani, 2014)

General Dosage Range Oral:

Infants, Children, and Adolescents: Furadantin, Macrodantin: 5 to 7 mg/kg/day divided every 6 hours (maximum: 400 mg daily) **or** 1 to 2 mg/kg/day as a single dose or divided every 12 hours (maximum: 100 mg daily)

Adolescents: Macrobid: 100 mg twice daily

Adults: Furadantin, Macrodantin: 50 to 100 mg every 6 hours **or** once daily; Macrobid: 100 mg twice daily

Mechanism of Action Nitrofurantoin is reduced by bacterial flavoproteins to reactive intermediates that inactivate or alter bacterial ribosomal proteins leading to inhibition of protein synthesis, aerobic energy metabolism, DNA, RNA, and cell wall synthesis. Nitrofurantoin is bactericidal in urine at therapeutic doses. The broad-based nature of this mode of action may explain the lack of acquired bacterial resistance to nitrofurantoin, as the necessary multiple and simultaneous mutations of the target macromolecules would likely be lethal to the bacteria.

Pharmacodynamics/Kinetics

Half-life Elimination 20-60 minutes; prolonged with renal impairment

Pregnancy Risk Factor B (contraindicated at term)

Pregnancy Considerations Adverse effects have not been observed in animal reproduction studies. Nitrofurantoin crosses the placenta (Perry, 1967) and maternal serum concentrations may be lower in pregnancy (Philipson, 1979). Current studies evaluating maternal use of nitrofurantoin during pregnancy and the development of birth defects have had mixed results (ACOG, 2011). An increased risk of neonatal jaundice was observed following maternal nitrofurantoin use during the last 30 days of pregnancy (Nordeng, 2013). Nitrofurantoin may be used to treat infections in pregnant women; use during the first trimester should be limited to situations where no alternative therapies are available. Prescriptions should be written when clinically appropriate and for the shortest effective duration for confirmed infections (ACOG, 2011). Nitrofurantoin is contraindicated in pregnant patients at term (38-42 weeks gestation), during labor and delivery, or when the onset of labor is imminent due to the possibility of hemolytic anemia in the neonate. Alternative antibiotics should be considered in pregnant women with G-6-PD deficiency (Nordeng, 2013).

Nitroglycerin (nye troe GLI ser in)

Related Information

Cardiovascular Diseases *on page* 1752

Brand Names: US GoNitro; Minitran; Nitro-Bid; Nitro-Dur; Nitro-Time; Nitrolingual; NitroMist; Nitronal [DSC]; Nitrostat; Rectiv

Brand Names: Canada Minitran; Mylan-Nitro Sublingual Spray; Nitro-Dur; Nitroglycerin Injection, USP; Nitrol; Nitrostat; Rho-Nitro Pump Spray; Transderm-Nitro; Trinipatch

Generic Availability (US) May be product dependent

Pharmacologic Category Antianginal Agent; Antidote, Extravasation; Vasodilator

Use Treatment or prevention of angina pectoris

Intravenous (IV) administration: Treatment or prevention of angina pectoris; acute decompensated heart failure (especially when associated with acute myocardial infarction); perioperative hypertension (especially during cardiovascular surgery); induction of intraoperative hypotension

Intra-anal administration (Rectiv ointment): Treatment of moderate-to-severe pain associated with chronic anal fissure

Local Anesthetic/Vasoconstrictor Precautions No information available to require special precautions

Effects on Dental Treatment Key adverse event(s) related to dental treatment: Xerostomia (normal salivary flow resumes upon discontinuation).

Effects on Bleeding No information available to require special precautions

Adverse Reactions

>10%: Central nervous system: Headache (patch, ointment: 50% to 64%; sublingual powder, lingual spray: >2%)

1% to 10%:

Cardiovascular: Hypotension (≤4%), syncope (≤4%), peripheral edema (lingual spray: ≤2%)

Central nervous system: Dizziness (>2% to 6%), paresthesia (>2%)

Gastrointestinal: Abdominal pain (lingual spray: ≤2%)

Neuromuscular & skeletal: Weakness (all sublingual forms: ≤2%)

Respiratory: Dyspnea (≤2%), pharyngitis (lingual spray: ≤2%), rhinitis (lingual spray: ≤2%)

Frequency not defined:

Cardiovascular: Bradycardia, exacerbation of angina pectoris, flushing, orthostatic hypotension

Dermatologic: Diaphoresis

Gastrointestinal: Vomiting

Miscellaneous: Drug tolerance

<1%, postmarketing, and/or case reports: Anaphylactoid reaction, application site irritation (patch), circulatory shock, contact dermatitis (ointment, patch), drowsiness, exfoliative dermatitis, fixed drug eruption (ointment, patch), hypersensitivity reaction, hypoxemia (transient), methemoglobinemia, nausea, pallor, palpitations, rebound hypertension, restlessness, skin rash, tachycardia, vertigo, vomiting

Dosing

Adult & Geriatric Note: Hemodynamic and antianginal tolerance often develop within 24 to 48 hours of continuous nitrate administration. Nitrate-free interval (10 to 12 hours/day) is recommended to avoid tolerance development; gradually decrease dose in patients receiving nitroglycerin for prolonged period to avoid withdrawal reaction.

Acute decompensated heart failure (off-label dose): IV: Initial: 10 to 20 mcg/minute, with subsequent titration (eg, 10 to 20 mcg/minute every 5 to 15 minutes) up to 200 mcg/minute (Coons 2011; Mebazaa 2016) **or** 0.3 to 0.5 mcg/**kg**/minute with titration (if SBP ≥90 mm Hg) in increments of 20 mcg/minute every 1 to 3 minutes up to 400 mcg/minute (Levy 2007). Patients who do not respond hemodynamically with doses of ~200 mcg/minute should be considered non-responders (Coons 2011).

Angina/coronary artery disease:

Oral: Initial: 2.5 to 6.5 mg 3 to 4 times daily; may titrate up to 26 mg 4 times daily

IV:

Manufacturer's labeling: 5 mcg/minute, increase by 5 mcg/minute every 3 to 5 minutes to 20 mcg/minute. If no response at 20 mcg/minute, may increase by 10 to 20 mcg/minute every 3 to 5 minutes (generally accepted maximum dose: 400 mcg/minute)

Alternate dosing: ACCF/AHA guidelines for STEMI: Initial: 10 mcg/minute, with subsequent titration to desired blood pressure effect (ACCF/AHA [O'Gara 2013]).

Sublingual powder (0.4 mg/packet):

Manufacturer's labeling: 1 to 2 packets under tongue every 5 minutes as needed for maximum of 3 packets in 15 minutes; may also use prophylactically 5 to 10 minutes prior to activities which may provoke an angina attack

Alternate dosing: ACCF/AHA guidelines for STEMI and AHA/ACC guidelines for the management of NSTE-ACS: 0.4 mg every 5 minutes up to 3 doses. Patients should be advised to take 1 dose promptly in response to chest pain. If pain is unrelieved or worsened 3 to 5 minutes after 1 dose, the patient or caregiver should call 9-1-1 immediately (ACC/AHA [Amsterdam 2014]; ACCF/AHA [O'Gara 2013]).

Sublingual tablet:

Manufacturer's labeling: 0.3 to 0.6 mg every 5 minutes for maximum of 3 tablets in 15 minutes; may also use prophylactically 5 to 10 minutes prior to activities which may provoke an attack.

Alternate dosing: ACCF/AHA guidelines for STEMI and AHA/ACC guidelines for the management of NSTE-ACS: 0.3 to 0.4 mg every 5 minutes up to 3 doses. Patients should be advised to take 1 dose promptly in response to chest pain. If pain is unrelieved or worsened 3 to 5 minutes after 1 dose, the patient or caregiver should call 9-1-1 immediately (ACC/AHA [Amsterdam 2014]; ACCF/AHA [O'Gara 2013]).

Topical 2% ointment: 1/2" upon rising and 1/2" 6 hours later; if necessary, the dose may be doubled to 1" and subsequently doubled again to 2" if response is inadequate. Doses of 1/2" to 2" were used in clinical trials. Recommended maximum: 2 doses/day; include a nitrate free-interval ~10 to 12 hours/day.

Topical patch, transdermal: 0.2 to 0.4 mg/hour initially and titrate to doses of 0.4 to 0.8 mg/hour. Tolerance is minimized by using a patch-on period of 12 to 14 hours/day and patch-off period of 10 to 12 hours/day.

Translingual 0.4 mg/spray:

Manufacturer's labeling: 1 to 2 sprays onto or under tongue approximately every 5 minutes for maximum of 3 sprays in 15 minutes, may also be used prophylactically 5 to 10 minutes prior to activities which may provoke an angina attack

Alternate dosing: ACCF/AHA guidelines for STEMI and AHA/ACC guidelines for the management of NSTE-ACS: 0.4 mg every 5 minutes up to 3 doses. Patients should be advised to take 1 dose promptly in response to chest pain. If pain is unrelieved or worsened 3 to 5 minutes after 1 dose, the patient or caregiver should call 9-1-1 immediately (ACC/AHA [Amsterdam 2014]; ACCF/AHA [O'Gara 2013]).

Anal fissure, chronic (0.4% ointment): Intra-anal: 1 inch (equals 1.5 mg of nitroglycerin) every 12 hours for up to 3 weeks

Esophageal spastic disorders (off-label use): Sublingual: 0.3 to 0.6 mg (Swamy, 1977)

Extravasation (sympathomimetic vasopressors), treatment (alternative to phentolamine; off-label use): Based on limited data in neonates; optimal dosing has not been established: Topical 2% ointment: 4 mm/kg applied as a thin ribbon to the affected area has been reported in a case series;

after 8 hours, if no improvement, the dose may be reapplied to the affected site (Wong, 1992). Application of a 1-inch strip on the affected site has also been described to be successful (Denkler, 1989); may also be considered for adults as an alternative to phentolamine (Hurst, 2004).

Gastroesophageal variceal hemorrhage (off-label use): IV infusion: Initial: 40 mcg/minute, increase by 40 mcg/minute every 15 minutes if systolic blood pressure is >90 to 100 mm Hg, up to a maximum of 400 mcg/minute (Garcia-Tsao, 2007; Gimson, 1986; Westaby, 1989). Coadminister with vasopressin and use at the highest effective dose for a maximum of 24 hours to minimize the development of adverse effects (Garcia-Tsao, 2007).

Uterine relaxation (off-label use): IV bolus: 100 to 200 mcg; may repeat dose every 2 minutes as necessary (Axemo, 1998; Chandraharan, 2005)

Pediatric Extravasation (sympathomimetic vasopressors), treatment (alternative to phentolamine; off-label use): Based on limited data in neonates; optimal dosing has not been established: Topical 2% ointment: 4 mm/kg applied as a thin ribbon to the affected area has been reported in a case series; after 8 hours, if no improvement, the dose may be reapplied to the affected site (Wong, 1992). Application of a 1-inch strip on the affected site has also been described to be successful (Denkler, 1989).

Renal Impairment There are no dosage adjustments provided in the manufacturer's labeling.

Hepatic Impairment There are no dosage adjustments provided in the manufacturer's labeling.

Mechanism of Action Nitroglycerin forms free radical nitric oxide. In smooth muscle, nitric oxide activates guanylate cyclase which increases guanosine 3'5' monophosphate (cGMP) leading to dephosphorylation of myosin light chains and smooth muscle relaxation. Produces a vasodilator effect on the peripheral veins and arteries with more prominent effects on the veins. Primarily reduces cardiac oxygen demand by decreasing preload (left ventricular end-diastolic pressure); may modestly reduce afterload; dilates coronary arteries and improves collateral flow to ischemic regions. For use in rectal fissures, intra-anal administration results in decreased sphincter tone and intra-anal pressure.

Contraindications

Hypersensitivity to nitroglycerin, other nitrates or nitrites, or any component of the formulation (includes adhesives for transdermal product); concurrent use with phosphodiesterase-5 (PDE-5) inhibitors (avanafil, sildenafil, tadalafil, or vardenafil); concurrent use with soluble guanylate cyclase (sGC) stimulators (eg, riociguat).

Additional contraindications for IV product: Hypersensitivity to corn or corn products (solutions containing dextrose); constrictive pericarditis; increased intracranial pressure; pericardial tamponade; restrictive cardiomyopathy; uncorrected hypovolemia

Additional contraindications for sublingual product and rectal ointment: Acute circulatory failure or shock (sublingual powder only); early myocardial infarction (sublingual tablet only; see **Note**); increased intracranial pressure; severe anemia

Additional contraindications for translingual product: Increased intracranial pressure; severe anemia; acute circulatory failure or shock (Nitrolingual only)

Canadian labeling: Additional contraindications for transdermal patch (not in US labeling): Acute circulatory failure associated with marked hypotension (shock and states of collapse); orthostatic hypotension; myocardial insufficiency due to obstruction (eg, presence of aortic or mitral stenosis or of constrictive pericarditis); increased intracranial pressure; increased intraocular pressure; severe anemia

Note: According to the American College of Cardiology Foundation/American Heart Association (ACCF/AHA) guidelines of the management of ST-elevation myocardial infarction (STEMI) and the ACC/AHA guidelines for the management of patients with non-ST-elevation acute coronary syndromes (NSTE-ACS), avoid nitrates in the following conditions: Hypotension (SBP <90 mm Hg or ≥30 mm Hg below baseline), marked bradycardia or tachycardia, and right ventricular infarction (ACC/AHA [Amsterdam 2014]; ACCF/AHA [O'Gara 2013]). Sublingual nitroglycerin may be used as initial treatment of ongoing chest pain in patients who may have STEMI or NSTE-ACS (ACC/AHA [Amsterdam 2014]; ACCF/AHA [O'Gara 2013]).

Warnings/Precautions Severe hypotension and shock may occur (even with small doses). Use with caution in volume depletion, preexisting hypotension, constrictive pericarditis, aortic or mitral stenosis, and extreme caution with inferior wall MI and suspected right ventricular involvement. According to the ACCF/AHA, avoid use in patients with severe hypotension (SBP <90 mm Hg or ≥30 mm Hg below baseline), marked bradycardia or tachycardia, and right ventricular MI (ACCF/AHA [O'Gara, 2013]). Avoid use in patients with hypertrophic cardiomyopathy (HCM) with outflow tract obstruction; nitrates may reduce preload, exacerbating obstruction and cause hypotension or syncope and/or worsening of heart failure (ACCF/AHA [Gersh 2011]).

Paradoxical bradycardia and increased angina pectoris may accompany hypotension. Orthostatic hypotension may also occur. Ethanol may accentuate this. Dose-related headaches may occur, especially during initial dosing. Tolerance may occur; cross tolerance to other nitro compounds have been reported; appropriate dosing is needed to minimize tolerance development. Avoid use of long-acting agents in acute MI or acute HF; cannot easily reverse effects. Nitrates may aggravate angina caused by hypertrophic cardiomyopathy. Nitroglycerin may precipitate or aggravate increased intracranial pressure and subsequently may worsen clinical outcomes in patients with neurologic injury (eg, intracranial hemorrhage, traumatic brain injury) (Rangel-Castilla 2008). Nitroglycerin transdermal patches may contain conducting metal (eg, aluminum); remove patch prior to MRI. Some dosage forms may contain propylene glycol; large amounts are potentially toxic and have been associated hyperosmolality, lactic acidosis, seizures and respiratory depression; use caution (AAP 1997; Zar 2007). Potentially significant drug-drug interactions may exist, requiring dose or frequency adjustment, additional monitoring, and/or selection of alternative therapy.

Use caution when treating rectal anal fissures with nitroglycerin ointment formulation in patients with suspected or known significant cardiovascular disorders (eg, cardiomyopathies, heart failure, acute MI); intra-anal nitroglycerin administration may decrease systolic blood pressure and decrease arterial vascular resistance.

Drug Interactions

Metabolism/Transport Effects None known.

Avoid Concomitant Use

Avoid concomitant use of Nitroglycerin with any of the following: Anticholinergic Agents; Ergot Derivatives; Phosphodiesterase 5 Inhibitors; Riociguat

Increased Effect/Toxicity

Nitroglycerin may increase the levels/effects of: Amifostine; Antipsychotic Agents (Second Generation [Atypical]); DULoxetine; Ergot Derivatives; Hypotension-Associated Agents; Levodopa; Nitroprusside; Prilocaine; Rilmenidine; Riociguat; Rosiglitazone; Sodium Nitrite

The levels/effects of Nitroglycerin may be increased by: Alcohol (Ethyl); Alfuzosin; Barbiturates; Blood Pressure Lowering Agents; Brimonidine (Topical); Dapoxetine; Dapsone (Topical); Diazoxide; Herbs (Hypotensive Properties); Lormetazepam; Molsidomine; Naftopidil; Nicergoline; Nicorandil; Nitric Oxide; Obinutuzumab; Pentoxifylline; Phosphodiesterase 5 Inhibitors; Prostacyclin Analogues; Quinagolide; Tetracaine (Topical)

Decreased Effect

Nitroglycerin may decrease the levels/effects of: Alteplase; Heparin

The levels/effects of Nitroglycerin may be decreased by: Anticholinergic Agents; Ergot Derivatives

Pharmacodynamics/Kinetics

Onset of Action Sublingual tablet: 1 to 3 minutes; Translingual spray: Similar to sublingual tablet; Extended release: ~60 minutes; Topical: 15 to 30 minutes; Transdermal: ~30 minutes; IV: Immediate

Peak effect: Sublingual powder: 7 minutes; Sublingual tablet: 5 minutes; Translingual spray: 4 to 15 minutes; Extended release: 2.5 to 4 hours; Topical: ~60 minutes; Transdermal: 120 minutes; IV: Immediate

Duration of Action Sublingual tablet: At least 25 minutes; Translingual spray: Similar to sublingual tablet; Extended release: 4 to 8 hours (Gibbons, 2002); Topical: 7 hours; Transdermal: 10 to 12 hours; IV: 3 to 5 minutes

Half-life Elimination ~1 to 4 minutes

Pregnancy Risk Factor B/C (product specific)

Pregnancy Considerations Animal reproduction studies have not been conducted with all products; adverse events were not observed in animal reproduction studies conducted using the ointment. Nitroglycerin crosses the placenta (David, 2000). Concentrations following application of a transdermal patch 0.4 mg/hour were low but detectable in the fetal serum (fetal/maternal ratio: 0.23) (Bustard, 2003). Nitroglycerin may be used in pregnancy when immediate relaxation of the uterus is needed (ACOG, 2006; Axemo, 1998; Chandraharan, 2005). Intravenous nitroglycerin may be used to treat pre-eclampsia with pulmonary edema (ESG, 2011).

Breastfeeding Considerations It is not known if nitroglycerin is excreted in breast milk. According to the manufacturer, the decision to continue or discontinue breastfeeding during therapy should take into account the risk of infant exposure, the benefits of breastfeeding to the infant, and benefits of treatment to the mother. Information related to the use of nitroglycerin and breastfeeding is limited (Böttiger 2010; O'Sullivan 2011).

Dosage Forms

Aerosol Solution, Translingual:

NitroMist: 400 mcg/spray (4.1 g, 8.5 g)

Generic: 400 mcg/spray (4.1 g, 8.5 g)

Capsule Extended Release, Oral:

Nitro-Time: 2.5 mg, 6.5 mg, 9 mg

Generic: 2.5 mg, 6.5 mg, 9 mg

Ointment, Rectal:

Rectiv: 0.4% (30 g)

Ointment, Transdermal:

Nitro-Bid: 2% (1 g, 30 g, 60 g)

Packet, Sublingual:

GoNitro: 400 mcg (1 ea, 36 ea)

Patch 24 Hour, Transdermal:

Minitran: 0.1 mg/hr (30 ea); 0.2 mg/hr (30 ea); 0.4 mg/hr (30 ea); 0.6 mg/hr (30 ea)

Nitro-Dur: 0.1 mg/hr (30 ea, 100 ea); 0.2 mg/hr (30 ea, 100 ea); 0.3 mg/hr (1 ea, 30 ea, 100 ea); 0.4 mg/hr (30 ea, 100 ea); 0.6 mg/hr (30 ea, 100 ea); 0.8 mg/hr (30 ea, 100 ea)

Generic: 0.1 mg/hr (30 ea, 4350 ea); 0.2 mg/hr (1 ea, 30 ea, 4350 ea); 0.4 mg/hr (1 ea, 30 ea, 4350 ea); 0.6 mg/hr (1 ea, 30 ea, 4350 ea)

Solution, Intravenous:

Generic: 25 mg (250 mL); 50 mg (250 mL, 500 mL); 100 mg (250 mL); 200 mg (500 mL); 5 mg/mL (10 mL)

Solution, Translingual:

Nitrolingual: 0.4 mg/spray (4.9 g, 12 g)

Generic: 0.4 mg/spray (4.9 g, 12 g)

Tablet Sublingual, Sublingual:

Nitrostat: 0.3 mg, 0.4 mg, 0.6 mg

Generic: 0.3 mg, 0.4 mg, 0.6 mg

Nitroprusside (nye troe PRUS ide)

Brand Names: US Nipride RTU; Nitropress

Brand Names: Canada Nipride

Pharmacologic Category Antihypertensive; Vasodilator

Use Management of hypertensive crises; acute decompensated heart failure (HF); used for controlled hypotension to reduce bleeding during surgery

Local Anesthetic/Vasoconstrictor Precautions No information available to require special precautions

Effects on Dental Treatment No significant effects or complications reported

Effects on Bleeding No information available to require special precautions

Adverse Reactions Frequency not defined.

Cardiovascular: Bradycardia, ECG changes, flushing, palpitations, severe hypotension, substernal pain, tachycardia

Central nervous system: Apprehension, dizziness, headache, increased intracranial pressure, restlessness

Dermatologic: Diaphoresis, skin rash

Endocrine & metabolic: Hypothyroidism

Gastrointestinal: Abdominal pain, intestinal obstruction, nausea, retching, vomiting

Hematologic & oncologic: Decreased platelet aggregation, methemoglobinemia

Local: Irritation at injection site

Neuromuscular & skeletal: Muscle twitching

General Dosage Range IV: *Children and Adults:* Initial: 0.3 mcg/kg/minute; Usual dose: 3 mcg/kg/minute (maximum: 10 mcg/kg/minute)

Mechanism of Action Causes peripheral vasodilation by direct action on venous and arteriolar smooth muscle, thus reducing peripheral resistance; will increase cardiac output by decreasing afterload; reduces aortal and left ventricular impedance

Pharmacodynamics/Kinetics

Onset of Action Hypotensive effect: <2 minutes

Duration of Action Hypotensive effect: 1-10 minutes

Half-life Elimination Nitroprusside, circulatory: ~2 minutes; Thiocyanate, elimination: ~3 days (may be doubled or tripled in renal failure)

Pregnancy Risk Factor C

Pregnancy Considerations Animal studies have shown that nitroprusside may cross the placental barrier and result in fetal cyanide levels that are dose-related to maternal nitroprusside levels. However, information related to use in pregnancy is limited.

Nitrous Oxide (NYE trus OKS ide)

Related Information

Management of the Patient With Anxiety or Depression *on page 1873*

Generic Availability (US) Yes

Pharmacologic Category Dental Gases; General Anesthetic

Dental Use Induction of sedation and analgesia in anxious dental patients

Use Sedation, analgesia, and amnesia; principal adjunct to inhalation and intravenous general anesthesia

Local Anesthetic/Vasoconstrictor Precautions No information available to require special precautions

Effects on Dental Treatment No significant effects or complications reported

Effects on Bleeding No information available to require special precautions

Adverse Reactions

Frequency not defined.

Cardiovascular: Hypotension

Central nervous system: Central nervous system stimulation, confusion, dizziness, headache

Gastrointestinal: Nausea and vomiting

Respiratory: Apnea

Dental Usual Dosage Sedation and analgesia: Children and Adults: Concentrations of 25% to 50% nitrous oxide with oxygen

Dosing

Adult & Geriatric

Surgical sedation and analgesia: Concentrations of 25% to 50% nitrous oxide with oxygen. For general anesthesia, concentrations of 40% to 70% via mask or endotracheal tube. Minimal alveolar concentration (MAC), which can be considered the ED_{50} of inhalational anesthetics, is 105%; therefore delivery in a hyperbaric chamber is necessary to use as a complete anesthetic. When administered at 70%, reduces the MAC of other anesthetics by half.

Dental: Sedation and analgesia: Concentrations of 25% to 50% nitrous oxide with oxygen

Pediatric Refer to adult dosing.

Mechanism of Action General CNS depressant action; may act similarly as inhalant general anesthetics by stabilizing axonal membranes to partially inhibit action potentials leading to sedation; may partially act on opiate receptor systems to cause mild analgesia; central sympathetic stimulating action supports blood pressure, systemic vascular resistance, and cardiac output; it does not depress carbon dioxide drive to breath. Nitrous oxide increases cerebral blood flow and intracranial pressure while decreasing hepatic and renal blood flow; has analgesic action similar to morphine.

Contraindications Hypersensitivity to nitrous oxide or any component of the formulation; nitrous oxide should not be administered without oxygen

Use is considered contraindicated in patients having undergone vitreoretinal surgery and presence of intraocular gas bubble (Lee, 2004; Fu, 2002).

Warnings/Precautions Nausea and vomiting occurs postoperatively in ~15% of patients. Prolonged use may produce bone marrow suppression and/or neurologic dysfunction. Oxygen should be briefly administered during emergence from prolonged anesthesia with nitrous oxide to prevent diffusion hypoxia. Patients with vitamin B_{12} deficiency (pernicious anemia) and those with other nutritional deficiencies (alcoholics) are at increased risk of developing neurologic disease and bone marrow suppression with exposure to nitrous oxide. May be associated with abuse and/or addiction.

Detached retina and other ocular disorders treated with vitreoretinal surgery where intraocular gas was used: Nitrous oxide can increase intraocular pressure which may result in retinal artery occlusion, ischemia, or optic nerve damage and vision loss in these patients. Nitrous oxide should not be used in patients who have had an intravitreal gas bubble unless it can be confirmed that the bubble has been completely resorbed (Fu, 2002; Lee, 2004). Avoid use in pneumothorax, pneumocephalus, middle ear surgery, or bowel obstruction (Miller 2010; Ohryn 1995; Sprehn 1992).

Drug Interactions

Metabolism/Transport Effects None known.

Avoid Concomitant Use

Avoid concomitant use of Nitrous Oxide with any of the following: Azelastine (Nasal); Orphenadrine; Oxomemazine; Paraldehyde; Thalidomide

Increased Effect/Toxicity

Nitrous Oxide may increase the levels/effects of: Alcohol (Ethyl); Analgesics (Opioid); Azelastine (Nasal); Blonanserin; Buprenorphine; CNS Depressants; Flunitrazepam; HYDROcodone; Methotrimeprazine; MetyroSINE; Mirtazapine; Orphenadrine; OxyCODONE; Paraldehyde; Piribedil; Pramipexole; ROPINIRole; Rotigotine; Selective Serotonin Reuptake Inhibitors; Suvorexant; Thalidomide; Zolpidem

The levels/effects of Nitrous Oxide may be increased by: Brimonidine (Topical); Cannabis; Chlormethiazole; Chlorphenesin Carbamate; Dimethindene (Topical); Doxylamine; Dronabinol; Droperidol; HydrOXYzine; Kava Kava; Lofexidine; Magnesium Sulfate; Methotrimeprazine; Minocycline; Nabilone; Oxomemazine; Perampanel; Rufinamide; Sodium Oxybate; Tapentadol; Tetrahydrocannabinol; Trimeprazine

Decreased Effect There are no known significant interactions involving a decrease in effect.

Pharmacodynamics/Kinetics

Onset of Action Inhalation: 2-5 minutes

Pregnancy Considerations Nitrous oxide crosses the placenta in concentrations ~80% of those in the maternal plasma. The half-life in the neonate is ~3 minutes and it is quickly eliminated from neonatal lungs with the onset of breathing (Rooks, 2011). Infertility, spontaneous abortion, and congenital abnormalities have been reported following prolonged occupational exposure (Becker, 2008; Brodsky, 1986; Rooks, 2011). Adverse events are related to dose and duration of exposure and risks may be decreased with proper administration procedures (Rooks, 2011). May be used when needed for dental treatments that cannot be postponed during pregnancy; use for labor analgesia is considered acceptable (Becker, 2008; Rooks, 2011). Avoid use in pregnant women during the first two trimesters of pregnancy, those with medical conditions that increase the risk of vitamin B_{12} deficiency, or infertile women undergoing *in vitro* fertilization (Brodsky, 1986; Rooks, 2011).

Dosage Forms

Supplied in blue cylinders

Nivolumab (nye VOL ue mab)

Brand Names: US Opdivo

Brand Names: Canada Opdivo

Pharmacologic Category Antineoplastic Agent, Anti-PD-1 Monoclonal Antibody; Antineoplastic Agent, Immune Checkpoint Inhibitor; Antineoplastic Agent, Monoclonal Antibody

Use

Head and neck cancer, squamous cell (recurrent or metastatic): Treatment of recurrent or metastatic squamous cell carcinoma of the head and neck in patients with disease progression on or after platinum-based therapy.

Hodgkin lymphoma, classical: Treatment of classical Hodgkin lymphoma (cHL) in patients that have relapsed or progressed following autologous hematopoietic stem cell transplant (HSCT) and post-transplant brentuximab vedotin

Melanoma, unresectable or metastatic: Treatment (as a single agent) of BRAF V600 wild-type or BRAF V600 mutation-positive unresectable or metastatic melanoma; treatment of unresectable or metastatic melanoma (in combination with ipilimumab)

Non-small cell lung cancer, metastatic, progressive: Treatment of metastatic non-small cell lung cancer (NSCLC) that has progressed on or after platinum-based chemotherapy. Patients with EGFR or ALK genomic tumor aberrations should have disease progression (on approved EGFR- or ALK-directed therapy) prior to receiving nivolumab.

Renal cell cancer, advanced: Treatment of advanced renal cell cancer in patients who have received prior anti-angiogenic therapy.

Urothelial carcinoma, locally advanced or metastatic: Treatment of locally advanced or metastatic urothelial carcinoma in patients with disease progression during or following a platinum-containing therapy or disease progression within 12 months of neoadjuvant or adjuvant treatment with a platinum-containing therapy.

Local Anesthetic/Vasoconstrictor Precautions

No information available to require special precautions

Effects on Dental Treatment No significant effects or complications reported

Effects on Bleeding No information available to require special precautions

Adverse Reactions

>10%:

Cardiovascular: Edema (≤13%), peripheral edema (≤13%)

Central nervous system: Fatigue (≤53%), malaise (≤46%), peripheral neuropathy (new onset and exacerberations: ≤21%), headache (12%)

Dermatologic: Skin rash (1% to 40%; immune-mediated: 9%), pruritus (10% to 25%), vitiligo (≤11%)

Endocrine & metabolic: Hyperglycemia (≤42%), hyponatremia (14% to 41%), increased serum triglycerides (32%), hyperkalemia (19% to 30%), hypocalcemia (11% to 26%), increased serum cholesterol (21%), hypercalcemia (2% to 19%), hypothyroidism (≤17%; including immune-mediated events), thyroiditis (≤17%; including immune-mediated events), hypomagnesemia (10% to 16%), hypokalemia (11% to 14%)

Gastrointestinal: Diarrhea (2% to 31%), increased serum lipase (16% to 29%), decreased appetite (22% to 28%), nausea (17% to 28%), constipation (9% to 23%), increased serum amylase (10% to 18%), vomiting (12% to 17%), abdominal pain (11% to 13%)

Genitourinary: Urinary tract infection (17%)

Hematologic & oncologic: Lymphocytopenia (24% to 42%; grade 3/4: 4% to 9%), anemia (22% to 40%; grade 3/4: 2% to 8%), neutropenia (29% to 37%; grade 3/4: 4% to 6%), thrombocytopenia (15% to 33%; grade 3/4: 2% to 3%), leukopenia (11%)

Hepatic: Increased serum AST (23% to 33%), increased serum alkaline phosphatase (10% to 33%), increased serum ALT (18% to 25%), increased serum bilirubin (9% to 13%)

Immunologic: Graft versus host disease (>10%; within 14 days of stem cell infusion: 20%), antibody development (11%; neutralizing: <1%; no evidence of altered pharmacokinetic profile)

Neuromuscular & skeletal: Weakness (≤56%), musculoskeletal pain (19% to 33%), back pain (21%), arthralgia (10% to 21%)

Renal: Increased serum creatinine (10% to 42%)

Respiratory: Upper respiratory tract infection (17% to 48%), cough (10% to 35%; includes productive cough), dyspnea (2% to 27%; includes exertional dyspnea), bronchopneumonia (≤19%), pneumonia (≤19%)

Miscellaneous: Febrile reaction (35%; events without an infectious cause that required steroids), fever (1% to 35%; may include tumor-associated fever), infusion related reaction (≤18%)

1% to 10%:

Cardiovascular: Pulmonary embolism (2% to 3%)

Central nervous system: Neuritis (<10%), paralysis (peroneal nerve palsy: <10%)

Dermatologic: Erythema (10%)

Endocrine & metabolic: Hyperthyroidism (3%; including immune-mediated events), adrenocortical insufficiency (1%; including immune-mediated events), increased gamma-glutamyl transferase

Gastrointestinal: Intestinal perforation (<10%), stomatitis (<10%), colitis (including immune-mediated events: 2% to 3%)

Hepatic: Hepatitis (immune-mediated: 2%)

Immunologic: Sjogren syndrome (<10%)

Neuromuscular & skeletal: Ankylosing spondylitis (spondyloarthropathy: <10%), myopathy (<10%),

Renal: Renal disease (7%), acute renal failure (≥2%), nephritis (≤1%; immune-mediated), renal insufficiency (≤1%; immune-mediated)

Respiratory: Interstitial pulmonary disease (5%), pleural effusion (1% to 5%), pneumonitis (1% to 3%; including immune-mediated events), respiratory failure (≥2%)

Frequency not defined:

Central nervous system: Migraine

Dermatologic: Palmar-plantar erythrodysesthesia

Endocrine & metabolic: Weight loss

Gastrointestinal: Abdominal distress

Neuromuscular & skeletal: Limb pain

<1%, postmarketing, and/or case reports: Demyelinating disease (immune-mediated), diabetic ketoacidosis, duodenitis (immune-mediated), encephalitis (limbic/lymphocytic/viral; may be immune-mediated),

facial paralysis (immune-mediated), gastritis (immune-mediated), Guillain-Barré syndrome (immune-mediated), hepatic veno-occlusive disease, hypophysitis (including immune-mediated events), iritis (immune-mediated), lymphadenitis (immune-mediated; histiocytic necrotizing lymphadenitis [Kikuchi lymphadenitis]), motor dysfunction (immune-mediated), myasthenia (myasthenic syndrome; immune-mediated), myocarditis (immune-mediated), myositis (immune-mediated), neuropathy (autoimmune; immune-mediated), pancreatitis (immune-mediated), pituitary insufficiency (immune-mediated), pneumonia due to *Pneumocystis carinii*, polymyalgia rheumatica (immune-mediated), rhabdomyolysis (immune-mediated), sarcoidosis (immune-mediated), sepsis (systemic inflammatory response), sixth nerve palsy (abducens nerve palsy; immune-mediated), type I diabetes mellitus (immune-mediated event), uveitis (immune-mediated), vasculitis

General Dosage Range IV: *Adults:* 1 mg/kg or 3 mg/kg or 240 mg once every 2 weeks

Mechanism of Action

Nivolumab is a fully human immunoglobulin G4 (IgG4) monoclonal antibody that selectively inhibits programmed cell death-1 (PD-1) activity by binding to the PD-1 receptor to block the ligands PD-L1 and PD-L2 from binding. The negative PD-1 receptor signaling that regulates T-cell activation and proliferation is therefore disrupted (Robert 2015). This releases PD-1 pathway-mediated inhibition of the immune response, including the antitumor immune response.

Combining nivolumab (anti-PD-1) with ipilimumab (anti-CTLA-4) results in enhanced T-cell function that is greater than that of either antibody alone, resulting in improved anti-tumor responses in metastatic melanoma.

Pharmacodynamics/Kinetics

Half-life Elimination ~25 days (single-agent and combination therapy with ipilimumab)

Pregnancy Considerations Adverse events were observed in animal reproduction studies. Nivolumab may be expected to cross the placenta; effects to the fetus may be greater in the second and third trimesters. Based on its mechanism of action, nivolumab is expected to cause fetal harm if used during pregnancy. Women of reproductive potential should use highly effective contraception during therapy and for at least 5 months after the last nivolumab dose.

Nizatidine (ni ZA ti deen)

Related Information

Gastrointestinal Disorders *on page 1775*

Brand Names: US Axid AR [OTC] [DSC]; Axid [DSC]

Brand Names: Canada Apo-Nizatidine; Axid; Gen-Nizatidine; Novo-Nizatidine; Nu-Nizatidine; PMS-Nizatidine

Pharmacologic Category Histamine H_2 Antagonist

Use

Duodenal ulcer: Treatment of active duodenal ulcer for up to 8 weeks and maintenance therapy after healing of active ulcer in adults.

Gastric ulcer, benign: Treatment of active benign gastric ulcer for up to 8 weeks in adults.

Gastroesophageal reflux disease: Treatment of endoscopically diagnosed esophagitis, including erosive and ulcerative esophagitis, and associated heartburn due to gastroesophageal reflux disease (GERD) for up to 12 weeks in adults (capsules and oral solution) and up to 8 weeks in children 12 years and older (oral solution only).

Local Anesthetic/Vasoconstrictor Precautions No information available to require special precautions

Effects on Dental Treatment Key adverse event(s) related to dental treatment: Xerostomia (normal salivary flow resumes upon discontinuation).

Effects on Bleeding No information available to require special precautions

Adverse Reactions

>10%: Central nervous system: Headache (16%)

1% to 10%:

Central nervous system: Anxiety, dizziness, drowsiness, insomnia, irritability (children), nervousness

Dermatologic: Pruritus, skin rash

Gastrointestinal: Abdominal pain, anorexia, constipation, diarrhea, flatulence, heartburn, nausea, vomiting, xerostomia

Respiratory: Cough (children), nasal congestion (children), nasopharyngitis (children)

Miscellaneous: Fever (children)

<1%, postmarketing, and/or case reports: Anaphylaxis, anemia, bronchospasm, confusion, eosinophilia, exfoliative dermatitis, gynecomastia, hepatitis, immune thrombocytopenia, increased serum alkaline phosphatase, increased serum ALT, increased serum AST, jaundice, laryngeal edema, serum sickness-like reaction, thrombocytopenia, vasculitis, ventricular tachycardia

General Dosage Range Dosage adjustment recommended in patients with renal impairment

Oral:

Children ≥12 years and Adolescents: 150 mg twice daily for GERD (maximum: 300 mg/day)

Adults: 300 mg/day in 1 or 2 divided doses

Mechanism of Action Competitive inhibition of histamine at H_2-receptors of the gastric parietal cells, which inhibits gastric acid secretion, gastric volume, and hydrogen ion concentration are reduced. Does not affect pepsin secretion, pentagastrin-stimulated intrinsic factor secretion, or serum gastrin.

Pharmacodynamics/Kinetics

Half-life Elimination 1 to 2 hours; prolonged with moderate to severe renal impairment

Time to Peak Plasma: 0.5 to 3 hours

Pregnancy Risk Factor B

Pregnancy Considerations Adverse events have not been observed in animal reproduction studies. Nizatidine crosses the placenta (Dicke 1988). Information related to the use of nizatidine in pregnancy is limited; other agents may be preferred (Richter 2005).

Nonoxynol 9 (non OKS i nole nine)

Brand Names: US Options Conceptrol [OTC]; Options Gynol II Contraceptive [OTC]; Shur-Seal Contraceptive [OTC]; Today Sponge [OTC]; VCF Vaginal Contraceptive [OTC]

Pharmacologic Category Contraceptive; Spermicide

Use Contraception: Prevention of pregnancy

Local Anesthetic/Vasoconstrictor Precautions No information available to require special precautions

Effects on Dental Treatment No significant effects or complications reported

Effects on Bleeding No information available to require special precautions

Adverse Reactions

Frequency not defined: Genitourinary: Mucous membrane disease (burning, irritation, pruritus; including vaginal/urethral)

General Dosage Range Intravaginal: *Adolescents and Adults: Females:* Insert 1 applicatorful, film, suppository, or sponge 10 minutes to 3 hours prior to intercourse (product specific).

Mechanism of Action

Nonoxynol 9 is a nonionic surfactant which prevents pregnancy by damaging the cell membrane of sperm; some product formulations may also provide a physical barrier

Pregnancy Considerations Use of spermicides has not been associated with birth defects (FDA 1986). The effectiveness of available nonoxynol 9-containing products in the prevention of pregnancy is similar (Raymond 2004). However the percentage of unintended pregnancies following use of these products is generally higher than with other methods of contraception; many can be used with a diaphragm and/or male condom. Consistent and correct use of the male latex condom is recommended to reduce the risk for sexually transmitted disease and HIV transmission and provides an additional method of contraception. Barrier contraceptives may not be appropriate for use in women in which the risk of pregnancy is unacceptable due to other health conditions, because of their relatively higher failure rate if not used correctly (CDC 2010).

Norepinephrine (nor ep i NEF rin)

Brand Names: US Levophed

Brand Names: Canada Levophed

Pharmacologic Category Alpha/Beta Agonist

Use Hypotension/shock: Treatment of shock which persists after adequate fluid volume replacement; severe hypotension

Note: Recommended as the first-choice vasopressor for the treatment of sepsis and septic shock in adult patients (Dellinger 2013)

Local Anesthetic/Vasoconstrictor Precautions

No information available to require special precautions

Effects on Dental Treatment No significant effects or complications reported

Effects on Bleeding Norepinephrine has been shown to cause platelet hyper-reactivity and enhance platelet-mediated coagulation associated with thrombotic risk.

Adverse Reactions Frequency not defined.

Cardiovascular: Bradycardia, cardiac arrhythmia, peripheral ischemia (digital)

Central nervous system: Anxiety, transient headache

Dermatologic: Skin necrosis (with extravasation)

Respiratory: Dyspnea

General Dosage Range Continuous IV infusion: *Adults:* Initial: 8 to 12 mcg/minute; Maintenance: Titrate to desired effect (usual maintenance range: 2 to 4 mcg/minute)

Mechanism of Action Stimulates $beta_1$-adrenergic receptors and alpha-adrenergic receptors causing increased contractility and heart rate as well as vasoconstriction, thereby increasing systemic blood pressure and coronary blood flow; clinically, alpha effects (vasoconstriction) are greater than beta effects (inotropic and chronotropic effects)

Pharmacodynamics/Kinetics

Onset of Action Very rapid acting

Duration of Action Vasopressor: 1 to 2 minutes

Pregnancy Risk Factor C

Pregnancy Considerations Animal reproduction studies have not been conducted. Norepinephrine is an endogenous catecholamine and crosses the placenta (Minzter 2010; Wang 1999). Medications used for the treatment of cardiac arrest in pregnancy are the same as in the non-pregnant woman. Appropriate medications should not be withheld due to concerns of fetal teratogenicity. Norepinephrine use during the post-resuscitation phase may be considered; however, the effects of vasoactive medications on the fetus should also be considered. Doses and indications should follow current Advanced Cardiovascular Life Support guidelines (Jeejeebhoy [AHA] 2015).

Norethindrone (nor ETH in drone)

Related Information

Endocrine Disorders and Pregnancy *on page 1781*

Brand Names: US Aygestin; Camila; Deblitane; Errin; Heather; Jencycla; Jolivette; Lyza; Nor-QD [DSC]; Nora-BE; Norlyroc; Ortho Micronor; Sharobel

Brand Names: Canada Jencycla; Micronor; Movisse; Norlutate

Pharmacologic Category Contraceptive; Progestin

Use

Abnormal uterine bleeding *(norethindrone acetate):* Treatment of abnormal uterine bleeding due to hormonal imbalance in absence of organic pathology, such as submucous fibroids or uterine cancer

Amenorrhea, secondary *(norethindrone acetate):* Treatment of secondary amenorrhea

Contraception *(norethindrone):* Prevention of pregnancy

Endometriosis *(norethindrone acetate):* Treatment of endometriosis

Limitations of use:

Norethindrone is not indicated for emergency contraception.

Norethindrone acetate is not indicated for use with estrogen therapy in postmenopausal women for endometrial protection.

Local Anesthetic/Vasoconstrictor Precautions

No information available to require special precautions

Effects on Dental Treatment Until we know more about the mechanism of interaction, caution is required in prescribing antibiotics to female dental patients taking progestin-only hormonal contraceptives.

Effects on Bleeding Norethindrone has been shown to enhance the risk of thrombosis, as assessed by significant increases in prothrombin fragments 1+2, thrombin-antithrombin complex, and D-dimer. These increases were higher during the first 3 months of therapy and gradually declined following prolonged therapy (>3 months). Medical consult is suggested for patients who are under active norethindrone treatment.

Adverse Reactions Frequency not defined.

Cardiovascular: Cerebral embolism, cerebral thrombosis, deep vein thrombosis, edema, pulmonary embolism, retinal thrombosis

Central nervous system: Depression, dizziness, fatigue, headache, insomnia, migraine, emotional lability, nervousness

Dermatologic: Acne vulgaris, alopecia, chloasma, pruritus, skin rash, urticaria

Endocrine & metabolic: Amenorrhea, hirsutism, hypermenorrhea, menstrual disease, weight gain

Gastrointestinal: Abdominal pain, nausea, vomiting

Genitourinary: Breakthrough bleeding, breast hypertrophy, breast tenderness, cervical erosion, change in cervical secretions, decreased lactation, genital discharge, mastalgia, spotting, vaginal hemorrhage

Hypersensitivity: Anaphylaxis, hypersensitivity

Hepatic: Cholestatic jaundice, hepatitis, abnormal hepatic function tests

Neuromuscular & skeletal: Arm pain, leg pain

Ophthalmic: Optic neuritis (with or without vision loss)

General Dosage Range Oral:

Norethindrone: *Children (postmenarche) and Adults:* 0.35 mg every day

Norethindrone acetate: *Adolescents and Adults:* 2.5 to 15 mg once daily

Mechanism of Action Once absorbed, systemic disposition of norethindrone acetate (NETA) and norethindrone (NET) is the same.

NET is used in preparations for progestin-only contraception. NET suppresses ovulation, thickens cervical mucus (which inhibits sperm penetration), alters follicle-stimulating hormone (FSH) and luteinizing hormone (LH) concentrations, slows the movement of ovum through the fallopian tubes, and alters the endometrium.

Progestogens, such as NETA in the doses used for abnormal uterine bleeding, amenorrhea, and endometriosis, lead to atrophy of the endometrial tissue. They may also suppress new growth and implantation. Pain associated with endometriosis is decreased. When treating endometriosis, NETA may be used in combination with gonadotropin-releasing hormone agonists to decrease side effects from hypoestrogenism (ASRM 2014).

Pharmacodynamics/Kinetics

Half-life Elimination ~8 to 9 hours

Time to Peak ~2 hours (varies by dose and use of concomitant estrogen (Orme 1983)

Pregnancy Risk Factor X (norethindrone acetate)

Pregnancy Considerations Use is contraindicated during pregnancy. First trimester exposure of progestins may cause genital abnormalities including hypospadias in male infants and mild virilization of external female genitalia. Changes in external genitalia have been reported in female infants exposed to norethindrone acetate (Fine 1963). Significant adverse events related to growth and development have not been observed following use of oral progestins in contraceptive doses (limited studies).

Norethindrone: Progestin-only contraceptives may be started immediately postpartum (CDC 2010; CDC 2013). A rapid return to fertility occurs when progestin-only contraceptives are discontinued.

Norethindrone acetate: The contraceptive dose of norethindrone acetate is not known. Barrier contraception is recommended to prevent unintended pregnancy (eg, when treating endometriosis) (Kaser 2012).

Norfloxacin (nor FLOKS a sin)

Brand Names: US Noroxin [DSC]

Brand Names: Canada Apo-Norflox; CO Norfloxacin; PMS-Norfloxacin; Teva-Norfloxacin

Pharmacologic Category Antibiotic, Fluoroquinolone

Use Uncomplicated and complicated urinary tract infections caused by susceptible gram-negative and gram-positive bacteria; sexually-transmitted disease (eg, uncomplicated urethral and cervical gonorrhea) caused by *N. gonorrhoeae*; prostatitis due to *E. coli*

Note: As of April 2007, the CDC no longer recommends the use of fluoroquinolones for the treatment of gonococcal disease.

Local Anesthetic/Vasoconstrictor Precautions Norfloxacin is one of the drugs confirmed to prolong the QT interval and is accepted as having a risk of causing torsade de pointes. The risk of drug-induced torsade de pointes is extremely low when a single QT interval prolonging drug is prescribed. In terms of epinephrine, it is not known what effect vasoconstrictors in the local anesthetic regimen will have in patients with a known history of congenital prolonged QT interval or in patients taking any medication that prolongs the QT interval. Until more information is obtained, it is suggested that the clinician consult with the physician prior to the use of a vasoconstrictor in suspected patients, and that the vasoconstrictor (epinephrine, mepivacaine and levonordefrin [Carbocaine® 2% with Neo-Cobefrin®]) be used with caution.

Effects on Dental Treatment No significant effects or complications reported

Effects on Bleeding Norfloxacin has been shown to alter leukocyte populations (reduce neutrophils and increase eosinophils). In more than 1 in 1000 patients, norfloxacin has been shown to reduce clotting ability through reduction in blood platelet concentrations. May also reduce the erythrocyte concentration following extended treatment.

Adverse Reactions

>1% to 10%:

Central nervous system: Dizziness (2% to 3%), headache (2% to 3%)

Gastrointestinal: Nausea (3% to 4%), abdominal cramping (2%)

Hematologic & oncologic: Eosinophilia (1% to 2%)

Hepatic: Liver enzymes increased (1% to 2%)

≥0.3% to 1%:

Central nervous system: Drowsiness

Dermatologic: Hyperhidrosis, pruritus, rash

Endocrine & metabolic: Decreased WBC count (1%), increased serum alkaline phosphatase (1%)

Gastrointestinal: Abdominal pain, anorectal pain, anorexia, constipation, diarrhea, dyspepsia, flatulence, loose stools, vomiting, xerostomia

Genitourinary: Proteinuria (1%)

Hematologic and oncologic: Decreased platelet count (1%), leukopenia (1%), thrombocytopenia (1%), decreased hematocrit, decreased hemoglobin

Neuromuscular & skeletal: Weakness (1%), back pain

Miscellaneous: Fever

<0.3%, postmarketing, and/or case reports: Abdominal swelling, acute renal failure, agranulocytosis, albuminuria, anaphylactoid reaction, anaphylaxis, angioedema, anxiety, arthralgia, arthritis, ataxia, bitter taste, blurred vision, bursitis, candiduria, casts in urine, chest pain, chills, cholestatic jaundice, *Clostridium difficile*-associated diarrhea, confusion, crystalluria, depression, diplopia, DRESS syndrome, dysgeusia, dysmenorrhea, dyspnea, edema, erythema, erythema multiforme, exacerbation of myasthenia gravis, exfoliative dermatitis, gastrointestinal hemorrhage, glycosuria, Guillain-Barré syndrome, hearing loss, heartburn, hematuria, hemolytic anemia (sometimes associated with G6PD deficiency), hepatic failure, hepatic necrosis, hepatitis, hepatotoxicity (idiosyncratic) (Chalasani 2014), hypercholesterolemia, hyperglycemia, hyperkalemia, hypersensitivity angiitis, hypersensitivity reaction, hypertriglyceridemia, hypoesthesia, hypoglycemia, increased blood urea nitrogen, increased creatine phosphokinase, increased intracranial pressure, increased lactate dehydrogenase, increased serum creatinine, insomnia, interstitial nephritis, jaundice, muscle spasm,

myalgia, myocardial infarction, myoclonus, neutropenia, nystagmus, oral mucosa ulcer, orthostatic hypotension, palpitations, pancreatitis (rare), paresthesia, peripheral edema, peripheral neuropathy (may be irreversible), phototoxicity, prolonged prothrombin time, prolonged Q-T interval on ECG, pruritus ani, pseudotumor cerebri, psychotic reaction, renal colic, rupture of tendon, seizure, skin photosensitivity, Stevens-Johnson syndrome, stomatitis, tendonitis, tingling of the fingers, tinnitus, torsades de pointes, toxic epidermal necrolysis, tremor, urticaria, uveitis, vasculitis, ventricular arrhythmia, vulvovaginal candidiasis

General Dosage Range Dosage adjustment recommended in patients with renal impairment

Oral: *Adults:* 400 mg every 12 hours **or** 800 mg as a single dose

Mechanism of Action Norfloxacin is a DNA gyrase inhibitor. DNA gyrase is an essential bacterial enzyme that maintains the superhelical structure of DNA. DNA gyrase is required for DNA replication and transcription, DNA repair, recombination, and transposition; bactericidal

Pharmacodynamics/Kinetics

Half-life Elimination 3 to 4 hours; Renal impairment (CrCl ≤30 mL/minute): 6.5 hours; Elderly: 4 hours

Time to Peak Serum: 1 to 2 hours

Pregnancy Risk Factor C

Pregnancy Considerations Adverse events have been observed in some animal reproduction studies. Norfloxacin crosses the placenta, distributing to cord blood and amniotic fluid (Wise 1984). Based on available data, an increased risk of teratogenic effects has not been observed following norfloxacin use during pregnancy (Bar-Oz 2009; Padberg 2014).

Product Availability Noroxin is no longer available in the US.

Dental Comment See Local Anesthetic/Vasoconstrictor Precautions

Nortriptyline (nor TRIP ti leen)

Related Information

Vasoconstrictor Interactions With Antidepressants *on page 1913*

Brand Names: US Pamelor

Brand Names: Canada Apo-Nortriptyline; Ava-Nortriptyline; Aventyl; Gen-Notriptyline; Norventyl; Nu-Nortriptyline; PMS-Nortriptyline; Ratio-Nortriptyline; Teva-Nortriptyline

Generic Availability (US) Yes

Pharmacologic Category Antidepressant, Tricyclic (Secondary Amine)

Dental Use Treatment of myofascial pain, neuralgia, burning mouth syndrome

Use Depression: Treatment of symptoms of depression

Local Anesthetic/Vasoconstrictor Precautions Nortriptyline is one of the drugs confirmed to prolong the QT interval and is accepted as having a risk of causing torsade de pointes. In terms of epinephrine, it is not known what effect vasoconstrictors in the local anesthetic regimen will have in patients with a known history of congenital prolonged QT interval or in patients taking any medication that prolongs the QT interval. Until more information is obtained, it is suggested that the clinician consult with the physician prior to the use of a vasoconstrictor in suspected patients, and that the vasoconstrictor (epinephrine, mepivacaine and levonordefrin [Carbocaine® 2% with Neo-Cobefrin®]) be used with caution. See Dental Comment.

Effects on Dental Treatment Key adverse event(s) related to dental treatment: Xerostomia (normal salivary flow resumes upon discontinuation), black tongue, and unpleasant taste. Long-term treatment with TCAs, such as nortriptyline, increases the risk of caries by reducing salivation and salivary buffer capacity.

Effects on Bleeding No information available to require special precautions

Adverse Reactions Frequency not defined. Some reactions listed are based on reports for other agents in this same pharmacologic class and may not be specifically reported for nortriptyline.

Cardiovascular: Cardiac arrhythmia, cerebrovascular accident, edema, flushing, heart block, hypertension, hypotension, myocardial infarction, palpitations, tachycardia

Central nervous system: Agitation, anxiety, ataxia, confusion, delusions, disorientation, dizziness, drowsiness, drug fever, EEG pattern changes, extrapyramidal reaction, fatigue, hallucination, headache, hypomania, insomnia, nightmares, numbness, panic, peripheral neuropathy, psychosis (exacerbation), restlessness, seizure, tingling of extremities, tingling sensation, withdrawal symptoms

Dermatologic: Alopecia, diaphoresis (excessive), pruritus, skin photosensitivity, skin rash, urticaria

Endocrine & metabolic: Decreased libido, decreased serum glucose, galactorrhea, gynecomastia, increased libido, increased serum glucose, SIADH, weight gain, weight loss

Gastrointestinal: Abdominal cramps, anorexia, constipation, diarrhea, epigastric distress, melanoglossia, nausea, paralytic ileus, parotid gland enlargement, stomatitis, sublingual adenitis, unpleasant taste, vomiting, xerostomia

Genitourinary: Breast hypertrophy, impotence, nocturia, testicular swelling, urinary hesitance, urinary retention, urinary tract dilation

Hematologic & oncologic: Agranulocytosis, eosinophilia, petechia, purpura, thrombocytopenia

Hepatic: Abnormal hepatic function tests, cholestatic jaundice

Neuromuscular & skeletal: Tremor, weakness

Ophthalmic: Accommodation disturbance, blurred vision, eye pain, mydriasis

Otic: Tinnitus

Renal: Polyuria

Postmarketing and/or case reports: Angle-closure glaucoma, serotonin syndrome, suicidal ideation, suicidal tendencies

Dental Usual Dosage Myofascial pain, neuralgia, burning mouth syndrome (off-label use): Adults: Initial: 10-25 mg at bedtime; dosage may be increased by 25 mg/day weekly, if tolerated; usual maintenance dose: 75 mg as a single bedtime dose or 2 divided doses

Dosing

Adult

Depression: Oral: Initial: 25 mg 3 to 4 times/day; adjust dose based on response and tolerability up to 150 mg/day; total daily doses may be given once daily.

Chronic pain (off-label use): Oral: Initial: 10 to 25 mg once daily at bedtime; may increase as tolerated as soon as every 3 days up to 150 mg/day (APS 2008; Atkinson 1998; Orbai 2010). Patients with neuropathic pain and an inadequate response to nortriptyline alone may benefit from a combination with gabapentin (Gilron 2009).

Myofascial pain (off-label use): Oral: Initial: 12.5 mg once daily at bedtime; may increase as tolerated up to 35 mg/day. If after 4 weeks at 25 to 35 mg/day there is no change in pain intensity, then consider alternative therapy (Haviv 2015).

Orofacial pain (off-label use): Oral: Initial: 10 to 30 mg once daily at bedtime; gradually titrated up to 100 mg/day as tolerated (Feinmann 1993; Romero-Reyes 2014).

Postherpetic neuralgia (off-label use): Oral: Initial: 10 to 20 mg once daily at bedtime; may increase as needed every 3 to 5 days in 10 mg once daily increments up to 160 mg/day (Raja 2002; Watson 1998).

Smoking cessation (off-label use): Oral: Initial: 25 mg once daily begun 10 to 28 days prior to selected "quit" date; titrate dose to 75 to 100 mg/day; continue therapy for ≥12 weeks after "quit" day (PHS 2008)

Discontinuation of therapy: Upon discontinuation of antidepressant therapy, gradually taper the dose to minimize the incidence of withdrawal symptoms and allow for the detection of re-emerging symptoms. Evidence supporting ideal taper rates is limited. APA and NICE guidelines suggest tapering therapy over at least several weeks with consideration to the half-life of the antidepressant; antidepressants with a shorter half-life may need to be tapered more conservatively. In addition for long-term treated patients, WFSBP guidelines recommend tapering over 4 to 6 months. If intolerable withdrawal symptoms occur following a dose reduction, consider resuming the previously prescribed dose and/or decrease dose at a more gradual rate (APA 2010; Bauer 2002; Haddad 2001; NCCMH 2010; Schatzberg 2006; Shelton 2001; Warner 2006).

MAO inhibitor recommendations:

Switching to or from an MAO inhibitor intended to treat psychiatric disorders:

Allow 14 days to elapse between discontinuing an MAO inhibitor intended to treat psychiatric disorders and initiation of nortriptyline.

Allow 14 days to elapse between discontinuing nortriptyline and initiation of an MAO inhibitor intended to treat psychiatric disorders.

Geriatric

Depression: Oral: Initial: 30 to 50 mg/day, given as a single daily dose or in divided doses.

Discontinuation of therapy: Refer to adult dosing.

MAO inhibitor recommendations: Refer to adult dosing.

Renal Impairment There are no dosage adjustments provided in the manufacturer's labeling. Nortriptyline is eliminated renally; use with caution.

Hepatic Impairment There are no dosage adjustments provided in the manufacturer's labeling. Nortriptyline is metabolized hepatically; use with caution.

Mechanism of Action Traditionally believed to increase the synaptic concentration of serotonin and/or norepinephrine in the central nervous system by inhibition of their reuptake by the presynaptic neuronal membrane. Inhibits the activity of histamine, 5-hydroxytryptamine, and acetylcholine. It increases the pressor effect of norepinephrine but blocks the pressor response of phenethylamine. However, additional receptor effects have been found including desensitization of adenyl cyclase, down regulation of beta-adrenergic receptors, and down regulation of serotonin receptors.

Contraindications Hypersensitivity to nortriptyline and similar chemical class dibenzazepines, or any component of the formulation; use in a patient during the acute recovery phase of MI; use of MAO inhibitors intended to treat psychiatric disorders (concurrently or within 14 days of discontinuing either nortriptyline or the MAO inhibitor); initiation of nortriptyline in a patient receiving linezolid or intravenous methylene blue

Warnings/Precautions [US Boxed Warning]: Antidepressants increase the risk of suicidal thinking and behavior in children, adolescents, and young adults (18 to 24 years of age) with major depressive disorder (MDD) and other psychiatric disorders; consider risk prior to prescribing. Short-term studies did not show an increased risk in patients >24 years of age and showed a decreased risk in patients ≥65 years. Closely monitor for clinical worsening, suicidality, or unusual changes in behavior, particularly during the initial 1 to 2 months of therapy or during periods of dosage adjustments (increases or decreases); the patient's family or caregiver should be instructed to closely observe the patient and communicate condition with healthcare provider. A medication guide should be dispensed with each prescription. **Nortriptyline is not FDA approved for use in children.**

The possibility of a suicide attempt is inherent in major depression and may persist until remission occurs. Use caution in high-risk patients. Worsening depression and severe abrupt suicidality that are not part of the presenting symptoms may require discontinuation or modification of drug therapy. The patient's family or caregiver should be alerted to monitor patients for the emergence of suicidality and associated behaviors (such as agitation, irritability, hostility, impulsivity, and hypomania) and call healthcare provider.

May precipitate a shift to mania or hypomania in patients with bipolar disorder. Patients presenting with depressive symptoms should be screened for bipolar disorder. Monotherapy in patients with bipolar disorder should be avoided. **Nortriptyline is not FDA approved for the treatment of bipolar depression.**

Potentially life-threatening serotonin syndrome (SS) has occurred with serotonergic agents (eg, SSRIs, SNRIs), particularly when used in combination with other serotonergic agents (eg, triptans, TCAs, fentanyl, lithium, tramadol, buspirone, St John wort, tryptophan) or agents that impair metabolism of serotonin (eg, MAO inhibitors intended to treat psychiatric disorders, other MAO inhibitors [ie, linezolid and intravenous methylene blue]). Discontinue treatment (and any concomitant serotonergic agent) immediately if signs/symptoms arise. TCAs may rarely cause bone marrow suppression; monitor for any signs of infection and obtain CBC if symptoms (eg, fever, sore throat) evident. The risk of sedation and orthostatic effects are low relative to other antidepressants (APA 2010; Bauer 2013). However, nortriptyline may impair physical or mental abilities; patients must be cautioned about performing tasks that require mental alertness (eg, operating machinery or driving). The degree of anticholinergic blockade produced by this agent is moderate relative to other cyclic antidepressants, however, caution should still be used in patients with urinary retention, benign prostatic hyperplasia, narrow-angle glaucoma, xerostomia, visual problems, constipation, or history of bowel obstruction. May cause orthostatic hypotension (risk is low relative to other antidepressants) or conduction disturbances (APA 2010). Use with caution in patients with a history of cardiovascular disease (including previous MI, stroke, tachycardia, or conduction abnormalities). The risk conduction abnormalities with this agent is moderate relative to other antidepressants (APA 2010). May cause mild pupillary dilation which in susceptible individuals can lead to an episode of narrow-angle glaucoma. Consider evaluating patients who have not had an iridectomy for narrow-angle glaucoma risk factors.

Recommended by the manufacturer to discontinue prior to elective surgery; risks exist for drug interactions with anesthesia and for cardiac arrhythmias. However, definitive drug interactions have not been widely reported in the literature and continuation of tricyclic antidepressants is generally recommended as long as precautions are taken to reduce the significance of any adverse events that may occur (Pass 2004). May alter glucose regulation - use caution in patients with diabetes (APA 2010). Use caution in patients with a history of seizures. May increase the risks associated with electroconvulsive therapy. Bone fractures have been associated with antidepressant treatment. Consider the possibility of a fragility fracture if an antidepressant-treated patient presents with unexplained bone pain, point tenderness, swelling, or bruising (Rabenda 2013; Rizzoli 2012). Use with caution in patients with hepatic or renal dysfunction.

Benzyl alcohol and derivatives: Some dosage forms may contain sodium benzoate/benzoic acid; benzoic acid (benzoate) is a metabolite of benzyl alcohol; large amounts of benzyl alcohol (≥99 mg/kg/day) have been associated with a potentially fatal toxicity ("gasping syndrome") in neonates; the "gasping syndrome" consists of metabolic acidosis, respiratory distress, gasping respirations, CNS dysfunction (including convulsions, intracranial hemorrhage), hypotension, and cardiovascular collapse (AAP ["Inactive" 1997]; CDC 1982); some data suggests that benzoate displaces bilirubin from protein binding sites (Ahlfors 2001); avoid or use dosage forms containing benzyl alcohol derivative with caution in neonates. See manufacturer's labeling.

Abrupt discontinuation or interruption of antidepressant therapy has been associated with a discontinuation syndrome. Symptoms arising may vary with antidepressant however commonly include nausea, vomiting, diarrhea, headaches, lightheadedness, dizziness, diminished appetite, sweating, chills, tremors, paresthesias, fatigue, somnolence, and sleep disturbances (eg, vivid dreams, insomnia). Greater risks for developing a discontinuation syndrome have been associated with antidepressants with shorter half-lives, longer durations of treatment, and abrupt discontinuation. For antidepressants of short or intermediate half-lives, symptoms may emerge within 2 to 5 days after treatment discontinuation and last 7 to 14 days (APA 2010; Fava 2006; Haddad 2001; Shelton 2001; Warner 2006).

Drug Interactions

Metabolism/Transport Effects **Substrate** of CYP1A2 (minor), CYP2C19 (minor), CYP2D6 (major), CYP3A4 (minor); **Note:** Assignment of Major/Minor substrate status based on clinically relevant drug interaction potential; **Inhibits** CYP2E1 (weak)

Avoid Concomitant Use

Avoid concomitant use of Nortriptyline with any of the following: Aclidinium; Azelastine (Nasal); Cimetropium; Dapoxetine; Dronedarone; Eluxadoline; Glucagon; Glycopyrrolate (Oral Inhalation); Iobenguane I 123; Ipratropium (Oral Inhalation); Levosulpiride; Linezolid; MAO Inhibitors; Methylene Blue; Moxonidine; Nitroglycerin; Orphenadrine; Oxatomide; Oxomemazine; Paraldehyde; Potassium Chloride; Thalidomide; Tiotropium; Umeclidinium

Increased Effect/Toxicity

Nortriptyline may increase the levels/effects of: AbobotulinumtoxinA; Alcohol (Ethyl); Alpha-/Beta-Agonists (Direct-Acting); Alpha1-Agonists; Amphetamines; Analgesics (Opioid); Anticholinergic Agents; Antipsychotic Agents; Azelastine (Nasal); Beta2-Agonists; Blonanserin; Buprenorphine; Cimetropium; Citalopram; CNS Depressants; Desmopressin; Dronedarone; Eluxadoline; Escitalopram; Flunitrazepam; Glucagon; Glycopyrrolate (Oral Inhalation); Highest Risk QTc-Prolonging Agents; HYDROcodone; Iohexol; Iomeprol; Iopamidol; Methotrimeprazine; Methylene Blue; MetyroSINE; Mirabegron; Mirtazapine; Moderate Risk QTc-Prolonging Agents; Nicorandil; OnabotulinumtoxinA; Orphenadrine; OxyCODONE; Paraldehyde; Perhexiline; Piribedil; Potassium Chloride; Pramipexole; QuiNIDine; Ramosetron; RimabotulinumtoxinB; ROPINIRole; Rotigotine; Selective Serotonin Reuptake Inhibitors; Serotonin Modulators; Sodium Phosphates; Sulfonylureas; Suvorexant; Thalidomide; Thiazide and Thiazide-Like Diuretics; Tiotropium; Topiramate; Vitamin K Antagonists; Yohimbine; Zolpidem

The levels/effects of Nortriptyline may be increased by: Abiraterone Acetate; Aclidinium; Altretamine; Antiemetics (5HT3 Antagonists); Antipsychotic Agents; Asunaprevir; Brimonidine (Topical); BuPROPion; Cannabis; Chloral Betaine; Chlormethiazole; Chlorphenesin Carbamate; Cimetidine; Cinacalcet; Citalopram; Cobicistat; CYP2D6 Inhibitors (Moderate); CYP2D6 Inhibitors (Strong); Dapoxetine; Darunavir; Dexmethylphenidate; Dimethindene (Topical); Doxylamine; Dronabinol; Droperidol; DULoxetine; Escitalopram; FLUoxetine; FluvoxaMINE; HydrOXYzine; Imatinib; Ipratropium (Oral Inhalation); Kava Kava; Linezolid; Lithium; Magnesium Sulfate; MAO Inhibitors; Metaxalone; Methotrimeprazine; Methylene Blue; Methylphenidate; Metoclopramide; MetyroSINE; Mianserin; MiFEPRIStone; Minocycline; Nabilone; Oxatomide; Oxomemazine; Panobinostat; PARoxetine; Peginterferon Alfa-2b; Perampanel; Perhexiline; Pramlintide; Protease Inhibitors; QuiNIDine; Rufinamide; Sertraline; Sodium Oxybate; Tapentadol; Tedizolid; Terbinafine (Systemic); Tetrahydrocannabinol; Thyroid Products; Trimeprazine; Umeclidinium; Valproate Products

Decreased Effect

Nortriptyline may decrease the levels/effects of: Acetylcholinesterase Inhibitors; Alpha1-Agonists; Alpha2-Agonists; Alpha2-Agonists (Ophthalmic); Gastrointestinal Agents (Prokinetic); Iobenguane I 123; Itopride; Levosulpiride; Moxonidine; Nitroglycerin; Secretin

The levels/effects of Nortriptyline may be decreased by: Acetylcholinesterase Inhibitors; Barbiturates; CarBAMazepine; Peginterferon Alfa-2b; St John's Wort

Pharmacodynamics/Kinetics

Onset of Action Depression: Individual responses may vary; however, 4 to 8 weeks of treatment are needed before determining if a patient with depression is partially or non-responsive (APA 2010)

Half-life Elimination

Adults: 14 to 51 hours (mean: 26 hours) (Dawling 1980)

Elderly: 23.5 to 79 hours (mean: 45 hours) (Dawling 1980)

Time to Peak Serum: 4 to 9 hours (Alexanderson 1972)

Pregnancy Considerations Animal reproduction studies are inconclusive. Nortriptyline and its metabolites cross the human placenta and can be detected in cord blood (Loughhead 2006). Tricyclic antidepressants may be associated with irritability, jitteriness, and convulsions (rare) in the neonate (Yonkers 2009).

The ACOG recommends that therapy for depression during pregnancy be individualized; treatment should incorporate the clinical expertise of the mental health clinician, obstetrician, primary health care provider, and pediatrician (ACOG 2008). According to the American Psychiatric Association (APA), the risks of medication treatment should be weighed against other treatment options and untreated depression. For women who discontinue antidepressant medications during pregnancy and who may be at high risk for postpartum depression, the medications can be restarted following delivery (APA 2010). Treatment algorithms have been developed by the ACOG and the APA for the management of depression in women prior to conception and during pregnancy (Yonkers 2009).

Pregnant women exposed to antidepressants during pregnancy are encouraged to enroll in the National Pregnancy Registry for Antidepressants (NPRAD). Women 18 to 45 years of age or their health care providers may contact the registry by calling 844-405-6185. Enrollment should be done as early in pregnancy as possible.

Breastfeeding Considerations Nortriptyline is excreted into breast milk and the M/P ratio ranged from 0.87 to 3.71 in one case report (Matheson 1988). Based on available information, nortriptyline has not been detected in the serum of nursing infants; however, low levels of the active metabolite E-10-hydroxynortriptyline have been detected in the serum of newborns following breastfeeding (Wisner 1991). Based on information from one mother-infant pair, following maternal use of nortriptyline 125 mg/day, the estimated exposure to the breastfeeding infant would be 0.6% to 3% of the weight-adjusted maternal dose. Adverse events have not been reported in nursing infants. Infants should be monitored for signs of adverse events; routine monitoring of infant serum concentrations is not recommended (Fortinguerra 2009).

Dosage Forms

Capsule, Oral:

Pamelor: 10 mg, 25 mg, 50 mg, 75 mg

Generic: 10 mg, 25 mg, 50 mg, 75 mg

Solution, Oral:

Generic: 10 mg/5 mL (473 mL)

Dental Comment See Local Anesthetic/Vasoconstrictor Precautions

Nystatin (Oral) (nye STAT in)

Related Information

Fungal Infections *on page 1847*

Related Sample Prescriptions

Fungal Infections - Sample Prescriptions *on page 35*

Brand Names: US Bio-Statin

Brand Names: Canada PMS-Nystatin

Generic Availability (US) Yes

Pharmacologic Category Antifungal Agent, Oral Nonabsorbed/Partially Absorbed

Dental Use Treatment of susceptible cutaneous, mucocutaneous, and oral cavity fungal infections normally caused by the *Candida* species; treatment of removable intraoral appliances in patients who experience oral cavity fungal infections

Use Treatment of susceptible cutaneous, mucocutaneous, and oral cavity fungal infections normally caused by the *Candida* species

Local Anesthetic/Vasoconstrictor Precautions No information available to require special precautions

Effects on Dental Treatment No significant effects or complications reported

Effects on Bleeding No information available to require special precautions

Adverse Reactions

1% to 10%: Gastrointestinal: Diarrhea, nausea, stomach pain, vomiting

<1%, postmarketing, and/or case reports: Hypersensitivity reaction

Dental Usual Dosage Oral candidiasis: Suspension (swish and swallow orally):

Premature infants: 100,000 units 4 times/day; paint suspension into recesses of the mouth

Infants: 200,000 units 4 times/day or 100,000 units to each side of mouth 4 times/day; paint suspension into recesses of the mouth

Children and Adults: 400,000 to 600,000 units 4 times/day; swish in the mouth and retain for as long as possible (several minutes) before swallowing. For patients wearing a removable intraoral appliance, some experts recommend to also treat the oral appliance with the oral suspension overnight for 2 to 5 days.

Dosing

Adult & Geriatric

Oral candidiasis: Suspension (swish and swallow): 400,000-600,000 units 4 times/day; swish in the mouth and retain for as long as possible (several minutes) before swallowing

Intestinal infections: Oral tablets: 500,000-1,000,000 units every 8 hours

Note: Powder for compounding: 1/8 teaspoon (500,000 units) to equal approximately 1/2 cup of water; give 4 times/day

Pediatric Oral candidiasis:

Suspension:

Premature infants: 100,000 units 4 times/day; paint suspension into recesses of the mouth

Infants: 200,000 units 4 times/day or 100,000 units to each side of mouth 4 times/day; paint suspension into recesses of the mouth

Children: 400,000-600,000 units 4 times/day; swish in the mouth and retain for as long as possible (several minutes) before swallowing

Powder for compounding: Children: Refer to adult dosing.

Renal Impairment No dosage adjustment provided in manufacturer's labeling.

Hepatic Impairment No dosage adjustment provided in manufacturer's labeling.

Mechanism of Action Binds to sterols in fungal cell membrane, changing the cell wall permeability allowing for leakage of cellular contents

Contraindications Hypersensitivity to nystatin or any component of the formulation

Drug Interactions

Metabolism/Transport Effects None known.

Avoid Concomitant Use

Avoid concomitant use of Nystatin (Oral) with any of the following: Saccharomyces boulardii

Increased Effect/Toxicity There are no known significant interactions involving an increase in effect.

Decreased Effect

Nystatin (Oral) may decrease the levels/effects of: Saccharomyces boulardii

Pharmacodynamics/Kinetics

Onset of Action Symptomatic relief from candidiasis: 24-72 hours

Pregnancy Risk Factor C

Pregnancy Considerations Animal reproduction studies have not been conducted. Adverse events in the fetus or newborn have not been reported following maternal use of vaginal nystatin during pregnancy. Absorption following oral use is poor.

Breastfeeding Considerations Excretion into breast milk is not known; however, absorption following oral use is poor.

Dosage Forms

Capsule, Oral [preservative free]:
Bio-Statin: 500,000 units, 1,000,000 units

Powder, Oral:
Bio-Statin: (1 ea)

Suspension, Mouth/Throat:
Generic: 100,000 units/mL (5 mL, 60 mL, 473 mL, 480 mL)

Tablet, Oral:
Generic: 500,000 units

Nystatin (Topical) (nye STAT in)

Related Information

Fungal Infections *on page* 1847

Related Sample Prescriptions

Fungal Infections - Sample Prescriptions *on page* 35

Brand Names: US Nyamyc; Nyata; Nystop; Pedi-Dri [DSC]; Pediaderm AF Complete [DSC]

Brand Names: Canada Nyaderm; Ratio-Nystatin

Generic Availability (US) May be product dependent

Pharmacologic Category Antifungal Agent, Topical

Dental Use Treatment of cutaneous and mucocutaneous fungal infections caused by *Candida albicans* and other susceptible *Candida* species.

Use Fungal infections (cutaneous and mucocutaneous): Treatment of cutaneous and mucocutaneous fungal infections caused by *Candida albicans* and other susceptible *Candida* species.

Local Anesthetic/Vasoconstrictor Precautions No information available to require special precautions

Effects on Dental Treatment No significant effects or complications reported

Effects on Bleeding No information available to require special precautions

Adverse Reactions

Frequency not defined: Dermatologic: Contact dermatitis, Stevens-Johnson syndrome

<1%, postmarketing, and/or case reports: Hypersensitivity reaction

Dental Usual Dosage Mucocutaneous fungal infections: Children and Adults: Topical: Apply 2 to 3 times/day to affected areas

Dosing

Adult & Geriatric Fungal infections (cutaneous and mucocutaneous): Topical: **Note:** Cream is usually preferred to ointment for intertriginous areas; very moist lesions are best treated with topical powder

Cream, ointment: Apply to the affected areas twice daily or as indicated until healing is complete

Powder: Apply to the affected areas 2 to 3 times daily until healing is complete

Pediatric Fungal infections (cutaneous and mucocutaneous): Infants, Children, and Adolescents: Topical: Refer to adult dosing.

Renal Impairment There are no dosage adjustments provided in the manufacturer's labeling. However, dosage adjustment unlikely due to low systemic absorption

Hepatic Impairment There are no dosage adjustments provided in the manufacturer's labeling. However, dosage adjustment unlikely due to low systemic absorption

Mechanism of Action Binds to sterols in fungal cell membrane, changing the cell wall permeability allowing for leakage of cellular contents

Contraindications Hypersensitivity to nystatin or any component of the formulation

Warnings/Precautions For topical use only; not for systemic, oral, intravaginal, or ophthalmic use. Hypersensitivity reactions may occur; immediately discontinue if signs of a hypersensitivity reaction occurs. Discontinue use if irritation occurs.

Drug Interactions

Metabolism/Transport Effects None known.

Avoid Concomitant Use

Avoid concomitant use of Nystatin (Topical) with any of the following: Progesterone

Increased Effect/Toxicity There are no known significant interactions involving an increase in effect.

Decreased Effect

Nystatin (Topical) may decrease the levels/effects of: Progesterone

Pharmacodynamics/Kinetics

Onset of Action Symptomatic relief from candidiasis: 24 to 72 hours

Pregnancy Risk Factor C

Pregnancy Considerations Animal reproduction studies have not been conducted. Absorption following oral use is poor and nystatin is not absorbed following application to mucous membranes or intact skin.

Breastfeeding Considerations It is not known if nystatin is excreted in breast milk; however, absorption following oral use is poor and nystatin is not absorbed following application to mucous membranes or intact skin. The manufacturer recommends that caution be exercised when administering nystatin to nursing women.

Dosage Forms Considerations

Nyata Kit contains nystatin powder and Curatin exfoliating serum.

Pediaderm AF Complete Kit contains nystatin cream and Pediaderm Diaper Defense cream.

Dosage Forms

Cream, External:
Generic: 100,000 units/g (15 g, 30 g)

Ointment, External:
Generic: 100,000 units/g (15 g, 30 g)

Powder, External:
Nyamyc: 100,000 units/g (15 g, 30 g, 60 g)
Nyata: 100,000 units/g (45 g)
Nystop: 100,000 units/g (15 g, 30 g, 60 g)
Generic: 100,000 units/g (15 g, 30 g, 60 g)

Obeticholic Acid (oh bet i KOE lik AS id)

Brand Names: US Ocaliva

Pharmacologic Category Farnesoid X Receptor Agonist

Use **Primary biliary cholangitis:** Treatment of primary biliary cholangitis (PBC) in combination with ursodiol (ursodeoxycholic acid) in adults with an inadequate response to ursodiol, or as monotherapy in adults unable to tolerate ursodiol.

Local Anesthetic/Vasoconstrictor Precautions No information available to require special precautions

Effects on Dental Treatment Key adverse event(s) related to dental treatment: Oropharyngeal pain has been reported

Effects on Bleeding No information available to require special precautions

Adverse Reactions

>10%:

- Central nervous system: Fatigue (19% to 25%)
- Dermatologic: Pruritus (56% to 70%; severe: 19% to 23%)
- Endocrine & metabolic: Decreased HDL cholesterol (9% to 20%)
- Gastrointestinal: Abdominal pain (19%)

1% to 10%:

- Cardiovascular: Peripheral edema (7%), palpitations (3% to 7%)
- Central nervous system: Dizziness (7%)
- Dermatologic: Skin rash (10%), eczema (3% to 6%)
- Endocrine & metabolic: Thyroid dysfunction (4% to 6%)
- Gastrointestinal: Constipation (7%)
- Neuromuscular & skeletal: Arthralgia (6% to 10%)
- Respiratory: Oropharyngeal pain (7% to 8%)
- Miscellaneous: Fever (7%)

Frequency not defined:

- Gastrointestinal: Cholangitis (primary biliary)
- Hepatic: Ascites (worsening), jaundice

General Dosage Range Dosage adjustment recommended in patients with hepatic impairment and in patients who develop toxicities.

Oral: *Adults:* 5 to 10 mg once daily (maximum: 10 mg/day).

Mechanism of Action Obeticholic acid is a farnesoid X receptor agonist; activation of FXR suppresses de novo synthesis of bile acids from cholesterol and increases transport of bile acids out of the hepatocytes, limiting the overall size of the circulating bile acid pool while promoting choleresis.

Pharmacodynamics/Kinetics

Time to Peak Plasma: Obeticholic acid: ~1.5 hours; glyco- and tauro- obeticholic acid: 10 hours

Pregnancy Considerations Adverse events have not been observed in animal reproduction studies.

Obinutuzumab (oh bi nue TOOZ ue mab)

Brand Names: US Gazyva

Brand Names: Canada Gazyva

Pharmacologic Category Antineoplastic Agent, Anti-CD20; Antineoplastic Agent, Monoclonal Antibody

Use

Chronic lymphocytic leukemia: Treatment of patients with previously untreated chronic lymphocytic leukemia (CLL) in combination with chlorambucil

Follicular lymphoma: Treatment of follicular lymphoma (in combination with bendamustine followed by obinutuzumab monotherapy) in patients who relapsed after, or are refractory to, a rituximab-containing regimen.

Local Anesthetic/Vasoconstrictor Precautions No information available to require special precautions

Effects on Dental Treatment Key adverse event(s) related to dental treatment: Monoclonal antibodies used to treat chronic lymphocytic leukemia are known to cause stomatitis and mucositis.

Effects on Bleeding Chemotherapy may result in significant myelosuppression, including thrombocytopenia. In patients who are under active treatment, a medical consult is suggested.

Adverse Reactions Adverse reactions reported in combination with chlorambucil or bendamustine in addition to reaction incidence during the monotherapy phase.

>10%:

- Endocrine & metabolic: Hypophosphatemia (25% to 41%), hypocalcemia (37% to 38%;), hyperkalemia (33%), hyponatremia (26%), hypoalbuminemia (23%), hypokalemia (14%)
- Gastrointestinal: Constipation (8% to 19%)
- Hematologic & oncologic: Lymphocytopenia (80% to 99%; grades 3/4: 39% to 93%), leukopenia (6% to 86%; grades 3/4: 4% to 47%), neutropenia (11% to 76%; grades 3/4: 10% to 52%; onset ≥28 days after completion of treatment: 16%; lasting ≥28 days: 3%), decreased hemoglobin (50%), thrombocytopenia (11% to 48%; grades 3/4: 1% to 13% onset within 24 hours of infusion: 4%), anemia (12% to 39%; grades 3/4: 1% to 10%), hemorrhage (11%; grades 3/4: 5%)
- Hepatic: Increased serum AST (24% to 27%), increased serum ALT (21% to 35%), increased serum alkaline phosphatase (18%)
- Infection: Infection (38% to 66%)
- Neuromuscular & skeletal: Musculoskeletal signs and symptoms (18% to 41%; including pain), back pain (5%), arthralgia (7% to 12%), weakness (11%)
- Renal: Decreased creatinine clearance (43% to 58%), increased serum creatinine (30%)
- Respiratory: Cough (10% to 26%), upper respiratory tract infection (12% to 13%), sinusitis (10% to 12%)

1% to 10%:

- Central nervous system: Fatigue (8%)
- Dermatologic: Pruritus (9%)
- Gastrointestinal: Diarrhea (8% to 10%), nausea (8%), dyspepsia (5%)
- Genitourinary: Urinary tract infection (5% to 10%)
- Endocrine & metabolic: Hyperphosphatemia, hyperuricemia
- Gastrointestinal: Diarrhea (10%; grades 3/4: 2%), constipation (8%), vomiting
- Genitourinary: Urinary tract infection (5% to 6%; grades 3/4: 1% to 2%)
- Hematologic & oncologic: Tumor lysis syndrome, febrile neutropenia
- Hepatic: Increased liver enzymes (4%; may be secondary or exacerbated by premedications)
- Immunologic: Antibody development (1% to 7%)
- Infection: Sepsis
- Neuromuscular & skeletal: Limb pain (9%)
- Respiratory: Nasopharyngitis (6% to 9%), bronchitis (7%), nasal congestion (7%)
- Miscellaneous: Infusion related reaction (initial infusion: 53% to 69%; grades 3/4: 9% to 20%; second infusion: 3% to 25%; subsequent infusions: ≤8%), fever (6% to 18%)

Frequency Not Defined:

- Cardiovascular: Exacerbation of cardiac disease
- Central nervous system: Progressive multifocal leukoencephalopathy

Infection: JCV (John Cunningham virus) infection, reactivation of HBV, viral infection (new or reactivation)

General Dosage Range Dosage adjustment recommended in patients who develop toxicities

IV: *Adults:* Dosage varies greatly depending on indication

Mechanism of Action Obinutuzumab is a glycoengineered type II anti-CD20 monoclonal antibody. The CD20 antigen is expressed on the surface of pre B- and mature B-lymphocytes; upon binding to CD20, obinutuzumab activates complement-dependent cytotoxicity, antibody-dependent cellular cytotoxicity and antibody-dependent cellular phagocytosis, resulting in cell death (Sehn 2012).

Pharmacodynamics/Kinetics

Half-life Elimination ~26.4 to 36.8 days

Pregnancy Considerations Adverse effects were observed in animal reproduction studies. Monoclonal antibodies are known to cross the placenta. Based on the mechanism of action and on animal data, if exposure occurs during pregnancy, B-cell counts may be depleted and immunologic function may be affected in the neonate after birth. Administration of live vaccines to neonates and infants exposed in utero should be avoided until after B-cell recovery. It has been recommended that women of childbearing potential use effective contraception during therapy and for 18 months after the last treatment (Gazyva Canadian product labeling 2016).

Octreotide (ok TREE oh tide)

Brand Names: US SandoSTATIN; SandoSTATIN LAR Depot

Brand Names: Canada Ocphyl; Octreotide Acetate Omega; Octreotide Injection; Sandostatin; Sandostatin LAR

Pharmacologic Category Antidiarrheal; Antidote; Somatostatin Analog

Use

Acromegaly:

Injection solution: To reduce blood levels of growth hormone (GH) and insulin-like growth factor 1 (IGF-1) in patients with inadequate response to or who cannot be treated with surgical resection, pituitary irradiation, and bromocriptine mesylate at maximally tolerated doses; goal of therapy is to achieve normalization of GH and IGF-1 levels.

LAR depot suspension: Long-term maintenance treatment of acromegaly in patients with an inadequate response to surgery and/or radiotherapy (or for whom surgery/radiotherapy are not options) with a goal of therapy to reduce GH and IGF-1 levels to normal.

Carcinoid tumors:

Injection solution: Management of symptoms (diarrhea and flushing) in patients with metastatic carcinoid tumors.

LAR depot suspension: Long-term treatment of severe diarrhea and flushing episodes associated with metastatic carcinoid tumors.

Vasoactive intestinal peptide-secreting tumors:

Injection solution: Treatment of profuse watery diarrhea associated with vasoactive intestinal peptide-secreting tumors (VIPomas).

LAR depot suspension: Long-term treatment of profuse watery diarrhea associated with VIPomas.

Limitations of use: The effects of octreotide (injection solution and LAR depot suspension) on tumor size, rate of growth, and development of metastases in patients with carcinoid syndrome and VIPomas have not been determined.

Local Anesthetic/Vasoconstrictor Precautions Octreotide is one of the drugs confirmed to prolong the QT interval and is accepted as having a risk of causing torsade de pointes. The risk of drug-induced torsade de pointes is extremely low when a single QT interval prolonging drug is prescribed. In terms of epinephrine, it is not known what effect vasoconstrictors in the local anesthetic regimen will have in patients with a known history of congenital prolonged QT interval or in patients taking any medication that prolongs the QT interval. Until more information is obtained, it is suggested that the clinician consult with the physician prior to the use of a vasoconstrictor in suspected patients, and that the vasoconstrictor (epinephrine, mepivacaine and levonordefrin [Carbocaine® 2% with Neo-Cobefrin®]) be used with caution.

Effects on Dental Treatment Key adverse event(s) related to dental treatment: Xerostomia (normal salivary flow resumes upon discontinuation), gingivitis, glossitis, stomatitis, taste perversion, and dysphagia.

Effects on Bleeding No information available to require special precautions

Adverse Reactions Adverse reactions vary by route of administration and dosage form. Frequency of cardiac, endocrine, and gastrointestinal adverse reactions was generally higher in patients with acromegaly.

>10%:

Cardiovascular: Sinus bradycardia (19% to 25%), chest pain (≤20%; non-depot formulations), palpitations (5% to 15%), peripheral edema (5% to 15%), hypertension (≤13%)

Central nervous system: Fatigue (1% to 32%), headache (6% to 30%), malaise (16% to 20%), dizziness (5% to 20%), anxiety (5% to 15%), confusion (5% to 15%), hypoesthesia (5% to 15%), insomnia (5% to 15%), paresthesia (5% to 15%), rigors (5% to 15%), pain (4% to 15%)

Dermatologic: Pruritus (≤18%), skin rash (15%; depot formulation), diaphoresis (5% to 15%), alopecia (≤13%)

Endocrine & metabolic: Hyperglycemia (2% to 27%), hypothyroidism (≤12%; non-depot formulations)

Gastrointestinal: Diarrhea (34% to 61%), abdominal pain (5% to 61%), loose stools (5% to 61%), nausea (5% to 61%), flatulence (≤38%), cholelithiasis (13% to 38%; length of therapy-dependent), gallbladder sludge (24%; length of therapy-dependent), constipation (9% to 21%), vomiting (4% to 21%), biliary obstruction (duct dilatation: 12%), anorexia (5% to 15%), abdominal cramps (5% to 15%)

Hematologic & oncologic: Anemia (≤15%; non-depot formulations: <1%)

Hypersensitivity: Hypersensitivity reaction (5% to 15%)

Immunologic: Antibody development (≤25%; to octreotide; no efficacy change)

Local: Pain at injection site (2% to 50%; formulation-related)

Neuromuscular & skeletal: Back pain (1% to 27%), arthropathy (8% to 19%), myalgia (≤18%), arthralgia (1% to 15%), weakness (5% to 15%)

Otic: Otalgia (5% to 15%)

Renal: Nephrolithiasis (5% to 15%)

Respiratory: Upper respiratory tract infection (10% to 23%), dyspnea (≤20%; non-depot formulations), flu-like symptoms (1% to 20%), cough (5% to 15%), pharyngitis (5% to 15%), rhinitis (5% to 15%), sinusitis (5% to 15%)

Miscellaneous: Fever (16% to 20%)

1% to 10%:

Cardiovascular: Cardiac conduction disturbance (9% to 10%), cardiac arrhythmia (3% to 9%), angina pectoris (1% to 4%), cardiac failure (1% to 4%), edema (1% to 4%), flushing (1% to 4%), phlebitis (1% to 4%)

Central nervous system: Abnormal gait (1% to 4%), amnesia (1% to 4%), depression (1% to 4%), drowsiness (1% to 4%), hallucination (1% to 4%), hypertonia (1% to 4%), nervousness (1% to 4%), neuralgia (1% to 4%), neuropathy (1% to 4%), vertigo (1% to 4%), voice disorder (1% to 4%)

Dermatologic: Acne vulgaris (1% to 4%), cellulitis (1% to 4%)

Endocrine & metabolic: Goiter (≤8%; non-depot formulations), hypoglycemia (2% to 4%), albuminuria (1% to 4%), hypokalemia (1% to 4%), gout (1% to 4%), cachexia (1% to 4%)

Gastrointestinal: Dyspepsia (4% to 6%), fecal discoloration (4% to 6%), steatorrhea (4% to 6%), tenesmus (4% to 6%), colitis (1% to 4%), diverticulitis (1% to 4%), dysgeusia (1% to 4%), dysphagia (1% to 4%), gastritis (1% to 4%), gastroenteritis (1% to 4%), gingivitis (1% to 4%), glossitis (1% to 4%), malabsorption (fat: 1% to 4%), melena (1% to 4%), stomatitis (1% to 4%), xerostomia (1% to 4%)

Genitourinary: Impotence (1% to 4%), mastalgia (1% to 4%), pollakiuria (1% to 4%; non-depot formulations), urinary incontinence (1% to 4%), urinary tract infection (1% to 4%)

Hematologic & oncologic: Bruise (1% to 4%), hematoma (1% to 4%), hypoproteinemia (1% to 4%)

Infection: Abscess (renal: 1% to 4%), bacterial infection (1% to 4%), candidiasis (1% to 4%), cold symptoms (1% to 4%)

Local: Hematoma at injection site (1% to 4%)

Neuromuscular & skeletal: Hyperkinesia (1% to 4%), tremor (1% to 4%)

Ophthalmic: Blurred vision (1% to 4%), visual disturbance (1% to 4%)

Otic: Tinnitus (1% to 4%)

Respiratory: Bronchitis (1% to 4%), epistaxis (1% to 4%)

<1%, postmarketing, and/or case reports: Adrenocortical insufficiency, amenorrhea, anaphylactic shock, anaphylactoid reaction, aneurysm, aphasia, appendicitis, arthritis, ascites, atrial fibrillation, basal cell carcinoma, Bell's palsy, biliary obstruction, breast carcinoma, cardiac failure, cerebrovascular disease, cholangitis (ascending), cholecystitis, cholestatic hepatitis, cyanocobalamin deficiency, deafness, decreased libido, diabetes insipidus, diabetes mellitus, erythema (with wheal), facial edema, galactorrhea, gastrointestinal hemorrhage, gastrointestinal ulcer, glaucoma, gynecomastia, hematuria, hemiparesis, hemorrhoids, hepatitis, hyperesthesia, hypoxia (children), increased creatine phosphokinase, increased intraocular pressure, increased liver enzymes, increased serum creatinine, intestinal obstruction, intracranial hemorrhage, iron deficiency, ischemia, jaundice, joint effusion, liver steatosis, malignant hyperthermia, menstrual disease (polymenorrhea), migraine, myocardial infarction, necrotizing enterocolitis (neonates), nephrolithiasis, neuritis, nodule (pulmonary), oligomenorrhea, orthostatic hypotension, pancreatitis, pancytopenia, paranoia, paresis, petechia, pituitary apoplexy, pleural effusion, pneumonia, pneumothorax, polyp (gallbladder), prolonged Q-T interval on ECG, pulmonary embolism, pulmonary hypertension, Raynaud's phenomenon, rectal hemorrhage, renal failure, renal insufficiency, scotoma, seizure, status asthmaticus, syncope, tachycardia, thrombocytopenia, thrombophlebitis, thrombosis (including retinal vein), urticaria, vaginitis, visual field defect, weight loss

General Dosage Range Dosage adjustment recommended in patients with hepatic or renal impairment

IM: *Adults:* Depot: 20 mg every 4 weeks (maximum: 40 mg every 4 weeks)

IV, SubQ: *Adults:* 50 to 1500 mcg/day in 2 to 4 divided doses

Mechanism of Action Mimics natural somatostatin by inhibiting serotonin release, and the secretion of gastrin, VIP, insulin, glucagon, secretin, motilin, and pancreatic polypeptide. Decreases growth hormone and IGF-1 in acromegaly. Octreotide provides more potent inhibition of growth hormone, glucagon, and insulin as compared to endogenous somatostatin. Also suppresses LH response to GnRH, secretion of thyroid-stimulating hormone and decreases splanchnic blood flow.

Pharmacodynamics/Kinetics

Duration of Action SubQ: 6 to 12 hours; when using Sandostatin LAR® Depot formulation, steady-state levels are achieved after 3 injections (3 months of therapy)

Half-life Elimination 1.7 to 1.9 hours; Increased in elderly patients; Cirrhosis: Up to 3.7 hours; Fatty liver disease: Up to 3.4 hours; Renal impairment: Up to 3.1 hours

Time to Peak Plasma: SubQ: 0.4 hours (0.7 hours acromegaly); IM: 1 hour

Pregnancy Risk Factor B

Pregnancy Considerations Adverse events have not been observed in animal reproduction studies. Octreotide crosses the placenta and can be detected in the newborn at delivery (Caron 1995; Fassnacht 2001; Maffei 2010); data concerning use in pregnancy is limited. In case reports of acromegalic women who received normal doses of octreotide during pregnancy, no congenital malformations were reported. Because normalization of IGF-1 and GH may restore fertility in women with acromegaly, women of childbearing potential should use adequate contraception during treatment. Long-acting formulations should be discontinued ~2 months prior to a planned pregnancy; use short acting octreotide as needed until conception. Octreotide therapy may be considered in pregnant women with worsening symptoms if needed. Monitoring of IGF-1 and/or GH is not recommended during pregnancy (Katznelson 2014).

Dental Comment See Local Anesthetic/Vasoconstrictor Precautions

Ofatumumab (oh fa TOOM yoo mab)

Brand Names: US Arzerra

Brand Names: Canada Arzerra

Pharmacologic Category Antineoplastic Agent, Anti-CD20; Antineoplastic Agent, Monoclonal Antibody

Use

Chronic lymphocytic leukemia, previously untreated: Treatment of previously untreated chronic lymphocytic leukemia (CLL) (in combination with chlorambucil) when fludarabine-based therapy is considered inappropriate

Chronic lymphocytic leukemia, relapsed : Treatment of relapsed CLL (in combination with fludarabine and cyclophosphamide).

Chronic lymphocytic leukemia, refractory: Treatment of CLL refractory to fludarabine and alemtuzumab

Chronic lymphocytic leukemia, extended treatment: Extended treatment of patients who are in complete or partial response after at least two lines of therapy for recurrent or progressive CLL

Local Anesthetic/Vasoconstrictor Precautions No information available to require special precautions

Effects on Dental Treatment No significant effects or complications reported

Effects on Bleeding Thrombocytopenia is not frequently observed (<1%) although it can rarely be seen. Neutropenia may be prolonged >2 weeks. In patients who are under active treatment with this agent, medical consult is suggested.

Adverse Reactions

>10%:

Central nervous system: Fatigue (15%)

Dermatologic: Skin rash (14%)

Gastrointestinal: Diarrhea (18%), nausea (11%)

Hematologic & oncologic: Neutropenia (24%; ≥grade 3: >22%; may be prolonged >2 weeks), anemia (16%; grades 3/4: 5%)

Infection: Infection (65% to 70%; includes bacterial, fungal, or viral), serious infection (20%)

Respiratory: Pneumonia (8% to 23%), cough (19%), upper respiratory tract infection (11% to 19%), dyspnea (14%), bronchitis (9% to 11%)

Miscellaneous: Infusion related reaction (46%; day 1 reactions: 25% to 44%; subsequent infusions: 2% to 29%), fever (20%)

1% to 10%:

Cardiovascular: Peripheral edema (9%), hypertension (5%), hypotension (5%), tachycardia (5%)

Central nervous system: Chills (8%), insomnia (5% to 7%), headache (6%)

Dermatologic: Urticaria (8%), hyperhidrosis (5%)

Hematologic & oncologic: Hypogammaglobulinemia (5%; grades 3/4: <1%)

Infection: Sepsis (8%), influenza (6%), herpes zoster (5% to 6%)

Neuromuscular & skeletal: Back pain (5% to 8%), muscle spasm (5%)

Respiratory: Nasopharyngitis (8%), sinusitis (5%)

<1%, postmarketing, and/or case reports: Antibody development, hepatitis B (new-onset or reactivation), porphyria cutanea tarda, progressive multifocal leukoencephalopathy, Stevens Johnson syndrome, tumor lysis syndrome

General Dosage Range Dosage adjustment recommended in patients who develop toxicities

IV: *Adults:* Dosage varies greatly depending on indication

Mechanism of Action Ofatumumab is a monoclonal antibody which binds specifically the extracellular (large and small) loops of the CD20 molecule (which is expressed on normal B lymphocytes and in B-cell CLL) resulting in potent complement-dependent cell lysis and antibody-dependent cell-mediated toxicity in cells that overexpress CD20.

Pharmacodynamics/Kinetics

Half-life Elimination 17.6 days (following repeated infusions)

Pregnancy Considerations Adverse events were observed in some animal reproduction studies. Based on animal data, prolonged depletion of circulating B cells may occur; avoid administering live vaccines to newborns exposed to ofatumumab in utero until B cell recovery occurs.

Ofloxacin (Systemic) (oh FLOKS a sin)

Related Information

Clinical Risk Related to Drugs Prolonging QT Interval *on page 1772*

Brand Names: Canada Apo-Oflox; Novo-Ofloxacin

Pharmacologic Category Antibiotic, Fluoroquinolone

Use

Treatment of acute exacerbations of chronic bronchitis, community-acquired pneumonia, skin and skin structure infections (uncomplicated), urethral and cervical gonorrhea (acute, uncomplicated), urethritis and cervicitis (nongonococcal) due to *Chlamydia trachomatis* infection, mixed infections of the urethra and cervix, pelvic inflammatory disease (acute), cystitis (uncomplicated), urinary tract infections (complicated), prostatitis

Note: As of April 2007, the CDC no longer recommends the use of fluoroquinolones for the treatment of gonococcal disease.

Local Anesthetic/Vasoconstrictor Precautions Ofloxacin (Systemic) is one of the drugs confirmed to prolong the QT interval and is accepted as having a risk of causing torsade de pointes. The risk of drug-induced torsade de pointes is extremely low when a single QT interval prolonging drug is prescribed. In terms of epinephrine, it is not known what effect vasoconstrictors in the local anesthetic regimen will have in patients with a known history of congenital prolonged QT interval or in patients taking any medication that prolongs the QT interval. Until more information is obtained, it is suggested that the clinician consult with the physician prior to the use of a vasoconstrictor in suspected patients, and that the vasoconstrictor (epinephrine, mepivacaine and levonordefrin [Carbocaine® 2% with Neo-Cobefrin®]) be used with caution.

Effects on Dental Treatment Key adverse event(s) related to dental treatment: Xerostomia (normal salivary flow resumes upon discontinuation) and abnormal taste.

Effects on Bleeding Quinolone antibiotic administration has not been shown to independently effect bleeding; however, ofloxacin has been shown to potentiate the hypoprothrombinemic effect of warfarin and other coumarin anticoagulants. The hypoprothrombinemic mechanism may involve inhibition of coumarin metabolism and/or depletion of certain clotting factors due to suppression of vitamin K-producing intestinal flora.

Adverse Reactions

1% to 10%:

Cardiovascular: Chest pain (1% to 3%)

Central nervous system: Headache (1% to 9%), insomnia (3% to 7%), dizziness (1% to 5%), fatigue (1% to 3%), drowsiness (1% to 3%), sleep disorder (1% to 3%), nervousness (1% to 3%), pain (trunk)

Dermatologic: Pruritus (≤3%), skin rash (≤3%), genital pruritus (women: 1% to 3%)

Gastrointestinal: Nausea (3% to 10%), diarrhea (1% to 4%), vomiting (1% to 4%), abdominal cramps (1% to 3%), constipation (1% to 3%), decreased appetite (1% to 3%), dysgeusia (1% to 3%), flatulence (1% to

3%), gastrointestinal distress (1% to 3%), xerostomia (1% to 3%)
Genitourinary: Vaginitis (1% to 5%)
Ophthalmic: Visual disturbance (1% to 3%)
Respiratory: Pharyngitis (1% to 3%)
Miscellaneous: Fever (1% to 3%)

<1%, postmarketing, and/or case reports: Abnormal dreams, anaphylaxis, anxiety, auditory disturbance (decreased acuity), blurred vision, chills, cognitive dysfunction, cough, depression, ecchymosis, edema, erythema nodosum, euphoria, exacerbation of myasthenia gravis, Gilles de la Tourette's syndrome, hallucination, hepatic insufficiency, hepatic failure, hepatitis, hepatotoxicity (idiosyncratic; Chalasani 2014), hyperglycemia, hypoglycemia, hypertension, increased intracranial pressure, increased thirst, interstitial nephritis, limb pain, malaise, palpitations, paresthesia, peripheral neuropathy, photophobia, pneumonitis, pseudotumor cerebri, psychotic reaction, rhabdomyolysis, rupture of tendon, seizure, skin photosensitivity, Stevens-Johnson syndrome, syncope, tendonitis, tinnitus, torsades de pointes, toxic epidermal necrolysis, vasculitis, vasodilatation, vertigo, weakness, weight loss

General Dosage Range Dosage adjustment recommended in patients with hepatic or renal impairment

Oral: *Adults:* 200 to 400 mg every 12 hours

Mechanism of Action Ofloxacin is a DNA gyrase inhibitor. DNA gyrase is an essential bacterial enzyme that maintains the superhelical structure of DNA. DNA gyrase is required for DNA replication and transcription, DNA repair, recombination, and transposition; bactericidal

Pharmacodynamics/Kinetics

Half-life Elimination ~9 hours (biphasic: 4 to 5 hours [6.4 to 7.4 hours in elderly patients] and 20 to 25 hours [accounts for <5%]); prolonged with renal impairment

Time to Peak Serum: 1 to 2 hours

Pregnancy Risk Factor C

Pregnancy Considerations Adverse events have been observed in some animal reproduction studies. Ofloxacin crosses the placenta and produces measurable concentrations in the amniotic fluid. Serum concentrations of ofloxacin may be lower during pregnancy than in nonpregnant patients (Giamarellou 1989). Based on available data, an increased risk of teratogenic effects has not been observed following ofloxacin use during pregnancy (Padberg 2014).

Dental Comment See Local Anesthetic/Vasoconstrictor Precautions

OLANZapine (oh LAN za peen)

Brand Names: US ZyPREXA; ZyPREXA Relprevv; ZyPREXA Zydis

Brand Names: Canada ACT Olanzapine; ACT Olanzapine ODT; Apo-Olanzapine; Apo-Olanzapine ODT; Auro-Olanzapine ODT; JAMP Olanzapine FC; JAMP-Olanzapine ODT; Mar-Olanzapine; Mar-Olanzapine ODT; Mint-Olanzapine ODT; Mylan-Olanzapine; Mylan-Olanzapine ODT; Olanzapine for injection; Olanzapine ODT; PHL-Olanzapine; PHL-Olanzapine ODT; PMS-Olanzapine; PMS-Olanzapine ODT; RAN-Olanzapine; RAN-Olanzapine ODT; Riva-Olanzapine; Riva-Olanzapine ODT; Sandoz-Olanzapine; Sandoz-Olanzapine ODT; Teva-Olanzapine; Teva-Olanzapine ODT; Van-Olanzapine; Zyprexa; Zyprexa Intramuscular; Zyprexa Zydis

Generic Availability (US) May be product dependent

Pharmacologic Category Antimanic Agent; Second Generation (Atypical) Antipsychotic

Use

Oral: Treatment of the manifestations of schizophrenia; treatment of acute or mixed mania episodes associated with bipolar I disorder (as monotherapy or in combination with lithium or valproate); maintenance treatment of bipolar I disorder; in combination with fluoxetine for treatment-resistant or bipolar I depression

IM, extended-release (Zyprexa Relprevv): Treatment of schizophrenia

IM, short-acting (Zyprexa IntraMuscular): Treatment of acute agitation associated with schizophrenia and bipolar I mania

Local Anesthetic/Vasoconstrictor Precautions No information available to require special precautions

Effects on Dental Treatment No significant effects or complications reported

Effects on Bleeding No information available to require special precautions

Adverse Reactions

Oral: Unless otherwise noted, adverse events are reported for placebo-controlled trials in adult patients on monotherapy:

>10%:

Cardiovascular: Orthostatic hypotension (3% to ≥20%)

Central nervous system: Drowsiness (dose dependent; adolescents and adults 20% to 39%), extrapyramidal reaction (dose dependent; adults ≤32%; adolescents ≤10%), akathisia (adolescents and adults 3% to 27%), parkinsonian-like syndrome (14% to 20%; includes akinesia, cogwheel rigidity, extrapyramidal syndrome, hypertonia, hypokinesia, maked facies, and tremor), dizziness (adults 11% to 18%; adolescents 7% to 8%), headache (adolescents 17%), fatigue (dose dependent; adolescents and adults 2% to 14%), insomnia (12%)

Endocrine & metabolic: Increased serum prolactin (adolescents 47%; adults 30%), weight gain (adults 5% to 6%; has been reported as high as 40%; adolescents 29% to 31%)

Gastrointestinal: Increased appetite (adolescents 17% to 29%; adults 3% to 6%), xerostomia (dose dependent; adults 3% to 22%; adolescents 4% to 7%), dyspepsia (adults 7% to 11%; adolescents 3%), constipation (adolescents and adults 4% to 11%)

Hepatic: Increased serum AST (adolescents 28%), decreased serum bilirubin (adolescents 22%), increased serum ALT (≥3 x ULN; adolescents and adults 5% to 12%)

Neuromuscular & skeletal: Weakness (dose dependent; 8% to 20%)

Miscellaneous: Accidental injury (12%)

1% to 10%:

Cardiovascular: Chest pain (3%), peripheral edema (3%), tachycardia (3%), hypertension (2%)

Central nervous system: Personality disorder (5% to 8%), abnormal gait (6%), hypertonia (3%), restlessness (adolescents 3%), falling (older adults ≥2%), articulation impairment (2%)

Endocrine & metabolic: Increased gamma-glutamyl transferase (adolescents 10%; adults 2%), increased uric acid (4%), menstrual disease (2%; including amenorrhea, hypomenorrhea, delayed menstruation, oligomenorrhea), breast changes (male and female adolescents ≤2%; including discharge, enlargement, galactorrhea, gynecomastia, lactation disorder)

Gastrointestinal: Abdominal pain (6%; adolescents), vomiting (≤4%), diarrhea (3%; adolescents)

Genitourinary: Urinary incontinence (adults and older adults ≥2%), sexual disorder (2%; adolescents ≤1%; anorgasmia, delayed ejaculation, erectile dysfunction, changes in libido, abnormal orgasm, sexual dysfunction), urinary tract infection (2%)

Hematologic & oncologic: Bruise (5%)

Hepatic: Increased liver enzymes (adolescents ≤8%), increased serum alkaline phosphatase (≥1%)

Neuromuscular & skeletal: Tremor (4% to 7%; dose dependent), limb pain (adolescents and adults 5% to 6%), arthralgia (adults 5%; adolescents 2%), back pain (5%), muscle rigidity (2%; adolescents), dyskinesia (1%)

Ophthalmic: Amblyopia (3%)

Respiratory: Rhinitis (7%), cough (6%), nasopharyngitis (adolescents 4%), pharyngitis (4%), epistaxis (adolescents 3%), respiratory tract infection (adolescents 3%), sinusitis (adolescents 3%)

Miscellaneous: Fever (≤6%)

<1%, postmarketing, and/or case reports: Abdominal distension, accommodation disturbance, agranulocytosis, alopecia, anaphylactoid reaction, angioedema, ataxia, cerebrovascular accident, chills, coma, confusion, diabetes mellitus, diabetic ketoacidosis, diabetic coma, difficulty in micturition, dry eye syndrome, dysarthria, facial edema, hangover effect, hepatic injury (cholestatic or mixed), hepatitis, hyperbilirubinemia, hypercholesterolemia, hyperglycemia, hyperlipidemia, hypermenorrhea, hypertriglyceridemia, hypoproteinemia, impotence, intestinal obstruction, jaundice, ketosis, leukocytosis (eosinophilia), leukopenia, liver steatosis, mastalgia, mydriasis, myopathy, nausea, neuroleptic malignant syndrome, neutropenia, osteoporosis, pancreatitis, polyuria, priapism, pruritus, pulmonary edema, pulmonary embolism, rhabdomyolysis, seizure, skin photosensitivity, skin rash, stupor, suicidal tendencies, syncope, tardive dyskinesia, thrombocytopenia, tongue edema, transient ischemic attacks, urinary frequency, urinary retention, urinary urgency, urticaria, vasodilation, venous thrombosis, withdrawal syndrome

Injection: Frequency not always defined. Unless otherwise noted, adverse events are reported for placebo-controlled trials in adult patients on extended release IM injection (Zyprexa Relprevv). Also refer to adverse reactions noted with oral therapy.

Cardiovascular: Hypertension (2% to 3%), hypotension (short-acting solution for IM injection 2%), prolonged Q-T interval on ECG (2%), orthostatic hypotension (short-acting solution for IM injection 1%)

Central nervous system: Headache (13% to 18%), sedation (8% to 13%), drowsiness (both IM injection formulations 5% to 6%), akathisia (short-acting solution for IM injection 5%), dizziness (both IM injection formulations 4%), fatigue (3% to 4%), extrapyramidal reaction (solution for IM injection 2% to 4%), abnormality in thinking (3%), auditory hallucination (3%), parkinsonian-like syndrome (short-acting solution for IM injection 3%), restlessness (3%), pain (2% to 3%), abnormal dreams (2%), procedural pain (2%), sleep disorder (2%), dysarthria (1% to 2%)

Dermatologic: Acne vulgaris (2%)

Endocrine & metabolic: Weight gain (6% to 7%)

Gastrointestinal: Diarrhea (5% to 7%), vomiting (6%), xerostomia (2% to 6%), increased appetite (1% to 6%), nausea (long-acting IM formula 4% to 5%; short-acting solution for injection <1%), tooth infection (4%), toothache (3% to 4%), abdominal pain (3%), flatulence (1% to 2%)

Genitourinary: Vaginal discharge (4%)

Hepatic: Increased liver enzymes (3% to 4%)

Infection: Viral infection (2%)

Local: Pain at injection site (both IM injection formulations 1% to 4%), abscess at injection site

Neuromuscular & skeletal: Arthralgia (3%), back pain (5%), muscle spasm (1% to 3%), stiffness (4%), tremor (long-acting IM formula 3%; short-acting solution for injection 1%)

Otic: Otalgia (4%)

Respiratory: Cough (9%), nasal congestion (7%), nasopharyngitis (3% to 6%), upper respiratory tract infection (3% to 4%), pharyngolaryngeal pain (3%), sneezing (2%)

Miscellaneous: Fever (2%)

<1%, postmarketing, and/or case reports (limited to important or life-threatening): Delirium, increased creatine phosphokinase, postinjection delirium/sedation syndrome, sleep apnea syndrome (obstructive) (Health Canada 2016, Shirani 2011), syncope (short-acting solution for injection)

Dosing

Adult & Geriatric

Schizophrenia:

Oral: Initial: 5 to 10 mg once daily (increase to 10 mg once daily within 5 to 7 days); thereafter, adjust by 5 mg daily at 1-week intervals, up to a recommended maximum of 20 mg/day. Maintenance: 10 to 20 mg once daily. Doses up to 60 mg daily have been used in treatment-resistant schizophrenia; however, supporting evidence is limited (APA [Lehman 2004]).

Special risk patients: Initial: 5 mg once daily is recommended in patients who are debilitated, who have a predisposition to hypotensive reactions, who exhibit a combination of factors that may result in slower metabolism of olanzapine (eg, nonsmoking female patients ≥65 years), or who may be more pharmacodynamically sensitive to olanzapine; increase dose with caution as clinically indicated.

Extended-release IM injection: **Note:** Establish tolerance to oral olanzapine prior to changing to extended-release IM injection. Maximum dose: 300 mg every 2 weeks or 405 mg every 4 weeks

Patients established on oral olanzapine 10 mg daily: Initial dose: 210 mg every 2 weeks for 4 doses or 405 mg every 4 weeks for 2 doses; Maintenance dose: 150 mg every 2 weeks or 300 mg every 4 weeks

Patients established on oral olanzapine 15 mg daily: Initial dose: 300 mg every 2 weeks for 4 doses; Maintenance dose: 210 mg every 2 weeks or 405 mg every 4 weeks

Patients established on oral olanzapine 20 mg daily: Initial and maintenance dose: 300 mg every 2 weeks

Special risk patients: Initial: 150 mg every 4 weeks is recommended in patients who are debilitated, who have a predisposition to hypotensive reactions, who exhibit a combination of factors that may result in slower metabolism of olanzapine (eg, nonsmoking female patients ≥65 years), or who may be more pharmacodynamically sensitive to olanzapine; increase dose with caution as clinically indicated.

Bipolar I (acute mixed or manic episodes: Oral:

Monotherapy: Initial: 10 to 15 mg once daily; increase by 5 mg daily at intervals of not less than 24 hours. Maintenance: 5 to 20 mg daily; recommended maximum dose: 20 mg/day.

Combination therapy (with lithium or valproate): Initial: 10 mg once daily; dosing range: 5 to 20 mg daily

Agitation (acute, associated with bipolar disorder or schizophrenia): Short-acting IM injection: Initial dose: 10 mg (a lower dose of 5 to 7.5 mg may be considered when clinical factors warrant); additional doses (up to 10 mg) may be considered; however, 2 hours after the initial dose and 4 hours after the second dose should be allowed between doses to evaluate response (maximum total dose: 30 mg/day)

Special risk patients: Consider a lower dose of 2.5 mg in patients who are debilitated, who have a predisposition to hypotensive reactions, or who may be more pharmacodynamically sensitive to olanzapine.

Depression:

Depression associated with bipolar disorder (in combination with fluoxetine): Oral: Initial: 5 mg in the evening; adjust as tolerated to usual range of 5 to 12.5 mg daily. See **"Note."**

Treatment-resistant depression (in combination with fluoxetine): Oral: Initial: 5 mg in the evening; adjust as tolerated to range of 5 to 20 mg daily. See **"Note."**

Note (olanzapine/fluoxetine combination [Symbyax]): When using individual components of fluoxetine with olanzapine rather than fixed dose combination product (Symbyax), approximate dosage correspondence is as follows:

Olanzapine 2.5 mg + fluoxetine 20 mg = Symbyax 3/25

Olanzapine 5 mg + fluoxetine 20 mg = Symbyax 6/25

Olanzapine 12.5 mg + fluoxetine 20 mg = Symbyax 12/25

Olanzapine 5 mg + fluoxetine 50 mg = Symbyax 6/50

Olanzapine 12.5 mg + fluoxetine 50 mg = Symbyax 12/50

Special risk patients: Initial: 2.5 to 5 mg once daily is recommended in patients who have a predisposition to hypotensive reactions, who have hepatic impairment, who exhibit a combination of factors that may result in slower metabolism of olanzapine (eg, female, elderly, nonsmoking status), or who may be more pharmacodynamically sensitive to olanzapine; increase dose with caution as clinically indicated.

Chemotherapy-associated acute and delayed nausea or vomiting, prevention (off-label use): Oral: 10 mg on the day of chemotherapy (day 1) followed by 10 mg once daily days 2 to 4 (in combination with dexamethasone and palonosetron on day 1 only) (Navari 2007; Navari 2011).

Chemotherapy-associated breakthrough nausea or vomiting (off-label use): Oral: 10 mg once daily for 3 days (Navari 2013).

Delirium (off-label use): Oral: 5 mg once daily for up to 5 days (NICE 2010)

Delusional parasitosis (off-label use): Oral: Initial: 2.5 mg once daily; increase gradually based on response and tolerability up to 5 to 10 mg/day. Maximum: 20 mg/day (Freudenmann 2008; Heller 2013). Additional data may be necessary to further define the role of olanzapine in this condition.

Post-traumatic stress disorder (off-label use): Oral: Initial: 5 to 10 mg daily; adjust dose based on response and tolerability every 1 to 2 weeks, up to 20 mg daily (Carey 2012; Stein 2002).

Tourette syndrome (off-label use): Initial: 2.5 to 5 mg daily; increase gradually based on response and tolerability to a usual dosage range of 2.5 to 20 mg daily (Pringsheim 2012; Roessner 2011). After initial dosage, increments of 2.5 to 5 mg weekly or biweekly were commonly used for dosage adjustments in clinical trials up to a maximum dosage of 20 mg/day (Budman 2001; Onofrj 2000; Stamenkovic 2000).

Discontinuation of therapy: American Psychiatric Association (APA), Canadian Psychiatric Association (CPA), and World Federation of Societies of Biological Psychiatry (WFSBP) guidelines recommend gradually tapering antipsychotics to avoid withdrawal symptoms and minimize the risk of relapse (APA [Lehman 2004]; Cerovecki 2013; CPA [Addington 2005]; WFSBP [Hasan 2012]); risk for withdrawal symptoms may be highest with highly anti-cholinergic or dopaminergic antipsychotics (Cerovecki 2013). When stopping antipsychotic therapy in patients with schizophrenia, the CPA guidelines recommend a gradual taper over 6 to 24 months, and the APA guidelines recommend reducing the dose by 10% each month (APA [Lehman 2004]; CPA [Addington 2005]). Continuing anti-parkinsonism agents for a brief period after discontinuation may prevent withdrawal symptoms (Cerovecki 2013). When switching antipsychotics, 3 strategies have been suggested: cross-titration (gradually discontinuing the first antipsychotic while gradually increasing the new antipsychotic), overlap and taper (maintaining the dose of the first antipsychotic while gradually increasing the new antipsychotic, then tapering the first antipsychotic), and abrupt change (abruptly discontinuing the first antipsychotic and either increasing the new antipsychotic gradually or starting it at a treatment dose). Evidence supporting ideal switch strategies and taper rates is limited, and results are conflicting (Cerovecki 2013; Remington 2005).

Pediatric

Bipolar I (acute mixed or manic episodes): Adolescents ≥13 years: Oral: Initial: 2.5 to 5 mg once daily; adjust by 2.5 to 5 mg daily to target dose of 10 mg daily; dosing range: 2.5 to 20 mg daily

Depression associated with bipolar I disorder (in combination with fluoxetine): Children and Adolescents 10 to 17 years: Oral: Initial: 2.5 mg once daily in the evening (in combination with fluoxetine); adjust dose, if needed, as tolerated; safety of doses >12 mg of olanzapine in combination with fluoxetine doses >50 mg has not been studied in pediatrics. Refer to adult dosing for **"Note"** for olanzapine/fluoxetine combination (Symbyax).

Schizophrenia: Adolescents ≥13 years: Oral: Initial: 2.5 to 5 mg once daily; adjust by 2.5 to 5 mg daily to target dose of 10 mg daily; dosing range: 2.5 to 20 mg daily

Chemotherapy-associated breakthrough or refractory nausea or vomiting (off-label use): Infants, Children, and Adolescents: Oral: 0.1 mg/kg/dose once daily (maximum 10 mg/dose); if necessary, may increase to 0.14 mg/kg/dose once daily (maximum 10 mg/dose) (Flank 2016).

Tourette syndrome (off-label use): Children and Adolescents: Initial: 2.5 to 5 mg once daily; increase gradually based on response and tolerability to a usual dosage of 2.5 to 12.5 mg once daily (AACAP [Murphy 2013]; Pringsheim 2012). After initial dosage, increments of 2.5 to 5 mg weekly or biweekly were used for dosage adjustments in clinical trials up to a maximum dosage of 20 mg/day (McCracken 2008; Stephens 2004)

Renal Impairment No dosage adjustment necessary. Not removed by dialysis.

Hepatic Impairment There are no dosage adjustments provided in the manufacturer's labeling except when used in combination with fluoxetine (as separate components) the initial olanzapine dose should be limited to 2.5 to 5 mg daily. Use with caution (cases of hepatitis and liver injury have been reported with olanzapine use).

Mechanism of Action Olanzapine is a second generation thienobenzodiazepine antipsychotic which displays potent antagonism of serotonin 5-HT_{2A} and 5-HT_{2C}, dopamine D_{1-4}, histamine H_1, and alpha$_1$-adrenergic receptors. Olanzapine shows moderate antagonism of 5-HT_3 and muscarinic M_{1-5} receptors, and weak binding to GABA-A, BZD, and beta-adrenergic receptors. Although the precise mechanism of action in schizophrenia and bipolar disorder is not known, the efficacy of olanzapine is thought to be mediated through combined antagonism of dopamine and serotonin type 2 receptor sites.

Contraindications There are no contraindications listed in the manufacturer's labeling.

Canadian labeling: Hypersensitivity to olanzapine or any component of the formulation

Warnings/Precautions [US Boxed Warning]: Elderly patients with dementia-related psychosis treated with antipsychotics are at an increased risk of death compared with placebo. Most deaths appeared to be either cardiovascular (eg, heart failure, sudden death) or infectious (eg, pneumonia) in nature. In addition, an increased incidence of cerebrovascular effects (eg, transient ischemic attack, stroke) has been reported in studies of placebo-controlled trials of olanzapine in elderly patients with dementia-related psychosis. Use with caution in patients with Lewy body dementia or Parkinson disease dementia due to greater risk of adverse effects, increased sensitivity to extrapyramidal effects, and association with irreversible cognitive decompensation or death. (APA [Reus 2016]). Olanzapine is not approved for the treatment of dementia-related psychosis.

May cause CNS depression, which impair physical and mental abilities; patients must be cautioned about performing tasks that require mental alertness (eg, operating machinery, driving). May be moderate to highly sedating in comparison with other antipsychotics (APA [Lehman 2004]); dose-related effects have been observed. Use caution in patients with cardiac disease. Use with caution in Parkinson disease, predisposition to seizures, or severe hepatic or renal disease. Life-threatening arrhythmias have occurred with therapeutic doses of some neuroleptics. May induce orthostatic hypotension; use caution with history of cardiovascular disease, hemodynamic instability, prior myocardial infarction, or ischemic heart disease. Dose-related increases in cholesterol and triglycerides have been noted. Use with caution in patients with preexisting abnormal lipid profile. Esophageal dysmotility and aspiration have been associated with antipsychotic use; use with caution in patients at risk of aspiration pneumonia. May cause dose-related increases in prolactin levels; clinical significance of hyperprolactinemia in patients with breast cancer or other prolactin-dependent tumors is unknown. Clinical manifestations of increased prolactin levels included menstrual-, sexual- and breast-related events. Significant dose-related weight gain (>7% of baseline weight) may occur; monitor waist circumference and BMI. Impaired core body temperature regulation may occur; caution with strenuous exercise, heat exposure, dehydration, and concomitant medication possessing anticholinergic effects.

Leukopenia, neutropenia, and agranulocytosis (sometimes fatal) have been reported in clinical trials and postmarketing reports with antipsychotic use; presence of risk factors (eg, preexisting low WBC or history of drug-induced leuko-/neutropenia) should prompt periodic blood count assessment. Discontinue therapy at first signs of blood dyscrasias or if absolute neutrophil count <1,000/mm^3. Multiorgan hypersensitivity reactions (drug reaction with eosinophilia and systemic symptoms [DRESS]): Potentially serious, sometimes fatal, multiorgan hypersensitivity reactions (DRESS) have been reported. Symptoms may include a cutaneous reaction (rash or exfoliative dermatitis), eosinophilia, fever, and/or lymphadenopathy with systemic complications (eg, hepatitis, nephritis, pneumonitis, myocarditis, pericarditis). Discontinue olanzapine if DRESS is suspected.

May cause anticholinergic effects; use with caution in patients with decreased gastrointestinal motility, urinary retention, BPH, xerostomia, or narrow-angle glaucoma. Relative to other neuroleptics, olanzapine has a moderate potency of cholinergic blockade. May cause extrapyramidal symptoms (EPS), although risk of these reactions is lower relative to other neuroleptics. Risk of dystonia (and probably other EPS) may be greater with increased doses, use of conventional antipsychotics, males, and younger patients. Factors associated with greater vulnerability to tardive dyskinesia include older in age, female gender combined with postmenopausal status, Parkinson disease, pseudoparkinsonism symptoms, affective disorders (particularly major depressive disorder), concurrent medical diseases such as diabetes, previous brain damage, alcoholism, poor treatment response, and use of high doses of antipsychotics (APA [Lehman 2004]; Soares-Weiser 2007). Consider therapy discontinuation with signs/symptoms of tardive dyskinesia. May increase the risk for falls due to somnolence, orthostatic hypotension and motor or sensory instability. Complete fall risk assessments at baseline and periodically during treatment in patients with diseases or on medications that may also increase fall risk. May be associated with neuroleptic malignant syndrome (NMS). May cause extreme and life-threatening hyperglycemia; use with caution in patients with diabetes or other disorders of glucose regulation; monitor. Olanzapine levels may be lower in patients who smoke. Smokers may require a daily dose 30% higher than nonsmokers in order to obtain an equivalent olanzapine concentration (Tsuda 2014); however, the manufacturer does not routinely recommend dosage adjustments.

Use in adolescent patients ≥13 years of age may result in increased weight gain and sedation, as well as greater increases in LDL cholesterol, total cholesterol, triglycerides, prolactin, and liver transaminase levels when compared with adults. Adolescent patients should be maintained on the lowest dose necessary.

The possibility of a suicide attempt is inherent in psychotic illness or bipolar disorder; use caution in high-risk patients during initiation of therapy. Prescriptions should be written for the smallest quantity consistent with good patient care.

Some dosage forms may contain polysorbate 80 (also known as Tweens). Hypersensitivity reactions, usually a delayed reaction, have been reported following exposure to pharmaceutical products containing polysorbate 80 in certain individuals (Isaksson 2002; Lucente 2000; Shelley 1995). Thrombocytopenia, ascites, pulmonary deterioration, and renal and hepatic failure have been reported in premature neonates after receiving parenteral products containing polysorbate 80 (Alade 1986; CDC 1984). See manufacturer's labeling.

There are two Zyprexa formulations for intramuscular injection: Zyprexa Relprevv is an extended-release formulation and Zyprexa Intramuscular is short-acting:

Extended-release IM injection (Zyprexa Relprevv): **[US Boxed Warning]: Sedation (including coma) and delirium (including agitation, anxiety, confusion, disorientation) have been observed following use of *Zyprexa Relprevv*.** Administer at a registered health care facility where patients should be continuously monitored (≥3 hours) for symptoms of olanzapine overdose; symptom development highest in first hour but may occur within or after 3 hours; risk of syndrome is cumulative with each injection; recovery expected by 72 hours. Upon determining alert status, patient should be escorted to their destination and not drive or operate heavy machinery for the remainder of the day.

Two unexplained deaths in patients who received *Zyprexa Relprevv* have been reported. The patients died 3 to 4 days after receiving an appropriate dose of the drug. Both patients were found to have high blood concentrations of olanzapine postmortem. It is unclear if these deaths were the result of post-injection delirium sedation syndrome (PDSS) (FDA Safety Communication 2013).

Zyprexa Relprevv is only available under a restricted distribution program. Only prescribers, health care facilities, and pharmacies registered with the program are able to prescribe, distribute, or dispense *Zyprexa Relprevv* for patients who are enrolled in and meet all conditions of the program.

Short-acting IM injection (Zyprexa IntraMuscular): Patients should remain recumbent if drowsy/dizzy until hypotension, bradycardia, and/or hypoventilation have been ruled out. Concurrent use of IM/IV benzodiazepines is not recommended (fatalities have been reported, though causality not determined).

When discontinuing antipsychotic therapy, the American Psychiatric Association (APA), Canadian Psychiatric Association (CPA), and World Federation of Societies of Biological Psychiatry (WFSBP) guidelines recommend gradually tapering antipsychotics to avoid physical withdrawal symptoms, including anorexia, anxiety, diaphoresis, diarrhea, dizziness, dyskinesia, headache, myalgia, nausea, paresthesia, restlessness, tremulousness and vomiting (APA [Lehman 2004]; CPA [Addington 2005]; Lambert 2007; WFSBP [Hasan 2012]). The risk of withdrawal symptoms is highest following abrupt discontinuation of highly anti-cholinergic or dopaminergic antipsychotics (Cerovecki 2013). Additional factors such as duration of antipsychotic exposure, the indication for use, medication half-life and risk for relapse should be consider. In schizophrenia, there is no reliable indicator to differentiate the minority who will not from the majority who will relapse with drug discontinuation. However, studies in which the medication of well-stabilized patients were discontinued indicate that 75% of patients relapse within 6 to 24 months. Indefinite maintenance antipsychotic medication is generally recommended, and especially for patients who have had multiple prior episodes or two episodes within 5 years (APA [Lehman 2004]).

Drug Interactions

Metabolism/Transport Effects **Substrate** of CYP1A2 (major), CYP2D6 (minor); **Note:** Assignment of Major/Minor substrate status based on clinically relevant drug interaction potential; **Inhibits** CYP1A2 (weak), CYP2C9 (weak)

Avoid Concomitant Use

Avoid concomitant use of OLANZapine with any of the following: Aclidinium; Amisulpride; Azelastine (Nasal); Benzodiazepines; Cimetropium; Eluxadoline; Glucagon; Glycopyrrolate (Oral Inhalation); Ipratropium (Oral Inhalation); Levosulpiride; Metoclopramide; Nitroglycerin; Orphenadrine; Oxatomide; Oxomemazine; Paraldehyde; Piribedil; Potassium Chloride; Sulpiride; Thalidomide; Tiotropium; Umeclidinium

Increased Effect/Toxicity

OLANZapine may increase the levels/effects of: AbobotulinumtoxinA; Alcohol (Ethyl); Amisulpride; Analgesics (Opioid); Anticholinergic Agents; Azelastine (Nasal); Benzodiazepines; Blonanserin; Buprenorphine; Cimetropium; CloZAPine; CNS Depressants; Eluxadoline; Glucagon; Glycopyrrolate (Oral Inhalation); Highest Risk QTc-Prolonging Agents; HYDROcodone; Iohexol; Iomeprol; Iopamidol; Mequitazine; Methotrimeprazine; Methylphenidate; MetyroSINE; Mirabegron; Mirtazapine; Moderate Risk QTc-Prolonging Agents; OnabotulinumtoxinA; Orphenadrine; OxyCODONE; Paraldehyde; Potassium Chloride; Ramosetron; RimabotulinumtoxinB; Selective Serotonin Reuptake Inhibitors; Serotonin Modulators; Sulpiride; Suvorexant; Thalidomide; Thiazide and Thiazide-Like Diuretics; Tiotropium; TiZANidine; Topiramate; Zolpidem

The levels/effects of OLANZapine may be increased by: Abiraterone Acetate; Acetylcholinesterase Inhibitors (Central); Aclidinium; Blood Pressure Lowering Agents; Brimonidine (Topical); Cannabis; Chloral Betaine; Chlormethiazole; Chlorphenesin Carbamate; CYP1A2 Inhibitors (Moderate); CYP1A2 Inhibitors (Strong); Deferasirox; Dimethindene (Topical); Doxylamine; Dronabinol; Droperidol; FluvoxaMINE; HydrOXYzine; Ipratropium (Oral Inhalation); Kava Kava; LamoTRIgine; Lithium; Lofexidine; Magnesium Sulfate; Methotrimeprazine; Methylphenidate; Metoclopramide; MetyroSINE; Mianserin; MiFEPRIStone; Minocycline; Nabilone; Obeticholic Acid; Oxatomide; Oxomemazine; Peginterferon Alfa-2b; Perampanel; Pramlintide; Rufinamide; Serotonin Modulators; Sodium Oxybate; Tapentadol; Tetrahydrocannabinol; Trimeprazine; Umeclidinium; Vemurafenib

Decreased Effect

OLANZapine may decrease the levels/effects of: Acetylcholinesterase Inhibitors; Amphetamines; Antidiabetic Agents; Anti-Parkinson Agents (Dopamine Agonist); Gastrointestinal Agents (Prokinetic); Itopride; Levosulpiride; Nitroglycerin; Piribedil; Quinagolide; Secretin

The levels/effects of OLANZapine may be decreased by: Acetylcholinesterase Inhibitors; Antihepaciviral Combination Products; Cannabis; CYP1A2 Inducers

(Strong); Cyproterone; Lithium; Piribedil; Ritonavir; Teriflunomide; Valproate Products

Dietary Considerations Tablets may be taken without regard to meals. Some products may contain phenylalanine.

Pharmacodynamics/Kinetics

Onset of Action Within 1 to 2 weeks for control of aggression, agitation, insomnia; 3 to 6 weeks for control of mania and positive psychotic symptoms. Adequate trial: Typically 6 weeks at maximum tolerated doses

Half-life Elimination

Oral and IM (short-acting): Children: (10 to 18 years; n=8): 37.2 ± 5.1 hours (Grothe 2000); Adults: 30 hours [21 to 54 hours (5th to 95th percentile)]; approximately 1.5 times greater in elderly

Extended-release injection: ~30 days

Time to Peak Maximum plasma concentrations after IM administration are 5 times higher than maximum plasma concentrations produced by an oral dose.

Extended-release injection: ~7 days

Short-acting injection: 15 to 45 minutes

Oral: Children (10 to 18 years; n=8): 4.7 ± 3.7 hours (Grothe 2000); Adults: ~6 hours

Pregnancy Risk Factor C

Pregnancy Considerations Adverse events were observed in animal reproduction studies. Olanzapine crosses the placenta and can be detected in cord blood at birth (Newport 2007). Information related to olanzapine use in pregnancy is limited (Goldstein 2000). Antipsychotic use during the third trimester of pregnancy has a risk for abnormal muscle movements (extrapyramidal symptoms [EPS]) and/or withdrawal symptoms in newborns following delivery. Symptoms in the newborn may include agitation, feeding disorder, hypertonia, hypotonia, respiratory distress, somnolence, and tremor; these effects may be self-limiting or require hospitalization. Olanzapine may cause hyperprolactinemia, which may decrease reproductive function in both males and females.

The ACOG recommends that therapy during pregnancy be individualized; treatment with psychiatric medications during pregnancy should incorporate the clinical expertise of the mental health clinician, obstetrician, primary healthcare provider, and pediatrician. Safety data related to atypical antipsychotics during pregnancy is limited and routine use is not recommended. However, if a woman is inadvertently exposed to an atypical antipsychotic while pregnant, continuing therapy may be preferable to switching to a typical antipsychotic that the fetus has not yet been exposed to; consider risk: benefit (ACOG 2008). Evaluate risk factors for gestational diabetes and weight gain if considering use of olanzapine in a pregnant woman (NICE 2007).

Healthcare providers are encouraged to enroll women 18 to 45 years of age exposed to olanzapine during pregnancy in the Atypical Antipsychotics Pregnancy Registry (1-866-961-2388 or http://www.womensmentalhealth.org/pregnancyregistry).

Breastfeeding Considerations Olanzapine is excreted into breast milk. At steady-state concentrations, it is estimated that a breast-fed infant may be exposed to ~2% of the maternal dose. In one study, the median time to peak milk concentration was ~5 hours after the maternal dose and serum concentrations in the nursing infants were low (<5 ng/mL; n=5) (Gardiner 2003). An increased risk of adverse events in nursing infants has not been reported (Gardiner 2003; Gilad 2011). breastfeeding is not recommended by the manufacturer.

Prescribing and Access Restrictions As a requirement of the REMS program, only prescribers, healthcare facilities, and pharmacies registered with the Zyprexa Relprevv Patient Care Program are able to prescribe, distribute, or dispense Zyprexa Relprevv for patients who are enrolled in and meet all conditions of the program. Zyprexa Relprevv must be administered at a registered healthcare facility. Prescribers will need to be recertified every 3 years. Contact the Zyprexa Relprevv Patient Care Program at 1-877-772-9390.

Dosage Forms

Solution Reconstituted, Intramuscular:

ZyPREXA: 10 mg (1 ea)

Generic: 10 mg (1 ea)

Suspension Reconstituted, Intramuscular:

ZyPREXA Relprevv: 210 mg (1 ea); 300 mg (1 ea); 405 mg (1 ea)

Tablet, Oral:

ZyPREXA: 2.5 mg, 5 mg, 7.5 mg, 10 mg, 15 mg, 20 mg

Generic: 2.5 mg, 5 mg, 7.5 mg, 10 mg, 15 mg, 20 mg

Tablet Dispersible, Oral:

ZyPREXA Zydis: 5 mg, 10 mg, 15 mg, 20 mg

Generic: 5 mg, 10 mg, 15 mg, 20 mg

Dosage Forms: Canada Note: Refer to Dosage Forms. ZyPREXA Relprevv is not available in Canada.

Olaparib (oh LAP a rib)

Brand Names: US Lynparza

Brand Names: Canada Lynparza

Pharmacologic Category Antineoplastic Agent, PARP Inhibitor

Use Ovarian cancer, advanced: Treatment (monotherapy) of deleterious or suspected deleterious germline BRCA-mutated (as detected by an approved test) advanced ovarian cancer in patients who have been treated with 3 or more prior lines of chemotherapy

Local Anesthetic/Vasoconstrictor Precautions No information available to require special precautions

Effects on Dental Treatment No significant effects or complications reported

Effects on Bleeding Chemotherapy may result in significant myelosuppression, potentially including reduction in platelet counts (thrombocytopenia) and altered hemostasis. In patients who are under active treatment with this agent, medical consult is suggested.

Adverse Reactions

≥10%:

Cardiovascular: Peripheral edema (10% to <20%)

Central nervous system: Fatigue (including weakness; 66% to 68%), headache (10% to 25%), dizziness (10% to <20%)

Dermatologic: Skin rash (10% to 25%)

Gastrointestinal: Nausea (64% to 75%), abdominal pain (43%), vomiting (32% to 43%), diarrhea (28% to 31%), dyspepsia (25%), decreased appetite (22% to 25%), dysgeusia (10% to 21%), constipation (10% to <20%)

Genitourinary: Urinary tract infection (10% to <20%)

Hematologic & oncologic: Decreased hemoglobin (85% to 90%; grades 3/4: 8% to 15%), increased MCV (57% to 85%), decreased absolute lymphocyte count (56%; grades 3/4: 17%), anemia (25% to 34%; grades 3/4: 4% to 18%), decreased neutrophils (25% to 32%; grades 3/4: 7% to 8%), decreased platelet count (26% to 30%; grades 3/4: 3% to 6%)

Neuromuscular & skeletal: Musculoskeletal pain (21% to 32%), myalgia (22% to 25%), back pain (10% to 25%)
Renal: Increased serum creatinine (26% to 30%)
Respiratory: Upper respiratory tract infection (26% to 43%), cough (10% to 21%), dyspnea (10% to <20%)

1% to ≤10%:
Cardiovascular: Hypertension, venous thrombosis (including pulmonary embolism)
Central nervous system: Anxiety, depression, insomnia, peripheral neuropathy
Dermatologic: Pruritus, xeroderma (including eczema)
Endocrine & metabolic: Hot flash, hyperglycemia, hypomagnesemia
Gastrointestinal: Stomatitis
Genitourinary: Dysuria, urinary incontinence, vulvovaginal disease
Hematologic & oncologic: Myelodysplastic syndrome (acute myeloid leukemia; 2%), leukopenia
Miscellaneous: Fever

<1%, postmarketing, and/or case reports: Pneumonitis

General Dosage Range Dosage adjustment recommended in patients with renal impairment or on concomitant therapy.

Oral: *Adults:* 400 mg twice daily

Mechanism of Action Olaparib is a poly (ADP-ribose) polymerase (PARP) enzyme inhibitor, including PARP1, PARP2, and PARP3. PARP enzymes are involved in DNA transcription, cell cycle regulation, and DNA repair. Olaparib is a potent oral PARP inhibitor which induces synthetic lethality in BRCA1/2 deficient tumor cells through the formation of double-stranded DNA breaks which cannot be accurately repaired, which leads to disruption of cellular homeostasis and cell death (Ledermann 2012).

Pharmacodynamics/Kinetics

Half-life Elimination Terminal: 11.9 ± 4.8 hours

Time to Peak 1 to 3 hours

Pregnancy Considerations Adverse events were observed in animal reproduction studies at doses less than human exposure. Based on animal reproduction studies and the mechanism of action, olaparib may be expected to cause adverse events to the fetus. Women of reproductive potential should use highly effective contraception during therapy and for at least 6 months after the last olaparib dose. In women of reproductive potential, pregnancy testing is recommended prior to treatment initiation.

Prescribing and Access Restrictions Olaparib is available only through the designated specialty pharmacy Biologics, Inc. For further information on patient assistance, product availability, and prescribing instructions, please refer to the following website: http://myaccess360.com/hcp/reimbursement/Oncology.aspx?product=lynparza or call 1-844-275-2360.

Olaratumab (oh lar AT ue mab)

Brand Names: US Lartruvo

Pharmacologic Category Antineoplastic Agent, Monoclonal Antibody; Antineoplastic Agent, PDGFR-alpha Blocker

Use Soft tissue sarcoma: Treatment (in combination with doxorubicin) of adults with soft tissue sarcoma (STS) with a histologic subtype for which an anthracycline-containing regimen is appropriate and which is not amenable to curative treatment with radiotherapy or surgery.

Local Anesthetic/Vasoconstrictor Precautions No information available to require special precautions

Effects on Dental Treatment Key adverse event(s) related to dental treatment: Mucositis

Effects on Bleeding Chemotherapy may result in significant myelosuppression. Higher incidence of grades 3 and 4 lymphopenia and neutropenia has been reported with olaratumab in combination with doxorubicin. Thrombocytopenia (all grades) also has a higher incidence.

Adverse Reactions

>10%:
Central nervous system: Fatigue (69%), neuropathy (22%), headache (20%), anxiety (11%)
Dermatologic: Alopecia (52%)
Endocrine & metabolic: Hyperglycemia (52%), hypokalemia (21%), hypophosphatemia (21%), hypomagnesemia (16%)
Gastrointestinal: Nausea (73%), mucositis (53%), vomiting (45%), diarrhea (34%), decreased appetite (31%), abdominal pain (23%)
Hematologic & oncologic: Lymphocytopenia (77%, grades 3/4: 44%), neutropenia (65%, grades 3/4: 48%), thrombocytopenia (63%, grades 3/4: 6%), prolonged partial thromboplastin time (33%, grades 3/4: 5%)
Hepatic: Increased serum alkaline phosphatase (16%)
Neuromuscular & skeletal: Musculoskeletal pain (64%)
Ophthalmic: Xerophthalmia (11%)
Miscellaneous: Infusion related reaction (13% to 14%)

1% to 10%: Immunologic: Development of IgG antibodies (4%; all patients had neutralizing antibodies; however, therapeutic effects of antibodies could not be assessed)

General Dosage Range IV: *Adults:* 15 mg/kg on days 1 and 8 every 3 weeks

Mechanism of Action Olaratumab is a human (recombinant) IgG1 antibody which expressly binds to platelet-derived growth receptor alpha (PDGFR-α) to prevent binding of PDGF-AA, PDGF-BB, and PDGF-CC and block receptor activation and disrupt PDGF receptor signaling. The PDGF-alpha receptor has a role in cell differentiation, growth, and angiogenesis and has demonstrated antitumor activity in sarcomas (Tap 2016).

Pharmacodynamics/Kinetics

Half-life Elimination ~11 days (range: 6 to 24 days)

Pregnancy Considerations Based on its mechanism of action, olaratumab would be expected to cause fetal harm if administered to a pregnant woman. Animal reproduction studies have not been conducted. Adequate contraception during therapy and for 3 months following the last dose is recommended in women of reproductive potential.

Olmesartan (ole me SAR tan)

Related Information

Cardiovascular Diseases *on page 1752*

Brand Names: US Benicar

Brand Names: Canada Olmetec

Pharmacologic Category Angiotensin II Receptor Blocker; Antihypertensive

Use

Hypertension: Treatment of hypertension with or without concurrent use of other antihypertensive agents

Guideline recommendations:

Hypertension: The 2014 guideline for the management of high blood pressure in adults (Eighth Joint National Committee [JNC 8; James 2013]) recommends initiation of pharmacologic treatment to lower blood pressure for the following patients:

- Patients ≥60 years of age with systolic blood pressure (SBP) ≥150 mm Hg or diastolic blood pressure (DBP) ≥90 mm Hg. Goal of therapy is SBP <150 mm Hg and DBP <90 mm Hg.
- Patients <60 years of age with SBP ≥140 mm Hg or DBP ≥90 mm Hg. Goal of therapy is SBP <140 mm Hg and DBP <90 mm Hg.
- Patients ≥18 years of age with diabetes and SBP ≥140 mm Hg or DBP ≥90 mm Hg. Goal of therapy is SBP <140 mm Hg and DBP <90 mm Hg.
- Patients ≥18 years of age with chronic kidney disease (CKD) and SBP ≥140 mm Hg or DBP ≥90 mm Hg. Goal of therapy is SBP <140 mm Hg and DBP <90 mm Hg.

Chronic kidney disease (CKD) and hypertension: Regardless of race or diabetes status, the use of an ACE inhibitor (ACEI) or angiotensin receptor blocker (ARB) as initial therapy is recommended to improve kidney outcomes. In the general nonblack population (without CKD), including those with diabetes, initial antihypertensive treatment should consist of a thiazide-type diuretic, calcium channel blocker, ACEI, or ARB. In the general black population (without CKD), including those with diabetes, initial antihypertensive treatment should consist of a thiazide-type diuretic or a calcium channel blocker instead of an ACEI or ARB.

Coronary artery disease (CAD) and hypertension: The American Heart Association, American College of Cardiology, and American Society of Hypertension (AHA/ACC/ASH) 2015 scientific statement for the treatment of hypertension in patients with CAD recommends the use of an ARB (or ACE inhibitor) as part of a regimen in patients with hypertension and chronic stable angina if there is prior MI, LV systolic dysfunction, diabetes mellitus, or CKD. A BP target of <140/90 mm Hg is reasonable for the secondary prevention of cardiovascular events. A lower target BP (<130/80 mm Hg) may be appropriate in some individuals with CAD, previous MI, stroke or transient ischemic attack, or CAD risk equivalents (AHA/ACC/ASH [Rosendorff 2015]).

Local Anesthetic/Vasoconstrictor Precautions No information available to require special precautions

Effects on Dental Treatment Key adverse event(s) related to dental treatment: Patients may experience orthostatic hypotension as they stand up after treatment; especially if lying in dental chair for extended periods of time. Use caution with sudden changes in position during and after dental treatment.

Effects on Bleeding No information available to require special precautions

Adverse Reactions

1% to 10%:

Central nervous system: Dizziness (3%), headache

Endocrine & metabolic: Hyperglycemia, hypertriglyceridemia

Gastrointestinal: Diarrhea

Genitourinary: Hematuria

Neuromuscular & skeletal: Back pain, increased creatine phosphokinase

Respiratory: Bronchitis, flu-like symptoms, pharyngitis, rhinitis, sinusitis

<1%, postmarketing, and/or case reports: Abdominal pain, acute renal failure, alopecia, anaphylaxis, angioedema, arthralgia, arthritis, chest pain, cough, dyspepsia, facial edema, gastroenteritis, hypercholesterolemia, hyperkalemia, hyperuricemia, increased liver enzymes, increased serum bilirubin, increased serum creatinine, myalgia, nausea, peripheral edema, pruritus, rhabdomyolysis, skin rash, sprue-like symptoms, tachycardia, urticaria, vertigo, vomiting, weakness

General Dosage Range Oral:

Children 6 to 16 years:

20 kg to <35 kg: Initial: 10 mg once daily (maximum: 20 mg once daily)

≥35 kg: Initial: 20 mg once daily (maximum: 40 mg once daily)

Adolescents >16 years and Adults: Initial: 20 mg once daily; Maintenance: 20 to 40 mg once daily

Elderly: Initial: 5 to 20 mg once daily

Mechanism of Action As a selective and competitive, nonpeptide angiotensin II receptor antagonist, olmesartan blocks the vasoconstrictor and aldosterone-secreting effects of angiotensin II; olmesartan interacts reversibly at the AT1 and AT2 receptors of many tissues and has slow dissociation kinetics; its affinity for the AT1 receptor is 12,500 times greater than the AT2 receptor. Angiotensin II receptor antagonists may induce a more complete inhibition of the renin-angiotensin system than ACE inhibitors, they do not affect the response to bradykinin, and are less likely to be associated with nonrenin-angiotensin effects (eg, cough and angioedema). Olmesartan increases urinary flow rate and, in addition to being natriuretic and kaliuretic, increases excretion of chloride, magnesium, uric acid, calcium, and phosphate.

Pharmacodynamics/Kinetics

Half-life Elimination Terminal: 13 hours

Time to Peak 1 to 2 hours

Pregnancy Risk Factor D

Pregnancy Considerations [U.S. Boxed Warning]: Drugs that act on the renin-angiotensin system can cause injury and death to the developing fetus. Discontinue as soon as possible once pregnancy is detected. The use of drugs which act on the renin-angiotensin system are associated with oligohydramnios. Oligohydramnios, due to decreased fetal renal function, may lead to fetal lung hypoplasia and skeletal malformations. Use is also associated with anuria, hypotension, renal failure, skull hypoplasia, and death in the fetus/neonate. The exposed fetus should be monitored for fetal growth, amniotic fluid volume, and organ formation. Infants exposed *in utero* should be monitored for hyperkalemia, hypotension, and oliguria (exchange transfusions or dialysis may be needed). These adverse events are generally associated with maternal use in the second and third trimesters.

Untreated chronic maternal hypertension is also associated with adverse events in the fetus, infant, and mother. The use of angiotensin II receptor blockers is not recommended to treat chronic uncomplicated hypertension in pregnant women and should generally be avoided in women of reproductive potential (ACOG, 2013).

Olopatadine (Nasal) (oh la PAT a deen)

Brand Names: US Patanase

Pharmacologic Category Histamine H_1 Antagonist; Histamine H_1 Antagonist, Second Generation; Piperidine Derivative

Use Treatment of the symptoms of seasonal allergic rhinitis

Local Anesthetic/Vasoconstrictor Precautions No information available to require special precautions

Effects on Dental Treatment Key adverse event(s) related to dental treatment: Taste perversion.

Effects on Bleeding No information available to require special precautions

Adverse Reactions

>10%:

Central nervous system: Bitter taste (13%; children: 1%)

Respiratory: Epistaxis (3% to 25%)

1% to 10%:

Central nervous system: Depression (2%), drowsiness (1%), fatigue (1%)

Dermatologic: Skin rash (children: 1%)

Endocrine & metabolic: Weight gain (1%)

Gastrointestinal: Xerostomia (1%)

Genitourinary: Urinary tract infection (1%)

Infection: Influenza (1%)

Neuromuscular & skeletal: Increased creatine phosphokinase (1%)

Respiratory: Nasal mucosa ulcer (9% to 10%), upper respiratory tract infection (children: 3%), pharyngolaryngeal pain (2%), post nasal drip (2%), cough (1%), throat irritation (1%)

<1%, postmarketing, and/or case reports: Altered sense of smell, anosmia, dizziness, dysgeusia, nasal discomfort, oropharyngeal pain

General Dosage Range Intranasal:

Children 6-11 years: 1 spray into each nostril twice daily

Children ≥12 years, Adolescents, and Adults: 2 sprays into each nostril twice daily

Mechanism of Action Selective histamine H_1-antagonist; inhibits release of histamine from mast cells.

Pharmacodynamics/Kinetics

Onset of Action 30 minutes in seasonal allergy patients

Half-life Elimination 8-12 hours

Time to Peak Serum: 15 minutes to 2 hours

Pregnancy Risk Factor C

Pregnancy Considerations Adverse effects were observed in animal reproduction studies. Until additional information is available, other agents may be preferred for the treatment of rhinitis in pregnant women (Scadding 2008).

Olopatadine (Ophthalmic) (oh la PAT a deen)

Brand Names: US Pataday; Patanol; Pazeo

Brand Names: Canada ACT-Olopatadine; Apo-Olopatadine; CO Olopatadine; Pataday; Patanol; Pazeo; Sandoz-Olopatadine

Pharmacologic Category Histamine H_1 Antagonist; Histamine H_1 Antagonist, Second Generation; Piperidine Derivative

Use Allergic conjunctivitis: Treatment of the signs and symptoms of allergic conjunctivitis

Local Anesthetic/Vasoconstrictor Precautions No information available to require special precautions

Effects on Dental Treatment No significant effects or complications reported

Effects on Bleeding No information available to require special precautions

Adverse Reactions

Central nervous system: Headache (≤5%)

Gastrointestinal: Dysgeusia (2% to 5%), nausea (≤5%)

Infection: Cold symptoms (≤10%)

Neuromuscular & skeletal: Back pain (≤5%), weakness (≤5%)

Ocular: Abnormal sensation in eyes (2% to 5%), blurred vision (2% to 5%), dry eye syndrome (2% to 5%), superficial punctate keratitis (2% to 5%), burning sensation of eyes (≤5%), conjunctivitis (≤5%), eyelid edema (≤5%), eye pain (≤5%), eye pruritus (≤5%), foreign body sensation (≤5%), keratitis (≤5%), stinging of eyes (≤5%), hyperemia

Respiratory: Pharyngitis (≤10%), cough (≤5%), rhinitis (≤5%), sinusitis (≤5%)

Miscellaneous: Flu-like symptoms (≤5%), hypersensitivity (≤5%), infection (≤5%)

General Dosage Range Ophthalmic:

Children ≥2 years, Adolescents, and Adults (Pataday, Pazeo): Instill 1 drop into each affected eye once daily

Children ≥3 years, Adolescents, and Adults (Patanol): Instill 1 drop into each affected eye twice daily

Mechanism of Action Selective histamine H_1-antagonist; inhibits release of histamine from mast cells. Inhibits histamine induced effects on conjunctival epithelial cells.

Pharmacodynamics/Kinetics

Half-life Elimination ~3 hours

Pregnancy Risk Factor C

Pregnancy Considerations Olopatadine has minimal systemic absorption following ophthalmic administration. Systemic absorption would be required in order for olopatadine to cross the placenta and reach the fetus.

Olsalazine (ole SAL a zeen)

Brand Names: US Dipentum

Brand Names: Canada Dipentum®

Pharmacologic Category 5-Aminosalicylic Acid Derivative

Use Maintenance of remission of ulcerative colitis in patients intolerant to sulfasalazine

Local Anesthetic/Vasoconstrictor Precautions No information available to require special precautions

Effects on Dental Treatment No significant effects or complications reported

Effects on Bleeding No information available to require special precautions

Adverse Reactions

>10%: Gastrointestinal: Diarrhea (11% to 17%; dose related)

1% to 10%:

Central nervous system: Depression (2%), dizziness/vertigo (1%)

Dermatologic: Rash (2%), pruritus (1%)

Gastrointestinal: Abdominal pain/cramps (10%), nausea (5%), bloating (2%), stomatitis (1%), vomiting (1%)

Neuromuscular & skeletal: Arthralgia (4%)

Respiratory: Upper respiratory infection (2%)

<1%, postmarketing, and/or case reports: Alkaline phosphatase increased, Alopecia, ALT increased, anemia, angioedema, aplastic anemia, AST increased, bilirubin increased, blood in stool, blurred vision, bronchospasm, cholestatic hepatitis, cholestatic jaundice, chest pain, chills, cirrhosis, dehydration, dry eyes, dyspnea, dysuria, eosinophilia, epigastric discomfort, erythema, erythema nodosum, fever, flare

of symptoms, flatulence, GGT increased, heart block (second degree), hematuria, hemolytic anemia, hepatitis, hepatic failure, hepatic necrosis, hot flashes, hypertension, impotence, insomnia, interstitial nephritis, interstitial pneumonia, irritability, jaundice, Kawasaki-like syndrome, LDH increased, leukopenia, lymphopenia, menorrhagia, mood swings, muscle cramps, myalgia, myocarditis, nephrotic syndrome, neutropenia, orthostatic hypotension, palpitation, pancreatitis, pancytopenia, paresthesia, pericarditis, peripheral edema, peripheral neuropathy, photosensitivity, proteinuria, rectal bleeding, rectal discomfort, reticulocytosis, rigors, tachycardia, thrombocytopenia, tinnitus, tremor, urinary frequency, watery eyes, xerostomia

General Dosage Range Oral: *Adults:* 1 g/day in 2 divided doses

Mechanism of Action Mesalamine (5-aminosalicylic acid) is the active component of olsalazine; the specific mechanism of action of mesalamine is unknown; however, it is thought that it modulates local chemical mediators of the inflammatory response, especially leukotrienes, and is also postulated to be a free radical scavenger or an inhibitor of tumor necrosis factor (TNF); action appears topical rather than systemic.

Pharmacodynamics/Kinetics

Half-life Elimination 54 minutes

Time to Peak ~1 hour

Pregnancy Risk Factor C

Pregnancy Considerations Animal studies have demonstrated fetal developmental toxicities. There are no well-controlled studies in pregnant women. Use during pregnancy only if clearly necessary.

Omacetaxine (oh ma se TAX een)

Brand Names: US Synribo

Pharmacologic Category Antineoplastic Agent, Cephalotaxine; Antineoplastic Agent, Protein Synthesis Inhibitor

Use Chronic myeloid leukemia: Treatment of chronic or accelerated phase chronic myeloid leukemia (CML) in adult patients resistant and/or intolerant to ≥2 tyrosine kinase inhibitors

Local Anesthetic/Vasoconstrictor Precautions Use vasoconstrictor with caution; patients may experience tachycardia and palpitations when taking omacetaxine

Effects on Dental Treatment Key adverse event(s) related to dental treatment: Abnormal taste, aphthous stomatitis, gingival bleeding, gingival pain, gingivitis, mouth ulceration, mouth hemorrhage, mucosal inflammation, oral pain, stomatitis, and xerostomia (normal salivary flow resumes upon discontinuation) have been reported.

Effects on Bleeding Chemotherapy may result in significant myelosuppression, potentially including significant reduction in platelet counts. Thrombocytopenia has been reported (grades 3/4: 49% to 88%). Gingival and GI bleeding have been reported. In patients who are under active treatment with these agents, medical consult is suggested.

Adverse Reactions

>10%:

Cardiovascular: Peripheral edema (16%)

Central nervous system: Fatigue (29% to 31%), headache (13% to 20%), chills (13%), insomnia (12%)

Dermatologic: Alopecia (15%), skin rash (11%)

Endocrine & metabolic: Increased uric acid (grades 3/4: 56% to 57%), hyperglycemia (grades 3/4: 10% to 15%; hyperosmolar nonketotic hyperglycemia <1%)

Gastrointestinal: Diarrhea (35% to 41%), nausea (29% to 35%), abdominal pain (16% to 23%), vomiting (12% to 15%), constipation (14%), anorexia (10% to 13%)

Hematologic & oncologic: Thrombocytopenia (58% to 76%; grades 3/4: 49% to 88%), neutropenia (20% to 53%; grades 3/4: 18% to 81%), anemia (51% to 61%; grades 3/4: 36% to 80%), leukocyte disorder (decreased: grades 3/4: 61% to 72%), febrile neutropenia (10% to 20%; grades 3/4: 10% to 16%), lymphocytopenia (17%; grades 3/4: 16%)

Infection: Infection (46% to 56%; grades 3/4: 11% to 20%)

Local: Injection site reaction (22% to 35%; includes edema, erythema, hematoma, hemorrhage, hypersensitivity, induration, inflammation, infusion related reaction, irritation, mass, pruritus, rash)

Neuromuscular & skeletal: Weakness (23% to 24%), arthralgia (19%), limb pain (11% to 13%), back pain (12%), myalgia (11%)

Renal: Increased serum creatinine (grades 3/4: 9% to 16%)

Respiratory: Epistaxis (11% to 17%), cough (≤16%), dyspnea (11%)

Miscellaneous: Fever (25% to 29%)

1% to 10%:

Cardiovascular: Acute coronary syndrome, angina pectoris, bradycardia, cardiac arrhythmia, chest pain, edema, hypertension, hypotension, palpitations, tachycardia, ventricular premature contractions

Central nervous system: Agitation, anxiety, cerebral hemorrhage, confusion, depression, dizziness, hyperthermia, hypoesthesia, lethargy, malaise, mental status changes, mouth pain, myasthenia, pain, paresthesia, sciatica, seizure, voice disorder

Dermatologic: Burning sensation of skin, dermal ulcer, desquamation, erythema, hyperhidrosis, hyperpigmentation, night sweats, pruritus, skin lesion, xeroderma

Endocrine & metabolic: Decreased serum glucose (grades 3/4: 6% to 8%), dehydration, diabetes mellitus, gout, hot flash

Gastrointestinal: Abdominal distention, anal fissure, aphthous stomatitis, decreased appetite, dysgeusia, dyspepsia, dysphagia, gastritis, gastroesophageal reflux disease, gastrointestinal hemorrhage, gingival hemorrhage, gingival pain, gingivitis, hemorrhoids, melena, mucosal inflammation, oral mucosa ulcer, stomatitis, xerostomia

Genitourinary: Dysuria

Hematologic & oncologic: Bone marrow failure (10%; grades 3/4: 10%), bruise, hematoma, hemorrhage (ear), oral hemorrhage, petechia, purpura

Hepatic: Increased serum bilirubin (grades 3/4: 6% to 9%), increased serum ALT (grades 3/4: 2% to 6%)

Hypersensitivity: Hypersensitivity reaction, transfusion reaction

Neuromuscular & skeletal: Muscle spasm, musculoskeletal chest pain, musculoskeletal pain (or discomfort), ostealgia, stiffness, tremor

Ophthalmic: Blurred vision, cataract, conjunctival hemorrhage, conjunctivitis, diplopia, eyelid edema, eye pain, increased lacrimation, xerophthalmia

Otic: Otalgia, tinnitus

Respiratory: Flu-like symptoms, hemoptysis, nasal congestion, pharyngolaryngeal pain, rales, rhinorrhea, sinus congestion

General Dosage Range SubQ: *Adults:* Induction: 1.25 mg/m^2 twice daily for 14 days of a 28-day treatment cycle; Maintenance: 1.25 mg/m^2 twice daily for 7 consecutive days of a 28-day treatment cycle

Mechanism of Action Omacetaxine is a reversible protein synthesis inhibitor which binds to the A-site cleft of the ribosomal subunit to interfere with chain elongation and inhibit protein synthesis. It acts independently of BCR-ABL1 kinase-binding activity, and has demonstrated activity against tyrosine kinase inhibitor-resistant BCR-ABL mutations.

Pharmacodynamics/Kinetics

Onset of Action

Chronic phase CML: Mean time to major cytogenetic response: 3.5 months

Accelerated phase CML: Mean time to response: 2.3 months

Duration of Action

Chronic phase CML: Median duration of major cytogenetic response: 12.5 months

Accelerated phase CML: Median duration of major hematologic response: 4.7 months

Half-life Elimination ~6 hours

Time to Peak SubQ: ~30 minutes

Pregnancy Risk Factor D

Pregnancy Considerations Adverse events were observed in animal reproduction studies at doses less than the equivalent human dose (based on BSA). Based on the mechanism of action, omacetaxine may cause fetal harm if administered during pregnancy. Women of reproductive potential should avoid pregnancy during therapy. Omacetaxine may impair fertility in males.

Omalizumab (oh mah lye ZOO mab)

Related Information

Respiratory Diseases *on page 1777*

Brand Names: US Xolair

Brand Names: Canada Xolair

Pharmacologic Category Monoclonal Antibody, Anti-Asthmatic

Use

Asthma: Treatment of moderate to severe persistent asthma in adults and patients 6 years and older who have a positive skin test or *in vitro* reactivity to a perennial aeroallergen and whose symptoms are inadequately controlled with inhaled corticosteroids.

Guideline recommendations:

The 2007 National Asthma Education and Prevention Program asthma guidelines recommend use be considered as adjunctive therapy in patients with severe persistent asthma who have allergies and in patients with severe persistent asthma that is inadequately controlled with a combination of a high-dose inhaled corticosteroid and a long-acting beta$_2$-agonist (NAEPP 2007).

The Global Initiative for Asthma suggests use be considered as adjunctive therapy in patients with moderate or severe allergic asthma that is uncontrolled with a combination of a medium- to high-dose inhaled corticosteroid and a long-acting beta$_2$-agonist (GINA 2016).

Chronic idiopathic urticaria: Treatment of chronic idiopathic urticaria in adults and adolescents 12 years and older who remain symptomatic despite H_1 antihistamine treatment.

Local Anesthetic/Vasoconstrictor Precautions No information available to require special precautions

Effects on Dental Treatment No significant effects or complications reported

Effects on Bleeding No information available to require special precautions

Adverse Reactions

Asthma:

>10%: Local: Injection site reaction (45%; severe 12%; includes bruising, redness, warmth, burning, stinging, itching, hive formation, pain, indurations, mass, and inflammation). Most reactions occurred within 1 hour, lasted <8 days, and decreased in frequency with additional dosing.

1% to 10%:

Cardiovascular: Pulmonary embolism (≤3%), venous thrombosis (≤3%), myocardial infarction (2%), unstable angina pectoris (2%)

Central nervous system: Pain (7%), dizziness (3%), fatigue (3%)

Dermatologic: Dermatitis (2%), pruritus (2%)

Neuromuscular & skeletal: Arthralgia (8%), leg pain (4%), arm pain (2%), bone fracture (2%)

Otic: Otalgia (2%)

Chronic idiopathic urticaria:

>10%: Central nervous system: Headache (6% to 12%)

1% to 10%:

Cardiovascular: Peripheral edema (≥2%)

Central nervous system: Anxiety (≥2%), migraine (≥2%)

Dermatologic: Alopecia (≥2%)

Gastrointestinal: Toothache (≥2%)

Genitourinary: Urinary tract infection (≥2%)

Infection: Fungal infection (≥2%)

Local: Injection site reaction (3%)

Neuromuscular & skeletal: Arthralgia (3%), limb pain (≥2%), musculoskeletal pain (≥2%), myalgia (≥2%)

Respiratory: Nasopharyngitis (9%), sinusitis (5%), upper respiratory tract infection (3%), asthma (≥2%), oropharyngeal pain (≥2%), sinus headache (≥2%), cough (2%), viral upper respiratory tract infection (≤2%)

Miscellaneous: Fever (≥2%)

All indications: <1%, postmarketing, and/or case reports: Alopecia, anaphylaxis, antibody development, arthritis, bronchospasm, chest tightness, Churg-Strauss syndrome, cough, dyspnea, eosinophilia, fever, hypotension, lymphadenopathy, malignant neoplasm, pharyngeal edema, pulmonary hypertension, skin edema, skin rash, swollen tongue, syncope, thrombocytopenia, transient ischemic attacks, urticaria

General Dosage Range SubQ: *Children ≥6 years, Adolescents, and Adults:* Dosage varies greatly depending on indication

Mechanism of Action

Asthma: Omalizumab is an IgG monoclonal antibody (recombinant DNA derived) which inhibits IgE binding to the high-affinity IgE receptor on mast cells and basophils. By decreasing bound IgE, the activation and release of mediators in the allergic response (early and late phase) is limited. Serum free IgE levels and the number of high-affinity IgE receptors are decreased. Long-term treatment in patients with allergic asthma showed a decrease in asthma exacerbations and corticosteroid usage.

Chronic idiopathic urticaria: Omalizumab binds to IgE and lowers free IgE levels. Subsequently, IgE receptors (FcεRI) on cells down-regulate. The mechanism by which these effects of omalizumab result in an improvement of chronic idiopathic urticaria symptoms is unknown.

Pharmacodynamics/Kinetics

Onset of Action Response to therapy: ~12 to 16 weeks (87% of patients had measurable response in 12 weeks)

Half-life Elimination 26 days (asthma patients); 24 days (chronic idiopathic urticaria patients)

Time to Peak 7-8 days

Pregnancy Considerations

Adverse events have not been observed in animal reproduction studies. IgG molecules are known to cross the placenta. Information related to the use of omalizumab in pregnancy is available from case reports of women with severe asthma (Kupryś-Lipińska 2014) or chronic idiopathic urticaria (some also with asthma) (Cuervo-Pardo 2016; Ghazanfar 2015). In addition, preliminary data from the Xolair Pregnancy Registry (EXPECT) has been published. Based on data collected from 191 women September 2006 through November 2012, the incidence of the adverse events monitored (major congenital malformations, prematurity, low birth weight, small for gestational age) are within the rates of those reported for women with severe asthma (Namazy 2015). The pregnancy registry has closed; however, new cases of exposure may be reported to the manufacturer (Genentech 888-835-2555).

Uncontrolled asthma is associated with adverse events on pregnancy (increased risk of perinatal mortality, preeclampsia, preterm birth, low-birth-weight infants). Optimal control of asthma prior to and during pregnancy is recommended (GINA 2016; NAEPP 2005).

Ombitasvir, Paritaprevir, and Ritonavir

(om BIT as vir, par i TA pre vir, & ri TOE na vir)

Brand Names: US Technivie

Brand Names: Canada Technivie

Pharmacologic Category Antihepaciviral, NS5A Inhibitor; Antihepaciviral, Protease Inhibitor (Anti-HCV); Cytochrome P-450 Inhibitor

Use Chronic hepatitis C: Treatment of chronic hepatitis C virus (HCV) genotype 4 infection without cirrhosis or with compensated cirrhosis, in combination with ribavirin.

Local Anesthetic/Vasoconstrictor Precautions No information available to require special precautions

Effects on Dental Treatment No significant effects or complications reported

Effects on Bleeding No information available to require special precautions

Adverse Reactions Frequency not always defined.

- Central nervous system: Fatigue (7%), insomnia (5%)
- Dermatologic: Allergic skin reaction (5%), pruritus (5%)
- Gastrointestinal: Nausea (9%)
- Hematologic & oncologic: Anemia, decreased hemoglobin
- Hepatic: Increased serum ALT
- Neuromuscular & skeletal: Weakness (25%)
- Miscellaneous: Tachyphylaxis
- <1%, postmarketing, and/or case reports: Hepatic failure (in patients with underlying cirrhosis; FDA Safety Alert, October 22, 2015), hypersensitivity reaction (including angioedema), liver decompensation (in patients with underlying cirrhosis; FDA Safety Alert, October 22, 2015), reactivation of HBV (FDA Safety Alert Dec. 8, 2016)

General Dosage Range

Oral: *Adults:* Ombitasvir/paritaprevir/ritonavir tablet: Two tablets once daily (every morning)

Mechanism of Action

Combines 2 direct-acting hepatitis C virus antiviral agents with distinct mechanisms of action. Ombitasvir inhibits HCV NS5A, and interferes with viral RNA replication and virion assembly. Paritaprevir inhibits HCV NS3/4A protease and interferes with HCV coded polyprotein cleavage necessary for viral replication.

Ritonavir is not active against HCV. Ritonavir is a potent CYP3A inhibitor that increases peak and trough plasma drug concentrations of paritaprevir and overall drug exposure (ie, AUC).

Pharmacodynamics/Kinetics

Half-life Elimination Ombitasvir: 21 to 25 hours; Paritaprevir: 5.5 hours; Ritonavir: 4 hours

Time to Peak Ombitasvir, paritaprevir, ritonavir: 4 to 5 hours

Pregnancy Considerations

Use of this product in combination with ribavirin is contraindicated in pregnant women and men whose female partners are pregnant.

Adverse events were not observed in animal reproduction studies using the individual agents. If used in combination with ribavirin, all warnings related to the use of ribavirin and pregnancy and/or contraception should be followed. Mother-to-child transmission of HCV does not occur if the woman is not viremic, therefore, HCV-infected women of childbearing potential should postpone pregnancy until therapy is complete. Treatment of HCV is not recommended for women who are already pregnant (AASLD/IDSA 2015).

Ombitasvir, Paritaprevir, Ritonavir, and Dasabuvir

(om BIT as vir, par i TA pre vir, ri TOE na vir, & da SA bue vir)

Brand Names: US Viekira Pak; Viekira XR

Brand Names: Canada Holkira Pak

Pharmacologic Category Antihepaciviral, NS5A Inhibitor; Antihepaciviral, Polymerase Inhibitor (Anti-HCV); Antihepaciviral, Protease Inhibitor (Anti-HCV); Cytochrome P-450 Inhibitor; NS3/4A Inhibitor; NS5A Inhibitor; NS5B RNA Polymerase Inhibitor

Use Chronic hepatitis C: Treatment of adults with chronic hepatitis C virus (HCV) infection genotype 1a and genotype 1b without cirrhosis or with compensated cirrhosis.

Local Anesthetic/Vasoconstrictor Precautions No information available to require special precautions

Effects on Dental Treatment No significant effects or complications reported

Effects on Bleeding No information available to require special precautions

Adverse Reactions Also see individual agents.

1% to 10%:

- Central nervous system: Insomnia (5%)
- Dermatologic: Pruritus (7%), skin rash (7%)
- Gastrointestinal: Nausea (8%)
- Hepatic: Increased serum bilirubin (≥2 x ULN; 2%), increased serum ALT (>5 x ULN; 1%)
- Neuromuscular & skeletal: Weakness (4%)

<1%, postmarketing, and/or case reports: Angioedema, hepatic failure, hypersensitivity reaction, liver

decompensation, reactivation of HBV (FDA Safety Alert Dec. 8, 2016)

General Dosage Range

Oral: *Adults:*

Immediate release: Ombitasvir/paritaprevir/ritonavir tablet: Two tablets every morning **and** Dasabuvir tablet: One tablet twice daily.

Extended release: Three tablets once daily.

Mechanism of Action

Combines 3 direct-acting hepatitis C virus antiviral agents with distinct mechanisms of action. Ombitasvir inhibits HCV NS5A, and interferes with viral RNA replication and virion assembly. Paritaprevir inhibits HCV NS3/4A protease and interferes with HCV coded polyprotein cleavage necessary for viral replication. Dasabuvir inhibits HCV RNA-dependent RNA polymerase (encoded by the NS5B gene) which is also necessary for viral replication.

Ritonavir is not active against HCV. Ritonavir is a potent CYP3A inhibitor that increases peak and trough plasma drug concentrations of paritaprevir and overall drug exposure (ie, AUC).

Pharmacodynamics/Kinetics

Half-life Elimination Ombitasvir: 21 to 25 hours; Paritaprevir: 5.5 hours; Ritonavir: 4 hours; Dasabuvir 5.5 to 6 hours

Time to Peak

Ombitasvir: ~5 hours

Paritaprevir: ~4 to 5 hours

Ritonavir: ~4 to 5 hours

Dasabuvir: ~4 hours (immediate release); 8 hours (ER)

Pregnancy Considerations

Use of this product in combination with ribavirin is contraindicated in pregnant women and men whose female partners are pregnant.

Adverse events were not observed in animal reproduction studies using the individual agents. If used in combination with ribavirin, all warnings related to the use of ribavirin and pregnancy and/or contraception should be followed. Mother-to-child transmission of HCV does not occur if the woman is not viremic, therefore, HCV-infected women of childbearing potential should postpone pregnancy until therapy is complete. Treatment of HCV is not recommended for women who are already pregnant (AASLD/IDSA 2015).

Omega-3 Fatty Acids

(oh MEG a three FAT tee AS ids)

Related Information

Cardiovascular Diseases *on page 1752*

Brand Names: US Dialyvite Omega-3 Concentrate [OTC]; Expecta LIPIL [OTC] [DSC]; Fish Oil Ultra [OTC] [DSC]; High Potency Fish Oil [OTC] [DSC]; Lovaza; Maximum Red Krill [OTC]; Ocean Blue Mini-Caps Omega-3 [OTC]; Omega Power [OTC]; Omega-3 2100 [OTC]; Omega-3 Fish Oil Ex St [OTC]; Omega-3 IQ [OTC]; Pro Nutrients Omega 3 [OTC]; Salmon Oil-1000 [OTC]; Sam-E.P.A. [OTC]; Sea-Omega [OTC]; Systane Omega-3 Healthy Tears [OTC] [DSC]; Vascepa

Generic Availability (US) May be product dependent

Pharmacologic Category Antilipemic Agent, Omega-3 Fatty Acids

Use

Dietary supplement: As dietary supplements for patients at early risk of coronary artery disease primarily because of effects on platelets and lipids.

Note: The American Heart Association recommends that consumers without documented coronary heart disease eat a variety of fish, preferably oily fish (eg, salmon), at least twice a week. Fish oil supplements should only be considered for individuals with heart disease or high triglyceride levels in consultation with a physician (AHA 2014).

Hypertriglyceridemia (Lovaza, Omtryg, Epanova, and Vascepa): As an adjunct to diet to reduce triglyceride levels in adults with severe (≥500 mg/dL) hypertriglyceridemia.

Note: The Endocrine Society recommends that omega-3 fatty acids may be considered for triglyceride levels >1,000 mg/dL and may be used alone or in combination with HMG-CoA reductase inhibitors (Berglund 2012). A number of OTC formulations containing omega-3 fatty acids are marketed as nutritional supplements; these do not have FDA-approved indications and may not contain the same amounts of the active ingredient.

Local Anesthetic/Vasoconstrictor Precautions No information available to require special precautions

Effects on Dental Treatment No significant effects or complications reported

Effects on Bleeding Prolongation of bleeding time has been observed in some clinical studies; however, there is no scientific evidence to warrant discontinuance prior to dental surgery. The clinician should anticipate the potential for slower clotting times.

Adverse Reactions

>10%: Gastrointestinal: Diarrhea (7% to 15%)

1% to 10%:

Gastrointestinal: Nausea (4% to 6%), abdominal pain (3% to 5%), dysgeusia (4%), eructation (3% to 4%), dyspepsia (3%)

Neuromuscular & skeletal: Arthralgia (2%)

Frequency not defined:

Central nervous system: Fatigue

Dermatologic: Pruritus, skin rash

Endocrine & metabolic: Increased LDL cholesterol

Gastrointestinal: Abdominal distension, constipation, flatulence, gastrointestinal disease, vomiting

Hematologic & oncologic: Prolonged bleeding time

Hepatic: Increased serum ALT, increased serum AST

Respiratory: Nasopharyngitis, oropharyngeal pain

<1%, postmarketing, and/or case reports: Anaphylaxis, cardiac arrhythmia, hemorrhagic diathesis

Dosing

Adult & Geriatric

Hypertriglyceridemia: Oral:

Epanova: 2 g (2 capsules) or 4 g (4 capsules) once daily

Lovaza: 4 g (4 capsules) once daily or 2 g (2 capsules) twice daily

Omtryg: 4.8 g (4 capsules) once daily with meals or 2.4 g (2 capsules) twice daily with meals

Vascepa: 2 g (2 [1 gram] capsules or 4 [0.5 g] capsules) twice daily with meals

Treatment of IgA nephropathy (off-label use): Oral: Lovaza: 4 g (4 capsules) once daily (Donadio 2001)

Renal Impairment There are no dosage adjustments provided in the manufacturer's labeling (has not been studied). EPA and DHA are not renally eliminated.

Hepatic Impairment There are no dosage adjustments provided in the manufacturer's labeling (has not been studied). Periodic monitoring of ALT and AST is recommended.

Mechanism of Action Reduction in the hepatic production of triglyceride-rich very low-density lipoproteins (VLDL). Possible cellular mechanisms include inhibition of acyl CoA:1,2 diacylglycerol acyltransferase, increased hepatic mitochondrial and peroxisomal beta-oxidation, and a reduction in the hepatic synthesis of triglycerides.

Contraindications Hypersensitivity (eg, anaphylactic reaction) to omega-3 fatty acids or any component of formulation.

Warnings/Precautions Use with caution in patients with known allergy or sensitivity to fish and/or shellfish. Should be used as an adjunct to diet therapy and exercise and only in those with very high triglyceride levels (≥500 mg/dL). Secondary causes of hyperlipidemia should be ruled out prior to therapy. ALT may be increased without ALT increasing. May increase LDL levels; periodically monitor LDL levels. Prolongation of bleeding time not exceeding normal limits has been observed in some clinical studies with omega-3 fatty acids; use with caution in patients with coagulopathy or in those receiving therapeutic anticoagulation or antiplatelet therapy. Monitor for changes in INR following initiation and dosage changes of omega-3 fatty acids in patients receiving warfarin. Omega-3 fatty acids are not indicated for the treatment of atrial fibrillation (AF) or flutter; recurrent AF or flutter may occur in patients with symptomatic paroxysmal or persistent AF treated with omega-3 fatty acids; more frequent occurrences were observed with omega-3 fatty acids in the first 2 to 3 months of therapy compared to placebo in clinical trials. However, the clinical significance of these results is uncertain. The effect, if any, of omega-3 fatty acids on the risk of pancreatitis or cardiovascular mortality and morbidity in patients with severe hypertriglyceridemia is not known. Manage concurrent conditions (eg, diabetes, hypothyroidism, excessive alcohol intake) that may contribute to lipid abnormalities.

Drug Interactions

Metabolism/Transport Effects None known.

Avoid Concomitant Use There are no known interactions where it is recommended to avoid concomitant use.

Increased Effect/Toxicity

Omega-3 Fatty Acids may increase the levels/effects of: Agents with Antiplatelet Properties; Anticoagulants; Ibrutinib

Decreased Effect There are no known significant interactions involving a decrease in effect.

Dietary Considerations Dietary modification is important in the control of severe hypertriglyceridemia. Maintain standard cholesterol-lowering diet during therapy.

Pharmacodynamics/Kinetics

Half-life Elimination EPA: ~37 to 89 hours; DHA: ~46 hours

Time to Peak

Plasma:

Omega-3-carboxylic acids: Following repeat dosing with low-fat meals for ~2 weeks (steady state): EPA: 5 to 8 hours; DHA: 5 to 9 hours

Icosapent ethyl: EPA: ~5 hours

Pregnancy Risk Factor C

Pregnancy Considerations Adverse events have been observed in animal reproduction studies. Maternal dietary consumption of omega-3 fatty acids (containing eicosapentaenoic acid [EPA] and docosahexaenoic acid [DHA]) influences fetal concentrations (Coletta 2010; Miles 2011). Information specific to the therapeutic use of these products in pregnancy has not been located; however, the use of omega-3 fatty acids to manage elevated triglycerides in pregnancy has been described in case reports (Goldberg 2012; Papadakis 2011).

Breastfeeding Considerations Omega-3 fatty acids are excreted in breast milk. According to the manufacturer, the decision to continue or discontinue breastfeeding during therapy should take into account the risk of infant exposure, the benefits of breastfeeding to the infant, and benefits of treatment to the mother.

Product Availability

Epanova: FDA approved May 2014; anticipated availability is currently unknown.

Omtryg: FDA approved April 2014; anticipated availability is currently unknown.

Dosage Forms Considerations

Epanova: Each 1 g capsule contains at least 850 mg of polyunsaturated fatty acids, including multiple omega-3 fatty acids (EPA and DHA being the most abundant).

Lovaza, Omtryg: Each 1 g (Lovaza) or 1.2 g (Omtryg) capsule contains the combination of eicosapentaenoic acid (EPA; ~465 mg) and docosahexaenoic acid (DHA; ~375 mg) ethyl esters.

Vascepa: Icosapent ethyl contains ethyl esters of an omega-3 fatty acid, eicosapentaenoic acid (EPA), obtained from fish oil. It contains ≥96% EPA and does **not** contain docosahexaenoic acid (DHA). Historically, mixtures containing both EPA and DHA have increased LDL cholesterol in patients with severe hypertriglyceridemia. However, studies have suggested that icosapent ethyl has not caused significant increases in LDL cholesterol while significantly decreasing triglyceride levels (Bays, 2011; Miller, 2011).

Dosage Forms

Capsule, Oral:

Dialyvite Omega-3 Concentrate [OTC]: 600 mg
Lovaza: 1 g
Ocean Blue MiniCaps Omega-3 [OTC]: 350 mg
Omega Power [OTC]: 1050 mg
Omega-3 2100 [OTC]: 1050 mg
Vascepa: 0.5 g, 1 g
Generic: 300 mg, 500 mg, 1000 mg, 1 g

Capsule, Oral [preservative free]:

Maximum Red Krill [OTC]: 300 mg
Omega-3 Fish Oil Ex St [OTC]: 880 mg
Salmon Oil-1000 [OTC]: 200 mg
Sam-E.P.A. [OTC]: 200-300 MG
Sea-Omega [OTC]: 1000 mg
Generic: 200 mg, 1000 mg, 1200 mg

Capsule Delayed Release, Oral:

Pro Nutrients Omega 3 [OTC]: 332.5 mg
Generic: 1000 mg

Tablet Chewable, Oral:

Omega-3 IQ [OTC]: 240 mg

Omeprazole (oh MEP ra zole)

Related Information

Esomeprazole *on page 604*
Gastrointestinal Disorders *on page 1775*

Brand Names: US First-Omeprazole; Omeprazole +Syrspend SF Alka; PriLOSEC; PriLOSEC OTC [OTC]

Brand Names: Canada Apo-Omeprazole; Auro-Omeprazole; Dom-Omeprazole DR; JAMP-Omeprazole DR; Losec; Mylan-Omeprazole; Olex; PMS-Omeprazole; PMS-Omeprazole DR; Q-Omeprazole; RAN-Omeprazole; ratio-Omeprazole; Riva-Omeprazole DR; Sandoz-Omeprazole; Teva-Omeprazole

Generic Availability (US) May be product dependent

Pharmacologic Category Proton Pump Inhibitor; Substituted Benzimidazole

Use

Duodenal ulcer (Rx only): Short-term treatment (4 to 8 weeks) of active duodenal ulcer in adults.

Gastric ulcer (Rx only): Short-term treatment (4 to 8 weeks) of active benign gastric ulcer in adults.

Gastroesophageal reflux disease (Rx only):

Treatment of erosive esophagitis: Short-term treatment (4 to 8 weeks) of erosive esophagitis (EE) due to acid-mediated gastroesophageal reflux disease (GERD) diagnosed by endoscopy in patients ≥1 year; short-term treatment (up to 6 weeks) of EE due to acid-mediated GERD in pediatric patients 1 month to <1 year.

Maintenance healing of erosive esophagitis: Maintenance healing of EE due to acid-mediated GERD in patients ≥1 year.

Symptomatic gastroesophageal reflux disease: Treatment of heartburn and other symptoms associated with GERD for up to 4 weeks in patients ≥1 year.

Heartburn (OTC only): Treatment of frequent, uncomplicated heartburn (occurring ≥2 or more days per week) in adults.

***Helicobacter pylori* eradication (Rx only):**

Dual therapy: Treatment of *H. pylori* infection and duodenal ulcer disease (active or up to 1-year history) in combination with clarithromycin to eradicate *H. pylori* in adults.

Triple therapy: Treatment of *H. pylori* infection and duodenal ulcer disease (active or up to 1-year history) in combination with clarithromycin and amoxicillin to eradicate *H. pylori* in adults.

Pathological hypersecretory conditions (Rx only): Long-term treatment of pathological hypersecretory conditions (eg, Zollinger-Ellison syndrome, multiple endocrine adenomas, systemic mastocytosis) in adults.

Local Anesthetic/Vasoconstrictor Precautions No information available to require special precautions

Effects on Dental Treatment Key adverse event(s) related to dental treatment: Taste perversion, dry mouth, esophageal candidiasis, and mucosal atrophy (tongue).

Effects on Bleeding No information available to require special precautions

Adverse Reactions

1% to 10%:

Central nervous system: Headache (7%), dizziness (2%)

Dermatologic: Skin rash (2%)

Gastrointestinal: Abdominal pain (5%), diarrhea (4%), nausea (4%), flatulence (3%), vomiting (3%), acid regurgitation (2%), constipation (2%)

Neuromuscular & skeletal: Back pain (1%), weakness (1%)

Respiratory: Upper respiratory infection (2%), cough (1%)

<1%, postmarketing, and/or case reports (adverse event occurrence may vary based on formulation): Abdominal swelling, abnormal dreams, aggression, agitation, agranulocytosis, allergic reactions, alopecia, anaphylaxis, anemia, angina pectoris, angioedema, anorexia, anxiety, apathy, arthralgia, atrophic gastritis, benign gastric polyps, blurred vision, bone fracture, bradycardia, bronchospasm, chest pain, cholestatic hepatitis, chronic renal disease (Lazarus 2016), *Clostridium difficile*-associated diarrhea (CDAD), confusion, depression, dermatitis, diplopia, drowsiness, dysgeusia, epistaxis, erythema multiforme, esophageal candidiasis, fatigue, fecal discoloration, fever, gastroduodenal carcinoids, glycosuria, gynecomastia, hallucination, hematuria, hemolytic anemia, hepatic disease (hepatocellular, cholestatic, mixed), hepatic encephalopathy, hepatic failure, hepatic necrosis, hepatitis, hepatocellular hepatitis, hepatotoxicity (idiosyncratic) (Chalasani 2014), hyperhidrosis, hypersensitivity, hypertension, hypocalcemia, hypoglycemia, hypokalemia, hypomagnesemia, hyponatremia, increased gamma glutamyl transferase, increased serum alkaline phosphatase, increased serum bilirubin, increased serum creatinine, increased serum transaminases, insomnia, interstitial nephritis, irritable bowel syndrome, jaundice, leg pain, leukocytosis, leukopenia, malaise, microscopic colitis, microscopic pyuria, mucosal atrophy (tongue), muscle cramps, myalgia, myasthenia, nervousness, neutropenia, ocular irritation, optic atrophy, optic neuritis, optic neuropathy (anterior ischemic), osteoporosis-related fracture, pain, palpitation, pancreatitis, pancytopenia, paresthesia, peripheral edema, petechiae, photophobia, pneumonia, proteinuria, pruritus, psychiatric disturbance, purpura, sleep disturbance, sore throat, Stevens-Johnson syndrome, stomatitis, systemic lupus erythematosus, tachycardia, testicular pain, thrombocytopenia, tinnitus, toxic epidermal necrolysis, tremor, urinary frequency, urinary tract infection, urticaria, vertigo, weight gain, xeroderma, xerophthalmia, xerostomia

Dosing

Adult

Duodenal ulcer: Oral: 20 mg once daily for 4 weeks; some patients may require an additional 4 weeks. Up to 40 mg once daily has been used in patients with ulcers refractive to other therapies (eg, H2 antagonists) (Bardhan 1991).

Gastric ulcers: Oral: 40 mg once daily for 4 to 8 weeks; in clinical trials, healing rates of ulcers ≤1 cm at 4 and 8 weeks were similar between omeprazole 20 mg and 40 mg; for ulcers >1 cm omeprazole 40 mg was significantly more effective at 8 weeks.

Erosive esophagitis: Oral:

Treatment:

Manufacturer's labeling: 20 mg once daily for 4 to 8 weeks; may continue for an additional 4 weeks if no response to 8 weeks of treatment. With recurrence of erosive esophagitis or GERD symptoms (eg, heartburn), an additional 4 to 8 weeks of treatment may be considered.

Alternate recommendations: For patients with partial response to usual dosing, may consider a dose increase to 20 mg twice daily (ACG [Katz 2013]; Kahrilas 2008) or 40 mg once or twice daily (NICE 2014).

Maintenance of healing: 20 mg once daily; 10 mg once daily is recommended for Asian patients.

GERD, symptomatic (without esophageal lesions): Oral: 20 mg once daily for up to 4 weeks

GERD, refractory (off-label dose): Oral: For patients with partial response to usual dosing, may consider a dose increase to 20 mg twice daily for 8 weeks (ACG [Katz 2013]; Herschovici 2010).

***Helicobacter pylori* eradication:** Oral: Dose varies with regimen:

Manufacturer labeling:

Dual therapy: 40 mg once daily administered with clarithromycin 500 mg 3 times daily for 14 days. In patients with presence of ulcer at time of therapy initiation, continue omeprazole 20 mg once daily for an additional 14 days after completion of dual therapy.

Triple therapy: 20 mg twice daily administered with amoxicillin 1000 mg *and* clarithromycin 500 mg twice daily for 10 days. In patients with presence of ulcer at time of therapy initiation, continue omeprazole 20 mg once daily for an additional 18 days after completion of triple therapy.

American College of Gastroenterology guidelines (Chey 2007):

Nonpenicillin allergy: 20 mg twice daily administered with amoxicillin 1000 mg *and* clarithromycin 500 mg twice daily for 10 to 14 days

Penicillin allergy: 20 mg twice daily administered with clarithromycin 500 mg *and* metronidazole 500 mg twice daily for 10 to 14 days **or** 20 mg once or twice daily administered with bismuth subsalicylate 525 mg *and* metronidazole 250 mg *plus* tetracycline 500 mg 4 times daily for 10 to 14 days

Pathological hypersecretory conditions: Oral: Initial: 60 mg once daily; doses up to 120 mg 3 times daily have been administered; administer daily doses >80 mg in divided doses. Treat as long as clinically indicated; some patients have been treated continuously for >5 years.

NSAID-induced ulcer treatment (off-label use): Oral: 20 mg once daily for 4 to 8 weeks; Maintenance: 20 mg once daily for up to 6 months (Hawkey 1998)

NSAID-induced ulcer prophylaxis (off-label use): Oral: 20 mg once daily for up to 6 months (Cullen 1998)

Stress ulcer prophylaxis, ICU patients (off-label use): Oral: 40 mg once daily (Levy 1997) or may administer 40 mg loading dose followed by 20 to 40 mg once daily (ASHP 1999). **Note:** Intended for patients with associated risk factors (eg, coagulopathy, mechanical ventilation for ≥48 hours, severe sepsis); discontinue use once risk factors have resolved (Dellinger 2013). Omeprazole 20 mg via NG tube once daily may be less effective in some critically ill populations compared to 40 mg via NG tube once daily (Balaban 1997).

Heartburn (OTC only): Oral: 20 mg once daily for 14 days; treatment may be repeated after 4 months if needed.

Geriatric Refer to adult dosing. Bioavailability may be increased in elderly patients.

Pediatric

Symptomatic GERD: Children ≥1 year to Adolescents ≤16 years: Oral:

5 kg to <10 kg: 5 mg once daily for up to 4 weeks
10 kg to <20 kg: 10 mg once daily for up to 4 weeks
≥20 kg: 20 mg once daily for up to 4 weeks

Erosive esophagitis, treatment:

Infants 1 month to <1 year: Oral:

3 kg to <5 kg: 2.5 mg once daily for up to 6 weeks
5 kg to <10 kg: 5 mg once daily for up to 6 weeks
≥10 kg: 10 mg once daily for up to 6 weeks

Children ≥1 year to Adolescents ≤16 years: Oral: **Note:** Duration of therapy is up to 4 to 8 weeks; may continue for an additional 4 weeks if no response to 8 weeks of treatment. With recurrence of erosive esophagitis or GERD symptoms (eg, heartburn), an additional 4 to 8 week course may be considered.

5 kg to <10 kg: 5 mg once daily
10 kg to <20 kg: 10 mg once daily
≥20 kg: 20 mg once daily

Erosive esophagitis maintenance of healing: Children ≥1 year to Adolescents ≤16 years: Oral: **Note:** Studies do not extend beyond 12 months.

5 kg to <10 kg: 5 mg once daily
10 kg to <20 kg: 10 mg once daily
≥20 kg: 20 mg once daily

Renal Impairment No dosage adjustment necessary.

Hepatic Impairment Mild to severe impairment (Child-Pugh class A, B, or C): 10 mg once daily when used for maintenance of healing of erosive esophagitis. There are no dosage adjustments provided for the other indications. Alternatively, a maximum dose of 20 mg/day regardless of indication, has been recommended (Losec Canadian product labeling 2016). In a very small study, omeprazole systemic exposure and half-life increased ~2- and ~3-fold respectively, in patients with mild to severe hepatic impairment.

Mechanism of Action Proton pump inhibitor; suppresses gastric basal and stimulated acid secretion by inhibiting the parietal cell H+/K+ ATP pump

Contraindications

Hypersensitivity (eg, anaphylaxis, anaphylactic shock, angioedema, bronchospasm, interstitial nephritis, urticaria) to omeprazole, other substituted benzimidazole proton pump inhibitors, or any component of the formulation; concomitant use with products that contain rilpivirine

OTC labeling: When used for self-medication (OTC), do not use if trouble or pain when swallowing food; vomiting with blood, or bloody or black stools; heartburn with lightheadedness, dizziness, or sweating; chest pain or shoulder pain with shortness of breath, sweating, pain spreading to arms, neck or shoulders, or lightheadedness; frequent chest pain.

Warnings/Precautions Use of proton pump inhibitors (PPIs) may increase the risk of gastrointestinal infections (eg, *Salmonella, Campylobacter*). Relief of symptoms does not preclude the presence of a gastric malignancy. In long-term (2-year) studies in rats, omeprazole produced a dose-related increase in gastric carcinoid tumors. While available endoscopic evaluations and histologic examinations of biopsy specimens from human stomachs have not detected a risk from short-term exposure to omeprazole, further human data on the effect of sustained hypochlorhydria and hypergastrinemia are needed to rule out the possibility of an increased risk for the development of tumors in humans receiving long-term therapy. Use of PPIs may increase risk of *Clostridium difficile*-associated diarrhea (CDAD), especially in hospitalized patients; consider CDAD diagnosis in patients with persistent diarrhea that does not improve. Use the lowest dose and shortest duration of PPI therapy appropriate for the condition being treated.

PPIs may diminish the therapeutic effect of clopidogrel, thought to be due to reduced formation of the active metabolite of clopidogrel. The manufacturer of clopidogrel recommends either avoidance both omeprazole (even when scheduled 12 hours apart) and esomeprazole or use of a PPI with comparatively less effect on the active metabolite of clopidogrel (eg, pantoprazole). In contrast to these warnings, others have recommended the continued use of PPIs, regardless of the degree of inhibition, in patients with a history of GI bleeding or multiple risk factors for GI bleeding who are also receiving clopidogrel since no evidence has established clinically meaningful differences in outcome; however, a clinically significant interaction cannot be excluded in those who are poor metabolizers of clopidogrel (Abraham, 2010; Levine, 2011). Potentially significant interactions may exist, requiring dose or frequency adjustment, additional monitoring, and/or selection of alternative therapy.

Increased incidence of osteoporosis-related bone fractures of the hip, spine, or wrist may occur with PPI therapy. Patients on high-dose (multiple daily doses) or long-term (≥1 year) therapy should be monitored. Use the lowest effective dose for the shortest duration of time, use vitamin D and calcium supplementation, and follow appropriate guidelines to reduce risk of fractures in patients at risk. Acute interstitial nephritis has been observed in patients taking PPIs; may occur at any time during therapy and is generally due to an idiopathic hypersensitivity reaction. Discontinue if acute interstitial nephritis develops.

Cutaneous and systemic lupus erythematosus has been reported as new onset or exacerbation of existing autoimmune disease; most cases were cutaneous lupus erythematosus (CLE), most commonly, subacute CLE (occurring within weeks to years after continuous therapy). Systemic lupus erythematosus (SLE) is less common (typically occurs within days to years after initiating treatment) and occurred primarily in young adults up to the elderly. Discontinue therapy if signs or symptoms of CLE or SLE occur and refer to specialist for evaluation; most patients improve 4 to 12 weeks after discontinuation of omeprazole.

Hypomagnesemia, reported rarely, usually with prolonged PPI use of ≥3 months (most cases >1 year of therapy); may be symptomatic or asymptomatic; severe cases may cause tetany, seizures, and cardiac arrhythmias. Consider obtaining serum magnesium concentrations prior to beginning long-term therapy, especially if taking concomitant digoxin, diuretics, or other drugs known to cause hypomagnesemia; and periodically thereafter. Hypomagnesemia may be corrected by magnesium supplementation, although discontinuation of omeprazole may be necessary; magnesium levels typically return to normal within 1 week of stopping. Serum chromogranin A levels may be increased if assessed while patient on omeprazole; may lead to diagnostic errors related to neuroendocrine tumors.

Prolonged treatment (>3 years) may lead to vitamin B_{12} malabsorption and subsequent vitamin B_{12} deficiency. The magnitude of the deficiency is dose-related and the association is stronger in females and those younger in age (<30 years); prevalence is decreased after discontinuation of therapy (Lam, 2013). Serum chromogranin A (CgA) levels increase secondary to drug-induced decreases in gastric acid; may cause false-positive results in diagnostic investigations for neuroendocrine tumors. Temporarily stop omeprazole treatment at least 14 days before CgA test; if initial CgA levels are high, repeat test to confirm. Use same commercial laboratory for testing to prevent variable results.

Decreased *H. pylori* eradication rates have been observed with short-term (≤7 days) combination therapy. The American College of Gastroenterology recommends 10 to 14 days of therapy (triple or quadruple) for eradication of *H. pylori* (Chey, 2007). Bioavailability may be increased in Asian populations and patients with hepatic impairment (Child-Pugh class A, B, or C); dosage reduction is recommended, especially for maintenance healing of erosive esophagitis. Bioavailability may be increased in the elderly.

When used for self-medication (OTC), notify health care provider before use if any of the following are present: heartburn for >3 months; frequent wheezing, particularly with heartburn; unexplained weight loss; nausea or vomiting; or stomach pain. Discontinue use and notify health care provider if heartburn continues or worsens; diarrhea occurs; if >14 days of therapy is needed; or if >1 course of therapy is needed every 4 months.

Benzyl alcohol and derivatives: Some dosage forms may contain benzyl alcohol; large amounts of benzyl alcohol (≥99 mg/kg/day) have been associated with a potentially fatal toxicity ("gasping syndrome") in neonates; the "gasping syndrome" consists of metabolic acidosis, respiratory distress, gasping respirations, CNS dysfunction (including convulsions, intracranial hemorrhage), hypotension, and cardiovascular collapse (AAP ["Inactive" 1997]; CDC, 1982); some data suggests that benzoate displaces bilirubin from protein binding sites (Ahlfors, 2001); avoid or use dosage forms containing benzyl alcohol with caution in neonates. See manufacturer's labeling.

Drug Interactions

Metabolism/Transport Effects **Substrate** of CYP2A6 (minor), CYP2C19 (major), CYP2C9 (minor), CYP2D6 (minor), CYP3A4 (minor); **Note:** Assignment of Major/Minor substrate status based on clinically relevant drug interaction potential; **Inhibits** CYP1A2 (weak), CYP2C19 (weak), CYP2C9 (moderate); **Induces** CYP1A2 (weak/moderate)

Avoid Concomitant Use

Avoid concomitant use of Omeprazole with any of the following: Dasatinib; Delavirdine; Erlotinib; Nelfinavir; PAZOPanib; RifAMPin; Rilpivirine; Risedronate; St John's Wort; Velpatasvir

Increased Effect/Toxicity

Omeprazole may increase the levels/effects of: Amphetamine; Bosentan; Cannabis; Carvedilol; Cilostazol; Citalopram; CloBAZam; CloZAPine; CycloSPORINE (Systemic); CYP2C9 Substrates; Dexmethylphenidate; Dextroamphetamine; Dronabinol; Escitalopram; Fosphenytoin; Methotrexate; Methylphenidate; Phenytoin; Raltegravir; Risedronate; Saquinavir; Tacrolimus (Systemic); Tetrahydrocannabinol; TiZANidine; Vitamin K Antagonists; Voriconazole

The levels/effects of Omeprazole may be increased by: Fluconazole; Ketoconazole (Systemic); Voriconazole

Decreased Effect

Omeprazole may decrease the levels/effects of: Atazanavir; Bisphosphonate Derivatives; Bosutinib; Capecitabine; Cefditoren; Clopidogrel; CloZAPine; Cysteamine (Systemic); Dabigatran Etexilate; Dabrafenib; Dasatinib; Delavirdine; Erlotinib; Gefitinib; Indinavir; Iron Salts; Itraconazole; Ketoconazole (Systemic); Ledipasvir; Mesalamine; Multivitamins/Minerals (with ADEK, Folate, Iron); Mycophenolate; Nalmefene; Nelfinavir; Nilotinib; PAZOPanib; Posaconazole; Rilpivirine; Riociguat; Risedronate; Velpatasvir

The levels/effects of Omeprazole may be decreased by: Antihepaciviral Combination Products; Dabrafenib; Darunavir; Enzalutamide; Fosphenytoin; Lumacaftor; Phenytoin; RifAMPin; St John's Wort; Tipranavir

Food Interactions Prolonged treatment (≥2 years) may lead to malabsorption of dietary vitamin B_{12} and subsequent vitamin B_{12} deficiency (Lam, 2013).

Pharmacodynamics/Kinetics

Onset of Action Antisecretory: ~1 hour; Peak effect: Within 2 hours

Duration of Action Up to 72 hours; 50% of maximum effect at 24 hours; after stopping treatment, secretory activity gradually returns over 3 to 5 days; Maximum secretory inhibition: 4 days

Half-life Elimination 0.5 to 1 hour; hepatic impairment: ~3 hours

Time to Peak Plasma: 0.5 to 3.5 hours

Pregnancy Considerations An increased risk of hypospadias was reported following maternal use of proton pump inhibitors (PPIs) during pregnancy (Anderka 2012), but this was based on a small number of exposures and the same association was not found in another study (Erichsen 2012). Most available studies have not shown an increased risk of major birth defects following maternal use of omeprazole during pregnancy (Diav-Citrin 2005; Källén 2001; Lalkin 1998; Matok 2012; Pasternak 2010). When treating GERD in pregnancy, PPIs may be used when clinically indicated (ACT [Katz 2013]).

Breastfeeding Considerations Omeprazole is excreted in breast milk.

The relative infant dose (RID) of omeprazole is 0.2% to 0.43% when calculated using the highest average breast milk concentration located and compared to an infant therapeutic dose of 0.7 to 1.5 mg/kg/day. In general, breastfeeding is considered acceptable when the RID is <10%; when an RID is >25% breastfeeding should generally be avoided (Anderson 2016; Ito 2000). Using the highest average milk concentration (20.03 mcg/L), the estimated daily infant dose via breast milk is 0.003 mg/kg/day. This milk concentration was obtained following maternal chronic administration of oral omeprazole 20 mg/day; the peak breast milk concentration occurred 3 hours after the dose. (Marshall 1998)

No adverse effects were noted in one infant exposed to omeprazole following maternal administration of oral omeprazole 20 mg/day for 3 months; the authors of this case report noted that the acidic content of a breastfed infants' stomach may potentially inactivate any ingested omeprazole (Marshall 1998).

According to the manufacturer, the decision to continue or discontinue breastfeeding during therapy should take into account the risk of infant exposure, the benefits of breastfeeding to the infant, and benefits of treatment to the mother.

Dosage Forms Considerations

First-Omeprazole and Omeprazole+Syrspend Alka oral suspensions are compounding kits. Refer to manufacturer's labeling for compounding instructions.

Dosage Forms

Capsule Delayed Release, Oral:
Generic: 10 mg, 20 mg, 40 mg, 20 mg

Packet, Oral:
PriLOSEC: 2.5 mg (30 ea); 10 mg (30 ea)

Suspension, Oral:
First-Omeprazole: 2 mg/mL (90 mL, 150 mL, 300 mL)
Omeprazole+Syrspend SF Alka: 2 mg/mL (100 mL, 120 mL, 240 mL)

Tablet Delayed Release, Oral:
PriLOSEC OTC [OTC]: 20 mg
Generic: 20 mg

Omeprazole, Clarithromycin, and Amoxicillin

(oh MEP ra zole, kla RITH roe mye sin, & a moks i SIL in)

Related Information

Amoxicillin *on page* 121
Clarithromycin *on page* 377
Omeprazole *on page* 1233

Brand Names: US Omeclamox-Pak®

Pharmacologic Category Antibiotic, Macrolide Combination; Antibiotic, Penicillin; Gastrointestinal Agent, Miscellaneous; Proton Pump Inhibitor; Substituted Benzimidazole

Use *Helicobacter pylori* eradication: Eradication of *H. pylori* infection to reduce the risk of recurrent duodenal ulcer in adults with active or 1-year history of duodenal ulcer

Local Anesthetic/Vasoconstrictor Precautions Clarithromycin is one of the drugs confirmed to prolong the QT interval and is accepted as having a risk of causing torsade de pointes. In terms of epinephrine, it is not known what effect vasoconstrictors in the local anesthetic regimen will have in patients with a known history of congenital prolonged QT interval or in patients taking any medication that prolongs the QT interval. Until more information is obtained, it is suggested that the clinician consult with the physician prior to the use of a vasoconstrictor in suspected patients, and that the vasoconstrictor (epinephrine, mepivacaine and levonordefrin [Carbocaine® 2% with Neo-Cobefrin®]) be used with caution. See Dental Comment.

Effects on Dental Treatment No significant effects or complications reported

Effects on Bleeding No information available to require special precautions

Adverse Reactions Frequencies noted refer to experience with combination therapy. Also see individual agents.

>10%: Gastrointestinal: Diarrhea (14%)

1% to 10%:
- Central nervous system: Headache (7%)
- Gastrointestinal: Dysgeusia (10%)

<1%, postmarketing, and/or case reports: Hepatotoxicity (idiosyncratic) (Chalasani 2014)

General Dosage Range Oral: *Adults:* Omeprazole 20 mg, clarithromycin 500 mg, and amoxicillin 1000 mg twice daily

Mechanism of Action

Omeprazole: A proton pump inhibitor, suppresses gastric acid secretion via inhibition of the parietal cell H+/K+ ATP pump.

Clarithromycin: An antibacterial agent, binds to the 50s ribosomal subunit of susceptible microorganisms resulting in inhibition of protein synthesis.

Amoxicillin: An antibacterial agent, inhibits bacterial cell wall synthesis.

Pregnancy Considerations Adverse events have been observed in animal reproduction studies using clarithromycin or omeprazole. Refer to individual monographs.

Dental Comment See Local Anesthetic/Vasoconstrictor Precautions

OnabotulinumtoxinA

(oh nuh BOT yoo lin num TOKS in aye)

Brand Names: US Botox; Botox Cosmetic

Brand Names: Canada Botox; Botox Cosmetic

Generic Availability (US) No

Pharmacologic Category Neuromuscular Blocker Agent, Toxin; Ophthalmic Agent, Toxin

Use

Axillary hyperhidrosis (Botox): Treatment of severe primary axillary hyperhidrosis in adults not adequately managed with topical agents.

Cervical dystonia (Botox): Treatment of cervical dystonia in patients ≥16 years to reduce the severity of abnormal head position and neck pain.

Chronic migraine (Botox): Prophylaxis of chronic migraine headaches (≥ 15 days/month with headache lasting ≥4 hours/day) in adults.

Glabellar lines (Botox Cosmetic): Temporary improvement in the appearance of moderate to severe glabellar lines associated with corrugator and/or procerus muscle activity in adults.

Lateral canthal lines (Botox Cosmetic): Temporary improvement in the appearance of moderate to severe lateral canthal lines associated with orbicularis oculi activity in adults.

Lower limb spasticity (Botox): Treatment of lower limb spasticity in adults to decrease the severity of increased muscle tone in ankle and toe flexors (gastrocnemius, soleus, tibialis posterior, flexor hallucis longus, and flexor digitorum longus).

Overactive bladder (Botox): Treatment of overactive bladder with symptoms of urge urinary incontinence, urgency, and frequency in adults who have an inadequate response to or who are intolerant to an anticholinergic medication.

Strabismus and blepharospasm associated with dystonia (Botox): Treatment of strabismus and blepharospasm associated with dystonia, including benign essential blepharospasm or VII nerve disorders, in patients ≥12 years.

Upper limb spasticity (Botox): Treatment of upper limb spasticity in adults to decrease the severity of increased muscle tone in elbow flexors (biceps), wrist flexors (flexor carpi radialis and flexor carpi ulnaris), finger flexors (flexor digitorum profundus and flexor digitorum sublimis), and thumb flexors (adductor pollicis and flexor pollicis longus).

Urinary incontinence due to detrusor overactivity (Botox): Treatment of urinary incontinence due to detrusor overactivity associated with a neurologic condition (eg, spinal cord injury [SCI], multiple sclerosis [MS]) in adults who have an inadequate response to or are intolerant of an anticholinergic medication.

Canadian labeling: Additional use (not in US labeling): Dynamic equinus foot deformity in pediatric cerebral palsy patients; treatment of forehead lines in adults

Local Anesthetic/Vasoconstrictor Precautions No information available to require special precautions

Effects on Dental Treatment Key adverse event(s) related to dental treatment: Xerostomia (normal salivary flow resumes upon discontinuation), facial pain, and facial weakness. Effects occur in ~1 week and may last up to several months.

Effects on Bleeding No information available to require special precautions

Adverse Reactions Adverse effects usually occur in 1 week and may last up to several months. Frequency not always defined.

>10%:

Bladder dysfunction:

Genitourinary: Urinary tract infection (18% to 49%), urinary retention (6% to 17%)

Cervical dystonia:

Central nervous system: Headache (11%)

Gastrointestinal: Dysphagia (19%)

Neuromuscular & skeletal: Neck pain (11%)

Respiratory: Upper respiratory tract infection (12%)

Other indications (blepharospasm, glabellar lines, lateral canthal lines, primary axillary hyperhidrosis, strabismus):

Ophthalmic: Blepharoptosis (blepharospasm: 21%; strabismus: 1% to 38%; glabellar lines: 3%), vertical deviation of eyes (strabismus 17%)

1% to 10%:

Bladder dysfunction:

Central nervous system: Myasthenia (4%), abnormal gait (3%), falling (3%)

Gastrointestinal: Constipation (4%)

Genitourinary: Dysuria (4% to 9%), bacteriuria (4%), hematuria (4%), increased post-void residual urine volume (not requiring catheterization: 3%)

Neuromuscular & skeletal: Muscle spasm (2%)

Cervical dystonia:

Central nervous system: Dizziness (2% to 10%), hypertonia (2% to 10%), numbness (2% to 10%), speech disturbance (2% to 10%), drowsiness

Gastrointestinal: Nausea (2% to 10%), xerostomia (2% to 10%)

Immunologic: Antibody development (1%)

Local: Injection site reaction: Soreness (2% to 10%)

Neuromuscular & skeletal: Back pain (2% to 10%), stiffness (2% to 10%), weakness (2% to 10%)

Ophthalmic: Blepharoptosis (2% to 10%), diplopia (2% to 10%)

Respiratory: Cough (2% to 10%), dyspnea (2% to 10%), flu-like symptoms (2% to 10%), rhinitis (2% to 10%)

Miscellaneous: Fever (2% to 10%)

Chronic migraines:

Cardiovascular: Hypertension (2%)

Central nervous system: Headache (5%), exacerbation of migraine headache (4%), facial paresis (2%)

Local: Pain at injection site (3%)

Neuromuscular & skeletal: Neck pain (9%), myasthenia (4%), stiffness (4%), musculoskeletal pain (3%), myalgia (3%), muscle spasm (2%)

Ophthalmic: Blepharoptosis (4%)

Respiratory: Bronchitis (3%)

Lower limb spasticity:

Local: Pain at injection site (2%)

Neuromuscular & skeletal: Arthralgia (3%), back pain (3%), myalgia (2%)

Respiratory: Upper respiratory tract infection (2%)

Upper limb spasticity:

Central nervous system: Fatigue (2% to 3%)

Gastrointestinal: Nausea (2% to 3%)

Neuromuscular & skeletal: Limb pain (5% to 9%), myasthenia (2% to 4%)

Respiratory: Bronchitis (2% to 3%)

Other indications (blepharospasm, glabellar lines, lateral canthal lines, primary axillary hyperhidrosis, reduction of glabellar lines, strabismus):

Central nervous system: Facial pain (1%), facial paresis (1%), anxiety, dizziness, headache, pain

Dermatologic: Diaphoresis (nonaxillary), pruritus, skin rash

Gastrointestinal: Nausea

Immunologic: Antibody development (2%)

Infection: Infection

Local: Injection site reaction: Hemorrhage, pain, soreness

Neuromuscular & skeletal: Weakness (1%), back pain, neck pain
Ophthalmic: Dry eye syndrome (6%), eyelid edema (1%), diplopia, ectropion, entropion, eye irritation (includes dry eye, lagophthalmos, photophobia), keratitis, lacrimation, superficial punctate keratitis
Respiratory: Flu-like symptoms, pharyngitis
Miscellaneous: Fever

<1%, postmarketing, and/or case reports: *Any indication:* Abdominal pain, acute angle closure glaucoma, alopecia, anaphylaxis, anorexia, antibody development (neutralizing), aspiration pneumonia, asthma, blurred vision, brachial plexopathy, cardiac arrhythmia, corneal perforation, corneal ulceration, denervation, dermatitis, diarrhea, dysarthria, erythema, erythema multiforme, exacerbation of myasthenia gravis, eye infection, facial paresis, focal facial paralysis, hyperhidrosis, hypersensitivity reaction, hypoacusis, hypoesthesia, inflammation at injection site, jaw pain, lagophthalmos, madarosis, malaise, myalgia, myocardial infarction, paresthesia, peripheral neuropathy, pneumonia, psoriasiform eruption, radiculopathy, reduced blinking, respiratory depression, respiratory failure, retinal vein occlusion, retrobulbar hemorrhage, seizure, serum sickness, syncope, tinnitus, urinary incontinence, urticaria, vertigo, visual disturbance, voice disorder, vomiting

Dosing

Adult Note: The lowest recommended dose should be used when initiating treatment (regardless of indication). In adults treated for more than one indication, the maximum cumulative dose should be ≤400 units/3 months for Botox or ≤360 units/3 months for Botox Cosmetic. Canadian labeling recommends a maximum cumulative dose of 6 units/kg (up to 360 units) over 3 months in adult patients receiving additional treatment for noncosmetic indications.

Bladder dysfunction: Intradetrusor: **Note:** Prophylactic antimicrobial therapy (excluding aminoglycosides) should be administered 1 to 3 days prior to, on the day of, and for 1 to 3 days following onabotulinumtoxinA administration to decrease risk of urinary tract infection (UTI). Discontinue antiplatelet therapy at least 3 days prior to administration.

Detrusor overactivity associated with neurologic condition: 30 injections of 1 mL (recommended concentration: ~6.7 units/mL) for a total dose of 200 units/30 mL (maximum: 200 units); for the final injection, ~1 mL of sterile NS should be injected to ensure that the remaining medication in the needle is delivered to the bladder; may consider re-treatment with diminishing effect but no sooner than 12 weeks from previous administration (median time until second treatment in studies: 42 to 48 weeks).

Overactive bladder: 20 injections of 0.5 mL (recommended concentration: 10 units/mL) for a total dose of 100 units/10 mL (maximum: 100 units); for the final injection, ~1 mL of sterile NS should be injected to ensure that the remaining medication in the needle is delivered to the bladder; may consider re-treatment with diminishing effect but no sooner than 12 weeks from the previous administration (median time until second treatment in studies: ~24 weeks)

Blepharospasm: IM:
Botox: Initial dose: 1.25 to 2.5 units injected into the medial and lateral pretarsal orbicularis oculi of the upper lid and lateral pretarsal orbicularis oculi of lower lid

Dose may be increased up to twice the previous dose if the response from the initial dose lasted ≤2 months; maximum dose per site: 5 units. Tolerance may occur if treatments are given more often than every 3 months, but the effect is not usually permanent. Cumulative dose:
US labeling: ≤200 units in 30-day period
Canadian labeling (not in US labeling): Botox: ≤200 units in 2-month period

Cervical dystonia: IM: For dosing guidance, the mean dose is 236 units (25th to 75th percentile range 198 to 300 units) divided among the affected muscles in patients previously treated with botulinum toxin (maximum: ≤50 units/site). Initial dose in previously untreated patients should be lower. Sequential dosing should be based on the patient's head and neck position, localization of pain, muscle hypertrophy, patient response, and previous adverse reactions. The total dose injected into the sternocleidomastoid muscles should be ≤100 units to decrease the occurrence of dysphagia.

Canadian labeling (not in US labeling): IM: Botox: Effective range of 200 to 360 units has been used in clinical practice; administer no more frequently than every 2 months

Chronic migraine: IM: Administer 5 units/0.1 mL per site. Recommended total dose is 155 units once every 12 weeks. Each 155 unit dose should be equally divided and administered bilaterally, into 31 total sites as described below (refer to prescribing information for specific diagrams of recommended injection sites):
Corrugator: 5 units to each side (2 sites)
Procerus: 5 units (1 site only)
Frontalis: 10 units to each side (divided into 2 sites/side)
Temporalis: 20 units to each side (divided into 4 sites/side)
Occipitalis: 15 units to each side (divided into 3 sites/side)
Cervical paraspinal: 10 units to each side (divided into 2 sites/side)
Trapezius: 15 units to each side (divided into 3 sites/side)

Spasticity: IM: Individualize dose based on patient size, extent, and location of muscle involvement, degree of spasticity, local muscle weakness, and response to prior treatment. May repeat therapy at ≥3 months with appropriate dosage based upon the clinical condition of patient at time of re-treatment. Single session doses of ≤1,200 units (off-label dose) have been reported; however, safety and efficacy of routine use of doses >500 units has not been evaluated (Francisco, 2004). Single site doses of ≤400 units (off-label dose) in a lower limb (off-label use) have been reported (Nalysnyk, 2013).

Lower limb spasticity: The lowest recommended starting dose should be used and ≤50 units/site should be administered. **Note:** Dose listed is total dose administered as divided separate intramuscular injection(s):
Flexor digitorum longus: 50 units (divided into 2 sites)
Flexor hallucis longus: 50 units (divided into 2 sites)
Gastrocnemius lateral head: 75 units (divided into 3 sites)
Gastrocnemius medial head: 75 units (divided into 3 sites)

Soleus: 75 units (divided into 3 sites)
Tibialis posterior: 75 units (divided into 3 sites)

Upper limb spasticity. The lowest recommended starting dose should be used and ≤50 units/site should be administered. **Note:** Dose listed is total dose administered as individual or separate intramuscular injection(s):

Adductor pollicis: 20 units (1 site)
Biceps brachii: 100 to 200 units (divided into 4 sites)
Flexor digitorum profundus: 30 to 50 units (1 site)
Flexor digitorum sublimes: 30 to 50 units (1 site)
Flexor carpi radialis: 12.5 to 50 units (1 site)
Flexor carpi ulnaris: 12.5 to 50 units (1 site)
Flexor pollicis longus: 20 units (1 site)

Suggested guidelines for the treatment of stroke-related upper limb spasticity: *Canadian labeling:* **Note:** Dose listed is total dose administered as individual or separate intramuscular injection(s):

Adductor pollicis: 20 units (1 to 2 sites)
Biceps brachii: 100 to 200 units (up to 4 sites)
Flexor digitorum profundus: 15 to 50 units (1 to 2 sites)
Flexor digitorum sublimes: 15 to 50 units (1 to 2 sites)
Flexor carpi radialis: 15 to 60 units (1 to 2 sites)
Flexor carpi ulnaris: 10 to 50 units (1 to 2 sites)
Flexor pollicis longus: 20 units (1 to 2 sites)

Strabismus: IM: **Note:** Several minutes prior to injection, administration of local anesthetic and ocular decongestant drops are recommended.

Initial dose:

Vertical muscles and for horizontal strabismus <20 prism diopters: 1.25 to 2.5 units in any one muscle

Horizontal strabismus of 20 to 50 prism diopters: 2.5 to 5 units in any one muscle

Persistent VI nerve palsy ≥1 month: 1.25 to 2.5 units in the medial rectus muscle

Re-examine patients 7 to 14 days after each injection to assess the effect of that dose. Subsequent doses for patients experiencing incomplete paralysis of the target may be increased up to twice the previous administered dose. The maximum recommended dose as a single injection for any one muscle is 25 units. Do not administer subsequent injections until the effects of the previous dose are gone.

Primary axillary hyperhidrosis: Intradermal: 50 units/axilla. Injection area should be defined by standard staining techniques. Injections should be evenly distributed into multiple sites (10 to 15), administered in 0.1 to 0.2 mL aliquots, ~1 to 2 cm apart. May repeat when clinical effect diminishes.

Cosmetic uses:

Reduction of glabellar lines: Adults: IM: An effective dose is determined by gross observation of the patient's ability to activate the superficial muscles injected. The location, size, and use of muscles may vary markedly among individuals. Inject 0.1 mL (4 units) dose into each of five sites, two in each corrugator muscle and one in the procerus muscle for a total dose 0.5 mL (20 units) administered no more frequently than every 3 to 4 months. **Note:** Treatment of adults >65 years is approved in the Canadian labeling.

Reduction of lateral canthus lines:

US labeling: Adults: IM: Inject 0.1 mL (4 units) into 3 injection sites per side (6 total injection points) in the lateral orbicularis oculi muscle for a total dose of 0.6 mL (24 units) administered no more frequently than every 3 months.

Canadian labeling: Adults: IM: Inject 2 to 6 units into each of 1 to 3 injection sites, lateral to the lateral orbital rim.

Reduction of forehead lines *(Canadian labeling; not in US labeling):* IM: Inject 2 to 6 units into each of four sites in the frontalis muscle every 1 to 2 cm along either side of forehead crease and 2 to 3 cm above eyebrows for total dose of 24 units.

Geriatric Initiate therapy at lowest recommended dose. Refer to adult dosing.

Pediatric Note: The lowest recommended dose should be used when initiating treatment (regardless of indication). Canadian labeling (not in US labeling) recommends a maximum cumulative dose of 6 units/kg (up to 200 units) over 3 months in pediatric patients receiving treatment for more than 1 indication.

Blepharospasm/strabismus: Children ≥12 years: Refer to adult dosing.

Cervical dystonia: Children ≥16 years: Refer to adult dosing.

Spasticity (cerebral palsy related [dynamic equinus foot deformity]): Botox: *Canadian labeling (not approved in US labeling):* Children ≥2 years: IM: 4 units/kg (total dose) divided into two injections into medial and lateral heads of the gastrocnemius of affected leg; if clinically indicated, may repeat every 2 months (maximum dose: 200 units); in diplegia, the recommended dose is 6 units/kg (total dose) divided between affected limbs

Renal Impairment There are no dosage adjustments provided in the manufacturer's labeling.

Hepatic Impairment There are no dosage adjustments provided in the manufacturer's labeling.

Mechanism of Action OnabotulinumtoxinA (previously known as botulinum toxin type A) is a neurotoxin produced by *Clostridium botulinum*, spore-forming anaerobic bacillus, which appears to affect only the presynaptic membrane of the neuromuscular junction in humans, where it prevents calcium-dependent release of acetylcholine and produces a state of denervation. Muscle inactivation persists until new fibrils grow from the nerve and form junction plates on new areas of the muscle-cell walls. Intradetrusor injection affects efferent pathways of detrusor activity by inhibiting release of acetylcholine. Intradermal injection results in temporary sweat gland denervation, reducing local sweating.

Contraindications

Hypersensitivity to botulinum toxin, or any component of the formulation; infection at the proposed injection site(s).

Botox: Additional contraindications: Intradetrusor injection in patients with overactive bladder or detrusor overactivity with a neurologic condition who have a urinary tract infection; intradetrusor injection in patients with urinary retention and in patients with post-void residual (PVR) urine volume >200 mL who are not routinely performing clean intermittent self-catheterization

Warnings/Precautions [US Boxed Warning]: Distant spread of botulinum toxin beyond the site of injection has been reported; dysphagia and breathing difficulties have occurred and may be life threatening; other symptoms reported include blurred vision, diplopia, dysarthria, dysphonia, generalized muscle weakness, ptosis, and urinary incontinence which may develop within hours or weeks following

injection. The risk is likely greatest in children treated for the unapproved use of spasticity, but symptoms can also occur in adults treated for spasticity and other conditions. Systemic effects have occurred following use in approved and unapproved uses, including doses comparable to or lower than doses used to treat cervical dystonia and upper limb spasticity. Immediate medical attention required if respiratory disorder, speech, or swallowing difficulties appear. Higher doses or more frequent administration may result in neutralizing antibody formation and loss of efficacy. Use caution in patients with bleeding disorders and/or receiving anticoagulation therapy. May impair ability to drive and/or operate machinery; if loss of strength, muscle weakness, or impaired vision occurs, patients should avoid driving or engaging in other hazardous activities.

Product contains albumin and may carry a remote risk of virus transmission. Use caution if there is inflammation or excessive weakness or atrophy at the proposed injection site(s); use is contraindicated if infection is present at injection site. Serious events (including fatalities) have been observed with direct injection into the esophagus, stomach, salivary glands and oro-lingual-pharyngeal region. Use caution when administering in close proximity to the lungs (especially the apices); pneumothorax has been reported following administration near the thorax. Have appropriate support in case of anaphylactic reaction. Use with caution in patients with neuromuscular diseases (such as myasthenia gravis or Lambert-Eaton syndrome), neuropathic disorders (such as amyotrophic lateral sclerosis), patients taking aminoglycosides, neuromuscular-blocking agents, or other drugs that interfere with neuromuscular transmission. Arrhythmia and myocardial infarction (some fatal) have been reported following administration. Some of these patients had risk factors including preexisting cardiovascular disease. The exact relationship to onabotulinumtoxinA has not been established. Long-term effects of chronic therapy are unknown. Botulinum products (abobotulinumtoxinA, onabotulinumtoxinA, rimabotulinumtoxinB) are not interchangeable; potency units are specific to each preparation and cannot be compared or converted to any other botulinum product. Serious and/or immediate hypersensitivity reactions (eg, anaphylaxis, serum sickness, urticaria, soft tissue edema, and dyspnea) have occurred. If a reaction occurs, discontinue and institute immediate treatment.

Serious adverse reactions, including excessive weakness, dysphagia, and aspiration pneumonia, including fatalities, have been reported in patients who have received injections for unapproved uses. In these cases, the reactions were not necessarily related to distant spread of toxin, but may have resulted from administration to the site of injection and/or adjacent structures; several patients had preexisting dysphagia or other significant disabilities. Bronchitis and upper respiratory infection have been reported more frequently in patients treated for upper or lower limb spasticity.

Cervical dystonia: Dysphagia is common. It may be severe requiring alternative feeding methods and may persist anywhere from 2 weeks up to 5 months after administration. In severe cases (some fatal), patients may require alternative feeding methods (eg, feeding tube). Risk factors include smaller neck muscle mass, bilateral injections into the sternocleidomastoid muscle, or injections into the levator scapulae. Risk of aspiration resulting from severe dysphagia is increased in patients when swallowing is already compromised. Limiting the dose injected into the sternocleidomastoid muscle may reduce the occurrence of dysphagia. Use extreme caution in patients with preexisting respiratory disease; may weaken accessory muscles that are necessary for these patients to maintain adequate ventilation. Serious breathing difficulties, including respiratory failure have been reported. Risk of aspiration resulting from severe dysphagia is increased in patients with decreased respiratory function.

Bladder dysfunction (overactive bladder or detrusor overactivity associated with a neurologic condition): Rule out acute urinary tract infection (UTI) prior to treatment; appropriate prophylactic antimicrobial therapy is required prior to, during, and following treatment. Discontinue antiplatelet therapy at least 3 days prior to administration. An increased incidence of urinary retention and need for catheterization has been observed in patients receiving therapy for bladder dysfunction; due to the risk of urinary retention, treatment should only be used in patients able and willing to initiate post-treatment catheterization, if required. Therapy in patients with overactive bladder increases the incidence of urinary tract infections; clinical trials for overactive bladder excluded patients with >2 UTIs in the previous 6 months and those taking chronic antibiotics for prophylaxis of recurrent UTIs. Consider risks vs. benefits when contemplating use in these patients or patients experiencing recurrent UTIs during treatment. Patients with diabetes had an increased incidence of urinary retention and urinary tract infection. Patients experiencing difficulty in voiding should be instructed to consult their healthcare provider. Autonomic dysreflexia has been observed with therapy in patients with detrusor overactivity associated with a neurologic condition; acts as stimuli to trigger an exaggerated sympathetic and parasympathetic response. Clinical presentation often includes headache, a marked increase in blood pressure, and diaphoresis; prompt treatment may be required in patients presenting with severe symptoms (eg, hypertensive crisis).

Episodic migraines: Safety and efficacy have not been established in patients with 14 or fewer headaches per month.

Ocular disease: Blepharospasm: Reduced blinking from injection of the orbicularis muscle can lead to corneal exposure and ulceration. Strabismus: Retrobulbar hemorrhages may occur from needle penetration into orbit. Spatial disorientation, double vision, or past-pointing may occur if one or more extraocular muscles are paralyzed. Covering the affected eye may help. Careful testing of corneal sensation, avoidance of lower lid injections, and treatment of epithelial defects are necessary. Use with caution in angle closure glaucoma.

Primary axillary hyperhidrosis: Evaluate for secondary causes prior to treatment (eg, hyperthyroidism). Safety and efficacy for treatment of hyperhidrosis in other areas of the body have not been established.

Temporary reduction in glabellar lines: Do not use more frequently than every 3 months (Canadian labeling states not to use more frequently than every 2 months). Patients with marked facial asymmetry, ptosis, excessive dermatochalasis, deep dermal scarring, thick sebaceous skin, or the inability to substantially lessen glabellar lines by physically spreading them apart were excluded from clinical trials. Use with caution in patients with surgical alterations to the facial anatomy. Reduced blinking from injection of the orbicularis muscle can lead to corneal exposure and ulceration. Spatial disorientation, double vision, or past pointing may occur if one or more extraocular muscles are paralyzed.

Upper or lower limb spasticity: Safety and effectiveness of other upper or lower limb muscle groups have not been established. Treatment has not been shown to improve upper extremity functional abilities, or range of motion at a joint affected by a fixed contracture.

Drug Interactions

Metabolism/Transport Effects None known.

Avoid Concomitant Use There are no known interactions where it is recommended to avoid concomitant use.

Increased Effect/Toxicity

OnabotulinumtoxinA may increase the levels/effects of: AbobotulinumtoxinA; RimabotulinumtoxinB

The levels/effects of OnabotulinumtoxinA may be increased by: Aminoglycosides; Anticholinergic Agents; Neuromuscular-Blocking Agents

Decreased Effect There are no known significant interactions involving a decrease in effect.

Pharmacodynamics/Kinetics

Onset of Action Blepharospasm: ~3 to 4 days; Cervical dystonia: ~2 weeks; Detrusor overactivity associated with neurologic condition: ~2 weeks; Reduction of glabellar lines (Botox Cosmetic): 1 to 2 days, increasing in intensity during first week; Spasticity: Focal and cerebral palsy related: <2 weeks; Strabismus: ~1 to 2 days

Duration of Action Blepharospasm: ~3 to 4 months; Cervical dystonia: ≤3 to 4 months; Detrusor overactivity associated with neurologic condition: ~42 to 48 weeks; Reduction of glabellar lines (Botox Cosmetic): ~3 to 4 months; Spasticity: ~3 to 3.5 months; Strabismus: ~2 to 6 weeks; Primary axillary hyperhidrosis: 201 days (mean)

Time to Peak Blepharospasm: 1 to 2 weeks; Cervical dystonia: ~6 weeks; Spasticity (focal): 4 to 6 weeks; Strabismus: Within first week

Pregnancy Risk Factor C

Pregnancy Considerations Adverse events have been observed in animal reproduction studies.

Breastfeeding Considerations It is not known if onabotulinumtoxinA is excreted in breast milk. The manufacturer recommends that caution be exercised when administering onabotulinumtoxinA to nursing women.

Dosage Forms

Solution Reconstituted, Injection:

Botox: 100 units (1 ea)

Solution Reconstituted, Injection [preservative free]:

Botox: 200 units (1 ea)

Solution Reconstituted, Intramuscular:

Botox Cosmetic: 100 units (1 ea)

Solution Reconstituted, Intramuscular [preservative free]:

Botox Cosmetic: 50 units (1 ea)

Dosage Forms: Canada

Injection, powder for reconstitution [preservative free]:

Botox: Botulinum toxin A 50 units, 100 units, 200 units

Botox Cosmetic: Botulinum toxin A 50 unit, 100 units, 200 units

Dental Comment Cote and associates, published a paper describing all serious adverse reactions reported to the FDA (Cote, 2005). Included in the 217 serious effects reported, there were 28 deaths and 17 seizures. The deaths were attributed to heart attacks, cerebrovascular accident, pulmonary embolisms, pneumonia, or unknown causes. There were 1031 adverse effects reported after cosmetic use, 36 were of a serious nature. These included focal facial paralysis, muscle weakness, dysphagia, flu-like symptoms, and allergic reactions.

In contrast to the Cote study, the Naumann study reviewed the adverse reactions described and reported in randomized, controlled trials of onabotulinumtoxinA. They reviewed 36 studies involving 2309 subjects through the years 1966-2003. Of the 2309 subjects, 1425 received onabotulinumtoxinA treatment. No study reported severe adverse events. The only adverse event occurring significantly more often than with placebo was focal weakness.

Ondansetron (on DAN se tron)

Related Information

Clinical Risk Related to Drugs Prolonging QT Interval *on page 1772*

Brand Names: US Zofran; Zofran ODT; Zuplenz

Brand Names: Canada ACT Ondansetron; AG-Ondansetron; Apo-Ondansetron; Bio-Ondansetron; Dom-Ondansetron; IPG-Ondansetron; JAMP-Ondansetron; Mar-Ondansetron; Mint-Ondansetron; Mylan-Ondansetron; NAT-Ondansetron; Nu-Ondansetron; Ondansetron Hydrochloride Dihydrate Injection; Ondansetron Injection; Ondansetron Injection USP; Ondansetron-Omega; Ondissolve ODF; PHL-Ondansetron; PMS-Ondansetron; Priva-Ondansetron; RAN-Ondansetron; ratio-Ondansetron; Sandoz-Ondansetron; Sandoz-Ondansetron ODT; Septa-Ondansetron; Teva-Ondansetron; Vanc-Ondansetron; Zofran ODT

Pharmacologic Category Antiemetic; Selective 5-HT_3 Receptor Antagonist

Use

Cancer chemotherapy-induced nausea and vomiting:

IV: Prevention of nausea and vomiting associated with initial and repeat courses of emetogenic cancer chemotherapy (including high-dose cisplatin)

Oral:

Prevention of nausea and vomiting associated with highly emetogenic cancer chemotherapy (including cisplatin ≥50 mg/m^2).

Prevention of nausea and vomiting associated with initial and repeat courses of moderately emetogenic cancer chemotherapy.

Radiotherapy-associated nausea and vomiting: Oral: Prevention of nausea and vomiting associated with radiotherapy in patients receiving either total body irradiation, single high-dose fraction to the abdomen, or daily fractions to the abdomen.

Postoperative nausea and/or vomiting: IV and Oral: Prevention of postoperative nausea and/or vomiting (PONV). If nausea/vomiting occur in a patient who had not received prophylactic ondansetron, IV ondansetron may be administered to prevent further episodes.

Limitations of use: Routine prophylaxis for PONV in patients with minimal expectation of nausea and/or vomiting is not recommended, although use is recommended in patients when nausea and vomiting must be avoided in the postoperative period, even if the incidence of PONV is low.

Local Anesthetic/Vasoconstrictor Precautions Ondansetron is one of the drugs confirmed to prolong the QT interval and is accepted as having a risk of causing torsade de pointes. The risk of drug-induced torsade de pointes is extremely low when a single QT interval prolonging drug is prescribed. In terms of epinephrine, it is not known what effect vasoconstrictors in the local anesthetic regimen will have in patients with a known history of congenital prolonged QT interval or in patients taking any medication that prolongs the QT interval. Until more information is obtained, it is suggested that the clinician consult with the physician prior to the use of a vasoconstrictor in suspected patients, and that the vasoconstrictor (epinephrine, mepivacaine and levonordefrin [Carbocaine® 2% with Neo-Cobefrin®]) be used with caution.

Effects on Dental Treatment Ondansetron is an alternative to phenothiazines (ie, promethazine) for the treatment of moderate-to-severe postoperative nausea and vomiting. Ondansetron prolongs the QT interval in a dose-dependent manner. Avoid ondansetron in patients with congenital long QT syndrome.

Effects on Bleeding No information available to require special precautions

Adverse Reactions Note: Percentages reported in adult patients unless otherwise specified.

>10%:

Central nervous system: Headache (oral: 9% to 27%; IV: 17%), fatigue (oral: ≤9% to 13%), malaise (oral: ≤9% to 13%)

Gastrointestinal: Constipation (6% to 11%)

1% to 10%:

Central nervous system: Drowsiness (IV: ≤8%), sedation (IV: ≤8%), (dizziness (7%), agitation (oral: ≤6%), anxiety (oral: ≤6%), paresthesia (IV: 2%), sensation of cold (IV: 2%)

Dermatologic: Pruritus (2% to 5%), skin rash (1%)

Gastrointestinal: Diarrhea (oral: 6% to 7%; IV: Children 1 to 24 months of age: 2%)

Genitourinary: Gynecologic disease (oral: 7%), urinary retention (oral: 5%)

Hepatic: Increased serum ALT (>2 times ULN: 1% to 5%; transient), increased serum AST (>2 times ULN: 1% to 5%; transient)

Local: Injection site reaction (IV: 4%; includes burning sensation at injection site, erythema at injection site, injection site pain)

Respiratory: Hypoxia (oral: 9%)

Miscellaneous: Fever (2% to 8%)

<1%, postmarketing, and/or case reports: Abdominal pain, accommodation disturbance, anaphylactoid reaction, anaphylaxis, angina pectoris, angioedema, atrial fibrillation, bradycardia, bronchospasm, bullous skin disease, cardiac arrhythmia, cardiorespiratory arrest (IV), chest pain, chills, depression of ST segment on ECG, dyspnea, dystonic reaction, ECG changes, extrapyramidal reaction (IV), flushing, hepatic failure (when used with other hepatotoxic medications), hiccups, hypersensitivity reaction, hypokalemia, hypotension, ischemic heart disease, laryngeal edema, laryngospasm (IV), liver enzyme disorder, mucosal tissue reaction, myocardial infarction, neuroleptic malignant syndrome, oculogyric crisis, palpitations, positive lymphocyte transformation test, prolonged Q-T interval on ECG (dose dependent), second-degree atrioventricular block, serotonin syndrome, shock (IV), Stevens-Johnson syndrome, stridor, supraventricular tachycardia, syncope, tachycardia, tonic-clonic seizures, torsades de pointes, toxic epidermal necrolysis, transient blindness (lasted ≤48 hours), transient blurred vision (following infusion), urticaria, vascular occlusive events, ventricular premature contractions, ventricular tachycardia, weakness, xerostomia

General Dosage Range Dosage adjustment recommended in patients with hepatic impairment

IM: *Adults:* 4 mg as a single dose

IV:

Infants 1 to 6 months: 0.1 mg/kg as a single dose

Children 6 months to 12 years and ≤40 kg: 0.1 mg/kg as a single dose **or** 0.15 mg/kg/dose (maximum: 16 mg/dose) for 3 doses

Children 6 months to 12 years and >40 kg and Children >12 years to 18 years: 4 mg as a single dose **or** 0.15 mg/kg/dose (maximum: 16 mg/dose) for 3 doses

Adults: 0.15 mg/kg/dose (maximum: 16 mg/dose) for 3 doses **or** 4 mg as a single dose

Oral:

Children 4 to 11 years: 4 mg every 4 hours for 3 doses (day 1), then 4 mg every 8 hours for 1 to 2 days

Children ≥12 years: 8 mg every 4 hours for 3 doses (day 1), then 8 mg every 8 hours for 1 to 2 days **or** 8 mg every 8 hours for 2 doses (day 1) then 8 mg twice a day for 1 to 2 days

Adults: 16 mg or 24 mg as a single dose **or** 8 mg every 8 to 12 hours

Mechanism of Action Selective 5-HT_3-receptor antagonist, blocking serotonin, both peripherally on vagal nerve terminals and centrally in the chemoreceptor trigger zone

Pharmacodynamics/Kinetics

Onset of Action ~30 minutes

Half-life Elimination

Children:

Cancer patients: Children and Adolescents: 4 to 18 years: 2.8 hours

Surgical patients: Infants 1 to 4 months: 6.7 hours; Infants and Children 5 months to 12 years: 2.9 hours

Adults: 3 to 6 hours; Mild-to-moderate hepatic impairment (Child-Pugh classes A and B): 12 hours; Severe hepatic impairment (Child-Pugh class C): 20 hours

Time to Peak Oral: ~2 hours; Oral soluble film: ~1 hour

Pregnancy Risk Factor B

Pregnancy Considerations

Adverse events were not observed in animal reproduction studies. Ondansetron readily crosses the human placenta in the first trimester of pregnancy and can be detected in fetal tissue (Siu 2006). Due to pregnancy-induced physiologic changes, clearance of ondansetron may increase as pregnancy progresses (Lemon 2016).

Although ondansetron has been evaluated for the treatment of nausea and vomiting of pregnancy, current guidelines note data related to fetal safety is conflicting (ACOG 2015); ondansetron is generally reserved for use when other agents have failed (Arsenault 2002). Because a dose-dependent QT-interval prolongation occurs with use, the manufacturer recommends ECG monitoring in patients with electrolyte abnormalities (which can be associated with some cases of NVP; Koren 2012). An international consensus panel recommends that 5-HT_3 antagonists (including ondansetron) should not be withheld in pregnant patients receiving chemotherapy for the treatment of gynecologic cancers, when chemotherapy is given according to general recommendations for chemotherapy use during pregnancy (Amant 2010).

Dental Comment Ondansetron is a safer alternative than phenothiazines (ie, promethazine) for the treatment of moderate-to-severe postoperative nausea and vomiting. The cost can be a limitation.

Also see Local Anesthetic/Vasoconstrictor Precautions

Oritavancin (or it a VAN sin)

Brand Names: US Orbactiv

Pharmacologic Category Glycopeptide

Use Acute bacterial skin and skin structure infections: Treatment of adult patients with acute bacterial skin and skin structure infections (ABSSSI) caused by susceptible isolates of the following gram-positive microorganisms: *Staphylococcus aureus* (including methicillin-susceptible and methicillin-resistant isolates); *Streptococcus pyogenes; Streptococcus agalactiae; Streptococcus dysgalactiae, Streptococcus anginosus* group (including *S. anginosus, S. intermedius, S. constellatus*); and *Enterococcus faecalis* (vancomycin-susceptible isolates only)

Local Anesthetic/Vasoconstrictor Precautions No information available to require special precautions

Effects on Dental Treatment Key adverse event(s) related to dental treatment: Use may result in fungal or bacterial superinfection within the oral cavity

Effects on Bleeding No information available to require special precautions

Adverse Reactions

1% to 10%:

Cardiovascular: Tachycardia (3%), hypersensitivity angiitis(<2%; leucocytoclastic vasculitis), peripheral edema (<2%)

Central nervous system: Headache (7%), dizziness (3%)

Dermatologic: Erythema multiforme (<2%), pruritus (<2%), skin rash (<2%), urticaria (<2%)

Endocrine & metabolic: Hyperuricemia (<2%), hypoglycemia (<2%)

Gastrointestinal: Nausea (10%), vomiting (5%), diarrhea (4%)

Hematologic & oncologic: Anemia (<2%), eosinophilia (<2%)

Hepatic: Increased serum ALT (3%), increased serum AST (2%), increased total serum bilirubin (<2%)

Hypersensitivity: Angioedema (<2%), hypersensitivity (<2%)

Infection: Abscess (subcutaneous and limb; 4%)

Local: Injection site phlebitis (3%), injection site reaction (2%), erythema at injection site (<2%), extravasation (<2%), induration at injection site (<2%)

Neuromuscular & skeletal: Myalgia (<2%), osteomyelitis (<2%), tenosynovitis (<2%)

Respiratory: Bronchospasm (<2%), wheezing (<2%)

<1%, postmarketing, and/or case reports: *Clostridium difficile*-associated diarrhea, hypersensitivity reaction

General Dosage Range IV: *Adults:* 1200 mg as a single dose.

Mechanism of Action Oritavancin is a lipoglycopeptide with concentration-dependent bactericidal activity. It inhibits cell wall biosynthesis by inhibiting the polymerization step by binding to stem peptides of peptidoglycan precursors, by inhibiting crosslinking by binding to bridging segments, and by disrupting bacterial membrane integrity, leading to cell death.

Pharmacodynamics/Kinetics

Half-life Elimination ~245 hours

Pregnancy Risk Factor C

Pregnancy Considerations Adverse events were not observed in animal reproduction studies.

Orlistat (OR li stat)

Brand Names: US Alli [OTC]; Xenical

Brand Names: Canada Xenical

Pharmacologic Category Lipase Inhibitor

Use Obesity management:

OTC: Weight loss in overweight adults when used along with a reduced-calorie and low-fat diet.

Rx: Obesity management, including weight loss and weight maintenance, when used in conjunction with a reduced-calorie diet; to reduce the risk for weight regain after prior weight loss.

Limitations of use: Orlistat is indicated for obese patients with an initial body mass index of ≥30 kg/m^2 or ≥27 kg/m^2 in the presence of other risk factors (eg, hypertension, diabetes, dyslipidemia).

Local Anesthetic/Vasoconstrictor Precautions No information available to require special precautions

Effects on Dental Treatment No significant effects or complications reported

Effects on Bleeding No information available to require special precautions

Adverse Reactions The frequency of most adverse reactions (especially gastrointestinal effects) decreases over time. Frequency not always defined.

Cardiovascular: Pedal edema (≤3%)

Central nervous system: Headache (≤31%), fatigue (3% to 7%), anxiety (3% to 5%), sleep disorder (≤4%)

Dermatologic: Xeroderma (≤2%)

Endocrine & metabolic: Menstrual disease (≤10%), hypoglycemia (in patients with diabetes)

Gastrointestinal: Oily rectal leakage (4% to 27%), abdominal distress (≤26%), abdominal pain (≤26%), flatulence with discharge (2% to 24%), bowel urgency (3% to 22%), steatorrhea (6% to 20%), oily evacuation (2% to 12%), frequent bowel movements (3% to 11%), nausea (4% to 8%), fecal incontinence (2% to 8%), infectious diarrhea (≤5%), rectal pain (3% to 5%), gingival disease (4%), cholelithiasis (3%), abdominal distension (in patients with diabetes)

Genitourinary: Urinary tract infection (6% to 8%), vaginitis (3%)

Infection: Influenza (≤40%)

Neuromuscular & skeletal: Back pain (≤14%), leg pain (≤11%), myalgia (≤4%)

Otic: Otitis (4%)

Respiratory: Upper respiratory tract infection (38%), lower respiratory tract infection (≤8%)

<1%, postmarketing, and/or case reports: Acute renal failure, anaphylaxis, angioedema, bronchospasm, bullous skin disease, calcium oxalate nephrolithiasis, gastrointestinal hemorrhage (lower), hepatic failure, hepatitis, hypersensitivity, hypersensitivity angiitis, increased serum alkaline phosphatase, increased serum transaminases, pancreatitis, pruritus, renal disease (secondary to increased urinary oxalate excretion), skin rash, urticaria

General Dosage Range Oral:

Children ≥12 years, Adolescents, and Adults: Xenical: 120 mg 3 times daily.

Adults: Alli (OTC labeling): 60 mg 3 times daily (maximum dose: 180 mg/day).

Mechanism of Action A reversible inhibitor of gastric and pancreatic lipases, thus inhibiting absorption of dietary fats by 30%.

Pharmacodynamics/Kinetics

Onset of Action 24-48 hours

Duration of Action 48-72 hours

Half-life Elimination 1-2 hours

Time to Peak Serum: ~8 hours

Pregnancy Risk Factor X

Pregnancy Considerations Adverse events have not been observed in animal reproduction studies. Although orlistat is minimally absorbed, weight-loss therapy is not recommended for pregnant women. Obese and overweight women should be encouraged to participate in weight reduction programs prior to attempting pregnancy; weight gain during pregnancy should be determined by their prepregnancy BMI and current guidelines (ADA, 2009; IOM, 2009). Use of orlistat is contraindicated in pregnant women.

Orphenadrine (or FEN a dreen)

Related Information

Temporomandibular Dysfunction (TMD), Chronic Pain, and Fibromyalgia *on page 1868*

Brand Names: US Norflex [DSC]

Brand Names: Canada Norflex; Orphenace; Rhoxal-orphendrine

Generic Availability (US) Yes

Pharmacologic Category Skeletal Muscle Relaxant

Use Treatment of muscle spasm associated with acute painful musculoskeletal conditions

Local Anesthetic/Vasoconstrictor Precautions No information available to require special precautions

Effects on Dental Treatment The peripheral anticholinergic effects of orphenadrine may decrease or inhibit salivary flow; normal salivation will return with cessation of drug therapy.

Effects on Bleeding No information available to require special precautions

Adverse Reactions Frequency not defined.

Cardiovascular: Palpitations, tachycardia

Central nervous system: Agitation, confusion, dizziness, drowsiness, euphoria, hallucination, headache

Dermatologic: Pruritus, urticaria

Gastrointestinal: Constipation, gastric irritation, nausea, vomiting, xerostomia

Genitourinary: Urinary retention, urination hesitancy

Hypersensitivity: Hypersensitivity reaction

Neuromuscular & skeletal: Tremor, weakness

Ophthalmic: Blurred vision, increased intraocular pressure, mydriasis, nystagmus

Respiratory: Nasal congestion

<1%, postmarketing, and/or case reports: Anaphylaxis (injection), aplastic anemia

Dosing

Adult & Geriatric Muscle spasms:

Oral: 100 mg twice daily

IM, IV: 60 mg every 12 hours

Renal Impairment No dosage adjustment provided in manufacturer's labeling.

Hepatic Impairment No dosage adjustment provided in manufacturer's labeling.

Mechanism of Action Indirect skeletal muscle relaxant thought to work by central atropine-like effects; has some euphorigenic and analgesic properties

Contraindications Hypersensitivity to orphenadrine or any component of the formulation; glaucoma; GI obstruction, stenosing peptic ulcer; prostatic hypertrophy, bladder neck obstruction; cardiospasm; myasthenia gravis

Warnings/Precautions Use with caution in patients with heart failure, cardiac decompensation, coronary insufficiency, tachycardia or cardiac arrhythmias. May cause CNS depression, which may impair physical or mental abilities. Effects may be potentiated when used with other sedative drugs or ethanol. Potential for abuse; use with caution in patients with history of drug abuse or acute alcoholism. Euphoria may occur at therapeutic doses. Solution for injection contains sodium bisulfite which may cause allergic reaction in some individuals. Has not been evaluated for continuous long-term use; monitor closely.

Drug Interactions

Metabolism/Transport Effects Substrate of CYP1A2 (minor), CYP2B6 (minor), CYP2D6 (minor), CYP3A4 (minor); **Note:** Assignment of Major/Minor substrate status based on clinically relevant drug interaction potential; **Inhibits** CYP1A2 (weak), CYP2A6 (weak), CYP2C9 (weak), CYP2E1 (weak)

Avoid Concomitant Use

Avoid concomitant use of Orphenadrine with any of the following: Aclidinium; Alcohol (Ethyl); Azelastine (Nasal); Cimetropium; CNS Depressants; Eluxadoline; Glucagon; Glycopyrrolate (Oral Inhalation); Ipratropium (Oral Inhalation); Levosulpiride; Nitroglycerin; Oxatomide; Oxomemazine; Paraldehyde; Potassium Chloride; Thalidomide; Tiotropium; Umeclidinium

Increased Effect/Toxicity

Orphenadrine may increase the levels/effects of: AbobotulinumtoxinA; Anticholinergic Agents; Azelastine (Nasal); Cimetropium; Eluxadoline; Glucagon; Glycopyrrolate (Oral Inhalation); MetyroSINE; Mirabegron; OnabotulinumtoxinA; Paraldehyde; Piribedil; Potassium Chloride; Pramipexole; Ramosetron; RimabotulinumtoxinB; ROPINIRole; Rotigotine; Selective Serotonin Reuptake Inhibitors; Thalidomide; Thiazide and Thiazide-Like Diuretics; Tiotropium

The levels/effects of Orphenadrine may be increased by: Aclidinium; Alcohol (Ethyl); Brimonidine (Topical); Cannabis; Chlorphenesin Carbamate; CNS Depressants; Dimethindene (Topical); Dronabinol; Ipratropium (Oral Inhalation); Kava Kava; Lofexidine; Magnesium Sulfate; Minocycline; Nabilone; Oxatomide; Oxomemazine; Pramlintide; Rufinamide; Tetrahydrocannabinol; Tolperisone; Umeclidinium

Decreased Effect

Orphenadrine may decrease the levels/effects of: Acetylcholinesterase Inhibitors; Gastrointestinal Agents (Prokinetic); Itopride; Levosulpiride; Nitroglycerin; Secretin

The levels/effects of Orphenadrine may be decreased by: Acetylcholinesterase Inhibitors

Pharmacodynamics/Kinetics

Onset of Action Peak effect: Oral: Within 2 to 4 hours

Duration of Action 4 to 6 hours

Half-life Elimination 14 to 16 hours

Pregnancy Risk Factor C

Pregnancy Considerations Animal reproduction studies have not been conducted.

Dosage Forms

Solution, Injection:

Generic: 30 mg/mL (2 mL)

Solution, Injection [preservative free]:

Generic: 30 mg/mL (2 mL)

Tablet Extended Release 12 Hour, Oral:

Generic: 100 mg

Orphenadrine, Aspirin, and Caffeine
(or FEN a dreen, AS pir in, & KAF een)

Related Information

Aspirin *on page 168*

Caffeine *on page 276*

Orphenadrine *on page 1245*

Pharmacologic Category Skeletal Muscle Relaxant

Use Relief of discomfort associated with skeletal muscular conditions

Local Anesthetic/Vasoconstrictor Precautions No information available to require special precautions

Effects on Dental Treatment Key adverse event(s) related to dental treatment: The peripheral anticholinergic effects of orphenadrine may decrease or inhibit salivary flow; normal salivation will return with cessation of drug therapy.

Aspirin: As with all drugs which may affect hemostasis, bleeding is associated with aspirin. Hemorrhage may occur at virtually any site; risk is dependent on multiple variables including dosage, concurrent use of multiple agents which alter hemostasis, and patient susceptibility. Many adverse effects of aspirin are dose related, and are rare at low dosages. Other serious reactions are idiosyncratic, related to allergy or individual sensitivity (see Dental Comment).

Aspirin as sole antiplatelet agent: Patients taking aspirin for ischemic stroke prevention are safe to continue it during dental procedures (Armstrong, 2013).

Concurrent aspirin use with other antiplatelet agents: Aspirin in combination with clopidogrel (Plavix®), prasugrel (Effient®), or ticagrelor (Brilinta™) is the primary prevention strategy against stent thrombosis after placement of drug-eluting metal stents in coronary patients. Premature discontinuation of combination antiplatelet therapy (ie, dual antiplatelet therapy) strongly increases the risk of a catastrophic event of stent thrombosis leading to myocardial infarction and/or death, so says a science advisory issued in January 2007 from the American Heart Association in collaboration with the American Dental Association and other professional healthcare organizations. The advisory stresses a 12-month therapy of dual antiplatelet therapy after placement of a drug-eluting stent in order to prevent thrombosis at the stent site. Any elective surgery should be postponed for 1 year after stent implantation, and if surgery must be performed, consideration should be given to continuing the antiplatelet therapy during the perioperative period in high-risk patients with drug-eluting stents.

This advisory was issued from a science panel made up of representatives from the American Heart Association (AHA), the American College of Cardiology, the Society for Cardiovascular Angiography and Interventions, the American College of Surgeons, the American Dental Association (ADA), and the American College of Physicians (Grines, 2007).

Effects on Bleeding Aspirin irreversibly inhibits platelet aggregation which can prolong bleeding. Upon discontinuation, normal platelet function returns only when new platelets are released (~7-10 days). However, in the case of dental surgery, there is no scientific evidence to support discontinuation of aspirin. This was recently supported by the American Academy of Neurology in patients with ischemic cerebrovascular disease (Armstrong, 2013). A recent study compared blood loss after a single tooth extraction in coronary artery disease patients who were either on aspirin (100 mg daily) or off aspirin for the extraction. The mean volume of bleeding was not statistically different between the groups. Local hemostatic measures were sufficient to control bleeding and there were no reported episodes of hemorrhaging intra- or postoperatively (Medeiros, 2011).

General Dosage Range Oral: *Adults:* 1 to 2 tablets 3 to 4 times/day

Pregnancy Considerations See individual agents.

Dental Comment There is no scientific evidence to warrant discontinuance of aspirin prior to dental surgery. Patients taking one aspirin tablet daily as an antithrombotic and who require dental surgery should be given special consideration in consultation with the physician before removal of the aspirin relative to prevention of postoperative bleeding.

Oseltamivir (oh sel TAM i vir)

Related Information

Systemic Viral Diseases *on page 1806*

Brand Names: US Tamiflu

Brand Names: Canada Tamiflu

Pharmacologic Category Antiviral Agent; Neuraminidase Inhibitor

Use

Prophylaxis of influenza: Prophylaxis of influenza (A or B) infection in patients ≥1 year of age.

Treatment of influenza: Treatment of uncomplicated acute illness due to influenza (A or B) infection in patients ≥2 weeks of age who have been symptomatic for no more than 48 hours.

The Advisory Committee on Immunization Practices (ACIP) recommends that **treatment** be considered for the following:

- Persons with severe, complicated or progressive illness
- Hospitalized persons
- Persons at higher risk for influenza complications:
  - Children <2 years of age (highest risk in children <6 months of age)
  - Adults ≥65 years of age
  - Persons with chronic disorders of the pulmonary (including asthma) or cardiovascular systems (except hypertension)
  - Persons with chronic metabolic diseases (including diabetes mellitus), hepatic disease, renal dysfunction, hematologic disorders (including sickle cell disease), or immunosuppression (including immunosuppression caused by medications or HIV)
  - Persons with neurologic/neuromuscular conditions (including conditions such as spinal cord injuries, seizure disorders, cerebral palsy, stroke, mental retardation, moderate to severe developmental delay, or muscular dystrophy) which may compromise respiratory function, the handling of respiratory secretions, or that can increase the risk of aspiration
  - Pregnant or postpartum women (≤2 weeks after delivery)
  - Persons <19 years of age on long-term aspirin therapy
  - American Indians and Alaskan Natives
  - Persons who are morbidly obese (BMI ≥40)
  - Residents of nursing homes or other chronic care facilities
- Use may also be considered for previously healthy, nonhigh-risk outpatients with confirmed or suspected

influenza based on clinical judgment when treatment can be started within 48 hours of illness onset.

The ACIP recommends that **prophylaxis** be considered for the following:

- Postexposure prophylaxis may be considered for family or close contacts of suspected or confirmed cases, who are at higher risk of influenza complications, and who have not been vaccinated against the circulating strain at the time of the exposure.
- Postexposure prophylaxis may be considered for unvaccinated healthcare workers who had occupational exposure without protective equipment.
- Pre-exposure prophylaxis should only be used for persons at very high risk of influenza complications who cannot be otherwise protected at times of high risk for exposure.
- Prophylaxis should also be administered to all eligible residents of institutions that house patients at high risk when needed to control outbreaks.

The ACIP recommends that treatment and prophylaxis be given to children <1 year of age when indicated.

Limitations of use: Not a substitute for annual influenza vaccination. Consider available information on influenza drug susceptibility patterns and treatment effects when deciding whether to use oseltamivir phosphate oral. Not recommended for patients with end-stage renal disease not undergoing dialysis.

Local Anesthetic/Vasoconstrictor Precautions No information available to require special precautions

Effects on Dental Treatment No significant effects or complications reported

Effects on Bleeding No information available to require special precautions

Adverse Reactions

>10%:

Central nervous system: Headache (adolescents and adults: 2% to 17%)

Gastrointestinal: Vomiting (2% to 16%)

1% to 10%:

Central nervous system: Pain (adolescents and adults: 4%)

Gastrointestinal: Nausea (adolescents and adults: 8% to 10%)

<1%, postmarketing, and/or case reports: Abnormal behavior, abnormal hepatic function tests, accidental injury, agitation, anaphylactoid reaction, anaphylaxis, anxiety, cardiac arrhythmia, confusion, delirium, delusions, dermatitis, eczema, erythema multiforme, exacerbation of diabetes mellitus, facial edema, gastrointestinal hemorrhage, hallucination, hemorrhagic colitis, hepatitis, hypersensitivity reaction, hypothermia, impaired consciousness, nightmares, seizure, skin rash, Stevens-Johnson syndrome, swollen tongue, toxic epidermal necrolysis, urticaria

General Dosage Range Dosage adjustment recommended in patients with renal impairment

Oral:

Infants ≥2 weeks: 3 mg/kg/dose twice daily

Children 1-12 years and ≤15 kg: 30 mg once or twice daily

Children 1-12 years and >15 to ≤23 kg: 45 mg once or twice daily

Children 1-12 years and >23 to ≤40 kg: 60 mg once or twice daily

Children 1-12 years and >40 kg, Adolescents, and Adults: 75 mg once or twice daily

Mechanism of Action Oseltamivir, a prodrug, is hydrolyzed to the active form, oseltamivir carboxylate (OC). OC inhibits influenza virus neuraminidase, an enzyme known to cleave the budding viral progeny from its cellular envelope attachment point (neuraminic acid) just prior to release.

Pharmacodynamics/Kinetics

Half-life Elimination Oseltamivir: 1 to 3 hours; Oseltamivir carboxylate: 6 to 10 hours

Pregnancy Risk Factor C

Pregnancy Considerations Adverse events were observed in some animal reproduction studies. Oseltamivir phosphate and its active metabolite oseltamivir carboxylate cross the placenta (Meijer, 2012). An increased risk of adverse neonatal or maternal outcomes has generally not been observed following maternal use of oseltamivir during pregnancy (CDC, 60[1], 2011; CDC, March 13, 2014).

Untreated influenza infection is associated with an increased risk of adverse events to the fetus and an increased risk of complications or death to the mother. Neuraminidase inhibitors are currently recommended for the treatment or prophylaxis of influenza in pregnant women and women up to 2 weeks postpartum (CDC 60 [1] 2011; CDC March 13, 2014; January 2015).

Osimertinib (oh si mer ti nib)

Brand Names: US Tagrisso

Brand Names: Canada Tagrisso

Pharmacologic Category Antineoplastic Agent, Epidermal Growth Factor Receptor (EGFR) Inhibitor; Antineoplastic Agent, Tyrosine Kinase Inhibitor

Use Non-small cell lung cancer, metastatic: Treatment of metastatic epidermal growth factor receptor (EGFR) T790M mutation-positive non-small cell lung cancer (NSCLC), as detected by an approved test, in patients who have progressed on or after EGFR tyrosine kinase inhibitor (TKI) therapy

Local Anesthetic/Vasoconstrictor Precautions Osimertinib is one of the drugs confirmed to prolong the QT interval and is accepted as having a risk of causing torsade de points. In terms of epinephrine, it is not known what effect vasoconstrictors in the local anesthetic regimen will have in patients with a known history of congenital prolonged QT interval or in patients taking any medication that prolongs the QT interval. Until more information is obtained, it is suggested that the clinician consult with the physician prior to the use of a vasoconstrictor in suspected patients, and that the vasoconstrictor be used with caution.

Effects on Dental Treatment Key adverse event(s) related to dental treatment: Stomatitis has been reported

Effects on Bleeding Chemotherapy may result in significant myelosuppression, potentially including significant reduction in platelet counts (thrombocytopenia 54% grades 3/4: 1%) and altered hemostasis. In patients who are under active treatment with these agents, medical consult is suggested.

Adverse Reactions

>10%:

Central nervous system: Fatigue (14%), headache (10%)

Dermatologic: Skin rash (41%, including erythematous rash, macular rash, maculopapular rash, papular rash, pustular rash, erythema, folliculitis, acne vulgaris, dermatitis, dermatitis acneiform), xeroderma (31%), nail disease (25%), pruritus (14%)

Endocrine & metabolic: Hyponatremia (26%), hypermagnesemia (20%)

Gastrointestinal: Diarrhea (42%), nausea (17%), decreased appetite (16%), constipation (15%), stomatitis (12%)
Hematologic & oncologic: Lymphocytopenia (63%, grades 3/4: 3%), thrombocytopenia (54%, grades 3/4: 1%), anemia (44%, grades 3/4: <1%), neutropenia (33%, grades 3/4: 3%)
Neuromuscular & skeletal: Back pain (13%)
Ophthalmic: Eye disorder (19%, including dry eyes, blurred vision, keratitis, cataract, eye irritation, blepharitis, eye pain, increased lacrimation, vitreous floaters, <1% other ocular toxicity)
Respiratory: Cough (14%)

1% to 10%:
Cardiovascular: Venous thromboembolism (7%, including deep vein thrombosis, internal jugular thrombosis), cerebrovascular accident (3%), prolonged Q-T interval on EKG (≤3%; prolonged from baseline), pulmonary embolism (≤2%), reduced ejection fraction (<2%), cardiomyopathy (≤1%)
Respiratory: Pneumonia (≤4%; grade 3/4: 2%), interstitial pneumonitis (3%)

General Dosage Range Dosage adjustment recommended for patients on concomitant therapy or who develop toxicities.

Oral: *Adults:* 80 mg once daily

Mechanism of Action Osimertinib is an irreversible epidermal growth factor receptor (EGFR) tyrosine kinase inhibitor which binds to select mutant forms of EGFR, including T790M, L858R, and exon 19 deletion at lower concentrations than wild-type. Osimertinib exhibits less activity against wild-type EGFR (as compared to other EGFR inhibitors) and is selective for sensitizing mutations and the T790M resistance mutation, which is the most common mechanism of resistance to EGFR tyrosine kinase inhibitors (Janne 2015).

Pharmacodynamics/Kinetics

Half-life Elimination Mean (estimated): 48 hours

Time to Peak Median: 6 hours (range: 3 to 24 hours)

Pregnancy Considerations Based on data from animal reproduction studies and the mechanism of action, use during pregnancy is expected to cause fetal harm. Women of reproductive potential should use effective contraception during therapy and for 6 weeks after the last dose. Males with female partners of reproductive potential should also use effective contraception during therapy and for 4 months after the last dose.

Prescribing and Access Restrictions
Available through specialty pharmacies and distributors. Further information may be obtained from the manufacturer, Astra Zeneca, at 1-844-275-2360 or at https://www.tagrisso.com.

Ospemifene (os PEM i feen)

Brand Names: US Osphena

Pharmacologic Category Selective Estrogen Receptor Modulator (SERM)

Use Treatment of moderate-to-severe dyspareunia due to vulvar and vaginal atrophy (VVA) of menopause

Local Anesthetic/Vasoconstrictor Precautions
No information available to require special precautions

Effects on Dental Treatment No significant effects or complications reported

Effects on Bleeding Ospemifene has been associated with thromboembolic adverse events. There is no information available to require special precautions for dental procedures.

Adverse Reactions
1% to 10%:
Dermatologic: Hyperhidrosis (2%)
Endocrine & metabolic: Hot flash (8%)
Genitourinary: Proliferative endometrium (9%), endometrial hyperplasia (without atypia, 6%), vaginal discharge (4%), genital discharge (1%)
Neuromuscular & skeletal: Muscle spasm (3%)

<1%: Angioedema, deep vein thrombosis, endometrial polyps, erythematous rash, hemorrhagic stroke, hypersensitivity, myocardial infarction, pruritus, skin rash, thrombotic stroke, urticaria

General Dosage Range Oral: *Adults (postmenopausal females):* 60 mg once daily

Mechanism of Action Ospemifene is a selective estrogen receptor modulator (SERM); it activates estrogen pathways in some tissues and blocks estrogen pathways in others, and specifically has agonistic effects on the endometrium. In women with VVA, ospemifene was shown to improve vaginal changes associated with the decrease in natural estrogen production associated with menopause (improves vaginal maturation index, decreases vaginal pH) and significantly decreased the most bothersome moderate-to-severe subjective findings reported by women (vaginal dryness and dyspareunia) after 12 weeks of therapy (Bachmann, 2010).

Pharmacodynamics/Kinetics

Onset of Action A significant decrease in vaginal dryness and dyspareunia were observed after 12 weeks of therapy (Bachmann, 2010).

Half-life Elimination ~26 hours

Time to Peak ~2 hours (range: 1-8 hours)

Pregnancy Risk Factor X

Pregnancy Considerations Adverse events were observed in animal reproduction studies. Use is contraindicated in women who are or may become pregnant. Ospemifene is currently approved only for the treatment of moderate-to-severe dyspareunia due to vulvar and vaginal atrophy (VVA) of menopause.

Oxacillin (oks a SIL in)

Brand Names: US Bactocill in Dextrose

Pharmacologic Category Antibiotic, Penicillin

Use

Staphylococcal infections: Treatment of infections caused by penicillinase-producing staphylococci that have demonstrated susceptibility to the drug; empiric therapy in suspected cases of resistant staphylococcal infections.

Limitations of use: Oxacillin should not be used in infections caused by organisms susceptible to penicillin G.

Local Anesthetic/Vasoconstrictor Precautions
No information available to require special precautions

Effects on Dental Treatment Key adverse event(s) related to dental treatment: Prolonged use of penicillins may lead to development of oral candidiasis.

Effects on Bleeding No information available to require special precautions

Adverse Reactions Frequency not defined.
Dermatologic: Skin rash
Gastrointestinal: Diarrhea, nausea, vomiting
Genitourinary: Hematuria
Hematologic & oncologic: Agranulocytosis, eosinophilia, leukopenia, neutropenia, thrombocytopenia
Hepatic: Hepatotoxicity, increased serum AST
Immunologic: Serum sickness-like reaction

Renal: Acute interstitial nephritis
Miscellaneous: Fever

General Dosage Range IM, IV:

Children: 50 to 200 mg/kg/day in divided doses every 6 hours (maximum: 12 **g/day**)

Adults: 250 to 2,000 mg every 4 to 6 hours

Mechanism of Action Inhibits bacterial cell wall synthesis by binding to one or more of the penicillin-binding proteins (PBPs); which in turn inhibits the final transpeptidation step of peptidoglycan synthesis in bacterial cell walls, thus inhibiting cell wall biosynthesis. Bacteria eventually lyse due to ongoing activity of cell wall autolytic enzymes (autolysins and murein hydrolases) while cell wall assembly is arrested.

Pharmacodynamics/Kinetics

Half-life Elimination

Neonates (PNA: 8 to 15 days): 1.6 hours
Infants and Children ≤2 years: 0.9 to 1.8 hours
Adults: 20 to 30 minutes; prolonged with renal impairment

Time to Peak Serum: IM: 30 minutes; IV: 5 minutes

Pregnancy Considerations Adverse events have not been observed in animal reproduction studies. Oxacillin is distributed into the amniotic fluid and is detected in cord blood. Maternal use of penicillins has generally not resulted in an increased risk of adverse fetal effects.

Oxaliplatin (ox AL i pla tin)

Brand Names: US Eloxatin [DSC]

Brand Names: Canada Eloxatin; Oxaliplatin Injection; PMS-Oxaliplatin

Pharmacologic Category Antineoplastic Agent, Alkylating Agent; Antineoplastic Agent, Platinum Analog

Use

Colon cancer, stage III (adjuvant therapy): Adjuvant treatment of stage III colon cancer (in combination with infusional fluorouracil and leucovorin) after complete resection of primary tumor.

Colorectal cancer, advanced: Treatment of advanced colorectal cancer (in combination with infusional fluorouracil and leucovorin).

Local Anesthetic/Vasoconstrictor Precautions No information available to require special precautions

Effects on Dental Treatment Key adverse event(s) related to dental treatment: Stomatitis, dysphagia, mucositis, and taste perversion.

Effects on Bleeding Chemotherapy may result in significant myelosuppression, potentially including significant reduction in platelet counts (infrequent, <1%) and altered hemostasis. In patients who are under active treatment with these agents, medical consult is suggested.

Adverse Reactions Percentages reported with monotherapy.

>10%:

Central nervous system: Peripheral neuropathy (may be dose limiting; 76% to 92%; acute 65%; grades 3/4: 5%; persistent 43%; grades 3/4: 3%), fatigue (61%), pain (14%), headache (13%), insomnia (11%)

Gastrointestinal: Nausea (64%), diarrhea (46%), vomiting (37%), abdominal pain (31%), constipation (31%), anorexia (20%), stomatitis (14%)

Hematologic & oncologic: Anemia (64%; grades 3/4: 1%), thrombocytopenia (30%; grades 3/4: 3%), leukopenia (13%)

Hepatic: Increased serum AST (54%; grades 3/4: 4%), increased serum ALT (36%; grades 3/4: 1%), increased serum bilirubin (13%; grades 3/4: 5%)

Neuromuscular & skeletal: Back pain (11%)

Respiratory: Dyspnea (13%), cough (11%)

Miscellaneous: Fever (25%)

1% to 10%:

Cardiovascular: Edema (10%), chest pain (5%), peripheral edema (5%), flushing (3%), thromboembolism (2%)

Central nervous system: Rigors (9%), dizziness (7%)

Dermatologic: Skin rash (5%), alopecia (3%), palmar-plantar erythrodysesthesia (1%)

Endocrine & metabolic: Dehydration (5%), hypokalemia (3%)

Gastrointestinal: Dyspepsia (7%), dysgeusia (5%), flatulence (3%), hiccups (2%), mucositis (2%), dysphagia (acute 1% to 2%), gastroesophageal reflux disease (1%)

Genitourinary: Dysuria (1%)

Hematologic & oncologic: Neutropenia (7%)

Hypersensitivity: Hypersensitivity reaction (3%; includes urticaria, pruritus, facial flushing, shortness of breath, bronchospasm, diaphoresis, hypotension, syncope: grades 3/4: 2% to 3%)

Local: Injection site reaction (9%; redness, swelling, pain)

Neuromuscular & skeletal: Arthralgia (7%)

Ocular: Abnormal lacrimation (1%)

Renal: Increased serum creatinine (5% to 10%)

Respiratory: Upper respiratory tract infection (7%), rhinitis (6%), epistaxis (2%), pharyngitis (2%), pharyngolaryngeal dysesthesia (grades 3/4: 1% to 2%)

<1%, postmarketing, and/or case reports (reported with mono- and combination therapy): Abnormal gait, acute renal failure, anaphylaxis, anaphylactic shock, anaphylactoid reaction, angioedema, aphonia, ataxia, blepharoptosis, cerebral hemorrhage, colitis, cranial nerve palsy, decreased deep tendon reflex, deafness, decreased visual acuity, diplopia, dysarthria, eosinophilic pneumonitis, fasciculations, febrile neutropenia, hematuria, hemolysis, hemolytic anemia (immuno-allergic), hemolytic-uremic syndrome, hemorrhage, hepatic failure, hepatic fibrosis (perisinusoidal), hepatic sinusoidal obstruction syndrome (SOS; veno-occlusive disease), hepatitis, hepatotoxicity, hypertension, hypomagnesemia, hypoxia, idiopathic noncirrhotic portal hypertension (nodular regenerative hyperplasia), increased INR, increased serum alkaline phosphatase, infusion related reaction (extravasation [including necrosis]), interstitial nephritis (acute), interstitial pulmonary disease, intestinal obstruction, laryngospasm, Lhermitte's sign, metabolic acidosis, muscle spasm, myoclonus, neutropenic enterocolitis, neutropenic infection (sepsis), optic neuritis, pancreatitis, prolonged Q-T interval on ECG, prolonged prothrombin time, pulmonary fibrosis, purpura, rectal hemorrhage, renal tubular necrosis, reversible posterior leukoencephalopathy syndrome (RPLS), rhabdomyolysis, seizure, sepsis, septic shock, temporary vision loss, thrombocytopenia (immuno-allergic), torsades de pointes, trigeminal neuralgia, ventricular arrhythmia, visual field loss, voice disorder

General Dosage Range Dosage adjustment recommended in patients with renal impairment or who develop toxicities

IV: *Adults:* 85 mg/m^2 every 2 weeks

Mechanism of Action Oxaliplatin, a platinum derivative, is an alkylating agent. Following intracellular hydrolysis, the platinum compound binds to DNA forming cross-links which inhibit DNA replication and transcription, resulting in cell death. Cytotoxicity is cell-cycle nonspecific.

Pharmacodynamics/Kinetics

Half-life Elimination

Children: Oxaliplatin ultrafilterable platinum (terminal): Median: 293 hours; range: 187 to 662 hours (Beaty 2010)

Adults: Oxaliplatin ultrafilterable platinum: Distribution: Alpha phase: 0.4 hours; Beta phase: 16.8 hours; Terminal: 391 hours

Pregnancy Risk Factor D

Pregnancy Considerations Adverse events were observed in animal reproduction studies at one-tenth the equivalent human dose. Women of childbearing potential should be advised to avoid pregnancy and use effective contraception during treatment.

Canadian labeling: Use in pregnant women is contraindicated in the Canadian labeling. Males should be advised not to father children during and for up to 6 months following therapy. May cause permanent infertility in males. Prior to initiating therapy, advise males desiring to father children, to seek counseling on sperm storage.

Oxandrolone (oks AN droe lone)

Brand Names: US Oxandrin

Pharmacologic Category Androgen

Use Adjunctive therapy to promote weight gain after weight loss following extensive surgery, chronic infections, or severe trauma, and in some patients who, without definite pathophysiologic reasons, fail to gain or to maintain normal weight; to offset protein catabolism with prolonged corticosteroid administration; relief of bone pain associated with osteoporosis

Local Anesthetic/Vasoconstrictor Precautions No information available to require special precautions

Effects on Dental Treatment No significant effects or complications reported

Effects on Bleeding No information available to require special precautions

Adverse Reactions Frequency not defined.

Cardiovascular: Edema

Central nervous system: Deepening of the voice (females), depression, excitement, habituation, insomnia

Dermatologic: Acne vulgaris (females and prepubertal males), androgenetic alopecia (females)

Endocrine & metabolic: Changes in libido, decreased glucose tolerance, decreased HDL cholesterol, electrolyte disturbance, gynecomastia, hirsutism (females), increased LDL cholesterol, inhibition of gonadotropin secretion, menstrual disease (females)

Genitourinary: Clitoromegaly (females), epididymitis (postpubertal males), erectile dysfunction (prepubertal males; increased or persistent erections), impotence (postpubertal males), inhibition of testicular function (postpubertal males), irritable bladder (postpubertal males), oligospermia (postpubertal males), phallic enlargement (prepubertal males), priapism (chronic; postpubertal males), testicular atrophy (postpubertal males)

Hematologic & oncologic: Clotting factors suppression, prolonged prothrombin time

Hepatic: Cholestatic jaundice, hepatocellular neoplasm, increased serum alkaline phosphatase, increased serum ALT, increased serum AST, increased serum bilirubin, peliosis hepatitis (long-term therapy)

Neuromuscular & skeletal: Increased creatine phosphokinase, premature epiphyseal closure (children)

Renal: Increased creatinine clearance

<1%, postmarketing, and/or case reports: Hepatic necrosis, hepatotoxicity (idiosyncratic; Chalasani 2014)

General Dosage Range Oral:

Children: ≤0.1 mg/kg/day

Adults: 2.5-20 mg daily in 2-4 divided doses

Elderly: 5 mg twice daily

Mechanism of Action Synthetic testosterone derivative with similar androgenic and anabolic actions

Pharmacodynamics/Kinetics

Half-life Elimination 10 to 13 hours

Time to Peak Concentration: ~1 hour (Orr 2004)

Pregnancy Risk Factor X

Pregnancy Considerations Use is contraindicated in women who are or may become pregnant; masculinization of the fetus has been reported.

Controlled Substance C-III

Oxaprozin (oks a PROE zin)

Related Information

Rheumatoid Arthritis, Osteoarthritis, and Osteoporosis *on page 1792*

Temporomandibular Dysfunction (TMD), Chronic Pain, and Fibromyalgia *on page 1868*

Brand Names: US Daypro

Brand Names: Canada Apo-Oxaprozin

Pharmacologic Category Analgesic, Nonopioid; Nonsteroidal Anti-inflammatory Drug (NSAID), Oral

Use

Juvenile rheumatoid arthritis: Relief of signs and symptoms of juvenile rheumatoid arthritis (JRA).

Osteoarthritis: Relief of signs and symptoms of osteoarthritis.

Rheumatoid arthritis: Relief of signs and symptoms of rheumatoid arthritis.

Local Anesthetic/Vasoconstrictor Precautions No information available to require special precautions

Effects on Dental Treatment The dentist should be aware of the potential of abnormal coagulation. Caution should also be exercised in the use of NSAIDs in patients already on anticoagulant therapy with drugs such as warfarin (Coumadin®). See Effects on Bleeding.

Effects on Bleeding Nonselective NSAIDs, such as oxaprozin, inhibit platelet aggregation and prolong bleeding time in some patients. Unlike aspirin, the NSAID effect on platelet function is quantitatively less, of shorter duration, and reversible. Normal platelet function should occur in ~5 elimination half-lives or in <10 hours after discontinuation of oxaprozin. Concomitant use of other NSAIDs should be avoided.

Adverse Reactions

1% to 10%:

Cardiovascular: Edema

Central nervous system: Confusion, depression, disturbed sleep, dizziness, drowsiness, headache, sedation

Dermatologic: Pruritus, skin rash

Gastrointestinal: Abdominal distress, abdominal pain, anorexia, constipation, diarrhea, dyspepsia, flatulence, gastrointestinal perforation (with gross bleeding), gastrointestinal ulcer, heartburn, nausea, vomiting

Genitourinary: Dysuria, urinary frequency

Hematologic & oncologic: Anemia, prolonged bleeding time

Hepatic: Increased liver enzymes

Otic: Tinnitus

Renal: Renal insufficiency

<1%, postmarketing, and/or case reports: Hepatotoxicity (idiosyncratic; Chalasani 2014)

General Dosage Range Dosage adjustment recommended in patients with renal impairment

Oral:

Children 6 to 16 years and 22 to 31 kg: 600 mg once daily

Children 6 to 16 years and 32 to 54 kg: 900 mg once daily

Children 6 to 16 years and ≥55 kg: 1200 mg once daily

Adults: 600 to 1,800 mg once daily (maximum: 1200 mg daily [<50 kg]; 1,800 mg daily or 26 mg/kg/day (whichever lower) [>50 kg])

Mechanism of Action Reversibly inhibits cyclooxygenase-1 and 2 (COX-1 and 2) enzymes, which results in decreased formation of prostaglandin precursors; has antipyretic, analgesic, and anti-inflammatory properties.

Other proposed mechanisms not fully elucidated (and possibly contributing to the anti-inflammatory effect to varying degrees) include inhibiting chemotaxis, altering lymphocyte activity, inhibiting neutrophil aggregation/activation, and decreasing proinflammatory cytokine levels.

Pharmacodynamics/Kinetics

Onset of Action Maximum effect: Due to its long half-life, several days of treatment are required for oxaprozin to reach its full effect

Half-life Elimination 41 to 55 hours

Time to Peak 2.4 to 3.1 hours

Pregnancy Considerations NSAID exposure during the first trimester is not strongly associated with congenital malformations; however, cardiovascular anomalies and cleft palate have been observed following NSAID exposure in some studies. The use of an NSAID close to conception may be associated with an increased risk of miscarriage. Nonteratogenic effects have been observed following NSAID administration during the third trimester including myocardial degenerative changes, prenatal constriction of the ductus arteriosus, fetal tricuspid regurgitation, failure of the ductus arteriosus to close postnatally; renal dysfunction or failure, oligohydramnios; gastrointestinal bleeding or perforation, increased risk of necrotizing enterocolitis; intracranial bleeding (including intraventricular hemorrhage), platelet dysfunction with resultant bleeding; pulmonary hypertension. Because they may cause premature closure of the ductus arteriosus, use of NSAIDs late in pregnancy should be avoided (use after 31 or 32 weeks gestation is not recommended by some clinicians). The chronic use of NSAIDs in women of reproductive age may be associated with infertility that is reversible upon discontinuation of the medication. A registry is available for pregnant women exposed to autoimmune medications including oxaprozin. For additional information, contact the Organization of Teratology Information Specialists, OTIS Autoimmune Diseases Study, at 877-311-8972.

Oxazepam (oks A ze pam)

Related Information

Dentin Hypersensitivity, Acid Erosion, High Caries Index, Management of Alveolar Osteitis, and Xerostomia *on page 1857*

Brand Names: Canada Apo-Oxazepam; Bio-Oxazepam; Novoxapram; Oxpam; Oxpram; PMS-Oxazepam; Riva-Oxazepam

Generic Availability (US) Yes

Pharmacologic Category Benzodiazepine

Use Management of anxiety disorders, including anxiety associated with depression; management of ethanol withdrawal

Local Anesthetic/Vasoconstrictor Precautions No information available to require special precautions

Effects on Dental Treatment Key adverse event(s) related to dental treatment: Xerostomia (normal salivary flow resumes upon discontinuation).

Effects on Bleeding No information available to require special precautions

Adverse Reactions Frequency not defined.

Cardiovascular: Edema, hypotension, syncope

Central nervous system: Amnesia, ataxia, dizziness, drowsiness, drug dependence, dysarthria, euphoria, headache, lethargy, memory impairment, slurred speech, vertigo

Dermatologic: Maculopapular rash, morbilliform rash, urticaria

Endocrine & metabolic: Decreased libido, menstrual disease

Gastrointestinal: Nausea

Genitourinary: Urinary incontinence

Hematologic & oncologic: Hematologic disease, leukopenia

Hepatic: Jaundice

Hypersensitivity: Fixed drug eruption

Neuromuscular & skeletal: Hyporeflexia, tremor

Ophthalmic: Blurred vision, diplopia

Miscellaneous: Paradoxical central nervous system stimulation, paradoxical excitation

Dosing

Adult

Anxiety, mild-to-moderate: Oral: 10-15 mg 3-4 times daily

Anxiety, severe or associated with depression: Oral: 15-30 mg 3-4 times daily

Ethanol withdrawal: Oral: 15-30 mg 3-4 times daily

Geriatric Anxiety: Oral: Initial: 10 mg 3 times daily. If necessary, increase cautiously to 15 mg 3-4 times daily. Dose titration should be slow to evaluate sensitivity.

Pediatric Children >12 years and Adolescents: Refer to adult dosing.

Renal Impairment

No dosage adjustment provided in manufacturer's labeling

Hemodialysis: Not dialyzable (0% to 5%) (Greenblatt, 1981; Mokhlesi, 2003)

Hepatic Impairment No dosage adjustment provided in manufacturer's labeling; however, pharmacokinetic studies have shown that hepatic dysfunction is not expected to significantly decrease clearance (Furlan, 1999; Greenblatt, 1981).

Mechanism of Action Binds to stereospecific benzodiazepine receptors on the postsynaptic GABA neuron at several sites within the central nervous system, including the limbic system, reticular formation. Enhancement of the inhibitory effect of GABA on neuronal excitability results by increased neuronal membrane permeability to chloride ions. This shift in chloride ions results in hyperpolarization (a less excitable state) and stabilization. Benzodiazepine receptors and effects appear to be linked to the GABA-A receptors. Benzodiazepines do not bind to GABA-B receptors.

Contraindications Hypersensitivity to oxazepam or any component of the formulation (cross-sensitivity with other benzodiazepines may exist)

Warnings/Precautions May cause hypotension (rare) - use with caution in patients with cardiovascular or cerebrovascular disease, or in patients who would not tolerate transient decreases in blood pressure.

Use with caution in elderly or debilitated patients, patients with hepatic disease (including alcoholics). Relative to other benzodiazepines, oxazepam possesses a short half-life and lacks an active metabolite which may be preferable in the elderly if benzodiazepine use is required for anxiety (Flint, 2005). Kinetics were not altered in patients of advanced age compared to younger patients, except in patients >80 years of age where an increased half-life was observed due to an increased volume of distribution and a decrease in unbound clearance. Use with caution in patients with respiratory disease or impaired gag reflex.

May cause CNS depression which may impair physical and mental capabilities. Patients must be cautioned about performing tasks which require mental alertness (eg, operating machinery or driving). Use with caution in patients receiving other CNS depressants or psychoactive agents; effects with other sedative drugs or ethanol may be potentiated. Benzodiazepines have been associated with falls and traumatic injury and should be used with extreme caution in patients who are at risk of these events.

Use caution in patients with depression, particularly if suicidal risk may be present. Use with caution in patients with a history of drug abuse or acute alcoholism; potential for drug dependency exists. Tolerance, psychological and physical dependence may occur with prolonged use. Rebound or withdrawal symptoms may occur following abrupt discontinuation or large decreases in dose. Use caution when reducing dose or withdrawing therapy; decrease slowly and monitor for withdrawal symptoms. Flumazenil may cause withdrawal in patients receiving long-term benzodiazepine therapy. Oxazepam is a short half-life benzodiazepine. Tolerance does not develop to the anxiolytic effects (Vinkers, 2012). Chronic use of this agent may increase the perioperative benzodiazepine dose needed to achieve desired effect.

Benzodiazepines have been associated with transient amnesia. Paradoxical reactions, including hyperactive or aggressive behavior have been reported with benzodiazepines, particularly in adolescent/pediatric or psychiatric patients. Does not have analgesic, antidepressant, or antipsychotic properties; not indicated for use in the treatment of psychosis.

Drug Interactions

Metabolism/Transport Effects None known.

Avoid Concomitant Use

Avoid concomitant use of Oxazepam with any of the following: Azelastine (Nasal); Methadone; OLANZapine; Orphenadrine; Oxomemazine; Paraldehyde; Sodium Oxybate; Thalidomide

Increased Effect/Toxicity

Oxazepam may increase the levels/effects of: Alcohol (Ethyl); Analgesics (Opioid); Azelastine (Nasal); Blonanserin; Buprenorphine; CloZAPine; CNS Depressants; Flunitrazepam; Fosphenytoin; HYDROcodone; Methadone; Methotrimeprazine; MetyroSINE; Mirtazapine; Orphenadrine; OxyCODONE; Paraldehyde; Phenytoin; Piribedil; Pramipexole; ROPINIRole; Rotigotine; Selective Serotonin Reuptake Inhibitors; Sodium Oxybate; Suvorexant; Thalidomide; Zolpidem

The levels/effects of Oxazepam may be increased by: Brimonidine (Topical); Cannabis; Chlormethiazole; Chlorphenesin Carbamate; Dimethindene (Topical); Doxylamine; Dronabinol; Droperidol; HydrOXYzine; Kava Kava; Lofexidine; Magnesium Sulfate; Methotrimeprazine; Minocycline; Nabilone; OLANZapine; Oxomemazine; Perampanel; Rufinamide; Tapentadol; Teduglutide; Tetrahydrocannabinol; Trimeprazine

Decreased Effect

The levels/effects of Oxazepam may be decreased by: Theophylline Derivatives; Yohimbine

Pharmacodynamics/Kinetics

Half-life Elimination ~8 hours (range: 6 to 11 hours)

Time to Peak Serum: ~3 hours

Pregnancy Considerations Oxazepam crosses the placenta. Teratogenic effects have been observed with some benzodiazepines; however, additional studies are needed. The incidence of premature birth and low birth weights may be increased following maternal use of benzodiazepines; hypoglycemia and respiratory problems in the neonate may occur following exposure late in pregnancy. Neonatal withdrawal symptoms may occur within days to weeks after birth and "floppy infant syndrome" (which also includes withdrawal symptoms) have been reported with some benzodiazepines (Bergman, 1992; Iqbal, 2002; Kangas, 1980; Wikner, 2007).

Breastfeeding Considerations Benzodiazepines are excreted into breast milk. Drowsiness, lethargy, or weight loss in nursing infants have been observed in case reports following maternal use of some benzodiazepines (Iqbal, 2002).

Controlled Substance C-IV

Dosage Forms

Capsule, Oral:

Generic: 10 mg, 15 mg, 30 mg

OXcarbazepine (ox car BAZ e peen)

Related Information

Temporomandibular Dysfunction (TMD), Chronic Pain, and Fibromyalgia *on page 1868*

Brand Names: US Oxtellar XR; Trileptal

Brand Names: Canada Jamp-Oxcarbazepine; Trileptal

Pharmacologic Category Anticonvulsant, Miscellaneous

Use

Partial seizures:

Immediate-release:

US labeling: Monotherapy or adjunctive therapy in the treatment of partial seizures in adults, as monotherapy in the treatment of partial seizures in children 4 years and older with epilepsy, and as adjunctive therapy in children 2 years and older with partial seizures.

Canadian labeling: Monotherapy or adjunctive therapy in the treatment of partial seizures in patients 6 years and older.

Extended-release: Adjunctive therapy in the treatment of partial seizures in adults and in children 6 to 17 years of age.

Local Anesthetic/Vasoconstrictor Precautions No information available to require special precautions

Effects on Dental Treatment No significant effects or complications reported

Effects on Bleeding No information available to require special precautions

Adverse Reactions Frequency not always defined. Incidence in children was similar.

>10%:

Central nervous system: Dizziness (20% to 49%), drowsiness (12% to 36%), headache (8% to 32%), ataxia (2% to 31%), abnormal gait (≤17%), fatigue (3% to 15%), vertigo (2% to 15%)

Gastrointestinal: Vomiting (7% to 36%), nausea (15% to 29%), abdominal pain (10% to 13%)

Neuromuscular & skeletal: Tremor (4% to 16%)

Ophthalmic: Diplopia (10% to 40%), nystagmus (3% to 26%), visual disturbance (1% to 14%)

1% to 10%:

Cardiovascular: Lower extremity edema (2%), hypotension (≤2%), bradycardia, cardiac failure, flushing, hypertension, orthostatic hypotension, palpitations, syncope, tachycardia

Central nervous system: Equilibrium disturbance (7%), nervousness (2% to 5%), amnesia (4%), emotional lability (4%), falling (4%), abnormality in thinking (≤4%), insomnia (2% to 4%), dysmetria (1% to 3%), speech disorder (1% to 3%), agitation (2%), confusion (2%), convulsions (2%), lack of concentration (2%), abnormal electroencephalogram (≤2%), feeling abnormal (≤2%), myasthenia (1% to 2%), aggressive behavior, anxiety, apathy, aphasia, aura, cerebral hemorrhage, delirium, delusion, depression, dystonia, euphoria extrapyramidal reaction, hemiplegia, hyperkinesia, hyperreflexia, hypertonia, hypokinesia, hyporeflexia, hypotonia, hysteria, impaired consciousness, intoxicated feeling, malaise, manic behavior, migraine, neuralgia, nightmares, oculogyric crisis, panic disorder, paralysis, personality disorder, precordial pain, psychosis, rigors, seizure (aggravated), stupor, voice disorder

Dermatologic: Skin rash (4%), diaphoresis (3%), acne vulgaris (1% to 2%), alopecia, contact dermatitis, eczema, erythematosus rash, facial rash, folliculitis, genital pruritus, maculopapular rash, miliaria, psoriasis, skin photosensitivity, urticaria, vitiligo

Endocrine & metabolic: Decreased serum sodium (<135 mEq/L: 7% to 9%), hyponatremia (1% to 3%), weight gain (2%), change in libido, hot flash, hyperglycemia, hypermenorrhea, hypocalcemia, hypoglycemia, hypokalemia, increased gamma-glutamyl transferase, intermenstrual bleeding, weight loss

Gastrointestinal: Diarrhea (7%), dyspepsia (≤6%), constipation (4% to 6%), dysgeusia (5%), xerostomia (3%), gastritis (≤3%), upper abdominal pain (≤3%), aphthous stomatitis, biliary colic, bloody stools, cholelithiasis, colitis, duodenal ulcer, dysphagia, enteritis, eructation, esophagitis, flatulence, gastric ulcer, gingival hemorrhage, gingival hyperplasia, hematemesis, hemorrhoids, hiccups, increased appetite, retching, sialadenitis, stomatitis

Genitourinary: Urinary frequency (2%), dysuria, hematuria, leukorrhea, priapism, urinary tract pain

Hematologic & oncologic: Bruise (2%), purpura, rectal hemorrhage, thrombocytopenia

Hepatic: Increased liver enzymes

Hypersensitivity: Hypersensitivity reaction (2%), angioedema

Neuromuscular & skeletal: Weakness (2% to 7%), back pain (4%), muscle spasm (2%), sprain (≤2%), right hypochondrium pain, systemic lupus erythematosus, tetany

Ophthalmic: Blurred vision (4%), accommodation disturbance (≤2%), blepharoptosis, cataract, conjunctival hemorrhage, hemianopia, mydriasis, ocular edema, photophobia, scotoma, xerophthalmia

Otic: Otitis externa, tinnitus

Renal: Nephrolithiasis, polyuria, renal pain

Respiratory: Rhinitis (5% to 10%), upper respiratory tract infection (7%), pulmonary infection (4%), epistaxis (4%), sinusitis (≤4%), nasopharyngitis (≤3%), pneumonia (2%), asthma, dyspnea, laryngismus, pleurisy

Miscellaneous: Fever (3%)

Postmarketing and/or case reports: Abnormal thyroid function test (decreased total T_4 and/or free T_4), acute generalized exanthematous pustulosis, agranulocytosis, anaphylaxis, aplastic anemia, bone fracture (long-term therapy), decreased bone mineral density (long-term therapy), DRESS syndrome, erythema multiforme, folate deficiency, hepatic failure, hepatitis (Hsu 2010), hypoesthesia, hypothyroidism, increased serum amylase, increased serum lipase, leukopenia, multiorgan hypersensitivity (eosinophilia, arthralgia, rash, fever, lymphadenopathy), osteopenia (long-term therapy), osteoporosis (long-term therapy), pancreatitis, pancytopenia, Stevens-Johnson syndrome, suicidal ideation, suicidal tendencies, toxic epidermal necrolysis

General Dosage Range Dosage adjustment recommended in patients with renal impairment

Oral:

Children 2 to 3 years and <20 kg: Immediate release: Initial: 8 to 20 mg/kg/day (maximum: 600 mg/day) in 2 divided doses; Maintenance: maximum of 60 mg/kg/day in 2 divided doses

Children 2 to 3 years and ≥20 kg: Immediate release: Initial: 8 to 10 mg/kg/day (maximum: 600 mg/day) in 2 divided doses; Maintenance: maximum of 60 mg/kg/day in 2 divided doses

Children 4 to 16 years: Immediate release: Initial: 8 to 10 mg/kg/day (maximum: 600 mg/day) in 2 divided doses; Maintenance: Dependent on patient weight and indication

Children 6 to 17 years and ≤29 kg: Extended release: Initial: 8 to 10 mg/kg once daily (maximum: 600 mg/day in the first week); Maintenance: up to 900 mg once daily

Children 6 to 17 years and ≥29.1 to 39 kg: Extended release: Initial: 8 to 10 mg/kg once daily (maximum: 600 mg/day in the first week); Maintenance: up to 1,200 mg once daily

Children 6 to 17 years and >39 kg: Extended release: Initial: 8 to 10 mg/kg once daily (maximum: 600 mg/day in the first week); Maintenance: up to 1,800 mg once daily

Children >16 years and Adults: Immediate release: Initial: 600 mg daily in 2 divided doses; Maintenance: 1,200 to 2,400 mg daily in 2 divided doses (maximum: 2,400 mg/day)

Children >17 years and Adults: Extended release: Initial: 600 mg once daily; Maintenance: 1,200 to 2,400 mg once daily (maximum: 2,400 mg/day)

Mechanism of Action Pharmacological activity results from both oxcarbazepine and its monohydroxy metabolite (MHD). Precise mechanism of anticonvulsant effect has not been defined. Oxcarbazepine and MHD block voltage-sensitive sodium channels, stabilizing hyperexcited neuronal membranes, inhibiting repetitive firing, and decreasing the propagation of synaptic impulses. These actions are believed to prevent the spread of seizures. Oxcarbazepine and MHD also increase potassium conductance and modulate the activity of high-voltage activated calcium channels.

Pharmacodynamics/Kinetics

Half-life Elimination

Children (Rey, 2004): 2 to 5 years: MHD: Single dose: Mean range: 4.8 to 6.7 hours; 6 to 12 years: MHD: Single dose: Mean range: 7.2 to 9.3 hours

Adults: Immediate release: Parent drug: 2 hours; MHD: 9 hours; renal impairment (CrCl 30 mL/minute): MHD: 19 hours; Extended release: Parent drug: 7 to 11 hours; MHD: 9 to 11 hours

Time to Peak

Children 2 to 12 years: Immediate release: Oxcarbazepine: 1 hour; MHD: 3 to 4 hours (Rey 2004)

Adults: Immediate release: MHD: Tablets: Median: 4.5 hours (range: 3 to 13 hours); Suspension: Median 6 hours; Extended release: MHD: 7 hours

Pregnancy Risk Factor C

Pregnancy Considerations

Adverse events have been observed in animal reproduction studies. Oxcarbazepine, the active metabolite MHD and the inactive metabolite DHD, crosses the placenta and can be detected in the newborn (Myllynen 2001). According to the manufacturer, data from a limited number of pregnancies collected from pregnancy registries suggest congenital malformations associated with oxcarbazepine monotherapy, including craniofacial defects and cardiac malformations. In general, the risk of teratogenic effects is higher with AED polytherapy than monotherapy (Harden 2009). Plasma concentrations of MHD gradually decrease due to physiologic changes which occur during pregnancy; patients should be monitored during pregnancy and postpartum. Oxcarbazepine may decrease plasma concentrations of hormonal contraceptives.

Data collection to monitor pregnancy and infant outcomes following exposure to oxcarbazepine is ongoing. Patients exposed to oxcarbazepine during pregnancy are encouraged to enroll themselves into the NAAED Pregnancy Registry by calling 1-888-233-2334. Additional information is available at www.aedpregnancyregistry.org.

Oxiconazole (oks i KON a zole)

Brand Names: US Oxistat

Brand Names: Canada Oxistat®

Pharmacologic Category Antifungal Agent, Imidazole Derivative; Antifungal Agent, Topical

Use

Cream: Treatment of tinea pedis (athlete's foot), tinea cruris (jock itch), tinea corporis (ringworm), and tinea (pityriasis) versicolor

Lotion: Treatment of tinea pedis (athlete's foot), tinea cruris (jock itch), tinea corporis (ringworm)

Local Anesthetic/Vasoconstrictor Precautions No information available to require special precautions

Effects on Dental Treatment No significant effects or complications reported

Effects on Bleeding No information available to require special precautions

Adverse Reactions

1% to 10%:

Central nervous system: Localized burning (≤1%)

Dermatologic: Pruritus (<2%)

<1%, postmarketing, and/or case reports: Allergic contact dermatitis, dyshidrotic eczema, erythema, exfoliation of skin, folliculitis, maceration of the skin, nodule, pain, papule, skin fissure, skin irritation, skin rash, stinging of the skin, tingling of skin

General Dosage Range Topical: *Children ≥12 years, Adolescents, and Adults:* Apply to affected areas 1-2 times daily

Mechanism of Action The cytoplasmic membrane integrity of fungi is destroyed by oxiconazole which exerts a fungicidal activity through inhibition of ergosterol synthesis. Effective for treatment of tinea pedis, tinea cruris, tinea corporis, and tinea versicolor. Active against *Trichophyton rubrum*, *Trichophyton mentagrophytes*, *Trichophyton violaceum*, *Microsporum canis*, *Microsporum audouinii*, *Microsporum gypseum*, *Epidermophyton floccosum*, *Candida albicans*, and *Malassezia furfur*.

Pregnancy Risk Factor B

Pregnancy Considerations When administered orally, teratogenic effects were not observed in animal reproduction studies.

Oxybutynin (oks i BYOO ti nin)

Related Information

Dentin Hypersensitivity, Acid Erosion, High Caries Index, Management of Alveolar Osteitis, and Xerostomia *on page 1857*

Brand Names: US Ditropan XL; Gelnique; Gelnique Pump; Oxytrol; Oxytrol For Women [OTC]

Brand Names: Canada Apo-Oxybutynin; Ditropan XL; Dom-Oxybutynin; Gelnique; Mylan-Oxybutynin; Oxybutyn; Oxybutynine; Oxytrol; PHL-Oxybutynin; PMS-Oxybutynin; Riva-Oxybutynin; Teva-Oxybutynin

Pharmacologic Category Antispasmodic Agent, Urinary

Use Treatment of symptoms associated with overactive uninhibited neurogenic or reflex neurogenic bladder (eg, urgency, frequency, leakage, urge incontinence, dysuria); treatment of symptoms associated with detrusor overactivity due to a neurological condition (eg, spina bifida) (extended release tablet only)

Local Anesthetic/Vasoconstrictor Precautions No information available to require special precautions

Effects on Dental Treatment Key adverse event(s) related to dental treatment: Xerostomia and changes in salivation (normal salivary flow resumes upon discontinuation), and taste perversion.

Effects on Bleeding No information available to require special precautions

Adverse Reactions

Oral:

>10%:

Central nervous system: Dizziness (5% to 17%), drowsiness (6% to 14%)

Gastrointestinal: Xerostomia (35% to 71%; dose related), constipation (9% to 15%), nausea (5% to 12%)

1% to 10%:

Cardiovascular: Cardiac arrhythmia (sinus; 1% to <5%), decreased blood pressure (1% to <5%), edema (1% to <5%), flushing (1% to <5%), hypertension (1% to <5%), palpitations (1% to <5%), peripheral edema (1% to <5%)

Central nervous system: Headache (8%), nervousness (7%), insomnia (3% to 6%), confusion (1% to <5%), falling (1% to 5%), fatigue (1% to <5%), flank pain (1% to <5%), pain (1% to <5%)

Dermatologic: Pruritus (1% to <5%), xeroderma (1% to <5%)

Endocrine & metabolic: Fluid retention (1% to <5%), hyperglycemia (1% to <5%), increased thirst (1% to <5%)

Gastrointestinal: Diarrhea (1% to 8%), dyspepsia (5% to 6%), abdominal pain (1% to <5%), dysphagia (1% to <5%), eructation (1% to <5%), flatulence (1% to <5%), unpleasant taste (1% to <5%), vomiting (1% to <5%), gastroesophageal reflux disease (≤1%)

Genitourinary: Urinary hesitancy (2% to 9%), urinary tract infection (7%), urinary retention (1% to 6%), cystitis (1% to <5%), dysuria (1% to <5%), pollakiuria (1% to <5%)

Infection: Fungal infection (1% to <5%)

Neuromuscular & skeletal: Arthralgia (1% to <5%), back pain (1% to <5%), limb pain (1% to <5%), weakness (1% to <5%)

Ophthalmic: Blurred vision (4% to 10%), eye irritation (1% to <5%), keratoconjunctivitis sicca (1% to <5%), xerophthalmia (3%)

Respiratory: Asthma (1% to <5%), bronchitis (1% to <5%), cough (1% to <5%), dry throat (1% to <5%), hoarseness (1% to <5%), nasal congestion (1% to <5%), dry nose (1% to <5%), nasopharyngitis (1% to <5%), pharyngolaryngeal pain (1% to <5%), sinus congestion (1% to <5%), upper respiratory tract infection (1% to <5%)

Topical gel:

>10%:

Gastrointestinal: Xerostomia (8% to 12%)

Local: Application site reaction (6% to 14%, includes anesthesia, irritation, pain, papules)

1% to 10%:

Central nervous system: Dizziness (3%), fatigue (2%), headache (2%)

Dermatologic: Pruritus (1%)

Gastrointestinal: Constipation (1%)

Genitourinary: Urinary tract infection (7%)

Local: Application site erythema (4%), application site rash (3%), application site pruritus (2% to 3%), application site dermatitis (2%)

Ophthalmic: Blurred vision (<2%), xerophthalmia (<2%)

Respiratory: Nasopharyngitis (3%)

Transdermal:

>10%: Local: Application site pruritus (14% to 17%)

1% to 10%:

Gastrointestinal: Xerostomia (4% to 10%), constipation (3%), diarrhea (3%)

Genitourinary: Dysuria (2%)

Local: Application site erythema (6% to 8%), application site vesicles (3%), application site rash (3%)

Ophthalmic: Visual disturbance (3%)

<1%, postmarketing, and/or case reports: Agitation, anaphylaxis, angioedema, anorexia, chest discomfort, cycloplegia, decreased gastrointestinal motility, decreased lactation, frequent bowel movements, glaucoma, hallucination, hot flash, hypersensitivity reaction, hypohidrosis, impotence, memory impairment, mydriasis, prolonged Q-T interval on ECG, psychotic reaction, seizure, skin rash, tachycardia, voice disorder

General Dosage Range

Oral:

Extended release:

Children ≥6 years and Adolescents: 5 mg once daily (maximum: 20 mg daily)

Adults: Initial: 5 to 10 mg once daily; Maintenance: 5 to 30 mg once daily (maximum: 30 mg daily)

Immediate release:

Children ≥5 years and Adolescents: 5 mg 2 to 3 times daily (maximum: 15 mg daily)

Adults: 5 mg 2 to 4 times daily (maximum: 20 mg daily)

Elderly: 2.5 mg 2 to 3 times daily

Topical gel: *Adults:* Gelnique 3%: Apply 3 pumps (84 mg) once daily; Gelnique 10%: Apply contents of 1 sachet (100 mg/g) once daily

Transdermal: *Adults:* Apply one 3.9 mg/day patch twice weekly

Mechanism of Action Direct antispasmodic effect on smooth muscle, also inhibits the action of acetylcholine on smooth muscle (exhibits 1/5 the anticholinergic activity of atropine, but has 4-10 times the antispasmodic activity); does not block effects at skeletal muscle or at autonomic ganglia; increases bladder capacity, decreases uninhibited contractions, and delays desire to void, therefore, decreases urgency and frequency

Pharmacodynamics/Kinetics

Onset of Action Oral: Immediate release: 30 to 60 minutes; Peak effect: 3 to 6 hours; Extended release: Peak effect: 3 days

Duration of Action Oral: Immediate release: 6 to 10 hours; Extended release: Up to 24 hours; Transdermal 96 hours

Half-life Elimination IV: ~2 hours (parent drug), 7 to 8 hours (metabolites); Oral: Immediate release: ~2 to 3 hours; Extended release: ~13 hours; Transdermal: 30 to 64 hours

Time to Peak Serum: Oral: Immediate release: ~60 minutes; Extended release: 4 to 6 hours; Transdermal: 24 to 48 hours

Pregnancy Risk Factor B

Pregnancy Considerations Adverse events were not observed in animal reproduction studies.

OxyCODONE (oks i KOE done)

Related Information

Management of the Chemically Dependent Patient *on page 1821*

Oral Pain *on page 1830*

Brand Names: US Oxaydo; Oxecta [DSC]; OxyCONTIN; Roxicodone; Xtampza ER

Brand Names: Canada ACT Oxycodone CR; Apo-Oxycodone CR; Oxy.IR; OxyNEO; PMS-Oxycodone; PMS-Oxycodone CR; Supeudol

Generic Availability (US) May be product dependent

Pharmacologic Category Analgesic, Opioid

Dental Use Treatment of postoperative pain

Use Pain management:

Immediate-release formulations: Management of acute or chronic moderate to severe pain where the use of an opioid analgesic is appropriate.

Extended-release formulations:

Capsules: Management of pain severe enough to require daily, around-the-clock, long-term opioid treatment and for which alternative treatment options are inadequate in adults

Tablets: Management of pain severe enough to require daily, around-the-clock, long-term opioid treatment and for which alternative treatment options are inadequate in adults and opioid-tolerant pediatric patients ≥11 years of age who are already receiving and tolerating a minimum daily opioid dose of at least 20 mg oxycodone orally or its equivalent.

Limitations of use: Reserve for use in patients for whom alternative treatment options (eg, nonopioid analgesics, opioid combination products) are ineffective, not tolerated, or would be otherwise inadequate to provide sufficient management of pain. Oxycodone ER is not indicated as an as-needed analgesic.

Local Anesthetic/Vasoconstrictor Precautions No information available to require special precautions

Effects on Dental Treatment Key adverse event(s) related to dental treatment: Xerostomia (normal salivary flow resumes upon discontinuation).

Effects on Bleeding No information available to require special precautions

Adverse Reactions Unless otherwise noted, frequency of adverse reactions is shown as reported for adult patients receiving OxyContin.

>10%:

Central nervous system: Drowsiness (adults: 23%; Xtampza ER: 9%; children and adolescents 11 to 16 years: 1% to <5%), headache (children and adolescents 11 to 16 years: 14%; Xtampza ER: 14%), dizziness (children ≥11 years, adolescents, and adults: 9% to 13%; Xtampza ER: 2% to 6%)

Dermatologic: Pruritus (children ≥11 years, adolescents, and adults: 6% to 13%; Xtampza ER: 3% to 7%)

Gastrointestinal: Nausea (children ≥11 years, adolescents, and adults: 15% to 23%; Xtampza ER: 11% to 17%), constipation (adults 23%; Xtampza ER: 5% to 13%; children and adolescents 11 to 16 years: 9%), vomiting (children ≥11 years, adolescents, and adults: 12% to 21%; Xtampza ER: 4% to 6%)

Miscellaneous: Fever (children ≥11 years, adolescents, and adults: 1% to 11%; Xtampza ER: 1% to 5%)

1% to 10%:

Cardiovascular: Edema (<1% [including facial and peripheral]; Xtampza ER: 1% to 5%), flushing (Xtampza ER: 1% to 5%), hypertension (Xtampza ER: 1% to 5%), orthostatic hypotension (1% to 5%), decreased oxygen saturation (children and adolescents 11 to 16 years: 1% to <5%), tachycardia (children and adolescents 11 to 16 years: 1% to <5%)

Central nervous system: Abnormal dreams (1% to 5%; Xtampza ER: <1%), abnormality in thinking (1% to 5%), anxiety (children ≥11 years, adolescents, and adults: 1% to 5%; Xtampza ER: 1% to 5%), chills (children and adolescents 11 to 16 years: 1% to 5%; Xtampza ER: 1% to 5%), confusion (1% to 5%), drug withdrawal (Xtampza ER: 1% to 5%), dysphoria (1% to 5%), euphoria (1% to 5%; Xtampza ER: <1%), fatigue (children and adolescents 11 to 16 years: 1% to 5%; Xtampza ER: 1% to 5%), insomnia (children ≥11 years, adolescents, and adults: 1% to 5%; Xtampza ER: 1% to 5%), irritability (Xtampza ER: 1% to 5%), lethargy (children and adolescents 11 to 16 years: 1% to <5%; Xtampza ER: <1%), migraine (<1%; Xtampza ER: 1% to 5%), nervousness (1% to 5%), twitching (1% to 5%), withdrawal syndrome (<1%; Xtampza ER: 1% to 5%), agitation (children and adolescents: 1% to <5%; adults: <1%), depression (children and adolescents: 1% to <5%; adults: <1%), hypoesthesia (children and adolescents: 1% to <5%; adults: <1%), pain (children and adolescents 11 to 16 years: 1% to <5%), paresthesia (children and adolescents: 1% to <5%; adults: <1%), procedural pain (children and adolescents 11 to 16 years: 1% to <5%)

Dermatologic: Diaphoresis (5%), excoriation (Xtampza ER: 1% to 5%), hyperhidrosis (Xtampza ER: 1% to 5%; children and adolescents 11 to 16 years: 1% to <5%), skin rash (children ≥11 years, adolescents, and adults: 1% to 5%; Xtampza ER: 1% to 5%)

Endocrine & metabolic: Hyperglycemia (Xtampza ER: 1% to 5%), hypochloremia (children and adolescents 11 to 16 years: 1% to <5%), hyponatremia (children and adolescents 11 to 16 years: 1% to <5%), weight loss (children and adolescents 11 to 16 years: 1% to <5%)

Gastrointestinal: Xerostomia (6%), diarrhea (children ≥11 years, adolescents, and adults: 1% to 6%; Xtampza ER: 1% to 5%), decreased appetite (children and adolescents 11 to 16 years: 5%; Xtampza ER: 1% to 5%), abdominal pain (children ≥11 years, adolescents, and adults: 1% to 5%; Xtampza ER: 1% to 5%), anorexia (1% to 5%), dyspepsia (1% to 5%), gastritis (1% to 5%), gastroesophageal reflux disease (children and adolescents 11 to 16 years: 1% to 5%; Xtampza ER: 1% to 5%), hiccups (1% to 5%), upper abdominal pain (Xtampza ER: 1% to 5%)

Genitourinary: Dysuria (children and adolescents: 1% to <5%; adults: <1%), urinary retention

Hematologic & oncologic: Decreased hemoglobin (children and adolescents 11 to 16 years: 1% to <5%), decreased neutrophils (children and adolescents 11 to 16 years: 1% to <5%), decreased platelet count (children and adolescents 11 to 16 years: 1% to <5%), decreased red blood cells (children and adolescents 11 to 16 years: 1% to <5%), febrile neutropenia (children and adolescents 11 to 16 years: 1% to <5%), neutropenia (children and adolescents 11 to 16 years: 1% to <5%)

Hepatic: Increased serum ALT (children and adolescents 11 to 16 years: 1% to <5%)

Neuromuscular & skeletal: Weakness (children ≥11 years, adolescents, and adults: 1% to 6%), arthralgia (Xtampza ER: 1% to 5%), back pain (Xtampza ER: 1% to 5%), musculoskeletal pain (Xtampza ER: 1% to 5%; children and adolescents 11 to 16 years: 1% to <5%), myalgia (Xtampza ER: 1% to 5%), tremor (<1%; Xtampza ER: 1% to 5%), limb pain (children and adolescents 11 to 16 years: 1% to <5%)

Ophthalmic: Blurred vision (Xtampza ER: 1% to 5%)

Respiratory: Cough (<1%; Xtampza ER: 1% to 5%), dyspnea (1% to 5%; Xtampza ER: <1%), oropharyngeal pain (Xtampza ER: 1% to 5%; children and adolescents 11 to 16 years: 1% to <5%)

Miscellaneous: Seroma (children and adolescents 11 to 16 years: 1% to <5%)

<1%, postmarketing, and/or case reports (any population): Abnormal gait, abnormal stools (tablet in stool [some controlled release dosage forms]; Anderson 2002), aggressive behavior, amenorrhea, amnesia, anaphylactoid reaction, anaphylaxis, chest pain, choking sensation (due to properties of controlled release tablets), cholestasis, cough, dehydration, dental caries, depersonalization, depression of ST segment on ECG, disturbed sleep, diverticulitis (exacerbation), drug abuse, drug dependence, dysgeusia, dysphagia (or other swallowing difficulties due to properties of controlled release tablets), emotional lability, eructation, exfoliative dermatitis, flatulence, gag reflex (due to properties of controlled release tablets), hallucination, hematuria, histamine release, hyperalgesia, hyperkinesia, hypertonia, hypogonadism (Brennan 2013; Debono 2011), hyponatremia, hypotonia, impotence, increased appetite, increased gamma-glutamyl transferase, increased heart rate, increased intracranial pressure, increased liver enzymes, increased thirst, intestinal obstruction, lymphadenopathy, malaise, memory impairment, mood changes, night sweats, palpitations, polyuria, restlessness, seizure, SIADH, speech disturbance, stomatitis, stupor,

suicidal ideation, suicidal tendencies, syncope, tinnitus, urticaria, vasodilatation, vertigo, visual disturbance, voice disorder, xeroderma

Dental Usual Dosage Postoperative pain: Adults: Oral: 5 mg every 6 hours as needed

Dosing

Adult

Pain management: Oral: **Note:** All doses should be titrated to appropriate effect.

Immediate release: Initial: 5 to 15 mg every 4 to 6 hours as needed; dosing range: 5 to 20 mg per dose (APS 6th edition). For severe chronic pain, administer on a regularly scheduled basis, every 4 to 6 hours, at the lowest dose that will achieve adequate analgesia.

Extended release:

Note: Oxycodone ER capsules are not bioequivalent to ER tablets. Dose of ER capsules is expressed as oxycodone base and the dose of ER tablets is expressed as oxycodone hydrochloride. Oxycodone ER 60 mg and 80 mg tablets are intended for use in opioid-tolerant patients only. Single doses >40 mg (ER tablets) or >36 mg (ER capsules), or a total dose of >80 mg daily (ER tablets) or >72 mg daily (ER capsules) are for use only in opioid-tolerant patients. Opioid tolerance is defined as: Patients already taking at least morphine 60 mg orally daily, oxymorphone 25 mg orally daily, transdermal fentanyl 25 mcg per hour, oxycodone 30 mg orally daily, hydromorphone 8 mg orally daily, hydrocodone 60 mg orally daily or an equivalent dose of another opioid for at least 1 week.

Opioid naive (use as the first opioid analgesic or use in patients who are not opioid tolerant): Initial:
ER tablet: 10 mg every 12 hours
ER capsules: 9 mg every 12 hours

Conversion from other oral oxycodone formulations to oxycodone ER: Initiate oxycodone ER with 50% of the total daily oral oxycodone daily dose (mg/day) administered every 12 hours.

Conversion from other opioids to oxycodone ER: Discontinue all other around-the-clock opioids when oxycodone ER is initiated. Initiate with 10 mg (ER tablets) or 9 mg (ER capsules) every 12 hours. Substantial interpatient variability exists due to patient specific factors, relative potency of different opioids, and dosage forms; therefore, it is preferable to underestimate the initial 24 hour oral oxycodone requirements and utilize rescue medication (immediate-release opioid).

Conversion from transdermal fentanyl patch to oxycodone ER: Note: Remove fentanyl patch at least 18 hours prior to starting oxycodone ER. The manufacturer suggests using the conservative conversion factor of oxycodone ER tablets 10 mg or oxycodone ER capsules 9 mg every 12 hours for each fentanyl 25 mcg/hour transdermal patch; systematic assessment of this suggested conversion has not been completed; monitor patients closely.

Conversion from methadone to oxycodone ER: Close monitoring is required when converting methadone to another opioid. Ratio between methadone and other opioid agonists varies widely according to previous dose exposure. Methadone has a long half-life and can accumulate in the plasma.

Maintenance dose: Dosage adjustment (titration): After initiation of oxycodone ER, adjust dose in increments (25% to 50%) no more frequently than every 1 to 2 days until desired pain control. Recommended maximum dose of ER capsules is 288 mg/day. Patients may require rescue doses of an immediate-release analgesic during dose titration. Observe for signs and symptoms of opioid withdrawal or signs of over sedation/toxicity; if unacceptable adverse reactions occur, the subsequent dose may be reduced. **Note:** Some clinicians have reported that in certain chronic pain patients, more frequent dosing (ie, every 8 hours) is required for effective pain relief (Gallagher 2007; Marcus 2004; Nicholson 2006), although dosing more frequently than every 12 hours is not recommended by the manufacturer, and safety and efficacy has not been established.

Dosage adjustment for concomitant therapy: Concomitant CNS depressants: Initiate oxycodone ER with 33% to 50% of the calculated recommended dose. If reduced dose is less than smallest available dosage form consider alternative analgesic.

Discontinuation of therapy:

Immediate release: Decrease previous daily dose by 25% to 50% every 2 to 4 days; monitor carefully for signs/symptoms of withdrawal. If patient displays withdrawal symptoms, increase dose to previous dose and then reduce dose more slowly by increasing interval between dose reductions, decreasing amount of daily dose reduction, or both.

Extended release: Gradually titrate dose downward to prevent withdrawal signs/symptoms. Do not abruptly discontinue.

Dosage adjustment in debilitated patients (non-opioid tolerant):

Immediate release: Initial: There are no specific dosage adjustments provided in the manufacturer's labeling; use caution and with a reduced dose.

Extended release: Initial: Initiate oxycodone ER with 33% to 50% of the calculated recommended dose. If reduced dose is less than smallest available dosage form consider alternative analgesic.

Geriatric Refer to adult dosing. Initiate therapy at low end of dosing range and use caution.

Pediatric

Pain management: Children and Adolescents: Oral:

Moderate to severe pain (off-label use): *Immediate release:* Initial dose: 0.1 to 0.2 mg/kg/dose (moderate pain) or 0.2 mg/kg/dose (severe pain) (APS 6th edition). For severe chronic pain, administer on a regularly scheduled basis, every 4 to 6 hours, at the lowest dose that will achieve adequate analgesia.

Severe pain requiring around-the-clock long-term opioid therapy: *Extended release tablets:* **Note:** Use only in pediatric patients ≥11 years of age who are already receiving opioid therapy for at least 5 consecutive days, tolerating a minimum daily opioid dose of at least 20 mg oxycodone orally or its equivalent at least for the two days immediately prior to starting oxycodone ER, and for which alternative treatment options are inadequate. Prior to initiation of oxycodone ER, all other around-the-clock opioid therapy must be discontinued. Extended-release capsules are not approved for use in pediatric patients.

Initial dose: Children ≥11 years and Adolescents: Oral: Initial dose based on current opioid regimen dose; use the conversion factor table to convert from the current opioid(s) daily dose to the oxycodone ER daily dose according to the following equation. **Note:** Substantial interpatient variability exists due to patient specific factors, relative potency of different opioids, and dosage forms; therefore, it is preferable to underestimate the initial 24 hour oral oxycodone requirements and utilize rescue medication (immediate-release opioid):

Dose of oxycodone ER administered every 12 hours = (mg/day of current opioid regimen X conversion factor)/2

Dose calculations or adjustments for specific clinical scenarios:

If rounding is necessary, numerical value should be rounded **down** to the nearest tablet strength. If calculated dose is <20 mg, do not start oxycodone ER as there is no safe tablet strength available.

If more than one opioid in the regimen, calculate the approximate oxycodone dose for each opioid and sum the totals for the approximate oxycodone ER **daily** dose, then divided by 2 for the every 12 hours oxycodone ER dose.

If current opioid regimen includes a fixed-dose opioid/nonopioid dosage form (eg, hydrocodone/acetaminophen), only the mg of opioid should be used in the conversion calculations.

If patient receiving concomitant CNS depressants, initiate oxycodone ER with 33% to 50% of the calculated recommended dose.

If using asymmetric dosing, the higher dose should be scheduled as the morning dose, and the lower dose 12 hours later.

Note: The following conversion table should ONLY be used to convert opioid doses to oxycodone ER tablets (not from oxycodone ER to other opioids; it is NOT a table of equianalgesic doses as it may overestimate initial dose).

Conversion Factor for Calculating Initial Oxycodone ER Tablet Dose in Pediatric Patients ≥11 years

Current opioid regimen to be converted to oxycodone ER tablet	Conversion Factor	
	Oral	Parenteral[1]
Oxycodone	1	
Hydrocodone	0.9	
Hydromorphone	4	20
Morphine	0.5	3
Tramadol	0.17	0.2

[1]For patients receiving high-dose parenteral opioids, a more conservative conversion factor should be applied (ie, lower numerical conversion factor); for example, for high-dose parenteral morphine, a conversion of 1.5 should be used for calculations instead of 3.

Conversion from fentanyl patch to oxycodone ER: Limited data available: **Note:** Remove fentanyl patch at least 18 hours prior to starting oxycodone ER. Initial dose based on current opioid regimen dose; the manufacturer suggests using the conservative conversion factor of oxycodone ER 10 mg every 12 hours for each fentanyl 25 mcg/hour transdermal patch; systematic assessment of this suggested conversion has not be completed; monitor patients closely

Maintenance dose: Dosage adjustment (titration): After initiation of oxycodone ER, adjust dose in small increments (up to 25%) no more frequently than every 1 to 2 days until desired pain control; patients may require rescue doses of an immediate-release analgesic during dose titration. Observe for signs and symptoms of opioid withdrawal or signs of over sedation/toxicity; if unacceptable adverse reactions occur, the subsequent dose may be reduced.

Renal Impairment

CrCl ≥60 mL/minute: There are no dosage adjustments provided in the manufacturer's labeling.

CrCl <60 mL/minute: Serum concentrations are increased ~50%. Initiate at the low end of the dosage range (use caution); adjust dose as clinically indicated. Alternatively, for both immediate- and extended-release forms, doses of 33% to 50% of usual initial dosing have been recommended (Oxy IR Canadian product labeling 2015; OxyNeo Canadian product labeling 2014). For ER tablets and capsules, if the reduced dose is less than smallest available dosage form, consider alternative analgesic.

Hepatic Impairment

Immediate release (Adults): Initiate therapy at 33% to 50% the usual dosage and titrate carefully.

Extended release tablets (Children ≥11 years, Adolescents, and Adults) or *Extended release capsules* (Adults): Initial: Initiate oxycodone ER with 33% to 50% of the calculated recommended dose. If reduced dose is less than smallest available dosage form consider alternative analgesic.

Mechanism of Action Binds to opiate receptors in the CNS, causing inhibition of ascending pain pathways, altering the perception of and response to pain; produces generalized CNS depression

Contraindications

Hypersensitivity (eg, anaphylaxis, angioedema) to oxycodone or any component of the formulation; significant respiratory depression; hypercarbia; acute or severe bronchial asthma in an unmonitored setting or in the absence of resuscitative equipment; GI obstruction, including paralytic ileus (known or suspected).

Documentation of allergenic cross-reactivity for opioids is limited. However, because of similarities in chemical structure and/or pharmacologic actions, the possibility of cross-sensitivity cannot be ruled out with certainty.

Canadian labeling: Additional contraindications (not in US labeling): Hypersensitivity to other opioids; suspected surgical abdomen (eg, acute appendicitis or pancreatitis); any disease/condition that affects bowel transit; mild pain that can be managed with other pain medications (immediate release); mild, intermittent or short duration pain that can be managed with other pain medications or acute pain (extended release); chronic obstructive airway; status asthmaticus; cor pulmonale; acute alcoholism; delirium tremens; convulsive disorders; severe CNS depression; increased cerebrospinal or intracranial pressure; head injury; monoamine oxidase (MAO) inhibitors (concomitant use or within 14 days of therapy); pregnant women or during labor and delivery; breastfeeding

Warnings/Precautions May cause CNS depression, which may impair physical or mental abilities; patients must be cautioned about performing tasks which require mental alertness (eg, operating machinery or driving). Potentially significant drug-drug interactions may exist, requiring dose or frequency adjustment, additional monitoring, and/or selection of alternative therapy. Use with caution in patients with hypersensitivity reactions to other phenanthrene derivative opioid agonists (morphine, hydrocodone, hydromorphone, levorphanol, oxymorphone). Use with caution in pancreatitis or biliary tract disease, delirium tremens, morbid obesity, adrenocortical insufficiency (including Addison disease), history of seizure disorders, thyroid dysfunction, prostatic hyperplasia, urinary stricture, and toxic psychosis. Long-term opioid use may cause secondary hypogonadism, which may lead to sexual dysfunction, infertility, mood disorders, and osteoporosis (Brennan 2013). Use with caution and monitor for respiratory depression in patients with significant chronic obstructive pulmonary disease or cor pulmonale, and those with a substantially decreased respiratory reserve, hypoxia, hypercapnia, or preexisting respiratory depression, particularly when initiating and titrating therapy; critical respiratory depression may occur, even at therapeutic dosages. Consider the use of alternative nonopioid analgesics in these patients. Use opioids with caution for chronic pain and titrate dosage cautiously in patients with risk factors for sleep-disordered breathing, including HF and obesity. Avoid opioids in patients with moderate to severe sleep-disordered breathing (Dowell [CDC 2016]). May obscure diagnosis or clinical course of patients with acute abdominal conditions. Avoid use in patients with impaired consciousness or coma. Use with caution in patients with a history of drug abuse or acute alcoholism; potential for drug dependency exists. Other factors associated with increased risk for misuse include younger age, concomitant depression (major), and psychotropic medication use. Consider offering naloxone prescriptions in patients with factors associated with an increased risk for overdose, such as history of overdose or substance use disorder, higher opioid dosages (≥50 morphine milligram equivalents/day orally), and concomitant benzodiazepine use (Dowell [CDC 2016]). Use opioids with caution for chronic pain in patients with mental health conditions (eg, depression, anxiety disorders, post-traumatic stress disorder) due to increased risk for opioid use disorder and overdose; more frequent monitoring is recommended (Dowell [CDC 2016]).

Use with caution in cachectic or debilitated patients, and in hepatic or severe renal impairment. Use opioids for chronic pain with caution in older adults; monitor closely due to an increased potential for risks, including certain risks such as falls/fracture, cognitive impairment, and constipation. Clearance may also be reduced in older adults (with or without renal impairment) resulting in a narrow therapeutic window and increasing the risk for respiratory depression or overdose (Dowell [CDC 2016]). May cause severe hypotension (including orthostatic hypotension and syncope); use with caution in patients with hypovolemia, cardiovascular disease (including acute MI), or drugs which may exaggerate hypotensive effects (including phenothiazines or general anesthetics). Monitor for symptoms of hypotension following initiation or dose titration. Avoid use in patients with circulatory shock. Use with extreme caution in patients with head injury, intracranial lesions, or elevated intracranial pressure; exaggerated elevation of ICP may occur. May cause constipation which may be problematic in patients with unstable angina and patients post-myocardial infarction. Concurrent use of mixed agonist/antagonist analgesics (eg, pentazocine, nalbuphine, butorphanol) or partial agonist (eg, buprenorphine) analgesics may precipitate withdrawal symptoms and/or reduced analgesic efficacy in patients following prolonged therapy with mu opioid agonists. Use with caution in the perioperative setting; individualize treatment when transitioning from parenteral to oral analgesics. Taper dose gradually when discontinuing. Opioids decrease bowel motility; monitor for decreased bowel motility in postop patients receiving opioids. Use with caution in the perioperative setting; individualize treatment when transitioning from parenteral to oral analgesics. An opioid-containing analgesic regimen should be tailored to each patient's needs and based upon the type of pain being treated (acute versus chronic), the route of administration, degree of tolerance for opioids (naive versus chronic user), age, weight, and medical condition. The optimal analgesic dose varies widely among patients; doses should be titrated to pain relief/prevention.

Chronic pain: Opioids should **not** be used as first-line therapy for chronic pain management (pain >3-month duration or beyond time of normal tissue healing) due to limited short-term benefits, undetermined long-term benefits, and association with serious risks (eg, overdose, MI, auto accidents, risk of developing opioid use disorder). Preferred management includes nonpharmacologic therapy and nonopioid therapy (eg, NSAIDs, acetaminophen, certain anticonvulsants and antidepressants). If opioid therapy is initiated, it should be combined with nonpharmacologic and nonopioid therapy, as appropriate. Prior to initiation, known risks of opioid therapy should be discussed and realistic treatment goals for pain/function should be established, including consideration for discontinuation if benefits do not outweigh risks. Therapy should be continued only if clinically meaningful improvement in pain/function outweighs risks. Therapy should be initiated at the lowest effective dosage using immediate-release opioids (instead of extended-release/long-acting opioids). Risk associated with use increases with higher opioid dosages. Risks and benefits should be re-evaluated when increasing dosage to ≥50 morphine milligram equivalents (MME)/day orally; dosages ≥90 MME/day orally should be avoided unless carefully justified (Dowell [CDC 2016]).

[US Boxed Warning]: Serious, life-threatening, or fatal respiratory depression may occur. Monitor closely for respiratory depression, especially during initiation or dose escalation. Swallow ER tablets whole; crushing, chewing, or dissolving can cause rapid release and a potentially fatal dose. Carbon dioxide retention from opioid-induced respiratory depression can exacerbate the sedating effects of opioids. **[US Boxed Warning]: Use with all CYP3A4 inhibitors may result in an increase in oxycodone plasma concentrations, which could increase or prolong adverse drug effects and may cause potentially fatal respiratory depression. In addition, discontinuation of a concomitant CYP 3A4 inducer may result in increased oxycodone concentrations. Monitor patients receiving oxycodone and any CYP 3A4 inhibitor or inducer. [US Boxed Warning]: Concomitant use of opioids with benzodiazepines or other CNS depressants, including alcohol, may result in profound sedation, respiratory depression, coma, and death. Reserve concomitant prescribing**

of oxycodone and benzodiazepines or other CNS depressants for use in patients for whom alternative treatment options are inadequate. Limit dosage and durations to the minimum required and follow patients for signs and symptoms of respiratory depression and sedation. [US Boxed Warning]: Oxycodone exposes patients and other users to the risks of addiction, abuse, and misuse, potentially leading to overdose and death. Assess each patient's risk prior to prescribing; monitor all patients regularly for development of these behaviors or conditions. [US Boxed Warning]: Accidental ingestion of even one dose, especially in children, can result in a fatal overdose of oxycodone. [US Boxed Warning]: Prolonged use of opioids during pregnancy can cause neonatal withdrawal syndrome, which may be life-threatening if not recognized and treated according to protocols developed by neonatology experts. If opioid use is required for a prolonged period in a pregnant woman, advise the patient of the risk of neonatal opioid withdrawal syndrome and ensure that appropriate treatment will be available. Signs and symptoms include irritability, hyperactivity and abnormal sleep pattern, high pitched cry, tremor, vomiting, diarrhea and failure to gain weight. Onset, duration and severity depend on the drug used, duration of use, maternal dose, and rate of drug elimination by the newborn.

[US Boxed Warning]: Ensure accuracy when prescribing, dispensing, and administering oxycodone oral solution. Dosing errors due to confusion between mg and mL, and other oxycodone oral solutions of different concentrations can results in accidental overdose.

Extended release tablets may be difficult to swallow and could become lodged in throat; patients with swallowing difficulties may be at increased risk. Cases of intestinal obstruction or diverticulitis exacerbation have also been reported, including cases requiring medical intervention to remove the tablet; patients with an underlying GI disease (eg, esophageal cancer, colon cancer) may be at increased risk.

Some dosage forms may contain sodium benzoate/benzoic acid; benzoic acid (benzoate) is a metabolite of benzyl alcohol; large amounts of benzyl alcohol (≥99 mg/kg/day) have been associated with a potentially fatal toxicity ("gasping syndrome") in neonates; the "gasping syndrome" consists of metabolic acidosis, respiratory distress, gasping respirations, CNS dysfunction (including convulsions, intracranial hemorrhage), hypotension, and cardiovascular collapse (AAP ["Inactive" 1997]; CDC 1982); some data suggests that benzoate displaces bilirubin from protein binding sites (Ahlfors 2001); avoid or use dosage forms containing benzyl alcohol derivative with caution in neonates. See manufacturer's labeling.

Drug Interactions

Metabolism/Transport Effects **Substrate** of CYP2D6 (minor), CYP3A4 (major); **Note:** Assignment of Major/Minor substrate status based on clinically relevant drug interaction potential

Avoid Concomitant Use

Avoid concomitant use of OxyCODONE with any of the following: Azelastine (Nasal); Conivaptan; Eluxadoline; Fusidic Acid (Systemic); Idelalisib; Mixed Agonist / Antagonist Opioids; Orphenadrine; Oxomemazine; Paraldehyde; Thalidomide

Increased Effect/Toxicity

OxyCODONE may increase the levels/effects of: Alvimopan; Azelastine (Nasal); Blonanserin; Desmopressin; Diuretics; Eluxadoline; Flunitrazepam; HYDROcodone; MAO Inhibitors; Methotrimeprazine; MetyroSINE; Orphenadrine; Paraldehyde; Piribedil; Pramipexole; Ramosetron; ROPINIRole; Rotigotine; Selective Serotonin Reuptake Inhibitors; Serotonin Modulators; Suvorexant; Thalidomide; Zolpidem

The levels/effects of OxyCODONE may be increased by: Amphetamines; Anticholinergic Agents; Aprepitant; Brimonidine (Topical); Cannabis; Chlormethiazole; Chlorphenesin Carbamate; CNS Depressants; Conivaptan; CYP3A4 Inhibitors (Moderate); CYP3A4 Inhibitors (Strong); Dasatinib; Dimethindene (Topical); Dronabinol; Droperidol; Fosaprepitant; Fusidic Acid (Systemic); Idelalisib; Ivacaftor; Kava Kava; Lofexidine; Magnesium Sulfate; Methotrimeprazine; MiFEPRIStone; Minocycline; Nabilone; Netupitant; Oxomemazine; Palbociclib; Perampanel; Rufinamide; Simeprevir; Sodium Oxybate; Stiripentol; Succinylcholine; Tapentadol; Tetrahydrocannabinol; Voriconazole

Decreased Effect

OxyCODONE may decrease the levels/effects of: Diuretics; Gastrointestinal Agents (Prokinetic); Pegvisomant

The levels/effects of OxyCODONE may be decreased by: Bosentan; CYP3A4 Inducers (Moderate); CYP3A4 Inducers (Strong); Dabrafenib; Deferasirox; Enzalutamide; Mitotane; Mixed Agonist / Antagonist Opioids; Nalmefene; Naltrexone; RifAMPin; Siltuximab; St John's Wort; Tocilizumab

Dietary Considerations Instruct patient to avoid high-fat meals when taking some products (food has no effect on the reformulated OxyContin).

Pharmacodynamics/Kinetics

Onset of Action Pain relief: Immediate release: 10 to 15 minutes; Peak effect: Immediate release: 0.5 to 1 hour

Duration of Action Immediate release: 3 to 6 hours; Extended release: ≤12 hours

Half-life Elimination

Apparent: Immediate release: 3.2 to ~4 hours; Extended release tablet: 4.5 hours; Extended release capsule: 5.6 hours

Elimination: Children 2 to 10 years: 1.8 hours (range: 1.2 to 3 hours); Adults: 3.7 hours

Adults with CrCl <60 mL/minute: Half-life increases by 1 hour, but peak oxycodone concentrations increase by 50% and AUC increases by 60%

Adults with mild to moderate hepatic impairment: Half-life increases by 2.3 hours, peak oxycodone concentrations increase by 50%, and AUC increases by 95%

Time to Peak

Plasma: Immediate release: 1.2 to 1.9 hours; Extended release: 4 to 5 hours

Pregnancy Considerations Adverse events have been observed in some animal reproduction studies. Opioids cross the placenta. Oxycodone should not be used immediately prior to or during labor.

[US Boxed Warning]: Prolonged use of opioids during pregnancy can cause neonatal withdrawal syndrome, which may be life-threatening if not recognized and treated according to protocols developed by neonatology experts. If opioid use is required for a prolonged period in a pregnant woman, advise the patient of the risk of neonatal

opioid withdrawal syndrome and ensure that appropriate treatment will be available. If chronic opioid exposure occurs in pregnancy, adverse events in the newborn (including withdrawal) may occur; monitoring of the neonate is recommended. The minimum effective dose should be used if opioids are needed (Chou 2009). Neonatal abstinence syndrome following opioid exposure may present with autonomic (eg, fever, temperature instability), gastrointestinal (eg, diarrhea, vomiting, poor feeding/weight gain), or neurologic (eg, high-pitched crying, increased muscle tone, irritability, seizure, tremor) symptoms (Dow 2012; Hudak 2012).

Long-term opioid use may cause secondary hypogonadism, which may lead to sexual dysfunction or infertility (Brennan 2013).

Breastfeeding Considerations Oxycodone is excreted in breast milk.

The actual amount received by a nursing infant varies and is dependent upon maternal plasma concentration, volume of milk ingested by the infant, and the extent of first pass metabolism.

The time to maximum milk concentration varied in available studies; however, oxycodone continued to be measurable in breast milk up to 37 hours after multiple doses (Marx 1986; Seaton 2007).

Sedation and/or respiratory depression may occur in the infant; symptoms of opioid withdrawal may occur following the cessation of breastfeeding. Caution should be used in a woman who may be an ultrarapid metabolizer; oxycodone is a substrate for CYP2D6 and their breastfeeding infants may be at higher risk for adverse events (Montgomery 2012).

Current guidelines note that nonopioid analgesics are preferred for postpartum pain in breastfeeding women (Montgomery 2012). When use of an opiate is needed, agents other than oxycodone are recommended by some guidelines (Sachs 2013). Other guidelines note oxycodone may be useful to treat pain in some postpartum women (Montgomery 2012). In general, a single, occasional dose of an opioid analgesic may be compatible with breastfeeding. **Note:** Not all dosage forms are appropriate for intermittent pain in patients who are not opioid tolerant. Mothers should closely monitor their nursing infants (WHO 2002). breastfeeding is not recommended by some manufacturers.

Controlled Substance C-II

Prescribing and Access Restrictions As a requirement of the REMS program, healthcare providers who prescribe extended-release and long-acting (ER/LA) opioid analgesics need to receive training on the proper use and potential risks of these agents including oxycodone ER. For training, please refer to http://www.er-la-opioidrems.com.

Dosage Forms Considerations

Xtampza ER: Strength is expressed in terms of oxycodone base.

9 mg equivalent to 10 mg oxycodone hydrochloride
13.5 mg equivalent to 15 mg oxycodone hydrochloride
18 mg equivalent to 20 mg oxycodone hydrochloride
36 mg equivalent to 40 mg oxycodone hydrochloride

Dosage Forms

Capsule, Oral:
Generic: 5 mg

Capsule ER 12 Hour Abuse-Deterrent, Oral:
Xtampza ER: 9 mg (100 ea); 13.5 mg (100 ea); 18 mg (100 ea); 27 mg (100 ea); 36 mg (100 ea)

Concentrate, Oral:
Generic: 100 mg/5 mL (15 mL, 30 mL)

Solution, Oral:
Generic: 5 mg/5 mL (5 mL, 15 mL, 473 mL, 500 mL)

Tablet, Oral:
Roxicodone: 5 mg, 15 mg, 30 mg
Generic: 5 mg, 10 mg, 15 mg, 20 mg, 30 mg

Tablet Abuse-Deterrent, Oral:
Oxaydo: 5 mg, 7.5 mg

Tablet ER 12 Hour Abuse-Deterrent, Oral:
OxyCONTIN: 10 mg, 15 mg, 20 mg, 30 mg, 40 mg, 60 mg, 80 mg
Generic: 10 mg, 15 mg, 20 mg, 30 mg, 40 mg, 60 mg, 80 mg

Dosage Forms: Canada

Tablet, Oral:
Oxy IR: 5 mg, 10 mg, 20 mg
Supeudol: 5 mg, 10 mg, 20 mg

Tablet Controlled Release, Oral:
OxyNeo: 10 mg, 15 mg, 20 mg, 30 mg, 40 mg, 60 mg, 80 mg

Oxycodone and Acetaminophen

(oks i KOE done & a seet a MIN oh fen)

Related Information

Acetaminophen *on page 56*
Oral Pain *on page 1830*
OxyCODONE *on page 1255*

Related Sample Prescriptions

Oral Pain - Sample Prescriptions *on page 28*

Brand Names: US Endocet; Percocet; Primlev; Roxicet [DSC]; Xartemis XR; Xolox [DSC]

Brand Names: Canada Apo-Oxycodone/Acet; Endocet; Percocet; Percocet-Demi; PMS-Oxycodone-Acetaminophen; Ratio-Oxycocet; Rivacocet; Sandoz-Oxycodone/Acetaminophen

Generic Availability (US) Yes: Excludes solution

Pharmacologic Category Analgesic Combination (Opioid); Analgesic, Opioid

Dental Use Treatment of moderate to moderately-severe postoperative dental pain

Use

Pain management

Extended-release: Management of acute pain, severe enough to require opioid treatment and for which alternative treatment options are inadequate.

Immediate-release: Management of moderate to moderately severe pain, severe enough to require an opioid analgesic and for which alternative treatments are inadequate.

Limitations of use: Reserve oxycodone/acetaminophen for use in patients for whom alternative treatment options (eg, nonopioid analgesics) are ineffective, not tolerated, or would be otherwise inadequate.

Local Anesthetic/Vasoconstrictor Precautions No information available to require special precautions

Effects on Dental Treatment Key adverse event(s) related to dental treatment: Nausea, sedation, constipation, and xerostomia (normal salivary flow resumes upon discontinuation) (see Dental Comment).

Effects on Bleeding As a single agent, acetaminophen does not appear to affect bleeding or platelet aggregation. Acetaminophen may prolong the INR and increase bleeding in patients taking warfarin (Coumadin). For patients taking warfarin, single acetaminophen doses or acetaminophen therapy of short duration should be safe, but if large (>1.3 g/day) doses are administered for longer than 10-14 days, then the INR should be monitored (see Dental Comment).

Adverse Reactions Also see individual agents. Frequency not always defined.

>10%:

Central nervous system: Dizziness (13%)

Gastrointestinal: Nausea (31%)

1% to 10%:

Cardiovascular: Peripheral edema (1%), circulatory depression, hypotension, shock

Central nervous system: Headache (10%), drowsiness (4%), fatigue (≥1%), insomnia (≥1%), dysphoria

Dermatologic: Skin rash (2%) erythema (1%), excoriation (1%), pruritus (1%), skin blister (1%), erythematous dermatitis

Endocrine & metabolic: Hot flash (1%)

Gastrointestinal: Vomiting (9%), constipation (4%), diarrhea (≥1%), dyspepsia (≥1%), xerostomia (≥1%)

Genitourinary: Dysuria (1%)

Hematologic & oncologic: Hemolytic anemia, neutropenia, pancytopenia, thrombocytopenia

Hepatic: Increased liver enzymes (≥1%)

Respiratory: Cough (≥1%), apnea, respiratory arrest, respiratory depression

<1%, postmarketing, and/or case reports: Abdominal distress, abdominal pain, abnormal hepatic function tests, acidosis, agitation, alkalosis, altered mental status, anaphylactoid reaction, anaphylaxis (acute), angioedema, anxiety, arthralgia, aspiration, asthma, blurred vision, bradycardia, bronchospasm, bruise, cardiac arrhythmia, cerebral edema, chest discomfort, chest pain, chills, cognitive dysfunction, confusion, decreased appetite, dehydration, depression, dermatitis, diaphoresis, disorientation, drug abuse, drug dependence, drug overdose (accidental and nonaccidental), dysgeusia, dyspnea, ecchymoses, emotional lability, esophageal spasm, euphoria, eye redness, falling, fever, flatulence, flushing, hallucination, hearing loss, hepatic disease, hepatic failure, hepatitis, hepatotoxicity, hiccups, hyperglycemia, hyperhidrosis, hyperkalemia, hypersensitivity, hypersensitivity reaction, hypertension, hypoesthesia, hypoglycemia, hypothermia, hypoventilation, impaired consciousness, increased blood pressure, increased gamma-glutamyl transferase, increased lactate dehydrogenase, increased serum alanine aminotransferase, increased serum aspartate aminotransferase, increased serum bilirubin, increased thirst, interstitial nephritis, intestinal obstruction, jaundice, jitteriness, laryngeal edema, lethargy, malaise, memory impairment, metabolic acidosis, migraine, miosis, musculoskeletal stiffness, myalgia, myoclonus, nervousness, noncardiac chest pain, obstructive sleep apnea hypopnea syndrome, oropharyngeal pain, orthostatic hypotension, palpitations, pancreatitis, paresthesia, proteinuria, pulmonary edema, renal failure, renal insufficiency, renal papillary necrosis, respiratory alkalosis, reduced urine flow, rhabdomyolysis, sedation, seizure, sleep disorder, stupor, suicide, tachycardia, tachypnea, throat irritation, tinnitus, tremor, urinary retention, urticaria, visual disturbance, weakness, withdrawal syndrome

Dental Usual Dosage

Note: Initial dose is based on the **oxycodone** content; however, the maximum daily dose is based on the **acetaminophen** content.

Management of pain: Doses should be given every 4-6 hours as needed and titrated to appropriate analgesic effects.

Mild-to-moderate pain:

Children: Initial dose, **based on oxycodone content:** 0.05-0.1 mg/kg/dose

Maximum acetaminophen dose: Children <45 kg: 90 mg/kg/day; children >45 kg: 4 g/day

Adults: Initial dose, **based on oxycodone content:** 2.5-5 mg

Severe pain:

Children: Initial dose, **based on oxycodone content:** 0.3 mg/kg/dose

Adults: Initial dose, **based on oxycodone content:** 10-30 mg. Do not exceed acetaminophen 4 g/day.

Elderly: Doses should be titrated to appropriate analgesic effects: Initial dose, **based on oxycodone content:** 2.5-5 mg every 6 hours. Do not exceed acetaminophen 4 g/day.

Dosage adjustment in hepatic impairment: Dose should be reduced in patients with severe liver disease.

Dosing

Adult Note: Initial dose is based on the **oxycodone** content; however, the maximum daily dose is based on the **acetaminophen** content.

Pain management:

Extended-release: Oral: Usual dose: 2 tablets every 12 hours; the second initial dose may be administered as early as 8 hours after the first initial dose if needed; subsequent doses are to be administered 2 tablets every 12 hours. Do not exceed acetaminophen 4 g/day. **NOTE:** Oxycodone/acetaminophen ER is not interchangeable with other oxycodone/acetaminophen products because of differing pharmacokinetic profiles that affect the frequency of administration.

Discontinuation of therapy: Decrease dose by 25% to 50% every 2 to 4 days to prevent signs and symptoms of withdrawal. If patient displays withdrawal symptoms, increase dose to previous dose and then reduce dose more slowly by increasing interval between dose reductions, decreasing amount of daily dose reduction, or both.

Immediate release: Oral: Doses should be titrated to appropriate analgesic effects.

Manufacturer's labeling: Moderate to moderately severe pain: Initial dose, **based on oxycodone content**: 2.5 to 10 mg every 6 hours as needed. Titrate according to pain severity and individual response. Do not exceed acetaminophen 4 g/day.

Alternate recommendations (APS 2008):

Moderate pain (off-label): Initial dose, **based on oxycodone content**: 5 mg. Doses typically given every 4 to 6 hours as needed; manufacturer's labeling recommends every 6 hours as needed. Do not exceed acetaminophen 4 g/day.

Severe pain (off-label): Initial dose, **based on oxycodone content**: 10 to 20 mg. Doses typically given every 4 to 6 hours as needed; manufacturer's labeling recommends every 6 hours as needed. Do not exceed acetaminophen 4 g/day.

Geriatric Pain management: Oral: There are no dosage adjustments provided in the manufacturer's labeling; however, use with caution and begin at the lower end of the dosing range.

Immediate release: *Severe pain:* Elderly >70 years (off-label dosing): Consider decreasing the initial dose **(based on oxycodone content)** by 25% to 50%, then titrating the dose upward or downward as needed; monitor frequently during titration. Do not exceed acetaminophen 4 g/day (APS, 2008).

Pediatric

Note: Initial dose is based on the **oxycodone** content; however, the maximum daily dose is based on the **acetaminophen** content.

Pain management: Children and Adolescents (off-label; American Pain Society [APS] 2008): Oral: **Immediate-release:** Doses should be titrated to appropriate analgesic effects:

Moderate pain: Initial dose, **based on oxycodone content**: 0.1 to 0.2 mg/kg/dose. Doses typically given every 4 to 6 hours as needed; manufacturer's labeling recommends every 6 hours as needed; maxi mum initial oxycodone dose: 5 mg/dose. Do not exceed maximum daily acetaminophen dose: Children <45 kg: 90 mg/kg/day; Children ≥45 kg: 4 g/day

Severe pain: Initial dose, **based on oxycodone content**: 0.2 mg/kg/dose. Doses typically given every 4 to 6 hours as needed; manufacturer's labeling recommends every 6 hours as needed; maximum initial oxycodone dose: 10 mg. Do not exceed maximum daily acetaminophen dose: Children <45 kg: 90 mg/kg/day; Children ≥45 kg: 4 g/day

Renal Impairment

Extended-release: Initial dose: One tablet every 12 hours; adjust dose as needed.

Immediate-release: There are no dosage adjustments provided in the manufacturer's labeling. Use with caution; reduced clearance in severe impairment may require dosage adjustment.

Hepatic Impairment

Extended-release: Initial dose: One tablet every 12 hours; adjust dose as needed.

Immediate-release: There are no dosage adjustments provided in the manufacturer's labeling. Use with caution; reduced clearance in severe impairment may require dosage adjustment.

Mechanism of Action

Oxycodone: Blocks pain perception in the cerebral cortex by binding to specific receptor molecules (opiate receptors) within the neuronal membranes of synapses. This binding results in a decreased synaptic chemical transmission throughout the CNS thus inhibiting the flow of pain sensations into the higher centers. Mu and kappa are the two subtypes of the opiate receptor to which oxycodone binds to cause analgesia.

Acetaminophen: Inhibits the synthesis of prostaglandins in the CNS and peripherally blocks pain impulse generation; produces antipyresis from inhibition of hypothalamic heat-regulating center.

Contraindications

Hypersensitivity (eg, anaphylaxis) to oxycodone, acetaminophen, or any component of the formulation; significant respiratory depression; acute or severe bronchial asthma (in an unmonitored setting or in the absence of resuscitative equipment); hypercarbia; GI obstruction, including paralytic ileus (known or suspected)

Documentation of allergenic cross-reactivity for opioids is limited. However, because of similarities in chemical structure and/or pharmacologic actions, the possibility of cross-sensitivity cannot be ruled out with certainty.

Warnings/Precautions Hypersensitivity and anaphylactic reactions have been reported with acetaminophen use; discontinue immediately if symptoms of allergic or hypersensitivity reactions occur. Serious and potentially fatal skin reactions, including acute generalized exanthematous pustulosis (AGEP), Stevens-Johnson syndrome (SJS), and toxic epidermal necrolysis (TEN), have occurred rarely with acetaminophen use; discontinue therapy at the first appearance of skin rash. Use with caution in patients with hepatic or renal impairment; thyroid dysfunction; adrenal insufficiency, including Addison disease; seizure disorder; toxic psychosis; delirium tremens; morbid obesity; biliary tract impairment; acute pancreatitis; prostatic hyperplasia; or urethral stricture. Use with caution in patients with known G6PD deficiency. May obscure diagnosis or clinical course of patients with acute abdominal conditions. Avoid use in patients with impaired consciousness or coma. Some preparations contain sulfites which may cause allergic reactions. May cause CNS depression, which may impair physical or mental abilities; caution must be used in performing tasks which require alertness (eg, operating machinery or driving). May cause severe hypotension (including orthostatic hypotension and syncope); use with caution in patients with hypovolemia, cardiovascular disease (including acute MI), or drugs which may exaggerate hypotensive effects (including phenothiazines or general anesthetics). Monitor for symptoms of hypotension following initiation or dose titration. Avoid use in patients with circulatory shock. Oxycodone decreases bowel motility, monitor for decreased bowel motility in postop patients receiving opioids. Concurrent use of mixed agonist/antagonist analgesics (eg, pentazocine, nalbuphine, butorphanol) or partial agonist (eg, buprenorphine) analgesics may precipitate withdrawal symptoms and/or reduced analgesic efficacy in patients following prolonged therapy with mu opioid agonists. Abrupt discontinuation following prolonged use may also lead to withdrawal symptoms. Taper dose gradually when discontinuing. Use with caution in patients with hypersensitivity reactions to other phenanthrene-derivative opioid agonists (codeine, hydrocodone, hydromorphone, levorphanol, oxymorphone).

Use opioids with caution for chronic pain in patients with mental health conditions (eg, depression, anxiety disorders, post-traumatic stress disorder) due to increased risk for opioid use disorder and overdose; more frequent monitoring is recommended (Dowell [CDC 2016]). **[US Boxed Warning]: Serious, life-threatening, or fatal respiratory depression may occur. Monitor closely for respiratory depression, especially during initiation or dose escalation. Swallow oxycodone/acetaminophen ER whole; crushing, chewing, or dissolving oxycodone/acetaminophen ER can cause rapid release and absorption of a potentially fatal dose of oxycodone.** Carbon dioxide retention from opioid-induced respiratory depression can exacerbate the sedating effects of opioids. Use with caution and monitor for respiratory depression in patients with significant chronic obstructive pulmonary disease or cor pulmonale, and those with a substantially decreased respiratory reserve, hypoxia, hypercapnia, or preexisting respiratory depression, particularly when initiating and titrating therapy; critical respiratory depression may occur, even at therapeutic dosages. Consider the use of alternative nonopioid analgesics in these patients. Use opioids with caution for chronic pain and titrate dosage cautiously in patients with risk factors for sleep-disordered breathing, including HF and obesity. Avoid opioids in patients with moderate to severe sleep-disordered breathing (Dowell [CDC 2016]). Use with extreme caution in patients with head injury, intracranial lesions, or increased intracranial pressure. Risk of respiratory depression is increased in elderly and cachectic or debilitated patients. Oxycodone clearance may be slightly reduced in the elderly; use with caution and consider dosage adjustments or the use of alternative nonopioid analgesics in these patients. Use opioids for chronic pain with caution in older adults and monitor closely due to an increased potential for risks, including certain risks such as falls/fracture, cognitive impairment, and constipation (Dowell [CDC 2016]). Use with caution in patients with alcoholic liver disease; consuming ≥3 alcoholic drinks/day may increase the risk of liver damage. Limit acetaminophen dose from all sources (prescription and OTC) to <4 g/day in adults. Do not use oxycodone/acetaminophen concomitantly with other acetaminophen-containing products. Oxycodone may cause constipation which may be problematic in patients with unstable angina and patients post- myocardial infarction.

Potentially significant drug-drug interactions may exist, requiring dose or frequency adjustment, additional monitoring, and/or selection of alternative therapy. **[US Boxed Warning]: Concomitant use of opioids with benzodiazepines or other CNS depressants, including alcohol, may result in profound sedation, respiratory depression, coma, and death. Reserve concomitant prescribing of oxycodone/acetaminophen and benzodiazepines or other CNS depressants for use in patients for whom alternative treatment options are inadequate. Limit dosage and durations to the minimum required and follow patients for signs and symptoms of respiratory depression and sedation.**

[US Boxed Warning]: Prolonged use of opioids during pregnancy can cause neonatal withdrawal syndrome in the newborn which may be life-threatening if not recognized and treated according to protocols developed by neonatology experts. If opioid use is required for a prolonged period in a pregnant woman, advise the patient of the risk of neonatal opioid withdrawal syndrome and ensure that appropriate treatment will be available. Signs and symptoms include irritability, hyperactivity and abnormal sleep pattern, high pitched cry, tremor, vomiting, diarrhea and failure to gain weight. Onset, duration and severity depend on the drug used, duration of use, maternal dose, and rate of drug elimination by the newborn.

[US Boxed Warning]: Use exposes patients and other users to the risks of opioid addiction, abuse, and misuse, which can lead to overdose and death. Assess each patient's risk prior to prescribing oxycodone/acetaminophen, and monitor all patients regularly for the development of these behaviors or conditions. Use with caution in patients with a history of drug abuse or acute alcoholism; potential for drug dependency exists. Other factors associated with increased risk for misuse include younger age, concomitant depression (major), and psychotropic medication use. Consider offering naloxone prescriptions in patients with factors associated with an increased risk for overdose, such as history of overdose or substance use disorder, higher opioid dosages (≥50 morphine milligram equivalents/day orally), and concomitant benzodiazepine use (Dowell [CDC 2016]). Abuse or misuse of ER tablets by crushing, chewing, snorting, or injecting the dissolved product will result in the uncontrolled delivery of the oxycodone and can result in overdose and death.

Chronic pain: Opioids should **not** be used as first-line therapy for chronic pain management (pain >3-month duration or beyond time of normal tissue healing) due to limited short-term benefits, undetermined long-term benefits, and association with serious risks (eg, overdose, MI, auto accidents, risk of developing opioid use disorder). Preferred management includes nonpharmacologic therapy and nonopioid therapy (eg, NSAIDs, acetaminophen, certain anticonvulsants and antidepressants). If opioid therapy is initiated, it should be combined with nonpharmacologic and nonopioid therapy, as appropriate. Prior to initiation, known risks of opioid therapy should be discussed and realistic treatment goals for pain/function should be established, including consideration for discontinuation if benefits do not outweigh risks. Therapy should be continued only if clinically meaningful improvement in pain/function outweighs risks. Therapy should be initiated at the lowest effective dosage using immediate-release opioids (instead of extended-release/long-acting opioids). Risk associated with use increases with higher opioid dosages. Risks and benefits should be re-evaluated when increasing dosage to ≥50 morphine milligram equivalents (MME)/day orally; dosages ≥90 MME/day orally should be avoided unless carefully justified (Dowell [CDC 2016]).

[US Boxed Warning]: Acetaminophen has been associated with cases of acute liver failure, at times resulting in liver transplant and death. Most of the cases of liver injury are associated with the use of acetaminophen at doses that exceed 4 g/day, and often involve more than 1 acetaminophen-containing product. Risk is increased with alcohol use, preexisting liver disease, and intake of more than one source of acetaminophen-containing medications. Chronic daily dosing in adults has also resulted in liver damage in some patients.

[US Boxed Warning]: Accidental ingestion of oxycodone/acetaminophen, especially in children, can result in a fatal overdose of oxycodone/acetaminophen. Do not to presoak, lick or otherwise wet ER tablets prior to placing in the mouth; take one tablet at a time with enough water to ensure complete swallowing. Oxycodone/acetaminophen ER is not interchangeable with other oxycodone/acetaminophen products because of differing pharmacokinetic profiles that affect the frequency of administration. Do not abruptly stop ER tablets in patients who may be physically dependent; gradually decrease dose by 50% every 2 to 4 days to prevent signs and symptoms of withdrawal. Due to characteristics of the ER formulation that cause the tablets to swell and become sticky when wet, consider use of an alternative analgesic in patients who have difficulty swallowing and patients at risk for underlying GI disorders resulting in a small GI lumen.

[US Boxed Warning]: The concomitant use of oxycodone/acetaminophen with all cytochrome P450 3A4 inhibitors may result in an increase in oxycodone plasma concentrations, which could increase or prolong adverse reactions and may cause potentially fatal respiratory depression. In addition, discontinuation of a concomitantly used cytochrome P450 3A4 inducer may result in an increase in oxycodone plasma concentration. Monitor patients receiving oxycodone/acetaminophen and any CYP3A4 inhibitor or inducer.

An opioid-containing analgesic regimen should be tailored to each patient's needs and based upon the type of pain being treated (acute versus chronic), the route of administration, degree of tolerance for opioids (naive versus chronic user), age, weight, and medical condition. The optimal analgesic dose varies widely among patients; doses should be titrated to pain relief/prevention. Opioids decrease bowel motility; monitor for decrease bowel motility in postop patients receiving opioids. Use with caution in the perioperative setting; individualize treatment when transitioning from parenteral to oral analgesics. Some dosage forms may contain sodium benzoate/benzoic acid; benzoic acid (benzoate) is a metabolite of benzyl alcohol; large amounts of benzyl alcohol (≥99 mg/kg/day) have been associated with a potentially fatal toxicity ("gasping syndrome") in neonates; the "gasping syndrome" consists of metabolic acidosis, respiratory distress, gasping respirations, CNS dysfunction (including convulsions, intracranial hemorrhage), hypotension, and cardiovascular collapse (AAP ["Inactive" 1997]; CDC 1982); some data suggests that benzoate displaces bilirubin from protein binding sites (Ahlfors 2001); avoid or use dosage forms containing benzyl alcohol derivative with caution in neonates. See manufacturer's labeling.

Drug Interactions

Metabolism/Transport Effects Refer to individual components.

Avoid Concomitant Use

Avoid concomitant use of Oxycodone and Acetaminophen with any of the following: Azelastine (Nasal); Conivaptan; Eluxadoline; Fusidic Acid (Systemic); Idelalisib; Mixed Agonist / Antagonist Opioids; Orphenadrine; Oxomemazine; Paraldehyde; Thalidomide

Increased Effect/Toxicity

Oxycodone and Acetaminophen may increase the levels/effects of: Alvimopan; Azelastine (Nasal); Blonanserin; Busulfan; Dasatinib; Desmopressin; Diuretics; Eluxadoline; Flunitrazepam; HYDROcodone; Imatinib; MAO Inhibitors; Methotrimeprazine; MetyroSINE; Mipomersen; Orphenadrine; Paraldehyde; Phenylephrine (Systemic); Piribedil; Pramipexole; Prilocaine; Ramosetron; ROPINIRole; Rotigotine; Selective Serotonin Reuptake Inhibitors; Serotonin Modulators; Sodium Nitrite; SORAfenib; Suvorexant; Thalidomide; Vitamin K Antagonists; Zolpidem

The levels/effects of Oxycodone and Acetaminophen may be increased by: Amphetamines; Anticholinergic Agents; Aprepitant; Brimonidine (Topical); Cannabis; Chlormethiazole; Chlorphenesin Carbamate; CNS Depressants; Conivaptan; CYP3A4 Inhibitors (Moderate); CYP3A4 Inhibitors (Strong); Dapsone (Topical); Dasatinib; Dimethindene (Topical); Dronabinol; Droperidol; Fosaprepitant; Fusidic Acid (Systemic); Idelalisib; Isoniazid; Ivacaftor; Kava Kava; Lofexidine; Magnesium Sulfate; Methotrimeprazine; MetyraPONE; MiFEPRIStone; Minocycline; Nabilone; Netupitant; Nitric Oxide; Oxomemazine; Palbociclib; Perampanel; Probenecid; Rufinamide; Simeprevir; Sodium Oxybate; SORAfenib; Stiripentol; Succinylcholine; Tapentadol; Tetracaine (Topical); Tetrahydrocannabinol; Voriconazole

Decreased Effect

Oxycodone and Acetaminophen may decrease the levels/effects of: Diuretics; Gastrointestinal Agents (Prokinetic); Pegvisomant

The levels/effects of Oxycodone and Acetaminophen may be decreased by: Bosentan; Cholestyramine Resin; CYP3A4 Inducers (Moderate); CYP3A4 Inducers (Strong); Dabrafenib; Deferasirox; Enzalutamide; Mitotane; Mixed Agonist / Antagonist Opioids; Nalmefene; Naltrexone; RifAMPin; Siltuximab; St John's Wort; Tocilizumab

Pharmacodynamics/Kinetics

Onset of Action Within 10 to 15 minutes; Peak effect: Within 1 hour

Duration of Action 3 to 6 hours

Pregnancy Considerations

Animal reproduction studies have not been conducted with this combination. Refer to individual monographs.

[US Boxed Warning]: Prolonged use of opioids during pregnancy can result in neonatal opioid withdrawal syndrome, which may be life-threatening if not recognized and requires management according to protocols developed by neonatology experts. If opioid use is required for a prolonged period in a pregnant woman, advise the patient of the risk of neonatal opioid withdrawal syndrome and ensure appropriate treatment will available.

Breastfeeding Considerations Oxycodone and acetaminophen are excreted in breast milk. Due to the potential for serious adverse reactions in the nursing infant, breastfeeding is not recommended by the manufacturer. Refer to individual monographs.

Controlled Substance C-II

Dosage Forms

Solution, Oral:

Generic: Oxycodone 5 mg and acetaminophen 325 mg per 5 mL

Tablet, Oral:

Endocet 2.5/325: Oxycodone 2.5 mg and acetaminophen 325 mg

Endocet 5/325 [scored]: Oxycodone 5 mg and acetaminophen 325 mg

Endocet 7.5/325: Oxycodone 7.5 mg and acetaminophen 325 mg

Endocet 10/325: Oxycodone 10 mg and acetaminophen 325 mg

Percocet 2.5/325: Oxycodone 2.5 mg and acetaminophen 325 mg

Percocet 5/325 [scored]: Oxycodone 5 mg and acetaminophen 325 mg

Percocet 7.5/325: Oxycodone 7.5 mg and acetaminophen 325 mg

Percocet 10/325: Oxycodone 10 mg and acetaminophen 325 mg

Primlev 5/300: Oxycodone 5 mg and acetaminophen 300 mg

Primlev 7.5/300: Oxycodone 7.5 mg and acetaminophen 300 mg

Primlev 10/300: Oxycodone 10 mg and acetaminophen 300 mg

Generic: 2.5/325: Oxycodone hydrochloride 2.5 mg and acetaminophen 325 mg; 5/325: Oxycodone hydrochloride 5 mg and acetaminophen 325 mg; 7.5/325: Oxycodone hydrochloride 7.5 mg and acetaminophen 325 mg; 10/325: Oxycodone hydrochloride 10 mg and acetaminophen 325 mg

Tablet, Extended Release, Oral:

Xartemis XR: Oxycodone hydrochloride 7.5 mg and acetaminophen 325 mg

Dental Comment Although the ***OTC product labeling*** for acetaminophen products state to limit the maximum dose to 3,000 mg daily (for extra strength) or 3,250 mg (for regular strength) (see this site for details: http://www.tylenolprofessional.com/extra-strength-tylenol-dosage-faq.html), it is still appropriate for patients to take up to 4,000 mg daily "under the direction of a healthcare provider" (http://www.tylenolprofessional.com/assets/v4/faqs-new-dosing.pdf).

Oxycodone, as with other opioid analgesics, is recommended only for limited acute dosing (ie, 3 days or less). Oxycodone has an addictive liability, especially when given long-term. The acetaminophen component requires use with caution in patients who use alcohol, with preexisting liver disease, and those receiving more than one source of acetaminophen-containing medication.

Hepatotoxicity caused by acetaminophen is potentiated by chronic alcohol consumption. People who are taking acetaminophen, even at therapeutic doses, and consume alcohol are at risk of developing hepatotoxicity.

Acetaminophen may increase the levels and enhance the anticoagulant effects of vitamin K antagonists acenocoumarol and warfarin (Coumadin). Studies have reported that acetaminophen has increased the INR in warfarin treated patients with daily acetaminophen doses as low as 2 g, particularly when taking acetaminophen for >1 week (Antlitz, 1968; Boeijinga, 1982; Gebauer, 2003; Hylek, 1998; Rubin, 1984). In addition, case reports of bleeding as a result of increased INR have been published (Bagheri, 1999; Bartle, 1991). There is no known mechanism of the interaction; furthermore, some studies have failed to demonstrate this interaction (Gadisseur, 2003; Kwan, 1995; van den Bemt, 2002). In terms of risk, the data suggest that acetaminophen and warfarin could interact in some clinically significant manner but that the benefits of concomitant use of acetaminophen for pain control in dental patients taking warfarin usually outweigh the risks. An appropriate monitoring plan should be in place to identify potential negative effects and dosage adjustments may be necessary in a minority of patients. The interaction may be more likely to occur with daily acetaminophen doses of >1.3 g for >1 week.

There are no reports of acetaminophen interacting with antiplatelet drugs such as aspirin, clopidogrel (Plavix), or prasugrel (Effient). Also, there are no reports of acetaminophen in combination with hydrocodone, codeine, or oxycodone interacting with warfarin (Coumadin).

Oxycodone and Naloxone

(oks i KOE done & nal OKS one)

Related Information

Naloxone *on page 1164*

OxyCODONE *on page 1255*

Brand Names: Canada Targin

Pharmacologic Category Analgesic, Opioid; Opioid Antagonist

Use

Pain management: Management of pain severe enough to require daily, around-the-clock, long-term opioid treatment and for which alternative treatment options are inadequate.

Limitations of use: Reserve for use in patients whom alternative treatment options (eg, nonopioid analgesics, immediate-release opioids) are ineffective, not tolerated, or would be otherwise inadequate to provide sufficient management of pain. Not indicated as an as-needed analgesic.

Local Anesthetic/Vasoconstrictor Precautions No information available to require special precautions

Effects on Dental Treatment Key adverse event(s) related to dental treatment: Nausea and xerostomia (normal salivary flow resumes upon discontinuation)

Effects on Bleeding No information available to require special precautions

Adverse Reactions

1% to 10%:

Cardiovascular: Peripheral edema (2% to 5%)

Central nervous system: Withdrawal syndrome (7%), fatigue (5%), headache (5%), depression (2%), dizziness (2%), drowsiness (1%), migraine (1%)

Dermatologic: Hyperhidrosis (7%), skin rash (1%)

Endocrine & metabolic: Increased serum glucose (2%), hyperglycemia (1%), hyperlipidemia (1%), hyperuricemia (1%), increased gamma-glutamyl transferase (1%)

Gastrointestinal: Nausea (3% to 8%), abdominal pain (<1% to 8%), anorexia (<1% to 8%), constipation (3% to 7%), vomiting (1% to 7%), xerostomia (3%), abdominal distention (2%), diarrhea (2%), gastroenteritis (2%)

Genitourinary: Urinary tract infection (4%)

Hematologic & oncologic: Anemia (5%), decreased hemoglobin (≤5%)

Infection: Viral infection (2%), influenza (1%)

Neuromuscular & skeletal: Weakness (7%), osteoarthritis (1%), tremor (1%)

Respiratory: Bronchitis (2%), sinusitis (1%)

<1%, postmarketing, and/or case reports: Abnormal dreams, abnormality in thinking, anal fissure, angina pectoris, anorectal pain, antisocial behavior, anxiety, biliary obstruction, blurred vision, candidiasis, cellulitis, chest pain, cholelithiasis, cold extremities, confusion, cough, deafness, decreased blood pressure, decreased hematocrit, decreased platelet count, decreased red blood cells, disorientation, diverticulitis, dry eye syndrome, dysgeusia, dysmenorrhea, dyspnea, dyspnea on exertion, ECG abnormality, eczema, epistaxis, equilibrium disturbance, erectile dysfunction, eructation, euphoria, falling, first degree atrioventricular block, furuncle, gastritis, gastroesophageal reflux disease, gastrointestinal hemorrhage, glossitis, gout, gouty arthritis, hallucination, hemoptysis, hypersensitivity, hypertensive crisis, hypogonadism (Brennan, 2013; Debono, 2011), hyponatremia, hypophosphatemia, hypotension, impacted cerumen, increased blood pressure, increased heart rate, increased lacrimation, increased lactate dehydrogenase, increased liver enzymes, increased serum alt, increased serum bilirubin, irritability, joint swelling, laceration, lack of concentration, lipoma, loss of libido, lower abdominal pain, memory impairment, muscle injury, muscle spasm, muscle twitching, musculoskeletal chest pain, myalgia, neuromuscular blockade, night sweats, nightmares, otitis externa, palpitations, panic attack, paresthesia, periodontitis, photopsia, pneumonia, pollakiuria, polyarthritis, polyneuropathy, pruritic rash, pruritus, respiratory depression, restless leg syndrome, restless sleep, rhinitis, right bundle branch block, sedation, sensation of cold, shoulder pain, speech disturbance, sprain, stiffness, stupor, syncope, tenosynovitis, tension headache, thrombophlebitis, thrombosis, tinnitus, tonic-clonic seizures, urinary incontinence, urinary retention, urinary urgency, vaginal hemorrhage, visual disturbance, weight loss, yawning

Dosing

Adult Pain management: Oral:

Note: Do not exceed oxycodone 80 mg/naloxone 40 mg daily. Single doses greater than oxycodone 40 mg/naloxone 20 mg or a total dose greater than oxycodone 80 mg/naloxone 40 mg daily are for use only in opioid-tolerant patients. Opioid tolerance is defined as: Patients already taking at least 60 mg of oral morphine daily, 25 mcg of transdermal fentanyl per hour, 30 mg of oral oxycodone daily, 8 mg oral hydromorphone daily, 25 mg oral oxymorphone daily, 60 mg oral hydrocodone daily or an equivalent dose of another opioid for at least 1 week.

Opioid-naive or not opioid tolerant: Initial: Oxycodone 10 mg/naloxone 5 mg every 12 hours

Converting from other opioids:

Currently on other oral oxycodone formulations: Administer 50% of the patient's total daily oral oxycodone dose as oxycodone/naloxone every 12 hours.

Currently on other oral opioids: Discontinue all other around-the-clock opioids; convert the patient's current total daily opioid dose(s) to an equivalent daily oral morphine dose (see manufacturer's labeling for conversion instructions). After equivalent daily oral morphine dose is determined, initiate oxycodone/naloxone as follows:

Oxycodone 10 mg/naloxone 5 mg every 12 hours (for patients with an equivalent daily oral morphine dose of 20 to <70 mg).

Oxycodone 20 mg/naloxone 10 mg every 12 hours (for patients with an equivalent daily oral morphine dose of 70 to <110 mg).

Oxycodone 30 mg/naloxone 15 mg every 12 hours (for patients with an equivalent daily oral morphine dose of 110 to <150 mg)

Oxycodone 40 mg/naloxone 20 mg every 12 hours (for patients with an equivalent daily oral morphine dose of 150 to 160 mg)

Currently on transdermal fentanyl: Initial: Oxycodone 10 mg/naloxone 5 mg every 12 hours substituted for each 25 mcg/hour fentanyl transdermal patch beginning 18 hours after removal of the transdermal fentanyl patch. Monitor closely during conversion.

Currently on transdermal buprenorphine: Initial: Oxycodone 10 mg/naloxone 5 mg every 12 hours for patients receiving transdermal buprenorphine (≤20 mcg/hour). Monitor closely during conversion.

Dose adjustment: Dose is individualized; titrate dose cautiously in increments of oxycodone 10 mg/naloxone 5 mg every 12 hours every 1 to 2 days until satisfactory response and acceptable adverse effects. Repeated pain at the end of the dosing interval may indicate the need for a dose adjustment rather than adjusting the dosing interval.

Patients requiring rescue medication: Patients who experience breakthrough pain may require a rescue medication with an appropriate dose of an immediate-release analgesic. **Note:** Rescue medications used in clinical trials were immediate release oxycodone or combination products containing codeine.

There are no specific recommendations made in the manufacturer's US labeling; however, the following recommendations have been made: Administer 1 dose of an immediate release opioid approximately one-sixth of the equivalent daily dose of oxycodone. Patients requiring >2 doses daily of rescue medication should have oxycodone/naloxone dose titrated upward every 1 to 2 days until satisfactory response is achieved (not to exceed recommended maximum dosing). Dosing interval (every 12 hours) should not be adjusted. (Targin Canadian product labeling 2016)

Dosage adjustment for concomitant therapy: Concomitant CNS depressants: Initiate oxycodone/naloxone with 33% to 50% of the calculated recommended dose and consider using a lower concomitant CNS depressant dose.

Discontinuation of therapy: Decrease dose by 25% to 50% each day every 2 to 4 days; monitor carefully for signs/symptoms of withdrawal. If patient displays withdrawal symptoms, increase dose to previous dose and then reduce dose more slowly by increasing interval between dose reductions, decreasing amount of daily dose reduction, or both. See manufacturer's labeling for detailed instruction.

Geriatric Refer to adult dosing. Initiate therapy at low end of dosing range; titrate dose cautiously to lowest dose that provides adequate pain relief with acceptable side effects.

Renal Impairment Reduce dose to 50% of the usual starting dose; titrate cautiously; consider use of alternative treatments without naloxone in patients with severe renal impairment.

Hepatic Impairment

Mild impairment: Initial: Reduce dose to 33% to 50% of the usual starting dose; titrate cautiously.

Moderate to severe impairment: Use is contraindicated.

Mechanism of Action

Oxycodone: Binds to opiate receptors in the CNS, causing inhibition of ascending pain pathways, altering the perception of and response to pain; produces generalized CNS depression; also binds to opiate receptors in peripheral organs including the gut to induce constipation.

Naloxone: Pure opioid antagonist that competes and displaces opioids at opioid receptor sites, including gut opioid receptors, which counteracts opioid-induced constipation.

Contraindications

Hypersensitivity (eg, anaphylaxis) to oxycodone, naloxone, or any component of the formulation; significant respiratory depression; acute or severe bronchial asthma in an unmonitored setting or in the absence of resuscitative equipment; GI obstruction, including paralytic ileus (known or suspected); moderate-to-severe hepatic impairment.

Documentation of allergenic cross-reactivity for opioids is limited. However, because of similarities in chemical structure and/or pharmacologic actions, the possibility of cross-sensitivity cannot be ruled out with certainty.

Canadian labeling: Additional contraindications (not in US labeling): Hypersensitivity to other opioids; rectal administration; suspected surgical abdomen (eg, acute appendicitis or pancreatitis); mild, intermittent, or short duration pain that can be managed with other pain medications; management of acute pain, including use in outpatient or day surgeries; management of perioperative pain; obstructive airway (other than bronchial asthma); cor pulmonale; hypercapnia; acute alcoholism, delirium tremens, and convulsive disorders; severe CNS depression, increased cerebrospinal or intracranial pressure, and head injury; severe renal impairment; concurrent use or use within 14 days of monoamine oxidase (MAO) inhibitors; opioid-dependent patients and for opioid withdrawal treatment; use in women who are breastfeeding, pregnant, or during labor and delivery

Warnings/Precautions [US Boxed Warning]: Serious, life-threatening, or fatal respiratory depression may occur with use of oxycodone/naloxone ER.

Monitor for respiratory depression, especially during initiation of therapy or following a dose increase. Carbon dioxide retention from opioid-induced respiratory depression can exacerbate the sedating effects of opioids. Use with caution and monitor for respiratory depression in patients with significant chronic obstructive pulmonary disease or cor pulmonale, and those with a substantially decreased respiratory reserve, hypoxia, hypercapnia, or preexisting respiratory depression, particularly when initiating and titrating therapy; critical respiratory depression may occur, even at therapeutic dosages. Consider the use of alternative nonopioid analgesics in these patients.

[US Boxed Warning]: Accidental ingestion of even one dose of oxycodone/naloxone ER, especially in children, can result in a fatal overdose of oxycodone.

[US Boxed Warning]: Use exposes patients and other users to the risks of opioid addiction, abuse, and misuse, which can lead to overdose and death. Assess each patient's risk prior to prescribing oxycodone/naloxone ER, and monitor all patients regularly for the development of these behaviors or conditions. Crushing, chewing, or dissolving the product can cause rapid release and absorption of a potentially fatal dose of oxycodone. Use with caution in patients with a history of drug abuse, acute alcoholism, or mental illness (eg, major depression); potential for drug dependency exists. Tolerance, psychological, and physical dependence may occur with prolonged use. Other factors associated with increased risk include younger age and psychotropic medication use. Consider offering naloxone prescriptions in patients with factors associated with an increased risk for overdose, such as history of overdose or substance use disorder, higher opioid dosages (≥50 morphine milligram equivalents/day orally), and concomitant benzodiazepine use (Dowell [CDC 2016]).

Chronic pain: Opioids should **not** be used as first-line therapy for chronic pain management (pain >3-month duration or beyond time of normal tissue healing) due to limited short-term benefits, undetermined long-term benefits, and association with serious risks (eg, overdose, MI, auto accidents, risk of developing opioid use disorder). Preferred management includes nonpharmacologic therapy and nonopioid therapy (eg, NSAIDs, acetaminophen, certain anticonvulsants and antidepressants). If opioid therapy is initiated, it should be combined with nonpharmacologic and nonopioid therapy, as appropriate. Prior to initiation, known risks of opioid therapy should be discussed and realistic treatment goals for pain/function should be established, including consideration for discontinuation if benefits do not outweigh risks. Therapy should be continued only if clinically meaningful improvement in pain/function outweighs risks. Therapy should be initiated at the lowest effective dosage using immediate-release opioids (instead of extended-release/long-acting opioids). Risk associated with use increases with higher opioid dosages. Risks and benefits should be re-evaluated when increasing dosage to ≥50 morphine milligram equivalents (MME)/day orally; dosages ≥90 MME/day orally should be avoided unless carefully justified (Dowell [CDC 2016]).

[US Boxed Warning]: Concomitant use of all CYP450 3A4 inhibitors may result in an increase in oxycodone plasma concentrations, which could increase or prolong adverse drug effects and may cause potentially fatal respiratory depression. In addition, discontinuation of a concomitantly used CYP450 3A4 inducer may result in an increase in oxycodone plasma concentration. Monitor patients receiving oxycodone/naloxone ER and any CYP3A4 inhibitor or inducer. Potentially significant interactions may exist requiring dose or frequency adjustment, additional monitoring, and/or selection of alternative therapy. **[US Boxed Warning]: Concomitant use of opioids with benzodiazepines or other CNS depressants, including alcohol, may result in profound sedation, respiratory depression, coma, and death. Reserve concomitant prescribing of oxycodone/naloxone ER and benzodiazepines or other CNS depressants for use in patients for whom alternative treatment options are inadequate. Limit dosage and durations to the minimum required and follow patients for signs and symptoms of respiratory depression and sedation.**

[US Boxed Warning]: Prolonged use of opioids during pregnancy can result in neonatal opioid withdrawal syndrome, which may be life-threatening if not recognized and requires management according to protocols developed by neonatology experts. If opioid use is required for a prolonged period in a pregnant woman, advise the patient of the risk of neonatal opioid withdrawal syndrome and ensure appropriate treatment will be available. Signs and symptoms include irritability, hyperactivity and abnormal sleep pattern, high pitched cry, tremor, vomiting, diarrhea and failure to gain weight. Onset, duration and severity depend on the drug used, duration of use, maternal dose, and rate of drug elimination by the newborn.

Tablets must be swallowed whole; tablets that are broken, crushed, chewed, or dissolved may result in a rapid release and absorption of a potentially fatal dose of oxycodone. Do not exceed maximum recommended doses and limit use to patients in whom alternative treatment options (eg, nonopioid analgesics or immediate-release opioids) are ineffective, not tolerated, or otherwise inadequate to provide sufficient pain relief. Not indicated as an as-needed analgesic. Limit use of the 40 mg/20 mg tablet dosage form to patients with established tolerance to an opioid of comparable potency **(single doses >40 mg or daily doses >80 mg of oxycodone may cause fatal respiratory depression in patients who are not tolerant to the respiratory depressant effects of opioids)**.

May cause CNS depression, which may impair physical or mental abilities; patients must be cautioned about performing tasks which require mental alertness (eg, operating machinery or driving). Use with extreme caution in patients with head injury, intracranial lesions, or elevated intracranial pressure; exaggerated elevation of ICP may occur. Avoid use in patients with impaired consciousness or coma.

May cause severe hypotension (including orthostatic hypotension and syncope); use with caution in patients with hypovolemia, cardiovascular disease (including acute MI), or drugs which may exaggerate hypotensive effects (including phenothiazines or general anesthetics). Monitor for symptoms of hypotension following initiation or dose titration; dose adjustment may be warranted. Avoid use in patients with circulatory shock. Use with caution in patients with hypersensitivity reactions to other phenanthrene-derivative opioid agonists (codeine, hydrocodone, hydromorphone, levorphanol, oxymorphone).

Use opioids with caution for chronic pain in patients with mental health conditions (eg, depression, anxiety disorders, post-traumatic stress disorder) due to increased risk for opioid use disorder and overdose; more frequent monitoring is recommended (Dowell [CDC 2016]). Use with caution in patients with adrenal insufficiency (including Addison disease), biliary tract dysfunction, acute pancreatitis, prostatic hyperplasia and/or urinary stricture, history of seizure disorders, thyroid dysfunction, delirium tremens, toxic psychosis, and those who are morbidly obese. Use opioids with caution for chronic pain and titrate dosage cautiously in patients with risk factors for sleep-disordered breathing, including HF and obesity. Avoid opioids in patients with moderate to severe sleep-disordered breathing (Dowell [CDC 2016]). Use with caution in cachetic, debilitated patients and in the elderly; consider the use of alternative nonopioid analgesics in these patients. Use opioids for chronic pain with caution in older adults; monitor closely due to an increased potential for risks, including certain risks such as falls/fracture, cognitive impairment, and constipation. Clearance may also be reduced in older adults (with or without renal impairment) resulting in a narrow therapeutic window and increasing the risk for respiratory depression or overdose (Dowell [CDC 2016]).

Use with caution in patients with mild hepatic impairment; use is contraindicated with moderate to severe hepatic impairment. Use with caution in patients with renal impairment. May obscure diagnosis or clinical course of patients with acute abdominal conditions. Oxycodone may cause constipation which may be problematic in patients with unstable angina and patients post-myocardial infarction. Consider preventive measures (eg, stool softener, increased fiber) to reduce the potential for constipation.

Opioids decrease bowel motility; monitor for decreased bowel motility in postoperative patients receiving opioids. Patients interrupting therapy to undergo pain-relieving procedures (eg, chordotomy) may require a dosage adjustment when resuming therapy after the postoperative recovery period.

An opioid-containing analgesic regimen should be tailored to each patient's needs and based upon the type of pain being treated (acute versus chronic), the route of administration, degree of tolerance for opioids (naive versus chronic user), age, weight, and medical condition. The optimal analgesic dose varies widely among patients; doses should be titrated to pain relief/prevention. Concurrent use of agonist/antagonist (eg, pentazocine, nalbuphine, butorphanol) or partial agonist (eg, buprenorphine) analgesics may precipitate withdrawal symptoms and/or reduced analgesic efficacy in patients following prolonged therapy with mu opioid agonists. Taper dose gradually when discontinuing.

Drug Interactions

Metabolism/Transport Effects Refer to individual components.

Avoid Concomitant Use

Avoid concomitant use of Oxycodone and Naloxone with any of the following: Azelastine (Nasal); Conivaptan; Eluxadoline; Fusidic Acid (Systemic); Idelalisib; Methylnaltrexone; Mixed Agonist / Antagonist Opioids; Naldemedine; Naloxegol; Orphenadrine; Oxomemazine; Paraldehyde; Thalidomide

Increased Effect/Toxicity

Oxycodone and Naloxone may increase the levels/effects of: Alvimopan; Azelastine (Nasal); Blonanserin; Desmopressin; Diuretics; Eluxadoline; Flunitrazepam; HYDROcodone; MAO Inhibitors; Methotrimeprazine; MetyroSINE; Naldemedine; Naloxegol; Orphenadrine; Paraldehyde; Piribedil; Pramipexole; Ramosetron; ROPINIRole; Rotigotine; Selective Serotonin Reuptake Inhibitors; Serotonin Modulators; Suvorexant; Thalidomide; Zolpidem

The levels/effects of Oxycodone and Naloxone may be increased by: Amphetamines; Anticholinergic Agents; Aprepitant; Brimonidine (Topical); Cannabis; Chlormethiazole; Chlorphenesin Carbamate; CNS Depressants; Conivaptan; CYP3A4 Inhibitors (Moderate); CYP3A4 Inhibitors (Strong); Dasatinib; Dimethindene (Topical); Dronabinol; Droperidol; Fosaprepitant; Fusidic Acid (Systemic); Idelalisib; Ivacaftor; Kava Kava; Lofexidine; Magnesium Sulfate; Methotrimeprazine; Methylnaltrexone; MiFEPRIStone; Minocycline; Nabilone; Netupitant; Oxomemazine; Palbociclib; Perampanel; Rufinamide; Simeprevir; Sodium Oxybate; Stiripentol; Succinylcholine; Tapentadol; Tetrahydrocannabinol; Voriconazole

Decreased Effect

Oxycodone and Naloxone may decrease the levels/effects of: Diuretics; Gastrointestinal Agents (Prokinetic); Pegvisomant

The levels/effects of Oxycodone and Naloxone may be decreased by: Bosentan; CYP3A4 Inducers (Moderate); CYP3A4 Inducers (Strong); Dabrafenib; Deferasirox; Enzalutamide; Mitotane; Mixed Agonist / Antagonist Opioids; Nalmefene; Naltrexone; RifAMPin; Siltuximab; St John's Wort; Tocilizumab

Pharmacodynamics/Kinetics

Duration of Action Oxycodone (controlled release): ≤12 hours

Half-life Elimination

Naloxone: ~4 to 17 hours

Oxycodone (controlled release): ~4 to 5 hours

Time to Peak Oxycodone (controlled release): Plasma: 3 to 4 hours

Pregnancy Considerations [US Boxed Warning]: Prolonged use of opioids during pregnancy can result in neonatal opioid withdrawal syndrome, which may be life-threatening if not recognized and requires management according to protocols developed by neonatology experts. If opioid use is required for a prolonged period in a pregnant woman, advise the patient of the risk of neonatal opioid withdrawal syndrome and ensure appropriate treatment will be available. Animal reproduction studies have not been conducted with this combination. See individual agents.

Breastfeeding Considerations Oxycodone is excreted in breast milk; it is not known if naloxone is excreted in breast milk. Due to the potential for serious adverse reactions in the nursing infant, breastfeeding is not recommended by the manufacturer. See individual agents.

Product Availability Targiniq ER: FDA approved July 2014; anticipated availability is currently unknown.

Controlled Substance C-II

Dosage Forms: Canada

Tablet, controlled release, oral:

Targin:

Oxycodone 5 mg and naloxone 2.5 mg
Oxycodone 10 mg and naloxone 5 mg
Oxycodone 20 mg and naloxone 10 mg
Oxycodone 40 mg and naloxone 20 mg

Oxycodone and Naltrexone

(oks i KOE done & nal TREKS one)

Pharmacologic Category Analgesic, Opioid; Opioid Antagonist

Use

Pain management: Management of pain severe enough to require daily, around-the-clock, long-term opioid treatment and for which alternative treatment options are inadequate

Limitations of use: Reserve for use in patients for whom alternative treatment options (eg, nonopioid analgesics, immediate-release opioids) are ineffective, not tolerated, or would be otherwise inadequate to provide sufficient management of pain. Oxycodone/naltrexone ER is not indicated as an as-needed ("prn") analgesic.

Local Anesthetic/Vasoconstrictor Precautions No information available to require special precautions

Effects on Dental Treatment Key adverse event(s) related to dental treatment: Nausea (>10%)

Effects on Bleeding No information available to require special precautions

Adverse Reactions Also see individual agents.

>10%: Gastrointestinal: Nausea (14%)

1% to 10%:

Cardiovascular: Peripheral edema (2%), bradycardia (<2%), chest pain (<2%), edema (<2%), increased blood pressure (<2%), palpitations (<2%), tachycardia (<2%)

Central nervous system: Dizziness (4%), drug withdrawal (3%), fatigue (3%), hypoesthesia (2%), abnormal dreams (<2%), chills (<2%), confusion (<2%), disorientation (<2%), disturbance in attention (<2%), drug abuse (<2%), irritability (<2%), lethargy (<2%), malaise (<2%), migraine (<2%), pain (<2%), paresthesia (<2%), vertigo (<2%), voice disorder (<2%)

Dermatologic: Hyperhidrosis (3%), pruritus (2%), skin rash (<2%), urticaria (<2%)

Endocrine & metabolic: Decreased libido (<2%), decreased plasma testosterone (<2%), gout (<2%), increased serum glucose (<2%)

Gastrointestinal: Diarrhea (6%), vomiting (6%), constipation (3%), decreased appetite (<2%), dysgeusia (<2%), dyspepsia (<2%)

Genitourinary: Dysuria (<2%), hematuria (<2%)

Hematologic & oncologic: Anemia (<2%), lymphadenopathy (<2%)

Hepatic: Abnormal hepatic function tests (<2%)

Hypersensitivity: Hypersensitivity reaction (<2%)

Neuromuscular & skeletal: Muscle spasm (3%), arthralgia (2%), arthritis (<2%), muscle twitching (<2%), myalgia (<2%), stiffness (<2%, musculoskeletal)

Ophthalmic: Increased lacrimation (<2%)

Otic: Tinnitus (<2%)

Respiratory: Oropharyngeal pain (3%), chronic bronchitis (<2%), dyspnea (<2%), flu-like symptoms (<2%), rhinorrhea (<2%)

Miscellaneous: Fever (<2%)

<1%, postmarketing, and/or case reports: Respiratory depression

Dosing

Adult

Pain management: Oral: **Note:** Individualize treatment using the lowest effective dose for the shortest duration based on patient's pain severity, response, prior analgesic treatment experience, and risk factors for addiction/abuse/misuse. Oxycodone 60 mg/naltrexone 7.2 mg, oxycodone 80 mg/naltrexone 9.6 mg, single doses >oxycodone 40 mg/naltrexone 4.8 mg or a total daily dose >oxycodone 80 mg/naltrexone 9.6 mg should only be used in opioid-tolerant patients. Opioid tolerance is defined as: Patients already taking at least 60 mg/day of oral morphine, 25 mcg/hour of transdermal fentanyl, 30 mg/day of oral oxycodone, 8 mg/day of oral hydromorphone, 25 mg/day of oral oxymorphone, 60 mg/day of oral hydrocodone, or an equianalgesic dose of another opioid. Patients who experience breakthrough pain may require a rescue medication with an appropriate dose of an immediate-release analgesic.

Opioid-naive or not opioid tolerant: Initial: Oxycodone 10 mg/naltrexone 1.2 mg every 12 hours.

Converting from other opioids: Monitor closely during conversion:

Currently on other oral oxycodone formulations: Administer 50% of the patient's total daily oral oxycodone dose as oxycodone/naltrexone ER every 12 hours.

Currently on other oral opioids: Discontinue all other around-the-clock opioids; convert the patient's current total daily opioid dose(s) to an equivalent daily oxycodone dose (see manufacturer's labeling for conversion instructions). After equivalent daily oxycodone dose is determined, reduce the estimated total daily oxycodone dose by 50% and then divide the daily dose in half to obtain the 12 hour dose of oxycodone/naltrexone ER needed. If the total daily opioid requirement is ≤20 mg, initiate therapy with oxycodone 10 mg/naltrexone 1.2 mg every 12 hours.

Currently on transdermal fentanyl: Initial: Oxycodone 10 mg/naltrexone 1.2 mg every 12 hours substituted for each 25 mcg/hour fentanyl transdermal patch beginning at least 18 hours after removal of the transdermal fentanyl patch.

Currently on transdermal buprenorphine or tramadol: Initial: Oxycodone 10 mg/naltrexone 1.2 mg every 12 hours (initiated after discontinuing the around-the-clock buprenorphine or tramadol).

Dose adjustment: Dose is individualized; titrate dose cautiously in increments of oxycodone 20 mg/naltrexone 2.4 mg every 2 to 3 days based on patient response.

Discontinuation of therapy: Dose should be gradually tapered by 25% to 50% every 2 to 4 days; do not abruptly discontinue.

Geriatric Refer to adult dosing. Initiate therapy at low end of dosing range; titrate dose cautiously to lowest dose that provides adequate pain relief with acceptable side effects.

Renal Impairment There are no dosage adjustments provided in the manufacturer's labeling. Use with caution; monitor closely for signs of CNS or respiratory depression due to elevated levels of oxycodone and for signs of withdrawal due to elevated levels of naltrexone and adjust dose based on clinical response.

Hepatic Impairment There are no dosage adjustments provided in the manufacturer's labeling. Use with caution; monitor patients closely for signs of CNS or respiratory depression due to elevated levels of oxycodone and for signs of withdrawal due to elevated levels of naltrexone and adjust dose based on clinical response.

Mechanism of Action

Oxycodone: Binds to opiate receptors in the CNS, causing inhibition of ascending pain pathways, altering the perception of and response to pain; produces generalized CNS depression.

Naltrexone: Pure opioid antagonist; reverses the subjective and analgesic effects of mu-opioid receptor agonists by competitively binding at mu-opioid receptors.

Contraindications

Hypersensitivity (eg, anaphylaxis) to oxycodone, naltrexone, or any component of the formulation; significant respiratory depression; acute or severe bronchial asthma in an unmonitored setting or in the absence of resuscitative equipment; GI obstruction, including paralytic ileus (known or suspected).

Documentation of allergenic cross-reactivity for opioids is limited. However, because of similarities in chemical structure and/or pharmacologic actions, the possibility of cross-sensitivity cannot be ruled out with certainty.

Warnings/Precautions [US Boxed Warning]: Serious, life-threatening, or fatal respiratory depression may occur. Monitor closely for respiratory depression, especially during initiation or dose escalation. Swallow tablets whole or sprinkle the contents of the capsule on applesauce and swallow immediately without chewing, crushing, chewing, or dissolving can cause rapid release and a potentially fatal dose. Carbon dioxide retention from opioid-induced respiratory depression can exacerbate the sedating effects of opioids. Use with caution and monitor for respiratory depression in patients with significant chronic obstructive pulmonary disease or cor pulmonale and patients having a substantially decreased respiratory reserve, hypoxia, or preexisting respiratory depression, particularly when initiating therapy and titrating; critical respiratory depression may occur, even at therapeutic dosages. Consider the use of alternative non-opioid analgesics in these patients. Avoid the use of oxycodone in patients with impaired consciousness or coma.

[US Boxed Warning]: Concomitant use of opioids with benzodiazepines or other CNS depressants, including alcohol, may result in profound sedation, respiratory depression, coma, and death. Reserve concomitant prescribing of oxycodone/naltrexone ER and benzodiazepines or other CNS depressants for use in patients for whom alternative treatment options are inadequate. Limit dosage and durations to the minimum required and follow patients for signs and symptoms of respiratory depression and sedation. [US Boxed Warning]: Concomitant use of oxycodone/naltrexone ER with all CYP450 3 A4 inhibitors may result in an increase in oxycodone plasma concentrations, which could increase or prolong adverse drug effects and may cause potentially fatal respiratory depression. In addition, discontinuation of a concomitantly used CYP450 3 A4 inducer may result in an increase in oxycodone plasma concentration. Monitor patients receiving oxycodone/naltrexone ER and any CYP3A4 inhibitor or inducer. Potentially significant interactions may exist requiring dose or frequency adjustment, additional monitoring, and/or selection of alternative therapy.

May cause CNS depression, which may impair physical or mental abilities; patients must be cautioned about performing tasks which require mental alertness (eg, operating machinery or driving). Oxycodone may cause constipation which may be problematic in patients with unstable angina and patients post-myocardial infarction. Consider preventive measures (eg, stool softener, increased fiber) to reduce the potential for constipation. May cause severe hypotension (including orthostatic hypotension and syncope); use with caution in patients with hypovolemia, cardiovascular disease (including acute MI), or drugs which may exaggerate hypotensive effects (including phenothiazines or general anesthetics). Monitor for symptoms of hypotension following initiation or dose titration; dose adjustment may be warranted. Avoid use in patients with circulatory shock. Use with caution in patients with hypersensitivity reactions to other phenanthrene-derivative opioid agonists (codeine, hydrocodone, hydromorphone, levorphanol, oxymorphone).

May obscure diagnosis or clinical course of patients with acute abdominal conditions. Opioids decrease bowel motility; monitor for decreased bowel motility in postoperative patients receiving opioids. Patients interrupting therapy to undergo pain-relieving procedures (eg, chordotomy) may require a dosage adjustment when resuming therapy after the postoperative recovery period. Use with caution in patients with hepatic impairment; oxycodone is extensively metabolized in the liver its clearance may decrease and an increase in naltrexone AUC in patients with compensated and decompensated liver cirrhosis has been reported. Monitor patients closely for signs of CNS or respiratory depression due to elevated levels of oxycodone and for signs of withdrawal due to elevated levels of naltrexone and adjust dose based on clinical response. Use opioids with caution for chronic pain in patients with mental health conditions (eg, depression, anxiety disorders, post-traumatic stress disorder) due to increased risk for opioid use disorder and overdose; more frequent monitoring is recommended (Dowell [CDC 2016]).

[US Boxed Warning]: Prolonged use of opioids during pregnancy can result in neonatal opioid withdrawal syndrome, which may be life-threatening if not recognized and requires management according to protocols developed by neonatology experts. If opioid use is required for a prolonged period in a pregnant woman, advise the patient of the risk of neonatal opioid withdrawal syndrome and ensure appropriate treatment will be available. Signs and symptoms include irritability, hyperactivity and abnormal sleep pattern, high pitched cry, tremor, vomiting, diarrhea, and failure to gain weight. Onset, duration, and severity depend on the drug used, duration of use, maternal dose, and rate of drug elimination by the newborn. **[US Boxed Warning]: Use exposes patients and other users to the risks of opioid addiction, abuse, and misuse, which can lead to overdose and death. Assess each patient's risk prior to prescribing oxycodone/naltrexone ER, and monitor all patients regularly for the development of these behaviors or conditions. Crushing, chewing, or dissolving the product can cause rapid release and absorption of a potentially fatal dose of oxycodone.** Use with caution in patients with a history of drug abuse, acute alcoholism, or mental illness (eg, major depression); potential for drug dependency exists. Tolerance, psychological, and physical dependence may occur with prolonged use. Other factors associated with increased risk include younger age and psychotropic medication use. Consider offering naloxone prescriptions in patients with factors associated with an increased risk for overdose, such as history of overdose or substance use disorder, higher opioid dosages (≥50 morphine milligram equivalents/day orally), and concomitant benzodiazepine use (Dowell [CDC 2016]). **[US Boxed Warning]: Accidental ingestion of even one dose of oxycodone/naltrexone ER, especially in children, can result in a fatal overdose of oxycodone.**

An opioid-containing analgesic regimen should be tailored to each patient's needs and based upon the type of pain being treated (acute versus chronic), the route of administration, degree of tolerance for opioids (naive versus chronic user), age, weight, and medical condition. The optimal analgesic dose varies widely among patients; doses should be titrated to pain relief/prevention. Concurrent use of agonist/antagonist analgesics (eg, pentazocine, nalbuphine, butorphanol) or partial agonist (eg, buprenorphine) may precipitate withdrawal symptoms and/or reduced analgesic efficacy in patients following prolonged therapy with mu opioid agonists. Taper dose gradually when discontinuing. Use with caution in patients with renal impairment; elimination of oxycodone is impaired and naltrexone plasma concentrations may be increased in patients with renal impairment. Monitor patients closely for signs of CNS or respiratory depression due to elevated levels of oxycodone and for signs of withdrawal due to elevated levels of naltrexone and adjust dose based on clinical response. Use with caution in patients with adrenocortical insufficiency, including Addison disease, biliary tract dysfunction, including acute pancreatitis, prostatic hyperplasia and/or urinary stricture, seizure disorders, thyroid dysfunction, delirium tremens, toxic psychosis, and in patients who are morbidly obese. Use with extreme caution in patients with head injury, intracranial lesions, or elevated intracranial pressure (ICP).

Use opioids with caution for chronic pain and titrate dosage cautiously in patients with risk factors for sleep-disordered breathing, including HF and obesity. Avoid opioids in patients with moderate to severe sleep-disordered breathing (Dowell [CDC 2016]). Use with caution in cachectic or debilitated patients; there is a greater potential for respiratory depression, even at therapeutic dosages. Consider the use of alternative nonopioid analgesics in these patients. Use with caution in the elderly; may be more sensitive to adverse effects. Use opioids for chronic pain with caution in this age group; monitor closely due to an increased potential for risks, including certain risks such as falls/fracture, cognitive impairment, and constipation. Clearance may also be reduced in older adults (with or without renal impairment) resulting in a narrow therapeutic window and increasing the risk for respiratory depression or overdose (Dowell [CDC 2016]).

Chronic pain (outside of end-of-life or palliative care, active cancer treatment, sickle cell disease, or medication-assisted treatment for opioid use disorder) in outpatient setting in adults: Opioids should not be used as first-line therapy for chronic pain management (pain >3-month duration or beyond time of normal tissue healing) due to limited short-term benefits, undetermined long-term benefits, and association with serious risks (eg, overdose, MI, auto accidents, risk of developing opioid use disorder). Preferred management includes nonpharmacologic therapy and nonopioid therapy (eg, NSAIDs, acetaminophen, certain anticonvulsants and antidepressants). If opioid therapy is initiated, it should be combined with nonpharmacologic and nonopioid therapy, as appropriate. Prior to initiation, known risks of opioid therapy should be discussed and realistic treatment goals for pain/function should be established, including consideration for discontinuation if benefits do not outweigh risks. Therapy should be continued only if clinically meaningful improvement in pain/function outweighs risks. Therapy should be initiated at the lowest effective dosage using immediate-release opioids (instead of extended-release/long-acting opioids). Risk associated with use increases with higher opioid dosages. Risks and benefits should be re-evaluated when increasing dosage to ≥50 morphine milligram equivalents (MME)/day orally; dosages ≥90 MME/day orally should be avoided unless carefully justified (Dowell [CDC 2016]).

Drug Interactions

Metabolism/Transport Effects Refer to individual components.

Avoid Concomitant Use

Avoid concomitant use of Oxycodone and Naltrexone with any of the following: Azelastine (Nasal); Conivaptan; Eluxadoline; Fusidic Acid (Systemic); Idelalisib; Mixed Agonist / Antagonist Opioids; Orphenadrine; Oxomemazine; Paraldehyde; Thalidomide

Increased Effect/Toxicity

Oxycodone and Naltrexone may increase the levels/effects of: Alvimopan; Azelastine (Nasal); Blonanserin; Desmopressin; Diuretics; Eluxadoline; Flunitrazepam; HYDROcodone; MAO Inhibitors; Methotrimeprazine; MetyroSINE; Orphenadrine; Paraldehyde; Piribedil; Pramipexole; Ramosetron; ROPINIRole; Rotigotine; Selective Serotonin Reuptake Inhibitors; Serotonin Modulators; Suvorexant; Thalidomide; Zolpidem

The levels/effects of Oxycodone and Naltrexone may be increased by: Amphetamines; Anticholinergic Agents; Aprepitant; Brimonidine (Topical); Cannabis; Chlormethiazole; Chlorphenesin Carbamate; CNS Depressants; Conivaptan; CYP3A4 Inhibitors (Moderate); CYP3A4 Inhibitors (Strong); Dasatinib; Dimethindene (Topical); Dronabinol; Droperidol; Fosaprepitant; Fusidic Acid (Systemic); Idelalisib; Ivacaftor; Kava Kava; Lofexidine; Magnesium Sulfate; Methotrimeprazine; MiFEPRIStone; Minocycline; Nabilone; Netupitant; Oxomemazine; Palbociclib; Perampanel; Rufinamide; Simeprevir; Sodium Oxybate; Stiripentol; Succinylcholine; Tapentadol; Tetrahydrocannabinol; Voriconazole

Decreased Effect

Oxycodone and Naltrexone may decrease the levels/effects of: Diuretics; Gastrointestinal Agents (Prokinetic); Pegvisomant

The levels/effects of Oxycodone and Naltrexone may be decreased by: Bosentan; CYP3A4 Inducers (Moderate); CYP3A4 Inducers (Strong); Dabrafenib; Deferasirox; Enzalutamide; Mitotane; Mixed Agonist / Antagonist Opioids; Nalmefene; Naltrexone; RifAMPin; Siltuximab; St John's Wort; Tocilizumab

Food Interactions Refer to individual agents.

Pregnancy Considerations [US Boxed Warning]: Prolonged use of opioids during pregnancy can cause neonatal withdrawal syndrome, which may be life-threatening if not recognized and treated according to protocols developed by neonatology experts. If opioid use is required for a prolonged period in a pregnant woman, advise the patient of the risk of neonatal opioid withdrawal syndrome and ensure appropriate treatment will be available. The naltrexone component may precipitate withdrawal in the fetus. Refer to individual monographs.

Breastfeeding Considerations Oxycodone and naltrexone are excreted in breast milk. Due to the potential for serious adverse events in a nursing infant, breastfeeding is not recommended by the manufacturer. Refer to individual monographs.

Product Availability Troxyca ER: FDA approved August 2016; anticipated availability is currently undetermined.

Controlled Substance C-II

Oxymetazoline (Nasal) (oks i met AZ oh leen)

Related Information

Bacterial Infections *on page 1835*

Related Sample Prescriptions

Sinus Infection Treatment - Sample Prescriptions *on page 38*

Brand Names: US 12 Hour Nasal Relief Spray [OTC]; 12 Hour Nasal Spray [OTC]; Afrin 12 Hour [OTC]; Afrin Extra Moisturizing [OTC] [DSC]; Afrin Menthol Spray [OTC]; Afrin Nasal Spray [OTC]; Afrin NoDrip Extra Moisture [OTC]; Afrin NoDrip Original [OTC]; Afrin NoDrip Sinus [OTC]; Afrin Sinus [OTC]; Dristan Spray [OTC]; Long Lasting Nasal Spray [OTC]; Mucinex Nasal Spray Full Force [OTC]; Mucinex Nasal Spray Moisture [OTC]; Mucinex Sinus-Max Full Force [OTC]; Mucinex Sinus-Max Moist Smart [OTC] [DSC]; Nasal Decongestant Spray [OTC]; Nasal Spray 12 Hour [OTC]; Nasal Spray Extra Moisturizing [OTC]; Nasal Spray Max Strength [OTC]; Neo-Synephrine 12 Hour Spray [OTC]; NRS Nasal Relief [OTC] [DSC]; QlearQuil [OTC]; Sinus Nasal Spray [OTC]; Vicks Sinex 12 Hour Decongest [OTC]; Vicks Sinex Moisturizing [OTC]; Vicks Sinex Severe Decongest [OTC]; Vicks Sinex [OTC]

Brand Names: Canada Claritin Allergic Decongestant; Dristan Long Lasting Nasal; Drixoral Nasal

Generic Availability (US) Yes

Pharmacologic Category Adrenergic Agonist Agent; Decongestant; Imidazoline Derivative

Use Nasal congestion: Temporary relief of nasal congestion (due to a cold, hay fever, or other upper respiratory allergies) and sinus congestion/pressure.

Local Anesthetic/Vasoconstrictor Precautions No information available to require special precautions

Effects on Dental Treatment No significant effects or complications reported

Effects on Bleeding No information available to require special precautions

Adverse Reactions Frequency not defined.

Respiratory: Dry nose, nasal congestion (rebound; chronic use), nasal mucosa irritation (temporary), sneezing

Dosing

Adult & Geriatric Nasal congestion: Intranasal: Instill 2 to 3 sprays into each nostril twice daily for ≤3 days (maximum dose: 2 doses/24 hours)

Pediatric Nasal congestion: Intranasal: Children ≥6 years and Adolescents: Refer to adult dosing.

Renal Impairment There are no dosage adjustments provided in manufacturer's labeling.

Hepatic Impairment There are no dosage adjustments provided in manufacturer's labeling.

Mechanism of Action Stimulates alpha-adrenergic receptors in the arterioles of the nasal mucosa to produce vasoconstriction

Contraindications

OTC labeling: When used for self-medication, do not use for more than 3 days.

Documentation of allergenic cross-reactivity for ophthalmic sympathomimetics is limited. However, because of similarities in chemical structure and/or pharmacologic actions, the possibility of cross-sensitivity cannot be ruled out with certainty.

Warnings/Precautions Frequent or prolonged use may cause nasal congestion to recur or worsen Use with caution in the presence of hypertension, diabetes, hyperthyroidism, heart disease, or benign prostatic hyperplasia/urinary obstruction. Temporary discomfort such as burning, stinging, sneezing, or an increased nasal discharge may occur.

Accidental ingestion by children of over-the-counter (OTC) imidazoline-derivative eye drops and nasal sprays may result in serious harm. Serious adverse reactions (eg, coma, bradycardia, respiratory depression, sedation) requiring hospitalization have been reported in children ≤5 years of age who had ingested even small amounts (eg, 1 to 2 mL). Contact a poison control center and seek emergency medical care immediately for accidental ingestion (FDA Drug Safety Communication 2012).

Benzyl alcohol and derivatives: Some dosage forms may contain benzyl alcohol; large amounts of benzyl alcohol (≥99 mg/kg/day) have been associated with a potentially fatal toxicity ("gasping syndrome") in neonates; the "gasping syndrome" consists of metabolic acidosis, respiratory distress, gasping respirations, CNS dysfunction (including convulsions, intracranial hemorrhage), hypotension, and cardiovascular collapse (AAP ["Inactive" 1997]; CDC 1982); some data suggests that benzoate displaces bilirubin from protein binding sites (Ahlfors 2001); avoid or use dosage forms containing benzyl alcohol with caution in neonates. See manufacturer's labeling.

Some dosage forms may contain polysorbate 80 (also known as Tweens). Hypersensitivity reactions, usually a delayed reaction, have been reported following exposure to pharmaceutical products containing polysorbate 80 in certain individuals (Isaksson 2002; Lucente 2000; Shelley 1995). Thrombocytopenia, ascites, pulmonary deterioration, and renal and hepatic failure have been reported in premature neonates after receiving parenteral products containing polysorbate 80 (Alade 1986; CDC 1984). See manufacturer's labeling.

Potentially significant interactions may exist, requiring dose or frequency adjustment, additional monitoring, and/or selection of alternative therapy.

Drug Interactions

Metabolism/Transport Effects None known.

Avoid Concomitant Use

Avoid concomitant use of Oxymetazoline (Nasal) with any of the following: Ergot Derivatives; Iobenguane I 123; MAO Inhibitors

Increased Effect/Toxicity

Oxymetazoline (Nasal) may increase the levels/effects of: Doxofylline; Sympathomimetics

The levels/effects of Oxymetazoline (Nasal) may be increased by: AtoMOXetine; Cannabinoid-Containing Products; Cocaine; Ergot Derivatives; Linezolid; MAO Inhibitors; Tedizolid; Tricyclic Antidepressants

Decreased Effect

Oxymetazoline (Nasal) may decrease the levels/effects of: FentaNYL; Iobenguane I 123

The levels/effects of Oxymetazoline (Nasal) may be decreased by: Alpha1-Blockers; Tricyclic Antidepressants

Pharmacodynamics/Kinetics

Onset of Action Within 10 minutes (Chua 1989)

Duration of Action Up to 12 hours (Chua 1989)

Pregnancy Considerations Adverse fetal or neonatal effects have not been observed following normal maternal doses of oxymetazoline during the third trimester of pregnancy. Adverse events have been noted in case reports following large doses or extended use. Decongestants are not the preferred agents for the treatment of rhinitis during pregnancy. Short-term (<3 days) use of intranasal oxymetazoline may be beneficial to some patients although its safety during pregnancy has not been studied (Wallace 2008).

Dosage Forms

Solution, Nasal:

12 Hour Nasal Relief Spray [OTC]: 0.05% (15 mL, 30 mL)
12 Hour Nasal Spray [OTC]: 0.05% (30 mL)
Afrin 12 Hour [OTC]: 0.05% (30 mL)
Afrin Menthol Spray [OTC]: 0.05% (15 mL)
Afrin Nasal Spray [OTC]: 0.05% (15 mL, 20 mL, 30 mL)
Afrin NoDrip Extra Moisture [OTC]: 0.05% (15 mL)
Afrin NoDrip Original [OTC]: 0.05% (15 mL)
Afrin NoDrip Sinus [OTC]: 0.05% (15 mL)
Afrin Sinus [OTC]: 0.05% (15 mL)
Dristan Spray [OTC]: 0.05% (15 mL)
Long Lasting Nasal Spray [OTC]: 0.05% (30 mL)
Mucinex Nasal Spray Full Force [OTC]: 0.05% (22 mL)
Mucinex Nasal Spray Moisture [OTC]: 0.05% (22 mL)
Mucinex Sinus-Max Full Force [OTC]: 0.05% (22 mL)
Nasal Decongestant Spray [OTC]: 0.05% (15 mL, 30 mL)
Nasal Spray 12 Hour [OTC]: 0.05% (30 mL)
Nasal Spray Extra Moisturizing [OTC]: 0.05% (30 mL)
Nasal Spray Max Strength [OTC]: 0.05% (30 mL)
Neo-Synephrine 12 Hour Spray [OTC]: 0.05% (15 mL)
QlearQuil [OTC]: 0.05% (15 mL)
Sinus Nasal Spray [OTC]: 0.05% (30 mL)
Vicks Sinex [OTC]: 0.05% (15 mL)
Vicks Sinex 12 Hour Decongest [OTC]: 0.05% (15 mL)
Vicks Sinex Moisturizing [OTC]: 0.05% (15 mL)
Vicks Sinex Severe Decongest [OTC]: 0.05% (15 mL)
Generic: 0.05% (30 mL)

Oxymetholone (oks i METH oh lone)

Brand Names: US Anadrol-50

Pharmacologic Category Anabolic Steroid

Use Treatment of anemias caused by deficient red cell production

Local Anesthetic/Vasoconstrictor Precautions No information available to require special precautions

Effects on Dental Treatment No significant effects or complications reported

Effects on Bleeding No information available to require special precautions

Adverse Reactions

Frequency not defined.

Cardiovascular: Coronary artery disease, peripheral edema

Central nervous system: Chills, deepening of the voice (females), excitement, insomnia

Dermatologic: Acne vulgaris, androgenetic alopecia (postpubertal males, females), hyperpigmentation

Endocrine & metabolic: Amenorrhea, change in libido (decreased/increased), decreased glucose tolerance, decreased HDL cholesterol, gynecomastia, hirsutism (women), hypercalcemia, hyperchloremia, hyperkalemia, hypernatremia, hyperphosphatemia, increased LDL cholesterol, menstrual disease

Gastrointestinal: Diarrhea, nausea, vomiting

Genitourinary: Benign prostatic hypertrophy (elderly males), clitoromegaly, decreased ejaculate volume, epididymitis, erectile dysfunction (increased erections; prepubertal males), impotence, irritable bladder, oligospermia, phallic enlargement, priapism, testicular atrophy, testicular disease, virilization (females)

Hematologic & oncologic: Clotting factors suppression (II, V, VII, X), hemorrhage, increased INR, iron deficiency anemia, leukemia, malignant neoplasm of prostate, prolonged prothrombin time

Hepatic: Cholestatic hepatitis, cholestatic jaundice, hepatic failure, hepatic necrosis, hepatocellular neoplasm (including carcinoma), increased serum alkaline phosphatase, increased serum bilirubin, increased serum transaminases, peliosis hepatitis

Neuromuscular & skeletal: Increased creatine phosphokinase, premature epiphyseal closure (children)

Renal: Increased serum creatinine

Respiratory: Hoarseness (females)

<1%, postmarketing, and/or case reports: Hepatotoxicity (idiosyncratic; Chalasani 2014)

General Dosage Range Oral: *Children and Adults:* 1-5 mg/kg once daily

Mechanism of Action Enhances production of erythropoietin in patients with anemias which are due to bone marrow failure; stimulates erythropoiesis in anemias due to deficient red cell production

Pharmacodynamics/Kinetics

Onset of Action Response is not often immediate; a minimum trial of 3 to 6 months is recommended

Pregnancy Risk Factor X

Pregnancy Considerations Oligospermia or amenorrhea may occur resulting in an impairment of fertility. Use is contraindicated in women who are or may become pregnant.

Controlled Substance C-III

OxyMORphone (oks i MOR fone)

Related Information

Oral Pain *on page 1830*

Brand Names: US Opana; Opana ER

Pharmacologic Category Analgesic, Opioid

Use Pain management:

Parenteral: Management of pain severe enough to require an opioid analgesic and for which alternative treatments are inadequate; obstetrical analgesia; preoperative medication; anesthesia support; relief of anxiety in patients with dyspnea associated with pulmonary edema secondary to acute left ventricular failure.

Oral, immediate release: Management of acute pain severe enough to require an opioid analgesic and for which alternative treatments are inadequate.

Oral, extended release: Management of pain severe enough to require daily, around-the-clock, long-term opioid treatment and for which alternative treatment options are inadequate.

Limitations of use: Reserve oxymorphone for use in patients for whom alternative treatment options (eg, nonopioid analgesics, opioid combination products) are ineffective, not tolerated, or would be otherwise inadequate to provide sufficient pain management. Oxymorphone ER is not indicated as an as-needed analgesic.

Local Anesthetic/Vasoconstrictor Precautions No information available to require special precautions

Effects on Dental Treatment Key adverse event(s) related to dental treatment: Xerostomia (normal salivary flow resumes upon discontinuation). Anticholinergic side effects can cause a reduction of saliva production or secretion, contributing to discomfort and dental disease (ie, caries, oral candidiasis, and periodontal disease).

Effects on Bleeding No information available to require special precautions

Adverse Reactions Incidence usually on higher end with extended release (ER) tablet.

>10%:

Central nervous system: Drowsiness (9% to 19%), dizziness (7% to 18%), headache (7% to 12%)

Dermatologic: Pruritus (8% to 15%)

Gastrointestinal: Nausea (19% to 33%), constipation (4% to 28%), vomiting (9% to 16%)

Miscellaneous: Fever (1% to 14%)

1% to 10%:

Cardiovascular: Edema (<10%), flushing (<10%), hypertension (<10%), hypotension (<10%), tachycardia (<10%)

Central nervous system: Depression (<10%), disorientation (<10%), lethargy (<10%), nervousness (<10%), restlessness (<10%), anxiety (1% to <10%), sedation (1% to <10%), fatigue (≤1%), insomnia (≤4%), confusion (3%)

Dermatologic: Diaphoresis (1% to <10%)

Endocrine & metabolic: Dehydration (<10%), weight loss (<10%)

Gastrointestinal: Abdominal distention (<10%), dyspepsia (<10%), flatulence (1% to <10%), xerostomia (1% to <10%), diarrhea (≤4%), abdominal pain (≤3%), decreased appetite (≤3%)

Neuromuscular & skeletal: Weakness (<10%)

Ophthalmic: Blurred vision (<10%)

Respiratory: Dyspnea (<10%), hypoxia (<10%)

<1%, postmarketing, and/or case reports: Agitation, apnea (injection), atelectasis (injection), biliary colic, bradycardia, bronchospasm (injection), cold and clammy skin, dermatitis, difficulty in micturition, diplopia (injection), drug dependence, dysphoria, euphoria, hallucination, hot flash, hypersensitivity, hypersensitivity reaction, hypogonadism (Brennan 2013; Debono 2011), increased serum prolactin (Molitch 2008; Vuong 2010), injection site reaction, intestinal obstruction, miosis, oliguria (injection), orthostatic hypotension, palpitations, respiratory depression, syncope, thrombotic thrombocytopenic purpura (inappropriate injection of ER tablet), ureteral spasm (injection), urinary retention, urticaria

General Dosage Range Dosage adjustment recommended in patients with hepatic or renal impairment

IM, SubQ: *Adults:* Initial: 0.5 mg; Maintenance: 1 to 1.5 mg every 4 to 6 hours as needed

IV: *Adults:* Initial: 0.5 mg

Oral:

Extended release: *Adults (opioid-naive):* Initial: 5 mg every 12 hours; Maintenance: Titrate upward with 5 to 10 mg every 12 hours at 3 to 7 day intervals until desired response

Immediate release: *Adults (opioid-naive):* Initial: 5 to 10 mg every 4 to 6 hours; Maintenance: Titrate upward to desired response

Mechanism of Action Oxymorphone is a potent opioid analgesic with uses similar to those of morphine. The drug is a semisynthetic derivative of morphine (phenanthrene derivative) and is closely related to hydromorphone chemically (Dilaudid).

Pharmacodynamics/Kinetics

Onset of Action Parenteral: 5 to 10 minutes

Duration of Action Analgesic: Parenteral: 3 to 6 hours

Half-life Elimination Oral: Immediate release: 7 to 9 hours; Extended release: 9 to 11 hours

Pregnancy Considerations Adverse events have been observed in some animal reproduction studies. Opioids cross the placenta. When used for pain relief during labor, opioids may temporarily affect the heart rate of the fetus (ACOG 2002). Oxymorphone injection is indicated for analgesia during labor. Neonates should be monitored for respiratory depression.

[US Boxed Warning]: Prolonged use of opioids during pregnancy can cause neonatal withdrawal syndrome, which may be life-threatening if not recognized and treated according to protocols developed by neonatology experts. If opioid use is required for a prolonged period in a pregnant woman, ensure treatment is available and warn patient of risk to the neonate. If chronic opioid exposure occurs in pregnancy, adverse events in the newborn (including withdrawal) may occur; monitoring of the neonate is recommended. The minimum effective dose should be used if opioids are needed (Chou 2009). Neonatal abstinence syndrome following opioid exposure may present with autonomic (eg, fever, temperature instability), gastrointestinal (eg, diarrhea, vomiting, poor feeding/weight gain), or neurologic (eg, high-pitched crying, increased muscle tone, irritability, seizure, tremor) symptoms (Dow 2012; Hudak 2012).

Long-term opioid use may cause secondary hypogonadism, which may lead to sexual dysfunction or infertility (Brennan 2013).

Controlled Substance C-II

Oxytocin (oks i TOE sin)

Brand Names: US Pitocin

Brand Names: Canada Oxytocin for injection

Pharmacologic Category Oxytocic Agent

Use

Antepartum: Induction of labor in patients with a medical indication (eg, Rh problems, maternal diabetes, preeclampsia, at or near term); stimulation or reinforcement of labor (as in selected cases of uterine inertia); adjunctive therapy in management of incomplete or inevitable abortion

Postpartum: To produce uterine contractions during the third stage of labor and to control postpartum bleeding or hemorrhage.

Local Anesthetic/Vasoconstrictor Precautions No information available to require special precautions

Effects on Dental Treatment No significant effects or complications reported

Effects on Bleeding No information available to require special precautions

Adverse Reactions

Frequency not defined.

Cardiovascular: Cardiac arrhythmia (including premature ventricular contraction), hypertension, subarachnoid hemorrhage

Central nervous system: Hypertonia (uterine)

Endocrine & metabolic: Water intoxication (severe water intoxication with seizure and coma is associated with a slow oxytocin infusion over 24 hours)

Gastrointestinal: Nausea, vomiting

Genitourinary: Postpartum hemorrhage, tetanic uterine contractions, uterine rupture, uterine spasm
Hematologic & oncologic: Pelvic hematoma
Hypersensitivity: Anaphylaxis

General Dosage Range

IM: *Adults:* 10 units after delivery of the placenta

IV: *Adults:* Dosage varies greatly depending on indication

Mechanism of Action Oxytocin stimulates uterine contraction by activating G-protein-coupled receptors that trigger increases in intracellular calcium levels in uterine myofibrils. Oxytocin also increases local prostaglandin production, further stimulating uterine contraction.

Pharmacodynamics/Kinetics

Onset of Action Uterine contractions: IM: 3 to 5 minutes; IV: ~1 minute

Duration of Action IM: 2 to 3 hours; IV: 1 hour

Half-life Elimination 1 to 6 minutes; decreased in late pregnancy and during lactation

Pregnancy Risk Factor C (manufacturer specific)

Pregnancy Considerations [U.S. Boxed Warning]: To be used for medical rather than elective induction of labor. Animal reproduction studies have not been conducted. When used as indicated, teratogenic effects would not be expected. Nonteratogenic adverse reactions are reported in the neonate as well as the mother.

PACLitaxel (Conventional)

(pac li TAKS el con VEN sha nal)

Brand Names: Canada Apo-Paclitaxel; Paclitaxel for Injection; Paclitaxel Injection USP

Pharmacologic Category Antineoplastic Agent, Antimicrotubular; Antineoplastic Agent, Taxane Derivative

Use

Breast cancer: Adjuvant treatment of node-positive breast cancer; treatment of metastatic breast cancer after failure of combination chemotherapy or relapse within 6 months of adjuvant chemotherapy (prior therapy should have included an anthracycline)

Kaposi sarcoma (AIDS-related): Second-line treatment of AIDS-related Kaposi sarcoma

Non-small cell lung cancer: First-line treatment of non-small cell lung cancer (in combination with cisplatin) in patients who are not candidates for potentially curative surgery and/or radiation therapy

Ovarian cancer: Subsequent therapy for treatment of advanced ovarian cancer; first-line therapy of ovarian cancer (in combination with cisplatin)

Local Anesthetic/Vasoconstrictor Precautions No information available to require special precautions

Effects on Dental Treatment Key adverse event(s) related to dental treatment: Severe, potentially dose-limiting mucositis and stomatitis.

Effects on Bleeding Chemotherapy may result in significant myelosuppression, potentially including significant reduction in platelet counts (thrombocytopenia grades 3/4: 1% to 7%) and altered hemostasis. Bleeding in seen in ~14% of patients. In patients who are under active treatment with these agents, medical consult is suggested.

Adverse Reactions Percentages reported with single-agent therapy.

>10%:

Cardiovascular: Flushing (28%), ECG abnormality (14% to 23%), edema (21%), hypotension (4% to 12%)
Central nervous system: Peripheral neuropathy (42% to 70%; grades 3/4: ≤7%)
Dermatologic: Alopecia (87%), skin rash (12%)
Gastrointestinal: Nausea (≤52%), vomiting (≤52%), diarrhea (38%), mucositis (17% to 35%), stomatitis (15%; most common at doses >390 mg/m^2), abdominal pain (with intraperitoneal administration)
Hematologic & oncologic: Neutropenia (78% to 98%; grade 4: 14% to 75%; onset: 8 to 10 days; median nadir: 11 days; recovery: 15 to 21 days), leukopenia (90%; grade 4: 17%), anemia (47% to 90%; grades 3/4: 2% to 16%), thrombocytopenia (4% to 20%; grades 3/4: 1% to 7%), hemorrhage (14%)
Hepatic: Increased serum alkaline phosphatase (22%), increased serum AST (19%)
Hypersensitivity: Hypersensitivity reaction (31% to 45%; grades 3/4: ≤2%)
Infection: Infection (15% to 30%)
Local: Injection site reaction (erythema at injection site, skin discoloration at injection site, swelling at injection site, tenderness at injection site: 13%)
Neuromuscular & skeletal: Arthralgia (≤60%), myalgia (≤60%), weakness (17%)
Renal: Increased serum creatinine (observed in Kaposi sarcoma patients only: 18% to 34%, severe: 5% to 7%)

1% to 10%:

Cardiovascular: Bradycardia (3%), tachycardia (2%), hypertension (1%), cardiac arrhythmia (1%), syncope (1%), venous thrombosis (1%)
Dermatologic: Changes in nails (2%)
Hematologic & oncologic: Febrile neutropenia (2%)
Hepatic: Increased serum bilirubin (7%)
Respiratory: Dyspnea (2%)

<1%, postmarketing, and/or case reports: Anaphylaxis, ataxia, atrial fibrillation, atrioventricular block, back pain, brain disease (neurological), cardiac conduction disturbance, cardiac failure, cellulitis, chills, conjunctivitis, dehydration, desquamation, enterocolitis, exacerbation of scleroderma, fibrosis at injection site, hepatic encephalopathy, hepatic necrosis, increased lacrimation, induration at injection site, intestinal obstruction, intestinal perforation, interstitial pneumonitis, ischemic colitis, ischemic heart disease, maculopapular rash, malaise, myocardial infarction, neutropenic enterocolitis, ototoxicity (tinnitus and hearing loss), pancreatitis, paralytic ileus, phlebitis, pneumonitis, pruritus, pulmonary embolism, pulmonary fibrosis, radiation recall phenomenon, radiation pneumonitis, renal insufficiency, seizure, skin edema (diffuse), skin necrosis, skin sclerosis, Stevens-Johnson syndrome, supraventricular tachycardia, thickening of skin, toxic epidermal necrolysis, typhlitis (neutropenic), ventricular tachycardia (asymptomatic), visual disturbance (scintillating scotomata)

General Dosage Range Dosage adjustment recommended in patients with hepatic impairment or who develop toxicities

IV: *Adults:* Dosage varies greatly depending on indication

Mechanism of Action Paclitaxel promotes microtubule assembly by enhancing the action of tubulin dimers, stabilizing existing microtubules, and inhibiting their disassembly, interfering with the late G_2 mitotic phase, and inhibiting cell replication. In addition, the drug can distort mitotic spindles, resulting in the breakage of chromosomes. Paclitaxel may also suppress cell proliferation and modulate immune response.

Pharmacodynamics/Kinetics

Half-life Elimination

Children: 4.6 to 17 hours (varies with dose and infusion duration)

Adults:

3-hour infusion: Mean (terminal): ~13 to 20 hours

24-hour infusion: Mean (terminal): ~16 to 53 hours

Pregnancy Risk Factor D

Pregnancy Considerations Adverse events (embryotoxicity, fetal toxicity, and maternal toxicity) have been observed in animal reproduction studies at doses less than the recommended human dose. An *ex vivo* human placenta perfusion model illustrated that paclitaxel crossed the placenta at term. Placental transfer was low and affected by the presence of albumin; higher albumin concentrations resulted in lower paclitaxel placental transfer (Berveiller, 2012). Some pharmacokinetic properties of paclitaxel may be altered in pregnant women (van Hasselt, 2014). Women of childbearing potential should be advised to avoid becoming pregnant. A pregnancy registry is available for all cancers diagnosed during pregnancy at Cooper Health (877-635-4499).

PACLitaxel (Protein Bound)

(pac li TAKS el PROE teen bownd)

Brand Names: US Abraxane

Brand Names: Canada Abraxane for Injectable Suspension

Pharmacologic Category Antineoplastic Agent, Antimicrotubular; Antineoplastic Agent, Taxane Derivative

Use

US labeling:

Breast cancer, metastatic: Treatment of refractory (metastatic) or relapsed (within 6 months of adjuvant therapy) breast cancer after failure of combination chemotherapy (including anthracycline-based therapy unless clinically contraindicated)

Non-small cell lung cancer (NSCLC): First-line treatment of locally advanced or metastatic NSCLC (in combination with carboplatin) in patients ineligible for curative surgery or radiation therapy

Pancreatic adenocarcinoma: First-line treatment of metastatic adenocarcinoma of the pancreas (in combination with gemcitabine)

Canadian labeling:

Breast cancer, metastatic: Treatment of metastatic breast cancer

Pancreatic adenocarcinoma: First-line treatment of metastatic adenocarcinoma of the pancreas (in combination with gemcitabine)

Local Anesthetic/Vasoconstrictor Precautions No information available to require special precautions

Effects on Dental Treatment Key adverse event(s) related to dental treatment: Mucositis.

Effects on Bleeding Chemotherapy may result in significant myelosuppression, potentially including significant reduction in platelet counts (thrombocytopenia grades 3/4: <1%) and altered hemostasis. In patients who are under active treatment with these agents, medical consult is suggested.

Adverse Reactions Frequency may vary based on indication and/or concomitant therapy.

>10%:

Cardiovascular: ECG abnormality (60%; 35% in patients with a normal baseline), peripheral edema (10% to 46%)

Central nervous system: Peripheral sensory neuropathy (71%; grades 3/4: 10%; dose dependent; cumulative), fatigue (25% to 59%), peripheral neuropathy (48% to 54%; grade 3: 3% to 17%), headache (14%), depression (12%)

Dermatologic: Alopecia (50% to 90%), skin rash (10% to 30%)

Endocrine & metabolic: Dehydration (21%), increased gamma-glutamyl transferase (grades 3/4: 14%), hypokalemia (12%)

Gastrointestinal: Nausea (27% to 54%; grades 3/4: 3% to 6%), diarrhea (15% to 44%; grades 3/4: ≤6%), decreased appetite (17% to 36%), vomiting (12% to 36%; grades 3/4: 4% to 6%), constipation (16%), dysgeusia (16%)

Genitourinary: Urinary tract infection (11%)

Hematologic & oncologic: Anemia (33% to 98%; grades 3/4: 1% to 28%), neutropenia (73% to 85%; grades 3/4: 34% to 47%), thrombocytopenia (2% to 74%; grades 3/4: <1% to 18%), bone marrow depression (dose-related)

Hepatic: Increased serum AST (39%), increased serum alkaline phosphatase (36%)

Infection: Infection (24%; primarily included oral candidiasis, respiratory tract infection, and pneumonia)

Neuromuscular & skeletal: Weakness (16% to 47%; severe: 8%), musculoskeletal pain (10% to 44%; myalgia/arthralgia), limb pain (11%)

Ophthalmic: Visual disturbance (13%; severe [keratitis, blurred vision]: 1%)

Renal: Increased serum creatinine (11%; severe 1%)

Respiratory: Cough (7% to 17%), epistaxis (7% to 15%), dyspnea (12%)

Miscellaneous: Fever (41%)

1% to 10%:

Cardiovascular: Edema (10%), cardiac failure (<10%), hypotension (5%), significant cardiovascular event (grades 3/4: 3%; included chest pain, cardiac arrest, supraventricular tachycardia, thrombosis, pulmonary thromboembolism, pulmonary emboli, and hypertension)

Gastrointestinal: Mucositis (7% to 10%; grades 3/4: ≤1%)

Hematologic & oncologic: Hemorrhage (2%), febrile neutropenia (2%)

Hepatic: Increased serum bilirubin (7%)

Hypersensitivity: Hypersensitivity reaction (4%, includes anaphylactic reactions, chest pain, dyspnea, flushing, hypotension; severe: <1%)

Infection: Sepsis (5%)

Ophthalmic: Cystoid macular edema (<10%)

Respiratory: Pneumonitis (4%)

<1%, postmarketing, and/or case reports: Atrioventricular block, autonomic neuropathy, bradycardia, cardiac arrhythmia, cerebrovascular accident, cranial nerve palsy, decreased visual acuity, embolism, erythema, hepatic encephalopathy, hepatic necrosis, injection site reaction (mild), intestinal obstruction, intestinal perforation, ischemic colitis, ischemic heart disease, left ventricular dysfunction, maculopapular rash, myocardial infarction, nail discoloration, neutropenic sepsis, optic nerve damage (rare), palmar-plantar erythrodysesthesia (in patients previously exposed to capecitabine), pancreatitis, pancytopenia, paralytic ileus, peripheral motor neuropathy, pneumonia, pneumothorax, pruritus, pulmonary embolism, radiation pneumonitis (with concurrent radiation therapy), radiation recall phenomenon, skin photosensitivity, Stevens-Johnson syndrome, thrombosis, toxic epidermal necrolysis, transient ischemic attacks, ventricular dysfunction, vocal cord paralysis

General Dosage Range Dosage adjustment recommended in patients with hepatic impairment or who develop toxicities

IV: *Adults:* Dosage varies greatly depending on indication.

Mechanism of Action Albumin-bound paclitaxel nanoparticle formulation; paclitaxel promotes microtubule assembly by enhancing the action of tubulin dimers, stabilizing existing microtubules, and inhibiting their disassembly, interfering with the late G_2 mitotic phase, and inhibiting cell replication. May also distort mitotic spindles, resulting in the breakage of chromosomes. Paclitaxel may also suppress cell proliferation and modulate immune response.

Pharmacodynamics/Kinetics

Half-life Elimination Terminal: 13 to 27 hours

Pregnancy Risk Factor D

Pregnancy Considerations Adverse events were observed in animal reproduction studies. An *ex vivo* human placenta perfusion model illustrated that paclitaxel (non-protein bound preparation) crossed the placenta at term. Placental transfer was low and affected by the presence of albumin; higher albumin concentrations resulted in lower paclitaxel placental transfer (Berveiller 2012). Women of childbearing potential should be advised to avoid becoming pregnant during therapy; may cause fetal harm if administered during pregnancy. Additionally, testicular atrophy/degeneration was observed in animal studies; males should be advised to not father a child during therapy. A pregnancy registry is available for all cancers diagnosed during pregnancy at Cooper Health (877-635-4499).

Palbociclib (pal boe SYE klib)

Brand Names: US Ibrance

Brand Names: Canada Ibrance

Pharmacologic Category Antineoplastic Agent, Cyclin-Dependent Kinase Inhibitor

Use

Breast cancer, advanced (initial endocrine-based therapy): Treatment of hormone receptor (HR)-positive, human epidermal growth factor receptor 2 (HER2)-negative advanced or metastatic breast cancer (in combination with letrozole) in postmenopausal women as initial endocrine-based therapy

Breast cancer, advanced (second-line endocrine-based therapy): Treatment of HR-positive, HER2-negative advanced or metastatic breast cancer (in combination with fulvestrant) in women with disease progression following endocrine therapy

Local Anesthetic/Vasoconstrictor Precautions No information available to require special precautions

Effects on Dental Treatment Key adverse event(s) related to dental treatment: Stomatitis reported (25% incidence)

Effects on Bleeding Chemotherapy may result in significant myelosuppression, potentially including significant reduction in platelet counts (thrombocytopenia [17%; grade 3: 2%]); and altered hemostasis.

Adverse Reactions Percentages reported as part of combination therapy.

>10%:

Central nervous system: Fatigue (41%), headache (26%), peripheral neuropathy (13%)

Dermatologic: Alopecia (18% to 22%), skin rash (17%)

Gastrointestinal: Nausea (25% to 34%), stomatitis (25% to 28%), diarrhea (21% to 24%), constipation (20%), vomiting (15% to 19%), decreased appetite (16%)

Hematologic & oncologic: Neutropenia (75% to 83%; grade 3: 48% to 55%; grade 4: 6% to 11%), decreased absolute lymphocyte count (81%; grade 3: 17%; grade 4: 1%), anemia (30% to 78%; grade 3: 3% to 5%; grade 4: ≤1%), leukopenia (43% to 53%; grade 3: 19% to 30%; grade 4: ≤1%), thrombocytopenia (17% to 23%; grade 3: 2%; grade 4: ≤1%)

Infection: Infection (47% to 55%)

Neuromuscular & skeletal: Weakness (8% to 13%)

Respiratory: Upper respiratory tract infection (31%), epistaxis (7% to 11%)

Miscellaneous: Fever (13%)

1% to 10%:

Cardiovascular: Pulmonary embolism (1% to 5%)

Dermatologic: Xeroderma (6%)

Gastrointestinal: Dysgeusia (7%)

Hematologic & oncologic: Febrile neutropenia (1%; grade 3: 1%)

Ophthalmic: Blurred vision (6%), increased lacrimation (6%), dry eye syndrome (4%)

General Dosage Range Dosage adjustment recommended in patients on concomitant therapy or who develop toxicities.

Oral: *Adults:* 125 mg once daily for 21 days of a 28-day treatment cycle (3 weeks on, 1 week off).

Mechanism of Action Palbociclib is a reversible small molecule cyclin-dependent kinase (CDK) inhibitor which is selective for CDK 4 and 6. CDKs have a role in regulating progression through the cell cycle at the G1/S phase by blocking retinoblastoma (Rb) hyperphosphorylation (Finn 2015). Palbociclib reduces proliferation of breast cancer cell lines by preventing progression from the G1 to the S cell cycle phase. The combination of palbociclib and letrozole provides for increased inhibition of Rb phosphorylation, downstream signaling, and tumor growth compared with each agent alone.

Pharmacodynamics/Kinetics

Half-life Elimination 29 ± 5 hours

Time to Peak 6 to 12 hours

Pregnancy Considerations Adverse events were observed in animal reproduction studies. Based on the mechanism of action, palbociclib may be expected to cause fetal harm if used during pregnancy. Women of reproductive potential should use effective contraception during treatment and for at least 3 weeks after the last dose. Males with female partners of reproductive potential should use effective contraception during treatment and for at least 3 months after the last dose. Although not approved for use in men, animal data suggests that palbociclib may affect male fertility.

Prescribing and Access Restrictions Palbociclib is available through specialty pharmacies. For more information, refer to http://www.ibrance.com/getting-ibrance

Palifermin (pal ee FER min)

Brand Names: US Kepivance

Pharmacologic Category Chemoprotective Agent; Keratinocyte Growth Factor

Use

Oral mucositis: To decrease the incidence and duration of severe oral mucositis associated with hematologic malignancies in patients receiving myelotoxic therapy in the setting of autologous hematopoietic stem cell support (when the preparative regimen is expected to result in mucositis ≥ grade 3 in most patients).

Limitations of use: Use (safety and efficacy) is not established for nonhematologic malignancies; use is not recommended with conditioning regimens containing melphalan 200 mg/m^2. Palifermin was not effective in decreasing the incidence of severe mucositis in patients with hematologic malignancies receiving myelotoxic therapy in the setting of allogeneic hematopoietic stem cell support.

Local Anesthetic/Vasoconstrictor Precautions No information available to require special precautions

Effects on Dental Treatment Key adverse event(s) related to dental treatment: Taste alteration, mouth/ tongue discoloration or thickness. See Dental Comment.

Effects on Bleeding No information available to require special precautions

Adverse Reactions

>10%:

Cardiovascular: Edema (28%)

Central nervous system: Pain (16%), dysesthesia (12%; includes hypoesthesia, oral hyperesthesia, paresthesia)

Dermatologic: Skin rash (62%; grade 3: 3%), pruritus (35%), erythema (32%)

Gastrointestinal: Increased serum amylase (62%, grades 3/4: 38%), increased serum lipase (28%, grades 3/4: 11%), mouth discoloration (≤17%), swelling of mouth (≤17%), tongue discoloration (≤17%), tongue edema (≤17%), dysgeusia (16%)

Miscellaneous: Fever (39%)

1% to 10%:

Immunologic: Antibody development (2%)

Neuromuscular & skeletal: Arthralgia (10%)

<1%, postmarketing, and/or case reports: Cataract, cough, genital edema (vaginal), hyperpigmentation (flexural), palmar-plantar erythrodysesthesia (hand-foot syndrome), perineal pain, rhinitis, vaginal disease (erythema)

General Dosage Range IV: *Adults:* 60 mcg/kg/day for 3 consecutive days before and after myelotoxic therapy

Mechanism of Action Palifermin is a recombinant keratinocyte growth factor (KGF) produced in *E. coli*. Endogenous KGF is produced by mesenchymal cells in response to epithelial tissue injury. KGF binds to the KGF receptor resulting in proliferation, differentiation and migration of epithelial cells in multiple tissues, including (but not limited to) the tongue, buccal mucosa, esophagus, and salivary gland.

Pharmacodynamics/Kinetics

Onset of Action Epithelial cell proliferation (dose-dependent): 48 hours

Half-life Elimination 4.5 hours (range: 3.3 to 5.7 hours)

Pregnancy Risk Factor C

Pregnancy Considerations Adverse events were observed in animal reproduction studies.

Dental Comment Palifermin works at the cellular level by protecting the epithelial cells lining the mouth and throat from damage caused by chemotherapy and radiation and by stimulating the growth and development of new epithelial cells to build up the mucosal barrier.

Paliperidone (pal ee PER i done)

Related Information

Clinical Risk Related to Drugs Prolonging QT Interval *on page 1772*

Brand Names: US Invega; Invega Sustenna; Invega Trinza

Brand Names: Canada Invega; Invega Sustenna; Invega Trinza

Pharmacologic Category Second Generation (Atypical) Antipsychotic

Use

Schizophrenia: Treatment of schizophrenia

Schizoaffective disorder (oral and monthly IM paliperidone): Treatment of schizoaffective disorder as monotherapy and as an adjunct to mood stabilizers or antidepressants

Local Anesthetic/Vasoconstrictor Precautions Paliperidone is one of the drugs confirmed to prolong the QT interval and is accepted as having a risk of causing torsade de pointes. The risk of drug-induced torsade de pointes is extremely low when a single QT interval prolonging drug is prescribed. In terms of epinephrine, it is not known what effect vasoconstrictors in the local anesthetic regimen will have in patients with a known history of congenital prolonged QT interval or in patients taking any medication that prolongs the QT interval. Until more information is obtained, it is suggested that the clinician consult with the physician prior to the use of a vasoconstrictor in suspected patients, and that the vasoconstrictor (epinephrine, mepivacaine and levonordefrin [Carbocaine® 2% with Neo-Cobefrin®]) be used with caution.

Effects on Dental Treatment Key adverse event(s) related to dental treatment: Significant xerostomia and changes in salivation (normal salivary flow resumes upon discontinuation).

Effects on Bleeding No information available to require special precautions

Adverse Reactions Unless otherwise noted, frequency of adverse effects is reported for the oral/IM formulation in adults. Frequency not always defined.

>10%:

Cardiovascular: Tachycardia (adolescents and adults: ≤14%)

Central nervous system: Extrapyramidal reaction (adolescents: 4% to 40%; adults: ≤3% to 26%; dose dependent), drowsiness (adolescents: 9% to 26%; adults: 4% to 12%; dose dependent), parkinsonian-like syndrome (adolescents and adults: 3% to 18%; dose dependent), akathisia (adolescents and adults: 4% to 17%; dose dependent), headache (adolescents and adults: 6% to 15%), dystonia (adolescents and adults: 1% to 14%; dose dependent)

Endocrine & metabolic: Decreased HDL cholesterol (adolescents and adults: 14% to 29%), weight gain (adolescents and adults; ≥7% from baseline: 2% to 19%), abnormal triglycerides (adolescents and adults: 5% to 13%), altered serum glucose (adolescents and adults: 4% to 11%), blood cholesterol abnormal (adolescents and adults: 4% to 11%)

Gastrointestinal: Vomiting (adolescents and adults: 5% to 11%)

Hematologic & oncologic: Change in LDL (adolescents and adults: 4% to 14%)

Neuromuscular & skeletal: Hyperkinesia (adolescents and adults: 4% to 17%; dose dependent), tremor (adolescents and adults: 1% to 12%)

1% to 10%:

Cardiovascular: Orthostatic hypotension (2% to 4%; dose dependent), bundle branch block (≤3%), first degree atrioventricular block (2%), hypertension (≤2%), sinus arrhythmia (≤2%), bradycardia (adolescents and adults: <2%), edema (adolescents and adults: <2%), palpitations (adolescents and adults: <2%)

Central nervous system: Agitation (≤10%), anxiety (adolescents and adults: ≤9%), dizziness (adolescents and adults: 2% to 6%), dysarthria (1% to 4%; dose dependent), fatigue (adolescents and adults: 4%), lethargy (adolescents: ≤3%), sleep disorder (≤3%), nightmares (≤2%), insomnia (adolescents and adults: <2%), opisthotonus (adolescents and adults: <2%), tonic-clonic seizures

Dermatologic: Pruritus (adolescents and adults: <2%), skin rash (adolescents and adults: <2%)

Endocrine & metabolic: Amenorrhea (adolescents and adults: ≤6%), galactorrhea (adolescents and adults: ≤4%), gynecomastia (adolescents and adults: ≤3%)

Gastrointestinal: Nausea (4% to 8%), dyspepsia (5% to 6%), sialorrhea (adolescents and adults: ≤6%; dose dependent), constipation (4% to 5%), abdominal pain (≤2% to 4%), increased appetite (2% to 3%), toothache (2% to 3%), xerostomia (adolescents and adults: 2% to 3%), diarrhea (≤3%), swollen tongue (adolescents: ≤3%), stomach discomfort (2%), decreased appetite (1% to 2%), flatulence (adolescents and adults: <2%)

Genitourinary: Urinary tract infection (≤3%), retrograde ejaculation (adolescents and adults:<2%)

Hepatic: Increased serum ALT (adolescents and adults: <2%), increased serum AST (adolescents and adults: <2%)

Hypersensitivity: Anaphylaxis (adolescents and adults: <2%)

Local: Injection site reaction (3% to 10%), erythema at injection site (≤2%), swelling at injection site (≤2%)

Neuromuscular & skeletal: Dyskinesia (adolescents and adults: <1% to 9%), myalgia (≤4%; dose dependent), weakness (adolescents and adults: ≤4%), back pain (1% to 3%), limb pain (≤3%), tongue paralysis (adolescents: ≤3%), stiffness (2%), arthralgia (adolescents and adults: <2%)

Ophthalmic: Blurred vision (adolescents and adults: ≤3%), abnormal eye movements (adolescents and adults: <2%)

Respiratory: Upper respiratory tract infection (2% to 10%), nasopharyngitis (adolescents and adults: 2% to 5%; dose dependent), cough (2% to 3%; dose dependent), rhinitis (1% to 3%; dose dependent), pharyngolaryngeal pain (1% to 2%; dose dependent), epistaxis (≤2%), nasal congestion (adolescents and adults: <2%)

Frequency not defined:

Cardiovascular: Cerebrovascular accident, hypotension, ischemia, peripheral edema, postural orthostatic tachycardia, prolonged Q-T interval on ECG, transient ischemic attacks

Central nervous system: Drooling, hypertonia, psychomotor agitation, restlessness, seizure, vertigo

Dermatologic: Papular rash

Endocrine & metabolic: Menstrual disease

Gastrointestinal: Intestinal obstruction

Genitourinary: Breast disease (includes discharge, engorgement, pain, tenderness), erectile dysfunction, sexual disorder

Neuromuscular & skeletal: Neck stiffness

Ophthalmic: Oculogyric crisis

Respiratory: Aspiration pneumonia

<1%, postmarketing, and/or case reports: Abnormal gait, abscess at injection site, agranulocytosis, alopecia, angioedema, antiemetic effect, atrial fibrillation, bradykinesia, cellulitis at injection site, cogwheel rigidity, deep vein thrombosis, diabetes mellitus, diabetic ketoacidosis, dysgeusia, ECG abnormality, granulocytopenia, gynecomastia, hyperglycemia, hyperinsulinism, hyperprolactinemia, hypersensitivity, hypoglycemia, hypothermia, intraoperative floppy iris syndrome, jaundice, lethargy, leukopenia, mania, muscle spasm, muscle twitching, musculoskeletal pain, neuroleptic malignant syndrome, neutropenia, orthostatic dizziness, pancreatitis, priapism, pulmonary embolism, sedation, SIADH, sleep apnea, syncope, tardive dyskinesia, thrombocytopenia, thrombotic thrombocytopenic purpura, torticollis, trismus, urinary incontinence, urinary retention, urticaria, venous thromboembolism, water intoxication

General Dosage Range Dosage adjustment recommended in patients with renal impairment

Monthly IM: *Adults:* Initial: 234 mg, then 156 mg 1 week later; Maintenance: 39 to 234 mg monthly

Three-month IM: *Adults:* Maintenance: 273 to 819 mg every 3 months

Oral: *Adolescents 12 to 17 years and Adults:* 3 to 12 mg once daily (maximum: 12 mg daily)

Mechanism of Action Paliperidone is considered a benzisoxazole atypical antipsychotic as it is the primary active metabolite of risperidone. As with other atypical antipsychotics, its therapeutic efficacy is believed to result from mixed central serotonergic and dopaminergic antagonism. The addition of serotonin antagonism to dopamine antagonism (classic neuroleptic mechanism) is thought to improve negative symptoms of psychoses and reduce the incidence of extrapyramidal side effects (Huttunen 1995). Similar to risperidone, paliperidone demonstrates high affinity to α_1, α_2, D_2, H_1, and 5-HT_{2A} receptors and low affinity for muscarinic receptors. In contrast to risperidone, paliperidone displays nearly 10-fold lower affinity for α_2 and 5-HT_{2A} receptors, and nearly three- to fivefold less affinity for 5-HT_{1A} and 5-HT_{1D}, respectively.

Pharmacodynamics/Kinetics

Half-life Elimination

Oral: 23 hours; 24 to 51 hours with renal impairment (CrCl <80 mL/minute)

Monthly IM (following a single-dose administration): Range: 25 to 49 days

3-month IM: Deltoid injection range: 84 to 95 days; gluteal injection range: 118 to 139 days

Time to Peak Oral: ~24 hours; Monthly IM: 13 days; 3-month IM: 30 to 33 days

Pregnancy Risk Factor C

Pregnancy Considerations Adverse events have not been observed in animal reproduction studies. Antipsychotic use during the third trimester of pregnancy has a risk for extrapyramidal symptoms (EPS) and/or withdrawal symptoms in newborns following delivery. Symptoms in the newborn may include agitation, feeding disorder, hypertonia, hypotonia, respiratory distress, somnolence, and tremor. These effects may be self-limiting and allow recovery within hours or days with no specific treatment, or they may be severe requiring prolonged hospitalization.

Paliperidone may cause hyperprolactinemia, which may decrease reproductive function in both males and females. Paliperidone is the active metabolite of risperidone; refer to Risperidone monograph for additional information.

The ACOG recommends that therapy during pregnancy be individualized; treatment with psychiatric medications during pregnancy should incorporate the clinical expertise of the mental health clinician, obstetrician, primary healthcare provider, and pediatrician. Safety data related to atypical antipsychotics during pregnancy is limited and routine use is not recommended. However, if a woman is inadvertently exposed to an atypical antipsychotic while pregnant, continuing therapy may be preferable to switching to a typical antipsychotic that the fetus has not yet been exposed to; consider risk: benefit (ACOG, 2008).

Healthcare providers are encouraged to enroll women 18 to 45 years of age exposed to paliperidone during pregnancy in the Atypical Antipsychotics Pregnancy Registry (1-866-961-2388 or http://www.-womensmentalhealth.org/pregnancyregistry).

Dental Comment See Local Anesthetic/Vasoconstrictor Precautions

Palivizumab (pah li VIZ u mab)

Brand Names: US Synagis

Brand Names: Canada Synagis

Pharmacologic Category Monoclonal Antibody

Use Respiratory syncytial virus prophylaxis: Prevention of serious lower respiratory tract disease caused by respiratory syncytial virus (RSV) in pediatric patients at high risk of RSV disease. Safety and efficacy were established in infants with bronchopulmonary dysplasia (BPD), infants with a history of premature birth (≤35 weeks gestational age), and children with hemodynamically significant congenital heart disease (CHD).

The American Academy of Pediatrics (AAP, 2014) recommends RSV prophylaxis with palivizumab during RSV season for:

- Infants born at ≤28 weeks 6 days gestational age and <12 months at the start of RSV season
- Infants <12 months of age with chronic lung disease (CLD) of prematurity
- Infants ≤12 months of age with hemodynamically significant congenital heart disease (CHD)
- Infants and children <24 months of age with CLD of prematurity necessitating medical therapy (eg, supplemental oxygen, bronchodilator, diuretic, or chronic steroid therapy) within 6 months prior to the beginning of RSV season

AAP also suggests that palivizumab prophylaxis may be considered in the following circumstances:

- Infants <12 months of age with congenital airway abnormality or neuromuscular disorder that decreases the ability to manage airway secretions
- Infants <12 months of age with cystic fibrosis with clinical evidence of CLD and/or nutritional compromise
- Children <24 months with cystic fibrosis with severe lung disease (previous hospitalization for pulmonary exacerbation in the first year of life or abnormalities on chest radiography or chest computed tomography that persist when stable) or weight for length less than the 10th percentile
- Infants and children <24 months who are profoundly immunocompromised
- Infants and children <24 months undergoing cardiac transplantation during RSV season

Limitations of use: Safety and efficacy have not been established for treatment of RSV disease.

Local Anesthetic/Vasoconstrictor Precautions No information available to require special precautions

Effects on Dental Treatment No significant effects or complications reported

Effects on Bleeding No information available to require special precautions

Adverse Reactions

>10%:

- Dermatologic: Skin rash (12%)
- Miscellaneous: Fever (27%)

1% to 10%: Immunologic: Antibody development (1% to 2%)

<1%, postmarketing, and/or case reports: Anaphylaxis (very rare; includes angioedema, dyspnea, hypotonia, pruritus, respiratory failure, unresponsiveness, urticaria), hypersensitivity reaction, injection site reaction, thrombocytopenia

General Dosage Range IM: *Children <2 years:* 15 mg/kg monthly

Mechanism of Action Exhibits neutralizing and fusion-inhibitory activity against RSV; these activities inhibit RSV replication in laboratory and clinical studies

Pharmacodynamics/Kinetics

Half-life Elimination Infants and Children <24 months: 20 days

Time to Peak Time to achieve adequate serum antibody titers: 48 hours

Pregnancy Risk Factor C

Pregnancy Considerations Not for adult use; reproduction studies have not been conducted

Palonosetron (pal oh NOE se tron)

Brand Names: US Aloxi

Pharmacologic Category Antiemetic; Selective 5-HT_3 Receptor Antagonist

Use

Chemotherapy-induced nausea and vomiting: Prevention of acute and delayed nausea and vomiting associated with initial and repeat courses in patients treated with moderately emetogenic cancer chemotherapy in adults; prevention of acute nausea and vomiting associated with initial and repeat courses in patients treated with highly emetogenic cancer chemotherapy in adults; prevention of acute nausea and vomiting associated with initial and repeat courses of emetogenic cancer chemotherapy (including highly emetogenic chemotherapy) in pediatric patients 1 month to <17 years.

Postoperative nausea and vomiting: Prevention of postoperative nausea and vomiting (PONV) for up to 24 hours following surgery in adults.

Limitations of use: Routine prophylaxis for PONV in patients with minimal expectation of nausea and/or vomiting is not recommended, although use is recommended in patients when nausea and vomiting must be avoided in the postoperative period, even if the incidence of PONV is low.

Local Anesthetic/Vasoconstrictor Precautions No information available to require special precautions

Effects on Dental Treatment No significant effects or complications reported

Effects on Bleeding No information available to require special precautions

Adverse Reactions Frequencies reported for both indications (chemotherapy-associated nausea and vomiting and postoperative nausea and vomiting) and in adults unless otherwise noted.

1% to 10%:

Cardiovascular: Prolonged Q-T interval on ECG (PONV 1% to 5%; chemotherapy-associated <1%), bradycardia (chemotherapy-associated 1%), sinus bradycardia (PONV: 1%), tachycardia (may be nonsustained; 1%), hypotension (≤1%)

Central nervous system: Headache (chemotherapy-associated: Adults 9%; infants, children, and adolescents <1%), anxiety (chemotherapy-associated: 1%), dizziness (infants, children, adolescents, and adults ≤1%)

Dermatologic: Pruritus (PONV: 1%)

Endocrine & metabolic: Hyperkalemia (chemotherapy-associated: 1%)

Gastrointestinal: Constipation (chemotherapy-associated: 5%), diarrhea (≤1%), flatulence (≤1%)

Genitourinary: Urinary retention (≤1%)

Hepatic: Increased serum ALT (≤1%; may be transient), increased serum AST (≤1%; may be transient)

Neuromuscular & skeletal: Weakness (chemotherapy-associated: 1%)

<1%, postmarketing, and/or case reports: Abdominal pain, allergic dermatitis, amblyopia, anaphylactic shock (very rare), anaphylaxis (very rare), anasarca, anemia, anorexia, arthralgia, cardiac arrhythmia, chills, decreased appetite, decreased blood pressure, decreased gastrointestinal motility, decreased platelet count, dermatological disease (infants, children, and adolescents), distended vein, drowsiness, dyskinesia (infants, children, and adolescents), dyspepsia, electrolyte disturbance, epistaxis, erythema, euphoria, extrasystoles, eye irritation, fatigue, fever, flattened T wave on ECG, flu-like symptoms, glycosuria, hiccups, hot flash, hyperglycemia, hypersensitivity (very rare), hypersomnia, hypertension, hypokalemia, hypoventilation, increased bilirubin (transient), increased liver enzymes, infusion site pain (infants, children, and adolescents), injection site reaction (very rare; includes burning sensation at injection site, discomfort at injection site, induration at injection site, pain at injection site), insomnia, ischemic heart disease, laryngospasm, limb pain, metabolic acidosis, motion sickness, paresthesia, serotonin syndrome, sialorrhea, sinus arrhythmia, sinus tachycardia, skin rash, supraventricular extrasystole, tinnitus, vein discoloration, ventricular premature contractions, xerostomia

General Dosage Range IV:

Infants ≥1 month, Children, and Adolescents <17 years: 20 **mcg**/kg as a single dose (maximum dose: 1.5 **mg**)

Adults: 0.25 mg **or** 0.075 mg as a single dose

Mechanism of Action Selective 5-HT_3 receptor antagonist, blocking serotonin, both on vagal nerve terminals in the periphery and centrally in the chemoreceptor trigger zone

Pharmacodynamics/Kinetics

Half-life Elimination IV: Children 1 month to 17 years: Median: 29.5 hours (range: 20 to 30 hours); Adults: ~40 hours

Pregnancy Risk Factor B

Pregnancy Considerations Adverse events have not been observed in animal reproduction studies. Use during pregnancy only if clearly needed.

Pamidronate (pa mi DROE nate)

Related Information

Osteonecrosis of the Jaw *on page 1796*

Brand Names: Canada Aredia; Pamidronate Disodium; Pamidronate Disodium Omega; PMS-Pamidronate

Pharmacologic Category Bisphosphonate Derivative

Use Hypercalcemia of malignancy: Treatment of moderate or severe hypercalcemia associated with malignancy, with or without bone metastases, in conjunction with adequate hydration.

Osteolytic bone metastases of breast cancer and osteolytic lesions of multiple myeloma: Treatment of osteolytic bone metastases of breast cancer and osteolytic lesions of multiple myeloma in conjunction with standard antineoplastic therapy.

Paget disease: Treatment of patients with moderate to severe Paget disease of bone.

Local Anesthetic/Vasoconstrictor Precautions No information available to require special precautions

Effects on Dental Treatment Osteonecrosis of the jaw (ONJ), generally associated with local infection and/or tooth extraction and often with delayed healing, has been reported in patients taking bisphosphonates. Symptoms included nonhealing extraction socket or an exposed jawbone. Most reported cases of bisphosphonate-associated osteonecrosis have been in cancer patients treated with intravenous bisphosphonates. However, some have occurred in patients with postmenopausal osteoporosis taking oral bisphosphonates. Dental surgery, particularly tooth extraction, may increase the risk for ONJ. Patients who develop ONJ while on bisphosphonate therapy should receive care by an oral surgeon. See Dental Comment.

Effects on Bleeding No information available to require special precautions

Adverse Reactions Note: Actual percentages may vary by indication and duration of infusion; treatment for multiple myeloma is associated with higher percentage.

>10%:

Central nervous system: Fatigue (≤37%), headache (≤26%), insomnia (≤22%)

Endocrine & metabolic: Hypophosphatemia (≤18%), hypokalemia (4% to 18%), hypocalcemia (≤3% to 17%), hypomagnesemia (10% to 12%)

Gastrointestinal: Nausea (≤54%), vomiting (≤36%), anorexia (≤26%), abdominal pain (≤23%), dyspepsia (≤23%)

Genitourinary: Urinary tract infection (≤19%)

Hematologic & oncologic: Anemia (≤43%), metastases (21% to 31%), granulocytopenia (≤20%)

Local: Infusion site reaction (≤18%; includes induration, pain, redness, and swelling)

Neuromuscular & skeletal: Myalgia (≤26%), weakness (≤22%), arthralgia (≤14%), osteonecrosis of the jaw (cancer patients: 1% to 11%)

Renal: Increased serum creatinine (≤19%)

Respiratory: Dyspnea (≤30%), cough (≤26%), upper respiratory tract infection (≤24%), sinusitis (≤16%), pleural effusion (≤11%)

Miscellaneous: Fever (18% to 39%; transient)

1% to 10%:

Cardiovascular: Atrial fibrillation (≤6%), hypertension (≤6%), syncope (≤6%), tachycardia (≤6%), atrial flutter (≤1%), cardiac failure (≤1%), edema (≤1%)

Central nervous system: Drowsiness (≤6%), psychosis (≤4%), seizure (≤2%)

Endocrine & metabolic: Hypothyroidism (≤6%)
Gastrointestinal: Constipation (≤6%), gastrointestinal hemorrhage (≤6%), diarrhea (≤1%), stomatitis (≤1%)
Genitourinary: Uremia (≤4%)
Hematologic & oncologic: Leukopenia (≤4%), neutropenia (≤1%), thrombocytopenia (≤1%)
Infection: Candidiasis (≤6%)
Neuromuscular & skeletal: Back pain, ostealgia
Respiratory: Rales (≤6%), rhinitis (≤6%)

<1%, postmarketing, and/or case reports: Acute renal failure, anaphylactic shock, angioedema, bronchospasm, cardiac failure, confusion, conjunctivitis, electrolyte disturbance, episcleritis, flu-like symptoms, focal segmental glomerulosclerosis (including collapsing variant), hallucination (visual), hematuria, herpes virus infection (reactivation), hyperkalemia, hypernatremia, hypersensitivity reaction, hypervolemia, hypotension, inflammation at injection site, injection site phlebitis, iridocyclitis, iritis, left heart failure, lymphocytopenia, malaise, mineral abnormalities, nephrotic syndrome, osteonecrosis (other than jaw), paresthesia, pruritus, renal failure, renal insufficiency, scleritis, skin rash, tetany, uveitis, xanthopsia

General Dosage Range Dosage adjustment recommended in patients with renal impairment

IV: *Adults:* 60 to 90 mg as a single dose, may repeat every 3 to 4 weeks **or** 30 mg daily for 3 consecutive days

Mechanism of Action Nitrogen-containing bisphosphonate; inhibits bone resorption and decreases mineralization by disrupting osteoclast activity (Gralow 2009; Rogers 2011)

Pharmacodynamics/Kinetics

Onset of Action

Hypercalcemia of malignancy (HCM): Reduction of albumin-corrected serum calcium: Children: ~48 hours (Kerdudo, 2005); Adults: ≤24 hours for decrease in albumin-corrected serum calcium; maximum effect: ≤7 days

Paget disease: ~1 month for ≥50% decrease in serum alkaline phosphatase

Maximum effect: Hypercalcemia of malignancy: ≤7 days

Duration of Action HCM: 7 to 14 days; Paget disease: 1 to 372 days

Half-life Elimination 28 ± 7 hours

Pregnancy Risk Factor D

Pregnancy Considerations Adverse events were observed in animal reproduction studies. It is not known if bisphosphonates cross the placenta, but fetal exposure is expected (Djokanovic, 2008; Stathopoulos, 2011). Bisphosphonates are incorporated into the bone matrix and gradually released over time. The amount available in the systemic circulation varies by dose and duration of therapy. Theoretically, there may be a risk of fetal harm when pregnancy follows the completion of therapy; however, available data have not shown that exposure to bisphosphonates during pregnancy significantly increases the risk of adverse fetal events (Djokanovic, 2008; Levy, 2009; Stathopoulos, 2011). Until additional data is available, most sources recommend discontinuing bisphosphonate therapy in women of reproductive potential as early as possible prior to a planned pregnancy; use in premenopausal women should be reserved for special circumstances when rapid bone loss is occurring (Bhalla, 2010; Pereira, 2012; Stathopoulos, 2011). Because hypocalcemia has been described following *in utero* bisphosphonate exposure, exposed infants should be monitored for hypocalcemia after birth (Djokanovic, 2008; Stathopoulos, 2011).

Dental Comment The American Association of Oral and Maxillofacial Surgeons position paper on bisphosphonate-related osteonecrosis of the jaws, 2009 update, stated that IV bisphosphonate exposure in the setting of managing malignancy remains the major risk factor for the development of ONJ. After reviewing case series, case-controlled studies, and cohort studies, the estimates of the cumulative incidence of IV bisphosphonate-associated ONJ ranges from 0.8% to 12%.

Two reports have attempted to assess more accurately the percent of cancer patients developing ONJ after bisphosphonate treatment. Maerevoet et al, reported that among 194 patients treated with Zometa® every 3-4 weeks, nine developed ONJ. Before receiving Zometa®, six had received Aredia® 90 mg every 3-4 weeks. The median duration of treatment with Aredia® was 39 months and for Zometa® 18 months. The incidence of ONJ in these patients was calculated to be 4.6%. Durie et al, described the results of a survey by the International Myeloma Foundation in 2004 to assess the risk factors of ONJ. Out of 1203 respondents, 904 had myeloma and 299 had breast cancer. Of the myeloma patients, 62 developed ONJ and 54 had suspicious findings. Of the breast cancer patients, 13 had ONJ and 23 had suspicious findings. The total number of cases of either ONJ or suspicious findings was 152. ONJ developed in 10% of 211 patients receiving Zometa® compared to 4% of 413 receiving Aredia®. The mean time to onset of ONJ among patients taking Zometa® was 18 months; the mean time to onset after Aredia® was 6 years. It should be noted that an early report by authors from Novartis Pharmaceuticals Corporation stressed that Aredia® and Zometa® had been used in 2.5 million patients world wide and reports of ONJ during their extensive use had been rare (Tarassoff, 2003). In addition, these authors stated that review of the reported cases revealed multiple risk factors for avascular necrosis. McMahon et al, followed up with a report that, along with other factors, bisphosphonates are additional stressors of bone health that can tip the balance to osteonecrosis. They suggested that the prevention of ONJ should be stressed such as the elimination of chronic dental infections prior to chemotherapy and bisphosphonate use in cancer patients.

The most comprehensive review to date on osteonecrosis of the jaw bone (ONJ) has been published in the *Journal of Bone and Mineral Research* (Khan 2015), and written by an International Task Force of authors, totaling 34, from academe; industry; clinical medical and dental practice; oral and maxillofacial surgery; bone and mineral research; epidemiology; medical and dental oncology; orthopedic surgery; osteoporosis research; muscle and bone research; endocrinology and diagnostic sciences. The work provides a systematic review of the literature and international consensus on the classification, incidence, pathophysiology, diagnosis, and management of ONJ in both oncology and osteoporosis patient populations. This review of the literature from January 2003 to April 2014, with 299 references, offers recommendations for management of ONJ based on multidisciplinary international consensus.

Incidence of ONJ in oncology patients from the Task Force report:

The incidence of ONJ ranges from 1% to 15% in the oncology patient population where high doses of BPs are used at frequent intervals. The oncology patient with bone metastasis is exposed to more osteoclastic inhibition than those with osteoporosis, thus the incidence of ONJ is much higher.

Panitumumab (pan i TOOM yoo mab)

Brand Names: US Vectibix

Brand Names: Canada Vectibix

Pharmacologic Category Antineoplastic Agent, Epidermal Growth Factor Receptor (EGFR) Inhibitor; Antineoplastic Agent, Monoclonal Antibody

Use

Colorectal cancer, metastatic: Treatment of patients with wild-type *KRAS* (exon 2 in codons 12 or 13) metastatic colorectal cancer (mCRC), either as first-line therapy in combination with FOLFOX (fluorouracil, leucovorin, and oxaliplatin) or as a single agent following disease progression after prior treatment with fluoropyrimidine-, oxaliplatin-, and irinotecan-containing chemotherapy regimens

Limitations of use: Panitumumab is not indicated for the treatment of patients with *RAS*-mutant mCRC or for whom *RAS* mutation status is unknown.

Local Anesthetic/Vasoconstrictor Precautions No information available to require special precautions

Effects on Dental Treatment Key adverse event(s) related to dental treatment: Stomatitis and mucositis.

Effects on Bleeding Although significant myelosuppression with associated altered hemostasis has been reported for many chemotherapeutic agents, myelosuppression is not common with panitumumab and no specific precautions appear to necessary.

Adverse Reactions

Monotherapy:

>10%:

Central nervous system: Fatigue (26%)

Dermatologic: Skin toxicity (90%; grades 3/4: 15%), erythema (66%; grades 3/4: 6%), pruritus (58%; grades 3/4: 3%), acneiform eruption (57%; grades 3/4: 7%), paronychia (25%; grades 3/4: 2%), rash (22%; grades 3/4: 1%), skin fissure (20%; grades 3/4: 1%), exfoliative dermatitis (18%; grades 3/4: 2%), acne vulgaris (14%; grades 3/4: 1%)

Endocrine & metabolic: Hypomagnesemia (grades 3/4: 7%)

Gastrointestinal: Nausea (23%), diarrhea (21%; grades 3/4: 2%), vomiting (19%)

Ophthalmic: Ocular toxicity (16%)

Respiratory: Dyspnea (18%), cough (15%)

Miscellaneous: Fever (17%)

1% to 10%:

Cardiovascular: Pulmonary embolism (1%)

Central nervous system: Chills (3%)

Dermatologic: Nail toxicity (10%), xeroderma (10%), desquamation (9%; grades 3/4: <1%), dermal ulcer (6%; grades 3/4: <1%), pustular rash (4%), papular rash (2%)

Endocrine & metabolic: Dehydration (3%)

Gastrointestinal: Mucositis (7%), stomatitis (7%), xerostomia (5%)

Immunologic: Antibody formation (≤5%)

Ophthalmic: Abnormal eyelash growth (6%), conjunctivitis (5%)

Respiratory: Epistaxis (4%), interstitial pulmonary disease (1%)

Miscellaneous: Infusion related reaction (3%; grades 3/4: <1%)

<1%: Hypersensitivity reaction, pulmonary fibrosis

Combination therapy with FOLFOX:

>10%:

Dermatologic: Skin rash (56%; grades 3/4: 17% to 26%), acneiform eruption (32%; grades 3/4: 10%), pruritus (23%; grades 3/4: <1%), paronychia (21%; grades 3/4: 3%), xeroderma (21%; grades 3/4: 2%), erythema (16%; grades 3/4: 2%), skin fissure (16%; grades 3/4: <1%), alopecia (15%), acne vulgaris (14%; grades 3/4: 3%)

Endocrine & metabolic: Hypomagnesemia (30%), hypokalemia (21%), weight loss (18%)

Gastrointestinal: Diarrhea (62%), anorexia (36%), abdominal pain (28%), stomatitis (27%), mucosal inflammation (25%)

Neuromuscular & skeletal: Weakness (25%)

Ophthalmic: Conjunctivitis (18%)

Respiratory: Epistaxis (14%)

1% to 10%:

Cardiovascular: Deep vein thrombosis (5%)

Central nervous system: Fatigue (≥1%), paresthesia (≥1%)

Dermatologic: Nail disorder (10%; grades 3/4: 1%), palmar-plantar erythrodysesthesia (9%; grades 3/4: 1%), cellulitis (3%)

Endocrine & metabolic: Dehydration (8%), hypocalcemia (6%)

Hypersensitivity: Hypersensitivity (≥1%)

Local: Localized infection (4%)

<1%: Antibody development

Postmarketing and/or case reports (mono- and combination therapy): Abscess, angioedema, bullous skin disease (mucocutaneous), corneal ulcer, keratitis, necrotizing fasciitis, sepsis, skin necrosis, Stevens-Johnson syndrome, toxic epidermal necrolysis

General Dosage Range Dosage adjustment recommended in patients who develop toxicities

IV: *Adults:* 6 mg/kg every 14 days

Mechanism of Action Recombinant human IgG2 monoclonal antibody which binds specifically to the epidermal growth factor receptor (EGFR, HER1, c-ErbB-1) and competitively inhibits the binding of epidermal growth factor (EGF) and other ligands. Binding to the EGFR blocks phosphorylation and activation of intracellular tyrosine kinases, resulting in inhibition of cell survival, growth, proliferation and transformation. EGFR signal transduction may result in *KRAS* and *NRAS* wild-type activation; cells with *RAS* mutations appear to be unaffected by EGFR inhibition.

Pharmacodynamics/Kinetics

Half-life Elimination ~7.5 days (range: 4 to 11 days)

Pregnancy Risk Factor C

Pregnancy Considerations Animal reproduction studies have demonstrated adverse fetal effects. Based on animal studies, panitumumab may disrupt normal menstrual cycles. IgG is known to cross the placenta; therefore, it is possible the developing fetus may be exposed to panitumumab. Because panitumumab inhibits epidermal growth factor (EGF), a component of fetal development, adverse effects on pregnancy would be expected. Men and women of childbearing potential should use effective contraception during and for 6 months after treatment. In the US and Canada, women who become pregnant during panitumumab treatment are encouraged to enroll in Amgen's Pregnancy Surveillance Program (US: 1-800-772-6436; Canada: 1-866-512-6436).

Panobinostat (pan oh BIN oh stat)

Brand Names: US Farydak

Pharmacologic Category Antineoplastic Agent, Histone Deacetylase (HDAC) Inhibitor

Use Multiple myeloma: Treatment of multiple myeloma (in combination with bortezomib and dexamethasone) in patients who have received at least 2 prior regimens, including bortezomib and an immunomodulatory agent.

Local Anesthetic/Vasoconstrictor Precautions Panobinostat is one of the drugs confirmed to prolong the QT interval and is accepted as having a risk of causing torsade de pointes. The risk of drug-induced torsade de pointes is extremely low when a single QT interval prolonging drug is prescribed. In terms of epinephrine, it is not known what effect vasoconstrictors in the local anesthetic regimen will have in patients with a known history of congenital prolonged QT interval or in patients taking any medication that prolongs the QT interval. Until more information is obtained, it is suggested that the clinician consult with the physician prior to the use of a vasoconstrictor in suspected patients, and that the vasoconstrictor (epinephrine, mepivacaine, and levonordefrin [Carbocaine 2% with Neo-Cobefrin]) be used with caution.

Effects on Dental Treatment No significant effects or complications reported

Effects on Bleeding Chemotherapy may result in significant myelosuppression, potentially including significant reduction in platelet counts (thrombocytopenia) and altered hemostasis. In patients who are under active treatment with these agents, medical consult is suggested.

Adverse Reactions Frequency not always defined.

>10%:

Cardiovascular: Abnormal T waves on ECG (40%), peripheral edema (29%; grades 3/4: 2%), depression of ST segment on ECG (22%), cardiac arrhythmia (12%; grades 3/4: 3%)

Central nervous system: Fatigue (≤60%, grades 3/4: ≤25%), lethargy (≤60%; grades 3/4: ≤25%), malaise (≤60%; grades 3/4: ≤25%)

Endocrine & metabolic: Hypocalcemia (67%; grades 3/4: 5%), hypoalbuminemia (63%; grades 3/4: 2%), hypophosphatemia (63%; grades 3/4: 20%), hypokalemia (52%; grades 3/4: 18%), hyponatremia (49%; grades 3/4: 13%), hyperphosphatemia (29%; grades 3/4: 2%), hypermagnesemia (27%; grades 3/4: 5%), weight loss (12%; grades 3/4: 2%)

Gastrointestinal: Diarrhea (68%; grades 3/4: 25%), nausea (36%; grades 3/4: 6%), decreased appetite (28%; grades 3/4: 3%), vomiting (26%; grades 3/4: 7%)

Hematologic & oncologic: Thrombocytopenia (97%; grades 3/4: 67%), lymphocytopenia (82%; grades 3/4: 53%), leukopenia (81%; grades 3/4: 23%), neutropenia (75%; grades 3/4: 34%), anemia (62%; grades 3/4: 18%)

Hepatic: Hyperbilirubinemia (21%; grades 3/4: 1%)

Infection: Severe infection (31%; includes bacterial, fungal, and viral infections)

Neuromuscular & skeletal: Weakness (≤60%; grades ≥3: ≤25%)

Renal: Increased serum creatinine (41%; grades 3/4: 1%)

Miscellaneous: Fever (26%)

1% to 10%:

Cardiovascular: Hypertension (>2% to <10%), hypotension (>2% to <10%), orthostatic hypotension (>2% to <10%), palpitations (>2% to <10%), syncope (>2% to <10%), ischemic heart disease (4%), ECG changes, prolonged Q-T interval on ECG

Central nervous system: Chills (>2% to <10%), dizziness (>2% to <10%), headache (>2% to <10%), insomnia (>2% to <10%)

Dermatologic: Cheilitis (>2% to <10%), erythema (>2% to <10%), skin lesion (>2% to <10%), skin rash (>2% to <10%)

Endocrine & metabolic: Dehydration (>2% to <10%), fluid retention (>2% to <10%), hyperglycemia (>2% to <10%), hyperuricemia (>2% to <10%), hypomagnesemia (>2% to <10%), hypothyroidism (>2% to <10%)

Gastrointestinal: Abdominal distention (>2% to <10%), abdominal pain (>2% to <10%), colitis (>2% to <10%), dysgeusia (>2% to <10%), dyspepsia (>2% to <10%), flatulence (>2% to <10%), gastritis (>2% to <10%), gastrointestinal pain (>2% to <10%), xerostomia (>2% to <10%), gastrointestinal toxicity

Genitourinary: Urinary incontinence (>2% to <10%)

Hematologic & oncologic: Hemorrhage (grades 3/4: 4%)

Hepatic: Hepatitis B (>2% to <10%), increased serum alkaline phosphatase (>2% to <10%), increased aminotransferases, increased serum bilirubin

Infection: Sepsis (6%)

Neuromuscular & skeletal: Joint swelling (>2% to <10%), tremor (>2% to <10%)

Renal: Increased blood urea nitrogen (>2% to <10%), mean glomerular filtration rate decreased (>2% to <10%), renal failure (>2% to <10%)

Respiratory: Cough (>2% to <10%), dyspnea (>2% to <10%), rales (>2% to <10%), respiratory failure (>2% to <10%), wheezing (>2% to <10%)

General Dosage Range Dose reduction recommended in patients with hepatic impairment, on concomitant therapy, or who develop toxicities.

Oral: *Adults:* 20 mg once every other day for 3 doses each week during weeks 1 and 2 of a 21-day treatment cycle

Mechanism of Action Panobinostat is a histone deacetylase (HDAC) inhibitor; inhibits enzymatic activity of HDACs resulting in increased acetylation of histone proteins. Accumulation of acetylated histones and other proteins induces cell cycle arrest and/or apoptosis of some transformed cells. Panobinostat has minimal activity in multiple myeloma as a single-agent; however, synergistic activity is demonstrated when combined with bortezomib and dexamethasone (San-Miguel 2014).

Pharmacodynamics/Kinetics

Half-life Elimination ~37 hours

Time to Peak Within 2 hours

Pregnancy Considerations Adverse events were observed in animal reproduction studies. Pregnancy should be ruled out prior to treatment. Women of reproductive potential should avoid pregnancy and use an effective contraceptive during therapy and for at least 3 months after the last panobinostat dose. Males should use condoms during therapy and for at least 6 months after the last dose of panobinostat.

Pantoprazole (pan TOE pra zole)

Related Information

Gastrointestinal Disorders *on page 1775*

Brand Names: US Protonix

Brand Names: Canada ACT Pantoprazole; Apo-Pantoprazole; Dom-Pantoprazole; JAMP-Pantoprazole; Mar-Pantoprazole; Mint-Pantoprazole; Mylan-Pantoprazole; Panto I.V.; Pantoloc; Pantoprazole for Injection; Pantoprazole Magnesium; Pantoprazole Sodium for Injection; PMS-Pantoprazole; Priva-Pantoprazole; Ran-Pantoprazole; Riva-Pantoprazole; Sandoz-Pantoprazole; Tecta; Teva-Pantoprazole; Teva-Pantoprazole Magnesium

Pharmacologic Category Proton Pump Inhibitor; Substituted Benzimidazole

Use

Oral:

Erosive esophagitis associated with gastroesophageal reflux disease: Short-term treatment (up to 8 weeks) in the healing and symptomatic relief of erosive esophagitis in adults and pediatric patients 5 years and older.

Maintenance of healing of erosive esophagitis: Maintenance of healing of erosive esophagitis and reduction in relapse rates of daytime and nighttime heartburn symptoms in adult patients with gastroesophageal reflux disease (GERD).

Pathological hypersecretory conditions, including Zollinger-Ellison syndrome: Long-term treatment of pathological hypersecretory conditions, including Zollinger-Ellison syndrome.

IV:

Gastroesophageal reflux disease associated with a history of erosive esophagitis: Short-term treatment (7 to 10 days) of adult patients with gastroesophageal reflux disease (GERD) and a history of erosive esophagitis.

Pathological hypersecretion associated with Zollinger-Ellison syndrome: Treatment of adult patients with pathological hypersecretory conditions, including Zollinger-Ellison syndrome.

Canadian labeling: Additional use (not in US labeling): Oral: Peptic ulcer disease (eg, duodenal or gastric ulcer); adjunct treatment with antibiotics for *Helicobacter pylori* eradication; NSAID-induced ulcer prophylaxis (Pantoloc)

Local Anesthetic/Vasoconstrictor Precautions No information available to require special precautions

Effects on Dental Treatment No significant effects or complications reported

Effects on Bleeding No information available to require special precautions

Adverse Reactions

>10%: Central nervous system: Headache (adults 12%; children >4%)

1% to 10%:

Cardiovascular: Facial edema (≤4%), edema (≤2%)

Central nervous system: Dizziness (≤4%), vertigo (≤4%), depression (≤2%)

Dermatologic: Skin rash (adults ≤2%; children >4%), urticaria (≤4%), pruritus (≤2%), skin photosensitivity (≤2%)

Endocrine & metabolic: Increased serum triglycerides (≤4%)

Gastrointestinal: Diarrhea (≤9%), abdominal pain (children >4%), vomiting (≥4%), constipation (≤4%), flatulence (children ≤4%), nausea (children ≤4%), xerostomia (≤2%)

Hematologic & oncologic: Leukopenia (≤2%), thrombocytopenia (≤2%)

Hepatic: Abnormal hepatic function tests (≤4%), hepatitis (≤2%)

Hypersensitivity: Hypersensitivity reaction (≤4%)

Local: Inflammation at injection site (≤2%)

Neuromuscular & skeletal: Arthralgia (≤4%), myalgia (≤4%), increased creatine phosphokinase (≤4%)

Ophthalmic: Blurred vision (≤2%)

Respiratory: Upper respiratory tract infection (children >4%)

Miscellaneous: Fever (adults ≤2%; children >4%)

<1%, postmarketing, and/or case reports: Ageusia, agranulocytosis, anaphylaxis (including anaphylactic shock), angioedema, bone fracture, chronic renal disease (Lazarus 2016), *Clostridium difficile*-associated diarrhea, confusion, contact dermatitis, cutaneous lupus erythematous, decreased libido, diabetes mellitus, drowsiness, dysgeusia, ECG abnormality, eosinophilia, erythema multiforme, esophagitis, fatigue, gastric ulcer, gastrointestinal carcinoma, hallucination, hematuria, hepatic failure, hepatotoxicity (idiosyncratic) (Chalasani 2014), hyperbilirubinemia, hypertension, hypokinesia, hypomagnesemia, hyponatremia, impotence, increased appetite, increased serum alkaline phosphatase, interstitial nephritis, ischemic heart disease, jaundice, leukocytosis, malaise, neoplasm, nervousness, optic neuropathy (including anterior ischemic), pancreatitis, pancytopenia, paresthesia, pneumonia (Eom 2011), rhabdomyolysis, Stevens-Johnson syndrome, systemic lupus erythematosus, thrombosis, tinnitus, tongue discoloration, toxic epidermal necrolysis, tremor, visual disturbance, weakness, weight changes

General Dosage Range

IV: *Adults:* Erosive gastritis: 40 mg once daily; Hypersecretory disorders: 160 to 240 mg daily in divided doses

Oral:

Children ≥5 years: ≥15 to <40 kg: 20 mg once daily; ≥40 kg: 40 mg once daily

Adults: 20 to 40 mg once or twice daily; doses up to 240 mg daily have been administered (for treatment of hypersecretory conditions)

Mechanism of Action Proton pump inhibitor, suppresses gastric acid secretion by inhibiting the parietal cell H^+/K^+ ATP pump

Pharmacodynamics/Kinetics

Onset of Action

Onset of action: Acid secretion: Oral: 2.5 hours; IV: 15 to 30 minutes

Maximum effect: IV: 2 hours

Duration of Action Oral, IV: 24 hours

Half-life Elimination

Neonates (PMA: 37 to 44 weeks): ~3 hours (Ward 2010)

Children and Adolescents (Kearns 2008): IV: 2 to 16 years: 1.22 ± 0.68 hours; Oral: 5 to 16 years: 1.27 ± 1.29 hours

Adults: 1 hour; increased to 3.5 to 10 hours with CYP2C19 deficiency

Time to Peak

Children and Adolescents (Kearns 2008): IV: 2 to 16 years: 0.34 ± 0.12 hours; Oral: 5 to 16 years: 2.54 ± 0.72 hours

Adults: Oral: 2.5 hours

Pregnancy Risk Factor B

Pregnancy Considerations Adverse events have not been observed in animal reproduction studies. Most available studies have not shown an increased risk of major birth defects following maternal use of proton pump inhibitors during pregnancy (Diav-Citrin, 2005; Erichsen, 2012; Matok, 2012; Pasternak, 2010). When treating GERD in pregnancy, PPIs may be used when clinically indicated (Katz, 2013).

Papaverine (pa PAV er een)

Pharmacologic Category Vasodilator

Use Various vascular spasms associated with smooth muscle spasms as in myocardial infarction, angina, peripheral and pulmonary embolism, peripheral vascular disease; cerebral angiospastic states; visceral spasms (ureteral, biliary, and GI colic). **Note:** Labeled uses have fallen out of favor; safer and more effective alternatives are available.

Local Anesthetic/Vasoconstrictor Precautions No information available to require special precautions

Effects on Dental Treatment No significant effects or complications reported

Effects on Bleeding No information available to require special precautions

Adverse Reactions Frequency not defined.

Cardiovascular: Cardiac arrhythmia (with rapid IV use), flushing, hypertension (mild), tachycardia

Central nervous system: Headache, malaise, sedation, vertigo

Dermatologic: Diaphoresis, skin rash

Gastrointestinal: Abdominal distress, anorexia, constipation, diarrhea, nausea

Hepatic: Hepatic cirrhosis

Hypersensitivity: Hypersensitivity reaction (hepatic)

Respiratory: Apnea (with rapid IV use)

<1%, postmarketing, and/or case reports: Hepatitis

General Dosage Range IM, IV: *Adults:* 30-120 mg, may repeat dose every 3 hours

Mechanism of Action Smooth muscle spasmolytic producing a generalized smooth muscle relaxation including: vasodilatation, gastrointestinal sphincter relaxation, bronchiolar muscle relaxation, and potentially a depressed myocardium (with large doses); muscle relaxation may occur due to inhibition or cyclic nucleotide phosphodiesterase, increasing cyclic AMP; muscle relaxation is unrelated to nerve innervation; papaverine increases cerebral blood flow in normal subjects; oxygen uptake is unaltered

Pharmacodynamics/Kinetics

Onset of Action Oral: Rapid

Half-life Elimination 30 to 120 minutes

Pregnancy Risk Factor C

Pregnancy Considerations Teratogenic effects have not been observed in animal reproduction studies.

Papillomavirus (Types 6, 11, 16, 18) Vaccine (Human, Recombinant)

(pap ih LO ma VYE rus typs six e LEV en SIX teen AYE teen vak SEEN YU man ree KOM be nant)

Brand Names: US Gardasil

Brand Names: Canada Gardasil

Pharmacologic Category Vaccine; Vaccine, Inactivated (Viral)

Use

Prevention of human papillomavirus infection:

US labeling:

Females 9 to 26 years of age:

For the prevention of the following diseases: Cervical, vulvar, vaginal, and anal cancer caused by HPV types 16 and 18; genital warts (condyloma acuminatum) caused by HPV types 6 and 11;

For the prevention of the following precancerous or dysplastic lesions caused by HPV types 6, 11, 16, and 18: Cervical intraepithelial neoplasia (CIN) grade 2/3 and cervical adenocarcinoma in situ; CIN grade 1; vulvar intraepithelial neoplasia grade 2 and 3; vaginal intraepithelial neoplasia grade 2 and 3; and anal intraepithelial neoplasia grades 1, 2, and 3.

Males 9 through 26 years of age:

For the prevention of the following diseases: Anal cancer caused by HPV types 16 and 18; genital warts (condyloma acuminata) caused by HPV types 6 and 11;

For the prevention of anal intraepithelial neoplasia grades 1, 2, and 3 caused by HPV types 6, 11, 16, and 18.

Limitations of use: Does not provide protection against vaccine HPV types to which a person has already been previously exposed, or HPV types not contained in the vaccine; does not prevent CIN grade 2/3 or worse in women >26 years. Not intended for the treatment of active external genital lesions or cervical, vulvar, vaginal, and anal cancers.

Canadian labeling:

Females ≥9 years and ≤26 years: Prevention of anal cancer caused by HPV types 16 and 18; anal intraepithelial neoplasia caused by HPV types 6, 11, 16, and 18

Females ≥9 years and ≤45 years: Prevention of cervical, vulvar, and vaginal cancer caused by HPV types 16 and 18; genital warts caused by HPV types 6 and 11; cervical adenocarcinoma *in situ*, vulvar, vaginal, or cervical intraepithelial neoplasia caused by HPV types 6, 11, 16, and 18

Males ≥9 years and ≤26 years: Prevention of anal cancer caused by HPV types 16 and 18; anal intraepithelial neoplasia caused by HPV types 6, 11, 16, and 18; genital warts caused by HPV types 6 and 11

The Advisory Committee on Immunization Practices (ACIP) recommends routine vaccination for females and males 11 to 12 years; for patients with any history of sexual abuse or assault, vaccination should be started at 9 years of age. Catch-up vaccination is recommended for females and transgender persons 13 to 26 years and males 13 to 21 years. Vaccination for males 22 through 26 years is recommended if immunocompromised (including HIV) and for men who have sex with men and may be considered for any other male in this age group (CDC/ACIP [Meites 2016]).

Local Anesthetic/Vasoconstrictor Precautions No information available to require special precautions

Effects on Dental Treatment No significant effects or complications reported (see Dental Comment)

Effects on Bleeding No information available to require special precautions

Adverse Reactions

>10%:

Central nervous system: Headache (12% to 28%)

Local: Pain at injection site (61% to 84%), erythema at injection site (17% to 25%), swelling at injection site (14% to 25%)
Miscellaneous: Fever (8% to 13%)

1% to 10%:
Central nervous system: Dizziness (1% to 4%), insomnia (1%), malaise (1%)
Dermatologic: Injection site pruritus (3%)
Gastrointestinal: Nausea (2% to 7%), diarrhea (3% to 4%), toothache (2%), vomiting (1% to 2%)
Local: Bruising at injection site (3%), hematoma at injection site (1%)
Neuromuscular & skeletal: Arthralgia (1%), myalgia (≤1%)
Respiratory: Pharyngolaryngeal pain (3%), cough (2%), nasal congestion (1%)

<1%, postmarketing, and/or case reports: Acute disseminated encephalomyelitis, acute renal failure, anaphylactoid reaction, anaphylaxis, appendicitis, arthritis, arthropathy (impaired joint movement at injection site), asthma, autoimmune disease, autoimmune hemolytic anemia, bronchospasm, cardiac arrhythmia, cellulitis, cerebrovascular accident, chills, deep vein thrombosis, fatigue, gastroenteritis, Guillain-Barré syndrome, hypersensitivity reaction, hyperthyroidism, hypothyroidism, immune thrombocytopenia, juvenile rheumatoid arthritis, lymphadenopathy, demyelinating disease, pancreatitis, paralysis, partial alopecia (alopecia areata), pelvic inflammatory disease, pulmonary embolism, rheumatoid arthritis, seizure, sepsis, syncope (may result in falls with injury or be associated with tonic-clonic movements), transverse myelitis, urticaria, weakness

General Dosage Range IM: *Children ≥9 years, Adolescents, and Adults ≤26 years:* 0.5 mL at 0, 2 and 6 months

Mechanism of Action

Contains inactive human papillomavirus (HPV) proteins HPV 6 L1, HPV 11 L1, HPV 16 L1, and HPV 18 L1 which produce neutralizing antibodies to prevent cervical cancer, cervical adenocarcinoma, cervical, vaginal and vulvar neoplasia, and genital warts caused by HPV. The vaccine has not been shown to provide cross-protective efficacy to HPV types not contained in the vaccine. Immunogenicity has been measured by the percentage of persons who became seropositive for antibodies contained in the vaccine; the minimum anti-HPV antibody concentration needed to protect against disease has not been determined. The population benefit to vaccination is influenced by the prevalence of HPV within the geographic area and subject characteristics (eg, lifetime sexual partners).

Efficacy: Vaccination with 4vHPV reduced the incidence of CIN 2/3 and AIS by 98% to 100% in several randomized clinical trials. Efficacy against vulvar or vaginal intraepithelial neoplasia grades 2/3 was 100%. Against HPV 6- and 11-related genital warts, 4vHPV vaccination reduced incidence in women by 99% in several clinical trials. In men and boys, 4vHPV vaccination reduced the incidence of the following end points: external genital warts, 89% penile intraepithelial neoplasia of any severity, 100%; anal intraepithelial neoplasia (AIN) of any severity, 78% (CDC/ACIP [Markowitz 2014]).

Pharmacodynamics/Kinetics

Onset of Action Peak seroconversion was observed 1 month following the last dose of vaccine

Duration of Action Not well defined; at least 8 years

Pregnancy Risk Factor B

Pregnancy Considerations Teratogenic effects were not observed in animal reproduction studies. In clinical trials, women who were found to be pregnant before the completion of the 3-dose regimen were instructed to defer any remaining dose until pregnancy resolution. Pregnancies detected within 30 days of vaccination had a higher rate of congenital anomalies (pyloric stenosis, congenital megacolon, congenital hydronephrosis, hip dysplasia, club foot) than the placebo group. Pregnancies with onset beyond 30 days of vaccination had a rate of congenital anomalies consistent with the general population. Overall, the types of teratogenic events were the same as those generally observed for this age group. Administration of the vaccine in pregnancy is not recommended; until additional information is available, the vaccine series (or completion of the series) should be delayed until pregnancy is completed. Pregnancy testing is not required prior to administration of the vaccine (CDC/ACIP [Petrosky 2015]).

A registry has been established for women exposed to the HPV vaccine during pregnancy (1-877-888-4231).

Dental Comment Human papilloma virus is widespread and serotypes 16 and 18 have been associated with cervical cancer. Although most types that cause oral HPV lesions are not of these serotypes, the clinician should recommend appropriate surgical removal of all such lesions. Lesions in the posterior oral pharyngeal region are of particular concern. Pre-exposure vaccination is one of the most effective methods for preventing transmission of some serotypes of HPV. Quadrivalent HPV vaccine (Gardasil) and the bivalent HPV vaccine (Cervarix) are available. Gardasil is indicated for the prevention of a number of diseases caused by oncogenic human papillomavirus (HPV) types 16 and 18 and approved for use in girls and women 9-26 years of age. Gardasil is also indicated in boys and men 9-26 years of age for the prevention of a number of diseases caused by HPV types (see Use).

Details regarding HPV vaccination are available at www.cdc.gov/std/hpv. Vaccines for other STDs (eg, HIV and herpes simplex virus) are under development or undergoing clinical trials. Vaccines are not available for bacterial or fungal STDs.

Papillomavirus (Types 16, 18) Vaccine (Human, Recombinant)

(pap ih LO ma VYE rus typs SIX teen AYE teen vak SEEN YU man ree KOM be nant)

Brand Names: US Cervarix [DSC]

Brand Names: Canada Cervarix

Pharmacologic Category Vaccine; Vaccine, Inactivated (Viral)

Use

Prevention of human papillomavirus infection:

US labeling: Prevention in females 9 to 25 years of age of the following diseases caused by oncogenic HPV types 16 and 18: Cervical cancer, cervical intraepithelial neoplasia (CIN) grade 2 or higher and adenocarcinoma in situ, and CIN grade 1.

The Advisory Committee on Immunization Practices (ACIP) recommends routine vaccination for females 11 to 12 years; for patients with any history of sexual abuse or assault, vaccination should be started at 9 years. Catch-up vaccination is recommended for females 13 to 26 years (CDC/ACIP [Meites 2016]).

Canadian labeling: Females 9 through 45 years of age: Prevention of cervical cancer, cervical adenocarcinoma *in situ*, and cervical intraepithelial neoplasia caused by human papillomavirus (HPV) types 16, 18

The National Advisory Committee on Immunization (NACI) recommends routine vaccination for females between 9 and 26 years of age. It should not be administered in females <9 years but may be administered to females >26 years who are at ongoing risk of exposure (NACI [CCDR 2012]).

Local Anesthetic/Vasoconstrictor Precautions No information available to require special precautions

Effects on Dental Treatment No significant effects or complications reported (see Dental Comment)

Effects on Bleeding No information available to require special precautions

Adverse Reactions

>10%:

Central nervous system: Fatigue (55%)

Local: Pain at injection site (92%), erythema at injection site (48%), swelling at injection site (44%)

Neuromuscular & skeletal: Myalgia (49%), arthralgia (21%)

1% to 10%:

Dermatologic: Urticaria (7%), injection site pruritus (1%)

Genitourinary: Vaginal infection (1%)

Infection: Influenza (3%), infection (chlamydia: 2%)

Respiratory: Nasopharyngitis (4%), pharyngolaryngeal pain (3%), upper respiratory tract infection (2%), pharyngitis (1%)

<1%, postmarketing, and/or case reports: Anaphylactoid reaction, anaphylaxis, angioedema, erythema multiforme, hypersensitivity reaction, lymphadenopathy, syncope (may be associated with tonic-clonic movements), vasodepressor syncope

General Dosage Range IM: *Children ≥9 years, Adolescents, and Adults ≤25 years: Females:* 0.5 mL per dose for a total of 3 doses; administer the second and third doses at 1 and 6 months after initial dose

Mechanism of Action

Contains inactive human papillomavirus (HPV) proteins HPV 16 L1, and HPV 18 L1 which produce neutralizing antibodies to prevent cervical cancer, cervical adenocarcinoma, and cervical neoplasia cause by HPV.

Efficacy: Moderate- to high-grade cervical intraepithelial neoplasia (CIN 2/3) and adenocarcinoma in situ (AIS) are the immediate and necessary precursors of squamous cell carcinoma and adenocarcinoma of the cervix, respectively. Vaccination with 2vHPV reduced the incidence of CIN 2/3 and AIS by 87% to 98% in several randomized clinical trials. (CDC/ACIP [Markowitz, 2014]).

Pharmacodynamics/Kinetics

Onset of Action Peak seroconversion was observed 1 month following the last dose of vaccine (CDC/ACIP [Markowitz, 2014])

Duration of Action Not well defined; >8 to 10 years (CDC/ACIP [Markowitz, 2014])

Pregnancy Risk Factor B

Pregnancy Considerations Adverse events were not observed in animal reproduction studies. In clinical trials, pregnancy testing was conducted prior to each vaccine administration and vaccination was discontinued if the woman was found to be pregnant; women were also instructed to avoid pregnancy for 2 months after receiving the vaccine. Pregnancies with vaccination within 1 month of their last menstrual period (LMP) had a higher rate of spontaneous abortions. The association between vaccination and spontaneous abortion occurring between gestation weeks 1 to 19 was evaluated in a postmarketing study. Women who were vaccinated within 1 month of their LMP were compared to women vaccinated 18 months prior to and 120 days after their LMP. The rate of spontaneous abortion was not statistically significant (HR 1.26, 95% CI 0.77 to 2.09). Based on available registry data, the rate of major birth defects is within the reported background rates (CDC/ACIP [Markowitz, 2014]).

Administration of the vaccine in pregnancy is not recommended; until additional information is available, the vaccine series (or completion of the series) should be delayed until pregnancy is completed. Pregnancy testing is not required prior to administration of the vaccine (CDC/ACIP [Petrosky, 2015]).

Dental Comment Human papilloma virus is widespread and serotypes 16 and 18 have been associated with cervical cancer. Although most types that cause oral HPV lesions are not of these serotypes, the clinician should recommend appropriate surgical removal of all such lesions. Lesions in the posterior oral pharyngeal region are of particular concern. Pre-exposure vaccination is one of the most effective methods for preventing transmission of some serotypes of HPV. Quadrivalent HPV vaccine (Gardasil) and the bivalent HPV vaccine (Cervarix) are available. Cervarix is indicated for the prevention of a number of diseases caused by oncogenic human papillomavirus (HPV) types 16 and 18 and approved for use in females 9-25 years of age (see Use).

Details regarding HPV vaccination are available at www.cdc.gov/std/hpv. Vaccines for other STDs (eg, HIV and herpes simplex virus) are under development or undergoing clinical trials. Vaccines are not available for bacterial or fungal STDs.

Parathyroid Hormone (par a THYE roid HOR mone)

Brand Names: US Natpara

Pharmacologic Category Parathyroid Hormone Analog

Use

Hypoparathyroidism: Adjunct to calcium and vitamin D to control hypocalcemia in patients with hypoparathyroidism

Limitations of use: Because of the potential risk of osteosarcoma, recommended only for patients who cannot be well-controlled on calcium supplements and active forms of vitamin D alone; has not been studied in patients with hypoparathyroidism caused by calcium-sensing receptor mutations or in patients with acute postsurgical hypoparathyroidism

Local Anesthetic/Vasoconstrictor Precautions No information available to require special precautions

Effects on Dental Treatment No significant effects or complications reported

Effects on Bleeding No information available to require special precautions

Adverse Reactions Frequency not always defined.

>10%:

Central nervous system: Paresthesia (31%), headache (25%), hypoesthesia (14%)

Endocrine & metabolic: Hypocalcemia (27%), hypercalcemia (19%)

Gastrointestinal: Diarrhea (12%), vomiting (12%)

Genitourinary: Hypercalciuria (11%)

Immunologic: Immunogenicity (6% to 16%; drug efficacy not affected)
Neuromuscular & skeletal: Arthralgia (11%)
1% to 10%:
Cardiovascular: Hypertension (6%)
Central nervous system: Peripheral pain (10%)
Endocrine & metabolic: Inhibited conversion of vitamin d3 to 25-hydroxy-d3 (6%)
Gastrointestinal: Upper abdominal pain (7%), facial numbness (6%)
Hematologic & oncologic: Osteosarcoma
Neuromuscular & skeletal: Neck pain (6%)
Respiratory: Upper respiratory tract infection (8%), sinusitis (7%)
Miscellaneous: Drug toxicity (risk when used concomitantly with digoxin and other drugs known to increase serum calcium)

General Dosage Range *SubQ:* Adults: 25 to 100 mcg/day

Mechanism of Action Exogenous parathyroid hormone; parathyroid hormone raises serum calcium concentrations by increasing renal tubular calcium reabsorption, increasing intestinal calcium absorption, and by increasing bone turnover, which releases calcium into the circulation.

Pharmacodynamics/Kinetics

Onset of Action Peak effect: 10 to 12 hours

Duration of Action >24 hours

Half-life Elimination ~3 hours

Time to Peak 5 to 30 minutes

Pregnancy Risk Factor C

Pregnancy Considerations Adverse events were observed in animal reproduction studies.

Prescribing and Access Restrictions As a requirement of the REMS program, access to this medication is restricted. Natpara is only available to certified health care prescribers and can only be dispensed by certified pharmacies under the Natpara REMS program. Further information is available at www.NATPARAREMS.com or by telephone at 1-855-NATPARA.

Paregoric (par e GOR ik)

Pharmacologic Category Analgesic, Opioid; Antidiarrheal

Use Diarrhea: Treatment of diarrhea

Local Anesthetic/Vasoconstrictor Precautions No information available to require special precautions

Effects on Dental Treatment No significant effects or complications reported

Effects on Bleeding No information available to require special precautions

Adverse Reactions Frequency not defined.
Cardiovascular: Hypotension, peripheral vasodilation
Central nervous system: Central nervous system depression, depression, dizziness, drowsiness, drug dependence (physical and psychological), dysphoria, euphoria, headache, increased intracranial pressure, insomnia, malaise, restlessness, sedation
Dermatologic: Pruritus
Gastrointestinal: Anorexia, biliary tract spasm, constipation, nausea, stomach cramps, vomiting
Genitourinary: Decreased urine output, ureteral spasm
Hepatic: Increased liver enzymes
Hypersensitivity: Histamine release
Neuromuscular & skeletal: Weakness
Ophthalmic: Miosis
Respiratory: Respiratory depression
Postmarketing and/or case reports: Hypogonadism (Brennan, 2013; Debono, 2011)

General Dosage Range Oral:
Children and Adolescents: 0.25 to 0.5 mL/kg 1 to 4 times daily
Adults: 5 to 10 mL 1 to 4 times daily

Mechanism of Action Increases smooth muscle tone in GI tract, decreases motility and peristalsis, diminishes digestive secretions

Pregnancy Risk Factor C

Pregnancy Considerations Animal reproduction studies have not been conducted. Paregoric contains morphine; refer to the Morphine (Systemic) monograph for additional information. In addition, this preparation contains large amounts of alcohol (47%).

Controlled Substance C-III

Paricalcitol (pah ri KAL si tole)

Brand Names: US Zemplar

Brand Names: Canada Zemplar

Pharmacologic Category Vitamin D Analog

Use
IV: Prevention and treatment of secondary hyperparathyroidism associated with stage 5 chronic kidney disease (CKD)
Oral: Prevention and treatment in adults and pediatric patients 10 years and older with secondary hyperparathyroidism associated with stage 3 and 4 CKD and stage 5 CKD patients on hemodialysis or peritoneal dialysis

Local Anesthetic/Vasoconstrictor Precautions No information available to require special precautions

Effects on Dental Treatment Key adverse event(s) related to dental treatment: Xerostomia (normal salivary flow resumes upon discontinuation).

Effects on Bleeding No information available to require special precautions

Adverse Reactions As reported in adults, unless otherwise noted.
>10%:
Gastrointestinal: Nausea (children, adolescents, and adults: 5% to 13%), diarrhea (7% to 12%)
Infection: Infection (bacterial, fungal, viral: 3% to 15%)
Respiratory: Rhinitis (children and adolescents: 17%)
1% to 10%:
Cardiovascular: Hypertension (7%), edema (6% to 7%), hypotension (5%), palpitations (3%), chest pain (3%), peripheral edema (3%), syncope (3%), atrial flutter (<2%), cardiac arrhythmia (<2%), cerebrovascular accident (<2%), chest discomfort (<2%), ischemic bowel disease (<2%)
Central nervous system: Dizziness (5% to 7%), chills (5%), insomnia (5%), vertigo (5%), headache (3% to 5%), anxiety (3%), depression (3%), fatigue (3%), malaise (3%), abnormal gait (<2%), agitation (<2%), confusion (<2%), delirium (<2%), hypoesthesia (<2%), myoclonus (<2%), nervousness (<2%), paresthesia (<2%), restlessness (<2%)
Dermatologic: Skin rash (4% to 6%), dermal ulcer (3%), ecchymoses (3%), acne vulgaris (<2%), alopecia (<2%), burning sensation of skin (<2%), extravasation reactions (<2%), night sweats (<2%), pruritus (<2%), urticaria (<2%)
Endocrine & metabolic: Hypervolemia (5%), dehydration (3%), hypoglycemia (3%), hirsutism (<2%), hypercalcemia (<2%), hyperkalemia (<2%), hyperparathyroidism (<2%), hyperphosphatemia (<2%),

hypocalcemia (<2%), hypoparathyroidism (<2%), increased thirst (<2%), weight loss (<2%)

Gastrointestinal: Vomiting (5% to 8%), gastrointestinal hemorrhage (5%), peritonitis (5%), constipation (4% to 5%), abdominal pain (4%), dyspepsia (3%), xerostomia (3%), decreased appetite (<2%), dysgeusia (<2%), dysphagia (<2%), gastritis (<2%), gastroesophageal reflux disease (<2%)

Genitourinary: Urinary urgency (children and adolescents: 6%), chronic renal failure (3%), uremia (3%), urinary tract infection (3%), erectile dysfunction (<2%), mastalgia (<2%), vaginal infection (<2%)

Hematologic & oncologic: Anemia (<2%), lymphadenopathy (<2%), malignant neoplasm of breast (<2%), prolonged bleeding time (<2%), rectal hemorrhage (<2%)

Hepatic: Abnormal hepatic function tests (<2%), increased serum AST (<2%)

Hypersensitivity: Hypersensitivity reaction (6%)

Infection: Influenza (5%), sepsis (5%)

Local: Pain at injection site (<2%)

Neuromuscular & skeletal: Arthralgia (5%), arthritis (5%), weakness (3% to 5%), back pain (3% to 4%), leg cramps (3%), muscle spasm (3%), joint stiffness (<2%), muscle twitching (<2%), myalgia (<2%)

Ophthalmic: Conjunctivitis (children and adolescents: 6%, adults: <2%), glaucoma (<2%), ocular hyperemia (<2%)

Otic: Otalgia (<2%)

Respiratory: Nasopharyngitis (8%), asthma (children and adolescents: 6%), pneumonia (5%), oropharyngeal pain (4%), bronchitis (3%), cough (3%), sinusitis (3%), dyspnea (<2%), orthopnea (<2%), pulmonary edema (<2%), upper respiratory tract infection (<2%), wheezing (<2%)

Miscellaneous: Fever (3% to 5%), laboratory test abnormality (<2%), swelling (<2%)

<1%, postmarketing, and/or case reports: Angioedema (including laryngeal edema), Increased serum creatinine

General Dosage Range

IV: *Children ≥5 years, Adolescents, and Adults:* 0.04 to 0.24 mcg/kg (2.8 to 16.8 mcg) every other day during dialysis

Oral:

Children >10 to Adolescents ≤16 years: Initial: 1 mcg 3 times/week

Adults: 1 to 2 mcg once daily **or** 2 to 4 mcg 3 times/week

Mechanism of Action Decreased renal conversion of vitamin D to its primary active metabolite (1,25-hydroxyvitamin D) in chronic renal failure leads to reduced activation of vitamin D receptor (VDR), which subsequently removes inhibitory suppression of parathyroid hormone (PTH) release; increased serum PTH (secondary hyperparathyroidism) reduces calcium excretion and enhances bone resorption. Paricalcitol is a synthetic vitamin D analog which binds to and activates the VDR in kidney, parathyroid gland, intestine and bone, thus reducing PTH levels and improving calcium and phosphate homeostasis.

Pharmacodynamics/Kinetics

Half-life Elimination

Healthy subjects: Oral: 4 to 6 hours; IV: 5 to 7 hours

Stage 3 and 4 CKD: Oral: 17 to 20 hours

Stage 5 CKD (on HD or PD): Oral: 14 to 18 hours; IV: 14 to 15 hours

Time to Peak Plasma: 3 hours: Delayed by food

Pregnancy Risk Factor C

Pregnancy Considerations Adverse events have been observed in some animal reproduction studies.

Paromomycin (par oh moe MYE sin)

Brand Names: Canada Humatin

Pharmacologic Category Amebicide

Use

Intestinal amebiasis: Treatment of acute and chronic intestinal amebiasis (not effective for extraintestinal amebiasis).

Hepatic coma: Management (adjunctive) of hepatic coma.

Local Anesthetic/Vasoconstrictor Precautions No information available to require special precautions

Effects on Dental Treatment No significant effects or complications reported

Effects on Bleeding No information available to require special precautions

Adverse Reactions

1% to 10%: Gastrointestinal: Abdominal cramps, diarrhea, heartburn, nausea, vomiting

<1%, postmarketing, and/or case reports: Enterocolitis (secondary), eosinophilia, headache, ototoxicity, pruritus, steatorrhea, vertigo

General Dosage Range

Oral:

Children and Adolescents: 25-35 mg/kg/day in 3 divided doses for 5-10 days

Adults: 25-35 mg/kg/day in 3 divided doses for 5-10 days **or** 4 g daily in divided doses (at regular intervals) for 5-6 days

Mechanism of Action Acts directly on ameba; has antibacterial activity against normal and pathogenic organisms in the GI tract; interferes with bacterial protein synthesis by binding to 30S ribosomal subunits

Pregnancy Considerations Paromomycin is poorly absorbed when given orally. Information related to the use of paromomycin in pregnancy is limited (Kreutner 1981). Use may be considered for the treatment of giardiasis throughout pregnancy (Gardner 2001) or cryptosporidiosis after the first trimester (DHHS 2013) in pregnant women.

PARoxetine (pa ROKS e teen)

Related Information

Dentin Hypersensitivity, Acid Erosion, High Caries Index, Management of Alveolar Osteitis, and Xerostomia *on page 1857*

Management of the Patient With Anxiety or Depression *on page 1873*

Vasoconstrictor Interactions With Antidepressants *on page 1913*

Brand Names: US Brisdelle; Paxil; Paxil CR; Pexeva

Brand Names: Canada Apo-Paroxetine; Auro-Paroxetine; CO Paroxetine; Dom-Paroxetine; JAMP-Paroxetine; Mylan-Paroxetine; Novo-Paroxetine; Paxil; Paxil CR; PHL-Paroxetine; PMS-Paroxetine; Q-Paroxetine; ratio-Paroxetine; Riva-Paroxetine; Sandoz-Paroxetine; Teva-Paroxetine

Generic Availability (US) May be product dependent

Pharmacologic Category Antidepressant, Selective Serotonin Reuptake Inhibitor

Use

Generalized anxiety disorder (immediate release): For the treatment of generalized anxiety disorder (GAD)

Major depressive disorder (immediate and controlled release): For the treatment of major depressive disorder (MDD)

Obsessive-compulsive disorder (immediate release): For the treatment of obsessions and compulsions in patients with obsessive-compulsive disorder (OCD)

Panic disorder (immediate and controlled release): For the treatment of panic disorder, with or without agoraphobia

Post-traumatic stress disorder (immediate release): For the treatment of post-traumatic stress disorder (PTSD)

Premenstrual dysphoric disorder (controlled release): For the treatment of premenstrual dysphoric disorder (PMDD)

Social anxiety disorder (immediate and controlled release): For the treatment of social anxiety disorder, also known as social phobia

Vasomotor symptoms of menopause (Brisdelle only): For the treatment of moderate to severe vasomotor symptoms associated with menopause

Local Anesthetic/Vasoconstrictor Precautions Although caution should be used in patients taking tricyclic antidepressants, no interactions have been reported with vasoconstrictor and paroxetine, a nontricyclic antidepressant which acts to increase serotonin; no precautions appear to be needed

Effects on Dental Treatment Key adverse event(s) related to dental treatment: Xerostomia and changes in salivation (normal salivary flow resumes upon discontinuation), and abnormal taste. Patients may experience orthostatic hypotension as they stand up after treatment; especially if lying in dental chair for extended periods of time. Use caution with sudden changes in position during and after dental treatment. Problems with SSRI-induced bruxism have been reported and may preclude their use; clinicians attempting to evaluate any patient with bruxism or involuntary muscle movement, who is simultaneously being treated with an SSRI drug, should be aware of the potential association. Prolonged use may decrease or inhibit salivary flow; normal salivation resumes upon discontinuation. See Effects on Bleeding.

Effects on Bleeding May impair platelet aggregation resulting in increased risk of bleeding events, particularly if used concomitantly with aspirin, NSAIDs, warfarin, or other anticoagulants. Bleeding related to SSRI use has been reported to range from relatively minor bruising and epistaxis to life-threatening hemorrhage. Routine interruption of therapy for most dental procedures is not warranted. In medically complicated patients or extensive oral surgery, the decision to interrupt therapy must be based on the risk to benefit in an individual patient and a medical consult is suggested. If therapy is continued without interruption, the clinician should anticipate the potential for a prolonged bleeding time.

Adverse Reactions Frequency varies by dose and indication. Adverse reactions reported as a composite of all indications.

>10%:

Central nervous system: Drowsiness (15% to 24%), insomnia (11% to 24%), headache (6% to 18%), dizziness (6% to 14%)

Dermatologic: Diaphoresis (5% to 14%)

Endocrine & metabolic: Decreased libido (3% to 15%)

Gastrointestinal: Nausea (19% to 26%), xerostomia (9% to 18%), constipation (5% to 16%), diarrhea (9% to 12%)

Genitourinary: Ejaculatory disorder (13% to 28%)

Neuromuscular & skeletal: Weakness (12% to 22%), tremor (4% to 11%)

1% to 10%:

Cardiovascular: Vasodilatation (2% to 4%), chest pain (3%), palpitations (2% to 3%), hypertension (≥1%), tachycardia (≥1%)

Central nervous system: Nervousness (4% to 9%), anxiety (5%), fatigue (5%), agitation (3% to 5%), paresthesia (4%), abnormal dreams (3% to 4%), lack of concentration (3% to 4%), yawning (2% to 4%), depersonalization (≤3%), myoclonus (2% to 3%), amnesia (2%), chills (2%), emotional lability (≥1%), vertigo (≥1%), confusion (1%), myasthenia (1%)

Dermatologic: Skin rash (2% to 3%), pruritus (≥1%)

Endocrine & metabolic: Weight gain (≥1%)

Gastrointestinal: Decreased appetite (5% to 9%), dyspepsia (2% to 5%), flatulence (4%), abdominal pain (4%), nausea and vomiting (4%), increased appetite (2% to 4%), vomiting (2% to 3%), dysgeusia (2%)

Genitourinary: Male genital disease (10%), female genital tract disease (2% to 9%), impotence (2% to 9%), orgasm disturbance (2% to 9%), dysmenorrhea (5%), urinary frequency (2% to 3%), urinary tract infection (2%)

Infection: Infection (5% to 6%)

Neuromuscular & skeletal: Myalgia (2% to 4%), back pain (3%), myopathy (2%), arthralgia (≥1%)

Ophthalmic: Blurred vision (4%), visual disturbance (2% to 4%)

Otic: Tinnitus (≥1%)

Respiratory: Dyspnea (≤7%), pharyngitis (4%), sinusitis (≤4%), rhinitis (3%)

<1%, postmarketing, and/or case reports: Abnormal erythrocytes, abnormal hepatic function tests, acute renal failure, adrenergic syndrome, aggressive behavior, agranulocytosis, akathisia, akinesia, anaphylactoid reaction, anaphylaxis, anemia (various), angina pectoris, angioedema, angle-closure glaucoma, aphasia, aphthous stomatitis, aplastic anemia, asthma, atrial fibrillation, behavioral problems (various), bloody diarrhea, bone marrow aplasia, bradycardia, bronchitis, bulimia nervosa, bundle branch block, cardiac failure, cataract, cellulitis, cerebral ischemia, cerebrovascular accident, change in platelet count, cholelithiasis, colitis, deafness, dehydration, delirium, depression, diabetes mellitus, disorientation, drug dependence, dyskinesia, dysphagia, dyspnea, dystonia, ecchymoses, eclampsia, emphysema, erythema, esophageal achalasia, exfoliative dermatitis, extrapyramidal reaction, fecal impaction, fungal dermatitis, gastroenteritis, goiter, Guillain-Barre syndrome, hallucination, hematemesis, hematologic disease, hematoma, hemoptysis, hemorrhage (eye, gingival, rectal, retinal, vaginal), hemorrhagic pancreatitis, hepatic failure, hepatic necrosis, hepatitis, hepatotoxicity, homicidal ideation, hyperbilirubinemia, hypercholesteremia, hypergammaglobulinemia, hyperglycemia, hyperhidrosis, hypersensitivity reaction, hyperthyroidism, hypoglycemia, hyponatremia, hypotension, hypothyroidism, immune thrombocytopenia, increased blood urea nitrogen, increased creatine phosphokinase, increased lactate dehydrogenase, increased serum alkaline phosphatase, intestinal obstruction, ischemic heart disease, jaundice, ketosis, low cardiac output, lymphadenopathy, malaise, meningitis, migraine, mydriasis, myelitis, myocardial infarction, neuroleptic malignant syndrome (Stevens, 2008), neuropathy, nodal arrhythmia, osteoarthritis, osteoporosis, pancreatitis, pancytopenia, peptic ulcer, peritonitis, phlebitis, pneumonia, prolonged bleeding time, pulmonary edema,

pulmonary embolism, pulmonary fibrosis, pulmonary hypertension, restlessness, seizure, sepsis, serotonin syndrome, status epilepticus, Stevens-Johnson syndrome, suicidal ideation, suicidal tendencies, syncope, tetany, thrombophlebitis, thrombosis, tongue edema, torsades de pointes, toxic epidermal necrolysis, uncontrolled diabetes mellitus, vasculitis, ventricular arrhythmia, ventricular fibrillation, ventricular tachycardia, withdrawal syndrome (including increased dreaming/nightmares, muscle cramps/spasms/twitching, headache, nervousness/anxiety, fatigue/tiredness, restless feeling in legs, and trouble sleeping/insomnia)

Dosing

Adult

Major depressive disorder (MDD): Oral:

Paxil, Pexeva: Initial: 20 mg once daily, preferably in the morning; increase if needed by 10 mg/day increments at intervals of at least 1 week; maximum dose: 50 mg/day

Paxil CR: Initial: 25 mg once daily; increase if needed by 12.5 mg/day increments at intervals of at least 1 week; maximum dose: 62.5 mg/day

Generalized anxiety disorder (GAD) *(Paxil, Pexeva)*: Oral: Initial: 20 mg once daily, preferably in the morning (if dose is increased, adjust in increments of 10 mg/day at 1-week intervals); doses of 20-50 mg/day were used in clinical trials, however, no greater benefit was seen with doses >20 mg.

Obsessive-compulsive disorder (OCD) *(Paxil, Pexeva)*: Oral: Initial: 20 mg once daily, preferably in the morning; increase if needed by 10 mg/day increments at intervals of at least 1 week; recommended dose: 40 mg/day; range: 20-60 mg/day; maximum dose: 60 mg/day

Panic disorder: Oral:

Paxil, Pexeva: Initial: 10 mg once daily, preferably in the morning; increase if needed by 10 mg/day increments at intervals of at least 1 week; recommended dose: 40 mg/day; range: 10-60 mg/day; maximum dose: 60 mg/day

Paxil CR: Initial: 12.5 mg once daily; increase if needed by 12.5 mg/day at intervals of at least 1 week; maximum dose: 75 mg/day

Premenstrual dysphoric disorder (PMDD) *(Paxil CR)*: Oral: Initial: 12.5 mg once daily in the morning; may be increased to 25 mg/day; dosing changes should occur at intervals of at least 1 week. May be given daily throughout the menstrual cycle or limited to the luteal phase.

Post-traumatic stress disorder (PTSD) *(Paxil)*: Oral: Initial: 20 mg once daily, preferably in the morning; increase if needed by 10 mg/day increments at intervals of at least 1 week; range: 20-50 mg. Limited data suggest doses of 40 mg/day were not more efficacious than 20 mg/day.

Social anxiety disorder: Oral:

Paxil: Initial: 20 mg once daily, preferably in the morning; recommended dose: 20 mg/day; range: 20-60 mg/day; doses >20 mg may not have additional benefit

Paxil CR: Initial: 12.5 mg once daily, preferably in the morning; may be increased by 12.5 mg/day at intervals of at least 1 week; maximum dose: 37.5 mg/day

Vasomotor symptoms of menopause:

Brisdelle: 7.5 mg once daily at bedtime

Paxil CR (off-label use): 12.5-25 mg once daily (Stearns, 2003)

Discontinuation of therapy: Upon discontinuation of antidepressant therapy, gradually taper the dose to minimize the incidence of withdrawal symptoms and allow for the detection of re-emerging symptoms. Evidence supporting ideal taper rates is limited. APA and NICE guidelines suggest tapering therapy over at least several weeks with consideration to the half-life of the antidepressant; antidepressants with a shorter half-life may need to be tapered more conservatively. In addition for long-term treated patients, WFSBP guidelines recommend tapering over 4-6 months. If intolerable withdrawal symptoms occur following a dose reduction, consider resuming the previously prescribed dose and/or decrease dose at a more gradual rate (APA, 2010; Bauer, 2002; Haddod, 2001; NCCMH, 2010; Schatzberg, 2006; Shelton, 2001; Warner, 2006).

MAO inhibitor recommendations:

Switching to or from an MAO inhibitor intended to treat psychiatric disorders:

Allow 14 days to elapse between discontinuing an MAO inhibitor intended to treat psychiatric disorders and initiation of paroxetine.

Allow 14 days to elapse between discontinuing paroxetine and initiation of an MAO inhibitor intended to treat psychiatric disorders.

Use with other MAO inhibitors (linezolid or IV methylene blue):

Do not initiate paroxetine in patients receiving linezolid or IV methylene blue; consider other interventions for psychiatric condition.

If urgent treatment with linezolid or IV methylene blue is required in a patient already receiving paroxetine and potential benefits outweigh potential risks, discontinue paroxetine promptly and administer linezolid or IV methylene blue. Monitor for serotonin syndrome for 2 weeks or until 24 hours after the last dose of linezolid or IV methylene blue, whichever comes first. May resume paroxetine 24 hours after the last dose of linezolid or IV methylene blue.

Geriatric

Major depressive disorder (MDD), obsessive compulsive disorder (OCD), panic attack, social anxiety disorder:

Paxil, Pexeva: Oral: Initial: 10 mg/day; increase if needed by 10 mg/day increments at intervals of at least 1 week; maximum dose: 40 mg/day

Paxil CR: Initial: 12.5 mg/day; increase if needed by 12.5 mg/day increments at intervals of at least 1 week; maximum dose: 50 mg/day

Discontinuation of therapy: Refer to adult dosing.

MAO inhibitor recommendations: Refer to adult dosing.

Pediatric

Obsessive-compulsive disorder (OCD) (off-label use): Children and Adolescents 7-17 years: Oral: Initial: 10 mg daily; titrate every 7-14 days in increments of 10 mg daily as necessary to a maximum of 60 mg daily; trials have typically continued for a 10- to 12-week treatment course (Geller, 2004; Rosenberg, 1999)

Social anxiety disorder (off-label use): Children and Adolescents 8-17 years: Oral: Initial: 10 mg once daily; titrate at intervals of at least 7 days in increments of 10 mg daily; maximum daily dose: 50 mg daily; trials have typically continued for a 16-week treatment course (Wagner, 2004)

Discontinuation of therapy: Refer to adult dosing.

MAO inhibitor recommendations: Refer to adult dosing.

Renal Impairment Adults:

Brisdelle: No dosage adjustment necessary.

Paxil, Paxil CR, Pexeva:

CrCl 30-60 mL/minute: Plasma concentration is 2 times that seen in normal function. There are no dosage adjustments provided in manufacturer's labeling.

Severe impairment (CrCl <30 mL/minute): Mean plasma concentration is ~4 times that seen in normal function.

Paxil, Pexeva: Initial: 10 mg/day; increase if needed by 10 mg/day increments at intervals of at least 1 week; maximum dose: 40 mg/day

Paxil CR: Initial: 12.5 mg/day; increase if needed by 12.5 mg/day increments at intervals of at least 1 week; maximum dose: 50 mg/day

Hepatic Impairment Adults: In hepatic dysfunction, plasma concentration is 2 times that seen in normal function.

Brisdelle: No dosage adjustment necessary.

Paxil, Paxil CR, Pexeva:

Mild-to-moderate impairment: There are no dosage adjustments provided in manufacturer's labeling.

Severe impairment:

Paxil, Pexeva: Initial: 10 mg/day; increase if needed by 10 mg/day increments at intervals of at least 1 week; maximum dose: 40 mg/day

Paxil CR: Initial: 12.5 mg/day; increase if needed by 12.5 mg/day increments at intervals of at least 1 week; maximum dose: 50 mg/day

Mechanism of Action Paroxetine is a selective serotonin reuptake inhibitor, chemically unrelated to tricyclic, tetracyclic, or other antidepressants; presumably, the inhibition of serotonin reuptake from brain synapse stimulated serotonin activity in the brain

Contraindications Concurrent use with or within 14 days of MAOIs intended to treat psychiatric disorders; initiation in patients being treated with linezolid or methylene blue IV; concomitant use with pimozide or thioridazine; hypersensitivity to paroxetine or any of its inactive ingredients; pregnancy (Brisdelle only).

Warnings/Precautions [U.S. Boxed Warning]: Antidepressants increase the risk of suicidal thinking and behavior in children, adolescents, and young adults (18 to 24 years of age) with major depressive disorder (MDD) and other psychiatric disorders; consider risk prior to prescribing. Short-term studies did not show an increased risk in patients >24 years of age and showed a decreased risk in patients ≥65 years. Closely monitor patients for clinical worsening, suicidality, or unusual changes in behavior, particularly during the initial 1 to 2 months of therapy or during periods of dosage adjustments (increases or decreases); the patient's family or caregiver should be instructed to closely observe the patient and communicate condition with healthcare provider. A medication guide concerning the use of antidepressants should be dispensed with each prescription. **Paroxetine is not FDA approved for use in children.**

The possibility of a suicide attempt is inherent in major depression and may persist until remission occurs. Use caution in high-risk patients. Worsening depression and severe abrupt suicidality that are not part of the presenting symptoms may require discontinuation or modification of drug therapy. The patient's family or caregiver should be alerted to monitor patients for the emergence of suicidality and associated behaviors (such as agitation, irritability, hostility, impulsivity, and hypomania) and call health care provider.

May worsen psychosis in some patients or precipitate a shift to mania or hypomania in patients with bipolar disorder. Patients presenting with depressive symptoms should be screened for bipolar disorder. Monotherapy in patients with bipolar disorder should be avoided. **Paroxetine is not FDA approved for the treatment of bipolar depression.**

Potentially life-threatening serotonin syndrome (SS) has occurred with serotonergic agents (eg, SSRIs, SNRIs), particularly when used in combination with other serotonergic agents (eg, triptans, TCAs, fentanyl, lithium, tramadol, buspirone, St John's wort, tryptophan) or agents that impair metabolism of serotonin (eg, MAO inhibitors intended to treat psychiatric disorders, other MAO inhibitors [ie, linezolid and intravenous methylene blue]). Discontinue treatment (and any concomitant serotonergic agent) immediately if signs/symptoms arise.

Paroxetine may increase the risks associated with electroconvulsive therapy. Has a low potential to impair cognitive or motor performance - use caution when operating hazardous machinery or driving. Symptoms of agitation and/or restlessness may occur during initial few weeks of therapy. Low potential for sedation or anticholinergic effects relative to cyclic antidepressants. Bone fractures have been associated with SSRI treatment. Consider the possibility of a fragility fracture if an SSRI-treated patient presents with unexplained bone pain, point tenderness, swelling, or bruising.

Use caution in patients with a previous seizure disorder or condition predisposing to seizures such as brain damage or alcoholism. Use with caution in patients with hepatic dysfunction. May cause SIADH; volume depletion and/or diuretics may increase risk. Potentially significant drug-drug interactions may exist, requiring dose or frequency adjustment, additional monitoring, and/or selection of alternative therapy. Use with caution in patients with renal insufficiency or other concurrent illness (due to limited experience); dose reduction recommended with severe renal impairment. May cause or exacerbate sexual dysfunction. May cause mild pupillary dilation, which can lead to an episode of narrow-angle glaucoma in susceptible individuals. Consider evaluating patients who have not had an iridectomy for narrow-angle glaucoma risk factors. Avoid use in the first trimester of pregnancy. Menopausal vasomotor symptoms do not occur during pregnancy; therefore, the use of paroxetine for the treatment of menopausal vasomotor symptoms is contraindicated in pregnant women.

Brisdelle contains a lower dose than what is required for the treatment of psychiatric conditions. Patients who require paroxetine for the treatment of psychiatric conditions should discontinue Brisdelle and begin treatment with a paroxetine-containing medication which provides an adequate dosage.

Abrupt discontinuation or interruption of antidepressant therapy has been associated with a discontinuation syndrome. Symptoms arising may vary with antidepressant however commonly include nausea, vomiting, diarrhea, headaches, lightheadedness, dizziness, diminished appetite, sweating, chills, tremors, paresthesias, fatigue, somnolence, and sleep disturbances (eg, vivid dreams, insomnia). Greater risks for developing a discontinuation syndrome have been associated with antidepressants with shorter half-lives, longer durations of treatment, and abrupt discontinuation. For antidepressants of short or intermediate half-lives, symptoms may emerge within 2 to 5 days after treatment discontinuation and last 7 to 14 days (APA, 2010; Fava, 2006; Haddod, 2001; Shelton, 2001; Warner, 2006).

Some dosage forms may contain polysorbate 80 (also known as Tweens). Hypersensitivity reactions, usually a delayed reaction, have been reported following exposure to pharmaceutical products containing polysorbate 80 in certain individuals (Isaksson, 2002; Lucente 2000; Shelley, 1995). Thrombocytopenia, ascites, pulmonary deterioration, and renal and hepatic failure have been reported in premature neonates after receiving parenteral products containing polysorbate 80 (Alade, 1986; CDC, 1984). See manufacturer's labeling.

Drug Interactions

Metabolism/Transport Effects **Substrate** of CYP2D6 (major); **Note:** Assignment of Major/Minor substrate status based on clinically relevant drug interaction potential; **Inhibits** CYP1A2 (weak), CYP2C9 (weak), CYP2D6 (strong)

Avoid Concomitant Use

Avoid concomitant use of PARoxetine with any of the following: Dapoxetine; Dosulepin; Iobenguane I 123; Linezolid; MAO Inhibitors; Mequitazine; Methylene Blue; Pimozide; Tamoxifen; Thioridazine; Tryptophan; Urokinase

Increased Effect/Toxicity

PARoxetine may increase the levels/effects of: Agents with Antiplatelet Properties; Anticoagulants; Antidepressants (Serotonin Reuptake Inhibitor/Antagonist); Antipsychotic Agents; Apixaban; ARIPiprazole; ARIPiprazole Lauroxil; Asenapine; Aspirin; AtoMOXetine; Beta-Blockers; Blood Glucose Lowering Agents; Brexpiprazole; BusPIRone; Cephalothin; CloZAPine; Collagenase (Systemic); CYP2D6 Substrates; Dabigatran Etexilate; Deoxycholic Acid; Desmopressin; Dextromethorphan; Dosulepin; DOXOrubicin (Conventional); DULoxetine; Edoxaban; Eliglustat; Fesoterodine; Galantamine; Highest Risk QTc-Prolonging Agents; Ibritumomab; Iloperidone; Indoramin; Mequitazine; Methylene Blue; Metoprolol; Mexiletine; Moderate Risk QTc-Prolonging Agents; Nebivolol; Nicergoline; NSAID (COX-2 Inhibitor); NSAID (Nonselective); Obinutuzumab; Perhexiline; Pimozide; Propafenone; Rivaroxaban; Salicylates; Serotonin Modulators; Tamsulosin; Tetrabenazine; Thiazide and Thiazide-Like Diuretics; Thioridazine; Thrombolytic Agents; Timolol (Ophthalmic); TIZANidine; Tositumomab and Iodine I 131 Tositumomab; TraMADol; Tricyclic Antidepressants; Tropisetron; Urokinase; Vitamin K Antagonists; Vortioxetine

The levels/effects of PARoxetine may be increased by: Abiraterone Acetate; Alcohol (Ethyl); Analgesics (Opioid); Antiemetics (5HT3 Antagonists); Antipsychotic Agents; ARIPiprazole; Asenapine; Asunaprevir; BuPROPion; BusPIRone; Cimetidine; Clarithromycin; CNS Depressants; Cobicistat; CYP2D6 Inhibitors (Moderate); CYP2D6 Inhibitors (Strong); Dapoxetine; Dasatinib; DULoxetine; Glucosamine; Herbs (Anticoagulant/Antiplatelet Properties); Ibrutinib; Imatinib; Limaprost; Linezolid; Lithium; MAO Inhibitors; Metaxalone; Methylene Blue; Methylphenidate; Metoclopramide; MetyroSINE; MiFEPRIStone; Multivitamins/Fluoride (with ADE); Multivitamins/Minerals (with ADEK, Folate, Iron); Multivitamins/Minerals (with AE, No Iron); Omega-3 Fatty Acids; Panobinostat; Peginterferon Alfa-2b; Pentosan Polysulfate Sodium; Pentoxifylline; Pravastatin; Prostacyclin Analogues; Tedizolid; TraMADol; Tryptophan; Vitamin E (Systemic)

Decreased Effect

PARoxetine may decrease the levels/effects of: Aprepitant; Codeine; Fosaprepitant; HYDROcodone; Iloperidone; Iobenguane I 123; Ioflupane I 123; Nicergoline; Tamoxifen; Thyroid Products; TraMADol

The levels/effects of PARoxetine may be decreased by: Aprepitant; Cyproheptadine; Darunavir; Fosamprenavir; Fosaprepitant; NSAID (COX-2 Inhibitor); NSAID (Nonselective); Peginterferon Alfa-2b

Food Interactions Peak concentration is increased, but bioavailability is not significantly altered by food. Management: Administer without regard to meals.

Dietary Considerations May be taken without regard to meals.

Pharmacodynamics/Kinetics

Onset of Action Depression: The onset of action is within a week, however, individual response varies greatly and full response may not be seen until 8-12 weeks after initiation of treatment; antiobsessional and antipanic effects: Up to several weeks

Half-life Elimination Paxil: 21 hours; Paxil CR: 15 to 20 hours; Pexeva: 33.2 hours

Time to Peak

Capsules: Median: 6 hours (range: 3 to 8 hours)

Tablets, oral suspension: Immediate release: Mean: 5.2 to 8.1 hours

Tablets: Controlled release: 6-10 hours

Pregnancy Risk Factor D/X (product specific)

Pregnancy Considerations Studies in pregnant women have demonstrated a risk to the fetus. Paroxetine crosses the placenta. An increased risk of teratogenic effects, including cardiovascular defects, may be associated with maternal use of paroxetine or other SSRIs; however, available information is conflicting. Nonteratogenic effects in the newborn following SSRI/SNRI exposure late in the third trimester include respiratory distress, cyanosis, apnea, seizures, temperature instability, feeding difficulty, vomiting, hypoglycemia, hypo- or hypertonia, hyper-reflexia, jitteriness, irritability, constant crying, and tremor. Symptoms may be due to the toxicity of the SSRIs/SNRIs or a discontinuation syndrome and may be consistent with serotonin syndrome associated with SSRI treatment. Persistent pulmonary hypertension of the newborn (PPHN) has also been reported with SSRI exposure. The long-term effects of in utero SSRI exposure on infant development and behavior are not known.

Due to pregnancy-induced physiologic changes, some pharmacokinetic parameters of paroxetine may be altered. The maternal CYP2D6 genotype also influences paroxetine plasma concentrations during pregnancy.

The manufacturer suggests discontinuing paroxetine or switching to another antidepressant unless the benefits of therapy justify continuing treatment during pregnancy; consider other treatment options for women who are planning to become pregnant. The ACOG recommends that therapy with SSRIs or SNRIs during pregnancy be individualized; treatment of depression during pregnancy should incorporate the clinical expertise of the mental health clinician, obstetrician, primary health care provider, and pediatrician. The ACOG also recommends that therapy with paroxetine be avoided during pregnancy if possible and that fetuses exposed in early pregnancy be assessed with a fetal echocardiography. According to the American Psychiatric Association (APA), the risks of medication treatment should be weighed against other treatment options and untreated depression. The use of paroxetine is not recommended as first line therapy during pregnancy. For women who discontinue antidepressant medications during pregnancy and who may be at high risk for postpartum depression, the medications can be restarted following delivery. Treatment algorithms have been developed by the ACOG and the APA for the management of depression in women prior to conception and during pregnancy. Menopausal vasomotor symptoms do not occur during pregnancy; therefore, the use of paroxetine for the treatment of menopausal vasomotor symptoms is contraindicated in pregnant women.

Pregnant women exposed to antidepressants during pregnancy are encouraged to enroll in the National Pregnancy Registry for Antidepressants (NPRAD). Women 18 to 45 years of age or their health care providers may contact the registry by calling 844-405-6185. Enrollment should be done as early in pregnancy as possible.

Breastfeeding Considerations Paroxetine is excreted in breast milk and concentrations in the hindmilk are higher than in foremilk. Paroxetine has not been detected in the serum of nursing infants. Adverse reactions have been reported in nursing infants exposed to some SSRIs. The manufacturer recommends that caution be exercised when administering paroxetine to nursing women. Maternal use of an SSRI during pregnancy may cause delayed milk secretion. The American Academy of Breastfeeding Medicine suggests that paroxetine may be considered for the treatment of postpartum depression in appropriately selected women who are nursing. Mothers should be monitored for changes in symptoms and infants should be monitored for growth. The long-term effects on development and behavior have not been studied.

Dosage Forms

Capsule, Oral:
Brisdelle: 7.5 mg

Suspension, Oral:
Paxil: 10 mg/5 mL (250 mL)

Tablet, Oral:
Paxil: 10 mg, 20 mg, 30 mg, 40 mg
Pexeva: 10 mg, 20 mg, 30 mg, 40 mg
Generic: 10 mg, 20 mg, 30 mg, 40 mg

Tablet Extended Release 24 Hour, Oral:
Paxil CR: 12.5 mg, 25 mg, 37.5 mg
Generic: 12.5 mg, 25 mg, 37.5 mg

Dosage Forms: Canada Note: Refer to Dosage Forms. Capsule, oral suspension, and tablet (as mesylate) are not available in Canada.

Pasireotide (pas i REE oh tide)

Related Information

Clinical Risk Related to Drugs Prolonging QT Interval *on page 1772*

Brand Names: US Signifor; Signifor LAR

Brand Names: Canada Signifor; Signifor LAR

Pharmacologic Category Somatostatin Analog

Use

Acromegaly (Signifor LAR): Treatment of patients with acromegaly who have had an inadequate response to surgery and/or for whom surgery is not an option.

Cushing disease (Signifor): Treatment of Cushing disease in patients for whom pituitary surgery is not an option or has not been curative

Local Anesthetic/Vasoconstrictor Precautions Pasireotide is one of the drugs confirmed to prolong the QT interval and is accepted as having a risk of causing torsade de pointes. In terms of epinephrine, it is not known what effect vasoconstrictors in the local anesthetic regimen will have in patients with a known history of congenital prolonged QT interval or in patients taking any medication that prolongs the QT interval. Until more information is obtained, it is suggested that the clinician consult with the physician prior to the use of a vasoconstrictor in suspected patients, and that the vasoconstrictor (epinephrine, mepivacaine and levonordefrin [Carbocaine® 2% with Neo-Cobefrin®]) be used with caution.

Effects on Dental Treatment No significant effects or complications reported

Effects on Bleeding No information available to require special precautions

Adverse Reactions

>10%:

Cardiovascular: Peripheral edema (10% to 11%)

Central nervous system: Headache (3% to 29%), fatigue (10% to 24%), insomnia (4% to 14%), anxiety (6% to 11%)

Dermatologic: Alopecia (2% to 18%)

Endocrine & metabolic: Hyperglycemia (29% to 43%), diabetes mellitus (6% to 31%), hypoglycemia (3% to 15%), increased gamma-glutamyl transferase (9% to 12%), hypercholesterolemia (9% to 11%)

Gastrointestinal: Diarrhea (16% to 59%), nausea (3% to 58%), cholelithiasis (10% to 30%), increased serum lipase (1% to 30%), abdominal pain (8% to 25%), increased serum amylase (2% to 20%), upper abdominal pain (6% to 12%), abdominal distension (5% to 12%), decreased appetite (9% to 11%)

Hematologic & oncologic: Prolonged prothrombin time (2% to 47%; minimal elevation), elevated glycosylated hemoglobin (6% to 12%)

Hepatic: Increased serum ALT (≤13%)

Infection: Influenza (6% to 11%)

Local: Injection site reactions (7% to 18%; including pain, erythema, hematoma, hemorrhage, pruritus)

Neuromuscular & skeletal: Weakness (6% to 16%), increased creatine phosphokinase (13%), myalgia (5% to 12%)

Respiratory: Nasopharyngitis (6% to 16%)

1% to 10%:

Cardiovascular: Hypertension (8% to 10%), sinus bradycardia (3% to 10%), hypotension (6% to 8%), atrioventricular block (6%), prolonged Q-T interval on ECG (4% to 6%)

Central nervous system: Dizziness (2% to 10%), vertigo (5% to 8%)

Dermatologic: Pruritus (7% to 9%), xeroderma (6%)

Endocrine & metabolic: Increased serum glucose (4% to 8%), hypokalemia (5% to 7%), adrenal insufficiency (≤6%), weight loss (5%), impaired glucose tolerance (1% to 5%), hypothyroidism (4%)

Gastrointestinal: Increased serum amylase (2% to 20%), vomiting (4% to 10%), constipation (5% to 9%), pancreatitis (1%)

Hematologic & oncologic: Anemia (3% to 6%)

Hepatic: Increased serum AST (≤7%), increased serum bilirubin (2%)

Neuromuscular & skeletal: Arthralgia (6% to 10%), back pain (5% to 8%), limb pain (5% to 7%)

Respiratory: Upper respiratory tract infection (7%), cough (5%)

General Dosage Range Dosage adjustment recommended in patients with hepatic impairment.

IM: *Adults: Signifor LAR*: Initial: 40 mg once every 28 days; after 3 months, may increase to a maximum of 60 mg.

SubQ: *Adults: Signifor*: Initial: 0.6 mg or 0.9 mg twice daily; titrate based on response and tolerability. Recommended maintenance dosage range: 0.3 to 0.9 mg twice daily.

Mechanism of Action Pasireotide is a cyclohexapeptide somatostatin analog, which is a peptide inhibitor of multiple endocrine, neuroendocrine, and exocrine mechanisms. In patients with Cushing disease, pasireotide binds to somatostatin receptor (sst_{1-5}), with high affinity for the sst_1, sst_2, sst_3 subtypes, and highest affinity for the sst_5 subtype, resulting in inhibition of ACTH secretion which leads to decreased cortisol secretion. In patients with acromegaly, pasireotide binds to sst_2 and sst_5, resulting in decreased GH and IGF-1.

Pharmacodynamics/Kinetics

Half-life Elimination Subcutaneous: ~12 hours

Time to Peak Plasma: Subcutaneous: 0.25 to 0.5 hours

Pregnancy Risk Factor C

Pregnancy Considerations Adverse events have been observed in animal reproduction studies.

Prescribing and Access Restrictions In Canada, patients prescribed Signifor must be enrolled in the Access Program for Signifor (Novartis Canada).

PAZOPanib (paz OH pa nib)

Related Information

Clinical Risk Related to Drugs Prolonging QT Interval *on page 1772*

Brand Names: US Votrient

Brand Names: Canada Votrient

Pharmacologic Category Antineoplastic Agent, Tyrosine Kinase Inhibitor; Antineoplastic Agent, Vascular Endothelial Growth Factor (VEGF) Inhibitor

Use

Renal cell carcinoma, advanced: Treatment of advanced renal cell carcinoma

Soft tissue sarcoma, advanced: Treatment of advanced soft tissue sarcoma (in patients who have received prior chemotherapy)

Limitations of use: The efficacy of pazopanib for the treatment of adipocytic soft tissue sarcoma or gastrointestinal stromal tumors (GIST) has not been demonstrated.

Local Anesthetic/Vasoconstrictor Precautions Hypertension can occur with the use of this drug, particularly early in the treatment course. Monitor for hypertension prior to using local anesthetic with vasoconstrictor; medical consult if necessary.

Pazopanib is one of the drugs confirmed to prolong the QT interval and is accepted as having a risk of causing torsade de pointes. The risk of drug-induced torsade de pointes is extremely low when a single QT interval prolonging drug is prescribed. In terms of epinephrine, it is not known what effect vasoconstrictors in the local anesthetic regimen will have in patients with a known history of congenital prolonged QT interval or in patients taking any medication that prolongs the QT interval. Until more information is obtained, it is suggested that the clinician consult with the physician prior to the use of a vasoconstrictor in suspected patients, and that the vasoconstrictor (epinephrine, mepivacaine and levonordefrin [Carbocaine® 2% with Neo-Cobefrin®]) be used with caution.

Effects on Dental Treatment Key adverse event(s) related to dental treatment: Taste alteration.

Effects on Bleeding Chemotherapy may result in significant myelosuppression, potentially including significant reduction in platelet counts (thrombocytopenia grades 3/4: <1%) and altered hemostasis. Hemorrhagic events have been reported. In patients who are under active treatment with these agents, medical consult is suggested.

Adverse Reactions

>10%:

Cardiovascular: Hypertension (40% to 42%; grade 3: 4% to 7%, early in treatment), bradycardia (2% to 19%), peripheral edema (STS: 14%), cardiac insufficiency (11% to 13%)

Central nervous system: Fatigue (19%, grade 3: 2%; STS: 65%, grades 3/4: 1% to 13%), tumor pain (STS: 29%, grade 3: 8%), headache (10%; STS: 23%, grade 3: 1%), dizziness (11%)

Dermatologic: Hair discoloration (38% to 39%, grade 3: <1%), exfoliative dermatitis (STS: 18%, grade 3: <1%), alopecia (8% to 12%), dermatological disease (STS: 11%, grade 3: 2%), hypopigmentation (STS, skin: 11%), palmar-plantar erythrodysesthesia (6% to 11%)

Endocrine & metabolic: Weight loss (9%, STS: 48%, grade 3: 4%), increased serum glucose (41% to 45%, grade 3: <1%), increased thyroid-stimulating hormone (TSH), decreased serum albumin (STS: 34%, grade 3: 1%), decreased serum phosphate (34%, grade 3: 4%), decreased serum sodium (31%, grade 3: 1% to 4%), decreased serum magnesium (26%, grades 3/4: ≤1%), decreased serum glucose (17%, grade 4: <1%), increased serum potassium (STS: 16%, grade 3: 1%)

Gastrointestinal: Diarrhea (52% to 59%; grades 3/4: ≤5%), nausea (26%, grade 3: <1%; STS: 56%, grade 3: 3%), decreased appetite (STS: 40%, grade 3: 6%), anorexia (22%, grade 3: 2%), vomiting (21%, grades 3/4: ≤2%; STS: 33%, grade 3: 3%), dysgeusia (8%, STS: 28%), increased serum lipase (27%, grades 3/4: 4%), gastrointestinal pain (STS: 23%, grade 3: 3%), abdominal pain (11%, grade 3: 2%), mucositis (STS: 12%, grade 3: 2%), stomatitis (STS: 11%, grade 3: <1%)

Hematologic & oncologic: Leukopenia (37% to 44%; STS, grade 3: 1%), lymphocytopenia (31%; grades 3/4: ≤4%; STS: 43%, grade 3: 10%), thrombocytopenia (32% to 36%; grades 3/4: ≤6%; grade 4: ≤1%), neutropenia (33% to 34%; grades 3/4 [in patients of East Asian descent]: 12%; grades 3/4 [in patients of non-East Asian descent]: ≤4%), hemorrhage (13% to 22%, including pulmonary, gastrointestinal, and genitourinary, grade 4: 1%, including intracranial, subarachnoid, and peritoneal)

Hepatic: Increased serum AST (51% to 53%; grades 3/4: ≤7%), increased serum ALT (4% to 53%; grades 3/4: 2% to 10%), increased serum bilirubin (29% to 36%; grades 3/4: ≤3%), increased serum alkaline phosphatase (STS: 32%, grade 3: 3%)

Neuromuscular & skeletal: Musculoskeletal pain (STS: 23%, grade 3: 2%), myalgia (STS: 23%, grade 3: 2%), weakness (14%, grade 3: 3%)

Respiratory: Dyspnea (STS: 20%, grades 3/4: ≤5%), cough (STS: 17%)

Miscellaneous: Tumor pain (29%)

1% to 10%:

Cardiovascular: Chest pain (5% to 10%; STS, grade 3: 2%), left ventricular systolic dysfunction (STS: 8%), venous thrombosis (STS: 5%), ischemia (≤2%), myocardial infarction (≤2%), prolonged Q-T interval on ECG (2%), facial edema (RCC: 1%), transient ischemic attacks (RCC: 1%)

Central nervous system: Insomnia (STS: 9%), voice disorder (4% to 8%), chills (STS: 5%)

Dermatologic: Skin rash (RCC: 8%), skin depigmentation (RCC: 3%), xeroderma (STS: 6%), nail disease (STS: 5%)

Endocrine & metabolic: Hypothyroidism (4% to 8%)

Gastrointestinal: Dyspepsia (5% to 7%), anal hemorrhage (STS: 2%), gastrointestinal fistula (≤1%), gastrointestinal perforation (≤1%)

Genitourinary: Proteinuria (1% to 9%), hematuria (RCC: 4%)

Hematologic & oncologic: Oral hemorrhage (STS: 3%), rectal hemorrhage (RCC: 1%)

Ophthalmic: Blurred vision (STS: 5%)

Respiratory: Epistaxis (2% to 8%), pneumothorax (≤3%), hemoptysis (RCC: 2%)

Frequency not defined:

Cardiovascular: Decreased left ventricular ejection fraction, hypertensive crisis

Central nervous system: Reversible posterior leukoencephalopathy syndrome

Hematologic & oncologic: Hemolytic-uremic syndrome, neutropenic infection, thrombotic thrombocytopenic purpura

Hepatic: Hepatotoxicity, severe hepatotoxicity

Infection: Serious infection

Neuromuscular & skeletal: Arthralgia (RCC), muscle spasm (RCC)

<1%, postmarketing, and/or case reports: Cardiac disease, cerebral hemorrhage, cerebrovascular accident, congestive heart failure, interstitial pneumonitis, nephrotic syndrome, pancreatitis, retinal changes (tear), retinal detachment, torsades de pointes

General Dosage Range Dosage adjustment recommended in patients with hepatic impairment, on concomitant therapy, or who develop toxicities

Oral: *Adults:* 800 mg once daily

Mechanism of Action Tyrosine kinase (multikinase) inhibitor; limits tumor growth via inhibition of angiogenesis by inhibiting cell surface vascular endothelial growth factor receptors (VEGFR-1, VEGFR-2, VEGFR-3), platelet-derived growth factor receptors (PDGFR-alpha and -beta), fibroblast growth factor receptor (FGFR-1 and -3), cytokine receptor (cKIT), interleukin-2 receptor inducible T-cell kinase, leukocyte-specific protein tyrosine kinase (Lck), and transmembrane glycoprotein receptor tyrosine kinase (c-Fms)

Pharmacodynamics/Kinetics

Half-life Elimination ~31 hours

Time to Peak Plasma: 2 to 4 hours

Pregnancy Risk Factor D

Pregnancy Considerations Adverse effects were observed in animal reproduction studies. Based on its mechanism of action, pazopanib would be expected to cause fetal harm if administered to a pregnant woman. Women of reproductive potential should avoid becoming pregnant during treatment and use effective contraception during therapy and for at least 2 weeks after the last pazopanib dose.

Dental Comment See Local Anesthetic/Vasoconstrictor Precautions

Pegaptanib (peg AP ta nib)

Brand Names: US Macugen

Brand Names: Canada Macugen

Pharmacologic Category Ophthalmic Agent; Vascular Endothelial Growth Factor (VEGF) Inhibitor

Use Macular degeneration (neovascular age-related): Treatment of neovascular (wet) age-related macular degeneration (AMD)

Local Anesthetic/Vasoconstrictor Precautions No information available to require special precautions

Effects on Dental Treatment No significant effects or complications reported

Effects on Bleeding No information available to require special precautions

Adverse Reactions

>10%:

Cardiovascular: Hypertension

Ophthalmic: Anterior chamber inflammation, blurred vision, cataract, conjunctival hemorrhage, corneal edema, decreased visual acuity, eye discharge, eye discomfort, eye irritation, eye pain, increased intraocular pressure, punctate keratitis, visual disturbance, vitreous opacity

1% to 10%:

Cardiovascular: Cerebrovascular accident (1% to 5%), chest pain (1% to 5%), occlusive arterial disease (carotid artery: 1% to 5%), transient ischemic attacks (1% to 5%)

Central nervous system: Dizziness (6% to 10%), headache (6% to 10%), vertigo (1% to 5%)

Dermatologic: Contact dermatitis (1% to 5%)

Endocrine & metabolic: Diabetes mellitus (1% to 5%)

Gastrointestinal: Diarrhea (6% to 10%), nausea (6% to 10%), dyspepsia (1% to 5%), vomiting (1% to 5%)

Genitourinary: Urinary tract infection (6% to 10%), urinary retention (1% to 5%)

Hematologic & oncologic: Bruise (1% to 5%), periorbital hematoma (1% to 5%), vitreous hemorrhage (1% to 5%)

Local: Local inflammation (eye: 1% to 5%), local irritation (eyelid: 1% to 5%)

Neuromuscular & skeletal: Arthritis (1% to 5%), bone spur (1% to 5%)

Ophthalmic: Blepharitis (6% to 10%), conjunctivitis (6% to 10%), photopsia (6% to 10%), vitreous disorder (6% to 10%; includes inflammation), allergic conjunctivitis (1% to 5%), conjunctival edema (1% to 5%), corneal abrasion (1% to 5%), corneal deposits (1% to 5%), epithelial keratopathy (1% to 5%), endophthalmitis (1% to 5%), meibomianitis (1% to 5%), mydriasis (1% to 5%), retinal edema (1% to 5%), swelling of eye (1% to 5%)

Otic: Auditory impairment (1% to 5%)

Respiratory: Bronchitis (6% to 10%), pleural effusion (1% to 5%)

<1%, postmarketing, and/or case reports: Accidental injury, anaphylactoid reaction, anaphylaxis, angioedema, arthropathy, blindness, choroidal detachment, colonic polyps, decreased white blood cell count, dysphagia, feeling abnormal, foreign body sensation of eye, giant-cell arteritis, hematochezia, hemoptysis, hemorrhage, iatrogenic traumatic cataracts, immune thrombocytopenia, increased heart rate, inflammation, intracranial hemorrhage, iridocyclitis, iritis, loss of consciousness, mass (pulmonary), musculoskeletal chest pain, myalgia, neuritis, non-small-cell lung carcinoma (adenocarcinoma), obstructive pulmonary disease, ocular hyperemia, pain, pain at injection site, prolonged partial thromboplastin time, pulmonary disease, pulmonary hemorrhage, retinal detachment, retinal hole without detachment, sclera disease, skin rash, sprue-like symptoms, subretinal neovascularization, syncope, tremor, urticaria, uveitis (intermediate)

General Dosage Range Intravitreous: *Adults:* 0.3 mg into affected eye once every 6 weeks

Mechanism of Action Pegaptanib is an apatamer, an oligonucleotide covalently bound to polyethylene glycol, which can adopt a three-dimensional shape and bind to vascular endothelial growth factor (VEGF). Pegaptanib binds to extracellular VEGF, selectively inhibiting VEGF from binding to its receptors and thereby suppressing neovascularization and slowing vision loss.

Pharmacodynamics/Kinetics

Half-life Elimination Plasma: 10 ± 4 days

Pregnancy Risk Factor B

Pregnancy Considerations Adverse events have not been observed in animal reproduction studies.

Pegaspargase (peg AS par jase)

Related Information

Asparaginase (*E. coli*) *on page 166*

Brand Names: US Oncaspar

Pharmacologic Category Antineoplastic Agent, Enzyme; Antineoplastic Agent, Miscellaneous

Use

Acute lymphoblastic leukemia and hypersensitivity to asparaginase: Treatment of acute lymphoblastic leukemia (ALL) in patients with hypersensitivity to native forms of L-asparaginase (as a component of a multiagent chemotherapy regimen)

Acute lymphoblastic leukemia, first-line: First-line treatment of ALL (as a component of a multiagent chemotherapy regimen)

Local Anesthetic/Vasoconstrictor Precautions No information available to require special precautions

Effects on Dental Treatment No significant effects or complications reported

Effects on Bleeding Although significant myelosuppression with associated altered hemostasis has been reported for many chemotherapeutic agents, myelosuppression is not common with pegaspargase and no specific precautions appear to necessary.

Adverse Reactions

>10%:

Hepatic: Increased serum transaminases (ALT, AST; grades 3/4: 3% to 11%)

Hypersensitivity: Hypersensitivity reaction (grades 3/4: 1%, includes anaphylaxis, bronchospasm, erythema, hives, hypotension, laryngeal edema, skin rash, swelling, urticaria; relapsed acute lymphoblastic leukemia [ALL] with no prior asparaginase hypersensitivity: 10%; relapsed ALL with prior asparaginase hypersensitivity: 32%)

1% to 10%:

Cardiovascular: Thrombosis (4%)

Central nervous system: Cerebral thrombosis (or hemorrhage of the brain: 2%; grades 3/4: 3%)

Endocrine & metabolic: Hyperglycemia (3% [some patients required insulin therapy]; grades 3/4: 5%)

Gastrointestinal: Pancreatitis (1%; grades 3/4: 2% [includes 3 deaths])

Hematologic: Blood coagulation disorder (grades 3/4: 2% to 7%; includes prolonged prothrombin time or partial thromboplastin time or decreased serum fibrogen)

Hepatic: Abnormal hepatic function tests (grades 3/4: 5%), hyperbilirubinemia (grades 3/4: 1% to 2%)

Immunologic: Hypersensitivity to L-asparaginase (grades 3/4: 2%)

<1%, postmarketing, case reports, and/or frequency not defined: Abdominal pain, anemia, anorexia, antithrombin III deficiency, arthralgia, ascites, bacteremia, bronchospasm, bruise, chest pain, chills, coagulation time increased, colitis, confusion, constipation, cough, deep vein thrombosis, disseminated intravascular coagulation, dizziness, dyspnea, edema, emotional lability, endocarditis, epistaxis, facial edema, fatigue, fever, gastrointestinal pain, headache, hematuria, hemolytic anemia, hemorrhagic cystitis, hepatic failure, hepatomegaly, hyperammonemia, hypertension, hyperuricemia, hypoalbuminemia, hypoglycemia, hyponatremia, increased blood urea nitrogen, increased serum amylase, increased serum creatinine, increased serum lipase, increased thirst, injection site pain, jaundice, leukopenia, lip edema, liver steatosis, malaise, metabolic acidosis, myalgia, nausea, night sweats, ostealgia, pancytopenia, paresthesia, petechial rash, prolonged prothrombin time, proteinuria, purpura, renal failure, renal function abnormality, sagittal sinus thrombosis, seizure, sepsis, septic shock, subacute bacterial endocarditis, superficial venous thrombosis, tachycardia, thrombocytopenia, uric acid nephropathy, urticaria, vomiting

General Dosage Range IM, IV: *Children, Adolescents, and Adults:* 2500 units/m^2 every 14 days

Mechanism of Action Pegaspargase is a modified version of L-asparaginase, conjugated with polyethylene glycol. In leukemic cells, asparaginase hydrolyzes L-asparagine to ammonia and L-aspartic acid, leading to depletion of asparagine. Leukemia cells, especially lymphoblasts, require exogenous asparagine; normal cells can synthesize asparagine. Asparagine depletion in leukemic cells leads to inhibition of protein synthesis and apoptosis. Asparaginase is cycle-specific for the G_1 phase of the cell cycle.

Pharmacodynamics/Kinetics

Onset of Action

Asparagine depletion: IM: Within 4 days

Duration of Action Asparagine depletion: IV (in asparaginase naive adults): 2 to 4 weeks (Douer 2007); IM: ~21 days

Half-life Elimination

IM: Children: 5.8 days; Adults: 5.5-6 days; 3.2 ± 1.8 days in patients who previously had a hypersensitivity reaction to native L-asparaginase

IV: Adults (asparaginase naive): 7 days (Douer 2007)

Time to Peak IM: 3 to 4 days

Pregnancy Risk Factor C

Pregnancy Considerations Animal reproduction studies have not been conducted with pegaspargase.

Pegfilgrastim (peg fil GRA stim)

Brand Names: US Neulasta; Neulasta Onpro

Brand Names: Canada Neulasta

Pharmacologic Category Colony Stimulating Factor; Hematopoietic Agent

Use

US labeling:

Prevention of chemotherapy-induced neutropenia: To decrease the incidence of infection (as manifested by febrile neutropenia), in patients with nonmyeloid malignancies receiving myelosuppressive cancer chemotherapy associated with a clinically significant incidence of febrile neutropenia.

Limitation of use: Pegfilgrastim is not indicated for mobilization of peripheral blood progenitor cells for hematopoietic stem cell transplant.

Hematopoietic radiation injury syndrome (acute): To increase survival in patients acutely exposed to myelosuppressive doses of radiation.

Canadian labeling:

Prevention of chemotherapy-induced neutropenia: To decrease the incidence of infection (as manifested by febrile neutropenia), in adult patients with nonmyeloid malignancies receiving myelosuppressive cancer chemotherapy.

Local Anesthetic/Vasoconstrictor Precautions No information available to require special precautions

Effects on Dental Treatment No significant effects or complications reported

Effects on Bleeding No information available to require special precautions. Medical consultation may be necessary to confirm adequate platelet counts.

Adverse Reactions

Neuromuscular & skeletal: Ostealgia (31%), limb pain (9%)

<1%, postmarketing, and/or case reports: Acute respiratory distress syndrome (ARDS), alopecia, anaphylaxis, antibody development, arthralgia, back pain, bruising at injection site, capillary leak syndrome, chest pain, constipation, diarrhea, erythema, fatigue, fever, flushing, glomerulonephritis, headache, hypersensitivity angiitis, hypertonia, increased serum alkaline phosphatase, increased uric acid, influenza, injection site reaction, leukocytosis, musculoskeletal pain, myalgia, neck pain, pain, pain at injection site, periorbital edema, peripheral edema, polyarthralgia, polymyalgia rheumatica, rhinitis, severe sickle cell crisis, skeletal pain, splenic rupture, splenomegaly, Sweet syndrome, urticaria, vomiting, weakness

General Dosage Range SubQ: *Adults:* 6 mg once per chemotherapy cycle

Mechanism of Action Stimulates the production, maturation, and activation of neutrophils, pegfilgrastim activates neutrophils to increase both their migration and cytotoxicity. Pegfilgrastim has a prolonged duration of effect relative to filgrastim and a reduced renal clearance.

Pharmacodynamics/Kinetics

Half-life Elimination SubQ: Pediatrics (100 mcg/kg dose): 0 to 5 years: 30.1 ± 38.2 hours; 6 to 11 years: 20.2 ± 11.3 hours; 12 years and older: 21.2 ± 16 hours; Adults: 15 to 80 hours. Pharmacokinetics (in adults) were comparable between manual subcutaneous injection and the On-body injector system.

Pregnancy Risk Factor C

Pregnancy Considerations Adverse events were observed in some animal reproduction studies.

Women who are exposed to Neulasta during pregnancy are encouraged to enroll in the Amgen Pregnancy Surveillance Program (800-772-6436).

Peginterferon Alfa-2a

(peg in ter FEER on AL fa too aye)

Related Information

Systemic Viral Diseases *on page 1806*

Brand Names: US Pegasys; Pegasys ProClick

Brand Names: Canada Pegasys

Pharmacologic Category Interferon

Use

Chronic hepatitis B: Treatment of adults with hepatitis B e antigen (HBeAg)-positive and HBeAg-negative chronic hepatitis B virus (HBV) infection who have compensated liver disease and evidence of viral replication and liver inflammation

Chronic hepatitis C:

Combination therapy: Treatment of adults with chronic hepatitis C (CHC) with compensated liver disease as part of a combination regiment with other hepatitis C virus (HCV) antiviral drugs; treatment of pediatric patients 5 years and older with CHC and compensated liver disease in combination with ribavirin

Monotherapy (for patients with contraindications or who are intolerant to other HCV antiviral drugs): Treatment (as a single agent) of chronic hepatitis C in patients with compensated liver disease in patients with contraindications or significant intolerance to other HCV antiviral drugs. **Note:** Monotherapy with peginterferon is not recommended in HCV treatment guidelines (treatment naïve or treatment-experienced patients) (AASLD/IDSA 2015).

Limitations of use: Peginterferon alfa-2a alone or in combination with ribavirin without additional HCV antiviral drugs is not recommended for treatment of patients with chronic HCV who previously failed therapy with an interferon alfa. Peginterferon alfa-2a is not recommended for treatment of patients with CHC who have had solid organ transplantation.

Local Anesthetic/Vasoconstrictor Precautions No information available to require special precautions

Effects on Dental Treatment Key adverse event(s) related to dental treatment: Xerostomia (normal salivary flow resumes upon discontinuation).

Effects on Bleeding Thrombocytopenia may occur in patients. Monitor for the potential for increased bleeding.

Adverse Reactions

>10%:

Central nervous system: Headache (27% to 54%), fatigue (24% to 56%), rigors (35%; hepatitis B: 25% to 27%), insomnia (19%), anxiety (≤19%), irritability (≤19%), nervousness (≤19%), depression (18%), dizziness (16%), pain (11%)

Dermatologic: Alopecia (18% to 23%), pruritus (12%)

Endocrine & metabolic: Growth suppression (children, percentile decrease (≥15 percentiles), weight [43%], height [25%])

Gastrointestinal: Nausea (≤24%), vomiting (≤24%), anorexia (16% to 17%), diarrhea (16%), abdominal pain (15%)

Hematologic & oncologic: Neutropenia (21%)

Hepatic: Increased serum ALT (hepatitis B: 5 to 10x ULN: 25% to 27%; >10x ULN: 12% to 18%; hepatitis C: 5 to 10x ULN: 1%)

Local: Injection site reaction (22%)

Neuromuscular & skeletal: Weakness (≤56%), myalgia (37%), arthralgia (28%)

Miscellaneous: Fever (37%; hepatitis B: 54%)

1% to 10%:

Central nervous system: Lack of concentration (8%), memory impairment (5%), mood changes (3%)

Dermatologic: Dermatitis (8%), diaphoresis (6%), skin rash (5%), xeroderma (4%), eczema (1%)

Endocrine & metabolic: Weight loss (4%), hypothyroidism (3% to 4%), hyperthyroidism (≤1%)

Gastrointestinal: Xerostomia (6%)

Hematologic & oncology: Thrombocytopenia (5%), lymphocytopenia (3%), anemia (2%)

Hepatic: Hepatic decompensation (2% in CHC/HIV)

Infection: Bacterial infection (3% to ≤5%)

Neuromuscular & skeletal: Back pain (9%)

Ophthalmic: Blurred vision (4%)

Respiratory: Cough (4%), dyspnea (4%)

≤1%, postmarketing, and/or case reports: Aggressive behavior, anaphylaxis, angina pectoris, angioedema, aplastic anemia, auditory impairment, autoimmune disorders, bipolar mood disorder, bronchiolitis obliterans, bronchoconstriction, cardiac arrhythmia, cerebral hemorrhage, chest pain, cholangitis, colitis, coma, corneal ulcer, dehydration, diabetes mellitus, dyspepsia, endocarditis, erythema multiforme major, dyspnea on exertion, exfoliative dermatitis, gastrointestinal hemorrhage, hallucination, hearing loss, hematocrit decreased, hemoglobin decreased, hepatic insufficiency, exacerbation of hepatitis B, graft rejection (hepatic, renal), hyperglycemia, hyperpigmentation, hypersensitivity reaction, hypertension, hypoglycemia, increased serum triglycerides, influenza, interstitial pneumonitis, liver steatosis, macular edema, mania, myocardial infarction, myositis, optic neuritis, pancreatitis, papilledema, peptic ulcer, peripheral neuropathy, pneumonia, psychiatric disturbance, psychosis, pulmonary embolism, pulmonary infiltrates, pure red cell aplasia, retinal thrombosis (in artery or vein), retinal cotton-wool spot, retinal detachment, retinal hemorrhage, retinopathy, rheumatoid arthritis, sarcoidosis, seizures, Stevens-Johnson syndrome, substance overdose, suicidal ideation, suicide, supraventricular arrhythmia, systemic lupus erythematosus, thrombotic thrombocytopenic purpura, urticaria, vesiculobullous reaction, vision loss

General Dosage Range Dosage adjustment recommended in patients with hepatic or renal impairment or who develop toxicities

SubQ:

Children ≥5 years and Adolescents: 180 mcg/1.73 m^2 x BSA once weekly (maximum dose: 180 mcg)

Adults: 180 mcg once weekly

Mechanism of Action Alpha interferons are a family of proteins, produced by nucleated cells that have antiviral, antiproliferative, and immune-regulating activity. There are 16 known subtypes of alpha interferons. Interferons interact with cells through high affinity cell surface receptors. Following activation, multiple effects can be detected including induction of gene transcription. Interferons inhibit cellular growth, alter the state of cellular differentiation, interfere with oncogene expression, alter cell surface antigen expression, increase phagocytic activity of macrophages, and augment cytotoxicity of lymphocytes for target cells.

Pharmacodynamics/Kinetics

Half-life Elimination Terminal: 50-160 hours; increased with renal dysfunction

Time to Peak Serum: 72 to 96 hours

Pregnancy Risk Factor C / X in combination with ribavirin

Pregnancy Considerations Use with ribavirin is contraindicated in pregnant women and males whose female partners are pregnant.

Combination therapy with ribavirin may cause birth defects and/or fetal mortality; avoid pregnancy in females and female partners of male patients. Female patients of childbearing potential and male patients with female partners of childbearing potential must use 2 forms of contraception along with monthly pregnancy tests during therapy and for 6 months after therapy has been discontinued. If used in combination with ribavirin, all warnings related to the use of ribavirin and pregnancy and/or contraception should be followed.

Reproduction studies with pegylated interferon alfa have not been conducted. Animal studies with nonpegylated interferon alfa-2b have demonstrated abortifacient effects. Disruption of the normal menstrual cycle was also observed in animal studies; therefore, the manufacturer recommends that reliable contraception is used in women of childbearing potential. Alfa interferon is endogenous to normal amniotic fluid (Lebon 1982). In vitro administration studies have reported that when administered to the mother, it does not cross the placenta (Waysbort 1993). Case reports of use in pregnant women are limited.

The HHS Perinatal HIV Guidelines do not recommend that peginterferon-alfa be used during pregnancy (HHS [perinatal] 2016). Mother-to-child transmission of HCV does not occur if the woman is not viremic, therefore, HCV-infected women of childbearing potential should postpone pregnancy until therapy is complete. Treatment of HCV is not recommended for women who are already pregnant (AASLD/IDSA 2015).

A pregnancy registry has been established for women inadvertently exposed to ribavirin while pregnant (800-593-2214).

Peginterferon Alfa-2a and Ribavirin

(peg in ter FEER on AL fa too aye & rye ba VYE rin)

Related Information

Peginterferon Alfa-2a *on page 1300*

Ribavirin (Systemic) *on page 1430*

Systemic Viral Diseases *on page 1806*

Brand Names: Canada Pegasys RBV

Pharmacologic Category Antihepaciviral, Nucleoside (Anti-HCV); Interferon

Use Note: Not approved in the US

Hepatitis C: Combination therapy for the treatment of chronic hepatitis C (HCV) in patients without cirrhosis and patients with compensated cirrhosis; includes patients coinfected with stable HIV disease

Guideline recommendations: Peginterferon and ribavirin (**without** the addition of another HCV antiviral agent) is **not** recommended in HCV treatment guidelines (treatment naïve or treatment-experienced; with or without cirrhosis), including those co-infected with HIV. Current AASLD/IDSA recommendations do not specify a particular peginterferon (eg, 2a or 2b); however, guideline recommendations are based on clinical trials that used peginterferon alfa-2a (AASLD/IDSA 2015). Hepatitic C treatment guidelines are constantly changing with the advent of new treatment therapies and information; consult current clinical practice guidelines for the most recent treatment recommendations.

Local Anesthetic/Vasoconstrictor Precautions No information available to require special precautions

Effects on Dental Treatment Key adverse event(s) related to dental treatment: Xerostomia (normal salivary flow resumes upon discontinuation), glossitis, stomatitis, mouth ulcerations, taste disturbances, and cheilitis.

Effects on Bleeding Thrombocytopenia may occur in patients. Monitor for the potential for increased bleeding.

Adverse Reactions Adverse reactions as reported with use of the combination product. Also see individual agents.

>10%:

Central nervous system: Fatigue (40% to 49%), headache (35% to 48%), insomnia (19% to 32%), rigors (16% to 30%), irritability (15% to 28%), depression (17% to 22%), dizziness (7% to 15%)

Dermatologic: Alopecia (10% to 25%), pruritus (4% to 25%), dermatitis (1% to 16%), xeroderma (4% to 13%)

Endocrine & metabolic: Weight loss (2% to 16%)
Gastrointestinal: Nausea (24% to 29%), anorexia (20% to 27%), diarrhea (14% to 16%)
Hematologic & oncologic: Hemolytic anemia (≤14%), neutropenia (3% to 11%)
Local: Injection site reaction (10% to 28%)
Neuromuscular & skeletal: Myalgia (32% to 42%), weakness (≥1% to 26%), arthralgia (16% to 22%)
Respiratory: Cough (3% to 13%), dyspnea (3% to 13%)
Miscellaneous: Fever (37% to 41%)

1% to 10%:

Cardiovascular: Chest pain (≥1% to ≤5%), flushing (≥1% to ≤5%), hypertension (≥1% to ≤5%), palpitations (≥1% to ≤5%), peripheral edema (≥1% to ≤5%), syncope (≥1% to ≤5%), tachycardia (≥1% to ≤5%)
Central nervous system: Pain (6% to 10%), lack of concentration (2% to 10%), anxiety (8%), mood changes (<1% to 8%), malaise (3% to 6%), emotional disturbance (<1% to 5%), aggressive behavior (≥1% to ≤5%), confusion (≥1% to ≤5%), drowsiness (≥1% to ≤5%), drug abuse (≥1% to ≤5%), hyperesthesia (≥1% to ≤5%), hypoesthesia (≥1% to ≤5%), lethargy (≥1% to ≤5%), migraine (≥1% to ≤5%), myasthenia (≥1% to ≤5%), nightmares (≥1% to ≤5%), paresthesia (≥1% to ≤5%), suicidal ideation (≥1% to ≤5%), vertigo (≥1% to ≤5%), memory impairment (1% to 5%), nervousness (1% to 3%), apathy (HIV-HCV coinfection: ≥1% to ≤3%), emotional lability (HIV-HCV coinfection: ≥1% to ≤3%)
Dermatologic: Skin rash (5% to 9%), diaphoresis (2% to 5%), dermatological reaction (≥1% to ≤5%), eczema (≥1% to ≤5%), night sweats (≥1% to ≤5%), psoriasis (≥1% to ≤5%), skin photosensitivity (≥1% to ≤5%), urticaria (≥1% to ≤5%), cheilitis (HIV-HCV coinfection: ≥1% to ≤3%)
Endocrine & metabolic: Decreased libido (2% to 5%), dehydration (≥1% to ≤5%), hot flash (≥1% to ≤5%), hyperthyroidism (≥1% to ≤5%), increased thirst (≥1% to ≤5%), hypothyroidism (<1% to 4%), lactic acidosis (HIV-HCV coinfection: ≥1% to ≤3%), lipodystrophy (HIV-HCV coinfection: ≥1% to ≤3%)
Gastrointestinal: Abdominal pain (7% to 10%), nausea and vomiting (7% to 8%), xerostomia (5% to 8%), decreased appetite (≤7%), dyspepsia (2% to 6%), constipation (≥1% to ≤5%), dental bleeding (≥1% to ≤5%), dysgeusia (≥1% to ≤5%), dysphagia (≥1% to ≤5%), flatulence (≥1% to ≤5%), glossitis (≥1% to ≤5%), oral candidiasis (≥1% to ≤5%), oral mucosa ulcer (≥1% to ≤5%), sore throat (≥1% to ≤5%), stomatitis (≥1% to ≤5%)
Genitourinary: Impotence (≥1% to ≤5%), urine discoloration (HIV-HCV coinfection: ≥1% to ≤3%)
Hematologic & oncologic: Thrombocytopenia (≥1% to 8%), lymphadenopathy (≥1% to ≤5%)
Infection: Herpes virus infection (≥1% to ≤5%), influenza (HIV-HCV coinfection: ≥1% to ≤3%)
Neuromuscular & skeletal: Back pain (3% to 5%), arthritis (≥1% to ≤5%), muscle cramps (≥1% to ≤5%), musculoskeletal pain (≥1% to ≤5%), neck pain (≥1% to ≤5%), ostealgia (≥1% to ≤5%), tremor (≥1% to ≤5%)
Ophthalmic: Blurred vision (≥1% to ≤5%), eye pain (≥1% to ≤5%), uveitis (≥1% to ≤5%), xerophthalmia (≥1% to ≤5%)
Otic: Otalgia (≥1% to ≤5%), tinnitus (≥1% to ≤5%)
Respiratory: Bronchitis (≥1% to ≤5%), epistaxis (≥1% to ≤5%), flu-like symptoms (≥1% to ≤5%), nasal congestion (≥1% to ≤5%), nasopharyngitis (≥1% to ≤5%), pharyngolaryngeal pain (≥1% to ≤5%), rhinitis (≥1% to ≤5%), sinus congestion (≥1% to ≤5%), upper respiratory tract infection (≥1% to ≤5%), dyspnea on exertion (3% to 4%), pneumonia (HIV-HCV coinfection: ≥1% to ≤3%)

<1%, postmarketing, and/or case reports (reported with other interferon preparations and/or ribavirin): Abdominal distention, acute psychosis, anaphylaxis, angioedema, aplastic anemia (rare), atrial fibrillation, bacterial infection (including sepsis), Bell's palsy, brain disease, bronchoconstriction, cardiac arrhythmia, cardiomyopathy, cerebral hemorrhage, cerebral ischemia, cerebrovascular hemorrhage, cholangitis, coma, congestive heart failure, corneal ulcer, deafness (rare), decreased platelet count, decreased white blood cell count, dental disorders, diabetes mellitus, endocarditis, erythema multiforme, fungal infection, gastrointestinal hemorrhage, gout, hallucination, hepatic insufficiency, hepatitis, hepatotoxicity, homicidal ideation, hyperglycemia, hypersensitivity reaction, hypertriglyceridemia, hypoglycemia, hypotension, increased indirect serum bilirubin, increased serum ALT, increased uric acid, interstitial nephritis, interstitial pneumonitis, ischemic colitis, ischemic heart disease, leukopenia, liver steatosis, macular edema, malignant neoplasm (hepatic), myocardial infarction, myositis, nephrotic syndrome, obtundation, optic neuritis, otitis externa, pancreatitis, pancytopenia, panic attack, papilledema, peptic ulcer, pericarditis, periodontal disease, peripheral neuropathy, pneumonitis, psychiatric signs and symptoms, pulmonary embolism, pulmonary infiltrates, pure red cell aplasia, renal failure, renal insufficiency, retinal blood vessel occlusion, retinal cotton-wool spot, retinal detachment, retinal hemorrhage, rhabdomyolysis, sarcoidosis (including exacerbation), seizure, skin infection, Stevens-Johnson syndrome, suicidal tendencies, thrombotic thrombocytopenic purpura, thyroid dysfunction, thyroiditis, tissue necrosis at injection site, toxic epidermal necrolysis, ulcerative colitis, viral infection

Use of alfa interferons has been associated with rare cases of autoimmune disease, including immune thrombocytopenia (ITP), thyroiditis, rheumatoid arthritis, systemic lupus erythematosus, vasculitis, and Vogt-Koyanagi-Harada syndrome

General Dosage Range Dosage adjustment recommended in patients with hepatic or renal impairment or who develop toxicities

SubQ: Peginterferon Alfa-2a: *Adults:* 180 mcg weekly

Oral: Ribavirin:

Adults <75 kg: 800 to 1000 mg daily in 2 divided doses
Adults ≥75 kg: 800 to 1200 mg daily in 2 divided doses

Mechanism of Action

Peginterferon Alfa-2a: Alpha interferons are a family of proteins, produced by nucleated cells that have antiviral, antiproliferative, and immune-regulating activity. There are 16 known subtypes of alpha interferons. Interferons interact with cells through high affinity cell surface receptors. Following activation, multiple effects can be detected including induction of gene transcription. Inhibits cellular growth, alters the state of cellular differentiation, interferes with oncogene expression, alters cell surface antigen expression, increases phagocytic activity of macrophages, and augments cytotoxicity of lymphocytes for target cells.

Ribavirin: Inhibits replication of RNA and DNA viruses; inhibits influenza virus RNA polymerase activity and inhibits the initiation and elongation of RNA fragments resulting in inhibition of viral protein synthesis.

Pregnancy Considerations Use is contraindicated in females who are pregnant or males whose female partners are pregnant. Abortifacient and teratogenic effects have been reported in women receiving interferons. Negative pregnancy test is required before initiation and monthly thereafter. Avoid pregnancy in female patients and female partners of male patients during therapy by using two effective forms of contraception; continue contraceptive measures for at least 6 months after completion of therapy. If female patients or female partners of male patients become pregnant during treatment, she should be counseled about potential risks of exposure.

Mother-to-child transmission of HCV does not occur if the woman is not viremic, therefore, HCV-infected women of childbearing potential should postpone pregnancy until therapy is complete. Treatment of HCV is not recommended for women who are already pregnant (AASLD/IDSA 2015).

Product Availability Not available in the US

Peginterferon Alfa-2b

(peg in ter FEER on AL fa too bee)

Related Information

Systemic Viral Diseases *on page 1806*

Brand Names: US Peg-Intron Redipen; Peg-Intron Redipen Pak 4; PegIntron; Sylatron

Brand Names: Canada PegIntron

Pharmacologic Category Antineoplastic Agent, Biological Response Modulator; Biological Response Modulator; Immunomodulator, Systemic; Interferon

Use

Chronic hepatitis C (CHC): Peg-Intron: Treatment of chronic hepatitis C (CHC) in compensated liver disease:

Combination therapy with ribavirin and an approved hepatitis C virus [HCV] NS3/4A protease inhibitor in adult patients with HCV genotype 1 infection. **Note:** Regimen is **not** recommended for hepatitis C virus (HCV) genotype 1 in HCV treatment guidelines (treatment-naive or treatment-experienced) (AASLD/IDSA 2015).

Combination therapy with ribavirin in adult patients with HCV genotypes other than 1, in pediatric patients (3 to 17 years), or in patients with HCV genotype 1 with contraindications or intolerance to HCV NS3/4A protease inhibitor use. **Note:** Combination therapy with ribavirin (**without** the addition of another preferred HCV antiviral agent) is **not** recommended for HCV genotypes other than 1 (ie, genotypes 2, 3, 4, 5, or 6) in HCV adult treatment guidelines (treatment-naive or treatment-experienced) (AASLD/IDSA 2015).

Monotherapy in adult patients with contraindications or significant intolerance to ribavirin if previously untreated. **Note:** Monotherapy with peginterferon is **not** recommended in HCV treatment guidelines (treatment-naive or treatment-experienced) (AASLD/IDSA 2015).

Limitations of use: *Manufacturer's labeling:* Combination therapy with ribavirin provides substantially better response rates than monotherapy.

Guideline recommendations: Current AASLD/IDSA recommendations do not specify a particular peginterferon (eg, 2a or 2b); however, guideline recommendations are based on clinical trials that used peginterferon alfa-2a (AASLD/IDSA 2015). Hepatitis C treatment guidelines are constantly changing with the advent of new treatment therapies and information; consult current clinical practice guidelines for the most recent treatment recommendations.

Melanoma: Sylatron: Adjuvant treatment of melanoma (with microscopic or gross nodal involvement within 84 days of definitive surgical resection, including complete lymphadenectomy)

Local Anesthetic/Vasoconstrictor Precautions No information available to require special precautions

Effects on Dental Treatment Key adverse event(s) related to dental treatment: Xerostomia (normal salivary flow resumes upon discontinuation).

Effects on Bleeding Thrombocytopenia may occur in patients. Monitor for the potential for increased bleeding.

Adverse Reactions

Antiviral:

>10%:

Central nervous system: Headache (56%), fatigue (including asthenia; ≤52%), depression (29%), anxiety (≤28%), emotional lability (≤28%), irritability (≤28%), insomnia (23%), rigors (23%), dizziness (12%)

Dermatologic: Alopecia (22%), pruritus (12%)

Endocrine & metabolic: Weight Loss (11%)

Gastrointestinal: Nausea (26%), anorexia (20%), diarrhea (18%), abdominal pain (15%)

Infection: Viral infection (11%)

Local: Inflammation at injection site (47%), injection site reaction (47%)

Neuromuscular & skeletal: Myalgia (54%), weakness (52%), musculoskeletal pain (28%), arthralgia (23%)

Miscellaneous: Fever (22%)

1% to 10%:

Cardiovascular: Chest pain (6%), flushing (6%)

Central nervous system: Lack of concentration (10%), right upper quadrant pain (8%), malaise (7%), nervousness (4%), agitation (2%), suicidal ideation (≤2%)

Dermatologic: Diaphoresis (6%), skin rash (6%)

Endocrine & metabolic: Hypothyroidism (5%), menstrual disease (4%), hyperthyroidism (3%)

Gastrointestinal: Vomiting (7%), dyspepsia (6%), xerostomia (6%), constipation (1%)

Hematologic & oncologic: Thrombocytopenia (7%), neutropenia (6%)

Hepatic: Increased serum ALT (10%), hepatomegaly (6%)

Immunologic: Antibody development (neutralizing: 2%)

Local: Pain at injection site (2% to 3%)

Ophthalmic: Conjunctivitis (4%), blurred vision (2%)

Respiratory: Pharyngitis (10%), cough (8%), sinusitis (7%), dyspnea (4%), rhinitis (2%)

Antineoplastic:

>10%:

Central nervous system: Fatigue (94%), headache (70%), chills (63%), depression (59%, grades 3/4: 7%), dizziness (35%), neuropathy (olfactory) (23%), paresthesia (21%)

Dermatologic: Exfoliative rash (36%), alopecia (34%)

Endocrine & metabolic: Weight loss (11%)

Gastrointestinal: Anorexia (69%), nausea (64%), dysgeusia (38%), diarrhea (37%), vomiting (26%)

Hepatic: Increased serum ALT (≤77%, grades 3/4: ≤11%), increased serum AST (≤77%, grades 3/4: ≤11%), increased serum alkaline phosphatase (23%)

Immunologic: Antibody development (binding antibodies: 35%)
Local: Injection site reaction (62%)
Neuromuscular & skeletal: Myalgia (68%), arthralgia (51%)
Miscellaneous: Fever (75%)

1% to 10%:
Cardiovascular: Bundle branch block (≤4%), myocardial infarction (≤4%), supraventricular cardiac arrhythmia (≤4%), ventricular tachycardia (≤4%)
Endocrine & metabolic: Increased gamma-glutamyl transferase (8%, grades 3/4: 4%)
Genitourinary: Proteinuria (7%)
Hematologic & oncologic: Anemia (6%)
Respiratory: Dyspnea (6%), cough (5%)

<1%, postmarketing, and/or case reports: Aggressive behavior, amnesia, anaphylaxis, angina pectoris, angioedema, aphthous stomatitis, aplastic anemia, auditory impairment, bacterial infection, bipolar mood disorder, brain disease (including exacerbations), bronchiolitis obliterans, bronchoconstriction, cardiac arrest, cardiac arrhythmia, cardiomyopathy, cerebrovascular accident, colitis, cytopenia, dehydration, diabetes mellitus, diabetic ketoacidosis, drug dependence (including relapse), drug overdose, dysgeusia, erythema multiforme, exacerbation of autoimmune disease, fungal infection, hallucination, hearing loss, hemorrhagic colitis, homicidal ideation, hyperglycemia, hypersensitivity reaction, hypertension, hypertriglyceridemia, hypotension, immune thrombocytopenia, interstitial nephritis, interstitial pneumonitis, ischemic colitis, leukopenia, lupus-like syndrome, macular edema, mania, migraine, myositis, optic neuritis, palpitations, pancreatitis, papilledema, paresthesia, peripheral neuropathy, pneumonia, psoriasis, pulmonary fibrosis, pulmonary hypertension, pulmonary infiltrates, pure red cell aplasia, renal failure, renal insufficiency (includes increases in serum creatinine), retinal cotton-wool spot, retinal detachment, retinal hemorrhage, retinal thrombosis, retinopathy, rhabdomyolysis, rheumatoid arthritis, sarcoidosis, seizure, sepsis, Stevens-Johnson syndrome, systemic lupus erythematosus, tachycardia, thrombotic thrombocytopenic purpura, thyroiditis, toxic epidermal necrolysis, ulcerative colitis, urticaria, vertigo, vision loss, visual disturbance, Vogt-Koyanagi-Harada syndrome

General Dosage Range Dosage adjustment recommended in patients with renal impairment or who develop toxicities

SubQ: Melanoma:
Adults: Initial: 6 mcg/kg/week; Maintenance: 3 mcg/kg/week

SubQ: Chronic hepatitis C:
Children ≥3 years: 60 mcg/m^2/week (in combination with ribavirin)
Adults: Peginterferon monotherapy (based on average weekly dose of 1 mcg/kg):
Adults ≤45 kg: 40 mcg once weekly
Adults 46 to 56 kg: 50 mcg once weekly
Adults 57 to 72 kg: 64 mcg once weekly
Adults 73 to 88 kg: 80 mcg once weekly
Adults 89 to 106 kg: 96 mcg once weekly
Adults 107 to 136 kg: 120 mcg once weekly
Adults 137 to 160 kg: 150 mcg once weekly
Adults: Combination therapy with ribavirin (based on average weekly dose of 1.5 mcg/kg):
Adults <40 kg: 50 mcg once weekly (with ribavirin 800 mg/day)
Adults 40 to 50 kg: 64 mcg once weekly (with ribavirin 800 mg/day)
Adults 51 to 60 kg: 80 mcg once weekly (with ribavirin 800 mg/day)
Adults 61 to 65 kg: 96 mcg once weekly (with ribavirin 800 mg/day)
Adults 66 to 75 kg: 96 mcg once weekly (with ribavirin 1000 mg/day)
Adults 76 to 80 kg: 120 mcg once weekly (with ribavirin 1000 mg/day)
Adults 81 to 85 kg: 120 mcg once weekly (with ribavirin 1200 mg/day)
Adults 86 to 105 kg: 150 mcg once weekly (with ribavirin 1200 mg/day)
Adults >105 kg: 1.5 mcg/kg once weekly (with ribavirin 1400 mg/day)

Mechanism of Action Alpha interferons are a family of proteins, produced by nucleated cells, that have antiviral, antiproliferative, and immune-regulating activity. There are 16 known subtypes of alpha interferons. Interferons interact with cells through high affinity cell surface receptors. Following activation, multiple effects can be detected including induction of gene transcription. Inhibits cellular growth, alters the state of cellular differentiation, interferes with oncogene expression, alters cell surface antigen expression, increases phagocytic activity of macrophages, and augments cytotoxicity of lymphocytes for target cells.

Pharmacodynamics/Kinetics

Half-life Elimination CHC: ~40 hours (range: 22 to 60 hours); Melanoma: ~43 to 51 hours

Time to Peak CHC: 15 to 44 hours

Pregnancy Risk Factor C / X in combination with ribavirin

Pregnancy Considerations

Use with ribavirin is contraindicated in pregnant women and males whose female partners are pregnant.

[US Boxed Warning]: Combination therapy with ribavirin may cause birth defects and/or fetal mortality; avoid pregnancy in females and female partners of male patients. Two forms of contraception should be used along with monthly pregnancy tests during combination therapy and for 6 months after therapy has been discontinued. If used in combination with ribavirin, all warnings related to the use of ribavirin and pregnancy and/or contraception should be followed.

Reproduction studies with pegylated interferon alfa have not been conducted. Animal reproduction studies with nonpegylated interferon alfa-2b have demonstrated abortifacient effects. Disruption of the normal menstrual cycle was also observed in animal studies; therefore, the manufacturer recommends that reliable contraception is used in women of childbearing potential. Alfa interferon is endogenous to normal amniotic fluid (Lebon 1982). In vitro administration studies have reported that when administered to the mother, it does not cross the placenta (Waysbort 1993). Case reports of use in pregnant women are limited.

The HHS Perinatal HIV Guidelines do not recommend that peginterferon alfa be used during pregnancy (HHS [perinatal] 2016). Mother-to-child transmission of HCV does not occur if the woman is not viremic, therefore, HCV-infected women of childbearing potential should postpone pregnancy until therapy is complete. Treatment of HCV is not recommended for women who are already pregnant (AASLD/IDSA 2015).

A pregnancy registry has been established for women inadvertently exposed to ribavirin while pregnant (800-593-2214).

Pegloticase (peg LOE ti kase)

Brand Names: US Krystexxa

Pharmacologic Category Enzyme; Enzyme, Urate-Oxidase (Recombinant)

Use

Gout: Treatment of chronic gout in adults refractory to conventional therapy

Limitations of use: Not for the treatment of asymptomatic hyperuricemia

Local Anesthetic/Vasoconstrictor Precautions No information available to require special precautions

Effects on Dental Treatment No significant effects or complications reported

Effects on Bleeding No information available to require special precautions

Adverse Reactions

>10%:

Dermatologic: Urticaria (11%)

Endocrine & metabolic: Gout (flare: 74%; within the first 3 months)

Gastrointestinal: Nausea (12%)

Hematologic & oncologic: Bruise (11%)

Immunologic: Antibody development (antipegloticase antibodies: 92%; anti-PEG antibodies: 42%)

Miscellaneous: Infusion-related reaction (26%)

1% to 10%:

Cardiovascular: Chest pain (6% to 10%)

Dermatologic: Erythema (10%), pruritus (10%)

Gastrointestinal: Constipation (6%), vomiting (5%)

Hypersensitivity: Anaphylaxis (≤7%)

Respiratory: Dyspnea (7%), nasopharyngitis (7%)

Frequency not defined:

Central nervous system: Headache

Gastrointestinal: Diarrhea

Hematologic & oncologic: Anemia

Neuromuscular & skeletal: Muscle spasm

Renal: Nephrolithiasis

General Dosage Range IV: *Adults:* 8 mg every 2 weeks

Mechanism of Action Pegloticase is a pegylated recombinant form of urate-oxidase enzyme, also known as uricase (an enzyme normally absent in humans and high primates), which converts uric acid to allantoin (an inactive and water soluble metabolite of uric acid); it does not inhibit the formation of uric acid.

Pharmacodynamics/Kinetics

Onset of Action ~24 hours following the first dose, serum uric acid concentrations decreased

Duration of Action >300 hours (12.5 days)

Half-life Elimination Median: ~14 days

Pregnancy Risk Factor C

Pregnancy Considerations Adverse events have been observed in some animal reproduction studies.

Pembrolizumab (pem broe LIZ ue mab)

Brand Names: US Keytruda

Brand Names: Canada Keytruda

Pharmacologic Category Antineoplastic Agent, Anti-PD-1 Monoclonal Antibody; Antineoplastic Agent, Monoclonal Antibody

Use

Head and neck cancer, squamous cell (recurrent or metastatic): Treatment of recurrent or metastatic squamous cell carcinoma of the head and neck in patients with disease progression on or after platinum-containing chemotherapy.

Hodgkin lymphoma, classical (relapsed or refractory): Treatment of adult and pediatric patients with refractory classical Hodgkin lymphoma or patients who have relapsed after 3 or more prior lines of therapy.

Melanoma (unresectable or metastatic): Treatment of unresectable or metastatic melanoma.

Non-small cell lung cancer (metastatic):

First-line treatment of metastatic non-small cell lung cancer in patients with tumors with high PD-L1 expression (tumor proportion score [TPS] ≥50%), as determined by an approved test, and with no EGFR or ALK genomic tumor aberrations.

Treatment of metastatic non-small cell lung cancer in patients with tumors with PD-L1 expression (TPS ≥1%), as determined by an approved test, and with disease progression on or following platinum-containing chemotherapy. Patients with EGFR or ALK genomic tumor aberrations should have disease progression (on approved EGFR- or ALK-directed therapy) prior to receiving pembrolizumab.

Local Anesthetic/Vasoconstrictor Precautions No information available to require special precautions

Effects on Dental Treatment No significant effects or complications reported

Effects on Bleeding No information available to require special precautions

Adverse Reactions Incidence of adverse reactions include unapproved dosing regimens.

>10%:

Cardiovascular: Facial edema (10%)

Central nervous system: Fatigue (43%)

Dermatologic: Pruritus (28%), skin rash (24%; immune-mediated: 1%)

Endocrine & metabolic: Hyperglycemia (49%), hypoalbuminemia (37%), hyponatremia (37%), hypertriglyceridemia (33%), decreased serum bicarbonate (22%), hypocalcemia (21%)

Gastrointestinal: Constipation (22%), nausea (22%), decreased appetite (20%), diarrhea (20%), abdominal pain (13%), vomiting (13%)

Hematologic & oncologic: Anemia (44%; grades 3/4: 10%), lymphocytopenia (40%; grades 3/4: 9%)

Hepatic: Increased serum alkaline phosphatase (26%), increased serum AST (24%), increased serum ALT (21%)

Neuromuscular & skeletal: Arthralgia (14%)

Respiratory: Dyspnea (≥20%), cough (18%)

Miscellaneous: Fever (14%)

1% to 10%:

Central nervous system: Confusion (≥2%), peripheral neuropathy (2%)

Endocrine & metabolic: Hypothyroidism (immune-mediated; 9%), hyperthyroidism (immune-mediated; 3%)

Gastrointestinal: Colitis (immune-mediated; 2%)

Immunologic: Antibody development (2%)

Neuromuscular & skeletal: Weakness (10%), arthritis (immune-mediated; 2%)

Respiratory: Pneumonitis (3%), pleural effusion (≥2%), pneumonia (≥2%), respiratory failure (≥2%)

<1%, postmarketing, and/or case reports: Adrenocortical insufficiency (immune-mediated), bullous pemphigoid (immune-mediated), chronic inflammatory demyelinating polyradiculoneuropathy (Maleissye 2016), diabetic ketoacidosis, exfoliative dermatitis (immune-mediated), Guillain-Barré syndrome

(immune-mediated), hemolytic anemia (immune-mediated), hepatitis (including autoimmune hepatitis), hypophysitis, infusion-related reaction, interstitial nephritis (with renal failure), myasthenia gravis (immune-mediated), myositis (immune-mediated), nephritis (autoimmune), pancreatitis (immune-mediated), partial epilepsy (immune-mediated; in a patient with inflammatory foci in brain parenchyma), thyroiditis, type 1 diabetes mellitus, uveitis (immune-mediated), vasculitis (immune-mediated)

General Dosage Range

IV:

Children ≥2 years and Adolescents: 2 **mg/kg** once every 3 weeks (maximum: 200 mg/dose)

Adults: 2 **mg/kg** once every 3 weeks or 200 **mg** once every 3 weeks

Mechanism of Action Highly selective anti-PD-1 humanized monoclonal antibody which inhibits programmed cell death-1 (PD-1) activity by binding to the PD-1 receptor on T-cells to block PD-1 ligands (PD-L1 and PD-L2) from binding. Blocking the PD-1 pathway inhibits the negative immune regulation caused by PD-1 receptor signaling (Hamid 2013). Anti-PD-1 antibodies (including pembrolizumab) reverse T-cell suppression and induce antitumor responses (Robert 2014).

Pharmacodynamics/Kinetics

Half-life Elimination 23 days

Pregnancy Considerations Animal reproduction studies have not been conducted. Immunoglobulins are known to cross the placenta; therefore fetal exposure to pembrolizumab is expected. Based on the mechanism of action, pembrolizumab may cause fetal harm if administered during pregnancy; an alteration in the immune response or immune mediated disorders may develop following in utero exposure. Women of reproductive potential should use highly effective contraception during therapy and for at least 4 months after treatment is complete.

PEMEtrexed (pem e TREKS ed)

Brand Names: US Alimta

Brand Names: Canada Alimta

Pharmacologic Category Antineoplastic Agent, Antimetabolite; Antineoplastic Agent, Antimetabolite (Antifolate)

Use

Mesothelioma: Treatment of unresectable malignant pleural mesothelioma (in combination with cisplatin)

Non-small cell lung cancer (NSCLC), nonsquamous: Treatment of locally advanced or metastatic **non**squamous NSCLC (as initial treatment in combination with cisplatin; as maintenance treatment after 4 cycles of initial platinum-based first-line therapy; as single-agent treatment after prior chemotherapy)

Limitation of use: Not indicated for the treatment of **squamous** cell NSCLC

Local Anesthetic/Vasoconstrictor Precautions No information available to require special precautions

Effects on Dental Treatment Key adverse event(s) related to dental treatment: Dysphagia, esophagitis, odynophagia, and stomatitis.

Effects on Bleeding Chemotherapy may result in significant myelosuppression, potentially including significant reduction in platelet counts (thrombocytopenia grades 3/4: 2%) and altered hemostasis. In patients who are under active treatment with these agents, medical consult is suggested.

Adverse Reactions

>10%:

Central nervous system: Fatigue (18% to 34%; dose-limiting)

Dermatologic: Desquamation (≤14%), skin rash (≤14%)

Gastrointestinal: Nausea (12% to 31%), anorexia (19% to 22%), vomiting (6% to 16%), stomatitis (5% to 15%), diarrhea (5% to 13%)

Hematologic & oncologic: Anemia (15% to 19%; grades 3/4: 3% to 5%), leukopenia (6% to 12%; grades 3/4: 2% to 4%), neutropenia (6% to 11%; grades 3/4: 3% to 5%; dose-limiting; nadir: 8 to 10 days; recovery: 4 to 8 days after nadir)

Respiratory: Pharyngitis (15%)

1% to 10%:

Cardiovascular: Edema (1% to 5%)

Central nervous system: Neuropathy (sensory: ≤9%; motor: ≤5%)

Dermatologic: Pruritus (1% to 7%), alopecia (1% to 6%), erythema multiforme (≤5%)

Endocrine & metabolic: Weight loss (1%)

Gastrointestinal: Constipation (1% to 6%), abdominal pain (≤5%)

Hematologic & oncologic: Thrombocytopenia (1% to 8%; grades 3/4: 2%; dose-limiting), febrile neutropenia (grades 3/4: 2%)

Hepatic: Increased serum ALT (8% to 10%; grades 3/4: ≤2%), increased serum AST (7% to 8%; grades 3/4: ≤1%)

Hypersensitivity: Hypersensitivity reaction (≤5%)

Infection: Infection (≤5%), sepsis (1%)

Ophthalmic: Conjunctivitis (≤5%), increased lacrimation (≤5%)

Renal: Decreased creatinine clearance (≤5%), increased serum creatinine (≤5%)

Miscellaneous: Fever (1% to 8%)

<1%, postmarketing, and/or case reports: Cardiac arrhythmia, chest pain, colitis, dehydration, depression, esophagitis, gastrointestinal obstruction, hemolytic anemia, hepatobiliary disease (failure), hypertension, increased gamma-glutamyl transferase, interstitial pneumonitis, pain, pancreatitis, pancytopenia, peripheral ischemia, pulmonary embolism, radiation recall phenomenon (median onset: 6 days; range: 1 to 35 days), renal failure, Stevens-Johnson syndrome, supraventricular cardiac arrhythmia, syncope, thromboembolism, toxic epidermal necrolysis, ventricular tachycardia

General Dosage Range Dosage adjustment recommended in patients with hepatic impairment, on concomitant therapy, or who develop toxicities

IV: *Adults:* 500 mg/m^2 on day 1 of each 21-day cycle

Mechanism of Action Antifolate; disrupts folate-dependent metabolic processes essential for cell replication. Inhibits thymidylate synthase (TS), dihydrofolate reductase (DHFR), glycinamide ribonucleotide formyltransferase (GARFT), and aminoimidazole carboxamide ribonucleotide formyltransferase (AICARFT), the enzymes involved in folate metabolism and DNA synthesis, resulting in inhibition of purine and thymidine nucleotide and protein synthesis.

Pharmacodynamics/Kinetics

Half-life Elimination Normal renal function: 3.5 hours

Pregnancy Risk Factor D

Pregnancy Considerations Adverse effects were observed in animal reproduction studies. Based on the mechanism of action, pemetrexed may cause fetal harm if administered to a pregnant woman. Women of childbearing potential should use effective contraceptive measures to avoid becoming pregnant during treatment. A negative serum pregnancy test prior to treatment is recommended in the Canadian labeling. The Canadian labeling also recommends that males receiving therapy use effective contraceptive measures and not father a child during, and for up to 6 months after, therapy. Additionally, the Canadian labeling recommends counseling on sperm storage prior to treatment, as irreversible infertility has been reported in males.

Penbutolol (pen BYOO toe lole)

Brand Names: US Levatol [DSC]

Brand Names: Canada Levatol

Pharmacologic Category Antihypertensive; Beta-Blocker With Intrinsic Sympathomimetic Activity

Use

Hypertension: Treatment of mild-to-moderate arterial hypertension

The 2014 guideline for the management of high blood pressure in adults (JNC 8) recommends initiation of pharmacologic treatment to lower blood pressure for the following patients (JNC8 [James, 2013]):

- Patients ≥60 years of age, with systolic blood pressure (SBP) ≥150 mm Hg or diastolic blood pressure (DBP) ≥90 mm Hg. Goal of therapy is SBP <150 mm Hg and DBP <90 mm Hg.
- Patients <60 years of age, with SBP ≥140 mm Hg or DBP is ≥90 mm Hg. Goal of therapy is SBP <140 mm Hg and DBP <90 mm Hg.
- Patients ≥18 years of age with diabetes, with SBP ≥140 mm Hg or DBP ≥90 mm Hg. Goal of therapy is SBP <140 mm Hg and DBP <90 mm Hg.
- Patients ≥18 years of age with chronic kidney disease (CKD), with SBP ≥140 mm Hg or DBP ≥90 mm Hg. Goal of therapy is SBP <140 mm Hg and DBP <90 mm Hg.

In patients with chronic kidney disease (CKD), regardless of race or diabetes status, the use of an ACE inhibitor (ACEI) or angiotensin receptor blocker (ARB) as initial therapy is recommended to improve kidney outcomes. In the general nonblack population (without CKD) including those with diabetes, initial antihypertensive treatment should consist of a thiazide-type diuretic, calcium channel blocker, ACEI, or ARB. In the general black population (without CKD) including those with diabetes, initial antihypertensive treatment should consist of a thiazide-type diuretic or a calcium channel blocker **instead of** an ACEI or ARB.

Local Anesthetic/Vasoconstrictor Precautions No information available to require special precautions

Effects on Dental Treatment Key adverse event(s) related to dental treatment: Xerostomia (normal salivary flow resumes upon discontinuation). Penbutolol is a nonselective beta-blocker and may enhance the pressor response to epinephrine, resulting in hypertension and bradycardia. Many nonsteroidal anti-inflammatory drugs, such as ibuprofen and indomethacin, can reduce the hypotensive effect of beta-blockers after 3 or more weeks of therapy with the NSAID. Short-term NSAID use (ie, 3 days) requires no special precautions in patients taking beta-blockers.

Effects on Bleeding No information available to require special precautions

Adverse Reactions

>10%: Cardiovascular: Bradycardia (<60 beats/minute: 25%; <50 beats/minute: 1%)

1% to 10%:

Cardiovascular: Cardiac arrhythmia, cardiac failure

Central nervous system: Headache (8%), dizziness (5%), fatigue (4%), insomnia (2%)

Dermatologic: Diaphoresis (2%)

Gastrointestinal: Constipation (4%; Schoenberger, 1989), nausea (4%), diarrhea (3%), dyspepsia (3%)

Genitourinary: Impotence (1%)

Neuromuscular & skeletal: Limb pain (2%), weakness (2%)

Renal: Mean glomerular filtration rate decreased

Respiratory: Nasal congestion (1% to 4%; Schoenberger, 1989), cough (2%), dyspnea (2%)

<1%: Arterial mesenteric thrombosis, atrioventricular block, bronchospasm, cold extremities, confusion, depression, edema, hypoglycemia, hypotension, ischemic colitis, lethargy, nightmares, purpura, Raynaud's phenomenon, thrombocytopenia

General Dosage Range Oral: *Adults:* Initial: 20 mg once daily; Maintenance: 10-40 mg once daily (maximum: 80 mg/day)

Mechanism of Action Blocks both beta$_1$- and beta$_2$-receptors and has mild intrinsic sympathomimetic activity; has negative inotropic and chronotropic effects and can significantly slow AV nodal conduction. Also shows affinity for the 5-HT$_{1A}$ receptor (autoreceptor and post-synaptic); clinical implications are unknown (Rabiner, 2000).

Pharmacodynamics/Kinetics

Onset of Action Peak effect: 1.5-3 hours

Duration of Action >20 hours

Half-life Elimination Penbutolol: 5 hours; Conjugated metabolite: ~20 hours with normal renal function, 100 hours with end-stage renal disease

Time to Peak Plasma: 2-3 hours

Pregnancy Risk Factor C

Pregnancy Considerations Adverse events were observed in some animal reproduction studies.

Adverse events, such as fetal/neonatal bradycardia, hypoglycemia, and reduced birth weight, have been observed following in utero exposure to beta-blockers as a class. Adequate facilities for monitoring infants at birth is generally recommended. Protein binding of penbutolol is decreased during the 2nd and 3rd trimesters of pregnancy (Aquirre 1988).

Untreated chronic maternal hypertension and preeclampsia are also associated with adverse events in the fetus, infant, and mother (ACOG 2015; Magee 2014). Although beta-blockers may be used when treatment of hypertension in pregnancy is indicated, agents other than penbutolol are preferred (ACOG 2013; Magee 2014; Regitz-Zagrosek 2011).

Penciclovir (pen SYE kloe veer)

Related Information

Systemic Viral Diseases *on page 1806*

Viral Infections *on page 1849*

Related Sample Prescriptions

Viral Infections - Sample Prescriptions *on page 40*

Brand Names: US Denavir

Generic Availability (US) No

Pharmacologic Category Antiviral Agent

Dental Use Topical treatment of recurrent herpes simplex labialis (cold sores)

Use Herpes labialis (cold sores): Topical treatment of recurrent herpes labialis (cold sores)

Local Anesthetic/Vasoconstrictor Precautions No information available to require special precautions

Effects on Dental Treatment No significant effects or complications reported

Effects on Bleeding No information available to require special precautions

Adverse Reactions

>10%: Dermatologic: Erythema (50%; mild)

1% to 10%:

Central nervous system: Headache (5%)

Local: Application site reaction (1%)

<1%, postmarketing, and/or case reports: Altered sense of smell, erythematous rash, local anesthesia, localized edema, oropharyngeal edema, pain, paresthesia, pruritus, skin discoloration, urticaria

Dental Usual Dosage Treatment of herpes simplex labialis (cold sores): Children ≥12 years and Adults: Topical: Apply cream at the first sign or symptom of cold sore (eg, tingling, swelling); apply every 2 hours during waking hours for 4 days

Dosing

Adult & Geriatric Herpes labialis (cold sores): Topical: Apply cream at the first sign or symptom of cold sore (eg, tingling, swelling) or appearance of lesion; apply every 2 hours during waking hours for 4 days.

Pediatric Herpes labialis (cold sores): Children ≥12 years and Adolescents: Refer to adult dosing.

Renal Impairment There are no dosage adjustments provided in the manufacturer's labeling. However, dosage adjustment unlikely due to low systemic absorption.

Hepatic Impairment There are no dosage adjustments provided in the manufacturer's labeling. However, dosage adjustment unlikely due to low systemic absorption.

Mechanism of Action In cells infected with HSV-1 or HSV-2, viral thymidine kinase phosphorylates penciclovir to a monophosphate form which, in turn, is converted to penciclovir triphosphate by cellular kinases. Penciclovir triphosphate inhibits HSV polymerase competitively with deoxyguanosine triphosphate. Consequently, herpes viral DNA synthesis and, therefore, replication are selectively inhibited

Contraindications Hypersensitivity to the penciclovir or any component of the formulation

Warnings/Precautions Penciclovir should only be used on herpes labialis on the lips and face; because no data are available, application to mucous membranes is not recommended. Avoid application in or near eyes since it may cause irritation. The effect of penciclovir has not been established in immunocompromised patients.

Drug Interactions

Metabolism/Transport Effects None known.

Avoid Concomitant Use There are no known interactions where it is recommended to avoid concomitant use.

Increased Effect/Toxicity There are no known significant interactions involving an increase in effect.

Decreased Effect

Penciclovir may decrease the levels/effects of: Talimogene Laherparepvec

Pharmacodynamics/Kinetics

Onset of Action Resolution of pain: Adults: 3.5 days (Spruance 1997); Cutaneous healing: Adults: 4.8 days (Spruance 1997)

Pregnancy Risk Factor B

Pregnancy Considerations Adverse events have not been observed in animal reproduction studies following intravenous administration.

Breastfeeding Considerations According to the manufacturer, the decision to continue or discontinue breastfeeding during therapy should take into account the risk of exposure to the infant and the benefits of treatment to the mother.

Dosage Forms

Cream, External:

Denavir: 1% (5 g)

PenicillAMINE (pen i SIL a meen)

Brand Names: US Cuprimine; Depen Titratabs

Brand Names: Canada Cuprimine

Pharmacologic Category Chelating Agent

Use Treatment of Wilson's disease, cystinuria; adjunctive treatment of severe, active rheumatoid arthritis

Canadian labeling: Additional use (not in U.S. labeling): Treatment of chronic lead poisoning

Local Anesthetic/Vasoconstrictor Precautions No information available to require special precautions

Effects on Dental Treatment Key adverse event(s) related to dental treatment: Oral ulcerations, glossitis, gingivostomatitis, and taste alteration.

Effects on Bleeding No information available to require special precautions

Adverse Reactions Frequency may vary by indication.

>10%:

Gastrointestinal: Diarrhea (17%), dysgeusia (12%)

1% to 10%:

Dermatologic: Skin rash (early and late: 5%)

Genitourinary: Proteinuria (6%)

Hematologic & oncologic: Thrombocytopenia (4%), leukopenia (2%)

Frequency not defined.

Cardiovascular: Local thrombophlebitis, vasculitis (including renal vasculitis)

Central nervous system: Anxiety, agitation, dystonia, Guillain-Barre syndrome, hyperpyrexia, myasthenia (including extraocular muscles), myasthenia gravis, neurological deterioration, neuropathy, psychiatric disturbance

Dermatologic: Alopecia, cheilosis, exfoliative dermatitis, fragile skin (friability increased), lichen planus, papule (white papules at venipuncture and surgical sites), pemphigus, pruritus, skin atrophy (anetoderma), toxic epidermal necrolysis, urticaria, wrinkling of skin (excessive), yellow nail syndrome

Endocrine & metabolic: Hypoglycemia, increased lactate dehydrogenase, thyroiditis

Gastrointestinal: Anorexia, epigastric pain, glossitis, nausea, oral mucosa ulcer, pancreatitis, peptic ulcer (reactivation), stomatitis (gingivostomatitis), vomiting

Genitourinary: Breast disease (mammary hyperplasia), Goodpasture's syndrome, hematuria, nephrotic syndrome

Hematologic & oncologic: Agranulocytosis, aplastic anemia, change in platelet count (increase), eosinophilia, hemolytic anemia, increased monocytes, leukocytosis, lymphadenopathy, positive ANA titer, pure red cell aplasia, sideroblastic anemia, thrombotic thrombocytopenic purpura

Hepatic: Increased serum alkaline phosphatase, hepatic failure, intrahepatic cholestasis, toxic hepatitis

Neuromuscular & skeletal: Arthralgia, connective tissue disease (elastosis perforans serpiginosa), dermatomyositis, lupus-like syndrome, polyarthralgia (migratory, often with objective synovitis), polymyositis

Ophthalmic: Blepharoptosis, diplopia, optic neuritis, visual disturbance

Otic: Tinnitus
Renal: Renal failure
Respiratory: Asthma, bronchiolitis obliterans, hypersensitivity pneumonitis, interstitial pneumonitis, pulmonary fibrosis
Miscellaneous: Fever

General Dosage Range Dosage adjustment recommended in patients with renal impairment

Oral:

Children: 30 mg/kg/day in 4 divided doses

Adults: Dosage varies greatly depending on indication

Mechanism of Action Chelates with lead, copper, mercury and other heavy metals to form stable, soluble complexes that are excreted in urine; depresses circulating IgM rheumatoid factor, depresses T-cell but not B-cell activity; combines with cystine to form a compound which is more soluble, thus cystine calculi are prevented

Pharmacodynamics/Kinetics

Onset of Action Rheumatoid arthritis: 2 to 3 months; Wilson disease: 1 to 3 months

Half-life Elimination 1.7 to 7 hours (Roberts 2008)

Time to Peak Serum: 1 to 3 hours

Pregnancy Risk Factor D

Pregnancy Considerations Birth defects, including congenital cutix laxa and associated defects, have been reported in infants following penicillamine exposure during pregnancy. Use for the treatment of rheumatoid arthritis during pregnancy is contraindicated. Use for the treatment of cystinuria only if the possible benefits to the mother outweigh the potential risks to the fetus. Continued treatment of Wilson's disease during pregnancy protects the mother against relapse. Discontinuation has detrimental maternal and fetal effects. Daily dosage should be limited to 750 mg. For planned cesarean section, reduce dose to 250 mg/day for the last 6 weeks of pregnancy, and continue at this dosage until wound healing is complete.

Penicillin G Benzathine

(pen i SIL in jee BENZ a theen)

Related Information

Sexually-Transmitted Diseases *on page 1804*

Brand Names: US Bicillin L-A

Brand Names: Canada Bicillin L-A

Pharmacologic Category Antibiotic, Penicillin

Use Acute glomerulonephritis: Prophylaxis (secondary) in patients with a history of acute glomerulonephritis

Respiratory tract infections: Treatment of mild to moderate upper respiratory tract infections caused by streptococci susceptible to low, prolonged serum concentrations of penicillin G

Rheumatic fever and chorea: Prophylaxis (secondary) of rheumatic fever and/or chorea

Rheumatic heart disease: Prophylaxis (secondary) in patients with rheumatic heart disease

Syphilis and other venereal diseases: Treatment of syphilis, yaws, bejel, and pinta

Local Anesthetic/Vasoconstrictor Precautions No information available to require special precautions

Effects on Dental Treatment No significant effects or complications reported

Effects on Bleeding No information available to require special precautions

Adverse Reactions

Frequency not defined.

Cardiovascular: Cerebrovascular accident, hypotension, palpitations, syncope, tachycardia, vasodilatation, vasospasm, vasodepressor syncope
Central nervous system: Anxiety, coma, confusion, dizziness, drowsiness, euphoria, fatigue, headache, localized warm feeling, nervousness, numbness, pain, seizure, transverse myelitis
Dermatologic: Diaphoresis, gangrene of skin or other tissue, pallor, skin mottling, skin ulceration at injection site
Gastrointestinal: Bloody stools, intestinal necrosis, nausea, vomiting
Genitourinary: Bladder dysfunction (neurogenic bladder), hematuria, impotence, priapism, proteinuria
Hematologic & oncologic: Local hemorrhage (at injection site), lymphadenopathy
Hepatic: Increased serum AST
Hypersensitivity: Hypersensitivity reaction
Immunologic: Jarisch-Herxheimer reaction
Local: Abscess at injection site, atrophy at injection site, bruising at injection site, cellulitis at injection site, localized edema (at injection site), inflammation at injection site, injection site reaction (neurovascular damage), pain at injection site, residual mass at injection site, tissue necrosis at injection site
Neuromuscular & skeletal: Arthropathy, exacerbation of arthritis, periosteal disease (periostitis), rhabdomyolysis, tremor, weakness
Ophthalmic: Blindness, blurred vision
Renal: Increased blood urea nitrogen, increased serum creatinine, myoglobinuria, renal failure
Respiratory: Cyanosis

General Dosage Range IM:

Children: Dosage varies greatly depending on indication.

Adults: 1.2 to 2.4 million units as a single dose

Mechanism of Action Interferes with bacterial cell wall synthesis during active multiplication, causing cell wall death and resultant bactericidal activity against susceptible bacteria

Pharmacodynamics/Kinetics

Duration of Action Dose dependent: 1 to 4 weeks; larger doses result in more sustained levels

Time to Peak Serum: Within 12 to 24 hours; serum levels are usually detectable for 1 to 4 weeks depending on the dose; larger doses result in more sustained levels rather than higher levels

Pregnancy Considerations Adverse events have not been observed in animal reproduction studies. Penicillin G benzathine crosses the placenta (Nathan 1993; Weeks 1997). Maternal use of penicillins has generally not resulted in an increased risk of adverse fetal effects. Penicillin G is the drug of choice for treatment of syphilis during pregnancy (CDC [Workowski 2015]).

Penicillin G Benzathine and Penicillin G Procaine

(pen i SIL in jee BENZ a theen & pen i SIL in jee PROE kane)

Related Information

Penicillin G Benzathine *on page 1309*
Penicillin G Procaine *on page 1311*

Brand Names: US Bicillin C-R; Bicillin C-R 900/300

Pharmacologic Category Antibiotic, Penicillin

Use

Pneumococcal infections: Treatment of moderately severe pneumonia and otitis media due to susceptible *Pneumococcus* spp. (eg, *Streptococcus pneumoniae*)

Streptococcal infections, group A: Treatment of moderately severe to severe infections, without associated bacteremia, of the upper respiratory tract, scarlet fever, erysipelas, and skin and soft tissue infections due to group A streptococci

Note: Bicillin C-R 900/300 is only indicated in pediatric patients.

Limitations of use: Do not use in the treatment of sexually transmitted diseases, including syphilis, gonorrhea, yaws, bejel, and pinta. When high, sustained serum levels are required, use penicillin G sodium or potassium, either IM or IV.

Local Anesthetic/Vasoconstrictor Precautions No information available to require special precautions

Effects on Dental Treatment No significant effects or complications reported

Effects on Bleeding No information available to require special precautions

Adverse Reactions See individual agents.

General Dosage Range IM:

Infants and Children <14 kg: 600,000 units/dose (Bicillin C-R); 1.2 million units/dose (Bicillin C-R 900/300)

Children and Adolescents 14 to 27 kg: 900,000 units to 1.2 million units as a single dose (Bicillin C-R); 1.2 million units/dose (Bicillin C-R 900/300)

Children (>27 kg) and Adolescents: 2.4 million units/dose (Bicillin C-R); 1.2 million units/dose (Bicillin C-R 900/300)

Adults: 1.2 to 2.4 million units/dose (Bicillin C-R)

Mechanism of Action Inhibits bacterial cell wall synthesis by binding to one or more of the penicillin-binding proteins (PBPs); which in turn inhibits the final transpeptidation step of peptidoglycan synthesis in bacterial cell walls, thus inhibiting cell wall biosynthesis. Bacteria eventually lyse due to ongoing activity of cell wall autolytic enzymes (autolysins and murein hydrolases) while cell wall assembly is arrested.

Pharmacodynamics/Kinetics

Time to Peak Serum: IM: Within 3 hours

Pregnancy Considerations Adverse events have not been observed in animal reproduction studies. Maternal use of penicillins has generally not resulted in an increased risk of adverse fetal effects. See individual agents

Penicillin G (Parenteral/Aqueous)

(pen i SIL in jee, pa REN ter al, AYE kwee us)

Related Information

Sexually-Transmitted Diseases *on page 1804*

Brand Names: US Pfizerpen-G

Brand Names: Canada Crystapen

Pharmacologic Category Antibiotic, Penicillin

Use Serious gram-positive infections: Treatment of septicemia, empyema, pneumonia, pericarditis, endocarditis, and meningitis caused by *Streptococcus pyogenes* (group A beta-hemolytic streptococcus), other beta-hemolytic streptococci including groups C, H, G, L and M, *Streptococcus pneumoniae* and *Staphylococcus* species (nonpenicillinase-producing strains)

Anthrax: Treatment of anthrax caused by *Bacillus anthracis*

Actinomycosis: Treatment of actinomycosis (cervicofacial disease and thoracic and abdominal disease) caused by *Actinomyces israelii*

Clostridial infections: Treatment of botulism (adjunctive therapy to antitoxin), gas gangrene, and tetanus (adjunctive therapy to human tetanus immune globulin) caused by *Clostridium* spp.

Diphtheria: Treatment of diphtheria (adjunctive therapy to antitoxin and prevention of the carrier state) caused by *Corynebacterium diphtheriae*

Erysipelothrix endocarditis: Treatment of erysipelothrix endocarditis caused by *Erysipelothrix rhusiopathiae*

Fusospirochetosis: Treatment of fusospirochetosis, including severe infections of the oropharynx [Vincent], lower respiratory tract and genital area, caused by *Fusobacterium* spp. and spirochetes

Listeria infections: Treatment of listeria infections, including meningitis and endocarditis, caused by *Listeria monocytogenes*

Meningococcal infection: Treatment of meningococcal meningitis and/or septicemia caused by *Neisseria meningitidis*

Pasteurella infections: Treatment of pasteurella infections, including bacteremia and meningitis, caused by *Pasteurella multocida*

Rat bite fever: Treatment of rat bite fever (including Haverhill fever) caused by *Spirillum minus* or *S. moniliformis*

Syphilis: Treatment of syphilis (congenital and neurosyphilis) caused by *Treponema pallidum*

Local Anesthetic/Vasoconstrictor Precautions No information available to require special precautions

Effects on Dental Treatment No significant effects or complications reported

Effects on Bleeding No information available to require special precautions

Adverse Reactions Frequency not defined.

Cardiovascular: Localized phlebitis, local thrombophlebitis

Central nervous system: Coma (high doses), hyperreflexia (high doses), myoclonus (high doses), seizure (high doses)

Dermatologic: Contact dermatitis, skin rash

Endocrine & metabolic: Electrolyte disturbance (high doses)

Gastrointestinal: Pseudomembranous colitis

Hematologic & oncologic: Neutropenia, positive direct Coombs test (rare, high doses)

Hypersensitivity: Anaphylaxis, hypersensitivity reaction (immediate and delayed), serum sickness

Immunologic: Jarisch-Herxheimer reaction

Local: Injection site reaction

Renal: Acute interstitial nephritis (high doses), renal tubular disease (high doses)

General Dosage Range Dosage adjustment recommended in patients with renal impairment

IM, IV:

Infants, Children and Adolescents: 100,000 to 300,000 units/kg/day in divided doses every 4 to 6 hours (maximum: 24 million units/day)

Adults: 2 to 24 million units/day in divided doses every 4 to 6 hours

Mechanism of Action Interferes with bacterial cell wall synthesis during active multiplication, causing cell wall death and resultant bactericidal activity against susceptible bacteria

Pharmacodynamics/Kinetics

Half-life Elimination

Neonates: <6 days of age: 3.2 hours; ≥14 days of age: 1.4 hours

Adults: Normal renal function: 31 to 50 minutes

End-stage renal disease (ESRD): 6 to 20 hours (Aronoff 2007)

Time to Peak Serum: IV: Immediately after infusion

Pregnancy Risk Factor B

Pregnancy Considerations Adverse events have not been observed in animal reproduction studies. Penicillin G crosses the placenta. Maternal use of penicillins has generally not resulted in an increased risk of adverse fetal effects. Penicillin G is the drug of choice for treatment of syphilis during pregnancy and penicillin G (parenteral/aqueous) is the drug of choice for the prevention of early-onset Group B Streptococcal (GBS) disease in newborns (consult current guidelines) (CDC (RR-10) 2010; CDC [Workowski 2015]). When IV therapy is required for anthrax infection in pregnant and postpartum women, penicillin G may be used as an alternative agent (Meaney-Delman 2014).

Penicillin G Procaine (pen i SIL in jee PROE kane)

Brand Names: Canada Pfizerpen-AS; Wycillin

Pharmacologic Category Antibiotic, Penicillin

Use

Anthrax, prophylaxis: To reduce the incidence of the disease following exposure to aerosolized *Bacillus anthracis*.

Anthrax, treatment: Treatment of anthrax, including post-exposure inhalational disease due to aerosolized *B. anthracis*.

Diphtheria: As an adjunct to antitoxin for prevention of the carrier stage of diphtheria caused by susceptible *Corynebacterium diphtheriae*.

Endocarditis, subacute: Treatment of subacute bacterial endocarditis, only in extremely sensitive infections, caused by susceptible group A streptococci.

Erysipeloid: Treatment of erysipeloid caused by susceptible *Erysipelothrix rhusiopathiae*.

Fusospirochetosis: Treatment of fusospirochetosis (Vincent gingivitis and pharyngitis) in conjunction with dental care, and moderately severe infections of the oropharynx caused by susceptible fusiform bacilli and spirochetes.

Pneumococcal infection: Treatment of moderately severe infections of the respiratory tract caused by susceptible pneumococci.

Limitations of use: Severe pneumonia, empyema, bacteremia, pericarditis, meningitis, peritonitis, and arthritis of pneumococcal etiology are better treated with aqueous penicillin G during the acute stage.

Rat bite fever: Treatment of rat bite fever caused by susceptible *Streptobacillus moniliformis* and *Spirillum minus* organisms.

Skin and soft tissue infection: Treatment of moderately severe infections of the skin and soft tissues caused by susceptible staphylococci (penicillin G-susceptible).

Streptococcal Infections: Treatment of moderately severe to severe infections of the upper respiratory tract, skin and soft tissue infections, scarlet fever, and erysipelas caused by susceptible streptococci (group A, without bacteremia).

Limitations of use: Some streptococcal groups, including group D (enterococcus), are resistant. Aqueous penicillin is recommended for streptococcal infections with bacteremia.

Syphilis: Treatment of syphilis (all stages) caused by susceptible *Treponema pallidum*.

Yaws, bejel, and pinta: Treatment of yaws, bejel, and pinta caused by susceptible organisms.

Limitations of use: When high, sustained serum levels are required, use aqueous penicillin G, either intramuscularly (IM) or intravenously (IV). Do not use in the treatment of beta-lactamase-producing organisms, which includes most strains of *Neisseria gonorrhea*.

Local Anesthetic/Vasoconstrictor Precautions No information available to require special precautions

Effects on Dental Treatment No significant effects or complications reported

Effects on Bleeding No information available to require special precautions

Adverse Reactions Frequency not defined.

Cardiovascular: Cardiac conduction disturbance, cardiac insufficiency, thrombophlebitis, vasodilatation

Central nervous system: Central nervous system stimulation, confusion, drowsiness, myoclonus, seizure

Hematologic & oncologic: Hemolytic anemia, neutropenia, positive direct Coombs test

Hypersensitivity: Anaphylactoid reaction, hypersensitivity reaction, serum sickness

Immunologic: Jarisch-Herxheimer reaction

Local: Pain at injection site, sterile abscess at injection site

Renal: Interstitial nephritis

General Dosage Range

IM:

Children: 25,000 to 50,000 units/kg/day in divided doses 1 to 2 times daily (maximum: 4.8 million units daily)

Adults: 0.6 to 4.8 million units/day in divided doses every 12 to 24 hours

Mechanism of Action Inhibits bacterial cell wall synthesis by binding to one or more of the penicillin-binding proteins (PBPs); which in turn inhibits the final transpeptidation step of peptidoglycan synthesis in bacterial cell walls, thus inhibiting cell wall biosynthesis. Bacteria eventually lyse due to ongoing activity of cell wall autolytic enzymes (autolysins and murein hydrolases) while cell wall assembly is arrested.

Pharmacodynamics/Kinetics

Duration of Action Therapeutic: 15 to 24 hours

Time to Peak Serum: Within 1 to 4 hours and can persist within the therapeutic range for 15 to 24 hours

Pregnancy Risk Factor B

Pregnancy Considerations Adverse events have not been observed in animal reproduction studies. Penicillin G crosses the placenta. Maternal use of penicillins has generally not resulted in an increased risk of adverse fetal effects. Penicillin G procaine may be used in the treatment of syphilis during pregnancy (consult current guidelines) (CDC [Workowski 2015]). Penicillin G procaine is also approved for the management of *Bacillus anthracis*, however other agents are preferred for use in pregnant women (Meaney-Delman 2014).

Penicillin V Potassium
(pen i SIL in vee poe TASS ee um)

Related Information

Bacterial Infections *on page 1835*

Viral Infections *on page 1849*

Related Sample Prescriptions

Bacterial Infections and Periodontal Diseases - Sample Prescriptions *on page 32*

Brand Names: Canada Apo-Pen VK; Novo-Pen-VK; Nu-Pen-VK

Generic Availability (US) Yes

Pharmacologic Category Antibiotic, Penicillin

Dental Use Treatment of common orofacial infections caused by aerobic gram-positive cocci and anaerobes. These orofacial infections include cellulitis, periapical abscess, periodontal abscess, acute suppurative pulpitis, oronasal fistula, pericoronitis, osteitis, osteomyelitis, postsurgical and post-traumatic infection.

Use

Fusospirochetosis (Vincent gingivitis and pharyngitis): Treatment of fusospirochetosis (Vincent gingivitis and pharyngitis), in conjunction with dental care for infections involving gum tissue.

Pneumococcal infections: Treatment of mild to moderately severe pneumococcal respiratory tract infections, including otitis media.

Rheumatic fever and/or chorea prophylaxis: Prophylaxis (chronic, secondary) of rheumatic fever and/or chorea.

Staphylococcal infections (penicillin G-sensitive): Treatment of mild infections of the skin and soft tissues.

Streptococcal infections (without bacteremia): Treatment of mild to moderate streptococcal infections of the upper respiratory tract, scarlet fever, and mild erysipelas.

Local Anesthetic/Vasoconstrictor Precautions No information available to require special precautions

Effects on Dental Treatment Key adverse event(s) related to dental treatment: Oral candidiasis (prolonged use).

Effects on Bleeding No information available to require special precautions

Adverse Reactions

>10%: Gastrointestinal: Melanoglossia, mild diarrhea, nausea, oral candidiasis, vomiting

<1%: Acute interstitial nephritis, anaphylaxis, convulsions, exfoliative dermatitis, fever, hemolytic anemia, hypersensitivity reaction, positive direct Coombs test, serum-sickness like reaction

Dental Usual Dosage

Orofacial infections: Oral:

Children <12 years: 25 to 50 mg/kg/day in divided doses every 6 to 8 hours (maximum dose: 3,000 mg daily)

Children ≥12 years and Adults: 125 to 500 mg every 6 to 8 hours

Dosing

Adult & Geriatric

Usual dosage range: Oral: 125 to 500 mg every 6 to 8 hours

Actinomycosis (off-label use): Oral: **Note:** Duration is dependent upon disease location and patient-specific factors; complicated infections requiring surgical intervention usually initiate IV therapy with penicillin G until disease subsidence followed by long term oral therapy (Hsieh 1993, Sudhakar 2004):

2 to 4 g/day in divided doses every 6 hours (Smego 1998)

Bite wounds (animal) (off-label use): Oral: 500 mg 4 times daily in combination with dicloxacillin (IDSA [Stevens 2014])

Cutaneous anthrax, community-acquired (off-label use): Oral: 500 mg 4 times daily for 7 to 10 days (IDSA [Stevens 2014])

Cutaneous erysipeloid (off-label use): Oral: 500 mg 4 times daily for 7 to 10 days (IDSA [Stevens 2014])

Erysipelas: Oral:

Manufacturer's labeling: 125 to 250 mg every 6 to 8 hours for 10 days

Alternate dosing: 500 mg 4 times daily (IDSA [Stevens 2014])

Fusospirochetosis (Vincent infection): Oral: 250 to 500 mg every 6 to 8 hours

Pharyngitis (streptococcal): Oral:

Acute treatment, group A streptococci:

Manufacturer's labeling: Acute treatment, group A streptococci: 125 to 250 mg every 6 to 8 hours for 10 days

Alternate dosing: 500 mg 2 to 3 times daily for 10 days (Gerber 2009) **or** 250 mg 4 times daily or 500 mg twice daily for 10 days (Shulman 2012)

Chronic carrier treatment, group A streptococcal: 500 mg 4 times daily (maximum: 2,000 mg daily) for 10 days in combination with oral rifampin (Shulman 2012)

Prophylaxis of recurrent rheumatic fever infections: Oral: 250 mg twice daily (Gerber 2009)

Prosthetic joint infection (off-label use): *Chronic oral antimicrobial suppression (Enterococcus spp [penicillin-susceptible], streptococci [beta-hemolytic], Propionibacterium spp):* Oral: 500 mg 2 to 4 times daily (Osmon 2013)

Streptococcal skin infection (off-label dose): Oral: 250 to 500 mg every 6 hours (IDSA [Stevens 2014])

Pediatric

General dosing, susceptible infections:

Infants and Children <12 years: Mild to moderate infection: Oral: 25 to 75 mg/kg/day in divided doses every 6 to 8 hours (maximum daily dose: 2,000 mg/**day**) (*Red Book* [AAP 2015])

Children ≥12 years and Adolescents: Oral:

Manufacturer's labeling (fixed dosing): 125 to 500 mg every 6 to 8 hours

Alternate dosing (weight-based): Mild to moderate infection: 25 to 75 mg/kg/day in divided doses every 6 to 8 hours (maximum daily dose: 2,000 mg/**day** [*Red Book* (AAP 2015)])

Indication-specific dosing:

Anthrax (cutaneous), community-acquired (off-label use): Infants, Children, and Adolescents: Oral: 25 to 50 mg/kg/day in divided doses 2 **or** 4 times daily; maximum single dose: 500 mg (Stevens 2005)

Fusospirochetosis (Vincent infection), mild to moderately severe infections: Children ≥12 years and Adolescents: Oral: Refer to adult dosing.

Tonsillopharyngitis; Group A streptococcal infection, treatment and primary prevention of rheumatic fever:

Acute treatment (Gerber 2009; Shulman 2012; WHO 2004):

Children ≤27 kg: Oral: 250 mg 2 to 3 times daily for 10 days

Children >27 kg and Adolescents: Oral: 500 mg 2 to 3 times daily for 10 days; in adolescents, 250 mg 4 times daily has also been suggested

Chronic carrier treatment (Group A *streptococci*) (off-label use): Children and Adolescents: 50 mg/kg/day in 4 divided doses for 10 days in combination with oral rifampin; maximum daily dose: 2,000 mg/**day** (Shulman 2012)

Recurrent rheumatic fever, prophylaxis (off-label): Children and Adolescents: 250 mg twice daily (Gerber 2009)

Pneumococcal infection prophylaxis for anatomic or functional asplenia (eg, sickle cell disease [SCD]) (off-label use) (AAP 2002; Kavanagh 2011; NHLBI 2014):

Infants (as soon as SCD diagnosed or asplenic) and Children <3 years: Oral: 125 mg twice daily

Children ≥3 years: Oral: 250 mg twice daily; the decision to discontinue penicillin prophylaxis after 5 years of age in children who have not experienced invasive pneumococcal infection and have received recommended pneumococcal immunizations is patient and clinician dependent

Pneumonia, community-acquired; Group A *Streptococcus*, mild infection or step-down therapy (off-label use): Infants ≥3 months, Children, and Adolescents: Oral: 50 to 75 mg/kg/day in 3 to 4 divided doses (Bradley 2011); maximum daily dose: 2,000 mg/**day**

Renal Impairment There are no dosage adjustments provided in manufacturer's labeling. Use with caution; excretion is prolonged in patients with renal impairment.

Hepatic Impairment There are no dosage adjustments provided in manufacturer's labeling.

Mechanism of Action Inhibits bacterial cell wall synthesis by binding to one or more of the penicillin-binding proteins (PBPs); which in turn inhibits the final transpeptidation step of peptidoglycan synthesis in bacterial cell walls, thus inhibiting cell wall biosynthesis. Bacteria eventually lyse due to ongoing activity of cell wall autolytic enzymes (autolysins and murein hydrolases) while cell wall assembly is arrested.

Contraindications Hypersensitivity to penicillin or any component of the formulation

Warnings/Precautions Use with caution in patients with severe renal impairment or history of seizures. Serious and occasionally severe or fatal hypersensitivity (anaphylactio) reactions have been reported in patients on penicillin therapy, especially with a history of beta lactam hypersensitivity or history of sensitivity to multiple allergens. e with caution in asthmatic patients. If a serious reaction occurs, treatment with supportive care measures and airway protection should be instituted immediately. Extended duration of therapy or use associated with high serum concentrations may be associated with an increased risk for some adverse reactions. Prolonged use may result in fungal or bacterial superinfection, including *C. difficile*-associated diarrhea (CDAD) and pseudomembranous colitis; CDAD has been observed >2 months postantibiotic treatment. Potentially significant interactions may exist, requiring dose or frequency adjustment, additional monitoring, and/or selection of alternative therapy.

Benzyl alcohol and derivatives: Some dosage forms may contain sodium benzoate/benzoic acid; benzoic acid (benzoate) is a metabolite of benzyl alcohol; large amounts of benzyl alcohol (≥99 mg/kg/day) have been associated with a potentially fatal toxicity ("gasping syndrome") in neonates; the "gasping syndrome" consists of metabolic acidosis, respiratory distress, gasping respirations, CNS dysfunction (including convulsions, intracranial hemorrhage), hypotension, and cardiovascular collapse (AAP ["Inactive" 1997]; CDC, 1982); some data suggests that benzoate displaces bilirubin from protein binding sites (Ahlfors 2001); avoid or use dosage forms containing benzyl alcohol derivative with caution in neonates. See manufacturer's labeling.

Drug Interactions

Metabolism/Transport Effects None known.

Avoid Concomitant Use

Avoid concomitant use of Penicillin V Potassium with any of the following: BCG (Intravesical); Cholera Vaccine

Increased Effect/Toxicity

Penicillin V Potassium may increase the levels/effects of: Methotrexate; Vitamin K Antagonists

The levels/effects of Penicillin V Potassium may be increased by: Probenecid

Decreased Effect

Penicillin V Potassium may decrease the levels/effects of: BCG (Intravesical); BCG Vaccine (Immunization); Cholera Vaccine; Lactobacillus and Estriol; Mycophenolate; Sodium Picosulfate; Typhoid Vaccine

The levels/effects of Penicillin V Potassium may be decreased by: Tetracycline Derivatives

Food Interactions Food decreases drug absorption rate; decreases drug serum concentration. Management: Take on an empty stomach 1 hour before or 2 hours after meals around-the-clock to promote less variation in peak and trough serum levels.

Pregnancy Considerations Penicillin crosses the placenta. Maternal use of penicillins has generally not resulted in an increased risk of adverse fetal effects. Due to pregnancy-induced physiologic changes, some pharmacokinetic parameters of penicillin V may be altered in the second and third trimester (Heikkilä 1993). If treatment for the management of *Bacillus anthracis* is needed in pregnant women, other agents are preferred (Meaney-Delman 2014)

Breastfeeding Considerations Penicillin V is excreted into breast milk and may be detected in the urine of some breastfeeding infants. Loose stools and rash have been reported in nursing infants (Matheson 1988).

Dosage Forms

Solution Reconstituted, Oral:

Generic: 125 mg/5 mL (100 mL, 200 mL); 250 mg/5 mL (100 mL, 200 mL)

Tablet, Oral:

Generic: 250 mg, 500 mg

Pentastarch (PEN ta starch)

Brand Names: Canada Pentaspan [DSC]

Pharmacologic Category Plasma Volume Expander, Colloid

Use Note: Not approved in the US

Adjunctive treatment in the management of shock

Local Anesthetic/Vasoconstrictor Precautions No information available to require special precautions

Effects on Dental Treatment No significant effects or complications reported

Effects on Bleeding No information available to require special precautions

Adverse Reactions Frequency not defined.

Cardiovascular: Angina pectoris, edema, tachycardia

Central nervous system: Anxiety, chills, dizziness, fatigue, headache, insomnia, malaise, paresthesia, shakiness

Dermatologic: Acne vulgaris

Endocrine & metabolic: Weight gain (temporary)

Gastrointestinal: Diarrhea, increased serum amylase, nausea

Hematologic & oncologic: Blood coagulation disorder, hemorrhage

Hepatic: Increased serum bilirubin

Hypersensitivity: Anaphylactoid reaction, anaphylaxis, hypersensitivity reaction (includes hypotension, urticaria, wheezing)

Neuromuscular & skeletal: Weakness

Respiratory: Nasal congestion

Miscellaneous: Fever

<1%, postmarketing, and/or case reports: Renal disease

Mechanism of Action Produces plasma volume expansion by virtue of its highly colloidal starch structure

Pharmacodynamics/Kinetics

Onset of Action Volume expansion: Within 1 hour

Duration of Action 18-24 hours (improves hemodynamic status for 12-18 hours)

Half-life Elimination ~2 days

Pregnancy Considerations Adverse events were observed in animal reproduction studies.

Product Availability Not available in the US; All Canadian dosage forms have been discontinued for more than 1 year.

Pentazocine (pen TAZ oh seen)

Brand Names: US Talwin

Brand Names: Canada Talwin

Pharmacologic Category Analgesic, Opioid; Analgesic, Opioid Partial Agonist

Use

Anesthesia: Sedative prior to surgery; supplement to surgical anesthesia.

Pain management: Management of pain severe enough to require an opioid analgesic and for which alternative treatments are inadequate.

Limitations of use: Reserve pentazocine for use in patients for whom alternative treatment options (eg, nonopioid analgesics, opioid combination products) are ineffective, not tolerated, or would be otherwise inadequate to provide sufficient management of pain.

Local Anesthetic/Vasoconstrictor Precautions No information available to require special precautions

Effects on Dental Treatment Key adverse event(s) related to dental treatment: Xerostomia (normal salivary flow resumes upon discontinuation).

Effects on Bleeding No information available to require special precautions

Adverse Reactions Frequency not defined.

Cardiovascular: Circulatory depression, facial edema, flushing, hypertension, hypotension, increased peripheral vascular resistance, shock, syncope, tachycardia

Central nervous system: Central nervous system depression, chills, confusion, disorientation, dizziness, drowsiness, drug dependence (physical and psychological), euphoria, excitement, hallucination, headache, insomnia, irritability, malaise, nightmares, paresthesia, sedation

Dermatologic: Dermatitis, diaphoresis, erythema multiforme, pruritus, skin rash, Stevens-Johnson syndrome, toxic epidermal necrolysis, urticaria

Gastrointestinal: Abdominal distress, anorexia, constipation, diarrhea, dysgeusia, nausea, vomiting, xerostomia

Genitourinary: Urinary retention

Hematologic & oncologic: Agranulocytosis (rare), decreased white blood cell count, eosinophilia

Hypersensitivity: Anaphylaxis

Local: Injection site reaction (tissue damage and irritation)

Neuromuscular & skeletal: Tremor, weakness

Ophthalmic: Blurred vision, diplopia, miosis, nystagmus

Otic: Tinnitus

Respiratory: Dyspnea, respiratory depression (rare)

Postmarketing and/or case reports: Hypogonadism (Brennan, 2013; Debono, 2011)

General Dosage Range

IM:

Children ≥1 years and Adolescents ≤16 years: 0.5 mg/kg preoperatively

Adults: 30 to 60 mg every 3 to 4 hours (maximum: 360 mg/day; 60 mg/dose) **or** 30 mg once

IV: *Adults:* 30 mg every 3 to 4 hours (maximum: 360 mg/day; 30 mg/dose) **or** 20 mg every 2 to 3 hours as needed (maximum total dose: 60 mg)

SubQ: *Adults:* 30 mg every 3 to 4 hours (maximum: 360 mg/day; 60 mg/dose)

Mechanism of Action Agonist of kappa opiate receptors and partial agonist of mu opiate receptors in the CNS, causing inhibition of ascending pain pathways, altering the perception of and response to pain; produces analgesia, respiratory depression and sedation similar to opioids

Pharmacodynamics/Kinetics

Onset of Action IM, SubQ: 15 to 20 minutes; IV: 2 to 3 minutes

Duration of Action 2 to 3 hours

Half-life Elimination Prolonged with hepatic impairment

Neonates: 8 to 12 hours (estimated; Osifo 2008)

Children 4 to 8 years (mean ± SD): 3 ± 1.5 hours (Hanunen 1993)

Adults: 2 to 3 hours

Pregnancy Considerations

Adverse events have been observed in animal reproduction studies. Pentazocine is approved for pain relief during labor. When used for pain relief during labor, opioids may temporarily affect the heart rate of the fetus (ACOG 2002).

[US Boxed Warning]: Prolonged use of opioids during pregnancy can cause neonatal withdrawal syndrome, which may be life-threatening if not recognized and treated according to protocols developed by neonatology experts. If opioid use is required for a prolonged period in a pregnant woman, advise the patient of the risk of neonatal opioid withdrawal opioid withdrawal syndrome and ensure that appropriate treatment will be available. If chronic opioid exposure occurs in pregnancy, adverse events in the newborn (including withdrawal) may occur; monitoring of the neonate is recommended. The minimum effective dose should be used if opioids are needed (Chou 2009). Neonatal abstinence syndrome following opioid exposure may present with autonomic (eg, fever, temperature instability), gastrointestinal (eg, diarrhea, vomiting, poor feeding/weight gain), or neurologic (eg, high-pitched crying, increased muscle tone, irritability, seizure, tremor) symptoms (Dow 2012; Hudak 2012). Neonatal abstinence syndrome has been reported following prolonged use of pentazocine during pregnancy.

Long-term opioid use may cause secondary hypogonadism, which may lead to sexual dysfunction or infertility (Brennan 2013).

Controlled Substance C-IV

Pentazocine and Acetaminophen
(pen TAZ oh seen & a seet a MIN oh fen)

Related Information

Acetaminophen *on page 56*

Pentazocine *on page 1314*

Generic Availability (US) Yes

Pharmacologic Category Analgesic Combination (Opioid); Analgesic, Opioid; Analgesic, Opioid Partial Agonist

Use Relief of mild-to-moderate pain

Local Anesthetic/Vasoconstrictor Precautions No information available to require special precautions

Effects on Dental Treatment No significant effects or complications reported (see Dental Comment)

Effects on Bleeding As a single agent, acetaminophen does not appear to affect bleeding or platelet aggregation. Acetaminophen may prolong the INR and increase bleeding in patients taking warfarin (Coumadin). For patients taking warfarin, single acetaminophen doses or acetaminophen therapy of short duration should be safe, but if large (>1.3 g/day) doses are administered for longer than 10-14 days, then the INR should be monitored (see Dental Comment).

Adverse Reactions Adverse reactions attributed to pentazocine 50 mg. Frequency not defined. See Acetaminophen monograph for acetaminophen-related reactions.

Cardiovascular: Circulatory depression, facial edema, flushing, hypertension, hypotension, syncope, tachycardia

Central nervous system: Chills, confusion, depression, disorientation, dizziness, drowsiness, drug dependence (physical and physological), euphoria, excitement, hallucination, headache, increased intracranial pressure, insomnia, irritability, nightmares, paresthesia, sedation, seizure, withdrawal syndrome

Dermatologic: Dermatitis, diaphoresis, erythema multiforme, pruritus, skin rash, Stevens-Johnson syndrome, toxic epidermal necrolysis, urticaria

Gastrointestinal: Abdominal distress, anorexia, biliary colic, constipation, diarrhea, nausea, vomiting, xerostomia

Genitourinary: Urinary retention

Hematologic & oncologic: Agranulocytosis, decreased white blood cell count, eosinophilia

Hypersensitivity: Anaphylaxis

Neuromuscular & skeletal: Tremor, weakness

Ophthalmic: Blurred vision, miosis

Otic: Tinnitus

Respiratory: Respiratory depression

Postmarketing and/or case reports: Hypogonadism (Brennan, 2013; Debono, 2011)

Dosing

Adult Note: Maximum daily intake of acetaminophen from all sources should not exceed 4 g.

Analgesic: Oral: One caplet (pentazocine 25 mg/ acetaminophen 650 mg) every 4 hours as needed (maximum: 6 caplets/day)

Geriatric Refer to adult dosing. Use with caution; may be more sensitive to analgesic and sedative effects.

Pediatric Analgesic: Oral: Children ≥12 years: Refer to adult dosing.

Renal Impairment No dosage adjustment provided in manufacturer's labeling. Use with caution.

Hepatic Impairment No dosage adjustment provided in manufacturer's labeling. However, dosage adjustment may be necessary due to decreased metabolism and predisposition to adverse effects. Use with caution.

Mechanism of Action

Pentazocine: Agonist of kappa opiate receptors and partial agonist of mu opiate receptors in the CNS, causing inhibition of ascending pain pathways, altering the perception of and response to pain; produces analgesia, respiratory depression and sedation similar to opioids

Acetaminophen: Inhibits the synthesis of prostaglandins in the central nervous system and peripherally blocks pain impulse generation

Contraindications Hypersensitivity to pentazocine, acetaminophen, or any component of the formulation; hypersensitivity to sulfites (contains metabisulfite)

Warnings/Precautions See individual agents.

Drug Interactions

Metabolism/Transport Effects Refer to individual components.

Avoid Concomitant Use

Avoid concomitant use of Pentazocine and Acetaminophen with any of the following: Analgesics (Opioid); Azelastine (Nasal); Buprenorphine; Eluxadoline; Orphenadrine; Oxomemazine; Paraldehyde; Thalidomide

Increased Effect/Toxicity

Pentazocine and Acetaminophen may increase the levels/effects of: Alvimopan; Azelastine (Nasal); Blonanserin; Busulfan; Dasatinib; Desmopressin; Diuretics; Eluxadoline; Flunitrazepam; Imatinib; Methotrimeprazine; MetyroSINE; Mipomersen; Orphenadrine; Paraldehyde; Phenylephrine (Systemic); Piribedil; Pramipexole; Prilocaine; Ramosetron; ROPINIRole; Rotigotine; Selective Serotonin Reuptake Inhibitors; Serotonin Modulators; Sodium Nitrite; SORAfenib; Suvorexant; Thalidomide; Vitamin K Antagonists; Zolpidem

The levels/effects of Pentazocine and Acetaminophen may be increased by: Amphetamines; Anticholinergic Agents; Brimonidine (Topical); Cannabis; Chlormethiazole; Chlorphenesin Carbamate; CNS Depressants; Dapsone (Topical); Dasatinib; Dimethindene (Topical); Dronabinol; Droperidol; Isoniazid; Kava Kava; Lofexidine; Magnesium Sulfate; Methotrimeprazine; MetyraPONE; Minocycline; Nabilone; Nitric Oxide; Oxomemazine; Perampanel; Probenecid; Rufinamide; Sodium Oxybate; SORAfenib; Succinylcholine; Tetracaine (Topical); Tetrahydrocannabinol

Decreased Effect

Pentazocine and Acetaminophen may decrease the levels/effects of: Analgesics (Opioid); Buprenorphine; Diuretics; Gastrointestinal Agents (Prokinetic); Pegvisomant

The levels/effects of Pentazocine and Acetaminophen may be decreased by: Cholestyramine Resin; Nalmefene; Naltrexone

Pregnancy Risk Factor C

Pregnancy Considerations See individual agents.

Breastfeeding Considerations See individual agents.

Controlled Substance C-IV

Dental Comment Although the ***OTC product labeling*** for acetaminophen products state to limit the maximum dose to 3,000 mg daily (for extra strength) or 3,250 mg (for regular strength) (see this site for details: http://www.tylenolprofessional.com/extra-strength-tylenol-dosage-faq.html), it is still appropriate for patients to take up to 4,000 mg daily "under the direction of a healthcare provider" (http://www.tylenolprofessional.com/assets/v4/faqs-new-dosing.pdf).

The acetaminophen component requires use with caution in patients who use alcohol, with preexisting liver disease, and those receiving more than one source of acetaminophen-containing medication.

Hepatotoxicity caused by acetaminophen is potentiated by chronic alcohol consumption. People who are taking acetaminophen, even at therapeutic doses, and consume alcohol are at risk of developing hepatotoxicity.

Acetaminophen may increase the levels and enhance the anticoagulant effects of vitamin K antagonists acenocoumarol and warfarin (Coumadin®). Studies have reported that acetaminophen has increased the INR in warfarin treated patients with daily acetaminophen doses as low as 2 g, particularly when taking acetaminophen for >1 week (Antlitz, 1968; Boeijinga, 1982; Gebauer, 2003; Hylek, 1998; Rubin, 1984). In addition, case reports of bleeding as a result of increased INR have been published (Bagheri, 1999; Bartle, 1991). There is no known mechanism of the interaction; furthermore, some studies have failed to demonstrate this interaction (Gadisseur, 2003; Kwan, 1995; van den Bemt, 2002). In terms of risk, the data suggest that acetaminophen and warfarin could interact in some clinically significant manner but that the benefits of concomitant use of acetaminophen for pain control in dental patients taking warfarin usually outweigh the risks. An appropriate monitoring plan should be in place to identify potential negative effects and dosage adjustments may be necessary in a minority of patients. The interaction may be more likely to occur with daily acetaminophen doses of >1.3 g for >1 week.

There are no reports of acetaminophen interacting with antiplatelet drugs such as aspirin, clopidogrel (Plavix®), or prasugrel (Effient™). Also, there are no reports of acetaminophen in combination with hydrocodone, codeine, or oxycodone interacting with warfarin (Coumadin®).

PENTobarbital (pen toe BAR bi tal)

Brand Names: US Nembutal

Brand Names: Canada Nembutal Sodium

Pharmacologic Category Anticonvulsant, Barbiturate; Barbiturate

Use Sedative/hypnotic; status epilepticus (refractory)

Local Anesthetic/Vasoconstrictor Precautions No information available to require special precautions

Effects on Dental Treatment No significant effects or complications reported

Effects on Bleeding No information available to require special precautions

Adverse Reactions

Frequency not defined.

Cardiovascular: Bradycardia, hypotension, syncope

Central nervous system: Abnormality in thinking, agitation, anxiety, ataxia, central nervous system stimulation, confusion, depression, dizziness, drowsiness, hallucination, headache, insomnia, nervousness, nightmares, psychiatric disturbance

Dermatologic: Exfoliative dermatitis, skin rash

Gastrointestinal: Constipation, nausea, vomiting

Hematologic & oncologic: Megaloblastic anemia

Hepatic: Hepatotoxicity

Hypersensitivity: Angioedema, hypersensitivity reaction

Local: Injection site reaction

Neuromuscular & skeletal: Hyperkinesia, laryngospasm

Respiratory: Apnea (especially with rapid IV use), hypoventilation, respiratory depression

Miscellaneous: Fever

General Dosage Range

IM:

Children: 2-6 mg/kg (maximum: 100 mg/dose)

Adults: 150-200 mg

IV:

Children:

Hypnotic/sedative: 1-6 mg/kg

Refractory status epilepticus: Loading dose: 5-15 mg/kg; Maintenance infusion: 0.5-5 mg/kg/hour

Adults:

Hypnotic/sedative: 100 mg; may repeat (maximum total dose: 500 mg)

Refractory status epilepticus: Loading dose: 10-15 mg/kg; Maintenance infusion: 0.5-10 mg/kg/hour

Mechanism of Action Barbiturate with sedative, hypnotic, and anticonvulsant properties. Barbiturates depress the sensory cortex, decrease motor activity, alter cerebellar function, and produce drowsiness, sedation, and hypnosis. In high doses, barbiturates exhibit anticonvulsant activity; barbiturates produce dose-dependent respiratory depression; reduce brain metabolism and cerebral blood flow in order to decrease intracranial pressure

Pharmacodynamics/Kinetics

Onset of Action Krauss 2006: Children and Adults: Sedation: IM: 10 to 15 minutes; IV: Almost immediate, within 3 to 5 minutes; Oral, Rectal: 15 to 60 minutes

Duration of Action Krauss 2006: Children and Adults: Sedation: IM: 1 to 2 hours; IV: 15 to 45 minutes; Oral, Rectal: 1 to 4 hours

Half-life Elimination Terminal: Children: 26 ± 16 hours (Schaible 1982); Adults: Healthy: 22 hours (average) (Ehrnebo 1974); Range: 15 to 50 hours; dose dependent

Pregnancy Risk Factor D

Pregnancy Considerations Barbiturates can be detected in the placenta, fetal liver and fetal brain. Fetal and maternal blood concentrations may be similar following parenteral administration. An increased incidence of fetal abnormalities may occur following maternal use. When used during the third trimester of pregnancy, withdrawal symptoms may occur in the neonate including seizures and hyperirritability; symptoms may be delayed up to 14 days. Use during labor does not impair uterine activity; however, respiratory depression may occur in the newborn; resuscitation equipment should be available, especially for premature infants.

Controlled Substance C-II

Pentosan Polysulfate Sodium

(PEN toe san pol i SUL fate SOW dee um)

Brand Names: US Elmiron

Brand Names: Canada Elmiron®

Pharmacologic Category Analgesic, Urinary

Use Relief of bladder pain or discomfort due to interstitial cystitis

Local Anesthetic/Vasoconstrictor Precautions No information available to require special precautions

Effects on Dental Treatment No significant effects or complications reported

Effects on Bleeding Pentosan polysulfate sodium is a low-molecular weight heparin-like compound with anticoagulant and fibrinolytic effects. Medical consult is suggested.

Adverse Reactions

1% to 10%:

Central nervous system: Headache (3%), dizziness (1%)

Dermatologic: Alopecia (4%), skin rash (3%)

Gastrointestinal: Diarrhea (4%), nausea (4%), abdominal pain (2%), dyspepsia (2%)

Hematologic & oncologic: Rectal hemorrhage (6%)

Hepatic: Abnormal hepatic function tests (1%; dose-related)

<1%, postmarketing, and/or case reports: Amblyopia, anemia, anorexia, colitis, conjunctivitis, constipation,

dehydration, depression, diaphoresis, dyspnea, ecchymoses, emotional lability, epistaxis, esophagitis, flatulence, gastritis, gingival hemorrhage, hyperkinesia, hypersensitivity reaction, insomnia, leukopenia, optic neuritis, oral mucosa ulcer, pharyngitis, prolonged partial thromboplastin time, prolonged prothrombin time, pruritus, retinal hemorrhage, rhinitis, skin photosensitivity, thrombocytopenia, tinnitus, urticaria, vomiting

General Dosage Range Oral: *Children ≥16 years and Adults:* 100 mg 3 times/day

Mechanism of Action Although pentosan polysulfate sodium is a low-molecular weight heparinoid, it is not known whether these properties play a role in its mechanism of action in treating interstitial cystitis; the drug appears to adhere to the bladder wall mucosa where it may act as a buffer to protect the tissues from irritating substances in the urine.

Pharmacodynamics/Kinetics

Half-life Elimination 20-27 hours

Time to Peak Serum: 2 hours (range: 0.6-120 hours)

Pregnancy Risk Factor B

Pregnancy Considerations No adverse events were noted in animal reproduction studies; however, reversible limb bud abnormalities were noted during *in vitro* animal studies. There are no adequate and well-controlled studies in pregnant women. Use with caution and only if clearly needed during pregnancy. Based on limited data, pentosan polysulfate does not appear to cross the placenta.

Pentostatin (pen toe STAT in)

Brand Names: US Nipent

Brand Names: Canada Nipent

Pharmacologic Category Antineoplastic Agent, Antimetabolite; Antineoplastic Agent, Antimetabolite (Purine Analog)

Use Hairy cell leukemia: Treatment (as a single-agent) of untreated and interferon-refractory hairy cell leukemia in patients with active disease (clinically significant anemia, neutropenia, thrombocytopenia, or disease-related symptoms)

Local Anesthetic/Vasoconstrictor Precautions No information available to require special precautions

Effects on Dental Treatment Key adverse event(s) related to dental treatment: Stomatitis.

Effects on Bleeding Chemotherapy may result in significant myelosuppression, potentially including significant reduction in platelet counts (thrombocytopenia: 6% to 32%) and altered hemostasis. In patients who are under active treatment with these agents, medical consult is suggested.

Adverse Reactions

>10%:

Central nervous system: Fatigue (29% to 42%), pain (8% to 20%), chills (11% to 19%), headache (13% to 17%), central nervous system toxicity (1% to 11%)

Dermatologic: Skin rash (26% to 43%), pruritus (10% to 21%), skin changes (4% to 17%)

Gastrointestinal: Nausea (≤63%), vomiting (≤63%), diarrhea (15% to 17%), anorexia (13% to 16%), abdominal pain (4% to 16%), stomatitis (5% to 12%)

Hematologic & oncologic: Leukopenia (22% to 60%), anemia (8% to 35%), thrombocytopenia (6% to 32%), bone marrow depression (nadir: 7 days; recovery: 10 to 14 days)

Hepatic: Increased serum transaminases (2% to 19%)

Hypersensitivity: Hypersensitivity reaction (2% to 11%)

Infection: Infection (7% to 36%)

Neuromuscular & skeletal: Myalgia (11% to 19%), weakness (10% to 12%)

Respiratory: Cough (17% to 20%), upper respiratory tract infection (13% to 16%), rhinitis (10% to 11%), dyspnea (8% to 11%)

Miscellaneous: Fever (42% to 46%)

1% to 10%:

Cardiovascular: Chest pain (3% to 10%), facial edema (3% to 10%), hypotension (3% to 10%), peripheral edema (3% to 10%), angina pectoris (<3%), atrioventricular block (<3%), bradycardia (<3%), cardiac arrhythmia (<3%), cardiac failure (<3%), deep vein thrombophlebitis (<3%), hypertension (<3%), localized phlebitis (<3%), pericardial effusion (<3%), sinoatrial arrest (<3%), syncope (<3%), tachycardia (<3%), vasculitis (<3%), ventricular premature contractions (<3%)

Central nervous system: Anxiety (3% to 10%), confusion (3% to 10%), depression (3% to 10%), dizziness (3% to 10%), drowsiness (3% to 10%), insomnia (3% to 10%), nervousness (3% to 10%), paresthesia (3% to 10%), abnormal dreams (<3%), abnormality in thinking (<3%), amnesia (<3%), ataxia (<3%), dysarthria (<3%), emotional lability (<3%), encephalitis (<3%), hallucination (<3%), hostility (<3%), meningism (<3%), neuralgia (<3%), neuritis (<3%), neuropathy (<3%), paralysis (<3%), psychoneurosis (<3%), seizure (<3%), twitching (<3%), vertigo (<3%)

Dermatologic: Diaphoresis (8% to 10%), cellulitis (6%), furunculosis (4%), xeroderma (3% to 10%), urticaria (3% to 10%), acne vulgaris (<3%), alopecia (<3%), eczema (<3%), skin photosensitivity (<3%)

Endocrine & metabolic: Amenorrhea (<3%), decreased libido (<3%), hypercalcemia (<3%), hyponatremia (<3%), gout (<3%), loss of libido (<3%)

Gastrointestinal: Dyspepsia (3% to 10%), flatulence (3% to 10%), gingivitis (3% to 10%), constipation (<3%), dysgeusia (<3%), dysphagia (<3%), glossitis (<3%), intestinal obstruction (<3%), oral candidiasis (2%)

Genitourinary: Urinary tract infection (3%), impotence (<3%)

Hematologic & oncologic: Agranulocytosis (3% to 10%), hemorrhage (3% to 10%), acute leukemia (<3%), aplastic anemia (<3%), hemolytic anemia (<3%), petechia (<3%)

Infection: Herpes zoster (8%), viral infection (≤8%), bacterial infection (5%), herpes simplex infection (4%), sepsis (3%), abscess (2%)

Neuromuscular & skeletal: Arthralgia (3% to 10%), arthritis (<3%), hyperkinesia (<3%), osteomyelitis (1%)

Ophthalmic: Conjunctivitis (4%), amblyopia (<3%), lacrimal dysfunction (<3%), nonreactive pupils (<3%), photophobia (<3%), retinopathy (<3%), visual disturbance (<3%), watery eyes (<3%), xerophthalmia (<3%)

Otic: Deafness (<3%), labyrinthitis (<3%), otalgia (<3%), tinnitus (<3%)

Renal: Increased serum creatinine (3% to 10%), nephrolithiasis (<3%), renal disease (<3%), renal failure (<3%), renal function abnormality (<3%), renal insufficiency (<3%)

Respiratory: Pharyngitis (8% to 10%), sinusitis (6%), pneumonia (5%), asthma (3% to 10%), bronchitis (3%), bronchospasm (<3%), flu-like symptoms

(<3%), laryngeal edema (<3%), pulmonary embolism (<3%)

<1%, postmarketing, and/or case reports: Dysuria, fungal skin infection, hematuria, lethargy, pulmonary edema, pulmonary toxicity (in combination with fludarabine), uveitis, vision loss

General Dosage Range Dosage adjustment recommended in patients with renal impairment

IV: *Adults:* 4 mg/m^2 every 2 weeks

Mechanism of Action Pentostatin is a purine antimetabolite that inhibits adenosine deaminase, preventing the deamination of adenosine to inosine. Accumulation of deoxyadenosine (dAdo) and deoxyadenosine 5′-triphosphate (dATP) results in a reduction of purine metabolism which blocks DNA synthesis and leads to cell death.

Pharmacodynamics/Kinetics

Half-life Elimination

Terminal: ~6 hours; Renal impairment (CrCl <50 mL/minute): 18 hours (range: 11 to 23 hours [Lathia, 2002])

Pregnancy Risk Factor D

Pregnancy Considerations Adverse events were observed in animal reproduction studies. Women of childbearing potential should be advised to avoid becoming pregnant during treatment.

Pentoxifylline (pen toks IF i lin)

Brand Names: US TRENtal [DSC]

Brand Names: Canada Pentoxifylline SR

Pharmacologic Category Blood Viscosity Reducer Agent

Use

Intermittent claudication: Treatment of intermittent claudication on the basis of chronic occlusive arterial disease of the limbs.

Limitations of use: May improve function and symptoms, but not intended to replace more definitive therapy. **Note:** The American College of Chest Physicians (ACCP) discourages the use of pentoxifylline for the treatment of intermittent claudication refractory to exercise therapy (and smoking cessation) (Guyatt, 2012).

Local Anesthetic/Vasoconstrictor Precautions No information available to require special precautions

Effects on Dental Treatment No significant effects or complications reported

Effects on Bleeding Pentoxifylline is a methylxanthine derivative with potent hemorrheologic properties. Pentoxifylline has been shown to decrease platelet aggregation and adhesion, and enhances plasminogen activator while decreasing fibrinogen and alpha$_2$-antiplasmin.

Adverse Reactions

1% to 10%: Gastrointestinal: Nausea (2%), vomiting (1%)

<1%, postmarketing, and/or case reports: Anaphylactic shock, anaphylactoid reaction, anaphylaxis, angioedema, angina pectoris, anorexia, anxiety, aplastic anemia, aseptic meningitis, bloating, blurred vision, cardiac arrhythmia, chest pain, cholecystitis, confusion, conjunctivitis, constipation, decreased serum fibrinogen, depression, dysgeusia, dyspnea, edema, epistaxis, eructation, flatulence, flu-like symptoms, hallucination, hepatitis, hypotension, increased liver enzymes, jaundice, laryngitis, leukemia, leukopenia, malaise, nail disease (brittle fingernails), nasal congestion, otalgia, pancytopenia, pruritus, purpura, scotoma, seizure, sialorrhea, skin rash, sore throat, tachycardia, thrombocytopenia, tremor, urticaria, weight changes, xerostomia

General Dosage Range Dosage adjustment recommended in patients with renal impairment

Oral: *Adults:* 400 mg 2 to 3 times daily

Mechanism of Action Pentoxifylline increases blood flow to the affected microcirculation. Although the precise mechanism of action is not well-defined, blood viscosity is lowered, erythrocyte flexibility is increased, leukocyte deformability is increased, and neutrophil adhesion and activation are decreased. Overall, tissue oxygenation is significantly increased.

Pharmacodynamics/Kinetics

Onset of Action 2 to 4 weeks with multiple doses

Half-life Elimination Parent drug: 24 to 48 minutes; Metabolites: 60 to 96 minutes

Time to Peak Serum: 2 to 4 hours

Pregnancy Risk Factor C

Pregnancy Considerations Adverse events have been observed in animal reproduction studies. Information related to use in pregnant women has not been located. Pentoxifylline may be used to test sperm viability when evaluating nonfertile males (ASRM, 2012). It has also been evaluated for the treatment of infertility due to endometriosis, but use for this purpose is not currently recommended (Lu, 2012).

Peramivir (pe RA mi veer)

Brand Names: US Rapivab

Brand Names: Canada Rapivab

Pharmacologic Category Antiviral Agent; Neuraminidase Inhibitor

Use

Influenza: Treatment of acute, uncomplicated influenza in adults who have been symptomatic ≤2 days.

Limitations of use:

Efficacy has not been established for patients with serious influenza requiring hospitalization.

Efficacy is based on clinical trials in which influenza A was the predominant virus; a limited number of subjects with influenza B have been studied.

Local Anesthetic/Vasoconstrictor Precautions No information available to require special precautions

Effects on Dental Treatment No significant effects or complications reported

Effects on Bleeding No information available to require special precautions

Adverse Reactions

1% to 10%:

Cardiovascular: Hypertension (2%)

Central nervous system: Insomnia (3%)

Endocrine: Increased serum glucose (>160 mg/dL: 5%)

Gastrointestinal: Diarrhea (8%), constipation (4%)

Hematologic and oncologic: Neutropenia (<1 x 10^9/L: 8%)

Hepatic: Increased serum ALT (>2.5 x ULN: 3%), increased serum AST (3%)

Neuromuscular & skeletal: Increased creatine phosphokinase (≥6 x ULN: 4%)

<1%, postmarketing, and/or case reports: Abnormal behavior, anaphylactoid reaction, anaphylaxis, delirium, erythema multiforme, exfoliative dermatitis, hallucination, skin rash, Stevens-Johnson syndrome

General Dosage Range

Dosage adjustment recommended in patients with renal impairment

IV: *Adults:* 600 mg as a single dose

Mechanism of Action Peramivir, a cyclopentane analogue, selectively inhibits the influenza virus neuraminidase enzyme, preventing the release of viral particles from infected cells.

Pharmacodynamics/Kinetics

Half-life Elimination ~20 hours

Pregnancy Risk Factor C

Pregnancy Considerations Adverse events were observed in some animal reproduction studies. Information related to the use of peramivir in pregnancy is limited (Hernandez 2011; Sorbello 2012). Based on information from one case, the pharmacokinetics of peramivir may be changed with pregnancy (Clay 2011).

Untreated influenza infection is associated with an increased risk of adverse events to the fetus and an increased risk of complications or death to the mother (CDC 62[07], 2013). Neuraminidase inhibitors are currently recommended for the treatment or prophylaxis of influenza in pregnant women and women up to 2 weeks postpartum (CDC 60[1], 2011; CDC March 13, 2014; CDC January 2015).

Perampanel (per AM pa nel)

Brand Names: US Fycompa

Brand Names: Canada Fycompa

Pharmacologic Category AMPA Glutamate Receptor Antagonist; Anticonvulsant, Miscellaneous

Use

Partial-onset seizures: Adjunctive therapy for the treatment of partial-onset seizures with or without secondarily generalized seizures in patients with epilepsy who are ≥12 years of age.

Primary generalized tonic-clonic seizures: Adjunctive therapy for the treatment of primary generalized tonic-clonic seizures in patients with epilepsy who are ≥12 years of age.

Local Anesthetic/Vasoconstrictor Precautions No information available to require special precautions

Effects on Dental Treatment Key adverse event(s) related to dental treatment: Cough, upper respiratory tract infection, and oropharyngeal pain

Effects on Bleeding No information available to require special precautions

Adverse Reactions Many adverse effects are dose-related. Frequency not always defined.

Cardiovascular: Peripheral edema (2%)

Central nervous system: Dizziness (16% to ≤47%), vertigo (3% to ≤47%), hostility (≤12% to ≤20%), aggressive behavior (2% to ≤20%), drowsiness (9% to 18%), abnormal gait (4% to 16%), fatigue (8% to 15%), headache (12% to 13%), irritability (2% to 12%), falling (5% to 10%), ataxia (≤8%), equilibrium disturbance (3% to 5%), anxiety (2% to 5%), dysarthria (1% to 4%), hypoesthesia (3%), hypersomnia (1% to 3%), anger (1% to 3%), memory impaired (2%), paresthesia (2%), confusion (1% to 2%), euphoria (≤2%), mood changes (1% to 2%), agitation, altered mental status, delusion, disorientation, emotional lability, homicidal ideation, paranoia, psychiatric disturbance (worsening)

Dermatologic: Skin rash (4%)

Endocrine & metabolic: Weight gain (4% to 9%), hyponatremia (2%)

Gastrointestinal: Vomiting (4% to 9%), nausea (6% to 8%), abdominal pain (5%), constipation (3%)

Genitourinary: Urinary tract infection (4%)

Hematologic & oncologic: Bruise (2% to 6%)

Neuromuscular & skeletal: Back pain (5%), sprain (4%), myalgia (3%), arthralgia (2% to 3%), limb pain (2% to 3%), musculoskeletal pain (2%), weakness (2%)

Ophthalmic: Blurred vision (3% to 4%), diplopia (3%)

Respiratory: Cough (4%), upper respiratory tract infection (4%), oropharyngeal pain (2%)

Miscellaneous: Head trauma (3%), laceration (2%), limb injury (1% to 2%)

<1%, postmarketing, and/or case reports: Acute psychosis, delirium, DRESS syndrome, hallucination, increased serum triglycerides, suicidal ideation

General Dosage Range Dosage adjustment recommended in patients with hepatic impairment or on concomitant therapy.

Oral: *Children ≥12 years, Adolescents, and Adults*: Initial: 2 or 4 mg once daily at bedtime; maintenance dose: 8 to 12 mg once daily

Mechanism of Action The exact mechanism by which perampanel exerts antiseizure activity is not definitively known; it is a noncompetitive antagonist of the ionotropic alpha-amino-3-hydroxy-5-methyl-4-isoxazolepropionic acid (AMPA) glutamate receptor on postsynaptic neurons. Glutamate is a primary excitatory neurotransmitter in the central nervous center causing many neurological disorders from neuronal over excitation.

Pharmacodynamics/Kinetics

Half-life Elimination ~105 hours

Time to Peak 0.5 to 2.5 hours; delayed ~1 to 3 hours with food

Pregnancy Risk Factor C

Pregnancy Considerations Adverse events have been observed in animal reproduction studies at doses equivalent to the human dose (based on BSA). Contraceptives containing levonorgestrel may be less effective; additional nonhormonal forms of contraception are recommended during perampanel therapy and for 1 month after discontinuation of therapy.

Patients exposed to perampanel during pregnancy are encouraged to enroll in the North American Antiepileptic Drug (NAAED) Pregnancy Registry by calling 1-888-233-2334. Additional information is available at www.aedpregnancyregistry.org.

Controlled Substance C-III

Periciazine (per ee CYE ah zeen)

Brand Names: Canada Neuleptil

Pharmacologic Category First Generation (Typical) Antipsychotic

Use Note: Not approved in the US

Psychosis: Adjunctive therapy in select psychotic patients to control prevailing hostility, impulsivity, or aggression

Local Anesthetic/Vasoconstrictor Precautions Periciazine is one of the drugs confirmed to prolong the QT interval and is accepted as having a risk of causing torsade de pointes. The risk of drug-induced torsade de pointes is extremely low when a single QT interval prolonging drug is prescribed. In terms of epinephrine, it is not known what effect vasoconstrictors in the local anesthetic regimen will have in patients with a known history of congenital prolonged QT interval or in patients taking any medication that prolongs the QT interval. Until more information is obtained, it is suggested that the clinician consult with the physician prior to the use of a vasoconstrictor in suspected patients, and that the vasoconstrictor (epinephrine, mepivacaine and levonordefrin [Carbocaine 2% with Neo-Cobefrin]) be used with caution.

Effects on Dental Treatment Key adverse event(s) related to dental treatment:

Significant hypotension may occur, especially when the drug is administered parenterally. Patients may experience orthostatic hypotension as they stand up after treatment; especially if lying in dental chair for extended periods of time. Use caution with sudden changes in position during and after dental treatment. Orthostatic hypotension is due to alpha-receptor blockade; elderly are at greater risk.

Tardive dyskinesia: Prevalence rate may be 40% in elderly; development of the syndrome and the irreversible nature are proportional to duration and total cumulative dose over time. Extrapyramidal reactions are more common in elderly with up to 50% developing these reactions after 60 years of age. Drug-induced Parkinson's syndrome occurs often; akathisia is the most common extrapyramidal reaction in elderly.

Increased confusion, memory loss, psychotic behavior, and agitation frequently occur as a consequence of anticholinergic effects. Antipsychotic-associated sedation in nonpsychotic patients is extremely unpleasant due to feelings of depersonalization, derealization, and dysphoria.

Effects on Bleeding No information available to require special precautions

Adverse Reactions Frequency not defined; listing includes adverse reactions reported with other agents from the phenothiazine class.

Cardiovascular: Atrioventricular block, cardiac arrhythmias, ECG changes, edema, hypotension, orthostatic hypotension, prolonged Q-T interval on ECG, pulmonary embolism, sinus tachycardia, tachycardia, venous thromboembolism, ventricular fibrillation

Central nervous system: Aggressive behavior, agitation, disruption of body temperature regulation, disturbed sleep, dizziness, drowsiness, EEG pattern changes, extrapyramidal reaction (tremor, akathisia, dystonia, dyskinesia, oculogyric, opisthotonos, hyper-reflexia, pseudo-Parkinsonism, rigidity, sialorrhea), headache, hyperpyrexia, insomnia, neuroleptic malignant syndrome, psychomotor retardation, psychosis (paradoxical), seizure, tardive dyskinesia, temperature regulation impaired

Dermatologic: Diaphoresis, skin photosensitivity, skin pigmentation (prolonged therapy)

Endocrine & metabolic: Change in libido, diabetic ketoacidosis, galactorrhea, gynecomastia, hyperglycemia, menstrual disease (including delayed ovulation), weight changes

Gastrointestinal: Cholestasis, constipation, diarrhea, fecal impaction, increased appetite, nausea, paralytic ileus, vomiting, xerostomia

Genitourinary: Ejaculatory disorder, false positive pregnancy test, priapism, urinary incontinence

Hematologic & oncologic: Agranulocytosis

Hepatic: Cholestatic jaundice

Hypersensitivity: Angioedema

Ophthalmic: Blurred vision, corneal deposits (prolonged therapy), glaucoma, pigment deposits on lens

Respiratory: Asthma, laryngeal edema, nasal congestion, pneumonia, pneumonitis

General Dosage Range Oral:

Children ≥5 years and Adolescents: Initial: 2.5 to 10 mg in the morning, followed by 5 to 30 mg in the evening

Adults: Initial: 5 to 20 mg in the morning, followed by 10 to 40 mg in the evening

Elderly: Initial: 5 mg/day; may increase dose gradually based on effect and tolerance. Doses >30 mg/day are rarely needed.

Mechanism of Action Phenothiazine of the piperidine group with sedative and weak antipsychotic properties; blocks subcortical dopamine receptors in the brain; depresses the release of hypothalamic and hypophyseal hormones

Pregnancy Considerations Use of antipsychotic agents during the third trimester may increase the risk of extrapyramidal and/or withdrawal symptoms (eg, agitation, feeding disorder, hypertonia, hypotonia, respiratory distress, somnolence, and tremor) in newborns. Reported adverse events have ranged from self-limiting to severe.

Product Availability Not available in the US

Dental Comment This drug is known to prolong the QT interval. The QT interval is measured as the time and distance between the Q point of the QRS complex and the end of the T wave in the ECG tracing. After adjustment for heart rate, the QT interval is defined as prolonged if it is more than 450 msec in men and 460 msec in women. A long QT syndrome was first described in the 1950s and 60s as a congenital syndrome involving QT interval prolongation and syncope and sudden death. Some of the congenital long QT syndromes were characterized by a peculiar electrocardiographic appearance of the QRS complex involving a premature atria beat followed by a pause, then a subsequent sinus beat showing marked QT prolongation and deformity. This type of cardiac arrhythmia was originally termed "torsade de pointes" (translated from the French as "twisting of the points").

Prolongation of the QT interval is thought to result from delayed ventricular repolarization. The repolarization process within the myocardial cell is due to the efflux of intracellular potassium. The channels associated with this current can be blocked by many drugs and predispose the electrical propagation cycle to torsade de pointes.

Periciazine is one of the drugs confirmed to prolong the QT interval and is accepted as having a risk of causing torsade de pointes. The risk of drug-induced torsade de pointes is extremely low when a single QT interval prolonging drug is prescribed. In terms of epinephrine, it is not known what effect vasoconstrictors in the local anesthetic regimen will have in patients with a known history of congenital prolonged QT interval or in patients taking any medication that prolongs the QT interval. Until more information is obtained, it is suggested that the clinician consult with the physician prior to the use of a vasoconstrictor in suspected patients, and that the vasoconstrictor (epinephrine, levonordefrin [Neo-Cobefrin®]) be used with caution.

Perindopril (per IN doe pril)

Related Information

Cardiovascular Diseases *on page 1752*

Brand Names: US Aceon

Brand Names: Canada Coversyl

Pharmacologic Category Angiotensin-Converting Enzyme (ACE) Inhibitor; Antihypertensive

Use

Treatment of hypertension; reduction of cardiovascular mortality or nonfatal myocardial infarction in patients with stable coronary artery disease

Guideline recommendations:

Hypertension: The 2014 guideline for the management of high blood pressure in adults (Eighth Joint National Committee [JNC 8]) recommends initiation of pharmacologic treatment to lower blood pressure for the following patients:

- Patients ≥60 years of age with systolic blood pressure (SBP) ≥150 mm Hg or diastolic blood pressure (DBP) ≥ 90 mm Hg. Goal of therapy is SBP <150 mm Hg and DBP <90 mm Hg.
- Patients <60 years of age with SBP ≥140 mm Hg or DBP is ≥90 mm Hg. Goal of therapy is SBP <140 mm Hg and DBP <90 mm Hg.
- Patients ≥18 years of age with diabetes and SBP ≥140 mm Hg or DBP ≥90 mm Hg. Goal of therapy is SBP <140 mm Hg and DBP <90 mm Hg.
- Patients ≥18 years of age with chronic kidney disease (CKD) and SBP ≥140 mm Hg or DBP ≥90 mm Hg. Goal of therapy is SBP <140 mm Hg and DBP <90 mm Hg.

Chronic kidney disease (CKD) and hypertension: Regardless of race or diabetes status, the use of an ACE inhibitor (ACEI) or angiotensin receptor blocker (ARB) as initial therapy is recommended to improve kidney outcomes. In the general nonblack population (without CKD) including those with diabetes, initial antihypertensive treatment should consist of a thiazide-type diuretic, calcium channel blocker, ACEI, or ARB. In the general black population (without CKD) including those with diabetes, initial antihypertensive treatment should consist of a thiazide-type diuretic or a calcium channel blocker **instead of** an ACEI or ARB.

Coronary artery disease (CAD) and hypertension: The American Heart Association, American College of Cardiology, and American Society of Hypertension (AHA/ACC/ASH) 2015 scientific statement for the treatment of hypertension in patients with CAD recommends the use of an ACE inhibitor (or an ARB) as part of a regimen in patients with hypertension and chronic stable angina if there is prior MI, LV systolic dysfunction, diabetes mellitus, or CKD. A BP target of <140/90 mm Hg is reasonable for the secondary prevention of cardiovascular events. A lower target BP (<130/80 mm Hg) may be appropriate in some individuals with CAD, previous MI, stroke or transient ischemic attack, or CAD risk equivalents (AHA/ACC/ASH [Rosendorff 2015]).

Heart failure: The ACCF/AHA 2013 heart failure guidelines recommend the use of ACE inhibitors, along with other guideline-directed medical therapies, to prevent HF in patients with a reduced ejection fraction who have a history of MI (stage B HF), to prevent HF in any patient with a reduced ejection fraction (stage B HF), or to treat those with HF and reduced ejection fraction (stage C HFrEF) (ACCF/AHA [Yancy 2013])

Local Anesthetic/Vasoconstrictor Precautions No information available to require special precautions

Effects on Dental Treatment Key adverse event(s) related to dental treatment: Patients may experience orthostatic hypotension as they stand up after treatment; especially if lying in dental chair for extended periods of time. Use caution with sudden changes in position during and after dental treatment.

An angiotensin-converting enzyme (ACE) inhibitor cough is a dry, hacking, nonproductive cough that can potentially interfere with longer dental procedures if patient has this side effect.

Effects on Bleeding No information available to require special precautions

Adverse Reactions

Some reactions occurred at an incidence of >1% but ≤ placebo.

>10%:

Central nervous system: Headache (24%)

Respiratory: Cough (12%; incidence higher in women, 3:1)

1% to 10%:

Cardiovascular: Edema (4%), chest pain (2%), ECG abnormality (2%), palpitations (1%)

Central nervous system: Hypertonia (3%), sleep disorder (3%), depression (2%), paresthesia (2%), drowsiness (1%), nervousness (1%)

Dermatologic: Skin rash (2%)

Endocrine & metabolic: Increased serum triglycerides (1%), menstrual disease (1%)

Gastrointestinal: Diarrhea (4%), abdominal pain (3%), dyspepsia (2%), nausea (2%), vomiting (2%), flatulence (1%)

Genitourinary: Urinary tract infection (3%), proteinuria (2%), sexual disorder (male: 1%)

Hepatic: Increased serum ALT (2%)

Hypersensitivity: Seasonal allergy (2%)

Infection: Viral infection (3%)

Neuromuscular & skeletal: Weakness (8%), back pain (6%), leg pain (5%), arm pain (3%), arthralgia (1%), arthritis (1%), myalgia (1%), neck pain (1%)

Otic: Tinnitus (2%), otic infection (1%)

Respiratory: Upper respiratory tract infection (9%), sinusitis (5%), rhinitis (5%), pharyngitis (3%)

Miscellaneous: Fever (2%)

<1%, postmarketing, and/or case reports: Amnesia, anaphylaxis, angioedema, anxiety, arthralgia, bronchitis, bruise, cardiac conduction disturbance, cerebrovascular accident, chills, conjunctivitis, constipation, diaphoresis, dyspnea, epistaxis, erythema, facial edema, flank pain, fluid retention, gastroenteritis, gout, heart murmur, hematoma, hematuria, hyperglycemia, hypokalemia, hypotension, increased appetite, increased serum alkaline phosphatase, increased serum AST, increased serum cholesterol, increased serum creatinine, increased uric acid, leukopenia, malaise, migraine, myocardial infarction, nephrolithiasis, neutropenia, orthostatic hypotension, otalgia, pain, pruritus, psychological disorder (psychosexual disorder), pulmonary fibrosis, purpura, rhinorrhea, sneezing, syncope, tinea, urinary frequency, urinary retention, vaginitis, vasodilatation, ventricular premature contractions, vertigo, visual hallucination (Doane 2013), xeroderma, xerostomia

General Dosage Range Dosage adjustment recommended in patients with renal impairment

Oral: *Adults:* Initial: 2-4 mg once daily; Maintenance: 4-8 mg/day in 1-2 divided doses (maximum: 16 mg/day)

Mechanism of Action Perindopril is a prodrug for perindoprilat, which acts as a competitive inhibitor of angiotensin-converting enzyme (ACE); prevents conversion of angiotensin I to angiotensin II, a potent vasoconstrictor; results in lower levels of angiotensin II which, in turn, causes an increase in plasma renin activity and a reduction in aldosterone secretion

Pharmacodynamics/Kinetics

Onset of Action Peak effect: 1-2 hours

Half-life Elimination Parent drug: 1.5-3 hours; Metabolite: Effective: 3-10 hours, Terminal: 30-120 hours

Time to Peak Chronic therapy: Perindopril: 1 hour; Perindoprilat: 3-7 hours (maximum perindoprilat serum levels are 2-3 times higher and T_{max} is shorter following chronic therapy); CHF: Perindoprilat: 6 hours

Pregnancy Risk Factor D

Pregnancy Considerations [US Boxed Warning]: Drugs that act on the renin-angiotensin system can cause injury and death to the developing fetus. Discontinue as soon as possible once pregnancy is detected. Drugs that act on the renin-angiotensin system are associated with oligohydramnios. Oligohydramnios, due to decreased fetal renal function, may lead to fetal lung hypoplasia and skeletal malformations. Their use in pregnancy is also associated with anuria, hypotension, renal failure, skull hypoplasia, and death in the fetus/neonate. Teratogenic effects may occur following maternal use of an ACE inhibitor during the first trimester, although this finding may be confounded by maternal disease. Because adverse fetal events are well documented with exposure later in pregnancy, ACE inhibitor use in pregnant women is not recommended (Seely 2014; Weber 2014). Infants exposed to an ACE inhibitor in utero should be monitored for hyperkalemia, hypotension, and oliguria. Oligohydramnios may not appear until after irreversible fetal injury has occurred. Exchange transfusions or dialysis may be required to reverse hypotension or improve renal function, although data related to the effectiveness in neonates is limited.

Chronic maternal hypertension itself is also associated with adverse events in the fetus/infant and mother. ACE inhibitors are not recommended for the treatment of uncomplicated hypertension in pregnancy (ACOG 2013) and they are specifically contraindicated for the treatment of hypertension and chronic heart failure during pregnancy by some guidelines (Regitz-Zagrosek 2011). In addition, ACE inhibitors should generally be avoided in women of reproductive age (ACOG, 2013). If treatment for hypertension or chronic heart failure in pregnancy is needed, other agents should be used (ACOG 2013; Regitz-Zagrosek 2011).

Permethrin (per METH rin)

Brand Names: US Acticin [DSC]; Elimite

Brand Names: Canada Kwellada-P [OTC]; Nix [OTC]

Pharmacologic Category Antiparasitic Agent, Topical; Pediculocide; Scabicidal Agent

Use

Head lice (lotion/cream rinse): Treatment of head lice (*Pediculus humanus capitis*) and its nits (eggs).

Scabies (cream): Treatment of scabies (*Sarcoptes scabiei*) infestation.

Local Anesthetic/Vasoconstrictor Precautions No information available to require special precautions

Effects on Dental Treatment No significant effects or complications reported

Effects on Bleeding No information available to require special precautions

Adverse Reactions

1% to 10%:

Central nervous system: Local discomfort (scalp), localized burning, localized numbness, tingling of skin

Dermatologic: Pruritus, erythema, skin rash (scalp), stinging of the skin

Local: Localized edema

General Dosage Range Topical:

Cream 5%: *Infants ≥2 months, Children, Adolescents, and Adults:* Thoroughly massage cream from head to soles of feet, leave on 8 to 14 hours before removing (shower or bath); may repeat if living mites are observed 14 days after first treatment

Lotion or cream rinse 1%: *Infants ≥2 months, Children, Adolescents, and Adults:* Apply a sufficient amount to saturate the hair and scalp, leave on hair for no longer than 10 minutes before rinsing off with warm water; may repeat 7 days after first treatment if lice or nits still present.

Mechanism of Action Inhibits sodium ion influx through nerve cell membrane channels in parasites resulting in delayed repolarization and thus paralysis and death of the pest

Pregnancy Risk Factor B

Pregnancy Considerations Adverse events have not been observed in oral animal reproduction studies. The amount of permethrin available systemically following topical application is ≤2%. The CDC considers the use of permethrin or pyrethrins with piperonyl butoxide the drugs of choice for the treatment of pubic lice during pregnancy; permethrin is the preferred treatment of scabies during pregnancy (CDC [Workowski 2015]).

Perphenazine (per FEN a zeen)

Brand Names: Canada Apo-Perphenazine

Pharmacologic Category Antiemetic; First Generation (Typical) Antipsychotic; Phenothiazine Derivative

Use

Nausea/vomiting: Control of severe nausea and vomiting in adults

Schizophrenia: Treatment of schizophrenia

Local Anesthetic/Vasoconstrictor Precautions No information available to require special precautions

Effects on Dental Treatment Key adverse event(s) related to dental treatment:

Significant hypotension may occur, especially when the drug is administered parenterally; Patients may experience orthostatic hypotension as they stand up after treatment; especially if lying in dental chair for extended periods of time. Use caution with sudden changes in position during and after dental treatment. Orthostatic hypotension is due to alpha-receptor blockade, the elderly are at greater risk for orthostatic hypotension.

Tardive dyskinesia: Prevalence rate may be 40% in elderly; development of the syndrome and the irreversible nature are proportional to duration and total cumulative dose over time. Extrapyramidal reactions are more common in elderly with up to 50% developing these reactions after 60 years of age. Drug-induced Parkinson's syndrome occurs often; akathisia is the most common extrapyramidal reaction in elderly.

Effects on Bleeding No information available to require special precautions

Adverse Reactions

Frequency not defined.

Cardiovascular: Bradycardia, ECG changes, hypertension, hypotension, orthostatic hypotension, peripheral edema, tachycardia

Central nervous system: Bizarre dream, catatonic-like state, cerebral edema, confusion (nocturnal), disruption of body temperature regulation, dizziness, drowsiness, extrapyramidal reaction (akathisia, dystonia, Parkinsonian-like syndrome, tardive dyskinesia), headache, hyperactivity, hyperpyrexia, insomnia, lethargy, myasthenia, neuroleptic malignant syndrome (NMS), paradoxical excitation, paranoia, restlessness, seizure

Dermatologic: Diaphoresis, pallor, skin discoloration (blue-gray), skin photosensitivity

Endocrine & metabolic: Amenorrhea, change in libido, galactorrhea, glycosuria, gynecomastia, hyperglycemia, hypoglycemia, menstrual disease, SIADH (syndrome of inappropriate antidiuretic hormone secretion), weight gain

Gastrointestinal: Anorexia, constipation, diarrhea, fecal impaction, increased appetite, nausea, obstipation, paralytic ileus, salivation, vomiting, xerostomia

Genitourinary: Bladder paralysis, breast hypertrophy, ejaculatory disorder, lactation, urinary incontinence, urinary retention

Hematologic & oncologic: Agranulocytosis, eosinophilia, hemolytic anemia, immune thrombocytopenic purpura, leukopenia, pancytopenia

Hepatic: Hepatotoxicity, jaundice

Hypersensitivity: Hypersensitivity reaction

Neuromuscular & skeletal: Lupus-like syndrome

Ophthalmic: Blurred vision, corneal changes, epithelial keratopathy, glaucoma, lens disease, miosis, mydriasis, photophobia, retinitis pigmentosa

Renal: Polyuria

Respiratory: Nasal congestion

<1%, postmarketing, and/or case reports: Parotid gland enlargement

General Dosage Range Oral: *Children ≥12, Adolescents, and Adults:* 4 to 16 mg 2 to 4 times/day (maximum: 64 mg/day)

Mechanism of Action

Perphenazine is a piperazine phenothiazine antipsychotic which blocks dopamine, subtype 2 (D_2), receptors in mesolimbocortical and nigrostriatal areas of the brain (APA [Lehman, 2004]).

Pharmacodynamics/Kinetics

Onset of Action 2 to 4 weeks for control of psychotic symptoms (hallucinations, disorganized thinking or behavior, delusions); adequate trial: 6 weeks at moderate to high dose based on tolerability (APA [Lehman 2004])

Half-life Elimination Perphenazine: 9 to 12 hours; 7-hydroxyperphenazine: 10 to 19 hours

Time to Peak Serum: Perphenazine: 1 to 3 hours; 7-hydroxyperphenazine: 2 to 4 hours

Pregnancy Considerations Jaundice or hyper- or hyporeflexia have been reported in newborn infants following maternal use of phenothiazines. Antipsychotic use during the third trimester of pregnancy has a risk for abnormal muscle movements (extrapyramidal symptoms [EPS]) and withdrawal symptoms in newborns following delivery. Symptoms in the newborn may include agitation, feeding disorder, hypertonia, hypotonia, respiratory distress, somnolence, and tremor; these effects may be self-limiting or require hospitalization. If needed, the minimum effective maternal dose should be used in order to decrease the risk of EPS (ACOG 2008).

Pertuzumab (per TU zoo mab)

Brand Names: US Perjeta

Brand Names: Canada Perjeta

Pharmacologic Category Antineoplastic Agent, Anti-HER2; Antineoplastic Agent, Monoclonal Antibody

Use

Breast cancer, metastatic: Treatment of human epidermal growth factor receptor 2 (HER2)-positive metastatic breast cancer (in combination with trastuzumab and docetaxel) in patients who have not received prior anti-HER2 therapy or chemotherapy to treat metastatic disease.

Breast cancer, neoadjuvant treatment: Neoadjuvant treatment of locally advanced, inflammatory, or early stage HER2-positive, breast cancer (either greater than 2 cm in diameter or node positive) in combination with trastuzumab and docetaxel (as part of a complete treatment regimen for early breast cancer).

Limitations of use: The safety of pertuzumab as part of a doxorubicin-containing regimen has not been established; the safety of pertuzumab administered for more than 6 cycles for early breast cancer has not been established.

Local Anesthetic/Vasoconstrictor Precautions No information available to require special precautions

Effects on Dental Treatment Key adverse event(s) related to dental treatment: A significant number of patients have experienced mucosal inflammation (28%), stomatitis (19%), or abnormal taste (18%)

Effects on Bleeding Although significant myelosuppression with associated altered hemostasis has been reported for many chemotherapeutic agents, myelosuppression is not common with pertuzumab and no specific precautions appear necessary.

Adverse Reactions Note: Reactions reported in combination therapy with trastuzumab and docetaxel unless otherwise noted.

>10%:

Central nervous system: Fatigue (26% to 38%), headache (11% to 21%), decreased left ventricular ejection fraction (8% to 16%), insomnia (8% to 13%), dizziness (3% to 13%)

Dermatologic: Alopecia (52% to 65%), skin rash (11% to 34%; grades 3/4: <1%), pruritus (4% to 14%), palmar-plantar erythrodysesthesia (11%), xeroderma (9% to 11%)

Gastrointestinal: Diarrhea (46% to 67%; grades 3/4: 5% to 8%), nausea (39% to 53%; monotherapy 24%), vomiting (13% to 36%; monotherapy 15%), decreased appetite (11% to 29%), constipation (23%), mucositis (20% to 28%), stomatitis (17% to 19%), dysgeusia (13% to 18%), abdominal pain (monotherapy 12%)

Hematologic & oncologic: Neutropenia (47% to 53%; grades 3/4: 43% to 49%), anemia (3% to 23%; grades 3/4: 3% to 4%), leukopenia (9% to 16%; grades 3/4: 5% to 12%), febrile neutropenia (8% to 14%; grades 3/4: 9% to 13%)

Hypersensitivity: Hypersensitivity (1% to 11%; grades 3/4: 2%)

Neuromuscular & skeletal: Weakness (15% to 26%), myalgia (11% to 23%), arthralgia (10% to 12%)

Respiratory: Upper respiratory tract infection (4% to 17%; grades 3/4: <1%), epistaxis (11%)

Miscellaneous: Fever (9% to 19%; grades 3/4: 1%), infusion reactions (13%; grades 3/4: <1%)

1% to 10%:

Cardiovascular: Left ventricular dysfunction (3% to 4%), peripheral edema (3% to 4%)

Central nervous system: Peripheral sensory neuropathy (8%; grades 3/4: 1%), peripheral neuropathy (1%)

Dermatologic: Nail disease (7%), paronychia (1% to 7%)

Gastrointestinal: Dyspepsia (8%), anorexia (monotherapy 5%)

Hematologic & oncologic: Thrombocytopenia (1%)

Hepatic: Increased serum ALT (3%)

Ophthalmic: Increased lacrimation (4% to 5%)

Respiratory: Dyspnea (5% to 8%), nasopharyngitis (7%), oropharyngeal pain (7%), cough (5%)

<1%, postmarketing, and/or case reports with combination therapy: Heart failure, pleural effusion, sepsis

General Dosage Range IV: *Adults:* Initial: 840 mg; Maintenance: 420 mg every 3 weeks

Mechanism of Action Pertuzumab is a recombinant humanized monoclonal antibody which targets the extracellular human epidermal growth factor receptor 2 protein (HER2) dimerization domain. Inhibits HER2 dimerization and blocks HER downstream signaling halting cell growth and initiating apoptosis. Pertuzumab binds to a different HER2 epitope than trastuzumab so that when pertuzumab is combined with trastuzumab, a more complete inhibition of HER2 signaling occurs (Baselga, 2012).

Pharmacodynamics/Kinetics

Half-life Elimination Terminal: 18 days

Pregnancy Considerations [US Boxed Warning]: Pertuzumab exposure during pregnancy may result in embryo-fetal mortality and birth defects. Advise patients of the risks and the need for effective contraception. Verify pregnancy status prior to treatment initiation (in women of reproductive potential). Based on the mechanism of action of pertuzumab and data from similar agents, oligohydramnios or oligohydramnios sequence may occur resulting in pulmonary hypoplasia, skeletal anomalies, and neonatal death. Monitor for oligohydramnios if exposure occurs during pregnancy or within 7 months prior to conception; conduct appropriate fetal testing if oligohydramnios occurs. Effective contraception should be used during therapy and for 7 months after the last dose (of pertuzumab in combination with trastuzumab) for women of childbearing potential. Advise patients to immediately report to healthcare provider if pregnancy is suspected during treatment. If pertuzumab exposure occurs during pregnancy or exposure to pertuzumab in combination with trastuzumab occurs within 7 months prior to conception, healthcare providers should report the exposure to the Genentech Adverse Event Line (888-835-2555).

Women exposed to pertuzumab during pregnancy or exposed to pertuzumab in combination with trastuzumab within 7 months prior to conception are encouraged to enroll in MotHER Pregnancy Registry (1-800-690-6720 or www.motherpregnancyregistry.com).

European Society for Medical Oncology (ESMO) guidelines for cancer during pregnancy recommend delaying treatment with HER2-targeted agents until after delivery in pregnant patients with HER2-positive disease (Peccatori 2013).

Phenazopyridine (fen az oh PEER i deen)

Brand Names: US Azo-Gesic [OTC] [DSC]; Baridium [OTC]; Pyridium; Urinary Pain Relief [OTC]

Pharmacologic Category Analgesic, Urinary

Use Dysuria, symptomatic relief: Symptomatic relief of pain, burning, urgency, frequency, and other discomforts arising from irritation of the lower urinary tract mucosa caused by infection, trauma, surgery, endoscopic procedures, or the passage of sounds or catheters.

Local Anesthetic/Vasoconstrictor Precautions No information available to require special precautions

Effects on Dental Treatment No significant effects or complications reported

Effects on Bleeding No information available to require special precautions

Adverse Reactions

1% to 10%:

Central nervous system: Headache, dizziness

Gastrointestinal: Stomach cramps

<1%, postmarketing, and/or case reports: Acute renal failure, hemolytic anemia, hepatitis, methemoglobinemia, skin pigmentation, skin rash, vertigo

General Dosage Range

Oral:

Children ≥12 years, Adolescents, and Adults: OTC labeling: Two tablets (190 mg) 3 times daily.

Adults: Rx labeling: 200 mg 3 times daily.

Mechanism of Action An azo dye which exerts local anesthetic or analgesic action on urinary tract mucosa through an unknown mechanism

Pregnancy Risk Factor B

Pregnancy Considerations Adverse events have not been observed in animal reproduction studies. Phenazopyridine crosses the placenta and can be detected in amniotic fluid (Meyer, 1991).

Phendimetrazine (fen dye ME tra zeen)

Brand Names: US Bontril PDM [DSC]

Pharmacologic Category Anorexiant; Sympathomimetic

Use Obesity: Management of exogenous obesity as a short-term adjunct (a few weeks) in a regimen of weight reduction based on caloric restriction.

Local Anesthetic/Vasoconstrictor Precautions Use vasoconstrictor with caution in patients taking phendimetrazine. Phendimetrazine can enhance the sympathomimetic response to epinephrine leading to potential hypertension and cardiotoxicity.

Effects on Dental Treatment Key adverse event(s) related to dental treatment: Xerostomia (normal salivary flow resumes upon discontinuation).

Effects on Bleeding No information available to require special precautions

Adverse Reactions Frequency not defined.

Cardiovascular: Flushing, hypertension, ischemic events, palpitations, tachycardia, valvular disease (regurgitant)

Central nervous system: Agitation, dizziness, headache, insomnia, overstimulation, psychosis, restlessness

Endocrine & metabolic: Changes in libido

Gastrointestinal: Constipation, diarrhea, nausea, stomach pain, xerostomia

Genitourinary: Dysuria, urinary frequency

Neuromuscular & skeletal: Tremor

Ocular: Blurred vision, mydriasis

Respiratory: Primary pulmonary hypertension

Miscellaneous: Diaphoresis, tachyphylaxis

<1%, postmarketing, and/or case reports: Dilated cardiomyopathy, retinal vein occlusion (Cho 2016)

General Dosage Range Oral:

Extended-release: *Adolescents ≥17 years and Adults:* 105 mg once daily 30 to 60 minutes before morning meal.

Immediate-release: *Adults:* 35 mg 2 or 3 times daily, 1 hour before meals (maximum: 70 mg 3 times daily)

Mechanism of Action Phendimetrazine is a sympathomimetic amine with pharmacologic properties similar to the amphetamines. The mechanism of action in reducing appetite appears to be secondary to CNS effects, including stimulation of the hypothalamus to release norepinephrine.

Pharmacodynamics/Kinetics

Half-life Elimination ~3.7 hours

Pregnancy Risk Factor X/C (product dependent)

Pregnancy Considerations Animal reproduction studies have not been conducted. Use is contraindicated by some manufacturers in pregnant women (lack of potential benefit and possible fetal harm). An increased risk of adverse maternal and fetal outcomes is associated with obesity; however, medications for weight loss therapy are not recommended at conception or during pregnancy (ACOG 156 2015).

Controlled Substance C-III

Phenelzine (FEN el zeen)

Related Information

Dentin Hypersensitivity, Acid Erosion, High Caries Index, Management of Alveolar Osteitis, and Xerostomia *on page 1857*

Vasoconstrictor Interactions With Antidepressants *on page 1913*

Brand Names: US Nardil

Brand Names: Canada Nardil

Pharmacologic Category Antidepressant, Monoamine Oxidase Inhibitor

Use Depression: Treatment of atypical,"nonendogenous, or neurotic depression.

Local Anesthetic/Vasoconstrictor Precautions Attempts should be made to avoid use of vasoconstrictor due to possibility of hypertensive episodes with monoamine oxidase inhibitors

Effects on Dental Treatment Key adverse event(s) related to dental treatment: Xerostomia and changes in salivation (normal salivary flow resumes upon discontinuation). Avoid use as an analgesic due to toxic reactions with MAO inhibitors. Patients may experience orthostatic hypotension as they stand up after treatment; especially if lying in dental chair for extended periods of time. Use caution with sudden changes in position during and after dental treatment.

Effects on Bleeding No information available to require special precautions

Adverse Reactions

Frequency not defined.

Cardiovascular: Edema, orthostatic hypotension

Central nervous system: Anxiety (acute), ataxia, cardiac insufficiency (following ECT; transient), coma, delirium, dizziness, drowsiness, euphoria, fatigue, headache, hyperreflexia, hypersomnia, insomnia, mania, myoclonus, paresthesia, schizophrenia, seizure, twitching, withdrawal syndrome (nausea, vomiting, malaise)

Dermatologic: Diaphoresis, pruritus, skin rash

Endocrine & metabolic: Hypernatremia, weight gain

Gastrointestinal: Constipation, glottis edema, xerostomia

Genitourinary: Sexual disorder (anorgasmia, ejaculatory disorder, impotence), urinary retention

Hematologic & oncologic: Leukopenia

Hepatic: Increased serum transaminases, jaundice

Neuromuscular & skeletal: Lupus-like syndrome, tremor, weakness

Ophthalmic: Blurred vision, glaucoma, nystagmus

Respiratory: Respiratory depression (following ECT; transient)

Miscellaneous: Fever

<1%, postmarketing, and/or case reports: Hepatic necrosis

General Dosage Range Oral: *Adults:* Initial: 45 mg/day in 3 divided doses; Maintenance: 15 to 90 mg/day in 1 to 3 divided doses

Mechanism of Action Thought to act by increasing endogenous concentrations of norepinephrine, dopamine, and serotonin through inhibition of the enzyme (monoamine oxidase) responsible for the breakdown of these neurotransmitters (Wimbiscus 2011).

Pharmacodynamics/Kinetics

Onset of Action Therapeutic: 4 weeks or more

Duration of Action May continue to have a therapeutic effect and interactions 2 weeks after discontinuing therapy (Feinberg 1981)

Half-life Elimination 11.6 hours

Time to Peak 43 minutes

Pregnancy Considerations Adverse events have been observed in animal reproduction studies. Information related to the use of phenelzine in pregnancy is limited (Frayne 2014; Gracious 1997; Pavy 1995).

Pregnant women exposed to antidepressants during pregnancy are encouraged to enroll in the National Pregnancy Registry for Antidepressants (NPRAD). Women 18 to 45 years of age or their health care providers may contact the registry by calling 844-405-6185. Enrollment should be done as early in pregnancy as possible.

PHENobarbital (fee noe BAR bi tal)

Brand Names: Canada Phenobarb

Pharmacologic Category Anticonvulsant, Barbiturate; Barbiturate

Use

Sedation: Use as a sedative

Seizures: Management of generalized tonic-clonic, status epilepticus, and partial seizures

Note: Use to treat insomnia is not recommended (Schutte-Rodin 2008)

Local Anesthetic/Vasoconstrictor Precautions No information available to require special precautions

Effects on Dental Treatment No significant effects or complications reported

Effects on Bleeding No information available to require special precautions

Adverse Reactions Frequency not defined.

Cardiovascular: Bradycardia, hypotension, syncope, thrombophlebitis (IV)

Central nervous system: Agitation, anxiety, ataxia, central nervous system stimulation, central nervous system depression, confusion, dizziness, drowsiness, hallucination, hangover effect, headache, impaired judgement, insomnia, lethargy, nervousness, nightmares

Dermatologic: Exfoliative dermatitis, skin rash, Stevens-Johnson syndrome

Gastrointestinal: Constipation, nausea, vomiting

Genitourinary: Oliguria

Hematologic & oncologic: Agranulocytosis, thrombocytopenia, megaloblastic anemia

Local: Pain at injection site

Neuromuscular & skeletal: Hyperkinesia, laryngospasm

Respiratory: Apnea (especially with rapid IV use), hypoventilation, respiratory depression

General Dosage Range Dosage adjustment recommended in patients with renal impairment

IM, IV, Oral: *Infants, Children, Adolescents, and Adults:* Dosage varies greatly depending on indication

Mechanism of Action Long-acting barbiturate with sedative, hypnotic, and anticonvulsant properties. Barbiturates depress the sensory cortex, decrease motor activity, alter cerebellar function, and produce drowsiness, sedation, and hypnosis. In high doses, barbiturates exhibit anticonvulsant activity; barbiturates produce dose-dependent respiratory depression.

Pharmacodynamics/Kinetics

Onset of Action Oral: ≥60 minutes; IV: 5 minutes; Peak effect: IV: CNS depression: ≥15 minutes

Duration of Action Oral: 10 to 12 hours; IV: >6 hours

Half-life Elimination Neonates (<48 hours old), Infants, and Children: ~110 hours (60 to 180 hours); Adults: ~79 hours (range: 53 to 118 hours)

Time to Peak Serum: Oral: 1.4 hours (0.5 to 4 hours) (Pasalos 2008)

Pregnancy Risk Factor D

Pregnancy Considerations Phenobarbital crosses the placenta (Harden 2009b). Barbiturates can be detected in the placenta, fetal liver, and fetal brain. Fetal and maternal blood concentrations may be similar following parenteral administration. An increased incidence of fetal abnormalities may occur following maternal use. When used during the third trimester of pregnancy, withdrawal symptoms may occur in the neonate, including seizures and hyperirritability; symptoms of withdrawal may be delayed in the neonate up to 14 days after birth. Use during labor does not impair uterine activity; however, respiratory depression may occur in the newborn; resuscitation equipment should be available, especially for premature infants. Use for the treatment of epilepsy should be avoided during pregnancy (Harden 2009a).

A registry is available for women exposed to phenobarbital during pregnancy: Pregnant women may enroll themselves into the North American Antiepileptic Drug (AED) Pregnancy Registry (888-233-2334 or http://www.aedpregnancyregistry.org).

Controlled Substance C-IV

Phenoxybenzamine (fen oks ee BEN za meen)

Brand Names: US Dibenzyline

Pharmacologic Category Alpha$_1$ Blocker; Antidote

Use Pheochromocytoma: Treatment of sweating and hypertension associated with pheochromocytoma.

Local Anesthetic/Vasoconstrictor Precautions No information available to require special precautions

Effects on Dental Treatment Key adverse event(s) related to dental treatment: Xerostomia (normal salivary flow resumes upon discontinuation).

Effects on Bleeding No information available to require special precautions

Adverse Reactions Frequency not defined.

Cardiovascular: Orthostatic hypotension, tachycardia

Central nervous system: Drowsiness, fatigue, inhibited ejaculation

Gastrointestinal: Gastrointestinal irritation

Ophthalmic: Miosis

Respiratory: Nasal congestion

General Dosage Range Oral: *Adults:* Initial: 10 mg twice daily; Maintenance: 20 to 40 mg 2 to 3 times/day

Mechanism of Action Produces long-lasting noncompetitive alpha-adrenergic blockade of postganglionic synapses in exocrine glands and smooth muscle; relaxes urethra and increases opening of the bladder

Pharmacodynamics/Kinetics

Onset of Action Within 2 hours; Maximum effect: Within 4 to 6 hours

Duration of Action IV: ≥3 to 4 days

Half-life Elimination IV: ~24 hours

Pregnancy Risk Factor C

Pregnancy Considerations Adequate animal reproduction studies have not been conducted. It is not known whether phenoxybenzamine can cause fetal harm when administered to a pregnant woman or can affect reproduction capacity.

Phentermine (FEN ter meen)

Brand Names: US Adipex-P; Lomaira; Suprenza [DSC]

Pharmacologic Category Anorexiant; Central Nervous System Stimulant; Sympathomimetic

Use Obesity (short-term adjunct): Short-term (few weeks) adjunct in a regimen of weight reduction based on exercise, behavioral modification and caloric restriction in the management of exogenous obesity with an initial body mass index (BMI) ≥30 kg/m^2 or ≥27 kg/m^2 in the presence of other risk factors (eg, diabetes, hyperlipidemia, controlled hypertension).

Local Anesthetic/Vasoconstrictor Precautions Use vasoconstrictor with caution in patients taking phentermine. Amphetamines enhance the sympathomimetic response of epinephrine and norepinephrine leading to potential hypertension and cardiotoxicity.

Effects on Dental Treatment Key adverse event(s) related to dental treatment: Phentermine causes tachycardia, increases in blood pressure, and palpitations. Consider monitoring blood pressure prior to using local anesthetic with a vasoconstrictor. Symptoms associated with bruxism have been observed in some patients.

Effects on Bleeding No information available to require special precautions

Adverse Reactions Frequency not defined.

Cardiovascular: Hypertension, ischemia, palpitations, tachycardia

Central nervous system: Dizziness, dysphoria, euphoria, headache, insomnia, overstimulation, psychosis, restlessness

Dermatologic: Urticaria

Endocrine & metabolic: Change in libido

Gastrointestinal: Constipation, diarrhea, gastrointestinal distress, unpleasant taste, xerostomia

Genitourinary: Impotence

Neuromuscular & skeletal: Tremor

<1%, postmarketing, and/or case reports: Acquired valvular heart disease (regurgitant), primary pulmonary hypertension

General Dosage Range Oral: *Adolescents >16 years and Adults:* 15 to 37.5 mg/day or 8 mg 3 times daily

Mechanism of Action Phentermine is a sympathomimetic amine with pharmacologic properties similar to the amphetamines. The mechanism of action in reducing appetite appears to be secondary to CNS effects, including stimulation of the hypothalamus to release norepinephrine.

Pharmacodynamics/Kinetics

Half-life Elimination ~20 hours

Time to Peak 3 to 4.4 hours

Pregnancy Risk Factor X

Pregnancy Considerations Use is contraindicated during pregnancy (lack of potential benefit and possible fetal harm). The risks of using appetite suppressing drugs in pregnant women are not known (NHLBI 1998) and limited information is available about the use of phentermine in pregnancy (Jones 2002; McElhatton 2006). Weight loss therapy is generally not recommended for pregnant women. Obese and overweight women should be encouraged to participate in weight reduction programs prior to attempting pregnancy; weight gain during pregnancy should be determined by their prepregnancy BMI and current guidelines (ACOG 2013; ADA 2009).

Controlled Substance C-IV

Dental Comment Many diet physicians have prescribed fenfluramine ("fen") and phentermine ("phen"). When taken together the combination is known as "fen-phen". The diet drug dexfenfluramine (Redux®) is chemically similar to fenfluramine (Pondimin®) and was also used in combination with phentermine called "Redux-phen". While each of the three drugs alone had approval from the FDA for sale in the treatment of obesity, neither combination had an official approval. The use of the combinations in the treatment of obesity was considered an "off-label" use. Reports in medical literature have been accumulating for some years about significant side effects associated with fenfluramine and dexfenfluramine. In 1997, the manufacturers, at the urging of the FDA, agreed to voluntarily withdraw the drugs from the market. The action was based on findings from physicians who evaluated patients taking fenfluramine and dexfenfluramine with echocardiograms. The findings indicated that approximately 30% of patients had abnormal echocardiograms, even though they had no symptoms. This was a much higher than expected percentage of abnormal test results. This conclusion was based on a sample of 291 patients examined by five different physicians. Under normal conditions, fewer than 1% of patients would be expected to show signs of heart valve disease. The findings suggested that fenfluramine and dexfenfluramine were the likely cause of heart valve problems of the type that promoted FDA's earlier warnings concerning "fen-phen". The earlier warning included the following: The mitral valve and other valves in the heart are damaged by a strange white coating and allow blood to flow back, causing heart muscle damage. In several cases, valve replacement surgery has been done. As a rule, the person must, thereafter for life, be on a blood thinner to prevent clots from the mechanical valve. This type of valve damage had only been seen before in persons who were exposed to large amounts of serotonin. The fenfluramine increases the availability of serotonin.

Phentermine and Topiramate

(FEN ter meen & toe PYRE a mate)

Related Information

Phentermine *on page 1326*

Topiramate *on page 1582*

Brand Names: US Qsymia

Pharmacologic Category Anorexiant; Anticonvulsant, Miscellaneous; Sympathomimetic

Use Chronic weight management, as an adjunct to a reduced-calorie diet and increased physical activity, in patients with either an initial body mass index (BMI) of ≥30 kg/m^2 **or** an initial BMI of ≥27 kg/m^2 and at least one weight-related comorbid condition (eg, hypertension, dyslipidemia, type 2 diabetes)

Local Anesthetic/Vasoconstrictor Precautions Use vasoconstrictor with caution in patients taking phentermine and topiramate. Phentermine is a sympathomimetic amine with pharmacologic properties similar to amphetamines. The phentermine component may enhance the sympathomimetic response of epinephrine and levonordefrin leading to potential hypertension and cardiotoxicity.

Effects on Dental Treatment Key adverse event(s) related to dental treatment: The following effects were reported more frequently than placebo during 1 year of treatment (n=1580): Paresthesia (experienced by ≤20% of patients), dysgeusia (metallic taste, experienced by ≤9% of patients), and dry mouth (experienced by ≤19% of patients). The paresthesia was characterized as tingling in hands, feet, or face.

Effects on Bleeding No information available to require special precautions

Adverse Reactions As reported with combination product (also see individual agents):

>10%:

- Cardiovascular: Increased heart rate (>5 bpm: 70% to 78%; >10 bpm: 50% to 56%; >15 bpm: 33% to 37%; >20 bpm: 14% to 20%)
- Central nervous system: Paresthesia (4% to 20%), headache (10% to 11%), insomnia (6% to 11%)
- Endocrine & metabolic: Decreased serum bicarbonate (6% to 13%; marked reductions [to <17 mEq/L] ≤1%)
- Gastrointestinal: Xerostomia (7% to 19%), constipation (8% to 16%)
- Respiratory: Upper respiratory tract infection (14% to 16%), nasopharyngitis (9% to 13%)

1% to 10%:

- Cardiovascular: Palpitations (≤2%), chest discomfort (≤2%)
- Central nervous system: Dizziness (3% to 9%), depression (3% to 8%), anxiety (2% to 8%), cognitive dysfunction (including problems with concentration, memory, and language [word finding]; 2% to 8%), fatigue (4% to 6%), hypoesthesia (4%), disturbance in attention (2% to 4%), irritability (2% to 4%), oral paresthesia (≤2%)
- Dermatologic: Alopecia (2% to 4%), skin rash (2% to 3%)
- Endocrine & metabolic: Decreased serum potassium (<3.5 mEq/L: 4% to 5%; <3 mEq/L: <1%), hypokalemia (≤3%), increased thirst (2%)
- Gastrointestinal: Dysgeusia (metallic taste; 1% to 9%), nausea (4% to 7%), diarrhea (5% to 6%), gastroesophageal reflux disease (3%), dyspepsia (2% to 3%), gastroenteritis (2% to 3%), decreased appetite (2%)
- Genitourinary: Urinary tract infection (5%), dysmenorrhea (≤2%)
- Infection: Influenza (4% to 8%)
- Neuromuscular & skeletal: Back pain (5% to 7%), muscle spasm (3%), musculoskeletal pain (2% to 3%), neck pain (1% to 2%)
- Ophthalmic: Blurred vision (4% to 6%), dry eye syndrome (≤3%), eye pain (2%)
- Renal: Increased serum creatinine (≥0.3 mg/dL: 2% to 8%; ≥50% over baseline: ≤3%), nephrolithiasis (≤1%)
- Respiratory: Sinusitis (7% to 8%), bronchitis (4% to 7%), cough (4% to 5%), pharyngolaryngeal pain (2% to 3%), sinus congestion (2% to 3%), nasal congestion (1% to 2%)

Postmarketing and/or case reports: Acute angle-closure glaucoma, suicidal ideation

General Dosage Range Dosage adjustment recommended in patients with renal impairment or hepatic impairment.

Oral: *Adults:* Phentermine 3.75-15 mg/topiramate 23-92 mg once daily.

Mechanism of Action

Phentermine: A sympathomimetic amine with pharmacologic properties similar to amphetamines. The mechanism of action in reducing appetite appears to be secondary to CNS effects, including stimulation of the hypothalamus to release norepinephrine.

Topiramate: Effect on weight management may be due to its effects on appetite suppression and satiety enhancement and based on a combination of potential mechanisms: blocks neuronal voltage-dependent sodium channels, enhances GABA(A) activity, antagonizes AMPA/kainite glutamate receptors, and weakly inhibits carbonic anhydrase.

Pregnancy Risk Factor X

Pregnancy Considerations Use of this combination product is contraindicated in pregnant women. Based on human data, topiramate may cause fetal harm if used during pregnancy. An increased risk of adverse maternal and fetal outcomes is associated with obesity; however, medications for weight loss therapy are not recommended at conception or during pregnancy (ACOG 156 2015).

Females of reproductive potential should have a negative pregnancy test prior to and monthly during therapy. Effective contraception should be used during treatment. If irregular bleeding or spotting occurs while using hormonal contraceptives during therapy, patients should be instructed to continue the contraceptive (contraceptive failure is not expected) and notify their health care provider if symptoms become troubling. Refer to individual monographs for additional information.

Health care providers are encouraged to enroll women exposed to Qsymia during pregnancy in the Qsymia Pregnancy Surveillance Program (888-998-4887).

Controlled Substance C-IV

Prescribing and Access Restrictions As a requirement of the REMS program, prescriptions for Qsymia may only be filled by certified retail pharmacies or certified mail order pharmacies. For a listing of certified pharmacies, refer to http://www.qsymiarems.com/certified-pharmacy-network.aspx.

Dental Comment According to product labeling, phentermine and topiramate can cause an increase in resting heart rate. A higher percentage of overweight and obese adults taking phentermine and topiramate experienced heart rate increases from baseline of more than 5, 10, 15, and 20 beats per minute compared to placebo-treated overweight and obese adults. The clinical significance of a heart rate elevation with treatment is presently unclear. Regular measurement of resting heart rate is recommended for all patients taking phentermine and topiramate. Product labeling states that patients should inform healthcare provider of palpitations or feelings of a racing heartbeat while at rest during treatment.

Phentolamine (fen TOLE a meen)

Related Information

Oral Pain *on page 1830*

Brand Names: US OraVerse

Brand Names: Canada OraVerse; Rogitine

Generic Availability (US) Yes

Pharmacologic Category Alpha$_1$ Blocker; Antidote, Extravasation; Antihypertensive

Dental Use Reversal of soft tissue anesthesia and the associated functional deficits resulting from a local dental anesthetic containing a vasoconstrictor

Use

Pheochromocytoma: Diagnosis of pheochromocytoma via the phentolamine-blocking test (see "**Note**"); prevention and management of hypertensive episodes associated with pheochromocytoma resulting from stress or manipulation during the perioperative period

Extravasation management: Prevention and treatment of dermal necrosis/sloughing after extravasation of norepinephrine

Local anesthesia reversal (OraVerse): Reversal of soft tissue (lip, tongue) anesthesia and the associated functional deficits resulting from an intraoral submucosal injection of a local anesthetic containing a vasoconstrictor in adult and pediatric patients ≥3 years.

Note: The phentolamine-blocking test for the diagnosis of pheochromocytoma has largely been supplanted by the measurement of catecholamine concentrations and catecholamine metabolites (eg, metanephrine) in the plasma and urine; reserve phentolamine for cases when additional confirmation is necessary to determine diagnosis.

Local Anesthetic/Vasoconstrictor Precautions Although the alpha-adrenergic blocking effects could antagonize epinephrine, there is no information available to require special precautions

Effects on Dental Treatment Key adverse event(s) related to dental treatment: The most common reaction that was greater than controls was injection site pain (~4% to 6%). A few incidences of paresthesia associated with OraVerse have been reported. These incidences were mild and transient, and resolved during the same time period. Patients may experience orthostatic hypotension as they stand up after treatment; especially if lying in dental chair for extended periods of time. Use caution with sudden changes in position during and after dental treatment.

Effects on Bleeding No information available to require special precautions

Adverse Reactions Frequency not always defined.

Cardiovascular: Bradycardia (OraVerse 2% to 4%), hypertension (OraVerse <3%), cerebrovascular occlusion, hypotension, myocardial infarction

Central nervous system: Mouth pain (OraVerse ≤19%), headache (OraVerse 6%), paresthesia (OraVerse <3%; mild, transient), cerebrovascular spasm

Dermatologic: Facial swelling (OraVerse <3%), pruritus (OraVerse <3%)

Gastrointestinal: Diarrhea (OraVerse <3%), upper abdominal pain (OraVerse <3%), vomiting (OraVerse <3%), nausea

Local: Pain at injection site (OraVerse 6%)

Neuromuscular & skeletal: Jaw pain (OraVerse <3%)

Miscellaneous: Postinjection pain (10%)

Postmarketing and/or case reports: Cardiac arrhythmia, dizziness, flushing, nasal congestion, orthostatic hypotension, weakness

Dental Usual Dosage

Reversal of soft tissue (lip, tongue) anesthesia (OraVerse): Infiltration or block technique:submucosal oral injection:

Children: 15 to 30 kg: 0.2 mg maximum dose

Children >30 kg and <12 years: 0.4 mg maximum dose

Adults: **Note:** Dose is based upon the number of cartridges of local anesthetic administered. Infiltration or block injection:

0.2 mg if one-half cartridge of anesthesia was administered

0.4 mg if 1 cartridge of anesthesia was administered

0.8 mg if 2 cartridges of anesthesia were administered

Dosing

Adult & Geriatric

Extravasation of norepinephrine, management (manufacturer's labeling): Local infiltration: Inject 5 to 10 mg (diluted in 10 mL 0.9% sodium chloride) into extravasation area (as soon as possible after extravasation is noted but within 12 hours of extravasation).

Extravasation of other sympathomimetic vasopressors, management (off-label use): Infiltrate extravasation site with 5 to 10 mg diluted in 10 to 15 mL 0.9% sodium chloride as soon as possible after extravasation (AHA [Peberdy 2010]).

Diagnosis of pheochromocytoma (phentolamine-blocking test): Note: The phentolamine-blocking test for the diagnosis of pheochromocytoma has largely been supplanted by the measurement of catecholamine concentrations and catecholamine metabolites (eg, metanephrine) in the plasma and urine; reserve phentolamine for cases when additional confirmation is necessary to determine diagnosis: IM, IV: 5 mg

Hypertensive episodes associated with pheochromocytoma, prevention and management: Note: In the perioperative period, the use of other agents may be preferred due to slow onset of action and prolonged duration of phentolamine in comparison to the other agents (eg, nitroprusside) (Miller 2010).

Preoperative: IM, IV: 5 mg given 1 to 2 hours before surgery and repeat if needed.

Intraoperative: IV: Administer 5 mg as indicated to prevent or control paroxysms of hypertension, tachycardia, respiratory depression, seizure, or other effects associated with epinephrine intoxication resulting from tumor manipulation or other stressor (eg, intubation) (Miller 2010).

Hypertensive crisis (off-label use): Note: Generally used in the setting of catecholamine excess (eg, pheochromocytoma) (Marik 2007): IV: 1 to 5 mg bolus; maximum single dose: 15 mg. A continuous infusion may be administered after initial bolus dosing (eg, 1 mg/hour titrated to blood pressure response) to a maximum infusion rate of 40 mg/hour (McMillian 2011).

Reversal of oral soft tissue (lip, tongue) anesthesia (OraVerse): Infiltration or block technique: Submucosal oral injection: **Note:** Dose is based upon the number of cartridges of local anesthetic administered. Infiltration or block injection:

0.1 mg if one-quarter cartridge of anesthesia was administered

0.2 mg if one-half cartridge of anesthesia was administered

0.4 mg if 1 cartridge of anesthesia was administered

0.8 mg if 2 cartridges of anesthesia were administered

Pediatric

Extravasation of sympathomimetic vasopressors, treatment:

Manufacturer's labeling: *Norepinephrine extravasation:* Children and Adolescents: Local infiltration: Infiltrate area of extravasation with a small amount of a 0.5 to 1 mg/mL solution as soon as extravasation is noted but within 12 hours of extravasation

Alternate dosing: *Extravasation of dopamine, epinephrine, norepinephrine, phenylephrine:* Limited data available: Infants, Children, and Adolescents: SubQ: Infiltrate area of extravasation with a small amount (eg, 1 mL given in 0.2 mL aliquots) of a 0.5 to 1 mg/mL solution within 12 hours of extravasation (Flemmer 1993; Hill 1991; MacCara 1983; Montgomery 1999). Total dose required depends on the size of extravasation; dose may be repeated if required. When reported, the total dose needed was 1 to 5 mL of a 1 mg/mL solution; however, other concentrations could be used (Montgomery 1999).

Diagnosis of pheochromocytoma (phentolamine blocking test): Note: The phentolamine-blocking test for the diagnosis of pheochromocytoma has largely been supplanted by the measurement of catecholamine concentrations and catecholamine metabolites (eg, metanephrine) in the plasma and urine; reserve phentolamine for cases when additional confirmation is necessary to determine diagnosis:

Manufacturer's labeling: Children and Adolescents:
IM: 3 mg
IV: 1 mg

Alternate dosing: Limited data available: Children and Adolescents: IV: 0.05 to 0.1 mg/kg/dose, maximum single dose: 5 mg (Kliegman 2007)

Hypertensive episodes associated with pheochromocytoma, prevention and treatment: Note: In the perioperative period, the use of other agents may be preferred due to slow onset of action and prolonged duration of phentolamine in comparison to the other agents (eg, nitroprusside) (Miller 2010).

Preoperative: Children and Adolescents: IM, IV: 1 mg given 1 to 2 hours before surgery and repeat if needed

Intraoperative:

Manufacturer's labeling: Children and Adolescents: IV: 1 mg as indicated to prevent or control paroxysms of hypertension, tachycardia, respiratory depression, seizure, or other effects associated with epinephrine intoxication resulting from tumor manipulation

Alternate dosing: Limited data available: Infants, Children, and Adolescents: IV: 0.05 to 0.1 mg/kg/dose (Coté 2013). **Note:** Usual adult dose is 5 mg/dose (Miller 2010).

Reversal of oral soft tissue (lip, tongue) anesthesia (OraVerse): Note: Dose is based upon the number of cartridge(s) of local anesthetic administered; location and administration technique (infiltration or block injection) should be the same as used for local anesthetic administration.

Children ≥3 years weighing ≥15 kg and Adolescents: Submucosal oral injection: Infiltration or block technique:

Amount of Local Anesthetic Administered	Dose of OraVerse
1/4 Cartridge	1/4 Cartridge (0.1 mg)
1/2 Cartridge	1/2 Cartridge (0.2 mg)
1 Cartridge	1 Cartridge (0.4 mg)
2 Cartridges	2 Cartridges (0.8 mg)

Maximum dose:

15 to <30 kg: 0.2 mg/dose

≥30 kg: 0.8 mg/dose; **Note:** A dose of >0.4 mg has not been studied in children <4 years

Renal Impairment There are no dosage adjustments provided in the manufacturer's labeling.

Hepatic Impairment There are no dosage adjustments provided in the manufacturer's labeling.

Mechanism of Action Competitively blocks alpha-adrenergic receptors (nonselective) to produce brief antagonism of circulating epinephrine and norepinephrine to reduce hypertension caused by alpha effects of these catecholamines and minimizes tissue injury due to extravasation of these and other sympathomimetic vasoconstrictors (eg, dopamine, phenylephrine); also has a positive inotropic and chronotropic effect on the heart thought to be due to presynaptic alpha-2 receptor blockade which results in release of presynaptic norepinephrine (Hoffman 1980)

OraVerse: Causes vasodilation and increased blood flow in injection area via alpha-adrenergic blockade to accelerate reversal of soft tissue anesthesia

Contraindications

Hypersensitivity to phentolamine, any component of the formulation, or related compounds; MI (or history of MI), coronary insufficiency, angina, or other evidence suggestive of coronary artery disease (excluding OraVerse)

Canadian labeling: Additional contraindications (not in US labeling): Hypotension

Warnings/Precautions MI, cerebrovascular spasm, and cerebrovascular occlusion have been reported following administration, usually associated with hypotensive episodes producing shock-like states. Tachycardia and cardiac arrhythmias may occur. Use with caution in patients with a history of cardiovascular disease. Discontinue if symptoms of angina occur or worsen. The use of phentolamine as a blocking agent in the screening of patients with hypertension has predominantly been replaced with urinary/biochemical assays; phentolamine use should be reserved for situations where additional confirmation is necessary and after risks associated with use have been considered. Potentially significant drug-drug interactions may exist, requiring dose or frequency adjustment, additional monitoring, and/or selection of alternative therapy.

Drug Interactions

Metabolism/Transport Effects None known.

Avoid Concomitant Use

Avoid concomitant use of Phentolamine with any of the following: Alpha1-Blockers

Increased Effect/Toxicity

Phentolamine may increase the levels/effects of: Alpha1-Blockers; Amifostine; Antipsychotic Agents (Second Generation [Atypical]); Calcium Channel Blockers; DULoxetine; Hypotension-Associated Agents; Levodopa; Nitroprusside; Rilmenidine

The levels/effects of Phentolamine may be increased by: Barbiturates; Benperidol; Beta-Blockers; Brimonidine (Topical); Dapoxetine; Diazoxide; Herbs (Hypotensive Properties); Lormetazepam; Molsidomine; Nicorandil; Obinutuzumab; Pentoxifylline; Phosphodiesterase 5 Inhibitors; Prostacyclin Analogues; Quinagolide

Decreased Effect

Phentolamine may decrease the levels/effects of: Alpha-/Beta-Agonists; Alpha1-Agonists

The levels/effects of Phentolamine may be decreased by: Amphetamines; Herbs (Hypertensive Properties); Methylphenidate; Yohimbine

Pharmacodynamics/Kinetics

Onset of Action IM: 15 to 20 minutes; IV: 1 to 2 minutes (Chobanian 2003)

Peak effect: OraVerse: 10 to 20 minutes

Duration of Action IM: 30 to 45 minutes; IV: 10 to 30 minutes (Chobanian 2003)

Half-life Elimination IV: 19 minutes; Submucosal injection: ~2 to 3 hours

Pregnancy Risk Factor C

Pregnancy Considerations Adverse events have been observed in some oral animal reproduction studies. Diagnosing and treating pheochromocytoma is critical for favorable maternal and fetal outcomes (Schenker 1971; Schenker 1982).

Breastfeeding Considerations It is not known if phentolamine is excreted in breast milk. Due to the potential for serious adverse reaction in the nursing infant, the decision to discontinue phentolamine or discontinue breastfeeding during treatment should take in account the benefits of treatment to the mother. The manufacturer of OraVerse recommends the developmental and health benefits of breastfeeding be considered along with the mother's clinical need for phentolamine and any potential adverse effects on the breast-fed infant from phentolamine, or from the underlying maternal condition.

Dosage Forms

Solution, Injection [preservative free]:

OraVerse: 0.4 mg/1.7 mL (1.7 mL)

Solution Reconstituted, Injection:

Generic: 5 mg (1 ea)

Dental Comment OraVerse (solution for injection/dental cartridge) is administered as a submucosal injection and is not to be confused with phentolamine used as an intramuscular or intravenous injection for the treatment of hypertension associated with pheochromocytoma.

In adolescents >12 years and adults, OraVerse reduced the median time to recovery of normal sensation in the lower lip by 85 minutes compared to control. OraVerse reduced the median time to recovery of normal sensation in the upper lip by 83 minutes. Within 1 hour after administration, 41% of patients reported normal lower lip sensation as compared to 7% in the control group and 59% of patients given OraVerse reported normal upper lip sensation as compared to 12% in the control group.

In children 6 to 11 years of age, the median time to normal sensation was reduced by 75 minutes after OraVerse administration, a 56% acceleration of the time to normal sensation.

While dental treatment is attainable using local anesthesia without the use of this reversal agent phentolamine, research suggests its use prevents self-inflicted soft tissue trauma in pediatric patients visiting a portable dental clinic. Such post-procedural soft tissue injuries are more likely in pediatric patients receiving local anesthesia with one or more of the following factors: Attention deficit disorder, obesity and/or the use of an inferior alveolar nerve block (Boynes 2013).

Phenylephrine (Systemic) (fen il EF rin)

Brand Names: US Little Colds Decongestant [OTC]; Medi-Phenyl [OTC] [DSC]; Nasal Decongestant PE Max St [OTC]; Nasal Decongestant [OTC]; Non-Pseudo Sinus Decongestant [OTC]; Sudafed PE Childrens [OTC]; Sudafed PE Congestion [OTC]; Sudafed PE

Maximum Strength [OTC] [DSC]; Sudogest PE [OTC]; Vazculep

Pharmacologic Category Alpha-Adrenergic Agonist

Use

Treatment of hypotension, vascular failure in shock (see "**Note**"); as a vasoconstrictor in regional analgesia; as a decongestant [OTC]

Note: Not recommended for routine use in the treatment of septic shock; use should be limited until more evidence demonstrating positive clinical outcomes becomes available (SCCM [Rhodes 2017]).

Local Anesthetic/Vasoconstrictor Precautions Use with caution since phenylephrine is a sympathomimetic amine which could interact with epinephrine to cause a pressor response

Effects on Dental Treatment Key adverse event(s) related to dental treatment: Tachycardia, palpitations (use vasoconstrictor with caution), and xerostomia (normal salivary flow resumes upon discontinuation).

Effects on Bleeding No information available to require special precautions

Adverse Reactions Frequency not defined.

Injection:

Cardiovascular: Cardiac arrhythmia (rare), exacerbation of angina, hypertension, hypertensive crisis, ischemia, localized blanching, low cardiac output, peripheral vasoconstriction (severe), reflex bradycardia, visceral vasoconstriction (severe), worsening of heart failure

Central nervous system: Anxiety, dizziness, excitability, headache, insomnia, nervousness, paresthesia, precordial pain (or discomfort), restlessness

Dermatologic: Pallor, piloerection, pruritus

Endocrine & metabolic: Metabolic acidosis

Gastrointestinal: Epigastric pain, gastric irritation, nausea, vomiting

Genitourinary: Decreased renal blood flow, decreased urine output

Hypersensitivity: Hypersensitivity reaction (including skin rash, urticaria, leukopenia, agranulocytosis, thrombocytopenia)

Local: Extravasation which may lead to necrosis and sloughing of surrounding tissue

Neuromuscular & skeletal: Neck pain, tremor, weakness

Ophthalmic: Blurred vision

Respiratory: Dyspnea, exacerbation of pulmonary arterial hypertension, respiratory distress

Oral: Central nervous system: Anxiety, dizziness, excitability, headache, insomnia, nervousness, restlessness

General Dosage Range

IV:

Children: Bolus: 5 to 20 mcg/kg/dose every 10 to 15 minutes as needed; Infusion: 0.1 to 0.5 mcg/kg/minute

Adults: Bolus: 40 to 500 mcg/dose every 10 to 15 minutes as needed (maximum: 500 mcg); Infusion: Initial: 10 to 180 mcg/minute

Oral:

Children 4 to <6 years: 2.5 mg every 4 hours as needed (maximum: 15 mg/24 hours)

Children 6 to <12 years: 5 mg every 4 hours as needed (maximum: 30 mg/24 hours)

Children ≥12 years and Adults: 10 mg every 4 hours as needed (maximum: 60 mg/24 hours)

Mechanism of Action Potent, direct-acting alpha-adrenergic agonist with virtually no beta-adrenergic activity; produces systemic arterial vasoconstriction. Such increases in systemic vascular resistance result in dose dependent increases in systolic and diastolic blood pressure and reductions in heart rate and cardiac output especially in patients with heart failure.

Pharmacodynamics/Kinetics

Onset of Action

Blood pressure increase/vasoconstriction: IM, SubQ: 10 to 15 minutes; IV: Immediate

Nasal decongestant: Oral: 15 to 30 minutes (Kollar 2007)

Duration of Action

Blood pressure increase/vasoconstriction: IM: 1 to 2 hours; IV: ~15 to 20 minutes; SubQ: 50 minutes

Nasal decongestant: Oral: ≤4 hours (Kollar 2007)

Half-life Elimination Alpha phase: ~5 minutes; Terminal phase: 2 to 3 hours (Hengstmann 1982; Kanfer 1993)

Time to Peak Oral: 0.75 to 2 hours (Kanfer 1993)

Pregnancy Risk Factor C

Pregnancy Considerations Animal reproduction studies have not been conducted. Phenylephrine crosses the placenta at term. Maternal use of phenylephrine during the first trimester of pregnancy is not strongly associated with an increased risk of fetal malformations; maternal dose and duration of therapy were not reported in available publications. Phenylephrine is available over-the-counter (OTC) for the symptomatic relief of nasal congestion. Decongestants are not the preferred agents for the treatment of rhinitis during pregnancy. Oral phenylephrine should be avoided during the first trimester of pregnancy; short-term use (<3 days) of intranasal phenylephrine may be beneficial to some patients although its safety during pregnancy has not been studied. Phenylephrine injection is used at delivery for the prevention and/or treatment of maternal hypotension associated with spinal anesthesia in women undergoing cesarean section. Phenylephrine may be associated with a more favorable fetal acid base status than ephedrine; however, overall fetal outcomes appear to be similar. Nausea or vomiting may be less with phenylephrine than ephedrine but is also dependent upon blood pressure control. Phenylephrine may be preferred in the absence of maternal bradycardia.

Phenylephrine (Topical) (fen il EF rin)

Brand Names: US Anu-Med [OTC]; GRX Hemorrhoidal [OTC]; Hem-Prep [OTC] [DSC]; Hemorrhoidal [OTC]; Major-Prep Hemorrhoidal [OTC]; Preparation H [OTC]; Rectacaine [OTC]

Pharmacologic Category Alpha-Adrenergic Agonist; Antihemorrhoidal Agent

Use For OTC use as treatment of hemorrhoids

Local Anesthetic/Vasoconstrictor Precautions No information available to require special precautions

Effects on Dental Treatment No significant effects or complications reported

Effects on Bleeding No information available to require special precautions

Adverse Reactions Rare systemic effects may occur.

General Dosage Range Rectal: *Children >12 years and Adults:* Ointment: Apply up to 4 times/day; Suppository: Insert 1 up to 4 times/day

Mechanism of Action Potent, direct-acting alpha-adrenergic agonist with virtually no beta-adrenergic activity; produces local vasoconstriction.

Pregnancy Considerations When administered intravenously, phenylephrine crosses the placenta. Refer to the Phenylephrine (Systemic) monograph for details.

There is limited information available supporting the use of topical agents for the treatment of hemorrhoids. Products containing phenylephrine should be used with caution in pregnant women, especially patients with hypertension or diabetes.

Phenytoin (FEN i toyn)

Related Information

Fosphenytoin *on page 774*

Brand Names: US Dilantin; Dilantin Infatabs; Phenytek; Phenytoin Infatabs

Brand Names: Canada Dilantin; Novo-Phenytoin; Taro-Phenytoin; Tremytoine Inj

Generic Availability (US) Yes

Pharmacologic Category Anticonvulsant, Hydantoin

Use

Seizures (non-emergent use): Control of generalized tonic-clonic and complex partial (psychomotor, temporal lobe) seizures; prevention and treatment of seizures occurring during or following neurosurgery (capsule, chewable tablet, and injection only).

Status epilepticus (injection only): Treatment of generalized tonic-clonic status epilepticus.

Local Anesthetic/Vasoconstrictor Precautions No information available to require special precautions

Effects on Dental Treatment Gingival hyperplasia is a common problem observed during the first 6 months of phenytoin therapy appearing as gingivitis or gum inflammation. To minimize severity and growth rate of gingival tissue begin a program of professional cleaning and patient plaque control within 10 days of starting anticonvulsant therapy.

Effects on Bleeding No information available to require special precautions

Adverse Reactions Frequency not defined.

Cardiovascular: Atrial conduction depression (IV administration), bradycardia (IV administration), cardiac arrhythmia (IV administration), circulatory shock (IV administration), hypotension (IV administration), periarteritis nodosa, ventricular conduction depression (IV administration), ventricular fibrillation (IV administration)

Central nervous system: Ataxia, cerebral atrophy (elevated serum levels and/or long-term use), cerebral dysfunction (elevated serum levels and/or long-term use), confusion, dizziness, drowsiness, headache, insomnia, mood changes, nervousness, paresthesia, peripheral neuropathy (associated with chronic treatment), slurred speech, twitching, vertigo

Dermatologic: Bullous dermatitis, exfoliative dermatitis, hypertrichosis, morbilliform rash (most common), scarlatiniform rash, skin or other tissue necrosis (IV administration), skin rash, Stevens-Johnson syndrome, toxic epidermal necrolysis

Endocrine & metabolic: Hyperglycemia, vitamin D deficiency (associated with chronic treatment)

Gastrointestinal: Constipation, dysgeusia (metallic taste), enlargement of facial features (lips), gingival hyperplasia, nausea, vomiting

Genitourinary: Peyronie disease

Hematologic & oncologic: Agranulocytosis, granulocytopenia, Hodgkin lymphoma, immunoglobulin abnormality, leukopenia, lymphadenopathy, macrocytosis, malignant lymphoma, megaloblastic anemia, pancytopenia, pseudolymphoma, purpuric dermatitis, thrombocytopenia

Hepatic: Acute hepatic failure, hepatic injury, hepatitis, toxic hepatitis

Hypersensitivity: Anaphylaxis

Immunologic: DRESS syndrome

Local: Injection site reaction ("purple glove syndrome"; edema, discoloration, and pain distal to injection site), local inflammation (IV administration), local irritation (IV administration), localized tenderness (IV administration), local tissue necrosis (IV administration)

Neuromuscular & skeletal: Coarsening of facial features, osteomalacia, systemic lupus erythematosus, tremor

Ophthalmic: Nystagmus

Miscellaneous: Fever, tissue sloughing (IV administration)

<1%, postmarketing, and/or case reports: Dyskinesia, hepatotoxicity (idiosyncratic) (Chalasani 2014)

Dosing

Adult Note: Phenytoin base (eg, oral suspension, chewable tablets) contains ~8% more drug than phenytoin sodium (~92 mg base is equivalent to 100 mg phenytoin sodium). Dosage adjustments and closer serum monitoring may be necessary when switching dosage forms.

Status epilepticus: IV:

Neurocritical Care Society recommendation: Loading dose: 20 mg/kg at a maximum rate of 50 mg/minute; if necessary, may give an additional dose of 5 to 10 mg/kg 10 minutes after the loading dose (NCS [Brophy 2012])

Manufacturer recommendation: Loading dose: 10 to 15 mg/kg at a maximum rate of 50 mg/minute; initial maintenance dose: IV or Oral: 100 mg every 6 to 8 hours

Seizures (non-emergent use): Oral:

Immediate release:

Tablet: Initial: 100 mg 3 times daily, individualize dosage with dosage adjustments at no less than 7- to 10-day intervals; maintenance dose: 300 to 400 mg/day; an increase to 600 mg/day may be necessary

Suspension: Initial: 125 mg 3 times daily, individualize dosage with dosage adjustments at no less than 7- to 10-day intervals; an increase to 625 mg/day may be necessary

Extended release:

Loading dose: 1 g divided into 3 doses (400, 300, 300 mg) administered at 2-hour intervals; begin maintenance dosage 24 hours after loading dose. **Note:** Do not use loading dose regimen in patients with a history of renal or hepatic disease. Reserve for patients who require rapid steady state serum levels, when IV administration is not desirable, and for patients in a clinic or hospital setting where phenytoin levels can be closely monitored.

Initial dosage (treatment naïve): 100 mg 3 times daily; adjust dosage at no less than 7- to 10-day intervals

Maintenance dose: 100 mg 3 to 4 times daily, doses up to 200 mg 3 times a day may be necessary. May consider converting patients established on 100 mg 3 times daily to 300 mg once daily

Geriatric Clearance is decreased in geriatric patients; lower doses or less frequent dosing may be required.

Pediatric Note: Phenytoin base (eg, oral suspension, chewable tablets) contains ~8% more drug than phenytoin sodium (~92 mg base is equivalent to 100 mg phenytoin sodium). Dosage adjustments and closer serum monitoring may be necessary when switching dosage forms.

Status epilepticus: Infants, Children, Adolescents: IV:

Neurocritical Care Society recommendation: Loading dose: 20 mg/kg at a maximum rate of 1 mg/kg/minute; if necessary, may give an additional dose of 5 to 10 mg/kg 10 minutes after the loading dose (NCS [Brophy 2012])

Manufacturer recommendation: Loading dose: 15 to 20 mg/kg at a maximum rate of 1 to 3 mg/kg/minute or 50 mg/minute (whichever is slower), followed by maintenance therapy

Seizures (non-emergent use): Oral:

Immediate release: Children and Adolescents: Tablet and suspension: Initial: 5 mg/kg/day in 2 to 3 equally divided doses, individualize dosage with dosage adjustments at no less than 7- to 10-day intervals; maintenance dose: 4 to 8 mg/kg/day (maximum: 300 mg/day). Some experts suggest higher maintenance doses may be necessary in infant and young children (range: 8 to 10 mg/kg/day in divided doses) (Guerrini 2006).

Extended release: Children and Adolescents: Initial: 5 mg/kg/day in 2 or 3 equally divided doses, individualize dosage with dosage adjustments at no less than 7- to 10-day intervals; maintenance dose: 4 to 8 mg/kg/day (maximum: 300 mg/day)

Renal Impairment There are no dosage adjustments provided in the manufacturer's labeling; <5% excreted as unchanged drug. Serum concentration may be difficult to interpret in renal failure. Monitoring of free (unbound) concentrations or adjustment to allow interpretation is recommended.

Hemodialysis: Dose supplementation may be required with high-efficiency dialyzers; monitor serum concentrations. Serum concentration may be difficult to interpret in renal failure (Asconapé 2014; Diaz 2012; Israni 2006).

Hepatic Impairment There are no dosage adjustments provided in the manufacturer's labeling; undergoes hepatic metabolism and clearance may be decreased. Monitor free phenytoin levels closely. Dosage adjustments may be necessary.

Obesity

Adults: Evidence from one small study in adult patients (n=24) with obesity (range: 71 to 197 kg) demonstrated that the volume of distribution (V_d) was 0.68 ± 0.03 L/kg (range: 0.53 to 0.85 L/kg) and distribution into weight in excess of IBW is disproportionately greater (by a factor of 1.33) (Abernethy 1985). Based on this evidence, the following dosing strategies have been suggested:

Loading dose:

14 mg/kg (IBW) + 19 mg/kg (weight in excess of IBW); maximum dose: 2 g (Abernethy 1985; Erstad 2004)

For example: For a patient with a total body weight (TBW) of 300 lb (136 kg) and an IBW of 73 kg

Loading dose = 14 mg/kg (73 kg) + 19 mg/kg (136 kg minus 73 kg) = 2219 mg; administer the maximum dose of 2,000 mg

OR

May also target a specific concentration (eg, 15 to 20 mg/L) by using the V_d obtained from patients with obesity (Abernethy 1985; Burton 2006). Therefore, the concentration desired (in mg/L) may be multiplied by this V_d (obesity) (in L) which is determined using the patient's total and ideal body weights.

V_d (obesity) = 0.65 L/kg (IBW) + 1.33 (TBW-IBW)

Loading dose = Calculated V_d (obesity) (target concentration)

For example: For a patient with a total body weight (TBW) of 300 lb (136 kg) and an IBW of 73 kg

V_d (obesity) = 0.65 L/kg (73 kg) + 1.33 (136 kg-73 kg) = 131 L; then,

Loading dose = 131 L x 15 mg/L = 1,965 mg

Maintenance dose: Base on ideal body weight if using weight-based regimens or use conventional daily doses with adjustments based upon therapeutic drug monitoring and clinical effectiveness. (Abernethy 1985; Erstad 2002; Erstad 2004)

Note: Additional data are necessary to further define dosing strategies in the obese patient.

Mechanism of Action Stabilizes neuronal membranes and decreases seizure activity by increasing efflux or decreasing influx of sodium ions across cell membranes in the motor cortex during generation of nerve impulses; prolongs effective refractory period and suppresses ventricular pacemaker automaticity, shortens action potential in the heart

Contraindications

Hypersensitivity to phenytoin, other hydantoins, or any component of the formulation; concurrent use of delavirdine; history of prior acute hepatotoxicity attributable to phenytoin

Injection: Additional contraindications: Sinus bradycardia, sinoatrial block, second- and third-degree heart block, Adams-Stokes syndrome

Warnings/Precautions

Antiepileptics are associated with an increased risk of suicidal behavior/thoughts with use (regardless of indication); patients should be monitored for signs/symptoms of depression, suicidal tendencies, and other unusual behavior changes during therapy and instructed to inform their healthcare provider immediately if symptoms occur.

[US Boxed Warning]: Phenytoin must be administered slowly. Intravenous administration should not exceed 50 mg/minute in adult patients. In pediatric patients, intravenous administration rate should not exceed 1-3 mg/kg/minute or 50 mg/minute whichever is slower. Hypotension and severe cardiac arrhythmias (eg, heart block, ventricular tachycardia, ventricular fibrillation) may occur with rapid administration; adverse cardiac events have been reported at or below the recommended infusion rate. Cardiac monitoring is necessary during and after administration of intravenous phenytoin; reduction in rate of administration or discontinuation of infusion may be necessary. For non-emergency use, intravenous phenytoin should be administered more slowly; the use of oral phenytoin should be used whenever possible. Vesicant (intravenous administration); ensure proper catheter or needle position prior to and during infusion; avoid extravasation; IV form may cause soft tissue irritation and inflammation, and skin necrosis at IV site; avoid IV administration in small veins. The "purple glove syndrome" (ie, discoloration with edema and pain of distal limb) may occur following peripheral IV administration of phenytoin; may or may not be associated with drug extravasation; symptoms may resolve spontaneously; however, skin necrosis and limb ischemia may occur; interventions such as fasciotomies, skin grafts, and amputation (rare) may be required. Use with caution in patients with porphyria; discontinue if rash or lymphadenopathy occurs; a spectrum of hematologic effects have been reported with use (eg, agranulocytosis, leukopenia, granulocytopenia, thrombocytopenia, and pancytopenia with or without bone marrow suppression) and may be fatal; use with caution in patients with hepatic dysfunction, renal dysfunction, hypothyroidism, or underlying cardiac disease; IV use is contraindicated in patients with sinus bradycardia, sinoatrial block, or second- and third-degree heart block; use with caution in elderly or debilitated patients, or in any condition associated with low serum albumin levels, which will increase the free fraction of phenytoin in the serum and, therefore, the pharmacologic response. Use free (unbound) serum concentrations to monitor patients with hepatic impairment, renal impairment, and hypoalbuminemia. Plasma concentrations of phenytoin sustained above the optimal range may produce confusional states referred to as delirium, psychosis, or encephalopathy, or rarely, irreversible cerebellar dysfunction and/or cerebellar atrophy. Measure plasma phenytoin concentrations at the first sign of acute toxicity; dosage reduction is indicated if phenytoin concentrations are excessive; if symptoms persist, discontinue administration. Anticonvulsants should not be discontinued abruptly because of the possibility of increasing seizure frequency; therapy should be withdrawn gradually to minimize the potential of increased seizure frequency, unless safety concerns require a more rapid withdrawal.

Severe reactions, including toxic epidermal necrolysis (TEN) and Stevens-Johnson syndrome (some fatal) have been reported; the onset of symptoms is usually within 28 days of treatment, but can occur later. Discontinue phenytoin if there are any signs of rash and evaluate for signs and symptoms of drug reaction with eosinophilia and systemic symptoms (DRESS). Data suggests a genetic susceptibility for serious skin reactions in patients of Asian descent. Asian patients with the variant HLA-B*1502 may be at an increased risk of developing Stevens-Johnson syndrome and/or TEN. **Note:** Carbamazepine, another antiepileptic with a chemical structure similar to phenytoin, includes in the manufacturer labeling a recommendation to screen patients of Asian descent for the HLA-B*1502 allele prior to initiating therapy; this is not a current recommendation in the phenytoin manufacturer labeling. Patients with a positive result should avoid phenytoin. Potentially serious, sometimes fatal multiorgan hypersensitivity reactions (also known as drug reaction with eosinophilia and systemic symptoms [DRESS]) have been reported with some antiepileptic drugs; including phenytoin; monitor for signs and symptoms of possible manifestations associated with lymphatic, hepatic, renal, and/or hematologic organ systems; gradual discontinuation and conversion to alternate therapy may be required. Chronic use of phenytoin has been associated with decreased bone mineral density (osteopenia, osteoporosis, and osteomalacia) and bone fractures. Chronic use may result in decreased vitamin D concentrations due to hepatic enzyme induction and may lead to vitamin D deficiency, hypocalcemia and hypophosphatemia; monitor as appropriate and consider implementing vitamin D and calcium supplementation. Cases of acute hepatotoxicity, including infrequent cases of acute hepatic failure, have been reported. Other manifestations include jaundice, hepatomegaly, elevated serum transaminase levels, leukocytosis, and eosinophilia. The clinical course of acute phenytoin hepatotoxicity ranges from prompt recovery to fatal outcomes. Immediately discontinue phenytoin in patients who develop acute hepatotoxicity and do not readminister. Consider alternative therapy in patients who have experienced hypersensitivity to structurally similar drugs such as carboxamides (eg, carbamazepine), barbiturates, succinimides, and oxazolidinediones (eg, trimethadione). Lymphadenopathy may occur (local or generalized), including benign lymph node hyperplasia, pseudolymphoma, lymphoma, and Hodgkin disease; cause and effect relationship has not been established. Use with caution in patients with diabetes mellitus; phenytoin may inhibit insulin release and increase serum glucose in patients with diabetes. Phenytoin is not indicated for the treatment of absence seizures or seizures due to hypoglycemia or other metabolic causes. Potentially significant interactions may exist, requiring dose or frequency adjustment, additional monitoring, and/or selection of alternative therapy.

Benzyl alcohol and derivatives: Some dosage forms may contain sodium benzoate/benzoic acid; benzoic acid (benzoate) is a metabolite of benzyl alcohol; large amounts of benzyl alcohol (≥99 mg/kg/day) have been associated with a potentially fatal toxicity ("gasping syndrome") in neonates; the "gasping syndrome" consists of metabolic acidosis, respiratory distress, gasping respirations, CNS dysfunction (including convulsions, intracranial hemorrhage), hypotension, and cardiovascular collapse (AAP ["Inactive" 1997]; CDC 1982); some data suggests that benzoate displaces bilirubin from protein binding sites (Ahlfors 2001); avoid or use dosage forms containing benzyl alcohol derivative with caution in neonates. See manufacturer's labeling.

Propylene glycol: Some dosage forms may contain propylene glycol; large amounts are potentially toxic and have been associated hyperosmolality, lactic acidosis, seizures and respiratory depression; use caution (AAP 1997; Zar 2007).

Drug Interactions

Metabolism/Transport Effects **Substrate** of CYP2C19 (major), CYP2C9 (major), CYP3A4 (minor); **Note:** Assignment of Major/Minor substrate status based on clinically relevant drug interaction potential; **Induces** CYP2B6 (weak), CYP2C8 (strong), CYP2C9 (strong), CYP3A4 (strong), P-glycoprotein, UGT1A1

Avoid Concomitant Use

Avoid concomitant use of Phenytoin with any of the following: Abiraterone Acetate; Antihepaciviral Combination Products; Apixaban; Apremilast; Aprepitant; Artemether; Asunaprevir; Axitinib; Azelastine (Nasal); Bedaquiline; Boceprevir; Bortezomib; Bosutinib; Cariprazine; Ceritinib; CloZAPine; Cobicistat; Cobimetinib; Crizotinib; Dabigatran Etexilate; Dabrafenib; Daclatasvir; Dasabuvir; Deflazacort; Delamanid; Delavirdine; Dienogest; Dolutegravir; Dronedarone; Eliglustat; Elvitegravir; Enzalutamide; Erlotinib; Etravirine; Everolimus; Flibanserin; Grazoprevir; Ibrutinib; Idelalisib; Irinotecan Products; Isavuconazonium Sulfate; Itraconazole; Ivabradine; Ivacaftor; Ixazomib; Lapatinib; Ledipasvir; Lumefantrine; Lurasidone; Macitentan; MiFEPRIStone; Naldemedine; Naloxegol; Netupitant; NIFEdipine; Nilotinib; NiMODipine; Nintedanib; Nisoldipine; Olaparib; Ombitasvir, Paritaprevir, Ritonavir, and Dasabuvir; Orphenadrine; Oxomemazine; Palbociclib; Panobinostat; Paraldehyde; PAZOPanib; PONATinib; Praziquantel; Ranolazine; Regorafenib; Ribociclib; Rilpivirine; Rivaroxaban; Roflumilast; RomiDEPsin; Simeprevir; Sofosbuvir; Sonidegib; SORAfenib; Stiripentol; Suvorexant; Tasimelteon; Telaprevir; Tenofovir Alafenamide; Thalidomide; Ticagrelor; Tofacitinib; Tolvaptan; Toremifene; Trabectedin; Ulipristal; Vandetanib; Velpatasvir;

Vemurafenib; Venetoclax; VinCRIStine (Liposomal); Vinflunine; Vorapaxar

Increased Effect/Toxicity

Phenytoin may increase the levels/effects of: Analgesics (Opioid); Azelastine (Nasal); Blonanserin; Buprenorphine; Chloramphenicol; Clarithromycin; CNS Depressants; Doxercalciferol; Flunitrazepam; Fosamprenavir; HYDROcodone; Ifosfamide; Lithium; Methotrexate; Methotrimeprazine; MetyroSINE; Neuromuscular-Blocking Agents (Nondepolarizing); Orphenadrine; OxyCODONE; Paraldehyde; PHENobarbital; Piribedil; Pramipexole; Prilocaine; ROPINIRole; Rotigotine; Selective Serotonin Reuptake Inhibitors; Sodium Nitrite; Thalidomide; Vitamin K Antagonists; Zolpidem

The levels/effects of Phenytoin may be increased by: Alcohol (Ethyl); Amiodarone; Antifungal Agents (Azole Derivatives, Systemic); Benzodiazepines; Brimonidine (Topical); Brivaracetam; Calcium Channel Blockers; Cannabis; Capecitabine; CarBAMazepine; Carbonic Anhydrase Inhibitors; CeFAZolin; Chloramphenicol; Chlormethiazole; Chlorphenesin Carbamate; Chlorpheniramine; Cimetidine; Clarithromycin; Cosyntropin; CYP2C19 Inhibitors (Moderate); CYP2C9 Inhibitors (Moderate); CYP2C9 Inhibitors (Strong); Dapsone (Topical); Delavirdine; Dexamethasone (Systemic); Dexketoprofen; Dexmethylphenidate; Dimethindene (Topical); Disulfiram; Doxylamine; Dronabinol; Droperidol; Efavirenz; Erlotinib; Eslicarbazepine; Ethosuximide; Felbamate; Floxuridine; Fluconazole; Fluorouracil (Systemic); Fluorouracil (Topical); FLUoxetine; FluvoxaMINE; Halothane; HydrOXYzine; Isoniazid; Kava Kava; Lofexidine; Lumacaftor; Magnesium Sulfate; Methotrimeprazine; Methylphenidate; MetroNIDAZOLE (Systemic); Miconazole (Oral); Minocycline; Nabilone; NIFEdipine; Nitric Oxide; Omeprazole; OXcarbazepine; Oxomemazine; Phenylbutazone; Rufinamide; Sertraline; Sodium Oxybate; Sulfamethoxazole; Sulthiame; Tacrolimus (Systemic); Tapentadol; Tegafur; Telaprevir; Tetracaine (Topical); Tetrahydrocannabinol; Ticlopidine; Topiramate; TraZODone; Trimeprazine; Trimethoprim; Valproate Products; Vitamin K Antagonists

Decreased Effect

Phenytoin may decrease the levels/effects of: Abiraterone Acetate; Acetaminophen; Afatinib; Albendazole; Amiodarone; Antifungal Agents (Azole Derivatives, Systemic); Antihepaciviral Combination Products; Apixaban; Apremilast; Aprepitant; ARIPiprazole; ARIPiprazole Lauroxil; Artemether; Asunaprevir; Axitinib; Bazedoxifene; Bedaquiline; Benperidol; Boceprevir; Bortezomib; Bosutinib; Brentuximab Vedotin; Brexpiprazole; Brivaracetam; Busulfan; Cabozantinib; Calcifediol; Calcium Channel Blockers; Canagliflozin; Cannabidiol; Cannabis; CarBAMazepine; Cariprazine; Caspofungin; Ceritinib; Chloramphenicol; Clarithromycin; Clindamycin (Systemic); CloZAPine; Cobicistat; Cobimetinib; Contraceptives (Estrogens); Contraceptives (Progestins); Corticosteroids (Systemic); Crizotinib; CycloSPORINE (Systemic); CYP2C8 Substrates; CYP2C9 Substrates; CYP3A4 Substrates; Dabigatran Etexilate; Dabrafenib; Daclatasvir; Dasabuvir; Dasatinib; Deferasirox; Deflazacort; Delamanid; Delavirdine; Dexamethasone (Systemic); Diclofenac (Systemic); Dienogest; Diethylstilbestrol; Disopyramide; Dolutegravir; Doxofylline; DOXOrubicin (Conventional); Doxycycline; Dronabinol; Dronedarone; Efavirenz; Eliglustat; Elvitegravir; Enzalutamide; Erlotinib; Eslicarbazepine; Estriol (Systemic); Estriol (Topical); Ethosuximide; Etizolam; Etoposide; Etoposide Phosphate; Etravirine; Everolimus; Exemestane; Ezogabine; Felbamate; Flibanserin; Flunarizine; Gefitinib; Gestrinone; Grazoprevir; GuanFACINE; HMG-CoA Reductase Inhibitors; Hydrocortisone (Systemic); Ibrutinib; Idelalisib; Ifosfamide; Imatinib; Irinotecan Products; Isavuconazonium Sulfate; Itraconazole; Ivabradine; Ivacaftor; Ixabepilone; Ixazomib; Lacosamide; LamoTRIgine; Lapatinib; Ledipasvir; Levodopa; Linagliptin; Loop Diuretics; Lopinavir; Lumefantrine; Lurasidone; Macitentan; Manidipine; Maraviroc; Mebendazole; Meperidine; Methadone; MethylPREDNISolone; MetroNIDAZOLE (Systemic); MetyraPONE; Mexiletine; Mianserin; MiFEPRIStone; Mirodenafil; Naldemedine; Naloxegol; Nelfinavir; Netupitant; Neuromuscular-Blocking Agents (Nondepolarizing); NIFEdipine; Nilotinib; NiMODipine; Nintedanib; Nisoldipine; Olaparib; Ombitasvir, Paritaprevir, Ritonavir, and Dasabuvir; Omeprazole; Osimertinib; OXcarbazepine; Palbociclib; Paliperidone; Panobinostat; PAZOPanib; Perampanel; P-glycoprotein/ABCB1 Substrates; Pimavanserin; PONATinib; Praziquantel; PrednisoLONE (Systemic); PredniSONE; Primidone; Propacetamol; Propafenone; QUEtiapine; QuiNIDine; QuiNINE; Radotinib; Ramelteon; Ranolazine; Reboxetine; Regorafenib; Ribociclib; Rilpivirine; Ritonavir; Rivaroxaban; Roflumilast; Rolapitant; RomiDEPsin; Rufinamide; SAXagliptin; Sertraline; Simeprevir; Sirolimus; Sofosbuvir; Sonidegib; SORAfenib; SUNItinib; Suvorexant; Tacrolimus (Systemic); Tadalafil; Tasimelteon; Telaprevir; Temsirolimus; Teniposide; Tenofovir Alafenamide; Tetrahydrocannabinol; Theophylline Derivatives; Thyroid Products; TiaGABine; Ticagrelor; Tipranavir; Tofacitinib; Tolvaptan; Topiramate; Topotecan; Toremifene; Trabectedin; TraZODone; Treprostinil; Trimethoprim; Tropisetron; Udenafil; Ulipristal; Valproate Products; Vandetanib; Velpatasvir; Vemurafenib; Venetoclax; Vilazodone; VinCRIStine; VinCRIStine (Liposomal); Vinflunine; Vorapaxar; Vortioxetine; Zaleplon; Zonisamide; Zuclopenthixol

The levels/effects of Phenytoin may be decreased by: Alcohol (Ethyl); Amphetamines; Bleomycin; CarBAMazepine; Ciprofloxacin (Systemic); Colesevelam; CYP2C9 Inducers (Strong); Darunavir; Dexamethasone (Systemic); Diazoxide; Enzalutamide; Folic Acid; Fosamprenavir; Leucovorin Calcium-Levoleucovorin; Levomefolate; Lopinavir; Lumacaftor; Mefloquine; Methotrexate; Methylfolate; Mianserin; Multivitamins/Minerals (with ADEK, Folate, Iron); Nelfinavir; Orlistat; PHENobarbital; Platinum Derivatives; Pyridoxine; RifAMPin; Ritonavir; Stiripentol; Theophylline Derivatives; Tipranavir; Vigabatrin; VinCRIStine; Vindesine

Food Interactions

Ethanol:

Acute use: Ethanol inhibits metabolism of phenytoin and may also increase CNS depression. Management: Monitor patients. Caution patients about effects.

Chronic use: Ethanol stimulates metabolism of phenytoin. Management: Monitor patients.

Food: If phenytoin is administered with enteral feeding preparations and/or related nutritional supplements, serum concentrations of phenytoin may be decreased. Management: Do not administer phenytoin concomitantly with an enteral feeding preparation.

Dietary Considerations

Folic acid: Phenytoin may decrease mucosal uptake of folic acid; to avoid folic acid deficiency and megaloblastic anemia, some clinicians recommend giving patients on anticonvulsants prophylactic doses of folic acid and cyanocobalamin (Belcastro 2012). Folic acid 0.5 mg/day has been shown to reduce the incidence of phenytoin-induced gingival overgrowth in children (Arya 2011). However, folate supplementation may increase seizures in some patients (dose dependent). Discuss with healthcare provider prior to using any supplements.

Calcium: Hypocalcemia has been reported in patients taking prolonged high-dose therapy with an anticonvulsant. Some clinicians have given an additional 4000 units/week of vitamin D (especially in those receiving poor nutrition and getting no sun exposure) to prevent hypocalcemia.

Vitamin B: Phenytoin use has been associated with low serum concentrations of vitamin B_2 (riboflavin), B_6 (pyridoxine) and B_{12} (cyanocobalamin), which may contribute to hyperhomocysteinemia. Hyperhomocysteinemia may contribute to cardiovascular disease, venous thromboembolic disease, dementia, neuropsychiatric symptoms and poor seizure control. Some clinicians recommend administering riboflavin, pyridoxine and cyanocobalamin supplements in patients taking phenytoin (Apeland 2003; Apeland 2008; Belcastro 2012; Bochyńska 2012).

Vitamin D: Phenytoin interferes with vitamin D metabolism and osteomalacia may result; may need to supplement with vitamin D

Tube feedings: Tube feedings decrease phenytoin absorption. To avoid decreased serum levels with continuous NG feeds, hold feedings for 1 to 2 hours prior to and 1-2 hours after phenytoin administration, if possible. The manufacturer recommends not to administer concomitantly with an enteral feeding preparation. There is a variety of opinions on how to administer phenytoin with enteral feedings. Be **consistent** throughout therapy.

Injection may contain sodium.

Pharmacodynamics/Kinetics

Onset of Action IV: ~0.5 to 1 hour

Half-life Elimination Range: 7 to 42 hours; newborns (PNA <7 days): Apparent half-life greatly prolonged (clearance decreased) and then rapidly accelerates to infant levels by 5 weeks of life. **Note:** Elimination is not first-order (ie, follows Michaelis-Menten pharmacokinetics); half-life increases with increasing phenytoin concentrations; best described using parameters such as V_{max} and K_m.

Time to Peak Serum (formulation dependent): Oral: Extended-release capsule: 4 to 12 hours; Immediate release preparation: 1.5 to 3 hours

Pregnancy Considerations Phenytoin crosses the placenta (Harden and Pennell 2009). An increased risk of congenital malformations and adverse outcomes may occur following *in utero* phenytoin exposure. Reported malformations include orofacial clefts, cardiac defects, dysmorphic facial features, nail/digit hypoplasia, growth abnormalities including microcephaly, and mental deficiency. Isolated cases of malignancies (including neuroblastoma) and coagulation defects in the neonate (may be life threatening) following delivery have also been reported. Maternal use of phenytoin should be avoided when possible to decrease the risk of cleft palate and poor cognitive outcomes. Polytherapy may also increase the risk of congenital malformations; monotherapy is recommended (Harden and Meader 2009). The maternal use of folic acid throughout pregnancy is recommended to reduce the risk of major congenital malformations (Harden and Pennell 2009). Potentially life-threatening bleeding disorders in the newborn may also occur due to decreased concentrations of vitamin K-dependent clotting factors following phenytoin exposure in utero; vitamin K administration to the mother prior to delivery and the newborn after birth is recommended.

Total plasma concentrations of phenytoin are decreased in the mother during pregnancy; unbound plasma (free) concentrations are also decreased and plasma clearance is increased. Due to pregnancy-induced physiologic changes, women who are pregnant may require dose adjustments of phenytoin in order to maintain clinical response; monitoring during pregnancy should be considered (Harden and Pennell 2009). For women with epilepsy who are planning a pregnancy in advance, baseline serum concentrations should be measured once or twice prior to pregnancy during a period when seizure control is optimal. Monitoring can then be continued once each trimester during pregnancy and postpartum; more frequent monitoring may be needed in some patients. Monitoring of unbound plasma concentrations is recommended (Patsalos 2008). In women taking phenytoin who are trying to avoid pregnancy, potentially significant interactions may exist with hormone-containing contraceptives; consult drug interactions database for more detailed information.

Patients exposed to phenytoin during pregnancy are encouraged to enroll themselves into the North American Antiepileptic Drug (NAAED) Pregnancy Registry by calling 1-888-233-2334. Additional information is available at https:\\aedpregnancyregistry.org.

Breastfeeding Considerations Phenytoin is excreted in breast milk. According to the manufacturer, the decision to breastfeed during therapy should consider the risk of infant exposure, the benefits of breastfeeding to the infant, and benefits of treatment to the mother.

Dosage Forms Considerations The capsule dosage form represents *Extended Phenytoin Sodium Capsules,* USP, a designation differentiating the drug from *Prompt Phenytoin Sodium Capsules,* USP (no longer available) as the extended form was characterized by a slow and extended rate of absorption when the two were compared.

Dosage Forms

Capsule, Oral:

Dilantin: 30 mg, 100 mg
Phenytek: 200 mg, 300 mg
Generic: 100 mg, 200 mg, 300 mg

Solution, Injection:

Generic: 50 mg/mL (2 mL, 5 mL)

Suspension, Oral:

Dilantin: 125 mg/5 mL (237 mL)
Generic: 125 mg/5 mL (4 mL, 237 mL)

Tablet Chewable, Oral:

Dilantin Infatabs: 50 mg
Phenytoin Infatabs: 50 mg
Generic: 50 mg

Physostigmine (fye zoe STIG meen)

Pharmacologic Category Acetylcholinesterase Inhibitor; Antidote

Use

Reversal of central nervous system anticholinergic syndrome

Note: Physostigmine should only be used to reverse toxic, life-threatening delirium caused by pure anticholinergic agents (ie, atropine, diphenhydramine, dimenhydrinate, *Atropa belladonna* [deadly nightshade], or jimson weed [*Datura* spp]). Consultation with a clinical toxicologist or poison control center is recommended in patients who require physostigmine administration.

Local Anesthetic/Vasoconstrictor Precautions No information available to require special precautions

Effects on Dental Treatment Key adverse event(s) related to dental treatment: Salivation.

Effects on Bleeding No information available to require special precautions

Adverse Reactions Frequency not defined.

Cardiovascular: Asystole, bradycardia, palpitations

Central nervous system: Hallucination, nervousness, restlessness, seizure, twitching

Dermatologic: Diaphoresis

Gastrointestinal: Diarrhea, frequent bowel movements, nausea, salivation, stomach pain, vomiting

Genitourinary: Urinary frequency

Hypersensitivity: Hypersensitivity reaction

Ophthalmic: Lacrimation, miosis

Respiratory: Bronchospasm, dyspnea, pulmonary edema, respiratory distress, respiratory paralysis

General Dosage Range

IM:

Infants, Children, and Adolescents: Initial: 0.02 mg/kg, may repeat every 5-10 minutes until response occurs (maximum total dose: 2 mg)

Adults: Initial: 0.5-2 mg, may repeat every 10-30 minutes until response occurs

IV:

Infants, Children, and Adolescents: Initial: 0.02 mg/kg, may repeat every 5-10 minutes until response occurs (maximum total dose: 2 mg)

Adults: Initial: 0.5-2 mg, may repeat every 10-30 minutes until response occurs

Mechanism of Action Physostigmine is a carbamate which inhibits the enzyme acetylcholinesterase and prolongs the central and peripheral effects of acetylcholine

Pharmacodynamics/Kinetics

Onset of Action Within 3 to 8 minutes

Duration of Action 45 to 60 minutes

Half-life Elimination 1 to 2 hours

Pregnancy Considerations In general, medications used as antidotes should take into consideration the health and prognosis of the mother; antidotes should be administered to pregnant women if there is a clear indication for use and should not be withheld because of fears of teratogenicity (Bailey, 2003).

Phytonadione (fye toe na DYE one)

Brand Names: US Mephyton

Brand Names: Canada AquaMEPHYTON; Konakion; Mephyton

Pharmacologic Category Vitamin, Fat Soluble

Use Prevention and treatment of hypoprothrombinemia caused by vitamin K antagonist (VKA)-induced (eg, warfarin-induced) or other drug-induced vitamin K deficiency, altered activity, or altered metabolism; hypoprothrombinemia caused by malabsorption or inability to synthesize vitamin K; prophylaxis and treatment of hemorrhagic disease of the newborn

Local Anesthetic/Vasoconstrictor Precautions No information available to require special precautions

Effects on Dental Treatment Key adverse event(s) related to dental treatment: Abnormal taste.

Effects on Bleeding Phytonadione is a synthetic form of vitamin K and has been used as an antidote to reverse warfarin-induced bleeding complications or endogenous vitamin K deficiencies.

Adverse Reactions

Frequency not defined.

Cardiovascular: Flushing, hypertension, hypotension

Central nervous system: Dizziness

Dermatologic: Diaphoresis, erythematous rash, pruritus

Gastrointestinal: Dysgeusia, nausea

Hypersensitivity: Anaphylactoid reaction (non-immunologic anaphylaxis), hypersensitivity reaction

Local: Fibrosis at injection site, injection site reaction

Respiratory: Cyanosis, dyspnea

General Dosage Range

IM:

Newborns: Prophylaxis: 0.5 to 1 mg within 1 hour of birth; Treatment: 1 mg/dose/day

Adults: Initial: 2.5 to 25 mg/dose (maximum: 50 mg)

IV: *Adults:* Initial: 2.5 to 25 mg/dose (maximum: 50 mg)

Oral: *Adults:* Initial: 2.5 to 25 mg/dose (maximum: 50 mg)

SubQ:

Newborns: 1 mg/dose/day

Adults: Initial: 2.5 to 25 mg/dose (maximum: 50 mg)

Mechanism of Action Promotes liver synthesis of clotting factors (II, VII, IX, X); however, the exact mechanism as to this stimulation is unknown. Menadiol is a water soluble form of vitamin K; phytonadione has a more rapid and prolonged effect than menadione; menadiol sodium diphosphate (K_4) is half as potent as menadione (K_3).

Pharmacodynamics/Kinetics

Onset of Action

Onset of action: Increased coagulation factors: Oral: 6 to 10 hours; IV: 1 to 2 hours

Peak effect: INR values return to normal: Oral: 24 to 48 hours; IV: 12 to 14 hours

Pregnancy Risk Factor C

Pregnancy Considerations Animal reproduction studies have not been conducted. Phytonadione crosses the placenta in limited concentrations (Kazzi, 1990). The dietary requirements of vitamin K are the same in pregnant and nonpregnant women (IOM, 2000). In general, medications used as antidotes should take into consideration the health and prognosis of the mother; antidotes should be administered to pregnant women if there is a clear indication for use and should not be withheld because of fears of teratogenicity (Bailey, 2003).

Pilocarpine (Systemic) (pye loe KAR peen)

Related Information

Dentin Hypersensitivity, Acid Erosion, High Caries Index, Management of Alveolar Osteitis, and Xerostomia *on page 1857*

Perioral Premalignant Lesions and Management of Patients Undergoing Cancer Therapy *on page 1875*

Brand Names: US Salagen

Brand Names: Canada Salagen

Generic Availability (US) Yes

Pharmacologic Category Cholinergic Agonist

Dental Use Treatment of xerostomia caused by radiation therapy in patients with head and neck cancer and from Sjögren's syndrome

Use Xerostomia: Treatment of symptoms of dry mouth from salivary gland hypofunction caused by radiotherapy for cancer of the head and neck; treatment of symptoms of dry mouth in patients with Sjögren syndrome.

Local Anesthetic/Vasoconstrictor Precautions No information available to require special precautions

Effects on Dental Treatment Key adverse event(s) related to dental treatment: Increased salivation (therapeutic effect) (see Dental Comment)

Effects on Bleeding No information available to require special precautions

Adverse Reactions

>10%:

Cardiovascular: Flushing (8% to 13%)

Central nervous system: Chills (3% to 15%), dizziness (5% to 12%), headache (11%)

Gastrointestinal: Nausea (6% to 15%)

Genitourinary: Urinary frequency (9% to 12%)

Neuromuscular & skeletal: Weakness (2% to 12%)

Respiratory: Rhinitis (5% to 14%)

Miscellaneous: Diaphoresis (29% to 68%)

1% to 10%:

Cardiovascular: Edema (<1% to 5%), facial edema, hypertension (3%), palpitation, tachycardia

Central nervous system: Pain (4%), fever, somnolence

Dermatologic: Pruritus, rash

Gastrointestinal: Diarrhea (4% to 7%), dyspepsia (7%), vomiting (3% to 4%), constipation, flatulence, glossitis, salivation increased, stomatitis, taste perversion

Genitourinary: Vaginitis, urinary incontinence

Neuromuscular & skeletal: Myalgias, tremor

Ocular: Lacrimation (6%), amblyopia (4%), abnormal vision, blurred vision, conjunctivitis

Otic: Tinnitus

Respiratory: Cough increased, dysphagia, epistaxis, sinusitis

Miscellaneous: Allergic reaction, voice alteration

<1%: Abnormal dreams, abnormal thinking, alopecia, angina pectoris, anorexia, anxiety, aphasia, appetite increased, arrhythmia, arthralgia, arthritis, bilirubinemia, body odor, bone disorder, bradycardia, breast pain, bronchitis, cataract, cholelithiasis, colitis, confusion, contact dermatitis, cyst, deafness, depression, dry eyes, dry mouth, dry skin, dyspnea, dysuria, ear pain, ECG abnormality, eczema, emotional lability, eructation, erythema nodosum, esophagitis, exfoliative dermatitis, eye hemorrhage, eye pain, gastritis, gastroenteritis, gastrointestinal disorder, gingivitis, glaucoma, hematuria, hepatitis, herpes simplex, hiccup, hyperkinesias, hypoesthesia, hypoglycemia, hypotension, hypothermia, insomnia, intracranial hemorrhage, laryngismus, laryngitis, leg cramps, leukopenia, liver function test abnormal, lymphadenopathy, mastitis, melena, menorrhagia, metrorrhagia, migraine, moniliasis, myasthenia, MI, neck pain, photosensitivity reaction, nervousness, ovarian disorder, pancreatitis, paresthesia, parotid gland enlargement, peripheral edema, platelet abnormality, pneumonia, pyuria, salivary gland enlargement, salpingitis, seborrhea, skin ulcer, speech disorder, sputum increased, stridor, syncope, taste loss, tendon disorder, tenosynovitis, thrombocythemia, thrombocytopenia, thrombosis, tongue disorder, twitching, urethral pain, urinary impairment, urinary urgency, vaginal hemorrhage, vaginal moniliasis, vesiculobullous rash, WBC abnormality, yawning

Dental Usual Dosage Treatment of xerostomia: Adults: Oral: Following head and neck cancer: 5 mg 3 times daily, titration up to 10 mg 3 times daily may be considered for patients who have not responded adequately; do not exceed 2 tablets per dose

Sjögren's syndrome: 5 mg 3 to 4 times daily

Dosing

Adult & Geriatric

Xerostomia: Oral:

Associated with head and neck cancer: Initial: 5 mg 3 times daily; may titrate dose based on response and tolerability; usual dosage range: 15 to 30 mg/day; maximum: 10 mg/dose

Sjögren syndrome: 5 mg 4 times daily

Renal Impairment There are no dosage adjustments provided in the manufacturer's labeling.

Hepatic Impairment

Mild impairment (Child-Pugh score 5 to 6): No dosage adjustment necessary.

Moderate impairment (Child-Pugh score 7 to 9): Initial: 5 mg twice daily; adjust dose based on response and tolerability.

Severe impairment (Child-Pugh score 10 to 15): Use is not recommended.

Mechanism of Action Binds to muscarinic (cholinergic) receptors, causing an increase in secretion of exocrine glands (such as salivary and sweat glands) and increase tone of smooth muscle in gastrointestinal and urinary tracts

Contraindications Hypersensitivity to pilocarpine or any component of the formulation; uncontrolled asthma; when miosis is undesirable (eg, acute iritis, angle-closure glaucoma)

Warnings/Precautions Use caution with significant cardiovascular disease; patients may have difficulty compensating for transient changes in hemodynamics or rhythm induced by pilocarpine. Use with caution in patients with controlled asthma, chronic bronchitis, or COPD; may increase airway resistance, bronchial smooth muscle tone, and bronchial secretions. Use with caution in patients with cholelithiasis, biliary tract disease, and nephrolithiasis; may induce smooth muscle spasms, precipitating renal colic or ureteral reflux in patients with nephrolithiasis. Use with caution in patients with moderate hepatic impairment; dosage adjustment recommended; use is not recommended in patients with severe hepatic impairment.

Drug Interactions

Metabolism/Transport Effects **Inhibits** CYP2A6 (weak), CYP2E1 (weak)

Avoid Concomitant Use There are no known interactions where it is recommended to avoid concomitant use.

Increased Effect/Toxicity

The levels/effects of Pilocarpine (Systemic) may be increased by: Acetylcholinesterase Inhibitors; Beta-Blockers

Decreased Effect

Pilocarpine (Systemic) may decrease the levels/effects of: Cimetropium

Food Interactions Fat decreases the rate of absorption, maximum concentration and increases the time it takes to reach maximum concentration. Management: Avoid administering with a high-fat meal.

Pharmacodynamics/Kinetics

Onset of Action 20 minutes; Maximum effect: 1 hour

Duration of Action 3 to 5 hours

Half-life Elimination 0.76 to 1.35 hours; Mild to moderate hepatic impairment: 2.1 hours

Time to Peak Serum: 0.85 to 1.25 hours (increased to 1.47 hours with a high-fat meal)

Pregnancy Risk Factor C

Pregnancy Considerations Adverse events have been observed in some animal reproduction studies.

Breastfeeding Considerations It is not known if pilocarpine is excreted in breast milk. Due to the potential for serious adverse reactions in the nursing infant, the manufacturer recommends a decision be made to discontinue nursing or to discontinue the drug, taking into account the importance of treatment to the mother.

Dosage Forms

Tablet, Oral:

Salagen: 5 mg, 7.5 mg

Generic: 5 mg, 7.5 mg

Dental Comment Pilocarpine may have potential as a salivary stimulant in individuals suffering from xerostomia induced by antidepressants and other medications. At the present time however, the FDA has not approved pilocarpine for use in drug-induced xerostomia (clinical studies required). In an attempt to discern the efficacy of pilocarpine as a salivary stimulant in patients suffering from Sjögren's syndrome (SS), Rhodus and Schuh studied 9 patients with SS given daily doses of pilocarpine over a 6-week period. A dose of 5 mg daily produced a significant overall increase in both whole unstimulated salivary flow and parotid stimulated salivary flow. These results support the use of pilocarpine to increase salivary flow in patients with SS.

Pimavanserin (pim a VAN ser in)

Brand Names: US Nuplazid

Pharmacologic Category Second Generation (Atypical) Antipsychotic

Use Parkinson disease psychosis: Treatment of hallucinations and delusions associated with Parkinson disease psychosis

Local Anesthetic/Vasoconstrictor Precautions Pimavanserin is one of the drugs confirmed to prolong the QT interval and is accepted as having a risk of causing torsades de pointes. The risk of drug-induced torsades de pointes is extremely low when a single QT interval prolonging drug is prescribed. In terms of epinephrine, it is not known what effect vasoconstrictors in the local anesthetic regimen will have in patients with a known history of congenital prolonged QT interval or in patients taking any medication that prolongs the QT interval. Until more information is obtained, it is suggested that the clinician consult with the physician prior to the use of a vasoconstrictor in suspected patients, and that the vasoconstrictor (epinephrine, mepivacaine, and levonordefrin [Carbocaine 2% with Neo-Cobefrin]) be used with caution.

Effects on Dental Treatment Key adverse event(s) related to dental treatment: May cause orthostatic hypotension; monitor patient rising from dental chair for signs of dizziness.

Effects on Bleeding No information available to require special precautions

Adverse Reactions

1% to 10%:

- Cardiovascular: Peripheral edema (7%)
- Central nervous system: Confusion (6%), hallucination (5%), abnormal gait (2%)
- Gastrointestinal: Nausea (7%), constipation (4%)

Frequency not defined: Cardiovascular: Prolonged Q-T interval on ECG

Mechanism of Action Pimavanserin acts as an inverse agonist and antagonist with high affinity for 5-HT_{2A} receptors and low affinity for 5-HT_{2C} and sigma 1 receptors; no affinity for 5-HT_{2B}, dopaminergic (including D_2), muscarinic, histaminergic, or adrenergic receptors, or to calcium channels.

Pharmacodynamics/Kinetics

Half-life Elimination Pimavanserin: ~57 hours; N-desmethylated metabolite: ~200 hours

Time to Peak 6 hours (median: 4 to 24 hours)

Pregnancy Considerations Adverse events were observed in some animal reproduction studies.

Pimecrolimus (pim e KROE li mus)

Brand Names: US Elidel

Brand Names: Canada Elidel

Generic Availability (US) No

Pharmacologic Category Calcineurin Inhibitor; Immunosuppressant Agent; Topical Skin Product

Use Atopic dermatitis: Second-line therapy for short-term and noncontinuous long-term treatment of mild to moderate atopic dermatitis in nonimmunocompromised patients 2 years and older who have failed to respond adequately to other topical prescription treatments, or when those treatments are not advisable.

Local Anesthetic/Vasoconstrictor Precautions No information available to require special precautions

Effects on Dental Treatment No significant effects or complications reported

Effects on Bleeding No information available to require special precautions

Adverse Reactions

>10%:

- Central nervous system: Headache (children and adolescents 11% to 25%; adults 7%), fever (children and adolescents 13%; adults 1%)
- Infection: Influenza (3% to 13%)
- Local: Local burning (adults 26%; children and adolescents 2% to 8%; tends to resolve/improve as lesions resolve), application site reaction (adults 15%; children and adolescents 2%)
- Respiratory: Nasopharyngitis (infants, children, and adolescents 10% to 27%; adults 8%), upper respiratory tract infection (children and adolescents 14% to 19%; adults 4%), cough (children and adolescents 9% to 16%; adults 2%), bronchitis (children and adolescents ≤11%; adults ≤2%)

1% to 10%:

- Dermatologic: Folliculitis (adults 6%; children and adolescents 1%), skin infection (5% to 6%), impetigo (4%), warts (children and adolescents ≤3%), acne vulgaris (≤2%), herpes simplex dermatitis (≤2%), molluscum contagiosum (children and adolescents ≤2%), urticaria (≤1%)
- Gastrointestinal: Diarrhea (children and adolescents 1% to 8%; adults ≤2%), gastroenteritis (children and adolescents ≤7%; adults 2%), vomiting (1% to 4%), constipation (children and adolescents ≤4%), abdominal pain (≤3%), toothache (≤3%), nausea (1% to 2%)
- Genitourinary: Dysmenorrhea (1% to 2%)
- Hypersensitivity: Hypersensitivity (3% to 5%)
- Infection: Viral infection (children and adolescents ≤7%), herpes simplex infection (≤4%), bacterial infection (1% to 2%), staphylococcal infection (1% to 2%), varicella (≤1%)
- Local: Local irritation (adults ≤6%; children and adolescents ≤1%), local pruritus (1% to 6%), localized erythema (≤2%)
- Neuromuscular & skeletal: Arthralgia (≤2%), back pain (≤2%)

Ocular: Conjunctivitis (≤2% to 3%), eye infection (≤1%)

Otic: Otic infection (1% to 6%), otitis media (1% to 3%)

Respiratory: Sore throat (4% to 8%), pharyngitis (children and adolescents 1% to 8%; adults 1%), tonsillitis (children and adolescents ≤6%; adults <1%), asthma (3% to 4%), asthma aggravated (children and adolescents ≤4%), streptococcal pharyngitis (children and adolescents 3%), nasal congestion (1% to 3%), sinusitis (1% to 3%), epistaxis (≤3%), dyspnea (≤2%), flu-like symptoms (≤2%), pneumonia (≤2%), rhinitis (≤2%), rhinorrhea (children and adolescents ≤2%), viral upper respiratory tract infection (≤2%), wheezing (children and adolescents ≤1%)

Miscellaneous: Laceration (children and adolescents ≤2%)

<1%, postmarketing, and/or case reports: Anaphylaxis, angioedema, eczema (herpeticum), eye irritation (following application near eyes), facial edema, flushing (ethanol-associated), lymphadenopathy, malignant neoplasm (basal cell carcinoma, squamous cell carcinoma, malignant melanoma, malignant lymphoma), skin discoloration

Dosing

Adult & Geriatric

Atopic dermatitis (mild to moderate): Topical: Apply thin layer to affected area twice daily. **Note:** Limit application to involved areas. Discontinue use when symptoms have resolved; re-evaluate if symptoms persist >6 weeks.

Oral lichen planus (off-label use): Topical: Apply twice daily for 1 month (Passeron 2007; Swift 2005; Volz 2008)

Psoriasis (off-label use): Topical: Apply twice daily (Gribetz 2004; Menter 2009)

Vitiligo (off-label use): Topical: Apply twice daily for 6 months. Treatment beyond 12 months may be useful; long-term safety has not been established. (Esfandiarpour 2009; Stinco 2009; Taieb 2013)

Pediatric Atopic dermatitis (mild-to-moderate): Children ≥2 years and Adolescents: Topical: Refer to adult dosing.

Mechanism of Action Penetrates inflamed epidermis to inhibit T cell activation by blocking transcription of proinflammatory cytokine genes such as interleukin-2, interferon gamma (Th1-type), interleukin-4, and interleukin-10 (Th2-type). Pimecrolimus binds to the intracellular protein FKBP-12, inhibiting calcineurin, which blocks cytokine transcription and inhibits T-cell activation. Prevents release of inflammatory cytokines and mediators from mast cells *in vitro* after stimulation by antigen/IgE.

Contraindications Hypersensitivity to pimecrolimus or any component of the formulation

Warnings/Precautions [US Boxed Warning]: Topical calcineurin inhibitors (including pimecrolimus) have been associated with rare cases of lymphoma and skin malignancy. Avoid use on malignant or premalignant skin conditions (eg, cutaneous T-cell lymphoma). **[US Boxed Warning]: Continuous long-term use of calcineurin inhibitors (including pimecrolimus) should be avoided and application of cream should be limited to areas of involvement with atopic dermatitis. Safety of intermittent use for >1 year has not been established.** Diagnosis should be reconfirmed if sign/symptoms do not improve within 6 weeks of treatment.

May cause local symptoms (eg, burning, pruritus, soreness, stinging) during first few days of treatment; usually self-resolving as atopic dermatitis lesions heal. Should not be used in immunocompromised patients, including patients on concomitant systemic immunosuppressive therapy. Patients with atopic dermatitis are predisposed to skin infections; therapy has been associated with an increased risk of developing eczema herpeticum, varicella zoster, and herpes simplex. Do not apply to areas of active bacterial or viral infection; local infections at the treatment site should be resolved prior to therapy. Skin papilloma (warts) have been observed with use; discontinue use if there is worsening of skin papillomas or they do not respond to conventional treatment. Pimecrolimus may be associated with development of lymphadenopathy; possible infectious causes should be investigated. Discontinue use in patients with unknown cause of lymphadenopathy or acute infectious mononucleosis. Not recommended for use in patients with skin disease which may increase the potential for systemic absorption (eg, Netherton's syndrome). Avoid artificial or natural sunlight exposure, even when pimecrolimus is not on the skin. Safety not established in patients with generalized erythroderma. **[US Boxed Warning]: The use of pimecrolimus in children <2 years of age is not recommended,** particularly since the effect on immune system development is unknown.

Benzyl alcohol and derivatives: Some dosage forms may contain benzyl alcohol; large amounts of benzyl alcohol (≥99 mg/kg/day) have been associated with a potentially fatal toxicity ("gasping syndrome") in neonates; the "gasping syndrome" consists of metabolic acidosis, respiratory distress, gasping respirations, CNS dysfunction (including convulsions, intracranial hemorrhage), hypotension, and cardiovascular collapse (AAP ["Inactive" 1997]; CDC, 1982); some data suggests that benzoate displaces bilirubin from protein binding sites (Ahlfors, 2001); avoid or use dosage forms containing benzyl alcohol with caution in neonates. See manufacturer's labeling.

Drug Interactions

Metabolism/Transport Effects Substrate of CYP3A4 (minor); **Note:** Assignment of Major/Minor substrate status based on clinically relevant drug interaction potential

Avoid Concomitant Use

Avoid concomitant use of Pimecrolimus with any of the following: Immunosuppressants

Increased Effect/Toxicity

Pimecrolimus may increase the levels/effects of: Immunosuppressants

The levels/effects of Pimecrolimus may be increased by: CYP3A4 Inhibitors (Moderate); CYP3A4 Inhibitors (Strong)

Decreased Effect There are no known significant interactions involving a decrease in effect.

Pharmacodynamics/Kinetics

Onset of Action Time to significant improvement: 8 days

Half-life Elimination Terminal: 30 to 40 hours

Time to Peak Serum: Topical: 2 to 6 hours

Pregnancy Risk Factor C

Pregnancy Considerations Adverse events were not observed in animal reproduction studies following topical application.

Breastfeeding Considerations It is not known if pimecrolimus is excreted in breast milk. Due to the potential for serious adverse reactions in the nursing infant, the manufacturer recommends a decision be made whether to discontinue nursing or to discontinue the drug, taking into account the importance of treatment to the mother.

Dosage Forms

Cream, External:

Elidel: 1% (30 g, 60 g, 100 g)

Pimozide (PI moe zide)

Related Information

Clinical Risk Related to Drugs Prolonging QT Interval *on page 1772*

Brand Names: US Orap

Brand Names: Canada Apo-Pimozide; Orap; PMS-Pimozide

Pharmacologic Category First Generation (Typical) Antipsychotic

Use Tourette disorder: Suppression of severe motor and phonic tics in patients with Tourette disorder who have failed to respond satisfactorily to standard treatment

Local Anesthetic/Vasoconstrictor Precautions Pimozide is one of the drugs confirmed to prolong the QT interval and is accepted as having a risk of causing torsade de pointes. The risk of drug-induced torsade de pointes is extremely low when a single QT interval prolonging drug is prescribed. In terms of epinephrine, it is not known what effect vasoconstrictors in the local anesthetic regimen will have in patients with a known history of congenital prolonged QT interval or in patients taking any medication that prolongs the QT interval. Until more information is obtained, it is suggested that the clinician consult with the physician prior to the use of a vasoconstrictor in suspected patients, and that the vasoconstrictor (epinephrine, mepivacaine and levonordefrin [Carbocaine® 2% with Neo-Cobefrin®]) be used with caution.

Effects on Dental Treatment Key adverse event(s) related to dental treatment: Tourette's disorder: Xerostomia and increased salivation (normal salivary flow resumes upon discontinuation), taste disturbance, and dysphagia.

Effects on Bleeding No information available to require special precautions

Adverse Reactions

Frequencies as reported in adults (limited data) and/or children with Tourette's disorder.

>10%:

Central nervous system: Sedation (70%), akathisia (40%), drowsiness (35%; children: ≤25%), behavioral changes (22% to 25%), hypertonia (15%)

Gastrointestinal: Xerostomia (25%), constipation (20%)

Genitourinary: Impotence (15%)

Neuromuscular & skeletal: Akinesia (40%), weakness (14%)

Ophthalmic: Decreased accommodation (20%), visual disturbance (3% to 20%)

1% to 10%:

Cardiovascular: ECG abnormality (3%)

Central nervous system: Depression (10%), insomnia (10%), speech disturbance (10%), nervousness (5% to 6%), writing difficulty (handwriting change: 5%), headache (3% to 5%), abnormal dreams (3%)

Dermatologic: Skin rash (3%)

Endocrine & metabolic: Increased thirst (5%)

Gastrointestinal: Sialorrhea (6%), diarrhea (5%), dysgeusia (5%), increased appetite (5%), dysphagia (3%)

Neuromuscular & skeletal: Muscle rigidity (10%), stooped posture (10%), hyperkinesia (3%), myalgia (3%), torticollis (3%), tremor (3%)

Ophthalmic: Photophobia (5%)

Frequency not defined (some reported for disorders other than Tourette's disorder):

Cardiovascular: Chest pain, hypertension, hypotension, orthostatic hypotension, prolonged Q-T interval on ECG, syncope, tachycardia, ventricular arrhythmia

Central nervous system: Dizziness, excitement, drug-induced extrapyramidal reaction (dystonia, pseudoparkinsonism, tardive dyskinesia), neuroleptic malignant syndrome, palpitations, seizure

Dermatologic: Diaphoresis, skin irritation

Endocrine & metabolic: Decreased libido, hyponatremia, weight changes (gain/loss)

Gastrointestinal: Anorexia, gastrointestinal distress, nausea, vomiting

Genitourinary: Nocturia

Hematologic & oncologic: Hemolytic anemia

Ophthalmic: Blurred vision, cataract, periorbital edema

Renal: Polyuria

<1%, postmarketing, and/or case reports: Gingival hyperplasia

General Dosage Range Dosage adjustment recommended in patients who develop toxicities or those with a CYP2D6 poor metabolizer status.

Oral:

Children 2 to 12 years: Initial: 0.05 mg/kg once daily (preferably bedtime); Maintenance: 2 to 4 mg once daily (maximum: 10 mg/day [0.2 mg/kg/day])

Children >12 years and Adults: Initial: 1 to 2 mg in divided doses (maximum: 10 mg/day [0.2 mg/kg/day])

Mechanism of Action Pimozide, a diphenylbutylperidine conventional antipsychotic, is a potent centrally-acting dopamine-receptor antagonist resulting in its characteristic neuroleptic effects

Pharmacodynamics/Kinetics

Onset of Action Within 1 week; Maximum effect: 4 to 6 weeks

Duration of Action Variable

Half-life Elimination

Tourette disorder (Sallee 1987): Children 6 to 13 years (n=4): Mean ± SD: 66 ± 49 hours; Adults 23 to 39 years (n=7): Mean ± SD: 111 ± 57 hours

Schizophrenia: Adults: Mean: 55 hours

Time to Peak Serum: 6 to 8 hours (range: 4 to 12 hours)

Pregnancy Risk Factor C

Pregnancy Considerations Adverse events were observed in some animal reproduction studies. Antipsychotic use during the third trimester of pregnancy has a risk for abnormal muscle movements (extrapyramidal symptoms [EPS]) and withdrawal symptoms in newborns following delivery. Symptoms in the newborn may include agitation, feeding disorder, hypertonia, hypotonia, respiratory distress, somnolence, and tremor; these effects may be self-limiting or require hospitalization.

Dental Comment See Local Anesthetic/Vasoconstrictor Precautions

Pindolol (PIN doe lole)

Related Information

Cardiovascular Diseases *on page 1752*

Brand Names: Canada Apo-Pindol; Dom-Pindolol; PMS-Pindolol; Sandoz-Pindolol; Teva-Pindolol; Visken

Pharmacologic Category Antihypertensive; Beta-Blocker With Intrinsic Sympathomimetic Activity

Use

Hypertension: Treatment of hypertension, alone or in combination with other agents

The 2014 guideline for the management of high blood pressure in adults (Eighth Joint National Committee [JNC 8]) recommends initiation of pharmacologic treatment to lower blood pressure for the following patients:

- Patients ≥60 years of age with systolic blood pressure (SBP) ≥150 mm Hg or diastolic blood pressure (DBP) ≥90 mm Hg. Goal of therapy is SBP <150 mm Hg and DBP <90 mm Hg.
- Patients <60 years of age with SBP ≥140 mm Hg or DBP ≥90 mm Hg. Goal of therapy is SBP <140 mm Hg and DBP <90 mm Hg.
- Patients ≥18 years of age with diabetes and SBP ≥140 mm Hg or DBP ≥90 mm Hg. Goal of therapy is SBP <140 mm Hg and DBP <90 mm Hg.
- Patients ≥18 years of age with chronic kidney disease (CKD) and SBP ≥140 mm Hg or DBP ≥90 mm Hg. Goal of therapy is SBP <140 mm Hg and DBP <90 mm Hg.

In patients with CKD, regardless of race or diabetes status, the use of an ACE inhibitor (ACEI) or angiotensin receptor blocker (ARB) as initial therapy is recommended to improve kidney outcomes. In the general nonblack population (without CKD) including those with diabetes, initial antihypertensive treatment should consist of a thiazide-type diuretic, calcium channel blocker, ACEI, or ARB. In the general black population (without CKD) including those with diabetes, initial antihypertensive treatment should consist of a thiazide-type diuretic or a calcium channel blocker **instead of** an ACEI or ARB.

Local Anesthetic/Vasoconstrictor Precautions Use with caution; epinephrine has interacted with nonselective beta-blockers to result in initial hypertensive episode followed by bradycardia

Effects on Dental Treatment Pindolol is a nonselective beta-blocker and may enhance the pressor response to epinephrine, resulting in hypertension and bradycardia. Many nonsteroidal anti-inflammatory drugs, such as ibuprofen and indomethacin, can reduce the hypotensive effect of beta-blockers after 3 or more weeks of therapy with the NSAID. Short-term NSAID use (ie, 3 days) requires no special precautions in patients taking beta-blockers.

Effects on Bleeding No information available to require special precautions

Adverse Reactions

>10%: Cardiovascular: Edema (6% to 16%)

1% to 10%:

Cardiovascular: Bradycardia (≤2%), claudication (≤2%), cold extremities (≤2%), heart block (≤2%), hypotension (≤2%), syncope (≤2%), tachycardia (≤2%), palpitations (≤1%)

Central nervous system: Insomnia (10%), dizziness (9%), fatigue (8%), nervousness (7%), abnormal dreams (5%), anxiety (≤2%), lethargy (≤2%)

Dermatologic: Hyperhidrosis (≤2%), pruritus (1%)

Endocrine & metabolic: Weight gain (≤2%)

Gastrointestinal: Nausea (5%), diarrhea (≤2%), vomiting (≤2%)

Genitourinary: Impotence (≤2%), pollakiuria (≤2%)

Hepatic: Increased serum ALT (7%), increased serum AST (7%)

Neuromuscular & skeletal: Myalgia (10%), arthralgia (7%), weakness (4%), muscle cramps (3%)

Ophthalmic: Burning sensation of eyes (≤2%), eye discomfort (≤2%), visual disturbance (≤2%)

Renal: Polyuria (≤2%)

Respiratory: Dyspnea (5%), wheezing (≤2%)

<1%, postmarketing, and/or case reports: Cardiac failure, hallucination, hyperuricemia, increased lactic acid dehydrogenase, increased serum alkaline phosphatase

General Dosage Range Dosage adjustment recommended in patients with hepatic impairment

Oral:

Adults: Initial: 5 mg twice daily; Maintenance: 10 to 40 mg twice daily (maximum: 60 mg daily)

Elderly: Initial: 5 mg once daily

Mechanism of Action Blocks both $beta_1$- and $beta_2$-receptors and has mild intrinsic sympathomimetic activity; pindolol has negative inotropic and chronotropic effects and can significantly slow AV nodal conduction. Augmentive action of antidepressants thought to be mediated via a serotonin 1A autoreceptor antagonism.

Pharmacodynamics/Kinetics

Half-life Elimination 3 to 4 hours; prolonged in the elderly (average 7 hours; up to 15 hours reported), and cirrhosis (range: 2.5 to 30 hours)

Time to Peak Serum: ~1 hour

Pregnancy Risk Factor B

Pregnancy Considerations Adverse effects were not observed in animal reproduction studies. Pindolol crosses the placenta and is measurable in the cord blood and amniotic fluid (Gonçalves 2007). The clearance and volume of distribution of pindolol are increased during pregnancy (Gonçalves 2002).

Adverse events, such as fetal/neonatal bradycardia, hypoglycemia, and reduced birth weight, have been observed following in utero exposure to beta-blockers as a class. Adequate facilities for monitoring infants at birth is generally recommended.

Untreated chronic maternal hypertension and preeclampsia are also associated with adverse events in the fetus, infant, and mother (ACOG 2015; Magee 2014). When treatment of hypertension in pregnancy is indicated, beta-blockers may be used. Specific recommendations vary by guideline. Although other agents are preferred (ACOG 2013), use of pindolol may be considered (Magee 2014).

Pioglitazone (pye oh GLI ta zone)

Related Information

Endocrine Disorders and Pregnancy *on page 1781*

Brand Names: US Actos

Brand Names: Canada Accel-Pioglitazone; ACH-Pioglitazone; ACT Pioglitazone; Actos; Apo-Pioglitazone; Auro-Pioglitazone; Dom-Pioglitazone; JAMP-Pioglitazone; Mint-Pioglitazone; Mylan-Pioglitazone; PHL-Pioglitazone; PMS-Pioglitazone; PRO-Pioglitazone; RAN-Pioglitazone; Sandoz-Pioglitazone; Teva-Pioglitazone; Van-Pioglitazone

Pharmacologic Category Antidiabetic Agent, Thiazolidinedione

Use Diabetes mellitus, type 2: As an adjunct to diet and exercise, to improve glycemic control in adults with type 2 diabetes mellitus

Local Anesthetic/Vasoconstrictor Precautions No information available to require special precautions

Effects on Dental Treatment Key adverse event(s) related to dental treatment: Pioglitazone-dependent diabetics should be appointed for dental treatment in morning in order to minimize chance of stress-induced hypoglycemia.

Effects on Bleeding No information available to require special precautions

Adverse Reactions Adverse reactions and incidences reported are associated with monotherapy unless otherwise stated.

>10%:

Cardiovascular: Edema (combination trials: ≤27%)

Endocrine and metabolic: Hypoglycemia (combination trials: ≤27%)

Respiratory: Upper respiratory tract infection (13%)

1% to 10%:

Cardiovascular: Cardiac failure (combination trials: ≤8%)

Central nervous system: Headache (9%)

Neuromuscular & skeletal: Bone fracture (females: ≤5%), myalgia (5%)

Respiratory: Sinusitis (6%), pharyngitis (5%)

Frequency not defined:

Endocrine & metabolic: Decreased serum triglycerides, increased HDL-cholesterol, weight gain, weight loss

Hematologic & oncologic: Decreased hematocrit, decreased hemoglobin

<1%, postmarketing, and/or case reports: Bladder carcinoma, blurred vision, decreased visual acuity, dyspnea (associated with weight gain and/or edema), hepatic failure (very rare), hepatitis, increased creatine phosphokinase, increased serum transaminases, macular edema (new-onset or worsening), pulmonary edema, rhabdomyolysis

General Dosage Range Dosage adjustment recommended in patients on concomitant therapy.

Oral: *Adults:* Initial: 15 to 30 mg once daily; Maintenance: 15 to 45 mg once daily (maximum: 45 mg/day)

Mechanism of Action Thiazolidinedione antidiabetic agent that lowers blood glucose by improving target cell response to insulin, without increasing pancreatic insulin secretion. It has a mechanism of action that is dependent on the presence of insulin for activity. Pioglitazone is a potent and selective agonist for peroxisome proliferator-activated receptor-gamma (PPARgamma). Activation of nuclear PPARgamma receptors influences the production of a number of gene products involved in glucose and lipid metabolism. PPARgamma is abundant in the cells within the renal collecting tubules; fluid retention results from stimulation by thiazolidinediones which increases sodium reabsorption.

Pharmacodynamics/Kinetics

Onset of Action Delayed; Peak effect: Glucose control: Several weeks

Half-life Elimination Parent drug: 3 to 7 hours; M-III and M-IV metabolites: 16 to 24 hours

Time to Peak ~2 hours; delayed with food

Pregnancy Considerations Information related to the use of pioglitazone in pregnant women is limited (Glueck 2003; Ortega-Gonzalez 2005; Ota 2008). Thiazolidinediones may cause ovulation in anovulatory premenopausal women, increasing the risk of pregnancy. Adequate contraception in premenopausal women is recommended.

In women with diabetes, maternal hyperglycemia can be associated with congenital malformations as well as adverse effects in the fetus, neonate, and the mother (ACOG 2005; ADA 2016d; Kitzmiller 2008; Metzger 2007). To prevent adverse outcomes, prior to conception and throughout pregnancy maternal blood glucose and HbA_{1c} should be kept as close to target goals as possible but without causing significant hypoglycemia (ACOG 2013; ADA 2016d; Blumer 2013; Kitzmiller 2008).

Agents other than pioglitazone are currently recommended to treat diabetes in pregnant women (ACOG 2013; Blumer 2013).

Pioglitazone and Glimepiride

(pye oh GLI ta zone & GLYE me pye ride)

Related Information

Glimepiride *on page 797*

Pioglitazone *on page 1342*

Brand Names: US Duetact

Pharmacologic Category Antidiabetic Agent, Sulfonylurea; Antidiabetic Agent, Thiazolidinedione

Use Diabetes mellitus, type 2: Management of type 2 diabetes mellitus (noninsulin dependent, NIDDM) as an adjunct to diet and exercise in adult patients already treated with a thiazolidinedione and a sulfonylurea or who have inadequate control on either agent alone

Local Anesthetic/Vasoconstrictor Precautions No information available to require special precautions

Effects on Dental Treatment Key adverse event(s) related to dental treatment: Patients with diabetes should be questioned by the dental professional at each dental visit to assess their risk for stress-induced hypoglycemia. The dental professional should inquire about the patient's routine (ie, work, sleep schedule, eating patterns), history of hypoglycemia, time of last medication dose, last meal, and most recent blood sugar assessment. Keep a supply of glucose tablets and other carbohydrates in the office to prepare for a hypoglycemic event. Seek medical attention when necessary (American Diabetes Association, 2014).

Effects on Bleeding No information available to require special precautions

Adverse Reactions Also see individual agents.

>10%:

Cardiovascular: Peripheral edema (6% to 12%)

Endocrine & metabolic: Hypoglycemia (13% to 16%), weight gain (9% to 13%)

Respiratory: Upper respiratory tract infection (12% to 15%)

1% to 10%:

Central nervous system: Headache (4% to 7%)

Gastrointestinal: Diarrhea (4% to 6%), nausea (4% to 5%)

Genitourinary: Urinary tract infection (6% to 7%)

Hematologic & oncologic: Anemia (≤2%)

Neuromuscular & skeletal: Limb pain (4% to 5%)

<1%, postmarketing, and/or case reports: Bladder carcinoma (FDA Safety Alert, Dec. 19, 2016)

General Dosage Range Oral: *Adults:*

Patients inadequately controlled on **glimepiride** alone: Initial dose: Pioglitazone 30 mg/glimepiride 2 to 4 mg once daily (maximum: pioglitazone 45 mg/glimepiride 8 mg once daily)

Patients inadequately controlled on **pioglitazone** alone: Initial dose: Pioglitazone 30 mg/glimepiride 2 mg once daily (maximum: pioglitazone 45 mg/glimepiride 8 mg once daily)

Mechanism of Action

Pioglitazone: A thiazolidinedione that lowers blood glucose by improving target cell response to insulin, without increasing pancreatic insulin secretion. It has a mechanism of action that is dependent on the presence of insulin for activity.

Glimepiride: A sulfonylurea that stimulates insulin release from the pancreatic beta cells; reduces glucose output from the liver; insulin sensitivity is increased at peripheral target sites.

Pregnancy Considerations Use pioglitazone with caution in premenopausal, anovulatory women; may result in a resumption of ovulation, increasing the risk of pregnancy. See individual agents.

Pioglitazone and Metformin

(pye oh GLI ta zone & met FOR min)

Related Information

MetFORMIN *on page 1069*

Pioglitazone *on page 1342*

Brand Names: US Actoplus Met; Actoplus Met XR

Pharmacologic Category Antidiabetic Agent, Biguanide; Antidiabetic Agent, Thiazolidinedione

Use Diabetes mellitus, type 2: As an adjunct to diet and exercise to improve glycemic control in adults with type 2 diabetes mellitus when treatment with both pioglitazone and metformin is appropriate.

Local Anesthetic/Vasoconstrictor Precautions No information available to require special precautions

Effects on Dental Treatment Pioglitazone-dependent patients with diabetes (noninsulin dependent, type 2) or metformin-dependent patients with diabetes (noninsulin dependent, type 2) should be appointed for dental treatment in morning in order to minimize chance of stress-induced hypoglycemia.

Effects on Bleeding No information available to require special precautions

Adverse Reactions Percentages of adverse effects as reported with the combination product. Also see individual agents.

>10%:

Cardiovascular: Lower extremity edema (3% to 11%)

Respiratory: Upper respiratory tract infection (12% to 16%)

1% to 10%:

Central nervous system: Headache (2% to 6%), dizziness (5%)

Endocrine & metabolic: Weight gain (3% to 7%)

Gastrointestinal: Diarrhea (5% to 6%), nausea (4% to 6%)

Genitourinary: Urinary tract infection (5% to 6%)

Hematologic & oncologic: Anemia (≤2%)

Respiratory: Sinusitis (4% to 5%)

<1%, postmarketing, and/or case reports: Bladder carcinoma (FDA Safety Alert, Dec. 19, 2016)

General Dosage Range Dosage adjustment recommended in patients on concomitant therapy.

Oral: *Adults:*

Immediate-release tablet: Pioglitazone 15 to 45 mg/day and metformin 500 to 2,550 mg/day (maximum daily dose: Pioglitazone 45 mg/metformin 2,550 mg)

Extended-release tablet: Pioglitazone 15 to 45 mg/day and metformin 1,000 to 2,000 mg/day (maximum daily dose: Pioglitazone 45 mg/metformin 2,000 mg)

Mechanism of Action

Pioglitazone is a thiazolidinedione antidiabetic agent that lowers blood glucose by improving target cell response to insulin, without increasing pancreatic insulin secretion. It has a mechanism of action that is dependent on the presence of insulin for activity.

Metformin decreases hepatic glucose production, decreasing intestinal absorption of glucose, and improves insulin sensitivity (increases peripheral glucose uptake and utilization).

Pregnancy Considerations Use pioglitazone with caution in premenopausal, anovulatory women; may result in a resumption of ovulation, increasing the risk of pregnancy. Use of adequate contraception in premenopausal women is recommended. Refer to individual agents.

Piperacillin and Tazobactam

(pi PER a sil in & ta zoe BAK tam)

Brand Names: US Zosyn

Brand Names: Canada AJ-PIP/TAZ; Piperacillin and Tazobactam for Injection; Tazocin

Pharmacologic Category Antibiotic, Penicillin

Use

Community-acquired pneumonia: Treatment of moderate severity community-acquired pneumonia (CAP) caused by beta-lactamase-producing strains of *Haemophilus influenzae*. Infectious Diseases Society of America/American Thoracic Society (IDSA/ATS) guidelines only recommend piperacillin/tazobactam for CAP caused by *P. aeruginosa* or due to aspiration (Mandell 2007).

Intra-abdominal infections: Treatment of appendicitis complicated by rupture or abscess and peritonitis caused by beta-lactamase-producing strains of *Escherichia coli*, *Bacteroides fragilis*, *Bacteroides ovatus*, *Bacteroides thetaiotaomicron*, or *Bacteroides vulgatus*.

Nosocomial pneumonia: Treatment of moderate to severe nosocomial pneumonia caused by beta-lactamase-producing strains of *Staphylococcus aureus* and by piperacillin/tazobactam-susceptible *Acinetobacter baumanii*, *H. influenzae*, *Klebsiella pneumoniae*, and *Pseudomonas aeruginosa*.

Pelvic infections: Treatment of postpartum endometriosis or pelvic inflammatory disease caused by beta-lactamase-producing strains of *E. coli*.

Skin and skin structure infections: Treatment of skin and skin structure infections, including cellulitis, cutaneous abscesses, and ischemic/diabetic foot infections caused by beta-lactamase–producing strains of *S. aureus*.

Local Anesthetic/Vasoconstrictor Precautions No information available to require special precautions

Effects on Dental Treatment Key adverse event(s) related to dental treatment: Prolonged use of penicillins may lead to development of oral candidiasis.

Effects on Bleeding May inhibit platelet aggregation (dose related). The clinical significance may be greater with those penicillins that are combined with a beta-lactamase inhibitor and/or with agents that have greater activity against specific enteric bacterial species.

Adverse Reactions Frequency not always defined. Also see piperacillin monograph.

Cardiovascular: Phlebitis (1%), flushing (≤1%), hypotension (≤1%), thrombophlebitis (≤1%)

Central nervous system: Headache (8%), insomnia (7%), rigors (≤1%)

Dermatologic: Skin rash (4%), pruritus (3%), purpura (≤1%)

Endocrine & metabolic: Hypoglycemia (≤1%), decreased serum albumin, decreased serum glucose, decreased serum total protein, electrolyte disturbance (increases and decreases in sodium, potassium, and calcium), hyperglycemia, hypokalemia, increased gamma-glutamyl transferase

Gastrointestinal: Diarrhea (11%), constipation (8%), nausea (7%), dyspepsia (3%), vomiting (3%), abdominal pain (1%), pseudomembranous colitis (≤1%)
Hematologic & oncologic: Decreased hematocrit, decreased hemoglobin, eosinophilia, leukopenia, neutropenia, positive direct Coombs test, prolonged bleeding time, prolonged partial thromboplastin time, prolonged prothrombin time, thrombocythemia, thrombocytopenia
Hepatic: Increased serum alkaline phosphatase, increased serum ALT, increased serum AST, increased serum bilirubin
Hypersensitivity: Anaphylaxis (≤1%)
Infection: Candidiasis (2%)
Local: Injection site reaction (≤1%)
Neuromuscular & skeletal: Arthralgia (≤1%), myalgia (≤1%)
Renal: Increased blood urea nitrogen, increased serum creatinine
Respiratory: Epistaxis (≤1%)
Miscellaneous: Fever (2%)
<1%, postmarketing, and/or case reports: Acute generalized exanthemous pustulosis, agranulocytosis, anaphylactoid reaction, *Clostridium difficile* associated diarrhea, convulsions, DRESS syndrome, eosinophilic pneumonitis, erythema multiforme, exfoliative dermatitis, hemolytic anemia, hepatitis, hypersensitivity reaction, interstitial nephritis, jaundice, pancytopenia, shock, Stevens-Johnson syndrome, toxic epidermal necrolysis

General Dosage Range Dosage adjustment recommended in patients with renal impairment.

IV:

Infants 2 to 9 months: 80 mg piperacillin/kg/dose every 8 hours
Infants >9 months, Children, and Adolescents: 100 mg piperacillin/kg/dose every 8 hours (maximum: 16 g piperacillin/day)
Adults: 3.375 g every 6 hours **or** 4.5 g every 6 hours (maximum: 16 g piperacillin daily)

Mechanism of Action Piperacillin inhibits bacterial cell wall synthesis by binding to one or more of the penicillin-binding proteins (PBPs); which in turn inhibits the final transpeptidation step of peptidoglycan synthesis in bacterial cell walls, thus inhibiting cell wall biosynthesis. Bacteria eventually lyse due to ongoing activity of cell wall autolytic enzymes (autolysins and murein hydrolases) while cell wall assembly is arrested. Piperacillin exhibits time-dependent killing. Tazobactam inhibits many beta-lactamases, including staphylococcal penicillinase and Richmond-Sykes types 2, 3, 4, and 5, including extended spectrum enzymes; it has only limited activity against class 1 beta-lactamases other than class 1C types.

Pharmacodynamics/Kinetics

Half-life Elimination Note: Pediatric data: Reed 1994

Piperacillin:
Infants 2 to 5 months: 1.4 hours
Infants and Children 6 to 23 months: 0.9 hour
Children 2 to 12 years: 0.7 hour
Adults: 0.7 to 1.2 hours
Metabolite: 1 to 1.5 hours
Tazobactam:
Infants 2 to 5 months: 1.6 hours
Infants and Children 6 to 23 months: 1 hour
Children 2 to 12 years: 0.8 to 0.9 hour
Adults: 0.7 to 0.9 hour

Time to Peak Immediately following completion of 30-minute infusion

Pregnancy Risk Factor B

Pregnancy Considerations Adverse events have not been observed in animal reproduction studies. Piperacillin and tazobactam both cross the placenta and are found in the fetal serum, placenta, amniotic fluid, and fetal urine. When used during pregnancy, the clearance and volume of distribution of piperacillin/tazobactam are increased; half-life and AUC are decreased (Bourget, 1998). Piperacillin/tazobactam is approved for the treatment of postpartum gynecologic infections, including endometritis or pelvic inflammatory disease, caused by susceptible organisms.

Pipotiazine (pip oh TYE a zeen)

Brand Names: Canada Piportil L_4

Pharmacologic Category First Generation (Typical) Antipsychotic

Use Note: Not approved in the US

Schizophrenia: Maintenance treatment of non-agitated patients with chronic schizophrenia

Local Anesthetic/Vasoconstrictor Precautions No information available to require special precautions

Effects on Dental Treatment Key adverse event(s) related to dental treatment: Xerostomia and changes in salivation (normal salivary flow resumes upon discontinuation).

Effects on Bleeding No information available to require special precautions

Adverse Reactions Frequency not defined.

Cardiovascular: Hypotension, prolonged Q-T interval on ECG, syncope, tachycardia
Central nervous system: Abnormal proteins in cerebrospinal fluid, agitation, anxiety, bizarre dream, depression, disturbed sleep, dizziness, drowsiness, excitement, extrapyramidal reaction (akathisia, dyskinesia, dystonia, hyper-reflexia, oculogyric crisis, opisthotonos, pseudoparkinsonism, rigidity, sialorrhea, tremor), fatigue, insomnia, psychosis (paradoxical), restlessness, tardive dyskinesia
Dermatologic: Dermatitis, pruritus, skin pigmentation (prolonged therapy), skin rash
Endocrine & metabolic: Change in libido, decreased glucose tolerance, diabetic ketoacidosis, hyperglycemia, increased thirst, menstrual disease, weight changes
Gastrointestinal: Anorexia, cholestasis, constipation, increased appetite, nausea, paralytic ileus, vomiting, xerostomia
Genitourinary: Impotence, urinary incontinence
Hepatic: Cholestatic jaundice
Ophthalmic: Blurred vision, corneal deposits (prolonged therapy), pigment deposits on lens, retinal changes (prolonged therapy)
Respiratory: Nasal congestion
Miscellaneous: Fever

General Dosage Range IM:

Adults: Initial: 50-100 mg; Maintenance: 25-250 mg every 3-4 weeks
Elderly >50 years: Initial: <50 mg is recommended

Mechanism of Action Blocks postsynaptic mesolimbic dopaminergic receptors in the brain; depresses the release of hypothalamic and hypophyseal hormones. Relative to other piperidine phenothiazines, pipotiazine appears to be less sedating, with less potential to potentiate other CNS depressants, and may possess a lower propensity to cause hypotension. However, it has a relatively high propensity for cause extrapyramidal reactions. Pipotiazine palmitate is an ester of pipotiazine with a prolonged duration of action.

Pharmacodynamics/Kinetics

Onset of Action IM: 2 to 3 days

Duration of Action 3 to 6 weeks

Time to Peak

Serum: 1 day (Spanaerello 2014)

Pregnancy Considerations Adverse events have been observed in some animal reproductive studies. Antipsychotic use during the third trimester of pregnancy has a risk for abnormal muscle movements (extrapyramidal symptoms [EPS]) and withdrawal symptoms in newborns following delivery. Symptoms in the newborn may include agitation, feeding disorder, hypertonia, hypotonia, respiratory distress, somnolence, and tremor; these effects may be self-limiting or require hospitalization.

Product Availability Not available in the US

Pirfenidone (pir FEN i done)

Brand Names: US Esbriet

Brand Names: Canada Esbriet

Pharmacologic Category Anti-inflammatory Agent; Antifibrotic Agent

Use Idiopathic pulmonary fibrosis: Treatment of idiopathic pulmonary fibrosis (IPF)

Local Anesthetic/Vasoconstrictor Precautions No information available to require special precautions

Effects on Dental Treatment No significant effects or complications reported

Effects on Bleeding No information available to require special precautions

Adverse Reactions

>10%:

Central nervous system: Fatigue (22% to 26%), headache (10% to 22%), dizziness (9% to 18%)

Dermatologic: Skin rash (29% to 30%; Japanese patients: 9%), skin photosensitivity (9% to 12%; Japanese patients: 51%)

Gastrointestinal: Nausea (33% to 36%), diarrhea (22% to 26%), abdominal pain (5% to 24%), dyspepsia (17% to 19%), anorexia (9% to 13%), vomiting (9% to 13%), gastroesophageal reflux disease (6% to 11%)

Respiratory: Upper respiratory tract infection (3% to 27%), sinusitis (1% to 11%)

≥3% to 10%:

Central nervous system: Insomnia (4% to 10%), noncardiac chest pain (1% to 5%), drowsiness (3%)

Dermatologic: Pruritus (4% to 8%), macular eruption (4%), sunburn (4%), erythema (3%)

Endocrine & metabolic: Weight loss (6% to 10%), increased gamma-glutamyl transferase (5%), hot flash (3%)

Gastrointestinal: Abdominal distension (9%), decreased appetite (8%), abdominal distress (3% to 8%), dysgeusia (1% to 6%), flatulence (5%)

Hepatic: Increased serum ALT (4%), increased serum transaminases (ALT and AST; ≥3 x ULN: 4%)

Neuromuscular & skeletal: Arthralgia (1% to 10%), weakness (6%)

Respiratory: Dyspnea (4%)

≥1% to <3%:

Central nervous system: Lethargy, malaise, paresthesia

Cardiovascular: Angina pectoris

Dermatologic: Desquamation, erythematous rash, hyperhidrosis, maculopapular rash, urticaria, xeroderma

Endocrine & metabolic: Dyslipidemia, fluid retention, gout, hyperglycemia, hyperlipidemia, hypertriglyceridemia, hypoglycemia, hypokalemia, hyponatremia, increased lactate dehydrogenase, vitamin D deficiency

Gastrointestinal: Frequent bowel movements, gastritis, increased appetite

Genitourinary: Urinary tract infection, vaginal infection

Hepatic: Abnormal hepatic function tests

Infection: Influenza

Neuromuscular & skeletal: Increased creatinine phosphokinase, myalgia, tremor

Respiratory: Cough, throat irritation

Miscellaneous: Fever

<1%, postmarketing, and/or case reports: Agranulocytosis, anemia, angioedema, atrial fibrillation, atrioventricular block (first and second degree), bradycardia, candidiasis, cholecystitis, decreased hemoglobin, decreased platelet count, dehydration, esophagitis, febrile neutropenia, flushing, hepatitis, herpes zoster, hyperbilirubinemia, hyperkalemia, increased blood urea nitrogen, increased C-reactive protein, increased troponin, intestinal obstruction, leukopenia, neutropenia, palpitations, pneumonia, pneumonitis, pneumothorax, prolonged QT-interval on ECG, pulmonary aspergillosis, renal insufficiency, respiratory failure, supraventricular tachycardia, ulcer with hemorrhage (gastric), ventricular tachycardia, viral respiratory tract infection, xanthoderma

Mechanism of Action Precise mechanisms of action have not been fully elucidated; however, pirfenidone may exert antifibrotic properties by decreasing fibroblast proliferation and the production of fibrosis-associated proteins and cytokines; may decrease the formation and accumulation of extracellular matrix (ie, collagen) in response to transforming growth factor-beta and platelet derived growth factor. Pirfenidone is also believed to exert anti-inflammatory properties by decreasing the accumulation of inflammatory cells resulting from a variety of stimuli.

Pharmacodynamics/Kinetics

Half-life Elimination ~3 hours

Time to Peak Plasma: Median: 0.5 hours (fasting); 3 hours (with food)

Pregnancy Considerations Adverse events have been observed in animal reproduction studies.

Piroxicam (peer OKS i kam)

Related Information

Rheumatoid Arthritis, Osteoarthritis, and Osteoporosis *on page 1792*

Temporomandibular Dysfunction (TMD), Chronic Pain, and Fibromyalgia *on page 1868*

Brand Names: US Feldene

Brand Names: Canada Apo-Piroxicam; Dom-Piroxicam; PMS-Piroxicam; PMS-Piroxicam Suppositories; Teva-Piroxicam

Pharmacologic Category Analgesic, Nonopioid; Nonsteroidal Anti-inflammatory Drug (NSAID), Oral

Use

Arthritis: Relief of signs and symptoms of osteoarthritis and rheumatoid arthritis.

Canadian labeling: Additional use (not in US labeling): Symptomatic treatment of ankylosing spondylitis

Local Anesthetic/Vasoconstrictor Precautions No information available to require special precautions

Effects on Dental Treatment The dentist should be aware of the potential of abnormal coagulation. Caution should also be exercised in the use of NSAIDs in patients already on anticoagulant therapy with drugs such as warfarin (Coumadin®). See Effects on Bleeding.

Effects on Bleeding Nonselective NSAIDs, such as piroxicam, inhibit platelet aggregation and prolong bleeding time in some patients. Unlike aspirin, the NSAID effect on platelet function is quantitatively less, of shorter duration, and reversible. Normal platelet function should occur in ~5 elimination half-lives or in <10 hours after discontinuation of piroxicam. Concomitant use of other NSAIDs should be avoided.

Adverse Reactions

1% to 10%:

Cardiovascular: Edema

Central nervous system: Dizziness, headache

Dermatologic: Pruritus, skin rash

Gastrointestinal: Abdominal pain, anorexia, constipation, diarrhea, dyspepsia, flatulence, gastrointestinal hemorrhage, gastrointestinal perforation, heartburn, nausea, ulcer (gastric, duodenal), vomiting

Hematologic & oncologic: Anemia, prolonged bleeding time

Hepatic: Increased liver enzymes

Otic: Tinnitus

Renal: Renal function abnormality

<1%, postmarketing, and/or case reports: Abnormal dreams, agranulocytosis, akathisia, alopecia, anaphylactoid reactions, anaphylaxis, angioedema, anxiety, aplastic anemia, aseptic meningitis, asthma, blurred vision, bone marrow depression, bruise, cardiac arrhythmia, cardiac failure, change in appetite, colic, coma, confusion, conjunctivitis, cystitis, depression, desquamation, diaphoresis, drowsiness, dyspnea, dysuria, ecchymoses, eosinophilia, epistaxis, eructation, erythema, erythema multiforme, esophagitis, exacerbation of angina pectoris, exfoliative dermatitis, fever, fluid retention, flu-like symptoms, gastritis, GI inflammation, glomerulonephritis, glossitis, hallucination, hearing loss, hematemesis, hematuria, hemolytic anemia, hepatic failure, hepatitis, hepatotoxicity (idiosyncratic) (Chalasani 2014), hyperglycemia, hyperkalemia, hypertension, hypoglycemia, hypotension, infection, insomnia, interstitial nephritis, jaundice, leukopenia, lymphadenopathy, malaise, melena, meningitis, mood changes, myocardial infarction, nephrotic syndrome, nervousness, oliguria, onycholysis, palpitations, pancreatitis, pancytopenia, paresthesia, petechial rash, pneumonia, polydipsia, polyuria, positive ANA titer, proteinuria, purpura, rectal hemorrhage, reduced fertility (female), renal failure, respiratory depression, seizure, sepsis, serum sickness, skin photosensitivity, Stevens-Johnson syndrome, stomatitis, swelling of eye, syncope, tachycardia, thrombocytopenia, toxic epidermal necrolysis, tremor, urticaria, vasculitis, vertigo, vesiculobullous reaction, weakness, weight changes, xerostomia

General Dosage Range Oral: *Adults:* 20 mg once daily

Mechanism of Action Reversibly inhibits cyclooxygenase-1 and 2 (COX-1 and 2) enzymes, which results in decreased formation of prostaglandin precursors; has antipyretic, analgesic, and anti-inflammatory properties

Other proposed mechanisms not fully elucidated (and possibly contributing to the anti-inflammatory effect to varying degrees), include inhibiting chemotaxis, altering lymphocyte activity, inhibiting neutrophil aggregation/activation, and decreasing proinflammatory cytokine levels.

Pharmacodynamics/Kinetics

Onset of Action Analgesia: Oral: Within 1 hour; Maximum effect: 3 to 5 hours

Half-life Elimination

Children and Adolescents 7 to 16 years: 32.6 hours; Range: 22 to 40 hours (Makela 1991)

Adults: 50 hours

Time to Peak 3 to 5 hours; Suppository [Canadian product]: ~10 hours

Pregnancy Risk Factor C (first and second trimester)/ D (third trimester)

Pregnancy Considerations Adverse events were observed in some animal reproduction studies. NSAID exposure during the first trimester is not strongly associated with congenital malformations; however, cardiovascular anomalies and cleft palate have been observed following NSAID exposure in some studies (Ericson, 2001; Källén, 2003; Ofori, 2006). The use of a NSAID close to conception may be associated with an increased risk of miscarriage (Li, 2003; Nielsen, 2001; Nielsen, 2004). Nonteratogenic effects have been observed following NSAID administration during the third trimester including: Myocardial degenerative changes, prenatal constriction of the ductus arteriosus, fetal tricuspid regurgitation, failure of the ductus arteriosus to close postnatally; renal dysfunction or failure, oligohydramnios; gastrointestinal bleeding or perforation, increased risk of necrotizing enterocolitis; intracranial bleeding (including intraventricular hemorrhage), platelet dysfunction with resultant bleeding; pulmonary hypertension (Van den Veyver, 1993). Because they may cause premature closure of the ductus arteriosus, use of NSAIDs late in pregnancy should be avoided (use after 31 or 32 weeks gestation is not recommended by some clinicians) (Moise, 1993; Van den Veyver, 1993; Vermillion, 1997; Vermillion, 1998). The chronic use of NSAIDs in women of reproductive age may be associated with infertility that is reversible upon discontinuation of the medication (Smith, 1996).

Pitavastatin (pi TA va sta tin)

Related Information

Cardiovascular Diseases *on page 1752*

Brand Names: US Livalo

Pharmacologic Category Antilipemic Agent, HMG-CoA Reductase Inhibitor

Use Primary hyperlipidemia and mixed dyslipidemia: As an adjunctive therapy to diet to reduce elevated total cholesterol, low-density lipoprotein cholesterol (LDL-C), apolipoprotein B (apo B), and triglycerides (TG), and to increase high-density lipoprotein cholesterol (HDL-C) in adults with primary hyperlipidemia or mixed dyslipidemia

Local Anesthetic/Vasoconstrictor Precautions No information available to require special precautions

Effects on Dental Treatment Key adverse event(s) related to dental treatment: Assess unusual presentations of muscle weakness or myopathy resulting from lipid therapy such as patient having a difficult time brushing teeth or weakness with chewing. Refer patient back to their physician for evaluation and adjustment of lipid therapy.

Effects on Bleeding No information available to require special precautions

Adverse Reactions

1% to 10%:

Central nervous system: Headache (<2%)

Endocrine & metabolic: Increased serum glucose (<2%)

Gastrointestinal: Constipation (4%), diarrhea (3%)

Hepatic: Increased serum alkaline phosphatase (<2%), increased serum bilirubin (<2%), increased serum transaminases (<2%; usually transient)

Infection: Influenza (<2%)

Neuromuscular & skeletal: Back pain (4%), myalgia (2% to 3%), arthralgia (<2%), increased creatine phosphokinase (<2%)

Respiratory: Nasopharyngitis (<2%)

<1%, postmarketing, and/or case reports: Abdominal distress, abdominal pain, cognitive dysfunction (reversible; including amnesia, confusion, forgetfulness, memory impairment), depression, dizziness, elevated glycosylated hemoglobin (Hb A1c), erectile dysfunction, fatigue, hepatic failure, hepatitis, hypoesthesia, immune-mediated necrotizing myopathy, insomnia, interstitial pulmonary disease, jaundice, malaise, muscle spasm, nausea, peripheral neuropathy, pruritus, myopathy, rhabdomyolysis (with acute renal failure), skin rash, urticaria, weakness

General Dosage Range Dosage adjustment recommended in patients with renal impairment or on concomitant therapy

Oral: *Adults:* Initial: 2 mg once daily; Maintenance: 1 to 4 mg once daily (maximum: 4 mg/day)

Mechanism of Action Inhibitor of 3-hydroxy-3-methylglutaryl coenzyme A (HMG-CoA) reductase, the rate-limiting enzyme in cholesterol synthesis (reduces the production of mevalonic acid from HMG-CoA); this then results in a compensatory increase in the expression of LDL receptors on hepatocyte membranes and a stimulation of LDL catabolism. In addition to the ability of HMG-CoA reductase inhibitors to decrease levels of high-sensitivity C-reactive protein (hsCRP), they also possess pleiotropic properties including improved endothelial function, reduced inflammation at the site of the coronary plaque, inhibition of platelet aggregation, and anticoagulant effects (de Denus, 2002; Ray, 2005).

Pharmacodynamics/Kinetics

Half-life Elimination ~12 hours

Time to Peak ~1 hour

Pregnancy Considerations Adverse events have been observed in some animal reproduction studies. There are reports of congenital anomalies following maternal use of HMG-CoA reductase inhibitors in pregnancy; however, maternal disease, differences in specific agents used, and the low rates of exposure limit the interpretation of the available data (Godfrey 2012; Lecarpentier 2012). Cholesterol biosynthesis may be important in fetal development; serum cholesterol and triglycerides increase normally during pregnancy. The discontinuation of lipid lowering medications temporarily during pregnancy is not expected to have significant impact on the long term outcomes of primary hypercholesterolemia treatment.

Use of pitavastatin is contraindicated in pregnancy. HMG-CoA reductase inhibitors should be discontinued prior to pregnancy (ADA 2013). If treatment of dyslipidemias is needed in pregnant women or in women of reproductive age, other agents are preferred (Berglund 2012; Stone 2013). The manufacturer recommends administration to women of childbearing potential only when conception is highly unlikely and patients have been informed of potential hazards.

Plecanatide (ple KAN a tide)

Brand Names: US Trulance

Pharmacologic Category Gastrointestinal Agent, Miscellaneous; Guanylate Cyclase-C (GC-C) Agonist

Use Chronic idiopathic constipation: Treatment of chronic idiopathic constipation (CIC) in adults

Local Anesthetic/Vasoconstrictor Precautions No information available to require special precautions

Effects on Dental Treatment No significant effects or complications reported

Effects on Bleeding No information available to require special precautions

Adverse Reactions

1% to 10%:

Gastrointestinal: Diarrhea (5%), abdominal distension (<2%), abdominal tenderness (<2%), flatulence (<2%)

Hepatic: Increased serum ALT (<2%), increased serum AST (<2%)

Respiratory: Sinusitis (<2%), upper respiratory tract infection (<2%)

General Dosage Range Oral: *Adults:* 3 mg once daily

Mechanism of Action Plecanatide and its active metabolite bind and agonize guanylate cyclase-C on the luminal surface of intestinal epithelium. Intracellular and extracellular cyclic guanosine monophosphate (cGMP) concentrations are subsequently increased resulting in chloride and bicarbonate secretion into the intestinal lumen. Intestinal fluid increases and GI transit time is decreased.

Pregnancy Considerations Plecanatide and its metabolite are not measurable in plasma when used at recommended doses. Maternal use is not expected to result in fetal exposure.

Plerixafor (pler IX a fore)

Brand Names: US Mozobil

Brand Names: Canada Mozobil

Pharmacologic Category Hematopoietic Agent; Hematopoietic Stem Cell Mobilizer

Use Peripheral stem cell mobilization: Mobilization of hematopoietic stem cells (HSC) for collection and subsequent autologous transplantation (in combination with filgrastim) in patients with non-Hodgkin lymphoma (NHL) and multiple myeloma (MM)

Local Anesthetic/Vasoconstrictor Precautions No information available to require special precautions

Effects on Dental Treatment Key adverse event(s) related to dental treatment: Xerostomia (normal salivary flow resumes upon discontinuation).

Effects on Bleeding No information available to require special precautions

Adverse Reactions Adverse reactions reported with filgrastim combination therapy.

>10%:

Central nervous system: Fatigue (27%), headache (22%), dizziness (11%)

Gastrointestinal: Diarrhea (37%), nausea (34%)

Local: Injection site reaction (34%, including edema, erythema, hematoma, hemorrhage, induration, inflammation, irritation, pain, paresthesia, pruritus, skin rash, urticaria)

Neuromuscular & skeletal: Arthralgia (13%)

5% to 10%:

Central nervous system: Insomnia (7%)

Gastrointestinal: Vomiting (10%), flatulence (7%)

Hematologic & oncologic: Hyperleukocytosis (7%)

<5%, postmarketing, and/or case reports: Abdominal distension, abdominal distress, abdominal pain, abnormal dreams, anaphylaxis, constipation, diaphoresis, dyspepsia, dyspnea, hypersensitivity reaction, hypoxia, leukocytosis, malaise, musculoskeletal pain, nightmares, oral hypoesthesia, orthostatic hypotension, periorbital swelling, syncope, thrombocytopenia, xerostomia

General Dosage Range Dosage adjustment recommended in patients with renal impairment

SubQ: *Adults:* 20 mg fixed dose or 0.24 mg/kg/day (maximum dose: 40 mg daily)

Mechanism of Action Reversibly inhibits binding of stromal cell-derived factor-1-alpha (SDF-1α), expressed on bone marrow stromal cells, to the CXC chemokine receptor 4 (CXCR4), resulting in mobilization of hematopoietic stem and progenitor cells from bone marrow into peripheral blood. Plerixafor used in combination with filgrastim results in synergistic increase in CD34+ cell mobilization. Mobilized CD34+ cells are capable of engrafting with extended repopulating capacity.

Pharmacodynamics/Kinetics

Onset of Action Peak CD34+ mobilization (healthy volunteers): Plerixafor monotherapy: 6 to 9 hours after administration; Plerixafor + filgrastim: 10 to14 hours

Duration of Action Sustained elevation in CD34+ cells (healthy volunteers): 4 to 18 hours after administration

Half-life Elimination Terminal: 3 to 5 hours

Time to Peak Plasma: SubQ: 30 to 60 minutes

Pregnancy Risk Factor D

Pregnancy Considerations Adverse effects have been observed in animal reproduction studies. May cause fetal harm if administered to pregnant women. Women of childbearing potential should use effective contraceptive measures to avoid becoming pregnant during treatment.

Pneumococcal Conjugate Vaccine (10-Valent) (noo moe KOK al KON ju gate vak SEEN, ten vay lent)

Brand Names: Canada Synflorix

Pharmacologic Category Vaccine; Vaccine, Inactivated (Bacterial)

Use Note: Not approved in the US

Pneumococcal disease prevention: Immunization of infants ≥ 6 weeks and children through 5 years against *Streptococcus pneumoniae* invasive diseases, pneumonia, and acute otitis media caused by serotypes included in the vaccine

Local Anesthetic/Vasoconstrictor Precautions No information available to require special precautions

Effects on Dental Treatment No significant effects or complications reported

Effects on Bleeding No information available to require special precautions

Adverse Reactions *Incidence not specifically defined, but reported in the range of 1% to 10%.

>10%:

Central nervous system: Irritability (51% to 66%), drowsiness (33% to 58%)

Gastrointestinal: Anorexia (17% to 31%)

Local: Pain at injection site (23% to 57%), erythema at injection site (38% to 53%), swelling at injection site (28% to 37%)

Miscellaneous: Fever (rectal; ≥38°C ages <2 years: 26% to 37%; >39°C ages <2 years: 2% to 3%; >39°C ages 2 to 5 years: <1%; >40°C ages <2 years: <1%; ≥38°C ages 2 to 5 years*)

1% to 10%:

Local: Induration at injection site

<1%, postmarketing, and/or case reports: Apnea (in premature infants ≤28 weeks gestation), bleeding at injection site, crying (abnormal), diarrhea, hematoma at injection site, hypersensitivity reaction (allergic dermatitis, atopic dermatitis, eczema), injection site nodule, seizure (febrile and nonfebrile), skin rash, urticaria, vomiting

General Dosage Range IM:

Infants 6 weeks to 6 months: 0.5 mL dose at 2, 4 and 6 months (minimum interval of 1 month between each of the first 3 doses), followed by booster dose of 0.5 mL administered at 12-15 months (minimum interval of 6 months between doses 3 and 4) **or** 0.5 mL dose at 2 and 4 months (minimum interval of 2 months between doses 1 and 2), followed by an additional 0.5 mL dose at 11-12 months (minimum interval of 6 months between doses 2 and 3)

Infants 7-11 months (previously unvaccinated): 0.5 mL for 2 doses administered at least 1 month apart, followed by a third dose administered after 1 year of age (minimum interval of 2 months between doses 2 and 3)

Children 12 months to <6 years (previously unvaccinated): 0.5 mL for a total of 2 doses administered at least 2 months apart

Mechanism of Action Promotes active immunization against invasive disease caused by *S. pneumoniae* capsular serotypes 1, 4, 5, 6B, 7F, 9V, 14, 18C, 19F, and 23F, all which are individually conjugated to a carrier protein (protein D, tetanus toxoid, or diphtheria toxoid); the aluminum salt, a mineral adjuvant, enhances the antibody response.

Pregnancy Considerations Animal reproduction studies have not been conducted. Inactivated vaccines have not been shown to cause increased risks to the fetus (NCIRD/ACIP 2011). This product is indicated for use in infants and children.

Product Availability Not available in the US

Pneumococcal Conjugate Vaccine (13-Valent)

(noo moe KOK al KON ju gate vak SEEN, thur TEEN vay lent)

Brand Names: US Prevnar 13

Brand Names: Canada Prevnar 13

Pharmacologic Category Vaccine; Vaccine, Inactivated (Bacterial)

Use

Pneumococcal disease prevention:

Active immunization of infants ≥6 weeks, children, adolescents, and adults for prevention of invasive disease caused by *Streptococcus pneumoniae* serotypes contained in the vaccine

Active immunization of infants ≥6 weeks and children less than 6 years for the prevention of otitis media caused by *S. pneumoniae* serotypes 4, 6B, 9V, 14, 18C, 19F, and 23F

Active immunization of adolescents ≥18 years and adults for the prevention of pneumonia caused by *S. pneumoniae* serotypes contained in the vaccine

The Advisory Committee on Immunization Practices (ACIP) recommends routine vaccination for the following (ACIP [Kobayashi 2015]; CDC/ACIP [Nuorti 2010]):

All infants and children age 2 to 59 months

Children 60 to 71 months with underlying medical conditions including:

Immunocompetent children with chronic heart disease (particularly cyanotic congenital heart disease and heart failure), chronic lung disease (including asthma if treated with high dose corticosteroids), diabetes, cerebrospinal fluid leaks, or cochlear implants

Children with functional or anatomic asplenia, including sickle cell disease or other hemoglobinopathies, congenital or acquired asplenia, or splenic dysfunction.

Children with immunocompromising conditions including congenital immunodeficiency (includes B or T cell deficiency, compliment deficiencies and phagocytic disorders; excludes chronic granulomatous disease), HIV infection, chronic renal failure, nephrotic syndrome, leukemia, lymphoma, Hodgkin disease, generalized malignancies, solid organ transplant, or other diseases requiring immunosuppressive drugs (including long term systemic corticosteroids and radiation therapy)

Children who received ≥1 dose of PCV7

Note: Routine use is not recommended for healthy children ≥5 years.

Children ≥6 years and Adolescents ≤18 years (CDC/ACIP, 62[25] 2013), and Adults ≥19 years (CDC/ACIP, 61[40] 2012): The ACIP also recommends routine vaccination for persons with the following underlying medical conditions:

Immunocompetent persons with cerebrospinal fluid leaks or cochlear implants

Persons with functional or anatomic asplenia, including sickle cell disease or other hemoglobinopathies, congenital or acquired asplenia

Persons with immunocompromising conditions including congenital or acquired immunodeficiency (includes B or T cell deficiency, compliment deficiencies and phagocytic disorders; excludes chronic granulomatous disease), HIV infection, chronic renal failure, nephrotic syndrome, leukemia, lymphoma, Hodgkin disease, generalized malignancies, solid organ transplant, multiple myeloma, or other diseases requiring immunosuppressive drugs (including long term systemic corticosteroids and radiation therapy)

All adults ≥65 years (CDC/ACIP [Tomczyk 2014])

Local Anesthetic/Vasoconstrictor Precautions No information available to require special precautions

Effects on Dental Treatment No significant effects or complications reported

Effects on Bleeding No information available to require special precautions

Adverse Reactions

>10%:

Central nervous system: Chills (adults), drowsiness, fatigue (adults), headache (adults), insomnia, irritability (infants and children)

Dermatologic: Skin rash (adults: >10%; children and infants: >1%; including urticaria-like rash)

Gastrointestinal: Decreased appetite

Local: Erythema at injection site, pain at injection site (adults), swelling at injection site, tenderness at injection site

Neuromuscular & skeletal: Arthralgia (adults), decreased range of motion (arm), myalgia (adults)

Miscellaneous: Fever

1% to 10%:

Dermatologic: Urticaria

Gastrointestinal: Diarrhea, vomiting

<1%, postmarketing, and/or case reports: Anaphylactic shock, anaphylactoid reaction, anaphylaxis, angioedema, apnea, injection site inflammation (dermatitis), injection-site pruritus, crying (abnormal), cyanosis, erythema multiforme, febrile seizures, hypersensitivity reaction (bronchospasm, dyspnea, facial edema), hypotonia, lymphadenopathy (injection site), pallor, seizure, urticaria at injection site

General Dosage Range IM:

Infants and Children 6 weeks to <2 years: 0.5 mL at approximately 2-month intervals for 3 consecutive doses, followed by a fourth dose of 0.5 mL at 12 to 15 months of age

Infants 7 to 11 months (previously unvaccinated): 0.5 mL for a total of 3 doses, 2 doses at least 4 weeks apart, followed by a third dose at 12 to 15 months (at least 2 months after second dose)

Children 12 to 23 months (previously unvaccinated) and Children 24 to 71 months (previously unvaccinated) with underlying conditions: 0.5 mL for a total of 2 doses, separated by at least 8 weeks

Healthy Children 24 to 59 months (previously unvaccinated) and Children 6 to 18 years at high risk for invasive pneumococcal disease: 0.5 mL as a single dose

Children 14 to 59 months and Children 60 to 71 months with an underlying medical condition (previously completing vaccination with PCV7): 0.5 mL supplemental dose

Children 6 through 17 years: 0.5 mL as a single dose

Adults: 0.5 mL as a single dose

Mechanism of Action Promotes active immunization against invasive disease caused by *S. pneumoniae* capsular serotypes 1, 3, 4, 5, 6A, 6B, 7F, 9V, 14, 18C, 19A, 19F, and 23F, all which are individually conjugated to CRM197 protein

Pregnancy Considerations Animal reproduction studies have not shown adverse fetal effects. Inactivated vaccines have not been shown to cause increased risks to the fetus (NCIRD/ACIP 2011).

Podofilox (poe DOF il oks)

Brand Names: US Condylox

Brand Names: Canada Condyline; Wartec

Pharmacologic Category Keratolytic Agent; Topical Skin Product

Use Treatment of external genital warts (solution and gel) and perianal warts (gel only)

Local Anesthetic/Vasoconstrictor Precautions No information available to require special precautions

Effects on Dental Treatment No significant effects or complications reported

Effects on Bleeding No information available to require special precautions

Adverse Reactions

Gel, topical:

>10%:

Central nervous system: Localized burning (12% to 37%), local pain (12% to 24%)

Dermatologic: Skin erosion (9% to 27%)

Hematologic & oncologic: Local hemorrhage (<1% to 19%)

Local: Local inflammation (9% to 32%), local pruritus (8% to 32%)

1% to 10%:

Central nervous system: Headache (7%)

Dermatologic: Stinging of the skin (7%), erythema (5%)

<1%, postmarketing, and/or case reports: Crusted skin, dermal ulcer, desquamation, edema, skin blister, skin discoloration, skin fissure, skin rash, skin tenderness, tingling of skin, xeroderma

Solution, topical:

>10%:

Central nervous system: Localized burning (female 78%; male 64%), local pain (female 72%; male 50%)

Dermatologic: Skin erosion (67%)

Local: Local inflammation (male 71%; female 63%), local pruritus (female 65%; male 50%)

<1%, postmarketing, and/or case reports: Body odor, dermal ulcer, dizziness, hematuria, insomnia, local hemorrhage, localized edema, localized vesiculation, pain, skin tenderness, tingling of skin, vomiting, xeroderma

General Dosage Range Topical: *Adults:* Apply twice daily for 3 consecutive days, then withhold use for 4 consecutive days; may repeat cycle up to 4 times

Mechanism of Action Exact mechanism of action is unknown; causes necrosis of visible wart tissue

Pregnancy Risk Factor C

Pregnancy Considerations Teratogenic events have not been observed in animal reproduction studies with topical administration. Podofilox should not be used during pregnancy (CDC [Workowski 2015])

Polidocanol (pol i DOE kuh nol)

Brand Names: US Asclera; Varithena

Brand Names: Canada Varithena

Pharmacologic Category Sclerosing Agent

Use Varicose veins:

Asclera: Treatment of uncomplicated spider veins (varicose veins 1 mm or less in diameter) and uncomplicated reticular veins (varicose veins 1 to 3 mm in diameter) in the lower extremity.

Varithena: Treatment of incompetent great saphenous veins, accessory saphenous veins, and visible varicosities of the great saphenous vein system above and below the knee.

Local Anesthetic/Vasoconstrictor Precautions No information available to require special precautions

Effects on Dental Treatment No significant effects or complications reported

Effects on Bleeding No information available to require special precautions

Adverse Reactions

>10%: Local: Hematoma at injection site (42%), irritation at injection site (41%), local discoloration (38%), pain at injection site (24%), local pruritus (19%), warm sensation at injection site (16%)

1% to 10%: Local: Venous thrombosis at injection site (6%)

<1%, postmarketing, and/or case reports: Allergic dermatitis, anaphylactic shock, angioedema, asthma, cerebrovascular accident, circulatory shock, confusion, deep vein thrombosis, dizziness, dyspnea, fever, flushing, hypertrichosis, loss of consciousness, migraine, neurologic injury, palpitations, paresthesia, pulmonary embolism, skin hyperpigmentation, tissue necrosis at injection site, urticaria, vasculitis, vasodepressor syncope

General Dosage Range IV: *Adults:* Asclera: 0.1 to 0.3 mL injection (0.5% or 1% solution) per session (maximum: 10 mL/session); Varithena: Up to 5 mL injection (1% solution) per session (maximum: 5 mL per injection; 15 mL per session)

Mechanism of Action Acts by irritation of the vein intimal endothelium and causes thrombosis formation leading to occlusion of the injected vein

Pharmacodynamics/Kinetics

Half-life Elimination

Asclera: 90 minutes

Varithena: 102 to 153 minutes

Pregnancy Risk Factor C

Pregnancy Considerations Adverse events have been observed in animal reproduction studies. Do not use polidocanol during pregnancy.

Poliovirus Vaccine (Inactivated)

(POE lee oh VYE rus vak SEEN, in ak ti VAY ted)

Brand Names: US IPOL

Brand Names: Canada Imovax Polio

Pharmacologic Category Vaccine; Vaccine, Inactivated (Viral)

Use Poliovirus prevention:

Active immunization of infants (≥6 weeks [US labeling]; ≥2 months [Canadian labeling]), children, adolescents, and adults for prevention of poliomyelitis caused by poliovirus types 1, 2, and 3.

US labeling: Infants (as young as 6 weeks), children, adolescents, and adults

Canadian labeling: Infants (as young as 2 months), children, adolescents, and adults

The Advisory Committee on Immunization Practices (ACIP) recommends routine vaccination for the following:

- All infants and children (first dose given at 2 months of age) (CDC/ACIP, 58[30] 2009)

Routine immunization of adults in the United States is generally not recommended. Adults with previous wild poliovirus disease, who have never been immunized, or those who are incompletely immunized may receive inactivated poliovirus vaccine if they fall into one of the following categories (CDC/ACIP [Prevots 2000]):

- Travelers to regions or countries where poliomyelitis is endemic or epidemic
- Healthcare workers in close contact with patients who may be excreting poliovirus
- Laboratory workers handling specimens that may contain poliovirus
- Members of communities or specific population groups with diseases caused by wild poliovirus
- Incompletely vaccinated or unvaccinated adults in a household or with other close contact with children receiving oral poliovirus (may be at increased risk of vaccine associated paralytic poliomyelitis)

Local Anesthetic/Vasoconstrictor Precautions No information available to require special precautions

Effects on Dental Treatment No significant effects or complications reported

Effects on Bleeding No information available to require special precautions

Adverse Reactions

Percentages noted with concomitant administration of DTP or DTaP vaccine and observed within 48 hours of injection.

>10%:

Central nervous system: Irritability (7% to 65%; most common in infants 2 months of age), fatigue (4% to 61%)

Gastrointestinal: Anorexia (1% to 17%)

Local: Tenderness at injection site (≤29%), swelling at injection site (≤11%)

1% to 10%:

Central nervous system: Excessive crying (≤1%; reported within 72 hours)

Gastrointestinal: Vomiting (1% to 3%)

Local: Erythema at injection site (≤3%)

Miscellaneous: Fever (>39°C: ≤4%)

<1%, postmarketing, and/or case reports: Agitation, anaphylactic shock, anaphylaxis, arthralgia, drowsiness, febrile seizures, headache, hypersensitivity reaction, lymphadenopathy, myalgia, paresthesia, seizure, skin rash, urticaria

General Dosage Range IM, SubQ:

Children: Primary immunization: Administer three 0.5 mL doses at 2, 4, and 6 to 18 months of age. Booster dose: 0.5 mL at 4 to 6 years of age; Minimum interval between booster and previous dose is 6 months.

Adults (previously unvaccinated): Administer 0.5 mL per dose for a total of 3 doses given as follows: Two 0.5 mL doses administered at 1- to 2-month intervals followed by a third dose 6 to 12 months later.

Mechanism of Action As an inactivated virus vaccine, poliovirus vaccine induces active immunity against poliovirus types 1, 2, and 3 infection

Pregnancy Considerations Animal reproduction studies have not been conducted. Although adverse effects of IPV have not been documented in pregnant women or their fetuses, vaccination of pregnant women should be avoided on theoretical grounds. Pregnant women at increased risk for infection and requiring immediate protection against polio may be administered the vaccine (CDC/ACIP [Prevots 2000]).

Polycarbophil (pol i KAR boe fil)

Brand Names: US Fiber Laxative [OTC]; Fiber-Caps [OTC]; Fiber-Lax [OTC]; FiberCon [OTC]; FiberGen [OTC]; Konsyl Fiber [OTC]

Pharmacologic Category Antidiarrheal; Fiber Supplement; Laxative, Bulk-Producing

Use Treatment of constipation or diarrhea

Local Anesthetic/Vasoconstrictor Precautions No information available to require special precautions

Effects on Dental Treatment Oral medication should be given at least 1 hour prior to taking the bulk-producing laxative in order to prevent decreased absorption of medication.

Effects on Bleeding No information available to require special precautions

Adverse Reactions

Frequency not defined: Gastrointestinal: Gastrointestinal fullness

General Dosage Range Oral:

Children 6-12 years: 625 mg calcium polycarbophil 1-4 times/day

Children ≥12 years and Adults: 1250 mg calcium polycarbophil 1-4 times/day

Mechanism of Action Restoring a more normal moisture level and providing bulk in the patient's intestinal tract

Pregnancy Considerations When administered with adequate fluids, use is considered safe for the treatment of occasional constipation during pregnancy (Wald, 2003).

Polyethylene Glycol 3350

(pol i ETH i leen GLY kol 3350)

Brand Names: US GaviLAX [OTC]; GlycoLax [OTC]; HealthyLax [OTC]; MiraLax [OTC]; PEGyLAX

Brand Names: Canada Lax-A-Day; Peg 3350; Pegalax; Relaxa

Pharmacologic Category Laxative, Osmotic

Use Occasional constipation: Treatment of occasional constipation

Local Anesthetic/Vasoconstrictor Precautions No information available to require special precautions

Effects on Dental Treatment No significant effects or complications reported

Effects on Bleeding No information available to require special precautions

Adverse Reactions

Frequency not defined.

Dermatologic: Urticaria

Gastrointestinal: Abdominal cramps, bloating of the stomach, diarrhea, flatulence, nausea

General Dosage Range Oral: *Adolescents ≥17 years and Adults:* 17 g (~1 heaping tablespoon) dissolved in 120 to 240 mL (4 to 8 ounces) of beverage once daily

Mechanism of Action An osmotic agent, polyethylene glycol 3350 causes water retention in the stool; increases stool frequency.

Pharmacodynamics/Kinetics

Onset of Action Oral: 24 to 96 hours

Pregnancy Considerations Polyethylene glycol (PEG) has minimal systemic absorption and would be unlikely to cause fetal malformations. However, until additional information is available, use to treat constipation in pregnancy should be avoided unless other preferred methods are inadequate (Mahadevan 2006). Use as a bowel preparation prior to colonoscopy in pregnant women may be considered (Wexner 2006).

Polyethylene Glycol-Electrolyte Solution

(pol i ETH i leen GLY kol ee LEK troe lite soe LOO shun)

Brand Names: US Colyte; GaviLyte-C; GaviLyte-G; GaviLyte-N; GoLYTELY; MoviPrep; NuLYTELY; TriLyte

Brand Names: Canada Colyte; Klean-Prep; PegLyte

Pharmacologic Category Laxative, Osmotic

Use Bowel cleansing prior to colonoscopy or barium enema X-ray examination

Local Anesthetic/Vasoconstrictor Precautions No information available to require special precautions

Effects on Dental Treatment No significant effects or complications reported

Effects on Bleeding No information available to require special precautions

Adverse Reactions

>10%:

Central nervous system: Sleep disorder (35%; evening prep vs oral sodium phosphate solution [90 mL]), rigors (34%; evening prep vs oral sodium phosphate solution [90 mL]), malaise (18% to 27%; MoviPrep split dose vs 4 L PEG with electrolytes [18%]; evening dose vs oral sodium phosphate solution [90 mL] [53%])

Endocrine & metabolic: Increased thirst (<47%)

Gastrointestinal: Abdominal distention (<60%; evening prep vs oral sodium phosphate solution [90 mL]), anorectal pain (<52%; evening prep vs oral sodium phosphate solution [90 mL]), bloating (≤50%), nausea (14% to ≤50%; split dose vs 4 L PEG with electrolytes [20%]; evening prep vs oral sodium phosphate solution [90 mL] [47%]), abdominal pain (6% to 39%; evening prep vs oral sodium phosphate solution [90 mL] [32%]; split dose vs PEG with electrolytes [6%]), hunger (30%; evening prep vs oral sodium phosphate solution [90 mL]), vomiting (7% to 12%; evening MoviPrep vs oral sodium phosphate solution (90 mL) [8%]; split dose vs PEG with electrolytes [13%])

1% to 10%:

Central nervous system: Dizziness (3% to 7%; evening prep vs oral sodium phosphate solution [90 mL]), headache (2%; evening prep vs oral sodium phosphate solution [90 mL])

Endocrine & metabolic: Hypokalemia (children 0%; evening prep vs oral sodium phosphate solution [90 mL] [6%])

Gastrointestinal: Dyspepsia (1% to 3%)

Frequency not defined, postmarketing, and/or case reports: Abdominal cramps, anaphylaxis, angioedema, aspiration, asystole (older adults >60 years), chest tightness, chills, dehydration, dermatitis, dyspnea, epigastric fullness, esophageal perforation (older adults >60 years), facial edema, fever, flatulence, hypersensitivity reaction, ischemic colitis, lip edema, Mallory-Weiss syndrome (older adults >60 years), pruritus, pulmonary edema (older adults >60 years), rhinorrhea, seizure, shock, skin rash, tightness in chest and throat, tongue edema, upper gastrointestinal hemorrhage (older adults >60 years), urticaria

General Dosage Range

Nasogastric:

Infants ≥6 months, Children, and Adolescents (GaviLyte-N, NuLYTELY, TriLyte): 25 mL/kg/hour until the rectal effluent is clear (maximum total dose: 4 L)

Adults (CoLyte, GaviLyte-C, GaviLyte-G, GaviLyte-N, GoLYTELY, NuLYTELY, TriLyte): 20-30 mL/minute (1.2-1.8 L/hour) until 4 L are administered or the rectal effluent is clear

Oral:

Infants ≥6 months, Children, and Adolescents (GaviLyte-N, NuLYTELY, TriLyte): 25 mL/kg/hour until the rectal effluent is clear (maximum total dose: 4 L)

Adults: CoLyte, GaviLyte-C, GaviLyte-G, GaviLyte-N, GoLYTELY, NuLYTELY, TriLyte: 240 mL (8 oz) every 10 minutes, until 4 L are consumed or the rectal effluent is clear; MoviPrep: 240 mL (8 oz) every 15 minutes until 1 L consumed; repeat 1 time

Mechanism of Action Induces catharsis by strong electrolyte and osmotic effects

Pharmacodynamics/Kinetics

Onset of Action Oral: ~1 hour

Pregnancy Risk Factor C

Pregnancy Considerations Animal reproduction studies have not been conducted. Information related to the use of polyethylene glycol-electrolyte solution in pregnancy is limited (Neri, 2004). Colonoscopy in pregnant women is generally reserved for strong indications or life-threatening emergencies; until additional safety data for polyethylene glycol-electrolyte solution is available, other agents may be preferred for this purpose (Siddiqui, 2006; Wexner, 2006).

Polymyxin B (pol i MIKS in bee)

Pharmacologic Category Antibiotic, Irrigation; Antibiotic, Miscellaneous

Use

Infections, acute:

Pseudomonal infections: Treatment of infections of the urinary tract, meninges, and bloodstream caused by susceptible strains of *Pseudomonas aeruginosa*

Serious infections: Treatment of serious infections caused by susceptible strains of the following organisms, when less potentially toxic drugs are ineffective or contraindicated: *H. influenzae*, specifically meningeal infections; *Escherichia coli*, specifically urinary tract infections; *Aerobacter aerogenes*, specifically bacteremia; *Klebsiella pneumoniae*, specifically bacteremia

In meningeal infections, polymyxin B sulfate should be administered only by the intrathecal route.

Local Anesthetic/Vasoconstrictor Precautions No information available to require special precautions

Effects on Dental Treatment No significant effects or complications reported

Effects on Bleeding No information available to require special precautions

Adverse Reactions

Frequency not defined.

Cardiovascular: Facial flushing

Central nervous system: Neurotoxicity (includes ataxia, blurred vision, drowsiness, irritability, numbness of extremities oral paresthesia), dizziness, drug fever, meningitis (intrathecal administration)

Dermatologic: Urticaria

Endocrine & metabolic: Hypocalcemia, hypochloremia, hypokalemia, hyponatremia

Genitourinary: Nephrotoxicity

Hypersensitivity: Anaphylactoid reaction

Local: Pain at injection site

Neuromuscular & skeletal: Neuromuscular blockade, weakness

General Dosage Range Manufacturer's prescribing information recommends a dosage adjustment in patients with renal impairment.

IM:

Infants and Children <2 years: Up to 40,000 units/kg/day divided every 6 hours

Children ≥2 years, Adolescents, and Adults: 25,000 to 30,000 units/kg/day divided every 4 to 6 hours

IV:

Infants and Children <2 years: Up to 40,000 units/kg/day divided every 12 hours

Children ≥2 years, Adolescents, and Adults: 15,000 to 25,000 units/kg/day divided every 12 hours

Intrathecal:

Infants and Children <2 years: 20,000 units daily for 3 to 4 days, then 25,000 units every other day

Children ≥2 years, Adolescents, and Adults: 50,000 units daily for 3 to 4 days, then every other day

Ophthalmic: *Children ≥2 years, Adolescents, and Adults:* Initial: 1 to 3 drops per hour; Reduce frequency as clinically indicated

Mechanism of Action Binds to phospholipids, alters permeability, and damages the bacterial cytoplasmic membrane permitting leakage of intracellular constituents

Pharmacodynamics/Kinetics

Half-life Elimination 6 hours, increased with reduced renal function (Evans 1999)

Time to Peak Serum: IM: Within 2 hours (Hoeprich 1970)

Pregnancy Considerations [US Boxed Warning]: Safety in pregnant women has not been established. Animal reproduction studies are lacking. A teratogenic potential has not been identified for polymyxin b, but very limited data is available (Heinonen 1977; Kazy 2005). Based on the relative toxicity compared to other antibiotics, systemic use in pregnancy is not recommended (Knothe 1985). Due to poor tissue diffusion, topical use would be expected to have only minimal risk to the mother or fetus (Leachman 2006).

Polysaccharide-Iron Complex

(pol i SAK a ride-EYE ern KOM pleks)

Brand Names: US EZFE 200 [OTC]; Ferrex 150 [OTC]; Ferric x-150 [OTC]; FerUS [OTC] [DSC]; iFerex 150 [OTC]; Myferon 150 [OTC]; NovaFerrum 125 [OTC]; NovaFerrum 50 [OTC]; NovaFerrum Pediatric Drops [OTC]; Nu-Iron [OTC]; PIC 200 [OTC]; Poly-Iron 150 [OTC]

Pharmacologic Category Iron Salt

Use Iron deficiency anemia: Management (prevention and treatment) of iron deficiency anemia

Local Anesthetic/Vasoconstrictor Precautions No information available to require special precautions

Effects on Dental Treatment No significant effects or complications reported

Effects on Bleeding No information available to require special precautions

Adverse Reactions

>10%: Gastrointestinal: Constipation, darkening of stools, epigastric pain, gastrointestinal irritation, nausea, stomach cramps, vomiting

1% to 10%:

Gastrointestinal: Dental discoloration, diarrhea, heartburn

Genitourinary: Urine discoloration

<1%, postmarketing, and/or case reports: Local irritation

General Dosage Range Oral:

Infants and Children <4 years: 15 mg daily

Children ≥12 years: 50 mg daily

Adults: 100-300 mg daily

Pharmacodynamics/Kinetics

Onset of Action Hematologic response: Red blood cells form within 3 to 10 days; similar onset as parenteral iron salts; Maximum effect: Peak reticulocytosis occurs in 5 to 10 days, and hemoglobin values increase within 2 to 4 weeks

Pregnancy Considerations It is recommended that pregnant women meet the dietary requirements of iron with diet and/or supplements in order to prevent adverse events associated with iron deficiency anemia in pregnancy. Treatment of iron deficiency anemia in pregnant women is the same as in nonpregnant women and in most cases, oral iron preparations may be used. Except in severe cases of maternal anemia, the fetus achieves normal iron stores regardless of maternal concentrations.

Polyvinylpyrrolidone and Sodium Hyaluronate

(pol e VI nil pi ROL i don & SOW dee um hye al yoor ON ate)

Brand Names: US Ameseal™

Generic Availability (US) No

Pharmacologic Category Protectant, Topical

Dental Use Treatment of mouth ulcers

Local Anesthetic/Vasoconstrictor Precautions No information available to require special precautions

Effects on Dental Treatment No significant effects or complications reported

Effects on Bleeding No information available to require special precautions

Dental Usual Dosage Spray: Direct the spray applicator towards the lesions and spray 3 times or as needed to cover the affected area. Repeat throughout the day as necessary.

Mechanism of Action Polyvinylpyrrolidone (PVP) sets up a barrier at application site to protect ulcer from irritants and irritation

Dosage Forms Excipient information presented when available (limited, particularly for generics); consult specific product labeling.

Solution, topical [spray]: 15 mL

Pomalidomide (poe ma LID oh mide)

Brand Names: US Pomalyst

Brand Names: Canada Pomalyst

Pharmacologic Category Angiogenesis Inhibitor; Antineoplastic Agent; Immunomodulator, Systemic

Use Multiple myeloma, relapsed/refractory: Treatment of multiple myeloma (in combination with dexamethasone) in patients who have received at least 2 prior therapies, including lenalidomide and a proteasome inhibitor, and have demonstrated disease progression on or within 60 days of completion of the last therapy.

Local Anesthetic/Vasoconstrictor Precautions No information available to require special precautions

Effects on Dental Treatment No significant effects or complications reported

Effects on Bleeding Chemotherapy may result in significant myelosuppression, neutropenia (50% to 52%; grades 3/4: 43% to 47%), anemia (38%; grades 3/4: 22%), thrombocytopenia (25%; grades 3/4: 22%), leukopenia (11%; grades 3/4: 6%). In patients who are under active treatment with these agents, medical consult is suggested.

Adverse Reactions Frequency not always defined.

Cardiovascular: Peripheral edema (25%), angina pectoris, congestive cardiac failure, hypotension, myocardial infarction, septic shock, syncope

Central nervous system: Fatigue (≤58%), dizziness (22%; grades 3/4: <5%), peripheral neuropathy (22%), neuropathy (18%; grades 3/4: 2%), headache (15%), anxiety (13%), confusion (12%; grades 3/4: 6%), chills (10%), insomnia (7%), pain (6%), altered mental status, depression, falling, noncardiac chest pain

Dermatologic: Skin rash (21%), pruritus (15%), xeroderma (9%), hyperhidrosis (8%), cellulitis

Endocrine & metabolic: Hypercalcemia (22%; grades 3/4: 10%), hypokalemia (12%; grades 3/4: <5%), hyperglycemia (11%; grades 3/4: <5%), hyponatremia (11%; grades 3/4: <5%), dehydration (<10%; grade 3/4: 5%), hypocalcemia (6%), weight gain (≤5%)

Gastrointestinal: Constipation (36%), nausea (36%), diarrhea (35%), decreased appetite (23%), weight loss (15%), vomiting (14%), abdominal pain, *Clostridium difficile*, increased serum alanine aminotransferase

Genitourinary: Urinary tract infection (10%, grades 3/4: 2%), urosepsis

Hematologic & oncologic: Neutropenia (53%; grades 3/4: 48%), anemia (38%; grades 3/4: 23%), thrombocytopenia (26%; grades 3/4: 22%), leukopenia (13%; grades 3/4: 7%), febrile neutropenia (<10%), lymphocytopenia (4%; grades 3/4: 2%), decreased hemoglobin

Infection: Sepsis (<10%), bacteremia, pneumonia due to *Streptococcal* species, viral infection

Neuromuscular & skeletal: Weakness (≤58%), back pain (35%), musculoskeletal chest pain (23%), muscle spasm (22%), arthralgia (17%), myasthenia (14%), musculoskeletal pain (12%), ostealgia (12%), tremor (10%), limb pain (8%), fracture, vertebral compression fracture

Renal: Increased serum creatinine (19%), renal failure (15%)

Respiratory: Upper respiratory tract infection (37%), dyspnea (36%), pneumonia (28%), cough (17%), epistaxis (17%), productive cough (9%), oropharyngeal pain (6%), bronchospasm, lobar pneumonia, pulmonary infection

Miscellaneous: Fever (23%), night sweats (5%), failure to thrive, multiorgan failure, physical health deterioration

<1%, postmarketing, and/or case reports: Acute cytolytic hepatitis, acute hepatoxicity, acute myelocytic leukemia, atrial fibrillation, hepatic failure, hepatitis, hepatitis (cytolytic), hyperbilirubinemia, hyperkalemia, hypersensitivity reaction, increased liver enzymes, increased serum ALT, interstitial pulmonary disease, liver steatosis, neutropenic sepsis, pancytopenia, pelvic pain, pneumonia (*Pneumocystis jiroveci*), pneumonitis, prolonged prothrombin time, pulmonary fibrosis, respiratory syncytial virus infection, thrombosis, tumor lysis syndrome, urinary retention, vertigo, weight gain

General Dosage Range Dosage adjustment recommended in patients with renal or hepatic impairment, who develop toxicities or who are on concomitant therapy.

Oral: *Adults:* 4 mg once daily on days 1 to 21 of 28-day cycles

Mechanism of Action Induces cell cycle arrest and apoptosis directly in multiple myeloma cells; enhances T cell- and natural killer (NK) cell-mediated cytotoxicity; inhibits production of proinflammatory cytokines tumor necrosis factor-α (TNF-α), IL-1, IL-6, and IL-12; inhibits angiogenesis (Zhu 2013)

Pharmacodynamics/Kinetics

Half-life Elimination ~9.5 hours (healthy subjects); ~7.5 hours (multiple myeloma patients)

Time to Peak 2 to 3 hours

Pregnancy Considerations [US Boxed Warning]: Pomalidomide is an analogue of thalidomide (a known human teratogen) and may cause severe birth defects or embryo-fetal death if taken during pregnancy. Pomalidomide cannot be used in women who are pregnant or may become pregnant during therapy. Obtain 2 negative pregnancy tests prior to initiation of treatment; 2 forms of contraception (or abstain from heterosexual intercourse) must be used at least 4 weeks prior to, during, and for ≥4 weeks after pomalidomide treatment (and during treatment interruptions) in females of reproductive potential. In order to decrease the risk of embryo-fetal exposure, pomalidomide is available only through a restricted distribution program (Pomalyst REMS).

Studies in animals have shown evidence of fetal abnormalities and use is contraindicated in women who are or may become pregnant. Women of childbearing potential should be treated only if they are able to comply with the conditions of the Pomalyst REMS Program. Reliable contraception is required even with a history of infertility (unless due to hysterectomy or if ≥24 consecutive months postmenopausal (natural). Reliable methods of birth control include one highly effective method (eg, tubal ligation, IUD, hormonal [birth control pills, injections, hormonal patches, vaginal rings, or implants], or partner's vasectomy) and one additional effective method (eg, male latex or synthetic condom, diaphragm, or cervical cap). Pregnancy tests should be performed 10 to 14 days and 24 hours prior to beginning therapy; weekly for the first 4 weeks and then every 4 weeks (every 2 weeks if menstrual cycle irregular) thereafter and during therapy interruptions for at least 4 weeks after discontinuation. Pomalidomide must be immediately discontinued for a missed period, abnormal pregnancy test or abnormal menstrual bleeding; refer patient to a reproductive toxicity specialist if pregnancy occurs during treatment. Pomalidomide is present in the semen of males taking this medication. Males (including those vasectomized) should use a latex or synthetic condom during any sexual contact with women of childbearing age during treatment, during treatment interruptions, and for 28 days after discontinuation. Male patients should not donate sperm. Any suspected fetal exposure should be reported to the FDA via the MedWatch program (1-800-332-1088) and to Celgene Corporation (1-888-423-5436).

Prescribing and Access Restrictions

As a requirement of the REMS program, access to this medication is restricted. Pomalidomide is approved for marketing in the US only under a Food and Drug Administration (FDA) approved, restricted distribution program called Pomalyst REMS (celgeneriskmanagement.com or 1-888-423-5436). Prescribers and pharmacies must be certified with the program to prescribe or dispense pomalidomide; patients must comply with the program requirements. No more than a 4-week supply should be dispensed. Prescriptions must be filled within 7 days (for females of reproductive potential) or within 30 days (for all other patients) after the authorization number is obtained. Subsequent prescriptions may be filled only if fewer than 7 days of therapy remain on the previous prescription. A new prescription is required for further dispensing (a telephone prescription may not be accepted). Pregnancy testing with a sensitivity of at least 50 milliunits/mL is required for females of childbearing potential.

In Canada, pomalidomide is only available through a restricted distribution program called RevAid. Only physicians and pharmacists registered with the program are authorized to prescribe or dispense pomalidomide. Patients must also be registered and meet all conditions of the program. Two negative pregnancy tests with a sensitivity of at least 25 milliunits/mL are required prior to initiating therapy in women of childbearing potential. Further information is available at 1-888-738-2431 or www.RevAid.ca.

PONATinib (poe NA ti nib)

Brand Names: US Iclusig

Brand Names: Canada Iclusig

Pharmacologic Category Antineoplastic Agent, BCR-ABL Tyrosine Kinase Inhibitor; Antineoplastic Agent, Tyrosine Kinase Inhibitor

Use

Acute lymphoblastic leukemia: Treatment of Philadelphia chromosome-positive acute lymphoblastic leukemia (Ph+ ALL) in patients for whom no other tyrosine kinase inhibitor therapy is indicated or who are T315I-positive.

Chronic myeloid leukemia: Treatment of chronic myeloid leukemia (CML) in chronic, accelerated, or blast phase in patients for whom no other tyrosine kinase inhibitor therapy is indicated or who are T315I-positive.

Limitations of use: Ponatinib is not indicated and not recommended for treatment of newly diagnosed chronic phase CML.

Local Anesthetic/Vasoconstrictor Precautions Ponatinib may cause hypertension; monitor blood pressure prior to vasoconstrictor use

Effects on Dental Treatment Key adverse event(s) related to dental treatment: Oral mucositis

Effects on Bleeding Chemotherapy may result in significant myelosuppression, potentially including significant reduction in platelet counts (thrombocytopenia grades 3/4: 36% to 57%) and altered hemostasis. In patients who are under active treatment with these agents, medical consult is suggested.

Adverse Reactions

>10%:

Cardiovascular: Hypertension (53% to 71%), peripheral edema (13% to 22%; grades 3/4: ≤1%), arterial ischemia (3% to 20%; grades 3/4: ≤11%; including cardiac, cerebrovascular, and peripheral-vascular ischemia), cardiac failure (6% to 15%; including congestive heart failure, reduced ejection fraction, pulmonary edema, cardiogenic shock, cardiorespiratory arrest, right ventricular failure), myocardial infarction (12%)

Central nervous system: Fatigue or weakness (31% to 39%), headache (25% to 39%), pain (6% to 16%), chills (7% to 13%), insomnia (7% to 12%), dizziness (3% to 11%)

Dermatologic: Skin rash (34% to 54%), xeroderma (24% to 39%), cellulitis (≤11%)

Endocrine & metabolic: Increased serum glucose (58%), decreased serum phosphate (57%), decreased serum calcium (52%), decreased serum sodium (29%), decreased serum glucose (24%), decreased serum potassium (16%), increased serum potassium (15%), decreased serum bicarbonate (11%)

Gastrointestinal: Abdominal pain (34% to 49%), constipation (24% to 47%), increased serum lipase (41%; grades 3/4: 15%), nausea (22% to 32%), decreased appetite (8% to 31%), diarrhea (13% to 26%), vomiting (13% to 24%), stomatitis (9% to 23%), weight loss (5% to 13%), gastrointestinal hemorrhage (2% to 11%; grades 3/4: ≤6%)

Genitourinary: Urinary tract infection (≤12%)

Hematologic & oncologic: Neutropenia (grades 3/4: 24% to 63%), leukopenia (grades 3/4: 14% to 63%), thrombocytopenia (grades 3/4: 36% to 57%), anemia (grades 3/4: 9% to 55%), bone marrow depression (severe grade 3 or 4: 48%), lymphocytopenia (grades 3/4: 10% to 37%), febrile neutropenia (1% to 25%), hemorrhage (24%; including cerebral hemorrhage and gastrointestinal hemorrhage)

Hepatic: Increased serum ALT (53%; grades 3/4: 8%), increased serum AST (41%; grades 3/4: 4%), increased serum alkaline phosphatase (37%), decreased serum albumin (28%), increased serum bilirubin (19%)

Infection: Sepsis (1% to 22%)

Miscellaneous: Fever (23% to 32%)

Neuromuscular & skeletal: Arthralgia (13% to 31%), myalgia (6% to 22%), limb pain (9% to 17%), back pain (11% to 16%), peripheral neuropathy (6% to 16%; including burning sensation), muscle spasm (5% to 13%), ostealgia (9% to 12%)

Respiratory: Dyspnea (6% to 21%), pleural effusion (3% to 19%; grades 3/4: ≤3%), cough (6% to 18%), pneumonia (3% to 13%), nasopharyngitis (3% to 12%), upper respiratory tract infection (≤11%)

1% to 10%:

Cardiovascular: Peripheral ischemia (8%), supraventricular tachycardia (5%), venous thromboembolism (5%); atrial fibrillation (4%), pericardial effusion (1% to 3%), cerebral hemorrhage (2%), bradycardia (1%; symptomatic)

Endocrine & metabolic: Increased serum sodium (10%), hyperuricemia (7%), increased serum calcium (5%), increased serum triglycerides (3%)

Gastrointestinal: Pancreatitis (6%; grade 3: 5%), increased serum amylase (3%)

Ophthalmic: Blurred vision (6%), retinal toxicity (3%, including macular edema, retinal vein occlusion, retinal hemorrhage)

Renal: Increased serum creatinine (7%)

Frequency not defined:

Cardiovascular: Cerebrovascular accident

Gastrointestinal: Mouth pain, oral mucosa ulcer, oropharyngeal pain, throat ulcer, tongue ulcer

Ophthalmic: Cataract, conjunctival irritation, corneal ulcer, dry eye syndrome, eye pain, glaucoma, iridocyclitis, iritis, keratitis

<1%, postmarketing, and/or case reports: Acute hepatic failure, ascites, atrial flutter, atrial tachycardia, cerebral edema, complete atrioventricular block, gastrointestinal fistula, gastrointestinal perforation, mesenteric artery occlusion, pulmonary embolism, retinal vein thrombosis, sick sinus syndrome, tumor lysis syndrome (serious)

General Dosage Range Dosage adjustment recommended in patients with hepatic impairment, on concomitant therapy or who develop toxicities.

Oral: *Adults:* 45 mg once daily

Mechanism of Action Ponatinib is a pan-BCR-ABL tyrosine kinase inhibitor with *in vitro* activity against cells expressing native or mutant BCR-ABL (including T315I); it also inhibits VEGFR, FGFR, PDGFR, EPH, and SRC kinases, as well as KIT, RET, TIE2, and FLT3.

Pharmacodynamics/Kinetics

Half-life Elimination ~24 hours (range: 12 to 66 hours)

Time to Peak ≤6 hours

Pregnancy Considerations Based on animal data and its mechanism of action, ponatinib is expected to cause fetal harm if used during pregnancy. Verify pregnancy status prior to initiating ponatinib treatment. Women of childbearing potential should use effective contraception during treatment and for 3 weeks after the last dose.

Prescribing and Access Restrictions Patient access and support is available through the ARIAD PASS program. Information regarding program enrollment may be found at http://www.ariadpass.com or by calling 1-855-447-PASS (7277). In Canada, ponatinib is available through the Iclusig Controlled Distribution Program; information about the program may be found at www.iclusigcdp.ca or by calling 1-888-867-7426.

Poractant Alfa (por AKT ant AL fa)

Brand Names: US Curosurf

Brand Names: Canada Curosurf

Pharmacologic Category Lung Surfactant

Use Respiratory distress syndrome (RDS): Treatment (rescue) of respiratory distress syndrome (RDS) in premature infants; reduces mortality and pneumothoraces associated with RDS.

Local Anesthetic/Vasoconstrictor Precautions No information available to require special precautions

Effects on Dental Treatment No significant effects or complications reported

Effects on Bleeding No information available to require special precautions

Adverse Reactions All reported adverse reactions occurred in premature neonates as safety and efficacy has not been established in full term neonates and older pediatric patients with respiratory failure. Frequency not always defined.

Cardiovascular: Patent ductus arteriosus (60%), bradycardia, hypotension

Hematologic & oncologic: Oxygen desaturation

Miscellaneous: Obstruction of endotracheal tube

<1%, postmarketing, and/or case reports: Pulmonary hemorrhage

General Dosage Range Intratracheal: *Neonates:* Initial: 2.5 mL/kg of birth weight, may administer up to 2 additional doses of 1.25 mL/kg birth weight at 12-hour intervals if needed. Maximum total dose: 5 mL/kg birth weight

Mechanism of Action Endogenous pulmonary surfactant reduces surface tension at the air-liquid interface of the alveoli during ventilation and stabilizes the alveoli against collapse at resting transpulmonary pressures. A deficiency of pulmonary surfactant in preterm infants results in respiratory distress syndrome characterized by poor lung expansion, inadequate gas exchange, and atelectasis. Poractant alfa compensates for the surfactant deficiency and restores surface activity to the infant's lungs. It reduces mortality and pneumothoraces associated with RDS.

Pregnancy Considerations This drug is not indicated for use in adults.

Porfimer (POR fi mer)

Brand Names: US Photofrin

Brand Names: Canada Photofrin

Pharmacologic Category Antineoplastic Agent, Miscellaneous

Use

Barrett esophagus dysplasia (photodynamic therapy): Ablation of high-grade dysplasia in Barrett esophagus (in patients who do not undergo esophagectomy)

Endobronchial cancer (photodynamic therapy): Treatment of microinvasive endobronchial non-small cell lung cancer (NSCLC) in patients for whom surgery and radiation therapy are not indicated; reduction of obstruction and symptom palliation in patients with obstructing (partial or complete) endobronchial NSCLC

Esophageal cancer (photodynamic therapy): Palliation of completely obstructing esophageal cancer, or partially obstructing esophageal cancer in patients who cannot be treated satisfactorily with Nd:YAG laser therapy.

Local Anesthetic/Vasoconstrictor Precautions No information available to require special precautions

Effects on Dental Treatment Key adverse event(s) related to dental treatment: Dysphagia.

Effects on Bleeding No information available to require special precautions

Adverse Reactions

>10%:

Cardiovascular: Chest pain (8% to 22%)

Central nervous system: Confusion (5% to 24%), pain (5% to 22%), insomnia (5% to 14%)

Dermatologic: Skin photosensitivity (19% to 69%)

Gastrointestinal: Esophageal stenosis (6% to 38%), nausea (24%), constipation (5% to 24%), abdominal pain (20%), vomiting (17%), dysphagia (10%)

Hematologic & oncologic: Anemia (esophageal cancer: 32%)

Neuromuscular & skeletal: Back pain (3% to 11%)

Respiratory: Pleural effusion (5% to 32%), dyspnea (7% to 30%), bronchial obstruction (≤21%; includes bronchial stenosis), bronchial plugs (≤21%), pneumonia (12% to 18%), hemoptysis (16%; massive: 10%), cough (7% to 15%), bronchoconstriction (bronchostenosis: 11%), pharyngitis (11%)

Miscellaneous: Fever (16% to 31%), serous drainage (22%)

1% to 10%:

Cardiovascular: Atrial fibrillation (10%), hypotension (7%), peripheral edema (5% to 7%), cardiac failure (esophageal carcinoma and endobronchial cancer: ≤7%), hypertension (6%), tachycardia (6%), edema (5%), substernal pain (5%), angina pectoris (<5%), bradycardia (<5%), myocardial infarction (<5%), pulmonary embolism (<5%), sick sinus syndrome (<5%), supraventricular tachycardia (<5%), thrombosis (pulmonary: <5%)

Central nervous system: Anxiety (6% to 7%), voice disorder (5%)

Endocrine & metabolic: Weight loss (9%), dehydration (7%)

Gastrointestinal: Anorexia (8%), disease of esophagus (esophageal edema: 8%), hematemesis (8%), tracheoesophageal fistula (6%), dyspepsia (2% to 6%), diarrhea (5%), eructation (5%), esophagitis (5%), melena (5%), esophageal perforation (<5%), gastric ulcer (<5%), intestinal obstruction (<5%), peritonitis (<5%)

Genitourinary: Urinary tract infection (7%)

Hematologic & oncologic: Tumor hemorrhage (8%), pulmonary hemorrhage (<5%)

Hepatic: Jaundice (<5%)

Infection: Candidiasis (9%), abscess (lung: <5%)

Neuromuscular & skeletal: Weakness (6%)

Ophthalmic: Diplopia (<5%), eye pain (<5%), photophobia (<5%), visual disturbance (<5%)

Respiratory: Bronchitis (≤10%), respiratory insufficiency (5% to 10%), airway obstruction (including laryngotracheal edema: <5%), bronchospasm (<5%), pneumonitis (<5%), pulmonary edema (<5%), respiratory failure (<5%), stridor (<5%)

Miscellaneous: Ulcer (bronchial: 9%), postoperative complication (5%)

<1%, postmarketing, and/or case reports: Cataract, cerebrovascular accident, cutaneous nodule, disturbance in fluid balance, fragile skin, gastrointestinal disease (gastroesophageal fistula, gastroesophageal perforation), hemorrhage, hypertrichosis, infusion related reaction (including dizziness and urticaria), pseudoporphyria, sepsis, skin discoloration, thromboembolism, wrinkling of skin

General Dosage Range IV: *Adults:* 2 mg/kg, followed by endoscopic exposure to the appropriate laser light

Mechanism of Action Porfimer's cytotoxic activity is dependent on light and oxygen. Following administration, the drug is selectively retained in neoplastic tissues. Exposure of the drug to laser light at wavelengths >630 nm results in the production of oxygen free-radicals. Release of thromboxane A_2, leading to vascular occlusion and ischemic necrosis, may also occur.

Pharmacodynamics/Kinetics

Half-life Elimination First dose: 17 days; Second dose: 30 days

Pregnancy Risk Factor C

Pregnancy Considerations Adverse events were observed in animal reproduction studies.

Posaconazole (poe sa KON a zole)

Related Information

Fungal Infections *on page 1847*

Related Sample Prescriptions

Fungal Infections - Sample Prescriptions *on page 35*

Brand Names: US Noxafil

Brand Names: Canada Posanol

Generic Availability (US) No

Pharmacologic Category Antifungal Agent, Oral

Dental Use Treatment of oropharyngeal candidiasis (including patients refractory to itraconazole and/or fluconazole)

Use

Prophylaxis of invasive *Aspergillus* and *Candida* infections: Suspension and delayed-release tablets (13 years and older) and injection (18 years and older): Prophylaxis of invasive *Aspergillus* and *Candida* infections in patients who are at high risk of developing these infections due to being severely immunocompromised (eg, hematopoietic stem cell transplant [HSCT] recipients with graft-versus-host disease [GVHD] or those with prolonged neutropenia secondary to chemotherapy for hematologic malignancies).

Oropharyngeal candidiasis: Suspension (13 years and older): Treatment of oropharyngeal candidiasis (including patients refractory to itraconazole and/or fluconazole)

Local Anesthetic/Vasoconstrictor Precautions No information available to require special precautions

Effects on Dental Treatment Key adverse event(s) related to dental treatment: Xerostomia (normal salivary flow resumes upon discontinuation), abnormal taste, mucositis.

Effects on Bleeding No information available to require special precautions

Adverse Reactions

>10%:

Cardiovascular: Thrombophlebitis (intravenous via peripheral venous catheter: 60%), hypertension (8% to 18%), peripheral edema (12% to 16%), lower extremity edema (oral: 15%), hypotension (oral: 14%), tachycardia (oral: 12%)

Central nervous system: Headache (8% to 28%), rigors (oral: ≤20%), fatigue (3% to 17%), insomnia (oral: 1% to 17%), chills (10% to 16%), dizziness (oral: 11%)

Dermatologic: Skin rash (3% to 24%), pruritus (oral: 11%)

Endocrine & metabolic: Hypokalemia (oral: ≤30%), hypomagnesemia (10% to 18%), hyperglycemia (oral: 11%)

Gastrointestinal: Diarrhea (10% to 42%), nausea (9% to 38%), vomiting (7% to 29%), abdominal pain (5% to 27%), constipation (8% to 21%), anorexia (oral: 2% to 15%), mucositis (oral: 14%), decreased appetite (10% to 12%), upper abdominal pain (6% to 11%)

Hematologic & oncologic: Thrombocytopenia (≤29%), anemia (2% to 25%), neutropenia (oral: 4% to 23%), petechia (8% to 11%)

Hepatic: Increased serum ALT (oral: ≤17%)

Neuromuscular & skeletal: Musculoskeletal pain (oral: 16%), arthralgia (oral: 11%), weakness (oral: 2% to 10%)

Respiratory: Cough (3% to 24%), dyspnea (1% to 20%), epistaxis (14% to 17%), pharyngitis (oral: 12%)

Miscellaneous: Fever (21% to 45%)

1% to 10%:

Cardiovascular: Edema (oral: 9%), pulmonary embolism (<5%), torsades de pointes (<5%)

Central nervous system: Paresthesia (<5%), pain (oral: 1%)

Dermatologic: Diaphoresis (oral: 2%)

Endocrine & metabolic: Hypocalcemia (9%), adrenocortical insufficiency (<5%), dehydration (oral: 1%), weight loss (oral: 1%)

Gastrointestinal: Dyspepsia (10%), oral candidiasis (oral: 1%)

Genitourinary: Vaginal hemorrhage (oral: 10%)

Hematologic & oncologic: Hemolytic-uremic syndrome (<5%), thrombotic thrombocytopenic purpura (<5%)

Hepatic: Hyperbilirubinemia (≤10%), hepatic insufficiency (<5%), hepatitis (<5%), hepatomegaly (<5%), increased liver enzymes (<5%), jaundice (<5%), increased serum AST (≤4%), increased serum alkaline phosphatase (oral: ≤3%)

Hypersensitivity: Hypersensitivity reaction (<5%)

Infection: Herpes simplex infection (oral: 3%)

Neuromuscular & skeletal: Back pain (oral: 10%)

Renal: Acute renal failure (<5%)

Respiratory: Pneumonia (oral: 3%)

<1%, postmarketing, and/or case reports: Cholestasis, prolonged Q-T interval on ECG

Dental Usual Dosage Children ≥13 years and Adults: Oral:

Oropharyngeal infection: Suspension: Initial: 100 mg twice daily on day 1; Maintenance: 100 mg once daily on day 2 and thereafter for 13 days

Oropharyngeal infection (refractory to fluconazole):

Suspension: 400 mg twice daily for 3 days, then 400 mg once daily for up to 28 days (IDSA [Pappas 2016])

Note: The delayed-release tablet and oral suspension are not to be used interchangeably due to dosing differences for each formulation. Since the delayed-release tablet is easier to administer, better tolerated, and more reliably absorbed, the use of delayed-release tablets are preferred. The bioavailability of a once daily 300 mg dose given as the delayed-release tablet appears to be similar or greater than the bioavailability of 200 mg given 3 to 4 times daily, based upon available pharmacokinetic studies (Cumpston 2015; Durani 2015).

Dosing

Adult & Geriatric

Note: The delayed-release tablet and oral suspension are not to be used interchangeably due to dosing differences for each formulation. Since the delayed-release tablet is easier to administer, better tolerated, and more reliably absorbed, the use of delayed-release tablets are preferred. The bioavailability of a once daily 300 mg dose given as the delayed-release tablet appears to be similar or greater than the bioavailability of 200 mg given 3 to 4 times daily, based upon available pharmacokinetic studies (Cumpston 2015; Durani 2015).

Aspergillosis, invasive:

Prophylaxis (immunocompromised host):

Oral:

Suspension: 200 mg 3 times daily; duration of therapy is based on recovery from neutropenia or immunosuppression. In patients with acute myelogenous leukemia (AML) or myelodysplastic syndromes (MDS), posaconazole was initiated at the time of chemotherapy initiation (or if receiving anthracyclines, 24 hours after the last anthracycline dose) and was continued until recovery from neutropenia, until complete remission, or for up to 12 weeks, whichever occurred first (Cornely 2007). In patients with graft-versus-host disease (GVHD) receiving immunosuppressive therapy, posaconazole was continued for 112 days (Ullmann 2007), although the optimal duration in GVHD has not been fully defined (Tomblyn 2009). It is recommended to continue throughout the duration of immunosuppression (ie, corticosteroid equivalent of >1 mg/kg/day of prednisone for >2 weeks and/or the use of other anti-GVHD therapies) (IDSA [Patterson 2016]).

Tablets (delayed release): Initial: 300 mg twice daily on day 1 followed by 300 mg once daily on day 2 and thereafter. Duration is based on recovery from neutropenia or immunosuppression.

Missed doses: Take as soon as remembered. If it is <12 hours until the next dose, skip the missed does and return to the regular schedule. Do not double doses.

IV: Loading dose: 300 mg twice a day on day 1 followed by 300 mg once daily on day 2 and thereafter. Duration is based on recovery from neutropenia or immunosuppression.

Treatment (refractory to or intolerant of conventional therapy) (off-label use):

Oral:

Suspension: 200 mg 3 times daily (IDSA [Patterson 2016])

Tablets (delayed release): Initial dose: 300 mg twice daily on day 1; Maintenance dose: 300 mg once daily (IDSA [Patterson 2016])

IV: Loading dose: 300 mg twice daily on day 1; Maintenance dose: 300 mg once daily (IDSA [Patterson 2016])

Duration of therapy: Minimum of 6 to 12 weeks, although duration is highly dependent on degree/duration of immunosuppression, disease site, and evidence of disease improvement (IDSA [Patterson 2016])

Alternative dosing recommendations (Posanol Canadian product labeling 2016):

Oral:

Suspension: 400 mg twice daily; in patients unable to tolerate food or nutritional supplement, administer 200 mg 4 times daily; duration of therapy is based on severity of underlying disease, recovery from immunosuppression, and clinical response.

Tablets (delayed release): Initial: 300 mg twice daily on day 1; Maintenance dose: 300 mg once daily; duration of therapy is based on disease severity, recovery from immunosuppression, and clinical response.

IV: Loading dose: 300 mg twice daily on day 1; Maintenance dose: 300 mg once daily on day 2 and thereafter. Duration of therapy is based on disease severity, recovery from immunosuppression, and clinical response.

Candidal infections:

Prophylaxis (disseminated candidiasis, immunocompromised host):

Oral:

Suspension: 200 mg 3 times daily; duration of therapy is based on recovery from neutropenia or immunosuppression

Tablets (delayed release): Oral: Initial: 300 mg twice daily on day 1; Maintenance dose: 300 mg once daily on day 2 and thereafter; duration of therapy is based on recovery from neutropenia or immunosuppression

Missed doses: Take as soon as remembered. If it is <12 hours until the next dose, skip the missed does and return to the regular schedule. Do not double doses.

IV: Initial: 300 mg twice daily on day 1; Maintenance dose: 300 mg once daily on day 2 and thereafter; duration of therapy is based on recovery from neutropenia or immunosuppression.

Treatment:

Oral:

Oropharyngeal infection: Suspension: Initial: 100 mg twice daily on day 1; Maintenance: 100 mg once daily on day 2 and thereafter for 13 days

Oropharyngeal infection (refractory to fluconazole):

Manufacturer's labeling: Suspension: 400 mg twice daily; duration of therapy is based on underlying disease and clinical response

Alternate dosing: Suspension: 400 mg twice daily for 3 days, then 400 mg once daily for up to 28 days (IDSA [Pappas 2016])

HIV-infected patients (alternative to fluconazole or azole refractory): Suspension: 400 mg twice daily on day 1, then 400 mg once daily for 7 to 14 days for initial episodes (continue for 28 days in azole refractory patients) (HHS [OI adult 2015])

Esophageal infections (off-label use):

Fluconazole-refractory (alternate therapy):

Tablets, delayed-release: 300 mg once daily (IDSA [Pappas 2016])

Suspension: 400 mg twice daily (IDSA [Pappas 2016])

HIV-infected patients (azole refractory): Suspension: 400 mg twice daily for 28 days. **Note:** If patient has frequent or severe recurrences, may continue for suppressive therapy; consider discontinuing when CD4 >200/mm^3 (HHS [OI adult 2015])

Coccidioidomycosis in HIV-infected patients (alternative to preferred therapy) (off-label use) (HHS [OI adult 2015]; Anstead 2005; Schein 2011; Stevens 2007):

Mild infections (eg, focal pneumonia): Oral: Suspension: 200 to 400 mg twice daily; patients who complete initial therapy should be considered for lifelong suppressive therapy.

Chronic suppressive therapy: Oral: Suspension: 200 mg twice daily

Mucormycosis, salvage and step-down therapy (off-label use): Oral:

Suspension: 800 mg daily in 2 or 4 divided doses; duration of therapy is based on response and risk of relapse due to immunosuppression (Danion 2015; ECIL [Skiada 2013]; ESCMID/ECMM [Cornely 2014]; Greenberg 2006)

Tablets (delayed release): 300 mg once daily (Danion 2015)

Cryptococcal infections:

Pulmonary, nonimmunosuppressed (off-label use): Oral: Suspension: 400 mg twice daily. **Note:** Fluconazole is considered first-line treatment (Perfect 2010; Raad 2006).

Salvage treatment of relapsed infection (off-label use): Oral: Suspension: 400 mg twice daily (or 200 mg 4 times daily) for 10 to 12 weeks. **Note:** Salvage treatment should only be started after an appropriate course of an induction regimen (Perfect 2010; Pitisuttitihum 2005).

Pediatric

Note: The delayed-release tablet and oral suspension are not to be used interchangeably due to dosing differences for each formulation.

Candidal infections: Oral: Adolescents ≥13 years: Refer to adult dosing.

Coccidioidomycosis in HIV-infected patients (alternative to preferred therapy) (off-label use): Adolescents: Oral: Refer to adult dosing.

Primary antifungal prophylaxis in allogeneic HSCT with grades 2 to 4 acute graft-versus-host-disease (GVHD) or chronic extensive GVHD (guideline recommendation): Adolescents ≥13 years: Oral: Suspension: 200 mg 3 times daily beginning with GVHD diagnosis, continue until GVHD resolves (Science 2014)

Primary antifungal prophylaxis in AML or MDS in centers with a high local incidence of mold infections (alternative to fluconazole; guideline recommendation): Adolescents ≥13 years: Oral: Suspension: 200 mg 3 times daily during chemotherapy-associated neutropenia (Science 2014)

Renal Impairment

Delayed-release tablets and oral suspension:

eGFR 20 to 80 mL/minute/1.73 m^2: No dosage adjustment necessary.

eGFR <20 mL/minute/1.73 m^2: No dosage adjustment necessary; however, monitor for breakthrough fungal infections due to variability in posaconazole exposure.

Intravenous infusion:

eGFR ≥50 mL/minute/1.73 m^2: No dosage adjustment recommended

eGFR<50 mL/minute/1.73 m^2: Avoid use unless risk/benefit has been assessed; the intravenous vehicle (cyclodextrin) may accumulate. Monitor serum creatinine levels; if increases occur, consider oral therapy.

Continuous venovenous hemofiltration (CVVH): In a critically ill patient undergoing CVVH, IV posaconazole administered at standard dosing demonstrated no evidence of SBECD accumulation; however, no specific dosing recommendations can be made (Morris 2015).

Hepatic Impairment

Preexisting mild-to-severe impairment (Child-Pugh class A, B, or C): No dosage adjustment necessary.

Hepatotoxicity during treatment: There are no dosage adjustments provided in the manufacturer's labeling; consider discontinuing therapy.

Mechanism of Action Interferes with fungal cytochrome P450 (lanosterol-14α-demethylase) activity, decreasing ergosterol synthesis (principal sterol in fungal cell membrane) and inhibiting fungal cell membrane formation.

Contraindications Coadministration with sirolimus, ergot alkaloids (eg, ergotamine, dihydroergotamine), HMG-CoA reductase inhibitors that are primarily metabolized through CYP3A4 (eg, atorvastatin, lovastatin, simvastatin), or CYP3A4 substrates that prolong the QT interval (eg, pimozide, quinidine); hypersensitivity to posaconazole, other azole antifungal agents, or any component of the formulation.

Warnings/Precautions The delayed-release tablet and oral suspension are not to be used interchangeably due to dosing differences for each formulation. Hepatic dysfunction has occurred, ranging from mild/moderate increases of ALT, AST, alkaline phosphatase, total bilirubin, and/or clinical hepatitis to severe reactions (cholestasis, hepatic failure including death). Consider discontinuation of therapy in patients who develop clinical evidence of liver disease that may be secondary to posaconazole. Elevations in liver function tests have been generally reversible after posaconazole has been discontinued; some cases resolved without drug interruption. More severe reactions have been observed in patients with underlying serious medical conditions (eg, hematologic malignancy) and primarily with suspension total daily doses of 800 mg. Monitor liver function tests at baseline and periodically during therapy. If increases occur, monitor for severe hepatic injury development. Use caution in patients with an increased risk of arrhythmia (long QT syndrome, concurrent QTc-prolonging drugs, drugs metabolized through CYP3A4, hypokalemia). Correct electrolyte abnormalities (eg, potassium, magnesium, and calcium) before initiating therapy. Potentially significant drug-drug interactions may exist, requiring dose or frequency adjustment, additional monitoring, and/or selection of alternative therapy.

Consider alternative therapy or closely monitor for breakthrough fungal infections in patients receiving drugs that decrease absorption or increase the metabolism of posaconazole or in any patient unable to eat or tolerate an oral liquid nutritional supplement or acidic carbonated beverage (eg, ginger ale). Do not give IV formulation as an intravenous bolus injection. Avoid/limit use of IV formulation in patients with eGFR <50 mL/minute/1.73 m^2; injection contains excipient cyclodextrin (sulfobutyl ether beta-cyclodextrin [SBECD]), which may accumulate although the clinical significance of this finding is uncertain (Luke 2010); consider using oral posaconazole in these patients unless benefit of injection outweighs the risk. Evaluate renal function (particularly serum creatinine) at baseline and periodically during therapy. If increases occur, consider oral therapy. Monitor for breakthrough fungal infections. Patients weighing >120 kg may have lower plasma drug exposure; monitor closely for breakthrough fungal infections.

Benzyl alcohol and derivatives: Some dosage forms may contain sodium benzoate/benzoic acid; benzoic acid (benzoate) is a metabolite of benzyl alcohol; large amounts of benzyl alcohol (≥99 mg/kg/day) have been associated with a potentially fatal toxicity ("gasping syndrome") in neonates; the "gasping syndrome" consists of metabolic acidosis, respiratory distress, gasping respirations, CNS dysfunction (including convulsions, intracranial hemorrhage), hypotension, and cardiovascular collapse (AAP ["Inactive" 1997]; CDC 1982); some data suggests that benzoate displaces bilirubin from protein binding sites (Ahlfors 2001); avoid or use dosage forms containing benzyl alcohol derivative with caution in neonates. See manufacturer's labeling.

Polysorbate 80: Some dosage forms may contain polysorbate 80 (also known as Tweens). Hypersensitivity reactions, usually a delayed reaction, have been reported following exposure to pharmaceutical products containing polysorbate 80 in certain individuals (Isaksson 2002; Lucente 2000; Shelley 1995). Thrombocytopenia, ascites, pulmonary deterioration, and renal and hepatic failure have been reported in premature neonates after receiving parenteral products containing polysorbate 80 (Alade 1986; CDC 1984). See manufacturer's labeling.

Drug Interactions

Metabolism/Transport Effects **Substrate** of UGT1A4; **Inhibits** CYP3A4 (strong)

Avoid Concomitant Use

Avoid concomitant use of Posaconazole with any of the following: Ado-Trastuzumab Emtansine; Alfuzosin; Aprepitant; Astemizole; Asunaprevir; AtorvaSTATin; Avanafil; Axitinib; Barnidipine; Blonanserin; Bosutinib; Bromocriptine; Budesonide (Systemic); Ceritinib; Cisapride; Cobimetinib; Conivaptan; Crizotinib; Dabrafenib; Dapoxetine; Dihydroergotamine; Dofetilide; Domperidone; Dronedarone; Efavirenz; Eletriptan; Eplerenone; Ergoloid Mesylates; Ergonovine; Ergotamine; Everolimus; Flibanserin; Halofantrine; Ibrutinib; Irinotecan Products; Isavuconazonium Sulfate; Ivabradine; Lapatinib; Lercanidipine; Lomitapide; Lovastatin; Lumacaftor; Lurasidone; Macitentan; Methadone; Methylergonovine; Naloxegol; Nilotinib; NiMODipine; Nisoldipine; Olaparib; Palbociclib; Pimozide; QuiNIDine; Radotinib; Ranolazine; Red Yeast Rice; Regorafenib; Rupatadine; Saccharomyces boulardii; Salmeterol; Silodosin; Simeprevir; Simvastatin; Sirolimus; Sonidegib; Suvorexant; Tamsulosin; Terfenadine; Ticagrelor; Tolvaptan; Toremifene; Trabectedin; Udenafil; Ulipristal; Vemurafenib; VinCRIStine (Liposomal); Vinflunine; Vorapaxar

Increased Effect/Toxicity

Posaconazole may increase the levels/effects of: Ado-Trastuzumab Emtansine; Alfuzosin; Alitretinoin (Systemic); Almotriptan; Alosetron; Antineoplastic Agents (Vinca Alkaloids); Apixaban; Aprepitant; ARIPiprazole; ARIPiprazole Lauroxil; Astemizole; Asunaprevir; Atazanavir; AtorvaSTATin; Avanafil; Axitinib; Barnidipine; Bedaquiline; Benperidol; Blonanserin; Boceprevir; Bortezomib; Bosentan; Bosutinib; Brentuximab Vedotin; Brexpiprazole; Brinzolamide; Bromocriptine; Budesonide (Nasal); Budesonide (Oral Inhalation); Budesonide (Systemic); Budesonide (Topical); Buprenorphine; BusPIRone; Busulfan; Cabazitaxel; Cabozantinib; Calcifediol; Calcium Channel Blockers; Cannabidiol; Cannabis; Cariprazine; Ceritinib; Cilostazol; Cisapride; CloZAPine; Cobimetinib; Colchicine; Conivaptan; Corticosteroids (Orally Inhaled); Corticosteroids (Systemic); Crizotinib; CycloSPORINE (Systemic); CYP3A4 Substrates; Dabrafenib; Daclatasvir; Dapoxetine; Dasatinib; Deflazacort; Delamanid; Dienogest; Digoxin; Dihydroergotamine; DOCEtaxel; Dofetilide; Domperidone; DOXOrubicin (Conventional); Dronabinol; Dronedarone; Drospirenone; Dutasteride; Eletriptan; Eliglustat; Enzalutamide; Eplerenone; Ergoloid Mesylates; Ergonovine; Ergotamine; Erlotinib; Estazolam; Eszopiclone; Etizolam; Etravirine; Everolimus; FentaNYL; Fesoterodine; Flibanserin; Fluticasone (Nasal); Fluticasone (Oral Inhalation); Fosamprenavir; Fosphenytoin; Gefitinib; GlipiZIDE; GuanFACINE; Halofantrine; Highest Risk QTc-Prolonging Agents; HYDROcodone; HydrOXYzine; Ibrutinib; Idelalisib; Iloperidone; Imatinib; Imidafenacin; Irinotecan Products; Isavuconazonium Sulfate; Ivabradine; Ivacaftor; Ixabepilone; Lacosamide; Lapatinib; Lercanidipine; Levobupivacaine; Levomilnacipran; Lomitapide; Losartan; Lovastatin; Lurasidone; Macitentan; Manidipine; Maraviroc; MedroxyPROGESTERone; Methadone; Methylergonovine; MethylPREDNISolone; MiFEPRIStone; Mirodenafil; Moderate Risk QTc-Prolonging Agents; Naldemedine; Naloxegol; Nilotinib; NiMODipine; Nisoldipine; Olaparib; Ospemifene; Oxybutynin; OxyCODONE; Palbociclib; Panobinostat; Parecoxib; Paricalcitol; PAZOPanib; Phenytoin; Pimavanserin; Pimecrolimus; Pimozide; PONATinib; Pranlukast; Praziquantel; PrednisoLONE (Systemic); PredniSONE; Propafenone; QUEtiapine; QuiNIDine; Radotinib; Ramelteon; Ranolazine; Reboxetine; Red Yeast Rice; Regorafenib; Repaglinide; Retapamulin; Ribociclib; Rifamycin Derivatives; Rilpivirine; Ritonavir; RomiDEPsin; Rupatadine; Ruxolitinib; Salmeterol; SAXagliptin; Sildenafil; Silodosin; Simeprevir; Simvastatin; Sirolimus; Solifenacin; Sonidegib; SORAfenib; SUNItinib; Suvorexant; Tacrolimus (Systemic); Tacrolimus (Topical); Tadalafil; Tamsulosin; Tasimelteon; Telaprevir; Telithromycin; Temsirolimus; Terfenadine; Tetrahydrocannabinol; Ticagrelor; Tofacitinib; Tolterodine; Tolvaptan; Toremifene; Trabectedin; TraMADol; Udenafil; Ulipristal; Vardenafil; Vemurafenib; Venetoclax; Vilazodone; VinCRIStine (Liposomal); Vinflunine; Vitamin K Antagonists; Vorapaxar; Zolpidem; Zopiclone; Zuclopenthixol

The levels/effects of Posaconazole may be increased by: Boceprevir; Etravirine; MiFEPRIStone; Telaprevir

Decreased Effect

Posaconazole may decrease the levels/effects of: Amphotericin B; Doxercalciferol; Ifosfamide; Prasugrel; Saccharomyces boulardii; Ticagrelor

The levels/effects of Posaconazole may be decreased by: Didanosine; Efavirenz; Etravirine; Fosamprenavir; Fosphenytoin; H2-Antagonists; Lumacaftor; Metoclopramide; Phenytoin; Proton Pump Inhibitors; Rifamycin Derivatives

Food Interactions

Suspension: Bioavailability increased ~3 times when posaconazole suspension was administered with a nonfat meal or an oral liquid nutritional supplement; increased ~4 times when administered with a high-fat meal. Management: Suspension must be administered with or within 20 minutes of a full meal, an oral liquid nutritional supplement, or an acidic carbonated beverage (eg, ginger ale). Consider alternative antifungal therapy in patients with inadequate oral intake or severe diarrhea/vomiting.

Tablets (delayed-release): Following administration of posaconazole delayed-release tablets, the AUC increased 51% when given with a high-fat meal compared with a fasted state. Management: Take tablet with food when possible. Consider alternative antifungal therapy in patients with severe diarrhea/vomiting.

Dietary Considerations

Tablets (delayed release): Take with food.

Suspension: Give during or within 20 minutes following a full meal, liquid nutritional supplement, or an acidic carbonated beverage (eg, ginger ale).

Consider alternative antifungal therapy in patients with inadequate oral intake or severe diarrhea/vomiting; if alternative therapy is not an option, closely monitoring for breakthrough fungal infections.

Adequate posaconazole absorption from GI tract and subsequent plasma concentrations are dependent on food for efficacy. Lower average plasma concentrations have been associated with an increased risk of treatment failure.

Pharmacodynamics/Kinetics

Half-life Elimination Suspension: 35 hours (range: 20 to 66 hours); Tablets: 26 to 31 hours; Injection: ~27 hours

Time to Peak Plasma: Suspension: ~3 to 5 hours; Tablets: ~4 to 5 hours

Pregnancy Considerations Adverse events have been observed in animal reproduction studies.

Breastfeeding Considerations It is not known if posaconazole is excreted in breast milk. Due to the potential for serious adverse reactions in the nursing infant, the manufacturer recommends a decision be made to discontinue nursing or the drug, taking into account the importance of treatment to the mother.

Dosage Forms

Solution, Intravenous:

Noxafil: 300 mg/16.7 mL (16.7 mL)

Suspension, Oral:

Noxafil: 40 mg/mL (105 mL)

Tablet Delayed Release, Oral:

Noxafil: 100 mg

Dental Comment This drug is known to prolong the QT interval. The QT interval is measured as the time and distance between the Q point of the QRS complex and the end of the T wave in the ECG tracing. After adjustment for heart rate, the QT interval is defined as prolonged if it is more than 450 msec in men and 460 msec in women. A long QT syndrome was first described in the 1950s and 60s as a congenital syndrome involving QT interval prolongation and syncope and sudden death. Some of the congenital long QT syndromes were characterized by a peculiar electrocardiographic appearance of the QRS complex involving a premature atria beat followed by a pause, then a subsequent sinus beat showing marked QT prolongation and deformity. This type of cardiac arrhythmia was originally termed "torsade de pointes" (translated from the French as "twisting of the points").

Prolongation of the QT interval is thought to result from delayed ventricular repolarization. The repolarization process within the myocardial cell is due to the efflux of intracellular potassium. The channels associated with this current can be blocked by many drugs and predispose the electrical propagation cycle to torsade de pointes.

Posaconazole is one of the drugs confirmed to prolong the QT interval and is accepted as having a risk of causing torsade de pointes. The risk of drug-induced torsade de pointes is extremely low when a single QT interval prolonging drug is prescribed. In terms of epinephrine, it is not known what effect vasoconstrictors in the local anesthetic regimen will have in patients with a known history of congenital prolonged QT interval or in patients taking any medication that prolongs the QT interval. Until more information is obtained, it is suggested that the clinician consult with the physician prior to the use of a vasoconstrictor in suspected patients, and that the vasoconstrictor (epinephrine, levonordefrin [Neo-Cobefrin®]) be used with caution.

Potassium Chloride (poe TASS ee um KLOR ide)

Brand Names: US K-Sol [DSC]; K-Tab; K-Vescent [DSC]; Klor-Con; Klor-Con 10; Klor-Con M10; Klor-Con M15; Klor-Con M20; Klor-Con Sprinkle; Micro-K

Brand Names: Canada Apo-K; K-10; K-Dur; Micro-K Extencaps; Roychlor; Slo-Pot; Slow-K

Pharmacologic Category Electrolyte Supplement, Oral; Electrolyte Supplement, Parenteral

Use Treatment or prevention of hypokalemia

Local Anesthetic/Vasoconstrictor Precautions No information available to require special precautions

Effects on Dental Treatment No significant effects or complications reported

Effects on Bleeding No information available to require special precautions

Adverse Reactions Frequency not defined.

Dermatologic: Skin rash

Endocrine & metabolic: Hyperkalemia

Gastrointestinal: Abdominal pain, abdominal distress, diarrhea, flatulence, gastrointestinal hemorrhage (oral), gastrointestinal obstruction (oral), gastrointestinal perforation (oral), nausea, vomiting

General Dosage Range

IV:

Children: Initial: 0.5-1 mEq/kg/dose (maximum dose: 40 mEq); repeat as needed based on lab values

Adults: Intermittent infusion: ≤10 mEq/hour; repeat as needed based on lab values (maximum: 200 mEq/day)

Oral:

Children: 1-2 mEq/kg/day in 1-2 divided doses or as needed based on lab values

Adults: Initial: 6-10 mEq/dose (maximum: 40 mEq/dose); Maintenance: 40-100 mEq/day in divided doses or as needed based on lab values

Mechanism of Action Potassium is the major cation of intracellular fluid and is essential for the conduction of nerve impulses in heart, brain, and skeletal muscle; contraction of cardiac, skeletal and smooth muscles; maintenance of normal renal function, acid-base balance, carbohydrate metabolism, and gastric secretion

Pregnancy Risk Factor C

Pregnancy Considerations Reproduction studies have not been conducted. Potassium requirements are the same in pregnant and nonpregnant women. Adverse events have not been observed following use of potassium supplements in healthy women with normal pregnancies. Use caution in pregnant women with other medical conditions (eg, pre-eclampsia; may be more likely to develop hyperkalemia) (IOM, 2004). Potassium supplementation (that does not cause maternal hyperkalemia) would not be expected to cause adverse fetal events.

Potassium Iodide (poe TASS ee um EYE oh dide)

Related Information

Endocrine Disorders and Pregnancy *on page 1781*

Brand Names: US iOSAT [OTC]; SSKI; ThyroSafe [OTC]; ThyroShield [OTC] [DSC]

Pharmacologic Category Antidote; Antithyroid Agent; Expectorant

Use

Antidote: Block thyroidal uptake of radioactive isotopes of iodine in a nuclear radiation emergency.

Expectorant: Expectorant for the symptomatic treatment of chronic pulmonary diseases complicated by mucous.

Local Anesthetic/Vasoconstrictor Precautions No information available to require special precautions

Effects on Dental Treatment Key adverse event(s) related to dental treatment: Metallic taste.

Effects on Bleeding No information available to require special precautions

Adverse Reactions Frequency not defined.

Cardiovascular: Cardiac arrhythmias, numbness, vasculitis

Central nervous system: Confusion, fatigue, fever, numbness, tingling sensation

Dermatologic: Acne vulgaris, dermatitis, urticaria

Endocrine & metabolic: Goiter, hyperthyroidism (prolonged use), hypothyroidism (prolonged use), myxedema

Gastrointestinal: Diarrhea, enlargement of salivary glands, gastric distress, gastrointestinal hemorrhage, gingival pain, metallic taste, nausea, stomach pain, toothache, vomiting

Hematologic & oncologic: Eosinophilia, lymphedema, thyroid adenoma

Hypersensitivity: Hypersensitivity reaction (angioedema, cutaneous and mucosal hemorrhage, serum sickness-like symptoms)

Neuromuscular & skeletal: Arthralgia, weakness

Respiratory: Dyspnea, rhinitis, wheezing

Miscellaneous: Iodine poisoning (with prolonged treatment/high doses)

General Dosage Range Oral:

Infants ≤1 month: iOSAT, ThyroSafe, ThyroShield: 16.25 mg once daily

Infants >1 month and Children ≤3 years: iOSAT, ThyroSafe, ThyroShield: 32.5 mg once daily

Children >3 years to ≤12 years: 65 mg once daily

Children >12 years and Adolescents weighing <68 kg: iOSAT, ThyroSafe, ThyroShield: 65 mg once daily

Children >12 years and Adolescents weighing ≥68 kg: iOSAT, ThyroSafe, ThyroShield: 130 mg once daily

Adults: SSKI: 300 to 600 mg 3 to 4 times daily

Mechanism of Action Reduces viscosity of mucus by increasing respiratory tract secretions; inhibits secretion of thyroid hormone, fosters colloid accumulation in thyroid follicles. Following radioactive iodine exposure, potassium iodide blocks the uptake of radioactive iodine by the thyroid, reducing the risk of thyroid cancer.

Pharmacodynamics/Kinetics

Onset of Action Hyperthyroidism: 24 to 48 hours (Nayak 2006); Peak effect: ~2 weeks after continuous therapy (Nayak 2006)

Duration of Action Radioactive iodine exposure: Each dose has a duration of ~24 hours

Pregnancy Risk Factor D

Pregnancy Considerations Iodide crosses the placenta (may cause hypothyroidism and goiter in fetus/newborn). Use as an expectorant during pregnancy is contraindicated by the AAP (AAP 1976). Use for protection against thyroid cancer secondary to radioactive iodine exposure is considered acceptable based upon risk:benefit, keeping in mind the dose and duration (AAP 2003). In general, medications used as antidotes should take into consideration the health and prognosis of the mother; antidotes should be administered to pregnant women if there is a clear indication for use and should not be withheld because of fears of teratogenicity (Bailey, 2003). Pregnant women should take as instructed by public officials and contact their physician. Repeat dosing should be avoided if possible (AAP 2003). Refer to Iodine monograph for additional information.

Potassium Iodide and Iodine

(poe TASS ee um EYE oh dide & EYE oh dine)

Related Information

Iodine *on page 912*

Potassium Iodide *on page 1362*

Pharmacologic Category Antiseptic, Topical; Antithyroid Agent

Use Topical antiseptic

Local Anesthetic/Vasoconstrictor Precautions No information available to require special precautions

Effects on Dental Treatment Key adverse event(s) related to dental treatment: Metallic taste.

Effects on Bleeding No information available to require special precautions

Adverse Reactions

Frequency not defined.

Cardiovascular: Cardiac arrhythmia, myxedema

Central nervous system: Confusion, fatigue, metallic taste, numbness, tingling sensation

Dermatologic: Skin rash

Endocrine & metabolic: Goiter, hyperthyroidism, hypothyroidiom

Gastrointestinal: Diarrhea, enlargement of salivary glands, gastric distress, gastrointestinal hemorrhage, nausea, salivary gland disease (tenderness), stomach pain, vomiting

Hematologic & oncologic: Adenopathy, thyroid adenoma

Hypersensitivity: Hypersensitivity reaction (angioedema, cutaneous and mucosal hemorrhage, serum sickness-like symptoms)

Neuromuscular & skeletal: Arthralgia, weakness

Respiratory: Pharyngeal edema

Miscellaneous: Drug overdose (with prolonged treatment/high doses), fever, iodism

General Dosage Range Topical: *Adults:* Apply directly to area(s) requiring antiseptic

Mechanism of Action In hyperthyroidism, iodine temporarily inhibits thyroid hormone synthesis and secretion into the circulation; use also decreases thyroid gland size and vascularity. Serum T_4 and T_3 concentrations can be reduced for several weeks with use but effect will not be maintained.

Following radioactive iodine exposure, potassium iodide blocks uptake of radioiodine by the thyroid, reducing the risk of thyroid cancer.

Pharmacodynamics/Kinetics

Onset of Action Hyperthyroidism: 24-48 hours; Peak effect: 10-15 days after continuous therapy

Pregnancy Risk Factor D (potassium iodide)

Pregnancy Considerations Iodide crosses the placenta (may cause hypothyroidism and goiter in fetus/newborn). Use for protection against thyroid cancer secondary to radioactive iodine exposure is considered acceptable based upon risk:benefit, keeping in mind the dose and duration. Repeat dosing should be avoided if possible. Refer to Iodine for additional information.

Potassium P-Aminobenzoate

(poe TASS ee um pe a mee noe BEN zoe ate)

Brand Names: US M2 Potassium [OTC] [DSC]; Potaba

Pharmacologic Category Vitamin, Water Soluble

Use Presently, all indications are classified by the FDA as "possibly effective."

Treatment of scleroderma, dermatomyositis, morphea, linear scleroderma, pemphigus, Peyronie's disease

Local Anesthetic/Vasoconstrictor Precautions No information available to require special precautions

Effects on Dental Treatment No significant effects or complications reported

Effects on Bleeding No information available to require special precautions

Adverse Reactions Frequency not defined.

Dermatologic: Skin rash
Gastrointestinal: Anorexia, nausea
Hypersensitivity: Hypersensitivity reaction
Miscellaneous: Fever

General Dosage Range Oral:

Children: 1 g/10 pounds of weight/day in divided doses
Adults: 12 g/day in 4-6 divided doses

Mechanism of Action P-aminobenzoate is a member of the vitamin B complex family. It may have an antifibrotic effect due to increased oxygen uptake at the tissue level.

Pregnancy Considerations Safety for use in pregnancy has not been established.

Povidone-Iodine (Topical)

(POE vi done EYE oh dyne)

Related Information

Perioral Premalignant Lesions and Management of Patients Undergoing Cancer Therapy *on page 1875*

Brand Names: US Betadine Skin Cleanser [OTC]; Betadine Spray [OTC] [DSC]; Betadine Surgical Scrub [OTC]; Betadine Swab Aid [OTC]; Betadine Swabsticks [OTC]; Betadine [OTC]; ExCel AP [OTC]; GRX Dyne Scrub [OTC] [DSC]; GRX Dyne [OTC] [DSC]; Nasal Antiseptic [OTC]; NuPrep 5% Povidone-Iodine [OTC]; Operand Povidone-Iodine [OTC]; Operand Scrub [OTC]; PVP Prep [OTC]; Summers Eve Disp Medicated [OTC]

Brand Names: Canada Betadine®; Proviodine

Pharmacologic Category Antiseptic, Topical; Antiseptic, Vaginal; Topical Skin Product

Use External antiseptic with broad microbicidal spectrum for the prevention or treatment of topical infections associated with surgery, burns, minor cuts/scrapes; relief of minor vaginal irritation

Local Anesthetic/Vasoconstrictor Precautions No information available to require special precautions

Effects on Dental Treatment No significant effects or complications reported

Effects on Bleeding No information available to require special precautions

Adverse Reactions Frequency not defined. Also refer to Iodine monograph.

Local: Edema, irritation, pruritus, rash

General Dosage Range

Intravaginal: *Adults:* Insert 0.3% solution vaginally once daily

Topical: *Adults:* Apply to affected area as needed **or** apply to wet skin or hands, scrub for ~5 minutes, then rinse

Mechanism of Action Povidone-iodine is known to be a powerful broad spectrum germicidal agent effective against a wide range of bacteria, viruses, fungi, protozoa, and spores.

Pregnancy Considerations Vaginal products should not be used during pregnancy. Povidine-iodine is absorbed systemically as iodine following topical administration to the vaginal mucosa (Velasco 2009; Vorherr 1980). Following vaginal administration as a douche, iodine concentrations are increased in the maternal urine, amniotic fluid, cord blood and fetal thyroid (Bachrach 1984; Mahillon 1989). Transient hypothyroidism in the newborn has been reported following topical use prior to delivery (Danziger 1984). Refer to Iodine for additional information.

PRALAtrexate (pral a TREX ate)

Brand Names: US Folotyn

Pharmacologic Category Antineoplastic Agent, Antimetabolite; Antineoplastic Agent, Antimetabolite (Antifolate)

Use Peripheral T-cell lymphoma: Treatment of relapsed or refractory peripheral T-cell lymphoma (PTCL)

Local Anesthetic/Vasoconstrictor Precautions No information available to require special precautions

Effects on Dental Treatment Key adverse event(s) related to dental treatment: Mucositis and stomatitis

Effects on Bleeding No information available to require special precautions

Adverse Reactions

>10%:

Cardiovascular: Edema (30%)
Central nervous system: Fatigue (36%)
Dermatologic: Skin rash (15%), pruritus (14%; grade 3: 2%), night sweats (11%)
Endocrine & metabolic: Hypokalemia (15%)
Gastrointestinal: Mucositis (70%; grade 3: 17%; grade 4: 4%), nausea (40%), constipation (33%), vomiting (25%), diarrhea (21%), anorexia (15%), abdominal pain (12%)
Hematologic & oncologic: Thrombocytopenia (41%; grade 3: 14%; grade 4: 19%), anemia (34%; grade 3: 15%; grade 4: 2%), neutropenia (24%; grade 3: 13%; grade 4: 7%), leukopenia (11%; grade 3: 3%; grade 4: 4%)
Hepatic: Increased serum transaminases (13%; grade 3: 5%)
Infection: Infection
Neuromuscular & skeletal: Limb pain (12%), back pain (11%)
Respiratory: Cough (28%), epistaxis (26%), dyspnea (19%), pharyngolaryngeal pain (14%)
Miscellaneous: Fever (32%)

1% to 10%:

Cardiovascular: Tachycardia (10%)
Endocrine & metabolic: Severe dehydration (>3%)
Hematologic & oncologic: Febrile neutropenia (serious: >3%)
Infection: Sepsis (serious: >3%)
Neuromuscular & skeletal: Weakness (10%)
Respiratory: Upper respiratory tract infection (10%)

<1%, postmarketing, and/or case reports: Dermal ulcer, desquamation, intestinal obstruction, lymphocytopenia, odynophagia, pancytopenia, toxic epidermal necrolysis, tumor lysis syndrome

General Dosage Range Dosage adjustment recommended in patients with renal impairment, hepatic impairment, or who develop toxicities.

IV: *Adults:* 30 mg/m^2 once weekly for 6 weeks of a 7-week treatment cycle

Mechanism of Action Antifolate analog; inhibits DNA, RNA, and protein synthesis by selectively entering cells expressing reduced folate carrier (RFC-1), is polyglutamylated by folylpolyglutamate synthetase (FPGS) and then competes for the DHFR-folate binding site to inhibit dihydrofolate reductase (DHFR)

Pharmacodynamics/Kinetics

Half-life Elimination 12 to 18 hours

Pregnancy Risk Factor D

Pregnancy Considerations Adverse effects were observed in animal reproduction studies. May cause fetal harm if administered to a pregnant woman.

Pramipexole (pra mi PEKS ole)

Brand Names: US Mirapex; Mirapex ER

Brand Names: Canada ACT-Pramipexole; Apo-Pramipexole; Auro-Pramipexole; Ava-Pramipexole; Dom-Pramipexole; Mirapex; Mylan-Pramipexole; PMS-Pramipexole; Sandoz-Pramipexole; Teva-Pramipexole

Pharmacologic Category Anti-Parkinson Agent, Dopamine Agonist

Use

Parkinson disease: Treatment of Parkinson disease.

Restless legs syndrome (immediate release only): Treatment of moderate to severe primary restless legs syndrome (RLS).

Local Anesthetic/Vasoconstrictor Precautions No information available to require special precautions

Effects on Dental Treatment Key adverse event(s) related to dental treatment: Xerostomia (normal salivary flow resumes upon discontinuation) and dysphagia.

Effects on Bleeding No information available to require special precautions

Adverse Reactions Actual frequency may be dependent on dose and/or formulation. All adverse reactions are as reported for Parkinson disease unless otherwise noted.

>10%:

Cardiovascular: Orthostatic hypotension (3% to 53%; dose related)

Central nervous system: Drowsiness (Parkinson disease: 9% to 36%; dose related; restless leg syndrome: 6%), extrapyramidal reaction (28%), insomnia (Parkinson disease: 4% to 27%; restless leg syndrome: 13%), dizziness (2% to 26%), hallucination (5% to 17%), headache (restless leg syndrome: 16%; Parkinson disease: 4% to 7%), worsening of restless leg syndrome (augmentation; 12%), abnormal dreams (Parkinson disease: 11%; restless leg syndrome: 8%)

Gastrointestinal: Nausea (Parkinson disease: 11% to 28%; dose related; restless leg syndrome: 11% to 27%), constipation (Parkinson disease: 6% to 14%; dose related; restless leg syndrome: 4%)

Neuromuscular & skeletal: Dyskinesia (17% to 47%), weakness (3% to 14%)

Miscellaneous: Accidental injury (17%)

1% to 10%:

Cardiovascular: Peripheral edema (2% to 8%), edema (4% to 5%), chest pain (3%)

Central nervous system: Worsening of restless leg syndrome (rebound; 10%), confusion (4% to 10%), fatigue (restless leg syndrome: 7% to 9%; Parkinson disease: 6%), dystonia (2% to 8%), abnormal gait (7%), hypertonia (7%), amnesia (4% to 6%; dose related), narcolepsy (2% to 6%), falling (4%), impulse control disorder (3% to 4%; eg, binge eating, hypersexuality, pathological gambling, shopping), vertigo (2% to 4%), hypoesthesia (3%), abnormality in thinking (2% to 3%), akathisia (2% to 3%), malaise (2% to 3%), sleep disorder (1% to 3%), equilibrium disturbance (2%), paranoia (2%), depression (2%), delusions (1%), myasthenia (1%), myoclonus (1%)

Dermatologic: Dermatological disease (2%)

Endocrine & metabolic: Weight loss (2%), decreased libido (1%)

Gastrointestinal: Xerostomia (Parkinson disease: 4% to 7%; restless leg syndrome: 3%), diarrhea (restless leg syndrome: 1% to 7%; Parkinson disease: 2%), anorexia (4% to 5%), vomiting (4%), upper abdominal pain (3% to 4%), dyspepsia (3%), increased appetite (2% to 3%), dysphagia (2%), sialorrhea (2%), abdominal distress (1% to 2%)

Genitourinary: Urinary frequency (6%), urinary tract infection (4%), impotence (2%), urinary incontinence (2%)

Infection: Influenza (restless leg syndrome: 3% to 7%)

Neuromuscular & skeletal: Limb pain (restless leg syndrome: 3% to 7%), muscle spasm (5%), arthritis (3%), tremor (3%), back pain (2% to 3%), bursitis (2%), muscle twitching (2%), elevated creatinine phosphokinase (1%)

Ophthalmic: Accommodation disturbance (4%), visual disturbance (3%), diplopia (1%)

Respiratory: Nasal congestion (restless leg syndrome: 3% to 6%), dyspnea (4%), cough (3%), rhinitis (3%), pneumonia (2%)

Miscellaneous: Fever (1%)

<1%, postmarketing, and/or case reports: Aggressive behavior, agitation, altered mental status, behavioral changes, cardiac failure, delirium, delusions, disorientation, fibrothorax, increased libido, paranoia, retroperitoneal fibrosis, psychotic symptoms, pulmonary fibrosis, rhabdomyolysis, SIADH, syncope, weight gain

General Dosage Range Dosage adjustment recommended in patients with renal impairment

Oral: Immediate release: *Adults:* Initial: 0.125 mg 3 times daily **or** 0.125 mg once daily before bedtime; Maintenance: 0.5 to 1.5 mg 3 times daily **or** 0.125 to 0.5 mg once daily before bedtime

Oral: Extended release: *Adults:* 0.375 to 4.5 mg once daily

Mechanism of Action Pramipexole is a nonergot dopamine agonist with specificity for the D_2 subfamily dopamine receptor, and has also been shown to bind to D_3 and D_4 receptors. By binding to these receptors, it is thought that pramipexole can stimulate dopamine activity on the nerves of the striatum and substantia nigra.

Pharmacodynamics/Kinetics

Half-life Elimination 8.5 hours; Elderly: 12 hours

Time to Peak Serum: Immediate release: ~2 hours; Extended release: 6 hours

Pregnancy Considerations Adverse events were observed in animal reproduction studies. Information related to the use of pramipexole for the treatment of Parkinson's disease (Benbir, 2013; Mucchiut 2004) or restless legs syndrome (RLS) (Dostal, 2013) in pregnant women is limited. Current guidelines note that the available information is insufficient to make a recommendation for the treatment of RLS in pregnant women (Aurora, 2012).

Pramlintide (PRAM lin tide)

Related Information

Endocrine Disorders and Pregnancy *on page 1781*

Brand Names: US SymlinPen 120; SymlinPen 60

Pharmacologic Category Amylinomimetic; Antidiabetic Agent

Use Type 1 and type 2 diabetes: Adjunct treatment in patients with type 1 or type 2 diabetes who use mealtime insulin therapy and who have failed to achieve desired glucose control despite optimal insulin therapy.

Local Anesthetic/Vasoconstrictor Precautions No information available to require special precautions

Effects on Dental Treatment No significant effects or complications reported

Effects on Bleeding No information available to require special precautions

Adverse Reactions

>10%:

Central nervous system: Headache (5% to 13%)

Endocrine & metabolic: Severe hypoglycemia (type 1 diabetes ≤17%)

Gastrointestinal: Nausea (28% to 48%), anorexia (≤17%), vomiting (7% to 11%)

Miscellaneous: Accidental injury (8% to 14%)

1% to 10%:

Central nervous system: Fatigue (3% to 7%), dizziness (2% to 6%)

Endocrine & metabolic: Severe hypoglycemia (type 2 diabetes ≤8%)

Gastrointestinal: Abdominal pain (2% to 8%)

Hypersensitivity: Hypersensitivity reaction (≤6%)

Neuromuscular & skeletal: Arthralgia (2% to 7%)

Respiratory: Cough (2% to 6%), pharyngitis (3% to 5%)

Postmarketing and/or case reports: Injection site reaction, pancreatitis

General Dosage Range SubQ: *Adults:*

Type 1 diabetes mellitus: Initial: 15 mcg immediately prior to major meals; Target dose: 30 to 60 mcg prior to major meals

Type 2 diabetes mellitus: Initial: 60 mcg immediately prior to major meals; after 3 days may increase to 120 mcg prior to major meals

Mechanism of Action Synthetic analog of human amylin cosecreted with insulin by pancreatic beta cells; reduces postprandial glucose increases via the following mechanisms: 1) prolongation of gastric emptying time, 2) reduction of postprandial glucagon secretion, and 3) reduction of caloric intake through centrally-mediated appetite suppression

Pharmacodynamics/Kinetics

Duration of Action ~3 hours

Half-life Elimination ~48 minutes

Time to Peak 20 minutes

Pregnancy Risk Factor C

Pregnancy Considerations Adverse events have been observed in animal reproduction studies. Based on in vitro data, pramlintide has a low potential to cross the placenta.

In women with diabetes, maternal hyperglycemia can be associated with congenital malformations as well as adverse effects in the fetus, neonate, and the mother (ACOG 2005; ADA 2016; Kitzmiller 2008; Metzger 2007). To prevent adverse outcomes, prior to conception and throughout pregnancy maternal blood glucose and HbA_{1c} should be kept as close to target goals as possible but without causing significant hypoglycemia (ACOG 2013; ADA 2016; Blumer 2013; Kitzmiller 2008). Agents other than pramlintide are currently recommended to treat diabetes in pregnant women (ACOG 2013; Blumer 2013).

Pramoxine (pra MOKS een)

Brand Names: US Calaclear [OTC]; Caladryl Clear [OTC]; Callergy Clear [OTC]; CeraVe Itch Relief [OTC]; Itch-X [OTC]; Ivy Wash Poison Ivy Cleanser [OTC]; PrameGel [OTC]; Pramox; Prax [OTC]; Proctofoam [OTC]; Sarna Sensitive [OTC]

Pharmacologic Category Antihemorrhoidal Agent; Local Anesthetic

Use Temporary relief of pain and itching associated with hemorrhoids, burns, minor cuts, scrapes, or minor skin irritations

Local Anesthetic/Vasoconstrictor Precautions No information available to require special precautions

Effects on Dental Treatment No significant effects or complications reported

Effects on Bleeding No information available to require special precautions

General Dosage Range Topical:

Children ≥2 years and Adults: Lotion, cream: Apply up to 3-4 times daily

Children ≥12 years and Adults: Hemorrhoidal foam, ointment, wipes: Apply up to 5 times daily

Mechanism of Action Pramoxine, like other anesthetics, decreases the neuronal membrane's permeability to sodium ions; both initiation and conduction of nerve impulses are blocked, thus depolarization of the neuron is inhibited

Pharmacodynamics/Kinetics

Onset of Action 3-5 minutes

Prasterone (PRAS ter one)

Pharmacologic Category Steroid, Synthetic

Use Dyspareunia: Treatment of moderate to severe dyspareunia (a symptom of vulvar and vaginal atrophy due to menopause)

Local Anesthetic/Vasoconstrictor Precautions No information available to require special precautions

Effects on Dental Treatment No significant effects or complications reported

Effects on Bleeding No information available to require special precautions

Adverse Reactions

>10%: Genitourinary: Vaginal discharge (6% to 14%)

1% to 10%: Genitourinary: Abnormal pap smear (2%)

General Dosage Range Intravaginal: *Adults (females):* 6.5 mg once daily at bedtime

Mechanism of Action An inactive steroid that is converted into active androgens and/or estrogens; the mechanism of action in postmenopausal women with vulvar and vaginal atrophy is unknown.

Pregnancy Considerations Animal reproduction studies have not been conducted with this preparation; this product is only approved for use in postmenopausal women.

Other formulations of prasterone (dehydroepiandrosterone [DHEA]) have been evaluated to improve pregnancy outcomes in women with diminished ovarian reserve (Gleicher 2011; Narkwichean 2013).

Product Availability Intrarosa: FDA approved November 2016; anticipated availability is currently undetermined

Prasugrel (PRA soo grel)

Related Information

Antiplatelet and Anticoagulation Considerations in Dentistry *on page 1764*

Cardiovascular Diseases *on page 1752*

Brand Names: US Effient

Brand Names: Canada Effient

Generic Availability (US) No

Pharmacologic Category Antiplatelet Agent; Antiplatelet Agent, Thienopyridine

Use Acute coronary syndrome to be managed with percutaneous coronary intervention (PCI): To reduce the rate of thrombotic cardiovascular events (including stent thrombosis) in patients with acute coronary syndrome (ACS) who are to be managed with PCI for unstable angina (UA), non-ST-segment elevation MI (NSTEMI), or ST-elevation MI (STEMI).

Local Anesthetic/Vasoconstrictor Precautions No information available to require special precautions

Effects on Dental Treatment Key adverse event(s) related to dental treatment: May cause bleeding during invasive dental procedures and medical consultation is suggested prior to any consideration of discontinuation. If possible, manage bleeding without discontinuing therapy; premature discontinuation of treatment may increase the risk for cardiac adverse effects.

Aspirin in combination with clopidogrel (Plavix®), prasugrel (Effient®), or ticagrelor (Brilinta™) is the primary prevention strategy against stent thrombosis after placement of drug-eluting metal stents in coronary patients. Premature discontinuation of combination antiplatelet therapy (ie, dual antiplatelet therapy) strongly increases the risk of a catastrophic event of stent thrombosis leading to myocardial infarction and/or death, so says a science advisory issued in January 2007 from the American Heart Association in collaboration with the American Dental Association and other professional healthcare organizations. The advisory stresses a 12-month therapy of dual antiplatelet therapy after placement of a drug-eluting stent in order to prevent thrombosis at the stent site. Any elective surgery should be postponed for 1 year after stent implantation, and if surgery must be performed, consideration should be given to continuing the antiplatelet therapy during the perioperative period in high-risk patients with drug-eluting stents.

This advisory was issued from a science panel made up of representatives from the American Heart Association (AHA), the American College of Cardiology, the Society for Cardiovascular Angiography and Interventions, the American College of Surgeons, the American Dental Association (ADA), and the American College of Physicians (Grines, 2007).

Effects on Bleeding Prasugrel blocks platelet aggregation and may prolong bleeding time. Inhibition is irreversible; on discontinuation of prasugrel, normal platelet function returns only when new platelets are released from the bone marrow. Normal platelet function will occur within 5-9 days of discontinuation. There is no scientific evidence to warrant the discontinuance of prasugrel prior to dental surgery.

Dual antiplatelet therapy: Aspirin irreversibly inhibits platelet aggregation which can prolong bleeding. Upon discontinuation, normal platelet function returns only when new platelets are released (~7-10 days). However, in the case of dental surgery, there is no scientific evidence to support discontinuation of aspirin. The discontinuation of aspirin may place the patient at risk for a thrombotic event or other cardiovascular complication. In particular, aspirin should **not** be discontinued in patients with cardiac stents that have not completed their full course of dual antiplatelet therapy (eg, aspirin and clopidogrel [prasugrel or ticagrelor]); patient-specific situations need to be discussed with cardiologist. When feasible, postponement of dental surgery until the completion of dual antiplatelet therapy should be considered. Any modification of aspirin therapy should be discussed with the prescribing physician.

Adverse Reactions

1% to 10%:

Cardiovascular: Hypertension (8%), hypotension (4%), atrial fibrillation (3%), bradycardia (3%), peripheral edema (3%)

Central nervous system: Headache (6%), dizziness (4%), fatigue (4%), noncardiac chest pain (3%)

Dermatologic: Skin rash (3%)

Endocrine & metabolic: Hypercholesterolemia (≤7%), hyperlipidemia (≤7%)

Gastrointestinal: Nausea (5%), diarrhea (2%), gastrointestinal hemorrhage (2%)

Hematologic & oncologic: Leukopenia (3%), anemia (2%), major hemorrhage (2%), minor hemorrhage (2%), major hemmorhage (life-threatening: 1%)

Neuromuscular & skeletal: Back pain (5%), limb pain (3%)

Respiratory: Epistaxis (6%), dyspnea (5%), cough (4%)

Miscellaneous: Fever (3%)

<1%, postmarketing, and/or case reports: Abnormal hepatic function tests, anaphylaxis, angioedema, hematoma, hemoptysis, hemorrhage (requiring inotropes or transfusion), hypersensitivity reaction, intracranial hemorrhage (symptomatic), re-operation due to bleeding, thrombocytopenia, thrombotic thrombocytopenic purpura

Dosing

Adult Acute coronary syndrome (ACS): Oral:

Percutaneous coronary intervention (PCI) for ACS: Loading dose: 60 mg administered promptly (as soon as coronary anatomy is known) and no later than 1 hour after PCI; Maintenance dose: 10 mg once daily (in combination with aspirin) (ACCF/AHA [O'Gara, 2013]; AHA/ACC [Amsterdam 2014]; Levine 2011). For patients with STEMI, a loading dose may also be administered if PCI is performed >24 hours after treatment with a fibrin-specific thrombolytic (ie, alteplase, reteplase, tenecteplase) (ACCF/AHA [O'Gara, 2013]).

Maintenance dosing in low body weight (ie, <60 kg) Individuals: Due to a higher incidence of bleeding in patients weighing <60 kg, a maintenance dose of 5 mg once daily may be considered. In aspirin-treated patients weighing <60 kg (mean: 56.4 ± 3.7 kg) with stable coronary artery disease, the use of prasugrel 5 mg once daily was shown to reduce platelet reactivity to a similar extent as prasugrel 10 mg administered once daily to patients >60 kg (mean: 84.7 ± 14.9 kg); clinical events were not evaluated (Erlinge 2012). In patients with ACS (medically managed) treated with aspirin, a 5 mg daily maintenance dose (after a 30 mg loading dose) in patients <60 kg did not demonstrate a significant difference in the composite primary end point of death from cardiovascular causes, MI, or stroke compared to patients >60 kg treated with a 10 mg maintenance dose; bleeding risk was not increased (Roe 2012).

Duration of prasugrel (in combination with aspirin) after stent placement: **Premature interruption of therapy may result in stent thrombosis, MI, and death.** According to the ACC/AHA Duration of Dual Antiplatelet Therapy (DAPT) guidelines, at least 12 months of a $P2Y_{12}$ inhibitor (eg, prasugrel) is recommended for those with ACS receiving either stent type (bare metal [BMS] or drug eluting stent [DES]). The DAPT score may be useful in determining whether to prolong or extend DAPT in patients with stent placement (Yeh 2016). In addition, in patients with DES placement with a high risk of bleeding or significant overt bleeding on DAPT, it may be reasonable to discontinue prasugrel after 6 months of therapy instead (ACC/AHA [Levine 2016]).

Conversion from clopidogrel to prasugrel: Beginning 24 hours after the last clopidogrel dose (loading or maintenance), may initiate prasugrel 10 mg once daily or a 60 mg loading dose followed in 24 hours with 10 mg once daily (Angiolillo 2010; Payne 2008; Wiviott 2007).

Geriatric Refer to adult dosing. Patients ≥75 years: Use not recommended; may be considered in high-risk situations (eg, patients with diabetes or history of MI).

Renal Impairment No dosage adjustment necessary; use caution in moderate to severe impairment (patients are generally at higher risk of bleeding).

Hepatic Impairment

Mild to moderate hepatic impairment (Child-Pugh class A and B): No dosage adjustment necessary for mild-to-moderate hepatic impairment.

Severe hepatic impairment (Child-Pugh class C): There are no dosage adjustments provided in the manufacturer's labeling (has not been studied); use caution (patients are generally at higher risk of bleeding).

Mechanism of Action Prasugrel, an inhibitor of platelet activation and aggregation, is a prodrug that is metabolized to both active (R-138727) and inactive metabolites. The active metabolite irreversibly blocks the $P2Y_{12}$ component of ADP receptors on the platelet, which prevents activation of the GPIIb/IIIa receptor complex, thereby reducing platelet activation and aggregation

Contraindications Hypersensitivity (eg, anaphylaxis) to prasugrel or any component of the formulation; active pathological bleeding (eg, peptic ulcer, intracranial hemorrhage); prior TIA or stroke.

Warnings/Precautions [US Boxed Warning]: May cause significant, sometimes fatal, bleeding. Do not use prasugrel in patients with active pathological bleeding or a history of TIA or stroke. Additional risk factors for bleeding include body weight <60 kg, propensity to bleed (eg, recent trauma, recent surgery, recent or recurrent GI bleeding, active peptic ulcer disease, severe hepatic impairment, or moderate to severe renal impairment), and concomitant use of medications that increase the risk of bleeding (eg, warfarin, heparin, fibrinolytic therapy, long-term use of NSAIDs). Suspect bleeding in any patient who is hypotensive and has recently undergone coronary angiography, PCI, CABG, or other surgical procedures in the setting of prasugrel. If possible, manage bleeding without discontinuing prasugrel. Discontinuing prasugrel, particularly in the first few weeks after ACS, increases the risk of subsequent cardiovascular events. Management of bleeding episodes includes the use of PRBCs and platelet transfusion.

[US Boxed Warning]: In patients ≥75 years, use is generally not recommended due to increased risk of fatal and intracranial bleeding and uncertain benefit, except in high-risk situations (patients with diabetes or a history of MI) in which its effect appears to be greater and its use may be considered. [US Boxed Warning]: Do not initiate therapy in patients likely to undergo urgent CABG surgery; when possible, discontinue ≥7 days prior to any surgery; increased risk of bleeding. The American College of Chest Physicians (ACCP) recommends discontinuing prasugrel 5 days before surgery (Guyatt, 2012). When urgent CABG is necessary, the ACCF/AHA CABG guidelines suggest that it may be reasonable to perform surgery within 7 days of discontinuing prasugrel especially if the benefits of prompt revascularization outweigh the risks of bleeding (ACCF/AHA [Hillis, 2011]; ACCF/AHA [O'Gara, 2013]).

Hypersensitivity, including angioedema, has been reported, including in patients with a previous history of thienopyridine hypersensitivity. Because of structural similarities, cross-reactivity is possible among the thienopyridines (clopidogrel, prasugrel, and ticlopidine); use with caution or avoid in patients with previous history of thienopyridine hypersensitivity. Use of prasugrel is contraindicated in patients with hypersensitivity (eg, anaphylaxis) to prasugrel. If necessary, discontinue therapy for active bleeding, elective surgery, stroke, or TIA; reinitiate therapy as soon as possible unless patient suffers stroke or TIA where subsequent use is contraindicated. If possible, manage bleeding without discontinuing prasugrel. Potentially significant drug-drug interactions may exist, requiring dose or frequency adjustment, additional monitoring, and/or selection of alternative therapy. Use with caution in patients with recent or recurrent GI bleeding or active peptic ulcer disease, severe hepatic impairment or moderate to severe renal impairment (patients are generally are at higher risk of bleeding). Cases of thrombotic thrombocytopenic purpura (TTP) (usually occurring within the first 2 weeks of therapy), resulting in some fatalities, have been reported with prasugrel; urgent plasmapheresis is required. In patients <60 kg, risk of bleeding increased; consider lower maintenance dose.

Drug Interactions

Metabolism/Transport Effects Substrate of CYP2B6 (minor), CYP3A4 (minor); **Note:** Assignment of Major/Minor substrate status based on clinically relevant drug interaction potential; **Inhibits** CYP2B6 (weak)

Avoid Concomitant Use

Avoid concomitant use of Prasugrel with any of the following: Urokinase

Increased Effect/Toxicity

Prasugrel may increase the levels/effects of: Agents with Antiplatelet Properties; Anticoagulants; Apixaban; Cephalothin; Collagenase (Systemic); Dabigatran Etexilate; Deoxycholic Acid; Edoxaban; Ibritumomab; Obinutuzumab; Rivaroxaban; Salicylates; Thrombolytic Agents; Tositumomab and Iodine I 131 Tositumomab; Urokinase

The levels/effects of Prasugrel may be increased by: Dasatinib; Glucosamine; Herbs (Anticoagulant/Antiplatelet Properties); Ibrutinib; Limaprost; Multivitamins/Fluoride (with ADE); Multivitamins/Minerals (with ADEK, Folate, Iron); Multivitamins/Minerals (with AE, No Iron); Omega-3 Fatty Acids; Pentosan

Polysulfate Sodium; Pentoxifylline; Prostacyclin Analogues; Tipranavir; Vitamin E (Systemic)

Decreased Effect

The levels/effects of Prasugrel may be decreased by: Cangrelor; CYP3A4 Inhibitors (Strong); Morphine (Liposomal); Morphine (Systemic); RaNITIdine; RifAMPin

Pharmacodynamics/Kinetics

Onset of Action Inhibition of platelet aggregation (IPA): Dose dependent: 60 mg loading dose: <30 minutes; median time to reach ≥20% IPA: 30 minutes (Brandt, 2007)

Peak effect: Time to maximal IPA: Dose-dependent: **Note:** Degree of IPA based on adenosine diphosphate (ADP) concentration used during light aggregometry: 60 mg loading dose: Occurs ~4 hours post administration; Mean IPA (ADP 5 micromol/L): ~84.1%; Mean IPA (ADP 20 micromole/L): ~78.8% (Brandt, 2007)

Duration of Action Duration of effect: Platelet aggregation gradually returns to baseline values over 5-9 days after discontinuation; reflective of new platelet production

Half-life Elimination Half-life elimination: Active metabolite: ~7 hours (range: 2-15 hours)

Time to Peak Active metabolite: ~30 minutes; With high-fat/high-calorie meal: 1.5 hours

Pregnancy Considerations Adverse events have not been observed in animal reproduction studies. Information related to use during pregnancy is limited (Tello-Montoliu, 2012).

Breastfeeding Considerations It is not known if prasugrel is excreted in breast milk. According to the manufacturer, the decision to continue or discontinue breastfeeding during therapy should take into account the risk of infant exposure, the benefits of breastfeeding to the infant, and benefits of treatment to the mother.

Dosage Forms

Tablet, Oral:

Effient: 5 mg, 10 mg

Dental Comment There is no scientific evidence to warrant the discontinuance of prasugrel prior to dental surgery. Patients requiring dental surgery who are taking 1 tablet daily as an antithrombotic or taking 1 tablet daily in combination with aspirin should be given special consideration in consultation with their healthcare provider.

Pravastatin (prav a STAT in)

Related Information

Cardiovascular Diseases *on page 1752*

Brand Names: US Pravachol

Brand Names: Canada ACT Pravastatin; Apo-Pravastatin; Dom-Pravastatin; JAMP-Pravastatin; Mint-Pravastatin; Mylan-Pravastatin; PMS-Pravastatin; Pravachol; RAN-Pravastatin; Riva-Pravastatin; Sandoz-Pravastatin; Teva-Pravastatin

Generic Availability (US) Yes

Pharmacologic Category Antilipemic Agent, HMG-CoA Reductase Inhibitor

Use

Hyperlipidemia

Dysbetalipoproteinemia: Treatment of primary dysbetalipoproteinemia (Fredrickson type III) in patients who do not respond adequately to diet.

Heterozygous familial hypercholesterolemia: Adjunct to diet in children ≥8 years and adolescents with heterozygous familial hypercholesterolemia (HeFH) if after an adequate trial of diet therapy the following findings are present: LDL-C ≥190 mg/dL or LDL ≥160 mg/dL with positive family history of premature cardiovascular disease (CVD), or with 2 or more other CVD risk factors.

Hypercholesterolemia and mixed dyslipidemia: Adjunct to diet to reduce elevated total cholesterol, LDL-C, apo B, and triglyceride (TG) levels and to increase HDL-C in patients with primary hypercholesterolemia and mixed dyslipidemia (Fredrickson Types IIa and IIb).

Limitations of use: Has not been studied in conditions where the major lipid abnormality is elevation of chylomicrons (Fredrickson types I and V).

Prevention of cardiovascular disease

Primary prevention of cardiovascular disease: To reduce the risk of myocardial infarction, revascularization procedures and cardiovascular mortality in hypercholesterolemic patients without established coronary heart disease (CHD).

Secondary prevention of cardiovascular disease: To slow the progression of coronary atherosclerosis; to reduce the risk of myocardial infarction, revascularization procedures, and total mortality; and to reduce the risk of stroke and transient ischemic attacks (TIA) in patients with established CHD.

Guideline recommendations: Primary and secondary prevention of atherosclerotic cardiovascular disease (ASCVD) to reduce the risk of ASCVD in select adult patients (ACC/AHA [Stone 2013]; NLA [Jacobson 2015]). Refer to respective guideline for specific recommendations.

Local Anesthetic/Vasoconstrictor Precautions No information available to require special precautions

Effects on Dental Treatment Key adverse event(s) related to dental treatment: Assess unusual presentations of muscle weakness or myopathy resulting from lipid therapy such as patient having a difficult time brushing teeth or weakness with chewing. Refer patient back to their physician for evaluation and adjustment of lipid therapy.

Effects on Bleeding No information available to require special precautions

Adverse Reactions As reported in short-term trials; safety and tolerability with long-term use were similar to placebo.

1% to 10%:

Cardiovascular: Chest pain (4%)

Central nervous system: Headache (2% to 6%), fatigue (4%), dizziness (1% to 3%)

Dermatologic: Skin rash (4%)

Gastrointestinal: Nausea (≤7%), vomiting (≤7%), diarrhea (6%), heartburn (3%)

Genitourinary: Cystitis (interstitial; Huang 2015)

Hepatic: Increased serum transaminases (>3x normal on 2 occasions: 1%)

Infection: Influenza (2%)

Neuromuscular & skeletal: Myalgia (2%)

Respiratory: Cough (3%)

<1%, postmarketing, and/or case reports: Alopecia, amnesia (reversible), anaphylaxis, angioedema, cataract, change in libido, cholestatic jaundice, cognitive dysfunction (reversible), confusion (reversible), cranial nerve dysfunction, decreased appetite, dermatitis, dermatomyositis, dysgeusia, edema, erythema multiforme, fever, flushing, fulminant hepatic necrosis, gynecomastia, hemolytic anemia, hepatic cirrhosis, hepatic neoplasm, hepatitis, hypersensitivity reaction, increased erythrocyte sedimentation rate, insomnia, lupus-like syndrome, memory impairment (reversible), myasthenia, myopathy, neuropathy, pancreatitis,

paresthesia, peripheral nerve palsy, polymyalgia rheumatica, positive ANA titer, pruritus, purpura, rhabdomyolysis, sexual disorder, Stevens-Johnson syndrome, tremor, urticaria, vasculitis, vertigo, xeroderma

Dosing

Adult & Geriatric Note: Doses should be individualized according to the baseline LDL-cholesterol levels, the recommended goal of therapy, and patient response; adjustments should be made at intervals of 4 weeks or more; doses may need adjusted based on concomitant medications.

Hyperlipidemias, primary prevention of coronary events, secondary prevention of cardiovascular events (also see ACC/AHA Blood Cholesterol Guideline recommendations): Oral: Initial: 40 mg once daily; titrate dosage to response (maximum dose: 80 mg/day)

Prevention of cardiovascular disease/reduce the risk of ASCVD:

ACC/AHA Blood Cholesterol Guideline recommendations (ACC/AHA [Stone 2013]): Adults ≥21 years:

Primary prevention:

LDL-C ≥190 mg/dL: High intensity therapy necessary; use alternate statin therapy (eg, atorvastatin or rosuvastatin)

Type 1 or 2 diabetes and age 40 to 75 years: Moderate intensity therapy: 40 to 80 mg once daily

Type 1 or 2 diabetes, age 40 to 75 years, and an estimated 10-year ASCVD risk ≥7.5%: High intensity therapy necessary; use alternate statin therapy (eg, atorvastatin or rosuvastatin)

Age 40 to 75 years and an estimated 10-year ASCVD risk ≥7.5%: Moderate to high intensity therapy: 40 to 80 mg once daily or consider using high intensity statin therapy (eg, atorvastatin or rosuvastatin)

Secondary prevention:

Patient has clinical ASCVD (eg, coronary heart disease, stroke/TIA, or peripheral arterial disease presumed to be of atherosclerotic origin) or is post-CABG (AHA [Kulik 2015]) **and**:

Age ≤75 years: High intensity therapy necessary; use alternate statin therapy (eg, atorvastatin or rosuvastatin)

Age >75 years or not a candidate for high intensity therapy: Moderate intensity therapy: 40 to 80 mg once daily

NLA Dyslipidemia Guideline recommendations (NLA [Jacobson 2015]): Adults ≥20 years:

Primary or secondary prevention: Note: Treatment initiation using either moderate- or high-intensity statin therapy is recommended in qualifying patients based on ASCVD risk assessment criteria **and** baseline non-HDL-C and LDL-C values. Dosage should be individualized based on patient characteristics, tolerance to therapy, and with consideration for non-HDL-C and LDL-C treatment goals.

Moderate-intensity therapy (30% to 50% reduction of LDL-C generally): 40 to 80 mg once daily

High-intensity therapy (≥50% reduction of LDL-C generally): Use alternate statin therapy (eg, atorvastatin or rosuvastatin)

Dosage adjustment for pravastatin with concomitant medications:

Clarithromycin: Maximum pravastatin dose: 40 mg/day.

Cyclosporine: Initial pravastatin dose: 10 mg once daily, titrate with caution (maximum dose: 20 mg/day)

Pediatric

Heterozygous familial hypercholesterolemia (HeFH): Oral:

Children and Adolescents 8 to 13 years: 20 mg once daily

Adolescents 14 to 18 years: 40 mg once daily

Dosage adjustment for pravastatin with concomitant medications (clarithromycin, cyclosporine): Refer to adult dosing.

Note: Doses should be individualized according to the baseline LDL-cholesterol levels, the recommended goal of therapy, and patient response; adjustments should be made at intervals of 4 weeks or more; doses may need adjusted based on concomitant medications.

Renal Impairment Mild to moderate impairment: There are no dosage adjustments provided in the manufacturer's labeling; use with caution.

Severe impairment: Initial: 10 mg once daily

Hepatic Impairment Active hepatic disease or unexplained persistent elevations of serum transaminases: Use is contraindicated.

Adjustment for Toxicity

Severe muscle symptoms or fatigue: Promptly discontinue use; evaluate CPK, creatinine, and urinalysis for myoglobinuria (Stone 2013).

Mild to moderate muscle symptoms: Discontinue use until symptoms can be evaluated; evaluate patient for conditions that may increase the risk for muscle symptoms (eg, hypothyroidism, reduced renal or hepatic function, rheumatologic disorders such as polymyalgia rheumatica, steroid myopathy, vitamin D deficiency, primary muscle diseases). Upon resolution, resume the original or lower dose of pravastatin. If muscle symptoms recur, discontinue pravastatin use. After muscle symptom resolution, may then use a low dose of a different statin; gradually increase if tolerated. In the absence of continued statin use, if muscle symptoms or elevated CPK continues after 2 months, consider other causes of muscle symptoms. If determined to be due to another condition aside from statin use, may resume statin therapy at the original dose (Stone 2013).

Mechanism of Action Pravastatin is a competitive inhibitor of 3-hydroxy-3-methylglutaryl coenzyme A (HMG-CoA) reductase, which is the rate-limiting enzyme involved in *de novo* cholesterol synthesis. In addition to the ability of HMG-CoA reductase inhibitors to decrease levels of high-sensitivity C-reactive protein (hsCRP), they also possess pleiotropic properties including improved endothelial function, reduced inflammation at the site of the coronary plaque, inhibition of platelet aggregation, and anticoagulant effects (de Denus 2002; Ray 2005).

Contraindications Hypersensitivity to pravastatin or any component of the formulation; active liver disease; unexplained persistent elevations of serum transaminases; pregnancy; breastfeeding

Warnings/Precautions Has not been studied in homozygous familial hypercholesterolemia (statins may be less effective due to lack of functional LDL receptors). Secondary causes of hyperlipidemia should be ruled out prior to therapy. Liver function must be monitored by periodic laboratory assessment. Rhabdomyolysis with acute renal failure secondary to myoglobinuria and/or myopathy have been reported; patients should be monitored closely. This risk is dose-related and is increased with concurrent use of erythromycin, cyclosporine, fibric acid derivatives (eg, gemfibrozil), or niacin (doses ≥1 g/day). Temporarily withhold therapy in patients experiencing conditions predisposing to the development of renal failure secondary to rhabdomyolysis (eg, sepsis, hypotension, major surgery, trauma, uncontrolled epilepsy; severe metabolic, endocrine, or electrolyte disorders). Discontinue therapy in any patient in which CPK levels are markedly elevated (>10 times ULN) or if myopathy is suspected/diagnosed. Use caution in patients with inadequately treated hypothyroidism and those taking other drugs associated with myopathy (eg, colchicine); these patients are predisposed to myopathy. Patients should be instructed to report unexplained muscle pain, tenderness, weakness, or brown urine. Immune-mediated necrotizing myopathy (IMNM), an autoimmune-mediated myopathy, has been reported (rarely) with HMG-CoA reductase inhibitor therapy. IMNM presents as proximal muscle weakness with elevated CPK levels, which persists despite discontinuation of HMG-CoA reductase inhibitor therapy; additionally, muscle biopsy may show necrotizing myopathy with limited inflammation; immunosuppressive therapy (eg, corticosteroids, azathioprine) may be used for treatment. The manufacturer recommends temporary discontinuation for elective major surgery, acute medical or surgical conditions, or in any patient experiencing an acute or serious condition predisposing to renal failure (eg, sepsis, hypotension, trauma, uncontrolled seizures). Based on current research and clinical guidelines (Fleisher 2009), HMG-CoA reductase inhibitors should be continued in the perioperative period. Postoperative discontinuation of statin therapy is associated with an increased risk of cardiac morbidity and mortality.

Reduced cholesterol synthesis as a result of therapy could theoretically lead to reduced adrenal or gonadal steroid hormone production; clinical trial data is inconsistent in regards to the effect on basal steroid hormone levels. Patients with signs/symptoms of endocrine dysfunction should be evaluated as clinically indicated; use caution with concomitant medications (eg, spironolactone, cimetidine, ketoconazole) that may reduce steroid hormone levels/activity. Use with caution in patients with advanced age and/or renal impairment; these patients are predisposed to myopathy. Use caution in patients with previous liver disease or heavy ethanol use. If serious hepatotoxicity with clinical symptoms and/or hyperbilirubinemia or jaundice occurs during treatment, interrupt therapy. If an alternate etiology is not identified, do not restart pravastatin. Liver enzyme tests should be obtained at baseline and as clinically indicated; routine periodic monitoring of liver enzymes is not necessary. Increases in HbA_{1c} and fasting blood glucose have been reported with HMG-CoA reductase inhibitors; however, the benefits of statin therapy far outweigh the risk of dysglycemia. Potentially significant drug-drug interactions may exist, requiring dose or frequency adjustment, additional monitoring, and/or selection of alternative therapy.

Drug Interactions

Metabolism/Transport Effects **Substrate** of CYP3A4 (minor), P-glycoprotein, SLCO1B1; **Note:** Assignment of Major/Minor substrate status based on clinically relevant drug interaction potential; **Inhibits** CYP2C9 (weak)

Avoid Concomitant Use

Avoid concomitant use of Pravastatin with any of the following: Fusidic Acid (Systemic); Gemfibrozil; Red Yeast Rice

Increased Effect/Toxicity

Pravastatin may increase the levels/effects of: CycloSPORINE (Systemic); DAPTOmycin; PARoxetine; PAZOPanib; Repaglinide; Trabectedin; Vitamin K Antagonists

The levels/effects of Pravastatin may be increased by: Acipimox; Antihepaciviral Combination Products; Asunaprevir; Bezafibrate; Boceprevir; Ciprofibrate; Clarithromycin; Colchicine; CycloSPORINE (Systemic); Daclatasvir; Darunavir; Eltrombopag; Erythromycin (Systemic); Fenofibrate and Derivatives; Fusidic Acid (Systemic); Gemfibrozil; Itraconazole; Niacin; Niacinamide; Raltegravir; Red Yeast Rice; Rupatadine; Simeprevir; Telaprevir; Telithromycin; Teriflunomide

Decreased Effect

Pravastatin may decrease the levels/effects of: Lanthanum

The levels/effects of Pravastatin may be decreased by: Antacids; Bile Acid Sequestrants; Efavirenz; Fosphenytoin; Nelfinavir; Phenytoin; Rifamycin Derivatives; Saquinavir

Dietary Considerations Before initiation of therapy, patients should be placed on a standard cholesterol-lowering diet for 6 weeks and the diet should be continued during drug therapy.

Red yeast rice contains variable amounts of several compounds that are structurally similar to HMG-CoA reductase inhibitors, primarily monacolin K (or mevinolin) which is structurally identical to lovastatin; concurrent use of red yeast rice with HMG-CoA reductase inhibitors may increase the incidence of adverse and toxic effects (Lapi 2008; Smith 2003).

Pharmacodynamics/Kinetics

Onset of Action Several days; Peak effect: 4 weeks; LDL-reduction: 40 mg/day: 34% (for each doubling of this dose, LDL-C is lowered by ~6%)

Half-life Elimination

Children and Adolescents (4.9-15.6 years): 1.6 hours; range: 0.85 to 4.2 hours (Hedman 2003)

Adults: 77 hours (including all metabolites); Pravastatin: ~2 to 3 hours (Pan 1990); 3 alpha hydroxy-isopravastatin: ~1.5 hours (Gustavson 2005)

Time to Peak Serum: 1-1.5 hours

Pregnancy Risk Factor X

Pregnancy Considerations

Use of pravastatin is contraindicated in pregnancy.

Adverse events were observed in some animal reproduction studies. Pravastatin was found to cross the placenta in an ex vivo study using term human placentas (Nanovskaya 2013). There are reports of congenital anomalies following maternal use of HMG-CoA reductase inhibitors in pregnancy; however, maternal disease, differences in specific agents used, and the low rates of exposure limit the interpretation of the available data (Godfrey 2012; Lecarpentier 2012). Cholesterol biosynthesis may be important in fetal development; serum cholesterol and triglycerides increase normally during pregnancy. The discontinuation of lipid lowering medications temporarily during pregnancy is not expected to have significant impact on the long term outcomes of primary hypercholesterolemia treatment.

HMG-CoA reductase Inhibitors should be discontinued prior to pregnancy (ADA 2013). If treatment of dyslipidemias is needed in pregnant women or in women of reproductive age, other agents are preferred (Berglund 2012; Stone 2013). The manufacturer recommends administration to women of childbearing potential only when conception is highly unlikely and patients have been informed of potential hazards.

Breastfeeding Considerations
Use of pravastatin in breastfeeding women is contraindicated.

A small amount of pravastatin is excreted into breast milk. Data is available from eight lactating females administered pravastatin 20 mg twice daily for 2.5 days. After the fifth dose, maximum maternal serum concentrations were ~40 ng/mL (pravastatin) and ~26 ng/mL (metabolite) and maximum milk concentrations were ~3.9 ng/mL (pravastatin) and ~2.1 ng/mL (metabolite). Maximum milk concentrations were detected ~3 hours after the dose (Pan 1988).

Dosage Forms
Tablet, Oral:
Pravachol: 20 mg, 40 mg, 80 mg
Generic: 10 mg, 20 mg, 40 mg, 80 mg

Praziquantel (pray zi KWON tel)

Brand Names: US Biltricide
Brand Names: Canada Biltricide
Pharmacologic Category Anthelmintic
Use
Helminths: Treatment of infections caused by the following: All species of *Schistosoma* (eg, *Schistosoma mekongi*, *S. japonicum*, *S. mansoni*, *S. hematobium*) and the liver flukes *Clonorchis sinensis*/*Opisthorchis viverrini*

Local Anesthetic/Vasoconstrictor Precautions
No information available to require special precautions

Effects on Dental Treatment No significant effects or complications reported

Effects on Bleeding No information available to require special precautions

Adverse Reactions Frequency not defined. May be more frequent and/or serious in patients with a heavy worm burden.
Central nervous system: Dizziness, headache, malaise
Dermatologic: Urticaria
Gastrointestinal: Abdominal distress, nausea
Miscellaneous: Fever
<1%, postmarketing and/or case reports: Abdominal pain, anorexia, atrioventricular block, bloody diarrhea, bradycardia, cardiac arrhythmia, drowsiness, ectopic beats, eosinophilia, fatigue, hypersensitivity, hypersensitivity reaction, increased liver enzymes (minimal), myalgia, paradoxical reaction (in schistosomiasis), polyserositis, pruritus, seizure, serum sickness (in schistosomiasis; Jarisch-Herxheimer-like reaction), skin rash, ventricular fibrillation, vertigo, vomiting, weakness

General Dosage Range Oral: *Children ≥4 years, Adolescents, and Adults:* 20 mg/kg/dose 2-3 times daily at 4- to 6-hour intervals for 1 day **or** 25 mg/kg 3 times daily at 4- to 6-hour intervals for 1 day

Mechanism of Action Increases the cell permeability to calcium in schistosomes, causing strong contractions and paralysis of worm musculature leading to detachment of suckers from the blood vessel walls and to dislodgment

Pharmacodynamics/Kinetics
Half-life Elimination Parent drug: 0.8-1.5 hours; Metabolites: 4.5 hours
Time to Peak Serum: 1-3 hours

Pregnancy Risk Factor B

Pregnancy Considerations Adverse effects have not been observed in animal reproduction studies. Use in pregnant women only if clearly needed.

Prazosin (PRAZ oh sin)

Related Information
Cardiovascular Diseases *on page 1752*
Brand Names: US Minipress
Brand Names: Canada Apo-Prazo; Minipress; Teva-Prazosin
Pharmacologic Category Alpha$_1$ Blocker; Antihypertensive
Use
Hypertension: Treatment of hypertension
The 2014 guideline for the management of high blood pressure in adults (Eighth Joint National Committee [JNC 8]) does **not** recommend the use of prazosin in the treatment of hypertension (James 2013).

Local Anesthetic/Vasoconstrictor Precautions
No information available to require special precautions

Effects on Dental Treatment Key adverse event(s) related to dental treatment: Significant xerostomia (normal salivary flow resumes upon discontinuation); Patients may experience orthostatic hypotension as they stand up after treatment; especially if lying in dental chair for extended periods of time. Use caution with sudden changes in position during and after dental treatment.

Effects on Bleeding No information available to require special precautions

Adverse Reactions
>4%:
Cardiovascular: Palpitations (5%)
Central nervous system: Dizziness (10%), drowsiness (8%), headache (8%), decreased energy (7%)
Gastrointestinal: Nausea (5%)
Neuromuscular & skeletal: Weakness (7%)
1% to 4%:
Cardiovascular: Edema, orthostatic hypotension, syncope
Central nervous system: Depression, nervousness, vertigo
Dermatologic: Skin rash
Gastrointestinal: Constipation, diarrhea, vomiting, xerostomia
Genitourinary: Urinary frequency
Ophthalmic: Blurred vision, injected sclera
Respiratory: Dyspnea, epistaxis, nasal congestion
<1%, postmarketing, and/or case reports: Abdominal distress, abnormal hepatic function tests, alopecia, angina pectoris, arthralgia, bradycardia, cataplexy, cataract (both development of cataract and disappearance have been reported), diaphoresis, eye pain, fever, flushing, gynecomastia, hallucination, hypersensitivity reaction, impotence, insomnia, leukopenia, lichen planus, malaise, myocardial infarction, narcolepsy (worsened), pain, pancreatitis, paresthesia, positive ANA titer, priapism, pruritus, retinal pigment changes (mottled), retinopathy (serous), systemic lupus erythematosus, tachycardia, tinnitus, urinary incontinence, urticaria, vasculitis

General Dosage Range Oral: *Adults:* Initial: 1 mg/dose 2 or 3 times daily; may increase up to 20 mg daily in divided doses

Mechanism of Action Competitively inhibits postsynaptic alpha-adrenergic receptors which results in vasodilation of veins and arterioles and a decrease in total peripheral resistance and blood pressure

Pharmacodynamics/Kinetics

Onset of Action Antihypertensive: Within 2 hours; Peak effect: 2 to 4 hours

Duration of Action 10 to 24 hours

Half-life Elimination 2 to 3 hours, prolonged with CHF

Time to Peak Plasma: ~3 hours

Pregnancy Risk Factor C

Pregnancy Considerations Adverse events were observed in some animal reproduction studies. Prazosin crosses the placenta and its pharmacokinetics may be slightly altered during pregnancy (Bourget 1995; Rubin 1983). Limited use in pregnant women has not demonstrated any fetal abnormalities or adverse effects (Dommisse 1983).

Untreated chronic maternal hypertension is associated with adverse events in the fetus, infant, and mother. If treatment for hypertension during pregnancy is needed, other agents are generally preferred (ACOG 2013).

Prednicarbate (pred ni KAR bate)

Brand Names: US Dermatop

Brand Names: Canada Dermatop

Pharmacologic Category Corticosteroid, Topical

Use Dermatoses: Relief of the inflammatory and pruritic manifestations of corticosteroid-responsive dermatoses (medium potency topical corticosteroid)

Local Anesthetic/Vasoconstrictor Precautions No information available to require special precautions

Effects on Dental Treatment No significant effects or complications reported

Effects on Bleeding No information available to require special precautions

Adverse Reactions

1% to 10%: Dermatologic: Skin atrophy (children: 3% to 8%; adults: 1%), telangiectasia (mild; children: 5%), taut and shiny skin (children: 3%)

<1%, postmarketing, and/or case reports: Acneiform eruption, allergic contact dermatitis, atrophic striae, burning sensation of skin, edema, folliculitis, hypopigmentation, miliaria, paresthesia, perioral dermatitis, pruritus, secondary infection, skin rash, urticaria

General Dosage Range Topical:

Children ≥1 year, Adolescents, and Adults: Cream: Apply a thin film to affected area twice daily

Children ≥10 year, Adolescents, and Adults: Ointment: Apply a thin film to affected area twice daily

Mechanism of Action Topical corticosteroids have anti-inflammatory, antipruritic, and vasoconstrictive properties. May depress the formation, release, and activity of endogenous chemical mediators of inflammation (kinins, histamine, liposomal enzymes, prostaglandins) through the induction of phospholipase A_2 inhibitory proteins (lipocortins) and sequential inhibition of the release of arachidonic acid. Prednicarbate has intermediate range potency.

Pregnancy Risk Factor C

Pregnancy Considerations Adverse events have been observed in animal reproduction studies. Topical corticosteroids are not recommended for extensive use, in large quantities, or for long periods of time in pregnant women (Koutroulis, 2011; Leachman, 2006).

PrednisoLONE (Systemic) (pred NISS oh lone)

Related Information

PredniSONE *on page 1377*
Respiratory Diseases *on page 1777*

Brand Names: US Flo-Pred [DSC]; Millipred; Millipred DP; Millipred DP 12-Day; Orapred ODT; Orapred [DSC]; Pediapred; Veripred 20

Brand Names: Canada Pediapred; PMS-Prednisolone

Generic Availability (US) May be product dependent

Pharmacologic Category Corticosteroid, Systemic

Use

Allergic states: Control of severe or incapacitating allergic conditions intractable to adequate trials of conventional treatment in asthma, atopic dermatitis, drug hypersensitivity reactions, seasonal or perennial allergic rhinitis, and serum sickness.

Dermatologic diseases: Bullous dermatitis herpetiformis; contact dermatitis; exfoliative erythroderma; exfoliative dermatitis; mycosis fungoides; pemphigus; severe erythema multiforme (Stevens-Johnson syndrome); severe psoriasis; severe seborrheic dermatitis.

Endocrine disorders: Congenital adrenal hyperplasia; hypercalcemia associated with cancer; nonsuppurative thyroiditis; primary or secondary adrenocortical insufficiency (hydrocortisone or cortisone is the first choice; synthetic analogs may be used in conjunction with mineralocorticoids where applicable).

GI diseases: During acute episodes of Crohn disease or ulcerative colitis.

Hematologic disorders: Acquired (autoimmune) hemolytic anemia; congenital (erythroid) hypoplastic anemia (Diamond-Blackfan anemia); erythroblastopenia (RBC anemia); idiopathic thrombocytopenic purpura, pure red cell aplasia; secondary thrombocytopenia

Neoplastic diseases: Treatment of acute leukemia and aggressive lymphomas.

Nervous system: Acute exacerbations of multiple sclerosis; cerebral edema associated with primary or metastatic brain tumor, craniotomy, or head injury. **Note:** Treatment guidelines recommend the use of high dose IV or oral methylprednisolone for acute exacerbations of multiple sclerosis (AAN [Scott 2011]; NICE 2014).

Ophthalmic diseases: Allergic conjunctivitis; allergic corneal marginal ulcers; anterior segment inflammation; chorioretinitis; diffuse posterior uveitis and choroiditis; herpes zoster ophthalmicus; iritis and iridocyclitises; keratitis; optic neuritis; sympathetic ophthalmia; uveitis and other ocular inflammatory conditions unresponsive to topical corticosteroids.

Renal disorders: To induce diuresis or remission of proteinuria in nephrotic syndrome, without uremia, of the idiopathic type or that due to lupus erythematosus.

Respiratory diseases: Acute exacerbations of chronic obstructive pulmonary disease (COPD); allergic bronchopulmonary aspergillosis; aspiration pneumonitis; asthma; berylliosis; fulminating or disseminated pulmonary tuberculosis when used concurrently with appropriate antituberculous chemotherapy; hypersensitivity pneumonitis; idiopathic bronchiolitis obliterans with organizing pneumonia; idiopathic eosinophilic pneumonias; idiopathic pulmonary fibrosis; Loeffler syndrome (not manageable by other means); *Pneumocystis carinii* pneumonia (PCP) associated with hypoxemia occurring in an HIV-positive individual who is also under treatment with appropriate anti-PCP antibiotics; symptomatic sarcoidosis.

Rheumatic disorders: As adjunctive therapy for short-term administration in acute and subacute bursitis, acute gouty arthritis, acute nonspecific tenosynovitis, ankylosing spondylitis, epicondylitis, polymyalgia rheumatica/temporal arteritis, posttraumatic osteoarthritis, psoriatic arthritis, relapsing polychondritis, rheumatoid arthritis (including juvenile rheumatoid arthritis), synovitis of osteoarthritis, acute rheumatic carditis, systemic lupus erythematosus, dermatomyositis/polymyositis, Sjogren syndrome, and certain cases of vasculitis.

Miscellaneous: Acute or chronic solid organ rejection; trichinosis with neurologic or myocardial involvement; tuberculous meningitis with subarachnoid block or impending block, tuberculosis with enlarged mediastinal lymph nodes causing respiratory difficulty, tuberculosis with pleural or pericardial effusion (use appropriate antituberculous chemotherapy concurrently when treating any tuberculosis complications).

Local Anesthetic/Vasoconstrictor Precautions

No information available to require special precautions

Effects on Dental Treatment Key adverse event(s) related to dental treatment: Ulcerative esophagitis.

Effects on Bleeding No information available to require special precautions

Adverse Reactions

Frequency not defined.

Cardiovascular: Cardiac failure, cardiomyopathy, edema, facial edema, hypertension

Central nervous system: Headache, insomnia, malaise, myasthenia, nervousness, pseudotumor cerebri, psychological disorder, seizure, vertigo

Dermatologic: Diaphoresis, facial erythema, skin atrophy, suppression of skin test reaction, urticaria

Endocrine & metabolic: Cushing's syndrome, diabetes mellitus, growth suppression, hirsutism, HPA-axis suppression, hyperglycemia, hypernatremia, hypokalemia, hypokalemic alkalosis, menstrual disease, negative nitrogen balance, weight gain

Gastrointestinal: Abdominal distention, carbohydrate intolerance, dyspepsia, increased appetite, nausea, pancreatitis, peptic ulcer, ulcerative esophagitis

Hematologic & oncologic: Bruise, petechia

Hepatic: Increased liver enzymes (usually reversible)

Neuromuscular & skeletal: Amyotrophy, arthralgia, aseptic necrosis of bones (humeral/femoral heads), bone fracture, rupture of tendon, weakness

Ophthalmic: Cataract, exophthalmos, eye irritation, eyelid edema, glaucoma, increased intraocular pressure

Respiratory: Epistaxis

Miscellaneous: Wound healing impairment

<1%, postmarketing, and/or case reports: Venous thrombosis (Johannesdottir 2013)

Dosing

Adult Dose depends upon condition being treated and response of patient. Consider alternate day therapy for long-term therapy. Discontinuation of long-term therapy requires gradual withdrawal by tapering the dose.

Usual dose (range): Oral: 5 to 60 mg daily

Asthma exacerbations:

Global Initiative for Asthma guidelines (GINA 2016):

Management in primary care or acute care facility: 1 mg/kg/day (maximum: 50 mg daily) as a single daily dose usually given for 5 to 7 days

National Asthma Education and Prevention Program guidelines (NAEPP 2007):

Asthma exacerbations (emergency care or hospital doses): 40 to 80 mg/day in a single dose or in 2 divided doses until peak expiratory flow is 70% of predicted or personal best

Short-course outpatient "burst" (acute asthma): 40 to 60 mg/day in a single dose or in 2 divided doses for 5 to 10 days. **Note:** Burst should be continued until symptoms resolve and peak expiratory flow is at least 80% of personal best; usually requires 3 to 10 days of treatment; longer treatment may be required

Long-term treatment: 7.5 to 60 mg daily given as a single dose in the morning or every other day as needed for asthma control

Multiple sclerosis:

Note: Treatment guidelines recommend the use of high dose IV or oral methylprednisolone for acute exacerbations of multiple sclerosis (AAN [Scott 2011]; NICE 2014).

Oral: 200 mg daily for 1 week followed by 80 mg every other day for 1 month

Acute exacerbations of chronic obstructive pulmonary disease (COPD) (off-label use): Oral: 30 to 40 mg daily for 10 to 14 days (GOLD guidelines 2013)

Bell's palsy (off-label use): Oral: 60 mg once daily for 5 days, then taper dose downward by 10 mg daily for 5 days (total treatment duration: 10 days) (Engstrom 2008; Berg 2012) **or** 50 mg daily (in 1 or 2 divided doses) for 10 days (begin within 72 hours of onset of symptoms) (Baugh 2013; Sullivan 2007)

Primary adrenal insufficiency, chronic (physiologic replacement) (off-label dose; alternative to preferred therapy): Oral: 3 to 5 mg daily in 1 to 2 divided doses (ES [Bornstein 2016]).

Severe alcoholic hepatitis (Maddrey Discriminant Function [MDF] score ≥32) (off-label use): Oral: 40 mg daily for 28 days, followed by a 2-week taper (O'Shea 2010)

Geriatric Refer to adult dosing; use lowest effective dose.

Pediatric Dose depends upon condition being treated and response of patient; dosage for infants and children should be based on disease severity and patient response rather than by rigid adherence to dosage guidelines indicated by age, weight, or body surface area. Consider alternate day therapy for long-term therapy. Discontinuation of long-term therapy requires gradual withdrawal by tapering the dose.

Asthma exacerbations:

Global Initiative for Asthma guidelines (GINA 2016):

Management in primary care or acute care facility:

Children ≤2 years: 1 to 2 mg/kg/day (maximum: 20 mg daily) for up to 5 days

Children 3 to 5 years: 1 to 2 mg/kg/day (maximum: 30 mg daily) for up to 5 days

Children 6 to 11 years: 1 to 2 mg/kg/day (maximum: 40 mg daily) usually given for 3 to 5 days

Children ≥12 years and Adolescents: Refer to adult dosing.

National Asthma Education and Prevention Program guidelines (NAEPP 2007):

Children <12 years:

Asthma exacerbations (emergency care or hospital doses): 1 to 2 mg/kg/day in 2 divided doses (maximum: 60 mg/day) until peak expiratory flow is 70% of predicted or personal best

Short-course "burst" (acute asthma): 1 to 2 mg/kg/day in single dose or 2 divided doses for 3 to 10 days; maximum dose: 60 mg/day. **Note:** Burst should be continued until symptoms resolve or patient achieves peak expiratory flow 80% of personal best; usually requires 3 to 10 days of treatment; longer treatment may be required

Long-term treatment: 0.25 to 2 mg/kg/day given as a single dose in the morning or every other day as needed for asthma control; maximum dose: 60 mg/day

Children ≥12 years and Adolescents: Refer to adult dosing.

Anti-inflammatory or immunosuppressive dose: Children and Adolescents: Oral: 0.1 to 2 mg/kg/day in 3 or 4 divided dose

Nephrotic syndrome; steroid sensitive (SSNS): Oral: Children and Adolescents: Note: Obese patients should be dosed based on ideal body weight:

Initial episode: 2 mg/kg/day or 60 mg/m^2/day once daily, maximum daily dose: 60 mg/day for 4 to 6 weeks; then adjust to an alternate-day schedule of 1.5 mg/kg/dose or 40 mg/m^2/dose on alternate days as a single dose, maximum dose: 40 mg/dose (Gipson 2009; KDIGO 2012; KDOQI 2013); duration of therapy based on patient response.

Relapse: 2 mg/kg/day or 60 mg/m^2/day once daily, maximum daily dose: 60 mg/day; continue until complete remission for at least 3 days; then adjust to an alternate-day schedule of 1.5 mg/kg/dose or 40 mg/m^2/dose on alternate days as a single dose, maximum dose: 40 mg/dose, recommended duration of alternate day dosing is variable: may continue for at least 4 weeks then taper. Longer duration of treatment may be necessary in patients who relapse frequently, some patients may require up to 3 months of treatment (Gipson 2009; KDIGO 2012; KDOQI 2013).

Maintenance therapy for frequently relapsing SSNS: Taper previous dose down to lowest effective dose which maintains remission using an alternate day schedule; usual effective range: 0.1 to 0.5 mg/kg/dose on alternating days; other patients may require doses up to 0.7 mg/kg/dose every other day (KDIGO 2012, KDOQI 2013).

Bell's palsy (off-label use): Adolescents ≥16 years: Oral: 50 mg daily (in 1 or 2 divided doses) for 10 days; treatment should begin within 72 hours of onset of symptoms (Baugh 2013; Sullivan 2007).

Renal Impairment There are no dosage adjustments provided in the manufacturer's labeling. Use with caution.

Hemodialysis: Slightly dialyzable (7% to 17.5%) (Frey 1990).

Intermittent hemodialysis: Supplemental dose necessary (Aronoff 2007).

Peritoneal dialysis: Supplemental dose is not necessary (Aronoff 2007).

Hepatic Impairment There are no dosage adjustments provided in the manufacturer's labeling. Use with caution.

Mechanism of Action Decreases inflammation by suppression of migration of polymorphonuclear leukocytes and reversal of increased capillary permeability; suppresses the immune system by reducing activity and volume of the lymphatic system

Contraindications

Hypersensitivity to prednisolone or any component of the formulation; live or attenuated virus vaccines (with immunosuppressive doses of corticosteroids); systemic fungal infections

Documentation of allergenic cross-reactivity for corticosteroids is limited. However, because of similarities in chemical structure and/or pharmacologic actions, the possibility of cross-sensitivity cannot be ruled out with certainty.

Warnings/Precautions May cause hypercorticism or suppression of hypothalamic-pituitary-adrenal (HPA) axis, particularly in younger children or in patients receiving high doses for prolonged periods. HPA axis suppression may lead to adrenal crisis. Withdrawal and discontinuation of a corticosteroid should be done slowly and carefully. Particular care is required when patients are transferred from systemic corticosteroids to inhaled products due to possible adrenal insufficiency or withdrawal from steroids, including an increase in allergic symptoms. Patients receiving >20 mg per day of prednisone (or equivalent) may be most susceptible. Fatalities have occurred due to adrenal insufficiency in asthmatic patients during and after transfer from systemic corticosteroids to aerosol steroids; aerosol steroids do **not** provide the systemic steroid needed to treat patients having trauma, surgery, or infections.

Acute myopathy has been reported with high dose corticosteroids, usually in patients with neuromuscular transmission disorders; may involve ocular and/or respiratory muscles; monitor creatine kinase; recovery may be delayed. Corticosteroid use may cause psychiatric disturbances, including severe depression, euphoria, insomnia, mood swings, and personality changes to frank psychotic manifestations. Preexisting psychiatric conditions may be exacerbated by corticosteroid use. Prolonged use of corticosteroids may also increase the incidence of secondary infection, mask acute infection (including fungal infections) or prolong or exacerbate viral infections or limit response to killed or inactivated vaccines. Exposure to chickenpox or measles should be avoided; corticosteroids should not be used to treat ocular herpes simplex. Corticosteroids should not be used for cerebral malaria or viral hepatitis. Close observation is required in patients with latent tuberculosis and/or TB reactivity; restrict use in active TB (only fulminating or disseminated TB in conjunction with antituberculosis treatment). Amebiasis should be ruled out in any patient with recent travel to tropic climates or unexplained diarrhea prior to initiation of corticosteroids. Use with extreme caution in patients with *Strongyloides* infections; hyperinfection, dissemination and fatalities have occurred. Increased intraocular pressure, open-angle glaucoma, and cataracts have occurred with prolonged use. Use with caution in patients with a history of ocular herpes simplex; corneal perforation has occurred; do not use in active ocular herpes simplex. Not recommended for the treatment of optic neuritis; may increase frequency of new episodes. Consider routine eye exams in chronic users. Prolonged treatment with corticosteroids has been associated with the development of Kaposi sarcoma (case reports); if noted, discontinuation of therapy should be considered (Goedert 2002). Rare cases of anaphylactoid reactions have been observed in patients receiving corticosteroids.

Use with caution in patients with thyroid disease, hepatic impairment, renal impairment, heart failure, hypertension, diabetes, glaucoma, cataracts, myasthenia gravis, patients at risk for osteoporosis, patients at risk for seizures, or GI diseases (diverticulitis, fresh intestinal anastomoses, active or latent peptic ulcer, ulcerative colitis, abscess or other pyogenic infection). Use caution following acute MI (corticosteroids have been associated with myocardial rupture). Use cautiously in the elderly with the smallest possible effective dose for the shortest duration. Withdraw therapy with gradual tapering of dose. May affect growth velocity; growth should be routinely monitored in pediatric patients. Patients may require higher doses when subject to stress (ie, trauma, surgery, severe infection). Potentially significant drug-drug interactions may exist, requiring dose or frequency adjustment, additional monitoring, and/or selection of alternative therapy.

Benzyl alcohol and derivatives: Some dosage forms may contain sodium benzoate/benzoic acid; benzoic acid (benzoate) is a metabolite of benzyl alcohol; large amounts of benzyl alcohol (≥99 mg/kg/day) have been associated with a potentially fatal toxicity ("gasping syndrome") in neonates; the "gasping syndrome" consists of metabolic acidosis, respiratory distress, gasping respirations, CNS dysfunction (including convulsions, intracranial hemorrhage), hypotension, and cardiovascular collapse (AAP ["Inactive" 1997]; CDC 1982); some data suggests that benzoate displaces bilirubin from protein binding sites (Ahlfors 2001); avoid or use dosage forms containing benzyl alcohol derivative with caution in neonates. See manufacturer's labeling.

Propylene glycol: Some dosage forms may contain propylene glycol; large amounts are potentially toxic and have been associated hyperosmolality, lactic acidosis, seizures, and respiratory depression; use caution (AAP 1997; Zar 2007).

Drug Interactions

Metabolism/Transport Effects **Substrate** of CYP3A4 (minor); **Note:** Assignment of Major/Minor substrate status based on clinically relevant drug interaction potential

Avoid Concomitant Use

Avoid concomitant use of PrednisoLONE (Systemic) with any of the following: Aldesleukin; BCG (Intravesical); Desmopressin; Indium 111 Capromab Pendetide; MiFEPRIStone; Natalizumab; Pimecrolimus; Tacrolimus (Topical); Tofacitinib

Increased Effect/Toxicity

PrednisoLONE (Systemic) may increase the levels/effects of: Acetylcholinesterase Inhibitors; Amphotericin B; Androgens; Ceritinib; CycloSPORINE (Systemic); Deferasirox; Desirudin; Desmopressin; Fingolimod; Leflunomide; Loop Diuretics; Natalizumab; Nicorandil; NSAID (COX-2 Inhibitor); NSAID (Nonselective); Quinolone Antibiotics; Thiazide and Thiazide-Like Diuretics; Tofacitinib; Vaccines (Live); Warfarin

The levels/effects of PrednisoLONE (Systemic) may be increased by: Aprepitant; Boceprevir; CycloSPORINE (Systemic); CYP3A4 Inhibitors (Strong); Denosumab; DilTIAZem; Estrogen Derivatives; Fosaprepitant; Indacaterol; MiFEPRIStone; Neuromuscular-Blocking Agents (Nondepolarizing); Ocrelizumab; Pimecrolimus; Ritonavir; Roflumilast; Salicylates; Tacrolimus (Topical); Telaprevir; Trastuzumab

Decreased Effect

PrednisoLONE (Systemic) may decrease the levels/effects of: Aldesleukin; Antidiabetic Agents; BCG (Intravesical); Calcitriol (Systemic); Coccidioides immitis Skin Test; Corticorelin; CycloSPORINE (Systemic); Hyaluronidase; Indium 111 Capromab Pendetide; Isoniazid; Nivolumab; Salicylates; Sipuleucel-T; Telaprevir; Tertomotide; Urea Cycle Disorder Agents; Vaccines (Inactivated); Vaccines (Live)

The levels/effects of PrednisoLONE (Systemic) may be decreased by: Antacids; Bile Acid Sequestrants; Carbimazole; CYP3A4 Inducers (Strong); Echinacea; MethIMAzole; MiFEPRIStone; Mitotane

Dietary Considerations Should be taken after meals or with food or milk to decrease GI upset; increase dietary intake of pyridoxine, vitamin C, vitamin D, folate, calcium, and phosphorus.

Pharmacodynamics/Kinetics

Duration of Action 18 to 36 hours (Pickup 1979)

Half-life Elimination 2 to 4 hours; reduced in children and prolonged in hepatic disease (Pickup 1979)

Time to Peak Plasma: 1 to 2 hours; prolonged with food

Pregnancy Risk Factor C/D (manufacturer specific)

Pregnancy Considerations Adverse events have been observed with corticosteroids in animal reproduction studies. Prednisolone crosses the placenta; prior to reaching the fetus, prednisolone is converted by placental enzymes to prednisone. As a result, the amount of prednisolone reaching the fetus is ~8 to 10 times lower than the maternal serum concentration (healthy women at term; similar results observed with preterm pregnancies complicated by HELLP syndrome) (Beitins 1972; van Runnard Heimel 2005). Some studies have shown an association between first trimester systemic corticosteroid use and oral clefts (Park-Wyllie 2000; Pradat 2003). Systemic corticosteroids may also influence fetal growth (decreased birth weight); however, information is conflicting (Lunghi 2010). Hypoadrenalism may occur in newborns following maternal use of corticosteroids in pregnancy; monitor.

When systemic corticosteroids are needed in pregnancy, it is generally recommended to use the lowest effective dose for the shortest duration of time, avoiding high doses during the first trimester (Leachman 2006; Lunghi 2010; Makol 2011; Østensen 2009). Inhaled corticosteroids are preferred for the treatment of asthma during pregnancy. Oral corticosteroids, such as prednisolone, may be used for the treatment of severe persistent asthma if needed; the lowest dose administered on alternate days (if possible) should be used (NAEPP 2005). Prednisolone may be used (alternative agent) to treat primary adrenal insufficiency (PAI) in pregnant women. Pregnant women with PAI should be monitored at least once each trimester (Bornstein 2016). Prednisolone may be used to treat women during pregnancy who require therapy for congenital adrenal hyperplasia (Speiser 2010). Topical agents are preferred for managing atopic dermatitis in pregnancy; for severe symptomatic or recalcitrant atopic dermatitis, a short course of prednisolone may be used during the third trimester (Koutroulis 2011).

Breastfeeding Considerations Prednisolone is excreted in breast milk. In one study (n=6), milk concentrations were 5% to 25% of the maternal serum concentration with peak concentrations occurring ~1 hour after the maternal dose. The milk/plasma ratio was found to be 0.2 with doses ≥30 mg/day and 0.1 with doses <30 mg/day. Following a maternal dose of prednisolone 80 mg/day, it was calculated that a breastfeeding infant would ingest <0.1% of the maternal dose (Ost 1985). One manufacturer notes that when used systemically, maternal use of corticosteroids have the potential to cause adverse events in a nursing infant (eg, growth suppression, interfere with endogenous corticosteroid production) and therefore caution should be used when administered to nursing women. In order to decrease potential exposure to a nursing infant, one manufacturer recommends administering the dose after nursing, at the time of day with the longest interval between feeds. Other sources recommend waiting 4 hours after the maternal dose before breastfeeding (Bae 2012; Leachman 2006; Makol 2011; Ost 1985). Other guidelines note that maternal use of systemic corticosteroids is not a contraindication to breastfeeding (NAEPP 2005).

Dosage Forms Considerations

Orapred oral solution contains fructose.
Orapred ODT dispersible tablets contain sucrose.
Prelone oral syrup contains sucrose.

Dosage Forms

Solution, Oral:
Millipred: 10 mg/5 mL (237 mL)
Pediapred: 5 mg/5 mL (120 mL)
Veripred 20: 20 mg/5 mL (237 mL)
Generic: 10 mg/5 mL (237 mL); 15 mg/5 mL (237 mL, 240 mL, 480 mL); 20 mg/5 mL (237 mL); 25 mg/5 mL (237 mL); 5 mg/5 mL (120 mL)

Syrup, Oral:
Generic: 15 mg/5 mL (240 mL, 480 mL)

Tablet, Oral:
Millipred: 5 mg
Millipred DP: 5 mg
Millipred DP 12-Day: 5 mg

Tablet Dispersible, Oral:
Orapred ODT: 10 mg, 15 mg, 30 mg
Generic: 10 mg, 15 mg, 30 mg

PredniSONE (PRED ni sone)

Related Information

PrednisoLONE (Systemic) *on page 1373*
Respiratory Diseases *on page 1777*
Rheumatoid Arthritis, Osteoarthritis, and Osteoporosis *on page 1792*
Ulcerative, Erosive, and Painful Oral Mucosal Disorders *on page 1853*

Related Sample Prescriptions

Ulcerative and Erosive Disorders - Sample Prescriptions *on page 43*

Brand Names: US Deltasone; PredniSONE Intensol; Rayos

Brand Names: Canada Apo-Prednisone; JAA-Prednisone; Teva-Prednisone; Winpred

Generic Availability (US) May be product dependent

Pharmacologic Category Corticosteroid, Systemic

Use

Allergic states: Control of severe or incapacitating allergic conditions intractable to adequate trials of conventional treatment in drug hypersensitivity reactions, seasonal or perennial allergic rhinitis; serum sickness.

Dermatologic diseases: Atopic dermatitis; bullous dermatitis herpetiformis; contact dermatitis; exfoliative dermatitis/erythroderma; mycosis fungoides; pemphigus; severe erythema multiforme (Stevens-Johnson syndrome).

Immediate-release only: Severe psoriasis, severe seborrheic dermatitis.

Endocrine disorders: Congenital adrenal hyperplasia; hypercalcemia of malignancy; nonsuppurative thyroiditis; primary or secondary adrenocortical insufficiency (hydrocortisone or cortisone is the first choice; synthetic analogues may be used in conjunction with mineralocorticoids where applicable.

GI diseases: During acute episodes in regional enteritis (Crohn disease) and ulcerative colitis.

Hematologic disorders: Acquired (autoimmune) hemolytic anemia; congenital (erythroid) hypoplastic anemia/Diamond-Blackfan anemia; idiopathic thrombocytopenic purpura in adults; secondary thrombocytopenia in adults.

Delayed-release only: Pure red cell aplasia.

Immediate-release only: Erythroblastopenia (red blood cell anemia).

Neoplastic diseases:

Delayed-release only: Treatment of acute leukemia and aggressive lymphomas.

Immediate-release only: Palliative management of leukemias and lymphomas in adults; acute leukemia of childhood.

Nervous system (delayed-release only): Acute exacerbations of multiple sclerosis; cerebral edema associated with primary or metastatic brain tumor, craniotomy, or head injury. **Note**: Treatment guidelines recommend the use of high dose IV or oral methylprednisolone for acute exacerbations of multiple sclerosis (Scott 2011; NICE 2014).

Ophthalmic diseases:

Delayed-release only: Severe acute and chronic allergic and inflammatory processes involving the eye and its adnexa, such as sympathetic ophthalmia; uveitis and ocular inflammatory conditions unresponsive to topical steroids.

Immediate-release only: Severe acute and chronic allergic and inflammatory processes involving the eye and its adnexa, such as allergic conjunctivitis, allergic corneal marginal ulcers, anterior segment inflammation, chorioretinitis, diffuse posterior uveitis and choroiditis, herpes zoster ophthalmicus, iridocyclitis, iritis, keratitis, optic neuritis, sympathetic ophthalmia.

Renal diseases: To induce a diuresis or remission of proteinuria in the nephrotic syndrome, without uremia, of the idiopathic type or that is caused by lupus erythematosus.

Respiratory diseases: Aspiration pneumonitis; asthma; fulminating or disseminated pulmonary tuberculosis when used concurrently with appropriate chemotherapy; symptomatic sarcoidosis.

Delayed-release only: Acute exacerbations of chronic obstructive pulmonary disease (COPD); allergic bronchopulmonary aspergillosis; hypersensitivity pneumonitis; idiopathic bronchiolitis obliterans with organizing pneumonia; idiopathic eosinophilic pneumonias; idiopathic pulmonary fibrosis; *Pneumocystis carinii* pneumonia (PCP) associated with hypoxemia occurring in an HIV-positive individual who is also under treatment with appropriate anti-PCP antibiotics.

Immediate-release only: Berylliosis; Loeffler syndrome not manageable by other means.

Rheumatic disorders:

Maintenance therapy:

Delayed-release only: During an exacerbation or as maintenance therapy in selected cases of ankylosing spondylitis, dermatomyositis/polymyositis, polymyalgia rheumatica, psoriatic arthritis, relapsing polychondritis, rheumatoid arthritis including juvenile rheumatoid arthritis, Sjögren syndrome, systemic lupus erythematosus, vasculitis.

Immediate-release only: During an exacerbation or as maintenance therapy in selected cases of acute rheumatic carditis, systemic dermatomyositis (polymyositis), systemic lupus erythematosus.

Short-term therapy:

Delayed release only: As adjunctive therapy for short-term administration in acute gouty arthritis.

Immediate-release only: As adjunctive therapy for short-term administration in acute and subacute bursitis; acute gouty arthritis; acute nonspecific tenosynovitis; ankylosing spondylitis; epicondylitis; posttraumatic osteoarthritis; psoriatic arthritis; rheumatoid arthritis including juvenile rheumatoid arthritis; synovitis of osteoarthritis.

Miscellaneous: Trichinosis with neurologic or myocardial involvement; tuberculous meningitis with subarachnoid block or impending block when used concurrently with appropriate antituberculous chemotherapy.

Delayed-release only: Acute or chronic solid organ rejection.

Local Anesthetic/Vasoconstrictor Precautions No information available to require special precautions

Effects on Dental Treatment No significant effects or complications reported (see Dental Comment)

Effects on Bleeding No information available to require special precautions

Adverse Reactions

Frequency not defined.

Cardiovascular: Cardiac failure (in susceptible patients), hypertension

Central nervous system: Emotional lability, headache, increased intracranial pressure (with papilledema), myasthenia, psychiatric disturbance (including euphoria, insomnia, mood swings, personality changes, severe depression), seizure, vertigo

Dermatologic: Diaphoresis, facial erythema, skin atrophy, urticaria

Endocrine & metabolic: Cushing's syndrome, decreased serum potassium, diabetes mellitus, fluid retention, growth suppression (children), hypokalemic alkalosis, hypothyroidism (enhanced), menstrual disease, negative nitrogen balance (due to protein catabolism), sodium retention

Gastrointestinal: Abdominal distention, carbohydrate intolerance, pancreatitis, peptic ulcer (with possible perforation and hemorrhage), ulcerative esophagitis

Hematologic & oncologic: Bruise, Kaposi's sarcoma, petechia

Hepatic: Increased serum alkaline phosphatase, increased serum ALT, increased serum AST

Hypersensitivity: Anaphylaxis, hypersensitivity reaction

Infection: Infection

Neuromuscular & skeletal: Amyotrophy, aseptic necrosis of bones (femoral and humeral heads), osteoporosis, pathological fracture (long bones), rupture of tendon (particularly Achilles tendon), steroid myopathy, vertebral compression fracture

Ophthalmic: Exophthalmos, glaucoma, increased intraocular pressure, subcapsular posterior cataract

Miscellaneous: Wound healing impairment

<1%, postmarketing, and/or case reports: Venous thrombosis (Johannesdottir 2013)

Dosing

Adult General dosing; anti-inflammatory/immunosuppressive/endocrine disorders: Oral: Initial: 5 to 60 mg daily:

Note: Dose depends upon condition being treated and response of patient. Consider alternate day therapy for long-term therapy. Discontinuation of long-term therapy requires gradual withdrawal by tapering the dose.

Prednisone taper (other regimens also available):

Day 1: 30 mg divided as 10 mg before breakfast, 5 mg at lunch, 5 mg at dinner, 10 mg at bedtime

Day 2: 5 mg at breakfast, 5 mg at lunch, 5 mg at dinner, 10 mg at bedtime

Day 3: 5 mg 4 times daily (with meals and at bedtime)

Day 4: 5 mg 3 times daily (breakfast, lunch, bedtime)

Day 5: 5 mg 2 times daily (breakfast, bedtime)

Day 6: 5 mg before breakfast

Indication-specific dosing:

Acute asthma (off-label dose): Oral: 40 to 60 mg/day for 3 to 10 days; administer as single or 2 divided doses (NAEPP 2007).

Acute exacerbations of chronic obstructive pulmonary disease (COPD) (off-label use for immediate release products; off-label dose): Oral: 40 mg once daily for 5 days (GOLD 2014).

Acute gout (off-label dose): Oral: Initial: ≥0.5 mg/kg for 5 to 10 days (ACR guidelines [Khanna 2012])

Anaphylaxis, adjunctive treatment (off-label dose): Oral: 0.5 mg/kg (Lieberman 2005)

Antineoplastic: Oral: Usual range: 10 mg daily to 100 mg/m^2/day (depending on indication). Refer to specific protocol for dosing and administration details.

Autoimmune hepatitis (off-label use): Oral: Initial: 60 mg daily for 1 week, *followed by* 40 mg daily for 1 week, *then* 30 mg daily for 2 weeks, *then* 20 mg daily. Half this dose should be given when used in combination with azathioprine (AASLD [Manns 2010]).

Bell palsy (off-label use): Oral: 60 mg daily for 5 days, followed by a 5-day taper. Treatment should begin within 72 hours of onset of symptoms (OHNS [Baugh 2013]).

Crohn disease, moderate/severe (off-label dose): Oral: 40 to 60 mg daily until resolution of symptoms and resumption of weight gain (usual duration: 7 to 28 days) (Lichtenstein 2009).

Dermatomyositis/polymyositis (off-label dose): Oral: 1 mg/kg daily (range: 0.5 to 1.5 mg/kg/day), often in conjunction with steroid-sparing therapies; depending on response/tolerance, consider slow tapering after 2 to 8 weeks depending on response; taper regimens vary widely, but often involve 5 to 10 mg decrements per week and may require 6 to 12 months to reach a low once-daily or every-other-day dose to prevent disease flare (Briemberg 2003; Hengstman 2009; Iorizzo 2008; Wiendl 2008).

Giant cell arteritis (off-label use): Oral: Initial: 40 to 60 mg daily; typically requires 1 to 2 years of treatment, but may begin to taper after 2 to 3 months; alternative dosing of 30 to 40 mg daily has demonstrated similar efficacy (Hiratzka 2010).

Glucocorticoid remediable aldosteronism, treatment (off-label use): Oral: Initial: 2.5 to 5 mg once daily preferably at bedtime to suppress early morning ACTH surge (Funder 2016)

Graves ophthalmopathy prophylaxis (off-label use): Oral: 0.4 to 0.5 mg/kg/day, starting 1 to 3 days after radioactive iodine treatment, and continued for 1 month, then gradually taper over 2 months (Bahn 2011).

Herpes zoster (off-label use): Oral: 60 mg daily for 7 days, *followed by* 30 mg daily for 7 days, *then* 15 mg daily for 7 days (Dworkin 2007).

Immune thrombocytopenia (ITP) (off-label dose): Oral: 1 to 2 mg/kg/day (American Society of Hematology 1997).

Lupus nephritis, induction (off-label dose): Oral:

Class III-IV lupus nephritis: 0.5 to 1 mg/kg/day (after glucocorticoid pulse) tapered after a few weeks to lowest effective dose, in combination with an immunosuppressive agent (Hahn 2012).

Class V lupus nephritis: 0.5 mg/kg/day for 6 months in combination mycophenolate mofetil; if not improved after 6 months, use 0.5 to 1 mg/kg/day (after a glucocorticoid pulse) for an additional 6 months in combination with cyclophosphamide (Hahn 2012).

Multiple sclerosis, acute exacerbations:

Note: Treatment guidelines recommend the use of high dose IV or oral methylprednisolone for acute exacerbations of multiple sclerosis (AAN [Scott 2011]; NICE 2014).

Oral: 200 mg daily for 1 week, followed by 80 mg every other day for 1 month.

Pericarditis (off-label use):

Recurrent pericarditis : Oral: 1 to 1.5 mg/kg once daily for at least 1 month; taper dose over a 3-month period (Maisch 2004)

Tuberculosis pericarditis : Oral: 1 to 2 mg/kg once daily for 5 to 7 days followed by 6 to 8 weeks of tapering (Maisch 2004) **or** 60 mg once daily for 4 weeks, followed by 30 mg once daily for 4 weeks, 15 mg once daily for 2 weeks, and 5 mg once daily for 1 week (Reuter 2006).

***Pneumocystis* pneumonia (adjunctive therapy) in HIV-infected patients (off-label dose):** Oral: 40 mg twice daily for 5 days beginning as early as possible and within 72 hours of PCP therapy, followed by 40 mg once daily on days 6 through 10, followed by 20 mg once daily on days 11 through 21 (DHHS [adult] 2015).

Polymyalgia rheumatica (off-label dose): Oral: Evidence to support an optimal dose and duration are lacking; recommendations provided are general guidelines only. Individualize therapy using the minimum effective dose and duration (Dejaco [EULAR/ACR 2015]):

Initial: Dosage range: 12.5 to 25 mg daily; consider higher doses within this range for patients at high risk of relapse and low risk of adverse events; consider lower doses within this range for patients with high risk factors for side effects (eg, diabetes, osteoporosis, glaucoma). Single daily doses are preferred over divided daily doses. Avoid initial doses ≤7.5 mg/day or >30 mg/day.

Tapering: For initial dosing, taper to a dose of 10 mg/day within 4 to 8 weeks. If relapse occurs, increase dosing to the prerelapse dose and gradually taper back to the dose which relapse occurred within 4 to 8 weeks. Once remission is achieved (initial or relapse therapy), taper daily dose by 1 mg every 4 weeks (or by 1.25 mg decrements if using schedules such as 10 mg and 7.5 mg on alternate days) until discontinuation.

Prostate cancer, metastatic (off-label use): Oral: 5 mg twice daily (in combination with abiraterone) until disease progression or unacceptable toxicity (de Bono 2011; Ryan 2015) **or** 10 mg once daily (in combination with cabazitaxel) for up to 10 cycles (de Bono 2010) **or** 5 mg twice daily (in combination with docetaxel) for up to 10 cycles (Berthold 2008; Tannock 2004).

Rheumatoid arthritis (off-label dose): Oral: ≤10 mg daily (American College of Rheumatology 2002).

Subacute thyroiditis (off-label use): Oral: 40 mg daily for 1 to 2 weeks; gradually taper over 2 to 4 weeks or longer depending on clinical response. **Note:** NSAIDs should be considered first-line therapy in such patients (Bahn 2011).

Takayasu arteritis (off-label use): Oral: Initial: 40 to 60 mg daily; taper to lowest effective dose when ESR and CRP levels are normal; usual duration: 1 to 2 years (Hiratzka 2010).

Thyrotoxicosis (type II amiodarone-induced; off-label use): Oral: 40 mg daily for 14 to 28 days; gradually taper over 2 to 3 months depending on clinical response (Bahn 2011).

Tuberculosis, severe, paradoxical reactions (off-label dose): Oral: 1 mg/kg/day, gradually reduce after 1 to 2 weeks (AIDS*info* guidelines 2008).

Geriatric Refer to adult dosing; use the lowest effective dose.

Pediatric

General dosing; anti-inflammatory/immunosuppressive/endocrine disorders: Children and Adolescents: Oral: Refer to adult dosing.

Note: Dose depends upon condition being treated and response of patient; dosage for infants and children should be based on severity of the disease and response of the patient rather than on strict adherence to dosage indicated by age, weight, or body surface area. Consider alternate day therapy for long-term therapy. Discontinuation of long-term therapy requires gradual withdrawal by tapering the dose.

Indication-specific dosing:

Acute asthma (off-label dose): Oral:

Infants and Children <12 years: 1 to 2 mg/kg/day for 3 to 10 days (maximum: 60 mg/day) (NAEPP 2007).

Children ≥12 years and Adolescents: Refer to adult dosing.

Antineoplastic: Children and Adolescents: Oral: Refer to adult dosing or to specific protocol.

Autoimmune hepatitis (monotherapy or in combination with azathioprine) (off-label use): Infants, Children, and Adolescents: Oral: Initial: 1 to 2 mg/kg/day for 2 weeks (maximum: 60 mg/day), followed by a taper over 6 to 8 weeks to a dose of 0.1 to 0.2 mg/kg/day or 2.5 to 5 mg daily (AASLD [Manns 2010]; Della Corte 2012).

Bell palsy (off-label use):

Infants, Children, and Adolescents <16 years: Oral: 1 mg/kg/day for 1 week, then taper over 1 week; ideally start within the 72 hours of onset of symptoms; maximum daily dose: 60 mg/day

Adolescents ≥16 years: Oral: Refer to adult dosing.

Nephrotic syndrome; steroid sensitive (SSNS) (off-label dose): Children and Adolescents: Oral:

Initial episode: 2 mg/kg/day or 60 mg/m^2/day once daily, maximum daily dose: 60 mg/day for 4 to 6 weeks; then adjust to an alternate-day schedule of 1.5 mg/kg/dose or 40 mg/m^2/dose on alternate days as a single dose, maximum dose: 40 mg/dose (Gipson 2009; KDIGO 2012; KDOQI 2013); duration of therapy based on patient response.

Relapse: 2 mg/kg/day or 60 mg/m^2/day once daily, maximum daily dose: 60 mg/day, continue until complete remission for at least 3 days; then adjust to an alternate-day schedule of 1.5 mg/kg/dose or 40 mg/m^2/dose on alternate days as a single dose, maximum dose: 40 mg/dose, recommended duration of alternate day dosing is variable: may continue for at least 4 weeks then taper. Longer duration of treatment may be necessary in patients who relapse frequently, some patients may require up to 3 months of treatment (Gipson 2009; KDIGO 2012; KDOQI 2013).

Maintenance therapy for frequently relapsing SSNS: Taper previous dose down to lowest effective dose which maintains remission using an alternate day schedule; usual effective range: 0.1 to 0.5 mg/kg/day on alternating days; other patients may require doses up to 0.7 mg/kg/dose every other day (KDIGO 2012; KDOQI 2013).

***Pneumocystis* pneumonia (adjunctive therapy) in HIV-infected patients (off-label dose):** Oral:

Infants and Children: 1 mg/kg twice daily on days 1 to 5, *followed by* 0.5 to 1 mg/kg twice daily on days 6 to 10, *followed by* 0.5 mg/kg once daily on days 11 through 21 (DHHS [pediatric] 2013).

Adolescents: Refer to adult dosing.

Renal Impairment There are no dosage adjustments provided in the manufacturer's labeling.

Hemodialysis: Supplemental dose is not necessary.

Hepatic Impairment There are no dosage adjustments provided in the manufacturer's labeling.

Mechanism of Action Decreases inflammation by suppression of migration of polymorphonuclear leukocytes and reversal of increased capillary permeability; suppresses the immune system by reducing activity and volume of the lymphatic system; suppresses adrenal function at high doses. Antitumor effects may be related to inhibition of glucose transport, phosphorylation, or induction of cell death in immature lymphocytes. Antiemetic effects are thought to occur due to blockade of cerebral innervation of the emetic center via inhibition of prostaglandin synthesis.

Contraindications Hypersensitivity to prednisone or any component of the formulation; administration of live or live attenuated vaccines with immunosuppressive doses of prednisone; systemic fungal infections

Documentation of allergenic cross-reactivity for corticosteroids is limited. However, because of similarities in chemical structure and/or pharmacologic actions, the possibility of cross-sensitivity cannot be ruled out with certainty.

Warnings/Precautions May cause hypercorticism or suppression of hypothalamic-pituitary-adrenal (HPA) axis, particularly in younger children or in patients receiving high doses for prolonged periods. HPA axis suppression may lead to adrenal crisis. Withdrawal and discontinuation of a corticosteroid should be done slowly and carefully. Particular care is required when patients are transferred from systemic corticosteroids to inhaled products due to possible adrenal insufficiency or withdrawal from steroids, including an increase in allergic symptoms. Patients receiving >20 mg per day of prednisone (or equivalent) may be most susceptible. Fatalities have occurred due to adrenal insufficiency in asthmatic patients during and after transfer from systemic corticosteroids to aerosol steroids; aerosol steroids do **not** provide the systemic steroid needed to treat patients having trauma, surgery, or infections.

Acute myopathy has been reported with high dose corticosteroids, usually in patients with neuromuscular transmission disorders; may involve ocular and/or respiratory muscles; monitor creatine kinase; recovery may be delayed. Prolonged use of corticosteroids may increase the incidence of secondary infection, mask acute infection (including fungal infections), prolong or exacerbate viral infections, or limit response to killed or inactivated vaccines. Exposure to chickenpox or measles should be avoided. Corticosteroids should not be used to treat viral hepatitis or cerebral malaria. Close observation is required in patients with latent tuberculosis and/or TB reactivity; restrict use in active TB (only fulminating or disseminated TB in conjunction with antituberculosis treatment). Latent or active amebiasis should be ruled out in any patient with recent travel to tropic climates or unexplained diarrhea prior to corticosteroid initiation. Use with extreme caution in patients with Strongyloides infections; hyperinfection, dissemination and fatalities have occurred. Prolonged treatment with corticosteroids has been associated with the development of Kaposi sarcoma (case reports); if noted, discontinuation of therapy should be considered (Goedert 2002). Use with caution in patients with cataracts and/or glaucoma; increased intraocular pressure, open-angle glaucoma, and cataracts have occurred with prolonged use. Use with caution in patients with a history of ocular herpes simplex; corneal perforation has occurred; do not use in active ocular herpes simplex. Consider routine eye exams in chronic users. Corticosteroid use may cause psychiatric disturbances, including euphoria, insomnia, mood swings, personality changes, severe depression or frank psychotic manifestations. Pre-existing psychiatric conditions may be exacerbated by corticosteroid use. Rare cases of anaphylactoid reactions have been observed in patients receiving corticosteroids.

Use with caution in patients with HF, hypertension, diabetes, GI diseases (diverticulitis, fresh intestinal anastomoses, active or latent peptic ulcer, ulcerative colitis [nonspecific]), hepatic impairment, myasthenia gravis, MI, patients with or who are at risk for osteoporosis, renal impairment, seizure disorders or thyroid disease. May affect growth velocity; growth and development should be routinely monitored in pediatric patients. Use with caution in the elderly in the smallest possible effective dose for the shortest duration.

Withdraw therapy with gradual tapering of dose. Increased mortality was observed in patients receiving high-dose IV methylprednisolone; high-dose corticosteroids should not be used for the management of head injury. Patients may require higher doses when subject to stress (ie, trauma, surgery, severe infection). Potentially significant drug-drug interactions may exist, requiring dose or frequency adjustment, additional monitoring, and/or selection of alternative therapy.

Some dosage forms may contain sodium benzoate/benzoic acid; benzoic acid (benzoate) is a metabolite of benzyl alcohol; large amounts of benzyl alcohol (≥99 mg/kg/day) have been associated with a potentially fatal toxicity ("gasping syndrome") in neonates; the "gasping syndrome" consists of metabolic acidosis, respiratory distress, gasping respirations, CNS dysfunction (including convulsions, intracranial hemorrhage), hypotension, and cardiovascular collapse (AAP ["Inactive" 1997]; CDC, 1982); some data suggests that benzoate displaces bilirubin from protein binding sites (Ahlfors 2001); avoid or use dosage forms containing benzyl alcohol derivative with caution in neonates. See manufacturer's labeling.

Some dosage forms may contain propylene glycol; large amounts are potentially toxic and have been associated hyperosmolality, lactic acidosis, seizures, and respiratory depression; use caution (AAP ["Inactive" 1997]; Zar 2007).

Drug Interactions

Metabolism/Transport Effects Substrate of CYP3A4 (minor); **Note:** Assignment of Major/Minor substrate status based on clinically relevant drug interaction potential

Avoid Concomitant Use

Avoid concomitant use of PredniSONE with any of the following: Aldesleukin; BCG (Intravesical); Desmopressin; Indium 111 Capromab Pendetide; MiFEPRIStone; Natalizumab; Pimecrolimus; Tacrolimus (Topical); Tofacitinib

Increased Effect/Toxicity

PredniSONE may increase the levels/effects of: Acetylcholinesterase Inhibitors; Amphotericin B; Androgens; Ceritinib; CycloSPORINE (Systemic); Deferasirox; Desirudin; Desmopressin; Fingolimod; Leflunomide; Loop Diuretics; Natalizumab; Nicorandil; NSAID (COX-2 Inhibitor); NSAID (Nonselective); Quinolone Antibiotics; Thiazide and Thiazide-Like Diuretics; Tofacitinib; Vaccines (Live); Warfarin

The levels/effects of PredniSONE may be increased by: Aprepitant; Boceprevir; CycloSPORINE (Systemic); CYP3A4 Inhibitors (Strong); Denosumab; DilTIAZem; Estrogen Derivatives; Fluconazole; Fosaprepitant; Indacaterol; MiFEPRIStone; Neuromuscular-Blocking Agents (Nondepolarizing); Ocrelizumab; Pimecrolimus; Ritonavir; Roflumilast; Salicylates; Tacrolimus (Topical); Telaprevir; Trastuzumab

Decreased Effect

PredniSONE may decrease the levels/effects of: Aldesleukin; Antidiabetic Agents; BCG (Intravesical); Calcitriol (Systemic); Coccidioides immitis Skin Test; Corticorelin; CycloSPORINE (Systemic); Hyaluronidase; Indium 111 Capromab Pendetide; Isoniazid; Nivolumab; Salicylates; Sipuleucel-T; Telaprevir; Tertomotide; Urea Cycle Disorder Agents; Vaccines (Inactivated); Vaccines (Live)

The levels/effects of PredniSONE may be decreased by: Antacids; Bile Acid Sequestrants; CYP3A4 Inducers (Strong); Echinacea; MiFEPRIStone; Mitotane; Somatropin; Tesamorelin

Dietary Considerations May require increased dietary intake of pyridoxine, vitamin C, vitamin D, folate, calcium, and phosphorus; may require decreased dietary intake of sodium and potassium supplementation

Pharmacodynamics/Kinetics

Half-life Elimination 2 to 3 hours

Time to Peak Oral: Immediate-release tablet: 2 hours; Delayed-release tablet: 6 to 6.5 hours

Pregnancy Risk Factor C/D (product specific)

Pregnancy Considerations Adverse events have been observed with corticosteroids in animal reproduction studies. Prednisone and its metabolite, prednisolone, cross the human placenta. In the mother, prednisone is converted to the active metabolite prednisolone by the liver. Prior to reaching the fetus, prednisolone is converted by placental enzymes back to prednisone. As a result, the level of prednisone remaining in the maternal serum and reaching the fetus are similar; however, the amount of prednisolone reaching the fetus is ~8 to 10 times lower than the maternal serum concentration (healthy women at term) (Beitins 1972).

Some studies have shown an association between first trimester systemic corticosteroid use and oral clefts or decreased birth weight; however, information is conflicting and may be influenced by maternal dose/indication for use (Lunghi 2010; Park-Wyllie 2000; Pradat 2003). Hypoadrenalism may occur in newborns following maternal use of corticosteroids in pregnancy; monitor.

When systemic corticosteroids are needed in pregnancy for rheumatic disorders, it is generally recommended to use the lowest effective dose for the shortest duration of time, avoiding high doses during the first trimester (Götestam Skorpen 2016; Makol 2011; Østensen 2009).

For dermatologic disorders in pregnant women, systemic corticosteroids are generally not preferred for initial therapy; should be avoided during the first trimester; and used during the second or third trimester at the lowest effective dose (Bae 2012; Leachman 2006). Prednisone is preferred by some guidelines when an oral corticosteroid is needed because placental enzymes limit passage to the embryo (Murase 2014).

Pregnant women with poorly controlled asthma or asthma exacerbations may have a greater fetal/maternal risk than what is associated with appropriately used medications. Uncontrolled asthma is associated with an increased risk of perinatal mortality, preeclampsia, preterm birth, and low birth weight infants. Inhaled corticosteroids are recommended for the treatment of asthma during pregnancy; however, systemic corticosteroids, including prednisone, should be used to control acute exacerbations or treat severe persistent asthma (ACOG 2008; GINA 2016; Namazy 2016).

Prednisone may be used to treat lupus nephritis in pregnant women who have active nephritis or substantial extrarenal disease activity (Hahn 2012). Prednisone may be used (alternative agent) to treat primary adrenal insufficiency (PAI) in pregnant women. Pregnant women with PAI should be monitored at least once each trimester (Bornstein 2016).

The National Transplantation Pregnancy Registry (NTPR) is a registry which follows pregnancies which occur in maternal transplant recipients or those fathered by male transplant recipients. The NTPR encourages reporting of pregnancies following solid organ transplant by contacting them at 877-955-6877 or NTPR@giftoflifeinstitute.org.

Breastfeeding Considerations Prednisone and its metabolite, prednisolone, are present in breast milk. Actual concentrations are dependent upon maternal dose (Berlin 1979; Katz 1975; Sagraves 1981). Peak concentrations of prednisone and prednisolone in breast milk occur ~2 hours after an oral maternal dose (Berlin 1979; Sagraves 1981); the half-life in breast milk is 1.9 hours (prednisone) and 4.2 hours (prednisolone) (Sagraves 1981).

In a study which included six mother-infant pairs, adverse events were not observed in nursing infants (maternal prednisone dose not provided) (Ito 1993).

The manufacturer notes that when used systemically, maternal use of corticosteroids have the potential to cause adverse events in a breastfeeding infant (eg, growth suppression, interfere with endogenous corticosteroid production) and therefore, a decision should be made whether to discontinue nursing or to discontinue the drug, taking into account the importance of treatment to the mother. Corticosteroids are generally considered acceptable in breastfeeding women when used in usual doses (Götestam Skorpen 2016; WHO 2002);

however, monitoring of the breastfeeding infant is recommended (WHO 2002). Prednisone is one of the oral corticosteroids preferred for use in breastfeeding women (Butler 2014). If there is concern about exposure to the infant, some guidelines recommend waiting 4 hours after the maternal dose of an oral systemic corticosteroid before breastfeeding in order to decrease potential exposure to the breastfeeding infant (based on a study using prednisolone) (Bae 2012; Butler 2014; Götestam Skorpen 2016; Leachman 2006; Makol 2011; Ost 1985).

Dosage Forms

Concentrate, Oral:
PredniSONE Intensol: 5 mg/mL (30 mL)

Solution, Oral:
Generic: 5 mg/5 mL (5 mL, 120 mL, 500 mL)

Tablet, Oral:
Deltasone: 20 mg
Generic: 1 mg, 2.5 mg, 5 mg, 10 mg, 20 mg, 50 mg, 10 mg, 5 mg

Tablet Delayed Release, Oral:
Rayos: 1 mg, 2 mg, 5 mg

Tablet Therapy Pack, Oral:
Generic: 10 mg (21 ea, 48 ea); 5 mg (21 ea, 48 ea)

Dental Comment Preoperative steroid use, particularly in patient on longer term corticosteroids (>2 weeks), increases the risk of infection and delays wound healing.

Pregabalin (pre GAB a lin)

Brand Names: US Lyrica

Brand Names: Canada ACT Pregabalin; Apo-Pregabalin; Auro-Pregabalin; Dom-Pregabalin; GD-Pregabalin; JAMP-Pregabalin; Lyrica; Mar-Pregabalin; Mint-Pregabalin; MYL Pregabalin; PMS-Pregabalin; RAN-Pregabalin; Riva-Pregabalin; Sandoz-Pregabalin; Teva-Pregabalin

Generic Availability (US) No

Pharmacologic Category Anticonvulsant, Miscellaneous

Use

Fibromyalgia: For the management of fibromyalgia

Neuropathic pain associated with diabetic peripheral neuropathy: For the management of neuropathic pain associated with diabetic peripheral neuropathy

Neuropathic pain associated with spinal cord injury: For the management of neuropathic pain associated with spinal cord injury

Partial-onset seizures, adjunctive therapy: Adjunctive therapy for adult patients with partial-onset seizures

Postherpetic neuralgia: For the management of postherpetic neuralgia

Local Anesthetic/Vasoconstrictor Precautions No information available to require special precautions

Effects on Dental Treatment Key adverse event(s) related to dental treatment: Xerostomia and changes in salivation (normal salivary flow resumes upon discontinuation).

Effects on Bleeding May be associated with thrombocytopenia (3%). No information available to require routine special precautions

Adverse Reactions Frequency of adverse effects may be influenced by dose or concurrent therapy. In add-on trials in epilepsy, frequency of CNS and visual adverse effects were higher than those reported in pain management trials. Range noted below is inclusive of all trials.

>10%:

Cardiovascular: Peripheral edema (≤16%)

Central nervous system: Dizziness (8% to 45%), drowsiness (4% to 36%), ataxia (1% to 20%), headache (5% to 14%), fatigue (5% to 11%)

Endocrine & metabolic: Weight gain (≤16%)

Gastrointestinal: Xerostomia (1% to 15%)

Infection: Infection (3% to 14%)

Neuromuscular & skeletal: Tremor (≤11%)

Ophthalmic: Blurred vision (1% to 12%), diplopia (≤12%)

Miscellaneous: Accidental injury (2% to 11%)

1% to 10%:

Cardiovascular: Edema (≤8%), chest pain (1% to 4%), facial edema (≤3%), hypertension (2%), hypotension (2%)

Central nervous system: Abnormality in thinking (≤9%), equilibrium disturbance (2% to 9%), neuropathy (2% to 9%), abnormal gait (≤8%), confusion (≤7%), euphoria (≤7%), speech disturbance (≤7%), amnesia (≤6%), disturbance in attention (4% to 6%), twitching (≤5%), pain (2% to 5%), insomnia (4%), myoclonus (≤4%), memory impairment (1% to 4%), vertigo (1% to 4%), hypoesthesia (2% to 3%), feeling abnormal (1% to 3%), anxiety (2%), paresthesia (2%), disorientation (≤2%), intoxicated feeling (1% to 2%), lethargy (1% to 2%), anorgasmia (≥1%), depersonalization (≥1%), hypertonia (≥1%), sedation (≥1%), stupor (≥1%), myasthenia (1%), nervousness (≤1%)

Dermatologic: Decubitus ulcer (3%), pruritus (≥1%)

Endocrine & metabolic: Fluid retention (2% to 3%), hypoglycemia (1% to 3%), decreased libido (≥1%)

Gastrointestinal: Constipation (≤10%), increased appetite (2% to 7%), nausea (5%), flatulence (≤3%), vomiting (1% to 3%), abdominal distension (2%), abdominal pain (≥1%), gastroenteritis (≥1%)

Genitourinary: Urinary incontinence (≤3%), impotence (≥1%), urinary frequency (≥1%)

Hematologic & oncologic: Bruise (≥1%), thrombocytopenia (≥1%)

Hypersensitivity: Hypersensitivity reaction (≥1%; including erythema, skin blister, skin rash, urticaria, wheezing)

Neuromuscular & skeletal: Weakness (2% to 7%), arthralgia (3% to 6%), back pain (≤4%), muscle spasm (2% to 4%), increased creatine phosphokinase (3%), limb pain (3%), neck pain (3%), joint swelling (2%), leg cramps (≥1%), myalgia (≥1%)

Ophthalmic: Visual disturbance (≤5%), eye disease (≤2%), conjunctivitis (≥1%), nystagmus (≥1%)

Otic: Otitis media (≥1%), tinnitus (≥1%)

Respiratory: Nasopharyngitis (8%), sinusitis (4% to 7%), bronchitis (≤3%), dyspnea (≤3%), pharyngolaryngeal pain (1% to 3%), flu-like symptoms (1% to 2%)

Miscellaneous: Fever (≥1%)

<1%, postmarketing, and/or case reports: Abscess, acute renal failure, ageusia, agitation, albuminuria, alopecia, altered sense of smell, amenorrhea, anaphylactoid reaction, anemia, angioedema, anisocoria, apathy, aphasia, aphthous stomatitis, apnea, arthropathy, ascites, atelectasis, blepharitis, blepharoptosis, blindness, brain disease, bronchiolitis, cardiac failure, cellulitis, cerebellar syndrome, cervicitis, chills, cholecystitis, cholelithiasis, chondrodystrophy, cogwheel rigidity, colitis, coma, corneal ulcer, cutaneous nodule, decreased glucose tolerance, delirium, delusions, depression of ST segment on ECG, dermal ulcer, diarrhea, drug dependence, dysarthria, dysautonomia,

dysgeusia, dyskinesia, dysmenorrhea, dyspareunia, dysphagia, dystonia, dysuria, eczema, ejaculatory disorder, eosinophilia, epididymitis, esophageal ulcer, esophagitis, exfoliative dermatitis, exophthalmos, extraocular palsy, extrapyramidal reaction, gastritis, gastrointestinal hemorrhage, glomerulonephritis, granuloma, Guillain-Barre syndrome, gynecomastia, hallucination, hematuria, hemophthalmos, hirsutism, hostility, hyperacusis, hyperalgesia, hyperesthesia, hyperkinesia, hypokinesia, hypoprothrombinemia, hypotonia, increased libido, intracranial hypertension, iritis, keratitis, keratoconjunctivitis, lactation (female), laryngismus, leukocytosis, leukopenia, leukorrhea, lichenoid dermatitis, lymphadenopathy, malaise, malignant neoplasm of bladder, manic reaction, melanosis, melena, miosis, mydriasis, myelofibrosis, neck stiffness, nephritis, nephrolithiasis, neuralgia, nocturnal amblyopia, oliguria, ophthalmoplegia, optic atrophy, oral mucosa ulcer, oral paresthesia, orthostatic hypotension, pancreatitis, papilledema, paranoia, pelvic pain, periodontal abscess, peripheral neuritis, personality disorder, photophobia, polycythemia, psychotic depression, pulmonary edema, pulmonary fibrosis, purpura, pyelonephritis, rectal hemorrhage, retinal edema, retinal vascular disease, retroperitoneal fibrosis, rhabdomyolysis, schizophrenia, shock, skin atrophy, skin necrosis, skin photosensitivity, skin rash (petechial rash, purpuric rash, pustular rash, vesiculobullous dermatitis), Stevens-Johnson syndrome, subcutaneous nodule, syncope, thrombocythemia, thrombophlebitis, tongue edema, torticollis, trismus, urate crystalluria, urinary retention, urticaria, uveitis, ventricular fibrillation, xerophthalmia

Dosing

Adult & Geriatric Note: When discontinuing, taper off gradually over at least 1 week.

Fibromyalgia: Oral: Initial: 150 mg daily in divided doses (75 mg twice daily); may be increased to 300 mg daily (150 mg twice daily) within 1 week based on tolerability and effect; may be further increased to 450 mg daily (225 mg twice daily). Maximum dose: 450 mg daily (dosages up to 600 mg daily were evaluated with no significant additional benefit and an increase in adverse effects)

Neuropathic pain, diabetes-associated: Oral: Initial: 150 mg daily in divided doses (50 mg 3 times daily); may be increased within 1 week based on tolerability and effect; maximum dose: 300 mg daily in 3 divided doses (dosages up to 600 mg daily were evaluated with no significant additional benefit and an increase in adverse effects)

Neuropathic pain, spinal cord injury associated: Oral: Initial: 150 mg daily in divided doses (75 mg twice daily); may be increased to 300 mg daily (150 mg twice daily) within 1 week based on tolerability and effect; further titration to 600 mg daily (300 mg twice daily) after 2 to 3 weeks may be considered in patients who do not experience sufficient relief of pain provided they are able to tolerate pregabalin. Maximum dose: 600 mg daily

Partial-onset seizures (adjunctive therapy): Oral: Initial: 150 mg daily in divided doses (75 mg twice daily or 50 mg 3 times daily); may be increased based on tolerability and effect (optimal titration schedule has not been defined). Maximum dose: 600 mg daily

Postherpetic neuralgia: Oral: Initial: 150 mg daily in divided doses (75 mg twice daily or 50 mg 3 times daily); may be increased to 300 mg daily within 1 week based on tolerability and effect; further titration (to 600 mg daily) after 2 to 4 weeks may be considered in patients who do not experience sufficient relief of pain provided they are able to tolerate pregabalin. Maximum dose: 600 mg daily

Generalized anxiety disorder (off-label use): Oral: Initial: 150 mg/day in 2 to 3 divided doses; based on response and tolerability, adjust dose at weekly intervals in increments of 150 mg to a maximum dose of 600 mg/day (Frampton 2014; WFSBP [Bandelow 2008]).

Hot flashes (off-label use): Oral: Initial: 50 mg daily at bedtime; increase to 50 mg twice daily after 1 week and then increase to 75 mg twice daily after 1 week. Dose can be increased to 150 mg twice daily after 1 week, based on response and tolerability (Loprinzi 2010).

Restless legs syndrome (off-label use): Oral: Initial: 75 mg daily, 1 to 3 hours before bedtime; then increase to 150 mg daily on day 6. On or after day 11, dosage may be further increased to 300 mg daily. Usual effective dose: 150 to 450 mg/day (Allen 2010; Allen 2014; Garcia-Borreguero 2014).

Social anxiety disorder (off-label use): Oral: Initial: 300 mg/day in 3 divided doses; on day 4, based on response and tolerability, increase dose to 450 mg/day. On or after day 6, dosage may be further increased to 600 mg/day. In clinical trials, efficacy for response and relapse prevention was found at doses of 450 and 600 mg/day (Feltner 2011; Greist 2011; Pande 2004).

Renal Impairment Renal function may be estimated using the Cockcroft-Gault formula. Then determine recommended dosage regimen based on the indication-specific total daily dose for normal renal function (CrCl ≥60 mL/minute). For example, if the indication-specific daily dose is 450 mg daily for normal renal function, the daily dose should be reduced to 225 mg daily (in 2 to 3 divided doses) for a creatinine clearance of 30 to 60 mL/minute (see table).

Pregabalin Renal Impairment Dosing

CrCl (mL/minute)	Total Pregabalin Daily Dose (mg/day)				Dosing Frequency
≥60 (normal renal function)	150	300	450	600	2 to 3 divided doses
30 to 60	75	150	225	300	2 to 3 divided doses
15 to 30	25 to 50	75	100-150	150	1 to 2 divided doses
<15	25	25 to 50	50 to 75	75	Single daily dose

Posthemodialysis supplementary dosage (as a single additional dose):
25 mg/day schedule: Single supplementary dose of 25 mg **or** 50 mg
25 to 50 mg/day schedule: Single supplementary dose of 50 mg **or** 75 mg
50 to 75 mg/day schedule: Single supplementary dose of 75 mg **or** 100 mg
75 mg/day schedule: Single supplementary dose of 100 mg **or** 150 mg

Hepatic Impairment No dosage adjustment provided in manufacturer's labeling. However, no adjustment expected since undergoes minimal hepatic metabolism.

Mechanism of Action Binds to alpha$_2$-delta subunit of voltage-gated calcium channels within the CNS and modulates calcium influx at the nerve terminals, thereby inhibiting excitatory neurotransmitter release including glutamate, norepinephrine (noradrenaline), serotonin, dopamine, substance P, and calcitonin gene-related peptide (Gajraj, 2007; McKeage, 2009). Although structurally related to GABA, it does not bind to GABA or benzodiazepine receptors. Exerts antinociceptive and anticonvulsant activity. Pregabalin may also affect descending noradrenergic and serotonergic pain transmission pathways from the brainstem to the spinal cord.

Contraindications Hypersensitivity to pregabalin or any component of the formulation

Warnings/Precautions Pooled analysis if trials involving various antiepileptics (regardless of indication) showed an increased risk of suicidal thoughts/behavior (incidence rate: 0.43% treated patients compared to 0.24% patients receiving placebo); risk observed as early as one week after initiation and continued through duration of trials (most trials ≤24 weeks). Monitor all patients for notable changes in behavior that might indicate suicidal thoughts or depression; notify healthcare provider immediately if symptoms occur. Angioedema has been reported; may be life threatening; use with caution in patients with a history of angioedema episodes. Concurrent use with other drugs known to cause angioedema (eg, ACE inhibitors) may increase risk. Hypersensitivity reactions, including skin redness, blistering, hives, rash, dyspnea, and wheezing have been reported; discontinue treatment if hypersensitivity occurs. Dizziness and somnolence are commonly reported; effects generally occur shortly after initiation and occur more frequently at higher doses. Patients must be cautioned about performing tasks which require mental alertness (eg, operating machinery or driving). Visual disturbances (blurred vision, decreased acuity and visual field changes) have been associated with pregabalin therapy; patients should be instructed to notify their physician if these effects are noted.

Pregabalin has been associated with increases in CPK and rare cases of rhabdomyolysis. Patients should be instructed to notify their prescriber if unexplained muscle pain, tenderness, or weakness, particularly if fever and/or malaise are associated with these symptoms. Use may cause weight gain; weight gain generally associated with dose and duration (average weight gain was 5.2 kg for diabetic patients receiving pregabalin for ≥2 years); weight gain was not limited to patients with edema and did not appear to be associated with baseline BMI, gender, age, or loss of glycemic control in diabetic patients. Use may cause peripheral edema; use with caution in patients with heart failure (NYHA Class III or IV) due to limited data in this patient population. In addition, effect on weight gain/edema may be additive with the thiazolidinedione class of antidiabetic agents; use caution when coadministering these agents, particularly in patients with prior cardiovascular disease. In a scientific statement from the American Heart Association, pregabalin has been determined to be an agent that may exacerbate underlying myocardial dysfunction (magnitude: minor to moderate) (AHA [Page 2016]). May decrease platelet count (extremely rare) or prolong PR interval (clinical significance unknown).

Has been noted to be tumorigenic (increased incidence of hemangiosarcoma) in animal studies; significance of these findings in humans is unknown. Anticonvulsants should not be discontinued abruptly because of the possibility of increasing seizure frequency; therapy should be withdrawal gradually unless safety concerns require a more rapid withdrawal. Tapering over at least 1 week is recommended. Abrupt discontinued with pregabalin has been associated with anxiety, diarrhea, headache, hyperhidrosis, insomnia and nausea. Use caution in renal impairment; dosage adjustment required. Potentially significant drug-drug interactions may exist, requiring dose or frequency adjustment, additional monitoring, and/or selection of alternative therapy.

Drug Interactions

Metabolism/Transport Effects None known.

Avoid Concomitant Use

Avoid concomitant use of Pregabalin with any of the following: Azelastine (Nasal); Orphenadrine; Oxomemazine; Paraldehyde; Thalidomide

Increased Effect/Toxicity

Pregabalin may increase the levels/effects of: Alcohol (Ethyl); Analgesics (Opioid); Antidiabetic Agents (Thiazolidinedione); Azelastine (Nasal); Blonanserin; Buprenorphine; CNS Depressants; Flunitrazepam; HYDROcodone; Methotrimeprazine; MetyroSINE; Mirtazapine; Orphenadrine; OxyCODONE; Paraldehyde; Piribedil; Pramipexole; ROPINIRole; Rotigotine; Selective Serotonin Reuptake Inhibitors; Suvorexant; Thalidomide; Zolpidem

The levels/effects of Pregabalin may be increased by: ACE Inhibitors; Brimonidine (Topical); Cannabis; Chlormethiazole; Chlorphenesin Carbamate; Dimethindene (Topical); Doxylamine; Dronabinol; Droperidol; HydrOXYzine; Kava Kava; Lofexidine; Magnesium Sulfate; Methotrimeprazine; Minocycline; Nabilone; Oxomemazine; Perampanel; Rufinamide; Sodium Oxybate; Tapentadol; Tetrahydrocannabinol; Trimeprazine

Decreased Effect

The levels/effects of Pregabalin may be decreased by: Mefloquine; Mianserin; Orlistat

Dietary Considerations May be taken with or without food.

Pharmacodynamics/Kinetics

Onset of Action Pain management: Effects may be noted as early as the first week of therapy

Half-life Elimination 6.3 hours

Time to Peak 1.5 hours (3 hours with food)

Pregnancy Considerations Adverse events have been observed in animal reproduction studies. Pregabalin crosses the human placenta (Ohman 2011). Outcome data following maternal use of pregabalin during pregnancy is limited (Veiby 2014).

In study conducted in males, pregabalin was found to temporarily decrease mean sperm concentrations; no effects on sperm morphology or motility were observed. Concentrations increased after pregabalin was discontinued. The clinical relevance of this is not known.

Patients exposed to pregabalin during pregnancy are encouraged to enroll themselves into the North American Antiepileptic Drug (NAAED) Pregnancy Registry by calling 1-888-233-2334. Additional information is available at www.aedpregnancyregistry.org.

Breastfeeding Considerations Pregabalin is excreted in breast milk (Ohman 2011). Data is available from 10 women at least 12 weeks postpartum who were given pregabalin 150 mg every 12 hours for 4 doses. Milk concentrations of pregabalin were 76% of those found in maternal serum. The estimated exposure to the nursing infant was calculated to be 7% of the weight adjusted maternal dose. The infants were not breastfed during the study period. Breastfeeding is not recommended by the manufacturer.

Controlled Substance C-V

Dosage Forms

Capsule, Oral:

Lyrica: 25 mg, 50 mg, 75 mg, 100 mg, 150 mg, 200 mg, 225 mg, 300 mg

Solution, Oral:
Lyrica: 20 mg/mL (473 mL)

Prilocaine (PRIL oh kane)

Related Information
Oral Pain *on page 1830*

Brand Names: US Citanest Plain Dental

Brand Names: Canada Citanest Plain Dental; Dentsply 4% Prilocaine Hydrochloride Dental Injection

Generic Availability (US) No

Pharmacologic Category Local Anesthetic

Dental Use Amide-type anesthetic used for local infiltration anesthesia; injection near nerve trunks to produce nerve block

Use

Local anesthesia: Production of local anesthesia in dentistry by nerve block or infiltration techniques.

Local Anesthetic/Vasoconstrictor Precautions
No information available to require special precautions

Effects on Dental Treatment It is common to misinterpret psychogenic responses to local anesthetic injection as an allergic reaction. Intraoral injections are perceived by many patients as a stressful procedure in dentistry. Common symptoms to this stress are diaphoresis, palpitations, hyperventilation, generalized pallor and a fainting feeling.

Degree of adverse effects in the CNS and cardiovascular system is directly related to blood levels of prilocaine (frequency not defined; more likely to occur after systemic administration rather than infiltration): Bradycardia and reduction in cardiac output, hypersensitivity reactions (may be manifest as dermatologic reactions and edema at injection site), asthmatic syndromes

High blood levels: Anxiety, restlessness, disorientation, confusion, dizziness, tremors, and seizures, followed by CNS depression, resulting in somnolence, unconsciousness and possible respiratory arrest; nausea and vomiting

In some cases, symptoms of CNS stimulation may be absent and the primary CNS effects are somnolence and unconsciousness.

Effects on Bleeding No information available to require special precautions

Adverse Reactions Degree of adverse effects in the central nervous system and cardiovascular system are directly related to the blood levels of local anesthetic. The effects below are more likely to occur after systemic administration rather than infiltration.

Frequency not defined.

Cardiovascular: Bradycardia, cardiac arrest, cardiovascular signs and symptoms (stimulation/depression), circulatory shock, edema, hypotension

Central nervous system: Apprehension, confusion, convulsions, dizziness, drowsiness, euphoria, localized warm feeling, loss of consciousness, nervousness, numbness, oral paresthesia (may be persistent), sensation of cold, twitching

Dermatologic: Dermal ulcer, urticaria

Gastrointestinal: Vomiting

Hematologic & oncologic: Methemoglobinemia

Hypersensitivity: Anaphylactoid reaction, hypersensitivity reaction

Neuromuscular & skeletal: Tremor

Ophthalmic: Blurred vision, diplopia

Otic: Tinnitus

Respiratory: Respiratory arrest, respiratory depression

Dental Usual Dosage Dental anesthesia: Infiltration or conduction block:

Children <10 years: Doses >40 mg (1 mL) as a 4% solution per procedure rarely needed for procedures involving a single tooth, in a maxillary infiltration for 2 to 3 teeth, or for an entire quadrant with a mandibular block.

Children ≥10 years, Adolescents, and Adults: Initial: 40 to 80 mg (1 to 2 mL) as a 4% solution. AAPD guidelines, 2009 maximum recommended dose within a 2-hour period:

<70 kg: 6 mg/kg (400 mg)

≥70 kg: 400 mg or 5 to 6 cartridges

Note: The effective anesthetic dose varies with procedure, intensity of anesthesia needed, duration of anesthesia required and physical condition of the patient. Always use the lowest effective dose along with careful aspiration.

The following numbers of dental carpules (1.8 mL) provide the indicated amounts of prilocaine hydrochloride 4%. See table.

Prilocaine

# of Cartridges (1.8 mL)	mg Prilocaine (4%)
1	72
2	144
3	216
4	288
5	360
6	432
7	504
8	576

Note: Adult and children doses of prilocaine hydrochloride cited from http://www.aapd.org/media/Policies_Guidelines/G_LocalAnesthesia.pdf.

Dosing

Adult & Geriatric Dental anesthesia: Infiltration or conduction block: Initial: 40 to 80 mg (1 to 2 mL) as a 4% solution. AAPD guidelines, 2009 maximum recommended dose within a 2-hour period:

<70 kg: 6 mg/kg (400 mg)

≥70 kg: 400 mg or 5 to 6 cartridges

Note: The effective anesthetic dose varies with procedure, intensity of anesthesia needed, duration of anesthesia required and physical condition of the patient. Always use the lowest effective dose along with careful aspiration.

Pediatric Dental anesthesia: Infiltration or conduction block:

Children <10 years: Doses >40 mg (1 mL) as a 4% solution per procedure rarely needed for procedures involving a single tooth, in a maxillary infiltration for 2 to 3 teeth, or for an entire quadrant with a mandibular block.

Children ≥10 years and Adolescents: Refer to adult dosing.

Renal Impairment There are no dosage adjustments provided in the manufacturer's labeling. Undergoes renal metabolism; use with caution.

Hepatic Impairment There are no dosage adjustments provided in the manufacturer's labeling. Undergoes hepatic metabolism; use with caution.

Mechanism of Action Local anesthetics bind selectively to the intracellular surface of sodium channels to block influx of sodium into the axon. As a result, depolarization necessary for action potential propagation and subsequent nerve function is prevented. The block at the sodium channel is reversible. When drug diffuses away from the axon, sodium channel function is restored and nerve propagation returns.

Contraindications

Hypersensitivity to local anesthetics of the amide type or any component of the formulation; patients with congenital or idiopathic methemoglobinemia

Canadian labeling: Additional contraindications (not in US labeling): Citanest Plain Dental: Severe shock or heart block; inflammation or sepsis in the region of proposed injection

Warnings/Precautions Methemoglobinemia has been reported with local anesthetics including prilocaine; clinically significant methemoglobinemia requires immediate treatment. Use with caution in patients who are very young, have glucose-6-phosphate deficiencies, or in patients taking concurrent drugs that can cause methemoglobinemia. Use is contraindicated in patients with congenital or idiopathic methemoglobinemia. Careful and constant monitoring of the patient's state of consciousness should be done following each local anesthetic injection; at such times, restlessness, anxiety, tinnitus, dizziness, blurred vision, tremors, depression, or drowsiness may be early warning signs of CNS toxicity. Treatment is primarily symptomatic and supportive. Intravascular injections should be avoided. Prilocaine may potentially trigger malignant hyperthermia; follow standard protocol for identification and treatment. Local anesthetics have also been associated with rare occurrences of sudden respiratory arrest, seizures, and cardiac arrest. Use with caution in patients with cardiovascular disease, severe shock, or heart block. Use with caution in patients with hepatic impairment; amide-type anesthetics are metabolized hepatically. Use with caution in acutely ill, debilitated, pediatric or elderly patients. Aspirate the syringe after tissue penetration and before injection to minimize chance of direct vascular injection. Resuscitative equipment, oxygen, and other resuscitative drugs should be available for immediate use. Potentially significant drug-drug interactions may exist, requiring dose or frequency adjustment, additional monitoring, and/or selection of alternative therapy.

Drug Interactions

Metabolism/Transport Effects None known.

Avoid Concomitant Use

Avoid concomitant use of Prilocaine with any of the following: Bupivacaine (Liposomal)

Increased Effect/Toxicity

Prilocaine may increase the levels/effects of: Bupivacaine (Liposomal); Neuromuscular-Blocking Agents; Sodium Nitrite

The levels/effects of Prilocaine may be increased by: Dapsone (Topical); Hyaluronidase; Methemoglobinemia Associated Agents; Nitric Oxide; Tetracaine (Topical)

Decreased Effect

Prilocaine may decrease the levels/effects of: Technetium Tc 99m Tilmanocept

Pharmacodynamics/Kinetics

Onset of Action Infiltration: <2 minutes; Inferior alveolar nerve block: <3 minutes

Duration of Action Infiltration: Complete anesthesia for procedures lasting 20 minutes; Inferior alveolar nerve block: ~2.5 hours

Half-life Elimination 1.6 hours; may be prolonged with hepatic or renal impairment

Pregnancy Risk Factor B

Pregnancy Considerations Adverse events have not been observed in animal reproduction studies. Prilocaine crosses the placenta.

Breastfeeding Considerations It is not known if prilocaine is excreted in breast milk. The manufacturer recommends that caution be exercised when administering prilocaine to nursing women.

Dosage Forms

Solution, Injection:

Citanest Plain Dental: 4% (1.8 mL)

Primaquine (PRIM a kween)

Pharmacologic Category Aminoquinoline (Antimalarial); Antimalarial Agent

Use Malaria: Radical cure (prevention of relapse) of vivax malaria

Local Anesthetic/Vasoconstrictor Precautions No information available to require special precautions

Effects on Dental Treatment No significant effects or complications reported

Effects on Bleeding No information available to require special precautions.

Adverse Reactions Frequency not defined.

Cardiovascular: Cardiac arrhythmia, dizziness, prolonged Q-T interval on ECG

Dermatologic: Pruritus, skin rash

Gastrointestinal: Abdominal cramps, epigastric distress, nausea, vomiting

Hematologic & oncologic: Anemia, hemolytic anemia (in patients with G6PD deficiency), leukopenia, methemoglobinemia (in NADH-methemoglobin reductase-deficient individuals)

General Dosage Range Oral: *Adults:* 15 mg once daily for 14 days (maximum dose: 15 mg/day)

Mechanism of Action Primaquine is an antiprotozoal agent active against exoerythrocytic stages of *Plasmodium ovale* and *P. vivax*, also active against the primary exoerythrocytic stages of *P. falciparum* and gametocytes of *Plasmodia*; disrupts mitochondria and binds to DNA

Pharmacodynamics/Kinetics

Half-life Elimination 7 hours; reported range: 3.7 to 9.6 hours

Time to Peak Serum: 1 to 3 hours

Pregnancy Considerations

Primaquine is contraindicated in pregnant women.

Malaria infection in pregnant women may be more severe than in nonpregnant women and has a high risk of maternal and perinatal morbidity and mortality. Therefore, pregnant women and women who are likely to become pregnant are advised to avoid travel to malaria-risk areas. When treatment is needed, other agents are preferred (CDC Yellow Book 2016). Consult current CDC guidelines for the treatment of malaria during pregnancy.

Primidone (PRI mi done)

Brand Names: US Mysoline

Brand Names: Canada Apo-Primidone

Pharmacologic Category Anticonvulsant, Miscellaneous; Barbiturate

Use Management of grand mal, psychomotor, and focal seizures

Local Anesthetic/Vasoconstrictor Precautions No information available to require special precautions

Effects on Dental Treatment No significant effects or complications reported

Effects on Bleeding Primidone has been associated with clotting factor defects in children, including elevated prothrombin time, elevated partial thromboplastin time, and diminished factors V, VII, or X. These defects are reversible; clotting factors return to normal after discontinuation of primidone.

Adverse Reactions

Frequency not defined.

Central nervous system: Ataxia, drowsiness, emotional disturbance, fatigue, hyperirritability, suicidal ideation, vertigo

Dermatologic: Morbilliform rash

Gastrointestinal: Anorexia, nausea, vomiting

Genitourinary: Impotence

Hematologic & oncologic: Agranulocytosis, granulocytopenia, megaloblastic anemia (idiosyncratic), pure red cell aplasia, red cell hypoplasia

Ophthalmic: Diplopia, nystagmus

General Dosage Range Dosage adjustment recommended in patients with renal impairment

Oral:

Children <8 years: Initial: 50 mg once daily at bedtime; Maintenance: 375 to 750 mg/day (10 to 25 mg/kg/day) in 3 to 4 divided doses

Children ≥8 years and Adults: Initial: 100 to 125 mg/day at bedtime; Maintenance: 750 to 1,500 mg/day in 3 to 4 divided doses (maximum: 2 g/day)

Mechanism of Action Decreases neuron excitability, raises seizure threshold similar to phenobarbital; primidone has two active metabolites, phenobarbital and phenylethylmalonamide (PEMA); PEMA may enhance the activity of phenobarbital

Pharmacodynamics/Kinetics

Half-life Elimination Primidone: 5 to16 hours (variable); PEMA: 16 to 50 hours (variable); Phenobarbital: 50 to 150 hours (Bourgeois 2000, Neels 2004)

Time to Peak Serum: 0.5 to 9 hours (variable) (Neels 2004)

Pregnancy Considerations Primidone and its metabolites (PEMA, phenobarbital, and p-hydroxyphenobarbital) cross the placenta; neonatal serum concentrations at birth are similar to those in the mother. Withdrawal symptoms may occur in the neonate and may be delayed due to the long half-life of primidone and its metabolites. Use may be associated with birth defects and adverse events; the use of folic acid throughout pregnancy and vitamin K during the last month of pregnancy is recommended. Epilepsy itself, number of medications, genetic factors, or a combination of these probably influence the teratogenicity of anticonvulsant therapy.

Patients exposed to primidone during pregnancy are encouraged to enroll themselves into the NAAED Pregnancy Registry by calling 1-888-233-2334. Additional information is available at www.aedpregnancyregistry.org.

Probenecid (proe BEN e sid)

Brand Names: Canada Benuryl

Pharmacologic Category Uricosuric Agent

Use Treatment of hyperuricemia associated with gout or gouty arthritis; prolongation and elevation of beta-lactam plasma levels

Local Anesthetic/Vasoconstrictor Precautions

No information available to require special precautions

Effects on Dental Treatment Key adverse event(s) related to dental treatment: Sore gums.

Effects on Bleeding No information available to require special precautions

Adverse Reactions

Frequency not defined.

Cardiovascular: Flushing

Central nervous system: Dizziness, headache, pain (costovertebral)

Dermatologic: Alopecia, dermatitis, pruritus, skin rash

Endocrine & metabolic: Gouty arthritis (acute)

Gastrointestinal: Anorexia, dyspepsia, gastroesophageal reflux disease, gingival pain, nausea, vomiting

Genitourinary: Hematuria, nephrotic syndrome

Hematologic & oncologic: Anemia, aplastic anemia, hemolytic anemia (in G6PD deficiency), leukopenia

Hepatic: Hepatic necrosis

Hypersensitivity: Anaphylaxis, hypersensitivity reaction

Renal: Polyuria, renal colic

Miscellaneous: Fever

General Dosage Range Avoid use if CrCl <30 mL/minute.

Oral:

Children ≥2 years and Adolescents ≤14 years: Prolong penicillin (PCN) serum levels: Initial: 25 mg/kg then 40 mg/kg/day given 4 times/day (maximum: 500 mg/dose)

Adolescents ≥15 years (and >50 kg) and Adults: Prolong PCN levels: 500 mg 4 times/day

Adults: Gout: Initial: 250 mg twice daily (maximum: 2 g/day)

Mechanism of Action Competitively inhibits the reabsorption of uric acid at the proximal convoluted tubule, thereby promoting its excretion and reducing serum uric acid levels; increases plasma levels of weak organic acids (penicillins, cephalosporins, or other beta-lactam antibiotics) by competitively inhibiting their renal tubular secretion

Pharmacodynamics/Kinetics

Onset of Action Effect on penicillin levels: 2 hours; Uric acid renal clearance: 30 minutes

Half-life Elimination Dose dependent: Normal renal function: 6 to 12 hours

Time to Peak Serum: 2 to 4 hours

Pregnancy Considerations Probenecid crosses the placenta. Based on available data, an increased risk of adverse fetal events have not been reported (Gutman, 2012).

Procainamide (pro KANE a mide)

Related Information

Clinical Risk Related to Drugs Prolonging QT Interval *on page 1772*

Brand Names: Canada Apo-Procainamide; Procainamide Hydrochloride Injection, USP; Procan SR

Pharmacologic Category Antiarrhythmic Agent, Class Ia

Use

Intravenous: Treatment of life-threatening ventricular arrhythmias

Oral [Canadian product]: Treatment of supraventricular arrhythmias. **Note:** In the treatment of atrial fibrillation, use only when preferred treatment is ineffective or cannot be used. Use in paroxysmal atrial tachycardia when reflex stimulation or other measures are ineffective.

Local Anesthetic/Vasoconstrictor Precautions

Procainamide is one of the drugs confirmed to prolong the QT interval and is accepted as having a risk of causing torsade de pointes. The risk of drug-induced torsade de pointes is extremely low when a single QT interval prolonging drug is prescribed. In terms of epinephrine, it is not known what effect vasoconstrictors in the local anesthetic regimen will have in patients with a known history of congenital prolonged QT interval or in patients taking any medication that prolongs the QT interval. Until more information is obtained, it is suggested that the clinician consult with the physician prior to the use of a vasoconstrictor in suspected patients, and that the vasoconstrictor (epinephrine, mepivacaine and levonordefrin [Carbocaine® 2% with Neo-Cobefrin®]) be used with caution.

Effects on Dental Treatment Key adverse event(s) related to dental treatment: Taste disorder.

Effects on Bleeding Patients may develop procainamide-induced syndrome, which causes prolonged thrombin and Reptilase® clotting times of plasma. Clinical manifestations of procainamide-induced syndrome subside following procainamide cessation.

Adverse Reactions

>10%:

Hematologic & oncologic: Positive ANA titer (≤50%)

Neuromuscular & skeletal: Lupus-like syndrome (≤30%, increased incidence with long-term therapy or slow acetylators; syndrome may include abdominal pain, arthralgia, arthritis, chills, fever, hepatomegaly, myalgia, pericarditis, pleural effusion, pulmonary infiltrates, skin rash)

1% to 10%:

Cardiovascular: Hypotension (intravenous: ≤5%)

Dermatologic: Skin rash

Gastrointestinal: Diarrhea (oral: 3% to 4%), dysgeusia (oral: 3% to 4%), nausea (oral: 3% to 4%), vomiting (oral: 3% to 4%)

<1%, postmarketing, and/or case reports: Agranulocytosis, angioedema, anorexia, aplastic anemia, arthralgia, asystole, bone marrow depression, cerebellar ataxia, confusion, demyelinating disease (demyelinating polyradiculoneuropathy), depression, depression of myocardial contractility, disorientation, dizziness, drug fever, exacerbation of cardiac arrhythmia, exacerbation of myasthenia gravis, fever, first degree atrioventricular block, flushing, gastrointestinal pseudo-obstruction, granulomatous hepatitis, hallucination, hemolytic anemia, hepatic failure, hyperbilirubinemia, hypoplastic anemia, increased serum alkaline phosphatase, increased serum transaminases, intrahepatic cholestasis, leukopenia, maculopapular rash, mania, myocarditis, myopathy, neuromuscular blockade, neutropenia, pancreatitis, pancytopenia, peripheral neuropathy, pleural effusion, polyneuropathy, positive direct Coombs test, prolonged Q-T interval on ECG, psychosis, pruritus, pulmonary embolism, second degree atrioventricular block, tachycardia, thrombocytopenia, torsades de pointes, urticaria, vasculitis, ventricular fibrillation, ventricular tachycardia (paradoxical; in atrial fibrillation/flutter), weakness

General Dosage Range Dosage adjustment recommended in patients with hepatic or renal impairment

IM:

Children: 20 to 30 mg/kg/day divided every 4 to 6 hours (maximum: 4 g/day)

Adults: 50 mg/kg/day divided every 3 to 6 hours **or** 0.5 to 1 g every 4 to 8 hours

IV:

Children: Loading dose: 3 to 6 mg/kg/dose over 5 minutes (maximum: 100 mg/dose), may repeat every 5 to 10 minutes to maximum of 15 mg/kg/load; Infusion: 20 to 80 mcg/kg/minute (maximum: 2 g/day)

Adults: Loading dose: 15 to 18 mg/kg administered as slow infusion over 25 to 30 minutes **or** 100 mg/dose at a rate not to exceed 50 mg/minute repeated every 5 minutes as needed (maximum total dose: 1 g); Infusion: 1 to 4 mg/minute

Mechanism of Action Decreases myocardial excitability and conduction velocity and may depress myocardial contractility, by increasing the electrical stimulation threshold of ventricle, His-Purkinje system and through direct cardiac effects

Pharmacodynamics/Kinetics

Onset of Action IM 10 to 30 minutes

Half-life Elimination

Procainamide (hepatic acetylator, phenotype, cardiac and renal function dependent): Children: 1.7 hours; Adults: 2.5 to 4.7 hours; Anephric: 11 hours

NAPA (renal function dependent): Children: 6 hours; Adults: 6 to 8 hours; Anephric: 42 hours

Time to Peak Serum: IM: 15 to 60 minutes

Pregnancy Risk Factor C

Pregnancy Considerations Animal reproduction studies have not been conducted. Procainamide crosses the placenta (Dumesic 1982; Oudijk 2002); procainamide and its active metabolite (N-acetyl procainamide) can be detected in the cord blood and neonatal serum (Pittard 1983). Intravenous procainamide may be considered for the acute treatment of SVT in pregnant women. Due to adverse events (lupus-like syndrome), long term therapy should be avoided unless other options are not available (Page [ACC/AHA/HRS 2015]).

Dental Comment See Local Anesthetic/Vasoconstrictor Precautions

Procarbazine (proe KAR ba zeen)

Brand Names: US Matulane

Brand Names: Canada Matulane; Natulan

Pharmacologic Category Antineoplastic Agent, Alkylating Agent

Use Treatment of Hodgkin lymphoma

Local Anesthetic/Vasoconstrictor Precautions No information available to require special precautions

Effects on Dental Treatment Key adverse event(s) related to dental treatment: Xerostomia (normal salivary flow resumes upon discontinuation), stomatitis, and dysphagia.

Effects on Bleeding Chemotherapy may result in significant myelosuppression, potentially including significant reduction in platelet counts and altered hemostasis. In patients who are under active treatment with these agents, medical consult is suggested.

Adverse Reactions Frequency not always defined.

Cardiovascular: Edema, flushing, hypotension, syncope, tachycardia

Central nervous system: Apprehension, ataxia, chills, coma, confusion, depression, dizziness, drowsiness, falling, fatigue, hallucination, headache, hyporeflexia, insomnia, lethargy, nervousness, neuropathy, nightmares, pain, paresthesia, seizure, slurred speech, unsteadiness

Dermatologic: Alopecia, dermatitis, diaphoresis, hyperpigmentation, pruritus, skin rash, urticaria

Endocrine & metabolic: Gynecomastia (in prepubertal and early pubertal males)

Gastrointestinal: Nausea and vomiting (60% to 90%; increasing the dose in a stepwise fashion over several days may minimize), abdominal pain, anorexia, constipation, diarrhea, dysphagia, hematemesis, melena, stomatitis, xerostomia

Genitourinary: Reduced fertility (>10%), azoospermia (reported with combination chemotherapy), hematuria, nocturia

Hematologic & oncologic: Malignant neoplasm (2% to 15%; secondary; nonlymphoid; reported with combination therapy), anemia, bone marrow depression, eosinophilia, hemolysis (in patients with G6PD deficiency), hemolytic anemia, pancytopenia, petechia, purpura, thrombocytopenia

Hepatic: Hepatic insufficiency, jaundice

Hypersensitivity: Hypersensitivity reaction

Infection: Herpes virus infection, increased susceptibility to infection

Neuromuscular & skeletal: Arthralgia, foot-drop, myalgia, tremor, weakness

Ophthalmic: Accommodation disturbance, diplopia, nystagmus, papilledema, photophobia, retinal hemorrhage

Otic: Hearing loss

Renal: Polyuria

Respiratory: Cough, epistaxis, hemoptysis, hoarseness, pleural effusion, pneumonitis, pulmonary toxicity (<1%)

Miscellaneous: Fever

General Dosage Range Dosage adjustment recommended in patients who develop toxicities and those with hepatic impairment.

Oral: *Children and Adults:* Dosage varies greatly depending on indication

Mechanism of Action Inhibits DNA, RNA, and protein synthesis by inhibiting transmethylation of methionine into transfer RNA; may also damage DNA directly through alkylation.

Pharmacodynamics/Kinetics

Half-life Elimination ~1 hour

Time to Peak ≤1 hour

Pregnancy Risk Factor D

Pregnancy Considerations Adverse events were observed in animal reproduction studies. There are case reports of fetal malformations in the offspring of pregnant women exposed to procarbazine as part of a combination chemotherapy regimen. Women of reproductive potential should avoid becoming pregnant during treatment.

Prochlorperazine (proe klor PER a zeen)

Related Information

Dentin Hypersensitivity, Acid Erosion, High Caries Index, Management of Alveolar Osteitis, and Xerostomia *on page 1857*

Management of the Patient With Anxiety or Depression *on page 1873*

Brand Names: US Compazine [DSC]; Compro

Brand Names: Canada Apo-Prochlorperazine; Nu-Prochlor; PMS-Prochlorperazine; Sandoz-Prochlorperazine

Pharmacologic Category Antiemetic; First Generation (Typical) Antipsychotic; Phenothiazine Derivative

Use Nausea/vomiting: Management of severe nausea and vomiting

Local Anesthetic/Vasoconstrictor Precautions May lower seizure threshold; use caution when administering prochlorperazine in combination with other agents that reduce seizure threshold (ie, local anesthetics). Due to prochlorperazine induced alpha-adrenergic blockade, administration of local anesthetics containing vasoconstrictors (epinephrine or levonordefrin), causes unopposed stimulation of beta-adrenergic receptors in heart and peripheral blood vessels that may result in tachycardia, peripheral vasodilation, or hypotension. Effects on blood pressure are greater in combination with epinephrine than levonordefrin.

Effects on Dental Treatment Key adverse event(s) related to dental treatment: Xerostomia and changes in salivation (normal salivary flow resumes upon discontinuation).

Significant hypotension may occur, especially when the drug is administered parenterally or following administration of local anesthetics containing vasoconstrictors (ie, epinephrine or levonordefrin); Patients may experience orthostatic hypotension as they stand up after treatment; especially if lying in dental chair for extended periods of time. Use caution with sudden changes in position during and after dental treatment. Orthostatic hypotension is due to alpha-receptor blockade, the elderly are at greater risk for orthostatic hypotension.

Significant sedation can occur and may be increased in the elderly and in patients taking other CNS depressants (ie, opioid analgesics or benzodiazepines).

Extrapyramidal effects including akathisia (motor restlessness), acute dystonia (spasmodic contractures), pseudoparkinsonism, and tardive dyskinesia can occur with 1 dose. These effects are more likely in the elderly, patients taking other dopamine antagonists (including antipsychotic agents and some antiemetic agents), and patients with Parkinson's disease.

Due to increased risk of adverse effects and drug interactions especially with opioid analgesics, reserve use for patients with moderate-to-severe postoperative nausea and vomiting, who cannot afford ondansetron, and for whom promethazine did not provide adequate control.

Effects on Bleeding No information available to require special precautions

Adverse Reactions Frequency not defined. Reactions listed are based on reports for other agents in this same pharmacologic class and may not be specifically reported for prochlorperazine.

Cardiovascular: ECG abnormality (Q wave and T wave distortions), hypotension, peripheral edema

Central nervous system: Agitation, altered cerebrospinal proteins, catatonia, cerebral edema, coma, decreased cough reflex, disruption of body temperature regulation, dizziness, drowsiness, dystonia (carpopedal spasm, protrusion of tongue, torticollis, trismus), extrapyramidal reaction (akathisia, dystonias, hyperreflexia, pseudoparkinsonism, tardive dyskinesia), headache, hyperpyrexia, insomnia, neuroleptic malignant syndrome (NMS), opisthotonos, restlessness, seizure

Dermatologic: Contact dermatitis, diaphoresis, erythema, eczema, exfoliative dermatitis, pruritus, skin photosensitivity, skin pigmentation, urticaria

Endocrine & metabolic: Amenorrhea, change in libido, galactorrhea, gynecomastia, glycosuria, hyperglycemia, hypoglycemia, menstrual disease, weight gain

Gastrointestinal: Atony of colon, cholestasis, increased appetite, constipation, intestinal obstruction, nausea, obstipation, vomiting, xerostomia

Genitourinary: Ejaculatory disorder, impotence, lactation, priapism, urinary retention

Hematologic & oncologic: Agranulocytosis, aplastic anemia, eosinophilia, hemolytic anemia, immune thrombocytopenia, leukopenia, pancytopenia

Hepatic: Cholestatic jaundice, hepatotoxicity
Hypersensitivity: Angioedema, hypersensitivity reaction
Neuromuscular & skeletal: Lupus-like syndrome, tremor
Ophthalmic: Blurred vision, cataract, epithelial keratopathy, corneal deposits, miosis, mydriasis, oculogyric crisis, retinitis pigmentosa
Respiratory: Asphyxia, asthma, laryngeal edema, nasal congestion
Miscellaneous: Fever (mild; intramuscular administration)

General Dosage Range

IM (as edisylate):

Children ≥2 years and ≥9 kg: 0.13 mg/kg/dose; change to oral as soon as possible

Adults: Nausea/vomiting: 5 to 10 mg every 3 to 4 hours **or** *5 to 10 mg as a single dose with surgery, may repeat (maximum: 40 mg/day)*

IV (as edisylate): *Adults:* 2.5 to 10 mg every 3 to 4 hours as needed (maximum: 40 mg/day) **or** 5 to 10 mg as a single dose with surgery, may repeat once

Oral:

Children ≥2 years and ≥9 kg: Nausea/vomiting:

9 to 13 kg: 2.5 mg 1 to 2 times/day as needed (maximum: 7.5 mg/day)

>13 to 18 kg: 2.5 mg 2 to 3 times/day as needed (maximum: 10 mg/day)

>18 to 39 kg: 2.5 mg 3 times/day or 5 mg 2 times/day as needed (maximum: 15 mg/day)

Adults: 5 to 10 mg 3 to 4 times/day (maximum: 40 mg/day)

Rectal: *Adults:* 25 mg twice daily

Mechanism of Action Prochlorperazine is a piperazine phenothiazine antipsychotic which blocks postsynaptic mesolimbic dopaminergic D_1 and D_2 receptors in the brain, including the chemoreceptor trigger zone; exhibits a strong alpha-adrenergic and anticholinergic blocking effect and depresses the release of hypothalamic and hypophyseal hormones; believed to depress the reticular activating system, thus affecting basal metabolism, body temperature, wakefulness, vasomotor tone and emesis

Pharmacodynamics/Kinetics

Onset of Action Oral: 30 to 40 minutes; IM: 10 to 20 minutes; Rectal: ~60 minutes; Peak antiemetic effect: IV: 30 to 60 minutes

Duration of Action Rectal: 3 to 12 hours; IM, Oral: 3 to 4 hours

Half-life Elimination Oral: 6 to 10 hours (single dose), 14 to 22 hours (repeated dosing) (Isah 1991); IV: 6 to 10 hours (Isah 1991; Taylor 1987)

Pregnancy Considerations Jaundice or hyper- or hyporeflexia have been reported in newborn infants following maternal use of phenothiazines. Antipsychotic use during the third trimester of pregnancy has a risk for abnormal muscle movements (extrapyramidal symptoms [EPS]) and withdrawal symptoms in newborns following delivery. Symptoms in the newborn may include agitation, feeding disorder, hypertonia, hypotonia, respiratory distress, somnolence, and tremor; these effects may be self-limiting or require hospitalization. Use may interfere with pregnancy tests, causing false positive results. Prochlorperazine has been used for the treatment of nausea and vomiting associated with pregnancy (Arsenault 2002).

Procyclidine (proe SYE kli deen)

Brand Names: Canada PDP-Procyclidine

Pharmacologic Category Anti-Parkinson Agent, Anticholinergic; Anticholinergic Agent

Use Note: Not available in the US

Parkinson disease: Treatment of parkinsonism, including postencephalitic, arteriosclerotic, and idiopathic types.

Extrapyramidal side effects: Relieves symptoms (eg, dystonia, dyskinesia, akathisia, and parkinsonism) induced by phenothiazine or rauwolfia compounds during treatment of mental depression.

Local Anesthetic/Vasoconstrictor Precautions No information available to require special precautions

Effects on Dental Treatment Key adverse event(s) related to dental treatment: Xerostomia (normal salivary flow resumes upon discontinuation) and dry throat and nose. Prolonged use of antidyskinetics may decrease or inhibit salivary flow, contributing to discomfort and dental disease (ie, caries, oral candidiasis, and periodontal disease).

Effects on Bleeding No information available to require special precautions

Adverse Reactions Frequency not defined.

Central nervous system: Dizziness
Dermatologic: Skin rash
Gastrointestinal: Constipation, epigastric distress, nausea, vomiting, xerostomia
Hypersensitivity: Hypersensitivity reaction
Neuromuscular & skeletal: Weakness
Ophthalmic: Blurred vision, mydriasis
<1%, postmarketing, and/or case reports: Suppurative parotitis (acute)

General Dosage Range Oral:

Adults: Initial: 2.5 mg 3 times daily; Maintenance: Up to 5 mg 4 times daily

Mechanism of Action Thought to act by blocking excess acetylcholine at cerebral synapses; many of its effects are due to its pharmacologic similarities with atropine; it exerts an antispasmodic effect on smooth muscle, is a potent mydriatic; inhibits salivation

Pharmacodynamics/Kinetics

Onset of Action 45 to 60 minutes (Whiteman 1985)

Duration of Action Significant autonomic effects have been observed up to 12 hours (Whiteman 1985)

Half-life Elimination ~12.6 hours (Whiteman 1985)

Time to Peak ~1.1 hour (Whiteman 1985)

Pregnancy Considerations Safe use during pregnancy or in women considering pregnancy has not been established.

Product Availability Not available in the US

Progesterone (proe JES ter one)

Brand Names: US Crinone; EC-RX Progesterone; Endometrin; First-Progesterone VGS 100; First-Progesterone VGS 200; First-Progesterone VGS 25 [DSC]; First-Progesterone VGS 400 [DSC]; First-Progesterone VGS 50 [DSC]; Prometrium

Brand Names: Canada ACT Progesterone Injection; Crinone; Endometrin; Gesterol in Oil; PMS-Progesterone Injection; Prometrium; TEVA-Progesterone

Pharmacologic Category Progestin

Use

Oral: Prevention of endometrial hyperplasia in nonhysterectomized, postmenopausal women who are receiving conjugated estrogens; treatment of secondary amenorrhea

IM: Treatment of amenorrhea or abnormal uterine bleeding due to hormonal imbalance in the absence of organic pathology, such as submucous fibroids or uterine cancer

Intravaginal gel: Part of assisted reproductive technology (ART) for infertile women with progesterone deficiency; treatment of secondary amenorrhea
Vaginal insert: To support embryo implantation and early pregnancy by supplementation of corpus luteal function as part of ART for infertile women

Local Anesthetic/Vasoconstrictor Precautions No information available to require special precautions

Effects on Dental Treatment Key adverse event(s) related to dental treatment: Progestins may predispose the patient to gingival bleeding.

Effects on Bleeding No information available to require special precautions

Adverse Reactions

Intramuscular injection

Frequency not defined:
Cardiovascular: Cerebral thrombosis, edema, pulmonary embolism, retinal thrombosis
Central nervous system: Cerebral edema, depression, drowsiness, insomnia
Dermatologic: Acne vulgaris, alopecia, hirsutism, pruritus, skin rash, urticaria
Endocrine & metabolic: Amenorrhea, change in menstrual flow, galactorrhea, weight gain, weight loss
Gastrointestinal: Nausea
Genitourinary: Breakthrough bleeding, breast tenderness, cervical erosion, change in cervical secretions, spotting
Hepatic: Cholestatic jaundice
Hypersensitivity: Anaphylactoid reaction
Local: Erythema at injection site, irritation at injection site, pain at injection site
Ophthalmic: Optic neuritis
Miscellaneous: Fever
<1%, postmarketing, and/or case reports: Allergic dermatitis

Oral (percentages reported when used in combination with or cycled with conjugated estrogens):
>10%:
Central nervous system: Headache (16% to 31%), dizziness (15% to 24%), depression (19%)
Endocrine & metabolic: Breast tenderness (27%), mastalgia (6% to 16%)
Gastrointestinal: Abdominal pain (10% to 20%), bloating (8% to 12%)
Genitourinary: Urination disorder (11%)
Infection: Viral infection (12%)
Neuromuscular & skeletal: Arthralgia (20%), musculoskeletal pain (12%)
1% to 10%:
Cardiovascular: Chest pain (7%)
Central nervous system: Anxiety (8%), fatigue (8%), irritability (8%)
Gastrointestinal: Nausea (≤8%), vomiting (≤8%), diarrhea (7% to 8%), cholecystectomy (<5%), constipation (<5%)
Genitourinary: Vaginal discharge (10%)
Hematologic & oncologic: Malignant neoplasm of breast (<5%)
Respiratory: Cough (8%)
<1%, postmarketing and/or case reports: Abnormal gait, acute pancreatitis, aggressive behavior, alopecia, anaphylaxis, arthralgia, asthma, blurred vision, choking sensation, cholestasis, cholestatic hepatitis, circulatory shock, confusion, depersonalization, diplopia, disorientation, dysarthria, dysphagia, dyspnea, endometrial carcinoma, facial edema, feeling abnormal, increased liver enzymes, hepatic failure, hepatic necrosis, hepatitis, hyperglycemia, hypermenorrhea, hypersensitivity reaction, hypertension, hypotension, impaired consciousness, intoxicated feeling, jaundice, loss of consciousness, menstrual disease, muscle cramps, ovarian cyst, paresthesia, pharyngeal edema, pruritus, sedation, seizure, slurred speech, stupor, suicidal ideation, syncope, tachycardia, tinnitus, tongue edema, transient ischemic attacks, urticaria, uterine hemorrhage, vertigo, visual disturbance, weight gain, weight loss

Vaginal gel (percentages reported with ART):
>10%:
Central nervous system: Drowsiness (27%), headache (13% to 17%), nervousness (16%), depression (11%)
Endocrine & metabolic: Decreased libido (11%)
Gastrointestinal: Constipation (27%), nausea (7% to 22%), abdominal cramps (15%), abdominal pain (12%)
Genitourinary: Breast hypertrophy (40%), perineal pain (17%), mastalgia (13%), nocturia (13%)
1% to 10%:
Central nervous system: Pain (8%), dizziness (5%)
Dermatologic: Genital pruritus (5%)
Gastrointestinal: Diarrhea (8%), bloating (7%), vomiting (5%)
Genitourinary: Vaginal discharge (7%), dyspareunia (6%), genital candidiasis (5%)
Neuromuscular & skeletal: Arthralgia (8%)

Vaginal insert (percentages reported with ART):
>10%:
Central nervous system: Pain (post-oocyte retrieval pain: 25% to 28%)
Gastrointestinal: Abdominal pain (12%)
1% to 10%:
Central nervous system: Headache (3% to 4%), fatigue (2% to 3%)
Endocrine & metabolic: Ovarian hyperstimulation syndrome (7%)
Gastrointestinal: Nausea (7% to 8%), abdominal distention (4%), constipation (2% to 3%), vomiting (2% to 3%)
Genitourinary: Uterine spasm (3% to 4%), vaginal hemorrhage (3%), urinary tract infection (1% to 2%)
<1%, postmarketing, and/or case reports: Genital pruritus, local discomfort, peripheral edema, urticaria, vulvovaginal burning, vulvovaginal irritation

General Dosage Range

IM: *Adults (females):* 5 to 10 mg/day for 6 to 8 doses

Intravaginal: *Adults (females):*
ART: 90 mg (8% gel) once or twice daily or 100 mg (vaginal insert) 2 to 3 times daily
Secondary amenorrhea: 45 mg (4% gel) every other day, may increase to 90 mg (8% gel) every other day if needed (maximum: 6 doses)

Oral: *Adults (females):*
Amenorrhea: 400 mg once daily at bedtime for 10 days
Endometrial hyperplasia, prevention: 200 mg once daily at bedtime for 12 days sequentially per 28-day cycle

Mechanism of Action Natural steroid hormone that induces secretory changes in the endometrium, promotes mammary gland development, relaxes uterine smooth muscle, blocks follicular maturation and ovulation, and maintains pregnancy. When used as part of an ART program in the luteal phase, progesterone supports embryo implantation.

Pharmacodynamics/Kinetics

Half-life Elimination Vaginal gel: 5 to 20 minutes

Time to Peak Oral: Within 3 hours; IM: ~8 hours; Intravaginal gel: 3.55 ± 2.48 to 7 ± 2.88 hours; Vaginal insert: 17.3 to 24 hours

Pregnancy Risk Factor B (oral)

Pregnancy Considerations

The oral capsules are contraindicated for use during pregnancy.

Adverse events have not been observed following oral administration in animal reproduction studies. Adverse events following maternal use in pregnancy (eg, hypospadias, congenital heart disease, cleft lip/palate) have been noted in postmarketing data; however, a causal relationship has not been clearly established. Use of vaginal progesterone may be considered to decrease the risk of recurrent spontaneous preterm birth in women with a singleton pregnancy and prior spontaneous preterm singleton birth (therapy may begin at 16 to 24 weeks, regardless of cervical length). It may also be used to prevent spontaneous preterm birth in women with a singleton pregnancy who have a cervix <20 mm before or at 24 weeks' gestation. Use is not recommended as an intervention for women with multiple gestations (ACOG 2012). The vaginal gel and insert are indicated for use in ART.

Promethazine (proe METH a zeen)

Brand Names: US Phenadoz; Phenergan; Promethegan

Brand Names: Canada Bioniche Promethazine; Histantil; Phenergan; PMS-Promethazine

Pharmacologic Category Antiemetic; Histamine H_1 Antagonist; Histamine H_1 Antagonist, First Generation; Phenothiazine Derivative

Use

Allergic conditions, treatment: Perennial and seasonal allergic rhinitis; vasomotor rhinitis; allergic conjunctivitis due to inhalant allergens and foods; mild, uncomplicated allergic skin manifestations of urticaria and angioedema; amelioration of allergic reactions to blood or plasma; dermographism; anaphylactic reactions, as adjunctive therapy to epinephrine and other standard measures, after the acute manifestations have been controlled

Nausea and vomiting: Prevention and control of nausea and vomiting associated with certain types of anesthesia and surgery; antiemetic therapy in postoperative patients

Motion sickness: Active and prophylactic treatment of motion sickness

Surgical analgesia/hypnotic; pre-/postoperative adjunct: Adjunctive therapy with analgesics and/or anesthesia

Sedation: Preoperative, postoperative, and obstetric sedation; for sedation, relief of apprehension, and production of light sleep from which the patient can be easily aroused

Local Anesthetic/Vasoconstrictor Precautions

Due to promethazine-induced alpha-adrenergic blockade, administration of local anesthetics containing the vasoconstrictors epinephrine or levonordefrin, causes unopposed stimulation of beta-adrenergic receptors in heart and peripheral blood vessels that may result in tachycardia and peripheral vasodilation causing hypotension. Effects on blood pressure are greater in combination with epinephrine than levonordefrin.

Effects on Dental Treatment Key adverse event(s) related to dental treatment: Xerostomia (normal salivary flow resumes upon discontinuation).

Significant hypotension may occur, especially when the drug is administered parenterally or following administration of local anesthetics containing vasoconstrictors (ie, epinephrine or levonordefrin); Patients may experience orthostatic hypotension as they stand up after treatment; especially if lying in dental chair for extended periods of time. Use caution with sudden changes in position during and after dental treatment. Orthostatic hypotension is due to alpha-receptor blockade, the elderly are at greater risk for orthostatic hypotension.

Significant sedation can occur and may be increased in the elderly and in patients taking or administered other CNS depressants (ie, opioid analgesics or benzodiazepines).

Extrapyramidal effects including akathisia (motor restlessness), acute dystonia (spasmodic contractures), pseudoparkinsonism, and tardive dyskinesia can occur with a single dose. These effects are more likely in the elderly, patients taking other dopamine antagonists (including antipsychotic agents and some antiemetic agents), and patients with Parkinson's disease.

Promethazine is a less expensive alternative for moderate-to-severe postoperative nausea than ondansetron but with a greater chance of adverse effects and drug interactions especially with opioid analgesics.

Effects on Bleeding No information available to require special precautions

Adverse Reactions

Frequency not defined.

Cardiovascular: Bradycardia, ECG changes (nonspecific QT changes) hypertension, hypotension, local thrombophlebitis, localized phlebitis, orthostatic hypotension, tachycardia, vasospasm (distal to injection site), venous thrombosis (local)

Central nervous system: Agitation, akathisia, ataxia, catatonia, confusion, delirium, disorientation, dizziness, drowsiness, dystonia, euphoria, excitement, extrapyramidal reaction, fatigue, hallucination, hysteria, insomnia, lassitude, paralysis (local), Parkinsonian-like syndrome, tardive dyskinesia, nervousness, neuroleptic malignant syndrome, nightmares, sedation, seizure, sensory disturbance (local sensory loss)

Dermatologic: Dermatitis, gangrene of skin or other tissue (local), skin photosensitivity, skin pigmentation (slate gray), urticaria

Endocrine & metabolic: Amenorrhea, gynecomastia, hyperglycemia

Gastrointestinal: Constipation, nausea, vomiting, xerostomia

Genitourinary: Breast engorgement, ejaculatory disorder, impotence, lactation, urinary retention

Hematologic & oncologic: Agranulocytosis, immune thrombocytopenia, leukopenia, thrombocytopenia

Hepatic: Jaundice

Hypersensitivity: Angioedema

Local: Abscess at injection site, injection site reaction (burning sensation at injection site, edema at injection site, erythema at injection site, pain at injection site), local tissue necrosis

Neuromuscular & skeletal: Tremor

Ophthalmic: Blurred vision, corneal changes, diplopia, epithelial keratopathy, lens disease (changes), retinitis pigmentosa

Otic: Tinnitus

Respiratory: Apnea, asthma, nasal congestion, respiratory depression

General Dosage Range

IM, IV:

Children ≥2 years and Adolescents:

Nausea and vomiting: 0.25 to 1 mg/kg/dose every 4 to 6 hours as needed (maximum dose: 25 mg)

Surgical analgesia/hypnotic; pre-/postoperative adjunct: 0.25 to 1.1 mg/kg once in combination with an analgesic or hypnotic

Adults: 12.5 to 75 mg/dose as a single dose **or** 12.5 to 50 mg every 4 to 6 hours as needed

Oral, rectal:

Children ≥2 years and Adolescents:

Allergic conditions, treatment: 0.125 mg/kg/dose every 6 hours (maximum dose: 12.5 mg) during the day as needed and 0.5 mg/kg/dose (maximum dose: 25 mg) at bedtime as needed

Motion sickness: 0.5 mg/kg/dose 30 minutes to 1 hour before departure, then every 12 hours as needed (maximum dose: 25 mg)

Nausea and vomiting: 0.25 to 1 mg/kg/dose every 4 to 6 hours as needed (maximum dose: 25 mg).

Adults: 6.25 to 25 mg every 4 to 8 hours as needed **or** 12.5 to 50 mg as a single dose **or** 25 mg 30 to 60 minutes before departure, 8 to 12 hours later, then 25 mg twice daily as needed

Mechanism of Action Phenothiazine derivative; blocks postsynaptic mesolimbic dopaminergic receptors in the brain; exhibits a strong alpha-adrenergic blocking effect and depresses the release of hypothalamic and hypophyseal hormones; competes with histamine for the H_1-receptor; muscarinic-blocking effect may be responsible for antiemetic activity; reduces stimuli to the brainstem reticular system

Pharmacodynamics/Kinetics

Onset of Action Oral, IM: ~20 minutes; IV: ~5 minutes

Duration of Action Usually 4 to 6 hours (up to 12 hours)

Half-life Elimination IM: ~10 hours; IV: 9 to 16 hours; Suppositories, syrup: 16 to 19 hours (range: 4 to 34 hours) (Strenkoski-Nox, 2000)

Time to Peak Maximum serum concentration (Brunton 2011): Oral (syrup): 2.8 ± 1.4 hours; Rectal: 8.2 ± 3.4 hours

Pregnancy Risk Factor C

Pregnancy Considerations Adverse effects have not been observed in animal reproduction studies. Promethazine crosses the placenta (Potts 1961). Platelet aggregation may be inhibited in newborns following maternal use of promethazine within 2 weeks of delivery. Promethazine is approved for use as an antiemetic; however, other agents are recommended as initial therapy for the treatment of nausea and vomiting of pregnancy (ACOG 2015). Promethazine is indicated for use during labor for obstetric sedation and may be used alone or as an adjunct to opioid analgesics. Although promethazine is approved for the treatment of allergic conditions (eg, allergic rhinitis, urticaria), other agents are preferred for use in pregnant women (Scadding 2008; Wallace 2008; Zuberbier 2014).

Dental Comment Sedation: When used alone as a sedative agent the degree of sedation is often mild. As a sedative agent, promethazine is effective in managing pediatric patients that require mild anxiety control. It is ineffective when used alone in children with extreme apprehension or for the disruptive, unmanageable child. A more profound sedation will occur if promethazine is administered in combination with an opioid or benzodiazepine. If promethazine is combined with an opioid, the dose of the opioid should be decreased by 25% to 50%.

Promethazine and Codeine

(proe METH a zeen & KOE deen)

Related Information

Codeine *on page 410*

Promethazine *on page 1392*

Pharmacologic Category Analgesic, Opioid; Antitussive; Histamine H_1 Antagonist; Histamine H_1 Antagonist, First Generation; Phenothiazine Derivative

Use Cough and upper respiratory symptoms: Temporary relief of coughs and upper respiratory symptoms associated with allergy or the common cold.

Local Anesthetic/Vasoconstrictor Precautions No information available to require special precautions

Effects on Dental Treatment Although promethazine is a phenothiazine derivative, extrapyramidal reactions or tardive dyskinesias are not seen with the use of this drug.

Effects on Bleeding No information available to require special precautions

Adverse Reactions Also see individual agents.

Postmarketing and/or case reports: Hypogonadism (Brennan 2013; Debono 2011)

General Dosage Range Oral:

Children 6 to <12 years: 2.5 to 5 mL (promethazine 3.125 to 6.25 mg/codeine 5 to 10 mg) every 4 to 6 hours (maximum: 30 mL [promethazine 37.5 mg/ codeine 60 mg] per 24 hours)

Children ≥12 years, Adolescents, and Adults: 5 mL (promethazine 6.25 mg/codeine 10 mg) every 4 to 6 hours (maximum: 30 mL [promethazine 37.5 mg/ codeine 60 mg] per 24 hours)

Mechanism of Action

Codeine: Binds to opioid receptors in the CNS, causing inhibition of ascending pain pathways, altering the perception of and response to pain; causes cough suppression by direct central action in the medulla; produces generalized CNS depression.

Promethazine: Phenothiazine derivative; blocks postsynaptic mesolimbic dopaminergic receptors in the brain; exhibits a strong alpha-adrenergic blocking effect and depresses the release of hypothalamic and hypophyseal hormones, competes with histamine for the H1-receptor; muscarinic-blocking effect may be responsible for antiemetic activity; reduces stimuli to the brainstem reticular system.

Pregnancy Risk Factor C

Pregnancy Considerations Animal reproduction studies have not been conducted with this combination. See individual agents.

Controlled Substance C-V

Propafenone (pro PAF en one)

Related Information

Cardiovascular Diseases *on page 1752*

Clinical Risk Related to Drugs Prolonging QT Interval *on page 1772*

Dentin Hypersensitivity, Acid Erosion, High Caries Index, Management of Alveolar Osteitis, and Xerostomia *on page 1857*

Brand Names: US Rythmol SR; Rythmol [DSC]

Brand Names: Canada Apo-Propafenone; Mylan-Propafenone; PMS-Propafenone; Rythmol

Pharmacologic Category Antiarrhythmic Agent, Class Ic

Use

Treatment of life-threatening ventricular arrhythmias; to prolong the time to recurrence of paroxysmal atrial fibrillation/flutter (PAF) or paroxysmal supraventricular tachycardia (PSVT) in patients with disabling symptoms without structural heart disease

Guideline recommendations: Due to safety risks, propafenone should be reserved for use in patients with symptomatic supraventricular tachycardias (SVTs) (atrioventricular nodal reentrant tachycardia [AVNRT], atrioventricular reentrant tachycardia [AVRT], focal atrial tachycardia [AT]) in patients without structural or ischemic heart disease who are not candidates for, or prefer not to undergo catheter ablation and in whom other therapies have failed or are contraindicated (ACC/AHA/HRS [Page 2015]).

Extended release capsule: Prolong the time to recurrence of symptomatic atrial fibrillation in patients without structural heart disease

Local Anesthetic/Vasoconstrictor Precautions In some patients, propafenone has been reported to induce new or worsened arrhythmias (proarrhythmic effect). It is suggested that vasoconstrictors be used with caution since epinephrine has the potential to stimulate the heart rate when given in the anesthetic regimen. The manufacturer notes that propafenone may increase the QT interval; however, due to QRS prolongation; changes in the QT interval are difficult to interpret. Cases of torsade de pointes have been reported. The risk of drug-induced torsade de pointes is extremely low when a single QT interval prolonging drug is prescribed. In terms of epinephrine, it is not known what effect vasoconstrictors in the local anesthetic regimen will have in patients with a known history of congenital prolonged QT interval or in patients taking any medication that prolongs the QT interval. Until more information is obtained, it is suggested that the clinician consult with the physician prior to the use of a vasoconstrictor in suspected patients, and that the vasoconstrictor (epinephrine, mepivacaine and levonordefrin [Carbocaine® 2% with Neo-Cobefrin®]) be used with caution.

Effects on Dental Treatment Key adverse event(s) related to dental treatment: Unusual taste and significant xerostomia (normal salivary flow resumes upon discontinuation).

Effects on Bleeding No information available to require special precautions

Adverse Reactions

>10%:

Central nervous system: Unusual taste (3% to 23%), dizziness (4% to 15%)

Gastrointestinal: Nausea (≤11%), vomiting (≤11%)

1% to 10%:

Cardiovascular: Cardiac arrhythmia (2% to 10%; new or worsened; proarrhythmic effect), angina pectoris (2% to 5%), cardiac failure (1% to 4%), first degree atrioventricular block (1% to 3%), palpitations (1% to 3%), ventricular tachycardia (1% to 3%), bradycardia (1% to 2%), chest pain (1% to 2%), widened QRS complex on ECG (1% to 2%), syncope (1% to 2%), ventricular premature contractions (1% to 2%), atrial fibrillation (1%), bundle branch block (≤1%), edema (≤1%), cardiac conduction delay (≤1%; intraventricular), hypotension (≤1%)

Central nervous system: Fatigue (2% to 6%), headache (2% to 5%), ataxia (≤2%), insomnia (≤2%), anxiety (1% to 2%), drowsiness (1%)

Dermatologic: Skin rash (1% to 3%), diaphoresis (1%)

Gastrointestinal: Constipation (2% to 7%), diarrhea (1% to 3%), dyspepsia (1% to 3%), abdominal pain (1% to 2%), anorexia (1% to 2%), xerostomia (1% to 2%), flatulence (≤1%)

Neuromuscular & skeletal: Weakness (1% to 2%), arthralgia (≤1%), tremor (≤1%)

Ophthalmic: Blurred vision (1% to 6%)

Respiratory: Dyspnea (2% to 5%)

<1%, postmarketing, and/or case reports: Abnormal dreams, agranulocytosis, alopecia, altered sense of smell, amnesia, anemia, apnea, asystole, atrioventricular block (second or third degree), atrioventricular dissociation, cardiac failure, cholestasis, coma, confusion, depression, eye irritation, flushing, gastroenteritis, granulocytopenia, hepatitis, hyperglycemia, hyponatremia, impotence, increased serum transaminases, leukopenia, lupus erythematosus, mania, muscle cramps, myasthenia, nephrotic syndrome, numbness, pain, paresthesia, peripheral neuropathy, positive ANA titer, prolongation P-R interval on ECG, prolonged bleeding time, pruritus, psychosis, purpura, renal failure, seizure, SIADH (syndrome of inappropriate antidiuretic hormone secretion), sinoatrial arrest, sinus node dysfunction, speech disturbance, thrombocytopenia, tinnitus, torsades de pointes, ventricular fibrillation, vertigo, visual disturbance

General Dosage Range

Oral:

Extended release: *Adults:* Initial: 225 mg every 12 hours; Maintenance: 225 to 425 mg every 12 hours

Immediate release: *Adults:* Initial: 150 mg every 8 hours; Maintenance: 150 to 300 mg every 8 hours

Mechanism of Action Propafenone is a class 1c antiarrhythmic agent which possesses local anesthetic properties, blocks the fast inward sodium current, and slows the rate of increase of the action potential. Prolongs conduction and refractoriness in all areas of the myocardium, with a slightly more pronounced effect on intraventricular conduction; it prolongs effective refractory period, reduces spontaneous automaticity and exhibits some beta-blockade activity.

Pharmacodynamics/Kinetics

Half-life Elimination Extensive metabolizers: 2-10 hours; Poor metabolizers: 10-32 hours

Time to Peak Serum: IR: 3.5 hours; ER: 3-8 hours

Pregnancy Risk Factor C

Pregnancy Considerations Adverse events were observed in some animal reproduction studies. Propafenone and its metabolite cross the placenta and can be detected in the newborn (Libardoni 1991). Guidelines are available for use during pregnancy (ESG [Regitz-Zagrosek 2011]). Propafenone may be used for the ongoing management of pregnant women with highly symptomatic SVT. The lowest effective dose is recommended; avoid use during the first trimester if possible (Page [ACC/AHA/HRS 2015]).Until more information is available, when treatment of AF or long term treatment of SVT is needed in pregnant women, propafenone is generally reserved for use when other agents are not effective (ESG [Regitz-Zagrosek 2011]).

Dental Comment See Local Anesthetic/Vasoconstrictor Precautions

Propantheline (proe PAN the leen)

Generic Availability (US) Yes

Pharmacologic Category Anticholinergic Agent

Dental Use Induce dry field (xerostomia) in oral cavity

Use Peptic ulcer: Adjunctive therapy in the treatment of peptic ulcer

Local Anesthetic/Vasoconstrictor Precautions No information available to require special precautions

Effects on Dental Treatment Key adverse event(s) related to dental treatment: Significant xerostomia (therapeutic effect; normal salivary flow resumes upon discontinuation), dry throat, nasal dryness, and dysphagia.

Effects on Bleeding No information available to require special precautions

Adverse Reactions

Frequency not defined.

Cardiovascular: Palpitations, tachycardia

Central nervous system: Confusion, dizziness, drowsiness, headache, insomnia, nervousness

Dermatologic: Hypohidrosis

Gastrointestinal: Ageusia, bloating, constipation, nausea, vomiting, xerostomia

Genitourinary: Decreased lactation, impotence, urinary hesitancy, urinary retention

Hypersensitivity: Anaphylaxis, hypersensitivity reaction

Neuromuscular & skeletal: Weakness

Ophthalmic: Blurred vision, cycloplegia, increased intraocular pressure, mydriasis

Dental Usual Dosage Antisecretory (off-label use); Treatment of Salivary Hypersecretion/Sialorrhea: Oral:

Children: 1-2 mg/kg/day in 3-4 divided doses

Adults: 15 mg 3 times/day before meals or food and 30 mg at bedtime

Elderly: 7.5 mg 3 times/day before meals and at bedtime

Dosing

Adult Peptic ulcer: Oral: 15 mg 3 times daily before meals or food and 30 mg at bedtime; adjust dosage according to patient response and tolerance.

Geriatric Refer to adult dosing; use with caution.

Renal Impairment There are no dosage adjustments provided in the manufacturer's labeling; use with caution

Hepatic Impairment There are no dosage adjustments provided in the manufacturer's labeling; use with caution

Mechanism of Action Competitively blocks the action of acetylcholine at postganglionic parasympathetic receptor sites and inhibits gastrointestinal motility

Contraindications Glaucoma; obstructive disease of the gastrointestinal tract (eg, pyloroduodenal stenosis, achalasia, paralytic ileus); obstructive uropathy (eg, bladder-neck obstruction due to prostatic hypertrophy); intestinal atony of elderly or debilitated patients; severe ulcerative colitis or toxic megacolon complicating ulcerative colitis; unstable cardiovascular adjustment in acute hemorrhage; myasthenia gravis.

Warnings/Precautions May cause drowsiness and/or blurred vision, which may impair physical or mental abilities; patients must be cautioned about performing tasks which require mental alertness (eg, operating machinery or driving). Use with caution in patients with hyperthyroidism, hiatal hernia with reflux esophagitis, autonomic neuropathy, hepatic, or renal disease. Use with caution in patients with coronary artery disease, tachyarrhythmias, heart failure, or hypertension. Heat prostration may occur in the presence of increased environmental temperature; use caution in hot weather and/or exercise. Use with caution in patients with ulcerative colitis; large doses may suppress intestinal motility. Diarrhea may be a sign of incomplete intestinal obstruction, discontinue treatment if this occurs. Use with caution in elderly patients. Potentially significant interactions may exist, requiring dose or frequency adjustment, additional monitoring, and/or selection of alternative therapy.

Polysorbate 80: Some dosage forms may contain polysorbate 80 (also known as Tweens). Hypersensitivity reactions, usually a delayed reaction, have been reported following exposure to pharmaceutical products containing polysorbate 80 in certain individuals (Isaksson 2002; Lucente 2000; Shelley 1995). Thrombocytopenia, ascites, pulmonary deterioration, and renal and hepatic failure have been reported in premature neonates after receiving parenteral products containing polysorbate 80 (Alade 1986; CDC 1984). See manufacturer's labeling.

Propylene glycol: Some dosage forms may contain propylene glycol; large amounts are potentially toxic and have been associated with hyperosmolality, lactic acidosis, seizures and respiratory depression; use caution (AAP 1997; Zar 2007). See manufacturer's labeling.

Drug Interactions

Metabolism/Transport Effects None known.

Avoid Concomitant Use

Avoid concomitant use of Propantheline with any of the following: Aclidinium; Cimetropium; Eluxadoline; Glucagon; Glycopyrrolate (Oral Inhalation); Ipratropium (Oral Inhalation); Levosulpiride; Nitroglycerin; Oxatomide; Potassium Chloride; Tiotropium; Umeclidinium

Increased Effect/Toxicity

Propantheline may increase the levels/effects of: AbobotulinumtoxinA; Analgesics (Opioid); Anticholinergic Agents; Cannabinoid-Containing Products; Cimetropium; Eluxadoline; Glucagon; Glycopyrrolate (Oral Inhalation); Mirabegron; OnabotulinumtoxinA; Potassium Chloride; Ramosetron; RimabotulinumtoxinB; Thiazide and Thiazide-Like Diuretics; Tiotropium; Topiramate

The levels/effects of Propantheline may be increased by: Aclidinium; Chloral Betaine; Ipratropium (Oral Inhalation); Mianserin; Oxatomide; Pramlintide; Umeclidinium

Decreased Effect

Propantheline may decrease the levels/effects of: Acetylcholinesterase Inhibitors; Gastrointestinal Agents (Prokinetic); Itopride; Levosulpiride; Nitroglycerin; Secretin

The levels/effects of Propantheline may be decreased by: Acetylcholinesterase Inhibitors

Dietary Considerations Some products may contain lactose.

Pharmacodynamics/Kinetics

Duration of Action 6 hours

Half-life Elimination Serum: ~1.6 hours

Time to Peak

Plasma: ~1 hour

Pregnancy Risk Factor C

Pregnancy Considerations Animal reproduction studies have not been conducted.

Breastfeeding Considerations It is not known if propantheline is excreted in breast milk. Suppression of lactation may occur with anticholinergics. The manufacturer recommends that caution be exercised when administering propantheline to nursing women.

Dosage Forms

Tablet, Oral:

Generic: 15 mg

Proparacaine (proe PAR a kane)

Brand Names: US Alcaine [DSC]; Parcaine [DSC]
Brand Names: Canada Alcaine®; Diocaine®
Pharmacologic Category Local Anesthetic, Ophthalmic
Use Topical anesthesia for tonometry, gonioscopy; suture removal from cornea; removal of corneal foreign body; short operative procedure involving the cornea and conjunctiva
Local Anesthetic/Vasoconstrictor Precautions No information available to require special precautions
Effects on Dental Treatment No significant effects or complications reported
Effects on Bleeding No information available to require special precautions
Adverse Reactions Frequency not defined.
Dermatologic: Allergic contact dermatitis
Hypersensitivity: Hypersensitivity reaction (corneal; characterized by acute, intense, and diffuse epithelial keratitis; gray, ground glass appearance; exfoliation of skin; corneal filaments; and can include iritis with descemetitis)
Ophthalmic: Burning sensation of eyes, conjunctival hemorrhage, conjunctival hyperemia, corneal erosion, cycloplegia, eye redness, mydriasis, stinging of eyes
General Dosage Range Ophthalmic: *Children, Adolescents, and Adults:* Instill 1-2 drops in eye(s) once **or** instill 1 drop in eye(s) every 5-10 minutes for 5-7 doses
Mechanism of Action Prevents initiation and transmission of impulse at the nerve cell membrane by decreasing ion permeability through stabilizing
Pharmacodynamics/Kinetics
Onset of Action Within 20 seconds of instillation
Duration of Action ~10-20 minutes
Pregnancy Risk Factor C
Pregnancy Considerations Animal reproduction studies have not been conducted.

Propofol (PROE po fole)

Brand Names: US Diprivan; Fresenius Propoven
Brand Names: Canada Diprivan; PMS-Propofol; Propofol Injection; Propofol-II Injection
Pharmacologic Category General Anesthetic
Use Induction of anesthesia in patients ≥3 years of age; maintenance of anesthesia in patients >2 months of age; in adults, for monitored anesthesia care sedation during procedures; in adults, for sedation in intubated, mechanically-ventilated ICU patients

Note: Consult local regulations and individual institutional policies and procedures.
Local Anesthetic/Vasoconstrictor Precautions No information available to require special precautions
Effects on Dental Treatment No significant effects or complications reported
Effects on Bleeding No information available to require special precautions
Adverse Reactions
>10%:
Cardiovascular: Hypotension (adults: 3% to 26%; children: 17%)
Central nervous system: Involuntary body movements (children: 17%; adults: 3% to 10%)
Local: Burning sensation at injection site (adults: ≤18%; children: ≤10%), pain at injection site (includes stinging; adults: ≤18%; children: ≤10%)
Respiratory: Apnea (30 to 60 seconds duration: adults: 24%, children: 10%; >60 seconds duration: adults: 12%, children: 5%)
1% to 10%:
Cardiovascular: Hypertension (children: 8%), bradycardia (1% to 3%), cardiac arrhythmia (1% to 3%), low cardiac output (1% to 3%; concurrent opioid use increases incidence), tachycardia (1% to 3%)
Dermatologic: Skin rash (children: 5%; adults: 1% to 3%), pruritus (1% to 3%)
Endocrine & metabolic: Hypertriglyceridemia (3% to 10%), respiratory acidosis (during weaning; 3% to 10%)
<1%, postmarketing, and/or case reports: Agitation, amblyopia, anaphylaxis, anaphylactoid reaction, anticholinergic syndrome, asystole, atrial arrhythmia, atrial premature contractions, bigeminy, chills, cloudy urine, cough, decreased lung function, delirium, dizziness, drowsiness, fever, flushing, hair discoloration (green), hemorrhage, hypertonia, hypomagnesemia, hypoxia, infusion-related reaction (propofol-related infusion syndrome), infusion site reaction (including pain, swelling, blisters and/or tissue necrosis following accidental extravasation), laryngospasm, leukocytosis, limb pain, loss of consciousness (postoperative; with or without increased muscle tone), myalgia, myoclonus (rarely including seizure and opisthotonos), nail discoloration (nailbeds green), nausea, pancreatitis, paresthesia, phlebitis, pulmonary edema, rhabdomyolysis, sialorrhea, syncope, thrombosis, urine discoloration (green), ventricular premature contractions, visual disturbance, wheezing
General Dosage Range IV: *Children and Adults:* Dosage varies greatly depending on indication
Mechanism of Action Propofol is a short-acting, lipophilic intravenous general anesthetic. The drug is unrelated to any of the currently used barbiturate, opioid, benzodiazepine, arylcyclohexylamine, or imidazole intravenous anesthetic agents. Propofol causes global CNS depression, presumably through agonism of $GABA_A$ receptors and perhaps reduced glutamatergic activity through NMDA receptor blockade.
Pharmacodynamics/Kinetics
Onset of Action Anesthetic: Bolus infusion (dose dependent): 9 to 51 seconds (average: 30 seconds)
Duration of Action 3 to 10 minutes depending on the dose, rate and duration of administration; with prolonged use (eg, 10 days ICU sedation), propofol accumulates in tissues and redistributes into plasma when the drug is discontinued, so that the time to awakening (duration of action) is increased; however, if dose is titrated on a daily basis, so that the minimum effective dose is utilized, time to awakening may be within 10 to 15 minutes even after prolonged use
Half-life Elimination Biphasic: Initial: 40 minutes; Terminal: 4 to 7 hours (after 10-day infusion, may be up to 1 to 3 days)
Pregnancy Risk Factor B
Pregnancy Considerations Propofol crosses the placenta and may be associated with neonatal CNS and respiratory depression. Propofol is not recommended by the manufacturer for obstetrics, including cesarean section deliveries.

Propranolol (proe PRAN oh lole)

Related Information

Cardiovascular Diseases *on page 1752*

Endocrine Disorders and Pregnancy *on page 1781*

Brand Names: US Hemangeol; Inderal LA; Inderal XL; InnoPran XL

Brand Names: Canada Apo-Propranolol; Dom-Propranolol; Inderal LA; PMS-Propranolol; Propranolol Hydrochloride Injection, USP; Teva-Propranolol

Generic Availability (US) Yes

Pharmacologic Category Antianginal Agent; Antiarrhythmic Agent, Class II; Antihypertensive; Beta-Adrenergic Blocker, Nonselective

Use Management of hypertension; angina pectoris; pheochromocytoma; essential tremor; supraventricular arrhythmias (such as atrial fibrillation and flutter, AV nodal re-entrant tachycardias), ventricular tachycardias (catecholamine-induced arrhythmias, digoxin toxicity); prevention of myocardial infarction; migraine headache prophylaxis; symptomatic treatment of obstructive hypertrophic cardiomyopathy (formerly known as hypertrophic subaortic stenosis); treatment of proliferating infantile hemangioma requiring systemic therapy (Hemangeol only)

Guideline recommendations:

Hypertension: The 2014 guideline for the management of high blood pressure in adults (JNC 8) recommends initiation of pharmacologic treatment to lower blood pressure for the following patients (JNC8 [James 2013]):

- Patients ≥60 years of age, with systolic blood pressure (SBP) ≥150 mm Hg or diastolic blood pressure (DBP) ≥90 mm Hg. Goal of therapy is SBP <150 mm Hg and DBP <90 mm Hg.
- Patients <60 years of age, with SBP ≥140 mm Hg or DBP ≥90 mm Hg. Goal of therapy is SBP <140 mm Hg and DBP <90 mm Hg.
- Patients ≥18 years of age with diabetes, with SBP ≥140 mm Hg or DBP ≥90 mm Hg. Goal of therapy is SBP <140 mm Hg and DBP <90 mm Hg.
- Patients ≥18 years of age with chronic kidney disease (CKD), with SBP ≥140 mm Hg or DBP ≥90 mm Hg. Goal of therapy is SBP <140 mm Hg and DBP <90 mm Hg.

Chronic kidney disease (CKD) and hypertension: Regardless of race or diabetes status, the use of an ACE inhibitor (ACEI) or angiotensin receptor blocker (ARB) as initial therapy is recommended to improve kidney outcomes. In the general nonblack population (without CKD) including those with diabetes, initial antihypertensive treatment should consist of a thiazide-type diuretic, calcium channel blocker, ACEI, or ARB. In the general black population (without CKD) including those with diabetes, initial antihypertensive treatment should consist of a thiazide-type diuretic or a calcium channel blocker **instead of** an ACEI or ARB. Beta-blockers are no longer recommended as first-line therapy in the general patient population.

Coronary artery disease (CAD) and hypertension: The American Heart Association, American College of Cardiology, and American Society of Hypertension (AHA/ACC/ASH) 2015 scientific statement for the treatment of hypertension in patients with CAD recommends the use of a beta blocker as part of a regimen in patients with hypertension and chronic stable angina with a history of prior MI. A BP target of <140/90 mm Hg is reasonable for the secondary prevention of cardiovascular events. A lower target BP (<130/80 mm Hg) may be appropriate in some individuals with CAD, previous MI, stroke or transient ischemic attack, or CAD risk equivalents (AHA/ACC/ASH [Rosendorff 2015]).

Local Anesthetic/Vasoconstrictor Precautions Use with caution; epinephrine has interacted with nonselective beta-blockers to result in initial hypertensive episode followed by bradycardia

Effects on Dental Treatment Propranolol is a nonselective beta-blocker and may enhance the pressor response to epinephrine, resulting in hypertension and bradycardia. Many nonsteroidal anti-inflammatory drugs, such as ibuprofen and indomethacin, can reduce the hypotensive effect of beta-blockers after 3 or more weeks of therapy with the NSAID. Short-term NSAID use (ie, 3 days) requires no special precautions in patients taking beta-blockers.

Effects on Bleeding No information available to require special precautions

Adverse Reactions Frequency not always defined.

Cardiovascular: Cold extremities (infants: 7% to 8%), angina pectoris, atrioventricular conduction disturbance, bradycardia, cardiogenic shock, congestive heart failure, hypotension, ineffective myocardial contractions, syncope

Central nervous system: Sleep disorder (infants: 16% to 18%), agitation (infants: 5% to 9%), fatigue (5% to 7%), dizziness (4% to 7%), nightmares (infants: 2% to 6%), irritability (infants: 1% to 6%), drowsiness (infants: 1% to 5%), amnesia, carpal tunnel syndrome (rare), catatonia, cognitive dysfunction, confusion, hypersomnia, lethargy, paresthesia, psychosis, vertigo

Dermatologic: Changes in nails, contact dermatitis, dermal ulcer, eczematous rash, erosive lichen planus, hyperkeratosis, pruritus, skin rash

Endocrine & metabolic: Hyperglycemia, hyperkalemia, hyperlipidemia, hypoglycemia

Gastrointestinal: Diarrhea (infants: 5% to 6%), abdominal pain (infants: ≤4%), decreased appetite (infants: 3% to 4%), constipation (1% to 3%), anorexia, stomach discomfort

Genitourinary: Oliguria (rare), proteinuria (rare)

Hematologic & oncologic: Immune thrombocytopenia, thrombocytopenia

Hepatic: Increased serum alkaline phosphatase, increased serum transaminases

Neuromuscular & skeletal: Arthropathy, oculomucocutaneous syndrome, polyarthritis

Ophthalmic: Conjunctival hyperemia, decreased visual acuity, mydriasis

Renal: Increased blood urea nitrogen, interstitial nephritis (rare)

Respiratory: Bronchitis (infants: 8% to 13%; associated with cough, fever, diarrhea, and vomiting), bronchiolitis (infants; associated with cough, fever, diarrhea, and vomiting), bronchospasm, dyspnea, pulmonary edema, wheezing

Miscellaneous: Ulcer

<1%, postmarketing, and/or case reports: Abdominal cramps, agranulocytosis, alopecia, altered mental status, arterial insufficiency, arterial mesenteric thrombosis, decreased heart rate (infants), decreased serum glucose (infants), depression, emotional lability, epigastric distress, erythema multiforme, erythematous rash, exfoliative dermatitis, fever combined with generalized ache, sore throat, laryngospasm, and respiratory distress), hallucination, hypersensitivity reaction (including anaphylaxis, anaphylactoid reaction), impotence, insomnia, ischemic colitis, lassitude, lupus-like

syndrome, myotonia, myopathy, nausea, nonthrombocytopenic purpura, peripheral arterial disease (exacerbation), Peyronie's disease, pharyngitis, psoriasiform eruption, purpura, Raynaud's phenomenon, second degree atrioventricular block (infants; in a patient with an underlying conduction disorder), Stevens-Johnson syndrome, systemic lupus erythematosus, temporary amnesia, tingling of extremities (hands), toxic epidermal necrolysis, urticaria, visual disturbance, vivid dream, vomiting, weakness, xerophthalmia

Dosing

Adult

Essential tremor: Oral: Immediate-release formulations: 40 mg twice daily initially; maintenance doses: Usually 120 to 320 mg/day

Hypertension: Oral:

Immediate-release formulations: 40 mg twice daily; increase dosage every 3 to 7 days; usual dose: 120 to 240 mg divided in 2 to 3 doses/day; maximum daily dose: 640 mg; usual dosage range (ASH/ISH [Weber 2014]): 40 to 160 mg twice daily

Extended-release formulations:

Inderal LA: Initial: 80 mg once daily; usual maintenance: 120 to 160 mg once daily; maximum daily dose: 640 mg

Inderal XL, InnoPran XL: Initial: 80 mg once daily at bedtime; if initial response is inadequate, may be increased at 2 to 3 week intervals to a maximum daily dose of 120 mg

Migraine headache prophylaxis: Oral:

Immediate-release formulations: Initial: 80 mg/day divided every 6 to 8 hours; increase by 20 to 40 mg/dose every 3 to 4 weeks to a maximum of 160 to 240 mg/day given in divided doses every 6 to 8 hours; if satisfactory response not achieved within 6 weeks of starting therapy, drug should be withdrawn gradually over several weeks

Inderal LA: Initial: 80 mg once daily; effective dose range: 160 to 240 mg once daily

Obstructive hypertrophic cardiomyopathy: Oral:

Immediate-release formulations: 20 to 40 mg 3 to 4 times/day

Inderal LA: 80 to 160 mg once daily

Pheochromocytoma: Oral: Immediate-release formulations: 30 to 60 mg/day in divided doses

Post-MI mortality reduction: Oral: Immediate-release formulations: Initial: 40 mg 3 times/day; usual dosage range: 180 to 240 mg/day in 3 to 4 divided doses

Stable angina: Oral:

Immediate-release formulations: 80 to 320 mg/day in doses divided 2 to 4 times/day

Inderal LA: Initial: 80 mg once daily; maximum dose: 320 mg once daily

Supraventricular tachycardia:

Acute treatment (off-label dose): IV: Initial: 1 mg over 1 minute, may repeat 1 mg after 2-minute intervals, up to 3 doses (ACC/AHA/HRS [Page 2015])

Ongoing management (off-label use): Oral: Initial: 30 to 60 mg daily in divided doses (immediate-release) or once daily (extended-release); maximum maintenance dose: 160 mg daily in divided doses (immediate-release) or once daily (extended-release) (ACC/AHA/HRS [Page 2015])

Tachyarrhythmias:

Oral: Immediate-release formulations: 10 to 30 mg/dose every 6 to 8 hours or a usual maintenance dose of 10 to 40 mg three or four times daily for rate control in patients with atrial fibrillation (AHA/ACC/HRS [January 2014]).

IV: 1 to 3 mg/dose slow IVP; repeat every 2-5 minutes up to a total of 5 mg; titrate initial dose to desired response. **Note:** Once response achieved or maximum dose administered, additional doses should not be given for at least 4 hours.

or

0.5 to 1 mg over 1 minute; may repeat, if necessary, up to a total maximum dose of 0.1 mg/kg (ACLS guidelines 2010)

or

1 mg over 1 minute; may be repeated every 2 minutes up to 3 doses for rate control in patients with atrial fibrillation (AHA/ACC/HRS [January 2014]).

Akathisia, antipsychotic-induced (off-label use): Oral: Immediate-release formulations: Initial: 10 mg twice daily **or** 10 mg 3 times daily; adjust dose based on response and tolerability up to 120 mg/day (Adler 1986; Adler 1993; Kane 2009; Kramer 1989). Treatment guidelines recommend doses of 30 to 90 mg/day (APA [Lehman 2004]; WFSBP [Hasan 2013].

Performance anxiety (off-label use): Oral: Immediate-release formulations: 40 mg 60 to 90 minutes prior to anxiety-provoking event (Hartley 1983). Additional data may be necessary to further define the role of propranolol in this condition.

Thyroid storm (off-label use):

Oral: Immediate-release formulations: 60 to 80 mg every 4 hours; may consider the use of an intravenous shorter-acting beta-blocker (ie, esmolol) (Bahn 2011)

IV: 0.5 to 1 mg administered over 10 minutes every 3 hours (Gardner 2011)

Thyrotoxicosis (off-label use): Oral: Immediate-release formulations: 10 to 40 mg/dose every 6 to 8 hours; may also consider administering extended or sustained release formulations (Bahn 2011)

Tremor, lithium-induced (off-label use): Oral: Immediate-release formulations: 30 to 80 mg/day in divided doses; adjust dose based on response and tolerability (Gelenberg 1995; Kirk 1973; Lapierre 1976). Additional data may be necessary to further define the role of propranolol in this condition.

Variceal hemorrhage prophylaxis (off-label use) (AASLD [Garcia-Tsao 2007]): Oral:

Primary prophylaxis: Immediate-release formulations: Initial: 20 mg twice daily; adjust to maximal tolerated dose. **Note:** Risk factors for hemorrhage include Child-Pugh class B/C or variceal red wale markings on endoscopy.

Secondary prophylaxis: Immediate-release formulations: Initial: 20 mg twice daily; adjust to maximal tolerated dose

Geriatric

IV: Use caution; initiate at lower end of the dosing range.

Oral:

Hypertension: Consider lower initial doses and titrate to response (Aronow 2011)

Tachyarrhythmias: Immediate-release formulations: Initial: 10 mg twice daily; increase dosage every 3 to 7 days; usual dose range: 10 to 320 mg/day given in 1 to 2 divided doses.

Refer to adult dosing for additional uses.

Pediatric

Proliferating infantile hemangioma (Hemangeol): Infants ≥2 kg: Oral: **Note:** Initiate treatment at age

5 weeks to 5 months; doses should be administered at least 9 hours apart. Refer to product labeling for detailed weight-based dosing tabulation.

Week 1: 0.15 mL/kg (~0.6 mg/kg) twice daily

Week 2: 0.3 mL/kg (~1.1 mg/kg) twice daily

Week 3 (maintenance): 0.4 mL/kg (~1.7 mg/kg) twice daily; maintain this dose for 6 months. Readjust dose periodically as the child's weight increases. Treatment may be reinitiated if hemangiomas recur.

Hypertension (off-label use): Children and Adolescents: Oral: Immediate-release formulations: Initial: 1 to 2 mg/kg/day divided in 2 to 3 doses/day; titrate dose to effect; maximum dose: 4 mg/kg/day up to 640 mg/day; sustained-release formulation may be dosed once daily (NHBPEP 2004; NHLBI 2011).

Thyrotoxicosis (off-label use): Adolescents: Oral: Refer to adult dosing.

Renal Impairment There are no dosage adjustments provided in the manufacturer's labeling. However, renal impairment increases systemic exposure to propranolol. Use with caution.

Not dialyzable (0% to 5%); supplemental dose is not necessary.

Peritoneal dialysis effects: Supplemental dose is not necessary.

Hepatic Impairment There are no dosage adjustments provided in the manufacturer's labeling. However, hepatic impairment increases systemic exposure to propranolol. Use with caution.

Mechanism of Action Nonselective beta-adrenergic blocker (class II antiarrhythmic); competitively blocks response to $beta_1$- and $beta_2$-adrenergic stimulation which results in decreases in heart rate, myocardial contractility, blood pressure, and myocardial oxygen demand. Nonselective beta-adrenergic blockers (propranolol, nadolol) reduce portal pressure by producing splanchnic vasoconstriction ($beta_2$ effect) thereby reducing portal blood flow.

Contraindications

Hypersensitivity to propranolol, beta-blockers, or any component of the formulation; uncompensated congestive heart failure (unless the failure is due to tachyarrhythmias being treated with propranolol), cardiogenic shock; severe sinus bradycardia, sick sinus syndrome, or heart block greater than first-degree (except in patients with a functioning artificial pacemaker); bronchial asthma

Hemangeol (additional contraindications): Premature infants with corrected age <5 weeks; infants weighing <2 kg; heart rate <80 bpm; blood pressure <50/30 mm Hg; pheochromocytoma; history of bronchospasm

Canadian labeling: Additional contraindications (not in US labeling): Cor pulmonale; allergic rhinitis during pollen season; patients prone to hypoglycemia; hypotension (blood pressure parameters not specified in labeling); metabolic acidosis; vasospastic angina (also referred to as Prinzmetal angina or variant angina); severe peripheral arterial circulatory disturbance

Warnings/Precautions Consider preexisting conditions such as sick sinus syndrome before initiating. Administer cautiously in compensated heart failure and monitor for a worsening of the condition (efficacy of propranolol in HF has not been demonstrated). **[US Boxed Warning]: Beta-blocker therapy should not be withdrawn abruptly (particularly in patients with CAD), but gradually tapered to avoid acute tachycardia, hypertension, and/or ischemia.** Beta-blockers without alpha1-adrenergic receptor blocking activity should be avoided in patients with Prinzmetal variant angina (Mayer 1998). Chronic beta-blocker therapy should not be routinely withdrawn prior to major surgery. May precipitate or aggravate symptoms of arterial insufficiency in patients with PVD and Raynaud's disease; use with caution and monitor for progression of arterial obstruction. Bradycardia may be observed more frequently in elderly patients (>65 years of age); dosage reductions may be necessary. Potentially significant drug-drug interactions may exist, requiring dose or frequency adjustment, additional monitoring, and/or selection of alternative therapy. Cigarette smoking may decrease plasma levels of propranolol by increasing metabolism. Patients should be advised to avoid smoking.

Use cautiously in patients with diabetes because it can mask prominent hypoglycemic symptoms. May mask signs of hyperthyroidism (eg, tachycardia); if hyperthyroidism is suspected, carefully manage and monitor; abrupt withdrawal may exacerbate symptoms of hyperthyroidism or precipitate thyroid storm. May alter thyroid-function tests. Use with caution in myasthenia gravis or psychiatric disease (may cause CNS depression). Use cautiously in renal and hepatic dysfunction; dosage adjustment may be required in hepatic impairment. In general, patients with bronchospastic disease should not receive beta-blockers; if used at all, should be used cautiously with close monitoring. Adequate alpha-blockade is required prior to use of any beta-blocker for patients with untreated pheochromocytoma. May induce or exacerbate psoriasis. Use caution with history of severe anaphylaxis to allergens; patients taking beta-blockers may become more sensitive to repeated challenges. Treatment of anaphylaxis (eg, epinephrine) in patients taking beta-blockers may be ineffective or promote undesirable effects.

Considerations when treating infantile hemangioma: Bradycardia and/or hypotension may occur or be worsened; monitor heart rate and blood pressure after propranolol initiation or increase in dose; discontinue treatment if severe (<80 bpm) or symptomatic bradycardia or hypotension (systolic blood pressure <50 mm Hg) occurs. Infants with large facial infantile hemangioma should be investigated for potential arteriopathy associated with PHACE syndrome prior to propranolol therapy; decreases in blood pressure caused by propranolol may increase risk of stroke in PHACE syndrome patients with cerebrovascular anomalies. May potentiate hypoglycemia and/or mask signs and symptoms. Withhold the dose in infants or children who are not feeding regularly or who are vomiting; discontinue therapy and seek immediate treatment if hypoglycemia occurs. May cause bronchospasm. Interrupt therapy in infants or children with lower respiratory tract infection associated with dyspnea or wheezing.

Drug Interactions

Metabolism/Transport Effects Substrate of CYP1A2 (major), CYP2C19 (minor), CYP2D6 (major), CYP3A4 (minor); **Note:** Assignment of Major/Minor substrate status based on clinically relevant drug interaction potential; **Inhibits** CYP1A2 (weak)

Avoid Concomitant Use

Avoid concomitant use of Propranolol with any of the following: Beta2-Agonists; Ceritinib; Floctafenine; Methacholine; Rivastigmine

Increased Effect/Toxicity

Propranolol may increase the levels/effects of: Alpha-/Beta-Agonists (Direct-Acting); Alpha1-Blockers; Alpha2-Agonists; Amifostine; Antipsychotic Agents (Phenothiazines); Antipsychotic Agents (Second

Generation [Atypical]); Bradycardia-Causing Agents; Bupivacaine; Cardiac Glycosides; Ceritinib; Cholinergic Agonists; CloZAPine; Disopyramide; Doxofylline; DULoxetine; Ergot Derivatives; Fingolimod; Grass Pollen Allergen Extract (5 Grass Extract); Hypotension-Associated Agents; Insulin; Ivabradine; Lacosamide; Levodopa; Lidocaine (Systemic); Lidocaine (Topical); Mepivacaine; Methacholine; Midodrine; Nitroprusside; Perhexiline; Rizatriptan; Sulfonylureas; TiZANidine; ZOLMitriptan

The levels/effects of Propranolol may be increased by: Abiraterone Acetate; Acetylcholinesterase Inhibitors; Ajmaline; Alcohol (Ethyl); Alfuzosin; Alpha2-Agonists; Aminoquinolines (Antimalarial); Amiodarone; Anilidopiperidine Opioids; Antipsychotic Agents (Phenothiazines); Asunaprevir; Barbiturates; Benperidol; Bretylium; Brimonidine (Topical); Calcium Channel Blockers (Nondihydropyridine); Cobicistat; CYP1A2 Inhibitors (Moderate); CYP1A2 Inhibitors (Strong); CYP2D6 Inhibitors (Moderate); CYP2D6 Inhibitors (Strong); Darunavir; Deferasirox; Diazoxide; Dipyridamole; Disopyramide; Dronedarone; Floctafenine; FluvoxaMINE; Herbs (Hypotensive Properties); Imatinib; Lacidipine; Lormetazepam; Lumefantrine; Methoxyflurane; Molsidomine; Naftopidil; Nicergoline; Nicorandil; NIFEdipine; Obeticholic Acid; Obinutuzumab; Panobinostat; Peginterferon Alfa-2b; Pentoxifylline; Perhexiline; Phosphodiesterase 5 Inhibitors; Propafenone; Prostacyclin Analogues; Quinagolide; QuiNIDine; QuiNINE; Regorafenib; Reserpine; Rivastigmine; Ruxolitinib; Selective Serotonin Reuptake Inhibitors; Tofacitinib; Vemurafenib; Zileuton

Decreased Effect

Propranolol may decrease the levels/effects of: Beta2-Agonists; Lacidipine; Theophylline Derivatives

The levels/effects of Propranolol may be decreased by: Alcohol (Ethyl); Amphetamines; Barbiturates; Bile Acid Sequestrants; Cannabis; CYP1A2 Inducers (Strong); Cyproterone; Herbs (Hypertensive Properties); Methylphenidate; Nonsteroidal Anti-Inflammatory Agents; Peginterferon Alfa-2b; Rifamycin Derivatives; Teriflunomide; Yohimbine

Food Interactions

Ethanol: Ethanol may increase or decrease plasma levels of propranolol. Reports are variable and have shown both enhanced as well as inhibited hepatic metabolism (of propranolol). Management: Caution advised with consumption of ethanol and monitor for heart rate and/or blood pressure changes.

Food: Propranolol serum levels may be increased if taken with food. Protein-rich foods may increase bioavailability; a change in diet from high carbohydrate/low protein to low carbohydrate/high protein may result in increased oral clearance. Management: Tablets (immediate release) should be taken on an empty stomach. Capsules (extended release) may be taken with or without food, but be consistent with regard to food.

Dietary Considerations Tablets (immediate release) should be taken on an empty stomach; capsules (extended release) may be taken with or without food, but should always be taken consistently (with food or on an empty stomach). Hemangeol should be administered during or right after a feeding to reduce the risk of hypoglycemia; skip dose if child is not eating or is vomiting.

Pharmacodynamics/Kinetics

Onset of Action Beta-blockade: Oral: 1 to 2 hours; Peak effect: Hypertension: A few days to several weeks

Duration of Action Immediate release: 6 to 12 hours; Extended-release formulations: ~24 to 27 hours

Half-life Elimination Neonates: Possible increased half-life; Infants (35 to 150 days of age): Median 3.5 hours; Children: 3.9 to 6.4 hours; Adults: Immediate release formulation: 3 to 6 hours; Extended-release formulations: 8 to 10 hours

Time to Peak Immediate release: Adults: 1 to 4 hours; Infants: ≤2 hours (Hemangeol); Extended release capsule (Inderal XL, InnoPran XL): 12 to 14 hours; Long acting capsule (Inderal LA): 6 hours

Pregnancy Risk Factor C

Pregnancy Considerations Adverse events have been observed in some animal reproduction studies. Propranolol crosses the placenta and is measurable in the newborn serum following maternal use during pregnancy (Taylor 1981). According to the manufacturer, congenital abnormalities have been reported following maternal use of propranolol. Bradycardia, hypoglycemia, and/or respiratory depression have been observed in neonates following in utero exposure to propranolol at parturition. Reduced birth weight has also been observed following in utero exposure to beta-blockers as a class. Adequate facilities for monitoring infants at birth should be available.

Untreated chronic maternal hypertension and preeclampsia are also associated with adverse events in the fetus, infant, and mother (ACOG 2015; Magee 2014). When treatment of hypertension in pregnancy is indicated, beta-blockers may be used. Specific recommendations vary by guideline. Although other agents are preferred (ACOG 2013), use of propranolol may be considered (Magee 2014). Use of propranolol may be considered for some arrhythmias, including SVT, when use of a beta-blocker is needed during pregnancy (ACC/AHA/HRS [Page 2015]; ESC [Regitz-Zagrosek 2011]). Propranolol is recommended for use in controlling hypermetabolic symptoms of thyrotoxicosis in pregnancy (Stagnaro-Green 2011). Propranolol may be used if prophylaxis of migraine is needed in pregnant women; it should be discontinued 2 to 3 days prior to delivery to decrease the risk of adverse events to the fetus/neonate and potential reductions in uterine contraction (Pringsheim 2012).

Breastfeeding Considerations Propranolol is present in breast milk.

The relative infant dose (RID) of propranolol is 1% when calculated using the highest breast milk concentration located and compared to an infant therapeutic dose of 1 mg/kg/day. In general, breastfeeding is considered acceptable when the RID is <10%; when an RID is >25% breastfeeding should generally be avoided (Anderson 2016; Ito 2000). Using the highest milk concentration (0.075 mcg/mL), the estimated daily infant dose via breast milk is 11.25 mcg/kg/day. This milk concentration was obtained following maternal administration of propranolol 1.2 mg/kg/day. Using data collected from three women, the same study found the overall half-life of propranolol in breast milk to be 6.5 ± 3.4 hours (Smith Livingstone Hooper 1983). Peak milk concentrations are reported to occur between 2 to 3 hours after an oral dose (Bauer 1979).

In general, propranolol may be compatible with breastfeeding when used at usual doses. Mothers should closely monitor their breastfeeding infants for bradycardia, cyanosis, and hypoglycemia (WHO 2002).

Prescribing and Access Restrictions Prescriptions for Hemangeol may be obtained via the Hemangeol Patient Access program. Visit http://www.hemangeol.com/hcp/hemangeol-direct/ or call 855-618-4950 for ordering information.

Dosage Forms

Capsule Extended Release 24 Hour, Oral:
Inderal LA: 60 mg, 80 mg, 120 mg, 160 mg
Inderal XL: 80 mg, 120 mg
InnoPran XL: 80 mg, 120 mg
Generic: 60 mg, 80 mg, 120 mg, 160 mg

Solution, Intravenous:
Generic: 1 mg/mL (1 mL)

Solution, Oral:
Hemangeol: 4.28 mg/mL (120 mL)
Generic: 20 mg/5 mL (500 mL); 40 mg/5 mL (500 mL)

Tablet, Oral:
Generic: 10 mg, 20 mg, 40 mg, 60 mg, 80 mg

Propylthiouracil (proe pil thye oh YOOR a sil)

Related Information
Endocrine Disorders and Pregnancy *on page 1781*

Brand Names: Canada Propyl-Thyracil

Pharmacologic Category Antithyroid Agent; Thioamide

Use Hyperthyroidism: Treatment of hyperthyroidism in patients with Graves' disease or toxic multinodular goiter who are intolerant of methimazole and for whom surgery or radioactive iodine therapy is not an appropriate treatment regimen; amelioration of hyperthyroid symptoms in preparation for thyroidectomy or radioactive iodine therapy (in patients who are intolerant of methimazole).

Local Anesthetic/Vasoconstrictor Precautions No information available to require special precautions

Effects on Dental Treatment Key adverse event(s) related to dental treatment: Loss of taste perception.

Effects on Bleeding Propylthiouracil administration may cause a bishydroxycoumarin-like hypocoagulable condition that is clinically observed by hemorrhagic diathesis. The syndrome is usually responsive to vitamin K therapy. It is suggested that all patients receiving propylthiouracil have their prothrombin times evaluated.

Adverse Reactions Frequency not defined.

Cardiovascular: Edema, periarteritis, vasculitis (ANCA-positive, cutaneous, leukocytoclastic)

Central nervous system: Drowsiness, drug fever, headache, neuritis, paresthesia, vertigo

Dermatologic: Alopecia, dermal ulcer, erythema nodosum, exfoliative dermatitis, pruritus, skin pigmentation, skin rash, Stevens-Johnson syndrome, toxic epidermal necrolysis, urticaria

Gastrointestinal: Ageusia, dysgeusia, nausea, salivary gland disease, stomach pain, vomiting

Hematologic & oncologic: Agranulocytosis, aplastic anemia, granulocytopenia, hemorrhage, hypoprothrombinemia, leukopenia, lymphadenopathy, splenomegaly, thrombocytopenia

Hepatic: Acute hepatic failure, hepatitis, hepatotoxicity (idiosyncratic) (Chalasani 2014), jaundice

Neuromuscular & skeletal: Arthralgia, lupus-like syndrome, myalgia

Renal: Acute renal failure, glomerulonephritis, nephritis

Respiratory: Interstitial pneumonitis, pulmonary alveolar hemorrhage

Miscellaneous: Fever

General Dosage Range Oral: *Adults:* Initial: 300 to 900 mg daily in 3 equally divided doses; Maintenance: 100 to 150 mg daily in 3 equally divided doses

Mechanism of Action Inhibits the synthesis of thyroid hormones by blocking the conversion of thyroxine to triiodothyronine in peripheral tissues (does not inactivate existing thyroxine and triiodothyronine stores in circulating blood and the thyroid and does not interfere with replacement thyroid hormones).

Pharmacodynamics/Kinetics

Onset of Action For significant therapeutic effects 24 to 36 hours are required; remission of hyperthyroidism usually does not occur before 4 months of continued therapy

Duration of Action 12 to 24 hours (Clark 2006)

Half-life Elimination ~1 hour (Clark 2006)

Time to Peak 1 to 2 hours (Clark 2006)

Pregnancy Risk Factor D

Pregnancy Considerations Propylthiouracil has been found to readily cross the placenta. Teratogenic effects have not been observed; however, nonteratogenic adverse effects, including fetal and neonatal hypothyroidism, goiter, and hyperthyroidism, have been reported following maternal propylthiouracil use. The transfer of thyroid-stimulating immunoglobulins can stimulate the fetal thyroid in utero and transiently after delivery and may increase the risk of fetal or neonatal hyperthyroidism (De Groot 2012; Peleg 2002).

Antithyroid treatment is recommended for the control of hyperthyroidism during pregnancy (Casey 2006; De Groot 2012). Uncontrolled maternal hyperthyroidism may result in adverse neonatal outcomes (eg, prematurity, low birth weight) and adverse maternal outcomes (eg, preeclampsia, congestive heart failure, stillbirth, and abortion). To prevent adverse fetal and maternal events, normal maternal thyroid function should be maintained prior to conception and throughout pregnancy (De Groot 2012).

[US Boxed Warning]: Because of the risk of fetal abnormalities associated with methimazole, propylthiouracil may be the treatment of choice when an antithyroid drug is indicated during or just prior to the first trimester of pregnancy. Due to an increased risk of liver toxicity with propylthiouracil, the use of methimazole may be preferred during the second and third trimesters. If drug therapy is changed, maternal thyroid function should be monitored after 2 weeks and then every 2 to 4 weeks (De Groot 2012). Propylthiouracil, along with other medications, is used for the treatment of thyroid storm in pregnant women (ACOG 2015).

The pharmacokinetics of propylthiouracil are not changed significantly during pregnancy; however, the severity of hyperthyroidism may fluctuate throughout pregnancy (DeGroot 2012; Sitar 1979; Sitar 1982). Doses of propylthiouracil may be decreased as pregnancy progresses and discontinued weeks to months prior to delivery.

Protamine (PROE ta meen)

Pharmacologic Category Antidote

Use Heparin overdose: Treatment of heparin overdosage

Local Anesthetic/Vasoconstrictor Precautions No information available to require special precautions

Effects on Dental Treatment No significant effects or complications reported

Effects on Bleeding Administration reverses the effect of heparin anticoagulants to permit general surgical treatment (eg, abdominal or orthopedic surgery). Risk of bleeding is dependent on multiple variables, including the intensity of anticoagulation and patient susceptibility. The need to address the effects of anticoagulation for dental surgery is based on a complex risk to benefit assessment; medical consult is suggested.

Adverse Reactions Frequency not defined.

Cardiovascular: Bradycardia, flushing, hypotension, sudden decrease of blood pressure

Central nervous system: Lassitude

Gastrointestinal: Nausea, vomiting

Hematologic & oncologic: Hemorrhage

Hypersensitivity: Hypersensitivity reaction

Respiratory: Dyspnea, pulmonary hypertension

General Dosage Range IV: *Children and Adults:* 1 mg of protamine neutralizes ~100 units of heparin (maximum dose: 50 mg)

Mechanism of Action Protamine, a highly alkaline protein molecule with a large positive charge, has weak anticoagulant activity when administered alone. When protamine is given in the presence of heparin (strongly acidic and negatively charged), a stable salt is formed and the anticoagulant activity of both drugs is nullified (Pai 2012). In the presence of LMWH, protamine incompletely reverses the antifactor Xa activity of LMWH (Makris 2000; Massonnet-Castel 1986; Racanelli 1985).

Pharmacodynamics/Kinetics

Onset of Action IV: Heparin neutralization: ~5 minutes

Half-life Elimination ~7 minutes

Pregnancy Risk Factor C

Pregnancy Considerations Animal reproduction studies have not been conducted. In general, medications used as antidotes should take into consideration the health and prognosis of the mother; antidotes should be administered to pregnant women if there is a clear indication for use and should not be withheld because of fears of teratogenicity (Bailey, 2003). Protamine sulfate may be used during delivery to reduce the risk of bleeding following maternal use of heparin or low molecular weight heparin (LMWH) (Bates, 2012).

Protein C Concentrate (Human)

(PROE teen cee KON suhn trate HYU man)

Brand Names: US Ceprotin

Pharmacologic Category Blood Product Derivative; Enzyme; Protein C

Use Severe congenital protein C deficiency: Prevention and treatment of venous thrombosis and purpura fulminans in adults and pediatric patients with severe congenital protein C deficiency.

Local Anesthetic/Vasoconstrictor Precautions No information available to require special precautions

Effects on Dental Treatment No significant effects or complications reported

Effects on Bleeding As with all drugs which may affect hemostasis, bleeding may be associated with protein C administration. Risk is dependent on multiple variables. Medical consult is suggested.

Adverse Reactions As with all drugs which may affect hemostasis, bleeding may be associated with protein C administration. Hemorrhage may occur at virtually any site. Risk is dependent on multiple variables, including the concurrent use of multiple agents that alter hemostasis and patient susceptibility. Frequency not defined.

Central nervous system: Dizziness

Hematologic & oncologic: Hemorrhage

Hypersensitivity: Hypersensitivity reaction (pruritus and rash)

<1%, postmarketing, and/or case reports: Fever, hemothorax, hypotension, hyperhidrosis, restlessness

General Dosage Range IV: *Infants, Children, Adolescents, and Adults:* Initial: 100 to 120 units, followed by 60 to 80 units every 6 hours for 3 doses; maintenance: 45 to 60 units every 6 hours (short-term) or every 12 hours (short-to-long term)

Mechanism of Action Converted to activated protein C (APC). APC is a serine protease which inactivates factors Va and VIIIa, limiting thrombotic formation. *In vitro* data also suggest inhibition of plasminogen activator inhibitor-1 (PAF-1) resulting in profibrinolytic activity, inhibition of macrophage production of tumor necrosis factor, blocking of leukocyte adhesion, and limitation of thrombin-induced inflammatory responses.

Pharmacodynamics/Kinetics

Onset of Action 30 minutes

Half-life Elimination Median: 9.8 hours; range: 4.9 to 14.7 hours

Time to Peak Plasma: T_{max}: 0.5 hours; range: 0.17 to 1.33 hours

Pregnancy Risk Factor C

Pregnancy Considerations Animal reproductive studies have not been conducted.

Protriptyline (proe TRIP ti leen)

Related Information

Dentin Hypersensitivity, Acid Erosion, High Caries Index, Management of Alveolar Osteitis, and Xerostomia *on page 1857*

Vasoconstrictor Interactions With Antidepressants *on page 1913*

Brand Names: US Vivactil [DSC]

Pharmacologic Category Antidepressant, Tricyclic (Secondary Amine)

Use Depression: Treatment of depression

Local Anesthetic/Vasoconstrictor Precautions Use with caution; epinephrine and levonordefrin have been shown to have an increased pressor response in combination with TCAs. Protriptyline is one of the drugs confirmed to prolong the QT interval and is accepted as having a risk of causing torsade de pointes. The risk of drug-induced torsade de pointes is extremely low when a single QT interval prolonging drug is prescribed. In terms of epinephrine, it is not known what effect vasoconstrictors in the local anesthetic regimen will have in patients with a known history of congenital prolonged QT interval or in patients taking any medication that prolongs the QT interval. Until more information is obtained, it is suggested that the clinician consult with the physician prior to the use of a vasoconstrictor in suspected patients, and that the vasoconstrictor (epinephrine, mepivacaine and levonordefrin [Carbocaine® 2% with Neo-Cobefrin®]) be used with caution.

Effects on Dental Treatment Key adverse event(s) related to dental treatment: Xerostomia and changes in salivation (normal salivary flow resumes upon discontinuation), unpleasant taste, and trouble with gums. Long-term treatment with TCAs, such as protriptyline, increases the risk of caries by reducing salivation and salivary buffer capacity.

Effects on Bleeding No information available to require special precautions

Adverse Reactions Frequency not defined. Some reactions listed are based on reports for other agents in this same pharmacologic class and may not be specifically reported for protriptyline.

Cardiovascular: Cardiac arrhythmia, cerebrovascular accident, edema, flushing, heart block, hypertension, hypotension, myocardial infarction, orthostatic hypotension, palpitations, tachycardia

Central nervous system: Agitation, anxiety, ataxia, confusion, delusions, disorientation, dizziness, drowsiness, drug fever, EEG pattern changes, extrapyramidal reaction, fatigue, hallucination, headache, hyperpyrexia, hypomania, insomnia, nightmares, numbness, panic, peripheral neuropathy, psychosis (exacerbation), restlessness, seizure, tingling of extremities, tingling sensation, withdrawal syndrome

Dermatologic: Alopecia, diaphoresis (excessive), pruritus, skin photosensitivity, skin rash, urticaria

Endocrine & metabolic: Decreased libido, decreased serum glucose, galactorrhea, gynecomastia, increased libido, increased serum glucose, SIADH, weight gain, weight loss

Gastrointestinal: Abdominal cramps, anorexia, constipation, diarrhea, epigastric distress, melanoglossia, nausea, paralytic ileus, parotid gland enlargement, stomatitis, sublingual adenitis, unpleasant taste, vomiting, xerostomia

Genitourinary: Breast hypertrophy, impotence, nocturia, testicular swelling, urinary hesitancy, urinary retention, urinary tract dilation

Hematologic & oncologic: Agranulocytosis, eosinophilia, leukopenia, petechia, purpura, thrombocytopenia

Hepatic: Abnormal hepatic function tests, cholestatic jaundice

Neuromuscular & skeletal: Tremor, weakness

Ophthalmic: Accommodation disturbance, blurred vision, eye pain, increased intraocular pressure

Otic: Tinnitus

Renal: Polyuria

Postmarketing and/or case reports: Angle-closure glaucoma, suicidal ideation, suicidal tendencies

General Dosage Range Oral:

Adolescents: 15 to 20 mg daily in 3 divided doses; maximum 60 mg daily

Adults: 10 to 60 mg daily in 3 to 4 divided doses; maximum 60 mg daily

Elderly: 15 to 20 mg daily in 3 divided doses; maximum 60 mg daily

Mechanism of Action Increases the synaptic concentration of serotonin and/or norepinephrine in the central nervous system by inhibition of their reuptake by the presynaptic neuronal membrane

Pharmacodynamics/Kinetics

Onset of Action Individual responses may vary; 4 to 8 weeks of treatment are needed before determining if a patient with depression is partially or nonresponsive (APA 2010)

Duration of Action 1 to 2 days

Half-life Elimination 54 to 92 hours (average: 74 hours) (Ziegler 1978)

Time to Peak Serum: ~6 to 12 hours (Ziegler 1978)

Pregnancy Considerations Adverse events have not been observed in animal reproduction studies. Tricyclic antidepressants may be associated with irritability, jitteriness, and convulsions (rare) in the neonate (Yonkers 2009).

The ACOG recommends that therapy for depression during pregnancy be individualized; treatment should incorporate the clinical expertise of the mental health clinician, obstetrician, primary health care provider, and pediatrician (ACOG 2008). According to the American Psychiatric Association (APA), the risks of medication treatment should be weighed against other treatment options and untreated depression. For women who discontinue antidepressant medications during pregnancy and who may be at high risk for postpartum depression, the medications can be restarted following delivery (APA 2010). Treatment algorithms have been developed by the ACOG and the APA for the management of depression in women prior to conception and during pregnancy (Yonkers 2009).

Pregnant women exposed to antidepressants during pregnancy are encouraged to enroll in the National Pregnancy Registry for Antidepressants (NPRAD). Women 18 to 45 years of age or their health care providers may contact the registry by calling 844-405-6185. Enrollment should be done as early in pregnancy as possible.

Dental Comment See Local Anesthetic/Vasoconstrictor Precautions

Prucalopride (proo KAL oh pride)

Brand Names: Canada Resotran

Pharmacologic Category Serotonin 5-HT_4 Receptor Agonist

Use Note: Not approved in the US

Chronic idiopathic constipation: Treatment of chronic idiopathic constipation in adult females with inadequate response to laxatives

Local Anesthetic/Vasoconstrictor Precautions No information available to require special precautions

Effects on Dental Treatment No significant effects or complications reported

Effects on Bleeding No information available to require special precautions

Adverse Reactions

>10%:

Central nervous system: Headache (22%)

Gastrointestinal: Nausea (17%), abdominal pain (12%), diarrhea (12%)

1% to 10%:

Central nervous system: Dizziness (4%), fatigue (3%), malaise (1%)

Genitourinary: Pollakiuria (1%)

Gastrointestinal: Upper abdominal pain (5%), flatulence (5%), vomiting (5%), dyspepsia (3%), abnormal bowel sounds (2%), anorexia (1%), gastroenteritis (1%)

Neuromuscular & skeletal: Muscle spasm (2%)

Miscellaneous: Fever (1%)

<1%, postmarketing, and/or case reports: Angina pectoris, anxiety, atrial arrhythmia, bronchitis, cardiac arrhythmia, chest pain, cholecystitis, cholelithiasis, confusion, constipation, depression, dyspnea, hyperhidrosis, migraine, myocardial infarction, ovarian cyst, pancreatitis, pneumonia, sinusitis, stomach discomfort, supraventricular tachycardia, syncope, tremor, urinary incontinence, urinary tract infection, vaginal hemorrhage

General Dosage Range Dosage adjustment recommended in patients with renal or hepatic impairment.

Oral:

Adults (females): 2 mg once daily

Elderly (females >65 years): Initial: 1 mg once daily; maintenance: 1 to 2 mg once daily

Mechanism of Action Prucalopride is a selective, high affinity 5-HT_4 receptor agonist whose action at the receptor site promotes cholinergic and nonadrenergic, noncholinergic neurotransmission by enteric neurons leading to stimulation of the peristaltic reflex, intestinal secretions, and gastrointestinal motility.

Pharmacodynamics/Kinetics

Half-life Elimination ~24 hours; terminal half-life increases to 34, 43, and 47 hours in mild, moderate, and severe renal impairment, respectively

Time to Peak 2 to 3 hours

Pregnancy Considerations Adverse events have not been observed in animal reproduction studies. Spontaneous abortion has been observed in pregnant women during clinical trials, although a causal association with prucalopride has not been established. Use during pregnancy is not recommended. Women of childbearing potential should employ effective contraception during therapy. An additional method of contraception is recommended for patients experiencing severe diarrhea and receiving oral contraceptives due to the potential for decreased efficacy of the oral contraceptive; cases of unintended pregnancies have been reported with prucalopride.

Product Availability Not available in the US

Pseudoephedrine (soo doe e FED rin)

Related Information

Bacterial Infections *on page 1835*

Related Sample Prescriptions

Sinus Infection Treatment - Sample Prescriptions *on page 38*

Brand Names: US Childrens Silfedrine [OTC]; Decongestant 12Hour Max St [OTC]; ElixSure Congestion [OTC] [DSC]; Genaphed [OTC]; Nasal Decongestant [OTC]; Nexafed [OTC]; Psudatabs [OTC] [DSC]; Shopko Nasal Decongestant Max [OTC]; Shopko Nasal Decongestant [OTC]; Simply Stuffy [OTC]; Sudafed 12 Hour [OTC]; Sudafed 24 Hour [OTC]; Sudafed Childrens [OTC]; Sudafed Congestion [OTC]; Sudafed [OTC]; Sudanyl [OTC] [DSC]; SudoGest 12 Hour [OTC]; SudoGest [OTC]; Suphedrine [OTC] [DSC]; Zephrex-D [OTC]

Brand Names: Canada Balminil Decongestant; Benylin® D for Infants; Contac® Cold 12 Hour Relief Non Drowsy; Drixoral® ND; Eltor®; PMS-Pseudoephedrine; Pseudofrin; Robidrine®; Sudafed® Decongestant

Generic Availability (US) May be product dependent

Pharmacologic Category Alpha/Beta Agonist; Decongestant

Use Temporary symptomatic relief of nasal congestion due to common cold, upper respiratory allergies, and sinusitis; also promotes nasal or sinus drainage

Local Anesthetic/Vasoconstrictor Precautions Use with caution since pseudoephedrine is a sympathomimetic amine which could interact with epinephrine to cause a pressor response

Effects on Dental Treatment Key adverse event(s) related to dental treatment: Xerostomia (normal salivary flow resumes upon discontinuation).

Effects on Bleeding No information available to require special precautions

Adverse Reactions

Frequency not defined.

Cardiovascular: Cardiac arrhythmia, chest tightness, circulatory shock (with hypotension), hypertension, palpitations, tachycardia

Central nervous system: Ataxia, central nervous system stimulation (transient), chills, confusion, dizziness, drowsiness, excitability, fatigue, hallucination, headache, insomnia, nervousness, neuritis, restlessness, seizure, vertigo

Dermatologic: Diaphoresis, skin photosensitivity, skin rash, urticaria

Gastrointestinal: Anorexia, constipation, diarrhea, dry throat, ischemic colitis, nausea, vomiting, xerostomia

Genitourinary: Difficulty in micturition, dysuria, urinary retention

Hematologic & oncologic: Agranulocytosis, hemolytic anemia, thrombocytopenia

Hypersensitivity: Anaphylaxis

Neuromuscular & skeletal: Tremor, weakness

Ophthalmic: Blurred vision, diplopia

Otic: Tinnitus

Renal: Polyuria

Respiratory: Dry nose, dyspnea, nasal congestion, pharyngeal edema, thickening of bronchial secretions, wheezing

Dosing

Adult Nasal congestion: General dosing guidelines: Oral: Immediate release: 60 mg every 4-6 hours; Extended release: 120 mg every 12 hours **or** 240 mg every 24 hours; maximum: 240 mg/24 hours

Geriatric Nasal congestion: Use caution in this population; initiate using immediate release formulation: 30-60 mg every 6 hours as needed

Pediatric Nasal congestion: General dosing guidelines: Oral:

Children:

4-5 years: 15 mg every 4-6 hours; maximum: 60 mg/24 hours

6-12 years: 30 mg every 4-6 hours; maximum: 120 mg/24 hours

>12 years: Refer to adult dosing.

Renal Impairment No dosage adjustment provided in manufacturer's labeling.

Hepatic Impairment No dosage adjustment provided in manufacturer's labeling.

Mechanism of Action Directly stimulates alpha-adrenergic receptors of respiratory mucosa causing vasoconstriction; directly stimulates beta-adrenergic receptors causing bronchial relaxation, increased heart rate and contractility

Contraindications Hypersensitivity to pseudoephedrine or any component of the formulation; with or within 14 days of MAO inhibitor therapy

Warnings/Precautions Use with caution in the elderly; may be more sensitive to adverse effects; administer with caution to patients with hypertension, hyperthyroidism, diabetes mellitus, cardiovascular disease, ischemic heart disease, increased intraocular pressure, prostatic hyperplasia, seizure disorders, or renal impairment. When used for self-medication (OTC), notify healthcare provider if symptoms do not improve within 7 days or are accompanied by fever. Discontinue and contact healthcare provider if nervousness, dizziness, or sleeplessness occur. Some products may contain sodium. Not for OTC use in children <4 years of age.

Benzyl alcohol and derivatives: Some dosage forms may contain sodium benzoate/benzoic acid; benzoic acid (benzoate) is a metabolite of benzyl alcohol; large amounts of benzyl alcohol (≥99 mg/kg/day) have been associated with a potentially fatal toxicity ("gasping syndrome") in neonates; the "gasping syndrome" consists of metabolic acidosis, respiratory distress, gasping respirations, CNS dysfunction (including convulsions, intracranial hemorrhage), hypotension, and cardiovascular collapse (AAP ["Inactive" 1997]; CDC, 1982); some data suggests that benzoate displaces bilirubin from protein binding sites (Ahlfors, 2001); avoid or use dosage forms containing benzyl alcohol derivative with caution in neonates. See manufacturer's labeling.

Drug Interactions

Metabolism/Transport Effects None known.

Avoid Concomitant Use

Avoid concomitant use of Pseudoephedrine with any of the following: Ergot Derivatives; Iobenguane I 123; MAO Inhibitors

Increased Effect/Toxicity

Pseudoephedrine may increase the levels/effects of: Doxofylline; Sympathomimetics

The levels/effects of Pseudoephedrine may be increased by: Alkalinizing Agents; AtoMOXetine; Cannabinoid-Containing Products; Carbonic Anhydrase Inhibitors; Cocaine; Ergot Derivatives; Linezolid; MAO Inhibitors; Serotonin/Norepinephrine Reuptake Inhibitors; Tedizolid

Decreased Effect

Pseudoephedrine may decrease the levels/effects of: Benzylpenicilloyl Polylysine; FentaNYL; Iobenguane I 123

The levels/effects of Pseudoephedrine may be decreased by: Alpha1-Blockers; Spironolactone; Urinary Acidifying Agents

Food Interactions Onset of effect may be delayed if pseudoephedrine is taken with food. Management: Administer without regard to food.

Dietary Considerations Some products may contain sodium. May be taken with or without food.

Pharmacodynamics/Kinetics

Onset of Action Decongestant: Oral: 30 minutes (Chua, 1989); Peak effect: Decongestant: Oral: ~1-2 hours (Chua, 1989)

Duration of Action Immediate release tablet: 3-8 hours (Chua, 1989)

Half-life Elimination Varies by urine pH and flow rate; alkaline urine decreases renal elimination of pseudoephedrine (Kanfer, 1993)

Children: ~3 hours (urine pH ~6.5) (Simons, 1996)

Adults: 9-16 hours (pH 8); 3-6 hours (pH 5) (Chua, 1989)

Time to Peak

Children (immediate release) ~2 hours (Simons, 1996)

Adults (immediate release): 1-3 hours (dose dependent) (Kanfer, 1993)

Pregnancy Considerations Use of pseudoephedrine during the first trimester may be associated with a possible risk of gastroschisis, small intestinal atresia, and hemifacial microsomia due to pseudoephedrine's vasoconstrictive effects; additional studies are needed to define the magnitude of risk. Single doses of pseudoephedrine were not found to adversely affect the fetus during the third trimester of pregnancy (limited data); however, fetal tachycardia was noted in a case report following maternal use of an extended release product for multiple days. Decongestants are not the preferred agents for the treatment of rhinitis during pregnancy. Oral pseudoephedrine should be avoided during the first trimester.

Breastfeeding Considerations Pseudoephedrine is excreted into breast milk in concentrations that are ~4% of the weight adjusted maternal dose. The time to maximum milk concentration is ~1-2 hours after the maternal dose. Irritability has been reported in nursing infants (limited data; dose, duration, relationship to breastfeeding not provided). Milk production may be decreased in some women.

Dosage Forms

Liquid, Oral:

Childrens Silfedrine [OTC]: 15 mg/5 mL (118 mL, 237 mL)

Nasal Decongestant [OTC]: 30 mg/5 mL (118 mL)

Sudafed Childrens [OTC]: 15 mg/5 mL (118 mL)

Syrup, Oral:

Nasal Decongestant [OTC]: 30 mg/5 mL (473 mL)

Tablet, Oral:

Genaphed [OTC]: 30 mg

Nasal Decongestant [OTC]: 30 mg

Shopko Nasal Decongestant Max [OTC]: 30 mg

Simply Stuffy [OTC]: 30 mg

Sudafed [OTC]: 30 mg

Sudafed Congestion [OTC]: 30 mg

SudoGest [OTC]: 30 mg, 60 mg

Generic: 30 mg, 60 mg

Tablet Abuse-Deterrent, Oral:

Nexafed [OTC]: 30 mg

Zephrex-D [OTC]: 30 mg

Tablet Extended Release 12 Hour, Oral:

Decongestant 12Hour Max St [OTC]: 120 mg

Shopko Nasal Decongestant [OTC]: 120 mg

Sudafed 12 Hour [OTC]: 120 mg

SudoGest 12 Hour [OTC]: 120 mg

Generic: 120 mg

Tablet Extended Release 24 Hour, Oral:

Sudafed 24 Hour [OTC]: 240 mg

Pseudoephedrine and Ibuprofen

(soo doe e FED rin & eye byoo PROE fen)

Related Information

Ibuprofen *on page 851*

Pseudoephedrine *on page 1404*

Brand Names: US Advil Cold & Sinus [OTC]

Brand Names: Canada Advil Cold & Sinus; Advil Cold & Sinus Daytime; Children's Advil Cold; Sudafed Sinus Advance

Pharmacologic Category Decongestant/Analgesic

Use Cold, sinus, and flu symptoms: Temporary relief of common cold, sinus, and flu symptoms (including nasal congestion, sinus pressure, headache, minor body aches and pains, and fever)

Local Anesthetic/Vasoconstrictor Precautions Use with caution since pseudoephedrine is a sympathomimetic amine which could interact with epinephrine to cause a pressor response

Effects on Dental Treatment Key adverse event(s) related to dental treatment: Pseudoephedrine: Xerostomia (normal salivary flow resumes upon discontinuation).

The dentist should be aware of the potential of abnormal coagulation. Caution should also be exercised in the use of NSAIDs in patients already on anticoagulant therapy with drugs such as warfarin (Coumadin®). See Effects on Bleeding.

Effects on Bleeding Nonselective NSAIDs, such as pseudoephedrine and ibuprofen, inhibit platelet aggregation and prolong bleeding time in some patients. Unlike aspirin, the NSAID effect on platelet function is quantitatively less, of shorter duration, and reversible. Normal platelet function should occur in ~5 elimination half-lives or in <10 hours after discontinuation of pseudoephedrine and ibuprofen. Concomitant use of other NSAIDs should be avoided.

Adverse Reactions See individual agents.

General Dosage Range Oral: *Children ≥12 years, Adolescents, and Adults:* 1 to 2 capsules/tablets (pseudoephedrine 30 mg/ibuprofen 200 mg per capsule/tablet) every 4 to 6 hours; (maximum: 6 tablets/capsules per 24 hours [pseudoephedrine 180 mg/ibuprofen 1,200 mg per 24 hours]).

Mechanism of Action

Ibuprofen: Reversibly inhibits cyclooxygenase-1 and 2 (COX-1 and 2) enzymes, which results in decreased formation of prostaglandin precursors; has antipyretic, analgesic, and anti-inflammatory properties.

Pseudoephedrine: Directly stimulates alpha-adrenergic receptors of respiratory mucosa causing vasoconstriction; directly stimulates beta-adrenergic receptors causing bronchial relaxation, increased heart rate and contractility.

Pregnancy Considerations Refer to individual agents.

Pyrantel Pamoate (pi RAN tel PAM oh ate)

Brand Names: US Pamix [OTC] [DSC]; Pin-X [OTC] [DSC]; Reeses Pinworm Medicine [OTC]

Brand Names: Canada Combantrin

Pharmacologic Category Anthelmintic

Use Pinworms: Treatment of pinworms caused by *Enterobius vermicularis* (alternative agent; not preferred therapy)

Local Anesthetic/Vasoconstrictor Precautions
No information available to require special precautions

Effects on Dental Treatment No significant effects or complications reported

Effects on Bleeding No information available to require special precautions

Adverse Reactions Frequency not defined.

Central nervous system: Dizziness, headache

Gastrointestinal: Abdominal cramps, diarrhea, nausea, vomiting

General Dosage Range Oral: *Children ≥2 years, Adolescents, and Adults:* 11 mg/kg as a single dose (maximum: 1 g per dose)

Mechanism of Action Causes the release of acetylcholine and inhibits cholinesterase; acts as a depolarizing neuromuscular blocker, paralyzing the helminths

Pharmacodynamics/Kinetics

Time to Peak Serum: 1 to 3 hours

Pregnancy Considerations Pyrantel pamoate has minimal systemic absorption. Systemic absorption would be required in order for pyrantel pamoate to cross the placenta and reach the fetus.

Pyrazinamide (peer a ZIN a mide)

Brand Names: Canada Tebrazid™

Pharmacologic Category Antitubercular Agent

Use Adjunctive treatment of tuberculosis in combination with other antituberculosis agents

Local Anesthetic/Vasoconstrictor Precautions
No information available to require special precautions

Effects on Dental Treatment No significant effects or complications reported

Effects on Bleeding No information available to require special precautions

Adverse Reactions

1% to 10%:

Central nervous system: Malaise

Gastrointestinal: Anorexia, nausea, vomiting

Neuromuscular & skeletal: Arthralgia, myalgia

<1%, postmarketing, and/or case reports: Acne vulgaris, acquired blood coagulation disorder (anticoagulant effect), angioedema (rare), dysuria, fever, gout, hepatotoxicity, interstitial nephritis, porphyria, pruritus, sideroblastic anemia, skin photosensitivity, skin rash, thrombocytopenia, urticaria

General Dosage Range Dosage adjustment recommended in patients with renal impairment

Oral:

Children: 15-30 mg/kg once daily (maximum: 2 g/day) **or** 50 mg/kg/dose twice weekly (maximum: 2 g/dose)

Adults 40-55 kg: 1000 mg once daily **or** 2000 mg twice weekly **or** 1500 mg 3 times/week

Adults 56-75 kg: 1500 mg once daily **or** 3000 mg twice weekly **or** 2500 mg 3 times/week

Adults 76-90 kg: 2000 mg once daily (maximum dose regardless of weight) **or** 4000 mg twice weekly (maximum dose regardless of weight) **or** 3000 mg 3 times/week (maximum dose regardless of weight)

Mechanism of Action Converted to pyrazinoic acid in susceptible strains of *Mycobacterium* which lowers the pH of the environment; exact mechanism of action has not been elucidated

Pharmacodynamics/Kinetics

Half-life Elimination 9 to 10 hours, prolonged with reduced renal or hepatic function

Time to Peak Serum: Within 2 hours

Pregnancy Risk Factor C

Pregnancy Considerations Teratogenic effects have not been observed in animal reproduction studies. Due to the risk of tuberculosis to the fetus, treatment is recommended when the probability of maternal disease is moderate to high. Although not recommended as the initial treatment regimen, the use of pyrazinamide during pregnancy is recommended by The World Health Organization (Blumberg, 2003).

Pyrethrins and Piperonyl Butoxide
(pye RE thrins & pi PER oh nil byo TOKS ide)

Brand Names: US A-200 Lice Treatment Kit [OTC]; A-200 Maximum Strength [OTC]; LiceMD Complete [OTC]; LiceMD Treatment [OTC]; Licide [OTC]; Pronto Plus Complete Lice Removal System [OTC]; RID Lice Elimination Essentials [OTC]; RID Lice Killing [OTC]; RID Lice Treatment Complete [OTC]

Brand Names: Canada Pronto Lice Control; R & C II; R & C Shampoo/Conditioner; RID Mousse

Pharmacologic Category Antiparasitic Agent, Topical; Pediculocide; Shampoo, Pediculocide

Use *Pediculus humanus* infestations: Treatment of *Pediculus humanus* infestations (head lice, body lice, pubic lice, and their eggs)

Local Anesthetic/Vasoconstrictor Precautions
No information available to require special precautions

Effects on Dental Treatment No significant effects or complications reported

Effects on Bleeding No information available to require special precautions

Adverse Reactions Frequency not defined.

Central nervous system: Localized burning

Dermatologic: Burning sensation of skin, pruritus, skin irritation (with repeat use), stinging of the skin

General Dosage Range Topical: *Children ≥2 years, Adolescents, and Adults:* Apply to dry hair and/or other infested area; allow to remain on area for 10 minutes and then wash and rinse; repeat treatment in 7 to 10 days

Mechanism of Action Pyrethrins are derived from flowers that belong to the chrysanthemum family. The mechanism of action on the neuronal membranes of lice is similar to that of DDT. Piperonyl butoxide is usually added to pyrethrin to enhance the product's activity by decreasing the metabolism of pyrethrins in arthropods.

Pregnancy Considerations Pregnant women may be treated with pyrethrins and piperonyl butoxide (CDC [Workowski 2015]).

Pyridostigmine (peer id oh STIG meen)

Brand Names: US Mestinon; Regonol

Brand Names: Canada Mestinon; Mestinon-SR

Pharmacologic Category Acetylcholinesterase Inhibitor

Use

Myasthenia gravis (oral only): Treatment of myasthenia gravis.

Reversal of nondepolarizing muscle relaxants (injection only): Reversal agent or antagonist to the neuromuscular blocking effects of nondepolarizing muscle relaxants.

Military use: Pretreatment for Soman nerve gas exposure

Local Anesthetic/Vasoconstrictor Precautions No information available to require special precautions

Effects on Dental Treatment Key adverse event(s) related to dental treatment: Dysphagia.

Effects on Bleeding No information available to require special precautions

Adverse Reactions

1% to 10%:

Central nervous system: Twitching (3%), hyperesthesia (2%)

Dermatologic: Xeroderma (2%)

Gastrointestinal: Abdominal pain (7%), diarrhea (7%)

Genitourinary: Dysmenorrhea (5%), urinary frequency (2%)

Neuromuscular & skeletal: Myalgia (2%), neck pain (2%)

Ophthalmic: Amblyopia (2%)

Respiratory: Epistaxis (2%)

Frequency not defined:

Cardiovascular: Bradycardia (transient), chest tightness, decreased heart rate, increased blood pressure

Central nervous system: Confusion, depressed mood, disturbed sleep, drowsiness, headache, hypertonia, lack of concentration, lethargy, localized warm feeling, numbness of tongue, tingling of extremities, vertigo

Dermatologic: Alopecia, diaphoresis, skin rash

Gastrointestinal: Abdominal cramps, bloating, borborygmi, flatulence, increased peristalsis, nausea, salivation, vomiting

Hypersensitivity: Hypersensitivity reaction

Neuromuscular & skeletal: Fasciculations, muscle cramps, weakness

Ophthalmic: Eye pain, lacrimation, miosis, visual disturbance

Respiratory: Acute bronchitis (exacerbation), exacerbation of asthma, increased bronchial secretions

<1%, postmarketing, and/or case reports: Fecal incontinence, loss of consciousness, pallor (postsyncopal), stiffness (arms or upper torso), thrombophlebitis, urinary incontinence

General Dosage Range

IV: *Adults:* 0.1 to 0.25 mg/kg/dose

Oral: *Adults:*

Immediate-release: 60 to 1,500 mg/day in 5 to 6 divided doses (usual: 600 mg/day)

Extended release: 180 to 540 mg once or twice daily (doses separated by at least 6 hours)

Mechanism of Action Inhibits destruction of acetylcholine by acetylcholinesterase which facilitates transmission of impulses across neuromuscular junction

Pharmacodynamics/Kinetics

Onset of Action

Recovery from vincristine neurotoxicity: Onset of action: 1 to 2 weeks (Akbayram 2010)

Myasthenia gravis: Oral: Within 30 minutes (Maggi 2011); IM: 15 to 30 minutes; IV: Within 2 to 5 minutes

Duration of Action Oral: 3 to 4 hours in the daytime (Maggi 2011); IM, IV: 2 to 3 hours

Half-life Elimination

Oral: 1 to 2 hours; renal failure: ~6 hours (Aquilonius 1986)

IV: 1.5 hours (Aquilonius 1986)

Time to Peak Oral: 1 to 2 hours (Aquilonius 1986)

Pregnancy Risk Factor B/C (manufacturer dependent)

Pregnancy Considerations Adverse events have not been observed in animal reproduction studies. Pyridostigmine may cross the placenta (Buckley 1968). Use of pyridostigmine may be continued during pregnancy for the treatment of myasthenia gravis (Norwood 2013; Skie 2010) and its use should be continued during labor (Norwood 2013). Transient neonatal myasthenia gravis may occur in 10% to 20% of neonates due to placental transfer of maternal antibodies (Skie 2010; Varner 2013).

In general, medications used as antidotes should take into consideration the health and prognosis of the mother; antidotes should be administered to pregnant women if there is a clear indication for use and should not be withheld because of fears of teratogenicity (Bailey 2003).

Pyridoxine (peer i DOKS een)

Brand Names: US Neuro-K-250 T.D. [OTC]; Neuro-K-250 Vitamin B6 [OTC]; Neuro-K-50 [OTC]; Neuro-K-500 [OTC]; Pyri 500 [OTC]

Pharmacologic Category Vitamin, Water Soluble

Use Pyridoxine deficiency: Treatment and prevention of pyridoxine (vitamin B_6) deficiency.

Local Anesthetic/Vasoconstrictor Precautions No information available to require special precautions

Effects on Dental Treatment No significant effects or complications reported

Effects on Bleeding No information available to require special precautions

Adverse Reactions Frequency not defined.

Central nervous system: Ataxia, drowsiness, headache, neuropathy, paresthesia, seizure (following very large IV doses)

Endocrine & metabolic: Acidosis, folate deficiency

Gastrointestinal: Nausea

Hepatic: Increased serum AST

Hypersensitivity: Hypersensitivity reaction

General Dosage Range
IM, IV: *Adults:* 10 to 20 mg/day
Oral:
Infants 1 to 6 months: Adequate intake: 0.1 mg/day
Infants 7 to 12 months: Adequate intake: 0.3 mg/day
Children 1 to 3 years: RDA: 0.5 mg
Children 4 to 8 years: RDA: 0.6 mg
Children and Adolescents 9 to 13 years: RDA: 1 mg
Adolescents 14 to 18 years: RDA: 1.2 mg (females); 1.3 mg (males)
Adults 19 to 50 years: RDA: 1.3 mg
Adults ≥51 years: RDA: 1.5 mg (females); 1.7 mg (males)
Pregnancy: RDA: 1.9 mg
Lactation: RDA: 2 mg

Mechanism of Action Precursor to pyridoxal, which functions in the metabolism of proteins, carbohydrates, and fats; pyridoxal also aids in the release of liver and muscle-stored glycogen and in the synthesis of GABA (within the central nervous system) and heme

Pharmacodynamics/Kinetics
Half-life Elimination Biologic: 15 to 20 days

Pregnancy Risk Factor A

Pregnancy Considerations Water soluble vitamins cross the placenta. Maternal pyridoxine plasma concentrations may decrease as pregnancy progresses and requirements may be increased in pregnant women (IOM 1998). Pyridoxine is used to treat nausea and vomiting of pregnancy (Neibyl 2010). In general, medications used as antidotes should take into consideration the health and prognosis of the mother; antidotes should be administered to pregnant women if there is a clear indication for use and should not be withheld because of fears of teratogenicity (Bailey 2003).

Pyrimethamine (peer i METH a meen)

Brand Names: US Daraprim
Brand Names: Canada Daraprim [DSC]
Pharmacologic Category Antimalarial Agent

Use
Malaria chemoprophylaxis: Chemoprophylaxis of malaria due to susceptible strains of plasmodia.
Limitations of use: Resistance to pyrimethamine is prevalent worldwide; it is not suitable as a prophylactic agent for travelers to most areas.
Malaria treatment: Treatment (in combination with a sulfonamide) of acute malaria due to susceptible strains of plasmodia.
Toxoplasmosis: Treatment of toxoplasmosis (in combination with a sulfonamide).

Local Anesthetic/Vasoconstrictor Precautions No information available to require special precautions

Effects on Dental Treatment Key adverse event(s) related to dental treatment: Xerostomia (normal salivary flow resumes upon discontinuation). Atrophic glossitis has been reported.

Effects on Bleeding No information available to require special precautions

Adverse Reactions
Frequency not defined.
Cardiovascular: Cardiac arrhythmia (large doses)
Dermatologic: Erythema multiforme, skin rash, Stevens-Johnson syndrome, toxic epidermal necrolysis
Gastrointestinal: Anorexia, glossitis (atrophic), vomiting
Hematologic & oncologic: Leukopenia, megaloblastic anemia, pancytopenia, thrombocytopenia
Genitourinary: Hematuria
Hypersensitivity: Anaphylaxis
Respiratory: Eosinophilic pneumonitis

General Dosage Range Dosage varies greatly depending on indication

Mechanism of Action Inhibits parasitic dihydrofolate reductase, resulting in inhibition of vital tetrahydrofolic acid synthesis

Pharmacodynamics/Kinetics
Half-life Elimination 80 to 95 hours (White 1985)
Time to Peak Serum: 2 to 6 hours

Pregnancy Risk Factor C

Pregnancy Considerations Adverse events have been observed in animal reproduction studies. If administered during pregnancy (ie, for toxoplasmosis), supplementation of folate is strongly recommended. Pregnancy should be avoided during therapy.

Prescribing and Access Restrictions
As of June 2015, pyrimethamine is no longer available in retail pharmacies in the United States. It is available through a special pharmacy program (http://www.-daraprimdirect.com/healthcare-providers).
Alternate availability information for a compounded formulation may be found at http://www.hivma.org/Pyrimethamine_Alternatives/.

Quazepam (KWAZ e pam)

Related Information
Dentin Hypersensitivity, Acid Erosion, High Caries Index, Management of Alveolar Osteitis, and Xerostomia *on page 1857*

Brand Names: US Doral
Brand Names: Canada Doral
Pharmacologic Category Benzodiazepine

Use Insomnia: For the treatment of insomnia characterized by difficulty in falling asleep, frequent nocturnal awakenings, and/or early morning

Local Anesthetic/Vasoconstrictor Precautions No information available to require special precautions

Effects on Dental Treatment Key adverse event(s) related to dental treatment: Xerostomia (normal salivary flow resumes upon discontinuation) and abnormal taste perception.

Effects on Bleeding No information available to require special precautions

Adverse Reactions
>10%: Central nervous system: Daytime sedation (12%)
<10%:
Central nervous system: Headache (5%), dizziness (2%), fatigue (2%)
Gastrointestinal: Xerostomia (2%), dyspepsia (1%)
Frequency not defined.
Cardiovascular: Palpitations
Central nervous system: Abnormality in thinking, agitation, amnesia, anxiety, apathy, ataxia, confusion, depression, drug dependence, euphoria, malaise, nervousness, nightmares, paranoia, speech disturbance
Dermatologic: Pruritus, skin rash
Endocrine & metabolic: Decreased libido
Gastrointestinal: Abdominal pain, anorexia, constipation, diarrhea, dysgeusia, nausea
Genitourinary: Impotence, urinary incontinence
Neuromuscular & skeletal: Hyperkinesia, hypokinesia, tremor, weakness
Ophthalmic: Cataract, visual disturbance
<1%, postmarketing, and/or case reports: Anaphylaxis, angioedema, sleep disorder (complex sleep-related behavior, eg, cooking while sleeping, eating food while

sleeping, making phone calls while sleeping, sleep driving)

General Dosage Range Oral:

Adults: 7.5 to 15 mg at bedtime

Elderly: Initial: 7.5 mg at bedtime

Mechanism of Action Binds to stereospecific benzodiazepine receptors on the postsynaptic GABA neuron at several sites within the central nervous system, including the limbic system, reticular formation. Enhancement of the inhibitory effect of GABA on neuronal excitability results by increased neuronal membrane permeability to chloride ions. This shift in chloride ions results in hyperpolarization (a less excitable state) and stabilization. Benzodiazepine receptors and effects appear to be linked to the GABA-A receptors. Benzodiazepines do not bind to GABA-B receptors.

Pharmacodynamics/Kinetics

Half-life Elimination Serum: Quazepam, 2-oxoquazepam: 39 hours; N-desalkyl-2-oxoquazepam: 73 hours

Time to Peak ~2 hours

Pregnancy Risk Factor C

Pregnancy Considerations Although information specific to the use of quazepam has not been located, all benzodiazepines are assumed to cross the placenta. Teratogenic effects have been observed with some benzodiazepines; hypoglycemia and respiratory problems in the neonate may occur following exposure late in pregnancy. Maternal use of quazepam later in pregnancy may also be associated with difficulty feeding, hypothermia, hypotonia, and respiratory depression in neonates. Neonatal withdrawal symptoms may occur within days to weeks after birth and "floppy infant syndrome" (which also includes withdrawal symptoms) has been reported with some benzodiazepines (Bergman, 1992; Iqbal, 2002; Wikner, 2007).

Controlled Substance C-IV

QUEtiapine (kwe TYE a peen)

Related Information

Clinical Risk Related to Drugs Prolonging QT Interval *on page 1772*

Brand Names: US SEROquel; SEROquel XR

Brand Names: Canada Abbott-Quetiapine; ACT-Quetiapine; Apo-Quetiapine; Auro-Quetiapine; Dom-Quetiapine; JAMP-Quetiapine; Mar-Quetiapine; Mylan-Quetiapine; PHL-Quetiapine; PMS-Quetiapine; PRO-Quetiapine; Quetiapine XR; RAN-Quetiapine; Riva-Quetiapine; Sandoz-Quetiapine; Sandoz-Quetiapine XRT; Seroquel; Seroquel XR; Teva-Quetiapine; Teva-Quetiapine XR

Pharmacologic Category Second Generation (Atypical) Antipsychotic

Use

Bipolar disorder: Acute treatment of manic (both immediate release and extended release [ER]) or mixed (ER only) episodes associated with bipolar I disorder, both as monotherapy and as an adjunct to lithium or divalproex; maintenance treatment of bipolar I disorder, as an adjunct to lithium or divalproex; acute treatment of depressive episodes associated with bipolar disorder

Major depressive disorder (ER only): Adjunctive therapy to antidepressants for the treatment of major depressive disorder.

Schizophrenia: Treatment of schizophrenia.

Local Anesthetic/Vasoconstrictor Precautions Quetiapine is one of the drugs confirmed to prolong the QT interval and is accepted as having a risk of causing torsade de pointes. The risk of drug-induced torsade de pointes is extremely low when a single QT interval prolonging drug is prescribed. In terms of epinephrine, it is not known what effect vasoconstrictors in the local anesthetic regimen will have in patients with a known history of congenital prolonged QT interval or in patients taking any medication that prolongs the QT interval. Until more information is obtained, it is suggested that the clinician consult with the physician prior to the use of a vasoconstrictor in suspected patients, and that the vasoconstrictor (epinephrine, mepivacaine and levonordefrin [Carbocaine 2% with Neo-Cobefrin]) be used with caution.

Effects on Dental Treatment Key adverse event(s) related to dental treatment: Xerostomia (normal salivary flow resumes upon discontinuation).

Effects on Bleeding No information available to require special precautions

Adverse Reactions Actual frequency may be dependent upon dose and/or indication. Unless otherwise noted, frequency of adverse effects is reported for adult patients; spectrum and incidence of adverse effects similar in children (with significant exceptions noted).

>10%:

Cardiovascular: Increased diastolic blood pressure (≥10 mm Hg; children and adolescents: 41% to 47%), increased systolic blood pressure (≥20 mm Hg; children and adolescents: 7% to 15%), tachycardia (1% to 11%)

Central nervous system: Drowsiness (16% to 57%), headache (17% to 21%), agitation (6% to 20%), dizziness (7% to 19%), fatigue (3% to 14%), extrapyramidal reaction (1% to 13%)

Endocrine & metabolic: Weight gain (dose related; 3% to 28%), increased serum triglycerides (≥200 mg/dL, 14% to 22%), decreased HDL cholesterol (≤40 mg/dL, 9% to 20%), total cholesterol increased (≥240 mg/dL, 7% to 18%), increased LDL cholesterol (≥160 mg/dL, 4% to 12%), hyperglycemia (≥200 mg/dL post glucose challenge or fasting glucose ≥126 mg/dL, 2% to 3%)

Gastrointestinal: Xerostomia (adults: 9% to 44%; children and adolescents 4% to 10%), increased appetite (2% to 12%), constipation (2% to 11%)

1% to 10%:

Cardiovascular: Orthostatic hypotension (2% to 7%; children and adolescents <1%), palpitations (4%), peripheral edema (4%), increased heart rate (2% to 4%), hypotension (3%), hypertension (adults 2%), hypertension (1% to 2%), syncope (1% to 2%)

Central nervous system: Pain (7%), drug-induced Parkinson disease (2% to ≤6%), lethargy (2% to 5%), dysarthria (2% to 5%), irritability (2% to 5%), akathisia (1% to 5%), hypertonia (4%), twitching (4%), anxiety (2% to 4%), abnormal dreams (2% to 3%), hypersomnia (2% to 3%), paresthesia (2% to 3%), aggressive behavior (children and adolescents 1% to 3%), depression (1% to 3%), dystonic reaction (1% to 3%), abnormality in thinking (2%), ataxia (2%), confusion (2%), decreased mental acuity (2%), disorientation (2%), disturbance in attention (2%), falling (2%), hypoesthesia (2%), lack of concentration (2%), migraine (2%), restless leg syndrome (2%), restlessness (2%), vertigo (2%)

Dermatologic: Skin rash (4%), acne vulgaris (children and adolescents 2% to 3%), diaphoresis (2%), pallor (children and adolescents 1% to 2%)

Endocrine & metabolic: Hyperprolactinemia (4%), increased thirst (children and adolescents 2%), decreased libido (≤2%), hypothyroidism (≤2%)

Gastrointestinal: Nausea (5% to 10%), vomiting (1% to 8%), dyspepsia (dose related; 2% to 7%), abdominal pain (1% to 7%), gastroenteritis (2% to 4%), toothache (2% to 3%), anorexia (1% to 3%), periodontal abscess (adolescents 1% to 3%), decreased appetite (2%), dysphagia (2%), gastroesophageal reflux disease (2%)

Genitourinary: Pollakiuria (2%), urinary tract infection (2%)

Hematologic & oncologic: Neutropenia (≤2%), leukopenia (≥1%)

Hepatic: Increased serum transaminases (1% to 6%)

Hypersensitivity: Seasonal allergy (2%)

Neuromuscular & skeletal: Weakness (1% to 10%), tremor (2% to 8%), back pain (1% to 5%), dyskinesia (3% to 4%), arthralgia (1% to 4%), muscle rigidity (3%), muscle spasm (1% to 3%), stiffness (children and adolescents 3%), limb pain (2%), myalgia (2%), neck pain (2%)

Ophthalmic: Blurred vision (1% to 4%), amblyopia (2% to 3%)

Otic: Otalgia (2%)

Respiratory: Pharyngitis (4% to 6%), nasal congestion (3% to 6%), rhinitis (3% to 4%), epistaxis (adolescents 3%), sinus congestion (2% to 3%), upper respiratory tract infection (2% to 3%), cough (≥1% to 3%), dyspnea (≥1% to 3%), sinus headache (2%), sinusitis (2%), influenza (1% to 2%)

Miscellaneous: Fever (2% to 4%)

<1%, postmarketing, and/or case reports: Abnormal gait, abnormality of accommodation, abnormal T waves on ECG, abnormal vision, acute renal failure, agranulocytosis, alcohol intolerance, amenorrhea, amnesia, anaphylaxis, anemia, angina pectoris, apathy, aphasia, arthritis, asthma, atrial arrhythmia, atrial fibrillation, atrioventricular block, blepharitis, bone pain, bradycardia, bruxism, buccoglossal syndrome, bundle branch block, candidiasis, cardiomyopathy, cataract, catatonic reaction, cerebral ischemia, cerebrovascular accident, chills, choreoathetosis, conjunctivitis, contact dermatitis, cyanosis, cystitis, deafness, deep vein thrombophlebitis, dehydration, delirium, delusions, dental caries, depersonalization, DRESS syndrome, dysmenorrhea, diabetes mellitus, dysuria, ecchymosis, eczema, ejaculatory disorder, emotional lability, enlargement of abdomen, eosinophilia, euphoria, exfoliative dermatitis, eye pain, facial edema, fecal incontinence, first degree atrioventricular block, flattened T wave on ECG, flatulence, flu-like symptoms, galactorrhea, gastritis, gingival hemorrhage, gingivitis, glaucoma, glossitis, glycosuria, gout, gynecomastia, hallucination, hand edema, hematemesis, hemiplegia, hemolysis, hemorrhoids, hiccups, hyperkinesia, hyperlipemia, hypersensitivity reaction, hyperthyroidism, hyperventilation, hypochromic anemia, hypoglycemia, hypokalemia, hyponatremia, hypothermia, impotence, increased creatinine phosphokinase, increased gamma-glutamyl transferase, increased libido, increased serum alkaline phosphatase, increased serum creatinine, increased ST segment on ECG, increased salivation, increased ST segment on ECG, insomnia, intestinal obstruction, inversion T wave on ECG, involuntary body movements, irregular pulse, lactation (females), leg cramps, leukocytosis, leukorrhea, lymphadenopathy, maculopapular rash, malaise, manic reaction, melena, mouth ulceration, myasthenia, myocarditis, myoclonus, neuralgia, neuroleptic malignant syndrome, nightmares, nocturia, orchitis, pancreatitis, paranoid reaction, pathological fracture, pelvic pain, pneumonia, polyuria, priapism, prolonged Q-T interval on ECG, pruritus, psoriasis, psychosis, psychosis, rectal hemorrhage, retrograde amnesia, rhabdomyolysis, seborrhea, seizure, skin discoloration, skin photosensitivity, skin ulcer, SIADH, sleep apnea syndrome (obstructive) (Health Canada 2016, Shirani 2011), somnambulism, Stevens-Johnson syndrome, stomatitis, ST segment changes on ECG, stupor, stuttering, subdural hematoma, suicidal ideation, suicidal tendencies, tardive dyskinesia, taste perversion, thrombocytopenia, thrombophlebitis, tinnitus, tongue edema, toxic epidermal necrolysis, urinary frequency, urinary Incontinence, urinary retention, uterine hemorrhage, vaginal hemorrhage, vaginitis, vasodilatation, vulvovaginal moniliasis, vulvovaginitis, water intoxication, weight loss, widened QRS complex on ECG, xerophthalmia

General Dosage Range Dosage adjustment recommended in patients with hepatic impairment and during concomitant therapy with CYP3A4 inhibitors and CYP3A4 inducers.

Oral:

Immediate release:

Children ≥10 to ≤12 years: Initial: 25 mg twice daily; Usual dosage range: 400 to 600 mg daily in 2 to 3 divided doses; maximum: 600 mg daily

Adolescents ≥13 to ≤17 years: Initial: 25 mg twice daily; Usual dosage range: 400 to 800 mg daily in 2 to 3 divided doses; maximum: 800 mg daily

Adults: Initial: 25 to 50 mg twice daily **or** 50 mg once daily; Usual dosage range: 150 to 800 mg daily in 2 to 3 divided doses

Elderly: Initial: 50 mg daily

Extended release:

Children ≥10 to ≤12 years: Initial: 50 mg once daily; Usual dosage range: 400 to 600 mg once daily; maximum: 600 mg once daily

Adolescents ≥13 to ≤17 years: Initial: 50 mg once daily; Usual dosage range: 400 to 800 mg once daily; maximum: 800 mg once daily

Adults: Initial: 50 to 300 mg once daily; Usual dosage range: 150 to 800 mg daily

Elderly: Initial: 50 mg once daily

Mechanism of Action Quetiapine is a dibenzothiazepine atypical antipsychotic. It has been proposed that this drug's antipsychotic activity is mediated through a combination of dopamine type 2 (D_2) and serotonin type 2 ($5\text{-}HT_2$) antagonism. It is an antagonist at multiple neurotransmitter receptors in the brain: Serotonin $5\text{-}HT_{1A}$ and $5\text{-}HT_2$, dopamine D_1 and D_2, histamine H_1, and adrenergic alpha$_1$- and alpha$_2$-receptors; but appears to have no appreciable affinity at cholinergic muscarinic and benzodiazepine receptors. Norquetiapine, an active metabolite, differs from its parent molecule by exhibiting high affinity for muscarinic M1 receptors.

Antagonism at receptors other than dopamine and $5\text{-}HT_2$ with similar receptor affinities may explain some of the other effects of quetiapine. The drug's antagonism of histamine H_1-receptors may explain the somnolence observed. The drug's antagonism of adrenergic alpha$_1$-receptors may explain the orthostatic hypotension observed.

Pharmacodynamics/Kinetics

Half-life Elimination

Children and Adolescents 12 to 17 years: Quetiapine: 5.3 hours (McConville 2000)

Adults: Mean: Terminal: Quetiapine: ~6 hours; Extended release: ~7 hours
Metabolite: N-desalkyl quetiapine: 12 hours

Time to Peak
Children and Adolescents 12 to 17 years: Immediate release: 0.5-3 hours (McConville 2000)
Adults: Plasma: Immediate release: 1.5 hours; Extended release: 6 hours

Pregnancy Risk Factor C

Pregnancy Considerations Adverse events were observed in animal reproduction studies. Quetiapine crosses the placenta and can be detected in cord blood (Newport 2007). Congenital malformations have not been observed in humans (based on limited data). Antipsychotic use during the third trimester of pregnancy has a risk for abnormal muscle movements (extrapyramidal symptoms [EPS]) and/or withdrawal symptoms in newborns following delivery. Symptoms in the newborn may include agitation, feeding disorder, hypertonia, hypotonia, respiratory distress, somnolence, and tremor; these effects may be self-limiting or require hospitalization. Quetiapine may cause hyperprolactinemia, which may decrease reproductive function in both males and females.

Treatment algorithms have been developed by the ACOG and the APA for the management of depression in women prior to conception and during pregnancy (Yonkers 2009). The ACOG recommends that therapy during pregnancy be individualized; treatment with psychiatric medications during pregnancy should incorporate the clinical expertise of the mental health clinician, obstetrician, primary healthcare provider, and pediatrician. Safety data related to atypical antipsychotics during pregnancy is limited and routine use is not recommended. However, if a woman is inadvertently exposed to an atypical antipsychotic while pregnant, continuing therapy may be preferable to switching to a typical antipsychotic that the fetus has not yet been exposed to; consider risk:benefit (ACOG 2008).

Healthcare providers are encouraged to enroll women 18-45 years of age exposed to quetiapine during pregnancy in the Atypical Antipsychotics Pregnancy Registry (1-866-961-2388 or http://www.womensmentalhealth.org/pregnancyregistry).

Dental Comment See Local Anesthetic/Vasoconstrictor Precautions

Quinagolide (kwin AG o lide)

Brand Names: Canada Norprolac

Pharmacologic Category Hyperprolactinemia Agent, Dopamine (D_2) Agonist

Use Note: Not approved in the US
Hyperprolactinemia: Treatment of hyperprolactinemia (idiopathic or due to a prolactin-secreting pituitary microadenoma or macroadenoma)

Local Anesthetic/Vasoconstrictor Precautions No information available to require special precautions

Effects on Dental Treatment No significant effects or complications reported

Effects on Bleeding No information available to require special precautions

Adverse Reactions
>10%:
Central nervous system: Dizziness, fatigue, headache
Gastrointestinal: Nausea, vomiting

1% to 10%:
Cardiovascular: Edema (2%), flushing (1%), hypotension (1%), palpitations (1%), syncope (1%)
Central nervous system: Sedation (3%), insomnia (2%), emotional lability (1%), lack of concentration (1%), malaise (1%)
Gastrointestinal: Constipation (3%), abdominal pain (≤3%), abdominal distress (≤3%), anorexia (2%), dyspepsia (2%), diarrhea (1%)
Endocrine & metabolic: Weight gain (1%)
Genitourinary: Mastalgia (1%)
Neuromuscular & skeletal: Weakness (3%), limb pain (1%)
Respiratory: Nasal congestion (2%)
<1%, postmarketing, and/or case reports: Acute psychosis, decreased hematocrit, decreased hemoglobin, drowsiness, increased creatine phosphokinase, increased serum bilirubin, increased serum potassium, increased serum transaminases, increased serum triglycerides, neutropenia

General Dosage Range Oral: *Adults:* Initial: 0.025 mg once daily for 3 days followed by 0.05 mg once daily for 3 days; Maintenance (begin day 7): Usual range 0.075 to 0.15 mg/day (maximum: 0.9 mg/day)

Mechanism of Action Selective dopamine D_2 receptor agonist that exerts a direct inhibitory effect on cells (lactotrophs) in the anterior pituitary gland which synthesize and secrete prolactin; not an ergot alkaloid

Pharmacodynamics/Kinetics
Onset of Action 2 hours; maximum effect: 4 to 6 hours
Duration of Action >24 hours
Half-life Elimination 11.5 hours; steady state: 17 hours
Time to Peak 30 to 60 minutes

Pregnancy Considerations Adverse events have not been observed in animal reproduction studies. Fertility may be restored with treatment. Discontinue use with confirmed pregnancy unless medically necessary to continue. No increase in the incidence of abortion has been seen upon discontinuation of the drug during pregnancy. The reinstitution of therapy may be necessary in patients who display symptoms of tumor enlargement (headaches, visual field changes).

Product Availability Not available in the US

Quinapril (KWIN a pril)

Related Information
Cardiovascular Diseases *on page 1752*

Brand Names: US Accupril

Brand Names: Canada Accupril; Apo-Quinapril; GD-Quinapril; PMS-Quinapril

Pharmacologic Category Angiotensin-Converting Enzyme (ACE) Inhibitor; Antihypertensive

Use
Heart failure: Adjunctive treatment of heart failure (HF)
Hypertension: Treatment of hypertension

Guideline recommendations:
Heart failure: The ACCF/AHA 2013 heart failure guidelines recommend the use of ACE inhibitors, along with other guideline directed medical therapies, to prevent HF in patients with a reduced ejection fraction who have a history of MI (stage B HF), to prevent HF in any patient with a reduced ejection fraction (stage B HF), or to treat those with HF and reduced ejection fraction (stage C HFrEF) (ACCF/AHA [Yancy, 2013]).

Hypertension: The 2014 guideline for the management of high blood pressure in adults (Eighth Joint National Committee [JNC 8]) recommends initiation of pharmacologic treatment to lower blood pressure for the following patients:

- Patients ≥60 years of age with systolic blood pressure (SBP) ≥150 mm Hg or diastolic blood pressure (DBP) ≥ 90 mm Hg. Goal of therapy is SBP <150 mm Hg and DBP <90 mm Hg.
- Patients <60 years of age with SBP ≥140 mm Hg or DBP is ≥90 mm Hg. Goal of therapy is SBP <140 mm Hg and DBP <90 mm Hg.
- Patients ≥18 years of age with diabetes and SBP ≥140 mm Hg or DBP ≥90 mm Hg. Goal of therapy is SBP <140 mm Hg and DBP <90 mm Hg.
- Patients ≥18 years of age with chronic kidney disease (CKD) and SBP ≥140 mm Hg or DBP ≥90 mm Hg. Goal of therapy is SBP <140 mm Hg and DBP <90 mm Hg.

Chronic kidney disease (CKD) and hypertension: Regardless of race or diabetes status, the use of an ACE inhibitor (ACEI) or angiotensin receptor blocker (ARB) as initial therapy is recommended to improve kidney outcomes. In the general non-black population (without CKD) including those with diabetes, initial antihypertensive treatment should consist of a thiazide-type diuretic, calcium channel blocker, ACEI, or ARB. In the general black population (without CKD) including those with diabetes, initial antihypertensive treatment should consist of a thiazide-type diuretic or a calcium channel blocker **instead of** an ACEI or ARB.

Coronary artery disease (CAD) and hypertension: The American Heart Association, American College of Cardiology and American Society of Hypertension (AHA/ACC/ASH) 2015 scientific statement for the treatment of hypertension in patients with CAD recommends the use of an ACE inhibitor (or an ARB) as part of a regimen in patients with hypertension and chronic stable angina if there is prior MI, LV systolic dysfunction, diabetes mellitus, or CKD. A BP target of <140/90 mm Hg is reasonable for the secondary prevention of cardiovascular events. A lower target BP (<130/80 mm Hg) may be appropriate in some individuals with CAD, previous MI, stroke or transient ischemic attack, or CAD risk equivalents (AHA/ACC/ASH [Rosendorff 2015]).

Local Anesthetic/Vasoconstrictor Precautions No information available to require special precautions

Effects on Dental Treatment Key adverse event(s) related to dental treatment: Patients may experience orthostatic hypotension as they stand up after treatment; especially if lying in dental chair for extended periods of time. Use caution with sudden changes in position during and after dental treatment.

An angiotensin-converting enzyme (ACE) Inhibitor cough is a dry, hacking, nonproductive cough that can potentially interfere with longer dental procedures if patient has this side effect.

Effects on Bleeding No information available to require special precautions

Adverse Reactions Frequency ranges include data from hypertension and heart failure trials. Higher rates of adverse reactions have generally been noted in patients with CHF. However, the frequency of adverse effects associated with placebo is also increased in this population.

>10%: Respiratory: Cough (≤13%)

1% to 10%:

Cardiovascular: Hypotension (3%; first dose: ≤3%), chest pain (2%)

Central nervous system: Dizziness (4% to 8%), headache (2% to 6%), fatigue (3%)

Dermatologic: Skin rash (1%)

Endocrine & metabolic: Hyperkalemia (2%)

Gastrointestinal: Nausea (≤2%), vomiting (≤2%), diarrhea (2%)

Neuromuscular & skeletal: Myalgia (2% to 5%), back pain (1%)

Renal: Increased blood urea nitrogen (≤2%; transient elevations may occur with a higher frequency), increased serum creatinine (≤2%; transient elevations may occur with a higher frequency), renal insufficiency (worsening; in patients with bilateral renal artery stenosis or hypovolemia)

Respiratory: Dyspnea (2%), upper respiratory complaint

<1%, postmarketing, and/or case reports: Abnormal hepatic function tests, acute renal failure, agranulocytosis, alopecia, amblyopia, anaphylactoid reaction, angina pectoris, angioedema, arthralgia, back pain, cardiac arrhythmia, cardiac failure, cerebrovascular accident, constipation, depression, diaphoresis, drowsiness, edema, eosinophilic pneumonitis, exfoliative dermatitis, gastrointestinal hemorrhage, hemolytic anemia, hepatitis, hypertensive crisis, impotence, insomnia, malaise, myocardial infarction, nervousness, orthostatic hypotension, palpitations, pancreatitis, paresthesia, pemphigus, pharyngitis, polymyositis (dermatopolymyositis), pruritus, shock, skin photosensitivity, syncope, tachycardia, thrombocytopenia, vasodilatation, vertigo, viral infection, visual hallucination (Doane 2013), xerostomia

General Dosage Range Dosage adjustment recommended in patients with renal impairment

Oral:

Adults: Initial: 5 to 20 mg daily in 1 to 2 divided doses; Maintenance: 10 to 80 mg daily in 1 to 2 divided doses

Elderly: Initial: 10 mg daily

Mechanism of Action Competitive inhibitor of angiotensin-converting enzyme (ACE); prevents conversion of angiotensin I to angiotensin II, a potent vasoconstrictor; results in lower levels of angiotensin II which causes an increase in plasma renin activity and a reduction in aldosterone secretion; a CNS mechanism may also be involved in hypotensive effect as angiotensin II increases adrenergic outflow from CNS; vasoactive kallikreins may be decreased in conversion to active hormones by ACE inhibitors, thus reducing blood pressure

Pharmacodynamics/Kinetics

Onset of Action 1 hour; Peak effect: Antihypertensive: 2 to 4 hours postdose

Duration of Action 24 hours (chronic dosing)

Half-life Elimination

Infants and Children <7 years: Quinaprilat: 2.3 hours (Blumer 2003)

Adults: Quinapril: 0.8 hours; Quinaprilat: 3 hours; increases as CrCl decreases

Time to Peak

Infants and Children <7 years: 1.7 hours (range: 1 to 4 hours) (Blumer 2003)

Adults: Serum: Quinapril: 1 hour; Quinaprilat: ~2 hours

Pregnancy Risk Factor D

Pregnancy Considerations **[US Boxed Warning]: Drugs that act on the renin-angiotensin system can cause injury and death to the developing fetus.**

Discontinue as soon as possible once pregnancy is detected. Quinapril crosses the placenta. Drugs that act on the renin-angiotensin system are associated with oligohydramnios. Oligohydramnios, due to decreased fetal renal function, may lead to fetal lung hypoplasia and skeletal malformations. The use of these drugs in pregnancy is also associated with anuria, hypotension, renal failure, skull hypoplasia, and death in the fetus/neonate. Teratogenic effects may occur following maternal use of an ACE inhibitor during the first trimester, although this finding may be confounded by maternal disease. Because adverse fetal events are well documented with exposure later in pregnancy, ACE inhibitor use in pregnant women is not recommended (Seely 2014; Weber 2014). Infants exposed to an ACE inhibitor in utero should be monitored for hyperkalemia, hypotension, and oliguria. Oligohydramnios may not appear until after irreversible fetal injury has occurred. Exchange transfusions or dialysis may be required to reverse hypotension or improve renal function, although data related to the effectiveness in neonates is limited.

Chronic maternal hypertension itself is also associated with adverse events in the fetus/infant and mother. ACE inhibitors are not recommended for the treatment of uncomplicated hypertension in pregnancy (ACOG 2013) and they are specifically contraindicated for the treatment of hypertension and chronic heart failure during pregnancy by some guidelines (Regitz-Zagrosek 2011). In addition, ACE inhibitors should generally be avoided in women of reproductive age (ACOG 2013). If treatment for hypertension or chronic heart failure in pregnancy is needed, other agents should be used (ACOG 2013; Regitz-Zagrosek 2011).

QuiNIDine (KWIN i deen)

Related Information

Clinical Risk Related to Drugs Prolonging QT Interval *on page 1772*

Brand Names: Canada Apo-Quinidine; BioQuin Durules; Novo-Quinidin; Quinate

Pharmacologic Category Antiarrhythmic Agent, Class Ia; Antimalarial Agent

Use

Quinidine gluconate and sulfate salts: Conversion and prevention of relapse into atrial fibrillation and/or flutter; suppression of ventricular arrhythmias. **Note:** Due to proarrhythmic effects, use should be reserved for life-threatening arrhythmias. Moreover, the use of quinidine has largely been replaced by more effective/safer antiarrhythmic agents and/or nonpharmacologic therapies (eg, radiofrequency ablation).

Quinidine gluconate (IV formulation): Conversion of atrial fibrillation/flutter and ventricular tachycardia. **Note:** The use of IV quinidine gluconate for these indications has been replaced by more effective/safer antiarrhythmic agents (eg, amiodarone and procainamide).

Quinidine gluconate (IV formulation) and quinidine sulfate: Treatment of malaria (*Plasmodium falciparum*)

Local Anesthetic/Vasoconstrictor Precautions Quinidine is one of the drugs confirmed to prolong the QT interval and is accepted as having a risk of causing torsade de pointes. The risk of drug-induced torsade de pointes is extremely low when a single QT interval prolonging drug is prescribed. In terms of epinephrine, it is not known what effect vasoconstrictors in the local anesthetic regimen will have in patients with a known history of congenital prolonged QT interval or in patients taking any medication that prolongs the QT interval. Until more information is obtained, it is suggested that the clinician consult with the physician prior to the use of a vasoconstrictor in suspected patients, and that the vasoconstrictor (epinephrine, mepivacaine and levonordefrin [Carbocaine® 2% with Neo-Cobefrin®]) be used with caution.

Effects on Dental Treatment When taken over a long period of time, the anticholinergic side effects from quinidine can cause a reduction of saliva production or secretion contributing to discomfort and dental disease (ie, caries, oral candidiasis, and periodontal disease).

Effects on Bleeding Quinidine has been shown to induce thrombocytopenia through the generation of both drug-dependent and drug-independent antibodies. In general, quinidine-induced thrombocytopenia is reversible following 9 days of discontinuation.

Adverse Reactions

Frequency not always defined.

Cardiovascular: Palpitations (7%), angina pectoris (6%), cardiac arrhythmia (3%; new or worsened; proarrhythmic effect), ECG abnormality (3%), cerebral ischemia (2%), prolonged Q-T interval on ECG (modest prolongation is common; however, excessive prolongation is rare and indicates toxicity), syncope

Central nervous system: Dizziness (3% to 15%), fatigue (7%), headache (3% to 7%), disturbed sleep (3%), nervousness (2%), ataxia (1%)

Dermatologic: Skin rash (5% to 6%)

Gastrointestinal: Diarrhea (24% to 35%), gastrointestinal distress (upper; 22%), nausea and vomiting (3%), esophagitis

Neuromuscular & skeletal: Weakness (2% to 5%), tremor (2%)

Ophthalmic: Visual disturbance (3%)

Miscellaneous: Fever (6%)

<1%, postmarketing, and/or case reports: Acute psychosis, agranulocytosis, angioedema, arthralgia, bradycardia (exacerbated, in sick sinus syndrome), bronchospasm, cerebrovascular insufficiency (possibly resulting in ataxia, apprehension, and seizure), cinchonism (may include tinnitus, high-frequency hearing loss, deafness, vertigo, blurred vision, diplopia, photophobia, headache, confusion, and delirium; usually associated with chronic toxicity but may occur after brief exposure to a moderate dose), depression, dyschromia, exfoliative dermatitis, flushing, granulomatous hepatitis, hemolytic anemia, hepatotoxicity (rare), hypotension, immune thrombocytopenia, increased creatine phosphokinase, lupus-like syndrome, lymphadenopathy, myalgia, mydriasis, nocturnal amblyopia, optic neuritis, pneumonitis, pruritus, psoriasiform eruption, scotoma, skin photosensitivity, Sjogren's syndrome, thrombocytopenia, torsades de pointes, urticaria, uveitis, vasculitis, ventricular fibrillation, ventricular tachycardia (including paradoxical, during atrial fibrillation/flutter), visual field loss, vision color changes

General Dosage Range Dosages expressed in terms of the salt. Dosage adjustment recommended in patients with renal impairment.

IV: Quinidine gluconate: *Children and Adults:* 10 mg/kg bolus followed by 0.02 mg/kg/minute **or** 24 mg/kg bolus followed by 12 mg/kg every 8 hours

Oral:

Immediate release: Quinidine sulfate: *Adults:* Initial: 200 to 400 mg/dose every 6 hours

Extended release:

Quinidine gluconate: *Adults:* Initial: 324 mg every 8 to 12 hours

Quinidine sulfate: *Adults:* Initial: 300 mg every 8 to 12 hours

Mechanism of Action Class Ia antiarrhythmic agent; depresses phase O of the action potential; decreases myocardial excitability and conduction velocity, and myocardial contractility by decreasing sodium influx during depolarization and potassium efflux in repolarization; also reduces calcium transport across cell membrane

Pharmacodynamics/Kinetics

Half-life Elimination Plasma: Children: 2.5 to 6.7 hours; Adults: 6 to 8 hours; prolonged with elderly, cirrhosis, and congestive heart failure

Time to Peak Serum: Oral: Sulfate: Immediate release: 2 hours; Extended release: 6 hours; Gluconate: Extended release: 3 to 5 hours

Pregnancy Risk Factor C

Pregnancy Considerations Animal reproduction studies have not been conducted. Quinidine crosses the placenta and can be detected in the amniotic fluid, cord blood, and neonatal serum. Quinidine is indicated for use in the treatment of severe malaria infection in pregnant women (CDC, 2011; Smereck, 2011) and has also been used to treat arrhythmias in pregnancy when other agents are ineffective (European Society of Cardiology, 2003).

Dental Comment See Local Anesthetic/Vasoconstrictor Precautions

QuiNINE (KWYE nine)

Related Information

Clinical Risk Related to Drugs Prolonging QT Interval *on page 1772*

Brand Names: US Qualaquin

Brand Names: Canada Apo-Quinine; Novo-Quinine; Quinine-Odan

Pharmacologic Category Antimalarial Agent

Use In conjunction with other antimalarial agents, treatment of uncomplicated chloroquine-resistant *P. falciparum* malaria

Local Anesthetic/Vasoconstrictor Precautions Quinine is one of the drugs confirmed to prolong the QT interval and is accepted as having a risk of causing torsade de pointes. The risk of drug-induced torsade de pointes is extremely low when a single QT interval prolonging drug is prescribed. In terms of epinephrine, it is not known what effect vasoconstrictors in the local anesthetic regimen will have in patients with a known history of congenital prolonged QT interval or in patients taking any medication that prolongs the QT interval. Until more information is obtained, it is suggested that the clinician consult with the physician prior to the use of a vasoconstrictor in suspected patients, and that the vasoconstrictor (epinephrine, mepivacaine and levonordefrin [Carbocaine® 2% with Neo-Cobefrin®]) be used with caution.

Effects on Dental Treatment No significant effects or complications reported

Effects on Bleeding Quinine has been shown to induce platelet-reactive monoclonal antibodies responsible for immune thrombocytopenia, leading to prolonged bleeding times. This drug-dependent antibody generation leads to the destruction of endogenous platelets. Quinine-induced thrombocytopenia can be treated through the discontinuation of the drug. Severe cases require a platelet transfusion.

Adverse Reactions

Frequency not defined.

Cardiovascular: Appearance of U waves on ECB, atrial fibrillation, atrioventricular block, bradycardia, cardiac arrhythmia, chest pain, flushing, hypersensitivity angiitis, hypotension, nodal rhythm disorder (nodal escape beats), orthostatic hypotension, palpitations, prolonged Q-T interval on ECG, syncope, tachycardia, torsades de pointes, unifocal premature ventricular contractions, vasodilatation, ventricular fibrillation, ventricular tachycardia

Central nervous system: Altered mental status, aphasia, ataxia, chills, coma, confusion, disorientation, dizziness, dystonic reaction, headache, restlessness, seizure, vertigo

Dermatologic: Allergic contact dermatitis, bullous dermatitis, diaphoresis, exfoliative dermatitis, erythema multiforme, pruritus, skin necrosis (acral), skin photosensitivity, skin rash (papular rash, scarlatiniform rash, urticaria), Stevens-Johnson syndrome, toxic epidermal necrolysis

Endocrine & metabolic: Hypoglycemia

Gastrointestinal: Abdominal pain, anorexia, diarrhea, esophagitis, gastric irritation, nausea, vomiting

Genitourinary: Hemoglobinuria

Hematologic & oncologic: Agranulocytosis, aplastic anemia, blood coagulation disorder, bruise, disseminated intravascular coagulation, hemolysis (black water fever), hemolytic anemia, hemolytic-uremic syndrome, hemorrhage, hypoprothrombinemia, immune thrombocytopenia (ITP), leukopenia, neutropenia, pancytopenia, petechia, thrombocytopenia, thrombotic thrombocytopenic purpura

Hepatic: Abnormal hepatic function tests, granulomatous hepatitis, hepatitis, jaundice

Hypersensitivity: Hypersensitivity reaction

Immunologic: Antibody development (lupus anticoagulant syndrome)

Neuromuscular & skeletal: Lupus-like syndrome, myalgia, tremor, weakness

Ophthalmic: Blindness, blurred vision (with or without scotomata), diplopia, mydriasis, nocturnal amblyopia, optic neuritis, photophobia, vision color changes, vision loss (sudden), visual field loss

Otic: Auditory impairment, deafness, tinnitus

Renal: Acute interstitial nephritis, renal failure, renal insufficiency

Respiratory: Asthma, dyspnea, pulmonary edema

Miscellaneous: Fever

General Dosage Range Dosage adjustment recommended in patients with renal impairment

Oral:

Children: 30 mg/kg/day divided every 8 hours

Adults: 648 mg every 8 hours

Mechanism of Action Depresses oxygen uptake and carbohydrate metabolism; intercalates into DNA, disrupting the parasite's replication and transcription; cardiovascular effects similar to quinidine

Pharmacodynamics/Kinetics

Half-life Elimination

Children: ~3 hours in healthy subjects; ~12 hours with malaria

Healthy adults: 10 to 13 hours

Healthy elderly subjects: 18 hours

Time to Peak

Children: Serum: 2 hours in healthy subjects; 4 hours with malaria

Adults: Serum: 2 to 4 hours in healthy subjects; 1 to 11 hours with malaria

Pregnancy Risk Factor C

Pregnancy Considerations Teratogenic effects have been reported in some animal studies. Quinine crosses the human placenta. Cord plasma to maternal plasma quinine ratios have been reported as 0.18-0.46 and should not be considered therapeutic to the infant. Teratogenic effects, optic nerve hypoplasia, and deafness have been reported in the infant following maternal use of very high doses; however, therapeutic doses used for malaria are generally considered safe. Quinine may also cause significant hypoglycemia when used during pregnancy. Malaria infection in pregnant women may be more severe than in nonpregnant women. Because *P. falciparum* malaria can cause maternal death and fetal loss, pregnant women traveling to malaria-endemic areas must use personal protection against mosquito bites. Quinine may be used for the treatment of malaria in pregnant women; consult current CDC guidelines. Pregnant women should be advised not to travel to areas of *P. falciparum* resistance to chloroquine.

Dental Comment See Local Anesthetic/Vasoconstrictor Precautions

Quinupristin and Dalfopristin

(kwi NYOO pris tin & dal FOE pris tin)

Brand Names: US Synercid

Brand Names: Canada Synercid

Pharmacologic Category Antibiotic, Streptogramin

Use Skin and skin structure infections, complicated: Treatment of complicated skin and skin structure infections caused by methicillin-susceptible *Staphylococcus aureus* or *Streptococcus pyogenes*

Local Anesthetic/Vasoconstrictor Precautions No information available to require special precautions

Effects on Dental Treatment No significant effects or complications reported

Effects on Bleeding No information available to require special precautions

Adverse Reactions

>10%:

Hepatic: Hyperbilirubinemia (3% to 35%)

Local: Local pain (40% to 44%), local inflammation (at infusion site: 38% to 42%), localized edema (17% to 18%), infusion site reaction (12% to 13%)

Neuromuscular & skeletal: Arthralgia (≤47%), myalgia (≤47%)

1% to 10%:

Cardiovascular: Thrombophlebitis (2%)

Central nervous system: Pain (2% to 3%), headache (2%)

Dermatologic: Skin rash (3%), pruritus (2%)

Endocrine & metabolic: Increased lactate dehydrogenase (3%), increased gamma-glutamyl transferase (2%), hyperglycemia (1%)

Gastrointestinal: Nausea (3% to 5%), vomiting (3% to 4%), diarrhea (3%)

Hematologic & oncologic: Anemia (3%)

Neuromuscular & skeletal: Increased creatine phosphokinase (2%)

<1%, postmarketing, and/or case reports: Abdominal pain, anaphylactoid reaction, anxiety, apnea, blood coagulation disorder, brain disease, cardiac arrhythmia, chest pain, confusion, constipation, dermal ulcer, diaphoresis, dizziness, dysautonomia, dyspepsia, dyspnea, fever, gastrointestinal hemorrhage, gout, hematuria, hemolysis, hemolytic anemia, hepatitis, hyperkalemia, hypersensitivity reaction, hypertonia, hypoglycemia, hyponatremia, hypotension, hypoventilation, hypovolemia, increased blood urea nitrogen, increased serum creatinine, increased serum transaminases, infection, insomnia, leg cramps, maculopapular rash, mesenteric artery occlusion, myasthenia, neck stiffness, neuropathy, oral candidiasis, ostealgia, palpitations, pancreatitis, pancytopenia, paraplegia, paresthesia, pericarditis, peripheral edema, phlebitis, pleural effusion, pseudomembranous colitis, respiratory distress, seizure, shock, stomatitis, syncope, thrombocytopenia, tremor, urticaria, vaginitis, vasodilatation

General Dosage Range IV: *Children ≥12 years, Adolescents, and Adults:* 7.5 mg/kg every 12 hours

Mechanism of Action Quinupristin/dalfopristin inhibits bacterial protein synthesis by binding to different sites on the 50S bacterial ribosomal subunit thereby inhibiting protein synthesis

Pharmacodynamics/Kinetics

Half-life Elimination Quinupristin: 0.85 hour; Dalfopristin: 0.7 hour (mean elimination half-lives, including metabolites: 3 and 1 hours, respectively)

Pregnancy Considerations Adverse events have not been observed in animal reproduction studies.

RABEprazole (ra BEP ra zole)

Related Information

Gastrointestinal Disorders *on page 1775*

Brand Names: US Aciphex; AcipHex Sprinkle

Brand Names: Canada Apo-Rabeprazole; Pariet; Pat-Rabeprazole; PMS-Rabeprazole EC; PRO-Rabeprazole; Rabeprazole EC; RAN-Rabeprazole; Riva-Rabeprazole EC; Sandoz-Rabeprazole; Teva-Rabeprazole EC

Pharmacologic Category Proton Pump Inhibitor; Substituted Benzimidazole

Use

Duodenal ulcers (tablets only): Short-term (4 weeks or fewer) treatment in the healing and symptomatic relief of duodenal ulcers in adults.

Gastroesophageal reflux disease:

Erosive or ulcerative (tablets only): Short-term (4 to 8 weeks) treatment in the healing and symptomatic relief of erosive or ulcerative gastroesophageal reflux disease (GERD) in adults; for maintaining healing and reduction in relapse rates of heartburn symptoms in adults with erosive or ulcerative GERD.

Symptomatic: Treatment of symptomatic GERD for up to 4 weeks in adults (tablets only), up to 8 weeks in children ≥12 years and adolescents (tablets only), and up to 12 weeks in children 1 to 11 years of age (capsules only).

***Helicobacter pylori* eradication (tablets only):** In combination with amoxicillin and clarithromycin as a 3-drug regimen for the treatment of adults with *H. pylori* infection and duodenal ulcer disease (active or history of within the past 5 years) to eradicate *H. pylori*.

Pathological hypersecretory conditions (tablets only): Long-term treatment of pathological hypersecretory conditions, including Zollinger-Ellison syndrome in adults.

Canadian labeling: Additional uses (not in US labeling): Treatment of nonerosive reflux disease (NERD); treatment of gastric ulcers

Local Anesthetic/Vasoconstrictor Precautions No information available to require special precautions

Effects on Dental Treatment No significant effects or complications reported

Effects on Bleeding No information available to require special precautions

Adverse Reactions As reported in adults unless otherwise noted.

1% to 10%:

Cardiovascular: Peripheral edema (≥2%)

Central nervous system: Headache (≥2%; children & adolescents: 5% to 10%), pain (3%), dizziness (≥2%)

Gastrointestinal: Diarrhea (2%; children and adolescents: 5% to 21%), nausea (children & adolescents: 2% to 9%), abdominal pain (children: 16%; adolescents: 4%; adults: <2%), vomiting (children: 10% to 14%; adolescents: 4%), flatulence (3%), xerostomia (≥2%), constipation (2%)

Hepatic: Hepatic encephalopathy (≥2%), hepatitis (≥2%), increased liver enzymes (≥2%)

Infection: Increased susceptibility to infection (2%)

Neuromuscular & skeletal: Arthralgia (≥2%), myalgia (≥2%)

Respiratory: Pharyngitis (3%)

<1%, postmarketing, and/or case reports: Agitation, agranulocytosis, albuminuria, alopecia, amblyopia, anaphylaxis, anemia, angioedema, bone fracture, bullous rash, chest pain, cholecystitis, cholelithiasis, chronic renal disease (Lazarus 2016), *Clostridium difficile* associated diarrhea (CDAD), colitis, coma, delirium, disorientation, drowsiness, dysgeusia, dyspnea, erythema multiforme, facial swelling, fever, gynecomastia, hematuria, hemolytic anemia, hepatotoxicity (idiosyncratic) (Chalasani 2014), hyperammonemia, hypersensitivity reaction, hypertension, hypokalemia, hypomagnesemia, hyponatremia, hypotension, increased thyroid stimulating hormone level, interstitial nephritis, jaundice, leukocytosis, leukopenia, melena, migraine, neutropenia, osteoporosis, palpitation, pancreatitis, pancytopenia, pathological fracture due to osteoporosis, pneumonia, pruritus, rhabdomyolysis, sinus bradycardia, Stevens-Johnson syndrome, thrombocytopenia, toxic epidermal necrolysis, weakness

General Dosage Range Oral:

Children 1 to 11 years: 5 to 10 mg once daily

Children ≥12 years and Adolescents: 20 mg once daily

Adults: 10 to 20 mg once to twice daily **or** 60 mg once daily

Mechanism of Action Potent proton pump inhibitor; suppresses gastric acid secretion by inhibiting the parietal cell H+/K+ ATP pump

Pharmacodynamics/Kinetics

Onset of Action Within 1 hour

Duration of Action 24 hours

Half-life Elimination Dose dependent:

Adolescents: ~0.55 to 1 hour (James 2007)

Adults: 1 to 2 hours; two- to threefold higher in patients with mild-to-moderate hepatic impairment

Time to Peak Plasma:

Adolescents: Tablet: 3.3 to 4.1 hours (James 2007)

Adults: Tablet: 2 to 5 hours; Capsule: 1 to 6.5 hours

Pregnancy Considerations Available studies have not shown an increased risk of major birth defects following maternal use of proton pump inhibitors during pregnancy; however, information specific to rabeprazole is limited (Pasternak 2010); most information available for omeprazole. When treating GERD in pregnancy, PPIs may be used when clinically indicated (Katz 2013).

Rabies Immune Globulin (Human)

(RAY beez i MYUN GLOB yoo lin, HYU man)

Brand Names: US HyperRAB S/D; Imogam Rabies-HT

Brand Names: Canada HyperRAB S/D; Imogam Rabies Pasteurized

Pharmacologic Category Blood Product Derivative; Immune Globulin

Use

Rabies exposure: Part of postexposure prophylaxis of persons with suspected rabies exposure. Provides passive immunity until active immunity with rabies vaccine is established. Not for use in persons with a history of vaccination (preexposure or postexposure prophylaxis) and documentation of antibody response. Each exposure to possible rabies infection should be individually evaluated.

Factors to consider include: species of biting animal, circumstances of biting incident (provoked vs unprovoked bite), type of exposure to rabies infection (bite vs nonbite), vaccination status of biting animal, presence of rabies in the region. See product information for additional details.

Local Anesthetic/Vasoconstrictor Precautions No information available to require special precautions

Effects on Dental Treatment No significant effects or complications reported

Effects on Bleeding No information available to require special precautions

Adverse Reactions Frequency not defined.

Central nervous system: Headache, malaise

Dermatologic: Skin rash

Genitourinary: Nephrotic syndrome

Hypersensitivity: Anaphylaxis, angioedema

Local: Local soreness/soreness at injection site, pain at injection site, tenderness at injection site

Neuromuscular & skeletal: Stiffness (at injection site)

Miscellaneous: Fever (mild)

General Dosage Range Local wound infiltration/IM: *Infants, Children, Adolescents, and Adults:* 20 units/kg in a single dose

Mechanism of Action Rabies immune globulin is a solution of globulins dried from the plasma or serum of selected adult human donors who have been immunized with rabies vaccine and have developed high titers of rabies antibody. It generally contains 10% to 18% of protein of which not less than 80% is monomeric immunoglobulin G.

Pregnancy Risk Factor C

Pregnancy Considerations Animal reproduction studies have not been conducted. Pregnancy is not a contraindication to postexposure prophylaxis. Preexposure prophylaxis may be indicated during pregnancy if the risk for exposure to rabies is significant.

Rabies Vaccine (RAY beez vak SEEN)

Brand Names: US Imovax Rabies; RabAvert

Brand Names: Canada Imovax Rabies; RabAvert

Pharmacologic Category Vaccine; Vaccine, Inactivated (Viral)

Use Rabies disease prevention: Preexposure and postexposure vaccination against rabies

Factors to consider include: species of biting animal, circumstances of biting incident (provoked vs unprovoked bite), type of exposure to rabies infection (bite vs nonbite), vaccination status of biting animal, and presence of rabies in the region. Refer to local/state health department and CDC for more information.

The Advisory Committee on Immunization Practices (ACIP) recommends a primary course of prophylactic immunization (preexposure vaccination) for the following (ACIP [Manning 2008]):

- Persons with continuous risk of infection, including rabies research laboratory and biologics production workers
- Persons with frequent risk of infection, including rabies diagnostic laboratory workers, cavers, veterinarians and their staff, and animal control and wildlife workers in areas where rabies is enzootic; persons who frequently handle bats
- Persons with infrequent risk of infection, including veterinarians and animal control staff working with terrestrial animals in areas where rabies infection is rare, veterinary students, and travelers visiting areas where rabies is enzootic and immediate access to medical care and biologicals is limited

The ACIP recommends the use of postexposure vaccination for a particular person be assessed by the severity and likelihood versus the actual risk of acquiring rabies. Consideration should include the type of exposure, epidemiology of rabies in the area, species of the animal, circumstances of the incident, and the availability of the exposing animal for observation or rabies testing. Postexposure vaccination is used in both previously vaccinated and previously unvaccinated individuals (ACIP [Manning 2008]; ACIP [Rupprecht 2010]).

Local Anesthetic/Vasoconstrictor Precautions No information available to require special precautions

Effects on Dental Treatment No significant effects or complications reported

Effects on Bleeding No information available to require special precautions

Adverse Reactions

>10%:

Central nervous system: Dizziness, headache, malaise
Dermatologic: Injection site pruritus
Gastrointestinal: Abdominal pain, nausea
Hematologic & oncologic: Lymphadenopathy
Local: Erythema at injection site, pain at injection site, swelling at injection site
Neuromuscular & skeletal: Myalgia

Frequency not defined:

Cardiovascular: Cardiovascular toxicity, edema, palpitations, swelling of injected limb (extensive)
Central nervous system: Chills, encephalitis, fatigue, Guillain-Barre syndrome, meningitis, neuropathy, paralysis (may be transient; includes neuroparalysis), paresthesia (transient), retrobulbar neuritis, seizure, vertigo
Dermatologic: Pruritus, urticaria (including urticaria pigmentosa)
Endocrine & metabolic: Hot flash
Gastrointestinal: Diarrhea, vomiting
Hematologic & oncologic: Adenopathy
Hypersensitivity: Anaphylaxis, hypersensitivity reaction, serum sickness
Local: Hematoma at injection site
Neuromuscular & skeletal: Arthralgia, arthritis (one joint), limb pain, multiple sclerosis, myelitis, weakness
Ophthalmic: Visual disturbance
Respiratory: Bronchospasm, dyspnea, wheezing
Miscellaneous: Fever >38°C (100°F)

General Dosage Range IM: *All Ages:* 1 mL

Mechanism of Action Rabies vaccine is an inactivated virus vaccine which promotes immunity by inducing an active immune response. The production of specific antibodies requires about 7-10 days to develop. Rabies immune globulin or antirabies serum, equine (ARS) is given in conjunction with rabies vaccine to provide immune protection until an antibody response can occur.

Pharmacodynamics/Kinetics

Onset of Action IM: Rabies antibody: ~7 to 10 days; Peak effect: ~30 to 60 days

Duration of Action ≥1 year

Pregnancy Risk Factor C

Pregnancy Considerations Animal reproduction studies have not been conducted. Pregnancy is not a contraindication to postexposure prophylaxis. Preexposure prophylaxis during pregnancy may also be considered if risk of rabies is great. Inactivated vaccines have not been shown to cause increased risks to the fetus (NCIRD/ACIP 2011).

Raloxifene (ral OKS i feen)

Related Information

Endocrine Disorders and Pregnancy *on page 1781*
Rheumatoid Arthritis, Osteoarthritis, and Osteoporosis *on page 1792*

Brand Names: US Evista

Brand Names: Canada ACT Raloxifene; Apo-Raloxifene; Evista; PMS-Raloxifene; Teva-Raloxifene

Generic Availability (US) Yes

Pharmacologic Category Selective Estrogen Receptor Modulator (SERM)

Use

Osteoporosis: Treatment and prevention of osteoporosis in postmenopausal women

Risk reduction for invasive breast cancer: Risk reduction for invasive breast cancer in postmenopausal women with osteoporosis; risk reduction of invasive breast cancer in postmenopausal women with high risk for invasive breast cancer (high risk is defined as at least 1 breast biopsy showing lobular carcinoma in situ or atypical hyperplasia, one or more first-degree relatives with breast cancer, or a 5 year predicted risk of breast cancer 1.66% or more [based on the Gail model]; factors included in the modified Gail model include current age, number of first-degree relatives with breast cancer, number of breast biopsies, age at menarche, nulliparity, or age of first live birth).

Limitations of use: Raloxifene does not eliminate the risk of breast cancer; patients should have a breast exam and mammogram prior to initiating raloxifene and continue regular breast exams and mammograms as per current guideline recommendations. Raloxifene is not indicated for the treatment of invasive breast cancer or reduction of the risk of recurrence. Raloxifene is not indicated for the reduction of the risk of noninvasive breast cancer. There are no data available regarding the effect of raloxifene on invasive breast cancer incidence in women with inherited mutations BRCA1, BRCA2 to be able to make specific recommendations on the effectiveness of raloxifene.

Local Anesthetic/Vasoconstrictor Precautions No information available to require special precautions

Effects on Dental Treatment No significant effects or complications reported

Effects on Bleeding Has been associated with thromboembolic adverse events. No information available to require routine special precautions for dental procedures.

Adverse Reactions

>10%:

Cardiovascular: Peripheral edema (3% to 14%)
Endocrine & metabolic: Hot flash (8% to 29%)
Infection: Infection (11%)
Neuromuscular & skeletal: Arthralgia (11% to 16%), leg cramps (≤12%), muscle spasm (≤12%)
Respiratory: Flu-like symptoms (14% to 15%)

1% to 10%:

Cardiovascular: Chest pain (3%), syncope (<2%), venous thromboembolism (1% to 2%; includes deep vein thrombosis, pulmonary embolism, retinal vein thrombosis)
Central nervous system: Insomnia (6%), hypoesthesia (<2%), neuralgia (<2%)
Dermatologic: Skin rash (6%), diaphoresis (3%)
Endocrine & metabolic: Weight gain (9%)
Gastrointestinal: Abdominal pain (7%), vomiting (5%), gastrointestinal disease (3%), flatulence (2% to 3%), gastroenteritis (≤3%)
Genitourinary: Vaginal hemorrhage (3% to 6%), mastalgia (4%), leukorrhea (3%), urinary tract abnormality (3%), uterine disease (3%), endometrium disease (≤3%)
Neuromuscular & skeletal: Myalgia (8%), tendon disease (4%)
Respiratory: Bronchitis (10%), sinusitis (10%), pharyngitis (8%), pneumonia (3%), laryngitis (≤2%)

<1%, postmarketing, and/or case reports: Cerebrovascular accident, decreased LDL cholesterol (Delmas 1997; Walsh 1998), decreased serum cholesterol (Delmas 1997; Walsh 1998), decreased serum fibrinogen (Walsh 1998), hypertriglyceridemia (in women with a history of increased triglycerides in response to oral estrogens), retinal vein occlusion, superficial thrombophlebitis

Dosing

Adult & Geriatric

Osteoporosis: Females: Oral: 60 mg once daily

Risk reduction for invasive breast cancer: Females (postmenopausal): Oral: 60 mg once daily.

Duration of therapy for breast cancer risk reduction: 5 years; may be used longer than 5 years in women with osteoporosis where breast cancer risk reduction is a secondary benefit (Visvanathan 2013).

Renal Impairment CrCl ≤50 mL/minute: There are no dosage adjustments provided in the manufacturer's labeling; use with caution.

Hepatic Impairment There are no dosage adjustments provided in the manufacturer's labeling (has not been studied); use with caution.

Mechanism of Action Raloxifene is an estrogen agonist/antagonist (a selective estrogen receptor modulator [SERM]); selective binding activates estrogenic pathways in some tissues and antagonizes estrogenic pathways in other tissues. Raloxifene acts like an estrogen agonist in the bone to prevent bone loss and has estrogen antagonist activity to block some estrogen effects in the breast and uterine tissues. Raloxifene decreases bone resorption, increasing bone mineral density and decreasing fracture incidence.

Contraindications History of or current venous thromboembolic disorders (including deep vein thrombosis [DVT], pulmonary embolism [PE], and retinal vein thrombosis); pregnancy or women who could become pregnant; breastfeeding

Warnings/Precautions

[US Boxed Warning]: Raloxifene may increase the risk for DVT and PE; use is contraindicated in patients with history of or current venous thromboembolic disorders (including DVT, PE, or retinal vein thrombosis). Consider risks versus benefits in women at risk for thromboembolism (HF, superficial thrombophlebitis, active malignancy). The risk for DVT and PE are higher during the first 4 months of treatment. Superficial thrombophlebitis has also been reported. Discontinue raloxifene at least 72 hours prior to and during prolonged immobilization (postoperative recovery or prolonged bed rest); restart only once patient fully ambulatory. Advise patients to move periodically during prolonged travel.

[US Boxed Warning]: The risk of death due to stroke is increased in postmenopausal women with coronary heart disease or at increased risk for major coronary events; consider risks versus benefits in women at risk for stroke. Do not use for primary or secondary prevention of cardiovascular disease. Assess risks versus benefits in women at risk for stroke (eg, prior stroke, TIA, atrial fibrillation, hypertension, or smokers). Women with a history of marked elevated triglycerides (>5.6 mmol/L or >500 mg/dL) in response to treatment with oral estrogens (or estrogen/progestin) may also develop elevated triglycerides when treated with raloxifene; monitor triglycerides.

The use of raloxifene has not been adequately studied in women with a prior history of breast cancer. Safety has not been established in premenopausal women; use in premenopausal women is not indicated and not recommended. Raloxifene does not eliminate the risk of breast cancer; investigate unexplained breast abnormality that occurs during treatment. Raloxifene is not indicated for treatment of invasive breast cancer, to reduce the risk of recurrence of invasive breast cancer, or to reduce the risk of noninvasive breast cancer. The efficacy (for breast cancer risk reduction) in women with inherited BRCA1 and BRCA1 mutations has not been established. The American Society of Clinical Oncology (ASCO) guidelines for breast cancer risk reduction (Visvanathan 2013) recommend raloxifene (for 5 years) as an option to reduce the risk of ER-positive invasive breast cancer in postmenopausal women with a 5-year projected risk (based on NCI trial model) of ≥1.66%, or with lobular carcinoma in situ. Raloxifene should not be used in premenopausal women. Women with osteoporosis may use raloxifene beyond 5 years of treatment. Investigate unexplained uterine bleeding.

Use with caution in patients with hepatic or renal impairment; safety and efficacy have not been established. Safety and efficacy have not been established in men; raloxifene is not indicated for use in men. Potentially significant drug-drug interactions may exist, requiring dose or frequency adjustment, additional monitoring, and/or selection of alternative therapy. Concurrent use with systemic estrogen therapy is not recommended; safety has not been established.

Drug Interactions

Metabolism/Transport Effects None known.

Avoid Concomitant Use

Avoid concomitant use of Raloxifene with any of the following: Ospemifene

Increased Effect/Toxicity

Raloxifene may increase the levels/effects of: Ospemifene

Decreased Effect

Raloxifene may decrease the levels/effects of: Levothyroxine; Ospemifene

The levels/effects of Raloxifene may be decreased by: Bile Acid Sequestrants

Dietary Considerations Osteoporosis prevention or treatment: Ensure adequate calcium and vitamin D intake; if dietary intake is inadequate, dietary supplementation is recommended. Women and men should consume:

Calcium: 1,000 mg/day (men: 50 to 70 years) **or** 1,200 mg/day (women ≥51 years and men ≥71 years) (IOM 2011; NOF [Cosman 2014])

Vitamin D: 800 to 1,000 int. units daily (men and women ≥50 years) (NOF [Cosman 2014]). Recommended Dietary Allowance (RDA): 600 int. units daily (men and women ≤70 years) **or** 800 int. units daily (men and women ≥71 years) (IOM 2011).

Pharmacodynamics/Kinetics

Half-life Elimination 27.7 hours (following a single dose); 32.5 hours (following multiple doses)

Pregnancy Risk Factor X

Pregnancy Considerations Adverse events were observed in in animal reproduction studies. Raloxifene is contraindicated for use in women who are or may become pregnant.

Breastfeeding Considerations It is not known if raloxifene is excreted into breast milk. breastfeeding is contraindicated by the manufacturer.

Dosage Forms

Tablet, Oral:

Evista: 60 mg

Generic: 60 mg

Raltegravir (ral TEG ra vir)

Related Information

HIV Infection and AIDS *on page 1785*

Brand Names: US Isentress

Brand Names: Canada Isentress

Pharmacologic Category Antiretroviral, Integrase Inhibitor (Anti-HIV)

Use HIV-1 infection:

US labeling: Treatment of HIV-1 infection in combination with other antiretroviral agents in patients 4 weeks and older and weighing at least 3 kg

Canadian labeling: Treatment of HIV-1 infection in combination with other antiretroviral agents in patients ≥2 years of age

Local Anesthetic/Vasoconstrictor Precautions No information available to require special precautions

Effects on Dental Treatment No significant effects or complications reported

Effects on Bleeding No information available to require special precautions related to hemostasis.

Adverse Reactions

>10%:

Hepatic: Increased serum ALT (1% to 11%; incidence higher with hepatitis B and/or C coinfection)

2% to 10%:

Central nervous system: Insomnia (4%), headache (2% to 4%), dizziness (2%), fatigue (2%)

Endocrine & metabolic: Increased serum glucose (126 to 250 mg/dL: 7% to 10%; 251 to 500 mg/dL: 2% to 3%)

Gastrointestinal: Increased serum lipase (2% to 5%), increased serum amylase (2% to 4%), nausea (3%)

Hematologic: Abnormal absolute neutrophil count (2% to 3%), thrombocytopenia (1% to 3%)

Hepatic: Increased serum AST (1% to 9%; incidence higher with hepatitis B and/or C coinfection), hyperbilirubinemia (<1% to 6%), increased serum alkaline phosphatase (<1% to 2%)

Neuromuscular & skeletal: Increased creatine phosphokinase (10 to 19.9 x ULN: 4%; ≥20 x ULN: 3%)

<2%, postmarketing, and/or case reports: Abdominal pain, abnormal behavior (children), anemia, anxiety, cerebellar ataxia, decreased hemoglobin, depression (particularly in subjects with a pre-existing history of psychiatric illness), diarrhea, drug rash with eosinophilia and systemic symptoms (DRESS; Perry, 2013), dyspepsia, gastritis, hepatic failure, hepatitis, herpes genitalis, herpes zoster, hypersensitivity, immune reconstitution syndrome, myopathy, nephrolithiasis, paranoia, psychomotor agitation (children; grade 3), renal failure, rhabdomyolysis, skin rash, Stevens-Johnson syndrome, suicidal ideation, toxic epidermal necrolysis, vomiting, weakness

General Dosage Range Dosage adjustment recommended in patients on concomitant therapy

Oral:

Children 2 to <6 years: Chewable tablet: Weight-based dosing: 75 to 300 mg twice daily

Children 6 to <12 years: Chewable tablet: Weight-based dosing. 75 to 300 mg twice daily; if ≥25 kg, refer to weight-based dosing or adult dosing

Adolescents ≥12 years and Adults: Film-coated tablet: 400 mg twice daily

Mechanism of Action Incorporation of viral DNA into the host cell's genome is required to produce a self-replicating provirus and propagation of infectious virion particles. The viral cDNA strand produced by reverse transcriptase is subsequently processed and inserted into the human genome by the enzyme HIV-1 integrase (encoded by the pol gene of HIV). Raltegravir inhibits the catalytic activity of integrase, thus preventing integration of the proviral gene into human DNA.

Pharmacodynamics/Kinetics

Half-life Elimination ~9 hours

Time to Peak Film-coated tablet: ~3 hours

Pregnancy Risk Factor C

Pregnancy Considerations Adverse events were observed in some animal reproduction studies. Raltegravir has high transfer across the human placenta and can be detected in neonatal serum after delivery. Data collected by the antiretroviral pregnancy registry are insufficient to evaluate human teratogenic risk. Maternal antiretroviral therapy may increase the risk of preterm delivery, although available information is conflicting possibly due to variability of maternal factors (disease severity; initiation of therapy); however, maternal antiretroviral medication should not be withheld due to concerns of preterm birth. Information related to stillbirth, low birth weight, and small for gestational age infants is limited. Long-term follow-up is recommended for all infants exposed to antiretroviral medications; children who develop significant organ system abnormalities of unknown etiology (particularly of the CNS or heart) should be evaluated for potential mitochondrial dysfunction.

Combination antiretroviral therapy (cART) therapy is recommended for all HIV-infected pregnant women to keep the viral load below the limit of detection and reduce the risk of perinatal transmission. When HIV is diagnosed during pregnancy in a woman who has never received antiretroviral therapy, cART should begin as soon as possible after diagnosis. The Health and Human Services (HHS) Perinatal HIV Guidelines consider raltegravir to be the preferred integrase inhibitor for initial use in antiretroviral-naive pregnant patients and is useful when drug interactions with protease inhibitors are a concern. Because of its ability to rapidly suppress viral load, raltegravir may be useful in women who present late in pregnancy with high viral loads. Dose adjustments are not required in pregnant women. In general, women who become pregnant on a stable cART regimen may continue that regimen if viral suppression is effective, appropriate drug exposure can be achieved, contraindications for use in pregnancy are not present, and the regimen is well tolerated. Monitoring during pregnancy is more frequent than in non-pregnant adults; cART should be continued postpartum. Reversible elevation of liver enzymes occurred in a patient who initiated raltegravir late in pregnancy; monitor liver enzymes if used during pregnancy.

For HIV-infected couples planning a pregnancy, maximum viral suppression with cART is recommended prior to conception for the HIV-infected partner(s) and expert consultation is recommended; modification of therapy (if needed) and optimization of the woman's health should be done prior to conception. HIV-infected women not planning a pregnancy may use any available type of contraception, considering possible drug interactions and contraindications of the specific method. In addition, consistent use of condoms is also recommended (even during pregnancy) to prevent transmission of HIV or other sexually transmitted diseases.

Health care providers are encouraged to enroll pregnant women exposed to antiretroviral medications as early in pregnancy as possible in the Antiretroviral Pregnancy Registry (1-800-258-4263 or www.APRegistry.com). Health care providers caring for HIV-infected women and their infants may contact the National Perinatal HIV Hotline (888-448-8765) for clinical consultation (HHS [perinatal], 2016).

Ramelteon (ra MEL tee on)

Brand Names: US Rozerem

Pharmacologic Category Hypnotic, Miscellaneous; Melatonin Receptor Agonist

Use Insomnia: Treatment of insomnia characterized by difficulty with sleep onset

Local Anesthetic/Vasoconstrictor Precautions No information available to require special precautions

Effects on Dental Treatment Key adverse event(s) related to dental treatment: Taste perversion.

Effects on Bleeding No information available to require special precautions

Adverse Reactions 1% to 10%:

Central nervous system: Dizziness (4% to 5%), somnolence (3% to 5%), fatigue (3% to 4%), insomnia worsened (3%), depression (2%)

Endocrine & metabolic: Serum cortisol decreased (1%)

Gastrointestinal: Nausea (3%), taste perversion (2%)

Neuromuscular & skeletal: Myalgia (2%), arthralgia (2%)

Respiratory: Upper respiratory infection (3%)

Miscellaneous: Influenza (1%)

Postmarketing and/or case reports: Anaphylaxis, angioedema, complex sleep-related behavior (sleep-driving, cooking or eating food, making phone calls), prolactin levels increased, testosterone levels decreased

General Dosage Range Oral: *Adults:* 8 mg at bedtime

Mechanism of Action Potent, selective agonist of melatonin receptors MT_1 and MT_2 (with little affinity for MT_3) within the suprachiasmic nucleus of the hypothalamus, an area responsible for determination of circadian rhythms and synchronization of the sleep-wake cycle. Agonism of MT_1 is thought to preferentially induce sleepiness, while MT_2 receptor activation preferentially influences regulation of circadian rhythms. Ramelteon is eightfold more selective for MT_1 than MT_2 and exhibits nearly sixfold higher affinity for MT_1 than melatonin, presumably allowing for enhanced effects on sleep induction (Hatta 2014).

Pharmacodynamics/Kinetics

Onset of Action 30 minutes

Half-life Elimination Ramelteon: 1 to 2.6 hours; M-II: 2 to 5 hours

Time to Peak Median: 0.5 to 1.5 hours

Pregnancy Risk Factor C

Pregnancy Considerations Adverse events were observed in some animal reproduction studies. May cause disturbances of reproductive hormonal regulation (eg, disruption of menses or decreased libido).

Ramipril (RA mi pril)

Related Information

Cardiovascular Diseases *on page 1752*

Brand Names: US Altace

Brand Names: Canada ACT Ramipril; Altace; Apo-Ramipril; Auro-Ramipri; Dom-Ramipril; JAMP-Ramipril; Mar-Ramipril; Mint-Ramipril; Mylan-Ramipril; PMS-Ramipril; Pro-Ramipril; RAN-Ramipril; Sandoz-Ramipril; Teva-Ramipril; Van-Ramipril

Pharmacologic Category Angiotensin-Converting Enzyme (ACE) Inhibitor; Antihypertensive

Use

Heart failure post-myocardial infarction: Treatment of heart failure (HF) after myocardial infarction (MI)

Hypertension: Treatment of hypertension, alone or in combination with thiazide diuretics

Reduction in risk of MI, stroke, and death from cardiovascular causes: To reduce the risk of MI, stroke, and death in patients ≥55 years of age at high risk of developing major cardiovascular events

Guideline recommendations:

Heart failure: The 2013 American College of Cardiology Foundation/American Heart Association (ACCF/AHA) heart failure guidelines recommend the use of ACE inhibitors, along with other guideline-directed medical therapies, to prevent HF in patients with a reduced ejection fraction who have a history of MI (stage B HF), to prevent HF in any patient with a reduced ejection fraction (stage B HF), or to treat those with HF and reduced ejection fraction (stage C HFrEF) (Yancy, 2013)

Hypertension: The 2014 guideline for the management of high blood pressure in adults (Eighth Joint National Committee [JNC 8]) recommends initiation of pharmacologic treatment to lower blood pressure for the following patients:

- Patients ≥60 years of age with systolic blood pressure (SBP) ≥150 mm Hg or diastolic blood pressure (DBP) ≥ 90 mm Hg. Goal of therapy is SBP <150 mm Hg and DBP <90 mm Hg.

- Patients <60 years of age with SBP ≥140 mm Hg or DBP is ≥90 mm Hg. Goal of therapy is SBP <140 mm Hg and DBP <90 mm Hg.
- Patients ≥18 years of age with diabetes and SBP ≥140 mm Hg or DBP ≥90 mm Hg. Goal of therapy is SBP <140 mm Hg and DBP <90 mm Hg.
- Patients ≥18 years of age with chronic kidney disease (CKD) and SBP ≥140 mm Hg or DBP ≥90 mm Hg. Goal of therapy is SBP <140 mm Hg and DBP <90 mm Hg.

Chronic kidney disease (CKD) and hypertension: Regardless of race or diabetes status, the use of an ACE inhibitor (ACEI) or angiotensin receptor blocker (ARB) as initial therapy is recommended to improve kidney outcomes. In the general non-black population (without CKD) including those with diabetes, initial antihypertensive treatment should consist of a thiazide-type diuretic, calcium channel blocker, ACEI, or ARB. In the general black population (without CKD) including those with diabetes, initial antihypertensive treatment should consist of a thiazide-type diuretic or a calcium channel blocker **instead of** an ACEI or ARB.

Coronary artery disease (CAD) and hypertension: The American Heart Association, American College of Cardiology and American Society of Hypertension (AHA/ACC/ASH) 2015 scientific statement for the treatment of hypertension in patients with CAD recommends the use of an ACE inhibitor (or an ARB) as part of a regimen in patients with hypertension and chronic stable angina if there is prior MI, LV systolic dysfunction, diabetes mellitus, or CKD. A BP target of <140/90 mm Hg is reasonable for the secondary prevention of cardiovascular events. A lower target BP (<130/80 mm Hg) may be appropriate in some individuals with CAD, previous MI, stroke or transient ischemic attack, or CAD risk equivalents (AHA/ACC/ASH [Rosendorff 2015]).

STEMI: The 2013 ACCF/AHA guidelines for the management of patients with ST-elevation myocardial infarction (STEMI) state that an ACE inhibitor should be initiated within the first 24 hours after STEMI in patients with anterior MI, heart failure, or left ventricular ejection fraction (LVEF) ≤0.4. It is also reasonable to initiate an ACE inhibitor in all patients with STEMI (O'Gara, 2013).

Local Anesthetic/Vasoconstrictor Precautions No information available to require special precautions

Effects on Dental Treatment Key adverse event(s) related to dental treatment: Patients may experience orthostatic hypotension as they stand up after treatment; especially if lying in dental chair for extended periods of time. Use caution with sudden changes in position during and after dental treatment.

An angiotensin-converting enzyme (ACE) inhibitor cough is a dry, hacking, nonproductive cough that can potentially interfere with longer dental procedures if patient has this side effect.

Effects on Bleeding No information available to require special precautions

Adverse Reactions Frequency ranges include data from hypertension and heart failure trials. Higher rates of adverse reactions have generally been noted in patients with cardiac failure. However, the frequency of adverse effects associated with placebo is also increased in this population.

>10%:

Cardiovascular: Hypotension (11%)

Respiratory: Increased cough (7% to 12%)

1% to 10%:

Cardiovascular: Angina pectoris (≤3%), orthostatic hypotension (2%), syncope (≤2%)

Central nervous system: Headache (1% to 5%), dizziness (2% to 4%), fatigue (2%), vertigo (≤2%), noncardiac chest pain (1%)

Endocrine & metabolic: Hyperkalemia (1% to 10%)

Gastrointestinal: Nausea (≤2%), vomiting (≤2%)

Renal: Increased blood urea nitrogen (≤3%; transient increases may occur more frequently), increased serum creatinine (1% to 2%; transient increases may occur more frequently), renal insufficiency (1%)

Respiratory: Cough (1% to 10%)

<1%, postmarketing, and/or case reports: Abdominal pain, agitation, agranulocytosis, amnesia, anaphylactoid reaction, angioedema, anorexia, anxiety, arthralgia, arthritis, auditory impairment, bone marrow depression, cardiac arrhythmia, cerebrovascular disease, constipation, decreased hematocrit, decreased hemoglobin, depression, diaphoresis, diarrhea, drowsiness, dysgeusia, dyspepsia, dysphagia, dyspnea, edema, eosinophilia, epistaxis, erythema multiforme, gastroenteritis, hemolytic anemia, hepatitis, hypersensitivity reaction (fever, skin rash, urticaria), hyponatremia, impotence, increased serum transaminases, insomnia, malaise, myalgia, myocardial infarction, nervousness, neuralgia, neuropathy, onycholysis, palpitations, pancreatitis, pancytopenia, paresthesia, pemphigoid, pemphigus, proteinuria, purpura, seizure, sialorrhea, skin photosensitivity, Stevens-Johnson syndrome, symptomatic hypotension, thrombocytopenia, tinnitus, toxic epidermal necrolysis, tremor, visual disturbance, visual hallucination (Doane 2013), weight gain, xerostomia

General Dosage Range Dosage adjustment recommended in patients with renal impairment

Oral: *Adults:* 2.5-20 mg daily

Mechanism of Action Ramipril is an ACE inhibitor which prevents the formation of angiotensin II from angiotensin I and exhibits pharmacologic effects that are similar to captopril. Ramipril must undergo enzymatic saponification by esterases in the liver to its biologically active metabolite, ramiprilat. The pharmacodynamic effects of ramipril result from the high-affinity, competitive, reversible binding of ramiprilat to angiotensin-converting enzyme, thus preventing the formation of the potent vasoconstrictor angiotensin II. This isomerized enzyme-inhibitor complex has a slow rate of dissociation, which results in high potency and a long duration of action; a CNS mechanism may also be involved in the hypotensive effect as angiotensin II increases adrenergic outflow from CNS; vasoactive kallikreins may be decreased in conversion to active hormones by ACE inhibitors, thus reducing blood pressure

Pharmacodynamics/Kinetics

Onset of Action 1-2 hours

Duration of Action 24 hours

Half-life Elimination Ramiprilat: Effective: 13-17 hours; Terminal: >50 hours

Time to Peak Serum: Ramipril: ~1 hour; Ramiprilat: 2-4 hours

Pregnancy Risk Factor D

Pregnancy Considerations [US Boxed Warning]: Drugs that act on the renin-angiotensin system can cause injury and death to the developing fetus. Discontinue as soon as possible once pregnancy is detected. Ramipril crosses the placenta. Drugs that act on the renin-angiotensin system are associated with oligohydramnios. Oligohydramnios, due to decreased fetal renal function, may lead to fetal lung hypoplasia and skeletal malformations. The use of these drugs in pregnancy is also associated with anuria, hypotension, renal failure, skull hypoplasia, and death in the fetus/neonate. Teratogenic effects may occur following maternal use of an ACE inhibitor during the first trimester, although this finding may be confounded by maternal disease. Because adverse fetal events are well documented with exposure later in pregnancy, ACE inhibitor use in pregnant women is not recommended (Seely 2014; Weber 2014). Infants exposed to an ACE inhibitor in utero should be monitored for hyperkalemia, hypotension, and oliguria. Oligohydramnios may not appear until after irreversible fetal injury has occurred. Exchange transfusions or dialysis may be required to reverse hypotension or improve renal function, although data related to the effectiveness in neonates is limited.

Chronic maternal hypertension itself is also associated with adverse events in the fetus/infant and mother. ACE inhibitors are not recommended for the treatment of uncomplicated hypertension in pregnancy (ACOG 2013) and they are specifically contraindicated for the treatment of hypertension and chronic heart failure during pregnancy by some guidelines (Regitz-Zagrosek 2011). In addition, ACE inhibitors should generally be avoided in women of reproductive age (ACOG 2013). If treatment for hypertension or chronic heart failure in pregnancy is needed, other agents should be used (ACOG 2013; Regitz-Zagrosek 2011).

Ramucirumab (ra mue SIR ue mab)

Brand Names: US Cyramza

Brand Names: Canada Cyramza

Pharmacologic Category Antineoplastic Agent, Monoclonal Antibody; Antineoplastic Agent, Vascular Endothelial Growth Factor (VEGF) Inhibitor; Antineoplastic Agent, Vascular Endothelial Growth Factor Receptor 2 (VEGFR2) Inhibitor

Use

Colorectal cancer, metastatic: Treatment (in combination with FOLFIRI [irinotecan, leucovorin, and fluorouracil]) of metastatic colorectal cancer (mCRC) in patients with disease progression on or after prior therapy with bevacizumab, oxaliplatin, and a fluoropyrimidine.

Gastric cancer, advanced or metastatic: Treatment (single-agent or in combination with paclitaxel) of advanced or metastatic gastric or gastroesophageal junction adenocarcinoma in patients with disease progression on or following fluoropyrimidine- or platinum-containing chemotherapy

Non-small cell lung cancer, metastatic: Treatment (in combination with docetaxel) of metastatic non-small cell lung cancer (NSCLC) in patients with disease progression on or after platinum-based chemotherapy. Patients with EGFR or ALK genomic tumor aberrations should have disease progression on FDA-approved therapy for these aberrations prior to receiving ramucirumab.

Local Anesthetic/Vasoconstrictor Precautions No information available to require special precautions

Effects on Dental Treatment Key adverse event(s) related to dental treatment: Ramucirumab impairs wound healing (see Warnings/Precautions); medical consultation advised prior to dental surgery.

Effects on Bleeding Ramucirumab associated with an increased risk of hemorrhage, which may be severe and sometimes fatal.

Adverse Reactions As reported with monotherapy. Frequency not always defined.

Cardiovascular: Hypertension (16%; grades 3/4: 8%), arterial thrombosis (including myocardial infarction, cardiac arrest, cerebrovascular accident, and cerebral ischemia; 2%)

Central nervous system: Headache (9%)

Dermatologic: Skin rash (4%)

Endocrine & metabolic: Hyponatremia (6%)

Gastrointestinal: Diarrhea (14%), intestinal obstruction (2%)

Genitourinary: Proteinuria (8% to 17%; grade ≥3: 1%)

Hematologic & oncologic: Decreased red blood cells (requiring transfusion; 11%), neutropenia (5%), anemia (4%), hemorrhage (2% to 4%)

Immunologic: Antibody development (3%; neutralizing: 1%)

Respiratory: Epistaxis (5%)

Miscellaneous: Infusion related reaction (≤16%; reactions minimized with premedications)

<1% and frequency not defined: Gastrointestinal perforation, reversible posterior leukoencephalopathy syndrome

General Dosage Range Dosage adjustment recommended in patients who develop toxicities

IV: *Adults:* 8 to 10 mg/kg every 2 to 3 weeks

Mechanism of Action Ramucirumab is a recombinant monoclonal antibody which inhibits vascular endothelial growth factor receptor 2 (VEGFR2). Ramucirumab has a high affinity for VEGFR2 (Spratlin, 2010), binding to it and blocking binding of VEGFR ligands, VEGF-A, VEGF-C, and VEGF-D to inhibit activation of VEGFR2, thereby inhibiting ligand-induced proliferation and migration of endothelial cells. VEGFR2 inhibition results in reduced tumor vascularity and growth (Fuchs, 2014).

Pharmacodynamics/Kinetics

Half-life Elimination 14 days

Pregnancy Considerations Ramucirumab inhibits angiogenesis, which is of critical importance to human fetal development. Based on the mechanism of action, ramucirumab may cause fetal harm if administered during pregnancy. Women of reproductive potential should use effective contraception during and for at least 3 months after the last ramucirumab dose. Ramucirumab may impair fertility in women.

Ranibizumab (ra nib i ZUE mab)

Brand Names: US Lucentis

Brand Names: Canada Lucentis

Pharmacologic Category Angiogenesis Inhibitor; Monoclonal Antibody; Ophthalmic Agent; Vascular Endothelial Growth Factor (VEGF) Inhibitor

Use

Diabetic macular edema: Treatment of patients with diabetic macular edema (DME).

Diabetic retinopathy: Treatment of diabetic retinopathy (nonproliferative diabetic retinopathy [NPDR]) and proliferative diabetic retinopathy [PDR]) in patients with diabetic macular edema (DME)

Macular degeneration: Treatment of neovascular (wet) age-related macular degeneration (AMD)

Macular edema: Treatment of macular edema following retinal vein occlusion (RVO)

Myopic choroidal neovascularization: Treatment of myopic choroidal neovascularization (mCNV).

Local Anesthetic/Vasoconstrictor Precautions No information available to require special precautions

Effects on Dental Treatment No significant effects or complications reported

Effects on Bleeding No information available to require special precautions in dental procedures.

Adverse Reactions As reported with AMD, RVO, and DME studies:

>10%:

Cardiovascular: Arterial thromboembolism (AMD trials during first year: 2%; DME trials at 3 years: 11%)

Central nervous system: Foreign body sensation of eye (7% to 16%), headache (6% to 12%)

Hematologic & oncologic: Anemia (4% to 11%)

Neuromuscular & skeletal: Arthralgia (2% to 11%)

Ophthalmic: Conjunctival hemorrhage (47% to 74%), eye pain (17% to 35%), vitreous opacity (7% to 27%), increased intraocular pressure (7% to 24%), blurred vision (5% to 18%), intraocular inflammation (1% to 18%)

Note: Cataract, blepharitis, dry eye syndrome, eye irritation, increased lacrimation, maculopathy, ocular hyperemia, eye pruritus, and vitreous detachment occurred in >10% of patients, but also occurred either in similar percentages to the control or more often in the control in some studies.

Respiratory: Nasopharyngitis (5% to 16%), bronchitis (6% to 11%)

1% to 10%:

Cardiovascular: Peripheral edema (6%), atrial fibrillation (1% to 5%), cerebrovascular accident (AMD trials during 2 years: 3%; DME trials at 3 years: 2%)

Central nervous system: Peripheral neuropathy (1% to 5%)

Endocrine & metabolic: Hypercholesterolemia (3% to 7%)

Gastrointestinal: Nausea (9% to 10%), constipation (8%), gastroesophageal reflux disease (1% to 6%)

Genitourinary: Chronic renal failure (6%)

Immunologic: Antibody formation (1% to 9%), seasonal allergy (8%)

Infection: Influenza (3% to 7%)

Local: Bleeding at injection site (1% to 5%)

Ophthalmic: Retinal degeneration (1% to 8%)

Note: Conjunctival hyperemia, eye discomfort, posterior capsule opacification, and retinopathy occurred in 1% to 10% of patients, but also occurred in similar percentages to the control or more often in the control in some of the studies.

Renal: Renal failure (7%)

Respiratory: Upper respiratory tract infection (9%), cough (5% to 9%), sinusitis (3% to 8%), chronic obstructive pulmonary disease (3% to 6%)

Miscellaneous: Wound healing impairment (1%)

All indications: <1%, postmarketing, and/or case reports: Anterior chamber inflammation, anxiety, back pain, corneal edema, corneal erosion, coronary artery occlusion, decreased visual acuity, dizziness, endophthalmitis, epithelial keratopathy, eye discharge (lid margin), eyelid pain, hypoglycemia, iatrogenic traumatic cataracts, intestinal obstruction, photophobia, retinal pigment epithelium tear, rhegmatogenous retinal detachment, rhinorrhea, urticaria

As reported with choroidal neovascularization secondary to pathologic myopia (not in U.S. labeling):

>10%:

Ophthalmic: Conjunctival hemorrhage (11%)

Respiratory: Nasopharyngitis (11%)

1% to 10%:

Cardiovascular: Hypertension (3%)

Central nervous system: Headache (8%), migraine (2%)

Endocrine & metabolic: Diabetes mellitus (2%)

Gastrointestinal: Abdominal pain (3%), nausea (2%), toothache (2%), vomiting (2%)

Genitourinary: Urinary tract infection (3%), bacteriuria (2%)

Infection: Influenza (2%)

Local: Bleeding at injection site (4%)

Neuromuscular & skeletal: Back pain (2%), herniated disk (2%), limb pain (2%), osteoporosis (2%)

Ophthalmic: Punctate keratitis (8%), vitreous opacity (5%), dry eye syndrome (4%), eye pain (4%), increased intraocular pressure (3%), blepharitis (2%), conjunctivitis (2%), eyelid edema (2%), retinal hole without detachment (2%)

Respiratory: Upper respiratory tract infection (3%), pharyngitis (2%)

<1%: Allergic conjunctivitis, arthralgia, bronchitis, cataract, conjunctival edema, corneal erosion, cough, eye irritation, hepatic insufficiency, hypercholesterolemia, hypersensitivity, increased intracranial pressure, iridocyclitis, ocular hyperemia, pain at injection site, retinal hemorrhage, sciatica, tendonitis, uveitis, viral conjunctivitis (adenovirus), vitreous detachment

General Dosage Range Intravitreal: *Adults:* 0.3 mg or 0.5 mg once every 1 to 3 months

Mechanism of Action Ranibizumab is a recombinant humanized monoclonal antibody fragment which binds to and inhibits human vascular endothelial growth factor A (VEGF-A). Ranibizumab inhibits VEGF from binding to its receptors and thereby suppressing neovascularization and slowing vision loss.

Pharmacodynamics/Kinetics

Half-life Elimination Vitreous: ~9 days

Pregnancy Considerations Based on its mechanism of action, adverse effects on pregnancy would be expected. Information related to use in pregnancy is limited (Jouve 2015).

RaNITIdine (ra NI ti deen)

Related Information

Gastrointestinal Disorders *on page 1775*

Brand Names: US Acid Reducer Maximum Strength [OTC] [DSC]; Acid Reducer [OTC]; Deprizine FusePaq; Deprizine RapidPaq; GoodSense Acid Reducer [OTC]; Ranitidine Acid Reducer [OTC]; Zantac; Zantac 150 Maximum Strength [OTC]; Zantac 75 [OTC]; Zantac in NaCl [DSC]

Brand Names: Canada Acid Reducer; ACT Ranitidine; Apo-Ranitidine; Dom-Ranitidine; Myl-Ranitidine; Mylan-Ranitidine; PHL-Ranitidine; PMS-Ranitidine; RAN-Ranitidine; Ranitidine Injection, USP; Riva-Ranitidine; Sandoz-Ranitidine; Teva-Ranitidine; Zantac; Zantac 75; Zantac Maximum Strength Non-Prescription

Pharmacologic Category Histamine H_2 Antagonist

Use

Oral:

Duodenal ulcer: Short-term treatment of active duodenal ulcer and maintenance therapy after the healing of acute ulcers.

Erosive esophagitis: Treatment of endoscopically diagnosed erosive esophagitis; for the maintenance of healing of erosive esophagitis.

Gastric ulcer: Short-term treatment of active, benign gastric ulcer and maintenance therapy after the healing of acute ulcer.

Gastroesophageal reflux disease: Treatment of gastroesophageal reflux disease (GERD).

Pathological hypersecretory conditions: Treatment of pathological hypersecretory conditions (eg, Zollinger-Ellison syndrome, systemic mastocytosis).

Heartburn (OTC only): Relief and prevention of heartburn associated with acid indigestion and sour stomach.

Injection:

Duodenal ulcers: Indicated in some hospitalized patients with intractable duodenal ulcers.

Pathological hypersecretory conditions: Indicated in some hospitalized patients with pathological hypersecretory conditions (eg, Zollinger-Ellison).

Patients not able to take oral medication: As an alternative to the oral dosage form for short-term use in patients who are unable to take oral medication.

Local Anesthetic/Vasoconstrictor Precautions No information available to require special precautions

Effects on Dental Treatment No significant effects or complications reported

Effects on Bleeding No information available to require special precautions

Adverse Reactions

Frequency not defined.

Cardiovascular: Asystole, atrioventricular block, bradycardia (with rapid IV administration), tachycardia, vasculitis, ventricular premature contractions

Central nervous system: Agitation, confusion, dizziness, depression, drowsiness, hallucination, headache, insomnia, involuntary motor activity, malaise, vertigo

Dermatologic: Alopecia, erythema multiforme, injection site pruritus (transient), skin rash

Endocrine & metabolic: Acute porphyria, increased serum prolactin

Gastrointestinal: Abdominal distress, abdominal pain, constipation, diarrhea, nausea, necrotizing enterocolitis (very low weight neonates; Guillet 2006), pancreatitis, vomiting

Hematologic & oncologic: Agranulocytosis, aplastic anemia, granulocytopenia, hemolytic anemia (immune; acquired), leukopenia, pancytopenia, thrombocytopenia

Hepatic: Cholestatic hepatitis, hepatic failure, hepatitis, jaundice

Hypersensitivity: Anaphylaxis, angioedema, hypersensitivity reaction (eg, bronchospasm, eosinophilia, fever)

Local: Burning sensation at injection site (transient), pain at injection site (transient)

Neuromuscular & skeletal: Arthralgia, myalgia

Ophthalmic: Blurred vision

Renal: Acute interstitial nephritis, increased serum creatinine

Respiratory: Pneumonia (causal relationship not established)

General Dosage Range Dosage adjustment recommended in patients with renal impairment

IM: *Adolescents >16 years and Adults:* 50 mg every 6 to 8 hours

IV:

Infants, Children, and Adolescents ≤16 years: 2 to 4 mg/kg/day divided every 6 to 8 hours (maximum dose: 50 mg/dose)

Adolescents >16 years and Adults: 50 mg every 6 to 8 hours **or** Infusion: 6.25 mg/hour **or** 1 to 2.5 mg/kg/hour

Oral:

Infants and Children ≤11 years: 2 to 4 mg/kg once or twice daily **or** 5 to 10 mg/kg/day in 2 divided doses (maximum: 300 mg/day)

Children ≥12 and Adolescents ≤16 years: 2 to 4 mg/kg once or twice daily **or** 5 to 10 mg/kg/day in 2 divided doses (maximum: 300 mg/day); OTC dosing: 75 to 150 mg 30 to 60 minutes before eating or drinking (maximum: 2 doses/day)

Adolescents >16 years and Adults: 150 mg 1 to 4 times/day **or** 300 mg once daily depending on indication; OTC dosing: 75 to 150 mg 30 to 60 minutes before eating or drinking (maximum: 2 doses/day)

Mechanism of Action Competitive inhibition of histamine at H_2-receptors of the gastric parietal cells, which inhibits gastric acid secretion, gastric volume, and hydrogen ion concentration are reduced. Does not affect pepsin secretion, pentagastrin-stimulated intrinsic factor secretion, or serum gastrin.

Pharmacodynamics/Kinetics

Half-life Elimination

Neonates (receiving ECMO): IV: 6.6 hours

Infants, Children, and Adolescents: IV: 1.7 to 2.4 hours

Adults:

Oral: Normal renal function: 2.5 to 3 hours; Elderly: 3 to 4 hours

IV: Normal renal function: 2 to 2.5 hours; CrCl 25 to 35 mL/minute: 4.8 hours; Elderly: 3.1 hours

Time to Peak Serum: Oral: 2 to 3 hours; IM: ≤15 minutes

Pregnancy Risk Factor B

Pregnancy Considerations Ranitidine crosses the placenta (Armentano 1989). Histamine H_2 antagonists have been evaluated for the treatment of gastroesophageal reflux disease (GERD) as well as gastric and duodenal ulcers during pregnancy. If needed, ranitidine is the agent of choice (Cappell 2003; Richter 2003). Histamine H_2 antagonists may be used for aspiration prophylaxis prior to cesarean delivery (ASA 2007).

Ranolazine (ra NOE la zeen)

Related Information

Clinical Risk Related to Drugs Prolonging QT Interval *on page 1772*

Brand Names: US Ranexa

Pharmacologic Category Antianginal Agent; Cardiovascular Agent, Miscellaneous

Use Chronic angina: Treatment of chronic angina

Note: According to the 2012 ACCF/AHA/ACP/AATS/PCNA/SCAI/STS guidelines for patients with stable ischemic heart disease, ranolazine may be useful when prescribed as a substitute for beta blockers for relief of symptoms if initial treatment with beta blockers leads to unacceptable side effects, is less effective, or if initial treatment with beta blockers is contraindicated. May also be used in combination with beta blockers, for relief of symptoms when initial treatment with beta blockers is not successful (Fihn 2012).

Local Anesthetic/Vasoconstrictor Precautions Ranolazine is one of the drugs confirmed to prolong the QT interval and is accepted as having a risk of causing torsade de pointes. The risk of drug-induced torsade de pointes is extremely low when a single QT interval prolonging drug is prescribed. In terms of epinephrine, it is not known what effect vasoconstrictors in the local anesthetic regimen will have in patients with a known history of congenital prolonged QT interval or in patients taking any medication that prolongs the QT interval. Until more information is obtained, it is suggested that the clinician consult with the physician prior to the use of a vasoconstrictor in suspected patients, and that the vasoconstrictor (epinephrine, mepivacaine and levonordefrin [Carbocaine® 2% with Neo-Cobefrin®]) be used with caution.

Effects on Dental Treatment Key adverse event(s) related to dental treatment: Xerostomia (normal salivary flow resumes upon discontinuation).

Effects on Bleeding No information available to require special precautions

Adverse Reactions

>0.5% to 10%:

Cardiovascular: Bradycardia (≤4%), hypotension (≤4%), orthostatic hypotension (≤4%), palpitation (≤4%), peripheral edema (≤4%), prolonged QT interval on ECG (>500 msec: ≤1%)

Central nervous system: Dizziness (6%; may be dose-related), headache (≤6%), confusion (≤4%), syncope (≤4%), vertigo (≤4%)

Dermatologic: Hyperhidrosis (≤4%)

Gastrointestinal: Constipation (5%), abdominal pain (≤4%), anorexia (≤4%), dyspepsia (≤4%), nausea (≤4%; dose-related), vomiting (≤4%), xerostomia (≤4%)

Genitourinary: Hematuria (≤4%)

Neuromuscular: Weakness (≤4%)

Ophthalmic: Blurred vision (≤4%)

Otic: Tinnitus (≤4%)

Respiratory: Dyspnea (≤4%)

≤0.5%, postmarketing, and/or case reports: Angioedema, ataxia, decreased glycosylated hemoglobin, decreased T-wave amplitude, dysuria, eosinophilia, hallucination, hypoesthesia, hypoglycemia (diabetic patients), increased blood urea nitrogen, increased serum creatinine, leukopenia, pancytopenia, paresthesia, pruritus, pulmonary fibrosis, renal failure, skin rash, thrombocytopenia, torsade de pointes (Morrow 2007), tremor, T-wave changes (notched), urinary retention, urine discoloration

General Dosage Range Dosage adjustment recommended in patients on concomitant therapy

Oral: *Adults:* Initial: 500 mg twice daily; Maintenance: 500 to 1,000 mg twice daily (maximum: 2,000 mg daily)

Mechanism of Action Ranolazine exerts antianginal and anti-ischemic effects without changing hemodynamic parameters (heart rate or blood pressure). At therapeutic levels, ranolazine inhibits the late phase of the inward sodium channel (late I_{Na}) in ischemic cardiac myocytes during cardiac repolarization reducing intracellular sodium concentrations and thereby reducing calcium influx via Na^+-Ca^{2+} exchange. Decreased intracellular calcium reduces ventricular tension and myocardial oxygen consumption. It is thought that ranolazine produces myocardial relaxation and reduces anginal symptoms through this mechanism although this is uncertain. At higher concentrations, ranolazine inhibits the rapid delayed rectifier potassium current (I_{Kr}) thus prolonging the ventricular action potential duration and subsequent prolongation of the QT interval.

Pharmacodynamics/Kinetics

Half-life Elimination Ranolazine: Terminal: 7 hours; Metabolites (activity undefined): 6 to 22 hours

Time to Peak 2 to 5 hours

Pregnancy Considerations Adverse events have been observed in animal reproduction studies.

Dental Comment See Local Anesthetic/Vasoconstrictor Precautions

Rasagiline (ra SA ji leen)

Brand Names: US Azilect

Brand Names: Canada Apo-Rasagiline; Azilect

Pharmacologic Category Anti-Parkinson Agent, MAO Type B Inhibitor

Use Parkinson disease: Treatment of Parkinson disease

Local Anesthetic/Vasoconstrictor Precautions Rasagiline in approved doses of 0.5-1 mg daily should not inhibit type-A MAO; however, the possibility exists of nonselective MAO inhibition at higher doses and/or in certain sensitive individuals. Therefore, attempts should be made to avoid use of vasoconstrictors due to possibility of hypertensive episodes.

Effects on Dental Treatment Key adverse event(s) related to dental treatment: Xerostomia and changes in salivation (normal salivary flow resumes upon discontinuation). Anticholinergic side effects can cause a reduction of saliva production or secretion, contributing to discomfort and dental disease (ie, caries, oral candidiasis, and periodontal disease). Patients may experience orthostatic hypotension as they stand up after treatment; especially if lying in dental chair for extended periods of time. Use caution with sudden changes in position during and after dental treatment.

Effects on Bleeding No information available to require special precautions

Adverse Reactions Unless otherwise noted, the following adverse reactions are as reported for monotherapy. Spectrum of adverse events was generally similar with adjunctive therapy, though the incidence tended to be higher. Frequency not always defined.

>10%:

Cardiovascular: Orthostatic hypotension (adjunctive therapy 3% to 13%, adjunctive therapy dose-related 6% to 9%; adjunctive therapy, 1 mg dose 3%; mild to moderate systolic blood pressure decrease [≥20 mmHg], 1 mg dose 44%; mild to moderate diastolic blood pressure decrease [≥10 mmHg], 1 mg dose 40%; severe diastolic blood pressure decrease [≥20 mmHg], 1 mg dose 9%; severe systolic blood pressure decrease [≥40 mmHg], 1 mg dose 7%), hypotension (3% post-treatment [systolic <90 mmHg or diastolic <50 mmHg combined with significant decrease from baseline, systolic >30 mmHg or diastolic >20 mmHg])

Central nervous system: Headache (14%; adjunctive therapy 6% to 11%)

Gastrointestinal: Nausea (adjunctive therapy 6% to 12%)

Neuromuscular & skeletal: Dyskinesia (adjunctive therapy 18%)

Miscellaneous: Trauma (adjunctive therapy 8% to 12%)

1% to 10%:

Cardiovascular: Peripheral edema (7%), increased blood pressure (adjunctive therapy, significant increase, >180 mmHg systolic or >100 mmHg diastolic 4%; adjunctive therapy, post-treatment [>180 mmHg systolic or >100 mmHg diastolic combined with significant increase from baseline >30 mmHg systolic or >20 mmHg diastolic] 2%), angina, bundle branch block, chest pain

Central nervous system: Dizziness (7%), drowsiness (adjunctive therapy 4% to 6%), ataxia (adjunctive therapy 3% to 6%), depression (5%), falling (5%; adjunctive therapy 6% to 12%), abnormal dreams (adjunctive therapy 1% to 4%), dystonia (adjunctive therapy 2% to 3%), malaise (2%), paresthesia (2%; adjunctive therapy 2% to 5%), insomnia (adjunctive therapy 4%), hallucinations (1%; adjunctive therapy 4% to 5%), myasthenia (adjunctive therapy 2%), vertigo (2%), anxiety

Dermatologic: Skin rash (adjunctive therapy 3% to 6%), ecchymosis (2%; adjunctive therapy 2% to 5%), diaphoresis (adjunctive therapy 2% to 3%), alopecia, skin carcinoma, vesiculobullous rash

Endocrine & metabolic: Weight loss (adjunctive therapy, dose-related 2% to 9%), impotence, libido decreased

Gastrointestinal: Constipation (adjunctive therapy 4% to 9%), dyspepsia (7%; adjunctive therapy 4% to 5%), diarrhea (adjunctive therapy 5% to 7%), vomiting (adjunctive therapy 4% to 7%), xerostomia (adjunctive therapy, dose-related 2% to 6%), abdominal pain (adjunctive therapy 2% to 5%), anorexia (adjunctive therapy 2% to 5%), gastroenteritis (3%), gingivitis (adjunctive therapy 1% to 2%), hernia (adjunctive therapy 1% to 2%), gastrointestinal hemorrhage

Genitourinary: Hematuria, urinary incontinence

Hematologic and oncologic: Hemorrhage (adjunctive therapy 1% to 2%), leukopenia

Hepatic: Liver function tests increased

Infection: Infection (adjunctive therapy 2% to 3%)

Neuromuscular & skeletal: Arthralgia (7%; adjunctive therapy 5% to 8%), back pain (adjunctive therapy 4%), neck pain (2%; adjunctive therapy 1% to 3%), tenosynovitis (adjunctive therapy 1% to 3%), arthritis (2%), abnormal gait, hyperkinesias, hypertonia, neuropathy, weakness

Ophthalmic: Conjunctivitis (3%)

Renal: Albuminuria

Respiratory: Flu-like symptoms (5%), dyspnea (adjunctive therapy 3% to 5%), cough (adjunctive therapy 4%), upper respiratory tract infection (adjunctive therapy 4%), rhinitis (3%), asthma

Miscellaneous: Fever (3%), allergic reaction

<1%, postmarketing, case reports and/or frequency not defined: Abnormal behavior, abnormality in thinking, acute kidney failure, aggressive behavior, agitation, altered sense of smell, amyotrophy, aphasia, apnea, arterial thrombosis, atrial arrhythmia, atrioventricular block, bigeminy, blepharitis, blepharoptosis, blindness, cardiac failure, cerebral hemorrhage, cerebral ischemia, confusion, deafness, deep vein thrombophlebitis, delirium, delusions, diplopia, disorientation, dysautonomia, dysesthesia, emphysema, esophageal ulcer, exacerbation of hypertension, excessive daytime sleepiness (including during operation of motor vehicles), exfoliative dermatitis, facial paralysis, gastric ulcer, genitourinary disorders, glaucoma, gynecomastia, hematemesis, hemiplegia, hostility, hypocalcemia, hypotension (while supine), impulse control disorder (pathological gambling, hypersexuality, intense urges to spend money, binge eating, and/or other intense urges and the inability to control the urges), interstitial pneumonitis, intestinal obstruction, intestinal perforation, intestinal stenosis, jaundice, keratitis, large intestine perforation, laryngeal edema, laryngismus, leukoderma, leukorrhea, macrocytic anemia, manic depressive reaction, mania, megacolon, menstrual abnormalities, myelitis, myocardial infarction, nephrolithiasis, neuralgia, neuritis, (a complex resembling) neuroleptic malignant syndrome (associated with rapid dose reduction, withdrawal of or changes in medication; includes autonomic insufficiency, hyperthermia, impaired consciousness, muscle rigidity), nocturia, oral paresthesia, osteonecrosis, paranoia, personality disorder, pleural effusion, pneumothorax, polyuria, psychiatric disturbance (new or worsening mental status and behavioral changes that may be severe, including psychotic-like behavior during or after starting or increasing doses), psychoneurosis, psychotic symptoms, psychotic depression, pulmonary fibrosis, purpura, retinal degeneration, retinal detachment, seizure, strabismus, stupor, thrombocythemia, tongue edema, ventricular fibrillation, ventricular tachycardia, vestibular disturbance, visual field defect, vulvovaginal candidiasis

General Dosage Range Dosage adjustment recommended in patients with hepatic impairment or on concomitant CYP1A2 inhibitor therapy

Oral: *Adults:* 0.5 to 1 mg once daily

Mechanism of Action Potent, irreversible and selective inhibitor of brain monoamine oxidase (MAO) type B, which plays a major role in the catabolism of dopamine. Inhibition of dopamine depletion in the striatal region of the brain reduces the symptomatic motor deficits of Parkinson's disease. There is also experimental evidence of rasagiline conferring neuroprotective effects (antioxidant, antiapoptotic), which may delay onset of symptoms and progression of neuronal deterioration.

Pharmacodynamics/Kinetics

Duration of Action ~1 week (irreversible inhibition)

Half-life Elimination ~3 hours (no correlation with biologic effect due to irreversible inhibition)

Time to Peak ~1 hour

Pregnancy Risk Factor C

Pregnancy Considerations Adverse effects have been observed in animal reproduction studies.

Rasburicase (ras BYOOR i kayse)

Brand Names: US Elitek

Brand Names: Canada Fasturtec

Pharmacologic Category Enzyme; Enzyme, Urate-Oxidase (Recombinant)

Use

Hyperuricemia associated with malignancy: Initial management of uric acid levels in pediatric and adult patients with leukemia, lymphoma, and solid tumor malignancies receiving chemotherapy expected to result in tumor lysis and elevation of plasma uric acid

Limitations of use: Indicated only for a single course of treatment

Local Anesthetic/Vasoconstrictor Precautions No information available to require special precautions

Effects on Dental Treatment Key adverse event(s) related to dental treatment: Mucositis.

Effects on Bleeding No information available to require special precautions

Adverse Reactions

>10%:

Cardiovascular: Peripheral edema (50%)

Central nervous system: Headache (26%), anxiety (24%)

Dermatologic: Rash (13%; serious: <1%)

Endocrine & metabolic: Hypophosphatemia (17%), hypervolemia (12%)

Gastrointestinal: Nausea (27% to 58%), vomiting (38% to 50%), abdominal pain (20% to 22%), constipation (20%), diarrhea (20%), mucositis (15%)

Hepatic: Hyperbilirubinemia (16%), increased serum ALT (11%)

Immunologic: Antibody development (children: 11%; IgE: 6%), development of IgG antibodies (18%; neutralizing 8%)
Infection: Sepsis (12%; serious: 5%)
Respiratory: Pharyngolaryngeal pain (14%)
Miscellaneous: Fever (46%)

1% to 10%:
Cardiovascular: Ischemic heart disease (≥2%), supraventricular arrhythmia (≥2%)
Endocrine & metabolic: Hyperphosphatemia (10%)
Gastrointestinal: Gastrointestinal infection (≥2%)
Hematologic & oncologic: Pulmonary hemorrhage (≥2%)
Hypersensitivity: Hypersensitivity (4%)
Infection: Infection (abdominal, ≥2%)
Respiratory: Respiratory failure (≥2%)

<1%, postmarketing, and/or case reports: Anaphylaxis, hemolysis, methemoglobinemia, muscle spasm, seizure

General Dosage Range IV: *Children and Adults:* 0.2 mg/kg once daily

Mechanism of Action Rasburicase is a recombinant urate-oxidase enzyme, which converts uric acid to allantoin (an inactive and soluble metabolite of uric acid); it does not inhibit the formation of uric acid.

Pharmacodynamics/Kinetics

Onset of Action Uric acid levels decrease within 4 hours of initial administration

Half-life Elimination ~16 to 23 hours

Pregnancy Risk Factor C

Pregnancy Considerations Adverse effects were observed in animal reproduction studies. Use during pregnancy only if the benefit to the mother outweighs the potential risk to the fetus.

Regorafenib (re goe RAF e nib)

Brand Names: US Stivarga

Brand Names: Canada Stivarga

Pharmacologic Category Antineoplastic Agent, Tyrosine Kinase Inhibitor; Antineoplastic Agent, Vascular Endothelial Growth Factor (VEGF) Inhibitor

Use

Colorectal cancer, metastatic: Treatment of metastatic colorectal cancer in patients previously treated with fluoropyrimidine-, oxaliplatin-, and irinotecan-based chemotherapy, anti-VEGF therapy, and anti-EGFR therapy (if *RAS* wild type)

Gastrointestinal stromal tumors: Treatment of locally-advanced, unresectable, or metastatic gastrointestinal stromal tumor (GIST) in patients previously treated with imatinib and sunitinib

Local Anesthetic/Vasoconstrictor Precautions Use vasoconstrictor with caution; patients may experience significant hypertension when taking regorafenib

Effects on Dental Treatment Key adverse event(s) related to dental treatment: Mucositis, xerostomia (normal salivary flow resumes upon discontinuation), and taste disturbance

Effects on Bleeding Chemotherapy may result in significant myelosuppression, potentially including significant reduction in platelet counts and altered hemostasis. Thrombocytopenia has been reported (41%; grade 3: 2%; grade 4: <1%). Bleeding has been reported in 21% in patients. In patients who are under active treatment with these agents, medical consult is suggested.

Adverse Reactions

>10%:
Cardiovascular: Hypertension (30% to 59%; grade ≥3: 8% to 28%)
Central nervous system: Fatigue (52% to 64%), voice disorder (30% to 39%), pain (29%), headache (10% to 16%)
Dermatologic: Palmar-plantar erythrodysesthesia (45% to 67%; grade ≥3: 17% to 22%), skin rash (26% to 30%; grade ≥3: 6% to 7%), alopecia (24%)
Endocrine & metabolic: Hypocalcemia (17% to 59%), hypophosphatemia (55% to 57%), weight loss (14% to 32%), hyponatremia (30%), increased amylase (26%), hypokalemia (21% to 26%), hypothyroidism (18%)
Gastrointestinal: Diarrhea (43% to 47%), decreased appetite (31% to 47%), increased serum lipase (14% to 46%), mucositis (33% to 40%), nausea (20%), vomiting (17%)
Hematologic & oncologic: Anemia (79%; grade 3: 5%; grade 4: 1%), lymphocytopenia (30% to 54%; grade 3: 8% to 9%), thrombocytopenia (13% to 41%; grade 3: 1% to 2%; grade 4: <1%), increased INR (24%), hemorrhage (11% to 21%; grade ≥3: 2% to 4%), neutropenia (3% to 16%; grade 3: 1%)
Hepatic: Increased serum AST (58% to 65%; grade 3: 5%; grade 4: 1%), increased serum ALT (45%; grade 3: 4% to 5%; grade 4: 1%), hyperbilirubinemia (33% to 45%)
Infection: Infection (31% to 32%; grade ≥3: 5% to 9%)
Neuromuscular & skeletal: Stiffness (14%)
Renal: Proteinuria (33% to 60%)
Miscellaneous: Fever (21% to 28%)

1% to 10%:
Cardiovascular: Ischemic heart disease (≤1%), myocardial infarction (≤1%)
Gastrointestinal: Gastrointestinal fistula (≤2%), gastrointestinal perforation (≤2%)
Hepatic: Hepatic failure (≤2%)

<1%, postmarketing, and/or case reports: Erythema multiforme, hepatic injury (severe), hypersensitivity reaction, hypertensive crisis, keratoacanthoma, reversible posterior leukoencephalopathy syndrome (RPLS), squamous cell carcinoma of skin, Stevens-Johnson syndrome, toxic epidermal necrolysis

General Dosage Range Dosage adjustment recommended in patients who develop toxicities

Oral: *Adults:* 160 mg once daily

Mechanism of Action Regorafenib is a multikinase inhibitor; it targets kinases involved with tumor angiogenesis, oncogenesis, and maintenance of the tumor microenvironment which results in inhibition of tumor growth. Specifically, it inhibits VEGF receptors 1-3, KIT, PDGFR-alpha, PDGFR-beta, RET, FGFR1 and 2, TIE2, DDR2, TrkA, Eph2A, RAF-1. BRAF, $BRAF^{V600E}$, SAPK2, PTK5, and Abl.

Pharmacodynamics/Kinetics

Half-life Elimination Regorafenib: 28 hours (range: 14 to 58 hours); M-2 metabolite: 25 hours (range: 14 to 32 hours); M-5 metabolite: 51 hours (range: 32 to 70 hours)

Time to Peak 4 hours

Pregnancy Considerations In animal reproduction studies, teratogenic effects were observed with doses less than the equivalent human dose. Based on animal reproduction studies and the mechanism of action, regorafenib may cause fetal harm if administered during pregnancy. Patients (male and female) should use effective contraception during therapy and for at least 2 months following treatment.

Prescribing and Access Restrictions Regorafenib is available only through the REACH support program. Information regarding program enrollment may be found at http://www.stivarga-us.com/hcp/mcrc/support.html or by calling 1-866-639-2827.

Remifentanil (rem i FEN ta nil)

Brand Names: US Ultiva

Brand Names: Canada Remifentanil Hydrochloride for Injection

Pharmacologic Category Analgesic, Opioid; Anilidopiperidine Opioid

Use Anesthesia: Analgesic for use during the induction and maintenance of general anesthesia; continued analgesia into the immediate postoperative period in adults; analgesic component of monitored anesthesia in adults

Local Anesthetic/Vasoconstrictor Precautions No information available to require special precautions

Effects on Dental Treatment No significant effects or complications reported

Effects on Bleeding No information available to require special precautions

Adverse Reactions Frequency of adverse events may vary based on surgical procedures and rate of infusion.

>10%:

Cardiovascular: Hypotension (2% to 19%)

Central nervous system: Headache (<2% to 18%)

Dermatologic: Pruritus (<2% to 18%)

Gastrointestinal: Nausea (<36% to 44%), vomiting (<16% to 22%)

Neuromuscular & skeletal: Muscle rigidity (≤11%; includes chest wall rigidity)

1% to 10%:

Cardiovascular: Bradycardia (1% to 7%; dose-dependent), shivering (<5%), hypertension (1% to 2%; dose-dependent), flushing (1%), flushing sensation (1%), tachycardia (≤1%; dose-dependent)

Central nervous system: Dizziness (<5%), chills (1%), agitation (≤1%)

Dermatologic: Diaphoresis (6%)

Local: Pain at injection site (1%)

Respiratory: Respiratory depression (<7%), apnea (<3%), hypoxia (≤1%)

Miscellaneous: Fever (<5%), postoperative pain (<2%)

<1%, postmarketing, and/or case reports: Abdominal distress, amnesia, anaphylaxis, anxiety, awareness under anesthesia without pain, bronchitis, bronchospasm, cardiac arrhythmia, chest pain, confusion, constipation, cough, diarrhea, disorientation, disruption of body temperature regulation, dysphagia, dysphoria, dyspnea, dysuria, ECG changes, electrolyte disturbance, erythema, gastroesophageal reflux disease, hallucination, heart block, heartburn, hepatic insufficiency, hiccups, hyperglycemia, increased creatine phosphokinase, intestinal obstruction, involuntary body movements, laryngospasm, leukocytosis, lymphocytopenia, nasal congestion, nightmares, nystagmus, oliguria, paresthesia, pharyngitis, pleural effusion, prolonged emergence from anesthesia, pulmonary edema, rales, rapid awakening from anesthesia, rhinorrhea, rhonchi, seizure, skin rash, sleep disorder, stridor, syncope, thrombocytopenia, tremor, twitching, urinary incontinence, urinary retention, urticaria, xerostomia

General Dosage Range IV:

Neonates and Infants 1 to 2 months: Infusion: 0.4 to 1 mcg/kg/minute; Supplemental bolus dose: ≤1 mcg/kg

Children and Adolescents: Infusion: 0.05 to 1.3 mcg/kg/minute; Bolus: 1 mcg/kg every 2 to 5 minutes

Adults: Infusion: 0.025 to 4 mcg/kg/minute; Bolus: 0.5 to 1 mcg/kg every 2 to 5 minutes

Mechanism of Action Binds with stereospecific mu-opioid receptors at many sites within the CNS, increases pain threshold, alters pain reception, inhibits ascending pain pathways

Pharmacodynamics/Kinetics

Onset of Action IV: 1 to 3 minutes; Peak effect: 3 to 5 minutes

Duration of Action 3 to 10 minutes (Scott 2005)

Half-life Elimination Dose dependent:

Pediatric patients (Ross 2001): Effective:

Neonates ≤2 months: 5.4 minutes (range: 3 to 8 minutes)

Infants and Children >2 months to <2 years: 3.4 minutes (range: 2 to 6 minutes)

Children 2 to 6 years: 3.6 minutes (range: 1 to 6 minutes)

Children 7 to 12 years: 5.3 minutes (range: 3 to 7 minutes)

Adolescents: 13 to <16 years: 3.7 minutes (range: 2 to 5 minutes)

Adolescents 16 to 18 years: 5.7 minutes (range: 5 to 6 minutes)

Adults: Terminal: 10 to 20 minutes; Effective: 3 to 10 minutes

Time to Peak Intranasal: Children ≤7 years: ~3.5 minutes (Verghese 2008)

Pregnancy Considerations Adverse events have not been observed in animal reproduction studies. Remifentanil has been shown to cross the placenta; fetal and maternal concentrations may be similar. Use during labor and delivery is not recommended by the manufacturer.

Controlled Substance C-II

Repaglinide (re PAG li nide)

Related Information

Endocrine Disorders and Pregnancy *on page 1781*

Brand Names: US Prandin

Brand Names: Canada ACT-Repaglinide; Apo-Repaglinide; Auro-Repaglinide; GlucoNorm; PMS-Repaglinide; Sandoz-Repaglinide

Pharmacologic Category Antidiabetic Agent, Meglitinide Analog

Use Diabetes mellitus, type 2: Management of type 2 diabetes mellitus (noninsulin dependent, NIDDM) as an adjunct to diet and exercise; may be used in combination with metformin or thiazolidinediones (US labeling) or metformin or rosiglitazone (Canadian labeling)

Local Anesthetic/Vasoconstrictor Precautions No information available to require special precautions

Effects on Dental Treatment No significant effects or complications reported

Effects on Bleeding No information available to require special precautions

Adverse Reactions

>10%:

Central nervous system: Headache (9% to 11%)

Endocrine & metabolic: Hypoglycemia (16% to 31%)

Respiratory: Upper respiratory tract infection (10% to 16%)

1% to 10%:

Cardiovascular: Ischemia (4%), chest pain (2% to 3%)

Gastrointestinal: Diarrhea (4% to 5%), constipation (2% to 3%)

Genitourinary: Urinary tract infection (2% to 3%)

Hypersensitivity: Hypersensitivity reaction (1% to 2%)

Neuromuscular & skeletal: Back pain (5% to 6%), arthralgia (3% to 6%)

Respiratory: Sinusitis (3% to 6%), bronchitis (2% to 6%)

<1%, postmarketing, and/or case reports: Alopecia, anaphylactoid reaction, blurred vision (transient), cardiac arrhythmia, ECG abnormality, hemolytic anemia, hepatic insufficiency (severe), hepatitis, hypertension, increased liver enzymes, jaundice, leukopenia, myocardial infarction, palpitations, pancreatitis, Stevens-Johnson syndrome, thrombocytopenia, visual disturbance (transient)

General Dosage Range Oral: *Adults:* Initial: 0.5-2 mg before each meal; Maintenance: 0.5-4 mg before each meal (maximum: 16 mg/day)

Mechanism of Action Nonsulfonylurea hypoglycemic agent which blocks ATP-dependent potassium channels, depolarizing the membrane and facilitating calcium entry through calcium channels. Increased intracellular calcium stimulates insulin release from the pancreatic beta cells. Repaglinide-induced insulin release is glucose-dependent.

Pharmacodynamics/Kinetics

Onset of Action Single dose: Increased insulin levels: ~15-60 minutes

Duration of Action 4-6 hours

Half-life Elimination ~1 hour

Time to Peak Plasma: ~1 hour

Pregnancy Risk Factor C

Pregnancy Considerations Adverse events have been observed in some animal reproduction studies. Repaglinide was shown to have a low potential to cross the placenta using an *ex vivo* perfusion model (Tertti 2011). Information describing the effects of repaglinide on pregnancy outcomes is limited.

In women with diabetes, maternal hyperglycemia can be associated with congenital malformations as well as adverse effects in the fetus, neonate, and the mother (ACOG 2005; ADA 2016c; Kitzmiller 2008; Metzger 2007). To prevent adverse outcomes, prior to conception and throughout pregnancy maternal blood glucose and HbA_{1c} should be kept as close to target goals as possible but without causing significant hypoglycemia (ACOG 2013; ADA 2016c; Blumer 2013; Kitzmiller 2008). Agents other than repaglinide are currently recommended to treat diabetes in pregnant women (ACOG 2013; Blumer 2013).

Reslizumab (res LIZ ue mab)

Brand Names: US Cinqair

Pharmacologic Category Interleukin-5 Receptor Antagonist; Monoclonal Antibody, Anti-Asthmatic

Use

Asthma: Add-on maintenance treatment of severe asthma in adults with an eosinophilic phenotype

Limitations of use: Not indicated for treatment of other eosinophilic conditions or for the relief of acute bronchospasm or status asthmaticus.

Local Anesthetic/Vasoconstrictor Precautions No information available to require special precautions

Effects on Dental Treatment Key adverse event(s) related to dental treatment: Oropharyngeal pain has been reported

Effects on Bleeding No information available to require special precautions

Adverse Reactions

Immunologic: Antibody development (5%)

Neuromuscular & skeletal: Increased creatine phosphokinase (20%; transient), myalgia (1%)

Respiratory: Oropharyngeal pain (3%)

<1%, postmarketing, and/or case reports: Anaphylaxis

General Dosage Range IV: *Adults:* 3 mg/kg once every 4 weeks

Mechanism of Action Reslizumab is an interleukin-5 antagonist (IgG4 kappa). IL-5 is the major cytokine responsible for the growth and differentiation, recruitment, activation, and survival of eosinophils (a cell type associated with inflammation and an important component in the pathogenesis of asthma). Reslizumab, by inhibiting IL-5 signaling, reduces the production and survival of eosinophils; however, the mechanism of reslizumab action in asthma has not been definitively established.

Pharmacodynamics/Kinetics

Half-life Elimination ~24 days

Pregnancy Considerations Adverse events were not observed in animal reproduction studies. Monoclonal antibodies, including reslizumab, are expected to cross the placenta in a linear fashion as pregnancy progresses. The long half-life of reslizumab should be considered if required for a pregnant woman.

Retapamulin (re te PAM ue lin)

Brand Names: US Altabax

Pharmacologic Category Antibiotic, Pleuromutilin; Antibiotic, Topical

Use Impetigo: Treatment of impetigo due to *Staphylococcus aureus* (methicillin-susceptible isolates only) or *Streptococcus pyogenes* in adults and pediatric patients 9 months and older.

Local Anesthetic/Vasoconstrictor Precautions No information available to require special precautions

Effects on Dental Treatment No significant effects or complications reported

Effects on Bleeding No information available to require special precautions

Adverse Reactions

1% to 10%:

Central nervous system: Headache (1% to 2%)

Dermatologic: Eczema (infants, children & adolescents; 1%)

Gastrointestinal: Diarrhea (1% to 2%), nausea (1%)

Local: Application site irritation (adults: 2%), application site pruritus (infants, children & adolescents: 2%)

Respiratory: Nasopharyngitis (1% to 2%)

<1%, postmarketing, and/or case reports: Angioedema, application site burning, application site pain, contact dermatitis, epistaxis, erythema, hypersensitivity reaction, increased creatine phosphokinase

General Dosage Range Topical: *Infants ≥9 months, Children, Adolescents, and Adults:* Apply a thin layer to affected area twice daily for 5 days.

Mechanism of Action Primarily bacteriostatic; inhibits normal bacterial protein biosynthesis by binding at a unique site (protein L3) on the ribosomal 50S subunit; prevents formation of active 50S ribosomal subunits by inhibiting peptidyl transfer and blocking P-site interactions at this site

Pregnancy Risk Factor B

Pregnancy Considerations Adverse events have not been observed in animal reproduction studies.

Reteplase (RE ta plase)

Related Information

Cardiovascular Diseases *on page 1752*

Brand Names: US Retavase Half-Kit [DSC]; Retavase [DSC]

Brand Names: Canada Retavase

Pharmacologic Category Thrombolytic Agent

Use Management of ST-elevation myocardial infarction (STEMI) for the improvement of ventricular function, the reduction of the incidence of CHF, and the reduction of mortality following STEMI

Recommended criteria for treatment of STEMI (ACCF/AHA; O'Gara, 2013): Ischemic symptoms within 12 hours of treatment or evidence of ongoing ischemia 12-24 hours after symptom onset with a large area of myocardium at risk or hemodynamic instability.

STEMI ECG definition: New ST-segment elevation at the J point in at least 2 contiguous leads of ≥2 mm (0.2 mV) in men or ≥1.5 mm (0.15 mV) in women in leads V_2-V_3 and/or of ≥1 mm (0.1 mV) in other contiguous precordial leads or limb leads on ECG. New or presumably new left bundle branch block (LBBB) may interfere with ST-elevation analysis and should not be considered diagnostic in isolation.

At non-PCI-capable hospitals, the ACCF/AHA recommends thrombolytic therapy administration when the anticipated first medical contact (FMC)-to-device time at a PCI-capable hospital is >120 minutes due to unavoidable delays.

Local Anesthetic/Vasoconstrictor Precautions No information available to require special precautions

Effects on Dental Treatment Key adverse event(s) related to dental treatment: Bleeding is the most frequent adverse effect of reteplase. See Effects on Bleeding.

Effects on Bleeding Bleeding is the most frequent adverse effect associated with reteplase. It is unlikely that ambulatory patients presenting for dental treatment will be taking intravenous anticoagulant therapy.

Adverse Reactions Bleeding is the most frequent adverse effect associated with reteplase. Heparin and aspirin have been administered concurrently with reteplase in clinical trials. The incidence of adverse events is a reflection of these combined therapies, and is comparable to comparison thrombolytics.

>10%: Local: Bleeding at injection site (5% to 49%)

1% to 10%:

Gastrointestinal: Gastrointestinal hemorrhage (2% to 9%)

Hematologic & oncologic: Hemorrhage (genitourinary: 1% to 10%), anemia (1% to 3%)

<1%, postmarketing, and/or case reports: Anaphylactoid reaction, atheromatous embolism, hypersensitivity reaction, intracranial hemorrhage

General Dosage Range IV: *Adults:* 10 units; repeat after 30 minutes

Mechanism of Action Reteplase is a nonglycosylated form of tPA produced by recombinant DNA technology using *E. coli*; it initiates local fibrinolysis by binding to fibrin in a thrombus (clot) and converts entrapped plasminogen to plasmin

Pharmacodynamics/Kinetics

Onset of Action Thrombolysis: 30-90 minutes

Half-life Elimination 13-16 minutes

Pregnancy Risk Factor C

Pregnancy Considerations Adverse events have been observed in some animal reproduction studies. The risk of bleeding may be increased in pregnant women.

Product Availability Retavase and Retavase Half-Kit have been discontinued in the US for more than 1 year.

Ribavirin (Systemic) (rye ba VYE rin)

Brand Names: US Copegus; Moderiba; Moderiba 1200 Dose Pack; Moderiba 800 Dose Pack; Rebetol; Ribasphere; Ribasphere RibaPak; RibaTab [DSC]

Brand Names: Canada Ibavyr

Pharmacologic Category Antihepaciviral, Nucleoside (Anti-HCV)

Use

Oral capsule: In combination with interferon alfa 2b (pegylated or nonpegylated) injection for the treatment of chronic hepatitis C in interferon alfa-naive or experienced patients ≥3 years of age with compensated liver disease. Patients likely to fail re-treatment after a prior failed course include previous nonresponders, those who received previous pegylated interferon treatment, patients who have significant bridging fibrosis or cirrhosis, or those with genotype 1 infection.

Oral solution: In combination with interferon alfa-2b (pegylated or nonpegylated) injection for the treatment of chronic hepatitis C in interferon alfa-naive or experienced patients ≥3 years of age with compensated liver disease. Patients likely to fail re-treatment after a prior failed course include previous nonresponders, those who received previous pegylated interferon treatment, patients who have significant bridging fibrosis or cirrhosis, or those with genotype 1 infection.

Oral tablet: In combination with peginterferon alfa-2a for the treatment of adults (Copegus, Moderiba, Ribasphere) and patients ≥5 years of age (Copegus and Moderiba) with chronic HCV infection who have compensated liver disease and have not previously been treated with interferon alpha, and in adult chronic hepatitis C patients coinfected with HIV

Guideline recommendations: Peginterferon and ribavirin, **without** additional preferred HCV antiviral agent(s), is **not** recommended for hepatitis C virus (HCV) (regardless of genotype) in HCV adult treatment guidelines (treatment-naive or treatment-experienced). In addition, nonpegylated interferons are **not** included in any recommended HCV treatment regimens. Current AASLD/IDSA recommendations do not specify a particular peginterferon (eg, 2a or 2b) to combine with oral ribavirin and additional preferred HCV antiviral agent(s); however, guideline recommendations are based on clinical trials that used peginterferon alfa-2a (AASLD/IDSA 2015). Hepatitis C treatment guidelines are constantly changing with the advent of new treatment therapies and information; consult current clinical practice guidelines for the most recent treatment recommendations.

Local Anesthetic/Vasoconstrictor Precautions No information available to require special precautions

Effects on Dental Treatment Key adverse event(s) related to dental treatment: Xerostomia (normal salivary flow resumes upon discontinuation) and taste perversion.

Effects on Bleeding No information available to require special precautions

Adverse Reactions

All adverse reactions are documented while receiving combination therapy with alfa interferons; percentages as reported in adults unless noted, most common pediatric adverse reactions were similar to adults; asterisked (*) percentages are those similar to interferon therapy alone:

>10%:

Central nervous system: Fatigue (60% to 70% [30% in pediatric patients])*, headache (43% to 66%)*, fever (32% to 55%)*, insomnia (26% to 41% [9% in pediatric patients]), depression (20% to 36%)*, irritability (23% to 33%), dizziness (14% to 26%), impaired concentration (10% to 21%)*, pain (≤13%), emotional lability (7% to 12%)*, anxiety (11%)

Dermatologic: Alopecia (27% to 36% [17% in pediatric patients]), pruritus (13% to 29% [11% in pediatric patients]), rash (5% to 28%), dry skin (10% to 24%), dermatitis (≤16%)

Endocrine and metabolic: Growth suppression (pediatric) percentile decrease (≥15 percentiles: weight 43%; height 25%), hyperuricemia (33% to 38%)

Gastrointestinal: Nausea (25% to 47% [18% in pediatric patients]), anorexia (21% to 32%), weight decrease (10% to 29%), vomiting (9% to 25%)*, diarrhea (10% to 22%), dyspepsia (6% to 16%), abdominal pain (8% to 13% [21% in pediatric patients]), xerostomia (≤12%), RUQ pain (≤12%)

Hematologic: Leukopenia (6% to 45%), neutropenia (8% to 42%; grade 4: 2% to 11%; 40% with HIV coinfection), hemoglobin decreased (11% to 35%), anemia (11% to 17%), thrombocytopenia (<1% to 15%), lymphocytopenia (12% to 14%), hemolytic anemia (10% to 13%)

Hepatic: Bilirubin increase (10% to 32%)

Local: Injection site reaction (36% to 58%), inflammation at injection site (18% to 25%)

Neuromuscular & skeletal: Decreased linear skeletal growth (including lagging weight gain; 70% in pediatric patients), myalgia (40% to 64% [17% in pediatric patients])*, rigors (25% to 48%), arthralgia (21% to 34%)*, musculoskeletal pain (19% to 28% [35% in pediatric patients])

Respiratory: Upper respiratory tract infection (60% in pediatric patients), dyspnea (13% to 26%), cough (7% to 23%), pharyngitis (≤13%), sinusitis (≤12%)*

Miscellaneous: Flu-like syndrome (13% to 18% [up to 91% in pediatric patients])*, viral infection (≤12%), diaphoresis (≤11%)

1% to 10%:

Cardiovascular: Chest pain (5% to 9%)*, flushing (≤4%)

Central nervous system: Mood alteration (≤6%; 9% with HIV coinfection), agitation (5% to 8%), nervousness (6%)*, memory impairment (≤6%), malaise (≤6%), suicidal ideation (adolescents: 2%; adults: 1%)

Dermatologic: Eczema (4% to 5%)

Endocrine & metabolic: Menstrual disorder (≤7%), hypothyroidism (≤5%)

Gastrointestinal: Taste perversion (4% to 9%), constipation (5%)

Hepatic: Hepatomegaly (4%), transaminases increased (1% to 3%), hepatic decompensation (2% with HIV coinfection)

Neuromuscular & skeletal: Weakness (9% to 10%), back pain (5%)

Ocular: Blurred vision (≤6%), conjunctivitis (≤5%)

Respiratory: Rhinitis (≤8%), exertional dyspnea (≤7%)

Miscellaneous: Fungal infection (≤6%), bacterial infection (3% to 5%)

<1%: Aggression, angina, aplastic anemia, arrhythmia; autoimmune disorders (systemic lupus erythematosus, rheumatoid arthritis, sarcoidosis); cerebral hemorrhage, cholangitis, colitis, coma, corneal ulcer, diabetes mellitus, drug abuse relapse/overdose, fatty liver, gastrointestinal bleeding, gout, hallucination, hepatic dysfunction, hyper-/hypothyroidism, myositis, pancreatitis, peptic ulcer, peripheral neuropathy, psychosis, psychotic disorder, pulmonary dysfunction, pulmonary embolism, suicide, thrombotic thrombocytopenic purpura, thyroid function test abnormalities

Postmarketing and/or case reports: Bone marrow suppression, dehydration, dental disorders, exfoliative dermatitis, hearing impairment/loss, hypersensitivity (including anaphylaxis, angioedema, bronchoconstriction, and urticaria), macular edema, optic neuritis, papilledema, periodontal disorders, pneumonitis, pulmonary infiltrates, pure red cell aplasia; retinal artery/vein thrombosis, retinal detachment, retinal hemorrhage, retinopathy, sarcoidosis exacerbation; skin reactions (erythema multiforme, exfoliative dermatitis, urticaria, vesiculobullous eruptions); Stevens-Johnson syndrome; transplant rejection (kidney, liver); vertigo, vision loss

Note: Incidence of headache, fever, suicidal ideation, and vomiting are higher in children.

General Dosage Range Dosage adjustment recommended in patients with renal impairment and in patients who develop toxicities.

Oral capsules:

Children 47 to 59 kg: 800 mg daily
Children 60 to 73 kg: 1,000 mg daily
Children >73 kg: 1,200 mg daily
Adults: 800 to 1400 mg daily

Oral solution:

Children <47 kg: 15 mg/kg/day in 2 divided doses
Adults: 800 to 1400 mg daily

Oral tablet (Copegus, Moderiba):

Children 23 to 33 kg: 400 mg daily
Children 34 to 46 kg: 600 mg daily
Children 47 to 59 kg: 800 mg daily
Children 60 to 74 kg: 1,000 mg daily
Children ≥75 kg: 1,200 mg daily
Adults: 800 to 1,200 mg daily

Oral tablet (Ribasphere): *Adults:* 800 to 1,200 mg daily

Mechanism of Action Inhibits replication of RNA and DNA viruses; inhibits influenza virus RNA polymerase activity and inhibits the initiation and elongation of RNA fragments resulting in inhibition of viral protein synthesis

Pharmacodynamics/Kinetics

Half-life Elimination Plasma: Adults: Oral:

Capsule, single dose: 24 hours in healthy adults, 44 hours with chronic hepatitis C infection (increases to ~298 hours at steady state)

Tablet, single dose: ~120 to 170 hours

Time to Peak Serum: Oral capsule: Multiple doses: Children and Adolescents 3 to 16 years: ~2 hours; Adults: 3 hours; Tablet: 2 hours

Pregnancy Risk Factor X

Pregnancy Considerations

[US Boxed Warning]: Use is contraindicated in pregnant women or male partners of pregnant women. Significant teratogenic and/or embryocidal effects have been observed in all animal species

with adequate studies. Avoid pregnancy in female patients and female partners of male patients during therapy by using two effective forms of contraception; continue contraceptive measures for at least 6 months after completion of therapy. A negative pregnancy test is required immediately before initiation, monthly during therapy, and for 6 months after treatment is discontinued. If patient or female partner becomes pregnant during treatment, she should be counseled about potential risks of exposure.

Mother-to-child transmission of HCV does not occur if the woman is not viremic, therefore, HCV-infected women of childbearing potential should postpone pregnancy until therapy is complete. Treatment of HCV is not recommended for women who are already pregnant (AASLD/IDSA 2015).

Health care providers and patients are encouraged to enroll women exposed to ribavirin during pregnancy or within 6 months after treatment in the Ribavirin Pregnancy Registry (800-593-2214).

Ribavirin (Oral Inhalation) (rye ba VYE rin)

Brand Names: US Virazole
Brand Names: Canada Virazole
Pharmacologic Category Antiviral Agent
Use Respiratory syncytial virus: Treatment of hospitalized infants and young children with respiratory syncytial virus (RSV) infections; specially indicated for treatment of severe lower respiratory tract RSV infections in patients with an underlying compromising condition (prematurity, cardiopulmonary disease, or immunosuppression)
Local Anesthetic/Vasoconstrictor Precautions No information available to require special precautions
Effects on Dental Treatment Key adverse event(s) related to dental treatment: Xerostomia (normal salivary flow resumes upon discontinuation) and taste perversion.
Effects on Bleeding No information available to require special precautions
Adverse Reactions
Frequency not defined:
Cardiovascular: Bigeminy, bradycardia, chest pain, hypotension, tachycardia
Dermatologic: Skin rash
Ophthalmic: Conjunctivitis
Respiratory: Apnea, atelectasis, bacterial pneumonia, bronchospasm, cyanosis, dyspnea, hypoventilation, pneumothorax, pulmonary complications (ventilator dependence), pulmonary edema, severe dyspnea (worsening of respiratory status)
<1%, postmarketing, and/or case reports: Anemia, hemolytic anemia, reticulocytosis
General Dosage Range Inhalation: *Children:* 20 mg/mL (6 **g** in 300 mL) solution; continuous: 12 to 18 hours daily
Mechanism of Action Inhibits replication of RNA and DNA viruses; inhibits influenza virus RNA polymerase activity and inhibits the initiation and elongation of RNA fragments resulting in inhibition of viral protein synthesis
Pharmacodynamics/Kinetics
Half-life Elimination
Respiratory tract secretions: Infants and Children 6 weeks to 7 years: ~2 hours (Englund 1990)
Plasma: Infants and Children: Inhalation: 9.5 hours
Time to Peak Serum: Inhalation: At end of inhalation period
Pregnancy Risk Factor X
Pregnancy Considerations Use is contraindicated in females who are or may become pregnant. **[US Boxed Warning]: Significant teratogenic and/or embryocidal effects have been observed in all animal species with adequate studies.** The manufacturer recommends that pregnant health care workers take precautions to limit exposure to ribavirin aerosol; potential occupational exposure may be greatest if administration is via oxygen tent or hood, and lower if administered via mechanical ventilation. The minimum interval following exposure to ribavirin inhalation prior to pregnancy is not known.

Riboflavin (RYE boe flay vin)

Brand Names: US B-2-400 [OTC]
Pharmacologic Category Vitamin, Water Soluble
Use Dietary supplement
Local Anesthetic/Vasoconstrictor Precautions No information available to require special precautions
Effects on Dental Treatment No significant effects or complications reported
Effects on Bleeding No information available to require special precautions
Adverse Reactions
Frequency not defined: Genitourinary: Urine discoloration (yellow-orange)
General Dosage Range Oral: *Adults:* 100 mg once or twice daily
Mechanism of Action Component of flavoprotein enzymes that work together, which are necessary for normal tissue respiration; also needed for activation of pyridoxine and conversion of tryptophan to niacin
Pharmacodynamics/Kinetics
Half-life Elimination Biologic: 66 to 84 minutes
Pregnancy Considerations Water-soluble vitamins cross the placenta. Riboflavin requirements may be increased in pregnant women compared to nonpregnant women (IOM, 1998).

Riboflavin 5'-Phosphate
(RYE boe flay vin five FOS fate)

Brand Names: US Photrexa; Photrexa Viscous
Pharmacologic Category Corneal Collagen Cross-Linking Agent, Ophthalmic; Ophthalmic Agent
Use
Corneal ectasia following refractive surgery: Treatment of corneal ectasia following refractive surgery with the KXL System in corneal collagen cross-linking.
Keratoconus, progressive: Treatment of progressive keratoconus with the KXL System in corneal collagen cross-linking.
Local Anesthetic/Vasoconstrictor Precautions No information available to require special precautions
Effects on Dental Treatment No significant effects or complications reported
Effects on Bleeding No information available to require special precautions
Adverse Reactions
>10%:
Central nervous system: Foreign body sensation of eye (14% to 15%)
Ophthalmic: Corneal opacity (haze) (64% to 71%), corneal disease (3% to 28%), eye pain (17% to 26%), punctate keratitis (20% to 25%), corneal

edema (in progressive keratoconus patients: 24%; all other patients: 3% to 9%), photophobia (2% to 19%), blurred vision (16% to 17%), ocular hyperemia (8% to 14%), dry eye syndrome (6% to 14%), decreased visual acuity (10% to 11%)

1% to 10%:

Central nervous system: Headache (4% to 8%)

Ophthalmic: Increased lacrimation (5% to 10%), eye discomfort (9%), conjunctival edema (7%), eyelid edema (5% to 6%), anterior chamber inflammation (2% to 6%), visual impairment (3% to 4%), blepharitis (3%), keratitis (1% to 3%), asthenopia (2%), diplopia (2%), eye discharge (2%), eye pruritus (2%), vitreous detachment (2%), eye injury (associated with device; 1% to 2%), visual halos around lights (1% to 2%)

Mechanism of Action Photo enhancer that generates singlet oxygen in corneal collagen cross-linking.

Pregnancy Considerations Animal reproduction studies have not been conducted with riboflavin 5'-phosphate. The manufacturer recommends that the corneal collagen cross-linking procedure not be done during pregnancy. Pregnancy may be a risk factor for the progression of keratoconus (Bilgihan 2011).

Rifabutin (rif a BYOO tin)

Related Information

Systemic Viral Diseases *on page 1806*

Brand Names: US Mycobutin

Brand Names: Canada Mycobutin

Pharmacologic Category Antibiotic, Miscellaneous; Antitubercular Agent

Use ***Mycobacterium avium* complex (MAC), prophylaxis:** Prevention of disseminated MAC disease in patients with advanced human immunodeficiency virus (HIV) infection

Local Anesthetic/Vasoconstrictor Precautions No information available to require special precautions

Effects on Dental Treatment Key adverse event(s) related to dental treatment: Saliva (reddish orange). The reddish-orange color of the saliva may cause a unique coloration to plaque and calculus buildup. Some patients may want more regular cleanings to remove.

Effects on Bleeding No information available to require special precautions

Adverse Reactions

>10%:

Dermatologic: Skin rash (11%)

Genitourinary: Discoloration of urine (30%)

Hematologic & oncologic: Neutropenia (25%), leukopenia (10% to 17%)

1% to 10%:

Gastrointestinal: Nausea (≤6%), abdominal pain (4%), dysgeusia (3%), dyspepsia (3%), eructation (3%), vomiting (≤3%), flatulence (2%)

Hematologic & oncologic: Thrombocytopenia (5%)

Neuromuscular & skeletal: Myalgia (2%)

Miscellaneous: Fever (2%)

<1%, postmarketing, and/or case reports: Abnormal T waves on ECG, agranulocytosis, aphasia, arthralgia, bronchospasm, chest pain, *clostridium difficile* associated diarrhea, confusion, corneal deposits, dyspnea, flu-like symptoms, granulocytopenia, hemolysis, hepatitis, hypersensitivity, jaundice, lymphocytopenia, myositis, pancytopenia, paresthesia, pseudomembranous colitis, seizure, skin discoloration, thrombotic thrombocytopenic purpura, uveitis

General Dosage Range Dosage adjustment recommended in patients with renal impairment

Oral: *Adults:* 300 mg once daily or 150 mg twice daily

Mechanism of Action Inhibits DNA-dependent RNA polymerase at the beta subunit which prevents chain initiation

Pharmacodynamics/Kinetics

Half-life Elimination Terminal: 45 hours (range: 16 to 69 hours)

Time to Peak Serum: 2 to 4 hours

Pregnancy Risk Factor B

Pregnancy Considerations Adverse events were seen in some animal reproduction studies.

RifAMPin (rif AM pin)

Related Information

Rifapentine *on page 1434*

Brand Names: US Rifadin

Brand Names: Canada Rifadin; Rofact

Pharmacologic Category Antibiotic, Miscellaneous; Antitubercular Agent

Use Management of active tuberculosis in combination with other agents; elimination of meningococci from the nasopharynx in asymptomatic carriers

Local Anesthetic/Vasoconstrictor Precautions No information available to require special precautions

Effects on Dental Treatment Key adverse event(s) related to dental treatment: Saliva (reddish orange). The reddish-orange color of the saliva may cause a unique coloration to plaque and calculus buildup. Some patients may want more regular cleanings to remove.

Effects on Bleeding Rifampin doses >600 mg may be associated with more adverse events including hemolytic anemia and thrombocytopenia.

Adverse Reactions

>10%: Hepatic: Increased liver enzymes (≤14%)

1% to 10%:

Dermatologic: Skin rash (1% to 5%)

Gastrointestinal: Abdominal cramps (1% to 2%), anorexia (1% to 2%), diarrhea (1% to 2%), epigastric distress (1% to 2%), flatulence (1% to 2%), heartburn (1% to 2%), nausea (1% to 2%), pseudomembranous colitis (1% to 2%), pancreatitis (1% to 2%), vomiting (1% to 2%)

<1%, postmarketing, and/or case reports: Agranulocytosis, hepatitis

Frequency not defined:

Cardiovascular: Edema, flushing

Central nervous system: Ataxia, behavioral changes, confusion, dizziness, drowsiness, fatigue, headache, lack of concentration, numbness, psychosis

Dermatologic: Pemphigoid reaction, pruritus, urticaria

Endocrine & metabolic: Adrenocortical insufficiency, increased uric acid, menstrual disease

Genitourinary: Hemoglobinuria, hematuria

Hematologic & oncologic: Decreased hemoglobin, disseminated intravascular coagulation, eosinophilia, hemolysis, hemolytic anemia, leukopenia, thrombocytopenia (especially with high-dose therapy)

Hepatic: Jaundice

Neuromuscular & skeletal: Myalgia, osteomalacia, weakness

Ophthalmic: Conjunctivitis (exudative), visual disturbance

Renal: Acute renal failure, increased blood urea nitrogen, interstitial nephritis

Respiratory: Flu-like symptoms

Miscellaneous: Fever

General Dosage Range IV, Oral:
Children <12 years: 10 to 20 mg/kg/day in 1 to 2 divided doses **or** 10 to 20 mg/kg twice weekly (maximum: 600 mg/day)
Children ≥12 years and Adults: 10 mg/kg/day **or** 10 mg/kg 2 to 3 times/week **or** 600 mg every 12 to 24 hours

Mechanism of Action Inhibits bacterial RNA synthesis by binding to the beta subunit of DNA-dependent RNA polymerase, blocking RNA transcription

Pharmacodynamics/Kinetics
Duration of Action ≤24 hours
Half-life Elimination 3-4 hours, prolonged with hepatic impairment; End-stage renal disease: 1.8-11 hours
Time to Peak Serum: Oral: 2-4 hours

Pregnancy Risk Factor C

Pregnancy Considerations Adverse events have been observed in animal reproduction studies. Rifampin crosses the human placenta. Due to the risk of tuberculosis to the fetus, treatment is recommended when the probability of maternal disease is moderate to high (ATC/CDC 2003). Postnatal hemorrhages have been reported in the infant and mother with administration during the last few weeks of pregnancy.

Rifampin and Isoniazid
(rif AM pin & eye soe NYE a zid)

Related Information
Isoniazid *on page 925*
RifAMPin *on page 1433*

Brand Names: US Rifamate

Brand Names: Canada Rifamate

Pharmacologic Category Antibiotic, Miscellaneous

Use Management of active tuberculosis; see individual agents for additional information

Local Anesthetic/Vasoconstrictor Precautions No information available to require special precautions

Effects on Dental Treatment No significant effects or complications reported

Effects on Bleeding Rifampin doses >600 mg may be associated with more adverse events including hemolytic anemia and thrombocytopenia.

Adverse Reactions See individual agents.

General Dosage Range Oral: *Adolescents ≥15 years and Adults:* Two capsules (rifampin 300 mg/isoniazid 150 mg per capsule) once daily

Mechanism of Action
Rifampin inhibits bacterial RNA synthesis by binding to the beta subunit of DNA-dependent RNA polymerase, blocking transcription
Isoniazid inhibits mycolic acid synthesis resulting in disruption of the bacterial cell wall

Pregnancy Risk Factor C

Pregnancy Considerations Animal reproduction studies have not been conducted with this combination. Refer to individual agents.

Rifapentine (rif a PEN teen)

Related Information
RifAMPin *on page 1433*

Brand Names: US Priftin

Pharmacologic Category Antitubercular Agent

Use
Active pulmonary tuberculosis: Treatment of active pulmonary tuberculosis caused by *Mycobacterium tuberculosis* in adults and children 12 years and older; must be used in combination with one or more antituberculosis drugs to which the isolate is susceptible.
Limitations of use: Rifapentine should not be used once weekly in the continuation phase regimen in combination with isoniazid in HIV-infected patients with active pulmonary tuberculosis because of a higher rate of failure and/or relapse with rifampin-resistant organisms. Rifapentine has not been studied as part of the initial phase treatment regimen in HIV-infected patients with active pulmonary tuberculosis.
Latent tuberculosis infection: Treatment of latent tuberculosis infection caused by *Mycobacterium tuberculosis*, in combination with isoniazid, in adults and children 2 years and older at high risk of progression to tuberculosis disease. To identify candidates for latent tuberculosis infection treatment, refer to Centers for Disease Control and Prevention (CDC) guidelines for current recommendations.
Limitations of use: Rifapentine in combination with isoniazid is not recommended for individuals presumed to be exposed to rifamycin- or isoniazid-resistant *M. tuberculosis*.

Local Anesthetic/Vasoconstrictor Precautions No information available to require special precautions

Effects on Dental Treatment No significant effects or complications reported

Effects on Bleeding No information available to require special precautions

Adverse Reactions Frequency may vary based on treatment phase; adverse reaction data is based on rifapentine combination therapy.
>10%:
Endocrine & metabolic: Hyperuricemia (≤32%; most likely due to pyrazinamide from initiation phase)
Genitourinary: Pyuria (11% to 22%), hematuria (10% to 18%), urinary tract infection (7% to 13%)
Hematologic & oncologic: Neutropenia (6% to 13%), lymphocytopenia (3% to 13%), anemia (2% to 11%)
1% to 10%:
Cardiovascular: Chest pain (3% to 6%), edema (1%)
Central nervous system: Pain (3% to 6%), headache (≤3%), dizziness (≤1%), fatigue (≤1%)
Dermatologic: Diaphoresis (2% to 5%), skin rash (3% to 4%), acne vulgaris (≤3%), pruritus (≤3%), maculopapular rash (≤2%)
Endocrine & metabolic: Hypoglycemia (5% to 10%), hyperglycemia (1% to 4%), increased nonprotein nitrogen (1% to 3%), gout (1%), hyperphosphatemia (1%)
Gastrointestinal: Anorexia (3% to 4%), nausea (≤3%), constipation (1% to 2%), dyspepsia (1% to 2%), abdominal pain (≤2%), diarrhea (≤2%), vomiting (≤2%), hemorrhoids (1%)
Genitourinary: Casts in urine (4% to 8%), cystitis (1%)
Hematologic & oncologic: Leukopenia (4% to 7%), thrombocytosis (≤6%), leukocytosis (2% to 3%), neutrophilia (1% to 3%), thrombocythemia (1% to 3%), polycythemia (≤2%), lymphadenopathy (≤1%)
Hepatic: Increased serum ALT (2% to 7%), increased serum AST (2% to 6%), hepatotoxicity (≤2%)
Hypersensitivity: Hypersensitivity reaction (≤4%; children & adolescents 1%)
Infection: Influenza (3% to 8%), herpes zoster (1%), infection (1%)
Neuromuscular & skeletal: Back pain (4% to 7%), arthralgia (≤4%), osteoarthrosis (1%), tremor (1%)
Ophthalmic: Conjunctivitis (≤3%)

Respiratory: Hemoptysis (2% to 8%), cough (3% to 6%), bronchitis (3%), pharyngitis (1% to 2%), epistaxis (1%), pleurisy (1%)
Miscellaneous: Accidental injury (1% to 5%), fever (≤1%)
<1%, postmarketing, and/or case reports: Ageusia, allergic skin reaction, alopecia, anaphylaxis, anxiety, asthma, azotemia, bronchial hyperactivity, bronchospasm, chills, confusion, convulsions, decreased appetite, depression, diabetes mellitus, disorientation, drowsiness, dyspnea, dysuria, enlargement of salivary glands, erythematous rash, esophagitis, facial edema, fungal infection, gastritis, hematoma, hepatitis, hepatomegaly, hyperbilirubinemia, hypercalcemia, hyperhidrosis, hyperkalemia, hyperlipidemia, increased blood urea nitrogen, increased serum alkaline phosphatase, jaundice, jitteriness, laryngeal edema, laryngitis, leukorrhea, lymphocytosis, myalgia, myasthenia, myositis, oropharyngeal pain, orthostatic hypotension, palpitations, pancreatitis, paresthesia, pericarditis, peripheral neuropathy, pneumonitis, pulmonary fibrosis, pulmonary tuberculosis (exacerbation), purpura, pyelonephritis, rhabdomyolysis, seizure, skin discoloration, suicidal ideation, syncope, tachycardia, thrombosis, urinary incontinence, urticaria, vaginal hemorrhage, vaginitis, viral infection, voice disorder, vulvovaginal candidiasis, vulvovaginal pruritus, weakness, weight gain, weight loss, xerostomia

General Dosage Range Oral:
Children ≥2 years to <12 years: 300 to 900 mg once weekly
Children ≥12 years, Adolescents, and Adults: 600 mg once or twice weekly OR 300 to 900 mg once weekly

Mechanism of Action Inhibits DNA-dependent RNA polymerase in susceptible strains of *Mycobacterium tuberculosis* (MTB) (but not in mammalian cells). Rifapentine is bactericidal against both intracellular and extracellular MTB organisms.

Pharmacodynamics/Kinetics
Half-life Elimination Rifapentine: ~17 hours; 25-desacetyl rifapentine: ~24 hours
Time to Peak Serum: 3 to 10 hours

Pregnancy Risk Factor C

Pregnancy Considerations Adverse events have been observed in animal reproduction studies. Information related to the use of rifapentine in pregnant women is limited. Postnatal hemorrhages have been reported in the infant and mother with rifampin (another rifamycin) administration during the last few weeks of pregnancy. Due to the risk of tuberculosis to the fetus, treatment is recommended when the probability of maternal disease is moderate to high. The CDC does not recommend rifapentine as part of the treatment regimen due to insufficient data in pregnant women (CDC, 2003).

RifAXIMin (rif AX i min)

Brand Names: US Xifaxan
Brand Names: Canada Zaxine
Pharmacologic Category Antibiotic, Miscellaneous

Use
Hepatic encephalopathy: Reduction in the risk of overt hepatic encephalopathy recurrence in adults
Irritable bowel syndrome with diarrhea: Treatment of irritable bowel syndrome with diarrhea (IBS-D) in adults
Traveler's diarrhea: Treatment of traveler's diarrhea caused by noninvasive strains of *E. coli* in adults and pediatric patients ≥12 years of age
Limitations of use: Rifaximin should not be used in patients with diarrhea complicated by fever or blood in the stool or diarrhea caused by pathogens other than *E. coli*.

Local Anesthetic/Vasoconstrictor Precautions No information available to require special precautions

Effects on Dental Treatment No significant effects or complications reported

Effects on Bleeding No information available to require special precautions

Adverse Reactions Frequency of adverse events generally higher following treatment for hepatic encephalopathy (HE). Percentages are presented for HE unless otherwise stated.
>10%:
Cardiovascular: Peripheral edema (15%)
Central nervous system: Dizziness (13%), fatigue (12%)
Hepatic: Ascites (11%)
Gastrointestinal: Nausea (14%; irritable bowel syndrome with diarrhea 2% to 3%)
2% to 10%:
Central nervous system: Headache (travelers' diarrhea 10%), depression (7%)
Dermatological: Pruritus (9%), skin rash (5%)
Gastrointestinal: Abdominal pain (>2% to 9%), pseudomembranous colitis (<5%; travelers' diarrhea or irritable bowel syndrome with diarrhea <2%)
Hematologic & oncologic: Anemia (8%)
Hepatic: Increased serum ALT (irritable bowel syndrome with diarrhea 2%)
Neuromuscular & skeletal: Muscle spasm (9%), arthralgia (6%), increased creatine phosphokinase (<5%; travelers' diarrhea or irritable bowel syndrome with diarrhea <2%)
Respiratory: Nasopharyngitis (7%), dyspnea (6%), epistaxis (>2% to 5%)
Miscellaneous: Fever (6%)
All indications: <2%, postmarketing, and/or case reports: Anaphylaxis, angioedema, *Clostridium difficile* associated diarrhea, exfoliative dermatitis, flushing, hypersensitivity reaction, urticaria

General Dosage Range Oral:
Children ≥12 years and Adolescents: 200 mg 3 times daily
Adults: 200 mg 3 times daily or 550 mg 2 or 3 times daily

Mechanism of Action Rifaximin inhibits bacterial RNA synthesis by binding to bacterial DNA-dependent RNA polymerase.

Pharmacodynamics/Kinetics
Half-life Elimination Healthy subjects: 5.6 hours; IBS-D patients: 6 hours
Time to Peak Healthy subjects and ISB-D patients: ~1 hour

Pregnancy Considerations Adverse events have been observed in some animal reproduction studies. Due to the limited oral absorption of rifaximin in patients with normal hepatic function, exposure to the fetus is expected to be low.

Rilpivirine (ril pi VIR een)

Related Information

Clinical Risk Related to Drugs Prolonging QT Interval *on page 1772*

HIV Infection and AIDS *on page 1785*

Brand Names: US Edurant

Brand Names: Canada Edurant

Pharmacologic Category Antiretroviral, Reverse Transcriptase Inhibitor, Non-nucleoside (Anti-HIV)

Use HIV-1 infection: Treatment of HIV-1 infections in antiretroviral treatment-naive patients with HIV-1 RNA ≤100,000 copies/mL at the start of therapy in combination with at least 2 other antiretroviral agents

Local Anesthetic/Vasoconstrictor Precautions Rilpivirine is one of the drugs confirmed to prolong the QT interval and is accepted as having a risk of causing torsade de pointes. The risk of drug-induced torsade de pointes is extremely low when a single QT interval prolonging drug is prescribed. In terms of epinephrine, it is not known what effect vasoconstrictors in the local anesthetic regimen will have in patients with a known history of congenital prolonged QT interval or in patients taking any medication that prolongs the QT interval. Until more information is obtained, it is suggested that the clinician consult with the physician prior to the use of a vasoconstrictor in suspected patients, and that the vasoconstrictor (epinephrine, mepivacaine and levonordefrin [Carbocaine® 2% with Neo-Cobefrin®]) be used with caution.

Effects on Dental Treatment No significant effects or complications reported

Effects on Bleeding No information available to require special precautions

Adverse Reactions

>10%:

Central nervous system: Depression (5% to 9%; children and adolescents: 19%), headache (3%; children and adolescents: 19%), drowsiness (children and adolescents: 14%)

Endocrine & metabolic: Decreased plasma cortisol (7%; children and adolescents: 20%; decrease from baseline via ACTH stimulation test; clinical significance is unknown), increased serum cholesterol (7% to 17%), increased LDL cholesterol (5% to 14%)

Gastrointestinal: Nausea (1%; children and adolescents: 11%)

Hepatic: Increased serum ALT (5% to 18%), increased serum AST (4% to 16%)

1% to 10%:

Central nervous system: Dizziness (1%; children and adolescents: 8%), insomnia (3%), abnormal dreams (2%), fatigue (2%)

Dermatologic: Skin rash (3% to 6%)

Endocrine & metabolic: Increased serum triglycerides (2%)

Gastrointestinal: Abdominal pain (2%; children and adolescents: 8%), vomiting (1%; children and adolescents: 6%)

Hepatic: Increased serum bilirubin (3% to 5%)

Renal: Increased serum creatinine (1% to 6%)

<1%, postmarketing, and/or case reports (Limited to important or life-threatening): Angioedema, conjunctivitis, DRESS syndrome, facial edema, fever, hepatitis, hypersensitivity reaction, localized vesiculation, nephrotic syndrome, suicidal ideation

General Dosage Range Dosage adjustment recommended in patients on concomitant therapy.

Oral: *Children ≥12 years, Adolescents, and Adults ≥ 35 kg:* 25 mg once daily

Mechanism of Action As a non-nucleoside reverse transcriptase inhibitor, rilpivirine has activity against HIV-1 by binding to reverse transcriptase. It consequently blocks the RNA-dependent and DNA-dependent DNA polymerase activities, including HIV-1 replication. It does not require intracellular phosphorylation for antiviral activity.

Pharmacodynamics/Kinetics

Half-life Elimination ~50 hours

Time to Peak Plasma: 4 to 5 hours

Pregnancy Risk Factor B

Pregnancy Considerations Adverse events have not been observed in animal reproduction studies. Rilpivirine has moderate to high placental transfer. Available data in pregnant women are insufficient to evaluate the overall risk of birth defects. Maternal antiretroviral therapy may increase the risk of preterm delivery, although available information is conflicting possibly due to variability of maternal factors (disease severity; initiation of therapy); however, maternal antiretroviral medication should not be withheld due to concerns of preterm birth. Information related to stillbirth, low birth weight, and small for gestational age infants is limited. Long-term follow-up is recommended for all infants exposed to antiretroviral medications; children who develop significant organ system abnormalities of unknown etiology (particularly of the CNS or heart) should be evaluated for potential mitochondrial dysfunction. Hypersensitivity reactions (including hepatic toxicity and rash) are more common in women on NNRTI therapy; it is not known if pregnancy increases this risk.

Combination antiretroviral therapy (cART) therapy is recommended for all HIV-infected pregnant women to keep the viral load below the limit of detection and reduce the risk of perinatal transmission. When HIV is diagnosed during pregnancy in a woman who has never received antiretroviral therapy, cART should begin as soon as possible after diagnosis. The Health and Human Services (HHS) Perinatal HIV Guidelines recommend rilpivirine as a component in alternative regimens for initial use in antiretroviral-naïve pregnant women with a pre-treatment HIV RNA ≤100,000 copies/mL and CD4 cell count ≥200 cells/mm³. The pharmacokinetics are variably altered in pregnancy and although routine dosing adjustment is not suggested for all women, close monitoring is recommended. In general, women who become pregnant on a stable cART regimen may continue that regimen if viral suppression is effective, appropriate drug exposure can be achieved, contraindications for use in pregnancy are not present, and the regimen is well tolerated. Monitoring during pregnancy is more frequent than in non-pregnant adults; cART should be continued postpartum.

For HIV-infected couples planning a pregnancy, maximum viral suppression with cART is recommended prior to conception for the HIV-infected partner(s) and expert consultation is recommended; modification of therapy (if needed) and optimization of the woman's health should be done prior to conception. HIV-infected women not planning a pregnancy may use any available type of contraception, considering possible drug interactions and contraindications of the specific method. In addition, consistent use of condoms is also recommended (even during pregnancy) to prevent transmission of HIV or other sexually transmitted diseases.

Health care providers are encouraged to enroll pregnant women exposed to antiretroviral medications as early in pregnancy as possible in the Antiretroviral Pregnancy Registry (1-800-258-4263 or www.APRegistry.com). Health care providers caring for HIV-infected women and their infants may contact the National Perinatal HIV Hotline (888-448-8765) for clinical consultation (HHS [perinatal] 2016).

Dental Comment See Local Anesthetic/Vasoconstrictor Precautions

Riluzole (RIL yoo zole)

Brand Names: US Rilutek

Brand Names: Canada Apo-Riluzole; Mylan-Riluzole; Rilutek

Pharmacologic Category Glutamate Inhibitor

Use Amyotrophic lateral sclerosis: Treatment of patients with amyotrophic lateral sclerosis (ALS); may extend survival and/or time to tracheostomy

Local Anesthetic/Vasoconstrictor Precautions No information available to require special precautions

Effects on Dental Treatment Key adverse event(s) related to dental treatment: Oral *Candida* infection and stomatitis.

Effects on Bleeding No information available to require special precautions

Adverse Reactions

>10%:

Gastrointestinal: Nausea (16%)

Neuromuscular & skeletal: Weakness (19%)

1% to 10%:

Cardiovascular: Hypertension (5%), peripheral edema (3%), tachycardia (3%)

Central nervous system: Dizziness (4%), drowsiness (2%), vertigo (2%), malaise (1%)

Dermatologic: Pruritus (4%), eczema (2%), exfoliative dermatitis (1%)

Gastrointestinal: Abdominal pain (5%), vomiting (4%), flatulence (3%), oral paresthesia (2%), dental caries (1%), oral candidiasis (1%), stomatitis (1%)

Genitourinary: Urinary tract infection (3%), dysuria (1%)

Hepatic: Increased liver enzymes (>3 x ULN: 8%; >5 x ULN: 2%)

Neuromuscular & skeletal: Arthralgia (4%), tremor (1%)

Respiratory: Decreased lung function (10%), cough (3%)

<1%, postmarketing, and/or case reports (Limited to important or life-threatening): Amblyopia, anaphylactoid reaction, anaphylaxis, angioedema, aplastic anemia, arthropathy, asthma, ataxia, bradycardia, bundle branch block, cardiac failure, cataract, cerebral hemorrhage, deafness, dementia, diabetes mellitus, diabetes insipidus, drug-induced extrapyramidal reaction, edema, erythema multiforme, facial paralysis, gastrointestinal hemorrhage, gastrointestinal ulcer, glaucoma, hallucination, hematemesis, hematuria, hemoptysis, hepatitis, hypercalcemia, hypokalemia, hypokinesia, hyponatremia, hypotension, hypersensitivity pneumonitis, increased gamma-glutamyl transferase, increased lactate dehydrogenase, increased serum alkaline phosphatase, interstitial pulmonary disease, jaundice, leukocytosis, leukopenia, lymphadenopathy, mania, myoclonus, neutropenia, osteonecrosis, osteoporosis, pancreatitis, peripheral neuritis, pleural effusion, pseudomembranous colitis, purpura, respiratory acidosis, seizure, subarachnoid hemorrhage, thrombosis, urinary retention, urticaria, uterine hemorrhage, ventricular fibrillation, ventricular tachycardia

General Dosage Range Oral: *Adults:* 50 mg twice daily

Mechanism of Action Mechanism of action is not known. Pharmacologic properties include inhibitory effect on glutamate release, inactivation of voltage-dependent sodium channels; and ability to interfere with intracellular events that follow transmitter binding at excitatory amino acid receptors

Pharmacodynamics/Kinetics

Half-life Elimination 12 hours

Pregnancy Considerations Adverse events have been observed in animal reproduction studies. Use is contraindicated during pregnancy (Canadian labeling).

RimabotulinumtoxinB
(rime uh BOT yoo lin num TOKS in bee)

Related Information

Dentin Hypersensitivity, Acid Erosion, High Caries Index, Management of Alveolar Osteitis, and Xerostomia *on page 1857*

Brand Names: US Myobloc

Pharmacologic Category Neuromuscular Blocker Agent, Toxin

Use Cervical dystonia: Treatment of cervical dystonia (spasmodic torticollis)

Local Anesthetic/Vasoconstrictor Precautions No information available to require special precautions

Effects on Dental Treatment Key adverse event(s) related to dental treatment: Xerostomia (normal salivary flow resumes upon discontinuation), stomatitis, and abnormal taste.

Effects on Bleeding No information available to require special precautions

Adverse Reactions

>10%:

Central nervous system: Headache (10% to 16%), pain (≤13%)

Gastrointestinal: Dysphagia (10% to 25%; severe dysphagia: 3%), xerostomia (3% to 34%; severe xerostomia: 6%)

Local: Injection site pain (12% to 16%)

Neuromuscular & skeletal: Neck pain (≤17%)

Miscellaneous: Infection (≤19%), antibody formation (~10% to 18%, at 12 and 18 months, respectively)

1% to 10%:

Cardiovascular: Chest pain, edema, peripheral edema, vasolidation

Central nervous system: Dizziness (3% to 6%), anxiety, chills, confusion, fever, hyperesthesia, malaise, migraine, somnolence, tremor, vertigo

Dermatologic: Pruritus, bruising

Endocrine & metabolic: Hypercholesterolemia

Gastrointestinal: Nausea (≤10%), dyspepsia (≤10%,) glossitis, stomatitis, taste perversion, vomiting

Genitourinary: Cystitis, urinary tract infection, vaginal moniliasis

Hematologic: Serum neutralizing activity

Neuromuscular & skeletal: Torticollis (≤8%), arthralgia (≤7%), back pain (≤7%), myasthenia (≤6%), weakness (≤6%), arthritis, hernia

Ocular: Amblyopia, vision abnormal

Otic: Otitis media, tinnitus

Respiratory: Cough (3% to 7%; placebo 3%), dyspnea, pneumonia

Miscellaneous: Flu-like syndrome (6% to 9%), abscess, allergic reaction, cyst, neoplasm, viral infection

<1%, postmarketing, and/or case reports: Constipation

General Dosage Range IM: *Adults:* Initial: 2,500 to 5,000 units divided among the affected muscles

Mechanism of Action RimabotulinumtoxinB (previously known as botulinum toxin type B) is a neurotoxin produced by *Clostridium botulinum*, spore-forming anaerobic bacillus. It cleaves synaptic Vesicle Association Membrane Protein (VAMP; synaptobrevin) which is a component of the protein complex responsible for docking and fusion of the synaptic vesicle to the presynaptic membrane. By blocking neurotransmitter release, rimabotulinumtoxinB paralyzes the muscle.

Pharmacodynamics/Kinetics

Duration of Action 12-16 weeks

Pregnancy Risk Factor C (manufacturer)

Pregnancy Considerations Reproduction studies have not been conducted. Based on limited case reports using onabotulinumtoxinA, adverse fetal effects have not been observed with inadvertent administration during pregnancy. It is currently recommended to ensure adequate contraception in women of childbearing years.

RiMANTAdine (ri MAN ta deen)

Related Information

Systemic Viral Diseases *on page 1806*

Brand Names: US Flumadine

Pharmacologic Category Antiviral Agent; Antiviral Agent, Adamantane

Use

Influenza A virus, prophylaxis: Prophylaxis against influenza A virus in adults and children 1 year and older; also refer to current ACIP guidelines for recommendations during current influenza season.

Influenza A virus, treatment: Treatment of illness caused by influenza A virus in adults; also refer to current ACIP guidelines for recommendations during current influenza season.

Local Anesthetic/Vasoconstrictor Precautions No information available to require special precautions

Effects on Dental Treatment Key adverse event(s) related to dental treatment: Xerostomia (normal salivary flow resumes upon discontinuation).

Effects on Bleeding No information available to require special precautions

Adverse Reactions

1% to 10%:

Central nervous system: Insomnia (2% to 3%), lack of concentration (≤2%), dizziness (1% to 2%), nervousness (1% to 2%), fatigue (1%), headache (1%)

Gastrointestinal: Nausea (3%), anorexia (2%), vomiting (2%), xerostomia (2%), abdominal pain (1%)

Neuromuscular & skeletal: Weakness (1%)

<1%, postmarketing, and/or case reports: Abnormal gait, agitation, altered sense of smell, ataxia, bronchospasm, cardiac failure, confusion, cough, depression, diarrhea, drowsiness, dysgeusia, dyspepsia, dyspnea, euphoria, hallucination, heart block, hyperkinesia, hypertension, lactation, palpitations, pallor, pedal edema, seizure, skin rash, syncope, tachycardia, tinnitus, tremor

General Dosage Range Dosage adjustment recommended in patients with hepatic or renal impairment

Oral:

Children 1 to 9 years: 5 mg/kg/dose once daily (maximum: 150 mg/day)

Children and Adolescents ≥10 years and Adults: 100 mg twice daily

Elderly: 100 mg once daily

Mechanism of Action Exerts its inhibitory effect on three antigenic subtypes of influenza A virus (H1N1, H2N2, H3N2) early in the viral replicative cycle, possibly inhibiting the uncoating process; it has no activity against influenza B virus and is two- to eightfold more active than amantadine

Pharmacodynamics/Kinetics

Onset of Action Antiviral activity: No data exist establishing a correlation between plasma concentration and antiviral effect

Half-life Elimination

Children 5 to 8 years: 24.8 ± 9.4 hours (Anderson 1987)

Adults: 25.4 hours (range: 13 to 65 hours); Elderly (71 to 79 years of age): 32 hours (range: 20 to 65 hours)

Time to Peak 6 hours

Pregnancy Risk Factor C

Pregnancy Considerations Adverse events have been observed in animal reproduction studies. Untreated influenza infection is associated with an increased risk of adverse events to the fetus and an increased risk of complications or death to the mother. Neuraminidase inhibitors are currently recommended for the treatment or prophylaxis influenza in pregnant women and women up to 2 weeks postpartum. Appropriate antiviral agents are currently recommended as an adjunct to vaccination and should not be used as a substitute for vaccination in pregnant women (CDC 60 [1] 2011; CDC March 13, 2014; CDC January 2015).

Health care providers are encouraged to refer women exposed to influenza vaccine, or who have taken an antiviral medication during pregnancy to the Vaccines and Medications in Pregnancy Surveillance System (VAMPSS) by contacting The Organization of Teratology Information Specialists (OTIS) at 1-877-311-8972.

Rimexolone (ri MEKS oh lone)

Brand Names: US Vexol [DSC]

Pharmacologic Category Corticosteroid, Ophthalmic

Use Ophthalmic inflammatory conditions: Treatment of postoperative inflammation following ocular surgery; treatment of anterior uveitis

Local Anesthetic/Vasoconstrictor Precautions No information available to require special precautions

Effects on Dental Treatment No significant effects or complications reported

Effects on Bleeding No information available to require special precautions

Adverse Reactions

1% to 5%:

Central nervous system: Foreign body sensation of eye

Ophthalmic: Blurred vision, eye discharge, eye discomfort, eye pain, eye pruritus, increased intraocular pressure, ocular hyperemia

<2%:

Cardiovascular: Hypotension

Central nervous system: Headache

Gastrointestinal: Dysgeusia

Respiratory: Pharyngitis, rhinitis

Frequency not defined:

Infection: Secondary ocular infection

Ophthalmic: Cataract, eye disease (defects in visual activity), eye perforation, optic nerve damage

<1%, postmarketing, and/or case reports: Anterior chamber fibrin deposition, brow ache, conjunctival edema, corneal edema, corneal erosion, corneal infiltrates, corneal staining, corneal ulcer, crusting of eyelid, eye irritation, keratitis, lacrimation, ocular edema, photophobia, sticky sensation of eye, xerophthalmia

General Dosage Range Ophthalmic: *Adults:* Anterior uveitis: Instill 1 to 2 drops in affected eye every 1 to 2 hours during waking hours; Postoperative ocular inflammation: Instill 1 to 2 drops in affected eye 4 times daily

Mechanism of Action Suppresses the inflammatory response by inhibiting edema, capillary dilation, leukocyte migration and scar formation.

Pharmacodynamics/Kinetics

Half-life Elimination 1 to 2 hours

Pregnancy Risk Factor C

Pregnancy Considerations Adverse events have been observed in animal reproduction studies following subcutaneous administration. The amount of rimexolone absorbed systemically following ophthalmic administration is low (<80 to 470 pg/mL).

Riociguat (rye oh SIG ue at)

Brand Names: US Adempas

Brand Names: Canada Adempas

Pharmacologic Category Soluble Guanylate Cyclase (sGC) Stimulator

Use

Chronic thromboembolic pulmonary hypertension: Treatment of persistent/recurrent chronic thromboembolic pulmonary hypertension (CTEPH) (WHO group 4) after surgical treatment or inoperable CTEPH to improve exercise capacity and WHO functional class in adults.

Pulmonary arterial hypertension: Treatment of pulmonary arterial hypertension (PAH) (WHO group 1) to improve exercise capacity, improve WHO functional class and to delay clinical worsening in adults.

Local Anesthetic/Vasoconstrictor Precautions No information available to require special precautions

Effects on Dental Treatment No significant effects or complications reported

Effects on Bleeding Bleeding, some serious, including intra-abdominal and hematemesis has been reported. There is a risk of unanticipated bleeding during dental procedures in patients exposed to riociguat; medical consult suggested prior to dental surgery in order to discuss bleeding risks and postoperative management considerations.

Adverse Reactions Frequency not always defined.

Cardiovascular: Hypotension (3% to 10%; Ghofrani 2013), palpitations, peripheral edema

Central nervous system: Headache (27%), dizziness (20%)

Gastrointestinal: Dyspepsia (13% to 19%; Ghofrani 2013), nausea (14%), diarrhea (12%), vomiting (10%), gastritis (2% to 6%; Ghofrani 2013), constipation (5%), gastroesophageal reflux disease (5%), abdominal distention, dysphagia

Hematologic & oncologic: Anemia (7%), major hemorrhage (2%; including vaginal hemorrhage, catheter site hemorrhage, subdural hematoma, hematemesis, and intra-abdominal hemorrhage)

Respiratory: Hemoptysis (1%), epistaxis, nasal congestion

General Dosage Range Dosage adjustment recommended in patients on concomitant therapy, smokers, and in patients who develop toxicities.

Oral: *Adults:* 0.5 to 1 mg 3 times daily; maximum dose: 2.5 mg 3 times daily.

Mechanism of Action Riociguat has a dual mode of action. It sensitizes soluble guanylate cyclase (sGC) to endogenous nitric oxide (NO) by stabilizing the NO-sGC binding. Riociguat also directly stimulates sGC independent of NO. Riociguat stimulates the NO-sGC-cGMP pathway and leads to increased generation of cGMP with subsequent vasodilation.

Pharmacodynamics/Kinetics

Half-life Elimination Patients: 12 hours; Healthy subjects: 7 hours

Time to Peak Plasma: 1.5 hours

Pregnancy Risk Factor X

Pregnancy Considerations Use is contraindicated in pregnant women.

Reproduction studies in animals have shown evidence of fetal abnormalities. **[US Boxed Warnings]: Riociguat may cause fetal harm if given to pregnant women. Riociguat is available to females only through the restricted Adempas Risk Evaluation and Mitigation Strategy (REMS) Program. All females of reproductive potential should have a negative pregnancy test prior to beginning therapy and testing should continue monthly during treatment and one month after discontinuing therapy. Females of childbearing potential should not become pregnant during therapy or for 1 month following discontinuation riociguat.** All females regardless of their reproductive potential must be enrolled in the REMS program; prescribers and pharmacies must also be enrolled in the program. Females of reproductive potential must be able to comply with pregnancy testing and contraception requirements of the program. Women may use one highly effective form of contraception (intrauterine device, contraceptive implant, or tubal sterilization) or a combination of methods (hormonal contraceptive with a barrier method or two barrier methods). A hormonal contraceptive or barrier method must be used in addition to a partner's vasectomy, if that method is chosen. Females should be counseled on pregnancy prevention and planning and instructed to notify their prescriber immediately if a pregnancy should occur. Women with pulmonary arterial hypertension (PAH) are encouraged to avoid pregnancy (McLaughlin 2009; Taichman 2014).

Prescribing and Access Restrictions As a requirement of the REMS program, access to this medication is restricted. Female patients, prescribers, and pharmacies must register and be active in the Adempas REMS Program. Additional information, including certified pharmacies, is provided at www.adempasREMS.com or by calling 1-855-423-3672.

Risedronate (ris ED roe nate)

Related Information

Osteonecrosis of the Jaw *on page 1796*

Rheumatoid Arthritis, Osteoarthritis, and Osteoporosis *on page 1792*

Brand Names: US Actonel; Atelvia

Brand Names: Canada Actonel; Actonel DR; Apo-Risedronate; Auro-Risedronate; Dom-Risedronate; JAMP-Risedronate; Mylan-Risedronate; PMS-Risedronate; ratio-Risedronate; Riva-Risedronate; Sandoz-Risedronate; Teva-Risedronate

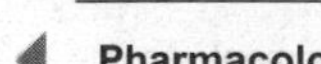

Pharmacologic Category Bisphosphonate Derivative

Use

Actonel:

Osteoporosis: Treatment and prevention of osteoporosis in postmenopausal women; treatment of osteoporosis in men; treatment and prevention of glucocorticoid-induced osteoporosis

Paget disease: Treatment of Paget disease of the bone

Atelvia, Actonel DR [Canadian product]:

Osteoporosis: Treatment of osteoporosis in postmenopausal women

Local Anesthetic/Vasoconstrictor Precautions No information available to require special precautions

Effects on Dental Treatment Osteonecrosis of the jaw (ONJ), generally associated with local infection and/or tooth extraction and often with delayed healing, has been reported in patients taking bisphosphonates. Symptoms included nonhealing extraction socket or an exposed jawbone. Most reported cases of bisphosphonate-associated osteonecrosis have been in cancer patients treated with intravenous bisphosphonates. However, some have occurred in patients with postmenopausal osteoporosis taking oral bisphosphonates. Dental surgery, particularly tooth extraction, may increase the risk for ONJ. Patients who develop ONJ while on bisphosphonate therapy should receive care by an oral surgeon. See Dental Comment.

Effects on Bleeding No information available to require special precautions

Adverse Reactions Frequency may vary with product, dose, and indication.

>10%:

Cardiovascular: Hypertension (11%)

Central nervous system: Headache (3% to 18%)

Dermatologic: Skin rash (8% to 12%)

Gastrointestinal: Gastrointestinal disease (perforations, ulcers, or bleeding; 51%), diarrhea (5% to 20%), nausea (4% to 13%), abdominal pain (2% to 12%)

Genitourinary: Urinary tract infection (11%)

Infection: Infection (31%)

Neuromuscular & skeletal: Arthralgia (7% to 33%), back pain (6% to 28%)

1% to 10%:

Cardiovascular: Peripheral edema (8%), chest pain (7%), cardiac arrhythmia (2%)

Central nervous system: Depression (7%), dizziness (3% to 7%)

Endocrine & metabolic: Increased parathyroid hormone (8% to 9%; >1.5 x ULN: ≤2%), hypocalcemia (≤5%), hypophosphatemia (<3% decrease from baseline)

Gastrointestinal: Dyspepsia (4% to 8%), constipation (3% to 7%), vomiting (2% to 5%), gastritis (1% to 3%), gastroesophageal reflux disease (1% to 2%), duodenitis (≤1%), glossitis (≤1%)

Genitourinary: Benign prostatic hyperplasia (5%), nephrolithiasis (3%)

Hypersensitivity: Acute phase reaction-like symptoms (≤8%; includes fever, influenza-like illness)

Infection: Influenza (6% to 7%)

Neuromuscular & skeletal: Arthropathy (7%), myalgia (1% to 7%), limb pain (2% to 4%), musculoskeletal pain (2%), muscle spasm (1% to 2%)

Ophthalmic: Cataract (7%)

Respiratory: Flu-like symptoms (10%), pharyngitis (6%), rhinitis (6%), bronchitis (4%), upper respiratory tract infection (3% to 4%)

<1%, postmarketing, and/or case reports: Abnormal hepatic function tests, angioedema, bullous skin reaction, cough, esophageal ulcer, esophagitis, exacerbation of asthma, femur fracture, gastric ulcer, hypersensitivity reaction, iritis, ostealgia, osteonecrosis (primarily of the jaw), Stevens-Johnson syndrome, toxic epidermal necrolysis, uveitis

General Dosage Range Oral: *Adults:* 5 mg or 30 mg once daily **or** 35 mg once weekly **or** 150 mg once a month

Mechanism of Action A bisphosphonate which inhibits bone resorption via actions on osteoclasts or on osteoclast precursors; decreases the rate of bone resorption, leading to an indirect increase in bone mineral density. In Paget's disease, characterized by disordered resorption and formation of bone, inhibition of resorption leads to an indirect decrease in bone formation; but the newly-formed bone has a more normal architecture.

Pharmacodynamics/Kinetics

Onset of Action May require weeks

Half-life Elimination Initial: 1.5 hours; Terminal: 480 to 561 hours

Time to Peak Serum: 1 to 3 hours

Pregnancy Risk Factor C

Pregnancy Considerations Adverse events were observed in some animal reproduction studies. It is not known if bisphosphonates cross the placenta, but fetal exposure is expected (Djokanovic, 2008; Stathopoulos, 2011). Bisphosphonates are incorporated into the bone matrix and gradually released over time. The amount available in the systemic circulation varies by dose and duration of therapy. Theoretically, there may be a risk of fetal harm when pregnancy follows the completion of therapy; however, available data have not shown that exposure to bisphosphonates during pregnancy significantly increases the risk of adverse fetal events (Djokanovic, 2008; Levy, 2009; Stathopoulos, 2011). Until additional data is available, most sources recommend discontinuing bisphosphonate therapy in women of reproductive potential as early as possible prior to a planned pregnancy; use in premenopausal women should be reserved for special circumstances when rapid bone loss is occurring (Bhalla, 2010; Pereira, 2012; Stathopoulos, 2011). Because hypocalcemia has been described following *in utero* bisphosphonate exposure, exposed infants should be monitored for hypocalcemia after birth (Djokanovic, 2008; Stathopoulos, 2011).

Dental Comment A review of 2,408 published cases of bisphosphonate-associated osteonecrosis of the jaw bone (BP-associated ONJ) was done by Filleul 2010. BP therapy was associated with 89% of the cases to treat malignancies and 11% of the cases to treat non-malignant conditions. Information on the specific bisphosphonate used was available for 1,694 of the patients. Intravenous therapy (primarily zoledronic acid) was received by 88% of the patients and 12% received oral treatment (primarily alendronate). Of all the cases of BP-associated ONJ, 67% were preceded by tooth extraction and for 26% of patients, there was no predisposing factor identified.

A 2010 retrospective case review reported the prevalence of BP-associated ONJ in patients using alendronate-type drugs was one out of 952 patients or ~0.1% (Lo 2010). Of the 8,572 respondents, nine cases of ONJ were identified; five had developed ONJ spontaneously and four developed ONJ after tooth extraction. When extrapolated to patient-years of bisphosphonate exposure, this prevalence rate of 0.1% equates to a frequency of 28 cases per 100,000 person-years of oral bisphosphonate treatment. An Australian group (Mavrokokki 2007), identified the frequency of BP-associated ONJ in osteoporotic patients, mainly taking weekly oral alendronate, was 1 in 8,470 to 1 in 2,260 (0.01% to 0.04%) patients. If extractions were carried out, the calculated frequency was 1 in 1,130 to 1 in 296 (0.09% to 0.34%) patients. The median time to onset of ONJ in alendronate patients was 24 months.

According to the 2011 report by the American Dental Association (ADA), the incidence of BP-associated ONJ remains low and the benefits of using oral bisphosphonates significantly outweighs the risk of developing BP-associated ONJ for treatment and prevention of osteoporosis and cancer treatment (Hellstein 2011). The full 47-page report can be accessed at http://www.ada.org/~/media/ADA/Member%20Center/FIles/topics_ARONJ_report.ashx.

The ADA review of 2011 stated the incidence of oral BP-associated ONJ was one case for every 1,000 individuals exposed to oral bisphosphonates (0.1%) (Hellstein 2011).

The most comprehensive review to date on osteonecrosis of the jaw bone (ONJ) has been published in the *Journal of Bone and Mineral Research* (Khan 2015), and written by an International Task Force of authors, totaling 34, from academe; industry; clinical medical and dental practice; oral and maxillofacial surgery; bone and mineral research; epidemiology; medical and dental oncology; orthopedic surgery; osteoporosis research; muscle and bone research; endocrinology and diagnostic sciences. The work provides a systematic review of the literature and international consensus on the classification, incidence, pathophysiology, diagnosis, and management of ONJ in both oncology and osteoporosis patient populations. This review of the literature from January 2003 to April 2014, with 299 references, offers recommendations for management of ONJ based on multidisciplinary international consensus.

Prevalence and incidence of ONJ in osteoporosis patients from the Task Force report:

Prevalence – the percent of osteoporotic population affected with ONJ

After reviewing all literature reports on this subject, the Task Force concluded that the prevalence of ONJ in patients prescribed oral BPs for the treatment of osteoporosis ranges from 0% to 0.04% with the majority being below 0.001%. However, the Task Force does cite the study of (Lo et al) that evaluated the Kaiser Permanente database and found the prevalence of ONJ in those receiving BPs for more than 2 years to range from 0.05% to 0.21% and appeared to be related to duration of exposure. As mentioned above, the American Dental Association has previously reported that the prevalence of ONJ in osteoporosis patients using oral BPs to be 1 out of 1,000 or 0.1% (Hellstein 2011).

Incidence - the rate at which ONJ occurs or the number of times it happens

From currently available data, the incidence of ONJ in the osteoporosis patient population appears to be low ranging from 0.15% to less than 0.001% person-years drug exposure. In terms of the osteoporosis patient population taking oral BPs, the incidence ranges from 1.04 to 69 per 100,000 patient years of drug exposure.

RisperiDONE (ris PER i done)

Related Information

Clinical Risk Related to Drugs Prolonging QT Interval *on page 1772*

Brand Names: US RisperDAL; RisperDAL Consta; RisperDAL M-TAB; RisperiDONE M-TAB

Brand Names: Canada ACT Risperidone; AG-Risperidone; Apo-Risperidone; Ava-Risperidone; Dom-Risperidone; IPG-Risperidone; JAMP-Risperidone; Mar-Risperidone; Mint-Risperidone; Mylan-Risperidone; Mylan-Risperidone ODT; NU-Risperidone; PHL-Risperidone; PHL-Risperidone ODT; PMS-Risperidone; PMS-Risperidone ODT; PRO-Risperidone; Q-Risperidone; RAN-Risperidone; ratio-Risperidone; Risperdal; Risperdal Consta; Risperdal M-Tab; Riva-Risperidone; Sandoz-Risperidone; Teva-Risperidone

Pharmacologic Category Antimanic Agent; Second Generation (Atypical) Antipsychotic

Use

Injection:

Bipolar disorder: As monotherapy or as adjunctive therapy to lithium or valproate for the maintenance treatment of bipolar I disorder.

Schizophrenia: Treatment of schizophrenia.

Oral:

Bipolar mania:

Monotherapy: For the treatment of acute manic or mixed episodes associated with bipolar I disorder in adults and in children and adolescents 10 to 17 years of age.

Adjunctive therapy: As adjunctive therapy with lithium or valproate for the treatment of adults with acute manic or mixed episodes associated with bipolar I disorder.

Irritability associated with autistic disorder: For the treatment of irritability associated with autistic disorder in children and adolescents 5 to 17 years of age, including symptoms of aggression toward others, deliberate self-injuriousness, temper tantrums, and quickly changing moods.

Schizophrenia: For the treatment of schizophrenia in adults and adolescents 13 to 17 years of age.

Local Anesthetic/Vasoconstrictor Precautions RisperiDONE is one of the drugs confirmed to prolong the QT interval and is accepted as having a risk of causing torsades de pointes. The risk of drug-induced torsades de pointes is extremely low when a single QT interval prolonging drug is prescribed. In terms of epinephrine, it is not known what effect vasoconstrictors in the local anesthetic regimen will have in patients with a known history of congenital prolonged QT interval or in patients taking any medication that prolongs the QT interval. Until more information is obtained, it is suggested that the clinician consult with the physician prior to the use of a vasoconstrictor in suspected patients, and that the vasoconstrictor (epinephrine, mepivacaine, and levonordefrin [Carbocaine 2% with Neo-Cobefrin]) be used with caution.

Effects on Dental Treatment Key adverse event(s) related to dental treatment: Significant xerostomia (normal salivary flow resumes upon discontinuation) and toothache.

Effects on Bleeding No information available to require special precautions

Adverse Reactions

>10%:

Central nervous system: Sedation (children 12% to 63%; adults 5% to 11%), parkinsonian-like syndrome (children 6% to 62%; adults 8% to 25%), drowsiness (adults 5% to 41%; children 4% to 11%), insomnia (≤32%), fatigue (children 18% to 31%; adults 1% to 9%), headache (12% to 21%), anxiety (≤8% to 16%), dizziness (3% to 16%), drooling (children 12%; adults <4%), akathisia (5% to 11%)

Endocrine & metabolic: Weight gain (≥7% kg increase from baseline: children 8% to 33%; adults 4% to 21%)

Gastrointestinal: Increased appetite (children 4% to 44%; adults 4%), vomiting (children 10% to 20%; adults <4%), constipation (5% to 17%), abdominal pain (children 6% to 16%; adults <4%), nausea (5% to 16%)

Genitourinary: Urinary incontinence (children 16%; adults <4%)

Neuromuscular & skeletal: Tremor (adults ≤24%; children ≤11%)

Respiratory: Nasopharyngitis (children 19%; adults ≤4%), cough (children ≤17%; adults ≤4%), rhinorrhea (children 12%; adults <4%)

Miscellaneous: Fever (children 16%; adults 1% to 2%)

1% to 10%:

Cardiovascular: Bradycardia (<4%), bundle branch block (<4%), buttock pain (<4%), chest pain (<4%), ECG changes (<4%), facial edema (<4%), first degree atrioventricular block (<4%), hypotension (<4%), orthostatic hypotension (<4%), palpitations (<4%), paresthesia (<4%), prolonged Q-T interval on ECG (<4%), tachycardia (adults <4%; children <1%), hypertension (≤3%), peripheral edema (≤3%), syncope (1% to 2%)

Central nervous system: Dystonia (2% to 6%), abnormal gait (4%), pain (1% to 4%), decreased attention span (≤4%), agitation (<4%), ataxia (<4%), depression (<4%), disturbed sleep (<4%), falling (<4%), lethargy (<4%), malaise (<4%), nervousness (<4%), orthostatic dizziness (<4%), seizure (<4%), tardive dyskinesia (<4%), vertigo (<4%), hypoesthesia (≤2%)

Dermatologic: Skin rash (<4% to 8%), eczema (<4%), pruritus (<4%), skin sclerosis (<4%), xeroderma (≤3%), acne vulgaris (<1% to 2%)

Endocrine & metabolic: Increased thirst (children ≤7%; adults <1%), weight loss (≤4%), amenorrhea (4%), decreased libido (<4%), galactorrhea (<4%), gynecomastia (<4%), hyperglycemia (<4%), hyperprolactinemia (<4%), increased gamma-glutamyl transferase (<4%), oligomenorrhea (<4%)

Gastrointestinal: Xerostomia (≤7% to 10%), dyspepsia (3% to 10%), sialorrhea (1% to 10%), diarrhea (<4% to 8%), decreased appetite (≤6%), anorexia (<4%), gastritis (<4%), gastroenteritis (<4%), toothache (≤3%)

Genitourinary: Menstruation (≤4%), cystitis (<4%), ejaculatory disorder (<4%), erectile dysfunction (<4%), glycosuria (<4%), irregular menses (<4%), mastalgia (<4%), sexual disorder (<4%), urinary tract infection (<4%)

Hematologic & oncologic: Anemia (<4%), neutropenia (<4%)

Hepatic: Increased serum ALT (<4%), increased serum AST (<4%)

Hypersensitivity: Hypersensitivity (<4%)

Infection: Infection (<4%), influenza (<4%), localized infection (<4%), subcutaneous abscess (<4%), viral infection (<4%)

Local: Induration at injection site (<4%), injection site reaction (<4%), pain at injection site (<4%), swelling at injection site (<4%)

Neuromuscular & skeletal: Limb pain (2% to 6%), dyskinesia (adults ≤6%; children <1%), back pain (≤4%), arthralgia (2% to 4%), abnormal posture (<4%), akinesia (<4%), hypokinesia (<4%), musculoskeletal chest pain (<4%), myalgia (<4%), neck pain (<4%), weakness (<4%), increased creatine phosphokinase (≤2%)

Ophthalmic: Blurred vision (2% to 7%), conjunctivitis (<4%), reduced visual acuity (<4%)

Otic: Otalgia (≤4%), otic infection (<4%)

Respiratory: Nasal congestion (≤6% to 10%), pharyngolaryngeal pain (3% to 10%), rhinitis (<4% to 9%), respiratory tract infection (≤6% to 8%), bronchitis (<4%), dyspnea (<4%), flu-like symptoms (<4%), pharyngitis (<4%), pneumonia (<4%), sinusitis (<4%), epistaxis (≤2%), sinus congestion (≤2%)

<1%, postmarketing, and/or case reports: Abnormal erythrocytes, abscess at injection site, acariasis, agranulocytosis, alopecia, anaphylaxis, angioedema, anorgasmia, apnea, aspiration, atrial fibrillation, atrial premature contractions, blepharospasm, blunted affect, breast hypertrophy, bronchopneumonia, cardiorespiratory arrest, cellulitis, cerebral ischemia, cerebrovascular accident, cerebrovascular disorder, cheilitis, chills, cholestatic hepatitis, cholinergic syndrome, cold extremities, coma, confusion, crusting of eyelid, cutaneous nodule, cyst, decreased hematocrit, decreased hemoglobin, dehydration, delirium, depression of ST segment on ECG, dermal ulcer, dermatological disease, desquamation, diabetes mellitus, diabetic coma, diabetic ketoacidosis, disruption of body temperature regulation, diverticulitis, dry eye syndrome, dysgeusia, dysphagia, dysuria, edema, eosinophilia, erythema, esophageal motility disorder, esophagitis, eye discharge, eye infection, eyelid edema, eye rolling, fecal incontinence, fecaloma, feeling abnormal, flushing, glaucoma, granulocytopenia, hematemesis, hematoma, hematuria, hemorrhage, hepatic failure, hepatic injury, hyperkeratosis, hyperphosphatemia, hyperthermia, hypertonia, hypertriglyceridemia, hyperuricemia, hyperventilation, hypoglycemia, hypokalemia, hypokinesia, hyponatremia, hypoproteinemia, hypothermia, impaired consciousness, increased serum cholesterol, increased serum transaminases, intestinal obstruction, intraoperative floppy iris syndrome, inversion T wave on ECG, jaundice, joint stiffness, joint swelling, lacrimation, leukocytosis, leukopenia, leukorrhea, lip edema, loss of balance, lower respiratory tract infection, lymphadenopathy, mania, mastitis, migraine, movement disorder, myocardial infarction, myocarditis, nasal mucosa swelling, neuroleptic malignant syndrome, nystagmus, ocular hyperemia, onychomycosis, pancreatitis, Pelger-Huët anomaly, phlebitis, photophobia, pitting edema, pituitary neoplasm, pollakiuria, polydipsia, precocious puberty, priapism, pulmonary congestion, pulmonary embolism, rales, renal insufficiency, respiratory congestion, respiratory distress, retinal artery occlusion, retrograde ejaculation, rhabdomyolysis, rigors, sarcoidosis, seborrhea, seborrheic dermatitis of scalp, SIADH, skin discoloration, skin lesion, sleep apnea, speech disturbance, stomatitis, stridor, swelling of eye, synostosis, thrombocytopenia, thrombophlebitis, thrombotic thrombocytopenic purpura,

tinnitus, tissue necrosis, tongue discoloration, tongue edema, tongue paralysis, tongue spasm, tonsillitis, torticollis, tracheobronchitis, transient ischemic attacks, unresponsive to stimuli, urinary retention, urticaria, vaginal discharge, ventricular premature contractions, ventricular tachycardia, voice disorder, water intoxication, wheezing, withdrawal syndrome, xerophthalmia

General Dosage Range Dosage adjustment recommended in patients with hepatic or renal impairment

IM: *Adults:* 25 mg every 2 weeks (range: 12.5 to 50 mg every 2 weeks; maximum: 50 mg every 2 weeks)

Oral:

Children ≥5 years: Irritability associated with autistic disorder: Initial: 0.25 mg daily (15 to <20 kg) or 0.5 mg daily (≥20 kg); dosing range 0.5 to 3 mg

Children 10 to 17 years: Bipolar disorder: Initial: 0.5 mg once daily; Recommended target dose: 1 to 2.5 mg daily; dosing range 1 to 6 mg daily

Children: 13 to 17 years: Schizophrenia: Initial: 0.5 mg once daily; Recommended target dose: 3 mg daily; dosing range 1 to 6 mg daily

Adults: Initial: 2 to 3 mg daily in 1 to 2 divided doses; Maintenance: 1 to 8 mg daily in 1 to 2 divided doses

Elderly: Initial: 0.5 mg twice daily

Mechanism of Action Risperidone is a benzisoxazole atypical antipsychotic with high 5-HT_2- dopamine-D_2 receptor antagonist activity. $Alpha_1$, $alpha_2$ adrenergic, and histaminergic receptors are also antagonized with high affinity. Risperidone has low to moderate affinity for 5-HT_{1C}, 5-HT_{1D}, and 5-HT_{1A} receptors, weak affinity for D_1 and no affinity for muscarinics or $beta_1$ and $beta_2$ receptors.

Pharmacodynamics/Kinetics

Half-life Elimination Active moiety (risperidone and its active metabolite 9-hydroxyrisperidone)

Oral: 20 hours (mean); prolonged in elderly patients

Extensive metabolizers: Risperidone: 3 hours; 9-hydroxyrisperidone: 21 hours

Poor metabolizers: Risperidone: 20 hours; 9-hydroxyrisperidone: 30 hours

Injection: 3 to 6 days; related to microsphere erosion and subsequent absorption of risperidone

Time to Peak Plasma: Oral: Risperidone: Within 1 hour; 9-hydroxyrisperidone: Extensive metabolizers: 3 hours; Poor metabolizers: 17 hours

Pregnancy Risk Factor C

Pregnancy Considerations Adverse events were observed in animal reproduction studies. In human studies, risperidone and its metabolite cross the placenta (Newport, 2007). An increased risk of teratogenic effects has not been observed following maternal use of risperidone (limited data) (Coppola, 2007). Agenesis of the corpus callosum has been noted in one case report of an infant exposed *in utero*; relationship to risperidone exposure is not known. Antipsychotic use during the third trimester of pregnancy has a risk for extrapyramidal symptoms (EPS) and/or withdrawal symptoms in newborns following delivery. Symptoms in the newborn may include agitation, feeding disorder, hypertonia, hypotonia, respiratory distress, somnolence, and tremor. These effects may be self-limiting and allow recovery within hours or days with no specific treatment, or they may be severe requiring prolonged hospitalization. When using Risperdal® Consta®, patients should notify healthcare provider if they become or intend to become pregnant during therapy or within 12 weeks of last injection. Risperidone may cause hyperprolactinemia, which may decrease reproductive function in both males and females.

The ACOG recommends that therapy during pregnancy be individualized; treatment with psychiatric medications during pregnancy should incorporate the clinical expertise of the mental health clinician, obstetrician, primary healthcare provider, and pediatrician. Safety data related to atypical antipsychotics during pregnancy is limited and routine use is not recommended. However, if a woman is inadvertently exposed to an atypical antipsychotic while pregnant, continuing therapy may be preferable to switching to a typical antipsychotic that the fetus has not yet been exposed to; consider risk: benefit (ACOG, 2008).

Healthcare providers are encouraged to enroll women 18 to 45 years of age exposed to risperidone during pregnancy in the Atypical Antipsychotics Pregnancy Registry (1-866-961-2388 or http://www.-womensmentalhealth.org/pregnancyregistry).

Dental Comment See Local Anesthetic/Vasoconstrictor Precautions

Ritonavir (ri TOE na veer)

Related Information

HIV Infection and AIDS *on page 1785*

Brand Names: US Norvir

Brand Names: Canada Norvir

Pharmacologic Category Antiretroviral, Protease Inhibitor (Anti-HIV)

Use HIV-1 infection: Treatment of HIV-1 infection in combination with other antiretroviral agents.

Local Anesthetic/Vasoconstrictor Precautions No information available to require special precautions

Effects on Dental Treatment Key adverse event(s) related to dental treatment: Xerostomia (normal salivary flow resumes upon discontinuation) and taste perversion.

Effects on Bleeding Increased bleeding has been noted with protease inhibitors in patients with hemophilia A or B. No information available to require routine special precautions relative to hemostasis in other patients.

Adverse Reactions Percentages as reported for combined experiences in both treatment-naive and experienced adults unless otherwise noted:

>10%:

Cardiovascular: Flushing (13%)

Central nervous system: Paresthesia (3% to 51%), fatigue (46%), dizziness (3% to 16%)

Dermatologic: Skin rash (≤28%), pruritus (12%)

Endocrine & metabolic: Hypercholesterolemia (3%; >240 mg/dL: 37% to 45%), increased serum triglycerides (9%; >800 mg/dL: 17% to 34%; >1500 mg/dL: 1% to 13%)

Gastrointestinal: Diarrhea (15% to 68%), nausea (26% to 57%), vomiting (14% to 32%), abdominal pain (6% to 26%), dysgeusia (7% to 16%) dyspepsia (≤12%)

Hepatic: Increased gamma-glutamyl transferase (5% to 20%)

Neuromuscular & skeletal: Musculoskeletal pain (arthralgia and back pain, ≤19%), weakness (10% to 15%), increased creatine phosphokinase (4% to 12%)

Respiratory: Cough (22%), oropharyngeal pain (16%)

2% to 10%:

Cardiovascular: Edema (including peripheral edema, ≤6%), hypertension (≤3%), syncope (1% to 3%), vasodilatation (2%)

Central nervous system: Peripheral neuropathy (10%), headache (6% to 7%), confusion (3%), disturbance in attention (3%), drowsiness (2% to 3%), insomnia (2% to 3%), depression (2%), anxiety (≤2%), malaise (1% to 2%)

Dermatologic: Acne vulgaris (4%), diaphoresis (2% to 3%)

Endocrine & metabolic: Increased uric acid (≤4%), lipodystrophy (acquired, 3%)

Gastrointestinal: Anorexia (2% to 8%), flatulence (1% to 8%), increased serum amylase (grades 3/4; pediatric: 7%), throat irritation (local, 2% to 3%), gastrointestinal hemorrhage (≤2%)

Hematologic & oncologic: Neutropenia (grades 3/4; pediatric: 9%), thrombocytopenia (<2%; grades 3/4; pediatric: 5%), anemia (<2%; grades 3/4; pediatric: 4%)

Hepatic: Increased serum AST (6% to 10%), increased serum ALT (8% to 9%), hepatitis (≤9%)

Hypersensitivity: Hypersensitivity reaction (≤8%)

Neuromuscular & skeletal: Myalgia (2% to 9%)

Ophthalmic: Blurred vision (6%)

Renal: Polyuria (4%)

Respiratory: Pharyngitis (≤1% to 3%)

Miscellaneous: Fever (1% to 5%)

<2%, postmarketing, and/or case reports: Adrenal suppression, adrenocortical insufficiency, amnesia, anaphylaxis, angioedema, aphasia, asthma, atrioventricular block (first, second, or third degree), bronchospasm, cachexia, cerebral ischemia, chest pain, cholestatic jaundice, cold extremities, coma, Cushing's syndrome, dehydration, dementia, depersonalization, diabetes mellitus, diabetic ketoacidosis, dyspnea, esophageal ulcer, gastroenteritis, gastroesophageal reflux disease, gout, hallucination, hematologic disease (myeloproliferative), hemorrhage (in patients with hemophilia A or B), hepatic coma, hepatitis, hepatomegaly, hepatosplenomegaly, hyperglycemia, hypotension, hypothermia, hypoventilation, immune reconstitution syndrome, increased serum bilirubin, intestinal obstruction, laryngeal edema, leukemia (acute myeloblastic), leukopenia, lymphadenopathy, lymphocytosis, malignant melanoma, manic behavior, myocardial infarction, neuropathy, orthostatic hypotension, palpitations, pancreatitis, paralysis, pneumonia, prolongation P-R interval on ECG, prolonged Q-T interval on ECG, pseudomembranous colitis, rectal hemorrhage, redistribution of body fat, renal failure, renal insufficiency, right bundle branch block, seizure, Stevens-Johnson syndrome, subdural hematoma, syncope, tachycardia, tongue edema, torsades de pointes, toxic epidermal necrolysis, ulcerative colitis, urticaria, vasospasm, venous thrombosis (cerebral), visual disturbance

General Dosage Range Dosage adjustment recommended in patients on concurrent therapy

Oral:

Infants >1 month and Children: Initial: 250 mg/m^2 twice daily; Maintenance: 350 to 400 mg/m^2 twice daily (maximum dose: 1200 mg/day)

Adolescents and Adults: 300 to 600 mg twice daily (maximum: 1200 mg/day)

Mechanism of Action Binds to the site of HIV-1 protease activity and inhibits cleavage of viral Gag-Pol polyprotein precursors into individual functional proteins required for infectious HIV. This results in the formation of immature, noninfectious viral particles.

Pharmacodynamics/Kinetics

Half-life Elimination Children: 2 to 4 hours; Adults: 3 to 5 hours

Time to Peak Oral solution: 2 hours (fasted); 4 hours (nonfasted)

Pregnancy Considerations Adverse events have been observed in animal reproduction studies only with doses which were also maternally toxic. Ritonavir has a low level of transfer across the human placenta; no increased risk of overall birth defects has been observed following first trimester exposure according to data collected by the antiretroviral pregnancy registry. A small increased risk of preterm birth has been associated with maternal use of protease inhibitor-based combination antiretroviral (cARV) therapy during pregnancy; however, the benefits of use generally outweigh this risk and protease inhibitors (PIs) should not be withheld if otherwise recommended. Hyperglycemia, new onset of diabetes mellitus, or diabetic ketoacidosis have been reported with protease inhibitors; it is not clear if pregnancy increases this risk. The HHS Perinatal HIV Guidelines consider ritonavir to be a preferred cARV component for use during pregnancy when used as a booster for other PIs (not recommended as a single protease inhibitor in ART naive pregnant women). The oral solution contains alcohol and propylene glycol and is not recommended for use in pregnancy. Early studies have shown lower plasma levels during pregnancy compared to postpartum, however dosage adjustment is not needed when used as a low-dose booster in pregnant women.

Combination antiretroviral therapy (cART) therapy is recommended for all HIV-infected pregnant women to keep the viral load below the limit of detection and reduce the risk of perinatal transmission. When HIV is diagnosed during pregnancy in a woman who has never received antiretroviral therapy, cART should begin as soon as possible after diagnosis. The Health and Human Services (HHS) Perinatal HIV Guidelines consider ritonavir, when used as a booster for other PIs, to be a preferred component of regimens for initial use in antiretroviral-naïve pregnant women (not recommended as initial therapy as a single protease inhibitor in ART naive pregnant women due to inferior efficacy and increased toxicity). The oral solution contains alcohol and therefore may not be the best formulation for use in pregnancy. Early studies have shown lower plasma levels during pregnancy compared to postpartum; however, dosage adjustment is not needed when used as a low-dose booster in pregnant women. In general, women who become pregnant on a stable cART regimen may continue that regimen if viral suppression is effective, appropriate drug exposure can be achieved, contraindications for use in pregnancy are not present, and the regimen is well tolerated. However, because treatment doses of ritonavir have a high risk of toxicity, women should be switched to a preferred or alternative regimen (ritonavir should only be used as a low-dose booster in pregnant women). Monitoring during pregnancy is more frequent than in non-pregnant adults; cART should be continued postpartum.

For HIV-infected couples planning a pregnancy, maximum viral suppression with cART is recommended prior to conception for the HIV-infected partner(s) and expert consultation is recommended; modification of therapy (if needed) and optimization of the woman's health should be done prior to conception. HIV-infected women not planning a pregnancy may use any available type of contraception, considering possible drug interactions and contraindications of the specific method. In addition, consistent use of condoms is also recommended (even during pregnancy) to prevent transmission of HIV or other sexually transmitted diseases.

Health care providers are encouraged to enroll pregnant women exposed to antiretroviral medications as early in pregnancy as possible in the Antiretroviral Pregnancy Registry (1-800-258-4263 or www.APRegistry.com). Health care providers caring for HIV-infected women and their infants may contact the National Perinatal HIV Hotline (888-448-8765) for clinical consultation (HHS [perinatal] 2016).

RiTUXimab (ri TUK si mab)

Brand Names: US Rituxan

Brand Names: Canada Rituxan; Rituxan SC

Pharmacologic Category Antineoplastic Agent, Anti-CD20; Antineoplastic Agent, Monoclonal Antibody; Antirheumatic Miscellaneous; Immunosuppressant Agent; Monoclonal Antibody

Use

Chronic lymphocytic leukemia: Treatment of previously untreated or previously treated CD20-positive chronic lymphocytic leukemia (CLL) (in combination with fludarabine and cyclophosphamide).

Granulomatosis with polyangiitis: Treatment of granulomatosis with polyangiitis (GPA; Wegener granulomatosis) (in combination with glucocorticoids).

Microscopic polyangiitis: Treatment of microscopic polyangiitis (MPA) (in combination with glucocorticoids).

Non-Hodgkin lymphomas: Treatment of CD20-positive non-Hodgkin lymphomas (NHL):

Relapsed or refractory, low-grade or follicular B-cell NHL (as a single agent)

Follicular B-cell NHL, previously untreated (in combination with first-line chemotherapy, and as single-agent maintenance therapy if response to first-line rituximab with chemotherapy)

Nonprogressing (including stable disease), low-grade B-cell NHL (as a single agent after first-line CVP treatment)

Diffuse large B-cell NHL, previously untreated (in combination with CHOP chemotherapy [or other anthracycline-based regimen])

Rheumatoid arthritis: Treatment of moderately to severely active rheumatoid arthritis (in combination with methotrexate) in adult patients with inadequate response to one or more TNF antagonist therapies.

Limitations of use: Rituximab is not recommended for use in patients with severe, active infections.

Local Anesthetic/Vasoconstrictor Precautions No information available to require special precautions

Effects on Dental Treatment No significant effects or complications reported

Effects on Bleeding Chemotherapy may result in significant myelosuppression, potentially including significant reduction in platelet counts (thrombocytopenia grades 3/4: 2% to 11%) and altered hemostasis. In patients who are under active treatment with these agents, medical consult is suggested.

Adverse Reactions Patients treated with rituximab for rheumatoid arthritis (RA) may experience fewer adverse reactions.

>10%:

Cardiovascular: Peripheral edema (8% to 16%), hypertension (6% to 12%)

Central nervous system: Fatigue (13% to 39%), chills (3% to 33%), neuropathy (≤30%), headache (17% to 19%), insomnia (≤14%), pain (12%)

Dermatologic: Skin rash (10% to 17%), pruritus (5% to 17%), night sweats (15%)

Endocrine & metabolic: Weight gain (11%)

Gastrointestinal: Nausea (8% to 23%), diarrhea (10% to 17%), abdominal pain (2% to 14%)

Hematologic & oncologic: Lymphocytopenia (48%; grades 3/4: 40%; median duration: 14 days), anemia (8% to 35%; grades 3/4: 3%), leukopenia (NHL: 14%, grades 3/4: 4%; CLL: grades 3/4: 23%; GPA/MPA: 10%), neutropenia (NHL: 14%, grades 3/4: 4% to 6%, median duration: 13 days; CLL: grades 3/4: 30% to 49%; late-onset: <1%, occurs >40 days after last dose), thrombocytopenia (12%; grades 3/4: 2% to 11%), cytopenia (may be prolonged), febrile neutropenia (CLL)

Hepatic: Increased serum ALT (≤13%)

Hypersensitivity: Angioedema (11%)

Immunologic: Antibody development (human antichimeric antibody [HACA] positive: 1% to 23%)

Infection: Infection (19% to 62%), bacterial infection (19%)

Neuromuscular & skeletal: Weakness (2% to 26%), muscle spasm (≤17%), arthralgia (6% to 13%)

Respiratory: Cough (13%), rhinitis (3% to 12%), epistaxis (≤11%)

Miscellaneous: Infusion related reaction (lymphoma: first dose: 77%, decreases with subsequent infusions and may include rigors; CLL: 59%, grades 3/4: 7% to 9%; RA: first infusion: 32%; GPA/MPA: 12%), fever (5% to 53%)

1% to 10%:

Cardiovascular: Hypotension (10%), flushing (5%)

Central nervous system: Dizziness (10%), anxiety (2% to 5%), migraine (RA: 2%), paresthesia (2%)

Dermatologic: Urticaria (2% to 8%)

Endocrine & metabolic: Hyperglycemia (9%), increased lactate dehydrogenase (7%)

Gastrointestinal: Vomiting (10%), dyspepsia (RA: 3%)

Infection: Viral infection (10%), fungal infection (1%)

Neuromuscular & skeletal: Back pain (10%), myalgia (10%)

Respiratory: Dyspnea (≤10%), throat irritation (2% to 9%), bronchospasm (8%), upper respiratory tract infection (RA: 7%), sinusitis (6%)

<1%, postmarketing and/or case reports: Acute mucocutaneous toxicity, acute renal failure, acute respiratory distress, anaphylactoid reaction, anaphylaxis, angina pectoris, aplastic anemia, arthritis (polyarticular), bone marrow depression, bronchiolitis obliterans, cardiac arrhythmia, cardiac failure, cardiogenic shock, encephalitis, fulminant hepatitis, gastrointestinal perforation, hemolytic anemia, hepatic failure, hepatitis, hypogammaglobulinemia (prolonged), hypoxia, increased serum immunoglobulins (hyperviscosity syndrome in Waldenstrom's macroglobulinemia), interstitial pneumonitis, intestinal obstruction, intestinal perforation, Kaposi's sarcoma (progression), laryngeal edema, lichenoid dermatitis, lupus-like syndrome, mucositis, myelitis, myocardial infarction, nephrotoxicity, optic neuritis, pancytopenia (prolonged), pemphigus (paraneoplastic; uncommon), pleurisy, pneumonia, pneumonitis, polymyositis, progressive multifocal leukoencephalopathy, pure red cell aplasia, reactivated tuberculosis, reactivation of HBV, reversible posterior leukoencephalopathy syndrome, serum sickness, Stevens-Johnson syndrome, supraventricular cardiac arrhythmia, toxic epidermal

necrolysis, tumor lysis syndrome, uveitis, vasculitic rash, vasculitis (systemic), ventricular fibrillation, ventricular tachycardia, vesiculobullous dermatitis, viral infection (reactivation; includes JC virus infection, cytomegalovirus, herpes simplex virus, parvovirus B19, varicella-zoster virus, West Nile disease, and hepatitis C), wheezing

General Dosage Range IV: *Adults:* Dosage varies greatly depending on indication

Mechanism of Action Rituximab is a monoclonal antibody directed against the CD20 antigen on the surface of B-lymphocytes. CD20 regulates cell cycle initiation; and, possibly, functions as a calcium channel. Rituximab binds to the antigen on the cell surface, activating complement-dependent B-cell cytotoxicity; and to human Fc receptors, mediating cell killing through an antibody-dependent cellular toxicity. B-cells are believed to play a role in the development and progression of rheumatoid arthritis. Signs and symptoms of RA are reduced by targeting B-cells and the progression of structural damage is delayed.

Pharmacodynamics/Kinetics

Onset of Action

Immune thrombocytopenia: Initial response: 7 to 56 days; Peak response: 14 to 180 days (Neunert 2011)

NHL: B-cell depletion: Within 3 weeks.

Rheumatoid arthritis (RA): B-cell depletion: Within 2 weeks.

Duration of Action

NHL: Detectable in serum 3 to 6 months after completion of treatment; B-cell depletion is sustained for up to 6 to 9 months and B-cell recovery begins ~6 months following completion of treatment; median B-cell levels return to normal by 12 months following completion of treatment

RA: B-cell depletion persists for at least 6 months.

Half-life Elimination

CLL: Median terminal half-life: 32 days (range: 14 to 62 days)

NHL: Median terminal half-life: 22 days (range: 6 to 52 days)

RA: Mean terminal half-life: 18 days (range: 5 to 78 days)

GPA/MPA: 23 days (range: 9 to 49 days)

Time to Peak SubQ: Median: 3 days (range: 2 to 4 days)

Pregnancy Risk Factor C

Pregnancy Considerations Animal reproduction studies have demonstrated adverse effects including decreased (reversible) B-cells and immunosuppression. Rituximab crosses the placenta and can be detected in the newborn. In one infant born at 41 weeks' gestation, in utero exposure occurred from week 16 to 37; rituximab concentrations were higher in the neonate at birth (32,095 ng/mL) than the mother (9,750 ng/mL) and still measurable at 18 weeks of age (700 ng/mL infant; 500 ng/mL mother) (Friedrichs 2006).

B-cell lymphocytopenia lasting <6 months may occur in exposed infants. Retrospective case reports of inadvertent pregnancy during rituximab treatment collected by the manufacturer (often combined with concomitant teratogenic therapies) describe premature births and infant hematologic abnormalities and infections; no specific pattern of birth defects has been observed (limited data) (Chakravarty 2010).

Effective contraception should be used in women of reproductive potential during and for 12 months following treatment with rituximab.

The European Society for Medical Oncology has published guidelines for diagnosis, treatment, and follow-up of cancer during pregnancy. The guidelines recommend referral to a facility with expertise in cancer during pregnancy and encourage a multidisciplinary team (obstetrician, neonatologist, oncology team). Based on limited data, if pregnancy occurs during rituximab treatment, the pregnancy may continue provided rituximab treatment is withheld. In general, although the risk of B-cell depletion in the newborn is increased, if postponing rituximab treatment would significantly compromise maternal outcome in patients diagnosed with B-cell lymphoma during pregnancy, rituximab use is not discouraged during the pregnancy (Peccatori 2013). An international consensus panel has published guidelines for hematologic malignancies during pregnancy. In patients with aggressive lymphomas, rituximab (as a component of the R-CHOP chemotherapy regimen) may be administered in the second and third trimesters, however, the cytotoxic portion of the regimen should not be administered within 3 weeks prior to anticipated delivery (Lishner 2016).

Other agents are preferred for treating lupus nephritis in pregnant women (Hahn 2012). When treating rheumatoid arthritis, it is recommended to discontinue use and switch to a safer medication prior to conception unless no other pregnancy compatible medication is able to control maternal disease (Götestam Skorpen 2016).

Data collection to monitor pregnancy and infant outcomes following exposure to rituximab is ongoing. A pregnancy registry is available for all cancers diagnosed during pregnancy at Cooper Health (877-635-4499).

Rivaroxaban (riv a ROX a ban)

Related Information

Antiplatelet and Anticoagulation Considerations in Dentistry *on page 1764*

Brand Names: US Xarelto; Xarelto Starter Pack

Brand Names: Canada Xarelto

Pharmacologic Category Anticoagulant; Anticoagulant, Factor Xa Inhibitor; Direct Oral Anticoagulant (DOAC)

Use

Deep vein thrombosis prophylaxis: Postoperative thromboprophylaxis of deep vein thrombosis (DVT) which may lead to pulmonary embolism in patients undergoing knee or hip replacement surgery.

Deep vein thrombosis treatment: Treatment of DVT.

Nonvalvular atrial fibrillation: Prevention of stroke and systemic embolism in patients with nonvalvular atrial fibrillation (AF).

Note: The 2014 American Heart Association/American College of Cardiology/Heart Rhythm Society guidelines for the management of AF recommend oral anticoagulation for patients with nonvalvular AF or atrial flutter with prior stroke, TIA, or a CHA_2DS_2-VASc score ≥2. As an alternative to warfarin, rivaroxaban may also be used for 3 weeks prior and 4 weeks after cardioversion in patients with AF or atrial flutter of ≥48 hours duration or when the duration is unknown. (January 2014).

Pulmonary embolism treatment: Treatment of pulmonary embolism.

Reduction in the risk (secondary prevention) of recurrent deep vein thrombosis and/or pulmonary embolism: Reduction in the risk of recurrence of DVT and pulmonary embolism following initial 6 months of treatment for DVT and/or pulmonary embolism.

Local Anesthetic/Vasoconstrictor Precautions No information available to require special precautions

Effects on Dental Treatment Key adverse event(s) related to dental treatment: Surgical site bleeding may occur. See Effects on Bleeding.

Effects on Bleeding Rivaroxaban inhibits platelet activation and fibrin clot formation via direct, selective, and reversible inhibition of factor Xa. As with all anticoagulants, bleeding is the major adverse effect of rivaroxaban. Hemorrhage may occur at virtually any site; risk is dependent on multiple variables including the intensity of anticoagulation and patient susceptibility. Medical consult is suggested.

Adverse Reactions Frequency not always defined.

Central nervous system: Fatigue (1%), syncope (1%)

Dermatologic: Wound secretion (3%), pruritus (2%), skin blister (1%)

Gastrointestinal: Nausea (1% to 3%), abdominal pain (2%), dyspepsia (1%), toothache (1%)

Genitourinary: Urinary tract infection (1%)

Hematologic & oncologic: Hemorrhage (DVT prophylaxis: 5% to 6% [major: <1%]; DVT/PE treatment: 28% [major: ≤1%]), pulmonary hemorrhage (with and without bronchiectasis)

Hepatic: Increased serum transaminases (>3 x ULN: 2% [Watkins 2011])

Neuromuscular & skeletal: Back pain (4%), limb pain (2%), osteoarthritis (2%), muscle spasm (1%)

Respiratory: Oropharyngeal pain (1%), sinusitis (1%)

<1%, postmarketing, and/or case reports: Agranulocytosis, allergic dermatitis, anaphylactic shock, anaphylaxis, angioedema, cerebral hemorrhage, cholestasis, decreased hemoglobin (≥2 g/dL), ecchymoses, epidural hematoma, gastrointestinal hemorrhage, hemiparesis, hemophthalmos, hepatitis, hepatic injury (Liakoni 2014), hypermenorrhea, hypersensitivity, hypotension, increased amylase, increased blood urea nitrogen, increased lactate dehydrogenase, increased serum alkaline phosphatase, increased serum creatinine, increased serum lipase, intracranial hemorrhage, jaundice, retroperitoneal hemorrhage, Stevens-Johnson syndrome, subdural hematoma, tachycardia, thrombocytopenia (<100,000/mm^3 or <50% baseline), urticaria, weakness, xerostomia

General Dosage Range Dosage adjustment recommended in patients with renal impairment.

Oral: *Adults:* 10 to 20 mg once daily or an initial dose of 15 mg twice daily followed by 20 mg once daily

Mechanism of Action Inhibits platelet activation and fibrin clot formation via direct, selective and reversible inhibition of factor Xa (FXa) in both the intrinsic and extrinsic coagulation pathways. FXa, as part of the prothrombinase complex consisting also of factor Va, calcium ions, factor II and phospholipid, catalyzes the conversion of prothrombin to thrombin. Thrombin both activates platelets and catalyzes the conversion of fibrinogen to fibrin.

Pharmacodynamics/Kinetics

Half-life Elimination Terminal: 5 to 9 hours; Elderly: 11 to 13 hours

Time to Peak Plasma: 2 to 4 hours

Pregnancy Risk Factor C

Pregnancy Considerations Adverse events have been observed in animal reproduction studies. Based on ex-vivo data, rivaroxaban crosses the placenta (Bapat 2015). Information related to the use of rivaroxaban during pregnancy (Hoeltzenbein 2015) and postpartum (Rudd 2015) is limited. Data are insufficient to evaluate the safety of oral factor Xa inhibitors during pregnancy; use during pregnancy should be avoided (Guyatt 2012). Use may increase the risk of pregnancy related hemorrhage. Clinicians should note that the anticoagulant effect cannot be easily monitored or readily reversed. Prompt clinical evaluation is warranted with any unexplained decrease in hemoglobin, hematocrit or blood pressure, or fetal distress. Pregnancy planning should be discussed if use is needed in women of reproductive potential.

Dental Comment At this time there are no coagulation parameters for rivaroxaban to predict the extent of bleeding. Increased bleeding may occur during invasive dental procedures in patients taking a 10 mg daily dose of rivaroxaban. Currently, postsurgical treatment with rivaroxaban is ~12 days for knee replacement patients and ~35 days for hip replacement patients. Medical consult is suggested prior to dental invasive procedures. There are no reports of interactions between the anticoagulant and amoxicillin, cephalexin, cefazolin, ampicillin, or clindamycin; therefore, any of these preprocedural antibiotics can safely be used in patients taking rivaroxaban.

Rivastigmine (ri va STIG meen)

Brand Names: US Exelon

Brand Names: Canada Apo-Rivastigmine; Exelon; Med-Rivastigmine; Mint-Rivastigmine; Mylan-Rivastigmine; Novo-Rivastigmine; PMS-Rivastigmine; ratio-Rivastigmine; Sandoz-Rivastigmine

Pharmacologic Category Acetylcholinesterase Inhibitor (Central)

Use

Alzheimer dementia:

Oral: Treatment of mild to moderate dementia of the Alzheimer type.

Transdermal: Treatment of mild, moderate, and severe dementia of the Alzheimer type.

Parkinson disease dementia: Treatment of mild to moderate dementia associated with Parkinson disease.

Local Anesthetic/Vasoconstrictor Precautions No information available to require special precautions

Effects on Dental Treatment No significant effects or complications reported

Effects on Bleeding No information available to require special precautions

Adverse Reactions

>10%:

Central nervous system: Dizziness (oral: 6% to 21%; transdermal: ≤6%), headache (oral: 4% to 17%; transdermal ≤4%), agitation (transdermal: 1% to 14%), falling (6% to 12%)

Endocrine & metabolic: Weight loss (3% to 26%)

Gastrointestinal: Nausea (oral: 17% to 47%; transdermal: 2% to 10%), vomiting (oral: 13% to 31%; transdermal: 3% to 9%), diarrhea (oral: 5% to 19%; transdermal: ≤7%), anorexia (oral: ≤17%; transdermal: ≤3%), abdominal pain (oral: 13%; transdermal: 2%)

Local: Application site erythema (transdermal: 1% to 13%)

Neuromuscular & skeletal: Tremor (oral: 4% to 23%; transdermal: 7%)

1% to 10%:

Cardiovascular: Hypertension (1% to 3%), syncope (oral: 3%)

Central nervous system: Fatigue (oral: 4% to 9%; transdermal: 2% to 4%), insomnia (1% to 9%), confusion (oral: 8%), depression (2% to 6%), drowsiness (4% to 6%), malaise (oral: 5%), anxiety (1% to 5%), hallucination (2% to 5%), abnormal gait (transdermal: 4%), psychomotor agitation (transdermal: 1% to 3%), aggressive behavior (1% to 3%), exacerbation of Parkinson disease (oral: 1% to 3%), cogwheel rigidity (oral: 1% to 3%), restlessness (oral: 1% to 3%), drug-induced Parkinson disease (oral: 2%)

Dermatologic: Diaphoresis (oral: 2% to 4%)

Endocrine & metabolic: Dehydration (1% to 2%)

Gastrointestinal: Dyspepsia (oral: 9%), decreased appetite (≤9%), upper abdominal pain (≤4%), sialorrhea (oral: 1% to 2%)

Genitourinary: Urinary tract infection (1% to 10%), urinary incontinence (≤3%)

Local: Application site pruritus (transdermal: ≤5%), application site irritation (transdermal: ≤3%), application site rash (transdermal: 2%)

Neuromuscular & skeletal: Weakness (2% to 6%;), bradykinesia (3% to 4%), hypokinesia (1% to 4%), dyskinesia (3%)

<1%, postmarketing, and/or case reports: Abnormal hepatic function tests, allergic dermatitis, atrial fibrillation, atrioventricular block, bradycardia, dermatitis (transdermal patch), dystonia, edema, extrapyramidal reaction, gastrointestinal hemorrhage, hepatic failure, hepatitis, hyperacidity, hypersensitivity reaction, nightmares, pancreatitis, seizure, severe vomiting (with esophageal rupture; following inappropriate reinitiation of dose), sick-sinus syndrome, skin blister, Stevens-Johnson syndrome, tachycardia, urticaria

General Dosage Range Dosage adjustment recommended (transdermal patch) in patients with hepatic impairment or who develop toxicities.

Oral: *Adults:* Initial: 1.5 mg twice daily; Maintenance: 1.5 to 6 mg twice daily (maximum: 12 mg daily)

Transdermal patch: *Adults:* Initial: 4.6 mg/24 hours; Maintenance: 9.5 to 13.3 mg/24 hours (maximum dose: 13.3 mg/24 hours)

Mechanism of Action A deficiency of cortical acetylcholine is thought to account for some of the symptoms of Alzheimer disease and the dementia of Parkinson disease; rivastigmine increases acetylcholine in the central nervous system through reversible inhibition of its hydrolysis by cholinesterase

Pharmacodynamics/Kinetics

Duration of Action Anticholinesterase activity (CSF): ~10 hours (6 mg oral dose)

Half-life Elimination Oral: 1.5 hours; Transdermal patch: ~3 hours (after removal)

Time to Peak Oral: 1 hour; Transdermal patch: 8 to 16 hours following first dose

Pregnancy Risk Factor B

Pregnancy Considerations Adverse events have not been observed in animal reproduction studies.

Product Availability Note: Exelon oral solution has been discontinued in the US for more than 1 year.

Rizatriptan (rye za TRIP tan)

Brand Names: US Maxalt; Maxalt-MLT

Brand Names: Canada ACT Rizatriptan; ACT Rizatriptan ODT; Apo-Rizatriptan; Apo-Rizatriptan RPD; Dom-Rizatriptan RDT; JAMP-Rizatriptan; JAMP-Rizatriptan IR; Mar-Rizatriptan; Maxalt; Maxalt RPD; Mint-Rizatriptan ODT; Mylan-Rizatriptan ODT; NAT-Rizatriptan ODT; PMS-Rizatriptan RDT; Riva-Rizatriptan ODT; Rizatriptan ODT; Rizatriptan RDT; Sandoz-Rizatriptan ODT; Teva-Rizatriptan ODT; Van-Rizatriptan

Pharmacologic Category Antimigraine Agent; Serotonin 5-$HT_{1B,\ 1D}$ Receptor Agonist

Use Migraine: Acute treatment of migraine with or without aura

Local Anesthetic/Vasoconstrictor Precautions No information available to require special precautions

Effects on Dental Treatment Key adverse event(s) related to dental treatment: Xerostomia (normal salivary flow resumes upon discontinuation).

Effects on Bleeding No information available to require special precautions

Adverse Reactions

1% to 10%:

Cardiovascular: Chest pain (≤3%), flushing (>1%), palpitations (>1%), flushing

Central nervous system: Dizziness (4% to 9%), drowsiness (4% to 8%), fatigue (adults: 4% to 7%; children: >1%), paresthesia (3% to 4%), pain (3%), feeling of heaviness (≤2%), headache (≤2%), euphoria (>1%), hypoesthesia (>1%)

Gastrointestinal: Nausea (4% to 6%), xerostomia (3%), sore throat (≤2%), abdominal distress (children: >1%), diarrhea (>1%), vomiting (>1%)

Neuromuscular & skeletal: Weakness (4% to 7%), jaw pain (≤2%), jaw pressure (≤2%), jaw tightness (≤2%), neck pain (≤2%), neck pressure (≤2%), neck tightness (≤2%), tremor (>1%)

Respiratory: Pharyngeal edema (≤2%), pressure on pharynx (≤2%), dyspnea (>1%)

<1%, postmarketing, and/or case reports: Abdominal distention, abnormal gait, agitation, anaphylaxis, anaphylactoid reaction, angina pectoris, angioedema, ataxia (children), auditory impairment (children), blurred vision, bradycardia, cardiac arrhythmia, cold extremities, confusion, diaphoresis, dysgeusia, dyspepsia, edema, erythema, facial edema, hallucination (children), hot flash, hypertensive crisis, increased blood pressure (diastolic/systolic), insomnia, ischemic heart disease, lack of concentration (children), memory impairment, muscle rigidity, muscle spasm, myalgia, myocardial infarction, pharyngeal edema, pruritus, seizure, skin rash, swelling of eye, syncope, tachycardia, tinnitus, tongue edema, toxic epidermal necrolysis, urticaria, vasospasm, vertigo, wheezing

General Dosage Range Oral:

Children 6-17 years: <40 kg: 5 mg as a single dose; ≥40 kg: 10 mg as a single dose

Adults: 5-10 mg once, repeat if needed (maximum: 30 mg/day)

Mechanism of Action Selective agonist for serotonin (5-HT_{1B} and 5-HT_{1D} receptors) in cranial arteries; causes vasoconstriction and reduces sterile inflammation associated with antidromic neuronal transmission correlating with relief of migraine

Pharmacodynamics/Kinetics

Onset of Action Most patients have response to treatment within 2 hours

Half-life Elimination 2-3 hours

Time to Peak Maxalt: 1 to 1.5 hours; Maxalt-MLT: 1.6 to 2.5 hours

Pregnancy Risk Factor C

Pregnancy Considerations Adverse events were observed in animal reproduction studies. Information related to rizatriptan use in pregnancy is limited (Källén, 2011; Nezvalová-Henriksen, 2010; Nezvalová-Henriksen, 2012).

A pregnancy registry has been established to monitor outcomes of women exposed to rizatriptan during pregnancy (800-986-8999). Preliminary data from the pregnancy registry (prospectively collected from 65 live births 1998-2004) does not show an increased risk of congenital malformations (Fiore, 2005). Until additional information is available, other agents are preferred for the initial treatment of migraine in pregnancy (Da Silva, 2012; MacGregor, 2012; Williams, 2012).

Roflumilast (roe FLUE mi last)

Brand Names: US Daliresp

Brand Names: Canada Daxas

Pharmacologic Category Phosphodiesterase-4 Enzyme Inhibitor

Use Chronic obstructive pulmonary disease: Reduce the risk of chronic obstructive pulmonary disease (COPD) exacerbations in patients with severe COPD associated with chronic bronchitis and a history of exacerbations

Local Anesthetic/Vasoconstrictor Precautions No information available to require special precautions

Effects on Dental Treatment No significant effects or complications reported

Effects on Bleeding No information available to require special precautions

Adverse Reactions

2% to 10%:

- Central nervous system: Headache (4%), dizziness (2%), insomnia (2%)
- Endocrine & metabolic: Weight loss (5% to 10% of body weight: 8% to 20%; >10% loss: 7%)
- Gastrointestinal: Diarrhea (10%), nausea (5%), decreased appetite (2%)
- Infection: Influenza (3%)
- Neuromuscular & skeletal: Back pain (3%)

<2%, postmarketing, and/or case reports: Abdominal pain, anemia, anxiety, arthralgia, arthritis, atrial fibrillation, constipation, depression, dysgeusia, dyspepsia, epistaxis, fatigue, gastritis, gastroesophageal reflux disease, gynecomastia, hematochezia, hypersensitivity, hypersensitivity reaction (including angioedema, urticaria, and rash), increased gamma-glutamyl transferase, increased lactate dehydrogenase, increased serum AST, limb pain, lung carcinoma, malaise, muscle spasm, myalgia, myasthenia, nervousness, pancreatitis, paresthesia, prostate carcinoma, renal failure, respiratory tract infection, rhinitis, sinusitis, suicidal ideation, suicidal tendencies, suicide, supraventricular cardiac arrhythmia, tremor, urinary tract infection, vertigo, vomiting, weakness

General Dosage Range Oral: *Adults:* 500 mcg once daily

Mechanism of Action Roflumilast and its active N-oxide metabolite selectively inhibit phosphodiesterase-4 (PDE4) leading to an accumulation of cyclic AMP (cAMP) within inflammatory and structural cells important in the pathogenesis of COPD. Anti-inflammatory effects include suppression of cytokine release and inhibition of lung infiltration by neutrophils and other leukocytes. Pulmonary remodeling and mucociliary malfunction are also attenuated.

Pharmacodynamics/Kinetics

Half-life Elimination 17 hours; N-oxide metabolite: 30 hours

Time to Peak ~1 hour (delayed by food); N-oxide metabolite: ~8 hours

Pregnancy Risk Factor C

Pregnancy Considerations Adverse events were observed in some animal reproduction studies. The Canadian labeling recommends avoiding use during pregnancy and in women of childbearing potential not using adequate contraception.

Rolapitant (roe LA pi tant)

Brand Names: US Varubi

Pharmacologic Category Antiemetic; Substance P/ Neurokinin 1 Receptor Antagonist

Use Chemotherapy-induced nausea and vomiting (CINV), prevention: Prevention of delayed nausea and vomiting associated with initial and repeat courses of emetogenic cancer chemotherapy, including, but not limited to, highly-emetogenic chemotherapy in adults (in combination with other antiemetic agents).

Local Anesthetic/Vasoconstrictor Precautions No information available to require special precautions

Effects on Dental Treatment Key adverse event(s) related to dental treatment: Stomatitis has been reported from clinical trials receiving combination therapy with dexamethasone and 5-HT3 receptor antagonist

Effects on Bleeding No information available to require special precautions

Adverse Reactions Clinical trials were conducted in patients receiving combination therapy with a 5-HT3 receptor antagonist and dexamethasone. It is not possible to correlate frequency of adverse events with rolaprepitant alone.

1% to 10%:

- Central nervous system: Dizziness (6%)
- Gastrointestinal: Decreased appetite (9%), hiccups (5%), dyspepsia (4%), stomatitis (4%), abdominal pain (3%)
- Genitourinary: Urinary tract infection (4%)
- Hematologic & oncologic: Neutropenia (7% to 9%), anemia (3%)

General Dosage Range Adults: *Oral:* 180 mg on day 1 of chemotherapy; Maximum: 180 mg every 14 days

Mechanism of Action Rolapitant prevents delayed nausea and vomiting associated with emetogenic chemotherapy by selectively and competitively inhibiting the substance P/neurokinin 1 (NK_1) receptor.

Pharmacodynamics/Kinetics

Half-life Elimination ~7 days (range: 169 to 183 hours)

Time to Peak Time to peak: ~4 hours

Pregnancy Considerations Adverse events were observed in some animal reproduction studies.

RomiDEPsin (roe mi DEP sin)

Related Information

Clinical Risk Related to Drugs Prolonging QT Interval *on page 1772*

Brand Names: US Istodax; Istodax (Overfill)

Brand Names: Canada Istodax

Pharmacologic Category Antineoplastic Agent, Histone Deacetylase (HDAC) Inhibitor

Use

Cutaneous T-cell lymphoma: Treatment of cutaneous T-cell lymphoma (CTCL) in patients who have received at least one prior systemic therapy

Peripheral T-cell lymphoma: Treatment of peripheral T-cell lymphoma (PTCL) in patients who have received at least one prior therapy

Local Anesthetic/Vasoconstrictor Precautions Romidepsin is one of the drugs confirmed to prolong the QT interval and is accepted as having a risk of causing torsade de pointes. The risk of drug-induced torsade de pointes is extremely low when a single QT interval prolonging drug is prescribed. In terms of epinephrine, it is not known what effect vasoconstrictors in the local anesthetic regimen will have in patients with a known history of congenital prolonged QT interval or in patients taking any medication that prolongs the QT interval. Until more information is obtained, it is suggested that the clinician consult with the physician prior to the use of a vasoconstrictor in suspected patients, and that the vasoconstrictor (epinephrine, mepivacaine and levonordefrin [Carbocaine® 2% with Neo-Cobefrin®]) be used with caution.

Effects on Dental Treatment Key adverse event(s) related to dental treatment: Taste alteration.

Effects on Bleeding Chemotherapy may result in significant myelosuppression, potentially including significant reduction in platelet counts (thrombocytopenia grades 3/4: ≤36%) and altered hemostasis. In patients who are under active treatment with these agents, medical consult is suggested.

Adverse Reactions

>10%:

Cardiovascular: ECG changes (ST-T wave changes: 2% to 63%), hypotension (7% to 23%)

Central nervous system: Fatigue (53% to 77%), headache (15% to 34%), chills (11% to 17%)

Dermatologic: Pruritus (7% to 31%), dermatitis (≤27%), exfoliative dermatitis (≤27%)

Endocrine & metabolic: Hypocalcemia (4% to 52%), hyperglycemia (2% to 51%), hypoalbuminemia (3% to 48%), hyperuricemia (≤33%), hypomagnesemia (22% to 28%), hypermagnesemia (≤27%), hypophosphatemia (≤27%), hyponatremia (≤20%), hypokalemia (6% to 20%), weight loss (10% to 15%)

Gastrointestinal: Nausea (56% to 86%), anorexia (23% to 54%), vomiting (34% to 52%), dysgeusia (15% to 40%), constipation (12% to 40%), diarrhea (20% to 36%), abdominal pain (13% to 14%)

Hematologic & oncologic: Anemia (19% to 72%; grades 3/4: 3% to 28%), thrombocytopenia (17% to 72%; grades 3/4: ≤36%), neutropenia (11% to 66%; grades 3/4: 4% to 47%), lymphocytopenia (4% to 57%; grades 3/4: ≤37%), leukopenia (4% to 55%; grades 3/4: ≤45%)

Hepatic: Increased serum AST (3% to 28%), increased serum ALT (3% to 22%)

Infection: Infection (46% to 54%; including infection of central line)

Neuromuscular & skeletal: Weakness (53% to 77%)

Respiratory: Cough (18% to 21%), dyspnea (13% to 21%)

Miscellaneous: Fever (20% to 47%)

1% to 10%:

Cardiovascular: Tachycardia (≤10%), peripheral edema (6% to 10%), chest pain, deep vein thrombosis, edema, prolonged Q-T interval on ECG, pulmonary embolism, supraventricular cardiac arrhythmia, syncope, ventricular arrhythmia

Dermatologic: Cellulitis

Endocrine & metabolic: Dehydration

Gastrointestinal: Stomatitis (6% to 10%)

Hematologic & oncologic: Tumor lysis syndrome (1% to 2%), febrile neutropenia

Hepatic: Hyperbilirubinemia

Hypersensitivity: Hypersensitivity reaction

Infection: Sepsis

Respiratory: Hypoxia, pneumonia, pneumonitis

<1%, postmarketing, and/or case reports: Acute renal failure, acute respiratory distress, atrial fibrillation, bacteremia, candidiasis, cardiac failure, cardiogenic shock, ischemic heart disease, multi-organ failure, reactivation of latent Epstein-Barr virus, respiratory failure, septic shock

General Dosage Range Dosage adjustment recommended in patients who develop toxicities

IV: *Adults:* 14 mg/m^2 days 1, 8, and 15 of a 28-day treatment cycle

Mechanism of Action Histone deacetylase inhibitor; catalyzes acetyl group removal from protein lysine residues (including histone and transcription factors). Inhibition of histone deacetylase results in accumulation of acetyl groups, leading to alterations in chromatin structure and transcription factor activation causing termination of cell growth (induces arrest in cell cycle at G_1 and G_2/M phases) leading to cell death.

Pharmacodynamics/Kinetics

Half-life Elimination ~3 hours

Pregnancy Risk Factor D

Pregnancy Considerations Adverse events were observed in animal reproduction studies. Based on the mechanism of action, romidepsin may cause fetal harm if administered during pregnancy.

Dental Comment See Local Anesthetic/Vasoconstrictor Precautions

RomiPLOStim (roe mi PLOE stim)

Brand Names: US Nplate

Brand Names: Canada Nplate

Pharmacologic Category Colony Stimulating Factor; Hematopoietic Agent; Thrombopoietic Agent

Use

Chronic immune thrombocytopenia: Treatment of thrombocytopenia in patients with chronic immune thrombocytopenia (ITP) who have had insufficient response to corticosteroids, immune globulin, or splenectomy

Limitations of use: Should be used only when the degree of thrombocytopenia and clinical condition increase the risk for bleeding; should not be used in attempt to normalize platelet counts; **not** indicated for the treatment of thrombocytopenia due to myelodysplastic syndrome or any cause of thrombocytopenia other than chronic ITP.

Local Anesthetic/Vasoconstrictor Precautions No information available to require special precautions

Effects on Dental Treatment No significant effects or complications reported

Effects on Bleeding Romiplostim is used for treatment of thrombocytopenia; dosing is established to increase platelet counts and reduce the risk of bleeding. Bleeding is not expected with therapy; however, upon discontinuation of therapy, rebound thrombocytopenia may occur and risk of bleeding is increased; monitor closely.

Adverse Reactions

>10%:

Central nervous system: Headache (35%), dizziness (17%), insomnia (16%)

Gastrointestinal: Abdominal pain (11%)
Neuromuscular & skeletal: Arthralgia (26%), myalgia (14%), limb pain (13%)

1% to 10%:

Central nervous system: Paresthesia (6%)
Gastrointestinal: Dyspepsia (7%)
Hematologic & oncologic: Thrombocytopenia (7%; rebound)
Immunologic: Antibody formation (≤4%; no correlation between antibody development and drug safety or efficacy has been established)
Neuromuscular & skeletal: Shoulder pain (8%)

Frequency not defined:

Hematologic & oncologic: Myelofibrosis (bone marrow reticulin formation/deposition)

<1%, postmarketing, and/or case reports: Angioedema, erythromelalgia, hypersensitivity reaction, myelofibrosis (marrow fibrosis with collagen), thromboembolism, thrombosis

General Dosage Range SubQ: *Adults:* Initial: 1 mcg/kg once weekly; adjust dose by 1 mcg/kg/week increments to achieve platelet count ≥50,000/mm^3 and reduce the risk of bleeding; Maximum: 10 mcg/kg/week

Mechanism of Action Thrombopoietin (TPO) peptide mimetic which increases platelet counts in ITP by binding to and activating the human TPO receptor.

Pharmacodynamics/Kinetics

Onset of Action Platelet count increase: SubQ: 4 to 9 days (Wang, 2004); Peak platelet count increase: Days 12 to 16 (Wang, 2004)

Duration of Action Platelet counts return to baseline by day 28 (Wang, 2004)

Half-life Elimination Median: 3.5 days (range: 1 to 34 days)

Time to Peak SubQ: Median: 14 hours (range: 7 to 50 hours)

Pregnancy Risk Factor C

Pregnancy Considerations Adverse events have been observed in animal reproduction studies. Use during pregnancy only if the potential benefit to the mother outweighs the potential risk to the fetus.

Women exposed to romiplostim during pregnancy are encouraged to enroll in the Nplate pregnancy (1-800-772-6436). In Canada, women who become pregnant during treatment are encouraged to enroll in Amgen's Pregnancy Surveillance Program (1-866-512-6436).

ROPINIRole (roe PIN i role)

Brand Names: US Requip; Requip XL

Brand Names: Canada ACT-Ropinirole; JAMP-Ropinirole; PMS-Ropinirole; RAN Ropinirole; Requip

Pharmacologic Category Anti-Parkinson Agent, Dopamine Agonist

Use

Parkinson disease: Treatment of Parkinson disease

Restless legs syndrome (immediate release only): Treatment of moderate to severe primary restless legs syndrome (RLS)

Local Anesthetic/Vasoconstrictor Precautions No information available to require special precautions

Effects on Dental Treatment Key adverse event(s) related to dental treatment: Xerostomia and dysphagia occur with use. Normal salivary flow resumes upon discontinuation of treatment.

Effects on Bleeding No information available to require special precautions

Adverse Reactions

Frequency not always defined. Data inclusive of trials in early Parkinson disease (without levodopa) and Restless Legs Syndrome.

>10%:

Cardiovascular: Hypotension (including orthostatic; 2% to 25%), syncope (1% to 12%)
Central nervous system: Drowsiness (11% to 40%), dizziness (6% to 40%), fatigue (including weakness, malaise; 9% to 16%)
Gastrointestinal: Nausea (immediate release: 40% to 60%; extended release: 19%), vomiting (11% to 12%)
Infection: Viral infection (11%)

1% to 10%:

Cardiovascular: Lower extremity edema (7%), dependent edema (6%), hypertension (5%), chest pain (4%), flushing (3%), palpitations (3%), peripheral ischemia (3%), atrial fibrillation (2%), extrasystoles (2%), peripheral edema (2%), tachycardia (2%)
Central nervous system: Pain (8%), headache (extended release: 6%), confusion (5%), hallucination (5%; dose related), hypoesthesia (4%), amnesia (3%), paresthesia (3%), yawning (3%), lack of concentration (2%), vertigo (2%), falling, insomnia
Dermatologic: Diaphoresis (6%), hyperhidrosis (3%)
Gastrointestinal: Dyspepsia (4% to 10%), abdominal pain (3% to 7%), constipation (5%), xerostomia (3% to 5%), diarrhea (5%), anorexia (4%), flatulence (3%)
Genitourinary: Urinary tract infection (5%), impotence (3%)
Hepatic: Increased serum alkaline (3%)
Infection: Influenza (3%)
Neuromuscular & skeletal: Arthralgia (4%), limb pain (3%), muscle cramps (3%), hyperkinesia (2%), muscle spasm, myalgia
Ophthalmic: Visual disturbance (6%), eye disease (3%), xerophthalmia (2%)
Respiratory: Nasopharyngitis (9%), pharyngitis (6%), rhinitis (4%), sinusitis (4%), bronchitis (3%), cough (3%), dyspnea (3%), nasal congestion (2%)
Miscellaneous: Fever

Advanced Parkinson disease (with levodopa):

>10%:

Cardiovascular: Decreased diastolic blood pressure (orthostatic; ≥10 mm Hg: 63%; ≥20 mm Hg: 10%; semi-supine; ≥20 mm Hg: 25%), systolic hypotension (orthostatic; ≥20 mm Hg: 38%; semi-supine; ≥40 mm Hg: 10%); decreased blood pressure (combined systolic and diastolic; orthostatic; mild to moderate: 23%), decreased heart rate (≥15 beats/minute: 19% to 24%), increased heart rate (≥15 beats/minute: 23%; ≥30 beats/minute: 2%)
Central nervous system: Dizziness (immediate release: 26%; extended release: 8%), drowsiness (immediate release: 20%, extended release: 7%), headache (6% to 17%)
Gastrointestinal: Nausea (immediate release: 30%; extended release: 11%)
Neuromuscular & skeletal: Dyskinesia (immediate release: 34%; extended-release: 13%; dose related)

1% to 10%:

Cardiovascular: Systolic hypertension (≥40 mm Hg: 8% to 9%), hypotension (≤7%; including orthostatic), peripheral edema (4%), syncope (1% to 3%), hypertension (3%; dose related), bradycardia
Central nervous system: Hallucination (6% to 10%; dose related), falling (2% to 10%; dose related), confusion (9%), anxiety (2% to 6%), amnesia (5%),

nervousness (5%), pain (5%), paresthesia (5%), vertigo (4%), abnormal dreams (3%), paresis (3%)

Dermatologic: Diaphoresis (5% to 7%)

Endocrine & metabolic: Weight loss (2%)

Gastrointestinal: Abdominal pain (6% to 9%), vomiting (7%), constipation (4% to 6%), diarrhea (3% to 5%), xerostomia (2% to 5%), dysphagia (2%), flatulence (2%), sialorrhea (2%)

Genitourinary: Urinary tract infection (6%), pyuria (2%), urinary incontinence (2%)

Hematologic & oncologic: Anemia (2%)

Infection: Viral infection

Neuromuscular & skeletal: Arthralgia (7%), tremor (6%), hypokinesia (5%), arthritis (3%), back pain (3%)

Ophthalmic: Diplopia (2%)

Respiratory: Upper respiratory tract infection (9%), dyspnea (3%), nasopharyngitis (≥2%)

Miscellaneous: Increased drug level (7%)

Postmarketing and/or case reports: Agitation, behavioral problems, delirium, delusion, heart valve disease, hypersensitivity reaction (angioedema, pruritus), impulse control disorder (eg, pathological gambling, hypersexuality, binge eating), interstitial pulmonary disease, mental status changes, paranoia, pleural effusion, pleuropulmonary fibrosis, psychiatric disturbance

General Dosage Range Oral: *Adults:*

Parkinson disease:

Immediate release: Initial: 0.25 mg 3 times daily; Maintenance: 0.75 to 24 mg/day in 3 divided doses

Extended release: Initial: 2 mg once daily; Maintenance: 2 to 24 mg once daily (maximum: 24 mg/day)

Restless legs syndrome: Immediate release: Initial: 0.25 mg prior to bedtime; Maintenance: 0.25 to 4 mg prior to bedtime

Mechanism of Action Ropinirole has a high relative *in vitro* specificity and full intrinsic activity at the D_2 and D_3 dopamine receptor subtypes, binding with higher affinity to D_3 than to D_2 or D_4 receptor subtypes; relevance of D_3 receptor binding in Parkinson disease is unknown. Ropinirole has moderate *in vitro* affinity for opioid receptors. Ropinirole and its metabolites have negligible *in vitro* affinity for dopamine D_1, 5-HT_1, 5-HT_2, benzodiazepine, GABA, muscarinic, alpha$_1$-, alpha$_2$-, and beta-adrenoreceptors. Although precise mechanism of action of ropinirole is unknown, it is believed to be due to stimulation of postsynaptic dopamine D_2-type receptors within the caudate putamen in the brain. Ropinirole caused decreases in systolic and diastolic blood pressure at doses >0.25 mg. The mechanism of ropinirole-induced postural hypotension is believed to be due to D_2-mediated blunting of the noradrenergic response to standing and subsequent decrease in peripheral vascular resistance.

Pharmacodynamics/Kinetics

Half-life Elimination ~6 hours

Time to Peak Immediate release: ~1-2 hours; Extended release: 6-10 hours; T_{max} increased by 2.5-3 hours when taken with a high-fat meal

Pregnancy Considerations Adverse events have been observed in animal reproduction studies. Information related to the use of ropinirole for the treatment of restless legs syndrome (RLS) in pregnant women is limited. Current guidelines note that the available information is insufficient to make a recommendation for use in pregnant women (Aurora, 2012; Dostal, 2013).

Ropivacaine (roe PIV a kane)

Related Information

Oral Pain *on page 1830*

Brand Names: US Naropin

Brand Names: Canada Naropin; Ropivacaine Hydrochloride Injection, USP

Pharmacologic Category Local Anesthetic

Use

Acute pain management: For acute pain management administered as an epidural continuous infusion, intermittent bolus (eg, postoperative or labor), or local infiltration.

Surgical anesthesia: For the production of local or regional anesthesia for surgery administered as an epidural block, including cesarean section, major nerve block, or local infiltration.

Local Anesthetic/Vasoconstrictor Precautions No information available to require special precautions (see Dental Comment)

Effects on Dental Treatment No significant effects or complications reported

Effects on Bleeding No information available to require special precautions

Adverse Reactions

>10%:

Cardiovascular: Hypotension (dose-related and age-related: 32% to 69%), bradycardia (6% to 20%)

Gastrointestinal: Nausea (11% to 29%), vomiting (7% to 14%)

Neuromuscular & skeletal: Back pain (7% to 16%)

1% to 10%:

Cardiovascular: Chest pain (1% to 5%), hypertension, tachycardia

Central nervous system: Headache (5% to 8%), paresthesia (2% to 6%), dizziness (3%), chills (2% to 3%), anxiety (1%), hypoesthesia, rigors, shivering

Dermatologic: Pruritus (1% to 5%)

Endocrine & metabolic: Hypokalemia

Gastrointestinal: Oral paresthesia

Genitourinary: Urinary retention (1% to 5%), urinary tract infection (1% to 5%), oliguria

Hematologic & oncologic: Anemia (6%)

Respiratory: Dyspnea

Miscellaneous: Fever (3% to 9%)

<1%, postmarketing, and/or case reports: Angioedema, apnea (usually associated with epidural block in head/neck region), bronchospasm, cardiac insufficiency, chondrolysis (continuous intra-articular administration), circulatory shock, dyskinesia, hallucination, hypersensitivity reaction, hyperthermia, laryngeal edema, myocardial infarction, seizure, skin rash, syncope, tinnitus, urticaria, ventricular arrhythmia

General Dosage Range

Epidural:

Lumbar: *Adults:* 10 to 30 mL of 0.2% to 1% solution **or** 15 to 25 mL of 0.75% solution; Infusion: 6 to 14 mL/hour of 0.2% solution, with incremental injections of 10 to 15 mL/hour of 0.2% solution

Thoracic: *Adults:* 5 to 15 mL of 0.5% or 0.75% solution; Infusion: 6 to 14 mL/hour of 0.2% solution

Field Block: *Adults:* 1 to 40 mL of 0.5% solution

Infiltration: *Adults:* 1 to 100 mL of 0.2% solution **or** 1 to 40 mL of 0.5% solution

Nerve Block: *Adults:* Major: 35 to 50 **mL** of 0.5% solution **or** 10 to 40 **mL** of 0.75% solution; Minor: 1 to 100 **mL** of 0.2% solution **or** 1 to 40 **mL** of 0.5% solution

Mechanism of Action Blocks both the initiation and conduction of nerve impulses by decreasing the neuronal membrane's permeability to sodium ions, which results in inhibition of depolarization with resultant blockade of conduction

Pharmacodynamics/Kinetics

Onset of Action Anesthesia (route dependent): 3 to 15 minutes

Duration of Action Dose and route dependent: 3 to 15 hours

Half-life Elimination

Children: Epidural: Terminal phase:4.9 hours (range: 3 to 6.7 hours) (Hansen 2000)

Adults: Epidural: 5 to 7 hours; IV: Terminal: 111 ± 62 minutes (Lee 1989)

Time to Peak Serum (dose and route dependent): Caudal:

Infants: Median: 60 minutes (range: 15 to 90 minutes) (Wulf 2000)

Children: Mean: 60 minutes (range: 12 to 249 minutes (Lonnqvist 2000)

Pregnancy Risk Factor B

Pregnancy Considerations Adverse events have not been observed in animal reproduction studies. When used for epidural block during labor and delivery, systemically absorbed ropivacaine may cross the placenta, resulting in varying degrees of fetal or neonatal effects (eg, CNS or cardiovascular depression). Fetal or neonatal adverse events include fetal bradycardia (12%), neonatal jaundice (8%), low Apgar scores (3%), fetal distress (2%), neonatal respiratory disorder (3%). Maternal hypotension may also result from systemic absorption. In cases of hypotension, position pregnant woman in left lateral decubitus position to prevent aortocaval compression by the gravid uterus. Epidural anesthesia may prolong the second stage of labor.

Dental Comment Not available with vasoconstrictor (epinephrine) and not available in dental (1.8 mL) carpules

Rosiglitazone (roh si GLI ta zone)

Related Information

Endocrine Disorders and Pregnancy *on page 1781*

Brand Names: US Avandia

Brand Names: Canada Avandia

Generic Availability (US) No

Pharmacologic Category Antidiabetic Agent, Thiazolidinedione

Use Type 2 diabetes: Adjunct to diet and exercise to improve glycemic control in adults with type 2 diabetes mellitus (noninsulin dependent, NIDDM); may be used as monotherapy or in combination with metformin or a sulfonylurea.

Limitations of use: Should not be used in patients with type 1 diabetes mellitus or diabetic ketoacidosis; use with insulin is not recommended.

Local Anesthetic/Vasoconstrictor Precautions No information available to require special precautions

Effects on Dental Treatment Rosiglitazone-dependent patients with diabetes should be appointed for dental treatment in morning in order to minimize chance of stress-induced hypoglycemia.

Effects on Bleeding Rosiglitazone has been demonstrated to induce severe thrombocytopenia (rare). Analysis of the patient's serum shows rosiglitazone-induced antibody, responsible for thrombocytopenia, confirming an immune-mediated platelet depletion.

Adverse Reactions Note: As reported in monotherapy studies; the rate of certain adverse reactions (eg, anemia, edema, hypoglycemia) may be higher with some combination therapies. Rare cases of hepatocellular injury have been reported in men in their 60s within 2 to 3 weeks after initiation of rosiglitazone therapy. LFTs in these patients revealed severe hepatocellular injury which responded with rapid improvement of liver function and resolution of symptoms upon discontinuation of rosiglitazone. Patients were also receiving other potentially hepatotoxic medications (Al-Salman 2000; Freid 2000).

>10%: Endocrine & metabolic: Increased HDL cholesterol, increased LDL cholesterol, increased serum cholesterol (total), weight gain

1% to 10%:

Cardiovascular: Edema (5%), hypertension (4%); cardiac failure (≤3% in patients receiving insulin; incidence likely higher in patients with pre-existing cardiac failure), ischemic heart disease (3%; incidence likely higher in patients with pre-existing CAD)

Central nervous system: Headache (6%)

Endocrine & metabolic: Hypoglycemia (1% to 3%; combination therapy with insulin: 12% to 14%)

Gastrointestinal: Diarrhea (3%)

Hematologic & oncologic: Anemia (2%)

Neuromuscular & skeletal: Bone fracture (≤9%; incidence greater in females; usually upper arm, hand, or foot), arthralgia (5%), back pain (4% to 5%)

Respiratory: Upper respiratory tract infection (4% to 10%), nasopharyngitis (6%)

Miscellaneous: Trauma (8%)

<1%, postmarketing, and/or case reports: Anaphylaxis, angina pectoris, angioedema, blurred vision, cardiac arrest, coronary artery disease, coronary thrombosis, decreased HDL cholesterol, decreased hematocrit, decreased hemoglobin, decreased visual acuity, decreased white blood cell count, dyspnea, hepatic failure, hepatitis, increased serum bilirubin, increased serum transaminases, jaundice (reversible), macular edema, myocardial infarction, pleural effusion, pruritus, pulmonary edema, skin rash, Stevens-Johnson syndrome, thrombocytopenia, urticaria, weight gain (rapid, excessive; usually due to fluid accumulation)

Dosing

Adult & Geriatric Type 2 diabetes: Oral: **Note:** All patients should be initiated at the lowest recommended dose.

Initial: 4 mg daily as a single daily dose or in divided doses twice daily. If response is inadequate after 8-12 weeks of treatment, the dosage may be increased to 8 mg daily (maximum dose) as a single daily dose or in divided doses twice daily. In clinical trials, the 4 mg twice-daily regimen resulted in the greatest reduction in fasting plasma glucose and HbA_{1c}.

Note: When used in combination therapy with other hypoglycemic agents, a dose reduction of the concurrent agent may be necessary if hypoglycemia occurs.

Renal Impairment No dosage adjustment necessary.

Hepatic Impairment There are no dosage adjustments provided in the manufacturer's labeling. Clearance is significantly lower in hepatic impairment; therapy should not be initiated if the patient exhibits active liver disease or increased transaminases (ALT >2.5 times the upper limit of normal) at baseline.

Mechanism of Action Thiazolidinedione antidiabetic agent that lowers blood glucose by improving target cell response to insulin, without increasing pancreatic insulin secretion. It has a mechanism of action that is dependent on the presence of insulin for activity. Rosiglitazone is an agonist for peroxisome proliferator-activated receptor-gamma (PPARgamma). Activation of nuclear PPARgamma receptors influences the production of a number of gene products involved in glucose and lipid metabolism. PPARgamma is abundant in the cells within the renal collecting tubules; fluid retention results from stimulation by thiazolidinediones which increases sodium reabsorption.

Contraindications

US labeling: Hypersensitivity to rosiglitazone or any component of the formulation; NYHA Class III/IV heart failure (initiation of therapy)

Canadian labeling: Hypersensitivity to rosiglitazone or any component of the formulation; any stage of heart failure (eg, NYHA Class I, II, III, IV); serious hepatic impairment; pregnancy

Warnings/Precautions [US Boxed Warning]: Thiazolidinediones, including rosiglitazone, may cause or exacerbate congestive heart failure; closely monitor for signs/symptoms of congestive heart failure (eg, rapid weight gain, dyspnea, edema), particularly after initiation or dose increases. If heart failure develops, treat accordingly and consider dose reduction or discontinuation. Not recommended for use in any patient with symptomatic heart failure. Initiation of therapy is contraindicated in patients with NYHA class III or IV heart failure. Use with caution in patients with edema; may increase plasma volume and/or cause fluid retention, leading to heart failure. Monitor for signs/symptoms of heart failure. Dose-related weight gain observed with use; mechanism unknown but likely associated with fluid retention and fat accumulation. Use may also be associated with an increased risk of angina and MI. Use caution in patients at risk for cardiovascular events and monitor closely. Discontinue if any deterioration in cardiac status occurs.

The risk of hypoglycemia is increased when rosiglitazone is combined with other hypoglycemic agents; dosage adjustment of concomitant hypoglycemic agents may be necessary. Monitor blood glucose and HbA1c as clinically necessary. Should not be used in diabetic ketoacidosis. Mechanism requires the presence of endogenous insulin; therefore, use in type 1 diabetes (insulin dependent, IDDM) is not recommended. Use with insulin is not recommended; may increase the risk of heart failure. It may be necessary to discontinue therapy and administer insulin if the patient is exposed to stress (fever, trauma, infection, surgery). Do not initiate in patients with stable ischemic heart disease due to an increased risk of cardiovascular complications (Fihn 2012).

Potentially significant drug-drug interactions may exist, requiring dose or frequency adjustment, additional monitoring, and/or selection of alternative therapy.

Use with caution in patients with elevated transaminases (AST or ALT); do not initiate in patients with active liver disease or ALT >2.5 times ULN at baseline; evaluate patients with ALT ≤2.5 times ULN at baseline or during therapy for cause of enzyme elevation; during therapy, if ALT >3 times ULN, reevaluate levels promptly and discontinue if elevation persists or if jaundice occurs at any time during use. Idiosyncratic hepatotoxicity has been reported with another thiazolidinedione agent (troglitazone); avoid use in patients who previously experienced jaundice during troglitazone therapy. Increased incidence of bone fractures in females treated with rosiglitazone was observed during analysis of long-term trial; majority of fractures occurred in the upper arm, hand, and foot (differing from the hip or spine fractures usually associated with postmenopausal osteoporosis). According to the American Diabetes Association guidelines, thiazolidinediones should be avoided in patients with fracture risk factors (ADA 2016a). May decrease hemoglobin/hematocrit and/or WBC count (slight); effects may be related to increased plasma volume and/or dose related. Changes in hemoglobin and hematocrit generally occurred during the first 3 months after initiation of therapy and after dose increases. Use with caution in patients with anemia.

Macular edema has been reported with thiazolidinedione use, including rosiglitazone; some patients with macular edema presented with blurred vision or decreased visual acuity, and most had peripheral edema at time of diagnosis. In addition, ophthalmological consultation should be initiated in these patients. Improvement in macular edema may occur with discontinuation of therapy. Use with caution in premenopausal, anovulatory women; may result in resumption of ovulation, increasing the risk of pregnancy. Use of adequate contraception in premenopausal women is recommended.

Drug Interactions

Metabolism/Transport Effects Substrate of CYP2C8 (major), CYP2C9 (minor); **Note:** Assignment of Major/Minor substrate status based on clinically relevant drug interaction potential; **Inhibits** CYP2C8 (moderate), CYP2C9 (weak)

Avoid Concomitant Use

Avoid concomitant use of Rosiglitazone with any of the following: Amodiaquine; Insulin

Increased Effect/Toxicity

Rosiglitazone may increase the levels/effects of: Amodiaquine; CYP2C8 Substrates; Hypoglycemia-Associated Agents; Sulfonylureas

The levels/effects of Rosiglitazone may be increased by: Abiraterone Acetate; Alpha-Lipoic Acid; Androgens; Atazanavir; CYP2C8 Inhibitors (Moderate); CYP2C8 Inhibitors (Strong); Deferasirox; Gemfibrozil; Insulin; Lumacaftor; MAO Inhibitors; MiFEPRIStone; Pegvisomant; Pregabalin; Prothionamide; Quinolone Antibiotics; Salicylates; Selective Serotonin Reuptake Inhibitors; Trimethoprim; Vasodilators (Organic Nitrates)

Decreased Effect

The levels/effects of Rosiglitazone may be decreased by: Cholestyramine Resin; CYP2C8 Inducers (Strong); Dabrafenib; Hyperglycemia-Associated Agents; Lumacaftor; Quinolone Antibiotics; RifAMPin; Thiazide and Thiazide-Like Diuretics

Dietary Considerations Management of type 2 diabetes mellitus (noninsulin dependent, NIDDM) should include diet control.

Pharmacodynamics/Kinetics

Onset of Action Delayed; Maximum effect: Up to 12 weeks

Half-life Elimination 3 to 4 hours; prolonged by approximately 2 hours in patients with moderate-to-severe hepatic impairment

Time to Peak 1 hour; delayed with food

Pregnancy Risk Factor C

Pregnancy Considerations Adverse effects were observed in initial animal reproduction studies. Rosiglitazone has been found to cross the placenta during the first trimester of pregnancy. Inadvertent use early in pregnancy has not been shown to increase the risk of adverse fetal effects, although in the majority of cases, the medication was stopped as soon as pregnancy was detected (Chan 2005; Kalyoncu 2005; Yaris 2004).

Thiazolidinediones may cause ovulation in anovulatory premenopausal women, increasing the risk of pregnancy. Adequate contraception in premenopausal women is recommended.

In women with diabetes, maternal hyperglycemia can be associated with congenital malformations as well as adverse effects in the fetus, neonate, and the mother (ACOG 2005; ADA 2016d; Kitzmiller 2008; Metzger 2007). To prevent adverse outcomes, prior to conception and throughout pregnancy maternal blood glucose and HbA_{1c} should be kept as close to target goals as possible but without causing significant hypoglycemia (ACOG 2013; ADA 2016d; Blumer 2013; Kitzmiller 2008).

Agents other than rosiglitazone are currently recommended to treat diabetes in pregnant women (ACOG 2013; Blumer 2013).

Breastfeeding Considerations It is not known if rosiglitazone is excreted in breast milk. Although breastfeeding is encouraged for all women, including those with diabetes, the safety of rosiglitazone during breastfeeding has not yet been established (Metzger 2007). The manufacturer recommends a decision be made whether to discontinue nursing or to discontinue the drug, taking into account the importance of treatment to the mother.

Prescribing and Access Restrictions Health Canada requires written informed consent for new and current patients receiving rosiglitazone.

Dosage Forms

Tablet, Oral:

Avandia: 2 mg, 4 mg

Dosage Forms: Canada

Tablet, Oral:

Avandia: 2 mg, 4 mg, 8 mg

Rosuvastatin (roe soo va STAT in)

Related Information

Cardiovascular Diseases *on page 1752*

Brand Names: US Crestor

Brand Names: Canada ACT-Rosuvastatin; Apo-Rosuvastatin; Crestor; Dom-Rosuvastatin; Jamp-Rosuvastatin; Mar-Rosuvastatin; Med-Rosuvastatin; Mint-Rosuvastatin; Mylan-Rosuvastatin; PMS-Rosuvastatin; RAN-Rosuvastatin; Riva-Rosuvastatin; Sandoz-Rosuvastatin; Teva-Rosuvastatin

Pharmacologic Category Antilipemic Agent, HMG-CoA Reductase Inhibitor

Use

Familial hypercholesterolemia:

Pediatric: Adjunct to diet to reduce total cholesterol, low-density lipoprotein cholesterol (LDL-C), and apolipoprotein B (apo B) levels in children and adolescents 8 to 17 years of age with heterozygous familial hypercholesteremia (HeFH) if after an adequate trial of diet therapy the following findings are present: LDL-C more than 190 mg/dL or more than 160 mg/dL and there is a positive family history of premature cardiovascular (CV) disease or 2 or more other CV disease risk factors; to reduce LDL-C, total-C, non–high-density lipoprotein cholesterol (non-HDL-C) and apo B in children and adolescents 7 to 17 years of age with homozygous familial hypercholesterolemia (HoFH), either alone or with other lipid-lowering treatments (eg, LDL apheresis).

Adult: To reduce LDL-C, total cholesterol, and apo B in adults with homozygous familial hypercholesterolemia as an adjunct to other lipid-lowering treatments (eg, LDL apheresis) or alone if such treatments are unavailable.

Hyperlipidemia and mixed dyslipidemia: Adjunctive therapy to diet to reduce elevated total cholesterol, LDL-C, apo B, non-HDL-C, and triglyceride levels, and to increase HDL-C in adults with primary hyperlipidemia or mixed dyslipidemia.

Hypertriglyceridemia: Adjunct to diet for the treatment of adults with hypertriglyceridemia.

Primary dysbetalipoproteinemia (type III hyperlipoproteinemia): Adjunct to diet for the treatment of adults with primary dysbetalipoproteinemia (type III hyperlipoproteinemia).

Prevention of cardiovascular disease:

Primary prevention: To reduce the risk of stroke, myocardial infarction, or arterial revascularization procedures in patients without clinically evident coronary heart disease but with all of the following: 1) an increased risk of cardiovascular disease based on age ≥50 years old in men and ≥60 years old in women, 2) hsCRP ≥2 mg/L, and 3) the presence of at least one additional cardiovascular disease risk factor such as hypertension, low HDL-C, smoking, or a family history of premature coronary heart disease.

Secondary prevention: Adjunctive therapy to diet to slow the progression of atherosclerosis in adults as part of a treatment strategy to lower total cholesterol and LDL-C to target levels.

Guideline recommendations: Primary and secondary prevention of atherosclerotic cardiovascular disease (ASCVD) to reduce the risk of ASCVD in select adult patients (ACC/AHA [Stone 2013]; NLA [Jacobson 2015]). Refer to respective guideline for specific recommendations.

Local Anesthetic/Vasoconstrictor Precautions No information available to require special precautions

Effects on Dental Treatment Key adverse event(s) related to dental treatment: Assess unusual presentations of muscle weakness or myopathy resulting from lipid therapy such as patient having a difficult time brushing teeth or weakness with chewing. Refer patient back to their physician for evaluation and adjustment of lipid therapy.

Effects on Bleeding No information available to require special precautions

Adverse Reactions

>10%: Neuromuscular & skeletal: Myalgia (2% to 13%)

1% to 10%:

Central nervous system: Headache (6% to 9%), dizziness (4%)

Endocrine & metabolic: Diabetes mellitus (new onset: 3%)

Gastrointestinal: Nausea (4% to 6%), constipation (3% to 5%)

Genitourinary: Cystitis (interstitial; Huang 2015)

Hepatic: Increased serum ALT (2%; >3 times ULN)

Neuromuscular & skeletal: Arthralgia (4% to 10%), increased creatine phosphokinase (3%; >10 x ULN: Children 3%), weakness (5%)

<1%, postmarketing, and/or case reports: Abnormal thyroid function test, cognitive dysfunction (reversible; includes amnesia, confusion, memory impairment), depression, elevated glycosylated hemoglobin

(HbA_{1c}), gynecomastia, hematuria (microscopic), hepatic failure, hepatitis, hypersensitivity reaction (including angioedema, pruritus, skin rash, urticaria), immune-mediated necrotizing myopathy, increased gamma-glutamyl transferase, increased serum alkaline phosphatase, increased serum bilirubin, increased serum glucose, increased serum transaminases, jaundice, myoglobinuria, myopathy, myositis, pancreatitis, peripheral neuropathy, proteinuria (dose related), renal failure, rhabdomyolysis, sleep disorder (including insomnia and nightmares), thrombocytopenia

General Dosage Range Dosage adjustment recommended in patients with severe renal impairment, on concomitant drug therapy, or who develop toxicities

Oral:

Children ≥7 years and Adolescents: HoFH: 20 mg once daily

Children 8 to <10 years: HeFH: 5 to 10 mg once daily (maximum: 10 mg/day).

Children ≥10 years and Adolescents: HeFH: 5 to 20 mg once daily (maximum: 20 mg/day).

Adults: Initial: 5 to 20 mg once daily; Maintenance: 5 to 40 mg once daily (maximum: 40 mg/day).

Mechanism of Action Inhibitor of 3-hydroxy-3-methylglutaryl coenzyme A (HMG-CoA) reductase, the rate-limiting enzyme in cholesterol synthesis (reduces the production of mevalonic acid from HMG-CoA); this then results in a compensatory increase in the expression of LDL receptors on hepatocyte membranes and a stimulation of LDL catabolism. In addition to the ability of HMG-CoA reductase inhibitors to decrease levels of high-sensitivity C-reactive protein (hsCRP), they also possess pleiotropic properties including improved endothelial function, reduced inflammation at the site of the coronary plaque, inhibition of platelet aggregation, and anticoagulant effects (de Denus 2002; Ray 2005).

Pharmacodynamics/Kinetics

Onset of Action Within 1 week; maximal at 4 weeks

Half-life Elimination 19 hours

Time to Peak Plasma: 3 to 5 hours

Pregnancy Considerations Adverse events have been observed in some animal reproduction studies. There are reports of congenital anomalies following maternal use of HMG-CoA reductase inhibitors in pregnancy; however, maternal disease, differences in specific agents used, and the low rates of exposure limit the interpretation of the available data (Godfrey 2012; Lecarpentier 2012). Cholesterol biosynthesis may be important in fetal development; serum cholesterol and triglycerides increase normally during pregnancy. The discontinuation of lipid lowering medications temporarily during pregnancy is not expected to have significant impact on the long term outcomes of primary hypercholesterolemia treatment.

Use of rosuvastatin is contraindicated in pregnancy. HMG-CoA reductase inhibitors should be discontinued prior to pregnancy (ADA 2013). If treatment of dyslipidemias is needed in pregnant women or in women of reproductive age, other agents are preferred (Berglund 2012; Stone 2013). The manufacturer recommends administration to women of childbearing potential only when conception is highly unlikely and patients have been informed of potential hazards.

Rotavirus Vaccine (ROE ta vye rus vak SEEN)

Brand Names: US Rotarix; RotaTeq

Brand Names: Canada Rotarix; RotaTeq

Pharmacologic Category Vaccine; Vaccine, Live (Viral)

Use

Rotavirus gastroenteritis prevention:

Rotarix: Prevention of rotavirus gastroenteritis in infants 6 to 24 weeks of age caused by the serotypes G1, G3, G4, and G9 when administered as a 2-dose series.

RotaTeq: Prevention of rotavirus gastroenteritis in infants 6 to 32 weeks of age caused by the serotypes G1, G2, G3, G4, and G9 when administered as a 3-dose series.

The Advisory Committee on Immunization Practices (ACIP) recommends routine vaccination of all infants (CDC/ACIP [Cortese 2009]).

Local Anesthetic/Vasoconstrictor Precautions No information available to require special precautions

Effects on Dental Treatment No significant effects or complications reported

Effects on Bleeding No information available to require special precautions

Adverse Reactions

Ranges reported; actual percentage may vary between products.

>10%:

Central nervous system: Irritability (≤52%)

Gastrointestinal: Diarrhea (4% to 24%), vomiting (3% to 15%)

Otic: Otitis media (15%)

Miscellaneous: Fussiness (≤52%)

1% to 10%:

Gastrointestinal: Flatulence (2%)

Respiratory: Nasopharyngitis (7%), bronchospasm (1%)

<1%, postmarketing, and/or case reports: Anaphylaxis, angioedema, gastroenteritis (with severe diarrhea and prolonged vaccine viral shedding in infants with SCID), hematochezia, immune thrombocytopenia (ITP), intussusception, Kawasaki syndrome, secondary infection (transmission of vaccine virus from recipient to nonvaccinated contacts), seizure, urticaria

General Dosage Range Oral:

Infants 6 to 24 weeks: Rotarix: A total of two 1 mL doses administered at 2 and 4 months of age

Infants 6 to 32 weeks: RotaTeq: A total of three 2 mL doses given at 2, 4, and 6 months of age

Mechanism of Action A live vaccine; replicates in the small intestine and promotes active immunity to rotavirus gastroenteritis. Rotarix is specifically indicated for prevention of rotavirus gastroenteritis caused by serotypes G1, G3, G4, and G9 and RotaTeq is specifically indicated for prevention of rotavirus gastroenteritis caused by serotypes G1, G2, G3, G4, and G9. However, these vaccines may provide immunity to other rotavirus serotypes.

Pharmacodynamics/Kinetics

Onset of Action Seroconversion:

Rotarix: Antirotavirus IgA antibodies were noted 1 to 2 months following completion of the 2-dose series in 77% to 87% of infants.

RotaTeq: A threefold increase in antirotavirus IgA was noted following completion of the 3-dose regimen in 93% to 100% of infants.

Duration of Action Following administration of rotavirus vaccine, efficacy of protecting against any grade of rotavirus gastroenteritis through two seasons was 71% to 79%.

Pregnancy Risk Factor C

Pregnancy Considerations Reproduction studies have not been conducted. Not indicated for use in women of reproductive age. Infants living in households with pregnant women may be vaccinated (CDC/ACIP [Cortese, 2009]).

Rotigotine (roe TIG oh teen)

Brand Names: US Neupro

Brand Names: Canada Neupro

Pharmacologic Category Anti-Parkinson's Agent, Dopamine Agonist

Use

Parkinson disease: For the treatment of Parkinson disease.

Restless legs syndrome: For the treatment of moderate to severe primary restless legs syndrome.

Local Anesthetic/Vasoconstrictor Precautions No information available to require special precautions

Effects on Dental Treatment Key adverse event(s) related to dental treatment: Xerostomia and changes in salivation (normal salivary flow resumes upon discontinuation). Dopamine agonists may cause syncope. Patients may experience orthostatic hypotension as they stand up after treatment; especially if lying in dental chair for extended periods of time. Use caution with sudden changes in position during and after dental treatment. Parkinson's disease patients should be carefully assisted from the chair and observed for signs of orthostatic hypotension.

Effects on Bleeding No information available to require special precautions

Adverse Reactions

>10%:

Cardiovascular: Systolic hypotension (13% to 32%), peripheral edema (dose related; 3% to 14%)

Central nervous system: Drowsiness (dose related; 5% to 32%), orthostatic hypotension (8% to 29%), dizziness (5% to 23%), headache (10% to 21%), fatigue (6% to 18%), sleep disorder (disturbance in initiating/maintaining sleep; dose related; 2% to 14%), malaise (≤14%), hallucination (dose related; 3% to 13%), insomnia (7% to 11%)

Dermatologic: Hyperhidrosis (dose related; 1% to 11%)

Endocrine & metabolic: Decreased serum glucose (1% to 15%)

Gastrointestinal: Nausea (dose related; 15% to 48%), vomiting (dose related; 2% to 20%)

Hematologic & oncologic: Decreased hematocrit (8% to 17%), decreased hemoglobin (8% to 15%)

Local: Application site reaction (dose related; 21% to 46%)

Neuromuscular & skeletal: Dyskinesia (dose related; 14% to 17%), weakness (≤14%), arthralgia (8% to 11%)

1% to 10%:

Cardiovascular: Increased diastolic blood pressure (4% to 8%), systolic hypertension (5%), hypertension (dose related; 1% to 5%), atrioventricular block (3%), abnormal T waves on ECG (≤3%), syncope

Central nervous system: Abnormal dreams (dose related; 1% to 7%), nightmares (dose related; 3% to 5%), depression (2% to 5%), paresthesia (dose related; 4%), vertigo (3% to 4%), equilibrium disturbance (2% to 3%), irritability (1% to 3%), sleep attacks (dose related; 1% to 2%)

Dermatologic: Pruritus (4% to 9%), erythema (dose related; 2% to 6%)

Endocrine & metabolic: Weight gain (2% to 9%), change in libido (4% to 6%), hot flash (3% to 4%), low serum ferritin (dose related; 2%), menstrual disorder (1% to 2%)

Gastrointestinal: Constipation (5% to 9%), anorexia (2% to 9%), xerostomia (dose related; 7%), diarrhea (5% to 7%), dyspepsia (dose related; 2% to 3%), viral gastroenteritis (1% to 2%)

Genitourinary: Change in WBC count (urine, ≤3%)

Hematologic & oncologic: Basal cell carcinoma (3%), leukocyturia (3%)

Infection: Herpes simplex infection (3%)

Neuromuscular & skeletal: Tremor (4%), muscle spasm (dose related; 3% to 4%)

Ophthalmic: Visual disturbance (3% to 5%)

Otic: Tinnitus (2% to 3%)

Renal: Increased blood urea nitrogen (3% to 11%)

Respiratory: Nasopharyngitis (8% to 10%), cough (3%), nasal congestion (3%), sinus congestion (2% to 3%), sinusitis (dose related; 2% to 3%)

Miscellaneous: Hiccups (dose related; 2% to 3%)

<1%, postmarketing, and/or case reports: Agitation, aggressive behavior, confusion, delirium, delusions, disorientation, impulse control disorder, increased creatine phosphokinase, neuroleptic malignant syndrome (resembling), paranoia, psychotic symptoms, skin rash

General Dosage Range

Transdermal: *Adults:* 1 to 4 mg/24 hours; Maintenance (usual): 1 to 8 mg/24 hours (maximum: varies by indication)

Mechanism of Action Rotigotine is a nonergot dopamine agonist with specificity for D_3-, D_2-, and D_1-dopamine receptors. Although the precise mechanism of action of rotigotine is unknown, it is believed to be due to stimulation of postsynaptic dopamine D_2-type auto receptors within the substantia nigra in the brain, leading to improved dopaminergic transmission in the motor areas of the basal ganglia, notably the caudate nucleus/putamen regions.

Pharmacodynamics/Kinetics

Half-life Elimination After removal of patch: ~5 to 7 hours

Time to Peak 15 to 18 hours; can occur 4 to 27 hours post application

Pregnancy Risk Factor C

Pregnancy Considerations Adverse events have been observed in animal reproduction studies.

Rufinamide (roo FIN a mide)

Brand Names: US Banzel

Brand Names: Canada Banzel

Pharmacologic Category Anticonvulsant, Triazole Derivative

Use Lennox-Gastaut syndrome: Adjunctive treatment of seizures associated with Lennox-Gastaut syndrome in adults and children 1 year and older

Local Anesthetic/Vasoconstrictor Precautions No information available to require special precautions

Effects on Dental Treatment No significant effects or complications reported

Effects on Bleeding No information available to require special precautions

Adverse Reactions

>10%:

Cardiovascular: Shortened QT interval (46% to 65%; dose related)

Central nervous system: Headache (adults 27%, children 16%), drowsiness (11% to 24%), dizziness (3% to 19%), fatigue (9% to 16%)

Gastrointestinal: Vomiting (children 17%, adults 5%), nausea (7% to 12%)

1% to 10%:

Central nervous system: Ataxia (4% to 5%), status epilepticus (≤4%), aggressive behavior (children 3%), anxiety (adults 3%), disturbance in attention (children 3%), hyperactivity (children 3%), vertigo (adults 3%), abnormal gait (1% to 3%), convulsions (children 2%)

Dermatologic: Skin rash (children 4%), pruritus (children 3%)

Gastrointestinal: Decreased appetite (children 5%), constipation (adults 3%), dyspepsia (adults 3%), upper abdominal pain (3%), increased appetite (≥1%)

Hematologic & oncologic: Leukopenia (4%), anemia (1%)

Infection: Influenza (children 5%)

Neuromuscular & skeletal: Tremor (adults 6%), back pain (adults 3%)

Ophthalmic: Diplopia (4% to 9%), blurred vision (adults 6%), nystagmus (adults 6%)

Otic: Otic infection (children 3%), pollakiuria (1%)

Respiratory: Nasopharyngitis (children 5%), bronchitis (children 3%), sinusitis (children 3%)

<1%, postmarketing, and/or case reports: Atrioventricular block (first degree), bundle branch block (right), dysuria, hematuria, hypersensitivity (multiorgan), iron-deficiency anemia, lymphadenopathy, nephrolithiasis, neutropenia, nocturia, polyuria, Stevens-Johnson syndrome, suicidal ideation, thrombocytopenia, urinary incontinence

General Dosage Range Oral:

Children and Adolescents <17 years: Initial: 10 mg/kg/day in 2 equally divided doses (maximum: 45 mg/kg/day, not to exceed 3,200 mg daily)

Adolescents ≥17 years and Adults: Initial: 400 to 800 mg daily in 2 equally divided doses (maximum: 3,200 mg daily)

Mechanism of Action A triazole-derivative antiepileptic whose exact mechanism is unknown. *In vitro*, it prolongs the inactive state of the sodium channels, thereby limiting repetitive firing of sodium-dependent action potentials mediating anticonvulsant effects.

Pharmacodynamics/Kinetics

Half-life Elimination ~6 to 10 hours

Time to Peak 4 to 6 hours

Pregnancy Risk Factor C

Pregnancy Considerations Adverse effects were seen in animal reproduction studies. Hormonal contraceptives may be less effective with concurrent rufinamide use; additional forms of nonhormonal contraceptives should be used.

Patients exposed to rufinamide during pregnancy are encouraged to enroll themselves into the AED Pregnancy Registry by calling 1-888-233-2334. Additional information is available at www.aedpregnancyregistry.org.

Ruxolitinib (rux oh LI ti nib)

Brand Names: US Jakafi

Brand Names: Canada Jakavi

Pharmacologic Category Antineoplastic Agent, Janus Associated Kinase Inhibitor; Antineoplastic Agent, Tyrosine Kinase Inhibitor; Janus Associated Kinase Inhibitor

Use

Myelofibrosis: Treatment of intermediate or high-risk myelofibrosis, including primary myelofibrosis, post-polycythemia vera myelofibrosis and post-essential thrombocythemia myelofibrosis

Polycythemia vera: Treatment of polycythemia vera with an inadequate response to or intolerance to hydroxyurea

Local Anesthetic/Vasoconstrictor Precautions
No information available to require special precautions

Effects on Dental Treatment No significant effects or complications reported

Effects on Bleeding Chemotherapy may result in significant myelosuppression, potentially including significant reduction in platelet counts and altered hemostasis. In patients who are under active treatment with these agents, medical consult is suggested.

Adverse Reactions

>10%:

Central nervous system: Dizziness (15% to 18%), headache (15% to 16%), fatigue (15%), insomnia (12%) (Verstovsek 2012)

Dermatologic: Bruise (23%), pruritus (14%)

Endocrine & metabolic: Increased serum cholesterol (17% to 35%), hypertriglyceridemia (15%)

Gastrointestinal: Diarrhea (15%), abdominal pain (15%)

Hematologic & oncologic: Anemia (72% to 96%; grade 3: ≤34%; grade 4: ≤11%), thrombocytopenia (27% to 70%; grade 3: 5% to 9%; grade 4: ≤4%), neutropenia (3% to 19%; grade 3: 5%; grade 4: ≤2%)

Hepatic: Increased serum ALT (25%; grade 3: <1%), increased serum AST (17% to 23%)

Neuromuscular & skeletal: Muscle spasm (12%)

Respiratory: Dyspnea (13%)

1% to 10%:

Cardiovascular: Edema (8%), hypertension (<6%)

Endocrine & metabolic: Weight gain (≤7%)

Gastrointestinal: Constipation (8%), nausea (6%), flatulence (5%), vomiting

Genitourinary: Urinary tract infection (≤9%)

Infection: Herpes zoster (2% to 6%)

Neuromuscular & skeletal: Weakness (7%)

Respiratory: Nasopharyngitis (9%), cough (8%), epistaxis (6%)

<1%, postmarketing, and/or case reports: Bradycardia, disseminated intravascular coagulation, fever, hemorrhagic diathesis, hypotension, multi-organ failure, myelofibrosis (symptom exacerbation), progressive multifocal leukoencephalopathy, prolonged Q-T interval on ECG, respiratory distress, systolic hypertension, tuberculosis, withdrawal syndrome

General Dosage Range Dosage adjustment recommended in patients with hepatic impairment, renal impairment, on concomitant strong CYP3A4 inhibitor therapy, or who develop toxicities.

Oral: *Adults:* 5 to 20 mg twice daily; maximum dose: 25 mg twice daily

Mechanism of Action Kinase inhibitor which selectively inhibits Janus Associated Kinases (JAKs), JAK1 and JAK2. JAK1 and JAK2 mediate signaling of cytokine and growth factors responsible for hematopoiesis and immune function; JAK mediated signaling involves recruitment of STATs (signal transducers and activators of transcription) to cytokine receptors which leads to modulation of gene expression. In myelofibrosis and polycythemia vera, JAK1/2 activity is dysregulated; ruxolitinib modulates the affected JAK1/2 activity.

Pharmacodynamics/Kinetics

Half-life Elimination Ruxolitinib: ~3 hours (hepatic impairment: 4.1 to 5 hours); Ruxolitinib + metabolites: ~5.8 hours

Pregnancy Risk Factor C

Pregnancy Considerations Increased resorptions (late) and reduced fetal weights were observed in animal reproduction studies.

Prescribing and Access Restrictions Available through specialty/network pharmacies. Further information may be obtained from the manufacturer, Incyte, at 1-855-452-5234 or at www.Jakafi.com.

Sacubitril and Valsartan

(sak UE bi tril & val SAR tan)

Brand Names: US Entresto

Brand Names: Canada Entresto

Pharmacologic Category Angiotensin II Receptor Blocker; Neprilysin Inhibitor

Use

Heart failure: Reduce the risk of cardiovascular death and hospitalization for heart failure in patients with chronic heart failure (NYHA Class II-IV) and reduced ejection fraction; usually administered in conjunction with other heart failure therapies, in place of an angiotensin converting enzyme (ACE) inhibitor or other angiotensin II receptor blocker (ARB)

Note: According to the ACC/AHA/HFSA heart failure guidelines, in patients with chronic symptomatic heart failure with reduced ejection fraction (HFrEF) NYHA Class II or III who tolerate an ACE inhibitor or ARB, replacement with sacubitril/valsartan is recommended (ACC/AHA/HFSA [Yancy 2016]). In addition, prior to enrollment in the PARADIGM-HF clinical trial, patients were already receiving a stable dose of an ACE inhibitor or ARB at daily doses equivalent to at least 10 mg of enalapril (McMurray 2014).

Local Anesthetic/Vasoconstrictor Precautions No information available to require special precautions

Effects on Dental Treatment Key adverse event(s) related to dental treatment: Hypotension in general and orthostatic hypotension has been reported; Patients may experience orthostatic hypotension as they stand up after treatment; especially if lying in dental chair for extended periods of time. Use caution with sudden changes in position during and after dental treatment.

Effects on Bleeding No information available to require special precautions

Adverse Reactions Also see individual agents.

>10%:

- Cardiovascular: Hypotension (18%)
- Endocrine & metabolic: Increased serum potassium (4% to 16%), hyperkalemia (12%)
- Renal: Increased serum creatinine (1% to 16%)

1% to 10%:

- Cardiovascular: Orthostatic hypotension (2%)
- Central nervous system: Dizziness (6%), falling (2%)
- Hematologic & oncologic: Decreased hematocrit (≤5%), decreased hemoglobin (≤5%)
- Hypersensitivity: Angioedema (black patients: 2%; others: <1%)
- Renal: Renal failure (5%)
- Respiratory: Cough (9%)

General Dosage Range Dosage adjustment recommended in patients with renal or hepatic impairment

Oral: *Adults:* Initial: Sacubitril 24 mg to 49 mg and valsartan 26 mg to 51 mg twice daily; Maintenance: Sacubitril 97 mg and valsartan 103 mg twice daily

Mechanism of Action

Sacubitril: Prodrug that inhibits neprilysin (neutral endopeptidase [NEP]) through the active metabolite LBQ657, leading to increased levels of peptides, including natriuretic peptides.

Valsartan: Produces direct antagonism of the angiotensin II (AT2) receptors. Displaces angiotensin II from the AT1 receptor; antagonizes AT1-induced vasoconstriction, aldosterone release, catecholamine release, arginine vasopressin release, water intake, and hypertrophic responses.

Pharmacodynamics/Kinetics

Half-life Elimination Sacubitril: 1.4 hours; LBQ657: 11.5 hours; Valsartan: 9.9 hours

Time to Peak Sacubitril: 0.5 hours; LBQ657: 2 hours; Valsartan: 1.5 hours

Pregnancy Considerations [US Boxed Warning]: Drugs that act on the renin-angiotensin system can cause injury and death to the developing fetus. Discontinue as soon as possible once pregnancy is detected. Refer to the valsartan monograph for additional information.

Salicylic Acid (sal i SIL ik AS id)

Brand Names: US Bensal HP; Betasal [OTC]; Clear Away 1-Step Wart Remover [OTC]; Corn Remover One Step [OTC]; Corn Remover Ultra Thin [OTC]; DHS Sal [OTC] [DSC]; Exuviance Blemish Treatment [OTC]; Gordofilm; Hydrisalic [OTC] [DSC]; Ionil [OTC]; Keralyt; Keralyt Scalp; Keralyt [OTC]; Mediplast [OTC]; Neutrogena Oil-Free Acne Wash [OTC]; One Step Callus Remover [OTC]; P & S [OTC]; Psoriasin [OTC]; Sal-Plant [OTC]; SalAc [OTC]; Salactic Film [OTC]; Salacyn; Salex; Salicylic Acid Wart Remover; Salisol; Salisol Forte; Salitech; Salitech Forte; Salkera [DSC]; Salvax; Scalpicin 2 in 1 [OTC]; Scholls Callus Removers [OTC] [DSC]; Scholls Corn Removers Extra [OTC] [DSC]; Scholls Corn Removers Small [OTC] [DSC]; Scholls Corn Removers [OTC] [DSC]; Sebasorb [OTC] [DSC]; Stri-Dex Maximum Strength [OTC]; Stri-Dex Sensitive Skin [OTC]; Stridex Essential [OTC]; UltraSal-ER; Virasal

Brand Names: Canada Duofilm; Duoforte 27; Occlusal-HP; Sebcur; Soluver; Soluver Plus; Trans-Plantar; Trans-Ver-Sal

Pharmacologic Category Acne Products; Keratolytic Agent; Topical Skin Product, Acne

Use

Acne: Topical management of acne

Dermatitis: Bensal HP: Treatment of inflammation and irritation associated with dermatitis, including eczematoid conditions and complications associated with pyodermas; treatment of insect bites, burns, and fungal infections

Hyperkeratotic skin disorders: Removal of excess keratin in various hyperkeratotic skin disorders and psoriasis (including affected areas of scalp, skin, and feet; treatment and removal of common and plantar warts

OTC labeling: Dandruff, psoriasis, or seborrheic dermatitis; removal of warts, calluses, or corns

Local Anesthetic/Vasoconstrictor Precautions No information available to require special precautions

Effects on Dental Treatment No significant effects or complications reported

Effects on Bleeding No information available to require special precautions

Adverse Reactions Frequency not defined.

Central nervous system: Confusion, dizziness, headache, localized burning (at site of exposure on normal tissue)
Dermatologic: Desquamation, exfoliation of skin
Local: Localized irritation (at site of exposure on normal tissue)
Otic: Tinnitus
Respiratory: Hyperventilation

General Dosage Range Topical: *Children, Adolescents, and Adults:* Dosage varies greatly depending on product; refer to manufacturer's labeling.

Mechanism of Action Produces desquamation of hyperkeratotic epithelium via dissolution of the intercellular cement which causes the cornified tissue to swell, soften, macerate, and desquamate. Salicylic acid is used for keratolytic skin disorders at concentrations of 3% to 6%; concentrations of 5% to 40% are used to remove corns and warts; concentrations up to 2% are used for acne (Akhavan 2003).

Pharmacodynamics/Kinetics

Onset of Action Treatment of warts: 1 to 2 weeks; full resolution may take >4 to 6 weeks.

Time to Peak Serum: Salicylic acid gel 6%: Within 5 hours of application with occlusion

Pregnancy Risk Factor C

Pregnancy Considerations Adverse events have been observed in animal reproduction studies when administered orally. Salicylates cross the placenta (Østensen 1998). Systemic absorption of topical salicylic acid occurs and varies depending on duration and vehicle (~9% to 25%) and is increased with occlusion (Akhavan 2003). Current guidelines do not recommend salicylic acid for the treatment of psoriasis in pregnant women due to limited safety data and the potential for systemic absorption (Bae 2012). For the topical treatment of acne or warts, salicylic acid can be used in pregnant women if the area of exposure and duration of therapy is limited, although other agents may be preferred (Murase, 2014). Consider maternal/fetal adverse events associated with aspirin if significant systemic exposure occurs (Akhavan 2003).

Saliva Substitute (sa LYE va SUB stee tute)

Related Information

Dentin Hypersensitivity, Acid Erosion, High Caries Index, Management of Alveolar Osteitis, and Xerostomia *on page 1857*
Perioral Premalignant Lesions and Management of Patients Undergoing Cancer Therapy *on page 1875*

Brand Names: US Aquoral; Biotene Moisturizing Mouth Spray [OTC]; Biotene Oral Balance [OTC]; Caphosol; Entertainer's Secret [OTC]; Moi-Stir [OTC]; Mouth Kote [OTC]; NeutraSal; Numoisyn; Oasis; SalivaMAX; SalivaSure [OTC]; Salivate Rx

Generic Availability (US) No

Pharmacologic Category Gastrointestinal Agent, Miscellaneous

Dental Use Relief of dry mouth and throat in xerostomia

Use

Mucositis (due to high-dose chemotherapy or radiation therapy): Adjunct to standard oral care in relief of symptoms associated with chemotherapy or radiation therapy-induced mucositis

Xerostomia: Relief of dry mouth and throat in xerostomia or hyposalivation

Local Anesthetic/Vasoconstrictor Precautions No information available to require special precautions

Effects on Dental Treatment No significant effects or complications reported

Effects on Bleeding No information available to require special precautions

Adverse Reactions Frequency not defined.

Central nervous system: Speech disturbance
Gastrointestinal: Dysgeusia, dysphagia, gastrointestinal disease (minor)

Dosing

Adult & Geriatric

Mucositis (due to high-dose chemotherapy or radiation therapy): Oral:

Caphosol, NeutraSal: Swish and spit 4 to 10 doses daily (use for the duration of chemo- or radiation therapy).

SalivateRx: Swish and spit 2 to 10 doses daily.

Xerostomia: Oral: Use as needed, or product-specific dosing:

Aquoral: 2 sprays 3 to 4 times daily.

Biotene Oral Balance gel: Apply one-half inch length onto tongue and spread evenly; repeat as often as needed.

Caphosol, NeutraSal, SalivateRx: Swish and spit 2 to 10 doses daily.

Entertainer's Secret: Spray as often as needed.

Mouth Kote spray: Spray 3 to 5 times, swish for 8 to 10 seconds, then spit or swallow; use as often as needed.

Numoisyn liquid: Use 2 mL as needed.

Numoisyn lozenges: Dissolve 1 lozenge slowly; maximum 16 lozenges/day.

Oasis mouthwash: Rinse mouth with ~30 mL twice daily or as needed; do not swallow.

Oasis spray: 1 to 2 sprays as needed; maximum 60 sprays/day.

SalivaSure: Dissolve 1 lozenge slowly as needed; for severe symptoms, 1 lozenge per hour is recommended.

Renal Impairment There are no dosage adjustments provided in the manufacturer's labeling.

Hepatic Impairment There are no dosage adjustments provided in the manufacturer's labeling.

Mechanism of Action Protein or electrolyte mixtures which restore/replace saliva, lubricate, moisten, clean, and/or provide a coating on oral mucosa

Contraindications Hypersensitivity to saliva substitute or any component of the formulation; fructose intolerance (Numoisyn lozenges only)

Drug Interactions

Metabolism/Transport Effects None known.

Avoid Concomitant Use There are no known interactions where it is recommended to avoid concomitant use.

Increased Effect/Toxicity There are no known significant interactions involving an increase in effect.

Decreased Effect There are no known significant interactions involving a decrease in effect.

Dietary Considerations

Caphosol: Contains sodium 75 mg/30 mL dose
Moi-Stir: Contains sodium: 6.47 mEq/120 mL, potassium: 1.93 mEq/120 mL, magnesium: 0.128 mEq/120 mL

Dosage Forms

Liquid, oral:

Biotene Oral Balance [OTC]: Water, starch, sunflower oil, propylene glycol, xylitol, glycerine, purified milk extract

Numoisyn: Water, sorbitol, linseed extract, *Chondrus crispus*, methylparaben, sodium benzoate, potassium sorbate, dipotassium phosphate, propylparaben

Lozenge, oral:

Numoisyn: Sorbitol 0.3 g/lozenge, polyethylene glycol, malic acid, sodium citrate, calcium phosphate dibasic, hydrogenated cottonseed oil, citric acid, magnesium stearate, silicon dioxide

SalivaSure [OTC]: Xylitol, citric acid, apple acid, sodium citrate dihydrate, sodium carboxymethylcellulose, dibasic calcium phosphate, silica colloidal, magnesium stearate, stearic acid

Powder, for reconstitution, oral:

NeutraSal: Calcium chloride, sodium bicarbonate, sodium chloride, and sodium phosphates

SalivaMAX: Calcium chloride, sodium bicarbonate, sodium chloride, and sodium phosphates

Salivate Rx: Calcium chloride, sodium bicarbonate, sodium chloride, and sodium phosphates

Solution, oral:

Caphosol: Dibasic sodium phosphate 0.032%, monobasic sodium phosphate 0.009%, calcium chloride 0.052%, sodium chloride 0.569%, purified water

Entertainer's Secret [OTC]: Sodium carboxymethylcellulose, aloe vera gel, glycerin (60 mL)

Solution, oral [mouthwash/gargle]:

Oasis: Water, glycerin, sorbitol, poloxamer 338, PEG-60, hydrogenated castor oil, copovidone, sodium benzoate, carboxymethylcellulose

Solution, oral [spray]:

Aquoral: Oxidized glycerol triesters and silicon dioxide

Biotene Moisturizing Mouth Spray [OTC]: Water, polyglycitol, propylene glycol, sunflower oil, xylitol, milk protein extract, potassium sorbate, acesulfame K, potassium thiocyanate, lysozyme, lactoferrin, lactoperoxidase

Moi-Stir [OTC]: Water, sorbitol, sodium carboxymethylcellulose, methylparaben, propylparaben, potassium chloride, dibasic sodium phosphate, calcium chloride, magnesium chloride, sodium chloride

Mouth Kote [OTC]: Water, xylitol, sorbitol, yerba santa, citric acid, ascorbic acid, sodium saccharin, sodium benzoate

Oasis: Glycerin, cetylpyridinium, copovidone

Salmeterol (sal ME te role)

Related Information

Respiratory Diseases *on page* 1777

Brand Names: US Serevent Diskus

Brand Names: Canada Serevent Diskhaler Disk; Serevent Diskus

Pharmacologic Category $Beta_2$ Agonist; $Beta_2$-Adrenergic Agonist, Long-Acting

Use

Asthma/Bronchospasm: Treatment of asthma and the prevention of bronchospasm (only as concomitant therapy with a long-term asthma control medication, such as an inhaled corticosteroid), in patients 4 years and older with reversible obstructive airway disease, including patients with symptoms of nocturnal asthma.

Chronic obstructive pulmonary disease: Maintenance treatment of bronchospasm associated with chronic obstructive pulmonary disease (COPD) (including emphysema and chronic bronchitis).

Exercise-induced bronchospasm: Prevention of exercise-induced bronchospasm (EIB) in patients 4 years and older (monotherapy may be indicated in patients without persistent asthma).

Limitations of use: Salmeterol is not indicated for the relief of acute bronchospasm.

Local Anesthetic/Vasoconstrictor Precautions No information available to require special precautions

Effects on Dental Treatment Key adverse event(s) related to dental treatment: Xerostomia (normal salivary flow resumes upon discontinuation), dental pain, and oropharyngeal candidiasis.

Effects on Bleeding No information available to require special precautions

Adverse Reactions

>10%: Central nervous system: Headache (13% to 17%), pain (1% to 12%)

1% to 10%:

Cardiovascular: Hypertension (4%), edema (1% to 3%)

Central nervous system: Dizziness (4%), sleep disorder (1% to 3%), anxiety (1% to 3%), migraine (1% to 3%), paresthesia (1% to 3%)

Dermatologic: Skin rash (1% to 4%), contact dermatitis (1% to 3%), eczema (1% to 3%), urticaria (3%), photodermatitis (1% to 2%), pallor

Endocrine & metabolic: Hyperglycemia (1% to 3%)

Gastrointestinal: Dyspepsia (1% to 3%), gastrointestinal infection (1% to 3%), nausea (1% to 3%), oropharyngeal candidiasis (1% to 3%), toothache (1% to 3%), xerostomia (1% to 3%)

Hepatic: Increased liver enzymes

Infection: Influenza (5%)

Neuromuscular & skeletal: Muscle cramps (≤3%), muscle spasm (≤3%), arthritis (1% to 3%), arthralgia (1% to 3%), muscle rigidity (1% to 3%)

Ophthalmic: Conjunctivitis (≤3%), keratitis (≤3%)

Respiratory: Nasal congestion (4% to 9%), bronchitis (≤7%), throat irritation (7%), tracheitis (≤7%; may be paradoxical), pharyngitis (≤6%), cough (5%), viral respiratory tract infection (5%), sinusitis (4% to 5%), rhinitis (4% to 5%), asthma (3% to 4%)

Miscellaneous: Fever (1% to 3%)

<1%, postmarketing, and/or case reports: Abdominal pain, agitation, aggressive behavior, anaphylaxis (some in patients with severe milk allergy), angioedema, aphonia, atrial fibrillation, bruise, cardiac arrhythmia, cataract, chest congestion, chest tightness, choking sensation, Churg-Strauss syndrome, Cushing's syndrome, Cushingoid appearance, decreased linear skeletal growth rate (children and adolescents), depression, dysmenorrhea, dyspnea, ecchymoses, edema (facial, oropharyngeal), eosinophilia, glaucoma, hypercorticoidism, hypersensitivity reaction (immediate and delayed), hypokalemia, hypothyroidism, increased intraocular pressure, irregular menses, laryngospasm, local irritation (larynx), myositis, oropharyngeal irritation, osteoporosis, otalgia, paradoxical bronchospasm, pelvic inflammatory disease, prolonged Q-T interval on ECG, restlessness, sinus pain (paranasal), stridor, supraventricular tachycardia, syncope, tremor, vaginitis, vulvovaginal candidiasis, vulvovaginitis, ventricular tachycardia, weight gain

General Dosage Range Inhalation: *Children ≥4 years and Adults:* 1 inhalation (50 mcg) twice daily

Mechanism of Action Relaxes bronchial smooth muscle by selective action on $beta_2$-receptors with little effect on heart rate; salmeterol acts locally in the lung.

Pharmacodynamics/Kinetics

Onset of Action Asthma: 30-48 minutes, COPD: 2 hours; Peak effect: Asthma: 3 hours, COPD: 2-5 hours

Duration of Action 12 hours

Half-life Elimination 5.5 hours

Time to Peak Serum: ~20 minutes

Pregnancy Risk Factor C

Pregnancy Considerations Adverse events were observed in some animal reproduction studies. Beta-agonists have the potential to affect uterine contractility if administered during labor.

Uncontrolled asthma is associated with adverse events on pregnancy (increased risk of perinatal mortality, pre-eclampsia, preterm birth, low birth weight infants). Although data related to its use in pregnancy is limited, salmeterol may be used when a long-acting beta agonist is needed to treat moderate persistent or severe persistent asthma in pregnant women (NAEPP, 2005).

Salsalate (SAL sa late)

Related Information

Temporomandibular Dysfunction (TMD), Chronic Pain, and Fibromyalgia *on page 1868*

Brand Names: US Disalcid

Generic Availability (US) Yes

Pharmacologic Category Salicylate

Use Rheumatic disorders: Treatment of signs and symptoms of osteoarthritis, rheumatoid arthritis, and related rheumatic disorders

Local Anesthetic/Vasoconstrictor Precautions No information available to require special precautions

Effects on Dental Treatment The dentist should be aware of the potential of abnormal coagulation. Caution should also be exercised in the use of NSAIDs in patients already on anticoagulant therapy with drugs such as warfarin (Coumadin®). See Effects on Bleeding.

Effects on Bleeding Nonacetylated salicylate formulations are known to reversibly decrease platelet aggregation via mechanisms different than observed with aspirin. Caution should also be exercised in the use of NSAIDs in patients already on anticoagulant therapy with drugs such as warfarin (Coumadin®). Unlike most salicylates/NSAIDs, salsalate does not interfere with platelet aggregation and presumably carries less risk of bleeding and/or effect on concurrent warfarin therapy.

With respect to surgery, dental practitioners should note that recommendations differ between general surgery (eg, appendectomy, hip replacement) and dental surgery. NSAIDs should be avoided (if possible) in general surgery patients for 3-5 half-lives of the drug (usually 1-3 days) prior to surgery to reduce the risk of excessive bleeding. However, there is no scientific evidence to warrant discontinuance of NSAIDs prior to dental surgery. In medically complicated patients or extensive oral surgery, the decision to interrupt therapy must be based on the risk to benefit in an individual patient and a medical consult is suggested. Routine interruption of NSAID therapy for most dental procedures is not warranted. If therapy is continued without interruption, the clinician should anticipate the potential for slower clotting times.

Adverse Reactions

Frequency not defined.

Cardiovascular: Hypotension

Central nervous system: Vertigo

Dermatologic: Skin rash, Stevens-Johnson syndrome, toxic epidermal necrolysis, urticaria

Gastrointestinal: Abdominal pain, diarrhea, gastrointestinal hemorrhage, gastrointestinal perforation, gastrointestinal ulcer, nausea

Hematologic & oncologic: Anemia

Hepatic: Abnormal hepatic function tests, hepatitis

Hypersensitivity: Anaphylactic shock, angioedema

Otic: Auditory impairment, tinnitus

Renal: Decreased creatinine clearance, nephritis

Respiratory: Bronchospasm

Dosing

Adult Rheumatic disorders: Oral: **Note:** Use the lowest effective dose for the shortest duration; after observing the response to initial therapy, adjust dose as needed. Usual dose: 3 g per day in 2 to 3 divided doses

Geriatric Refer to adult dosing. May require lower dosage.

Renal Impairment There are no dosage adjustments provided in the manufacturer's labeling. Use is not recommended in patients with advanced renal disease.

Hepatic Impairment There are no dosage adjustments provided in the manufacturer's labeling.

Mechanism of Action Salsalate inhibits prostaglandin synthesis providing, anti-inflammatory effects with less inhibition of platelet aggregation than aspirin

Contraindications

Hypersensitivity to salsalate or any component of the formulation; asthma, urticaria, or allergic reaction to aspirin or NSAIDs; perioperative pain in the setting of coronary artery bypass graft (CABG) surgery.

Documentation of allergenic cross-reactivity for salicylates is limited. However, because of similarities in chemical structure and/or pharmacologic actions, the possibility of cross-sensitivity cannot be ruled out with certainty.

Warnings/Precautions [U.S. Boxed Warning]: NSAIDs are associated with an increased risk of adverse cardiovascular thrombotic events, including fatal MI and stroke. Risk may be increased with duration of use or pre-existing cardiovascular risk factors or disease. Carefully evaluate individual cardiovascular risk profiles prior to prescribing. May cause new-onset hypertension or worsening of existing hypertension. Response to ACE inhibitors, thiazides, or loop diuretics may be impaired with concurrent use of NSAIDs. Use caution with fluid retention or heart failure. Concurrent administration of salsalate, and potentially other nonselective NSAIDs, may interfere with aspirin's cardioprotective effect. **[U.S. Boxed Warning]: Use is contraindicated for treatment of perioperative pain in the setting of coronary artery bypass graft (CABG) surgery.** Risk of MI and stroke may be increased with use following CABG surgery. Use the lowest effective dose for the shortest duration of time, consistent with individual patient goals, to reduce risk of cardiovascular or GI adverse events. Alternate therapies should be considered for patients at high risk.

NSAID use may compromise existing renal function; dose-dependent decreases in prostaglandin synthesis may result from NSAID use, reducing renal blood flow which may cause renal decompensation. Patients with impaired renal function, dehydration, heart failure, liver dysfunction, those taking diuretics, and ACE inhibitors, and the elderly are at greater risk of renal toxicity. Rehydrate patient before starting therapy; monitor renal function closely. Not recommended for use in patients with advanced renal disease. Long-term NSAID use may result in renal papillary necrosis.

[U.S. Boxed Warning]: NSAIDs may increase risk of gastrointestinal irritation, inflammation, ulceration, bleeding, and perforation. These events may occur at any time during therapy and without warning. Use caution with a history of GI disease (bleeding and/or ulcers), concurrent therapy with aspirin, anticoagulants and/or corticosteroids, smoking, use of ethanol, the elderly or debilitated patients. When used concomitantly with ≤325 mg of aspirin, a substantial increase in the risk of gastrointestinal complications (eg, ulcer) occurs; concomitant gastroprotective therapy (eg, proton pump inhibitors) is recommended (Bhatt, 2008).

Platelet adhesion and aggregation may be decreased; may prolong bleeding time; patients with coagulation disorders or who are receiving anticoagulants should be monitored closely. Anemia may occur; patients on long-term NSAID therapy should be monitored for anemia.

NSAIDs may cause serious skin adverse events including exfoliative dermatitis, Stevens-Johnson Syndrome (SJS) and toxic epidermal necrolysis (TEN); may be fatal; discontinue use at first sign of skin rash or hypersensitivity. Patients with sensitivity to tartrazine dyes, nasal polyps, and asthma may have an increased risk of salicylate sensitivity. Anaphylactoid reactions may occur, even without prior exposure to salsalate; patients with "aspirin triad" (bronchial asthma, aspirin intolerance, rhinitis) may be at increased risk. Do not use in patients who experience bronchospasm, asthma, rhinitis, or urticaria with NSAID or aspirin therapy. Use caution in other forms of asthma.

Use with caution in patients with decreased hepatic function. Closely monitor patients with any abnormal LFT. Severe hepatic reactions (eg, fulminant hepatitis, liver failure) have occurred with NSAID use, rarely; discontinue if signs or symptoms of liver disease develop, or if systemic manifestations occur.

Children and teenagers who have or are recovering from chickenpox or flu-like symptoms should not use this product. Potentially significant interactions may exist, requiring dose or frequency adjustment, additional monitoring, and/or selection of alternative therapy.

Drug Interactions

Metabolism/Transport Effects None known.

Avoid Concomitant Use

Avoid concomitant use of Salsalate with any of the following: Dexketoprofen; Influenza Virus Vaccine (Live/Attenuated); Sulfinpyrazone

Increased Effect/Toxicity

Salsalate may increase the levels/effects of: ACE Inhibitors; Ajmaline; Anticoagulants; Blood Glucose Lowering Agents; Carbonic Anhydrase Inhibitors; Corticosteroids (Systemic); Dexketoprofen; Methotrexate; PRALAtrexate; Salicylates; Thrombolytic Agents; Valproate Products; Varicella Virus-Containing Vaccines

The levels/effects of Salsalate may be increased by: Agents with Antiplatelet Properties; Ammonium Chloride; Ginkgo Biloba; Herbs (Anticoagulant/Antiplatelet Properties); Influenza Virus Vaccine (Live/Attenuated); Loop Diuretics; NSAID (Nonselective); Potassium Acid Phosphate

Decreased Effect

Salsalate may decrease the levels/effects of: ACE Inhibitors; Benzbromarone; Dexketoprofen; Hyaluronidase; Loop Diuretics; NSAID (Nonselective); Probenecid; Sulfinpyrazone

The levels/effects of Salsalate may be decreased by: Corticosteroids (Systemic); Dexketoprofen; NSAID (Nonselective)

Food Interactions Salsalate peak serum levels may be delayed if taken with food. Management: May administer with food to decrease GI distress.

Dietary Considerations May be taken with food to decrease GI distress.

Pharmacodynamics/Kinetics

Onset of Action Therapeutic: 3 to 4 days of continuous dosing

Half-life Elimination Salsalate: ~1 hour; Salicylic acid 3.5 to ≥16 hours (due to capacity limited biotransformation)

Pregnancy Risk Factor C

Pregnancy Considerations Adverse events have not been observed in animal reproduction studies. Due to the known effects of salicylates (closure of ductus arteriosus), use during late pregnancy should be avoided.

Breastfeeding Considerations Salsalate is metabolized to salicylic acid which is excreted in breast milk in concentrations equivalent to maternal blood concentrations. An infant may ingest up to 80% per kg body weight as the mother is taking. The manufacturer recommends that caution be exercised when administering salsalate to nursing women.

Dosage Forms

Tablet, Oral:

Disalcid: 500 mg, 750 mg

Generic: 500 mg, 750 mg

Saquinavir (sa KWIN a veer)

Related Information

Clinical Risk Related to Drugs Prolonging QT Interval *on page 1772*

HIV Infection and AIDS *on page 1785*

Brand Names: US Invirase

Brand Names: Canada Invirase

Pharmacologic Category Antiretroviral, Protease Inhibitor (Anti-HIV)

Use HIV-1 infection: Treatment of HIV-1 infection in adults (>16 years) in combination with ritonavir and other antiretroviral agents

Local Anesthetic/Vasoconstrictor Precautions Saquinavir is one of the drugs confirmed to prolong the QT interval and is accepted as having a risk of causing torsade de pointes. The risk of drug-induced torsade de pointes is extremely low when a single QT interval prolonging drug is prescribed. In terms of epinephrine, it is not known what effect vasoconstrictors in the local anesthetic regimen will have in patients with a known history of congenital prolonged QT interval or in patients taking any medication that prolongs the QT interval. Until more information is obtained, it is suggested that the clinician consult with the physician prior to the use of a vasoconstrictor in suspected patients, and that the vasoconstrictor (epinephrine, mepivacaine and levonordefrin [Carbocaine® 2% with Neo-Cobefrin®]) be used with caution.

Effects on Dental Treatment Key adverse event(s) related to dental treatment: Buccal mucosa ulceration and taste alteration.

Effects on Bleeding Increased bleeding has been noted with protease inhibitors in patients with hemophilia A or B. No information available to require routine special precautions relative to hemostasis in other patients.

Adverse Reactions

Incidence data for saquinavir soft gel capsule formulation (no longer available) in combination with ritonavir:

10%: Gastrointestinal: Nausea (11%)

1% to 10%:

Cardiovascular: Chest pain

Central nervous system: Fatigue (6%), anxiety, depression, headache, insomnia, pain, paresthesia

Dermatologic: Pruritus (3%), skin rash (3%), eczema (2%), cheilosis (≤2%), xeroderma (≤2%), warts

Endocrine & metabolic: Lipodystrophy (5%), hyperglycemia (3%), change in libido, hypoglycemia, hyperkalemia

Gastrointestinal: Diarrhea (8%), vomiting (7%), abdominal pain (6%), constipation (2%), abdominal distress, decreased appetite, dysgeusia, dyspepsia, flatulence, increased serum amylase, oral mucosa ulcer

Hepatic: Increased serum ALT, increased serum AST, increased serum bilirubin

Infection: Influenza (3%)

Neuromuscular & skeletal: Back pain (2%), increased creatine phosphokinase, weakness

Respiratory: Pneumonia (5%), bronchitis (3%), sinusitis (3%)

Miscellaneous: Fever (3%)

Frequency not defined; reported for hard or soft gel capsule with/without ritonavir:

Cardiovascular: Heart valve disease (including murmur), hypertension, hypotension, peripheral vasoconstriction, prolongation P-R interval on ECG, prolonged Q-T interval on ECG, syncope, thrombophlebitis

Central nervous system: Agitation, amnesia, ataxia, colic, confusion, drowsiness, hallucination, hyperreflexia, hyporeflexia, neuropathy, poliomyelitis, progressive multifocal leukoencephalopathy, psychosis, seizure, speech disturbance

Dermatologic: Alopecia, bullous dermatitis, dermal ulcer, dermatitis, erythema, maculopapular rash, skin photosensitivity, Stevens-Johnson syndrome, urticaria

Endocrine & metabolic: Dehydration, diabetes mellitus, electrolyte disturbance, increased gamma-glutamyl transferase, increased lactate dehydrogenase, increased thyroid stimulating hormone level

Gastrointestinal: Bloody stools, dysphagia, esophagitis, gastritis, intestinal obstruction, pancreatitis, stomatitis

Genitourinary: Benign prostatic hypertrophy, hematuria, impotence, urinary tract infection

Hematologic & oncologic: Acute myelocytic leukemia, anemia (including hemolytic), leukopenia, neutropenia, pancytopenia, rectal hemorrhage, splenomegaly, thrombocytopenia

Hepatic: Ascites, hepatic disease (exacerbation), hepatitis, hepatomegaly, hepatosplenomegaly, increased serum alkaline phosphatase, jaundice

Immunologic: Immune reconstitution syndrome

Infection: Infection (bacterial, fungal, viral)

Neuromuscular & skeletal: Arthritis

Ophthalmic: Blepharitis, visual disturbance

Otic: Auditory impairment, otitis, tinnitus

Renal: Nephrolithiasis

Respiratory: Cyanosis, dyspnea, hemoptysis, pharyngitis, upper respiratory tract infection

<1%, postmarketing, and/or case reports: Atrioventricular block (second or third degree), autoimmune disease, torsades de pointes

General Dosage Range

Oral: *Adolescents >16 years and Adults:* 1,000 mg twice daily in combination with ritonavir

Mechanism of Action Binds to the site of HIV-1 protease activity and inhibits cleavage of viral Gag-Pol polyprotein precursors into individual functional proteins required for infectious HIV. This results in the formation of immature, noninfectious viral particles.

Pharmacodynamics/Kinetics

Half-life Elimination Serum: 1 to 2 hours

Pregnancy Risk Factor B

Pregnancy Considerations Adverse events were not observed in animal reproduction studies. Saquinavir has a low level of transfer across the human placenta. Data collected by the antiretroviral pregnancy registry are insufficient to evaluate human teratogenic risk. A small increased risk of preterm birth has been associated with maternal use of protease inhibitor-based combination antiretroviral therapy during pregnancy; however, the benefits of use generally outweigh this risk and protease inhibitors (PIs) should not be withheld if otherwise recommended. Information related to stillbirth, low birth weight, and small for gestational age infants is limited. Long-term follow-up is recommended for all infants exposed to antiretroviral medications; children who develop significant organ system abnormalities of unknown etiology (particularly of the CNS or heart) should be evaluated for potential mitochondrial dysfunction. Hyperglycemia, new onset of diabetes mellitus, or diabetic ketoacidosis have been reported with PIs; it is not clear if pregnancy increases this risk.

Combination antiretroviral therapy (cART) therapy is recommended for all HIV-infected pregnant women to keep the viral load below the limit of detection and reduce the risk of perinatal transmission. When HIV is diagnosed during pregnancy in a woman who has never received antiretroviral therapy, cART should begin as soon as possible after diagnosis. The Health and Human Services (HHS) Perinatal HIV Guidelines do not recommend ritonavir-boosted saquinavir for initial use in antiretroviral-naive pregnant women due to potential toxicity, twice-daily dosing requirements, and limited data in pregnancy; use of saquinavir without ritonavir is **not** recommended in any patient. Based on available data, dose adjustments are not required in pregnant women. In general, women who become pregnant on a stable cART regimen may continue that regimen if viral suppression is effective, appropriate drug exposure can be achieved, contraindications for use in pregnancy are not present, and the regimen is well tolerated. Monitoring during pregnancy is more frequent than in non-pregnant adults; cART should be continued postpartum.

For HIV-infected couples planning a pregnancy, maximum viral suppression with cART is recommended prior to conception for the HIV-infected partner(s) and expert consultation is recommended; modification of therapy (if needed) and optimization of the woman's health should be done prior to conception. HIV-infected women not planning a pregnancy may use any available type of contraception, considering possible drug interactions and contraindications of the specific method. In addition, consistent use of condoms is also recommended (even during pregnancy) to prevent transmission of HIV or other sexually transmitted diseases.

Health care providers are encouraged to enroll pregnant women exposed to antiretroviral medications as early in pregnancy as possible in the Antiretroviral Pregnancy Registry (1-800-258-4263 or www.-APRegistry.com). Health care providers caring for HIV-infected women and their infants may contact the National Perinatal HIV Hotline (888-448-8765) for clinical consultation (HHS [perinatal] 2016).

Dental Comment See Local Anesthetic/Vasoconstrictor Precautions

Sargramostim (sar GRAM oh stim)

Brand Names: US Leukine

Brand Names: Canada Leukine

Pharmacologic Category Colony Stimulating Factor; Hematopoietic Agent

Use

Acute myeloid leukemia (AML; following induction chemotherapy): To shorten time to neutrophil recovery and to reduce the incidence of severe and life-threatening infections and infections resulting in death following induction chemotherapy in older adults (≥55 years of age)

Bone marrow transplant (allogeneic or autologous) failure or engraftment delay: For graft failure or engraftment delay in patients who have undergone allogeneic or autologous bone marrow transplantation, to prolong survival (survival benefit may be greater in patients with autologous bone marrow transplant failure or engraftment delay, no previous total body irradiation, malignancy other than leukemia, or multiple organ failure score ≤2)

Myeloid reconstitution after allogeneic bone marrow transplantation: To accelerate myeloid recovery in patients undergoing allogeneic bone marrow transplant from HLA-matched related donors (safe and effective in accelerating myeloid engraftment, reducing the incidence of bacteremia and other culture-positive infections, and shortening the median hospitalization duration)

Myeloid reconstitution after autologous bone marrow transplantation: To accelerate myeloid recovery following transplantation in non-Hodgkin lymphoma (NHL), acute lymphoblastic leukemia (ALL), Hodgkin lymphoma patients undergoing autologous bone marrow transplant (safe and effective in accelerating myeloid engraftment, reducing the median duration of antibiotic administration, reducing the median duration of infectious episodes, and shortening the median hospitalization duration)

Peripheral stem cell transplantation (autologous), mobilization and post-transplant: Mobilization of hematopoietic progenitor cells for collection by leukapheresis (increases the number of progenitor cells capable of engraftment and may lead to more rapid engraftment); to accelerate myeloid reconstitution following peripheral blood progenitor cell transplantation

Local Anesthetic/Vasoconstrictor Precautions No information available to require special precautions

Effects on Dental Treatment Key adverse event(s) related to dental treatment: Dysphagia.

Effects on Bleeding No information available to require special precautions. Medical consultation may be considered to confirm adequate platelet counts.

Adverse Reactions

>10%:

Cardiovascular: Hypertension (34%), edema (13% to 25%), pericardial effusion (4% to 25%), thrombosis (19%), chest pain (15%), peripheral edema (11%), tachycardia (11%)

Central nervous system: Malaise (57%), headache (26%), chills (25%), anxiety (11%), insomnia (11%)

Dermatologic: Skin rash (44% to 77%), pruritus (23%)

Endocrine & metabolic: Weight loss (37%), hyperglycemia (25%), hypercholesterolemia (17%), hypomagnesemia (15%)

Gastrointestinal: Diarrhea (81% to 89%), nausea (58% to 70%), vomiting (46% to 70%), gastric ulcer (50%), abdominal pain (38%), anorexia (13%), hematemesis (13%), dysphagia (11%), gastrointestinal hemorrhage (11%)

Hepatic: Hyperbilirubinemia (30%)

Neuromuscular & skeletal: Weakness (66%), ostealgia (21%), arthralgia (11% to 21%), myalgia (18%)

Ophthalmic: Retinal hemorrhage (11%)

Renal: Increased blood urea nitrogen (23%), increased serum creatinine (15%)

Respiratory: Pharyngitis (23%), epistaxis (17%), dyspnea (15%)

Miscellaneous: Fever (81%)

1% to 10%:

Immunologic: Antibody development (2%)

Respiratory: Pleural effusion (1%)

<1%, postmarketing, and/or case reports: Anaphylaxis, capillary leak syndrome, cardiac arrhythmia, dizziness, eosinophilia, flushing, hypotension, hypoxia, injection site reaction, lethargy, leukocytosis, liver function impairment (transient), pain, pericarditis, prolonged prothrombin time, respiratory distress, rigors, sore throat, supraventricular cardiac arrhythmia, syncope, thrombocythemia, thrombophlebitis

General Dosage Range

IV: *Adults:* Infusion: 250 mcg/m^2 once daily (maximum: 500 mcg/m^2/day)

SubQ: *Adults:* 250 mcg/m^2 once daily

Mechanism of Action Stimulates proliferation, differentiation and functional activity of neutrophils, eosinophils, monocytes, and macrophages.

Pharmacodynamics/Kinetics

Onset of Action Increase in WBC in 7 to 14 days

Duration of Action WBCs return to baseline within 1 to 2 weeks of discontinuing drug

Half-life Elimination

Children 6 months to 15 years: IV: Median: 1.6 hours; range: 0.9 to 2.5 hours; SubQ: Median: 2.3 hours (0.3 to 3.8 hours) (Stute 1995)

Adults: IV: ~60 minutes; SubQ: ~2.7 hours

Time to Peak Serum: SubQ: 1 to 3 hours

Pregnancy Risk Factor C

Pregnancy Considerations Animal reproduction studies have not been conducted.

SAXagliptin (sax a GLIP tin)

Related Information

Endocrine Disorders and Pregnancy *on page 1781*

Brand Names: US Onglyza

Brand Names: Canada Onglyza

Generic Availability (US) No

Pharmacologic Category Antidiabetic Agent, Dipeptidyl Peptidase 4 (DPP-4) Inhibitor

Use Diabetes mellitus, type 2: As an adjunct to diet and exercise to improve glycemic control in adults with type 2 diabetes mellitus (noninsulin dependent, NIDDM) as monotherapy or in combination therapy.

Local Anesthetic/Vasoconstrictor Precautions No information available to require special precautions

Effects on Dental Treatment Key adverse event(s) related to dental treatment: Saxagliptin dependent patients with diabetes should be appointed for dental treatment in the morning in order to minimize chance of stress-induced hypoglycemia.

Effects on Bleeding No information available to require special precautions

Adverse Reactions Frequencies and adverse reactions reported with monotherapy unless otherwise noted.

1% to 10%:

- Cardiovascular: Peripheral edema (≤4%; incidence increased in conjunction with thiazolidinediones: ≤8%)
- Central nervous system: Headache (7%)
- Endocrine & metabolic: Hypoglycemia (≤6%; incidence increased in conjunction with insulin secretagogues: ≤15%)
- Gastrointestinal: Abdominal pain (2%), gastroenteritis (2%), vomiting (2%)
- Genitourinary: Urinary tract infection (7%)
- Hematologic: Lymphocytopenia (≤2%; dose related)
- Hypersensitivity: Hypersensitivity reaction (2%; including facial edema and urticaria)
- Respiratory: Sinusitis (3%)

<1%, postmarketing, and/or case reports: Acute pancreatitis, anaphylaxis, angioedema, exfoliative dermatitis, immune thrombocytopenia, increased creatine phosphokinase, increased serum creatinine, severe arthralgia (FDA Safety Alert, Aug 28, 2015), skin rash

Dosing

Adult & Geriatric

Diabetes mellitus, type 2: Oral: 2.5 to 5 mg once daily

Concomitant use with strong CYP3A4/5 inhibitors (eg, atazanavir, clarithromycin, indinavir, itraconazole, ketoconazole, nefazodone, nelfinavir, ritonavir, saquinavir, telithromycin): 2.5 mg once daily

Concomitant use with insulin or insulin secretagogues: Reduced dose of insulin or insulin secretagogues (eg, sulfonylureas) may be needed

Renal Impairment

eGFR ≥45 mL/minute/1.73 m^2: No dosage adjustment necessary.

eGFR <45 mL/minute/1.73 m^2: 2.5 mg once daily.

ESRD requiring hemodialysis: 2.5 mg once daily; administer postdialysis

Peritoneal dialysis: There are no dosage adjustments provided in the manufacturer's labeling (has not been studied).

Hepatic Impairment Mild to severe impairment: No dosage adjustment necessary.

Mechanism of Action Saxagliptin inhibits dipeptidyl peptidase IV (DPP-IV) enzyme resulting in prolonged active incretin levels. Incretin hormones (eg, glucagon-like peptide-1 [GLP-1] and glucose-dependent insulinotropic polypeptide [GIP]) regulate glucose homeostasis by increasing insulin synthesis and release from pancreatic beta cells and decreasing glucagon secretion from pancreatic alpha cells. Decreased glucagon secretion results in decreased hepatic glucose production. Under normal physiologic circumstances, incretin hormones are released by the intestine throughout the day and levels are increased in response to a meal; incretin hormones are rapidly inactivated by the DPP-IV enzyme.

Contraindications

Hypersensitivity (eg, anaphylaxis, angioedema, exfoliative skin conditions) to saxagliptin or any component of the formulation

Canadian labeling: Additional contraindications (not in US labeling): Hypersensitivity to another DPP-4 inhibitor; diabetic ketoacidosis, diabetic coma/precoma, type 1 diabetes mellitus

Warnings/Precautions Use with caution in patients with moderate to severe renal dysfunction (eGFR <45 mL/minute/1.73 m^2) including end-stage renal disease (ESRD) requiring hemodialysis; dosing adjustment required. Heart failure that may require hospitalization has been reported in a multi-center, randomized, double-blind, placebo-controlled trial in patients with type 2 diabetes with a history of, or at risk for, cardiovascular events; risk was increased in patients with preexisting heart failure or renal impairment and during the first 12 months of therapy (Scirica 2013; Scirica 2014). However, a population-based retrospective study in an ambulatory setting with relatively lower baseline cardiovascular risk factors failed to demonstrate increased risk in patients on saxagliptin compared to other agents (eg, sitagliptin, pioglitazone, sulfonylureas, insulin) (Toh 2016). Monitor for signs and symptoms of heart failure during therapy and consider discontinuation if condition develops. In a scientific statement from the American Heart Association, saxagliptin has been determined to be an agent that may exacerbate underlying myocardial dysfunction (magnitude: major) (AHA [Page 2016]).

Severe and disabling arthralgia has been reported with DPP-IV inhibitor use; onset may occur within one day to years after treatment initiation and may resolve with discontinuation of therapy. Some patients may experience a recurrence of symptoms if DPP-IV inhibitor therapy resumed. DPP-4 inhibitor use has been associated with development of bullous pemphigoid; cases have typically resolved with topical or systemic immunosuppressive therapy and discontinuation of DPP-4 inhibitor therapy. Advise patients to report development of blisters or erosions. Discontinue therapy if bullous pemphigoid is suspected and consider referral to a dermatologist. Hypersensitivity reactions, including anaphylaxis, angioedema, and/or exfoliative dermatologic reactions have been reported; discontinue if signs/symptoms of severe hypersensitivity reactions occur. Cases of acute pancreatitis have been reported; discontinue immediately if suspected. Saxagliptin is not indicated for use in patients with type 1 diabetes mellitus (insulin dependent, IDDM) or for the treatment of diabetic ketoacidosis (DKA). Potentially significant drug-drug interactions may exist, requiring dose or frequency adjustment, additional monitoring, and/or selection of alternative therapy.

Drug Interactions

Metabolism/Transport Effects Substrate of CYP3A4 (major), P-glycoprotein; **Note:** Assignment of Major/Minor substrate status based on clinically relevant drug interaction potential

Avoid Concomitant Use

Avoid concomitant use of SAXagliptin with any of the following: Conivaptan; Fusidic Acid (Systemic); Idelalisib

Increased Effect/Toxicity

SAXagliptin may increase the levels/effects of: ACE Inhibitors; Hypoglycemia-Associated Agents; Insulin; Sulfonylureas

The levels/effects of SAXagliptin may be increased by: Alpha-Lipoic Acid; Androgens; Aprepitant; Conivaptan; CYP3A4 Inhibitors (Moderate); CYP3A4 Inhibitors (Strong); Dasatinib; Fosaprepitant; Fusidic Acid (Systemic); Idelalisib; Ivacaftor; Lumacaftor; MAO Inhibitors; MiFEPRIStone; Netupitant; Palbociclib; Pegvisomant; P-glycoprotein/ABCB1 Inhibitors; Prothionamide; Quinolone Antibiotics; Ranolazine;

Salicylates; Selective Serotonin Reuptake Inhibitors; Simeprevir; Stiripentol

Decreased Effect

The levels/effects of SAXagliptin may be decreased by: CYP3A4 Inducers (Strong); Hyperglycemia-Associated Agents; Lumacaftor; P-glycoprotein/ABCB1 Inducers; Quinolone Antibiotics; Thiazide and Thiazide-Like Diuretics

Dietary Considerations Individualized medical nutrition therapy (MNT) is an integral part of therapy (ADA 2013).

Pharmacodynamics/Kinetics

Duration of Action 24 hours

Half-life Elimination Saxagliptin: 2.5 hours; 5-hydroxy saxagliptin: 3.1 hours

Time to Peak Plasma: Saxagliptin: 2 hours; 5-hydroxy saxagliptin: 4 hours

Pregnancy Considerations In women with diabetes, maternal hyperglycemia can be associated with congenital malformations as well as adverse effects in the fetus, neonate, and the mother (ACOG 2005; ADA 2016c; Kitzmiller 2008; Metzger 2007). To prevent adverse outcomes, prior to conception and throughout pregnancy maternal blood glucose and HbA_{1c} should be kept as close to target goals as possible but without causing significant hypoglycemia (ACOG 2013; ADA 2016c; Blumer 2013; Kitzmiller 2008). Agents other than saxagliptin are currently recommended to treat diabetes in pregnant women (ACOG 2013; Blumer 2013).

Breastfeeding Considerations It is not known if saxagliptin is excreted in breast milk. According to the manufacturer, the decision to continue or discontinue breastfeeding during therapy should take into account the risk of infant exposure, the benefits of breastfeeding to the infant, and benefits of treatment to the mother

Dosage Forms

Tablet, Oral:

Onglyza: 2.5 mg, 5 mg

Saxagliptin and Metformin

(sax a GLIP tin & met FOR min)

Related Information

MetFORMIN *on page* 1009

SAXagliptin *on page* 1465

Brand Names: US Kombiglyze XR

Brand Names: Canada Kombiglyze

Pharmacologic Category Antidiabetic Agent, Biguanide; Antidiabetic Agent, Dipeptidyl Peptidase 4 (DPP-4) Inhibitor

Use Diabetes mellitus, type 2: Management of adults with type 2 diabetes mellitus (noninsulin dependent, NIDDM) as an adjunct to diet and exercise when treatment with both saxagliptin and metformin is appropriate.

Local Anesthetic/Vasoconstrictor Precautions No information available to require special precautions

Effects on Dental Treatment Key adverse event(s) related to dental treatment: Saxagliptin- and metformin-dependent patients with diabetes should be appointed for dental treatment in the morning in order to minimize chance of stress-induced hypoglycemia.

Effects on Bleeding No information available to require special precautions

Adverse Reactions See individual agents.

General Dosage Range Dosage adjustment recommended in patients on concomitant therapy

Oral: *Adults:* Saxagliptin 2.5 to 5 mg and metformin 500 to 1,000 mg once daily (maximum: saxagliptin 5 mg/metformin 2,000 mg ER per day)

Mechanism of Action

Saxagliptin inhibits dipeptidyl peptidase IV (DPP-IV) enzyme resulting in prolonged active incretin levels. Incretin hormones (eg, glucagon-like peptide-1 [GLP-1] and glucose-dependent insulinotropic polypeptide [GIP]) regulate glucose homeostasis by increasing insulin synthesis and release from pancreatic beta cells and decreasing glucagon secretion from pancreatic alpha cells. Decreased glucagon secretion results in decreased hepatic glucose production. Under normal physiologic circumstances, incretin hormones are released by the intestine throughout the day and levels are increased in response to a meal; incretin hormones are rapidly inactivated by the DPP-IV enzyme.

Metformin decreases hepatic glucose production, decreasing intestinal absorption of glucose and improves insulin sensitivity (increases peripheral glucose uptake and utilization).

Pregnancy Considerations Adverse events were not observed in animal reproduction studies conducted with this combination. Refer to individual monographs.

Scopolamine (Systemic) (skoe POL a meen)

Brand Names: US Transderm-Scop (1.5 MG)

Brand Names: Canada Buscopan; Scopolamine Hydrobromide Injection; Transderm-V

Pharmacologic Category Anticholinergic Agent

Use

Scopolamine base: Transdermal: Prevention of nausea/vomiting associated with motion sickness and recovery from anesthesia and surgery

Scopolamine hydrobromide: Injection: Preoperative medication to produce amnesia, sedation, tranquilization, antiemetic effects, and decrease salivary and respiratory secretions

Scopolamine butylbromide [Canadian product]: Oral/injection: Treatment of smooth muscle spasm of the genitourinary or gastrointestinal tract; injection may also be used prior to radiological/diagnostic procedures to prevent spasm

Local Anesthetic/Vasoconstrictor Precautions No information available to require special precautions

Effects on Dental Treatment Key adverse event(s) related to dental treatment: Significant xerostomia (normal salivary flow resumes upon discontinuation), dry throat (transdermal), and dysphagia.

Effects on Bleeding No information available to require special precautions

Adverse Reactions

Frequency not defined.

Cardiovascular: Bradycardia, flushing, orthostatic hypotension, tachycardia

Central nervous system: Amnesia, ataxia, confusion, disorientation, dizziness, drowsiness, fatigue, headache, heat intolerance, irritability, restlessness, sedation

Dermatologic: Dyshidrotic eczema, erythema, hypohidrosis, pruritus, skin rash (including drug eruption), urticaria, xeroderma

Endocrine & metabolic: Increased thirst

Gastrointestinal: Constipation, diarrhea, dysphagia, nausea, vomiting, xerostomia

Genitourinary: Dysuria, urinary retention

Hypersensitivity: Angioedema, hypersensitivity reaction

Neuromuscular & skeletal: Tremor, weakness

Ophthalmic: angle-closure glaucoma, blurred vision, conjunctival infection, cycloplegia, decreased accommodation, eye pain (intraocular), eye pruritus, mydriasis, photophobia, retinal pigment changes, xerophthalmia

Respiratory: Dry nose, dry throat, dyspnea

<1%, postmarketing, and/or case reports: Agitation, anaphylaxis, anaphylactic shock, delusions, hallucination, paranoia, toxic psychosis (acute)

General Dosage Range

IM, IV, SubQ:

Children 6 months to 3 years: 0.1-0.15 mg

Children 3-6 years: 0.2-0.3 mg

Adults: 0.3-0.65 mg (single dose) **or** 0.6 mg 3-4 times/day

Transdermal: *Adults:* Apply 1 patch every 3 days as needed

Mechanism of Action Blocks the action of acetylcholine at parasympathetic sites in smooth muscle, secretory glands and the CNS; increases cardiac output, dries secretions, antagonizes histamine and serotonin; at usual recommended doses, causes blockade of muscarinic receptors at the cardiac SA-node and is parasympatholytic (ie, blocks vagal activity increasing heart rate)

Pharmacodynamics/Kinetics

Onset of Action Oral, IM: 0.5 to 1 hour; IV: 10 minutes; Transdermal: 6 to 8 hours

Duration of Action IM: 4 to 6 hours; IV: 2 hours; Transdermal: 72 hours

Half-life Elimination Butylbromide: ~5 to 11 hours; Hydrobromide: ~1 to 4 hours; Scopolamine base: 9.5 hours

Time to Peak Hydrobromide: IM: ~20 minutes, SubQ: ~15 minutes; Butylbromide: Oral: ~2 hours; Scopolamine base: Transdermal: 24 hours

Pregnancy Risk Factor C

Pregnancy Considerations Adverse events were observed in some animal reproduction studies. Scopolamine crosses the placenta; may cause respiratory depression and/or neonatal hemorrhage when used during pregnancy. Transdermal scopolamine has been used as an adjunct to epidural anesthesia for cesarean delivery without adverse CNS effects on the newborn. Parenteral administration does not increase the duration of labor or affect uterine contractions. Except when used prior to cesarean section, use during pregnancy only if the benefit to the mother outweighs the potential risk to the fetus.

Product Availability Scopolamine injection is no longer available in the US.

Secukinumab (sek ue KIN ue mab)

Brand Names: US Cosentyx; Cosentyx 300 Dose; Cosentyx Sensoready 300 Dose; Cosentyx Sensoready Pen

Brand Names: Canada Cosentyx

Pharmacologic Category Antipsoriatic Agent; Interleukin-17A Receptor Antagonist; Monoclonal Antibody

Use

US labeling:

Ankylosing spondylitis: Treatment of active ankylosing spondylitis in adults.

Plaque psoriasis: Treatment of moderate to severe plaque psoriasis in adult patients who are candidates for systemic therapy or phototherapy.

Psoriatic arthritis: Treatment of active psoriatic arthritis in adults.

Canadian labeling:

Plaque psoriasis: Treatment of moderate to severe plaque psoriasis in adult patients who are candidates for systemic therapy or phototherapy.

Local Anesthetic/Vasoconstrictor Precautions No information available to require special precautions

Effects on Dental Treatment Key adverse event(s) related to dental treatment: Mucocutaneous candidiasis, oral herpes, and pharyngitis have been reported.

Effects on Bleeding No information available to require special precautions

Adverse Reactions Frequency not always defined.

Central nervous system: Headache (≥2%)

Dermatologic: Urticaria (≤1%), candidiasis

Endocrine & metabolic: Hypercholesterolemia (≥2%)

Gastrointestinal: Diarrhea (3% to 4%), nausea (≥2%), mucocutaneous candidiasis (1%), inflammatory bowel disease (≤1%), oral herpes (≤1%), exacerbation of inflammatory bowel disease

Hypersensitivity: Anaphylaxis, hypersensitivity

Infection: Infection (29% to 48%), serious infection (≤1%), herpes virus infection, staphylococcal infection

Respiratory: Nasopharyngitis (11% to 12%), upper respiratory tract infection (3%), pharyngitis (1%), rhinitis (1%), rhinorrhea (≤1%)

<1%, postmarketing, and/or case reports: Conjunctivitis, Crohn disease, exacerbation of Crohn disease, exacerbation of ulcerative colitis, immunogenicity (neutralizing antibodies not associated with drug efficacy), impetigo, increased serum transaminases, neutropenia, oral candidiasis, otitis externa, otitis media, sinusitis, tinea pedis, tonsillitis, ulcerative colitis

General Dosage Range SubQ: *Adults:* 150 to 300 mg per dose at weeks 0,1,2,3, and 4, then every 4 weeks thereafter **or** 150 to 300 mg every 4 weeks

Mechanism of Action Secukinumab is a human IgG1 monoclonal antibody that selectively binds to the interleukin-17A (IL-17A) cytokine and inhibits its interaction with the IL-17 receptor. IL-17A is a naturally occurring cytokine involved in normal inflammatory and immune responses. Secukinumab inhibits the release of proinflammatory cytokines and chemokines.

Pharmacodynamics/Kinetics

Half-life Elimination 22 to 31 days

Time to Peak ~6 days

Pregnancy Risk Factor B

Pregnancy Considerations Adverse events were not observed in animal reproduction studies. In general, maternal use of monoclonal antibodies during pregnancy may increase the risk of infection to the exposed infant or interfere with vaccine administration in the newborn (Mervic 2014). Other agents are currently preferred for the treatment of plaque psoriasis in pregnant women (Hsu 2012).

Selegiline (se LE ji leen)

Related Information

Dentin Hypersensitivity, Acid Erosion, High Caries Index, Management of Alveolar Osteitis, and Xerostomia *on page 1857*

Brand Names: US Eldepryl; Emsam; Zelapar

Brand Names: Canada Apo-Selegiline; Dom-Selegiline; Mylan-Selegiline; PMS-Selegiline; Teva-Selegiline

Pharmacologic Category Anti-Parkinson Agent, MAO Type B Inhibitor; Antidepressant, Monoamine Oxidase Inhibitor

Use

Parkinson disease: Adjunct in the management of patients with Parkinson disease being treated with levodopa/carbidopa who exhibit deterioration in the quality of their response to this therapy (oral products).

Major depressive disorder: Treatment of major depressive disorder (MDD) (transdermal patch)

Local Anesthetic/Vasoconstrictor Precautions Selegiline in doses of 10 mg a day or less does not inhibit type-A MAO. Therefore, there are no precautions with the use of vasoconstrictors.

Effects on Dental Treatment Key adverse event(s) related to dental treatment: Xerostomia and changes in salivation (normal salivary flow resumes upon discontinuation). Anticholinergic side effects can cause a reduction of saliva production or secretion, contributing to discomfort and dental disease (ie, caries, oral candidiasis, and periodontal disease).

Orally disintegrating tablet: Dysphagia, stomatitis, and taste perversion.

Effects on Bleeding No information available to require special precautions

Adverse Reactions Unless otherwise noted, the percentage of adverse events is reported for the transdermal patch (ODT = orally disintegrating tablet, Oral = capsule/tablet)

>10%:

Central nervous system: Headache (18%; ODT: 7%; oral: 4%), dizziness (oral: 14%; ODT: 11%), insomnia (12%; ODT: 7%)

Gastrointestinal: Nausea (oral: 20%; ODT: 11%)

Local: Application site reaction (24%)

1% to 10%:

Cardiovascular: Hypotension (3% to 10%; including orthostatic hypotension), hypertension (≥1%; ODT: 3%), chest pain (≥1%; ODT: 2%), palpitations (oral: 2%), peripheral edema (≥1%)

Central nervous system: Pain (ODT: 8%; oral: 2%), confusion (oral: 6%; ODT: 4%), hallucination (oral: 6%; ODT: 4%), vivid dream (oral: 4%), ataxia (<1%; ODT: 3%), drowsiness (ODT: 3%), depression (<1%; ODT: 2%), lethargy (oral: 2%), abnormality in thinking (≥1%), agitation (≥1%), amnesia (≥1%), paresthesia (≥1%)

Dermatologic: Skin rash (4%), acne vulgaris (≥1%), diaphoresis (≥1%), pruritus (≥1%)

Endocrine & metabolic: Weight loss (5%; oral: 2%), hypokalemia (ODT: 2%)

Gastrointestinal: Diarrhea (9%; ODT: 2%; oral: 2%), xerostomia (8%; oral: 6%; ODT: 4%), abdominal pain (oral: 8%), dyspepsia (4%; ODT: 5%), stomatitis (ODT: 5%), constipation (≥1%; ODT: 4%), vomiting (≥1%; ODT: 3%), dental caries (ODT: 2%), dysgeusia (>1%; ODT: 2%), dysphagia (ODT: 2%), flatulence (≥1%; ODT: 2%), anorexia (≥1%), gastroenteritis (≥1%)

Genitourinary: Urinary retention (oral: 2%), dysmenorrhea (≥1%), sexual disorder (≥1%), urinary frequency (≥1%), urinary tract infection (≥1%), uterine hemorrhage (≥1%)

Hematologic & oncologic: Bruise (≥1%; ODT: 2%)

Neuromuscular & skeletal: Dyskinesia (ODT: 6%), back pain (ODT: 5%; oral: 2%), leg cramps (ODT: 3%; oral: 2%), myalgia (≥1%; ODT: 3%), tremor (<1%; ODT: 3%), neck pain (≥1%)

Otic: Tinnitus (≥1%)

Respiratory: Rhinitis (ODT: 7%), pharyngitis (3%; ODT: 4%), dyspnea (<1%; ODT: 3%), sinusitis (3%), bronchitis (≥1%), cough (≥1%)

Frequency not defined:

Cardiovascular: Atrial fibrillation, bradycardia, cardiac arrhythmia, facial edema, myocardial infarction, peripheral vascular disease, syncope, tachycardia, vasodilatation

Central nervous system: Altered sense of smell, behavioral changes, chorea, delusions, depersonalization, emotional lability, euphoria, heatstroke, hostility, hyperesthesia, hypertonia, impulse control disorder (including binge eating, hypersexuality, pathological gambling), loss of balance, mania, migraine, mood changes, myasthenia, myoclonus, oral paresthesia, paranoia, psychoneurosis, twitching, vertigo

Dermatologic: Maculopapular rash, skin hypertrophy, urticaria, vesiculobullous dermatitis

Endocrine & metabolic: Dehydration, hypercholesterolemia, hyperglycemia, hypoglycemia, hyponatremia, increased lactate dehydrogenase, increased libido

Gastrointestinal: Colitis, eructation, gastritis, glossitis, increased appetite, melena, periodontal abscess, sialorrhea

Genitourinary: Benign prostatic hypertrophy, hematuria (females), hernia, mastalgia, pelvic pain, urinary urgency, urination disorder (males; impairment), vaginal hemorrhage, vaginitis, vulvovaginal candidiasis

Hematologic & oncologic: Benign skin neoplasm, breast neoplasm (female), leukocytosis, leukopenia, lymphadenopathy, neoplasm, rectal hemorrhage

Hepatic: Abnormal hepatic function tests, hyperbilirubinemia, increased serum alkaline phosphatase

Hypersensitivity: Tongue edema

Infection: Bacterial infection, candidiasis, fungal infection, parasitic infection, viral infection

Neuromuscular & skeletal: Bradykinesia, hyperkinesia, muscle spasm (generalized), osteoporosis, tenosynovitis

Ophthalmic: Visual field defect

Otic: Otitis externa

Renal: Nephrolithiasis (females), polyuria (females)

Respiratory: Asthma, epistaxis, laryngismus, pneumonia

Miscellaneous: Fever

General Dosage Range Dosage adjustment recommended for the orally disintegrating tablets in patients with hepatic impairment.

Oral:

Capsule, tablet: *Adults:* 5 mg twice daily (maximum: 10 mg/day)

Orally disintegrating tablet: *Adults:* Initial: 1.25 mg once daily; Maintenance: 1.25 to 2.5 mg once daily (maximum: 2.5 mg/day)

Transdermal:

Adults: Initial: 6 mg/24 hours once daily; Maintenance: 6 to 12 mg/24 hours once daily (maximum: 12 mg/24 hours)

Elderly: 6 mg/24 hours once daily

Mechanism of Action Potent, irreversible inhibitor of monoamine oxidase (MAO). Plasma concentrations achieved via administration of oral dosage forms in recommended doses confer selective inhibition of MAO type B, which plays a major role in the metabolism of dopamine, serotonin, norepinephrine, and epinephrine in the CNS; selegiline may also increase dopaminergic activity by interfering with dopamine reuptake at the synapse. When administered transdermally in recommended doses, selegiline achieves higher blood levels and effectively inhibits both MAO-A and MAO-B, an enzyme in the gut and liver that metabolizes dietary amines such as tyramine.

Pharmacodynamics/Kinetics

Half-life Elimination Oral: 10 hours

Pregnancy Risk Factor C

Pregnancy Considerations Adverse events have been observed in some animal reproduction studies.

Selenium (se LEE nee um)

Brand Names: US Aqueous Selenium [OTC]; Oceanic Selenium [OTC]; Se Aspartate [OTC]; Se-100 [OTC]; Se-Plus Protein [OTC]; Selenicaps-200 [OTC]; Selenimin [OTC]; Selenimin-200 [OTC]

Pharmacologic Category Trace Element, Parenteral

Use Trace metal supplement

Local Anesthetic/Vasoconstrictor Precautions No information available to require special precautions

Effects on Dental Treatment No significant effects or complications reported

Effects on Bleeding No information available to require special precautions

Adverse Reactions

Frequency not defined: Local: Local irritation

General Dosage Range

IV:

Children: 3 mcg/kg/day added to TPN

Adults: Metabolically stable: 20-40 mcg/day added to TPN; Deficiency from prolonged TPN support: 100 mcg/day

Oral:

Children: Adequate intake: 1-6 months: 15 mcg/day, 7-12 months: 20 mcg/day; Recommended daily allowance: 1-3 years: 20 mcg/day, 4-8 years: 30 mcg/day, 9-13 years 40 mcg/day, ≥14 years

Adults: Recommended daily allowance: 55 mcg/day; Pregnancy: 60 mcg/day; Lactation: 70 mcg/day

Mechanism of Action Part of glutathione peroxidase which protects cell components from oxidative damage due to peroxidases produced in cellular metabolism

Pregnancy Risk Factor C

Pregnancy Considerations Adverse events were seen with high doses in animal studies. Selenium is found in the placenta and cord blood. Teratogenic effects have not been observed with nontoxic doses in humans (IOM, 2000).

Selexipag (se LEX i pag)

Brand Names: US Uptravi

Pharmacologic Category Prostacyclin; Prostacyclin IP Receptor Agonist; Vasodilator

Use Pulmonary arterial hypertension: Treatment of pulmonary arterial hypertension (PAH) (WHO Group I) to delay disease progression and reduce the risk of hospitalization for PAH

Local Anesthetic/Vasoconstrictor Precautions No information available to require special precautions

Effects on Dental Treatment Key adverse event(s) related to dental treatment: Jaw pain reported in significant numbers of subjects (26%)

Effects on Bleeding No information available to require special precautions

Adverse Reactions

>10%:

Cardiovascular: Flushing (12%)

Central nervous system: Headache (65%)

Dermatologic: Skin rash (11%)

Gastrointestinal: Diarrhea (42%), nausea (33%), vomiting (18%)

Neuromuscular & skeletal: Jaw pain (26%), limb pain (17%), myalgia (16%), arthralgia (11%)

1% to 10%:

Endocrine & metabolic: Hyperthyroidism (1%)

Gastrointestinal: Decreased appetite (6%)

Hematologic & oncologic: Decreased hemoglobin (below 10 g/dL: 9%), anemia (8%)

Frequency not defined:

Endocrine & metabolic: TSH abnormalities

General Dosage Range Dosage adjustment required in patients with hepatic impairment.

Oral: *Adults:* Initial: 200 mcg twice daily; maximum dose: 1,600 mcg twice daily.

Mechanism of Action Selexipag is a selective prostacyclin IP receptor agonist. Prostacyclin is produced in the endothelial cells and induces vasodilation; also inhibits platelet aggregation. Patients with pulmonary arterial hypertension appear to have a dysregulation in the prostacyclin metabolic pathways (Galie 2013).

Pharmacodynamics/Kinetics

Half-life Elimination Terminal: Selexipag: 0.8 to 2.5 hours; Active metabolite: 6.2 to 13.5 hours

Time to Peak Selexipag: 1 to 3 hours; Active metabolite: 3 to 4 hours; Delayed with food

Pregnancy Considerations Adverse events have not been observed in animal reproduction studies. Women with pulmonary arterial hypertension (PAH) are encouraged to avoid pregnancy (McLaughlin 2009).

Senna (SEN na)

Brand Names: US Ex-Lax Maximum Strength [OTC]; Ex-Lax [OTC]; Geri-kot [OTC]; GoodSense Senna Laxative [OTC]; Perdiem Overnight Relief [OTC]; Senexon [OTC]; Senna Lax [OTC]; Senna Laxative [OTC]; Senna Maximum Strength [OTC]; Senna Smooth [OTC]; Senna-Gen [OTC] [DSC]; Senna-GRX [OTC]; Senna-Lax [OTC]; Senna-Tabs [OTC]; Senna-Time [OTC]; SennaCon [OTC]; Senno [OTC]; Senokot Extra Strength [OTC]; Senokot To Go [OTC] [DSC]; Senokot XTRA [OTC] [DSC]; Senokot [OTC]

Pharmacologic Category Laxative, Stimulant

Use Constipation: Relieves occasional constipation (irregularity); generally causes bowel movement in 6 to 12 hours

Local Anesthetic/Vasoconstrictor Precautions No information available to require special precautions

Effects on Dental Treatment No significant effects or complications reported

Effects on Bleeding No information available to require special precautions

Adverse Reactions Frequency not defined: Gastrointestinal: Abdominal cramps, diarrhea, nausea, vomiting

General Dosage Range Oral:

Children 2 to 6 years: Usual dose: 4.3 to 17.2 mg/day in 1 to 2 divided doses (maximum: 17.2 mg/day)

Children 6 to 12 years: Usual dose: 8.6 to 50 mg/day in 1 to 2 divided doses (maximum: 50 mg/day)

Children ≥12 years, Adolescents, and Adults: Usual dose: 17.2 to 100 mg/day in 1 to 2 divided doses (maximum: 100 mg/day)

Mechanism of Action The anthraquinone group of stimulant laxatives includes the plant-derived agents such as senna. Stimulant laxatives typically induce defecation by stimulating peristaltic activity on the intestine by direct action on intestinal mucosa or nerve plexus, therefore increasing motility.

Pharmacodynamics/Kinetics

Onset of Action Oral: Within 6 to 24 hours

Pregnancy Considerations An increased risk of congenital abnormalities was not observed following maternal use of senna during pregnancy (Acs, 2009). Short-term use of senna is generally considered safe during pregnancy (Mahadevan, 2006).

Sertaconazole (ser ta KOE na zole)

Brand Names: US Ertaczo

Pharmacologic Category Antifungal Agent, Imidazole Derivative; Antifungal Agent, Topical

Use Tinea pedis: Topical treatment of interdigital tinea pedis in immunocompetent patients 12 years of age and older, caused by *Trichophyton rubrum*, *Trichophyton mentagrophytes*, and *Epidermophyton floccosum*.

Local Anesthetic/Vasoconstrictor Precautions No information available to require special precautions

Effects on Dental Treatment No significant effects or complications reported

Effects on Bleeding No information available to require special precautions

Adverse Reactions

1% to 10%: Dermatologic: Burning sensation of skin, contact dermatitis, skin tenderness, xeroderma

<1%, postmarketing and/or case reports: Desquamation, erythema, hyperpigmentation, pruritus, skin vesicle

General Dosage Range Topical: *Children ≥12 years, Adolescents, and Adults:* Apply twice daily

Mechanism of Action Alters fungal cell wall membrane permeability; inhibits the CYP450-dependent synthesis of ergosterol

Pregnancy Risk Factor C

Pregnancy Considerations Adverse events were not observed in animal reproduction studies following oral administration.

Sertraline (SER tra leen)

Related Information

Management of the Patient With Anxiety or Depression *on page 1873*

Vasoconstrictor Interactions With Antidepressants *on page 1913*

Brand Names: US Zoloft

Brand Names: Canada ACT Sertraline; Apo-Sertraline; Auro-Sertraline; Dom-Sertraline; GD-Sertraline; JAMP-Sertraline; Mar-Sertraline; MINT-Sertraline; Mylan-Sertraline; PHL-Sertraline; PMS-Sertraline; Q-Sertraline; Ran-Sertraline; ratio-Sertraline; Riva-Sertraline; Sandoz-Sertraline; Teva-Sertraline; Zoloft

Generic Availability (US) Yes

Pharmacologic Category Antidepressant, Selective Serotonin Reuptake Inhibitor

Use

Major depressive disorder: Treatment of major depressive disorder (MDD) in adults.

Obsessive-compulsive disorder: Treatment of obsessions and compulsions in patients with obsessive-compulsive disorder (OCD).

Panic disorder: Treatment of panic disorder in adults with or without agoraphobia.

Post-traumatic stress disorder: Treatment of post-traumatic stress disorder (PTSD) in adults.

Premenstrual dysphoric disorder: Treatment of premenstrual dysphoric disorder (PMDD) in adults.

Social anxiety disorder: Treatment of social anxiety disorder (social phobia) in adults.

Local Anesthetic/Vasoconstrictor Precautions Although caution should be used in patients taking tricyclic antidepressants, no interactions have been reported with vasoconstrictor and sertraline, a nontricyclic antidepressant which acts to increase serotonin; no precautions appear to be needed

Effects on Dental Treatment Key adverse event(s) related to dental treatment: Xerostomia (normal salivary flow resumes upon discontinuation) (see Effects on Bleeding and Dental Comment).

Effects on Bleeding May impair platelet aggregation resulting in increased risk of bleeding events, particularly if used concomitantly with aspirin, NSAIDs, warfarin, or other anticoagulants. Bleeding related to SSRI use has been reported to range from relatively minor bruising and epistaxis to life-threatening hemorrhage. Routine interruption of therapy for most dental procedures is not warranted. In medically complicated patients or extensive oral surgery, the decision to interrupt therapy must be based on the risk to benefit in an individual patient and a medical consult is suggested. If therapy is continued without interruption, the clinician should anticipate the potential for a prolonged bleeding time.

Adverse Reactions

>10%:

Central nervous system: Insomnia (12% to 28%), headache (25%), dizziness (6% to 17%), fatigue (10% to 16%), drowsiness (2% to 15%)

Dermatologic: Diaphoresis (4% to 11%)

Endocrine & metabolic: Decreased libido (1% to 11%)

Gastrointestinal: Nausea (13% to 30%), diarrhea (13% to 24%), xerostomia (6% to 16%), dyspepsia (6% to 13%), anorexia (3% to 11%)

Genitourinary: Ejaculatory disorder (7% to 19%)

Neuromuscular & skeletal: Tremor (<1% to 11%)

1% to 10%:

Cardiovascular: Chest pain (≥1%), palpitations (≥1%)

Central nervous system: Malaise (7% to 9%), pain (3% to 6%), agitation (1% to 6%), nervousness (5%), paresthesia (2%), aggressive behavior (children ≥2%), hypertonia (≥1%), hypoesthesia (≥1%), yawning (≥1%), anxiety

Dermatologic: Skin rash (3%)

Endocrine & metabolic: Weight gain (≥1%)

Gastrointestinal: Constipation (5% to 8%), abdominal pain (6% to 7%), vomiting (4%), increased appetite (≥1%)

Genitourinary: Urinary incontinence (children ≥2%), impotence (≥1%)

Hematologic & oncologic: Purpura (children ≥2%)

Neuromuscular & skeletal: Hyperkinesia (children ≥2%), back pain (≥1%), myalgia(≥1%), weakness (≥1%)

Ophthalmic: Visual disturbance (3%)

Otic: Tinnitus (≥1%)

Respiratory: Epistaxis (children ≥2%), sinusitis (children ≥2%), rhinitis (≥1%)

Miscellaneous: Fever (children ≥2%)

<1%, postmarketing, and/or case reports: Acute renal failure, agranulocytosis, altered platelet function, anaphylactoid reaction, angioedema, angle-closure glaucoma, anterior chamber eye hemorrhage, aplastic anemia, apnea, ataxia, atrial arrhythmia, atrioventricular block, blindness, bradycardia, bradypnea, bronchitis, bullous rash, cataract, cerebrovascular spasm,

choreoathetosis, colitis, coma, cystitis, depression, diabetes mellitus, diverticulitis, dystonia, edema, esophagitis, extrapyramidal reaction, galactorrhea, gastroenteritis, gingival hyperplasia, gynecomastia, hallucination, hematuria, hemoptysis, hepatic failure, hepatitis, hepatomegaly, hyperglycemia, hyperprolactinemia, hypersensitivity reaction, hypertension, hypoglycemia, hyponatremia, hypothyroidism, increased INR, increased serum bilirubin, increased serum transaminases, jaundice, leukopenia, lupus-like syndrome, myocardial infarction, neuroleptic malignant syndrome (Stevens, 2008), nystagmus, oculogyric crisis, orthostatic hypotension, serotonin syndrome, SIADH, Stevens-Johnson syndrome (and other severe dermatologic reactions), optic neuritis, pancreatitis (rare), peptic ulcer bleed, peripheral ischemia, priapism, proctitis, prolonged prothrombin time, prolonged Q-T interval on ECG, psychosis, pulmonary hypertension, pyelonephritis, rectal hemorrhage, reversible cerebral vasoconstriction syndrome, seizure, serum sickness, skin photosensitivity, strangury, suicidal ideation, syncope, tachycardia, thrombocytopenia, torsades de pointes, upper respiratory tract infection, urinary frequency, vaginal hemorrhage, vasculitis, ventricular tachycardia, withdrawal syndrome

Pediatric patients: Additional adverse reactions reported in pediatric patients (frequency >2%)

Dosing

Adult

Depression/obsessive-compulsive disorder: Oral: Initial: 50 mg once daily; may increase dose in increments of 25 to 50 mg once weekly to a maximum of 200 mg/day

Panic disorder, post-traumatic stress disorder (PTSD), social anxiety disorder: Oral: Initial: 25 mg once daily; may increase dose in increments of 25 to 50 mg once weekly to a maximum of 200 mg/day

Premenstrual dysphoric disorder (PMDD): Oral: 50 mg daily either daily throughout menstrual cycle **or** limited to the luteal phase of menstrual cycle. Patients not responding to 50 mg daily may benefit from dose increases (50 mg increments per menstrual cycle) up to 150 mg/day when dosing throughout menstrual cycle **or** up to 100 mg/day when dosing during luteal phase only. If a 100 mg daily dose has been established with luteal phase dosing, a 50 mg daily titration step for 3 days should be utilized at the beginning of each luteal phase dosing period.

Binge-eating disorder (off-label use): Oral: Initial: 25 mg daily after lunch for 3 days; increase at 25 mg increments every 3 days based on response and tolerability. Usual dose range: 100 to 200 mg daily. Maximum dose: 200 mg/day (Leombruni 2008).

Bulimia nervosa (off-label use): Oral: Initial: 50 mg daily; increase at 50 mg increments each week based on response and tolerability. Maximum dose: 200 mg/day (Milano 2004; Sloan 2004).

Generalized anxiety disorder (GAD) off-label use): Oral: Initial dose: 25 mg once daily for 1 week; increase based on response and tolerability. Maximum dose: 200 mg/day (Ball 2005; Brawman, 2006; Dahl, 2005).

Discontinuation of therapy: Upon discontinuation of antidepressant therapy, gradually taper the dose to minimize the incidence of withdrawal symptoms and allow for the detection of re-emerging symptoms. Evidence supporting ideal taper rates is limited. APA and NICE guidelines suggest tapering therapy over at least several weeks with consideration to the half-life of the antidepressant; antidepressants with a shorter half-life may need to be tapered more conservatively. In addition for long-term treated patients, WFSBP guidelines recommend tapering over 4-6 months. If intolerable withdrawal symptoms occur following a dose reduction, consider resuming the previously prescribed dose and/or decrease dose at a more gradual rate (APA 2010; Bauer 2002; Haddad 2001; NCCMH 2010; Schatzberg 2006; Shelton 2001; Warner 2006).

MAO inhibitor recommendations:

Switching to or from an MAO inhibitor intended to treat psychiatric disorders:

Allow 14 days to elapse between discontinuing an MAO inhibitor intended to treat psychiatric disorders and initiation of sertraline.

Allow 14 days to elapse between discontinuing sertraline and initiation of an MAO inhibitor intended to treat psychiatric disorders.

Pediatric

Obsessive-compulsive disorder (OCD):

Children ≥6 years: Oral: Initial: 25 mg once daily; may increase dose in increments of 25 to 50 mg once weekly to a maximum of 200 mg/day

Adolescents: Oral: Initial: 50 mg once daily; may increase dose in increments of 25 to 50 mg once weekly to a maximum of 200 mg/day

Depression (off-label use):

Children ≥6 years: Oral: Initial: 12.5 to 25 mg once daily; titrate dose upwards if clinically needed; may increase by 25 to 50 mg daily increments at intervals of at least 1 week; mean final dose in 21 children (8 to 18 years) was 100 ± 53 mg or 1.6 mg/kg/day (n=11); range: 25 to 200 mg daily; maximum dose: 200 mg/day (Dopheide 2006; Tierney 1995); avoid excessive dosing

Adolescents: Oral: Initial 25 to 50 mg once daily; titrate dose upwards if clinically needed; may increase by 50 mg daily increments at intervals of at least 1 week; mean final dose in 13 adolescents was 110 ± 50 mg or about 2 mg/kg/day (McConville 1996); in another study using a slower titration, the mean dose at week 6 was 93 mg (n=41) and at week 10 was 127 mg (n=34) (Ambrosini, 1999); range: 25 to 200 mg daily; maximum dose: 200 mg/day (Dopheide 2006).

Discontinuation of therapy: Refer to adult dosing.

MAO inhibitor recommendations: Refer to adult dosing.

Renal Impairment No dosage adjustment necessary.

Hepatic Impairment

Mild impairment (Child-Pugh class A): Reduce dose to 50% of usual dose.

Moderate to severe impairment (Child-Pugh class B or C): Use is not recommended.

Mechanism of Action Antidepressant with selective inhibitory effects on presynaptic serotonin (5-HT) reuptake and only very weak effects on norepinephrine and dopamine neuronal uptake. *In vitro* studies demonstrate no significant affinity for adrenergic, cholinergic, GABA, dopaminergic, histaminergic, serotonergic, or benzodiazepine receptors.

Contraindications

Use of MAOIs including linezolid or methylene blue (concurrently or within 14 days of stopping an MAOI or sertraline); concurrent use with pimozide; hypersensitivity (eg, anaphylaxis, angioedema) to sertraline or any component of the formulation; concurrent use with disulfiram (oral concentrate only).

Documentation of allergenic cross-reactivity for SSRIs is limited. However, because of similarities in chemical structure and/or pharmacologic actions, the possibility of cross-sensitivity cannot be ruled out with certainty.

Warnings/Precautions [US Boxed Warning]: Antidepressants increase the risk of suicidal thinking and behavior in pediatric and young adult patients (18 to 24 years) in short-term studies; consider risk prior to prescribing. Short-term studies did not show an increased risk in patients >24 years of age and showed a decreased risk in patients ≥65 years. Closely monitor patients for clinical worsening, suicidality, or unusual changes in behavior, particularly during the initial 1 to 2 months of therapy or during periods of dosage adjustments (increases or decreases); the patient's family or caregiver should be instructed to closely observe the patient and communicate condition with health care provider. A medication guide concerning the use of antidepressants should be dispensed with each prescription.

The possibility of a suicide attempt is inherent in major depression and may persist until remission occurs. Use caution in high-risk patients. Worsening depression and severe abrupt suicidality that are not part of the presenting symptoms may require discontinuation or modification of drug therapy. The patient's family or caregiver should be alerted to monitor patients for the emergence of suicidality and associated behaviors (such as agitation, irritability, hostility, impulsivity, and hypomania) and call healthcare provider.

May precipitate a mixed/manic episode in patients at risk for bipolar disorder. Use with caution in patients with a family history of bipolar disorder, mania, or hypomania. Patients presenting with depressive symptoms should be screened for bipolar disorder. **Sertraline is not FDA approved for the treatment of bipolar depression.**

Potentially life-threatening serotonin syndrome (SS) has occurred with serotonergic agents (eg, SSRIs, SNRIs), particularly when used in combination with other serotonergic agents (eg, triptans, TCAs, fentanyl, lithium, tramadol, buspirone, St John's wort, tryptophan) or agents that impair metabolism of serotonin (eg, MAO inhibitors intended to treat psychiatric disorders, other MAO inhibitors [ie, linezolid and intravenous methylene blue]). Discontinue treatment (and any concomitant serotonergic agent) immediately if signs/symptoms arise. Has a very low potential to impair cognitive or motor performance. However, caution patients regarding activities requiring alertness until response to sertraline is known. May impair platelet aggregation resulting in increased risk of bleeding events, particularly if used concomitantly with aspirin, NSAIDs, warfarin or other anticoagulants. Bleeding related to SSRI use has been reported to range from relatively minor bruising and epistaxis to life-threatening hemorrhage. Bone fractures have been associated with antidepressant treatment. Consider the possibility of a fragility fracture if an antidepressant-treated patient presents with unexplained bone pain, point tenderness, swelling, or bruising (Rabenda 2013; Rizzoli 2012).

Use caution in patients with a previous seizure disorder or condition predisposing to seizures such as brain damage or alcoholism. May cause mild pupillary dilation which in susceptible individuals can lead to an episode of narrow-angle glaucoma. Consider evaluating patients who have not had an iridectomy for narrow-angle glaucoma risk factors. Avoid use in patients with untreated anatomically narrow angles. Use with caution in patients with hepatic impairment; clearance is decreased and plasma concentrations are increased; use reduced dose in mild impairment; use is not recommended in moderate or severe impairment. SSRIs and SNRIs have been associated with the development of SIADH; hyponatremia has been reported rarely (including severe cases with serum sodium <110 mmol/L), predominately in the elderly. Volume depletion and/or concurrent use of diuretics likely increases risk. Discontinue use if symptomatic hyponatremia occurs. May cause or exacerbate sexual dysfunction. Potentially significant drug-drug interactions may exist, requiring dose or frequency adjustment, additional monitoring, and/or selection of alternative therapy.

Use oral concentrate formulation with caution in patients with latex sensitivity; dropper dispenser contains dry natural rubber. Some dosage forms may contain polysorbate 80 (also known as Tweens). Hypersensitivity reactions, usually a delayed reaction, have been reported following exposure to pharmaceutical products containing polysorbate 80 in certain individuals (Isaksson 2002; Lucente 2000; Shelley, 1995). Thrombocytopenia, ascites, pulmonary deterioration, and renal and hepatic failure have been reported in premature neonates after receiving parenteral products containing polysorbate 80 (Alade 1986; CDC 1984). See manufacturer's labeling.

Monitor growth in pediatric patients. Given their lower body weight, lower doses are advisable in pediatric patients in order to avoid excessive plasma levels, despite slightly greater metabolism efficiency than adults.

Abrupt discontinuation or interruption of antidepressant therapy has been associated with a discontinuation syndrome. Symptoms arising may vary with antidepressant however commonly include nausea, vomiting, diarrhea, headaches, lightheadedness, dizziness, diminished appetite, sweating, chills, tremors, paresthesias, fatigue, somnolence, and sleep disturbances (eg, vivid dreams, insomnia). Greater risks for developing a discontinuation syndrome have been associated with antidepressants with shorter half-lives, longer durations of treatment, and abrupt discontinuation. For antidepressants of short or intermediate half-lives, symptoms may emerge within 2 to 5 days after treatment discontinuation and last 7 to 14 days (APA 2010; Fava 2006; Haddad 2001; Shelton 2001; Warner 2006).

Drug Interactions

Metabolism/Transport Effects Substrate of CYP2B6 (minor), CYP2C19 (minor), CYP2C9 (minor), CYP2D6 (minor), CYP3A4 (minor); **Note:** Assignment of Major/Minor substrate status based on clinically relevant drug interaction potential; **Inhibits** CYP1A2 (weak), CYP2C8 (weak), CYP2C9 (weak), CYP2D6 (weak)

Avoid Concomitant Use

Avoid concomitant use of Sertraline with any of the following: Amodiaquine; Dapoxetine; Disulfiram; Dosulepin; Iobenguane I 123; Linezolid; MAO Inhibitors; Methylene Blue; Pimozide; Tryptophan; Urokinase

Increased Effect/Toxicity

Sertraline may increase the levels/effects of: Agents with Antiplatelet Properties; Amodiaquine; Anticoagulants; Antidepressants (Serotonin Reuptake Inhibitor/Antagonist); Antipsychotic Agents; Apixaban; ARIPiprazole; Aspirin; Beta-Blockers; Blood Glucose

Lowering Agents; BusPIRone; Cephalothin; CloZAPine; Collagenase (Systemic); Dabigatran Etexilate; Deoxycholic Acid; Desmopressin; Dextromethorphan; Dosulepin; Edoxaban; Fosphenytoin; Galantamine; Highest Risk QTc-Prolonging Agents; Ibritumomab; Methylene Blue; Moderate Risk QTc-Prolonging Agents; NSAID (COX-2 Inhibitor); NSAID (Nonselective); Obinutuzumab; Perhexiline; Phenytoin; Pimozide; Propafenone; RisperiDONE; Rivaroxaban; Salicylates; Serotonin Modulators; Thiazide and Thiazide-Like Diuretics; Thrombolytic Agents; TiZANidine; Tositumomab and Iodine I 131 Tositumomab; TraMADol; Tricyclic Antidepressants; Urokinase; Vitamin K Antagonists

The levels/effects of Sertraline may be increased by: Alcohol (Ethyl); Analgesics (Opioid); Antiemetics (5HT3 Antagonists); Antipsychotic Agents; BusPIRone; Cimetidine; CNS Depressants; Dapoxetine; Dasatinib; Disulfiram; Erythromycin (Systemic); Glucosamine; Grapefruit Juice; Herbs (Anticoagulant/Antiplatelet Properties); Ibrutinib; Limaprost; Linezolid; Lithium; MAO Inhibitors; Metaxalone; Methylene Blue; Methylphenidate; Metoclopramide; MetyroSINE; MiFEPRIStone; Multivitamins/Fluoride (with ADE); Multivitamins/Minerals (with ADEK, Folate, Iron); Multivitamins/Minerals (with AE, No Iron); Omega-3 Fatty Acids; Pentosan Polysulfate Sodium; Pentoxifylline; Prostacyclin Analogues; Tedizolid; Tipranavir; TraMADol; Tryptophan; Vitamin E (Systemic)

Decreased Effect

Sertraline may decrease the levels/effects of: Iobenguane I 123; Ioflupane I 123; Thyroid Products

The levels/effects of Sertraline may be decreased by: CarBAMazepine; CYP3A4 Inducers (Strong); Cyproheptadine; Darunavir; Efavirenz; Fosphenytoin; NSAID (COX-2 Inhibitor); NSAID (Nonselective); Phenytoin

Pharmacodynamics/Kinetics

Onset of Action Depression: The onset of action is within a week, however, individual response varies greatly and full response may not be seen until 8 to 12 weeks after initiation of treatment (APA [Gelenberg 2010]).

Half-life Elimination

Sertraline: Mean: 26 hours; N-desmethylsertraline: 62 to 104 hours

- Children 6 to 12 years: Mean: 26.2 hours (Alderman 1998)
- Children 13 to 17 years: Mean: 27.8 hours (Alderman 1998)
- Adults 18 to 45 years: Mean: 27.2 hours (Alderman 1998)

Time to Peak Plasma: Sertraline: 4.5 to 8.4 hours

Pregnancy Considerations Sertraline crosses the human placenta. Available studies evaluating teratogenic effects following maternal use of sertraline in the first trimester have not shown an overall increased risk of major birth defects. Studies evaluating specific birth defects have provided inconsistent results. Nonteratogenic effects in the newborn following SSRI/SNRI exposure late in the third trimester include respiratory distress, cyanosis, apnea, seizures, temperature instability, feeding difficulty, vomiting, hypoglycemia, hypo- or hypertonia, hyper-reflexia, jitteriness, irritability, constant crying, and tremor. Symptoms may be due to the toxicity of the SSRIs/SNRIs or a discontinuation syndrome and may be consistent with serotonin syndrome associated with SSRI treatment. Persistent pulmonary hypertension of the newborn (PPHN) has also been reported with SSRI exposure. The long-term effects of in utero SSRI exposure on infant development and behavior are not known.

Due to pregnancy-induced physiologic changes, women who are pregnant may require adjusted doses of sertraline to achieve euthymia. The ACOG recommends that therapy with SSRIs or SNRIs during pregnancy be individualized; treatment of depression during pregnancy should incorporate the clinical expertise of the mental health clinician, obstetrician, primary health care provider, and pediatrician. According to the American Psychiatric Association (APA), the risks of medication treatment should be weighed against other treatment options and untreated depression. For women who discontinue antidepressant medications during pregnancy and who may be at high risk for postpartum depression, the medications can be restarted following delivery. Treatment algorithms have been developed by the ACOG and the APA for the management of depression in women prior to conception and during pregnancy (ACOG 2008; APA 2010; Yonkers 2009).

Pregnant women exposed to antidepressants during pregnancy are encouraged to enroll in the National Pregnancy Registry for Antidepressants (NPRAD). Women 18 to 45 years of age or their health care providers may contact the registry by calling 844-405-6185. Enrollment should be done as early in pregnancy as possible.

Breastfeeding Considerations Sertraline and desmethylsertraline are excreted in breast milk. Adverse events have been reported in nursing infants exposed to some SSRIs. The American Academy of Breastfeeding Medicine suggests that sertraline may be considered for the treatment of postpartum depression in appropriately selected women who are nursing. Infants exposed to sertraline while breastfeeding generally receive a low relative dose and serum concentrations are not detectable in most infants. Sertraline concentrations in the hindmilk are higher than in foremilk. If the benefits of the mother receiving the sertraline and breastfeeding outweigh the risks, the mother may consider pumping and discarding breast milk with the feeding 7-9 hours after the daily dose to decrease sertraline exposure to the infant. The long-term effects on development and behavior have not been studied. The manufacturer recommends that caution be exercised when administering sertraline to nursing women. Maternal use of an SSRI during pregnancy may cause delayed milk secretion.

Dosage Forms

Concentrate, Oral:

Zoloft: 20 mg/mL (60 mL)

Generic: 20 mg/mL (60 mL)

Tablet, Oral:

Zoloft: 25 mg, 50 mg, 100 mg

Generic: 25 mg, 50 mg, 100 mg

Dosage Forms: Canada

Capsule, Oral: 25 mg, 50 mg, 100 mg

Dental Comment Problems with SSRI-induced bruxism have been reported and may preclude their use; clinicians attempting to evaluate any patient with bruxism or involuntary muscle movement, who is simultaneously being treated with an SSRI drug, should be aware of the potential association.

Sevelamer (se VEL a mer)

Brand Names: US Renagel; Renvela

Brand Names: Canada Renagel; Renvela

Pharmacologic Category Phosphate Binder

Use Control of serum phosphorous: Control of serum phosphorous in patients with chronic kidney disease on hemodialysis

Local Anesthetic/Vasoconstrictor Precautions No information available to require special precautions

Effects on Dental Treatment No significant effects or complications reported

Effects on Bleeding No information available to require special precautions

Adverse Reactions

>10%:

Endocrine & metabolic: Metabolic acidosis (children: 34% [Pieper 2006]); adults: Frequency not defined)

Gastrointestinal: Vomiting (22%), nausea (20%), diarrhea (19%), dyspepsia (16%)

1% to 10%:

Endocrine & metabolic: Hypercalcemia (5% to 7%)

Gastrointestinal: Abdominal pain (9%), constipation (8%), flatulence (8%), peritonitis (peritoneal dialysis: 8%)

<1%, postmarketing, and/or case reports: Fecal impaction, hypersensitivity reaction, intestinal obstruction (rare), intestinal perforation (rare), pruritus, skin rash

General Dosage Range

Oral:

Children ≥6 years and Adolescents: Initial: 800 to 1,600 mg 3 times daily based on body surface area

Adults: Initial: 800 to 1,600 mg 3 times daily; Maintenance: Up to 2,400 to 14,000 mg/day in 3 divided doses

Mechanism of Action Sevelamer (a polymeric compound) binds phosphate within the intestinal lumen, limiting absorption and decreasing serum phosphate concentrations without altering calcium, aluminum, or bicarbonate concentrations.

Pharmacodynamics/Kinetics

Onset of Action Reduction in serum phosphorus has been demonstrated after 1-2 weeks (Burke 1997; Chertow 1997).

Pregnancy Risk Factor C

Pregnancy Considerations Adverse events have been observed in animal reproduction studies. Sevelamer is not absorbed systemically; however, it may cause a reduction in the absorption of fat soluble vitamins and folic acid.

Sildenafil (sil DEN a fil)

Brand Names: US Revatio; Viagra

Brand Names: Canada ACT-Sildenafil; Apo-Sildenafil; GD-Sildenafil; Jamp-Sildenafil; M-Sildenafil; Mint-Sildenafil; MYL-Sildenafil; PMS-Sildenafil; RAN-Sildenafil; ratio-Sildenafil R; Revatio; Sandoz-Sildenafil; Teva-Sildenafil; Viagra

Pharmacologic Category Phosphodiesterase-5 Enzyme Inhibitor

Use

Erectile dysfunction: Viagra: Treatment of erectile dysfunction (ED)

Pulmonary arterial hypertension: Revatio: Treatment of pulmonary arterial hypertension (PAH) (WHO Group I; efficacy established predominately in patients with WHO/NYHA functional class II and III) in adults to improve exercise ability and delay clinical worsening.

Local Anesthetic/Vasoconstrictor Precautions No information available to require special precautions

Effects on Dental Treatment No significant effects or complications reported

Effects on Bleeding No information available to require special precautions

Adverse Reactions Based upon normal doses for either indication or route. (Adverse effects such as flushing, diarrhea, myalgia, and visual disturbances may be increased with adult doses >100 mg/24 hours.)

>10%:

Cardiovascular: Flushing (10% to 19%)

Central nervous system: Headache (16% to 46%)

Gastrointestinal: Dyspepsia (3% to 17%; dose-related)

Ophthalmic: Visual disturbance (2% to 11%; including vision color changes, blurred vision, and photophobia; dose-related)

Respiratory: Epistaxis (9% to 13%)

2% to 10%:

Central nervous system: Insomnia (≤7%), dizziness (2% to 4%), paresthesia (≤3%)

Dermatologic: Erythema (6%), skin rash (1% to 3%)

Gastrointestinal: Diarrhea (3% to 9%), gastritis (≤3%), nausea (2% to 3%)

Genitourinary: Urinary tract infection (3%)

Hepatic: Increased liver enzymes (2% to 10%)

Neuromuscular & skeletal: Myalgia (2% to 7%), back pain (3% to 4%)

Respiratory: Nasal congestion (4% to 9%), exacerbation of dyspnea (≤7%), nasal congestion (4%), rhinitis (4%), sinusitis (3%)

Miscellaneous: Fever (6%)

<2%, postmarketing, and/or case reports (limited to important or life-threatening): Abdominal pain, abnormal dreams, abnormal hepatic function tests, absent reflexes, accidental injury, amnesia (transient global), anemia, angina pectoris, anorgasmia, anterior chamber eye hemorrhage, anterior ischemic optic neuropathy, anxiety, arthritis, asthma, ataxia, atrioventricular block, auditory impairment, basal cell carcinoma (Loeb 2015), bone pain, breast hypertrophy, bronchitis, burning sensation of eyes, cardiac arrest, cardiac failure, cardiomyopathy, cataract, cerebral hemorrhage, cerebral thrombosis, cerebrovascular hemorrhage, chest pain, chills, colitis, conjunctivitis, contact dermatitis, cystitis, depression, dermal ulcer, diaphoresis, diplopia, drowsiness, dry eye syndrome, dysphagia, ECG abnormality, edema, ejaculatory disorder, esophagitis, exfoliative dermatitis, eye pain, eye redness, facial edema, falling, gastroenteritis, genital edema, gingivitis, glossitis, gout, hearing loss, hematuria, hemorrhage, herpes simplex infection, hyperglycemia, hypernatremia, hypersensitivity reaction, hypertension, hypertonia, hyperuricemia, hypoesthesia, hypoglycemia, hypotension, increased bronchial secretions, increased cough, increased intraocular pressure, increased thirst, ischemic heart disease, leukopenia, laryngitis, malignant melanoma (Li 2014; Loeb 2015), migraine, myasthenia, mydriasis, myocardial infarction, neuralgia, neuropathy, nocturia, orthostatic hypotension, ostealgia, osteoarthritis, otalgia, pain, palpitations, peripheral edema, pharyngitis, photophobia, priapism, prolonged erection, pruritus, pulmonary hemorrhage, rectal hemorrhage, retinal edema, retinal hemorrhage, retinal vascular disease, rupture of tendon, seizure, severe sickle cell crisis (vaso-occlusive crisis in patients with pulmonary hypertension associated with sickle cell disease), shock, skin photosensitivity, stomatitis, subarachnoid hemorrhage, swelling of eye, syncope, synovitis, tachycardia, temporary vision loss, tenosynovitis, tinnitus, transient ischemic attacks, tremor, unstable

diabetes, urinary frequency, urinary incontinence, urticaria, ventricular arrhythmia, vertigo, visual field loss, vitreous detachment, vitreous traction, vomiting, weakness, xerostomia

General Dosage Range Dosage adjustment recommended in patients with hepatic or renal impairment or on concomitant therapy

IV: *Adults:* Revatio: 2.5 mg or 10 mg 3 times daily

Oral:

Adults: Revatio: 5 mg or 20 mg 3 times daily; Viagra: 25 to 100 mg once daily as needed

Elderly: Viagra: Initial: 25 mg once daily as needed

Mechanism of Action

Erectile dysfunction: Does not directly cause penile erections, but affects the response to sexual stimulation. The physiologic mechanism of erection of the penis involves release of nitric oxide (NO) in the corpus cavernosum during sexual stimulation. NO then activates the enzyme guanylate cyclase, which results in increased levels of cyclic guanosine monophosphate (cGMP), producing smooth muscle relaxation and inflow of blood to the corpus cavernosum. Sildenafil enhances the effect of NO by inhibiting phosphodiesterase type 5 (PDE-5), which is responsible for degradation of cGMP in the corpus cavernosum; when sexual stimulation causes local release of NO, inhibition of PDE-5 by sildenafil causes increased levels of cGMP in the corpus cavernosum, resulting in smooth muscle relaxation and inflow of blood to the corpus cavernosum; at recommended doses, it has no effect in the absence of sexual stimulation.

Pulmonary arterial hypertension (PAH): Inhibits phosphodiesterase type 5 (PDE-5) in smooth muscle of pulmonary vasculature where PDE-5 is responsible for the degradation of cyclic guanosine monophosphate (cGMP). Increased cGMP concentration results in pulmonary vasculature relaxation; vasodilation in the pulmonary bed and the systemic circulation (to a lesser degree) may occur.

Pharmacodynamics/Kinetics

Onset of Action Onset: Erectile dysfunction: ~60 minutes; Peak effect: Decrease blood pressure: Oral: 1 to 2 hours

Duration of Action Erectile dysfunction: 2 to 4 hours; Decrease blood pressure: <8 hours

Half-life Elimination

Sildenafil: Terminal:

Neonates: PNA 1 day: 55.9 hours (Mukherjee 2009)

Neonates: PNA 7 days: 47.7 hours (Mukherjee 2009)

Adults: 4 hours

Active N-desmethyl metabolite: Terminal:

Neonates: 11.9 hours (Mukherjee 2009)

Adults: 4 hours

Time to Peak Oral: Fasting: 30 to 120 minutes (median 60 minutes); delayed by 60 minutes with a high-fat meal

Pregnancy Risk Factor B

Pregnancy Considerations Adverse events were not observed in animal reproduction studies. Information related to the use of sildenafil for the treatment of pulmonary arterial hypertension (PAH) in pregnant women is limited (Hsu 2011). Women with pulmonary arterial hypertension are encouraged to avoid pregnancy (McLaughlin 2009; Taichman 2014). Less than 0.001% appears in the semen.

Silodosin (SI lo doe sin)

Brand Names: US Rapaflo

Brand Names: Canada Rapaflo®

Pharmacologic Category $Alpha_1$ Blocker

Use Treatment of signs and symptoms of benign prostatic hyperplasia (BPH)

Local Anesthetic/Vasoconstrictor Precautions No information available to require special precautions

Effects on Dental Treatment Key adverse event(s) related to dental treatment: Dizziness; nasal congestion or rhinitis; Patients may experience orthostatic hypotension as they stand up after treatment; especially if lying in dental chair for extended periods of time. Use caution with sudden changes in position during and after dental treatment.

Effects on Bleeding No information available to require special precautions

Adverse Reactions

>10%: Genitourinary: Retrograde ejaculation (28%)

1% to 10%:

Cardiovascular: Orthostatic hypotension (3%; increased in elderly ≥65 years up to 5%)

Central nervous system: Dizziness (3%), headache (2%), insomnia (1% to 2%)

Gastrointestinal: Diarrhea (3%), abdominal pain (1% to 2%)

Genitourinary: Prostate specific antigen increased (1% to 2%)

Neuromuscular & skeletal: Weakness (1% to 2%)

Respiratory: Nasal congestion (2%), rhinorrhea (1% to 2%), sinusitis (1% to 2%)

<1%, postmarketing, and/or case reports: Hepatic insufficiency, hypersensitivity reaction, increased serum transaminases, intraoperative floppy iris syndrome, jaundice, pharyngeal edema, priapism, pruritus, purpura, skin rash (including toxic), swollen tongue, syncope, urticaria

General Dosage Range Dosage adjustment recommended in patients with renal impairment

Oral: *Adults:* Males: 8 mg once daily

Mechanism of Action Silodosin is a selective antagonist of $alpha_{1A}$-adrenoreceptors in the prostate and bladder. Smooth muscle tone in the prostate is mediated by $alpha_{1A}$-adrenoreceptors; blocking them leads to relaxation of smooth muscle in the bladder neck and prostate causing an improvement of urine flow and decreased symptoms of BPH. Approximately 75% of the alpha1-receptors in the prostate are of the $alpha_{1A}$ subtype.

Pharmacodynamics/Kinetics

Half-life Elimination Healthy volunteers: Silodosin: ~13 hours (mean); KMD-3213G: ~24 hours

Time to Peak Silodosin: ~3 hours; KMD-3213G: ~5.5 hours (Lepor, 2010)

Pregnancy Risk Factor B

Pregnancy Considerations Teratogenic effects were not observed in animal studies; however, silodosin is not approved for use in women.

Siltuximab (sil TUX i mab)

Brand Names: US Sylvant

Brand Names: Canada Sylvant

Pharmacologic Category Antineoplastic Agent, Monoclonal Antibody; Interleukin-6 Receptor Antagonist

Use Castleman disease: Treatment of multicentric Castleman disease (MCD) in patients who are human immunodeficiency virus (HIV) negative and human herpesvirus-8 (HHV-8) negative

Limitations of use: Has not been studied in patients with MCD who are HIV positive or HHV-8 positive because in a nonclinical study, siltuximab did not bind to virally produced IL-6

Local Anesthetic/Vasoconstrictor Precautions No information available to require special precautions

Effects on Dental Treatment Key adverse event(s) related to dental treatment: Oropharyngeal pain and hypotension have been reported; Patients may experience orthostatic hypotension as they stand up after treatment; especially if lying in dental chair for extended periods of time. Use caution with sudden changes in position during and after dental treatment.

Effects on Bleeding No information available to require special precautions

Adverse Reactions

>10%:

Cardiovascular: Peripheral edema (16%)

Central nervous system: Fatigue (21%; long-term exposure)

Dermatologic: Pruritus (28%), skin rash (28%)

Endocrine & metabolic: Weight gain (19%), hyperuricemia (11%)

Gastrointestinal: Diarrhea (32%; long-term exposure), abdominal pain (12%)

Neuromuscular & skeletal: Arthralgia (21%; long-term exposure), limb pain (21%; long term exposure)

Respiratory: Upper respiratory tract infection (26%; long-term exposure: 63%)

1% to 10%:

Cardiovascular: Hypotension (4% to 6%; grades 3/4: 2% [anaphylactic reaction])

Central nervous system: Headache (8%)

Dermatologic: Eczema (4%), psoriasis (4%), skin hyperpigmentation (4%), xeroderma (4%)

Endocrine & metabolic: Hypertriglyceridemia (8%), dehydration (4%), hypercholesterolemia (4%)

Gastrointestinal: Constipation (8%), decreased appetite (4%)

Hematologic & oncologic: Thrombocytopenia (9%)

Renal: Renal insufficiency (8%)

Respiratory: Lower respiratory tract infection (8%), oropharyngeal pain (8%)

Miscellaneous: Infusion related reaction (5%)

<1%: Anaphylaxis, antibody development (non-neutralizing)

General Dosage Range IV: Adults: 11 mg/kg over 1 hour every 3 weeks until treatment failure

Mechanism of Action Chimeric monoclonal antibody which binds with high affinity and specificity to IL-6; prevents IL-6 from binding to both soluble and membrane-bound IL-6 receptors. Overproduction of IL-6 may lead to systemic manifestations in multicentric Castleman disease (MCD) patients by inducing C-reactive protein (CRP) synthesis (Kurzrock, 2010). Lowering serum IL-6 levels may improve systemic symptoms of Castleman disease.

Pharmacodynamics/Kinetics

Half-life Elimination ~21 days (range: 14.2 to 29.7 days)

Pregnancy Risk Factor C

Pregnancy Considerations Adverse events were not observed in animal reproduction studies. However, decreased globulin levels were detected in the pregnant animals and their offspring. Infants born to pregnant women treated with siltuximab may be at increased risk for infection. Use during pregnancy only if the potential benefit outweighs the possible risk to the fetus. Women of childbearing potential should use effective contraception during and for 3 months following treatment discontinuation.

Silver Nitrate (SIL ver NYE trate)

Generic Availability (US) Yes

Pharmacologic Category Antibiotic, Topical; Cauterizing Agent, Topical; Topical Skin Product, Antibacterial

Use Astringent, cauterization of wounds, germicidal, removal of granulation tissue, corns, and warts

Local Anesthetic/Vasoconstrictor Precautions No information available to require special precautions

Effects on Dental Treatment No significant effects or complications reported

Effects on Bleeding No information available to require special precautions

Adverse Reactions Frequency not defined.

Dermatologic: Burning sensation of skin, skin discoloration, skin irritation

Hematologic & oncologic: Methemoglobinemia

Dosing

Adult & Geriatric Antiseptic, wound cauterization:

Topical:

Sticks: Apply to mucous membranes and other moist skin surfaces only on area to be treated

Topical solution: Usual: Apply a cotton applicator dipped in solution on the affected area 2-3 times/ week for 2-3 weeks.

Pediatric Antiseptic, wound cauterization: Topical: Refer to adult dosing.

Mechanism of Action Free silver ions precipitate bacterial proteins by combining with chloride in tissue forming silver chloride; coagulates cellular protein to form an eschar; silver ions or salts or colloidal silver preparations can inhibit the growth of both gram-positive and gram-negative bacteria. This germicidal action is attributed to the precipitation of bacterial proteins by liberated silver ions. Silver nitrate coagulates cellular protein to form an eschar, and this mode of action is the postulated mechanism for control of benign hematuria, rhinitis, and recurrent pneumothorax.

Contraindications Hypersensitivity to silver nitrate or any component of the formulation; not for use on broken skin, cuts, or wounds

Warnings/Precautions Do not use applicator sticks on the eyes. Prolonged use may result in skin discoloration. Silver nitrate is a caustic agent and inappropriate use may cause chemical burns. Skin contact time with applicator sticks should be extremely short when used in neonates or on thin delicate skin contact.

Drug Interactions

Metabolism/Transport Effects None known.

Avoid Concomitant Use

Avoid concomitant use of Silver Nitrate with any of the following: BCG (Intravesical)

Increased Effect/Toxicity There are no known significant interactions involving an increase in effect.

Decreased Effect

Silver Nitrate may decrease the levels/effects of: BCG (Intravesical); BCG Vaccine (Immunization); Sodium Picosulfate

Dosage Forms

Applicator sticks, topical: Silver nitrate 75% and potassium 25%

Solution, topical: 0.5% (960 mL); 10% (30 mL); 25% (30 mL); 50% (30 mL)

Silver Sulfadiazine (SIL ver sul fa DYE a zeen)

Brand Names: US Silvadene; SSD; Thermazene [DSC]

Brand Names: Canada Flamazine

Pharmacologic Category Antibiotic, Topical

Use Burn treatment: As an adjunct for the prevention and treatment of wound sepsis in patients with second- and third-degree burns.

Local Anesthetic/Vasoconstrictor Precautions No information available to require special precautions

Effects on Dental Treatment No significant effects or complications reported

Effects on Bleeding No information available to require special precautions

Adverse Reactions Frequency not defined.

Dermatologic: Erythema multiforme, pruritus, skin discoloration, skin photosensitivity, skin rash

Hematologic & oncologic: Agranulocytosis, aplastic anemia, hemolytic anemia, leukopenia

Hepatic: Hepatitis

Hypersensitivity: Hypersensitivity reaction (may be related to sulfa component)

Renal: Interstitial nephritis

General Dosage Range Topical: *Infants ≥2 months, Children, Adolescents, and Adults:* Apply to a thickness of 1/16 inch once or twice daily

Mechanism of Action Acts upon the bacterial cell wall and cell membrane. Bactericidal for many gram-negative and gram-positive bacteria and is effective against yeast. Active against *Pseudomonas aeruginosa*, *Pseudomonas maltophilia*, *Enterobacter* species, *Klebsiella* species, *Serratia* species, *Escherichia coli*, *Proteus mirabilis*, *Morganella morganii*, *Providencia rettgeri*, *Proteus vulgaris*, *Providencia* species, *Citrobacter* species, *Acinetobacter calcoaceticus*, *Staphylococcus aureus*, *Staphylococcus epidermidis*, *Enterococcus* species, *Candida albicans*, *Corynebacterium diphtheriae*, and *Clostridium perfringens*

Pharmacodynamics/Kinetics

Half-life Elimination Sulfadiazine: ~24 hours (Sano 1982)

Pregnancy Considerations Adverse events were not observed in animal reproduction studies. Because of the theoretical increased risk for hyperbilirubinemia and kernicterus, silver sulfadiazine is contraindicated for use near term, on premature infants, or on newborn infants during the first 2 months of life (refer to Sulfadiazine monograph).

Simeprevir (sim E pre vir)

Related Information

Systemic Viral Diseases *on page 1806*

Brand Names: US Olysio

Brand Names: Canada Galexos

Pharmacologic Category Antihepaciviral, Protease Inhibitor (Anti-HCV); NS3/4A Inhibitor

Use

Chronic hepatitis C: Treatment of genotype 1 chronic hepatitis C in combination with peginterferon alfa and ribavirin **or** sofosbuvir in adults without cirrhosis or with compensated cirrhosis.

Limitations of use: Not recommended for use in patients who have previously failed a simeprevir-containing regimen or another regimen containing HCV protease inhibitors.

Local Anesthetic/Vasoconstrictor Precautions No information available to require special precautions

Effects on Dental Treatment No significant effects or complications reported

Effects on Bleeding No information available to require special precautions

Adverse Reactions Percentages reported for combination therapy with peginterferon alfa and ribavirin (Peg-IFN-alfa and RBV) unless otherwise noted.

>10%:

Central nervous system: Headache (with sofosbuvir 7% to 49%), fatigue (with sofosbuvir 10% to 47%), insomnia (with sofosbuvir 14%), dizziness (with sofosbuvir 5% to 10%)

Dermatologic: Skin photosensitivity (with sofosbuvir ≤5% to ≤34%; grade 3: ≤1%; with Peg-IFN-alfa and RBV ≤28%; grade 3: <1%), skin rash (with sofosbuvir ≤5% to ≤34%; grade 3: ≤1%; with Peg-IFN-alfa and RBV ≤28%; including erythema, eczema, maculopapular rash, urticaria, toxic skin eruption, dermatitis exfoliative, cutaneous vasculitis; grade 3: ≤1%), pruritus (with Peg-IFN-alfa and RBV 22%; with sofosbuvir 11%)

Endocrine & metabolic: Increased amylase (with sofosbuvir)

Gastrointestinal: Nausea (with sofosbuvir 4% to 40%; with Peg-IFN-alfa and RBV 22%), diarrhea (with sofosbuvir 5% to 18%)

Hepatic: Increased serum bilirubin (<66%), hyperbilirubinemia (with sofosbuvir)

Neuromuscular & skeletal: Myalgia (16%)

Respiratory: Dyspnea (12%)

1% to 10%:

Gastrointestinal: Increased serum lipase (with sofosbuvir)

Hepatic: Increased serum alkaline phosphatase

<1%, postmarketing, and/or case reports: Hepatic failure, liver decompensation, reactivation of HBV (FDA Safety Alert Dec. 8, 2016)

General Dosage Range

Oral: Adults: 150 mg once daily, as part of a combination regimen.

Mechanism of Action Simeprevir is an inhibitor of HCV NS3/4A protease, a protease that is essential for viral replication. It is considered a direct-acting antiviral treatment for HCV, also called a specifically targeted antiviral therapy for HCV (STAT-C).

Pharmacodynamics/Kinetics

Half-life Elimination Plasma: 10 to 13 hours (healthy volunteers); 41 hours (HCV-infected patients)

Time to Peak Serum: 4 to 6 hours

Pregnancy Considerations

Use of this product in combination with ribavirin is contraindicated in pregnant women and men whose female partners are pregnant.

Adverse events have been observed in animal reproduction studies. If used in combination with ribavirin, all warnings related to the use of ribavirin and pregnancy and/or contraception should be followed. Mother-to-child transmission of HCV does not occur if the woman is not viremic; therefore, HCV-infected women of childbearing potential should postpone pregnancy until therapy is complete. Treatment of HCV is not recommended for women who are already pregnant (AASLD/IDSA 2016).

Simethicone (sye METH i kone)

Brand Names: US Gas Free Extra Strength [OTC] [DSC]; Gas Relief Extra Strength [OTC]; Gas Relief Maximum Strength [OTC]; Gas Relief Ultra Strength [OTC]; Gas Relief [OTC]; Gas-X Childrens [OTC]; Gas-X Extra Strength [OTC]; Gas-X Infant Drops [OTC]; Gas-X Ultra Strength [OTC]; Gas-X [OTC]; GasAid [OTC] [DSC]; Infants Gas Relief [OTC]; Infants Simethicone [OTC]; Mi-Acid Gas Relief [OTC]; Mytab Gas Maximum Strength [OTC]; Mytab Gas [OTC]; Phazyme Maximum Strength [OTC]; Phazyme Ultra Strength [OTC]; Phazyme [OTC]

Brand Names: Canada Ovol, Phazyme

Pharmacologic Category Antiflatulent

Use Gas retention: Relief of pressure, bloating, fullness, and discomfort of gastrointestinal gas.

Local Anesthetic/Vasoconstrictor Precautions No information available to require special precautions

Effects on Dental Treatment No significant effects or complications reported

Effects on Bleeding No information available to require special precautions

Adverse Reactions No data reported

General Dosage Range Oral:

Infants and Children <2 years or <11 kg: 20 mg 4 times daily after meals and at bedtime, as needed (maximum: 240 mg/)

Children >2 years or >11 kg: 40 mg 4 times daily after meals and at bedtime, as needed (maximum: 480 mg/day)

Children, Adolescents >12 years, and Adults: Usual dose: 40 to 125 mg 4 times daily as needed after meals and at bedtime; may administer single doses of up to 160 to 500 mg after meals or at bedtime, not to exceed a maximum daily dose of 500 mg/day

Mechanism of Action Decreases the surface tension of gas bubbles thereby disperses and prevents gas pockets in the GI system

Pregnancy Considerations Simethicone is not absorbed systemically following oral administration. Systemic absorption would be required in order for simethicone to cross the placenta and reach the fetus (Mahadevan 2006).

Simvastatin (sim va STAT in)

Related Information

Cardiovascular Diseases *on page 1752*

Brand Names: US Zocor

Brand Names: Canada ACT-Simvastatin; Apo-Simvastatin; Auro-Simvastatin; Dom-Simvastatin; JAMP-Simvastatin; Mar-Simvastatin; Mint-Simvastatin; Mylan-Simvastatin; PHL-Simvastatin; PMS-Simvastatin; Q-Simvastatin; RAN-Simvastatin; Riva-Simvastatin; Sandoz-Simvastatin; Simvastatin-Odan; Teva-Simvastatin; Zocor

Generic Availability (US) Yes

Pharmacologic Category Antilipemic Agent, HMG-CoA Reductase Inhibitor

Use Used with dietary therapy for the following:

Secondary prevention of cardiovascular events in hypercholesterolemic patients with established coronary heart disease (CHD) or at high risk for CHD: To reduce cardiovascular morbidity (myocardial infarction, coronary/noncoronary revascularization procedures) and mortality; to reduce the risk of stroke

Hyperlipidemias: To reduce elevations in total cholesterol (total-C), LDL-C, apolipoprotein B, triglycerides, and VLDL-C, and to increase HDL-C in patients with primary hypercholesterolemia (elevations of 1 or more components are present in Fredrickson type IIa, IIb, III, and IV hyperlipidemias); treatment of homozygous familial hypercholesterolemia

Heterozygous familial hypercholesterolemia (HeFH): In adolescent patients (10-17 years of age, females >1 year postmenarche) with HeFH having LDL-C ≥190 mg/dL **or** LDL-C ≥160 mg/dL with positive family history of premature cardiovascular disease (CVD), or 2 or more CVD risk factors in the adolescent patient

Guideline recommendations: Primary and secondary prevention of atherosclerotic cardiovascular disease (ASCVD) to reduce the risk of ASCVD in select adult patients (ACC/AHA [Stone 2013]; NLA [Jacobson 2015]). Refer to respective guideline for specific recommendations.

Local Anesthetic/Vasoconstrictor Precautions No information available to require special precautions

Effects on Dental Treatment Key adverse event(s) related to dental treatment: Assess unusual presentations of muscle weakness or myopathy resulting from lipid therapy such as patient having a difficult time brushing teeth or weakness with chewing. Refer patient back to their physician for evaluation and adjustment of lipid therapy.

Effects on Bleeding No information available to require special precautions

Adverse Reactions Frequency not always defined.

Cardiovascular: Atrial fibrillation (6%), edema (3%)

Central nervous system: Headache (3% to 7%), vertigo (5%)

Dermatologic: Eczema (5%)

Gastrointestinal: Abdominal pain (7%), constipation (2% to 7%), gastritis (5%), nausea (5%)

Genitourinary: Cystitis (interstitial; Huang 2015)

Hepatic: Increased transaminases (>3 x ULN; 1%)

Neuromuscular & skeletal: Increased CPK (>3 x normal; 5%), myalgia (4%)

Respiratory: Upper respiratory infections (9%), bronchitis (7%)

<1%, postmarketing, and/or case reports: Alopecia, amnesia (reversible), anaphylaxis, anemia, angioedema, arthralgia, arthritis, chills, cognitive impairment (reversible), confusion (reversible), depression, dermatomyositis, diabetes mellitus (new onset), diarrhea, dizziness, dryness of skin/mucous membranes, dysgeusia (Tuccori 2011), dyspepsia, dyspnea, elevated glycosylated hemoglobin (HbA_{1c}), eosinophilia, erythema multiforme, fever, flatulence, flushing, hemolytic anemia, hepatic failure, hepatitis, hypersensitivity reaction, increased alkaline phosphatase, increased blood glucose, increased ESR, increased GGT, increased serum alkaline phosphatase, jaundice, leukopenia, malaise, memory impairment (reversible), muscle cramps, nail changes, nodules, pancreatitis, paresthesia, peripheral neuropathy, polymyalgia rheumatica, positive ANA, pruritus, purpura, rhabdomyolysis, skin discoloration, skin photosensitivity, skin rash, Stevens-Johnson syndrome, systemic lupus erythematosus-like syndrome, thrombocytopenia, toxic epidermal necrolysis, ulcerative colitis, urticaria, vasculitis, vomiting, weakness

Dosing

Adult Note: Doses should be individualized according to the baseline LDL-cholesterol levels, the recommended goal of therapy, and the patient's response;

adjustments should be made at intervals of 4 weeks or more; doses may need adjusted based on concomitant medications

Note: Dosing limitation: Simvastatin 80 mg is limited to patients that have been taking this dose for >12 consecutive months without evidence of myopathy and are not currently taking or beginning to take a simvastatin dose-limiting or contraindicated interacting medication. If patient is unable to achieve low-density lipoprotein-cholesterol (LDL-C) goal using the 40 mg dose of simvastatin, increasing to 80 mg dose is not recommended. Instead, switch patient to an alternative LDL-C-lowering treatment providing greater LDL-C reduction.

Homozygous familial hypercholesterolemia: Oral: 40 mg once daily in the evening

Prevention of cardiovascular events (also see ACC/AHA Blood Cholesterol Guideline recommendations), hyperlipidemias: Oral: 10 to 20 mg once daily in the evening; range: 5 to 40 mg/day

Patients requiring only moderate reduction of LDL-C: May be started at 5 to 10 mg once daily in the evening; adjust to achieve recommended LDL-C goal.

Patients requiring reduction of >40% of LDL-C: May be started at 40 mg once daily in the evening; adjust to achieve recommended LDL-C goal.

Patients with CHD or at high risk for cardiovascular events (patients with diabetes, PVD, history of stroke or other cerebrovascular disease): Dosing should be started at 40 mg once daily in the evening; start simultaneously with diet therapy.

Prevention of cardiovascular disease/reduce the risk of ASCVD:

ACC/AHA Blood Cholesterol Guideline recommendations (ACC/AHA [Stone 2013]): Adults ≥21 years:

Primary prevention:

LDL-C ≥190 mg/dL: High intensity therapy necessary; use alternate statin therapy (eg, atorvastatin or rosuvastatin)

Type 1 or 2 diabetes and age 40 to 75 years: Moderate intensity therapy: 20 to 40 mg once daily

Type 1 or 2 diabetes, age 40 to 75 years, and an estimated 10-year ASCVD risk ≥7.5%: High intensity therapy necessary; use alternate statin therapy (eg, atorvastatin or rosuvastatin)

Age 40 to 75 years and an estimated 10-year ASCVD risk ≥7.5%: Moderate to high intensity therapy: 20 to 40 mg once daily or consider using high intensity statin therapy (eg, atorvastatin or rosuvastatin)

Secondary prevention:

Patient has clinical ASCVD (eg, coronary heart disease, stroke/TIA, or peripheral arterial disease presumed to be of atherosclerotic origin) or is post-CABG (AHA [Kulik, 2015]) **and**:

Age ≤75 years: High intensity therapy necessary; use alternate statin therapy (eg, atorvastatin or rosuvastatin)

Age >75 years or not a candidate for high intensity therapy: Moderate intensity therapy: 20 to 40 mg once daily

NLA Dyslipidemia Recommendations (NLA [Jacobson 2015]): Adults ≥20 years:

Primary or secondary prevention: Note: Treatment initiation using either moderate- or high-intensity statin therapy is recommended in qualifying patients based on ASCVD risk assessment criteria **and** baseline non-HDL-C and LDL-C values. Dosage should be individualized based on patient characteristics, tolerance to therapy, and with consideration for non-HDL-C and LDL-C treatment goals.

Moderate-intensity therapy (30% to 50% reduction of LDL-C generally): 20 to 40 mg once daily

High-intensity therapy (≥50% reduction of LDL-C generally): Use alternate statin therapy (eg, atorvastatin or rosuvastatin)

Dosage adjustment for simvastatin with concomitant medications: Note: Patients currently tolerating and requiring a dose of simvastatin 80 mg who require initiation of an interacting drug with a dose cap for simvastatin should be switched to an alternative statin with less potential for drug-drug interaction.

Amiodarone, amlodipine, or ranolazine: Simvastatin dose should **not** exceed 20 mg/day

Diltiazem, dronedarone, or verapamil: Simvastatin dose should **not** exceed 10 mg/day

Lomitapide: Reduce simvastatin dose by 50% when initiating lomitapide. Simvastatin dose should not exceed 20 mg/day (or 40 mg daily for those who previously tolerated simvastatin 80 mg daily for ≥1 year without evidence of muscle toxicity)

Dosage adjustment in Chinese patients on niacin doses ≥1 g/day: Use caution with simvastatin doses exceeding 20 mg/day; because of an increased risk of myopathy, do not administer simvastatin 80 mg concurrently.

Geriatric Oral: Initial: Maximum reductions in LDL-cholesterol may be achieved with daily dose ≤20 mg.

Pediatric HeFH: Oral: Children 10 to 17 years (females >1 year postmenarche): 10 mg once daily in the evening; range: 10 to 40 mg/day (maximum: 40 mg/day)

Dosage adjustment with concomitant medications: With concomitant amiodarone, amlodipine, diltiazem, dronedarone, lomitapide, ranolazine, or verapamil: Refer to adult dosing.

Note: Doses should be individualized according to the baseline LDL-cholesterol levels, the recommended goal of therapy, and the patient's response; adjustments should be made at intervals of 4 weeks or more; doses may need adjusted based on concomitant medications

Renal Impairment Manufacturer's recommendations:

Mild to moderate renal impairment: No dosage adjustment necessary; simvastatin does not undergo significant renal excretion.

Severe renal impairment: CrCl <30 mL/minute: Initial: 5 mg/day with close monitoring.

Hepatic Impairment Use is contraindicated in the setting of active liver disease.

Adjustment for Toxicity

Severe muscle symptoms or fatigue: Promptly discontinue use; evaluate CPK, creatinine, and urinalysis for myoglobinuria (Stone, 2013).

Mild to moderate muscle symptoms: Discontinue use until symptoms can be evaluated; evaluate patient for conditions that may increase the risk for muscle symptoms (eg, hypothyroidism, reduced renal or hepatic function, rheumatologic disorders such as polymyalgia rheumatica, steroid myopathy, vitamin D deficiency, or primary muscle diseases). Upon resolution, resume the original or lower dose of simvastatin. If muscle symptoms recur, discontinue simvastatin use. After muscle symptom resolution, may then use a low dose of a different statin; gradually increase if tolerated. In the absence of continued statin use, if muscle symptoms or elevated CPK continues after 2 months, consider other causes of muscle symptoms. If determined to be due to another condition aside from statin use, may resume statin therapy at the original dose (Stone, 2013).

Mechanism of Action Simvastatin is a methylated derivative of lovastatin that acts by competitively inhibiting 3-hydroxy-3-methylglutaryl-coenzyme A (HMG-CoA) reductase, the enzyme that catalyzes the rate-limiting step in cholesterol biosynthesis. In addition to the ability of HMG-CoA reductase inhibitors to decrease levels of high-sensitivity C-reactive protein (hsCRP), they also possess pleiotropic properties including improved endothelial function, reduced inflammation at the site of the coronary plaque, inhibition of platelet aggregation, and anticoagulant effects (de Denus, 2002; Ray, 2005).

Contraindications Hypersensitivity to simvastatin or any component of the formulation; active liver disease; unexplained persistent elevations of serum transaminases; concomitant use of strong CYP3A4 inhibitors (eg, clarithromycin, erythromycin, itraconazole, ketoconazole, nefazodone, posaconazole, voriconazole, protease inhibitors [including boceprevir and telaprevir], telithromycin, cobicistat-containing products), cyclosporine, danazol, and gemfibrozil; pregnancy; breast-feeding

Warnings/Precautions Secondary causes of hyperlipidemia should be ruled out prior to therapy. Liver enzyme tests should be obtained at baseline and as clinically indicated; routine periodic monitoring of liver enzymes is not necessary. Use with caution in patients who consume large amounts of ethanol or have a history of liver disease; use is contraindicated with active liver disease and with unexplained transaminase elevations. Rhabdomyolysis with acute renal failure has occurred. Risk of rhabdomyolysis is dose-related and increased with high doses (80 mg), concurrent use of lipid-lowering agents which may also cause rhabdomyolysis (other fibrates or niacin doses ≥1 g/day), or moderate-to strong CYP3A4 inhibitors (eg, amiodarone, grapefruit juice in large quantities, or verapamil), age ≥65 years, female gender, uncontrolled hypothyroidism, and renal dysfunction. In Chinese patients, do not use high-dose simvastatin (80 mg) if concurrently taking niacin ≥1 g/day; may increase risk of myopathy. Immune-mediated necrotizing myopathy (IMNM), an autoimmune-mediated myopathy, has been reported (rarely) with HMG-CoA reductase inhibitor therapy. IMNM presents as proximal muscle weakness with elevated CPK levels, which persists despite discontinuation of HMG-CoA reductase inhibitor therapy; additionally, muscle biopsy may show necrotizing myopathy with limited inflammation; immunosuppressive therapy (eg, corticosteroids, azathioprine) may be used for treatment. Concomitant use of simvastatin with some drugs may require cautious use, may not be recommended, may require dosage adjustments, or may be contraindicated. If concurrent use of a contraindicated interacting medication is unavoidable, treatment with simvastatin should be suspended during use or consider the use of an alternative HMG-CoA reductase inhibitor void of CYP3A4 metabolism. Monitor closely if used with other drugs associated with myopathy (eg, colchicine). Increases in HbA_{1c} and fasting blood glucose have been reported with HMG-CoA reductase inhibitors; however, the benefits of statin therapy far outweigh the risk of dysglycemia. The manufacturer recommends temporary discontinuation for elective major surgery, acute medical or surgical conditions, or in any patient experiencing an acute or serious condition predisposing to renal failure (eg, sepsis, hypotension, trauma, uncontrolled seizures). Based on current research and clinical guidelines (Fleisher, 2009), HMG-CoA reductase inhibitors should be continued in the perioperative period. Use with caution in patients with severe renal impairment; initial dosage adjustment is necessary; monitor closely.

Drug Interactions

Metabolism/Transport Effects **Substrate** of CYP3A4 (major), SLCO1B1; **Note:** Assignment of Major/Minor substrate status based on clinically relevant drug interaction potential; **Inhibits** CYP2C8 (weak), CYP2C9 (weak)

Avoid Concomitant Use

Avoid concomitant use of Simvastatin with any of the following: Amodiaquine; Boceprevir; Clarithromycin; Conivaptan; CycloSPORINE (Systemic); CYP3A4 Inhibitors (Strong); Danazol; Erythromycin (Systemic); Fusidic Acid (Systemic); Gemfibrozil; Grapefruit Juice; Idelalisib; MiFEPRIStone; Protease Inhibitors; Red Yeast Rice; Telaprevir; Telithromycin

Increased Effect/Toxicity

Simvastatin may increase the levels/effects of: Amodiaquine; Dabigatran Etexilate; DAPTOmycin; DilTIAZem; PAZOPanib; Repaglinide; Trabectedin; Vitamin K Antagonists

The levels/effects of Simvastatin may be increased by: Acipimox; Amiodarone; AmLODIPine; Aprepitant; Asunaprevir; Azithromycin (Systemic); Bezafibrate; Boceprevir; Ciprofibrate; Clarithromycin; Colchicine; Conivaptan; CycloSPORINE (Systemic); CYP3A4 Inhibitors (Moderate); CYP3A4 Inhibitors (Strong); Cyproterone; Daclatasvir; Danazol; Dasatinib; DilTIAZem; Dronedarone; Elbasvir; Eltrombopag; Erythromycin (Systemic); Fenofibrate and Derivatives; Fluconazole; Fosaprepitant; Fusidic Acid (Systemic); Gemfibrozil; Grapefruit Juice; Grazoprevir; Green Tea; Idelalisib; Imatinib; Ivacaftor; Lercanidipine; Lomitapide; MiFEPRIStone; Netupitant; Niacin; Niacinamide; Palbociclib; Protease Inhibitors; QuiNINE; Raltegravir; Ranolazine; Red Yeast Rice; Rupatadine; Simeprevir; Stiripentol; Telaprevir; Telithromycin; Teriflunomide; Ticagrelor; Verapamil

Decreased Effect

Simvastatin may decrease the levels/effects of: Lanthanum

The levels/effects of Simvastatin may be decreased by: Antacids; Bosentan; CYP3A4 Inducers (Moderate); CYP3A4 Inducers (Strong); Dabrafenib; Deferasirox; Efavirenz; Enzalutamide; Eslicarbazepine; Etravirine; Fosphenytoin; Mitotane; Phenytoin; Rifamycin Derivatives; Siltuximab; St John's Wort; Tocilizumab

Food Interactions Simvastatin serum concentration may be increased when taken with grapefruit juice. Management: Avoid combination.

Dietary Considerations May be taken without regard to meals. Red yeast rice contains variable amounts of several compounds that are structurally similar to HMG-CoA reductase inhibitors, primarily monacolin K (or mevinolin) which is structurally identical to lovastatin; concurrent use of red yeast rice with HMG-CoA reductase inhibitors may increase the incidence of adverse and toxic effects (Lapi, 2008; Smith, 2003).

Pharmacodynamics/Kinetics

Onset of Action

Onset of action: >3 days; Peak effect: 2 weeks

LDL-C reduction: 20 to 40 mg/day: 35% to 41% (for each doubling of this dose, LDL-C is lowered ~6%)

Average HDL-C increase: 5% to 15%

Average triglyceride reduction: 7% to 30%

Half-life Elimination Unknown

Time to Peak 1.3 to 2.4 hours

Pregnancy Risk Factor X

Pregnancy Considerations Adverse events were not observed in animal reproduction studies. There are reports of congenital anomalies following maternal use of HMG-CoA reductase inhibitors in pregnancy; however, maternal disease, differences in specific agents used, and the low rates of exposure limit the interpretation of the available data (Godfrey, 2012; Lecarpentier, 2012). Cholesterol biosynthesis may be important in fetal development; serum cholesterol and triglycerides increase normally during pregnancy. The discontinuation of lipid lowering medications temporarily during pregnancy is not expected to have significant impact on the long term outcomes of primary hypercholesterolemia treatment.

Use of simvastatin is contraindicated in pregnancy. HMG-CoA reductase inhibitors should be discontinued prior to pregnancy (ADA, 2013). If treatment of dyslipidemias is needed in pregnant women or in women of reproductive age, other agents are preferred (Berglund, 2012; Stone, 2013). The manufacturer recommends administration to women of childbearing potential only when conception is highly unlikely and patients have been informed of potential hazards.

Breastfeeding Considerations It is not known if simvastatin is excreted into breast milk. Due to the potential for serious adverse reactions in a nursing infant, breastfeeding is contraindicated by the manufacturer.

Dosage Forms

Tablet, Oral:

Zocor: 5 mg, 10 mg, 20 mg, 40 mg, 80 mg

Generic: 5 mg, 10 mg, 20 mg, 40 mg, 80 mg

Sinecatechins (sin e KAT e kins)

Brand Names: US Veregen

Brand Names: Canada Veregen

Pharmacologic Category Immunomodulator, Topical; Topical Skin Product

Use

External genital and perianal warts (*Condyloma acuminatum*): Treatment of external genital and perianal warts (*Condyloma acuminatum*) in immunocompetent patients ≥18 years of age.

Local Anesthetic/Vasoconstrictor Precautions No information available to require special precautions

Effects on Dental Treatment No significant effects or complications reported

Effects on Bleeding No information available to require special precautions

Adverse Reactions

>10%:

Central nervous system: Localized burning (67%), local discomfort (≤56%)

Dermatologic: Erythema (70%), pruritus (69%), skin erosion (≤49%), skin sclerosis (35%), vesicular eruption (20%)

Local: Local pain (≤56%), dermal ulcer (≤49%), localized edema (45%)

1% to 10%:

Dermatologic: Desquamation (5%), dermatological reaction (2%), scarring (1%), skin rash (1%)

Genitourinary: Foreskin irretraction (3%; uncircumcised males)

Hematologic & oncologic: Lymphadenitis (3%; local), local hemorrhage (2%)

Hypersensitivity: Hypersensitivity reaction (2%)

Local: Application site discharge (3%), local irritation (1%)

<1%, postmarketing, and/or case reports: Dyschromia, eczema, facial rash, hyperesthesia, infection (perianal), local discoloration, local dryness, local tissue necrosis, papule, pelvic pain, staphylococcal bacteremia, urethritis, vulvitis

General Dosage Range Topical: *Adults:* Apply a thin layer (~0.5 cm strand) 3 times daily

Mechanism of Action The mechanism by which sinecatechins ointment aids in the clearance of genital and perianal warts is unknown. Antioxidant properties have been demonstrated *in vitro*; however, the significance of this finding is not known.

Pregnancy Risk Factor C

Pregnancy Considerations Adverse events have not been observed in animal reproduction studies. Sinecatechins ointment may weaken condoms and diaphragms. Sinecatechins should not be used during pregnancy (CDC [Workowski 2015])

Sipuleucel-T (si pu LOO sel tee)

Brand Names: US Provenge

Pharmacologic Category Cellular Immunotherapy, Autologous

Use Prostate cancer, metastatic: Treatment of asymptomatic or minimally symptomatic metastatic castrate-resistant (hormone-refractory) prostate cancer.

Local Anesthetic/Vasoconstrictor Precautions No information available to require special precautions

Effects on Dental Treatment No significant effects or complications reported

Effects on Bleeding No information available to require special precautions

Adverse Reactions Note: Initial infusion-related events usually present within the first 24 hours after administration.

>10%:

Central nervous system: Chills (53%; grades ≥3: 2%), fatigue (41%; grades ≥3: 1%), headache (18%; grades ≥3: <1%), dizziness (12%; grades ≥3: <1%), pain (12%)

Gastrointestinal: Nausea (22%; grades ≥3: <1%), vomiting (13% grades ≥3: <1%), constipation (12%; grades ≥3: <1%)

Hematologic: Anemia (13%)

Hypersensitivity: Severe infusion related reaction (71%; grade 3: 4%)

Neuromuscular & skeletal: Back pain (30%; grades ≥3: 3%), myalgia (12%; grades ≥3: <1%), weakness (11%; grades ≥3: 1%)

Miscellaneous: Fever (31%; grades ≥3: 1%), citrate toxicity (15%)

1% to 10%:

Cardiovascular: Hypertension (8% grades ≥3: <1%), hemorrhagic stroke (4%)

Dermatologic: Diaphoresis (5%; grades ≥3: <1%), skin rash (5%)

Gastrointestinal: Anorexia (7%), acute ischemic stroke (4%)

Genitourinary: Hematuria (8%)
Neuromuscular & skeletal: Musculoskeletal pain (9%; grades ≥3: <1%), muscle spasm (8%; grades ≥3: <1%), neck pain (6%), tremor (5%)
Renal: Hematuria (8%)
Respiratory: Flu-like symptoms (10%), dyspnea (9%; grades ≥3: 2%)

<1%, postmarketing, and/or case reports: Cerebrovascular accident, eosinophilia, hypotension, myasthenia gravis, myocardial infarction, myositis, paresthesia (grades ≥3), pulmonary embolism, rhabdomyolysis, sepsis, syncope, transient ischemic attacks, tumor flare, venous thrombosis

General Dosage Range IV: *Adults (males):* ≥50 million autologous CD54+ cells activated with PAP-GM-CSF; dose administered at ~2 week intervals for a total of 3 doses

Mechanism of Action Autologous cellular immunotherapy which stimulates an immune response against an antigen (PAP) expressed in most prostate cancer tissues. Peripheral blood is collected (~3 days prior to infusion) from the patient via leukapheresis, from which peripheral blood mononuclear cells (PBMCs) are isolated. Antigen presenting cell (APC) precursors, consisting of CD54-positive cells that include dendritic cells, are isolated from the PBMCs. The APCs are then activated (*in vitro*) with a recombinant human fusion protein, PAP-GM-CSF (also termed PA2024), composed of an antigen specific for prostate cancer, prostatic acid phosphatase (PAP) linked to granulocyte-macrophage colony-stimulating factor (GM-CSF) and cultured for ~40 hours. The final product, sipuleucel-T, is reinfused into the patient, inducing T-cell immunity to tumors that express PAP.

Pregnancy Considerations Animal reproduction studies have not been conducted. Not indicated for use in women.

Prescribing and Access Restrictions Patients may receive Sipuleucel-T at a participating site. Physicians must go through an inservice and register to prescribe the treatment; patients must also complete an enrollment form. Information on registration and enrollment is available at 1-877-336-3736.

Sirolimus (sir OH li mus)

Brand Names: US Rapamune

Brand Names: Canada Rapamune

Generic Availability (US) May be product dependent

Pharmacologic Category Immunosuppressant Agent; mTOR Kinase Inhibitor

Use

Lymphangioleiomyomatosis: Treatment of lymphangioleiomyomatosis. Therapeutic drug monitoring is recommended for all patients receiving sirolimus.

Renal transplantation: Prophylaxis of organ rejection in patients receiving renal transplants (in low-to-moderate immunologic risk patients in combination with cyclosporine and corticosteroids with cyclosporine withdrawn 2 to 4 months after transplant, and in high immunologic risk patients in combination with cyclosporine and corticosteroids for the first year after transplant). Therapeutic drug monitoring is recommended for all patients receiving sirolimus. High immunologic risk renal transplant patients are defined (per the manufacturer's labeling) as Black transplant recipients and/or repeat renal transplant recipients who lost a previous allograft based on an immunologic process and/or patients with high PRA (panel-reactive antibodies; peak PRA level >80%).

Limitations of use (renal transplantation): Cyclosporine withdrawal has not been studied in patients with Banff grade 3 acute rejection or vascular rejection prior to cyclosporine withdrawal, patients who are dialysis-dependent, patients with serum creatinine >4.5 mg/dL, Black patients, patients with multiorgan transplants or secondary transplants, or those with high levels of PRA. In patients at high immunologic risk, the safety and efficacy of sirolimus used in combination with cyclosporine and corticosteroids have not been studied beyond 1 year; therefore, after the first 12 months following transplantation, consider any adjustments to the immunosuppressive regimen on the basis of the clinical status of the patient. The safety and efficacy of sirolimus have not been established in patients younger than 13 years or in pediatric renal transplant patients younger than 18 years who are considered at high immunologic risk. The safety and efficacy of de novo use of sirolimus without cyclosporine have not been established in renal transplant patients. The safety and efficacy of conversion from calcineurin inhibitors to sirolimus in maintenance renal transplant patients have not been established.

Local Anesthetic/Vasoconstrictor Precautions No information available to require special precautions

Effects on Dental Treatment Key adverse event(s) related to dental treatment: Mouth ulceration, oral candida infection, stomatitis, gingival hyperplasia, gingivitis, and dysphagia (see Dental Comment)

Effects on Bleeding Thrombocytopenia (15% to 30%) has been associated with use; severe thrombocytopenia (rare) may be associated with delayed coagulation. Consultation to ensure adequate platelet counts may be considered in patients with signs/symptoms or a history of thrombocytopenia.

Adverse Reactions Incidence of many adverse effects is dose related. Reported events exclusive to renal transplant patients unless otherwise noted. Frequency not always defined.

Cardiovascular: Peripheral edema (≥20% to 58%, LAM and renal transplants), hypertension (49%), edema (18% to 20%), chest pain (LAM), deep vein thrombosis, pulmonary embolism, tachycardia
Central nervous system: Headache (≥20% to 34%, LAM and renal transplants), pain (29% to 33%), dizziness (LAM)
Dermatologic: Acne vulgaris (≥20% to 22%, LAM and renal transplants), skin rash (10% to 20%)
Endocrine & metabolic: Hypertriglyceridemia (45% to 57%), hypercholesterolemia (≥20% to 46%, LAM and renal transplants), amenorrhea, diabetes mellitus, hypermenorrhea, hypervolemia, hypokalemia, increased lactate dehydrogenase, menstrual disease, ovarian cyst
Gastrointestinal: Constipation (36% to 38%), abdominal pain (≥20% to 36%, LAM and renal transplants), diarrhea (≥20% to 35%, LAM and renal transplants), nausea (≥20% to 31%, LAM and renal transplants), stomatitis (3% to >20%)
Genitourinary: Urinary tract infection (33%)
Hematologic & oncologic: Anemia (23% to 33%), thrombocytopenia (14% to 30%), lymphoproliferative disorder (≤3%; including lymphoma), skin carcinoma (≤3%; includes basal cell carcinoma, squamous cell carcinoma, melanoma), hemolytic-uremic syndrome, leukopenia, lymphocele, thrombotic thrombocytopenic purpura

Infection: Herpes simplex infection, herpes zoster, sepsis
Neuromuscular & skeletal: Arthralgia (25% to 31%), myalgia (LAM), osteonecrosis
Renal: Increased serum creatinine (39% to 40%), pyelonephritis
Respiratory: Nasopharyngitis (LAM), epistaxis, pneumonia, upper respiratory tract infection (LAM)
Miscellaneous: Wound healing impairment
<3%, postmarketing, and/or case reports: Abnormal hepatic function tests, anaphylactoid reaction, anaphylaxis, angioedema, ascites, azoospermia, cardiac tamponade, cytomegalovirus, dehiscence (fascial), Epstein-Barr infection, exfoliative dermatitis, fluid retention, focal segmental glomerulosclerosis, gingival hyperplasia, hepatic necrosis, hepatotoxicity, hyperglycemia, hypersensitivity angiitis, hypersensitivity reaction, hypophosphatemia, incisional hernia, increased serum ALT, increased serum AST, increased susceptibility to infection (including opportunistic), interstitial pulmonary disease (dose related; includes pneumonitis, pulmonary fibrosis, and bronchiolitis obliterans organizing pneumonia with no identified infectious etiology), joint disorders, lymphedema, mycobacterium infection, nephrotic syndrome, neutropenia, pancreatitis, pancytopenia, pericardial effusion, pleural effusion, pneumonia due to *Pneumocystis carinii*, progressive multifocal leukoencephalopathy, proteinuria, pseudomembranous colitis, pulmonary alveolitis, pulmonary hemorrhage, renal disease (BK virus-associated), reversible posterior leukoencephalopathy syndrome, tuberculosis, weight loss, wound dehiscence

Dosing

Adult & Geriatric

Low-to-moderate immunologic risk renal transplant patients: Oral:
<40 kg: Loading dose: 3 mg/m^2 on day 1, followed by maintenance dosing of 1 mg/m^2 once daily
≥40 kg: Loading dose: 6 mg on day 1; maintenance: 2 mg once daily

High immunologic risk renal transplant patients: Oral: Loading dose: Up to 15 mg on day 1; maintenance: 5 mg/day; obtain trough concentration between days 5 to 7 and adjust accordingly. Continue concurrent cyclosporine/sirolimus/corticosteroid therapy for 1 year following transplantation. Further adjustment of the regimen must be based on clinical status.

Dosage adjustment for renal transplantation: Sirolimus dosages should be adjusted to maintain trough concentrations within desired range based on risk and concomitant therapy. Maximum daily dose: 40 mg. Dosage should be adjusted at intervals of 7 to 14 days to account for the long half-life of sirolimus. In general, dose proportionality may be assumed. New sirolimus dose **equals** current dose **multiplied by** (target concentration **divided by** current concentration). **Note:** If large dose increase is required, consider loading dose calculated as:

Loading dose **equals** (new maintenance dose **minus** current maintenance dose) **multiplied by** 3

Maximum dose in 1 day: 40 mg; if required dose is >40 mg (due to loading dose), divide loading dose over 2 days. Whole blood concentrations should not be used as the sole basis for dosage adjustment (monitor clinical signs/symptoms, tissue biopsy, and laboratory parameters).

Maintenance therapy after withdrawal of cyclosporine: Cyclosporine withdrawal is not recommended in high immunological risk patients. Following 2 to 4 months of combined therapy, withdrawal of cyclosporine may be considered in low-to-moderate immunologic risk patients. Cyclosporine should be discontinued over 4 to 8 weeks, and a necessary increase in the dosage of sirolimus (up to fourfold) should be anticipated due to removal of metabolic inhibition by cyclosporine and to maintain adequate immunosuppressive effects. Dose-adjusted trough target concentrations are typically 16 to 24 ng/mL for the first year post-transplant and 12 to 20 ng/mL thereafter (measured by chromatographic methodology).

Lymphangioleiomyomatosis: Adults: Oral: Initial: 2 mg once daily. Obtain trough concentration in 10 to 20 days; adjust dose to maintain a target concentration of 5 to 15 ng/mL.

Dosage adjustment for lymphangioleiomyomatosis: Once the maintenance dose is adjusted, further adjustments should be made at 7 to 14 day intervals to account for the long half-life of sirolimus. In general, dose proportionality may be assumed. New sirolimus dose **equals** current dose **multiplied by** (target concentration **divided by** current concentration). Once a stable dose is achieved, trough concentrations should be assessed at least every 3 months.

Graft-versus-host disease (GVHD): Oral:
GVHD prophylaxis (off-label use): 12 mg loading dose on day -3, followed by 4 mg daily (target trough level: 3 to 12 ng/mL); taper off after 6 to 9 months (Armand 2008; Cutler 2007)
Treatment of refractory acute GVHD (off-label use): 4 to 5 mg/m^2 for 14 days (no loading dose) (Benito 2001)
Treatment of chronic GVHD (off-label use): 6 mg loading dose, followed by 2 mg daily (target trough level: 7 to 12 ng/mL) for 6 to 9 months (Couriel 2005)

Heart transplantation (off-label use): Oral: **Note:** The use of sirolimus in the immediate post-cardiac transplant period (ie, *de novo* heart transplant) as a primary immunosuppressant has fallen out of favor due to adverse effects (eg, impaired wound healing and infection); however, patients may be converted to sirolimus from a calcineurin inhibitor (after at least 6 months from time of transplant [Costanzo 2010]) or may have sirolimus added to a calcineurin inhibitor to prevent or minimize further transplant related vasculopathy or renal toxicity due to calcineurin inhibitor use.

Conversion from a calcineurin inhibitor (CNI) (ie, cyclosporine, tacrolimus): Reduce cyclosporine by 25 mg twice daily or tacrolimus by 1 mg twice daily followed by initiation of sirolimus 1 mg once daily; adjust sirolimus dose to target trough level of 8 to 14 ng/mL, withdraw CNI, repeat biopsy 2 weeks after CNI withdrawal (Topilsky 2012). Alternatively, maintain CNI concentrations and initiate sirolimus 1 mg once daily for 1 week; adjust sirolimus to target trough levels of 10 to 15 ng/mL over 2 weeks, then reduce CNI to target 50% of therapeutic concentrations and after 2 weeks evaluate for rejection. If no rejection, continue same regimen for an additional month, then reduce CNI to 25% of therapeutic concentrations with repeat biopsy 2 weeks later; if no rejection, may discontinue CNI after 2 weeks and continue to maintain sirolimus trough levels of 10 to 15 ng/mL (usual doses required to maintain target levels: 1 to 8 mg daily) (Kushwaha 2005).

Conversion from antiproliferative drug (ie, azathioprine or mycophenolate) while maintaining calcineurin inhibitor: Upon discontinuation of antiproliferative, administer sirolimus 6 mg loading dose followed by 2 mg once daily titrated to a target trough level of 4 to 15 ng/mL (Mancini 2003) or 4 to 12 ng/mL per ISHLT recommendations (Costanzo 2010).

Renal angiomyolipoma (off-label use): Oral: Initial: 0.5 mg/m^2 once daily titrated to a target trough level of 3 to 6 ng/mL (may increase to target trough level of 6 to 10 ng/mL if <10% reduction in lesion diameters at 2 months) for 2 years (Davies 2011)

Pediatric

Low-to-moderate immunologic risk renal transplant patients: Adolescents ≥13 years: Oral: Refer to adult dosing.

Renal Impairment No dosage adjustment is necessary. However, adjustment of regimen (including discontinuation of therapy) should be considered when used concurrently with cyclosporine and elevated or increasing serum creatinine is noted.

Hepatic Impairment

Loading dose: No dosage adjustment is necessary.

Maintenance dose:

Mild to moderate impairment (Child Pugh classes A and B): Reduce maintenance dose by ~33%.

Severe impairment (Child-Pugh class C): Reduce maintenance dose by ~50%.

Mechanism of Action

Sirolimus inhibits T-lymphocyte activation and proliferation in response to antigenic and cytokine stimulation and inhibits antibody production. Its mechanism differs from other immunosuppressants. Sirolimus binds to FKBP-12, an intracellular protein, to form an immunosuppressive complex which inhibits the regulatory kinase, mTOR (mechanistic target of rapamycin). This inhibition suppresses cytokine mediated T-cell proliferation, halting progression from the G1 to the S phase of the cell cycle. It inhibits acute rejection of allografts and prolongs graft survival.

In lymphangioleiomyomatosis, the mTOR signaling pathway is activated through the loss of the tuberous sclerosis complex (TSC) gene function (resulting in cellular proliferation and release of lymphangiogenic growth factors). By inhibiting the mTOR pathway, sirolimus prevents the proliferation of lymphangioleiomyomatosis cells.

Contraindications Hypersensitivity to sirolimus or any component of the formulation

Warnings/Precautions

[US Boxed Warning]: Immunosuppressive agents, including sirolimus, increase the risk of infection and may be associated with the development of lymphoma. Immune suppression may also increase the risk of opportunistic infections including activation of latent viral infections (including BK virus-associated nephropathy), fatal infections, and sepsis. Prophylactic treatment for *Pneumocystis jirovecii* pneumonia (PCP) should be administered for 1 year post-transplant; prophylaxis for cytomegalovirus (CMV) should be taken for 3 months post-transplant in patients at risk for CMV. Progressive multifocal leukoencephalopathy (PML), an opportunistic CNS infection caused by reactivation of the JC virus, has been reported in patients receiving immunosuppressive therapy, including sirolimus. Clinical findings of PML include apathy, ataxia, cognitive deficiency, confusion, and hemiparesis; promptly evaluate any patient presenting with neurological changes; consider decreasing the degree of immunosuppression with consideration to the risk of organ rejection in transplant patients.

[US Boxed Warning]: Sirolimus is not recommended for use in liver or lung transplantation. Bronchial anastomotic dehiscence cases have been reported in lung transplant patients when sirolimus was used as part of an immunosuppressive regimen; most of these reactions were fatal. Studies indicate an association with an increased risk of hepatic artery thrombosis (HAT), graft failure, and increased mortality (with evidence of infection) in liver transplant patients when sirolimus is used in combination with cyclosporine and/or tacrolimus. Most cases of HAT occurred within 30 days of transplant.

In renal transplant patients, *de novo* use without cyclosporine has been associated with higher rates of acute rejection. Sirolimus should be used in combination with cyclosporine (and corticosteroids) initially when used in renal transplant patients. Cyclosporine may be withdrawn in low-to-moderate immunologic risk patients after 2 to 4 months, in conjunction with an increase in sirolimus dosage. In high immunologic risk patients, use in combination with cyclosporine and corticosteroids is recommended for the first year. Safety and efficacy of combination therapy with cyclosporine in high immunologic risk patients has not been studied beyond 12 months of treatment; adjustment of immunosuppressive therapy beyond 12 months should be considered based on clinical judgment. Monitor renal function closely when combined with cyclosporine; consider dosage adjustment or discontinue in patients with increasing serum creatinine.

May increase serum creatinine and decrease GFR. Use caution when used concurrently with medications which may alter renal function. May delay recovery of renal function in patients with delayed allograft function. Increased urinary protein excretion has been observed when converting renal transplant patients from calcineurin inhibitors to sirolimus during maintenance therapy. A higher level of proteinuria prior to sirolimus conversion correlates with a higher degree of proteinuria after conversion. In some patients, proteinuria may reach nephrotic levels; nephrotic syndrome (new onset) has been reported. Increased risk of BK viral-associated nephropathy which may impair renal function and cause graft loss; consider decreasing immunosuppressive burden if evidence of deteriorating renal function.

Use caution with hepatic impairment; a reduction in the maintenance dose is recommended. Has been associated with an increased risk of fluid accumulation and lymphocele; peripheral edema, lymphedema, ascites, and pleural and pericardial effusions (including significant effusions and tamponade) were reported; use with caution in patients in whom fluid accumulation may be poorly tolerated, such as in cardiovascular disease (heart failure or hypertension) and pulmonary disease. Cases of interstitial lung disease (ILD) (eg, pneumonitis, bronchiolitis obliterans organizing pneumonia [BOOP], pulmonary fibrosis) have been observed (some fatal); may be associated with pulmonary hypertension (including pulmonary arterial hypertension) and risk may be increased with higher trough levels. ILD may resolve with dose reduction or discontinuation of therapy. Potentially significant drug-drug interactions may exist, requiring dose or frequency adjustment, additional monitoring, and/or selection of alternative therapy. Concurrent use with a calcineurin inhibitor (cyclosporine, tacrolimus) may increase the risk of calcineurin inhibitor-induced hemolytic uremic syndrome/thrombotic thrombocytopenic purpura/thrombotic microangiopathy (HUS/TTP/TMA). Immunosuppressants may affect response to vaccination. Therefore, during treatment with sirolimus, vaccination may be less effective. The use of live vaccines should be avoided.

Hypersensitivity reactions, including anaphylactic/anaphylactoid reactions, angioedema, exfoliative dermatitis, and hypersensitivity vasculitis have been reported. Angioedema risk is increased in patients with elevated sirolimus levels and/or concurrent use with other drugs known to cause angioedema (eg, ACE inhibitors). Angioedema resolved following discontinuation or dose reduction in some cases. Immunosuppressant therapy is associated with an increased risk of skin cancer; limit sun and ultraviolet light exposure; use appropriate sun protection. May increase serum lipids (cholesterol and triglycerides); use with caution in patients with hyperlipidemia; monitor cholesterol/lipids; if hyperlipidemia occurs, follow current guidelines for management (diet, exercise, lipid lowering agents); antihyperlipidemic therapy may not be effective in normalizing levels. May be associated with wound dehiscence and impaired healing; use caution in the perioperative period. Patients with a body mass index (BMI) >30 kg/m^2 are at increased risk for abnormal wound healing.

Sirolimus tablets and oral solution are not bioequivalent, due to differences in absorption. Clinical equivalence was seen using 2 mg tablet and 2 mg solution. It is not known if higher doses are also clinically equivalent. Monitor sirolimus levels if changes in dosage forms are made. Some dosage forms may contain propylene glycol; large amounts are potentially toxic and have been associated hyperosmolality, lactic acidosis, seizures, and respiratory depression; use caution (AAP, 1997; Zar 2007). **[US Boxed Warning]: Should only be used by physicians experienced in immunosuppressive therapy and management of transplant patients. Adequate laboratory and supportive medical resources must be readily available.** Sirolimus concentrations are dependent on the assay method (eg, chromatographic and immunoassay) used; assay methods are not interchangeable. Variations in methods to determine sirolimus whole blood concentrations, as well as interlaboratory variations, may result in improper dosage adjustments, which may lead to subtherapeutic or toxic levels. Determine the assay method used to assure consistency (or accommodations if changes occur), and for monitoring purposes, be aware of alterations to assay method or reference range and that values from different assays may not be interchangeable.

Drug Interactions

Metabolism/Transport Effects **Substrate** of CYP3A4 (major), P-glycoprotein; **Note:** Assignment of Major/Minor substrate status based on clinically relevant drug interaction potential

Avoid Concomitant Use

Avoid concomitant use of Sirolimus with any of the following: Antihepaciviral Combination Products; BCG (Intravesical); Conivaptan; Crizotinib; Deferiprone; Dipyrone; Enzalutamide; Fusidic Acid (Systemic); Idelalisib; MiFEPRIStone; Natalizumab; Pimecrolimus; Posaconazole; Tacrolimus (Systemic); Tacrolimus (Topical); Tofacitinib; Vaccines (Live); Voriconazole

Increased Effect/Toxicity

Sirolimus may increase the levels/effects of: ACE Inhibitors; CloZAPine; CycloSPORINE (Systemic); Deferiprone; Fingolimod; Leflunomide; Natalizumab; Tacrolimus (Systemic); Tacrolimus (Topical); Tofacitinib; Vaccines (Live)

The levels/effects of Sirolimus may be increased by: Antihepaciviral Combination Products; Aprepitant; Boceprevir; Clotrimazole (Topical); Conivaptan; Crizotinib; CycloSPORINE (Systemic); CYP3A4 Inhibitors (Moderate); CYP3A4 Inhibitors (Strong); Dasatinib; Denosumab; Dipyrone; Fluconazole; Fosaprepitant; Fusidic Acid (Systemic); Idelalisib; Isavuconazonium Sulfate; Itraconazole; Ivacaftor; Ketoconazole (Systemic); Macrolide Antibiotics; Micafungin; MiFEPRIStone; Nelfinavir; Netupitant; Ocrelizumab; Palbociclib; P-glycoprotein/ABCB1 Inhibitors; Pimecrolimus; Posaconazole; Promazine; Ranolazine; Roflumilast; Stiripentol; Tacrolimus (Systemic); Tacrolimus (Topical); Telaprevir; Trastuzumab; Venetoclax; Voriconazole

Decreased Effect

Sirolimus may decrease the levels/effects of: Antidiabetic Agents; BCG (Intravesical); Coccidioides immitis Skin Test; Nivolumab; Sipuleucel-T; Tacrolimus (Systemic); Tertomotide; Vaccines (Inactivated); Vaccines (Live)

The levels/effects of Sirolimus may be decreased by: Bosentan; CYP3A4 Inducers (Moderate); CYP3A4 Inducers (Strong); Dabrafenib; Deferasirox; Echinacea; Efavirenz; Enzalutamide; Mitotane; Siltuximab; St John's Wort; Tocilizumab

Food Interactions Grapefruit juice may decrease clearance of sirolimus. Ingestion with high-fat meals decreases peak concentrations but increases AUC by 23% to 35%. Management: Avoid grapefruit juice. Take consistently (either with or without food) to minimize variability.

Pharmacodynamics/Kinetics

Half-life Elimination

Children: 13.7 ± 6.2 hours

Adults: Mean: 62 hours (range; 46 to 78 hours); extended in hepatic impairment (Child-Pugh class A or B) to 113 hours

Time to Peak Oral solution: 1 to 3 hours; Tablet: 1 to 6 hours

Pregnancy Risk Factor C

Pregnancy Considerations Adverse events have been observed in animal reproduction studies. Effective contraception must be initiated before therapy with sirolimus and continued for 12 weeks after discontinuation.

The National Transplantation Pregnancy Registry (NTPR) is a registry which follows pregnancies which occur in maternal transplant recipients or those fathered by male transplant recipients. The NTPR encourages reporting of pregnancies following solid organ transplant by contacting them at 877-955-6877 or NTPR@giftoflifeinstitute.org.

Breastfeeding Considerations It is not known if sirolimus is excreted in breast milk. Due to the potential for serious adverse reactions in the nursing infant, the manufacturer recommends a decision be made whether to discontinue nursing or to discontinue the drug, taking into account the importance of treatment to the mother.

Dosage Forms

Solution, Oral:

Rapamune: 1 mg/mL (60 mL)

Tablet, Oral:

Rapamune: 0.5 mg, 1 mg, 2 mg

Generic: 0.5 mg, 1 mg, 2 mg

Dental Comment Consider a medical consultation prior to any invasive dental procedure in patients who have received an organ transplant; delayed wound healing due to the immunosuppressive effects and an increased potential for postoperative infection may be of concern.

SITagliptin (sit a GLIP tin)

Related Information

Endocrine Disorders and Pregnancy *on page 1781*

Brand Names: US Januvia

Brand Names: Canada Januvia

Pharmacologic Category Antidiabetic Agent, Dipeptidyl Peptidase 4 (DPP-4) Inhibitor

Use Diabetes mellitus, type 2: As an adjunct to diet and exercise to improve glycemic control in adults with type 2 diabetes mellitus (noninsulin dependent) as monotherapy or combination therapy.

Local Anesthetic/Vasoconstrictor Precautions No information available to require special precautions

Effects on Dental Treatment Sitagliptin-dependent patients with diabetes should be appointed for dental treatment in morning in order to minimize chance of stress-induced hypoglycemia.

Effects on Bleeding No information available to require special precautions

Adverse Reactions Reported with monotherapy.

1% to 10%:

Cardiovascular: Peripheral edema (2%)

Endocrine & metabolic: Hypoglycemia (1%)

Gastrointestinal: Diarrhea (4%), constipation (3%), nausea (2%)

Neuromuscular & skeletal: Osteoarthritis (1%)

Respiratory: Nasopharyngitis (5%), pharyngitis (1%), upper respiratory tract infection (viral; 1%)

<1%, postmarketing, and/or case reports: Abdominal distress (includes abdominal pain, abdominal tenderness), acne rosacea, acute pancreatitis (including hemorrhagic or necrotizing forms with some fatalities), acute renal failure (possibly requiring dialysis), anaphylaxis, anemia, angioedema, anxiety, arthralgia, ataxia, back pain, bundle branch block, cough, decreased appetite, depression, dizziness, drowsiness, dysmenorrhea, dyspepsia, erectile dysfunction, erythema, exfoliative dermatitis, facial edema, fever, flatulence, gastritis (*Helicobacter*), gastroesophageal reflux disease, headache, hyperhidrosis, hypertension, hypersensitivity, hypersensitivity vasculitis, hypertonia, hypotension, increased liver enzymes, increased serum creatinine, increased uric acid, leukocytosis, limb pain, liver steatosis, malaise, migraine, myalgia, orthostatic hypotension, pain, palpitations, pemphigoid, peripheral neuropathy, pruritus, renal insufficiency, retching, severe arthralgia (FDA Safety Alert, Aug 28, 2015), sialorrhea, skin rash (including macular), Stevens-Johnson syndrome, urticaria, vomiting, xeroderma

General Dosage Range Dosage adjustment recommended in patients with renal impairment

Oral: *Adults:* 100 mg once daily

Mechanism of Action Sitagliptin inhibits dipeptidyl peptidase IV (DPP-IV) enzyme resulting in prolonged active incretin levels. Incretin hormones (eg, glucagon-like peptide-1 [GLP-1] and glucose-dependent insulinotropic polypeptide [GIP]) regulate glucose homeostasis by increasing insulin synthesis and release from pancreatic beta cells and decreasing glucagon secretion from pancreatic alpha cells. Decreased glucagon secretion results in decreased hepatic glucose production. Under normal physiologic circumstances, incretin hormones are released by the intestine throughout the day and levels are increased in response to a meal; incretin hormones are rapidly inactivated by the DPP-IV enzyme.

Pharmacodynamics/Kinetics

Half-life Elimination 12.4 hours

Time to Peak 1 to 4 hours

Pregnancy Risk Factor B

Pregnancy Considerations Adverse events have not been observed in animal reproduction studies.

In women with diabetes, maternal hyperglycemia can be associated with congenital malformations as well as adverse effects in the fetus, neonate, and the mother (ACOG 2005; ADA 2016c; Kitzmiller 2008; Metzger 2007). To prevent adverse outcomes, prior to conception and throughout pregnancy, maternal blood glucose and HbA_{1c} should be kept as close to target goals as possible but without causing significant hypoglycemia (ACOG 2013; ADA 2016c; Blumer 2013; Kitzmiller 2008). Agents other than sitagliptin are currently recommended to treat diabetes in pregnant women (ACOG 2013; Blumer 2013).

Health care providers are encouraged to enroll women exposed to sitagliptin during pregnancy in the registry (1-800-986-8999).

Sitagliptin and Metformin
(sit a GLIP tin & met FOR min)

Related Information

MetFORMIN *on page 1069*

SITagliptin *on page 1487*

Brand Names: US Janumet; Janumet XR

Brand Names: Canada Janumet; Janumet XR

Pharmacologic Category Antidiabetic Agent, Biguanide; Antidiabetic Agent, Dipeptidyl Peptidase 4 (DPP-4) Inhibitor

Use Diabetes mellitus, type 2: As an adjunct to diet and exercise to improve glycemic control in adults with type 2 diabetes mellitus when treatment with both sitagliptin and metformin is appropriate

Local Anesthetic/Vasoconstrictor Precautions No information available to require special precautions

Effects on Dental Treatment Sitagliptin- and metformin-dependent patients with diabetes (noninsulin dependent, Type 2) should be appointed for dental treatment in morning in order to minimize chance of stress-induced hypoglycemia.

Effects on Bleeding No information available to require special precautions

Adverse Reactions Also see individual agents.

1% to 10%:

Central nervous system: Headache (6%)

Gastrointestinal: Diarrhea (8%), nausea (5%), abdominal pain (3%), vomiting (2%)

Respiratory: Upper respiratory tract infection (6%)

<1%, postmarketing and/or case reports: Arthralgia, back pain, constipation, hypersensitivity reaction (including anaphylaxis, angioedema, skin rash, urticaria, hypersensitivity angiitis, exfoliative skin conditions

[including Stevens-Johnson syndrome]), increased liver enzymes, lactic acidosis, limb pain, myalgia, pancreatitis (including hemorrhagic or necrotizing), pemphigoid, pruritus, renal failure, renal insufficiency, severe arthralgia (FDA Safety Alert, Aug 28, 2015)

General Dosage Range Oral: *Adults:*

Immediate release: Sitagliptin 50 mg and metformin 500 to 1,000 mg twice daily (maximum: sitagliptin 100 mg/metformin 2,000 mg per day)

Extended release: Sitagliptin 100 mg and metformin 1,000 to 2,000 mg once daily (maximum: sitagliptin 100 mg/metformin 2,000 mg per day)

Mechanism of Action Sitagliptin inhibits dipeptidyl peptidase IV (DPP-IV) enzymes resulting in prolonged active incretin levels. Incretin hormones [eg, glucagon-like peptide-1 (GLP-1) and glucose-dependent insulinotropic polypeptide (GIP)] regulate glucose homeostasis by increasing insulin synthesis and release from pancreatic beta cells and decreasing glucagon secretion from pancreatic alpha cells. Decreased glucagon secretion results in decreased hepatic glucose production. Under normal physiologic circumstances, incretin hormones are released by the intestine throughout the day and levels are increased in response to a meal; incretin hormones are rapidly inactivated by DPP-IV enzymes.

Metformin decreases hepatic glucose production, decreasing intestinal absorption of glucose, and improves insulin sensitivity (increases peripheral glucose uptake and utilization).

Pregnancy Risk Factor B

Pregnancy Considerations

Animal reproduction studies have not been conducted with this combination. See individual agents.

Health professionals are encouraged to report any prenatal exposure to sitagliptin/metformin combination by contacting Merck's pregnancy registry (1-800-986-8999).

Sitagliptin and Simvastatin

(sit a GLIP tin & sim va STAT in)

Brand Names: US Juvisync™ [DSC]

Pharmacologic Category Antidiabetic Agent, Dipeptidyl Peptidase 4 (DPP-4) Inhibitor; Antilipemic Agent, HMG-CoA Reductase Inhibitor

Use For use when treatment with both sitagliptin and simvastatin is appropriate:

Sitagliptin: Management of type 2 diabetes mellitus (noninsulin dependent, NIDDM) as an adjunct to diet and exercise as monotherapy or in combination therapy with other antidiabetic agents

Simvastatin: Used with dietary therapy for the following:

Secondary prevention of cardiovascular events in hypercholesterolemic patients with established coronary heart disease (CHD) or at high risk for CHD: To reduce cardiovascular morbidity (myocardial infarction, coronary/noncoronary revascularization procedures) and mortality; to reduce the risk of stroke

Hyperlipidemias: To reduce elevations in total cholesterol (total-C), LDL-C, apolipoprotein B, triglycerides, and VLDL-C, and to increase HDL-C in patients with primary hypercholesterolemia (elevations of 1 or more components are present in Fredrickson type IIa, IIb, III, and IV hyperlipidemias); treatment of homozygous familial hypercholesterolemia

Primary and secondary prevention of atherosclerotic cardiovascular disease (ASCVD) according to the American College of Cardiology/American Heart Association: To reduce the risk of ASCVD in patients with clinical ASCVD (eg, coronary heart disease, stroke/TIA, or peripheral arterial disease presumed to be of atherosclerotic origin) who are greater than 75 years of age or not a candidate for high-intensity statin therapy; in patients without clinical ASCVD if LDL-C is 190 mg/dL or greater and not a candidate for high-intensity statin therapy; in patients without clinical ASCVD who have type 1 or type 2 diabetes and are between 40 and 75 years of age; in patients with an estimated 10-year ASCVD risk 7.5% or greater and who are between 40 and 75 years of age (Stone, 2013). Specific recommendations from the Kidney Disease: Improving Global Outcomes (KDIGO) organization have also been released for patients with chronic kidney disease (KDIGO [Tonelli, 2013]).

Local Anesthetic/Vasoconstrictor Precautions No information available to require special precautions

Effects on Dental Treatment Key adverse event(s) related to dental treatment: Assess unusual presentations of muscle weakness or myopathy resulting from lipid therapy such as patient having a difficult time brushing teeth or weakness with chewing. Refer patient back to their physician for evaluation and adjustment of lipid therapy. Sitagliptin-dependent patients with diabetes should be appointed for dental treatment in morning in order to minimize chance of stress-induced hypoglycemia.

Effects on Bleeding No information available to require special precautions

Adverse Reactions See individual agents.

General Dosage Range Dosage adjustment recommended in patients on concomitant therapy or with renal impairment.

Oral: *Adults:* Initial: Sitagliptin 100 mg and simvastatin 40 mg once daily

Mechanism of Action

Simvastatin: A methylated derivative of lovastatin that acts by competitively inhibiting 3-hydroxy-3-methylglutaryl-coenzyme A (HMG-CoA) reductase, the enzyme that catalyzes the rate-limiting step in cholesterol biosynthesis. In addition to the ability of HMG-CoA reductase inhibitors to decrease levels of high-sensitivity C-reactive protein (hsCRP), they also possess pleiotropic properties including improved endothelial function, reduced inflammation at the site of the coronary plaque, inhibition of platelet aggregation, and anticoagulant effects (de Denus, 2002; Ray, 2005).

Sitagliptin: Inhibits dipeptidyl peptidase IV (DPP-IV) enzyme resulting in prolonged active incretin levels. Incretin hormones (eg, glucagon-like peptide-1 [GLP-1] and glucose-dependent insulinotropic polypeptide [GIP]) regulate glucose homeostasis by increasing insulin synthesis and release from pancreatic beta cells and decreasing glucagon secretion from pancreatic alpha cells. Decreased glucagon secretion results in decreased hepatic glucose production. Under normal physiologic circumstances, incretin hormones are released by the intestine throughout the day and levels are increased in response to a meal; incretin hormones are rapidly inactivated by the DPP-IV enzyme.

Pregnancy Risk Factor X

Pregnancy Considerations Use is contraindicated in pregnant women. See individual agents.

Sodium Bicarbonate

(SOW dee um bye KAR bun ate)

Brand Names: US Neut

Pharmacologic Category Alkalinizing Agent; Antacid; Electrolyte Supplement, Oral; Electrolyte Supplement, Parenteral

Use

Management of metabolic acidosis; gastric hyperacidity; alkalinization of the urine; treatment of hyperkalemia; management of overdose of certain drugs, including tricyclic antidepressants and aspirin

Neutralizing additive (dental use): Improves onset of analgesia and reduces injection site pain by adjusting lidocaine with epinephrine solution to a more physiologic pH.

Local Anesthetic/Vasoconstrictor Precautions No information available to require special precautions

Effects on Dental Treatment Lidocaine with epinephrine when mixed with sodium bicarbonate, in a ratio of 10:1, accelerates analgesia onset and decreases the pain of injection.

Effects on Bleeding No information available to require special precautions

Adverse Reactions

Frequency not defined.

Cardiovascular: Edema, exacerbation of congestive heart failure

Central nervous system: Cerebral hemorrhage

Endocrine & metabolic: Acidosis (intracranial), hypernatremia, hypocalcemia, hypokalemia, metabolic alkalosis, milk-alkali syndrome (especially with renal dysfunction)

Gastrointestinal: Abdominal distention, eructation, flatulence (oral administration)

Neuromuscular & skeletal: Tetany

Respiratory: Pulmonary edema

General Dosage Range

IV: *Children and Adults:* Dosage varies greatly depending on indication

Oral:

Children: 1-10 mEq/kg/day as a single dose **or** divided every 4-6 hours

Adults <60 years: 0.5-200 mEq/kg/day in 4-5 divided doses **or** 325 mg to 2 g 1-4 times/day (maximum: 16 g [200 mEq] day)

Adults ≥60 years: 0.5-100 mEq/kg/day in 4-6 divided doses **or** 325 mg to 2 g 1-4 times/day (maximum: 8 g [100 mEq] day)

Mechanism of Action

Dissociates to provide bicarbonate ion which neutralizes hydrogen ion concentration and raises blood and urinary pH

Neutralizing additive (dental use): Increases pH of lidocaine and epinephrine solution to improve tolerability and increase tissue uptake

Pharmacodynamics/Kinetics

Onset of Action Oral: 15 minutes; IV: Rapid

Duration of Action Oral: 1 to 3 hours; IV: 8 to 10 minutes

Pregnancy Risk Factor C

Pregnancy Considerations Animal reproduction studies have not been conducted. Medications used for the treatment of cardiac arrest in pregnancy are the same as in the non-pregnant woman. Doses and indications should follow current Advanced Cardiovascular Life Support guidelines. Appropriate medications should not be withheld due to concerns of fetal teratogenicity (Campbell 2009; Jeejeebhoy [AHA] 2015). Antacids containing sodium bicarbonate should not be used during pregnancy due to their potential to cause metabolic alkalosis and fluid overload (Mahadevan 2007).

Sodium Chloride (SOW dee um KLOR ide)

Brand Names: US 4-Way Saline [OTC]; Afrin Saline Nasal Mist [OTC]; Allclenz [OTC] [DSC]; Altachlore [OTC]; Altamist Spray [OTC]; Atrapro Dermal Spray; Ayr Nasal Mist Allergy/Sinus [OTC]; Ayr Saline Nasal Drops [OTC]; Ayr Saline Nasal Gel [OTC]; Ayr Saline Nasal Neti Rinse [OTC]; Ayr Saline Nasal No-Drip [OTC]; AYR Saline Nasal Rinse [OTC]; Ayr Saline Nasal [OTC]; Ayr [OTC]; Baby Ayr Saline [OTC]; Broncho Saline [OTC]; Deep Sea Nasal Spray [OTC]; DiaB Klenz [OTC]; Elta Dermal Wound Cleanser [OTC]; Entsol Nasal Wash [OTC]; Entsol Nasal [OTC]; Entsol [OTC]; Humist [OTC]; HyperSal; MicroKlenz Wound Cleanser [OTC]; Muro 128 [OTC]; Na-Zone [OTC]; Nasal Moist [OTC]; Nebusal; Ocean Complete Sinus Rinse [OTC]; Ocean for Kids [OTC]; Ocean Nasal Moisturizer [OTC]; Ocean Nasal Spray [OTC]; Ocean Ultra Saline Mist [OTC]; Pretz Irrigation [OTC]; Pretz [OTC]; PulmoSal; RadiaKlenz [OTC]; Remedy 4-in-1 Body Cleanser [OTC]; Rhinaris [OTC]; Rhinase [OTC]; Safe Wash [OTC]; Saline Flush ZR; Saline Mist Spray [OTC]; Saljet Rinse [OTC]; Saljet [OTC]; Sea Soft Nasal Mist [OTC] [DSC]; Sea-Clens Wound Cleanser [OTC]; Sochlor [OTC]; Sodium Chloride Thermoject Syc [DSC]; SwabFlush Saline Flush; Ultra-Klenz [OTC]; Wound Wash Saline [OTC]

Pharmacologic Category Electrolyte Supplement, Parenteral; Genitourinary Irrigant; Irrigant; Lubricant, Ocular; Sodium Salt

Use

Parenteral: Restores sodium ion in patients with restricted oral intake (especially hyponatremia states or low salt syndrome).

Concentrated sodium chloride: Additive for parenteral fluid therapy

Hypertonic sodium chloride: For severe hyponatremia and hypochloremia

Hypotonic sodium chloride: Hydrating solution

Normal saline: Restores water/sodium losses

Ophthalmic: Reduces corneal edema

Inhalation: Restores moisture to pulmonary system; loosens and thins congestion caused by colds or allergies; diluent for bronchodilator solutions that require dilution before inhalation

Intranasal: Restores moisture to nasal membranes

Irrigation: Wound cleansing, irrigation, and flushing

Local Anesthetic/Vasoconstrictor Precautions No information available to require special precautions

Effects on Dental Treatment No significant effects or complications reported

Effects on Bleeding No information available to require special precautions

Adverse Reactions Frequency not defined.

Cardiovascular: Cardiac failure, hypotension (transient; especially with adult administration of 23.4% NaCl), localized phlebitis, thrombosis

Central nervous system: Osmotic demyelination syndrome (due to rapid correction of hyponatremia)

Endocrine & metabolic: Electrolyte disturbance (dilution of electrolytes), hypernatremia, hypervolemia, hypokalemia, water intoxication

Gastrointestinal: Nausea, vomiting (oral administration)

Respiratory: Bronchospasm (inhalation with hypertonic solutions), pulmonary edema

General Dosage Range

IV: *Children and Adults:* Dosage varies greatly depending on indication

Inhalation: *Children ≥2 years and Adults:* 1-3 sprays (1-3 mL)
Intranasal: *Children ≥2 years and Adults:* 2-3 sprays in each nostril as needed
Irrigation: *Children ≥2 years and Adults:* 1-3 L/day **or** spray affected area
Ophthalmic: *Adults:* Ointment: Apply once or more daily; Solution: Instill 1-2 drops into affected eye(s) every 3-4 hours

Mechanism of Action Principal extracellular cation; functions in fluid and electrolyte balance, osmotic pressure control, and water distribution

Pregnancy Risk Factor C

Pregnancy Considerations Animal reproduction studies have not been conducted. Sodium requirements do not change during pregnancy (IOM, 2004). Nasal saline rinses may be used for the treatment of pregnancy rhinitis (Wallace, 2008)

Sodium Hypochlorite

(SOW dee um hye poe KLOR ite)

Brand Names: US Anasept; Anasept Antimicrobial [OTC]; Anasept [OTC]; Di-Dak-Sol [OTC]; H-Chlor 12 [OTC]; H-Chlor 6 [OTC]; HySept [OTC]

Pharmacologic Category Disinfectant, Antibacterial (Topical)

Use Antiseptic: Treatment and prevention of skin and tissue infections; treatment of cuts, abrasions, and skin ulcers; use pre- and postsurgery.
Anasept, H-Chlor 6:
OTC use: Cleansing and removal of dirt, debris, and foreign material from skin abrasions, lacerations, minor irritations, cuts, exit sites, and intact skin (Anasept cleanser, H-Chlor 6), or management of conditions (Anasept gel).
Professional use: Cleansing of foreign materials (including microorganisms) from wounds (Anasept cleanser, H-Chlor 6) or management of wounds (Anasept gel, H-Chlor 6) such as stage I to IV pressure ulcers, diabetic foot and leg ulcers, post-surgical wounds, first- and second degree burns, and grafted and donor sites.

Local Anesthetic/Vasoconstrictor Precautions No information available to require special precautions

Effects on Dental Treatment No significant effects or complications reported

Effects on Bleeding No information available to require special precautions

Adverse Reactions Frequency not defined.
Dermatologic: Irritating to skin
Hematologic: Dissolves blood clots, delays clotting

General Dosage Range Topical: *Adults:*
Gel:
Indwelling catheter care: Apply sufficient amount to completely cover skin area around the indwelling catheter.
Ostomy care: Apply a thin layer.
Skin care: Apply a thin layer; repeat as needed.
Wound care: Apply thick layer (¼ to ½ inch) to entire wound bed; apply a thin layer to periwound skin area.
Liquid:
Skin cleansing: Apply to site.
Wound cleansing: Apply once daily (may be repeated up to a total of twice daily).
Solution 0.062%: Apply to wound and cover with dressing; repeat if necessary.
Solution 0.0125%, 0.125%, 0.25%, 0.5%:
Lightly to moderately exudative wounds: Apply once daily.
Highly exudative or contaminated wounds: Apply twice daily.

Sodium Iodide I^{131}

(SOW dee um EYE oh dide eye one THUR tee one)

Related Information
Endocrine Disorders and Pregnancy *on page 1781*

Brand Names: US Hicon

Pharmacologic Category Antithyroid Agent; Diagnostic Agent; Radiopharmaceutical

Use
Diagnostic agent: Diagnostic use in performance of radioactive iodide (RAI) uptake test to evaluate thyroid function.
Therapeutic agent: Treatment of hyperthyroidism and select cases of thyroid carcinomas (if the lesions take up iodide); palliative effects may be observed in patients with advanced thyroid malignancy if the metastatic lesions take up iodide.

Local Anesthetic/Vasoconstrictor Precautions No information available to require special precautions

Effects on Dental Treatment Key adverse event(s) related to dental treatment: Salivary gland pain and swelling; decreased salivation and taste, mucositis (see Dental Comment)

Effects on Bleeding No information available to require special precautions

Adverse Reactions Frequency not defined, dose dependent.
Cardiovascular: Chest pain, tachycardia
Central nervous system: Cerebral edema (in patients with iodine-avid brain metastases), metallic taste
Dermatologic: Alopecia, pruritus, skin lesion (ioderma), skin rash, urticaria
Endocrine & metabolic: Hyperthyroidism, hypoparathyroidism, hypothyroidism, thyroiditis, thyroid storm
Gastrointestinal: Gastritis, nausea (high dose used in treatment of thyroid cancer), odynophagia, salivary gland disease, sialadenitis, sore throat, unpleasant taste, vomiting
Genitourinary: Infertility (transient; may be permanent in males with repeated or high dose)
Hematologic & oncologic: Acute leukemia, anemia, bone marrow depression (high dose used in treatment of thyroid cancer), hematologic abnormality, leukopenia, solid tumor, thrombocytopenia
Hypersensitivity: Anaphylaxis, hypersensitivity reaction
Immunologic: Immunosuppression
Neuromuscular & skeletal: Neck discomfort (tenderness/swelling)
Ophthalmic: Lacrimation
Respiratory: Bronchospasm, cough, pulmonary fibrosis (in patients with iodine-avid lung metastases), radiation pneumonitis (in patients with iodine-avid lung metastases)
Miscellaneous: Chromosomal abnormality, local swelling, radiation injury
Postmarketing and/or case reports: Conjunctivitis, epiphora, neoplasm (rare; causative role not established), xerophthalmia, xerostomia (high dose used in treatment of thyroid cancer)

General Dosage Range Oral: *Adults:* Dosage varies greatly depending on product

Mechanism of Action Oral sodium iodide I^{131} is rapidly absorbed and distributed within the extracellular fluid of the body. Iodide is concentrated in the thyroid via the sodium/iodide symporter, and subsequently oxidized to iodine. Beta emission of sodium iodide I^{131} destroys thyroid tissue.

Pregnancy Risk Factor X

Pregnancy Considerations Use is contraindicated in pregnancy. Iodine-131 crosses the placenta and may cause severe and irreversible hypothyroidism in neonates. Pregnancy should be ruled out prior to therapy. Use of 2 effective methods of contraception is recommended (for females and males) during treatment and for at least 12 months following administration; if additional iodide I^{131} therapy or radionuclide imaging is anticipated, the use of 2 effective methods of contraception may be necessary for at least 1 year. Elective diagnostic procedures should be delayed until after delivery (Parker 2004).

Dental Comment Loss of saliva and sialolithiasis may develop. If this persists may lead to excessive dental caries. Immediately after treatment there may be pain and tenderness of the salivary gland, mucositis, and neck pain and swelling. All of these effects are dose-related and are typically temporary. Although very rare, other malignancies may develop including in the salivary glands. Hydration of patient and efforts to increase salivary flow may be advised after treatment.

Sodium Oxybate (SOW dee um ox i BATE)

Brand Names: US Xyrem

Brand Names: Canada Xyrem

Pharmacologic Category Central Nervous System Depressant

Use Narcolepsy: Treatment of cataplexy and excessive daytime sleepiness in patients with narcolepsy

Local Anesthetic/Vasoconstrictor Precautions No information available to require special precautions

Effects on Dental Treatment Key adverse event(s) related to dental treatment: Tooth ache (see Dental Comment).

Effects on Bleeding No information available to require special precautions

Adverse Reactions

>10%:

Central nervous system: Confusion (3% to 17%; dose-related), dizziness (9% to 15%)

Gastrointestinal: Nausea (8% to 20%, dose-related), vomiting (2% to 11%; dose-related)

1% to 10%:

Cardiovascular: Peripheral edema (≤3%)

Central nervous system: Drowsiness (8%), depression (3% to 7%), somnambulism (3% to 6%; dose-related), anxiety (2% to 6%), disturbance in attention (1% to 4%; dose-related), intoxicated feeling (3%; dose-related), irritability (3%; dose-related), pain (3%), sleep paralysis (3%), disorientation (2% to 3%; dose-related), paresthesia (2% to to 3%; dose-related), severe central nervous system depression (2%)

Dermatologic: Hyperhidrosis (1% to 3%)

Gastrointestinal: Diarrhea (3% to 4%), upper abdominal pain (3%)

Genitourinary: Urinary incontinence (3% to 7%; dose-related)

Neuromuscular & skeletal: Tremor (2% to 5%), limb pain (3%), cataplexy (2%)

Frequency not defined:

Central nervous system: Central nervous system depression

Respiratory: Respiratory depression

<1%, postmarketing, and/or case reports: Aggressive behavior, agitation, arthralgia, blurred vision, decreased appetite, falling, fluid retention, hallucination, hangover effect, headache, hypersensitivity reaction, hypertension, memory impairment, nocturia, panic attack, paranoia, psychosis, suicidal ideation, weight loss

General Dosage Range Dosage adjustment recommended in patients with hepatic impairment

Oral: *Adults:* Initial: 4.5 g nightly in 2 equal doses given at bedtime and 2.5 to 4 hours later; Maintenance (usual effective dose): 6 to 9 g daily (maximum: 9 g per night)

Mechanism of Action Sodium oxybate is derived from gamma aminobutyric acid (GABA) and acts as an inhibitory chemical transmitter in the brain. May function through specific receptors for gamma hydroxybutyrate (GHB) and GABA (B).

Pharmacodynamics/Kinetics

Half-life Elimination 30 to 60 minutes

Time to Peak 30 to 75 minutes

Pregnancy Risk Factor C

Pregnancy Considerations Adverse effects have been reported with maternal use. The injection formulation, when used as an anesthetic during labor and delivery, was shown to cross the placenta in concentrations ≤25% of maternal levels; a slight decrease in Apgar scores due to sleepiness in the neonate was observed. Sodium oxybate was not detected in infant blood 30 minutes after delivery.

Controlled Substance C-I (illicit use); C-III (medical use)

Prescribing and Access Restrictions

Sodium oxybate is deemed to have an approved REMS program. As a requirement of the REMS program, access to this medication is restricted. Sodium oxybate oral solution will be available only to prescribers and patients enrolled in the Xyrem REMS Program and dispensed to the patient only by the central pharmacy that is specially certified (http://www.xyremrems.com or 1-866-997-3688). Prior to dispensing the first prescription, prescribers will be sent educational materials to be reviewed with the patient and enrollment forms for the postmarketing surveillance program. Patients must be seen at least every 3 months; prescriptions can be written for a maximum of 3 months (the first prescription may only be written for a 1-month supply).

In Canada, access to sodium oxybate is restricted under the Xyrlem Success Program. The program is intended to educate prescribers, pharmacists, and patients on the safe use, storage, and handling of the drug, to maintain a registry of trained physicians, pharmacies, and patients, and to limit distribution through a single wholesaler to pharmacies on an as-needed basis after a prescription is received by the pharmacy. Initial dispensing of prescriptions should occur only after the prescriber, pharmacist, and patient have received and read the educational materials. Further information regarding the program may be obtained at 1-866-599-7365.

Dental Comment Sodium oxybate is a known substance of abuse. When used illegally, it has been referred to as a "date-rape drug". The dentist should be aware of patients showing signs of CNS depression, as with all other drugs in this class.

Sodium Phenylbutyrate

(SOW dee um fen il BYOO ti rate)

Brand Names: US Buphenyl

Brand Names: Canada Pheburane

Pharmacologic Category Urea Cycle Disorder (UCD) Treatment Agent

Use Urea cycle disorders: Adjunctive therapy in the chronic management of patients with urea cycle disorder involving deficiencies of carbamoylphosphate synthetase, ornithine transcarbamylase, or argininosuccinic acid synthetase; neonatal-onset deficiency (complete enzymatic deficiency, presenting within the first 28 days of life); late-onset disease (partial enzymatic deficiency, presenting after the first month of life) who have a history of hyperammonemic encephalopathy

Local Anesthetic/Vasoconstrictor Precautions No information available to require special precautions

Effects on Dental Treatment Key adverse event(s) related to dental treatment: Abnormal taste.

Effects on Bleeding No information available to require special precautions

Adverse Reactions

>10%: Endocrine & metabolic: Amenorrhea (≤23%), menstrual disease (≤23%), acidosis (14%), hypoalbuminemia (11%)

1% to 10%:

Cardiovascular: Syncope (≤2%)

Central nervous system: Depression (≤2%), headache (≤2%)

Dermatologic: Body odor (3%), skin rash (≤2%)

Endocrine & metabolic: Alkalosis (7%), hyperchloremia (7%), hypophosphatemia (6%), decreased serum total protein (3%), hyperuricemia (2%), hyperphosphatemia (2%), hypernatremia (1%), hypokalemia (1%)

Gastrointestinal: Anorexia (4%), dysgeusia (3%), abdominal pain (≤2%), gastritis (≤2%), nausea (≤2%), vomiting (≤2%)

Hematologic & oncologic: Anemia (9%), leukocytosis (4%), leukopenia (4%), thrombocytopenia (3%), thrombocythemia (1%)

Hepatic: Increased serum alkaline phosphatase (6%), increased serum transaminases (4%), hyperbilirubinemia (1%)

Renal: Renal tubular acidosis (≤2%)

<1%, postmarketing, and/or case reports: Aplastic anemia, bruise, cardiac arrhythmia, constipation, dizziness, drowsiness, edema, fatigue, memory impairment, neuropathy (exacerbation), pancreatitis, peptic ulcer, rectal hemorrhage

General Dosage Range Oral:

Children <20 kg: Powder: 450 to 600 mg/kg/day administered in equally divided doses with each meal or feeding, 3 to 6 times/day

Children ≥20 kg, Adolescents, and Adults: 9.9 to 13 g/m²/day, administered in equally divided doses with each meal, 3 to 6 times/day

Mechanism of Action Sodium phenylbutyrate is a prodrug which is rapidly converted to phenylacetate, followed by conjugation with glutamine to form phenylacetylglutamine; phenylacetylglutamine serves as a substitute for urea as it is clears nitrogenous waste from the body when excreted in the urine.

Pharmacodynamics/Kinetics

Half-life Elimination Phenylbutyrate (tablets and powder): 0.76 to 0.77 hours; Phenylacetate (tablets and powder): 1.15 to 1.29 hours

Time to Peak Plasma: Phenylbutyrate (tablets and powder): 1 to 1.35 hours; Phenylacetate (tablets and powder): 3.55 to 3.74 hours

Pregnancy Risk Factor C

Pregnancy Considerations Animal reproduction studies have not been conducted. Use during pregnancy is contraindicated in the Canadian labeling.

Sodium Phosphates (SOW dee um FOS fates)

Brand Names: US Fleet Enema Extra [OTC]; Fleet Enema [OTC]; Fleet Pedia-Lax Enema [OTC]; LaCrosse Complete [OTC]; OsmoPrep

Brand Names: Canada Fleet Enema

Pharmacologic Category Cathartic; Electrolyte Supplement, Parenteral; Laxative, Bowel Evacuant

Use

Oral solution, rectal: Short-term treatment of constipation

Oral tablets: Bowel cleansing prior to colonoscopy

IV: Source of phosphate in large volume IV fluids and parenteral nutrition; treatment and prevention of hypophosphatemia

Local Anesthetic/Vasoconstrictor Precautions No information available to require special precautions

Effects on Dental Treatment No significant effects or complications reported

Effects on Bleeding No information available to require special precautions

Adverse Reactions Frequency not always defined.

Central nervous system: Dizziness, headache

Gastrointestinal: Bloating (31% to 47%), nausea (26% to 35%), abdominal pain (23% to 30%), vomiting (4% to 7%), diarrhea, mucosal bleeding, superficial mucosal ulcerations

Endocrine & metabolic: Hyperphosphatemia (≤96%), hypocalcemia (on colonoscopy day; 47%), hypophosphatemia (2-3 days postcolonoscopy; 34%), hypokalemia (on colonoscopy day; 28%), hypernatremia

Postmarketing and/or case reports: Acute phosphate nephropathy, anaphylaxis, bronchospasm, calcium nephrolithiasis, cardiac arrhythmia, dehydration, dysphagia, dyspnea, facial edema, increased blood urea nitrogen, increased serum creatinine, ischemic colitis, lip edema, paresthesia, pharyngeal edema, pruritus, rectal bleeding, renal failure, renal insufficiency, renal tubular necrosis, seizure, skin rash, tightness in throat, tongue edema, urticaria

General Dosage Range

IV:

Children: 0.08-1 mmol phosphate/kg **or** Parenteral nutrition: Infusion: 0.5-2 mmol/kg/24 hours

Adults: 0.08-1 mmol phosphate/kg **or** Parenteral nutrition: Infusion: 20-40 mmol/24 hours

Oral:

Solution:

Children 5-9 years: 7.5 mL as a single dose (maximum single daily dose: 7.5 mL)

Children 10-11 years: 15 mL as a single dose (maximum single daily dose: 15 mL)

Children ≥12 years and Adults: 15 mL as a single dose (maximum single daily dose: 45 mL)

Tablet: *Adults*:

OsmoPrep: 32 tablets in divided doses as directed beginning evening before colonoscopy

Rectal:

Children 2-4 years: One-half contents of one 2.25 oz pediatric enema

Children 5-11 years: Contents of one 2.25 oz pediatric enema

Children ≥12 years and Adults: Contents of one 4.5-ounce enema as a single dose

Mechanism of Action As a laxative, exerts osmotic effect in the small intestine by drawing water into the lumen of the gut, producing distention and promoting peristalsis and evacuation of the bowel; phosphorous participates in bone deposition, calcium metabolism, utilization of B complex vitamins, and as a buffer in acid-base equilibrium

Pharmacodynamics/Kinetics

Onset of Action Cathartic: 3 to 6 hours; Rectal: 2 to 5 minutes

Pregnancy Risk Factor C

Pregnancy Considerations Reproduction studies have not been conducted with these products. Use with caution in pregnant women.

Sodium Picosulfate, Magnesium Oxide, and Citric Acid

(SOW dee um pye ko SUL fate mag NEE zhum OKS ide & SI trik AS id)

Brand Names: US Prepopik

Brand Names: Canada Oral Purgative; Pico-Salax; Picodan; Picoflo; Purg-Odan

Pharmacologic Category Laxative, Osmotic; Laxative, Stimulant

Use Bowel cleansing: Cleansing of colon prior to colonoscopy

Local Anesthetic/Vasoconstrictor Precautions No information available to require special precautions

Effects on Dental Treatment No significant effects or complications reported

Effects on Bleeding No information available to require special precautions

Adverse Reactions

>10%:

Endocrine & metabolic: Hypermagnesemia (9% to 12%)

Genitourinary: Decreased estimated GFR (eGFR, ≤48 hours after colonoscopy: 10% to 29%)

1% to 10%:

Central nervous system: Headache (2% to 3%)

Endocrine & metabolic: Hypokalemia (5% to 7%), hypochloremia (1% to 4%), hyponatremia (1% to 4%)

Gastrointestinal: Nausea (3%), vomiting (1%)

Renal: Increased serum creatinine (≤5%)

<1%, postmarketing, and/or case reports: Abdominal pain, diarrhea, disturbed sleep, dizziness, fecal incontinence, flatulence, hypersensitivity reaction, hypocalcemia, ischemic colitis, purpura, rectal pain, seizure, skin rash, ulcer (aphthoid ileal), urticaria

General Dosage Range Oral: *Adults:* Two 150 mL (5 oz) doses

Mechanism of Action

Sodium picosulfate, a prodrug, is hydrolyzed by colonic bacteria to an active metabolite which stimulates colonic peristalsis.

Magnesium oxide and citric acid react to create magnesium citrate which induces catharsis by the osmotic effects of the unabsorbed ions in the GI tract.

Pharmacodynamics/Kinetics

Half-life Elimination Sodium picosulfate: ~7.5 hours

Time to Peak Sodium picosulfate: ~7 hours; Magnesium: 10 hours

Pregnancy Risk Factor B

Pregnancy Considerations Adverse events were not observed in animal reproduction studies using doses similar to a human dose.

Sodium Tetradecyl Sulfate

(SOW dee um tetra DEK il SUL fate)

Brand Names: US Sotradecol

Brand Names: Canada Trombovar

Pharmacologic Category Sclerosing Agent

Use Treatment of small, uncomplicated varicose veins of the lower extremities

Local Anesthetic/Vasoconstrictor Precautions No information available to require special precautions

Effects on Dental Treatment No significant effects or complications reported

Effects on Bleeding No information available to require special precautions

Adverse Reactions Frequency not defined.

Central nervous system: Headache

Dermatologic: Discoloration at site of injection, sloughing and tissue necrosis following extravasation

Gastrointestinal: Nausea, vomiting

Local: Pain, itching, or ulceration at injection site

Miscellaneous: Allergic reaction (including hives, asthma, hay fever); anaphylactic shock

General Dosage Range IV: *Adults:* 0.5-2 mL in each vein (maximum: 10 mL per treatment session)

Mechanism of Action Acts by irritation of the vein intimal endothelium and causes thrombosis formation leading to occlusion of the injected vein

Pregnancy Risk Factor C

Pregnancy Considerations Reproduction studies have not been conducted.

Sodium Thiosulfate (SOW dee um thye oh SUL fate)

Pharmacologic Category Antidote; Antidote, Extravasation

Use Cyanide poisoning: Treatment of acute, life-threatening cyanide poisoning in combination with sodium nitrite. Consider consultation with a poison control center at 1-800-222-1222.

Local Anesthetic/Vasoconstrictor Precautions No information available to require special precautions

Effects on Dental Treatment No significant effects or complications reported

Effects on Bleeding No information available to require special precautions

Adverse Reactions Frequency not defined

Cardiovascular: Hypotension

Central nervous system: Disorientation, flushing sensation, headache, salty taste

Gastrointestinal: Nausea, vomiting

Hematologic & oncologic: Prolonged bleeding time

General Dosage Range IV:

Children: 250 mg/kg (1 mL/kg or ~30 to 40 mL/m^2 of a 25% solution) or 500 mg/kg (2 mL/kg of a 25% solution) (maximum: 12.5 g); may repeat at one-half the original dose if needed

Adults: 12.5 g; may repeat at one-half the original dose if needed

Mechanism of Action

Cyanide toxicity: Serves as a sulfur donor in rhodanese-catalyzed formation of thiocyanate (much less toxic than cyanide)

Extravasation management: Neutralizes the reactive species of mechlorethamine; reduces the formation of hydroxyl radicals which cause tissue injury

Pharmacodynamics/Kinetics

Half-life Elimination Thiosulfate: ~3 hours (Howland 2011); Thiocyanate: ~3 days; Renal impairment: ≤9 days

Pregnancy Risk Factor C

Pregnancy Considerations Teratogenic effects were not observed in animal reproduction studies of sodium thiosulfate. In general, medications used as antidotes should take into consideration the health and prognosis of the mother; antidotes should be administered to pregnant women if there is a clear indication for use and should not be withheld because of fears of teratogenicity (Bailey 2003).

Sofosbuvir (soe FOS bue vir)

Related Information

Systemic Viral Diseases *on page 1806*

Brand Names: US Sovaldi

Brand Names: Canada Sovaldi

Pharmacologic Category Antihepaciviral, Polymerase Inhibitor (Anti-HCV); NS5B RNA Polymerase Inhibitor

Use Chronic hepatitis C: Treatment of genotype 1, 2, 3, or 4 chronic hepatitis C virus (HCV) as a component of a combination antiviral treatment regimen.

Local Anesthetic/Vasoconstrictor Precautions No information available to require special precautions

Effects on Dental Treatment No significant effects or complications reported

Effects on Bleeding No information available to require special precautions

Adverse Reactions

Adverse reactions reported with combination therapy.

>10%:

Central nervous system: Fatigue (30% to 59%), headache (24% to 36%), insomnia (15% to 25%), chills (2% to 17%), irritability (10% to 13%)

Dermatologic: Pruritus (11% to 27%), skin rash (8% to 18%)

Gastrointestinal: Nausea (22% to 34%), decreased appetite (18%), diarrhea (9% to 12%)

Hematologic & oncologic: Decreased hemoglobin (<10 g/dL: 6% to 23%; <8.5 g/dL: ≤2%), anemia (6% to 21%), neutropenia (<1% [interferon-free regimen] to 17% [interferon-containing regimen]), decreased neutrophils (≥0.5 to <0.75 times 10^9/L: <1% [interferon-free regimen] to 15%; <0.5 times 10^9/L: ≤5%)

Neuromuscular & skeletal: Weakness (5% to 21%), myalgia (6% to 14%)

Respiratory: Flu-like symptoms (6% to 16%)

Miscellaneous: Fever (4% to 18%)

1% to 10%:

Gastrointestinal: Increased serum lipase (>3 times ULN: ≤2%)

Hematologic & oncologic: Thrombocytopenia (≤1%)

Hepatic: Increased serum bilirubin (>2.5 times ULN: 3%)

Renal: Increased creatine kinase (≥10 times ULN: 1% to 2%)

<1%, postmarketing, and/or case reports: Bradycardia, pancytopenia, reactivation of HBV (FDA Safety Alert Dec. 8, 2016), severe depression, suicidal ideation

Mechanism of Action Sofosbuvir, a direct-acting antiviral agent against the hepatitis C virus, is a prodrug converted to its pharmacologically active form (GS-461203) via intracellular metabolism. It inhibits HCV NS5B RNA-dependent RNA polymerase, essential for viral replication, and acts as a chain terminator.

Pharmacodynamics/Kinetics

Half-life Elimination 0.4 hours

Time to Peak ~0.5 to 2 hours

Pregnancy Risk Factor B

Pregnancy Considerations

Use in combination with ribavirin is contraindicated in pregnant women and males whose female partners are pregnant.

Adverse events were not observed in animal reproduction studies using sofosbuvir; however, sofosbuvir is only to be used in combination with ribavirin or peginterferon alfa/ribavirin for the treatment of hepatitis C virus (HCV) (according to the manufacturer's labeling), and ribavirin use is contraindicated in pregnancy. If used in combination with ribavirin, all warnings related to the use of ribavirin and pregnancy and/or contraception should be followed.

Mother-to-child transmission of HCV does not occur if the woman is not viremic, therefore, HCV-infected women of childbearing potential should postpone pregnancy until therapy is complete. Treatment of HCV is not recommended for women who are already pregnant (AASLD/IDSA 2016).

Sofosbuvir and Velpatasvir

(soe FOS bue vir & vel PAT as vir)

Brand Names: US Epclusa

Brand Names: Canada Epclusa

Pharmacologic Category Antihepaciviral, NS5A Inhibitor; Antihepaciviral, Polymerase Inhibitor (Anti-HCV); NS5A Inhibitor; NS5B RNA Polymerase Inhibitor

Use Chronic hepatitis C: Treatment of chronic hepatitis C (CHC) genotype 1, 2, 3, 4, 5, or 6 infection in adults without cirrhosis or with compensated cirrhosis or in combination with ribavirin in patients with decompensated cirrhosis.

Local Anesthetic/Vasoconstrictor Precautions No information available to require special precautions

Effects on Dental Treatment No significant effects or complications reported

Effects on Bleeding No information available to require special precautions

Adverse Reactions

>10%: Central nervous system: Headache (22%), fatigue (15%)

1% to 10%:

Central nervous system: Irritability (≥5%), insomnia (5%), depression (1%)

Dermatologic: Skin rash (2%)

Gastrointestinal: Nausea (9%), increased serum lipase (>3X ULN: 3% to 6%)

Neuromuscular & skeletal: Weakness (5%), increased creatine phosphokinase (≥10X ULN: 1% to 2%)

Frequency not defined: Hepatic: Increased indirect serum bilirubin (patients with HIV-1/HCV coinfection)

<1%, postmarketing, and/or case reports: Reactivation of HBV (FDA Safety Alert Dec. 8, 2016)

General Dosage Range Oral: *Adults:* One tablet once daily for 12 weeks

Mechanism of Action Velpatasvir inhibits the HCV NS5A protein necessary for viral replication; sofosbuvir is a prodrug converted to its pharmacologically active form (GS-461203), which inhibits NS5B RNA-dependent RNA polymerase, also essential for viral replication, and acts as a chain terminator.

Pharmacodynamics/Kinetics

Half-life Elimination Velpatasvir: 15 hours; Sofosbuvir: 0.5 hours

Time to Peak Velpatasvir: 3 hours; Sofosbuvir: 0.5 to 1 hour

Pregnancy Considerations Adverse events were not observed in animal reproduction studies using sofosbuvir or velpatasvir. Also refer to the sofosbuvir monograph (and the ribavirin monograph if used in combination with ribavirin) for additional information.

Solifenacin (sol i FEN a sin)

Brand Names: US VESIcare

Brand Names: Canada ACT Solifenacin; Auro-Solifenacin; JAMP-Solifenacin; PMS-Solifenacin; RAN-Solifenacin; Sandoz-Solifenacin; Teva-Solifenacin; VESIcare

Pharmacologic Category Anticholinergic Agent

Use Overactive bladder: Treatment of overactive bladder with symptoms of urinary frequency, urgency, or urge incontinence.

Local Anesthetic/Vasoconstrictor Precautions No information available to require special precautions

Effects on Dental Treatment Key adverse event(s) related to dental treatment: Xerostomia (normal salivary flow resumes upon discontinuation). Prolonged xerostomia may contribute to discomfort and dental disease (eg, caries, periodontal disease, and oral candidiasis).

Effects on Bleeding No information available to require special precautions

Adverse Reactions

>10%: Gastrointestinal: Xerostomia (11% to 28%; dose-related), constipation (5% to 13%; dose-related)

1% to 10%:

Cardiovascular: Edema (≤1%), hypertension (≤1%)

Central nervous system: Fatigue (1% to 2%), depression (≤1%)

Gastrointestinal: Dyspepsia (1% to 4%), nausea (2% to 3%), upper abdominal pain (1% to 2%)

Genitourinary: Urinary tract infection (3% to 5%), urinary retention (≤1%)

Ophthalmic: Blurred vision (4% to 5%), dry eye syndrome (≤2%)

Respiratory: Cough (≤1%)

Miscellaneous: Influenza (≤2%)

<1%, postmarketing, and/or case reports: Abnormal hepatic function tests, anaphylaxis, angioedema, atrial fibrillation, confusion, decreased appetite, delirium, drowsiness, erythema multiforme, exfoliative dermatitis, fecal impaction, gastroesophageal reflux disease, gastrointestinal obstruction, glaucoma, hallucination, headache, hyperkalemia, hypersensitivity reactions, intestinal obstruction, myasthenia, palpitations, prolonged Q-T interval on ECG, pruritus, renal insufficiency, skin rash, tachycardia, torsades de pointes, urticaria, voice disorder

General Dosage Range Dosage adjustment recommended in patients with hepatic or renal impairment and on concomitant therapy

Oral: *Adults:* Initial: 5 mg once daily; Maintenance: 5 to 10 mg once daily.

Mechanism of Action Inhibits muscarinic receptors resulting in decreased urinary bladder contraction, increased residual urine volume, and decreased detrusor muscle pressure.

Pharmacodynamics/Kinetics

Half-life Elimination 45 to 68 hours following chronic dosing; prolonged in severe renal (CrCl <30 mL/minute) or moderate hepatic (Child-Pugh class B) impairment

Time to Peak Plasma: 3 to 8 hours

Pregnancy Risk Factor C

Pregnancy Considerations Adverse events were observed in some animal reproduction studies.

Somatropin (soe ma TROE pin)

Brand Names: US Genotropin; Genotropin MiniQuick; Humatrope; Norditropin FlexPro; Norditropin NordiFlex Pen [DSC]; Nutropin AQ NuSpin 10; Nutropin AQ NuSpin 20; Nutropin AQ NuSpin 5; Nutropin AQ Pen [DSC]; Nutropin [DSC]; Omnitrope; Saizen; Saizen Click.Easy; Serostim; Tev-Tropin [DSC]; Zomacton; Zorbtive

Brand Names: Canada Genotropin GoQuick; Genotropin MiniQuick; Humatrope; Norditropin Nordiflex; Norditropin Simplexx; Nutropin AQ NuSpin; Nutropin AQ Pen; Omnitrope; Saizen; Serostim

Pharmacologic Category Growth Hormone

Use

Children:

Treatment of growth failure due to inadequate endogenous growth hormone secretion (Genotropin, Humatrope, Norditropin, Nutropin, Nutropin AQ, Omnitrope, Saizen, Tev-Tropin, Zomacton)

Treatment of growth failure associated with Turner syndrome (Genotropin, Humatrope, Norditropin, Nutropin, Nutropin AQ, Omnitrope)

Treatment of growth failure due to Prader-Willi syndrome (PWS) (Genotropin, Omnitrope)

Treatment of growth failure associated with chronic renal insufficiency (CRI) up until the time of renal transplantation (Nutropin, Nutropin AQ)

Treatment of growth failure in children born small for gestational age who fail to manifest catch-up growth by 2 years of age (Genotropin, Omnitrope) or by 2 to 4 years of age (Humatrope, Norditropin)

Treatment of idiopathic short stature (nongrowth hormone-deficient short stature) defined by height standard deviation score (SDS) ≤-2.25 and growth rate not likely to attain normal adult height (Genotropin, Humatrope, Nutropin, Nutropin AQ, Omnitrope)

Treatment of short stature or growth failure associated with short stature homeobox gene (SHOX) deficiency (Humatrope)

Treatment of short stature associated with Noonan syndrome (Norditropin)

Adults:

HIV patients with wasting or cachexia with concomitant antiviral therapy (Serostim)

Replacement of endogenous growth hormone in patients with adult growth hormone deficiency who meet both of the following criteria (Genotropin, Humatrope, Norditropin, Nutropin, Nutropin AQ, Omnitrope, Saizen):

Biochemical diagnosis of adult growth hormone deficiency by means of a subnormal response to a standard growth hormone stimulation test (peak growth hormone ≤5 mcg/L). Confirmatory testing may not be required in patients with congenital/genetic growth hormone deficiency or multiple other pituitary hormone deficiencies due to organic diseases.

and

Adult-onset: Patients who have adult growth hormone deficiency whether alone or with multiple hormone deficiencies (hypopituitarism) as a result of pituitary disease, hypothalamic disease, surgery, radiation therapy, or trauma

or

Childhood-onset: Patients who were growth hormone deficient during childhood as a result of congenital, genetic, acquired, or idiopathic causes, confirmed as an adult before replacement therapy is initiated

Treatment of short-bowel syndrome (Zorbtive)

Local Anesthetic/Vasoconstrictor Precautions No information available to require special precautions

Effects on Dental Treatment No significant effects or complications reported

Effects on Bleeding No information available to require special precautions

Adverse Reactions

>10%:

Cardiovascular: Peripheral edema (short bowel syndrome: 69% to 81%; HARS: 19% to 45%; HIV with wasting/cachexia: 26%), facial edema (short bowel syndrome: 44% to 50%), chest pain (short bowel syndrome: ≤19%), edema (≤13%)

Central nervous system: Pain (short bowel syndrome: 6% to 19%), hypoesthesia (HARS: 9% to 15%; HIV with wasting/cachexia: 5%), headache (≤14%), malaise (short bowel syndrome: ≤13%), paresthesia (8% to 13%), dizziness (short bowel syndrome: 6% to 13%)

Dermatologic: Diaphoresis (short bowel syndrome: ≤13%), skin rash (short bowel syndrome: 6% to 13%)

Endocrine & metabolic: Dehydration (short bowel syndrome: ≤19%)

Gastrointestinal: Nausea (short bowel syndrome: 13% to 31%; HIV with wasting/cachexia: 9%), flatulence (short bowel syndrome: 25%), abdominal pain (short bowel syndrome: 13% to 25%), vomiting (short bowel syndrome: 19%)

Infection: Infection (short bowel syndrome: ≤19%), candidiasis (short bowel syndrome: ≤13%)

Local: Pain at injection site (short bowel syndrome: ≤31%), injection site reaction (short bowel syndrome: 19% to 25%, idiopathic short stature: <1%)

Neuromuscular & skeletal: Arthralgia (HIV with wasting/cachexia: ≤78%; HARS, short bowel syndrome: 28% to 44%; idiopathic short stature, SHOX deficiency: 11%), arthropathy (HIV with wasting/cachexia: ≤78%; idiopathic short stature: 11%), myalgia (HIV with wasting/cachexia: ≤78%, idiopathic short stature: 24%; HARS, short bowel syndrome: ≤13%), scoliosis (idiopathic short stature: 19%; SHOX deficiency: 4%), limb pain (HARS: 5% to 19%)

Otic: Otitis media (Turner syndrome: 43%; idiopathic short stature: 16%), ear disease (Turner syndrome: 18%), auditory disturbance (short bowel syndrome: 13%)

Respiratory: Rhinitis (short bowel syndrome: ≤19%)

Miscellaneous: Surgery (Turner syndrome: 45%)

1% to 10%:

Cardiovascular: Hypertension (idiopathic short stature: 3%)

Dermatologic: Nevus (excessive; SHOX deficiency: 7%)

Endocrine & metabolic: Hyperlipidemia (idiopathic short stature: 8%), gynecomastia (≤8%)

Neuromuscular & skeletal: Hip pain (idiopathic short stature: 3%)

Frequency not defined:

Cardiovascular: Lower extremity edema (adults; growth hormone deficiency)

Central nervous system: Depression (adults; growth hormone deficiency), fatigue (adults; growth hormone deficiency), insomnia (adults; growth hormone deficiency), seizure (children; growth hormone deficiency)

Dermatologic: Acne vulgaris (adults; growth hormone deficiency), exacerbation of psoriasis (children; growth hormone deficiency)

Endocrine & metabolic: Decreased glucose tolerance (adults; growth hormone deficiency), glycosuria (growth hormone deficiency), hyperglycemia (mild; growth hormone deficiency, small for gestational age), hypertriglyceridemia (children; growth hormone deficiency), hypoglycemia (children; growth hormone deficiency), hypothyroidism (growth hormone deficiency), insulin resistance (adults; growth hormone deficiency)

Gastrointestinal: Gastritis (adults; growth hormone deficiency)

Genitourinary: Hematuria (children; growth hormone deficiency), precocious puberty (small for gestational age), urinary tract infection (Turner syndrome)

Hematologic & oncologic: Elevated glycosylated hemoglobin (children; growth hormone deficiency), eosinophilia (children; growth hormone deficiency), hematoma (children; growth hormone deficiency), leukemia (children; growth hormone deficiency), meningioma (children, growth hormone deficiency), neoplasm (intracranial; children; growth hormone deficiency)

Hepatic: Increased serum ALT (adults; growth hormone deficiency), increased serum AST (adults; growth hormone deficiency)

Immunologic: Antibody development (children; growth hormone deficiency)

Neuromuscular & skeletal: Back pain (adults; growth hormone deficiency), leg pain (children; growth hormone deficiency), lipoatrophy (children; growth hormone deficiency), muscle rigidity (adults; growth hormone deficiency), skeletal pain (adults; growth hormone deficiency), slipped capital femoral epiphysis (small for gestational age; children, growth hormone deficiency), weakness (growth hormone deficiency)

Ophthalmic: Papilledema (children; growth hormone deficiency), retinopathy (adults; growth hormone deficiency)

Respiratory: Bronchitis (adults; growth hormone deficiency), cough (adults; growth hormone deficiency), flu-like symptoms (adults; growth hormone deficiency), pharyngitis (adults, growth hormone deficiency), respiratory tract disease (Turner syndrome), upper respiratory tract infection (adults, growth hormone deficiency)

<1%, postmarketing, and/or case reports: Aggressive behavior (idiopathic short stature), alopecia (idiopathic short stature), carpal tunnel syndrome (small for gestational age), diabetes mellitus (idiopathic short stature, small for gestational age), enlargement of facial features (jaw prominence; small for gestational age), increased growth of pre-existing nevi (growth hormone deficiency, small for gestational age), pancreatitis (growth hormone deficiency), pseudotumor cerebri, scoliosis progression (small for gestational age)

General Dosage Range IM, SubQ: *Children, Adolescents, and Adults:* Dosage varies greatly depending on indication

Mechanism of Action Somatropin is a purified polypeptide hormones of recombinant DNA origin; somatropin contains the identical sequence of amino acids found in human growth hormone; human growth hormone assists growth of linear bone, skeletal muscle, and organs by stimulating chondrocyte proliferation and differentiation, lipolysis, protein synthesis, and hepatic glucose output; stimulates erythropoietin which increases red blood cell mass; exerts both insulin-like and diabetogenic effects; enhances the transmucosal transport of water, electrolytes, and nutrients across the gut

Pharmacodynamics/Kinetics

Duration of Action Maintains supraphysiologic levels for 18 to 20 hours

Half-life Elimination SubQ: Somatrem: 2.3 ± 0.42 hours; Somatropin: 3.8 hours; IM: Somatropin: 4.9 hours

Pregnancy Risk Factor B/C (depending upon manufacturer)

Pregnancy Considerations Adverse events have not observed in animal reproduction studies, however, reproduction studies have not been conducted with all agents. During normal pregnancy, maternal production of endogenous growth hormone decreases as placental growth hormone production increases. Data with somatropin use during pregnancy is limited.

Product Availability Nutropin (lyophilized powder) has been discontinued in the US for more than 1 year.

Sonidegib (soe ni DEG ib)

Brand Names: US Odomzo

Pharmacologic Category Antineoplastic Agent, Hedgehog Pathway Inhibitor

Use Basal cell carcinoma, locally advanced: Treatment of adult patients with locally advanced basal cell carcinoma (BCC) that has recurred following surgery or radiation therapy, or those who are not candidates for surgery or radiation therapy.

Local Anesthetic/Vasoconstrictor Precautions No information available to require special precautions

Effects on Dental Treatment No significant effects or complications reported

Effects on Bleeding No information available to require special precautions

Adverse Reactions

>10%:

Central nervous system: Fatigue (41%), headache (15%), pain (14%)

Dermatologic: Alopecia (53%)

Endocrine & metabolic: Hyperglycemia (51%), weight loss (30%), increased serum ALT (19%), increased serum AST (19%), increased amylase (16%)

Gastrointestinal: Dysgeusia (46%), increased serum lipase (43%), nausea (39%), diarrhea (32%), decreased appetite (23%), abdominal pain (18%), vomiting (11%)

Hematologic & oncologic: Anemia (32%), lymphocytopenia (28%, grades 3/4: 3%)

Neuromuscular & skeletal: Increased creatine phosphokinase (61%, grades 3/4: 8%), muscle spasm (54%; grade 3: 3%), musculoskeletal pain (32%, grade 3: 1%), myalgia (19%)

Renal: Increased serum creatinine (92%)

1% to 10%:

Dermatologic: Pruritus (10%)

<1%, postmarketing, and/or case reports: Amenorrhea, rhabdomyolysis

General Dosage Range Oral: *Adults:* 200 mg once daily

Mechanism of Action Basal cell cancer is associated with mutations in Hedgehog pathway components. Hedgehog regulates cell growth and differentiation in embryogenesis; while generally not active in adult tissue, Hedgehog mutations associated with basal cell cancer can activate the pathway resulting in unrestricted proliferation of skin basal cells (Von Hoff, 2009). Sonidegib is a selective Hedgehog pathway inhibitor which binds to and inhibits Smoothened homologue (SMO), the transmembrane protein involved in Hedgehog signal transduction.

Pharmacodynamics/Kinetics

Half-life Elimination ~28 days

Time to Peak 2 to 4 hour

Pregnancy Considerations [US Boxed Warning]: Sonidegib can cause embryo-fetal death or severe birth defects when administered to a pregnant woman. Sonidegib is embryotoxic, fetotoxic, and teratogenic in animals. Verify the pregnancy status of females of reproductive potential prior to initiating therapy. Advise females of reproductive potential to use effective contraception during treatment with sonidegib and for at least 20 months after the last dose. Advise males of the potential risk of exposure through semen and to use condoms with a pregnant partner or a female partner of reproductive potential during treatment with sonidegib and for at least 8 months after the last dose. It is not known if sonidegib is present in semen. Males with female partners of reproductive potential should use condoms even following a vasectomy. Advise male patients not to donate sperm during sonidegib treatment and for at least 8 months after the last sonidegib dose.

Health care providers should notify the manufacturer of pregnancies which may occur following exposure to sonidegib (888-669-6682).

SORAfenib (sor AF e nib)

Related Information

Osteonecrosis of the Jaw *on page 1796*

Brand Names: US NexAVAR

Brand Names: Canada Nexavar

Pharmacologic Category Antineoplastic Agent, Tyrosine Kinase Inhibitor; Antineoplastic Agent, Vascular Endothelial Growth Factor (VEGF) Inhibitor

Use

Hepatocellular cancer: Treatment of unresectable hepatocellular cancer (HCC)

Renal cell cancer, advanced: Treatment of advanced renal cell cancer (RCC)

Thyroid cancer, differentiated: Treatment of locally recurrent or metastatic, progressive, differentiated thyroid cancer (refractory to radioactive iodine treatment)

Local Anesthetic/Vasoconstrictor Precautions Sorafenib may cause hypertension; monitor blood pressure prior to vasoconstrictor use

Effects on Dental Treatment Key adverse event(s) related to dental treatment: Mouth pain, mucositis, stomatitis, xerostomia (normal salivary flow resumes upon discontinuation), and dysphagia.

Effects on Bleeding Chemotherapy may result in significant myelosuppression, potentially including significant reduction in platelet counts (thrombocytopenia grades 3/4: 1% to 4%) and altered hemostasis. In patients who are under active treatment with these agents, medical consult is suggested.

Adverse Reactions

>10%:

Cardiovascular: Hypertension (9% to 41%; grade 3: 3% to 4%; grade 4: <1%; grades 3/4: 10%, onset: ~3 weeks)

Central nervous system: Fatigue (37% to 46%), headache (≤10% to 17%), mouth pain (14%), voice disorder (13%), peripheral sensory neuropathy (≤13%), pain (11%)

Dermatologic: Palmar-plantar erythrodysesthesia (21% to 69%; grade 3: 6% to 8%; grades 3/4: 19%), alopecia (14% to 67%), skin rash (including desquamation; 19% to 40%; grade 3: ≤1%; grades 3/4: 5%), pruritus (14% to 20%), xeroderma (10% to 13%), erythema (≥10%)

Endocrine & metabolic: Hypoalbuminemia (≤59%), weight loss (10% to 49%), hypophosphatemia (35% to 45%; grade 3: 11% to 13%; grade 4: <1%), increased thyroid stimulating hormone level (>0.5 mU/L: 41%; due to impairment of exogenous thyroid suppression), hypocalcemia (12% to 36%), increased amylase (30% to 34% [usually transient])

Gastrointestinal: Diarrhea (43% to 68%; grade 3: 2% to 10%; grade 4: <1%), increased serum lipase (40% to 41% [usually transient]), abdominal pain (11% to 31%), decreased appetite (30%), anorexia (16% to 29%), stomatitis (24%), nausea (21% to 24%), constipation (14% to 16%), vomiting (11% to 16%)

Hematologic & oncologic: Lymphocytopenia (23% to 47%; grades 3/4: ≤13%), thrombocytopenia (12% to 46%; grades 3/4: 1% to 4%), increased INR (≤42%), neutropenia (≤18%; grades 3/4: ≤5%), hemorrhage (15% to 17%; grade 3: 2%), leukopenia

Hepatic: Increased serum ALT (59%; grades 3/4: 4%), increased serum AST (54%; grades 3/4: 2%), hepatic insufficiency (≤11%; grade 3: 2%; grade 4: 1%)

Infection: Infection

Neuromuscular & skeletal: Limb pain (15%), weakness (12%), myalgia

Respiratory: Dyspnea (≤14%), cough (≤13%)

Miscellaneous: Fever (11%)

1% to 10%:

Cardiovascular: Ischemic heart disease (including myocardial infarction; ≤3%), cardiac failure (2%, congestive), flushing

Central nervous system: Depression, glossalgia

Dermatologic: Hyperkeratosis (7%), acne vulgaris, exfoliative dermatitis, folliculitis

Endocrine & metabolic: Hypokalemia (5% to 10%), hyponatremia, hypothyroidism

Gastrointestinal: Dysgeusia (6%), dyspepsia, dysphagia, gastroesophageal reflux disease, mucositis, xerostomia

Genitourinary: Erectile dysfunction, proteinuria

Hematologic & oncologic: Squamous cell carcinoma of skin (3%; grades 3/4: 3%), anemia

Hepatic: Increased serum transaminases (transient)

Neuromuscular & skeletal: Muscle spasm (10%), arthralgia (≤10%), myalgia

Renal: Renal failure

Respiratory: Epistaxis (7%), flu-like symptoms, hoarseness, rhinorrhea

<1%, postmarketing, and/or case reports: Acute renal failure, anaphylaxis, angioedema, aortic dissection, amyotrophy, cardiac arrhythmia, cardiac failure, cerebral hemorrhage, cholangitis, cholecystitis, dehydration, eczema, erythema multiforme, gastritis, gastrointestinal hemorrhage, gastrointestinal perforation, gynecomastia, hepatic failure, hepatitis, hypersensitivity reaction (skin reaction, urticaria), hypertensive crisis, hyperthyroidism, increased serum alkaline phosphatase, increased serum bilirubin, interstitial pulmonary disease (acute respiratory distress, interstitial pneumonia, lung inflammation, pneumonitis, pulmonitis, radiation pneumonitis), jaundice, malignant neoplasm of skin (keratoacanthomas), nephrotic syndrome, ostealgia, osteonecrosis of the jaw, pancreatitis, pleural effusion, prolonged QT interval on ECG, respiratory tract hemorrhage, reversible posterior leukoencephalopathy syndrome, rhabdomyolysis, Stevens-Johnson syndrome, thromboembolism, tinnitus, toxic epidermal necrolysis, transient ischemic attacks, tumor lysis syndrome, tumor pain

General Dosage Range Dosage adjustments recommended in patients with hepatic or renal impairment, or who develop toxicities

Oral: *Adults:* 400 mg twice daily

Mechanism of Action Multikinase inhibitor; inhibits tumor growth and angiogenesis by inhibiting intracellular Raf kinases (CRAF, BRAF, and mutant BRAF), and cell surface kinase receptors (VEGFR-1, VEGFR-2, VEGFR-3, PDGFR-beta, cKIT, FLT-3, RET, and RET/PTC)

Pharmacodynamics/Kinetics

Half-life Elimination 25 to 48 hours

Time to Peak ~3 hours

Pregnancy Risk Factor D

Pregnancy Considerations Animal reproduction studies have demonstrated teratogenicity and fetal loss. Based on its mechanism of action and because sorafenib inhibits angiogenesis, a critical component of fetal development, adverse effects on pregnancy would be expected. Women of childbearing potential should be advised to avoid pregnancy. Men and women of reproductive potential should use effective birth control during treatment and for at least 2 weeks after treatment is discontinued.

Prescribing and Access Restrictions Available from specialty pharmacies. Further information may be obtained at 1-866-639-2827 or www.nexavar-us.-com.

Sorbitol (SOR bi tole)

Pharmacologic Category Genitourinary Irrigant; Laxative, Osmotic

Use Genitourinary irrigant in transurethral prostatic resection or other transurethral resection or other transurethral surgical procedures; diuretic; humectant; sweetening agent; hyperosmotic laxative; facilitate the passage of sodium polystyrene sulfonate through the intestinal tract

Local Anesthetic/Vasoconstrictor Precautions No information available to require special precautions

Effects on Dental Treatment Key adverse event(s) related to dental treatment: Xerostomia (normal salivary flow resumes upon discontinuation).

Effects on Bleeding No information available to require special precautions

Adverse Reactions Frequency not defined.

Cardiovascular: Edema

Endocrine & metabolic: Electrolyte depletion, hyperglycemia, hypovolemia, lactic acidosis

Gastrointestinal: Abdominal distress, diarrhea, nausea, vomiting, xerostomia

General Dosage Range

Oral:

Children 2-11 years: 2 mL/kg (70% solution) as a single dose

Children ≥12 years and Adults: 30-150 mL (70% solution) as a single dose

Rectal:

Children 2-11 years: 30-60 mL (25% to 30% solution) as a single dose

Children ≥12 years and Adults: 120 mL (25% to 30% solution) as a single dose

Topical: *Adults:* 3% to 3.3% as a transurethral irrigation

Mechanism of Action A polyalcoholic sugar with osmotic cathartic actions

Pharmacodynamics/Kinetics

Onset of Action Rectal: 0.25-1 hour

Pregnancy Risk Factor C

Pregnancy Considerations Animal reproduction studies have not been conducted.

Sotalol (SOE ta lole)

Related Information

Cardiovascular Diseases *on page 1752*

Clinical Risk Related to Drugs Prolonging QT Interval *on page 1772*

Brand Names: US Betapace; Betapace AF; Sorine; Sotylize

Brand Names: Canada Apo-Sotalol; CO Sotalol; Dom-Sotalol; Med Sotalol; Mylan Sotalol; Novo-Sotalol; Nu-Sotalol; PHL-Sotalol; PMS-Sotalol; PRO-Sotalol; ratio-Sotalol; Rhoxal-sotalol; Riva-Sotalol; Rylosol; Sandoz-Sotalol; ZYM-Sotalol

Pharmacologic Category Antiarrhythmic Agent, Class II; Antiarrhythmic Agent, Class III; Beta-Adrenergic Blocker, Nonselective

Use

Betapace/Betapace AF, Sorine, Sotylize: Treatment of documented ventricular arrhythmias (ie, sustained ventricular tachycardia), that in the judgment of the health care provider are life-threatening

Betapace/Betapace AF, Sotylize: Maintenance of normal sinus rhythm (delay in time to recurrence of atrial fibrillation/atrial flutter) in patients with symptomatic atrial fibrillation/atrial flutter who are currently in sinus rhythm. Manufacturer of Sorine states substitutions should not be made for sotalol AF due to significant differences in labeling (ie, patient package insert and safety information)

According to the American Heart Association/American College of Cardiology/Heart Rhythm Society (AHA/ACC/HRS), sotalol is not effective for conversion of atrial fibrillation to sinus rhythm but may be used to prevent atrial fibrillation (AHA/ACC/HRS [January 2014])

Injection: Substitution for oral sotalol in those who are unable to take sotalol orally

Local Anesthetic/Vasoconstrictor Precautions Use with caution; epinephrine has interacted with nonselective beta-blockers to result in initial hypertensive episode followed by bradycardia. Sotalol is one of the drugs confirmed to prolong the QT interval and is accepted as having a risk of causing torsade de pointes. The risk of drug-induced torsade de pointes is extremely low when a single QT interval prolonging drug is prescribed. In terms of epinephrine, it is not known what effect vasoconstrictors in the local anesthetic regimen will have in patients with a known history of congenital prolonged QT interval or in patients taking any medication that prolongs the QT interval. Until more information is obtained, it is suggested that the clinician consult with the physician prior to the use of a vasoconstrictor in suspected patients, and that the vasoconstrictor (epinephrine, mepivacaine and levonordefrin [Carbocaine 2% with Neo-Cobefrin]) be used with caution.

Effects on Dental Treatment Sotalol is a nonselective beta-blocker and may enhance the pressor response to epinephrine, resulting in hypertension and bradycardia. Many nonsteroidal anti-inflammatory drugs, such as ibuprofen and indomethacin, can reduce the hypotensive effect of beta-blockers after 3 or more weeks of therapy with the NSAID. Short-term NSAID use (ie, 3 days) requires no special precautions in patients taking beta-blockers.

Adverse Reactions There is minimal clinical experience with IV sotalol; however, since exposure is similar between IV and oral sotalol, adverse reactions are expected to be similar.

>10%:

Cardiovascular: Bradycardia (dose related; 8% to 16%), chest pain (3% to 16%), palpitations (3% to 14%)

Central nervous system: Fatigue (dose related; 5% to 20%), dizziness (3% to 20%), headache (2% to 12%)

Neuromuscular & skeletal: Weakness (4% to 13%)

Respiratory: Dyspnea (dose related; 5% to 21%)

1% to 10%:

Cardiovascular: Edema (2% to 8%), ECG abnormality (2% to 7%), hypotension (3% to 6%), congestive heart failure (1% to 5%; incidence may be higher in patients with risk factors), syncope (1% to 5%), proarrhythmia (<1% to 5%), torsades de pointes (dose related; 1% to 4%), peripheral vascular disorder (1% to 3%), angina pectoris (2%), presyncope (1% to 2%), cardiovascular signs and symptoms (<1% to 2%), worsened ventricular tachycardia (1%), cerebrovascular accident (≤1%), hypertension (≤1%), vasodilation (≤1%), prolonged Q-T interval on ECG (dose related)

Central nervous system: Sleep disorder (1% to 8%), insomnia (3% to 4%), anxiety (2% to 4%), depression (1% to 4%), paresthesia (1% to 4%), sensation of cold (2% to 3%), impaired consciousness (1% to 3%), mood changes (≤1%)

Dermatologic: Hyperhidrosis (5%), skin rash (2% to 5%), diaphoresis (1% to 3%)

Endocrine & metabolic: Weight changes (1%)

Gastrointestinal: Nausea and vomiting (4% to 10%), diarrhea (2% to 7%), abdominal pain (<1% to 4%), dyspepsia (2% to 3%), abdominal distention (<1% to 3%), decreased appetite (2%), change in appetite (1% to 2%), colonic disease (1% to 2%), flatulence (<1% to 2%)

Genitourinary: Sexual disorder (≤3%), genitourinary complaint (≤1%)

Hematologic & oncologic: Hemorrhage (<1% to 2%)

Infection: Infection (1% to 2%), influenza (1% to 2%)

Local: Local pain (1% to 2%)

Neuromuscular & skeletal: Limb pain (2% to 7%), musculoskeletal pain (3% to 4%), musculoskeletal chest pain (2% to 3%), back pain (<1% to 3%)

Ophthalmic: Visual disturbance (1% to 5%)

Respiratory: Upper respiratory complaint (1% to 8%), pulmonary disease (3% to 5%), tracheobronchitis (1% to 3%), asthma (<1% to 2%)

Miscellaneous: Fever (1% to 3%), laboratory test abnormality (1% to 3%), AICD discharge (<1% to 2%)

<1%, postmarketing and/or case reports: Alopecia, clouding of consciousness, emotional lability, eosinophilia, hyperlipidemia, incoordination, increased liver enzymes, leukopenia, myalgia, paralysis, skin

photosensitivity, pruritus, pulmonary edema, thrombocytopenia, vertigo

General Dosage Range Dosage adjustment recommended in patients with renal impairment or who develop toxicities

IV: *Adults:* Initial: 75 mg twice daily; Maintenance: 75 to 150 mg twice daily (maximum: 300 mg/day)

Oral:

Children ≤2 years: Dosage should be adjusted (decreased) by plotting of the child's age on a logarithmic scale; **Note:** Refer to manufacturer's package labeling

Children >2 years and Adolescents: Initial: 30 mg/m^2/dose every 8 hours; maximum: 60 mg/m^2/dose every 8 hours, up to 320 mg/day

Adults: Initial: 80 mg twice daily; Maintenance: 240 to 320 mg daily in 2 to 3 divided doses (maximum: 320 mg/day)

Mechanism of Action

Beta-blocker which contains both beta-adrenoreceptor-blocking (Vaughan Williams Class II) and cardiac action potential duration prolongation (Vaughan Williams Class III) properties

Class II effects: Increased sinus cycle length, slowed heart rate, decreased AV nodal conduction, and increased AV nodal refractoriness Sotalol has both beta$_1$- and beta$_2$-receptor blocking activity. The beta-blocking effect of sotalol is a noncardioselective (half maximal at about 80 mg/day and maximal at doses of 320 to 640 mg/day). Significant beta-blockade occurs at oral doses as low as 25 mg/day.

Class III effects: Prolongation of the atrial and ventricular monophasic action potentials, and effective refractory prolongation of atrial muscle, ventricular muscle, and atrioventricular accessory pathways in both the antegrade and retrograde directions. Sotalol is a racemic mixture of *d*- and *l*-sotalol; both isomers have similar Class III antiarrhythmic effects while the *l*-isomer is responsible for virtually all of the beta-blocking activity. The Class III effects are seen only at oral doses ≥160 mg/day.

Pharmacodynamics/Kinetics

Onset of Action

Oral: Rapid; at 1 to 2 hours post dosing (steady-state), reductions in heart rate and cardiac index seen (Winters 1993)

IV: When administered IV over 5 minutes for ongoing VT, onset of action is ~5 to 10 minutes (Ho 1994)

Half-life Elimination

Oral:

Neonates ≤1 month: 8.4 hours (Saul 2001b)

Infants and Children >1 month to 24 months: 7.4 hours (Saul 2001b)

Children >2 years to <7 years: 9.1 hours (Saul 2001b)

Children 7 to 12 years: 9.2 hours (Saul 2001b)

Adults: 12 hours

Adults with renal failure (anuric): Up to 69 hours

IV: Pharmacokinetics of the IV formulation (administered over 5 hours) are similar to the oral formulations (Somberg 2010).

Time to Peak Serum: Oral: Infants and Children 3 days to 12 years: Mean range: 2 to 3 hours; Adults: 2.5 to 4 hours

Pregnancy Risk Factor B

Pregnancy Considerations Adverse events were not observed in the initial animal reproduction studies. Sotalol crosses the placenta and is found in amniotic fluid. Adverse events, such as fetal/neonatal bradycardia, hypoglycemia, and reduced birth weight have been observed following in utero exposure to beta-blockers as a class. Adequate facilities for monitoring infants at birth are generally recommended.

Sotalol crosses the placenta in concentrations similar to the maternal serum and it is generally preferred for the treatment of fetal atrial flutter (Namouz-Haddad 2013).

The clearance of sotalol is increased during the third trimester of pregnancy, but other pharmacokinetic parameters do not significantly differ from nonpregnant values (O'Hare 1983). Use of sotalol may be considered for some cardiac arrhythmias when use of a beta-blocker is needed during pregnancy (ESC [Regitz-Zagrosek 2011]).

Dental Comment See Local Anesthetic/Vasoconstrictor Precautions

Spiramycin (speer a MYE sin)

Brand Names: Canada Rovamycine®

Pharmacologic Category Antibiotic, Macrolide

Use Note: Not approved in the US

Treatment of infections of the respiratory tract, buccal cavity, skin and soft tissues due to susceptible organisms. *N. gonorrhoeae*: as an alternate choice of treatment for gonorrhea in patients allergic to the penicillins. Before treatment of gonorrhea, the possibility of concomitant infection due to *T. pallidum* should be excluded

Local Anesthetic/Vasoconstrictor Precautions No information available to require special precautions

Effects on Dental Treatment No significant effects or complications reported

Effects on Bleeding No information available to require special precautions

Adverse Reactions Frequency not defined.

Dermatologic: Pruritus, skin rash, urticaria

Gastrointestinal: Diarrhea, nausea, vomiting

Hepatic: Increased serum transaminases

<1%, postmarketing, and/or case reports: Anaphylactic shock, angioedema, hepatotoxicity (idiosyncratic; Chalasani 2014), paresthesia, pseudomembranous colitis

General Dosage Range Oral:

Children: 150,000 units/kg/day in 2-3 divided doses

Adults: 6,000,000-15,000,000 units/day in 2 divided doses **or** 12,000,000-13,500,000 units as a single dose

Mechanism of Action Inhibits growth of susceptible organisms; mechanism not established.

Pregnancy Risk Factor Not assigned (other macrolides rated B); C per expert analysis

Pregnancy Considerations Crosses placenta. Specific safety information is not available. However, spiramycin has been used to treat *Toxoplasma gondii* to prevent transmission from mother to fetus.

Product Availability Not available in the US

Spironolactone (speer on oh LAK tone)

Related Information

Cardiovascular Diseases *on page 1752*

Brand Names: US Aldactone

Brand Names: Canada Aldactone; NTP-Spironolactone; Teva-Spironolactone

Pharmacologic Category Antihypertensive; Diuretic, Potassium-Sparing; Mineralocorticoid (Aldosterone) Receptor Antagonists

Use

Edema: Management of edema and sodium retention associated with heart failure unresponsive to other therapies; cirrhosis of liver accompanied by edema and/or ascites; or nephrotic syndrome unresponsive to other therapies.

Hypertension: Management of hypertension unresponsive to other therapies.

Guideline recommendations: According to the Eighth Joint National Committee (JNC 8) guidelines, aldosterone antagonists are not recommended for the initial treatment of hypertension.

Hypokalemia: Treatment of hypokalemia unresponsive to other therapies; prophylaxis of hypokalemia in patients taking digitalis.

Primary hyperaldosteronism: Establishing the diagnosis of primary hyperaldosteronism by therapeutic trial; short-term preoperative treatment of primary hyperaldosteronism; long-term maintenance therapy for patients with discrete aldosterone-producing adrenal adenomas who are judged to be poor operative risks or who decline surgery; long-term maintenance therapy for bilateral micro- or macronodular adrenal hyperplasia (idiopathic hyperaldosteronism).

Heart failure, severe: To increase survival and to reduce hospitalization for severe heart failure (New York Heart Association class III to IV) when used in addition to standard therapy.

Guideline recommendations: The American College of Cardiology Foundation/American Heart Association (ACCF/AHA) 2013 heart failure guidelines recommend the use of aldosterone antagonists, along with other guideline-directed medical therapies, to reduce morbidity and mortality in patients with heart failure (New York Heart Association [NYHA] class III to IV) with left ventricular ejection fraction (LVEF) 35% or less.

Local Anesthetic/Vasoconstrictor Precautions No information available to require special precautions

Effects on Dental Treatment No significant effects or complications reported

Effects on Bleeding No information available to require special precautions

Adverse Reactions Frequency not defined.

Cardiovascular: Vasculitis

Central nervous system: Ataxia, confusion, drowsiness, headache, lethargy

Dermatologic: Erythematous maculopapular rash, Stevens-Johnson syndrome, toxic epidermal necrolysis, urticaria

Endocrine & metabolic: Amenorrhea, gynecomastia, hyperkalemia

Gastrointestinal: Abdominal cramps, diarrhea, gastritis, gastrointestinal hemorrhage, gastrointestinal ulcer, nausea, vomiting

Genitourinary: Impotence, irregular menses, postmenopausal bleeding

Hematologic & oncologic: Agranulocytosis, malignant neoplasm of breast

Hepatic: Hepatotoxicity

Hypersensitivity: Anaphylaxis

Immunologic: DRESS syndrome

Renal: Increased blood urea nitrogen, renal failure, renal insufficiency

Miscellaneous: Fever

General Dosage Range

Oral:

Adults: 25 to 400 mg daily in single or divided doses

Mechanism of Action Competes with aldosterone for receptor sites in the distal renal tubules, increasing sodium chloride and water excretion while conserving potassium and hydrogen ions; may block the effect of aldosterone on arteriolar smooth muscle as well

Pharmacodynamics/Kinetics

Duration of Action 2 to 3 days

Half-life Elimination Spironolactone: ~1.4 hours; Canrenone: 16.5 hours (terminal); 7-alpha-spirolactone: 13.8 hours (terminal)

Time to Peak Serum: 2.6 to 4.3 hours (primarily as active metabolites)

Pregnancy Considerations Adverse events have been observed in some animal reproduction studies. The antiandrogen effects of spironolactone have been shown to cause feminization of the male fetus in animal studies. Spironolactone crosses the placenta (Regitz-Zagrosek 2011).

The treatment of heart failure is generally the same in pregnant and nonpregnant women; however, spironolactone should be avoided in the first trimester due to its antiandrogenic effects (Regitz-Zagrosek 2011). The use of mineralocorticoid receptor antagonists is not recommended to treat chronic uncomplicated hypertension in pregnant women and should generally be avoided in women of reproductive potential. When treatment for hypertension in pregnancy is needed, other agents are preferred (ACOG 2013). Use of diuretics to treat edema during normal pregnancies is not appropriate; use may be considered when edema is due to pathologic causes (as in the nonpregnant patient); monitor.

Stavudine (STAV yoo deen)

Related Information

HIV Infection and AIDS *on page 1785*

Brand Names: US Zerit

Brand Names: Canada Zerit

Pharmacologic Category Antiretroviral, Reverse Transcriptase Inhibitor, Nucleoside (Anti-HIV)

Use Treatment of HIV infection in combination with other antiretroviral agents

Local Anesthetic/Vasoconstrictor Precautions No information available to require special precautions

Effects on Dental Treatment No significant effects or complications reported

Effects on Bleeding No information available to require special precautions relative to hemostasis.

Adverse Reactions Adverse reactions reported below represent experience with combination therapy with other nucleoside analogues and protease inhibitors.

>10%:

Central nervous system: Headache (25% to 46%), peripheral neuropathy (8% to 21%)

Dermatologic: Skin rash (18% to 30%)

Endocrine & metabolic: Increased amylase (21% to 31%; grades 3/4: 4% to 8%), increased gamma-glutamyl transferase (15% to 28%; grades 3/4: 2% to 5%)

Gastrointestinal: Nausea (43% to 53%), diarrhea (34% to 45%), vomiting (18% to 30%), increased serum lipase (27%; grades 3/4: 5% to 6%)

Hepatic: Hyperbilirubinemia (65% to 68%; grades 3/4: 7% to 16%), increased serum AST (42% to 53%; grades 3/4: 5% to 7%), increased serum ALT (40% to 50%; grades 3/4: 6% to 8%)

<1%, postmarketing, and/or case reports: Abdominal pain, anemia, anorexia, chills, diabetes mellitus, fever, hepatic failure, hepatitis, hepatomegaly with steatosis (some fatal), hyperglycemia, hyperlipidemia, hypersensitivity reaction, immune reconstitution syndrome,

insomnia, insulin resistance, lactic acidosis (some fatal), leukopenia, lipoatrophy, lipotrophy, macrocytosis, myalgia, neutropenia, pancreatitis (some fatal), redistribution of body fat, severe weakness (severe neuromuscular weakness resembling Guillain-Barré), thrombocytopenia

General Dosage Range Dosage adjustment recommended in patients with renal impairment.

Oral:

Newborns (Birth to 13 days): 0.5 mg/kg every 12 hours

Children ≥14 days and <30 kg: 1 mg/kg every 12 hours

Children and Adults 30-59 kg: 30 mg every 12 hours

Children and Adults ≥60 kg: 40 mg every 12 hours

Mechanism of Action Stavudine is a thymidine analog which interferes with HIV viral DNA dependent DNA polymerase resulting in inhibition of viral replication; nucleoside reverse transcriptase inhibitor

Pharmacodynamics/Kinetics

Half-life Elimination

Note: Half-life is prolonged with renal dysfunction

Newborns (at birth): 5.3 ± 2 hours

Neonates 14 to 28 days old: 1.6 ± 0.3 hours

Children 5 weeks to 15 years: 0.9 ± 0.3 hours

Adults: 1.6 ± 0.2 hours

Intracellular: Adults: 3.5 to 7 hours

Time to Peak Serum: 1 hour

Pregnancy Risk Factor C

Pregnancy Considerations Adverse events were observed in some animal reproduction studies. Stavudine has a high level of transfer across the human placenta. No increased risk of overall birth defects has been observed following first trimester exposure according to data collected by the antiretroviral pregnancy registry. Maternal antiretroviral therapy may increase the risk of preterm delivery, although available information is conflicting possibly due to variability of maternal factors (disease severity; initiation of therapy); however, maternal antiretroviral medication should not be withheld due to concerns of preterm birth. Information related to stillbirth, low birth weight, and small for gestational age infants is limited. Long-term follow-up is recommended for all infants exposed to antiretroviral medications; children who develop significant organ system abnormalities of unknown etiology (particularly of the CNS or heart) should be evaluated for potential mitochondrial dysfunction.

[US Boxed Warning]: Fatal lactic acidosis has been reported in pregnant women using didanosine and stavudine in combination with other antiretroviral agents. Cases of lactic acidosis and hepatic steatosis related to mitochondrial toxicity have been reported with use of nucleoside reverse transcriptase inhibitors (NRTIs). These adverse events are similar to other rare but life-threatening syndromes which occur during pregnancy (eg, HELLP syndrome). In general nucleoside reverse transcriptase inhibitors are well tolerated and the benefits of use generally outweigh potential risk. However, due to reports of potentially fatal lactic acidosis, didanosine and stavudine should not be used in combination during pregnancy.

Combination antiretroviral therapy (cART) therapy is recommended for all HIV-infected pregnant women to keep the viral load below the limit of detection and reduce the risk of perinatal transmission. When HIV is diagnosed during pregnancy in a woman who has never received antiretroviral therapy, cART should begin as soon as possible after diagnosis. The Health and Human Services (HHS) Perinatal HIV Guidelines do not recommend stavudine for initial therapy in antiretroviral-naive pregnant women due to toxicity; do not use with didanosine or zidovudine. Pharmacokinetics of stavudine are not significantly altered during pregnancy; dose adjustments are not needed. In general, women who become pregnant on a stable cART regimen may continue that regimen if viral suppression is effective, appropriate drug exposure can be achieved, contraindications for use in pregnancy are not present, and the regimen is well tolerated. However, because stavudine has a high risk of toxicity, women should be switched to a preferred or alternative regimen. Monitoring during pregnancy is more frequent than in non-pregnant adults; cART should be continued postpartum.

For HIV-infected couples planning a pregnancy, maximum viral suppression with cART is recommended prior to conception for the HIV-infected partner(s) and expert consultation is recommended; modification of therapy (if needed) and optimization of the woman's health should be done prior to conception. HIV-infected women not planning a pregnancy may use any available type of contraception, considering possible drug interactions and contraindications of the specific method. In addition, consistent use of condoms is also recommended (even during pregnancy) to prevent transmission of HIV or other sexually transmitted diseases.

Health care providers are encouraged to enroll pregnant women exposed to antiretroviral medications as early in pregnancy as possible in the Antiretroviral Pregnancy Registry (1-800-258-4263 or www.APRegistry.com). Health care providers caring for HIV-infected women and their infants may contact the National Perinatal HIV Hotline (888-448-8765) for clinical consultation (HHS [perinatal] 2016).

Stiripentol (stir i PEN tol)

Brand Names: Canada Diacomit

Pharmacologic Category Anticonvulsant, Miscellaneous

Use Note: Not approved in the US

Dravet syndrome: Adjunctive treatment of refractory generalized tonic-clonic seizures in conjunction with clobazam and valproic acid in patients with severe myoclonic epilepsy in infancy (SMEI, Dravet syndrome) and whose seizures are not adequately controlled with clobazam and valproic acid alone

Local Anesthetic/Vasoconstrictor Precautions No information available to require special precautions

Effects on Dental Treatment No significant effects or complications reported

Effects on Bleeding No information available to require special precautions

Adverse Reactions Note: Adverse reactions reported with combination (valproate plus clobazam) therapy.

>10%:

Central nervous system: Drowsiness (58% to 71%), hypotonia (10% to 25%), hyperexcitability/agitation (17% to 24%), aggressive behavior/irritability (14% to 17%), ataxia (14%)

Endocrine & metabolic: Weight loss (17% to 29%), weight gain (24%)

Gastrointestinal: Anorexia (33% to 50%), nausea/vomiting (10% to 25%), sialorrhea (17%)

Hematologic & oncologic: Neutropenia (14%)

Neuromuscular & skeletal: Tremor (14%)

1% to 10%:

Central nervous system:

Dermatologic: Facial erythema (8%), urticaria (5%), xeroderma (5%)

Genitourinary: Dysuria (5%)

Hematologic & oncologic: Thrombocytopenia (10%), eosinophilia (5%)

Hepatic: Increased serum AST (8%)

<1%, postmarketing, and/or case reports: Apathy, coma, convulsions, delirium (rare), esophageal pain, hallucination (rare), hepatitis (cytolytic), hyperthermia, increased creatine phosphokinase, increased gamma-glutamyl transferase, increased serum ALT, increased serum transaminases, infection, movement disorder (including ataxia, hypotonia, tremor, hyperkinesia, dysarthria, and equilibrium disorders), muscle spasm (involuntary), pancreatitis, physical health deterioration, skin rash, Stevens-Johnson syndrome, testicular disease, thyroiditis

General Dosage Range Oral: *Children ≥3 years, Adolescents, and Adults:* Titrate dose upward over 3 days to 50 mg/kg daily given in 2 or 3 divided doses (maximum daily dose: 50 mg/kg)

Mechanism of Action Precise mechanism behind anticonvulsant effects is unknown. May enhance GABAergic inhibitory neurotransmission by weak partial agonism and/or positive allosteric modulation of gamma-aminobutyric acid (GABA)-A receptors (Fisher, 2009). Also inhibits multiple cytochrome P450 isoenzymes involved in the metabolism of other anticonvulsants; concurrent use may increase their systemic exposure and efficacy.

Pharmacodynamics/Kinetics

Half-life Elimination Adults: 4.5-13 hours (dose-dependent); clearance decreases with repeated administration possibly due to inhibition of cytochrome P450 isoenzymes and is markedly decreased at higher doses

Time to Peak 1.5 hours

Pregnancy Considerations Adverse effects have not been observed in animal reproduction studies. Use of stiripentol in pregnant women has not been studied; however, infants exposed to antiepileptic drugs in utero are at increased risk for malformations.

Product Availability Not available in the US

Streptomycin (strep toe MYE sin)

Brand Names: Canada Streptomycin for Injection

Pharmacologic Category Antibiotic, Aminoglycoside; Antitubercular Agent

Use

Tuberculosis:

Treatment of tuberculosis, in combination with other appropriate antituberculosis agents, when the primary agents (eg, isoniazid, rifampin, ethambutol, pyrazinamide) are contraindicated because of toxicity or intolerance.

Nontuberculosis infections:

Treatment of infections caused by susceptible bacteria that are not amenable to therapy with less potentially toxic agents,including sensitive *Yersinia pestis* (plague); *Francisella tularensis* (tularemia); *Brucella*; *Klebsiella granulomatis* (donovanosis, granuloma inguinale); *Haemophilus ducreyi* (chancroid); *Haemophilus influenzae* (in respiratory, endocardial, and meningeal infections, concomitantly with another antibacterial agent); *Klebsiella pneumoniae* pneumonia (concomitantly with another antibacterial agent); *Escherichia coli*, *Proteus* spp., *Enterobacter aerogenes*, *K. pneumoniae*, and *Enterococcus faecalis* in urinary tract infections; *Streptococcus viridans*; *E. faecalis* (in endocardial infections, concomitant with penicillin); and gram-negative bacillary bacteremia (concomitant with another antibacterial agent).

Local Anesthetic/Vasoconstrictor Precautions No information available to require special precautions

Effects on Dental Treatment No significant effects or complications reported

Effects on Bleeding No information available to require special precautions

Adverse Reactions

Frequency not defined.

Cardiovascular: Hypotension

Central nervous system: Drug fever, facial paresthesia, headache, neurotoxicity

Dermatologic: Exfoliative dermatitis, skin rash, urticaria

Gastrointestinal: Nausea, vomiting

Genitourinary: Azotemia, nephrotoxicity

Hematologic & oncologic: Eosinophilia, hemolytic anemia, leukopenia, pancytopenia, thrombocytopenia

Hypersensitivity: Anaphylaxis, angioedema

Neuromuscular & skeletal: Arthralgia, tremor, weakness

Ophthalmic: Amblyopia

Otic: Auditory ototoxicity, vestibular ototoxicity

Respiratory: Dyspnea

<1%, postmarketing, and/or case reports: DRESS syndrome (drug reaction with eosinophilia and systemic symptoms), toxic epidermal necrolysis

General Dosage Range Dosage adjustment recommended in patients with renal impairment

IM: Dosage varies greatly by indication.

Mechanism of Action Inhibits bacterial protein synthesis by binding directly to the 30S ribosomal subunits causing faulty peptide sequence to form in the protein chain

Pharmacodynamics/Kinetics

Half-life Elimination Newborns: 4 to 10 hours; Adults: ~2 to 4.7 hours; prolonged with renal impairment

Time to Peak IM: Within 1 to 2 hours

Pregnancy Risk Factor D

Pregnancy Considerations Streptomycin crosses the placenta. Streptomycin may cause fetal harm if administered to a pregnant woman. There are multiple reports of total irreversible bilateral congenital deafness in children whose mothers received streptomycin during pregnancy. Streptomycin should never be substituted as first line therapy for the treatment of tuberculosis in pregnant women (Blumberg 2003).

Streptozocin (strep toe ZOE sin)

Brand Names: US Zanosar

Brand Names: Canada Zanosar

Pharmacologic Category Antineoplastic Agent, Alkylating Agent; Antineoplastic Agent, Alkylating Agent (Nitrosourea)

Use Treatment of metastatic islet cell carcinoma of the pancreas (symptomatic or progressive disease)

Local Anesthetic/Vasoconstrictor Precautions No information available to require special precautions

Effects on Dental Treatment No significant effects or complications reported

Effects on Bleeding Chemotherapy may result in significant myelosuppression, potentially including significant reduction in platelet counts and altered hemostasis. In patients who are under active treatment with these agents, medical consult is suggested.

Adverse Reactions Frequency not defined.

Endocrine & metabolic: Decreased glucose tolerance, glycosuria, hyperglycemia, hypoalbuminemia, hypoglycemia, hypophosphatemia, increased lactate dehydrogenase

Gastrointestinal: Diarrhea, nausea, vomiting

Genitourinary: Anuria, azotemia, nephrotoxicity, proteinuria

Hepatic: Increased serum transaminases

Local: Injection site reaction (includes burning sensation at injection site, erythema at injection site, inflammation at injection site, irritation at injection site, swelling at injection site, tenderness at injection site)

Renal: Increased blood urea nitrogen, increased serum creatinine, renal insufficiency, renal tubular acidosis

<1%, postmarketing, and/or case reports: Anemia, bone marrow depression (nadir: 2 to 3 weeks), confusion, depression, diabetes insipidus, hepatic insufficiency, lethargy, leukopenia, metastases, thrombocytopenia

General Dosage Range Dosage adjustment recommended in patients with renal impairment or who develop toxicities.

IV: *Adults:* 500 mg/m^2 for 5 consecutive days every 6 weeks **or** 1000-1500 mg/m^2 once weekly (maximum dose: 1500 mg/m^2)

Mechanism of Action Inhibits DNA synthesis by alkylation and cross-linking the strands of DNA, and by possible protein modification; cell cycle nonspecific

Pharmacodynamics/Kinetics

Onset of Action 1500 mg/m^2 once weekly: Onset of response: 17 days; median time to maximum response: 35 days

Half-life Elimination <1 hour

Pregnancy Risk Factor D

Pregnancy Considerations Teratogenic events have been observed in animal reproduction studies.

Succinylcholine (suks in il KOE leen)

Brand Names: US Anectine; Quelicin; Quelicin-1000 [DSC]

Brand Names: Canada Quelicin

Pharmacologic Category Neuromuscular Blocker Agent, Depolarizing

Use

Neuromuscular blockade: As an adjunct to general anesthesia, to facilitate tracheal intubation, and to provide skeletal muscle relaxation during surgery or mechanical ventilation.

Note: Does not relieve pain or produce sedation

Local Anesthetic/Vasoconstrictor Precautions No information available to require special precautions

Effects on Dental Treatment No significant effects or complications reported

Effects on Bleeding No information available to require special precautions

Adverse Reactions

Frequency not defined.

Cardiovascular: Bradycardia (higher with second dose; more frequent in children), cardiac arrhythmia, hypertension, hypotension, malignant hyperthermia, tachycardia

Dermatologic: Skin rash

Endocrine & metabolic: Hyperkalemia

Gastrointestinal: Sialorrhea

Hypersensitivity: Anaphylaxis

Neuromuscular & skeletal: Fasciculations, jaw tightness, myalgia (postoperative), rhabdomyolysis (with possible myoglobinuric acute renal failure)

Ophthalmic: Increased intraocular pressure

Respiratory: Apnea, respiratory depression (prolonged)

<1%, postmarketing, and/or case reports: Abnormal bone growth (myositis ossificans; prolonged use), myopathy (acute quadriplegic myopathy syndrome; prolonged use)

General Dosage Range

IM: *Infants, Children, Adolescents, and Adults:* Up to 3 to 4 mg/kg (maximum: 150 mg total dose)

IV:

Neonates, Infants ≤6 months: Intubation: 2 to 3 mg/kg/dose

Infants >6 months and Children ≤ 2 years: Intubation: 1 to 2 mg/kg/dose

Older Children and Adolescents: Intubation: 1 mg/kg/dose

Adults: Intubation: 0.6 mg/kg (range: 0.3 to 1.1 mg/kg); Rapid sequence intubation: 1 to 1.5 mg/kg (Sluga, 2005; Weiss, 1997); Long surgical procedures (intermittent administration): Initial: 0.3 to 1.1 mg/kg; administer 0.04 to 0.07 mg/kg at appropriate intervals as needed.

Mechanism of Action Acts similar to acetylcholine, produces depolarization of the motor endplate at the myoneural junction which causes sustained flaccid skeletal muscle paralysis produced by state of accommodation that develops in adjacent excitable muscle membranes

Pharmacodynamics/Kinetics

Onset of Action

Dependent on route, age, and dose; data suggest faster onset with higher doses (Coté 2013):

IM: Infants and Children: 3 to 4 minutes (Lui 1981); Adults: 2 to 3 minutes

IV:

Neonates and Infants: ~30 seconds (range: 19 to 40 seconds [dose: 2 to 4 mg/kg]) (Meakin 1990)

Children and Adolescents: 35 to 55 seconds (Coté 2013); Dose-specific: 40 seconds (dose: 1.5 to 2 mg/kg); 50 seconds (dose: 1 mg/kg) (Coté 2013)

Adults: Flaccid paralysis rapid <60 seconds

Duration of Action Dependent on route, age, and dose:

IM: 10 to 30 minutes; observed to be shorter in infants than children

IV: ~4 to 6 minutes; faster recovery rate in infants and children compared to adults (Fisher 1975)

Pregnancy Risk Factor C

Pregnancy Considerations Animal reproduction studies have not been conducted. Small amounts cross the placenta. Sensitivity to succinylcholine may be increased due to a ~24% decrease in plasma cholinesterase activity during pregnancy and several days postpartum.

Sucralfate (soo KRAL fate)

Related Information

Perioral Premalignant Lesions and Management of Patients Undergoing Cancer Therapy *on page 1875*

Brand Names: US Carafate

Brand Names: Canada Apo-Sucralfate; Dom-Sucralfate; Novo-Sucralate; Nu-Sucralate; PMS-Sucralate; Sucralfate-1; Sulcrate®; Sulcrate® Suspension Plus; Teva-Sucralfate

Pharmacologic Category Gastrointestinal Agent, Miscellaneous

Use Short-term (≤8 weeks) management of duodenal ulcers; maintenance therapy for duodenal ulcers

Local Anesthetic/Vasoconstrictor Precautions No information available to require special precautions

Effects on Dental Treatment No significant effects or complications reported

Effects on Bleeding No information available to require special precautions

Adverse Reactions

1% to 10%: Gastrointestinal: Constipation (2%)

<1%, postmarketing, and/or case reports: Anaphylaxis, back pain, bezoar formation, bronchospasm, diarrhea, dizziness, drowsiness, dyspepsia, flatulence, headache; hypersensitivity (urticaria, angioedema, facial swelling, laryngospasm, respiratory difficulty, rhinitis); insomnia, nausea, pruritus, skin rash, stomach pain, vertigo, vomiting, xerostomia

General Dosage Range Oral: *Adults:* 1 g 2-4 times/day

Mechanism of Action Forms a complex by binding with positively charged proteins in exudates, forming a viscous paste-like, adhesive substance. This selectively forms a protective coating that acts locally to protect the gastric lining against peptic acid, pepsin, and bile salts.

Pharmacodynamics/Kinetics

Onset of Action Paste formation and ulcer adhesion: 1-2 hours; acid neutralizing capacity: 14-17 mEq/1 g dose of sucralfate

Duration of Action Up to 6 hours

Pregnancy Risk Factor B

Pregnancy Considerations Adverse events were not observed in animal reproduction studies. Sucralfate is only minimally absorbed following oral administration. Based on available data, use of sucralfate does not appear to increase the risk of adverse fetal events when used during the first trimester (Mahadevan, 2006).

Sucroferric Oxyhydroxide

(soo kroe FER ik ox ee hye DROX ide)

Brand Names: US Velphoro

Pharmacologic Category Phosphate Binder

Use Hyperphosphatemia: For control of serum phosphorus levels in patients with chronic kidney disease (CKD) receiving dialysis

Local Anesthetic/Vasoconstrictor Precautions No information available to require special precautions

Effects on Dental Treatment No significant effects or complications reported

Effects on Bleeding No information available to require special precautions

Adverse Reactions

>10%: Gastrointestinal: Diarrhea (4% to 24%), darkening of stools (12% to 16%)

1% to 10%: Gastrointestinal: Nausea (2% to 10%), dysgeusia (2%)

General Dosage Range Oral: *Adults:* Initial: 500 mg iron 3 times daily (1.5 g iron daily); usual maintenance: 1.5-2 g iron daily

Mechanism of Action Binds phosphate in the aqueous environment of the GI tract via ligand exchange between hydroxyl groups and/or water in sucroferric oxyhydroxide and dietary phosphate. Reduced dietary phosphate absorption results in reduced serum phosphorus levels and calcium-phosphorus product levels.

Pregnancy Risk Factor B

Pregnancy Considerations Adverse events were not observed in most animal reproduction studies. Maternal systemic absorption of sucroferric oxyhydroxide is low

SUFentanil (soo FEN ta nil)

Brand Names: Canada Sufenta; Sufentanil Citrate Injection, USP

Pharmacologic Category Analgesic, Opioid; Anilidopiperidine Opioid; General Anesthetic

Use

Epidural analgesia: For epidural administration as an analgesic combined with low-dose bupivacaine during labor and vaginal delivery.

Surgical analgesia: Analgesic adjunct for the maintenance of balanced general anesthesia in patients who are intubated and ventilated.

Surgical anesthesia: As a primary anesthetic agent for the induction and maintenance of anesthesia with 100% oxygen in patients undergoing major surgical procedures; in patients who are intubated and ventilated, such as cardiovascular surgery or neurosurgical procedures in the sitting position; to provide favorable myocardial and cerebral oxygen balance or when extended postoperative ventilation is anticipated.

Local Anesthetic/Vasoconstrictor Precautions No information available to require special precautions

Effects on Dental Treatment Key adverse event(s) related to dental treatment: Patients may experience orthostatic hypotension as they stand up after treatment; especially if lying in dental chair for extended periods of time. Use caution with sudden changes in position during and after dental treatment.

Effects on Bleeding No information available to require special precautions

Adverse Reactions

>10%: Dermatologic: Pruritus (epidural administration: 25%)

Frequency not defined:

Cardiovascular: Bradycardia, hypotension, peripheral vasodilation

Central nervous system: Drug dependence (physical and psychological; with prolonged use)

Gastrointestinal: Decreased gastrointestinal motility, nausea (dose-related), vomiting (dose-related)

Neuromuscular & skeletal: Muscle rigidity (dose-related)

Ophthalmic: Miosis

Respiratory: Apnea, respiratory depression (dose-related)

<1%, postmarketing, and/or case reports: Anaphylaxis

General Dosage Range

IV:

Children <12 years: 10 to 25 mcg/kg; Maintenance: Up to 25 to 50 mcg as needed

Adults: 1 to 30 mcg/kg (depending on length of surgical procedure); Maintenance: 10 to 25 mcg as needed

Epidural: *Adults:* 10 to 15 mcg (maximum: 3 doses)

Mechanism of Action Binds to opioid receptors throughout the CNS. Once receptor binding occurs, effects are exerted by opening K+ channels and inhibiting Ca++ channels. These mechanisms increase pain threshold, alter pain perception, inhibit ascending pain pathways; short-acting opioid; dose-related inhibition of catecholamine release (up to 30 mcg/kg) controls sympathetic response to surgical stress.

Pharmacodynamics/Kinetics

Onset of Action Analgesia: IV: 1 to 3 minutes; Epidural: 10 minutes

Duration of Action Dose dependent; Epidural: 10 to 15 mcg with bupivacaine 0.125%: 1.7 hours; Anesthesia adjunct doses: 5 minutes

Half-life Elimination Neonates: 7.2 ± 2.7 hours; Infants and Children (2 to 8 years): 97 ± 42 minutes; Adolescents 10-15 years: 76 ± 33 minutes; Adults: 164 minutes

Pregnancy Considerations Adverse event have been observed in some animal reproduction studies. Administration of epidural sufentanil with bupivacaine with or without epinephrine is indicated in labor and delivery. Intravenous use or larger epidural doses are not recommended in pregnant women. When used for pain relief during labor, opioids may temporarily affect the heart rate of the fetus (ACOG 2002).

Controlled Substance C-II

Sulconazole (sul KON a zole)

Brand Names: US Exelderm

Pharmacologic Category Antifungal Agent, Imidazole Derivative; Antifungal Agent, Topical

Use Fungal infections:

Cream: Treatment of tinea pedis (athlete's foot), tinea cruris, and tinea corporis caused by *Trichophyton rubrum*, *Trichophyton mentagrophytes*, *Epidermophyton floccosum*, and *Microsporum canis*; treatment of tinea versicolor

Solution: Treatment of tinea cruris and tinea corporis caused by *Trichophyton rubrum*, *Trichophyton mentagrophytes*, *Epidermophyton floccosum*, and *Microsporum canis*; treatment of tinea versicolor

Limitations of use: Effectiveness has not been proven in tinea pedis (athlete's foot).

Local Anesthetic/Vasoconstrictor Precautions No information available to require special precautions

Effects on Dental Treatment No significant effects or complications reported

Effects on Bleeding No information available to require special precautions

Adverse Reactions 1% to 10%:

Central nervous system: Localized burning

Dermatologic: Localized erythema, pruritus, stinging of the skin

General Dosage Range Topical: *Adults:* Apply a small amount to affected area once or twice daily

Mechanism of Action Substituted imidazole derivative which inhibits metabolic reactions necessary for the synthesis of ergosterol, an essential membrane component. The end result is usually fungistatic; however, sulconazole may act as a fungicide in *Candida albicans* and *Candida parapsilosis* during certain growth phases.

Pregnancy Risk Factor C

Pregnancy Considerations Adverse events have been observed in animal reproduction studies with large doses administered orally. Systemic absorption is limited following topical administration.

Sulfacetamide and Prednisolone
(sul fa SEE ta mide & pred NIS oh lone)

Brand Names: US Blephamide

Brand Names: Canada AK Cide Oph; Blephamide; Dioptimyd

Pharmacologic Category Antibiotic/Corticosteroid, Ophthalmic

Use Inflammatory ocular conditions: Treatment of steroid-responsive inflammatory ocular conditions (where either a superficial bacterial ocular infection or the risk of bacterial ocular infection exists) of the palpebral and bulbar conjunctiva, cornea, and anterior segment of the globe; chronic anterior uveitis; corneal injury from chemical, radiation, or thermal burns; penetration of foreign bodies

Local Anesthetic/Vasoconstrictor Precautions No information available to require special precautions

Effects on Dental Treatment No significant effects or complications reported

Effects on Bleeding No information available to require special precautions

Adverse Reactions Frequency not defined. Also see individual agents.

Dermatologic: Stevens-Johnson syndrome, toxic epidermal necrolysis

Hematologic & oncologic: Agranulocytosis, aplastic anemia

Hepatic: Fulminant hepatic necrosis

Hypersensitivity: Hypersensitivity reaction

Infection: Secondary infection (bacterial, fungal)

Local: Local irritation

Ophthalmic: Accommodation disturbance, anterior uveitis (acute), blepharoptosis, eye perforation, glaucoma, increased intraocular pressure, mydriasis, optic nerve damage (infrequent), subcapsular posterior cataract

Miscellaneous: Wound healing impairment

<1%, postmarketing, and/or case reports: Hypercorticoidism (systemic)

General Dosage Range Ophthalmic: *Children ≥6 years, Adolescents, and Adults:*

Ointment: Apply ~1/2 inch ribbon 3 to 4 times daily and 1 to 2 times at night

Solution: Instill 2 drops every 4 hours

Suspension: Instill 2 drops every 4 hours during the day and at bedtime

Mechanism of Action Interferes with bacterial growth by inhibiting bacterial folic acid synthesis through competitive antagonism of PABA; decreases inflammation by suppression of migration of polymorphonuclear leukocytes and reversal of increased capillary permeability; suppresses the immune system by reducing activity and volume of the lymphatic system

Pregnancy Considerations Animal reproduction studies have not been conducted with this combination. Use of systemic sulfonamides during pregnancy may cause kernicterus in the newborn. See individual agents.

SulfADIAZINE (sul fa DYE a zeen)

Pharmacologic Category Antibiotic, Sulfonamide Derivative

Use Treatment of chancroid, trachoma, inclusion conjunctivitis, nocardiosis, urinary tract infections, toxoplasmosis encephalitis, malaria, meningococcal meningitis, acute otitis media, meningitis (adjunctive); prophylaxis of rheumatic fever

Local Anesthetic/Vasoconstrictor Precautions No information available to require special precautions

Effects on Dental Treatment No significant effects or complications reported

Effects on Bleeding No information available to require special precautions

Adverse Reactions

Frequency not defined.

Cardiovascular: Allergic myocarditis, periarteritis nodosa
Central nervous system: Ataxia, chills, depression, hallucination, headache, insomnia, peripheral neuritis, seizure, vertigo
Dermatologic: Erythema multiforme, exfoliative dermatitis, pruritus, skin photosensitivity, skin rash, Stevens-Johnson syndrome, toxic epidermal necrolysis, urticaria
Endocrine & metabolic: Hypoglycemia, thyroid dysfunction
Gastrointestinal: Abdominal pain, anorexia, diarrhea, nausea, pancreatitis, stomatitis, vomiting
Genitourinary: Crystalluria, diuresis, toxic nephrosis (with anuria and oliguria)
Hematologic & oncologic: Agranulocytosis, aplastic anemia, hemolytic anemia, hypoprothrombinemia, leukopenia, methemoglobinemia, purpura, thrombocytopenia
Hepatic: Hepatitis
Hypersensitivity: Anaphylactoid reaction
Immunologic: Serum sickness-like reaction
Neuromuscular & skeletal: Arthralgia, lupus erythematosus
Ophthalmic: Conjunctival injection, injected sclera, periorbital edema
Otic: Tinnitus
Renal: Nephrolithiasis
Miscellaneous: Fever

General Dosage Range Oral:
Children >2 months: Initial: 75 mg/kg; Maintenance: 150 mg/kg/day (maximum: 6 g/24 hours)
Children <30 kg and Adults <30 kg: 0.5 g/day (rheumatic fever prophylaxis)
Children ≥30 kg and Adults ≥30 kg: 1 g/day (rheumatic fever prophylaxis)
Adults: 2-4 g/day in divided doses

Mechanism of Action Interferes with bacterial growth by inhibiting bacterial folic acid synthesis through competitive antagonism of PABA

Pharmacodynamics/Kinetics
Half-life Elimination 10 hours
Time to Peak Within 3-6 hours

Pregnancy Risk Factor C

Pregnancy Considerations Adverse events have been observed in animal reproduction studies. Sulfadiazine crosses the placenta (Speert, 1943). Available studies and case reports have failed to show an increased risk for congenital malformations after sulfadiazine use (Heinonen, 1977); however, studies with sulfonamides as a class have shown mixed results (ACOG, 2011).

Sulfadiazine is recommended for use in pregnant women to prevent *T. gondii* infection of the fetus, for the maternal treatment of *Toxoplasmic gondii* encephalitis, and as an alternative agent for the secondary prevention of rheumatic fever (CDC, 2009; DHHS, 2013; Gerber, 2009). Sulfonamides may be used to treat other infections in pregnant women when clinically appropriate for confirmed infections caused by susceptible organisms; use during the first trimester should be limited to situations where no alternative therapies are available (ACOG, 2011). Because safer options are available for the treatment of urinary tract infections in pregnant women, use of sulfonamide-containing products >32 weeks gestation should be avoided (Lee, 2008). Due to the theoretical increased risk for hyperbilirubinemia and kernicterus, sulfadiazine is contraindicated by the manufacturer for use near term. Neonatal healthcare providers should be informed if maternal sulfonamide therapy is used near the time of delivery (DHHS, 2013).

Sulfamethoxazole and Trimethoprim

(sul fa meth OKS a zole & trye METH oh prim)

Related Information
Trimethoprim *on page 1610*

Brand Names: US Bactrim; Bactrim DS; Sulfatrim Pediatric

Brand Names: Canada Apo-Sulfatrim; Apo-Sulfatrim DS; Apo-Sulfatrim Pediatric; Protrin DF; Septra Injection; Teva-Trimel; Teva-Trimel DS; Trisulfa; Trisulfa DS; Trisulfa S

Pharmacologic Category Antibiotic, Miscellaneous; Antibiotic, Sulfonamide Derivative

Use
Oral: Treatment of urinary tract infections due to *Escherichia coli, Klebsiella* and *Enterobacter* sp, *Morganella morganii, Proteus mirabilis* and *Proteus vulgaris*; acute otitis media; acute exacerbations of chronic bronchitis due to susceptible strains of *Haemophilus influenzae* or *Streptococcus pneumoniae*; treatment and prophylaxis of *Pneumocystis* pneumonia (PCP); traveler's diarrhea due to enterotoxigenic *E. coli*; treatment of Shigellosis caused by *Shigella flexneri* or *Shigella sonnei*
IV: Treatment of *Pneumocystis* pneumonia (PCP); treatment of Shigellosis caused by *Shigella flexneri* or *Shigella sonnei*; treatment of severe or complicated urinary tract infections due to *E. coli, Klebsiella* and *Enterobacter* spp, *M. morganii, P. mirabilis,* and *P. vulgaris*

Local Anesthetic/Vasoconstrictor Precautions No information available to require special precautions

Effects on Dental Treatment Key adverse event(s) related to dental treatment: Stomatitis.

Effects on Bleeding No information available to require special precautions

Adverse Reactions Frequency not defined:
Cardiovascular: Allergic myocarditis, periarteritis nodosa (rare)
Central nervous system: Apathy, aseptic meningitis, ataxia, chills, depression, fatigue, hallucination, headache, insomnia, nervousness, peripheral neuritis, seizure, vertigo
Dermatologic: Erythema multiforme (rare), exfoliative dermatitis (rare), pruritus, skin photosensitivity, skin rash, Stevens-Johnson syndrome (rare), toxic epidermal necrolysis (rare), urticaria
Endocrine & metabolic: Hyperkalemia (generally at high dosages), hypoglycemia (rare), hyponatremia
Gastrointestinal: Abdominal pain, anorexia, diarrhea, glottis edema, kernicterus (in neonates), nausea, pancreatitis, pseudomembranous colitis, stomatitis, vomiting
Genitourinary: Crystalluria, diuresis (rare), nephrotoxicity (in association with cyclosporine), toxic nephrosis (with anuria and oliguria)
Hematologic & oncologic: Agranulocytosis, anaphylactoid purpura (IgA vasculitis; rare), aplastic anemia, eosinophilia, hemolysis (with G6PD deficiency), hemolytic anemia, hypoprothrombinemia, leukopenia, megaloblastic anemia, methemoglobinemia, neutropenia, thrombocytopenia
Hepatic: Cholestatic jaundice, hepatotoxicity (including hepatitis, cholestasis, and hepatic necrosis), hyperbilirubinemia, increased transaminases

Hypersensitivity: Anaphylaxis, angioedema, hypersensitivity reaction, serum sickness
Neuromuscular & skeletal: Arthralgia, myalgia, rhabdomyolysis (mainly in AIDS patients), systemic lupus erythematosus (rare), weakness
Ophthalmic: Conjunctival injection, injected sclera
Otic: Tinnitus
Renal: Increased blood urea nitrogen, increased serum creatinine, interstitial nephritis, renal failure
Respiratory: Cough, dyspnea, pulmonary infiltrates
Miscellaneous: Fever
Postmarketing: Dysgeusia (Syed 2016), idiopathic thrombocytopenic purpura, prolonged Q-T interval on ECG, thrombotic thrombocytopenic purpura

General Dosage Range Dosage adjustment recommended in patients with renal impairment

IV: *Children >2 months and Adults:* 8-20 mg TMP/kg/day divided every 6-12 hours

Oral:

Children >2 months: 6-20 mg TMP/kg/day divided every 6-12 hours **or** 150 mg TMP/m^2/day in divided doses every 12-24 hours for 3-7 days/week (maximum: sulfamethoxazole 1600 mg/day; trimethoprim 320 mg/day)

Adults: 1 or 2 double-strength tablets (sulfamethoxazole 800-1600 mg; trimethoprim 160-320 mg) every 12-24 hours **or** 15-20 mg TMP/kg/day in 3-4 divided doses

Mechanism of Action Sulfamethoxazole interferes with bacterial folic acid synthesis and growth via inhibition of dihydrofolic acid formation from para-aminobenzoic acid; trimethoprim inhibits dihydrofolic acid reduction to tetrahydrofolate resulting in sequential inhibition of enzymes of the folic acid pathway

Pharmacodynamics/Kinetics

Half-life Elimination

TMP: Prolonged in renal failure
Newborns: ~19 hours; range: 11 to 27 hours (Springer 1982)
Infants 2 months to 1 year: ~4.6 hours; range: 3 to 6 hours (Hoppu 1989)
Children 1 to 10 years: 3.7 to 5.5 hours (Hoppu 1987)
Children and Adolescents >10 years: 8.19 hours
Adults: 6 to 11 hours
SMX: 9 to 12 hours, prolonged in renal failure

Time to Peak Serum: Oral: 1 to 4 hours

Pregnancy Risk Factor D

Pregnancy Considerations Adverse events have been observed in animal reproduction studies. Trimethoprim-sulfamethoxazole (TMP-SMX) crosses the placenta and distributes to amniotic fluid (Ylikorkala, 1973). An increased risk of congenital malformations (neural tube defects, cardiovascular malformations, urinary tract defects, oral clefts, club foot) following maternal use of TMP-SMX during pregnancy has been observed in some studies. Folic acid supplementation may decrease this risk (Crider 2009; Czeizel 2001; Hernandez-Diaz 2000; Hernandez-Diaz 2001; Matok 2009). Due to theoretical concerns that sulfonamides pass the placenta and may cause kernicterus in the newborn, neonatal healthcare providers should be informed if maternal sulfonamide therapy is used near the time of delivery (DHHS 2013).

The pharmacokinetics of TMP-SMX are similar to nonpregnant values in early pregnancy (Ylikorkala, 1973). TMP-SMX is recommended for the prophylaxis or treatment of *Pneumocystis jirovecii* pneumonia (PCP), prophylaxis of *Toxoplasmic gondii* encephalitis (TE), and for the acute and chronic treatment of Q fever in pregnancy (CDC 2013; DHHS 2013). Sulfonamides may also be used to treat other infections in pregnant women when clinically appropriate; use during the first trimester should be limited to situations where no alternative therapies are available (ACOG 2011). Because safer options are available for the treatment of urinary tract infections in pregnant women, use of TMP-containing products in the first trimester and sulfonamide-containing products >32 weeks gestation should be avoided (Lee 2008).

SulfaSALAzine (sul fa SAL a zeen)

Brand Names: US Azulfidine; Azulfidine EN-tabs

Brand Names: Canada Apo-Sulfasalazine; PMS-Sulfasalazine; Salazopyrin; Salazopyrin En-Tabs

Pharmacologic Category 5-Aminosalicylic Acid Derivative

Use

Juvenile rheumatoid arthritis: Delayed release: Treatment of pediatric patients with polyarticular-course juvenile rheumatoid arthritis who have responded inadequately to salicylates or other nonsteroidal anti-inflammatory drugs (NSAIDs).

Rheumatoid arthritis: Delayed release: Treatment of patients with rheumatoid arthritis who have responded inadequately to salicylates or other NSAIDs. **Note:** Treatment initiation with a disease-modifying antirheumatic drug (DMARD) is recommended in DMARD-naive patients with either early rheumatoid arthritis (RA) (disease duration <6 months) or established RA (disease duration ≥6 months) (Singh [ACR 2016]).

Ulcerative colitis: Immediate and delayed release: Treatment of mild to moderate ulcerative colitis; adjunctive therapy in severe ulcerative colitis; prolongation of the remission period between acute attacks of ulcerative colitis.

Local Anesthetic/Vasoconstrictor Precautions No information available to require special precautions

Effects on Dental Treatment No significant effects or complications reported

Effects on Bleeding Sulfasalazine has been shown to induce a rare but potentially serious autoimmune thrombocytopenia, as detected by a significant decrease in platelet counts. Sulfasalazine-induced thrombocytopenia can be resolved by discontinuation of the drug.

Adverse Reactions

>10%:
Central nervous system: Headache (RA 9%)
Dermatologic: Skin rash (RA 13%)
Gastrointestinal: Nausea (RA 19%), dyspepsia (RA 13%), anorexia, gastric distress, vomiting
Genitourinary: Oligospermia (reversible)

1% to 10%:
Central nervous system: Dizziness
Dermatologic: Pruritus (RA 4%), urticaria
Gastrointestinal: Abdominal pain (RA 8%), stomatitis (RA 4%)
Hematologic & oncologic: Leukopenia (RA 3%), thrombocytopenia (RA 1%), Heinz body anemia, hemolytic anemia
Hepatic: Abnormal hepatic function tests (RA 4%)
Respiratory: Cyanosis
Miscellaneous: Fever

<1%, postmarketing, and/or case reports (includes reactions reported with mesalamine or other sulfonamides): Agranulocytosis, alopecia, anaphylaxis, angioedema, aplastic anemia, arthralgia, ataxia, cauda equina syndrome, cholestasis, cholestatic hepatitis, cholestatic jaundice, conjunctival injection,

crystalluria, depression, diarrhea, DRESS syndrome, drowsiness, eosinophilia, exfoliative dermatitis, folate deficiency, fulminant hepatitis, Guillain-Barré syndrome, hallucination, hearing loss, hematologic abnormality, hematologic disease (pseudomononucleosis), hematuria, hemolytic-uremic syndrome, hepatic cirrhosis, hepatic failure, hepatic necrosis, hepatitis, hepatotoxicity (idiosyncratic) (Chalasani, 2014), hypoglycemia, hypoprothrombinemia, injected sclera, insomnia, interstitial nephritis, interstitial pulmonary disease, jaundice, Kawasaki syndrome (single case report), lupus-like syndrome, megaloblastic anemia, meningitis, methemoglobinemia, myelitis, myelodysplastic syndrome, myocarditis (allergic), nephritis, nephrolithiasis, nephrotic syndrome, neutropenia (congenital), neutropenic enterocolitis, oropharyngeal pain, pallor, pancreatitis, parapsoriasis varioliformis acuta, periarteritis nodosa, pericarditis, periorbital edema, peripheral neuropathy, pleurisy, pneumonia, pneumonitis, proteinuria, pulmonary alveolitis, purpura, renal disease (acute), rhabdomyolysis, seizure, sepsis, serum sickness-like reaction (children with JRA have frequent and severe reaction), skin discoloration, skin photosensitivity, Stevens-Johnson syndrome, thyroid function impairment, tinnitus, toxic epidermal necrolysis, toxic nephrosis, urinary tract infection, urine discoloration, vasculitis, vertigo

General Dosage Range Oral:

Delayed release:

Children ≥6 years: Initial: 1/4 to 1/3 of expected maintenance dose; Maintenance: 30 to 50 mg/kg/day in 2 divided doses (maximum: 2 g daily)

Adults: Initial: 0.5 to 1 g daily; Maintenance: 2 g/day in 2 divided doses (maximum: 3 g daily)

Immediate release:

Children ≥6 years: Initial: 40 to 60 mg/kg/day in 3 to 6 divided doses (maximum: 4 g/day); Maintenance: 30 mg/kg/day in 4 divided doses (maximum: 2 g/day)

Adults: Initial: 3 to 4 g daily in evenly divided doses at ≤8-hour intervals; Maintenance: 2 g daily in divided doses at ≤8-hour intervals

Mechanism of Action 5-aminosalicylic acid (5-ASA) is the active component of sulfasalazine; the specific mechanism of action of 5-ASA is unknown; however, it is thought that it modulates local chemical mediators of the inflammatory response, especially leukotrienes, and is also postulated to be a free radical scavenger or an inhibitor of tumor necrosis factor (TNF); action appears topical rather than systemic

Pharmacodynamics/Kinetics

Onset of Action JIA: Minimum trial of 3 months is necessary; Ulcerative colitis: >3 to 4 weeks

Half-life Elimination Sulfasalazine: 5.7 to 10 hours (prolonged in elderly); Sulfapyridine: 14.8 hours (slow acetylators) and 10.4 hours (fast acetylators)

Time to Peak Sulfasalazine: 3 to 12 hours (mean: 6 hours); Serum sulfapyridine (active metabolite): Within 6 to 24 hours

Pregnancy Risk Factor B

Pregnancy Considerations Adverse events have not been observed in animal reproduction studies. Sulfasalazine and sulfapyridine cross the placenta; a potential for kernicterus in the newborn exists. Agranulocytosis was noted in an infant following maternal use of sulfasalazine during pregnancy. Additionally, cases of neural tube defects have been reported (causation undetermined); sulfasalazine is known to inhibit the absorption and metabolism of folic acid and may diminish the effects of folic acid supplementation. Based on available data, an increase in fetal malformations has not been observed following maternal use of sulfasalazine for the treatment of inflammatory bowel disease or ulcerative colitis. When treatment for inflammatory bowel disease is needed during pregnancy, sulfasalazine may be used, although supplementation with folic acid is recommended (Habal, 2012; Mahadevan, 2009; Mottet, 2007).

Sulfur and Salicylic Acid

(SUL fyoor & sal i SIL ik AS id)

Related Information

Salicylic Acid *on page 1459*

Brand Names: US ala seb [OTC]; Pernox Lemon [OTC]; Pernox Regular [OTC]; Sebex [OTC]; Sebulex [OTC]

Pharmacologic Category Antiseborrheic Agent, Topical

Use Therapeutic shampoo for dandruff and seborrheic dermatitis; acne skin cleanser

Local Anesthetic/Vasoconstrictor Precautions No information available to require special precautions

Effects on Dental Treatment No significant effects or complications reported

Effects on Bleeding No information available to require special precautions

Adverse Reactions Local: Topical preparations containing 2% to 5% sulfur generally are well tolerated, local irritation may occur, concentration >15% is very irritating to the skin, higher concentration (eg, 10% or higher) may cause systemic toxicity (eg, headache, vomiting, muscle cramps, dizziness, collapse)

Mechanism of Action Salicylic acid works synergistically with sulfur in its keratolytic action to break down keratin and promote skin peeling

Pregnancy Considerations Refer to salicylic acid monograph.

Sulindac (SUL in dak)

Related Information

Rheumatoid Arthritis, Osteoarthritis, and Osteoporosis *on page 1792*

Temporomandibular Dysfunction (TMD), Chronic Pain, and Fibromyalgia *on page 1868*

Brand Names: Canada Apo-Sulin; Teva-Sulindac

Pharmacologic Category Analgesic, Nonopioid; Nonsteroidal Anti-inflammatory Drug (NSAID), Oral

Use

Acute gouty arthritis: Relief of signs and symptoms of acute gouty arthritis.

Ankylosing spondylitis: Relief of signs and symptoms of ankylosing spondylitis.

Arthritis: Relief of signs and symptoms of osteoarthritis and rheumatoid arthritis (RA).

Bursitis/tendinitis of the shoulder: Relief of signs and symptoms of acute painful shoulder (acute subacromial bursitis/supraspinatus tendinitis).

Local Anesthetic/Vasoconstrictor Precautions No information available to require special precautions

Effects on Dental Treatment The dentist should be aware of the potential of abnormal coagulation. Caution should also be exercised in the use of NSAIDs in patients already on anticoagulant therapy with drugs such as warfarin (Coumadin®). See Effects on Bleeding.

Effects on Bleeding Nonselective NSAIDs, such as sulindac, inhibit platelet aggregation and prolong bleeding time in some patients. Unlike aspirin, the NSAID ▶

effect on platelet function is quantitatively less, of shorter duration, and reversible. Normal platelet function should occur in ~5 elimination half-lives or in <10 hours after discontinuation of sulindac. Concomitant use of other NSAIDs should be avoided.

Adverse Reactions

1% to 10%:

Cardiovascular: Edema (1% to 3%)

Central nervous system: Dizziness (3% to 9%), headache (3% to 9%), nervousness (1% to 3%)

Dermatologic: Skin rash (3% to 9%), pruritus (1% to 3%)

Gastrointestinal: Gastrointestinal pain (10%), constipation (3% to 9%), diarrhea (3% to 9%), dyspepsia (3% to 9%), nausea (3% to 9%), abdominal cramps (1% to 3%), anorexia (1% to 3%), flatulence (1% to 3%), vomiting (1% to 3%)

Otic: Tinnitus (1% to 3%)

<1%, postmarketing, and/or case reports: Agranulocytosis, ageusia, alopecia, anaphylaxis, angioedema, aplastic anemia, aseptic meningitis, auditory impairment, bitter taste, blurred vision, bone marrow depression, bowel stricture, bronchospasm, bruise, cardiac arrhythmia, cardiac failure, cholestasis, colitis, conjunctivitis, crystalluria, depression, drowsiness, dry mucous membranes, dyspnea, dysuria, epistaxis, erythema multiforme, exfoliative dermatitis, fever, gastritis, gastrointestinal hemorrhage, gastrointestinal perforation, glossitis, gynecomastia, hematuria, hemolytic anemia, hepatic failure, hepatic insufficiency, hepatitis, hepatotoxicity (idiosyncratic; Chalasani 2014), hyperglycemia, hyperkalemia, hypersensitivity angiitis, hypersensitivity reaction (including hypersensitivity syndrome with chills, diaphoresis, fever, flushing), hypertension, insomnia, interstitial nephritis, jaundice, leukopenia, metallic taste, necrotizing fasciitis, nephrolithiasis, nephrotic syndrome, neuritis, neutropenia, palpitations, pancreatitis, paresthesia, peptic ulcer, proteinuria, psychosis, purpura, renal failure, renal insufficiency, retinopathy, seizure, skin photosensitivity, Stevens-Johnson syndrome, stomatitis, syncope, thrombocytopenia, toxic epidermal necrolysis, urine discoloration, urticaria, vaginal hemorrhage, vertigo, visual disturbance, weakness

General Dosage Range Oral: *Adults:* 150 to 200 mg twice daily (maximum: 400 mg/day)

Mechanism of Action

Reversibly inhibits cyclooxygenase-1 and 2 (COX-1 and 2) enzymes, which results in decreased formation of prostaglandin precursors; has antipyretic, analgesic, and anti-inflammatory properties.

Other proposed mechanisms not fully elucidated (and possibly contributing to the anti-inflammatory effect to varying degrees), include inhibiting chemotaxis, altering lymphocyte activity, inhibiting neutrophil aggregation/activation, and decreasing proinflammatory cytokine levels.

Pharmacodynamics/Kinetics

Onset of Action

Therapeutic response: Within 1 week

Half-life Elimination Sulindac: 7.8 hours; Sulfide metabolite: 16.4 hours

Time to Peak Sulindac: ~3 to 4 hours; Sulfide and sulfone metabolites: ~5 to 6 hours

Pregnancy Risk Factor C

Pregnancy Considerations Adverse events have not been observed in animal reproduction studies. Sulindac and the sulfide metabolite have been found to cross the placenta. NSAID exposure during the first trimester is not strongly associated with congenital malformations; however, cardiovascular anomalies and cleft palate have been observed following NSAID exposure in some studies. The use of an NSAID in the first trimester may be associated with an increased risk of miscarriage. Nonteratogenic effects have been observed following NSAID administration during the third trimester including myocardial degenerative changes, prenatal constriction of the ductus arteriosus, failure of the ductus arteriosus to close postnatally, and fetal tricuspid regurgitation; renal dysfunction or failure, oligohydramnios; gastrointestinal bleeding or perforation, increased risk of necrotizing enterocolitis; intracranial bleeding, platelet dysfunction with resultant bleeding; or pulmonary hypertension. Because they may cause premature closure of the ductus arteriosus, use of NSAIDs late in pregnancy should be avoided (use after 31-32 weeks gestation is not recommended by some clinicians). Sulindac has been used in the management of preterm labor. The chronic use of NSAIDs in women of reproductive age may be associated with infertility that is reversible upon discontinuation of the medication. A registry is available for pregnant women exposed to autoimmune medications including sulindac. For additional information contact the Organization of Teratology Information Specialists, OTIS Autoimmune Diseases Study, at (877) 311-8972.

SUMAtriptan (soo ma TRIP tan)

Related Information

Temporomandibular Dysfunction (TMD), Chronic Pain, and Fibromyalgia *on page 1868*

Brand Names: US Alsuma [DSC]; Imitrex; Imitrex STATdose Refill; Imitrex STATdose System; Onzetra Xsail; Sumavel DosePro; Zecuity [DSC]; Zembrace SymTouch

Brand Names: Canada ACT-Sumatriptan; Apo-Sumatriptan; Ava-Sumatriptan; Dom-Sumatriptan; Imitrex DF; Imitrex Injection; Imitrex Nasal Spray; Mylan-Sumatriptan; PHL-Sumatriptan; PMS-Sumatriptan; Sandoz-Sumatriptan; Sumatriptan DF; Taro-Sumatriptan; Teva-Sumatriptan; Teva-Sumatriptan DF

Pharmacologic Category Antimigraine Agent; Serotonin 5-$HT_{1B, 1D}$ Receptor Agonist

Use

Migraine: Intranasal, Oral, SubQ, Transdermal: Acute treatment of migraine with or without aura in adults

Cluster headache: SubQ (excluding Zembrace): Acute treatment of cluster headache episodes in adults

Local Anesthetic/Vasoconstrictor Precautions No information available to require special precautions

Effects on Dental Treatment Key adverse event(s) related to dental treatment: Bad taste, dysphagia, hyposalivation (tablet), mouth/tongue discomfort (injection).

Effects on Bleeding No information available to require special precautions

Adverse Reactions

Injection:

>10%:

Central nervous system: Tingling sensation (14%), paresthesia (5% to 14%), dizziness (12%), localized warm feeling (11%)

Local: Injection site reaction (≤86%; includes bleeding, bruising, swelling, and erythema), warm sensation at injection site (11%)

1% to 10%:

Cardiovascular: Flushing (7%), chest discomfort (2% to 5%), chest tightness (3%), chest pressure (2%)

Central nervous system: Burning sensation (7%), feeling of heaviness (7%), sensation of pressure (7%), numbness (5%), sensation of tightness (5%), drowsiness (3%), headache (2%), strange feeling (2%), tight feeling in the head (2%), nasal cavity pain (≤2%), anxiety (1%), cold sensation (1%), malaise (1%)
Dermatologic: Diaphoresis (2%)
Gastrointestinal: Nausea and vomiting (4%), sore throat (3%), abdominal distress (1%), dysphagia (1%)
Neuromuscular & skeletal: Neck pain (5%), numbness (5%), weakness (5%), jaw pain (2%), myalgia (2%), muscle cramps (1%)
Ophthalmic: Visual disturbance (1%)
Respiratory: Throat irritation (3%), nasal discomfort (2%), nasal signs and symptoms (2%), sinus discomfort (≤2%), bronchospasm (1%)

Nasal spray:
>10%: Gastrointestinal: Unpleasant taste (13% to 24%), nausea (11% to 13%), vomiting (11% to 13%)
1% to 10%:
Central nervous system: Dizziness (1% to 2%)
Gastrointestinal: Sore throat (1% to 2%)
Respiratory: Nasal signs and symptoms (2% to 4%)

Intranasal:
>10%:
Gastrointestinal: Dysgeusia (20%)
Respiratory: Nasal discomfort (11%)
1% to 10%: Respiratory: Rhinorrhea (5%), rhinitis (2%)

Tablet:
1% to 10%:
Cardiovascular: Hot and cold flashes (2% to 3%, placebo 2%), chest pain (1% to 2%), palpitations (1%), syncope (1%)
Central nervous system: Paresthesia (3% to 5%), malaise (2% to 3%), sensation of pressure (neck/throat/jaw: 2% to 3%; nonspecified: 1% to 3%, placebo 2%), pain (nonspecified; 1% to 2%, placebo 1%), vertigo (<1% to 2%), dizziness (>1%), drowsiness (>1%), headache (>1%), migraine (>1%), sleepiness (>1%), burning sensation (1%), hyperacusis (1%), numbness (1%)
Gastrointestinal: Nausea (>1%), reduced salivation (>1%), vomiting (>1%), diarrhea (1%)
Genitourinary: Hematuria (1%)
Hematologic & oncologic: Hemolytic anemia (1%), hemorrhage (ear: 1%; nose/throat: 1%)
Hypersensitivity: Hypersensitivity reaction (1%)
Neuromuscular & skeletal: Myalgia (1%)
Otic: Hearing loss (1%), tinnitus (1%)
Respiratory: Allergic rhinitis (1%), dyspnea (1%), rhinitis (1%), sinusitis (1%), upper respiratory tract inflammation (1%)

Transdermal system:
>10%: Local: Localized pain (26%)
1% to 10%:
Central nervous system: Localized warm feeling (6%), feeling abnormal (paresthesia, warm/cold sensation: 2%), sensation of pressure (chest/neck/throat/jaw: 2%)
Dermatologic: Skin discoloration (application site: 3% to 5%), allergic contact dermatitis (4%), skin vesicle (application site: 3%)
Hematologic & oncologic: Bruise (application site: 1% to 2%)
Local: Localized pruritus (8%), localized irritation (4%)
<1%, postmarketing, and/or case reports: Skin erosion (application site)

Route unspecified:
Frequency not defined:
Cardiovascular: Ischemia, Raynaud's phenomenon
Hematologic & oncologic: Splenic infarction
<1%, postmarketing, and/or case reports: Abdominal aortic aneurysm, abdominal distress, abnormal hepatic function tests, accommodation disturbance, acute renal failure, agitation, anaphylactoid reaction, anaphylaxis, anemia, angioedema, application site reaction (including serious burns with potential scarring, severe redness, pain, skin discoloration, blistering, and cracked skin; FDA Safety Alert June 2, 2016), arthralgia, atrial fibrillation, bronchospasm, cardiac arrhythmia, cardiomyopathy, cerebral ischemia, cerebrovascular accident, colonic ischemia, coronary artery vasospasm, cyanosis, deafness, decreased appetite, diarrhea, dyspepsia, dysphagia, dystonia, dystonic reaction, ECG changes, fluid retention, flushing, gastrointestinal pain, giant-cell arteritis, hallucination, heart block, hematuria, hemolytic anemia, hemorrhage (nose/throat), hiccups, hypersensitivity reaction, hypertension, hypertensive crisis, hypotension, increased intracranial pressure, increased serum transaminases, increased thyroid stimulating hormone level, intestinal obstruction, ischemic colitis, menstrual disease, muscle rigidity, myocardial infarction, myocardial ischemia (transient), numbness of tongue, optic neuropathy (ischemic), palpitations, pancytopenia, paresthesia, phlebitis, Prinzmetal angina, pruritus, psychomotor disturbance, pulmonary embolism, retinal blood vessel occlusion (artery), retinal thrombosis, seizure, sensation disorder, serotonin syndrome, shock, skin photosensitivity, skin rash, subarachnoid hemorrhage, syncope, thrombocytopenia, thrombophlebitis, thrombosis, toothache, tremor, vasculitis, ventricular fibrillation, ventricular tachycardia, vision loss, xerostomia

General Dosage Range Dosage adjustment recommended for oral route in patients with hepatic impairment

Intranasal:
Powder: *Adults:* 22 mg (11 mg in each nostril); may repeat after 2 hours (maximum: 44 mg [4 nosepieces]/day or 22 mg and one dose of another sumatriptan product separated by ≥2 hours/day).
Solution: *Adults:* 5 to 20 mg in one nostril as a single dose (may divide dose into both nostrils); may repeat after 2 hours (maximum: 40 mg/day)

Oral: *Adults:* 25 to 100 mg as a single dose; may repeat after 2 hours (maximum: 200 mg/day)

SubQ: *Adults:* Initial: Up to 6 mg; may repeat if needed ≥1 hour after initial dose (maximum: 3 or 6 mg per dose; two 6 mg injections per 24-hour period or four 3 mg injections per 24-hour period; or maximum cumulative dose of 12 mg in 24 hours, separated by at least 1 hour)

Transdermal: *Adults:* Initial: Apply one patch (provides 6.5 mg per 4 hours) a second patch may be applied no sooner than 2 hours after activation of the first patch (maximum: 2 patches per 24-hour period)

Mechanism of Action Selective agonist for serotonin ($5\text{-}HT_{1B}$ and $5\text{-}HT_{1D}$ receptors) on intracranial blood vessels and sensory nerves of the trigeminal system; causes vasoconstriction and reduces neurogenic inflammation associated with antidromic neuronal transmission correlating with relief of migraine

Pharmacodynamics/Kinetics

Onset of Action Oral: ~30 minutes; Intranasal: Solution: ~15 to 30 minutes; SubQ: ~10 minutes; Peak effect: Oral: 2 to 4 hours

Half-life Elimination Distribution: 15 minutes; Terminal: 2 hours; range: 1 to 4 hours

Time to Peak Oral: 2 to 2.5 hours; Intranasal: Powder: ~45 minutes; SubQ: 12 minutes (range: 4 to 20 minutes); Transdermal patch: ~1 hour

Pregnancy Risk Factor C

Pregnancy Considerations Adverse events have been observed in animal reproduction studies. In a study using full-term, healthy human placentas, limited amounts of sumatriptan were found to cross the placenta (Schenker 1995).

Pregnancy outcome information for sumatriptan is available from a pregnancy registry sponsored by GlaxoSmithKline. As of September 2012, data were available for 617 infants/fetuses exposed to sumatriptan (including seven also exposed to naratriptan). Following sumatriptan exposure, the risk of major birth defects following first trimester exposure was 4.2% and no consistent pattern of birth defects was observed. The pregnancy registry was closed to enrollment in January 2012 (Ephross 2014).

An analysis of data collected between 1995 and 2008 using the Swedish Medical Birth Register reported pregnancy outcomes following 5-HT1B/1D agonist exposure. An increased risk of major congenital malformations was not observed following sumatriptan exposure (2,229 exposed during the first trimester) (Källén 2011). An increased risk of major congenital malformations was not observed in the prospective Norwegian Mother and Child Cohort Study. The study included women with 5-HT1B/1D agonist exposure between 1999 and 2006 (n=455); of these, 217 were exposed to sumatriptan (Nezvalová-Henriksen 2010; Nezvalová-Henriksen 2012).

If treatment for cluster headaches is needed during pregnancy, sumatriptan may be used (Jürgens 2009). Other agents are preferred for the initial treatment of migraine in pregnancy (Da Silva 2012; MacGregor 2014; Williams 2012); however, sumatriptan may be considered if first-line agents fail (MacGregor 2014).

SUNItinib (su NIT e nib)

Related Information

Clinical Risk Related to Drugs Prolonging QT Interval *on page 1772*

Osteonecrosis of the Jaw *on page 1796*

Brand Names: US Sutent

Brand Names: Canada Sutent

Pharmacologic Category Antineoplastic Agent, Tyrosine Kinase Inhibitor; Antineoplastic Agent, Vascular Endothelial Growth Factor (VEGF) Inhibitor; Vascular Endothelial Growth Factor (VEGF) Inhibitor

Use

Gastrointestinal stromal tumor: Treatment of gastrointestinal stromal tumor (GIST) after disease progression on or intolerance to imatinib

Pancreatic neuroendocrine tumors, advanced: Treatment of progressive, well-differentiated pancreatic neuroendocrine tumors in patients with unresectable locally advanced or metastatic disease

Renal cell carcinoma, advanced: Treatment of advanced renal cell carcinoma

Local Anesthetic/Vasoconstrictor Precautions Hypertension can occur with the use of this drug, particularly early in the treatment course. Monitor for hypertension prior to using local anesthetic with vasoconstrictor; medical consult if necessary.

Sunitinib is one of the drugs confirmed to prolong the QT interval and is accepted as having a risk of causing torsade de pointes. The risk of drug-induced torsade de pointes is extremely low when a single QT interval prolonging drug is prescribed. In terms of epinephrine, it is not known what effect vasoconstrictors in the local anesthetic regimen will have in patients with a known history of congenital prolonged QT interval or in patients taking any medication that prolongs the QT interval. Until more information is obtained, it is suggested that the clinician consult with the physician prior to the use of a vasoconstrictor in suspected patients, and that the vasoconstrictor (epinephrine, mepivacaine and levonordefrin [Carbocaine® 2% with Neo-Cobefrin®]) be used with caution.

Effects on Dental Treatment Key adverse event(s) related to dental treatment: Xerostomia (normal salivary flow resumes upon discontinuation), mucositis/stomatitis, taste perversion, and oral pain.

Effects on Bleeding Chemotherapy may result in significant myelosuppression, potentially including significant reduction in platelet counts (thrombocytopenia grades 3/4: 5% to 9%) and altered hemostasis. Bleeding has been reported in 18% to 37% of patients. In patients who are under active treatment with these agents, medical consult is suggested.

Adverse Reactions

>10%:

Cardiovascular: Hypertension (27% to 34%, GIST: 8% to 15%; grade 3: 10% to 13%, GIST: 4%), decreased left ventricular ejection fraction (RCC: 16% to 27%, grade 3: 3% to 7%; GIST: 11%, grade 3: 1%), peripheral edema (RCC: 24%), chest pain (RCC: 13%), severe hypertension (4% to 10%; >200 mmHg systolic or 110 mmHg diastolic)

Central nervous system: Fatigue (RCC: 62%, pNET: 33%), glossalgia (pNET: ≤48%; RCC: 11%), mouth pain (pNET: ≤48%; RCC: 6% to 14%), headache (18% to 23%), insomnia (15% to 18%), chills (RCC: 14%), depression (RCC: 11%), dizziness (RCC: 11%)

Dermatologic: Skin discoloration (≤25% to 30%; yellow color), hair discoloration (20% to 29%; GIST: 7%), palmar-plantar erythrodysesthesia (23% to 29%, GIST: 14%; grades 3/4: 4% to 8%), xeroderma (15% to 23%), skin rash (14% to 18%; RCC: 29%), alopecia (5% to 14%), erythema (RCC: 12%), pruritus (RCC: 12%)

Endocrine & metabolic: Increased uric acid (RCC: 46%), decreased serum calcium (34% to 42%), decreased serum albumin (pNET: 41%, RCC: 28%), decreased serum phosphate (31% to 36%), increased serum glucose (RCC: 23%), decreased serum potassium (12% to 21%), decreased serum sodium (RCC: 20%), decreased serum magnesium (pNET: 19%), increased serum potassium (16% to 18%), hypothyroidism (4% to 7%; RCC: 16%), increased serum calcium (RCC: 13%), increased serum sodium (10% to 13%)

Gastrointestinal: Diarrhea (59% to 66%; GIST: 40%), nausea (RCC: 58%; pNET: 45%), increased serum lipase (17% to 25%; RCC: 56%; grades 3/4: 5% to 18%), anorexia (RCC: 48%; GIST: 33%), mucositis (47% to 48%, GIST: 29%; includes aphthous stomatitis, dry mucous membranes, gingival pain, gingivitis, glossitis, oral discomfort, oral mucosal ulcer, stomatitis, tongue ulceration), dysgeusia (21%; RCC: 47%), vomiting (34% to 39%), abdominal pain (30% to 39%), increased serum amylase (17% to 20%; RCC: 35%; grades 3/4: 4% to 6%), dyspepsia (RCC: 34%; pNET: 15%), constipation (20% to 23%), weight loss (16%), flatulence (RCC: 14%), xerostomia (RCC: 13%), gastroesophageal reflux disease (RCC: 12%)

Hematologic & oncologic: Decreased hemoglobin (RCC: 79%, pNET: 65%, GIST: 26%; grades 3/4: ≤8%), leukocyte disorder (decreased leukocytes; RCC: 78%; grades 3/4: 8%), decreased neutrophils (71% to 77%, GIST: 53%; grades 3/4: 10% to 17%), abnormal absolute lymphocyte count (decreased; RCC: 68%, pNET: 56%, GIST: 38%; grades 3/4: RCC: 18%, pNET: 7%), decreased platelet count (60% to 68%, GIST: 38%, GIST and RCC: grades 3/4: 5% to 9%), hemorrhage (18% to 22%; RCC: 37%; RCC and GIST, grades 3/4: 3% to 4%; includes hematemesis, hematochezia, hematoma, hemoptysis, melena, metrorrhagia)

Hepatic: Increased serum AST (pNET: 72%, RCC: 56%, GIST: ≤39%; grades 3/4: ≤2% to 5%), increased serum ALT (pNET: 61%; RCC: 51%; GIST: ≤39%; grades 3/4: ≤2% to 4%), increased serum alkaline phosphatase (RCC: 46%; GIST: 24%; grades 3/4: 2% to 4%), increased serum bilirubin (16% to 20%; pNET: 37%; RCC and GIST, grades 3/4: 1%), increased indirect serum bilirubin (RCC and GIST: 10% to 13%; grades 3/4: ≤1%)

Neuromuscular & skeletal: Increased creatine phosphokinase (RCC: 49%), limb pain (RCC: 40%; GIST: ≤14%), weakness (22% to 34%), arthralgia (RCC: 30%; pNET: 15%), back pain (RCC: 28%), myalgia (GIST: ≤14%)

Renal: Increased serum creatinine (RCC: 70%; GIST: 12%)

Respiratory: Cough (RCC: 27%), dyspnea (RCC: 26%), epistaxis (pNET: 20%), nasopharyngitis (RCC: 14%), oropharyngeal pain (RCC: 14%), upper respiratory tract infection (RCC: 11%)

Miscellaneous: Fever (RCC: 22%)

1% to 10%:

Cardiovascular: Deep vein thrombosis (≤3%), pulmonary embolism (≤3%)

Endocrine & metabolic: Hypoglycemia (2%; pNET: 10%)

Gastrointestinal: Hemorrhoids (RCC: 10%), pancreatitis (1%)

Respiratory: Flu-like symptoms (RCC: 5%)

<1%, postmarketing, and/or case reports: Acute renal failure, adrenocortical insufficiency, arterial thrombosis (includes cerebral infarction, cerebrovascular accident, transient ischemic attack), cardiac failure, cardiomyopathy, cerebral hemorrhage, cholecystitis (particularly acalculous), erythema multiforme, esophagitis, fistula (sometimes associated with tumor necrosis and/or regression), fulminant necrotizing fasciitis (including of the perineum), gastrointestinal hemorrhage, gastrointestinal perforation, hemolytic uremic syndrome, hepatic failure, hepatotoxicity, hypersensitivity (includes angioedema), hyperthyroidism, ischemic heart disease, myocardial infarction, myopathy (with/without acute renal failure), nephrotic syndrome, neutropenic infection, osteonecrosis of the jaw, preeclampsia (like syndrome with proteinuria and reversible hypertension) (Gallucci 2013; Patel 2008), prolonged Q-T interval on ECG (dose dependent), proteinuria, pulmonary hemorrhage, pyoderma gangrenosum (including positive dechallenges), renal insufficiency, respiratory tract hemorrhage, respiratory tract infection (may be serious), reversible posterior leukoencephalopathy syndrome, rhabdomyolysis (with/without acute renal failure), seizure, sepsis, septic shock, skin infection (may be serious), Stevens-Johnson syndrome, thrombotic thrombocytopenic purpura, thyroiditis (Feldt 2012), torsades de pointes, toxic epidermal necrolysis, tumor hemorrhage, tumor lysis syndrome, urinary tract hemorrhage, urinary tract infection (may be serious), ventricular arrhythmia, wound healing impairment

General Dosage Range Dosage adjustment recommended in patients with renal impairment, on concomitant therapy, or who develop toxicities

Oral: *Adults:* 50 mg once daily for 4 weeks of a 6-week treatment cycle **or** 37.5 mg once daily, continuous daily dosing

Mechanism of Action Exhibits antitumor and antiangiogenic properties by inhibiting multiple receptor tyrosine kinases, including platelet-derived growth factors (PDGFRα and PDGFRβ), vascular endothelial growth factors (VEGFR1, VEGFR2, and VEGFR3), FMS-like tyrosine kinase-3 (FLT3), colony-stimulating factor type 1 (CSF-1R), and glial cell-line-derived neurotrophic factor receptor (RET).

Pharmacodynamics/Kinetics

Half-life Elimination Terminal: Sunitinib: 40 to 60 hours; SU12662: 80 to 110 hours

Time to Peak 6 to 12 hours

Pregnancy Risk Factor D

Pregnancy Considerations Animal reproduction studies have demonstrated teratogenicity, embryotoxicity, and fetal loss. Because sunitinib inhibits angiogenesis, a critical component of fetal development, adverse effects on pregnancy would be expected. Women of childbearing potential should be advised to avoid pregnancy if receiving sunitinib.

Dental Comment See Local Anesthetic/Vasoconstrictor Precautions

Suvorexant (soo voe REX ant)

Brand Names: US Belsomra

Pharmacologic Category Hypnotic, Miscellaneous; Orexin Receptor Antagonist

Use Insomnia: Treatment of insomnia characterized by difficulties with sleep onset and/or sleep maintenance.

Local Anesthetic/Vasoconstrictor Precautions No information available to require special precautions

Effects on Dental Treatment Key adverse event(s) related to dental treatment: Xerostomia (normal salivary flow resumes after discontinuation)

Effects on Bleeding No information available to require special precautions

Adverse Reactions Frequency not always defined.

Central nervous system: Drowsiness (2% to 12%; dose dependent and more common in females), headache (7%; more common in females), dizziness (3%), abnormal dreams (2%; more common in females), abnormality in thinking, amnesia, anxiety, behavioral changes, central nervous system depression, drug abuse, drug dependence, exacerbation of depression, hallucination, hypnagogic hallucinations, sleep driving, suicidal ideation

Endocrine & metabolic: Increased serum cholesterol

Gastrointestinal: Diarrhea (2%), xerostomia (2%; more common in females)

Neuromuscular & skeletal: Lower extremity weakness, sleep paralysis
Respiratory: Cough (2%; more common in females), upper respiratory tract infection (2%; more common in females)

General Dosage Range Dosage adjustment recommended in patients on concomitant therapy.

Oral: *Adults:* Usual dose: 10 mg once daily, taken within 30 minutes of bedtime; maximum daily dose: 20 mg

Mechanism of Action Suvorexant blocks the binding of wake-promoting neuropeptides orexin A and orexin B to receptors OX1R and OX2R, which is thought to suppress wake drive. Antagonism of orexin receptors may also underlie potential adverse effects such as signs of narcolepsy/cataplexy.

Pharmacodynamics/Kinetics

Onset of Action ~30 minutes

Half-life Elimination ~12 hours; Half-life terminal: ~15 hours (healthy subjects, range: 10 to 22 hours), ~19 hours (moderate hepatic disease, range: 11 to 49 hours)

Time to Peak 2 hours (range: 30 minutes to 6 hours); Delayed approximately 1.5 hours when administered with a meal.

Pregnancy Risk Factor C

Pregnancy Considerations Adverse events have been observed in some animal reproduction studies.

Controlled Substance C-IV

Tacrolimus (Systemic) (ta KROE li mus)

Brand Names: US Astagraf XL; Envarsus XR; Hecoria [DSC]; Prograf

Brand Names: Canada Advagraf; Prograf; Sandoz-Tacrolimus

Generic Availability (US) May be product dependent

Pharmacologic Category Calcineurin Inhibitor; Immunosuppressant Agent

Use Organ rejection prophylaxis:

US labeling:

Astagraf XL: Prevention of organ rejection in kidney transplant recipients in combination with other immunosuppressants.

Envarsus XR: Prevention of organ rejection in kidney transplant recipients converted from tacrolimus immediate-release formulation, in combination with other immunosuppressants.

Hecoria and Prograf: Prevention of organ rejection in heart, kidney, and liver transplant recipients

Canadian labeling:

Advagraf: Prevention of organ rejection in kidney and liver transplant recipients

Prograf: Prevention of organ rejection in heart, kidney, or liver transplant recipients; treatment of refractory rejection in kidney or liver transplant recipients; treatment of active rheumatoid arthritis in adult patients nonresponsive to disease-modifying antirheumatic drug (DMARD) therapy or when DMARD therapy is inappropriate

Local Anesthetic/Vasoconstrictor Precautions No information available to require special precautions

Effects on Dental Treatment Key adverse event(s) related to dental treatment: Stomatitis, oral candida infection, dysphagia, and esophagitis (including ulcerative) (see Dental Comment)

Effects on Bleeding Thrombocytopenia (14% to 24%) has been associated with use; severe thrombocytopenia (rare) may be associated with delayed coagulation. Consultation to ensure adequate platelet counts may be considered in patients with signs/symptoms or a history of thrombocytopenia.

Adverse Reactions

>10%:

Cardiovascular: Angina pectoris, atrial fibrillation, atrial flutter, bradycardia, cardiac arrhythmia, cardiac failure, cerebral infarction, cerebral ischemia, chest pain, deep vein thrombophlebitis, deep vein thrombosis, ECG abnormality (QRS or ST segment or T wave), edema, flushing, hemorrhagic stroke, hypertension, hypertrophic cardiomyopathy, hypotension, ischemic heart disease, localized phlebitis, myocardial infarction, orthostatic hypotension, pericardial effusion, peripheral edema, peripheral vascular disease, phlebitis, syncope, tachycardia, thrombosis, vasodilatation, ventricular premature contractions

Central nervous system: Abnormal dreams, abnormality in thinking, agitation, amnesia, anxiety, aphasia, ataxia, brain disease, carpal tunnel syndrome, chills, confusion, depression, dizziness, drowsiness, emotional lability, excessive crying, falling, fatigue, flaccid paralysis, hallucination, headache, hypertonia, hypoesthesia, insomnia, mental status changes, mood elevation, myasthenia, myoclonus, nervousness, neurotoxicity, nightmares, pain, paresis, paresthesia, peripheral neuropathy, psychosis, seizure, vertigo, voice disorder, writing difficulty

Dermatologic: Acne vulgaris, alopecia, cellulitis, condyloma acuminatum, dermal ulcer, dermatitis (including fungal), dermatological reaction, diaphoresis, exfoliative dermatitis, pruritus, skin discoloration, skin photosensitivity, skin rash

Endocrine & metabolic: Acidosis, albuminuria, alkalosis, anasarca, Cushing's syndrome, decreased serum bicarbonate, decreased serum iron, dehydration, diabetes mellitus, gout, hirsutism, hypercalcemia, hypercholesterolemia, hyperkalemia, hyperphosphatemia, hypertriglyceridemia, hypervolemia, hypocalcemia, hypoglycemia, hypokalemia, hypomagnesemia, hyponatremia, hypophosphatemia, increased gamma-glutamyl transferase, increased lactate dehydrogenase, weight changes

Gastrointestinal: Abdominal pain, anorexia, dyspepsia, aphthous stomatitis, cholangitis, colitis, constipation, delayed gastric emptying, diarrhea, duodenitis, dysphagia, enlargement of abdomen, esophagitis (including ulcerative), flatulence, gastric ulcer, gastritis, gastroesophageal reflux disease, gastrointestinal hemorrhage, gastrointestinal perforation, hernia, hiccups, increased appetite, intestinal obstruction, nausea, oral candidiasis, pancreatic disease (pseudocyst), pancreatitis (including hemorrhagic and necrotizing), peritonitis, rectal disease, stomach cramps, stomatitis, vomiting

Genitourinary: Anuria, bladder spasm, cystitis, dysuria, hematuria, nocturia, oliguria, proteinuria, toxic nephrosis, urinary frequency, urinary incontinence, urinary retention, urinary tract infection, urinary urgency, vaginitis

Hematologic & oncologic: Anemia, blood coagulation disorder, bruise, decreased prothrombin time, hemolytic anemia, hemorrhage, hypochromic anemia, hypoproteinemia, increased hematocrit, increased INR, Kaposi's sarcoma, leukocytosis, leukopenia, malignant neoplasm of bladder, malignant neoplasm of thyroid (papillary), neutropenia, pancytopenia, polycythemia, skin neoplasm, thrombocytopenia

Hepatic: Abnormal hepatic function tests, ascites, cholestatic jaundice, hepatic injury, hepatitis (including acute, chronic, and granulomatous), hyperbilirubinemia, increased serum alkaline phosphatase, jaundice

Hypersensitivity: Hypersensitivity reaction

Immunologic: Graft complications

Infection: Abscess, infection, sepsis, tinea versicolor

Neuromuscular & skeletal: Arthralgia, arthropathy, back pain, leg cramps, muscle spasm, muscle weakness of the extremities, myalgia, neuropathy (including compression), osteoporosis, tremor, weakness

Ophthalmic: Amblyopia, blurred vision, conjunctivitis, visual disturbance

Otic: Hearing loss, otalgia, otitis externa, otitis media, tinnitus

Renal: Acute renal failure, hydronephrosis, increased blood urea nitrogen, increased serum creatinine, renal disease (BK nephropathy), renal function abnormality, renal tubular necrosis

Respiratory: Allergic rhinitis, asthma, atelectasis, cough, flu-like symptoms, pleural effusion, pneumothorax, pulmonary edema, respiratory tract infection

Miscellaneous: Fever, postoperative pain, postoperative wound complication, wound healing impairment

1% to 10%: Gastrointestinal: Gastroenteritis (2% to 7%)

<1%, postmarketing, and/or case reports: Adult respiratory distress syndrome, agranulocytosis, anaphylactoid reaction, anaphylaxis, angioedema, basal cell carcinoma, biliary tract disease (stenosis), blindness, cerebrovascular accident, coma, deafness, decreased serum fibrinogen, delirium, disseminated intravascular coagulation, dysarthria, graft versus host disease (acute and chronic), hemiparesis, hemolytic-uremic syndrome, hemorrhagic cystitis, hepatic cirrhosis, hepatic failure, hepatic necrosis, hepatic veno-occlusive disease, hepatosplenic T-cell lymphomas, hepatotoxicity, hyperpigmentation, immune thrombocytopenia, interstitial pulmonary disease, leukemia, leukoencephalopathy, liver steatosis, lymphoproliferative disorder (post-transplant or related to Epstein-Barr virus), malignant lymphoma, malignant melanoma, multiorgan failure, mutism, optic atrophy, osteomyelitis, photophobia, polyarthritis, progressive multifocal leukoencephalopathy (PML), prolonged partial thromboplastin time, prolonged Q-T interval on ECG, pulmonary hypertension, pure red cell aplasia, quadriplegia, reversible posterior leukoencephalopathy syndrome, rhabdomyolysis, septicemia, squamous cell carcinoma, status epilepticus, Stevens-Johnson syndrome, supraventricular extrasystole, supraventricular tachycardia, thrombotic thrombocytopenic purpura, torsades de pointes, toxic epidermal necrolysis, urticaria, venous thrombosis, ventricular fibrillation

Dosing

Adult

Immunosuppression after solid-organ transplant, sublingual administration: Sublingual (off-label route): Optimal dosing has not been determined. In dosing regimens using sublingual administration of the contents of tacrolimus capsules, the sublingual to oral dosing ratio has ranged from 1:3 to 1:1 (Collin 2010, Nasiri-Toosi 2012). However, most studies suggest a dosing ratio of 1:2 (or 50% of the oral dose given sublingually), and most centers use this approach in practice (Doligalski 2014, Watkins 2012). Adjust dose based on serum trough concentrations. Lower doses of sublingual tacrolimus may be required during coadministration of drugs that inhibit tacrolimus metabolism (Collin 2010, Reams 2002).

Prevention of organ rejection in transplant recipients: Note: The initial postoperative dose of tacrolimus (immediate release) should begin no sooner than 6 hours after liver and heart transplant and within 24 hours of kidney transplant (but may be delayed until renal function has recovered); titrate to target trough concentrations. Adjunctive therapy with corticosteroids is recommended early post-transplant. IV route should only be used in patients not able to take oral medications and continued only until oral medication can be tolerated; anaphylaxis has been reported with IV administration. If switching from IV to oral, the oral dose should be started 8 to 12 hours after stopping the infusion.

Liver transplant:

Oral:

Immediate release: Initial: 0.1 to 0.15 mg/kg/day in 2 divided doses, given every 12 hours (titrate to target trough concentrations)

Extended release: Canadian labeling (Advagraf): 0.1 to 0.2 mg/kg once daily in combination with corticosteroids; initiate within 12 to 18 hours of transplantation. Titrate to target trough concentrations.

Conversion from immediate release to extended release: Patients stable on immediate release tacrolimus may be converted to extended release by initiating extended-release treatment in a 1:1 ratio (mg:mg) using previously established total daily dose of immediate-release product. Administer once daily.

IV: Initial: 0.03 to 0.05 mg/kg/day as a continuous infusion

Heart transplant: Use in combination with azathioprine or mycophenolate mofetil is recommended.

Oral: Immediate release: Initial: 0.075 mg/kg/day in 2 divided doses, given every 12 hours (titrate to target trough concentrations)

IV: Initial: 0.01 mg/kg/day as a continuous infusion

Kidney transplant: Use in combination with azathioprine or mycophenolate mofetil is recommended. **Note:** African-American patients may require larger doses to attain trough concentration.

Oral:

US labeling:

Immediate release (Hecoria, Prograf): Initial: 0.2 mg/kg/day in combination with azathioprine or 0.1 mg/kg/day in combination with mycophenolate mofetil; titrate to target trough concentrations. Administer in 2 divided doses, given every 12 hours.

Extended release (Astagraf XL):

With basiliximab induction (prior to reperfusion or within 48 hours of transplant completion): 0.15 to 0.2 mg/kg once daily (in combination with corticosteroids and mycophenolate); titrate to target trough concentrations

Without basiliximab induction: Preoperative dose (administer within 12 hours prior to reperfusion): 0.1 mg/kg (in combination with corticosteroids and mycophenolate)

Without basiliximab induction: Postoperative dosing (administer at least 4 hours after preoperative dose and within 12 hours of reperfusion): 0.2 mg/kg once daily (in combination with corticosteroids and mycophenolate); titrate to target trough concentrations

Conversion from IV to extended release: Administer the first oral extended release dose 8 to 12 hours after discontinuation of IV tacrolimus

Conversion from immediate release to extended release: Initiate extended release treatment in a 1:1 ratio (mg:mg) using previously established total daily dose of immediate release (Van Hooff 2012). Administer once daily.

Extended release (Envarsus XR): Conversion from immediate release to extended release: Initiate extended-release treatment with a once-daily dose that is 80% of the total daily dose of the immediate-release tacrolimus

Canadian labeling:

Immediate release (Prograf): Initial: 0.2 to 0.3 mg/kg/day in 2 divided doses, given every 12 hours in combination with corticosteroids and other immunosuppressive agents; titrate to target trough concentrations

Extended release (Advagraf): Initial: 0.15 to 0.2 mg/kg once daily; titrate to target trough concentrations. Administer in combination with corticosteroids and mycophenolate mofetil (MMF) in *de novo* kidney transplant recipients. Antibody induction therapy should also be used.

Conversion from immediate release to extended release: Initiate extended release treatment in a 1:1 ratio (mg:mg) using previously established total daily dose of immediate release. Administer once daily.

IV: Initial: 0.03 to 0.05 mg/kg/day as a continuous infusion

Graft-versus-host disease (GVHD) (off-label use):

Prevention:

Oral: Convert from IV to immediate release oral dose (1:4 ratio): Multiply total daily IV dose times 4 and administer in 2 divided oral doses per day, every 12 hours (Uberti 1999; Yanik 2000).

IV: Initial: 0.03 mg/kg/day (based on lean body weight) as continuous infusion. Treatment should begin at least 24 hours prior to stem cell infusion and continued only until oral medication can be tolerated (Przepiorka 1999; Yanik 2000).

Treatment:

Oral: Immediate release: 0.06 mg/kg twice daily (Furlong 2000; Przepiorka 1999)

IV: Initial: 0.03 mg/kg/day (based on lean body weight) as continuous infusion (Furlong 2000; Przepiorka 1999)

Lung transplant (off-label use): Usually used in a combination regimen that contains a corticosteroid and either azathioprine or mycophenolate (Snell 2013).

Oral, nasogastric: Immediate release: 0.05 to 0.3 mg/kg/day in 2 divided doses, given every 12 hours (usual dose: 0.05 mg/kg every 12 hours); titrate to target trough concentrations (Treede 2001; Treede 2012; Zuckermann 2003). May also be administered sublingually at ~50% of the oral/NG dose (Doligalski 2014; Watkins 2012).

Note: May convert from twice-daily dosing to once-daily dosing (on a mg per mg basis) using the extended-release formulation (Astagraf XL [US] or Advagraf [Canada]) in stable lung transplant recipients (Mendez 2014).

IV: 0.01 to 0.05 mg/kg over 24 hours as a continuous IV infusion; titrate to target trough concentrations (Treede 2001; Treede 2012; Zuckermann 2003). For patients receiving the initial dose of tacrolimus intravenously, may begin immediately after transplantation, or up to 2 days postoperatively depending on renal function and hemodynamic stability (Treede 2001; Treede 2012; Witt 2013; Zuckermann 2003). When patient is able to take oral medication, may switch to an oral maintenance regimen (typically transitioned after extubation).

Rheumatoid arthritis: Canadian labeling (not in US labeling): Oral: Immediate release: 3 mg once daily; carefully monitor serum creatinine during therapy

Geriatric Refer to adult dosing. Use with caution; begin at the low end of dosing range.

Pediatric

Liver transplant:

Oral: Immediate release: Initial: 0.15-0.20 mg/kg/day in 2 divided doses, given every 12 hours (titrate to target trough concentrations)

IV: Initial: 0.03-0.05 mg/kg/day as a continuous infusion

Note: The initial postoperative dose of tacrolimus should begin no sooner than 6 hours after liver and heart transplant and within 24 hours of kidney transplant (but may be delayed until renal function has recovered). Adjunctive therapy with corticosteroids is recommended early post-transplant. IV route should only be used in patients not able to take oral medications and continued only until oral medication can be tolerated; anaphylaxis has been reported with IV administration. If switching from IV to oral, the oral dose should be started 8-12 hours after stopping the infusion. Patients without pre-existing renal or hepatic dysfunction have required (and tolerated) higher doses than adults to achieve similar blood concentrations. It is recommended that therapy be initiated at the **high end** of the recommended adult IV and oral dosing ranges; dosage adjustments may be required.

Prevention of graft-vs-host disease (GVHD) (off-label use): Oral, IV: Refer to adult dosing.

Renal Impairment Evidence suggests that lower doses should be used; patients should receive doses at the lowest value of the recommended IV and oral dosing ranges; further reductions in dose below these ranges may be required. May also require dose reductions due to nephrotoxicity.

Kidney transplant: Tacrolimus therapy in patients with postoperative oliguria should begin no sooner than 6 hours and within 24 hours (immediate release) or 48 hours (extended release) post-transplant, but may be delayed until renal function displays evidence of recovery.

Hemodialysis: Not removed by hemodialysis; supplemental dose is not necessary.

Peritoneal dialysis: Significant drug removal is unlikely based on physiochemical characteristics.

Hepatic Impairment Use of tacrolimus in liver transplant recipients experiencing post-transplant hepatic impairment may be associated with increased risk of developing renal insufficiency related to high whole blood levels of tacrolimus. The presence of moderate-to-severe hepatic dysfunction (serum bilirubin >2 mg/dL; Child-Pugh score ≥10) appears to affect the metabolism of tacrolimus. The half-life of the drug was prolonged and the clearance reduced after IV administration. The bioavailability of tacrolimus was also increased after oral administration. The higher plasma concentrations as determined by ELISA, in patients with severe hepatic dysfunction are probably due to the accumulation of metabolites of lower activity. These patients should be monitored closely and dosage adjustments should be considered. Some evidence indicates that lower doses could be used in these patients.

Mechanism of Action Suppresses cellular immunity (inhibits T-lymphocyte activation), by binding to an intracellular protein, FKBP-12 and complexes with calcineurin dependent proteins to inhibit calcineurin phosphatase activity

Contraindications Hypersensitivity to tacrolimus, polyoxyl 60 hydrogenated castor oil (HCO-60), or any other component of the formulation.

Warnings/Precautions

[US Boxed Warning]: Risk of developing infections (including bacterial, viral [including CMV], fungal, and protozoal infections [including opportunistic infections]) is increased. Latent viral infections may be activated, including BK virus (associated with polyoma virus-associated nephropathy [PVAN]) and JC virus (associated with progressive multifocal leukoencephalopathy [PML]); may result in serious adverse effects. Immunosuppression increases the risk for CMV viremia and/or CMV disease; the risk of CMV disease is increased for patients who are CMV-seronegative prior to transplant and receive a graft from a CMV-seropositive donor. Monitor for development of infection; consider reduction in immunosuppression if PVAN, PML, CMV viremia and/or CMV disease occurs. **[US Boxed Warning]: Immunosuppressive therapy may result in the development of lymphoma and other malignancies (predominantly skin malignancies).** The risk for new-onset diabetes and insulin-dependent post-transplant diabetes mellitus (PTDM) is increased with tacrolimus use after transplantation, including in patients without pretransplant history of diabetes mellitus; insulin dependence may be reversible; monitor blood glucose frequently; risk is increased in African-American and Hispanic kidney transplant patients. Nephrotoxicity (acute or chronic) may occur when used in high doses, in patients with impaired renal function, or with other nephrotoxic drugs (eg, sirolimus, cyclosporine) or when administered concomitantly with CYP3A inhibitors (due to increased tacrolimus concentrations). Monitor renal function and consider dosage reduction in nephrotoxicity occurs. Neurotoxicity may occur especially when used in high doses; tremor headache, coma and delirium have been reported and are associated with serum concentrations. Seizures may also occur. Posterior reversible encephalopathy syndrome (PRES) has been reported; symptoms (altered mental status, headache, hypertension, seizures, and visual disturbances) are reversible with dose reduction or discontinuation of therapy; stabilize blood pressure and reduce dose with suspected or confirmed PRES diagnosis.

Pure red cell aplasia (PRCA) has been reported in patients receiving tacrolimus. Use with caution in patients with risk factors for PRCA including parvovirus B19 infection, underlying disease, or use of concomitant medications associated with PRCA (eg, mycophenolate). Discontinuation of therapy should be considered with diagnosis of PRCA. Monitoring of serum concentrations (trough for oral therapy) is essential to prevent organ rejection and reduce drug-related toxicity. Use caution in renal or hepatic dysfunction, dosing adjustments may be required. Delay initiation of therapy in kidney transplant patients if postoperative oliguria occurs; begin therapy no sooner than 6 hours and within 24 hours post-transplant, but may be delayed until renal function has recovered. Mild-to-severe hyperkalemia may occur; monitor serum potassium levels. Hypertension may commonly occur; antihypertensive treatment may be necessary; avoid use of potassium-sparing diuretics due to risk of hyperkalemia; concurrent use of calcium channel blockers may require tacrolimus dosage adjustment. Gastrointestinal perforation may occur; all reported cases were considered to be a complication of transplant surgery or accompanied by infection, diverticulum, or malignant neoplasm. Myocardial hypertrophy has been reported (rare). Prolongation of the QT/QTc and torsade de pointes may occur; avoid use in patients with congenital long QT syndrome. Consider obtaining electrocardiograms and monitoring electrolytes (magnesium, potassium, calcium) periodically during treatment in patients with congestive heart failure, bradyarrhythmias, those taking certain antiarrhythmic medications or other medicinal products that lead to QT prolongation, and those with electrolyte disturbances such as hypokalemia, hypocalcemia, or hypomagnesemia. Potentially significant drug-drug/drug-food interactions may exist, requiring dose or frequency adjustment, additional monitoring, and/or selection of alternative therapy. Concomitant use with strong CYP3A inducers and/or inhibitors may alter tacrolimus whole blood concentrations, potentially leading to rejection and/or increased toxicity, respectively. Monitor tacrolimus whole blood trough concentrations closely. In liver transplantation, the tacrolimus dose and target range should be reduced to minimize the risk of nephrotoxicity when used in combination with everolimus. Extended release tacrolimus in combination with sirolimus is not recommended in renal transplant patients; the safety and efficacy of immediate release tacrolimus in combination with sirolimus has not been established in this patient population. Concomitant use was associated with increased mortality, graft loss, and hepatic artery thrombosis in liver transplant patients, as well as increased risk of renal impairment, wound healing complications, and PTDM in heart transplant recipients.

Immediate release and extended release capsules are NOT interchangeable or substitutable. The extended release formulation is a once daily preparation; and immediate release is intended for twice daily administration. Serious adverse events, including organ rejection may occur if inadvertently substituted. **[US Boxed Warning]: Astagraf XL was associated with increased mortality in female liver transplant recipients; the use of extended release tacrolimus is not approved for use in liver transplantation.** Mortality at 12 months was 10% higher in females who received extended release tacrolimus compared to females who received regular release tacrolimus. Each mL of injection contains polyoxyl 60 hydrogenated castor oil (HCO-60) (200 mg) and dehydrated alcohol USP 80% v/v.

Hypersensitivity reactions, including anaphylaxis, have been reported with tacrolimus injection. Tacrolimus injection contains polyoxyl 60 hydrogenated castor oil (HCO-60), a castor oil derivative. HCO-60 is a solubilizer similar to polyoxyethylated castor oil (also known as polyoxyl 35 castor oil or Cremophor EL); polyoxyethylated castor oil is associated with hypersensitivity reactions (Nicolai 2012). Tacrolimus intravenous (IV) use should be limited to patients unable to take oral capsules. Monitor patient for a minimum of 30 minutes after initiation of infusion and then at frequent intervals; discontinue infusion if anaphylaxis occurs. Patients should be transitioned from IV to oral tacrolimus as soon as the patient can tolerate oral administration. Patients should be brought up to date with all immunizations before initiating therapy. Patients should not be immunized with live vaccines during or shortly after treatment and should avoid close contact with recently vaccinated (live vaccine) individuals. Inactivated vaccines may be administered (response may be diminished). Oral formulations contain lactose; the Canadian labeling does not recommend use of these products in patients who may be lactose intolerant (eg, Lapp lactase deficiency, glucose-galactose malabsorption, galactose intolerance). Oral formulations contain lactose; the Canadian labeling does not recommend use of these products in patients who may be lactose intolerant (eg, Lapp lactase deficiency, glucose-galactose malabsorption, galactose intolerance). **[US Boxed Warning]: Should be administered under the supervision of a physician experienced in immunosuppressive therapy and organ transplantation in a facility appropriate for monitoring and managing therapy.**

Drug Interactions

Metabolism/Transport Effects **Substrate** of CYP3A4 (major), P-glycoprotein; **Note:** Assignment of Major/Minor substrate status based on clinically relevant drug interaction potential

Avoid Concomitant Use

Avoid concomitant use of Tacrolimus (Systemic) with any of the following: BCG (Intravesical); Conivaptan; Crizotinib; CycloSPORINE (Systemic); Deferiprone; Dipyrone; Enzalutamide; Eplerenone; Foscarnet; Fusidic Acid (Systemic); Grapefruit Juice; Idelalisib; MiFEPRIStone; Natalizumab; Nelfinavir; Ombitasvir, Paritaprevir, and Ritonavir; Ombitasvir, Paritaprevir, Ritonavir, and Dasabuvir; Pimecrolimus; Potassium-Sparing Diuretics; Sirolimus; Tacrolimus (Topical); Temsirolimus; Tofacitinib; Vaccines (Live)

Increased Effect/Toxicity

Tacrolimus (Systemic) may increase the levels/effects of: Afatinib; CloZAPine; CycloSPORINE (Systemic); Deferiprone; Dronedarone; Fenofibrate and Derivatives; Fingolimod; Fosphenytoin; Highest Risk QTc-Prolonging Agents; Leflunomide; Moderate Risk QTc-Prolonging Agents; Natalizumab; Phenytoin; Sirolimus; Temsirolimus; Tofacitinib; Vaccines (Live)

The levels/effects of Tacrolimus (Systemic) may be increased by: Alcohol (Ethyl); Antidepressants (Serotonin Reuptake Inhibitor/Antagonist); Aprepitant; Azithromycin (Systemic); Boceprevir; Calcium Channel Blockers (Dihydropyridine); Calcium Channel Blockers (Nondihydropyridine); Chloramphenicol; Clotrimazole (Oral); Clotrimazole (Topical); Conivaptan; Crizotinib; CycloSPORINE (Systemic); CYP3A4 Inhibitors (Moderate); CYP3A4 Inhibitors (Strong); Danazol; Dasatinib; Denosumab; Dipyrone; Dronedarone; Efonidipine; Eplerenone; Ertapenem; Erythromycin (Systemic); Fluconazole; Fosaprepitant; Foscarnet; Fusidic Acid (Systemic); Grapefruit Juice; Grazoprevir; Idelalisib; Isavuconazonium Sulfate; Itraconazole; Ivacaftor; Ketoconazole (Systemic); LevoFLOXacin (Systemic); MiFEPRIStone; Nelfinavir; Netupitant; Nonsteroidal Anti-Inflammatory Agents; Ocrelizumab; Ombitasvir, Paritaprevir, and Ritonavir; Ombitasvir, Paritaprevir, Ritonavir, and Dasabuvir; Palbociclib; P-glycoprotein/ABCB1 Inhibitors; Pimecrolimus; Posaconazole; Potassium-Sparing Diuretics; Promazine; Protease Inhibitors; Proton Pump Inhibitors; Ranolazine; Ritonavir; Roflumilast; Schisandra; Sirolimus; Stiripentol; Tacrolimus (Topical); Telaprevir; Temsirolimus; Tofisopam; Trastuzumab; Voriconazole

Decreased Effect

Tacrolimus (Systemic) may decrease the levels/effects of: Antidiabetic Agents; BCG (Intravesical); Coccidioides immitis Skin Test; Nivolumab; Sipuleucel-T; Tertomotide; Vaccines (Inactivated); Vaccines (Live)

The levels/effects of Tacrolimus (Systemic) may be decreased by: Bosentan; Caspofungin; Cinacalcet; CYP3A4 Inducers (Moderate); CYP3A4 Inducers (Strong); Dabrafenib; Deferasirox; Echinacea; Efavirenz; Enzalutamide; Fosphenytoin; Mitotane; Phenytoin; Rifamycin Derivatives; Sevelamer; Siltuximab; Sirolimus; St John's Wort; Temsirolimus; Tocilizumab

Food Interactions

Ethanol: Alcohol may increase the rate of release of extended-release tacrolimus and adversely affect tacrolimus safety and/or efficacy. Management: Avoid alcohol.

Food: Food decreases rate and extent of absorption. High-fat meals have most pronounced effect (37% and 25% decrease in AUC, respectively, and 77% and 25% decrease in C_{max}, respectively, for immediately release and extended release formulations). Grapefruit juice, a CYP3A4 inhibitor, may increase serum level and/or toxicity of tacrolimus. Management: Administer with or without food (immediate release), but be consistent. Administer extended release on an empty stomach. Avoid concurrent use of grapefruit juice.

Dietary Considerations Capsule: Administer immediate release with or without food; be consistent with timing and composition of meals, food decreases bioavailability. Administer extended release on an empty stomach 1 hour before or 2 hours after a meal. Avoid grapefruit and grapefruit juice. Avoid alcohol.

Pharmacodynamics/Kinetics

Half-life Elimination

Children: 7.7 to 15.3 hours

Adults: Immediate release: Variable, 23 to 46 hours in healthy volunteers; 2.1 to 36 hours in transplant patients; prolonged in patients with severe impairment

Adults: Extended release: 38 ± 3 hours; prolonged in patients with severe impairment

Time to Peak Oral: 0.5 to 6 hours

Pregnancy Risk Factor C

Pregnancy Considerations Adverse events were observed in animal reproduction studies. Tacrolimus crosses the human placenta and is measurable in the cord blood, amniotic fluid, and newborn serum. Tacrolimus concentrations in the placenta may be higher than the maternal serum (Jain 1997). Infants with lower birth weights have been found to have higher tacrolimus concentrations (Bramham 2013). Transient neonatal hyperkalemia and renal dysfunction have been reported.

Tacrolimus pharmacokinetics are altered during pregnancy. Whole blood concentrations decrease as pregnancy progresses; however, unbound concentrations increase. Measuring unbound concentrations may be preferred, especially in women with anemia or hypoalbuminemia. If unbound concentration measurement is not available, interpretation of whole blood concentrations should account for RBC count and serum albumin concentration (Hebert 2013; Zheng 2012).

In general, women who have had a kidney transplant should be instructed that fertility will be restored following the transplant but that pregnancy should be avoided for ~2 years. Tacrolimus may be used as an immunosuppressant during pregnancy. The risk of infection, hypertension, and pre-eclampsia may be increased in pregnant women who have had a kidney transplant (EPBG 2002).

The National Transplantation Pregnancy Registry (NTPR) is a registry which follows pregnancies which occur in maternal transplant recipients or those fathered by male transplant recipients. The NTPR encourages reporting of pregnancies following solid organ transplant by contacting them at 877-955-6877 or NTPR@giftoflifeinstitute.org.

Breastfeeding Considerations Tacrolimus is excreted into breast milk; concentrations are variable and lower than that of the maternal serum. The low bioavailability of tacrolimus following oral absorption may also decrease the amount of exposure to a nursing infant (Bramham 2013; French 2003; Gardiner 2006). In one study, tacrolimus serum concentrations in the infants did not differ between those who were bottle fed or breast-fed (all infants were exposed to tacrolimus throughout pregnancy) (Bramham 2013). Available information suggests that tacrolimus exposure to the nursing infant is ≤0.5% of the weight-adjusted maternal dose (Bramham 2013; French 2003; Gardiner 2006). The manufacturer recommends that nursing be discontinued, taking into consideration the importance of the drug to the mother.

Dosage Forms Considerations

Prograf injection contains polyoxyl 60 hydrogenated castor oil (HCO-60)

Dosage Forms

Capsule, Oral:

Prograf: 0.5 mg, 1 mg, 5 mg

Generic: 0.5 mg, 1 mg, 5 mg

Capsule Extended Release 24 Hour, Oral:

Astagraf XL: 0.5 mg, 1 mg, 5 mg

Solution, Intravenous:

Prograf: 5 mg/mL (1 mL)

Tablet Extended Release 24 Hour, Oral:

Envarsus XR: 0.75 mg, 1 mg, 4 mg

Dosage Forms: Canada

Capsule Extended Release 24 Hour, Oral:

Advagraf: 0.5 mg, 1 mg, 3 mg, 5 mg

Dental Comment Consider a medical consultation prior to any invasive dental procedure in patients who have received an organ transplant; delayed wound healing due to the immunosuppressive effects and an increased potential for postoperative infection may be of concern.

Tacrolimus (Topical) (ta KROE li mus)

Brand Names: US Protopic

Brand Names: Canada Protopic®

Generic Availability (US) Yes

Pharmacologic Category Calcineurin Inhibitor; Immunosuppressant Agent; Topical Skin Product

Dental Use Treatment of severe ulcerative or vesicobullous lesions (usually in consult with patient's physician)

Use Moderate-to-severe atopic dermatitis in immunocompetent patients not responsive to conventional therapy or when conventional therapy is not appropriate

Canadian labeling: Additional use (not in U.S. labeling): Maintenance therapy to prevent flares and extend flare-free intervals in patients with moderate-to-severe atopic dermatitis who are responsive to initial therapy and experiencing ≥5 flares per year

Local Anesthetic/Vasoconstrictor Precautions No information available to require special precautions

Effects on Dental Treatment No significant effects or complications reported

Effects on Bleeding No information available to require special precautions

Adverse Reactions As reported in children and adults, unless otherwise noted. Frequency not always defined.

Cardiovascular: Peripheral edema (adults 3% to 4%), hypertension (adults 1%)

Central nervous system: Headache (adults 19% to 20%), tingling of skin (2% to 8%), hyperesthesia (adults 3% to 7%), insomnia (adults 4%), paresthesia (adults 3%), depression (adults 2%), pain (1% to 2%)

Dermatologic: Burning sensation of skin (43% to 58%), pruritus (41% to 46%), erythema (25% to 28%), skin infection (adults 12%), acne vulgaris (adults 4% to 7%), urticaria (adults 3% to 6%), folliculitis (2% to 6%), skin rash (adults 2% to 5%), dermatological disease (children 4%), vesiculobullous dermatitis (children 4%), contact dermatitis (3% to 4%), pustular rash (adults 2% to 4%), contact eczema herpeticum (children 2%), fungal dermatitis (adults 1% to 2%), sunburn (adults 1% to 2%), alopecia (adults 1%), xeroderma (children 1%)

Gastrointestinal: Diarrhea (3% to 5%), dyspepsia (adults 1% to 4%), abdominal pain (children 3%), gastroenteritis (adults 2%), vomiting (adults 1%), nausea (children 1%)

Genitourinary: Dysmenorrhea (adults 4%), urinary tract infection (adults 1%)

Hematologic & oncologic: Lymphadenopathy (children 3%), malignant lymphoma, malignant neoplasm of skin

Hypersensitivity: Hypersensitivity reaction (adults 6% to 12%)

Infection: Herpes zoster (1% to 5%), varicella zoster infection (1% to 5%), infection (adults 1% to 2%)

Neuromuscular & skeletal: Myalgia (adults 2% to 3%), weakness (adults 2% to 3%), arthralgia (adults 1% to 3%), back pain (adults 2%)

Ocular: Conjunctivitis (adults 2%)

Otic: Otitis media (children 12%), otalgia (children 1%)

Respiratory: Flu-like symptoms (23% to 31%), increased cough (children 18%), asthma (adults 6%), rhinitis (children 6%), pharyngitis (adults 4%), sinusitis (adults 2% to 4%), bronchitis (adults 2%), pneumonia (adults 1%)

Miscellaneous: Fever (children 21%), allergic reaction (4% to 12%), alcohol intolerance (adults 3% to 7%), accidental injury (6%), cyst (adults 1% to 3%)

<1%, postmarketing, and/or case reports (Limited to important or life-threatening): Abnormality in thinking, abscess, acne rosacea, acute renal failure, aggravated tooth caries, anaphylactoid reaction, anemia, anorexia, anxiety, application site edema, arthritis, arthropathy, basal cell carcinoma, benign neoplasm (breast), blepharitis, bone disease, bursitis, candidiasis, cataract, chest pain, chills, colitis, conjunctival edema, constipation, cutaneous candidiasis, cystitis, dehydration, dermal ulcer, diaphoresis, dizziness, dry nose, dysgeusia, dyspnea, ear disease, ecchymoses, edema, epistaxis, eye pain, furunculosis, gastritis, gastrointestinal disease, heart valve disease, hernia, hyperbilirubinemia, hypercholesterolemia, hypertonia, hypothyroidism, impetigo (bullous), laryngitis, leukoderma, malaise, malignant lymphoma, malignant melanoma, migraine, muscle cramps, nail disease, neck pain, neoplasm (benign), oral candidiasis, oral mucosa ulcer, osteoarthritis, osteomyelitis, otitis externa, pulmonary disease, rectal disease, renal insufficiency, seborrhea, seizure, septicemia, skin

carcinoma, skin discoloration, skin hypertrophy, skin photosensitivity, squamous cell carcinoma, stomatitis, syncope, tachycardia, tendon disease, unintended pregnancy, vaginitis, vasodilatation, vertigo, visual disturbance, vulvovaginal candidiasis, xerophthalmia, xerostomia

Dosing

Adult & Geriatric

Atopic dermatitis (moderate-to-severe): Topical:

Treatment: Apply thin layer of 0.03% or 0.1% ointment to affected area twice daily; rub in gently and completely. Discontinue use when symptoms have cleared. If no improvement within 6 weeks, patients should be re-examined to confirm diagnosis.

Maintenance therapy (Canadian labeling; not in US labeling): Apply one application (thin layer of 0.03% or 0.1% ointment) to areas usually affected twice a week, allowing 2 to 3 days between applications (eg, one application on Monday and Thursday). Re-evaluate after 12 months. Safety of maintenance therapy >12 months has not been established.

Note: Patients experiencing flares should resume twice daily treatment.

Oral lichen planus (off-label use): Topical: Apply thin layer of 0.1% ointment to affected area up to 4 times daily; the treatment period in clinical trials ranged from 4 to 6 weeks (Corrocher 2008; Laeijendecker 2006; Radfar 2008).

Psoriasis (off-label use): Topical: Apply thin layer of 0.03% ointment twice daily; the treatment period in clinical trials was 6 weeks (Liao 2007).

Pyoderma gangrenosum (off-label use): Topical: Apply thin layer of 0.1% or 0.3% ointment to affected area once daily (Ghislain 2004; Lyon 2001); the treatment period in one clinical trial (0.3% ointment) was up to 10 weeks (Lyon 2001).

Vitiligo (off-label use): Topical: Apply thin layer of 0.1% ointment to affected area twice daily; may require several months for adequate response; the treatment period in clinical trials ranged from 10 weeks to 18 months (Majid 2010; Radakovic 2009; Taieb 2013).

Pediatric Moderate-to-severe atopic dermatitis:

Topical:

Treatment:

Children ≥2 to 15 years: Apply thin layer of 0.03% ointment to affected area twice daily; rub in gently and completely. Discontinue use when symptoms have cleared. If no improvement within 6 weeks, patients should be re-examined to confirm diagnosis.

Children >15 years: Refer to adult dosing.

Maintenance therapy (Canadian labeling; not in US labeling):

Children ≥2 to 15 years: Apply one application (thin layer of 0.03% ointment) to areas usually affected twice a week, allowing 2 to 3 days between applications (eg, one application on Monday and Thursday). Re-evaluate after 12 months. Safety of maintenance therapy >12 months has not been established.

Children >15 years: Refer to adult dosing.

Note: Patients experiencing flares should resume twice daily treatment.

Mechanism of Action Suppresses cellular immunity (inhibits T-lymphocyte activation), by binding to an intracellular protein, FKBP-12 and complexes with calcineurin dependent proteins to inhibit calcineurin phosphatase activity

Contraindications Hypersensitivity to tacrolimus or any component of the formulation

Warnings/Precautions

[US Boxed Warning]: Topical calcineurin inhibitors have been associated with rare cases of malignancy (including skin and lymphoma); therefore, it should be limited to short-term and intermittent treatment using the minimum amount necessary for the control of symptoms and only on involved areas. Use in children <2 years of age is not recommended, children ages 2-15 should only use the 0.03% ointment. Avoid use on malignant or premalignant skin conditions (eg,cutaneous T-cell lymphoma). Should not be used in immunocompromised patients. Do not apply to areas of active bacterial or viral infection; infections at the treatment site should be cleared prior to therapy. Topical calcineurin agents are considered second-line therapies in the treatment of atopic dermatitis/eczema, and should be limited to use in patients who have failed treatment with other therapies. Patients with atopic dermatitis are predisposed to skin infections, and tacrolimus therapy has been associated with risk of developing eczema herpeticum, varicella zoster, and herpes simplex. If atopic dermatitis is not improved in <6 weeks, re-evaluate to confirm diagnosis. May be associated with development of lymphadenopathy; possible infectious causes should be investigated. Discontinue use in patients with unknown cause of lymphadenopathy or acute infectious mononucleosis. Acute renal failure has been observed (rarely) with topical use. Not recommended for use in patients with skin disease which may increase systemic absorption (eg, Netherton's syndrome). Minimize sunlight exposure during treatment. Safety not established in patients with generalized erythroderma. Safety of intermittent use for >1 year has not been established, particularly since the effect on immune system development is unknown. Should not be used in immunocompromised patients; safety and efficacy have not been evaluated.

Drug Interactions

Metabolism/Transport Effects Substrate of CYP3A4 (minor), P-glycoprotein; **Note:** Assignment of Major/Minor substrate status based on clinically relevant drug interaction potential

Avoid Concomitant Use

Avoid concomitant use of Tacrolimus (Topical) with any of the following: CycloSPORINE (Systemic); Immunosuppressants; Sirolimus; Temsirolimus

Increased Effect/Toxicity

Tacrolimus (Topical) may increase the levels/effects of: Alcohol (Ethyl); CycloSPORINE (Systemic); Immunosuppressants; Sirolimus; Temsirolimus

The levels/effects of Tacrolimus (Topical) may be increased by: Antidepressants (Serotonin Reuptake Inhibitor/Antagonist); Antifungal Agents (Azole Derivatives, Systemic); Calcium Channel Blockers (Nondihydropyridine); CycloSPORINE (Systemic); Danazol; Grapefruit Juice; Macrolide Antibiotics; Ombitasvir, Paritaprevir, and Ritonavir; Ombitasvir, Paritaprevir, Ritonavir, and Dasabuvir; Protease Inhibitors; Sirolimus; Temsirolimus

Decreased Effect There are no known significant interactions involving a decrease in effect.

Pregnancy Risk Factor C

Pregnancy Considerations Adverse events were observed in animal reproduction studies. Tacrolimus crosses the human placenta and is measurable in the cord blood, amniotic fluid, and newborn serum following systemic use. Refer to the Tacrolimus (Systemic) monograph for additional information.

Breastfeeding Considerations Tacrolimus is excreted into breast milk following systemic administration. Refer to the Tacrolimus (Systemic) monograph for additional information.

Dosage Forms

Ointment, External:

Protopic: 0.03% (30 g, 60 g, 100 g); 0.1% (30 g, 60 g, 100 g)

Generic: 0.03% (30 g, 60 g, 100 g); 0.1% (30 g, 60 g, 100 g)

Tadalafil (tah DA la fil)

Brand Names: US Adcirca; Cialis

Brand Names: Canada Adcirca; Apo-Tadalafil PAH; Cialis

Pharmacologic Category Phosphodiesterase-5 Enzyme Inhibitor

Use

Benign prostatic hyperplasia (Cialis only): Treatment of the signs and symptoms of benign prostatic hyperplasia (BPH).

Erectile dysfunction (Cialis only): Treatment of erectile dysfunction

Erectile dysfunction and benign prostatic hyperplasia (Cialis only): Treatment of erectile dysfunction and the signs and symptoms of BPH.

Pulmonary arterial hypertension (Adcirca only): Treatment of pulmonary arterial hypertension (World Health Organization group 1) to improve exercise ability. Studies establishing effectiveness included predominately patients with New York Heart Association (NYHA) functional class II to III symptoms and etiologies of idiopathic or heritable pulmonary arterial hypertension (61%) or pulmonary arterial hypertension associated with connective tissue diseases (23%).

Local Anesthetic/Vasoconstrictor Precautions No information available to require special precautions

Effects on Dental Treatment No significant effects or complications reported

Effects on Bleeding No information available to require special precautions

Adverse Reactions Based upon usual doses for either indication. For erectile dysfunction, similar adverse events are reported with once-daily versus intermittent dosing, but are generally lower than with doses used intermittently.

>10%:

Cardiovascular: Flushing (1% to 13%; dose related)

Central nervous system: Headache (3% to 42%; dose related), pain (in extremities) (1% to 11%)

Gastrointestinal: Dyspepsia (1% to 13%), nausea (10% to 11%)

Neuromuscular & skeletal: Myalgia (1% to 14%; dose related), back pain (2% to 12%)

Respiratory: Respiratory tract infection (3% to 13%), nasopharyngitis (2% to 13%)

2% to 10%:

Cardiovascular: Hypertension (1% to 3%)

Gastrointestinal: Gastroenteritis (viral; 3% to 5%), gastroesophageal reflux disease (1% to 3%), abdominal pain (1% to 2%), diarrhea (1% to 2%)

Genitourinary: Urinary tract infection (≤2%)

Respiratory: Nasal congestion (≤9%), flu-like symptoms (2% to 5%), cough (2% to 4%), bronchitis (≤2%)

<2%, postmarketing, and/or case reports: Amnesia (transient global), angina pectoris, arthralgia, basal cell carcinoma, blurred vision, cerebrovascular accident, chest pain, conjunctival hyperemia, conjunctivitis, diaphoresis, dizziness, drowsiness, dysphagia, dyspnea, epistaxis, esophagitis, exfoliative dermatitis, eye pain, facial edema, fatigue, gastritis, hearing loss, hypoesthesia, hypotension, increased gamma-glutamyl transferase, increased liver enzymes, insomnia, lacrimation, malignant melanoma, migraine, myocardial infarction, neck pain, optic neuropathy (nonarteritic ischemic), orthostatic hypotension, pain, palpitations, paresthesia, periorbital swelling, peripheral edema, pharyngitis, priapism, pruritus, retinal artery occlusion, retinal vein occlusion, seizure, skin rash, spontaneous erections, Stevens-Johnson syndrome, syncope, tachycardia, tinnitus, urticaria, vertigo, vision color changes, visual field loss, vomiting, weakness, xerostomia

General Dosage Range Dosage adjustment recommended in patient with hepatic or renal impairment or on concomitant therapy

Oral: *Adults:* Benign prostatic hyperplasia: 5 mg once daily; Erectile dysfunction: As-needed dosing: 5 to 20 mg prior to anticipated sexual activity as a single dose (maximum: 1 dose/day); Once-daily dosing: 2.5 to 5 mg once daily; Pulmonary arterial hypertension: 40 mg once daily

Mechanism of Action

BPH: Exact mechanism unknown; effects likely due to PDE-5 mediated reduction in smooth muscle and endothelial cell proliferation, decreased nerve activity, and increased smooth muscle relaxation and tissue perfusion of the prostate and bladder

Erectile dysfunction: Does not directly cause penile erections, but affects the response to sexual stimulation. The physiologic mechanism of erection of the penis involves release of nitric oxide (NO) in the corpus cavernosum during sexual stimulation. NO then activates the enzyme guanylate cyclase, which results in increased levels of cyclic guanosine monophosphate (cGMP), producing smooth muscle relaxation and inflow of blood to the corpus cavernosum. Tadalafil enhances the effect of NO by inhibiting phosphodiesterase type 5 (PDE-5), which is responsible for degradation of cGMP in the corpus cavernosum; when sexual stimulation causes local release of NO, inhibition of PDE-5 by tadalafil causes increased levels of cGMP in the corpus cavernosum, resulting in smooth muscle relaxation and inflow of blood to the corpus cavernosum. At recommended doses, it has no effect in the absence of sexual stimulation.

PAH: Inhibits phosphodiesterase type 5 (PDE-5) in smooth muscle of pulmonary vasculature where PDE-5 is responsible for the degradation of cyclic guanosine monophosphate (cGMP). Increased cGMP concentration results in pulmonary vasculature relaxation; vasodilation in the pulmonary bed and the systemic circulation (to a lesser degree) may occur.

Pharmacodynamics/Kinetics

Onset of Action Within 1 hour; Peak effect: Pulmonary artery vasodilation: 75 to 90 minutes (Ghofrani 2004)

Duration of Action Erectile dysfunction: Up to 36 hours

Half-life Elimination 15 to 17.5 hours; Pulmonary hypertension (not receiving bosentan): 35 hours

Time to Peak Plasma: ~2 hours (range: 30 minutes to 6 hours)

Pregnancy Risk Factor B

Pregnancy Considerations Teratogenic events were not reported in animal reproduction studies. Postnatal development and pup survival was decreased at some doses. There are no adequate and well-controlled studies in pregnant women. Women with pulmonary arterial hypertension are encouraged to avoid pregnancy (McLaughlin 2009; Taichman 2014). Less than 0.0005% is found in the semen of healthy males.

Tafluprost (TA floo prost)

Brand Names: US Zioptan

Pharmacologic Category Ophthalmic Agent, Antiglaucoma; Prostaglandin, Ophthalmic

Use Elevated intraocular pressure: Reduction of intraocular pressure (IOP) in patients with open-angle glaucoma or ocular hypertension.

Local Anesthetic/Vasoconstrictor Precautions No information available to require special precautions

Effects on Dental Treatment No significant effects or complications reported

Effects on Bleeding No information available to require special precautions

Adverse Reactions

>10%: Ophthalmic: Conjunctival hyperemia (4% to 20%)

1% to 10%:

Central nervous system: Headache (6%)

Genitourinary: Urinary tract infection (2%)

Infection: Common cold (4%)

Ophthalmic: Eye irritation (≤7%), stinging of eyes (≤7%), conjunctivitis (5%), cataract (3%), eye pain (3%), xerophthalmia (3%), blurred vision (2%), hyperpigmentation of eyelashes (2%), increased eyelash length (2%)

Respiratory: Cough (3%)

<1%, postmarketing, and/or case reports: Dyspnea, exacerbation of asthma, iris hyperpigmentation, iritis, uveitis

General Dosage Range Ophthalmic: *Adults:* One drop in the affected eye(s) once daily

Mechanism of Action Tafluprost acid is a fluorinated prostaglandin F_2-alpha analog believed to reduce intraocular pressure by increasing outflow of aqueous humor via the uveoscleral pathway; exact mechanism by which it reduces IOP is unknown.

Pharmacodynamics/Kinetics

Onset of Action Reduction of intraocular pressure (IOP): 2 to 4 hours; Peak effect: Maximum reduction of IOP: ~12 hours

Time to Peak Plasma: ~10 minutes

Pregnancy Risk Factor C

Pregnancy Considerations Adverse events have been observed in animal reproduction studies. Effective contraception during treatment is recommended for women of childbearing potential.

Talimogene Laherparepvec
(tal IM oh jeen la her pa REP vek)

Brand Names: US Imlygic

Pharmacologic Category Antineoplastic Agent, Oncolytic Virus

Use

Melanoma, unresectable: Treatment (local) of unresectable cutaneous, subcutaneous, and nodal lesions in patients with melanoma recurrent after initial surgery

Limitations of use: Has not been shown to improve overall survival or have an effect on visceral metastases.

Local Anesthetic/Vasoconstrictor Precautions No information available to require special precautions

Effects on Dental Treatment Key adverse event(s) related to dental treatment: Oral herpes has been reported as an adverse effect (frequency not defined)

Effects on Bleeding No information available to require special precautions

Adverse Reactions Frequency not always defined. Most reactions resolved within 72 hours.

Cardiovascular: Vasculitis

Central nervous system: Fatigue (50%), chills (49%), headache (19%), dizziness (10%)

Dermatologic: Cellulitis, exacerbation of psoriasis, vitiligo

Endocrine & metabolic: Weight loss (6%)

Gastrointestinal: Nausea (36%), vomiting (21%), diarrhea (19%), constipation (12%), abdominal pain (9%), oral herpes

Infection: Bacterial infection (systemic), herpes virus infection

Local: Pain at injection site (28%), inflammation at injection site (tumor tissue ulceration), injection site lesion (plasmacytoma), injection site reaction (impaired healing; previous radiation or poorly vascularized lesion may increase risk), tissue necrosis at injection site

Neuromuscular & skeletal: Myalgia (18%), arthralgia (17%), pain in extremity (16%)

Renal: Glomerulonephritis

Respiratory: Flu-like symptoms (31%), oropharyngeal pain (6%), pneumonitis

Miscellaneous: Fever (43%)

General Dosage Range Intralesional: *Adults:* Inject up to 4 mL at a concentration of 10^6 (1 million) PFU/mL (initial treatment) or 10^8 (100 million) PFU/mL (subsequent treatment). Maximum volume (per treatment visit, for all injected lesions combined): 4 mL.

Mechanism of Action Talimogene laherparepvec is a genetically modified attenuated herpes simplex virus 1 (HSV) oncolytic virus which selectively replicates in and lyses tumor cells (Andtbacka 2015). Talimogene laherparepvec is modified through deletion of two nonessential viral genes. Deletion of the herpes virus neurovirulence factor gene ICP34.5 diminishes viral pathogenicity and increases tumor-selective replication; deletion of the ICP47 gene reduces virally mediated suppression of antigen presentation and increases the expression of the HSV US11 gene (Andtback, 2015). Virally derived GM-CSF recruits and activates antigen-presenting cells, leading to an antitumor immune response.

Pharmacodynamics/Kinetics

Time to Peak Peak levels of talimogene laherparepvec were detected in the urine on the day of treatment

Pregnancy Considerations Use is contraindicated in pregnant women.

Women of reproductive potential should use effective contraception during therapy. Talimogene laherparepvec is a live, attenuated, genetically modified herpes simplex virus type 1 (HSV-1). HSV-1 is known to cross the placenta, can be transmitted during birth, and produce infections in the fetus or neonate. It is not known if this can occur following exposure to talimogene laherparepvec. Pregnant women should not prepare or administer this medication. Pregnant women who are in close contact of patients treated with talimogene laherparepvec should not change dressings or clean injection sites, and should avoid direct contact with the injection site, dressings, or body fluids of patients.

Tamoxifen (ta MOKS i fen)

Brand Names: US Soltamox

Brand Names: Canada Apo-Tamox; Mylan-Tamoxifen; Nolvadex-D; PMS-Tamoxifen; Teva-Tamoxifen

Generic Availability (US) May be product dependent

Pharmacologic Category Antineoplastic Agent, Estrogen Receptor Antagonist; Selective Estrogen Receptor Modulator (SERM)

Use Treatment of metastatic (female and male) breast cancer; adjuvant treatment of breast cancer after primary treatment with surgery and radiation; reduce risk of invasive breast cancer in women with ductal carcinoma *in situ* (DCIS) after surgery and radiation; reduce the incidence of breast cancer in women at high risk

Local Anesthetic/Vasoconstrictor Precautions No information available to require special precautions

Effects on Dental Treatment No significant effects or complications reported

Effects on Bleeding Although significant myelosuppression with associated altered hemostasis has been reported for many chemotherapeutic agents, myelosup pression is not common with tamoxifen and no specific precautions appear to necessary.

Adverse Reactions

>10%:

Cardiovascular: Vasodilatation (41%), flushing (33%), hypertension (11%), peripheral edema (11%)

Central nervous system: Mood changes (12% to 18%), pain (3% to 16%), depression (2% to 12%)

Dermatologic: Skin changes (6% to 19%), skin rash (13%)

Endocrine & metabolic: Hot flash (3% to 80%), fluid retention (32%), menstrual disease (6% to 25%), weight loss (23%), amenorrhea (16%)

Gastrointestinal: Nausea (5% to 26%), vomiting (12%)

Genitourinary: Vaginal discharge (13% to 55%), vaginal hemorrhage (2% to 23%)

Hematologic & oncologic: Lymphedema (11%)

Neuromuscular & skeletal: Weakness (18%), arthritis (14%), arthralgia (11%)

Respiratory: Pharyngitis (14%)

1% to 10%:

Cardiovascular: Chest pain (5%), venous thrombosis (5%), edema (4%), ischemic heart disease (3%), angina pectoris (2%), deep vein thrombosis (≤2%), myocardial infarction (1%)

Central nervous system: Insomnia (9%), dizziness (8%), headache (8%), anxiety (6%), paresthesia (5%), fatigue (4%)

Dermatologic: Diaphoresis (6%), alopecia (≤5%)

Endocrine & metabolic: Oligomenorrhea (9%), weight gain (9%), hypercholesterolemia (4%), ovarian cyst (3%)

Gastrointestinal: Abdominal pain (9%), constipation (4% to 8%), diarrhea (7%), dyspepsia (6%), abdominal cramps (1%), anorexia (1%)

Genitourinary: Urinary tract infection (10%), leukorrhea (9%), mastalgia (6%), vaginitis (5%), vulvovaginitis (5%)

Hematologic & oncologic: Thrombocytopenia (≤10%), anemia (5%), breast neoplasm (5%), neoplasm (5%; second primary)

Hepatic: Increased serum AST (5%), increased serum bilirubin (2%)

Hypersensitivity: Hypersensitivity reaction (3%)

Infection: Infection (≤9%), sepsis (≤9%)

Neuromuscular & skeletal: Back pain (10%), ostealgia (6% to 10%), bone fracture (7%), osteoporosis (7%), arthropathy (5%), myalgia (5%), musculoskeletal pain (3%)

Ophthalmic: Cataract (7%)

Renal: Increased serum creatinine (≤2%)

Respiratory: Cough (4% to 9%), dyspnea (8%), flu-like symptoms (6%), bronchitis (5%), sinusitis (5%), throat irritation (oral solution: 5%)

Miscellaneous: Cyst (5%)

Frequency not defined:

Cardiovascular: Cerebrovascular accident, phlebitis (including superficial), pulmonary embolism, thrombosis (retinal vein)

Central nervous system: Tumor pain (during treatment of metastatic breast cancer; generally resolves with continuation)

Dermatologic: Pruritus vulvae

Endocrine & metabolic: Hypercalcemia, hyperlipidemia

Gastrointestinal: Cholestasis, dysgeusia

Genitourinary: Endometrial hyperplasia, endometrial polyps, endometriosis, vaginal dryness

Hematologic & oncologic: Endometrial carcinoma, tumor flare (during treatment of metastatic breast cancer; generally resolves with continuation; includes increased lesion size and erythema), uterine fibroids

Hepatic: Hepatic necrosis, hepatitis, liver steatosis

Ophthalmic: Corneal changes, retinopathy

<1%, postmarketing, and/or case reports: Angioedema, bullous pemphigoid, erythema multiforme, hypertriglyceridemia, impotence, interstitial pneumonitis, loss of libido (males), pancreatitis, Stevens-Johnson syndrome, vision color changes

Dosing

Adult & Geriatric Note: For the treatment of breast cancer, patients receiving both tamoxifen and chemotherapy should receive treatment sequentially, with tamoxifen following completion of chemotherapy.

Breast cancer treatment: Oral:

Adjuvant therapy (females): 20 mg once daily for 5 years

Premenopausal women: Duration of treatment is 5 years (Burstein 2010; NCCN Breast Cancer guidelines v.2.2013)

Postmenopausal women: Duration of tamoxifen treatment is 2-3 years followed by an aromatase inhibitor (AI) to complete 5 years; may take tamoxifen for the full 5 years (if contraindications or intolerance to AI) or extended therapy: 4.5 to 6 years of tamoxifen followed by 5 years of an AI (Burstein 2010; NCCN Breast Cancer guidelines v.2.2013)

ER-positive early breast cancer: Extended duration: Duration of treatment of 10 years demonstrated a reduced risk of recurrence and mortality (Davies 2012)

Metastatic (males and females): 20-40 mg daily (doses >20 mg should be given in 2 divided doses). **Note:** Although the FDA-approved labeling recommends dosing up to 40 mg daily, clinical benefit has not been demonstrated with doses above 20 mg daily (Bratherton 1984).

Ductal carcinoma in situ (DCIS) (females), to reduce the risk for invasive breast cancer: 20 mg once daily for 5 years

Breast cancer risk reduction (pre- and postmenopausal high-risk females): Oral: 20 mg once daily for 5 years

Endometrial carcinoma, recurrent, metastatic, or high-risk (endometrioid histologies only) (off-label use): Oral:

Monotherapy: 20 mg twice daily until disease progression or unacceptable toxicity (Thigpen 2001)

Combination therapy: 20 mg twice daily for 3 weeks (alternating with megestrol acetate every 3 weeks); continue alternating until disease progression or unacceptable toxicity) (Fiorica 2004)

Gynecomastia (off-label use): Oral: 20 mg once daily for up to 12 months (Boccardo 2005; Fradet 2007). The majority of published experiences have been in adult men with prostate cancer receiving bicalutamide. Use has also been reported in patients with idiopathic gynecomastia.

Induction of ovulation (off-label use): Oral: 20 mg once daily (range: 20-80 mg once daily) for 5 days (Steiner 2005)

Oligospermia (off-label use): Oral: 10 mg twice daily (Adamopoulos 1995; Adamopoulos 1997; Adamopoulos 2003; Buvat 1987); most effective when used in combination with testosterone (Adamopoulos 2003). The treatment period in clinical trials was up to 18 months (Buvat 1987). Although doses of 10 to 40 mg/day have been used, increasing dose after 6 months from 10 mg twice daily to 20 mg twice daily did not increase sperm count (Buvat 1987).

Ovarian cancer, advanced and/or recurrent (off-label use): Oral: 20 mg twice daily (Hatch 1991; Markman 1996)

Paget's disease of the breast (risk reduction; with DCIS or without associated cancer): Oral: 20 mg once daily for 5 years (NCCN Breast Cancer Guidelines v.2.2013)

Dosage adjustment for DVT, pulmonary embolism, cerebrovascular accident, or prolonged immobilization: Discontinue tamoxifen (NCCN Breast Cancer Risk Reduction Guidelines v.1.2013)

Pediatric Females: Precocious puberty secondary to McCune-Albright syndrome (off-label use): Oral: A dose of 20 mg daily has been reported in patients 2-10 years of age; safety and efficacy have not been established for treatment of longer than 1 year duration (Eugster, 2003)

Renal Impairment No dosage adjustment provided in manufacturer's labeling.

Chronic dialysis: No dosage adjustment necessary (Janus, 2013).

Hepatic Impairment No dosage adjustment provided in manufacturer's labeling (has not been studied).

Mechanism of Action Competitively binds to estrogen receptors on tumors and other tissue targets, producing a nuclear complex that decreases DNA synthesis and inhibits estrogen effects; nonsteroidal agent with potent antiestrogenic properties which compete with estrogen for binding sites in breast and other tissues; cells accumulate in the G_0 and G_1 phases; therefore, tamoxifen is cytostatic rather than cytocidal.

Contraindications Hypersensitivity to tamoxifen or any component of the formulation; concurrent warfarin therapy or history of deep vein thrombosis or pulmonary embolism (when tamoxifen is used for breast cancer risk reduction in women at high risk for breast cancer or with ductal carcinoma *in situ* [DCIS])

Warnings/Precautions [U.S. Boxed Warning]: Serious and life-threatening events (some fatal), including stroke, pulmonary emboli, and uterine or endometrial malignancies, have occurred at an incidence greater than placebo during use for breast cancer risk reduction in women at high-risk for breast cancer and in women with ductal carcinoma *in situ* (DCIS). In women already diagnosed with breast cancer, the benefits of tamoxifen treatment outweigh risks; evaluate risks versus benefits (and discuss with patients) when used for breast cancer risk reduction. An increased incidence of thromboembolic events, including DVT and pulmonary embolism, has been associated with use for breast cancer; risk is increased with concomitant chemotherapy; use with caution in individuals with a history of thromboembolic events. Thrombocytopenia and/or leukopenia may occur; neutropenia and pancytopenia have been reported rarely. Although the relationship to tamoxifen therapy is uncertain, rare hemorrhagic episodes have occurred in patients with significant thrombocytopenia. Use with caution in patients with hyperlipidemias; infrequent postmarketing cases of hyperlipidemias have been reported. Decreased visual acuity, retinal vein thrombosis, retinopathy, corneal changes, color perception changes, and increased incidence of cataracts (and the need for cataract surgery), have been reported. Hypercalcemia has occurred in some patients with bone metastasis, usually within a few weeks of therapy initiation; institute appropriate hypercalcemia management; discontinue if severe. Local disease flare and increased bone and tumor pain may occur in patients with metastatic breast cancer; may be associated with (good) tumor response.

Potentially significant drug-drug interactions may exist, requiring dose or frequency adjustment, additional monitoring, and/or selection of alternative therapy. Decreased efficacy and an increased risk of breast cancer recurrence has been reported with concurrent moderate or strong CYP2D6 inhibitors (Aubert, 2009; Dezentje, 2009). Concomitant use with select SSRIs may result in decreased tamoxifen efficacy. Strong CYP2D6 inhibitors (eg, fluoxetine, paroxetine) and moderate CYP2D6 inhibitors (eg, sertraline) are reported to interfere with transformation to the active metabolite endoxifen; when possible, select alternative medications with minimal or no impact on endoxifen levels (NCCN Breast Cancer Risk Reduction Guidelines v.1.2013; Sideras, 2010). Weak CYP2D6 inhibitors (eg, venlafaxine, citalopram) have minimal effect on the conversion to endoxifen (Jin, 2005; NCCN Breast Cancer Risk Reduction Guidelines v.1.2013); escitalopram is also a weak CYP2D6 inhibitor. In a retrospective analysis of breast cancer patients taking tamoxifen and SSRIs, concomitant use of paroxetine and tamoxifen was associated with an increased risk of death due to breast cancer (Kelly, 2010). Lower plasma concentrations of endoxifen have been observed in patients associated with reduced CYP2D6 activity (Jin, 2005; Schroth, 2009) and may be associated with reduced efficacy, although data is conflicting. Routine CYP2D6 testing is not recommended at this time in order to determine optimal endocrine therapy (NCCN Breast Cancer Guidelines v.2.2013; Visvanathan, 2009).

Tamoxifen use may be associated with changes in bone mineral density (BMD) and the effects may be dependent upon menstrual status. In postmenopausal women, tamoxifen use is associated with a protective effect on bone mineral density (BMD), preventing loss of BMD which lasts over the 5-year treatment period. In premenopausal women, a decline (from baseline) in BMD mineral density has been observed in women who continued to menstruate; may be associated with an increased risk of fractures. Liver abnormalities such as cholestasis, fatty liver, hepatitis, and hepatic necrosis have occurred. Hepatocellular carcinomas have been reported in some studies; relationship to treatment is unclear. Tamoxifen is associated with an increased incidence of uterine or endometrial cancers. Endometrial hyperplasia, polyps, endometriosis, uterine fibroids, and ovarian cysts have occurred. Monitor and promptly evaluate any report of abnormal vaginal bleeding. Amenorrhea and menstrual irregularities have been reported with tamoxifen use.

Drug Interactions

Metabolism/Transport Effects **Substrate** of CYP2A6 (minor), CYP2B6 (minor), CYP2C9 (major), CYP2D6 (major), CYP2E1 (minor), CYP3A4 (major); **Note:** Assignment of Major/Minor substrate status based on clinically relevant drug interaction potential; **Inhibits** CYP2C8 (moderate), CYP2C9 (weak)

Avoid Concomitant Use

Avoid concomitant use of Tamoxifen with any of the following: Amodiaquine; Conivaptan; CYP2D6 Inhibitors (Strong); Fusidic Acid (Systemic); Idelalisib; Ospemifene; Vitamin K Antagonists

Increased Effect/Toxicity

Tamoxifen may increase the levels/effects of: Amodiaquine; CYP2C8 Substrates; Highest Risk QTc-Prolonging Agents; Hydroxychloroquine; Mipomersen; Moderate Risk QTc-Prolonging Agents; Ospemifene; Vitamin K Antagonists

The levels/effects of Tamoxifen may be increased by: Abiraterone Acetate; Asunaprevir; Conivaptan; CYP2C9 Inhibitors (Moderate); CYP2C9 Inhibitors (Strong); CYP3A4 Inhibitors (Moderate); CYP3A4 Inhibitors (Strong); Dasatinib; Fosaprepitant; Fusidic Acid (Systemic); Idelalisib; Imatinib; Ivacaftor; MiFEPRIStone; Netupitant; Palbociclib; Panobinostat; Peginterferon Alfa-2b; Simeprevir; Stiripentol

Decreased Effect

Tamoxifen may decrease the levels/effects of: Anastrozole; Letrozole; Ospemifene

The levels/effects of Tamoxifen may be decreased by: Bexarotene (Systemic); Bosentan; CYP2C9 Inducers (Strong); CYP2D6 Inhibitors (Moderate); CYP2D6 Inhibitors (Strong); CYP3A4 Inducers (Moderate); CYP3A4 Inducers (Strong); Dabrafenib; Deferasirox; Enzalutamide; Mitotane; Peginterferon Alfa-2b; Rifamycin Derivatives; Siltuximab; St John's Wort; Tocilizumab

Food Interactions Grapefruit juice may decrease the metabolism of tamoxifen. Management: Avoid grapefruit juice.

Dietary Considerations Tablets and oral solution may be taken with or without food. Avoid grapefruit and grapefruit juice.

Pharmacodynamics/Kinetics

Half-life Elimination Tamoxifen: ~5 to 7 days; N-desmethyl tamoxifen: ~14 days

Time to Peak Serum: Children 2 to 10 years (female): ~8 hours; Adults: ~5 hours

Pregnancy Risk Factor D

Pregnancy Considerations Animal reproduction studies have demonstrated fetal adverse effects and fetal loss. There have been reports of vaginal bleeding, birth defects and fetal loss in pregnant women. Tamoxifen use during pregnancy may have a potential long term risk to the fetus of a DES-like syndrome. For sexually-active women of childbearing age, initiate during menstruation (negative β-hCG immediately prior to initiation in women with irregular cycles). Tamoxifen may induce ovulation. Barrier or nonhormonal contraceptives are recommended. Pregnancy should be avoided during treatment and for 2 months after treatment has been discontinued.

Breastfeeding Considerations It is not known if tamoxifen is excreted in breast milk, however, it has been shown to inhibit lactation. Due to the potential for adverse reactions, women taking tamoxifen should not breast-feed.

Dosage Forms

Solution, Oral:

Soltamox: 10 mg/5 mL (150 mL)

Tablet, Oral:

Generic: 10 mg, 20 mg

Tamsulosin (tam SOO loe sin)

Brand Names: US Flomax

Brand Names: Canada Apo-Tamsulosin CR; Flomax CR; Mylan-Tamsulosin; ratio-Tamsulosin; Sandoz-Tamsulosin; Tamsulosin CR; Teva-Tamsulosin; Teva-Tamsulosin CR

Pharmacologic Category Alpha$_1$ Blocker

Use

Benign prostatic hyperplasia: Treatment of signs and symptoms of benign prostatic hyperplasia (BPH)

Limitations of use: Not indicated for the treatment of hypertension.

Local Anesthetic/Vasoconstrictor Precautions No information available to require special precautions

Effects on Dental Treatment Key adverse event(s) related to dental treatment: Patients may experience orthostatic hypotension as they stand up after treatment; especially if lying in dental chair for extended periods of time. Use caution with sudden changes in position during and after dental treatment.

Effects on Bleeding No information available to require special precautions

Adverse Reactions

>10%:

Cardiovascular: Orthostatic hypotension (first dose: 6% to 19%; symptomatic orthostatic hypotension (chronic therapy) <1%)

Central nervous system: Headache (19% to 21%), dizziness (15% to 17%)

Genitourinary: Ejaculation failure (8% to 18%)

Infection: Infection (9% to 11%)

Respiratory: Rhinitis (13% to 18%)

1% to 10%:

Central nervous system: Drowsiness (3% to 4%), insomnia (1% to 2%), vertigo (≤1%)

Endocrine & metabolic: Loss of libido (2%)

Gastrointestinal: Diarrhea (6%), nausea (4%)

Neuromuscular & skeletal: Weakness (8% to 9%), back pain (7% to 8%)

Ophthalmic: Blurred vision (≤2%)

Respiratory: Pharyngitis (6%), cough (3% to 5%), sinusitis (4%)

<1%, postmarketing, and/or case reports: Constipation, decreased visual acuity, epistaxis, erythema multiforme, exfoliation of skin, exfoliative dermatitis, hypersensitivity reaction, hypotension, intraoperative floppy iris syndrome, palpitations, priapism, syncope, vomiting, xerostomia

General Dosage Range **Oral:** *Adults:* Initial: 0.4 mg once daily; Maintenance: 0.4 to 0.8 mg once daily

Mechanism of Action Tamsulosin is an antagonist of alpha$_{1A}$-adrenoreceptors in the prostate. Smooth muscle tone in the prostate is mediated by alpha$_{1A}$-adrenoreceptors; blocking them leads to relaxation of smooth muscle in the bladder neck and prostate causing an improvement of urine flow and decreased symptoms of BPH. Approximately 75% of the $alpha_1$-receptors in the prostate are of the $alpha_{1A}$ subtype.

Pharmacodynamics/Kinetics

Half-life Elimination Healthy volunteers: 9-13 hours; Target population: 14-15 hours

Time to Peak Fasting: 4-5 hours; With food: 6-7 hours

Steady-state: By the fifth day of once daily dosing

Pregnancy Risk Factor B

Pregnancy Considerations Adverse events were not observed in animal reproduction studies. For pregnant women with kidney stones, other treatments such as stents or ureteroscopy, are recommended if stone removal is needed (Preminger, 2007; Tan, 2013).

Tapentadol (ta PEN ta dol)

Related Information

Oral Pain *on page 1830*

Brand Names: US Nucynta; Nucynta ER

Brand Names: Canada Nucynta ER; Nucynta IR

Generic Availability (US) No

Pharmacologic Category Analgesic, Opioid

Dental Use Management of moderate-to-severe acute pain

Use

Neuropathic pain associated with diabetic peripheral neuropathy: Extended-release: Management of neuropathic pain associated with diabetic peripheral neuropathy (DPN) severe enough to require daily, around-the-clock, long-term opioid treatment and for which alternative treatment options are inadequate.

Pain management:

Immediate release: Management of acute pain severe enough to require an opioid analgesic and for which alternative treatments are inadequate in adults.

Extended release: Management of pain severe enough to require daily, around-the-clock, long-term opioid treatment and for which alternative treatments are inadequate.

Limitations of use: Reserve tapentadol for use in patients for whom alternative treatment options (eg, nonopioid analgesics, opioid combination products) are ineffective, not tolerated, or would be otherwise inadequate to provide sufficient management of pain. Tapentadol ER is not indicated as an as-needed analgesic.

Local Anesthetic/Vasoconstrictor Precautions Although part of the mechanism of tapentadol inhibits the reuptake of norepinephrine, there is no information available to require any special precautions.

Effects on Dental Treatment Key adverse effect(s) related to dental treatment: Xerostomia (normal salivary flow resumes upon discontinuation)

Effects on Bleeding No information available to require special precautions

Adverse Reactions

Immediate release:

>10%:

Central nervous system: Dizziness (24%), drowsiness (15%)

Gastrointestinal: Nausea (30%), vomiting (18%)

1% to 10%:

Central nervous system: Fatigue (3%), insomnia (2%), abnormal dreams (1%), anxiety (1%), confusion (1%), lethargy (1%)

Dermatologic: Pruritus (3% to 5%), hyperhidrosis (3%), skin rash (1%)

Endocrine & metabolic: Hot flash (1%)

Gastrointestinal: Constipation (8%), xerostomia (4%), decreased appetite (2%), dyspepsia (2%)

Genitourinary: Urinary tract infection (1%)

Neuromuscular & skeletal: Arthralgia (1%), tremor (1%)

Respiratory: Nasopharyngitis (1%), upper respiratory tract infection (1%)

<1%, postmarketing, and/or case reports: Abdominal distress, abnormality in thinking, agitation, angioedema, ataxia, cough, decreased blood pressure, decreased heart rate, delayed gastric emptying, diarrhea, disorientation, drug withdrawal, dysarthria, dyspnea, edema, euphoria, feeling of heaviness, flatulence, hallucination, headache, hypersensitivity, hypoesthesia, hypogonadism (Brennan, 2013; Debono, 2011), impaired consciousness, increased gamma-glutamyl transferase, increased heart rate, increased serum ALT, increased serum AST, intoxicated feeling, irritability, lack of concentration, memory impairment, muscle spasm, nervousness, oxygen desaturation, palpitations, paresthesia, pollakiuria, presyncope, respiratory depression, restlessness, sedation, seizure, syncope, urinary hesitancy, urticaria, visual disturbance

Extended release:

>10%:

Central nervous system: Dizziness (17% to 18%), headache (10% to 15%), drowsiness (12% to 14%)

Gastrointestinal: Nausea (21% to 27%), constipation (13% to 17%), vomiting (8% to 12%)

1% to 10%:

Cardiovascular: Hypotension (1%)

Central nervous system: Fatigue (9%), anxiety (2% to 5%), insomnia (4%), irritability (2%), lethargy (2%), abnormal dreams (1% to 2%), vertigo (1% to 2%), chills (1%), depression (1%), hypoesthesia (1%), lack of concentration (1%), nervousness (1%), sedation (1%), withdrawal syndrome (1%)

Dermatologic: Pruritus (1% to 8%), hyperhidrosis (3% to 5%), skin rash (1%)

Endocrine & metabolic: Hot flash (2% to 3%)

Gastrointestinal: Diarrhea (7%), xerostomia (7%), decreased appetite (2% to 6%), dyspepsia (1% to 3%), abdominal distress (1%)

Genitourinary: Erectile dysfunction (1%)

Neuromuscular & skeletal: Tremor (1% to 3%), weakness (2%)

Ophthalmic: Blurred vision (1%)

Respiratory: Dyspnea (1%)

<1%, postmarketing, and/or case reports: Abnormality in thinking, agitation, altered mental status, anaphylaxis, angioedema, ataxia, confusion, decreased blood pressure, decreased heart rate, delayed gastric emptying, disorientation, drug dependence, dysarthria, equilibrium disturbance, euphoria, feeling abnormal, hallucination, hypersensitivity, hypogonadism (Brennan, 2013; Debono, 2011), illusion, impaired consciousness, increased heart rate, intoxicated feeling, left bundle branch block, memory impairment, nightmares, palpitations, panic attack, paresthesia, pollakiuria, presyncope, respiratory depression, sexual difficulty, suicidal ideation, syncope, urinary hesitancy, urticaria, visual disturbance, weight loss

Dental Usual Dosage Adults: 50-100 mg every 4-6 hours as need for acute pain

Dosing

Adult Note: Dose and dosage intervals should be individualized according to pain severity with respect to patient's previous experience with similar opioid analgesics. In patients receiving tapentadol ER, immediate-release opioid or nonopioid medication may be used for rescue relief of breakthrough pain and during dosage adjustments. Opioid tolerance is defined as: Patients already taking at least morphine 60 mg orally daily, oxymorphone 25 mg orally daily, transdermal fentanyl 25 mcg per hour, oxycodone 30 mg orally daily, hydromorphone 8 mg orally daily, hydrocodone 60 mg orally daily or an equivalent dose of another opioid for at least 1 week.

Neuropathic pain associated with diabetic peripheral neuropathy: Oral: Extended release:

Opioid naive (use as the first opioid analgesic or use in patients who are **not** opioid tolerant): Initial: 50 mg every 12 hours

Conversion from other opioids to tapentadol ER: Initial: 50 mg every 12 hours

Conversion from tapentadol immediate release to ER: Convert using same total daily dose but divide into 2 equal doses and administer every 12 hours.

Conversion from methadone to tapentadol ER: Close monitoring is required when converting methadone to another opioid. Ratio between methadone and other opioid agonists varies widely according to previous dose exposure. Methadone has a long half-life and can accumulate in the plasma.

Dosage titration: Titrate in increments of 50 mg no more frequently than twice daily every 3 days to effective dose (therapeutic range: 100 to 250 mg every 12 hours).

Pain management: Oral:

Immediate release tablets and solution: Day 1: 50 to 100 mg (2.5 to 5 mL) every 4 to 6 hours as needed; may administer a second dose ≥1 hour after the initial dose (maximum dose on first day: 700 mg/day); Day 2 and subsequent dosing: 50 to 100 mg (2.5 to 5 mL) every 4 to 6 hours as needed (maximum: 600 mg/day).

Conversion from tapentadol immediate release to ER: Convert using same total daily dose but divide into 2 equal doses and administer every 12 hours.

Extended-release:

Opioid naive (use as the first opioid analgesic or use in patients who are **not** opioid tolerant): Initial: 50 mg every 12 hours

Conversion from other opioids to tapentadol ER: Initial: 50 mg every 12 hours

Conversion from tapentadol immediate release to ER: Convert using same total daily dose but divide into 2 equal doses and administer every 12 hours.

Conversion from methadone to extended release tapentadol: Close monitoring is required when converting methadone to another opioid. Ratio between methadone and other opioid agonists varies widely according to previous dose exposure. Methadone has a long half-life and can accumulate in the plasma.

Dosage titration: Titrate in increments of 50 mg no more frequently than twice daily every 3 days to effective dose (therapeutic range: 100 to 250 mg every 12 hours).

Discontinuation of therapy: Decrease previous daily dose by 25% to 50% each day every 2 to 4 days; monitor carefully for signs/symptoms of withdrawal. If patient displays withdrawal symptoms, increase dose to previous level and then reduce dose more slowly by increasing interval between dose reductions, decreasing amount of daily dose reduction, or both.

Geriatric Refer to adult dosing. Initiate therapy at low end of dosing range and use caution.

Renal Impairment

CrCl ≥30 mL/minute: No dosage adjustment necessary.

CrCl <30 mL/minute: Use not recommended.

Hepatic Impairment

Mild impairment (Child-Pugh class A): No dosage adjustment necessary.

Moderate impairment (Child-Pugh class B):

Immediate release: Initial: 50 mg every 8 hours or longer (maximum: 150 mg/24 hours). Further treatment for maintenance of analgesia may be achieved by either shortening or lengthening the dosing interval.

Extended release: Initial: 50 mg every 24 hours or longer; maximum: 100 mg/day

Severe impairment (Child-Pugh class C): Use not recommended.

Mechanism of Action Binds to μ-opiate receptors in the CNS causing inhibition of ascending pain pathways, altering the perception of and response to pain; also inhibits the reuptake of norepinephrine, which also modifies the ascending pain pathway

Contraindications

Hypersensitivity (eg, anaphylaxis, angioedema) to tapentadol or any component of the formulation; significant respiratory depression; acute or severe asthma or hypercapnia in unmonitored settings or in absence of resuscitative equipment; GI obstruction, including paralytic ileus (known or suspected); use with or within 14 days of MAO inhibitors.

Canadian labeling: Additional contraindications (not in US labeling): Hypersensitivity to opioids; acute respiratory depression, cor pulmonale; obstructive airway; known or suspected gastrointestinal obstruction or any disease/condition that affects bowel transit (eg, ileus of any type, strictures); suspected surgical abdomen (eg, acute appendicitis, pancreatitis); severe renal impairment (CrCl <30 mL/minute); severe hepatic impairment (Child-Pugh class C); mild, intermittent, or short-duration pain that can be managed with alternative pain medication; management of perioperative pain (extended-release tablets); acute alcoholism, delirium tremens, and seizure disorders; severe CNS depression, increased cerebrospinal or intracranial pressure or head injury; pregnancy; breastfeeding; use during labor/delivery

Warnings/Precautions [US Boxed Warning]: Serious, life-threatening, or fatal respiratory depression may occur. Monitor closely for respiratory depression, especially during initiation or dose escalation. Swallow ER tablets whole; crushing, chewing, or dissolving can cause rapid release and a potentially fatal dose. Carbon dioxide retention from opioid-induced respiratory depression can exacerbate the sedating effects of opioids. Use with caution and monitor for respiratory depression in patients with significant chronic obstructive pulmonary disease or cor pulmonale, and patients having a substantially decreased respiratory reserve, hypoxia, hypercarbia, or preexisting respiratory depression, particularly when initiating and titrating therapy; critical respiratory depression may occur, even at therapeutic dosages. Consider the use of alternative nonopioid analgesics in these patients. Avoid use in patients with impaired consciousness or coma as these patients are susceptible to intracranial effects of CO_2 retention. Potentially life-threatening serotonin syndrome (SS) has occurred with concomitant use of tapentadol and serotonergic agents (eg, SSRIs, SNRIs, triptans, TCAs, fentanyl, lithium, tramadol, buspirone, St John's wort, tryptophan) or agents that impair metabolism of serotonin (eg, MAO inhibitors intended to treat psychiatric disorders, other MAO inhibitors [ie, linezolid and intravenous methylene blue]). Discontinue treatment (and any concomitant serotonergic agent) immediately if signs/symptoms arise.

[US Boxed Warning]: Tapentadol exposes patients and other users to the risks of addiction, abuse, and misuse, potentially leading to overdose and death. Assess each patient's risk prior to prescribing; monitor all patients regularly for development of these behaviors or conditions. Use with caution in patients with a history of drug abuse or acute alcoholism; potential for drug dependency exists. Other factors associated with increased risk for misuse include younger age, concomitant depression (major), and psychotropic medication use. Consider offering naloxone prescriptions in patients with factors associated with an increased risk for overdose, such as history of overdose or substance use disorder, higher opioid dosages (≥50 morphine milligram equivalents/day orally), and concomitant benzodiazepine use (Dowell [CDC 2016]). Use opioids with caution for chronic pain in patients with mental health conditions (eg, depression, anxiety disorders, post-traumatic stress disorder) due to increased risk for opioid use disorder and overdose; more frequent monitoring is recommended (Dowell [CDC 2016]). **[US Boxed Warning]: Accidental ingestion of even one dose, especially in children, can result in a fatal overdose of tapentadol.**

May obscure diagnosis or clinical course of patients with acute abdominal conditions. May cause CNS depression, which may impair physical or mental abilities; patients must be cautioned about performing tasks which require mental alertness (eg, operating machinery or driving). **[US Boxed Warning]: Concomitant use of opioids with benzodiazepines or other CNS depressants, including alcohol, may result in profound sedation, respiratory depression, coma, and death. Reserve concomitant prescribing of tapentadol and benzodiazepines or other CNS depressants for use in patients for whom alternative treatment options are inadequate. Limit dosage and durations to the minimum required and follow patients for signs and symptoms of respiratory depression and sedation. [US Boxed Warning]: Patients should not consume alcoholic beverages or medication containing ethanol while taking tapentadol ER; ethanol may increase tapentadol plasma levels resulting in a potentially fatal overdose.**

Potentially significant drug-drug interactions may exist, requiring dose or frequency adjustment, additional monitoring, and/or selection of alternative therapy.

[US Boxed Warning]: Prolonged use of opioids during pregnancy can cause neonatal withdrawal syndrome, which may be life-threatening if not recognized and treated according to protocols developed by neonatology experts. If opioid use is required for a prolonged period in a pregnant woman, advise the patient of the risk of neonatal opioid withdrawal syndrome and ensure that appropriate treatment will be available. Signs and symptoms include irritability, hyperactivity and abnormal sleep pattern, high pitched cry, tremor, vomiting, diarrhea and failure to gain weight. Onset, duration and severity depend on the drug used, duration of use, maternal dose, and rate of drug elimination by the newborn.

Use with caution in patients who are morbidly obese. Use with caution in cachectic or debilitated patients and in the elderly; consider the use of nonopioid analgesics in these patients. Use with caution in patients with adrenal insufficiency (including Addison disease); biliary tract dysfunction or acute pancreatitis; delirium tremens; head injury, intracranial lesions, or elevated intracranial pressure (ICP); history of seizures or conditions predisposing patients to seizures; prostatic hyperplasia and/or urinary stricture; toxic psychosis; and/or thyroid dysfunction. Use opioids for chronic pain with caution in older adults; monitor closely due to an increased potential for risks, including certain risks such as falls/fracture, cognitive impairment, and constipation. Clearance may also be reduced in older adults (with or without renal impairment) resulting in a narrow therapeutic window and increasing the risk for respiratory depression or overdose (Dowell [CDC 2016]). Use opioids with caution for chronic pain and titrate dosage cautiously in patients with risk factors for sleep-disordered breathing, including HF and obesity. Avoid opioids in patients with moderate to severe sleep-disordered breathing (Dowell [CDC 2016]).Use with caution in patients with moderate hepatic impairment (dosage adjustment required). Not recommended for use in severe hepatic impairment. Use with caution in patients with mild-to-moderate renal impairment. Not recommended for use in severe renal impairment. May cause severe hypotension (including orthostatic hypotension and syncope); use with caution in patients with hypovolemia, cardiovascular disease (including acute MI), or drugs which may exaggerate hypotensive effects (including phenothiazines or general anesthetics). Monitor for symptoms of hypotension following initiation or dose titration. Avoid use in patients with circulatory shock.

An opioid-containing regimen should be tailored to each patient's needs with respect to degree of tolerance for opioids (naïve versus chronic user), age, weight, and medical condition. The optimal analgesic dose varies widely among patients; doses should be titrated to pain relief/prevention. Concurrent use of mixed agonist/antagonist analgesics (eg, pentazocine, nalbuphine, butorphanol) or partial agonist (eg, buprenorphine) analgesics may precipitate withdrawal symptoms and/or reduced analgesic efficacy in patients following prolonged therapy with mu opioid agonists. Taper dose gradually when discontinuing. In order to avoid dosing errors, include the dose in mL and mg when writing prescriptions. Instruct patients to always use the enclosed calibrated oral syringe to ensure the dose is measured and administered accurately. Opioids decrease bowel motility; monitor for decrease bowel motility in postop patients receiving opioids. Use with caution in the perioperative setting; individualize treatment when transitioning from parenteral to oral analgesics.

Chronic pain: Opioids should **not** be used as first-line therapy for chronic pain management (pain >3-month duration or beyond time of normal tissue healing) due to limited short-term benefits, undetermined long-term benefits, and association with serious risks (eg, overdose, MI, auto accidents, risk of developing opioid use disorder). Preferred management includes nonpharmacologic therapy and nonopioid therapy (eg, NSAIDs, acetaminophen, certain anticonvulsants and antidepressants). If opioid therapy is initiated, it should be combined with nonpharmacologic and nonopioid therapy, as appropriate. Prior to initiation, known risks of opioid therapy should be discussed and realistic treatment goals for pain/function should be established, including consideration for discontinuation if benefits do not outweigh risks. Therapy should be continued only if clinically meaningful improvement in pain/function outweighs risks. Therapy should be initiated at the lowest effective dosage using immediate-release opioids (instead of extended-release/long-acting opioids). Risk associated with use increases with higher opioid dosages. Risks and benefits should be re-evaluated when increasing dosage to ≥50 morphine milligram equivalents (MME)/day orally; dosages ≥90 MME/day orally should be avoided unless carefully justified (Dowell [CDC 2016]).

Drug Interactions

Metabolism/Transport Effects Substrate of CYP2C9 (minor), CYP2D6 (minor); **Note:** Assignment of Major/Minor substrate status based on clinically relevant drug interaction potential

Avoid Concomitant Use

Avoid concomitant use of Tapentadol with any of the following: Alcohol (Ethyl); Azelastine (Nasal); Dapoxetine; Eluxadoline; MAO Inhibitors; Methylene Blue; Mixed Agonist / Antagonist Opioids; Orphenadrine; Oxomemazine; Paraldehyde; Thalidomide

Increased Effect/Toxicity

Tapentadol may increase the levels/effects of: Alvimopan; Azelastine (Nasal); Blonanserin; CNS Depressants; Desmopressin; Diuretics; Eluxadoline; Flunitrazepam; HYDROcodone; MAO Inhibitors, Methotrimeprazine; Metoclopramide; MetyroSINE; Orphenadrine; OxyCODONE; Paraldehyde; Piribedil; Pramipexole; Ramosetron; ROPINIRole; Rotigotine; Selective Serotonin Reuptake Inhibitors; Serotonin Modulators; Suvorexant; Thalidomide; Zolpidem

The levels/effects of Tapentadol may be increased by: Alcohol (Ethyl); Amphetamines; Anticholinergic Agents; Brimonidine (Topical); Cannabis; Chlormethiazole; Chlorphenesin Carbamate; Dapoxetine; Dimethindene (Topical); Dronabinol; Droperidol; Kava Kava; Lofexidine; Magnesium Sulfate; Methotrimeprazine; Methylene Blue; Methylphenidate; Minocycline; Nabilone; Oxomemazine; Perampanel; Rufinamide; Sodium Oxybate; Succinylcholine; Tetrahydrocannabinol

Decreased Effect

Tapentadol may decrease the levels/effects of: Diuretics; Gastrointestinal Agents (Prokinetic); Pegvisomant

The levels/effects of Tapentadol may be decreased by: Antiemetics (5HT3 Antagonists); Mixed Agonist / Antagonist Opioids; Nalmefene; Naltrexone

Food Interactions

Ethanol: Concomitant use with alcohol can increase the bioavailability of extended release tablets. Management: Avoid use of alcohol during therapy.

Food: When administered after a high fat/calorie meal, the AUC and C_{max} increased by 25% and 16%, respectively. Management: May administer without regard to meals.

Pharmacodynamics/Kinetics

Half-life Elimination Immediate release: ~4 hours; Long acting formulations: ~5-6 hours

Time to Peak Plasma: Immediate release: 1.25 hours; Long acting formulations: 3-6 hours

Pregnancy Risk Factor C

Pregnancy Considerations

Adverse events have been observed in animal reproduction studies. Opioids cross the placenta. Tapentadol is not recommended for use during labor and delivery and if exposure occurs the neonate should be monitored for respiratory depression.

[US Boxed Warning]: Prolonged use of opioids during pregnancy can cause neonatal withdrawal syndrome, which may be life-threatening if not recognized and treated according to protocols developed by neonatology experts. If opioid use is required for a prolonged period in a pregnant woman, advise the patient of the risk of neonatal opioid withdrawal syndrome and ensure that appropriate treatment will be available. If chronic opioid exposure occurs in pregnancy, adverse events in the newborn (including withdrawal) may occur; monitoring of the neonate is recommended. The minimum effective dose should be used if opioids are needed (Chou 2009). Neonatal abstinence syndrome following opioid exposure may present with autonomic (eg, fever, temperature instability), gastrointestinal (eg, diarrhea, vomiting, poor feeding/weight gain), or neurologic (eg, high-pitched crying, increased muscle tone, irritability, seizure, tremor) symptoms (Dow 2012; Hudak 2012).

Long-term opioid use may cause secondary hypogonadism, which may lead to sexual dysfunction or infertility (Brennan 2013).

Breastfeeding Considerations Limited information is available on the excretion of tapentadol in human milk; however, data suggests it may be excreted in human milk. The possibility of sedation or respiratory depression in the nursing infant should be considered; withdrawal may occur when maternal therapy is stopped. According to the manufacturer, the decision to continue or discontinue breastfeeding during therapy should take into account the risk of infant exposure, the benefits of breastfeeding to the infant, and benefits of treatment to the mother.

Controlled Substance C-II

Dosage Forms

Tablet, Oral:

Nucynta: 50 mg, 75 mg, 100 mg

Tablet Extended Release 12 Hour, Oral:

Nucynta ER: 50 mg, 100 mg, 150 mg, 200 mg, 250 mg

Dosage Forms: Canada

Tablet, Oral:

Nucynta IR: 50 mg, 75 mg, 100 mg

Tablet, Controlled Release, Oral:

Nucynta ER: 50 mg, 100 mg, 150 mg, 200 mg, 250 mg

Dental Comment Tapentadol is classified as an opioid analgesic having a unique ability to bind to μ-opiate receptors and to also inhibit the reuptake of norepinephrine. It shares many properties of the traditional opioid drugs including addiction liability. A report by Kleinert et al, showed that single doses of tapentadol ≥75 mg effectively reduced moderate-to-severe postoperative dental pain in a dose related fashion and were well tolerated compared to 60 mg morphine. The study showed that tapentadol was a highly effective, centrally acting analgesic with a favorable side effect profile with rapid onset of action.

Tasimelteon (tas i MEL tee on)

Brand Names: US Hetlioz

Pharmacologic Category Hypnotic, Miscellaneous; Melatonin Receptor Agonist

Use Non-24-hour sleep-wake disorder: Treatment of non-24-hour sleep-wake disorder (non-24). **Note:** Efficacy was established in totally blind patients with non-24-hour sleep-wake disorder.

Local Anesthetic/Vasoconstrictor Precautions No information available to require special precautions

Effects on Dental Treatment No significant effects or complications reported

Effects on Bleeding No information available to require special precautions

Adverse Reactions

>10%: Central nervous system: Headache (17%)

1% to 10%:

Central nervous system: Abnormal dreams (10%)
Genitourinary: Urinary tract infection (7%)
Hepatic: Increased serum ALT (10%)
Respiratory: Upper respiratory tract infection (7%)

General Dosage Range Oral: *Adults:* 20 mg once daily before bedtime.

Mechanism of Action Agonist of melatonin receptors MT_1 and MT_2 (greater affinity for the MT_2 receptor than the MT_1 receptor). Agonism of MT_1 is thought to preferentially induce sleepiness, while MT_2 receptor activation preferentially influences regulation of circadian rhythms.

Pharmacodynamics/Kinetics

Onset of Action Effect may take weeks or months (due to individual differences in circadian rhythms)

Half-life Elimination ~1 to 2 hours

Time to Peak Fasting: ~0.5 to 3 hours (increased by ~1.75 hours with a high-fat meal)

Pregnancy Risk Factor C

Pregnancy Considerations Adverse events were observed in some animal reproduction studies.

Tazarotene (taz AR oh teen)

Brand Names: US Avage; Fabior; Tazorac

Brand Names: Canada Tazorac

Pharmacologic Category Acne Products; Keratolytic Agent; Topical Skin Product, Acne

Use

Acne (Fabior, Tazorac 0.1% cream, Tazorac 0.1% gel): Topical treatment of acne vulgaris in patients 12 years and older.

Psoriasis:

Tazorac 0.05% and 0.1% cream: Topical treatment of plaque psoriasis in patients 18 years and older (US labeling) or patients 12 years and older (Canadian labeling).

Tazorac 0.05% and 0.1% gel: Topical treatment of stable plaque psoriasis of up to 20% body surface area involvement in patients 12 years and older.

Wrinkling, hyper- and hypopigmentation, lentigines (Avage): Adjunctive agent for use in the mitigation (palliation) of facial fine wrinkling, facial mottled hyper- and hypopigmentation, and benign facial lentigines in patients 17 years and older who use comprehensive skin care and sunlight avoidance programs.

Limitations of use: Does not eliminate or prevent wrinkles, repair sun-damaged skin, reverse photoaging, or restore more youthful or younger skin. Has not demonstrated a mitigating effect on significant signs of chronic sunlight exposure such as coarse or deep wrinkling, tactile roughness, telangiectasia, skin laxity, keratinocytic atypia, melanocytic atypia, or dermal elastosis. Safety and effectiveness for the prevention or treatment of actinic keratoses, skin neoplasms, or lentigo maligna has not been established. Safe and effective daily use >52 weeks is not known.

Local Anesthetic/Vasoconstrictor Precautions No information available to require special precautions

Effects on Dental Treatment No significant effects or complications reported

Effects on Bleeding No information available to require special precautions

Adverse Reactions Percentage of incidence varies with formulation and/or strength:

>10%: Dermatologic: Desquamation (0.1% cream 40%; foam 6%), erythema (0.1% cream 34%; foam 6%), burning sensation of skin (26%), xeroderma (7% to 16%), skin irritation (10% to 14%), exacerbation of psoriasis, skin pain

1% to 10%:

Cardiovascular: Peripheral edema
Dermatologic: Pruritus (0.1% cream 10%; foam 1%), contact dermatitis (8%), stinging of the skin (3%), skin rash (≤3%), cheilitis (1%), dermatitis (1%), skin photosensitivity (1%), eczema, skin discoloration, skin fissure
Endocrine & metabolic: Hypertriglyceridemia
Local: Application site pain (1%), local hemorrhage
Ophthalmic: Ocular irritation (including edema, irritation, and inflammation of the eye or eyelid; 4%)

<1%, postmarketing, and/or case reports: Application site edema, impetigo, skin blister

General Dosage Range Topical: *Children ≥12 years, Adolescents, and Adults:* Apply a pea-sized amount or thin film **or** 2 mg/cm^2 once daily

Mechanism of Action Synthetic, acetylenic retinoid which modulates differentiation and proliferation of epithelial tissue and exerts some degree of anti-inflammatory and immunological activity

Pharmacodynamics/Kinetics

Onset of Action Psoriasis: 1 week

Duration of Action Therapeutic: Psoriasis: Effects have been observed for up to 3 months after a 3-month course of topical treatment

Half-life Elimination Cream, gel: ~81 hours (tazarotenic acid); Foam: 8.1 ± 3.7 hours

Pregnancy Risk Factor X

Pregnancy Considerations Use in pregnancy is contraindicated.

Adverse events have been observed in animal reproduction studies. A negative pregnancy test should be obtained within 2 weeks prior to treatment; treatment should begin during a normal menstrual period.

Tedizolid (ted eye ZOE lid)

Brand Names: US Sivextro

Pharmacologic Category Antibiotic, Oxazolidinone

Use Acute bacterial skin and skin structure infections: Treatment of adult patients with acute bacterial skin and skin structure infections (ABSSSI) caused by susceptible isolates of the following gram-positive microorganisms: *Staphylococcus aureus* (including methicillin-resistant [MRSA] and methicillin-susceptible [MSSA] isolates), *Streptococcus pyogenes, Streptococcus agalactiae, Streptococcus anginosus* group (including *Streptococcus anginosus, Streptococcus* *intermedius,* and *Streptococcus constellatus*), and *Enterococccus faecalis*

Local Anesthetic/Vasoconstrictor Precautions Tedizolid inhibits monoamine oxidase (MAO). Drug interactions warn that MAO inhibitors can interact with racemic epinephrine thus enhancing the hypertensive effect of epinephrine. Until more evidence is established, it is suggested that caution be exercised and the patient monitored when using local anesthetics with vasoconstrictor in patients receiving tedizolid.

Effects on Dental Treatment Key adverse event(s) related to dental treatment: Oral candidiasis, facial paralysis, and paresthesia have all been reported with prolonged use of tedizolid.

Effects on Bleeding No information available to require special precautions

Adverse Reactions

1% to 10%:

Cardiovascular: Flushing (<2%), hypertension (<2%), palpitations (<2%), tachycardia (<2%)

Central nervous system: Headache (6%), dizziness (2%), facial paralysis (<2%), hypoesthesia (<2%), insomnia (<2%), paresthesia (<2%), peripheral neuropathy (1%)

Dermatologic: Dermatitis (<2%), pruritus (<2%), urticaria (<2%)

Gastrointestinal: Nausea (8%), diarrhea (4%), vomiting (3%), oral candidiasis (<2%), pseudomembranous colitis (<2%)

Hematologic & oncologic: Decreased hemoglobin (males <10.1 g/dL; females <9 g/dL: 3%), decreased platelet count (<112,000/mm^3: 2%), anemia (<2%), decreased white blood cell count (<2%)

Hepatic: Increased serum transaminases (<2%)

Hypersensitivity: Hypersensitivity (<2%)

Infection: Fungal infection (vulvovaginal: <2%)

Ophthalmic: Asthenopia (<2%), blurred vision (<2%), visual impairment (<2%), vitreous opacity (<2%)

Miscellaneous: Infusion related reaction (<2%)

<1%, postmarketing, and/or case reports: *Clostridium difficile* associated diarrhea, decrease in absolute neutrophil count (<800/mm^3), optic neuropathy

General Dosage Range **Oral, IV:** *Adults:* 200 mg once daily

Mechanism of Action After conversion from the prodrug, tedizolid phosphate, tedizolid binds to the 50S bacterial ribosomal subunit. This prevents the formation of a functional 70S initiation complex that is essential for the bacterial translation process and subsequently inhibits protein synthesis. Tedizolid is bacteriostatic against enterococci, staphylococci, and streptococci (Kisgen, 2014).

Pharmacodynamics/Kinetics

Half-life Elimination ~12 hours

Time to Peak Oral: ~3 hours; IV: 1 to 1.5 hours

Pregnancy Risk Factor C

Pregnancy Considerations Adverse events were observed in animal reproduction studies.

Teduglutide (te due GLOO tide)

Brand Names: US Gattex

Brand Names: Canada Revestive

Pharmacologic Category Glucagon-Like Peptide-2 (GLP-2) Analog

Use **Short bowel syndrome:** Treatment of short bowel syndrome in adults who are dependent on parenteral support.

Local Anesthetic/Vasoconstrictor Precautions No information available to require special precautions

Effects on Dental Treatment No significant effects or complications reported

Effects on Bleeding No information available to require special precautions

Adverse Reactions

>10%:

Central nervous system: Headache (16%)

Endocrine & metabolic: Hypervolemia (12%)

Gastrointestinal: Abdominal pain (30% to 38%), nausea (18% to 25%), abdominal distension (14% to 20%), vomiting (12%)

Immunologic: Antibody development (3% to 48%; 3% at month 3, 18% at month 6, 25% at month 12, 31% at month 24, and 48% at month 30)

Local: Injection site reaction (12% to 22%)

Respiratory: Upper respiratory tract infection (12% to 26%)

Miscellaneous: Intestinal stoma complication (42%)

1% to 10%:

Central nervous system: Disturbed sleep (5%)

Dermatologic: Dermal hemorrhage (5%)

Gastrointestinal: Flatulence (9%), change in appetite (7%), intestinal obstruction (4%), intestinal polyps (2%)

Hypersensitivity: Hypersensitivity reaction (8%)

Respiratory: Cough (5%)

<1%, postmarketing, and/or case reports: Cardiac arrest, cardiac failure, cerebral hemorrhage, cholecystitis, cholelithiasis, cholestasis, congestive heart failure, gallbladder perforation, malignant neoplasm, pancreatic pseudocyst, pancreatitis

General Dosage Range Dosage adjustment recommended in patients with renal impairment.

SubQ: *Adults:* 0.05 mg/kg once daily

Mechanism of Action Teduglutide is an analog of glucagon-like peptide-2 (GLP-2), which is secreted in the distal intestine. Endogenous GLP-2 increases intestinal and portal blood flow while inhibiting gastric acid secretion, thereby reducing intestinal losses and improving intestinal absorption. Teduglutide binds and activates GLP-2 receptors, resulting in release of mediators including insulin-like growth factor (IGF)-1, nitric oxide and keratinocyte growth factor (KGF).

Pharmacodynamics/Kinetics

Half-life Elimination ~2 hours (healthy patients); 1.3 hours (short bowel syndrome patients)

Time to Peak Plasma: 3 to 5 hours

Pregnancy Risk Factor B

Pregnancy Considerations Adverse events were not observed in animal reproduction studies.

Tegaserod (teg a SER od)

Brand Names: US Zelnorm

Pharmacologic Category Serotonin 5-HT_4 Receptor Agonist

Use Emergency treatment of irritable bowel syndrome with constipation (IBS-C) and chronic idiopathic constipation (CIC) in women (<55 years of age) in which no alternative therapy exists

Local Anesthetic/Vasoconstrictor Precautions No information available to require special precautions

Effects on Dental Treatment No significant effects or complications reported

Effects on Bleeding No information available to require special precautions

Adverse Reactions
>10%:
Central nervous system: Headache (15%)
Gastrointestinal: Abdominal pain (12%)
1% to 10%:
Central nervous system: Dizziness (4%), migraine (2%)
Gastrointestinal: Diarrhea (9%; severe: <1%; severe diarrhea was complicated by hypovolemia, hypotension, syncope), nausea (8%), flatulence (6%)
Neuromuscular & skeletal: Back pain (5%), arthropathy (2%), leg pain (1%)
<1%, postmarketing, and/or case reports: Albuminuria, alopecia, angina pectoris, appendicitis, asthma, attempted suicide, breast carcinoma, bundle branch block, cardiac arrhythmia, cerebrovascular accident, cholecystitis (with or without increased serum transaminases), choledocholithiasis, depression, diaphoresis, emotional lability, eructation, facial edema, fecal incontinence, flushing, hepatitis, hypermenorrhea, hypersensitivity reaction, hypotension, increased appetite, increased creatine phosphokinase, increased serum ALT, increased serum AST, increased serum bilirubin, intestinal obstruction, irritable bowel syndrome, ischemic colitis, lack of concentration, local tissue necrosis (gangrenous bowel), mesenteric ischemia, muscle cramps, myocardial infarction, ovarian cyst, pain, polyuria, pruritus, rectal hemorrhage, renal pain, sleep disorder, spasm of sphincter of Oddi (suspected), supraventricular tachycardia, syncope, tenesmus, unstable angina pectoris, vertigo

General Dosage Range Oral: *Adults (females <55 years of age):* 6 mg twice daily

Mechanism of Action Tegaserod is a partial neuronal 5-HT_4 receptor agonist. Its action at the receptor site leads to stimulation of the peristaltic reflex and intestinal secretion, and moderation of visceral sensitivity.

Pharmacodynamics/Kinetics

Half-life Elimination IV: 11 ± 5 hours

Time to Peak 1 hour

Pregnancy Risk Factor B

Pregnancy Considerations Adverse events were not observed in animal reproduction studies. Pregnant women were excluded from clinical trials and outcome information following inadvertent pregnancy exposure is limited (Appel-Dingemanse, 2002).

Product Availability Zelnorm is only available in the US via an emergency investigational new drug (IND) process. Physicians with patients who may qualify can contact the FDA's Division of Drug Information at druginfo@fda.hhs.gov or 301-796-3400.

Prescribing and Access Restrictions Available in U.S. under an emergency investigational new drug (IND) process. Emergency situations are defined as immediately life-threatening or requiring hospitalization. Physicians with patients who may qualify can contact the FDA's Division of Drug Information at druginfo@fda.hhs.gov or 301-796-3400. The FDA may either deny the request or authorize shipment of Zelnorm® by Novartis. Additional information can be found at http://www.fda.gov/Drugs/DrugSafety/PostmarketDrugSafetyInformationforPatientsandProviders/ucm103223.htm.

Telavancin (tel a VAN sin)

Brand Names: US Vibativ
Pharmacologic Category Glycopeptide

Use
Complicated skin and skin structure infections: Treatment of complicated skin and skin structure infections caused by susceptible gram-positive organisms including methicillin-susceptible or -resistant *Staphylococcus aureus*, vancomycin-susceptible *Enterococcus faecalis*, and *Streptococcus pyogenes*, *Streptococcus agalactiae*, or *Streptococcus anginosus* group
Hospital-acquired and ventilator-associated bacterial pneumonia (HABP/VABP): Treatment of HABP/VABP caused by susceptible isolates of *Staphylococcus aureus* when alternative treatments are not appropriate

Local Anesthetic/Vasoconstrictor Precautions Telavancin is one of the drugs confirmed to prolong the QT interval and is accepted as having a risk of causing torsade de pointes. The risk of drug-induced torsade de pointes is extremely low when a single QT interval prolonging drug is prescribed. In terms of epinephrine, it is not known what effect vasoconstrictors in the local anesthetic regimen will have in patients with a known history of congenital prolonged QT interval or in patients taking any medication that prolongs the QT interval. Until more information is obtained, it is suggested that the clinician consult with the physician prior to the use of a vasoconstrictor in suspected patients, and that the vasoconstrictor (epinephrine, mepivacaine and levonordefrin [Carbocaine® 2% with Neo-Cobefrin®]) be used with caution.

Effects on Dental Treatment Key adverse event(s) related to dental treatment: Metallic or abnormal taste

Effects on Bleeding Although there are no reports of enhanced bleeding, telavancin may interfere with tests used to monitor coagulation (eg, prothrombin time, INR, activated partial thromboplastin time, activated clotting time, and coagulation-based factor Xa tests). Thrombocytopenia occurs in 7% of patients.

Adverse Reactions
>10%:
Central nervous system: Metallic taste (33%)
Gastrointestinal: Nausea (5% to 27%), vomiting (5% to 14%)
Renal: Increased serum creatinine (8% to 16%; ≥65 years of age: 11%; <65 years of age: 8%), foamy urine (13%)
1% to 10%:
Central nervous system: Dizziness (6%), infusion site pain (4%), rigors (4%)
Dermatologic: Pruritus (3% to 6%), skin rash (4%), localized erythema (3%)
Gastrointestinal: Diarrhea (7%), decreased appetite (3%), abdominal pain (2%)
Local: Infusion site reaction (3%)
Renal: Renal insufficiency (3%; ≥65 years of age: 9%; <65 years of age: 2%), acute renal failure (5%)
<1%, postmarketing, and/or case reports: *Clostridium difficile* associated diarrhea, flushing, hypersensitivity reaction (including anaphylaxis), nephrotoxicity, prolonged Q-T interval on ECG, transient flushing of upper body, urticaria

General Dosage Range Dosage adjustment recommended in patients with renal impairment
IV: *Adults:* 10 mg/kg every 24 hours

Mechanism of Action Exerts concentration-dependent bactericidal activity; inhibits bacterial cell wall synthesis by blocking polymerization and cross-linking of peptidoglycan by binding to D-Ala-D-Ala portion of cell wall. Unlike vancomycin, additional mechanism involves disruption of membrane potential and changes cell permeability due to presence of lipophilic side chain moiety.

Pharmacodynamics/Kinetics

Half-life Elimination 6.6-9.6 hours

Pregnancy Risk Factor C

Pregnancy Considerations [US Boxed Warning]: Based on animal data, adverse developmental outcomes have been observed. Prior to use, women of childbearing potential should have a serum pregnancy test. Use of telavancin is not recommended during pregnancy unless the potential benefit to the mother outweighs the possible risk to the fetus. Telavancin crosses the placenta (Nanovskaya, 2012). In women of childbearing potential, effective contraception should be used during therapy.

Healthcare providers are encouraged to enroll women exposed to telavancin during pregnancy in the Vibativ Pregnancy Registry (855-633-8479).

Dental Comment See Local Anesthetic/Vasoconstrictor Precautions

Telbivudine (tel BI vyoo deen)

Related Information

HIV Infection and AIDS *on page 1785*

Systemic Viral Diseases *on page 1806*

Brand Names: US Tyzeka [DSC]

Brand Names: Canada Sebivo®

Pharmacologic Category Antihepadnaviral, Reverse Transcriptase Inhibitor, Nucleoside (Anti-HBV)

Use Treatment of chronic hepatitis B with evidence of viral replication and either persistent transaminase elevations or histologically-active disease

Local Anesthetic/Vasoconstrictor Precautions No information available to require special precautions

Effects on Dental Treatment No significant effects or complications reported

Effects on Bleeding No information available to require special precautions regarding hemostasis.

Adverse Reactions

>10%:

Central nervous system: Fatigue (13%)

Neuromuscular & skeletal: Increased creatine phosphokinase (79%; grades 3/4: 16%, most asymptomatic and transient)

1% to 10%:

Central nervous system: Headache (10%), dizziness (4%), fever (4%), insomnia (3%)

Dermatologic: Skin rash (4%), pruritus (2%)

Endocrine & metabolic: Increased serum lipase (grades 3/4: 2%)

Gastrointestinal: Diarrhea (6%), abdominal pain (3% to 6%), nausea (5%), abdominal distension (3%), dyspepsia (3%)

Hematologic & oncologic: Neutropenia (grades 3/4: 2%)

Hepatic: Increased serum ALT (grades 3/4: 5% to 7%), increased serum AST (grades 3/4: 6%)

Infection: Exacerbation of hepatitis B (2%)

Neuromuscular & skeletal: Arthralgia (4%), back pain (4%), myalgia (3%)

Respiratory: Cough (6%), pharyngolaryngeal pain (5%)

<1%, postmarketing, and/or case reports: Hepatomegaly, hyperbilirubinemia, hypoesthesia, increased amylase, lactic acidosis, liver steatosis, myopathy, myositis, paresthesia, peripheral neuropathy, rhabdomyolysis, thrombocytopenia

General Dosage Range Dosage adjustment recommended in patients with renal impairment

Oral: *Children ≥16 years and Adults:* 600 mg once daily

Mechanism of Action Telbivudine, a synthetic thymidine nucleoside analogue (L-enantiomer of thymidine), is intracellularly phosphorylated to the active triphosphate form, which competes with the natural substrate, thymidine 5'-triphosphate, to inhibit hepatitis B viral DNA polymerase; enzyme inhibition blocks reverse transcriptase activity thereby reducing viral DNA replication.

Pharmacodynamics/Kinetics

Half-life Elimination Terminal: 40-49 hours

Time to Peak 1-4 hours

Pregnancy Risk Factor B

Pregnancy Considerations Adverse events were not observed in animal reproduction studies. Based on available information, telbivudine may be used to treat hepatitis b during pregnancy (Liu, 2013). Health professionals are encouraged to contact the antiretroviral pregnancy registry to monitor outcomes of pregnant women exposed to antiretroviral medications (1-800-258-4263).

Telithromycin (tel ith roe MYE sin)

Related Information

Clinical Risk Related to Drugs Prolonging QT Interval *on page 1772*

Brand Names: US Ketek [DSC]

Pharmacologic Category Antibiotic, Ketolide

Use Community-acquired pneumonia: Treatment of mild to moderate community-acquired pneumonia (CAP) due to *Streptococcus pneumoniae* (including multidrug-resistant isolates), *Haemophilus influenzae*, *Moraxella catarrhalis*, *Chlamydophila* (also known as *Chlamydia*) *pneumoniae*, or *Mycoplasma pneumoniae* in patients 18 years and older.

Local Anesthetic/Vasoconstrictor Precautions Telithromycin is one of the drugs confirmed to prolong the QT interval and is accepted as having a risk of causing torsade de pointes. The risk of drug-induced torsade de pointes is extremely low when a single QT interval prolonging drug is prescribed. In terms of epinephrine, it is not known what effect vasoconstrictors in the local anesthetic regimen will have in patients with a known history of congenital prolonged QT interval or in patients taking any medication that prolongs the QT interval. Until more information is obtained, it is suggested that the clinician consult with the physician prior to the use of a vasoconstrictor in suspected patients, and that the vasoconstrictor (epinephrine, mepivacaine and levonordefrin [Carbocaine® 2% with Neo-Cobefrin®]) be used with caution.

Effects on Dental Treatment Key adverse event(s) related to dental treatment: Xerostomia (normal salivary flow resumes upon discontinuation), glossitis, stomatitis, and tooth discoloration.

Effects on Bleeding No information available to require special precautions

Adverse Reactions

>10%: Gastrointestinal: Diarrhea (10% to 11%)

2% to 10%:

Central nervous system: Headache (2% to 6%), dizziness (3% to 4%)

Gastrointestinal: Nausea (7% to 8%), vomiting (2% to 3%), dysgeusia (2%), loose stools (2%)

≥0.2% to <2%:

Central nervous system: Drowsiness, fatigue, insomnia, vertigo

Dermatologic: Diaphoresis, skin rash

Gastrointestinal: Abdominal distension, abdominal pain, anorexia, constipation, dyspepsia, flatulence, gastric distress, gastritis, gastroenteritis, glossitis, oral candidiasis, stomatitis, xerostomia

Genitourinary: Fungal vaginosis, vaginitis, vulvovaginal candidiasis

Hematologic & oncologic: Thrombocythemia

Hepatic: Abnormal hepatic function tests, increased serum transaminases

Ophthalmic: Accommodation disturbance, blurred vision, diplopia

<0.2%, postmarketing, and/or case reports: Ageusia, altered sense of smell, anaphylaxis, angioedema, anosmia, anxiety, arthralgia, atrial arrhythmia, bradycardia, cardiac arrhythmia, confusion, convulsions, dyspnea, eczema, eosinophilia, erythema multiforme, exacerbation of myasthenia gravis, facial edema, flushing, hallucination, hepatic failure, hepatic injury (including necrosis), hepatitis, hypersensitivity reaction, hypotension, increased serum alkaline phosphatase, increased serum bilirubin, ischemic heart disease, jaundice, loss of consciousness (may be vagal-related), muscle cramps, myalgia, palpitations, pancreatitis, paresthesia, prolonged Q-T interval on ECG, pruritus, pseudomembranous colitis, respiratory failure, syncope, torsades de pointes, tremor, urticaria, urine discoloration, ventricular arrhythmia, ventricular tachycardia

General Dosage Range Dosage adjustment recommended in patients with renal impairment

Oral: *Adults:* 800 mg once daily

Mechanism of Action Inhibits bacterial protein synthesis by binding to two sites on the 50S ribosomal subunit. Telithromycin has also been demonstrated to alter secretion of IL-1alpha and TNF-alpha; the clinical significance of this immunomodulatory effect has not been evaluated.

Pharmacodynamics/Kinetics

Half-life Elimination 10 hours

Time to Peak Plasma: 1 hour

Pregnancy Risk Factor C

Pregnancy Considerations Adverse events have been observed in animal reproduction studies

Dental Comment See Local Anesthetic/Vasoconstrictor Precautions

Telmisartan (tel mi SAR tan)

Related Information

Cardiovascular Diseases *on page 1752*

Brand Names: US Micardis

Brand Names: Canada ACT Telmisartan; Apo-Telmisartan; Auro-Telmisartan; Micardis; Mylan-Telmisartan; PMS-Telmisartan; Ran-Telmisartan; Sandoz-Telmisartan; Teva-Telmisartan; Van-Telmisartan

Pharmacologic Category Angiotensin II Receptor Blocker; Antihypertensive

Use

Cardiovascular risk reduction: Cardiovascular risk reduction in patients ≥55 years of age unable to take ACE inhibitors and who are at high risk of major cardiovascular events (eg, MI, stroke, death)

Hypertension: For the treatment of hypertension, alone or in combination with other antihypertensive agents

Guideline recommendations:

Hypertension: The 2014 guideline for the management of high blood pressure in adults (Eighth Joint National Committee [JNC 8; James, 2013]) recommends initiation of pharmacologic treatment to lower blood pressure for the following patients:

- Patients ≥60 years of age with systolic blood pressure (SBP) ≥150 mm Hg or diastolic blood pressure (DBP) ≥90 mm Hg. Goal of therapy is SBP <150 mm Hg and DBP <90 mm Hg.
- Patients <60 years of age with SBP ≥140 mm Hg or DBP ≥90 mm Hg. Goal of therapy is SBP <140 mm Hg and DBP <90 mm Hg.
- Patients ≥18 years of age with diabetes and SBP ≥140 mm Hg or DBP ≥90 mm Hg. Goal of therapy is SBP <140 mm Hg and DBP <90 mm Hg.
- Patients ≥18 years of age with chronic kidney disease (CKD) and SBP ≥140 mm Hg or DBP ≥90 mm Hg. Goal of therapy is SBP <140 mm Hg and DBP <90 mm Hg.

Chronic kidney disease (CKD) and hypertension: Regardless of race or diabetes status, the use of an ACE inhibitor (ACEI) or angiotensin receptor blocker (ARB) as initial therapy is recommended to improve kidney outcomes. In the general nonblack population (without CKD), including those with diabetes, initial antihypertensive treatment should consist of a thiazide-type diuretic, calcium channel blocker, ACEI, or ARB. In the general black population (without CKD), including those with diabetes, initial antihypertensive treatment should consist of a thiazide-type diuretic or a calcium channel blocker instead of an ACEI or ARB.

Coronary artery disease and hypertension: The American Heart Association, American College of Cardiology and American Society of Hypertension (AHA/ACC/ASH) 2015 scientific statement for the treatment of hypertension in patients with coronary artery disease (CAD) recommends the use of an ARB (or ACE inhibitor) as part of a regimen in patients with hypertension and chronic stable angina if there is prior MI, LV systolic dysfunction, diabetes mellitus, or CKD. A BP target of <140/90 mm Hg is reasonable for the secondary prevention of cardiovascular events. A lower target BP (<130/80 mm Hg) may be appropriate in some individuals with CAD, previous MI, stroke or transient ischemic attack, or CAD risk equivalents (AHA/ACC/ASH [Rosendorff 2015]).

Local Anesthetic/Vasoconstrictor Precautions No information available to require special precautions

Effects on Dental Treatment Key adverse event(s) related to dental treatment: Patients may experience orthostatic hypotension as they stand up after treatment; especially if lying in dental chair for extended periods of time. Use caution with sudden changes in position during and after dental treatment.

Effects on Bleeding No information available to require special precautions

Adverse Reactions May be associated with worsening of renal function in patients dependent on renin-angiotensin-aldosterone system.

1% to 10%:

Cardiovascular: Intermittent claudication (7%), chest pain (≥1%), hypertension (≥1%), peripheral edema (≥1%)

Central nervous system: Dizziness (≥1%), fatigue (≥1%), headache (≥1%), pain (≥1%)

Dermatologic: Dermal ulcer (3%)

Gastrointestinal: Diarrhea (3%), abdominal pain (≥1%), dyspepsia (≥1%), nausea (≥1%)
Genitourinary: Urinary tract infection (≥1%)
Neuromuscular & skeletal: Back pain (3%), myalgia (≥1%)
Respiratory: Upper respiratory tract infection (7%), sinusitis (3%), cough (≥1%), pharyngitis (1%)

<1%, postmarketing, and/or case reports: Abscess, anaphylaxis, anemia, angina pectoris, angioedema, anxiety, arthralgia, arthritis, asthma, atrial fibrillation, bradycardia, bronchitis, cardiac failure, cerebrovascular disease, conjunctivitis, constipation, cystitis, decreased hemoglobin, depression, dermatitis, diabetes mellitus, diaphoresis, drowsiness, dyspnea, ECG abnormality, eczema, edema, enteritis, epistaxis, eosinophilia, erectile dysfunction, erythema, facial edema, fever, fixed drug eruption, flatulence, flushing, fungal infection, gastroenteritis, gastroesophageal reflux, gout, hemorrhoids, hepatic insufficiency, hypercholesterolemia, hyperkalemia, hypersensitivity reaction, hypoglycemia (diabetic patients), hypotension, impotence, increased creatine phosphokinase, increased blood urea nitrogen, increased liver enzymes, increased serum creatinine, increased uric acid, insomnia, malaise, migraine, muscle cramps, myocardial infarction, neoplasm, nervousness, orthostatic hypotension (more frequent in dialysis patients), otalgia, otitis media, palpitations, paresthesia, pruritus, renal failure, renal insufficiency, rhabdomyolysis, rhinitis, skin rash, syncope, tachycardia, tendon pain, tendonitis, tenosynovitis, thrombocytopenia, tinnitus, toothache, urinary frequency, urticaria, vertigo, visual disturbance, vomiting, weakness, xerostomia

General Dosage Range Oral: *Adults:* Initial: 40 to 80 mg once daily; Maintenance: 20 to 80 mg daily once daily

Mechanism of Action Angiotensin II acts as a vasoconstrictor. In addition to causing direct vasoconstriction, angiotensin II also stimulates the release of aldosterone. Once aldosterone is released, sodium as well as water is reabsorbed. The end result is an elevation in blood pressure. Telmisartan is a nonpeptide AT1 angiotensin II receptor antagonist. This binding prevents angiotensin II from binding to the receptor thereby blocking the vasoconstriction and the aldosterone secreting effects of angiotensin II.

Pharmacodynamics/Kinetics

Onset of Action 1 to 2 hours; Peak effect: 0.5 to 1 hours

Duration of Action Up to 24 hours

Half-life Elimination Terminal: 24 hours

Time to Peak Plasma: 0.5 to 1 hours

Pregnancy Risk Factor D

Pregnancy Considerations [U.S. Boxed Warning]: Drugs that act on the renin-angiotensin system can cause injury and death to the developing fetus. Discontinue as soon as possible once pregnancy is detected. The use of drugs which act on the renin-angiotensin system are associated with oligohydramnios. Oligohydramnios, due to decreased fetal renal function, may lead to fetal lung hypoplasia and skeletal malformations. Use is also associated with anuria, hypotension, renal failure, skull hypoplasia, and death in the fetus/neonate. The exposed fetus should be monitored for fetal growth, amniotic fluid volume, and organ formation. Infants exposed *in utero* should be monitored for hyperkalemia, hypotension, and oliguria (exchange transfusions or dialysis may be needed). These adverse events are generally associated with maternal use in the second and third trimesters.

Untreated chronic maternal hypertension is also associated with adverse events in the fetus, infant, and mother. The use of angiotensin II receptor blockers is not recommended to treat chronic uncomplicated hypertension in pregnant women and should generally be avoided in women of reproductive potential (ACOG, 2013).

Telmisartan and Amlodipine

(tel mi SAR tan & am LOE di peen)

Related Information

AmLODIPine *on page 117*
Telmisartan *on page 1534*

Brand Names: US Twynsta

Brand Names: Canada Twynsta

Pharmacologic Category Angiotensin II Receptor Blocker; Antianginal Agent; Antihypertensive; Calcium Channel Blocker; Calcium Channel Blocker, Dihydropyridine

Use Hypertension: Treatment of hypertension, including initial treatment in patients who will require multiple antihypertensives for adequate control

Local Anesthetic/Vasoconstrictor Precautions No information available to require special precautions

Effects on Dental Treatment Key adverse event(s) related to dental treatment: Patients may experience orthostatic hypotension as they stand up after treatment; especially if lying in dental chair for extended periods of time. Use caution with sudden changes in position during and after dental treatment.

Fewer reports of gingival hyperplasia reported with amlodipine use than with other calcium channel blockers (usually resolves upon discontinuation); consult with healthcare provider.

Effects on Bleeding No information available to require special precautions

Adverse Reactions Reactions/percentages reported with combination product; also see individual agents.

>10%: Cardiovascular: Peripheral edema (dose related: 1% to 11%)

1% to 10%:
Cardiovascular: Orthostatic hypotension (6%), edema (<2%), hypotension (<2%), syncope (<2%)
Central nervous system: Dizziness (3%)
Neuromuscular & skeletal: Back pain (2%)

General Dosage Range Oral: *Adults:* Amlodipine 5 to 10 mg/telmisartan 40 to 80 mg once daily (maximum: amlodipine 10 mg/telmisartan 80 mg per day)

Mechanism of Action

Telmisartan is a nonpeptide AT1 (angiotensin II type 1) receptor antagonist. Angiotensin II acts as a vasoconstrictor. In addition to causing direct vasoconstriction, angiotensin II also stimulates the release of aldosterone. Once aldosterone is released, sodium and water are reabsorbed. The end result is an elevation in blood pressure. Telmisartan binding to AT1 prevents angiotensin II from binding to the receptor thereby blocking the vasoconstriction and the aldosterone secreting effects of angiotensin II.

Amlodipine inhibits calcium ion from entering the "slow channels" or select voltage-sensitive areas of vascular smooth muscle and myocardium during depolarization, producing a relaxation of coronary vascular smooth muscle and coronary vasodilation; increases myocardial oxygen delivery in patients with vasospastic angina. Amlodipine directly acts on vascular smooth muscle to produce peripheral arterial vasodilation reducing peripheral vascular resistance and blood pressure.

Pregnancy Risk Factor D

Pregnancy Considerations [US Boxed Warning]: Drugs that act on the renin-angiotensin system can cause injury and death to the developing fetus. Discontinue as soon as possible once pregnancy is detected. Also see individual agents.

Temazepam (te MAZ e pam)

Related Information

Dentin Hypersensitivity, Acid Erosion, High Caries Index, Management of Alveolar Osteitis, and Xerostomia *on page 1857*

Brand Names: US Restoril

Brand Names: Canada Apo-Temazepam; Dom-Temazepam; PHL-Temazepam; PMS-Temazepam; Restoril; Temazepam-15; Temazepam-30; Teva-Temazepam

Pharmacologic Category Benzodiazepine

Use Insomnia: Short-term treatment of insomnia

Local Anesthetic/Vasoconstrictor Precautions No information available to require special precautions

Effects on Dental Treatment Key adverse event(s) related to dental treatment: Significant xerostomia (normal salivary flow resumes upon discontinuation).

Effects on Bleeding No information available to require special precautions

Adverse Reactions

1% to 10%:

Central nervous system: Drowsiness (9%), dizziness (5%), lethargy (5%), hangover effect (3%), euphoria (2%), anxiety, confusion, dysarthria, fatigue, headache, vertigo

Dermatologic: Diaphoresis, skin rash

Endocrine & metabolic: Decreased libido

Gastrointestinal: Diarrhea (2%)

Neuromuscular & skeletal: Weakness

Ophthalmic: Blurred vision

<1%, postmarketing, and/or case reports: Abnormal behavior, aggressive behavior, agitation, amnesia, anaphylaxis, angioedema, anorexia, ataxia, back pain, burning sensation of eyes, depersonalization, drug dependence, dyspnea, equilibrium disturbance, extroversion, hallucination, hematologic disease, hyperhidrosis, hyporeflexia, increased dream activity, menstrual disease, nausea, nystagmus, palpitations, paradoxical reaction, pharyngeal edema, sleep disorder (sleep-driving, cooking or eating food, making phone calls), tremor, vomiting

General Dosage Range Oral:

Adults: 7.5 to 30 mg at bedtime

Elderly: Initial: 7.5 mg at bedtime

Mechanism of Action Binds to stereospecific benzodiazepine receptors on the postsynaptic GABA neuron at several sites within the central nervous system, including the limbic system, reticular formation. Enhancement of the inhibitory effect of GABA on neuronal excitability results by increased neuronal membrane permeability to chloride ions. This shift in chloride ions results in hyperpolarization (a less excitable state) and stabilization. Benzodiazepine receptors and effects appear to be linked to the GABA-A receptors. Benzodiazepines do not bind to GABA-B receptors.

Pharmacodynamics/Kinetics

Half-life Elimination 3.5-18.4 hours

Time to Peak Serum: 1.2-1.6 hours

Pregnancy Risk Factor X

Pregnancy Considerations Adverse events were observed in animal reproduction studies. Although information specific to the use of temazepam has not been located, all benzodiazepines are assumed to cross the placenta. Teratogenic effects have been observed with some benzodiazepines; however, additional studies are needed. The incidence of premature birth and low birth weights may be increased following maternal use of benzodiazepines; hypoglycemia and respiratory problems in the neonate may occur following exposure late in pregnancy. Neonatal withdrawal symptoms may occur within days to weeks after birth and "floppy infant syndrome" (which also includes withdrawal symptoms) have been reported with some benzodiazepines (Bergman, 1992; Iqbal, 2002; Wikner, 2007). Use during pregnancy is contraindicated.

Controlled Substance C-IV

Temozolomide (te moe ZOE loe mide)

Brand Names: US Temodar

Brand Names: Canada ACH-Temozolomide; ACT Temozolomide; Temodal

Pharmacologic Category Antineoplastic Agent, Alkylating Agent (Triazene)

Use

Anaplastic astrocytoma: Treatment of refractory anaplastic astrocytoma (refractory to a regimen containing a nitrosourea and procarbazine)

Glioblastoma multiforme: Treatment of newly-diagnosed glioblastoma multiforme (initially in combination with radiotherapy, then as maintenance treatment)

Local Anesthetic/Vasoconstrictor Precautions No information available to require special precautions

Effects on Dental Treatment Key adverse event(s) related to dental treatment: Stomatitis, dysphagia, and taste perversion.

Effects on Bleeding Chemotherapy may result in significant myelosuppression, potentially including significant reduction in platelet counts and altered hemostasis. In patients who are under active treatment with these agents, medical consult is suggested.

Adverse Reactions Note: With CNS malignancies, it may be difficult to distinguish between CNS adverse events caused by temozolomide versus the effects of progressive disease.

>10%:

Cardiovascular: Peripheral edema (11%)

Central nervous system: Fatigue (34% to 61%), headache (23% to 41%), convulsions (6% to 23%), hemiparesis (18%), dizziness (5% to 12%), ataxia (8% to 11%)

Dermatologic: Alopecia (55%), skin rash (8% to 13%)

Gastrointestinal: Nausea (49% to 53%; grades 3/4: 1% to 10%), vomiting (29% to 42%; grades 3/4: 2% to 6%), constipation (22% to 33%), anorexia (9% to 27%), diarrhea (10% to 16%)

Hematologic & oncologic: Lymphocytopenia (grades 3/4: 55%), thrombocytopenia (grades 3/4: adults: 4% to 19%; children: 25%), neutropenia (grades 3/4: adults: 8% to 14%; children: 20%), leukopenia (grades 3/4: 11%)

Infection: Viral infection (11%)

Neuromuscular & skeletal: Weakness (7% to 13%)

Miscellaneous: Fever (13%)

1% to 10%:

Central nervous system: Amnesia (10%), insomnia (4% to 10%), drowsiness (9%), paresthesia (9%), paresis (8%), anxiety (7%), memory impairment

(7%), abnormal gait (6%), depression (6%), confusion (5%)

Dermatologic: Pruritus (5% to 8%), xeroderma (5%), erythema (1%)

Endocrine & metabolic: Hypercorticoidism (8%), weight gain (5%)

Gastrointestinal: Stomatitis (9%), abdominal pain (5% to 9%), dysphagia (7%), dysgeusia (5%)

Genitourinary: Urinary incontinence (8%), urinary tract infection (8%), mastalgia (females 6%), urinary frequency (6%)

Hematologic & oncologic: Anemia (grades 3/4: 4%)

Hypersensitivity: Hypersensitivity reaction (≤3%)

Neuromuscular & skeletal: Back pain (8%), arthralgia (6%), myalgia (5%)

Ophthalmic: Blurred vision (5% to 8%), diplopia (5%), visual disturbance (visual deficit/vision changes 5%)

Respiratory: Pharyngitis (8%), upper respiratory tract infection (8%), cough (5% to 8%), sinusitis (6%), dyspnea (5%)

Miscellaneous: Radiation injury (2% maintenance phase after radiotherapy)

<1%, postmarketing, and/or case reports (limited to important or life-threatening): Agitation, anaphylaxis, apathy, aplastic anemia, cholestasis, cytomegalovirus disease (primary and reactivation), diabetes insipidus, emotional lability, erythema multiforme, febrile neutropenia, flu-like symptoms, hallucination, hematoma, hemorrhage, hepatitis, hepatitis B (reactivation), hepatotoxicity, herpes simplex infection, herpes zoster, hyperbilirubinemia, hyperglycemia, hypersensitivity pneumonitis, hypokalemia, increased serum alkaline phosphatase, increased serum transaminases, injection site reaction (erythema, irritation, pain, pruritus, swelling, warmth), interstitial pneumonitis, metastases (including myeloid leukemia), myelodysplastic syndrome, neuropathy, opportunistic infection (including pneumocystosis), oral candidiasis, pancytopenia (may be prolonged), peripheral neuropathy, petechia, pneumonitis, pulmonary fibrosis, Stevens-Johnson syndrome, toxic epidermal necrolysis, weight loss

General Dosage Range Dosage adjustment recommended in patients who develop toxicities.

IV, Oral: *Adults:* Dosage varies greatly depending on indication

Mechanism of Action Temozolomide is a prodrug which is rapidly and nonenzymatically converted to the active alkylating metabolite MTIC [(methyl-triazene-1-yl)-imidazole-4-carboxamide]; this conversion is spontaneous, nonenzymatic, and occurs under physiologic conditions in all tissues to which it distributes. The cytotoxic effects of MTIC are manifested through alkylation (methylation) of DNA at the O^6, N^7 guanine positions which lead to DNA double strand breaks and apoptosis. Non-cell cycle specific.

Pharmacodynamics/Kinetics

Half-life Elimination Mean: Parent drug: Children: 1.7 hours; Adults: 1.6-1.8 hours

Time to Peak Oral: Empty stomach: 1 hour; with food (high-fat meal): 2.25 hours

Pregnancy Risk Factor D

Pregnancy Considerations Adverse events were observed in animal reproduction studies. May cause fetal harm when administered to pregnant women. Male and female patients should avoid pregnancy while receiving temozolomide.

Temsirolimus (tem sir OH li mus)

Brand Names: US Torisel

Brand Names: Canada Torisel

Pharmacologic Category Antineoplastic Agent, mTOR Kinase Inhibitor

Use Renal cell carcinoma, advanced: Treatment of advanced renal cell carcinoma (RCC)

Local Anesthetic/Vasoconstrictor Precautions No information available to require special precautions

Effects on Dental Treatment Key adverse event(s) related to dental treatment: Effects on oral cavity including mucositis, stomatitis, and taste disturbances.

Effects on Bleeding Thrombocytopenia has been associated with use; severe thrombocytopenia (grades 3/4: 1%) may be associated with delayed coagulation. Consultation to ensure adequate platelet counts may be considered in patients with signs/symptoms or a history of thrombocytopenia.

Adverse Reactions

>10%:

Cardiovascular: Edema (35%), chest pain (16%)

Central nervous system: Pain (28%), headache (15%), insomnia (12%)

Dermatologic: Skin rash (47%), pruritus (19%), nail disease (14%), xeroderma (11%)

Endocrine & metabolic: Increased serum glucose (89%; grades 3/4: 16%), increased serum cholesterol (87%, grades 3/4: 2%), hypertriglyceridemia (83%; grades 3/4: 44%), hypophosphatemia (49%; grades 3/4: 18%), hyperglycemia (26%), hyperlipidemia (≥30%), hypokalemia (21%; grades 3/4: 5%), weight loss (19%)

Gastrointestinal: Mucositis (41%), nausea (37%), anorexia (32%), diarrhea (27%), abdominal pain (21%; grades 3/4: 4%), constipation (20%), dysgeusia (20%), stomatitis (20%), vomiting (19%)

Genitourinary: Urinary tract infection (15%)

Hematologic & oncologic: Decreased hemoglobin (94%; grades 3/4: 20%), lymphocytopenia (53%; grades 3/4: 16%), thrombocytopenia (40%; grades 3/4: 1%; dose-limiting toxicity), decreased white blood cell count (32%; grades 3/4: 1%), anemia (≥30%), decreased neutrophils (19%; grades 3/4: 5%)

Hepatic: Increased serum alkaline phosphatase (68%; grades 3/4: 3%), increased serum AST (38%; grades 3/4: 2%)

Infection: Infection (20%; grades 3/4: 3%; includes abscess, bronchitis, cellulitis, herpes simplex, herpes zoster)

Neuromuscular & skeletal: Weakness (51%), back pain (20%), arthralgia (18%)

Renal: Increased serum creatinine (57%; grades 3/4: 3%)

Respiratory: Dyspnea (28%), cough (26%), epistaxis (12%), pharyngitis (12%)

Miscellaneous: Fever (24%; grades 3/4: 1%)

1% to 10%:

Cardiovascular: Hypertension (7%), venous thromboembolism (2%; includes deep vein thrombosis and pulmonary embolism), pericardial effusion (1%), thrombophlebitis (1%)

Central nervous system: Chills (8%), depression (4%), convulsions (1%)

Dermatologic: Acne vulgaris (10%)

Endocrine & metabolic: Diabetes mellitus (5%)

Gastrointestinal: Gastrointestinal hemorrhage (1%)

Hematologic & oncologic: Rectal hemorrhage (1%)

Hepatic: Hyperbilirubinemia (8%)

Infection: Sepsis (1%), wound infection (1%)

Neuromuscular & skeletal: Myalgia (8%)

Ophthalmic: Conjunctivitis (8%; including lacrimation disorder)
Respiratory: Rhinitis (10%), pneumonia (8%), upper respiratory tract infection (7%), pleural effusion (4%)
Miscellaneous: Wound healing impairment (1%)
<1%, postmarketing, and/or case reports: Acute renal failure, angioedema, causalgia, cholecystitis, cholelithiasis, decreased glucose tolerance, extravasation reactions (with pain, swelling, warmth, erythema), hypersensitivity reaction, interstitial pulmonary disease, intestinal perforation, pancreatitis, pneumonitis, rhabdomyolysis, seizure, Stevens-Johnson syndrome

General Dosage Range Dosage adjustment recommended in patients with hepatic impairment, on concomitant therapy, or who develop toxicities

IV: *Adults:* 25 mg once weekly

Mechanism of Action Temsirolimus and its active metabolite, sirolimus, are targeted inhibitors of mTOR (mechanistic target of rapamycin) kinase activity. Temsirolimus (and sirolimus) bind to FKBP-12, an intracellular protein, to form a complex which inhibits mTOR signaling, halting the cell cycle at the G1 phase in tumor cells. Inhibition of mTOR blocks downstream phosphorylation of p70S6k and S6 ribosomal proteins. In renal cell carcinoma, mTOR inhibition also exhibits anti-angiogenesis activity by reducing levels of HIF-1 and HIF-2 alpha (hypoxia inducible factors) and vascular endothelial growth factor (VEGF).

Pharmacodynamics/Kinetics

Half-life Elimination Temsirolimus: ~17 hours; Sirolimus: ~55 hours

Time to Peak Temsirolimus: At end of infusion; Sirolimus: 0.5 to 2 hours after temsirolimus infusion

Pregnancy Risk Factor D

Pregnancy Considerations Adverse events have been observed in animal reproduction studies. Based on its mechanism of action, temsirolimus may cause fetal harm if administered to a pregnant woman. Women of childbearing potential should be advised to avoid pregnancy. Men and women should use effective birth control during temsirolimus treatment, and continue for 3 months after temsirolimus discontinuation.

Tenecteplase (ten EK te plase)

Related Information

Cardiovascular Diseases *on page 1752*

Brand Names: US TNKase

Brand Names: Canada TNKase®

Pharmacologic Category Thrombolytic Agent

Use Management of ST-elevation myocardial infarction (STEMI) for the lysis of thrombi in the coronary vasculature to restore perfusion and reduce mortality.

Recommended criteria for treatment of STEMI (ACCF/AHA; O'Gara, 2013): Ischemic symptoms within 12 hours of treatment or evidence of ongoing ischemia 12-24 hours after symptom onset with a large area of myocardium at risk or hemodynamic instability.

STEMI ECG definition: New ST-segment elevation at the J point in at least 2 contiguous leads of ≥2 mm (0.2 mV) in men or ≥1.5 mm (0.15 mV) in women in leads V_2-V_3 and/or of ≥1 mm (0.1 mV) in other contiguous precordial leads or limb leads on ECG. New or presumably new left bundle branch block (LBBB) may interfere with ST-elevation analysis and should not be considered diagnostic in isolation.

At non-PCI-capable hospitals, the ACCF/AHA recommends thrombolytic therapy administration when the anticipated first medical contact (FMC)-to-device time at a PCI-capable hospital is >120 minutes due to unavoidable delays.

Local Anesthetic/Vasoconstrictor Precautions No information available to require special precautions

Effects on Dental Treatment Key adverse event(s) related to dental treatment: Bleeding is the most frequent adverse effect of tenecteplase. See Effects on Bleeding.

Effects on Bleeding Bleeding is the most frequent adverse effect associated with tenecteplase. It is unlikely that ambulatory patients presenting for dental treatment will be taking intravenous anticoagulant therapy.

Adverse Reactions

>10%:
Hematologic & oncologic: Hemorrhage (ASSENT-2 trial: minor: 22%; major: 5%), hematoma (local: minor: 12%; major: 2%)

1% to 10%:
Cardiovascular: Cerebrovascular accident (2%)
Gastrointestinal: Gastrointestinal hemorrhage (minor: 2%; major: 1%)
Genitourinary: Genitourinary tract hemorrhage (minor: 4%; major: <1%)
Hematologic & oncologic: Local hemorrhage (catheter puncture site: minor: 4%; major: <1%)
Respiratory: Pharyngeal bleeding (minor: 3%), epistaxis (minor: 2%)

Frequency not defined:
Cardiovascular: Atrioventricular block, cardiac arrhythmia, cardiac failure, cardiac tamponade, cardiogenic shock, embolism, hypotension, ischemic heart disease (recurrent), mitral valve insufficiency (regurgitation), myocardial reinfarction, myocardial rupture, pericardial effusion, pericarditis, pulmonary edema, thrombosis
Gastrointestinal: Nausea, vomiting
Miscellaneous: Fever

<1%, postmarketing, and/or case reports: Anaphylaxis, angioedema, intracranial hemorrhage, laryngeal edema, respiratory tract hemorrhage, retroperitoneal hemorrhage, skin rash, thrombolytic drug-induced cholesterol embolism (clinical features may include acute renal failure, bowel infarction, cerebral infarction, gangrenous digits, hypertension, livedo reticularis, myocardial infarction, pancreatitis, "purple toe" syndrome, retinal artery occlusion, rhabdomyolysis, spinal cord infarction), urticaria

General Dosage Range IV:
Adults <60 kg: 30 mg as a single dose
Adults ≥60 to <70 kg: 35 mg as a single dose
Adults ≥70 to <80 kg: 40 mg as a single dose
Adults ≥80 to <90 kg: 45 mg as a single dose
Adults ≥90 kg: 50 mg as a single dose

Mechanism of Action Promotes initiation of fibrinolysis by binding to fibrin and converting plasminogen to plasmin. Tenecteplase is essentially alteplase with the exception of 3 point mutations and is more fibrin specific, more resistant to plasminogen activator inhibitor -1 (PAI-1), with a longer duration of action compared to alteplase. Produced by recombinant DNA technology using a mammalian cell line (Chinese hamster ovary cells).

Pharmacodynamics/Kinetics

Half-life Elimination Biphasic: Initial: 20-24 minutes; Terminal: 90-130 minutes

Pregnancy Risk Factor C

Pregnancy Considerations Adverse events have been observed in some animal reproduction studies.

The risk of bleeding may be increased in pregnant women. Administer to pregnant women only if the potential benefits justify the risk to the fetus.

Teniposide (ten i POE side)

Brand Names: Canada Vumon

Pharmacologic Category Antineoplastic Agent, Podophyllotoxin Derivative; Antineoplastic Agent, Topoisomerase II Inhibitor

Use Acute lymphoblastic leukemia, refractory: Treatment of refractory childhood acute lymphoblastic leukemia (ALL) in combination with other chemotherapy

Local Anesthetic/Vasoconstrictor Precautions No information available to require special precautions

Effects on Dental Treatment Key adverse event(s) related to dental treatment: Mucositis.

Effects on Bleeding Chemotherapy may result in significant myelosuppression, including significant thrombocytopenia (85%), and altered hemostasis. In patients who are under active treatment with these agents, medical consult is suggested.

Adverse Reactions

>10%:

Gastrointestinal: Mucositis (76%), diarrhea (33%), nausea and vomiting (29%; mild to moderate)

Hematologic & oncologic: Neutropenia (95%), leukopenia (89%), anemia (88%), thrombocytopenia (85%), bone marrow depression (75%)

Infection: Infection (12%)

1% to 10%:

Cardiovascular: Hypotension (2%; may be intractable; associated with rapid [<30 minutes] infusions)

Dermatologic: Alopecia (9%; usually reversible), skin rash (3%)

Hematologic & oncologic: Hemorrhage (5%)

Hypersensitivity: Hypersensitivity reaction (5%; includes bronchospasm, chills, dyspnea, fever, flushing, hypertension, hypotension, tachycardia, or urticaria)

Miscellaneous: Fever (3%)

<1%, postmarketing, and/or case reports: Cardiac arrhythmia, central nervous system depression, confusion, fluid and electrolyte disturbance, headache, hepatic insufficiency, metabolic acidosis, neuropathy (severe), neurotoxicity, renal insufficiency, thrombophlebitis, weakness

General Dosage Range IV: *Children:* 165 mg/m^2 twice weekly for 8 to 9 doses **or** 250 mg/m^2 weekly for 4 to 8 weeks

Mechanism of Action Teniposide does not inhibit microtubular assembly; it has been shown to delay transit of cells through the S phase and arrest cells in late S or early G_2 phase, preventing cells from entering mitosis. Teniposide is a topoisomerase II inhibitor, and appears to cause DNA strand breaks by inhibition of strand-passing and DNA ligase action.

Pharmacodynamics/Kinetics

Half-life Elimination Children: 5 hours

Pregnancy Risk Factor D

Pregnancy Considerations Adverse effects were observed in animal reproduction studies. May cause fetal harm if administered during pregnancy. Women of childbearing potential should avoid becoming pregnant during teniposide treatment.

Tenofovir Alafenamide
(ten OF oh vir al a FEN a mide)

Brand Names: US Vemlidy

Pharmacologic Category Antihepadnaviral, Reverse Transcriptase Inhibitor, Nucleotide (Anti-HBV)

Use Chronic hepatitis B: Treatment of chronic hepatitis B virus (HBV) infection in adults with compensated liver disease

Local Anesthetic/Vasoconstrictor Precautions No information available to require special precautions

Effects on Dental Treatment No significant effects or complications reported

Effects on Bleeding No information available to require special precautions

Adverse Reactions

1% to 10%:

Central nervous system: Headache (9%), fatigue (6%)

Endocrine & metabolic: Increased LDL cholesterol (4%), glycosuria, increased amylase

Gastrointestinal: Abdominal pain (7%), nausea (5%)

Hepatic: Increased serum ALT, increased serum AST

Neuromuscular & skeletal: Decreased bone mineral density (3% to 6%), back pain (5%), increased serum creatine phosphokinase

Respiratory: Cough (6%)

General Dosage Range Oral: *Adults:* 25 mg once daily

Mechanism of Action Tenofovir alafenamide, an analog of adenosine 5'-monophosphate, is converted intracellularly by hydrolysis to tenofovir and subsequently phosphorylated to the active tenofovir diphosphate. The active moiety inhibits replication of HBV by inhibiting HBV polymerase.

Pharmacodynamics/Kinetics

Half-life Elimination Serum: 0.51 hours

Time to Peak Serum: 0.48 hours

Pregnancy Considerations

Adverse events were not observed in animal reproduction studies. Tenofovir alafenamide is rapidly converted to tenofovir. There have been no data reported to the antiretroviral registry related to the use of this drug in pregnancy. The Health and Human Services (HHS) Perinatal HIV Guidelines note data are insufficient to recommend tenofovir alafenamide for initial therapy in antiretroviral-naive pregnant women (HHS [perinatal] 2016).

Health care providers are encouraged to enroll pregnant women exposed to antiretroviral medications as early in pregnancy as possible in the Antiretroviral Pregnancy Registry (1-800-258-4263 or www.-APRegistry.com).

Tenofovir Disoproxil Fumarate
(ten OF oh vir dye soe PROX il FUE ma rate)

Related Information

HIV Infection and AIDS *on page 1785*

Systemic Viral Diseases *on page 1806*

Brand Names: US Viread

Brand Names: Canada Viread

Pharmacologic Category Antihepadnaviral, Reverse Transcriptase Inhibitor, Nucleotide (Anti-HBV); Antiretroviral, Reverse Transcriptase Inhibitor, Nucleotide (Anti-HIV)

Use

Chronic hepatitis B: Treatment of chronic hepatitis B virus (HBV) in patients ≥12 years of age

HIV infection: In combination with other antiretroviral agents for the treatment of HIV-1 infection in adults and pediatric patients ≥2 years of age

Local Anesthetic/Vasoconstrictor Precautions No information available to require special precautions

Effects on Dental Treatment No significant effects or complications reported

Effects on Bleeding No information available to require special precautions regarding hemostasis.

Adverse Reactions Includes data from both treatment-naive and treatment-experienced HIV patients and in chronic hepatitis B.

>10%:

Central nervous system: Insomnia (3% to 18%), headache (5% to 14%), pain (12% to 13%), dizziness (8% to 13%), depression (4% to 11%)

Dermatologic: Skin rash (includes maculopapular, pustular, or vesiculobullous rash; pruritus; or urticaria: 5% to 18%), pruritus (16%)

Endocrine & metabolic: Hypercholesterolemia (19% to 22%), increased serum triglycerides (1% to 4%)

Gastrointestinal: Abdominal pain (4% to 22%), nausea (8% to 20%), diarrhea (9% to 16%), vomiting (2% to 13%)

Neuromuscular & skeletal: Decreased bone mineral density (28%; ≥5% at spine or ≥7% at hip), increased creatine phosphokinase (2% to 12%), weakness (6% to 11%)

Miscellaneous: Fever (4% to 11%)

1% to 10%:

Cardiovascular: Chest pain (3%)

Central nervous system: Fatigue (9%), anxiety (6%), peripheral neuropathy (1% to 5%)

Dermatologic: Diaphoresis (3%)

Endocrine & metabolic: Weight loss (2% to 4%), glycosuria (grades 3/4: ≤3%), hyperglycemia (grades 3/4: 2% to 3%), lipodystrophy (1%)

Gastrointestinal: Increased serum amylase (grades 3/4: 4% to 9%), anorexia (3% to 4%), dyspepsia (3% to 4%), flatulence (3% to 4%)

Genitourinary: Hematuria (≤grades 3/4: 3% to 7%)

Hematologic & oncologic: Neutropenia (3%)

Hepatic: Increased serum ALT (2% to 10%), increased serum AST (3% to 5%), increased serum transaminases (2% to 5%), increased serum alkaline phosphatase (1%)

Neuromuscular & skeletal: Back pain (4% to 9%), arthralgia (5%), myalgia (4%)

Renal: Increased serum creatinine (9%), renal failure (7%)

Respiratory: Sinusitis (8%), upper respiratory tract infection (8%), nasopharyngitis (5%), pneumonia (2% to 5%)

Postmarketing and/or case reports: Angioedema, dyspnea, exacerbation of hepatitis B (following discontinuation), Fanconi's syndrome, hepatitis, hypersensitivity reaction, hypokalemia, hypophosphatemia, immune reconstitution syndrome, increased gamma-glutamyl transferase, interstitial nephritis, lactic acidosis, myasthenia, myopathy, nephrogenic diabetes insipidus, nephrotoxicity, osteomalacia, pancreatitis, polyuria, proteinuria, proximal tubular nephropathy, renal insufficiency, renal tubular necrosis, rhabdomyolysis, severe hepatomegaly with steatosis

General Dosage Range Dosage adjustment recommended in patients with renal impairment

Oral:

Children 2 to <12 years: 8 mg/kg once daily (maximum: 300 mg once daily)

Children ≥12 years (and ≥35 kg), Adolescents, and Adults: 300 mg once daily

Mechanism of Action Tenofovir disoproxil fumarate (TDF), a nucleotide reverse transcriptase inhibitor, is an analog of adenosine 5'-monophosphate; it interferes with the HIV viral RNA dependent DNA polymerase resulting in inhibition of viral replication. TDF is first converted intracellularly by hydrolysis to tenofovir and subsequently phosphorylated to the active tenofovir diphosphate. Tenofovir inhibits replication of HBV by inhibiting HBV polymerase.

Pharmacodynamics/Kinetics

Half-life Elimination Serum: 17 hours; intracellular: 10 to 50 hours

Time to Peak Serum: Fasting: 36-84 minutes; With high-fat meal: 96-144 minutes

Pregnancy Risk Factor B

Pregnancy Considerations Adverse events were observed in some animal reproduction studies. Tenofovir has a high level of transfer across the human placenta. No increased risk of overall birth defects has been observed following first trimester exposure according to data collected by the antiretroviral pregnancy registry. Maternal antiretroviral therapy may increase the risk of preterm delivery, although available information is conflicting possibly due to variability of maternal factors (disease severity; initiation of therapy); however, maternal antiretroviral medication should not be withheld due to concerns of preterm birth. Intrauterine growth has not been affected following use of tenofovir disoproxil fumarate, but data are conflicting about potential growth effects later in infancy. Clinical studies in children have shown bone demineralization with chronic use. Bone mineral content was also decreased in infants following in utero exposure. Long-term follow-up is recommended for all infants exposed to antiretroviral medications; children who develop significant organ system abnormalities of unknown etiology (particularly of the CNS or heart) should be evaluated for potential mitochondrial dysfunction. Cases of lactic acidosis and hepatic steatosis related to mitochondrial toxicity have been reported with use of nucleoside reverse transcriptase inhibitors (NRTIs). These adverse events are similar to other rare but life-threatening syndromes that occur during pregnancy (eg, HELLP syndrome). In general NRTIs are well tolerated and the benefits of use generally outweigh potential risk.

Combination antiretroviral therapy (cART) therapy is recommended for all HIV-infected pregnant women to keep the viral load below the limit of detection and reduce the risk of perinatal transmission. When HIV is diagnosed during pregnancy in a woman who has never received antiretroviral therapy, cART should begin as soon as possible after diagnosis. The Health and Human Services (HHS) Perinatal HIV Guidelines consider tenofovir disoproxil fumarate a component in preferred regimens for initial therapy in antiretroviral-naïve pregnant women. The guidelines also consider emtricitabine plus tenofovir disoproxil fumarate, or lamivudine plus tenofovir disoproxil fumarate as recommended dual NRTI backbone for HIV/HBV coinfected pregnant women. Hepatitis B flare may occur if tenofovir disporoxil fumarate is discontinued. Limited data indicate decreased maternal exposure during the third trimester; dose adjustments are not needed. In general, women who become pregnant on a stable cART regimen may continue that regimen if viral suppression is effective, appropriate drug exposure can be achieved, contraindications for use in pregnancy are not present, and the regimen is well tolerated. Monitoring during pregnancy is more frequent than in non-pregnant adults; cART should be continued postpartum.

For HIV-infected couples planning a pregnancy, maximum viral suppression with cART is recommended prior to conception for the HIV-infected partner(s) and expert consultation is recommended; modification of therapy (if needed) and optimization of the woman's health should be done prior to conception. HIV-infected women not planning a pregnancy may use any available type of contraception, considering possible drug interactions and contraindications of the specific method. In addition, consistent use of condoms is also recommended (even during pregnancy) to prevent transmission of HIV or other sexually transmitted diseases.

Health care providers are encouraged to enroll pregnant women exposed to antiretroviral medications as early in pregnancy as possible in the Antiretroviral Pregnancy Registry (1-800-258-4263 or www.-APRegistry.com). Health care providers caring for HIV-infected women and their infants may contact the National Perinatal HIV Hotline (888-448-8765) for clinical consultation (HHS [perinatal] 2016).

Terazosin (ter AY zoe sin)

Related Information

Cardiovascular Diseases *on page 1752*

Brand Names: Canada Apo-Terazosin; Dom-Terazosin; Hytrin; Nu-Terazosin; PHL-Terazosin; PMS-Terazosin; ratio-Terazosin; Teva-Terazosin

Pharmacologic Category Alpha$_1$ Blocker; Antihypertensive

Use

Benign prostatic hyperplasia: Treatment of symptomatic benign prostatic hyperplasia (BPH)

Hypertension: Management of hypertension (monotherapy or in combination with other antihypertensives).

Note: The 2014 guideline for the management of high blood pressure in adults (Eighth Joint National Committee [JNC 8]) does **not** recommend the use of terazosin in the treatment of hypertension (JNC8 [James, 2013]).

Local Anesthetic/Vasoconstrictor Precautions No information available to require special precautions

Effects on Dental Treatment Key adverse event(s) related to dental treatment: Xerostomia (normal salivary flow resumes upon discontinuation); Patients may experience orthostatic hypotension as they stand up after treatment; especially if lying in dental chair for extended periods of time. Use caution with sudden changes in position during and after dental treatment.

Effects on Bleeding No information available to require special precautions

Adverse Reactions

>10%:

Central nervous system: Dizziness (9% to 19%), myasthenia (7% to 11%)

1% to 10%:

Cardiovascular: Peripheral edema (1% to 6%), orthostatic hypotension (1% to 4%), palpitations (≤4%), tachycardia (≤2%), syncope (≤1%)

Central nervous system: Drowsiness (4% to 5%), paresthesia (≤3%), vertigo (1%)

Endocrine & metabolic: Decreased libido (≤1%), weight gain (≤1%)

Gastrointestinal: Nausea (2% to 4%)

Genitourinary: Impotence (≤2%)

Neuromuscular & skeletal: Limb pain (≤4%), back pain (≤2%)

Ophthalmic: Blurred vision (≤2%)

Respiratory: Nasal congestion (2% to 6%), dyspnea (2% to 3%), sinusitis (≤3%)

<1%, postmarketing, and/or case reports: Abdominal pain, anaphylaxis, anxiety, arthralgia, arthritis, arthropathy, atrial fibrillation, bronchitis, cardiac arrhythmia, chest pain, conjunctivitis, constipation, cough, diaphoresis, diarrhea, dyspepsia, epistaxis, facial edema, fever, flatulence, flu-like symptoms, gout, hypersensitivity reaction, insomnia, intraoperative floppy iris syndrome (IFIS), myalgia, neck pain, pharyngitis, polyuria, priapism, pruritus, rhinitis, shoulder pain, skin rash, thrombocytopenia, tinnitus, urinary incontinence, urinary tract infection, vasodilatation, visual disturbance, vomiting, xerostomia

General Dosage Range

Oral: *Adults:* Initial: 1 mg at bedtime; Maintenance: 1 to 20 mg once daily (maximum: 20 mg/day)

Mechanism of Action Alpha$_1$-specific blocking agent with minimal alpha$_2$ effects; this allows peripheral post-synaptic blockade, with the resultant decrease in arterial tone, while preserving the negative feedback loop which is mediated by the peripheral presynaptic alpha$_2$-receptors; terazosin relaxes the smooth muscle of the bladder neck, thus reducing bladder outlet obstruction

Pharmacodynamics/Kinetics

Onset of Action Antihypertensive effect: 15 minutes; Peak effect: Antihypertensive effect: 2 to 3 hours

Duration of Action Antihypertensive effect: 24 hours

Half-life Elimination ~12 hours

Time to Peak Plasma: ~1 hour; delayed ~40 minutes with food

Pregnancy Risk Factor C

Pregnancy Considerations Adverse events have not been observed in animal studies. Untreated chronic maternal hypertension is associated with adverse events in the fetus, infant, and mother. If treatment for hypertension during pregnancy is needed, other agents are generally preferred (ACOG 2013).

Terbinafine (Systemic) (TER bin a feen)

Brand Names: US LamISIL; Terbinex [DSC]

Brand Names: Canada Apo-Terbinafine; Auro-Terbinafine; CO Terbinafine; Dom-Terbinafine; GD-Terbinafine; JAMP-Terbinafine; Lamisil; Mylan-Terbinafine; PHL-Terbinafine; PMS-Terbinafine; Q-Terbinafine; Riva-Terbinafine; Sandoz-Terbinafine; Teva-Terbinafine

Pharmacologic Category Antifungal Agent, Oral

Use

Onychomycosis (tablets only): Treatment of onychomycosis of the toenail or fingernail caused by dermatophytes (tinea unguium).

Tinea capitis (granules only): Treatment of tinea capitis in patients 4 years and older.

Local Anesthetic/Vasoconstrictor Precautions No information available to require special precautions

Effects on Dental Treatment Key adverse event(s) related to dental treatment: Taste disturbance.

Effects on Bleeding No information available to require special precautions

Adverse Reactions Adverse events listed for tablets unless otherwise specified. Granules were studied in patients 4 to 12 years of age.

>10%: Central nervous system: Headache (13%; granules: 7%)

1% to 10%:

Dermatologic: Skin rash (6%; granules: 2%), pruritus (3%; granules: 1%), urticaria (1%)

Gastrointestinal: Diarrhea (6%; granules: 3%), vomiting (<1%; granules: 5%), dyspepsia (4%), dysgeusia (3%; may be severe and result in weight loss and depression), nausea (3%; granules: 2%), abdominal pain (2%; granules: 2% to 4%), flatulence (2%), sore throat (granules: 2%), toothache (granules: 1%)

Hepatic: Liver enzyme disorder (3%)

Infection: Influenza (granules: 2%)

Ophthalmic: Visual disturbance (1%)

Respiratory: Nasopharyngitis (granules: 10%), cough (granules: 6%), upper respiratory tract infection (granules: 5%), nasal congestion (granules: 2%), rhinorrhea (granules: 2%)

Miscellaneous: Fever (granules: 7%)

<1%, postmarketing, and/or case reports: Acute generalized exanthematous pustulosis, acute pancreatitis, agranulocytosis, alopecia, altered sense of smell, anaphylaxis, anemia, angioedema, arthralgia, auditory impairment, decreased appetite, depression, DRESS syndrome, exacerbation of psoriasis, exacerbation of systemic lupus erythematosus, fatigue, hepatic insufficiency, hepatic failure, hypersensitivity reaction, increased creatine phosphokinase, malaise, myalgia, neutropenia (severe), pancytopenia, psoriasiform eruption, retinal changes, rhabdomyolysis, serum sickness-like reaction, skin photosensitivity, Stevens-Johnson syndrome, thrombocytopenia, tinnitus, toxic epidermal necrolysis, vasculitis, vertigo, visual field defect, visual field loss, weight loss

General Dosage Range

Oral granules: *Children ≥4 years, Adolescents, and Adults:*

<25 kg: 125 mg once daily for 6 weeks

25 to 35 kg: 187.5 mg once daily for 6 weeks

>35 kg: 250 mg once daily for 6 weeks

Oral tablet: *Adults:* 250 mg once daily for 6 to 12 weeks

Mechanism of Action Synthetic allylamine derivative which inhibits squalene epoxidase, a key enzyme in sterol biosynthesis in fungi. This results in a deficiency in ergosterol within the fungal cell wall and results in fungal cell death.

Pharmacodynamics/Kinetics

Half-life Elimination Terminal half-life: 200 to 400 hours; very slow release of drug from skin and adipose tissues occurs; effective half-life: Children: 27 to 31 hours; Adults: ~36 hours

Time to Peak Plasma: Children and Adults: Within 2 hours

Pregnancy Risk Factor B

Pregnancy Considerations Adverse events were not observed in animal reproduction studies. Avoid use in pregnancy since treatment of onychomycosis is postponable.

Terbutaline (ter BYOO ta leen)

Brand Names: Canada Bricanyl Turbuhaler

Pharmacologic Category Antidote, Extravasation; $Beta_2$ Agonist

Use Asthma/Bronchospasm: Bronchodilator in reversible airway obstruction and bronchial asthma

Local Anesthetic/Vasoconstrictor Precautions No information available to require special precautions

Effects on Dental Treatment Key adverse event(s) related to dental treatment: Xerostomia (normal salivary flow resumes upon discontinuation) and bad taste in mouth.

Effects on Bleeding No information available to require special precautions

Adverse Reactions

>10%:

Central nervous system: Nervousness, restlessness

Endocrine & metabolic: Decreased serum potassium, increased serum glucose

Neuromuscular & skeletal: Tremor

1% to 10%:

Cardiovascular: Hypertension, tachycardia

Central nervous system: Dizziness, drowsiness, headache, insomnia

Dermatologic: Diaphoresis

Gastrointestinal: Dysgeusia, nausea, vomiting, xerostomia

Neuromuscular & skeletal: Muscle cramps, weakness

<1%, postmarketing, and/or case reports: Cardiac arrhythmia, chest pain, hyperglycemia (preterm labor), hypokalemia (preterm labor), hypotension (preterm labor), ischemic heart disease (preterm labor), myocardial infarction (preterm labor), paradoxical bronchospasm, pulmonary edema (preterm labor)

General Dosage Range

Oral:

Children 12 to 15 years: 2.5 mg every 6 hours 3 times/day (maximum: 7.5 mg/day)

Children >15 years and Adults: 2.5 to 5 mg every 6 hours 3 times/day (maximum: 15 mg/day)

SubQ:

Children <12 years: 0.005 to 0.01 mg/kg/dose to a maximum of 0.4 mg/dose; may repeat in 15 to 20 minutes

Children ≥12 years, Adolescents, and Adults: 0.25 mg/dose; may repeat in 15 to 30 minutes (maximum: 0.5 mg/4-hour period)

Mechanism of Action Relaxes bronchial and uterine smooth muscle by action on $beta_2$-receptors with less effect on heart rate

Pharmacodynamics/Kinetics

Onset of Action Oral: 30 to 45 minutes; SubQ: 6 to 15 minutes; Inhalation: 5 minutes (maximum effect: 15 to 60 minutes)

Duration of Action Oral: 4 to 8 hours; Oral inhalation: 3 to 6 hours; SubQ: 1.5 to 4 hours

Half-life Elimination 5.7 hours (range: 2.9 to 14 hours)

Time to Peak Serum: SubQ: 0.5 hours

Pregnancy Risk Factor C

Pregnancy Considerations

Adverse events have been observed in animal reproduction studies. Terbutaline crosses the placenta; umbilical cord concentrations are ~11% to 48% of maternal blood levels.

Uncontrolled asthma is associated with adverse events on pregnancy (increased risk of perinatal mortality, pre-eclampsia, preterm birth, low birth weight infants). Terbutaline is not recommended for the treatment of asthma during pregnancy; inhaled $beta_2$-receptor agonists are preferred (NAEPP 2005).

[US Boxed Warning]: Terbutaline is not FDA approved for and should not be used for prolonged tocolysis (>48 to 72 hours). Use for maintenance tocolysis should not be done in the outpatient setting. Adverse events observed in pregnant women include arrhythmias, increased heart rate, hyperglycemia (transient), hypokalemia, myocardial ischemia, and pulmonary edema. Heart rate may be increased in the fetus and hypoglycemia may occur in the neonate. Terbutaline has been used in the management of preterm labor. Tocolytics may be used for the short-term (48 hour) prolongation of pregnancy to allow for the administration of antenatal steroids and should not be used prior to fetal viability or when the risks of use to the fetus or mother are greater than the risk of preterm birth (ACOG 171 2016).

Terconazole (ter KONE a zole)

Brand Names: US Terazol 3 [DSC]; Terazol 7; Zazole

Brand Names: Canada Taro-Terconazole; Terazol 7

Pharmacologic Category Antifungal Agent, Azole Derivative; Antifungal Agent, Vaginal

Use Candidiasis: For the local treatment of vulvovaginal candidiasis (moniliasis). As terconazole is effective only for vulvovaginitis caused by the genus *Candida*, the diagnosis should be confirmed by KOH smears or cultures.

Local Anesthetic/Vasoconstrictor Precautions No information available to require special precautions

Effects on Dental Treatment No significant effects or complications reported

Effects on Bleeding No information available to require special precautions

Adverse Reactions

>10%: Central nervous system: Headache

1% to 10%:

Central nervous system: Chills, pain

Gastrointestinal: Abdominal pain

Genitourinary: Dysmenorrhea, vaginal discomfort (burning, irritation, or itching)

Miscellaneous: Fever

<1%, postmarketing, and/or case reports: Anaphylaxis, asthenia, bronchospasm, burning sensation of the penis, dizziness, facial edema, flu-like symptoms (including nausea, vomiting, myalgia, arthralgia, malaise), hypersensitivity, skin rash, toxic epidermal necrolysis, urticaria

General Dosage Range Intravaginal: *Adults, females:* Insert 1 applicatorful or suppository at bedtime

Mechanism of Action Terconazole is a triazole ketal antifungal agent; involves inhibition of fungal cytochrome P450. Specifically, terconazole inhibits cytochrome P450-dependent 14-alpha-demethylase which results in accumulation of membrane disturbing 14-alpha-demethylsterols and ergosterol depletion.

Pharmacodynamics/Kinetics

Half-life Elimination 6.4 to 8.5 hours

Time to Peak ~5 to 10 hours

Pregnancy Risk Factor C

Pregnancy Considerations Adverse events have been observed in some animal reproduction studies. Although the manufacturer recommends that use should be avoided during the first trimester of pregnancy (due to systemic absorption) and that use may be considered in the second or third trimesters if the benefits outweigh risks to the fetus, guidelines state that 7-day topical azole vaginal products are the preferred treatment of vulvovaginal candidiasis in pregnant women (CDC [Workowski 2015]. This product may weaken latex condoms and diaphragms (CDC [Workowski 2015]).

Teriflunomide (ter i FLOO noh mide)

Brand Names: US Aubagio

Brand Names: Canada Aubagio

Pharmacologic Category Pyrimidine Synthesis Inhibitor

Use Multiple sclerosis: Treatment of patients with relapsing forms of multiple sclerosis.

Local Anesthetic/Vasoconstrictor Precautions Use vasoconstrictor with caution; patients may experience significant hypertension and palpitations when taking teriflunomide

Effects on Dental Treatment Key adverse event(s) related to dental treatment: Abnormal taste, aphthous stomatitis, and toothache have been reported.

Effects on Bleeding Thrombocytopenia has been reported.

Adverse Reactions

>10%:

Central nervous system: Headache (16% to 18%)

Dermatologic: Alopecia (10% to 13%)

Endocrine & metabolic: Hypophosphatemia (4% to 18%)

Gastrointestinal: Diarrhea (13% to 14%), nausea (8% to 11%)

Hematologic & oncologic: Neutropenia (4% to 16%)

Hepatic: Increased serum ALT (6% to 15%)

1% to 10%:

Cardiovascular: Hypertension (3% to 4%)

Central nervous system: Paresthesia (8% to 9%)

Endocrine & metabolic: Hyperkalemia (1%)

Neuromuscular & skeletal: Arthralgia (6% to 8%), peripheral neuropathy (including carpal tunnel syndrome; 1% to 2%)

Renal: Renal failure (transient; 1%)

<1%, postmarketing, and/or case reports: Anaphylaxis, angioedema, cytomegalovirus disease (reactivation), hypersensitivity reaction, increased serum creatinine, interstitial pulmonary disease, jaundice, pancreatitis, Stevens-Johnson syndrome, thrombocytopenia, toxic epidermal necrolysis

General Dosage Range Oral: *Adults:* 7 mg or 14 mg once daily

Mechanism of Action Teriflunomide is an immunomodulatory agent that inhibits pyrimidine synthesis, resulting in antiproliferative and anti-inflammatory effects. It may reduce the number of activated lymphocytes in the CNS.

Pharmacodynamics/Kinetics

Half-life Elimination Median: 18-19 days; enterohepatic recycling appears to contribute to the long half-life of this agent, since activated charcoal and cholestyramine substantially reduce plasma half-life

Time to Peak Plasma: 1-4 hours

Pregnancy Considerations [US Boxed Warning]: Based on animal data, teriflunomide may cause major birth defects if used in pregnant women. Teriflunomide is contraindicated in pregnant women or women of childbearing potential who are not using effective contraception. Pregnancy must be avoided during therapy or prior to completing the accelerated elimination treatment protocol. Pregnancy must be excluded prior to initiating treatment. Women of childbearing potential should not receive therapy until pregnancy has been excluded, they have been counseled concerning fetal risk, and reliable contraceptive measures have been confirmed. Following treatment, pregnancy should be avoided until undetectable serum concentrations (<0.02 mg/L) are verified. This may be accomplished by the use of an enhanced drug elimination procedure using cholestyramine or activated charcoal powder. If pregnancy occurs during treatment, discontinue therapy and initiate the accelerated elimination procedure.

Teriflunomide is also found in semen. Males and their female partners should use reliable contraception during therapy. Males taking teriflunomide who wish to father a child should consider discontinuing therapy and using the accelerated elimination procedure to decrease the potential risk of fetal exposure. (**Note:** Without use of the accelerated elimination procedure, teriflunomide may remain in the serum for up to 2 years).

Pregnant women exposed to teriflunomide should be registered with the pregnancy registry (800-745-4447, option 2).

Teriparatide (ter i PAR a tide)

Related Information

Rheumatoid Arthritis, Osteoarthritis, and Osteoporosis *on page 1792*

Brand Names: US Forteo

Brand Names: Canada Forteo

Pharmacologic Category Parathyroid Hormone Analog

Use

Glucocorticoid-induced osteoporosis: Treatment of men and women with osteoporosis associated with sustained systemic glucocorticoid therapy (daily dosage equivalent to prednisone 5 mg or more) at high risk for fracture.

Osteoporosis in men: To increase bone mass in men with primary or hypogonadal osteoporosis who are at high risk for fracture.

Osteoporosis in postmenopausal women: Treatment of postmenopausal women with osteoporosis who are at high risk for fracture.

Local Anesthetic/Vasoconstrictor Precautions No information available to require special precautions

Effects on Dental Treatment Key adverse event(s) related to dental treatment: May have beneficial effects for treatment of osteoporosis in patients with osteonecrosis of the jaw due to bisphosphonates; however, teriparatide may have cost constraints.

Effects on Bleeding No information available to require special precautions

Adverse Reactions

>10%: Endocrine & metabolic: Hypercalcemia (transient increases noted 4 to 6 hours postdose [women 11%; men 6%])

1% to 10%:

Cardiovascular: Orthostatic hypotension (5%; transient), angina pectoris (3%), syncope (3%)

Central nervous system: Dizziness (8%), headache (8%), insomnia (5%), anxiety (4%), depression (4%), vertigo (4%)

Endocrine & metabolic: Hyperuricemia (3%)

Gastrointestinal: Nausea (9% to 14%), gastritis (7%), dyspepsia (5%), vomiting (3%)

Immunologic: Antibody development (3% of women in long-term treatment; hypersensitivity reactions or decreased efficacy were not associated in preclinical trials)

Infection: Herpes zoster (3%)

Neuromuscular & skeletal: Arthralgia (10%), weakness (9%), leg cramps (3%)

Respiratory: Rhinitis (10%), pharyngitis (6%), dyspnea (4% to 6%), pneumonia (3% to 6%)

<1%, postmarketing and/or case reports: Anaphylaxis, angioedema, chest pain, dyspnea (acute), facial edema, hypercalcemia (>13 mg/dL), hypersensitivity reaction, injection site reactions (bruising, pain, swelling), mouth edema, muscle spasm, osteosarcoma, urticaria

General Dosage Range

SubQ: *Adults:* 20 mcg once daily

Mechanism of Action Teriparatide is a recombinant formulation of endogenous parathyroid hormone (PTH), containing a 34-amino-acid sequence which is identical to the N-terminal portion of this hormone. The pharmacologic activity of teriparatide, which is similar to the physiologic activity of PTH, includes stimulating osteoblast function, increasing gastrointestinal calcium absorption, and increasing renal tubular reabsorption of calcium. Treatment with teriparatide results in increased bone mineral density, bone mass, and strength. In postmenopausal women, teriparatide has been shown to decrease osteoporosis-related fractures.

Pharmacodynamics/Kinetics

Half-life Elimination IV: 5 minutes; SubQ: ~1 hour

Time to Peak Serum: ~30 minutes

Pregnancy Risk Factor C

Pregnancy Considerations Adverse events were observed in animal studies; the effect on human fetal development has not been studied. Teriparatide is not indicated for use in pregnant or premenopausal women.

Testosterone (tes TOS ter one)

Brand Names: US Androderm; AndroGel; AndroGel Pump; Aveed; Axiron; Depo-Testosterone; EC-RX Testosterone; First-Testosterone; First-Testosterone MC; Fortesta; Natesto; Striant; Testim; Testopel; Vogelxo; Vogelxo Pump

Brand Names: Canada Andriol; Androderm; AndroGel; Axiron; Delatestryl; Depo-Testosterone; Natesto; PMS-Testosterone; Taro-Testosterone; Testim

Pharmacologic Category Androgen

Use

Breast cancer, metastatic: Injection (enanthate): Secondary treatment in women with advancing inoperable metastatic (skeletal) mammary cancer who are 1 to 5 years postmenopausal. Use may be considered in premenopausal women with breast cancer who have benefited from oophorectomy and have a hormone-responsive tumor.

Delayed puberty: Injection (enanthate); pellet: To stimulate puberty in carefully selected males with delayed puberty.

Hypogonadism, hypogonadotropic (congenital or acquired): Buccal; Gel (nasal, transdermal); Injection (cypionate, enanthate, undecanoate); Patch (transdermal); Pellet; Solution (transdermal): Gonadotropin or luteinizing hormone-releasing hormone deficiency, or pituitary-hypothalamic injury from tumors, trauma, or radiation.

Hypogonadism, primary (congenital or acquired): Buccal; Gel (nasal, transdermal); Injection (cypionate, enanthate, undecanoate); Patch (transdermal); Pellet; Solution (transdermal): Treatment of testicular failure due to cryptorchidism, bilateral torsion, orchitis, vanishing testis syndrome, orchiectomy, Klinefelter syndrome, chemotherapy, or toxic damage from alcohol or heavy metals.

Limitations of use: Safety and efficacy in men with age-related hypogonadism (or late-onset hypogonadism) has not been established.

Local Anesthetic/Vasoconstrictor Precautions No information available to require special precautions

Effects on Dental Treatment Key adverse event(s) related to dental treatment: Buccal administration: Bitter taste, gum edema, gum or mouth irritation, gum tenderness, and taste perversion.

Effects on Bleeding No information available to require special precautions

Adverse Reactions Frequency not always defined.

Cardiovascular: Hypertension (≥3%), increased blood pressure (1%), decreased blood pressure, deep vein thrombosis, edema, vasodilatation

Central nervous system: Headache (1% to ≥3%), fatigue (2%), irritability (2%), insomnia (≤2%), mood swings (≤2%), aggressive behavior (1%), taste disorder (1%), altered sense of smell (≤1%), abnormal dreams, amnesia, anxiety, chills, depression, dizziness, emotional lability, excitement, hostility, malaise, nervousness, outbursts of anger, paresthesia, seizure, sleep apnea, suicidal ideation

Dermatologic: Acne vulgaris (5%), hyperhidrosis (1%), alopecia, contact dermatitis, diaphoresis, erythema, folliculitis, hair discoloration, pruritus, seborrhea, skin rash, xeroderma

Endocrine & metabolic: Increased plasma estradiol concentration (3%), weight gain (1%), gynecomastia (≤1%), hot flash (≤1%), change in libido, decreased gonadotropin, fluid retention, hirsutism (increase in pubic hair growth), hypercalcemia, hyperchloremia, hypercholesterolemia, hyperglycemia, hyperkalemia, hyperlipidemia, hypernatremia, hypoglycemia, hypokalemia, inorganic phosphate retention, menstrual disease (including amenorrhea)

Gastrointestinal: Diarrhea (≥3%), gastroesophageal reflux disease, gastrointestinal hemorrhage, gastrointestinal irritation, increased appetite, nausea, vomiting

Following buccal administration (most common): Dysgeusia, gingival pain, gingival swelling, mouth irritation (including gums), unpleasant taste

Genitourinary: Prostate specific antigen increase (5% to 11%), prostatitis (≥3%), ejaculatory disorder (1%), prostate induration (1%), spontaneous erections (≤1%), benign prostatic hypertrophy, difficulty in micturition, hematuria, impotence, irritable bladder, mastalgia, oligospermia, priapism, testicular atrophy, urinary tract infection, virilization

Hepatic: Abnormal hepatic function tests, cholestatic hepatitis, cholestatic jaundice, hepatic insufficiency, hepatic necrosis, hepatocellular neoplasms, increased serum bilirubin, peliosis hepatis

Hematologic & oncologic: Increased hematocrit (1% to 3%), increased hemoglobin (2%), malignant neoplasm of prostate (1%), anemia, clotting factors suppression, hemorrhage, leukopenia, polycythemia, prostate carcinoma

Hypersensitivity: Anaphylactoid reaction, hypersensitivity reaction (including pulmonary oil microembolism)

Local: Pain at injection site (5%), erythema at injection site (1%), application site reaction (gel, solution), inflammation at injection site

Transdermal system: Application site pruritus (17% to 37%), application site vesicles (including burn-like blisters under system; 6% to 12%), application site erythema (≤7%), local allergic contact dermatitis (4%), application site burning (3%), application site induration (3%), local skin exfoliation (<3%)

Neuromuscular & skeletal: Arthralgia (≥3%), back pain (≥3%), abnormal bone growth (accelerated), hemarthrosis, hyperkinesia, weakness

Ophthalmic: Increased lacrimation

Renal: Increased serum creatinine, polyuria

Respiratory: Bronchitis (≥3%), nasopharyngitis (≥3%), sinusitis (≥3%), upper respiratory tract infection (≥3%), dyspnea

<1%, postmarketing, and/or case reports: Injection, gel: Abdominal pain, abnormal erythropoiesis, abscess at injection site, allergic dermatitis, anaphylactic shock, anaphylaxis, androgenetic alopecia, angina pectoris, angioedema, asthma, atrial fibrillation, breast induration, cardiac failure, cerebral infarction, cerebrovascular accident, cerebrovascular insufficiency, chest pain, chronic obstructive pulmonary disease, circulatory shock, cognitive dysfunction, confusion, coronary artery disease, coronary occlusion, cough, decreased libido, decreased plasma testosterone, decreased thyroxine binding globulin, decreased urinary calcium excretion, diabetes mellitus, dysuria, electrolyte disturbance, epididymitis, erectile dysfunction, hearing loss (sudden), hematoma at injection site, hepatic neoplasm, hepatotoxicity (idiosyncratic) (Chalasani 2014), hyperparathyroidism, hypersensitivity angiitis, hypertriglyceridemia, hyperventilation, impaired glucose tolerance, increased gamma-glutamyl transferase, increased intraocular pressure, increased serum ALT, increased serum AST, increased serum prolactin, increased serum transaminases, increased serum triglycerides, Korsakoff's psychosis (nonalcoholic), migraine, musculoskeletal chest pain, musculoskeletal pain, myalgia, myocardial infarction, nephrolithiasis, nipple tenderness, orgasm disturbance (male), osteopenia, osteoporosis, peripheral edema, personality disorder, pharyngeal edema, pharyngolaryngeal pain, prolonged partial thromboplastin time, prolonged prothrombin time, prostatic intraepithelial neoplasia, pulmonary embolism, pure red cell aplasia, renal colic, renal disease, renal pain, respiratory distress, restlessness, reversible ischemic neurological deficit, rhinitis, sleep disorder, snoring, spermatocele, syncope, systemic lupus erythematosus, tachycardia, testicular pain, thrombocytopenia, thromboembolism, thrombosis, tinnitus, transient ischemic attacks, urinary incontinence, urolithiasis, urticaria, venous insufficiency, venous thromboembolism, vesicobullous rash, virilization (of children, following secondary exposure to topical gel [advanced bone age, aggressive behavior, enlargement of clitoris requiring surgery, enlargement of penis, increased erections, increased libido, pubic hair development]), vitreous detachment, voice disorder

General Dosage Range

Buccal: *Adults (males):* 30 mg every 12 hours

IM: *Adolescents and Adults (males):* Testosterone enanthate or testosterone cypionate: 50 to 400 mg every 2 to 4 weeks; Testosterone undecanoate: Initial dose: 750 mg, followed by 750 mg administered 4 weeks later, then 750 mg administered every 10 weeks thereafter

Intranasal: *Adults (males):* 11 mg (2 pump actuations; 1 actuation per nostril) administered intranasally 3 times daily (6 to 8 hours apart)

SubQ: *Adolescents and Adults (males):* 150 to 450 mg every 3 to 6 months

Topical: *Adults (males):* AndroGel 1%: Apply 50 to 100 mg daily; AndroGel 1.62%: Apply 20.25 to 81 mg daily; Axiron: Apply 30 to 120 mg daily;

Fortesta: Apply 10 to 70 mg daily; Testim and Vogelxo: Apply 50 to 100 mg daily

Transdermal: *Adults (males):* Androderm: Apply 2 to 6 mg daily

Mechanism of Action Principal endogenous androgen responsible for promoting the growth and development of the male sex organs and maintaining secondary sex characteristics in androgen-deficient males

Pharmacodynamics/Kinetics

Duration of Action Route and ester dependent; IM: Cypionate and enanthate esters: 2 to 4 weeks; Undecanoate: 10 weeks; Transdermal gel: 24 hours

Half-life Elimination Variable: 10 to 100 minutes; Testosterone cypionate: ~8 days

Time to Peak IM (undecanoate): 7 days (median; range: 4 to 42 days); Intranasal: ~40 minutes; Transdermal system: 8 hours (range: 4 to 12 hours); Buccal system: 10 to 12 hours; Oral capsule [Canadian product]: 4 to 5 hours

Pregnancy Risk Factor X

Pregnancy Considerations Use is contraindicated in pregnant women or women who may become pregnant. Exposure to a fetus may cause virilization of varying degrees. Because of the potential for secondary exposure, all children and women should avoid skin-to-skin contact to areas where testosterone has been applied topically on another person.

Some products contain benzyl alcohol, which can cross the placenta.

Large doses of testosterone may suppress spermatogenesis. Treatment of hypogonadotropic hypogonadism is not recommended for men desiring fertility (Endocrine Society [Bhasin 2010]).

Controlled Substance C-III

Tetanus Immune Globulin (Human)

(TET a nus i MYUN GLOB yoo lin HYU man)

Brand Names: US HyperTET S/D

Brand Names: Canada HyperTET S/D

Pharmacologic Category Blood Product Derivative; Immune Globulin

Use

Tetanus prophylaxis: For prophylaxis against tetanus following injury in patients whose immunization is incomplete or uncertain

Tetanus treatment: Treatment of active tetanus

The Advisory Committee on Immunization Practices (ACIP) recommends passive immunization with TIG for the following:

- Persons with a wound that is not clean or minor and who have received ≤2 or an unknown number of adsorbed tetanus toxoid doses (CDC 55[RR3] 2006; CDC 55[RR17] 2006).
- Persons who are wounded in bombings or similar mass casualty events if no reliable history of completed primary vaccination with tetanus exists. In case of shortage, use should be reserved for persons ≥60 years of age and immigrants from regions other than Europe or North America (CDC 57 [RR6] 2008).

Local Anesthetic/Vasoconstrictor Precautions No information available to require special precautions

Effects on Dental Treatment No significant effects or complications reported

Effects on Bleeding No information available to require special precautions

Adverse Reactions Frequency not defined.

Central nervous system: Increased body temperature

Local: Local soreness/soreness at injection site, pain at injection site, tenderness at injection site

<1%, postmarketing, and/or case reports: Anaphylactic shock, angioedema, nephrotic syndrome

General Dosage Range IM:

Infants and Children <7 years: Prophylaxis: 4 units/kg

Children ≥7 years and Adolescents: Prophylaxis: 250 units; Treatment: 3,000 to 6,000 units

Adults: Prophylaxis: 250 units; Treatment: 3,000 to 6,000 units

Mechanism of Action Provides passive immunity towards tetanus by supplying antibodies to neutralize the free form of toxins produced by *Clostridium tetani*.

Pharmacodynamics/Kinetics

Half-life Elimination Individuals with normal IgG concentration: ~23 days

Time to Peak Plasma: IgG concentration: IM: ~2 days

Pregnancy Risk Factor C

Pregnancy Considerations Animal reproduction studies have not been conducted. Tetanus immune globulin and a tetanus toxoid containing vaccine are recommended by the ACIP as part of the standard wound management to prevent tetanus in pregnant women (CDC 57[RR6], 2008; CDC 62[7], 2013).

Tetrabenazine (tet ra BEN a zeen)

Related Information

Clinical Risk Related to Drugs Prolonging QT Interval *on page 1772*

Brand Names: US Xenazine

Brand Names: Canada Nitoman; PMS-Tetrabenazine

Pharmacologic Category Central Monoamine-Depleting Agent

Use Chorea associated with Huntington disease: Treatment of chorea associated with Huntington disease

Canadian labeling: Treatment of hyperkinetic movement disorders, including Huntington chorea, hemiballismus, senile chorea, Tourette syndrome, and tardive dyskinesia

Local Anesthetic/Vasoconstrictor Precautions Tetrabenazine is one of the drugs confirmed to prolong the QT interval and is accepted as having a risk of causing torsade de pointes. The risk of drug-induced torsade de pointes is extremely low when a single QT interval prolonging drug is prescribed. In terms of epinephrine, it is not known what effect vasoconstrictors in the local anesthetic regimen will have in patients with a known history of congenital prolonged QT interval or in patients taking any medication that prolongs the QT interval. Until more information is obtained, it is suggested that the clinician consult with the physician prior to the use of a vasoconstrictor in suspected patients, and that the vasoconstrictor (epinephrine, mepivacaine and levonordefrin [Carbocaine® 2% with Neo-Cobefrin®]) be used with caution.

Effects on Dental Treatment Key adverse event(s) related to dental treatment: Dysphagia; Patients may experience orthostatic hypotension as they stand up after treatment; especially if lying in dental chair for extended periods of time. Use caution with sudden changes in position during and after dental treatment.

Effects on Bleeding No information available to require special precautions

Adverse Reactions Note: Many adverse effects are dose-related and may resolve at lower dosages. Adverse effects reported for adults with chorea associated with Huntington disease.

>10%:

Central nervous system: Drowsiness (≤17% to ≤57%), sedation (≤17% to ≤57%), depression (19% to 35%), extrapyramidal reaction (15% to 33%), fatigue (22%), insomnia (22%), akathisia (19% to 20%), anxiety (15%), falling (15%)

Gastrointestinal: Nausea (13%)

Respiratory: Upper respiratory tract infection (11%)

1% to 10%:

Central nervous system: Drug-induced Parkinson's disease (3% to 10%), equilibrium disturbance (9%), irritability (9%), abnormal gait (4%), dizziness (4%), dysarthria (4%), headache (4%), obsessive rumination (4%)

Gastrointestinal: Dysphagia (4% to 10%), vomiting (6%), decreased appetite (4%), diarrhea (2%)

Genitourinary: Dysuria (4%)

Hematologic & oncologic: Bruise (6%)

Neuromuscular & skeletal: Bradykinesia (9%)

Respiratory: Bronchitis (4%), dyspnea (4%)

Miscellaneous: Laceration (6%, head)

<1%, postmarketing, and/or case reports: Aggressive behavior (worsening), aspiration pneumonia, confusion, hyperhidrosis, hyperprolactinemia, increased serum transaminases, orthostatic dizziness, orthostatic hypotension, neuroleptic malignant syndrome, pneumonia, prolonged QT interval on ECG, restlessness, skin rash, suicidal ideation, syncope, tremor

General Dosage Range Dosage adjustment recommended in patients on concomitant therapy or who develop toxicities

Oral: *Adults:* 12.5 mg once daily; Maintenance: 25 to 100 mg/day in 2 to 3 divided doses

Mechanism of Action Acts as a reversible inhibitor of the human vesicular monamine transporter type 2 (VMAT-2) and thereby decreases the uptake of monoamines (including dopamine, serotonin, norepinephrine, and histamine) into synaptic vesicles and depletes the monoamine stores; hydroxytetrabenazine (HTBZ) also inhibits VMAT-2; weak binding affinity for dopamine D_2 receptors.

Pharmacodynamics/Kinetics

Duration of Action 16 to 24 hours (at steady-state); chorea may recur within 12 to 18 hours after discontinuation

Half-life Elimination Alpha-HTBZ: 7 hours; 10 hours (hepatic impairment); Beta-HTBZ: 5 hours, 8 hours (hepatic impairment); Terabenazine: ~17.5 hours (hepatic impairment)

Time to Peak Metabolites: Within 1 to 1.5 hours

Pregnancy Risk Factor C

Pregnancy Considerations Adverse events were observed in some animal reproduction studies. Limited information related to the use of tetrabenazine in pregnancy has been located (Lubbe, 1983).

Prescribing and Access Restrictions Xenazine is available only through specialty pharmacies. For more information regarding the procurement of Xenazine, healthcare providers, patients, and caregivers may contact the Xenazine Information Center (XIC) at 1-888-882-6013 or at:

Health care providers: http://www.xenazineusa.com/HCP/PrescribingXenazine/Default.aspx

Patients and caregivers: http://www.xenazineusa.com/AboutXenazine/Getting-Your-Prescription.aspx

Dental Comment See Local Anesthetic/Vasoconstrictor Precautions

Tetracaine (Systemic) (TET ra kane)

Brand Names: Canada Pontocaine

Generic Availability (US) Yes

Pharmacologic Category Local Anesthetic

Dental Use Ester-type local anesthetic

Use Spinal anesthesia

Local Anesthetic/Vasoconstrictor Precautions No information available to require special precautions

Effects on Dental Treatment No significant effects or complications reported

Effects on Bleeding No information available to require special precautions

Adverse Reactions Frequency not defined. Adverse effects listed are those characteristics of local anesthetics. Systemic adverse effects are generally associated with excessive doses or rapid absorption.

Cardiovascular: Hypotension

Central nervous system: Chills, dizziness, drowsiness, loss of consciousness, nervousness, seizure

Dermatologic: Urticaria

Gastrointestinal: Nausea, vomiting

Hematologic & oncologic: Methemoglobinemia

Hypersensitivity: Anaphylaxis, hypersensitivity reaction

Neuromuscular & skeletal: Tremor

Ophthalmic: Blurred vision, miosis

Otic: Tinnitus

Dosing

Adult & Geriatric Spinal anesthesia: Injection: **Note:** Dosage varies with the anesthetic procedure, the degree of anesthesia required, and the individual patient response; it is administered by subarachnoid injection for spinal anesthesia.

Perineal anesthesia: 5 mg

Perineal and lower extremities: 10 mg

Anesthesia extending up to costal margin: 15 mg; doses up to 20 mg may be given, but are reserved for exceptional cases

Low spinal anesthesia (saddle block): 2-5 mg

Renal Impairment No dosage adjustment provided in manufacturer's labeling.

Hepatic Impairment No dosage adjustment provided in manufacturer's labeling.

Mechanism of Action Ester local anesthetic blocks both the initiation and conduction of nerve impulses by decreasing the neuronal membrane's permeability to sodium ions, which results in inhibition of depolarization with resultant blockade of conduction

Contraindications Hypersensitivity to tetracaine, ester-type anesthetics, aminobenzoic acid, or any component of the formulation; injection should not be used when spinal anesthesia is contraindicated

Warnings/Precautions Use with caution in patients with cardiac disease (especially rhythm disturbances, heart block, or shock), hyperthyroidism, and abnormal or decreased levels of plasma esterases. Use of the lowest effective dose is recommended. Acutely ill, elderly, debilitated, obstetric patients, or patients with increased intra-abdominal pressure may require decreased doses. Dental practitioners and/or clinicians using local anesthetic agents should be well-trained in diagnosis and management of emergencies that may arise from the use of these agents. Resuscitative equipment, oxygen, and other resuscitative drugs should be available for immediate use.

Drug Interactions

Metabolism/Transport Effects None known.

Avoid Concomitant Use

Avoid concomitant use of Tetracaine (Systemic) with any of the following: Bupivacaine (Liposomal)

Increased Effect/Toxicity

Tetracaine (Systemic) may increase the levels/effects of: Bupivacaine (Liposomal); Neuromuscular-Blocking Agents

The levels/effects of Tetracaine (Systemic) may be increased by: Hyaluronidase

Decreased Effect

Tetracaine (Systemic) may decrease the levels/effects of: Technetium Tc 99m Tilmanocept

Pharmacodynamics/Kinetics

Duration of Action 1.5 to 3 hours

Pregnancy Risk Factor C

Pregnancy Considerations Animal reproduction studies have not been conducted.

Breastfeeding Considerations It is not known if tetracaine (systemic) is excreted in breast milk. The manufacturer recommends that caution be exercised when administering tetracaine (systemic) to nursing women.

Dosage Forms

Solution, Injection [preservative free]:

Generic: 1% (2 mL)

Tetracaine (Topical) (TET ra kane)

Related Information

Oral Pain *on page 1830*

Ulcerative, Erosive, and Painful Oral Mucosal Disorders *on page 1853*

Brand Names: Canada Ametop; Pontocaine

Generic Availability (US) May be product dependent

Pharmacologic Category Local Anesthetic

Dental Use Ester-type local anesthetic; applied to throat for various diagnostic procedures and on cold sores and fever blisters for pain

Use Applied to nose and throat for diagnostic procedures

Local Anesthetic/Vasoconstrictor Precautions No information available to require special precautions

Effects on Dental Treatment No significant effects or complications reported

Effects on Bleeding No information available to require special precautions

Adverse Reactions Frequency not defined. Adverse effects listed are those characteristics of local anesthetics. Systemic adverse effects are generally associated with excessive doses or rapid absorption.

Cardiovascular: Hypotension

Central nervous system: Chills, dizziness, drowsiness, loss of consciousness, nervousness, seizure

Dermatologic: Urticaria

Gastrointestinal: Nausea, vomiting

Hematologic & oncologic: Methemoglobinemia

Hypersensitivity: Anaphylaxis, hypersensitivity reaction

Neuromuscular & skeletal: Tremor

Ophthalmic: Blurred vision, miosis

Otic: Tinnitus

Dental Usual Dosage Topical mucous membranes (rhinolaryngology): Adults: Used as a 0.25% or 0.5% solution by direct application or nebulization; total dose should not exceed 20 mg

Dosing

Adult & Geriatric Topical mucous membranes (rhinolaryngology): Used as a 0.25% or 0.5% solution by direct application or nebulization; total dose should not exceed 20 mg

Mechanism of Action Ester local anesthetic blocks both the initiation and conduction of nerve impulses by decreasing the neuronal membrane's permeability to sodium ions, which results in inhibition of depolarization with resultant blockade of conduction

Contraindications Hypersensitivity to tetracaine, ester-type anesthetics, aminobenzoic acid, or any component of the formulation

Warnings/Precautions For topical use only. Use with caution in patients with cardiac disease, hyperthyroidism, and abnormal or decreased levels of plasma esterases. Use of the lowest effective dose is recommended. Use caution in acutely ill, elderly, debilitated, or obstetric patients. Dental practitioners and/or clinicians using local anesthetic agents should be well trained in diagnosis and management of emergencies that may arise from the use of these agents. Resuscitative equipment, oxygen, and other resuscitative drugs should be available for immediate use.

Drug Interactions

Metabolism/Transport Effects None known.

Avoid Concomitant Use There are no known interactions where it is recommended to avoid concomitant use.

Increased Effect/Toxicity

Tetracaine (Topical) may increase the levels/effects of: Methemoglobinemia Associated Agents; Prilocaine; Sodium Nitrite

The levels/effects of Tetracaine (Topical) may be increased by: Dapsone (Topical); Nitric Oxide

Decreased Effect There are no known significant interactions involving a decrease in effect.

Pharmacodynamics/Kinetics

Onset of Action Anesthetic: Rhinolaryngology: 5-10 minutes

Duration of Action Rhinolaryngology: ~30 minutes

Pregnancy Risk Factor C

Pregnancy Considerations Animal reproduction studies have not been conducted.

Tetracaine and Oxymetazoline
(TET ra kane & oks i met AZ oh leen)

Pharmacologic Category Adrenergic Agonist Agent; Imidazoline Derivative; Local Anesthetic

Use Anesthesia, dental: Regional anesthesia when performing a restorative procedure on teeth 4-13 and A-J in adults and children who weigh 40 kg or more.

Local Anesthetic/Vasoconstrictor Precautions No information available to require special precautions

Effects on Dental Treatment Key adverse event(s) related to dental treatment: Nasal congestion, nasal discomfort, oropharyngeal pain, oral discomfort, and rhinorrhea have been observed; the oxymetazoline component is a sympathomimetic and hypertension may occur. Monitor patients for increased blood pressure. Not recommended in patients with uncontrolled hypertension. Tetracaine component may cause methemoglobinemia; use is not recommended in patients with a history of congenital or idiopathic methemoglobinemia. See Warnings/Precautions "Concerns related to adverse effects".

Effects on Bleeding No information available to require special precautions

Adverse Reactions Also see individual monographs.

>10%:

Ophthalmic: Increased lacrimation (13%)

Respiratory: Rhinorrhea (52%), nasal congestion (32%), nasal discomfort (26%), oropharyngeal pain (14%)

1% to 10%:

Cardiovascular: Increased systolic blood pressure (5%), bradycardia (3%), hypertension (3%), increased diastolic blood pressure (3%)

Central nervous system: Headache (10%), hypoesthesia (intranasal: 10%; pharyngeal: 10%), nasal cavity pain (6%), dizziness (3%), sensory disturbance (2%)

Gastrointestinal: Dysgeusia (8%), oral discomfort (2%), dysphagia (1%)

Respiratory: Throat irritation (9%), sneezing (4%), nasal mucosa ulcer (3%), sinus headache (3%), dry nose (2%), epistaxis (2%)

Dosing

Adult & Geriatric Anesthesia, dental: Intranasal: 2 sprays administered 4 to 5 minutes apart in the nostril ipsilateral (same side) to the maxillary tooth on which the dental procedure will be performed. Initiate the dental procedure 10 minutes after the second spray. May administer 1 additional spray 10 minutes after the second initial spray if inadequate anesthesia.

Pediatric Anesthesia, dental: Children and Adolescents ≥3 years and ≥40 kg: Intranasal: 2 sprays administered 4 to 5 minutes apart in the nostril ipsilateral (same side) to the maxillary tooth on which the dental procedure will be performed. Initiate the dental procedure 10 minutes after the second spray.

Renal Impairment There are no dosage adjustments provided in the manufacturer's labeling (has not been studied).

Hepatic Impairment There are no dosage adjustments provided in the manufacturer's labeling (has not been studied); use with caution in patients with severe impairment.

Mechanism of Action

Tetracaine: Local ester anesthetic that blocks both the initiation and conduction of nerve impulses by decreasing the neuronal membrane's permeability to sodium ions, which results in inhibition of depolarization with resultant blockade of conduction.

Oxymetazoline: Imidazoline derivative with sympathomimetic activity that stimulates alpha-adrenergic receptors in the arterioles of the nasal mucosa to produce vasoconstriction.

Contraindications Hypersensitivity to or intolerance of tetracaine, benzyl alcohol, other ester local anesthetics, *p*-aminobenzoic acid (PABA), oxymetazoline, or any component of the formulation.

Warnings/Precautions Tetracaine may cause methemoglobinemia, particularly when used in combination with other drugs associated with drug-induced methemoglobin (eg, acetaminophen, acetanilide, aniline dyes, benzocaine, chloroquine, dapsone, naphthalene, nitrates and nitrites, nitrofurantoin, nitroglycerin, nitroprusside, pamaquine, *p*-aminosalicylic acid, phenacetin, phenobarbital, phenytoin, primaquine, quinine, sulfonamides). Use with caution in patients with glucose-6-phosphate dehydrogenase deficiency; use is not recommended in patients with a history of congenital or idiopathic methemoglobinemia. Allergic or anaphylactoid reactions, including urticaria, angioedema, bronchospasm, and shock may occur. Dysphagia, epistaxis, and hypertension have been reported. Avoid use in patients with a history of frequent nose bleeds (≥5 per month). Use is not recommended in patients with uncontrolled hypertension. Patients with severe hepatic impairment or pseudocholinesterase deficiency may be at a greater risk of developing toxic plasma concentrations of tetracaine; monitor these patients for signs of local anesthetic toxicity. Use is not recommended in patients with inadequately controlled active thyroid disease.

Potentially significant interactions may exist, requiring dose or frequency adjustment, additional monitoring, and/or selection of alternative therapy. Avoid use with other intranasal products, including other oxymetazoline-containing nasal sprays. Discontinue oxymetazoline-containing products 24 hours prior to administration of tetracaine/oxymetazoline.

Some dosage forms may contain benzyl alcohol; large amounts of benzyl alcohol (≥99 mg/kg/day) have been associated with a potentially fatal toxicity ("gasping syndrome") in neonates; the "gasping syndrome" consists of metabolic acidosis, respiratory distress, gasping respirations, CNS dysfunction (including convulsions, intracranial hemorrhage), hypotension and cardiovascular collapse (AAP 1997; CDC 1982); some data suggests that benzoate displaces bilirubin from protein binding sites (Ahlfors 2001); avoid or use dosage forms containing benzyl alcohol with caution in neonates. See manufacturer's labeling.

Drug Interactions

Metabolism/Transport Effects None known.

Avoid Concomitant Use

Avoid concomitant use of Tetracaine and Oxymetazoline with any of the following: Ergot Derivatives; Iobenguane I 123; MAO Inhibitors

Increased Effect/Toxicity

Tetracaine and Oxymetazoline may increase the levels/effects of: Doxofylline; Methemoglobinemia Associated Agents; Prilocaine; Sodium Nitrite; Sympathomimetics

The levels/effects of Tetracaine and Oxymetazoline may be increased by: AtoMOXetine; Cannabinoid-Containing Products; Cocaine; Dapsone (Topical); Ergot Derivatives; Linezolid; MAO Inhibitors; Nitric Oxide; Tedizolid; Tricyclic Antidepressants

Decreased Effect

Tetracaine and Oxymetazoline may decrease the levels/effects of: FentaNYL; Iobenguane I 123

The levels/effects of Tetracaine and Oxymetazoline may be decreased by: Alpha1-Blockers; Tricyclic Antidepressants

Pharmacodynamics/Kinetics

Half-life Elimination

Pediatric patients 4 to 15 years of age: Oxymetazoline: ~1.6 to 4.3 hours; Tetracaine metabolite *p*-butylaminobenzoic acid (PBBA): ~1.6 to 2.8 hours.

Adults: Oxymetazoline: ~5.2 hours; Tetracaine metabolite (PBBA): ~2.6 hours.

Time to Peak Median:

Pediatric patients 4 to 15 years of age: Oxymetazoline: ~10 to 30 minutes; Tetracaine metabolite (PBBA): ~20 to 30 minutes.

Adults: Oxymetazoline: 5 minutes; Tetracaine metabolite (PBBA): 20 minutes.

Pregnancy Considerations Adverse events have been observed in some animal reproduction studies using this combination subcutaneously. See individual monographs.

Breastfeeding Considerations It is not known if tetracaine or oxymetazoline are excreted in breast milk following nasal administration. According to the manufacturer, the decision to continue or discontinue breastfeeding during therapy should take into account the risk of infant exposure, the benefits of breastfeeding to the infant, and benefits of treatment to the mother.

Product Availability Kovanaze: FDA approved July 2016; anticipated availability is currently undetermined.

Tetracycline (tet ra SYE kleen)

Related Information

Bacterial Infections *on page 1835*
Gastrointestinal Disorders *on page 1775*
Periodontal Diseases *on page 1844*
Ulcerative, Erosive, and Painful Oral Mucosal Disorders *on page 1853*

Brand Names: Canada Apo-Tetra; Nu-Tetra

Generic Availability (US) Yes

Pharmacologic Category Antibiotic, Tetracycline Derivative

Dental Use Treatment of periodontitis associated with presence of *Actinobacillus actinomycetemcomitans* (AA); as adjunctive therapy in recurrent aphthous ulcers

Use

Acute intestinal amebiasis: Adjunctive therapy in acute intestinal amebiasis caused by *Entamoeba histolytica*.

Acne: Adjunctive therapy for the treatment of severe acne.

Actinomycosis: Treatment of actinomycosis caused by *Actinomyces* species when penicillin is contraindicated.

Anthrax: Treatment of anthrax due to *Bacillus anthracis* when penicillin is contraindicated.

Campylobacter: Treatment of infections caused by *Campylobacter fetus*.

Cholera: Treatment of cholera caused by *Vibrio cholerae*.

Clostridium: Treatment of infections caused by *Clostridium* spp. when penicillin is contraindicated.

Gram-negative infections: Treatment of infections caused by *Escherichia coli*, *Enterobacter aerogenes*, *Shigella* spp., *Acinetobacter* spp., *Klebsiella* spp., and *Bacteroides* spp.

Listeriosis: Treatment of listeriosis due to *Listeria monocytogenes* when penicillin is contraindicated.

Ophthalmic infections: Treatment of inclusion conjunctivitis or trachoma caused by *Chlamydia trachomatis*.

Relapsing fever: Treatment of relapsing fever due to *Borrelia* spp.

Respiratory tract infection: Treatment of respiratory tract infections caused by *Haemophilus influenzae* (upper respiratory tract only), *Klebsiella* spp. (lower respiratory tract only), *Mycoplasma pneumoniae* (lower respiratory tract only), *Streptococcus pneumoniae*, or *Streptococcus pyogenes*.

Rickettsial infections: Treatment of Rocky Mountain spotted fever, typhus group infections, Q fever, and rickettsialpox caused by *Rickettsiae*.

Sexually transmitted diseases: Treatment of lymphogranuloma venereum or uncomplicated urethral, endocervical, or rectal infections caused by *C. trachomatis*; chancroid caused by *Haemophilus ducreyi*; granuloma inguinale (donovanosis) caused by *Klebsiella granulomatis*; syphilis caused by *Treponema pallidum*, when penicillin is contraindicated.

Limitations of use: Tetracycline is **not** a recommended alternative for uncomplicated gonorrhea according to the Centers for Disease Control and Prevention (CDC) sexually transmitted diseases guidelines (CDC [Workowski 2015]).

Skin and skin structure infections: Treatment of skin and skin structure infections caused by *Staphylococcus aureus* or *S. pyogenes*.

Urinary tract infections: Treatment of urinary tract infections caused by susceptible gram-negative organisms (eg, *E. coli*, *Klebsiella* spp.).

Vincent infection: Treatment of Vincent infection caused by *Fusobacterium fusiforme* when penicillin is contraindicated.

Yaws: Treatment of yaws caused by *Treponema pertenue* when penicillin is contraindicated.

Zoonotic infections: Treatment of psittacosis (ornithosis) due to *Chlamydophila psittaci*; plague due to *Yersinia pestis*; tularemia due to *Francisella tularensis*; brucellosis due to *Brucella* spp. (in conjunction with an aminoglycoside); bartonellosis due to *Bartonella bacilliformis*.

Local Anesthetic/Vasoconstrictor Precautions No information available to require special precautions

Effects on Dental Treatment Key adverse event(s) related to dental treatment: Esophagitis, superinfections, and candidal superinfection. Opportunistic "superinfection" with *Candida albicans*; tetracyclines are not recommended for use during pregnancy or in children ≤8 years of age since they have been reported to cause enamel hypoplasia and permanent teeth discoloration. The use of tetracyclines should only be used in these patients if other agents are contraindicated or alternative antimicrobials will not eradicate the organism. Long-term use associated with oral candidiasis.

Effects on Bleeding No information available to require special precautions

Adverse Reactions Frequency not defined.

Cardiovascular: Pericarditis, thrombophlebitis

Central nervous system: Bulging fontanel (infants), increased intracranial pressure, paresthesia, pseudotumor cerebri

Dermatologic: Exfoliative dermatitis, nail discoloration, pruritus, skin photosensitivity

Gastrointestinal: Abdominal cramps, anorexia, dental discoloration (young children), diarrhea, enamel hypoplasia (young children), esophagitis, nausea, pancreatitis, pseudomembranous colitis (antibiotic-associated), staphylococcal enterocolitis, vomiting

Genitourinary: Azotemia

Hepatic: Hepatotoxicity

Hypersensitivity: Anaphylaxis, hypersensitivity reaction

Infection: Fungal superinfection (candida), superinfection

Renal: Acute renal failure, renal insufficiency

<1%, postmarketing, and/or case reports: Dysgeusia (Syed 2016)

Dental Usual Dosage Periodontitis: Adults: Oral: 250 mg every 6 hours until improvement (usually 10 days)

Dosing

Adult & Geriatric

Usual dosage range: Oral: 250 to 500 mg every 6 to 12 hours

Acne: Oral: Initial dose: 1 g daily in divided doses; reduce gradually to 125 to 500 mg/day once improvement is noted (alternate day or intermittent therapy may be adequate in some patients). **Note:** The shortest possible duration should be used to minimize development of bacterial resistance; re-evaluate at 3 to 4 months (AAD [Zaenglein 2016])

***Helicobacter pylori* eradication (off-label use):** 500 mg 4 times daily for 10 to 14 days, in combination with bismuth subsalicylate, metronidazole, and either ranitidine or a proton pump inhibitor (Chey 2007)

Malaria, severe, treatment (off-label use): Oral: 250 mg 4 times daily for 7 days with quinidine gluconate. **Note:** Quinidine gluconate duration is region specific; consult CDC for current recommendations (CDC 2013).

Malaria, uncomplicated, treatment (off-label use): Oral: 250 mg 4 times daily for 7 days with quinine sulfate. **Note:** Quinine sulfate duration is region specific; consult CDC for current recommendations (CDC 2013).

Periodontitis (off-label use): Oral: 250 mg every 6 hours until improvement (usually 10 days)

Syphilis, penicillin-allergic patients: Note: Data to support the use of alternatives to penicillin are limited in primary and secondary syphilis and are not well documented in the treatment of latent syphilis (CDC [Workowski 2015])

Early syphilis (primary or secondary infection): 500 mg 4 times daily for 14 days.

Latent syphilis (late or of unknown duration): 500 mg 4 times daily for 28 days.

Tularemia (mild to moderate): Oral: 500 mg 4 times daily for at least 14 days (IDSA [Stevens 2014])

Vibrio cholerae: Oral: 500 mg 4 times daily for 3 days (Sack 1990)

Pediatric Usual dosage range: Children >8 years and Adolescents: Oral: 25 to 50 mg/kg/day in divided doses every 6 hours

Malaria, severe, treatment (off-label use): Children ≥8 years and Adolescents: Oral: 25 mg/kg/day in divided doses every 6 hours (maximum dose: 250 mg every 6 hours) for 7 days with quinidine gluconate. **Note:** Quinidine gluconate duration is region specific; consult CDC for current recommendations (CDC 2013).

Malaria, uncomplicated, treatment (off-label use): Children ≥8 years and Adolescents: Oral: 25 mg/kg/day in divided doses every 6 hours (maximum dose: 250 mg every 6 hours) for 7 days with quinine sulfate. **Note:** Quinine sulfate duration is region specific; consult CDC for current recommendations (CDC 2013).

Renal Impairment

Adults:

Manufacturer's labeling: There are no specific dosage adjustments provided in the manufacturer's labeling; decrease dose and/or extend dosing interval.

Alternative dosing (Aronoff 2007): Note: Renally adjusted dose recommendations are based on doses of 250 mg to 500 mg twice daily to 4 times daily.

GFR >50 mL/minute: Administer recommended dose based on indication every 8 to 12 hours.

GFR 10 to 50 mL/minute: Administer recommended dose based on indication every 12 to 24 hours.

GFR <10 mL/minute: Administer recommended dose based on indication every 24 hours.

Children >8 years and Adolescents: There are no specific dosage adjustments provided in the manufacturer's labeling; decrease dose and/or extend dosing interval.

Hepatic Impairment There are no dosage adjustments provided in the manufacturer's labeling.

Mechanism of Action Inhibits bacterial protein synthesis by binding with the 30S and possibly the 50S ribosomal subunit(s) of susceptible bacteria; may also cause alterations in the cytoplasmic membrane

Contraindications Hypersensitivity to any of the tetracyclines or any component of the formulation.

Warnings/Precautions Use with caution in patients with renal or hepatic impairment; dosage modification required in patients with renal impairment. May be associated with increases in serum urea nitrogen (BUN) secondary to antianabolic effects. Hepatotoxicity has been reported rarely; risk may be increased in patients with preexisting hepatic or renal impairment. Intracranial hypertension (headache, blurred vision, diplopia, vision loss, and/or papilledema) has been associated with use. Women of childbearing age who are overweight or have a history of intracranial hypertension are at greater risk. Concomitant use of isotretinoin (known to cause pseudotumor cerebri) and tetracycline should be avoided. Intracranial hypertension typically resolves after discontinuation of treatment; however, permanent visual loss is possible. If visual symptoms develop during treatment, prompt ophthalmologic evaluation is warranted. Intracranial pressure can remain elevated for weeks after drug discontinuation; monitor patients until they stabilize. May cause photosensitivity; discontinue if skin erythema occurs. Use skin protection and avoid prolonged exposure to sunlight; do not use tanning equipment. Prolonged use may result in fungal or bacterial superinfection, including *Clostridium difficile*–associated diarrhea (CDAD) and pseudomembranous colitis; CDAD has been observed >2 months postantibiotic treatment. May cause tissue hyperpigmentation, enamel hypoplasia, or permanent tooth discoloration; use of tetracyclines should be avoided during tooth development (children <8 years of age) unless other drugs are not likely to be effective or are contraindicated. Do not use during pregnancy. In addition to affecting tooth development, tetracycline use has been associated with retardation of skeletal development and reduced bone growth.

Appropriate use: Acne: The American Academy of Dermatology acne guidelines recommend tetracycline as adjunctive treatment for moderate and severe acne and forms of inflammatory acne that are resistant to topical treatments. Concomitant topical therapy with benzoyl peroxide or a retinoid should be administered with systemic antibiotic therapy (eg, tetracycline) and continued for maintenance after antibiotic course is completed (AAD [Zaenglein 2016])

Drug Interactions

Metabolism/Transport Effects Substrate of CYP3A4 (major); **Note:** Assignment of Major/Minor substrate status based on clinically relevant drug interaction potential

Avoid Concomitant Use

Avoid concomitant use of Tetracycline with any of the following: BCG (Intravesical); Cholera Vaccine; Mecamylamine; Methoxyflurane; Retinoic Acid Derivatives; Strontium Ranelate

Increased Effect/Toxicity

Tetracycline may increase the levels/effects of: Aminolevulinic Acid; Mecamylamine; Methoxyflurane; Mipomersen; Neuromuscular-Blocking Agents; Porfimer; QuiNINE; Retinoic Acid Derivatives; Verteporfin; Vitamin K Antagonists

Decreased Effect

Tetracycline may decrease the levels/effects of: Atovaquone; BCG (Intravesical); BCG Vaccine (Immunization); Cholera Vaccine; Iron Salts; Lactobacillus and Estriol; Penicillins; Sodium Picosulfate; Typhoid Vaccine

The levels/effects of Tetracycline may be decreased by: Antacids; Bile Acid Sequestrants; Bismuth Subcitrate; Bismuth Subsalicylate; Bosentan; Calcium Salts; CYP3A4 Inducers (Moderate); CYP3A4 Inducers (Strong); Dabrafenib; Deferasirox; Enzalutamide; Iron Salts; Lanthanum; Magnesium Salts; Mitotane; Multivitamins/Minerals (with ADEK, Folate, Iron); Multivitamins/Minerals (with AE, No Iron); Quinapril; Siltuximab; St John's Wort; Strontium Ranelate; Sucralfate; Sucroferric Oxyhydroxide; Tocilizumab; Zinc Salts

Food Interactions Serum concentrations may be decreased if taken with dairy products. Management: Take on an empty stomach 1 hour before or 2 hours after meals to increase total absorption. Administer around-the-clock to promote less variation in peak and trough serum levels.

Dietary Considerations Take on an empty stomach (ie, 1 hour prior to, or 2 hours after meals). Take at least 1-2 hours prior to, or 4 hours after antacid.

Pharmacodynamics/Kinetics

Half-life Elimination 6 to 11 hours (Agwuh 2006)

Time to Peak Serum: Oral: 2 to 4 hours (Agwuh 2006)

Pregnancy Risk Factor D

Pregnancy Considerations Tetracycline crosses the placenta (Leblanc 1967). Tetracyclines accumulate in developing teeth and long tubular bones (Mylonas 2011). Permanent discoloration of teeth (yellow, gray, brown) can occur following in utero exposure and is more likely to occur following long-term or repeated exposure. The pharmacokinetics of tetracycline are not altered in pregnant patients with normal renal function (Whalley 1966; Whalley 1970). Hepatic toxicity during pregnancy, potentially associated with tetracycline use, has been reported. Pregnant women with renal disease may be more likely to develop hepatic failure with tetracycline use.

As a class, tetracyclines are generally considered second-line antibiotics in pregnant women and their use should be avoided (Mylonas 2011). Many guidelines consider use of tetracycline to be contraindicated during pregnancy, or to be a relative contraindication in pregnant women if other agents are available and appropriate for use (Anderson 2013; CDC 2011; HHS [OI adult 2015]; Stevens 2014; Workowski [CDC 2015]; Wormser 2006). When systemic antibiotics are needed for dermatologic conditions in pregnant women, other agents are preferred (Kong 2013; Murase 2014).

Breastfeeding Considerations Tetracycline is excreted into breast milk (Knowles 1965; Matsuda 1984).

According to the manufacturer, the decision to continue or discontinue breastfeeding during therapy should take into account the risk of exposure to the infant and the benefits of treatment to the mother. The calcium in the maternal milk is expected to decrease the amount of tetracycline absorbed by the breastfeeding infant (Chung 2002).

As a class, tetracyclines have generally been avoided in nursing women due to theoretical concerns that they may permanently stain the teeth of the breastfeeding infant (Chung 2002). Some sources note that breastfeeding can continue during tetracycline therapy (Chung 2002; WHO 2002) but recommend use of alternative medications when possible (WHO 2002). Other sources note that short-term exposure may be acceptable; however, long-term use of tetracyclines (eg, for the treatment of acne) should be avoided in breastfeeding women (Pugashetti 2013). In general, antibiotics that are present in breast milk may cause nondose-related modification of bowel flora. Monitor infants for GI disturbances (Chung 2002; WHO 2002).

Dosage Forms

Capsule, Oral:

Generic: 250 mg, 500 mg

Tetrahydrocannabinol and Cannabidiol

(TET ra hye droe can NAB e nol & can nab e DYE ol)

Brand Names: Canada Sativex

Pharmacologic Category Analgesic, Nonopioid; Skeletal Muscle Relaxant

Use Note: Not approved in the US

Multiple sclerosis: Adjunctive treatment in adults with multiple sclerosis for the symptomatic relief of neuropathic pain and of spasticity that is nonresponsive to other therapy

Pain: Adjunctive analgesic treatment in adults with advanced cancer with moderate-to-severe pain at the highest tolerated dose of strong opioid therapy

Local Anesthetic/Vasoconstrictor Precautions No information available to require special precautions

Effects on Dental Treatment Key adverse event(s) related to dental treatment: Xerostomia and changes in salivation (normal salivary flow resumes upon discontinuation), abnormal taste, oral pain; administered as buccal spray, associated with irritation to the buccal (oral) mucosa. Patients may experience orthostatic hypotension as they stand up after treatment; especially if lying in dental chair for extended periods of time. Use caution with sudden changes in position during and after dental treatment.

Effects on Bleeding No information available to require special precautions

Adverse Reactions

>10%:

Central nervous system: Dizziness (12% to 25%), drowsiness (8% to 15%), fatigue (13%)

Gastrointestinal: Nausea (10% to 12%)

1% to 10%:

Cardiovascular: Hypotension (5%), palpitations (1%), syncope (1%), tachycardia (1%)

Central nervous system: Confusion (7%), vertigo (5% to 7%), disorientation (4%), disturbance in attention (3% to 4%), depression (3%), equilibrium disturbance (3%), feeling drunk (3%), headache (3%), insomnia (3%), panic attack (3%), euphoria (2% to 3%), hallucination (≤3%), depersonalization (2%), dysarthria (2%), falling (2%), feeling abnormal (2%), lethargy (2%), amnesia (1%), malaise (1%), memory impairment (1%), paranoia (1%), suicidal ideation (1%)

Gastrointestinal: Vomiting (4% to 8%), diarrhea (6% to 7%), xerostomia (6%), dysgeusia (3%), glossalgia (3%), oral candidiasis (3%), anorexia (2%), constipation (2%), dental discoloration (2%), oral mucosa changes (2%), oral mucosa ulcer (2%), abdominal pain (1%), increased appetite (1%), stomatitis (1%)

Genitourinary: Urinary retention (5%), hematuria (3%)

Hepatic: Abnormal hepatic function tests (5%)

Neuromuscular & skeletal: Weakness (5% to 6%)

Ophthalmic: Blurred vision (2%)

Respiratory: Throat irritation (1%)

<1%, postmarketing, frequency not defined, and/or case reports: Delusions, hypertension, illusion, oral leukoplakia, urinary tract infection

General Dosage Range Dosage adjustment recommended in patients who develop toxicities

Buccal: *Adults:* Initial: 1 spray twice daily; Maintenance: Usual: 4 to 8 sprays/day (usual maximum: 12 sprays/day)

Mechanism of Action Stimulates cannabinoid receptors CB1 and CB2 in the CNS and dorsal root ganglia as well as other sites in the body. Cannabinoid receptors in the pain pathways of the brain and spinal cord mediate cannabinoid-induced analgesia. Peripheral CB2 receptors modulate immune function through cytokine release.

Pharmacodynamics/Kinetics

Half-life Elimination Biphasic: Initial: 1 to 2 hours; Terminal: 24 to 36 hours (or longer) secondary to redistribution from fatty tissue

Time to Peak 2 to 4 hours

Pregnancy Considerations

Use is contraindicated during pregnancy, in women of childbearing potential not using reliable contraception, and in males intending to start a family.

Cannabinoids have been associated with reproductive toxicity. Animal studies indicate possible effects on fetal development and spermatogenesis. Women of childbearing potential and males who are capable of causing pregnancy should use a reliable form of contraception for the duration of treatment and for 3 months following discontinuation.

Product Availability Not available in the US

Controlled Substance CDSA-II

Tetrahydrozoline (Nasal)

(tet ra hye DROZ a leen)

Brand Names: US Tyzine

Pharmacologic Category Adrenergic Agonist Agent; Decongestant; Imidazoline Derivative

Use Symptomatic relief of nasal congestion

Local Anesthetic/Vasoconstrictor Precautions No information available to require special precautions

Effects on Dental Treatment No significant effects or complications reported

Effects on Bleeding No information available to require special precautions

Adverse Reactions

>10%: Respiratory: Sneezing, stinging sensation of the nose

1% to 10%:

Cardiovascular: Hypertension, palpitations, tachycardia

Central nervous system: Headache

Neuromuscular & skeletal: Tremor

Ophthalmic: Blurred vision

General Dosage Range Intranasal:

Children 2-6 years: Instill 2-3 drops (0.05%) into each nostril every 4-6 hours as needed (maximum: Every 3 hours)

Children >6 years and Adults: Instill 2-4 drops (0.1%) **or** 3-4 sprays (0.1%) into each nostril every 3-4 hours as needed (maximum: Every 3 hours)

Mechanism of Action Stimulates alpha-adrenergic receptors in the arterioles of the nasal mucosa to produce vasoconstriction

Pharmacodynamics/Kinetics

Onset of Action Decongestant: 4-8 hours

Pregnancy Risk Factor C

Pregnancy Considerations Animal reproduction studies have not been conducted.

Thalidomide (tha LI doe mide)

Related Information

HIV Infection and AIDS *on page 1785*

Ulcerative, Erosive, and Painful Oral Mucosal Disorders *on page 1853*

Brand Names: US Thalomid

Brand Names: Canada Thalomid

Generic Availability (US) No

Pharmacologic Category Angiogenesis Inhibitor; Antineoplastic Agent; Immunomodulator, Systemic

Use

Erythema nodosum leprosum: Acute treatment of cutaneous manifestations of moderate to severe erythema nodosum leprosum; maintenance treatment for prevention and suppression of cutaneous manifestations of erythema nodosum leprosum recurrence

Limitation of use: Thalidomide is not indicated as monotherapy for erythema nodosum leprosum treatment in the presence of moderate to severe neuritis.

Multiple myeloma: Treatment of newly diagnosed multiple myeloma (in combination with dexamethasone)

Local Anesthetic/Vasoconstrictor Precautions No information available to require special precautions

Effects on Dental Treatment Key adverse event(s) related to dental treatment: Oral *Candida* infection (HIV-seropositive patients), toothache, xerostomia (normal salivary flow resumes upon discontinuation), and aphthous stomatitis.

Effects on Bleeding No information available to require special precautions

Adverse Reactions

>10%:

Cardiovascular: Edema (57%), embolism (≤23%), thrombosis (≤23%), hypotension (16%)

Central nervous system: Fatigue (79%), neuropathy (8%; sensory: 54%; motor: 22%), myasthenia (40%), drowsiness (36% to 38%), dizziness (4% to 20%), confusion (28%), agitation (≤26%), anxiety (≤26%), headache (13% to 19%), paresthesia (6% to 16%)

Dermatologic: Desquamation (≤30%), skin rash (≤30%), xeroderma (21%), maculopapular rash (4% to 19%), diaphoresis (13%), acne vulgaris (3% to 11%)

Endocrine & metabolic: Hypocalcemia (72%), weight loss (23%), weight gain (22%)

Gastrointestinal: Constipation (3% to 55%), nausea (4% to 28%), anorexia (3% to 28%), diarrhea (4% to 19%), oral candidiasis (4% to 11%)

Genitourinary: Hematuria (11%)

Hematologic & oncologic: Leukopenia (17% to 35%), neutropenia (31%), anemia (6% to 13%), lymphadenopathy (6% to 13%)

Hepatic: Increased serum AST (3% to 25%), increased serum bilirubin (14%)

Neuromuscular & skeletal: Tremor (4% to 26%), weakness (6% to 22%), myalgia (17%), arthralgia (13%)

Respiratory: Dyspnea (42%)

Miscellaneous: Fever (19% to 23%)

1% to 10%:

Cardiovascular: Peripheral edema (3% to 8%), facial edema (4%)

Central nervous system: Insomnia (9%), nervousness (3% to 9%), malaise (8%), vertigo (8%), pain (3% to 8%)

Dermatologic: Fungal dermatitis (4% to 9%), pruritus (3% to 8%), nail disease (3% to 4%)

Endocrine & metabolic: Hyperlipidemia (6% to 9%), albuminuria (3% to 8%)
Gastrointestinal: Xerostomia (8% to 9%), flatulence (8%), toothache (4%)
Genitourinary: Impotence (3% to 8%)
Hepatic: Abnormal hepatic function tests (9%)
Infection: Infection (6% to 8%)
Neuromuscular & skeletal: Back pain (4% to 6%), neck pain (4%), neck stiffness (4%)
Respiratory: Pharyngitis (4% to 8%), sinusitis (3% to 8%), rhinitis (4%)

<1%, postmarketing, and/or case reports: Acute renal failure, amenorrhea, angioedema, aphthous stomatitis, atrial fibrillation, biliary obstruction, bradycardia, cardiac arrhythmia, carpal tunnel syndrome, cerebrovascular accident, change in prothrombin time, chronic myelocytic leukemia, deafness, decreased creatinine clearance, depression, diplopia, dysesthesia, ECG abnormality, eosinophilia, epistaxis, erythema multiforme, erythema nodosum, erythroleukemia, exfoliative dermatitis, febrile neutropenia, foot-drop, galactorrhea, gastric ulcer, granulocytopenia, gynecomastia, hearing loss, hepatomegaly, Hodgkin's lymphoma, hypercalcemia, hyperkalemia, hypersensitivity reaction, hypertension, hyperthyroidism, hyperuricemia, hypokalemia, hypomagnesemia, hyponatremia, hypoproteinemia, hypothyroidism, increased blood urea nitrogen, increased lactate dehydrogenase, increased serum alkaline phosphatase, increased serum ALT, increased serum creatinine, intestinal obstruction, intestinal perforation, interstitial pneumonitis, lethargy, leukocytosis, loss of consciousness, lymphedema, lymphocytopenia, mental status changes, metastases (AML, MDS, solid tumors), myocardial infarction, myxedema, nystagmus, oliguria, orthostatic hypotension, pancytopenia, petechia, peripheral neuritis, pleural effusion, psychosis, pulmonary embolism, pulmonary hypertension, purpura, Raynaud's phenomenon, renal failure, seizure, sepsis, septic shock, sexual disorder, sick sinus syndrome, skin photosensitivity, status epilepticus, Stevens-Johnson syndrome, stupor, syncope, tachycardia, thrombocytopenia, toxic epidermal necrolysis, transient ischemic attacks, tumor lysis syndrome, urinary incontinence, urticaria, uterine hemorrhage

Dosing

Adult

Erythema nodosum leprosum, acute cutaneous: Oral: Initial: 100 to 300 mg once daily at bedtime, continue until signs/symptoms subside (usually ~2 weeks), then taper off in 50 mg decrements every 2 to 4 weeks. For severe cases with moderate to severe neuritis, corticosteroids may be initiated with thalidomide (taper off and discontinue corticosteroids when neuritis improves).

Patients weighing <50 kg: Initiate at lower end of the dosing range

Severe cutaneous reaction or patients previously requiring high doses: May be initiated at up to 400 mg once daily at bedtime or in divided doses

Erythema nodosum leprosum, maintenance (prevention/suppression, or with flares during tapering attempts): Oral: Maintain on the minimum dosage necessary to control the reaction; efforts to taper off should be attempted every 3 to 6 months, in decrements of 50 mg every 2 to 4 weeks.

Multiple myeloma, newly diagnosed: Oral: 200 mg once daily at bedtime (in combination with dexamethasone)

Multiple myeloma (off-label dosing or combinations):

In combination with bortezomib and dexamethasone (off-label combination): Induction therapy: 100 mg once daily for the first 14 days, then 200 mg once daily for 3 (21-day) cycles (Cavo 2010) **or** 100 mg once daily for up to 8 (21-day) cycles (Kaufman 2010)

In combination with melphalan and prednisone (off-label combination): 200 to 400 mg once daily (Facon 2007) **or** 100 mg once daily (Palumbo 2008) **or** 50 to 100 mg once daily, depending on patient tolerance (Hulin 2009)

Multiple myeloma, maintenance (following autologous stem cell transplant; off-label use): Oral: 200 mg once daily starting 3 to 6 months after transplant; continue until disease progression or unacceptable toxicity (Brinker 2006) or 100 mg once daily starting 42 to 60 days following transplant; increase to 200 mg once daily after 2 weeks if tolerated; continue for up to 12 months (in combination with prednisolone) (Spencer 2009)

Multiple myeloma, salvage therapy: Initial: 200 mg once daily at bedtime; may increase daily dose by 200 mg every 2 weeks for 6 weeks (if tolerated) to a maximum of 800 mg once daily at bedtime (Singhal, 1999) **or** 100 mg once daily (in combination with dexamethasone) (Palumbo 2001) **or** 200 mg once daily (in combination with bortezomib and dexamethasone) for 1 year (Garderet 2012) **or** 400 mg once daily at bedtime (in combination with dexamethasone, cisplatin, doxorubicin, cyclophosphamide and etoposide) (Lee 2003)

AIDS-related aphthous stomatitis (off-label use): Oral: 200 mg once daily at bedtime for up to 8 weeks, if no response, then 200 mg twice daily for 4 weeks (Jacobson, 1997)

Chronic graft-versus-host disease (refractory), treatment (off-label second-line use; optimum dose not determined): Oral: Initial: 100 mg once daily at bedtime, with dose escalation up to 400 mg daily in 3 to 4 divided doses (Wolff 2010) **or** Initial: 50 to 100 mg 3 times daily; maximum dose: 600 to 1,200 mg daily (Kulkarni 2003) **or** 200 mg 4 times daily (dose adjusted to goal thalidomide concentration of ≥5 mcg/mL 2 hours postdose) (Vogelsang, 1992) **or** 100 to 300 mg 4 times daily (Parker, 1995)

Systemic light chain amyloidosis (off-label use): Oral: 200 mg once daily (starting dose 50 to 100 mg once daily; titrate at 4-week intervals) in combination with cyclophosphamide and dexamethasone (Wechalekar 2007)

Uremic pruritus, refractory (off-label use): Oral: 100 mg once daily at bedtime (Silva 1994). Additional data is necessary to further define the role of thalidomide in this condition; several other treatment modalities with more benign safety profiles are available.

Waldenström macroglobulinemia (off-label use): Oral: ≤200 mg once daily for up to 52 weeks (in combination with rituximab) (Treon 2008)

Geriatric Refer to adult dosing. A reduced initial dose may be appropriate (depending on patient tolerance) in patients ≥75 years (Hulin 2009).

Pediatric

Erythema nodosum leprosum, acute cutaneous: Children ≥12 years: Oral: Refer to adult dosing.

Erythema nodosum leprosum, maintenance (prevention/suppression, or with flares during

tapering attempts): Children ≥12 years: Oral: Refer to adult dosing.

Chronic graft-versus-host disease (refractory), treatment (off-label second-line use; limited data): Children ≥3 years: Oral: 3 mg/kg 4 times daily (dose adjusted to goal thalidomide concentration of ≥5 mcg/mL 2 hours postdose) (Vogelsang 1992) **or** Initial: 3 to 6 mg/kg/day in 2 to 4 divided doses; target dose 12 mg/kg/day; Maximum daily dose: 800 mg (Rovelli, 1998)

Renal Impairment No dosage adjustment necessary for patients with renal impairment and on dialysis (per manufacturer). In a study of 6 patients with end-stage renal disease on dialysis, although clearance was increased by dialysis, a supplemental dose was not needed (Eriksson 2003).

Multiple myeloma: An evaluation of 29 newly diagnosed myeloma patients with renal failure (serum creatinine ≥2 mg/dL) treated with thalidomide and dexamethasone (some also received cyclophosphamide) found that toxicities and efficacy were similar to patients with normal renal function (Seol 2010). A study evaluating induction therapy with thalidomide and dexamethasone in 31 newly diagnosed myeloma patients with renal failure (CrCl <50 mL/minute), including 16 patients with severe renal impairment (CrCl <30 mL/minute) and 7 patients on chronic hemodialysis found that toxicities were similar to patients without renal impairment and that thalidomide and dexamethasone could be administered safely (Tosi 2009). The International Myeloma Working Group (IMWG) suggests that thalidomide may be safely administered to patients with renal impairment, including those on dialysis (Dimopoulos 2016). The IMWG recommends the use of the Chronic Kidney Disease Epidemiology Collaboration (CKD-EPI) equation (preferred) or the Modification of Diet in Renal Disease (MDRD) formula to evaluate renal function estimation in multiple myeloma patients with a stable serum creatinine.

Hepatic Impairment There are no dosage adjustments provided in the manufacturer's labeling (has not been studied). However, thalidomide does not appear to undergo significant hepatic metabolism.

Adjustment for Toxicity

ANC ≤750/mm^3: Withhold treatment if clinically appropriate

Grade 3 or 4 adverse reactions: Consider dose reduction, delay or discontinuation (based on clinical judgment).

Multiple myeloma:

Constipation, oversedation: Temporarily withhold or continue with a reduced dose

Peripheral neuropathy:

The manufacturer recommends to temporarily withhold or continue with a reduced dose.

The follow adjustments have also been recommended (Richardson 2012):

Grade 1: Reduce dose by 50%

Grade 2: Temporarily interrupt therapy; once resolved to ≤ grade 1, resume therapy with a 50% dosage reduction (if clinically appropriate)

Grade 3 or higher: Discontinue therapy

Mechanism of Action Immunomodulatory and antiangiogenic characteristics; immunologic effects may vary based on conditions; may suppress excessive tumor necrosis factor-alpha production in patients with ENL, yet may increase plasma tumor necrosis factor-alpha levels in HIV-positive patients. In multiple myeloma, thalidomide is associated with an increase in natural killer cells and increased levels of interleukin-2 and interferon gamma. Other proposed mechanisms of action include suppression of angiogenesis, prevention of free-radical-mediated DNA damage, increased cell mediated cytotoxic effects, and altered expression of cellular adhesion molecules.

Contraindications

Hypersensitivity to thalidomide or any component of the formulation; pregnancy

Canadian labeling: Additional contraindications (not in the US labeling): Hypersensitivity to lenalidomide or pomalidomide; females at risk of becoming pregnant and male patients who are unable to follow or comply with conditions for use (refer to manufacturer labeling); breastfeeding

Warnings/Precautions

[US Boxed Warning]: Thalidomide use for the treatment of multiple myeloma is associated with an increased risk for venous thromboembolism (VTE), including deep vein thrombosis (DVT) and pulmonary embolism (PE); the risk is increased when used in combination with standard chemotherapy agents, including dexamethasone. In one controlled study, the incidence of VTE was 22.5% in patients receiving thalidomide in combination with dexamethasone, compared to 4.9% for dexamethasone alone. Monitor for signs and symptoms of thromboembolism (shortness of breath, chest pain, or arm or leg swelling) and instruct patients to seek prompt medical attention with development of these symptoms. Consider thromboprophylaxis based on risk factors. Ischemic heart disease, including MI and stroke, also occurred at a higher rate (compared to placebo) in myeloma patients receiving thalidomide plus dexamethasone who had not received prior treatment. Assess individual risk factors for thromboembolism and consider thromboprophylaxis. The American Society of Clinical Oncology guidelines for VTE prophylaxis and treatment recommend thromboprophylaxis for patients receiving thalidomide in combination with chemotherapy and/or dexamethasone; either aspirin or low molecular weight heparin (LMWH) are recommended for lower risk patient and LMWH is recommended for higher risk patients (Lyman 2013). Anticoagulant prophylaxis should be individualized and selected based on the venous thromboembolism risk of the combination treatment regimen, using the safest and easiest to administer (Palumbo 2008). Monitor for signs/symptoms of thromboembolism and advise patients to seek immediate care if symptoms (shortness of breath, chest pain, arm/leg swelling) develop. Other medications that are also associated with thromboembolism should be used with caution. In a scientific statement from the American Heart Association, thalidomide has been determined to be an agent that may exacerbate underlying myocardial dysfunction (magnitude: minor) (AHA [Page 2016]).

May cause leukopenia and neutropenia; avoid initiating therapy if ANC <750/mm^3. Persistent neutropenia may require treatment interruption. Thrombocytopenia (including grades 3 and 4) has been reported; may require dose reduction, treatment delay, or discontinuation. Monitor for signs and symptoms of bleeding (including petechiae, epistaxis, and gastrointestinal bleeding), especially if concomitant medication may increase the risk of bleeding. Monitor CBC with differential and platelets. Anemia has also been observed. May cause bradycardia; use with caution when administering concomitantly with medications that may also decrease heart rate. May require thalidomide dose reduction or discontinuation. Stevens-Johnson syndrome (SJS) and toxic epidermal necrolysis (TEN) have been reported (may be fatal); withhold therapy and evaluate if skin rash occurs; permanently discontinue if rash is exfoliative, purpuric, bullous or if SJS or TEN is suspected. Hypersensitivity, including erythematous macular rash, possibly associated with fever, tachycardia and hypotension has been reported. May require treatment interruption for severe reactions; discontinue if recurs with rechallenge. Abnormal liver function tests, hepatitis and cholestatic jaundice have been reported. Hepatotoxicity (including hepatocellular and cholestatic injury) has been observed rarely (case reports), with a mean time to development of 46 days; most events resolved after discontinuing thalidomide (Vilas-Boas 2012).

Increased incidence of second primary malignancies (SPMs), including acute myeloid leukemia (AML) and myelodysplastic syndrome (MDS), has been observed in previously untreated multiple myeloma patients receiving thalidomide in combination with melphalan, and prednisone. In addition to AML and MDS, solid tumors have been reported with thalidomide maintenance treatment for multiple myeloma (Usmani 2012). Carefully evaluate patients for SPMs prior to and during treatment and manage as clinically indicated.

Thalidomide is commonly associated with peripheral neuropathy; may be irreversible. Neuropathy generally occurs following chronic use (over months), but may occur with short-term use; onset may be delayed. Use caution with other medications that may also cause peripheral neuropathy. Monitor for signs/symptoms of neuropathy monthly for the first 3 months of therapy and regularly thereafter. Electrophysiological testing may be considered at baseline and every 6 months to detect asymptomatic neuropathy. To limit further damage, immediately discontinue (if clinically appropriate) in patients who develop neuropathy. Reinitiate therapy only if neuropathy returns to baseline; may require dosage reduction or permanent discontinuation. Seizures (including grand mal convulsions) have been reported in postmarketing data; monitor closely for clinical changes indicating potential seizure activity in patients with a history of seizures, concurrent therapy with drugs that alter seizure threshold, or conditions that predispose to seizures. May cause dizziness, drowsiness, and/or somnolence; caution patients about performing tasks that require mental alertness (eg, operating machinery or driving). Avoid ethanol and concomitant medications that may exacerbate these symptoms; dose reductions may be necessary for excessive drowsiness or somnolence. May cause orthostatic hypotension; use with caution in patients who would not tolerate transient hypotensive episodes. When arising from a recumbent position, advise patients to sit upright for a few minutes prior to standing. Constipation may commonly occur. May require treatment interruption or dosage reduction. Certain adverse reactions (constipation, fatigue, weakness, nausea, hypokalemia, hyperglycemia, DVT, pulmonary embolism, atrial fibrillation) are more likely in elderly patients. In studies conducted prior to the use of highly active antiretroviral therapy, thalidomide use was associated with increased viral loads in HIV infected patients. Monitor viral load after the 1st and 3rd months of therapy and every 3 months thereafter. Patients with a high tumor burden may be at risk for tumor lysis syndrome; monitor closely; institute appropriate management for hyperuricemia.

Potentially significant drug-drug interactions may exist, requiring dose or frequency adjustment, additional monitoring, and/or selection of alternative therapy. Patients should not donate blood during thalidomide treatment and for 4 weeks after therapy discontinuation.

[US Boxed Warning]: Thalidomide is contraindicated in pregnant women. Thalidomide may cause severe birth defects or embryo-fetal death if taken during pregnancy. Thalidomide cannot be used in women who are pregnant or may become pregnant during therapy as even a single dose may cause severe birth defects. In order to decrease the risk of fetal exposure, thalidomide is available only through a special restricted distribution program (Thalomid REMS). Use is also contraindicated in women who may become pregnant. Pregnancy must be excluded prior to therapy initiation with 2 negative pregnancy tests. Women of reproductive potential must avoid pregnancy beginning 4 weeks prior to therapy, during therapy, during therapy interruptions, and for ≥4 weeks after therapy is discontinued; two reliable methods of birth control, or abstinence from heterosexual intercourse, must be used. Males taking thalidomide (even those vasectomized) must use a latex or synthetic condom during any sexual contact with women of childbearing potential and for up to 28 days following discontinuation of therapy. Males taking thalidomide must not donate sperm. Some forms of contraception may not be appropriate in certain patients. An intrauterine device (IUD) or implantable contraceptive may increase the risk of infection or bleeding; estrogen containing products may increase the risk of thromboembolism.

Due to the embryo-fetal risk, thalidomide is only available through a restricted program under the Thalomid REMS program. Prescribers and pharmacies must be certified with the program to prescribe or dispense thalidomide. Patients must sign an agreement and comply with the REMS program requirements.

Drug Interactions

Metabolism/Transport Effects

None known.

Avoid Concomitant Use

Avoid concomitant use of Thalidomide with any of the following: Abatacept; Anakinra; Azelastine (Nasal); BCG (Intravesical); Canakinumab; Certolizumab Pegol; CNS Depressants; Deferiprone; Dipyrone; Natalizumab; Orphenadrine; Oxomemazine; Paraldehyde; Pimecrolimus; Rilonacept; Tacrolimus (Topical); Tocilizumab; Tofacitinib; Vaccines (Live); Vedolizumab

Increased Effect/Toxicity

Thalidomide may increase the levels/effects of: Abatacept; Amifostine; Anakinra; Azelastine (Nasal); Bisphosphonate Derivatives; Canakinumab; Certolizumab Pegol; Deferiprone; DULoxetine; Fingolimod; Hypotension-Associated Agents; Leflunomide; Levodopa; MetyroSINE; Natalizumab; Nitroprusside; Orphenadrine; Pamidronate; Paraldehyde; Piribedil; Pramipexole; Rilonacept; ROPINIRole; Rotigotine; Selective Serotonin Reuptake Inhibitors; Tofacitinib; Vaccines (Live); Vedolizumab; Zoledronic Acid

The levels/effects of Thalidomide may be increased by: Alfuzosin; Blood Pressure Lowering Agents; Brimonidine (Topical); Cannabis; Chlorphenesin Carbamate; CNS Depressants; Contraceptives (Estrogens); Contraceptives (Progestins); Denosumab; Dexamethasone (Systemic); Diazoxide; Dimethindene (Topical); Dipyrone; Dronabinol; Erythropoiesis-Stimulating Agents; Estrogen Derivatives; Herbs (Hypotensive Properties); Kava Kava; Lofexidine;

Magnesium Sulfate; Minocycline; Molsidomine; Nabilone; Naftopidil; Nicergoline; Nicorandil; Obinutuzumab; Ocrelizumab; Oxomemazine; Pentoxifylline; Phosphodiesterase 5 Inhibitors; Pimecrolimus; Prostacyclin Analogues; Quinagolide; Roflumilast; Rufinamide; Tacrolimus (Topical); Tetrahydrocannabinol; Tocilizumab; Trastuzumab

Decreased Effect

Thalidomide may decrease the levels/effects of: BCG (Intravesical); Coccidioides immitis Skin Test; Nivolumab; Sipuleucel-T; Tertomotide; Vaccines (Inactivated); Vaccines (Live)

The levels/effects of Thalidomide may be decreased by: Echinacea

Pharmacodynamics/Kinetics

Half-life Elimination 5.5 to 7.3 hours

Time to Peak Plasma: ~2 to 5 hours

Pregnancy Considerations [US Boxed Warning]: Thalidomide is contraindicated in pregnant women. Thalidomide may cause severe birth defects or embryo-fetal death if taken during pregnancy. Thalidomide cannot be used in women who are pregnant or may become pregnant during therapy as even a single dose may cause severe birth defects. In order to decrease the risk of fetal exposure, thalidomide is available only through a special restricted distribution program (Thalomid REMS). Reproduction studies in animals and data from pregnant women have shown evidence of fetal abnormalities; use is contraindicated in women who are or may become pregnant. Anomalies observed in humans include amelia, phocomelia, bone defects, ear and eye abnormalities, facial palsy, congenital heart defects, urinary and genital tract malformations; mortality in ~40% of infants at or shortly after birth has also been reported.

Women of reproductive potential must avoid pregnancy beginning 4 weeks prior to therapy, during therapy, during therapy interruptions, and for at least 4 weeks after therapy is discontinued. Two forms of effective/reliable contraception or total abstinence from heterosexual intercourse must be used by females who are not infertile or who have not had a hysterectomy. A negative pregnancy test (sensitivity of at least 50 milli-units/mL) 10 to 14 days prior to therapy, within 24 hours prior to beginning therapy, weekly during the first 4 weeks, and every 4 weeks (every 2 weeks for women with irregular menstrual cycles) thereafter is required for women of childbearing potential. Thalidomide must be immediately discontinued for a missed period, abnormal pregnancy test or abnormal menstrual bleeding; refer patient to a reproductive toxicity specialist if pregnancy occurs during treatment.

Females of reproductive potential (including health care workers and caregivers) must also avoid contact with thalidomide capsules.

Thalidomide is also present in the semen of males. Males (even those vasectomized) must use a latex or synthetic condom during any sexual contact with women of childbearing potential and for up to 28 days following discontinuation of therapy. Males taking thalidomide must not donate sperm.

The parent or legal guardian for patients between 12 to 18 years of age must agree to ensure compliance with the required guidelines.

A pregnancy exposure registry has been created to monitor outcomes in females exposed to thalidomide during pregnancy and female partners of male patients and to understand the root cause for the pregnancy. The pregnancy exposure registry may be contacted at 1-888-423-5436. If pregnancy occurs during treatment, thalidomide must be immediately discontinued and the patient referred to a reproductive toxicity specialist. Any suspected fetal exposure to thalidomide must be reported to the FDA via the MedWatch program (1-800-FDA-1088) and to Celgene Corporation (1-888-423-5436).

Breastfeeding Considerations It is not known if thalidomide is present in breast milk. Due to the potential for serious adverse reactions in the breastfed infant, breastfeeding is not recommended by the manufacturer.

Prescribing and Access Restrictions

US: As a requirement of the REMS program, access to this medication is restricted. Thalidomide is approved for marketing only under a special distribution program, the Thalomid REMS (https://www.celgeneriskmanagement.com or 1-888-423-5436), which has been approved by the FDA. Prescribers, patients, and pharmacies must be certified with the program to prescribe or dispense thalidomide. No more than a 4-week supply should be dispensed. Blister packs should be dispensed intact (do not repackage capsules). Prescriptions must be filled within 7 days (for females of reproductive potential) or within 30 days (for all other patients) after authorization number obtained. Subsequent prescriptions may be filled only if fewer than 7 days of therapy remain on the previous prescription. A new prescription is required for further dispensing (a telephone prescription may not be accepted.) Pregnancy testing is required for females of childbearing potential.

Canada: Access to thalidomide is restricted through a controlled distribution program called RevAid. Only physicians and pharmacists enrolled in this program are authorized to prescribe or dispense thalidomide. Patients must be enrolled in the program by their physicians. Further information is available at www.RevAid.ca or by calling 1-888-738-2431.

Dosage Forms

Capsule, Oral:

Thalomid: 50 mg, 100 mg, 150 mg, 200 mg

Theophylline (thee OFF i lin)

Related Information

Aminophylline *on page 114*

Respiratory Diseases *on page 1777*

Brand Names: US Elixophyllin; Theo-24; Theochron

Brand Names: Canada Apo-Theo LA®; Novo-Theophyl SR; PMS-Theophylline; Pulmophylline; ratio-Theo-Bronc; Teva-Theophylline SR; Theo ER; Theolair; Uniphyl

Pharmacologic Category Phosphodiesterase Enzyme Inhibitor, Nonselective

Use

Treatment of symptoms and reversible airway obstruction due to chronic asthma, or other chronic lung diseases

Guideline recommendations:

Asthma: The 2016 Global Initiative for Asthma Guidelines (GINA) and the 2007 National Heart, Lung and Blood Institute Asthma Guidelines do not recommend oral theophylline as a long-term control medication for asthma in children ≤5 years of age. Additionally, GINA guidelines do not recommend oral theophylline for asthma in children 6 to 11 years of age. Oral theophylline is a potential alternative option (not preferred) in adolescents and adults as a long-term control medication in mild asthma or as an add-on long-term control medication in moderate to severe asthma; however, a stepwise approach using inhaled corticosteroids (+/- inhaled long-acting beta agonists depending on asthma severity) is preferred to theophylline due to efficacy concerns and potential for adverse events (GINA 2015). Both guidelines recommend against theophylline for the treatment of asthma exacerbations due to poor efficacy and safety concerns (GINA 2016; NAEPP 2007).

COPD: The Global Initiative for Chronic Obstructive Lung Disease Guidelines (2013) suggest that while higher doses of slow release formulations of theophylline have been proven to be effective for use in COPD, it is not a preferred agent due to its potential for toxicity.

Local Anesthetic/Vasoconstrictor Precautions No information available to require special precautions

Effects on Dental Treatment Prescribe erythromycin products with caution to patients taking theophylline products. Erythromycin will delay the normal metabolic inactivation of theophyllines leading to increased blood levels; this has resulted in nausea, vomiting, and CNS restlessness. Azithromycin does not cause these effects in combination with theophylline products.

Effects on Bleeding No information available to require special precautions

Adverse Reactions Frequency not defined. Adverse events observed at therapeutic serum levels.

Cardiovascular: Cardiac flutter, tachycardia

Central nervous system: Headache, hyperactivity (children), insomnia, restlessness, seizure, status epilepticus (nonconvulsive)

Endocrine & metabolic: Hypercalcemia (with concomitant hyperthyroid disease)

Gastrointestinal: Gastroesophageal reflux (aggravation), gastrointestinal ulcer (aggravation), nausea, vomiting

Genitourinary: Difficulty in micturition (elderly males with prostatism), diuresis (transient)

Neuromuscular & skeletal: Tremor

General Dosage Range

IV:

Infants 6-52 weeks: mg/kg/hour = (0.008) (age in weeks) + 0.21

Children 1-9 years: 0.8 mg/kg/hour

Children 9-12 years and Adolescents 12-16 years (cigarette or marijuana smokers): 0.7 mg/kg/hour

Adolescents 12-16 years (nonsmokers): 0.5 mg/kg/hour; maximum: 900 mg/day unless serum levels indicate need for larger dose

Adults 16-60 years (otherwise healthy, nonsmokers): 0.4 mg/kg/hour; maximum: 900 mg/day unless serum levels indicate need for larger dose

Adults >60 years: 0.3 mg/kg/hour; maximum: 400 mg/day unless serum levels indicate need for larger dose

Oral solution:

Full-term Infants and Infants <26 weeks: Total daily dose (mg) = [(0.2 x age in weeks) +5] x (weight in kg); divide dose into 3 equal amounts and administer at 8-hour intervals

Full-term Infants and Infants ≥26 weeks and <52 weeks: Total daily dose (mg) = [(0.2 x age in weeks) +5] x (weight in kg); divide dose into 4 equal amounts and administer at 6-hour intervals

Children ≥1 year and <45 kg: Initial: 10-14 mg/kg/day in divided doses (maximum dose: 300 mg/day); titrate to maintenance dose: 20 mg/kg/day in divided doses every 4-6 hours (maximum dose: 600 mg/day)

Children >45 kg and Adults: Initial: 300 mg/day in divided doses; titrate to maintenance dose: 600 mg/day in divided doses every 6-8 hours

Oral extended release formulations:

Children ≥1 year and <45 kg: Initial: 10-14 mg/kg once daily (maximum dose: 300 mg/day); titrate to maintenance dose: 20 mg/kg once daily (maximum dose: 600 mg/day)

Children >45 kg and Adults: 300-600 mg once daily

Mechanism of Action Causes bronchodilatation, diuresis, CNS and cardiac stimulation, and gastric acid secretion by blocking phosphodiesterase which increases tissue concentrations of cyclic adenine monophosphate (cAMP) which in turn promotes catecholamine stimulation of lipolysis, glycogenolysis, and gluconeogenesis and induces release of epinephrine from adrenal medulla cells

Pharmacodynamics/Kinetics

Onset of Action IV: <30 minutes

Half-life Elimination Highly variable and age, liver and cardiac function, lung disease, and smoking history dependent (Hendeles 1995):

Premature infants, postnatal age 3 to 15 days: 30 hours (range: 17 to 43 hours)

Premature infants, postnatal age 25 to 57 days: 20 hours (range: 9.4 to 30.6 hours)

Term infants, postnatal age 1 to 2 days: 25 hours

Term infants, postnatal age 3 to 30 weeks: 11 hours

Children 1 to 4 years: 3.4 hours

Children 16 to 17 years: 3.7 hours (range: 1.5 to 5.9 hours)

Adults ≥18 years to ≤ 60 years (nonsmoking, asthmatic): 8.2 hours

Adults >60 years (nonsmoking, healthy): 9.8 hours

Acute pulmonary edema: 19 hours

Cystic fibrosis (14 to 28 years): 6 hours

Acute hepatitis: 19.2 hours

Cholestasis: 14.4 hours

Cirrhosis: 32 hours

Sepsis with multiorgan failure: 18.8 hours

Hypothyroid: 11.6 hours

Hyperthyroid: 4.5 hours

Time to Peak Serum: Oral: Liquid: 1 hour

Pregnancy Risk Factor C

Pregnancy Considerations Teratogenic effects were observed in animal reproduction studies. Theophylline crosses the placenta; adverse effects may be seen in the newborn. Use is generally safe when used at the recommended doses (serum concentrations 5-12 mcg/mL) however maternal adverse events may be increased and efficacy may be decreased in pregnant women. Theophylline metabolism may change during pregnancy; the half-life is similar to that observed in otherwise healthy, nonsmoking adults with asthma during the first and second trimesters (~8.7 hours), but may increase to 13 hours (range: 8-18 hours) during the third trimester. The volume of distribution is also increased during the third trimester. Monitor serum levels. The recommendations for the use of theophylline in pregnant women with asthma are similar to those used in nonpregnant adults (National Heart, Lung, and Blood Institute Guidelines 2004).

Thiamine (THYE a min)

Brand Names: Canada Betaxin

Pharmacologic Category Vitamin, Water Soluble

Use Treatment of thiamine deficiency including beriberi, Wernicke's encephalopathy, Korsakoff's syndrome, neuritis associated with pregnancy, or in alcoholic patients; dietary supplement

Local Anesthetic/Vasoconstrictor Precautions No information available to require special precautions

Effects on Dental Treatment Key adverse event(s) related to dental treatment: Tightness of the throat.

Effects on Bleeding No information available to require special precautions

Adverse Reactions Adverse reactions reported with injection. Frequency not defined.

Central nervous system: Flushing sensation, restlessness

Dermatologic: Diaphoresis, pruritus, skin sclerosis (at the injection site following IM administration), urticaria

Gastrointestinal: Nausea

Hematologic & oncologic: Hemorrhage (into the gastrointestinal tract)

Hypersensitivity: Anaphylaxis (following IV administration), angioedema, hypersensitivity reaction (following IV administration)

Local: Tenderness at injection site (following IM administration)

Neuromuscular & skeletal: Weakness

Respiratory: Cyanosis, pharyngeal edema, pulmonary edema

General Dosage Range

IM, IV:

Children: 10-25 mg/dose daily (thiamine deficiency)

Adults: 5-30 mg/dose 3 times/day (thiamine deficiency) **or** 50-250 mg/day (Wernicke's encephalopathy)

Oral:

Infants: 0.2-0.3 mg/day (adequate intake)

Children: 0.5-1.4 mg/day (recommended daily intake) **or** 5-50 mg/day (thiamine deficiency)

Adults: 1.1-1.4 mg/day (recommended daily intake) **or** 5-30 mg/day in 1-3 divided doses (thiamine deficiency)

Mechanism of Action An essential coenzyme in carbohydrate metabolism by combining with adenosine triphosphate to form thiamine pyrophosphate

Pregnancy Risk Factor A

Pregnancy Considerations Water soluble vitamins cross the placenta. Thiamine requirements may be increased during pregnancy (IOM, 1998). Severe nausea and vomiting (hyperemesis gravidarum) may lead to thiamine deficiency manifested as Wernicke's encephalopathy (Chiossi, 2006).

Thioguanine (thye oh GWAH neen)

Brand Names: US Tabloid

Brand Names: Canada Lanvis

Pharmacologic Category Antineoplastic Agent, Antimetabolite; Antineoplastic Agent, Antimetabolite (Purine Analog)

Use

Acute myeloid leukemia: Treatment (remission induction and consolidation) of acute myeloid (nonlymphocytic) leukemia (AML)

Limitations of use: The use of thioguanine for AML maintenance therapy or other similar long-term continuous treatments is not recommended due to the high risk of hepatotoxicity.

Local Anesthetic/Vasoconstrictor Precautions No information available to require special precautions

Effects on Dental Treatment Key adverse event(s) related to dental treatment: Stomatitis.

Effects on Bleeding Chemotherapy may result in significant myelosuppression, potentially including significant reduction in platelet counts and altered hemostasis. In patients who are under active treatment with these agents, medical consult is suggested.

Adverse Reactions Frequency not defined.

Cardiovascular: Esophageal varices, hepatic veno-occlusive disease (hepatic sinusoidal obstruction syndrome; SOS), portal hypertension

Endocrine & metabolic: Fluid retention, hyperuricemia (common), weight gain

Gastrointestinal: Anorexia, intestinal necrosis, intestinal perforation, nausea, stomatitis, vomiting

Hematologic & oncologic: Anemia (may be delayed), bone marrow hypoplasia, granulocytopenia, hemorrhage, leukopenia (common; may be delayed), pancytopenia, splenomegaly, thrombocytopenia (common; may be delayed)

Hepatic: Ascites, hepatic necrosis (centrilobular), hepatitis, hepatomegaly (tender), hepatotoxicity, hyperbilirubinemia, increased liver enzymes, jaundice

Infection: Infection

Mechanism of Action Purine analog that is incorporated into DNA and RNA resulting in the blockage of synthesis and metabolism of purine nucleotides

Pharmacodynamics/Kinetics

Half-life Elimination Terminal: 5 to 9 hours

Time to Peak Serum: Within 8 hours; predominantly metabolite(s)

Pregnancy Risk Factor D

Pregnancy Considerations Adverse effects have been observed in animal reproduction studies. May cause fetal harm if administered during pregnancy. Women of childbearing potential should avoid becoming pregnant during treatment.

Thioridazine (thye oh RID a zeen)

Related Information

Clinical Risk Related to Drugs Prolonging QT Interval *on page 1772*

Pharmacologic Category First Generation (Typical) Antipsychotic; Phenothiazine Derivative

Use Schizophrenia: Management of schizophrenic patients who fail to respond adequately to treatment with other antipsychotic drugs, either because of insufficient effectiveness or the inability to achieve an effective dose because of intolerable adverse effects from those medications. Before initiating treatment with thioridazine, it is strongly recommended that a patient be given at least 2 trials, each with a different antipsychotic drug product, at an adequate dose and for an adequate duration.

Local Anesthetic/Vasoconstrictor Precautions Thioridazine is one of the drugs confirmed to prolong the QT interval and is accepted as having a risk of causing torsade de pointes. The risk of drug-induced torsade de pointes is extremely low when a single QT interval prolonging drug is prescribed. In terms of epinephrine, it is not known what effect vasoconstrictors in the local anesthetic regimen will have in patients with a known history of congenital prolonged QT interval or in patients taking any medication that prolongs the QT interval. Until more information is obtained, it is suggested that the clinician consult with the physician prior to the use of a vasoconstrictor in suspected patients, and that the vasoconstrictor (epinephrine, mepivacaine and levonordefrin [Carbocaine® 2% with Neo-Cobefrin®]) be used with caution.

Effects on Dental Treatment Key adverse event(s) related to dental treatment: Xerostomia and changes in salivation (normal salivary flow resumes upon discontinuation). Significant hypotension may occur, especially when the drug is administered parenterally; orthostatic hypotension is due to alpha-receptor blockade, the elderly are at greater risk for orthostatic hypotension.

Tardive dyskinesia; Prevalence rate may be 40% in elderly; development of the syndrome and the irreversible nature are proportional to duration and total cumulative dose over time. Extrapyramidal reactions are more common in elderly with up to 50% developing these reactions after 60 years of age. Drug-induced Parkinson's syndrome occurs often; akathisia is the most common extrapyramidal reaction in elderly.

Effects on Bleeding No information available to require special precautions

Adverse Reactions Frequency not defined.

Cardiovascular: ECG changes, hypotension, orthostatic hypotension, peripheral edema, prolonged QT Interval on ECG, torsades de pointes

Central nervous system: Disruption of temperature regulation (Martinez 2002), drowsiness, drug-induced Parkinson disease, extrapyramidal reaction, headache, hyperactivity, lethargy, psychotic reaction, seizure, tardive dyskinesia (Lehman 2004)

Dermatologic: Dermatitis, hyperpigmentation (Lehman 2004), pallor, skin photosensitivity, skin rash, urticaria

Endocrine & metabolic: Amenorrhea, galactorrhea, weight gain (Lehman 2004)

Gastrointestinal: Constipation, diarrhea, nausea, parotid gland enlargement, vomiting, xerostomia

Genitourinary: Breast engorgement, ejaculatory disorder, priapism

Hematologic & oncologic: Agranulocytosis, leukopenia

Ophthalmic: Blurred vision, corneal opacity (Lehman 2004), retinitis pigmentosa

Respiratory: Nasal congestion

General Dosage Range Oral:

Children and Adolescents: Initial: 0.5 mg/kg/day in 2 to 4 divided doses (maximum: 3 mg/kg/day)

Adults: Initial: 50 to 100 mg 3 times daily; Usual dosage: 200 to 800 mg in 2 to 4 divided doses; maximum: 800 mg daily

Mechanism of Action Thioridazine is a piperidine phenothiazine which blocks postsynaptic mesolimbic dopaminergic receptors in the brain; also has activity at serotonin, noradrenaline, and histamine receptors (Fenton, 2007).

Pharmacodynamics/Kinetics

Half-life Elimination 5 to 27 hours (Martensson 1973; Muusze 1977; Vanderdeeren 1977)

Time to Peak Serum: ~1 to 4 hours (Martensson 1973)

Pregnancy Considerations Jaundice or hyper- or hyporeflexia have been reported in newborn infants following maternal use of phenothiazines. Antipsychotic use during the third trimester of pregnancy has a risk for abnormal muscle movements (extrapyramidal symptoms [EPS]) and withdrawal symptoms in newborns following delivery. Symptoms in the newborn may include agitation, feeding disorder, hypertonia, hypotonia, respiratory distress, somnolence, and tremor; these effects may be self-limiting or require hospitalization.

Dental Comment See Local Anesthetic/Vasoconstrictor Precautions

Thiotepa (thye oh TEP a)

Pharmacologic Category Antineoplastic Agent, Alkylating Agent

Use

Bladder cancer, papillary: Treatment of superficial papillary bladder cancer

Breast cancer: Palliative treatment of adenocarcinoma of the breast

Effusions: Controlling intracavitary effusions secondary to diffuse or localized disease of various serosal cavities

Ovarian cancer: Palliative treatment of adenocarcinoma of the ovary

Local Anesthetic/Vasoconstrictor Precautions No information available to require special precautions

Effects on Dental Treatment No significant effects or complications reported

Effects on Bleeding Chemotherapy may result in significant myelosuppression, potentially including significant reduction in platelet counts and altered hemostasis. In patients who are under active treatment with these agents, medical consult is suggested.

Adverse Reactions Frequency not defined.

Central nervous system: Chills, dizziness, fatigue, headache

Dermatologic: Alopecia, contact dermatitis, dermatitis, skin depigmentation (with topical treatment), skin rash, urticaria

Endocrine & metabolic: Amenorrhea

Gastrointestinal: Abdominal pain, anorexia, nausea, vomiting

Genitourinary: Dysuria, hematuria, inhibition of spermatogenesis, urinary retention

Hematologic & oncologic: Anemia, hemorrhage, leukopenia, thrombocytopenia

Hypersensitivity: Anaphylactic shock, hypersensitivity reaction

Infection: Infection

Local: Pain at injection site

Neuromuscular & skeletal: Weakness

Ophthalmic: Blurred vision, conjunctivitis

Respiratory: Asthma, epistaxis, laryngeal edema, wheezing

Miscellaneous: Fever

<1%, postmarketing, and/or case reports: Acute myelocytic leukemia (AML), cystitis (chemical; bladder instillation), hemorrhagic cystitis (bladder instillation), myelodysplastic syndrome

General Dosage Range Dosage adjustment recommended in patients who develop toxicities

Dosage varies greatly depending on indication

Mechanism of Action Thiotepa is an alkylating agent which produces cross-linking of DNA strands leading to inhibition of DNA, RNA, and protein synthesis; thiotepa is cell-cycle independent (Perry 2012)

Pharmacodynamics/Kinetics

Half-life Elimination Terminal: Thiotepa: 2.3 ± 0.3 to 2.4 ± 0.3 hours with dose-dependent clearance; TEPA: 15.7 ± 2.7 to 17.6 ± 3.6 hours

Pregnancy Risk Factor D

Pregnancy Considerations Adverse events were observed in animal reproduction studies. May cause harm if administered during pregnancy. Effective contraception is recommended for men and women of childbearing potential.

Thrombin (Topical) (THROM bin, TOP i kal)

Related Information

Antiplatelet and Anticoagulation Considerations in Dentistry *on page 1764*

Cardiovascular Diseases *on page 1752*

Brand Names: US Evithrom; Recothrom; Recothrom Spray Kit; Thrombi-Gel; Thrombi-Pad; Thrombin-JMI; Thrombin-JMI Epistaxis Kit; Thrombin-JMI Pump Spray Kit; Thrombin-JMI Syringe Spray Kit

Brand Names: Canada Recothrom

Generic Availability (US) No

Pharmacologic Category Blood Product Derivative; Hemostatic Agent

Dental Use Hemostasis whenever minor bleeding from capillaries and small venules is accessible

Use

Hemostasis aid:

Evithrom, Recothrom, Thrombin-JMI only: As an aid to hemostasis whenever oozing blood and minor bleeding from capillaries and small venules is accessible and control of bleeding by standard surgical techniques is ineffective or impractical.

Thrombi-Gel, Thrombi-Pad only: As a trauma dressing for temporary control of moderate to severe bleeding wounds; control of surface bleeding from vascular access sites and percutaneous catheters and tubes.

Local Anesthetic/Vasoconstrictor Precautions No information available to require special precautions

Effects on Dental Treatment No significant effects or complications reported

Effects on Bleeding General dental procedures and simple restorative procedures are not associated with bleeding; therefore, there is no contraindication to general dental treatment for most patients with bleeding disorders. However, after dental extractions and other dental surgeries including deep scaling, block anesthesia, and large fillings, in patients with hemophilia, drugs such as topical thrombin may be useful in controlling bleeding. A carefully coordinated strategy between the dental and medical team may be required to ensure adequate procedures for hemostasis.

Adverse Reactions Frequency not always defined.

Cardiovascular: Thromboembolism (1% to 9%)

Dermatologic: Pruritus

Gastrointestinal: Nausea, vomiting

Hematologic and oncologic: Increased INR, increased neutrophils, lymphocytopenia, prolonged partial thromboplastin time, prolonged prothrombin time

Hypersensitivity: Hypersensitivity reaction

Immunologic: Antibody development (≤2%)

Local: Postoperative wound complication

Dental Usual Dosage Topical: Hemostasis: **Note:** For topical use only; do not administer intravenously or intra-arterially:

Evithrom: Children and Adults: Dose depends on area to be treated; up to 10 mL was used with absorbable gelatin sponge in clinical studies

Recothrom: Adults: Dose depends on area to be treated

Thrombi-Gel 10, 40, 100: Adults: Wet product with up to 3 mL, 10 mL, or 20 mL, respectively, of 0.9% sodium chloride or SWFI; apply directly over source of the bleeding with manual pressure

Thrombi-Pad: Adults: Apply pad directly over source of bleeding; may apply dry or wetted with up to 10 mL of 0.9% sodium chloride. If desired, product may be left in place for up to 24 hours; do not leave in the body.

Thrombin-JMI: Adults:

Solution: Use 1000-2000 units/mL of solution where bleeding is profuse; use 100 units/mL for bleeding from skin or mucosal surfaces

Powder: May apply powder directly to the site of bleeding or on oozing surfaces

Dosing

Adult & Geriatric Hemostasis aid: Topical: **Note:** For topical use only; do not administer intravenously or intra-arterially:

Evithrom: Dose depends on area to be treated; for direct application, flood treatment area; up to 10 mL was used with absorbable gelatin sponge in clinical studies.

Recothrom: Dose depends on area to be treated. Apply to the bleeding site directly or in conjunction with absorbable gelatin sponge.

Thrombi-Gel: Apply directly over source of the bleeding with adjunct manual pressure until hemostasis is achieved.

Thrombin-JMI:

Solution: Apply 1,000 to 2,000 units/mL of solution where bleeding is profuse. Apply 100 units/mL for bleeding from skin or mucosal surfaces (eg, skin grafting, dental extractions, plastic surgery).

Powder: May apply dry powder directly to the site on oozing surfaces.

Thrombi-Pad: Apply dry or wetted pad directly over source of bleeding with adjunct manual pressure. If desired, product may be left in place for up to 24 hours; do not leave in the body.

Pediatric

Evithrom: Children and Adolescents: Refer to adult dosing.

Recothrom: Infants ≥1 month, Children, and Adolescents: Refer to adult dosing. Canadian labeling does not approve of use in patients <18 years.

Renal Impairment There are no dosage adjustments provided in the manufacturer's labeling.

Hepatic Impairment There are no dosage adjustments provided in the manufacturer's labeling.

Mechanism of Action Activates platelets and catalyzes the conversion of fibrinogen to fibrin to promote hemostasis.

Contraindications Known hypersensitivity to any component of the formulation.

Evithrom: Additional contraindications: Known anaphylactic or severe systemic reactions to blood products; treatment of severe or brisk arterial bleeding

Recothrom: Additional contraindications: Known hypersensitivity to hamster proteins; injection directly into the circulatory system; treatment of massive or brisk arterial bleeding.

Thrombi-Gel: Additional contraindications: Use in the closure of skin incisions.

Thrombin-JMI: Additional contraindications: Known sensitivity to material of bovine origin; injection directly into the circulatory system; re-exposure if there are known or suspected antibodies to bovine thrombin and/or factor V; treatment of severe or brisk arterial bleeding.

Thrombi-Pad: Additional contraindications: Known sensitivity to bovine-derived materials.

Warnings/Precautions For topical use only. Do not inject intravenously or intra-arterially. Intravascular clotting, possibly leading to death, may occur following injection. Powder and solution formulations may be used in combination with absorbable gelatin sponges. Hypersensitivity reactions, including anaphylaxis, may occur. Institute supportive measures and treat individual symptoms immediately.

[US Boxed Warning]: Thrombin topical (bovine) can cause fatal severe bleeding or thrombosis. Thrombosis may result from the development of antibodies against bovine thrombin. Bleeding may result from the development of antibodies against factor V. These may cross-react with human factor V and lead to its deficiency. Re-exposure of patients with known or suspected antibodies to bovine thrombin and/or factor V should be avoided. Monitor patients for abnormal coagulation laboratory values, bleeding, or thrombosis.

Evithrom is a product of human plasma; may potentially contain infectious agents, such as viruses and, theoretically the Creutzfeldt-Jacob disease agent, or an unknown infectious agent. Screening of donors, as well as testing and/or inactivation or removal of certain viruses, reduces the risk. Infections thought to be transmitted by this product should be reported to the manufacturer. Recothrom should be used with caution in patients with known hypersensitivity to snake or hamster proteins (manufacturing process uses a genetically modified hamster cell line and snake proteins); the potential for allergic reaction theoretically exists.

Do not use Thrombi-Gel or Thrombi-Pad in the presence of infection; use caution in areas of contamination. Thrombi-Pad is nonabsorbable and should not be used as a replacement for absorbable hemostats; do not leave in the body.

Drug Interactions

Metabolism/Transport Effects None known.

Avoid Concomitant Use There are no known interactions where it is recommended to avoid concomitant use.

Increased Effect/Toxicity There are no known significant interactions involving an increase in effect.

Decreased Effect There are no known significant interactions involving a decrease in effect.

Pregnancy Risk Factor C

Pregnancy Considerations Animal reproduction studies have not been conducted. Reproduction studies conducted with the solvent/detergent used in processing the human-derived product (Evithrom) showed adverse events in animals. Only residual levels of the solvent/detergent would be expected to remain in the finished product.

Breastfeeding Considerations It is not known if thrombin topical is excreted in breast milk. The manufacturer recommends that caution be exercised when administering thrombin topical to breastfeeding women.

Dosage Forms

Pad, topical [preservative free]:
Thrombi-Pad 3x3: ≥200 units

Powder for reconstitution, topical:
Thrombin-JMI: 5000 units, 20,000 units
Thrombin-JMI Epistaxis kit: 5000 units
Thrombin-JMI Pump Spray Kit: 20,000 units
Thrombin-JMI Syringe Spray Kit: 5000 units; 20,000 units

Powder for reconstitution, topical [preservative free]:
Recothrom: 5000 units; 20,000 units
Recothrom Spray Kit: 20,000 units

Solution, topical:
Evithrom: 800-1200 units/mL (2 mL, 5 mL, 20 mL)

Sponge, topical [preservative free]:
Thrombi-Gel10: ≥1000 units (10s)
Thrombi-Gel 40: ≥1000 units (5s)
Thrombi-Gel 100: ≥2000 units (5s)

Thyroid, Desiccated (THYE roid DES i kay tid)

Related Information

Endocrine Disorders and Pregnancy *on page 1781*

Brand Names: US Armour Thyroid; Nature-Throid; NP Thyroid; Westhroid; Westhroid-P [DSC]; WP Thyroid

Pharmacologic Category Thyroid Product

Use Replacement or supplemental therapy in hypothyroidism; pituitary TSH suppressants (thyroid nodules, thyroiditis, multinodular goiter, thyroid cancer)

Local Anesthetic/Vasoconstrictor Precautions No precautions with vasoconstrictor are necessary if patient is well controlled with thyroid preparations

Effects on Dental Treatment No significant effects or complications reported

Effects on Bleeding No information available to require special precautions

Adverse Reactions Adverse reactions are often indicative of excess thyroid replacement and/or hyperthyroidism.

<1%, postmarketing, and/or case reports: Abdominal cramps, alopecia, ataxia, cardiac arrhythmia, chest pain, constipation, diaphoresis, diarrhea, dyspnea, fever, headache, heat intolerance, increased appetite, insomnia, menstrual disease, myalgia, nervousness, palpitations, tachycardia, tremor, tremor of hands, vomiting, weight loss

General Dosage Range Oral:

Children 0-6 months: 15-30 mg/day **or** 4.8-6 mg/kg/day
Children 6-12 months: 30-45 mg/day **or** 3.6-4.8 mg/kg/day
Children 1-5 years: 45-60 mg/day **or** 3-3.6 mg/kg/day
Children 6-12 years: 60-90 mg/day **or** 2.4-3 mg/kg/day
Children >12 years: >90 mg/day **or** 1.2-1.8 mg/kg/day
Adults: Initial: 15-30 mg/day; Maintenance: 60-120 mg/day

Mechanism of Action The primary active compound is T_3 (triiodothyronine), which may be converted from T_4 (thyroxine) and then circulates throughout the body to influence growth and maturation of various tissues; exact mechanism of action is unknown; however, it is believed the thyroid hormone exerts its many metabolic effects through control of DNA transcription and protein synthesis; involved in normal metabolism, growth, and development; promotes gluconeogenesis, increases utilization and mobilization of glycogen stores and stimulates protein synthesis, increases basal metabolic rate

Pharmacodynamics/Kinetics

Onset of Action Liothyronine (T_3): ~3 hours

Half-life Elimination

T_4: Euthyroid: 6 to 7 days; Hyperthyroid: 3 to 4 days; Hypothyroid: 9 to 10 days
T_3: 0.75 days (Brent, 2011)

Time to Peak Serum: T_4: 2 to 4 hours; T_3: 2 to 3 days

Pregnancy Risk Factor A

Pregnancy Considerations Endogenous thyroid hormones minimally cross the placenta; the fetal thyroid becomes active around the end of the first trimester. Liothyronine has not been found to increase the risk of teratogenic or adverse effects following maternal use during pregnancy.

Uncontrolled maternal hypothyroidism may result in adverse neonatal and maternal outcomes. To prevent adverse events, normal maternal thyroid function should be maintained prior to conception and throughout pregnancy. Levothyroxine is considered the treatment of choice for the control of hypothyroidism during pregnancy.

Thyrotropin Alpha (thye roe TROH pin AL fa)

Brand Names: US Thyrogen
Brand Names: Canada Thyrogen
Pharmacologic Category Diagnostic Agent
Use

Diagnostic imaging: Adjunctive diagnostic tool for serum thyroglobulin (Tg) testing (with or without radioiodine imaging) in follow up of patients with well-differentiated thyroid cancer who have previously undergone thyroidectomy.

Limitations of use: Thyrotropin alfa-stimulated Tg levels are generally lower than and do not correlate with Tg levels after thyroid hormone withdrawal; even when thyrotropin alfa-stimulated Tg testing is performed in combination with radioiodine imaging, there is a risk of missing a thyroid cancer diagnosis or of underestimating disease extent; anti-Tg antibodies may confound Tg assay and render Tg levels uninterpretable, in such cases, even with a negative or low-stage thyrotropin alfa radioiodine scan, consider further patient evaluation.

Thyroid tissue remnant ablation: Adjunctive treatment for radioiodine ablation of thyroid tissue remnants after total or near-total thyroidectomy in patients with well-differentiated thyroid cancer without evidence of metastatic disease

Limitations of use: The effect of thyrotropin alfa on long-term thyroid cancer outcomes has not been determined. Due to relatively small clinical experience, it is not possible to conclude if long-term thyroid cancer outcomes would be equivalent after thyrotropin alfa use or withholding thyroid hormone for TSH elevation prior to remnant ablation.

Local Anesthetic/Vasoconstrictor Precautions No information available to require special precautions

Effects on Dental Treatment No significant effects or complications reported

Effects on Bleeding No information available to require special precautions

Adverse Reactions

>10%: Gastrointestinal: Nausea (11%)

1% to 10%:

Central nervous system: Headache (6%), dizziness (2%), fatigue (2%)

Gastrointestinal: Vomiting (2%)

Neuromuscular & skeletal: Weakness (1%)

Frequency not defined: Endocrine & metabolic: Altered thyroid hormone levels (increased)

<1%, postmarketing, and/or case reports: Cerebrovascular accident (with and without physiologic symptoms like unilateral weakness), flu-like symptoms (transient; including arthralgia, chills, fever, malaise, myalgia, shivering), hypersensitivity reaction (including dyspnea, flushing, pruritus, skin rash, urticaria)

General Dosage Range IM: *Adults:* 0.9 mg, followed 24 hours later by a second 0.9 mg dose

Mechanism of Action Thyrotropin alfa, derived from a recombinant DNA source, has the identical amino acid sequence as endogenous human thyroid stimulating hormone (TSH). As a diagnostic tool in conjunction with serum thyroglobulin (Tg) testing, thyrotropin alfa stimulates the secretion of Tg from any remaining thyroid tissues (remnants). Under conditions of successful thyroidectomy and complete ablation, very little serum Tg should be detected under TSH stimulatory conditions; conversely, elevated Tg levels suggest the presence of remnant thyroid tissues. Since the source of TSH is exogenous, stimulation of Tg synthesis can be achieved in euthyroid patients, avoiding the need for thyroid hormone withdrawal.

As an adjunctive agent for radioiodine ablation treatment of thyroid cancer tissue remnants, thyrotropin alfa binds to TSH receptors on these tissues, stimulating the uptake and organification of iodine, including radiolabeled iodine (I^{131}). Cancerous tissue is destroyed via gamma emission from the radioiodine concentrated in these tissues.

Pharmacodynamics/Kinetics

Half-life Elimination 25 ± 10 hours

Time to Peak Median: 10 hours (range: 3-24 hours)

Pregnancy Risk Factor C

Pregnancy Considerations Animal reproduction studies have not been conducted. Effects on the fetus or pregnant woman are unknown.

TiaGABine (tye AG a been)

Brand Names: US Gabitril
Pharmacologic Category Anticonvulsant, Miscellaneous
Use Partial seizures: Adjunctive therapy in adults and children ≥12 years in the treatment of partial seizures

Local Anesthetic/Vasoconstrictor Precautions No information available to require special precautions

Effects on Dental Treatment Key adverse event(s) related to dental treatment: Stomatitis, gingivitis, and mouth ulceration.

Effects on Bleeding No information available to require special precautions

Adverse Reactions

>10%:

Central nervous system: Dizziness (27% to 31%), drowsiness (18% to 21%), nervousness (10% to 14%), lack of concentration (7% to 14%)

Gastrointestinal: Nausea (11%)

Infection: Infection (19%)

Neuromuscular & skeletal: Weakness (18% to 23%), tremor (9% to 21%)

Miscellaneous: Accidental injury (21%)

1% to 10%:

Cardiovascular: Vasodilation (2%), chest pain (≥1%), edema (≥1%), hypertension (≥1%), palpitations (≥1%), peripheral edema (≥1%), syncope (≥1%), tachycardia (≥1%)

Central nervous system: Ataxia (5% to 9%), pain (5% to 7%), depression (1% to 7%), insomnia (5% to 6%), confusion (5%), status epilepticus (5%), abnormal gait (3% to 5%), hostility (2% to 5%), memory impairment (4%), paresthesia (4%), speech disturbance (4%), emotional lability (3%), chills (≥1%), depersonalization (≥1%), dysarthria (≥1%), euphoria (≥1%), hallucination (≥1%), hypertonia (≥1%), hypoesthesia (≥1%), hyporeflexia (≥1%), hypotonia (≥1%), malaise (≥1%), migraine (≥1%), myoclonus (≥1%), paranoia (≥1%), personality disorder (≥1%), stupor (≥1%), twitching (≥1%), vertigo (≥1%), agitation (1%), myasthenia (1%)

Dermatologic: Bruise (6%), skin rash (5%), pruritus (2%), alopecia (≥1%), xeroderma (≥1%)

Gastrointestinal: Diarrhea (7% to 10%), vomiting (7%), abdominal pain (5% to 7%), increased appetite (2%), gingivitis (≥1%), stomatitis (≥1%), oral mucosa ulcer (1%)

Endocrine & metabolic: Weight gain (≥1%), weight loss (≥1%)

Genitourinary: Urinary tract infection (5%), abnormal uterine bleeding (≥1%), dysmenorrhea (≥1%), dysuria (≥1%), urinary incontinence (≥1%), vaginitis (≥1%)

Hematologic & oncologic: Lymphadenopathy (≥1%)

Hypersensitivity: Hypersensitivity reaction (≥1%)

Neuromuscular & skeletal: Myalgia (5%), arthralgia (≥1%), hyperkinesia (≥1%), hypokinesia (≥1%), neck pain (≥1%)

Ophthalmic: Amblyopia (9%), nystagmus (2%), visual disturbance (≥1%)

Otic: Otalgia (≥1%), otitis media (≥1%), tinnitus (≥1%)

Respiratory: Flu-like symptoms (6% to 9%), pharyngitis (7% to 8%), increased cough (4%), bronchitis (≥1%), dyspnea (≥1%), epistaxis (≥1%), pneumonia (≥1%)

Miscellaneous: Language problems (2%), cyst (≥1%), diaphoresis (≥1%)

<1%, postmarketing, and/or case reports: Abnormal dreams, abnormal electroencephalogram, abnormal erythrocytes, abnormal hepatic function tests, abnormal pap smear, abnormal stools, abscess, ageusia, altered sense of smell, amenorrhea, anemia, angina pectoris, apathy, aphthous stomatitis, apnea, arthritis, asthma, benign skin neoplasm, blepharitis, blindness, blurred vision, brain disease, breast hypertrophy, bullous dermatitis, bursitis, cellulitis, cerebral ischemia, cholecystitis, cholelithiasis, CNS neoplasm, coma, contact dermatitis, cutaneous nodule, cystitis, deafness, dehydration, delusions, dental caries, dermal ulcer, dysgeusia, dysphagia, dystonia, ECG abnormality, eczema, eructation, esophagitis, exfoliative dermatitis, eye pain, facial edema, fecal incontinence, fibrocystic breast disease, furunculosis, gastritis, gastrointestinal hemorrhage, gingival hyperplasia, glossitis, goiter, halitosis, hematuria, hemiplegia, hemoptysis, hemorrhage, hepatomegaly, hernia, herpes simplex infection, herpes zoster, hiccups, hirsutism, hyperacusis, hypercholesteremia, hyperglycemia, hyperlipemia, hypermenorrhea, hyperreflexia, hyperventilation, hypoglycemia, hypokalemia, hyponatremia, hypotension, hypothyroidism, impotence, increased libido, increased thirst, keratoconjunctivitis, laryngitis, leg cramps, leukopenia, maculopapular rash, mastalgia, melena, movement disorder, muscle spasm, myocardial infarction, neck stiffness, neoplasm, neuritis, nocturia, oral paresthesia, orthostatic hypotension, osteoarthrosis, otitis externa, pallor, paralysis, pelvic pain, periodontal abscess, peripheral neuritis, peripheral vascular disease, petechia, phlebitis, photophobia, polyuria, psoriasis, psychoneurosis, psychosis, pyelonephritis, rectal hemorrhage, renal failure, salpingitis, seizure (in patients with or without underlying seizure disorder), sepsis, sialorrhea, skin carcinoma, skin discoloration, skin photosensitivity, status epilepticus, Stevens-Johnson syndrome, subcutaneous nodule, suicidal ideation, suicidal tendencies, tendinous contracture, thrombocytopenia, thrombophlebitis, urethritis, urinary retention, urinary urgency, urticaria, vaginal hemorrhage, vesiculobullous dermatitis, visual field defect, voice disorder, withdrawal seizures, xerostomia

General Dosage Range Dosage adjustment recommended in patients on concomitant therapy and with hepatic impairment.

Oral:

Children and Adolescents 12 to 18 years: Initial: 4 mg once daily; Maintenance: 8 to 32 mg/day in 2 to 4 divided doses

Adults: Initial: 4 mg once daily; Maintenance: 32 to 56 mg/day in 2 to 4 divided doses

Mechanism of Action The exact mechanism by which tiagabine exerts antiseizure activity is not definitively known; however, *in vitro* experiments demonstrate that it enhances the activity of gamma aminobutyric acid (GABA). It is thought that the binding of tiagabine to the GABA uptake carrier inhibits the uptake of GABA into presynaptic neurons, allowing an increased amount of GABA to be available to postsynaptic neurons; based on *in vitro* studies, tiagabine does not inhibit the uptake of dopamine, norepinephrine, serotonin, glutamate, or choline

Pharmacodynamics/Kinetics

Half-life Elimination

Children 3 to 10 years: Mean: 5.7 hours (range: 2 to 10 hours); receiving enzyme-inducing AEDs: Mean: 3.2 hours (range: 2 to 7.8 hours)

Adults: 7 to 9 hours; receiving enzyme-inducing AEDs: 2 to 5 hours

Time to Peak Plasma: Fasting state: 45 minutes

Pregnancy Risk Factor C

Pregnancy Considerations Adverse events were observed in animal reproduction studies. Information specific to the use of tiagabine in pregnancy is limited (Leppik 1999; Neppe 2000). Patients exposed to tiagabine during pregnancy are encouraged to enroll themselves into the North American Antiepileptic Drug (NAAED) Pregnancy Registry by calling 1-888-233-2334. Additional information is available at www.aedpregnancyregistry.org.

Ticagrelor (tye KA grel or)

Related Information

Antiplatelet and Anticoagulation Considerations in Dentistry *on page 1764*

Cardiovascular Diseases *on page 1752*

Brand Names: US Brilinta

Brand Names: Canada Brilinta

Pharmacologic Category Antiplatelet Agent; Antiplatelet Agent, Cyclopentyltriazolopyrimidine

Use Acute coronary syndrome: Reduction of the rate of cardiovascular death, myocardial infarction (MI), and stroke in patients with acute coronary syndrome (ACS) or a history of MI. Ticagrelor also reduces the rate of stent thrombosis in patients who have been stented for treatment of ACS.

Local Anesthetic/Vasoconstrictor Precautions No information available to require special precautions

Effects on Dental Treatment No significant effects or complications reported (see Dental Comment)

Aspirin in combination with clopidogrel (Plavix), prasugrel (Effient), or ticagrelor (Brilinta) is the primary prevention strategy against stent thrombosis after placement of drug-eluting metal stents in coronary patients. Premature discontinuation of combination antiplatelet therapy (ie, dual antiplatelet therapy) strongly increases the risk of a catastrophic event of stent thrombosis leading to myocardial infarction and/or death, so says a science advisory issued in January 2007 from the American Heart Association in collaboration with the American Dental Association and other professional healthcare organizations. The advisory stresses a 12-month therapy of dual antiplatelet therapy after placement of a drug-eluting stent in order to prevent thrombosis at the stent site. Any elective surgery should be postponed for 1 year after stent implantation, and if surgery must be performed, consideration should be given to continuing the antiplatelet therapy during the perioperative period in high-risk patients with drug-eluting stents.

This advisory was issued from a science panel made up of representatives from the American Heart Association (AHA), the American College of Cardiology, the Society for Cardiovascular Angiography and Interventions, the American College of Surgeons, the American Dental Association (ADA), and the American College of Physicians (Grines, 2007).

Effects on Bleeding Ticagrelor is an antiplatelet agent similar in actions to clopidogrel. Major bleeding has been reported with a frequency of 12% of individuals (as composite of major fatal or life-threatening and other major bleeding events). Minor bleeding has occurred in ~5% of patients; also reported have been anemia, hematoma, and postprocedural hemorrhage (2%).

Dual antiplatelet therapy: Aspirin irreversibly inhibits platelet aggregation which can prolong bleeding. Upon discontinuation, normal platelet function returns only when new platelets are released (~7-10 days). However, in the case of dental surgery, there is no scientific evidence to support discontinuation of aspirin. The discontinuation of aspirin may place the patient at risk for a thrombotic event or other cardiovascular complication. In particular, aspirin should **not** be discontinued in patients with cardiac stents that have not completed their full course of dual antiplatelet therapy (eg, aspirin and clopidogrel [prasugrel or ticagrelor]); patient-specific situations need to be discussed with cardiologist. When feasible, postponement of dental surgery until the completion of dual antiplatelet therapy should be considered. Any modification of aspirin therapy should be discussed with the prescribing physician.

Adverse Reactions As with all drugs which may affect hemostasis, bleeding is associated with ticagrelor. Hemorrhage may occur at virtually any site. Risk is dependent on multiple variables, including the concurrent use of multiple agents which alter hemostasis and patient susceptibility.

>10%: Respiratory: Dyspnea (14%)

1% to 10%:

Cardiovascular: ECG abnormality (ventricular pause; 2% to 6%), presyncope (≤2%), syncope (≤2%)

Central nervous system: Dizziness (5%), loss of consciousness (≤2%)

Gastrointestinal: Nausea (4%)

Hematologic & oncologic: Major hemorrhage (4%), minor hemorrhage (4%)

Renal: Increased serum creatinine (7%; transient; mechanism undetermined)

Frequency not defined: Endocrine & metabolic: Increased uric acid

<1%, postmarketing, and/or case reports: Angioedema, atrioventricular block, bradycardia, gout, hypersensitivity reaction, skin rash

General Dosage Range Oral: *Adults:* Loading dose: 180 mg; Maintenance: 60 to 90 mg twice daily

Mechanism of Action Reversibly and noncompetitively binds the adenosine diphosphate (ADP) $P2Y_{12}$ receptor on the platelet surface which prevents ADP-mediated activation of the GPIIb/IIIa receptor complex thereby reducing platelet aggregation. Due to the reversible antagonism of the $P2Y_{12}$ receptor, recovery of platelet function is likely to depend on serum concentrations of ticagrelor and its active metabolite.

Pharmacodynamics/Kinetics

Onset of Action Inhibition of platelet aggregation (IPA): 180 mg loading dose: ~41% within 30 minutes (similar to clopidogrel 600 mg at 8 hours); Peak effect: Time to maximal IPA: 180 mg loading dose: IPA ~88% at 2 hours post administration

Duration of Action

IPA: 180 mg loading dose: 87% to 89% maintained from 2 to 8 hours; 24 hours after the last maintenance dose, IPA is 58% (similar to maintenance clopidogrel)

Time after discontinuation when IPA is 30%: ~56 hours; IPA 10%: ~110 hours (Gurbel, 2009). Mean IPA observed with ticagrelor at 3 days post-discontinuation was comparable to that observed with clopidogrel at 5 days post discontinuation.

Half-life Elimination Parent drug: ~7 hours; active metabolite: ~9 hours

Time to Peak

Whole tablets: Parent drug: 1.5 hours (median; range: 1 to 4 hours); Active metabolite (AR-C124910XX): 2.5 hours (median; range: 1.5 to 5 hours)

Crushed tablets: Oral or nasogastric tube administration. Parent drug: ~1 hour (median; range: 1 to 4 hours); Active metabolite (AR-C124910XX): 2 hours (median; range: 1 to 8 hours). Note: Significantly higher concentrations of both ticagrelor and AR-C124910XX may appear at earlier time points (0.5 and 1 hour, respectively) when administered as crushed tablets (Teng 2015).

Pregnancy Risk Factor C

Pregnancy Considerations Adverse events have been observed in animal reproduction studies.

Dental Comment Premature discontinuation of ticagrelor therapy may increase the risk of cardiac events (eg, stent thrombosis with subsequent fatal or nonfatal myocardial infarction). Duration of therapy, in general, is determined by the type of stent placed (bare metal or drug eluting) and whether an acute coronary syndrome event was ongoing at the time of placement. Patient-specific situations need to be discussed with healthcare provider.

Patients taking ticagrelor may have shortness of breath.

If patient is taking aspirin along with ticagrelor, aspirin dose should not exceed 100 mg/day. Patient should also avoid taking any other medicine containing aspirin. The manufacturer implemented REMS components to alert physicians to the risk of using higher doses of aspirin while taking ticagrelor.

Ticarcillin and Clavulanate Potassium

(tye kar SIL in & klav yoo LAN ate poe TASS ee um)

Brand Names: US Timentin [DSC]

Pharmacologic Category Antibiotic, Penicillin

Use

Bone and joint infections: Treatment of bone and joint infections caused by beta-lactamase-producing isolates of *Staphylococcus aureus*.

Endometritis: Treatment of endometritis caused by beta-lactamase-producing isolates of *Prevotella melaninogenicus*, *Enterobacter* species (including *E. cloacae*), *Klebsiella pneumoniae*, *Escherichia coli*, *S. aureus*, or *Staphylococcus epidermidis*.

Lower respiratory tract infections: Treatment of lower respiratory tract infections caused by beta-lactamase-producing isolates of *S. aureus*, *Haemophilus influenzae*, or *Klebsiella* species.

Peritonitis: Treatment of peritonitis caused by beta-lactamase-producing isolates of *E. coli*, *K. pneumonia*, or *Bacteroides fragilis* group.

Septicemia: Treatment of septicemia (including bacteremia) caused by beta-lactamase-producing isolates of *Klebsiella* species, *E. coli*, *S. aureus*, or *Pseudomonas aeruginosa* (or other *Pseudomonas* species).

Skin and skin structure infections: Treatment of skin and skin structure infections caused by beta-lactamase-producing isolates of *S. aureus*, *Klebsiella* species, or *E. coli*.

Urinary tract infections: Treatment of complicated and uncomplicated urinary tract infections caused by beta-lactamase-producing isolates of *E. coli*, *Klebsiella* species, *P. aeruginosa* (and other *Pseudomonas* species), *Citrobacter* species, *Enterobacter cloacae*, *Serratia marcescens*, or *S. aureus*.

Local Anesthetic/Vasoconstrictor Precautions
No information available to require special precautions

Effects on Dental Treatment Key adverse event(s) related to dental treatment: Prolonged use of penicillins may lead to development of oral candidiasis.

Effects on Bleeding May inhibit platelet aggregation (dose related). No information available to require special precautions

Adverse Reactions Frequency not defined.

Cardiovascular: Local thrombophlebitis (with IV injection)

Central nervous system: Confusion, drowsiness, headache, seizure

Dermatologic: Skin rash

Endocrine & metabolic: Electrolyte disturbance, hypernatremia, hypokalemia

Gastrointestinal: *Clostridium difficile* diarrhea, diarrhea, nausea

Genitourinary: Proteinuria (false positive)

Hematologic & oncologic: Bleeding complication, eosinophilia, hemolytic anemia, positive direct Coombs' test (false positive)

Hepatic: Hepatotoxicity, increased serum ALT, increased serum AST, jaundice

Immunologic: Jarisch Herxheimer reaction

Infection: Superinfection (fungal or bacterial)

Renal: Interstitial nephritis (acute)

Miscellaneous: Anaphylaxis

Postmarketing and/or case reports: Abdominal pain, altered sense of smell, arthralgia, chest discomfort, chills, decreased hematocrit, decreased hemoglobin, decreased serum potassium, dizziness, dysgeusia, erythema multiforme, fever, flatulence, headache, hemorrhagic cystitis, hypersensitivity reaction, hypouricemia, increased blood urea nitrogen, increased lactate dehydrogenase, increased serum alkaline phosphatase, increased serum bilirubin, increased serum creatinine, injection site reaction (burning, induration, pain, swelling), leukopenia, myalgia, myclonus, neutropenia, prolonged prothrombin time, pruritus, pseudomembranous colitis (during or after antibacterial treatment), Stevens-Johnson syndrome, stomatitis, thrombocytopenia, toxic epidermal necrolysis, urticaria, vomiting

General Dosage Range Dosage adjustment recommended in patients with hepatic or renal impairment

IV: *Infants ≥3 months, Children, Adolescents, and Adults:*

<60 kg: 200-300 mg ticarcillin/kg/day in divided doses every 4-6 hours (maximum: 18 g daily)

≥60 kg: 3.1 g every 4-6 hours

Mechanism of Action Inhibits bacterial cell wall synthesis by binding to one or more of the penicillin-binding proteins (PBPs), which in turn inhibits the final transpeptidation step of peptidoglycan synthesis in bacterial cell walls, thus inhibiting cell wall biosynthesis. Bacteria eventually lyse due to ongoing activity of cell wall autolytic enzymes (autolysins and murein hydrolases) while cell wall assembly is arrested.

Pharmacodynamics/Kinetics

Half-life Elimination

Neonates: Ticarcillin: 4.4 hours; Clavulanic acid: 1.9 hours

Children (1 month to 9.3 years): Ticarcillin: 66 minutes; Clavulanic acid: 54 minutes

Adults: Ticarcillin: 66 to 72 minutes; 13 hours (in patients with renal failure); Clavulanic acid: 66 to 90 minutes; clavulanic acid does not affect the clearance of ticarcillin

Time to Peak Immediately following completion of 30-minute infusion

Pregnancy Risk Factor B

Pregnancy Considerations Adverse events were not observed in animal reproduction studies. Ticarcillin and clavulanate cross the placenta (Maberry, 1992). Maternal use of penicillins has generally not resulted in an increased risk of adverse fetal effects (Crider, 2009; Santos, 2011). Ticarcillin/clavulanate is approved for the treatment of postpartum gynecologic infections, including endometritis, caused by susceptible organisms.

Product Availability Not available in the US

Ticlopidine (tye KLOE pi deen)

Related Information

Antiplatelet and Anticoagulation Considerations in Dentistry *on page 1764*

Brand Names: Canada Apo-Ticlopidine; Dom-Ticlopidine; Gen-Ticlopidine; Mylan-Ticlopidine; Novo-Ticlopidine; Nu-Ticlopidine; PMS-Ticlopidine; Sandoz-Ticlopidine; Teva-Ticlopidine

Pharmacologic Category Antiplatelet Agent; Antiplatelet Agent, Thienopyridine

Use Platelet aggregation inhibitor that reduces the risk of thrombotic stroke in patients who have had a stroke or stroke precursors (**Note:** Due to its association with life-threatening hematologic disorders, ticlopidine should be reserved for patients who are intolerant to aspirin, or who have failed aspirin therapy); adjunctive therapy (with aspirin) following successful coronary stent implantation to reduce the incidence of subacute stent thrombosis.

Local Anesthetic/Vasoconstrictor Precautions
No information available to require special precautions

Effects on Dental Treatment No significant effects or complications reported; if a patient is to undergo elective surgery and an antiplatelet effect is not desired, ticlopidine should be discontinued at least 7 days prior to surgery.

Effects on Bleeding Ticlopidine blocks platelet aggregation and may prolong bleeding time. Inhibition is irreversible; on discontinuation, normal platelet function returns only when new platelets are released from the bone marrow. Dental practitioners should note that recommendations differ between general surgery (eg, appendectomy, hip replacement) and dental surgery. Prior to elective general surgery, it may be temporarily discontinued (usually for 5-10 days) to restore platelet function. However, routine interruption of therapy for noninvasive dental procedures is NOT warranted and there is no scientific evidence to warrant the discontinuance of ticlopidine prior to dental surgery. In particular, ticlopidine should NOT be discontinued in patients with cardiac stents that have not completed their full course of dual antiplatelet therapy (aspirin, clopidogrel/ticlopidine); patient specific situations need to be discussed with cardiologist. When feasible, postponement of dental surgery until the completion of dual antiplatelet therapy should be considered.

Adverse Reactions As with all drugs which may affect hemostasis, bleeding is associated with ticlopidine. Hemorrhage may occur at virtually any site. Risk is dependent on multiple variables, including the use of multiple agents which alter hemostasis and patient susceptibility.

>10%:

Endocrine & metabolic: Hyperlipidemia (8% to 10%; within 1 month of therapy), increased serum triglycerides

Gastrointestinal: Diarrhea (13%; may be chronic)

1% to 10%:

Central nervous system: Dizziness (1%)

Dermatologic: Skin rash (5%), pruritus (1%)

Gastrointestinal: Dyspepsia (7%), nausea (7%), gastrointestinal pain (4%), flatulence (2%), vomiting (2%), anorexia (1%)

Hematologic & oncologic: Neutropenia (2%), purpura (2%)

Hepatic: Increased serum alkaline phosphatase (>2 x upper limit of normal: 8%), abnormal hepatic function tests (1%)

<1%, postmarketing, and/or case reports: Agranulocytosis, anaphylaxis, angioedema, aplastic anemia, arthropathy, bone marrow depression, bronchiolitis obliterans organizing pneumonia, conjunctival hemorrhage, ecchymosis, eosinophilia, epistaxis, erythema multiforme, erythema nodosum, exfoliative dermatitis, gastrointestinal hemorrhage, headache, hematuria, hemolytic anemia, hepatic necrosis, hepatitis, hypermenorrhea, hypersensitivity pneumonitis, hyponatremia, increased serum bilirubin, intracranial hemorrhage, immune thrombocytopenia, increased serum creatinine, jaundice, maculopapular rash, myositis, nephrotic syndrome, pain, pancytopenia, peptic ulcer, peripheral neuropathy, positive ANA titer, renal failure, sepsis, serum sickness, Stevens-Johnson syndrome, systemic lupus erythematosus, thrombocythemia, thrombotic thrombocytopenic purpura (TTP), tinnitus, urticaria, vasculitis, weakness

General Dosage Range Oral: *Adults:* 250 mg twice daily

Mechanism of Action Ticlopidine requires *in vivo* biotransformation to an unidentified active metabolite. This active metabolite irreversibly blocks the P2Y12 component of ADP receptors, which prevents activation of the GPIIb/IIIa receptor complex, thereby reducing platelet aggregation. Platelets blocked by ticlopidine are affected for the remainder of their lifespan.

Pharmacodynamics/Kinetics

Onset of Action ~6 hours; Peak effect: 3-5 days; serum levels do not correlate with clinical antiplatelet activity

Half-life Elimination 13 hours

Time to Peak ~2 hours

Pregnancy Risk Factor B

Pregnancy Considerations Teratogenic effects have not been observed in animal reproduction studies; a case report has demonstrated the safe use of ticlopidine in pregnant women (Ueno, 2001).

Product Availability Ticlopidine is no longer available in the US.

Tigecycline (tye ge SYE kleen)

Brand Names: US Tygacil

Brand Names: Canada Tygacil

Pharmacologic Category Antibiotic, Glycylcycline

Use

Pneumonia, community-acquired bacterial:

US labeling: Treatment of community-acquired bacterial pneumonia in patients 18 years and older caused by *Streptococcus pneumoniae* (penicillin-susceptible isolates), including cases with concurrent bacteremia, *Haemophilus influenzae*, and *Legionella pneumophila*.

Canadian labeling: Treatment of mild or moderate community-acquired pneumonia in patients 18 years and older caused by *S. pneumoniae* (penicillin-susceptible isolates), *H. influenzae*, *Mycoplasma pneumoniae*, and *Chlamydia pneumoniae*.

Intra-abdominal infections, complicated: Treatment of complicated intra-abdominal infections in patients 18 years and older caused by *Citrobacter freundii*, *Enterobacter cloacae*, *Escherichia coli*, *Klebsiella oxytoca*, *Klebsiella pneumoniae*, *Enterococcus faecalis* (vancomycin-susceptible isolates), *Staphylococcus aureus* (methicillin-susceptible and methicillin-resistant isolates [US labeling] or methicillin-susceptible isolates [Canadian labeling]), *Streptococcus anginosus* group (includes *S. anginosus*, *Streptococcus intermedius*, and *Streptococcus constellatus*), *Bacteroides fragilis*, *Bacteroides thetaiotaomicron*, *Bacteroides uniformis*, *Bacteroides vulgatus*, *Clostridium perfringens*, and *Peptostreptococcus micros*.

Skin and skin structure infections, complicated: Treatment of complicated skin and skin structure infections in patients 18 years and older caused by *E. coli*, *E. faecalis* (vancomycin-susceptible isolates), *S. aureus* (methicillin-susceptible and methicillin-resistant isolates), *Streptococcus agalactiae*, *S. anginosus* group (includes *S. anginosus*, *S. intermedius*, and *S. constellatus*) [US labeling] or *S. anginosus* [Canadian labeling], *Streptococcus pyogenes*, *E. cloacae*, *K. pneumoniae*, and *B. fragilis*.

Local Anesthetic/Vasoconstrictor Precautions No information available to require special precautions

Effects on Dental Treatment Key adverse events(s) related to dental treatment: Tigecycline is structurally similar to tetracycline. Therefore, tigecycline is not recommended for use in pregnancy or in children ≤8 years of age. Permanent discoloration of the teeth may occur if used during tooth development.

Effects on Bleeding No information available to require special precautions

Adverse Reactions

>10%: Gastrointestinal: Nausea (24% to 35%), vomiting (16% to 20%), diarrhea (12%)

1% to 10%:

Cardiovascular: Localized phlebitis (≤3%), septic shock (<2%), thrombophlebitis (<2%)

Central nervous system: Headache (6%), dizziness (3%), chills (<2%)

Dermatologic: Skin rash (3%), pruritus (<2%)

Endocrine & metabolic: Increased amylase (3%), hyponatremia (2%), hypocalcemia (<2%), hypoglycemia (<2%)
Gastrointestinal: Abdominal pain (6%), dyspepsia (2%), abnormal stools (<2%), anorexia (<2%), dysgeusia (<2%)
Genitourinary: Leukorrhea (<2%), vaginitis (<2%), vulvovaginal candidiasis (<2%)
Hematologic & oncologic: Anemia (5%), hypoproteinemia (5%), eosinophilia (<2%), increased INR (<2%), prolonged partial thromboplastin time (<2%), prolonged prothrombin time (<2%), thrombocytopenia (<2%)
Hepatic: Increased serum ALT (5%), increased serum AST (4%), increased serum alkaline phosphatase (3%), hyperbilirubinemia (2%), jaundice (<2%)
Hypersensitivity: Hypersensitivity reaction (<2%)
Infection: Infection (7%), abscess (2%)
Local: Inflammation at injection site (<2%), injection site reaction (<2%), pain at injection site (<2%), swelling at injection site (<2%)
Neuromuscular & skeletal: Weakness (3%)
Renal: Increased blood urea nitrogen (3%), increased serum creatinine (<2%)
Respiratory: Pneumonia (2%)
Miscellaneous: Abnormal healing (3%)

<1%, postmarketing, and/or case reports: Acute pancreatitis, allergic skin reaction, anaphylactoid reaction, anaphylaxis, *Clostridium difficile* associated diarrhea, hepatic dysfunction, hepatic failure, hypersensitivity reaction, hypoglycemia signs and symptoms (diabetic and nondiabetic patients), intrahepatic cholestasis, Stevens-Johnson syndrome

General Dosage Range Dosage adjustment recommended in patients with hepatic impairment

IV: *Adults:* Initial: 100 mg as a single dose; Maintenance: 50 mg every 12 hours

Mechanism of Action A glycylcycline antibiotic that binds to the 30S ribosomal subunit of susceptible bacteria, thereby, inhibiting protein synthesis. Generally considered bacteriostatic; however, bactericidal activity has been demonstrated against isolates of *S. pneumoniae* and *L. pneumophila*. Tigecycline is a derivative of minocycline (9-t-butylglycylamido minocycline), and while not classified as a tetracycline, it may share some class-associated adverse effects. Tigecycline has demonstrated activity against a variety of gram-positive and -negative bacterial pathogens including methicillin-resistant staphylococci.

Pharmacodynamics/Kinetics

Half-life Elimination Single dose: 27 hours; following multiple doses: 42 hours; increased by 23% in moderate hepatic impairment and 43% in severe hepatic impairment

Pregnancy Risk Factor D

Pregnancy Considerations Because adverse effects were observed in animals and because of the potential for permanent tooth discoloration, tigecycline is classified pregnancy category D. Tigecycline frequently causes nausea and vomiting and, therefore, may not be ideal for use in a patient with pregnancy-related nausea.

Timolol (Ophthalmic) (TIM oh lol)

Brand Names: US Betimol; Istalol; Timoptic; Timoptic Ocudose; Timoptic-XE

Brand Names: Canada Apo-Timop; Dom-Timolol; Odan-Timol; PMS-Timolol; Sandoz-Timolol; Timolol Maleate-EX; Timoptic; Timoptic-XE

Pharmacologic Category Beta-Blocker, Nonselective; Ophthalmic Agent, Antiglaucoma

Use Elevated intraocular pressure: Treatment of elevated intraocular pressure (IOP) in patients with ocular hypertension or open-angle glaucoma

Local Anesthetic/Vasoconstrictor Precautions Epinephrine has interacted with nonselective beta-blockers, such as propranolol, to result in initial hypertensive episode followed by bradycardia. Timolol is also a nonselective beta-blocker. The significance of a potential systemic interaction with epinephrine is unknown. However, it is suggested that cautionary procedures be used, particularly if vasoconstrictor is used immediately following a dose of timolol taken by the patient.

Effects on Dental Treatment Key adverse event(s) related to dental treatment: Xerostomia (normal salivary flow resumes upon discontinuation).

Timolol is a nonselective beta-blocker and may enhance the pressor response to epinephrine, resulting in hypertension and bradycardia.

Effects on Bleeding No information available to require special precautions

Adverse Reactions

>10%: Ophthalmic: Burning sensation of eyes, stinging of eyes

Frequency not defined:
Cardiovascular: Angina pectoris, bradycardia, cardiac arrhythmia, cardiac failure, cerebral ischemia, cerebrovascular accident, claudication, cold extremities, edema, heart block, hypertension, hypotension, palpitations, Raynaud's phenomenon
Central nervous system: Amnesia, anxiety, confusion, depression, disorientation, dizziness, drowsiness, exacerbation of myasthenia gravis, hallucination, headache, insomnia, nervousness, nightmares, paresthesia
Dermatologic: Alopecia, exacerbation of psoriasis, pemphigoid-like lesion, psoriasiform eruption, skin rash, urticaria
Endocrine & metabolic: Hypoglycemia (masked), decreased libido
Gastrointestinal: Anorexia, diarrhea, dyspepsia, nausea, xerostomia
Genitourinary: Impotence, Peyronie's disease, retroperitoneal fibrosis
Hypersensitivity: Angioedema, hypersensitivity reaction
Neuromuscular & skeletal: Systemic lupus erythematosus
Ophthalmic: Blepharitis, blepharoptosis, blurred vision, cataract, choroidal detachment (following filtration surgery), conjunctival injection, conjunctivitis, cystoid macular edema, decreased corneal sensitivity, decreased visual acuity, diplopia, eye discharge, eye pain, eye pruritus, foreign body sensation of eye, hyperemia, keratitis, lacrimation, visual disturbance (including refractive changes), xerophthalmia
Otic: Tinnitus
Respiratory: Bronchospasm, cough, dyspnea, nasal congestion, pulmonary edema, respiratory failure

General Dosage Range Ophthalmic:

Gel-forming solution: *Adults:* Instill 1 drop (0.25% or 0.5%) once daily

Solution: *Children 2 years, Adolescents, and Adults:* Initial: Instill 1 drop (0.25%) twice daily; Maintenance: Instill 1 drop (0.25% or 0.5%) 1 to 2 times daily

Mechanism of Action Blocks both $beta_1$- and $beta_2$-adrenergic receptors and reduces intraocular pressure by reducing aqueous humor production or possibly increases the outflow of aqueous humor

Pharmacodynamics/Kinetics

Onset of Action Solution: Intraocular pressure reduction: 30 minutes; Peak effect: 1 to 2 hours

Duration of Action Solution: 24 hours

Half-life Elimination 4 hours

Pregnancy Risk Factor C

Pregnancy Considerations Adverse events were observed in some animal reproduction studies. Decreased fetal heart rate has been observed following maternal use of ophthalmic timolol during pregnancy (Wagenvoort 1998). Timolol is absorbed systemically following ophthalmic use; additional adverse effects observed with systemic administration may occur. If ophthalmic agents are needed to treat glaucoma in pregnancy, the minimum effective dose should be used in combination with punctal occlusion to decrease exposure to the fetus (Johnson 2001; Salim 2014; Wagenvoort 1998).

Tinidazole (tye NI da zole)

Brand Names: US Tindamax

Pharmacologic Category Amebicide; Antibiotic, Miscellaneous; Antiprotozoal, Nitroimidazole

Use

Amebiasis: Treatment of intestinal amebiasis and amebic liver abscess caused by *Entamoeba histolytica* in adults and pediatric patients older than 3 years.

Limitations of use: Not indicated for the treatment of asymptomatic cyst passage.

Bacterial vaginosis: Treatment of bacterial vaginosis (formerly referred to as *Haemophilus* vaginitis, *Gardnerella vaginitis*, nonspecific vaginitis, or anaerobic vaginosis) in nonpregnant women.

Giardiasis: Treatment of giardiasis caused by *Giardiasis duodenalis* (also termed *Giardiasis lamblia*) in adults and pediatric patients older than 3 years.

Trichomoniasis: Treatment of trichomoniasis caused by *T. vaginalis*; treat partners of infected patients simultaneously to prevent reinfection.

Local Anesthetic/Vasoconstrictor Precautions No information available to require special precautions

Effects on Dental Treatment Key adverse event(s) related to dental treatment: Xerostomia and changes in salivation (normal salivary flow resumes upon discontinuation), metallic/bitter taste, oral candidiasis, tongue discoloration, stomatitis, furry tongue. See Dental Comment.

Effects on Bleeding No information available to require special precautions

Adverse Reactions

1% to 10%:

Central nervous system: Fatigue (≤2%), malaise (≤2%), dizziness (≤1%), headache (≤1%)

Dermatologic: Body odor (vaginal: >2%)

Endocrine & metabolic: Hypermenorrhea (>2%)

Gastrointestinal: Dysgeusia (bitter taste, metallic taste: 4% to 6%), nausea (3% to 5%), anorexia (2% to 3%), decreased appetite (>2%), flatulence (>2%), dyspepsia (≤2%), abdominal cramps (≤2%), epigastric distress (≤2%), vomiting (1% to 2%), constipation (≤1%)

Genitourinary: Vulvovaginal candidiasis (5%), dysuria (>2%), pelvic pain (>2%), urine abnormality (>2%), vulvovaginal disease (discomfort) (>2%)

Neuromuscular & skeletal: Weakness (1% to 2%)

Renal: Urinary tract infection (>2%)

Respiratory: Upper respiratory tract infection (>2%)

Frequency not defined:

Cardiovascular: Flushing, palpitations

Central nervous system: Ataxia, burning sensation, drowsiness, insomnia, peripheral neuropathy (transient; includes numbness and paresthesia), seizure, vertigo

Dermatologic: Diaphoresis, pruritus, skin rash, urticaria

Endocrine & metabolic: Increased thirst

Gastrointestinal: Abdominal pain, diarrhea, oral candidiasis, salivation, stomatitis, tongue discoloration, xerostomia

Genitourinary: Dark urine, vaginal discharge

Hematologic & oncologic: Leukopenia (transient), neutropenia (transient)

Hepatic: Increased serum transaminases

Hypersensitivity: Angioedema

Infection: Candidiasis (overgrowth)

Neuromuscular & skeletal: Arthralgia, arthritis, myalgia

Miscellaneous: Fever

<1%, postmarketing, and/or case reports: Bronchospasm, coma, confusion, depression, dyspnea, erythema multiforme, hairy tongue, hypersensitivity reaction (acute, severe), pharyngitis, Stevens-Johnson syndrome, thrombocytopenia (reversible)

General Dosage Range Oral:

Children >3 years and Adolescents: 50 mg/kg/day (maximum: 2 g/day)

Adults: 1 to 2 g/day

Mechanism of Action After diffusing into the organism, it is proposed that tinidazole causes cytotoxicity by damaging DNA and preventing further DNA synthesis.

Pharmacodynamics/Kinetics

Half-life Elimination 13.2 hours

Time to Peak 1.6 hours (fasting, delayed ~2 hours when given with food)

Pregnancy Risk Factor C

Pregnancy Considerations The manufacturer contraindicates use of tinidazole during the first trimester of pregnancy. Adverse events have been observed in some animal reproduction studies. Tinidazole crosses the human placenta and enters the fetal circulation. The safety of tinidazole for the treatment of bacterial vaginosis or trichomoniasis in pregnant women has not been well evaluated. Other agents are preferred for use during pregnancy (CDC [Workowski 2015]).

Dental Comment Although this drug is a member of the metronidazole family, there is no specific dental indication for its use. Just as with metronidazole, alcohol in any form is contraindicated while the patient is on this medication because of the danger of a disulfiram-type reaction.

Tinzaparin (tin ZA pa rin)

Related Information

Cardiovascular Diseases *on page 1752*

Brand Names: Canada Innohep

Pharmacologic Category Anticoagulant; Anticoagulant, Low Molecular Weight Heparin

Use Note: Not available in the US

Anticoagulation in extracorporeal circuit during hemodialysis: Prevention of clotting in indwelling intravenous lines and extracorporeal circuit during hemodialysis (in patients without high bleeding risk)

Deep vein thrombosis/pulmonary embolus (treatment): Treatment of deep vein thrombosis (DVT) and/or pulmonary embolism (PE)

Postoperative thromboprophylaxis: Prevention of venous thromboembolism (VTE) following orthopedic surgery or following general surgery in patients at high risk of VTE; prevention of clotting in indwelling intravenous lines and extracorporeal circuit during hemodialysis (in patients without high bleeding risk)

Local Anesthetic/Vasoconstrictor Precautions No information available to require special precautions

Effects on Dental Treatment Key adverse event(s) related to dental treatment: Bleeding is the major adverse effect of tinzaparin. See Effects on Bleeding.

Effects on Bleeding As with all anticoagulants, bleeding is the major adverse effect of tinzaparin. Hemorrhage may occur at virtually any site; risk is dependent on multiple variables including the intensity of anticoagulation and patient susceptibility. At the recommended doses, LMWHS do not significantly influence platelet aggregation or affect global clotting time (ie, PT or aPTT). Medical consult is suggested.

Adverse Reactions As with all anticoagulants, bleeding is the major adverse effect of tinzaparin. Hemorrhage may occur at virtually any site. Risk is dependent on multiple variables.

>10%:

Hepatic: Increased serum ALT (≤13%)

Local: Hematoma at injection site

1% to 10%:

Cardiovascular: Chest pain (2%), angina pectoris (≥1%), cardiac arrhythmia (≥1%), coronary thrombosis (≥1%), myocardial infarction (≥1%), thromboembolism (≥1%)

Central nervous system: Headache (2%), pain (2%)

Dermatologic: Bullous rash (≥1%), erythematous rash (≥1%), maculopapular rash (≥1%), skin necrosis (≥1%)

Endrocrine & metabolic: Dependent edema (≥1%)

Gastrointestinal: Nausea (2%), abdominal pain (1%), constipation (1%), diarrhea (1%), vomiting (1%)

Genitourinary: Urinary tract infection (4%)

Hematologic & oncologic: Granulocytopenia (≥1%), hemorrhage (≥1%, including anorectal bleeding, gastrointestinal hemorrhage, hemarthrosis, hematemesis, hematuria, hemopericardium, injection site bleeding, melena, purpura, intra-abdominal bleeding, vaginal bleeding, wound hemorrhage; major: ≤3%, including intracranial, retroperitoneal, or bleeding into a major prosthetic joint), neoplasm (≥1%), thrombocytopenia (≥1%)

Hepatic: Increased serum AST (9%)

Hypersensitivity: Hypersensitivity reaction (≥1%)

Local: Cellulitis at injection site (≥1%)

Neuromuscular & skeletal: Back pain (2%)

Respiratory: Epistaxis (2%), dyspnea (1%)

Miscellaneous: Fever (2%)

<1%, postmarketing, and/or case reports: Agranulocytosis, angioedema, anaphylactoid reaction, epidural hematoma (spinal), hemophthalmos, hemoptysis, hyperkalemia, increased gamma-glutamyl transferase, increased, lactate dehydrogenase, increased serum lipase, metabolic acidosis, osteoporosis, priapism, pruritus, skin rash, Stevens-Johnson syndrome, suppression of aldosterone synthesis, thrombocythemia, toxic epidermal necrolysis, urticaria

General Dosage Range Dosage adjustment recommended in renal impairment and extended (>4 hours) hemodialysis sessions.

IV or added to hemodialysis circuit: *Adults:* 2,250 to 4,500 anti-Xa units

SubQ: *Adults:* 50 anti-Xa units/kg or 3,500 anti-Xa units/kg preoperatively; 50 to 3,500 anti-Xa units/kg once daily

Mechanism of Action Tinzaparin is a low molecular weight heparin (average molecular weight ranges between 5,500 and 7,500 daltons, distributed as <2,000 daltons [<10%], 2,000 to 8,000 daltons [60% to 72%], and >8,000 daltons [22% to 36%]) that binds antithrombin III, enhancing the inhibition of several clotting factors, particularly factor Xa. Tinzaparin anti-Xa activity (70 to 120 units/mg) is greater than anti-IIa activity (~55 units/mg) and it has a higher ratio of antifactor Xa to antifactor IIa activity compared to unfractionated heparin. Low molecular weight heparins have a small effect on the activated partial thromboplastin time.

Pharmacodynamics/Kinetics

Duration of Action Detectable anti-Xa activity persists for 24 hours

Half-life Elimination 82 minutes; prolonged in renal impairment

Time to Peak 4 to 6 hours

Pregnancy Considerations

Use is contraindicated in conditions involving increased risks of hemorrhage, including women with imminent abortion.

Tinzaparin does not cross the human placenta; increased risks of fetal bleeding or teratogenic effects have not been reported (Bates 2012). Low molecular weight heparin (LMWH) is recommended over unfractionated heparin for the treatment of acute venous thromboembolism (VTE) in pregnant women. LMWH is also recommended over unfractionated heparin for VTE prophylaxis in pregnant women with certain risk factors. LMWH should be discontinued prior to induction of labor or a planned cesarean delivery. For women undergoing cesarean section and who have additional risk factors for developing VTE, the prophylactic use of LMWH may be considered (Bates 2012). When choosing therapy, fetal outcomes (ie, pregnancy loss, malformations), maternal outcomes (ie, VTE, hemorrhage), burden of therapy, and maternal preference should be considered (Bates 2012).

Multiple-dose vials contain benzyl alcohol (avoid use in pregnant women due to association with gasping syndrome in premature infants); use of preservative-free formulation is recommended.

Tioconazole (tye oh KONE a zole)

Brand Names: US Vagistat-1 [OTC]

Pharmacologic Category Antifungal Agent, Imidazole Derivative; Antifungal Agent, Vaginal

Use Candidiasis, vulvovaginal: Local treatment of vulvovaginal candidiasis

Local Anesthetic/Vasoconstrictor Precautions No information available to require special precautions

Effects on Dental Treatment No significant effects or complications reported

Effects on Bleeding No information available to require special precautions

Adverse Reactions

Frequency not defined.

Central nervous system: Headache

Gastrointestinal: Abdominal pain

Dermatologic: Burning sensation of skin, exfoliation of skin

Genitourinary: Dyspareunia, dysuria, nocturia, vaginal discharge, vaginal pain, vaginitis, vulvar swelling, vulvovaginal irritation, vulvovaginal pruritus

General Dosage Range Intravaginal: *Children ≥12 years, Adolescents, and Adults:* Insert 1 applicatorful in vagina, as a single dose at bedtime

Mechanism of Action A 1-substituted imidazole derivative with a broad antifungal spectrum against a wide variety of dermatophytes and yeasts, including *Trichophyton mentagrophytes*, *T. rubrum*, *T. erinacei*, *T. tonsurans*, *Microsporum canis*, *Microsporum gypseum*, and *Candida albicans*. Both agents appear to be similarly effective against *Epidermophyton floccosum*.

Pharmacodynamics/Kinetics

Onset of Action Onset of action: Some improvement: Within 24 hours; Complete relief: Within 7 days

Pregnancy Considerations Following vaginal administration, small amounts of imidazoles are absorbed systemically. Single dose, topical azole regimens are not recommended for the treatment of vulvovaginal candidiasis; only topical azole products with 7-day regimens are recommended in pregnant women with vulvovaginal candidiasis. This product may weaken latex condoms and diaphragms (CDC [Workowski 2015]).

Tiopronin (tye oh PROE nin)

Brand Names: US Thiola

Pharmacologic Category Urinary Tract Product

Use

Prevention of kidney stone (cystine) formation in patients with severe homozygous cystinuria who have urinary cystine >500 mg/day who are resistant to treatment with high fluid intake, alkali and diet modification, or who have had adverse reactions to penicillamine.

Note: Based on the American Urologic Association (AUA) guidelines for the medical management of kidney stones (http://www.auanet.org/common/pdf/education/clinical-guidance/Medical-Management-of-Kidney-Stones.pdf), tiopronin is recommended as the agent of choice for the prevention of recurrent cystine stones in patients that are unresponsive to increased fluid intake, restriction of sodium and protein intake, and urinary alkalinization or who have large recurrent stone burdens (AUA [Pearle, 2014]; Pak 1986).

Local Anesthetic/Vasoconstrictor Precautions No information available to require special precautions

Effects on Dental Treatment No significant effects or complications reported

Effects on Bleeding No information available to require special precautions

Adverse Reactions Frequency not defined.

Central nervous system: Anosmia, chills, fatigue, myasthenia gravis

Dermatologic: Fragile skin, pemphigus, pruritus, skin rash, urticaria, warts, wrinkling of skin

Gastrointestinal: Abdominal pain, ageusia, anorexia, bloating, diarrhea, flatulence, nausea, oral mucosa ulcer, vomiting

Genitourinary: Goodpasture's syndrome, hematuria, nephrotic syndrome, proteinuria

Hematologic & oncologic: Anemia, bruise, eosinophilia, hemorrhage, leukopenia, lymphadenopathy, positive ANA titer, thrombocytopenia

Hepatic: Abnormal hepatic function tests, jaundice

Hypersensitivity: Hypersensitivity reaction

Neuromuscular & skeletal: Arthralgia, connective tissue disease (elastosis perforans serpiginosa), lupus-like syndrome, myalgia, weakness

Respiratory: Bronchiolitis, dyspnea, hemoptysis, laryngeal edema, pharyngitis, pulmonary infiltrates, respiratory distress

Miscellaneous: Fever

General Dosage Range Oral:

Children ≥9 years: Initial: 15 mg/kg/day in 3 divided doses

Adults: Initial: 800 mg/day in 3 divided doses; average dose: 1000 mg/day

Mechanism of Action As an active reducing agent, tiopronin undergoes thiol-disulfide exchange with cystine to form tiopronin-cystine disulfide, which is more water soluble than cystine. As a result, the amount of sparingly soluble cystine in the urine is decreased and the formation of cystine calculi is reduced.

Pregnancy Risk Factor C

Pregnancy Considerations Teratogenic effects, including skeletal defects and cleft palates, have been observed following penicillamine exposure in animal reproduction studies. Birth defects, including congenital cutix laxa and associated defects, have been reported in infants following penicillamine exposure during pregnancy. Similar effects may be expected with tiopronin; however, animal studies have not shown these same findings. Use is contraindicated during pregnancy; use only if the possible benefits to the mother outweigh the potential risks to the fetus.

Tiotropium (ty oh TRO pee um)

Related Information

Dentin Hypersensitivity, Acid Erosion, High Caries Index, Management of Alveolar Osteitis, and Xerostomia *on page 1857*

Respiratory Diseases *on page 1777*

Brand Names: US Spiriva HandiHaler; Spiriva Respimat

Brand Names: Canada Spiriva; Spiriva Respimat

Pharmacologic Category Anticholinergic Agent; Anticholinergic Agent, Long-Acting

Use

Asthma (Spiriva Respimat only): Maintenance treatment of asthma in patients ≥6 years.

Chronic obstructive pulmonary disease: Maintenance treatment of bronchospasm associated with chronic obstructive pulmonary disease (COPD), including chronic bronchitis and emphysema; reduction of COPD exacerbations.

Limitations of use: Not indicated for the relief of acute bronchospasm.

Local Anesthetic/Vasoconstrictor Precautions No information available to require special precautions

Effects on Dental Treatment Key adverse event(s) related to dental treatment: Xerostomia (normal salivary flow resumes upon discontinuation) and ulcerative stomatitis.

Effects on Bleeding No information available to require special precautions

Adverse Reactions Non-postmarketing incidences listed are for powder for inhalation unless otherwise specified.

>10%:

Gastrointestinal: Xerostomia (powder and solution: 4% to 16%)

Respiratory: Upper respiratory tract infection (41% to 43%), pharyngitis (powder and solution: 7% to 16%), sinusitis (powder and solution: 3% to 11%)

1% to 10%:

Cardiovascular: Chest pain (powder and solution: ≤7%), edema (dependent, 3% to 5%), angina pectoris (1% to 3%; includes exacerbation of angina pectoris), palpitations (powder and solution: ≤3%), hypertension (solution: 1% to 2%)

Central nervous system: Headache (powder and solution: 4% to 6%), depression (≤4%), insomnia (powder and solution: ≤4%), paresthesia (1% to 3%), dizziness (powder and solution: ≤3%), voice disorder (powder and solution: ≤3%)

Dermatologic: Skin rash (powder and solution: 1% to 4%), pruritus (powder and solution: ≤3%)

Endocrine & metabolic: Hypercholesterolemia (1% to 3%), hyperglycemia (1% to 3%)

Gastrointestinal: Abdominal pain (5% to 6%), dyspepsia (1% to 6%), constipation (powder and solution: 1% to 5%), vomiting (1% to 4%), gastrointestinal disease (not otherwise specified; 1% to 3%), gastroesophageal reflux disease (powder and solution: ≤3%), oropharyngeal candidiasis (powder and solution: ≤3%), stomatitis (includes ulcerative stomatitis; powder and solution: ≤3%), diarrhea (solution: 1% to 2%)

Genitourinary: Urinary tract infection (powder and solution: 1% to 7%)

Hypersensitivity: Hypersensitivity reaction (powder and solution: ≤3%)

Infection: Candidiasis (3% to 4%), infection (1% to 4%), herpes zoster (powder and solution: ≤3%)

Neuromuscular & skeletal: Arthralgia (powder and solution: ≤4%), myalgia (4%), arthritis (≥3%), leg pain (1% to 3%), skeletal pain (1% to 3%)

Ophthalmic: Cataract (1% to 3%)

Respiratory: Rhinitis (powder and solution: ≤6%), epistaxis (powder and solution: ≤4%), cough (powder: ≥3%; solution: 1% to 2%), flu-like symptoms (≥3%), bronchitis (solution: 3%), laryngitis (powder and solution: ≤3%), allergic rhinitis (solution: 1% to 2%)

Miscellaneous: Fever (solution: 1% to 2%)

<1%, postmarketing, and/or case reports: Abnormal hepatic function tests, anaphylaxis, angioedema, application site irritation (powder; includes glossitis, oral mucosa ulcer, pharyngolaryngeal pain), atrial fibrillation, blurred vision, bronchospasm, dehydration, dermal ulcer, dysphagia, dysuria, gingivitis, glaucoma, glossitis, hepatic insufficiency, hoarseness, increased intraocular pressure, intestinal obstruction (includes paralytic ileus), joint swelling, limb pain, muscle spasm, mydriasis (if powder comes in contact with eyes), oropharyngeal pain, paradoxical bronchospasm, skin infection, supraventricular tachycardia, tachycardia, throat irritation, tonsillitis, urinary retention, urticaria, xeroderma

General Dosage Range Oral Inhalation:

Asthma: Children ≥6 years, Adolescents, and Adults: Spiriva Respimat (1.25 mcg/actuation): Metered dose inhaler: 2 inhalations (2.5 mcg) once daily

COPD: Adults: Spiriva Handihaler: Dry powder inhaler: Contents of 1 capsule (18 mcg) once daily **or** Spiriva Respimat (2.5 mcg/actuation): Metered dose inhaler: Two inhalations (5 mcg) once daily

Mechanism of Action Competitively and reversibly inhibits the action of acetylcholine at type 3 muscarinic (M_3) receptors in bronchial smooth muscle causing bronchodilation

Pharmacodynamics/Kinetics

Half-life Elimination

Dry powder inhaler: COPD: ~25 hours

Metered dose inhaler: Asthma: 44 hours; COPD: 25 hours

Time to Peak

Dry powder inhaler: Plasma: 7 minutes (following inhalation)

Metered dose inhaler: Plasma: 5 to 7 minutes (following inhalation)

Pregnancy Risk Factor C

Pregnancy Considerations Adverse events have been observed in animal reproduction studies.

Tiotropium and Olodaterol

(ty oh TRO pee um & oh loe DA ter ol)

Brand Names: US Stiolto Respimat

Brand Names: Canada Inspiolto Respimat

Pharmacologic Category Anticholinergic Agent; Anticholinergic Agent, Long-Acting; $Beta_2$ Agonist; $Beta_2$ Agonist, Long-Acting

Use

Chronic obstructive pulmonary disease: Maintenance treatment of airflow obstruction in patients with chronic obstructive pulmonary disease (COPD), including chronic bronchitis and/or emphysema.

Limitations of use: Not indicated to treat acute deteriorations of COPD; not indicated to treat asthma (safety and effectiveness in asthma have not been established)

Local Anesthetic/Vasoconstrictor Precautions No information available to require special precautions

Effects on Dental Treatment Key adverse event(s) related to dental treatment: The anticholinrgic effect of tiopropium resulting in xerostomia should be anticipated. Normal salivary flow should resume upon discontinuation.

Effects on Bleeding No information available to require special precautions

Adverse Reactions

>10%:

Respiratory: Nasopharyngitis (12%)

1% to 10%:

Neuromuscular & skeletal: Back pain (4%)

Respiratory: Cough (4%)

≤3%, postmarketing, and/or case reports: Angioedema, arthralgia, atrial fibrillation, blurred vision, bronchospasm, constipation, dehydration, dermal ulcer, dizziness, dysphagia, dysuria, epistaxis, gastroesophageal reflux disease, gingivitis, glaucoma, glossitis, hypersensitivity (including immediate reactions), hypertension, increased intraocular pressure, insomnia, intestinal obstruction (including paralytic ileus), joint swelling, laryngitis, oropharyngeal candidiasis, palpitations, pharyngitis, pruritus, sinusitis, skin infection, skin rash, stomatitis, supraventricular tachycardia, tachycardia, urinary retention, urinary tract infection, urticaria, voice disorder, xeroderma, xerostomia

General Dosage Range Oral inhalation: *Adults:* Two inhalations once daily (maximum: 2 inhalations per day)

Mechanism of Action

Tiotropium: Competitively and reversibly inhibits the action of acetylcholine at type 3 muscarinic (M3) receptors in bronchial smooth muscle causing bronchodilation.

Olodaterol: Long acting $beta_2$-receptor agonist; activates $beta_2$ airway receptors, resulting in the stimulation of intracellular adenyl cyclase and a subsequent increase in the synthesis of cyclic-3',5' adenosine monophosphate (cAMP). Elevated cAMP levels induce bronchodilation by relaxation of airway smooth muscle cells. Has much greater affinity for $beta_2$-receptors than for $beta_1$- or $beta_3$-receptors.

Pregnancy Risk Factor C

Pregnancy Considerations Animal reproduction studies have not been conducted with this combination. See individual monographs.

Tipranavir (tip RA na veer)

Related Information

HIV Infection and AIDS *on page 1785*

Brand Names: US Aptivus

Brand Names: Canada Aptivus

Pharmacologic Category Antiretroviral, Protease Inhibitor (Anti-HIV)

Use HIV-1 infection: Treatment of HIV-1 infection in combination with ritonavir and other antiretroviral agents; limited to treatment-experienced or multiprotease inhibitor-resistant patients.

Local Anesthetic/Vasoconstrictor Precautions No information available to require special precautions

Effects on Dental Treatment No significant effects or complications reported

Effects on Bleeding Increased bleeding has been noted with protease inhibitors in patients with hemophilia A or B. No information available to require routine special precautions relative to hemostasis in other patients.

Adverse Reactions

>10%:

Dermatologic: Skin rash (children: 21%; adults: 3% to 10%)

Endocrine & metabolic: Hypertriglyceridemia (>400 mg/dL: 61%), hypercholesterolemia (>300 mg/dL: 22%)

Gastrointestinal: Diarrhea (15%; children: 4%)

Hepatic: Increased serum transaminases (>2.5 x ULN: 26% to 32%; grades 3/4: 10% to 20%)

Neuromuscular & skeletal: Increased creatine phosphokinase (children, grades 3/4: 11%)

1% to 10%:

Central nervous system: Fatigue (6%), headache (5%), dizziness, drowsiness, insomnia, intracranial hemorrhage, malaise, peripheral neuropathy, sleep disorder

Dermatologic: Pruritus

Endocrine & metabolic: Increased amylase (grade 3: 6% to 8%), weight loss (3%), dehydration (2%), increased gamma-glutamyl transferase (2%), diabetes mellitus, hyperglycemia, lipodystrophy (acquired), lipohypertrophy

Gastrointestinal: Nausea (5% to 9%), vomiting (6%), abdominal pain (4%), abdominal distension, anorexia, decreased appetite, dyspepsia, flatulence, gastroesophageal reflux disease, increased serum lipase, pancreatitis

Hematologic & oncologic: Hemorrhage (children: 8%), decreased white blood cell count (grade 3: 5%), anemia (3%), neutropenia (2%), thrombocytopenia

Hepatic: Increased serum ALT (2%, grades 3/4: 10%), increased serum AST (grades 3/4: 6%), hepatic failure, hepatitis, hyperbilirubinemia, liver steatosis

Hypersensitivity: Hypersensitivity reaction

Immunologic: Immune reconstitution syndrome

Neuromuscular & skeletal: Myalgia (2%), amyotrophy (facial), lipoatrophy, muscle cramps

Renal: Renal insufficiency

Respiratory: Cough (children: 6%), dyspnea (2%), epistaxis (children: 4%), flu-like symptoms

Miscellaneous: Fever (6% to 8%), drug toxicity (mitochondrial damage)

General Dosage Range Dosage adjustment recommended in patients on concomitant therapy

Oral:

Children ≥2 years and Adolescents: 12 to 14 mg/kg or 290 to 375 mg/m² (maximum: 500 mg/dose) twice daily

Adults: 500 mg twice daily

Mechanism of Action Binds to the site of HIV-1 protease activity and inhibits cleavage of viral Gag-Pol polyprotein precursors into individual functional proteins required for infectious HIV. This results in the formation of immature, noninfectious viral particles.

Pharmacodynamics/Kinetics

Half-life Elimination Children 2 to <6 years of age: ~8 hours, 6 to <12 years of age: ~7 hours, 12 to 18 years: ~5 hours; Adults: Males: 6 hours; Females: 5.5 hours

Time to Peak Children and Adolescents 2 to 18 years: 2.5 to 2.7 hours; Adults: 3 hours

Pregnancy Risk Factor C

Pregnancy Considerations Adverse events were observed in some animal reproduction studies. Tipranavir has a moderate level of transfer across the human placenta (based on one case). Data collected by the antiretroviral pregnancy registry are insufficient to evaluate human teratogenic risk. A small increased risk of preterm birth has been associated with maternal use of protease inhibitor-based combination antiretroviral therapy during pregnancy; however, the benefits of use generally outweigh this risk and protease inhibitors (PIs) should not be withheld if otherwise recommended. Information related to stillbirth, low birth weight, and small for gestational age infants is limited. Long-term follow-up is recommended for all infants exposed to antiretroviral medications; children who develop significant organ system abnormalities of unknown etiology (particularly of the CNS or heart) should be evaluated for potential mitochondrial dysfunction. Hyperglycemia, new onset of diabetes mellitus, or diabetic ketoacidosis have been reported with PIs; it is not clear if pregnancy increases this risk.

Combination antiretroviral therapy (cART) therapy is recommended for all HIV-infected pregnant women to keep the viral load below the limit of detection and reduce the risk of perinatal transmission. When HIV is diagnosed during pregnancy in a woman who has never received antiretroviral therapy, cART should begin as soon as possible after diagnosis. The Health and Human Services (HHS) Perinatal HIV Guidelines do not recommend tipranavir for initial use in antiretroviral-naive pregnant women. Available pharmacokinetic data are insufficient to make dosing recommendations. In general, women who become pregnant on a stable cART regimen may continue that regimen if viral suppression is effective, appropriate drug exposure can be achieved, contraindications for use in pregnancy are not present, and the regimen is well tolerated. Monitoring during pregnancy is more frequent than in non-pregnant adults; cART should be continued postpartum.

For HIV-infected couples planning a pregnancy, maximum viral suppression with cART is recommended prior to conception for the HIV-infected partner(s) and expert consultation is recommended; modification of therapy (if needed) and optimization of the woman's health should be done prior to conception. HIV-infected women not planning a pregnancy may use any available type of contraception, considering possible drug interactions and contraindications of the specific method. In addition, consistent use of condoms is also recommended (even during pregnancy) to prevent transmission of HIV or other sexually transmitted diseases.

Health care providers are encouraged to enroll pregnant women exposed to antiretroviral medications as early in pregnancy as possible in the Antiretroviral Pregnancy Registry (1-800-258-4263 or www.APRegistry.com). Health care providers caring for HIV-infected women and their infants may contact the National Perinatal HIV Hotline (888-448-8765) for clinical consultation (HHS [perinatal] 2016).

Tirofiban (tye roe FYE ban)

Related Information

Cardiovascular Diseases *on page 1752*

Brand Names: US Aggrastat

Brand Names: Canada Aggrastat

Pharmacologic Category Antiplatelet Agent, Glycoprotein IIb/IIIa Inhibitor

Use Unstable angina/non-ST-elevation myocardial infarction: To decrease the rate of thrombotic cardiovascular events (combined end point of death, MI, or refractory ischemia/repeat cardiac procedure) in patients with non-ST-elevation acute coronary syndrome (unstable angina/non-ST-elevation myocardial infarction [UA/NSTEMI]).

Local Anesthetic/Vasoconstrictor Precautions No information available to require special precautions

Effects on Dental Treatment Key adverse event(s) related to dental treatment: Bleeding is a potential adverse effect of tirofiban. See Effects on Bleeding.

Effects on Bleeding As with all anticoagulants, bleeding is a potential adverse effect of tirofiban during dental surgery; risk is dependent on multiple variables, including the intensity of anticoagulation and patient susceptibility. Medical consult is suggested. It is unlikely that ambulatory patients presenting for dental treatment will be taking intravenous anticoagulant therapy.

Adverse Reactions Bleeding is the major drug-related adverse effect. Patients received background treatment with aspirin and heparin. Adverse reactions reported are derived from both the high-dose bolus regimen **and** the dosing regimen used in studies that established the effectiveness of tirofiban. Frequency not always defined.

>10%: Hematologic & oncologic: Minor hemorrhage (TIMI criteria minor bleeding; 10.5% to 12%; transfusion required: 4% to 4.3%)

1% to 10%:

Cardiovascular: Coronary artery dissection (5%), bradycardia (4%), edema (2%), vasodepressor syncope (2%)

Central nervous system: Dizziness (3%), headache (>1%)

Dermatologic: Diaphoresis (2%)

Gastrointestinal: Nausea (>1%)

Genitourinary: Pelvic pain (6%)

Hematologic & oncologic: Major hemorrhage (TIMI criteria major bleeding: 1.4% to 2.2%; including hematoma [femoral]: 2% [Valgimigli, 2005], intracranial bleeding, GI bleeding, retroperitoneal bleeding [Aydin, 2003], GU bleeding, pulmonary alveolar hemorrhage [Guo, 2012], spinal-epidural hematoma), thrombocytopenia: <90,000/mm^3 (1.5% to 1.9%), <50,000/mm^3 (0.3% to 0.5%)

Neuromuscular & skeletal: Leg pain (3%)

Miscellaneous: Fever (>1%)

<1%, postmarketing, and/or case reports: Anaphylaxis, hemopericardium, hypersensitivity, skin rash, urticaria

General Dosage Range Dosage adjustment recommended in patients with renal impairment

IV: *Adults:* Loading dose: 25 mcg/kg administered over 5 minutes or less; Maintenance infusion: 0.15 mcg/kg/minute continued for up to 18 hours

Mechanism of Action A reversible antagonist of fibrinogen binding to the glycoprotein (GP) IIb/IIIa receptor, the major platelet surface receptor involved in platelet aggregation. When administered intravenously, it inhibits *ex vivo* platelet aggregation in a dose- and concentration-dependent manner. When given according to the recommended regimen, >90% inhibition is attained within 10 minutes after initiation. Platelet aggregation inhibition is reversible following cessation of the infusion.

Pharmacodynamics/Kinetics

Onset of Action >90% inhibition of platelet aggregation (reversible after discontinuation) seen within 10 minutes

Half-life Elimination 2 hours; **Note:** In ~90% of patients, *ex vivo* platelet aggregation returns to near baseline in 4 to 8 hours after discontinuation.

Pregnancy Risk Factor B

Pregnancy Considerations Adverse events have not been observed in animal reproduction studies. Information related to use in pregnancy is limited; successful use during pregnancy has been described in a case report (Boztosun, 2008).

TiZANidine (tye ZAN i deen)

Related Information

Dentin Hypersensitivity, Acid Erosion, High Caries Index, Management of Alveolar Osteitis, and Xerostomia *on page 1857*

Brand Names: US Zanaflex

Brand Names: Canada Apo-Tizanidine; Gen-Tizanidine; Mylan-Tizanidine; Pal-Tizanidine; Zanaflex

Pharmacologic Category Alpha$_2$-Adrenergic Agonist

Use Muscle spasticity: Management of spasticity; reserve treatment with tizanidine for daily activities and times when relief of spasticity is most important.

Local Anesthetic/Vasoconstrictor Precautions No information available to require special precautions

Effects on Dental Treatment Key adverse event(s) related to dental treatment: Significant xerostomia (normal salivary flow resumes upon discontinuation).

Effects on Bleeding No information available to require special precautions

Adverse Reactions Frequencies reported during multiple-dose studies.

>10%:

Cardiovascular: Hypotension (16% to 33%)

Central nervous system: Drowsiness (48%), dizziness (16%)

Gastrointestinal: Xerostomia (49%)

Neuromuscular & skeletal: Weakness (41%)

1% to 10%:

Cardiovascular: Bradycardia (2% to 10%)

Central nervous system: Nervousness (3%), speech disturbance (3%), delusions (≤3%), visual hallucination (≤3%), anxiety (1%), depression (1%), myasthenia (1%), paresthesia (1%)

Dermatologic: Dermal ulcer (1%), diaphoresis (1%), skin rash (1%)

Gastrointestinal: Constipation (4%), vomiting (3%), abdominal pain (1%), diarrhea (1%), dyspepsia (1%)
Genitourinary: Urinary tract infection (10%), urinary frequency (3%)
Hepatic: Increased liver enzymes (3% to 5%)
Infection: Infection (6%)
Neuromuscular & skeletal: Dyskinesia (3%), back pain (1%)
Ophthalmic: Blurred vision (3%)
Respiratory: Flu-like symptoms (3%), pharyngitis (3%), rhinitis (3%)
Miscellaneous: Fever (1%)
<1%, postmarketing, and/or case reports: Abnormal dreams, abnormality in thinking, abscess, acne vulgaris, adrenocortical insufficiency, agitation, albuminuria, alopecia, anemia, angina pectoris, arthralgia, arthritis, asthma, attempted suicide, bone fracture, bronchitis, bruise, bursitis, candidiasis, carcinoma (including skin), cardiac arrhythmia, cardiac failure, cellulitis, cholelithiasis, conjunctivitis, coronary artery disease, cystitis, deafness, dementia, depersonalization, dysphagia, dyslipidemia, edema, exfoliative dermatitis, eye pain, fecal impaction, flatulence, gastroenteritis, gastrointestinal hemorrhage, glaucoma, glycosuria, hematemesis, hematuria, hemiplegia, hepatic failure, hepatic neoplasm, hepatitis, hepatomegaly, herpes virus infection, hypercholesterolemia, hyperglycemia, hypermenorrhea, hypersensitivity reaction, hypokalemia, hyponatremia, hypoproteinemia, hypothyroidism, intestinal obstruction, iritis, jaundice, keratitis, leukopenia, leukocytosis, malaise, melena, migraine, myocardial infarction, neck pain, nephrolithiasis, neuralgia, neuropathy, optic atrophy, optic neuritis, orthostatic hypotension, otalgia, otitis media, palpitations, paralysis, petechia, personality disorder (various), phlebitis, pneumonia, pruritus, psychotic symptoms, pulmonary embolism, purpura, pyelonephritis, respiratory acidosis, retinal hemorrhage, seizure, sepsis, sinusitis, stupor, syncope, thrombocythemia, thrombocytopenia, tinnitus, tremor, urinary retention, urinary urgency, urticaria, uterine fibroid enlargement, uterine hemorrhage, vulvovaginal candidiasis, vaginitis, vasodilatation, ventricular premature contractions, ventricular tachycardia, vertigo, visual field defect, weight loss, xeroderma

General Dosage Range Oral: *Adults:* Initial: 2 mg up to 3 times daily (at 6- to 8-hour intervals); maximum: 36 mg daily

Mechanism of Action An alpha$_2$-adrenergic agonist agent which decreases spasticity by increasing presynaptic inhibition; effects are greatest on polysynaptic pathways; overall effect is to reduce facilitation of spinal motor neurons.

Pharmacodynamics/Kinetics

Onset of Action Single dose (8 mg): Peak effect: 1-2 hours

Duration of Action Single dose (8 mg): 3-6 hours

Half-life Elimination ~2.5 hours

Time to Peak

Fasting state: Capsule, tablet: 1 hour
Fed state: Capsule: 3-4 hours, Tablet: 1.5 hours

Pregnancy Risk Factor C

Pregnancy Considerations Adverse events were observed in some animal reproduction studies.

Tobramycin (Systemic) (toe bra MYE sin)

Brand Names: Canada JAMP-Tobramycin; Tobramycin For Injection; Tobramycin For Injection, USP; Tobramycin Injection; Tobramycin Injection, USP

Pharmacologic Category Antibiotic, Aminoglycoside

Use Treatment of documented or suspected infections caused by susceptible gram-negative bacilli, including *Pseudomonas aeruginosa*.

Local Anesthetic/Vasoconstrictor Precautions No information available to require special precautions

Effects on Dental Treatment No significant effects or complications reported

Effects on Bleeding No information available to require special precautions

Adverse Reactions Frequency not defined.

Central nervous system: Confusion, disorientation, dizziness, headache, lethargy, vertigo
Dermatologic: Exfoliative dermatitis, pruritus, skin rash, urticaria
Endocrine & metabolic: Decreased serum calcium, decreased serum magnesium, decreased serum potassium, decreased serum sodium, increased lactate dehydrogenase, increased nonprotein nitrogen
Gastrointestinal: Diarrhea, nausea, vomiting
Genitourinary: Casts in urine, oliguria, proteinuria
Hematologic & oncologic: Anemia, eosinophilia, granulocytopenia, leukocytosis, leukopenia, thrombocytopenia
Hepatic: Increased serum ALT, increased serum AST, increased serum bilirubin
Local: Pain at injection site
Otic: Auditory ototoxicity, hearing loss, tinnitus, vestibular ototoxicity
Renal: Increased blood urea nitrogen, increased serum creatinine
Miscellaneous: Fever
<1%, postmarketing, and/or case reports: Anaphylaxis, *clostridium difficile* associated diarrhea, erythema multiforme, Stevens-Johnson syndrome, toxic epidermal necrolysis

General Dosage Range Dosage adjustment recommended for the IM and IV routes in patients with renal impairment

IM:

Infants and Children <5 years: 2.5 mg/kg every 8 hours
Children ≥5 years: 2 to 3.3 mg/kg every 6 to 8 hours
Adults: 1 to 2.5 mg/kg every 8 to 12 hours (1 mg/kg used for synergy) **or** 4 to 7 mg/kg/day as a single daily dose
Elderly: 1.5 to 5 mg/kg/day in 1 to 2 divided doses

IV:

Infants and Children <5 years: 2.5 mg/kg every 8 hours
Children ≥5 years: 2 to 3.3 mg/kg every 6 to 8 hours
Adults: 1 to 2.5 mg/kg every 8 to 12 hours (1 mg/kg/dose used for synergy) **or** 4 to 7 mg/kg/day as a single daily dose
Elderly: 1.5 to 5 mg/kg/day in 1 to 2 divided doses **or** 5 to 7 mg/kg given every 24, 36, or 48 hours based on CrCl

Mechanism of Action Interferes with bacterial protein synthesis by binding to 30S and 50S ribosomal subunits, resulting in a defective bacterial cell membrane

Pharmacodynamics/Kinetics

Half-life Elimination

Neonates: ≤1,200 g: 11 hours; >1,200 g: 2 to 9 hours
Infants: 4 ± 1 hour
Children: 2 ± 1 hour
Adolescents: 1.5 ± 1 hour
Adults: IV: 2 to 3 hours; directly dependent upon glomerular filtration rate
Adults with impaired renal function: 5 to 70 hours

Time to Peak Serum: IM: 30 to 60 minutes; IV: ~30 minutes; **Note:** Distribution may be prolonged after larger doses. One study reported a 1.7-hour distribution period after a 60-minute, high-dose aminoglycoside infusion (Demczar 1997).

Pregnancy Risk Factor D

Pregnancy Considerations [US Boxed Warning]: Aminoglycosides may cause fetal harm if administered to a pregnant woman. Tobramycin crosses the placenta. There are several reports of total irreversible bilateral congenital deafness in children whose mothers received another aminoglycoside (streptomycin) during pregnancy. Although serious side effects to the fetus/infant have not been reported following maternal use of all aminoglycosides, a potential for harm exists.

Due to pregnancy-induced physiologic changes, some pharmacokinetic parameters of tobramycin may be altered (Bourget 1991). Tobramycin injection may be used for the management of cystic fibrosis in pregnant patients with *Pseudomonas aeruginosa* (inhalation is preferred unless risk of infection is great) (Edenborough 2008).

Tobramycin (Oral Inhalation)

(toe bra MYE sin)

Brand Names: US Bethkis; Kitabis Pak; Tobi; Tobi Podhaler; Tobramycin Pak [DSC]

Brand Names: Canada TOBI; TOBI Podhaler

Pharmacologic Category Antibiotic, Aminoglycoside

Use Management of cystic fibrosis patients with *Pseudomonas aeruginosa*.

Local Anesthetic/Vasoconstrictor Precautions No information available to require special precautions

Effects on Dental Treatment No significant effects or complications reported

Effects on Bleeding No information available to require special precautions

Adverse Reactions

>10%:

Central nervous system: Voice disorder (4% to 14%), headache (11% to 12%)

Respiratory: Cough (powder: 10% to 48%, solution: 31%), rhinitis (solution: 11% to 35%), pulmonary disease (30% to 34%; includes pulmonary or cystic fibrosis exacerbations), reduced forced expiratory volume (solution: 1% to 31%, powder: 4%), discoloration of sputum (21%), productive cough (18% to 20%), rales (solution: 6% to 19%, powder: 7%), dyspnea (12% to 16%), decreased lung function (7% to 16%), oropharyngeal pain (11% to 14%), hemoptysis (12% to 13%), pharyngolaryngeal pain (powder: 11%, solution: 3%)

Miscellaneous: Fever (12% to 16%)

1% to 10%:

Cardiovascular: Chest discomfort (3% to 7%)

Central nervous system: Malaise (6%)

Dermatologic: Skin rash (2%)

Endocrine: Increased serum glucose (powder: 3%, solution: <1%)

Gastrointestinal: Nausea (8% to 10%), dysgeusia (powder: 4% to 7%, solution: <1%), vomiting (6%), diarrhea (2% to 4%)

Hematologic & oncologic: Increased erythrocyte sedimentation rate (solution: 8%), eosinophilia (solution: 2%), increased serum immunoglobulins (solution: 2%)

Neuromuscular & skeletal: Musculoskeletal chest pain (<1% to 5%), myalgia (solution: ≤5%)

Otic: Hypoacusis (powder: 10%), tinnitus (2% to 3%), deafness (≤1%; including unilateral deafness, reported as mild to moderate hearing loss or increased hearing loss)

Respiratory: Upper respiratory tract infection (7% to 9%), nasal congestion (7% to 8%), wheezing (5% to 7%), throat irritation (2% to 5%), bronchospasm (≤1% to 5%), laryngitis (solution: ≤5%) bronchitis (solution: 3%), epistaxis (2% to 3%), tonsillitis (solution: 2%)

<1%, postmarketing, and/or case reports: Aphonia, decreased appetite, hypersensitivity reaction, increased bronchial secretions, pneumonitis, pruritus, pulmonary congestion, urticaria

General Dosage Range Inhalation: *Children ≥6 years, Adolescents, and Adults:* Bethkis, Kitabis Pak, Tobi: 300 mg every 12 hours; Tobi Podhaler: 112 mg every 12 hours

Mechanism of Action Interferes with bacterial protein synthesis by binding to 30S and 50S ribosomal subunits, resulting in a defective bacterial cell membrane

Pharmacodynamics/Kinetics

Half-life Elimination

Solution for inhalation: 4.4 hours

Powder for inhalation: ~3 hours (after a single 112 mg dose)

Time to Peak Serum: Powder for inhalation: 60 minutes

Pregnancy Risk Factor D

Pregnancy Considerations Aminoglycosides may cause fetal harm if administered to a pregnant woman. Tobramycin crosses the placenta when given by injection. There are several reports of total irreversible bilateral congenital deafness in children whose mothers received another aminoglycoside (streptomycin) during pregnancy. Although serious side effects to the fetus/infant have not been reported following maternal use of all aminoglycosides, a potential for harm exists.

Tobramycin inhalation may be used for the management of cystic fibrosis in pregnant patients with *Pseudomonas aeruginosa* (Edenborough 2008).

Tocilizumab (toe si LIZ oo mab)

Related Information

Rheumatoid Arthritis, Osteoarthritis, and Osteoporosis *on page 1792*

Brand Names: US Actemra

Brand Names: Canada Actemra

Pharmacologic Category Antirheumatic, Disease Modifying; Interleukin-6 Receptor Antagonist

Use

Polyarticular juvenile idiopathic arthritis: Treatment of active polyarticular juvenile idiopathic arthritis (PJIA) in patients 2 years and older.

Rheumatoid arthritis: Treatment of adults with moderately to severely active rheumatoid arthritis (RA) who have had an inadequate response to one or more disease-modifying antirheumatic drugs (DMARDs).

Systemic juvenile idiopathic arthritis: Treatment of active systemic juvenile idiopathic arthritis (SJIA) in patients 2 years and older.

Local Anesthetic/Vasoconstrictor Precautions No information available to require special precautions

Effects on Dental Treatment Key adverse event(s) related to dental treatment: Mouth ulcerations and stomatitis

Effects on Bleeding No information available to require special precautions

Adverse Reactions Incidence as reported for monotherapy, except where noted. Combination therapy refers to use in rheumatoid arthritis with nonbiological DMARDs or use in SJIA or PJIA in trials where most patients (~70% to 80%) were taking methotrexate at baseline.

>10%:

Endocrine & metabolic: Increased serum cholesterol (>240 mg/dL; 19% to 20%; >1.5-2 x ULN; combination therapy; children and adolescents <1% to 2%)

Hepatic: Increased serum ALT (≤36%; grades 3/4: <1%), increased serum AST (≤22%; grades 3/4: <1%)

Miscellaneous: Infusion-related reaction (combination therapy; 4% to 16%)

1% to 10%:

Cardiovascular: Hypertension (1% to 6%), peripheral edema (<2%)

Central nervous system: Headache (1% to 7%), dizziness (3%)

Dermatologic: Skin rash (2%), dermatological reaction (combination therapy; 1% [includes pruritus, urticaria])

Endocrine & metabolic: Increased LDL cholesterol (9% to 10%; >1.5-2 x ULN; combination therapy; children and adolescents <1% to 2%), hypothyroidism (<2%)

Gastrointestinal: Diarrhea (children and adolescents ≤5%), abdominal pain (2%), oral mucosa ulcer (2%), gastric ulcer (<2%), stomatitis (<2%), weight gain (<2%), gastritis (1%)

Hematologic & oncologic: Neutropenia (combination therapy; grade 3: 2% to 7%; grade 4: <1%), thrombocytopenia (combination therapy; 1% to 2%), leukopenia (<2%)

Hepatic: Increased serum bilirubin (<2%)

Immunologic: Antibody development (<2%)

Infection: Herpes simplex infection (<2%)

Local: Injection site reaction (SubQ: Including erythema, pruritus, pain, and hematoma, 4% to 10%)

Ophthalmic: Conjunctivitis (<2%)

Renal: Nephrolithiasis (<2%)

Respiratory: Upper respiratory tract infection (7%), nasopharyngitis (7%), bronchitis (3%), cough (<2%), dyspnea (<2%)

<1%, postmarketing, and/or case reports: Anaphylaxis, anaphylactoid reaction, angioedema, aspergillosis, candidiasis, cellulitis, chronic inflammatory demyelinating polyneuropathy, cryptococcosis, diverticulitis, gastroenteritis, gastrointestinal perforation, herpes zoster, hypersensitivity, hypersensitivity pneumonitis, hypertriglyceridemia, hypotension, increased HDL cholesterol, malignant neoplasm (including breast and colon cancer), multiple sclerosis, nausea, otitic media, pneumonia, pneumocystosis, reactivation of latent Epstein-Barr virus, septic arthritis, sepsis, Stevens-Johnson syndrome, tuberculosis, urinary tract infection, varicella

General Dosage Range Dosage adjustment recommended in patients who develop toxicities

IV:

Children ≥2 years and <30 kg: 12 mg/kg every 2 weeks **or** 10 mg/kg every 4 weeks

Children ≥2 years and ≥30 kg: 8 mg/kg every 2 weeks **or** 8 mg/kg every 4 weeks

Adults: 4 to 8 mg/kg every 4 weeks (maximum dose: 800 mg)

SubQ:

Adults <100 kg: 162 mg every other week or every week

Adults ≥100 kg: 162 mg every week

Mechanism of Action Antagonist of the interleukin-6 (IL-6) receptor. Endogenous IL-6 is induced by inflammatory stimuli and mediates a variety of immunological responses. Inhibition of IL-6 receptors by tocilizumab leads to a reduction in cytokine and acute phase reactant production.

Pharmacodynamics/Kinetics

Half-life Elimination

IV: Terminal, single dose: 6.3 days (concentration-dependent; may be increased up to 16 to 23 days [children] or 11 to 13 days [adults] at steady state)

SubQ: Concentration dependent: Adults: Up to 5 days (every other week dosing) or up to 13 days (every week dosing)

Pregnancy Considerations

Adverse events have been observed in some animal reproduction studies. As pregnancy progresses, monoclonal antibodies are increasingly transported across the placenta, with the largest amount transferred during the third trimester. Immune response in infants exposed to tocilizumab in utero may be affected. Consider risks/benefits prior to administering live or live-attenuated vaccines to infants exposed to tocilizumab during pregnancy.

A pregnancy registry has been established to monitor outcomes of women exposed to tocilizumab during pregnancy. Health care providers or pregnant patients are encouraged to register (877-311-8972).

Tofacitinib (toe fa SYE ti nib)

Related Information

Rheumatoid Arthritis, Osteoarthritis, and Osteoporosis *on page 1792*

Brand Names: US Xeljanz; Xeljanz XR

Brand Names: Canada Xeljanz

Pharmacologic Category Antirheumatic Miscellaneous; Antirheumatic, Disease Modifying; Janus Associated Kinase Inhibitor

Use

Rheumatoid arthritis: Treatment of moderately- to severely-active rheumatoid arthritis (as monotherapy or in combination with methotrexate or other nonbiologic disease-modifying antirheumatic drugs [DMARDs]) in adults who have had an inadequate response to, or are intolerant of, methotrexate

Limitations of use: The use of tofacitinib in combination with biologic DMARDs or with potent immunosuppressants (eg, azathioprine, cyclosporine) is not recommended.

Local Anesthetic/Vasoconstrictor Precautions No information available to require special precautions

Effects on Dental Treatment No significant effects or complications reported

Effects on Bleeding Active therapy with tofacitinib may result in significant myelosuppression; medical consult is suggested.

Adverse Reactions Incidences of adverse reactions include unapproved dosing regimens. Frequency not always defined.

Cardiovascular: Hypertension (2%), peripheral edema

Central nervous system: Headache (4%), fatigue, insomnia, paresthesia

Dermatologic: Erythema, pruritus, skin rash

Endocrine & metabolic: Dehydration

Gastrointestinal: Diarrhea (4%), abdominal pain, diverticulitis, dyspepsia, gastritis, nausea, vomiting

Genitourinary: Urinary tract infection (2%)

Hematologic & oncologic: Anemia, skin carcinoma (nonmelanoma)
Hepatic: Increased serum ALT (>3 x upper limit of normal; 1%), liver steatosis
Infection: Infection (20% to 22%), serious infection (2% to 3%)
Neuromuscular & skeletal: Arthralgia, joint swelling, musculoskeletal pain, tendonitis
Renal: Increased serum creatinine (<2%)
Respiratory: Upper respiratory tract infection (5%), nasopharyngitis (4%), cough, dyspnea, sinus congestion
Miscellaneous: Fever
<1%, postmarketing, and/or case reports: BK virus, cellulitis, cryptococcosis, cytomegalovirus disease, decreased heart rate, esophageal candidiasis, hepatotoxicity, herpes zoster, increased creatine kinase, increased serum AST, interstitial pulmonary disease, lymphocytopenia, malignant neoplasm, neutropenia, pneumocystosis, pneumonia, prolongation P-R interval on ECG, rhabdomyolysis, skin carcinoma, tuberculosis

General Dosage Range Dosage adjustment recommended in patients with renal impairment, hepatic impairment, on concomitant therapy, and who develop toxicities.

Oral: *Adults:* 5 mg twice daily

Mechanism of Action Tofacitinib inhibits Janus kinase (JAK) enzymes, which are intracellular enzymes involved in stimulating hematopoiesis and immune cell function through a signaling pathway. In response to extracellular cytokine or growth factor signaling, JAKs activate signal transducers and activators of transcription (STATs), which regulate gene expression and intracellular activity. Inhibition of JAKs prevents cytokine- or growth factor-mediated gene expression and intracellular activity of immune cells, reduces circulating CD16/56+ natural killer cells, serum IgG, IgM, IgA, and C-reactive protein, and increases B cells.

Pharmacodynamics/Kinetics

Half-life Elimination ~3 hours (immediate release); ~6 hours (extended release)

Time to Peak 0.5 to 1 hour (immediate release); 4 hours (extended release)

Pregnancy Risk Factor C

Pregnancy Considerations Adverse events have been observed in animal reproduction studies. Healthcare providers are encouraged to enroll women exposed to tofacitinib during pregnancy in the Xeljanz Pregnancy Registry (877-311-8972); patients may also enroll themselves. Canadian labeling recommends avoiding use during pregnancy.

Product Availability Xeljanz XR tablets: FDA approved February 2016; anticipated availability is currently unknown. Information pertaining to this product within the monograph is pending revision. Consult prescribing information for additional information.

Prescribing and Access Restrictions Available through specialty/network pharmacies. Further information may be obtained from the manufacturer, Pfizer Inc, at 1-855-493-5526 or at http://www.xeljanz.com/.

TOLAZamide (tole AZ a mide)

Related Information

Endocrine Disorders and Pregnancy *on page 1781*

Pharmacologic Category Antidiabetic Agent, Sulfonylurea

Use Adjunct to diet for the management of mild-to-moderately severe, stable, type 2 diabetes mellitus (noninsulin dependent, NIDDM)

Guideline recommendations: Tolbutamide is not listed as a treatment option for type 2 diabetes in the ADA diabetes guidelines (ADA 2017). If used, first generation sulfonylureas (eg, tolbutamide) should be used with caution; consider the use of other agents that are recommended in the ADA guidelines such as second generation sulfonylureas (eg, glyburide, glipizide, glimepiride).

Local Anesthetic/Vasoconstrictor Precautions No information available to require special precautions

Effects on Dental Treatment Key adverse event(s) related to dental treatment: Patients with diabetes should be questioned by the dental professional at each dental visit to assess their risk for stress-induced hypoglycemia. The dental professional should inquire about the patient's routine (ie, work, sleep schedule, eating patterns), history of hypoglycemia, time of last medication dose, last meal, and most recent blood sugar assessment. Keep a supply of glucose tablets and other carbohydrates in the office to prepare for a hypoglycemic event. Seek medical attention when necessary (American Diabetes Association, 2014).

Effects on Bleeding No information available to require special precautions

Adverse Reactions Frequency not defined.
Central nervous system: Disulfiram-like reaction, dizziness, fatigue, headache, malaise, vertigo
Dermatologic: Maculopapular rash, morbilliform rash, pruritus, skin photosensitivity, skin rash, urticaria
Endocrine & metabolic: Hepatic porphyria, hypoglycemia, hyponatremia, porphyria cutanea tarda, SIADH (syndrome of inappropriate antidiuretic hormone secretion)
Gastrointestinal: Anorexia, constipation, diarrhea, epigastric fullness, heartburn, nausea, vomiting
Genitourinary: Diuretic effect
Hematologic & oncologic: Agranulocytosis, aplastic anemia, hemolytic anemia, leukopenia, pancytopenia, thrombocytopenia
Hepatic: Cholestatic jaundice
Neuromuscular & skeletal: Weakness

General Dosage Range Oral: *Adults:* Initial: 100-250 mg/day with first main meal of day; Maintenance: 100-1000 mg/day in 1-2 (doses >500 mg) divided doses (maximum: 1 g/day)

Mechanism of Action Stimulates insulin release from the pancreatic beta cells; reduces glucose output from the liver; insulin sensitivity is increased at peripheral target sites

Pharmacodynamics/Kinetics

Onset of Action Hypoglycemic effect: 20 minutes; Peak hypoglycemic effect: 4-6 hours

Duration of Action 10-24 hours

Half-life Elimination 7 hours

Time to Peak Serum: 3-4 hours

Pregnancy Risk Factor C

Pregnancy Considerations Adverse events have been observed in animal reproduction studies. Severe hypoglycemia lasting 4 to 10 days has been noted in infants born to mothers taking a sulfonylurea at the time of delivery. Additional adverse events have been reported and may be influenced by maternal glycemic control (Piacquadio 1991)

In women with diabetes, maternal hyperglycemia can be associated with congenital malformations as well as adverse effects in the fetus, neonate, and the mother

(ACOG 2005; ADA 2016c; Kitzmiller 2008; Metzger 2007). To prevent adverse outcomes, prior to conception and throughout pregnancy maternal blood glucose and HbA_{1c} should be kept as close to target goals as possible but without causing significant hypoglycemia (ACOG 2013; ADA 2016c; Blumer 2013; Kitzmiller 2008). Agents other than tolazamide are currently recommended to treat diabetes in pregnant women (ACOG 2013; Blumer 2013). The manufacturer recommends if tolazamide is used during pregnancy, it should be discontinued at least 2 weeks before the expected delivery date.

TOLBUTamide (tole BYOO ta mide)

Related Information

Endocrine Disorders and Pregnancy *on page 1781*

Brand Names: Canada Apo-Tolbutamide®

Pharmacologic Category Antidiabetic Agent, Sulfonylurea

Use Adjunct to diet for the management of type 2 diabetes mellitus (noninsulin dependent, NIDDM)

Guideline recommendations: Tolbutamide is not listed as a treatment option for type 2 diabetes in the ADA diabetes guidelines (ADA 2017). If used, first generation sulfonylureas (eg, tolbutamide) should be used with caution; consider the use of other agents that are recommended in the ADA guidelines such as second generation sulfonylureas (eg, glyburide, glipizide, glimepiride).

Local Anesthetic/Vasoconstrictor Precautions No information available to require special precautions

Effects on Dental Treatment Key adverse event(s) related to dental treatment: Patients with diabetes should be questioned by the dental professional at each dental visit to assess their risk for stress-induced hypoglycemia. The dental professional should inquire about the patient's routine (ie, work, sleep schedule, eating patterns), history of hypoglycemia, time of last medication dose, last meal, and most recent blood sugar assessment. Keep a supply of glucose tablets and other carbohydrates in the office to prepare for a hypoglycemic event. Seek medical attention when necessary (American Diabetes Association, 2014).

Effects on Bleeding No information available to require special precautions

Adverse Reactions Frequency not defined.

Central nervous system: Disulfiram-like reaction, headache

Dermatologic: Erythema, maculopapular rash, morbilliform rash, pruritus, skin photosensitivity, urticaria

Endocrine & metabolic: Hepatic porphyria, hypoglycemia, hyponatremia, porphyria cutanea tarda, SIADH (syndrome of inappropriate antidiuretic hormone secretion)

Gastrointestinal: Dysgeusia, epigastric fullness, heartburn, nausea

Hematologic & oncologic: Agranulocytosis, aplastic anemia, hemolytic anemia, leukopenia, pancytopenia, thrombocytopenia

Hepatic: Cholestatic jaundice

Hypersensitivity: Hypersensitivity reaction

General Dosage Range Oral:

Adults: Initial: 1-2 g/day as a single dose or divided doses; Maintenance: 0.25-3 g/day as a single dose or divided doses

Elderly: Initial: 0.25 g 1-3 times/day; Maintenance: 0.5-2 g/day in 1-3 divided doses (maximum: 3 g/day)

Mechanism of Action Stimulates insulin release from the pancreatic beta cells; reduces glucose output from the liver; insulin sensitivity is increased at peripheral target sites, suppression of glucagon may also contribute

Pharmacodynamics/Kinetics

Onset of Action 1 hour

Duration of Action Oral: 6-24 hours

Half-life Elimination 4.5-6.5 hours (range: 4-25 hours)

Time to Peak Serum: 3-4 hours

Pregnancy Risk Factor C

Pregnancy Considerations Adverse events have been observed in animal reproduction studies. Tolbutamide crosses the placenta and can be measured in the serum of newborn infants following maternal use during pregnancy (Miller 1962). Severe hypoglycemia lasting 4 to 10 days has been noted in infants born to mothers taking a sulfonylurea at the time of delivery. Additional adverse events have been reported and may be influenced by maternal glycemic control (Larsson 1960; Saili 1991; Schiff 1970).

In women with diabetes, maternal hyperglycemia can be associated with congenital malformations as well as adverse effects in the fetus, neonate, and the mother (ACOG 2005; ADA 2016c; Kitzmiller 2008; Metzger 2007). To prevent adverse outcomes, prior to conception and throughout pregnancy maternal blood glucose and HbA_{1c} should be kept as close to target goals as possible but without causing significant hypoglycemia (ACOG 2013; ADA 2016c; Blumer 2013; Kitzmiller 2008). Agents other than tolbutamide are currently recommended to treat diabetes in pregnant women (ACOG 2013; Blumer 2013).

The manufacturer recommends if tolbutamide is used during pregnancy, it should be discontinued at least 2 weeks before the expected delivery date

Tolcapone (TOLE ka pone)

Brand Names: US Tasmar

Pharmacologic Category Anti-Parkinson Agent, COMT Inhibitor

Use Adjunct to levodopa and carbidopa for the treatment of signs and symptoms of idiopathic Parkinson's disease in patients with motor fluctuations not responsive to other therapies

Local Anesthetic/Vasoconstrictor Precautions No information available to require special precautions

Effects on Dental Treatment Key adverse event(s) related to dental treatment: Significant xerostomia (normal salivary flow resumes upon discontinuation).

Dopaminergic therapy in Parkinson's disease (ie, treatment with levodopa) is associated with orthostatic hypotension. Tolcapone enhances levodopa bioavailability and may increase the occurrence of hypotension/syncope in the dental patient. The patient should be carefully assisted from the chair and observed for signs of orthostatic hypotension.

Effects on Bleeding No information available to require special precautions

Adverse Reactions

>10%:

Cardiovascular: Orthostatic hypotension (17%)

Central nervous system: Drowsiness (14% to 32%), sleep disorder (24% to 25%), hallucination (8% to 24%), dystonia (19% to 22%), increased dream

activity (16% to 21%), dizziness (6% to 13%), confusion (10% to 11%), headache (10% to 11%)
Gastrointestinal: Nausea (28% to 50%), diarrhea (16% to 34%; severe: 3% to 4%), anorexia (19% to 23%)
Neuromuscular & skeletal: Dyskinesia (42% to 51%), muscle cramps (17% to 18%)

1% to 10%:

Cardiovascular: Syncope (4% to 5%), chest pain (1% to 3%), hypotension (2%), palpitations
Central nervous system: Fatigue (3% to 7%), loss of balance (2% to 3%), paresthesia (1% to 3%), burning sensation (1% to 2%), agitation (1%), euphoria (1%), hyperactivity (1%), malaise (1%), panic (1%), irritability (1%), mental deficiency (1%), depression, emotional lability, flank pain, hypoesthesia, speech disturbance, vertigo
Dermatologic: Diaphoresis (4% to 7%), alopecia (1%), skin rash
Gastrointestinal: Vomiting (8% to 10%), constipation (6% to 8%), abdominal pain (5% to 6%), xerostomia (5% to 6%), dyspepsia (3% to 4%), flatulence (2% to 4%)
Genitourinary: Urinary tract infection (5%), hematuria (4% to 5%), urine discoloration (2% to 3%), urination disorder (1% to 2%), impotence, urinary incontinence
Hematologic & oncologic: Hemorrhage (1%), skin neoplasm (1%), uterine neoplasm (1%)
Hepatic: Increased serum transaminases (1% to 3%; 3 x ULN, usually with first 6 months of therapy)
Infection: Influenza (3% to 4%), infection
Neuromuscular & skeletal: Hyperkinesia (≤3%), hypokinesia (≤3%), muscle rigidity (2%), neck pain (2%), arthritis (1% to 2%), myalgia, rhabdomyolysis, tremor
Ophthalmic: Cataract (1%), ophthalmic inflammation (1%)
Otic: Tinnitus
Respiratory: Upper respiratory tract infection (5% to 7%), dyspnea (3%), sinus congestion (1% to 2%), bronchitis, pharyngitis
Miscellaneous: Fever (1%), accidental injury

<1%, postmarketing, and/or case reports: Abnormal stools, abnormality in thinking, abscess, altered sense of smell, amnesia, anemia, antisocial behavior, apathy, apnea, arteriosclerosis, arthropathy, asthma, bacterial infection, bladder calculus, brain disease, breast neoplasm, carcinoma, cardiovascular signs and symptoms, cellulitis, cerebral ischemia, cerebrovascular accident, change in libido, chills, cholecystitis, cholelithiasis, choreoathetosis, colitis, cough, dehydration, delirium, delusions, dermatological disease, diabetes mellitus, diplopia, disease of the lacrimal apparatus, duodenal ulcer, dysphagia, dysuria, eczema, edema, epistaxis, erythema multiforme, esophagitis, extrapyramidal reaction, eye pain, facial edema, fungal infection, furunculosis, gastric atony, gastroenteritis, gastrointestinal carcinoma, gastrointestinal hemorrhage, genitourinary disease, glaucoma, hemiplegia, hemophthalmos, hernia, herpes simplex infection, herpes zoster, hiccups, hostility, hypercholesteremia, hypersensitivity reaction, hyperventilation, hypoxia, increased thirst, laryngitis, leukemia, manic reaction, meningitis, myoclonus, neoplasm, nephrolithiasis, nervousness, neuralgia, neuropathy, nocturia, oliguria, oral mucosa ulcer, otalgia, otitis media, ovarian carcinoma, pain, paranoia, pericardial effusion, polyuria, prostate carcinoma, prostatic disease, pruritus, psychosis, pulmonary edema, rectal disease, rhinitis, seborrhea, sialorrhea, skin discoloration, surgery, tenosynovitis, thrombocytopenia, thrombosis, tongue disease, twitching, urinary retention, urticaria, uterine atony, uterine disease, uterine hemorrhage, vaginitis, viral infection

General Dosage Range Oral: *Adults:* Initial: 100 mg 3 times daily; Maintenance: 100-200 mg 3 times daily

Mechanism of Action Tolcapone is a selective and reversible inhibitor of catechol-o-methyltransferase (COMT). In the presence of a decarboxylase inhibitor (eg, carbidopa), COMT is the major degradation pathway for levodopa. Inhibition of COMT leads to more sustained plasma levels of levodopa and enhanced central dopaminergic activity.

Pharmacodynamics/Kinetics

Half-life Elimination 2-3 hours

Time to Peak ~2 hours

Pregnancy Risk Factor C

Pregnancy Considerations Adverse events were observed in animal reproduction studies.

Prescribing and Access Restrictions A patient signed consent form acknowledging the risks of hepatic injury should be obtained by the treating physician.

Tolnaftate (tole NAF tate)

Brand Names: US Anti-Fungal [OTC]; Antifungal [OTC]; Athletes Foot Spray [OTC]; Dr Gs Clear Nail [OTC]; Fungi-Guard [OTC]; Fungoid-D [OTC]; Jock Itch Spray [OTC]; LamISIL AF Defense [OTC]; Medi-First Anti-Fungal [OTC]; Mycocide Clinical NS [OTC]; Podactin [OTC]; The Treatment Formula 3 [OTC]; Tinactin Deodorant [OTC]; Tinactin Jock Itch [OTC]; Tinactin [OTC]; Tinaspore [OTC]; Tolnaftate Antifungal [OTC] [DSC]

Brand Names: Canada Pitrex

Pharmacologic Category Antifungal Agent, Topical

Use Treatment of tinea pedis, tinea cruris, tinea corporis

Local Anesthetic/Vasoconstrictor Precautions No information available to require special precautions

Effects on Dental Treatment No significant effects or complications reported

Effects on Bleeding No information available to require special precautions

Adverse Reactions Frequency not defined.

Dermatologic: Contact dermatitis, pruritus, stinging of the skin
Local: Irritation

General Dosage Range Topical: *Children ≥2 years and Adults:* Apply to affected areas 2 times/day

Mechanism of Action Distorts the hyphae and stunts mycelial growth in susceptible fungi

Pharmacodynamics/Kinetics

Onset of Action 24-72 hours

Tolterodine (tole TER oh deen)

Brand Names: US Detrol; Detrol LA

Brand Names: Canada Detrol; Detrol LA; Mint-Tolterodine; Mylan-Tolterodine; Sandoz-Tolterodine; Teva-Tolterodine

Pharmacologic Category Anticholinergic Agent

Use Treatment of patients with an overactive bladder with symptoms of urinary frequency, urgency, or urge incontinence

Local Anesthetic/Vasoconstrictor Precautions No information available to require special precautions

Effects on Dental Treatment The anticholinergic effects of tolterodine are selective for the urinary bladder rather than salivary glands; xerostomia and changes in salivation (normal salivary flow resumes upon discontinuation).

Effects on Bleeding No information available to require special precautions

Adverse Reactions As reported with immediate release tablet, unless otherwise specified

>10%: Gastrointestinal: Xerostomia (35%; extended release capsules: 23%)

1% to 10%:

Cardiovascular: Chest pain (2%)

Central nervous system: Headache (7%; extended release capsules: 6%), dizziness (5%; extended release capsules: 2%), fatigue (4%; extended release capsules: 2%), drowsiness (immediate and extended release: 3%), anxiety (extended release capsules: 1%)

Dermatologic: Xeroderma (1%)

Endocrine & metabolic: Weight gain (1%)

Gastrointestinal: Constipation (7%; extended release capsules: 6%), abdominal pain (5%; extended release capsules: 4%), diarrhea (4%), dyspepsia (4%; extended release capsules: 3%)

Genitourinary: Dysuria (2%; extended-release capsules: 1%)

Infection: Infection (1%)

Neuromuscular & skeletal: Arthralgia (2%)

Ophthalmic: Xerophthalmia (immediate and extended release: 3%), visual disturbance (2%; extended release capsules: 1%)

Respiratory: Flu-like symptoms (3%), bronchitis (2%), sinusitis (extended release capsules: 2%)

<1%, postmarketing, and/or case reports: Anaphylaxis, angioedema, confusion, dementia (aggravated), disorientation, hallucination, memory impairment, palpitations, peripheral edema, prolonged Q-T interval on ECG, tachycardia

General Dosage Range Dosage adjustment recommended in patients with hepatic or renal impairment and on concomitant therapy

Oral: *Adults:* Extended release capsule: 2-4 mg once daily; Immediate release tablet: 1-2 mg twice daily

Mechanism of Action Tolterodine is a competitive antagonist of muscarinic receptors. In animal models, tolterodine demonstrates selectivity for urinary bladder receptors over salivary receptors. Urinary bladder contraction is mediated by muscarinic receptors. Tolterodine increases residual urine volume and decreases detrusor muscle pressure.

Pharmacodynamics/Kinetics

Half-life Elimination

Immediate release tablet: Extensive metabolizers: ~2 hours; Poor metabolizers: ~10 hours

Extended release capsule: Extensive metabolizers: ~7 hours; Poor metabolizers: ~18 hours

Time to Peak Immediate release tablet: 1-2 hours; Extended release capsule: 2-6 hours

Pregnancy Risk Factor C

Pregnancy Considerations Teratogenic effects were observed in some animal reproduction studies.

Tolvaptan (tol VAP tan)

Brand Names: US Samsca

Brand Names: Canada Jinarc; Samsca

Pharmacologic Category Vasopressin Antagonist

Use

Samsca:

Hypervolemic and euvolemic hyponatremia: Treatment of clinically significant hypervolemic or euvolemic hyponatremia (serum sodium <125 mEq/L or less marked hyponatremia that is symptomatic and resistant to fluid restriction), including patients with heart failure and Syndrome of Inappropriate Antidiuretic Hormone (SIADH).

Limitations of use: Not indicated for use when urgent treatment of hyponatremia is required to prevent or treat serious neurological symptoms. It has not been established that raising serum sodium with tolvaptan provides symptomatic benefit.

Jinarc [Canadian product]:

Autosomal dominant polycystic kidney disease (ADPKD): Slow the progression of kidney enlargement in patients with ADPKD.

Limitations of use: Clinical trials evaluated ADPKD patients having a total kidney volume ≥750 mL with relatively preserved renal function (eg, estimated creatinine clearance ≥60 mL/minute, generally corresponding to a CKD-EPI eGFR ≥30 mL/minute/1.73 m^2 at the time of therapy initiation).

Local Anesthetic/Vasoconstrictor Precautions No information available to require special precautions

Effects on Dental Treatment No significant effects or complications reported

Effects on Bleeding No information available to require special precautions

Adverse Reactions

>10%:

Endocrine & metabolic: Increased thirst (12% to 16%)

Gastrointestinal: Nausea (21%), xerostomia (7% to 13%)

Renal: Polyuria (including pollakiuria, 4% to 11%)

2% to 10%:

Endocrine & metabolic: Hyperglycemia (6%), hypernatremia (<2%)

Gastrointestinal: Gastrointestinal hemorrhage (cirrhosis patients 10%), constipation (7%), anorexia (4%)

Hepatic: Hepatotoxicity (≤4%)

Neuromuscular & skeletal: Weakness (9%)

Miscellaneous: Fever (4%)

<2%, postmarketing, and/or case reports: Anaphylactic shock, cerebrovascular accident, deep vein thrombosis, diabetic ketoacidosis, disseminated intravascular coagulation, hypersensitivity reaction, increased serum ALT, increased serum bilirubin, intracardiac thrombus, ischemic colitis, osmotic demyelination syndrome, prolonged prothrombin time, pulmonary embolism, respiratory failure, rhabdomyolysis, skin rash, urethral bleeding, vaginal hemorrhage, ventricular fibrillation

General Dosage Range **Oral:** *Adults:* 15 to 60 mg once daily

Mechanism of Action An arginine vasopressin (AVP) receptor antagonist with affinity for AVP receptor subtypes V_2 and V_{1a} in a ratio of 29:1. Antagonism of the V_2 receptor by tolvaptan promotes the excretion of free water (without loss of serum electrolytes) resulting in net fluid loss, increased urine output, decreased urine osmolality, and subsequent restoration of normal serum sodium levels.

Pharmacodynamics/Kinetics

Onset of Action 2 to 4 hour; Peak effect: 4 to 8 hours

Duration of Action 60% peak serum sodium elevation is retained at 24 hours; urinary excretion of free water is no longer elevated

Half-life Elimination ~12 hours; dominant half-life <12 hours

Time to Peak Plasma: 2 to 4 hours

Pregnancy Risk Factor C

Pregnancy Considerations Adverse events were observed in animal reproduction studies. Jinarc [Canadian product] is contraindicated in pregnant women and the manufacturer recommends women of childbearing potential use reliable contraception during therapy.

Prescribing and Access Restrictions Jinarc [Canadian product]: Only physicians experienced in the diagnosis and treatment of polycystic kidney disease should prescribe Jinarc. Prior to initiating therapy, a patient-prescriber agreement (PPAF) is required outlining relevant patient selection criteria for consideration, expected benefits and risks of treatment, and the need for mandatory hepatic function monitoring. Jinarc is available only through a hepatic safety monitoring and distribution program conducted and maintained by Otsuka Canada Pharmaceuticals Incorporated. All patients initiating therapy should be offered participation in the Canadian Jinarc patient outcomes registry.

Topiramate (toe PYRE a mate)

Brand Names: US Qudexy XR; Topamax; Topamax Sprinkle; Topiragen [DSC]; Trokendi XR

Brand Names: Canada Abbott-Topiramate; ACT Topiramate; Apo-Topiramate; AURO-Topiramate; Dom-Topiramate; Jamp-Topiramate; Mint-Topiramate; Mylan-Topiramate; PHL-Topiramate; PMS-Topiramate; PRO-Topiramate; RAN-Topiramate; Sandoz-Topiramate; TEVA-Topiramate; Topamax

Pharmacologic Category Anticonvulsant, Miscellaneous

Use

Epilepsy:

Monotherapy: As initial monotherapy in patients ≥2 years (immediate release and Qudexy XR) or ≥6 years (Trokendi XR) with partial-onset or primary generalized tonic-clonic seizures

Adjunctive therapy: As adjunctive therapy in patients ≥2 years (immediate release and Qudexy XR) or ≥6 years (Trokendi XR only) with partial-onset seizures, primary generalized tonic-clonic seizures, or seizures associated with Lennox-Gastaut syndrome

Migraine (immediate release only): Prophylaxis of migraine headache in adults and adolescents ≥12 years.

Local Anesthetic/Vasoconstrictor Precautions No information available to require special precautions

Effects on Dental Treatment Key adverse event(s) related to dental treatment: Gingivitis, dysphagia, glossitis, gum hyperplasia, and xerostomia (normal salivary flow resumes upon discontinuation).

Effects on Bleeding No information available to require special precautions

Adverse Reactions Adverse events are reported for adult and pediatric patients for various indications and regimens. **Note:** A wide range of dosages were studied. Incidence of adverse events was frequently lower in the pediatric population studied.

Epilepsy, monotherapy:

>10%:

Central nervous system: Paresthesia (adolescents ≥16 years and adults: 21% to 40%; children and adolescents 6 to <16 years: 2% to 16%), drowsiness (adolescents ≥16 years and adults: 9% to 15%), fatigue (14%), dizziness (adolescents ≥16 years and adults: 13% to 14%), memory impairment (adolescents ≥16 years and adults: 5% to 11%; children and adolescents 6 to <16 years: 1% to 3%), mood disorder (1% to 11%)

Endocrine & metabolic: Decreased serum bicarbonate (children ≥6 years, adolescents, and adults: 9% to 25%), weight loss (6% to 21%)

Gastrointestinal: Anorexia (4% to 14%), diarrhea (5% to 11%)

Respiratory: Upper respiratory tract infection (children and adolescents 6 to <16 years: 16% to 18%)

Miscellaneous: Fever (children and adolescents 6 to <16 years: ≤12%)

1% to 10%:

Cardiovascular: Flushing (children and adolescents 6 to <16 years: ≤5%), chest pain (adolescents ≥16 years and adults: 1% to 2%)

Central nervous system: Lack of concentration (7% to 10%), depression (≤9%), insomnia (adolescents ≥16 years and adults: 8% to 9%), cognitive dysfunction (≤7%), anxiety (adolescents ≥16 years and adults: 4% to 6%), hypoesthesia (adolescents ≥16 years and adults: 4% to 5%), nervousness (children and adolescents 10 to 16 years: 4% to 5%), psychomotor retardation (adolescents ≥16 years and adults: 3% to 5%), ataxia (adolescents ≥16 years and adults: 3% to 4%), confusion (≤4%), behavioral problems (children and adolescents 6 to <16 years: ≤3%), hypertonia (adolescents ≥16 years and adults: ≤3%), vertigo (children and adolescents 6 to <16 years: ≤3%)

Dermatologic: Alopecia (1% to 5%), pruritus (adolescents ≥16 years and adults: 1% to 4%), skin rash (1% to 4%), acne vulgaris (adolescents ≥16 years and adults: 2% to 3%)

Endocrine & metabolic: Increased gamma-glutamyl transferase (adolescents ≥16 years and adults: 1% to 3%), intermenstrual bleeding (children and adolescents 6 to <16 years: ≤3%)

Gastrointestinal: Dysgeusia (adolescents ≥16 years and adults: 3% to 5%), constipation (adolescents ≥16 years and adults: 1% to 4%), gastritis (adolescents ≥16 years and adults: ≤3%), xerostomia (adolescents ≥16 years and adults: 1% to 3%), gastroesophageal reflux disease (adolescents ≥16 years and adults: 1% to 2%)

Genitourinary: Decreased libido (adolescents ≥16 years and adults: ≤3%), urinary frequency (≤3%), vaginal hemorrhage (adolescents ≥16 years and adults: ≤3%), cystitis (adolescents ≥16 years and adults: 1% to 3%), urinary incontinence (children and adolescents 6 to <16 years: 1% to 3%), dysuria (adolescents ≥16 years and adults: ≤2%), urinary tract infection (adolescents ≥16 years and adults: 1% to 2%)

Hematologic & oncologic: Anemia (1% to 3%)

Infection: Viral infection (3% to 9%), infection (2% to 8%)

Neuromuscular & skeletal: Weakness (≤6%), muscle spasm (children and adolescents 6 to <16 years: ≤3%), leg pain (adolescents ≥16 years and adults: 2% to 3%)

Renal: Nephrolithiasis (adolescents ≥16 years and adults: ≤3%)

Respiratory: Rhinitis (2% to 7%), bronchitis (1% to 7%), sinusitis (children and adolescents 6 to <16 years: 1% to 5%), epistaxis (children and adolescents 6 to <16 years: ≤4%), dyspnea (adolescents ≥16 years and adults: 1% to 2%)

Migraine prophylaxis:

Frequency not always defined.

Central nervous system: Paresthesia (adults: 35% to 51%; children and adolescents ≥12 years: 19% to 20%; dose related), fatigue (8% to 15%; dose related), insomnia (6% to 9%), drowsiness (6% to 8%; dose related), memory impairment (adults 7%; dose related), hypoesthesia (adults 6% to 7%; dose related), dizziness (children and adolescents ≥12 years: 6%), lack of concentration (adults: 3% to 6%; children and adolescents ≥12 years: ≤2%), mood disorder (adults: 3% to 6%; dose related), anxiety (adults: 4% to 5%; dose related), headache (children and adolescents ≥12 years: 4%; adults: >1%), nervousness (4%), confusion (adults: 3%; dose related), psychomotor retardation (≤3%), agitation (adults: 2%), cognitive dysfunction (adults: 2%), exacerbation of depression (adults: 2%), ataxia (adults: 1% to 2%), pain (children and adolescents ≥12 years: >1%), sensory disturbance (adults: >1%), vertigo (adults: >1%), speech disturbance (adults: 1%; dose related)

Dermatologic: Pruritus (4%), alopecia (adults: >1%), skin rash (>1%)

Endocrine & metabolic: Decreased serum bicarbonate (23% to 39%), hyperammonemia (children and adolescents ≥12 years: 14% to 26%), weight loss (4% to 9%; dose related), menstrual disease (adults: 3%), increased thirst (adults: 2%), intermenstrual bleeding (adults: >1%), hyperchloremia, increased serum total protein, increased uric acid

Gastrointestinal: Anorexia (9% to 15%; dose related), abdominal pain (6% to 15%), dysgeusia (6% to 15%), nausea (8% to 13%), dyspepsia (adults: 4% to 5%), gastroenteritis (3%), xerostomia (adults: 3%; dose related), diarrhea (children and adolescents ≥12 years: 2%), constipation (adults: >1%), gastroesophageal reflux disease (adults: >1%), vomiting (children and adolescents ≥12 years: >1%), ageusia (adults: 1%)

Genitourinary: Urinary tract infection (4%), premature ejaculation (adults: ≤3%), genital candidiasis (adults: >1%), urinary incontinence (children and adolescents ≥12 years: >1%)

Hematologic & oncologic: Neoplasm (adults: 2%), abnormal phosphorus levels (decreased), thrombocythemia

Hypersensitivity: Hypersensitivity reaction (≤4%)

Infection: Viral infection (4% to 8%), infection (>1%)

Neuromuscular & skeletal: Arthralgia (adults: 3% to 7%), leg pain (children and adolescents ≥12 years: 2%), muscle spasm (adults: 2%; dose related), weakness (adults: 2%), back pain (children and adolescents ≥12 years: >1%), myalgia (>1%), tremor (adults: >1%)

Ophthalmic: Conjunctivitis (children and adolescents ≥12 years: 7%; adults: 2%), blurred vision (adults: 4%), visual disturbance (1% to 2%; dose related), accommodation disturbance (adults: >1%), eye pain (>1%)

Otic: Otitis media (adults: 1% to 2%)

Renal: Nephrolithiasis (adults: ≤1%; dose related), increased blood urea nitrogen, increased serum creatinine

Respiratory: Upper respiratory tract infection (children and adolescents ≥12 years: 23% to 26%; adults: 13% to 14%), sinusitis (4% to 10%), rhinitis (children and adolescents ≥12 years: 6% to 7%; adults: 2%), cough (2% to 7%), pharyngitis (5% to 6%), bronchitis (adults: 3%; children and adolescents ≥12 years: >1%), dyspnea (adults: 3%), epistaxis (2%), asthma (>1%), flu-like symptoms (children and adolescents ≥12 years: >1%), pneumonia (adults: >1%)

Miscellaneous: Accidental injury (9%), language problems (adults: 6% to 7%), fever (children and adolescents ≥12 years: 4% to 6%)

<1%, postmarketing, and/or case reports (**any indication**): Abnormal dreams, abnormal electroencephalogram, abnormal hair texture, acute myopia with secondary angle-closure glaucoma, albuminuria, alcohol intolerance, altered sense of smell, angina pectoris, apraxia, atrioventricular block, blepharoptosis, bone marrow depression, brain disease, bullous rash, cerebellar syndrome, chloasma, deep vein thrombosis, dehydration, delirium, delusions, diabetes mellitus, dyskinesia, dystonia, ejaculatory disorder, enlargement of abdomen, erythema multiforme, hepatic failure, hepatitis, hyperchloremic metabolic acidosis (nonanion gap), hyperesthesia, hyperglycemia, hyperlipidemia, hypernatremia, hyperthermia, hypocalcemia, hypocholesterolemia, hypohidrosis, hyponatremia, hypotension, hypothermia (with valproic acid, with or without hyperammonemia). impotence, increased libido, increased serum ALT, increased serum AST, iritis, lymphadenopathy, lymphocytopenia, lymphocytosis, maculopathy, manic reaction, melena, mydriasis, neuropathy, nipple discharge, oliguria, orthostatic hypotension, ostealgia, pancreatitis, pancytopenia, paranoia, pemphigus, phlebitis, photophobia, polycythemia, polyuria, psychosis, pulmonary embolism, renal pain, scotoma, skin photosensitivity, Stevens-Johnson syndrome, stomatitis, strabismus, suicidal ideation, suicidal tendencies, tongue edema, tongue paralysis, toxic epidermal necrolysis, upper motor neuron lesion, urinary retention, urticaria, vasodilatation, vasospasm, visual field defect, voice disorder, xerophthalmia

General Dosage Range Dosage adjustment recommended in patients with renal impairment

Oral:

Immediate release:

Epilepsy, monotherapy and adjunctive therapy:

Children 2 years to <10 years: Initial: 25 mg once daily **or** 1 to 3 mg/kg/day; Maintenance: 150 to 400 mg/day in 2 divided doses **or** 5 to 9 mg/kg/day in 2 divided doses.

Children ≥10 years and Adolescents <17 years: Initial: 25 mg once or twice daily **or** 1 to 3 mg/kg/day; Maintenance: 5 to 9 mg/kg/day in 2 divided doses **or** 25 to 200 mg twice daily

Adolescents ≥17 years: Initial: 25 mg once or twice daily; Maintenance: 100 to 200 mg twice daily

Adults: Initial: 25 to 50 mg daily in 1 to 2 divided doses; Maintenance: 50 to 200 mg twice daily

Migraine: *Adolescents ≥12 years and Adults:* Initial: 25 mg once daily (in evening); Maintenance: 100 mg daily in 2 divided doses

Extended release:

Epilepsy, monotherapy:

Children 2 to <10 years (Qudexy XR only): Initial: 25 mg once daily; Maintenance: 150 mg to 400 mg once daily

Children 6 to <10 years (Trokendi XR only): Initial: 25 mg once daily; Maintenance: 150 mg to 400 mg once daily.

Children ≥10 years and Adolescents: Initial: 50 mg daily; Maintenance 400 mg once daily

Adults: Initial: 50 mg daily once daily; Maintenance: 400 mg once daily

Epilepsy, adjunctive therapy:

Children 2 to <6 years (Qudexy XR only): Initial: 25 mg (1 to 3 mg/kg/day) once daily; Maintenance 5 to 9 mg/kg once daily

Children ≥6 years and Adolescents <17 years: Initial: 25 mg (1 to 3 mg/kg/day) once daily (in evening); Maintenance 5 to 9 mg/kg once daily

Adolescents ≥17 years and Adults: Initial: 25 to 50 mg daily once daily; Maintenance: 200 to 400 mg once daily

Mechanism of Action Anticonvulsant activity may be due to a combination of potential mechanisms: Blocks neuronal voltage-dependent sodium channels, enhances GABA(A) activity, antagonizes AMPA/kainate glutamate receptors, and weakly inhibits carbonic anhydrase.

Pharmacodynamics/Kinetics

Half-life Elimination

Immediate release:

Not receiving concomitant enzyme inducers or valproic acid:

Neonates (full-term) with hypothermia: ~43 hours (Fillipi 2009)

Infants and Children 9 months to <4 years: 10.4 hours (range: 8.5 to 15.3 hours) (Mikaeloff 2004)

Children 4 to 7 years: Mean range: 7.7 to 8 hours (Rosenfeld 1999)

Children 8 to 11 years: Mean range: 11.3 to 11.7 hours (Rosenfeld 1999)

Children and Adolescents 12 to 17 years: Mean range: 12.3 to 12.8 hours (Rosenfeld 1999)

Receiving concomitant enzyme inducers (eg, carbamazepine, phenytoin, phenobarbital):

Neonates (full-term) with hypothermia: 26.5 hours (Fillipi 2009)

Infants and Children 9 months to <4 years: 6.5 hours (range: 3.75 to 10.2 hours) (Mikaeloff 2004)

Children and Adolescents 4 to 17 years: 7.5 hours (Rosenfeld 1999)

Receiving valproic acid: Infants and Children 9 months to 4 years: 9.2 hours (range: 7.23 to 12 hours) (Mikaeloff 2004)

Adults: 19 to 23 hours (mean: 21 hours)

Adults with renal impairment: 59 ± 11 hours

Extended release: Qudexy XR: ~56 hours; Trokendi XR: ~31 hours

Time to Peak

Immediate release:

Neonates (full-term) with hypothermia: 3.8 hours (Fillipi 2009)

Infants and Children 9 months to <4 years: 3.7 hours (range: 1.5 to 10.2 hours) (Michealoff 2004)

Children 4 to 17 years: Mean range: 1 to 2.8 hours (Rosenfeld 1999)

Adults: 2 hours; range: 1.4 to 4.3 hours

Extended release: Qudexy XR: ~20 hours; Trokendi XR: ~24 hours

Pregnancy Risk Factor D

Pregnancy Considerations Adverse events have been observed in animal reproduction studies. Based on limited data (n=5), topiramate was found to cross the placenta and could be detected in neonatal serum (Ohman 2002). Topiramate may cause fetal harm if administered to a pregnant woman. An increased risk of oral clefts (cleft lip and/or palate) has been observed following first trimester exposure. Data from the North American Antiepileptic Drug (NAAED) Pregnancy Registry reported that the prevalence of oral clefts was 1.2% for infants exposed to topiramate during the first trimester of pregnancy, versus 0.39% to 0.46% for infants exposed to other antiepileptic drugs and 0.12% with no exposure. Although not evaluated during pregnancy, metabolic acidosis may be induced by topiramate. In general, metabolic acidosis during pregnancy may result in adverse effects and fetal death. Pregnant women and their newborns should be monitored for metabolic acidosis. Maternal serum concentrations may decrease during the second and third trimesters of pregnancy therefore therapeutic drug monitoring should be considered in pregnant women who require therapy (Ohman 2009; Westin 2009). Effective contraception should be used in women who are not planning a pregnancy; consider use of alternative medications in women who wish to become pregnant.

Patients exposed to topiramate during pregnancy are encouraged to enroll themselves into the AED Pregnancy Registry by calling 1-888-233-2334. Additional information is available at www.aedpregnancyregistry.org.

Topotecan (toe poe TEE kan)

Brand Names: US Hycamtin

Brand Names: Canada Hycamtin; Topotecan For Injection; Topotecan Hydrochloride For Injection

Pharmacologic Category Antineoplastic Agent, Camptothecin; Antineoplastic Agent, Topoisomerase I Inhibitor

Use

Cervical cancer, recurrent or resistant: Treatment of recurrent or resistant (stage IVB) cervical cancer (in combination with cisplatin) which is not amenable to curative treatment

Ovarian cancer, metastatic: Treatment of metastatic ovarian cancer (as a single agent) after disease progression on or after initial or subsequent chemotherapy

Small cell lung cancer, relapsed:

Injection: Treatment of small cell lung cancer (as a single agent) in patients with platinum-sensitive disease which has progressed at least 60 days after initiation of first-line chemotherapy

Oral: Treatment of relapsed small cell lung cancer in patients with a prior complete or partial response and who are at least 45 days from the end of first-line chemotherapy

Local Anesthetic/Vasoconstrictor Precautions No information available to require special precautions

Effects on Dental Treatment Key adverse event(s) related to dental treatment: Stomatitis.

Effects on Bleeding Chemotherapy may result in significant myelosuppression, potentially including significant thrombocytopenia (grade 4: 6% to 27%, nadir 15 days, duration 3-5 days) and altered hemostasis. In patients who are under active treatment with these agents, medical consult is suggested.

Adverse Reactions

>10%:

Central nervous system: Fatigue (oral: 11% to 19%)

Dermatologic: Alopecia (oral: 10% to 20%)

Gastrointestinal: Nausea (oral: 27% to 33%), anorexia (intravenous: 32%; oral: 7% to 14%), diarrhea (oral: 14% to 22%, grade 3: 4%, grade 4: ≤1%; intravenous: grades 3/4: 6%), vomiting (oral: 19% to 21%)

Hematologic & oncologic: Anemia (oral: 94% to 98%; grades 3/4: 25%; grade 3: 15% to 18%; grade 4: 7% to 10%; intravenous: grades 3/4: 37% to 42%), neutropenia (oral: 83% to 91%; grade 3: 24% to 28%; grade 4: 32% to 33%; intravenous: grade 4: 70% to 80%; nadir 12 to 15 days; duration: 7 days), thrombocytopenia (oral: 81%; grade 3: 29% to 30%; grade 4: 6% to 7%; intravenous: grade 4: 27% to

29%; nadir: 15 days; duration: 3 to 5 days), febrile neutropenia (intravenous: grade 3/4: 23% to 28%; oral: grade 4: 4%), neutropenic infection (13% to 17%)

1% to 10%:

Gastrointestinal: Abdominal pain (intravenous: grades 3/4: 5% to 6%)

Hepatic: Increased liver enzymes (intravenous: 8%; transient)

Neuromuscular & skeletal: Weakness (3% to 7%)

Respiratory: Dyspnea (intravenous: 6% to 9%)

Miscellaneous: Fever (oral: 5% to 7%), sepsis (intravenous: grades 3/4: 5%; oral: 2%)

<1%, postmarketing, and/or case reports: Anaphylactoid reactions, angioedema, arthralgia, chest pain, cough, dermatitis (severe), extravasation, headache, hemorrhage (severe, associated with thrombocytopenia), hypersensitivity reaction, interstitial pulmonary disease, leukopenia, myalgia, neutropenic enterocolitis, pancytopenia, paresthesia, pruritus (severe), skin rash, stomatitis, typhlitis

General Dosage Range Dosage adjustment recommended in patients with renal impairment or who develop toxicities

Oral: *Adults:* 2.3 mg/m^2/day for 5 days; repeated every 21 days

IV: *Adults:* IVPB: 1.5 mg/m^2/day for 5 days; repeated every 21 days **or** 0.75 mg/m^2/day for 3 days; repeated every 21 days

Mechanism of Action Binds to topoisomerase I and stabilizes the cleavable complex so that religation of the cleaved DNA strand cannot occur. This results in the accumulation of cleavable complexes and single-strand DNA breaks. Topotecan acts in S phase of the cell cycle.

Pharmacodynamics/Kinetics

Half-life Elimination

Pediatric patients (0-18 years): Lactone moiety: 2.58 hours ± 0.15 (range: 0.2-7.1 hours) (Santana 2005)

Adults: IV: 2 to 3 hours; renal impairment: ~5 hours; Oral: 3 to 6 hours

Time to Peak

Pediatric patients (1-18 years): Parenteral formulation (reconstituted lyophilized formulation): 0.75-2 hours (Zamboni 1999)

Adults: Oral: 1 to 2 hours; delayed with high-fat meal (1.5 to 4 hours)

Pregnancy Risk Factor D

Pregnancy Considerations Adverse effects were observed in animal reproduction studies. May cause fetal harm in pregnant women. Women of childbearing potential should use highly effective contraception to prevent pregnancy during treatment and for at least 1 month after therapy discontinuation. Males with female partners of childbearing potential should use highly effective contraception during treatment and for 3 months after therapy discontinuation. Topotecan may have both acute and long-term effects on fertility in women; fertility in males may be impaired due to effects on spermatogenesis.

Toremifene (tore EM i feen)

Related Information

Clinical Risk Related to Drugs Prolonging QT Interval *on page 1772*

Brand Names: US Fareston

Brand Names: Canada Fareston

Pharmacologic Category Antineoplastic Agent, Estrogen Receptor Antagonist; Selective Estrogen Receptor Modulator (SERM)

Use Breast cancer, metastatic: Treatment of metastatic breast cancer in postmenopausal women with estrogen receptor positive or estrogen receptor status unknown tumors

Local Anesthetic/Vasoconstrictor Precautions Toremifene is one of the drugs confirmed to prolong the QT interval and is accepted as having a risk of causing torsade de pointes. The risk of drug-induced torsade de pointes is extremely low when a single QT interval prolonging drug is prescribed. In terms of epinephrine, it is not known what effect vasoconstrictors in the local anesthetic regimen will have in patients with a known history of congenital prolonged QT interval or in patients taking any medication that prolongs the QT interval. Until more information is obtained, it is suggested that the clinician consult with the physician prior to the use of a vasoconstrictor in suspected patients, and that the vasoconstrictor (epinephrine, mepivacaine and levonordefrin [Carbocaine® 2% with Neo-Cobefrin®]) be used with caution.

Effects on Dental Treatment No significant effects or complications reported

Effects on Bleeding Although significant myelosuppression with associated altered hemostasis has been reported for many chemotherapeutic agents, myelosuppression is not common with toremifene and no specific precautions appear to necessary.

Adverse Reactions

>10%:

Dermatologic: Diaphoresis (20%)

Endocrine & metabolic: Hot flash (35%)

Gastrointestinal: Nausea (14%)

Genitourinary: Vaginal discharge (13%)

Hepatic: Increased serum alkaline phosphatase (8% to 19%), increased serum AST (5% to 19%)

1% to 10%:

Cardiovascular: Edema (5%), cardiac arrhythmia (≤2%), cerebrovascular accident (≤2%), local thrombophlebitis (≤2%), pulmonary embolism (≤2%), thrombosis (≤2%), transient ischemic attacks (≤2%), cardiac failure (≤1%), myocardial infarction (≤1%)

Central nervous system: Dizziness (9%)

Endocrine & metabolic: Hypercalcemia (≤3%)

Gastrointestinal: Vomiting (4%)

Genitourinary: Vaginal hemorrhage (2%)

Hepatic: Increased serum bilirubin (1% to 2%)

Ophthalmic: Cataract (≤10%), xerophthalmia (≤9%), visual field defect (≤4%), corneal disease (≤2%), glaucoma (≤2%), visual disturbance (≤2%), diplopia (≤2%)

<1%, postmarketing, and/or case reports: Alopecia, angina pectoris, anorexia, arthritis, ataxia, blurred vision, constipation, corneal opacity (reversible; including corneal verticulata), depression, dermatitis, dyspnea, endometrial carcinoma, endometrial hyperplasia, fatigue, jaundice, lethargy, leukopenia, paresis, prolonged Q-T interval on ECG, pruritus, rigors, skin discoloration, thrombocytopenia, toxic hepatitis, tremor, tumor flare, vertigo, weakness

General Dosage Range Oral: *Adults:* 60 mg once daily

Mechanism of Action Nonsteroidal, triphenylethylene derivative with potent antiestrogenic properties (also has estrogenic effects). Competitively binds to estrogen receptors on tumors and inhibits the growth stimulating effects of estrogen.

Pharmacodynamics/Kinetics

Half-life Elimination Toremifene: ~5 days, ~7 days (females >60 years); N-demethyltoremifene: 6 days

Time to Peak Serum: ≤3 hours

Pregnancy Risk Factor D

Pregnancy Considerations Adverse events were observed in animal reproduction studies. Based on the mechanism of action, may cause fetal harm if administered during pregnancy. Toremifene is only approved for use in postmenopausal women; however, if prescribed in premenopausal women, effective non-hormonal contraception should be used.

Dental Comment See Local Anesthetic/Vasoconstrictor Precautions

Torsemide (TORE se mide)

Related Information

Cardiovascular Diseases *on page 1752*

Brand Names: US Demadex

Pharmacologic Category Antihypertensive; Diuretic, Loop

Use

Edema: Treatment of edema associated with heart failure and hepatic or renal disease.

Hypertension: Management of hypertension (monotherapy or in combination with other antihypertensives).

Note: According to the Eighth Joint National Committee (JNC 8) guidelines, loop diuretics are not recommended for the initial treatment of hypertension (James, 2013). In patients with chronic kidney disease (ie, eGFR <30 mL/minute/1.73 m^2), the American Society of Hypertension/International Society of Hypertension (ASH/ISH) suggests that the use of a loop diuretic may be necessary (Weber, 2014).

Local Anesthetic/Vasoconstrictor Precautions No information available to require special precautions

Effects on Dental Treatment No significant effects or complications reported

Effects on Bleeding No information available to require special precautions

Adverse Reactions

1% to 10%:

Cardiovascular: ECG abnormality (2%), chest pain (1%)

Central nervous system: Nervousness (1%)

Gastrointestinal: Constipation (2%), diarrhea (2%), dyspepsia (2%), nausea (2%), sore throat (2%)

Neuromuscular & skeletal: Arthralgia (2%), myalgia (2%), weakness (2%)

Renal: Polyuria (7%)

Respiratory: Rhinitis (3%), cough (2%)

<1%, postmarketing, and/or case reports: Angioedema, arthritis, atrial fibrillation, esophageal hemorrhage, gastrointestinal hemorrhage, hyperglycemia, hyperuricemia, hypokalemia, hyponatremia, hypotension, hypovolemia, impotence, increased thirst, leukopenia, pancreatitis, rectal hemorrhage, shunt thrombosis, skin rash, Stevens-Johnson syndrome, syncope, thrombocytopenia, toxic epidermal necrolysis, ventricular tachycardia, vomiting

General Dosage Range

IV: *Adults:* 10 to 200 mg once daily

Oral: *Adults:* 5 to 200 mg once daily

Mechanism of Action Inhibits reabsorption of sodium and chloride in the ascending loop of Henle and distal renal tubule, interfering with the chloride-binding cotransport system, thus causing increased excretion of water, sodium, chloride, magnesium, and calcium; does not alter GFR, renal plasma flow, or acid-base balance

Pharmacodynamics/Kinetics

Onset of Action Diuresis: Oral: Within 1 hour; IV: 10 minutes; Peak effect: Diuresis: Oral: 1 to 2 hours; IV: Within 60 minutes; Antihypertensive: Oral: 4 to 6 weeks (up to 12 weeks)

Duration of Action Diuresis: Oral, IV: ~6 to 8 hours

Half-life Elimination ~3.5 hours

Time to Peak Plasma: Oral: Within 1 hour; delayed ~30 minutes when administered with food

Pregnancy Considerations Adverse events have been observed in animal reproduction studies.

Product Availability Torsemide injection has been discontinued in the US for more than 1 year.

TraMADol (TRA ma dole)

Related Sample Prescriptions

Oral Pain - Sample Prescriptions *on page 28*

Brand Names: US Active-Tramadol; ConZip; EnovaRX-Tramadol; Rybix ODT [DSC]; Synapryn FusePaq; Ultram; Ultram ER [DSC]

Brand Names: Canada Apo-Tramadol; Durela; Ralivia; Taro-Tramadol; Tridural; Ultram; Zytram XL

Generic Availability (US) May be product dependent

Pharmacologic Category Analgesic, Opioid

Dental Use Relief of moderate to moderately-severe dental pain

Use

Pain management: Management of pain severe enough to require daily, around-the-clock, long-term opioid treatment and for which alternative treatment options are inadequate.

Limitations of use: Reserve tramadol for use in patients for whom alternative treatment options (eg, nonopioid analgesics, opioid combination products) are ineffective, not tolerated, or would be otherwise inadequate to provide sufficient management of pain. Tramadol ER is not indicated as an as-needed analgesic.

Local Anesthetic/Vasoconstrictor Precautions No information available to require special precautions

Effects on Dental Treatment Key adverse event(s) related to dental treatment: Xerostomia and changes in salivation (normal salivary flow resumes upon discontinuation). See Dental Comment.

Effects on Bleeding No information available to require special precautions

Adverse Reactions

>10%:

Cardiovascular: Flushing (8% to 16%)

Central nervous system: Dizziness (10% to 33%), headache (4% to 32%), drowsiness (7% to 25%), central nervous system stimulation (7% to 14%), insomnia (2% to 11%)

Dermatologic: Pruritus (3% to 12%)

Gastrointestinal: Constipation (9% to 46%), nausea (15% to 40%), vomiting (5% to 17%), xerostomia (3% to 13%), dyspepsia (1% to 13%)

Neuromuscular & skeletal: Weakness (4% to 12%)

1% to 10%:

Cardiovascular: Orthostatic hypotension (2% to 5%), chest pain (1% to <5%), hypertension (1% to <5%), peripheral edema (1% to <5%), vasodilation (1% to <5%)

Central nervous system: Agitation (1% to <5%), anxiety (1% to <5%), apathy (1% to <5%), ataxia (1% to <5%), chills (1% to <5%), confusion (1% to <5%), depersonalization (1% to <5%), depression (1% to

<5%), euphoria (1% to <5%), hypertonia (1% to <5%), hypoesthesia (1% to <5%), lethargy (1% to <5%), malaise (<1% to <5%), nervousness (1% to <5%), pain (1% to <5%), paresthesia (1% to <5%), restlessness (1% to <5%), rigors (1% to <5%), sleep disorder (1% to <5%) withdrawal syndrome (1% to <5%), fatigue (2%), vertigo (2%)

Dermatologic: Diaphoresis (2% to 9%), dermatitis (1% to <5%), skin rash (1% to <5%)

Endocrine & metabolic: Hot flash (1% to <5%), hyperglycemia (1% to <5%), weight loss (1% to <5%)

Gastrointestinal: Diarrhea (5% to 10%), anorexia (1% to 6%), abdominal pain (1% to <5%), decreased appetite (1% to <5%), flatulence (<1% to <5%), sore throat (1% to <5%)

Genitourinary: Menopausal symptoms (1% to <5%), pelvic pain (1% to <5%), prostatic disease (1% to <5%), urine abnormality (1% to <5%), urinary tract infection (1% to <5%), urinary frequency (<1% to <5%), urinary retention (<1% to <5%)

Neuromuscular & skeletal: Arthralgia (1% to 5%), back pain (1% to <5%), increased creatine phosphokinase (1% to <5%), myalgia (1% to <5%), neck pain (1% to <5%), tremor (1% to <5%)

Ophthalmic: Blurred vision (1% to <5%), miosis (1% to <5%), visual disturbance (1% to <5%)

Respiratory: Bronchitis (1% to <5%), cough (1% to <5%), dyspnea (1% to <5%), nasopharyngitis (1% to <5%), pharyngitis (1% to <5%), respiratory congestion (1% to <5%), rhinitis (1% to <5%), rhinorrhea (1% to <5%), sinusitis (1% to <5%), sneezing (1% to <5%), upper respiratory tract infection (1% to <5%)

Miscellaneous: Accidental injury (<5%), fever (1% to <5%), flu-like syndrome (1% to <5%)

<1%, postmarketing, and/or case reports (limited to important or life-threatening): Abnormal dreams, abnormal gait, amnesia, anaphylactoid reaction, anaphylaxis, anemia, angioedema, appendicitis, bradycardia, bronchospasm, cataract, cellulitis, changes in ALT, changes in AST, cholecystitis, cholelithiasis, cognitive dysfunction, cold and clammy skin, convulsions, deafness, decreased hemoglobin, decreased libido, delirium, disorientation, diverticulitis, dysgeusia, dysphagia, dysuria, ECG abnormality, edema, fecal impaction, gastroenteritis, gastrointestinal hemorrhage, gout, hallucination, hematuria, hepatic failure, hepatitis, hypersensitivity, hypersensitivity reaction, hypoglycemia, hypotension, increased blood urea nitrogen, increased gamma-glutamyl transferase, increased liver enzymes, increased serum creatinine, irritability, ischemic heart disease, joint stiffness, lack of concentration, menstrual disease, migraine, movement disorder, muscle cramps, muscle spasm, muscle twitching, mydriasis, myocardial infarction, night sweats, otitis, palpitations, pancreatitis, peripheral edema, peripheral ischemia, pneumonia, proteinuria, pulmonary edema, pulmonary embolism, sedation, seizure, serotonin syndrome, shivering, skin vesicle, speech disturbance, Stevens-Johnson syndrome, stomatitis, suicidal tendencies, syncope, tachycardia, thrombocytopenia, tinnitus, toxic epidermal necrolysis, urticaria

Dental Usual Dosage Moderate-to-severe chronic pain: Oral:

Adults:

Immediate release formulation: 50-100 mg every 4-6 hours (not to exceed 400 mg/day)

For patients not requiring rapid onset of effect, tolerability may be improved by starting dose at 25 mg/day and titrating dose by 25 mg every 3 days, until reaching 25 mg 4 times/day. The total daily dose may then be increased by 50 mg every 3 days as tolerated, to reach dose of 50 mg 4 times/day. After titration, 50-100 mg may be given every 4-6 hours as needed up to a maximum 400 mg/day.

Extended release formulations:

Ultram ER:

Patients not currently on immediate-release: 100 mg once daily; titrate every 5 days (maximum: 300 mg/day)

Patients currently on immediate-release: Calculate 24-hour immediate release total and initiate total daily dose (round dose to the next lowest 100 mg increment); titrate (maximum: 300 mg/day)

Ralivia (Canadian labeling, not available in US): 100 mg once daily; titrate every 5 days as needed based on clinical response and severity of pain (maximum: 300 mg/day)

Tridural (Canadian labeling, not available in US): 100 mg once daily; titrate by 100 mg/day every 2 days as needed based on clinical response and severity of pain (maximum: 300 mg/day)

Zytram XL (Canadian labeling, not available in US): 150 mg once daily; if pain relief is not achieved may titrate by increasing dosage incrementally, with sufficient time to evaluate effect of increased dosage; generally not more often than every 7 days (maximum: 400 mg/day)

Elderly >75 years:

Immediate release: 50 mg every 6 hours (not to exceed 300 mg/day); see dosing adjustments for renal and hepatic impairment.

Extended release formulation: Use with great caution. See adult dosing.

Dosing

Adult Pain management: Oral: **Note:** Doses should be titrated to appropriate analgesic effect; use the lowest effective dose for the shortest period of time:

Immediate release: 50 to 100 mg every 4 to 6 hours (maximum: 400 mg/day). For patients not requiring rapid onset of effect, tolerability may be improved by initiating therapy at 25 mg once daily in the morning and titrating dose by 25 mg every 3 days until 25 mg 4 times daily is reached. Dose may then be increased by 50 mg every 3 days as tolerated to reach 50 mg 4 times daily. After titration, 50 to 100 mg may be given every 4 to 6 hours as needed (maximum: 400 mg/day).

Orally-disintegrating tablet (Rybix ODT): 50 to 100 mg every 4 to 6 hours (maximum: 400 mg/day). For patients not requiring rapid onset of effect, tolerability may be improved by initiating with 50 mg/day and titrating dose by 50 mg every 3 days, until reaching 50 mg 4 times daily. After titration, 50 to 100 mg may be given every 4 to 6 hours as needed (maximum: 400 mg/day).

Extended release: **Note:** For patients requiring around-the-clock pain management for an extended period of time.

US labeling:

Patients not currently on tramadol immediate-release: Initial: 100 mg once daily; titrate by 100 mg increments every 5 days as needed (maximum: 300 mg/day).

Patients currently on tramadol immediate-release: Calculate 24-hour tramadol immediate release total dose and initiate total extended release daily dose (round dose to the next lowest 100 mg increment); titrate as tolerated to desired effect (maximum: 300 mg/day).

Canadian labeling: **Note:** Patients currently on immediate-release tramadol: When switching to extended release, initiate at the same or lowest nearest total daily tramadol dose. Not to exceed recommended maximum daily dosing.

Durela, Ralivia, Tridural: Patients not currently on immediate-release tramadol or opioids: Initial: 100 mg once daily; titrate every 5 days (Durela, Ralivia) or every 2 days (Tridural) as needed based on clinical response and severity of pain (maximum: 300 mg/day)

Zytram XL: Patients not currently on immediate-release tramadol or opioids: 150 mg once daily; if pain relief is not achieved may titrate by increasing dosage incrementally, with sufficient time to evaluate effect of increased dosage; generally not more often than every 7 days (maximum: 400 mg/day)

Discontinuation of therapy: Decrease dose by 25% to 50% every 2 to 4 days; monitor carefully for signs/symptoms of withdrawal. If patient displays withdrawal symptoms, increase dose to previous dose and then reduce dose more slowly by increasing interval between dose reductions, decreasing amount of daily dose reduction, or both.

Restless legs syndrome (off-label use): Oral: 50 to 100 mg once daily at bedtime or during the night (Silber 2013). Doses as high as 150 mg/day have been used (Lauerma 1999).

Geriatric Elderly >65 years to ≤75 years: Refer to adult dosing; use with caution initiate at the low end of the dosing range.

Elderly >75 years:

Immediate release: Maximum: 300 mg/day.

Extended release: Use with extreme caution.

Pediatric

Moderate to severe pain: Oral:

Immediate release: Adolescents ≥17 years: Refer to adult dosing.

Extended release: Adolescents ≥18 years: Refer to adult dosing.

Renal Impairment

Immediate release:

CrCl ≥30 mL/minute: There are no dosage adjustments provided in the manufacturer's labeling; use with caution.

CrCl <30 mL/minute: Increase dosing interval to every 12 hours (maximum: 200 mg/day).

Dialysis: Dialyzable (7%); increase dosing interval to every 12 hours; (maximum: 200 mg/day); administer regular dose on the day of dialysis.

Extended release:

CrCl ≥30 mL/minute: There are no dosage adjustments provided in the manufacturer's labeling; use with caution.

CrCl <30 mL/minute: Avoid use.

Hepatic Impairment

Immediate release: There are no dosage adjustments provided in the manufacturer's labeling. In patients with cirrhosis, recommended dose is 50 mg every 12 hours.

Extended release:

Mild to moderate impairment (Child-Pugh Class A and B): There are no dosage adjustments provided in the manufacturer's labeling; use with caution.

Severe impairment (Child-Pugh class C): Avoid use.

Mechanism of Action Tramadol and its active metabolite (M1) binds to μ-opiate receptors in the CNS causing inhibition of ascending pain pathways, altering the perception of and response to pain; also inhibits the reuptake of norepinephrine and serotonin, which are neurotransmitters involved in the descending inhibitory pain pathway responsible for pain relief (Grond 2004)

Contraindications

Hypersensitivity (eg, anaphylaxis) to tramadol, opioids, or any component of the formulation; significant respiratory depression; acute or severe bronchial asthma in the absence of appropriately monitored settings and/or resuscitative equipment; GI obstruction, including paralytic ileus (known or suspected); concomitant use with or within 14 days following MAO inhibitor therapy

Canadian product labeling:

Tramadol is contraindicated during or within 14 days following MAO inhibitor therapy

Extended release formulations: Additional contraindications:

Ralivia, Tridural: Severe (CrCl <30 mL/minute) renal dysfunction, severe (Child-Pugh class C) hepatic dysfunction

Durela and Zytram XL: Severe (CrCl <30 mL/minute) renal dysfunction, severe (Child-Pugh class C) hepatic dysfunction; known or suspected mechanical GI obstruction or any disease/condition that affects bowel transit; mild, intermittent or short-duration pain that can be managed with other pain medication; management of perioperative pain; obstructive airway, acute respiratory depression, cor pulmonale, delirium tremens, seizure disorder, severe CNS depression, increased cerebrospinal or intracranial pressure, head injury, breastfeeding, pregnancy; use during labor and delivery

Warnings/Precautions [US Boxed Warning]: Serious, life-threatening, or fatal respiratory depression may occur. Monitor closely for respiratory depression, especially during initiation or dose escalation. Swallow ER tablets whole; crushing, chewing, or dissolving can cause rapid release and a potentially fatal dose. Carbon dioxide retention from opioid-induced respiratory depression can exacerbate the sedating effects of opioids. Use with caution and monitor for respiratory depression in patients with significant chronic obstructive pulmonary disease or cor pulmonale, and those with a substantially decreased respiratory reserve, hypoxia, hypercapnia, or preexisting respiratory depression, particularly when initiating and titrating therapy; critical respiratory depression may occur, even at therapeutic dosages. Consider the use of alternative nonopioid analgesics in these patients.

[US Boxed Warning]: Tramadol exposes patients and other users to the risks of addiction, abuse, and misuse, potentially leading to overdose and death. Assess each patient's risk prior to prescribing; monitor all patients regularly for development of these behaviors or conditions. Use with caution in patients with a history of drug abuse or acute alcoholism; potential for drug dependency exists. Other factors associated with increased risk for misuse include younger age, concomitant depression (major), and psychotropic medication use. Consider offering naloxone prescriptions in patients with factors associated with an increased risk for overdose, such as history of overdose or substance use disorder, higher opioid dosages (≥50 morphine milligram equivalents/day orally), and concomitant benzodiazepine use (Dowell [CDC 2016]). **[US Boxed Warning]: Accidental ingestion of even one dose of tramadol, especially in children, can result in a fatal overdose of tramadol.**

[US Boxed Warning]: Concomitant use of opioids with benzodiazepines or other CNS depressants, including alcohol, may result in profound sedation, respiratory depression, coma, and death. Reserve concomitant prescribing of tramadol and benzodiazepines or other CNS depressants for use in patients for whom alternative treatment options are inadequate. Limit dosage and durations to the minimum required and follow patients for signs and symptoms of respiratory depression and sedation. [US Boxed Warning]: Use with all CYP3A4 inhibitors may result in an increase in tramadol plasma concentrations, which could increase or prolong adverse drug effects and may cause potentially fatal respiratory depression. In addition, discontinuation of a concomitant CYP 3A4 inducer may result in increased tramadol concentrations. Monitor patients receiving tramadol and any CYP 3A4 inhibitor or inducer. Potentially significant interactions may exist, requiring dose or frequency adjustment, additional monitoring, and/or selection of alternative therapy.

Even when taken within the recommended dosage seizures may occur; risk is increased in patients receiving serotonin reuptake inhibitors (SSRIs), serotonin norepinephrine reuptake inhibitors (SNRIs), anorectics, other opioids, tricyclic antidepressants and other tricyclic compounds (eg, cyclobenzaprine, promethazine), neuroleptics, MAO inhibitors, other drugs which may lower seizure threshold, or drugs which impair metabolism of tramadol (eg, CYP2D6 and 3A4 inhibitors). Patients with a history of seizures, or with a risk of seizures (head trauma, metabolic disorders, CNS infection, malignancy, or during alcohol/drug withdrawal) are also at increased risk. Serious anaphylactoid reactions (including rare fatalities) often following initial dosing have been reported. Pruritus, hives, bronchospasm, angioedema, toxic epidermal necrolysis (TEN), and Stevens-Johnson syndrome have also been reported. Previous anaphylactoid reactions to opioids may increase risks for similar reactions to tramadol; avoid use in these patients. If anaphylaxis or other hypersensitivity occurs, discontinue permanently; do not rechallenge. May cause CNS depression, which may impair physical or mental abilities; patients must be cautioned about performing tasks which require mental alertness (eg, operating machinery or driving).

Hypoglycemia (including severe cases) has been reported (rare) particularly within the first 30 days of tramadol initiation (Fournier 2015). May cause severe hypotension (including orthostatic hypotension and syncope); use with caution in patients with hypovolemia, cardiovascular disease (including acute MI), or drugs which may exaggerate hypotensive effects (including phenothiazines or general anesthetics). Monitor for symptoms of hypotension following initiation or dose titration. Avoid use in patients with circulatory shock. Serotonin syndrome may occur with concomitant use of serotonergic agents (eg, SSRIs, SNRIs, triptans, TCAs), lithium, St John's wort, agents that impair metabolism of serotonin (eg, MAO inhibitors), or agents that impair metabolism of tramadol (eg, CYP2D6 and 3A4 inhibitors). May obscure diagnosis or clinical course of patients with acute abdominal conditions. Avoid use in patients with impaired consciousness or coma as these patients are susceptible to intracranial effects of CO_2 retention. Use with caution in patients who are morbidly obese. Use with caution in patients with adrenal insufficiency (including Addison disease); biliary tract dysfunction or acute pancreatitis; delirium tremens; head injury, intracranial lesions, or elevated intracranial pressure; prostatic hyperplasia and/or urinary stricture; toxic psychosis; and/or thyroid dysfunction.

Use with caution and reduce dosage in patients with mild-to-moderate renal or hepatic impairment; extended release formulations should not be used in severe renal (CrCl <30 mL/minute) or hepatic impairment (Child-Pugh class C). Use opioids with caution for chronic pain in patients with mental health conditions (eg, depression, anxiety disorders, post-traumatic stress disorder) due to increased risk for opioid use disorder and overdose; more frequent monitoring is recommended. Use opioids with caution for chronic pain and titrate dosage cautiously in patients with risk factors for sleep-disordered breathing, including HF and obesity. Avoid opioids in patients with moderate to severe sleep-disordered breathing (Dowell [CDC 2016]). Avoid use in patients who are suicidal; use with caution in patients taking tranquilizers and/or antidepressants, or those with an emotional disturbance including depression. Consider the use of alternative nonopioid analgesics in these patients. Use with caution in cachectic or debilitated patients; there is a greater potential for critical respiratory depression, even at therapeutic dosages; consider the use of alternative nonopioid analgesics in these patients.

Use opioids for chronic pain with caution in older adults; monitor closely due to an increased potential for risks, including certain risks such as falls/fracture, cognitive impairment, and constipation. Clearance may also be reduced in older adults (with or without renal impairment) resulting in a narrow therapeutic window and increasing the risk for respiratory depression or overdose (Dowell [CDC 2016]). Consider the use of alternative nonopioid analgesics in these patients.

[US Boxed Warning]: Prolonged use of opioids during pregnancy can cause neonatal withdrawal syndrome in the newborn which may be life-threatening if not recognized and treated according to protocols developed by neonatology experts. If opioid use is required for a prolonged period in a pregnant woman, advise the patient of the risk of neonatal opioid withdrawal syndrome and ensure that appropriate treatment will be available. Signs and symptoms include irritability, hyperactivity and abnormal sleep pattern, high pitched cry, tremor, vomiting, diarrhea and failure to gain weight. Onset, duration and severity depend on the drug used, duration of use, maternal dose, and rate of drug elimination by the newborn.

An opioid-containing analgesic regimen should be tailored to each patient's needs and based upon the type of pain being treated (acute versus chronic), the route of administration, degree of tolerance for opioids (naive versus chronic user), age, weight, and medical condition. The optimal analgesic dose varies widely among patients; doses should be titrated to pain relief/prevention. Opioids decrease bowel motility; monitor for decrease bowel motility in postop patients receiving opioids. Use with caution in the perioperative setting; individualize treatment when transitioning from parenteral to oral analgesics. Tolerance or drug dependence may result from extended use (withdrawal symptoms have been reported); abrupt discontinuation should be avoided. Tapering of dose at the time of discontinuation limits the risk of withdrawal symptoms. Some products may contain phenylalanine.Chronic pain: Opioids should **not** be used as first-line therapy for chronic pain management (pain >3-month duration or beyond time of normal tissue healing) due to limited short-term benefits, undetermined long-term benefits, and association with serious risks (eg, overdose, MI, auto accidents, risk of developing opioid use disorder). Preferred management includes nonpharmacologic therapy and nonopioid therapy (eg, NSAIDs, acetaminophen, certain anticonvulsants and antidepressants). If opioid therapy is initiated, it should be combined with nonpharmacologic and nonopioid therapy, as appropriate. Prior to initiation, known risks of opioid therapy should be discussed and realistic treatment goals for pain/function should be established, including consideration for discontinuation if benefits do not outweigh risks. Therapy should be continued only if clinically meaningful improvement in pain/function outweighs risks. Therapy should be initiated at the lowest effective dosage using immediate-release opioids (instead of extended-release/long-acting opioids). Risk associated with use increases with higher opioid dosages. Risks and benefits should be re-evaluated when increasing dosage to ≥50 morphine milligram equivalents (MME)/day orally; dosages ≥90 MME/day orally should be avoided unless carefully justified (Dowell [CDC 2016]).

Drug Interactions

Metabolism/Transport Effects Substrate of CYP2B6 (minor), CYP2D6 (major), CYP3A4 (major); **Note:** Assignment of Major/Minor substrate status based on clinically relevant drug interaction potential

Avoid Concomitant Use

Avoid concomitant use of TraMADol with any of the following: Azelastine (Nasal); CarBAMazepine; Dapoxetine; Eluxadoline; Methylene Blue; Mixed Agonist / Antagonist Opioids; Moclobemide; Orphenadrine; Oxomemazine; Paraldehyde; Thalidomide

Increased Effect/Toxicity

TraMADol may increase the levels/effects of: Alvimopan; Azelastine (Nasal); Blonanserin; CarBAMazepine; Desmopressin; Diuretics; Eluxadoline; Flunitrazepam; HYDROcodone; Iohexol; Iomeprol; Iopamidol; Methotrimeprazine; Metoclopramide; MetyroSINE; Moclobemide; Orphenadrine; OxyCODONE; Paraldehyde; Piribedil; Pramipexole; Ramosetron; ROPINIRole; Rotigotine; Serotonin Modulators; Suvorexant; Thalidomide; Vitamin K Antagonists; Zolpidem

The levels/effects of TraMADol may be increased by: Amphetamines; Anticholinergic Agents; Anti-Parkinson Agents (Monoamine Oxidase Inhibitor); Brimonidine (Topical); Cannabis; Chlormethiazole; Chlorphenesin Carbamate; CNS Depressants; CYP2D6 Inhibitors (Strong); CYP3A4 Inhibitors (Strong); Dapoxetine; Dimethindene (Topical); Dronabinol; Droperidol; Kava Kava; Linezolid; Lofexidine; Magnesium Sulfate; Methotrimeprazine; Methylene Blue; Methylphenidate; Minocycline; Nabilone; Oxomemazine; Perampanel; Ritonavir; Rufinamide; Serotonin Modulators; Sodium Oxybate; Succinylcholine; Tapentadol; Tedizolid; Tetrahydrocannabinol

Decreased Effect

TraMADol may decrease the levels/effects of: CarBAMazepine; Diuretics; Gastrointestinal Agents (Prokinetic); Pegvisomant

The levels/effects of TraMADol may be decreased by: Antiemetics (5HT3 Antagonists); Bosentan; CarBAMazepine; CYP2D6 Inhibitors (Moderate); CYP2D6 Inhibitors (Strong); CYP3A4 Inducers (Moderate); CYP3A4 Inducers (Strong); Dabrafenib; Deferasirox; Enzalutamide; Mitotane; Mixed Agonist / Antagonist Opioids; Nalmefene; Naltrexone; Ritonavir; Siltuximab; St John's Wort; Tocilizumab

Dietary Considerations Some products may contain phenylalanine.

Pharmacodynamics/Kinetics

Onset of Action Immediate release: Within 1 hour; Peak effect: 2 to 3 hours

Half-life Elimination

Immediate release: 6.3 ± 1.4 hours; active metabolite (M1): 7.4 ± 1.4 hours; prolonged in elderly

Extended release:

Capsules: ~10 hours; active metabolite (M1): ~11 hours

Tablets: ~7.9 hours; active metabolite (M1): 8.8 hours

Time to Peak

Immediate release: ~2 hours; active metabolite (M1): 3 hours

Extended release: ~4 to 12 hours; active metabolite (M1): ~5 to 15 hours

Pregnancy Risk Factor C

Pregnancy Considerations

Adverse events have been observed in animal reproduction studies. Tramadol has been shown to cross the human placenta when administered during labor. Tramadol is not recommended for use prior to or during labor and delivery.

[US Boxed Warning]: Prolonged use of opioids during pregnancy can cause neonatal withdrawal syndrome in the newborn which may be life-threatening if not recognized and treated according to protocols developed by neonatology experts. If opioid use is required for a prolonged period in a pregnant woman, advise the patient of the risk of neonatal opioid withdrawal syndrome and ensure that appropriate treatment will be available. If chronic opioid exposure occurs in pregnancy, adverse events in the newborn (including withdrawal) may occur; monitoring of the neonate is recommended (Chou 2009). Neonatal abstinence syndrome following opioid exposure may present with autonomic (eg, fever, temperature instability), gastrointestinal (eg, diarrhea, vomiting, poor feeding/weight gain), or neurologic (eg, high-pitched crying, increased muscle tone, irritability, seizure, tremor) symptoms (Dow 2012; Hudak 2012).

Long-term opioid use may cause secondary hypogonadism, which may lead to sexual dysfunction or infertility (Brennan 2013).

Breastfeeding Considerations Tramadol is excreted in breast milk. Sixteen hours following a single 100 mg IV dose, the amount of tramadol found in breast milk was 0.1% of the maternal dose. Due to the potential for serious adverse reactions in the breastfeeding infant, breastfeeding is not recommended by the manufacturer. breastfeeding infants exposed to large doses of opioids should be monitored for apnea and sedation (Montgomery 2012).

Controlled Substance C-IV

Dosage Forms Considerations

ConZip extended release capsules are formulated as a biphasic product, providing immediate and extended release components:

100 mg: 25 mg (immediate release) and 75 mg (extended release)

200 mg: 50 mg (immediate release) and 150 mg (extended release)

300 mg: 50 mg (immediate release) and 250 mg (extended release)

EnovaRX-Tramadol and Active-Tramadol creams are compounded from kits. Refer to manufacturer's labeling for compounding instructions.

Synapryn FusePaq is a compounding kit for the preparation of an oral suspension. Refer to manufacturer's labeling for compounding instructions.

Dosage Forms

Capsule Extended Release 24 Hour, Oral:
ConZip: 100 mg, 200 mg, 300 mg
Generic: 100 mg, 150 mg, 200 mg, 300 mg

Cream, External:
Active-Tramadol: 8% (120 g)
EnovaRX-Tramadol: 5% (60 g, 120 g)

Suspension Reconstituted, Oral:
Synapryn FusePaq: 10 mg/mL (500 mL)

Tablet, Oral:
Ultram: 50 mg
Generic: 50 mg

Tablet Extended Release 24 Hour, Oral:
Generic: 100 mg, 200 mg, 300 mg

Dosage Forms: Canada

Capsule Extended Release 24 Hour, Oral:
Durela: 100 mg, 200 mg, 300 mg

Tablet Extended Release 24 Hour, Oral:
Ralivia, Tridural: 100 mg, 200 mg, 300 mg
Zytram XL: 75 mg, 100 mg, 150 mg, 200 mg, 300 mg, 400 mg

Dental Comment Literature reports suggest that the efficacy of tramadol in oral surgery pain is equivalent to the combination of aspirin and codeine. One study (Olson, 1990) showed acetaminophen and dextropropoxyphene combination to be superior to tramadol and another study showed tramadol to be superior to acetaminophen and dextropropoxyphene combination. Tramadol appears to be at least equal to if not better than codeine alone. Seizures have been reported with the use of tramadol.

Trametinib (tra ME ti nib)

Brand Names: US Mekinist

Brand Names: Canada Mekinist

Pharmacologic Category Antineoplastic Agent, MEK Inhibitor

Use Melanoma, metastatic or unresectable: Treatment of unresectable or metastatic melanoma in patients with a BRAF V600E or BRAF V600K mutation (as detected by an approved test), either as a single-agent or in combination with dabrafenib.

Limitations of use: Trametinib is not indicated for use in patients who have received prior BRAF inhibitor therapy.

Local Anesthetic/Vasoconstrictor Precautions No information available to require special precautions

Effects on Dental Treatment No significant effects or complications reported

Effects on Bleeding No information available to require special precautions

Adverse Reactions

Adverse reactions reported with monotherapy:

>10%:

Cardiovascular: Hypertension (15%), cardiomyopathy (7% to 11%; defined as cardiac failure, decreased left ventricular ejection fraction, or left ventricular dysfunction)

Dermatologic: Skin toxicity (87%, most commonly dermatitis acneiform rash, palmar-plantar erythrodysesthesia, erythema, skin rash; severe: 12%; severe toxicity and secondary skin infection requiring hospitalization: 6%), skin rash (57%; grades 3/4: 8%), acneiform eruption (19%; grades 3/4: <1%), xeroderma (11%)

Endocrine & metabolic: Hypoalbuminemia (42%)

Gastrointestinal: Diarrhea (43%), stomatitis (15%), abdominal pain (13%)

Hematologic & oncologic: Anemia (38%; grades 3/4: 2%), lymphedema (32%; includes edema, peripheral edema; grades 3/4: 1%), hemorrhage (13%; includes epistaxis, gingival bleeding, hematochezia, rectal hemorrhage, melena, vaginal hemorrhage, hemorrhoidal hemorrhage, hematuria, conjunctival hemorrhage; grades 3/4: <1%)

Hepatic: Increased serum AST (60%), increased serum ALT (39%), increased serum alkaline phosphatase (24%)

1% to 10%:

Cardiovascular: Decreased left ventricular ejection fraction (5%, ≥20% below baseline), bradycardia

Central nervous system: Dizziness

Dermatologic: Paronychia (10%), pruritus (10%; grades 3/4: 2%), cellulitis, folliculitis, pustular rash

Gastrointestinal: Dysgeusia, xerostomia

Neuromuscular & skeletal: Rhabdomyolysis

Ophthalmic: Blurred vision, dry eye syndrome

Respiratory: Interstitial pulmonary disease (≤2%), pneumonitis (≤2%)

<1%, postmarketing, and/or case reports: Retinal detachment, retinal vein occlusion

Adverse reactions reported with dual therapy (trametinib plus dabrafenib):

>10%:

Cardiovascular: Hypertension (25% to 26%), peripheral edema (21% to 25%; includes edema and lymphedema; grades 3/4: ≤1%), prolonged Q-T Interval on ECG (4% QTcF increased >60 msec; <1% QTcF prolongation to >500 msec)

Central nervous system: Headache (30% to 33%), chills (31%; grades 3/4: <1%), dizziness (11% to 14%)

Dermatologic: Skin toxicity (55% any skin toxicity; severe toxicity: <1%), skin rash (32% to 42%; includes generalized rash, pruritic rash, erythematous rash, papular rash, vesicular rash, macular rash, maculopapular rash, folliculitis rash; grades 3/4: ≤1%), xeroderma (10% to 12%)

Endocrine & metabolic: Hyperglycemia (60% to 65%; grades 3/4: 5% to 6%), hypoalbuminemia (48% to 53%), hypophosphatemia (38%), exacerbation of diabetes mellitus (27%), hyponatremia (24% to 25%)

Gastrointestinal: Nausea (34% to 35%), diarrhea (30% to 31%), vomiting (25% to 27%), abdominal pain (18% to 26%), constipation (13%)

Hematologic & oncologic: Neutropenia (46% to 50%; grades 3/4: 6% to 7%), anemia (43%; grades 3/4: 2%), lymphocytopenia (32% to 38%; grades 3/4: 8% to 9%), thrombocytopenia (19% to 21%; grades 3/4: <1%), hemorrhage (18% to 19%; includes epistaxis, hematochezia, decreased hemoglobin, purpura, rectal hemorrhage; grades 3/4: 2%; includes hepatic hematoma, duodenal ulcer hemorrhage)

Hepatic: Increased serum AST (59% to 60%), increased serum alkaline phosphatase (49% to 50%), increased serum ALT (44% to 48%)

Neuromuscular & skeletal: Arthralgia (25% to 26%), myalgia (13% to 15%)

Respiratory: Cough (20% to 21%)

Miscellaneous: Fever (54% to 57%; grades 3/4: 5% to 7%), febrile reaction (complicated with dehydration: 2%, complicated with severe chills/rigors: <1%, complicated with renal failure: <1%, complicated with syncope: <1%)

1% to 10%:

Cardiovascular: Bradycardia (<10%), cardiomyopathy (6%), venous thromboembolism (3%; deep vein thrombosis, pulmonary embolism), hypertension

Central nervous system: Intracranial hemorrhage (1%)

Gastrointestinal: Gastrointestinal hemorrhage (6%), pancreatitis

Hematologic & oncologic: Basal cell carcinoma (3%), squamous cell carcinoma of skin (3%; including keratoacanthoma)

Neuromuscular & skeletal: Rhabdomyolysis (<10%)

Respiratory: Pneumonitis (1%)

<1%, postmarketing, and/or case reports: Malignant melanoma

General Dosage Range Dosage adjustment recommended in patients who develop toxicities.

Oral: *Adults:* 2 mg once daily

Mechanism of Action Reversibly and selectively inhibits mitogen-activated extracellular kinase (MEK) 1 and 2 activation and kinase activity. MEK is a downstream effector of the protein kinase B-raf (BRAF); BRAF V600 mutations result in constitutive activation of the BRAF pathway (including MEK1 and MEK2). Through inhibition of MEK 1 and 2 kinase activity, trametinib causes decreased cellular proliferation, cell cycle arrest, and increased apoptosis (Kim, 2013). The combination of trametinib and dabrafenib allows for greater inhibition of the MAPK pathway, resulting in BRAF V600 melanoma cell death (Flaherty, 2012).

Pharmacodynamics/Kinetics

Half-life Elimination 4 to 5 days

Time to Peak 1.5 hours; delayed with a high-fat, high-calorie meal

Pregnancy Considerations Adverse effects were observed in animal reproduction studies. Based on its mechanism of action, trametinib would be expected to cause fetal harm if administered to a pregnant woman. Females of reproductive potential should use a highly effective contraceptive during therapy and for 4 months after treatment is complete. When trametinib is used in combination with dabrafenib, a highly effective nonhormonal contraceptive method should be used (dabrafenib may diminish efficacy of hormonal contraceptives). Fertility may also be impaired in females. Due to a risk for impaired spermatogenesis, males who may want to father a child should seek fertility/family planning counseling prior to initiating combination therapy with dabrafenib.

Trandolapril (tran DOE la pril)

Related Information

Cardiovascular Diseases *on page 1752*

Brand Names: US Mavik

Brand Names: Canada Mavik

Pharmacologic Category Angiotensin-Converting Enzyme (ACE) Inhibitor; Antihypertensive

Use

Hypertension: Management of hypertension alone or in combination with other antihypertensive agents

Post-myocardial infarction (MI) heart failure or left-ventricular dysfunction: Treatment of post-MI heart failure (HF) in patients who are symptomatic from HF within the first few days after sustaining acute MI or post-MI left ventricular (LV) dysfunction in stable patients who have evidence of left-ventricular systolic dysfunction (identified by wall motion abnormalities).

Guideline recommendations:

Hypertension: The 2014 guideline for the management of high blood pressure in adults (Eighth Joint National Committee [JNC 8]) recommends initiation of pharmacologic treatment to lower blood pressure for the following patients:

- Patients ≥60 years of age with systolic blood pressure (SBP) ≥150 mm Hg or diastolic blood pressure (DBP) ≥90 mm Hg. Goal of therapy is SBP <150 mm Hg and DBP <90 mm Hg.
- Patients <60 years of age with SBP ≥140 mm Hg or DBP is ≥90 mm Hg. Goal of therapy is SBP <140 mm Hg and DBP <90 mm Hg.
- Patients ≥18 years of age with diabetes and SBP ≥140 mm Hg or DBP ≥90 mm Hg. Goal of therapy is SBP <140 mm Hg and DBP <90 mm Hg.
- Patients ≥18 years of age with chronic kidney disease (CKD) and SBP ≥140 mm Hg or DBP ≥90 mm Hg. Goal of therapy is SBP <140 mm Hg and DBP <90 mm Hg.

Chronic kidney disease (CKD) and hypertension: Regardless of race or diabetes status, the use of an ACE inhibitor (ACEI) or angiotensin receptor blocker (ARB) as initial therapy is recommended to improve kidney outcomes. In the general non-black population (without CKD) including those with diabetes, initial antihypertensive treatment should consist of a thiazide-type diuretic, calcium channel blocker, ACEI, or ARB. In the general black population (without CKD) including those with diabetes, initial antihypertensive treatment should consist of a thiazide-type diuretic or a calcium channel blocker **instead of** an ACEI or ARB.

Coronary artery disease (CAD) and hypertension: The American Heart Association, American College of Cardiology and American Society of Hypertension (AHA/ACC/ASH) 2015 scientific statement for the treatment of hypertension in patients with CAD recommends the use of an ACE inhibitor (or an ARB) as part of a regimen in patients with hypertension and chronic stable angina if there is prior MI, LV systolic dysfunction, diabetes mellitus, or CKD. A BP target of <140/90 mm Hg is reasonable for the secondary prevention of cardiovascular events. A lower target BP (<130/80 mm Hg) may be appropriate in some individuals with CAD, previous MI, stroke or transient ischemic attack, or CAD risk equivalents (AHA/ACC/ASH [Rosendorff 2015]).

Heart failure: The American College of Cardiology Foundation/American Heart Association (ACCF/AHA) 2013 heart failure guidelines recommend the use of ACE inhibitors, along with other guideline directed medical therapies, to prevent heart failure in patients with a reduced ejection fraction who have a history of MI (Stage B HF), to prevent heart failure in any patient with a reduced ejection fraction (Stage B HF), or to treat those with heart failure and reduced ejection fraction (Stage C HFrEF) (ACCF/AHA [Yancy 2013]).

STEMI: The 2013 ACCF/AHA guidelines for the management of patients with ST-elevation myocardial infarction (STEMI) states that an ACE inhibitor should be initiated within the first 24 hours after STEMI in patients with anterior MI, heart failure, or left ventricular ejection fraction (LVEF) of 0.4 or less.

It is also reasonable to initiate an ACE inhibitor in all patients with STEMI (O'Gara 2013).

Local Anesthetic/Vasoconstrictor Precautions No information available to require special precautions

Effects on Dental Treatment Key adverse event(s) related to dental treatment: Patient may experience orthostatic hypotension as they stand up after treatment; especially if lying in the dental chair for an extended period of time. Use caution with sudden changes in position during and after dental treatment.

An angiotensin-converting enzyme (ACE) inhibitor cough is a dry, hacking, nonproductive cough that can potentially interfere with longer dental procedures if patient has this side effect.

Effects on Bleeding No information available to require special precautions

Adverse Reactions Frequency ranges include data from hypertension and heart failure trials. Higher rates of adverse reactions have generally been noted in patients with heart failure. However, the frequency of adverse effects associated with placebo is also increased in this population.

>10%:

Cardiovascular: Hypotension (≤11%)

Central nervous system: Dizziness (1% to 23%)

Respiratory: Cough (2% to 35%)

1% to 10%:

Cardiovascular: Syncope (6%), bradycardia (≤5%), cardiogenic shock (4%), intermittent claudication (4%), cerebrovascular accident (3%)

Endocrine & metabolic: Hyperkalemia (5%), hypocalcemia (5%)

Gastrointestinal: Gastritis (4%), diarrhea (1%)

Neuromuscular & skeletal: Myalgia (5%), weakness (3%)

Renal: Increased blood urea nitrogen (9%), increased serum creatinine (1% to 5%)

<1%, postmarketing, and/or case reports: Abdominal distention, abdominal pain, agranulocytosis, alopecia, angina pectoris, angioedema, anxiety, bronchitis, cardiac arrhythmia, cardiac failure, chest pain, constipation, decreased libido, depression, diaphoresis, drowsiness, dyspepsia, dyspnea, edema, epistaxis, fever, first degree atrioventricular block, flushing, gout, hallucination, hepatitis, hyponatremia, impotence, increased serum ALT, increased serum AST, increased serum bilirubin, increased serum transaminases, insomnia, ischemic heart disease, jaundice, laryngeal edema, leukopenia, malaise, myalgia, myocardial infarction, nausea, neutropenia, palpitations, pancreatitis, pancytopenia, paresthesia, pemphigus, pharyngitis, pruritus, renal failure, skin rash, Stevens-Johnson syndrome, symptomatic hypotension, tachycardia, thrombocytopenia, toxic epidermal necrolysis, transient ischemic attacks, upper respiratory tract infection, ventricular tachycardia, vertigo, vomiting, xerostomia

General Dosage Range Dosage adjustment recommended in patients with hepatic and/or renal impairment

Oral: *Adults:* Initial: 1 to 2 mg once daily; Maintenance: 1 to 4 mg once daily

Mechanism of Action Trandolapril is an ACE inhibitor which prevents the formation of angiotensin II from angiotensin I. Trandolapril must undergo enzymatic hydrolysis, mainly in liver, to its biologically active metabolite, trandolaprilat. A CNS mechanism may also be involved in the hypotensive effect as angiotensin II increases adrenergic outflow from the CNS. Vasoactive kallikreins may be decreased in conversion to active hormones by ACE inhibitors, thus reducing blood pressure.

Pharmacodynamics/Kinetics

Half-life Elimination Trandolapril: ~6 hours; Trandolaprilat: Effective: 22.5 hours

Time to Peak Trandolapril: ~1 hour; Trandolaprilat: 4 to 10 hours

Pregnancy Risk Factor D

Pregnancy Considerations [US Boxed Warning]: Drugs that act on the renin-angiotensin system can cause injury and death to the developing fetus. Discontinue as soon as possible once pregnancy is detected. Drugs that act on the renin-angiotensin system are associated with oligohydramnios. Oligohydramnios, due to decreased fetal renal function, may lead to fetal lung hypoplasia and skeletal malformations. The use of these drugs in pregnancy is also associated with anuria, hypotension, renal failure, skull hypoplasia, and death in the fetus/neonate. Teratogenic effects may occur following maternal use of an ACE inhibitor during the first trimester, although this finding may be confounded by maternal disease. Because adverse fetal events are well documented with exposure later in pregnancy, ACE inhibitor use in pregnant women is not recommended (Seely 2014; Weber 2014). Infants exposed to an ACE inhibitor in utero should be monitored for hyperkalemia, hypotension, and oliguria. Oligohydramnios may not appear until after irreversible fetal injury has occurred. Exchange transfusions or dialysis may be required to reverse hypotension or improve renal function, although data related to the effectiveness in neonates is limited.

Chronic maternal hypertension itself is also associated with adverse events in the fetus/infant and mother. ACE inhibitors are not recommended for the treatment of uncomplicated hypertension in pregnancy (ACOG 2013) and they are specifically contraindicated for the treatment of hypertension and chronic heart failure during pregnancy by some guidelines (Regitz-Zagrosek 2011). In addition, ACE inhibitors should generally be avoided in women of reproductive age (ACOG 2013). If treatment for hypertension or chronic heart failure in pregnancy is needed, other agents should be used (ACOG 2013; Regitz-Zagrosek 2011).

Tranexamic Acid (tran eks AM ik AS id)

Related Information

Antiplatelet and Anticoagulation Considerations in Dentistry *on page 1764*

Brand Names: US Cyklokapron; Lysteda

Brand Names: Canada Cyklokapron; GD-Tranexamic Acid; Tranexamic Acid Injection; Tranexamic Acid Injection BP

Pharmacologic Category Antifibrinolytic Agent; Antihemophilic Agent; Hemostatic Agent; Lysine Analog

Use

US labeling:

Cyclic heavy menstrual bleeding (oral): Treatment of cyclic heavy menstrual bleeding.

Tooth extraction in patients with hemophilia (injection): Short-term use (2 to 8 days) in hemophilia patients to reduce or prevent hemorrhage and reduce need for replacement therapy during and following tooth extraction

Canadian labeling:

Bleeding: Treatment and/or prophylaxis of bleeding as a result of increased local fibrinolysis (hyperfibrinolysis) associated with cervical conization, dental extraction in patients with coagulopathies (in conjunction with antihemophilic factor), epistaxis, hyphema, or menorrhagia (hypermenorrhea).

Hereditary angioedema: Treatment of hereditary angioedema.

Local Anesthetic/Vasoconstrictor Precautions No information available to require special precautions

Effects on Dental Treatment No significant effects or complications reported. See Effects on Bleeding and Dental Comment.

Effects on Bleeding General dental procedures and simple restorative procedures are not associated with bleeding; therefore, there is no contraindication to general dental treatment for most patients with bleeding disorders. However, after dental extractions and other dental surgeries including deep scaling, block anesthesia, and large fillings, in patients with hemophilia, antifibrinolytic drugs such as tranexamic acid are useful in controlling bleeding. A carefully coordinated strategy between the dental and medical team may be required to ensure adequate procedures for hemostasis. As preparation for selected dental procedures tranexamic acid may be required.

Immediately before dental extraction in hemophilic patients, administer 10 mg/kg tranexamic acid IV together with replacement therapy.

Adverse Reactions

Injection: Frequency not defined.

Cardiovascular: Hypotension (with rapid IV injection)
Central nervous system: Dizziness
Dermatologic: Allergic dermatitis
Endocrine & metabolic: Menstrual disease (unusual menstrual discomfort)
Gastrointestinal: Diarrhea, nausea, vomiting
Ophthalmic: Blurred vision

Oral:

>10%:

Central nervous system: Headache (50%)
Gastrointestinal: Abdominal pain (20%)
Neuromuscular & skeletal: Back pain (21%), myalgia (11%)
Respiratory: Nasal signs and symptoms (25%; including sinus symptoms)

1% to 10%:

Central nervous system: Fatigue (5%)
Hematologic & oncologic: Anemia (6%)
Neuromuscular & skeletal: Arthralgia (7%), muscle cramps (≤7%), muscle spasm (≤7%)

All formulations: <1%, postmarketing, and/or case reports: Allergic skin reaction, anaphylactic shock, anaphylactoid reaction, cerebral thrombosis, deep vein thrombosis, diarrhea, dizziness, nausea, pulmonary embolism, renal cortical necrosis, retinal artery occlusion, retinal vein occlusion, seizure, ureteral obstruction, visual disturbances (including impaired color vision and vision loss), vomiting

General Dosage Range Dosage adjustment recommended in patients with renal impairment

IV: *Children, Adolescents, and Adults:* Initial: 10 mg/kg as a single dose; Maintenance: 10 mg/kg 3 to 4 times daily

Oral: *Children ≥12 years (postmenarche), Adolescents, and Adults:* 1,300 mg 3 times daily (3,900 mg/day)

Mechanism of Action Forms a reversible complex that displaces plasminogen from fibrin resulting in inhibition of fibrinolysis; it also inhibits the proteolytic activity of plasmin

With reduction in plasmin activity, tranexamic acid also reduces activation of complement and consumption of C1 esterase inhibitor (C1-INH), thereby decreasing inflammation associated with hereditary angioedema.

Pharmacodynamics/Kinetics

Half-life Elimination ~2 to 11 hours

Time to Peak Oral: 2.5 hours (range: 1 to 5 hours)

Pregnancy Risk Factor B

Pregnancy Considerations Adverse events have not been observed in animal reproduction studies. Tranexamic acid crosses the placenta and concentrations within cord blood are similar to maternal concentrations. Tranexamic acid has been evaluated for the treatment of postpartum hemorrhage (Ducloy-Bouthors 2011; Gungorduk 2011). Oral tranexamic acid (Lysteda) is not indicated for use in pregnant women.

Dental Comment Antifibrinolytic drugs are useful for the control of bleeding after dental extractions in patients with hemophilia because the oral mucosa and saliva are rich in plasminogen activators.

Tranylcypromine (tran il SIP roe meen)

Related Information

Vasoconstrictor Interactions With Antidepressants *on page 1913*

Brand Names: US Parnate

Brand Names: Canada Parnate

Pharmacologic Category Antidepressant, Monoamine Oxidase Inhibitor

Use Major depression: Treatment of major depressive episode without melancholia

Local Anesthetic/Vasoconstrictor Precautions Attempts should be made to avoid use of vasoconstrictor due to possibility of hypertensive episodes with monoamine oxidase inhibitors

Effects on Dental Treatment Key adverse event(s) related to dental treatment: Orthostatic hypotension. Avoid use as an analgesic due to toxic reactions with MAO inhibitors. Xerostomia (normal salivary flow resumes upon discontinuation).

Effects on Bleeding No information available to require special precautions

Adverse Reactions Frequency not defined.

Cardiovascular: Edema, orthostatic hypotension, palpitations, tachycardia
Central nervous system: Agitation, anxiety, chills, dizziness, drowsiness, headache, insomnia, mania, myoclonus, numbness, paresthesia, restlessness
Dermatologic: Diaphoresis, urticaria
Endocrine & metabolic: SIADH (syndrome of inappropriate antidiuretic hormone secretion)
Gastrointestinal: Abdominal pain, anorexia, constipation, diarrhea, nausea, xerostomia
Genitourinary: Sexual disorder (anorgasmia, ejaculatory disturbance, impotence), urinary retention
Hematologic & oncologic: Agranulocytosis, anemia, leukopenia, thrombocytopenia
Neuromuscular & skeletal: Muscle spasm, tremor, weakness
Ophthalmic: Blurred vision
Otic: Tinnitus
<1%, postmarketing, and/or case reports: Acne vulgaris (cystic acne), akinesia, alopecia, amnesia, ataxia, cheilitis (angular), confusion, disorientation, hepatitis, polyuria, scleroderma (localized), skin rash, urinary incontinence, withdrawal syndrome

General Dosage Range Oral: *Adults:* 30 to 60 mg/day in divided doses

Mechanism of Action Tranylcypromine is a nonhydrazine monoamine oxidase inhibitor. It increases endogenous concentrations of epinephrine, norepinephrine, and serotonin through inhibition of the enzyme (monoamine oxidase) responsible for the breakdown of these neurotransmitters.

Pharmacodynamics/Kinetics

Onset of Action Therapeutic: 2 days to 3 weeks continued dosing

Duration of Action MAO inhibition may persist for up to 10 days following discontinuation.

Half-life Elimination 2.5 hours (Mallinger 1990)

Time to Peak Serum: 1.5 hours (Mallinger 1990)

Pregnancy Considerations Information related to the use of tranylcypromine in pregnancy is limited (Kennedy 2000).

Pregnant women exposed to antidepressants during pregnancy are encouraged to enroll in the National Pregnancy Registry for Antidepressants (NPRAD). Women 18 to 45 years of age or their health care providers may contact the registry by calling 844-405-6185. Enrollment should be done as early in pregnancy as possible.

Trastuzumab (tras TU zoo mab)

Brand Names: US Herceptin

Brand Names: Canada Herceptin

Pharmacologic Category Antineoplastic Agent, Anti-HER2; Antineoplastic Agent, Monoclonal Antibody

Use

Breast cancer, adjuvant treatment: Treatment (adjuvant) of human epidermal growth receptor 2 (HER2)-overexpressing node positive or node negative (estrogen receptor/progesterone receptor negative or with 1 high risk feature) breast cancer as part of a treatment regimen consisting of doxorubicin, cyclophosphamide, and either paclitaxel or docetaxel; with docetaxel and carboplatin; or as a single agent following multimodality anthracycline-based therapy.

Breast cancer, metastatic: First-line treatment of HER2-overexpressing metastatic breast cancer (in combination with paclitaxel); single agent treatment of HER2-overexpressing breast cancer in patients who have received 1 or more chemotherapy regimens for metastatic disease.

Gastric cancer, metastatic: Treatment of HER2-overexpressing metastatic gastric or gastroesophageal junction adenocarcinoma (in combination with cisplatin and either capecitabine or 5-fluorouracil) in patients who have not received prior treatment for metastatic disease.

Local Anesthetic/Vasoconstrictor Precautions No information available to require special precautions

Effects on Dental Treatment No significant effects or complications reported

Effects on Bleeding Although significant myelosuppression with associated altered hemostasis has been reported for many chemotherapeutic agents, myelosuppression is not common with trastuzumab and no specific precautions appear to necessary.

Adverse Reactions Percentages reported with single-agent therapy.

>10%:

Cardiovascular: Decreased left ventricular ejection fraction (4% to 22%)

Central nervous system: Pain (47%), chills (5% to 32%), headache (10% to 26%), insomnia (14%), dizziness (4% to 13%)

Dermatologic: Skin rash (4% to 18%)

Gastrointestinal: Nausea (6% to 33%), diarrhea (7% to 25%), vomiting (4% to 23%), abdominal pain (2% to 22%), anorexia (14%)

Infection: Infection (20%)

Neuromuscular & skeletal: Weakness (4% to 42%), back pain (5% to 22%)

Respiratory: Cough (5% to 26%), dyspnea (3% to 22%), rhinitis (2% to 14%), pharyngitis (12%)

Miscellaneous: Infusion related reaction (21% to 40%, chills and fever most common; severe: 1%), fever (6% to 36%)

1% to 10%:

Cardiovascular: Peripheral edema (5% to 10%), edema (8%), cardiac failure (2% to 7%; severe: <1%), tachycardia (5%), hypertension (4%), arrhythmia (3%), palpitations (3%)

Central nervous system: Paresthesia (2% to 9%), depression (6%), peripheral neuritis (2%), neuropathy (1%)

Dermatologic: Acne vulgaris (2%), nail disease (2%), pruritus (2%)

Gastrointestinal: Constipation (2%), dyspepsia (2%)

Genitourinary: Urinary tract infection (3% to 5%)

Hematologic & oncologic: Anemia (4%; grade 3: <1%), leukopenia (3%)

Hypersensitivity: Hypersensitivity reaction (3%)

Infection: Influenza (4%), herpes simplex infection (2%)

Neuromuscular & skeletal: Arthralgia (6% to 8%), ostealgia (3% to 7%), myalgia (4%), muscle spasm (3%)

Respiratory: Flu-like symptoms (2% to 10%), sinusitis (2% to 9%), nasopharyngitis (8%), upper respiratory tract infection (3%), epistaxis (2%), pharyngolaryngeal pain (2%)

Miscellaneous: Accidental injury (6%)

<1%, postmarketing, and/or case reports (as a single-agent or with combination chemotherapy): Abnormality in thinking, adult respiratory distress syndrome, amblyopia, anaphylactic shock, anaphylactoid reaction, anaphylaxis, angioedema, apnea, ascites, asthma, ataxia, blood coagulation disorder, bradycardia, bronchitis, bronchospasm, cardiogenic shock, cardiomyopathy, cellulitis, cerebral edema, cerebrovascular accident, cerebrovascular disease, chest discomfort, colitis, coma, confusion, cystitis, deafness, dermal ulcer, dermatitis, dyspnea on exertion, dysuria, erysipelas, esophageal ulcer, febrile neutropenia, focal segmental glomerulosclerosis, gastritis, gastroenteritis, glomerulonephritis (membraneous, focal and fibrillary), glomerulopathy, hematemesis, hemorrhage, hemorrhagic cystitis, hepatic failure, hepatic injury, hepatitis, herpes zoster, hiccups, hydrocephalus, hydronephrosis, hypercalcemia, hypervolemia, hypoprothrombinemia, hypotension, hypothyroidism, hypoxia, immune thrombocytopenia, intestinal obstruction, interstitial pneumonitis, interstitial pulmonary disease, jaundice, laryngeal edema, laryngitis, lethargy, leukemia (acute), limb pain, lymphangitis, madarosis, mania, mastalgia, meningitis, musculoskeletal pain, myopathy, nephrotic syndrome, neutropenia, neutropenic sepsis, oligohydramnios, onychoclasis, osteonecrosis, oxygen desaturation, pancreatitis, pancytopenia, paresis, paroxysmal nocturnal dyspnea, pathological fracture, pericardial effusion, pericarditis, pleural effusion, pneumonitis, pneumothorax, pulmonary edema (noncardiogenic), pulmonary fibrosis, pulmonary hypertension, pulmonary infiltrates, pyelonephritis, radiation injury, renal

failure, respiratory distress, respiratory failure, seizure, sepsis, shock, syncope, stomatitis, thrombosis (including mural), thyroiditis (autoimmune), urticaria, vertigo, ventricular dysfunction, wheezing

General Dosage Range Dosage adjustment recommended in patients who develop toxicities

IV: *Adults:* Loading dose: 4 mg/kg; Maintenance: 2 mg/kg once weekly **or** Loading dose: 8 mg/kg; Maintenance: 6 mg/kg every 3 weeks

Mechanism of Action Trastuzumab is a monoclonal antibody which binds to the extracellular domain of the human epidermal growth factor receptor 2 protein (HER-2); it mediates antibody-dependent cellular cytotoxicity by inhibiting proliferation of cells which overexpress HER-2 protein.

Pregnancy Considerations Trastuzumab inhibits HER2 protein, which has a role in embryonic development. **[US Boxed Warning]: Trastuzumab exposure during pregnancy may result in oligohydramnios and oligohydramnios sequence (pulmonary hypoplasia, skeletal malformations and neonatal death). Advise patients of these risks and the need for effective contraception.** Oligohydramnios (reversible in some cases) has been reported with trastuzumab use alone or with combination chemotherapy. Monitor for oligohydramnios if trastuzumab exposure occurs during pregnancy or within 7 months prior to conception; conduct appropriate fetal testing if oligohydramnios occurs. Verify pregnancy status in women of reproductive potential prior to initiation of therapy. Women of reproductive potential should use effective contraception during treatment and for at least 7 months after the last trastuzumab dose. If trastuzumab is administered during pregnancy, or if a patient becomes pregnant during or within 7 months after treatment, report exposure to Genentech Adverse Events at 1-888-835-2555. Women exposed to trastuzumab during pregnancy (or within 7 months prior to conception) are encouraged to enroll in MotHER (the Herceptin Pregnancy Registry; 1-800-690-6720 or http://www.motherpregnancyregistry.com).

European Society for Medical Oncology (ESMO) guidelines for cancer during pregnancy recommend delaying treatment with trastuzumab (and other HER-2 targeted agents) until after delivery in pregnant patients with HER-2 positive disease (Peccatori 2013).

Travoprost (TRA voe prost)

Brand Names: US Travatan Z

Brand Names: Canada Apo-Travoprost Z; Sandoz-Travoprost; Teva-Travoprost Z Ophthalmic Solution; Travatan Z

Pharmacologic Category Ophthalmic Agent, Antiglaucoma; Prostaglandin, Ophthalmic

Use Elevated intraocular pressure: Reduction of elevated intraocular pressure in patients ≥16 years with open-angle glaucoma or ocular hypertension

Local Anesthetic/Vasoconstrictor Precautions No significant effects or complications reported

Effects on Dental Treatment No information available to require special precautions

Effects on Bleeding No information available to require special precautions

Adverse Reactions

>10%: Ophthalmic: Ocular hyperemia (30% to 50%)

1% to 10%:

Cardiovascular: Angina pectoris (1% to 5%), bradycardia (1% to 5%), chest pain (1% to 5%), hypertension (1% to 5%), hypotension (1% to 5%)

Central nervous system: Foreign body sensation of eye (5% to 10%), anxiety (1% to 5%), depression (1% to 5%), headache (1% to 5%), pain (1% to 5%)

Dermatologic: Hyperpigmentation of eyelashes, increased growth in number of eyelashes

Endocrine & metabolic: Hypercholesterolemia (1% to 5%)

Gastrointestinal: Dyspepsia (1% to 5%), gastrointestinal distress (1% to 5%)

Genitourinary: Prostatic disease (1% to 5%), urinary incontinence (1% to 5%), urinary tract infection (1% to 5%)

Hypersensitivity: Hypersensitivity reaction (1% to 5%)

Infection: Infection (1% to 5%)

Neuromuscular & skeletal: Arthritis (1% to 5%), back pain (1% to 5%)

Ophthalmic: Decreased visual acuity (5% to 10%), eye discomfort (5% to 10%), eye pain (5% to 10%), eye pruritus (5% to 10%), blepharitis (1% to 4%), blurred vision (1% to 4%), cataract (1% to 4%), conjunctivitis (1% to 4%), corneal staining (1% to 4%), crusting of eyelid (1% to 4%), dry eye syndrome (1% to 4%), hyperpigmentation of eyelids (periorbital; 1% to 4%), iris discoloration (1% to 4%), keratitis (1% to 4%), lacrimation (1% to 4%), ophthalmic inflammation (1% to 4%), photophobia (1% to 4%), subconjunctival hemorrhage (1% to 4%), visual disturbance (1% to 4%), increased eyelash length, increased eyelash thickness

Respiratory: Bronchitis (1% to 5%), flu-like symptoms (1% to 5%), sinusitis (1% to 5%)

<1%, postmarketing, and/or case reports: Abdominal pain, arthralgia, asthma, bacterial keratitis (due to solution contamination), chest discomfort, corneal edema, cystoid macular edema, diarrhea, dyspnea, dysuria, enophthalmos, erythema, iritis, macular edema, musculoskeletal pain, nausea, prostate specific antigen increase, pruritus, tachycardia, tinnitus, uveitis

General Dosage Range Ophthalmic: *Adolescents ≥16 years and Adults:* Instill 1 drop into affected eye(s) once daily

Mechanism of Action A selective FP prostanoid receptor agonist which lowers intraocular pressure by increasing trabecular meshwork and outflow

Pharmacodynamics/Kinetics

Onset of Action ~2 hours; Peak effect: 12 hours

Half-life Elimination 45 minutes (range: 17 to 86 minutes)

Pregnancy Risk Factor C

Pregnancy Considerations Adverse events have been observed in animal reproduction studies following systemic administration. If ophthalmic agents are needed during pregnancy, the minimum effective dose should be used in combination with punctual occlusion to decrease potential exposure to the fetus (Samples 1988).

TraZODone (TRAZ oh done)

Related Information

Clinical Risk Related to Drugs Prolonging QT Interval *on page 1772*

Management of the Patient With Anxiety or Depression *on page 1873*

Vasoconstrictor Interactions With Antidepressants *on page 1913*

Brand Names: US Oleptro [DSC]

Brand Names: Canada Apo-Trazodone; Apo-Trazodone D; Dom-Trazodone; Mylan-Trazodone; Novo-Trazodone; Nu-Trazodone; Nu-Trazodone D; Oleptro; PHL-Trazodone; PMS-Trazodone; ratio-Trazodone; Teva-Trazodone; Trazorel; ZYM-Trazodone

Pharmacologic Category Antidepressant, Serotonin Reuptake Inhibitor/Antagonist

Use Treatment of major depressive disorder

Local Anesthetic/Vasoconstrictor Precautions Trazodone inhibits reuptake of both serotonin and norepinephrine and also blocks some serotonin receptors. No precautions with vasoconstrictors appear to be necessary.

Trazodone is one of the drugs confirmed to prolong the QT interval and is accepted as having a risk of causing torsade de pointes. The risk of drug-induced torsade de pointes is extremely low when a single QT interval prolonging drug is prescribed. In terms of epinephrine, it is not known what effect vasoconstrictors in the local anesthetic regimen will have in patients with a known history of congenital prolonged QT interval or in patients taking any medication that prolongs the QT interval. Until more information is obtained, it is suggested that the clinician consult with the physician prior to the use of a vasoconstrictor in suspected patients, and that the vasoconstrictor (epinephrine, mepivacaine and levonordefrin [Carbocaine® 2% with Neo-Cobefrin®]) be used with caution.

Effects on Dental Treatment Key adverse event(s) related to dental treatment: Significant xerostomia (normal salivary flow resumes upon discontinuation).

Effects on Bleeding No information available to require special precautions

Adverse Reactions

>10%:

Central nervous system: Sedation (46%), headache (33%), dizziness (25%), fatigue (15%)

Gastrointestinal: Xerostomia (25%), nausea (21%)

1% to 10%:

Cardiovascular: Edema (≥1%)

Central nervous system: Agitation (≥1%), ataxia (≥1%), confusion (≥1%), disorientation (≥1%), memory impairment (≥1%), migraine (≥1%)

Dermatologic: Night sweats (≥1%)

Endocrine & metabolic: Decreased libido (2%)

Gastrointestinal: Constipation (8%), abdominal pain (≥1%), dysgeusia (≥1%), vomiting (≥1%)

Genitourinary: Ejaculatory disorder (2%), urinary urgency (≥1%)

Neuromuscular & skeletal: Back pain (5%), myalgia (≥1%), tremor (≥1%)

Ophthalmic: Blurred vision (5%), visual disturbance (≥1%)

Respiratory: Dyspnea (≥1%)

<1%, postmarketing, and/or case reports: Abnormal dreams, abnormal gait, acne vulgaris, akathisia, alopecia, anemia, angle-closure glaucoma, anxiety, aphasia, apnea, atrial fibrillation, bladder pain, bradycardia, breast engorgement, breast hypertrophy, cardiac arrest, cardiac arrhythmia, cardiac conduction disturbance, cardiac failure, cerebrovascular accident, chills, cholestasis, diplopia, dry eye syndrome, erectile dysfunction, esophageal achalasia, extrapyramidal reaction, eye pain, flatulence, flushing, hallucination, hemolytic anemia, hirsutism, hyperbilirubinemia, hyperhidrosis, hypersensitivity, hypersensitivity reaction, hypoesthesia, hypomania, hypotension, impotence, increased serum amylase, increased urine output, insomnia, jaundice, lack of concentration, lactation, leukocytosis, leukonychia, liver enzyme disorder, methemoglobinemia, muscle twitching, myocardial infarction, orgasm abnormal, orthostatic hypotension, palpitations, paranoia, paresthesia, photophobia, priapism, prolonged Q-T interval on ECG, pruritus, psoriasis, psychosis, reflux esophagitis, retrograde ejaculation, seizure, SIADH, sialorrhea, skin photosensitivity, skin rash, speech disturbance, stupor, syncope, tachycardia, tardive dyskinesia, tinnitus, torsades de pointes, urinary incontinence, urinary retention, urticaria, vasodilatation, ventricular ectopy, ventricular tachycardia, vertigo, vulvar pain, weakness

General Dosage Range Oral:

Adults: Immediate release: Initial: 150 mg daily in divided doses or once daily at bedtime; Maintenance: 150 to 600 mg daily in divided doses or once daily at bedtime; Maximum dose: 600 mg daily (inpatients); 400 mg daily (outpatients); Extended-release: Initial: 150 mg once daily; Maximum dose: 375 mg daily

Elderly: Immediate release: Initial: 25 to 50 mg at bedtime; Maintenance: 25 to 150 mg daily at bedtime

Mechanism of Action Inhibits reuptake of serotonin, causes adrenoreceptor subsensitivity, and induces significant changes in 5 HT presynaptic receptor adrenoreceptors. Trazodone also significantly blocks histamine (H_1) and alpha$_1$-adrenergic receptors.

Pharmacodynamics/Kinetics

Onset of Action Therapeutic (antidepressant): Up to 6 weeks; sleep aid: 1 to 3 hours

Half-life Elimination 5 to 9 hours, prolonged in obese patients

Time to Peak

Immediate release: 30 to 100 minutes; delayed with food (up to 2.5 hours)

Extended release: 9 hours; not significantly affected by food

Pregnancy Risk Factor C

Pregnancy Considerations Adverse effects were observed in some animal reproduction studies. When trazodone is taken during pregnancy, an increased risk of major malformations has not been observed in the limited number of pregnancies studied (Einarson 2003; Einarson 2009). The long-term effects of in utero trazodone exposure on infant development and behavior are not known.

The ACOG recommends that therapy with antidepressants during pregnancy be individualized; treatment of depression during pregnancy should incorporate the clinical expertise of the mental health clinician, obstetrician, primary health care provider, and pediatrician. According to the American Psychiatric Association (APA), the risks of medication treatment should be weighed against other treatment options and untreated depression. Consideration should be given to using agents with safety data in pregnancy. For women who discontinue antidepressant medications during pregnancy and who may be at high risk for postpartum depression, the medications can be restarted following delivery. Treatment algorithms have been developed by the ACOG and the APA for the management of depression in women prior to conception and during pregnancy (ACOG 2008; APA 2010; Yonkers 2009).

Pregnant women exposed to antidepressants during pregnancy are encouraged to enroll in the National Pregnancy Registry for Antidepressants (NPRAD). Women 18 to 45 years of age or their health care providers may contact the registry by calling 844-405-6185. Enrollment should be done as early in pregnancy as possible.

Product Availability Oleptro has been discontinued in the United States for more than 1 year.

Dental Comment See Local Anesthetic/Vasoconstrictor Precautions

Treprostinil (tre PROST in il)

Brand Names: US Orenitram; Remodulin; Tyvaso; Tyvaso Refill; Tyvaso Starter

Brand Names: Canada Remodulin

Pharmacologic Category Prostacyclin; Prostaglandin; Vasodilator

Use Pulmonary arterial hypertension:

Injection: Treatment of pulmonary arterial hypertension (PAH) (WHO Group I) in patients with NYHA class II-IV symptoms to decrease exercise-associated symptoms; to diminish clinical deterioration when transitioning from epoprostenol (IV)

Inhalation: Treatment of pulmonary arterial hypertension (PAH) (WHO Group I) in patients with NYHA class III symptoms to improve exercise ability. **Note:** Nearly all controlled clinical trial experience has been with concomitant bosentan or sildenafil.

Oral: Treatment of pulmonary arterial hypertension (PAH) (WHO Group 1) in patients with WHO functional class II-III symptoms to improve exercise capacity.

Local Anesthetic/Vasoconstrictor Precautions No information available to require special precautions

Effects on Dental Treatment No significant effects or complications reported. Treprostinil may enhance the risk of bleeding associated with other antiplatelet agents (aspirin or NSAIDs).

Effects on Bleeding Treprostinil is an inhibitor of platelet aggregation and may prolong bleeding times.

Adverse Reactions

>10%:

Cardiovascular: Flushing (11% to 15%)

Central nervous system: Headache (27% to 63%)

Dermatologic: Skin rash (14%)

Gastrointestinal: Diarrhea (25% to 30%), nausea (19% to 30%)

Local: Pain at injection site (SubQ: 85%; may improve after several months of therapy), infusion site reaction (SubQ: 83%)

Neuromuscular & skeletal: Limb pain (Oral: 14%), jaw pain (11% to 13%)

Respiratory: Cough (Inhalation: 54%), pharyngolaryngeal pain (Inhalation: 25%), throat irritation (Inhalation: 25%)

1% to 10%:

Cardiovascular: Edema (9%), syncope (Inhalation: 6%), hypotension (4%)

Central nervous system: Dizziness (9%)

Dermatologic: Pruritus (8%)

Endocrine & metabolic: Hypokalemia (Oral: 9%)

Gastrointestinal: Abdominal distress (Oral: 6%)

Respiratory: Epistaxis (Inhalation), hemoptysis, pneumonia, wheezing (Inhalation)

<1%, postmarketing, and/or case reports: Angioedema, anxiety, catheter infection (central venous), catheter sepsis (central venous), cellulitis, decreased platelet aggregation, hematoma, ostealgia, pain, paresthesia, restlessness, swelling of extremities, thrombocytopenia, thrombophlebitis

General Dosage Range Dosage adjustment recommended for the IV infusion, SubQ, and oral routes in patients with hepatic impairment; dosage adjustment recommended for the oral route in patients on strong CYP2C8 inhibitor concomitant therapy

Inhalation: *Adults:* Initial: 18 mcg (or 3 inhalations) every 4 hours 4 times/day; Maintenance: Maximum dose: 54 mcg (or 9 inhalations) 4 times/day

IV Infusion, SubQ: *Adults:* Initial: 0.625 to 1.25 ng/kg/minute; Maintenance: 1.25 to 40 ng/kg/minute

Oral: *Adults:* Initial: 0.125 every 8 hours or 0.25 mg every 12 hours

Mechanism of Action Treprostinil is a direct vasodilator of both pulmonary and systemic arterial vascular beds; also inhibits platelet aggregation.

Pharmacodynamics/Kinetics

Half-life Elimination Terminal: ~4 hours

Time to Peak Oral: 4 to 6 hours

Pregnancy Risk Factor B/C (product specific)

Pregnancy Considerations Adverse events have been observed in some animal reproduction studies. Women with pulmonary arterial hypertension (PAH) are encouraged to avoid pregnancy (McLaughlin 2009; Taichman 2014).

Tretinoin (Systemic) (TRET i noyn)

Brand Names: Canada Vesanoid

Pharmacologic Category Antineoplastic Agent, Retinoic Acid Derivative; Retinoic Acid Derivative

Use Acute promyelocytic leukemia (remission induction): Induction of remission in patients with acute promyelocytic leukemia, French American British (FAB) classification M3 (including the M3 variant) characterized by t(15;17) translocation and/or PML/RARα gene presence

Local Anesthetic/Vasoconstrictor Precautions No information available to require special precautions

Effects on Dental Treatment Key adverse event(s) related to dental treatment: Xerostomia (normal salivary flow resumes upon discontinuation).

Effects on Bleeding Although significant myelosuppression with associated altered hemostasis has been reported for many chemotherapeutic agents, myelosuppression is not common with tretinoin and no specific precautions appear to necessary.

Adverse Reactions Most patients will experience drug-related toxicity, especially headache, fever, weakness and fatigue. These are seldom permanent or irreversible and do not typically require therapy interruption.

>10%:

Cardiovascular: Peripheral edema (52%), chest discomfort (32%), edema (29%), cardiac arrhythmia (23%), flushing (23%), hypotension (14%), hypertension (11%), localized phlebitis (11%)

Central nervous system: Headache (86%), malaise (66%), shivering (63%), pain (37%), dizziness (20%), anxiety (17%), paresthesia (17%), depression (14%), insomnia (14%), confusion (11%)

Dermatologic: Xeroderma (≤77%), skin rash (54%), diaphoresis (20%), pruritus (20%), alopecia (14%), skin changes (14%)

Endocrine & metabolic: Hypercholesterolemia (≤60%), hypertriglyceridemia (≤60%), weight gain (23%), weight loss (17%)
Gastrointestinal: Dry mucous membranes (≤77%), nausea (≤57%), vomiting (≤57%), gastrointestinal hemorrhage (34%), abdominal pain (31%), mucositis (26%), diarrhea (23%), anorexia (17%), constipation (17%), dyspepsia (14%), abdominal distention (11%)
Hematologic & oncologic: Hemorrhage (60%), leukocytosis (40%), disseminated intravascular coagulation (26%)
Hepatic: Increased liver enzymes (50% to 60%)
Infection: Infection (58%)
Neuromuscular & skeletal: Ostealgia (77%), APL differentiation syndrome (≤25%), myalgia (14%)
Ophthalmic: Eye disease (17%), visual disturbance (17%)
Otic: Otalgia (23%; ear fullness)
Renal: Renal insufficiency (11%)
Respiratory: Upper respiratory complaint (63%), dyspnea (60%), respiratory insufficiency (26%), pleural effusion (20%), pneumonia (14%), rales (14%), wheezing (expiratory: 14%)
Miscellaneous: Fever (83%)

1% to 10%:
Cardiovascular: Cardiac failure (6%), facial edema (6%), cardiomegaly (3%), cardiomyopathy (3%), cerebrovascular accident (3%), heart murmur (3%), ischemia (3%), myocardial infarction (3%), myocarditis (3%), pericarditis (3%)
Central nervous system: Agitation (9%), cerebral hemorrhage (9%), flank pain (9%), intracranial hypertension (9%), hallucination (6%), abnormal gait (3%), agnosia (3%), aphasia (3%), asterixis (3%), ataxia (3%), brain disease (3%), cerebral edema (cerebellar: 3%), central nervous system depression (3%), coma (3%), dementia (3%), drowsiness (3%), dysarthria (3%), facial paralysis (3%), forgetfulness (3%), hemiplegia (3%), hyporeflexia (3%), hypothermia (3%), loss of consciousness (3%), seizure (3%), speech disturbance (3%)
Dermatologic: Cellulitis (8%), pallor (6%)
Endocrine & metabolic: Disturbance in fluid balance (6%), acidosis (3%)
Gastrointestinal: Gastrointestinal ulcer (3%)
Genitourinary: Dysuria (9%), benign prostatic hypertrophy (3%), urinary frequency (3%)
Hematologic & oncologic: Lymphatic disease (6%)
Hepatic: Hepatosplenomegaly (9%), ascites (3%), hepatitis (3%)
Local: Local inflammation (bone: 3%)
Neuromuscular & skeletal: Lower extremity weakness (3%), myelopathy (3%), tremor (3%)
Ophthalmic: Decreased visual acuity (6%), decreased pupillary reflex (3%), visual field defect (3%)
Otic: Hearing loss (6%; may be irreversible)
Renal: Acute renal failure (3%), renal tubular necrosis (3%)
Respiratory: Lower respiratory signs and symptoms (9%), pulmonary infiltrates (6%), asthma (3%), laryngeal edema (3%), pulmonary hypertension (3%)

<1%, postmarketing, and/or case reports: Arterial thrombosis, basophilia, erythema nodosum, histamine release (hyperhistaminemia), hypercalcemia, hypersensitivity angiitis, myositis, pancreatitis, pseudotumor cerebri, renal infarction, Sweet's syndrome, thrombocythemia, ulcer (genital), venous thrombosis

General Dosage Range Dosage adjustment recommended in patients who develop toxicities

Oral: *Children and Adults:* Induction: 45 mg/m^2/day in 2 divided doses (maximum duration of treatment: 90 days)

Mechanism of Action Tretinoin appears to bind one or more nuclear receptors and decreases proliferation and induces differentiation of APL cells; initially produces maturation of primitive promyelocytes and repopulates the marrow and peripheral blood with normal hematopoietic cells to achieve complete remission

Pharmacodynamics/Kinetics

Half-life Elimination Terminal: Parent drug: 0.5 to 2 hours

Time to Peak Serum: 1 to 2 hours

Pregnancy Risk Factor D

Pregnancy Considerations Adverse events were observed in animal reproduction studies. **[US Boxed Warning]: High risk of teratogenicity; if treatment with tretinoin is required in women of childbearing potential, two reliable forms of contraception should be used simultaneously during and for 1 month after discontinuation of treatment, unless abstinence is the chosen method. Within 1 week prior to starting therapy, serum or urine pregnancy test (sensitivity at least 50 milliunits/mL) should be collected. If possible, delay therapy until results are available. Repeat pregnancy testing and contraception counseling monthly throughout the period of treatment.** Contraception must be used even when there is a history of infertility or menopause, unless a hysterectomy has been performed. Tretinoin was detected in the serum of a neonate at birth following maternal use of standard doses during pregnancy (Takitani 2005). Use in humans for the treatment of acute promyelocytic leukemia (APL) is limited and exposure occurred after the first trimester in most cases (Valappil 2007). However, major fetal abnormalities and spontaneous abortions have been reported with other retinoids; some of these abnormalities were fatal. If the clinical condition of a patient presenting with APL during pregnancy warrants immediate treatment, tretinoin use should be avoided in the first trimester; treatment with tretinoin may be considered in the second and third trimester with careful fetal monitoring, including cardiac monitoring (Sanz 2009).

Tretinoin (Topical) (TRET i noyn)

Brand Names: US Atralin; Avita; Refissa; Renova; Renova Pump; Retin-A; Retin-A Micro; Retin-A Micro Pump; Tretin-X

Brand Names: Canada Retin-A; Retin-A Micro; Stieva-A; Vitamin A Acid

Pharmacologic Category Acne Products; Retinoic Acid Derivative; Topical Skin Product, Acne

Use

Acne vulgaris: Atralin, Avita, Retin-A, Retin-A Micro, Stieva-A [Canadian product], Tretin-X, Vitamin-A Acid [Canadian product]: Treatment of acne vulgaris.

Palliation of fine wrinkles: Renova: Adjunctive treatment for mitigation (palliation) of fine wrinkles in patients who use comprehensive skin care and sun avoidance programs.

Palliation of fine wrinkles, mottled hyperpigmentation, and facial skin roughness: Refissa: Adjunctive treatment for mitigation (palliation) of fine wrinkles, mottled hyperpigmentation, and tactile roughness of facial skin in patients who do not achieve such palliation using comprehensive skin care and sun avoidance programs alone.

Local Anesthetic/Vasoconstrictor Precautions No information available to require special precautions

Effects on Dental Treatment No significant effects or complications reported

Effects on Bleeding No information available to require special precautions

Adverse Reactions

1% to 10%:

Dermatologic: Burning sensation of the skin (gel: 8%), skin irritation (gel: 4% to 6%; severe: 1% to ≤3%), erythema (5%), dermatitis (gel: 4%)

Local: Skin edema

<1%, postmarketing, case reports, and frequency not defined: Acne flare (initial), contact dermatitis (rare), crusted skin, exfoliation of skin, hyperpigmentation or hypopigmentation (temporary), pharyngitis, pruritus, skin blister, skin pain, skin photosensitivity, xeroderma

General Dosage Range Topical: *Children ≥10 years, Adolescents, and Adults:* Apply once daily.

Mechanism of Action Tretinoin is a derivative of vitamin A. When used topically, it modifies epithelial growth and differentiation. In patients with acne, it decreases the cohesiveness of follicular epithelial cells and decreases micromedo formation. Additionally, tretinoin stimulates mitotic activity and increased turnover of follicular epithelial cells causing extrusion of the comedones.

Pharmacodynamics/Kinetics

Onset of Action

Acne: ≥2 weeks, may take ≥7 weeks; Facial wrinkles: Up to 6 months

Pregnancy Risk Factor C

Pregnancy Considerations Adverse events were observed in animal reproduction studies following topical application of tretinoin. Teratogenic effects were also observed in pregnant women following topical use; however, a causal association has not been established. When treatment for acne is needed during pregnancy, other agents are preferred (Kong, 2013). These products should not be used for palliation of fine wrinkles, mottled hyperpigmentation, and tactile roughness of facial skin in women who are pregnant, attempting to conceive, or at high risk for pregnancy.

Triamcinolone (Systemic) (trye am SIN oh lone)

Related Information

Respiratory Diseases *on page 1777*

Brand Names: US Aristospan Intra-Articular [DSC]; Aristospan Intralesional [DSC]; Arze-Ject-A; Kenalog; Pro-C-Dure 5; Pro-C-Dure 6; ReadySharp Triamcinolone

Brand Names: Canada Aristospan; Kenalog

Generic Availability (US) May be product dependent

Pharmacologic Category Corticosteroid, Systemic

Dental Use Adjunctive treatment and temporary relief of symptoms associated with oral inflammatory lesions and ulcerative lesions resulting from trauma

Use

Intra-articular or soft tissue administration: As adjunctive therapy for short-term administration in acute gouty arthritis, acute and subacute bursitis, acute nonspecific tenosynovitis, epicondylitis, rheumatoid arthritis (RA), or synovitis of osteoarthritis.

Intralesional administration (triamcinolone hexacetonide and triamcinolone acetonide [Kenalog-10 only]): Alopecia areata; discoid lupus erythematosus; keloids; localized hypertrophic, infiltrated, inflammatory lesions of granuloma annulare, lichen planus, lichen simplex chronicus (neurodermatitis), and psoriatic plaques; necrobiosis lipoidica diabeticorum; cystic tumors of an aponeurosis or tendon (ganglia).

Intramuscular administration (triamcinolone acetonide [Kenalog-40] only):

Allergic states: Control of severe or incapacitating allergic conditions intractable to adequate trials of conventional treatment in asthma, drug hypersensitivity reactions, perennial or seasonal allergic rhinitis, serum sickness, or transfusion reactions.

Dermatologic diseases: Atopic dermatitis, bullous dermatitis herpetiformis, contact dermatitis, exfoliative erythroderma, mycosis fungoides, pemphigus, or severe erythema multiforme (Stevens-Johnson syndrome).

Endocrine disorders: Primary or secondary adrenocortical insufficiency (hydrocortisone or cortisone is the drug of choice), congenital adrenal hyperplasia, hypercalcemia associated with cancer, or nonsuppurative thyroiditis.

GI diseases: To tide the patient over a critical period of disease in Crohn disease or ulcerative colitis.

Hematologic disorders: Acquired (autoimmune) hemolytic anemia, Diamond-Blackfan anemia, pure red cell aplasia, select cases of secondary thrombocytopenia.

Neoplastic diseases: Palliative management of leukemias and lymphomas.

Nervous system: Acute exacerbations of multiple sclerosis; cerebral edema associated with primary or metastatic brain tumor or craniotomy. **Note**: Treatment guidelines recommend the use of high dose IV or oral methylprednisolone for acute exacerbations of multiple sclerosis (AAN [Scott 2011]; NICE 2014).

Ophthalmic diseases: Sympathetic ophthalmia, temporal arteritis, uveitis, and ocular inflammatory conditions unresponsive to topical corticosteroids.

Renal diseases: To induce diuresis or remission of proteinuria in idiopathic nephrotic syndrome or that is caused by lupus erythematosus.

Respiratory diseases: Berylliosis, fulminating or disseminated pulmonary tuberculosis when used concurrently with appropriate antituberculous chemotherapy, idiopathic eosinophilic pneumonias, symptomatic sarcoidosis.

Rheumatic disorders: As adjunctive therapy for short-term administration in acute gouty arthritis; acute rheumatic carditis; ankylosing spondylitis; psoriatic arthritis; RA, including juvenile RA; treatment of dermatomyositis, polymyositis, and systemic lupus erythematosus.

Miscellaneous: Trichinosis with neurologic or myocardial involvement; tuberculous meningitis with subarachnoid block or impending block when used with appropriate antituberculous chemotherapy.

Local Anesthetic/Vasoconstrictor Precautions No information available to require special precautions

Effects on Dental Treatment Key adverse event(s) related to dental treatment: Ulcerative esophagitis, perioral dermatitis, atrophy of oral mucosa, burning, irritation, and oral monilia (oral inhaler).

Effects on Bleeding No information available to require special precautions

Adverse Reactions Frequency not defined. Reactions listed are based on reports for other agents in this same pharmacologic class and may not be specifically reported for systemic triamcinolone.

Cardiovascular: Bradycardia, cardiac arrhythmia, cardiac failure, cardiomegaly, cerebrovascular accident, circulatory shock, edema, hypertension, hypertrophic cardiomyopathy (premature infants), myocardial rupture (following recent myocardial infarction), syncope, tachycardia, thromboembolism, thrombophlebitis, vasculitis

Central nervous system: Arachnoiditis (intrathecal), depression, emotional lability, euphoria, headache, increased intracranial pressure, insomnia, malaise, meningitis (intrathecal), mood changes, neuritis, neuropathy, paraplegia, paresthesia, personality changes, pseudotumor cerebri (upon discontinuation), quadriplegia, seizure, spinal cord infarction, vertigo

Dermatologic: Acne vulgaris, allergic dermatitis, atrophic striae, diaphoresis, epidermal thinning, erythema, hyperpigmentation, hypertrichosis, hypopigmentation, skin atrophy (cutaneous/subcutaneous), skin rash, suppression of skin test reaction, thinning hair, xeroderma

Endocrine & metabolic: Calcinosis, cushingoid state, decreased glucose tolerance, diabetes mellitus, fluid retention, glycosuria, growth suppression (children), hirsutism, hypokalemia, hypokalemic alkalosis, lipodystrophy, menstrual disease, moon face, negative nitrogen balance, sodium retention, weight gain

Gastrointestinal: Abdominal distention, carbohydrate intolerance, gastrointestinal hemorrhage, gastrointestinal perforation, hiccups, increased appetite, nausea, pancreatitis, peptic ulcer, ulcerative esophagitis

Genitourinary: Spermatozoa disorder (motility altered)

Hematologic & oncologic: Bruise, petechiae, purpura

Hepatic: Hepatomegaly, increased liver enzymes

Hypersensitivity: Anaphylactoid reaction, anaphylaxis, angioedema

Infection: Infection, sterile abscess

Neuromuscular & skeletal: Amyotrophy, arthropathy (joint tissue damage), aseptic necrosis of bones (femoral and humeral heads), bone fracture, Charcot-like arthropathy, lupus erythematosus-like rash, myopathy, osteoporosis, rupture of tendon, vertebral compression fracture, weakness

Ophthalmic: Cataract, cortical blindness, exophthalmos, glaucoma, increased intraocular pressure, papilledema

Respiratory: Pulmonary edema

Miscellaneous: Wound healing impairment

Dosing

Adult & Geriatric Note: Aristospan Intra-Articular and Aristospan Intralesional have been discontinued in the US for more than 1 year.

Adjust dose depending upon condition being treated and response of patient. The lowest possible dose should be used to control the condition; when dose reduction is possible, the dose should be reduced gradually.

Dermatoses (steroid-responsive):

Acetonide (Kenalog-10): 1 mg Intralesional: Initial dose varies depending on the specific disease and lesion being treated; may be repeated at weekly or less frequent intervals; multiple sites may be injected if they are 1 cm or more apart

Hexacetonide (Aristospan 5 mg/mL): Intralesional, sublesional: Up to 0.5 mg/square inch of affected skin; range: 2 to 48 mg/day

Inflammatory/allergic conditions/other steroid-responsive systemic conditions: Acetonide (Kenalog-40): IM: Initial: 60 mg; adjust dose to a range of 40 to 80 mg. For patients with hay fever or pollen asthma who are not responding to pollen administration and other conventional therapy, a single injection of 40 mg to 100 mg per season may be given.

Multiple sclerosis (acute exacerbation):

Note: Treatment guidelines recommend the use of high dose IV or oral methylprednisolone for acute exacerbations of multiple sclerosis (AAN [Scott 2011]; NICE 2014).

Acetonide (Kenalog-40): IM: 160 mg daily for 1 week, followed by 64 mg every other day for 1 month.

Rheumatic conditions:

Intra-articular (or similar injection as designated):

Acetonide: Intra-articular, intrabursal, tendon sheaths: Initial: Smaller joints: 2.5 to 5 mg, larger joints: 5 to 15 mg; may require up to 10 mg for small joints and up to 40 mg for large joints; maximum dose/treatment (several joints at one time): 80 mg

Hexacetonide (Aristospan 20 mg/mL): Intra-articular: Average dose: 2 to 20 mg; smaller joints (interphalangeal, metacarpophalangeal): 2 to 6 mg; large joints (knee, hip, shoulder): 10 to 20 mg. Frequency of injection into a single joint is every 3 to 4 weeks as necessary; to avoid possible joint destruction use as infrequently as possible.

IM: Acetonide (Kenalog-40): Initial: 60 mg; range: 2.5 to 100 mg/day

Pericarditis (off-label use): Intrapericardial (off-label route): 300 mg/**m²** as a single dose (Maisch 2002) **or** 50 mg every 6 hours for 2 to 3 days (ESC [Maisch 2004]); may use in conjunction with oral colchicine therapy. Administration may be painful and appropriate analgesic premedication (eg, morphine) should be administered (Frasiolas 2010; Maisch 2002). Additional data may be necessary to further define the role of triamcinolone in this condition.

Pediatric Note: Aristospan Intra-Articular and Aristospan Intralesional have been discontinued in the US for more than 1 year.

Adjust dose depending upon condition being treated and response of patient. The lowest possible dose should be used to control the condition; when dose reduction is possible, the dose should be reduced gradually.

Dermatoses (steroid-responsive):

Acetonide (Kenalog-10): Intralesional: Children and Adolescents: Initial dose varies depending on the specific disease and lesion being treated; may be repeated at weekly or less frequent intervals; multiple sites may be injected if they are 1 cm or more apart

Hexacetonide (Aristospan 5 mg/mL): Intralesional, sublesional: Up to 0.5 mg/square inch of affected skin; initial range: 2 to 48 mg; frequency of dose is determined by clinical response

Inflammatory/allergic conditions/other steroid-responsive systemic conditions: Children and Adolescents:

Manufacturer's labeling: Acetonide (Kenolog-40): IM: Initial: 0.11 to 1.6 mg/kg/day (or 3.2 to 48 mg/m²/day) in 3 to 4 divided doses

Alternative dosing: Limited data available: Acetonide: Children 6 to 12 years: IM: 0.03 to 0.2 mg/kg/dose every 1 to 7 days (Kliegman, 2011)

Rheumatic conditions: Children and Adolescents: Intra-articular:

Manufacturer's labeling:

Acetonide: Initial: Smaller joints: 2.5 to 5 mg, larger joints: 5 to 15 mg; Up to 80 mg (total) has been given for single injections into several joints.

Hexacetonide (Aristospan 20 mg/mL): Average dose: 2 to 20 mg; small joints (interphalangeal, metacarpophalangeal): 2 to 6 mg; large joints (knee, hip, shoulder): 10 to 20 mg. Frequency of injection into a single joint is every 3 to 4 weeks as necessary; to avoid possible joint destruction use as infrequently as possible

Alternative dosing: Limited data available: Hexacetonide: Large joints (typically knees, ankles): 1 to 1.5 mg/kg/dose; maximum dose: 40 mg; doses greater than 1.5 mg/kg have not been associated with additional clinical benefit; similar dosing for the acetonide salt can be used; however, data show that the response is greater and lasts longer with hexacetonide (Bloom, 2011; Hashkes, 2005; Zulian, 2003; Zulian 2004)

Renal Impairment There are no dosage adjustments provided in the manufacturer's labeling; use with caution.

Hepatic Impairment There are no dosage adjustments provided in the manufacturer's labeling; use with caution.

Mechanism of Action A long acting corticosteroid with minimal sodium-retaining potential. Decreases inflammation by suppression of migration of polymorphonuclear leukocytes and reversal of increased capillary permeability; suppresses the immune system by reducing activity and volume of the lymphatic system; suppresses adrenal function at high doses

Contraindications

Hypersensitivity to triamcinolone or any component of the formulation; idiopathic thrombocytopenic purpura (IM administration only).

Documentation of allergenic cross-reactivity for corticosteroids is limited. However, because of similarities in chemical structure and/or pharmacologic actions, the possibility of cross-sensitivity cannot be ruled out with certainty.

Warnings/Precautions May cause hypercorticism or suppression of hypothalamic-pituitary-adrenal (HPA) axis, particularly in younger children or in patients receiving high doses for prolonged periods. HPA axis suppression may lead to adrenal crisis. Withdrawal and discontinuation of a corticosteroid should be done slowly and carefully. Particular care is required when patients are transferred from systemic corticosteroids to inhaled products due to possible adrenal insufficiency or withdrawal from steroids, including an increase in allergic symptoms. Patients receiving >20 mg per day of prednisone (or equivalent) may be most susceptible. Fatalities have occurred due to adrenal insufficiency in asthmatic patients during and after transfer from systemic corticosteroids to aerosol steroids; aerosol steroids do not provide the systemic steroid needed to treat patients having trauma, surgery, or infections.

Acute myopathy has been reported with high-dose corticosteroids, usually in patients with neuromuscular transmission disorders or when given concomitantly with neuromuscular blocking agents; may involve ocular and/or respiratory muscles; monitor creatine kinase; recovery may be delayed. Corticosteroid use may cause psychiatric disturbances, including severe depression, euphoria, insomnia, mood swings, and personality changes to frank psychotic manifestations. Preexisting psychiatric conditions may be exacerbated by corticosteroid use. Prolonged use of corticosteroids may also increase the incidence of secondary infection, cause activation of latent infections, mask acute infection (including fungal infections), prolong or exacerbate viral infections, or limit response to killed or inactivated vaccines. Exposure to chickenpox or measles should be avoided; corticosteroids should not be used to treat ocular herpes simplex, cerebral malaria, fungal infections, or viral hepatitis. Close observation is required in patients with latent tuberculosis and/or TB reactivity; restrict use in active TB (only fulminating or disseminated TB in conjunction with antituberculosis treatment). Amebiasis should be ruled out in any patient with recent travel to tropic climates or unexplained diarrhea prior to initiation of corticosteroids. Use with extreme caution in patients with *Strongyloides* infections; hyperinfection, dissemination, and fatalities have occurred. Prolonged treatment with corticosteroids has been associated with the development of Kaposi sarcoma (case reports); if noted, discontinuation of therapy should be considered (Goedert 2002). Increased mortality was observed in patients receiving high-dose IV methylprednisolone; high-dose corticosteroids should not be used for the management of head injury.

Use with caution in patients with thyroid disease, hepatic impairment, renal impairment, cardiovascular disease, diabetes, myasthenia gravis, osteoporosis, patients at risk for seizures, or GI diseases (diverticulitis, fresh intestinal anastomoses, active or latent peptic ulcer, ulcerative colitis, abscess or other pyogenic infection). Use cautiously in the elderly with the smallest possible effective dose for the shortest duration. Use with caution in patients with cataracts and/or glaucoma; increased intraocular pressure, open-angle glaucoma, and cataracts have occurred with prolonged use. Use with caution in patients with a history of ocular herpes simplex; corneal perforation has occurred; do not use in active ocular herpes simplex. Not recommended for the treatment of optic neuritis; may increase frequency of new episodes. Consider routine eye exams in chronic users.

Withdraw therapy with gradual tapering of dose. Administer products only via recommended route (depending on product used). Do **not** administer any triamcinolone product via the intrathecal route; serious adverse events, including fatalities, have been reported. Corticosteroids are not approved for epidural injection. Serious neurologic events (eg, spinal cord infarction, paraplegia, quadriplegia, cortical blindness, stroke), some resulting in death, have been reported with epidural injection of corticosteroids, with and without use of fluoroscopy. Septic arthritis may occur as a complication to intra-articular or soft tissue administration; institute appropriate antimicrobial therapy as required. Atrophy at the injection site has been reported. Avoid IM deltoid injection; subcutaneous atrophy may occur.

Rare cases of anaphylactoid reactions have been observed in patients receiving corticosteroids. Use may affect growth velocity; growth should be routinely monitored in pediatric patients. Patients may require higher doses when subject to stress (ie, trauma, surgery, severe infection). Potentially significant drug-drug interactions may exist, requiring dose or frequency adjustment, additional monitoring, and/or selection of alternative therapy.

Benzyl alcohol and derivatives: Some dosage forms may contain benzyl alcohol; large amounts of benzyl alcohol (≥99 mg/kg/day) have been associated with a potentially fatal toxicity ("gasping syndrome") in neonates; the "gasping syndrome" consists of metabolic acidosis, respiratory distress, gasping respirations, CNS dysfunction (including convulsions, intracranial hemorrhage), hypotension, and cardiovascular collapse (AAP ["Inactive" 1997]; CDC, 1982); some data suggests that benzoate displaces bilirubin from protein binding sites (Ahlfors, 2001); avoid or use dosage forms containing benzyl alcohol with caution in neonates. See manufacturer's labeling.

Polysorbate 80: Some dosage forms may contain polysorbate 80 (also known as Tweens). Hypersensitivity reactions, usually a delayed reaction, have been reported following exposure to pharmaceutical products containing polysorbate 80 in certain individuals (Isaksson, 2002; Lucente 2000; Shelley, 1995). Thrombocytopenia, ascites, pulmonary deterioration, and renal and hepatic failure have been reported in premature neonates after receiving parenteral products containing polysorbate 80 (Alade, 1986; CDC, 1984). See manufacturer's labeling.

Drug Interactions

Metabolism/Transport Effects **Substrate** of CYP3A4 (minor); **Note:** Assignment of Major/Minor substrate status based on clinically relevant drug interaction potential

Avoid Concomitant Use

Avoid concomitant use of Triamcinolone (Systemic) with any of the following: Aldesleukin; BCG (Intravesical); Desmopressin; Indium 111 Capromab Pendetide; Loxapine; MiFEPRIStone; Natalizumab; Pimecrolimus; Tacrolimus (Topical); Tofacitinib

Increased Effect/Toxicity

Triamcinolone (Systemic) may increase the levels/effects of: Acetylcholinesterase Inhibitors; Amphotericin B; Androgens; Ceritinib; Deferasirox; Desirudin; Desmopressin; Fingolimod; Leflunomide; Loop Diuretics; Loxapine; Natalizumab; Nicorandil; NSAID (COX-2 Inhibitor); NSAID (Nonselective); Quinolone Antibiotics; Thiazide and Thiazide-Like Diuretics; Tofacitinib; Vaccines (Live); Warfarin

The levels/effects of Triamcinolone (Systemic) may be increased by: Antihepaciviral Combination Products; Aprepitant; CYP3A4 Inhibitors (Strong); Denosumab; DilTIAZem; Estrogen Derivatives; Fosaprepitant; Indacaterol; MiFEPRIStone; Neuromuscular-Blocking Agents (Nondepolarizing); Ocrelizumab; Pimecrolimus; Ritonavir; Roflumilast; Salicylates; Tacrolimus (Topical); Telaprevir; Trastuzumab

Decreased Effect

Triamcinolone (Systemic) may decrease the levels/effects of: Aldesleukin; Antidiabetic Agents; BCG (Intravesical); Calcitriol (Systemic); Coccidioides immitis Skin Test; Corticorelin; Hyaluronidase; Indium 111 Capromab Pendetide; Isoniazid; Nivolumab; Salicylates; Sipuleucel-T; Telaprevir; Tertomotide; Urea Cycle Disorder Agents; Vaccines (Inactivated); Vaccines (Live)

The levels/effects of Triamcinolone (Systemic) may be decreased by: CYP3A4 Inducers (Strong); Echinacea; MiFEPRIStone; Mitotane

Dietary Considerations Ensure adequate intake of calcium and vitamins (or consider supplementation) in patients on medium-to-high doses of systemic corticosteroids.

Pharmacodynamics/Kinetics

Onset of Action IM (acetonide): Adrenal suppression: 24 to 48 hours

Duration of Action IM (acetonide): Adrenal suppression: 30 to 40 days

Half-life Elimination Plasma: 300 minutes (Asare 2007)

Pregnancy Risk Factor C

Pregnancy Considerations Adverse events have been observed with corticosteroids in animal reproduction studies. Some studies have shown an association between first trimester systemic corticosteroid use and oral clefts (Park-Wyllie, 2000; Pradat, 2003). Systemic corticosteroids may also influence fetal growth (decreased birth weight); however, information is conflicting (Lunghi, 2010). Hypoadrenalism may occur in newborns following maternal use of corticosteroids in pregnancy; monitor. When systemic corticosteroids are needed in pregnancy, it is generally recommended to use the lowest effective dose for the shortest duration of time, avoiding high doses during the first trimester (Leachman 2006; Lunghi 2010; Makol 2011; Østensen 2009).

Breastfeeding Considerations Corticosteroids are excreted in breast milk. The manufacturer notes that when used systemically, maternal use of corticosteroids have the potential to cause adverse events in a nursing infant (eg, growth suppression, interfere with endogenous corticosteroid production); therefore, caution should be used if administered to a nursing woman. A case report notes a decrease in milk production following a high-dose triamcinolone injection in a nursing mother with a previously abundant milk supply (McGuire, 2012). If there is concern about exposure to the infant, some guidelines recommend waiting 4 hours after the maternal dose of an oral systemic corticosteroid before breastfeeding in order to decrease potential exposure to the nursing infant (based on a study using prednisolone) (Bae, 2011; Leachman, 2006; Makol, 2011; Ost, 1985).

Product Availability

Aristospan Intra-Articular and Aristospan Intralesional have been discontinued in the US for more than 1 year.

Dosage Forms

Kit, Injection:

Arze-Ject-A: 40 mg/mL (3 x 1 mL)

Pro-C-Dure 5: 40 mg/mL (2 x 1 mL)

Pro-C-Dure 6: 40 mg/mL (3 x 1 mL)

ReadySharp Triamcinolone: 40 mg/mL (1 x 1 mL)

Suspension, Injection:

Kenalog: 10 mg/mL (5 mL); 40 mg/mL (1 mL, 5 mL, 10 mL)

Triamcinolone (Nasal) (trye am SIN oh lone)

Brand Names: US Nasacort Allergy 24HR Children [OTC]; Nasacort Allergy 24HR [OTC]; Nasacort AQ [DSC]; Nasal Allergy 24 Hour [OTC]

Brand Names: Canada Nasacort Allergy 24HR; Nasacort AQ

Pharmacologic Category Corticosteroid, Nasal

Use

Allergic rhinitis (Rx products): Management of seasonal and perennial allergic rhinitis in adults and children 2 years and older

Upper respiratory allergies (OTC products): Relief of hay fever and other upper respiratory allergies (eg, nasal congestion, runny nose, sneezing, itchy nose) in adults and children 2 years and older

Local Anesthetic/Vasoconstrictor Precautions No information available to require special precautions

Effects on Dental Treatment No significant effects or complications reported

Effects on Bleeding No information available to require special precautions

Adverse Reactions

>10%:

Central nervous system: Headache (2% to 51%)

Respiratory: Pharyngitis (5% to 25%)

1% to 10%:

Cardiovascular: Facial edema (1% to 3%)

Central nervous system: Pain (1% to 3%), voice disorder (1% to 3%)

Dermatologic: Skin photosensitivity (1% to 3%), skin rash (1% to 3%), burning sensation of the nose (≥2%; transient)

Endocrine & metabolic: Weight gain (1% to 3%), dysmenorrhea (≥2%)

Gastrointestinal: Dysgeusia (5% to 8%), dyspepsia (3% to 5%), abdominal pain (1% to 5%), nausea (2% to 3%), diarrhea (1% to 3%), oral candidiasis (1% to 3%), toothache (1% to 3%), vomiting (1% to 3%), xerostomia (1% to 3%)

Genitourinary: Cystitis (1% to 3%), urinary tract infection (1% to 3%), vulvovaginal candidiasis (1% to 3%)

Hypersensitivity: Hypersensitivity reaction (≥2%)

Infection: Infection (≥2%)

Neuromuscular & skeletal: Back pain (2% to 8%), bursitis (1% to 3%), myalgia (1% to 3%), tenosynovitis (1% to 3%)

Ophthalmic: Conjunctivitis (1% to 4%)

Otic: Otitis media (≥2%)

Respiratory: Flu-like symptoms (2% to 9%), sinusitis (2% to 9%), cough (≤8%), epistaxis (≤5%), bronchitis (children: 3%), chest congestion (1% to 3%), asthma (≥2%), rhinitis (≥2%), stinging sensation of the nose (≥2%; transient)

<1%, postmarketing, and/or case reports: Anaphylaxis, cataract, decreased bone mineral density (prolonged use), decreased plasma cortisol, dizziness, dry throat, dyspnea, fatigue, glaucoma, growth suppression, hoarseness, increased intraocular pressure, insomnia, nasal septum perforation, osteoporosis (prolonged use), pruritus, sneezing, throat irritation, urticaria, wheezing, wound healing impairment

General Dosage Range Intranasal:

Children 2 to <6 years: One spray (55 mcg) in each nostril once daily (maximum: 1 spray [55 mcg] in each nostril once daily)

Children 6 to <12 years: Initial: One spray (55 mcg) in each nostril once daily; Maintenance: 1 to 2 sprays (55 to 110 mcg) in each nostril once daily (maximum: 2 sprays [110 mcg] in each nostril once daily)

Children ≥12 years, Adolescents, and Adults: 1 to 2 sprays (55 to 110 mcg) in each nostril once daily (maximum: 2 sprays [110 mcg] in each nostril once daily)

Mechanism of Action Controls the rate of protein synthesis, depresses the migration of polymorphonuclear leukocytes and fibroblasts, reverses capillary permeability, and stabilizes lysosomal membranes at the cellular level to prevent or control inflammation

Pharmacodynamics/Kinetics

Half-life Elimination Biologic: 18-36 hours; Terminal (intranasal): 3.1 hours

Pregnancy Risk Factor C

Pregnancy Considerations Adverse events have been observed in some animal reproduction studies. Intranasal corticosteroids are recommended for the treatment of rhinitis during pregnancy; the lowest effective dose should be used (NAEPP, 2005; Wallace, 2008).

Triamcinolone (Topical) (trye am SIN oh lone)

Related Information

Ulcerative, Erosive, and Painful Oral Mucosal Disorders *on page 1853*

Related Sample Prescriptions

Ulcerative and Erosive Disorders - Sample Prescriptions *on page 43*

Brand Names: US Dermasorb TA; Dermazone; Kenalog; Oralone; Pediaderm TA [DSC]; Trianex; Triderm

Brand Names: Canada Kenalog; Oracort; Triaderm

Generic Availability (US) May be product dependent

Pharmacologic Category Corticosteroid, Topical

Dental Use Oral topical: Adjunctive treatment and temporary relief of symptoms associated with oral inflammatory lesions and ulcerative lesions resulting from trauma

Use

Dermatoses (corticosteroid-responsive): Topical: Relief of inflammatory and pruritic manifestations of corticosteroid-responsive dermatoses.

Oral inflammatory and ulcerative lesions: Oral paste: Adjunctive treatment and temporary relief of symptoms associated with oral inflammatory and ulcerative lesions resulting from trauma

Local Anesthetic/Vasoconstrictor Precautions No information available to require special precautions

Effects on Dental Treatment Key adverse event(s) related to dental treatment: Ulcerative esophagitis, perioral dermatitis, atrophy of oral mucosa, burning, and irritation.

Effects on Bleeding No information available to require special precautions

Adverse Reactions Frequency not defined.

Central nervous system: Localized burning

Dermatologic: Acneiform eruption, allergic contact dermatitis, atrophic striae, folliculitis, hypertrichosis, hypopigmentation, maceration of the skin, miliaria, perioral dermatitis, pruritus, secondary skin infection, skin atrophy, xeroderma

Endocrine & metabolic: HPA-axis suppression, hyperglycemia, hypokalemia

Local: Local irritation

Dental Usual Dosage Oral inflammatory lesions/ulcers: Adults: Oral topical: Press a small dab (about 1/4 inch) to the lesion until a thin film develops; a larger quantity may be required for coverage of some lesions. For optimal results, use only enough to coat the lesion with a thin film; do not rub in.

Dosing

Adult

Dermatoses (corticosteroid-responsive): Topical:

Note: Frequency of application based upon severity of condition

Cream, ointment: Apply thin film to affected areas 2 to 4 times daily

Lotion:

0.025%: Apply a thin film to affected area 3 to 4 times daily

0.1%: Apply a thin film to affected area 2 to 4 times daily

Aerosol solution: Apply to affected area 3 to 4 times daily

Oral inflammatory and ulcerative lesions: Oral paste: Press a small amount (about 1/4 inch) to the lesion at bedtime; a larger quantity may be required for coverage of some lesions. For severe lesions, may be used 2 or 3 times daily after meals.

Geriatric Refer to adult dosing. Use the lowest effective dose.

Pediatric

Dermatoses (corticosteroid-responsive): Children and Adolescents: Topical: **Note:** Frequency based upon severity of condition: Cream, ointment, lotion, aerosol solution: Refer to adult dosing.

Renal Impairment There are no dosage adjustments provided in the manufacturer's labeling.

Hepatic Impairment There are no dosage adjustments provided in the manufacturer's labeling.

Mechanism of Action Topical corticosteroids have anti-inflammatory, antipruritic, and vasoconstrictive properties. May depress the formation, release, and activity of endogenous chemical mediators of inflammation (kinins, histamine, liposomal enzymes, prostaglandins) through the induction of phospholipase A_2 inhibitory proteins (lipocortins) and sequential inhibition of the release of arachidonic acid. Triamcinolone has intermediate to high range potency (dosage-form dependent).

Contraindications

Hypersensitivity to triamcinolone or any component of the formulation; fungal, viral, or bacterial infections of the mouth or throat (oral topical formulation)

Oral topical formulations only: Fungal, viral, or bacterial infections of the mouth or throat

Warnings/Precautions For external use only; avoid contact with eyes. Do not apply oral paste to skin or eyes. Topical corticosteroids may be absorbed percutaneously. Absorption may cause manifestations of Cushing's syndrome, hyperglycemia, or glycosuria. Absorption is increased by the use of occlusive dressings, application to denuded skin, or application to large surface areas. Do not use occlusive dressings on weeping or exudative lesions and general caution with occlusive dressings should be observed; discontinue if skin irritation or contact dermatitis should occur; do not use in patients with decreased skin circulation. May cause hypercorticism or suppression of hypothalamic-pituitary-adrenal (HPA) axis, particularly in younger children or in patients receiving high doses for prolonged periods. HPA axis suppression may lead to adrenal crisis.

Prolonged use may result in fungal or bacterial superinfection; discontinue if dermatological infection persists despite appropriate antimicrobial therapy. Topical use has been associated with local sensitization (redness, irritation); discontinue if sensitization is noted. When used as a topical agent in the oral cavity, if significant regeneration or repair of oral tissues has not occurred in seven days, re-evaluation of the etiology of the oral lesion is advised.

Because of the risk of adverse effects associated with systemic absorption, topical corticosteroids should be used cautiously in the elderly in the smallest possible effective dose for the shortest duration. Children may absorb proportionally larger amounts after topical application and may be more prone to systemic effects. HPA axis suppression, intracranial hypertension, and Cushing syndrome have been reported in children receiving topical corticosteroids. Prolonged use may affect growth velocity; growth should be routinely monitored in pediatric patients. Some dosage forms may contain polysorbate 80 (also known as Tweens). Hypersensitivity reactions, usually a delayed reaction, have been reported following exposure to pharmaceutical products containing polysorbate 80 in certain individuals (Isaksson 2002; Lucente 2000; Shelley 1995). Thrombocytopenia, ascites, pulmonary deterioration, and renal and hepatic failure have been reported in premature neonates after receiving parenteral products containing polysorbate 80 (Alade 1986; CDC 1984). See manufacturer's labeling. Do not apply aerosol solution to underarms or groin unless directed by a health care professional; if improvement is not seen within 2 weeks, contact prescriber. Aerosol solution is flammable; avoid heat, smoking or flames when applying. Potentially significant interactions may exist, requiring dose or frequency adjustment, additional monitoring, and/or selection of alternative therapy.

Drug Interactions

Metabolism/Transport Effects None known.

Avoid Concomitant Use

Avoid concomitant use of Triamcinolone (Topical) with any of the following: Aldesleukin

Increased Effect/Toxicity

Triamcinolone (Topical) may increase the levels/effects of: Ceritinib; Deferasirox

Decreased Effect

Triamcinolone (Topical) may decrease the levels/effects of: Aldesleukin; Corticorelin; Hyaluronidase

Pharmacodynamics/Kinetics

Half-life Elimination Biologic: 18 to 36 hours

Pregnancy Risk Factor C

Pregnancy Considerations Corticosteroids were found to be teratogenic following topical application in animal reproduction studies. In general, the use of topical corticosteroids during pregnancy is not considered to have significant risk, however, intrauterine growth retardation in the infant has been reported (rare). The use of large amounts or for prolonged periods of time should be avoided.

Breastfeeding Considerations Corticosteroids are excreted in human milk; information specific to triamcinolone has not been located. The amount of triamcinolone absorbed systemically following topical administration is variable. Hypertension in the nursing infant has been reported following corticosteroid ointment applied to the nipples. Use with caution.

Dosage Forms Considerations

Dermazone therapy pack is a kit containing triamcinolone acetonide cream 0.1% (80 g) and silicone gel sheets.

Dosage Forms

Aerosol Solution, External:

Kenalog: 0.147 mg/g (63 g, 100 g)

Generic: 0.147 mg/g (63 g, 100 g)

Cream, External:

Triderm: 0.1% (28.4 g, 85.2 g)

Generic: 0.025% (15 g, 80 g, 453.6 g, 454 g); 0.1% (15 g, 30 g, 80 g, 453.6 g, 454 g); 0.5% (15 g)

Kit, External:

Dermasorb TA: 0.1%

Lotion, External:

Generic: 0.025% (60 mL); 0.1% (60 mL)

Ointment, External:

Trianex: 0.05% (430 g)

Generic: 0.025% (15 g, 80 g, 454 g); 0.1% (15 g, 30 g, 80 g, 453.6 g, 454 g); 0.5% (15 g)

Paste, Mouth/Throat:

Oralone: 0.1% (5 g)

Generic: 0.1% (5 g)

Therapy Pack, External:

Dermazone: 0.1% (1 ea)

Triamterene (trye AM ter een)

Related Information

Cardiovascular Diseases *on page 1752*

Brand Names: US Dyrenium

Pharmacologic Category Antihypertensive; Diuretic, Potassium-Sparing

Use Edema: For the treatment of edema associated with congestive heart failure, cirrhosis of the liver and the nephrotic syndrome; also in steroid-induced edema, idiopathic edema and edema due to secondary hyperaldosteronism.

Local Anesthetic/Vasoconstrictor Precautions No information available to require special precautions

Effects on Dental Treatment No significant effects or complications reported

Effects on Bleeding No information available to require special precautions

Adverse Reactions Frequency not defined.

Central nervous system: Dizziness, fatigue, headache

Dermatologic: Skin photosensitivity, skin rash

Endocrine & metabolic: Hyperkalemia, hypokalemia, increased uric acid, metabolic acidosis

Gastrointestinal: Diarrhea, nausea, vomiting, xerostomia

Genitourinary: Azotemia

Hematologic & oncologic: Hematologic abnormality, megaloblastic anemia, thrombocytopenia

Hepatic: Jaundice, liver enzyme disorder

Hypersensitivity: Anaphylaxis

Neuromuscular & skeletal: Weakness

Renal: Acute interstitial nephritis (rare), acute renal failure (rare), increased blood urea nitrogen, increased serum creatinine, nephrolithiasis

General Dosage Range Oral: *Adults:* 50 to 300 mg daily in 1 to 2 divided doses (maximum: 300 mg daily)

Mechanism of Action Blocks epithelial sodium channels in the late distal convoluted tubule (DCT) and collecting duct which inhibits sodium reabsorption from the lumen. This effectively reduces intracellular sodium, decreasing the function of Na+/K+ ATPase, leading to potassium retention and decreased calcium, magnesium, and hydrogen excretion. As sodium uptake capacity in the DCT/collecting duct is limited, the natriuretic, diuretic, and antihypertensive effects are generally considered weak.

Pharmacodynamics/Kinetics

Onset of Action Diuresis: 2 to 4 hours; **Note:** Maximum therapeutic effect may not occur until after several days of therapy

Duration of Action Diuresis: 7 to 9 hours

Time to Peak Plasma: ~3 hours

Pregnancy Risk Factor C

Pregnancy Considerations Adverse events have not been observed in animal reproduction studies. Triamterene crosses the placenta and is found in cord blood. Use of triamterene to treat edema during normal pregnancies is not appropriate; use may be considered when edema is due to pathologic causes (as in the nonpregnant patient); monitor.

Triazolam (trye AY zoe lam)

Related Information

Management of the Patient With Anxiety or Depression *on page 1873*

Related Sample Prescriptions

Sedation (Prior to Dental Treatment) - Sample Prescriptions *on page 42*

Brand Names: US Halcion

Generic Availability (US) Yes

Pharmacologic Category Benzodiazepine

Dental Use Oral premedication before dental procedures

Use Insomnia: Short-term (generally 7 to 10 days) treatment of insomnia

Local Anesthetic/Vasoconstrictor Precautions No information available to require special precautions

Effects on Dental Treatment No significant effects or complications reported (see Dental Comment)

Effects on Bleeding No information available to require special precautions

Adverse Reactions

>10%: Central nervous system: Drowsiness (14%)

1% to 10%:

Central nervous system: Headache (10%), dizziness (5% to 8%), ataxia (5%), nervousness (5%)

Gastrointestinal: Nausea (5%), vomiting (5%)

<1%, postmarketing, and/or case reports: Abnormal dreams, anaphylaxis, angioedema, anterograde amnesia, sleep disorder (complex sleep-related behavior including cooking or eating food while asleep, making phone calls while asleep, sleep driving), confusion, depression, dermatitis, dysesthesia, euphoria, fatigue, hepatic failure (fulminant), memory impairment, muscle cramps, nightmares, pain, paresthesia, tachycardia, violent behavior, visual disturbance, weakness, xerostomia

Dental Usual Dosage Preprocedure sedation (off-label use): Adults: Oral: 0.25 mg 1 hour before procedure; 0.125 mg used for elderly patients or patients sensitive to sedative effects of medications (Dionne, 2006)

Dosing

Adult

Insomnia (short-term use): Usual dose: 0.25 mg at bedtime; 0.125 mg at bedtime may be sufficient in some patients, such as those with low body weight; maximum dose: 0.5 mg daily

Dental preprocedure oral sedation (off-label use): 0.25 mg 1 hour before procedure; 0.125 mg used for elderly patients or patients sensitive to sedative effects (Dionne, 2006)

Geriatric Elderly and/or debilitated patients: Insomnia (short-term use): Oral: Initial: 0.125 mg at bedtime; maximum dose: 0.25 mg daily

Renal Impairment There are no dosage adjustments provided in the manufacturer's labeling; use with caution.

Hepatic Impairment There are no dosage adjustments provided in the manufacturer's labeling; use with caution.

Mechanism of Action Binds to stereospecific benzodiazepine receptors on the postsynaptic GABA neuron at several sites within the central nervous system, including the limbic system and reticular formation. Enhancement of the inhibitory effect of GABA on neuronal excitability results by increased neuronal membrane permeability to chloride ions. This shift in chloride ions results in hyperpolarization (a less excitable state) and stabilization. Benzodiazepine receptors and effects appear to be linked to the GABA-A receptors. Benzodiazepines do not bind to GABA-B receptors (Vinkers, 2012).

Contraindications Hypersensitivity to triazolam, other benzodiazepines, or any component of the formulation; concurrent therapy with cytochrome P450 3A (CYP 3A) inhibitors including itraconazole, ketoconazole, nefazodone, and several HIV protease inhibitors; pregnancy

Warnings/Precautions As a hypnotic, should be used only after evaluation of potential causes of sleep disturbance. Failure of sleep disturbance to resolve after 7 to 10 days may indicate psychiatric or medical illness. A worsening of insomnia or the emergence of new abnormalities of thought or behavior may represent unrecognized psychiatric or medical illness and requires immediate and careful evaluation. Prescription should be written for a maximum of 7 to 10 days and should not be prescribed in quantities exceeding a 1-month supply. Rebound insomnia or withdrawal symptoms may occur following abrupt discontinuation or large decreases in dose. Use caution when reducing dose or withdrawing therapy; decrease slowly and monitor for withdrawal symptoms. Flumazenil may cause withdrawal in patients receiving long-term benzodiazepine therapy. An increase in daytime anxiety may occur after as few as 10 days of continuous use, which may be related to withdrawal reaction in some patients.

Use with caution in elderly or debilitated patients, patients with hepatic disease (including alcoholics), or renal impairment. Use with caution in patients with respiratory compromise, COPD, or sleep apnea. Elderly patients experience greater sedation and increased psychomotor impairment (Greenblatt, 1991). In debilitated patients, benzodiazepines increase the risk for oversedation, impaired coordination, and dizziness with use. Reports of hypersensitivity reactions, including anaphylaxis and angioedema, have been reported with triazolam.

Causes CNS depression (dose-related) resulting in sedation, dizziness, confusion, or ataxia which may impair physical and mental capabilities. Patients must be cautioned about performing tasks which require mental alertness (eg, operating machinery or driving). Abnormal thinking and behavior changes including symptoms of decreased inhibition (eg, excessive aggressiveness and extroversion), bizarre behavior, agitation, hallucinations, and depersonalization have been reported with the use of benzodiazepine hypnotics. Some evidence suggests symptoms may be dose-related. Anterograde amnesia may occur at a higher rate with triazolam than with other benzodiazepines. An increased risk for hazardous sleep-related activities such as sleep-driving; cooking and eating food, having sex, and making phone calls while asleep have also been noted. Concurrent use of alcohol and other CNS depressants as well as exceeding the maximum recommended dose may increase the risk of these behaviors. Patients will often not remember doing these activities. Consider discontinuation of therapy for patients who report sleep-driving episodes. Benzodiazepines have been associated with falls and traumatic injury and should be used with extreme caution in patients who are at risk of these events (especially the elderly).

Use caution in patients with suicidal risk. Minimize risks of overdose by prescribing the least amount of drug that is feasible in suicidal patients. Worsening of depressive symptoms has also been reported with use of benzodiazepines. Use with caution in patients with a history of drug dependence. Paradoxical reactions, including hyperactive or aggressive behavior have been reported with benzodiazepines, particularly in adolescent/pediatric or psychiatric patients. Evaluate any new changes in behavior. Triazolam is a short half-life benzodiazepine. Tolerance develops to the hypnotic effects (Vinkers, 2012). Chronic use of this agent may increase the perioperative benzodiazepine dose needed to achieve desired effect. Does not have analgesic, antidepressant, or antipsychotic properties. Potentially significant drug-drug interactions may exist, requiring dose or frequency adjustment, additional monitoring, and/or selection of alternative therapy. **[US Boxed warning]: Concomitant use of benzodiazepines and opioids may result in profound sedation, respiratory depression, coma, and death. Reserve concomitant prescribing of these drugs for use in patients for whom alternative treatment options are inadequate. Limit dosages and durations to the minimum required. Follow patients for signs and symptoms of respiratory depression and sedation.**

Drug Interactions

Metabolism/Transport Effects **Substrate** of CYP3A4 (major); **Note:** Assignment of Major/Minor substrate status based on clinically relevant drug interaction potential; **Inhibits** CYP2C8 (weak), CYP2C9 (weak)

Avoid Concomitant Use

Avoid concomitant use of Triazolam with any of the following: Amodiaquine; Antihepaciviral Combination Products; Azelastine (Nasal); Boceprevir; Cobicistat; Conivaptan; Fusidic Acid (Systemic); Idelalisib; Itraconazole; Ketoconazole (Systemic); Methadone; OLANZapine; Orphenadrine; Oxomemazine; Paraldehyde; Protease Inhibitors; Sodium Oxybate; Telaprevir; Thalidomide

Increased Effect/Toxicity

Triazolam may increase the levels/effects of: Alcohol (Ethyl); Amodiaquine; Analgesics (Opioid); Azelastine (Nasal); Blonanserin; Buprenorphine; CloZAPine; CNS Depressants; Flunitrazepam; HYDROcodone; Methadone; Methotrimeprazine; MetyroSINE; Mirtazapine; Orphenadrine; OxyCODONE; Paraldehyde; Piribedil; Pramipexole; ROPINIRole; Rotigotine; Selective Serotonin Reuptake Inhibitors; Sodium Oxybate; Suvorexant; Thalidomide; Zolpidem

The levels/effects of Triazolam may be increased by: Antihepaciviral Combination Products; Aprepitant; Boceprevir; Brimonidine (Topical); Cannabis; Chlormethiazole; Chlorphenesin Carbamate; Cobicistat; Conivaptan; CYP3A4 Inhibitors (Moderate); CYP3A4 Inhibitors (Strong); Dasatinib; Dimethindene (Topical); Doxylamine; Dronabinol; Droperidol; Fosaprepitant; Fusidic Acid (Systemic); HydrOXYzine; Idelalisib; Itraconazole; Ivacaftor; Kava Kava; Ketoconazole (Systemic); Lofexidine; Macrolide Antibiotics; Magnesium Sulfate; Methotrimeprazine; MiFEPRIStone; Minocycline; Nabilone; Netupitant; OLANZapine; Oxomemazine; Palbociclib; Perampanel; Protease Inhibitors; Rufinamide; Simeprevir; Stiripentol; Tapentadol; Teduglutide; Telaprevir; Tetrahydrocannabinol; Trimeprazine

Decreased Effect

The levels/effects of Triazolam may be decreased by: Bosentan; CYP3A4 Inducers (Moderate); CYP3A4 Inducers (Strong); Dabrafenib; Deferasirox; Dexamethasone (Systemic); Enzalutamide; Mitotane;

Siltuximab; St John's Wort; Theophylline Derivatives; Tocilizumab; Yohimbine

Food Interactions Benzodiazepine serum concentrations may be increased by grapefruit juice. Management: Limit or avoid grapefruit juice (Sugimoto, 2006).

Pharmacodynamics/Kinetics

Onset of Action Hypnotic: 15 to 30 minutes (Pakes 1981)

Duration of Action Hypnotic: 6 to 7 hours

Half-life Elimination 1.5 to 5.5 hours

Time to Peak Oral: Within 2 hours

Pregnancy Risk Factor X

Pregnancy Considerations A case report describes placental transfer of triazolam following a maternal overdose. Teratogenic effects have been observed with some benzodiazepines; however, additional studies are needed. The incidence of premature birth and low birth weights may be increased following maternal use of benzodiazepines; hypoglycemia and respiratory problems in the neonate may occur following exposure late in pregnancy. Neonatal withdrawal symptoms may occur within days to weeks after birth and "floppy infant syndrome" (which also includes withdrawal symptoms) have been reported with some benzodiazepines (Bergman, 1992; Iqbal, 2002; Sakai, 1996; Wikner, 2007). Use of triazolam is contraindicated in pregnant women.

Breastfeeding Considerations Although information specific to triazolam has not been located, all benzodiazepines are expected to be excreted into breast milk. Drowsiness, lethargy, or weight loss in nursing infants have been observed in case reports following maternal use of some benzodiazepines (Iqbal, 2002). breastfeeding is not recommended by the manufacturer.

Controlled Substance C-IV

Dosage Forms

Tablet, Oral:

Halcion: 0.25 mg

Generic: 0.125 mg, 0.25 mg

Dental Comment An adult companion should accompany the patient to and from dental office.

Triazolam (0.25 mg) 1 hour prior to dental procedure has been used as an oral preop sedative. There has been recent interest in its use as an orally titratable sedative to render anxious patients at ease during difficult dental procedures. This technique has been referred to as enteral conscious sedation (ECS) and oral conscious sedation (OCS).

Triazolam has the shortest half-life of all the orally administered benzodiazepines. Although midazolam is shorter, it is used parenterally, not orally. The relatively fast onset of action (15 to 30 minutes) of triazolam offers an advantage in its use as an oral sedative. The clinician is reminded that no kinetic data has been reported with multiple titration doses of triazolam, a technique often used in the ECS/OCS regimen.

Trichloroacetic Acid (trye klor oh a SEE tik AS id)

Brand Names: US Tri-Chlor

Pharmacologic Category Keratolytic Agent

Use

Condylomata: To aid in the elimination of condylomata (external anogenital warts).

Limitations of use: The Centers for Disease Control (CDC) sexually transmitted guidelines recommend trichloroacetic acid as a health care provider-administered option for the treatment of external anogenital warts (eg, penis, groin, vulva, perineum, external anus, and perianus). Although trichloroacetic acid has been widely used for this, it has not been thoroughly investigated (CDC [Workowski 2015])

Local Anesthetic/Vasoconstrictor Precautions No information available to require special precautions

Effects on Dental Treatment No significant effects or complications reported

Effects on Bleeding No information available to require special precautions

General Dosage Range Topical: *Adults:* Applied by a health care provider; may repeat weekly if necessary

Pregnancy Considerations Effective when used topically for the treatment of genital condylomas in pregnant women (Schwartz 1988). However, other agents may be preferred for use (CDC [Workowski 2015])

Trifluoperazine (trye floo oh PER a zeen)

Pharmacologic Category First Generation (Typical) Antipsychotic; Phenothiazine Derivative

Use

Nonpsychotic anxiety: Short-term treatment of generalized nonpsychotic anxiety.

Schizophrenia: Management of schizophrenia.

Local Anesthetic/Vasoconstrictor Precautions No information available to require special precautions

Effects on Dental Treatment Key adverse event(s) related to dental treatment: Significant hypotension may occur, especially when the drug is administered parenterally; orthostatic hypotension is due to alpha-receptor blockade, the elderly are at greater risk for orthostatic hypotension. Xerostomia (normal salivary flow resumes upon discontinuation).

Tardive dyskinesia: Prevalence rate may be 40% in elderly; development of the syndrome and the irreversible nature are proportional to duration and total cumulative dose over time. Extrapyramidal reactions are more common in elderly with up to 50% developing these reactions after 60 years of age. Drug-induced Parkinson's syndrome occurs often; akathisia is the most common extrapyramidal reaction in elderly.

Effects on Bleeding No information available to require special precautions

Adverse Reactions

Frequency not defined.

Cardiovascular: Hypotension, orthostatic hypotension

Central nervous system: Decreased seizure threshold, dizziness, disruption of body temperature regulation, extrapyramidal reaction (akathisia, dystonia, Parkinsonian-like syndrome, tardive dyskinesia), headache, neuroleptic malignant syndrome (NMS)

Dermatologic: Skin discoloration (blue-gray), skin photosensitivity (includes increased sensitivity to sun), skin rash

Endocrine & metabolic: Change in libido, change in menstrual flow, galactorrhea, gynecomastia, hyperglycemia, hypoglycemia, weight gain

Gastrointestinal: Constipation, nausea, stomach pain, vomiting, xerostomia

Genitourinary: Difficulty in micturition, ejaculatory disorder, lactation, mastalgia, priapism, urinary retention

Hematologic & oncologic: Agranulocytosis, aplastic anemia, eosinophilia, hemolytic anemia, immune thrombocytopenia, leukopenia, pancytopenia

Hepatic: Cholestatic jaundice, hepatotoxicity

Neuromuscular & skeletal: Tremor

Ophthalmic: Corneal changes, lens disease, retinitis pigmentosa

Respiratory: Nasal congestion

General Dosage Range Oral:
Children 6 to 12 years: Initial: 1 mg once or twice daily; Usual dosage: 1 to 15 mg/day in 1 to 2 divided doses
Adolescents and Adults: Initial: 1 to 5 mg twice daily

Mechanism of Action Trifluoperazine is a piperazine phenothiazine antipsychotic which blocks dopamine, subtype 2 (D_2), receptors in mesolimbocortical and nigrostriatal areas of the brain (APA [Lehman, 2004]).

Pharmacodynamics/Kinetics

Onset of Action For control of agitation, aggression, hostility: 2 to 4 weeks; For control of psychotic symptoms (hallucinations, disorganized thinking or behavior, delusions): Within 1 week; Adequate trial: 6 weeks at moderate to high dose based on tolerability

Duration of Action Variable

Half-life Elimination 3 to 12 hours (Midha 1984)

Time to Peak Serum: 1.5 to 6 hours (Midha 1984)

Pregnancy Considerations Adverse events have not been observed in animal reproduction studies, except when using doses that were also maternally toxic. Prolonged jaundice, extrapyramidal signs, or hyporeflexia have been reported in newborn infants following maternal use of phenothiazines. Antipsychotic use during the third trimester of pregnancy has a risk for extrapyramidal and/or withdrawal symptoms in newborns following delivery. Symptoms in the newborn may include agitation, feeding disorder, hypertonia, hypotonia, respiratory distress, somnolence, and tremor; these effects may be self-limiting or require hospitalization.

Trifluridine (trye FLURE i deen)

Related Information
Systemic Viral Diseases *on page 1806*

Brand Names: US Viroptic

Brand Names: Canada Sandoz-Trifluridine; Viroptic®

Pharmacologic Category Antiviral Agent, Ophthalmic

Use Herpes keratoconjunctivitis, keratitis: Treatment of primary keratoconjunctivitis and recurrent epithelial keratitis due to herpes simplex virus, types 1 and 2

Local Anesthetic/Vasoconstrictor Precautions
No information available to require special precautions

Effects on Dental Treatment No significant effects or complications reported

Effects on Bleeding No information available to require special precautions

Adverse Reactions
1% to 10%:
Ophthalmic: Burning sensation of eyes (≤5%), stinging of eyes (≤5%), eyelid edema (3%)
Frequency not defined:
Hypersensitivity: Local ocular hypersensitivity reaction
Ophthalmic: Epithelial keratopathy, eye irritation, hyperemia, increased intraocular pressure, keratoconjunctivitis sicca, ocular stromal edema, superficial punctate keratitis

General Dosage Range Ophthalmic: *Children ≥6 years, Adolescents, and Adults:* Initial: Instill 1 drop into affected eye(s) every 2 hours while awake (maximum: 9 drops/day); After re-epithelialization of corneal ulcer: 1 drop every 4 hours (maximum: 21 days of treatment)

Mechanism of Action Interferes with viral replication by inhibiting thymidylate synthetase and incorporating into viral DNA in place of thymidine (Carmine 1982).

Pharmacodynamics/Kinetics

Half-life Elimination ~12 minutes

Pregnancy Considerations Adverse effects have not been observed during animal reproduction studies of the ophthalmic solution.

Trifluridine and Tipiracil
(trye FLURE i deen & tye PIR a sil)

Brand Names: US Lonsurf

Pharmacologic Category Antineoplastic Agent, Antimetabolite; Antineoplastic Agent, Antimetabolite (Pyrimidine Analog); Thymidine Phosphorylase Inhibitor

Use Colorectal cancer, metastatic: Treatment of metastatic colorectal cancer in patients who have been previously treated with fluoropyrimidine-, oxaliplatin- and irinotecan-based chemotherapy, an anti-VEGF biological therapy, and if RAS wild-type, an anti-EGFR therapy.

Local Anesthetic/Vasoconstrictor Precautions
No information available to require special precautions

Effects on Dental Treatment Key adverse event(s) related to dental treatment: Stomatitis

Effects on Bleeding Thrombocytopenia, neutropenia and anemia can occur during systemic therapy

Adverse Reactions
>10%:
Central nervous system: Fatigue (≤52%)
Gastrointestinal: Nausea (48%), decreased appetite (39%), diarrhea (32%), vomiting (28%), abdominal pain (21%)
Hematologic & oncologic: Anemia (77%; grade 3: 18%), neutropenia (67%; grade 3: 27%; grade 4: 11%), thrombocytopenia (42%; grade 3: 5%; grade 4: 1%)
Neuromuscular & skeletal: Weakness (≤52%)
Miscellaneous: Fever (19%)
1% to 10%:
Cardiovascular: Pulmonary embolism (2%)
Dermatologic: Alopecia (7%)
Gastrointestinal: Stomatitis (8%), dysgeusia (7%)
Genitourinary: Urinary tract infection (4%)
Respiratory: Nasopharyngitis (4%)
<1%, postmarketing, and/or case reports: Lung disease

General Dosage Range
Dosage adjustment recommended in patients who develop toxicities.
Oral: *Adults:* 35 mg/m^2 (based on the trifluridine component) twice daily on days 1 to 5 and days 8 to 12 of a 28-day cycle (maximum per dose: trifluridine 80 mg)

Mechanism of Action Trifluridine, the active cytotoxic component of trifluridine/tipiracil, is a thymidine-based nucleic acid analogue; the triphosphate form of trifluridine is incorporated into DNA which interferes with DNA synthesis and inhibits cell proliferation. Tipiracil is a potent thymidine phosphorylase inhibitor which prevents the rapid degradation of trifluridine, allowing for increased trifluridine exposure (Mayer 2015).

Pharmacodynamics/Kinetics

Half-life Elimination Trifluridine: 2.1 hours; Tipiracil: 2.4 hours

Time to Peak Plasma: ~2 hours

Pregnancy Considerations Based on the mechanism of action, use of trifluridine/tipiracil would be expected to cause fetal harm when used during pregnancy. Females of reproductive potential should use effective contraception during therapy. Males who have female partners of reproductive potential should use condoms during therapy and for ≥3 months following the final dose.

Trihexyphenidyl (trye heks ee FEN i dil)

Brand Names: Canada PMS-Trihexyphenidyl; Trihexyphenidyl

Pharmacologic Category Anti-Parkinson Agent, Anticholinergic; Anticholinergic Agent

Use

Drug-induced extrapyramidal disorders: Control of extrapyramidal disorders caused by CNS drugs (eg, dibenzoxazepines, phenothiazines, thioxanthenes, butyrophenones)

Parkinsonism: Treatment of all forms of parkinsonism (postencephalitic, arteriosclerotic, and idiopathic) as adjunctive therapy

Local Anesthetic/Vasoconstrictor Precautions No information available to require special precautions

Effects on Dental Treatment Key adverse event(s) related to dental treatment: Xerostomia, dry throat (normal salivary flow resumes upon discontinuation). Prolonged xerostomia may contribute to discomfort and dental disease (ie, caries, periodontal disease, and oral candidiasis).

Effects on Bleeding No information available to require special precautions

Adverse Reactions Frequency not defined.

Cardiovascular: Tachycardia

Central nervous system: Agitation, confusion, delusions, dizziness, drowsiness, euphoria, hallucination, headache, nervousness, paranoia, psychiatric disturbance

Dermatologic: Skin rash

Gastrointestinal: Constipation, intestinal obstruction, nausea, parotitis, toxic megacolon, vomiting, xerostomia

Genitourinary: Urinary retention

Neuromuscular & skeletal: Weakness

Ophthalmic: Blurred vision, glaucoma, increased intraocular pressure, mydriasis

General Dosage Range Oral: *Adults:* Initial: 1 mg/day; Maintenance: 3 to 15 mg/day in 3 to 4 divided doses

Mechanism of Action Exerts a direct inhibitory effect on the parasympathetic nervous system. It also has a relaxing effect on smooth musculature; exerted both directly on the muscle itself and indirectly through parasympathetic nervous system (inhibitory effect)

Pharmacodynamics/Kinetics

Half-life Elimination 33 hours (Brocks 1999)

Time to Peak Serum: 1.3 hours (Brocks 1999)

Pregnancy Risk Factor C

Pregnancy Considerations Animal reproduction studies have not been conducted. One case report did not show evidence of adverse events after trihexyphenidyl administration during pregnancy (Robottom, 2011).

Trimethoprim (trye METH oh prim)

Brand Names: US Primsol

Brand Names: Canada Trimethoprim

Pharmacologic Category Antibiotic, Miscellaneous

Use

Otitis media, acute (oral solution): Treatment of acute otitis media in pediatric patients due to susceptible strains of *Streptococcus pneumoniae* and *Haemophilus influenzae*.

Urinary tract infection (uncomplicated), treatment (tablets, oral solution): Treatment of initial episodes of uncomplicated urinary tract infections due to susceptible strains of *Escherichia coli*, *Proteus mirabilis*, *Klebsiella pneumoniae*, *Enterobacter* species and coagulase-negative *Staphylococcus* species, including *S. saprophyticus*.

Local Anesthetic/Vasoconstrictor Precautions No information available to require special precautions

Effects on Dental Treatment Key adverse event(s) related to dental treatment: Glossitis.

Effects on Bleeding Trimethoprim has been shown to induce acute thrombocytopenic purpura, as a consequence of immune-mediated platelet destruction. Platelet numbers as low as <5 x 10^9/L have been observed with normal white blood cell counts. A review of clinical case reports indicates the thrombocytopenic purpura risk typically occurs when trimethoprim is coadministered with sulfamethoxazole. Clinicians should be aware of this adverse effect and closely observe patients for cutaneous manifestations and bleeding attributable to thrombocytopenia in order to withdraw the drug promptly.

Adverse Reactions

Frequency not always defined.

Dermatologic: Maculopapular rash (200 mg/day: 3% to 7%; incidence higher with larger daily doses), phototoxicity, pruritus (common)

Endocrine & metabolic: Hyperkalemia, hyponatremia

Gastrointestinal: Epigastric distress, glossitis, nausea, vomiting

Hematologic & oncologic: Leukopenia, megaloblastic anemia, methemoglobinemia, neutropenia, thrombocytopenia

Hepatic: Increased liver enzymes

Hypersensitivity: Anaphylaxis, hypersensitivity reaction

Renal: Increased blood urea nitrogen, increased serum creatinine

Miscellaneous: Fever

1%, postmarketing, and/or case reports: Aseptic meningitis, cholestatic jaundice, erythema multiforme, exfoliative dermatitis, Stevens-Johnson syndrome, toxic epidermal necrolysis

General Dosage Range Dosage adjustment recommended in patients with renal impairment

Oral:

Infants ≥6 months, Children, and Adolescents: 10 mg/kg/day in divided doses every 12 hours

Adults: 100 mg every 12 hours **or** 200 mg every 24 hours

Mechanism of Action Inhibits folic acid reduction to tetrahydrofolate by reversible inhibition of dihydrofolate reductase, inhibiting bacterial synthesis of nucleic acids and proteins

Pharmacodynamics/Kinetics

Half-life Elimination

Prolonged with renal impairment

Newborns: 19 hours; range: 11 to 27 hours (Springer 1982)

Infants 2 months to 1 year: 4.6 hours; range: 3 to 6 hours (Hoppu 1989)

Children (Hoppu 1987): 1 to 3 years: 3.7 hours; 8 to 10 years: 5.4 hours

Adults, normal renal function: 8 to 10 hours

Time to Peak Serum: 1 to 4 hours

Pregnancy Risk Factor C

Pregnancy Considerations Adverse events have been observed in animal reproduction studies. Trimethoprim crosses the placenta and can be detected in the fetal serum and amniotic fluid (Reid 1975). Adverse events may be associated with trimethoprim use during pregnancy (Andersen 2012; Andersen 2013; Mølgaard-Nielsen 2012). Untreated urinary tract infections may cause adverse pregnancy outcomes (Nicolle 2005); because safer options are available for the treatment of UTIs in pregnant women, use of TMP containing products in the first trimester should be avoided (Lee 2008). Studies evaluating the effects of trimethoprim administration in pregnancy have also been conducted with Sulfamethoxazole and Trimethoprim (see the Sulfamethoxazole and Trimethoprim monograph for details).

Trimipramine (trye MI pra meen)

Related Information

Dentin Hypersensitivity, Acid Erosion, High Caries Index, Management of Alveolar Osteitis, and Xerostomia *on page 1857*

Vasoconstrictor Interactions With Antidepressants *on page 1913*

Brand Names: US Surmontil

Brand Names: Canada Apo-Trimip; Nu-Trimipramine; Rhotrimine; Surmontil

Pharmacologic Category Antidepressant, Tricyclic (Tertiary Amine)

Use Depression: Relief of symptoms of depression

Local Anesthetic/Vasoconstrictor Precautions Use with caution; epinephrine and levonordefrin have been shown to have an increased pressor response in combination with TCAs. Trimipramine is one of the drugs confirmed to prolong the QT interval and is accepted as having a risk of causing torsade de pointes. The risk of drug-induced torsade de pointes is extremely low when a single QT interval prolonging drug is prescribed. In terms of epinephrine, it is not known what effect vasoconstrictors in the local anesthetic regimen will have in patients with a known history of congenital prolonged QT interval or in patients taking any medication that prolongs the QT interval. Until more information is obtained, it is suggested that the clinician consult with the physician prior to the use of a vasoconstrictor in suspected patients, and that the vasoconstrictor (epinephrine, mepivacaine and levonordefrin [Carbocaine® 2% with Neo-Cobefrin®]) be used with caution.

Effects on Dental Treatment Key adverse event(s) related to dental treatment: Xerostomia (normal salivary flow resumes upon discontinuation) and unpleasant taste. Long-term treatment with TCAs, such as trimipramine, increases the risk of caries by reducing salivation and salivary buffer capacity.

Effects on Bleeding No information available to require special precautions

Adverse Reactions Frequency not defined.

Cardiovascular: Cardiac arrhythmia, cerebrovascular accident, facial edema, flushing, heart block, hypertension, hypotension, myocardial infarction, palpitations, tachycardia

Central nervous system: Abnormal electroencephalogram, agitation, anxiety, ataxia, confusion, delusions, disorientation, dizziness, drowsiness, exacerbation of psychosis, extrapyramidal reaction, fatigue, hallucination, headache, hypomania, insomnia, nightmares, numbness, paresthesia, peripheral neuropathy, restlessness, seizure, tingling sensation, withdrawal syndrome

Dermatologic: Alopecia, diaphoresis, pruritus, skin photosensitivity, skin rash, urticaria

Endocrine & metabolic: Change in libido, galactorrhea, gynecomastia, hyperglycemia, hypoglycemia, SIADH, weight gain, weight loss

Gastrointestinal: Abdominal cramps, anorexia, constipation, diarrhea, epigastric distress, melanoglossia, nausea, paralytic ileus, parotid gland enlargement, stomatitis, unpleasant taste, vomiting, xerostomia

Genitourinary: Breast hypertrophy, difficulty in micturition, impotence, testicular swelling, urinary retention

Hematologic & oncologic: Agranulocytosis, eosinophilia, petechia, purpura, thrombocytopenia

Hepatic: Cholestatic jaundice, increased liver enzymes

Hypersensitivity: Tongue edema

Neuromuscular & skeletal: Tremor, weakness

Ophthalmic: Accommodation disturbance, angle-closure glaucoma, blurred vision, mydriasis

Otic: Tinnitus

Renal: Polyuria

General Dosage Range

Oral:

Adolescents: Initial: A reduced dose of up to 50 mg daily; Maintenance: 50 to 100 mg daily

Adults: Initial: 25 to 100 mg daily; Maintenance: 75 to 300 mg daily

Elderly: Initial: A reduced dose of up to 50 mg daily; Maintenance: 50 to 100 mg daily

Mechanism of Action Antidepressant effects are proposed to result from postsynaptic sensitization to serotonin (Cournoyer, 1987).

Pharmacodynamics/Kinetics

Half-life Elimination 7 to 40 hours (Abernethy 1984; Bougerolle, 1989; Caille, 1980)

Time to Peak 1 to 6 hours (Abernethy, 1984; Bougerolle, 1989; Caille, 1980)

Pregnancy Risk Factor C

Pregnancy Considerations Adverse events have been observed in animal reproduction studies. Tricyclic antidepressants may be associated with irritability, jitteriness, and convulsions (rare) in the neonate (Yonkers 2009).

The ACOG recommends that therapy for depression during pregnancy be individualized; treatment should incorporate the clinical expertise of the mental health clinician, obstetrician, primary health care provider, and pediatrician (ACOG 2008). According to the American Psychiatric Association (APA), the risks of medication treatment should be weighed against other treatment options and untreated depression. For women who discontinue antidepressant medications during pregnancy and who may be at high risk for postpartum depression, the medications can be restarted following delivery (APA 2010). Treatment algorithms have been developed by the ACOG and the APA for the management of depression in women prior to conception and during pregnancy (Yonkers 2009).

Pregnant women exposed to antidepressants during pregnancy are encouraged to enroll in the National Pregnancy Registry for Antidepressants (NPRAD). Women 18 to 45 years of age or their health care providers may contact the registry by calling 844-405-6185. Enrollment should be done as early in pregnancy as possible.

Dental Comment See Local Anesthetic/Vasoconstrictor Precautions

Triprolidine (trye PROE li deen)

Brand Names: US Histex PD [OTC]; Histex [OTC]; M-Hist PD [OTC]

Pharmacologic Category Alkylamine Derivative; Histamine H_1 Antagonist; Histamine H_1 Antagonist, First Generation

Use Upper respiratory allergies: Temporary relief of runny nose; sneezing; itchy nose and throat; and itchy, watery eyes caused by hay fever (allergic rhinitis) or other upper respiratory allergies.

Local Anesthetic/Vasoconstrictor Precautions No information available to require special precautions

Effects on Dental Treatment No significant effects or complications reported

Effects on Bleeding No information available to require special precautions

Adverse Reactions There are no adverse reactions listed in the manufacturer's labeling.

General Dosage Range Oral:

Infants and Children 4 months to <2 years: 0.31 mg every 4 to 6 hours (maximum 1.25 mg/day)

Children 2 to <4 years: 0.63 mg every 4 to 6 hours (maximum 2.5 mg/day)

Children 4 to <6 years: 0.938 mg every 4 to 6 hours (maximum 3.75 mg/day)

Children 6 to <12 years: 1.25 mg every 4 to 6 hours (maximum 5 mg/day)

Children ≥12 years, Adolescents, and Adults: 2.5 mg every 4 to 6 hours (maximum 10 mg/day)

Mechanism of Action Triprolidine is an H_1-receptor antagonist, which provides dose-related suppression of histamine-induced wheel and flare reactions (Simmons 1986). It is useful for the prevention and suppression of the signs and symptoms of allergic rhinitis and other upper respiratory allergies.

Pharmacodynamics/Kinetics

Half-life Elimination ~2 hours (Simons 1986)

Time to Peak ~2 hours (Simons 1986)

Pregnancy Considerations Information related to the use of triprolidine in pregnancy is limited (Aldridge 2014; Gilboa 2009). Antihistamines may be used for the treatment of rhinitis in pregnant women, although agents other than triprolidine may be preferred (Wallace 2008).

Triptorelin (trip toe REL in)

Brand Names: US Trelstar; Trelstar Mixject

Brand Names: Canada Decapeptyl; Trelstar

Pharmacologic Category Gonadotropin Releasing Hormone Agonist

Use

Advanced prostate cancer: Palliative treatment of advanced prostate cancer

Assisted reproductive technologies: Decapeptyl [Canadian product]: Adjunctive therapy in women undergoing controlled ovarian hyperstimulation for assisted reproductive technologies (ART)

Local Anesthetic/Vasoconstrictor Precautions No information available to require special precautions

Effects on Dental Treatment No significant effects or complications reported

Effects on Bleeding Although significant myelosuppression with associated altered hemostasis has been reported for many chemotherapeutic agents, myelosuppression is not common with triptorelin and no specific precautions appear to necessary.

Adverse Reactions Prostate cancer: As reported with all strengths; frequency of effect may vary by strength:

>10%:

Endocrine & metabolic: Hot flash (59% to 72%), increased serum glucose, increased testosterone (peak: days 2-4; decline to low levels by weeks 3-4)

Hematologic & oncologic: Decreased hemoglobin, decreased red blood cells

Hepatic: Increased serum alkaline phosphatase (2% to >10%), increased serum ALT, increased serum AST

Neuromuscular & skeletal: Musculoskeletal pain (12% to 13%)

Renal: Increased blood urea nitrogen

1% to 10%:

Cardiovascular: Lower extremity edema (6%), hypertension (≤4%), chest pain (2%), dependent edema (2%), peripheral edema (≤1%)

Central nervous system: Headache (2% to 7%), pain (2% to 3%), dizziness (1% to 3%), fatigue (2%), insomnia (1% to ≤2%), emotional lability (1%)

Dermatologic: Skin rash (2%), pruritus (1%)

Endocrine & metabolic: Decreased libido (2%), gynecomastia (2%)

Gastrointestinal: Nausea (3%), anorexia (2%), constipation (2%), dyspepsia (2%), mastalgia (2%), vomiting (2%), abdominal pain (1%), diarrhea (1%)

Genitourinary: Erectile dysfunction (10%), testicular atrophy (8%), impotence (2% to 7%), dysuria (5%), urinary retention (≤1%), urinary tract infection (≤1%)

Hematologic & oncologic: Anemia (1%)

Local: Pain at injection site (4%)

Neuromuscular & skeletal: Leg pain (2% to 5%), back pain (≤3%), leg cramps (2%), arthralgia (≤2%), myalgia (1%), weakness (1%)

Ophthalmic: Conjunctivitis (1%), eye pain (1%)

Respiratory: Cough (2%), dyspnea (1%), pharyngitis (1%)

Reproductive studies:

>10%:

Central nervous system: Headache (4% to 27%)

Gastrointestinal: Abdominal pain (9% to 15%)

Genitourinary: Vaginal hemorrhage (2% to 24%)

Local: Inflammation at injection site (10% to 12%)

1% to 10%:

Cardiovascular: Flushing (4%)

Central nervous system: Dizziness (4% to 5%), fatigue (3% to 4%), malaise (2%)

Endocrine & metabolic: Spontaneous abortion (7%), dysmenorrhea (2% to 6%), ovarian hyperstimulation syndrome (3%), hot flash (2%), ovarian cyst (1%)

Gastrointestinal: Nausea (3% to 10%), vomiting (3%), abdominal distension (2%), diarrhea (2%)

Genitourinary: Pelvic pain (6%), gynecological pain (adnexa uteri, 2%), leukorrhea (2%)

Local: Pain at injection site (4% to 7%), bruising at injection site (3%), injection site reaction (2% to 3%)

Neuromuscular & skeletal: Postoperative pain (3% to 4%), back pain (3%)

Respiratory: Upper respiratory tract infection (4%), flu-like symptoms (3%), pharyngitis (3%), dyspnea (2%), rhinitis (2%)

Postmarketing and/or case reports (all indications): Anaphylactic shock, anaphylaxis, angioedema, bladder outflow obstruction, blurred vision, cerebrovascular accident, circulatory shock, deep vein thrombosis, dyspareunia, exacerbation of depression, hematuria, hypersensitivity reaction, increased appetite, limb pain, myocardial infarction, neuropathy, ostealgia, pituitary apoplexy, prolonged Q-T interval on ECG, pulmonary embolism, renal insufficiency, seizure, sleep disorder, spinal cord compression, thrombophlebitis, tissue necrosis at injection site, transient ischemic attacks, tumor flare, urethral obstruction, vaginal dryness

General Dosage Range IM: *Adults:* 3.75 mg once every 4 weeks **or** 11.25 mg once every 12 weeks **or** 22.5 mg once every 24 weeks

Mechanism of Action Triptorelin is an agonist analog of gonadotropin releasing hormone (GnRH) and causes suppression of ovarian and testicular steroidogenesis due to decreased levels of LH and FSH with subsequent decrease in testosterone (male) and estrogen (female) levels. After chronic and continuous administration, usually 2 to 4 weeks after initiation, a sustained decrease in LH and FSH secretion occurs. When used for ART, prevents premature LH surge in women undergoing controlled ovarian hyperstimulation.

Pharmacodynamics/Kinetics

Half-life Elimination 2.8 ± 1.2 hours

Moderate-to-severe renal impairment: 6.6 to 7.7 hours

Hepatic impairment: 7.6 hours

Time to Peak 1 to 3 hours

Pregnancy Risk Factor X

Pregnancy Considerations Use is contraindicated in pregnant women. When used for ART, pregnancy must be ruled out prior to therapy and nonhormonal contraception should be used until menses occurs. Due to the short half-life of triptorelin (formulations used for ART), it is not expected to be present in the maternal serum at the time of embryo transfer. In case reports, spontaneous abortion, congenital anomalies, and other adverse events have been reported following triptorelin (Decapeptyl) exposure during pregnancy.

Trolamine (TROLE a meen)

Brand Names: US Analgesic Creme Rub/Aloe [OTC] [DSC]; Arthricream [OTC]; Asper-Flex [OTC]; Mobisyl [OTC]; Myoflex [OTC]; Tru-micin [OTC]; Ultracin T [OTC]

Brand Names: Canada Antiphlogistine Rub A-535 No Odour; Myoflex

Pharmacologic Category Analgesic, Topical; Salicylate; Topical Skin Product

Use Relief of pain of muscular aches, rheumatism, neuralgia, sprains, arthritis on intact skin

Local Anesthetic/Vasoconstrictor Precautions No information available to require special precautions

Effects on Dental Treatment No significant effects or complications reported

Effects on Bleeding No information available to require special precautions

Adverse Reactions

1% to 10%:

Central nervous system: Confusion, drowsiness

Gastrointestinal: Diarrhea, nausea, vomiting

Respiratory: Hyperventilation

General Dosage Range Topical: *Children ≥12 years and Adults:* Apply to affected area as needed up to 3-4 times/day

Pregnancy Considerations Systemic absorption of salicylate occurs following topical administration of trolamine (Rabinowitz, 1984).

Tromethamine (troe METH a meen)

Brand Names: US Tham [DSC]

Pharmacologic Category Alkalinizing Agent, Parenteral

Use Correction of metabolic acidosis associated with cardiac bypass surgery or cardiac arrest; to correct excess acidity of stored blood that is preserved with acid citrate dextrose (ACD); indicated in infants needing alkalinization after receiving maximum sodium bicarbonate (8-10 mEq/kg/24 hours)

Local Anesthetic/Vasoconstrictor Precautions No information available to require special precautions

Effects on Dental Treatment No significant effects or complications reported

Effects on Bleeding No information available to require special precautions

Adverse Reactions Frequency not defined.

Cardiovascular: Localized phlebitis, venospasm

Endocrine & metabolic: Hyperkalemia, hypervolemia, hypoglycemia (usually doses >500 mg/kg administered over <1 hour)

Hepatic: Hepatic necrosis (resulted during delivery via umbilical venous catheter)

Local: Local irritation

Respiratory: Apnea, pulmonary edema, respiratory depression

General Dosage Range

IV: *Adults:* 3.6 to 10.8 g (111 to 333 mL of 0.3 M solution) **or** 9 mL/kg (maximum: 500 mg/kg) of 0.3 M solution **or** 15 to 77 mL of 0.3 M solution added to each 500 mL of ACD blood

Intraventricular: *Adults:* 2 to 6 g (62 to 185 mL of 0.3 M solution)

Mechanism of Action Acts as a proton acceptor, which combines with hydrogen ions, liberating bicarbonate buffer, to correct acidosis. It buffers both metabolic and respiratory acids, limiting carbon dioxide generation. Also an osmotic diuretic.

Pharmacodynamics/Kinetics

Half-life Elimination 5.6 hours

Pregnancy Risk Factor C

Pregnancy Considerations Animal studies have not been conducted. There are no adequate and well-controlled studies in pregnant women. Use only if potential benefit outweighs possible risk to the fetus.

Product Availability Tham solution is no longer available in the US.

Tropicamide (troe PIK a mide)

Brand Names: US Mydral [DSC]; Mydriacyl

Brand Names: Canada Diotrope; Mydriacyl

Pharmacologic Category Ophthalmic Agent, Mydriatic

Use Mydriasis/Cycloplegia: For mydriasis and cycloplegia in diagnostic procedures

Local Anesthetic/Vasoconstrictor Precautions No information available to require special precautions

Effects on Dental Treatment Key adverse event(s) related to dental treatment: Dryness of mouth.

Effects on Bleeding No information available to require special precautions

Adverse Reactions Frequency not defined.

Cardiovascular: Central nervous system dysfunction, tachycardia

Central nervous system: Headache

Dermatologic: Pallor

Gastrointestinal: Nausea, vomiting, xerostomia

Hypersensitivity: Hypersensitivity reaction

Neuromuscular & skeletal: Muscle rigidity

Ophthalmic: Blurred vision, photophobia, stinging of eyes (transient), superficial punctate keratitis

General Dosage Range Ophthalmic: *Children, Adolescents, and Adults:* 0.5%: Instill 1 to 2 drops 15 to 20 minutes before exam; 1%: Instill 1 to 2 drops, may repeat in 5 minutes

Mechanism of Action Prevents the sphincter muscle of the iris and the muscle of the ciliary body from responding to cholinergic stimulation; produces dilation and prevents accommodation.

Pharmacodynamics/Kinetics

Onset of Action Cycloplegic effect: Peak: 20 to 35 minutes; Mydriatic effect: ~20 to 40 minutes

Duration of Action Cycloplegic effect: <6 hour; Mydriatic effect: ~6 to 7 hours

Pregnancy Risk Factor C

Pregnancy Considerations Animal reproduction studies have not been conducted. If ophthalmic agents are needed during pregnancy, the minimum effective dose should be used in combination with punctual occlusion to decrease potential exposure to the fetus (Samples, 1988).

Trospium (TROSE pee um)

Related Information

Dentin Hypersensitivity, Acid Erosion, High Caries Index, Management of Alveolar Osteitis, and Xerostomia *on page 1857*

Brand Names: US Sanctura XR [DSC]; Sanctura [DSC]

Brand Names: Canada Sanctura XR; Trosec

Pharmacologic Category Anticholinergic Agent

Use Treatment of overactive bladder with symptoms of urgency, incontinence, and urinary frequency

Local Anesthetic/Vasoconstrictor Precautions No information available to require special precautions

Effects on Dental Treatment Key adverse event(s) related to dental treatment: Significant xerostomia and changes in salivation (normal salivary flow resumes upon discontinuation).

Effects on Bleeding No information available to require special precautions

Adverse Reactions

>10%: Gastrointestinal: Xerostomia (9% to 22%)

1% to 10%:

Cardiovascular: Tachycardia (<2%)

Central nervous system: Headache (4% to 7%), fatigue (2%)

Dermatologic: Skin rash (<2%), xeroderma

Gastrointestinal: Constipation (9% to 10%), abdominal pain (1% to 3%), dyspepsia (1% to 2%), flatulence (1% to 2%), abdominal distention (<2%), nausea (1%), dysgeusia, vomiting

Genitourinary: Urinary tract infection (1% to 7%), urinary retention (≤1%)

Infection: Influenza (2%)

Ophthalmic: Dry eye syndrome (1% to 2%), blurred vision (1%)

Respiratory: Nasopharyngitis (3%), dry nose (1%)

<1%, postmarketing, and/or case reports: Anaphylaxis, angioedema, back pain, chest pain, confusion, delirium, dizziness, drowsiness, fecal impaction, gastritis, hallucination, heat intolerance, hypertensive crisis, inversion T wave on ECG, palpitations, rhabdomyolysis, Stevens-Johnson syndrome, supraventricular tachycardia, syncope, visual disturbance

General Dosage Range Dosage adjustment recommended in patients with renal impairment

Oral:

Adults <75 years: Immediate release: 20 mg twice daily; Extended release: 60 mg once daily

Elderly ≥75 years: Immediate release: Initial: 20 mg; Extended release: 60 mg once daily

Mechanism of Action Trospium antagonizes the effects of acetylcholine on muscarinic receptors in cholinergically innervated organs. It reduces the smooth muscle tone of the bladder.

Pharmacodynamics/Kinetics

Half-life Elimination Immediate release formulation: 20 hours

Severe renal insufficiency (CrCl <30 mL/minute): ~33 hours; extended release formulation: ~35 hours

Time to Peak 5-6 hours

Pregnancy Risk Factor C

Pregnancy Considerations Adverse events were observed in animal studies. There are no adequate or well-controlled studies in pregnant women; use only if clearly needed.

Tuberculin Tests (too BER kyoo lin tests)

Brand Names: US Aplisol; Tubersol

Pharmacologic Category Diagnostic Agent

Use Tuberculosis skin test: An aid in the diagnosis of tuberculosis (TB) infection.

Local Anesthetic/Vasoconstrictor Precautions No information available to require special precautions

Effects on Dental Treatment No significant effects or complications reported

Effects on Bleeding No information available to require special precautions

Adverse Reactions

Frequency not defined:

Cardiovascular: Presyncope, syncope

Dermatologic: Erythematous rash, localized erythema, localized vesiculation, rash at injection site, skin rash, skin ulceration at injection site, urticaria at injection site

Hypersensitivity: Anaphylactoid reaction, anaphylaxis, angioedema, hypersensitivity reaction

Local: Injection site reactions, discomfort at injection site, hematoma at injection site, injection site scarring, local pruritus, localized edema, local tissue necrosis, pain at injection site

Respiratory: Dyspnea, stridor

Miscellaneous: Fever

General Dosage Range Intradermal: *Children, Adolescents, and Adults:* 5 units (0.1 mL)

Mechanism of Action Tuberculosis results in individuals becoming sensitized to certain antigenic components of the *M. tuberculosis* organism. Culture extracts called tuberculins are contained in tuberculin skin test preparations. Upon intracutaneous injection of these culture extracts, a classic delayed (cellular) hypersensitivity reaction occurs. This reaction is characteristic of a delayed course (peak occurs >24 hours after injection, induration of the skin secondary to cell infiltration, and occasional vesiculation and necrosis). Delayed hypersensitivity reactions to tuberculin may indicate infection with a variety of nontuberculosis mycobacteria, or vaccination with the live attenuated mycobacterial strain of *M. bovis* vaccine, BCG, in addition to previous natural infection with *M. tuberculosis.*

Pharmacodynamics/Kinetics

Onset of Action Delayed hypersensitivity reactions: 5-6 hours; Peak effect: 48-72 hours

Duration of Action Reactions subside over a few days

Pregnancy Risk Factor C

Pregnancy Considerations Animal reproduction studies have not been conducted. Pregnancy is not a contraindication to testing (CDC 2005).

Typhoid and Hepatitis A Vaccine

(TYE foid & hep a TYE tis aye vak SEEN)

Brand Names: Canada ViVAXIM

Pharmacologic Category Vaccine, Inactivated (Bacterial); Vaccine, Inactivated (Viral)

Use Note: Not approved in the US

***Salmonella typhi* and hepatitis A disease prevention**: Active immunization against typhoid fever caused by *Salmonella typhi* and against disease caused by hepatitis A virus (HAV) in adolescents ≥16 years and adults

National Advisory Committee on Immunizations (NACI) does not recommend use for routine vaccination but does recommend that immunization be considered in the following groups (NACI 2014; NACI 2016):

- Travelers to areas with a prolonged risk (>4 weeks) of exposure to *S. typhi* or travelers to areas with endemic hepatitis A
- Persons with intimate exposure to a *S. typhi* carrier or who are residing in communities with high endemic rates of hepatitis A virus or at risk of outbreaks
- Laboratory technicians with frequent exposure to *S. typhi* or individuals involved in hepatitis A research or production of hepatitis A vaccine
- Travelers with achlorhydria or hypochlorhydria
- Military personnel, relief workers, or others relocated to areas with high rates of hepatitis A infection
- Persons with lifestyle risks for hepatitis A infection (eg, drug abusers, homosexual men), chronic liver disease, receiving hepatotoxic medication or with disease(s) which may necessitate use of hepatotoxic medications
- Persons with hemophilia A or B treated with plasma-derived clotting factors
- Zookeepers, veterinarians, and researchers who handle nonhuman primates

Local Anesthetic/Vasoconstrictor Precautions No information available to require special precautions

Effects on Dental Treatment No significant effects or complications reported

Effects on Bleeding No information available to require special precautions

Adverse Reactions In Canada, adverse reactions may be reported to local provincial/territorial health agencies or to the Vaccine Safety Section at Public Health Agency of Canada (1-866-844-0018).

>10%:

Central nervous system: Headache (15%)

Local: Pain at injection site (90%), induration at injection site (≤28%), swelling at injection site (≤28%), erythema at injection site (10%)

Neuromuscular & skeletal: Weakness (17%), myalgia (16%)

1% to 10%:

Central nervous system: Malaise (3%), dizziness (1%)

Gastrointestinal: Diarrhea (3%), nausea (3%)

Miscellaneous: Fever (5%)

<1%, postmarketing, and/or case reports (reported with ViVAXIM): Arthralgia, pruritus, skin rash

General Dosage Range IM: Adolescents ≥*16 years and Adults:* 1 mL given at least 2 weeks prior to expected exposure; may administer 1 mL booster dose 3 years after previous dose when necessary

Mechanism of Action Provides active immunization against typhoid fever through production of antibodies (predominantly IgG) and against hepatitis A infection through production of antihepatitis A virus antibodies.

Pharmacodynamics/Kinetics

Onset of Action Seroprotection rate at 14 days: Hepatitis A: ~96%, typhoid: ~89%; Seroprotection at 28 days: Hepatitis A: ~100%, typhoid: ~90%

Duration of Action Kinetic models suggest antihepatitis A antibodies may persist ≥20 years (NACI 2016); Typhoid: 3 years

Pregnancy Considerations Animal reproduction studies have not been conducted. Although the safety of this combination vaccine during pregnancy has not been determined, consider use in high risk situations. Inactivated vaccines have not been shown to cause increased risks to the fetus (Canadian NACI 2015).

Product Availability Not available in the US

Typhoid Vaccine (TYE foid vak SEEN)

Brand Names: US Typhim Vi; Vivotif

Brand Names: Canada Typherix; Typhim Vi; Vivotif

Pharmacologic Category Vaccine; Vaccine, Inactivated (Bacterial); Vaccine, Live (Bacterial)

Use

Active immunization against typhoid fever caused by *Salmonella typhi*:

Oral: Immunization of adults and children >6 years of age; complete the vaccine regimen at least 1 week before potential exposure to typhoid bacteria.

Parenteral: Immunization of adults and children ≥2 years of age; complete the vaccine regimen at least 2 weeks before potential exposure to typhoid bacteria.

Not for routine vaccination. In the United States (CDC/ACIP [Jackson 2015]) and Canada, use should be limited to:

- Travelers to areas with a recognized risk of exposure to *S. typhi*
- Persons with intimate exposure to a household contact with *S. typhi* fever or a known carrier
- Laboratory technicians with frequent exposure to *S. typhi*

Additional recommendations: May consider administration to travelers with achlorhydria, or receiving acid suppression therapy; anatomic or functional asplenia (Canadian Immunization Guide)

Local Anesthetic/Vasoconstrictor Precautions No information available to require special precautions

Effects on Dental Treatment No significant effects or complications reported

Effects on Bleeding No information available to require special precautions

Adverse Reactions In the US, all serious adverse reactions must be reported to the Department of Health and Human Services (DHHS) Vaccine Adverse Event Reporting System (VAERS) 1-800-822-7967 or online at https://vaers.hhs.gov/esub/index. In Canada, adverse reactions may be reported to local provincial/territorial health agencies or to the Vaccine Safety Section at Public Health Agency of Canada (1-866-844-0018).

Injection (incidence may vary based on age and/or product used):

>10%:

Central nervous system: Malaise (4% to 24%), headache (16% to 20%), generalized ache (1% to 13%)

Local: Tenderness at injection site (97% to 98%), pain at injection site (27% to 41%), induration at injection site (5% to 15%)

Neuromuscular & skeletal: Muscle tenderness (≤16%)

Miscellaneous: Fever (undefined 2% to 32%)

1% to 10%:

Dermatologic: Pruritus (≤8%)

Gastrointestinal: Nausea (≤8%), vomiting (2%)

Local: Injection site: Erythema at injection site (≤5%), swelling at injection site (≤4%)

Neuromuscular & skeletal: Myalgia (3% to 7%)

Miscellaneous: Fever greater than 100 to 101 degrees (2%)

Postmarketing and/or case reports: Abdominal pain, anaphylaxis, angioedema, arthralgia, asthma, diarrhea, dizziness, flu-like symptoms, Guillain-Barré syndrome, hypersensitivity reaction, hypotension, inflammation at injection site (including angioedema and urticaria), intestinal perforation (jejunum), loss of consciousness, lymphadenopathy, malaise, neck pain, serum sickness, skin rash, syncope (with and without convulsions), tremor, urticaria, vasodilation, weakness

Oral:

1% to 10%:

Central nervous system: Headache (5%)

Dermatologic: Skin rash (1%)

Gastrointestinal: Abdominal pain (6%), nausea (6%), diarrhea (3%), vomiting (2%)

Miscellaneous: Fever (3%)

Postmarketing and/or case reports: Anaphylaxis, demyelinating disease, myalgia, pain, rheumatoid arthritis, sepsis, urticaria, weakness

General Dosage Range

IM: *Children ≥2 years, Adolescents, and Adults:* 0.5 mL given at least 2 weeks prior to expected exposure; may repeat every 2 years

Oral: *Children ≥6 years, Adolescents, and Adults:* One capsule on alternate days (day 1, 3, 5, and 7) for a total of 4 doses; may repeat full course every 5 years

Mechanism of Action Virulent strains of *Salmonella typhi* cause disease by penetrating the intestinal mucosa and entering the systemic circulation via the lymphatic vasculature. One possible mechanism of conferring immunity may be the provocation of a local immune response in the intestinal tract induced by oral ingesting of a live strain with subsequent aborted infection. The ability of *S. typhi* to produce clinical disease (and to elicit an immune response) is dependent on the bacteria having a complete lipopolysaccharide. The live attenuate Ty21a strain lacks the enzyme UDP-4-galactose epimerase so that lipopolysaccharide is only synthesized under conditions that induce bacterial autolysis. Thus, the strain remains avirulent despite the production of sufficient lipopolysaccharide to evoke a protective immune response. Despite low levels of lipopolysaccharide synthesis, cells lyse before gaining a virulent phenotype due to the intracellular accumulation of metabolic intermediates.

Efficacy: Based on a systematic review and meta-analysis, the estimated 2.5 to 3 year cumulative efficacy was 55% (95% confidence interval [CI]: 30% to 70%) for the injectable vaccine and 48% (CI: 34% to 58%) for the oral vaccine (CDC/ACIP [Jackson 2015]).

Pharmacodynamics/Kinetics

Onset of Action Immunity to *Salmonella typhi*: Oral: ~1 week after completing the series; Parenteral: Antibody response develops within 2 weeks after a single dose.

Duration of Action Immunity: Oral: >5 years; Parenteral: Typhim Vi: ~2 years, Typherix [Canadian product]: ~3 years

Pregnancy Risk Factor C

Pregnancy Considerations Animal reproduction studies have not been conducted. The manufacturer of the Typhim Vi injection suggests delaying vaccination until the second or third trimester if possible. Untreated typhoid fever may lead to miscarriage or vertical intrauterine transmission causing neonatal typhoid (rare).

Ulipristal (ue li PRIS tal)

Brand Names: US Ella

Brand Names: Canada Ella; Fibristal

Pharmacologic Category Contraceptive; Progestin Receptor Modulator

Use

Emergency contraceptive (Ella): Prevention of pregnancy following unprotected intercourse or a known or suspected contraceptive failure. Ulipristal is not intended for routine use as a contraceptive.

Uterine fibroids (Fibristal [Canadian product]):

Treatment of moderate to severe signs/symptoms of uterine fibroids in adult women of reproductive age who are eligible for surgery.

Intermittent treatment of moderate to severe signs/symptoms of uterine fibroids in adult women of reproductive age

Local Anesthetic/Vasoconstrictor Precautions No information available to require special precautions

Effects on Dental Treatment No significant effects or complications reported (see Dental Comment)

Effects on Bleeding No information available to require special precautions

Adverse Reactions

Emergency contraception (Ella):

>10%:

Central nervous system: Headache (18% to 19%)

Endocrine & metabolic: Suppressed menstruation (≥7 days later than expected: 19%)

Gastrointestinal: Abdominal pain (8% to 15%), nausea (12% to 13%)

Genitourinary: Dysmenorrhea (7% to 13%)

1% to 10%:

Central nervous system: Fatigue (6%), dizziness (5%)

Endocrine & metabolic: Intermenstrual bleeding (9%)

Genitourinary: Early menses (≥7 days earlier than expected: 7%)

Postmarketing and/or case reports: Acne vulgaris

Treatment of moderate-to-severe signs/symptoms of uterine fibroids (Fibristal [Canadian product]):

>10%:

Central nervous system: Headache (1% to 16%)

Endocrine & metabolic: Hot flash (1% to 25%)

1% to 10%:

Cardiovascular: Edema (≤1%), hypotension (≤1%), sinus bradycardia (≤1%)

Central nervous system: Fatigue (≤4%), vertigo (≤4%), insomnia (≤2%), dizziness (1%), aggressive behavior (≤1%), drowsiness (≤1%), emotional lability (≤1%), migraine (≤1%), sleep disorder (≤1%)

Dermatologic: Night sweats (≤2%), acne vulgaris (≤1%), alopecia (≤1%), seborrhea (≤1%), xeroderma (≤1%)
Endocrine & metabolic: Hypercholesterolemia (3%), hypertriglyceridemia (≤3%), hypothyroidism (≤2%), obesity (1%), amenorrhea (≤1%), increased gamma-glutamyl transferase (≤1%), ovarian cyst (≤1%), ovarian hyperstimulation (≤1%), thyroid disease (≤1%)
Gastrointestinal: Nausea (3%), constipation (1%), dyspepsia (≤1%), upper abdominal pain (≤1%)
Genitourinary: Mastalgia (2%), pelvic pain (1% to 2%), endometrial hyperplasia (≤2%), genital bleeding (≤2%), breast swelling (≤1%), breast tenderness (≤1%), genital discharge (≤1%), uterine disease (≤1%), uterine hemorrhage (≤1%), vaginal dryness (≤1%), vulvovaginal candidiasis (≤1%)
Infection: Herpes virus infection (≤1%)
Neuromuscular & skeletal: Arthralgia (2%), muscle spasm (≤2%), back pain (≤1%), limb pain (≤1%)
Respiratory: Dyspnea (≤1%), epistaxis (≤1%), pharyngitis (≤1%)
Miscellaneous: Fever (≤1%)

General Dosage Range Oral: *Adolescents (postpubertal) and Adults:* 30 mg as a single dose

Mechanism of Action Prevents progestin from binding to the progesterone receptor. Ulipristal postpones follicular rupture when administered prior to ovulation, thereby inhibiting or delaying ovulation. May also alter the normal endometrium, impairing implantation. When used for the treatment of signs and symptoms of uterine fibroids, ulipristal reduces the size of uterine fibroids by inhibiting cellular proliferation and inducing apoptosis.

Pharmacodynamics/Kinetics

Half-life Elimination Ulipristal: ~32 to 38 hours; Monodemethylated metabolite: ~27 hours

Time to Peak Serum: 1 hour (ulipristal and monodemethylated metabolite)

Pregnancy Risk Factor X

Pregnancy Considerations Adverse events have been observed in some animal reproduction studies. Exclude pregnancy prior to therapy; not indicated for terminating an existing pregnancy. A rapid return of fertility is expected following use for emergency contraception; routine contraceptive measures should be initiated or continued following use to ensure ongoing prevention of pregnancy. Barrier contraception is recommended immediately following emergency contraception and throughout the same menstrual cycle; efficacy of hormonal contraceptives may be decreased. The manufacturer labeling suggests that hormonal contraceptives may be less effective in females with BSA >30 kg/m^2. When ulipristal is used for treatment of uterine fibroids (Canadian labeling; not in US labeling) a nonhormonal method of contraception is recommended.

Health care providers are encouraged to enroll women who were exposed to ulipristal during the cycle pregnancy started or anytime during pregnancy in the Ellipse II study (forms available at www.ellipse2.com).

Dental Comment Current hormone contraceptives should not be considered a risk factor for gingival or periodontal disease (Preshaw, 2013).

Umeclidinium (ue me kli DIN ee um)

Brand Names: US Incruse Ellipta

Brand Names: Canada Incruse Ellipta

Pharmacologic Category Anticholinergic Agent; Anticholinergic Agent, Long-Acting

Use

Chronic obstructive pulmonary disease: Maintenance treatment of airflow obstruction in patients with chronic obstructive pulmonary disease (COPD), including chronic bronchitis and/or emphysema.

Limitations of use: Not indicated for relief of acutely deteriorating COPD.

Local Anesthetic/Vasoconstrictor Precautions No information available to require special precautions

Effects on Dental Treatment Key adverse event(s) related to dental treatment: Nasopharyngitis, toothache have been reported

Effects on Bleeding No information available to require special precautions

Adverse Reactions

1% to 10%:
Cardiovascular: Tachycardia (1%)
Gastrointestinal: Toothache (1%), upper abdominal pain (1%)
Hematologic & oncologic: Bruise (1%)
Neuromuscular & skeletal: Arthralgia (2%), myalgia (1%)
Respiratory: Nasopharyngitis (8%), upper respiratory tract infection (5%), cough (3%), pharyngitis (1%), viral upper respiratory tract infection (1%)

<1%, postmarketing, and/or case reports: Atrial fibrillation, dysgeusia

General Dosage Range Oral inhalation: *Adults:* One inhalation (62.5 mcg) once daily; maximum dose: 1 inhalation (62.5 mcg) once daily

Mechanism of Action Competitively and reversibly inhibits the action of acetylcholine at type 3 muscarinic (M_3) receptors in bronchial smooth muscle causing bronchodilation.

Pharmacodynamics/Kinetics

Half-life Elimination 11 hours

Time to Peak 5 to 15 minutes

Pregnancy Risk Factor C

Pregnancy Considerations Adverse events were not observed in animal reproduction studies. Systemic absorption following oral inhalation in negligible.

Umeclidinium and Vilanterol
(ue me kli DIN ee um & VYE lan ter ol)

Brand Names: US Anoro Ellipta

Brand Names: Canada Anoro Ellipta

Pharmacologic Category Anticholinergic Agent; Anticholinergic Agent, Long-Acting; Beta$_2$ Agonist; Beta$_2$-Adrenergic Agonist, Long-Acting

Use

Chronic obstructive pulmonary disease: Maintenance treatment of airflow obstruction in patients with chronic obstructive pulmonary disease (COPD), including chronic bronchitis and emphysema

Limitations of use: Not for the relief of acute bronchospasm or for asthma treatment

Local Anesthetic/Vasoconstrictor Precautions No information available to require special precautions

Effects on Dental Treatment No significant effects or complications reported

Effects on Bleeding No information available to require special precautions

Adverse Reactions Percentages as reported with combination product.

1% to 10%:
Cardiovascular: Chest pain (1%)

Central nervous system: Headache (≥1%), vertigo (≥1%)
Endocrine & metabolic: Diabetes mellitus (≥1%)
Gastrointestinal: Diarrhea (2%), abdominal pain (≥1%), nausea (≥1%), toothache (≥1%), constipation (1%)
Genitourinary: Urinary tract infection (≥1%)
Neuromuscular & skeletal: Limb pain (2%), arthralgia (≥1%), back pain (≥1%), muscle spasm (1%), neck pain (1%)
Respiratory: Pharyngitis (2%), cough (≥1%), lower respiratory tract infection (≥1%), pleuritic chest pain (≥1%), sinusitis (≥1%)

<1%, postmarketing, and/or case reports: Atrial fibrillation, anxiety, chest discomfort, conjunctivitis, dysgeusia, dyspepsia, gastroesophageal reflux disease, hypersensitivity reaction (including anaphylaxis, angioedema and urticaria), musculoskeletal chest pain, myocardial infarction, palpitations, pruritus, skin rash, supraventricular extrasystole, tremor, ventricular premature contractions, vomiting, weakness, xerostomia

General Dosage Range

Oral inhalation (dry powder inhaler): *Adults:* Umeclidinium 62.5 mcg/vilanterol 25 mcg: 1 inhalation once daily; maximum dose: 1 inhalation/day

Mechanism of Action

Umeclidinium: A long-acting anticholinergic, competitively and reversibly inhibits the action of acetylcholine at type 3 muscarinic (M_3) receptors in bronchial smooth muscle causing bronchodilation.

Vilanterol: A long-acting beta$_2$-agonist, relaxes bronchial smooth muscle by selective action on beta$_2$-receptors with little effect on heart rate.

Pharmacodynamics/Kinetics

Half-life Elimination 11 hours

Pregnancy Risk Factor C

Pregnancy Considerations Animal reproduction studies have not been conducted with this combination. Beta-agonists have the potential to affect uterine contractility if administered during labor.

Unoprostone (yoo noe PROS tone)

Brand Names: US Rescula

Pharmacologic Category Docosanoid, Synthetic; Ophthalmic Agent, Antiglaucoma

Use To lower intraocular pressure (IOP) in patients with open-angle glaucoma or ocular hypertension

Local Anesthetic/Vasoconstrictor Precautions No information available to require special precautions

Effects on Dental Treatment No significant effects or complications reported

Effects on Bleeding No information available to require special precautions

Adverse Reactions

>10%: Ophthalmic: Burning sensation of eyes (≤25%), stinging of eyes (≤25%), eye pruritus (10% to 25%), eye redness (10% to 25%), xerophthalmia (10% to 25%), increased eyelash length (10% to 14%; ≥1 mm at 12 months)

1% to 10%:

Cardiovascular: Hypertension
Central nervous system: Foreign body sensation of eye (5% to 10%), dizziness, headache, insomnia, pain
Endocrine & metabolic: Diabetes mellitus
Hypersensitivity: Hypersensitivity reaction
Neuromuscular & skeletal: Back pain
Ophthalmic: Abnormal lacrimation (5% to 10%), eyelid disease (5% to 10%), visual disturbance (5% to 10%), decreased eyelash length (7%), blepharitis, cataract, conjunctivitis, corneal lesion, eye discharge, eye irritation, eye pain, hemophthalmos, keratitis, photophobia, vitreous disorder
Respiratory: Flu-like symptoms (6%), bronchitis, cough, pharyngitis, rhinitis, sinusitis
Miscellaneous: Accidental injury

<1%, postmarketing, and/or case reports: Blepharoptosis, color blindness, corneal deposits, corneal edema, corneal opacity, diplopia, hyperpigmentation of eyelids, increased growth in number of eyelashes, increased intraocular pressure (acute), iris hyperpigmentation, iritis, optic atrophy, retinal hemorrhage, visual field defect

General Dosage Range Ophthalmic: *Adults:* Instill 1 drop into affected eye(s) twice daily

Mechanism of Action The exact mechanism of action is unknown; however, unoprostone likely decreases IOP by increasing the outflow of aqueous humor. Cardiovascular and pulmonary function were not affected in clinical studies. IOP was decreased by 3-4 mm Hg in patients with a mean baseline IOP of 23 mm Hg. IOP may also be lowered by increased trabecular meshwork outflow via stimulation of calcium-activated BK and ClC-2 type channels (Fung, 2014).

Pharmacodynamics/Kinetics

Half-life Elimination 14 minutes

Pregnancy Risk Factor C

Pregnancy Considerations In animal reproduction studies, adverse events were observed when administered subcutaneously at doses greater than the recommended human dose. Following ophthalmic administration, systemic absorption is minimal; systemic absorption would be required in order for unoprostone to cross the placenta and reach the fetus. If ophthalmic agents are needed during pregnancy, the minimum effective dose should be used in combination with punctual occlusion to decrease potential exposure to the fetus (Samples, 1988).

Urea (Systemic) (yoor EE a)

Brand Names: US Ure-Na

Pharmacologic Category Medical Food

Use

Hyponatremia: A medical food for the management of hyponatremia (euvolemic and hypervolemic).

Note: A medical food is formulated to be administered enterally under the supervision of a physician and is intended for the specific dietary management of a disease or condition for which distinctive nutritional requirements are established by medical evaluation. Medical foods are not drugs and, therefore, are not subject to any FDA regulatory requirements that specifically apply to drugs (eg, requirement for written/oral prescription prior to dispensing, premarket review or approval, proof of safety and efficacy).

Adverse Reactions Frequency not defined.

Endocrine & metabolic: Hypernatremia
Gastrointestinal: Mildly upset stomach

General Dosage Range

Oral: *Adults:* 15 to 45 g daily

Mechanism of Action Urea normalizes serum sodium levels by inducing osmotic excretion of free water. Urea also ameliorates hyponatremia in syndrome of inappropriate antidiuretic hormone secretion by a more specific effect, diminishing the natriuresis in association with increased medullary urea content.

Urea (Topical) (yoor EE a)

Brand Names: US Aluvea [DSC]; Aquaphilic/Carbamide [OTC]; Atrac-Tain [OTC]; Beta Care Betamide [OTC]; Carb-O-Lac5 [OTC] [DSC]; Carb-O-Philic/10 [OTC] [DSC]; Carb-O-Philic/20 [OTC] [DSC]; Carb-O-Philic/40 [DSC]; Carmol 10 [OTC]; Carmol 20 [OTC]; Carmol [OTC]; CEM-Urea; Cerovel; Dermal Therapy Finger Care [OTC]; Dermasorb XM; DPM [OTC] [DSC]; Gordons Urea; Gordons Urea [OTC]; Gormel 10 [OTC]; Gormel [OTC]; Hydro 35; Hydro 40; Kerafoam 42 [DSC]; Kerafoam [DSC]; Keralac; Lanaphilic/Urea [OTC]; Latrix; Latrix XM; Mycocide CX Callus Exfoliator [OTC]; Nutraplus [OTC]; Rea Lo 39; Rea Lo 40; Rea-Lo [OTC]; Remeven; Rynoderm; Salrix; U-Kera E [DSC]; Ultra Mide 25 [OTC]; Umecta; Umecta Mousse; Umecta Nail Film; Umecta PD [DSC]; Uramaxin; Uramaxin GT; Ure-K; Urea 20 Intensive Hydrating [OTC]; Urea Hydrating; Urea Nail; Urea-C40; Ureacin-10 [OTC]; Ureacin-20 [OTC]; Urevaz; Utopic; X-Viate [DSC]

Pharmacologic Category Keratolytic Agent; Topical Skin Product

Use Hyperkeratotic conditions: Debridement and promotion of normal healing of hyperkeratotic surface lesions, particularly where healing is retarded by local infection, necrotic tissue, fibrinous or purulent debris, or eschar; treatment of hyperkeratotic conditions, such as dry, rough skin; skin cracks and fissures; dermatitis; psoriasis; xerosis; ichthyosis; eczema; keratosis; keratoderma; corns and calluses; damaged, ingrown, and devitalized nails.

Local Anesthetic/Vasoconstrictor Precautions No information available to require special precautions

Effects on Dental Treatment No significant effects or complications reported

Effects on Bleeding No information available to require special precautions

Adverse Reactions Frequency not defined.

Central nervous system: Transient stinging of the skin

Dermatologic: Burning sensation of skin (transient), pruritus (transient)

Local: Local irritation

General Dosage Range Topical: *Adults:* Apply 1-3 times daily

Mechanism of Action Urea softens hyperkeratotic areas by dissolving the intracellular matrix, resulting in loosening the horny layer of the skin, or softening and debridement of the nail plate

Pregnancy Risk Factor B/C (manufacturer specific)

Pregnancy Considerations Reproduction studies have not been conducted with all products. When conducted, adverse events were not observed in animal studies.

Urea and Hydrocortisone

(yoor EE a & hye droe KOR ti sone)

Related Information

Hydrocortisone (Topical) *on page 836*

Urea (Topical) *on page 1619*

Brand Names: US Carmol-HC® [DSC]; U-Cort [DSC]

Brand Names: Canada Ti-U-Lac® H; Uremol® HC

Pharmacologic Category Corticosteroid, Topical

Use Inflammation of corticosteroid-responsive dermatoses

Local Anesthetic/Vasoconstrictor Precautions No information available to require special precautions

Effects on Dental Treatment No significant effects or complications reported

Effects on Bleeding No information available to require special precautions

General Dosage Range Topical: *Children and Adults:* Apply thin film and rub in well 2-4 times/day

Mechanism of Action See individual agents.

Pregnancy Risk Factor C

Pregnancy Considerations Teratogenic effects have been observed in animals administered potent topical corticosteroids. Topical products are not recommended for extensive use, in large quantities, or for long periods of time in pregnant women.

Urofollitropin (yoor oh fol li TROE pin)

Brand Names: US Bravelle

Brand Names: Canada Bravelle

Pharmacologic Category Gonadotropin; Ovulation Stimulator

Use

Multifollicular development during ART: Development of multiple follicles with assisted reproductive technologies (ART) in women who have previously received pituitary suppression.

Limitations of use: Prior to therapy, perform a complete gynecologic exam (including demonstration of tubal patency) and endocrinologic evaluation (cause of infertility should be diagnosed prior to ART); exclude the possibility of pregnancy; evaluate the fertility status of the male partner; exclude a diagnosis of primary ovarian failure.

Ovulation induction: Ovulation induction in women who previously received GnRH agonist or antagonist for pituitary suppression.

Local Anesthetic/Vasoconstrictor Precautions No information available to require special precautions

Effects on Dental Treatment No significant effects or complications reported

Effects on Bleeding Medical consult is suggested.

Adverse Reactions Percentage may vary by indication or route of administration.

>10%:

Central nervous system: Headache

Endocrine & metabolic: Ovarian hyperstimulation syndrome, ovary enlargement

Gastrointestinal: Abdominal cramps

1% to 10%:

Cardiovascular: Hypertension

Central nervous system: Depression, emotional lability, pain (including post-retrieval pain)

Dermatologic: Acne vulgaris, exfoliative dermatitis, skin rash

Endocrine & metabolic: Dehydration, hot flash, ovarian disease (cyst, pain), weight gain

Gastrointestinal: Abdominal pain, constipation, diarrhea, enlargement of abdomen, nausea, vomiting

Genitourinary: Breast tenderness, cervix disease, pelvic cramps, pelvic pain, spotting, urinary tract infection, uterine spasm, vaginal discharge, vaginal hemorrhage

Infection: Infection

Local: Injection site reaction

Neuromuscular & skeletal: Neck pain

Respiratory: Respiratory tract disease, sinusitis

Miscellaneous: Fever

General Dosage Range

IM: *Adults (females):* Initial: 150 units once daily for 5 days; Maintenance: Up to 450 units/day (maximum: 12 days therapy)

SubQ: *Adults (females):* Initial: 225 units once daily for 5 days; Maintenance: Up to 450 units/day (maximum: 12 days therapy)

Mechanism of Action Urofollitropin is a preparation of highly purified follicle-stimulating hormone (FSH) extracted from the urine of postmenopausal women. Follitropins stimulate ovarian follicular growth in women who do not have primary ovarian failure. FSH is required for normal follicular growth, maturation, gonadal steroid production, and spermatogenesis.

Pharmacodynamics/Kinetics

Half-life Elimination

IM: 37 hours (single dose), 15 hours (multiple doses)

SubQ: 32 hours (single dose), 21 hours (multiple doses)

Time to Peak

IM: 17 hours (single dose), 11 hours (multiple doses)

SubQ: 21 hours (single dose), 10 hours (multiple doses)

Pregnancy Risk Factor X

Pregnancy Considerations Ectopic pregnancy, congenital abnormalities, spontaneous abortion, and multifetal gestations/births have been reported. The incidence of congenital abnormality may be slightly higher after ART than with spontaneous conception; higher incidence may be related to parental characteristics (maternal age, genetics, sperm characteristics). Urofollitropin is used for the induction of ovulation and with ART; use is contraindicated in women who are already pregnant.

Ursodiol (ur soe DYE ol)

Brand Names: US Actigall; Urso 250; Urso Forte

Brand Names: Canada Dom-Ursodiol C; PHL-Ursodiol C; PMS-Ursodiol C; Urso; Urso DS

Pharmacologic Category Gallstone Dissolution Agent

Use

Gallstones (capsules only):

For patients with radiolucent, noncalcified gallbladder stones less than 20 mm in greatest diameter in whom elective cholecystectomy would be undertaken except for the presence of increased surgical risk caused by systemic disease, advanced age, idiosyncratic reaction to general anesthesia, or for those patients who refuse surgery. Safety for use of ursodiol beyond 24 months is not established.

For the prevention of gallstone formation in obese patients experiencing rapid weight loss.

Primary biliary cirrhosis (tablets only): For the treatment of patients with primary biliary cirrhosis (PBC).

Local Anesthetic/Vasoconstrictor Precautions No information available to require special precautions

Effects on Dental Treatment No significant effects or complications reported

Effects on Bleeding Medical consult is suggested.

Adverse Reactions

>10%:

Central nervous system: Headache (≤25%), dizziness (17%)

Gastrointestinal: Diarrhea (≤27%), constipation (≤26%), dyspepsia (≤17%), nausea (≤17%)

Neuromuscular & skeletal: Back pain (≤12%)

Respiratory: Upper respiratory tract infection (≤16%)

1% to 10%:

Dermatologic: Alopecia (5%), skin rash (3%)

Endocrine & metabolic: Hyperglycemia (1%)

Gastrointestinal: Vomiting (≤10%), peptic ulcer (1%)

Genitourinary: Urinary tract infection (7%)

Hematologic & oncologic: Leukopenia (3%), thrombocytopenia (1%)

Hepatic: Cholecystitis (5%)

Hypersensitivity: Hypersensitivity reaction (5%)

Infection: Viral infection (9%)

Neuromuscular & skeletal: Arthritis (6%), musculoskeletal pain (6%)

Renal: Increased serum creatinine (1%)

Respiratory: Pharyngitis (≤8%), bronchitis (7%), cough (7%), flu-like symptoms (7%)

<1%, postmarketing, and/or case reports: Abdominal distress, abdominal pain, abnormal hepatic function tests, angioedema, anorexia, biliary colic, esophagitis, facial edema, fever, hepatobiliary disease, increased gamma-glutamyl transferase, increased liver enzymes, increased serum alkaline phosphatase, increased serum ALT, increased serum AST, increased serum bilirubin, jaundice, laryngeal edema, malaise, metallic taste, myalgia, peripheral edema, pruritus, transaminases increased, urticaria, weakness

General Dosage Range Oral: *Adults:* 8-15 mg/kg/day in 2-4 divided doses **or** 300 mg twice daily

Mechanism of Action Decreases the cholesterol content of bile and bile stones by reducing the secretion of cholesterol from the liver and the fractional reabsorption of cholesterol by the intestines. Mechanism of action in primary biliary cirrhosis is not clearly defined.

Pregnancy Risk Factor B

Pregnancy Considerations Adverse events have not been observed in animal reproduction studies. Ursodiol (ursodeoxycholic acid) is the treatment of choice for intrahepatic cholestasis of pregnancy (Kremer, 2011).

Ustekinumab (yoo stek in YOO mab)

Brand Names: US Stelara

Brand Names: Canada Stelara

Pharmacologic Category Antipsoriatic Agent; Interleukin-12 Inhibitor; Interleukin-23 Inhibitor; Monoclonal Antibody

Use

Crohn disease: Treatment of moderately to severely active Crohn disease in adults who have failed or were intolerant to immunomodulatory or corticosteroid therapy, but never failed tumor necrosis factor (TNF) blocker therapy or who have failed or were intolerant to treatment with one or more TNF blockers.

Plaque psoriasis: Treatment of moderate to severe plaque psoriasis in adults who are candidates for phototherapy or systemic therapy

Psoriatic arthritis: Treatment of active psoriatic arthritis (as monotherapy or in combination with methotrexate) in adults

Local Anesthetic/Vasoconstrictor Precautions No information available to require special precautions

Effects on Dental Treatment No significant effects or complications reported

Effects on Bleeding No information available to require special precautions

Adverse Reactions

>10%:

Infection: Infection (psoriasis: 27% to 72%; severe infection: ≤3%)

Respiratory: Nasopharyngitis (Crohn's disease: 11%)

1% to 10%:

Central nervous system: Headache (psoriasis: 5%), fatigue (psoriasis: 3%), dizziness (psoriasis: 2%), depression (psoriasis: 1%)

Dermatologic: Pruritus (2% to 4%), acne vulgaris (Crohn's disease: 1%)

Gastrointestinal: Vomiting (Crohn's disease: 4%), nausea (psoriatic arthritis: 3%), dental disease (infection; 1%)

Genitourinary: Vaginal mycosis (Crohn's disease: ≤5%), vulvovaginal candidiasis (Crohn's disease: ≤5%), urinary tract infection (Crohn's disease: 4%)

Hematologic & oncologic: Skin carcinoma (nonmelanoma including squamous cell carcinoma; psoriasis: 2%)

Immunologic: Antibody development (<3% to 6%)

Local: Erythema at injection site (1% to 5%)

Neuromuscular & skeletal: Arthralgia (psoriatic arthritis: 3%), back pain (psoriasis: 2%), weakness (Crohn's disease: 1%)

Respiratory: Bronchitis (Crohn's disease: 5%), sinusitis (Crohn's disease: 3%), pharyngolaryngeal pain (psoriasis: 2%)

Frequency not defined:

Gastrointestinal: Appendicitis, cholecystitis, gastroenteritis

Genitourinary: Perirectal abscess

Infection: Sepsis, viral infection

Neuromuscular & skeletal: Osteomyelitis

Respiratory: Pneumonia

<1%, postmarketing, and/or case reports: Anaphylaxis, angina pectoris, angioedema, bacterial infection, bleeding at injection site, bruising at injection site, cellulitis, cerebrovascular accident, dactylitis, diverticulitis, erythrodermic psoriasis, fungal infection, herpes zoster, hypersensitivity reaction, hypertension, induration at injection site, irritation at injection site, itching at injection site, malignant neoplasm, meningitis due to listeria monocytogenes, myocardial infarction, nephrolithiasis, ocular herpes simplex, pain at injection site, pustular psoriasis, reversible posterior leukoencephalopathy syndrome, skin rash, swelling at injection site, urticaria

General Dosage Range

IV: Adults: Induction (single dose): ≤55 kg: 260 mg; >55 kg to 85 kg: 390 mg; >85 kg: 520 mg

SubQ: *Adults:* ≤100 kg: 45 mg at 0- and 4 weeks, and then every 12 weeks; >100 kg: 45 mg or 90 mg at 0- and 4 weeks, and then every 12 weeks or 90 mg every 8 weeks (non-weight based)

Mechanism of Action Ustekinumab is a human monoclonal antibody that binds to and interferes with the proinflammatory cytokines, interleukin (IL)-12 and IL-23. Biological effects of IL-12 and IL-23 include natural killer (NK) cell activation, CD4+ T-cell differentiation and activation. Ustekinumab also interferes with the expression of monocyte chemotactic protein-1 (MCP-1), tumor necrosis factor-alpha (TNF-α), interferon-inducible protein-10 (IP-10), and interleukin-8 (IL-8). Significant clinical improvement in psoriasis and psoriatic arthritis patients is seen in association with reduction of these proinflammatory signalers.

Pharmacodynamics/Kinetics

Half-life Elimination 10 to 126 days; Psoriasis: 14.9 ± 4.6 to 45.6 ± 80.2 days; Crohn disease: ~19 days

Time to Peak Plasma: 45 mg: 13.5 days; 90 mg: 7 days

Pregnancy Risk Factor B

Pregnancy Considerations Adverse events were not observed in animal reproduction studies. There is limited information related to the use of ustekinumab in pregnancy (Andrulonis, 2012). In general, other agents are preferred for the treatment of plaque psoriasis in pregnant women (Hsu, 2012). Patients exposed to ustekinumab during pregnancy are encouraged to enroll in the pregnancy registry by calling 877-311-8972.

Vaccinia Immune Globulin (Intravenous)

(vax IN ee a i MYUN GLOB yoo lin IN tra VEE nus)

Brand Names: US CNJ-016

Pharmacologic Category Blood Product Derivative; Immune Globulin

Use Vaccinia conditions: Treatment and/or modification of the following conditions:

- Aberrant infections induced by vaccinia virus that include its accidental implantation in eyes (except in cases of isolated keratitis), mouth, or other areas where vaccinia infection would constitute a special hazard.
- Eczema vaccinatum
- Progressive vaccinia
- Severe generalized vaccinia
- Vaccinia infections in individuals who have skin conditions such as burns, impetigo, varicella-zoster, or poison ivy; or in individuals who have eczematous skin lesions because of either the activity or extensiveness of such lesions

The Advisory Committee on Immunization Practices (ACIP) recommends the following (CDC 2009; CDC [Rotz 2001]; CDC [Wharton 2003]):

Use is recommended for:

- Inadvertent inoculation (considering severity, toxicity of affected person, and pain)
- Eczema vaccinatum
- Generalized vaccinia (severe form or if underlying illness is present)
- Progressive vaccinia

Use may be considered for:

- Severe ocular complications except isolated keratitis

Use is not recommended for:

- Inadvertent inoculation that is not severe
- Mild or limited generalized vaccinia
- Nonspecific rashes, erythema multiforme, or Stevens-Johnson syndrome
- Postvaccinial encephalitis or encephalomyelitis

Local Anesthetic/Vasoconstrictor Precautions No information available to require special precautions

Effects on Dental Treatment No significant effects or complications reported

Effects on Bleeding No information available to require special precautions

Adverse Reactions Frequency not defined. Actual frequency varies by dose and rate of infusion.

Cardiovascular: Peripheral edema

Central nervous system: Dizziness, fatigue, feeling hot, headache, pain, paresthesia, rigors, sensation of cold

Dermatologic: Diaphoresis, erythema, pallor

Gastrointestinal: Decreased appetite, nausea, vomiting

Local: Injection site reaction

Neuromuscular & skeletal: Back pain, muscle spasm, tremor, weakness

Miscellaneous: Fever

<1%, postmarketing, and/or case reports: Abdominal pain, acute intravascular hemolysis, acute renal failure, altered blood pressure, anaphylaxis, apnea, acute respiratory distress, arthralgia, aseptic meningitis, bronchospasm, bullous rash, chills, circulatory shock, coma, cyanosis, diarrhea, dyspnea, epidermolysis, erythema multiforme, flushing, hemolysis, hepatic insufficiency, hypersensitivity reaction, hypoxemia, hypotension, leukopenia, loss of consciousness, malaise, myalgia, pancytopenia, positive direct Coombs test, proximal tubular nephropathy, pulmonary edema, renal disease (osmotic nephropathy), renal insufficiency, seizure, Stevens-Johnson syndrome, syncope, tachycardia, thrombocytopenia, thromboembolism, transfusion-related acute lung injury (TRALI), urticaria, wheezing

General Dosage Range IV: *Adolescents ≥16 years and Adults:* Initial: 6,000 units/kg; may repeat 6,000 to 9,000 units/kg if needed

Mechanism of Action Antibodies obtained from pooled human plasma of individuals immunized with the smallpox vaccine provide passive immunity

Pharmacodynamics/Kinetics

Half-life Elimination 30 days (range: 13 to 67 days)

Time to Peak Plasma: 1.8 to 2.6 hours

Pregnancy Risk Factor C

Pregnancy Considerations Animal reproduction studies have not been conducted. Immune globulins cross the placenta in increased amounts after 30 weeks gestation. There are no adequate and well-controlled studies in pregnant women. Vaccinia immune globulin is currently not recommended for use in persons with contraindications to smallpox vaccine; inadvertent exposure to smallpox vaccine in high risk populations (eg,pregnant women) should be reported to the CDC so that standardized treatment may be provided.

Prescribing and Access Restrictions Vaccinia immune globulin is not available for general public use. All supplies are currently owned by the federal government for inclusion in the Strategic National Stockpile. The CDC Smallpox Adverse Events Clinical Consultation team will coordinate shipment. The State Health Department should be contacted first concerning severe or unexpected adverse events from smallpox vaccination.

ValACYclovir (val ay SYE kloe veer)

Related Information

Acyclovir (Systemic) *on page 73*
Systemic Viral Diseases *on page 1806*
Viral Infections *on page 1849*

Related Sample Prescriptions

Viral Infections - Sample Prescriptions *on page 40*

Brand Names: US Valtrex

Brand Names: Canada Apo-Valacyclovir; Auro-Valacyclovir; CO Valacyclovir; DOM-Valacyclovir; JAMP-Valacyclovir; Mar-Valacyclovir; Mylan-Valacyclovir; PHL-Valacyclovir; PMS-Valacyclovir; Priva-Valacyclovir; PRO-Valacyclovir; Riva-Valacyclovir; Sandoz-Valacyclovir; Teva-Valacyclovir; Valtrex

Generic Availability (US) Yes

Pharmacologic Category Antiviral Agent; Antiviral Agent, Oral

Dental Use Treatment of herpes labialis (cold sores)

Use Treatment of herpes zoster (shingles) in immunocompetent patients; treatment of first-episode and recurrent genital herpes in immunocompetent patients; suppression of recurrent genital herpes and reduction of transmission of genital herpes in immunocompetent patients; suppression of genital herpes in HIV-infected individuals; treatment of herpes labialis (cold sores); chickenpox in immunocompetent children

Local Anesthetic/Vasoconstrictor Precautions No information available to require special precautions

Effects on Dental Treatment No significant effects or complications reported (see Dental Comment)

Effects on Bleeding Medical consult is suggested.

Adverse Reactions

>10%:

Central nervous system: Headache (13% to 38%)
Gastrointestinal: Nausea (5% to 15%), abdominal pain (1% to 11%)
Hepatic: Increased serum AST (2% to 16%), increased serum ALT (≤14%)
Respiratory: Nasopharyngitis (≤16%)

1% to 10%:

Central nervous system: Fatigue (≤8%), depression (≤7%), dizziness (2% to 4%)
Dermatologic: Skin rash (≤8%)
Endocrine & metabolic: Dehydration (children: 2%)
Gastrointestinal: Vomiting (≤6%), diarrhea (children: 5%; adults: <1%)
Genitourinary: Dysmenorrhea (≤8%)
Hematologic & oncologic: Thrombocytopenia (≤3%), leukopenia (≤1%; mild)
Hepatic: Increased serum alkaline phosphatase (≤4%)
Infection: Herpes simplex infection (children: 2%)
Neuromuscular & skeletal: Arthralgia (≤6%)
Respiratory: Rhinorrhea (children: 2%)
Miscellaneous: Fever (children: 4%)

<1%, postmarketing, and/or case reports: Aggressive behavior, agitation, alopecia, anemia, aplastic anemia, ataxia, brain disease, coma, confusion, delirium, dysarthria, erythema multiforme, facial edema, hallucination (auditory and visual), hemolytic-uremic syndrome, hepatitis, hypersensitivity reaction (acute; includes anaphylaxis, angioedema, dyspnea, pruritus, skin rash, urticaria), hypertension, hypersensitivity angiitis, increased serum creatinine, loss of consciousness, mania, psychosis, renal failure, renal pain, seizure, skin photosensitivity, tachycardia, thrombotic thrombocytopenic purpura, tremor, urinary urgency, visual disturbance

Dental Usual Dosage

Herpes labialis (cold sores): Adolescents and Adults: Oral: 2 g twice daily for 1 day (separate doses by ~12 hours)

Chronic suppression of recurrent herpes labialis (cold sores) (off-label use): Immunocompetent adults: 500 mg once daily (Baker 2003)

Dosing

Adult & Geriatric

Herpes labialis (cold sores): Oral: 2 g every 12 hours for 1 day

Herpes labialis (cold sores) in HIV-infected patients (off-label use): Oral: 1 g twice daily for 5 to 10 days (HHS [OI adult 2016])

Herpes zoster (shingles): Oral:

Immunocompetent patients: 1 g 3 times daily for 7 days

HIV-infected patients, acute localized dermatomal (off-label use): 1 g 3 times daily for 7 to 10 days; consider longer duration if lesions resolve slowly (HHS [OI adult 2016])

Herpes simplex virus (HSV), genital infection: Oral:

Manufacturer's labeling:

Initial episode: Immunocompetent patients: 1 g twice daily for 10 days. **Note:** CDC STD guidelines recommend a treatment duration of 7 to 10 days (CDC [Workowski 2015]).

Recurrent episode: Immunocompetent patients: 500 mg twice daily for 3 days or alternatively (off-label dose), 1,000 mg once daily for 5 days (CDC [Workowski 2015])

Reduction of transmission: 500 mg once daily (source partner)

Suppressive therapy:

Immunocompetent patients: 1 g once daily (500 mg once daily in patients with ≤9 recurrences per year). **Note:** Safety and efficacy have been documented for up to 1 year (CDC [Workowski 2015]).

HIV-infected patients (CD4 ≥100 cells/mm^3): 500 mg twice daily

Alternate dosing: HIV-infected patients:

Initial or recurrent episodes (off-label use): 1 g twice daily for 5 to 10 days (HHS [OI adult 2016])

Chronic suppressive therapy: 500 mg twice daily; continue indefinitely regardless of CD4 count in patients with severe recurrences or in patients who want to minimize frequency of recurrences (HHS [OI adult 2016])

B virus, postexposure prophylaxis (off-label use): Oral: 1 g 3 times daily for 14 days (Tunkel 2008)

CMV reactivation (prevention in allogeneic HSCT recipients) (off-label use): Oral: 2 g 3 to 4 times daily; in combination with screening for CMV reactivation; begin at engraftment and continue to day 100 (Tomblyn 2009)

HSV keratitis (off-label use) (White 2014): Oral

Epithelial keratitis, dendritic: 500 mg twice daily for 7 to 10 days

Epithelial keratitis, geographic: 1 g 3 times daily for 14 to 21 days

Stromal keratitis, without epithelial ulceration: 500 mg once daily; use in combination with therapeutic dose of topical corticosteroid, for the duration of corticosteroid treatment

Stromal keratitis, with epithelial ulceration: 1 g 3 times daily for 7 to 10 days, then reduce to 500 mg once daily; use in combination with therapeutic dose of topical corticosteroid, for the duration of corticosteroid treatment

Endothelial keratitis: 500 mg twice daily for 7 to 10 days, then reduce to 500 mg once daily; use in combination with therapeutic dose of topical corticosteroid, for the duration of corticosteroid treatment.

HSV reactivation (prevention in seropositive HSCT recipients) (off-label use) (Tomblyn 2009): Oral:

Early reactivation: 500 mg once daily **or** 500 mg twice daily in highly immune-suppressed patients (eg, T cell depletion, anti-T cell antibodies, high-dose steroids). Initiate at the beginning of conditioning therapy and continue until engraftment or until mucositis resolves

Late reactivation: 500 mg twice daily

Varicella (chickenpox) in HIV-infected patients (off-label use): 1 g 3 times daily for 5 to 7 days in uncomplicated cases (HHS [OI adult 2016])

Varicella zoster virus (VZV) acute retinal necrosis (ARN) in HIV-infected patients (off-label use): Oral: 1 g 3 times daily for 6 weeks following initial treatment with acyclovir IV and intravitreal ganciclovir (HHS [OI adult 2016])

VZV, postexposure prophylaxis (HSCT recipients) (off-label use): Oral: 1 g 3 times daily; initiate within 96 hours (preferably, 48 hours) of exposure and continue until 22 days after exposure (Tomblyn 2009)

VZV reactivation (prevention in HSCT recipients) (off-label use): Oral: 500 mg twice daily for 1 year after HSCT (Tomblyn 2009)

Pediatric

Herpes labialis (cold sores): Children ≥12 years and Adolescents: Oral: Refer to adult dosing.

Herpes labialis (cold sores) in HIV-infected patients (off-label use): Adolescents: Oral: Refer to adult dosing.

Herpes simplex virus, genital infection in HIV-infected patients: Adolescents (off-label population): Oral:

Initial or recurrent episodes (off-label use): 1 g twice daily for 5 to 14 days (HHS [OI adult 2015])

Chronic suppressive therapy (off-label dose): 500 mg twice daily; continue indefinitely regardless of CD4 count in patients with severe recurrences or in patients who want to minimize frequency of recurrences (HHS [OI adult 2015])

Herpes zoster (shingles) in HIV-infected patients (off-label use): Adolescents: Oral: Refer to adult dosing.

Varicella (chickenpox):

Immunocompetent patients: Children ≥2 years and Adolescents: Oral: 20 mg/kg/dose 3 times daily for 5 days (maximum: 1 g 3 times daily)

HIV-infected patients (off-label use): Adolescents: Oral: Refer to adult dosing.

Renal Impairment

Herpes zoster: Adults:

CrCl 30 to 49 mL/minute: 1 g every 12 hours
CrCl 10 to 29 mL/minute: 1 g every 24 hours
CrCl <10 mL/minute: 500 mg every 24 hours

Genital herpes: Adults:

US labeling:

Initial episode:

CrCl 10 to 29 mL/minute: 1 g every 24 hours
CrCl <10 mL/minute: 500 mg every 24 hours

Recurrent episode: CrCl <29 mL/minute: 500 mg every 24 hours

Suppressive therapy: CrCl <29 mL/minute:

For usual dose of 1 g every 24 hours or 500 mg every 12 hours, decrease dose to 500 mg every 24 hours

For usual dose of 500 mg every 24 hours, decrease dose to 500 mg every 48 hours

Canadian labeling:

Initial episode:

CrCl 10 to 29 mL/minute: 1 g every 24 hours
CrCl <10 mL/minute: 500 mg every 24 hours

Recurrent episode:

CrCl 10 to 29 mL/minute: 500 mg every 24 hours
CrCl <10 mL/minute: 500 mg every 24 hours

Suppressive therapy:

CrCl 10 to 29 mL/minute:

Immunocompetent or HIV-infected patients: 500 mg every 24 hours

Immunocompetent patients with ≤9 recurrences/year: 500 mg every 48 hours

CrCl <10 mL/minute:

Immunocompetent or HIV-infected patients: 500 mg every 24 hours

Immunocompetent patients with ≤9 recurrences/year: 500 mg every 48 hours

Herpes labialis (cold sores): Adolescents and Adults *(US labeling)* or Adults *(Canadian labeling)*:

CrCl 30 to 49 mL/minute: 1 g every 12 hours for 2 doses

CrCl 10 to 29 mL/minute: 500 mg every 12 hours for 2 doses

CrCl <10 mL/minute: 500 mg as a single dose

Hemodialysis: Dialyzable (~33% removed during 4-hour session); administer dose postdialysis

Chronic ambulatory peritoneal dialysis/continuous arteriovenous hemofiltration dialysis: Pharmacokinetic parameters are similar to those in patients with ESRD; supplemental dose not needed following dialysis

Hepatic Impairment No dosage adjustment necessary.

Mechanism of Action Valacyclovir is rapidly and nearly completely converted to acyclovir by intestinal and hepatic metabolism. Acyclovir is converted to acyclovir monophosphate by virus-specific thymidine kinase then further converted to acyclovir triphosphate by other cellular enzymes. Acyclovir triphosphate inhibits DNA synthesis and viral replication by competing with deoxyguanosine triphosphate for viral DNA polymerase and being incorporated into viral DNA.

Contraindications Hypersensitivity to valacyclovir, acyclovir, or any component of the formulation

Warnings/Precautions Thrombotic thrombocytopenic purpura/hemolytic uremic syndrome has occurred in immunocompromised patients (at doses of 8 g/day). Safety and efficacy have not been established for treatment/suppression of recurrent genital herpes or disseminated herpes in patients with profound immunosuppression (eg, advanced HIV with CD4 <100 cells/mm^3). CNS adverse effects (including agitation, hallucinations, confusion, delirium, seizures, and encephalopathy) have been reported. Use caution in patients with renal impairment, the elderly, and/or those receiving nephrotoxic agents. Acute renal failure has been observed in patients with renal dysfunction; dose adjustment may be required. Precipitation in renal tubules may occur leading to urinary precipitation; adequately hydrate patient. For cold sores, treatment should begin at with earliest symptom (tingling, itching, burning). For genital herpes, treatment should begin as soon as possible after the first signs and symptoms (within 72 hours of onset of first diagnosis or within 24 hours of onset of recurrent episodes). For herpes zoster, treatment should begin within 72 hours of onset of rash. For chickenpox, treatment should begin with earliest sign or symptom. Use with caution in the elderly; CNS effects have been reported.

Drug Interactions

Metabolism/Transport Effects **Inhibits** CYP1A2 (weak)

Avoid Concomitant Use

Avoid concomitant use of ValACYclovir with any of the following: Foscarnet; Varicella Virus Vaccine; Zoster Vaccine

Increased Effect/Toxicity

ValACYclovir may increase the levels/effects of: CloZAPine; Mycophenolate; Tenofovir Products; TiZANidine; Zidovudine

The levels/effects of ValACYclovir may be increased by: Foscarnet; Mycophenolate; Tenofovir Products

Decreased Effect

ValACYclovir may decrease the levels/effects of: Talimogene Laherparepvec; Varicella Virus Vaccine; Zoster Vaccine

Pharmacodynamics/Kinetics

Half-life Elimination Normal renal function: Children: 1.3 to 2.5 hours, slower clearance with increased age; Adults: 2.5 to 3.3 hours (acyclovir), ~30 minutes (valacyclovir); End-stage renal disease: 14 to 20 hours (acyclovir); During hemodialysis: 4 hours

Time to Peak Children: 1.4 to 2.6 hours; Adults: 1.5 hours

Pregnancy Risk Factor B

Pregnancy Considerations Adverse events were not observed in animal reproduction studies. Valacyclovir is metabolized to acyclovir. In a pharmacokinetic study, maternal acyclovir serum concentrations were higher in pregnant women receiving valacyclovir than those given acyclovir for the suppression of recurrent herpes simplex virus (HSV) infection late in pregnancy. Amniotic fluid concentrations were also higher; however, there was no evidence that fetal exposure differed between the groups (Kimberlin 1998). Data from an acyclovir pregnancy registry has shown no increased rate of birth defects than that of the general population; however, the registry is small and the manufacturer notes that use during pregnancy is only warranted if the potential benefit to the mother justifies the risk of the fetus. Because more data is available for acyclovir, that agent is preferred for the treatment of genital herpes in pregnant women (CDC [Workowski 2015]); however, valacyclovir may be considered for use due to its simplified dosing schedule (HHS [OI adult 2015]). Pregnant women who have a history of genital herpes recurrence, suppressive therapy is recommended starting at 36-weeks gestation (HHS [OI adult 2016]).

Breastfeeding Considerations Valacyclovir is rapidly metabolized to acyclovir. Following administration of valacyclovir, acyclovir is present in breast milk; unchanged valacyclovir has not been detected in breast milk.

Following administration of valacyclovir, the relative infant dose (RID) of acyclovir is 5.1% when calculated using the highest average breast milk concentration located and compared to an infant therapeutic dose of intravenous acyclovir of 30 mg/kg/day. In general, breastfeeding is considered acceptable when the RID is <10%; when an RID is >25% breastfeeding should generally be avoided (Anderson 2016; Ito 2000). Using the highest average milk concentration (10.15 mcg/mL), the estimated daily infant acyclovir dose via breast milk is 1.52 mg/kg/day. This milk concentration was obtained following maternal administration of valacyclovir 500 mg twice daily (Drake 2012).

Peak acyclovir milk concentrations occurred 4 hours (range: 2 to 4 hours) following maternal administration of a single oral dose of valacyclovir 500 mg; the half-life of acyclovir in breast milk was ~2 hours (range: 1.3 to 12.2 hours) (Sheffield 2002). Acyclovir was able to be detected in the urine of breastfeeding infants following 5 days of treatment with valacyclovir 500 mg twice daily (Sheffield 2002).

The manufacturer recommends that caution be used if administered to a breastfeeding woman. Other sources note that women with HSV infection taking valacyclovir may breastfeed as long as there are not lesions on the breast, body lesions are covered, and strict hand hygiene is practiced (ACOG 2007; Jaiyeoba 2012).

Dosage Forms

Tablet, Oral:

Valtrex: 500 mg, 1 g

Generic: 500 mg, 1 g

Dental Comment Although some conflicting data, dental treatment may be a risk factor for asymptomatic viral shedding of herpes simplex virus type-1 (HSV-1) into human saliva in patients with previous exposure to the virus (Hyland 2007).

It is recommended to reappoint the patient if an active lesion is present. If the lesion is already "crusted" over, treatment will not induce spread of the virus but treatment is aimed at patient comfort during the procedure relating to the wound healing on their lip.

ValGANciclovir (val gan SYE kloh veer)

Related Information

Ganciclovir (Systemic) *on page 785*

Brand Names: US Valcyte

Brand Names: Canada Apo-Valganciclovir; Valcyte

Pharmacologic Category Antiviral Agent

Use

Cytomegalovirus, prophylaxis (solid organ transplant recipients):

Prevention of cytomegalovirus (CMV) in high-risk adult patients (donor CMV seropositive/recipient CMV seronegative) undergoing kidney, heart, or kidney/pancreas transplantation

Prevention of CMV in high risk pediatric patients undergoing kidney transplant (age 4 months to 16 years) or heart transplant (age 1 month to 16 years)

CMV retinitis, treatment (AIDS-related): Treatment of cytomegalovirus (CMV) retinitis in patients with acquired immunodeficiency syndrome (AIDS)

Local Anesthetic/Vasoconstrictor Precautions No information available to require special precautions

Effects on Dental Treatment No significant effects or complications reported

Effects on Bleeding Medical consult is suggested.

Adverse Reactions

>10%:

Cardiovascular: Hypertension (12% to 18%)

Central nervous system: Headache (6% to 22%), insomnia (6% to 20%)

Gastrointestinal: Diarrhea (16% to 41%), nausea (8% to 30%), vomiting (3% to 21%), abdominal pain (15%)

Hematologic: Anemia (≤31%), thrombocytopenia (≤22%), neutropenia (3% to 19%)

Immunologic: Graft rejection (24%)

Neuromuscular & skeletal: Tremor (12% to 28%)

Ophthalmic: Retinal detachment (15%)

Renal: Increased serum creatinine (S_{cr} >1.5 to 2.5 mg/dL: 12% to 50%; S_{cr} >2.5: 3% to 17%)

Miscellaneous: Fever (9% to 31%)

1% to 10%:

Cardiovascular: Edema (<5%), hypotension (<5%), peripheral edema (<5%)

Central nervous system: Peripheral neuropathy (9%), paresthesia (≤8%), agitation (<5%), confusion (<5%), depression (<5%), dizziness (<5%), fatigue (<5%), hallucination (<5%), pain (<5%), psychosis (<5%), seizure (<5%)

Dermatologic: Acne vulgaris (<5%), dermatitis (<5%), increased wound secretion (<5%), pruritus (<5%)

Endocrine & metabolic: Dehydration (<5%), hyperglycemia (<5%), hyperkalemia (<5%), hypocalcemia (<5%), hypokalemia (<5%), hypomagnesemia (<5%), hypophosphatemia (<5%)

Gastrointestinal: Abdominal distention (<5%), constipation (<5%), decreased appetite (<5%), dyspepsia (<5%)

Genitourinary: Dysuria (<5%), urinary tract infection (<5%)

Hematologic: Aplastic anemia (<5%), bone marrow depression (<5%), pancytopenia (<5%)

Hepatic: Ascites (<5%), hepatic insufficiency (<5%)

Hypersensitivity: Hypersensitivity reaction (<5%)

Immunologic: Organ transplant rejection (6% to 9%)

Infection: Localized infection (<5%), sepsis (<5%), wound infection (<5%)

Local: Catheter infection (3%)

Neuromuscular & skeletal: Arthralgia (<5%), back pain (<5%), limb pain (<5%), muscle cramps (<5%), weakness (<5%)

Renal: Decreased creatinine clearance (<5%), renal impairment (<5%)

Respiratory: Cough (<5%), dyspnea (<5%), nasopharyngitis (<5%), pharyngitis (<5%), pleural effusion (<5%), rhinorrhea (<5%), upper respiratory tract infection (<5%)

Miscellaneous: Postoperative complication (<5%), postoperative pain (<5%), wound dehiscence (<5%)

Postmarketing and/or case reports: Acute renal failure, anaphylaxis, bone marrow aplasia, reduced fertility (males)

General Dosage Range Dosage adjustment recommended in adult patients with renal impairment

Oral:

Infants, Children, and Adolescents 1 month to 16 years: Dose (mg) = 7 x body surface area x creatinine clearance once daily (maximum dose: 900 mg daily)

Adolescents >16 years and Adults: 900 mg once or twice daily

Mechanism of Action Valganciclovir is rapidly converted to ganciclovir in the body. The bioavailability of ganciclovir from valganciclovir is increased 10-fold compared to oral ganciclovir. A dose of 900 mg achieved systemic exposure of ganciclovir comparable to that achieved with the recommended doses of intravenous ganciclovir of 5 mg/kg. Ganciclovir is phosphorylated to a substrate which competitively inhibits the binding of deoxyguanosine triphosphate to DNA polymerase resulting in inhibition of viral DNA synthesis.

Pharmacodynamics/Kinetics

Half-life Elimination

Pediatric patients (heart, kidney, or liver transplant):

Mean range:

4 months to 2 years: 2.8 to 4.5 hours

2 to 12 years: 2.8 to 3.8 hours

12 to 16 years: 4.9 to 6 hours

Adults:

Ganciclovir: 4.08 hours, prolonged with renal impairment; Severe renal impairment: Up to 68 hours

Heart, kidney, kidney-pancreas, or liver transplant patients: Mean range: 6.18 to 6.77 hours

Time to Peak Ganciclovir: 1-3 hours

Pregnancy Considerations [U.S. Boxed Warning]: May cause temporary or permanent inhibition of spermatogenesis; has the potential to cause birth defects in humans. Valganciclovir is converted to ganciclovir and shares its reproductive toxicity. Ganciclovir crosses the placenta. Based on animal data, temporary or permanent impairment of fertility may occur in males and females. Ganciclovir is also teratogenic in animals. The manufacturer recommends females of reproductive potential undergo pregnancy testing prior to therapy. Females should use effective contraception during treatment and for 30 days after; males should use barrier contraception during treatment and for 90 days after.

Adverse events following congenital CMV infection may also occur. Hearing loss, mental retardation, microcephaly, seizures, and other medical problems have been observed. The indications for treating CMV retinitis during pregnancy are the same as in non-pregnant HIV infected woman; however systemic therapy should be avoided during the first trimester when possible. Use of valganciclovir is recommended to treat maternal infection, but not recommended for the treatment of asymptomatic maternal disease for the sole purpose of preventing infant infection. Monitoring of the fetus is recommended. Current recommendations for use of valganciclovir in HIV infected pregnant women are based on data from ganciclovir use in pregnant women following organ transplant or use late in pregnancy in non-HIV infected women [DHHS Adult OI, 2014].

Valproic Acid and Derivatives

(val PROE ik AS id & dah RIV ah tives)

Brand Names: US Depacon; Depakene; Depakote; Depakote ER; Depakote Sprinkles; Stavzor [DSC]

Brand Names: Canada Apo-Divalproex; Apo-Valproic; Depakene; Dom-Divalproex; Dom-Valproic Acid; Dom-Valproic Acid E.C.; Epival; Mylan-Divalproex; Mylan-Valproic; Novo-Valproic; PHL-Valproic Acid; PHL-Valproic Acid E.C.; PMS-Divalproex; PMS-Valproic Acid; PMS-Valproic Acid E.C.; ratio-Valproic; Sandoz-Valproic; Teva Divalproex

Pharmacologic Category Anticonvulsant, Miscellaneous; Antimanic Agent; Histone Deacetylase Inhibitor

Use

Oral, IV: Monotherapy and adjunctive therapy in the treatment of patients with complex partial seizures; monotherapy and adjunctive therapy of simple and complex absence seizures; adjunctive therapy in patients with multiple seizure types that include absence seizures

Additional indications: Depakote, Depakote ER, Stavzor, Epival [Canadian product]: Mania associated with bipolar disorder; migraine prophylaxis

Limitation of use: Do not administer to a woman of childbearing potential unless essential for the management of her condition.

Local Anesthetic/Vasoconstrictor Precautions No information available to require special precautions

Effects on Dental Treatment Key adverse event(s) related to dental treatment: Periodontal abscess and taste perversion.

Effects on Bleeding Has been associated with dose-related thrombocytopenia. Normal coagulation may generally be expected unless thrombocytopenia is present and severe.

Adverse Reactions As reported with oral administration, unless otherwise noted.

>10%:

Central nervous system: Headache (oral: 31%; intravenous: 3% to 4%), drowsiness (oral: 7% to 30%; intravenous: 2% to 11%), dizziness (oral: 12% to 25%; intravenous: 5% to 7%), insomnia (>1% to 15%), pain (oral: 11%; intravenous: 1%), nervousness (oral: 7% to 11%; intravenous: <1%)

Dermatologic: Alopecia (>1% to 24%)

Gastrointestinal: Nausea (oral: 15% to 48%; intravenous: 3% to 6%), vomiting (oral: 7% to 27%; intravenous: 1%), abdominal pain (oral: 7% to 23%; intravenous: 1%), diarrhea (oral: 7% to 23%; intravenous: <1%), dyspepsia (7% to 23%), anorexia (>1% to 12%)

Hematologic & oncologic: Thrombocytopenia (1% to 27%; dose related)

Infection: Infection (≤20%)

Neuromuscular & skeletal: Tremor (≤57%), weakness (6% to 27%; intravenous: 7%)

Ophthalmic: Diplopia (>1% to 16%), visual disturbance (amblyopia, blurred vision ≤1% to 12%)

Respiratory: Flu-like symptoms (>1% to 12%)

Miscellaneous: Accidental injury (>1% to 11%)

1% to 10%:

Cardiovascular: Peripheral edema (>1% to 8%), edema (>1% to 5%), facial edema (>1% to 5%), hypertension (>1% to 5%), hypotension (1% to 5%), orthostatic hypotension (1% to 5%), palpitations (>1% to 5%), vasodilatation (oral: >1% to 5%; intravenous: <1%), tachycardia (>1% to <5%), chest pain (2%)

Central nervous system: Ataxia (>1% to 8%), amnesia (>1% to 7%), paresthesia (≤7%), abnormality in thinking (>1% to 6%), emotional lability (>1% to 6%), abnormal dreams (>1% to 5%), abnormal gait (>1% to 5%), confusion (>1% to 5%), depression (>1% to 5%), hallucination (>1% to 5%), hypertonia (>1% to 5%), speech disturbance (>1% to 5%), tardive dyskinesia (>1% to 5%), agitation (1% to 5%), catatonia (1% to 5%), chills (1% to 5%), hyper-reflexia (1% to 5%), vertigo (1% to 5%), anxiety (>1% to <5%), malaise (>1% to <5%), myasthenia (>1% to <5%), personality disorder (>1% to <5%), twitching (>1% to <5%), sleep disorder (>1%)

Dermatologic: Skin rash (>1% to 6%), maculopapular rash (>1% to 5%), pruritus (>1% to 5%), xeroderma (>1% to 5%), diaphoresis (oral: >1%; intravenous: <1%), erythema nodosum (>1%), vesiculobullous dermatitis (>1%), furunculosis (1% to 5%), seborrhea (1% to 5%)

Endocrine & metabolic: Weight gain (>1% to 9%), weight loss (6%), amenorrhea (>1% to <5%), menstrual disease (>1%)

Gastrointestinal: Increased appetite (>1% to 6%), constipation (>1% to 5%), flatulence (>1% to 5%), periodontal abscess (>1% to 5%), fecal incontinence (1% to 5%), gastroenteritis (1% to 5%), glossitis (1% to 5%), stomatitis (1% to 5%), xerostomia (1% to 5%), eructation (>1% to <5%), hematemesis (>1% to <5%), pancreatitis (>1% to <5%), dysgeusia (2%), dysphagia (>1%), gingival hemorrhage (>1%), hiccups (>1%), oral mucosa ulcer (>1%)

Genitourinary: Cystitis (>1% to 5%), dysmenorrhea (>1% to 5%), dysuria (>1% to 5%), urinary incontinence (>1% to 5%), vaginal hemorrhage (>1% to 5%), urinary frequency (>1% to <5%), vaginitis (>1% to <5%)

Hematologic & oncologic: Ecchymoses (>1% to 5%), petechia (>1% to <5%), hypoproteinemia (>1%), prolonged bleeding time (>1%)

Hepatic: Increased serum ALT (>1% to <5%), increased serum AST (>1% to <5%)

Infection: Viral infection (>1% to 5%), fungal infection (>1%)

Local: Pain at injection site (intravenous: 3%), injection site reaction (intravenous: 2%)

Neuromuscular & skeletal: Back pain (>1% to 8%), arthralgia (>1% to 5%), discoid lupus erythematosus (>1% to 5%), leg cramps (>1% to 5%), hypokinesia (1% to 5%), neck pain (1% to 5%), neck stiffness (1% to 5%), osteoarthritis (1% to 5%), dysarthria (>1% to <5%), myalgia (>1% to <5%)

Ophthalmic: Nystagmus (1% to 8%), conjunctivitis (1% to 5%), dry eye syndrome (1% to 5%), eye pain (1% to 5%), photophobia (>1%)

Otic: Tinnitus (1% to 7%), deafness (>1% to 5%), otitis media (>1% to <5%)

Respiratory: Pharyngitis (oral: 2% to 8%; intravenous: <1%), bronchitis (5%), rhinitis (>1% to 5%), dyspnea (1% to 5%), cough (>1% to <5%), epistaxis (>1% to <5%), pneumonia (>1% to <5%), sinusitis (>1% to <5%)

Miscellaneous: Fever (>1% to 6%)

<1%, postmarketing, and/or case reports: Abnormal behavior, abnormalities in sperm motility, abnormal thyroid function tests, acute porphyria, aggressive behavior, agranulocytosis, anaphylaxis, anemia, aplastic anemia, azoospermia, bone fracture, bone marrow depression, bradycardia, brain disease (rare), breast hypertrophy, cerebral atrophy (reversible or irreversible), change in prothrombin time, changes of hair (color, texture), coma (rare), decreased bone mineral density, decreased plasma carnitine concentrations, decreased platelet aggregation, decreased spermatozoa motility, dementia, developmental delay, disturbance in attention, DRESS syndrome, eosinophilia, erythema multiforme, euphoria, Fanconi-like syndrome (rare, in children), galactorrhea, hemorrhage, hepatic failure, hepatotoxicity, hirsutism, hostility, hyperactivity, hyperammonemia, hyperammonemic encephalopathy (in patients with UCD), hyperandrogenism, hyperglycinemia, hypersensitivity angiitis, hypersensitivity reaction, hypoesthesia, hypofibrinogenemia, hyponatremia, hypothermia, increased testosterone level, injection site inflammation, leukopenia, lymphocytosis, macrocytosis, male infertility, myelodysplasia, nail bed changes, nail disease, oligospermia, ostealgia, osteopenia, osteoporosis, pancytopenia, parotid gland enlargement, polycystic ovary syndrome (rare), psychomotor disturbance, psychosis, severe hypersensitivity (with multiorgan dysfunction), SIADH, skin photosensitivity, sleep disorder, spermatozoa disorder (abnormal morphology), Stevens-Johnson syndrome, suicidal ideation, suicidal tendencies, toxic epidermal necrolysis (rare), urinary incontinence, urinary tract infection

General Dosage Range

IV:

Children: Initial: 15 mg/kg/day; Maximum: 60 mg/kg/day

Children ≥10 years and Adults: Initial: 10 to 15 mg/kg/day; Maximum: 60 mg/kg/day

Oral:

Children: Initial: 15 mg/kg/day; Maximum: 60 mg/kg/day; **Note:** Depakote ER is not recommended for use in children <10 years of age.

Children ≥10 years and Adults: Seizures: Initial: 10 to 15 mg/kg/day; Maximum: 60 mg/kg/day

Children ≥12 years and Adults: Migraine prophylaxis: (Stavzor) 250 mg twice daily; Maintenance: Up to 1,000 mg daily

Adults: Migraine prophylaxis (Depakote tablets): 250 mg twice daily, up to 1,000 mg daily

Adults: Migraine prophylaxis (Depakote ER): 500 to 1,000 mg once daily

Adults: Mania: Depakote tablet, Stavzor: Initial: 750 mg/day in divided doses (maximum recommended dose: 60 mg/kg/day); Depakote ER: Initial: 25 mg/kg/day given once daily (maximum recommended dose: 60 mg/kg/day)

Mechanism of Action Causes increased availability of gamma-aminobutyric acid (GABA), an inhibitory neurotransmitter, to brain neurons or may enhance the action of GABA or mimic its action at postsynaptic receptor sites. Divalproex sodium is a compound of sodium valproate and valproic acid; divalproex dissociates to valproate in the GI tract.

Pharmacodynamics/Kinetics

Half-life Elimination Increased in neonates, elderly, and patients with liver impairment

Newborns (exposed to VPA in utero): 30 to 60 hours

Neonates first week of life: 40 to 45 hours

Neonates <10 days: 10 to 67 hours

Infants and Children >2 months: 7 to 13 hours

Children and Adolescents 2 to 14 years: 9 hours (range: 3.5 to 20 hours) (Cloyd 1993)

Adults: 9 to 16 hours

Time to Peak

Oral: Depakote tablet and sprinkle capsules: ~4 hours; Depakote ER: 4 to 17 hours; Stavzor: 2 hours; Epival [Canadian product]: 4 hours

Rectal (off-label route): 1 to 3 hours (Graves 1987)

Pregnancy Risk Factor X (migraine prophylaxis)/D (all other indications)

Pregnancy Considerations Adverse events have been observed in animal reproduction studies and in human pregnancies. **[US Boxed Warning]: May cause major congenital malformations, such as neural tube defects (eg, spina bifida) and decreased IQ scores following in utero exposure. Use is contraindicated in pregnant women for the prevention of migraine. Use is not recommended in women of childbearing potential for any other condition unless valproate is essential to manage her condition and alternative therapies are not appropriate. Effective contraception should be used during therapy.**

Valproic acid crosses the placenta (Harden 2009b). Neural tube defects, craniofacial defects, cardiovascular malformations, hypospadias, and limb malformations have been reported. Information from the North American Antiepileptic Drug Pregnancy Registry notes the rate of major malformations to be 9% to 11% following an average exposure to valproate monotherapy 1,000 mg/day; this is an increase in congenital malformations when compared with monotherapy with other antiepileptic drugs (AED). Based on data from the CDC National Birth Defects Prevention Network, the risk of spinal bifida is approximately 1% to 2% following valproate exposure (general population risk estimated to be 0.06% to 0.07%).

Nonteratogenic adverse effects have also been reported. Decreased IQ scores have been noted in children exposed to valproate in utero when compared to children exposed to other antiepileptic medications or no antiepileptic medications; the risk of autism spectrum disorders may also be increased. Fatal hepatic failure and hypoglycemia in infants have been noted in case reports following in utero exposure to valproic acid.

Clotting factor abnormalities (hypofibrinogenemia, thrombocytopenia, or decrease in other coagulation factors) may develop in the mother following valproate use during pregnancy; close monitoring of coagulation factors is recommended.

Current guidelines recommend complete avoidance of valproic acid and derivatives for the treatment of epilepsy in pregnant women whenever possible (Harden

2009a), especially when used for conditions not associated with permanent injury or risk of death. Effective contraception should be used during treatment. When pregnancy is being planned, consider tapering off of therapy prior to conception if appropriate; abrupt discontinuation of therapy may cause status epilepticus and lead to maternal and fetal hypoxia. Folic acid decreases the risk of neural tube defects in the general population; supplementation with folic acid should be used prior to conception and during pregnancy in all women, including those taking valproate.

A pregnancy registry is available for women who have been exposed to valproic acid. Patients may enroll themselves in the North American Antiepileptic Drug (NAAED) Pregnancy Registry by calling (888) 233-2334. Additional information is available at www.aedpregnancyregistry.org.

Product Availability Stavzor has been discontinued in the US for more than 1 year.

Valrubicin (val ROO bi sin)

Brand Names: US Valstar

Brand Names: Canada Valtaxin

Pharmacologic Category Antineoplastic Agent, Anthracycline; Antineoplastic Agent, Topoisomerase II Inhibitor

Use Bladder cancer: Intravesical treatment of BCG-refractory bladder carcinoma in situ of the urinary bladder when cystectomy would be associated with unacceptable morbidity or mortality.

Local Anesthetic/Vasoconstrictor Precautions No information available to require special precautions

Effects on Dental Treatment No significant effects or complications reported

Effects on Bleeding This chemotherapy is administered locally and hematologic toxicity is not experienced.

Adverse Reactions In general, local adverse reactions occur during or shortly after instillation and resolve within 1 to 7 days.

>10%: Genitourinary: Irritable bladder (88%), urinary frequency (61%), urinary urgency (57%), dysuria (56%), bladder spasm (31%), hematuria (29%; microscopic: 3%; gross hematuria: 1%), bladder pain (28%), urinary incontinence (22%), cystitis (15%), urinary tract infection (15%), red urine discoloration

1% to 10%:

Cardiovascular: Chest pain (3%), vasodilatation (2%), peripheral edema (1%)

Central nervous system: Localized burning (5%), headache (4%), malaise (4%), dizziness (3%)

Dermatologic: Skin rash (3%)

Endocrine & metabolic: Hyperglycemia (1%)

Gastrointestinal: Abdominal pain (5%), nausea (5%), diarrhea (3%), vomiting (2%), flatulence (1%)

Genitourinary: Nocturia (7%), urinary retention (4%), urethral pain (3%), pelvic pain (1%)

Hematologic & oncologic: Anemia (2%)

Neuromuscular & skeletal: Weakness (4%), back pain (3%), myalgia (1%)

Respiratory: Pneumonia (1%)

Miscellaneous: Fever (2%)

<1%, postmarketing, and/or case reports: Ageusia, increased nonprotein nitrogen, pruritus, reduced urine flow, skin irritation (local), tenesmus, urethritis

General Dosage Range Dosage adjustment recommended in patients who develop toxicities

Intravesical: *Adults:* 800 mg once weekly for 6 weeks

Mechanism of Action Blocks function of DNA topoisomerase II; inhibits DNA synthesis, causes extensive chromosomal damage, and arrests cell development (G_2 phase); unlike other anthracyclines, does not appear to intercalate DNA; readily penetrates cells.

Pregnancy Risk Factor C

Pregnancy Considerations Adverse effects were observed in animal reproduction studies. Systemic exposure (eg, with bladder perforation) during human pregnancy may result in fetal harm. Women of childbearing potential should avoid becoming pregnant during treatment. All patients of reproductive age should use an effective method of contraception during the treatment period.

Valsartan (val SAR tan)

Related Information

Cardiovascular Diseases *on page 1752*

Brand Names: US Diovan

Brand Names: Canada ACT Valsartan; Apo-Valsartan; Auro-Valsartan; Ava-Valsartan; Diovan; Mylan-Valsartan; PMS-Valsartan; Ran-Valsartan; Sandoz-Valsartan; Teva-Valsartan

Pharmacologic Category Angiotensin II Receptor Blocker; Antihypertensive

Use

Heart failure: Treatment of heart failure (NYHA Class II to IV).

Hypertension: Management of hypertension (monotherapy or in combination with other antihypertensives).

Left ventricular dysfunction or failure after MI: Reduction of cardiovascular mortality in patients with left ventricular dysfunction or failure postmyocardial infarction.

Guideline recommendations:

Hypertension: The 2014 guideline for the management of high blood pressure in adults (Eighth Joint National Committee [JNC 8; James 2013]) recommends initiation of pharmacologic treatment to lower blood pressure for the following patients:

- Patients ≥60 years of age with systolic blood pressure (SBP) ≥150 mm Hg or diastolic blood pressure (DBP) ≥90 mm Hg. Goal of therapy is SBP <150 mm Hg and DBP <90 mm Hg.
- Patients <60 years of age with SBP ≥140 mm Hg or DBP ≥90 mm Hg. Goal of therapy is SBP <140 mm Hg and DBP <90 mm Hg.
- Patients ≥18 years of age with diabetes and SBP ≥140 mm Hg or DBP ≥90 mm Hg. Goal of therapy is SBP <140 mm Hg and DBP <90 mm Hg.
- Patients ≥18 years of age with chronic kidney disease (CKD) and SBP ≥140 mm Hg or DBP ≥90 mm Hg. Goal of therapy is SBP <140 mm Hg and DBP <90 mm Hg.

Chronic kidney disease (CKD) and hypertension: Regardless of race or diabetes status, the use of an ACE inhibitor (ACEI) or angiotensin receptor blocker (ARB) as initial therapy is recommended to improve kidney outcomes. In the general nonblack population (without CKD), including those with diabetes, initial antihypertensive treatment should consist of a thiazide-type diuretic, calcium channel blocker, ACEI, or ARB. In the general black population (without CKD), including those with diabetes, initial antihypertensive treatment should consist of a thiazide-type diuretic or a calcium channel blocker instead of an ACEI or ARB.

Coronary artery disease and hypertension: The American Heart Association, American College of Cardiology and American Society of Hypertension (AHA/ACC/ASH) 2015 scientific statement for the treatment of hypertension in patients with coronary artery disease (CAD) recommends the use of an ARB (or ACE inhibitor) as part of a regimen in patients with hypertension and chronic stable angina if there is prior MI, LV systolic dysfunction, diabetes mellitus, or CKD. A BP target of <140/90 mm Hg is reasonable for the secondary prevention of cardiovascular events. A lower target BP (<130/80 mm Hg) may be appropriate in some individuals with CAD, previous MI, stroke or transient ischemic attack, or CAD risk equivalents (AHA/ACC/ASH [Rosendorff 2015]).

Heart failure: The ACCF/AHA 2013 heart failure guidelines recommend the use of ARBs (ie, candesartan, losartan, and valsartan) in patients with HF with reduced ejection fraction who cannot tolerate ACE inhibitors (due to cough) to reduce morbidity and mortality. They also suggest that ARBs are reasonable first-line alternatives to ACE inhibitors in patients already maintained on an ARB for other indications (ACCF/AHA [Yancy 2013]).

Local Anesthetic/Vasoconstrictor Precautions No information available to require special precautions

Effects on Dental Treatment Key adverse event(s) related to dental treatment: Patients may experience orthostatic hypotension as they stand up after treatment; especially if lying in dental chair for extended periods of time. Use caution with sudden changes in position during and after dental treatment.

Effects on Bleeding No information available to require special precautions

Adverse Reactions

>10%:

Central nervous system: Dizziness (heart failure trials 17%)

Renal: Increased blood urea nitrogen (>50% increase; heart failure trials 17%)

1% to 10%:

Cardiovascular: Hypotension (heart failure trials 7%; MI trial 1%), orthostatic hypotension (heart failure trials 2%), syncope (up to >1%)

Central nervous system: Dizziness (hypertension trial 2% to 8%), fatigue (heart failure trials 3%; hypertension trial 2%), orthostatic dizziness (heart failure trials 2%), headache (heart failure trials >1%), vertigo (up to >1%)

Endocrine & metabolic: Increased serum potassium (>20% increase; 4% to 10%), hyperkalemia (heart failure trials 2%)

Gastrointestinal: Diarrhea (heart failure trials 5%), abdominal pain (2%), nausea (heart failure trials >1%), upper abdominal pain (heart failure trials >1%)

Hematologic & oncologic: Neutropenia (2%)

Infection: Viral infection (3%)

Neuromuscular & skeletal: Arthralgia (heart failure trials 3%), back pain (≤3%)

Ophthalmic: Blurred vision (heart failure trials >1%)

Renal: Increased serum creatinine (doubled: MI trial 4%; >50% increase: heart failure trials 4%), renal insufficiency (>1%)

Respiratory: Cough (1% to 3%)

All indications: <1%, postmarketing, and/or case reports: Alopecia, anaphylaxis, anemia, angioedema, anorexia, anxiety, bullous dermatitis, chest pain, constipation, decreased hematocrit, decreased hemoglobin, drowsiness, dyspepsia, flatulence, hepatitis (rare), hypersensitivity reaction, impotence, insomnia, liver function tests increased, microcytic anemia, muscle cramps, myalgia, palpitation, paresthesia, photosensitivity, pruritus, renal failure, rhabdomyolysis, skin rash, taste disorder, thrombocytopenia (very rare), vasculitis, vomiting, weakness, xerostomia

General Dosage Range Oral:

Children and Adolescents 6 to 16 years: Initial: 1.3 mg/kg once daily (maximum initial dose: 40 mg/day); Maintenance: Up to 2.7 mg/kg (160 mg) once daily.

Adults: Initial: 20 to 40 mg twice daily **or** 80 to 160 mg once daily; Maintenance: 80 to 160 mg twice daily (maximum: 320 mg/day).

Mechanism of Action Valsartan produces direct antagonism of the angiotensin II (AT2) receptors, unlike the ACE inhibitors. It displaces angiotensin II from the AT1 receptor and produces its blood pressure-lowering effects by antagonizing AT1-induced vasoconstriction, aldosterone release, catecholamine release, arginine vasopressin release, water intake, and hypertrophic responses. This action results in more efficient blockade of the cardiovascular effects of angiotensin II and fewer side effects than the ACE inhibitors.

Pharmacodynamics/Kinetics

Onset of Action ~2 hours

Duration of Action 24 hours

Half-life Elimination

Children 1 to 5 years: ~4 hours (Blumer 2009)

Children and Adolescents 6 to 16 years: ~5 hours (Blumer 2009)

Adults: ~6 hours; ~35% longer in elderly patients

Time to Peak Serum: Children and Adolescents 1 to 16 years: Oral suspension: 2 hours (Blumer 2009); Adults: 2 to 4 hours

Pregnancy Risk Factor D

Pregnancy Considerations [US Boxed Warning]: Drugs that act on the renin-angiotensin system can cause injury and death to the developing fetus. Discontinue as soon as possible once pregnancy is detected. The use of drugs which act on the renin-angiotensin system are associated with oligohydramnios. Oligohydramnios, due to decreased fetal renal function, may lead to fetal lung hypoplasia and skeletal malformations. Use is also associated with anuria, hypotension, renal failure, skull hypoplasia, and death in the fetus/neonate. in The exposed fetus should be monitored for fetal growth, amniotic fluid volume, and organ formation. Infants exposed *in utero* should be monitored for hyperkalemia, hypotension, and oliguria (exchange transfusions or dialysis may be needed). These adverse events are generally associated with maternal use In the second and third trimesters.

Untreated chronic maternal hypertension is also associated with adverse events in the fetus, infant, and mother. The use of angiotensin II receptor blockers is not recommended to treat chronic uncomplicated hypertension in pregnant women and should generally be avoided in women of reproductive potential (ACOG, 2013).

Vancomycin (van koe MYE sin)

Brand Names: US First-Vancomycin 25; First-Vancomycin 50; Vancocin HCl; Vancomycin+SyrSpend SF PH4

Brand Names: Canada JAMP-Vancomycin; PMS-Vancomycin; Sterile Vancomycin Hydrochloride, USP;

Val-Vancomycin; Vancocin; Vancomycin Hydrochloride for Injection; Vancomycin Hydrochloride for Injection, USP

Generic Availability (US) May be product dependent

Pharmacologic Category Glycopeptide

Use

***Clostridium difficile*-associated diarrhea/staphylococcal enterocolitis (oral):** Treatment of *C. difficile*-associated diarrhea (CDAD), pseudomembranous colitis, and staphylococcal enterocolitis

Endocarditis (injection):

Diphtheroid: Treatment of diphtheroid endocarditis in combination with either rifampin, an aminoglycoside, or both in early-onset prosthetic valve endocarditis caused by *Staphylococcus epidermidis* or diphtheroids

Enterococcal: Treatment of endocarditis caused by enterococci (eg, *Enterococcus faecalis*), in combination with an aminoglycoside

Staphylococcal: Treatment of staphylococcal endocarditis

Streptococcal: Treatment of endocarditis due to *Streptococcus viridans* or *Streptococcus bovis,* as monotherapy or in combination with an aminoglycoside

Staphylococcal infections (injection): Treatment of serious or severe infections (eg, septicemia, bone infections, lower respiratory tract infections, skin and skin structure infections) caused by susceptible strains of methicillin-resistant (beta-lactam-resistant) staphylococci; empiric therapy of infections when methicillin-resistant staphylococci are suspected

Local Anesthetic/Vasoconstrictor Precautions No information available to require special precautions

Effects on Dental Treatment Key adverse event(s) related to dental treatment: Bitter taste. "Red man syndrome", characterized by skin rash and hypotension, is not an allergic reaction but rather is associated with too rapid infusion of the drug. To alleviate or prevent the reaction, infuse vancomycin at a rate of ≥30 minutes for each 500 mg of drug being administered (eg, 1 g over ≥60 minutes); 1.5 g over ≥90 minutes.

Effects on Bleeding Vancomycin has been demonstrated to induce immune thrombocytopenia, causing a significant drop in platelet count following a short (ie, 12-15 hours) period of time after treatment. Both IgG and IgM vancomycin-dependent platelets have been identified post vancomycin administration. Discontinuation has shown to be an effective remedy, as platelet levels return to the pre-exposure counts within 4 days of drug withdrawal.

Adverse Reactions

Injection:

>10%:

Cardiovascular: Hypotension (accompanied by flushing)

Hypersensitivity: Red neck syndrome (infusion rate-related)

1% to 10%:

Cardiovascular: Local phlebitis

Central nervous system: Chills, drug fever

Dermatologic: Skin rash

Hematologic & oncologic: Eosinophilia, neutropenia (reversible)

<1%, postmarketing, and/or case reports: DRESS syndrome (drug rash with eosinophilia and systemic symptoms), ototoxicity (rare; use of other ototoxic agents may increase risk), renal failure (limited data suggesting direct relationship), Stevens-Johnson syndrome, thrombocytopenia, vasculitis

Oral:

>10%: Gastrointestinal: Abdominal pain, dysgeusia (with oral solution), nausea

1% to 10%:

Cardiovascular: Peripheral edema

Central nervous system: Fatigue, headache

Gastrointestinal: Diarrhea, flatulence, vomiting

Genitourinary: Urinary tract infection

Neuromuscular & skeletal: Back pain

Miscellaneous: Fever

<1%, postmarketing, and/or case reports: Increased serum creatinine, interstitial nephritis, ototoxicity, renal failure, renal insufficiency, thrombocytopenia, vasculitis

Dental Usual Dosage Prophylaxis against infective endocarditis: IV:

Infants >1 month and Children:

Dental, oral, or upper respiratory tract surgery: 20 mg/kg 1 hour prior to the procedure. **Note:** American Heart Association (AHA) guidelines now recommend prophylaxis only in patients undergoing invasive procedures and in whom underlying cardiac conditions may predispose to a higher risk of adverse outcomes should infection occur.

GI/GU procedure: 20 mg/kg plus gentamicin 2 mg/kg 1 hour prior to surgery. **Note:** As of April 2007, routine prophylaxis no longer recommended by the AHA.

Adults:

Dental, oral, or upper respiratory tract surgery: 1 g 1 hour before surgery. **Note:** AHA guidelines now recommend prophylaxis only in patients undergoing invasive procedures and in whom underlying cardiac conditions may predispose to a higher risk of adverse outcomes should infection occur

GI/GU procedure: 1 g plus 1.5 mg/kg gentamicin 1 hour prior to surgery. **Note:** As of April 2007, routine prophylaxis no longer recommended by the AHA.

Dosing

Adult & Geriatric

Usual dosage range: Note: Initial intravenous dosing should be based on actual body weight; subsequent dosing adjusted based on serum trough vancomycin concentrations.

IV:

Manufacturer's labeling: Usual dose: 500 mg every 6 hours **or** 1,000 mg every 12 hours

Alternate recommendations:

15 to 20 mg/kg/dose every 8 to 12 hours (ASHP/IDSA/SIDP [Rybak 2009])

Complicated infections in seriously ill patients: A loading dose of 25 to 30 mg/kg (based on actual body weight) may be used to rapidly achieve target concentrations (ASHP/IDSA/SIDP [Rybak 2009]).

Oral: 500 to 2,000 mg daily in divided doses every 6 hours. **Note:** Not appropriate for systemic infections due to low absorption.

Indication-specific dosing:

Bacteremia (*S. aureus* [methicillin-resistant]) (off-label dose): IV: 15 to 20 mg/kg/dose (based on actual body weight) every 8 to 12 hours for 2 to 6 weeks depending on severity. A loading dose of 25 to 30 mg/kg (based on actual body weight) may be used to rapidly achieve target concentrations in seriously ill patients (ASHP/IDSA/SIDP [Rybak 2009]; IDSA [Liu 2011]).

Brain abscess, subdural empyema, spinal epidural abscess (*S. aureus* [methicillin-resistant]) (off-label dose): IV: 15 to 20 mg/kg/dose (based on actual body weight) every 8 to 12 hours for 4 to 6 weeks (with or without rifampin). A loading dose of 25 to 30 mg/kg (based on actual body weight) may be used to rapidly achieve target concentrations in seriously ill patients (ASHP/IDSA/SIDP [Rybak 2009]; IDSA [Liu 2011]).

Catheter-related infections: Antibiotic lock technique (off-label use) (Mermel 2009): 2 mg/mL ± 10 units heparin/mL **or** 2.5 mg/mL ± 2,500 **or** 5,000 units heparin/mL **or** 5 mg/mL ± 5,000 units heparin/mL (preferred regimen); instill into catheter port with a volume sufficient to fill the catheter (2 to 5 mL). **Note:** May use SWFI/NS or D5W as diluents. Do not mix with any other solutions. Dwell times generally should not exceed 48 hours before renewal of lock solution. Remove lock solution prior to catheter use, then replace.

***C. difficile*-associated diarrhea (CDAD):** Oral:

Manufacturer's labeling: 125 mg 4 times daily for 10 days

Alternate dosing:

HIV-infected patients: 125 mg 4 times daily for 10 to 14 days (HHS [OI adult 2015])

Mild to moderate disease unresponsive to metronidazole: 125 mg 4 times daily for 10 days (ACG [Surawicz 2013])

Severe disease (defined as serum albumin <3 g/dL and either WBC ≥15,000 or abdominal tenderness): 125 mg 4 times daily for 10 days (ACG [Surawicz 2013])

Severe, complicated infection without abdominal distention: 125 mg 4 times daily with IV metronidazole (ACG [Surawicz 2013])

Severe, complicated infection: 500 mg 4 times daily for 10 to 14 days with or without concurrent IV metronidazole. May consider vancomycin retention enema (in patients with complete ileus) (SHEA/IDSA [Cohen 2010])

Severe, complicated infection with significant abdominal distention, ileus, and/or toxic colon: 500 mg 4 times daily plus rectal vancomycin in combination with IV metronidazole (ACG [Surawicz 2013])

Recurrent, severe infection (if initial regimen did not include vancomycin): 125 mg 4 times daily for 10 days (ACG [Surawicz 2013])

Rectal (off-label route): Retention enema:

Severe, complicated infection in patients with ileus: 500 mg every 6 hours (in 100 mL 0.9% sodium chloride) with oral vancomycin with or without concurrent IV metronidazole (SHEA/IDSA [Cohen 2010])

Severe and complicated disease with abdominal distention, ileus, and/or toxic colon: 500 mg 4 times daily (in 500 mL NS) in combination with oral vancomycin and IV metronidazole (ACG [Surawicz 2013])

Endocarditis, treatment (off-label dose):

Enterococcus (native or prosthetic valve; penicillin-resistant strains or patients unable to tolerate beta-lactams): IV: 15 mg/kg/dose every 12 hours in combination with gentamicin for 6 weeks; adjust dose to obtain a trough concentration of 10 to 20 mcg/mL (AHA [Baddour 2015])

S. aureus (methicillin-resistant): IV:

Native valve: 15 mg/kg/dose every 12 hours for 6 weeks; dose adjusted to obtain a serum trough concentration of 10 to 20 mcg/mL (AHA [Baddour 2015]) **or** 15 to 20 mg/kg/dose (based on actual body weight) every 8 to 12 hours for 6 weeks (IDSA [Lui 2011]).

Prosthetic valve: 15 mg/kg/dose every 12 hours; adjust dose to obtain a trough concentration of 10 to 20 mcg/mL (AHA [Baddour 2015]) **or** 15 to 20 mg/kg/dose (based on actual body weight) every 8 to 12 hours (IDSA [Lui 2011]). Duration of therapy: At least 6 weeks (combine with rifampin for the entire duration of therapy and gentamicin for the first 2 weeks) (AHA [Baddour 2015]; IDSA [Lui 2011]).

Viridans group streptococcus (VGS) and S. bovis (native or prosthetic valve; patients intolerant to penicillin or ceftriaxone): IV: 15 mg/kg/dose every 12 hours for 4 weeks (native valve) or 6 weeks (prosthetic valve); adjust dose to obtain a trough concentration of 10 to 15 mcg/mL (AHA [Baddour 2015])

Endophthalmitis (off-label use): Intravitreal (off-label): Usual dose: 1 mg/0.1 mL NS instilled into vitreum; may repeat administration, if necessary, in 2 to 3 days, usually in combination with ceftazidime or an aminoglycoside (Kelsey 1995). **Note:** Based on concerns for retinotoxicity, some clinicians have recommended using a lower dose of 0.2 mg/0.1mL; may repeat in 3 to 4 days, if necessary (Gan 2001).

Enterocolitis *(S. aureus)*: Oral: 500 to 2,000 mg/day in 3 to 4 divided doses for 7 to 10 days (usual dose: 125 to 500 mg every 6 hours)

Group B streptococcus (neonatal prophylaxis) (off-label use): IV: 1,000 mg every 12 hours until delivery. **Note:** Reserved for penicillin allergic patients at high risk for anaphylaxis if organism is resistant to clindamycin or where no susceptibility data are available (CDC 2010).

Intra-abdominal infection (off-label use): IV: 15 to 20 mg/kg/dose every 8 to 12 hours (Solomkin 2010)

Meningitis, bacterial (off-label use): IV: 15 to 20 mg/kg/dose (based on actual body weight) every 8 to 12 hours (for empiric therapy, use in combination with a third-generation cephalosporin; for patients >50 years, include ampicillin); duration of therapy should be individualized based upon clinical response (in general, 10 to 21 days). A loading dose of 25 to 30 mg/kg (based on actual body weight) may be used to rapidly achieve target concentration in seriously ill patients (ASHP/IDSA/SIDP [Rybak 2009]; IDSA [Tunkel 2004]). Note: For PCN-resistant *Streptococcus pneumoniae* (MIC ≥2 mcg/mL), combine with a third-generation cephalosporin (IDSA [Tunkel 2004]). For methicillin-resistant S. aureus, treat for 2 weeks (with or without rifampin) (IDSA [Liu 2011]).

Osteomyelitis (*S. aureus* [methicillin-resistant]) (off-label dose): IV: 15 to 20 mg/kg/dose (based on actual body weight) every 8 to 12 hours for a minimum of 8 weeks (with or without rifampin). A loading dose of 25 to 30 mg/kg (based on actual body weight) may be used to rapidly achieve target concentrations in seriously ill patients (ASHP/IDSA/SIDP [Rybak 2009]; IDSA [Liu 2011]).

Osteomyelitis, native vertebral: IV:

Staphylococci (oxacillin-resistant) (off-label dose): 15 to 20 mg/kg/dose (based on actual body weight) every 12 hours for 6 weeks. A loading dose may be considered (IDSA [Berbari 2015]).

Enterococcus spp (penicillin-susceptible or -resistant), beta-hemolytic streptococci, Propionibacterium acnes, or staphylococci (oxacillin-susceptible) (off-label use): 15 to 20 mg/kg/dose (based on actual body weight) every 12 hours for 6 weeks. A loading dose may be considered. **Note:** In patients with concurrent infective endocarditis due to *Enterococcus* spp, adjunctive aminoglycoside therapy for 4 to 6 weeks is recommended (IDSA [Berbari 2015])

Peritonitis, treatment (off-label use) (ISPD [Li 2016]): Intraperitoneal:

Continuous ambulatory peritoneal dialysis (CAPD):

Note: Intermittent administration is preferred; maintain serum vancomycin level above 15 mcg/mL.

Intermittent (one exchange daily): 15 to 30 mg/kg every 5 to 7 days (allow to dwell for ≥6 hours); supplemental doses may be needed for patients receiving automated peritoneal dialysis (APD).

Continuous (all exchanges): Loading dose: 30 mg/kg; maintenance dose: 1.5 mg/kg/bag.

Pneumonia, *S. aureus* (methicillin-resistant): IV:

Community-acquired pneumonia (CAP): 15 to 20 mg/kg/dose (based on actual body weight) every 8 to 12 hours for 7 to 21 days depending on severity. A loading dose of 25 to 30 mg/kg (based on actual body weight) may be used to rapidly achieve target concentrations in seriously ill patients (ASHP/IDSA/SIDP [Rybak 2009]; IDSA [Liu 2011]).

Hospital-acquired pneumonia or ventilator-associated pneumonia: 15 mg/kg/dose every 8 to 12 hours for 7 days; may consider shorter or longer duration depending on rate of clinical improvement. A loading dose of 25 to 30 mg/kg/ dose may be used in seriously ill patients. When used as empiric therapy, use in combination with an antipseudomonal agent (one or two antipseudomonal agents depending on patient and institution specific risk factors) (Kalil 2016).

Prosthetic joint infection (off-label use): IV:

Enterococcus spp (penicillin-susceptible or –resistant), Propionibacterium acnes, streptococci (beta-hemolytic): 15 mg/kg every 12 hours for 4 to 6 weeks, followed by an oral antibiotic suppressive regimen (IDSA [Osman 2013]).

Note: For penicillin-susceptible or -resistant *Enterococcus* spp, consider addition of an aminoglycoside; in penicillin-susceptible *Enterococcus*, beta-hemolytic streptococcus or *Propionibacterium acnes* infections, only use vancomycin if patient has penicillin allergy (IDSA [Osman 2013]).

Staphylococci (oxacillin-susceptible or –resistant): 15 mg/kg every 12 hours for 2 to 6 weeks in combination with rifampin followed by oral antibiotic treatment and suppressive regimens (IDSA [Osman 2013]).

Sepsis/Septic shock (empiric treatment or treatment for specific sensitive organism): IV: 15 to 20 mg/kg/dose (based on actual body weight) every 8 to 12 hours. A loading dose of 25 to 30 mg/kg (based on actual body weight) may be used to rapidly achieve target concentrations in seriously ill patients (ASHP/IDSA/SIDP [Rybak 2009]). The Society of Critical Care Medicine recommends administration of empiric antibiotics within 1 hour of identifying severe sepsis (SCCM [Dellinger 2013]).

Septic arthritis (*S. aureus* [methicillin-resistant]) (off-label dose): IV: 15 to 20 mg/kg/dose (based on actual body weight) every 8 to 12 hours for 3 to 4 weeks. A loading dose of 25 to 30 mg/kg (based on actual body weight) may be used to rapidly achieve target concentrations in seriously ill patients (ASHP/IDSA/SIDP [Rybak 2009]; IDSA [Liu 2011]).

Septic thrombosis of cavernous or dural venous sinus (*S. aureus* [methicillin-resistant]) (off-label dose): IV: 15 to 20 mg/kg/dose (based on actual body weight) every 8 to 12 hours for 4 to 6 weeks (with or without rifampin). A loading dose of 25 to 30 mg/kg (based on actual body weight) may be used to rapidly achieve target concentrations in seriously ill patients (ASHP/IDSA/SIDP [Rybak 2009]; IDSA [Liu 2011]).

Skin and skin structure infections (*S. aureus* [methicillin-resistant]) (off-label dose): IV: 15 to 20 mg/kg/dose every 8 to 12 hours for 7 to 14 days (IDSA [Liu 2011; Stevens 2014]). A loading dose of 25 to 30 mg/kg (based on actual body weight) may be used to rapidly achieve target concentrations in seriously ill patients (ASHP/IDSA/SIDP [Rybak 2009]; IDSA [Liu 2011]).

Skin and soft tissue necrotizing infections due to *S. aureus* (resistant strains) or polymicrobial (mixed) (off-label use): IV: 15 mg/kg/dose every 12 hours. **Note:** Give in combination with piperacillin/tazobactam for empiric therapy of polymicrobial [mixed] infections. Continue until further debridement is not necessary, patient has clinically improved, and patient is afebrile for 48 to 72 hours (IDSA [Stevens 2014]).

Surgical (perioperative) prophylaxis (off-label use): IV: 15 mg/kg within 120 minutes prior to surgical incision. May be administered in combination with other antibiotics depending upon the surgical procedure (ASHP/IDSA/SIS/SHEA [Bratzler 2013]).

Note: For patients known to be colonized with methicillin-resistant *S. aureus*, a single 15 mg/kg preoperative dose may be added to other recommended agents for the specific procedure (ASHP/IDSA/SIS/SHEA [Bratzler 2013]).

The Society of Thoracic Surgeons recommends 1,000 to 1,500 mg or 15 mg/kg over 60 minutes with completion within 1 hour of skin incision. Although not well established, a second dose of 7.5 mg/kg may be considered during cardiopulmonary bypass (STS [Engelman 2007]).

Surgical site infections (trunk or extremity [away from axilla or perineum]) (off-label use): IV: 15 mg/kg/dose every 12 hours (IDSA [Stevens 2014])

Pediatric

Usual dosage range: Note: Initial IV dosing should be based on actual body weight; subsequent dosing adjusted based on serum trough vancomycin concentrations.

Infants >1 month, Children, and Adolescents: IV:

Manufacturer's labeling: 10 mg/kg/dose every 6 hours

Alternate recommendations: 15 mg/kg/dose (maximum: 2,000 mg/dose) every 6 hours (IDSA [Liu 2011])

Indication-specific dosing:

Bacteremia (*S. aureus* [methicillin-resistant]) (off-label use): Children and Adolescents: IV: 15 mg/kg/dose every 6 hours for 2 to 6 weeks depending on severity (IDSA [Liu 2011])

Brain abscess, subdural empyema, spinal epidural abscess (*S. aureus* [methicillin-resistant]) (off-label use): Children and Adolescents: IV: 15 mg/kg/dose every 6 hours for 4 to 6 weeks (with or without rifampin) (IDSA [Liu 2011])

***C. difficile*-associated diarrhea (CDAD):** Infants >1 month, Children, and Adolescents: Oral:

Manufacturer's labeling: 40 mg/kg/day in 3 to 4 divided doses for 7 to 10 days (maximum: 2,000 mg/day)

Alternate dosing: Adolescents: HIV-infected patients: 125 mg 4 times daily for 10 to 14 days (HHS [OI adult 2015])

Endocarditis, treatment (off-label dose):

S. aureus (methicillin-resistant):

Native valve: Children and Adolescents: IV: 15 mg/kg/dose every 6 hours for 6 weeks (IDSA [Liu 2011])

Prosthetic valve: Children and Adolescents: IV: 15 mg/kg/dose every 6 hours for at least 6 weeks (combine with rifampin for the entire duration of therapy and gentamicin for the first 2 weeks) (IDSA [Liu 2011]).

Enterocolitis *(S. aureus)*: Infants >1 months, Children, and Adolescents: Oral: 40 mg/kg/day in 3 to 4 divided doses for 7 to 10 days (maximum: 2,000 mg/day)

Meningitis: Infants >1 month, Children, and Adolescents: IV: 15 mg/kg/dose every 6 hours (for empiric therapy, use in combination with a third-generation cephalosporin); duration of therapy should be individualized based upon clinical response (in general, 10 to 21 days) (IDSA [Tunkel 2004]). For methicillin-resistant *S. aureus*, treat for 2 weeks (with or without rifampin) (IDSA [Liu 2011]).

Osteomyelitis (*S. aureus* [methicillin-resistant]) (off-label use): Children and Adolescents: IV: 15 mg/kg/dose every 6 hours for 4 to 6 weeks (IDSA [Liu 2011]).

Pneumonia:

Community-acquired pneumonia (CAP) (IDSA/PIDS, 2011): Infants >3 months, Children, and Adolescents: IV: **Note:** In children ≥5 years, a macrolide antibiotic should be added if atypical pneumonia cannot be ruled out. Also consider if community-acquired MRSA suspected.

Group A *Streptococcus* (alternative to ampicillin or penicillin in beta-lactam allergic patients): 40 to 60 mg/kg/day divided every 6 to 8 hours

Presumed bacterial (in addition to recommended antibiotic therapy), *S. pneumoniae*, moderate to severe infection (MICs to penicillin ≤2.0 mcg/mL) (alternative to ampicillin or penicillin): 40 to 60 mg/kg/day divided every 6 to 8 hours

S. aureus (methicillin-susceptible) (alternative to cefazolin/oxacillin): 40 to 60 mg/kg/day divided every 6 to 8 hours

S. aureus, moderate to severe infection (methicillin-resistant +/- clindamycin susceptible) (preferred): 40 to 60 mg/kg/day divided every 6 to 8 hours **or** dosing to achieve AUC/MIC >400

Alternate regimen: 60 mg/kg/day divided every 6 hours for 7 to 21 days, depending on severity (Liu 2011)

S. pneumoniae, moderate to severe infection (MICs to penicillin ≥4.0 mcg/mL) (alternative to ceftriaxone in beta-lactam allergic patients): 40 to 60 mg/kg/day divided every 6 to 8 hours

Healthcare-associated pneumonia (HAP), S. aureus (methicillin-resistant): IV: Infants, Children, and Adolescents: 60 mg/kg/day divided every 6 hours for 7 to 21 days depending on severity (IDSA [Liu 2011])

Prophylaxis against infective endocarditis: Children and Adolescents: IV:

Dental, oral, or upper respiratory tract surgery: 20 mg/kg/dose administered 1 hour prior to the procedure. **Note:** American Heart Association (AHA) guidelines recommend prophylaxis only in patients undergoing invasive procedures and in whom underlying cardiac conditions may predispose to a higher risk of adverse outcomes should infection occur.

GI/GU procedure: 20 mg/kg (plus gentamicin 1.5 mg/kg) administered 1 hour prior to surgery. **Note:** Routine prophylaxis no longer recommended by the AHA.

Septic arthritis (*S. aureus* [methicillin-resistant]) (off-label use): Children and Adolescents: IV: 15 mg/kg/dose every 6 hours for minimum of 3 to 4 weeks (IDSA [Liu 2011])

Septic thrombosis of cavernous or dural venous sinus (*S. aureus* [methicillin-resistant]) (off-label use): Infants, Children, and Adolescents: IV: 15 mg/kg/dose every 6 hours for 4 to 6 weeks (with or without rifampin) (IDSA [Liu 2011])

Skin and skin structure infections, complicated (*S. aureus* [methicillin-resistant or methicillin sensitive in penicillin allergic patients]) (off-label use): Infants, Children, and Adolescents: IV:

Non-necrotizing infection: 10 mg/kg/dose every 6 hours (IDSA [Stevens 2014])

Necrotizing infection: 15 mg/kg/dose every 6 hours. Continue until further debridement is not necessary, patient has clinically improved, and patient is afebrile for 48 to 72 hours (IDSA [Stevens 2014]).

Alternate dosing: *S. aureus* (methicillin-resistant): 60 mg/kg/day divided every 6 hours for 7 to 14 days (IDSA [Liu 2011])

Surgical (perioperative) prophylaxis (off-label use): Children and Adolescents: IV: 15 mg/kg/dose within 120 minutes prior to surgical incision. May be administered in combination with other antibiotics depending upon the surgical procedure (ASHP/IDSA/SIS/SHEA [Bratzler 2013]).

Note: For patients known to be colonized with methicillin-resistant *S. aureus*, a single 15 mg/kg preoperative dose may be added to other recommended agents for the specific procedure (ASHP/IDSA/SIS/SHEA [Bratzler 2013]).

Renal Impairment

Oral: There are no dosage adjustments provided in the manufacturer's labeling. However, dosage adjustment unlikely due to low systemic absorption.

IV: Note: Vancomycin levels should be monitored in patients with any renal impairment: In critically ill patients with renal insufficiency, the initial loading dose (~25 mg/kg) should not be reduced. However, subsequent dosage adjustments should be made based on renal function and trough serum concentrations (Wang 2001).

Vancomycin Initial Dosage Regimens for Patients With Impaired Renal Function (Golightly 2013)

eGFR (mL/ minute per 1.73 m^2)	Actual Body Weight			
	<60 kg	60 to 80 kg	81 to 100 kg	>100 kg
>90	750 mg every 8 hours	1,000 mg every 8 hours	1,250 mg every 8 hours	1,500 mg every 8 hours
50 to 90	750 mg every 12 hours	1,000 mg every 12 hours	1,250 mg every 12 hours	1,000 mg every 8 hours
15 to 49	750 mg every 24 hours	1,000 mg every 24 hours	1,250 mg every 24 hours	1,500 mg every 24 hours
<15[a]	750 mg	1,000 mg	1,250 mg	1,500 mg

[a]Check a random vancomycin level in 24 hours after the dose. If random level is ≤20 mcg/mL, repeat the dose. If random level is >20 mcg/mL, do not re-dose; repeat random level in 12 hours.

Dialysis: Poorly dialyzable by intermittent hemodialysis; however, use of high-flux membranes and continuous renal replacement therapy (CRRT) increases vancomycin clearance, and generally requires replacement dosing (Launay-Vacher 2002).

End stage renal disease (ESRD) on intermittent hemodialysis (IHD) (administer after hemodialysis on dialysis days): Following loading dose of 15 to 25 mg/kg, give either 500 to 1,000 mg **or** 5 to 10 mg/kg after each dialysis session (Heintz 2009). **Note:** Dosing dependent on the assumption of 3 times/week, complete IHD sessions.

Redosing based on pre-HD concentrations:
- <10 mg/L: Administer 1,000 mg after HD
- 10 to 25 mg/L: Administer 500 to 750 mg after HD
- >25 mg/L: Hold vancomycin

Redosing based on post-HD concentrations: <10 to 15 mg/L: Administer 500 to 1,000 mg

Peritoneal dialysis (PD): 1 g every 4 to 7 days (Aronoff 2007)

Continuous renal replacement therapy (CRRT) (Heintz 2009; Trotman 2005): Drug clearance is highly dependent on the method of renal replacement, filter type, and flow rate. Appropriate dosing requires close monitoring of pharmacologic response, signs of adverse reactions due to drug accumulation, as well as drug concentrations in relation to target trough (if appropriate). The following are general recommendations only (based on dialysate flow/ultrafiltration rates of 1 to 2 L/hour and minimal residual renal function) and should not supersede clinical judgment:

CVVH: Loading dose of 15 to 25 mg/kg, followed by either 1,000 mg every 48 hours **or** 10 to 15 mg/kg every 24 to 48 hours

CVVHD: Loading dose of 15 to 25 mg/kg, followed by either 1,000 mg every 24 hours **or** 10 to 15 mg/kg every 24 hours

CVVHDF: Loading dose of 15 to 25 mg/kg, followed by either 1,000 mg every 24 hours **or** 7.5 to 10 mg/kg every 12 hours

Note: Consider redosing patients receiving CRRT for vancomycin concentrations <10 to 15 mg/L.

Hepatic Impairment

Oral: There are no dosage adjustments provided in the manufacturer's labeling. However, dosage adjustment unlikely due to low systemic absorption.

IV: There are no dosage adjustments provided in the manufacturer's labeling. However, degrees of hepatic dysfunction do not affect the pharmacokinetics of vancomycin (Marti, 1996).

Mechanism of Action Inhibits bacterial cell wall synthesis by blocking glycopeptide polymerization through binding tightly to D-alanyl-D-alanine portion of cell wall precursor

Contraindications Hypersensitivity to vancomycin or any component of the formulation

Warnings/Precautions May cause nephrotoxicity although limited data suggest direct causal relationship; usual risk factors include preexisting renal impairment, concomitant nephrotoxic medications, advanced age, and dehydration (nephrotoxicity has also been reported following treatment with oral vancomycin, typically in patients >65 years of age). If multiple sequential (≥2) serum creatinine concentrations demonstrate an increase of 0.5 mg/dL or ≥50% increase from baseline (whichever is greater) in the absence of an alternative explanation, the patient should be identified as having vancomycin-induced nephrotoxicity (Rybak 2009). Discontinue treatment if signs of nephrotoxicity occur; renal damage is usually reversible.

May cause neutropenia; prolonged therapy and use of concomitant drugs that cause neutropenia may increase the risk; monitor leukocyte counts periodically in these patients. Prompt reversal of neutropenia is expected after discontinuation of therapy.

Ototoxicity is rarely associated with monotherapy. It has been most frequently reported in patients receiving excessive doses, those who have underlying hearing loss, or those receiving concomitant ototoxic drugs (eg, aminoglycosides). Serial auditory function testing may be helpful to minimize risk. Ototoxicity may be transient or permanent; discontinue treatment if signs of ototoxicity occur. Prolonged therapy (>1 week) or total doses exceeding 25 g may increase the risk of neutropenia; prompt reversal of neutropenia is expected after discontinuation of therapy. Prolonged use may result in fungal or bacterial superinfection, including *C. difficile*-associated diarrhea (CDAD) and pseudomembranous colitis; CDAD has been observed >2 months postantibiotic treatment. Use with caution in patients with renal impairment or those receiving other nephrotoxic or ototoxic drugs; dosage modification required in patients with impaired renal function (especially elderly). Accumulation may occur after multiple oral doses of vancomycin in patients with renal impairment; consider monitoring trough concentrations in this circumstance.

IV vancomycin is an irritant and can cause thrombophlebitis; ensure proper needle or catheter placement prior to and during infusion; avoid extravasation. Pain, tenderness, and necrosis may occur with extravasation. If thrombophlebitis occurs, slow infusion rates, dilute solution (eg, 2.5 to 5 g/L) and rotate infusion sites.

Rapid IV administration (eg, over <60 minutes) may result in hypotension, flushing, erythema, urticaria, pruritus and, rarely, cardiac arrest. Reactions usually cease promptly after infusion is stopped. Frequency of infusion reactions may increase with concomitant administration of anesthetics. If used in conjunction with anesthesia, complete the vancomycin infusion prior to anesthesia induction. Oral vancomycin is only indicated for the treatment of pseudomembranous colitis due to *C. difficile* and enterocolitis due to *S. aureus* and is not effective for systemic infections; parenteral vancomycin is not effective for the treatment of colitis due to *C. difficile* and enterocolitis due to *S. aureus*. Clinically significant serum concentrations have been reported in patients with inflammatory disorders of the intestinal mucosa who have taken oral vancomycin (multiple doses) for the treatment of *C. difficile*-associated diarrhea. Although use may be warranted, the risk for adverse reactions may be higher in this situation; consider monitoring serum trough concentrations, especially with renal insufficiency, severe colitis, concurrent rectal vancomycin administration, and/or concomitant IV aminoglycosides. The Society for Healthcare Epidemiology of America (SHEA) and the Infectious Diseases Society of America (IDSA) suggest that it is appropriate to obtain trough concentrations when a patient is receiving long courses of ≥2 g/day in adults (SHEA/IDSA [Cohen 2010]). **Note:** The SHEA, the IDSA, and the American College of Gastroenterology (ACG) recommend the use of oral metronidazole for initial treatment of mild to moderate *C. difficile* infection and the use of oral vancomycin for initial treatment of severe *C. difficile* infection (SHEA/IDSA [Cohen 2010]; ACG [Surawicz 2013]). Use caution when administering intraperitoneally (IP); In some continuous ambulatory peritoneal dialysis (CAPD) patients, chemical peritonitis (cloudy dialysate, fever, severe abdominal pain) has occurred. Symptoms are self-limited and usually clear after vancomycin discontinuation.

Potentially significant interactions may exist, requiring dose or frequency adjustment, additional monitoring, and/or selection of alternative therapy.

Drug Interactions

Metabolism/Transport Effects None known.

Avoid Concomitant Use

Avoid concomitant use of Vancomycin with any of the following: BCG (Intravesical); Cholera Vaccine

Increased Effect/Toxicity

Vancomycin may increase the levels/effects of: Aminoglycosides; Colistimethate; Neuromuscular-Blocking Agents

The levels/effects of Vancomycin may be increased by: Nonsteroidal Anti-Inflammatory Agents; Piperacillin

Decreased Effect

Vancomycin may decrease the levels/effects of: BCG (Intravesical); BCG Vaccine (Immunization); Cholera Vaccine; Lactobacillus and Estriol; Sodium Picosulfate; Typhoid Vaccine

The levels/effects of Vancomycin may be decreased by: Bile Acid Sequestrants

Dietary Considerations May be taken with food.

Pharmacodynamics/Kinetics

Half-life Elimination Biphasic: Terminal:

Newborns: 6 to 10 hours

Neonates receiving ECMO: 6.53 ± 2.1 hours (Buck 1998); others have reported longer: 10.4 ± 6.7 hours (Mulla 2005)

Infants and Children 3 months to 4 years: 4 hours

Children and Adolescents >3 years: 2.2 to 3 hours

Adults: 4 to 6 hours; significantly prolonged with renal impairment

End-stage renal disease (ESRD): 7.5 days

Time to Peak Serum: IV: Immediately after completion of infusion

Pregnancy Risk Factor B (oral); C (injection)

Pregnancy Considerations Adverse events have not been observed in animal reproduction studies. Vancomycin crosses the placenta and can be detected in fetal serum, amniotic fluid, and cord blood (Bourget 1991; Reyes 1989). Adverse fetal effects, including sensorineural hearing loss or nephrotoxicity, have not been reported following maternal use during the second or third trimesters of pregnancy.

The pharmacokinetics of vancomycin may be altered during pregnancy and pregnant patients may need a higher dose of vancomycin. Maternal half-life is unchanged, but the volume of distribution and the total plasma clearance may be increased (Bourget 1991). Individualization of therapy through serum concentration monitoring may be warranted. Vancomycin is recommended for the treatment of mild, moderate, or severe *Clostridium difficile* infections in pregnant women (ACG [Surawicz 2013]). Vancomycin is recommended as an alternative agent to prevent the transmission of group B streptococcal (GBS) disease from mothers to newborns (ACOG 2011; CDC 2010).

Breastfeeding Considerations Vancomycin is excreted in human milk following IV administration. If given orally to the mother, the minimal systemic absorption of the dose would limit the amount available to pass into the milk. Vancomycin is recommended for the treatment of mild, moderate, or severe *Clostridium difficile* infections in breastfeeding women (ACG [Surawicz 2013]). Due to the potential for serious adverse reactions in the nursing infant, the manufacturer recommends a decision be made whether to discontinue nursing or to discontinue the drug, taking into account the importance of treatment to the mother. Nondose-related effects could include modification of bowel flora.

Dosage Forms Considerations

First-Vancomycin oral solution and Vancomycin+SyrSpend SF oral suspension are compounding kits. Refer to manufacturer's labeling for compounding instructions.

Dosage Forms

Capsule, Oral:

Vancocin HCl: 125 mg, 250 mg

Generic: 125 mg, 250 mg

Solution, Intravenous:

Generic: 1 g/200 mL (200 mL); 500 mg/100 mL (100 mL); 750 mg/150 mL (150 mL)

Solution, Oral:

First-Vancomycin 25: 25 mg/mL (150 mL, 300 mL)

First-Vancomycin 50: 50 mg/mL (150 mL, 210 mL, 300 mL)

Solution Reconstituted, Intravenous:

Generic: 500 mg (1 ea); 750 mg (1 ea); 1000 mg (1 ea); 5000 mg (1 ea); 10 g (1 ea)

Solution Reconstituted, Intravenous [preservative free]:

Generic: 500 mg (1 ea); 1000 mg (1 ea); 5000 mg (1 ea); 10 g (1 ea)

Suspension, Oral:

Vancomycin+SyrSpend SF PH4: 50 mg/mL (120 mL, 240 mL)

Vandetanib (van DET a nib)

Related Information

Clinical Risk Related to Drugs Prolonging QT Interval *on page 1772*

Brand Names: US Caprelsa

Brand Names: Canada Caprelsa

Pharmacologic Category Antineoplastic Agent, Epidermal Growth Factor Receptor (EGFR) Inhibitor; Antineoplastic Agent, Tyrosine Kinase Inhibitor; Antineoplastic Agent, Vascular Endothelial Growth Factor (VEGF) Inhibitor

Use Thyroid cancer, medullary (locally advanced or metastatic): Treatment of metastatic or unresectable locally-advanced medullary thyroid cancer (symptomatic or progressive)

Local Anesthetic/Vasoconstrictor Precautions Hypertension can occur with the use of this drug, particularly early in the treatment course. Monitor for hypertension prior to using local anesthetic with vasoconstrictor; medical consult if necessary.

Vandetanib is one of the drugs confirmed to prolong the QT interval and is accepted as having a risk of causing torsade de pointes. The risk of drug-induced torsade de pointes is extremely low when a single QT interval prolonging drug is prescribed. In terms of epinephrine, it is not known what effect vasoconstrictors in the local anesthetic regimen will have in patients with a known history of congenital prolonged QT interval or in patients taking any medication that prolongs the QT interval. Until more information is obtained, it is suggested that the clinician consult with the physician prior to the use of a vasoconstrictor in suspected patients, and that the vasoconstrictor (epinephrine, mepivacaine and levonordefrin [Carbocaine® 2% with Neo-Cobefrin®]) be used with caution.

Effects on Dental Treatment Key adverse event(s) related to dental treatment: Xerostomia (normal salivary flow resumes upon discontinuation), mucositis/stomatitis, taste perversion, and oral pain.

Effects on Bleeding Chemotherapy may result in significant myelosuppression, potentially including significant reduction in platelet counts (thrombocytopenia: 9%) and altered hemostasis. In patients who are under active treatment with these agents, medical consult is suggested.

Adverse Reactions

>10%:

Cardiovascular: Hypertension (33%; grades 3/4: 9%), prolonged Q-T interval on ECG (14%; grades 3/4: 8%)

Central nervous system: Headache (26%), fatigue (24%)

Dermatologic: Skin rash (53%), acne vulgaris (35%), xeroderma (15%), skin photosensitivity (13%), pruritus (11%)

Endocrine & metabolic: Hypocalcemia (11% to 57%), hypoglycemia (24%)

Gastrointestinal: Colitis (≤57%; grades 3/4: ≤11%), diarrhea (≤57%; grades 3/4: ≤11%), nausea (33%), abdominal pain (21%), decreased appetite (21%), vomiting (15%), dyspepsia (11%)

Hematologic & oncologic: Hemorrhage (grades ≤2: 14%)

Hepatic: Increased serum ALT (51%)

Ophthalmic: Corneal changes (13%)

Renal: Increased serum creatinine (16%)

Respiratory: Upper respiratory tract infection (23%)

1% to 10%:

Cardiovascular: Cerebral ischemia (1%)

Central nervous system: Depression (10%)

Dermatologic: Nail disease (9%), alopecia (8%)

Endocrine & metabolic: Hypomagnesemia (7%), hypothyroidism (6%)

Gastrointestinal: Xerostomia (9%), dysgeusia (8%)

Genitourinary: Proteinuria (10%)

Hematologic & oncologic: Neutropenia (10%), thrombocytopenia (9%)

Neuromuscular & skeletal: Muscle spasm (6%)

Ophthalmic: Blurred vision (9%)

Frequency not defined:

Cardiovascular: Torsades de pointes, ventricular tachycardia

Central nervous system: Reversible posterior leukoencephalopathy syndrome

Dermatologic: Stevens-Johnson syndrome, toxic epidermal necrolysis

Respiratory: Interstitial pulmonary disease, pneumonitis

<1%, postmarketing, and/or case reports: Intestinal perforation, pancreatitis

Mechanism of Action Multikinase inhibitor; inhibits tyrosine kinases including epidermal growth factor reception (EGFR), vascular endothelial growth factor (VEGF), rearranged during transfection (RET), protein tyrosine kinase 6 (BRK), TIE2, EPH kinase receptors and SRC kinase receptors, selectively blocking intracellular signaling, angiogenesis and cellular proliferation

Pharmacodynamics/Kinetics

Half-life Elimination 19 days

Time to Peak 6 hours (range: 4 to 10 hours)

Pregnancy Risk Factor D

Pregnancy Considerations Adverse events have been observed in animal reproduction studies. Because vandetanib inhibits angiogenesis, a critical component of fetal development, adverse effects on pregnancy would be expected. Women of childbearing potential should be advised to avoid pregnancy and use effective contraception during and for 4 months following treatment with vandetanib.

Prescribing and Access Restrictions As a requirement of the REMS program, access to vandetanib is restricted. Vandetanib is approved for marketing under a Food and Drug Administration (FDA) approved, risk management program, and through a restricted distribution program, the Vandetanib REMS Program (1-800-236-9933). Prescribers and pharmacies must be certified with the program to prescribe or dispense vandetanib.

In Canada, vandetanib is available only through the CAPRELSA Restricted Distribution Program. Prescribers and pharmacies must be certified with the program to prescribe or dispense vandetanib. Further information may be obtained at 1-800-668-6000.

Dental Comment See Local Anesthetic/Vasoconstrictor Precautions

Vardenafil (var DEN a fil)

Brand Names: US Levitra; Staxyn

Brand Names: Canada Levitra; Staxyn

Pharmacologic Category Phosphodiesterase-5 Enzyme Inhibitor

Use Erectile dysfunction: Treatment of erectile dysfunction (ED)

Local Anesthetic/Vasoconstrictor Precautions No information available to require special precautions

Effects on Dental Treatment No significant effects or complications reported

Effects on Bleeding No information available to require special precautions

Adverse Reactions

>10%:

Cardiovascular: Flushing (8% to 11%)

Central nervous system: Headache (14% to 15%)

2% to 10%:

Central nervous system: Dizziness (2%)

Gastrointestinal: Dyspepsia (3% to 4%), nausea (2%)

Neuromuscular & skeletal: Back pain (2%), increased creatine phosphokinase (2%)

Respiratory: Rhinitis (9%), flu-like symptoms (3%), nasal congestion (3%), sinusitis (3%)

<2%, postmarketing, and/or case reports: Abdominal pain, abnormal hepatic function tests, allergic edema, anaphylaxis, angina pectoris, angioedema, arthralgia, auditory impairment, basal cell carcinoma (Loeb 2015), blurred vision, chest pain, chromatopsia, conjunctivitis, decreased visual acuity, diaphoresis, diarrhea, drowsiness, dysesthesia, dysphagia, dyspnea, ejaculatory disorder, epistaxis, erythema, esophagitis, eye discomfort, eye pain, facial edema, gastritis, gastroesophageal reflux disease, glaucoma, hearing loss, hypersensitivity reaction, hypertension, hypertonia, hypoesthesia, hypotension, increased gamma-glutamyl transferase, increased intraocular pressure, insomnia, ischemic heart disease, laryngeal edema, malignant melanoma (Loeb 2015), muscle cramps, myalgia, myocardial infarction, neck pain, anterior ischemic optic neuropathy (nonarteritic; NAION), ocular hyperemia, orthostatic hypotension, pain, palpitations, paresthesia, pharyngitis, photophobia, priapism, pruritus, retinal vein occlusion, seizure, skin photosensitivity, skin rash, sleep disorder, syncope, tachycardia, temporary amnesia (global), tinnitus, ventricular tachyarrhythmia, vertigo, vision color changes, vision loss (temporary or permanent), visual disturbance (including dim vision), visual field defect, vomiting, watery eyes, weakness, xerostomia

General Dosage Range Dosage adjustment recommended in patients with hepatic impairment or on concomitant therapy

Oral:

Adults: Film-coated tablet (Levitra): 2.5 to 20 mg as a single dose (maximum: 1 dose/day); Oral disintegrating tablet (Staxyn): 10 mg as a single dose (maximum: 10 mg daily)

Elderly ≥65 years: Film-coated tablet (Levitra): 2.5 to 5 mg as a single dose (maximum: 1 dose daily)

Mechanism of Action Does not directly cause penile erections, but affects the response to sexual stimulation. The physiologic mechanism of erection of the penis involves release of nitric oxide (NO) in the corpus cavernosum during sexual stimulation. NO then activates the enzyme guanylate cyclase, which results in increased levels of cyclic guanosine monophosphate (cGMP), producing smooth muscle relaxation and inflow of blood to the corpus cavernosum. Vardenafil enhances the effect of NO by inhibiting phosphodiesterase type 5 (PDE-5), which is responsible for degradation of cGMP in the corpus cavernosum; when sexual stimulation causes local release of NO, inhibition of PDE-5 by vardenafil causes increased levels of cGMP in the corpus cavernosum, resulting in smooth muscle relaxation and inflow of blood to the corpus cavernosum; at recommended doses, it has no effect in the absence of sexual stimulation.

Pharmacodynamics/Kinetics

Onset of Action ~60 minutes

Half-life Elimination Terminal: Vardenafil and metabolite: 4 to 6 hours

Time to Peak Plasma: 0.5 to 2 hours

Pregnancy Risk Factor B

Pregnancy Considerations Teratogenic effects were not observed in animal studies; however, vardenafil is not indicated for use in women. No effects on sperm motility or morphology were observed in healthy males.

Varenicline (var e NI kleen)

Brand Names: US Chantix; Chantix Continuing Month Pak; Chantix Starting Month Pak

Brand Names: Canada Champix

Generic Availability (US) No

Pharmacologic Category Partial Nicotine Agonist; Smoking Cessation Aid

Use Smoking cessation: As an aid to smoking cessation treatment

Local Anesthetic/Vasoconstrictor Precautions No information available to require special precautions

Effects on Dental Treatment Key adverse event(s) related to dental treatment: Xerostomia (normal salivary flow resumes upon discontinuation).

Effects on Bleeding No information available to require special precautions

Adverse Reactions

>10%:

Central nervous system: Headache (15% to 19%), insomnia (10% to 19%), abnormal dreams (9% to 13%), irritability (11%), suicidal ideation (11%), depression (4% to 11%)

Gastrointestinal: Nausea (16% to 40%), vomiting (5% to 11%)

1% to 10%:

Cardiovascular: Angina pectoris (4%), chest pain (3%), peripheral edema (2%), myocardial infarction (≤1%)

Central nervous system: Agitation (7%), malaise (7%), sleep disorder (5%), tension (4%), drowsiness (3%), hostility (2% to 3%), lethargy (1% to 2%), nightmares (1% to 2%)

Dermatologic: Skin rash (3%)

Gastrointestinal: Flatulence (6% to 9%), constipation (5% to 8%), dysgeusia (5% to 8%), abdominal pain (7%), diarrhea (6%), xerostomia (6%), dyspepsia (5%), increased appetite (3% to 4%), anorexia (≤2%), decreased appetite (≤2%), gastroesophageal reflux disease (1%)

Respiratory: Upper respiratory tract infection (5% to 7%), dyspnea (2%), rhinorrhea (≤1%)

<1%, postmarketing, and/or case reports: Abnormal hepatic function tests, abnormality in thinking, abnormal urinalysis, accidental injury, acne vulgaris, acute coronary syndrome, acute renal failure, aggressive behavior, allergic rhinitis, altered sense of smell, amnesia, anemia, angioedema, anxiety, arthralgia, asthma, atrial fibrillation, back pain, behavioral changes, Bell's palsy, blurred vision, bradycardia, cardiac arrhythmia, cardiac flutter, cataract (subcapsular), cerebrovascular accident, chills, conjunctivitis, cor pulmonale, coronary artery disease, deafness, decreased libido, decreased mental acuity, decreased visual acuity, delusions, diabetes mellitus, difficulty thinking, disorientation, dissociative disorder,

dizziness, dysarthria, dysphagia, ECG abnormality, eczema, edema, elevation in serum levels of skeletal-muscle enzymes, emotional disturbance, emotional lability, enterocolitis, epistaxis, equilibrium disturbance, erectile dysfunction, eructation, erythema, erythema multiforme, esophagitis, euphoria, eye irritation, eye pain, fever, flu-like symptoms, flushing, gallbladder disease, gastric ulcer, gastritis, gastrointestinal hemorrhage, hallucination, homicidal ideation, hyperglycemia, hyperhidrosis, hyperlipidemia, hypersensitivity reaction, hypoglycemia, hypokalemia, intestinal obstruction, lack of concentration, leukocytosis, loss of consciousness, lymphadenopathy, mania, Meniere disease, menstrual disease, migraine, multiple sclerosis, muscle cramps, musculoskeletal pain, myalgia, myositis, nephrolithiasis, nocturia, nocturnal amblyopia, nystagmus, ophthalmic vascular disease, oral mucosa ulcer, osteoporosis, palpitations, pancreatitis, panic, paranoia, photophobia, pleurisy, pollakiuria, polyuria, psoriasis, psychomotor agitation, psychomotor retardation, psychosis, pulmonary embolism, respiratory tract disease, restless leg syndrome, seizure, sensory disturbance, sexual difficulty, skin photosensitivity, somnambulism, splenomegaly, Stevens-Johnson syndrome, syncope, tachycardia, thrombocytopenia, thrombosis, thyroid disease, tinnitus, toothache, transient blindness, transient ischemic attacks, tremor, upper respiratory tract inflammation, urethral disease, urinary retention, urine abnormality, urticaria, ventricular premature contractions, vertigo, visual field defect, vitreous opacity, weight gain, xeroderma, xerophthalmia

Dental Usual Dosage Smoking cessation: Oral:

Initial:

Days 1 to 3: 0.5 mg once daily

Days 4 to 7: 0.5 mg twice daily

Maintenance (≥ Day 8): 1 mg twice daily for 11 weeks

Note: Start 1 week before target quit date. Alternatively, patients may consider setting a quit date up to 35 days after initiation of varenicline (some data suggest that an extended pretreatment regimen may result in higher abstinence rates [Hajek, 2011]). If patient successfully quits smoking at the end of the 12 weeks, may continue for another 12 weeks to help maintain success. If not successful in first 12 weeks, then stop medication and reassess factors contributing to failure.

Dosing

Adult & Geriatric Smoking cessation: Oral:

Initial:

Days 1 to 3: 0.5 mg once daily

Days 4 to 7: 0.5 mg twice daily

Maintenance (≥ Day 8): 1 mg twice daily for 11 weeks; may consider a temporary or permanent dose reduction if usual dose is not tolerated.

Note: Start 1 week before target quit date. Alternatively, patients may consider setting a quit date up to 35 days after initiation of varenicline (some data suggest that an extended pretreatment regimen may result in higher abstinence rates [Hajek 2011]). For patients who are sure that they are not able or willing to quit abruptly, begin treatment with vareniciline and reduce smoking by 50% from baseline within the first 4 weeks, by an additional 50% in the next 4 weeks, and continue reducing with the goal of complete abstinence by 12 weeks. If patient successfully quits smoking at the end of the 12 weeks, may continue for another 12 weeks to help maintain success. Patients who are motivated to quit and do not succeed in stopping smoking during prior therapy, or who relapse after treatment, should be encouraged to make another attempt with varenicline once factors contributing to the failed attempt have been identified and addressed.

Renal Impairment

CrCl ≥30 mL/minute: No dosage adjustment necessary.

CrCl <30 mL/minute: Initiate: 0.5 mg once daily; maximum dose: 0.5 mg twice daily

End-stage renal disease (ESRD) (receiving hemodialysis): Maximum dose: 0.5 mg once daily

Hepatic Impairment No dosage adjustment necessary.

Adjustment for Toxicity Patients who cannot tolerate adverse events may require temporary (or permanent) reduction in dose.

Mechanism of Action Partial neuronal α_4 β_2 nicotinic receptor agonist; prevents nicotine stimulation of mesolimbic dopamine system associated with nicotine addiction. Also binds to 5-HT_3 receptor (significance not determined) with moderate affinity. Varenicline stimulates dopamine activity but to a much smaller degree than nicotine does, resulting in decreased craving and withdrawal symptoms.

Contraindications Serious hypersensitivity reactions or skin reactions to varenicline or any component of the formulation

Warnings/Precautions Post-marketing cases of serious neuropsychiatric events (including depression, suicidal thoughts, and suicide) have been reported in patients with or without preexisting psychiatric disease; some cases may have been complicated by symptoms of nicotine withdrawal following smoking cessation. Subsequent controlled trials in patients with or without psychiatric disorders; however, have not identified significant differences in neuropsychiatric effects for patients taking varenicline, bupropion, nicotine patches, or placebo (Anthenelli 2013; Anthenelli 2016; Gibbons 2013; Thomas 2015). Monitor all patients for behavioral changes and psychiatric symptoms (eg, agitation, depression, suicidal behavior, suicidal ideation); inform patients to discontinue treatment and contact their health care provider immediately if they experience any behavioral and/or mood changes. Of post-marketing cases, many resolved following therapy discontinuation.

Post-marketing reports of hypersensitivity reactions (including angioedema) and rare cases of serious skin reactions (including Stevens-Johnson syndrome and erythema multiforme) have been reported. Patients should be instructed to discontinue use and contact healthcare provider if signs/symptoms occur. Treatment may increase risk of cardiovascular events. A meta-analysis of 15 clinical trials, including a placebo-controlled trial in patients with stable cardiovascular disease, showed an increased incidence of major cardiovascular events (combined outcome of cardiovascular-related death, nonfatal MI, nonfatal stroke) in patients using varenicline compared with placebo. Cardiovascular events were uncommon in both the varenicline and placebo groups. These findings did not reach statistical significance, although data was consistent. Events occurred primarily in patients with known cardiovascular disease. The meta-analysis also showed a lower incidence of all-cause and cardiovascular mortality in varenicline-treated patients, although this was not statistically significant either. Seizures have been reported in patients with or without a history of seizures. Seizures generally occurred within the first month of therapy. Consider the risks against the benefits before initiating in patients with a history of seizures or other factors that can lower the seizure threshold; discontinue use if seizures occur during therapy. Dose-dependent nausea may occur; both transient and persistent nausea has been reported. Dosage reduction may be considered for intolerable nausea. May cause CNS depression, which may impair physical or mental abilities; patients must be cautioned about performing tasks which require mental alertness (eg, operating machinery or driving). There have been postmarketing reports of traffic accidents, near-miss incidents in traffic, or other accidental injuries in patients taking varenicline. Cases of somnambulism, involving harmful behavior to self, others or property, have been reported. Discontinue treatment if somnambulism occurs.

Use caution in renal dysfunction; dosage adjustment required with severe impairment. Potentially significant drug-drug interactions may exist, requiring dose or frequency adjustment, additional monitoring, and/or selection of alternative therapy. Consult drug interactions database for more detailed information.

Drug Interactions

Metabolism/Transport Effects Substrate of OCT2

Avoid Concomitant Use There are no known interactions where it is recommended to avoid concomitant use.

Increased Effect/Toxicity

Varenicline may increase the levels/effects of: Alcohol (Ethyl); Nicotine

The levels/effects of Varenicline may be increased by: BuPROPion; H2-Antagonists; Quinolone Antibiotics; Trimethoprim

Decreased Effect There are no known significant interactions involving a decrease in effect.

Dietary Considerations Take after eating and with a full glass of water to decrease gastric upset.

Pharmacodynamics/Kinetics

Half-life Elimination ~24 hours

Time to Peak Plasma: ~3 to 4 hours

Pregnancy Considerations Adverse events have been observed in animal reproduction studies.

Breastfeeding Considerations It is not known if varenicline is excreted in breast milk. Due to the potential for serious adverse reactions in the nursing infant, the manufacturer recommends a decision be made whether to discontinue nursing or to discontinue the drug, taking into account the importance of treatment to the mother.

Dosage Forms

Tablet, Oral:

Chantix: 0.5 mg, 1 mg
Chantix Continuing Month Pak: 1 mg
Chantix Starting Month Pak: 0.5 mg x 11 & 1 mg x 42

Dosage Forms: Canada

Tablet, Oral:

Champix: 0.5 mg, 1 mg

Varicella-Zoster Immune Globulin (Human)

(var i SEL a- ZOS ter i MYUN GLOB yoo lin HYU man)

Brand Names: US VariZIG

Brand Names: Canada VariZIG

Pharmacologic Category Blood Product Derivative; Immune Globulin

Use

US labeling: **Varicella prophylaxis:** Postexposure prophylaxis of varicella in high-risk individuals. High-risk groups include immunocompromised children and adults, newborns of mothers with varicella shortly before or after delivery, premature infants, neonates and infants <1 year, adults without evidence of immunity, and pregnant women.

Canadian labeling: **Prevention or reduction of maternal infection:** In pregnant women, for the prevention or reduction in severity of maternal infection within 4 days of exposure to the varicella zoster virus.

The Advisory Committee on Immunization Practices (ACIP) recommends varicella-zoster immune globulin (VZIG) to patients who are at high risk for severe varicella infection and complications; and who were exposed to varicella or herpes zoster; and for whom varicella vaccine is contraindicated. The decision to use VZIG should take into consideration if the patient lacks evidence of immunity; if exposure is likely to result in an infection; and if the patient is at greater risk for varicella complications than the general population. The following are patient groups for whom VZIG is recommended (CDC 2013):

- Immunocompromised patients without evidence of immunity (seronegative), including those with neoplastic disease (eg, leukemia or lymphoma); primary or acquired immunodeficiency; immunosuppressive therapy (including steroid therapy equivalent to prednisone ≥2 mg/kg or 20 mg/day)
- Newborn of mother who had onset of varicella (chickenpox) within 5 days before delivery or within 48 hours after delivery
- Hospitalized premature infants (≥28 weeks gestation) who were exposed during the neonatal period and whose mother has no evidence of immunity
- Hospitalized premature infants (<28 weeks gestation or ≤1000 g) regardless of maternal history and who were exposed during the neonatal period
- Pregnant women without evidence of immunity who have been exposed

Local Anesthetic/Vasoconstrictor Precautions No information available to require special precautions

Effects on Dental Treatment No significant effects or complications reported

Effects on Bleeding No information available to require special precautions

Adverse Reactions

U.S. labeling:

1% to 10%:

Central nervous system: Headache (2% to 4%), chills (≤2%), fatigue (≤2%)
Dermatologic: Skin rash (<2%)
Gastrointestinal: Nausea (<2%)
Local: Pain at injection site (2% to 9%)

<1%, postmarketing, and/or case reports: Deep vein thrombosis, hypersensitivity reaction, serum sickness, thrombosis

Canadian labeling:

>10%:

Central nervous system: Headache (7% to 11%)
Local: Pain at injection site (17% to 47%)

1% to 10%:

Cardiovascular: Flushing (≤2%)
Central nervous system: Dizziness (≤5%), pain (≤5%), chills (≤2%), fatigue (≤2%), insomnia (≤2%)
Dermatologic: Skin rash (≤5%), dermatitis (≤2%), erythematous rash (≤2%)

Gastrointestinal: Nausea (2% to 5%), dysgeusia (≤2%)
Local: Injection site reaction (bruising, itching, or tenderness ≤2%)
Neuromuscular & skeletal: Neck pain (≤5%), myalgia (≤2%)
Miscellaneous: Fever (≤5%)

General Dosage Range IM: *Infants, Children, Adolescents, and Adults:* Dose is based on body weight. Minimum dose: 62.5 units; maximum dose: 625 units

Mechanism of Action Antibodies obtained from pooled human plasma of individuals with high titers of varicella-zoster provide passive immunity.

Pharmacodynamics/Kinetics

Duration of Action ≥6 weeks

Half-life Elimination IV: 18 to 24 days; IM: 26.2 ± 4.6 days

Time to Peak IV: <3 hours; IM: 4.5 ± 2.8 days

Pregnancy Risk Factor C

Pregnancy Considerations Animal reproduction studies have not been conducted. Endogenous immune globulins cross the placenta. Clinical use of other immunoglobulins suggest that there are no adverse effects on the fetus. Women who do not have evidence of immunity to varicella may be at increased risk of complications if infected during pregnancy. Varicella infection in the mother can also lead to intrauterine infection in the fetus. VZIG is primarily used to prevent maternal complications, not fetal infection (CDC 2007).

Vasopressin (vay soe PRES in)

Brand Names: US Pitressin Synthetic [DSC]; Vasostrict

Brand Names: Canada Pressyn; Pressyn AR

Pharmacologic Category Antidiuretic Hormone Analog; Hormone, Posterior Pituitary

Use

Diabetes Insipidus (Pitressin Synthetic only): Treatment of central diabetes insipidus; differential diagnosis of diabetes insipidus

Vasodilatory shock (Vasostrict only): To increase blood pressure in adults with vasodilatory shock (eg, postcardiotomy or sepsis) who remain hypotensive despite fluids and catecholamines

Local Anesthetic/Vasoconstrictor Precautions No information available to require special precautions

Effects on Dental Treatment No significant effects or complications reported

Effects on Bleeding No information available to require special precautions

Adverse Reactions Frequency not defined.

Cardiovascular: Angina pectoris, atrial fibrillation, bradycardia, cardiac arrest, cardiac arrhythmia, ischemic heart disease, limb ischemia (distal), localized blanching, low cardiac output, myocardial infarction, right heart failure, shock, vasoconstriction (peripheral)
Central nervous system: Headache (pounding), vertigo
Dermatologic: Circumoral pallor, diaphoresis, gangrene of skin or other tissues, skin lesion (ischemic), urticaria
Endocrine & metabolic: Hyponatremia, hypovolemic shock, water intoxication
Gastrointestinal: Abdominal cramps, flatulence, mesenteric ischemia, nausea, vomiting
Hematologic & oncologic: Decreased platelet count, hemorrhage (intractable)
Hepatic: Increased serum bilirubin
Hypersensitivity: Anaphylaxis
Neuromuscular & skeletal: Tremor
Renal: Renal insufficiency
Respiratory: Bronchoconstriction

General Dosage Range

IV: *Adults:* Initial: 0.01 to 0.03 units per minute; Maximum dose: Post-cardiotomy shock: 0.1 units per minute; Septic shock: 0.07 units/minute.

IM, SubQ:

Children and Adolescents: 2.5 to 10 units 2 to 4 times daily as needed

Adults: 5 to 10 units 2 to 4 times daily as needed

Mechanism of Action Vasopressin stimulates a family of arginine vasopressin (AVP) receptors, oxytocin receptors, and purinergic receptors (Russell 2011). Vasopressin, at therapeutic doses used for vasodilatory shock, stimulates the AVPR1a (or V1) receptor and increases systemic vascular resistance and mean arterial blood pressure; in response to these effects, a decrease in heart rate and cardiac output may be seen. When the AVPR2 (or V2) receptor is stimulated, cyclic adenosine monophosphate (cAMP) increases which in turn increases water permeability at the renal tubule resulting in decreased urine volume and increased osmolality. Vasopressin, at pressor doses, also causes smooth muscle contraction in the GI tract by stimulating muscular V1 receptors and release of prolactin and ACTH via AVPR1b (or V3) receptors.

Pharmacodynamics/Kinetics

Onset of Action

Nasal: 1 hour
IV: Vasopressor effect: Rapid with peak effect occurring within 15 minutes of initiation of continuous IV infusion

Duration of Action Nasal: 3 to 8 hours; IM, SubQ: Antidiuretic: 2 to 8 hours; IV: Vasopressor effect: Within 20 minutes after IV infusion terminated

Half-life Elimination IM, IV, SubQ: 10 to 20 minutes (apparent half-life: ≤10 minutes)

Pregnancy Risk Factor C

Pregnancy Considerations Animal reproduction studies have not been conducted. Vasopressin may produce tonic uterine contractions; however, doses sufficient for diabetes insipidus are not likely to produce this effect.

Vedolizumab (ve doe LIZ ue mab)

Brand Names: US Entyvio

Brand Names: Canada Entyvio

Pharmacologic Category Gastrointestinal Agent, Miscellaneous; Monoclonal Antibody; Monoclonal Antibody, Selective Adhesion-Molecule Inhibitor

Use

Crohn disease: Treatment of moderately to severely active Crohn disease in patients who have had an inadequate response with, lost response to, or were intolerant to inhibitors of tumor necrosis factor-alpha (TNF-alpha) blocker or immunomodulator; or had an inadequate response with, were intolerant to, or demonstrated dependence on corticosteroids.

Ulcerative colitis Treatment of moderately to severely active ulcerative colitis in patients who have had an inadequate response with, were intolerant to inhibitors of tumor necrosis factor-alpha (TNF-alpha) blocker or immunomodulator; or had an inadequate response with, were intolerant to, or demonstrated dependence on corticosteroids.

Local Anesthetic/Vasoconstrictor Precautions No information available to require special precautions

Effects on Dental Treatment Key adverse event(s) related to dental treatment: Nasopharyngitis (13%), cough (5%), bronchitis (4%), oropharyngeal pain (3%), sinusitis (3%) have all been observed

Effects on Bleeding No information available to require special precautions

Adverse Reactions

>10%:

Central nervous system: Headache (12%)

Immunologic: Antibody development (4% to 13%; neutralizing: 2%)

Neuromuscular & skeletal: Arthralgia (12%)

Respiratory: Nasopharyngitis (13%)

1% to 10%:

Central nervous system: Fatigue (6%)

Dermatologic: Pruritus (3%), skin rash (3%)

Gastrointestinal: Nausea (9%)

Hepatic: Increased serum ALT (≥3 x ULN: <2%), increased serum AST (≥3 x ULN: <2%)

Infection: Influenza (4%)

Neuromuscular & skeletal: Back pain (4%), limb pain (3%)

Respiratory: Upper respiratory tract infection (7%), cough (5%), bronchitis (4%), oropharyngeal pain (3%), sinusitis (3%)

Miscellaneous: Fever (9%), infusion related reaction (4%)

<1%: Anaphylaxis, hepatitis, hypersensitivity reaction, increased serum bilirubin, increased serum transaminases, infection (including anal abscess, sepsis, tuberculosis, salmonella sepsis, listeria meningitis, giardiasis, cytomegaloviral colitis), malignant neoplasm (excluding dysplasia and basal cell carcinoma)

Mechanism of Action Vedolizumab is a humanized monoclonal antibody that binds to the alpha4beta7 integrin and blocks the interaction of alpha4beta7 integrin with mucosal addressin cell adhesion molecule-1 (MAdCAM-1) and inhibits the migration of memory T-lymphocytes across the endothelium into inflamed gastrointestinal parenchymal tissue. The interaction of the alpha4beta7 integrin with MAdCAM-1 has been implicated as an important contributor to the chronic inflammation that is a hallmark of ulcerative colitis and Crohn disease.

Pharmacodynamics/Kinetics

Half-life Elimination 25 days (serum, at 300 mg dosage)

Pregnancy Risk Factor B

Pregnancy Considerations Adverse events have not been observed in animal reproduction studies. Monoclonal antibodies are transported across the placenta in a linear fashion as pregnancy progresses, with the largest amount transferred during the third trimester. Any adverse pregnancy effect would likely be greater during the second and third trimesters of pregnancy.

Health care providers are encouraged to enroll women exposed to vedolizumab during pregnancy in a pregnancy exposure registry. Information about the registry can be obtained by calling 1-877-825-3327.

Vemurafenib (vem ue RAF e nib)

Related Information

Clinical Risk Related to Drugs Prolonging QT Interval *on page 1772*

Brand Names: US Zelboraf

Brand Names: Canada Zelboraf

Pharmacologic Category Antineoplastic Agent, BRAF Kinase Inhibitor

Use Melanoma, unresectable or metastatic: Treatment of unresectable or metastatic melanoma in patients with a BRAFV600E mutation (as detected by an approved test).

Local Anesthetic/Vasoconstrictor Precautions Vemurafenib is one of the drugs confirmed to prolong the QT interval and is accepted as having a risk of causing torsade de pointes. The risk of drug-induced torsade de pointes is extremely low when a single QT interval prolonging drug is prescribed. In terms of epinephrine, it is not known what effect vasoconstrictors in the local anesthetic regimen will have in patients with a known history of congenital prolonged QT interval or in patients taking any medication that prolongs the QT interval. Until more information is obtained, it is suggested that the clinician consult with the physician prior to the use of a vasoconstrictor in suspected patients, and that the vasoconstrictor (epinephrine, mepivacaine, and levonordefrin [Carbocaine® 2% with Neo-Cobefrin®]) be used with caution.

Effects on Dental Treatment Key adverse event(s) related to dental treatment: Taste alteration has been reported

Effects on Bleeding Does not cause significant hematologic toxicity.

Adverse Reactions

>10%:

Cardiovascular: Peripheral edema (17% to 23%)

Central nervous system: Fatigue (38% to 54%; grade 3: 2% to 4%), headache (23% to 27%)

Dermatologic: Skin rash (37% to 52%; grade 3: 7% to 8%), skin photosensitivity (33% to 49%; grade 3: 3%), alopecia (36% to 45%), pruritus (23% to 30%; grade 3: 2%), hyperkeratosis (24% to 28%; actinic: 8% to 17%; seborrheic: 10% to 14%; pilaris: ≤10%), maculopapular rash (9% to 21%; grade 3: 2% to 6%), xeroderma (16% to 19%), sunburn (10% to 14%), erythema (8% to 14%), papular rash (5% to 13%)

Gastrointestinal: Nausea (35% to 37%; grade 3: 2%), diarrhea (28% to 29%; grade 3: <1%), vomiting (18% to 26%; grade 3: 1% to 2%), decreased appetite (18% to 21%), constipation (12% to 16%), dysgeusia (11% to 14%)

Hematologic & oncologic: Cutaneous papilloma (21% to 30%), squamous cell carcinoma of skin (24%; grade 3: 22% to 24%)

Hepatic: Increased gamma-glutamyl transferase (5% to 15%)

Neuromuscular & skeletal: Arthralgia (53% to 67%; grade 3: 4% to 8%), myalgia (13% to 24%; grade 3: <1%), limb pain (9% to 18%), back pain (8% to 11%; grade 3: <1%), musculoskeletal pain (8% to 11%), weakness (2% to 11%)

Renal: Increased serum creatinine (up to 3x ULN: 26%; greater than 3x ULN: 1%)

Respiratory: Cough (8% to 12%)

Miscellaneous: Fever (17% to 19%)

1% to 10%:

Cardiovascular: Atrial fibrillation, hypotension, prolonged Q-T interval on ECG, retinal vein occlusion, vasculitis

Central nervous system: Cranial nerve palsy (facial), dizziness, peripheral neuropathy

Dermatologic: Erythema nodosum, folliculitis, palmar-plantar erythrodysesthesia, Stevens-Johnson syndrome, toxic epidermal necrolysis

Endocrine & metabolic: Weight loss

Hematologic & oncologic: Basal cell carcinoma, malignant melanoma (new primary), squamous cell carcinoma (oropharyngeal)

Hepatic: Increased serum alkaline phosphatase, increased serum ALT, increased serum AST, increased serum bilirubin
Hypersensitivity: Anaphylaxis, hypersensitivity
Neuromuscular & skeletal: Arthritis
Ophthalmic: Blurred vision, iritis, photophobia, uveitis

<1%, postmarketing, and/or case reports: Acute interstitial nephritis, acute renal failure, acute tubular necrosis, chronic myelomonocytic leukemia with NRAS mutation (progression of preexisting condition), drug reaction with eosinophilia and systemic symptoms (DRESS syndrome), febrile neutropenia, hepatic failure, local acneiform eruptions (Ansai 2016), neutropenia, pancreatitis, panniculitis, recall skin sensitization

General Dosage Range Dosage adjustment recommended in patients who develop toxicities.

Oral: *Adults:* 960 mg twice daily

Mechanism of Action BRAF kinase inhibitor (potent) which inhibits tumor growth in melanomas by inhibiting kinase activity of certain mutated forms of BRAF, including BRAF with V600E mutation, thereby blocking cellular proliferation in melanoma cells with the mutation. Does not have activity against cells with wild-type BRAF. BRAFV600E activating mutations are present in ~50% of melanomas; V600E mutation involves the substitution of glutamic acid for valine at amino acid 600.

Pharmacodynamics/Kinetics

Half-life Elimination 57 hours (range: 30 to 120 hours)

Time to Peak ~3 hours

Pregnancy Considerations Adverse effects were not demonstrated in animal reproduction studies. However, based on the mechanism of action, vemurafenib may cause fetal harm if administered during pregnancy or in patients who become pregnant during treatment. Women of reproductive potential should use effective contraception methods during treatment and for at least 2 weeks after the last dose.

Prescribing and Access Restrictions Available through specialty pharmacies. Further information may be obtained from the manufacturer, Genentech, at 1-888-249-4918, or at http://www.zelboraf.com.

Dental Comment See Local Anesthetic/Vasoconstrictor Precautions

Venetoclax (ven ET oh klax)

Brand Names: US Venclexta; Venclexta Starting Pack

Brand Names: Canada Venclexta

Pharmacologic Category Antineoplastic Agent; Antineoplastic Agent, BCL-2 Inhibitor

Use Chronic lymphocytic leukemia: Treatment of chronic lymphocytic leukemia (CLL) in patients with 17p deletion (as detected by an approved test) who have received at least one prior therapy.

Local Anesthetic/Vasoconstrictor Precautions No information available to require special precautions

Effects on Dental Treatment No significant effects or complications reported

Effects on Bleeding Chemotherapy may result in significant myelosuppression, potentially including significant reduction in platelet counts (thrombocytopenia grades 3/4:15%) and altered hemostasis. Since there is the potential for bleeding in patients under active treatment with venetoclax, medical consult is suggested.

Adverse Reactions

>10%:

Cardiovascular: Peripheral edema (11%; grades 3/4: <1%)
Central nervous system: Fatigue (21%; grades 3/4: 2%), headache (15%; grades 3/4: <1%)
Endocrine & metabolic: Hyperkalemia (20%; ≥ grade 3: 2%), hyperphosphatemia (15%; ≥ grade 3: 3%), hypokalemia (12%; grades 3/4: 4%)
Gastrointestinal: Diarrhea (35%; grades 3/4: <1%), nausea (33%; grades 3/4: <1%), vomiting (15%; grades 3/4: <1%), constipation (14%)
Hematologic & oncologic: Neutropenia (45%; grades 3/4: 41%), anemia (29%; grades 3/4: 18%), thrombocytopenia (22%; grades 3/4: 15%)
Respiratory: Upper respiratory tract infection (22%; grades 3/4: 1%), cough (13%)
Miscellaneous: Fever (16%; grades 3/4: <1%)

1% to 10%:

Endocrine & metabolic: Hypocalcemia (9%; ≥ grade 3: 3%), hyperuricemia (6%; ≥ grade 3: 2%)
Hematologic & oncologic: Tumor lysis syndrome (2 to 3 week ramp-up phase: 12%; 5 week ramp-up phase: 6%; ≥ grade 3: 6%), febrile neutropenia (5%; grades 3/4: 5%)
Neuromuscular & skeletal: Back pain (10%; grades 3/4: <1%)
Respiratory: Pneumonia (8%; grades 3/4: 5%)

General Dosage Range Dosage adjustment recommended in patients on concomitant therapy or who develop toxicities.

Oral: *Adults:* Initial: 20 mg once daily (week 1), then 50 mg once daily (week 2), then 100 mg once daily (week 3), then 200 mg once daily (week 4), then 400 mg once daily thereafter.

Mechanism of Action Venetoclax has cytotoxic activity in tumor cells which overexpress BCL-2. Venetoclax selectively inhibits the anti-apoptotic protein BCL-2, which is overexpressed in chronic lymphocytic leukemia (CLL) cells. BCL-2 mediates tumor cell survival and has been associated with chemotherapy resistance. Venetoclax binds directly to the BCL-2 protein, displacing pro-apoptotic proteins and restoring the apoptotic process.

Pharmacodynamics/Kinetics

Half-life Elimination ~26 hours

Time to Peak 5 to 8 hours

Pregnancy Considerations Based on the mechanism of action and data from animal reproduction studies, venetoclax is expected to cause fetal harm if administered during pregnancy. Females of reproductive potential should have a pregnancy test prior to therapy, and use effective contraception during treatment and for at least 30 days after the final dose. Based on animal data, venetoclax may compromise fertility in males.

Prescribing and Access Restrictions Available through specialty pharmacies and distributors. Further information may be obtained from the manufacturer.

Venlafaxine (ven la FAX een)

Related Information

Dentin Hypersensitivity, Acid Erosion, High Caries Index, Management of Alveolar Osteitis, and Xerostomia *on page 1857*
Vasoconstrictor Interactions With Antidepressants *on page 1913*

Brand Names: US Effexor XR

Brand Names: Canada ACT Venlafaxine XR; Apo-Venlafaxine XR; Dom-Venlafaxine XR; Effexor XR;

GD-Venlafaxine XR; Mylan-Venlafaxine XR; PMS-Venlafaxine XR; Ran-Venlafaxine XR; Riva-Venlafaxine XR; Sandoz-Venlafaxine XR; Teva-Venlafaxine XR; Venlafaxine XR

Pharmacologic Category Antidepressant, Serotonin/Norepinephrine Reuptake Inhibitor

Use

Generalized anxiety disorder (extended-release capsules only): Treatment of generalized anxiety disorder (GAD)

Major depressive disorder: Treatment of major depressive disorder (MDD)

Panic disorder (extended-release capsules only): Treatment of panic disorder, with or without agoraphobia

Social anxiety disorder (extended-release capsules and tablets only): Treatment of social anxiety disorder, also known as social phobia

Local Anesthetic/Vasoconstrictor Precautions Although venlafaxine is not a tricyclic antidepressant, it does block norepinephrine reuptake within CNS synapses as part of its mechanisms. It has been suggested that vasoconstrictor be administered with caution and to monitor vital signs in dental patients taking antidepressants that affect norepinephrine in this way. This is particularly important in patients taking venlafaxine, which has been noted to produce a sustained increase in diastolic blood pressure and heart rate as a side effect.

Effects on Dental Treatment Key adverse event(s) related to dental treatment: Significant xerostomia (normal salivary flow resumes upon discontinuation); may contribute to oral discomfort, especially in the elderly; taste perversion. See Effects on Bleeding.

Effects on Bleeding May impair platelet aggregation resulting in increased risk of bleeding events, particularly if used concomitantly with aspirin, NSAIDs, warfarin, or other anticoagulants. Bleeding related to SSRI use has been reported to range from relatively minor bruising and epistaxis to life-threatening hemorrhage. Routine interruption of therapy for most dental procedures is not warranted. In medically complicated patients or extensive oral surgery, the decision to interrupt therapy must be based on the risk to benefit in an individual patient and a medical consult is suggested. If therapy is continued without interruption, the clinician should anticipate the potential for a prolonged bleeding time.

Adverse Reactions Note: Actual frequency may be dependent upon formulation and/or indication.

>10%:

Central nervous system: Headache (38%), insomnia (15% to 24%), drowsiness (12% to 20%), dizziness (11% to 20%)

Dermatologic: Diaphoresis (10% to 14%)

Endocrine & metabolic: Weight loss (children & adolescents 18% to 47%; adults 2% to 7%)

Gastrointestinal: Nausea (21% to 35%), xerostomia (12% to 17%), anorexia (8% to 17%)

Genitourinary: Abnormal ejaculation (8% to 19%)

Neuromuscular & skeletal: Weakness (8% to 19%)

1% to 10%:

Cardiovascular: Vasodilation (3% to 4%), hypertension (dose related; 3% in patients receiving <100 mg/day, up to 13% in patients receiving >300 mg/day), palpitations (3%), chest pain (≥1%), edema (≥1%), tachycardia (≥1%)

Central nervous system: Nervousness (6% to 10%), abnormal dreams (3% to 7%), anxiety (5%), yawning (3% to 5%), agitation (3%), depression (3%), twitching (3%), anorgasmia (females: 2% to 4%; more common in males), paresthesia (2% to 3%), abnormality in thinking (≥1%), amnesia (≥1%), chills (≥1%), confusion (≥1%), depersonalization (≥1%), hypoesthesia (≥1%), migraine (≥1%), trismus (≥1%), vertigo (≥1%)

Dermatologic: Pruritus (1%), ecchymoses (≥1%)

Endocrine & metabolic: Decreased libido (3% to 8%), hypercholesterolemia (5%), orgasm abnormal (2% to 5%), albuminuria (≥1%), weight gain (≥1%), increased serum triglycerides

Gastrointestinal: Constipation (8% to 10%), diarrhea (8%), dyspepsia (7%), abdominal pain (6%), vomiting (3% to 5%), flatulence (4%), dysgeusia (≥1%), increased appetite (≥1%)

Genitourinary: Impotence (4% to 6%), urinary disorder (≥1%)

Neuromuscular & skeletal: Tremor (4% to 5%), neck pain (≥1%)

Ophthalmic: Visual disturbance (4% to 5%), accommodation disturbance (≥1%), mydriasis (≥1%)

Respiratory: Pharyngitis (7%), dyspnea (≥1%), increased cough (≥1%)

Miscellaneous: Accidental injury (4%), fever (≥1%)

<1%, postmarketing, and/or case reports: Abdominal distention, abnormal behavior, abnormal gait, abnormal healing, abortion, acne vulgaris, adjustment disorder, ageusia, agranulocytosis, akathisia, akinesia, alcohol abuse, alcohol intolerance, alcohol intoxication, alopecia, altered sense of smell, amenorrhea, anaphylaxis, anemia, angina pectoris, angioedema, angle-closure glaucoma, anuria, aortic aneurysm, apathy, aphasia, aplastic anemia, appendicitis, arteritis, arthritis, arthropathy, asthma, ataxia, atelectasis, atrophic striae, attempted suicide, bacteremia, balanitis, basophilia, bigeminy, biliary colic, bladder pain, blepharitis, bone spur, bradycardia, bradykinesia, breast engorgement, breast hypertrophy, bruxism, buccoglossal syndrome, bundle branch block, bursitis, candidiasis, capillary fragility, carcinoma, cardiac arrest, cardiac arrhythmia (including atrial fibrillation, supraventricular tachycardia, ventricular extrasystoles, ventricular fibrillation, ventricular tachycardia, and torsades de pointes), cardiovascular disease (mitral valve and circulatory disturbance), cataract, catatonia, cellulitis, central nervous system stimulation, cerebral ischemia, cerebrovascular accident, cervicitis, changes in LDH, cheilitis, chest congestion, chills, cholecystitis, cholelithiasis, chromatopsia, colitis, congenital anomalies, congestive heart failure, conjunctival edema, conjunctivitis, contact dermatitis, corneal lesion, coronary artery disease, crystalluria, cyanosis, cystitis, deafness, decreased pupillary reflex, deep vein thrombosis, dehydration, delirium, delusions, dementia, diabetes mellitus, diplopia, duodenitis, dysphagia, dyspnea, dystonia, dysuria, ECG abnormality (including QT prolongation), eczema, electric shock-like sensation, emotional lability, endometriosis, enlargement of salivary glands, eosinophilia, epistaxis, eructation, erythema multiforme, erythema nodosum, esophageal spasm, esophagitis, euphoria, exfoliative dermatitis, exophthalmos, extrapyramidal reaction, extrasystoles, eye pain, facial paralysis, fibrocystic breast disease, first degree atrioventricular block, furunculosis, galactorrhea, gastritis, gastroenteritis, gastroesophageal reflux disease, gastrointestinal ulcer, gingivitis, glossitis, glycosuria, goiter, gout, granuloma, Guillain-Barré syndrome, gynecomastia (male), hair discoloration, hallucination, hematemesis, hematoma, hematuria,

hemochromatosis, hemoptysis, hemorrhage (eye, GI, gum, mucocutaneous, rectal, retinal, subconjunctival, uterine, vaginal), hemorrhoids, hepatic effects (including GGT elevation; abnormalities of unspecified liver function tests; liver damage, necrosis, or failure; and fatty liver), hepatitis, hirsutism, homicidal ideation, hostility, hyperacidity, hyperacusis, hyperbilirubinemia, hypercalciuria, hyperesthesia, hyperglycemia, hyperkalemia, hyperkinesia, hyperlipidemia, hypermenorrhea, hyperphosphatemia, hyperreflexia, hyperthyroidism, hypertonia, hyperuricemia, hyperventilation, hypocholesterolemia, hypoglycemia, hypohidrosis, hypokalemia, hypokinesia, hypomenorrhea, hyponatremia, hypophosphatemia, hypoproteinemia, hyporeflexia, hypotension, hypothyroidism, hypotonia, hypoventilation, hypoxia, hysteria, ileitis, impulse control disorder, increased blood urea nitrogen, increased creatine phosphokinase, increased energy, increased intraocular pressure (open-angle glaucoma) (Botha 2016), increased libido, increased serum alkaline phosphatase, increased serum ALT, increased serum AST, increased serum creatinine, increased serum prolactin, increased thirst, intentional injury, interstitial pulmonary disease (including eosinophilic pneumonia), intestinal obstruction, involuntary body movements, jaundice, keratitis, labyrinthitis, lactation (female), laryngeal edema, laryngismus, laryngitis, leg cramps, leukocytosis, leukoderma, leukopenia, leukorrhea, lichenoid dermatitis, liver tenderness, loose stools, loss of consciousness, lymphadenopathy, lymphocytosis, maculopapular rash, malaise, manic reaction, mastalgia, mastitis, melena, menopause, miliaria, miosis, motion sickness, multiple myeloma, muscle cramps, muscle spasm, musculoskeletal stiffness, myasthenia, myocardial infarction, myoclonus, myopathy, neck stiffness, nephrolithiasis, neuralgia, neuritis, neuropathy, neutropenia, night sweats, nipple discharge, nocturia, nystagmus, oliguria, onychia sicca, oral candidiasis, oral mucosa ulcer, oral paresthesia, orchitis, orthostatic hypotension, ostealgia, osteoporosis, osteosclerosis, otitis externa, otitis media, ovarian cyst, pallor, pancreatitis, pancytopenia, panic, papilledema, paranoia, paresis, parotitis, pathological fracture, pelvic pain, periodontitis, peripheral vascular disease, petechial rash, plantar fasciitis, pleurisy, pneumonia, polyuria, proctitis, prolonged bleeding time, prolonged erection, prostatic disease, pruritic rash, psoriasis, psychosis, psychotic depression, pulmonary embolism, purpura, pustular rash, pyelonephritis, pyuria, rectal disease, renal failure, renal function abnormality, renal pain, rhabdomyolysis, rheumatoid arthritis, rupture of tendon, salpingitis, scleritis, seborrhea, seizure, serotonin syndrome, SIADH, sialorrhea, sinus arrhythmia, skin atrophy, skin discoloration, skin hypertrophy, skin photosensitivity, sleep apnea, speech disturbance, Stevens-Johnson syndrome, stomatitis, stupor, suicidal ideation (reported at a frequency up to 2% in children/adolescents with major depressive disorder), syncope, tenosynovitis, thrombocythemia, thrombocytopenia, thrombophlebitis, thyroiditis, thyroid nodule, tinnitus, tongue discoloration, tongue edema, torticollis, toxic epidermal necrolysis, uremia, urinary incontinence, urinary retention, urinary urgency, urolithiasis, urticaria, uterine spasm, uveitis, vaginal dryness, vaginitis, vesicobullous dermatitis, visual field defect, voice disorder, withdrawal syndrome, xeroderma, xerophthalmia

General Dosage Range Dosage adjustment recommended in patients with hepatic or renal impairment

Oral:

Extended release: *Adults:* Initial: 37.5 to 75 mg/day once daily; Usual dosage: 75 to 225 mg/day once daily (recommended maximum: 225 mg/day)

Immediate release: *Adults:* Initial: 75 mg/day in 2 to 3 divided doses; Usual dosage: 75 to 375 mg/day in 2 to 3 divided doses (recommended maximum: 375 mg/day)

Mechanism of Action Venlafaxine and its active metabolite, O-desmethylvenlafaxine (ODV), are potent inhibitors of neuronal serotonin and norepinephrine reuptake and weak inhibitors of dopamine reuptake. Venlafaxine and ODV have no significant activity for muscarinic cholinergic, H_1-histaminergic, or alpha$_2$-adrenergic receptors. Venlafaxine and ODV do not possess MAO-inhibitory activity. Venlafaxine functions like an SSRI in low doses (37.5 mg/day) and as a dual mechanism agent affecting serotonin and norepinephrine at doses above 225 mg/day (Harvey 2000; Kelsey 1996).

Pharmacodynamics/Kinetics

Half-life Elimination Venlafaxine: 5 ± 2 hours (immediate-release), 10.7 ± 3.2 hours (extended-release); ODV: 11 ± 2 hours (immediate-release), 12.5 ± 3 hours (extended-release); prolonged with cirrhosis (venlafaxine: ~30%, ODV: ~60%), renal impairment (venlafaxine: ~50%, ODV: ~40%), and during dialysis (venlafaxine: ~180%, ODV: ~142%)

Time to Peak

Immediate release: Venlafaxine: 2 hours, ODV: 3 hours

Extended release: Venlafaxine: 6.3 ± 2.3 hours, ODV: 11.6 ± 2.9 hours

Pregnancy Risk Factor C

Pregnancy Considerations Adverse events have been observed in some animal reproduction studies. Venlafaxine and its active metabolite ODV cross the human placenta. An increased risk of teratogenic effects following venlafaxine exposure during pregnancy has not been observed, based on available data. The risk of spontaneous abortion may be increased. Neonatal seizures and neonatal abstinence syndrome have been noted in case reports following maternal use of venlafaxine during pregnancy. Nonteratogenic effects in the newborn following SSRI/SNRI exposure late in the third trimester include respiratory distress, cyanosis, apnea, seizures, temperature instability, feeding difficulty, vomiting, hypoglycemia, hyper- or hypotonia, hyper-reflexia, jitteriness, irritability, constant crying, and tremor. Symptoms may be due to the toxicity of the SNRI or a discontinuation syndrome and may be consistent with serotonin syndrome associated with treatment. The long-term effects of in utero SNRI/SSRI exposure on infant development and behavior are not known.

Due to pregnancy-induced physiologic changes, some pharmacokinetic parameters of venlafaxine may be altered. Women should be monitored for decreased efficacy. The ACOG recommends that therapy with SSRIs or SNRIs during pregnancy be individualized; treatment of depression during pregnancy should incorporate the clinical expertise of the mental health clinician, obstetrician, primary health care provider, and pediatrician. According to the American Psychiatric Association (APA), the risks of medication treatment should be weighed against other treatment options and untreated depression. For women who discontinue antidepressant medications during pregnancy and who may be at high risk for postpartum depression, the medications can be restarted following delivery. Treatment algorithms have been developed by the ACOG and the APA for the management of depression in women prior to conception and during pregnancy.

Pregnant women exposed to antidepressants during pregnancy are encouraged to enroll in the National Pregnancy Registry for Antidepressants (NPRAD). Women 18 to 45 years of age or their health care providers may contact the registry by calling 844-405-6185. Enrollment should be done as early in pregnancy as possible.

Verapamil (ver AP a mil)

Related Information

Calcium Channel Blockers and Gingival Hyperplasia *on page 1908*

Cardiovascular Diseases *on page 1752*

Brand Names: US Calan; Calan SR; Isoptin SR [DSC]; Verelan; Verelan PM

Brand Names: Canada Alti-Verapamil; Apo-Verap; Apo-Verap SR; Covera-HS; Dom-Verapamil SR; Isoptin SR; Med Verapamil; Mylan-Verapamil; Mylan-Verapamil SR; Novo-Veramil; Novo-Veramil SR; Nu-Verap SR; Nu-Verp; Penta-Verapamil; PHL-Verapamil SR; PMS-Verapamil SR; PRO-Verapamil SR; Riva-Verapamil SR; Taro-Verapamil; Verapamil Hydrochloride Injection, USP; Verapamil SR; Verelan

Pharmacologic Category Antianginal Agent; Antiarrhythmic Agent, Class IV; Antihypertensive; Calcium Channel Blocker; Calcium Channel Blocker, Nondihydropyridine

Use

Angina: Immediate-release tablet: Treatment of angina at rest, including vasospastic (Prinzmetal variant) angina and unstable (crescendo, preinfarction) angina; treatment of chronic stable angina (classic effort-associated angina).

Atrial fibrillation (rate control):

Immediate-release tablet: To control ventricular rate at rest and during stress in chronic atrial flutter and/or fibrillation.

IV: Temporary control of rapid ventricular rate in atrial flutter and/or atrial fibrillation (except when the atrial flutter and/or atrial fibrillation are associated with accessory bypass tracts [Wolff-Parkinson-White and Lown-Ganong-Levine syndromes]).

Hypertension: Immediate release tablet/ER capsule and tablet: Management of hypertension.

Paroxysmal supraventricular tachycardia prophylaxis: Immediate-release tablet: Prophylaxis of repetitive paroxysmal supraventricular tachycardia (PSVT).

Supraventricular tachycardias: IV: Rapid conversion to sinus rhythm of PSVT, including those associated with accessory bypass tracts (Wolff-Parkinson-White and Lown-Ganong-Levine syndromes).

Guideline recommendations:

Acute coronary syndrome (ACS): The AHA/ACC guidelines for the management of non-ST-elevation ACS recommend a nondihydropyridine calcium channel blocker (eg, verapamil) to treat ongoing ischemia if beta-blocker therapy is ineffective or contraindicated and in the absence of left ventricular dysfunction, increased risk for cardiogenic shock, PR interval >0.24 seconds, or second- or third-degree AV block (without a pacemaker) (ACC/AHA [Amsterdam 2014]).

Hypertension: The 2014 guideline for the management of high blood pressure in adults (JNC 8) recommends initiation of pharmacologic treatment to lower blood pressure for the following patients (JNC 8 [James 2013]):

- Patients ≥60 years with systolic blood pressure (SBP) ≥150 mm Hg or diastolic blood pressure (DBP) ≥90 mm Hg. Goal of therapy is SBP <150 mm Hg and DBP <90 mm Hg.
- Patients <60 years with SBP ≥140 mm Hg or DBP ≥90 mm Hg. Goal of therapy is SBP <140 mm Hg and DBP <90 mm Hg.
- Patients ≥18 years with diabetes with SBP ≥140 mm Hg or DBP ≥90 mm Hg. Goal of therapy is SBP <140 mm Hg and DBP <90 mm Hg.
- Patients ≥18 years with chronic kidney disease (CKD) with SBP ≥140 mm Hg or DBP ≥90 mm Hg. Goal of therapy is SBP <140 mm Hg and DBP <90 mm Hg.

Chronic kidney disease (CKD) and hypertension: Regardless of race or diabetes status, the use of an ACE inhibitor (ACEI) or angiotensin receptor blocker (ARB) as initial therapy is recommended to improve kidney outcomes. In the general nonblack population (without CKD) including those with diabetes, initial antihypertensive treatment should consist of a thiazide-type diuretic, calcium channel blocker, ACEI, or ARB. In the general black population (without CKD) including those with diabetes, initial antihypertensive treatment should consist of a thiazide-type diuretic or a calcium channel blocker instead of an ACEI or ARB.

Coronary artery disease (CAD) and hypertension: The American Heart Association, American College of Cardiology and American Society of Hypertension (AHA/ACC/ASH) 2015 scientific statement for the treatment of hypertension in patients with coronary artery disease (CAD) recommends that a non-dihydropyridine CCB (verapamil, diltiazem) may be used as a substitute for a beta blocker in patients who have an intolerance or contraindication to beta blockers with ongoing ischemia, hypertension and chronic stable angina, or if angina or hypertension continues to be uncontrolled while receiving standard therapies (eg, beta blocker). However, a non-dihydropyridine CCB (eg, verapamil, diltiazem) should be avoided in patients with LV dysfunction or heart failure (with reduced ejection fraction). A BP target of <140/90 mm Hg is reasonable for the secondary prevention of cardiovascular events. A lower target BP (<130/80 mm Hg) may be appropriate in some individuals with CAD, previous MI, stroke or transient ischemic attack, or CAD risk equivalents (AHA/ACC/ASH [Rosendorff 2015]).

Supraventricular tachycardia: The American College of Cardiology, American Heart Association, and Heart Rhythm Society (ACC/AHA/HRS) supraventricular tachycardia (SVT) guidelines recommends IV verapamil for the acute treatment (ie, conversion) of a variety of SVTs (atrioventricular nodal reentrant tachycardia [AVNRT], atrioventricular reentrant tachycardia [AVRT], focal atrial tachycardia [AT], multifocal atrial tachycardia [MAT]) in hemodynamically stable patients. Oral verapamil is effective and recommended for the ongoing management of hemodynamically stable patients with symptomatic supraventricular tachycardia (AVNRT, AVRT, focal AT, MAT) without pre-excitation in patients who are not candidates for, or prefer not to undergo, catheter ablation. Oral verapamil may also be useful for acute rate control in hemodynamically-stable patients with atrial flutter (ACC/AHA/HRS [Page 2015])

Local Anesthetic/Vasoconstrictor Precautions No information available to require special precautions

Effects on Dental Treatment Key adverse event(s) related to dental treatment: Gingival hyperplasia. Calcium channel blockers (CCB) have been reported to cause gingival hyperplasia (GH). Verapamil-induced GH has appeared 11 months or more after subjects took daily doses of 240-360 mg. The severity of hyperplastic syndrome does not seem to be dose dependent. Gingivectomy is only successful if CCB therapy is discontinued. GH regresses markedly 1 week after CCB discontinuance with all symptoms resolving in 2 months. If a patient must continue CCB therapy, begin a program of professional cleaning and patient plaque control to minimize severity and growth rate of gingival tissue.

Effects on Bleeding No information available to require special precautions

Adverse Reactions

>10%:

Central nervous system: Headache (1% to 12%)

Gastrointestinal: Gingival hyperplasia (≤19%), constipation (7% to 12%)

1% to 10%:

Cardiovascular: Peripheral edema (1% to 4%), hypotension (3%), cardiac failure (≤2%), atrioventricular block (1% to 2%), bradycardia (heart rate <50 bpm: 1%), flushing (1%), angina pectoris (oral: ≤1%), atrioventricular dissociation (oral: ≤1%), cerebrovascular accident (oral: ≤1%), chest pain (oral: ≤1%), claudication (oral: ≤1%), ECG abnormality (oral: ≤1%), myocardial infarction (oral: ≤1%), palpitations (oral: ≤1%), syncope (oral: ≤1%)

Central nervous system: Fatigue (2% to 5%), dizziness (1% to 5%), lethargy (3%), pain (2%), paresthesia (1%), sleep disorder (1%), confusion (oral: ≤1%), drowsiness (oral: ≤1%; IV: <1%), equilibrium disturbance (oral: ≤1%), extrapyramidal reaction (oral: ≤1%), insomnia (oral: ≤1%), psychosis (oral: ≤1%), shakiness (oral: ≤1%)

Dermatologic: Skin rash (1% to 2%), alopecia (oral: ≤1%), diaphoresis (oral: ≤1%), erythema multiforme (oral: ≤1%), hyperkeratosis (oral: ≤1%), macular eruption (oral: ≤1%), Stevens-Johnson syndrome (oral: ≤1%), urticaria (oral: ≤1%)

Endocrine & metabolic: Galactorrhea (oral: ≤1%), gynecomastia (oral: ≤1%), hyperprolactinemia (oral: ≤1%), spotty menstruation (oral: ≤1%)

Gastrointestinal: Dyspepsia (3%), nausea (1% to 3%), diarrhea (2%), abdominal distress (oral: ≤1%), gastrointestinal distress (oral: ≤1%), xerostomia (oral: ≤1%)

Genitourinary: Impotence (oral: ≤1%)

Hematologic & oncologic: Bruise (oral: ≤1%), purpuric vasculitis (oral: ≤1%)

Hepatic: Increased liver enzymes (1%)

Neuromuscular & skeletal: Myalgia (1%), arthralgia (oral: ≤1%), muscle cramps (oral: ≤1%), weakness (oral: ≤1%)

Ophthalmic: Blurred vision (oral: ≤1%)

Otic: Tinnitus (oral: ≤1%)

Renal: Polyuria (oral: ≤1%)

Respiratory: Flu-like symptoms (4%), pulmonary edema (≤2%), dyspnea (1%)

<1%, postmarketing, and/or case reports: Asystole, bronchospasm (IV administration), depression (IV administration), diaphoresis (IV administration), drowsiness (IV administration), electromechanical dissociation, eosinophilia, exfoliative dermatitis, gastrointestinal obstruction, hair discoloration, laryngospasm (IV administration), muscle fatigue (IV administration), paralytic ileus, Parkinsonian-like syndrome, pruritus (IV administration), respiratory failure (IV administration), rotary nystagmus (IV administration), seizure (IV administration), shock, urticaria (IV administration), vertigo (IV administration), ventricular fibrillation

General Dosage Range

IV:

Children and Adolescents 1 to 15 years: 0.1 to 0.3 mg/kg/dose (maximum: 5 mg/dose); may repeat dose (maximum for second dose: 10 mg)

Adults: 0.075 to 0.15 mg/kg (usual dose: 5 to 10 mg); may give an additional 10 mg after 15 to 30 minutes

Oral:

Extended release:

Adults: Initial: 180 to 240 mg once daily (maximum: 480 mg/day)

Elderly: Initial: 120 mg once daily in the morning or 100 mg once daily at bedtime

Immediate release:

Adults: Maintenance: 80 to 480 mg/day in 3 to 4 divided doses (maximum: 480 mg/day)

Elderly: Initial: 40 mg 3 times daily

Mechanism of Action Inhibits calcium ion from entering the "slow channels" or select voltage-sensitive areas of vascular smooth muscle and myocardium during depolarization; produces relaxation of coronary vascular smooth muscle and coronary vasodilation; increases myocardial oxygen delivery in patients with vasospastic angina; slows automaticity and conduction of AV node.

Pharmacodynamics/Kinetics

Onset of Action Oral (immediate release tablets): Peak effect: Oral: Immediate release: 1 to 2 hours (Singh 1978); IV bolus: 3 to 5 minutes

Duration of Action Oral: Immediate release tablets: 6 to 8 hours; IV: 10 to 20 minutes (Singh 1978)

Half-life Elimination

Injection: Terminal: 2 to 5 hours.

Oral:

Immediate release: Single dose: 2.8 to 7.4 hours; Multiple doses: 4.5 to 12 hours

Extended release: ~12 hours

Severe hepatic impairment: 14 to 16 hours

Time to Peak Serum: Oral:

Immediate release: 1 to 2 hours

Extended release:

Calan SR: 5.21 hours

Verelan: 7 to 9 hours

Verelan PM: ~11 hours; Drug release delayed ~4 to 5 hours

Pregnancy Risk Factor C

Pregnancy Considerations Adverse events have been observed in some animal reproduction studies in doses, which also caused maternal toxicity. Verapamil crosses the placenta. Use during pregnancy may cause adverse fetal effects (bradycardia, heart block, hypotension) (Tan 2001). Women with hypertrophic cardiomyopathy who are controlled with verapamil prior to pregnancy may continue therapy, but increased fetal monitoring is recommended (Gersh 2011). Verapamil may be used IV for the acute treatment of supraventricular tachycardia (SVT) in pregnant women when adenosine or beta-blockers are ineffective or contraindicated. Verapamil may also be used for the ongoing management of SVT in highly symptomatic patients. The lowest effective dose is recommended; avoid use during the first trimester if possible (Page [ACC/AHA/HRS 2015]). Untreated chronic maternal hypertension is associated with adverse events in the fetus, infant, and mother. If treatment for hypertension during pregnancy is needed, other agents are preferred (ACOG 2013). Additional guidelines are available for management of cardiovascular diseases during pregnancy (ESG [Regitz-Zagrosek 2011]).

Verteporfin (ver te POR fin)

Brand Names: US Visudyne
Brand Names: Canada Visudyne
Pharmacologic Category Ophthalmic Agent
Use

Subfoveal choroidal neovascularization: Treatment of predominantly classic subfoveal choroidal neovascularization due to age-related macular degeneration, pathologic myopia, or presumed ocular histoplasmosis.

Limitations of use: There is insufficient evidence to indicate verteporfin for the treatment of predominantly occult subfoveal choroidal neovascularization.

Local Anesthetic/Vasoconstrictor Precautions No information available to require special precautions

Effects on Dental Treatment No significant effects or complications reported

Effects on Bleeding No information available to require special precautions

Adverse Reactions

>10%:

Local: Injection site reaction (including extravasation, inflammation at injection site, local discoloration, local edema, local hemorrhage, pain at injection site, rash at injection site)

Ophthalmic: Blurred vision, decreased visual acuity, photopsia, visual field defect (including scotoma)

1% to 10%:

Cardiovascular: Atrial fibrillation, hypertension, peripheral vascular disease, varicose veins

Central nervous system: Disturbed sleep, hypoesthesia, myasthenia, vertigo

Dermatologic: Eczema, skin photosensitivity

Endocrine & metabolic: Albuminuria

Gastrointestinal: Constipation, nausea

Genitourinary: Prostatic disease

Hematologic & oncologic: Anemia, gastrointestinal carcinoma, leukocytosis, leukopenia

Hepatic: Increased liver enzymes

Neuromuscular & skeletal: Arthralgia, arthropathy, back pain (primarily during infusion), weakness

Ophthalmic: Abnormal lacrimation, blepharitis (at treatment site), cataract (at treatment site), conjunctivitis (at treatment site), conjunctival injection (at treatment site), diplopia, eye pruritus (at treatment site), severe vision loss (1% to 5%; at treatment site, with or without subretinal/retinal or vitreous hemorrhage; decrease in 4 lines or more within 7 days of treatment), xerophthalmia (at treatment site)

Otic: Hearing loss

Renal: Increased serum creatinine

Respiratory: Cough, flu-like symptoms, pharyngitis, pneumonia

Miscellaneous: Fever

Frequency not defined:

Cardiovascular: Chest pain, vasodepressor syncope

Hypersensitivity: Hypersensitivity reaction

Neuromuscular & skeletal: Musculoskeletal pain (during infusion)

Ophthalmic: Retinal detachment (nonrhegmatogenous), retinal ischemia (retinal or choroidal vessel nonperfusion), retinal pigment epithelium tear

General Dosage Range IV: *Adults:* 6 mg/m^2 body surface area

Mechanism of Action Following intravenous administration, verteporfin is transported by lipoproteins to the neovascular endothelium in the affected eye(s), including choroidal neovasculature and the retina. Verteporfin then needs to be activated by nonthermal red light, which results in local damage to the endothelium, leading to temporary choroidal vessel occlusion.

Pharmacodynamics/Kinetics

Half-life Elimination Terminal: 5 to 6 hours, biexponential

Pregnancy Risk Factor C

Pregnancy Considerations Adverse events have been observed in some animal reproduction studies.

Vigabatrin (vye GA ba trin)

Brand Names: US Sabril
Brand Names: Canada Sabril
Pharmacologic Category Anticonvulsant, Miscellaneous
Use

Infantile spasms: As monotherapy for pediatric patients 1 month to 2 years of age with infantile spasms for whom the potential benefits outweigh the potential risk of vision loss.

Refractory complex partial seizures: As adjunctive therapy for adults and pediatric patients 10 years and older with refractory complex partial seizures who have inadequately responded to several alternative treatments and for whom the potential benefits outweigh the risk of vision loss.

Local Anesthetic/Vasoconstrictor Precautions No information available to require special precautions

Effects on Dental Treatment No significant effects or complications reported

Effects on Bleeding No information available to require special precautions

Adverse Reactions Adult and pediatric information is combined unless significantly different.

>10%:

Central nervous system: Drowsiness (infants: 17% to 45%; adults: 22% to 24%), headache (33%), fatigue (23% to 28%), dizziness (21% to 24%), irritability (infants: 16% to 23%; adults: 10%), sedation (infants: 17% to 19%; adults: 2% to 4%), insomnia (infants: 10% to 12%)

Dermatologic: Skin rash (infants: 8% to 11%)

Gastrointestinal: Vomiting (infants: 14% to 20%; adults: 7%), constipation (infants: 12% to 14%; adults: 6% to 8%), diarrhea (10% to 13%)

Infection: Viral infection (infants: 19% to 20%)

Neuromuscular & skeletal: Tremor (14% to 15%)

Ophthalmic: Visual field loss (≥30%), nystagmus (13% to 15%), blurred vision (11% to 13%)

Otic: Otitis media (infants: 10% to 44%)

Respiratory: Upper respiratory tract infection (infants: 46% to 51%; adults: 7% to 9%), bronchitis (infants: 30%), pharyngitis (13% to 14%), pneumonia (infants: 11% to 13%), nasal congestion (infants: 4% to 13%)

Miscellaneous: Fever (infants: 19% to 29%; adults: 4% to 5%)

1% to 10%:

Cardiovascular: Peripheral edema (2% to 5%), edema (1%)

Central nervous system: Memory impairment (7% to 10%), ataxia (7% to 9%), disturbance in attention (5% to 9%), depression (4% to 7%), lethargy (4% to 7%), seizure (infants: 4% to 7%), confusion (4% to 6%), hypotonia (infants: 4% to 6%), status epilepticus (2% to 6%), paresthesia (5%), hyporeflexia (4% to 5%), sensory disturbance (4% to 5%), anxiety (4%), hyperreflexia (4%), hypoesthesia (3% to 4%), abnormal behavior (3%), abnormality in thinking (3%), aggressive behavior (2%), dysarthria (2%), impaired consciousness (2%), vertigo (2%)

Endocrine & metabolic: Weight gain (6% to 8%), fluid retention (2%), increased thirst (2%)

Gastrointestinal: Nausea (9% to 10%), decreased appetite (infants: 7% to 9%), viral gastroenteritis (infants: 5% to 6%), abdominal pain (3% to 5%), dyspepsia (4%), abdominal distention (2%), increased appetite (2%), hemorrhoids (2%)

Genitourinary: Dysmenorrhea (7% to 9%), urinary tract infection (4% to 6%)

Hematologic & oncologic: Bruise (3% to 4%)

Infection: Candidiasis (infants: 3% to 8%), influenza (3% to 5%)

Neuromuscular & skeletal: Arthralgia (8% to 10%), limb pain (5% to 6%), back pain (4% to 6%), weakness (5%), myalgia (3%), muscle spasm (2% to 3%), joint swelling (2%), shoulder pain (2%)

Ophthalmic: Diplopia (3% to 7%), strabismus (5%), conjunctivitis (2% to 5%), asthenopia (2%)

Otic: Tinnitus (2%)

Respiratory: Pharyngolaryngeal pain (7% to 9%), sinusitis (infants: 5% to 9%), cough (2% to 8%), sinus headache (4% to 6%), croup (infants: 1% to 5%), dyspnea (2%)

<1%, postmarketing, and/or case reports: Acute psychosis, agitation (neonates), angioedema, apathy, brain disease, cholestasis, deafness, delirium, developmental delay, dyskinesia, dystonia, esophagitis, facial edema, gastrointestinal hemorrhage, hypertonia, hypomania, laryngeal edema, maculopapular rash, malignant hyperthermia, multi-organ failure, myoclonus, optic neuritis, pruritus, psychosis, pulmonary embolism, respiratory failure, sexual disorder (delayed puberty), Stevens-Johnson syndrome, stridor, toxic epidermal necrolysis

General Dosage Range Dosage adjustment recommended in patients with renal impairment

Oral:

Infants and Children 1 month to 2 years: 50 to 150 mg/kg/day in 2 divided doses

Children and Adolescents 10 to <17 years and 25 to 60 kg: 500 to 2,000 mg daily in 2 divided doses

Children ≥10 years and >60 kg, Adolescents ≥17 years, and Adults: 1 to 3 g daily in 2 divided doses

Mechanism of Action Irreversibly inhibits gamma-aminobutyric acid transaminase (GABA-T), increasing the levels of the inhibitory compound gamma amino butyric acid (GABA) within the brain. Duration of effect is dependent upon rate of GABA-T resynthesis.

Pharmacodynamics/Kinetics

Duration of Action Resynthesis of GABA-T dependent: Variable (not strictly correlated to serum concentrations)

Half-life Elimination

Prolonged in renal impairment

Pediatric patients:

5 months to 2 years: ~5.7 hours

4 to 14 years: ~5.5 hours (Sabril Canadian product monograph)

10 to 16 years: 9.5 hours

Adult patients: 10.5 hours

Time to Peak Infants and Children 5 months to 2 years: 2.5 hours; Children and Adolescents 10 to 16 years and Adults: 1 hour (2 hours with food)

Pregnancy Risk Factor C

Pregnancy Considerations

Adverse events were observed in animal reproduction studies. Vigabatrin crosses the placenta in humans (Tran 1998). Birth defects have been reported following use in pregnancy and include: cardiac defects, limb defects, male genital malformations, fetal anticonvulsant syndrome, renal and ear abnormalities. Time of exposure or maternal dosage was not reported and information is not available relating to the incidence or types of these outcomes in comparison to the general epilepsy population. Visual field examinations have been conducted following in utero exposure in a limited number of children tested at ≥6 years of age; no visual field loss was observed in 4 children and results were inconclusive in 2 others (Lawthorn 2009; Sorri 2005).

Patients exposed to vigabatrin during pregnancy are encouraged to enroll in the North American Antiepileptic Drug (NAAED) Pregnancy Registry by calling 1-888-233-2334. Additional information is available at www.aedpregnancyregistry.org.

Prescribing and Access Restrictions As a requirement of the REMS program, access to this medication is restricted. Vigabatrin is only available in the U.S. under a special restricted distribution program (Sabril REMS program). Under the Sabril REMS program, only prescribers and pharmacies registered with the program are able to prescribe and distribute vigabatrin. Vigabatrin may only be dispensed to patients who are enrolled in and meet all conditions of the Sabril REMS program. Contact the REMS program at 1-888-457-4273.

Vilazodone (vil AZ oh done)

Related Information

Vasoconstrictor Interactions With Antidepressants *on page 1913*

Brand Names: US Viibryd; Viibryd Starter Pack

Pharmacologic Category Antidepressant, Selective Serotonin Reuptake Inhibitor/5-HT_{1A} Receptor Partial Agonist

Use Major depressive disorder: Treatment of major depressive disorder (MDD)

Local Anesthetic/Vasoconstrictor Precautions Although caution should be used in patients taking tricyclic antidepressants, no interactions have been reported with vasoconstrictors and vilazodone, a non-tricyclic antidepressant which acts to increase serotonin; no precautions appear to be needed

Effects on Dental Treatment Key adverse event(s) related to dental treatment: Xerostomia (normal salivary flow resumes upon discontinuation) and abnormal taste (see Effects on Bleeding and Dental Comment)

Effects on Bleeding May impair platelet aggregation resulting in increased risk of bleeding events, particularly if used concomitantly with aspirin, NSAIDs, warfarin, or other anticoagulants. Bleeding related to SSRI use has been reported to range from relatively minor bruising and epistaxis to life-threatening hemorrhage. Routine interruption of therapy for most dental procedures is not warranted. In medically complicated patients or extensive oral surgery, the decision to interrupt therapy must be based on the risk to benefit in an individual patient and a medical consult is suggested. If therapy is continued without interruption, the clinician should anticipate the potential for a prolonged bleeding time.

Adverse Reactions

>10%:

Central nervous system: Headache (15%)

Gastrointestinal: Diarrhea (26% to 29%), nausea (22% to 24%)

1% to 10%:

Cardiovascular: Palpitations (1% to 2%)

Central nervous system: Dizziness (6% to 8%), insomnia (6% to 7%), drowsiness (4% to 5%), fatigue (4%), abnormal dreams (3%), restlessness (2% to 3%), paresthesia (2%), delayed ejaculation (1% to 2%), migraine (≥1%), sedation (>1%), panic attack (≤1%), ventricular premature contractions (≤1%)

Dermatologic: Hyperhidrosis (≤1%), night sweats (≤1%)

Endocrine & metabolic: Decreased libido (2% to 4%), weight gain (2%)

Gastrointestinal: Xerostomia (7% to 8%), abdominal pain (4% to 7%), vomiting (4% to 5%), dyspepsia (3%), flatulence (3%), increased appetite (3%), abdominal distension (2%), gastroenteritis (2%)

Genitourinary: Erectile dysfunction (≤3%), orgasm disturbance (1% to 2%)

Neuromuscular & skeletal: Arthralgia (2%), tremor (>1%)

Ophthalmic: Blurred vision (≤1%), xerophthalmia (≤1%)

<1%, postmarketing, and/or case reports: Acute pancreatitis, angle-closure glaucoma, cataract, hallucination, hyponatremia, irritability, mania, seizure, serotonin syndrome, skin rash, sleep paralysis, suicidal ideation, suicidal tendencies, urticaria

General Dosage Range Dosage adjustment recommended in patients on concomitant therapy

Oral: *Adults:* 10 to 40 mg once daily

Mechanism of Action Vilazodone inhibits CNS neuron serotonin uptake, minimal or no effect on reuptake of norepinephrine or dopamine. It also binds selectively with high affinity to 5-HT_{1A} receptors and is a 5-HT_{1A} receptor partial agonist. 5-HT_{1A} receptor activity may be altered in depression and anxiety.

Pharmacodynamics/Kinetics

Half-life Elimination Terminal: ~25 hours

Time to Peak Serum: 4 to 5 hours

Pregnancy Considerations Adverse events have been observed in animal reproduction studies. An increased risk of teratogenic effects may be associated with maternal use of other SSRIs. However, available information is conflicting and information specific to the use of vilazodone has not been located. Nonteratogenic effects in the newborn following SSRI/SNRI exposure late in the third trimester include respiratory distress, cyanosis, apnea, seizures, temperature instability, feeding difficulty, vomiting, hypoglycemia, hypo- or hypertonia, hyper-reflexia, jitteriness, irritability, constant crying, and tremor. Symptoms may be due to the toxicity of the SSRIs/SNRIs or a discontinuation syndrome and may be consistent with serotonin syndrome associated with SSRI treatment. Persistent pulmonary hypertension of the newborn (PPHN) has also been reported with SSRI exposure. The long-term effects of *in utero* SSRI exposure on infant development and behavior are not known.

The ACOG recommends that therapy with SSRIs or SNRIs during pregnancy be individualized; treatment of depression during pregnancy should incorporate the clinical expertise of the mental health clinician, obstetrician, primary healthcare provider, and pediatrician. According to the American Psychiatric Association (APA), the risks of medication treatment should be weighed against other treatment options and untreated depression. For women who discontinue antidepressant medications during pregnancy and who may be at high risk for postpartum depression, the medications can be restarted following delivery. Treatment algorithms have been developed by the ACOG and the APA for the management of depression in women prior to conception and during pregnancy. Consideration should be given to using an agent with some safety information in pregnant women.

Dental Comment Problems with SSRI-induced bruxism have been reported and may preclude their use; clinicians attempting to evaluate any patient with bruxism or involuntary muscle movement, who is simultaneously being treated with an SSRI drug, should be aware of the potential association.

VinBLAStine (vin BLAS teen)

Brand Names: Canada Vinblastine Sulphate Injection

Pharmacologic Category Antineoplastic Agent, Antimicrotubular; Antineoplastic Agent, Vinca Alkaloid

Use Treatment of Hodgkin lymphoma; lymphocytic lymphoma; histiocytic lymphoma; mycosis fungoides; testicular cancer; Kaposi sarcoma; histiocytosis X (Letterer-Siwe disease); has also been used for the treatment of refractory/resistant breast cancer and choriocarcinoma

Local Anesthetic/Vasoconstrictor Precautions No information available to require special precautions

Effects on Dental Treatment Key adverse event(s) related to dental treatment: Stomatitis, metallic taste, and jaw pain.

Effects on Bleeding Chemotherapy may result in significant myelosuppression, potentially including significant reduction in platelet counts and altered hemostasis. In patients who are under active treatment with these agents, medical consult is suggested.

Adverse Reactions

Frequency not defined.

Cardiovascular: Angina pectoris, cerebrovascular accident, ECG abnormality, hypertension (common), ischemic heart disease, limb ischemia, myocardial infarction, Raynaud's phenomenon

Central nervous system: Decreased deep tendon reflex, depression, dizziness, headache, malaise (common), metallic taste, neurotoxicity (duration: >24 hours), paresthesia, peripheral neuritis, seizure, tumor pain (common), vertigo

Dermatologic: Alopecia (common), dermatitis, skin blister, skin photosensitivity (rare), skin rash

Endocrine & metabolic: Hyperuricemia, SIADH (syndrome of inappropriate antidiuretic hormone secretion)

Gastrointestinal: Abdominal pain, anorexia, constipation (common), diarrhea, enterocolitis (hemorrhagic), gastrointestinal hemorrhage, intestinal obstruction, nausea (mild), paralytic ileus, stomatitis, toxic megacolon, vomiting (mild)

Genitourinary: Azoospermia, urinary retention

Hematologic & oncologic: Anemia, bone marrow depression (common), granulocytopenia (common; nadir: 5 to 10 days; recovery: 7 to 14 days; dose-limiting toxicity), hemolytic uremic syndrome, leukopenia (common; nadir: 5 to 10 days; recovery: 7 to 14 days; dose-limiting toxicity), rectal hemorrhage,

thrombocytopenia (recovery within a few days), thrombotic thrombocytopenic purpura
Local: Local irritation
Neuromuscular & skeletal: Jaw pain (common), myalgia, ostealgia (common), weakness
Ophthalmic: Nystagmus
Otic: Auditory disturbance, deafness, vestibular disturbance
Respiratory: Bronchospasm, dyspnea, pharyngitis
Miscellaneous: Radiation recall phenomenon

General Dosage Range Dosage adjustment recommended in patients with hepatic impairment

IV:

Children: Initial dose: 3 to 6.5 mg/m^2 every 7 days as needed

Adults: Initial: 3.7 mg/m^2; adjust dose every 7 days; Second dose: 5.5 mg/m^2; Third dose: 7.4 mg/m^2; Fourth dose: 9.25 mg/m^2; Fifth dose: 11.1 mg/m^2; Usual range: 5.5 to 7.4 mg/m^2 every 7 days; Maximum dose: 18.5 mg/m^2

Mechanism of Action Vinblastine binds to tubulin and inhibits microtubule formation, therefore, arresting the cell at metaphase by disrupting the formation of the mitotic spindle; it is specific for the M and S phases. Vinblastine may also interfere with nucleic acid and protein synthesis by blocking glutamic acid utilization.

Pharmacodynamics/Kinetics

Half-life Elimination Terminal: ~25 hours

Pregnancy Risk Factor D

Pregnancy Considerations Adverse effects were observed in animal reproduction studies. May cause fetal harm if administered during pregnancy. Women of childbearing potential should avoid becoming pregnant during vinblastine treatment. Aspermia has been reported in males who have received treatment with vinblastine.

VinCRIStine (vin KRIS teen)

Brand Names: US Vincasar PFS

Brand Names: Canada Vincristine Sulfate Injection; Vincristine Sulfate Injection USP

Pharmacologic Category Antineoplastic Agent, Antimicrotubular; Antineoplastic Agent, Vinca Alkaloid

Use Treatment of acute lymphocytic leukemia (ALL), Hodgkin lymphoma, non-Hodgkin lymphomas, Wilms' tumor, neuroblastoma, rhabdomyosarcoma

Local Anesthetic/Vasoconstrictor Precautions No information available to require special precautions

Effects on Dental Treatment Key adverse event(s) related to dental treatment: Oral ulceration, metallic taste, orthostatic hypotension or hypertension.

Effects on Bleeding Although significant myelosuppression with associated altered hemostasis has been reported for many chemotherapeutic agents, myelosuppression is not common with vincristine and no specific precautions appear to necessary.

Adverse Reactions Frequency not defined.

Cardiovascular: Edema, hepatic veno-occlusive disease (SOS; hepatic sinusoidal obstruction syndrome), hypertension, hypotension, ischemic heart disease, myocardial infarction, phlebitis
Central nervous system: Abnormal gait, ataxia, coma, cranial nerve dysfunction (auditory impairment, extraocular muscle impairment, laryngeal muscle impairment, motor dysfunction, paralysis, paresis, vestibular damage, vocal cord paralysis), decreased deep tendon reflex, dizziness, headache, neurotoxicity (dose-related), neuropathic pain (common), paralysis, paresthesia, parotid pain, peripheral neuropathy (common), seizure, sensorimotor neuropathy, sensory loss, vertigo
Dermatologic: Alopecia (common), skin rash
Endocrine & metabolic: Hyperuricemia, uric acid nephropathy (acute), weight loss
Gastrointestinal: Abdominal cramps, abdominal pain, anorexia, constipation (common), diarrhea, intestinal necrosis, intestinal perforation, nausea, oral mucosa ulcer, paralytic ileus, sore throat, vomiting
Genitourinary: Bladder atony, dysuria, urinary retention
Hematologic & oncologic: Anemia (mild), hemolytic uremic syndrome, leukopenia (mild), thrombocytopenia (mild), thrombotic thrombocytopenic purpura
Local: Local irritation (if infiltrated)
Neuromuscular & skeletal: Amyotrophy, back pain, footdrop, jaw pain, limb pain, myalgia, ostealgia
Ophthalmic: Cortical blindness (transient), nystagmus, optic atrophy with blindness
Otic: Deafness
Renal: Polyuria
Respiratory: Bronchospasm, dyspnea
Miscellaneous: Fever, tissue necrosis (if infiltrated)
<1%, postmarketing, and/or case reports: Anaphylaxis, hypersensitivity reaction, SIADH (syndrome of inappropriate antidiuretic hormone secretion)

General Dosage Range Dosage adjustment recommended in patients with hepatic impairment

IV:

Children ≤10 kg: 0.05 mg/kg once weekly (maximum: 2 mg/dose)

Children >10 kg: 1.5 to 2 mg/m^2/dose (maximum: 2 mg/dose)

Adults: 1.4 mg/m^2/dose (maximum: 2 mg/dose)

Mechanism of Action Binds to tubulin and inhibits microtubule formation, therefore, arresting the cell at metaphase by disrupting the formation of the mitotic spindle; it is specific for the M and S phases. Vincristine may also interfere with nucleic acid and protein synthesis by blocking glutamic acid utilization.

Pharmacodynamics/Kinetics

Half-life Elimination Terminal: 85 hours (range: 19-155 hours)

Pregnancy Risk Factor D

Pregnancy Considerations Animal reproduction studies have demonstrated teratogenicity and fetal loss. May cause fetal harm if administered during pregnancy. Women of childbearing potential should avoid becoming pregnant during treatment.

VinCRIStine (Liposomal)
(vin KRIS teen lye po SO mal)

Brand Names: US Marqibo

Pharmacologic Category Antineoplastic Agent, Antimicrotubular; Antineoplastic Agent, Vinca Alkaloid

Use Treatment of relapsed Philadelphia chromosome-negative (Ph-) acute lymphoblastic leukemia (ALL) in adult patients whose disease has progressed after two or more antileukemic therapies

Local Anesthetic/Vasoconstrictor Precautions No information available to require special precautions

Effects on Dental Treatment No significant effects or complications reported

Effects on Bleeding Although significant myelosuppression with associated altered hemostasis has been reported for many chemotherapeutic agents, myelosuppression is not common with vincristine and no specific precautions appear to necessary.

Adverse Reactions
>10%:
Central nervous system: Fatigue (41%), peripheral neuropathy (39%; grades 3/4: 17%), insomnia (32%)
Gastrointestinal: Constipation (57%), nausea (52%), diarrhea (37%), decreased appetite (33%)
Hematologic & oncologic: Febrile neutropenia (38%; grades 3/4: 31%), anemia (34%; grades 3/4: 17%), neutropenia (grades 3/4: 18%), thrombocytopenia (grades 3/4: 17%)
Hepatic: Increased serum AST (grades 3/4: 6% to 11%)
Miscellaneous: Fever (43%)
1% to 10%:
Cardiovascular: Hypotension (grades 3/4: 6%), septic shock (grades 3/4: 6%)
Central nervous system: Pain (grades 3/4: 8%), mental status changes (grades 3/4: 4%), myasthenia (grades 3/4: 1%)
Gastrointestinal: Abdominal pain (grades 3/4: 8%), intestinal obstruction (grades 3/4: 6%)
Infection: Staphylococcal bacteremia (grades 3/4: 6%)
Neuromuscular & skeletal: Weakness (grades 3/4: 5%)
Respiratory: Pneumonia (grades 3/4: 8%), respiratory distress (grades 3/4: 6%), respiratory failure (grades 3/4: 5%)

General Dosage Range Dosage adjustment recommended in patients with hepatic impairment or who develop toxicities.
IV: *Adults:* 2.25 mg/m^2 once every 7 days

Mechanism of Action Vincristine is a cell cycle specific agent which binds to tubulin, leading to microtubule depolymerization and cellular apoptosis. The liposomal formulation increases the half-life, allowing for enhanced cytotoxic activity in tumor cells.

Pharmacodynamics/Kinetics
Half-life Elimination 45 hours (urinary half-life); dependent on rate of vincristine release from sphingosome (Bedikian, 2006)

Pregnancy Risk Factor D

Pregnancy Considerations Adverse events (fetal malformations, decreased fetal weight, and fetal loss) were observed in animal reproduction studies at doses less than the recommended human dose. Given the mechanism of action, adverse fetal events would be expected to occur with use in pregnant women. Women of childbearing potential should avoid becoming pregnant during therapy.

Vinorelbine (vi NOR el been)

Brand Names: US Navelbine
Brand Names: Canada Navelbine; Vinorelbine Injection, USP; Vinorelbine Tartrate for Injection
Pharmacologic Category Antineoplastic Agent, Antimicrotubular; Antineoplastic Agent, Vinca Alkaloid
Use Treatment of non-small cell lung cancer (NSCLC)
Local Anesthetic/Vasoconstrictor Precautions No information available to require special precautions
Effects on Dental Treatment No significant effects or complications reported
Effects on Bleeding Chemotherapy may result in significant myelosuppression, potentially including significant reduction in platelet counts and altered hemostasis. In patients who are under active treatment with these agents, medical consult is suggested.
Adverse Reactions Reported with single-agent therapy.
>10%:
Central nervous system: Fatigue (27%), peripheral neuropathy (25%; grade 3: 1%; grade 4: <1%)
Dermatologic: Alopecia (12% to 30%)
Gastrointestinal: Nausea (31% to 44%; grade 3: 1% to 2%), constipation (35%; grade 3: 3%), vomiting (20% to 31%; grade 3: 1% to 2%), diarrhea (12% to 17%)
Hematologic & oncologic: Leukopenia (83% to 92%; grade 4: 6% to 15%), granulocytopenia (90%; grade 4: 36%; nadir: 7 to 10 days; recovery 14 to 21 days), neutropenia (85%; grade 4: 28%), anemia (83%; grades 3/4: 9%)
Hepatic: Increased serum AST (67%; grade 3: 5%; grade 4: 1%), increased serum bilirubin (total bilirubin: 5% to 13%; grade 3: 4%; grade 4: 3%)
Local: Injection site reaction (22% to 28%; includes erythema at injection site, vein discoloration), pain at injection site (16%)
Neuromuscular & skeletal: Weakness (36%)
Renal: Increased serum creatinine (13%)
1% to 10%:
Cardiovascular: Localized phlebitis (7% to 10%), chest pain (5%)
Central nervous system: Decreased deep tendon reflex (<5%)
Dermatologic: Skin rash (<5%)
Gastrointestinal: Paralytic ileus (1%)
Hematologic & oncologic: Febrile neutropenia (≤8%; grade 4: ≤4%), thrombocytopenia (3% to 5%; grades 3/4: 1%)
Infection: Sepsis (≤8%; grade 4: ≤4%)
Neuromuscular & skeletal: Arthralgia (<5%), myalgia (<5%), jaw pain (<5%)
Otic: Ototoxicity (≤1%)
Respiratory: Dyspnea (7%)
<1%, postmarketing, and/or case reports: Abdominal pain, anaphylaxis, angioedema, back pain, deep vein thrombosis, dysphagia, esophagitis, flushing, headache, hemolytic-uremic syndrome, hemorrhagic cystitis, hypersensitivity reaction, hypertension, hyponatremia, hypotension, intestinal necrosis, intestinal obstruction, intestinal perforation, interstitial pulmonary disease, ischemic heart disease, localized rash, mucositis, myasthenia, myocardial infarction (rare), pancreatitis, pneumonia, pruritus, pulmonary edema, pulmonary embolism, radiation recall phenomenon (dermatitis, esophagitis), skin blister, SIADH (syndrome of inappropriate antidiuretic hormone secretion), tachycardia, thromboembolism, thrombotic thrombocytopenic purpura, tumor pain, unsteady gait, urticaria, urticaria at injection site, vasodilatation

General Dosage Range Dosage adjustment recommended in patients with hepatic or renal impairment or who develop toxicities
IV: *Adults:* 25-30 mg/m^2 every 7 days

Mechanism of Action Semisynthetic vinca alkaloid which binds to tubulin and inhibits microtubule formation, therefore, arresting the cell at metaphase by disrupting the formation of the mitotic spindle; it is specific for the M and S phases. Vinorelbine may also interfere with nucleic acid and protein synthesis by blocking glutamic acid utilization.

Pharmacodynamics/Kinetics
Half-life Elimination Triphasic:
Children and Adolescents 2 to 17 years: Terminal: 16.5 ± 9.7 hours (Johansen 2006)
Adults: Terminal: 28 to 44 hours

Pregnancy Risk Factor D

Pregnancy Considerations Animal reproduction studies have demonstrated embryotoxicity, fetotoxicity, decreased fetal weight, and delayed ossification. May cause fetal harm if administered during pregnancy. Women of childbearing potential should avoid becoming pregnant during vinorelbine treatment.

Vismodegib (vis moe DEG ib)

Brand Names: US Erivedge
Brand Names: Canada Erivedge
Pharmacologic Category Antineoplastic Agent, Hedgehog Pathway Inhibitor
Use Basal cell carcinoma, metastatic or locally advanced: Treatment of metastatic basal cell carcinoma, or locally-advanced basal cell carcinoma that has recurred following surgery or in patients who are not candidates for surgery, and not candidates for radiation therapy
Local Anesthetic/Vasoconstrictor Precautions No information available to require special precautions
Effects on Dental Treatment Key adverse event(s) related to dental treatment: Abnormal taste and loss of taste perception have been reported (see Dental Comment)
Effects on Bleeding No information available to require special precautions
Adverse Reactions
>10%:
Central nervous system: Fatigue (40%)
Dermatologic: Alopecia (64%)
Endocrine & metabolic: Amenorrhea (≤30%)
Gastrointestinal: Dysgeusia (55%), weight loss (45%), nausea (30%), diarrhea (29%), decreased appetite (25%), constipation (21%), vomiting (14%), ageusia (11%)
Neuromuscular & skeletal: Muscle spasm (72%), arthralgia (16%)
1% to 10%:
Endocrine & metabolic: Hypokalemia, hyponatremia
Neuromuscular & skeletal: Increased creatinine phosphokinase
Renal: Azotemia
General Dosage Range Oral: *Adults:* 150 mg once daily
Mechanism of Action
Basal cell cancer is associated with mutations in Hedgehog pathway components. Hedgehog regulates cell growth and differentiation in embryogenesis; while generally not active in adult tissue, Hedgehog mutations associated with basal cell cancer can activate the pathway resulting in unrestricted proliferation of skin basal cells. Vismodegib is a selective Hedgehog pathway inhibitor which binds to and inhibits Smoothened homologue (SMO), the transmembrane protein involved in Hedgehog signal transduction.
Pharmacodynamics/Kinetics
Half-life Elimination Continuous daily dosing: ~4 days; Single dose: ~12 days
Time to Peak ~2.4 days (Graham 2011)
Pregnancy Considerations [US Boxed Warning]: May result in severe birth defects or embryo-fetal death. Teratogenic effects (severe midline defects, missing digits, and other irreversible malformations), embryotoxic, and fetotoxic events were observed in animal reproduction studies when administered in doses less than the normal human dose. Based on its mechanism of action adverse effects on pregnancy would be expected. **[US Boxed Warning]: Verify pregnancy status (in females of reproductive potential) within 7 days prior to initiating treatment and advise patients (female and male) of the risk of birth defects, the need for contraception and risk of exposure through semen and to use condoms with a pregnant partner or a female partner of childbearing potential.** In females of childbearing potential, obtain pregnancy test within 7 days prior to treatment initiation; after the negative pregnancy test, initiate highly effective contraception prior to the first vismodegib dose and continue during treatment and for 24 months after the final dose. During treatment (including treatment interruptions) and for 3 months after treatment, male patients should not donate sperm and should use condoms with spermicide (even after vasectomy) if their partner is of childbearing potential.

Women exposed to vismodegib during pregnancy (directly or via seminal fluid) are encouraged to participate in the Erivedge Pregnancy Pharmacovigilance program by contacting the Genentech Adverse Event Line (1-888-835-2555). Pregnancies occurring during or within 7 months after treatment should be reported to the Genentech Adverse Event Line.

In Canada, vismodegib is available only through a controlled distribution program (Erivedge Pregnancy Prevention Program). Female and male patients of reproductive potential must be registered with the program and comply with all requirements. Females of childbearing potential should use 2 simultaneous forms of effective contraception beginning at least 4 weeks prior to treatment initiation, during treatment (including treatment interruptions), and for 24 months after discontinuation. Pregnancy testing should be performed within 7 days prior to treatment initiation, monthly during treatment (including treatment interruptions), and for 24 months after discontinuation. For females of child bearing potential, a new prescription is required each month to allow for monthly pregnancy testing. During treatment (including treatment interruptions) and for 2 months after treatment, male patients should not donate sperm and should use condoms with spermicide (even after vasectomy) if their partner is of childbearing potential. Any suspected exposure (directly or via seminal fluid) during pregnancy should be immediately reported to the Erivedge Pregnancy Prevention Program at 1-888-748-8926.
Prescribing and Access Restrictions
US: Available at specialty pharmacies through the Erivedge Access Solutions program. Further information may be obtained from the manufacturer, Genentech, at 1-888-249-4918, or at www.ErivedgeAccessSolutions.com

Canada: Available through a controlled distribution program called Erivedge Pregnancy Prevention Program (EPPP). Registration with the program is required for participating prescribers and pharmacies. Patients must also be registered with the program and meet all necessary requirements to receive vismodegib. Consult product monograph for detailed information regarding program requirements. Further information may also be obtained at 1-888-748-8926 or at www.erivedge.ca.
Dental Comment Review head and neck exam for changes since previous visit; Refer patient back to dermatologist/physician if changes are noted.

Vitamin A (VYE ta min aye)

Brand Names: US A-25 [OTC]; AFirm 1X [OTC]; AFirm 2X [OTC]; AFirm 3X [OTC]; Aquasol A; Gordons-Vite A [OTC]; Vitamin A Fish [OTC]

Pharmacologic Category Vitamin, Fat Soluble

Use Treatment and prevention of vitamin A deficiency; parenteral (IM) route is indicated when oral administration is not feasible or when absorption is insufficient (malabsorption syndrome); dietary supplement (OTC)

Local Anesthetic/Vasoconstrictor Precautions No information available to require special precautions

Effects on Dental Treatment No significant effects or complications reported

Effects on Bleeding No information available to require special precautions

Adverse Reactions Frequency not defined: Hypersensitivity: Anaphylactic shock (following IV administration), hypersensitivity reaction (rare)

General Dosage Range IM, Oral: *Children and Adults:* Dosage varies greatly depending on indication

Mechanism of Action Vitamin A is a fat soluble vitamin needed for visual adaptation to darkness, maintenance of epithelial cells, immune function and embryonic development.

Pregnancy Risk Factor X

Pregnancy Considerations Adverse events have been observed in animal reproduction studies. In humans, the critical period of exposure is the first trimester of pregnancy. Excess vitamin A during pregnancy may cause craniofacial malformations, as well as CNS, heart, and thymus abnormalities. Maternal vitamin A deficiency also causes adverse effects in the fetus, and vitamin A requirements are increased in pregnant women (IOM, 2000). The manufacturer notes that the safety of doses >6000 units/day in pregnant women has not been established and doses greater than the RDA are contraindicated in pregnant women or those who may become pregnant. High doses are used in some areas of the world for supplementation where deficiency is a public health problem (eg, to prevent night blindness); however, single doses >25,000 units should be avoided within 60 days of conception. High-dose supplementation is otherwise not recommended as part of routine antenatal care (WHO, 2011c).

Vitamin B Complex Combinations

(VYE ta min bee KOM pleks kom bi NAY shuns)

Pharmacologic Category Vitamin

Use Dietary supplement

Local Anesthetic/Vasoconstrictor Precautions No information available to require special precautions

Effects on Dental Treatment No significant effects or complications reported

Effects on Bleeding No information available to require special precautions

General Dosage Range

Oral: *Adults:* Dosage varies greatly depending on product

Pregnancy Considerations Water soluble vitamins cross the placenta (IOM, 1998). Refer to individual vitamins for additional information and specific requirements during pregnancy.

Vitamin E (Systemic) (VYE ta min ee)

Brand Names: US Alph-E [OTC]; Alph-E-Mixed 1000 [OTC]; Alph-E-Mixed [OTC]; Aquasol E [OTC] [DSC]; Aquavit-E [OTC] [DSC]; Aqueous Vitamin E [OTC]; E-400 [OTC]; E-400-Clear [OTC]; E-400-Mixed [OTC]; E-Max-1000 [OTC]; E-Pherol [OTC]; Formula E 400 [OTC]; Natural Vitamin E [OTC]; Nutr-E-Sol [OTC]; Vita-Plus E [OTC]

Pharmacologic Category Vitamin, Fat Soluble

Use Dietary supplement

Note: According to the 2014 USPSTF recommendations for the primary prevention of cardiovascular disease and cancer, the use of vitamin E supplements are not recommended (Moyer 2014).

Local Anesthetic/Vasoconstrictor Precautions No information available to require special precautions

Effects on Dental Treatment No significant effects or complications reported

Effects on Bleeding High doses of vitamin E (800 to 1,200 int. units/day) may increase the overall risk of bleeding. Although the mechanism is unknown, it may affect the coagulation cascade and has the potential to enhance the anticoagulant effects of various anticoagulants.

Adverse Reactions There are no adverse reactions listed in the manufacturer's labeling.

General Dosage Range

Oral:

Infants 1 to 6 months: Adequate intake: 4 mg

Infants 7 to 12 months: Adequate intake: 5 mg

Children 1 to 3 years: RDA: 6 mg; upper limit of intake should not exceed 200 mg/day

Children 4 to 8 years: RDA: 7 mg; upper limit of intake should not exceed 300 mg/day

Children 9 to 13 years: RDA: 11 mg; upper limit of intake should not exceed 600 mg/day

Children 14 to 18 years: RDA: 15 mg; upper limit of intake should not exceed 800 mg/day

Adults: RDA: 15 mg; upper limit of intake should not exceed 1,000 mg/day

Pregnant female:

≤18 years: RDA: 15 mg; upper level of intake should not exceed 800 mg/day

19 to 50 years: RDA: 15 mg; upper level of intake should not exceed 1,000 mg/day

Lactating female:

≤18 years: RDA: 19 mg; upper level of intake should not exceed 800 mg/day

19 to 50 years: RDA: 19 mg; upper level of intake should not exceed 1,000 mg/day

Mechanism of Action Prevents oxidation of vitamin A and C; protects polyunsaturated fatty acids in membranes from attack by free radicals and protects red blood cells against hemolysis

Pregnancy Considerations Vitamin E crosses the placenta. Maternal serum concentrations of α tocopherol increase with lipid concentrations as pregnancy progresses; however, placental transfer remains constant. Additional supplementation is not needed in pregnant women without deficiency (IOM 2000).

Vitamins (Fluoride) (VYE ta mins, FLOOR ide)

Brand Names: US Poly-Vi-Flor®; Poly-Vi-Flor® With Iron; Soluvite-F; Tri-Vi-Flor®; Tri-Vi-Flor® with Iron; Vi-Daylin®/F + Iron [DSC]; Vi-Daylin®/F ADC [DSC]; Vi-Daylin®/F ADC + Iron [DSC]; Vi-Daylin®/F [DSC]

Pharmacologic Category Vitamin

Use Prevention/treatment of vitamin deficiency; products containing fluoride are used to prevent dental caries; labeled for OTC use as a dietary supplement

Local Anesthetic/Vasoconstrictor Precautions No information available to require special precautions

Effects on Dental Treatment No significant effects or complications reported

Contraindications Hypersensitivity to any component of the formulation; pre-existing hypervitaminosis

Warnings/Precautions Not all products can be used in children of all age groups; consult specific product labeling prior to use. Do not exceed recommended doses. Use caution with severe renal or hepatic dysfunction or failure. **[U.S. Boxed Warning]: Products may contain iron. Severe iron toxicity may occur in overdose, particularly when ingested by children; iron is a leading cause of fatal poisoning in children; store out of children's reach and in child-resistant containers.**

Dietary Considerations May take with food to decrease stomach upset.

Dosage Forms Content varies depending on product used. For more detailed information on ingredients in these and other multivitamins, please refer to package labeling.

Dental Comment Chronic overdose of fluoride may result in mottling of tooth enamel and osseous changes.

Vitamins (Multiple/Oral)

(VYE ta mins, MUL ti pul/OR al)

Brand Names: US Androvite [OTC]; BP Vit 3 Plus; CalciFol; CalciFolic-D; Centamin [OTC]; Centrum Cardio [OTC]; Centrum Flavor Burst [OTC]; Centrum MultiGummies [OTC]; Centrum Performance [OTC]; Centrum Silver Ultra Men's [OTC]; Centrum Silver Ultra Women's [OTC]; Centrum Silver [OTC]; Centrum Ultra Men's [OTC]; Centrum Ultra Women's [OTC]; Centrum [OTC]; Corvite 150; Diatx Zn; Drinkables Fruits and Vegetables [OTC]; Drinkables MultiVitamins [OTC]; Encora; FeRiva; FeRiva 21/7; FeRivaFA; Ferralet 90; Foltrin; Freedavite [OTC]; Fusion Plus; Fusion [OTC]; Geri-Freeda [OTC]; Geriation [OTC]; Geritol Complete [OTC]; Geritol Extend [OTC]; Geritol Tonic [OTC]; Glutofac-MX; Gynovite Plus [OTC]; Hemocyte Plus; Hi-Kovite [OTC]; Iberet-500 [OTC] [DSC]; K-Tan Plus; Monocaps [OTC]; Multilex [OTC]; Multilex-T&M [OTC]; Myadec [OTC]; Natalvirt FLT; Nicadan; Nicadan ZX; NicAzel Forte; NuFera; Nutrimin-Plus [OTC]; Ocuvel; Ocuvite Adult 50+ [OTC]; Ocuvite Extra [OTC]; Ocuvite Lutein [OTC]; Ocuvite [OTC]; One A Day Cholesterol Plus [OTC]; One A Day Energy [OTC]; One A Day Essential [OTC]; One A Day Maximum [OTC]; One A Day Men's 50+ Advantage [OTC]; One A Day Men's Health Formula [OTC]; One A Day Teen Advantage for Her [OTC]; One A Day Teen Advantage for Him [OTC]; One A Day Weight Smart Advanced [OTC]; One A Day Women's Active Mind & Body [OTC]; One A Day Women's [OTC]; One A Day® Women's 50+ Advantage [OTC]; Optivite P.M.T. [OTC]; PreserVision AREDS 2 Formula + Multivitamin [OTC]; PreserVision AREDS [OTC]; PreserVision Lutein [OTC]; Quintabs [OTC]; Quintabs-M Iron-Free [OTC]; Quintabs-M [OTC]; Replace Without Iron [OTC]; Replace [OTC]; Repliva 21/7; Strovite; Strovite Forte; Strovite Plus [DSC]; T-Vites [OTC]; Theramill Forte [OTC]; Ultra Freeda A-Free [OTC]; Ultra Freeda Iron-Free [OTC]; Ultra Freeda With Iron [OTC]; Viactiv Calcium Flavor Glides [OTC]; Viactiv Flavor Glides [OTC]; Viactiv for Teens [OTC]; Viactiv With Calcium [OTC]; Viactiv [OTC]; Vitafol; VP-Zel; Xtramins [OTC]; Yelets [OTC]

Pharmacologic Category Vitamin

Use Prevention/treatment of vitamin and mineral deficiencies; labeled for OTC use as a dietary supplement

Local Anesthetic/Vasoconstrictor Precautions No information available to require special precautions

Effects on Dental Treatment No significant effects or complications reported (see Dental Comment)

Effects on Bleeding No information available to require special precautions

Adverse Reactions See individual vitamin monographs.

General Dosage Range Oral: *Adults:* 1 tablet/capsule **or** 5-15 mL once daily

Pregnancy Considerations Refer to individual vitamin monographs for requirements during pregnancy.

Dental Comment Dentists may encourage good nutritional habits and may detect signs/symptoms of vitamin deficiency through the intraoral examination. Refer patient back to physician if exam suggests poor nutrition or possible vitamin deficiency.

von Willebrand Factor (Recombinant)

(von WILL le brand FAK tor ree KOM be nant)

Brand Names: US Vonvendi

Pharmacologic Category Antihemophilic Agent; Blood Product Derivative

Use von Willebrand disease: Treatment (on demand) and control of bleeding episodes in adults with von Willebrand disease (VWD).

Local Anesthetic/Vasoconstrictor Precautions No information available to require special precautions

Effects on Dental Treatment No significant effects or complications reported

Effects on Bleeding Due to underlying hemophilia, medical consultation is warranted

Adverse Reactions

Cardiovascular: Chest discomfort (2%), hypertension (2%), increased heart rate (2%), inversion T wave on ECG (2%), tachycardia (2%)

Central nervous system: Dizziness (2%)

Dermatologic: Pruritus (3%)

Endocrine & metabolic: Hot flash (2%)

Gastrointestinal: Dysgeusia (2%), nausea (2%)

Local: Infusion site reaction (paresthesia; 2%)

Neuromuscular & skeletal: Tremor (2%)

Postmarketing and/or case reports: Anaphylaxis, antibody development (neutralizing), cerebrovascular accident, disseminated intravascular coagulation, hypersensitivity reaction, myocardial infarction, pulmonary embolism, venous thrombosis

General Dosage Range IV: *Adults:* Initial: 40 to 80 units/kg; maintenance dose: 40 to 60 units/kg every 8 to 24 hours (as clinically required).

Mechanism of Action von Willebrand Factor (recombinant) promotes platelet aggregation and adhesion to damaged vascular endothelium and acts as a stabilizing carrier protein for factor VIII.

Pharmacodynamics/Kinetics

Half-life Elimination 19.1 to 21.9 hours.

Pregnancy Considerations

Animal reproduction studies have not been conducted.

In some women, von Willebrand Factor (VWF) concentrations may increase during pregnancy. However, bleeding complications in women with VWD may also be increased during pregnancy. Laboratory assays for FVIII and VWF:RCo should be done prior to invasive procedures and during the third trimester. FVIII and VWF:RCo concentrations of at least 50 units/dL should be achieved prior to delivery and for at least 3 to 5 days postpartum. Vaginal bleeding may be delayed once VWF levels return to baseline, 7 to 21 days after delivery (AGOG 580 2013; Nichols 2008).

Vorapaxar (vor a PAX ar)

Related Information

Antiplatelet and Anticoagulation Considerations in Dentistry *on page 1764*

Brand Names: US Zontivity

Brand Names: Canada Zontivity

Pharmacologic Category Antiplatelet Agent; Protease-Activated Receptor-1 (PAR-1) Antagonist

Use History of myocardial infarction or established peripheral arterial disease: To reduce thrombotic cardiovascular events (cardiovascular death, MI, stroke, urgent coronary revascularization) in patients with a history of myocardial infarction (MI) or with peripheral arterial disease (PAD)

Local Anesthetic/Vasoconstrictor Precautions No information available to require special precautions

Effects on Dental Treatment Key adverse event(s) related to dental treatment: Vorapaxar increases the risk of bleeding. The risk of bleeding is proportional to the patient's underlying bleeding risk. Older age is an underlying risk factor. See Warnings/Precautions. The clinician is reminded that the dosing of vorapaxar is usually taken in combination with aspirin and/or clopidogrel. Significant bleeding after invasive dental procedures should be expected. NSAIDs for postoperative pain control should be avoided if possible since NSAIDs may further enhance bleeding in combination with these antiplatelet agents.

Effects on Bleeding Vorapaxar is an antiplatetet agent that works through antagonism of the protease-activated receptor-1 (PAR-1) expressed on platelets, resulting in reduced platelet aggregation and enhanced bleeding. Greater than 10% incidence: Hemorrhage (any GUSTO [Global Utilization of Streptokinase and Tissue Plasminogen Activator for Occluded Arteries] bleeding [severe, moderate, mild]): 25%), major hemorrhage, life-threatening (13%; clinically significant bleeding, including any bleeding requiring medical attention such as intracranial hemorrhage, or clinically significant overt signs of hemorrhage associated with a drop in hemoglobin of ≥3 g/dL). One to 10% incidence: Major hemorrhage (GUSTO bleeding category "moderate or severe": 3%; GUSTO bleeding category "severe": 1%)

Adverse Reactions

>10%:

Hematologic and oncologic: Hemorrhage (any GUSTO [Global Utilization of Streptokinase and Tissue Plasminogen Activator for Occluded Arteries] bleeding [severe, moderate, mild]): 25%), major hemorrhage, life-threatening (13%; clinically significant bleeding, including any bleeding requiring medical attention such as intracranial hemorrhage, or clinically significant overt signs of hemorrhage associated with a drop in hemoglobin of ≥3 g/dL [or when hemoglobin is unavailable, an absolute drop in hematocrit of ≥15% or a fall in hematocrit of 9% to <15%])

1% to 10%:

Central nervous system: Depression (2%)

Dermatologic: Skin rash (2%, includes cutaneous eruptions and exanthemas)

Endocrine & metabolic: Iron deficiency (<2%)

Gastrointestinal: Gastrointestinal hemorrhage (4%)

Hematologic and oncologic: Anemia (5%), major hemorrhage (GUSTO bleeding category "moderate or severe": 3%; GUSTO bleeding category "severe": 1%)

Ophthalmic: Retinopathy (<2%)

<1%, postmarketing, and/or case reports: Diplopia (or oculomotor disturbance), hemorrhagic death, intracranial hemorrhage

Mechanism of Action Vorapaxar, an antagonist of the protease-activated receptor-1 (PAR-1) expressed on platelets, inhibits thrombin-induced and thrombin receptor agonist peptide (TRAP)-induced platelet aggregation. Due to the very long half-life, vorapaxar is effectively irreversible. Vorapaxar reversibly binds to the PAR-1 receptor with a long receptor dissociation half-life of approximately 20 hours; additionally, vorapaxar displays significant inhibition of platelet aggregation that remains for up to 4 weeks after discontinuation due to the very long elimination half-life (Ueno 2010).

Pharmacodynamics/Kinetics

Onset of Action ≥80% inhibition of TRAP-induced platelet aggregation within one week

Duration of Action Dose and concentration dependent; with the recommended dosing, inhibition of TRAP-induced platelet aggregation at a level of 50% can be expected 4 weeks after discontinuation

Half-life Elimination Effective half-life: 3 to 4 days; Terminal elimination half-life (vorapaxar and active metabolite): ~8 days (range: 5 to 13 days)

Time to Peak 1 to 2 hours

Pregnancy Risk Factor D

Pregnancy Considerations Adverse events have not been observed in animal reproduction studies.

Voriconazole (vor i KOE na zole)

Related Information

Clinical Risk Related to Drugs Prolonging QT Interval *on page 1772*

Fungal Infections *on page 1847*

Brand Names: US Vfend; Vfend IV

Brand Names: Canada Apo-Voriconazole; Sandoz-Voriconazole; Teva-Voriconazole; VFEND; VFEND For Injection; Voriconazole For Injection

Generic Availability (US) Yes

Pharmacologic Category Antifungal Agent, Oral; Antifungal Agent, Parenteral

Use Treatment of fungal infections: Treatment of invasive aspergillosis; treatment of esophageal candidiasis; treatment of candidemia (in non-neutropenic patients); treatment of disseminated *Candida* infections of the skin and abdomen, kidney, bladder wall and wounds; treatment of serious fungal infections caused by *Scedosporium apiospermum* and *Fusarium* spp (including *Fusarium solani*) in patients intolerant of, or refractory to, other therapy in children >12 years of age, adolescents and adults

Local Anesthetic/Vasoconstrictor Precautions Voriconazole is one of the drugs confirmed to prolong the QT interval and is accepted as having a risk of causing torsade de pointes. The risk of drug-induced torsade de pointes is extremely low when a single QT interval prolonging drug is prescribed. In terms of epinephrine, it is not known what effect vasoconstrictors in the local anesthetic regimen will have in patients with a known history of congenital prolonged QT interval or in patients taking any medication that prolongs the QT interval. Until more information is obtained, it is suggested that the clinician consult with the physician prior to the use of a vasoconstrictor in suspected patients, and that the vasoconstrictor (epinephrine, mepivacaine and levonordefrin [Carbocaine® 2% with Neo-Cobefrin®]) be used with caution.

Effects on Dental Treatment Key adverse event(s) related to dental treatment: Xerostomia (normal salivary flow resumes upon discontinuation).

Effects on Bleeding No information available to require special precautions

Adverse Reactions

>10%:

Central nervous system: Hallucination (2% to 12%; auditory and/or visual and likely serum concentration-dependent)

Ophthalmic: Visual disturbance (19%)

Renal: Increased serum creatinine (1% to 21%)

2% to 10%:

Cardiovascular: Tachycardia (≤2%)

Central nervous system: Chills (≤4%), headache (≤3%)

Dermatologic: Skin rash (≤7%)

Endocrine & metabolic: Hypokalemia (≤2%)

Gastrointestinal: Nausea (1% to 5%), vomiting (1% to 4%)

Hepatic: Increased serum alkaline phosphatase (4% to 5%), increased serum AST (2% to 4%), increased serum ALT (2% to 3%), cholestatic jaundice (1% to 2%)

Ophthalmic: Photophobia (2%)

Miscellaneous: Fever (≤6%)

<2%, postmarketing, and/or case reports (limited to important or life-threatening): Acute renal failure, adrenocortical insufficiency, agranulocytosis, alopecia, anaphylactoid reaction, anemia (aplastic, hemolytic, macrocytic, megaloblastic, or microcytic), angioedema, anorexia, anuria, arthritis, ascites, ataxia, atrial arrhythmia, atrial fibrillation, atrioventricular block, bacterial infection, bigeminy, blighted ovum, bone marrow depression, bradycardia, brain disease, bundle branch block, cardiac arrest, cardiac failure, cardiomegaly, cardiomyopathy, cellulitis, cerebral edema, cerebral hemorrhage, cerebral ischemia, cerebrovascular accident, chest pain, cholecystitis, cholelithiasis, cholestasis, chromatopsia, color blindness, coma, confusion, convulsions, corneal opacity, cyanosis, deafness, deep vein thrombophlebitis, deep vein thrombosis, delirium, dementia, dental fluorosis, depersonalization, depression, diabetes insipidus, diarrhea, discoid lupus erythematosus, disseminated intravascular coagulation, drowsiness, duodenal ulcer (active), duodenitis, dyspnea, eczema, edema, encephalitis, endocarditis, eosinophilia, erythema multiforme, esophageal ulcer, exfoliative dermatitis, extrapyramidal reaction, extrasystoles, fixed drug eruption, fungal infection, gastric ulcer, gastrointestinal hemorrhage, glucose tolerance decreased, graft versus host disease, Guillain-Barre syndrome, hematemesis, hemorrhagic cystitis, hepatic coma, hepatic failure, hepatitis, hepatomegaly, herpes simplex infection, hydronephrosis, hyperbilirubinemia, hypercholesterolemia, hyper-/hypocalcemia, hyper-/hypoglycemia, hyper-/hypomagnesemia, hyper-/hyponatremia, hyper-/hypotension, hyper-/hypothyroidism, hyperkalemia, hypersensitivity reaction, hyperuricemia, hypophosphatemia, hypoxia, impotence, increased blood urea nitrogen, increased gamma-glutamyl transferase, increased lactate dehydrogenase, increased susceptibility to infection, intestinal perforation, intracranial hypertension, jaundice, leukopenia, lymphadenopathy, lymphangitis, maculopapular rash, malignant melanoma, melanosis, multiorgan failure, myasthenia, myocardial infarction, myopathy, nephritis, nephrosis, neuropathy, nocturnal amblyopia, nodal arrhythmia, nodule, nystagmus, oculogyric crisis, optic atrophy, optic neuritis, orthostatic hypotension, osteomalacia, osteonecrosis, osteoporosis, otitis externa, palpitations, pancreatitis, pancytopenia, papilledema, paresthesia, perforated duodenal ulcer, periosteal disease, peripheral edema, peritonitis, petechia, pleural effusion, pneumonia, prolonged bleeding time, prolonged QT interval on ECG, pruritus, pseudomembranous colitis, pseudoporphyria, psoriasis, psychosis, pulmonary edema, pulmonary embolism, purpura, rectal hemorrhage, renal insufficiency, renal tubular necrosis, respiratory distress syndrome, respiratory tract infection, retinal hemorrhage, retinitis, seizure, sepsis, skin discoloration, skin photosensitivity, splenomegaly, squamous cell carcinoma, Stevens-Johnson syndrome, subconjunctival hemorrhage, substernal pain, suicidal ideation, supraventricular extrasystole, supraventricular tachycardia, syncope, thrombocytopenia, thrombophlebitis, thrombotic thrombocytopenic purpura, tongue edema, tonic-clonic seizures, torsades de pointes, toxic epidermal necrolysis, uremia, urinary incontinence, urinary retention, urinary tract infection, urticaria, uterine hemorrhage, uveitis, vaginal hemorrhage, vasodilation, ventricular arrhythmia, ventricular fibrillation, ventricular tachycardia, visual field defect

Dosing

Adult & Geriatric

Aspergillosis, invasive, including disseminated and extrapulmonary infection; treatment:

IV:

Initial: 6 mg/kg every 12 hours for 2 doses

Maintenance dose: 4 mg/kg every 12 hours

Oral: Maintenance dose:

Manufacturer's labeling: **Note:** If patient has inadequate clinical response, titrate in 50 mg/dose increments for weight <40 kg and 100 mg/dose increments for weight ≥40 kg.

Weight <40 kg: 100 mg every 12 hours

Weight ≥40 kg: 200 mg every 12 hours

Alternate recommendations: Oral: 200 to 300 mg every 12 hours **or** weight-based dosing (3 to 4 mg/kg) every 12 hours. **Note:** In patients able to tolerate oral administration, may consider oral in place of IV; however, IV administration is recommended in seriously ill patients (IDSA [Patterson 2016]).

Duration of therapy: Minimum of 6 to 12 weeks, although duration is highly dependent on degree/duration of immunosuppression, disease site, and evidence of disease improvement (IDSA [Patterson 2016]).

Aspergillosis, invasive (prophylaxis during prolonged neutropenia) (alternative therapy) (off-label use): Oral: 200 mg twice daily (IDSA [Patterson 2016])

Aspergillosis, ocular (off-label use):

Endophthalmitis: Intravitreal: 100 mcg/0.1 mL of an extemporaneously prepared solution administered intravitreally (need for a repeat dose is at physician discretion); concomitant systemic (IV or oral) voriconazole therapy is also recommended (Hariprasad 2008; Hoenigl 2013; Kramer 2006; IDSA [Patterson 2016]; Riddell 2011).

Keratitis: Ophthalmic: Dosing may vary; the following dosing regimen has been used in trials: 1 drop of an extemporaneously prepared 1% ophthalmic solution applied topically to the cornea of the affected eye every 1 hour while awake for 1 week, then every 2 hours while awake for 2 weeks; further continuation was at physician discretion (IDSA [Patterson 2016]; Prajna 2010; Prajna 2013)

Candidemia in non-neutropenic patients and disseminated *Candida* infections in skin, and infections in abdomen, kidney, bladder wall and wounds: Treatment should continue for a minimum of 14 days following resolution of symptoms or following last positive culture, whichever is longer.

IV:
- Initial: 6 mg/kg every 12 hours for 2 doses
- Maintenance: 3 to 4 mg/kg every 12 hours

Oral:
- *Manufacturer's labeling:* Maintenance dose: **Note:** If patient has inadequate clinical response, titrate in 50 mg/dose increments for weight <40 kg and 100 mg/dose increments for weight ≥40 kg
  - Weight <40 kg: 100 mg every 12 hours
  - Weight ≥40 kg: 200 mg every 12 hours
- *Alternate recommendations (IDSA [Pappas 2016]):*
  - Candidemia in non-neutropenic patients:
  - Initial therapy: 400 mg (6 mg/kg) IV every 12 hours for 2 doses, followed by 200 mg (3 mg/kg) IV or orally every 12 hours. **Note:** Voriconazole is considered alternative therapy and offers little advantage over fluconazole as first-line therapy of candidemia.
  - Step down therapy (after patient has responded to initial therapy): Oral:
    - Isolates of C. glabrata (voriconazole-susceptible isolates): 200 to 300 mg (3 to 4 mg/kg) twice daily
    - Isolates of C. krusei (selected cases): 200 mg every 12 hours
    - Duration: Continue for 14 days **after** first negative blood culture and resolution of signs/symptoms; step-down therapy to voriconazole (eg, after 5 to 7 days in nonneutropenic patients) is recommended only in select clinically stable patients with certain voriconazole-susceptible isolates and negative repeat cultures.

Candidiasis, endophthalmitis (with or without vitritis) (off-label use) (IDSA [Pappas 2016]): Voriconazole-susceptible isolates:
- *Systemic therapy:* Loading dose: 400 mg (6 mg/kg) IV twice daily for 2 doses, then 300 mg (4 mg/kg) IV or orally twice daily for at least 4 to 6 weeks until examination indicates resolution; for patients with vitritis or with macular involvement (with or without vitritis), an intravitreal injection of voriconazole or amphotericin B deoxycholate is also recommended.
- *Intravitreal therapy:* Patients with vitritis or with macular involvement (with or without vitritis): Intravitreal: 100 mcg of an extemporaneously prepared solution in 0.1 mL sterile water or NS; concomitant antifungal systemic therapy is also recommended.

Candidiasis, esophageal:
- *US labeling:* Oral: Treatment should continue for a minimum of 14 days, and for at least 7 days following resolution of symptoms. **Note:** If patient has inadequate clinical response, titrate in 50 mg/dose increments for weight <40 kg and 100 mg/dose increments for weight ≥40 kg
  - Weight <40 kg: 100 mg every 12 hours; maximum: 300 mg daily
  - Weight ≥40 kg: 200 mg every 12 hours; maximum: 600 mg daily
- *Alternative dosing:*
  - Fluconazole-refractory: Oral, IV (off-label route): 200 mg (3 mg/kg) twice daily for 14 to 21 days (IDSA [Pappas 2016])
  - HIV-positive patients (alternative to preferred therapy): Oral, IV (off-label route): 200 mg twice daily for 14 to 21 days (HHS [OI adult 2015])

Candidiasis, intravascular infections (off-label use) (IDSA [Pappas 2016]): Fluconazole-resistant/voriconazole-susceptible isolates:
- *Endocarditis, native or prosthetic valve:* Oral: 200 to 300 mg twice daily; voriconazole should only be used as step-down therapy in clinically stable, culture-negative patients following initial therapy with an amphotericin B lipid formulation (with or without flucytosine) or an echinocandin; antifungal therapy should continue for at least 6 weeks after valve replacement surgery (longer durations recommended in patients with perivalvular abscesses or other complications).
- *Implantable cardiac devices (eg, pacemaker. ICD, VAD):* Oral: 200 to 300 mg twice daily; voriconazole should only be used as step-down therapy in clinically stable, culture-negative patients following initial therapy with an amphotericin B lipid formulation (with or without flucytosine) or an echinocandin; antifungal therapy should continue for 4 to 6 weeks after device removal (4 weeks for infections limited to generator pockets and at least 6 weeks for infections involving the wires).

Candidiasis, oropharyngeal (fluconazole-refractory) (off-label use): Oral: 200 mg twice daily for up to 28 days (IDSA [Pappas 2016])

Coccidioidomycosis in HIV-infected patients (alternative to preferred therapy) (off-label use) (HHS [OI adult 2015]): Oral:
- Mild infections (eg, focal pneumonia): 200 mg twice daily; patients who complete initial therapy should be considered for lifelong suppressive therapy.
- Chronic suppressive therapy: 200 mg twice daily

Empiric antifungal therapy (neutropenic fever) (off-label use): IV: Initial: 6 mg/kg every 12 hours for 2 doses; maintenance dose: 4 mg/kg every 12 hours. **Note:** May consider oral therapy in place of IV therapy, with dosing of 200 to 300 mg orally every 12 hours **or** weight-based dosing (3 to 4 mg/kg) every 12 hours (IDSA [Patterson 2016])

Scedosporiosis, fusariosis:

IV:
- Initial: 6 mg/kg every 12 hours for 2 doses
- Maintenance dose: 4 mg/kg every 12 hours for >7 days

Oral: Maintenance dose: **Note:** If patient has inadequate clinical response, titrate in 50 mg/dose increments for weight <40 kg and 100 mg/dose increments for weight ≥40 kg.
- Weight <40 kg: 100 mg every 12 hours.
- Weight ≥40 kg: 200 mg every 12 hours.

Infection prophylaxis in graft-versus-host disease (GVHD) (high-risk patients) (off-label use) (Maertens 2011; Tomblyn 2009; Wingard 2010): Note: The optimal duration of prophylaxis in GVHD has not been determined.
- Oral: Weight >40 kg: 200 mg every 12 hours
- IV: Weight >40 kg: 4 mg/kg every 12 hours

Infection prophylaxis in standard- or high-risk patients with allogeneic hematopoietic stem cell transplant (HSCT) or certain autologous HSCT (off-label use) (Castagna 2012; Maertens 2011; Tomblyn 2009; Wingard 2010): Note: Begin prophylaxis at the start of chemotherapy or the day of transplantation. The ASBMT recommends continuing prophylaxis until engraftment (ie, 30 days) or for 7 days after the ANC reaches >1000 cells/mm^3 (Tomblyn 2009). The IDSA recommends anti-mold prophylaxis in allograft HSCT patients "through the neutropenic period and beyond," based on a demonstrated survival advantage in patients receiving prophylaxis for 75 days post-HSCT, or until cessation of immunosuppressive therapy (Freifeld 2011).

Oral: Weight >40 kg: 200 mg every 12 hours

IV: Weight >40 kg: 4 mg/kg every 12 hours.

Meningitis (secondary to contaminated [eg, *Exserohilum rostratum*] steroid products) (off-label use) (CDC [parameningeal] 2012; Kauffman 2013): Note: Consult an infectious disease specialist and current CDC guidelines for specific treatment recommendations. Therapy duration is ≥3 months; trough serum concentrations must be maintained between 2 to 5 mcg/mL.

IV: 6 mg/kg every 12 hours. If patient does not improve or has severe disease, consider adding amphotericin B (liposomal).

Oral (only in mild disease in adherent patients whose trough concentrations/response to therapy can be closely monitored): 6 mg/kg every 12 hours (CDC [parameningeal] 2012).

Osteoarticular infection involving the spine, discitis, epidural abscess or vertebral osteomyelitis (secondary to contaminated [eg, *Exserohilum rostratum*] steroid products) (off-label use) (CDC [osteoarticular] 2012; Kauffman 2013): IV: 6 mg/kg every 12 hours for ≥3 months. **Note:** Consult an infectious disease specialist and current CDC guidelines for specific treatment recommendations. Trough serum concentrations must be maintained between 2 to 5 mcg/mL. If patient has severe disease, consider adding amphotericin B (liposomal). Patients may be switched to oral therapy if condition has improved or stabilized.

Osteoarticular infection not involving the spine (secondary to contaminated [eg, *Exserohilum rostratum*] steroid products) (off-label use) (CDC [osteoarticular] 2012; Kauffman 2013): Note: Consult an infectious disease specialist and current CDC guidelines for specific treatment recommendations. Therapy duration is ≥3 months. Trough serum concentrations must be maintained between 2 to 5 mcg/mL.

IV: 6 mg/kg every 12 hours for 2 doses, then 4 mg/kg every 12 hours. If patient has severe disease, consider adding amphotericin B (liposomal)

Oral (only in mild disease in adherent patients whose trough concentrations/response to therapy can be closely monitored): 6 mg/kg every 12 hours for 2 doses, then 4 mg/kg every 12 hours

***Penicillium marneffei* infection in HIV-infected patients (off-label use) (HHS [OI adult 2015]):**

Acute infection in severely ill patients: 6 mg/kg IV every 12 hours for 2 doses, then 4 mg/kg IV every 12 hours for at least 3 days, followed by 200 mg orally twice daily for a maximum of 12 weeks; follow with itraconazole chronic maintenance therapy

Mild disease: Oral: 400 mg twice daily for 2 doses, then 200 mg twice daily for a maximum of 12 weeks; follow with itraconazole chronic maintenance therapy

Dosage adjustment in patients with inadequate response:

IV: Maintenance dose may be increased from 3 mg/kg every 12 hours to 4 mg/kg every 12 hours, depending upon condition.

Oral: Maintenance dose may be increased from 200 mg every 12 hours to 300 mg every 12 hours in patients weighing ≥40 kg (or to 150 mg every 12 hours in patients <40 kg), depending upon condition.

Dosage adjustment in patients unable to tolerate treatment:

IV: Maintenance dose may be reduced from 4 mg/kg every 12 hours to 3 mg/kg every 12 hours, depending upon condition.

Oral: Maintenance dose may be reduced in 50 mg decrements to a minimum dosage of 200 mg every 12 hours in patients weighing ≥40 kg (or to 100 mg every 12 hours in patients <40 kg), depending upon condition.

Dosage adjustment in patients receiving concomitant CYP450 enzyme inducers or substrates:

Efavirenz: Oral: Increase maintenance dose of voriconazole to 400 mg every 12 hours and reduce efavirenz dose to 300 mg once daily; upon discontinuation of voriconazole, return to the initial dose of efavirenz.

Phenytoin:

IV: Increase voriconazole maintenance dose to 5 mg/kg every 12 hours.

Oral: Increase voriconazole maintenance dose to 400 mg every 12 hours in patients ≥40 kg (200 mg every 12 hours in patients <40 kg).

Pediatric

Pediatric: **Note:** In pediatric patients <12 years, bioequivalence between the oral tablet and suspension has not been determined; due to possible shortened gastric transit time in infants and children, absorption of tablets may be different than adults; it is recommended that infants and children <12 years only receive oral suspension formulation [Vfend prescribing information (Europe Medicines Agency) 2013]. Data suggest higher doses (mg/kg) than adults are required in patients <15 years and weighing <50 kg. Although FDA approved for treatment of certain fungal infections in patients ≥12 years, the manufacturer's dosing may not achieve necessary therapeutic targets and possible suboptimal response in patients <15 years may occur (Friberg 2012).

General dosing, susceptible infection:

Infants and Children <2 years (off-label): IV, Oral (oral suspension): Initial: 9 mg/kg/dose every 12 hours followed by monitoring of serum trough concentrations typically initiated after 3 to 5 days; adjust dose to achieve target trough (>1 mcg/mL); median final dosage: 31.5 mg/kg/**day** (range: 12 to 71 mg/kg/**day**) divided every 12 hours; dosing based on 2 pharmacokinetic studies that included a total of 17 patients <2 years (Bartenlink 2013; Gerin 2011)

Children 2 to <12 years (off-label; *Red Book* [AAP 2015]):

Loading dose: IV: 9 mg/kg/dose every 12 hours for 2 doses on day 1

Maintenance:

IV: 8 mg/kg/dose every 12 hours; monitor serum concentrations to maintain trough >2 mcg/mL

Oral (oral suspension): 9 mg/kg/dose every 12 hours; maximum initial dose: 350 mg/dose; **Note:** In most patients, oral therapy has not been recommended as initial therapy for treatment; it has been recommended to convert from parenteral to oral therapy only after significant clinical improvement has been observed [Vfend prescribing information (Europe Medicines Agency) 2013].

Children ≥12 years and Adolescents ≤14 years (off-label; Friberg 2012): **Note:** In this age group, body weight is more important than age in predicting pharmacokinetics

IV:

<50 kg: Loading dose: 9 mg/kg/dose every 12 hours for 2 doses; followed by maintenance dose of 4 to 8 mg/kg/dose every 12 hours

≥50 kg: Loading dose: 6 mg/kg/dose every 12 hours for 2 doses; followed by maintenance dose of 3 to 4 mg/kg/dose every 12 hours

Oral: **Note:** Higher doses may be required if adequate trough concentrations are not achieved; monitor trough concentrations closely

<50 kg: 9 mg/kg/dose every 12 hours; maximum dose: 350 mg/dose

≥50 kg: 200 mg every 12 hours

Adolescents ≥15 years:

IV: Loading dose: 6 mg/kg/dose every 12 hours for 2 doses; followed by a maintenance dose of 3 to 4 mg/kg/dose every 12 hours

Oral: 200 mg every 12 hours

Aspergillosis, invasive, including disseminated and extrapulmonary infection; treatment: Note: Duration of therapy should be a minimum of 6 to 12 weeks, although duration is highly dependent on degree/duration of immunosuppression, disease site, and evidence of disease improvement. Monitor trough concentrations in patients with invasive aspergillosis; in pediatric patients <50 kg, therapeutic drug monitoring is critical to ensure efficacy and minimize toxicity; may consider switching to oral therapy once patient is stable and able to tolerate (IDSA [Patterson 2016]).

Children 2 to <12 years (off-label):

IV: Loading dose: 9 mg/kg/dose every 12 hours for 2 doses on day 1, followed by a maintenance dose of 8 mg/kg/dose every 12 hours (Friberg 2012; IDSA [Patterson 2016]; *Red Book* [AAP 2015])

Oral (oral suspension): 9 mg/kg/dose every 12 hours; maximum dose: 350 mg/dose; higher doses may be required if adequate trough concentrations are not achieved; monitor trough concentrations closely (Friberg 2012; IDSA [Patterson 2016])

Children ≥12 years and Adolescents ≤14 years (off-label): **Note:** In this age group, body weight is more important than age in predicting pharmacokinetics (Friberg 2012; IDSA [Patterson 2016]); monitor trough concentrations closely; higher doses may be required if adequate trough concentrations are not achieved.

<50 kg:

IV: Loading dose: 9 mg/kg/dose every 12 hours for 2 doses; followed by maintenance dose of 8 mg/kg/dose every 12 hours

Oral: 9 mg/kg/dose every 12 hours

≥50 kg:

IV: Loading dose: 6 mg/kg/dose every 12 hours for 2 doses; followed by maintenance dose of 4 mg/kg/dose every 12 hours

Oral: 200 to 300 mg every 12 hours **or** 3 to 4 mg/kg/dose every 12 hours

Adolescents ≥15 years (off-label; IDSA [Patterson 2016]):

IV: Loading dose: 6 mg/kg/dose every 12 hours for 2 doses; followed by maintenance dose of 4 mg/kg/dose every 12 hours

Oral: 200 to 300 mg every 12 hours **or** 3 to 4 mg/kg/dose every 12 hours

Candidiasis, prophylaxis for patients at high risk of invasive candidiasis (eg, AML, recurrent ALL, allogeneic HSCT) (off-label use):

Children 2 to <12 years (Dvorak 2012; ESCMID [Hope 2012]; Friberg 2012):

IV: Loading dose: 9 mg/kg/dose every 12 hours for 2 doses on day 1, followed by a maintenance dose of 8 mg/kg/dose every 12 hours

Oral (oral suspension): 9 mg/kg/dose every 12 hours; maximum dose: 350 mg/dose

Children ≥12 years and Adolescents ≤14 years: **Note:** In this age group, body weight is more important than age in predicting pharmacokinetics (Friberg 2012)

<50 kg:

IV: Loading dose: 9 mg/kg/dose every 12 hours for 2 doses; followed by maintenance dose of 8 mg/kg/dose every 12 hours (Dvorak 2012; ESCMID [Hope 2012]; Friberg 2012)

Oral: 9 mg/kg/dose every 12 hours; maximum dose: 350 mg/dose (ESCMID [Hope 2012]; Friberg 2012)

≥50 kg:

IV: 4 mg/kg/dose every 12 hours (Tomblyn 2009)

Oral: 200 mg every 12 hours (Tomblyn 2009; Wingard 2010)

Adolescents ≥15 years:

IV: 4 mg/kg/dose every 12 hours (Tomblyn 2009)

Oral: 200 mg every 12 hours (Tomblyn 2009; Wingard 2010)

Candidiasis, invasive; treatment: Note: Voriconazole is considered an alternative therapy and offers little advantage over fluconazole as first-line therapy of candidemia. Step-down therapy to oral voriconazole is recommended only in select clinically stable patients with certain voriconazole-susceptible isolates (eg, *C. krusei*) and negative repeat cultures (IDSA [Pappas 2016]).

Children 2 to <12 years (off-label; ESCMID [Hope 2012]; IDSA [Pappas 2016]):

IV: Loading dose: 9 mg/kg/dose every 12 hours for 2 doses on day 1, followed by a maintenance dose of 8 mg/kg/dose every 12 hours

Oral (oral suspension): 9 mg/kg/dose every 12 hours; maximum dose: 350 mg/dose

Children ≥12 years and Adolescents ≤14 years (off label): **Note:** In this age group, body weight is more important than age in predicting pharmacokinetics (Friberg 2012)

<50 kg:

IV: Loading dose: 9 mg/kg/dose every 12 hours for 2 doses; followed by maintenance dose of 8 mg/kg/dose every 12 hours (ESCMID [Hope 2012]; Friberg 2012; IDSA [Pappas 2016])

Oral: 9 mg/kg/dose every 12 hours; maximum dose: 350 mg/dose (ESCMID [Hope 2012]; Friberg 2012; IDSA [Pappas 2016])

≥50 kg:

IV: Loading dose: 400 mg (6 mg/kg/dose) every 12 hours for 2 doses, followed by 200 mg (3 mg/kg/dose) every 12 hours (ESCMID [Hope 2012]; Friberg 2012; IDSA [Pappas 2016])

Oral: 200 mg (3 mg/kg/dose) every 12 hours (ESCMID [Hope 2012]; Friberg 2012; IDSA [Pappas 2016])

Adolescents ≥15 years (off-label):

IV: Loading dose: 400 mg (6 mg/kg/dose) every 12 hours for 2 doses, followed by 200 mg (3 mg/kg/dose) every 12 hours (IDSA [Pappas 2016])

Oral: 200 mg (3 mg/kg/dose) every 12 hours (IDSA [Pappas 2016])

Candidiasis, esophageal (fluconazole-refractory); treatment: Treatment should continue for 14 to 21 days (IDSA [Pappas 2016])

Children 2 to <12 years:

IV (off-label): Loading dose: 9 mg/kg/dose every 12 hours for 2 doses; followed by maintenance dose of 8 mg/kg/dose every 12 hours (IDSA [Pappas 2016])

Oral (oral suspension): 9 mg/kg/dose every 12 hours; maximum dose: 350 mg/dose (IDSA [Pappas 2016])

Children ≥12 years and Adolescents ≤ 14 years: **Note:** In this age group, body weight is more important than age in predicting pharmacokinetics (Friberg 2012)

<50 kg:

IV (off-label): Loading dose: 9 mg/kg/dose every 12 hours for 2 doses; followed by maintenance dose of 8 mg/kg/dose every 12 hours (Friberg 2012; IDSA [Pappas 2016])

Oral: 9 mg/kg/dose every 12 hours; maximum dose: 350 mg/dose (Friberg 2012; IDSA [Pappas 2016])

≥50 kg: IV (off-label), Oral: 200 mg (3 mg/kg/dose) twice daily (IDSA [Pappas 2016])

Adolescents ≥15 years: IV (off-label), Oral: 200 mg (3 mg/kg/dose) twice daily (IDSA [Pappas 2016])

Candidiasis, intravascular infections (endocarditis/implantable cardiac devices [eg, pacemaker, ICD, VAD]); treatment (off-label use): Note: Voriconazole should only be used as step-down therapy in clinically stable, culture-negative patients following initial therapy

Children 2 to <12 years: Oral (oral suspension): 9 mg/kg/dose every 12 hours; maximum dose: 350 mg/dose (IDSA [Pappas 2016])

Children ≥12 years and Adolescents ≤14 years: **Note:** In this age group, body weight is more important than age in predicting pharmacokinetics (Friberg 2012)

<50 kg: Oral: 9 mg/kg/dose every 12 hours; maximum dose: 350 mg/dose (Friberg 2012; IDSA [Pappas 2016])

≥50 kg: Oral: 200 to 300 mg (3 to 4 mg/kg/dose) twice daily (Friberg 2012; IDSA [Pappas 2016])

Adolescents ≥15 years: Oral: 200 to 300 mg (3 to 4 mg/kg/dose) twice daily (IDSA [Pappas 2016])

Candidiasis, oropharyngeal (fluconazole-refractory); treatment (off-label use): Treatment should continue for up to 28 days (IDSA [Pappas 2016])

Children 2 to <12 years: Oral (oral suspension): 9 mg/kg/dose every 12 hours; maximum dose: 350 mg/dose (IDSA [Pappas 2016])

Children ≥12 years and Adolescents ≤14 years: **Note:** In this age group, body weight is more important than age in predicting pharmacokinetics (Friberg 2012)

<50 kg: Oral: 9 mg/kg/dose every 12 hours; maximum dose: 350 mg/dose (Friberg 2012; IDSA [Pappas 2016])

≥50 kg: Oral: 200 mg twice daily (Friberg 2012; IDSA [Pappas 2016])

Adolescents ≥15 years: Oral: 200 mg twice daily (IDSA [Pappas 2016])

Candidiasis, endophthalmitis (with or without vitritis): Voriconazole-susceptible isolates (off-label use):

Systemic therapy: **Note:** For patients with vitritis or with macular involvement (with or without vitritis), an intravitreal injection of voriconazole or amphotericin B deoxycholate is also recommended (IDSA [Pappas 2016]).

Children 2 to <12 years:

IV: Loading dose: 9 mg/kg/dose every 12 hours for 2 doses; followed by maintenance dose of 8 mg/kg/dose every 12 hours (IDSA [Pappas 2016])

Oral (oral suspension): 9 mg/kg/dose every 12 hours; maximum dose: 350 mg/dose (IDSA [Pappas 2016])

Children ≥12 years and Adolescents ≤14 years: **Note:** In this age group, body weight is more important than age in predicting pharmacokinetics (Friberg 2012)

<50 kg:

IV: Loading dose: 9 mg/kg/dose every 12 hours for 2 doses; followed by maintenance dose of 8 mg/kg/dose every 12 hours (Friberg 2012; IDSA [Pappas 2016])

Oral: 9 mg/kg/dose every 12 hours; maximum dose: 350 mg/dose (Friberg 2012; IDSA [Pappas 2016])

≥50 kg:

IV: Loading dose: 400 mg (6 mg/kg/dose) every 12 hours for 2 doses, followed by 300 mg (4 mg/kg/dose) twice daily (Friberg 2012; IDSA [Pappas 2016])

Oral: 300 mg (4 mg/kg/dose) twice daily (Friberg 2012; IDSA [Pappas 2016])

Adolescents ≥15 years:

IV: Loading dose: 400 mg (6 mg/kg/dose) every 12 hours for 2 doses, followed by 300 mg (4 mg/kg/dose) twice daily (IDSA [Pappas 2016])

Oral: 300 mg (4 mg/kg/dose) twice daily (IDSA [Pappas 2016])

Intravitreal therapy: Patients with vitritis or with macular involvement (with or without vitritis): Children ≥2 years and Adolescents: Intravitreal: 100 **mcg** of an extemporaneously prepared solution in 0.1 mL sterile water or NS; concomitant systemic antifungal therapy is also recommended.

Renal Impairment

IV:

CrCl ≥50 mL/minute: There are no dosage adjustments provided in the manufacturer's labeling.

CrCl <50 mL/minute: There are no specific dosage adjustments provided in the manufacturer's labeling. Due to accumulation of the intravenous vehicle (cyclodextrin), the manufacturer recommends the use of oral voriconazole in these patients unless an assessment of the benefit:risk justifies the use of IV voriconazole; if IV therapy is used, closely monitor serum creatinine and change to oral voriconazole when possible. IV therapy has been used in select patients with CrCl <50 mL/minute using varying doses (median duration of treatment 7 to 10 days) (Neofytos 2012; Oude Lashof 2012).

Oral:

Mild to severe impairment: No dosage adjustment necessary.

Dialysis: Poorly dialyzed; no supplemental dose or dosage adjustment necessary, including patients on intermittent hemodialysis (IHD) with thrice weekly sessions or peritoneal dialysis.

Continuous renal replacement therapy (CRRT) (Heintz 2009): Drug clearance is highly dependent on the method of renal replacement, filter type, and flow rate. Appropriate dosing requires close monitoring of pharmacologic response, signs of adverse reactions due to drug accumulation, as well as drug concentrations in relation to target trough (if appropriate). The following are general recommendations only (based on dialysate flow/ultrafiltration rates of 1 to 2 L/hour and minimal residual renal function) and should not supersede clinical judgment:

CVVH, CVVHD, and CVVHDF: Loading dose of 400 mg every 12 hours for 2 doses, followed by 200 mg every 12 hours.

Hepatic Impairment

Mild to moderate impairment (Child-Pugh class A or B): Following standard loading dose, reduce maintenance dosage by 50%

Severe impairment (Child-Pugh class C): There are no dosage adjustments provided in the manufacturer's labeling (has not been studied). Should only be used if benefit outweighs risk; monitor closely for toxicity

Obesity Use ideal body weight (IBW) for most obese patients in weight-based dosing calculations; consider using an adjusted body weight (adjusted body weight=0.4 [total body weight – IBW] + IBW) in obese patients with life-threatening invasive fungal infections. Confirm selection of an appropriate dose with therapeutic drug monitoring (Eljaaly 2016).

Mechanism of Action Interferes with fungal cytochrome P450 activity (selectively inhibits 14-alpha-lanosterol demethylation), decreasing ergosterol synthesis (principal sterol in fungal cell membrane) and inhibiting fungal cell membrane formation.

Contraindications Hypersensitivity to voriconazole or any component of the formulation; coadministration with astemizole, barbiturates (long acting), carbamazepine, cisapride, efavirenz (≥400 mg daily), ergot derivatives (ergotamine and dihydroergotamine), pimozide, quinidine, rifampin, rifabutin, ritonavir (>800 mg daily; also avoid low dose [eg, 200 mg daily] dosing if possible), sirolimus, St John's wort, terfenadine

Documentation of allergenic cross-reactivity for imidazole antifungals is limited. However, because of similarities in chemical structure and/or pharmacologic actions, the possibility of cross-sensitivity cannot be ruled out with certainty.

Warnings/Precautions

Visual changes, including blurred vision, changes in visual acuity, color perception, and photophobia, are commonly associated with treatment; postmarketing cases of optic neuritis and papilledema (lasting >1 month) have also been reported. Patients should be warned to avoid tasks which depend on vision, including operating machinery or driving. Changes are reversible on discontinuation following brief exposure/treatment regimens (≤28 days).

Serious (and rarely fatal) hepatic reactions (eg, hepatitis, cholestasis, fulminant failure) have been observed with voriconazole. In lung transplant recipients, median time to hepatic toxicity was 14 days with the majority occurring within 30 days of therapy initiation (Luong 2012). Use with caution in patients with serious underlying medical conditions (eg, hematologic malignancy); hepatic reactions have occurred in patients with no identifiable underlying risk factors. Liver dysfunction is usually reversible upon therapy discontinuation. Monitor serum transaminase and bilirubin at baseline and at least weekly for the first month of treatment. Monitoring frequency can then be reduced to monthly during continued use if no abnormalities are noted. If marked elevations occur compared to baseline, discontinue unless benefit/risk of treatment justifies continued use. Adjustments to maintenance dosing is required in mild to moderate hepatic cirrhosis (Child-Pugh class A and B).

Voriconazole tablets contain lactose; avoid administration in hereditary galactose intolerance, Lapp lactase deficiency, or glucose-galactose malabsorption. Suspension contains sucrose; use caution with fructose intolerance, sucrase-isomaltase deficiency, or glucose-galactose malabsorption. Avoid/limit use of intravenous formulation in patients with moderate to severe renal impairment (CrCl <50 mL/minute); injection contains excipient cyclodextrin (sulfobutyl ether beta-cyclodextrin [SBECD]), which may accumulate, although the clinical significance of this finding is uncertain (Luke 2010); consider using oral voriconazole in these patients unless benefit of injection outweighs the risk. If injection is used in patients CrCl <50 mL/minute, monitor serum creatinine closely; if increases occur, consider changing therapy to oral voriconazole.

Anaphylactoid-type reactions (eg, flushing, fever, sweating, tachycardia, chest tightness, dyspnea, nausea, pruritus, rash) may occur with IV infusion. Consider discontinuation of infusion should these reactions occur. Acute renal failure has been observed in severely ill patients; use with caution in patients receiving concomitant nephrotoxic medications. Evaluate renal function (particularly serum creatinine) at baseline and periodically during therapy.

Potentially significant drug-drug interactions may exist, requiring dose or frequency adjustment, additional monitoring, and/or selection of alternative therapy. QT interval prolongation has been associated with voriconazole use; rare cases of arrhythmia (including torsade de pointes), cardiac arrest, and sudden death have been reported, usually in seriously ill patients with comorbidities and/or risk factors (eg, prior cardiotoxic chemotherapy, cardiomyopathy [especially with concomitant heart failure], electrolyte imbalance, or concomitant QTc-prolonging drugs). Also use with caution in patients with potentially proarrhythmic conditions (eg, congenital or acquired QT syndrome, sinus bradycardia, or preexisting symptomatic arrhythmias); correct electrolyte abnormalities (eg, hypokalemia, hypomagnesemia, hypocalcemia) prior to initiating and during therapy. Do not infuse concomitantly with blood products or short-term concentrated electrolyte solutions, even if the two infusions are running in separate intravenous lines (or cannulas).

Rare cases of malignancy (melanoma, squamous cell carcinoma [SCC]) have been reported in patients with prior onset of severe photosensitivity reactions or exposure to standard dose long-term voriconazole therapy (in lung transplant recipients, SCC increased by ~6% per 60 days with a 28% absolute risk increase at 5 years [Singer 2012]). Other serious exfoliative cutaneous reactions, including Stevens-Johnson syndrome, toxic epidermal necrolysis, and erythema multiforme, have also been reported. Patients, including children, should avoid exposure to direct sunlight and should use protective clothing and high SPF sunscreen; may cause photosensitivity, especially with long-term use. If phototoxic reactions occur, referral to a dermatologist and voriconazole discontinuation should be considered. If therapy is continued, dermatologic evaluation should be performed on a systematic and regular basis to allow early detection and management of premalignant lesions. Pediatric patients are at particular risk for phototoxicity; stringent photoprotective measures are necessary in children due to the risk of squamous cell carcinoma. In children experiencing photoaging injuries (eg,lentigines or ephelides), avoidance of sun and dermatologic follow-up are warranted even after treatment is discontinued. Discontinue use in patients who develop an exfoliative cutaneous reaction or a skin lesion consistent with squamous cell carcinoma or melanoma. Periodic total body skin examinations should be performed, particularly with prolonged use. Fluorosis and/or periostitis may occur during long-term therapy. If patient develops skeletal pain and radiologic findings of fluorosis or periostitis, discontinue therapy.

Voriconazole demonstrates nonlinear pharmacokinetics. Dose modifications may result in unpredictable changes in serum concentrations and contribute to toxicity. It is important to note that cutoff trough threshold values ranged widely among studies; however, an upper limit of <5.0 mg/L would be reasonable for most disease states (see CDC recommendations for *Exserohilum rostratum* in Reference Range section) (CDC 2012). In patients >14 years of age or 12-14 years and weighing >50 kg, data suggest that pharmacokinetics are similar to adults (Friberg 2012). In patients <12 years of age, the full pharmacokinetic profile for voriconazole is not completely defined, and for patients <2 years, the data are sparse. In children 2 to <12 years, current data suggests voriconazole undergoes a high degree of variability in exposure with linear elimination at lower doses and nonlinear elimination at higher doses; therefore, to achieve similar AUC as adults, increased dosage is necessary in children (Friberg 2012; Karlsson 2009; Walsh 2004).

Correct electrolyte abnormalities (eg, hypokalemia, hypomagnesemia, hypocalcemia) prior to initiating and during therapy. Monitor pancreatic function in patients (children and adults) at risk for acute pancreatitis (eg, recent chemotherapy or hematopoietic stem cell transplantation). Pancreatitis has occurred in pediatric patients.

Benzyl alcohol and derivatives: Some dosage forms may contain sodium benzoate/benzoic acid; benzoic acid (benzoate) is a metabolite of benzyl alcohol; large amounts of benzyl alcohol (≥99 mg/kg/day) have been associated with a potentially fatal toxicity ("gasping syndrome") in neonates; the "gasping syndrome" consists of metabolic acidosis, respiratory distress, gasping respirations, CNS dysfunction (including convulsions, intracranial hemorrhage), hypotension, and cardiovascular collapse (AAP ["Inactive" 1997]; CDC 1982); some data suggests that benzoate displaces bilirubin from protein binding sites (Ahlfors 2001); avoid or use dosage forms containing benzyl alcohol derivative with caution in neonates. See manufacturer's labeling.

Drug Interactions

Metabolism/Transport Effects **Substrate** of CYP2C19 (major), CYP2C9 (major), CYP3A4 (minor); **Note:** Assignment of Major/Minor substrate status based on clinically relevant drug interaction potential; **Inhibits** CYP2C19 (moderate), CYP2C9 (moderate), CYP3A4 (strong)

Avoid Concomitant Use

Avoid concomitant use of Voriconazole with any of the following: Ado-Trastuzumab Emtansine; Alfuzosin; Aprepitant; Astemizole; Asunaprevir; Atazanavir; Avanafil; Axitinib; Barbiturates; Barnidipine; Blonanserin; Bosutinib; Bromocriptine; Budesonide (Systemic); CarBAMazepine; Ceritinib; Cisapride; Cobimetinib; Conivaptan; Crizotinib; Dabrafenib; Dapoxetine; Darunavir; Dihydroergotamine; Dofetilide; Domperidone; Dronedarone; Eletriptan; Eplerenone; Ergoloid Mesylates; Ergonovine; Ergotamine; Everolimus; Flibanserin; Fluconazole; Halofantrine; Ibrutinib; Irinotecan Products; Isavuconazonium Sulfate; Ivabradine; Lapatinib; Lercanidipine; Lomitapide; Lopinavir; Lovastatin; Lumacaftor; Lurasidone; Macitentan; Methylergonovine; Naloxegol; Nilotinib; NiMODipine; Nisoldipine; Olaparib; Palbociclib; Pimozide; QuiNIDine; Radotinib; Ranolazine; Red Yeast Rice; Regorafenib; Rifamycin Derivatives; Ritonavir; Rupatadine; Saccharomyces boulardii; Salmeterol; Silodosin; Simeprevir; Simvastatin; Sirolimus; Sonidegib; St John's Wort; Suvorexant; Tamsulosin; Terfenadine; Ticagrelor; Tolvaptan; Toremifene; Trabectedin; Udenafil; Ulipristal; Vemurafenib; VinCRIStine (Liposomal); Vinflunine; Vorapaxar

Increased Effect/Toxicity

Voriconazole may increase the levels/effects of: Ado-Trastuzumab Emtansine; Alfuzosin; Alitretinoin (Systemic); Almotriptan; Alosetron; Aminolevulinic Acid; Antineoplastic Agents (Vinca Alkaloids); Apixaban; Aprepitant; ARIPiprazole; ARIPiprazole Lauroxil; Astemizole; Asunaprevir; AtorvaSTATin; Avanafil; Axitinib; Barnidipine; Bedaquiline; Benperidol; Blonanserin; Boceprevir; Bortezomib; Bosentan; Bosutinib; Brentuximab Vedotin; Brexpiprazole; Brinzolamide; Bromocriptine; Budesonide (Nasal); Budesonide (Oral Inhalation); Budesonide (Systemic); Budesonide (Topical); Buprenorphine; BusPIRone; Busulfan; Cabazitaxel; Cabozantinib; Calcifediol; Calcium Channel Blockers; Cannabidiol; Cannabis; Cariprazine; Carvedilol; Ceritinib; Cilostazol; Cisapride; Citalopram; CloZAPine; Cobicistat; Cobimetinib; Colchicine; Conivaptan; Contraceptives (Estrogens); Contraceptives (Progestins); Corticosteroids (Orally Inhaled); Corticosteroids (Systemic); Crizotinib; CycloSPORINE (Systemic); CYP2C19 Substrates; CYP2C9 Substrates; CYP3A4 Substrates; Dabrafenib; Daclatasvir; Dapoxetine; Dasatinib; Deflazacort; Delamanid; Diclofenac (Systemic); Diclofenac (Topical); Dienogest; Dihydroergotamine; DOCEtaxel; Dofetilide; Domperidone; DOXOrubicin (Conventional); Dronabinol; Dronedarone; Drospirenone; Dutasteride; Efavirenz; Eletriptan; Eliglustat; Elvitegravir; Eplerenone; Ergoloid Mesylates; Ergonovine; Ergotamine; Erlotinib; Estazolam; Eszopiclone; Etizolam; Etravirine; Everolimus; FentaNYL; Fesoterodine; Flibanserin; Fluticasone (Nasal); Fluticasone (Oral Inhalation); Fosamprenavir; Fosphenytoin; Gefitinib; GuanFACINE; Halofantrine; Highest Risk QTc-Prolonging Agents; HYDROcodone; HydrOXYzine; Ibrutinib; Ibuprofen; Idelalisib; Iloperidone; Imatinib; Imidafenacin; Irinotecan Products; Isavuconazonium Sulfate; Ivabradine; Ivacaftor; Ixabepilone; Lacosamide; Lapatinib; Lercanidipine; Levobupivacaine; Levomilnacipran; Lomitapide; Losartan; Lovastatin; Lurasidone; Macitentan; Manidipine; Maraviroc; MedroxyPROGESTERone; Meloxicam; Methadone; Methylergonovine; MethylPREDNISolone; MiFEPRIStone; Mirodenafil; Moderate Risk QTc-Prolonging Agents; Naldemedine; Naloxegol; Nelfinavir; Nilotinib; NiMODipine;

Nisoldipine; Olaparib; Ospemifene; Oxybutynin; OxyCODONE; Palbociclib; Panobinostat; Parecoxib; Paricalcitol; PAZOPanib; Phenytoin; Pimavanserin; Pimecrolimus; Pimozide; PONATinib; Porfimer; Pranlukast; Praziquantel; PrednisoLONE (Systemic); PredniSONE; Propafenone; Proton Pump Inhibitors; QUEtiapine; QuiNIDine; Radotinib; Ramelteon; Ranolazine; Reboxetine; Red Yeast Rice; Regorafenib; Repaglinide; Retapamulin; Reverse Transcriptase Inhibitors (Non-Nucleoside); Ribociclib; Rifamycin Derivatives; Rilpivirine; RomiDEPsin; Rupatadine; Ruxolitinib; Salmeterol; SAXagliptin; Sildenafil; Silodosin; Simeprevir; Simvastatin; Sirolimus; Solifenacin; Sonidegib; SORAfenib; Sulfonylureas; SUNItinib; Suvorexant; Tacrolimus (Systemic); Tacrolimus (Topical); Tadalafil; Tamsulosin; Tasimelteon; Telaprevir; Telithromycin; Terfenadine; Tetrahydrocannabinol; Ticagrelor; Tofacitinib; Tolterodine; Tolvaptan; Toremifene; Trabectedin; TraMADol; Udenafil; Ulipristal; Vardenafil; Vemurafenib; Venetoclax; Venlafaxine; Verteporfin; Vilazodone; VinCRIStine (Liposomal); Vinflunine; Vitamin K Antagonists; Vorapaxar; Zolpidem; Zopiclone; Zuclopenthixol

The levels/effects of Voriconazole may be increased by: Atazanavir; Boceprevir; Chloramphenicol; Cobicistat; Contraceptives (Estrogens); Contraceptives (Progestins); CYP2C19 Inhibitors (Moderate); CYP2C9 Inhibitors (Moderate); CYP2C9 Inhibitors (Strong); Etravirine; Fluconazole; Fosamprenavir; MIFEPRIStone; Proton Pump Inhibitors; Telaprevir

Decreased Effect

Voriconazole may decrease the levels/effects of: Amphotericin B; Atazanavir; Clopidogrel; Doxercalciferol; Ifosfamide; Prasugrel; Saccharomyces boulardii; Ticagrelor

The levels/effects of Voriconazole may be decreased by: Antihepaciviral Combination Products; Atazanavir; Barbiturates; CarBAMazepine; CYP2C9 Inducers (Strong); Darunavir; Dexamethasone (Systemic); Didanosine; Efavirenz; Enzalutamide; Etravirine; Fosphenytoin; Lopinavir; Lumacaftor; Phenytoin; Reverse Transcriptase Inhibitors (Non-Nucleoside); Rifamycin Derivatives; Ritonavir; St John's Wort; Telaprevir

Food Interactions Food may decrease voriconazole absorption. Management: Oral voriconazole should be taken 1 hour before or 1 hour after a meal. Maintain adequate hydration unless instructed to restrict fluid intake.

Pharmacodynamics/Kinetics

Half-life Elimination Variable, dose-dependent. **Note:** Steady-state trough concentrations are achieved within 1 day when an IV loading dose is administered and 5 days if no loading dose is used.

Time to Peak Oral:

Children 2 to <12 years: Median: 1.1 hours (range: 0.73-8.03 hours) (Driscoll 2011) Adults: 1 to 2 hours

Pregnancy Risk Factor D

Pregnancy Considerations Voriconazole can cause fetal harm when administered to a pregnant woman. Voriconazole was teratogenic and embryotoxic in animal studies, and lowered plasma estradiol in animal models. Women of childbearing potential should use effective contraception during treatment. Should be used in pregnant woman only if benefit to mother justifies potential risk to the fetus.

Breastfeeding Considerations It is not known if voriconazole is excreted in breast milk. Due to the potential for serious adverse reactions in the nursing infant, the manufacturer recommends a decision be made whether to discontinue nursing or to discontinue the drug, taking into account the importance of treatment to the mother.

Dosage Forms

Solution Reconstituted, Intravenous:
Generic: 200 mg (1 ea)

Solution Reconstituted, Intravenous [preservative free]:
Vfend IV: 200 mg (1 ea)
Generic: 200 mg (1 ea)

Suspension Reconstituted, Oral:
Vfend: 40 mg/mL (75 mL)
Generic: 40 mg/mL (75 mL)

Tablet, Oral:
Vfend: 50 mg, 200 mg
Generic: 50 mg, 200 mg

Dental Comment See Local Anesthetic/Vasoconstrictor Precautions

Vorinostat (vor IN oh stat)

Brand Names: US Zolinza

Brand Names: Canada Zolinza

Pharmacologic Category Antineoplastic Agent, Histone Deacetylase (HDAC) Inhibitor

Use Cutaneous T-cell lymphoma: Treatment of cutaneous manifestations of cutaneous T-cell lymphoma (CTCL) with progressive, persistent, or recurrent disease on or following 2 systemic treatments

Local Anesthetic/Vasoconstrictor Precautions Vorinostat is one of the drugs confirmed to prolong the QT interval and is accepted as having a risk of causing torsade de pointes. The risk of drug-induced torsade de pointes is extremely low when a single QT interval prolonging drug is prescribed. In terms of epinephrine, it is not known what effect vasoconstrictors in the local anesthetic regimen will have in patients with a known history of congenital prolonged QT interval or in patients taking any medication that prolongs the QT interval. Until more information is obtained, it is suggested that the clinician consult with the physician prior to the use of a vasoconstrictor in suspected patients, and that the vasoconstrictor (epinephrine, mepivacaine and levonordefrin [Carbocaine® 2% with Neo-Cobefrin®]) be used with caution.

Effects on Dental Treatment Key adverse event(s) related to dental treatment: High incidence of xerostomia (normal salivary flow resumes upon discontinuation) and taste perversion (see Dental Comment)

Effects on Bleeding Chemotherapy may result in significant myelosuppression, potentially including significant reduction in platelet counts (thrombocytopenia grades 3/4: 6%) and altered hemostasis. In patients who are under active treatment with these agents, medical consult is suggested.

Adverse Reactions

>10%:

Cardiovascular: Peripheral edema (13%)

Central nervous system: Fatigue (52%), chills (16%), dizziness (15%), headache (12%)

Dermatologic: Alopecia (19%), pruritus (12%)

Endocrine & metabolic: Hyperglycemia (8% to 69%; grade 3: 5%), weight loss (21%), dehydration (1% to 16%)

Gastrointestinal: Diarrhea (52%), nausea (41%), dysgeusia (28%), anorexia (24%), xerostomia (16%), constipation (15%), vomiting (15%), decreased appetite (14%)

Genitourinary: Proteinuria (51%)

Hematologic & oncologic: Thrombocytopenia (26%; grades 3/4: 6%), anemia (14%; grades 3/4: 2%)
Neuromuscular & skeletal: Muscle spasm (20%)
Renal: Increased serum creatinine (16% to 47%)
Respiratory: Cough (11%), upper respiratory tract infection (11%)
Miscellaneous: Fever (11%)

1% to 10%:

Cardiovascular: Pulmonary embolism (5%), prolonged Q-T interval on ECG (3% to 4%)
Hematologic & oncologic: Squamous cell carcinoma of skin (4%)

<1%, postmarketing, and/or case reports: Abdominal pain, acute ischemic stroke, angioedema, bacteremia (streptococcal), blurred vision, chest pain, cholecystitis, deafness, deep vein thrombosis, diverticulitis, dysphagia, exfoliative dermatitis, gastrointestinal hemorrhage, Guillain-Barre syndrome, hemoptysis, hypertension, hypokalemia, hyponatremia, infection, infection due to enterococcus, lethargy, leukopenia, myocardial infarction, neutropenia, pneumonia, renal failure, sepsis, spinal cord injury, syncope, T-cell lymphoma, tumor hemorrhage, ureteral obstruction, obstructive uropathy (ureteropelvic junction), urinary retention, vasculitis, weakness

General Dosage Range Dosage adjustment recommended in patients who develop toxicities and those with hepatic impairment

Oral: *Adults:* 400 mg once daily

Mechanism of Action Inhibits histone deacetylase enzymes, HDAC1, HDAC2, HDAC3, and HDAC6, which catalyze acetyl group removal from protein lysine residues (including histones and transcription factors). Histone deacetylase inhibition results in accumulation of acetyl groups, which alters chromatin structure and transcription factor activation; cell growth is terminated and apoptosis occurs.

Pharmacodynamics/Kinetics

Half-life Elimination ~2 hours

Time to Peak Plasma: With high-fat meal: ~4 hours (range: 2 to 10 hours)

Pregnancy Risk Factor D

Pregnancy Considerations Adverse events were observed in animal reproduction studies. Based on the mechanism of action, may cause fetal harm if administered during pregnancy. Inform patient of potential hazard if used during pregnancy or if pregnancy occurs during treatment.

Dental Comment This drug is known to prolong the QT interval (see Local Anesthetic/Vasoconstrictor Precautions)

Vortioxetine (vor tye OX e teen)

Brand Names: US Brintellix [DSC]; Trintellix

Brand Names: Canada Trintellix

Pharmacologic Category Antidepressant, Selective Serotonin Reuptake Inhibitor; Serotonin 5-HT_{1A} Receptor Agonist; Serotonin 5-HT_3 Receptor Antagonist

Use Major depressive disorder: Treatment of major depressive disorder (MDD)

Local Anesthetic/Vasoconstrictor Precautions Although caution should be used in patients taking tricyclic antidepressants, no interactions have been reported with vasoconstrictors and vortioxetine, a nontricyclic antidepressant which acts to increase serotonin; no precautions appear to be needed.

Effects on Dental Treatment Key adverse event(s) related to dental treatment: Xerostomia (normal salivary flow resumes upon discontinuation) (see Dental Comment)

Effects on Bleeding Bleeding risk: SSRIs have been reported to impair platelet aggregation resulting in increased risk of bleeding events, particularly if used concomitantly with aspirin, NSAIDs, warfarin, or other anticoagulants. Bleeding related to antidepressant use has been reported to range from relatively minor bruising and epistaxis to life-threatening hemorrhage.

Adverse Reactions

>10%:

Central nervous system: Female sexual disorder (self-reporting: 1% to 2%; Arizona Sexual Experience Scale: 22% to 34%), male sexual disorder (self-reporting: 3% to 5%; Arizona Sexual Experience Scale: 16% to 29%)
Gastrointestinal: Nausea (dose-related, females >males, 21% to 32%; commonly occurs within the first week of treatment, then decreases in frequency but can persist in some patients)

1% to 10%:

Central nervous system: Dizziness (8% to 9%), abnormal dreams (2% to 3%)
Dermatologic: Pruritus (2% to 3%)
Gastrointestinal: Diarrhea (7% to 10%), xerostomia (7% to 8%), constipation (5% to 6%), vomiting (3% to 6%), flatulence (2% to 3%)

<1%, postmarketing, and/or case reports: Acute pancreatitis, angle-closure glaucoma, dysgeusia, dyspepsia, flushing, hypomania, hyponatremia, mania, serotonin syndrome, vertigo, weight gain, withdrawal syndrome

General Dosage Range Oral: *Adults:* Initial: 10 mg once daily; Maintenance: 5-20 mg once daily.

Mechanism of Action Inhibits reuptake of serotonin (5-HT); also has agonist activity at the 5-HT_{1A} receptor and antagonist activity at the 5-HT_3 receptor.

Pharmacodynamics/Kinetics

Onset of Action Therapeutic: 2-4 weeks

Half-life Elimination ~66 hours

Time to Peak 7-11 hours

Pregnancy Considerations Nonteratogenic effects in the newborn following SSRI/SNRI exposure late in the third trimester include respiratory distress, cyanosis, apnea, seizures, temperature instability, feeding difficulty, vomiting, hypoglycemia, hypo- or hypertonia, hyper-reflexia, jitteriness, irritability, constant crying, and tremor. Symptoms may be due to the toxicity of the SSRIs/SNRIs or a discontinuation syndrome and may be consistent with serotonin syndrome associated with SSRI treatment. Persistent pulmonary hypertension of the newborn (PPHN) has also been reported with SSRI exposure.

The ACOG recommends that therapy with SSRIs or SNRIs during pregnancy be individualized; treatment of depression during pregnancy should incorporate the clinical expertise of the mental health clinician, obstetrician, primary health care provider, and pediatrician (ACOG 2008). According to the American Psychiatric Association (APA), the risks of medication treatment should be weighed against other treatment options and untreated depression. For women who discontinue antidepressant medications during pregnancy and who may be at high risk for postpartum depression, the medications can be restarted following delivery (APA 2010). Treatment algorithms have been developed by the ACOG and the APA for the management of depression in women prior to conception and during pregnancy (Yonkers 2009).

Pregnant women exposed to antidepressants during pregnancy are encouraged to enroll in the National Pregnancy Registry for Antidepressants (NPRAD). Women 18 to 45 years of age or their health care providers may contact the registry by calling 844-405-6185. Enrollment should be done as early in pregnancy as possible.

Dental Comment Problems with SSRI-induced bruxism have been reported and may preclude their use; clinicians attempting to evaluate any patient with bruxism or involuntary muscle movement, who is simultaneously being treated with an SSRI drug, should be aware of the potential association.

Warfarin (WAR far in)

Related Information

Antiplatelet and Anticoagulation Considerations in Dentistry *on page 1764*

Cardiovascular Diseases *on page 1752*

Brand Names: US Coumadin; Jantoven

Brand Names: Canada Apo-Warfarin; Coumadin; Mylan-Warfarin; Novo-Warfarin; Taro-Warfarin

Generic Availability (US) May be product dependent

Pharmacologic Category Anticoagulant; Anticoagulant, Vitamin K Antagonist

Use

Thromboembolic complications: Prophylaxis and treatment of thromboembolic disorders (eg, venous, pulmonary) and embolic complications arising from atrial fibrillation or cardiac valve replacement:

Nonvalvular AF or atrial flutter: The 2014 American Heart Association/American College of Cardiology/Heart Rhythm Society guidelines for the management of AF recommend oral anticoagulation for patients with nonvalvular AF or atrial flutter with prior stroke, TIA, or a CHA_2DS_2-VASc score ≥2. In patients with AF or atrial flutter of >48 hours duration or when the duration is unknown, anticoagulation with warfarin is recommended for at least 3 weeks prior to and 4 weeks after cardioversion regardless of the CHA_2DS_2-VASc score and method used to restore sinus rhythm (AHA/ACC [January 2014]).

Valvular AF: The 2014 American Heart Association/American Stroke Association (AHA/ASA) guidelines for the primary prevention of stroke recommend chronic oral anticoagulation with warfarin for patients with valvular atrial fibrillation at high risk for stroke, defined as a CHA2DS2-VASc score of ≥2, and acceptably low risk for hemorrhagic complications (AHA/ASA [Meschia 2014]).

Mechanical prosthetic cardiac valves: The 2014 American Heart Association/American Stroke Association (AHA/ASA) guidelines for the primary prevention of stroke recommend warfarin and low-dose aspirin in the patients who have received an aortic mechanical prosthetic valve (with or without risk factors) or any mitral mechanical prosthetic valve. Target INRs vary depending on valve position and/or risk factors (AHA/ASA [Meschia 2014]).

Myocardial infarction: Adjunct to reduce risk of systemic embolism (eg, recurrent MI, stroke) after myocardial infarction:

According to the American College of Cardiology/American Heart Association (ACCF/AHA) guidelines for the management of patients with ST-elevation myocardial infarction (STEMI), warfarin should be administered to patients with STEMI and AF and a $CHADS_2$ score of 2 or more, mechanical valve, venous thromboembolism, or hypercoagulable disorder. Use is reasonable in patients with STEMI and asymptomatic LV mural thrombi and may be considered in patients with STEMI and anterior apical akinesis or dyskinesis (O'Gara 2013).

Limitations of use: Warfarin has no direct effect on an established thrombus and does not reverse ischemic tissue damage. The goal of anticoagulant therapy is to prevent further extension of an already formed thrombus and to prevent secondary thromboembolic complications that may result in serious and potentially fatal sequelae.

Local Anesthetic/Vasoconstrictor Precautions
No information available to require special precautions

Effects on Dental Treatment Key adverse event(s) related to dental treatment: Mouth ulcers and taste disturbance.

Signs of warfarin overdose may first appear as bleeding from gingival tissue (see Effects on Bleeding and Dental Comment)

For stroke patients undergoing dental procedures (see Effects on Bleeding and Dental Comment)

Effects on Bleeding As with all anticoagulants, bleeding is a potential adverse effect of warfarin during dental surgery; risk is dependent on multiple variables, including the intensity of anticoagulation and patient susceptibility. Consultation with prescribing physician is advisable prior to surgery to determine if temporary dose reduction or withdrawal of medication is indicated. Stroke patients maintained on warfarin should continue therapy during dental procedures as warfarin is unlikely to increase bleeding risk (Armstrong, 2013)

Tooth extraction: A recent study assessed the amount of bleeding during a single tooth extraction in patients who remained on warfarin during the procedure versus those who discontinued warfarin (Karsli, 2011). All patients had coronary artery disease. There was no significant difference in bleeding with or without warfarin. The mean blood loss was 2486 ± 1408 g in the warfarin group, compared to 1736 ± 876 g in the patients who stopped warfarin. The mean INR value in the warfarin group was 2.6 ± 0.7. Hemostasis was successfully established locally by packing the extraction sockets with oxidized cellulose (Surgicel) and suturing with 3-0 silk sutures.

Concurrent antibiotic use: A retrospective study evaluating over 38,000 patients ≥65 years of age showed exposure to any antibiotic agent was associated with at least a 2-fold increased risk of bleeding that required hospitalization among continuous warfarin users (Baillargeon, 2012). All five antibiotic drug classes examined (macrolides, quinolones, cotrimoxazole, penicillins, and cephalosporins) were associated with an increased risk of bleeding. Exposure to an azole antifungal (fluconazole, ketoconazole, or miconazole) while on warfarin was associated with a 4-fold increased risk of bleeding.

Adverse Reactions Bleeding is the major adverse effect of warfarin. Hemorrhage may occur at virtually any site. Risk is dependent on multiple variables, including the intensity of anticoagulation and patient susceptibility.

1% to 10%:

Hematologic & oncologic: Major hemorrhage (≤5%; INR 2.5 to 4.0 generally associated with more bleeding)

Frequency not defined:

Cardiovascular: Purple-toe syndrome, systemic cholesterol micro-embolism, vasculitis

Central nervous system: Chills
Dermatologic: Alopecia, bullous rash, dermatitis, pruritus, skin necrosis, urticaria
Gastrointestinal: Abdominal pain, bloating, diarrhea, dysgeusia, flatulence, nausea, vomiting
Hematologic & oncologic: Minor hemorrhage
Hepatic: Hepatitis
Hypersensitivity: Anaphylaxis, hypersensitivity reaction
Renal: Acute renal failure (in patients with altered glomerular integrity or with a history of kidney disease)
Respiratory: Tracheobronchial calcification
<1%, postmarketing, and/or case reports: Gangrene of skin or other tissue, skin necrosis, vascular calcification (calcium uremic arteriolopathy and calciphylaxis)

Dosing

Adult Note: Coumadin injection has been discontinued in the US for more than 1 year.

Note: Labeling identifies genetic factors which may increase patient sensitivity to warfarin. Specifically, genetic variations in the proteins CYP2C9 and VKORC1, responsible for warfarin's primary metabolism and pharmacodynamic activity, respectively, have been identified as predisposing factors associated with decreased dose requirement and increased bleeding risk. Genotyping tests are available, and may provide guidance on initiation of anticoagulant therapy. The American College of Chest Physicians recommends against the use of routine pharmacogenomic testing to guide dosing (Guyatt 2012). For management of elevated INRs as a result of warfarin therapy, see Additional Information/Pharmacotherapy Pearls for guidance.

Thromboembolic complications (prophylaxis/treatment) or myocardial infarction (risk reduction):

IV (administer as a slow bolus injection): 2 to 5 mg/day

Oral: Initial dosing must be individualized. Consider the patient (hepatic function, cardiac function, age, nutritional status, concurrent therapy, risk of bleeding) in addition to prior dose response (if available) and the clinical situation. Start 2 to 5 mg once daily **or** for healthy individuals, 10 mg once daily for 2 days; lower doses (eg, 5 mg once daily) recommended for patients with confirmed HIT once platelet recovery has occurred (Guyatt 2012). In patients with acute venous thromboembolism, initiation may begin on the first or second day of low molecular weight heparin or unfractionated heparin therapy (Guyatt 2012). Adjust dose according to INR results; usual maintenance dose ranges from 2 to 10 mg daily (individual patients may require loading and maintenance doses outside these general guidelines).

Note: Lower starting doses may be required for patients with hepatic impairment, poor nutrition, CHF, elderly, high risk of bleeding, or patients who are debilitated, or those with reduced function genomic variants of the catabolic enzymes CYP2C9 (*2 or *3 alleles) or VKORC1 (-1639 polymorphism); see table. Higher initial doses may be reasonable in selected patients (ie, receiving enzyme-inducing agents and with low risk of bleeding). Overlapping a parenteral anticoagulant and warfarin therapy by at least 5 days is necessary in treatment of DVT/PE even if the INR is therapeutic earlier. Although an elevation in INR (due to factor VII depletion) may be seen early (within the first 24 to 48 hours) in warfarin therapy, it does not represent adequate anticoagulation. Factors II and X must also be depleted which takes considerably longer (ACCP [Guyatt 2012]).

Range[1] of Expected Therapeutic Maintenance Dose Based on CYP2C9[2] and VKORC1[3] Genotypes

VKORC1	CYP2C9					
	*1/*1	*1/*2	*1/*3	*2/*2	*2/*3	*3/*3
GG	5-7 mg	5-7 mg	3-4 mg	3-4 mg	3-4 mg	0.5-2 mg
AG	5-7 mg	3-4 mg	3-4 mg	3-4 mg	0.5-2 mg	0.5-2 mg
AA	3-4 mg	3-4 mg	0.5-2 mg	0.5-2 mg	0.5-2 mg	0.5-2 mg

Note: Must also take into account other patient related factors when determining initial dose (eg, age, body weight, concomitant medications, comorbidities). The American College of Chest Physicians recommends against the use of routine pharmacogenomic testing to guide dosing (Guyatt, 2012).

[1]Ranges derived from multiple published clinical studies.

[2]Patients with CYP2C9 *1/*3, *2/*2, *2/*3, and *3/*3 alleles may take up to 4 weeks to achieve maximum INR with a given dose regimen.

[3]VKORC1 -1639G>A (rs 9923231) variant is used in this table; other VKORC1 variants may also be important determinants of dose.

Geriatric Thromboembolic complications (prophylaxis/treatment) or myocardial infarction (risk reduction): Oral: Initial dose ≤5 mg. Usual maintenance dose: 2 to 5 mg/day. Patients >60 years of age tend to require lower dosages to produce a therapeutic level of anticoagulation (due to changes in the pattern of warfarin metabolism).

Pediatric Note: Coumadin injection has been discontinued in the US for more than 1 year.

Note: Labeling identifies genetic factors which may increase patient sensitivity to warfarin. Specifically, genetic variations in the proteins CYP2C9 and VKORC1, responsible for warfarin's primary metabolism and pharmacodynamic activity, respectively, have been identified as predisposing factors associated with decreased dose requirement and increased bleeding risk. Genotyping tests are available, and may provide guidance on initiation of anticoagulant therapy. The American College of Chest Physicians recommends against the use of routine pharmacogenomic testing to guide dosing (Guyatt 2012). For management of elevated INRs as a result of warfarin therapy, see Additional Information/Pharmacotherapy Pearls for guidance.

Prevention/treatment of thrombosis: Infants and Children (off-label use): Oral: Initial loading dose (if baseline INR is 1-1.3): 0.2 mg/kg (maximum: 10 mg/dose); adjust dose based on INR (reported ranges to maintain INR of 2 to 3: 0.09 to 0.33 mg/kg/day). Infants <12 months of age may require doses at or near the high end of this range; consistent anticoagulation may be difficult to maintain in children <5 years of age (Monagle 2012).

Renal Impairment No dosage adjustment necessary. However, patients with renal impairment have an increased risk for bleeding diathesis; monitor INR closely.

Hepatic Impairment There are no dosage adjustments provided in the manufacturer's labeling. However, the response to oral anticoagulants may be markedly enhanced in obstructive jaundice, hepatitis, and cirrhosis. INR should be closely monitored.

Mechanism of Action Hepatic synthesis of coagulation factors II (half-life 42 to 72 hours), VII (half-life 4 to 6 hours), IX, and X (half-life 27 to 48 hours), as well as proteins C and S, requires the presence of vitamin K.

These clotting factors are biologically activated by the addition of carboxyl groups to key glutamic acid residues within the proteins' structure. In the process, "active" vitamin K is oxidatively converted to an "inactive" form, which is then subsequently reactivated by vitamin K epoxide reductase complex 1 (VKORC1). Warfarin competitively inhibits the subunit 1 of the multi-unit VKOR complex, thus depleting functional vitamin K reserves and hence reduces synthesis of active clotting factors.

Contraindications Hypersensitivity to warfarin or any component of the formulation; hemorrhagic tendencies (eg, active GI ulceration, patients bleeding from the GI, respiratory, or GU tract; cerebral aneurysm; CNS hemorrhage; dissecting aortic aneurysm; spinal puncture and other diagnostic or therapeutic procedures with potential for significant bleeding); recent or potential surgery of the eye or CNS; major regional lumbar block anesthesia or traumatic surgery resulting in large, open surfaces; blood dyscrasias; malignant hypertension; pericarditis or pericardial effusion; bacterial endocarditis; unsupervised patients with conditions associated with a high potential for noncompliance; eclampsia/preeclampsia, threatened abortion, pregnancy (except in women with mechanical heart valves at high risk for thromboembolism)

Warnings/Precautions

Use care in the selection of patients appropriate for this treatment. Ensure patient cooperation especially from the alcoholic, illicit drug user, demented, or psychotic patient; ability to comply with routine laboratory monitoring is essential. Use with caution in trauma, acute infection, prolonged dietary insufficiencies, moderate-severe hypertension, polycythemia vera, vasculitis, open wound, active TB, any disruption in normal GI flora, history of PUD, anaphylactic disorders, indwelling catheters, severe diabetes, and menstruating and postpartum women. Use with caution in patients with thyroid disease; warfarin responsiveness may increase (Ageno 2012). Use with caution in protein C deficiency. Use with caution in patients with heparin-induced thrombocytopenia and DVT. Warfarin monotherapy is contraindicated in the initial treatment of active HIT. Reduced liver function, regardless of etiology, may impair synthesis of coagulation factors leading to increased warfarin sensitivity. Use with caution in patients with renal impairment; these patients are at an increased risk for bleeding diathesis; frequent INR monitoring is recommended. Acute kidney injury, possibly as a result of episodes of excessive anticoagulation and hematuria, may occur in patients with a history of kidney disease or in patients with altered glomerular integrity.

[US Boxed Warning]: May cause major or fatal bleeding. Perform regular INR monitoring in all treated patients. INR levels achieved with warfarin therapy may be affected by concomitant medication, dietary modifications and/or other factors (eg, smoking). Risk factors for bleeding include high intensity anticoagulation (INR >4), age (>65 years), variable INRs, history of GI bleeding, hypertension, cerebrovascular disease, serious heart disease, anemia, malignancy, trauma, renal insufficiency, drug-drug interactions, long duration of therapy, or known genetic deficiency in CYP2C9 activity. Patient must be instructed to report bleeding, accidents, or falls. Unrecognized bleeding sites (eg, colon cancer) may be uncovered by anticoagulation. Patient must also report any new or discontinued medications, herbal or alternative products used, or significant changes in smoking or dietary habits. Necrosis or gangrene of the skin and other tissue can occur, usually in conjunction with protein C or S deficiency. Consider alternative therapies if anticoagulation is necessary. Warfarin therapy may release atheromatous plaque emboli; symptoms depend on site of embolization, most commonly kidneys, pancreas, liver, and spleen. In some cases may lead to necrosis or death. "Purple toes syndrome," due to cholesterol microembolization, may rarely occur. The elderly may be more sensitive to anticoagulant therapy.

Fatal and serious calciphylaxis (calcium uremic arteriolopathy) has been reported in patients with and without end-stage renal disease. If calciphylaxis is diagnosed, discontinue therapy and treat calciphylaxis as appropriate. Consider alternative anticoagulation therapy.

Presence of the CYP2C9*2 or *3 allele and/or polymorphism of the vitamin K oxidoreductase (VKORC1) gene may increase the risk of bleeding. Lower doses may be required in these patients; genetic testing may help determine appropriate dosing.

When temporary interruption is necessary before surgery, discontinue for approximately 5 days before surgery; when there is adequate hemostasis, may reinstitute warfarin therapy ~12 to 24 hours after surgery (evening of or next morning). Decision to safely continue warfarin therapy through the procedure and whether or not bridging of anticoagulation is necessary is dependent upon risk of perioperative bleeding and risk of thromboembolism, respectively. If risk of thromboembolism is elevated, consider bridging warfarin therapy with an alternative anticoagulant (eg, unfractionated heparin, LMWH) (Guyatt 2012).

Drug Interactions

Metabolism/Transport Effects Substrate of CYP1A2 (minor), CYP2C19 (minor), CYP2C9 (major), CYP3A4 (minor); **Note:** Assignment of Major/Minor substrate status based on clinically relevant drug interaction potential; **Inhibits** CYP2C9 (weak)

Avoid Concomitant Use

Avoid concomitant use of Warfarin with any of the following: Hemin; MiFEPRIStone; Omacetaxine; Oxatomide; Streptokinase; Tamoxifen; Urokinase; Vorapaxar

Increased Effect/Toxicity

Warfarin may increase the levels/effects of: Collagenase (Systemic); Deferasirox; Deoxycholic Acid; Desirudin; Ethotoin; Fosphenytoin; Ibritumomab; Nintedanib; Obinutuzumab; Omacetaxine; Phenytoin; Regorafenib; Sulfonylureas; Tositumomab and Iodine I 131 Tositumomab

The levels/effects of Warfarin may be increased by: Acetaminophen; Agents with Antiplatelet Properties; Allopurinol; Amiodarone; Androgens; Anticoagulants; Atazanavir; Benzbromarone; Bicalutamide; Bifonazole; Boceprevir; Capecitabine; Cephalosporins; Ceritinib; Chenodiol; Chloral Betaine; Chloral Hydrate; Chloramphenicol; Chondroitin Sulfate; Cimetidine; Clopidogrel; Cloxacillin; Cobicistat; Coenzyme Q-10; Corticosteroids (Systemic); Cranberry; CYP2C9 Inhibitors (Moderate); CYP2C9 Inhibitors (Strong); Dasatinib; Desvenlafaxine; Dexmethylphenidate; Disulfiram; Dronabinol; Dronedarone; Econazole; Efavirenz; Erlotinib; Erythromycin (Ophthalmic); Esomeprazole; Ethacrynic Acid; Ethotoin; Etoposide; Etoposide Phosphate; Exenatide; Fenofibrate and Derivatives; Fenugreek; Fibric Acid Derivatives; Fluconazole; Fluorouracil (Systemic); Fluorouracil (Topical); Fosamprenavir; Fosphenytoin; Fusidic Acid (Systemic); Gefitinib; Gemcitabine; Ginkgo Biloba; Glucagon;

Glucosamine; Green Tea; Hemin; Herbs (Anticoagulant/Antiplatelet Properties); HMG-CoA Reductase Inhibitors; Ibrutinib; Ifosfamide; Imatinib; Itraconazole; Ivermectin (Systemic); Ketoconazole (Systemic); Lansoprazole; Leflunomide; LevOCARNitine; Levomilnacipran; Limaprost; Lomitapide; Lumacaftor; Macrolide Antibiotics; Methylphenidate; Metreleptin; MetroNIDAZOLE (Systemic); Miconazole (Oral); Miconazole (Topical); MiFEPRIStone; Milnacipran; Mirtazapine; Multivitamins/Fluoride (with ADE); Multivitamins/Minerals (with ADEK, Folate, Iron); Multivitamins/Minerals (with AE, No Iron); Nelfinavir; Neomycin; Nonsteroidal Anti-Inflammatory Agents; NSAID (COX-2 Inhibitor); NSAID (Nonselective); Omega-3 Fatty Acids; Omeprazole; Oritavancin; Orlistat; Oxatomide; Penicillins; Pentosan Polysulfate Sodium; Pentoxifylline; Phenytoin; Posaconazole; Proguanil; Propacetamol; Propafenone; Prostacyclin Analogues; QuiNIDine; QuiNINE; Quinolone Antibiotics; RaNITIdine; RomiDEPsin; Roxithromycin; Salicylates; Salicylates (Topical); Saquinavir; Selective Serotonin Reuptake Inhibitors; SORAfenib; Streptokinase; Sugammadex; Sulfinpyrazone; Sulfonamide Derivatives; Sulfonylureas; Tamoxifen; Tegafur; Telaprevir; Tetracycline Derivatives; Thrombolytic Agents; Thyroid Products; Tibolone; Tigecycline; Tipranavir; Tolterodine; Toremifene; Torsemide; TraMADol; Tranilast (Systemic); Tricyclic Antidepressants; Urokinase; Vemurafenib; Venetoclax; Venlafaxine; Vitamin E (Systemic); Vorapaxar; Voriconazole; Vorinostat; Zafirlukast; Zileuton

Decreased Effect

The levels/effects of Warfarin may be decreased by: Adalimumab; Alcohol (Ethyl); Antihepaciviral NS5B RNA Polymerase Inhibitors; Antithyroid Agents; Aprepitant; AzaTHIOprine; Barbiturates; Bile Acid Sequestrants; Boceprevir; Bosentan; CarBAMazepine; Cloxacillin; Coenzyme Q-10; Contraceptives (Estrogens); Contraceptives (Progestins); CYP2C9 Inducers (Strong); Dabrafenib; Darunavir; Dicloxacillin; Efavirenz; Enzalutamide; Eslicarbazepine; Estrogen Derivatives; Fat Emulsion (Fish Oil Based); Flucloxacillin; Fosaprepitant; Ginseng (American); Glutethimide; Green Tea; Griseofulvin; Leflunomide; Lopinavir; Lumacaftor; Menadiol Diphosphate; Mercaptopurine; Metreleptin; Multivitamins/Minerals (with ADEK, Folate, Iron); Nafcillin; Nelfinavir; Nevirapine; Obeticholic Acid; Phytonadione; Progestins; Ribavirin (Systemic); Rifamycin Derivatives; Ritonavir; St John's Wort; Sucralfate; Telaprevir; Telavancin; Teriflunomide; Tranilast (Systemic); TraZODone

Food Interactions

Ethanol: Acute ethanol ingestion (binge drinking) decreases the metabolism of oral anticoagulants and increases PT/INR. Chronic daily ethanol use increases the metabolism of oral anticoagulants and decreases PT/INR. Management: Avoid ethanol.

Food: The anticoagulant effects of warfarin may be decreased if taken with foods rich in vitamin K. Vitamin E may increase warfarin effect. Cranberry juice may increase warfarin effect. Management: Maintain a consistent diet; consult prescriber before making changes in diet. Take warfarin at the same time each day.

Dietary Considerations Foods high in vitamin K (eg, leafy green vegetables) inhibit anticoagulant effect. The list of usual foods with high vitamin K content is well known, however, some unique ones include green tea (*Camellia sinensis*), chewing tobacco, a variety of oils (canola, corn, olive, peanut, safflower, sesame seed, soybean, and sunflower) (Booth, 1999; Kuykendall, 2004; Nutescu, 2011). Snack foods containing Olestra have 80 mcg of vitamin K added to each ounce (Harrell, 1999). Some natural products may contain hidden sources of vitamin K (Nutescu, 2006). Avoid drastic changes in diet (eg, intake of large amounts of alfalfa, asparagus, broccoli, Brussels sprouts, cabbage, cauliflower, green teas, kale, lettuce, spinach, turnip greens, watercress) which decrease efficacy of warfarin. A balanced diet with a consistent intake of vitamin K is essential. The recommended dietary allowance for vitamin K in adults is 75 to 120 mcg/day (USDA Dietary Reference Intake).

Pharmacodynamics/Kinetics

Onset of Action Anticoagulation: Oral: 24-72 hours; Peak effect: Full therapeutic effect: 5-7 days; INR may increase in 36-72 hours

Duration of Action 2-5 days

Half-life Elimination 20-60 hours; Mean: 40 hours; highly variable among individuals

Time to Peak Oral: ~4 hours

Pregnancy Risk Factor D (women with mechanical heart valves)/X (other indications)

Pregnancy Considerations Warfarin crosses the placenta; concentrations in the fetal plasma are similar to maternal values. Teratogenic effects have been reported following first trimester exposure and may include coumarin embryopathy (nasal hypoplasia and/or stippled epiphyses; limb hypoplasia may also be present). Adverse CNS events to the fetus have also been observed following exposure during any trimester and may include CNS abnormalities (including ventral midline dysplasia, dorsal midline dysplasia). Spontaneous abortion, fetal hemorrhage, and fetal death may also occur. Use is contraindicated during pregnancy (or in women of reproductive potential) except in women with mechanical heart valves who are at high risk for thromboembolism; use is also contraindicated in women with threatened abortion, eclampsia, or preeclampsia. Frequent pregnancy tests are recommended for women who are planning to become pregnant and adjusted-dose heparin or low molecular weight heparin (LMWH) should be substituted as soon as pregnancy is confirmed or adjusted-dose heparin or LMWH should be used instead of warfarin prior to conception.

In pregnant women with high-risk mechanical heart valves, the benefits of warfarin therapy should be discussed with the risks of available treatments (ACCP [Bates 2012]; AHA/ACC [Nishimura 2014]); when possible avoid warfarin use during the first trimester (ACCP [Bates 2012]) and close to delivery (ACCP [Bates 2012]; AHA/ACC [Nishimura 2014]). Use of warfarin during the first trimester may be considered if the therapeutic INR can be achieved with a dose ≤5 mg/day (AHA/ACC [Nishimura 2014]). Adjusted-dose LMWH or adjusted-dose heparin may be used throughout pregnancy or until week 13 of gestation when therapy can be changed to warfarin. LMWH or heparin should be resumed close to delivery. In women who are at a very high risk for thromboembolism (older generation mechanical prosthesis in mitral position or history of thromboembolism), warfarin can be used throughout pregnancy and replaced with LMWH or heparin near term; the use of low-dose aspirin is also recommended (ACCP [Bates 2012] AHA/ACC [Nishimura 2014]). Women who require long-term anticoagulation with warfarin and who are considering pregnancy, LMWH substitution should be done prior to conception when possible. If anti-Xa monitoring cannot be done, do not use LMWH therapy in pregnant patients with a mechanical prosthetic valve (AHA/ACC [Nishimura 2014]). When choosing therapy, fetal outcomes (ie, pregnancy loss, malformations), maternal outcomes (ie, VTE, hemorrhage), burden of therapy, and maternal preference should be considered (ACCP [Bates 2012]).

Breastfeeding Considerations Based on available data, warfarin is not present in breast milk.

Breastfeeding women may be treated with warfarin. According to the American College of Chest Physicians (ACCP), warfarin may be used in lactating women who wish to breastfeed their infants (ACCP [Bates 2012]). The manufacturer recommends monitoring of breastfeeding infants for bruising or bleeding.

Product Availability Coumadin injection has been discontinued in the US for more than 1 year.

Dosage Forms

Tablet, Oral:

Coumadin: 1 mg, 2 mg, 2.5 mg, 3 mg, 4 mg, 5 mg, 6 mg, 7.5 mg, 10 mg

Jantoven: 1 mg, 2 mg, 2.5 mg, 3 mg, 4 mg, 5 mg, 6 mg, 7.5 mg, 10 mg

Generic: 1 mg, 2 mg, 2.5 mg, 3 mg, 4 mg, 5 mg, 6 mg, 7.5 mg, 10 mg

Dental Comment It is important to discuss patient with physician or to ask for recent INR result to ensure that patient is within a reasonable range prior to an invasive dental procedure. One clue to determining how stable a patient is on warfarin therapy is to assess how often the patient gets INRs drawn. Recent frequent blood draws may suggest poor control on the patient's warfarin regimen. Surgery is generally acceptable for patients on warfarin with an INR between 2 to 3.

Zafirlukast (za FIR loo kast)

Related Information

Respiratory Diseases *on page* 1777

Brand Names: US Accolate

Brand Names: Canada Accolate

Pharmacologic Category Leukotriene-Receptor Antagonist

Use Asthma: Prophylaxis and chronic treatment of asthma in adults and children 5 years and older.

Local Anesthetic/Vasoconstrictor Precautions No information available to require special precautions

Effects on Dental Treatment No significant effects or complications reported

Effects on Bleeding No information available to require special precautions

Adverse Reactions Incidences reported in children ≥12 years and adults unless otherwise specified.

>10%: Central nervous system: Headache (13%; children 5 to 11 years: 5%)

1% to 10%:

Central nervous system: Dizziness (2%), pain (2%)

Gastrointestinal: Nausea (3%), diarrhea (3%), abdominal pain (2%; children 5 to 11 years: 3%), vomiting (2%), dyspepsia (1%)

Hepatic: Increased serum ALT (2%)

Infection: Infection (4%)

Neuromuscular & skeletal: Back pain (2%), myalgia (2%), weakness (2%)

Miscellaneous: Fever (2%)

<1%, postmarketing, and/or case reports: Agranulocytosis, angioedema, arthralgia, bruise, depression, edema, eosinophilia (systemic), eosinophilic pneumonitis, hemorrhage, hepatic failure, hepatitis, hyperbilirubinemia, hypersensitivity reaction, insomnia, malaise, pruritus, skin rash, urticaria, vasculitis (with clinical features of Churg-Strauss syndrome; rare)

General Dosage Range Oral:

Children 5 to 11 years: 10 mg twice daily

Children ≥12 years and Adults: 20 mg twice daily

Mechanism of Action Zafirlukast is a selectively and competitive leukotriene-receptor antagonist (LTRA) of leukotriene D4 and E4 (LTD4 and LTE4), components of slow-reacting substance of anaphylaxis (SRSA). Cysteinyl leukotriene production and receptor occupation have been correlated with the pathophysiology of asthma, including airway edema, smooth muscle constriction, and altered cellular activity associated with the inflammatory process, which contribute to the signs and symptoms of asthma.

Pharmacodynamics/Kinetics

Onset of Action Asthma symptom improvement: Peak effect: 2 to 6 weeks

Duration of Action Asthma symptom improvement: 12 hours

Half-life Elimination ~10 hours (range: 8 to 16 hours)

Time to Peak Serum:

Children: 2 to 2.5 hours

Adults: 3 hours

Pregnancy Risk Factor B

Pregnancy Considerations Adverse events were not observed in animal reproduction studies except with doses that were also maternally toxic. Based on limited data, an increased risk of teratogenic effects has not been observed with zafirlukast use in pregnancy (Bakhireva, 2007). Uncontrolled asthma is associated with adverse events on pregnancy (increased risk of perinatal mortality, pre-eclampsia, preterm birth, low birth weight infants). Zafirlukast may be considered for use in women who had a favorable response prior to becoming pregnant; however, initiating a leukotriene receptor antagonist during pregnancy is an alternative (but not preferred) treatment option for mild persistent asthma (NAEPP, 2005).

Zaleplon (ZAL e plon)

Brand Names: US Sonata

Pharmacologic Category Hypnotic, Miscellaneous

Use Insomnia: Short-term treatment of insomnia.

Local Anesthetic/Vasoconstrictor Precautions No information available to require special precautions

Effects on Dental Treatment Key adverse event(s) related to dental treatment: Xerostomia (normal salivary flow resumes upon discontinuation) (see Dental Comment)

Effects on Bleeding No information available to require special precautions

Adverse Reactions

>10%: Central nervous system: Headache (30% to 42%)

1% to 10%:

Cardiovascular: Chest pain (≥1%), peripheral edema (≤1%)

Central nervous system: Dizziness (7% to 9%), drowsiness (5% to 6%), amnesia (2% to 4%), paresthesia (3%), altered sense of smell (<1% to 2%), depersonalization (<1% to 2%), hyperacusis (1% to 2%), hypoesthesia (<1% to 2%), malaise (<1% to 2%), abnormality in thinking (≥1%), anxiety (≥1%), depression (≥1%), migraine (≥1%), nervousness (≥1%), hypertonia (1%), confusion (≤1%), hallucination (≤1%), vertigo (≤1%)

Dermatologic: Pruritus (≥1%), skin rash (≥1%), skin photosensitivity (≤1%)
Gastrointestinal: Nausea (6% to 8%), abdominal pain (6%), anorexia (<1% to 2%), constipation (≥1%), dysgeusia (≥1%), dyspepsia (≥1%), xerostomia (≥1%), colitis (≤1%)
Genitourinary: Dysmenorrhea (3% to 4%)
Neuromuscular & skeletal: Weakness (5% to 7%), tremor (2%), arthralgia (≥1%), arthritis (≥1%), back pain (≥1%), myalgia (≥1%)
Ophthalmic: Eye pain (3% to 4%), visual disturbance (<1% to 2%), conjunctivitis (≥1%)
Otic: Otalgia (≤1%)
Respiratory: Bronchitis (≥1%), epistaxis (≤1%)
Miscellaneous: Fever (≥1%)

<1%, postmarketing, and/or case reports: Abnormal gait, abnormal hepatic function tests, accommodation disturbance, ageusia, agitation, alopecia, anaphylaxis, anemia, angina pectoris, angioedema, apathy, aphthous stomatitis, apnea, asthma, ataxia, bigeminy, biliary colic, blepharitis, blepharoptosis, bruxism, bundle branch block, bursitis, cataract, central nervous system stimulation, cerebral ischemia, cholelithiasis, conjunctival hyperemia (subconjunctival hemorrhage), contact dermatitis, corneal erosion, cyanosis, cystitis, deafness, decreased libido, delusions, diabetes mellitus, diaphoresis, diplopia, dry eye syndrome, duodenal ulcer, dysarthria, dysphagia, dyspnea, dystonia, dysuria, ecchymoses, eczema, edema, emotional lability, eosinophilia, eructation, esophageal achalasia, esophagitis, euphoria, facial paralysis, flatulence, gastritis, gastroenteritis, gingival hemorrhage, gingivitis, glaucoma, glossitis, goiter, gout, hangover effect, hematuria, hemorrhage, hyperbilirubinemia, hypercholesterolemia, hyperesthesia, hyperglycemia, hyperkinesia, hypermenorrhea, hyperreflexia, hypertension, hyperuricemia, hyperventilation, hypoglycemia, hypokinesia, hyporeflexia, hypotension, hypothyroidism, hypotonia, impotence, increased appetite, increased bronchial secretions, increased serum ALT, increased serum AST, increased thirst, insomnia, intestinal obstruction, irregular menses, ketosis, lactose intolerance, laryngitis, leukocytosis, leukorrhea, lymphadenopathy, lymphocytosis, maculopapular rash, mastalgia, melanosis, melena, menstrual disease, myasthenia, myoclonus, myositis, neck stiffness, nephrolithiasis, neuralgia, neuropathy, nightmares, nystagmus, orthostatic hypotension, osteoporosis, palpitations, paradoxical central nervous system stimulation, peptic ulcer, pericardial effusion, photophobia, pleural effusion, pneumonia, psoriasis, psychomotor retardation, pulmonary embolism, purpura, pustular rash, rectal hemorrhage, renal pain, retinal detachment, sialorrhea, sinus bradycardia, skin discoloration, skin hypertrophy, skin rash, sleep talking, slurred speech, snoring, somnambulism (complex sleep-related behavior [sleep-driving, sleep- cooking, sleep-eating, sleep-talking on the phone]), stupor, substernal pain, syncope, tenosynovitis, thrombophlebitis, tinnitus, tongue discoloration, tongue edema, transient perioral paresthesia, trismus, urethritis, urinary frequency, urinary incontinence, urinary retention, urinary urgency, urticaria, vaginal hemorrhage, vaginitis, vasodilatation, ventricular premature contractions, ventricular tachycardia, vesicobullous dermatitis, visual field defect, voice disorder, weight gain, weight loss, xeroderma

General Dosage Range Dosage adjustment recommended in patients with hepatic impairment

Oral:
Adults: 5 to 20 mg immediately before bedtime (maximum dose: 20 mg daily)
Debilitated/Elderly: 5 mg immediately before bedtime (maximum dose: 10 mg daily)

Mechanism of Action Zaleplon is unrelated to benzodiazepines, barbiturates, or other hypnotics. However, it interacts with the benzodiazepine GABA receptor complex. Nonclinical studies have shown that it binds selectively to the brain omega-1 receptor situated on the alpha subunit of the GABA-A receptor complex.

Pharmacodynamics/Kinetics
Onset of Action Rapid
Half-life Elimination ~1 hour
Time to Peak Serum: ~1 hour

Pregnancy Risk Factor C

Pregnancy Considerations Teratogenic effects were not observed in animal reproduction studies. Adverse effects, including stillbirth, postnatal mortality, and decreased growth and physical development, were observed near the end of gestation. A small study of pregnant women did not show an increased risk of teratogenic effects when used early in pregnancy (Wiker, 2011). Use during pregnancy is not recommended by the manufacturer.

Controlled Substance C-IV

Dental Comment An adult companion should accompany the patient to and from dental office.

Zanamivir (za NA mi veer)

Related Information
Systemic Viral Diseases *on page 1806*

Brand Names: US Relenza Diskhaler

Brand Names: Canada Relenza

Pharmacologic Category Antiviral Agent; Neuraminidase Inhibitor

Use Influenza:
Prophylaxis: Prophylaxis of influenza in adults and pediatric patients 5 years and older (US labeling) or 7 years and older (Canadian labeling).
Treatment: Treatment of uncomplicated acute illness caused by influenza A and B virus in adults and pediatric patients 7 years and older who have been symptomatic for no more than 2 days.

The Advisory Committee on Immunization Practices (ACIP) recommends that **treatment** be considered for the following:
- Persons with severe, complicated or progressive illness
- Hospitalized persons
- Persons at higher risk for influenza complications:
  - Children <2 years of age (highest risk in children <6 months of age)
  - Adults ≥65 years of age
  - Persons with chronic disorders of the pulmonary (including asthma) or cardiovascular systems (except hypertension)
  - Persons with chronic metabolic diseases (including diabetes mellitus), hepatic disease, renal dysfunction, hematologic disorders (including sickle cell disease), or immunosuppression (including immunosuppression caused by medications or HIV)
  - Persons with neurologic/neuromuscular conditions (including conditions such as spinal cord injuries, seizure disorders, cerebral palsy, stroke, mental retardation, moderate to severe developmental delay, or muscular dystrophy) which may compromise respiratory function, the handling of

respiratory secretions, or that can increase the risk of aspiration
- Pregnant or postpartum women (≤2 weeks after delivery)
- Persons <19 years of age on long-term aspirin therapy
- American Indians and Alaskan Natives
- Persons who are morbidly obese (BMI ≥40)
- Residents of nursing homes or other chronic care facilities

• Use may also be considered for previously healthy, nonhigh-risk outpatients with confirmed or suspected influenza based on clinical judgment when treatment can be started within 48 hours of illness onset.

The ACIP recommends that **prophylaxis** be considered for the following:

• Postexposure prophylaxis may be considered for family or close contacts of suspected or confirmed cases, who are at higher risk of influenza complications, and who have not been vaccinated against the circulating strain at the time of the exposure.
• Postexposure prophylaxis may be considered for unvaccinated healthcare workers who had occupational exposure without protective equipment.
• Pre-exposure prophylaxis should only be used for persons at very high risk of influenza complications who cannot be otherwise protected at times of high risk for exposure.
• Prophylaxis should also be administered to all eligible residents of institutions that house patients at high risk when needed to control outbreaks.

Local Anesthetic/Vasoconstrictor Precautions No information available to require special precautions

Effects on Dental Treatment No significant effects or complications reported

Effects on Bleeding No information available to require special precautions

Adverse Reactions Most adverse reactions occurred at a frequency that was less than or equal to the control (lactose vehicle).

>10%:

Central nervous system: Headache (prophylaxis: 13% to 24%; treatment: 2%)

Gastrointestinal: Sore throat (or discomfort; prophylaxis: ≤19%)

Infection: Viral infection (prophylaxis: 3% to 13%)

Respiratory: Nasal signs and symptoms (prophylaxis: 12% to 20%; treatment: 2%), tonsil disease (discomfort or pain; prophylaxis: ≤19%), cough (prophylaxis: 7% to 17%; treatment: ≤2%)

1% to 10%:

Central nervous system: Chills (prophylaxis: ≤9%; treatment: <2%), fatigue (prophylaxis: 5% to 8%; treatment: <2%), malaise (prophylaxis: 5% to 8%; treatment: <2%), dizziness (treatment: 1% to 2%)

Dermatologic: Urticaria (treatment: <2%)

Gastrointestinal: Anorexia (prophylaxis: ≤4%), decreased appetite (prophylaxis: ≤4%), increased appetite (prophylaxis: 2% to 4%), nausea (prophylaxis: 1% to 2%; treatment: ≤3%), diarrhea (2% to 3%), vomiting (1% to 2%), abdominal pain (treatment: <2%)

Neuromuscular & skeletal: Myalgia (prophylaxis: 3% to 8%; treatment: <2%), musculoskeletal pain (prophylaxis: 6%), arthralgia (≤2%), rheumatic disease (prophylaxis: ≤2%)

Respiratory: ENT infection (treatment: 1% to 5%; prophylaxis: 2%), sinusitis (treatment: 3%), bronchitis (treatment: 2%), rhinitis (prophylaxis: 1%)

Miscellaneous: Fever (prophylaxis: ≤9%; treatment: <2%)

<1%, postmarketing and/or case reports: Abnormal behavior, agitation, anxiety, asthma, bronchospasm, cardiac arrhythmia, delusions, dyspnea, facial edema, hallucination, hemorrhage (ear/nose/throat), hypersensitivity reaction (or hypersensitivity-like reaction; includes oropharyngeal edema), impaired consciousness, nightmares, psychiatric disturbance (confusion, delirium, self-injury), seizure, skin rash (including serious cutaneous reactions [eg, erythema multiforme, Stevens-Johnson syndrome, toxic epidermal necrolysis]), syncope

General Dosage Range Oral inhalation:

Children ≥5 years, Adolescents, and Adults: Prophylaxis: 10 mg once daily

Children ≥7 years, Adolescents, and Adults: Treatment: 10 mg twice daily

Mechanism of Action Zanamivir inhibits influenza virus neuraminidase enzymes, potentially altering virus particle aggregation and release.

Pharmacodynamics/Kinetics

Half-life Elimination Serum: 2.5 to 5.1 hours; Mild to moderate renal impairment: 4.7 hours; Severe renal impairment: 18.5 hours

Time to Peak 1-2 hours

Pregnancy Risk Factor C

Pregnancy Considerations Adverse events have not been observed in animal reproduction studies. An increased risk of adverse neonatal or maternal outcomes has not been observed following use of zanamivir during pregnancy. Untreated influenza infection is associated with an increased risk of adverse events to the fetus and an increased risk of complications or death to the mother. Neuraminidase inhibitors are currently recommended for the treatment or prophylaxis of influenza in pregnant women and women up to 2 weeks postpartum (CDC 60[1] 2011; CDC March 13 2014; January 2015).

Prescribing and Access Restrictions Zanamivir *aqueous solution* intended for intravenous (IV) administration is **not** currently approved for use. Data on safety and efficacy via this route of administration are limited. However, limited supplies of zanamivir aqueous solution may be made available through the Zanamivir Compassionate Use Program for qualifying patients for the treatment of serious influenza illness. For information, contact the GlaxoSmithKline Clinical Support Help Desk at 1-866-341-9160 or gskclinicalsupport-HD@gsk.com.

Ziconotide (zi KOE no tide)

Brand Names: US Prialt

Pharmacologic Category Analgesic, Nonopioid; Calcium Channel Blocker, N-Type

Use Management of severe chronic pain in patients requiring intrathecal therapy and who are intolerant or refractory to other therapies

Local Anesthetic/Vasoconstrictor Precautions No information available to require special precautions

Effects on Dental Treatment Key adverse event(s) related to dental treatment: Xerostomia (normal salivary flow resumes upon discontinuation) and taste perversion.

Effects on Bleeding No information available to require special precautions

Adverse Reactions

>10%:

Central nervous system: Dizziness (46%), confusion (15% to 33%), memory impairment (7% to 22%), drowsiness (17%), abnormal gait (14%), ataxia (14%), speech disorder (14%), headache (13%), aphasia (12%), hallucination (12%; including auditory and visual)

Gastrointestinal: Nausea (40%), diarrhea (18%), vomiting (16%)

Neuromuscular & skeletal: Increased creatine phosphokinase (40%; ≥3 x ULN: 11%), weakness (18%)

Ophthalmic: Blurred vision (12%)

2% to 10%:

Cardiovascular: Hypotension, orthostatic hypotension, peripheral edema

Central nervous system: Abnormality in thinking (8%), amnesia (8%), anxiety (8%), dysarthria (7%), paresthesia (7%), rigors (7%), vertigo (7%), insomnia (6%), paranoia (3%), delirium (2%), hostility (2%), stupor (2%), absent reflexes, agitation, burning sensation, decreased mental acuity, depression, disorientation, disturbance in attention, fatigue, hypoesthesia, irritability, lethargy, loss of balance, mood disorder, myasthenia, nervousness, pain, sedation

Dermatologic: Pruritus (7%), diaphoresis (5%)

Gastrointestinal: Anorexia (6%), dysgeusia (5%), abdominal pain, constipation, decreased appetite, xerostomia

Genitourinary: Urinary retention (9%), dysuria, urinary hesitancy

Neuromuscular & skeletal: Tremor (7%), muscle spasm (6%), limb pain (5%), muscle cramps, myalgia

Ophthalmic: Nystagmus (8%), diplopia, visual disturbance

Respiratory: Sinusitis (5%)

Miscellaneous: Fever (5%)

<2%, postmarketing, and/or case reports: Acute renal failure, aspiration pneumonia (<1%), atrial fibrillation, attempted suicide (<1%), cerebrovascular accident, ECG abnormality, incoherence, loss of consciousness, mania, meningitis, myoclonus, psychosis (1%), respiratory distress, rhabdomyolysis, seizure (clonic and grand mal), sepsis, suicidal ideation

General Dosage Range Dosage adjustment recommended in patients who develop toxicities

Intrathecal: *Adults:* Initial dose: ≤2.4 mcg/day (0.1 mcg/hour); Maintenance range: 2.4-19.2 mcg/day (0.1-0.8 mcg/hour) (maximum: 19.2 mcg/day [0.8 mcg/hour])

Mechanism of Action Ziconotide selectively binds to N-type voltage-sensitive calcium channels located on the nociceptive afferent nerves of the dorsal horn in the spinal cord. This binding is thought to block N-type calcium channels, leading to a blockade of excitatory neurotransmitter release and reducing sensitivity to painful stimuli.

Pharmacodynamics/Kinetics

Half-life Elimination IV: 1-1.6 hours (plasma); Intrathecal: 2.9-6.5 hours (CSF)

Pregnancy Risk Factor C

Pregnancy Considerations Adverse events and maternal toxicity were observed in animal reproduction studies.

Zidovudine (zye DOE vyoo deen)

Related Information

HIV Infection and AIDS *on page 1785*

Brand Names: US Retrovir

Brand Names: Canada Apo-Zidovudine; AZT; Novo-AZT; Retrovir; Retrovir (AZT)

Pharmacologic Category Antiretroviral, Reverse Transcriptase Inhibitor, Nucleoside (Anti-HIV)

Use

HIV-1 infection: Treatment of HIV-1 infection in combination with at least two other antiretroviral agents.

Perinatal HIV-1 transmission: Prevention of perinatal HIV-1 transmission.

Local Anesthetic/Vasoconstrictor Precautions No information available to require special precautions

Effects on Dental Treatment Key adverse event(s) related to dental treatment: Taste perversion, oral mucosa pigmentation, dysphagia, and mouth ulcer.

Effects on Bleeding No information available to require special precautions relative to hemostasis.

Adverse Reactions Percentages noted with adults unless otherwise stated.

>10%:

Central nervous system: Headache (63%), malaise (53%)

Dermatologic: Skin rash (children: 12%)

Gastrointestinal: Nausea (adults: 51%; children: 8%), anorexia (20%), vomiting (adults: 17%; children: 8%)

Hematologic & oncologic: Macrocytosis (children: >50%), anemia (neonates: 22%; children: 4%; adults: 1%; onset: 2 to 4 weeks)

Hepatic: Hepatomegaly (children: 11%)

Respiratory: Cough (children: 15%)

Miscellaneous: Fever (children: 25%)

1% to 10%:

Cardiovascular: Cardiac failure (children: <6%), ECG abnormality (children: <6%), edema (children: <6%), left ventricular dilation (children: <6%)

Central nervous system: Irritability (children: <6%), nervousness (children: <6%), chills (≥5%), fatigue (≥5%), insomnia (≥5%), neuropathy (≥5%)

Endocrine & metabolic: Weight loss (children: <6%)

Gastrointestinal: Diarrhea (children: 8%), constipation (6%), abdominal cramps (≥5%), abdominal pain (≥5%), dyspepsia (≥5%)

Genitourinary: Hematuria (children: <6%)

Hematologic & oncologic: Neutropenia (children: 8%), granulocytopenia (2%; onset 6 to 8 weeks), thrombocytopenia (children: 1%)

Hepatic: Increased serum transaminases (1% to 3%)

Neuromuscular & skeletal: Weakness (9%), arthralgia (≥5%), musculoskeletal pain (≥5%), myalgia (≥5%)

Otic: Auricular edema (≤7%), ear redness (≤7%), ear residue, debris or precipitate (≤7%), otalgia (≤7%)

<1%, postmarketing and/or case reports: Amblyopia, anaphylaxis, angioedema, anxiety, aplastic anemia, back pain, cardiomyopathy, chest pain, confusion, decreased mental acuity, depression, diabetes mellitus, diaphoresis, dizziness, drowsiness, dyschromia (blue pigmentation of nails and skin), dysgeusia, dyslipidemia, dysphagia, dyspnea, flatulence, flu-like symptoms, gynecomastia, hearing loss, hemolytic anemia, hepatitis, hepatomegaly with steatosis, hyperbilirubinemia, hypersensitivity reaction, immune reconstitution syndrome, increased creatine phosphokinase, increased lactate dehydrogenase, insulin resistance, jaundice, lactic acidosis, leukopenia, lymphadenopathy, macular edema, mania, muscle

spasm, myopathy, myositis, oral mucosa hyperpigmentation, oral mucosa ulcer, pancreatitis, pancytopenia (with marrow hypoplasia), paresthesia, photophobia, pruritus, pure red cell aplasia, redistribution of body fat, rhabdomyolysis, rhinitis, seizure, sinusitis, Stevens-Johnson syndrome, syncope, toxic epidermal necrolysis, tremor, urinary frequency, urinary hesitancy, urticaria, vasculitis, vertigo

General Dosage Range Dosage adjustment recommended in patients with renal impairment or who develop toxicities

IV:

Infants ≤6 weeks: 1.5 mg/kg every 6 hours

Infants >6 weeks and Children <12 years: 120 mg/m^2/dose every 6 hours **or** 20 mg/m^2/hour as a continuous infusion

Adolescents and Adults: 1 mg/kg/dose every 4 hours around-the-clock **or** 2 mg/kg bolus followed by 1 mg/kg/hour continuous infusion during labor and delivery

Oral:

Neonates and Infants ≤6 weeks: 2 mg/kg every 6 hours

Infants, Children, and Adolescents: 240 mg/m^2 every 12 hours (maximum: 300 mg every 12 hours) **or** 160 mg/m^2/dose every 8 hours (maximum: 200 mg every 8 hours)

4 to <9 kg: 12 mg/kg/dose twice daily **or** 8 mg/kg/dose 3 times daily

≥9 to <30 kg: 9 mg/kg/dose twice daily **or** 6 mg/kg/dose 3 times daily

≥30 kg: 300 mg twice daily **or** 200 mg 3 times daily

Adults: 300 mg twice daily

Mechanism of Action Zidovudine is a thymidine analog which interferes with the HIV viral RNA-dependent DNA polymerase resulting in inhibition of viral replication; nucleoside reverse transcriptase inhibitor

Pharmacodynamics/Kinetics

Half-life Elimination Terminal:

Premature neonate: 6.3 hours

Full-term neonates: 3.1 hours

Infants 14 days to 3 months: 1.9 hours

Infants 3 months to Children 12 years: 1.5 hours

Adults: 0.5 to 3 hours (mean 1.1 hours)

Time to Peak Serum: 30 to 90 minutes

Pregnancy Considerations Zidovudine has a high level of transfer across the human placenta and the placenta also metabolizes zidovudine to the active metabolite. No increased risk of overall birth defects has been observed following first trimester exposure according to data collected by the antiretroviral pregnancy registry. Maternal antiretroviral therapy may increase the risk of preterm delivery, although available information is conflicting possibly due to variability of maternal factors (disease severity; initiation of therapy); however, maternal antiretroviral medication should not be withheld due to concerns of preterm birth. Information related to stillbirth, low birth weight, and small for gestational age infants is limited. Long-term follow-up is recommended for all infants exposed to antiretroviral medications; children who develop significant organ system abnormalities of unknown etiology (particularly of the CNS or heart) should be evaluated for potential mitochondrial dysfunction. Cases of lactic acidosis and hepatic steatosis related to mitochondrial toxicity have been reported with use of nucleoside reverse transcriptase inhibitors (NRTIs). These adverse events are similar to other rare but life-threatening syndromes that occur during pregnancy (eg, HELLP syndrome). In general, NRTIs are well tolerated and the benefits of use generally outweigh potential risk.

Combination antiretroviral therapy (cART) therapy is recommended for all HIV-infected pregnant women to keep the viral load below the limit of detection and reduce the risk of perinatal transmission. When HIV is diagnosed during pregnancy in a woman who has never received antiretroviral therapy, cART should begin as soon as possible after diagnosis. The Health and Human Services (HHS) Perinatal HIV Guidelines consider zidovudine a component in alternative regimens for initial therapy in antiretroviral-naïve pregnant women. Zidovudine should be administered IV near delivery regardless of antepartum regimen or mode of delivery in women with HIV RNA >1,000 copies/mL or unknown HIV RNA status (even in cases of documented zidovudine resistance), unless there is a history of hypersensitivity. The pharmacokinetics of zidovudine are not significantly altered in pregnancy and dosing adjustment is not needed. In general, women who become pregnant on a stable cART regimen may continue that regimen if viral suppression is effective, appropriate drug exposure can be achieved, contraindications for use in pregnancy are not present, and the regimen is well tolerated. Monitoring during pregnancy is more frequent than in non-pregnant adults; cART should be continued postpartum.

For HIV-infected couples planning a pregnancy, maximum viral suppression with cART is recommended prior to conception for the HIV-infected partner(s) and expert consultation is recommended; modification of therapy (if needed) and optimization of the woman's health should be done prior to conception. HIV-infected women not planning a pregnancy may use any available type of contraception, considering possible drug interactions and contraindications of the specific method. In addition, consistent use of condoms is also recommended (even during pregnancy) to prevent transmission of HIV or other sexually transmitted diseases.

Health care providers are encouraged to enroll pregnant women exposed to antiretroviral medications as early in pregnancy as possible in the Antiretroviral Pregnancy Registry (1-800-258-4263 or www.APRegistry.com). Health care providers caring for HIV-infected women and their infants may contact the National Perinatal HIV Hotline (888-448-8765) for clinical consultation (HHS [perinatal] 2016).

Zileuton (zye LOO ton)

Related Information

Respiratory Diseases *on page 1777*

Brand Names: US Zyflo; Zyflo CR

Pharmacologic Category 5-Lipoxygenase Inhibitor

Use Prophylaxis and chronic treatment of asthma

Local Anesthetic/Vasoconstrictor Precautions No information available to require special precautions

Effects on Dental Treatment No significant effects or complications reported

Effects on Bleeding No information available to require special precautions

Adverse Reactions

>10%: Central nervous system: Headache (23% to 25%)

1% to 10%:

Cardiovascular: Chest pain

Central nervous system: Pain (8%), dizziness, drowsiness, hypertonia, insomnia, malaise, nervousness
Dermatologic: Pruritus, skin rash
Gastrointestinal: Dyspepsia (8%), nausea (5% to 6%), abdominal pain (5%), diarrhea (5%), constipation, flatulence, vomiting
Genitourinary: Urinary tract infection, vaginitis
Hematologic & oncologic: Leukopenia (1% to 3%), lymphadenopathy
Hepatic: Increased serum ALT (≥3 x ULN: 2% to 5%), hepatotoxicity
Hypersensitivity: Hypersensitivity reaction
Neuromuscular & skeletal: Myalgia (7%), weakness (4%), arthralgia, neck pain, neck stiffness
Ophthalmic: Conjunctivitis
Respiratory: Upper respiratory tract infection (9%), sinusitis (7%), pharyngolaryngeal pain (5%)
Miscellaneous: Fever

<1%, postmarketing, and/or case reports: Behavioral changes, hepatic failure, hepatitis, hyperbilirubinemia, jaundice, mood changes, sleep disorder, suicidal tendencies, urticaria

General Dosage Range Oral:
Extended release: *Children ≥12 years and Adults:* 1200 mg twice daily
Immediate release: *Children ≥12 years and Adults:* 600 mg 4 times/day

Mechanism of Action Specific 5-lipoxygenase inhibitor which inhibits leukotriene formation. Leukotrienes augment neutrophil and eosinophil migration, neutrophil and monocyte aggregation, leukocyte adhesion, increased capillary permeability, and smooth muscle contraction (which contribute to inflammation, edema, mucous secretion, and bronchoconstriction in the airway of the asthmatic.)

Pharmacodynamics/Kinetics
Half-life Elimination ~3 hours
Time to Peak Immediate release: 1.7 hours

Pregnancy Risk Factor C

Pregnancy Considerations Adverse events were observed in animal reproduction studies. If a leukotriene modifier is needed during pregnancy, other agents are preferred (ACOG, 2008).

Zinc Oxide (zink OKS ide)

Brand Names: US AmeriDerm PeriShield [OTC]; Ammens® Original Medicated [OTC]; Ammens® Shower Fresh [OTC]; Balmex® [OTC]; Boudreaux's® Butt Paste [OTC]; Critic-Aid Skin Care® [OTC]; Desitin Maximum Strength Original [OTC]; Desitin Rapid Relief [OTC]; Dr. Smith's Diaper Rash [OTC]; Elta Seal Moisture Barrier [OTC]; PeriGuard [OTC]; Pharmabase Barrier [OTC]

Brand Names: Canada Zincofax®

Pharmacologic Category Topical Skin Product

Use Protective coating for mild skin irritations and abrasions; soothing and protective ointment to promote healing of chapped skin, diaper rash

Local Anesthetic/Vasoconstrictor Precautions No information available to require special precautions

Effects on Dental Treatment No significant effects or complications reported

Effects on Bleeding No information available to require special precautions

Adverse Reactions
1% to 10%:
Hypersensitivity: Local hypersensitivity reaction
Local: Local irritation

General Dosage Range Topical: *Children and Adults:* Apply as required to affected areas several times daily

Mechanism of Action Mild astringent with weak antiseptic properties

Pregnancy Considerations Zinc oxide is not expected to be absorbed systemically following topical administration to healthy skin (Newman, 2009). Systemic absorption would be required in order for zinc oxide to cross the placenta and reach the fetus.

Ziprasidone (zi PRAS i done)

Related Information
Clinical Risk Related to Drugs Prolonging QT Interval *on page 1772*

Brand Names: US Geodon

Brand Names: Canada Zeldox

Pharmacologic Category Second Generation (Atypical) Antipsychotic

Use Treatment of schizophrenia; treatment of acute manic or mixed episodes associated with bipolar disorder with or without psychosis; maintenance treatment of bipolar disorder as an adjunct to lithium or valproate; acute agitation in patients with schizophrenia

Local Anesthetic/Vasoconstrictor Precautions Ziprasidone is one of the drugs confirmed to prolong the QT interval and is accepted as having a risk of causing torsade de pointes. The risk of drug-induced torsade de pointes is extremely low when a single QT interval prolonging drug is prescribed. In terms of epinephrine, it is not known what effect vasoconstrictors in the local anesthetic regimen will have in patients with a known history of congenital prolonged QT interval or in patients taking any medication that prolongs the QT interval. Until more information is obtained, it is suggested that the clinician consult with the physician prior to the use of a vasoconstrictor in suspected patients, and that the vasoconstrictor (epinephrine, mepivacaine and levonordefrin [Carbocaine® 2% with Neo-Cobefrin®]) be used with caution.

Effects on Dental Treatment Key adverse event(s) related to dental treatment: Xerostomia and changes in salivation (normal salivary flow resumes upon discontinuation), orthostatic hypotension, tongue edema, and dysphagia.

Effects on Bleeding No information available to require special precautions

Adverse Reactions Frequencies represent oral administration unless otherwise indicated. **Note:** Although minor QTc prolongation (mean: 10 msec at 160 mg/day) may occur more frequently (incidence not specified), clinically relevant prolongation (>500 msec) was rare (0.06%) and less than placebo (0.23%).

>10%:
Central nervous system: Drowsiness (oral and IM: 8% to 31%; may be dose-related), extrapyramidal reaction (oral: 1% to 31%), headache (oral and IM: 5% to 18%), dizziness (oral and IM: 3% to 16%; includes lightheadedness; may be dose-related)
Gastrointestinal: Nausea (oral and IM: 8% to 12%)

1% to 10%:
Cardiovascular: Orthostatic hypotension (IM: ≤5%, oral: ≥1%; may be dose-related), chest pain (3%), hypertension (oral and IM: 1% to 3%), tachycardia (1% to 2%), bradycardia (oral and IM: ≤2%), facial edema (≥1%), angina pectoris (≤1%), peripheral edema (≤1%)
Central nervous system: Akathisia (oral: 8% to 10%; IM: ≤2%), anxiety (oral: 5%; may be dose-related),

hypoesthesia (1% to 2%), agitation (oral: ≥1%, IM: ≤2%), personality disorder (IM: ≤2%), speech disturbance (oral and IM: ≤2%), amnesia (≥1%), ataxia (≥1%), chills (≥1%), confusion (≥1%), delirium (≥1%), dystonia (≥1%; may be dose-related), falling (≥1%), flank pain (≥1%), hostility (≥1%), hypothermia (≥1%), vertigo (≥1%), withdrawal syndrome (≥1%), anorgasmia (≤1%), atrial fibrillation (≤1%), male sexual disorder (≤1%), paralysis (≤1%), insomnia

Dermatologic: Skin rash (1% to 5%; may be dose-related), fungal dermatitis (1% to 2%), diaphoresis (IM: ≤2%), furunculosis (IM: ≤2%), skin photosensitivity (≥1%), alopecia (≤1%), contact dermatitis (≤1%), ecchymoses (≤1%), eczema (≤1%), exfoliative dermatitis (≤1%), maculopapular rash (≤1%), urticaria (≤1%), vesiculobullous dermatitis (≤1%)

Endocrine & metabolic: Weight gain (4% to 16%), albuminuria (≤1%), amenorrhea (≤1%), dehydration (≤1%), glycosuria (≤1%), hypercholesterolemia (≤1%), hyperglycemia (≤1%), hypermenorrhea (≤1%), hypokalemia (≤1%), increased lactate dehydrogenase (≤1%), increased thirst (≤1%)

Gastrointestinal: Constipation (oral: 9%, IM: ≤2%), dyspepsia (oral: 8%, IM: 2% to 3%), vomiting (oral and IM: 1% to 5%), xerostomia (oral: 4% to 5%; may be dose-related), diarrhea (oral and IM: ≤5%), sialorrhea (4%; may be dose-related), abdominal pain (oral and IM: ≤2%), anorexia (oral and IM: ≤2%; may be dose-related), dysmenorrhea (IM: ≤2%), dysphagia (≤2%), buccoglossal syndrome (≥1%)

Genitourinary: Hematuria (≤1%), impotence (≤1%), lactation (female: ≤1%), priapism (IM: ≤1%), urinary retention (≤1%)

Hematologic & oncologic: Rectal hemorrhage (oral and IM: ≤2%), anemia (≤1%), eosinophilia (≤1%), leukocytosis (≤1%), leukopenia (≤1%), lymphadenopathy (≤1%)

Hepatic: Increased serum alkaline phosphatase (≤1%), increased serum transaminases (≤1%)

Hypersensitivity: Tongue edema (≤3%)

Local: Pain at injection site (IM: 7% to 8%)

Neuromuscular & skeletal: Weakness (oral: 5% to 6%; may be dose-related), myalgia (1% to 2%), paresthesia (oral and IM: ≤2%), abnormal gait (≥1%), akinesia (≥1%), choreoathetosis (≥1%), dysarthria (≥1%), dyskinesia (≥1%), hyperkinesia (≥1%), hypokinesia (≥1%), hypotonia (≥1%), neuropathy (≥1%), tremor (≥1%; may be dose-related), twitching (≥1%), cogwheel rigidity (oral: ≥1%), hypertonia (≥1%), increased creatine phosphokinase (≤1%), tenosynovitis (≤1%)

Ophthalmic: Visual disturbance (3% to 6%; may be dose-related), diplopia (≥1%), oculogyric crisis (≥1%), blepharitis (≤1%), cataract (≤1%), conjunctivitis (≤1%), photophobia (≤1%), xerophthalmia (≤1%)

Otic: Tinnitus (≤1%)

Renal: Polyuria (≤1%)

Respiratory: Respiratory tract infection (8%), rhinitis (oral: 4%), cough (3%), pharyngitis (3%), dyspnea (1% to 2%), flu-like symptoms (oral: ≥1%), epistaxis (≤1%), pneumonia (≤1%)

Miscellaneous: Accidental injury (4%), fever (≥1%), motor vehicle accident (≥1%)

<1%, postmarketing, and/or case reports: Agranulocytosis, angioedema, arthralgia, basophilia, bundle branch block, cardiomegaly, cerebral infarction, cerebrovascular accident, cholestatic jaundice, decreased glucose tolerance, deep vein thrombophlebitis, diabetic coma, DRESS syndrome, ejaculatory disorder, facial droop, fecal impaction, female sexual disorder, first degree atrioventricular block, galactorrhea, gingival hemorrhage, gout, granulocytopenia, gynecomastia, hematemesis, hemophthalmos, hemoptysis, hepatitis, hepatomegaly, hyperchloremia, hyperkalemia, hyperreflexia, hypersensitivity reaction (including allergic dermatitis, orofacial edema), hyperthyroidism, hyperuricemia, hypocalcemia, hypochloremia, hypocholesterolemia, hypochromic anemia, hypoglycemia, hypomagnesemia, hypomania, hyponatremia, hypoproteinemia, hypothyroidism, increased blood urea nitrogen, increased gamma-glutamyl transferase, increased monocytes, increased serum creatinine, increased serum prolactin, jaundice, keratitis, keratoconjunctivitis, ketosis, laryngismus, liver steatosis, lymphedema, lymphocytosis, mania, melena, myocarditis, myoclonus, myopathy, neuroleptic malignant syndrome, neutropenia, nocturia, nystagmus, oliguria, opisthotonos, oral leukoplakia, oral paresthesia, phlebitis, polycythemia, prolonged Q-T interval on ECG, pulmonary embolism, respiratory alkalosis, seizure, serotonin syndrome (with or without serotonergic medications), sleep apnea syndrome (obstructive) (Health Canada 2016, Shirani 2011), Stevens-Johnson syndrome, swollen tongue, syncope, tardive dyskinesia, thrombocythemia, thrombocytopenia, thrombophlebitis, thyroiditis, torsade de pointes, torticollis, trismus, urinary incontinence, vaginal hemorrhage, venous thromboembolism, visual field defect

General Dosage Range

IM: *Adults:* 10 mg every 2 hours **or** 20 mg every 4 hours (maximum: 40 mg daily)

Oral: *Adults:* Initial: 20 to 40 mg twice daily; Maintenance: 20 to 100 mg twice daily

Mechanism of Action Ziprasidone is a benzylisothiazolylpiperazine antipsychotic. The exact mechanism of action is unknown. However, *in vitro* radioligand studies show that ziprasidone has high affinity for D_2, D_3, $5\text{-}HT_{2A}$, $5\text{-}HT_{1A}$, $5\text{-}HT_{2C}$, $5\text{-}HT_{1D}$, and $alpha_1$-adrenergic; moderate affinity for histamine H_1 receptors; and no appreciable affinity for $alpha_2$-adrenergic receptors, beta-adrenergic, $5\text{-}HT_3$, $5\text{-}HT_4$, cholinergic, mu, sigma, or benzodiazepine receptors. Ziprasidone functions as an antagonist at the D_2, $5\text{-}HT_{2A}$, and $5\text{-}HT_{1D}$ receptors and as an agonist at the $5\text{-}HT_{1A}$ receptor. Ziprasidone moderately inhibits the reuptake of serotonin and norepinephrine.

Pharmacodynamics/Kinetics

Half-life Elimination

Oral: Mean terminal half-life:

Children: Mean: 3.3 to 4.1 hours (Sallee 2006)

Adults: 7 hours

IM: Mean half-life: 2 to 5 hours

Time to Peak

Oral: Children: Mean: 5 to 5.5 hours (Sallee 2006); Adults: 6 to 8 hours

IM: ≤60 minutes

Pregnancy Risk Factor C

Pregnancy Considerations Adverse events were observed in animal reproduction studies. Antipsychotic use during the third trimester of pregnancy has a risk for abnormal muscle movements (extrapyramidal symptoms [EPS]) and/or withdrawal symptoms in newborns following delivery. Symptoms in the newborn may include agitation, feeding disorder, hypertonia, hypotonia, respiratory distress, somnolence, and tremor; these effects may be self-limiting or require hospitalization. Ziprasidone may cause hyperprolactinemia, which may decrease reproductive function in both males and females.

The ACOG recommends that therapy during pregnancy be individualized; treatment with psychiatric medications during pregnancy should incorporate the clinical expertise of the mental health clinician, obstetrician, primary healthcare provider, and pediatrician. Safety data related to atypical antipsychotics during pregnancy is limited and routine use is not recommended. However, if a woman is inadvertently exposed to an atypical antipsychotic while pregnant, continuing therapy may be preferable to switching to a typical antipsychotic that the fetus has not yet been exposed to; consider risk: benefit (ACOG, 2008).

Healthcare providers are encouraged to enroll women 18-45 years of age exposed to ziprasidone during pregnancy in the Atypical Antipsychotics Pregnancy Registry (1-866-961-2388 or http://www.womensmentalhealth.org/pregnancyregistry).

Dental Comment See Local Anesthetic/Vasoconstrictor Precautions

Ziv-Aflibercept (Systemic) (ziv a FLIB er sept)

Brand Names: US Zaltrap

Pharmacologic Category Antineoplastic Agent; Vascular Endothelial Growth Factor (VEGF) Inhibitor

Use Colorectal cancer, metastatic: Treatment of metastatic colorectal cancer (in combination with fluorouracil, leucovorin, and irinotecan [FOLFIRI]) in patients who are resistant to or have progressed on an oxaliplatin-based regimen

Local Anesthetic/Vasoconstrictor Precautions Use vasoconstrictor with caution; patients may experience significant hypertension when taking Ziv-Aflibercept (Systemic)

Effects on Dental Treatment Key adverse event(s) related to dental treatment: Stomatitis has been reported in ≤50% of patients

Effects on Bleeding The risk of hemorrhage is increased; GI tract bleeding has been reported

Adverse Reactions Note: Reactions reported in combination therapy with fluorouracil, leucovorin, and irinotecan (FOLFIRI).

>10%:

Cardiovascular: Hypertension (41%; grade 3: 19%; grade 4: <1%)

Central nervous system: Fatigue (48%), voice disorder (25%; grades 3/4: <1%), headache (22%)

Dermatologic: Palmar-plantar erythrodysesthesia (11%)

Endocrine & metabolic: Weight loss (32%)

Gastrointestinal: Diarrhea (69%; grades 3/4: 19%), stomatitis (50%), decreased appetite (32%), abdominal pain (27%), upper abdominal pain (11%)

Genitourinary: Proteinuria (62%, grades 3/4: 8%)

Hematologic: Leukopenia (78%; grades 3/4: 16%), neutropenia (67%; grades 3/4: 37%), thrombocytopenia (48%; grades 3/4: 3%), hemorrhage (38%; grades 3/4: 3%)

Hepatic: Increased serum AST (62%), increased serum ALT (50%)

Infection: Infection (46%, grades 3/4: 12%)

Neuromuscular & skeletal: Weakness (18%; grades 3/4: 5%)

Renal: Increased serum creatinine (23%)

Respiratory: Epistaxis (28%; grades 3/4: <1%), dyspnea (12%)

1% to 10%:

Cardiovascular: Venous thromboembolic events (9%), pulmonary embolism (5%), arterial thromboembolism (3%; grades 3/4: 2%)

Central nervous system: Reversible posterior encephalopathy syndrome (1%)

Dermatologic: Hyperpigmentation (8%)

Endocrine & metabolic: Dehydration (9%; grades 3/4: 4%)

Gastrointestinal: Hemorrhoids (6%), proctalgia (5%), rectal hemorrhage (5%; grades 3/4: <1%), rectal pain (5%)

Genitourinary: Urinary tract infection (9%), nephrotic syndrome (1%)

Hematologic: Febrile neutropenia (grades 3/4: 4%)

Immunologic: Immunogenicity (3%)

Infection: Neutropenic sepsis

Respiratory: Oropharyngeal pain (8%), rhinorrhea (6%)

Miscellaneous: Fistula formation (2%; grades 3/4: <1%)

Frequency not defined:

Central nervous system: Intracranial hemorrhage (severe)

Hematologic & oncologic: Pulmonary hemorrhage

<1%, postmarketing, and/or case reports: Osteonecrosis of the jaw, reduced ejection fracture, thrombotic thrombocytopenic purpura, wound healing impairment

General Dosage Range Dosage adjustment recommended in patients who develop toxicities.

IV: *Adults:* 4 mg/kg every 2 weeks

Mechanism of Action Also known as VEGF-trap, ziv-aflibercept is a recombinant fusion protein which is comprised of portions of binding domains for vascular endothelial growth factor (VEGF) receptors 1 and 2, attached to the Fc portion of human IgG1. Ziv-aflibercept acts as a decoy receptor for VEGF-A, VEGF-B, and placental growth factor (PlGF) which prevent VEGF receptor binding/activation to their receptors (an action critical to angiogenesis), thus leading to antiangiogenesis and tumor regression.

Pharmacodynamics/Kinetics

Half-life Elimination ~6 days (range: 4 to 7 days)

Pregnancy Risk Factor C

Pregnancy Considerations Adverse events were observed in animal reproduction studies with doses providing systemic exposure equivalent to ~30% of a human dose. The incidence of fetal malformations increased with increasing doses. Patients (male and female) should use effective contraception during therapy and for at least 3 months following treatment.

Zoledronic Acid (zoe le DRON ik AS id)

Related Information

Osteonecrosis of the Jaw *on page 1796*

Rheumatoid Arthritis, Osteoarthritis, and Osteoporosis *on page 1792*

Brand Names: US Reclast; Zometa

Brand Names: Canada Aclasta; Taro-Zoledronic Acid; Taro-Zoledronic Acid Concentrate; Zoledronic Acid Injection; Zoledronic Acid for Injection; Zoledronic Acid Z; Zometa Concentrate

Generic Availability (US) Yes

Pharmacologic Category Bisphosphonate Derivative

Use

Bone metastases from solid tumors (Zometa): Treatment of documented bone metastases from solid tumors (in conjunction with standard antineoplastic therapy); prostate cancer should have progressed following treatment with at least one hormonal therapy.

Glucocorticoid-induced osteoporosis (Reclast, Aclasta [Canadian product]): Treatment and prevention of glucocorticoid-induced osteoporosis in men and women who are initiating or continuing systemic glucocorticoids in a daily dose equivalent to 7.5 mg or more of prednisone and who are expected to remain on glucocorticoids for at least 12 months.

Hypercalcemia of malignancy (Zometa): Treatment of hypercalcemia (albumin-corrected serum calcium ≥12 mg/dL) of malignancy.

Multiple myeloma (Zometa): Treatment of osteolytic lesions of multiple myeloma.

Osteoporosis in men (Reclast, Aclasta [Canadian product]): To increase bone mass in men with osteoporosis.

Paget disease of bone (Reclast, Aclasta [Canadian product]): Treatment of Paget disease of bone in men and women. **Note:** In patients without contraindications, zoledronic acid is recommended as the treatment of choice per Endocrine Society guidelines (Singer 2014).

Postmenopausal osteoporosis (Reclast, Aclasta [Canadian product]): Treatment and prevention of osteoporosis in postmenopausal women.

Limitations of use: Safety and efficacy for treatment of hypercalcemia associated with hyperparathyroidism or with other non-tumor-related conditions have not been established. Safety and efficacy for osteoporosis treatment is based on clinical data of 3 years duration; the optimal duration has not been determined. All patients on bisphosphonate therapy for the treatment of osteoporosis should be re-evaluated periodically for the need to continue therapy; consider discontinuing after 3 to 5 years in patients at low-risk for fracture; re-evaluate fracture risk periodically in patients who discontinue therapy.

Local Anesthetic/Vasoconstrictor Precautions No information available to require special precautions

Effects on Dental Treatment Key adverse event(s) related to dental treatment: Mucositis, dysphagia, stomatitis, and sore throat.

Osteonecrosis of the jaw (ONJ), generally associated with local infection and/or tooth extraction and often with delayed healing, has been reported in patients taking bisphosphonates. Symptoms included nonhealing extraction socket or an exposed jawbone. Most reported cases of bisphosphonate-associated osteonecrosis have been in cancer patients treated with intravenous bisphosphonates. However, some have occurred in patients with postmenopausal osteoporosis taking oral bisphosphonates. Dental surgery, particularly tooth extraction, may increase the risk for ONJ. Patients who develop ONJ while on bisphosphonate therapy should receive care by an oral surgeon. See Dental Comment.

Effects on Bleeding Zoledronic acid has been shown to induce thrombotic thrombocytopenia purpura-hemolytic uremic syndrome (TTP-HUS). In a clinical report, zoledronic acid therapy caused acute anemia and thrombocytopenia, with reticulocyte count at 6% and bilirubin at 1.6 mg/dL, with few fragmented erythrocytes. Treatment for this thrombocytopenia complication is discontinuation of the drug and plasma exchange therapy to increase platelet count.

Adverse Reactions

Oncology indications:

>10%:

Cardiovascular: Lower extremity edema (5% to 21%), hypotension (11%)

Central nervous system: Fatigue (39%), headache (5% to 19%), dizziness (18%), insomnia (15% to 16%), depression (14%), anxiety (11% to 14%), agitation (13%), confusion (7% to 13%), hypoesthesia (12%), rigors (11%)

Dermatologic: Alopecia (12%), dermatitis (11%)

Endocrine & metabolic: Dehydration (5% to 14%), hypophosphatemia (13%), hypokalemia (12%), hypomagnesemia (11%)

Gastrointestinal: Nausea (29% to 46%), vomiting (14% to 32%), constipation (27% to 31%), diarrhea (17% to 24%), anorexia (9% to 22%), weight loss (16%), abdominal pain (14% to 16%), decreased appetite (13%)

Genitourinary: Urinary tract infection (12% to 14%)

Hematologic & oncologic: Anemia (22% to 33%), progression of cancer (16% to 20%), neutropenia (12%)

Infection: Candidiasis (12%)

Neuromuscular & skeletal: Ostealgia (55%), weakness (5% to 24%), myalgia (23%), arthralgia (5% to 21%), back pain (15%), paresthesia (15%), limb pain (14%), skeletal pain (12%)

Renal: Renal insufficiency (8% to 17%; up to 40% in patients with abnormal baseline creatinine)

Respiratory: Dyspnea (22% to 27%), cough (12% to 22%)

Miscellaneous: Fever (32% to 44%; most common symptom of acute phase reaction)

1% to 10%:

Cardiovascular: Chest pain (5% to 10%)

Central nervous system: Somnolence (5% to 10%)

Endocrine & metabolic: Hypocalcemia (5% to 10%; grades 3/4: ≤1%), hypermagnesemia (grade 3: 2%)

Gastrointestinal: Dyspepsia (10%), dysphagia (5% to 10%), mucositis (5% to 10%), sore throat (8%), stomatitis (8%)

Hematologic & oncologic: Granulocytopenia (5% to 10%), pancytopenia (5% to 10%), thrombocytopenia (5% to 10%)

Infection: Infection (nonspecific; 5% to 10%)

Renal: Increased serum creatinine (grades 3/4: ≤2%)

Respiratory: Upper respiratory tract infection (10%)

Nononcology indications:

>10%:

Cardiovascular: Hypertension (5% to 13%)

Central nervous system: Pain (2% to 24%), fever (9% to 22%), headache (4% to 20%), chills (2% to 18%), fatigue (2% to 18%), flank pain (≤2%)

Endocrine & metabolic: Hypocalcemia (≤3%; Paget's disease 21%), dehydration (3%)

Gastrointestinal: Nausea (5% to 18%), upper abdominal pain (5%), abdominal distension (≤2%)

Immunologic: Infusion related reaction (4% to 25%)

Neuromuscular & skeletal: Arthralgia (9% to 27%), myalgia (5% to 23%), back pain (4% to 18%), limb pain (3% to 16%), musculoskeletal pain (≤12%), osteoarthritis (6%)

Respiratory: Flu-like symptoms (1% to 11%)

1% to 10%:

Cardiovascular: Chest pain (1% to 8%), peripheral edema (3% to 6%), atrial fibrillation (1% to 3%), palpitations (≤3%)

Central nervous system: Dizziness (2% to 9%), rigors (8%), malaise (1% to 7%), hypoesthesia (≤6%), lethargy (3% to 5%), vertigo (1% to 4%), paresthesia (2%), hyperthermia (≤2%)

Dermatologic: Skin rash (2% to 3%), hyperhidrosis (≤3%)

Gastrointestinal: Abdominal pain (1% to 9%), diarrhea (5% to 8%), vomiting (2% to 8%), constipation (6% to 7%), dyspepsia (2% to 7%), abdominal discomfort (1% to 2%), anorexia (1% to 2%)

Hematologic & oncologic: Change in serum protein (C-reactive protein increased; ≤5%)

Neuromuscular & skeletal: Ostealgia (3% to 9%), arthritis (2% to 9%), neck pain (1% to 7%), shoulder pain (≤7%), muscle spasm (2% to 6%), weakness (2% to 6%), stiffness (1% to 5%), jaw pain (2% to 4%), joint swelling (≤3%)

Ophthalmic: Eye pain (≤2%)

Renal: Increased serum creatinine (2%)

Respiratory: Dyspnea (5% to 7%)

All indications: <1%, postmarketing, and/or case reports: Acute phase reaction-like symptoms (including pyrexia, fatigue, bone pain, arthralgia, myalgia, chills, influenza-like illness; usually resolves within 3 to 4 days of onset, although may take up to 14 days to resolve), acute renal failure (requiring hospitalization/dialysis), acute renal tubular necrosis (toxic), anaphylactic shock, anaphylaxis, angioedema, arthralgia (sometimes severe and/or incapacitating), blurred vision, bradycardia, bronchoconstriction, bronchospasm, cardiac arrhythmia, cerebrovascular accident, conjunctivitis, diaphoresis, drowsiness, dysgeusia, episcleritis, exacerbation of asthma, femur fracture (diaphyseal or subtrochanteric), hematuria, hyperesthesia, hyperkalemia, hypernatremia, hyperparathyroidism, hypersensitivity reaction, hypertension, injection site reaction (eg, itching, pain, redness), interstitial pulmonary disease, iridocyclitis, iritis, muscle cramps, myalgia (sometimes severe and/or incapacitating), numbness, osteonecrosis (primarily of the jaws), periorbital edema, periorbital swelling, prolonged QT interval on ECG, proteinuria, pruritus, renal insufficiency, scleritis, seizure, skin rash, Stevens-Johnson syndrome, tetany, toxic epidermal necrolysis, tremor, urticaria, uveitis, weight gain, xerostomia

Dosing

Adult & Geriatric Note: Acetaminophen administration after the infusion may reduce symptoms of acute-phase reactions. Patients treated for bone metastases from solid tumors, multiple myeloma, and Paget disease should receive a daily calcium and vitamin D supplement, and patients with osteoporosis should receive calcium and vitamin D supplementation if dietary intake is inadequate.

Bone metastases from solid tumors (Zometa): IV: 4 mg once every 3 to 4 weeks

Bone metastases due to breast cancer or prostate cancer (off-label dosing): IV: 4 mg once every 12 weeks; dosing once every 12 weeks (compared to once every 4 weeks) did not result in an increased risk of skeletal events within 2 years in patients with at least 1 site of bone involvement (Himmelstein 2017).

Hypercalcemia of malignancy (albumin-corrected serum calcium ≥12 mg/dL) (Zometa): IV: 4 mg (maximum) given as a single dose. Wait at least 7 days before considering re-treatment.

Multiple myeloma osteolytic lesions (Zometa): IV: 4 mg once every 3 to 4 weeks

Multiple myeloma (off-label dosing): IV: 4 mg once every 12 weeks; dosing once every 12 weeks (compared to once every 4 weeks) did not result in an increased risk of skeletal events within 2 years in patients with at least 1 site of bone involvement (Himmelstein 2017).

Osteoporosis, glucocorticoid-induced, treatment and prevention (Reclast, Aclasta [Canadian product]): IV: 5 mg once a year

Osteoporosis, prevention (Reclast): IV: 5 mg once every 2 years

Canadian labeling (Aclasta): 5 mg as a single (one-time) dose

Osteoporosis, treatment (Reclast, Aclasta [Canadian product]): IV: 5 mg once a year; consider discontinuing after 3 to 5 years of use in patients at low risk for fracture

Paget disease (Reclast, Aclasta [Canadian product]): IV: 5 mg as a single dose.

Re-treatment: Data concerning retreatment is not available; retreatment may be considered for relapse (increase in alkaline phosphatase) if appropriate, for inadequate response, or in patients who are symptomatic.

Canadian labeling (Aclasta): Data concerning retreatment is limited; retreatment with 5 mg (single dose) may be considered for relapse after an interval of at least 1 year from initial treatment.

The Endocrine Society guidelines suggest re-treatment is seldom required within 5 years (Singer 2014).

Postrenal transplant bone loss (prevention) (off-label use): IV: 4 mg at week 2 and month 3 after engraftment (Haas 2003; Schwarz 2004). Additional data may be necessary to further define the role of zoledronic acid in this condition.

Bone loss associated with androgen deprivation therapy in prostate cancer, prevention (off-label use): IV: 4 mg once every 3 months for 1 year (Smith, 2003) or 4 mg every 12 months (Michaelson 2007)

Bone loss associated with aromatase inhibitor therapy in women with breast cancer, prevention (off-label use): IV: 4 mg once every 6 months for 5 years (Brufsky 2012)

Renal Impairment Note: Prior to each dose, obtain serum creatinine and calculate the creatinine clearance using the Cockcroft-Gault formula.

***Nononcology uses:* Note:** Use actual body weight in the Cockcroft-Gault formula when calculating clearance for nononcology uses.

CrCl ≥35 mL/minute: No dosage adjustment is necessary.

CrCl <35 mL/minute: Use is contraindicated.

Oncology uses:

Multiple myeloma and bone metastases:

CrCl >60 mL/minute: 4 mg (no dosage adjustment is necessary)

CrCl 50 to 60 mL/minute: Reduce dose to 3.5 mg

CrCl 40 to 49 mL/minute: Reduce dose to 3.3 mg

CrCl 30 to 39 mL/minute: Reduce dose to 3 mg

CrCl <30 mL/minute: Use is not recommended.

Hypercalcemia of malignancy:

Mild to moderate impairment: No dosage adjustment is necessary.

Severe impairment (serum creatinine >4.5 mg/dL): Evaluate risk versus benefit

Dosage adjustment for renal toxicity (during treatment):

Hypercalcemia of malignancy: Evidence of renal deterioration: Evaluate risk versus benefit.

Multiple myeloma and bone metastases: Evidence of renal deterioration: Withhold dose until renal function returns to within 10% of baseline; renal deterioration defined as follows:

Normal baseline creatinine: Increase of 0.5 mg/dL

Abnormal baseline creatinine: Increase of 1 mg/dL

Reinitiate therapy at the same dose administered prior to treatment interruption.

Multiple myeloma: Albuminuria >500 mg/24 hours (unexplained): Withhold dose until return to baseline, then reevaluate every 3 to 4 weeks; consider reinitiating with a longer infusion time of at least 30 minutes (Kyle 2007).

Hepatic Impairment There are no dosage adjustments provided in the manufacturer's labeling (has not been studied); however, zoledronic acid is not metabolized hepatically.

Mechanism of Action A bisphosphonate which inhibits bone resorption via actions on osteoclasts or on osteoclast precursors; inhibits osteoclastic activity and skeletal calcium release induced by tumors. Decreases serum calcium and phosphorus, and increases their elimination. In osteoporosis, zoledronic acid inhibits osteoclast-mediated resorption, therefore reducing bone turnover.

Contraindications

US labeling:

Hypersensitivity to zoledronic acid or any component of the formulation; hypocalcemia (Reclast only); CrCl <35 mL/minute and in those with evidence of acute renal impairment (Reclast only).

Canadian labeling:

All indications: Hypersensitivity to zoledronic acid or other bisphosphonates, or any component of the formulation; uncorrected hypocalcemia at the time of infusion; pregnancy, breastfeeding

Nononcology uses: Additional contraindications: Use in patients with CrCl <35 mL/minute and use in patients with evidence of acute renal impairment due to an increased risk of renal failure

Documentation of allergenic cross-reactivity for bisphosphonates is limited. However, because of similarities in chemical structure and/or pharmacologic actions, the possibility of cross-sensitivity cannot be ruled out with certainty.

Warnings/Precautions

Osteonecrosis of the jaw (ONJ), also referred to as medication-related osteonecrosis of the jaw (MRONJ), has been reported in patients receiving bisphosphonates. Known risk factors for MRONJ include invasive dental procedures (eg, tooth extraction, dental implants, bony surgery), cancer diagnosis, concomitant therapy (eg, chemotherapy, corticosteroids, angiogenesis inhibitors), poor oral hygiene, ill-fitting dentures, and comorbid disorders (anemia, coagulopathy, infection, preexisting dental disease). Risk may increase with duration of bisphosphonate use and/or may be reported at a greater frequency based on tumor type (eg, advanced breast cancer or multiple myeloma). According to a position paper by the American Association of Maxillofacial Surgeons (AAOMS), MRONJ has been associated with bisphosphonates and other antiresorptive agents (denosumab), and antiangiogenic agents (eg, bevacizumab, sunitinib) used for the treatment of osteoporosis or malignancy; risk is significantly higher in cancer patients receiving antiresorptive therapy compared to patients receiving osteoporosis treatment (regardless of medication used or dosing schedule). MRONJ risk is also increased with monthly IV antiresorptive therapy compared to the minimal risk associated with oral bisphosphonate use, although risk appears to increase with oral bisphosphonates when duration of therapy exceeds 4 years. The manufacturer's labeling states that there are no data to suggest whether discontinuing bisphosphonates in patients requiring invasive dental procedures reduces the risk of ONJ. The manufacturer recommends a dental exam and preventive dentistry be performed prior to placing patients with risk factors on chronic bisphosphonate therapy and that during therapy, invasive dental procedures be avoided, if possible. The AAOMS suggests that if medically permissible, initiation of IV bisphosphonates for cancer therapy should be delayed until optimal dental health is attained (if extractions are required, antiresorptive therapy should delayed until the extraction site has mucosalized or until after adequate osseous healing). Once IV bisphosphonate therapy is initiated for oncologic disease, procedures that involve direct osseous injury and placement of dental implants be avoided. Patients developing ONJ during therapy should receive care by an oral surgeon (AAOMS [Ruggiero 2014]).

Atypical, low-energy, or low-trauma femur fractures have been reported in patients receiving bisphosphonates. The fractures include subtrochanteric femur (bone just below the hip joint) and diaphyseal femur (long segment of the thigh bone). Some patients experience prodromal pain weeks or months before the fracture occurs. It is unclear if bisphosphonate therapy is the cause for these fractures; atypical femur fractures have also been reported in patients not taking bisphosphonates, and in patients receiving glucocorticoids. Patients receiving long-term (>3 to 5 years) bisphosphonate therapy may be at an increased risk. Patients presenting with thigh or groin pain with a history of receiving bisphosphonates should be evaluated for femur fracture. Consider interrupting bisphosphonate therapy in patients who develop a femoral shaft fracture; assess for fracture in the contralateral limb.

Infrequently, severe (and occasionally debilitating) musculoskeletal (bone, joint, and/or muscle) pain have been reported during bisphosphonate treatment. The onset of pain ranged from a single day to several months. Consider discontinuing therapy in patients who experience severe symptoms; symptoms usually resolve upon discontinuation. Some patients experienced recurrence when rechallenged with same drug or another bisphosphonate; avoid use in patients with a history of these symptoms in association with bisphosphonate therapy.

Hypocalcemia (including severe and life-threatening cases) has been reported with use; patients with Paget disease may be at significant risk for hypocalcemia after treatment with zoledronic acid (because pretreatment rate of bone turnover may be elevated); severe and life-threatening hypocalcemia has also been reported with oncology-related uses. Measure serum calcium prior to treatment initiation. Correct preexisting hypocalcemia before initiation of therapy in patients with Paget disease, osteoporosis, or oncology indications. Use with caution with other medications known to cause hypocalcemia (severe hypocalcemia may develop). Ensure adequate calcium and vitamin D supplementation during therapy. Use caution in patients with disturbances of calcium and mineral metabolism (eg, hypoparathyroidism, thyroid/parathyroid, surgery, malabsorption syndromes, excision of small intestine).

Nononcology indications: Use is contraindicated in patients with CrCl <35 mL/minute and in patients with evidence of acute renal impairment due to an increased risk of renal failure. Do not use single doses >5 mg and do not infuse over less than 15 minutes. Obtain serum creatinine and calculate creatinine clearance (using actual body weight) with the Cockcroft-Gault formula prior to each administration. In the management of osteoporosis, reevaluate the need for continued therapy periodically; the optimal duration of treatment has not yet been determined. Consider discontinuing after 3 to 5 years of use in patients at low risk for fracture; following discontinuation, reevaluate fracture risk periodically.

Oncology indications: Use caution in mild to moderate renal dysfunction; dosage adjustment required. In cancer patients, do not use single doses >4 mg and do not infuse over less than 15 minutes (renal toxicity has been reported with doses >4 mg or infusions administered over less than 15 minutes). Risk factors for renal deterioration include preexisting renal insufficiency and repeated doses of zoledronic acid and other bisphosphonates. Dehydration and the use of other nephrotoxic drugs which may contribute to renal deterioration should be identified and managed. Use is not recommended in patients with severe renal impairment (serum creatinine >3 mg/dL or CrCl <30 mL/minute) and bone metastases (limited data); use in patients with hypercalcemia of malignancy and severe renal impairment (serum creatinine >4.5 mg/dL for hypercalcemia of malignancy) should only be done if the benefits outweigh the risks. Diuretics should not be used before correcting hypovolemia. Renal deterioration, resulting in renal failure and dialysis has occurred in patients treated with zoledronic acid after single and multiple infusions at recommended doses of 4 mg over 15 minutes. Assess renal function (eg, serum creatinine) prior to each dose and withhold for renal deterioration [increase in serum creatinine of 0.5 mg/dL (if baseline level normal) or increase of 1 mg/dL (if baseline level abnormal)]; treatment should be withheld until renal function returns to within 10% of baseline.

Adequate hydration is required during treatment (urine output ~2 L/day); avoid overhydration, especially in patients with heart failure. Preexisting renal compromise, severe dehydration, and concurrent use with diuretics or other nephrotoxic drugs may increase the risk for renal impairment. Single and multiple infusions in patients with both normal and impaired renal function have been associated with renal deterioration, resulting in renal failure and dialysis or death (rare). Patients with underlying moderate to severe renal impairment, increased age, concurrent use of nephrotoxic or diuretic medications, or severe dehydration prior to or after zoledronic acid administration may have an increased risk of acute renal impairment or renal failure. Others with increased risk include patients with renal impairment or dehydration secondary to fever, sepsis, gastrointestinal losses, or diuretic use. If history or physical exam suggests dehydration, treatment should not be given until the patient is normovolemic. Transient increases in serum creatinine may be more pronounced in patients with impaired renal function; consider monitoring creatinine clearance in at-risk patients taking other renally eliminated drugs.

Conjunctivitis, uveitis, episcleritis, iritis, scleritis, and orbital inflammation have been reported (infrequently) with use; further ophthalmic evaluation (and possibly therapy discontinuation) may be necessary in patients with complicated infection. Use caution in patients with aspirin-sensitive asthma (may cause bronchoconstriction) and elderly patients (because decreased renal function occurs more commonly in elderly patients). Rare cases of urticaria and angioedema and very rare cases of anaphylactic reactions/shock have been reported. Do not administer Zometa and Reclast (Aclasta [Canadian product]) to the same patient for different indications.

Breast cancer (metastatic): The American Society of Clinical Oncology (ASCO) updated guidelines on the role of bone-modifying agents (BMAs) in the prevention and treatment of skeletal-related events for metastatic breast cancer patients (Van Poznak 2011). The guidelines recommend initiating a BMA (denosumab, pamidronate, zoledronic acid) in patients with metastatic breast cancer to the bone. There is currently no literature indicating the superiority of one particular BMA. Optimal duration is not yet defined; however, the guidelines recommend continuing therapy until substantial decline in patient's performance status. The ASCO guidelines are in alignment with prescribing information for dosing, renal dose adjustments, infusion times, prevention and management of osteonecrosis of the jaw, and monitoring of laboratory parameter recommendations. BMAs are not the first-line therapy for pain. BMAs are to be used as adjunctive therapy for cancer-related bone pain associated with bone metastasis, demonstrating a modest pain control benefit. BMAs should be used in conjunction with agents such as NSAIDS, opioid and nonopioid analgesics, corticosteroids, radiation/surgery, and interventional procedures.

Multiple myeloma: The American Society of Clinical Oncology (ASCO) has published guidelines on bisphosphonate use for prevention and treatment of bone disease in multiple myeloma (Kyle, 2007). Bisphosphonate (pamidronate or zoledronic acid) use is recommended in multiple myeloma patients with lytic bone destruction or compression spine fracture from osteopenia. Bisphosphonates may also be considered in patients with pain secondary to osteolytic disease, adjunct therapy to stabilize fractures or impending fractures, and for multiple myeloma patients with osteopenia but no radiographic evidence of lytic bone disease. Bisphosphonates are not recommended in patients with solitary plasmacytoma, smoldering (asymptomatic) or indolent myeloma, or monoclonal gammopathy of undetermined significance. The guidelines recommend monthly treatment for a period of 2 years. At that time, consider discontinuing in responsive and stable patients, and reinitiate if a new-onset skeletal-related event occurs. The ASCO guidelines are in alignment with prescribing information for dosing, renal dose adjustments, infusion times, prevention and management of osteonecrosis of the jaw, and monitoring of laboratory parameter recommendations. According to the guidelines, in patients with a serum creatinine >3 mg/dL or CrCl <30 mL/minute or extensive bone disease, an alternative bisphosphonate (pamidronate) should be used. Monitor for albuminuria every 3 to 6 months; in patients with unexplained albuminuria >500 mg/24 hours, withhold the dose until level returns to baseline, then recheck every 3 to 4 weeks. Upon reinitiation, the guidelines recommend considering increasing the zoledronic acid infusion time to at least

30 minutes; however, one study has demonstrated that extending the infusion to 30 minutes did not change the safety profile (Berenson, 2011).

Drug Interactions

Metabolism/Transport Effects None known.

Avoid Concomitant Use There are no known interactions where it is recommended to avoid concomitant use.

Increased Effect/Toxicity

Zoledronic Acid may increase the levels/effects of: Deferasirox

The levels/effects of Zoledronic Acid may be increased by: Aminoglycosides; Calcitonin; Nonsteroidal Anti-Inflammatory Agents; Systemic Angiogenesis Inhibitors; Thalidomide

Decreased Effect

The levels/effects of Zoledronic Acid may be decreased by: Proton Pump Inhibitors

Dietary Considerations

Multiple myeloma or metastatic bone lesions from solid tumors: Take daily calcium supplement (500 mg) and daily multivitamin (with 400 units vitamin D).

Osteoporosis: Ensure adequate calcium and vitamin D intake; if dietary intake is inadequate, dietary supplementation is recommended. Women and men should consume:

Calcium: 1,000 mg/day (men: 50 to 70 years) **or** 1200 mg/day (women ≥51 years and men ≥71 years) (IOM 2011; NOF [Cosman 2014])

Vitamin D: 800 to 1,000 int. units/day (men and women ≥50 years) (NOF 2014). Recommended Dietary Allowance (RDA): 600 int. units/day (men and women ≤70 years) **or** 800 int. units/day (men and women ≥71 years) (IOM 2011).

Paget disease: Take elemental calcium 1500 mg/day (750 mg twice daily or 500 mg 3 times/day) and vitamin D 800 units/day, particularly during the first 2 weeks after administration.

Pharmacodynamics/Kinetics

Half life Elimination Triphasic; Terminal: 146 hours

Pregnancy Risk Factor D

Pregnancy Considerations Adverse events were observed in animal reproduction studies. It is not known if bisphosphonates cross the placenta, but fetal exposure is expected (Djokanovic, 2008; Stathopoulos, 2011). Bisphosphonates are incorporated into the bone matrix and gradually released over time. The amount available in the systemic circulation varies by dose and duration of therapy. Theoretically, there may be a risk of fetal harm when pregnancy follows the completion of therapy; however, available data have not shown that exposure to bisphosphonates during pregnancy significantly increases the risk of adverse fetal events (Djokanovic, 2008; Levy, 2009; Stathopoulos, 2011). Until additional data is available, most sources recommend discontinuing bisphosphonate therapy in women of reproductive potential as early as possible prior to a planned pregnancy; use in premenopausal women should be reserved for special circumstances when rapid bone loss is occurring (Bhalla, 2010; Pereira, 2012; Stathopoulos, 2011). Because hypocalcemia has been described following *in utero* bisphosphonate exposure, exposed infants should be monitored for hypocalcemia after birth (Djokanovic, 2008; Stathopoulos, 2011).

Breastfeeding Considerations It is not known if zoledronic acid is excreted into breast milk. Due to the potential for serious adverse reactions in the nursing infant, the manufacturer recommends a decision be made to discontinue nursing or to discontinue the drug, taking into account the importance of treatment to the mother.

Dosage Forms

Concentrate, Intravenous:
Zometa: 4 mg/5 mL (5 mL)
Generic: 4 mg/5 mL (5 mL)

Concentrate, Intravenous [preservative free]:
Generic: 4 mg/5 mL (5 mL)

Solution, Intravenous:
Reclast: 5 mg/100 mL (100 mL)
Zometa: 4 mg/100 mL (100 mL)
Generic: 5 mg/100 mL (100 mL)

Solution, Intravenous [preservative free]:
Generic: 4 mg/100 mL (100 mL); 5 mg/100 mL (100 mL)

Dosage Forms: Canada

Concentrate, Intravenous:
Zometa: 4 mg/5 mL (5 mL)

Infusion, Solution [premixed]:
Aclasta: 5 mg/100 mL

Dental Comment Zoledronic acid (Reclast) is administered once annually for the treatment of osteoporosis. A single, large prospective, placebo-controlled study established its efficacy for this indication through 3 years of treatment (Black 2007). Two cases of ONJ were reported, one each in the treatment and control groups, suggesting a low risk of ONJ with this treatment protocol through 3 years.

The American Association of Oral and Maxillofacial Surgeons position paper on bisphosphonate-related osteonecrosis of the jaws, 2009 update, stated that IV bisphosphonate exposure in the setting of managing malignancy remains the major risk factor for the development of ONJ. After reviewing case series, case-controlled studies, and cohort studies, the estimates of the cumulative incidence of IV bisphosphonate-associated ONJ ranges from 0.8% to 12%.

Two reports have attempted to assess more accurately the percent of cancer patients developing ONJ after bisphosphonate treatment. Maerevoet et al, reported that among 194 patients treated with Zometa every 3 to 4 weeks, nine developed ONJ. Before receiving Zometa, six had received Aredia 90 mg every 3 to 4 weeks. The median duration of treatment with Aredia was 39 months and for Zometa 18 months. The incidence of ONJ in these patients was calculated to be 4.6%. Durie et al, described the results of a survey by the International Myeloma Foundation in 2004 to assess the risk factors of ONJ. Out of 1,203 respondents, 904 had myeloma and 299 had breast cancer. Of the myeloma patients, 62 developed ONJ and 54 had suspicious findings. Of the breast cancer patients, 13 had ONJ and 23 had suspicious findings. The total number of cases of either ONJ or suspicious findings was 152. ONJ developed in 10% of 211 patients receiving Zometa compared to 4% of 413 receiving Aredia. The mean time to onset of ONJ among patients taking Zometa was 18 months; the mean time to onset after Aredia was 6 years. It should be noted that an early report by authors from Novartis Pharmaceuticals Corporation stressed that Aredia and Zometa had been used in 2.5 million patients world wide and reports of ONJ during their extensive use had been rare (Tarassoff 2003). In addition, these authors stated that review of the reported cases revealed multiple risk factors for avascular necrosis. McMahon et al, followed up with a report that, along with other factors, bisphosphonates are additional stressors of bone health that can tip the balance to osteonecrosis. They suggested that the prevention of ONJ should be stressed such as the elimination of chronic dental infections prior to chemotherapy and bisphosphonate use in cancer patients.

The most comprehensive review to date on osteonecrosis of the jaw bone (ONJ) has been published in the *Journal of Bone and Mineral Research* (Khan 2015), and written by an International Task Force of authors, totaling 34, from academe; industry; clinical medical and dental practice; oral and maxillofacial surgery; bone and mineral research; epidemiology; medical and dental oncology; orthopedic surgery; osteoporosis research; muscle and bone research; endocrinology and diagnostic sciences. The work provides a systematic review of the literature and international consensus on the classification, incidence, pathophysiology, diagnosis, and management of ONJ in both oncology and osteoporosis patient populations. This review of the literature from January 2003 to April 2014, with 299 references, offers recommendations for management of ONJ based on multidisciplinary international consensus.

Incidence of ONJ in oncology patients from the Task Force report:

The incidence of ONJ ranges from 1% to 15% in the oncology patient population where high doses of BPs are used at frequent intervals. The oncology patient with bone metastasis is exposed to more osteoclastic inhibition than those with osteoporosis, thus the incidence of ONJ is much higher.

ZOLMitriptan (zohl mi TRIP tan)

Related Information

Temporomandibular Dysfunction (TMD), Chronic Pain, and Fibromyalgia *on page 1868*

Brand Names: US Zomig; Zomig ZMT

Brand Names: Canada Dom-Zolmitriptan; JAMP-Zolmitriptan; JAMP-Zolmitriptan ODT; Mar-Zolmitriptan; Mint-Zolmitriptan; Mint-Zolmitriptan ODT; Mylan-Zolmitriptan; Mylan-Zolmitriptan ODT; NAT-Zolmitriptan; PMS-Zolmitriptan; PMS-Zolmitriptan ODT; Riva-Zolmitriptan; Sandoz-Zolmitriptan; Sandoz-Zolmitriptan ODT; Septa-Zolmitriptan ODT; Teva-Zolmitriptan; Teva-Zolmitriptan OD; Zolmitriptan ODT; Zomig; Zomig Nasal Spray; Zomig Rapimelt

Pharmacologic Category Antimigraine Agent; Serotonin 5-$HT_{1B,\ 1D}$ Receptor Agonist

Use Migraines:

Nasal inhalation: Acute treatment of migraine with or without aura in adults and pediatric patients ≥12 years.

Oral: Acute treatment of migraine with or without aura in adults.

Local Anesthetic/Vasoconstrictor Precautions No information available to require special precautions

Effects on Dental Treatment Key adverse event(s) related to dental treatment: Xerostomia (normal salivary flow resumes upon discontinuation) and dysphagia.

Effects on Bleeding No information available to require special precautions

Adverse Reactions

>10%: Gastrointestinal: Unpleasant taste (nasal: adults: 17% to 21%; children & adolescents: 6% to 10%)

1% to 10%:

Cardiovascular: Chest pain (oral: 2% to 4%), chest pressure (nasal: 1% to <2%), facial edema (nasal: 1% to <2%), palpitations (nasal: 1% to <2%), cardiac arrhythmia (≤1%), hypertension (≤1%), syncope (≤1%), tachycardia (≤1%)

Central nervous system: Dizziness (adults: 6% to 10%; children & adolescents: 2%), paresthesia (5% to 10%), drowsiness (4% to 8%), local alterations in temperature sensations (oral: 5% to 7%), sensation of pressure (oral: 2% to 5%), hyperesthesia (nasal: 1% to 5%), (1% to 5%), flushing sensation (nasal: 4%), pain (nasal: 2% to 4%), vertigo (oral: 2%), chills (nasal: 1% to <2%), depersonalization (nasal: 1% to <2%), headache (1% to <2%), agitation (≤1%), amnesia (≤1%), anxiety (≤1%), depression (≤1%), emotional lability (oral: ≤1%), insomnia (≤1%), nervousness (nasal: ≤1%)

Dermatologic: Diaphoresis (oral: 2% to 3%), pruritus (≤1%), skin rash (≤1%), urticaria (≤1%)

Gastrointestinal: Nausea (adults: 4% to 9%; children & adolescents: 2%), xerostomia (2% to 5%), dyspepsia (oral: 2% to 3%), dysphagia (1% to 2%), abdominal pain (nasal: 1% to <2%), vomiting (1% to <2%)

Genitourinary: Urinary frequency (oral: ≤1%), urinary urgency (≤1%)

Hypersensitivity: Hypersensitivity reaction (≤1%)

Local: Local pain (4% to 10%; neck/throat/jaw), application site irritation (nasal: 3%)

Neuromuscular & skeletal: Weakness (oral: 5% to 9%; nasal: 3%), arthralgia (nasal: 1% to <2%), myalgia (nasal: 1% to <2%)

Otic: Tinnitus (≤1%)

Renal: Polyuria (≤1%)

Respiratory: Nasal discomfort (nasal: 3%), constriction of the pharynx (nasal: 2%), pressure on pharynx (nasal: 1% to <2%), bronchitis (nasal: ≤1%), cough (nasal: ≤1%), dyspnea (nasal: ≤1%), epistaxis (nasal: ≤1%), laryngeal edema (nasal: ≤1%), pharyngitis (nasal: ≤1%), rhinitis (nasal: ≤1%), sinusitis (nasal: ≤1%)

<1%, postmarketing, and/or case reports: Abnormal dreams, abnormality in thinking, altered sense of smell, amblyopia, anaphylactoid reaction, anaphylaxis, angina pectoris, angioedema, apathy, ataxia, atrial fibrillation, back pain, bradycardia, breast carcinoma, breast neoplasm, bruise, cellulitis, cerebral ischemia, colitis, confusion, conjunctivitis, constipation, convulsions, coronary artery vasospasm, cyanosis, cyst, cystitis, diarrhea, dry eye syndrome, dysmenorrhea, eczema, eructation, erythema, erythema multiforme, euphoria, eye pain, fever, fibrocystic breast disease, flu-like symptoms, gastritis, gastrointestinal carcinoma, gastrointestinal infarction, gastrointestinal necrosis, genitourinary neoplasm, gingivitis, hallucination, hepatic neoplasm, hiccups, hypertensive crisis, hyperthyroidism, hypertonia, hyperventilation, increased appetite, increased bronchial secretions, increased thirst, infection, intestinal obstruction, irritability, ischemic colitis, ischemic heart disease, lacrimation, laryngitis, leukopenia, mania, menorrhagia, myocardial infarction, neoplasm, neuropathy, otalgia, photophobia, pneumonia, psychosis, pyelonephritis, renal pain, salivation, seizure, serotonin syndrome, sialadenitis, skin neoplasm, splenic infarction, stomatitis, tardive dyskinesia, tenosynovitis, thrombophlebitis, thyroid edema, tongue edema, tremor, twitching, urinary tract infection, uterine fibroid enlargement, uterine hemorrhage, vaginitis, vasodilatation, ventricular fibrillation, ventricular tachycardia, visual field defect, voice disorder, yawning

General Dosage Range Dosage adjustment recommended in patients with hepatic impairment

Nasal inhalation: *Children ≥12 years, Adolescents, and Adults:* 2.5 mg at the onset of migraine headache; may repeat in 2 hours if no relief (maximum: 10 mg daily)

Oral: *Adults:* 1.25 to 2.5 mg at the onset of migraine headache; may repeat in 2 hours if no relief (maximum: 10 mg daily)

Mechanism of Action Selective agonist for serotonin (5-HT_{1B} and 5-HT_{1D} receptors) in cranial arteries and sensory nerves of the trigeminal system; causes vasoconstriction and reduces inflammation associated with antidromic neuronal transmission correlating with relief of migraine

Pharmacodynamics/Kinetics

Half-life Elimination 3 hours

Time to Peak Serum: Tablet: 1.5 hours; Orally-disintegrating tablet and nasal spray: 3 hours

Pregnancy Risk Factor C

Pregnancy Considerations Adverse events were observed in animal reproduction studies. Information related to zolmitriptan use in pregnancy is limited (Källén, 2011; Nezvalová-Henriksen, 2010; Nezvalová-Henriksen, 2012). Until additional information is available, other agents are preferred for the initial treatment of migraine in pregnancy (Da Silva, 2012; MacGregor, 2012; Williams, 2012).

Zolpidem (zole PI dem)

Brand Names: US Ambien; Ambien CR; Edluar; Intermezzo; Zolpimist

Brand Names: Canada Sublinox

Generic Availability (US) May be product dependent

Pharmacologic Category Hypnotic, Miscellaneous

Use Insomnia:

Immediate release and sublingual tablets (Edluar only) and oral spray: Short-term treatment of insomnia with difficulty of sleep onset

Extended release tablet: Treatment of insomnia with difficulty of sleep onset and/or sleep maintenance

Sublingual tablet (Intermezzo only): "As needed" treatment of insomnia when middle-of-the-night awakening is followed by difficulty returning to sleep and the patient has ≥4 hours of sleep time remaining

Sublingual tablet (Sublinox only [Canadian product]): Short-term treatment of insomnia (with difficulty of sleep onset, frequent awakenings, and/or early awakenings)

Local Anesthetic/Vasoconstrictor Precautions No information available to require special precautions

Effects on Dental Treatment Key adverse event(s) related to dental treatment: Xerostomia (normal salivary flow resumes upon discontinuation) (see Dental Comment)

Effects on Bleeding No information available to require special precautions

Adverse Reactions As reported with oral administration, unless otherwise noted.

>10%: Central nervous system: Headache (oral: 7% to 19%; sublingual: 3%), drowsiness (2% to 15%), dizziness (1% to 12%)

1% to 10%:

Cardiovascular: Palpitations (2%), chest discomfort (1%), chest pain (1%), increased blood pressure (1%), edema (≤1%), hypertension (≤1%), orthostatic hypotension (≤1%), syncope (≤1%), tachycardia (≤1%)

Central nervous system: Anxiety (2% to 6%), hallucination (≤4%), disorientation (3%), drugged feeling (3%), fatigue (oral: 3%; sublingual: 1%), lethargy (3%), memory impairment (3%), equilibrium disturbance (2%), psychomotor retardation (2%), vertigo (2%), hypoesthesia (≤2%), lack of concentration (≤2%), depression (2%), confusion (>1%), insomnia (>1%), abnormal dreams (1%), amnesia (1%), ataxia (1%), disinhibition (1%), eating disorder (1%; binge eating), euphoria (1%), increased body temperature (1%), sleep disorder (1%), stress (1%), agitation (≤1%), apathy (≤1%), cerebrovascular disease (≤1%), cognitive dysfunction (≤1%), depersonalization (≤1%), dysarthria (≤1%), emotional lability (≤1%), falling (≤1%), illusion (≤1%), malaise (≤1%), migraine (≤1%), nervousness (≤1%), paresthesia (≤1%), speech disturbance (≤1%), stupor (≤1%)

Dermatologic: Skin rash (1% to 2%), diaphoresis (≤1%), pallor (≤1%), pruritus (≤1%), urticaria (≤1%), wrinkling of skin (1%)

Endocrine & metabolic: Hypermenorrhea (1%), hyperglycemia (≤1%), increased thirst (≤1%), menstrual disease (≤1%)

Gastrointestinal: Nausea (7%), xerostomia (3%), diarrhea (1% to 3%), constipation (2%), dyspepsia (>1%), hiccups (>1%), abdominal distress (1%), abdominal tenderness (1%), change in appetite (1%), frequent bowel movements (1%), gastroesophageal reflux disease (1%), anorexia (≤1%), dysgeusia (≤1%), flatulence (≤1%), gastroenteritis (≤1%), vomiting (≤1%)

Genitourinary: Urinary tract infection (>1%), cystitis (≤1%), dysuria (≤1%), urinary incontinence (≤1%), vaginitis (≤1%)

Hematologic & oncologic: Bruise (1%)

Hepatic: Abnormal hepatic function tests (≤1%), increased serum ALT (≤1%)

Hypersensitivity: Hypersensitivity reaction (4%)

Infection: Influenza (3%), infection (≤1%)

Neuromuscular & skeletal: Myalgia (4%), back pain (3% to 4%), neck pain (2%), arthralgia (>1%), weakness (1%), arthritis (≤1%), leg cramps (≤1%), tremor (≤1%)

Ophthalmic: Visual disturbance (1% to 3%; including altered depth perception), blurred vision (2%), eye redness (2%), diplopia (>1%), asthenopia (1%), eye irritation (≤1%), eye pain (≤1%), scleritis (≤1%)

Otic: Labyrinthitis (1%), tinnitus (≤1%)

Respiratory: Sinusitis (4%), pharyngitis (3%), flu-like symptoms (1% to 2%), lower respiratory tract infection (>1%), upper respiratory tract infection (>1%), throat irritation (1%), bronchitis (≤1%), cough (≤1%), dyspnea (≤1%), rhinitis (≤1%)

Miscellaneous: Fever (≤1%), trauma (≤1%)

<1%, postmarketing, and/or case reports: Abnormal gait, abnormal lacrimation, abnormality in thinking, abscess, accommodation disturbance, acne vulgaris, acute renal failure, aggressive behavior, alteration of saliva, altered sense of smell, anaphylactic shock, anaphylaxis, anemia, angina pectoris, angioedema (including tongue, glottis, larynx), arteritis, behavioral changes, breast fibroadenosis, breast neoplasm, bronchospasm, bullous rash, cardiac arrhythmia, circulatory shock, conjunctivitis, corneal ulcer, decreased libido, delusions, dementia, dental caries, dermatitis, drug tolerance, dysphagia, dysphasia, enteritis, epistaxis, eructation, esophageal spasm, exacerbation of hypertension, extrasystoles, facial edema, furunculosis, gastritis, glaucoma, gout, hemorrhoids, hepatic encephalopathy (in patients with hepatic insufficiency), hepatitis (mixed pattern, hepatocellular, and cholestatic; with or without jaundice), herpes simplex

infection, herpes zoster, hot flash, hyperbilirubinemia, hypercholesteremia, hyperhemoglobinemia, hyperlipidemia, hypokinesia, hypotension, hypotonia, hypoxia, hysteria, impotence, increased appetite, increased blood urea nitrogen, increased erythrocyte sedimentation rate, increased serum alkaline phosphatase, increased serum AST, inflammation at injection site, intestinal obstruction, intoxicated feeling, laryngitis, leukopenia, lymphadenopathy, macrocytic anemia, manic reaction, mastalgia, myasthenia, myocardial infarction, neuralgia, neuritis, neuropathy, nocturia, numbness of tongue, oral bullae (sublingual tablet), oral inflammation (sublingual tablet), oral mucosa ulcer (sublingual tablet), osteoarthritis, pain, otitis externa, otitis media, panic disorder, paresis, periorbital edema, personality disorder, phlebitis, photopsia, pneumonia, polyuria, psychoneurosis, pulmonary edema, pulmonary embolism, purpura, pyelonephritis, rectal hemorrhage, renal pain, respiratory depression, restless leg syndrome, rigors, sciatica, skin photosensitivity, sleep driving, somnambulism, strange feeling, suicidal ideation, suicidal tendencies, tendonitis, tenesmus, tetany, thrombosis, urinary frequency, urinary retention, varicose veins, ventricular tachycardia, weight loss, yawning

Dosing

Adult Insomnia: Oral: **Note:** The lowest effective dose should be used; higher doses may be more likely to impair next morning activities.

Immediate release tablet, spray: 5 mg (females) or 5 to 10 mg (males) immediately before bedtime; maximum dose: 10 mg daily

Extended release tablet: 6.25 mg (females) or 6.25 to 12.5 mg (males) immediately before bedtime; maximum dose: 12.5 mg daily

Sublingual tablet:

Edluar, Sublinox [Canadian product]: 5 mg (females) or 5 to 10 mg (males) immediately before bedtime; if 5 mg dose is ineffective may increase to 10 mg (maximum dose: 10 mg daily)

Intermezzo: **Note:** Take in bed only if ≥4 hours left before waking and there is difficulty in returning to sleep

Females: 1.75 mg once per night as needed (maximum: 1.75 mg/night)

Males: 3.5 mg once per night as needed (maximum: 3.5 mg/night)

Dosage adjustment with concomitant CNS depressants: Females and males: 1.75 mg once per night as needed; dose adjustment of concomitant CNS depressant(s) may be necessary.

Debilitated:

Immediate release tablet, spray: 5 mg immediately before bedtime

Sublingual tablet:

Edluar, Sublinox [Canadian product]: 5 mg immediately before bedtime

Extended release tablet: 6.25 mg immediately before bedtime

Geriatric Oral:

Immediate release tablet, spray: 5 mg immediately before bedtime

Sublingual tablet:

Edluar, Sublinox [Canadian product]: 5 mg immediately before bedtime

Intermezzo: Females and males: 1.75 mg once per night as needed (maximum: 1.75 mg/night). **Note:** Take in bed only if ≥4 hours left before waking and there is difficulty in returning to sleep.

Extended release tablet: 6.25 mg immediately before bedtime

Renal Impairment No dosage adjustment necessary.

Hemodialysis: Not dialyzable

Hepatic Impairment

Immediate release tablet:

Mild to moderate impairment: 5 mg immediately before bedtime

Severe impairment: Avoid use

Extended release tablet:

Mild to moderate impairment: 6.25 mg immediately before bedtime

Severe impairment: Avoid use

Oral spray: 5 mg immediately before bedtime

Sublingual tablet:

Edluar: 5 mg immediately before bedtime

Intermezzo: Females and males: 1.75 mg once per night as needed. **Note:** Take in bed only if ≥4 hours left before waking and there is difficulty in returning to sleep.

Sublinox [Canadian product]:

Mild to moderate impairment: 5 mg immediately before bedtime

Severe impairment: Use is contraindicated.

Mechanism of Action Zolpidem, an imidazopyridine hypnotic that is structurally dissimilar to benzodiazepines, enhances the activity of the inhibitory neurotransmitter, γ-aminobutyric acid (GABA), via selective agonism at the benzodiazepine-1 (BZ_1) receptor; the result is increased chloride conductance, neuronal hyperpolarization, inhibition of the action potential, and a decrease in neuronal excitability leading to sedative and hypnotic effects. Because of its selectivity for the BZ_1 receptor site over the BZ_2 receptor site, zolpidem exhibits minimal anxiolytic, myorelaxant, and anticonvulsant properties (effects largely attributed to agonism at the BZ_2 receptor site).

Contraindications

Hypersensitivity to zolpidem or any component of the formulation

Canadian labeling: Additional contraindications (not in U.S. labeling): Significant obstructive sleep apnea syndrome and acute and/or severe impairment of respiratory function; myasthenia gravis; severe hepatic impairment; personal or family history of sleep-walking

Warnings/Precautions Should be used only after evaluation of potential causes of sleep disturbance. Failure of sleep disturbance to resolve after 7-10 days may indicate the need for psychiatric and/or medical illness reevaluation. Hypnotics/sedatives have been associated with abnormal thinking and behavior changes including decreased inhibition (eg, aggressiveness and extroversion that seemed out of character), bizarre behavior, agitation, visual and auditory hallucinations, and depersonalization. These changes may occur unpredictably and may indicate previously unrecognized psychiatric disorders; evaluate appropriately. Sedative/hypnotics may produce withdrawal symptoms following abrupt discontinuation or rapid dose decrease. Use with caution in patients with depression; worsening of depression, including suicide or suicidal ideation has been reported with the use of hypnotics. Intentional overdose may be an issue in this population. The minimum dose that will effectively treat the individual patient should be used. Prescriptions should be written for the smallest quantity consistent with good patient care. May cause CNS depression impairing physical and mental capabilities; patients must be cautioned about performing tasks which require mental alertness (operating machinery or driving). An increased risk of next-day psychomotor impairment is increased if patient is unable to stay in bed for a full night of sleep (7 to 8 hours); if coadministered with other CNS depressants and/or taken with other drugs that increase blood levels of zolpidem; or if a higher than recommended dose is taken. Dose adjustment may be necessary if taking concomitant CNS depressants; use with alcohol is not recommended.

Potentially significant drug-drug interactions may exist, requiring dose or frequency adjustment, additional monitoring, and/or selection of alternative therapy.

Use caution in patients with myasthenia gravis. Avoid use in patients with sleep apnea or a history of sedative-hypnotic abuse. Hypersensitivity reactions including anaphylaxis as well as angioedema have been reported after taking the first or subsequent doses. Do not rechallenge patient if such reactions occur. An increased risk for hazardous sleep-related activities such as sleep-driving; cooking and eating food, making phone calls or having sex while asleep have also been noted; amnesia, anxiety, and other neuropsychiatric symptoms may also occur. Patients usually do not remember these events. The use of alcohol, other CNS depressants, and exceeding the recommended maximum dose may increase the risk of these activities. Discontinue treatment in patients who report any sleep-driving episodes. Use with caution in patients with a history of drug dependence. Risk of abuse is increased in patients with a history or family history of alcohol or drug abuse or mental illness.

Use caution with respiratory disease. GABA agonists, including zolpidem, have been associated with precipitation of hepatic encephalopathy in patients with hepatic impairment. Patients with hepatic impairment do not clear zolpidem as rapidly as patients with normal hepatic function. Use with caution in patients with mild to moderate hepatic impairment; dose adjustment recommended. Avoid use of immediate and extended-release tablets in patients with severe hepatic impairment; may result in encephalopathy. Because of the rapid onset of action, administer Intermezzo immediately prior to bedtime, after the patient has gone to bed and is having difficulty falling asleep, or during the middle of the night when at least 4 hours are left before waking.

Use with caution in elderly patients; dose adjustment recommended. Monitor for impaired cognitive and/or motor performance, confusion, and potential for falling. Use with caution in debilitated patients; potential for oversedation, impaired coordination, and confusion with use; dosage adjustment recommended.

Dosage adjustment is recommended for females; pharmacokinetic studies involving zolpidem showed a significant increase in maximum concentration and exposure in females compared to males at the same dose. When studied for the unapproved use of insomnia associated with ADHD in children, a higher incidence (~7%) of hallucinations was reported. In addition, sleep latency did not decrease compared to placebo.

Some dosage forms may contain polysorbate 80 (also known as Tweens). Hypersensitivity reactions, usually a delayed reaction, have been reported following exposure to pharmaceutical products containing polysorbate 80 in certain individuals (Isaksson 2002; Lucente 2000; Shelley 1995). Thrombocytopenia, ascites, pulmonary deterioration, and renal and hepatic failure have been reported in premature neonates after receiving parenteral products containing polysorbate 80 (Alade 1986; CDC 1984). See manufacturer's labeling.

Drug Interactions

Metabolism/Transport Effects **Substrate** of CYP1A2 (minor), CYP2C19 (minor), CYP2C9 (minor), CYP2D6 (minor), CYP3A4 (major); **Note:** Assignment of Major/Minor substrate status based on clinically relevant drug interaction potential

Avoid Concomitant Use

Avoid concomitant use of Zolpidem with any of the following: Azelastine (Nasal); Orphenadrine; Oxomemazine; Paraldehyde; RifAMPin; Sodium Oxybate; St John's Wort; Thalidomide

Increased Effect/Toxicity

Zolpidem may increase the levels/effects of: Azelastine (Nasal); Blonanserin; Buprenorphine; CarBAMazepine; Flunitrazepam; HYDROcodone; Methotrimeprazine; MetyroSINE; Orphenadrine; OxyCODONE; Paraldehyde; Piribedil; Pramipexole; ROPINIRole; Rotigotine; Selective Serotonin Reuptake Inhibitors; Sodium Oxybate; Suvorexant; Thalidomide

The levels/effects of Zolpidem may be increased by: Brimonidine (Topical); Cannabis; Chlormethiazole; Chlorphenesin Carbamate; Ciprofloxacin (Systemic); CNS Depressants; CYP3A4 Inhibitors (Strong); Dimethindene (Topical); Dronabinol; Droperidol; FluvoxaMINE; Itraconazole; Kava Kava; Ketoconazole (Systemic); Lofexidine; Magnesium Sulfate; Methotrimeprazine; Minocycline; Nabilone; Oxomemazine; Perampanel; Ritonavir; Rufinamide; Tapentadol; Tetrahydrocannabinol

Decreased Effect

The levels/effects of Zolpidem may be decreased by: Bosentan; CarBAMazepine; CYP3A4 Inducers (Moderate); CYP3A4 Inducers (Strong); Dabrafenib; Deferasirox; Enzalutamide; Flumazenil; Mitotane; RifAMPin; Siltuximab; St John's Wort; Telaprevir; Tocilizumab

Food Interactions Maximum plasma concentration and bioavailability are decreased with food; time to peak plasma concentration is increased; half-life remains unchanged. Grapefruit juice may decrease the metabolism of zolpidem. Management: Do not administer with (or immediately after) a meal. Avoid grapefruit juice.

Dietary Considerations Do not administer with or immediately after a meal (may delay onset).

Pharmacodynamics/Kinetics

Onset of Action Immediate release: 30 minutes

Duration of Action Immediate release: 6 to 8 hours

Half-life Elimination

Children 2 to 6 years: Immediate release: 1.8 hours (Blumer 2008)

Children >6 years and Adolescents: Immediate release: 2.3 hours (Blumer 2008)

Adults:

Immediate release, Extended release: ~2.5 hours (range: 1.4 to 4.5 hours); Cirrhosis: Up to 9.9 hours; Elderly: Prolonged up to 32%

Spray: ~3 hours (range: 1.7 to 8.4)

Sublingual tablet: ~3 hours (range: 1.4 to 6.7 hours)

Time to Peak

Children 2 to 6 years: Immediate release: 0.9 hours (Blumer 2008)

Children >6 to 12 years: Immediate release: 1.1 hours (Blumer 2008)

Adolescents: Immediate release: 1.3 hours (Blumer 2008)
Adults:
Immediate release: 1.6 hours; 2.2 hours with food
Extended release: 1.5 hours; 4 hours with food
Spray: ~0.9 hours
Sublingual tablet: Edluar: ~1.4 hours, ~1.8 hours with food; Intermezzo: 0.6 to 1.3 hours, ~3 hours with food

Pregnancy Risk Factor C

Pregnancy Considerations Adverse events were observed in some animal reproduction studies. Zolpidem crosses the placenta (Juric, 2009). Severe neonatal respiratory depression has been reported when zolpidem was used at the end of pregnancy, especially when used concurrently with other CNS depressants. Children born of mothers taking sedative/hypnotics may be at risk for withdrawal; neonatal flaccidity has been reported in infants following maternal use of sedative/hypnotics during pregnancy. Additional adverse effects to the fetus/newborn have been noted in some studies (Wang, 2010; Wikner, 2011).

Breastfeeding Considerations Zolpidem is excreted in breast milk. The manufacturer recommends that caution be exercised when administering zolpidem to nursing women.

Controlled Substance C-IV

Dosage Forms

Solution, Oral:
Zolpimist: 5 mg/actuation (4.5 mL, 7.7 mL)

Tablet, Oral:
Ambien: 5 mg, 10 mg
Generic: 5 mg, 10 mg

Tablet Extended Release, Oral:
Ambien CR: 6.25 mg, 12.5 mg
Generic: 6.25 mg, 12.5 mg

Tablet Sublingual, Sublingual:
Edluar: 5 mg, 10 mg
Intermezzo: 1.75 mg, 3.5 mg
Generic: 1.75 mg, 3.5 mg

Dosage Forms: Canada

Tablet, sublingual:
Sublinox: 5 mg, 10 mg

Dental Comment An adult companion should accompany the patient to and from dental office.

Zonisamide (zoe NIS a mide)

Brand Names: US Zonegran

Pharmacologic Category Anticonvulsant, Miscellaneous

Use Partial seizures: Adjunct treatment of partial seizures in adolescents >16 years of age and adults with epilepsy

Local Anesthetic/Vasoconstrictor Precautions No information available to require special precautions

Effects on Dental Treatment Key adverse event(s) related to dental treatment: Xerostomia (normal salivary flow resumes upon discontinuation) and abnormal taste.

Effects on Bleeding No information available to require special precautions

Adverse Reactions Frequency not always defined. Frequencies noted in patients receiving other anticonvulsants:

>10%:
Central nervous system: Drowsiness (17%), dizziness (13%)
Gastrointestinal: Anorexia (13%)

1% to 10%:
Cardiovascular: Facial edema (1%)
Central nervous system: Headache (10%), agitation (9%), irritability (9%), fatigue (7% to 8%), tiredness (7%), confusion (6%), depression (6%), insomnia (6%), lack of concentration (6%), memory impairment (6%), ataxia (≥1% to 6%), speech disturbance (5%), decreased mental acuity (4%), anxiety (3%), nervousness (2%), schizophreniform disorder (2%), speech disturbance (2%), convulsions (≥1%), hyperesthesia (≥1%), seizure (1%), status epilepticus (1%), hypotonia (≤1%), hyperthermia
Dermatologic: Skin rash (1% to 3%), bruising (2%), pruritus (≥1%), hypohidrosis (children), Stevens-Johnson syndrome, toxic epidermal necrolysis
Endocrine & metabolic: Metabolic acidosis
Gastrointestinal: Nausea (9%), abdominal pain (6%), diarrhea (5%), dyspepsia (3%), weight loss (3%), constipation (2%), dysgeusia (2%), xerostomia (2%), vomiting (≥1%)
Hematologic & oncologic: Agranulocytosis, aplastic anemia
Neuromuscular & skeletal: Paresthesia (4%), abnormal gait (≥1%), tremor (≥1%), weakness (≥1%)
Ophthalmic: Diplopia (6%), nystagmus (4%), amblyopia (≥1%)
Otic: Tinnitus (≥1%)
Renal: Nephrolithiasis (4%, children 3% to 8%), increased blood urea nitrogen
Respiratory: Rhinitis (2%), increased cough (≥1%), pharyngitis (≥1%)
Miscellaneous: Flu-like syndrome (4%), accidental injury (≥1%)

<1%, postmarketing, and/or case reports: Abnormal dreams, acne vulgaris, albuminuria, alopecia, altered sense of smell, amenorrhea, anemia, aphthous stomatitis, apnea, arthralgia, arthritis, atrial fibrillation, bladder calculus, bladder pain, bradycardia, brain disease, cardiac failure, cerebrovascular accident, chest pain, cholangitis, cholecystitis, cholelithiasis, cholestatic jaundice, colitis, conjunctivitis, deafness, decreased libido, dehydration, diaphoresis, DRESS syndrome, duodenitis, dysarthria, dyskinesia, dysphagia, dyspnea, dystonia, dysuria, eczema, edema, esophagitis, euphoria, facial paralysis, fecal incontinence, flank pain, flatulence, gastritis, gastroenteritis, gastrointestinal ulcer, gingival hemorrhage, gingival hyperplasia, gingivitis, glaucoma, glossitis, gynecomastia, hematemesis, hematuria, hemoptysis, hirsutism, hyperkinesia, hypermenorrhea, hyperreflexia, hypersensitivity reaction, hypertension, hypertonia, hypoglycemia, hypokinesia, hyponatremia, hypotension, immunodeficiency, impotence, increased creatine phosphokinase, increased lactic dehydrogenase, increased serum alkaline phosphatase, increased serum ALT, increased serum creatinine, increased thirst, iritis, leg cramps, leukopenia, lupus erythematosus, lymphadenopathy, maculopapular rash, malaise, mastitis, melena, microcytic anemia, movement disorder, myalgia, myasthenia, myoclonus, neck stiffness, neuropathy, nocturia, oculogyric crisis, oral mucosa ulcer, palpitation, pancreatitis, peripheral edema, peripheral neuritis, petechia, photophobia, polyuria, psychomotor disturbance, pulmonary embolism, pustular rash, rectal hemorrhage, rhabdomyolysis, stomatitis, suicidal behavior, suicidal ideation, syncope, tachycardia, thrombocytopenia, thrombophlebitis, twitching, urinary frequency, urinary incontinence, urinary incontinence, urinary retention, urinary urgency, urticaria, vascular insufficiency,

ventricular premature contractions, vertigo, vesiculobullous dermatitis, visual field defect, weight gain, xeroderma

General Dosage Range Oral: *Adolescents >16 years and Adults:* Initial: 100 mg/day; Maintenance: 100 to 600 mg/day

Mechanism of Action Stabilizes neuronal membranes and suppresses neuronal hypersynchronization through action at sodium and calcium channels; does not affect GABA activity.

Pharmacodynamics/Kinetics

Half-life Elimination Plasma: ~63 hours (range: 50 to 68 hours)

Time to Peak 2 to 6 hours

Pregnancy Risk Factor C

Pregnancy Considerations Teratogenic effects were observed in animal reproduction studies. Zonisamide crosses the placenta and can be detected in the newborn following delivery (Kawada 2002; Shimoyama 1999). Information related to pregnancy outcomes following maternal use of zonisamide is limited (Hernández-Díaz 2014; Kanemoto 2007; Kondo 1996; Ohtahara 2007). Metabolic acidosis is an adverse effect of zonisamide therapy; newborns exposed to zonisamide in utero should be monitored for transient metabolic acidosis after birth and pregnant women taking zonisamide should be monitored and treated as nonpregnant patients. In general, maternal polytherapy with antiepileptic drugs may increase the risk of congenital malformations; monotherapy with the lowest effective dose is recommended. Newborns of women taking antiepileptic medications may be at an increased risk of adverse events (Harden and Meader 2009).

Zonisamide clearance may increase during pregnancy, requiring dosage adjustment (Oles 2008; Reisinger 2013). Women of childbearing potential are advised to use effective contraception during therapy. Until additional data is available, other agents may be preferred for the treatment of epilepsy in pregnant women (Ohtahara 2007).

Patients exposed to zonisamide during pregnancy are encouraged to enroll themselves into the NAAED Pregnancy Registry by calling 1-888-233-2334. Additional information is available at http://www.aedpregnancyregistry.org.

Zopiclone (ZOE pi clone)

Brand Names: Canada ACT Zopiclone; Apo-Zopiclone; Dom-Zopiclone; Imovane; JAMP-Zopiclone; Mar-Zopiclone; Mint-Zopiclone; Mylan-Zopiclone; Novo-Zopiclone; PHL-Zopiclone; PMS-Zopiclone; Priva-Zopiclone; PRO-Zopiclone; Q-Zopiclone; RAN-Zopiclone; ratio-Zopiclone; Rhovane; Riva-Zopiclone; Sandoz-Zopiclone; Septa-Zopiclone

Pharmacologic Category Hypnotic, Miscellaneous

Use Note: Not approved in the US

Insomnia: Short-term and symptomatic relief of insomnia (typically treatment should not exceed 7 to 10 consecutive days).

Local Anesthetic/Vasoconstrictor Precautions No information available to require special precautions

Effects on Dental Treatment Key adverse event(s) related to dental treatment: Coated tongue, dry mouth, halitosis, taste alteration (bitter taste, common).

Effects on Bleeding No information available to require special precautions

Adverse Reactions Frequency not defined. Some incidences tend to be higher in geriatric patients.

Cardiovascular: Palpitations

Central nervous system: Aggressiveness behavior, anterograde amnesia (rare; dose-related; elderly are at particular risk), anxiety, ataxia, bitter taste, confusion, depression, dizziness, drowsiness, euphoria, hypotonia, impaired morning arousal, intoxicated feeling, memory impairment, nervousness, speech disturbance

Dermatological: Diaphoresis

Gastrointestinal: Anorexia, constipation, coated tongue, halitosis, increased appetite, sialorrhea, xerostomia

Neuromuscular & skeletal: Tremor, weakness

<1%, postmarketing, and/or case reports: Abnormal behavior (possibly associated with amnesia), anaphylactoid reaction, anaphylaxis, angioedema (rare; includes angioedema of the tongue, oropharyngeal edema, laryngeal edema), constriction of the pharynx (has occurred with angioedema; suggests anaphylaxis), delusions, diplopia, disinhibition, disturbance in attention, drug dependence, dyspepsia, dyspnea (has occurred with angioedema; suggests anaphylaxis), hostility, increased serum alkaline phosphatase (mild to moderate; very rare), increased serum transaminases (mild to moderate; very rare), lack of concentration, myasthenia, nausea (has occurred with angioedema; suggests anaphylaxis), paresthesia (not associated with withdrawal), psychotic symptoms (includes agitation, depersonalization, hallucination, irritability, nightmares), rebound insomnia (upon withdrawal), respiratory depression, restlessness, sleep disorder (complex sleep-related behaviors, usually without recall of the event; includes sleep driving, sleep eating, preparing food, and making telephone calls while not fully awake), somnambulism, vomiting (has occurred with angioedema; suggests anaphylaxis), withdrawal syndrome

General Dosage Range Dosage adjustment recommended in patients with hepatic and renal impairment, debilitated patients, and patients with chronic respiratory insufficiency.

Oral:

Adults: 3.75 to 7.5 mg once daily at bedtime

Elderly: 3.75 to 5 mg once daily at bedtime

Mechanism of Action Zopiclone is a cyclopyrrolone derivative and has a pharmacological profile similar to benzodiazepines. Zopiclone reduces sleep latency, increases duration of sleep, and decreases the number of nocturnal awakenings.

Pharmacodynamics/Kinetics

Half-life Elimination ~5 hours; Elderly: ~7 hours, Hepatic impairment: ~12 hours

Time to Peak Serum: <2 hours; Hepatic impairment: 3.5 hours

Pregnancy Considerations There is insufficient data on safety in pregnancy; however, benzodiazepines may cause congenital malformations during the 1st trimester and neonatal CNS depression during the last few weeks of pregnancy; it is expected zopiclone may do the same. Use is not recommended during pregnancy.

Product Availability Not available in the US

Zoster Vaccine (ZOS ter vak SEEN)

Related Information

Systemic Viral Diseases *on page 1806*

Brand Names: US Zostavax

Brand Names: Canada Zostavax

Pharmacologic Category Vaccine; Vaccine, Live (Viral)

Use

Herpes zoster prevention: Prevention of herpes zoster (shingles) in patients ≥50 years of age

The Advisory Committee on Immunization Practices (ACIP) recommends:

Routine vaccination of **all patients ≥60 years of age, including** patients who report a previous episode of zoster; patients with chronic medical conditions (eg, chronic renal failure, diabetes mellitus, rheumatoid arthritis, chronic pulmonary disease) unless those conditions are contraindications; and residents of nursing homes and other long-term care facilities ≥60 years of age without contraindications (CDC/ACIP [Harpaz, 2008]).

Limitations of use: Not indicated for treatment of zoster or postherpetic neuralgia (PHN); not indicated for prophylaxis of primary varicella infection (chickenpox).

Local Anesthetic/Vasoconstrictor Precautions No information available to require special precautions

Effects on Dental Treatment No significant effects or complications reported

Effects on Bleeding No information available to require special precautions

Adverse Reactions All serious adverse reactions must be reported to the U.S. Department of Health and Human Services (DHHS) Vaccine Adverse Event Reporting System (VAERS) 1-800-822-7967 or online at https://vaers.hhs.gov/esub/index.

>10%: Local: Pain at injection site (≤34 to 54%), erythema at injection site (36% to 48%), swelling at injection site (26% to 40%), localized tenderness (≤34%), itching at injection site (7% to 11%)

1% to 10%:

Cardiovascular: Congestive cardiac failure (≤2%)

Central nervous system: Headache (1% to 9%)

Gastrointestinal: Diarrhea (2%)

Local: Warm sensation at injection site (2% to 4%), hematoma at injection site (2%), induration at injection site (1%)

Neuromuscular & skeletal: Weakness (1%), limb pain (1%)

Respiratory: Pulmonary edema (≤2%), respiratory tract disease (1%)

<1%, postmarketing, and/or case reports: Anaphylaxis, arthralgia, exacerbation of asthma, fever, herpes zoster, hypersensitivity reaction, lymphadenopathy (transient), myalgia, nausea, necrotizing retinitis (patients on immunosuppressive therapy), polymyalgia rheumatica, rash at injection site, skin rash (noninjection site), urticaria at injection site

General Dosage Range SubQ: *Adults ≥50 years:* 0.65 mL as a single dose

Mechanism of Action A decline in VZV-specific immunity increases the risk of developing zoster infection. As a live, attenuated vaccine (Oka/Merck strain of varicella-zoster virus), zoster virus vaccine stimulates active immunity to disease caused by the varicella-zoster virus. Administration has been demonstrated to protect against the development of herpes zoster, with the highest efficacy in patients 60-69 years of age. It may also reduce the severity of complications, including postherpetic neuralgia, in patients who develop zoster following vaccination.

Zoster vaccine reduced the incidence of zoster by ~70% in those 50 to 59 years of age, 64% in those 60-69 years of age, 41% in those 70-79 years of age, and 18% in those 80 years and older. The overall efficacy for those 60 years and older was 51%. Additional benefit was afforded to vaccine recipients who developed zoster by reduction in the incidence of PHN: 5% for those 60-69 years of age, 55% for those 70-79 years of age, and 26% for those 80 years and older. Other prespecified zoster-related complications were reported less frequently in subjects who received zoster vaccine compared with subjects who received placebo.

Pharmacodynamics/Kinetics

Onset of Action Seroconversion: ~6 weeks (CDC/ACIP [Harpaz, 2008])

Duration of Action Not established; protection has been demonstrated for at least 4 years

Pregnancy Considerations Use during pregnancy is contraindicated. Women should avoid becoming pregnant for 3 months after vaccination (4 weeks per CDC). Risk to the fetus following exposure to wild-type varicella zoster virus is small and risk following exposure from the attenuated vaccine is probably even less (CDC/ACIP [Harpaz, 2008]). Based on information collected from 1995-2013 using the manufacturer's pregnancy registry, of 820 women who received a varicella-containing vaccine, there were no infants born with abnormalities consistent with congenital varicella syndrome. Any exposures to the vaccine during pregnancy or within 3 months prior to pregnancy should be reported to the manufacturer (Merck & Co, 877-888-4231) or to VAERS (800-822-7967) as suspected adverse reactions.

Zucapsaicin (zu kap SAY sin)

Brand Names: Canada ZUACTA

Pharmacologic Category Analgesic, Topical; Topical Skin Product; Transient Receptor Potential Vanilloid 1 (TRPV1) Agonist

Use Note: Not approved in the US

Osteoarthritis of the knee: In conjunction with an oral NSAID or COX-2 inhibitor for short-term (≤3 months) treatment of severe pain associated with osteoarthritis of the knee that is not controlled by NSAID or COX-2 inhibitor monotherapy

Local Anesthetic/Vasoconstrictor Precautions No information available to require special precautions

Effects on Dental Treatment The safety and efficacy of zucapsaicin have only been assessed in treating pain associated with osteoarthritis of the knee; its use as a topical application in treating pain of the temporomandibular joint in the patient with temporomandibular dysfunction has not been studied and is not recommended (see Warnings/Precautions)

Effects on Bleeding No information available to require special precautions

Adverse Reactions

>10%: Local: Application site burning (22% to 35%)

1% to 10%:

Central nervous system: Localized warm feeling (4% to 6%), localized numbness (3%)

Dermatologic: Burning sensation of skin (2%)

Local: Application site reaction (4%; includes application site edema, application site erythema, application site pain, cold sensation, dryness), application site irritation (1%), application-site pruritus (1%), application site rash (1%)

Neuromuscular & skeletal: Arthralgia (1%)

Ophthalmic: Eye irritation (1%)

Respiratory: Cough (2%), sneezing (1%)

<1%, postmarketing, and/or case reports: Arthropathy, dyspnea, flushing, headache, limb pain, nasal

congestion, nasal mucosa irritation, osteoarthritis (aggravated), skin photosensitivity, skin rash, skin blister, skin discoloration, throat irritation

Dosing

Adult & Geriatric Pain relief in osteoarthritis of knee: Topical: Apply a pea-sized amount to 3 locations around affected knee 3 times daily; allow at least 4 hours between applications (maximum: 3 applications/day). Therapy should be limited to ≤3 months.

Missed dose: Apply the dose as soon as possible, but not within four hours of the next dose.

Renal Impairment There are no dosage adjustments provided in the manufacturer's labeling; however, dosage adjustment does not appear to be necessary since there is no systemic absorption following topical administration of zucapsaicin.

Hepatic Impairment There are no dosage adjustments provided in the manufacturer's labeling; however, dosage adjustment does not appear to be necessary since there is no systemic absorption following topical administration of zucapsaicin.

Mechanism of Action Actions are thought to be similar to other capsaicinoids, such as capsaicin, which is a transient receptor potential vanilloid 1 receptor (TRPV1) agonist, that activates TRPV1 ligand-gated cation channels on nociceptive nerve fibers, resulting in depolarization, initiation of action potential, and pain signal transmission to the spinal cord; capsaicin exposure results in subsequent desensitization of the sensory axons, depletion of proinflammatory neuropeptides (eg, calcitonin gene-related peptide, substance P) and inhibition of pain transmission initiation. In arthritis, capsaicin induces release of substance P, the principal chemomediator of pain impulses from the periphery to the CNS, from peripheral sensory neurons; after repeated application, capsaicin depletes the neuron of substance P and prevents reaccumulation. The functional link between substance P and the capsaicin receptor, TRPV1, is not well understood.

Contraindications Hypersensitivity to zucapsaicin or any component of the formulation; application to broken or irritated skin or areas with a compromised skin barrier

Warnings/Precautions May induce cough; do not apply to the face. Wash hands thoroughly after each application. Avoid contact with eyes, lips, genital areas, broken or irritated skin or on areas with a compromised skin barrier. Avoid application of other topical products to zucapsaicin treated areas. Do not use under occlusive dressings. Avoid hot baths or showers just prior to or right after application to avoid a possible burning sensation. Safety and efficacy have only been evaluated in the treatment of osteoarthritis of the knee; has not been evaluated and is not recommended for use in other arthritic, inflammatory, or painful musculoskeletal conditions, in severe neurological or vascular disease, and/or in osteoarthritis of the knee secondary to other pathological processes.

Drug Interactions

Metabolism/Transport Effects None known.

Avoid Concomitant Use There are no known interactions where it is recommended to avoid concomitant use.

Increased Effect/Toxicity There are no known significant interactions involving an increase in effect.

Decreased Effect There are no known significant interactions involving a decrease in effect.

Pregnancy Considerations Adverse events have not been observed in animal reproduction studies. Zucapsaicin is not absorbed systemically following topical administration. Use during pregnancy is not expected to result in significant exposure to the fetus.

Breastfeeding Considerations It is not known if zucapsaicin is excreted in breast milk. The manufacturer recommends that caution be exercised when administering zucapsaicin to nursing women.

Product Availability Not available in the US

Dosage Forms: Canada

Cream, External

Zuacta: 0.075% (30 g, 60 g)

ALPHABETICAL LISTING OF NATURAL PRODUCTS

Acacia

Clinical Overview

Uses

Acacia gum has been used in pharmaceuticals as a demulcent. It is used topically for healing wounds and inhibits the growth of periodontic bacteria and the early deposition of plaque.

A probiotic effect (bifidogenic) of gum acacia has been reported along with increased satiety and decreased body weight in a limited number of clinical trials; however, no effect on lipid or glucose profiles has been demonstrated.

Dosing

Clinical trials are generally lacking. One trial used gum arabic (as A. senegal) 30 g daily for 6 weeks as a dietary supplement to reduce weight.

Contraindications

Contraindications have not yet been identified.

Pregnancy/Lactation

Information regarding safety and efficacy in pregnancy and lactation is lacking.

Interactions

None well documented.

Adverse Reactions

Allergic reactions have been reported. Adverse effects reported in clinical trials include unfavorable sensation in the mouth, early morning nausea, mild diarrhea, and bloating.

Toxicology

Acacia is essentially nontoxic when ingested and is generally recognized as safe (GRAS).

Local Anesthetic/Vasoconstrictor Precautions

No information available to require special precautions

Effects on Bleeding None reported

Acai

Clinical Overview

Uses

Antioxidant and anti-inflammatory activity of acai has been documented. Potential exists for use in treating cancer and metabolic syndrome; however, clinical information is limited.

Dosing

Clinical evidence on which to base dosing guidelines is lacking. A pilot study used acai pulp 100 g daily for 1 month.

Contraindications

Hypersensitivity to acai palm or any of its components.

Pregnancy/Lactation

Avoid use. Information regarding safety and efficacy in pregnancy and lactation is lacking.

Interactions

None well documented.

Adverse Reactions

Limited clinical studies exist; however, no adverse events have been reported.

Toxicology

One study reported mutagenicity in the Salmonella typhimurium TA97 assay and clastogenicity when using highly concentrated pulp.

Local Anesthetic/Vasoconstrictor Precautions

No information available to require special precautions

Effects on Bleeding None reported

Agrimony

Clinical Overview

Uses

Agrimony is used as a tea and gargle for sore throat, and externally as a mild antiseptic and astringent.

Dosing

There is no published clinical evidence for a safe or effective dose; however, the German Komission E recommended a daily dose of 3 g of the herb for internal use. Agrimony also is used as a poultice from a 10% decoction of the herb.

Contraindications

Contraindications have not yet been identified.

Pregnancy/Lactation

Information regarding safety and efficacy in pregnancy and lactation is lacking.

Interactions

None well documented.

Adverse Reactions

Agrimony reportedly can produce photodermatitis.

Toxicology

No data.

Local Anesthetic/Vasoconstrictor Precautions

No information available to require special precautions

Effects on Bleeding None reported

Alfalfa

Clinical Overview

Uses

Alfalfa may be useful in lowering cholesterol and treating menopausal symptoms. It also may have hypoglycemic and anti-inflammatory effects; however, clinical information supporting these indications is limited.

Dosing

A general dosing regimen is 5 to 10 g of the dried herb taken 3 times daily. For the treatment of high cholesterol, the seeds may be taken at a dose of 40 g 3 times daily.

Contraindications

The US Food and Drug Administration (FDA) issued an advisory indicating that children, the elderly, and people with compromised immune systems should not consume alfalfa sprouts because they are frequently contaminated with bacteria. Use should be avoided in people with a personal or family history of systemic lupus erythematous (SLE) because of possible effects on immunoregulatory cells by canavanine, a component of alfalfa.

Pregnancy/Lactation

Avoid use. Documented adverse effects of alfalfa during pregnancy include possible uterine stimulation. Although alfalfa has been anecdotally recommended to stimulate milk production, evidence is lacking.

Interactions

Because of its high vitamin K content, alfalfa may antagonize and therefore reduce the effects of warfarin. Alfalfa may interact with immunosuppressant agents, such as cyclosporine, because of its immunostimulatory effects.

Adverse Reactions

Alfalfa seeds and fresh sprouts can be contaminated with bacteria, such as Salmonella enterica and Escherichia coli. The FDA issued an advisory indicating that children, the elderly, and people with compromised immune systems should avoid eating alfalfa sprouts. Ingestion of dried alfalfa preparations is generally safe in healthy adults. Because of its high potassium content, alfalfa may cause hyperkalemia.

Toxicology

Alfalfa tablets have been associated with the reactivation of SLE in at least 2 patients.

Local Anesthetic/Vasoconstrictor Precautions

No information available to require special precautions

Effects on Bleeding As a single agent, alfalfa has no effect on bleeding. Due to the vitamin K content found in alfalfa, it has the potential to reduce the anticoagulant effect of warfarin.

Almond

Clinical Overview

Uses

Almonds are used as a dietary source of protein, unsaturated fats, minerals, micronutrients, phytochemicals, alpha-tocopheral, and fiber, as well as in confectioneries. The efficacy of almonds in altering the lipid profile is weakly supported by the literature; larger, more robust clinical trials of longer duration are required. The almond derivative laetrile/amygdalin has been used as an alternative cancer treatment, but there is no clinical evidence to support this use. Laetrile is banned by the US Food and Drug Administration (FDA) and in Europe for use in cancer therapy.

Dosing

Trials of almond dietary supplementation in adults have used 25 to 168 g of almonds per day. The American Heart Association (AHA) recommends the daily intake of nuts (28.35 to 56.7 g) as part of a healthy diet. There is no widely accepted standard for laetrile/amygdalin dosing due to the potential for toxicity and no evidence for efficacy.

Contraindications

Allergy to almonds or its products

Pregnancy/Lactation

Consumption of bitter almond or laetrile is not recommended in pregnant or breastfeeding women because of insufficient data and a theoretical risk of birth defects. Consumption of sweet almond has generally recognized as safe (GRAS) status when used as food. Avoid dosages above those found in food because safety is unproven.

Interactions

None well documented.

Adverse Reactions

Adverse reactions similar to those of cyanide poisoning have been reported.

Toxicology

Cyanide poisoning and death have resulted from laetrile and bitter almond consumption.

Local Anesthetic/Vasoconstrictor Precautions

No information available to require special precautions

Effects on Bleeding None reported

Aloe

Clinical Overview

Uses

Topical aloe appears to inhibit infection and promote healing of minor burns and wounds, frostbite, as well as in skin affected by diseases such as psoriasis and seborrheic dermatitis, although studies have had conflicting results. Dried aloe latex should be ingested with caution as a drastic cathartic, but its use is not recommended. In 2002, the US Food and Drug Administration required all over-the-counter aloe laxative products to be removed from the US market or reformulated because manufacturers have not provided the necessary safety data.

Dosing

As a gel, A. vera may be applied externally. The resin product is cathartic and not recommended for internal use.

Contraindications

Ingestion is contraindicated in pregnant and breastfeeding women, children younger than 12 years of age, patients with inflammatory bowel disease, and elderly patients with suspected intestinal obstruction.

Pregnancy/Lactation

Documented adverse effects with ingestion; do not use. Cathartic, reputed abortifacient.

Interactions

Potential interactions between ingested aloe resin and the following medications have been identified: digoxin, furosemide, thiazide diuretics, sevoflurane stimulant laxatives, and antidiabetic agents.

Adverse Reactions

There has been 1 report that aloe gel as standard wound therapy delayed healing. The gel may cause burning sensations in dermabraded skin, and redness and itching also can occur. Use caution with cosmetic products containing A. vera gel. A case of acute hepatitis induced by aloe vera ingestion has been reported.

Toxicology

The resin product is cathartic at doses of 250 mg and is not recommended for internal use.

Local Anesthetic/Vasoconstrictor Precautions

No information available to require special precautions.

Effects on Bleeding None reported

Alpha-Lipoic Acid

Clinical Overview

Uses

Alpha-lipoic acid (ALA) has been used as an antioxidant for the treatment of diabetes and HIV. It also has been used for cancer, liver ailments, and various other conditions.

Dosing

Oral dosage of alpha-lipoic acid given in numerous clinical studies ranges from 300 to 1,800 mg daily. It also is given intravenously at similar daily dosages.

Contraindications

Contraindications have not yet been determined.

Pregnancy/Lactation

Information regarding safety and efficacy in pregnancy and lactation is lacking.

Interactions

None well documented.

Adverse Reactions

No adverse reactions have been reported.

Toxicology

No data.

Local Anesthetic/Vasoconstrictor Precautions

No information available to require special precautions

Effects on Bleeding None reported

Andrographis

Clinical Overview

Uses

Kalmegh has been used for liver complaints and fever, and as an anti-inflammatory and immunostimulant. In clinical trials, Andrographis extract has been studied for use as an immunostimulant in upper respiratory tract infections and HIV infection. The potential of andrographolide as an anticancer agent is being investigated. However, clinical evidence to support the use of Kalmegh for any indication is lacking.

Dosing

The usual daily dose of andrographolides for common cold, sinusitis, and tonsillitis is 60 mg. Doses of 10 mg/kg resulted in the discontinuation of a clinical trial because of adverse reactions. Clinical trials in children with upper respiratory tract infection reported the use of andrographolide 30 mg daily for 10 days.

Contraindications

Contraindications have not been identified.

Pregnancy/Lactation

Documented adverse reactions. Abortifacient. Avoid use.

Interactions

None well documented.

Adverse Reactions

Headache, fatigue, rash, bitter/metallic taste, diarrhea, pruritus, and decreased sex drive were reported in 1 clinical trial. One HIV-positive participant experienced an anaphylactic reaction. Doses used in this trial were 10 mg/kg body weight.

Toxicology

Data are limited. Male reproductive adverse reaction studies have been equivocal.

Local Anesthetic/Vasoconstrictor Precautions No information available to require special precautions

Effects on Bleeding None reported

Angelica

Clinical Overview

Uses

Angelica may have applications in treating epilepsy and anxiety; however, clinical trials are lacking to support therapeutic applications, and its use should be balanced against the possibility of increased formation of amyloid beta peptides. Antioxidant activity has also been reported.

Dosing

Angelica root typically is given at doses of 3 to 6 g/day of the crude root, but clinical trials are lacking regarding dosage recommendations.

Contraindications

Crude fruit extract is not recommended; safety and efficacy have not been established.

Pregnancy/Lactation

Avoid use. Adverse effects and emmenagogue effects have been documented.

Interactions

Angelica sinensis exhibits antiplatelet aggregating activity.

Adverse Reactions

Limited clinical trials provide information on adverse effects. A small clinical trial found no increase in blood pressure or heart rate during 8 weeks of leaf extract use. Allergic dermatitis has been reported, and photosensitization is possible.

Toxicology

Poisoning has been reported with high doses of angelica oils. The constituent imperatorin has been shown to accelerate the formation of amyloid-beta peptide in vitro.

Local Anesthetic/Vasoconstrictor Precautions No information available to require special precautions

Effects on Bleeding Angelica root has the potential to increase the risk of bleeding or potentiate the effects of warfarin.

Anise

Clinical Overview

Uses

Anise has been used as a flavoring in alcohols, liqueurs, dairy products, gelatins, puddings, meats, and candies, and as a scent in perfumes, soaps, and sachets. The oil has been used to treat lice, scabies, and psoriasis. Anise frequently is used as a carminative and expectorant. Anise also is used to decrease bloating and settle the digestive tract in children. In high doses, it is used as an antispasmodic and an antiseptic and for the treatment of cough, asthma, and bronchitis. However, research reveals no clinical data regarding the use of anise for any of these applications.

Dosing

There are no recent clinical studies to guide use of anise; however, typical use in dyspepsia is 0.5 to 3 g of seed, or 0.1 to 0.3 mL of the essential oil.

Contraindications

Anise is not recommended for use in pregnancy.

Pregnancy/Lactation

Aniseed is a reputed abortifacient. Excessive use is not recommended in pregnancy.

Interactions

None well documented.

Adverse Reactions

Anise may cause allergic reactions of the skin, respiratory tract, and gastrointestinal tract.

Toxicology

Ingestion of the oil may result in pulmonary edema, vomiting, and seizures.

Local Anesthetic/Vasoconstrictor Precautions No information available to require special precautions

Effects on Bleeding None reported

Arnica

Clinical Overview

Uses

Arnica and its extracts have been widely used in folk and homeopathic medicine as a treatment for acne, boils, bruises, rashes, sprains, pains, and wounds. There does not appear to be sufficient evidence to support the use of arnica as an anti-inflammatory or analgesic agent or in the prevention of bruising. Heterogeneity of doses, delivery forms, and indications in available clinical studies also makes generalization difficult.

Dosing

Arnica is classified as an unsafe herb by the US Food and Drug Administration (FDA) because of its toxicity and should not be administered orally or applied to broken skin where absorption can occur. No consensus exists on topical dosing, and evidence from clinical trials is lacking to support therapeutic dosing. In homeopathic use, less concentrated strengths, such as 12C, 200C, 1M (1,000C), and 10M (10,000C) (C = centisimal dilution [1 part in 100]; M = millesimal dilution [1 part in 1,000]), are recommended for use before and after surgery.

Contraindications

Contraindications have not been identified.

Pregnancy/Lactation

Avoid use. Uterine stimulation has been documented.

Interactions

None well documented.

Adverse Reactions

Homeopathic doses of arnica are unlikely to result in any adverse reactions because of the small amount ingested. Arnica irritates mucous membranes and causes stomach pain, diarrhea, and vomiting. Allergy and contact dermatitis have been reported.

Toxicology

The plant is poisonous and ingestion can cause gastroenteritis, dyspnea, cardiac arrest, and death. The flowers and roots of the plant have caused vomiting, drowsiness, and coma when eaten by children.

Local Anesthetic/Vasoconstrictor Precautions

May cause serious interactions with anesthetic drugs

Effects on Bleeding May see increased bleeding due to inhibition of platelet aggregation

Artichoke

Clinical Overview

Uses

Artichoke has been used for its antioxidant and GI soothing effects. It may also have moderately hypoglycemic and hypolipidemic properties; however, clinical information for any use is lacking.

Dosing

A range of divided doses from 600 to 3,200 mg/day have been used in clinical trials.

Contraindications

Allergy to Asteraceae family plants (eg, daisy, chrysanthemum, marigold, Echinacea, ragweed); bile duct obstruction.

Pregnancy/Lactation

Artichoke heads are generally recognized as safe (GRAS) when used as food. Information is lacking for artichoke leaf extract; caution is warranted.

Interactions

None well documented.

Adverse Reactions

Mild, transient, and infrequent adverse reactions generally limited to GI complaints. Allergic reactions and a case of hepatotoxicity have been reported.

Toxicology

Specific toxicological studies are limited. No toxicity was observed in vitro in a study of artichoke leaf extract on human umbilical endothelial cells and hamster ovary cells. Some genotoxicity was demonstrated in vitro on bone marrow cells at the highest dose administered.

Local Anesthetic/Vasoconstrictor Precautions

No information available to require special precautions

Effects on Bleeding None reported

Ashwagandha

Clinical Overview

Uses

Ashwagandha has been used as an adaptogen, diuretic, and sedative and is available in the United States as a dietary supplement. Trials supporting its clinical use are limited; however, many in vitro and animal experiments suggest effects on the immune and CNS systems, as well as in the pathogenesis of cancer and inflammatory conditions.

Dosing

Dosing information is limited. W. somnifera root powder has generally been used at dosages of 450 mg to 2 g in combination with other preparations.

Contraindications

Contraindications have not been identified.

Pregnancy/Lactation

Abortifacient properties have been reported for ashwagandha. Avoid use.

Interactions

None well documented.

Adverse Reactions

Limited clinical trials are available and case reports are lacking.

Toxicology

Acute toxicity of W. somnifera is modest; at reasonable doses, ashwagandha is nontoxic.

Local Anesthetic/Vasoconstrictor Precautions

No information available to require special precautions

Effects on Bleeding None reported

Asparagus

Clinical Overview

Uses

Asparagus stalks are commonly eaten as a vegetable. Roots, seeds, and extracts have been used as a treatment for various illnesses and as a diuretic, despite the lack of clinical evidence. Other species, such as Asparagus racemosus, are used in traditional Chinese and Ayurvedic medicine systems.

Dosing

There is insufficient clinical evidence to guide the dosage of asparagus. A maximum of 2.4 g daily of dried asparagus root in divided doses contained in a combination preparation with parsley has been evaluated for antihypertensive effect; however, adverse reactions led to significant participant withdrawal from the study.

Contraindications

Contraindications have not yet been identified.

Pregnancy/Lactation

Generally recognized as safe when used as food. Avoid dosages above those found in food because safety and efficacy are unknown.

Interactions

None well documented.

Adverse Reactions

Symptoms of allergy, including rhinitis, occupational asthma, oral allergic syndrome, allergic contact dermatitis, and anaphylaxis, are well documented. Exacerbation of gout with excessive consumption has been reported.

Toxicology

Information is lacking.

Local Anesthetic/Vasoconstrictor Precautions

No information available to require special precautions

Effects on Bleeding None reported

Astragalus

Clinical Overview

Uses

Most evidence suggests that astragalus root may modulate immune function and reported benefits are derived from this action, although studies are older and of limited quality. Evidence in the literature for other purported therapeutic uses is lacking.

Dosing

There is no recent clinical evidence to guide dosage of astragalus products; however, recommendations of 2 to 6 g daily of the powdered root are typical.

Contraindications

Contraindications have not yet been identified.

Pregnancy/Lactation

Information regarding safety and efficacy in pregnancy and lactation is lacking.

Interactions

None well documented.

Adverse Reactions

Allergy has been reported. A case report exists of increased carbohydrate antigen 19-9 and induction of reversible liver and kidney cysts in a woman consuming A. membranaceus daily for 1 month.

Toxicology

Evidence is equivocal; however, mutagenicity has been shown in the Ames test.

Local Anesthetic/Vasoconstrictor Precautions

No information available to require special precautions

Effects on Bleeding Astragalus may increase the risk of bleeding.

Barberry

Clinical Overview

Uses

Clinical applications may include use in treating diabetes and dyslipidemia, although clinical trials are limited and are often of poor quality. Other activity includes antimicrobial, antioxidant, and anti-inflammatory effects. No clinical trials exist to support uses related to effects on the cardiovascular and central nervous systems or treating cancer.

Dosing

Daily doses of 2 g of the berries and 1.5 to 3 g daily of dry bark have been used; however, there are limited clinical studies to substantiate barberry's varied uses.

Contraindications

Caution is warranted in the presence of cardiac arrhythmia. Use in children has not been validated.

Pregnancy/Lactation

Avoid use. There are documented adverse effects, including uterine stimulant effects.

Interactions

Case reports are lacking; however, barberry exhibits anti-cytochrome P450 3A4 (CYP3A4) activity similar to that of grapefruit. Caution is warranted with coadministration of potentially toxic medicines such as cyclosporine.

Adverse Reactions

GI symptoms (eg, nausea, vomiting, diarrhea), dizziness, and fainting have been reported. Effects on the cardiovascular system (eg, hypotension, decreased heart rate) and decreased respiration may occur with high dosages. The German Commission E reports that lower doses of berberine are well tolerated. Hypersensitivity has been documented.

Toxicology

Symptoms of poisoning are characterized by lethargy, stupor and daze, vomiting and diarrhea, and nephritis. A median lethal dose (LD_{50}) for berberine was noted as 27.5 mg/kg in humans. Berberine showed mutagenicity in yeast cells and Ames test, while a phototoxic reaction between berberine alkaloid and ultraviolet A (UVA) light has been described.

Local Anesthetic/Vasoconstrictor Precautions

No information available to require special precautions

Effects on Bleeding None reported

Beta Sitosterol

Clinical Overview

Uses

Beta-sitosterol has been used to lower low-density lipoprotein (LDL) cholesterol and improve symptoms in mild-to-moderate benign prostatic hypertrophy (BPH). Beta-sitosterol has also been investigated for its immunomodulatory and anticancer effects.

Dosing

Beta sitosterol is incorporated in margarine, yogurt, or other foods to give a daily intake of 1.5-3 g.

Contraindications

Avoid plant sterols such as beta-sitosterol in patients with sitosterolemia, a condition in which high plasma concentrations of plant sterols can lead to tendon xanthomas, premature atherosclerosis, and hemolytic anemia.

Pregnancy/Lactation

Beta-sitosterol should be avoided in pregnant women due to demonstrated uterine stimulant effects.

Interactions

Plant sterols reduce the absorption of the fat-soluble vitamins beta-carotene, alpha-carotene, and vitamin E. No effects on vitamins A and K have been noted. Beta-sitosterol levels may decrease in patients receiving ezetimibe through its inhibition of intestinal absorption of plant sterols.

Adverse Reactions

A review of the literature suggests that beta-sitosterol may cause GI adverse effects as well as impotence. In one study, adverse reactions deemed related to beta-sitosterol use were flatulence, discoloration of the feces, appetite changes, dyspepsia, leg cramps, skin rash, and leukopenia. A 1-year study in healthy patients consuming 1.6 g/day of plant sterols contained in a dietary spread demonstrated cholesterol-lowering effects as well as general tolerability with long-term consumption.

Toxicology

Clinical data are lacking.

Local Anesthetic/Vasoconstrictor Precautions

No information available to require special precautions

Effects on Bleeding None reported

Bilberry

Clinical Overview

Uses

Clinical studies are limited. Interest has focused on antioxidant potential in cancer and cardiovascular conditions, and other applications may exist in diabetes, as well as in inflammatory bowel and ocular conditions.

Dosing

Typical bilberry products are standardized to 25% anthocyanoside content, and 100 g of fresh fruit contains anthocyanin content 300 to 700 mg. Limited clinical studies have evaluated supplemental bilberry 100 to 400 g over 4 to 8 weeks' duration.

Contraindications

Contraindications have not yet been identified.

Pregnancy/Lactation
Generally recognized as safe (GRAS) when used as food. Avoid doses above those found in food because safety and efficacy are unproven.

Interactions
None well documented.

Adverse Reactions
Information is lacking.

Toxicology
Information is lacking. Long-term use of bilberry leaves is suspected to lead to adverse effects.

Local Anesthetic/Vasoconstrictor Precautions
No information available to require special precautions

Effects on Bleeding May increase risk of bleeding by inhibiting platelet aggregation

Bitter Melon

Clinical Overview

Uses
There is insufficient evidence from quality clinical trials to recommend the use of bitter melon as a therapeutic option in type 2 diabetes.

Dosing
Bitter melon juice has been recommended for diabetes at daily doses of 50 to 100 mL; 900 mg of fruit given 3 times/day has also been given for the same indication. There is insufficient clinical trial evidence to substantiate these doses.

Contraindications
Patients deficient in glucose-6-phosphate dehydrogenase should avoid consumption of bitter melon preparations due to the presence of vicine in the seeds.

Pregnancy/Lactation
Documented adverse reactions include emmenagogue and abortifacient effects. Avoid use.

Interactions
None well documented.

Adverse Reactions
Bitter melon generally causes few adverse reactions. GI effects (eg, abdominal pain, diarrhea) and headache have been reported in clinical trials. Case reports exist of hypoglycemic coma and atrial fibrillation associated with bitter melon intake. Increases in liver enzymes have been observed experimentally, but without histological changes. Bitter melon should be used with caution in patients with impaired hepatic function.

Toxicology
The red arils around bitter melon seeds are toxic to children.

Local Anesthetic/Vasoconstrictor Precautions
No information available to require special precautions

Effects on Bleeding None reported

Bitter Orange

Clinical Overview

Uses
Pharmacological actions for C. aurantium include antispasmodic, sedative, demulcent, digestive, tonic, and vascular stimulant; as an anti-inflammatory, antibacterial, and antifungal agent; and for reducing cholesterol. Clinical data are limited. Most medical literature focuses on the plant's safety and efficacy in OTC weight loss supplement formulations, with studies using small sample sizes and often focusing on combination products. Therefore, no recommendations for any indication can be made.

Dosing
Follow manufacturer's dosage guidelines because synephrine content may vary in supplement formulations.

Contraindications
Because of potentially additive effects, avoid synephrine use in patients with hypertension, tachyarrhythmia, hyperthyroidism, or narrow-angle glaucoma.

Pregnancy/Lactation
Avoid use. Information regarding safety and efficacy in pregnancy and lactation is lacking.

Interactions
C. aurantium inhibits intestinal CYP3A4 and intestinal efflux in the small intestine and may interact with numerous drugs, including amiodarone, anxiolytics, antidepressants, antiviral agents, calcium channel blockers, dextromethorphan, GI prokinetic agents, vasoconstrictors, and weight loss formulas.

Adverse Reactions
Bitter orange may cause photosensitization, particularly in people with fair skin. There are numerous case reports of adverse cardiac reactions associated with C. aurantium extract use.

Toxicology
Bitter orange is considered generally recognized as safe (GRAS) by the US Food and Drug Administration (FDA) when consumed in amounts found in foods. Medical literature primarily documents cardiovascular toxicity, especially due to the stimulant amines synephrine, octopamine, and N-methyltyramine, which may cause vasoconstriction as well as increased heart rate and blood pressure.

Local Anesthetic/Vasoconstrictor Precautions
Synephrine, the main chemical constituent in the fruit, is a sympathomimetic amine having properties of vasoconstriction and tachycardia. Use vasoconstrictor with caution; synephrine may interact with epinephrine and levonordefrin to cause a pressor response.

Effects on Bleeding None reported

Bittersweet Nightshade

Clinical Overview

Uses
Bittersweet nightshade has been used as a traditional external remedy for skin abrasions and inflammation. The stems were approved by the German Commission E for external use as supportive therapy in chronic eczema (see Toxicology).

Dosing
Traditional use of the stem has been at a dosage of 1 to 3 g/day, usually given as a decoction or infusion in 250 mL of water.

Contraindications
Contraindications have not yet been identified.

Pregnancy/Lactation
Documented teratogenic effects of the glycoalkaloids in animals. Avoid use.

Interactions
None well documented.

Adverse Reactions
No data.

Toxicology
The plant is toxic. Ingestion of unripened berries should be considered a medical emergency. Symptoms may be delayed for several hours.

Local Anesthetic/Vasoconstrictor Precautions No information available to require special precautions

Effects on Bleeding None reported

Black Cohosh

Clinical Overview

Uses

Black cohosh has been used to help manage some symptoms of menopause and as an alternative to hormone replacement therapy (HRT). It may be useful for treatment of hypercholesteremia or peripheral arterial disease. Clinical studies do not support these uses.

Dosing

On the basis of clinical studies, the currently recommended daily dose of black cohosh is a 40% to 60% ethanol or isopropanol extract of 40 to 80 mg herbal drug that is standardized to contain 1 mg of triterpene 27-deoxyactein per 20 mg tablet. Counsel patients that therapeutic effects generally begin after 2 weeks, with maximum effects usually observed within 8 weeks.

Contraindications

Patients with aspirin sensitivity because it contains salicylates.

Pregnancy/Lactation

Black cohosh is contraindicated in pregnancy and may cause premature birth in large doses. Avoid black cohosh during lactation.

Interactions

None well documented.

Adverse Reactions

There is a low incidence of adverse reactions.

Toxicology

Overdose of black cohosh may cause nausea, vomiting, dizziness, nervous system and visual disturbances, reduced pulse rate, and increased perspiration. Case reports primarily document hepatic toxicity; however, cardiovascular and circulatory disorders and 1 case of convulsions have been documented.

Local Anesthetic/Vasoconstrictor Precautions No information available to require special precautions

Effects on Bleeding None reported

Black Currant

Clinical Overview

Uses

Based on limited published data, black currant oil and juice extracts might be useful as an antioxidant source and in treating rheumatoid arthritis, as well as for night- and fatigue-related visual impairment; the oil and juice extracts also exhibit limited antimicrobial and anticancer properties.

Dosing

A tea can be made from 2 to 4 g of chopped leaves and administered several times per day.

Contraindications

Contraindications have not been identified.

Pregnancy/Lactation

Information regarding safety and efficacy in pregnancy and lactation is lacking.

Interactions

None well documented.

Adverse Reactions

No adverse reactions have been reported. Although no direct evidence is available, black currant should be used with caution in epileptic patients because of reports of lowered seizure threshold with evening primrose oil.

Toxicology

No toxicity, carcinogenicity, or teratogenicity has been reported.

Local Anesthetic/Vasoconstrictor Precautions No information available to require special precautions

Effects on Bleeding None reported

Black Walnut

Clinical Overview

Uses

Black walnut has many traditional uses; however, there are no human trials to support these effects. Black walnuts are a good dietary source of essential fatty acids.

Dosing

No clinical trials are available to support dosage recommendations.

Contraindications

None well documented.

Pregnancy/Lactation

Avoid use. Documented adverse reactions (mutagenic properties).

Interactions

None well documented.

Adverse Reactions

Allergic reactions have occurred.

Toxicology

The quinones juglone and plumbagin found in black walnut are regarded as toxins.

Local Anesthetic/Vasoconstrictor Precautions No information available to require special precautions

Effects on Bleeding None reported

Blessed Thistle

Clinical Overview

Uses

Blessed thistle has been traditionally used to stimulate secretion of gastric juices and saliva, to increase appetite and facilitate digestion, and to stimulate the flow of bile. It is a common ingredient in combination formulas for gastric health. Anti-inflammatory, antimicrobial, and cytotoxic activities have been reported and thought to be due to the chemical constituent cnicin. However, there are no clinical trials to support these potential uses.

Dosing

No clinical studies exist to provide dosing recommendations for blessed thistle. Doses of 4 to 6 g daily have been traditionally used.

Contraindications

Blessed thistle is contraindicated in patients with gastric ulcers or other inflammatory bowel conditions, such as Crohn disease.

Pregnancy/Lactation

Avoid use. Blessed thistle should not be used in pregnancy. Information regarding safety and efficacy in lactation is lacking.

Interactions

None well documented.

Adverse Reactions

Allergy and cross sensitization have been reported with other members of the Asteraceae family. Stimulation of gastric acid secretion has been reported. Emesis is likely with high dosages.

Toxicology

Clinical information is limited. Emesis is likely with high dosages (5 g or more).

Local Anesthetic/Vasoconstrictor Precautions

No information available to require special precautions

Effects on Bleeding None reported

Blue Cohosh

Clinical Overview

Uses

Blue cohosh has been used to induce uterine contractions; however there are no quality clinical trials to support any therapeutic application for blue cohosh, and concerns of toxicity outweigh any potential clinical benefit.

Dosing

Despite widespread knowledge or use of blue cohosh, there are no clinical trials on which to base dosage recommendations.

Contraindications

Contraindications have not yet been identified.

Pregnancy/Lactation

Avoid use; adverse effects have been documented.

Interactions

None well documented.

Adverse Reactions

Information is limited; clinical trials are lacking. Potential for toxicity appears to outweigh any medical benefit.

Toxicology

Blue cohosh root is potentially toxic to humans and fetuses.

Local Anesthetic/Vasoconstrictor Precautions

No information available to require special precautions

Effects on Bleeding None reported

Boldo

Clinical Overview

Uses

In vitro and animal studies suggest boldo leaf extract and its constituent, boldine, possess antioxidant, anti-inflammatory, and antimicrobial effects, as well as potential applications in diabetes, GI disorders, and cancer. However, clinical trials are lacking to support any therapeutic application.

Dosing

No quality clinical trials exist to support therapeutic dosing of boldo leaf extract. Traditional doses include 1 to 2 teaspoons (2 to 3 g) of dry leaf per cup of water; 0.1 to 0.3 mL of liquid extract (1:1 in 45% alcohol) 3 times a day. Commercial preparations may contain ascaridole, a toxic constituent.

Contraindications

Contraindicated in liver disease and diseases of the bile duct, including gallstones.

Pregnancy/Lactation

Avoid use. Adverse effects have been noted in animal studies.

Interactions

Boldo ingestion may enhance the anticoagulant effect of warfarin; caution is warranted.

Adverse Reactions

Boldo-related adverse events described in case reports included anaphylaxis, prolonged QT interval and ventricular tachycardia, and hepatotoxicity.

Toxicology

High doses are necessary for toxic effects; animal studies documented neurotoxicity, hepatotoxicity, and mutagenicity.

Local Anesthetic/Vasoconstrictor Precautions

No information available to require special precautions

Effects on Bleeding As a single agent, boldo has no effect on bleeding. Boldo may enhance the anticoagulant effects of warfarin when taken simultaneously. This effect has not been confirmed.

Boneset

Clinical Overview

Uses

Boneset has chiefly been used to treat fevers.

Dosing

There is no recent clinical evidence to guide dosage of boneset. Traditional use was at a dose of 2 g of leaves and flowers. Internal use should be tempered by the occurrence of hepatotoxic pyrrolizidine alkaloids in this plant.

Contraindications

Contraindications have not yet been identified.

Pregnancy/Lactation

Documented adverse effects, including cytotoxic constituents. Avoid use.

Interactions

None well documented.

Adverse Reactions

The FDA has classified boneset as an "Herb of Undefined Safety."

Toxicology

The ingestion of large amounts of teas or extracts may result in severe diarrhea. The identification of pyrrolizidine alkaloids in related Eupatorium species is cause for concern until detailed phytochemical investigations are carried out on boneset. This class of alkaloids is known to cause hepatic impairment after long-term ingestion. While direct evidence for a hepatotoxic effect from boneset does not exist, there is sufficient evidence to indicate that any plant containing unsaturated pyrrolizidine alkaloids should not be ingested.

Local Anesthetic/Vasoconstrictor Precautions

No information available to require special precautions

Effects on Bleeding None reported

Borage

Clinical Overview

Uses

Borage has been used in European herbal medicine since the Middle Ages, alone and in combination with fish oil in rheumatoid arthritis, atopic eczema, and osteoporosis, although limited clinical evidence is available to support these uses.

Dosing

Borage seed oil 1 to 3 g/day has been given in clinical trials (1 g/day has been used in children and up to 3 g/day in adults). The content of gamma-linolenic acid is between 20% and 26% of the oil.

Contraindications

Contraindications have not been identified.

Pregnancy/Lactation

Documented adverse effects (pyrrolizidine alkaloids). Avoid use.

Interactions

None well documented.

Adverse Reactions

No adverse effects have been reported. Although no direct evidence is available, caution is advised in patients with epilepsy because of reports of lowered seizure threshold with evening primrose oil.

Toxicology

The presence of unsaturated pyrrolizidine alkaloids in leaves, flowers, and seeds of borage suggests a potential for hepatotoxicity, although the total plant alkaloid content is low.

Local Anesthetic/Vasoconstrictor Precautions

No information available to require special precautions

Effects on Bleeding None reported

Boron

Clinical Overview

Uses

Boric acid is a topical astringent, mild disinfectant and eye wash. Sprinkled in crevices and corners, boric acid powder controls rodents and insects. Sodium borate is used in cold creams, eye washes and mouth rinses. Boron compounds are used to enhance the cell selectivity of radiation therapy.

Dosing

Boron has been studied in several clinical studies at a wide range of doses. Daily dosage of 2.5 to 6 mg as boron has been administered for osteoarthritis and strength conditioning. Intravaginal boric acid (600 mg daily) was administered for vulvovaginal candidiasis. A single dose of 102.6 mg sodium tetraborate was studied for its effects on factor VIIa.

Contraindications

Contraindications have not yet been identified.

Pregnancy/Lactation

Information regarding safety and efficacy in pregnancy and lactation is lacking.

Interactions

None well documented.

Adverse Reactions

There is little or no clinical data about the adverse effects of boron; boron compounds can be toxic to humans.

Toxicology

While boric acid, borates, and other compounds containing boron are used medicinally, they are potentially toxic if ingested or absorbed through nonintact skin.

Local Anesthetic/Vasoconstrictor Precautions

No information available to require special precautions

Effects on Bleeding None reported

Bovine Colostrum

Clinical Overview

Uses

Bovine colostrum has been used to treat diarrhea, to improve GI health, to boost the immune system.

Dosing

Bovine colostrum is a difficult preparation to standardize because its antibody content may vary widely. Some clinical studies have been performed with hyperimmune colostrum, which may have a specific antibody titer; however, most products do not meet this criterion. Studies administering 25 to 125 mL of liquid formulations or 10 to 20 g of dry powder have been reported.

Contraindications

Contraindications have not yet been identified.

Pregnancy/Lactation

Information regarding safety and efficacy in pregnancy and lactation is lacking.

Interactions

None well documented.

Adverse Reactions

Bovine colostrum is well tolerated. A few symptoms, including mild nausea and flatulence have been reported.

Toxicology

Bovine colostrum appears to be safe and effective. There is no data in the literature concerning any toxicities.

Local Anesthetic/Vasoconstrictor Precautions

No information available to require special precautions

Effects on Bleeding None reported

Brahmi

Clinical Overview

Uses

Brahmi is used for its antioxidant activity. It has been investigated for use in improving cognition.

Dosing

Numerous dosage forms and commercial products are available and marketed for improved short- and long-term memory. A typical commercially available regimen is 2 oral capsules (500 mg; herbal extract of brahmi ratio, 10:1) twice a day with water after meals. Each capsule contains 500 mg (herbal extract of brahmi ratio is 10:1). Brahmi extracts have been used in clinical trials at dosages of 300 to 450 mg per day.

Contraindications

Avoid use with hypersensitivity to any of the components of brahmi.

Pregnancy/Lactation

Avoid use. Information regarding safety and efficacy in pregnancy and lactation is lacking.

Interactions

None well documented.

Adverse Reactions

Commonly reported adverse effects are flu-like symptoms, GI irritation, nausea, increased intestinal motility, and muscle fatigue.

Toxicology

No clinical data are available regarding toxicity.

Local Anesthetic/Vasoconstrictor Precautions

No information available to require special precautions

Effects on Bleeding None reported

Brewer's yeast

Clinical Overview

Uses

Brewer's yeast is traditionally used as a source of vitamin B, selenium, and chromium, especially by vegetarians. Clinical trials have evaluated yeast for a role in immunomodulation, respiratory infections, prevention of postsurgical infections (as beta-glucan), and as a source of dietary fiber to improve the lipid profile. However, there is a lack of quality trials.

Dosing

Upper respiratory tract infections: S. cerevisiae 500 mg daily has been used in clinical trials over 12 weeks to treat respiratory infections and allergic rhinitis.

Laxative: 6 to 50 g of fresh baker's yeast over 3 days was used in a study for the treatment of cancer-related constipation.

Acute diarrhea: 500 mg daily of brewer's yeast is recommended in the German Commission E Monographs.

Contraindications

Crohn disease; concomitant monoamine oxidase inhibitor (MAOI) therapy.

Pregnancy/Lactation

Information regarding safety and efficacy in pregnancy and lactation is lacking.

Interactions

Brewer's yeast contains tyramine. Avoid concurrent use with MAOIs.

Adverse Reactions

Mild GI symptoms, including flatulence.

Toxicology

Information is limited. Baker's yeast has Food and Drug Administration (FDA) GRAS (generally recognized as safe) status.

Local Anesthetic/Vasoconstrictor Precautions

No information available to require special precautions

Effects on Bleeding None reported

Buchu

Clinical Overview

Uses

Buchu has been used to treat inflammation and kidney and urinary tract infections; as a diuretic and as a stomach tonic. Other uses include carminative action and treatment of cystitis, urethritis, prostatitis and gout. It has also been used for leukorrhea and yeast infections.

Dosing

There is no recent clinical evidence to guide dosage of buchu. Classical doses were from 1 to 2 g of the leaves daily.

Contraindications

Contraindications have not yet been identified.

Pregnancy/Lactation

Documented adverse effects, including uterine stimulant effects. Avoid use.

Interactions

None well documented.

Adverse Reactions

Buchu can cause stomach and kidney irritation and can be an abortifacient. It can also induce increased menstrual flow. Buchu is not recommended during pregnancy.

Toxicology

Poisoning has not been reported. Buchu contains the hepatotoxin pulegone, also known to be present in pennyroyal.

Local Anesthetic/Vasoconstrictor Precautions

No information available to require special precautions

Effects on Bleeding None reported

Bupleurum

Clinical Overview

Uses

Bupleurum is being investigated for its antipyretic, immunomodulatory, GI tract, and hepatoprotective effects, as well as its potential in the prevention and treatment of cancers. Clinical trials are generally lacking.

Dosing

No clinical trials exist.

Contraindications

Contraindications have not been identified.

Pregnancy/Lactation

Information regarding safety and efficacy in pregnancy and lactation is lacking.

Interactions

None well documented.

Adverse Reactions

Mild lassitude, sedation, and drowsiness. Large doses may increase flatulence and bowel movements. Allergy to injected bupleurum has been reported.

Toxicology

The toxicity profile appears to be low; however, information is limited.

Local Anesthetic/Vasoconstrictor Precautions

No information available to require special precautions

Effects on Bleeding None reported

Bur Marigold

Clinical Overview

Uses

Several Bidens spp. have been used extensively in traditional medicine. Bur marigold may possess anti-inflammatory, antimicrobial, cardiovascular, and cytotoxic activity; however, clinical studies are lacking to support recommendations for use. A B. pilosa extract has been investigated for use in the management of diabetes.

Dosing

Clinical studies are lacking to provide dosing recommendations.

Contraindications

Contraindications have not been identified.

Pregnancy/Lactation

Avoid use. Information regarding safety and efficacy during pregnancy and lactation is lacking.

Interactions

None well documented.

Adverse Reactions

Clinical data regarding adverse effects of bur marigold are lacking; however, a small clinical study reported no adverse effects following administration of a B. pilosa formulation for 90 days. Cross-sensitivity to other members of the Asteraceae family may exist.

Toxicology

Clinical data are limited, especially regarding long-term toxicity.

Local Anesthetic/Vasoconstrictor Precautions

No information available to require special precautions

Effects on Bleeding None reported

Butcher's Broom

Clinical Overview

Uses

Butcher's broom has been used in many forms as a laxative, diuretic, treatment for circulatory disease, and cytotoxic agent, although limited results from clinical trials are available.

Dosing

Butchers broom has been used in clinical trials for chronic venous insufficiency standardized to 7 to 11 mg of ruscogenin. Hesperidin methyl chalcone has also been used as a marker for standardization in the product Cyclo 3 Fort. Extracts have been dosed at 16 mg daily for chronic phlebopathy, while a topical cream formulation was used to apply 64 to 96 mg of extract daily.

Contraindications

Contraindications have not yet been identified.

Pregnancy/Lactation
Information regarding safety and efficacy in pregnancy and lactation is lacking. Avoid use.

Interactions
None well documented.

Adverse Reactions
No adverse reactions have been reported.

Toxicology
Not known to be toxic.

Local Anesthetic/Vasoconstrictor Precautions
No information available to require special precautions

Effects on Bleeding None reported

Calendula

Clinical Overview

Uses
Potential uses for calendula include the treatment of inflammatory skin disorders, wound healing, and the treatment of other skin conditions. It may also be ingested for its anti-inflammatory and antispasmolytic effects. However, clinical trials to support these uses are limited. Use of calendula for dental purposes is increasing.

Dosing
A preparation can be made by steeping 5 to 10 mL of the herb in 1 cup of boiling water for 10 minutes and then gargled as a mouthwash for oral sores, consumed for its antispasmodic effects, or applied topically for skin conditions. Topical products typically contain 2 to 5 g of the herb per 100 g of the product.

Contraindications
Contraindications have not been identified.

Pregnancy/Lactation
Information regarding safety and efficacy in pregnancy and lactation is lacking. A study in rats demonstrated a reduction in maternal weight gain when administered during pregnancy.

Interactions
None well documented.

Adverse Reactions
Allergic reactions, contact sensitization, and 1 case of anaphylaxis have been reported.

Toxicology
Calendula appears to have a low potential for toxicity.

Local Anesthetic/Vasoconstrictor Precautions
No information available to require special precautions

Effects on Bleeding None reported

Capsicum Peppers

Clinical Overview

Uses
Many varieties are eaten as vegetables, condiments, and spices. The component capsaicin is an irritant and analgesic used in self-defense sprays, and in a variety of conditions associated with pain. Other studies have evaluated a role in weight loss, GI conditions, postoperative nausea, and rhinitis, although limited information is available.

Dosing
For external uses, capsaicin and Capsicum creams are available in several strengths, from 0.025% to 0.075% capsaicin. Clinical trials are lacking to guide dosage for other uses.

Contraindications
None clearly established.

Pregnancy/Lactation
Generally recognized as safe (GRAS) when used as food. Safety and efficacy for dosages above those in foods are unproven and should be avoided. Studies in animals have shown both positive and negative effects.

Interactions
Use of capsaicin by patients receiving captopril or other angiotensin-converting enzyme (ACE) inhibitors may cause or exacerbate ACE inhibitor-induced cough. Nonheme iron absorption may be inhibited by concomitant chili consumption.

Adverse Reactions
Topical, mucosal, and GI irritations are common. Allergies and cross-sensitization to other allergens have been reported.

Toxicology
Toxicity is evidenced in animal experiments in higher dosages. Controversy exists regarding capsaicin's mutagenicity and tumorigenicity. Toxicity from long-term exposure to chili powder has not been found, and the use of defense sprays likewise has not resulted in reports of toxicity.

Local Anesthetic/Vasoconstrictor Precautions
No information available to require special precautions

Effects on Bleeding May have some antiplatelet effects

Cascara

Clinical Overview

Uses
Limited clinical studies exist for cascara aside from those of its laxative effects. Attention has shifted to studying the effects of its constituent emodin, particularly with regard to possible therapeutic applications in the treatment of cancer.

Dosing
Cascara sagrada over-the-counter (OTC) laxative products were declared no longer safe and effective by the US Food and Drug Administration (FDA) in 2002. Typical doses of cascara are 1 g of bark, 2 to 6 mL of fluid extract or 325 mg of dried extract.

Contraindications
Cascara is contraindicated in ileus of any origin and in inflammatory diseases of the colon, including ulcerative colitis, irritable bowel syndrome (IBS), and Crohn disease.

Pregnancy/Lactation
Documented emmenagogue and abortifacient effects. Avoid use. Anthranoid metabolites may be excreted in breast milk.

Interactions
None well documented.

Adverse Reactions
Extended use may cause chronic diarrhea and consequent electrolyte imbalance.

Toxicology
Overdose of anthraquinone laxatives results in intestinal pain and severe diarrhea with consequent electrolyte imbalance and dehydration. No causal relationship between long-term use of cascara and colorectal cancer has been established. The carcinogenicity of emodin has been studied with equivocal results.

Local Anesthetic/Vasoconstrictor Precautions
No information available to require special precautions

Effects on Bleeding None reported

Catnip

Clinical Overview

Uses

There is little clinical data to support any use of catnip in humans, except as an insect repellant.

Dosing

There is no clinical evidence to guide dosage of catnip. Traditional doses for sedation require 4 g of dried herb, usually given as a tea. A 15% lotion of the essential oil has been used as an insect repellant.

Contraindications

None well documented.

Pregnancy/Lactation

Documented adverse effects when consumed (eg, emmenagogue and abortifacient effects). Avoid use.

Interactions

None well documented.

Adverse Reactions

Headache and malaise have been reported.

Toxicology

Information is lacking.

Local Anesthetic/Vasoconstrictor Precautions

No information available to require special precautions

Effects on Bleeding None reported

Cat's Claw

Clinical Overview

Uses

Despite multiple purported effects, controlled clinical trials are lacking. Suggested anti-inflammatory, anticancer, and immunostimulant properties are largely based on in vitro and limited animal studies.

Dosing

One gram of root bark given 2 to 3 times daily is a typical dose, while 20 to 30 mg of a root bark extract has been recommended. Clinical trials are generally lacking to support appropriate dosages. A standardized extract containing 8% to 10% carboxy alkyl esters and less than 0.5% oxindole alkaloids has been used in clinical studies in doses of 250 to 300 mg.

Contraindications

Cat's claw products should be avoided before and after surgery, as well as by those using immunosuppressant therapy and in children due to lack of safety data.

Pregnancy/Lactation

Information regarding safety and efficacy during pregnancy and lactation is lacking.

Interactions

Case reports are generally lacking; however, there is a reported interaction with protease inhibitors.

Adverse Reactions

Although reports of adverse effects are rare, GI complaints (nausea, diarrhea, stomach discomfort), renal effects, neuropathy, and an increased risk of bleeding with anticoagulant therapy are possible.

Toxicology

Historical ethnomedicinal evidence and current use by consumers suggest low toxicity; however, toxicological studies are limited.

Local Anesthetic/Vasoconstrictor Precautions

No information available to require special precautions

Effects on Bleeding May cause increased bleeding due to inhibition of platelet aggregation

Chamomile

Clinical Overview

Uses

Chamomile is used topically in skin and mucous membrane inflammations and skin diseases. It can be inhaled for respiratory tract inflammations or irritations; used in baths as irrigation for anogenital inflammation; and used internally for GI spasms and inflammatory diseases. However, clinical trials supporting any use of chamomile are limited.

Dosing

Chamomile has been used as a tea for various conditions and as a topical cream. Typical oral doses are 9 to 15 g/day. Gargles made from 8 g chamomile flowers in 1,000 mL of water have been used in clinical trials.

Contraindications

The use of chamomile-containing preparations is contraindicated in persons with hypersensitivity to ragweed pollens.

Pregnancy/Lactation

Unreferenced adverse reactions have been cited. Avoid use during pregnancy. No clinical data are available on use during lactation.

Interactions

Possible interactions have been reported with warfarin or cyclosporine. Because warfarin and cyclosporine have a narrow therapeutic index, patients taking either of these medications in other than modest amounts should avoid concurrent use of chamomile.

Adverse Reactions

Use of the tea and essential oil has resulted in anaphylaxis, contact dermatitis, and other severe hypersensitivity reactions. Cross-reactivity to asters, chrysanthemums, ragweed, and other members of the Asteraceae family exists.

Toxicology

Animal studies report low toxicity with oral ingestion of chamomile.

Local Anesthetic/Vasoconstrictor Precautions

No information available to require special precautions

Effects on Bleeding None reported

Chaparral

Clinical Overview

Uses

Chaparral has been traditionally used for the treatment of cancer, acne, rheumatism, and diabetes. It has also been promoted for its antioxidant effects by inhibiting free radicals. Chaparral has also been used as a blood purifier and a weight loss agent. However, clinical trials are lacking to support any of these uses.

Dosing

Because chaparral has been documented as hepatotoxic at doses of crude herb from 1.5 to 3.5 g/day, its use is discouraged.

Contraindications

Chaparral was removed from the US Food and Drug Administration's Generally Recognized as Safe (GRAS) list in 1968. Increased risk for hepatotoxicity is expected in patients with hepatic dysfunction. Chaparral is not recommended for use in patients with renal dysfunction due to a risk for accumulation of chaparral and toxicity.

Pregnancy/Lactation
Documented adverse effects (uterine activity, hepatotoxic). Avoid use.

Interactions
None well documented.

Adverse Reactions
The creosote bush can induce contact dermatitis.

Toxicology
Chaparral may cause liver damage, stimulate some malignancies, and cause contact dermatitis.

Local Anesthetic/Vasoconstrictor Precautions
No information available to require special precautions

Effects on Bleeding Nordihydroguaiaretic acid (NDGA), believed to be responsible for the biological activity of chaparral, is a platelet aggregation inhibitor; there is potential for an increased risk of bleeding in patients undergoing invasive dental procedures, particularly in patients taking concomitant anticoagulants, antiplatelet drugs, or any drugs or herbals with antiplatelet properties.

Chaste Tree

Clinical Overview

Uses
Chaste tree extract has been used to manage symptoms related to premenstrual syndrome (PMS) and cyclic mastalgia and may be a suitable alternative to standard pharmacological management. Although the Complete German Commission E Monographs supports its use for PMS and cyclic mastalgia, there are limited clinical trials to support these uses. Limited evidence exists for its use in menopause.

Dosing
Daily doses of chaste tree fruit extract are typically 20 to 40 mg.

Contraindications
Patients who have an allergy to or are hypersensitive to V. agnus-castus or patients who are pregnant or breastfeeding should avoid use. Safe use in children has not been established.

Pregnancy/Lactation
Information regarding safety and efficacy in pregnancy and lactation is lacking. However, chaste tree may have estrogenic, progesterogenic, and/or uterine stimulant activity and should be avoided in pregnancy and while breastfeeding.

Interactions
None well documented.

Adverse Reactions
Generally regarded as safe; mild and reversible adverse effects include GI reactions, itching, rash, headache, fatigue, acne, and menstrual disturbances.

Toxicology
Information is limited and safety has not been determined in children.

Local Anesthetic/Vasoconstrictor Precautions
No information available to require special precautions

Effects on Bleeding None reported

Chinese Cucumber

Clinical Overview

Uses
Chinese cucumber root extract has been traditionally used to induce abortion. Antiviral activity and potential application in cancer therapy is being investigated; however, a lack of clinical trials and toxicity of the plant's root limit use.

Dosing
In traditional Chinese medicine, Chinese cucumber is most commonly administered as part of a polyherbal preparation. In a clinical trial in HIV patients, trichosanthin 1.2 mg intravenously (IV) weekly, then monthly, was used. In another study, the plant seeds (20 g of seed kernels per day for 28 days) were eaten as a dietary source of conjugated linolenic acid.

Contraindications
Pregnancy.

Pregnancy/Lactation
Avoid use. Extracts of the root possess abortifacient activity and are toxic to the fetus.

Interactions
None well documented.

Adverse Reactions
Available published clinical studies are limited. However, one trial reported myalgia, fever, elevated liver function tests, and mild to moderate anaphylactic reactions.

Toxicology
Extracts of the Chinese cucumber are extremely toxic (death has occurred), particularly with parenteral use.

Local Anesthetic/Vasoconstrictor Precautions
No information available to require special precautions

Effects on Bleeding None reported

Chinese Foxglove

Clinical Overview

Uses
Rehmannia rhizome extracts are used extensively in traditional Chinese medicine. Clinical trials to support documented uses are lacking, and because the preparation is often used in combination with other agents, it is difficult to attribute any benefits to the plant. Catalpol, a chemical constituent of the root, is being evaluated for its potential in treating CNS diseases and its effects on aging.

Dosing
None validated by clinical data. Common prescription products range from Rehmannia root 55 to 350 mg extract in polyherbal mixtures.

Contraindications
Chronic liver disease and GI disease, including diarrhea.

Pregnancy/Lactation
Avoid use. Rehmannia has been used traditionally as an emmenagogue.

Interactions
None well documented.

Adverse Reactions
Minor and transient adverse reactions have been reported and include GI discomfort (eg, mild nausea, loose bowels, flatulence), allergy, headache, dizziness, heart palpitations, fatigue, and vertigo.

Toxicology
None well documented.

Local Anesthetic/Vasoconstrictor Precautions
No information available to require special precautions

Effects on Bleeding None reported

Chitosan

Clinical Overview

Uses
There is some evidence of the effect of chitosan on lowering cholesterol and body weight, but the effect is unlikely to be of clinical importance. To some extent,

chitosan is used in the emergency setting to control bleeding. Chitosan has been used in various drug delivery systems. Antimicrobial and other effects are being evaluated for use in dentistry.

Dosing

Chitosan has been administered at wide-ranging doses in clinical studies. In studies evaluating weight loss, 2.4 g/day is commonly used.

Contraindications

None well established.

Pregnancy/Lactation

Information regarding safety and efficacy in pregnancy and lactation is lacking.

Interactions

Data are limited. Potentiation of the anticoagulant effect of warfarin was reported in a patient receiving chitosan 2.4 g/day.

Adverse Reactions

The potential for allergy exists in individuals allergic to shellfish. Clinical trials report few adverse events, generally limited to flatulence and constipation.

Toxicology

Chitosan's toxicity profile is relatively low.

Local Anesthetic/Vasoconstrictor Precautions

No information available to require special precautions

Effects on Bleeding None reported

Chondroitin

Clinical Overview

Uses

Chondroitin sulfate has been studied for the treatment of arthritis; however, information on its effectiveness is conflicting. It is commonly given in combination with other agents, such as glucosamine sulfate or glucosamine hydrochloride. It has also been studied for use in drug delivery, antithrombotic and extravasation therapy, and treatment of dry eyes and interstitial cystitis.

Dosing

Chondroitin sulfate has been administered orally for treatment of arthritis at a dosage of 800 to 1,200 mg/day. Positive results often require several months to manifest, and a posttreatment effect has been observed. Animal studies have suggested that the bioavailability of chondroitin sulfate may be increased when given multiple times a day.

Contraindications

Contraindications have not been identified.

Pregnancy/Lactation

Information regarding safety and efficacy in pregnancy and lactation is lacking.

Interactions

An increase in the international normalized ratio (INR) may occur in patients taking anticoagulants, such as warfarin (eg, Coumadin), with either chondroitin alone or in combination with glucosamine.

Adverse Reactions

Potential adverse reactions associated with chondroitin sulfate include alopecia, constipation, diarrhea, epigastralgia, extrasystoles, eyelid edema, lower limb edema, and skin symptoms. Chondroitin sulfate may also exacerbate asthma.

Toxicology

There is little information regarding the long-term effects of chondroitin. Most reports conclude that it is safe.

Local Anesthetic/Vasoconstrictor Precautions

No information available to require special precautions

Effects on Bleeding None reported

Chromium

Clinical Overview

Uses

Chromium supplementation has been studied for a variety of indications, especially diabetes and weight loss, but clinical studies have shown inconsistent results. The role of supplemental chromium remains controversial.

Dosing

The currently accepted value for chromium dietary intake is 25 mcg/day for women and 35 mcg/day for men. Daily dosages used in clinical trials for periods of up to 9 months range as follows: brewer's yeast up to 400 mcg/day; chromium chloride 50 to 600 mcg/day; chromium nicotinate 200 to 800 mcg/day; chromium picolinate 60 to 1,000 mcg/day. The potential for genotoxic effects exists at higher dosages.

Contraindications

None well documented. Renal failure may be considered a relative contraindication.

Pregnancy/Lactation

Information regarding safety and efficacy in pregnancy and lactation is lacking. Limited animal experimentation showed skeletal and neurological defects in the offspring of mice fed chromium picolinate.

Interactions

None well documented.

Adverse Reactions

Ingestion or exposure to certain forms of chromium may cause or contribute to GI irritation and ulcers, dermatitis, hemorrhage, circulatory shock, and renal tubule damage.

Toxicology

No risk of genotoxicity at low dosages over the short-term exists for chromium as a dietary supplement. However, at higher dosages, such as those used in trials evaluating the efficacy of chromium in glycemic control, concern exists for potential genotoxic effects.

Local Anesthetic/Vasoconstrictor Precautions

No information available to require special precautions

Effects on Bleeding None reported

Cinnamon

Clinical Overview

Uses

Cinnamon is used as a spice and aromatic. Traditionally, the bark or oil has been used to combat microorganisms, diarrhea, and other GI disorders, and dysmenorrhea, although there is limited data to sup port these uses. Evidence is lacking to support the use of cinnamon in the management of diabetes. Research has focused on anti-inflammatory, antioxidant, and antimicrobial activity.

Dosing

Ground cinnamon is generally given at dosages of 1 to 1.5 g/day in studies of diabetes without reported adverse reactions.

Contraindications

Contraindicated in people who are allergic to cinnamon or Peru balsam. Further contraindications have not yet been identified.

Pregnancy/Lactation

Data are insufficient for adequate risk-to-benefit analysis. Cinnamon is generally recognized as safe when used in food.

Interactions
None well documented.

Adverse Reactions
Heavy exposure may cause skin irritation and allergic reactions.

Toxicology
Information is lacking.

Local Anesthetic/Vasoconstrictor Precautions
No information available to require special precautions

Effects on Bleeding None reported

Clove

Clinical Overview

Uses
Clove has historically been used for its antiseptic and analgesic effects. Clove and clove oils are used safely in foods, beverages, and toothpastes. Clove oil cream has been used in the treatment of anal fissures and an extract has exhibited aphrodisiac action in rats; however, there are limited studies supporting clinical applications for clove oil.

Dosing
There are limited studies to support therapeutic dosing for clove oil.

Contraindications
Contraindications have not been identified.

Pregnancy/Lactation
Information regarding safety and efficacy in pregnancy and lactation is lacking.

Interactions
None well documented.

Adverse Reactions
Contact dermatitis has been noted.

Toxicology
Toxicity has been observed following ingestion of the oil, but is rare and poorly documented.

Local Anesthetic/Vasoconstrictor Precautions
No information available to require special precautions

Effects on Bleeding Clove has been reported to have antiplatelet effects; however, case reports and clinical data are lacking. Presently, there is no information available to require special precautions.

Cocoa

Clinical Overview

Uses
Cocoa solid, cocoa butter, and chocolate are all rich sources of antioxidants. Epidemiological studies show an inverse association between the consumption of cocoa and the risk of cardiovascular disease. The likely mechanisms are antioxidant activity; improvement in endothelial function, vascular function, and insulin sensitivity; as well as attenuation of platelet reactivity and reduction in blood pressure.

Dosing
No specific dosing recommendations can be made. Further studies characterizing the polyphenol content of cocoa products and method of measurement are needed. In one study, an inverse relationship was demonstrated between cocoa intake and blood pressure, as well as a 15-year cardiovascular and all-cause mortality; the median cocoa intake among users was 2.11 g/day.

Contraindications
None known.

Pregnancy/Lactation
Generally recognized as safe (GRAS) when used in moderate amounts or in amounts used in foods. Avoid dosages greater than those found in food because safety and efficacy are unproven. Caffeine content should be restricted during pregnancy.

Interactions
None well documented.

Adverse Reactions
Children consuming large amounts of chocolate and caffeinated beverages may exhibit tics or restlessness. Ingredients in chocolate may precipitate migraine headaches, and cocoa products may be allergenic.

Toxicology
Cocoa is nontoxic when ingested in typical confectionery amounts.

Local Anesthetic/Vasoconstrictor Precautions
No information available to require special precautions

Effects on Bleeding None reported

Comfrey

Clinical Overview

Uses
Therapeutic use of comfrey is limited because of its toxicity. A limited number of clinical trials show short-term efficacy of topically applied, alkaloid-free comfrey preparations in skin abrasions and inflammatory conditions. Although not examined in clinical trials, comfrey may possess antifungal and anticancer activity.

Dosing
Oral use of comfrey is not supported because of potential hepatotoxicity. Additionally, because externally applied alkaloids are well absorbed and detected in the urine, topical use of comfrey should not exceed an alkaloid exposure of 100 mcg/day. Limited trials have evaluated the efficacy of alkaloid-free preparations for topical use; however, these studies do not report on hepatic laboratory indices of study participants.

Contraindications
Comfrey is not recommended for internal use because of the hepatotoxic pyrrolizidine alkaloid content. Patients with hypersensitivity or allergic reactions to the plant should avoid external use. Use is contraindicated during pregnancy and lactation, in infants, and in patients with liver or kidney disease.

Pregnancy/Lactation
Contraindicated because of documented adverse effects. Pyrrolizidine alkaloids have abortifacient effects and increase the risk of fatal hepatic veno-occlusive disease. Animal experiments have detected alkaloids in breast milk.

Interactions
None well documented.

Adverse Reactions
Neither internal nor extensive topical use of comfrey is recommended because of numerous reports of liver toxicity (see Toxicology). Case reports show hepatic veno-occlusive disease and pulmonary hypertension related to comfrey use. Infants are more susceptible to pyrrolizidine-related, veno-occlusive disease; therefore, the use of comfrey in this population is contraindicated.

Toxicology
The Food and Drug Administration (FDA) released an advisory in July 2001 recommending that comfrey products be removed from the market because of

cases of hepatic veno-occlusive disease. Comfrey is generally considered unsafe, with numerous toxicological effects in animals and humans.

Local Anesthetic/Vasoconstrictor Precautions No information available to require special precautions

Effects on Bleeding None reported

Cordyceps

Clinical Overview

Uses

Well-controlled clinical trials are lacking.

Dosing

Dosing supported by product quality data is unavailable, and many herbal supplements on the market contain varying undefined levels of this product. Cordyceps 3 to 6 g/day has been used in patients with chronic renal failure for periods ranging from days to years.

Contraindications

Contraindications have not been identified.

Pregnancy/Lactation

Information regarding safety and efficacy in pregnancy and lactation is lacking.

Interactions

None well documented.

Adverse Reactions

Mild GI discomfort, including diarrhea, dry mouth, and nausea, has been reported.

Toxicology

Cordyceps is generally considered safe.

Local Anesthetic/Vasoconstrictor Precautions No information available to require special precautions

Effects on Bleeding Cordyceps has been reported to have antiplatelet effects; however, case reports and clinical data are lacking. Presently, there is no information available to require special precautions.

Cranberry

Clinical Overview

Uses

Some evidence exists for the use of cranberry in preventing, but not treating, urinary tract infections (UTIs). Other possible uses for cranberry, with limited evidence, include reduction of the risk of cardiovascular disease and cancer.

Dosing

Cranberry juice, juice concentrate, and dried extract have been studied in UTIs; however, consistency in dosage regimens is lacking. Doses of juice cocktail (25% pure cranberry juice) have ranged from 120 to 1,000 mL/day in divided doses. Concentrated cranberry extract in the form of tablets and capsules is available and 600 to more than 1,200 mg/day in divided doses have been used in studies in UTIs.

Contraindications

Predisposition to or history of nephrolithiasis (kidney stones).

Pregnancy/Lactation

Information is limited; however, when ingested at normal food consumption amounts, cranberry is considered relatively safe in pregnancy. Safety during lactation is unknown.

Interactions

An interaction between cranberry and warfarin has been suggested based on case reports; however, evidence for a causal relationship is lacking from clinical trials.

Adverse Reactions

The berries and juice have few adverse reactions associated with their consumption. Large daily doses may produce GI symptoms, such as diarrhea. Concentrated cranberry tablets may predispose patients to nephrolithiasis. Cranberry juice should not be used to clear enteral feeding tubes.

Toxicology

Information is lacking.

Local Anesthetic/Vasoconstrictor Precautions No information available to require special precautions

Effects on Bleeding None reported

Creatine

Clinical Overview

Uses

Creatine has enhanced performance in short-duration, high-intensity exercise in limited trials. Creatine supplementation has been extensively studied in myopathies and neurodegenerative disorders, but with limited efficacy. Further trials are ongoing.

Dosing

Dosage regimens in clinical trials vary from 2 to 20 g daily, and from 1 to 6 weeks and longer.

Contraindications

Patients with a history of renal impairment or those taking nephrotoxic agents should avoid concomitant creatine supplementation or be monitored closely if supplementation is necessary.

Pregnancy/Lactation

Information regarding safety and efficacy in pregnancy and lactation is lacking.

Interactions

None well documented.

Adverse Reactions

Few adverse reactions have been reported in clinical studies among patients with neurological or muscle disorders, or in healthy individuals

Concerns regarding renal and hepatic toxicity exist; unequivocal proof of safety is lacking and caution is warranted.

Case reports of adverse reactions among athletes include dehydration, electrolyte imbalance, and muscle cramping. Minor GI upset (diarrhea, GI pain, nausea), dizziness, and short-term loss in body mass have also been reported. The safety of creatine in children has not been established.

Toxicology

Information is limited; however, the French Agency for Food, Environmental and Occupational Health & Safety (ANSES) has warned of the potential for production of cytotoxic compounds, especially at high dosages.

Local Anesthetic/Vasoconstrictor Precautions No information available to require special precautions

Effects on Bleeding None reported

Cumin

Clinical Overview

Uses

Cumin seeds are used in cooking and the oil is used to flavor food and scent cosmetics. Components may have antioxidant, anticancer, hypoglycemic, antiepileptic, antiosteoporotic, ophthalmic, antibacterial, and larvicidal effects; however, there is no clinical evidence to support these claims. Cumin is generally recognized as safe for human consumption as a spice and flavoring.

Dosing

There are no recent clinical studies of cumin that provide a basis for dosage recommendations.

Contraindications

Contraindications have not yet been identified.

Pregnancy/Lactation

Information regarding safety and efficacy in pregnancy and lactation is lacking.

Interactions

None well documented.

Adverse Reactions

The oil may have photosensitizing effects. Cumin may also cause hypoglycemia.

Toxicology

No data are available.

Local Anesthetic/Vasoconstrictor Precautions
No information available to require special precautions

Effects on Bleeding A study published in 1989 showed that cumin inhibits human platelet aggregation in *in vitro* testing; the clinical significance of this effect is unknown at this time.

Damiana

Clinical Overview

Uses

Clinical studies evaluating the effect of T. diffusa are lacking. Studies in rodents suggest damiana has aphrodisiac and anxiolytic effects.

Dosing

There are no recent clinical studies of damiana to provide dosage recommendations. Traditionally, damiana extract British Pharmaceutical Codex (BPC) has been used at a dosage of 0.3 to 0.6 g.

Contraindications

Contraindications have not been identified.

Pregnancy/Lactation

Avoid use. Documented adverse effects include cyanogenic glycosides and risk of cyanide toxicity with high doses of damiana.

Interactions

None well documented.

Adverse Reactions

There is limited clinical information regarding adverse reactions associated with damiana use. The possibility of convulsions, especially in relation to excess alcohol consumption, exists. Damiana-induced hallucinations are unlikely.

Toxicology

Research reveals little or no information regarding toxicity with damiana use. T. diffusa contains potentially toxic chemicals including arbutin, tannins, and cyanogenic glycosides.

Local Anesthetic/Vasoconstrictor Precautions
No information available to require special precautions

Effects on Bleeding None reported

Dandelion

Clinical Overview

Uses

Dandelion has been used for its nutritional value. Other traditional uses include regulation of blood glucose, treatment of liver and gallbladder disorders, appetite stimulation, treatment of dyspeptic complaints, and as a diuretic. However, limited clinical studies are available to provide evidence to support such claims.

Dosing

Clinical trials on which to base dosing are limited. Fresh roots and leaves are often consumed in salads. The *German Commission E Monographs* recommends 3 to 4 g of the root or 10 to 15 drops of root tincture twice a day, or 4 to 10 g of the leaves or 2 to 5 mL of leaf tincture 3 times a day.

Contraindications

Contraindications have not yet been identified.

Pregnancy/Lactation

Generally recognized as safe (GRAS) by the US Food and Drug Administration or used as food. Avoid dosages above those in foods; safety and efficacy of such dosages are unproven.

Interactions

None well documented.

Adverse Reactions

Allergy and mild gastric discomfort have been reported.

Toxicology

The acute toxicity of dandelion is considered low. Decreased fertility in male rats has been observed.

Local Anesthetic/Vasoconstrictor Precautions
No information available to require special precautions

Effects on Bleeding None reported

Danshen

Clinical Overview

Uses

Danshen has been used extensively in Chinese medicine for many years. Limited studies have shown efficacy in coronary artery disease and acute ischemic stroke, but the quality of methodology limits the validity of the findings.

Dosing

Active components in commercially available preparations vary greatly. Commonly cited dosages include the following: 10 "dripping" pills taken 3 times a day (oral or sublingual), 3 Fu Fang Dan Shen tablets taken orally 3 times a day, or danshen 20 mg/kg capsules. Doses of 100 mg/kg as a bolus injection have been used in children.

Contraindications

Data are lacking.

Pregnancy/Lactation

Information regarding safety and efficacy in pregnancy and lactation is lacking.

Interactions

Danshen may interfere with laboratory digoxin plasma levels and increase the anticoagulant effect of warfarin. It may reduce midazolam plasma concentrations, decreasing the pharmacologic effects, and inhibits numerous cytochrome P450 (CYP-450) enzymes in vitro.

Adverse Reactions

Adverse reactions appear to be limited to allergy, dizziness, headache, mild GI symptoms, and reversible thrombocytopenia.

Toxicology

Information is limited.

Local Anesthetic/Vasoconstrictor Precautions
No information available to require special precautions

Effects on Bleeding Danshen has been shown to inhibit platelet aggregation *in vitro* in animals and is suggested to inhibit platelet aggregation in humans; the clinical significance of this effect is unknown at this time. Case reports described increased anticoagulation in patients taking warfarin, but this appears to be a result of a pharmacokinetic/pharmacodynamic interaction rather than any anticoagulation activity on the part of danshen.

Dehydroepiandrosterone

Clinical Overview

Uses

Adequately powered, long-term clinical trials are lacking to support a place in therapy for dehydroepiandrosterone (DHEA) and dehydroepiandrosterone sulfate (DHEAS) supplementation (henceforth, jointly referred to as DHEA/S). Reviews of clinical trials found no convincing evidence to support a place in therapy for postmenopausal symptoms in women, in improving cognitive function or physical strength in elderly patients, in hyperlipidemia or insulin resistance, or in schizophrenia or cancer. Some evidence exists to support the use of DHEA/S supplementation in women with diminished ovarian reserves, in subpopulations of elderly women with osteoporosis, and in mild systemic lupus erythematosus.

Dosing

Orally administered DHEA has a less than 10% bioavailability and is converted into inactive DHEAS, which can then act as a reservoir for the body to utilize. Daily dosing of DHEA 25 mg has been suggested in postmenopausal women because this dose minimizes the adverse androgenic effects; however, only studies in which at least 50 mg/day were used demonstrated positive outcomes. Dosages used in clinical studies of assisted reproduction were in the range of 50 to 75 mg/day (in divided doses). In adrenal insufficiency, DHEA 50 mg/day for 3 months is considered a replacement dose, while 200 mg/day achieves supraphysiological circulating levels and would thus be considered a pharmacological dose.

Contraindications

Contraindications have not been identified. Use of DHEA or DHEAS is not recommended in breast or prostate cancer.

Pregnancy/Lactation

Information regarding safety and efficacy in pregnancy and lactation is lacking. DHEA supplementation has been evaluated to improve oocyte production in infertility.

Interactions

None well documented.

Adverse Reactions

Studies in adrenal insufficiency suggest DHEA is generally well tolerated. However, data from long-term studies are lacking. Observed adverse effects include acne, hirsutism, and decreased high-density lipoprotein (HDL) levels.

Toxicology

Information in humans is limited. DHEA has been shown to be carcinogenic as well as protective against certain cancers in rodents.

Local Anesthetic/Vasoconstrictor Precautions

No information available to require special precautions

Effects on Bleeding None reported

Devil's Claw

Clinical Overview

Uses

Devil's claw is a folk remedy used for an extensive range of diseases, including arthritis and rheumatism. Clinical trials are generally supportive of its use as an anti-inflammatory and analgesic in low back pain and osteoarthritis.

Dosing

Devil's claw has been studied for low back pain, muscle pain, and osteoarthritis using daily doses of crude tuber up to 9 g, 1 to 3 g of extract, or harpagoside 50 to 100 mg.

Contraindications

Because of the bitterness of the preparation and consequent increase in gastric secretion, devil's claw is contraindicated in patients with gastric or duodenal ulcers.

Pregnancy/Lactation

Documented oxytoxic adverse effects. Avoid use.

Interactions

None well documented.

Adverse Reactions

Rare, generally consisting of headache, tinnitus, or anorexia.

Toxicology

Clinically important toxicity has not been observed in limited, short-term use.

Local Anesthetic/Vasoconstrictor Precautions

No information available to require special precautions

Effects on Bleeding Purpura has occurred in a patient taking warfarin and Devil's Claw concurrently, suggesting over anticoagulation.

Dong Quai

Clinical Overview

Uses

Dong quai is used in combination with other plant extracts in Chinese traditional medicine as an analgesic for rheumatism, an allergy suppressant, and in the treatment of menstrual disorders. Dong quai and its chemical constituents possess antiasthmatic, antispasmodic, anti-inflammatory, and anticoagulant properties. Clinical trials supporting traditional uses are limited. It has also been used to flavor liqueurs and confections.

Dosing

Several forms of the plant exist and dosages vary widely: crude root extract by decoction ranges from 3 to 15 g/day; while in combination, preparations 75 mg to 500 mg may be taken up to 6 times a day.

Contraindications

Relative contraindications in patients receiving warfarin, heparin, or other anticoagulant/antiplatelet therapy, in those with breast cancer, or in the first trimester of pregnancy.

Pregnancy/Lactation

Avoid use. Uterine stimulant and relaxant activity have been reported with A. sinensis, while a related species, Angelica archangelica L., was a reported abortifacient and affected the menstrual cycle.

Interactions

Warfarin, heparin, and other antiplatelet therapy due to anticoagulant/antiplatelet action of A. sinensis.

Adverse Reactions

Case reports exist of fever, gynaecomastia, and bleeding with concurrent warfarin use. A risk of photosensitization exists.

Toxicology

Data are limited. Chemical constituents have demonstrated cytotoxic properties.

Local Anesthetic/Vasoconstrictor Precautions
No information available to require special precautions

Effects on Bleeding May inhibit platelet aggregation and therefore increase bleeding

Du Zhong

Clinical Overview

Uses

The medical literature includes numerous studies on the use of *Eucommia ulmoides* (du zhong) for treating diabetes, inflammation, and obesity. One clinical study exists for its use in treating hypertension.

Dosing

E. ulmoides is commercially available as a combination product or alone as a capsule, tablet, powder, or tea, primarily for treating hypertension. *Tablets*: 3 to 5 (100 mg) tablets 3 times per day with warm water after meals. One clinical study used a 500 mg standardized extract 3 times daily for 8 weeks.

Contraindications

Avoid use in patients who are hypersensitive to any components of *E. ulmoides*. The herb may be contraindicated in patients diagnosed with estrogen-dependent cancers.

Pregnancy/Lactation

Information regarding safety and efficacy in pregnancy and lactation is lacking.

Interactions

None well documented.

Adverse Reactions

One clinical study of *E. ulmoides* documented moderately severe headache, dizziness, edema, and onset of a cold.

Toxicology

No information in humans is available.

Local Anesthetic/Vasoconstrictor Precautions
No information available to require special precautions

Effects on Bleeding
No information available to require special precautions

Echinacea

Clinical Overview

Uses

Although evidence of efficacy in the treatment of infections is limited, use of echinacea as prophylaxis for upper respiratory tract infections has been reported. Use of echinacea for the treatment of anxiety and cancer has been investigated. Specific recommendations for use are unreliable due to variations in the composition of commercial products and inconsistent clinical trial results.

Dosing

A major limitation of available dosing information is the lack of standardization of echinacea preparations. Commercial preparations contain echinacea components derived from different plant parts, species, and varieties. Recommended dosing includes the following: 300 mg of dry powdered extract (standardized to echinacoside 3.5%), 0.25 to 1.25 mL of liquid extract (1:1 in alcohol 45%), 1 to 2 mL of tincture (1:5 in alcohol 45%), 2 to 3 mL of expressed juice of E. purpurea, and 0.5 to 1 g of dried root or tea (all administered 3 times daily). Long-term use of echinacea or use for longer than 10 days in acute infections in otherwise healthy individuals is not recommended. Parenteral use is not recommended.

Contraindications

Avoid use with known hypersensitivity to plants of the Asteraceae/Compositae family. Echinacea is also contraindicated in patients with rheumatoid arthritis, systemic lupus erythematosus, leukosis, multiple sclerosis, tuberculosis, and HIV infection.

Pregnancy/Lactation

Information regarding safety and efficacy in pregnancy and lactation is lacking. Limited clinical evidence, expert opinion, and long-term traditional use suggest that oral echinacea use is safe during pregnancy at normal dosages. Echinacea should be used with caution during lactation.

Interactions

Specific case reports of interactions are limited, although one report describes an interaction with etoposide. Data regarding echinacea effects on the cytochrome P450 (CYP-450) enzyme system are conflicting.

Adverse Reactions

Adverse reactions with echinacea are rare. The most commonly reported reactions were allergy, GI upset, and rash. A case report of leukopenia, possibly caused by long-term echinacea use, has been published. Due to conflicting data, echinacea should not be used in any condition potentially affected by immune stimulation or suppression such as HIV, tuberculosis, multiple sclerosis, and immunosuppressive therapy.

Toxicology

There is little evidence regarding toxicity with echinacea, despite its widespread use. Echinacea has not been associated with acute or chronic toxic effects. Patients with hepatic impairment should use echinacea with caution, as case reports of hepatotoxicity exist.

Local Anesthetic/Vasoconstrictor Precautions
No information available to require special precautions

Effects on Bleeding None reported

Elderberry

Clinical Overview

Uses

Limited clinical trials have been conducted. Elderberry extracts may have some value in the treatment of influenza and appear to have antioxidant potential.

Dosing

The bioavailability of active constituents in elderberry extracts is considered to be poor. Trials are lacking to provide dosing information. For the treatment of influenza, 15 mL of syrup taken 4 times per day for 5 days has been used in clinical trials.

Contraindications

Contraindications have not been identified.

Pregnancy/Lactation

Information regarding safety and efficacy in pregnancy and lactation is lacking.

Interactions

None well documented.

Adverse Reactions

Consumption of uncooked berries may result in vomiting and diarrhea. Commercial preparations generally do not cause adverse reactions at the recommended dosage. Type 1 allergy to elderberry (positive skin prick tests) has been recorded.

Toxicology

Poisonous alkaloids, lectins, and cyanogenic glycosides are present in some plant parts. Short-term use of elderberry extract preparations appears to be relatively safe; however, long-term toxicological studies are lacking.

Local Anesthetic/Vasoconstrictor Precautions

No information available to require special precautions

Effects on Bleeding None reported

Ephedra

Clinical Overview

Uses

The whole Ephedra sinica plant has traditionally been used to treat symptoms of bronchial asthma, colds, influenza, allergies, and hives in teas or tinctures. Because of adverse events and lack of efficacy, use is not recommended for weight loss or increased athletic performance. Ephedra-containing supplements are banned for sale in the United States.

Dosing

Ephedra-containing dietary supplements are currently banned in the United States. Dosages of ephedra more than 32 mg/day have resulted in adverse reactions.

Contraindications

Cardiovascular and cerebrovascular adverse events have been documented in case reports.

Pregnancy/Lactation

Documented adverse reactions. Avoid use.

Interactions

Interactions are likely to be similar to those established for synthetic ephedrine and include monoamine oxidase inhibitors (MAOIs), the anesthetic propofol, cholinergic agents such as tricyclic antidepressants, caffeine, theophylline, and steroids such as dexamethasone.

Adverse Reactions

Reported adverse reactions include arrhythmia and sudden death, myocardial infarction, stroke, psychiatric symptoms, autonomic hyperactivity, seizures, and ischemic colitis and gastric mucosal injury.

Toxicology

Toxicological data are limited. Periconceptional use of ephedra-containing products has been associated with an increased adjusted odds ratio for anencephaly.

Local Anesthetic/Vasoconstrictor Precautions

Use vasoconstrictor with caution since ephedrine may enhance cardiostimulation and vasopressor effects of sympathomimetics such as epinephrine and levonordefrin.

Effects on Bleeding None reported

Evening Primrose Oil

Clinical Overview

Uses

Evidence suggests that evening primrose oil may be effective for treating rheumatoid arthritis and diabetic neuropathy, but is lacking to support its place in the treatment of atopic dermatitis, menopausal vasomotor symptoms, mastalgia, or multiple sclerosis.

Dosing

Evening primrose oil has been administered orally in clinical trials at doses between 6 and 8 g/day in adults and 2 and 4 g/day in children. The typical content of gamma-linolenic acid (GLA) in the oil is 8% to 10%.

Contraindications

No contraindications have been identified.

Pregnancy/Lactation

Information regarding safety and efficacy in pregnancy and lactation is lacking. A case report exists of transient petechiae in a newborn following oral and intravaginal use of evening primrose oil for cervical ripening for a week prior to the infant's birth. Both linoleic and GLA are normally present in breast milk, and it is reasonable to assume that evening primrose oil may be taken while breastfeeding.

Interactions

A case report exists of an interaction between evening primrose oil and lopinavir in which lopinavir plasma concentrations were elevated to toxic levels.

Adverse Reactions

Evening primrose oil was previously suspected to lower the seizure threshold in schizophrenic patients; however, this is now disputed.

Toxicology

No toxicity, carcinogenicity, or teratogenicity have been reported.

Local Anesthetic/Vasoconstrictor Precautions

No information available to require special precautions

Effects on Bleeding Contains gamma-linolenic acid which can inhibit platelet aggregation and prolong bleeding.

Eyebright

Clinical Overview

Uses

Although eyebright preparations have been used to treat a variety of conditions, specifically inflammatory eye disease, clinical trials are lacking.

Dosing

Clinical studies are lacking to provide guidance. Single-dose homeopathic eye drops are available commercially and are used up to 5 times/day. Tinctures and extracts of the fresh herb have been used, and an oral form was administered in 1 study evaluating use in preventing conjunctivitis.

Contraindications

None well documented.

Pregnancy/Lactation

Avoid use. Information regarding safety and efficacy in pregnancy and lactation is lacking.

Interactions

None well documented.

Adverse Reactions

Multiple adverse symptoms, including nausea and constipation, confusion, weakness, sneezing, rhinitis, cough, dyspnea, insomnia, polyuria, and diaphoresis from 10 to 60 drops of eyebright tincture have been reported. Only sterile ophthalmic preparations should be used. Homeopathic doses are unlikely to exert any adverse reactions because of the minimal amounts ingested.

Toxicology

Information regarding toxicology is limited.

Local Anesthetic/Vasoconstrictor Precautions

No information available to require special precautions

Effects on Bleeding None reported

Fennel

Clinical Overview

Uses

Fennel has been used as a flavoring agent, a scent, and an insect repellent, as well as an herbal remedy for poisoning and GI conditions. It has also been used as a stimulant to promote lactation and menstruation. However, clinical evidence to support the use of fennel for any indication is lacking.

Dosing

Fennel seed and fennel seed oil have been used as stimulant and carminative agents in doses of 5 to 7 g and 0.1 to 0.6 mL, respectively.

Contraindications

Contraindications have not been identified.

Pregnancy/Lactation

There are documented adverse reactions and emmenagogue effects. Avoid use.

Interactions

One study suggested that the fennel constituent 5-methoxypsoralen has the ability to inhibit cytochrome P450 3A4. Therefore, fennel should be used cautiously with medications requiring this isoenzyme as a substrate.

Adverse Reactions

Fennel may cause photodermatitis, contact dermatitis, and cross reactions. The oil may induce reactions, such as hallucinations and seizures. Four case reports of premature thelarche (breast development) in girls have been reported with the use of fennel. Poison hemlock may be mistaken for fennel.

Toxicology

Fennel oil is genotoxic in the Bacillus subtilis DNA repair test. Estragole, present in the volatile oil, has caused tumors in animals.

Local Anesthetic/Vasoconstrictor Precautions

No information available to require special precautions

Effects on Bleeding May see increased bleeding

Fenugreek

Clinical Overview

Uses

Limited clinical trial data suggest fenugreek extracts may have a role in the therapy of dyslipidemia, diabetes, and Parkinson disease; however, studies were limited and provided inconsistent dosing information, making it difficult to provide recommendations. Anti-inflammatory, antioxidant, and cytotoxic properties have yet to be fully explored.

Dosing

Wide-ranging dosages and differing preparations have been used in clinical studies. A standardized hydroalcoholic extract of fenugreek seeds is available, and a trial evaluated its use in patients with Parkinson disease at 300 mg twice daily for a period of 6 months. Studies in patients with type 2 diabetes and hypercholesterolemia have used 5 g/day of seeds or 1 g/day of a hydroalcoholic extract of fenugreek.

Contraindications

Contraindications have not yet been identified. Avoid if an allergy to any member of the Fabaceae family exists. Cross-reactivity to chickpea, peanut, or coriander allergy is possible.

Pregnancy/Lactation

Avoid use in pregnancy. Fenugreek has documented uterine stimulant effects and has been used in traditional medicine to induce childbirth. Studies in pregnant mice have shown intrauterine growth retardation and fetal malformations related to fenugreek seed consumption. Fenugreek has been used to stimulate milk production in breastfeeding mothers; however, the extent of transmission of fenugreek-derived constituents into breast milk is unknown.

Interactions

Interactions with anticoagulant and hypoglycemic agents are possible; monitor therapy.

Adverse Reactions

Dyspepsia and mild abdominal distention have been reported in studies using large doses of the seeds. When ingested in culinary quantities, fenugreek is usually devoid of adverse reactions. Allergy to fenugreek is recognized.

Toxicology

The acute toxicity from large doses of fenugreek has not been characterized, although hypoglycemia is possible.

Local Anesthetic/Vasoconstrictor Precautions

No information available to require special precautions

Effects on Bleeding As a single agent, fenugreek has no effect on bleeding. Fenugreek may enhance the anticoagulant effects of warfarin when taken simultaneously. This effect has not been confirmed.

Feverfew

Clinical Overview

Uses

Feverfew is primarily known for use in prophylactic treatment of migraine headaches and associated nausea and vomiting; however, evidence to support this use is inconclusive. Feverfew has numerous other pharmacological actions, including inhibition of prostaglandin synthesis, blockage of platelet granule secretion, effects on smooth muscle, antitumor activity, inhibition of serotonin release, inhibition of histamine release, and mast cell inhibition, but information from clinical trials is limited.

Dosing

Feverfew is generally given for migraine headaches at a daily dosage of 50 to 150 mg of dried leaves, 2.5 fresh leaves with or after food, or 5 to 20 drops of a 1:5, 25% ethanol tincture. Though optimal doses of feverfew have not been established, an adult dosage of parentholide 0.2 to 0.6 mg/day is recommended for the prevention of migraine. However, parthenolide has not been confirmed as a major active principle for migraine. Numerous feverfew products are commercially available; most are standardized to parthenolide 0.7% in tablet or capsule dosage forms.

Contraindications

Feverfew is contraindicated in patients allergic to other members of the Asteraceae family, such as aster, chamomile, chrysanthemum, ragweed, sunflower, tansy, and yarrow. Due to its potential antiplatelet effects, it is not recommended for use in patients undergoing surgery. Patients with blood-clotting disorders should consult their health care provider prior to using products containing feverfew.

Pregnancy/Lactation

Avoid use because of documented adverse effects. Pregnant women should not use the plant because the leaves possess emmenagogue activity (ejection of the placenta and fetal membranes) and may induce abortion. It is not recommended for breastfeeding mothers or for use in children younger than 2 years of age.

Interactions
None well documented.

Adverse Reactions
Patients withdrawn from feverfew may experience ill effects often known as "postfeverfew" syndrome. Handling fresh feverfew leaves may cause allergic contact dermatitis. Swelling of the lips, tongue, and oral mucosa, in addition to mouth ulceration, have been reported with feverfew use. GI effects, such as abdominal pain, nausea, vomiting, diarrhea, indigestion, and flatulence, may also occur.

Toxicology
No studies of chronic toxicity have been performed on the plant. The safety of long-term use has not been established.

Local Anesthetic/Vasoconstrictor Precautions
No information available to require special precautions

Effects on Bleeding May see increased bleeding due to inhibition of platelet aggregation

Flax

Clinical Overview

Uses
Flaxseed and flaxseed oil contain various essential fatty acids but are particularly rich in alpha linolenic acid (ALA). Flaxseed (but not flaxseed oil) also has a high fiber content that may have health benefits similar to those of other high-fiber products and phytoestrogens. Historically, linseed oil, derived from flaxseed, has been used as a topical demulcent and emollient, as a laxative, and as a treatment for coughs, colds, and urinary tract infections. Interest in flaxseed centers on atherosclerosis, cancer, diabetes, and to a lesser extent, menopause, attention deficit hyperactivity disorder, bipolar disorder, and systemic lupus erythematosus (SLE).

Dosing
Flaxseed (whole or ground) has been used in clinical trials at doses from 5 to 50 g/day or 60 mL flaxseed oil daily, and has been used in children at doses equivalent to 400 mg of ALA in divided doses.

Eight grams of ground flaxseed (or 2.5 g of flaxseed oil) per day provides a daily intake of 1.1 g of ALA for women and 1.6 g for men.

Contraindications
Contraindicated in patients with known hypersensitivity to flaxseed.

Pregnancy/Lactation
The use of flaxseed and flaxseed oil during pregnancy and lactation is not recommended.

Interactions
None well documented.

Adverse Reactions
Flaxseed and flaxseed oil appear to be well tolerated, with few adverse reactions reported except allergy.

Toxicology
The US Food and Drug Administration has not granted GRAS (Generally Recognized as Safe) status to flaxseed or flaxseed oil. The safety of ingested amounts greater than 50 g/day of flaxseed is not established.

Local Anesthetic/Vasoconstrictor Precautions
No information available to require special precautions

Effects on Bleeding None reported

Forskolin

Clinical Overview

Uses
Forskolin has multiple sites of action and should be used with caution. Forskolin derivatives have been developed for use in cardiovascular conditions. Quality clinical trials are lacking to substantiate claims made of the weight loss properties of forskolin, and clinical studies conducted with oral and inhaled forskolin in patients with asthma are limited.

Dosing
Asthma: Oral forskolin has been studied using 10 mg daily over 2 to 6 months.

Obesity: 250 mg of a 10% forskolin extract twice daily for 12 weeks has been studied.

Contraindications
Case reports are lacking.

Pregnancy/Lactation
Information regarding safety and efficacy in pregnancy and lactation is lacking. P. barbatus has been traditionally used as an emmenagogue and oral contraceptive.

Interactions
None well documented.

Adverse Reactions
Clinical trial data are generally lacking. Adverse events reported with the use of colforsin (a forskolin derivative) include tachycardia and arrhythmias. Forskolin should be avoided in patients with polycystic kidney disease.

Toxicology
Information is limited. Embryo-related toxicity has been reported.

Local Anesthetic/Vasoconstrictor Precautions
No information available to require special precautions

Effects on Bleeding Forskolin has been shown *in vitro* to inhibit platelet aggregation. Clinical relevance of this effect is unknown. There are no current published reports of any anticoagulant effect in patients taking Forskolin.

Forsythia

Clinical Overview

Uses
Forsythia has been used for treatment of bacterial infections and upper respiratory tract infections, although the clinical evidence supporting its use is limited.

Dosing
There are no recent clinical studies of forsythia to provide a basis for dosage recommendations.

Contraindications
Contraindications have not yet been identified.

Pregnancy/Lactation
Documented adverse effects. Uterine stimulant, emmenagogue. Avoid use.

Interactions
None well documented.

Adverse Reactions
Forsythia is contraindicated in pregnancy.

Toxicology
Forsythia has minimal potential for toxicity.

Local Anesthetic/Vasoconstrictor Precautions
No information available to require special precautions

Effects on Bleeding None reported

Frankincense, Indian

Clinical Overview

Uses

The extract of Indian frankincense tree has anti-inflammatory activity. Boswellic acids may play a role in preventing formation of anaphylatoxins during severe acute allergic reactions.

Dosing

An extract of frankincense (H15) was studied in arthritis at a dose of 3.6 g daily. The gum resin of frankincense has been used at a daily dose of 900 mg for bronchial asthma.

Contraindications

Contraindications have not yet been identified.

Pregnancy/Lactation

Information regarding safety and efficacy in pregnancy and lactation is lacking.

Interactions

None well documented.

Adverse Reactions

Although data are limited, no side effects have been reported that necessitated stopping treatment.

Toxicology

No data.

Local Anesthetic/Vasoconstrictor Precautions

No information available to require special precautions

Effects on Bleeding None reported

Fruit Acids

Clinical Overview

Uses

Fruit acids have been used to treat a range of dermatological conditions, including acne, photoaging, dry skin, psoriasis, actinic keratosis, and melasma. Additionally, they have been investigated as a treatment for fibromyalgia.

Dosing

For dry skin disorders, alpha hydroxy acid 8% to 10% cream or lotion is applied 2 to 3 times daily to the affected area. If the dry skin persists after 2 weeks, the concentration can be increased by 2% to 4%. Once the skin appears healthy, the frequency can be reduced to every 2 to 3 days. For fibromyalgia, clinical data suggest the use of 3 Super Malic tablets (each containing malic acid 200 mg) twice daily. Dosing for chemical peels involving glycolic acid will depend on a variety of factors, including the condition being treated, patient expectations, patient age, cumulative sun exposure, skin type, area being treated, peeling agent used, concentration of peel agent, frequency of application, quantity applied, and length of time applied. Typically, on the first visit, glycolic acid is applied for approximately 2 to 3 minutes to determine sensitivity and provide guidance for future length of exposure. Intervals between peels are generally 2 to 4 weeks, and 6 to 8 peels are required for most patients.

Contraindications

Hypersensitive individuals and those with irritated skin should use alpha hydroxy acids cautiously. Patients who have undergone recent cosmetic surgeries, patients with open wounds, and those who have used isotretinoin therapy within the last 6 to 12 months should not receive alpha hydroxy acid peels. In patients who have a history of recurrent or active herpes simplex lesions, treatment with an oral antiviral agent should occur before undergoing chemical peels.

Pregnancy/Lactation

Information regarding safety and efficacy in pregnancy and lactation is lacking.

Interactions

Use of isotretinoin causes a reduction in the number and size of pilosebaceous units in the skin and may cause a delay in wound healing and increase the risk of scarring. It is advised that patients wait at least 6 to 12 months after receiving isotretinoin to begin chemical peels. Antimetabolites and corticosteroids may delay wound healing in patients using chemical peels. Use of hormone replacement therapy and oral contraceptives may cause postinflammatory hyperpigmentation in some patients using chemical peels. Following a chemical peel with glycolic acid, there may be an increase in risk of photosensitivity in patients using photosensitizing agents, such as tetracyclines and other photosensitizing agents.

Adverse Reactions

Dryness, scaling, burning, erythema, and similar effects may occur in sensitive individuals or with prolonged use.

Toxicology

In rats, long-term ingestion of malic acid was found to reduce body weight gains and feed consumption when given for a period of 2 years.

Local Anesthetic/Vasoconstrictor Precautions

No information available to require special precautions

Effects on Bleeding None reported

Garcinia (hydroxycitric acid)

Clinical Overview

Uses

The medical literature primarily documents weight loss and lipid-lowering activity for Garcinia cambogia, although trials supporting its use are limited. In short-term clinical trials lasting 12 weeks or less, G. cambogia was ineffective or moderately effective for weight loss in overweight subjects. Results have been inconsistent in studies evaluating the effect of G. cambogia on lipids.

Dosing

The dosages of G. cambogia extract used in clinical trials ranged from 1,500 to 4,667 mg/day (25 to 78 mg/kg/day). The equivalent HCA dosage in the trials ranged from 900 to 2,800 mg/day (15 to 47 mg/kg/day). G. cambogia is available in capsule or tablet form with a maximum dosage of 1,500 mg/day.

Contraindications

Avoid use if there is a known allergy or hypersensitivity to any components of G. cambogia.

Pregnancy/Lactation

Avoid use during pregnancy and lactation. Information regarding safety and efficacy in pregnancy and lactation is lacking.

Interactions

The herb has documented drug interactions.

Adverse Reactions

Fifteen clinical studies involving approximately 900 patients documented very mild adverse reactions, with the most common adverse reactions including headache, dizziness, dry mouth, and GI complaints such as nausea and diarrhea. Hydroxycut dietary supplements for weight loss were voluntarily recalled from the US market in 2009 because of concerns about hepatotoxicity. Although G. cambogia was an ingredient in some formulations of Hydroxycut, its role in cases of hepatotoxicity associated with Hydroxycut is unclear.

Toxicology

Toxicology studies showed no toxicity or deaths in animals given dosages of HCA 5,000 mg/kg, equivalent to HCA 350 g in humans, or 233 times the maximum recommended human dosage of HCA 1.5 g/day.

Local Anesthetic/Vasoconstrictor Precautions No information available to require special precautions

Effects on Bleeding None reported

Garlic

Clinical Overview

Uses

Evidence suggests that garlic may produce modest but not clinically significant effects in the treatment of dyslipidemia and hypertension. Traditionally, it has been used for its antiseptic and antibacterial properties, as well as for treating the common cold, upper respiratory tract infections, mild bronchitis, and rhinitis, and to relieve cough and congestion. Other potential uses include treatment of atherosclerosis, benign prostatic hyperplasia, diabetes, gastrointestinal (GI) disorders, and stomach and colon cancer; however, evidence is lacking.

Dosing

The following doses are recommended: 2 to 5 g of fresh raw garlic; 0.4 to 1.2 g of dried garlic powder; 2 to 5 mg garlic oil; 300 to 1,000 mg of garlic extract (as solid material). Other preparations should correspond to 4 to 12 mg of alliin or approximately 2 to 5 mg of allicin, an active constituent of garlic. However, dosage is complicated by the volatility and instability of important constituents in various products (eg, aged extracts, deodorized garlic, distilled oils). Administer garlic preparations with food to minimize GI upset. Because garlic is widely consumed, dosage will remain a matter of personal tolerance.

Contraindications

Contraindicated if known allergy to garlic and its constituents.

Pregnancy/Lactation

Garlic may be used safely in pregnancy and breastfeeding. However, consumption by breastfeeding mothers may impact the infant's behavior during breastfeeding, causing prolonged attachment to the breast and increased sucking. There have been documented emmenagogue effects.

Interactions

Garlic may reduce saquinavir plasma concentrations. Caution patients taking saquinavir to limit ingestion of garlic and to avoid taking garlic supplements without consulting their health care provider. Based on available reports, no special precautions are necessary in patients eating garlic and taking warfarin. However, because warfarin has a narrow therapeutic index, caution patients against use of alternative medicines without consulting their health care provider and to report any signs of bleeding. Based on an initial study, garlic does not appear to interact with alprazolam, dextromethorphan, docetaxel, or ritonavir.

Adverse Reactions

Body odor and malodorous breath are the most common complaints after ingesting garlic preparations. Mild GI adverse reactions (eg, bloating, flatulence, nausea) have been commonly reported with use. Ingestion of a single 25 mL dose of fresh garlic extract has caused burning of the mouth, esophagus, and stomach; nausea; sweating; and light-headedness. The safety of repeated doses of this amount has not been defined. Alterations in coagulation have also been reported. Ingestion of large amounts may increase the risk of postoperative and spontaneous bleeding. Ingestion as a food or supplement or topical use may cause allergic reactions (contact dermatitis, anaphylaxis, angioedema, generalized urticaria, pemphigus, and photoallergy). Topical exposure to crushed, uncooked garlic cloves for 3 to 5 minutes has resulted in toxic contact dermatitis. Repeated exposure to garlic dust can induce asthmatic reactions.

Toxicology

Research reveals little or no information regarding the toxicology of garlic.

Local Anesthetic/Vasoconstrictor Precautions No information available to require special precautions

Effects on Bleeding Causes platelet dysfunction and prolonged bleeding time

Gelsemium

Clinical Overview

Uses

Gelsemium has been traditionally used to treat pain and respiratory ailments.

Dosing

There are no recent clinical studies of gelsemium to provide a basis for dosage recommendations. Classical use of this herb indicated 30 mg of the rhizome. Current use is primarily homeopathic.

Contraindications

No longer considered safe.

Pregnancy/Lactation

Documented adverse effects. Avoid use.

Interactions

None well documented.

Adverse Reactions

Research reveals little or no information regarding adverse reactions with the use of this product.

Toxicology

All parts of the gelsemium are toxic and can cause death when ingested.

Local Anesthetic/Vasoconstrictor Precautions No information available to require special precautions

Effects on Bleeding None reported

Ginger

Clinical Overview

Uses

There are many traditional uses for ginger, but recent interest centers on the prevention and management of nausea. However, information to support ginger's use for nausea, especially in pregnancy, is lacking. Ginger may possess anti-inflammatory and analgesic effects, and has been effective in dysmenorrhea in limited studies.

Dosing

Ginger has been used in clinical trials in dosages of 250 mg to 1 g 3 to 4 times daily.

Contraindications

Contraindications have not been identified.

Pregnancy/Lactation

Avoid use. Despite trials conducted to determine its effectiveness in pregnancy-related nausea, data on fetal outcomes are lacking.

Interactions

Anticoagulants (eg, warfarin), agents with antiplatelet properties, nonsteroidal anti-inflammatory agents, salicylates or thrombolytic agents, antihypertensives, and hypoglycemic agents interact with ginger.

Adverse Reactions

The US Food and Drug Administration (FDA) lists ginger as generally recognized as safe (GRAS), but large doses carry the potential for adverse reactions. Mild GI effects (eg, heartburn, diarrhea, mouth irritation) have been reported, and case reports of arrhythmia and immunoglobulin E (IgE) allergic reaction are documented.

Toxicology

Toxicological information regarding the use of ginger in humans is limited, and mutagenicity is contested.

Local Anesthetic/Vasoconstrictor Precautions
No information available to require special precautions

Effects on Bleeding No information available to require special precautions

Ginkgo biloba

Clinical Overview

Uses

Ginkgo has been studied extensively in diverse medical conditions. Evidence is lacking to support a protective role in cardiovascular conditions and stroke, and a definitive place in therapy for dementia and schizophrenia, although promising, is yet to be established. The findings from 2 large trials are pivotal in evaluating the efficacy of G. biloba extracts.

Dosing

Standardized ginkgo leaf extracts, such as EGb 761 (Tebonin forte, Schwabe), have been used in clinical trials for cognitive and circulatory disorders at daily doses of 120 to 240 mg of extract.

Contraindications

Absolute contraindications have not been established.

Pregnancy/Lactation

Evidence is lacking on the safety of ginkgo; preparations should not be used during pregnancy and lactation.

Interactions

Ginkgo interacts with the human cytochrome P450 (CYP-450) system and its isoenzymes, which may affect the metabolism of various drugs. Case reports of various interactions exist; however, consistent data are limited.

Adverse Reactions

Severe adverse reactions are rare; possible reactions include headache, dizziness, heart palpitations, and GI and dermatologic reactions. Ginkgo pollen can be strongly allergenic. Contact with the fleshy fruit pulp may cause allergic dermatitis similar to poison ivy.

Toxicology

A toxic syndrome has been recognized in Asian children who have ingested ginkgo seeds.

Local Anesthetic/Vasoconstrictor Precautions
No information available to require special precautions

Effects on Bleeding Spontaneous bleeding is a concerning side effect. Significant peri- and postoperative bleeding have been reported. Chronic use inhibits platelet aggregation and prolongs bleeding.

Ginseng

Clinical Overview

Uses

Ginseng root is widely used for its adaptogenic, immunomodulatory, antineoplastic, cardiovascular, CNS, endocrine, and ergogenic effects, but these uses have not been confirmed by clinical trials.

Dosing

According to the Complete German Commission E Monographs, crude preparations of dried root powder 1 to 2 g can be taken daily for up to 3 months. In numerous clinical trials, the dosage of crude root has ranged from 0.5 to 3 g/day and the dose of extracts has generally ranged from 100 to 400 mg.

Contraindications

Contraindications have not been established aside from known hypersensitivity.

Pregnancy/Lactation

Information regarding safety and efficacy in pregnancy and lactation is lacking.

Interactions

Limited evidence exists for any established interactions, with most data derived from laboratory studies and healthy volunteers. Very few case reports exist; however, exercise caution when using the following medicines: antidiabetic drugs/insulin, antipsychotic drugs, caffeine and other stimulants, furosemide, imatinib, monoamine oxidase inhibitors (MAOIs), and nifedipine. Interactions with warfarin and antiviral drugs are conflicting.

Adverse Reactions

It is estimated that more than 6 million people ingest ginseng regularly in the United States. There have been few reports of severe reactions and a very low incidence of adverse events has been reported in clinical trials. Hypersensitivity and anaphylaxis have been reported. Inappropriate use of P. ginseng or ginseng abuse syndrome includes symptoms such as hypertension, diarrhea, sleeplessness, mastalgia, skin rash, confusion, and depression.

Toxicology

None known.

Local Anesthetic/Vasoconstrictor Precautions
Has potential to interact with epinephrine and levonordefrin to result in increased BP; use vasoconstrictor with caution

Effects on Bleeding May prolong thrombin time (TT) and activated partial thromboplastin time (aPTT).

Glucosamine

Clinical Overview

Uses

Glucosamine is being investigated extensively for its action in osteoarthritis. However, there is a lack of consensus in clinical trials regarding its efficacy.

Dosing

In clinical studies of arthritis, glucosamine dosage has typically been 1.5 g/day, as a single dose or in divided doses.

Contraindications

No absolute contraindications have been identified.

Pregnancy/Lactation

Information regarding safety and efficacy in pregnancy and lactation is lacking.

Interactions

None well documented.

Adverse Reactions
Glucosamine is generally considered safe. Use caution when administering to persons with poorly controlled diabetes.

Toxicology
Mutagenicity studies are limited and conflicting.

Local Anesthetic/Vasoconstrictor Precautions
No information available to require special precautions

Effects on Bleeding None reported

Goat's Rue

Clinical Overview

Uses
Goat's rue and its derivatives have been used in the management of diabetes mellitus to reduce blood sugar levels. Goat's rue has also been used for its lactogenic effects to increase milk production. It has tonic, liver protectant, and platelet aggregation inhibitory effects, and has been evaluated for its diuretic and weight loss effects. However, limited clinical trials exist to support these uses.

Dosing
Diabetes: Information is lacking to provide dosing recommendations for goat's rue in diabetes. Clinical dosing information focuses on metformin, which is derived from goat's rue.

Galactorrhea: 1 teaspoon (5 mL) of dried herb steeped in 1 cup (240 mL) of water administered twice daily or 1 to 2 mL of tincture administered 3 times daily.

Contraindications
Use caution if administering goat's rue during surgical procedures due to a potential increased risk of bleeding.

Pregnancy/Lactation
Avoid use. Information regarding safety and efficacy in pregnancy is lacking. Silymarin in combination with galega enhances milk production in breastfeeding mothers.

Interactions
Hypoglycemic medications: Additive blood glucose-lowering effects may occur if using goat's rue concomitantly with other hypoglycemic medications such as insulin and sulfonylureas.

Antiplatelet/Anticoagulant medications: Because goat's rue inhibits platelet aggregation, the risk of bleeding may be increased when given concomitantly with other antiplatelet medications or anticoagulants.

Adverse Reactions
Headache, jitteriness, or weakness may occur. Because of its ability to inhibit platelet aggregation, there may be an increased risk of bleeding and bruising with administration of goat's rue.

Toxicology
Toxicity has been observed with other guanidine derivatives.

Local Anesthetic/Vasoconstrictor Precautions
No information available to require special precautions

Effects on Bleeding None reported

Goji Berry

Clinical Overview

Uses
Limited quality clinical trials exist to support therapeutic claims. In vitro and animal experiments suggest antioxidant, hypoglycemic, immune-enhancing, and neuro-, hepato-, and ophthalmic-protective effects.

Dosing
Data are lacking to guide dosage in the clinical setting.

Contraindications
Contraindications have not been identified.

Pregnancy/Lactation
Information regarding safety and efficacy in pregnancy and lactation is lacking.

Interactions
Case reports of interactions with warfarin exist.

Adverse Reactions
Clinical trials report few or no adverse reactions. Information is limited.

Toxicology
Information is lacking.

Local Anesthetic/Vasoconstrictor Precautions
No information available to require special precautions

Effects on Bleeding None reported

Goldenseal

Clinical Overview

Uses
Traditional uses of goldenseal are not validated by clinical studies, although it may be of use in diabetes, dyslipidemia, cardiovascular conditions, and cancer.

Dosing
Clinical evidence is lacking; few well-controlled clinical trials are available to guide dosage for goldenseal root extract.

Recommended dosages vary considerably, from 250 mg to 1 g 3 times daily. Some product labeling suggests higher dosages.

Traditional dosages include 0.5 to 1 g dried rhizomes 3 times daily, and 0.3 to 1 mL 1:1 liquid extract in 60% ethanol 3 times daily.

Contraindications
None well defined.

Pregnancy/Lactation
Avoid use; activity as a uterine stimulant has been documented. Safety in lactation has not been established.

Interactions
Goldenseal may affect the cytochrome CYP-450 (CYP450) system. The clinical importance of this interaction has not been established.

Adverse Reactions
Information from clinical studies is lacking, but adverse reactions with common doses are rare. Very high doses of goldenseal may rarely induce nausea, anxiety, depression, seizures, or paralysis.

Toxicology
Toxicological concerns have been reported, with some evidence of carcinogenicity in rodents.

Local Anesthetic/Vasoconstrictor Precautions
No information available to require special precautions

Effects on Bleeding None reported

Gossypol

Clinical Overview

Uses
According to Chinese studies, gossypol is effective as a nonhormonal male contraceptive; however, it has been documented to have irreversible effects on male fertility. It is being studied for clinical applications in cancer therapy.

Dosing

Antifertility: Trials have used 5 to 10 mg daily for 2 to 3 months to achieve azoospermia, with a lower maintenance dose for up to 2 years.

Cancer: Maximum tolerated dosages appear to be 40 mg of gossypol (as AT-101) per day.

Contraindications

None well documented.

Pregnancy/Lactation

Documented abortifacient effects. Avoid use.

Interactions

None well documented.

Adverse Reactions

Nausea, emesis, anorexia, diarrhea, altered taste sensation, small intestine obstruction, and fatigue have been recorded in clinical trials. The irreversible effects of gossypol on male fertility have been well documented, as has the incidence of hypokalemia.

Toxicology

Gossypol is potentially toxic.

Local Anesthetic/Vasoconstrictor Precautions

No information available to require special precautions

Effects on Bleeding None reported

Gotu Kola

Clinical Overview

Uses

Gotu kola has been traditionally used as treatment for a variety of conditions and as an aphrodisiac. There is potential efficacy in treating wounds, varicose veins, skin disorders, venous insufficiency, and to enhance memory, although there is little clinical information to support these claims.

Dosing

Dosages of gotu kola in crude form range from 1.5 to 4 g/day. Various extracts standardized to asiaticoside content also are available and have been studied in clinical trials in venous insufficiency and wound healing at doses of 30 to 90 mg/day. Wound-healing studies have involved topical application of a hydrogel ointment containing a titrated extract of C. asiatica (TECA). Commercial manufacturers have numerous dosage regimens listed for gotu kola.

Contraindications

Avoid use if hypersensitive to any of the ingredients of C. asiatica or gotu kola.

Pregnancy/Lactation

Avoid use during pregnancy and lactation, because gotu kola may have emmenagogue effects.

Interactions

None well documented.

Adverse Reactions

Contact dermatitis is documented in some clinical trials.

Toxicology

Three cases of hepatotoxicity have been reported with patients using C. asiatica for 20 to 60 days.

Local Anesthetic/Vasoconstrictor Precautions

No information available to require special precautions

Effects on Bleeding None reported

Grapefruit

Clinical Overview

Uses

Clinical trials are generally lacking for therapeutic applications. Grapefruit or its juice have potential in influencing weight loss and promoting cholesterol reduction, and have demonstrated antibacterial activity in the urinary tract.

Dosing

Quality clinical trials upon which to base therapeutic dosing recommendations are limited. Improved lipid profiles were achieved with consumption of 1 grapefruit daily for 30 days. Grapefruit juice 8 oz (237 mL), or half of a fresh grapefruit, 3 times a day before each meal for 12 weeks resulted in weight loss in a clinical trial evaluating the effect on metabolic syndrome.

Contraindications

None well defined. In patients with major myocardial structural disorders, pink grapefruit should probably be avoided due to proarrhythmic effects. The potential for drug interaction with grapefruit should be considered in cases where an increase or decrease of the available drug is clinically important.

Pregnancy/Lactation

GRAS (generally recognized as safe) for use as food. Safety and efficacy for dosages above those in foods are unproven.

Interactions

Grapefruit juice has been reported to interact with numerous drugs; however, case reports of significant interactions are rare. Interactions between grapefruit and cyclosporine and some, but not all, calcium channel antagonists and HMG-CoA reductase inhibitors are considered relevant. However, the potential for an interaction with grapefruit should be considered in cases where an increase or decrease of the available drug is clinically important.

Adverse Reactions

Reports of adverse reactions to grapefruit consumption are limited and are largely related to drug interactions. Case reports exist of allergy to pectin and pectin-induced asthma.

Toxicology

Toxicological studies on whole grapefruit are lacking. A meta-analysis of 3 landmark studies evaluating the association of grapefruit consumption and risk of breast cancer found no increased risk. The constituent d-limonene in grapefruit has GRAS status. Grapefruit seed extract has been shown to be toxic to human skin fibroblast cells.

Local Anesthetic/Vasoconstrictor Precautions

No information available to require special precautions

Effects on Bleeding None reported

Grape Seed

Clinical Overview

Uses

Grape seed is known for its antioxidant properties. Limited studies suggest possible cardiovascular, chemopreventive, and cytoprotective effects.

Dosing

Extracts of grape seeds containing mostly proanthocyanidin have been studied for antioxidant and cardiovascular properties, as well as for venous insufficiency and ophthalmologic disorders at doses of 50 to 300 mg/day. A maximum of 900 mg/day has been used.

Contraindications

Contraindicated in patients with known hypersensitivity to grape seed.

Pregnancy/Lactation

Information regarding safety and efficacy in pregnancy and lactation is lacking.

Interactions

Caution is advised when administering supplements containing grape seed polyphenols concomitantly with vitamin C to hypertensive patients because increases in blood pressure may occur.

Adverse Reactions

None well documented. It is contraindicated in patients with known hypersensitivity to grape seed. Gastralgia, headache, and an allergic reaction have been reported in the literature. Additional clinical studies are recommended.

Toxicology

No toxicity in humans has been reported.

Local Anesthetic/Vasoconstrictor Precautions

No information available to require special precautions

Effects on Bleeding None reported

Green Tea

Clinical Overview

Uses

Tea is traditionally consumed as a beverage. Evidence from clinical trials suggests that green tea plays a role in metabolic syndrome because it may have an impact on body weight, glucose homeostasis, and other cardiovascular risk factors. It has yet to be determined whether green tea is an agent in cancer prevention; however, a role in the prevention of stroke has been suggested. Topical applications have been studied for protection from ultraviolet (UV) damage, and a commercial preparation has been approved for use in the treatment of anogenital warts.

Dosing A daily intake of 3 to 5 cups/day (1,200 mL) of green tea will provide at least 250 mg/day of catechins. Green tea extract should not be taken on an empty stomach due to the potential for hepatotoxicity from excessive levels of epigallocatechin gallate.

Anogenital warts: topical application of sinecatechins 3 times a day for a maximum of 6 weeks.

Cardiovascular effect: 400 to 716 mg/day of catechins have been used in trials in divided dosages.

Diabetes: Dosages of epigallocatechin gallate range from 84 to 386 mg/day in trials evaluating glucose homeostasis.

Obesity: Dosage ranges used in trials include 270 to 800 mg/day of epigallocatechin gallate, or 125 to 625 mg/day of catechins.

Contraindications

Contraindications have not been identified; however, use caution when hepatic failure is present.

Pregnancy/Lactation

The US Food and Drug Administration (FDA) advises those who are or may become pregnant to avoid caffeine.

Interactions

Vitamin K present in green tea may antagonize the anticoagulant effect of warfarin. Green tea consumption reduces the bioavailability of folic acid and may interfere with the absorption of iron.

Adverse Reactions

There are no reports of clinical toxicity from daily tea consumption as a beverage. Adverse events include headache, dizziness, and GI symptoms. Hepatotoxicity, including 1 fatality, has been associated with high plasma levels of epigallocatechin gallate or its metabolites.

Toxicology

Multidose pharmacokinetic studies suggest a daily dosage of 800 mg/day of epigallocatechin gallate capsules for up to 4 weeks to be safe and well tolerated. High-dose oral green tea extract and catechins were hepatotoxic in rats.

Local Anesthetic/Vasoconstrictor Precautions

No information available to require special precautions

Effects on Bleeding Caffeine in green tea may have antiplatelet effects

Guggul

Clinical Overview

Uses

Guggul has been used in the traditional Ayurvedic medical system for centuries and has been studied extensively in India. Commercial products are promoted for use in hyperlipidemia; however, clinical studies do not substantiate this claim. Anti-inflammatory and cardiovascular effects are being evaluated, as well as use in cancer, obesity, and diabetes.

Dosing

Clinical trials are lacking to provide dosage guidelines; however, in a US clinical trial of hyperlipidemia, 75 to 150 mg of standardized guggulsterones were administered daily. In a study evaluating the anti-inflammatory effect of guggul, 500 mg of gum guggul was taken 3 times per day.

Contraindications

None identified. Caution may be warranted in patients previously experiencing adverse effects to statins.

Pregnancy/Lactation

Information regarding safety and efficacy in pregnancy and lactation is lacking.

Interactions

None well documented.

Adverse Reactions

Although generally accepted as relatively safe, case reports of adverse events exist. Moderate to severe generalized acute eczematous reactions to oral guggul have been reported, and caution may be warranted. A case report exists of rhabdomyolysis possibly caused by guggul consumption.

Toxicology

Research reveals little information regarding toxicology with the use of guggul.

Local Anesthetic/Vasoconstrictor Precautions

No information available to require special precautions

Effects on Bleeding None reported

Gymnema

Clinical Overview

Uses

The plant has been used in traditional medicine, most notably to control blood glucose. Use as a lipid-lowering agent, for weight loss, and for the inhibition of caries have also been investigated, primarily in rodent studies. However, little to no clinical information is available to support the use of gymnema for any indication.

Dosing

Limited controlled studies exist. Clinical studies investigating antidiabetic effects have typically used 200 or 400 mg extract daily standardized to contain 25% gymnemic acids.

Contraindications

None established.

Pregnancy/Lactation

Information regarding safety and efficacy in pregnancy and lactation is lacking.

Interactions

None well documented.

Adverse Reactions

A case report of hepatotoxicity exists.

Toxicology

Information is lacking.

Local Anesthetic/Vasoconstrictor Precautions No information available to require special precautions

Effects on Bleeding None reported

Hawthorn

Clinical Overview

Uses

Hawthorn may have a role as adjunctive therapy in mild heart failure and exhibits some advantages over digoxin. In more severe cases of congestive heart failure (CHF), its place in therapy is less clear. Studies in animals suggest that hawthorn extracts exert effects on the CNS, including anxiolytic and analgesic action; however, clinical studies are limited. Although limited clinical studies have shown improvement in hyperlipidemia with hawthorn extracts, specific, well-designed trials are needed before hawthorn extracts can be recommended.

Dosing

Trials have evaluated dosages ranging from 160 to 1,800 mg/day standardized extracts (mostly WS 1442) in divided doses over 3 to 24 weeks. A minimum effective dose for adjunctive therapy in mild CHF is suggested to be standardized extract 300 mg daily, and maximum benefit appears after 6 to 8 weeks of therapy. Clinical trials conducted in patients with class II and III CHF found hawthorn extract 900 mg daily to be safe, but not superior to placebo.

Contraindications

Known allergy to members of the rose family.

Pregnancy/Lactation

In the absence of clear data, hawthorn extracts should be avoided in pregnancy and during lactation. Animal studies, however, have not shown any adverse effect on embryonic development.

Interactions

None well documented.

Adverse Reactions

Serious adverse reactions are rarely reported. Mild to moderate dizziness, headache, rash, palpitations, and nausea and other GI symptoms have been reported.

Toxicology

Hawthorn is reportedly toxic in high doses; low doses of hawthorn usually lack adverse effects. No increase in the frequency of fetal malformations or teratogenicity has been found in animal studies.

Local Anesthetic/Vasoconstrictor Precautions No information available to require special precautions

Effects on Bleeding None reported

Holy Basil

Clinical Overview

Uses

Limited evidence suggests potential applications in treating stress, anxiety disorders, diabetes, and cancer. Anti-inflammatory and antimicrobial activities have also been demonstrated. However, few clinical trials have been conducted to support these uses.

Dosing

Limited clinical trials are available to provide dosing recommendations for holy basil.

CNS disorders: 300 mg/day of an ethanolic leaf extract for 30 days was used in a study evaluating use of holy basil for enhancement of cognition. Dosages of 1,000 mg/day for 8 weeks or 1,200 mg/day for 6 weeks were used in studies evaluating the effects of holy basil extract on stress disorders.

Diabetes/Metabolic syndrome: One clinical trial used 2.5 g of the leaves as a dried powder mixed in 200 mL of water daily for 2 months to produce a hypoglycemic effect.

Contraindications

Contraindications have not been identified.

Pregnancy/Lactation

Avoid use. Information regarding safety and efficacy in pregnancy and lactation is lacking. Emmenagogue and abortifacient effects have been reported for the related species Ocimum basilicum.

Interactions

None well documented.

Adverse Reactions

Clinical information is lacking.

Toxicology

No data.

Local Anesthetic/Vasoconstrictor Precautions No information available to require special precautions

Effects on Bleeding None reported

Honeybee Products

Clinical Overview

Uses

Honeybee products have been used topically and internally for hundreds of years worldwide as remedies for a variety of illnesses; however, clinical trials are lacking for most uses. Honey and royal jelly exhibit antibacterial properties, and there is some evidence that honey might have a role in wound healing. Discrepancies among studies evaluating honey for wounds may be due to variations in the source and preparation of the honey. Bee pollen is most often used for its nutritional properties, and although it is nutritionally rich, claims that it enhances everyday and athletic performance have not been reliably verified. Data supporting the use of honeybee products for other indications are not well substantiated.

Dosing

Honey is a common food and there are no dose restrictions on its use. It has been ingested and used topically.

The ideal dose of bee pollen is unknown, with doses varying among products because tablets contain differing amounts. Manufacturers' recommendations on product labeling may provide more guidance.

Clinical trials are generally lacking to recommend dosage for royal jelly. Small clinical trials have used royal jelly 6 to 10 g/day for 14 to 28 days when evaluating the effect on hyperlipidemia.

Contraindications

Honey should be used with caution in infant formulations. Allergy to bee venom is considered a relative contraindication to royal jelly. Other contraindications have not been identified for honey, bee pollen, or royal jelly.

Pregnancy/Lactation

Clinical data regarding safety and efficacy of these products in pregnancy and lactation are lacking. Honey is generally recognized as safe (GRAS) during pregnancy and lactation when used as food.

Interactions
None well documented for honey or bee pollen. Case reports of hematuria due to potentiation of warfarin have been documented with royal jelly.

Adverse Reactions
Allergic reactions may occur to pollen in honey when ingested. Attempts to hyposensitize patients by administering bee pollen may produce severe anaphylaxis and other acute or chronic responses. Although rare, bee pollen can cause serious, sometimes fatal, adverse reactions. Some case reports of acute hepatitis and photosensitivity following ingestion of bee pollen have been reported. In many allergic patients, skin tests are positive for royal jelly. Case reports exist of allergy, acute exacerbation of asthma, anaphylaxis, and death.

Toxicology
Contaminated honey containing botulism spores can poison infants. The American Academy of Pediatrics and the World Health Organization recommend that honey should not be given to an infant younger than 12 months due to the potential for botulism. Honey made from the nectar of poisonous plants can be poisonous. Information on the toxicology of bee pollen or royal jelly is lacking.

Local Anesthetic/Vasoconstrictor Precautions
No information available to require special precautions

Effects on Bleeding None reported

Hops

Clinical Overview

Uses
Hops have been used for flavoring; hops and lupulin have been used as a digestive aid, for mild sedation, diuresis, and treating menstrual problems, but no clinical studies are available to confirm these uses.

Dosing
Hops has been used as a mild sedative or sleep aid, with the dried strobile given in doses of 1.5 to 2 g. An extract combination with valerian, Ze 91019 (ReDormin, Ivel) has been studied at a hops dose of 60 mg for insomnia.

Contraindications
Contraindications have not yet been identified.

Pregnancy/Lactation
Information regarding safety and efficacy in pregnancy and lactation is lacking.

Interactions
None well documented.

Adverse Reactions
There are no reported side effects when used in moderation.

Toxicology
Malignant hyperthermic reactions have been observed in dogs that consumed boiled hops residues. A wide safety margin for humans has been extrapolated from animal experiments.

Local Anesthetic/Vasoconstrictor Precautions
No information available to require special precautions

Effects on Bleeding None reported

Horehound

Clinical Overview

Uses
Clinical studies regarding therapeutic uses of horehound are limited. Research has centered on the potential for use in cardiovascular disease, diabetes, and pain and inflammation; however, no clinical evidence supports the use of horehound in these roles or in cough preparations.

Dosing
Clinical trials are lacking to provide dosing guidance. One clinical study evaluating the effect of horehound in type 2 diabetes used horehound infusions prepared with the leaves of M. vulgare and administered in 1 g envelopes, 3 times a day for 21 days.

Dosages of 4.5 g daily as the crude herb and 30 to 60 mL as pressed juice from the herb have been traditionally used.

Contraindications
Use in pregnancy is contraindicated.

Pregnancy/Lactation
Avoid use. Horehound reportedly has emmenagogue and abortifacient effects.

Interactions
None well documented.

Adverse Reactions
In a small clinical study, nausea, dry mouth, excessive salivation, dizziness, and anorexia were reported by some patients drinking a prepared infusion solution of dry leaves of the plant.

Toxicology
Marrubiin, one of the main constituents of *M. vulgare*, has a median lethal dose (LD_{50}) of 370 mg/kg when administered orally to rats and an LD_{50} of 100 mg/kg when injected in mice; marrubiin was not cytotoxic to any of 66 cell lines tested. *M. vulgare* was given to rats at increasing doses of up to 1,000 mg/kg daily for 3 weeks, with no signs of toxicity. As a flavoring agent and essential oil, horehound has been granted generally recognized as safe (GRAS) status by the US Food and Drug Administration (FDA).

Local Anesthetic/Vasoconstrictor Precautions
No information available to require special precautions

Effects on Bleeding None reported

Horse Chestnut

Clinical Overview

Uses
Oral horse chestnut seed extract is effective in the short-term treatment of mild to moderate long-term venous insufficiency. Other investigations focus on the role of the major component aescin in antiobesity and anti-inflammatory effects, as well as potential cancer treatment. Aescin gel has been evaluated for use in bruising.

Dosing
Aescin 20 to 120 mg taken orally has been used for venous insufficiency and is available in tablet form. Oral tinctures and topical gels containing aescin 2% are also available.

Contraindications
Renal or hepatic impairment may be relative contraindications to the use of aescin or horse chestnut derivatives.

Pregnancy/Lactation
Avoid use. Information regarding safety and efficacy in pregnancy and lactation is lacking.

Interactions
None well documented.

Adverse Reactions
The most commonly cited adverse effects include nausea and stomach discomfort, which may be minimized by the use of film-coated tablets. Other mild and infrequent complaints include headache, dizziness,

and pruritus. Rare cases of allergy and anaphylaxis have been reported.

Toxicology

All parts of plants in the Aesculus family are potentially toxic, especially the seeds (nuts). Horse chestnut has been classified by the Food and Drug Administration (FDA) as an unsafe herb.

Local Anesthetic/Vasoconstrictor Precautions
No information available to require special precautions

Effects on Bleeding Contains esculin which has antithrombotic effects and may increase the risk of bleeding or bruising.

Horseradish

Clinical Overview

Uses

Horseradish has been used internally as a condiment, GI stimulant, diuretic, and a vermifuge, and externally for sciatica and facial neuralgia. However, there are no clinical trials to support any therapeutic use for horseradish. Animal data suggest potential antibacterial and hypotensive effects.

Dosing

Traditional use for colds and respiratory infections was 20 g/day of fresh root. Externally, preparations with 2% mustard oil have been used.

Contraindications

Contraindicated in patients with GI ulcers and in those with kidney impairment. Not recommended for children younger than 4 years of age.

Pregnancy/Lactation

Documented adverse effects. Avoid use. Use should be avoided during pregnancy and lactation because the allylisothiocyanates are toxic mucosal irritants. Horseradish has abortifacient effects.

Interactions

None well documented.

Adverse Reactions

Irritant effects on GI mucosa. External use may cause erythematous rash. Horseradish is part of the cabbage and mustard family; therefore, it may suppress thyroid function. The isothiocyanates may irritate mucous membranes on contact or if inhaled.

Toxicology

Ingestion of large amounts can cause bloody vomiting and diarrhea.

Local Anesthetic/Vasoconstrictor Precautions
No information available to require special precautions

Effects on Bleeding None reported

Horsetail

Clinical Overview

Uses

Horsetail has been used as a diuretic, in the treatment of kidney and bladder ailments, as an astringent to stop bleeding and stimulate healing, as an antitubercular drug, and as a cosmetic component, although there is a lack of clinical trials.

Dosing

A water extract of horsetail was used in a clinical study as a hypoglycemic in type 2 diabetes at 0.33 g/kg via the oral route.

Contraindications

No longer considered safe for use.

Pregnancy/Lactation

Information regarding safety and efficacy in pregnancy and lactation is lacking. Avoid use.

Interactions

None well documented.

Adverse Reactions

No data.

Toxicology

Horsetail is of undefined safety and may be toxic, especially to children. Avoid use during pregnancy.

Local Anesthetic/Vasoconstrictor Precautions
No information available to require special precautions

Effects on Bleeding None reported

5-HTP

Clinical Overview

Uses

Clinical trials of 5-HTP conducted in various conditions have resulted in limited evidence suggesting a place in therapy for anxiety, depression, and neurological conditions in which a serotonin deficiency is a contributory factor. 5-HTP may also be an effective appetite suppressant, but further clinical trials are needed.

Dosing

Recent clinical trials do not provide adequate dosing guidelines. Studies in depression have used 5-HTP 200 to 300 mg/day given in 3 to 4 divided doses to prevent possible nausea.

Contraindications

The potential for serotonin syndrome exists with concomitant use of selective serotonin reuptake inhibitors (SSRIs) or monoamine oxidase inhibitors (MAOIs).

Pregnancy/Lactation

Information regarding safety and efficacy in pregnancy and lactation is lacking.

Interactions

The potential for serotonin syndrome exists with concomitant use of SSRIs or MAOIs. 5-HTP augments the effect of citalopram and clomipramine, while carbidopa increases the bioavailability of 5-HTP.

Adverse Reactions

Nausea and vomiting are the most common dose-related adverse events. Diarrhea, abdominal pain, mild headache, and sleepiness have also been reported.

Toxicology

There is little information on the toxicology of 5-HTP. A possible association with fatal eosinophilia-myalgia syndrome in the 1980s and 1990s has now been attributed to contaminated L-tryptophan.

Local Anesthetic/Vasoconstrictor Precautions
No information available to require special precautions

Effects on Bleeding None reported

Human Chorionic Gonadotropin

Clinical Overview

Uses

Existing evidence does not support the use of human chorionic gonadotropin (hCG) in weight reduction, and the use of hCG for this purpose is not supported by the American Medical Association (AMA) or the American Society of Bariatric Physicians. Homeopathic preparations of hCG do not contain significant amount of the active ingredient, and clinical trials have not been conducted to provide evidence for effect.

Dosing

Recommendations for dosing for indications other than those approved for hCG cannot be made because evidence to support efficacy is lacking.

Contraindications
Precocious puberty, prostatic carcinoma or other androgen-dependent neoplasia, prior allergic reaction to chorionic gonadotropin, and pregnancy.

Pregnancy/Lactation
hCG is contraindicated in pregnant women. Avoid use in lactation.

Interactions
None well documented.

Adverse Reactions
Arterial thromboembolism, headache, irritability and other CNS symptoms, genitourinary effects, and hypersensitivity have been reported.

Toxicology
Defects of forelimbs and the CNS, as well as alterations in sex ratio, have been reported in mice on combined gonadotropin and hCG regimens. No mutagenic effect has been clearly established in humans.

Local Anesthetic/Vasoconstrictor Precautions
No information available to require special precautions

Effects on Bleeding None reported

Huperzine A

Clinical Overview

Uses
Historically, club moss has been used for the treatment of bruises, strains, swelling, rheumatism, and colds, to relax muscles and tendons, and to improve blood circulation. Because of its anticholinesterase activity, huperzine A, a constituent of the whole plant, has been studied for potential use in treating Alzheimer disease and other CNS disorders; however, there is still insufficient evidence to support its routine use.

Dosing
Huperzine A has been studied at oral dosages of 0.2 to 0.4 mg/day for Alzheimer disease.

Contraindications
Contraindications have not been identified.

Pregnancy/Lactation
Information regarding safety and efficacy in pregnancy and lactation is lacking.

Interactions
None well documented.

Adverse Reactions
In clinical trials, cholinergic adverse reactions have been noted, including hyperactivity, nasal obstruction, nausea, vomiting, diarrhea, insomnia, anxiety, dizziness, thirst, and constipation. One trial reported abnormalities in electrocardiogram (ECG) patterns (cardiac ischemia and arrhythmia).

Toxicology
Symptoms of acute toxicity are similar to those of other cholinergic inhibitors and include muscular tremor, drooling, tears, increased bronchial secretions, and incontinence. No mutagenicity or teratogenicity were found in rodent studies.

Local Anesthetic/Vasoconstrictor Precautions
No information available to require special precautions

Effects on Bleeding None reported

Hyssop

Clinical Overview

Uses
Toxic effects of hyssop essential oil limit therapeutic applications. Although no clinical evidence supports use, animal research indicates the potential for use of hyssop extract in diabetes and for its antimicrobial and CNS effects.

Dosing
No clinical evidence is available to determine hyssop dosing recommendations.

Contraindications
Contraindications have not been identified.

Pregnancy/Lactation
Avoid use. Documented adverse effects.

Interactions
None well documented.

Adverse Reactions
Information is limited; however, case reports of seizures exist.

Toxicology
Convulsant toxic effects of the essential oil have been established in rodents.

Local Anesthetic/Vasoconstrictor Precautions
No information available to require special precautions

Effects on Bleeding None reported

Iboga

Clinical Overview

Uses
Iboga has been used ritually as a hallucinogen. Studies suggest that ibogaine, one of the Iboga alkaloids, has potential in the treatment of addiction to several substances. The US Drug Enforcement Agency (DEA) has placed ibogaine into Schedule I of the Controlled Substances Act (CSA).

Dosing
Strict medical supervision is necessary. Ibogaine has been used in single doses of 500 to 800 mg in a clinical study, and 17 mg/kg in a drug dependency treatment center.

Contraindications
Fatalities have been associated with the use of ibogaine; concomitant opioid use and comorbidities (eg, cardiovascular disease, depression, posttraumatic stress disorder, anxiety, stress, schizophrenia, epilepsy, or other imbalances in the autonomic nervous system) increase the risk of life-threatening complications including sudden cardiac death. Ibogaine should only be used under the supervision of an experienced health care provider.

Pregnancy/Lactation
Avoid use. Information regarding the safety and efficacy in pregnancy and lactation is lacking.

Interactions
None well documented.

Adverse Reactions
Mild acute effects occur frequently and include nausea, vomiting, ataxia, tremors, headaches, and mental confusion. Manic episodes lasting 1 to 2 weeks have also been reported and manifested as sleeplessness, irritability, impulsivity, emotional lability, grandiose delusions, rapid tangential speech, aggressive behavior, and suicidal ideation.

Toxicology
Large doses of iboga can induce agitation, hallucinations, vomiting, ataxia, muscle spasms, weakness, seizures, paralysis, arrhythmias, urinary retention, respiratory insufficiency, and cardiac arrest.

Local Anesthetic/Vasoconstrictor Precautions
No information available to require special precautions

Effects on Bleeding None reported

Ipecac

Clinical Overview

Uses

Ipecac has been used as an emetic and treatment for dysentery. It has amebicidal components. It currently is not recommended as an emetic for childhood poisonings. Activated charcoal now is the treatment of choice. Always consult a health care professional or poison control center when an accidental poisoning occurs.

Dosing

Ipecac syrup, which contains total alkaloids123 to 157 mg per 100 mL, has been used to induce vomiting. The usual dose range for the syrup is 10 to 30 mL, yielding a dose of alkaloids of 12 to 48 mg. Do not confuse the syrup with the fluid extract of ipecac, which is 14 times stronger. Cumulative toxicity requires administration of emetine for amebic dysentery in low doses for a short time with intervals of several weeks before further treatment.

Contraindications

Do not administer ipecac when a patient has a decreased level of consciousness or has ingested either a corrosive substance or hydrocarbon with a high aspiration potential.

Pregnancy/Lactation

Documented adverse effects include uterine stimulation. Avoid use.

Interactions

None well documented.

Adverse Reactions

Repeated exposure to powdered ipecac may cause rhinitis or asthma. Emetine can irritate skin if applied topically. Diarrhea, lethargy, drowsiness, and prolonged vomiting may occur.

Toxicology

Ipecac extracts may be highly toxic; do not confuse with syrup of ipecac. Emetine is a cardiotoxin and has been associated with serious cardiotoxicity.

Local Anesthetic/Vasoconstrictor Precautions

No information available to require special precautions

Effects on Bleeding None reported

Jiaogulan

Clinical Overview

Uses

Limited clinical studies have been conducted to support therapeutic applications. Jiaogulan may have a role in the management of type 2 diabetes, fatty liver disease, immune response (such as asthma), and cancer. *G. pentaphyllum* extracts may also have a place in beneficial antioxidant therapy.

Dosing

Clinical information is lacking. Jiaogulan tea (aqueous extract) 6 g/day, in divided doses twice a day 30 minutes before meals, has been studied in 2 clinical trials in patients with type 2 diabetes.

Contraindications

Contraindications have not yet been identified.

Pregnancy/Lactation

Information regarding safety and efficacy in pregnancy and lactation is lacking.

Interactions

None well documented.

Adverse Reactions

Severe nausea and increased bowel movements are possible.

Toxicology

No data available for human toxicity.

Local Anesthetic/Vasoconstrictor Precautions

No information available to require special precautions

Effects on Bleeding None reported

Jojoba

Clinical Overview

Uses

The toxicity of the constituent simmondsin in jojoba seed meal and some oil components limits the likelihood of clinical applications. Jojoba oil is commonly used in dermatological preparations.

Dosing

There is no clinical evidence to guide dosage of jojoba or its oil; it is primarily used as a vehicle for oxidation-sensitive substances in ointments.

Contraindications

Although absolute contraindications have not been identified, jojoba should not be ingested by humans due to potential toxicity.

Pregnancy/Lactation

Information regarding safety and efficacy in pregnancy and lactation is lacking. Adverse toxicological studies in rodents and birds exist.

Interactions

None well documented.

Adverse Reactions

Case reports of contact dermatitis, confirmed by skin patch tests, exist for jojoba oil.

Toxicology

Constituents of jojoba are toxic. Studies demonstrate hematological toxicity, histological abnormalities, and other adverse effects.

Local Anesthetic/Vasoconstrictor Precautions

No information available to require special precautions

Effects on Bleeding None reported

Juniper

Clinical Overview

Uses

Juniper berries have been used as a flavoring for beverages and as a seasoning for cooking, as well as in traditional medicine. Limited clinical evidence exists for efficacy or harm, and use should be limited to low concentrations.

Dosing

There are no clinical studies of juniper to guide dosage.

Contraindications

Avoid in renal impairment.

Pregnancy/Lactation

Avoid use. Possible anti-implantation, abortifacient, and emmenagogue effects based on animal studies.

Interactions

None well documented.

Adverse Reactions

Allergy is common.

Toxicology

Information is limited. Juniper tar and related cade oil should be considered toxic, especially in infants.

Local Anesthetic/Vasoconstrictor Precautions

No information available to require special precautions

Effects on Bleeding None reported

Kava

Clinical Overview

Uses

A number of meta-analyses and systematic reviews of kava use in anxiety have found in favor of kava over placebo, but results are not consistent. Kava has also been studied for effects on cognitive function and for potential cancer applications. However, concerns over hepatotoxicity have limited clinical studies.

Dosing

A maximum daily dose of kavalactones 250 mg is suggested to avoid potential hepatotoxicity. Studies in children are lacking, and use is not recommended.

Contraindications

Kava and kava-containing products are not recommended for use in children or in patients with hepatic disease. Kava should be used cautiously in patients with renal or liver disease, blood disorders, Parkinson disease, or depression.

Pregnancy/Lactation

Documented adverse effects. Avoid use.

Interactions

Kava extracts have been shown to interfere with cytochrome P450 (CYP-450) enzymes; however, specific reports on the metabolism of pharmaceuticals are sparse. Case reports exist on interactions with alprazolam, alcohol, barbiturates, and levodopa. Concomitant administration of kava with haloperidol, risperidone, and metoclopramide, among other drugs, may be associated with adverse reactions.

Adverse Reactions

Heavy kava use may cause a scaly skin rash. A variety of adverse reactions, including visual disturbances, urinary retention, GI discomfort, exacerbation of Parkinson disease, extrapyramidal effects, and rhabdomyolysis, have been reported.

Toxicology

Rare cases of severe liver toxicity have been reported.

Local Anesthetic/Vasoconstrictor Precautions
No information available to require special precautions

Effects on Bleeding None reported

Kudzu

Clinical Overview

Uses

Current interest in kudzu centers on its use as therapy for alcoholism, although sufficient and consistent clinical trials are lacking. Estrogenic activity of kudzu is also being investigated, although clinical trials are limited.

Dosing

Kudzu extract 3 g daily with 25% isoflavone content has been studied in adult heavy drinkers. In another study, 2.4 g kudzu root was given daily.

Contraindications

Contraindications have not yet been identified.

Pregnancy/Lactation

Information regarding safety in pregnancy and lactation is lacking.

Interactions

None well documented.

Adverse Reactions

A few case reports of allergy exist.

Toxicology

Limited data available.

Local Anesthetic/Vasoconstrictor Precautions
No information available to require special precautions

Effects on Bleeding None reported

Lady's Mantle

Clinical Overview

Uses

Lady's mantle has been traditionally used both topically and internally as a treatment for wounds, GI complaints, and female ailments (eg, menstrual or menopausal complaints); however, clinical studies are lacking to support these uses. Animal studies do not support the use of lady's mantle in diabetes, and limited studies of use in wound healing have been conducted.

Dosing

Clinical studies are lacking to support specific dosing recommendations for lady's mantle. A gel made from the leaves has been used topically for mouth ulcers. Oral dosages of 5 to 10 g of the herb in 1 L of water daily, or of 2 to 4 mL of the liquid herb extract have been traditionally used for the treatment of diarrhea.

Contraindications

Contraindications have not been identified.

Pregnancy/Lactation

Avoid use. Information regarding safety and efficacy in pregnancy and lactation is lacking.

Interactions

None well documented.

Adverse Reactions

None known with use at low doses.

Toxicology

No data.

Local Anesthetic/Vasoconstrictor Precautions
No information available to require special precautions

Effects on Bleeding None reported

Laminaria

Clinical Overview

Uses

Laminaria has been used traditionally as a hygroscopic cervical dilator and inducer of labor, and commercial products are available for this purpose. The basal parts of the blades of Laminaria japonica and Laminaria angustata have been used as a hypotensive agent (ne-kombu) in Japanese folk medicine.

Dosing

Clinical trials are lacking to provide dosing information for uses other than mechanical cervical dilation.

Contraindications

Use is contraindicated during pregnancy.

Pregnancy/Lactation

Laminaria dilators have been used to dilate the cervix and to induce labor in abortions. Information on the use of laminaria for other purposes during pregnancy is lacking. Avoid use.

Interactions

None well documented.

Adverse Reactions

There is a risk of laminaria dilators becoming trapped and fragmenting.

Toxicology

Information is lacking.

Local Anesthetic/Vasoconstrictor Precautions
No information available to require special precautions

Effects on Bleeding None reported

L-arginine

Clinical Overview

Uses

L-arginine is a nonessential amino acid that may play an important role in the treatment of cardiovascular disease due to its antiatherogenic, anti-ischemic, antiplatelet, and antithrombotic properties. It has been promoted as a growth stimulant and as a treatment for erectile dysfunction in men.

Dosing

L-arginine has been studied at oral doses of 6 to 30 g/day for a variety of conditions. Parenteral, enteral, intramural, and topical formulations have been used.

Contraindications

Absolute contraindications have not yet been identified. L-arginine is not recommended in patients following an acute myocardial infarction.

Pregnancy/Lactation

Specific information regarding safety and efficacy in pregnancy and lactation is lacking, although several trials have been conducted in pregnant women without notable ill effects.

Interactions

L-arginine has unpredictable effects on insulin and cholesterol-lowering agents. L-arginine may potentiate the effects of isosorbide mononitrate and other nitric oxide donors, such as glyceryl trinitrate and sodium nitroprusside.

Adverse Reactions

L-arginine has few reported adverse reactions. Nausea and diarrhea have been reported infrequently. Bitter taste may occur with higher doses. Due to its vasodilatory effects, hypotension may occur. Intravenous (IV) preparations containing L-arginine hydrochloride have a high chloride content that may increase the risk for metabolic acidosis in patients with electrolyte imbalances. Hyperkalemia and elevations in serum urea nitrogen (BUN) levels may occur in patients with renal and/or hepatic impairment.

Toxicology

High concentrations of nitric oxide are considered toxic to brain tissue.

Local Anesthetic/Vasoconstrictor Precautions

No information available to require special precautions

Effects on Bleeding None reported

Lavender

Clinical Overview

Uses

Lavender has been used for restlessness, insomnia, anxiety, diabetes, GI distress, perineal discomfort following childbirth, chemoprevention, as an insect repellant, and as a food flavoring agent. However, there are limited clinical trials to support any therapeutic use for lavender.

Dosing

Aromatherapy for a bath: 6 drops (120 mg) added to 20 L of bath water or 20 to 100 g of the dried herb in 20 L of bath water.

Inhalational aromatherapy: 2 to 4 drops in 2 to 3 cups (480 to 720 mL) of boiling water or used in an aromatic diffuser and inhaled.

Massage: 1 to 4 drops/Tbsp (15 mL) of base or carrier oil may be used or it may be mixed with other oils.

Tea: 1 to 2 tsp (5 to 10 mL) of lavender per cup (240 mL) of water.

Oil for ingestion: 1 to 4 drops (20 mg to 80 mg), often given on a sugar cube.

Contraindications

Cautious use or avoidance is warranted in patients with known allergy/hypersensitivity to lavender.

Pregnancy/Lactation

Information regarding safety and efficacy in pregnancy and lactation is lacking. Lavender may possess emmenagogue properties, and excessive internal use should be avoided in pregnancy.

Interactions

CNS depressants and anticonvulsants may increase or potentiate narcotic and sedative effects when given in combination with lavender-containing products. Anticoagulants may increase the risk of bleeding when given concomitantly with lavender. Lavender may also cause additive cholesterol-lowering effects when given along with other drugs that lower cholesterol (eg, statins, nicotinic acid, fibric acid derivatives).

Adverse Reactions

Lavender may cause allergic contact dermatitis and photosensitization. Large oral doses have been associated with nausea, vomiting, and anorexia. Additionally, 3 case reports suggest a possible association between topical application of lavender and tea tree oils and prepubertal gynecomastia.

Toxicology

A case report describes an accidental ingestion of lavandin resulting in central nervous system depression in an 18-month-old child. The child's neurological state normalized within 6 hours of ingestion.

Local Anesthetic/Vasoconstrictor Precautions

No information available to require special precautions

Effects on Bleeding None reported

Lecithin

Clinical Overview

Uses

Lecithin is used for its emulsifying properties in the food, pharmaceutical, and cosmetic industries. Proposed pharmacological use of lecithin includes treatment for hypercholesterolemia, neurologic disorders, manic disorders, and liver ailments. It has also been used to modify the immune system by activating specific and nonspecific defense systems. However, no quality clinical trials exist to support lecithin's use for these indications.

Dosing

Studies of lecithin in cognitive impairment have used a wide range of dosages, from 1 to 35 g daily. In a study of patients with bipolar disorder, 10 mg given 3 times daily was found to improve symptoms of mania.

Contraindications

Contraindications have not yet been identified.

Pregnancy/Lactation

Information regarding safety and efficacy in pregnancy and lactation is lacking.

Interactions

None well documented.

Adverse Reactions

Adverse effects are usually not associated with lecithin. However, there have been reports of anorexia, nausea, sweating, increased salivation, other GI effects, and hepatitis.

Toxicology

Information regarding toxicology with the use of this lecithin is limited.

Local Anesthetic/Vasoconstrictor Precautions No information available to require special precautions

Effects on Bleeding None reported

Lemon Balm

Clinical Overview

Uses

Primary interest in lemon balm surrounds its effects on the central nervous system. One small study demonstrated decreased stress and agitation in patients with dementia and Alzheimer disease. Lemon balm cream has shown some efficacy in herpes virus lesions in a few small placebo-controlled trials.

Dosing

Crude lemon balm herb is typically dosed at 1.5 to 4.5 g/day. Doses of 600 to 1,600 mg extract have been studied in trials. A standardized preparation of lemon balm (80 mg) and valerian extract (160 mg) has been given 2 or 3 times/day as a sleep aid, and has also been studied in children. A 1% extract cream has been studied as a topical agent for treatment of herpes virus lesions.

Contraindications

Contraindications have not yet been identified.

Pregnancy/Lactation

Information regarding safety and efficacy in pregnancy and lactation is lacking.

Interactions

None well documented.

Adverse Reactions

Clinical trials generally report no adverse reactions.

Toxicology

Research reveals little or no information regarding toxicology with the use of this product.

Local Anesthetic/Vasoconstrictor Precautions No information available to require special precautions

Effects on Bleeding None reported

Lemongrass

Clinical Overview

Uses

Lemongrass is used as a fragrance and flavoring and for a wide variety of ailments in folk medicine. However, clinical trials are lacking to support these uses. Limited studies have demonstrated antifungal and insecticide efficacy, as well as potential anticarcinogenic activity, while suggested hypotensive and hypoglycemic actions have not been confirmed.

Dosing

Information from clinical trials is lacking.

Contraindications

Contraindications have not yet been identified.

Pregnancy/Lactation

Information regarding safety and efficacy in pregnancy and lactation is lacking. Avoid use.

Interactions

None well documented.

Adverse Reactions

Rare cases of hypersensitivity have been reported. Toxic alveolitis has been associated with inhalation of the oil.

Toxicology

Lemongrass is considered to be of low toxicity at low doses.

Local Anesthetic/Vasoconstrictor Precautions No information available to require special precautions

Effects on Bleeding None reported

Licorice

Clinical Overview

Uses

Used historically for GI complaints, licorice is primarily used as a flavoring agent in the tobacco and candy industries and to some extent in the pharmaceutical and beverage industries today. The chemical compounds found in licorice have been investigated as cancer therapy as well as for their antiviral activity.

Dosing

Licorice root has been used in daily doses from 2 to 15 g for ulcer and gastritis. Higher doses given for extended periods of time may pose a risk of hyperkalemia. The acceptable daily intake (ADI) for glycyrrhizin is suggested to be 0.2 mg/kg/day.

Contraindications

Contraindications have not yet been identified.

Pregnancy/Lactation

Use during pregnancy should be avoided. Licorice exhibits estrogenic activity and has reputed abortifacient effects. There is no clinical evidence to support the use of licorice tea as a galactogogue.

Interactions

Glycyrrhizin in licorice may alter prednisolone plasma concentrations and may increase the risk of digitalis toxicity.

Adverse Reactions

At lower dosages or normal consumption levels, few adverse reactions are evident. Ocular effects and hypersensitivity have been described. Hypertension and hypokalemia are recognized effects of excessive licorice consumption.

Toxicology

Toxicity from excessive licorice ingestion is well established. Mutagenicity and teratogenicity studies have generally shown no ill effects.

Local Anesthetic/Vasoconstrictor Precautions No information available to require special precautions

Effects on Bleeding None reported

Lobelia

Clinical Overview

Uses

L. inflata and its major alkaloid, lobeline, have been used in smoking cessation programs and have been proposed for treatment of other drug dependencies; however, clinical evidence is limited.

Dosing

There is no recent clinical evidence to support the use of lobelia. The sale of OTC lobeline products for smoking cessation was prohibited by the US Food and Drug Administration (FDA) in 1993.

Traditional use of the leaf (eg, as an expectorant) suggests 100 mg of dry herb up to 3 times a day. However, there are no clinical trials to support this use. Doses of 0.6 to 1 g leaf are considered toxic, while 4 g of leaf is considered to be fatal.

Contraindications

Contraindications have not been defined; however, the sale of lobelia OTC products for smoking cessation is prohibited by the FDA due to a lack of efficacy and safety evidence.

Pregnancy/Lactation

Avoid use. Documented adverse effects, including loss of uterine tone and lack of safety evidence.

Interactions

None well documented.

Adverse Reactions

Lobelia and lobeline are capable of inducing nausea, vomiting, tremors, and dizziness at high doses. Lobelia alkaloids are cardioactive, and cardiotoxicities, including hypotension, tachycardia, and convulsion, have been reported. Contact dermatitis has also been reported.

Toxicology

Toxic dosages of the plant have been described: 1 g of leaf is toxic, while 4 g of leaf is considered to be a fatal dose. The alkaloid lobeline was not genotoxic or mutagenic in 1 study, and liver and kidney biochemistry in mice appeared unaffected.

Local Anesthetic/Vasoconstrictor Precautions

No information available to require special precautions

Effects on Bleeding None reported

Lycopene

Clinical Overview

Uses

Scientific literature documents lycopene's antioxidant activity and its use in cancer prevention (breast and prostate), as well as its use in the prevention of cardiovascular disease.

Dosing

Lycopene administered as a pure compound has been studied in clinical trials at dosages of 8 to 75 mg/day. Lycopene is primarily available in capsule and softgel form, with dosage guidelines from manufacturers ranging from 10 to 30 mg taken twice daily with meals. Lycopene is also incorporated in multivitamin and multimineral products.

Contraindications

Avoid with hypersensitivity to lycopene or to any of its food sources, especially tomatoes. Tomato-based products are acidic and may irritate stomach ulcers.

Pregnancy/Lactation

Information regarding safety and efficacy in pregnancy and lactation is lacking. The amount of lycopene in food is assumed to be safe. Tomato consumption increases lycopene concentration in the breast milk and plasma of lactating women.

Interactions

None well documented.

Adverse Reactions

In general, tomato-based products and lycopene supplements are well tolerated. Some GI complaints (eg, diarrhea, dyspepsia, gas, nausea, vomiting) are documented. One trial reported a cancer-related hemorrhage in a patient taking lycopene, but causality was unclear.

Toxicology

None known.

Local Anesthetic/Vasoconstrictor Precautions

No information available to require special precautions

Effects on Bleeding None reported

Maitake

Clinical Overview

Uses

Maitake has been used for its antiviral action and to treat diabetes, high blood pressure, cholesterol, and obesity. Maitake has been studied to a limited extent for treating cancer; however, the information available is not sufficient to recommend it for this use.

Dosing

Disease-prevention doses of commercial preparations range from 12 to 25 mg of the extract and 200 to 250 mg or 500 to 2,500 mg of whole powder daily. A trial among HIV-positive patients used doses of 6 g/day whole powder or 20 mg purified extract with 4 g whole maitake powder.

Contraindications

Contraindications have not been identified.

Pregnancy/Lactation

Information regarding safety and efficacy during pregnancy and lactation is lacking.

Interactions

None well documented.

Adverse Reactions

Information is limited.

Toxicology

Information is limited.

Local Anesthetic/Vasoconstrictor Precautions

No information available to require special precautions

Effects on Bleeding None reported

Marijuana

Clinical Overview

Uses

The use of medical marijuana for the management of chemotherapy-induced nausea, glaucoma, spasticity in multiple sclerosis, and neuropathic pain has been clinically demonstrated to some extent. Undesirable adverse reactions limit its applications, and therapeutic use may be limited to either concomitant therapy or when conventional therapy has failed. Clinical studies in the United States have been limited by legal factors.

Dosing

Clinical studies use a wide range of preparations and usually allow dosage titration for effect, making standard dosage recommendations difficult to determine. A large, multicenter trial used initial oral doses of delta-9-tetrahydrocannabinol (THC) 5 mg daily, self-titrated up to THC 25 mg daily for up to 52 weeks in multiple sclerosis. Estimates of relative efficacy for the treatment of pain with THC compared with codeine are THC 10 mg to codeine 60 mg.

Contraindications

Contraindications have not been identified. The benefits versus risks of the use of cannabis extracts should be carefully weighed in individuals with psychosocial disorders.

Pregnancy/Lactation

Avoid use. Information regarding safety and efficacy in pregnancy and lactation is lacking. In retrospective studies, marijuana had a modest effect on fetal growth. THC crosses the placental barrier and is excreted in breast milk.

Interactions

Marijuana may interact with the following agents: Alcohol, anticholinergic agents, azelastine, CNS depressants, cocaine, droperidol, hydroxyzine, magnesium sulfate, methotrimeprazine, metyrosine, mirtazapine, paraldehyde, perampanel, pramipexole, ropinirole, rotigotine, SSRIs, sodium oxybate, sympathomimetics, and zolpidem.

Adverse Reactions

The use of medical marijuana or cannabinoid preparations is mainly considered safe and devoid of major adverse reactions. Impairments in cognitive and motor function may limit its use.

Toxicology

There is a lack of consensus as to the risk of lung cancer from smoked medical marijuana, or the risk of psychotic events from oral cannabinoid consumption. All risk factors should be considered in the context of applications for medical marijuana in intractable diseases. The risks of long-term toxicity due to nonmedical (recreational) cannabis include increased incidence of psychotic, respiratory, and cardiovascular events, as well as cancers of the lung, head and neck, brain, cervix, prostate, and testis.

Local Anesthetic/Vasoconstrictor Precautions
No information available to require special precautions

Effects on Bleeding None reported

Maritime Pine

Clinical Overview

Uses

Pine bark extract demonstrates antioxidant and anti-inflammatory actions and has been studied for a wide range of clinical conditions, including chronic venous insufficiency, cardiovascular conditions, and erectile dysfunction. However, many clinical studies have been limited in size, with nonrandomized or open-label designs conducted by a limited pool of researchers.

Dosing

Doses of pine bark extract have been studied in clinical trials, most commonly at 150 mg of Pycnogenol per day.

Contraindications

Contraindications have not been identified.

Pregnancy/Lactation

Information regarding safety and efficacy during pregnancy and lactation is lacking.

Interactions

None well documented.

Adverse Reactions

Pine bark extract is generally well tolerated, with minor gastric discomfort, dizziness, nausea, and headache occasionally noted. Clinical studies using Pycnogenol report no clinically important adverse events.

Toxicology

Pine bark extract is generally recognized as safe (GRAS), based on data from clinical trials. Limited toxicological data are available.

Local Anesthetic/Vasoconstrictor Precautions
No information available to require special precautions

Effects on Bleeding May see increased bleeding due to inhibition of platelet aggregation

Marshmallow

Clinical Overview

Uses

A. officinalis has been traditionally used for cough, inflammation of the mouth and stomach, and peptic ulcers. It appears to have antimicrobial and anti-inflammatory properties and may be used topically to increase epithelialization of wounds. However, there are no recent clinical trials to support these uses.

Dosing

Root: 6 g/day.

Leaf: 10 g/day.

Marshmallow syrup: 10 g/day.

Topical: 5 to 10 g in an ointment or cream base or 5% powdered marshmallow leaf applied 3 times daily.

Gargle: 2 g soaked in 240 mL of cold water for 2 hours then gargled. Hot water should not be used.

Contraindications

Contraindications have not been identified.

Pregnancy/Lactation

Avoid use. Information regarding safety and efficacy in pregnancy and lactation is lacking.

Interactions

Oral medications: When taken with other oral medications, marshmallow may delay the absorption of the other medications.

Oral hypoglycemic agents/Insulin: Due to potential additive hypoglycemic effects, marshmallow should be used cautiously in patients receiving oral hypoglycemic agents and insulin.

Topical corticosteroids: Marshmallow may enhance the effects of topical corticosteroids. Use caution.

Aminoglycosides: Use caution or avoid use of marshmallow in patients receiving aminoglycosides such as gentamicin.

Adverse Reactions

Anecdotal evidence suggests potential allergic reactions and hypoglycemia.

Toxicology

The acute median lethal dose (LD_{50}) of A. officinalis in mice was greater than 5,000 mg/kg.

Local Anesthetic/Vasoconstrictor Precautions
No information available to require special precautions

Effects on Bleeding None reported

Mastic

Clinical Overview

Uses

The pharmacology and medicinal use of mastic is diverse. The resin has been used in cancer, infection, surgical wound adhesion, and ulcers. Studies also document its use as an antioxidant and an insecticide, and for treatment of high cholesterol, Crohn disease, diabetes, and hypertension. However, clinical trials to support these uses are limited.

Dosing

Mastic resin has been studied as a treatment for ulcers at a dosage of 1 g daily. Various commercial products are available including Mastika, which contains mastic gum 250 mg in capsule form. The manufacturer's dosage guidelines are 4 capsules by mouth before bed or on an empty stomach for 4 weeks, followed by a maintenance dosage of 2 capsules daily to maintain GI health.

Contraindications

Avoid use with hypersensitivity to any ingredients of mastic gum as well as with pollen hypersensitivity.

Pregnancy/Lactation

Information regarding safety and efficacy in pregnancy and lactation is lacking.

Interactions

None well documented.

Adverse Reactions

Most adverse reactions are associated with hypersensitivity to the plant or to allergic reactions.

Toxicology

Most toxicity involves allergic reactions.

Local Anesthetic/Vasoconstrictor Precautions
No information available to require special precautions

Effects on Bleeding None reported

Meadowsweet

Clinical Overview

Uses

Meadowsweet has been used for colds, respiratory problems, acid indigestion, peptic ulcers, arthritis and rheumatism, skin diseases, and diarrhea.

Dosing

Doses of 2.5 to 3.5 g/day of flower and 4 to 5 g of herb are considered conventional; however, no clinical trials support the safety or efficacy of these dosages. A tea may be prepared from 4 to 6 g of the dried herb and taken 3 times daily.

Contraindications

Patients with salicylate or sulfite sensitivity. Use with caution in patients with asthma.

Pregnancy/Lactation

Documented adverse effects. Uteroactivity from meadowsweet has been observed in vitro; avoid administration during pregnancy and lactation.

Interactions

Because meadowsweet contains salicylates, it may increase the risk of bleeding when given concomitantly with antiplatelet or anticoagulant drugs, with nonsteroidal anti-inflammatory drugs (NSAIDs), or with any alternative medicines with antiplatelet properties.

Adverse Reactions

Meadowsweet may cause GI bleeding.

Toxicology

Few toxic events have been reported.

Local Anesthetic/Vasoconstrictor Precautions

No information available to require special precautions

Effects on Bleeding Limited evidence suggests an anticoagulant effect *in vitro* and *in vivo* by meadowsweet flowers and seeds. Clinical relevance of this effect is unknown. There are no current published reports of any anticoagulant effect in patients taking meadowsweet.

Melatonin

Clinical Overview

Uses

A large amount of clinical trial data exists to support melatonin's role in reducing sleep onset latency in many sleep-related disorders in both adults and children. Evidence is less clear for improvements in sleep duration or quality. Clinical trial data suggest that melatonin may increase survival rates in solid tumor cancers and decrease the adverse effects of chemotherapy. Increased healing rates in gastric and duodenal ulcers have been found in a small number of studies when melatonin was used as adjunctive therapy. Treatment of infertility, hypertension, anxiety, headache, and tinnitus has also been studied.

Dosing

Adjunctive therapy in cancer: Dosages of up to 20 mg/day have been used in trials.

Insomnia: 3 to 5 mg daily in the evening over 4 weeks. Independent studies have not yet clarified the efficacy of sustained-release preparations.

Jet lag: In general, lower doses (0.5 to 2 mg) preflight and higher doses (5 mg) postflight over a period of up to 4 days appear to be adequate.

Pediatric: Melatonin 2 to 5 mg has been used in children

Contraindications

Until it is studied more thoroughly, melatonin is contraindicated for patients with an autoimmune disease.

Pregnancy/Lactation

Information regarding safety and efficacy in pregnancy and lactation is lacking.

Interactions

Melatonin has been used in many conditions as an adjunct to standard therapy with few reports of interactions. Caffeine and fluvoxamine may increase the effects of melatonin. Exogenous melatonin may potentiate the effects of warfarin.

Adverse Reactions

Possible adverse effects include dizziness, enuresis, excessive daytime somnolence, headache, nausea, and transient depression. Drowsiness may be experienced within 30 minutes after taking melatonin and may persist for approximately 1 hour; as a result, melatonin may affect driving ability.

Toxicology

Studies are limited. There is little or no evidence of major toxicities with melatonin, even at high doses.

Local Anesthetic/Vasoconstrictor Precautions

No information available to require special precautions

Effects on Bleeding None reported

Methylsulfonylmethane (MSM)

Clinical Overview

Uses

MSM is commonly used for osteoarthritis, but may also benefit in alleviating GI upset, musculoskeletal pain, and allergies; boosting the immune system; and fighting antimicrobial infection. Clinical trials are needed to verify these potential uses.

Dosing

MSM commonly is given as 2 to 6 g/day in 2 to 3 divided doses for arthritis and other joint conditions.

Contraindications

Contraindications have not been identified.

Pregnancy/Lactation

Information regarding safety and efficacy in pregnancy and lactation in humans is lacking.

Interactions

None well documented.

Adverse Reactions

No conclusive data on adverse reactions with MSM have been reported.

Toxicology

No toxicity was noted in animal studies.

Local Anesthetic/Vasoconstrictor Precautions

No information available to require special precautions

Effects on Bleeding None reported

Milk Thistle

Clinical Overview

Uses

Although sufficient evidence from prospective clinical trial data is lacking, studies suggest potential applications for silymarin (a flavonoid lignan complex from milk thistle) in treating alcohol-related hepatitis, toxicity due to Amanita mushroom poisoning, diabetes, and cancer.

Dosing

Oral consumption of milk thistle (standardized to 70% to 80% silymarin) at 420 mg/day in divided doses is considered safe for up to 41 months based on clinical trial data. One source suggests 12 to 15 g of drug fruits or 200 to 400 mg of silymarin extract as effective doses. Higher doses have been used in clinical trials.

Contraindications

Allergy to any plant in the Asteraceae family. Avoid use of aboveground parts of the plant in women with hormone-sensitive conditions due to the extract's possible estrogenic effects. These conditions include breast, uterine, and ovarian cancers, endometriosis, and uterine fibroids.

Pregnancy/Lactation

Avoid use because information is limited. Use in pregnant and breastfeeding women has been reported in limited clinical studies without apparent ill-effect, but further data are needed.

Interactions

Milk thistle should be used with caution at high doses.

Adverse Reactions

In most clinical trials, the incidence of adverse reactions was approximately equal in milk thistle and control groups. No serious adverse events were reported at recommended dosages. The most common effects after oral ingestion were brief GI disturbances.

Toxicology

There are no documented milk thistle toxicities in humans, and toxicity appears to be low in laboratory animals.

Local Anesthetic/Vasoconstrictor Precautions

No information available to require special precautions

Effects on Bleeding None reported

Mistletoe

Clinical Overview

Uses

Mistletoe has been used to treat cancer, although there is a lack of quality clinical trials and no evidence of an effect. Further study is needed. In folk medicine, it has been used for its cardiovascular properties. Clinical efficacy has not been established. Injectable mistletoe extract is widely used in Europe but is not licensed for use in the United States.

Dosing

Crude mistletoe fruit or herb is used to make a tea to treat hypertension at a dosage of 10 g/day. There are a number of proprietary extracts containing low levels of mistletoe lectin-I (ML-I) used as adjuvant cancer therapies. These extracts usually are given by intravenous (IV) or subcutaneous injection at dosages of 0.1 to 30 mg several times per week. Mistletoe preparations, produced according to anthroposophical methods, are given in incrementally increasing dosages depending on the patient's general condition and response to the injection. Use in pediatric patients has been reported. The pharmacokinetics in healthy adults has been determined.

Contraindications

Data are limited. Use of mistletoe extracts in patients with primary or secondary brain tumors, leukemia, or malignant lymphoma is contraindicated.

Pregnancy/Lactation

Mistletoe contains toxic constituents. Avoid use during pregnancy or lactation.

Interactions

None well documented.

Adverse Reactions

Local reactions following injection include redness, itching, inflammation, and induration at the injection site. Systemic reactions include mild fever or flu-like symptoms. Anaphylaxis has been reported.

Toxicology

Poison centers report toxicity of the whole plant, but especially mistletoe berries. The use of preparations standardized to small doses of ML-I or depleted of lectins may reduce toxicity.

Local Anesthetic/Vasoconstrictor Precautions

No information available to require special precautions

Effects on Bleeding None reported

Muira Puama

Clinical Overview

Uses

P. olacoides is used as a tonic for neuromuscular problems. A root decoction is used externally in massages and baths for paralysis and beriberi. Oral use of tea made from the roots for sexual impotence, rheumatism, and GI problems has been noted. Muira puama is currently promoted as a male aphrodisiac or as a treatment for impotence.

Dosing

Muira puama leaves, stem, and roots typically are used at a dose of 0.5 to 1.5 g/day, although there are no clinical studies supporting this dose.

Contraindications

Contraindications have not yet been identified.

Pregnancy/Lactation

Information regarding safety and efficacy in pregnancy and lactation is lacking.

Interactions

None well documented.

Adverse Reactions

Research reveals little or no information about adverse reactions of muira puama.

Toxicology

Muira puama does not appear to have the serious side effect potential of yohimbine.

Local Anesthetic/Vasoconstrictor Precautions

No information available to require special precautions

Effects on Bleeding None reported

Mullein

Clinical Overview

Uses

Although mullein has been used traditionally, therapeutic applications have not been defined by clinical studies. Animal data has investigated potential antimicrobial, cytotoxic, and anti-inflammatory properties.

Dosing

No recent clinical evidence supports specific dosage of mullein; however, traditional uses of the herb suggest 3 to 4 g of flowers daily and 15 to 30 mL of fresh leaf or 2 to 3 g of dry leaf.

Contraindications

Contraindications have not been identified.

Pregnancy/Lactation

Information regarding safety and efficacy in pregnancy and lactation is lacking.

Interactions

None well documented.

Adverse Reactions

Information is limited. Occupational airborne dermatitis has been reported for both American and European mullein.

Toxicology

Information is limited.

Local Anesthetic/Vasoconstrictor Precautions
No information available to require special precautions
Effects on Bleeding None reported

Nettles

Clinical Overview

Uses

Nettles are primarily used in the management of benign prostatic hyperplasia (BPH), diabetes, and arthritis. However, clinical trials are limited.

Dosing

Clinical trials for BPH have used aqueous extracts of U. dioica root in dosages of 360 mg daily over 6 months and methanol root extract in dosages of 600 to 1,200 mg daily for 6 to 9 weeks. Dosages of 600 mg of freeze-dried nettle leaf have been used in a clinical trial for allergic rhinitis. Standardization of commercial preparations is lacking.

Contraindications

Due to the effects on androgen and estrogen metabolism, nettle preparations are contraindicated in pregnancy and lactation and should not be used in children younger than 12 years.

Pregnancy/Lactation

Avoid use. Adverse effects have been documented.

Interactions

None well documented.

Adverse Reactions

Nettles are primarily known for their ability to induce acute urticaria following contact with exposed skin. Radix urticae extracts and other nettle preparations are generally well tolerated; minor and transient gastric effects, including diarrhea, gastric pain, and nausea, have been reported.

Toxicology

The possibility of oral toxicity with nettle preparations is considered low. Mutagenicity and carcinogenicity studies using the aqueous extract have been negative.

Local Anesthetic/Vasoconstrictor Precautions
No information available to require special precautions
Effects on Bleeding None reported

Nutmeg

Clinical Overview

Uses

Nutmeg and mace, widely accepted as flavoring agents, have been used in higher doses for their aphrodisiac and psychoactive properties.

Dosing

There are no clinical trials to support therapeutic dosing. Consumption of nutmeg at 1 to 2 mg/kg body weight was reported to induce CNS effects. Toxic overdose occurred at a 5 g dose.

Contraindications

Contraindications have not been identified. The excessive use of nutmeg or mace is not recommended in people with psychiatric conditions.

Pregnancy/Lactation

Generally recognized as safe when used in food as a flavoring agent. Safety for doses above those found in foods is unproven; avoid because of possible abortifacient effects.

Interactions

None well documented.

Adverse Reactions

Allergy, contact dermatitis, and asthma have been reported.

Toxicology

CNS excitation with anxiety/fear, cutaneous flushing, decreased salivation, GI symptoms, and tachycardia. Acute psychosis and anticholinergic-like episodes have been documented; death has rarely been reported following the ingestion of large doses of nutmeg.

Local Anesthetic/Vasoconstrictor Precautions
No information available to require special precautions
Effects on Bleeding None reported

Octacosanol

Clinical Overview

Uses

Octacosanol, which has been studied mainly as a constituent of policosanol (see Policosanol monograph), may have a role to play in the management of dyslipidemia and may achieve antiplatelet effects similar to those of aspirin. Although octacosanol has been protective in rats with induced parkinsonism, clinical studies in humans have not documented these effects. Clinical trials are lacking to support claims of enhanced athletic performance due to supplemental octacosanol.

Dosing

Limited clinical trials have been conducted with octacosanol. In one pharmacokinetic study, octacosanol 30 mg daily for 4 weeks did not result in measurable serum concentration changes, whereas octacosanol 50 mg was detected in the serum within 8 hours.

Contraindications

Contraindications have not been identified.

Pregnancy/Lactation

Information regarding safety and efficacy in pregnancy and lactation is lacking.

Interactions

None well documented.

Adverse Reactions

Limited clinical trials have been conducted with octacosanol; however, one surveillance study found long-term tolerability with policosanol supplementation.

Toxicology

No data.

Local Anesthetic/Vasoconstrictor Precautions
No information available to require special precautions
Effects on Bleeding None reported

Oleander

Clinical Overview

Uses

Oleander has been used in the treatment of cardiac illness, asthma, diabetes mellitus, corns, scabies, cancer, and epilepsy. However, in none of these conditions is there good evidence for use.

Dosing

There is no clinical evidence to support specific doses of oleander. Extreme caution should be used because of its acute cardiotoxicity.

Contraindications

No longer considered safe.

Pregnancy/Lactation

Information regarding safety and efficacy in pregnancy and lactation is lacking. Avoid use.

Interactions

None well documented.

Adverse Reactions

Phytodermatitis caused by contact with oleander has been reported frequently.

Toxicology

Oleander is extremely toxic. Major toxicity includes disturbances in heart rhythm and death. Other signs of toxicity include pain in the oral cavity, nausea, emesis, abdominal pain, cramping, and diarrhea.

Local Anesthetic/Vasoconstrictor Precautions

No information available to require special precautions

Effects on Bleeding None reported

Olive Leaf

Clinical Overview

Uses

Interest in olive leaf use centers on antioxidant and antiviral activity, as well as its possible role in diabetes and cardiovascular conditions. However, clinical trials do not support its use for any indication.

Dosing

Traditional dosages of olive leaf include 7 to 8 g of dry leaf in 150 mL water. In 1 clinical trial, patients with stage 1 hypertension were administered 500 mg of olive leaf extract twice daily for 8 weeks. A clinical trial in overweight men used oleuropein 51.1 mg and hydroxytyrosol 9.7 mg daily for 12 weeks.

Contraindications

Contraindications have not been identified. Caution may be warranted in hepatic disease.

Pregnancy/Lactation

Information regarding safety and efficacy during pregnancy and lactation is lacking.

Interactions

None well documented.

Adverse Reactions

None well documented. Diabetic patients should be supervised carefully because of potential hypoglycemic effects.

Toxicology

Information is limited.

Local Anesthetic/Vasoconstrictor Precautions

No information available to require special precautions

Effects on Bleeding None reported

Onion

Clinical Overview

Uses

Onion has potential in treating cardiovascular disease, hyperglycemia, and stomach cancer, although few quality clinical trials are available to support these uses. Topical preparations have been evaluated for the prevention of surgical scarring with varying results.

Dosing

Clinical trials are lacking to provide dosage recommendations. Average daily doses of 50 g of fresh onion, 50 g of fresh onion juice, or 20 g of dried onion have been suggested. Topical onion extract gels have been used in studies evaluating the effect on scarring and are generally applied 3 times daily.

Contraindications

Contraindications have not been identified.

Pregnancy/Lactation

Generally recognized as safe when used as food. Avoid dosages above those found in foods because safety is unproven.

Interactions

None well documented.

Adverse Reactions

Few reported.

Toxicology

Information is limited.

Local Anesthetic/Vasoconstrictor Precautions

No information available to require special precautions

Effects on Bleeding None reported

Pantothenic Acid

Clinical Overview

Uses

Clinical studies are limited. Pantothenic acid and its derivatives may have a role in the management of dyslipidemia and in wound healing.

Dosing

The US recommended dietary allowance (RDA) for pantothenic acid in nutritional supplements and foods is age dependent and ranges from 0.2 mg/kg in infants to 5 mg in adults. The RDA during pregnancy and lactation is slightly higher, at 6 and 7 mg daily, respectively.

Clinical studies have used pantethine 600 to 1200 mg/day for dyslipidemia.

Contraindications

Avoid use if hypersensitivity to pantothenic acid exists.

Pregnancy/Lactation

Pantothenic acid has been assigned US Food and Drug Administration (FDA) Pregnancy Category A (studies have failed to demonstrate risk). When dosed above the recommended dietary allowance (6 to 7 mg/day), pantothenic acid is designated Category C.

Interactions

None well documented. Caution may be warranted with concomitant use of biotin.

Adverse Reactions

In high doses, pantothenic acid may inhibit the absorption of biotin produced by the microflora in the large intestine. Diarrhea may occur with large doses of pantothenic acid. Allergic contact dermatitis has been reported with topical use of dexpanthenol.

Toxicology

A tolerable upper intake level for pantothenic acid has not been set because reports of adverse effects are lacking. An oral median lethal dose of 10 g/kg for mice has been reported.

Local Anesthetic/Vasoconstrictor Precautions

No information available to require special precautions

Effects on Bleeding None reported

Papaya

Clinical Overview

Uses

In some developing countries, the traditional use of papaya is being investigated as an alternative to standard treatments for a range of ailments. C. papaya has a wide range of purported medicinal properties including antiseptic, antimicrobial, antiparasitic, anti-inflammatory, antihypertensive, diuretic, antihyperlipidemic, antidiabetic, and contraceptive activity. While there are only limited data to support most of these uses, there is some evidence for use in healing decubitus ulcers and other wounds and in treating intestinal worms in humans.

Dosing

A commercially produced debriding ointment is available by prescription in the United States. Each 1 g contains 8.3 × 10^5 USP units papain and 100 mg of urea. There are very little data available to make specific recommendations regarding systemic doses of papaya. One study used a 4 g dose of air-dried papaya seeds in 20 mL of honey to treat helminthiasis. In the United States, the fruit is generally recognized as safe (GRAS status) when used as a food.

Contraindications

Papaya may cause severe allergic reactions and is therefore contraindicated in sensitive people.

Pregnancy/Lactation

Possibly unsafe depending on the part of the plant being used and dose administered. Avoid use.

Interactions

None documented.

Adverse Reactions

Papaya may cause severe allergic reactions in sensitive people. Topically, papaya latex can be a severe irritant and vesicant. Papaya juice and papaya seeds are unlikely to cause adverse effects when taken orally; however, papaya leaves at high doses may cause gastric irritation.

Toxicology

There are parts of the plant (eg, seeds) that contain benzyl isothiocyanate, which may cause toxicity at high doses.

Local Anesthetic/Vasoconstrictor Precautions

No information available to require special precautions

Effects on Bleeding None reported

Parsley

Clinical Overview

Uses

Parsley, in addition to being a source of certain vitamins and minerals, has been used in the treatment of prostate, liver and spleen diseases, as well as anemia, arthritis, and microbial infections. It has also been found useful as a diuretic and laxative. However, there have been no clinical trials to confirm these uses.

Dosing

Parsley has been used at daily doses of 6 g, however, no clinical studies have been found that support this dose. The essential oil should not be used because of toxicity.

Contraindications

Contraindications have not yet been identified.

Pregnancy/Lactation

Generally recognized as safe or used as food. Safety and efficacy for dosages above those in foods are unproven and should be avoided. Emmenagogue and abortifacient effects in higher doses.

Interactions

None well documented.

Adverse Reactions

Adverse effects from the ingestion of parsley oil include headache, giddiness, loss of balance, convulsions, and renal damage.

Toxicology

While no major toxicities have been reported with the use of parsley, pregnant women should not take parsley because of possible uterotonic effects.

Local Anesthetic/Vasoconstrictor Precautions

No information available to require special precautions

Effects on Bleeding None reported

Passion Flower

Clinical Overview

Uses

Passion flower has been used to treat sleep disorders and historically in homeopathic medicine to treat pain, insomnia related to neurasthenia or hysteria, and nervous exhaustion.

Dosing

No clinical trials of passion flower as a single agent have been reported; however, a daily dose of 4 to 8 g is typical.

Contraindications

Contraindications have not yet been identified.

Pregnancy/Lactation

Documented adverse effects. Avoid use. Passion flower is a known uterine stimulant.

Interactions

None well documented.

Adverse Reactions

Though no adverse effects of passion flower have been reported, large doses may result in CNS depression.

Toxicology

No major clinical trials have been conducted to assess the plant's toxicity.

Local Anesthetic/Vasoconstrictor Precautions

No information available to require special precautions

Effects on Bleeding None reported

Pectin

Clinical Overview

Uses

Pectin has been used in antidiarrheal products and to lower blood lipoprotein levels. Pectin also has been investigated for its effects on cancer, diabetes, and gastroesophageal reflux disease/gastric ulceration. However, quality clinical trials are lacking.

Dosing

Pectin and/or modified pectin have been used in clinical studies in doses of 10 to 20 g daily.

Contraindications

Contraindications have not yet been identified.

Pregnancy/Lactation

Information regarding safety and efficacy in pregnancy and lactation is lacking.

Interactions

Coadministration of pectin with beta-carotene–containing foods or supplements can reduce blood levels of beta-carotene by more than 50%.

Adverse Reactions

Pectin is generally well tolerated when ingested. Occupational asthma has been associated with the inhalation of pectin dust. A cross-sensitivity to cashew and pistachio nuts may exist.

Toxicology

No major toxicities have been reported with the use of pectin.

Local Anesthetic/Vasoconstrictor Precautions

No information available to require special precautions

Effects on Bleeding None reported

Peppermint

Clinical Overview

Uses

In addition to use as a seasoning and flavoring, peppermint is used to treat irritable bowel syndrome (IBS) and other GI conditions. Menthol is available in numerous commercial preparations used to treat respiratory tract infections and topically for its cooling and warming action to relieve pain. However, there is limited clinical information supporting its use for these conditions.

Dosing

Peppermint oil has been used as a carminative at doses of 0.1 to 0.24 mL. Up to 1,200 mg of the oil in enteric-coated tablets has been used to treat IBS. Peppermint oil (40 mL) has been added to barium suspensions and also administered intraluminally (8 mL) during colonoscopy.

Contraindications

Peppermint oil should not be administered to patients with gastroesophageal reflux or active gastric ulcers because the oil decreases esophageal sphincter pressure. Peppermint oil should not be applied to the face, especially under the nose of a child or infant. Enteric-coated preparations are not recommended for use in children younger than 8 years.

Pregnancy/Lactation

Documented adverse reactions. Avoid use because of emmenagogue effects.

Interactions

Peppermint oil may influence metabolism of certain drugs, including felodipine and simvastatin, via inhibition of the cytochrome P450 (CYP-450) enzyme system, increasing pharmacologic and adverse reactions. Absorption of caffeine may be delayed by menthol. Decreased cyclosporine levels have been reported with consumption of a tea containing peppermint and 8 other herbs.

Adverse Reactions

Peppermint oil may cause allergic reactions characterized by contact dermatitis, flushing, and headache and may worsen the symptoms of heartburn, hiatus hernias, and stomach ulcers.

Toxicology

Peppermint is GRAS (generally recognized as safe) in amounts used in seasoning or flavoring, although medicinal uses of the plant can cause adverse reactions. (See Adverse Reactions.)

Local Anesthetic/Vasoconstrictor Precautions

No information available to require special precautions

Effects on Bleeding None reported

Periwinkle

Clinical Overview

Uses

Periwinkle alkaloids have been used to treat certain cancers; however, use of the plant for this purpose is not recommended without consulting a health care provider.

Periwinkle has been studied for potential antimicrobial and antiprotozoal applications, as well as for use in diabetes and wound healing; however, there is not enough reliable information to recommend the plant for these uses.

Dosing

There is no recent clinical evidence to support specific doses of periwinkle for medicinal use. Traditional doses have included 10 leaves and 10 flowers boiled in water as a tea, or 9 pink flowers in 0.5 L of water for 3 hours ("solar tea") sipped throughout the day. Therapeutic doses for preparations of the pure alkaloids vincristine and vinblastine are available.

Contraindications

Contraindications have not been identified.

Pregnancy/Lactation

Avoid use. Abortifacient effects have been documented.

Interactions

None well documented.

Adverse Reactions

Clinical information is lacking.

Toxicology

Severe, systemic adverse events are associated with the use of the alkaloids vincristine and vinblastine.

Local Anesthetic/Vasoconstrictor Precautions

No information available to require special precautions

Effects on Bleeding None reported

Peru Balsam

Clinical Overview

Uses

Peru balsam has been used in the treatment of dry socket in dentistry, topically as a treatment for wounds and ulcers, and in suppositories for hemorrhoids. However, there are only older, small case studies to support this use. The material is not used internally.

Dosing

Peru balsam has been used topically in 5% to 20% formulations for wounds and burns. Case reports and small clinical studies report the efficacy of balsam combined with other ingredients in the management of certain wounds; however, there are no recent, well-controlled clinical studies to support appropriate dosing.

Contraindications

Contraindications have not been identified.

Pregnancy/Lactation

Information regarding safety and efficacy in pregnancy and lactation is lacking. Systemic toxicity following application of Peru balsam to the nipples of breast-feeding mothers has been reported.

Interactions

None well documented.

Adverse Reactions

Peru balsam is an allergen.

Toxicology

Information is lacking.

Local Anesthetic/Vasoconstrictor Precautions

No information available to require special precautions

Effects on Bleeding None reported

Pineapple

Clinical Overview

Uses

Few well-controlled clinical trials have been published to support the wide range of therapeutic claims for bromelain, a crude, aqueous extract of pineapple. Evidence exists primarily for the use of bromelain in debridement of burns and as an anti-inflammatory agent.

Dosing

Two slices of pineapple contain approximately 100 mg of ascorbic acid (vitamin C). The usual dosage of bromelain is 40 mg taken 3 or 4 times daily. Pineapple products are available commercially in liquid, tablet, and capsule doseforms. Most products contain bromelain 500 mg; manufacturers suggest a dose of 500 to 1,000 mg daily.

Contraindications

Hypersensitivity to any of the components in pineapple. Cross-reaction with honeybee venom, olive tree pollen, celery, cypress pollen, bromelain, and papain have been reported.

Pregnancy/Lactation

Information regarding safety and efficacy in pregnancy and lactation is lacking. Data is lacking to support the historical use of pineapple as an emmenagogue and abortifacient.

Interactions

Potentiation of amoxicillin and tetracycline because of increased volume of distribution by bromelain has been documented.

Adverse Reactions

The juice from unripe pineapples can act as a violent purgative. Bromelain ingestion is associated with a low incidence of adverse reactions, including diarrhea, menorrhagia, nausea, skin rash, and vomiting. Angular stomatitis/cheilitis can result from eating large amounts of the fruit.

Toxicology

Bromelain has very low toxicity.

Local Anesthetic/Vasoconstrictor Precautions

No information available to require special precautions

Effects on Bleeding May cause increased bleeding due to inhibition of platelet aggregation

Plantain

Clinical Overview

Uses

The psyllium in plantain has been used as GI therapy, to treat hyperlipidemia for anticancer effects, respiratory treatment, and other uses.

Dosing

Plantain leaves have been given as a tea for cold and cough at 3 to 6 g/day.

Contraindications

Contraindications have not yet been identified.

Pregnancy/Lactation

Documented adverse effects. Avoid use. Uterine activity, laxative.

Interactions

Patients taking lithium or carbamazepine should avoid coadministration of plantain. Caution patients receiving lithium or carbamazepine to consult their health care provider before using herbal products.

Adverse Reactions

Adverse events include anaphylaxis, chest congestion, sneezing and watery eyes, occupational asthma, and a situation involving the occurrence of a giant phytobezoar composed of psyllium seed husks.

Toxicology

The pollen contains allergenic glycoproteins that react with concanavalin A, as well as components that bind IgE. IgE antibodies have been demonstrated. The IgE-mediated sensitization has contributes to seasonal allergy.

Local Anesthetic/Vasoconstrictor Precautions

No information available to require special precautions

Effects on Bleeding None reported

Poinsettia

Clinical Overview

Uses

Poinsettias are used primarily as Christmas ornamentation but have been used traditionally to treat skin conditions, warts, and toothaches; however, clinical studies are lacking to support these uses.

Dosing

No recent clinical evidence exists to support specific dosing of poinsettia in a therapeutic context.

Contraindications

Contraindications have not been identified.

Pregnancy/Lactation

Avoid use. Information regarding safety and efficacy in pregnancy and lactation is lacking.

Interactions

None well documented.

Adverse Reactions

Allergy and contact dermatitis have been reported. Minor GI irritation following ingestion is possible requiring only supportive therapy.

Toxicology

Although many published reports have warned of the plant's toxicity, there is little clinical evidence to support this claim.

Local Anesthetic/Vasoconstrictor Precautions

No information available to require special precautions

Effects on Bleeding None reported

Pokeweed

Clinical Overview

Uses

Young pokeweed leaves and berries may be eaten as food, but only after being cooked properly by boiling in several changes of water.

Dosing

At doses of 1 g, dried pokeweed root is emetic and purgative. At lower doses of 60 to 100 mg/day, the root and berries have been used to treat rheumatism and for immune stimulation; however, there are no clinical trials that support these uses or doses.

Contraindications

Contraindications have not yet been identified.

Pregnancy/Lactation

Documented adverse effects. Avoid use. Uterine stimulant with toxic constituents; is reputed to affect menstrual cycle.

Interactions

None well documented.

Adverse Reactions

GI distress, possibly leading to severe toxicities (see Toxicology).

Toxicology

Ingestion of poisonous parts of the plant may cause severe stomach cramping, nausea with persistent diarrhea and vomiting, slow and difficult breathing, weakness, spasms, hypotension, severe convulsions, and death.

Local Anesthetic/Vasoconstrictor Precautions

No information available to require special precautions

Effects on Bleeding None reported

Policosanol

Clinical Overview

Uses

Cholesterol-lowering effects previously attributed to policosanol have not been validated by more recent trials. Policosanol has been studied in platelet aggregation and intermittent claudication, but data are insufficient to support this use.

Dosing

Policosanol is typically initiated at 5 mg/day and titrated up to 20 mg/day for hypercholesterolemia.

Contraindications

Contraindications have not been identified.

Pregnancy/Lactation

Information regarding safety and efficacy in pregnancy and lactation is lacking. Studies in rats and mice demonstrated no adverse effects on fertility, reproduction, teratogenesis, or development at doses equivalent to 1,500 times the normal human dose of 20 mg/kg/day.

Interactions

Because of policosanol's possible effects on platelet aggregation, caution is warranted if policosanol is used concurrently with anticoagulants (eg, warfarin) or antiplatelet agents (eg, aspirin, clopidogrel, prasugrel). In a study in healthy men, policosanol did not affect the pharmacokinetics of warfarin.

Adverse Reactions

Animal and human studies have demonstrated few adverse reactions from policosanol.

Toxicology

Limited animal and human studies have found policosanol to be safe.

Local Anesthetic/Vasoconstrictor Precautions

No information available to require special precautions

Effects on Bleeding May see increased bleeding due to inhibition of platelet aggregation

Prickly Pear

Clinical Overview

Uses

Prickly pear is widely cultivated and commercially used in juices, jellies, candies, teas, and alcoholic drinks. American Indians used prickly pear juice to treat burns, and prickly pear has a long history in traditional Mexican folk medicine for treating diabetes. Its use in treating diabetes, lipid disorders, inflammation, and ulcers, as well as its other pharmacologic effects, have been documented. However, there is limited clinical information to support these uses.

Dosing

Prickly pear is commercially available in numerous doseforms, including capsules, tablets, powders, and juices, and as food. Follow manufacturers' suggested guidelines if using commercial products. Typical dosage regimens are two 250 mg capsules by mouth 3 times a day or every 8 hours.

Contraindications

Hypersensitivity to any components of prickly pear.

Pregnancy/Lactation

Avoid use during pregnancy and lactation because of the lack of clinical studies.

Interactions

None well documented.

Adverse Reactions

Dermatitis is the most common adverse reaction to prickly pear.

Toxicology

Little information is available.

Local Anesthetic/Vasoconstrictor Precautions

No information available to require special precautions

Effects on Bleeding None reported

Pygeum

Clinical Overview

Uses

Pygeum has been used to improve symptoms of benign prostatic hyperplasia (BPH) and to improve sexual function. However, only studies comparing pygeum to placebo are available.

Dosing

Benign prostatic hyperplasia: 25 to 200 mg/day of P. africana extract standardized to 14% total sterols. The usual dosage is 100 mg/day in 6- to 8-week cycles.

Contraindications

Contraindications have not been identified.

Pregnancy/Lactation

Avoid use. Information regarding safety and efficacy in pregnancy and lactation is lacking.

Interactions

None well documented.

Adverse Reactions

GI irritation and headache have been reported.

Toxicology

A low incidence of toxicity has been demonstrated.

Local Anesthetic/Vasoconstrictor Precautions

No information available to require special precautions

Effects on Bleeding None reported

Quassia

Clinical Overview

Uses

Quassia has a variety of uses, including treatment for measles, diarrhea, fever, and lice. Quassia has antibacterial, antifungal, antifertility, antitumor, antileukemic, and insecticidal actions as well. However, efficacy in clinical trials has not been proven.

Dosing

Quassia wood has been used as a bitter tonic, with a typical oral dose of 500 mg. No studies have been performed to support this dose. Several recent studies of topical quassia tincture for head lice have been reported.

Contraindications

Contraindications have not yet been identified.

Pregnancy/Lactation

Documented adverse reactions. Avoid use.

Interactions

None well documented.

Adverse Reactions

Quassia is used in a number of food products and is considered safe by the FDA. If taken in large doses, this product can irritate the GI tract and cause vomiting. It is not recommended for pregnant women.

Toxicology

Quassia is listed as generally regarded as safe (GRAS) by the FDA. Parenteral administration of quassin is toxic, leading to cardiac irregularities, tremors, and paralysis.

Local Anesthetic/Vasoconstrictor Precautions No information available to require special precautions

Effects on Bleeding None reported

Queen's Delight

Clinical Overview

Uses

With the exception of prostratin, the other Stillingia factors are likely to be tumor promoters and to possess the typical pleiotropic effects possessed by most other phorbol esters.

Dosing

There is no clinical evidence to support specific dosage recommendations for queen's delight. Classical use of queen's delight called for 2 g of the root, however the documented presence of irritant and tumor-promoting phorbol esters in this plant contraindicates therapeutic use.

Contraindications

No longer considered safe.

Pregnancy/Lactation

Documented adverse effects. Not to be used while nursing. Avoid use.

Interactions

None well documented.

Adverse Reactions

Do not ingest or use topically in human medicine. Observe particular caution with the fresh root, which appears to be more toxic than the dried product. Stillingia root is a purgative and irritant product that should be avoided because of a high likelihood of tumor promotion and documented severe irritancy to skin.

Toxicology

There are reports of sheep poisoned by Stillingia in Florida. Because of the reported phorbol esters, this plant should not be ingested or used topically in human medicine. Observe particular caution with the fresh root, which appears to be more toxic than the dried product.

Local Anesthetic/Vasoconstrictor Precautions No information available to require special precautions

Effects on Bleeding None reported

Raspberry

Clinical Overview

Uses

There is little pharmacologic evidence to support the use of raspberry leaf in pregnancy, menstruation, or during childbirth. Raspberry fruit and leaf extracts have shown activity on cancer cell lines, possibly due to an antioxidant effect; however, no clinical trials exist.

Dosing

Traditional dosages include 5-10 mg (1-2 tsp) crushed leaf per 240 mL of water up to 6 times per day, or up to 12 g dry leaf. Substantiated clinical applications for dosage recommendations are lacking.

Contraindications

Contraindications have not yet been identified.

Pregnancy/Lactation

Avoid use during pregnancy; adverse effects have been documented. Information regarding safety during lactation is lacking.

Use of raspberry leaf preparations has been promoted by nurse-midwives for strengthening the uterus and shortening the duration of labor. However, there are too few studies upon which to substantiate either the efficacy or the safety of this practice.

Interactions

None well documented.

Adverse Reactions

Information regarding adverse reactions with the use of raspberry fruit is limited. No adverse events were reported in a clinical study evaluating the effect of raspberry tea during pregnancy.

Toxicology

Information is generally lacking for raspberry leaf; raspberry fruit is considered nontoxic.

Local Anesthetic/Vasoconstrictor Precautions No information available to require special precautions

Effects on Bleeding None reported

Red Clover

Clinical Overview

Uses

Red clover flowers have been used traditionally as a sedative, to purify the blood, and to treat respiratory conditions; topical preparations have been used for psoriasis, eczema, and rashes, and to accelerate wound healing. However, there is no clinical evidence to support any of these uses or for use in menopause-related conditions. Safety of use in treating breast cancer has not been determined, and the epidemiological association of isoflavone consumption in protecting against prostate cancer has not yet been confirmed by clinical trials.

Dosing

Red clover blossoms for sedation were formerly used at doses of 4 g, but is now used primarily as a source of isoflavones. The usual dose is 40 to 80 mg/day of standardized isoflavones, typically containing biochanin A, formononetin, genistein, and daidzein. Several commercial preparations are available.

Contraindications

Red clover is contraindicated in patients with hormonal disorders, estrogen-dependent breast cancer (or risk of), and during pregnancy or lactation. Red clover supplementation is not advised in children younger than 12 years.

Pregnancy/Lactation

Avoid use; red clover has estrogenic activity.

Interactions

Isoflavonoids may interfere with hormonal agents; avoid use with oral contraceptives, estrogen, or progesterone therapies. Case reports are lacking; however, caution is warranted with concomitant use of tamoxifen or letrozole.

Adverse Reactions

Few adverse reactions have been reported in doses used in clinical trials. High doses of isoflavones have been associated with loss of appetite, pedal edema, and abdominal tenderness.

Toxicology

The phytoestrogens in red clover may be expected to act through estrogenic mechanisms, with the associated risk of estrogen-like adverse effects, including increased incidence of endometrial, ovarian, and breast cancers.

Local Anesthetic/Vasoconstrictor Precautions No information available to require special precautions

Effects on Bleeding Red clover contains coumarins; it may enhance the anticoagulant effects of warfarin when taken simultaneously. This effect has not been confirmed.

Red Yeast Rice

Clinical Overview

Uses

M. purpureus is a natural source of mevinolin, the active ingredient of the drug lovastatin, therefore, having beneficial effects in the treatment of hyperlipidemia. However, red yeast rice should not be used in place of lovastatin and regular medical care because no studies directly compare its use with a statin. Evidence also exists for its antibacterial and anticancer effects, as well as its activity on glycemic metabolism.

Dosing

Red yeast rice is available commercially, primarily as a 600 mg capsule. Most manufacturers suggest an oral dosage of 2 capsules twice a day for a total dose of 2,400 mg/day. Commercial over-the-counter products often contain coenzyme Q_{10} to supplement low levels of this enzyme in patients with statin myopathy. Clinical trials have used dosages of 2,400 mg/day.

Contraindications

Hypersensitivity to any components of red yeast rice. Anaphylactic reactions in certain populations are documented. Because red yeast rice depletes tissue of coenzyme Q_{10}, which may increase the risk of statin-induced myopathy, patients with muscle damage caused by statins should avoid its use.

Pregnancy/Lactation

Avoid use during pregnancy and lactation. The major ingredient in red yeast rice is monacolin K, which is also known as mevinolin or lovastatin and has statin-like activity. Statins are potential teratogens based on theoretical considerations and in small case studies. CNS and limb defects have been reported in newborns exposed to statins in utero.

Interactions

There are many possible drug interactions associated with red yeast rice. Consult a health care provider before using any dietary supplement.

Adverse Reactions

Meta-analysis of the efficacy of 3 red yeast rice preparations (Cholestin, Xuezhikang, and Zhibituo) from 93 randomized trials (9,625 patients) documented no serious adverse reactions. The most common adverse reactions included dizziness, decreased appetite, nausea, stomachache, abdominal distension, and diarrhea. A small number of patients experienced increased serum blood urea nitrogen (BUN) and ALT levels.

Toxicology

The nephrotoxic mycotoxin citrinin has been isolated from some strains of M. purpureus and Monascus ruber. No severe toxicities at high doses have been reported. Not recommended for use in patients with liver or kidney disease.

Local Anesthetic/Vasoconstrictor Precautions

No information available to require special precautions

Effects on Bleeding None reported

Reishi Mushroom

Clinical Overview

Uses

The polysaccharide content of reishi mushroom is responsible for possible anticancer and immunostimulatory effects. Reishi may also provide hepatoprotective action, antiviral activity, and beneficial effect on the cardiovascular system, rheumatoid arthritis, chronic fatigue syndrome, and diabetes. Few clinical trials have been conducted.

Dosing

The Pharmacopoeia of the People's Republic of China recommends 6 to 12 g reishi extract daily. Ganopoly (a Ganoderma lucidum polysaccharide extract) in doses up to 5.4 g daily (equivalent to 81 g of the fruiting body) for 12 weeks has been used in a few clinical trials.

Contraindications

Contraindications have not been identified.

Pregnancy/Lactation

Information regarding safety and efficacy in pregnancy and lactation is lacking.

Interactions

None well documented.

Adverse Reactions

Adverse reactions are mild and may include dizziness, GI upset, and skin irritation.

Toxicology

There are few reports of toxicity with the use of reishi mushroom.

Local Anesthetic/Vasoconstrictor Precautions

No information available to require special precautions

Effects on Bleeding Reishi mushroom may have an antiplatelet effect. Clinical significance of this property is unknown.

Rhubarb

Clinical Overview

Uses

Rhubarb is extensively used in traditional Chinese medicine. Rhubarb has been studied for the management of GI and renal function disorders, and for the treatment of hyperlipidemia and cancer. However, sound clinical evidence for its use is lacking.

Dosing

Dried rhubarb extract 20 to 50 mg/kg daily has been used in clinical trials.

Contraindications

Contraindications have not been identified.

Pregnancy/Lactation

Avoid dosages higher than those found in food because safety and efficacy are unproven.

Interactions

Interaction with cardiac glycosides (digoxin) and a reduction in the absorption of orally administered drugs have been noted when rhubarb is taken in large quantities.

Adverse Reactions

A few reactions, primarily GI effects, have been reported in clinical trials.

Toxicology

The leaf blades (but not the stalks) of rhubarb contain enough oxalic acid to cause poisoning. Acute renal failure has been associated with long-term anthraquinone use.

Local Anesthetic/Vasoconstrictor Precautions

No information available to require special precautions

Effects on Bleeding None reported

Rose Hips

Clinical Overview

Uses

Rose hips provide vitamin C supplements. Rose hips have been used for diuretic actions, to reduce thirst, to alleviate gastric inflammation, and to flavor teas and jams.

Dosing

There is no recent clinical evidence upon which dosage recommandations can be based. Classical use of rose petals was 3 to 6 g daily.

Contraindications

Contraindications have not yet been identified.

Pregnancy/Lactation

Information regarding safety and efficacy in pregnancy and lactation is lacking.

Interactions

None well documented.

Adverse Reactions

There have been no reported side effects except in those exposed to rose hips dust who have developed severe respiratory allergies.

Toxicology

No data.

Local Anesthetic/Vasoconstrictor Precautions
No information available to require special precautions

Effects on Bleeding None reported

Rue

Clinical Overview

Uses

Rue extract is potentially useful as a potassium channel blocker. It has been used to treat many neuromuscular problems and to stimulate the onset of menstruation. Because rue has an antispasmodic effect at relatively low doses, it should be taken with caution. However, considering rue's potential for severe adverse effects, clinical trials are limited.

Dosing

There is no recent clinical evidence to support dosing recommendations for rue. Traditional use calls for 0.5 to 1 g of the herb daily or 65 mg of the essential oil. In larger doses, rue is an emmenagogue, an aphrodisiac, and an abortifacient, and should be considered dangerous.

Contraindications

Contraindications have not yet been identified.

Pregnancy/Lactation

Documented adverse effects, including emmenagogue and abortifacient effects. Avoid use.

Interactions

None well documented.

Adverse Reactions

Rue extracts are mutagenic and furocoumarins have been associated with photosensitization. If ingested, rue oil may result in kidney damage and hepatic degeneration. Large doses can cause violent gastric pain, vomiting, and systemic complications, including death. Because of possible abortifacient effects, the plant should never be ingested by women of childbearing potential. Toxic hepatitis due to Ruta has been reported.

Toxicology

Rue should only be taken with extreme caution. A case report describes multiorgan toxicity in a 78-year-old woman ingesting R. graveolens for cardiovascular protection. After 3 days of use, the patient entered the emergency department with bradycardia, acute renal failure with hyperkalemia necessitating hemodialysis, and coagulopathy.

Local Anesthetic/Vasoconstrictor Precautions
No information available to require special precautions

Effects on Bleeding None reported

Safflower

Clinical Overview

Uses

Safflower has been used as a laxative and as a dietary supplement to modify lipid profiles and treat fever. However, there is no supporting evidence for these uses from clinical trials.

Dosing

Safflower oil 8 g/day has been associated with improvement in glycemic control.

Contraindications

Contraindications have not yet been identified.

Pregnancy/Lactation

Avoid use. Not recommended for use in pregnancy; abortifacient and emmenagogue effects have been suggested.

Interactions

None well documented.

Adverse Reactions

Allergy to the flowers has been reported. Safflower oil was generally well tolerated when used as a control in clinical trials.

Toxicology

Research reveals limited information regarding toxicity with the use of safflower oil.

Local Anesthetic/Vasoconstrictor Precautions
No information available to require special precautions

Effects on Bleeding None reported

Salvia divinorum

Clinical Overview

Uses

Salvia divinorum is a hallucinogen and is illegal in some jurisdictions. Check individual state legislation.

Dosing

200 to 500 mcg of salvinorin A, or several leaves, smoked or absorbed perorally, is sufficient to cause hallucinations.

Contraindications

S. divinorum should not be used in people with any mental disease.

Pregnancy/Lactation

Use during pregnancy or lactation is not recommended.

Interactions

None well documented.

Adverse Reactions

None systematically reported.

Toxicology

No toxicity was observed in a 2-week study in mice.

Local Anesthetic/Vasoconstrictor Precautions
No information available to require special precautions

Effects on Bleeding None reported

SAMe

Clinical Overview

Uses

SAMe has been studied for the treatment of depressive disorders. Although it has been shown to be equivalent to tricyclics, it has not been compared with newer agents. Information regarding its use in osteoarthritis is conflicting and information regarding its use in liver disorders and hepatitis is limited.

Dosing

Depression: 200 to 1,600 mg/day. *Liver disease:* 800 to 1,000 mg/day. *Osteoarthritis:* 1,200 mg/day initially; then maintenance 400 mg/day.

Contraindications

SAMe should not be used in patients with bipolar depression because of reports of increased anxiety and mania.

Pregnancy/Lactation

Trials conducted in pregnant women documented no harmful effects.

Interactions

None well documented.

Adverse Reactions

Available data indicate nausea, diarrhea, constipation, mild insomnia, dizziness, irritability, anxiety, and sweating to be the most commonly reported adverse reactions associated with the use of SAMe. Data from long-term use are lacking.

Toxicology

Toxicological studies concluded that SAMe is safe even at the highest doses.

Local Anesthetic/Vasoconstrictor Precautions No information available to require special precautions

Effects on Bleeding None reported

Sarsaparilla

Clinical Overview

Uses

Extracts of the roots may be effective in treating gout and metabolic syndrome; however, evidence is based largely on animal studies and clinical trials are limited. Sarsaparilla has been traditionally used for treating syphilis, leprosy, and psoriasis; however, evidence to support these uses is lacking. Evidence is also lacking for purported ergogenic/adaptogenic effects. Interest in cytotoxic potential in treating cancer exists.

Dosing

Clinical trials are lacking to provide guidance on therapeutic dosages. Typical sarsaparilla doses for a variety of uses range from 0.3 to 2 g/day of the powdered root.

Contraindications

Contraindications have not yet been identified.

Pregnancy/Lactation

Avoid use. Information regarding safety and efficacy in pregnancy and lactation is lacking. Estrogenic and antiestrogenic activities have been described for extracts of at least one of the species.

Interactions

None well documented.

Adverse Reactions

GI irritation and increased diuresis have been reported. Clinical studies are lacking to provide evidence (or lack of evidence) of harm.

Toxicology

Information regarding toxicology with the use of sarsaparilla is limited.

Local Anesthetic/Vasoconstrictor Precautions No information available to require special precautions

Effects on Bleeding None reported

Sassafras

Clinical Overview

Uses

Sassafras has been used for a variety of illnesses, but the safrole in sassafras root bark and oil has been banned by the US Food and Drug Administration (FDA), including for use as a flavoring or fragrance. The constituent safrole has been used in the illegal production of 3,4-methylene-dioxymethamphetamine (MDMA), also known by the street names "ecstasy" or "Molly," and the sale of safrole and sassafras oil is monitored by the US Drug and Enforcement Administration (DEA).

Dosing

Clinical applications are lacking to provide guidance. Long-term use should be avoided due to the potential carcinogenicity of its constituent safrole. Sassafras root bark has been traditionally used at doses of 10 g.

Contraindications

No longer considered safe for use.

Pregnancy/Lactation

Avoid use. Documented emmenagogue and abortifacient effects. Information on use during breastfeeding is lacking.

Interactions

None well documented.

Adverse Reactions

Diaphoresis, hot flashes, and dermatitis have been reported.

Toxicology

Sassafras oil and safrole have demonstrated carcinogenicity in animal studies. Symptoms of sassafras oil poisoning in humans include vomiting, stupor, lowering of body temperature, exhaustion, tachycardia, spasms, hallucinations, and paralysis, and may also be fatal.

Local Anesthetic/Vasoconstrictor Precautions No information available to require special precautions

Effects on Bleeding None reported

Saw Palmetto

Clinical Overview

Uses

Saw palmetto has been used to treat symptoms of benign prostatic hyperplasia (BPH), but evidence from quality clinical trials and a meta-analysis does not support this use. Data suggesting a positive effect on erectile dysfunction are limited, and results from studies evaluating the effect of saw palmetto on outcomes of transurethral resection of the prostate surgery are equivocal. Some effects on in vitro prostate cancer cells have been described; however, clinical trials are lacking.

Dosing

Benign prostatic hyperplasia: 320 mg/day standardized extract.

Contraindications

Contraindications have not been identified. Use in children younger than 12 years is not recommended.

Pregnancy/Lactation

Information regarding safety and efficacy in pregnancy and lactation is lacking. Effects on androgen and estrogen metabolism have been identified, as well as a lack of rationale for its use in pregnancy, and suggest that saw palmetto should not be used.

Interactions

Case reports of interactions are lacking. Caution may be warranted with concomitant coagulation therapy.

Adverse Reactions

Results from clinical trials note that saw palmetto products are generally well tolerated, with occasional reports of adverse GI effects and headache.

Toxicology
Information is limited.

Local Anesthetic/Vasoconstrictor Precautions
No information available to require special precautions

Effects on Bleeding None reported

Schisandra

Clinical Overview

Uses
Schisandra has been used as a tonic and restorative, as well as for liver protection, nervous system effects, respiratory treatment, and GI therapy. However, there are limited clinical trials to support these uses.

Dosing
Schisandra fruit is used as an adaptogen at dosages of 1.5 to 6 g/day. A standardized extract containing 3.4% schisandrin has been used in a clinical trial for improved athletic performance at 91 mg/day of extract. Examples of various doses used in Russia include the following: ***Tinctura Fructum***: Schisandrae prepared with air-dried fruits and 95% ethanol given as 20 to 30 drops twice daily; ***Tinctura Seminum***: Schizandrae prepared with dried seeds and 95% ethanol given as 20 to 30 drops twice daily; ***Infusion Fructum***: Schizandrae prepared with air-dried fruits and water (1:20 w/v) given as 150 mL twice daily; ***Fructum Schizandrae***: contains air-dried fruits given at a dose of 0.5 to 1.5 g twice daily; ***Schizandra seed powder***: given as 0.5 to 1.5 g twice daily before lunch and dinner over 20 to 30 days; ***Schizandra seed extract***: prepared with air-dried seed and 95% ethanol given as a single dose of 0.05 or 0.2 mL/kg.

Contraindications
Contraindications have not been identified.

Pregnancy/Lactation
Information regarding safety and efficacy in pregnancy and lactation is lacking. Various compounds from the stem of Schisandra propinqua were found to be cytotoxic against rat luteal cells and human decidual cells in vitro.

Interactions
Because of its documented effects on hepatic and gastric enzyme activity, particularly CYP3A, it is possible that schisandra may interfere with the metabolism of coadministered drugs (eg, midazolam). Findings from a study of healthy volunteers suggest patients receiving schisandra while concomitantly taking drugs that are P-glycoprotein (P-gp) substrates (eg, tacrolimus) may require a dosage adjustment.

Adverse Reactions
Research does not report any incidence of adverse effects.

Toxicology
The minimal toxic dose when given orally to mice is 3.6 g/kg. The acute toxicity was studied in mice, and following intraperitoneal administration, no effects on blood pressure, breath, or motility were noted; however, high doses caused convulsions (median effective dose [ED_{50}] = 175 mg/kg) and paresis (ED_{50} = 370 mg/kg).

Local Anesthetic/Vasoconstrictor Precautions
No information available to require special precautions

Effects on Bleeding None reported

Scullcap

Clinical Overview

Uses
Scullcap traditionally has been used as a sedative for nervousness and anxiety, although there is little to no data to support any of these uses.

Dosing Limit doses of American skullcap to no more than the package recommendation. Typical doses (see individual product information):
Dried herb: 1 to 2 grams 3 times/day.
Tea: 240 mL 3 times/day (Pour 250 mL of boiling water over 5 to 10 mL of the dried herb and steep for 10 to 15 minutes).
Tincture: 2 to 4 mL 3 times/day.

Contraindications
Contraindications have not yet been identified.

Pregnancy/Lactation
Documented adverse effects in pregnancy. Avoid use. May inhibit pituitary and chorionic gonadotropins, as well as prolactin.

Interactions
None well documented, though it may exaggerate the effects of other drugs that cause drowsiness.

Adverse Reactions
If taken according to the manufacturer's directions, scullcap does not seem to exhibit any adverse effects.

Toxicology
An overdose of the tincture causes giddiness, stupor, confusion, twitching of the limbs, intermission of the pulse, and other symptoms similar to epilepsy.

Local Anesthetic/Vasoconstrictor Precautions
No information available to require special precautions

Effects on Bleeding None reported

Sea Buckthorn

Clinical Overview

Uses
Numerous pharmacological effects are documented in the scientific literature, including antimicrobial, antiulcerogenic, antioxidant, anticancer, radioprotective activity, platelet aggregation, liver injury, cardiovascular risk factors, and effects on skin and mucosa.

Dosing
Five to 45 g of seed oil and 300 mL/day of juice have been studied in clinical trials.

Contraindications
None well documented.

Pregnancy/Lactation
Avoid use during pregnancy and lactation because clinical trial data are lacking.

Interactions
Sea buckthorn oil reportedly induces the cytogenetic activity of cyclophosphamide and farmorubicin.

Adverse Reactions
None well documented.

Toxicology
Sea buckthorn has been used as a food in Asia and in Europe. Toxicological studies in animals suggest seed oil and oil from the fruit's soft parts are safe. Acute and chronic toxicity of blood, liver, and heart as well as mutagenicity and teratogenicity of sea buckthorn oils have been studied.

Local Anesthetic/Vasoconstrictor Precautions
No information available to require special precautions

Effects on Bleeding Sea buckthorn inhibits platelet aggregation *in vitro*. One clinical report showed an inhibition of platelet aggregation in 12 healthy volunteers with daily ingestion of sea buckthorn berry oil. The clinician should anticipate that ingestion of sea buckthorn may pose some increased risk of bleeding.

Seaweed

Clinical Overview

Uses

Clinical trials are generally lacking to support definitive therapeutic recommendations for seaweeds. However, seaweeds are an important nutritional source of minerals and elements and are low in sodium. Applications may exist for use in cardiovascular conditions due to potential in cholesterol reduction and appetite suppression. Alginates extracted from seaweed have been used in wound dressings.

Dosing

Clinical trials have used an oral dosage range of 4 to 12 g seaweed daily for up to 2 months.

Contraindications

Contraindications have not been identified.

Pregnancy/Lactation

Information regarding safety and efficacy in pregnancy and lactation is lacking.

Interactions

Patients taking warfarin and consuming a large quantity of food containing seaweed may experience a change in international normalized ratio (INR) because of seaweed's high vitamin K content.

Adverse Reactions

Contact dermatitis, goiter, and, occasionally, GI effects may occur.

Toxicology

Excessive intake of dried seaweed may result in increased serum thyroid-stimulating hormone (TSH). There have been case reports of carotenodermia (yellowing of the skin) with excessive seaweed consumption.

Local Anesthetic/Vasoconstrictor Precautions

No information available to require special precautions

Effects on Bleeding May see increased bleeding due to anticoagulant effects.

Shark Derivatives

Clinical Overview

Uses

The shark cartilage was thought to be a cancer control agent, but no studies have proven this theory. Squalamine has been used as a potent antibiotic with fungicidal and antiprotozoal activity.

Dosing

A standardized shark cartilage product has been marketed under the name Neovastat (AE-941). Clinical trials in cancer angiogenesis have used doses of 60 to 240 mL daily, while another trial of a liquid shark cartilage product used only 7 to 21 mL daily.

Contraindications

Contraindications have not yet been identified.

Pregnancy/Lactation

Information regarding safety and efficacy in pregnancy and lactation is lacking.

Interactions

None well documented.

Adverse Reactions

Research reveals little or no information regarding adverse reactions with the use of shark derivatives.

Toxicology

Research reveals little or no information regarding toxicology with the use of shark derivatives.

Local Anesthetic/Vasoconstrictor Precautions

No information available to require special precautions

Effects on Bleeding None reported

Shark Liver Oil

Clinical Overview

Uses

Shark liver oil (SLO) has been used to help treat cancer, skin conditions, and respiratory ailments, as well as to reduce recurrent aphthous stomatitis and prevent radiation sickness. However, limited clinical data are available. Alkylglycerols have been studied as an immune system stimulant. Animal data suggest SLO may improve fertility.

Dosing

SLO marketed under the name isolutrol has been studied in a clinical trial of acne at a topical concentration of 0.15 g per 100 mL.

Contraindications

Contraindications have not been identified.

Pregnancy/Lactation

Information regarding safety and efficacy in pregnancy and lactation is lacking.

Interactions

None well documented.

Adverse Reactions

Few toxic effects have been reported. SLO supplements may have an unpleasant taste and/or odor. There have been reports of SLO-induced pneumonia in humans and pigs.

Toxicology

No adverse reactions or effects on mortality were noted in rats receiving short- and long-term doses of a supercritical fluid extract of SLO at doses 100 to 200 times that of normal human consumption. In Sweden, a SLO product (Ecomer) was prohibited for use by the National Board of Health and Welfare because of suspected adverse effects.

Local Anesthetic/Vasoconstrictor Precautions

No information available to require special precautions

Effects on Bleeding None reported

Slippery Elm

Clinical Overview

Uses

The mucilaginous property of slippery elm has been used in traditional medicine to treat multiple conditions; however, no clinical studies exist to support these applications. Although limited studies have investigated the antioxidant and anti-inflammatory potential of slippery elm, the information from these studies does not provide any recommendations for use.

Dosing

No clinical studies exist to support dosage guidelines. Traditional use suggests a dosage of 1 to 3 tsp of slippery elm powder in 240 mL of water, up to 3 times a day.

Contraindications

Contraindications have not been identified.

Pregnancy/Lactation

Avoid use in pregnancy. Abortifacient effects have been described, although they may be related to vaginal use of whole bark pieces to induce abortion.

Information regarding safety and efficacy in pregnancy and lactation is lacking.

Interactions

None well documented. Because the mucilaginous property of slippery elm may decrease absorption rates of other medicines, it may be beneficial to separate slippery elm doses from those of other medicines by 2 to 3 hours.

Adverse Reactions

Oleoresins from several Ulmus species have been reported to cause contact dermatitis, and the pollen of slippery elm is a known allergen.

Toxicology

Research regarding the toxicity of slippery elm is limited.

Local Anesthetic/Vasoconstrictor Precautions

No information available to require special precautions

Effects on Bleeding None reported

Soy

Clinical Overview

Uses

Soy is commonly used as a source of fiber, protein, and minerals. A number of meta-analyses are now available; however, evidence is lacking to support a definitive place in therapy for menopausal symptoms, osteoporosis, diabetes, or heart disease. Epidemiologic data suggest an association with a lower incidence of certain cancers with higher intake of dietary soy.

Dosing

A large number of clinical trials have been conducted for conditions (eg, menopause, osteoporosis, breast cancer, cardiovascular diseases) using daily doses of isoflavones from 40 to 120 mg.

Contraindications

Contraindications have not been identified.

Pregnancy/Lactation

Generally recognized as safe (GRAS) when used as food. Avoid dosages above those found in food because safety and efficacy are unproven.

Interactions

None well documented. A decrease in the anticoagulated effect of warfarin has been reported in 1 patient.

Adverse Reactions

Soybeans and their products are generally well tolerated. Minor GI disturbances have been reported. The National Toxicology Program (US Department of Health and Human Services) has concluded that there is minimal concern for developmental effects in infants fed soy infant formula.

Toxicology

Evidence exists from animal studies on the adverse effects of the isoflavone genistein on the developing female reproductive tract.

Local Anesthetic/Vasoconstrictor Precautions

No information available to require special precautions

Effects on Bleeding None reported

Spirulina

Clinical Overview

Uses

Spirulina is sold in the United States as a health food or supplement. Diverse claims exist for its immunostimulatory, hypolipidemic, antiviral, and anticancer effects; however, there is limited evidence to support these indications.

Dosing

Doses in clinical studies have ranged from 1 to 10 g/day.

Contraindications

Phenylketonuria; however, this has not been substantiated.

Pregnancy/Lactation

Information regarding safety and efficacy in pregnancy and lactation is lacking. Because of possible mercury and other heavy metal contamination, spirulina should be avoided during pregnancy.

Interactions

None well documented.

Adverse Reactions

Few reports of adverse reactions are available. However, spirulina-associated hepatotoxicity and reactions from heavy metal contamination are possible.

Toxicology

Spirulina is considered nontoxic to humans at usual levels of consumption; however, information is limited.

Local Anesthetic/Vasoconstrictor Precautions

No information available to require special precautions

Effects on Bleeding None reported

Stevia

Clinical Overview

Uses

Stevia leaf is used as a sweetening agent and contains several sweet glycosides. The glycoside rebaudioside A is used in commercially available products in the United States and has not shown any pharmacologic effects. Stevioside and stevia preparations have shown conflicting data, indicating possible effects as hypotensive and hypoglycemic agents and possible bactericidal properties.

Dosing

Stevia leaf is used for sweetening foods.

Contraindications

Contraindications have not yet been identified.

Pregnancy/Lactation

Information regarding safety and efficacy in pregnancy and lactation is lacking.

Interactions

None well documented.

Adverse Reactions

No major contraindications, warnings, or adverse reactions have been documented.

Toxicology

Stevioside, a main glycoside of stevia, was found to be nontoxic in acute toxicity studies in a variety of laboratory animals.

Local Anesthetic/Vasoconstrictor Precautions

No information available to require special precautions

Effects on Bleeding None reported

St. John's Wort

Clinical Overview

Uses

Meta-analyses of quality clinical trials support Hypericum 's place in the treatment of depression. Effectiveness is comparable with standard antidepressants, while adverse events are lower than with conventional antidepressants. Interactions with other drugs and quality control issues may limit use. Other areas of therapeutic research for St. John's wort include smoking cessation, premenstrual symptoms, somatoform disorder, and attention deficit hyperactivity disorder, as well as its possible role in treating cancer and HIV.

Dosing

Preparations vary greatly in chemical content and quality, and may be standardized to quantity of hyperforin (commonly 3% to 5%) or hypericin (commonly 0.3%). Clinical trials evaluating the efficacy of St. John's wort in depression have commonly used 900 mg of extract daily in 3 divided doses, both in short-term treatment and for ongoing therapy, for periods of up to 1 year (range, 600 to 1,200 mg/day).

Contraindications

Use with cyclosporine, tacrolimus, irinotecan, and imatinib mesylate, as well as protease inhibitors and nonnucleoside reverse transcriptase inhibitors in HIV treatment, is contraindicated.

Pregnancy/Lactation

Avoid use. The use of St. John's wort in perinatal depression has been considered; however, insufficient data on efficacy or safety exist to support its use. St. John's wort should be avoided during pregnancy and lactation until further long-term studies demonstrate a lack of toxicity in the developing fetus and breastfeeding newborn.

Interactions

St. John's wort has been reported to interact with numerous drugs. Drugs with a narrow therapeutic window should be monitored closely. Patients should be cautioned on the potential for interactions and the need to consult their health care provider before taking St. John's wort with prescription or nonprescription drugs. Drugs that are most prominently affected, and therefore for which concomitant use with St. John's wort should be avoided, include protease inhibitors (eg, saquinavir) and nonnucleoside reverse transcriptase inhibitors (eg, nevirapine) used in HIV, and cyclosporine, tacrolimus, irinotecan, and imatinib mesylate. Ethinyl estradiol is metabolized by CYP3A4; therefore, a high possibility of interaction exists. The risk of developing serotonin syndrome and other CNS adverse reactions cannot be ruled out; extreme caution is needed with combinations of psychotropic medications. Reviews of interactions with St. John's wort are available.

Adverse Reactions

Adverse reactions are usually mild. Potential adverse reactions include dry mouth, dizziness, constipation, and other GI symptoms, and confusion. Photosensitization also may occur. In clinical trials, adverse reactions and discontinuation with St. John's wort were usually less than those observed with standard antidepressants. Other possible rare adverse reactions include induction of mania and effects on male and female reproductive capabilities.

Toxicology

Limited information on genotoxicity exists. Potent inhibition of sperm motility was observed in vitro. A case report exists of an overdose of St. John's wort in a 16-year-old patient consuming 15 tablets (300 mcg strength) per day for 2 weeks, requiring management in an intensive care unit.

Local Anesthetic/Vasoconstrictor Precautions

No information available to require special precautions

Effects on Bleeding None reported

Syrian Rue

Clinical Overview

Uses

In several countries the plant has been traditionally used as an hallucinogen in ceremonies, and has found its way into modern day recreational use. Although in vitro and animal experiments suggest a role as an antimicrobial, vasorelaxant, antidepressant, analgesic, or cytotoxic agent, clinical studies are lacking to support any therapeutic application.

Dosing

Clinical applications are lacking to provide therapeutic dosages. Consumption of decoctions made from 100 to 150 g of seeds has resulted in toxic effects.

Contraindications

Harmala alkaloids (specifically harmine and harmaline) are reversible monoamine oxidase inhibitors (MAOI), thus concomitant use with MAOI medicines and tyramine-containing foods is not advised.

Pregnancy/Lactation

Documented adverse reactions. Avoid use.

Interactions

None well documented.

Adverse Reactions

Case reports of toxicity include nausea and vomiting, visual and auditory hallucinations, confusion, agitation, locomotor ataxia, tremors and convulsions, and life-threatening respiratory depression and coma. Severe gastrointestinal distress, vomiting blood, gastric ulceration, and convulsions have also been reported, as well as bradycardia and low blood pressure. Symptoms are generally of short duration (a few hours) and supportive therapy is recommended.

Toxicology

Information is limited. Elevated renal and liver function tests have been reported.

Local Anesthetic/Vasoconstrictor Precautions

Long-term use of syrian rue has been associated with hypertension, tachycardia, tachypnea, and heart block. Use vasoconstrictor with caution in order to minimize risk of hypertension or tachycardia.

Effects on Bleeding None reported

Tea Tree Oil

Clinical Overview

Uses

Despite an abundance of commercial preparations promoted for antimicrobial use, sound clinical trials are limited. Trials have been conducted in conditions including nail infections, athlete's foot, fungal skin infections, acne, and methicillin-resistant Staphylococcus aureus. Case reports exist for use in other conditions.

Dosing

Decolonization of methicillin-resistant S. aureus: Tea tree oil as a nasal cream (4% to 10%) applied 3 times a day for 5 days and 5% body wash for 5 days. Acne vulgaris: 5% tea tree oil gel applied for 20 minutes twice daily, then washed off. Onchomycosis (fungal nail infections): 100% tea tree oil applied for 6 months. Tinea pedis (athlete's foot): 25% to 50% tea tree oil for 4 weeks.

Contraindications

Oral ingestion is contraindicated.

Pregnancy/Lactation
Information regarding safety and efficacy in pregnancy and lactation is lacking.

Interactions
None well documented.

Adverse Reactions
Case reports exist of dermatitis associated with topical tea tree oil.

Toxicology
Tea tree oil is toxic when ingested orally. Some case studies of accidental and intentional poisoning exist; however, no deaths have been reported to the American Association of Poison Control Centers through 2006. Mutagenicity of tea tree oil appears to be low; however, chemical constituents have been shown to be cytotoxic and embryotoxic.

Local Anesthetic/Vasoconstrictor Precautions
No information available to require special precautions

Effects on Bleeding None reported

Thunder God Vine

Clinical Overview

Uses
Thunder god vine has been evaluated for use primarily in rheumatoid arthritis (RA); however, its adverse event profile and limited quality trials restrict any recommendations for clinical use. Antifertility properties in men have been described, while amenorrhea was observed in women.

Dosing
In RA trials, 60 mg/day of T2 (a chloroform-methanol extract of Tripterygium wilfordii) for 12 weeks has been evaluated, as well as ethanol/ethyl alcohol root extract 180 to 360 mg/day. Several long-term studies have evaluated the use of 1 mg/kg/day of T2 for up to 5 years; however, adequate safety data during the same time period are limited.

Contraindications
Contraindications have not been determined. Due to immune suppression, thunder god vine preparations should not be used in immune-compromised patients.

Pregnancy/Lactation
Avoid use. Embryotoxicity has been demonstrated in mice.

Interactions
None well documented.

Adverse Reactions
Clinically important adverse events have been reported in clinical trials. GI upset, male and female infertility, and immune suppression are common side effects of thunder god vine.

Toxicology
Information is limited. Embryotoxicity was demonstrated in mice, including neural effects, absence of limb buds, and ophthalmic-related effects.

Local Anesthetic/Vasoconstrictor Precautions
No information available to require special precautions

Effects on Bleeding None reported

Thyme

Clinical Overview

Uses
Thyme has primarily culinary uses. Thyme extracts and thymol have been used in cough mixtures and mouthwashes, as well as for skin conditions, especially fungal infections. Clinical trials are lacking to support these uses.

Dosing
Studies are lacking to guide clinical dosages.

Contraindications
Information is lacking.

Pregnancy/Lactation
Information regarding safety and efficacy in pregnancy and lactation is lacking.

Interactions
None well documented.

Adverse Reactions
Contact dermatitis and systemic allergy have been reported.

Toxicology
Information is lacking.

Local Anesthetic/Vasoconstrictor Precautions
No information available to require special precautions

Effects on Bleeding An extract from thyme has been shown to have antiplatelet aggregating activity. The clinical significance of this effect is unknown.

Tolu Balsam

Clinical Overview

Uses
Tolu balsam is best known for its fragrance and use as flavoring in pharmaceutical products, although it also has mild antiseptic and expectorant properties. There are no clinical data to support its use in any condition.

Dosing
There is no recent clinical evidence to support specific dosing of tolu balsam. Traditional dosage of the herb for colds has been 0.6 g daily.

Contraindications
Contraindications have not yet been determined.

Pregnancy/Lactation
Information regarding safety and efficacy in pregnancy and lactation is lacking.

Interactions
None well documented.

Adverse Reactions
Allergic reactions have been reported.

Toxicology
Information is lacking.

Local Anesthetic/Vasoconstrictor Precautions
No information available to require special precautions

Effects on Bleeding None reported

Turmeric

Clinical Overview

Uses
Use of curcumin (tumeric) as a pharmacologic agent is limited due to its low systemic bioavailability following oral dosing. Curcumin is used as a spice in curry powders and mustard. It is marketed with claims of potent antioxidant activity, improving bone and joint health, and reducing inflammation, but clinical trials are limited. Its efficacy in treating numerous cancers has been investigated.

Dosing
Curcumin is primarily available in capsule form from commercial manufacturers. The most common regimen is one to three 500 mg capsules daily with or without food. Powdered turmeric root has traditionally been used as a stimulant and carminative at dosages of 0.5 to 3 g/day. Dosages of 3 to 6 g/day have been investigated for protective effects against ulcers. Daily oral doses of curcumin 3,600 mg have been typically used in clinical trials, but dosages of up to curcumin

8 g/day have also been used. Higher doses are associated with adverse GI effects.

Contraindications

Avoid use if hypersensitive to any of the components of curcumin. Avoid use during pregnancy and lactation due to emmenagogue and uterine stimulant effects. The herb should not be used in patients with gall stones or bile duct or passage obstruction.

Pregnancy/Lactation

Avoid use. Documented emmenagogue and abortifacient effects.

Interactions

None well documented.

Adverse Reactions

Clinical trials report few adverse reactions. Rare cases of contact dermatitis and anaphylaxis have been reported.

Toxicology

Limited clinical data are available. The oral median lethal dose (LD_{50}) of curcumin in rats and mice was higher than 2,000 mg/kg body weight.

Local Anesthetic/Vasoconstrictor Precautions No information available to require special precautions

Effects on Bleeding May see increased bleeding due to inhibition of platelet aggregation

Ubiquinone

Clinical Overview

Uses

Ubiquinone may have applications in cardiovascular disease, especially congestive heart failure (CHF), although there is a lack of consensus. Studies in neurological disorders are less promising. Limited clinical trials have been conducted to support its widespread use for other conditions.

Dosing

Cardiovascular and neurologic trials predominantly use ubiquinone dosages of 300 mg/day or idebenone dosages of 5 mg/kg/day. Higher dosages of ubiquinone (up to 3,000 mg/day) have been used. Pharmacokinetic studies suggest split dosing is superior to single daily dosing.

Contraindications

Absolute contraindications have not been identified.

Pregnancy/Lactation

Information regarding safety and efficacy in pregnancy and lactation is lacking.

Interactions

Findings are conflicting. Case reports show ubiquinone decreases the anticoagulant effect of warfarin; however, a randomized clinical trial found no effect on the international normalized ratio (INR).

Adverse Reactions

Adverse effects are rare and include diarrhea, GI discomfort, headache, loss of appetite, and nausea. Allergic reactions have been reported.

Toxicology

An observed intake safety level of 1,200 mg/day is based on clinical data; however, dosages exceeding this amount have been used with no apparent adverse effect. No accumulation in plasma or tissue following cessation of coenzyme Q10 consumption has been noted.

Local Anesthetic/Vasoconstrictor Precautions No information available to require special precautions

Effects on Bleeding May increase the risk of bleeding

Uva Ursi

Clinical Overview

Uses

Uva ursi has been traditionally used to treat symptoms of mild urinary tract infections. However, there are no clinical trials demonstrating the safety, efficacy, or toxicity of its use. In vitro research supports its use as a urinary antiseptic.

Dosing

Dosing and formulations of uva ursi products available in the United States vary. Doses of arbutin 400 to 840 mg have been used.

Contraindications

Uva ursi is contraindicated during pregnancy and lactation.

Pregnancy/Lactation

Avoid use. Uva ursi is contraindicated during pregnancy and lactation.

Interactions

Uva ursi should not be administered with foods or drugs that acidify the urine.

Adverse Reactions

Ingestion of the dried leaves of uva ursi may cause a greenish brown discoloration of the urine. Ingestion of uva ursi leaves may cause nausea and vomiting due to its high tannin content. Bull's eye maculopathy has been reported with long-term ingestion (3 years).Topical application has caused leukoderma, erythema, and allergic contact dermatitis.

Toxicology

While uva ursi leaves are not carcinogenic, hydroquinone, a primary constituent of the plant, may be carcinogenic. A recommended therapeutic human daily dose of bearberry leaf extract (420 mg of hydroquinone derivatives calculated as anhydrous arbutin) liberates free hydroquinone in urine at a maximum exposure level of 11 mcg/kg of body weight per day. However, the daily exposure dose, below which there is negligible risk to humans, is 100 mcg/kg.

Local Anesthetic/Vasoconstrictor Precautions No information available to require special precautions

Effects on Bleeding None reported

Valerian

Clinical Overview

Uses

The evidence to support the common use of valerian in insomnia remains weak. However, as valerian preparations seem to have a wide margin of safety, further trials for insomnia and anxiety may be warranted.

Dosing

Anxiety: Valeprotriates 150 mg/day in 3 divided doses for 4 weeks has been used in a clinical trial. Other trials used the dried herb 0.5 to 2 g, extract 0.5 to 2 mL, and valerian tincture 2 to 4 mL for anxiety. Insomnia: Valerian extract 400 to 600 mg/day taken 1 hour before bedtime for 2 to 4 weeks has been used in clinical trials. Single-dose studies have consistently found no effect for single doses of valerian in insomnia.

Contraindications

Contraindications have not been identified.

Pregnancy/Lactation

Information regarding safety and efficacy in pregnancy and lactation is lacking.

Interactions

None well documented.

Adverse Reactions

In general, clinical studies have found valerian to have a wide margin of safety, be devoid of adverse effects, and have fewer adverse reactions than positive control drugs, such as diazepam. Headache and diarrhea have been reported in clinical trials, but hangover is seldom reported.

Toxicology

Valerian has been classified as GRAS (generally recognized as safe) in the United States for food use; extracts and the root oil are used as flavorings in foods and beverages. The observed in vitro cytotoxicity of valepotriate compounds may not be relevant in vivo because of limited absorption.

Local Anesthetic/Vasoconstrictor Precautions

No information available to require special precautions

Effects on Bleeding None reported

Vinpocetine

Clinical Overview

Uses

Vinpocetine is used to enhance memory and increase brain metabolism. It has also been used for ischemia and reperfusion injury, and is considered a neuroprotective agent. However, there are few robust clinical studies to support the use of vinpocetine in stroke, dementia, or other diseases of the CNS.

Dosing

Most clinical studies have used between 5 and 20 mg vinpocetine, given 3 times daily due to a short half-life (2 to 4 hours).

Contraindications

V. minor whole plant or extract is potentially contraindicated in constipation and hypotension.

Pregnancy/Lactation

Avoid use. Information regarding safety and efficacy in pregnancy and lactation is lacking. Traditional uses for lesser periwinkle include antilactagogue and emmenagogue effects.

Interactions

Caution is warranted in patients on anticoagulant medications.

Adverse Reactions

Vinpocetine is well tolerated. Minor adverse reactions include facial flushing, dry mouth, drowsiness, headache, insomnia, anxiety, dizziness, nausea, and indigestion.

Toxicology

None well documented.

Local Anesthetic/Vasoconstrictor Precautions

No information available to require special precautions

Effects on Bleeding Vinpocetine has the potential to increase the risk of bleeding or potentiate the effects of warfarin. Clinical relevance of this effect is unknown.

Vitamin D

Clinical Overview

Uses

Vitamin D, long recognized as playing a role in bone and calcium homeostasis, is being investigated for use in cardiovascular disease, cancer, diabetes, infections, multiple sclerosis, psoriasis, respiratory health, and other conditions. More clinical trials are needed.

Dosing

The American Academy of Pediatrics recommends 400 units/day of vitamin D in infants and adolescents. Clinical data are not yet sufficiently robust to make definitive recommendations for therapeutic dosages of vitamin D; however, in the elderly, 700 to 1,000 units/day have been shown to reduce the risk of falls.

Contraindications

Contraindications have not been identified.

Pregnancy/Lactation

Routine use of supplemental vitamin D during pregnancy is not supported by safety evidence. However, adequate maternal intake of vitamin D-containing foods during lactation ensures that breast-fed infants receive sufficient vitamin D.

Interactions

The use of statins has been shown to increase serum vitamin D levels. Corticosteriods decrease the metabolism of vitamin D and orlistat reduces its absorption; phenobarbital and phenytoin increase the hepatic metabolism of vitamin D.

Adverse Reactions

High doses of vitamin D have rarely produced adverse events in clinical trials.

Toxicology

Toxicity due to vitamin D is considered to manifest at serum levels greater than 150 ng/mL of 25-hydroxyvitamin D. Symptoms of hypervitaminosis D include fatigue, nausea, vomiting, and weakness associated with hypercalcemia.

Local Anesthetic/Vasoconstrictor Precautions

No information available to require special precautions

Effects on Bleeding None reported

Wild Yam

Clinical Overview

Uses

Clinical trials are generally lacking for topical formulations of Dioscorea for menopausal symptoms. Chinese yam polysaccharides have been evaluated in laboratory studies for potential as prebiotics, with varying results. Dioscorea oppositifolia tubers have been used as a saliva substitute.

Dosing

There are inadequate clinical trials on which to base dosing guidelines.

Contraindications

Contraindications have not been identified.

Pregnancy/Lactation

Information regarding safety and efficacy in pregnancy and lactation is lacking.

Interactions

None well documented.

Adverse Reactions

A clinical study evaluating the daily consumption of wild yam reported no adverse events. Topical preparations of wild yam extract are relatively free from adverse effects. Based on a single study in rats, oral D. villosa should be avoided in people with compromised renal function.

Toxicology

Topical D. villosa (with an upper limit of 3.5% diosgenin) was not found to be systemically toxic or genotoxic.

Local Anesthetic/Vasoconstrictor Precautions

No information available to require special precautions

Effects on Bleeding None reported

Willow Bark

Clinical Overview

Uses

Willow bark can be an effective analgesic if the salicylate content is adequate. Anticancer, antioxidant, and anti-inflammatory activity has been documented in limited trials. Clinical trials have shown that willow has moderate efficacy in treating lower back pain but very little efficacy in treating arthritic conditions.

Dosing

Willow is available in several dosage forms, including tablets, capsules, powder, and liquid. Willow bark has been used for analgesia at daily doses of 1 to 3 g of bark, corresponding to salicin 60 to 120 mg. A clinical study of patients with lower back pain used willow bark at a dose of salicin 120 to 240 mg/day. A proprietary extract of willow bark, Assalix, was standardized to contain 15% salicin. The pharmacokinetics of salicylic acid delivered from willow bark have been studied, and plasma half-life is approximately 2.5 hours. Another pharmacokinetic study of salicylic acid from salicin found peak levels within 2 hours after oral administration.

Contraindications

Patients with known hypersensitivity to aspirin should avoid any willow-containing product. This caution also applies to patients with asthma, impaired thrombocyte function, vitamin K antagonistic treatment, diabetes, gout, kidney or liver conditions, peptic ulcer disease, and in any other medical conditions in which aspirin is contraindicated.

Pregnancy/Lactation

Avoid use because of the lack of information regarding safety and efficacy during pregnancy and lactation.

Interactions

In general, drug interactions associated with salicylates may apply to willow-containing products. Therefore, avoid use with alcohol, barbiturates, sedatives, and other salicylate-containing products because of additive irritant effects and adverse reactions on the GI tract and blood platelets. Willow may also interact with oral anticoagulants (eg, warfarin), seizure medications (eg, phenytoin, valproate acid), and other medications (eg, methotrexate).

Adverse Reactions

Reports from clinical trials primarily document GI discomfort, such as nausea and stomachache, as well as dizziness and rash. An anaphylactic reaction to willow bark has been reported.

Toxicology

There is little or no toxicity information on the use of willow bark. However, the same toxicity associated with salicylates applies to willow. Patients should monitor for blood in stools, tinnitus, nausea or vomiting, and stomach or kidney irritation.

Local Anesthetic/Vasoconstrictor Precautions

No information available to require special precautions

Effects on Bleeding Salicylate derivatives of willow bark had little effect on platelet aggregation when compared with a daily cardioprotective dose of acetylsalicylate 100 mg. The total serum salicylate concentration of salicin, one of the principle salicylates of willow, was bioequivalent to acetylsalicylate 50 mg. There are no reports of bleeding caused by willow bark.

Wormwood

Clinical Overview

Uses

Wormwood was traditionally used to treat worm infestations, although no clinical data support this use. Anti-inflammatory, antipyretic, and chemotherapeutic activity are documented in nonhuman studies. Initial studies suggest that wormwood may improve Crohn disease symptoms, but information regarding the plant's use in immunoglobulin A (IgA) nephropathy is limited. In Germany, woodworm is used to treat loss of appetite, dyspepsia, and biliary dyskinesia. Wormwood is also used as a flavoring agent.

Dosing

Wormwood is commercially available as an essential oil, as well as in capsule, tablet, tincture, and aqueous extract dosage forms. However, no recent clinical evidence supports dosing recommendations. Traditional use of the herb for treating dyspepsia was dosed as an infusion of 2 to 3 g daily.

Contraindications

Avoid use with hypersensitivity to any of the components of wormwood, particularly the essential oil. It may be contraindicated in patients with an underlying defect of hepatic heme synthesis, because thujone is a porphyrogenic terpenoid.

Pregnancy/Lactation

Avoid use. Documented abortifacient and emmenagogue effects.

Interactions

A single case report suggests that wormwood may increase the international normalized ratio (INR) with warfarin.

Adverse Reactions

The volatile oil thujone in wormwood produces a state of excitement and is a powerful convulsant. Repeated ingestion of wormwood may result in absinthism, a syndrome characterized by digestive disorders, thirst, restlessness, vertigo, trembling of the limbs, numbness of the extremities, loss of intellect, delirium, paralysis, and death.

Toxicology

Wormwood is classified as an unsafe herb by the US Food and Drug Administration (FDA) because of the neurotoxic potential of thujone and its derivatives; it is generally regarded as safe if it is thujone free. The safety of wormwood is poorly documented despite its long history as a food additive. Convulsions, dermatitis, and renal failure have been reported.

Local Anesthetic/Vasoconstrictor Precautions

No information available to require special precautions

Effects on Bleeding None reported

Xylitol

Clinical Overview

Uses

Medical literature documents the use of xylitol in medical conditions and applications, including acute otitis media, dental caries, intravenous (IV) nutrition, and osteoporosis, although limited clinical trials exist.

Dosing

Dosage regimens vary. In one study to prevent ear infections in children, the daily dose varied from 8.4 g in chewing gum to 10 g in syrup. Xylitol oral solution at dosages of 5 g orally 3 times a day and 7.5 g orally once a day was well tolerated in young children. Xylitol chewing gum was effective in reducing dental caries when divided into at least 3 consumption periods per day for a total dose of 6 to 10 g. For adults 21 years and older at high risk of caries, consideration may be given for daily use of five 1 gram xylitol lozenges.

Contraindications

Avoid use if allergic to xylitol. Hypersensitivity reactions are documented.

Pregnancy/Lactation

Pregnancy: Category B. Xylitol is considered safe in pregnancy and during breastfeeding, according to the US Food and Drug Administration (FDA). The use of xylitol chewing gum in mothers lowered maternal oral bacterial load and reduced transmission of mutans streptococci to infants late in pregnancy and during the postpartum period.

Interactions

None well documented.

Adverse Reactions

The main adverse effects reported from oral xylitol use at a dosage exceeding 40 to 50 g/day included nausea, bloating, borborygmi (rumbling sounds of gas moving through the intestine), colic, diarrhea, and increased total bowel movement frequency.

Toxicology

Xylitol is generally nontoxic based on various clinical studies and its historical use in foods, pharmaceuticals, and nutraceuticals. Animal studies also confirm its overall safety profile. Renocerebral oxalosis with renal failure is documented with large doses of IV administered xylitol.

Local Anesthetic/Vasoconstrictor Precautions

No information available to require special precautions

Effects on Bleeding None reported

Yarrow

Clinical Overview

Uses

Clinical studies are limited.

Dosing

Traditionally, yarrow herb 4.5 g/day has been used for various conditions. However, there are no quality clinical studies to validate this dosing.

Contraindications

Yarrow use is contraindicated in known allergies to any members of the Aster family. Data for reported contraindications in epilepsy are lacking.

Pregnancy/Lactation

Avoid use. Documented adverse effects.

Interactions

None well documented.

Adverse Reactions

Contact dermatitis is the most commonly reported adverse reaction, but high doses may be associated with anticholinergic effects.

Toxicology

Yarrow is not generally considered toxic; however, an antispermatogenic effect has been reported, and safety data are insufficient to support use of the herb in cosmetic products.

Local Anesthetic/Vasoconstrictor Precautions

No information available to require special precautions

Effects on Bleeding None reported

Yohimbe

Clinical Overview

Uses

Yohimbine has been used primarily in the treatment of sexual dysfunction, weight (body fat) loss, and xerostomia (dry mouth). It has also been used in studies investigating autonomic failure and orthostatic hypotension.

Dosing

Yohimbine 6 mg given 3 times a day has been used in xerostomia trials. A mean dose of 0.4 mg/kg body weight or 30 mg daily, and a maximum of 50 mg, has been used in erectile dysfunction studies. In studies investigating effects on body mass, yohimbine 20 mg daily has been used.

Contraindications

This drug should not be used in the presence of renal or hepatic function impairment.

Pregnancy/Lactation

Do not use during pregnancy or lactation.

Interactions

None well documented.

Adverse Reactions

Clinical trials report few serious adverse reactions. There are case reports of rash, lupus-like syndrome, bronchospasm, severe hypotension, dysrhythmia, heart failure, and death. Increased anxiety, irritability, and excitability have also been reported. Animal studies suggest yohimbine may increase motor activity and seizures at higher dosages. Yohimbe may precipitate psychoses in predisposed individuals.

Toxicology

No data.

Local Anesthetic/Vasoconstrictor Precautions

Has potential to interact with epinephrine and levonordefrin to result in increased BP; use vasoconstrictor with caution

Effects on Bleeding None reported

ORAL MEDICINE TOPICS

PART I:
DENTAL MANAGEMENT AND THERAPEUTIC CONSIDERATIONS IN MEDICALLY-COMPROMISED PATIENTS

This first part of the chapter focuses on common medical conditions and their associated drug therapies with which the dentist must be familiar. Patient profiles with commonly associated drug regimens are described.

TABLE OF CONTENTS

CARDIOVASCULAR DISEASES

Cardiovascular disease is the most prevalent human disease affecting over 60 million Americans, accounting for >50% of all deaths in the United States. Surgical and pharmacological therapies have resulted in many cardiovascular patients living healthy and profitable lives. Consequently, patients presenting to the dental office may require treatment planning modifications related to the medical management of their cardiovascular disease. For the purposes of this text, we will cover coronary artery disease (CAD) including angina pectoris, myocardial infarction, cardiac arrhythmias, heart failure, and hypertension.

CARDIOVASCULAR DRUGS: DENTAL CONSIDERATIONS

Some of the drug listings are redundant because the drugs are used to treat more than one cardiovascular disorder. As a convenience to the reader, each table has been constructed as a stand alone listing of drugs for the given disorder.

CORONARY ARTERY DISEASE (CAD)

Any long-term decrease in the delivery of oxygen to the heart muscle can lead to the condition ischemic heart disease. Often arteriosclerosis and atherosclerosis result in a narrowing of the coronary vessels' lumina and are the most common causes of vascular ischemic heart disease. Other causes such as previous infarct, mitral valve regurgitation, and ruptured septa may also lead to ischemia in the heart muscle. The two most common major conditions that result from ischemic heart disease are angina pectoris and myocardial infarction. Sudden death can likewise result from ischemia.

To the physician, the most common presenting sign or symptom of ischemic heart disease is chest pain. This chest pain can be of a transient nature as in angina pectoris or the result of a myocardial infarction. This pain pattern is the more typical presentation in men; women may have more subtle signs of fatigue and general malaise. It is now believed that sudden death represents a separate occurrence that essentially involves the development of a lethal cardiac arrhythmia or coronary artery spasm leading to an acute shutdown of the heart muscle blood supply. Risk factors in patients for coronary atherosclerosis include age (males ≥45, females ≥55 years), family history of premature development, hypertension, hypercholesterolemia, low HDL, cigarette smoking, and diabetes mellitus.

CAD is the cause of about half of all deaths in the United States. CAD has been shown to be correlated with the levels of plasma cholesterol and/or triacylglycerol-containing lipoprotein particles. Primary prevention focuses on averting the development of CAD. In contrast, secondary prevention of CAD focuses on therapies to reduce morbidity and mortality in patients with clinically documented CAD.

Lipid-lowering and cardioprotective drugs provide significant risk-reducing benefits in the secondary prevention of CAD. By reducing the levels of total and low density cholesterol through the inhibition of hydroxymethylglutaryl-coenzyme A (HMG-CoA) reductase, statin drugs significantly improve survival. Cardioprotective drug therapy includes antiplatelet/anticoagulant agents to inhibit platelet adhesion; aggregation and blood coagulation; beta-blockers to lower heart rate, contractility and blood pressure; and the angiotensin-converting enzyme (ACE) inhibitors to lower peripheral resistance and workload. For a listing of lipid lowering drugs, see Table 1.

Table 1. Drugs Used in the Treatment of Hyperlipidemia

Reduction of Total and Low-Density Cholesterol Levels

HMG-CoA Reductase Inhibitors

Fluvastatin on page 757
Lovastatin on page 1027
Pitavastatin on page 1347
Pravastatin on page 1369
Rosuvastatin on page 1455
Simvastatin on page 1479
AtorvaSTATin on page 182

Fibrate Group

Fenofibrate and Derivatives on page 692
Gemfibrozil on page 791

Bile Acid Sequestrants

Cholestyramine Resin on page 355
Colesevelam on page 415
Colestipol on page 417

Nicotinic Acid

Niacin on page 1186

Cholesterol Absorption Inhibitor

Ezetimibe on page 680

Antilipemic Agent, Microsomal Triglyceride Transfer Protein (MTP) Inhibitor

Lomitapide on page 1015

Table 1. Drugs Used in the Treatment of Hyperlipidemia *(continued)*

PCSK9 Inhibitor

Alirocumab on page 96

Evolocumab on page 678

Miscellaneous

Omega-3-Acid Ethyl Esters

ANGINA PECTORIS (Emphasis on Unstable Angina)

Numerous physiologic triggers can initiate the rupture of plaque in coronary blood vessels. Rupture leads to the activation, adhesion and aggregation of platelets, and the activation of the clotting cascade, resulting in the formation of occlusive thrombus. If this process leads to the complete occlusion of the artery, acute myocardial infarction with ST-segment elevation occurs. Alternatively, if the process leads to severe stenosis but the artery remains partially patent, unstable angina can occur. Triggers which induce unstable angina include physical exertion, mechanical stress due to an increase in cardiac contractility, pulse rate, blood pressure, and vasoconstriction.

Recently, the non-ST-elevation Acute Coronary Syndrome guidelines have been updated by the American Heart Association and the American College of Cardiology Foundation (Amsterdam 2014). These guidelines may be helpful in outlining treatment strategies.

Pharmacologic therapy to treat unstable angina includes antiplatelet drugs, antithrombin therapy, and conventional antianginal therapy with beta-blockers (or non-dihydropyridine calcium channel blockers [eg, diltiazem]) and nitrates. These drug groups and selected agents are listed in Table 2 and see Antiplatelet and Anticoagulation Considerations in Dentistry on page 1764.

Conventional Antianginal Therapy: Beta-Blockers, Nitrates, Calcium Channel Blockers

The pharmacotherapeutic strategy in treating angina is directed at improving myocardial oxygen supply and/or decreasing myocardial oxygen demand. Myocardial oxygen supply can be increased through enhancing coronary blood flow. Myocardial oxygen demand can be reduced by decreasing heart rate, contractility, and myocardial wall tension. Preload, afterload, and myocardial wall thickness are determinants of myocardial wall tension.

Organic Nitrates

Organic nitrates benefit angina by enhancing coronary blood flow via vasodilation of both large epicardial vessels and neighboring collateral vessels and decreasing myocardial oxygen demand by dilating veins and reducing preload. In order to be effective for the chronic prevention of angina, organic nitrates need to be dosed in a manner that does not induce nitrate tolerance.

Beta-Blockers

Beta-blockers are beneficial in treating angina since they decrease heart rate and contractility. Beta-blockers without intrinsic sympathomimetic activity (ISA) are preferred and those with ISA generally should be avoided when treating angina (such beta-blockers may actually increase myocardial workload). Beta-blockers are useful in the treatment of stable and unstable angina; but, since they can induce coronary vasospasm, they should be avoided in patients with vasospastic angina (aka, Prinzmetal's or variant angina).

Beta-blockers are the preferred initial choice, often used in conjunction with an organic nitrate to more positively address the hemodynamic imbalances causing the angina. If the patient cannot tolerate the beta-blocker or if the beta-blocker therapy is contraindicated, a non-dihydropyridine calcium channel blocker (eg, diltiazem) with or without an organic nitrate can be considered. If combination therapy (ie, beta-blocker with an organic nitrate) is ineffective, a calcium channel blocker may be added. Type of calcium channel blocker chosen becomes important when combining with a beta-blocker. Since the combination of a beta-blocker and either of the non-dihydropyridine calcium channel blockers, verapamil or diltiazem, frequently induces undesirable bradycardia, a dihydropyridine calcium channel blocker is often selected in combination with a beta-blocker, unless the patient is experiencing unstable angina. Caution should be used when using beta-blockers in patients with difficult-to-control diabetes mellitus, bronchospastic disease, or peripheral vascular disease. The medications may be dosed as high as possible without inducing symptomatic bradycardia, hypotension, and/or heart blocks. Some patients on beta-blockers will experience fatigue and other adverse effects related to the central nervous system. Abrupt withdrawal of beta-blockers in patients with angina has been known to cause excessive tachycardia, ischemia, and cardiac arrhythmias.

Calcium Channel Blockers

Two categories of agents comprise the calcium channel blockers: Non-dihydropyridines (eg, diltiazem and verapamil) and the dihydropyridine family (eg, nifedipine). These agents are useful in treating stable and unstable angina and are the drugs of choice in treating variant angina. All three agents increase coronary blood flow. Verapamil and diltiazem reduce contractility, heart rate, and, to some extent, afterload (thus reducing wall tension). Dihydropyridines (eg, nifedipine) are potent afterload reducers and have no impact on reducing heart rate. In fact, dihydropyridines may actually increase heart rate in patients not on a beta-blocker and may increase ischemia in patients experiencing unstable angina.

Stable and Unstable Angina

Since stable and unstable angina are nearly always related to CAD, patients should be placed on aspirin and an angiotensin-converting enzyme inhibitor (especially if the patient has heart failure) in addition to antianginal therapy. Clopidogrel or prasugrel may be considered if the patient is allergic to aspirin. If applicable, weight reduction, smoking cessation, and following an appropriate low-cholesterol, low-fat diet should be encouraged as well as an effort to reduce other CAD risk factors. In addition to these lifestyle changes, the patient should be placed on a moderate or high dose statin if no contraindications exist. Titrating statins to LDL-C or non-HDL-C goals as primary or secondary prevention is no longer recommended by the ACC/AHA Blood Cholesterol Guidelines due to insufficient supporting evidence (Stone 2013).

Patients with cardiac stents who have not completed their full course of dual antiplatelet therapy should not have their antiplatelet agents discontinued even if only briefly. Premature interruption of therapy may result in stent thrombosis with subsequent MI. Discussion with the patient's cardiologist is required especially if urgent dental procedures are necessary.

Dental Management

The dental management of the patient with angina pectoris may include sedation techniques for complicated procedures (see the Sedation section in Management of the Patient With Anxiety or Depression on page 1873), to limit the extent of procedures, and to limit the use of local anesthesia containing 1:100,000 epinephrine to two carpules. Anesthesia without a vasoconstrictor might also be selected. The appropriate use of a vasoconstrictor in anesthesia, however, should be weighed against the necessity to maximize anesthesia. Complete history, appropriate referral, and consultation with the patient's physician should be done for patients who are known to be at risk for angina pectoris.

MYOCARDIAL INFARCTION

Myocardial infarction is the leading cause of death in the United States. It is an acute irreversible ischemic event that produces an area of myocardial necrosis in the heart tissue. If a patient has a previous history of myocardial infarction, he/she may be taking a variety of drugs (ie, antihypertensives, lipid lowering drugs, ACE inhibitors or angiotensin receptor blockers, and antianginal medications) to not only prevent a second infarct, but to treat the long-term effects associated ischemic heart disease. Postmyocardial infarction patients are often taking anticoagulants, such as warfarin, or antiplatelet agents, such as aspirin, clopidogrel, or prasugrel. Consultation with the prescribing physician by the dentist is necessary prior to invasive procedures. Temporary dose reduction may allow the dentist to proceed with very invasive procedures. Most procedures, however, can be accomplished without changing the anticoagulant or antiplatelet therapy at all, using local hemostasis techniques and thereby keeping the thromboembolic risk to a minimum.

Aspirin on page 168
Warfarin on page 1665

Thrombolytic drugs, which might dissolve hemostatic plugs, may also be given on a short-term basis immediately following a myocardial infarction and include:

Alteplase on page 104
Reteplase on page 1430
Tenecteplase on page 1538

Following myocardial infarction and rehabilitation, outpatients may be placed on antiplatelet agents, beta-adrenergic blockers, ACE inhibitors or angiotensin receptor blockers, lipid-lowering therapies, and possibly aldosterone inhibitors and diuretics, if significant heart failure is associated with the MI, or even anticoagulants (such as warfarin) when significant thromboembolic risk coexists. Depending on the presence or absence of continued angina pectoris, patients may also be taking nitrates, beta-blockers, or calcium channel blockers as indicated for treatment of angina.

Beta-Adrenergic Blocking Agents Categorized According to Specific Properties

Alpha-Adrenergic Blocking Activity

Carvedilol on page 304
Labetalol on page 953

Intrinsic Sympathomimetic Activity

Acebutolol on page 55
Pindolol on page 1341

Long Duration of Action and Fewer CNS Effects

Atenolol on page 179
Betaxolol (Systemic) on page 223
Nadolol on page 1160

Beta-1 Receptor Selectivity

Atenolol on page 179
Betaxolol (Systemic) on page 223
Metoprolol on page 1106
Nebivolol on page 1176

Nonselective (blocks both beta-1 and beta-2 receptors)

Nadolol on page 1160
Propranolol on page 1397
Timolol (Systemic)

ARRHYTHMIAS

Abnormal cardiac rhythm can develop spontaneously and survivors of a myocardial infarction are often left with an arrhythmia. An arrhythmia is any alteration or disturbance in the normal rate, rhythm, or conduction through the cardiac tissue. Abnormalities in rhythm can occur in either the atria or the ventricles. Various valvular deformities, drug effects, and chemical derangements can initiate arrhythmias. These arrhythmias can be a slowing of the heart rate (<60 beats/minute) as defined in bradycardia or tachycardia resulting in a rapid heart beat (usually >150 beats/minute). The dentist will encounter a variety of treatments for management of arrhythmias. Usually, underlying causes such as reduced cardiac output, hypertension, and irregular ventricular beats will require treatment. Pacemaker therapy is also sometimes used. Indwelling pacemakers may require supplementation with antibiotics, and consultation with the physician is certainly appropriate.

Beta-blockers are often used to slow cardiac rate and diazepam may be helpful when anxiety is a contributing factor in arrhythmia. When atrial flutter and atrial fibrillation are diagnosed, drug therapy is usually required.

Atrial fibrillation (AF) is an arrhythmia characterized by multiple electrical activations in the atria resulting in scattered and disorganized depolarization and repolarization of the myocardium. Atrial contraction can lead to an irregular and rapid rate of ventricular contraction. The prevalence of AF within the US population ranges between 1% and 4%, with the incidence increasing with age. It is often associated with rheumatic valvular disease and nonvalvular conditions including CAD, heart failure, and hypertension. CAD is present in about one-half of the patients with AF. Atrial fibrillation is a major risk factor for cerebral embolism. It is thought that thrombi develop as a result of stasis in the dilated left atrium and are dislodged by sudden changes in cardiac rhythm. About 10% of all strokes in patients >60 years of age are caused by AF.

The cornerstones of drug therapy for atrial fibrillation are the restoration and maintenance of a normal sinus rhythm through the use of antiarrhythmic drugs, ventricular rate control through the use of beta-blockers, digoxin, or calcium channel blockers, and stroke prevention through the use of anticoagulants.

Antiarrhythmic Drugs

Cardiac rhythm is conducted through the sinoatrial (SA) and atrioventricular (AV) nodes, bundle branches, and Purkinje fibers. Electrical impulses are transmitted within this system by the opening and closing of sodium and potassium channels. Antiarrhythmic drugs are classified by which primary channel they act upon, a classification known as Vaughan Williams. The Class I agents act primarily on sodium channels, and the Class III agents act on potassium channels. In addition, there are subclassifications within the Class I agents according to effects of the drug on conduction and refractoriness within the Purkinje and ventricular tissues. Class IA agents show moderate depression of conduction and prolongation of repolarization.

Atrial Fibrillation: Restoring and Maintaining Normal Sinus Rhythm

Pharmacologic cardioversion may be attempted in hemodynamically stable patients whose ventricular rate is controlled. If a patient has been in atrial fibrillation for ≥48 hours, anticoagulation with warfarin should be considered prior to cardioversion and for at least 4 weeks after cardioversion. Drugs recommended for pharmacologic cardioversion include amiodarone, dofetilide (must be initiated within the hospital), flecainide, or propafenone, depending upon patient's specific characteristics (eg, heart failure).

Ventricular Rate Control

It is accepted practice to treat patients with medication when the resting ventricular rate is >110 beats/minute. Non-dihydropyridine calcium channel blockers and beta-adrenergic blockers are recommended to regulate ventricular rate. Although commonly used, digoxin should be reserved for patients with concurrent heart failure. Digoxin increases the vagal tone to the AV node, non-dihydropyridine calcium channel blockers slow the AV nodal conduction, and the beta-adrenergic blocking drugs decrease the sympathetic activation of AV nodal conduction.

Anticoagulants Useful in Arrhythmias

Warfarin (Coumadin) elicits its anticoagulant effect by interfering with the hepatic synthesis of vitamin K-dependent coagulation factors II, VII, IX, and X. Although warfarin appears to be somewhat effective after myocardial infarction in preventing death or recurrent myocardial infarction, its effectiveness in the treatment of acute coronary syndrome is questionable. Combination therapy with aspirin and heparin, followed by warfarin, has resulted in reduced incidence of recurrent angina, myocardial infarction, death, or all three at 14 days, compared to aspirin alone. In contrast, another study failed to show any additional benefit in the treatment of acute coronary syndrome using a combination of aspirin and warfarin, compared to aspirin alone (Douketis 2012).

Recently, the FDA approved dabigatran (Pradaxa), rivaroxaban (Xarelto), apixaban (Eliquis), and edoxaban (Savavsa) for the prevention of stroke and systemic embolism in patients with atrial fibrillation. Dabigatran was the first FDA-approved replacement available for warfarin. Dabigatran is an anticoagulant that acts by inhibiting thrombin, an enzyme in the blood that is involved in blood clotting. Thrombin (serine protease) enables the conversion of fibrinogen to fibrin during the coagulation cascade, preventing the development of thrombus. Caution is required for patients with mild renal impairment (creatinine clearance 50 to 80 mL/minute), dosage adjustments are required for patients with moderate to severe renal impairment (creatinine clearance 15 to 50 mL/minute), and use is considered contraindicated in patients with a creatinine clearance of <15 mL/minute or those on hemodialysis. Until recently, there have been no direct reversal agents for the novel oral anticoagulant drugs. Idarucizumab (Praxbind) has been approved by the Food and Drug Administration for reversing the anticoagulant effects of dabigatran. Specifically, idarucizumab is intended for use in patients who, while taking dabigatran, require reversal of anticoagulation for emergency surgery/urgent procedures, or those experiencing life-threatening or uncontrolled bleeding. The other novel oral anticoagulants which inhibit Factor X (ie, apixaban, edoxaban, and rivaroxaban) do not currently have approved reversal agents available.

Dental clinicians should consider consultation with the patient's health care provider prior to invasive therapies. However, recent reviews have argued that inappropriate adjustments in anticoagulation therapy places the patient at far greater risk of stroke than hemorrhage during most dental procedures (Armstrong 2013; Douketis 2012; Jeske 2003). Therefore, scientific evidence does not support changing regimens of anticoagulation therapy in most instances.

Table 2. Antithrombotic Drugs Used to Manage Unstable Angina

Antiplatelet Drugs

Aspirin on page 168

Clopidogrel on page 400

Prasugrel on page 1367

Ticagrelor on page 1564

Ticlopidine on page 1566

Glycoprotein IIb/IIIa Receptor Antagonists

Abciximab on page 51

Eptifibatide on page 590

Tirofiban on page 1574

Antithrombin Drugs

Indirect Thrombin Inhibitors

Heparin (unfractionated) on page 812

Low molecular weight heparins

Dalteparin on page 444

Enoxaparin on page 576

Nadroparin on page 1161

Direct Thrombin Inhibitors

Bivalirudin on page 231

Factor Xa Inhibitors

Fondaparinux on page 766

REFERENCES

Albert NM. Use of novel oral anticoagulants for patients with atrial fibrillation: systematic review and clinical implications. *Heart Lung*. 2014;43(1):48-59.

American Diabetes Association. Standards of medical care in diabetes − 2013. *Diabetes Care*. 2013;36(Suppl 1):11-66.

Amin H, Nowak RJ, Schindler JL. Cardioembolic stroke: practical considerations for patient risk management and secondary prevention. *Postgrad Med*. 2014;126(1):55-65.

Amsterdam EA, Wenger NK, Brindis RG, et al; ACC/AHA Task Force Members. 2014 AHA/ACC guideline for the management of patients with non-ST-elevation acute coronary syndromes: a report of the American College of Cardiology/American Heart Association Task Force on Practice Guidelines. *Circulation*. 2014; 130(25):e344-426.

Armstrong MJ, Gronseth G, Anderson DC, et al. Summary of evidence-based guideline: periprocedural management of antithrombotic medications in patients with ischemic cerebrovascular disease: report of the Guideline Development Subcommittee of the American Academy of Neurology. Neurology. 2013;80(22):2065-2069.

Aspirin may prevent blood clots in the legs from recurring. *Harvard Heart Lett*. 2013;23(6):8.

Brunzell JD, Davidson M, Furberg CD, et al. Lipoprotein management in patients with cardiometabolic risk: consensus statement from the American Diabetes Association and the American College of Cardiology Foundation. *Diabetes Care*. 2008;31(4):811-822.

Douketis JD. Contra: "bridging anticoagulation is needed during warfarin interruption when patients require elective surgery." *Thromb Haemost*. 2012;108(2):210-212.

Fihn SD, Blankenship JC, Alexander KP, et al. 2014 ACC/AHA/AATS/PCNA/SCAI/STS focused update of the guideline for the diagnosis and management of patients with stable ischemic heart disease: a report of the American College of Cardiology/American Heart Association Task Force on Practice Guidelines, and the American Association for Thoracic Surgery, Preventive Cardiovascular Nurses Association, Society for Cardiovascular Angiography and Interventions, and Society of Thoracic Surgeons. *Circulation*. 2014;130(19):1749-1767.

Fihn SD, Gardin JM, Abrams J, et al. 2012 ACCF/AHA/ACP/AATS/PCNA/SCAI/STS guideline for the diagnosis and management of patients with stable ischemic heart disease: a report of the American College of Cardiology Foundation/American Heart Association Task Force on Practice Guidelines, and the American College of Physicians, American Association for Thoracic Surgery, Preventive Cardiovascular Nurses Association, Society for Cardiovascular Angiography and Interventions, and Society of Thoracic Surgeons. *Circulation*. 2012;126(25):e354-e471.

Gaziano M, Ridker PM, Libby P. Primary and secondary prevention of coronary heart disease. In: Bonow RO, Mann DL, Zipes DP, Libby P, eds. *Braunwald'sHeart Disease: A Textbook of Cardiovascular Medicine*. 9th ed. Saunders; 2011:chap 49.

Heart Failure Society of America, Lindenfeld J, Albert NM, et al. HFSA 2010 comprehensive heart failure practice guideline. *J Card Fail*. 2010;16(6):e1-e194.

Jeske AH, Suchko GD; ADA Council on Scientific Affairs and Division of Science; Journal of the American Dental Association. Lack of a scientific basis for routine discontinuation of oral anticoagulation therapy before dental treatment. *J Am Dent Assoc*. 2003;134(11):1492-1497.

Lee TH, Lee RT. Ask the doctors. There is a long list of drugs and substances that interact with Coumadin (warfarin). Does this mean they make Coumadin more effective, or less effective? *Harvard Heart Lett*. 2013;24(1):2.

New alternatives to warfarin. New drugs may be best when starting treatment for atrial fibrillation, but don't switch if warfarin works for you. *Harvard Heart Lett*. 2013;24(1):4-5.

O'Gara PT, Kushner FG, Ascheim DD, et al. 2013 ACCF/AHA guideline for the management of ST-elevation myocardial infarction: a report of the American College of Cardiology Foundation/American Heart Association Task Force on Practice Guidelines. *Circulation*. 2013;127(4):e362-e425.

Skanes AC, Healey JS, Cairns JA, et al. Focused 2012 update of the Canadian Cardiovascular Society atrial fibrillation guidelines: recommendations for stroke prevention and rate/rhythm control. *Can J Cardiol*. 2012;28(2):125-136.

Smith SC Jr, Benjamin EJ, Bonow RO, et al. AHA/ACCF secondary prevention and risk reduction therapy for patients with coronary and other atherosclerotic vascular sisease: 2011 update: a guideline from the American Heart Association and American College of Cardiology Foundation. *Circulation*. 2011;124(22):2458-2473.

Stone NJ, Robinson J, Lichtenstein AH, et al. 2013 ACC/AHA guideline on the treatment of blood cholesterol to reduce atherosclerotic cardiovascular risk in adults: a report of the American College of Cardiology/American Heart Association Task Force on Practice Guidelines. *Circulation*. 2014; 129 (25 Suppl 2):S1-45.

Vandvik PO, Lincoff AM, Gore JM, et al. Primary and secondary prevention of cardiovascular disease: Antithrombotic Therapy and Prevention of Thrombosis, 9th ed: American College of Chest Physicians Evidence-Based Clinical Practice Guidelines. *Chest*. 2012;141(2 Suppl):e637S-68S.

Wann LS, Curtis AB, January CT, et al. 2011 ACCF/AHA/HRS focused update on the management of patients with atrial fibrillation (updating the 2006 guideline): a report of the American College of Cardiology Foundation/American Heart Association Task Force on Practice Guidelines. *Circulation*. 2011;123(1):104-123.

Yancy CW. ACC/AHA task force on practice guidelines. Circulation. 2013;128(16):e240e327.

HEART FAILURE

Heart failure is a condition in which the heart is unable to pump sufficient blood to meet the metabolic demand of the body. It is caused by impairment of cardiac muscle contraction or ventricular filling. Most frequently, the underlying cause of heart failure is ischemic heart disease. Other major contributory causes include hypertension, idiopathic dilated cardiomyopathy, and valvular heart disease. It is estimated that heart failure affects approximately 5 million Americans. The New York Heart Association functional classification is regarded as the standard measure to describe the severity of a patient's symptom. Class I is characterized by having no limitation of physical activity. There is no dyspnea, fatigue, palpitations, or angina with ordinary physical activity. There is no objective evidence of cardiovascular dysfunction. Class II includes those patients having slight limitation of physical activity. These patients experience fatigue, palpitations, dyspnea, or angina with ordinary physical activity, but are comfortable at rest. There is evidence of minimal cardiovascular dysfunction. Class III is characterized by marked limitation of activity. Less-than-ordinary physical activity causes fatigue, palpitations, dyspnea, or angina, but patients are comfortable at rest. There is objective evidence of moderately severe cardiovascular dysfunction. Class IV is characterized by the inability to carry out any physical activity without discomfort. Symptoms of heart failure may be present even at rest, and any physical activity undertaken increases discomfort. There is objective evidence of severe cardiovascular dysfunction. Drug classes and the specific agents used to treat heart failure are listed in Table 3.

Table 3. Drugs Used in the Treatment of Heart Failure

Table 3. Drugs Used in the Treatment of Heart Failure *(continued)*

Supplemental Agents
Direct-Acting Vasodilators
HydrALAZINE on page 820
Isosorbide Dinitrate on page 926
Isosorbide Mononitrate on page 926
Nitroglycerin on page 1202

[a]Regarded as the cornerstone of heart failure treatment and should be used routinely and early in all patients.

Drug Classes and Specific Agents Used to Treat Heart Failure

Angiotensin-converting enzyme (ACE) inhibitors reduce left ventricular volume and filling pressure while decreasing total peripheral resistance. They improve cardiac output (modestly) and natriuresis. ACE inhibitors are usually used in all patients with heart failure if no contraindication or intolerance exists. This group of drugs is considered the cornerstone of treatment and is used routinely and early if pharmacologic treatment is indicated. Angiotensin receptor blockers may be used if a patient cannot tolerate an ACE inhibitor or in rare instances used with an ACE inhibitor when persistent symptoms or progressive worsening occurs despite optimal ACE inhibitor and beta-blocker therapy.

Beta-adrenergic receptor blocking drugs (beta-blockers), specifically carvedilol, bisoprolol, and metoprolol extended release, are used in the treatment of heart failure because of their beneficial effect in reducing mortality.

Diuretics increase sodium chloride and water excretion resulting in reduction of preload, thus relieving the symptoms of pulmonary congestion associated with heart failure. They may also reduce myocardial oxygen demand. The thiazides, loop diuretics, and potassium-sparing agents are all useful in reducing preload by way of their diuretic actions.

Digitalis glycosides have been used in the treatment of heart failure for >200 years. Digitalis drugs increase cardiac output by a direct positive inotropic action on the myocardium. This increased cardiac output results in decreased venous pressure, reduced heart size, and diminished compensatory tachycardia.

Other drugs used in the treatment of heart failure include aldosterone blockers and direct-acting vasodilators. Direct-acting vasodilators (hydralazine, isosorbide) may be used in place of an ACE inhibitor or angiotensin receptor blocker. The direct-acting vasodilators reduce excessive vasoconstriction and reduce workload of the failing heart. Aldosterone blockers may be used in severe forms of heart failure to enhance survival; close attention to introduction and monitoring is essential to prevent hyperkalemia.

HYPERTENSION

In the United States, almost 50 million adults 25 to 74 years of age have hypertension. Hypertension is defined as systolic blood pressure ≥140 mm Hg, and/or diastolic pressure >90 mm Hg. People with blood pressure above normal are considered at increased risk of developing damage to the heart, kidney, brain, and eyes, resulting in premature morbidity and mortality.

Hypertension is one of the most common systemic conditions seen in primary care medicine and can lead to myocardial infarction, stroke, renal failure, and death if not detected early and treated appropriately. The Eighth Joint National Committee (JNC 8) Report on Prevention, Detection, Evaluation and Treatment of High Blood Pressure convened in 2008 to begin work on revisions of the JNC 7 which had been in place since 2003. The committee used evidence based principles to determine suggested changes in how HBP is managed. Other international organizations may have slightly different guidelines but the overreaching goals are the same, ie, to recommend lifestyle modifications and pharmacologic regimens that reduce BP to levels that lower these risks. The definitions of high blood pressure have not changed.

The recommendations are very detailed into nine specifics and for practicing dentists the primary changes over the JNC 7 report relate to relaxing the treatment targets for otherwise healthy patients >60 years of age and suggesting other drugs such as angiotensin-converting enzyme inhibitors, angiotensin receptor blockers and calcium channel blockers as alternative first line therapy as alternatives in addition to thiazide-type diuretics.

The suggested initial goals of drug therapy are the maintenance of an arterial pressure of ≤140/90 mm Hg with concurrent control of other modifiable cardiovascular risk factors. Further reduction to 130/85 mm Hg should be pursued if cardiovascular and cerebrovascular function is not compromised. The Hypertension Optimal Treatment (HOT) randomized trial using patients 50 to 80 years of age found that the lowest incidence of major cardiovascular events and the lowest risk of cardiovascular mortality occurred at a mean diastolic blood pressure of 82.6 and 86.5 mm Hg, respectively. The target blood pressure for patients with diabetes or chronic kidney disease is <130/90 mm Hg.

Table 4. Classification of Blood Pressure for Adults ≥18 Years of Age

BP Classification	Systolic BP (mm Hg)		Diastolic BP (mm Hg)
Normotensive	<120	and	<80
Prehypertension[a]	120 to 139	or	80 to 89
Stage 1 hypertension[b]	140 to 159	or	90 to 99
Stage 2 hypertension[c]	≥160	or	≥100

[a]Not taking antihypertensive drugs and not acutely ill. When systolic and diastolic blood pressures fall into different categories, the higher category should be selected to classify the individual's blood pressure status. In addition to classifying stages of hypertension on the basis of average blood pressure levels, clinicians should specify presence or absence of target organ disease and additional risk factors. The specificity is important for risk classification and treatment.

[b]Optimal blood pressure with respect to cardiovascular risk is below 120/80 mm Hg. However, unusually low readings should be evaluated for clinical significance.

[c]Based on the average of two or more readings taken at each of two or more visits after an initial screening.

Adapted from: Weber MA, Schiffrin EL, White WB, et al. Clinical practice guidelines for the management of hypertension in the community: a statement by the American Society of Hypertension and the International Society of Hypertension. *J Clin Hypertens (Greenwich)*. 2014;16(1):14-26.

James PA, Oparil S, Carter BL, et al, 2014 evidence-based guideline for the management of high blood pressure in adults. Report from the panel members appointed to the eighth joint national committee (JNC8). *JAMA*. Published online December 18, 2013.

Table 5. Lifestyle Modifications to Manage Hypertension[a,b,c,j]

Modification	Recommendation	Approximate Systolic Reduction (Range)
Weight reduction	Maintain normal body weight (body mass index 18.5 to 24.9 kg/m^2)	5 to 20 mm of Hg/10 kg weight loss[d]
Adopt DASH[5] eating plan	Consume a diet rich in fruits, vegetables, and low-fat dairy products with a reduced content of saturated and total fat	8 to 14 mm Hg[f]
Dietary sodium reduction	Reduce dietary sodium intake to ≤100 mmol/day (2.4 g sodium or 6 g sodium chloride)	2 to 8 mm Hg[g]
Physical activity	Engage in regular aerobic physical activity such as brisk walking (≥30 minutes/day, most days of the week)	4 to 9 mm Hg[h]
Moderation of alcohol consumption	Limit consumption to ≤2 drinks (1 oz or 30 mL ethanol); (eg, 24 oz beer, 10 oz wine, or 3 oz 80 proof whiskey) per day in most men and to ≤1 drink/day in women and lighter weight people	2 to 4 mm Hg[i]

[a]Adapted from: US Department of Health and Human Services; National Institutes of Health; National Heart, Lung, and Blood Institute; National High Blood Pressure Education Program

[b]Overall cardiovascular risk education can be achieved by cessation of smoking

[c]The effects of implementing these modifications are dose- and time-dependent and could be greater for some people.

[d]The trials of Hypertension Prevention Collaborative Research Group; He and colleagues

[e]DASH: Dietary Approaches to Stop Hypertension

[f]Sacks and colleagues; Vollmer and colleagues

[g]Sacks and colleagues; Vollmer and colleagues; Chobanian and Hill

[h]Kelley and Kelley; Whelton and colleagues

[i]Xin and colleagues

[j]Eckel RH, Jakicic JM, Ard JD, et al. 2013 AHA/ACC guideline on lifestyle management to reduce cardiovascular risk: a report of the American College of Cardiology/American Heart Association task force on practice guidelines. *Circulation*. 2013.

Table 6. Drug Categories and Representative Agents Used in the Treatment of Hypertension[a]

Diuretics

Thiazide Types

Chlorothiazide on page 348

Chlorthalidone on page 353

HydroCHLOROthiazide on page 820

Indapamide on page 880

Methyclothiazide

MetOLazone on page 1105

Loops

Bumetanide on page 250

Furosemide on page 777

Torsemide on page 1586

Potassium-Sparing

AMILoride on page 111

Eplerenone on page 586

Table 6. Drug Categories and Representative Agents Used in the Treatment of Hypertension[a] *(continued)*

Table 6. Drug Categories and Representative Agents Used in the Treatment of Hypertension[a] *(continued)*

Direct-Acting Peripheral Vasodilator

HydrALAZINE on page 820

Minoxidil (Systemic) on page 1130

Current Thinking Regarding Antihypertensive Drug Selection

Medications in the first eight categories in Table 6 were held to be equally effective in two large-scale studies reported in the *New England Journal of Medicine* and the *Journal of the American Medical Association*, and that any of the medications could be used initially for monotherapy. The JNC 8 panel determined that there is strong evidence to support treating hypertensive persons ≥60 years of age to a BP goal of <150/90 mm Hg and hypertensive persons 30 to 59 years of age to a diastolic goal of <90 mm Hg. However, there is insufficient evidence in hypertensive persons <60 years of age for a systolic goal, or in those <30 years of age for a diastolic goal, so the panel recommends a BP of <140/90 mm Hg for those groups based on expert opinion. The same thresholds and goals are recommended for hypertensive adults with diabetes or nondiabetic chronic kidney disease (CKD) as for the general hypertensive population <60 years of age. There is moderate evidence to support initiating drug treatment with an angiotensin-converting enzyme inhibitor, angiotensin receptor blocker, calcium channel blocker, or thiazide-type diuretic in the nonblack hypertensive population, including those with diabetes. In the black hypertensive population, including those with diabetes, a calcium channel blocker or thiazide-type diuretic is recommended as initial therapy. There is moderate evidence to support initial or add-on antihypertensive therapy with an angiotensin-converting enzyme inhibitor or angiotensin receptor blocker in persons with CKD to improve kidney outcomes.

These guidelines provide evidence-based recommendations for the management of high BP and should meet the clinical needs of most patients. They are not a substitute for clinical judgment, and all clinicians' decisions about care should incorporate the clinical characteristics and co-morbidities of each individual patient.

Beta-blockers are the agents of choice in patients with coronary artery disease or supraventricular arrhythmia, and in young patients with hyperdynamic circulation. Beta-blockers are alternatives for initial therapy and are more effective in white patients than in black patients. Beta-blockers are not considered first choice drugs in elderly patients with uncomplicated hypertension. The beta-blocking drug carvedilol also selectively blocks alpha-1 receptors.

Alpha-1 adrenergic blocking agents (eg, prazosin) can be used as initial therapy in patients with benign prostatic hypertrophy (BPH).

ACE inhibitors are the preferred drugs for patients with coexisting heart failure. They are useful as initial therapy in hypertensive patients with kidney damage or diabetes mellitus with proteinuria, and in non-black patients. No clinically relevant differences have been found among the available ACE inhibitors. The ACE inhibitors are well-tolerated by young, physically active patients and elderly patients. The most common adverse effect of the ACE inhibitors is dry cough. Angiotensin II receptor blockers produce hemodynamic effects similar to ACE inhibitors while avoiding dry cough. These agents are similar to the ACE inhibitors in potency and are useful for initial therapy.

Calcium channel blocking agents are effective as initial therapy in both black and non-black patients, and are well-tolerated by elderly patients. These agents inhibit entry of calcium ion into cardiac cells and smooth muscle cells of the coronary and systemic vasculature. The dihydropyridine calcium channel blockers, nifedipine (Procardia) and amlodipine (Norvasc), are more potent as peripheral vasodilators than diltiazem (Cardizem).

Supplemental antihypertensive agents include the centrally-acting alpha-2 agonists and direct-acting vasodilators. These agents are less commonly prescribed for initial therapy because of the impressive effectiveness of the other drug groups. Clonidine (Catapres) lowers blood pressure by activating inhibitory alpha-2 receptors in the CNS, thus reducing sympathetic outflow. It lowers both supine and standing blood pressure by reducing total peripheral resistance.

The most common oral side effects of the management of the hypertensive patient are related to the antihypertensive drug therapy. A dry, sore mouth can be caused by diuretics and centrally-acting adrenergic inhibitors. Occasionally, lichenoid reactions can occur in patients taking methyldopa. The thiazides are occasionally also implicated. Lupus-like face rashes can be seen in patients taking calcium channel blockers as well.

REFERENCES

American Diabetes Association. Standards of medical care in diabetes — 2013. *Diabetes Care.* 2013;36(suppl 1):S11-S66.

Benavente OR, Coffey CS, Conwit R, et al; SPS3 Study Group. Blood-pressure targets in patients with recent lacunar stroke: the SPS3 randomised trial. *Lancet.* 2013;382(9891):507-515.

Cushman WC, Evans GW, Byington RP, et al; ACCORD Study Group. Effects of intensive blood-pressure control in type 2 diabetes mellitus. *N Engl J Med.* 2010;362(17):1575-1585.

Eckel RH, Jakicic JM, Ard JD, et al. AHA/ACC guideline on lifestyle management to reduce cardiovascular risk: a report of the American College of Cardiology/American Heart Association task force on practice guidelines. *Circulation.* 2013.

Flack JM, Sica DA, Bakris G, et al; International Society on Hypertension in Blacks. Management of high blood pressure in blacks: an update of the International Society on hypertension in blacks consensus statement. *Hypertension.* 2010;56(5):780-800.

Gibbons GH, Harold JG, Jessup M, Robertson RM, OetgenWJ. The next steps in developing clinical practice guidelines for prevention. *J AmColl Cardiol.* 2013;62(15):1399-1400.

Gibbons GH, Shurin SB, Mensah GA, Lauer MS. Refocusing the agenda on cardiovascular guidelines: an announcement from the National Heart, Lung, and Blood Institute. *Circulation.* 2013;128(15):1713-1715.

Hypertension without compelling indications: 2013 CHEP recommendations. Hypertension Canada website. http://www.hypertension.ca/hypertension-without-compelling-indications. Accessed October 30, 2013.

Institute of Medicine. Clinical Practice Guidelines We Can Trust.Washington, DC: National Academies Press; 2011. http://www.iom.edu/Reports/2011/Clinical-Practice-Guidelines-We-Can-Trust.aspx.

James PA, Oparil S, Carter BL, et al. MPH 2014 Evidence-based guideline for the management of high blood pressure in adults report from the panel members appointed to the eighth Joint National Committee (JNC 8). *JAMA.* Published online December 18, 2013.

Kidney Disease; Improving Global Outcomes (KDIGO) Blood Pressure Work Group. KDIGO clinical practice guideline for the management of blood pressure in chronic kidney disease. *Kidney Int Suppl.* 2012;2(5):337-414.

Lindenfeld J, Albert NM, Boehmer JP, et al. HFSA 2010 comprehensive heart failure practice guideline. *J Card Fail.* 2010;16(6):e1-e194.

Mancia G, Fagard R, Narkiewicz K, et al. 2013 ESH/ESC guidelines for the management of arterial hypertension: the task force for the management of arterial hypertension of the european society of hypertension (ESH) and of the european society of cardiology (ESC). *Eur Heart J.* 2013;34 (28):2159-2219.

Pickering TG, Hall JE, Appel LJ, et al. Recommendations for blood pressure measurement in humans and experimental animals: part 1: blood pressure measurement in humans: a statement for professionals from the Subcommittee of Professional and Public Education of the American Heart Association Council on High Blood Pressure Research. *Circulation.* 2005;111(5):697-716.

Verdecchia P, Staessen JA, Angeli F, et al. Cardio-Sis investigators. Usual versus tight control of systolic blood pressure in non-diabetic patients with hypertension (Cardio-Sis): an open-label randomised trial. *Lancet.* 2009;374(9689): 525-533.

Weber MA, Schiffrin EL, White WB, et al. Clinical practice guidelines for the management of hypertension in the community: a statement by the American Society of Hypertension and the International Society of Hypertension. *J Clin Hypertens (Greenwich).* 2014;16(1):14-26.

Yancy CW, Jessup M, Bozkurt B, et al; American College of Cardiology Foundation/American Heart Association Task Force on Practice Guidelines. 2013 ACCF/AHA guideline for the management of heart failure: a report of the American College of Cardiology Foundation/American Heart Association Task Force on practice guidelines. *Circulation.* 2013;128(16):e240-e327.

CARDIOVASCULAR DISEASE IN WOMEN

American Heart Association Guidelines for Reducing Cardiovascular Risk in Women

Most cardiovascular disease (CVD) in women is preventable, according to the American Heart Association (AHA). In 1999, the AHA published a set of guidelines based on a 1997 review of the literature that described risk factor management and occurrence of CVD in women. The American College of Cardiology has a new guideline for the prevention of cardiovascular disease in women (Mosca 2011).

Cardiovascular disease is the largest single cause of death among women worldwide and accounts for one-third of all deaths. New reports have shown that in the United States, more women than men die every year of CVD.

In general the women who are at risk of CVD are those that have more than one major risk factor for CVD including:

- Cigarette smoking
- Poor diet
- Physical inactivity
- Obesity
- Family history of CVD at <55 years of age in male relative and <65 years of age in female relative
- Hypertension
- Dyslipidemia
- Evidence of subclinical vascular disease (eg, coronary calcification)
- Metabolic syndrome
- Poor exercise capacity on treadmill test
- Abnormal heart rate recovery after stopping exercise

Specific Recommendations

Aspirin:

Aspirin use in high-risk women

As a preventive drug intervention in women, aspirin therapy at a dose of 75 to 162 mg/day should be used in high-risk women unless contraindicated. High-risk women were defined as those with established coronary artery disease, cerebrovascular disease, or peripheral artery disease.

Aspirin use for other at-risk or healthy women

In women ≥65 years of age, consider aspirin therapy 81 mg/day if blood pressure is controlled and benefit for ischemic stroke and myocardial infarction (MI) prevention is likely to outweigh the risk of gastrointestinal bleeding and hemorrhagic stroke. However, the new guidelines suggested that the routine use of aspirin in healthy women <65 years of age is not recommended to prevent MI. It was noted in these new guidelines that previous guidelines by the AHA did not recommend aspirin at all in lower-risk or healthy women.

Smoking Cessation: The guidelines suggest smokers try behavioral modification programs, counseling, nicotine replacement therapy, or prescription smoking cessation medications such as bupropion (Zyban). Also, women should avoid environmental tobacco smoke.

Exercise: Women should accumulate a minimum of 30 minutes of moderate-intensity physical activity on most, and preferably all, days of the week.

Obesity and Exercise: Women who need to lose weight or sustain weight loss should accumulate a minimum of 60 to 90 minutes of moderate-intensity physical activity, such as brisk walking, on most days of the week.

Dietary Intake: Consume a diet rich in fruits and vegetables. Choose whole grain, high fiber foods. Consume fish, especially oily fish such as mackerel or salmon, at least twice a week. Limit intake of dietary saturated fat to <10% of caloric intake, cholesterol intake to <300 mg/day, sodium intake to no more than 1 teaspoonful daily, and consumption of trans-fatty acids to <1% of caloric intake.

Alcohol Consumption: Limit to no more than one drink per day. A drink is equivalent to a 12 ounce bottle of beer, a 5 ounce glass of wine, or a 1.5 ounce shot of 80 proof spirit. It does not matter what form of alcohol is consumed. In contrast to the recommendations by the AHA for moderate alcohol intake as part of the updated guidelines for heart disease prevention in women, a recent report showed that alcohol consumption increases the risk of breast cancer. One to two drinks per day increased the risk of breast cancer by 10% and excessive drinking defined as three or more drinks per day increased the risk by 30%. The researchers examined data from 70,033 women who gave health information during medical examinations during 1978 to 1985. In 2004, follow ups indicated that 2,829 of the women in the study were diagnosed with breast cancer. The study examined alcohol preferences, frequency of drinking one type of alcohol, and overall alcohol consumption. High consumption of any alcohol was linked with a significant increased risk of being diagnosed with breast cancer.

Omega-3 Fatty Acids: As an adjunct to diet, omega-3 fatty acids in capsule form (~850 to 1,000 mg of EPA [eicosapentaenoic acid] and DHA [docosahexaenoic acid] should be considered in those with coronary heart disease and for treatment of women with high triglyceride levels.

In addition, the new guidelines suggested that the following interventions were not useful and may be harmful for CVD or MI in women.

Menopausal Therapy: Hormone replacement therapy, such as Premarin and Prempro, and selective estrogen-receptor modulators (SERMs), such as raloxifene (Evista), should not be used for the primary prevention or secondary prevention of CVD.

Antioxidant Supplements: Antioxidant vitamin supplements such as vitamin E, C, or beta-carotene should not be used for the primary or secondary prevention of CVD.

Folic Acid: Folic acid, with or without vitamin B_6 and B_{12} supplementation, should not be used for the primary or secondary prevention of CVD.

REFERENCES

Bushnell C, McCullough LD, Awad IA, et al. American Heart Association Stroke Council; Council on Cardiovascular and Stroke Nursing; Council on Clinical Cardiology; Council on Epidemiology and Prevention; Council for High Blood Pressure Research. Guidelines for the prevention of stroke in women: a statement for healthcare professionals from the American Heart Association/American Stroke Association. *Stroke*. 2014; 45 (5):1545-1588.

Mehta LS, Beckie TM, DeVon HA, et al. American Heart Association Cardiovascular Disease in Women and Special Populations Committee of the Council on Clinical Cardiology, Council on Epidemiology and Prevention, Council on Cardiovascular and Stroke Nursing, and Council on Quality of Care and Outcomes Research. Acute myocardial infarction in women: a scientific statement from the American Heart Association. *Circulation*. 2016; 133(9):916-947.

Mosca L, Benjamin EJ, Berra K, et al. Effectiveness-based guidelines for the prevention of cardiovascular disease in women – 2011 update: a guideline from the American Heart Association. *J Am Coll Cardiol*. 2011;57(12):1404-1423. Available at http://circ.ahajournals.org/content/123/11/1243.full.pdf

Mosca L, Linfante AH, Benjamin EJ, et al. National study of physician awareness and adherence to cardiovascular disease prevention guidelines. *Circulation*. 2005;111(4):499-510.

ANTIPLATELET AND ANTICOAGULATION CONSIDERATIONS IN DENTISTRY

Over the last 30 years, there has been an increasing use of drugs that relate to the clotting mechanisms in patients. These drugs have included the widespread use of aspirin, as well as an increasing use of anticoagulants found in warfarin and synthetic drugs that also have anticoagulation effects. Many patients with ischemic heart disease, atherosclerosis, atrial fibrillation, cerebrovascular disease, and in patients at high risk for stroke, we find the increased use of these anticoagulants. Large numbers of these patients are receiving oral anticoagulation therapy as outpatients. The dental clinician is often faced with the decision as to how to manage these patients prior to dental procedures. Key factors regarding the patient receiving any form of anticoagulation therapy include:

- Is the surgery urgent or elective?
- Can the procedure be done safely without discontinuing the drug?
- Does the patient understand the nature of the dental procedure and the risks associated with continuing or discontinuing the drug?
- What degree of risk are the patient and the provider willing to accept?
- Is the patient on a single antiplatelet drug or on combination therapy with another drug?
- What is the thromboembolic risk for this patient?
- What is the bleeding risk of the dental procedure planned?
- If an invasive procedure is planned in the face of a high thromboembolic risk, what is the managing physician's opinion on altering the dosage of anticoagulation therapy?

Often, in order to determine these factors, consultation with a patient's physician is necessary. However, recent reviews have argued that inappropriate adjustments in anticoagulation therapy create far greater risk for the patient than the risk of hemorrhage during most dental procedures (Jeske 2003 and others in the reference list). Therefore, the scientific evidence does not support changing regimens of anticoagulation therapy in most instances. This decision can only be determined by weighing the factors described above and discussing the situation with the patient's physician.

Antiplatelet Drugs Used in Cardiovascular Diseases

Aspirin reduces platelet aggregation by blocking platelet cyclo-oxygenase through irreversible acetylation. This action prevents the formation of thromboxane A_2. A number of studies have confirmed that aspirin reduces the risk of death from cardiac causes and fatal and nonfatal myocardial infarction by ~50% to 70% in patients presenting with unstable angina (see Aspirin Alert Update for Dentistry at the end of this chapter).

Clopidogrel (Plavix) inhibits platelet aggregation by affecting the ADP-dependent activation of the glycoprotein IIb/IIIa complex. Clopidogrel is chemically related to ticlopidine but has fewer side effects.

Prasugrel is a prodrug and has no biological activity but is metabolized in the body to an active molecule exhibiting antiplatelet action. The active compound irreversibly blocks P2Y12 component of adenosine diphosphate (ADP) receptors on the platelet for their lifespan, inhibiting activation and decreasing subsequent platelet aggregation. Normal platelet aggregation returns only when new platelets are produced (5 to 9 days after discontinuation of prasugrel).

Ticagrelor (Brilinta) is also a newly released platelet aggregation inhibitor similar to clopidogrel produced by AstraZeneca. Ticagrelor is used along with low-dose aspirin to help prevent myocardial infarction and stroke in people with unstable angina or previous heart attack. It may also be used to prevent heart attack or stroke after certain cardiac surgeries (eg, stent placement, coronary artery bypass graft-CABG, or angioplasty). Trade names include Brilinta, Brilique, Possia. Ticagrelor and its major metabolite reversibly interacts with the platelet $P2Y_{12}$ ADP-receptor to prevent signal transduction and platelet activation.

Platelet Glycoprotein IIb / IIIa Receptor Antagonists

Antagonists of glycoprotein IIb/IIIa, a receptor on the platelet for adhesive proteins, inhibit the final common pathway involved in adhesion, activation, and aggregation. Presently, there exist three classes of inhibitors. One class is murine-human chimeric antibodies of which abciximab is the prototype. The other two classes are the synthetic peptide forms (eg, eptifibatide) and the synthetic nonpeptide forms (eg, tirofiban). These agents, in combination with heparin and aspirin, have been used to treat unstable angina, significantly reducing the incidence of death or myocardial infarction.

Antithrombin Drugs

Unfractionated heparin, in combination with aspirin, is used to treat unstable angina. Unfractionated heparin consists of polysaccharide chains which bind to antithrombin III, causing a conformational change that accelerates the inhibition of thrombin and factor Xa. Unfractionated heparin is therefore an indirect thrombin inhibitor. Unfractionated heparin can only be administered intravenously. Low-molecular-weight heparins (LMWH) have a more predictable pharmacokinetic profile than unfractionated heparin and can be administered subcutaneously. These heparins have a mechanism of action and use similar to unfractionated heparin.

The direct antithrombins decrease thrombin activity in a manner independent of any actions on antithrombin III. Argatroban is a direct antithrombin that is highly specific. It binds directly to thrombin (circulating and clot bound) and inhibits thrombogenic activity.

Until recently there have been no direct reversal agents for the novel new anticoagulation drugs. Idarucizumab has been approved by the Food and Drug Administration for reversing the effects of dabigatran, a novel oral anticoagulant. Specifically, idarucizumab (Praxbind) is intended for use in patients who are taking dabigatran (Pradaxa) during emergency situations when there is a need to reverse its blood-thinning effects. Both drugs are marketed by Boehringer Ingelheim. The other novel anticoagulants, edoxaban (Savaysa), rivaroxaban (Xarelto), and apixaban (Eliquis) that inhibit factor Xa, do not currently have approved reversal agents available.

Warfarin (Coumadin) elicits its anticoagulant effect by interfering with the hepatic synthesis of vitamin K-dependent coagulation factors II, VII, IX, and X. Although warfarin appears to be somewhat effective after myocardial infarction in preventing death or recurrent myocardial infarction, its effectiveness in the treatment of acute coronary syndrome is questionable. Combination therapy with aspirin and heparin, followed by warfarin, has resulted in reduced incidence of recurrent angina, myocardial infarction, death, or all three at 14 days as compared with aspirin alone. In contrast, another study failed to show any additional benefit in the treatment of acute coronary syndrome using a combination of aspirin and warfarin compared to aspirin alone.

Recently, the FDA approved Dabigatran (Pradaxa) for the prevention of stroke and systemic embolism in patients with atrial fibrillation. Dabigatran is the first FDA-approved replacement available for warfarin. Dabigatran is an anticoagulant that acts by inhibiting thrombin, an enzyme in the blood that is involved in blood clotting. Thrombin (serine protease) enables the conversion of fibrinogen to fibrin during the coagulation cascade preventing the development of thrombus. The recommended oral dose is 150 mg twice daily for patients with a creatinine clearance >30 mL/minute. For patients with a creatinine clearance 15 to 30 mL/minute, the recommended oral dose is 75 mg twice daily.

It is quite common for a patient to be taking both warfarin and low-molecular-weight heparins, such as Dalteparin (Fragmin) or Enoxaparin (Lovenox). Low-molecular-weight heparins begin working right away, while warfarin does not. In fact, in the short period of time when a patient first begins taking warfarin, the drug may actually increase the risk of clots. Therefore, warfarin and low-molecular-weight heparins are often taken together. The low-molecular-weight heparins prevent clots while the warfarin begins working. The low-molecular-weight heparins can be stopped once the INR is in the appropriate range.

A similar situation sometimes occurs in patients who have been taking warfarin for a while. If a PT/INR test shows that the patient is at a high risk for clots, a health care provider may recommend using low-molecular-weight heparins as a "bridge therapy" while the warfarin dose is being adjusted. The aPTT is the appropriate test to evaluate the effects of heparin. Bridging guidelines and their application in dental surgery must be discussed with the health care provider on a case-by-case basis.

Dental clinicians should consider consultation with patient's health care provider prior to invasive therapies. However, adjustments in anticoagulation therapy may place the patient at greater risk of stroke than hemorrhage during most dental procedures (Douketis 2012; Jeske 2003). Therefore, scientific evidence does not support changing regimens of anti-coagulation therapy in most instances. Given the minimal bleeding risks, stroke patients undergoing dental procedures should routinely continue warfarin (Armstrong 2013).

Evaluating Antiplatelet Response

Partial thromboplastin time and bleeding time (IVY) are appropriate measures for platelet dysfunction. Aspirin, clopidogrel (Plavix), ticagrelor (Brilinta), prasugrel (Effient), and other drugs, such as ticlopidine (Ticlid) are considered antiplatelet drugs, whereas oral Coumadin is considered an oral anticoagulant. Aspirin works by inhibiting cyclo-oxygenase which is an enzyme involved in the platelet system associated with clot formation. As little as one aspirin (300 mg dose) can result in an alteration in this enzyme pathway. Although aspirin is cleared from the circulation very quickly (within 15 to 30 minutes), the effect on the life of the platelet may last up to 7 to 10 days. Most routine dental procedures can be accomplished with no change in these medications using aggressive local hemostasis efforts and prudent treatment planning. The benefit of stroke prevention outweighs the risk of bleeding during most dental treatment. Specifically, the American Academy of Neurology recommends that patients taking aspirin for ischemic stroke prevention continue the aspirin therapy when undergoing any dental procedure (Armstrong 2013).

Evaluating Coumadin Response

The effects of Coumadin on the coagulation within patients occur by way of the vitamin K-dependent clotting mechanism and are generally monitored by measuring the prothrombin time known as the PT. Often, to prevent venous thrombosis, a patient will be maintained at ~2.5 times their normal prothrombin time. Other anticoagulant goals, such as prevention of arterial thromboembolism as in patients with artificial heart valves, may require 2.5 to 3.5 times the normal prothrombin time. It is important for the clinician to obtain the International Normalized Ratio (INR) for the patient. This ratio is calculated by dividing the patient's PT by the mean normal PT for the laboratory, which is determined by using the International Sensitivity Index (ISI) to adjust for the lab's reagents.

The response to oral anticoagulants varies greatly in patients and should be monitored regularly. The dental clinician planning an invasive procedure should consider not only what the patient can tell them from a historical point-of-view, but also when the last monitoring test was performed. In general, all dental procedures can be performed in patients that are 3 times normal or less. Most researchers further suggest that even less than 4 times normal pose little risk in most dental patients and procedures, but these values may be misleading unless the INR is also determined at a time close to the actual planned dental procedure. When in doubt, the prudent dental clinician will consult with the patient's physician and obtain current prothrombin time and INR in order to evaluate fully and plan for his patients.

At recommended therapeutic doses, dabigatran (Pradaxa) prolongs the activated partial thromboplastin time (aPTT). For an oral dose of 150 mg twice daily, the median peak aPTT is approximately twice that of control values. Twelve hours after the last dose, the median aPTT is 1.5 times the control values. The INR test is relatively insensitive to the activity of dabigatran and may not be elevated in patients on this medication.

Regarding dental management patients that are already taking warfarin, the use of analgesics is implicated as a potential source of drug interaction. Hayek, in *JAMA*, found that patients taking warfarin had dangerously elevated INRs and were taking acetaminophen (not necessarily with their physician's recommendation). Additional factors independently influence the INR, as well as a potential interaction with acetaminophen. Effects on the INR are greatest in patients taking acetaminophen at high doses over a protracted time period. Short-term pain management with acetaminophen poses little risk. Other factors influencing INR include advanced malignancy, patients who did not take their warfarin properly (therefore, took more than was necessary), changes in oral intake of liquids or solids, acute diarrhea leading to dehydration, alcohol consumption, and vitamin K intake.

The mechanisms of these augmenting factors for enhancement of the INR are that the cytochrome P450 system is also affected by changes in metabolism associated with these factors. For instance, the metabolism of alcohol in the liver alters its ability to manage the CYP450 enzyme system necessary for warfarin; therefore, enhancing its presence and potentially increasing the half-life of warfarin. As oral intake of nutrients declines in patients with either diarrhea or reduced intake of liquids and/or solids, absorption of vitamin K is reduced and the vitamin K-dependent system of metabolism of warfarin changes, therefore increases warfarin blood levels. These factors, along with the liver metabolism of acetaminophen, have resulted in the increased concern that patients, who may be taking acetaminophen as an analgesic or for other reasons, may be at risk for enhancing or elevating, inadvertently, their anticoagulation effect of warfarin. The dentist should be aware of these potential interactions in prescribing any drug containing acetaminophen or in recommending that a patient use an analgesic for relief of even mild pain on a prolonged basis.

Acetaminophen on page 56

It should also be noted that as we learn more about herbal and nutritional supplements, we will find that some of these products have effects on coagulation. Patients sometimes do not include this information in their normal history and it is important for the practitioner to delve into all types of over-the-counter, as well as prescription drugs, that the patient may be taking.

Although not used specifically for this purpose, numerous herbal medicines and natural dietary supplements have been associated with inhibition of platelet aggregation or other anticoagulation effects, and therefore may lead to increased bleeding during invasive dental procedures. Current reports include bilberry, bromelain, cat's claw, devil's claw, dong quai, evening primrose, feverfew, garlic (irreversible inhibition), ginger (only at very high doses), ginkgo biloba, ginseng, grape seed, green tea, horse chestnut, and turmeric.

ASPIRIN ALERT UPDATE FOR DENTISTRY

There are three special alerts provided by the FDA of clinical importance relative to the aspirin patient:

Special Alert 1: Sudden aspirin discontinuation may elevate the risk of myocardial infarction

It was reported in 2004 by Collett et al, that patients with acute coronary syndrome (ACS) who discontinued aspirin use had worse short-term outcomes than individuals not previously on aspirin therapy. Fischer et al, have also reported similar findings and have suggested that discontinuation of aspirin by daily aspirin users may increase the risk of myocardial infarction. A Harvard Health Letter in 2005 also stated that quitting aspirin "cold turkey" could be dangerous and studies have linked aspirin withdrawal to heart attacks.

A more recent review updated the risks associated with discontinuing aspirin antiplatelet therapy and the bleeding risks associated with continuing aspirin during surgical procedures (Lordkipanidze 2009). The article review confirmed the possibility of a pharmacological rebound phenomenon which could lead to adverse ischemic events and supports the warning against premature discontinuation of aspirin issued previously. An analysis of data obtained from 50,279 patients, reported that the increased risk of major adverse cardiac events attributed to aspirin withdrawal/nonadherence was approximately threefold (Biondi-Zoccai 2006).

Special Alert 2: Ibuprofen may interfere with aspirin's cardioprotection

In a statement released on September 8, 2006, the Food and Drug Administration (FDA) notified consumers and health care professionals that the administration of ibuprofen for pain relief to patients taking aspirin for cardioprotection may interfere with aspirin's cardiovascular benefits. The report stated that ibuprofen can interfere with the antiplatelet effect of low-dose aspirin (81 mg daily). This could result in diminished effectiveness of aspirin as used for cardioprotection and stroke prevention. The FDA added that although ibuprofen and aspirin can be taken together, it is recommended that consumers talk with their health care providers for additional information.

Special Alert 3: Strong advisory warning against the discontinuation of dual aspirin and clopidogrel (Plavix) antiplatelet therapy in patients with coronary artery stents

Aspirin and clopidogrel (Plavix) in combination is the primary prevention strategy against stent thrombosis after placement of drug-eluting metal stents in coronary patients (Grines 2007). Premature discontinuation of this drug combination strongly increases the risk of a catastrophic event of stent thrombosis leading to myocardial infarction and/or death (Grines 2007). Discontinuation of Brilinta will increase the risk of MI, stroke, and death. When possible, interrupt therapy with Brilinta for 5 days prior to surgery that has a major risk of bleeding. If Brilinta must be temporarily discontinued, restart as soon as possible.

The AHA stresses a 12-month therapy of aspirin and Plavix combination after placement of a drug-eluting stent in order to prevent thrombosis at the stent site. The AHA also stresses educating both the patient and the health care provider about the hazards of premature antiplatelet drug discontinuation. Any elective surgery should be postponed for 1 year after stent implantation, and if surgery must be performed, consideration should be given to continuing the antiplatelet therapy during the perioperative period in high risk patients with drug-eluting stents.

The recommendations from the AHA advisory panel were summarized for the dental professional according to the following:

Dental professionals and other health care providers who perform invasive or surgical procedures and are concerned about periprocedural and postoperative bleeding must be made aware of the potential catastrophic risks of premature discontinuation of dual antiplatelet (aspirin, Plavix, or drugs like Brilinta) therapy. The dental professional should contact the patient's cardiologist if issues regarding the patient's antiplatelet therapy are unclear, in order to discuss optimal patient management strategy.

Elective procedures for which there is significant risk of perioperative or postoperative bleeding should be deferred until patients have completed an appropriate course of dual antiplatelet therapy. The course of this therapy is suggested as 12 months after drug-eluting stent implantation if patient is not at high risk of bleeding.

Agents Useful to Aid in Hemostasis During or Prior to Perioperative Bleeding

Aluminum Chloride on page 106
Aminocaproic Acid on page 112
Cellulose (Oxidized Regenerated) on page 332
Collagen (Absorbable/Dental) on page 417
Collagen Hemostat on page 419
Fibrin Sealant on page 714
Gelatin (Absorbable) on page 789
Thrombin (Topical) on page 1561
Tranexamic Acid on page 1593

Hemostatic agents inhibit the activation of plasminogen to plasmin, producing antifibrinolytic activity. These agents have been used systemically and locally for treatment and prevention of various bleeding disorders. The oral mucosa tissues are rich in plasminogen activators, making hemostatic agents potentially effective for controlling oral bleeding. Although many hemostatic agents are available, only tranexamic acid and epsilon aminocaproic acid can be prepared and used as mouthwashes. Tranexamic acid is available as an intravenous injection (100 mg/mL). Aminocaproic acid is available as a 500 mg tablet, an injectable solution (250 mg/mL), and a raspberry-flavored oral syrup (250 mg/mL). A potentially critical difference between these drugs is that tranexamic acid is 6 to 10 times more potent that aminocaproic acid, as show in both in vitro and in vivo assays. Neither agent is commercially available as a mouthwash. The EACA oral syrup is most readily usable as a mouthwash; however, due to cost the tablet is usually compounded to form a mouthwash. In addition, the solution for injection may be diluted with sterile water and used as a mouthwash. To ensure stability and sterility, this is commonly prepared the day of surgery. The adverse effects of these agents are dose dependent and generally manifest as nausea, vomiting, abdominal pain, and diarrhea. Theoretically, adverse effects are more likely to occur with systemic use than with local use.

Clinicians managing antithrombotic medications periprocedurally must weigh bleeding risks from drug continuation against thromboembolic risks from discontinuation or interruption in therapy. Data suggesting specific stopping and restarting times are based on drug metabolism, half-life, and excretion rates and may apply to extensive surgical procedures, but most dental manipulations are not in this category. There is a lack of scientific basis for routine discontinuation of oral anticoagulation or antiplatelet therapy before dental treatment. Dental therapy for patients with medical conditions requiring anticoagulation or antiplatelet therapy must provide for potential excess bleeding with local measures and/or appropriate reversal agents as described. Routine discontinuation of these drugs before dental care, however, can place patients at unnecessary medical risk for thromboembolic events and therefore, any changes in anticoagulant therapy must be undertaken in collaboration with the patient's prescribing physician.

Oral Anticoagulant Comparison Chart

Medication	Mechanism of Action	Metabolism	Monitoring Parameters	Pharmacotherapy Pearls	Reversal Strategies[a]
Warfarin	Inhibits formation of vitamin K-dependent clotting factors II, VII, IX, X, and proteins C and S	CYP2C9 CYP1A2 CYP3A4 CYP2C19	PT/INR (individualized; depends on INR stability)	CYP1A2, 3A4, 2C9, and 2C19 drug interactions and vitamin K-containing food interactions Full therapeutic effect usually seen within 5 to 7 days Half-life is ~40 hours	Vitamin K (route and dose will depend on clinical situation and INR) For major bleeding (at any INR): Consider PCC with vitamin K ± FFP
Dabigatran (Pradaxa)	Directly inhibits thrombin	Hepatic glucuronidation P-gp substrate	Routine lab monitoring not required; aPTT, ECT (if available), TT (most sensitive) may be used to detect presence of dabigatran Renal function	Compliance issues (BID dosing) Specific conversions to/from warfarin, parenteral anticoagulants Renal dosing adjustment required; per ACCP, contraindicated with CrCl ≤30 mL/minute Use with caution in patients ≥80 years of age Dose reduction or avoidance required if used with dronedarone, ketoconazole, P-gp inhibitors P-gp drug interactions Half-life is 12 to 17 hours; considerably prolonged with severe renal impairment	IdaruCIZUmab Dabigatran is ~60% dialyzable Activated charcoal may be used if ingestion occurred <2 hours prior to presentation
Edoxaban (Savaysa)	Directly inhibits factor Xa	CYP3A4 (minor) Hydrolysis (minimal) P-gp substrate	Routine lab monitoring not required	Specific conversions to/from warfarin, parenteral anticoagulants DVT/PE: Dose reduction necessary for patients <60 kg, concomitant P-gp inhibitor, or if CrCl 15 to 50 mL/minute. Not recommended if CrCl <15 mL/minute NVAF: **Do not use if CrCl >95 mL/minute.** Dose reduction necessary if CrCl 15 to 50 mL/minute. Not recommended if CrCl <15 mL/minute	No specific antidote Edoxaban is **not** dialyzable

Oral Anticoagulant Comparison Chart *continued*

Medication	Mechanism of Action	Metabolism	Monitoring Parameters	Pharmacotherapy Pearls	Reversal Strategies[a]
Rivaroxaban (Xarelto)	Directly inhibits factor Xa	CYP3A4 CYP3A5 CYP2J2 P-gp substrate	Routine lab monitoring not required; may use PT to detect presence of rivaroxaban Renal and hepatic function	Administer doses ≥15 mg/day with food Dosing frequency depends on indication Specific conversions to/from warfarin, parenteral anticoagulants Renal dosing adjustment required Avoid in moderate or severe hepatic impairment CYP3A4 and P-gp drug interactions Half-life is 5 to 9 hours; slightly prolonged with renal impairment	No specific antidote; for major bleeding, may consider PCC, activated PCC (ie, FEIBA NF), or recombinant factor VIIa[b] Rivaroxaban is **not** dialyzable
Apixaban (Eliquis)	Directly inhibits factor Xa	CYP3A4 P-gp substrate	Routine lab monitoring not required; PT, INR, and aPTT may be used to detect presence of apixaban	Compliance issues (BID dosing) Specific conversions to/from warfarin, parenteral anticoagulants Renal dosing adjustment required (NVAF); the AHA/ASA recommends to avoid use with CrCl <25 mL/minute Not recommended in patients with severe liver impairment CYP3A4 and P-gp drug interactions Half-life is ~8 to 15 hours; slightly prolonged with renal impairment	No specific antidote; for major bleeding, may consider PCC, activated PCC (ie, FEIBA NF), or recombinant factor VIIa Apixaban is **not** dialyzable Activated charcoal may be used if ingestion occurred within 2 to 6 hours of presentation

Abbreviations: ACCP = American College of Chest Physicians, AHA/ASA = American Heart Association/American Stroke Association, aPTT = activated partial thromboplastin time, BID = twice daily, DVT = deep venous thrombosis, ECT = ecarin clotting time, FFP = fresh frozen plasma, INR = international normalized ratio, NVAF = nonvalvular atrial fibrillation, PCC = prothrombin complex concentrate, PE = pulmonary embolism, P-gp = P-glycoprotein, PT = prothrombin time, TT = thrombin time

Note: Recommendations listed reflect only the US labeling or US clinical practice guidelines.

[a]Management of anticoagulant-associated bleeding requires careful consideration of the indication for anticoagulant therapy and bleeding extent (eg, epistaxis vs intracranial hemorrhage); minor bleeding may only require local hemostasis.

[b]The evidence in support of these reversal strategies is limited; an exception to this may be the use of a 4-factor PCC for rivaroxaban reversal. The only available 4-factor PCC currently in the US is Kcentra. Other 4-factor PCCs **not** available in the US include Beriplex P/N, Cofact, and Octaplex. Bebulin VH and Profilnine SD **do not** contain adequate levels of factor VII and are considered 3-factor PCCs.

Armstrong MJ, Gronseth G, Anderson DC, et al. Summary of evidence-based guideline: periprocedural management of antithrombotic medications in patients with ischemic cerebrovascular disease: report of the Guideline Development Subcommittee of the American Academy of Neurology. *Neurology*. 2013;80(22):2065-2069.

Furie KL, Goldstein LB, Albers GW, et al. Oral antithrombotic agents for the prevention of stroke in nonvalvular atrial fibrillation: a science advisory for health care professionals from the American Heart Association/American Stroke Association. *Stroke*. 2012;43(12):3442-3453.

Guyatt GH, Akl EA, Crowther M, et al. Executive summary: antithrombotic therapy and prevention of thrombosis, 9th ed: American College of Chest Physicians evidence-based clinical practice guidelines. *Chest*. 2012;141(2 Suppl):7S-47S.

Kaatz S, Kouides PA, Garcia DA, et al. Guidance on the emergent reversal of oral thrombin and factor Xa inhibitors. *Am J Hematol*. 2012;87(Suppl 1):S141-S145.

Levi M, Eerenberg E, Kamphuisen PW. Bleeding risk and reversal strategies for old and new anticoagulants and antiplatelet agents. *J Thromb Haemost*. 2011;9(9):1705-1712.

Poulsen BK, Grove EL, Husted SE. New oral anticoagulants: a review of the literature with particular emphasis on patients with impaired renal function. *Drugs*. 2012;72(13):1739-1753.

Wolzt M, Levi M, Sarich TC, et al. Effect of recombinant factor VIIa on melagatran-induced inhibition of thrombin generation and platelet activation in healthy volunteers. *Thromb Haemost*. 2004;91(6):1090-1096.

Oral Antiplatelet Comparison Chart

Medication	Mechanism of Action	Reversible Platelet Inhibition	Prodrug	Metabolism	Pharmacotherapy Pearls	Reversal Strategies[a]
Aspirin	Inhibits cyclooxygenase-1 and 2	No	No	CYP2C9	Chronic NSAID use can compromise antiplatelet effects Monitor for GI ulceration	No specific antidote Consider platelet transfusion ± DDAVP Normal platelet function returns within 7 to 10 days after discontinuation
Cilostazol (Pletal)	Inhibits platelet phosphodiesterase III	Yes	No	CYP3A4 CYP2C19 CYP1A2 CYP2D6	Administer before or 2 hours after meals Contraindicated in patients with heart failure of any severity CYP3A4 and 2C19 drug interactions	No specific antidote Normal platelet function returns within 4 days after discontinuation
Clopidogrel (Plavix)	Inhibits $P2Y_{12}$ component of ADP receptors	No	Yes	CYP2C19 CYP3A4	CYP2C19 inhibitors may reduce concentrations of active metabolite CYP2C19 polymorphisms may affect clopidogrel efficacy	No specific antidote Consider platelet transfusion ± DDAVP Normal platelet function returns within 7 to 10 days after discontinuation
Prasugrel (Effient)	Inhibits $P2Y_{12}$ component of ADP receptors	No	Yes	CYP3A4 CYP2B6	Reduce maintenance dose to 5 mg in patients <60 kg Contraindicated in patients with history of stroke, TIA Not recommended in patients ≥75 years of age	No specific antidote Consider platelet transfusion ± DDAVP Normal platelet function returns within 5 to 9 days after discontinuation
Ticagrelor (Brilinta)	Inhibits $P2Y_{12}$ component of ADP receptors	Yes	No	CYP3A4 CYP3A5	Used in combination with aspirin; daily maintenance aspirin dose should not exceed 81 mg CYP3A4 drug interactions BID dosing Monitor closely for dyspnea, bradyarrhythmia (including ventricular pauses)	No specific antidote Consider aminocaproic acid, tranexamic acid, recombinant factor VIIa Normal platelet function returns within 3 to 5 days after discontinuation
Ticlopidine	Inhibits $P2Y_{12}$ component of ADP receptors	No	Yes	CYP3A4	Black Box warning on hematologic toxicities (aplastic anemia, TTP) Frequent CBC monitoring required BID dosing	No specific antidote Consider platelet transfusion ± DDAVP Normal platelet function returns within 5 to 10 days after discontinuation
Vorapaxar	Inhibits PAR-1	Yes[b]	No	CYP3A4 CYP2J2	Use in combination with aspirin and/or clopidogrel Contraindicated in patients with history of stroke, TIA, or ICH Extremely long effective half-life of 3 to 5 days	No specific antidote Significant inhibition of platelet aggregation remains 4 weeks after discontinuation

[a]Management of antiplatelet-associated bleeding requires careful consideration of the indication for antiplatelet therapy and bleeding extent (eg, epistaxis vs intracranial hemorrhage); minor bleeding may only require local hemostasis.

[b]Due to the very long half-life, vorapaxar is effectively irreversible.

Armstrong MJ, Gronseth G, Anderson DC, et al. Summary of evidence-based guideline: periprocedural management of antithrombotic medications in patients with ischemic cerebrovascular disease: report of the Guideline Development Subcommittee of the American Academy of Neurology. *Neurology.* 2013;80(22):2065-2069.
Hillis LD, Smith PK, Anderson JL, et al. 2011 ACCF/AHA guideline for coronary artery bypass graft surgery: executive summary: a report of the American College of Cardiology Foundation/American Heart Association task force on practice guidelines. *Circulation.* 2011;124(23):2610-2642.
Levi M, Eerenberg E, Kamphuisen PW. Bleeding risk and reversal strategies for old and new anticoagulants and antiplatelet agents. *J Thromb Haemost.* 2011;9(9):1705-1712.
Patrono C, Andreotti F, Arnesen H, et al. Antiplatelet agents for the treatment and prevention of atherothrombosis. *Eur Heart J.* 2011;32(23):2922-2932.

REFERENCES

American College of Chest Physicians Evidence-Based Clinical Practice Guidelines (8th Edition). Perioperative Management of Antithrombotic Therapy. *CHEST.* 2008;133:299–339S.

Armstrong MJ, Gronseth G, Anderson DC, et al. Summary of evidence-based guideline: Periprocedural management of antithrombotic medications in patients with ischemic cerebrovascular disease: Report of the Guideline Development Subcommittee of the American Academy of Neurology. *Neurology.* 2013;80(22):2065-2069.

Aspirin: quitting cold turkey could be dangerous. Studies have linked aspirin withdrawal to heart attacks. *Harv Health Lett.* 2005;30(12):6.

Biondi-Zoccai GG, Lotrionte M, Agostoni P, et al. A systematic review and meta-analysis on the hazards of discontinuing or not adhering to aspirin among 50,279 patients at risk for coronary artery disease. *Eur Heart J.* 2006;27(22):2667-2674.

Brennan MT, Wynn RL, Miller CS. Aspirin and bleeding in dentistry: an update and recommendations. *Oral Surg Oral Med Oral Pathol Oral Radiol Endod.* 2007;104(3):316-323.

Connolly SJ, Ezekowitz MD, Yusuf S, et al. Dabigatran versus warfarin in patients with atrial fibrillation. *N Engl J Med.* 2009;361(12):1139-1151.

Douketis JD, Spyropoulos AC, Spencer FA, et al. Perioperative management of antithrombotic therapy: antithrombotic therapy and prevention of thrombosis, 9th ed: American College of Chest Physicians evidence-based clinical practice guidelines. *Chest.* 2012;141(2 Suppl):e326S-e350S.

du Breuil AL, Umland EM. Outpatient management of anticoagulation therapy. *Am Fam Physician.* 2007;75(7):1031-1042.

Eisenberg MJ, Richard PR, Libersan D, Filion KB. Safety of short-term discontinuation of antiplatelet therapy in patients with drug-eluting stents. *Circulation.* 2009;119(12):1634-1642.

FDA. Ibuprofen and aspirin taken together. http://www.fda.gov/Safety/MedWatch/SafetyInformation/SafetyAlertsforHumanMedicalProducts/ucm150611.htm

Friedlander AH, Yoshikawa TT, Chang DS, Feliciano Z, Scully C. Atrial fibrillation: Pathogenesis, medical-surgical management and dental implications. *J Am Dent Assoc.* 2009;140(2):167-177.

Jeske AH, Suchko GD, ADA Council on Scientific Affairs and Division of Science, Journal of the American Dental Association. Lack of a scientific basis for routine discontinuation of oral anticoagulation therapy before dental treatment. *J Am Dent Assoc.* 2003;134(11):1492-1497.

Lockhart PB, Gibson J, Pond SH, Leitch J. Dental management considerations for the tatient with an acquired coagulopathy. Part 2: coagulopathies from drugs. *Br Dent J.* 2003;195(9):495-501.

Lordkipanidzé M, Diodati JG, Pharand C. Possibility of a rebound phenomenon following antiplatelet therapy withdrawal: a look at the clinical and pharmacological evidence. *Pharmacol Ther.* 2009;123(2):178-186.

Managing anticoagulation in the perioperative period: ACCP guidelines. 9th ed; 2012.

CLINICAL RISK RELATED TO DRUGS PROLONGING QT INTERVAL

The QT interval is measured as the time and distance between the Q point of the QRS complex and the end of the T wave in the ECG tracing. After adjustment for heart rate, the QT interval is defined as prolonged if it is more than 450 msec in men and 460 msec in women. A long QT syndrome was first described in the 1950s and 60s as a congenital syndrome involving QT interval prolongation, syncope, and sudden death. Some of the congenital long QT syndromes were characterized by a peculiar electrocardiographic appearance of the QRS complex involving a premature atria beat, followed by a pause, then a subsequent sinus beat showing marked QT prolongation and deformity. This type of cardiac arrhythmia was originally termed "torsade de pointes" (translated from the French as "twisting of the points").

Prolongation of the QT interval is thought to result from delayed ventricular repolarization. The repolarization process within the myocardial cell is due to the efflux of intracellular potassium. The channels associated with this current can be blocked by many drugs and predispose the electrical propagation cycle to torsade de pointes. In fact there is a wide array of drugs that have been implicated in the prolongation of the QT interval. Some of these drugs have either been restricted or withdrawn from the market due to the increased incidence of fatal polymorphic ventricular tachycardia. The list of drugs that cause QT prolongation continues to grow, and an updated list of specific drugs that prolong the QT interval can be found at www.qtdrugs.org.

Erythromycin, a drug often associated as a dental antibiotic, is considered to have a risk of causing torsade de pointes. Drug-induced torsade de pointes, a specific type of ventricular arrhythmia associated with prolongation of the QT interval, is a well understood form of drug toxicity. The evidence for risk of this event varies among the many drugs associated with torsade de pointes and with the patients' characteristics. The risk of drug-induced torsade de pointes is extremely low when a single QT interval prolonging drug is prescribed. It is not known what effect vasoconstrictors in the local anesthetic regimen will have in patients with a known history of congenital prolonged QT interval or in patients taking any medication that prolongs the QT interval. Until more information is obtained, it is suggested that the clinician consult with the physician prior to the use of a vasoconstrictor in suspected patients, and that the vasoconstrictor (epinephrine, levonordefrin [Neo-Cobefrin]) be used with caution. Other drugs commonly used in oral diseases that have been associated with significant QT interval changes include fluconazole, azithromycin, and levofloxacin, each having variable risk. In May 2012, the FDA notified health care providers that it is aware of the study published in the *New England Journal of Medicine* (May 17) reporting a small increase in cardiovascular deaths and in the risk of death from any cause in patients treated with a 5 day course of azithromycin (Zithromax) compared to patients treated with amoxicillin, ciprofloxacin, or no drug. The FDA is reviewing the results from this study and will communicate any new information on azithromycin and this study or the potential risk of QT interval prolongation after the agency has completed its review.

Patients taking azithromycin should not stop taking their medicine without talking to their health care provider. Health care providers should be aware of the potential for QT interval prolongation and heart arrhythmias when prescribing or administering any macrolide antibiotic.

Thioridazine is another drug confirmed to prolong the QT interval and is accepted as having a risk of causing torsade de pointes. The risk of drug-induced torsade de pointes is extremely low when a single QT interval prolonging drug is prescribed. In terms of epinephrine, it is not known what effect vasoconstrictors in the local anesthetic regimen will have in patients with a known history of congenital prolonged QT interval or in patients taking any medication that prolongs the QT interval. Until more information is obtained, it is suggested that the clinician consult with the physician prior to the use of a vasoconstrictor in suspected patients, and that the vasoconstrictor (epinephrine, levonordefrin [Neo-Cobefrin]) be used with caution.

Drugs Generally Accepted as Having a Risk of Causing Torsade de Pointes

Generic Name	Brand Name	Use
Alfuzosin	Uroxatral	Alpha-1 Blocker
Amiodarone	Cordarone	Antiarrhythmic
Arsenic Trioxide	Trisenox	Antileukemic agent
Artemether and Lumefantrine	Coartem	Antimalarial Agent
Asenapine	Saphris	Antipsychotic
Azithromycin (Systemic)	**Zithromax**	**Antibiotic**
Bedaquiline	-	Antitubercular Agent
Chloroquine	Aralen	Antimalarial
ChlorproMAZINE	-	Antipsychotic
Citalopram	CeleXA	Antidepressant
Clarithromycin	**Biaxin**	**Antibiotic**
Crizotinib	Xalkori	Antineoplastic
Disopyramide	Norpace	Antiarrhythmic
Dofetilide	Tikosyn	Antiarrhythmic

Drugs Generally Accepted as Having a Risk of Causing Torsade de Pointes *(continued)*

Generic Name	Brand Name	Use
Dolasetron	Anzemet	Antiemetic
Dronedarone	Multaq	Antiarrhythmic
Droperidol	-	Antiemetic
Erythromycin (Systemic)	**Various brand names available**	**Antibiotic**
Escitalopram	Lexapro	Antidepressant
Flecainide	Tambocor	Antiarrhythmic
Fluconazole	**Diflucan**	**Antifungal**
FLUoxetine	PROzac	Antidepressant
Gemifloxacin	Factive	Antibiotic
Granisetron	Granisol, Sancuso	Antiemetic
Haloperidol	Haldol	Antipsychotic
Ibutilide	Corvert	Antiarrhythmic
Iloperidone	Fanapt	Antipsychotic
Lapatinib	Tykerb	Antineoplastic
LevoFLOXacin (Systemic)	**Levaquin**	**Antibiotic**
Methadone	Various brand names available	Analgesic, Opioid
MiFEPRIStone	Korlym, Mifeprex	Abortifacient, Cortisol Receptor Blocker
Moxifloxacin (Systemic)	**Avelox**	**Antibiotic**
Nilotinib	Tasigna	Antineoplastic
Ofloxacin (Systemic)	-	Antibiotic
Ondansetron	Zofran, Zofran ODT, Zuplenz	Antiemetic
Paliperidone	Invega, Invega Sustenna	Antipsychotic
Pasireotide	Signifor	Somatostatin Analog
PAZOPanib	Votrient	Antineoplastic Agent, Tyrosine Kinase Inhibitor
Pentamidine	NebuPent	Antibiotic
Pimozide	Orap	Antipsychotic
Procainamide	Procanbid	Antiarrhythmic
Propafenone	Rythmol, Rythmol SR	Antiarrhythmic
Rilpivirine	Edurant	Antiretroviral Agent
QUEtiapine	SEROquel	Antipsychotic
QuiNIDine	-	Antiarrhythmic
QuiNINE	Qualaquin	Antimalarial Agent
Ranolazine	Ranexa	Antianginal
RisperiDONE	RisperDAL	Antipsychotic
RomiDEPsin	Istodax	Antineoplastic Agent, Histone Deacetylase Inhibitor
Saquinavir	Invirase	Antiretroviral Agent
Sotalol	Betapace	Antiarrhythmic
SUNItinib	Sutent	Antineoplastic
Telithromycin	**Ketek**	**Antibiotic**
Tetrabenazine	Xenazine	Huntington's Disease
Thioridazine	-	Antipsychotic
Toremifene	Fareston	Antineoplastic
TraZODone	Oleptro	Antidepressant
Vandetanib	-	Medullary thyroid cancer (symptomatic or progressive)
Vemurafenib	Zelboraf	Antineoplastic
Voriconazole	**VFEND**	**Antifungal**
Ziprasidone	Geodon	Antipsychotic
Zuclopenthixol	Clopixol	Antipsychotic

Note: Dental drugs are identified by bold print. This is not a comprehensive list; additional resources should be consulted.

REFERENCES

Barsheshet A, Peterson DR, Moss AJ, et al. Genotype-specific QT correction for heart rate and the risk of life-threatening cardiac events in adolescents with congenital long-QT syndrome. *Heart Rhythm.* 2011;8(8):1207-1213.

Hedley PL, Jorgensen P, Schlamowitz S, Wangari R, Moolman-Smook J, Brink PA, Kanters JK, et al. The genetic basis of long QT and short QT syndromes: a mutation update. *Hum Mutat.* 2009;30(11): 1486–1511.

Long QT syndrome. *National Heart, Lung, and Blood Institute.* http://www.nhlbi.nih.gov/health/dci/Diseases/qt/qt_. Feb. 10, 2012.

Madias C, Fitzgibbons TP, Alsheikh-Ali AA, et al. Acquired long QT syndrome from stress cardiomyopathy is associated with ventricular arrhythmias and *torsades de pointes*. *Heart Rhythm.* 2011;8(4):555-561.

Mauriello DA, Johnson JN, Ackerman MJ. Holter monitoring in the evaluation of congenital long QT syndrome. *Pacing Clin Electrophysiol.* 2011;34 (9):1100-1104.

Morita H, Wu J, Zipes DP. The QT syndromes: long and short. *Lancet.* 2008;372(9640):750–763.

Nachimuthu S, Assar MD, Schussler JM. Drug-induced QT interval prolongation: mechanisms and clinical management. *Ther Adv Drug Saf.* 2012; 3 (5):241–253.

Torekov SS, Iepsen E, Christiansen M, Linneberg A, Pedersen O, Holst JJ, Kanters JK, et al. KCNQ1 long QT syndrome patients have hyperinsulinemia and symptomatic hypoglycemia. *Diabetes.* 2014;63(4):1315-1325.

GASTROINTESTINAL DISORDERS

The oral cavity and related structures comprise the first part of the gastrointestinal tract. Diseases affecting the oral cavity are often reflected in GI disturbances. In addition, the oral cavity may indeed reflect diseases of the GI tract, including ulcers, polyps, and liver and gallbladder diseases. The first oral condition that may reflect or be reflected in GI disturbances is taste. Typically, complaints of taste abnormalities are presented to the dentist. The sweet, saline, sour, and bitter taste sensations all vary in quality and intensity and are affected by the olfactory system. Often, anemic conditions are reflected in changes in the tongue, also resulting in potential taste aberrations.

Gastric and duodenal ulcers represent the primary diseases that can be reflected in the oral cavity. Gastroesophageal reflux disease (GERD), also known as gastroesophageal reflux disease (GORD), gastric reflux disease, or acid reflux disease, is a chronic symptom of mucosal damage caused by stomach acid coming up from the stomach into the esophagus. GERD is caused by changes in the barrier between the stomach and the esophagus, including abnormal relaxation of the lower esophageal sphincter, which normally holds the top of the stomach closed, impaired expulsion of gastric reflux from the esophagus, or a hiatal hernia. These changes may be permanent or temporary. When attempting diagnosis of oral diseases, such as taste aberrations, halitosis, and Burning Mouth Syndrome, GERD should be considered as a potential complicating or causative factor.

Another kind of acid reflux, which can cause respiratory and laryngeal signs and symptoms, is called extraesophageal reflux disease (EERD). Unlike GERD, EERD is unlikely to produce heartburn, and is sometimes called "silent reflux." Crohn's disease and ulcerative colitis have also been associated with these conditions and should be ruled out in a differential diagnostic work-up. Chronic recurring oral ulcerations are sometimes associated with Crohn's disease and this association should be considered in patients with a history of both conditions.

Gastric reflux and problems with food metabolism often present as acid erosions to the teeth and occasionally as changes in the mucosal surface as well, resulting in chronic oral ulcerations. In some studies, this has also been associated with burning mouth syndrome. Patients may be identified, upon diagnosis, as harboring the organism *Helicobacter pylori*. Treatment with antibiotics can oftentimes aid in correcting the ulcerative disease.

Celiac disease is a permanent intolerance to certain proteins (collectively called 'gluten') that are present in wheat, rye, and barley and related grains. Ingestion of gluten causes damage to the small intestine through an autoimmune mechanism in genetically susceptible individuals. It can develop at any age when gluten is present in the diet, but if it develops in children while the permanent teeth are developing, abnormalities in the structure of the dental enamel can occur. Common oral and dental manifestations of celiac disease may include the following:

- Enamel defects
- Delayed eruption
- Recurrent aphthous ulcers

Both hypoplasia and hypomineralization of the enamel can occur. A band of hypoplastic enamel is common, often with intact cusps. A break in the enamel and dentine formation can occur at a developmental stage which corresponds with the onset of gastrointestinal symptoms. Specific enamel defects can include pitting and grooving. Sometimes there is complete loss of enamel.

PROTON PUMP AND GASTRIC ACID SECRETION INHIBITORS

Dexlansoprazole on page 481
Esomeprazole on page 604
Lansoprazole on page 961
Lansoprazole, Amoxicillin, and Clarithromycin on page 964
Omeprazole on page 1233
Omeprazole and Sodium Bicarbonate
Pantoprazole on page 1286
RABEprazole on page 1415

HISTAMINE H_2 ANTAGONIST

Cimetidine on page 362
Famotidine on page 688
Nizatidine on page 1208
RaNITIdine on page 1423

The oral aspects of gastrointestinal disease are often nonspecific and are related to the patient's gastric reflux problems. Intestinal polyps occasionally present as part of the "Peutz-Jeghers Syndrome," resulting in pigmented areas of the perioral region that resemble freckles. The astute dentist will need to differentiate these from melanin pigmentation, while at the same time encouraging the patient to seek evaluation for an intestinal disorder.

Diseases of the liver and gallbladder system are complex. Most of the disorders of interest to the dentist are covered in the section on Systemic Viral Diseases on page 1806. All of the new drugs, including interferons, are mentioned in this section.

Multiple Drug Regimens for the Treatment of *H. pylori* Infection in Adult Patients

Medication Regimen	Dosages	Duration of Therapy
First-Line Therapy (Option 1)		
H_2-Receptor antagonist (H_2RA) **or** proton pump inhibitor (PPI)	Standard dose of H_2RA or PPI[a]	10 to 14 days
plus		
Bismuth subsalicylate on page 229	525 mg 4 times/day	10 to 14 days
plus		
MetroNIDAZOLE on page 1110	250 mg 4 times/day	10 to 14 days
plus		
Tetracycline on page 1550	500 mg 4 times/day	10 to 14 days
First-Line Therapy (Option 2)		
PPI	Standard dose[a]	10 to 14 days
plus		
Clarithromycin on page 377	500 mg 2 times/day	10 to 14 days
plus		
Amoxicillin on page 121	1,000 mg 2 times/day	10 to 14 days
First-Line Therapy (Option 3)		
PPI	Standard dose[a]	10 to 14 days
plus		
Clarithromycin on page 377	500 mg 2 times/day	10 to 14 days
plus		
MetroNIDAZOLE on page 1110	500 mg 2 times/day	10 to 14 days
Salvage Therapy for Persistent Infection (Option 1)		
PPI (once daily), bismuth, metroNIDAZOLE, and tetracycline (4 times/day) for 7 to 14 days		
Salvage Therapy for Persistent Infection (Option 2)		
PPI (standard dose[a]), levofloxacin 500 mg (once daily), and amoxicillin 1,000 mg (2 times/day) for 10 days		

[a]Standard proton pump inhibitor dose: Esomeprazole = 40 mg once daily, lansoprazole = 30 mg 2 times/day, omeprazole = 20 mg 2 times/day, RABEprazole = 20 mg 2 times/day

REFERENCES

Cheng J, Malahias T, Brar P, Minaya MT, Green PH.The association between celiac disease, dental enamel defects, and aphthous ulcers in a United States cohort. *J Clin Gastroenterol.* 2010:44(3):191-194.

Chey WD, Wong BC, Practice Parameters Committee of the American College of Gastroenterology. American College of Gastroenterology guideline on the management of *Helicobacter pylori* infection. *Am J Gastroenterol.* 2007;102(8):1808-1825.

Cobrin GM, Abreu MT. Defects in mucosal immunity leading to Crohn disease. *Immunol Rev.* 2005;206:277-295.

Daley TD, Armstrong JE. Oral manifestations of gastrointestinal diseases. *Can J Gastroenterol.* 2007;21(4):241-244.

Franch AM, Jimenez-Soriano Y, Sarrion-Pérez MG. Dental management of patients with inflammatory bowel disease. *J Clin Exp Dent.* 2010;2(4): e191-195.

Karthik R, Karthik KS, David C, Ameerunnisa, Keerthi G. Oral adverse effects of gastrointestinal drugs and considerations for dental management in patients with gastrointestinal disorders. *J Pharm Bioallied Sci.* 2012;4(Suppl 2):S239–S241.

Pastore L, Carroccio A, Compilato D, Panzarella V, Serpico R, Lo Muzio L. Oral manifestations of celiac disease. *J Clin Gastroenterol.* 2008;42 (3):224-232.

Permin H, Andersen LP. Inflammation, immunity, and vaccines for *Helicobacter* infection. *Helicobacter.* 2005;10(Suppl 1):21-25.

Rashid M, Zarkadas M, Anca A, Limeback H. Oral manifestations of celiac disease: A clinical guide for dentists. *J Can Dent Assoc.* 2011;77:b39.

Saad RJ, Schoenfeld P, Kim HM, Chey WD. Levofloxacin-based triple therapy versus bismuth-based quadruple therapy for persistent *Helicobacter pylori* infection: a meta-analysis. *Am J Gastroenterol.* 2006;101(3):488-496.

Schreiber S, Rosenstiel P, Albrecht M, Hampe J, Krawczak M. Genetics of Crohn disease, an archetypal inflammatory barrier disease. *Nat Rev Genet.* 2005;6(5):376-388.

Tummala S, Keates S, Kelly CP. Update on the immunologic basis of *Helicobacter pylori* gastritis. *Curr Opin Gastroenterol.* 2004;20(6):592-597.

Yuan Y, Padol IT, Hunt RH. Peptic ulcer disease today. *Nat Clin Pract Gastroenterol Hepatol.* 2006;3(2):80-89.

RESPIRATORY DISEASES

Diseases of the respiratory system put dental patients at increased risk in the dental office because of their decreased pulmonary reserve, the medications they may be taking, drug interactions between these medications, medications the dentist may prescribe, and in some patients with infectious respiratory diseases, a risk of disease transmission.

The respiratory system consists of the nasal cavity, the nasopharynx, the trachea, and the components of the lung, including the bronchi, the bronchioles, and the alveoli. The diseases that affect the lungs and the respiratory system can be separated by location of affected tissue. Diseases that affect the lower respiratory tract are often chronic, although infections can also occur. Three major diseases that affect the lower respiratory tract are often encountered in the medical history for dental patients. These include chronic bronchitis, emphysema, and asthma. Diseases that affect the upper respiratory tract are usually of the infectious nature and include sinusitis and the common cold. The upper respiratory tract infections may also include a wide variety of nonspecific infections, most of which are also caused by viruses. Influenza produces upper respiratory type symptoms and is often caused by orthomyxoviruses. Herpangina is caused by the Coxsackie type viruses and results in upper respiratory infections in addition to pharyngitis or sore throat. One serious condition, known as croup, has been associated with *Haemophilus influenzae* infections. Other more serious infections might include respiratory syncytial virus, adenoviruses, and parainfluenza viruses.

The respiratory symptoms that are often encountered in both upper respiratory and lower respiratory disorders include cough, dyspnea (difficulty in breathing), the production of sputum, hemoptysis (coughing up blood), a wheeze, and occasionally chest pain. One additional symptom, orthopnea (difficulty in breathing when lying down), is often used by the dentist to assist in evaluating the patient with the condition pulmonary edema. This condition results from either respiratory disease or congestive heart failure.

No effective drug treatments are available for the management of many of the upper respiratory tract viral infections. However, amantadine (Symmetrel) is a synthetic drug given orally (200 mg/day) and has been found to be effective against some strains of influenza. Treatment other than for influenza includes supportive care products, available over-the-counter. These might include antihistamines for symptomatic relief of the upper respiratory congestion, antibiotics to combat secondary bacterial infections, and in severe cases, fluids, when patients have become dehydrated during the illness (see Pharmacologic Category Index for selection).

SINUSITIS

Sinusitis represents an upper respiratory condition that often comes under the purview of the practicing dentist. Acute sinusitis is characterized by nasal obstruction, fever, chills, and midface head pain. Oftentimes there is only evidence of inflammation rather than true infection. This condition may be discovered as part of a differential workup for other facial or dental pain since the symptoms are often referred to teeth adjacent to the affected sinus. Chronic sinusitis may likewise produce similar dental symptoms. Dental drugs of choice may include ephedrine or nasal drops, antihistamines, and analgesics. When infection accompanies the inflammation of sinusitis, antibiotics may be required. Most commonly, broad spectrum antibiotics such as amoxicillin (often supplemented with clavulanate acid as Augmentin) are prescribed. Levofloxacin (Levoquin) has been specifically approved for sinusitis and has become popular. Antibiotic therapies are often combined with antral lavage to re-establish drainage from the sinus area. Surgical intervention, such as a Caldwell-Luc procedure opening into the sinus, is rarely necessary and many of the second generation antibiotics, such as cephalosporins, are used successfully in treating the acute and chronic sinusitis patient (see Antibiotic Prophylaxis on page 1812).

LOWER RESPIRATORY DISEASES

Lower respiratory tract diseases, including asthma, chronic bronchitis, and emphysema are often identified in dental patients. Asthma is an intermittent respiratory disorder that produces recurrent bronchial smooth muscle spasm, inflammation of the bronchial mucosa, and hypersecretion of mucus. The incidence of childhood asthma appears to be increasing and may be related to the presence of pollutants such as sulfur dioxide and indoor cigarette smoke. The end result is widespread narrowing of the airways and decreased ventilation with increased airway resistance, especially to expiration. Asthmatic patients often suffer asthmatic attacks when stimulated by respiratory tract infections, exercise, and cold air. Medications such as aspirin and some NSAIDs, as well as cholinergic and beta-adrenergic blocking drugs, can also trigger asthmatic attacks in addition to chemicals, smoke, and emotional anxiety.

The classic chronic obstructive pulmonary diseases (COPD) of chronic bronchitis and emphysema are both characterized by chronic airflow obstructions during normal ventilation efforts. They often occur in combination in the same patient and their treatment is similar. One common finding is that the patient is often a smoker. The dentist can play a role in reinforcement of smoking cessation in patients with chronic respiratory diseases.

Treatments include a variety of drugs depending on the severity of the symptoms and the respiratory compromise upon full respiratory evaluation. Patients who are having acute and chronic obstructive pulmonary attacks may be susceptible to infection and antibiotics such as penicillin, ampicillin, tetracycline, or sulfamethoxazole-trimethoprim are often used to eradicate susceptible infective organisms. Corticosteroids, as well as a wide variety of respiratory stimulants, are available in inhalant and/or oral forms. In patients using inhalant medication, oral candidiasis is occasionally encountered. Aclidinium bromide (Tudorza Pressair) has been approved for the long-term maintenance treatment of bronchospasm (narrowing of the airways in the lung) associated with chronic obstructive pulmonary disease (COPD), including chronic bronchitis and emphysema. Aclidinium bromide is a long-acting anticholinergic and, as such, becomes the second approved inhaled long-acting muscarinic antagonist (LAMA), along with tiotropium. Both drugs produce bronchodilation by inhibiting acetylcholine's effect on the muscarinic M3 receptor in the airway smooth muscle. Both drugs are inhaled as dry powders.

Analgesics
Antibiotics
Antihistamines
Decongestants

SPECIFIC DRUGS USED IN THE TREATMENT OF CHRONIC RESPIRATORY CONDITIONS

Beta-2-Selective Agonists

Methylxanthines

Mast Cell Stabilizer

Corticosteroids

Anticholinergics

Leukotriene Receptor Antagonists

5-Lipoxygenase Inhibitors

Monoclonal Antibody, Antiasthmatic

OBSTRUCTIVE SLEEP APNEA

Obstructive sleep apnea is a condition in which the flow of air pauses or decreases during breathing while you are asleep because the airway has become narrowed, blocked, or floppy. A pause in breathing is called an apnea episode. A decrease in airflow during breathing is called a hypopnea episode. Almost everyone has brief apnea episodes while they sleep. Normally, the upper throat still remains open enough during sleep to let air pass by. However, some people have a narrower throat area. When the muscles in their upper throat relax during sleep, their breathing can stop for a period of time (often more than 10 seconds). This is called apnea. Snoring in people with obstructive sleep apnea is caused by the air trying to squeeze through the narrowed or blocked airway. However, everyone who snores does not have sleep apnea.

Other factors that may also increase your risk include:

- A lower jaw that is short compared to the upper jaw (retrognathia)
- Certain shapes of the palate or airway that cause the airway to be narrower or collapse more easily
- Large neck or collar size (≥17 inches in men and ≥16 inches in women)
- Large tongue, which may fall back and block the airway
- Obesity
- Large tonsils and adenoids in children that can block the airway

At this time, the most effective treatments for sleep apnea are devices that deliver slightly pressurized air to keep the throat open during the night. There are a number of such devices available.

Continuous Positive Airflow Pressure (CPAP)

The best treatment for obstructive sleep apnea is a system known as continuous positive airflow pressure (CPAP). It is safe and effective for people of all ages, including children. Patients with obstructive sleep apnea who use CPAP feel better rested, have less daytime sleepiness, and have improved concentration and memory. In addition, CPAP may potentially reduce the risks for heart problems such as high blood pressure. For maximum benefit, CPAP should be used for at least 6 to 7 hours each night.

CPAP works in the following way:

- The device itself is a machine weighing about 3 pounds that fits on a bedside table.
- A mask containing a tube connects to the device and fits over just the nose.
- The machine supplies a steady stream of air through a tube and applies sufficient air pressure to prevent the tissues from collapsing during sleep.

The standard CPAP machine delivers a fixed, constant flow of air. Variations on CPAP include:

- Autotitrating positive airway pressure (APAP) devices automatically respond to changes in the sleeper's breathing patterns by adjusting and varying the air pressure flow throughout the night. Some patients find this makes CPAP easier to tolerate.
- Bilevel positive airway pressure (BPAP) systems deliver two different pressures, a higher one for inhalation (breathing in) and a lower one for exhalation (breathing out).

OTHER RESPIRATORY DISEASES

Other respiratory diseases include tuberculosis and sarcoidosis which are considered to be restrictive granulomatous respiratory diseases. Sarcoidosis is a relatively rare acquired systemic granulomatous disease affecting multiple organs and tissues. The respiratory system is most commonly affected, with approximately 90% of patients presenting pulmonary findings during the course of their disease. Cutaneous manifestations occur in ~25% of cases but are more common in chronic forms. Head and neck lesions of sarcoidosis are manifested in 10% to 15% of patients. In the maxillofacial region, the salivary glands are frequently involved, with xerostomia and bilateral parotid swelling present. Lesions that occur in the soft tissues of the oral cavity and/or in the jaws are not common but may be the initial presenting findings of sarcoidosis. The diagnosis of sarcoidosis is established by biopsy and the histopathological evidence of typical noncaseating granulomas. These findings are usually supported by elevated serum angiotensin converting enzyme (ACE) levels. Any patient with cutaneous sarcoidosis should be evaluated for the possibility of systemic disease. Testing should include a complete physical exam, chest x-ray, pulmonary function test, electrocardiogram, tuberculin skin testing, a urinalysis, and several blood studies.

Sarcoidosis is a condition that at one time was thought to be similar to tuberculosis; however, it is a multisystem disorder of unknown origin which has a characteristic lymphocytic and mononuclear phagocytic accumulation in epithelioid granulomas within the lung. It occurs worldwide but shows a slight increased prevalence in temperate climates. The treatment of sarcoidosis is usually one that corresponds to its usually benign course; however, many patients are placed on corticosteroids at the level of 40 to 60 mg of prednisone daily. This treatment is continued for a protracted period of time. As in any disease requiring steroid therapy, consideration of adrenal suppression is necessary. Alteration of steroid dosage prior to stressful dental procedures may be necessary, usually increasing the steroid dosage prior to and during the stressful procedures and then gradually returning the patient to the original dosage over several days. Many dentists prefer to use the Medrol Dosepak; however, consultation with the patient's physician regarding dose selection is always advised. Even in the absence of evidence of adrenal suppression, consultation with the prescribing physician for appropriate dosing and timing of procedures is advisable.

PredniSONE on page 1377

Relative Potency of Endogenous and Synthetic Corticosteroids

Agent	Equivalent Dose (mg)
Short-Acting (8 to 12 hours)	
Cortisol	20
Cortisone acetate	25
Intermediate-Acting (18 to 36 hours)	
PrednisoLONE	5
PredniSONE	5
MethylPREDNISolone	4
Triamcinolone	4
Long-Acting (36 to 54 hours)	
Betamethasone	0.75
Dexamethasone	0.75

Potential drug interactions for the respiratory disease patient exist. Check a patient's medical regimen to identify any potential interactions that may affect dental prescribing or a planned dental procedure. An acute sensitivity to aspirin-containing drugs and some of the nonsteroidal anti-inflammatory drugs is a threat for the asthmatic patient. Benzodiazepines may require adjustments, especially if respiratory reserve is limited. Patients that are taking steroid preparations as part of their respiratory therapy may require alteration in dosing prior to stressful dental procedures.

E-Cigarettes

Electronic cigarettes have been available for many years. In the last 5 years, however, these devices have been advocated as a highly recommended alternative to conventional cigarette smoking and have been marketed to adolescents and young adults as an option opposed to conventional smoking products. The safety of E-cigarettes has come into question in the last few years because of concern over the excessive nicotine that is provided through the device. The devices are generally supplied with flavorings and refillable cartridges, making them potentially desirable for adolescent use as well as adult use. There is very little reliable data available regarding the long-term risks of E-cigarettes, regarding their addictive potential and as a potential inducer of premalignant changes in the oral mucosa and the respiratory tract due to chronic exposure to the E-cigarette vapors. Some E-cigarettes also incorporate a concentration of formaldehyde, which by some estimates could deliver exceedingly high concentrations to the user, further increasing the cancer risk. As more information comes available the dentist should be aware of this potential risk and as always be concerned regarding any oral mucosal changes that could indicate premalignancy. More evidence-based risk assessment will be available in the future.

REFERENCES AND SELECTED READINGS

Aurora RN, Casey KR, Kristo D, et al. Practice parameters for the surgical modifications of the upper airway for obstructive sleep apnea in adults. *Sleep.* 2010;33:1408-1413.

de Almeida FR, Lowe AA, Tsuiki S, et al. Long-term compliance and side effects of oral appliances used for the treatment of snoring and obstructive sleep apnea syndrome. *J Clin Sleep Med.* 2005;1(2):143-152.

Dincer HE, O'Neill W. Deleterious effects of sleep-disordered breathing on the heart and vascular system. *Respiration.* 2006;73(1):124-130.

Epstein LJ, Kristo D, Strollo PJ Jr, et al. Adult Obstructive Sleep Apnea Task Force of the American Academy of Sleep Medicine: clinical guideline for the evaluation, management, and long-term care of obstructive sleep apnea in adults. *J Clin Sleep Med.* 2009;5(3):263-276.

Ferguson KA, Cartwright R, Rogers R, Schmidt-Nowara W. Oral appliances for snoring and obstructive sleep apnea: a review. *Sleep.* 2006;29(2):244-262.

Gay P, Weaver T, Loube D, et al. Evaluation of positive airway pressure treatment for sleep related breathing disorders in adults. *Sleep.* 2006;29(3):381-401.

Global Initiative for COPD Science Committee. Global strategy for diagnosis, management, and prevention of COPD. 2011. Available at http://www.goldcopd.org/guidelines-global-strategy-for-diagnosis-management.html

Global Initiative for COPD Science Committee. Global strategy for diagnosis, management, and prevention of COPD. 2013. Available at http://www.goldcopd.org/guidelines-global-strategy-for-diagnosis-management.html

Goniewicz ML, Knysak J, Gawron M, et al. Levels of selected carcinogens and toxicants in vapour from electronic cigarettes. *Tob Control.* 2014; 23(2):133-139.

Goniewicz ML, Kuma T, Gawron M, Knysak J, Kosmider L. Nicotine levels in electronic cigarettes. *Nicotine Tob Res.* 2013; 15(1):158-166.

Hu S, Pallonen U, McAlister AL, et al. Knowing how to help tobacco users. Dentists' familiarity and compliance with the clinical practice guideline. *J Am Dent Assoc.* 2006;137(2):170-179.

Kasai T, Bradley TD. Obstructive sleep apnea and heart failure: pathophysiologic and therapeutic implications. *J Am Coll Cardiol.* 2011;57(2):119-127.

Kowalczyk JP, Ricotti CA, de Araujo T, Drosou A, Nousari CH. "Strawberry gums" in sarcoidosis. *J Am Acad Dermatol.* 2008;59(5 Suppl):S118-S120.

Lodha S, Sanchez M, Prystowsky S. Sarcoidosis of the skin: a review for the pulmonologist. *Chest.* 2009;136(2):583-596.

McArdle N, Singh B, Murphy M, et al. Continuous positive airway pressure titration for obstructive sleep apnoea: automatic versus manual titration. *Thorax.* 2010;65(7):606-611.

Patil SP, Schneider H, Schwartz AR, Smith PL. Adult obstructive sleep apnea: pathophysiology and diagnosis. *Chest.* 2007;132:325-337.

Popova L, Ling PM. Alternative tobacco product use and smoking cessation: a national study. *Am J Public Health.* 2013; 103(5):923-930.

Schwab R, Kuna S, Remmers JE. Anatomy and physiology of upper airway obstruction. *Principles and Practice of Sleep Medicine.* 4th ed. Kryger MH, Roth T, Dement WC. Philadelphia, PA: Elsevier; 2005;983-1000.

Suresh L, Radfar L. Oral sarcoidosis: a review of literature. *Oral Dis.* 2005;11(3):138-145.

The International Classification of Sleep Disorders: Diagnostic and Coding Manual. 2nd ed. Westchester, IL: American Academy of Sleep Medicine; 2005.

Tomfohr LM, Ancoli-Israel S, Loredo JS, Dimsdale JE. Effects of continuous positive airway pressure on fatigue and sleepiness in patients with obstructive sleep apnea: data from a randomized controlled trila. *Sleep.* 2011;34(1):121-126.

ENDOCRINE DISORDERS AND PREGNANCY

The human endocrine system manages metabolism and homeostasis. Numerous glandular tissues produce hormones that act in broad reactions with tissues throughout the body. Cells in various organ systems may be sensitive to the hormone, or they release, in reaction to the hormone, a second hormone that acts directly on another organ. Diseases of the endocrine system may have importance in dentistry. For the purposes of this section, we will limit our discussion to diseases of the thyroid tissues, diabetes mellitus, conditions requiring the administration of synthetic hormones, and pregnancy.

THYROID

Thyroid diseases can be classified into conditions that cause the thyroid to be overactive (hyperthyroidism) and those that cause the thyroid to be underactive (hypothyroidism). Clinical signs and symptoms associated with hyperthyroidism may include goiter, heat intolerance, tremor, weight loss, diarrhea, and hyperactivity. Thyroid hormone production can be tested by TSH levels and additional screens may include radioactive iodine uptake or a pre-T_4 (tetraiodothyronine, thyroxine) assay or iodine index or total serum T_3 (triiodothyronine). The results of thyroid function tests may be altered by ingestion of antithyroid drugs such as propylthiouracil, estrogen-containing drugs, and organic and inorganic iodides. When a diagnosis of hyperthyroidism has been made, treatment usually begins with antithyroid drugs which may include propranolol coupled with radioactive iodides, as well as surgical procedures, to reduce thyroid tissue. Generally, the beta-blockers are used to control cardiovascular effects of excessive T_4. Propylthiouracil or methimazole are the most common antithyroid drugs used. The dentist should be aware that epinephrine is definitely contraindicated in patients with uncontrolled hyperthyroidism.

Diseases and conditions associated with hypothyroidism may include bradycardia, drowsiness, cold intolerance, thick dry skin, and constipation. Generally, hypothyroidism is treated with replacement thyroid hormone until a euthyroid state is achieved. Various preparations are available, the most common of which is levothyroxine and is generally the drug of choice for thyroid replacement therapy.

Drugs to Treat Hypothyroidism

Levothyroxine on page 985
Liothyronine on page 1004
Liotrix on page 1005
Thyroid, Desiccated on page 1562

Drugs to Treat Hyperthyroidism

MethIMAzole on page 1076
Potassium Iodide on page 1362
Propranolol on page 1397
Propylthiouracil on page 1401
Sodium Iodide I^{131} on page 1490

DIABETES

Diabetes mellitus refers to a condition of prolonged hyperglycemia associated with either abnormal production or lack of production of insulin. Commonly known as Type 1 diabetes, insulin-dependent diabetes (IDDM) is a condition where there are absent or deficient levels of circulating insulin therefore triggering tissue reactions associated with prolonged hyperglycemia. The kidney's attempt to excrete the excess glucose and the organs that do not receive adequate glucose essentially are damaged. Small vessels and arterial vessels in the eye, kidney, and brain are usually at the greatest risk. Generally, fasting blood sugar levels between 70 to 120 mg/dL are considered to be normal although blood sugar levels greater than 100 mg/dL are considered to be prediabetic and nonpharmacologic interventions are usually recommended at the very least. Inadequate insulin levels allow glucose to rise to greater than the renal threshold which is 180 mg/dL, and such elevations prolonged lead to organ damage.

The goals of treatment of the diabetic are to maintain metabolic control of the blood glucose levels and to reduce the morbid effects of periodic hyperglycemia. Insulin therapy is the primary mechanism to attain management of consistent insulin levels. Insulin preparations are categorized according to their duration of action. Generally, intermediate-acting insulin and long-acting insulin can be used in combination with short-acting or rapid-acting insulins to maintain levels consistent throughout the day.

In Type 2 or noninsulin-dependent diabetes (NIDDM), the receptor for insulin in the tissues is generally down regulated; therefore, the glucose is not utilized at an appropriate rate. There is perhaps a stronger genetic basis for noninsulin-dependent diabetes than for Type 1. Treatment of the diabetes Type 2 patient is generally directed toward early nonpharmacologic intervention, mainly weight reduction, moderate exercise, and lower plasma-glucose concentrations. Oral hypoglycemic agents as seen in the following list are often used to maintain blood sugar levels. Thirty percent of Type 2 diabetics require insulin, as well as oral hypoglycemics, in order to manage their diabetes. Generally, the two classes of oral hypoglycemics are the sulfonylureas and the biguanides. The sulfonylureas are prescribed more frequently. They stimulate beta cell production of insulin, increase glucose utilization, and tend to normalize glucose metabolism in the liver. The uncontrolled diabetic may represent a challenge to the dental practitioner.

Glycosylated hemoglobin or glycol-hemoglobin assays have emerged as a "gold standard" by which glycemic control is measured in diabetic patients. The test does not rely on the patient's ability to monitor their daily blood glucose levels and is not influenced by acute changes in blood glucose or by the interval since the last meal. Glycohemoglobin is formed when glucose reacts with hemoglobin A in the blood and is composed of several fractions. Numerous assay methods have been developed, however, they vary in their precision. Dental clinicians are advised to be aware of the laboratory's particular standardization procedures when requesting glycosylated hemoglobin values. One major advantage of the glycosylated hemoglobin assay is that it provides an overview of the level of glucose in the life span of the red blood cell population in the patient, and therefore is a measure of overall glycemic control for the previous six to twelve weeks. Thus, clinicians use glycosylated hemoglobin values to determine whether their patient is under good control, on average. These assays have less value in medication dosing decisions. Blood glucose monitoring methods are actually better in that respect. The values of glycosylated hemoglobin are expressed as a percentage of the total hemoglobin in the red blood cell population and a normal value is considered to be <6%. The goal is generally for diabetic patients to remain at <7% with a treatment goal of <6%. Values >8% constitute a worrisome signal. Medical conditions such as anemias or any red blood cell disease, numerous levels of myelosuppression, or pregnancy can artificially lower glycosylated hemoglobin values.

Rapid-Acting Insulins

Insulin Lispro (HumaLOG) on page 899
Insulin Aspart (NovoLOG) on page 892
Insulin Glulisine (Apidra) on page 898

Short-Acting Insulin

Insulin Regular on page 903

Intermediate-Acting Insulin

Insulin NPH on page 901

Intermediate- to Long-Acting Insulin

Insulin Detemir on page 896

Long-Acting Insulin

Insulin Glargine on page 897

Oral Hypoglycemic Agents

Acarbose on page 54
Alogliptin on page 100
Canagliflozin on page 283
ChlorproPAMIDE on page 352
Dapagliflozin on page 448
Exenatide on page 679
Glimepiride on page 797
GlipiZIDE on page 798
GlyBURIDE on page 800
Linagliptin on page 1002
Liraglutide on page 1005
MetFORMIN on page 1069
Miglitol on page 1125
Nateglinide on page 1176
Pioglitazone on page 1342
Pramlintide on page 1365
Repaglinide on page 1428
Rosiglitazone on page 1453
SAXagliptin on page 1465
SITagliptin on page 1487
TOLAZamide on page 1578
TOLBUTamide on page 1579

Neuropathic pain can be a significant problem in the management of diabetes. Recently, Tapentadol (Nucynta ER) received approval for use in the management of neuropathic pain in patients with diabetic peripheral neuropathy (DPN). Tapentadol is a dual-acting agent that combines a strong opioid agonist action together with inhibition of norepinephrine and serotonin reuptake. Essentially, it functions in a similar way to combining a schedule II opioid (ie, morphine, oxycodone) with a tricyclic or SNRI antidepressant. Serotonin and especially norepinephrine are important for reducing pain signal transmission in the spinal cord as part of the descending pathways for pain modulation. Opioids also produce spinal analgesia, directly on spinal cord neurons, but also by stimulating the activity of the descending pathways (primarily serotonin). Neuropathic pain is a complex disorder that usually affects ascending pathways initially, but, over time, descending pain pathways can also become damaged or less efficient in pain modulation. Other approved drugs for diabetic neuropathy include pregabalin (Lyrica) and duloxetine (Cymbalta). Unlabeled use of gabapentin (Neurontin) has also shown some efficacy.

Other oral manifestations of uncontrolled diabetes require aggressive dental management and might include abnormal neutrophil function, resulting in a poor response to periodontal pathogens. Increased risk of gingivitis and periodontitis in these patients is common. Candidiasis is also a frequent occurrence. Denture-sore mouth may be more common. Poor wound-healing following extractions may be one of the complications encountered.

HORMONAL THERAPY

Two uses of hormonal supplementation include oral contraceptives and estrogen replacement therapy. Drugs used for contraception interfere with fertility by inhibiting release of follicle stimulating hormone, luteinizing hormone, and by preventing ovulation. There are few oral side effects; however, moderate gingivitis, similar to that seen during pregnancy, has been reported.

Drugs commonly encountered include:

Estradiol and Dienogest on page 610
Estradiol and Norethindrone on page 611
Estradiol and Norgestimate on page 612
Ethinyl Estradiol and Drospirenone on page 630
Ethinyl Estradiol and Ethynodiol Diacetate on page 633
Ethinyl Estradiol and Etonogestrel on page 636
Ethinyl Estradiol and Levonorgestrel on page 640
Ethinyl Estradiol and Norethindrone on page 648
Ethinyl Estradiol and Norgestimate on page 655
Ethinyl Estradiol and Norgestrel on page 659
Ethinyl Estradiol, Drospirenone, and Levomefolate on page 662
MedroxyPROGESTERone on page 1043
Norethindrone on page 1209
Norethindrone and Mestranol

Estrogens or derivatives are usually prescribed as replacement therapy following menopause or cyclic irregularities and to inhibit osteoporosis. The following list of drugs may interact with antidepressants and barbiturates. New tissue-specific estrogens like Evista may help with the problem of osteoporosis.

Estradiol (Systemic) on page 609
Estradiol and Levonorgestrel on page 611
Estrogens (Conjugated/Equine, Systemic) on page 614
Estrogens (Conjugated A/Synthetic)
Estrogens (Conjugated B/Synthetic) on page 613
Estrogens (Esterified) on page 619
Estrogens (Conjugated/Equine) and Medroxyprogesterone on page 618
Estrogens (Esterified) and Methyltestosterone on page 620
Estropipate on page 620
Raloxifene on page 1417

PREGNANCY

Normal endocrine and physiologic functions are altered during pregnancy. Endogenous estrogens and progesterone increase and placental hormones are secreted. Thyroid stimulating hormone and growth hormone also increase. Cardiovascular changes can result and increased blood volume can lead to blood pressure elevations and transient heart murmurs. Generally, in a normal pregnancy, oral gingival changes will be limited to gingivitis. Alteration of treatment plans might include limiting administration of all drugs to emergency procedures only during the first and third trimesters and medical consultation regarding the patients' status for all elective procedures. Limiting dental care throughout pregnancy to preventive procedures is reasonable. The effects on dental treatment of the "morning after pill" (Plan B and PREVEN) and the abortifacient, mifepristone on page 1123, have not been documented at this time. Consultation with the patient's internist and obstetrician for evaluation of medication safety in pregnancy is advised.

Hypertensive Disorders and Pregnancy

Hypertensive disorders, including chronic or pre-existing hypertension and the development of hypertension during pregnancy, occur in 12% to 22% of pregnant women. Oral health professionals should consult with patient's prenatal care provider before initiating dental procedures due to increased bleeding with uncontrolled severe hypertension (blood pressure values ≥160/110 mm Hg).

Diabetes and Pregnancy

Gestational diabetes occurs in 2% to 5% of pregnant women in the US. It is usually diagnosed after 24 weeks of gestation. Any inflammatory process, including acute and chronic periodontal infection, may make diabetes control more difficult. Poorly controlled diabetes is associated with adverse pregnancy outcomes, such as pre-eclampsia, congenital anomalies, and large-for-gestational-age newborns. Meticulous control to avoid or minimize dental infection is important for pregnant women with diabetes. Regulating all sources of acute or chronic inflammation helps manage diabetes.

REFERENCES AND SELECTED READINGS

American Diabetes Association. Standards of medical care in diabetes − 2013. *Diabetes Care*. 2013;36(Suppl 1):S11-S66.
Bertagna X, Guignat L, Groussin L, Bertherat J. Cushing's disease. *Best Pract Res Clin Endocrinol Metab*. 2009;23:607-623.
Carlos-Fabue L, Jimenez-Soriano Y, Sarrion-Perez MG. Dental management of patients with endocrine disorders. *J Clin Exp Dent*. 2010;2(4)e:196–203.
De Groot L, Abalovich M, Alexander EK, et al. Management of thyroid dysfunction during pregnancy and postpartum: an Endocrine Society clinical practice guideline. *J Clin Endocrinol Metab*. 2012;97(8):2543-2565.
Gibson N, Ferguson JW. Steroid cover for dental patients on longterm steroid medication: proposed clinical guidelines based upon a critical review of the literature. *Br Dent J*. 2004;197(11):681-685.
Handelsman Y, Mechanick JI, Blonde L, et al. American Association of Clinical Endocrinologists medical guidelines for clinical practice for developing a diabetes mellitus comprehensive care plan. *Endocr Pract*. 2011;17(Suppl 2):1-53.
Huber MA, Terézhalmy GT. Risk stratification and dental management of the patient with thyroid dysfunction. *Quintessence Int*. 2008;39(2):139-150.

Kelly A, Pomarico L, de Souza IP. Cessation of dental development. in a child with idiopathic hypoparathyroidism: a 5-year follow-up. *Oral Surg Oral Med Oral Pathol Oral Radiol Endod*. 2009;107(5):673-677.

Michalowicz BS, DiAngelis AJ, Novak MJ, et al. Examining the safety of dental treatment in pregnant women. *J Am Dent Assoc*. 2008;139 (6):685-695.

Michalowicz BS, Hodges JS, DiAngelis AJ, et al. Treatment of periodontal disease and the risk of preterm birth. *N Engl J Med*. 2006;355 (18):1885-1894.

Nathan DM, Buse JB, Davidson MB. Medical management of hyperglycemia in type 2 diabetes: a consensus algorithm for the initiation and adjustment of therapy: a consensus statement of the American Diabetes Association and the European Association for the Study of Diabetes. *Diabetes Care*. 2009;32(1):193-203.

Rodbard HW, Jellinger PS, Davidson JA. Statement by an American Association of Clinical Endocrinologists/American College of Endocrinology consensus panel on type 2 diabetes mellitus: an algorithm for glycemic control. *Endocr Pract*. 2009;15(6):540-559.

Stagnaro-Green A, Abalovich M, Alexander E. Guidelines of the American Thyroid Association for the diagnosis and management of thyroid disease during pregnancy and postpartum. *Thyroid*. 2011;21(10):1081-1125.

HIV INFECTION AND AIDS

Human immunodeficiency virus (HIV) represents agents HIV-1 and HIV-2 that produce a devastating systemic disease. The virus causes disease by leading to elevated risk of infections in patients and, from our experience over the last 18 years, there clearly are oral manifestations associated with these patients. Also, there has been a revolution in infection control in our dental offices over the last two decades due to our expanding knowledge of this infectious agent. Infection control practices have been elevated to include all of the infectious agents with which dentists often come into contact. These might include, in addition to HIV, hepatitis viruses (of which the serotypes include A, B, C, D, E, F, and G); the herpes viruses (see Systemic Viral Diseases on page 1806); and STDs such as syphilis, gonorrhea, and papillomavirus (see Sexually-Transmitted Diseases on page 1804).

Acquired immunodeficiency syndrome (AIDS) has been recognized since early 1981 as a unique clinical syndrome manifest by opportunistic infections or by neoplasms complicating the underlying defect in the cellular immune system. These defects are now known to be brought on by infection and pathogenesis with human immunodeficiency virus 1 or 2 (HIV-1 is the predominant serotype identified). The major cellular defect brought on by infection with HIV is a depletion of T-cells, primarily the subtype, T-helper cells, known as CD4+ cells. When the CD4 cell count falls below 200 cells/µL, patients are at high risk for life-threatening AIDS-defining opportunistic infections (eg, *Pneumocystis jiroveci* pneumonia, *Toxoplasma gondii* encephalitis, disseminated *Mycobacterium avium* complex disease, tuberculosis, bacterial pneumonia). Over these years, our knowledge regarding HIV infection and the oral manifestations often associated with patients with HIV or AIDS, has increased dramatically. Populations of individuals known to be at high risk of HIV transmission include homosexuals, intravenous drug abuse patients, transfusion recipients, patients with other sexually transmitted diseases, and patients practicing promiscuous sex.

The definitions of AIDS have also evolved over this period of time. The natural history of HIV infection along with some of the oral manifestations can be reviewed in Table 1. The risk of developing these opportunistic infections increases as the patient progresses to AIDS.

Table 1. Natural History of HIV Infection/Oral Manifestations

Time From Transmission (Average)	Observation	CD4 Cell Count
0	Viral transmissions	Normal: 1,000 (±500/mm^3)
2 to 4 weeks	Self-limited infectious mononucleosis-like illness with fever, rash, leukopenia, mucocutaneous ulcerations (mouth, genitals, etc), thrush	Transient decrease
6 to 12 weeks	Seroconversion (rarely requires ≥3 months for seroconversion)	Normal
0 to 8 years	Healthy/asymptomatic HIV infection; peripheral/persistent generalized lymphadenopathy; HPV, thrush, OHL; RAU, periodontal diseases, salivary gland diseases; dermatitis	≥500/mm^3 gradual reduction with average decrease of 50 to 80/mm^3/year
4 to 8 years	Early symptomatic HIV infection previously called (AIDS-related complex): Thrush, vaginal candidiasis (persistent, frequent and/or severe), cervical dysplasia/CA Hodgkin lymphoma, B-cell lymphoma, oral hairy leukoplakia, salivary gland diseases, ITP, xerostomia, dermatitis, shingles; RAU, herpes simplex, HPV, bacterial infections, periodontal diseases, molluscum contagiosum, other physical symptoms: fever, weight loss, fatigue	≥300 to 500/mm^3
6 to 10 years	AIDS: Wasting syndrome, *Candida* esophagitis, Kaposi's sarcoma, HIV-associated dementia, disseminated *M. avium*, Hodgkin's or B-cell lymphoma, herpes simplex >30 days; PCP; cryptococcal meningitis, other systemic fungal infections; CMV	<200/mm^3

Natural history indicates course of HIV infection in absence of antiretroviral treatment. Adapted from: Bartlett JG. A guide to HIV care from the AIDS Care Program of the Johns Hopkins Medical Institutions. 2nd ed.

PCP = *Pneumocystis carinii* pneumonia, ITP = immune thrombocytopenia (formerly known as idiopathic thrombocytopenic purpura), HPV = human papilloma virus, OHL = oral hairy leukoplakia, RAU = recurrent aphthous ulcer

Patients with HIV infection and/or AIDS are seen in dental offices throughout the country. In general, it is the dentist's obligation to treat HIV individuals including patients of record and other patients who may seek treatment when the office is accepting new patients. These patients are protected under the Americans with Disabilities Act and the dentist has an obligation as described. Two excellent publications, one by the American Dental Association and the other by the American Academy of Oral Medicine, outline the dentist's responsibility as well as a very detailed explanation of dental management protocols for HIV patients. These protocols, however, are evolving just as our knowledge of HIV has evolved. New drugs and their interactions present the dentist with continuous need for updates regarding the appropriate management of HIV patients. Diagnostic tests, including determining viral load in combination with the CD4 status, now are used to modify a patient's treatment in ways that allow them to remain relatively illness-free for longer periods of time. This places more of a responsibility on the dental practice team to be aware of drug changes, of new drugs, and of the appropriate oral management in such patients.

Our knowledge of AIDS allows us to properly treat these patients while protecting ourselves, our staff, and other patients in the office. All types of infectious disease require consistent practices in our dental offices known as Standard/Universal Precautions. These agents include sexually transmitted disease agents, the highly virulent hepatitis viruses, and the less virulent but always worrisome HIV. In general, an office that is practicing standard/universal precautions is one that is considered safe for patients and staff. Throughout this spectrum, HIV is placed somewhere in the middle, in terms of infection risk in the dental office. Other sexually transmitted diseases and infectious diseases such as tuberculosis represent a greater threat to the dentist than HIV itself. However, due to the grave danger of HIV infection, many of our precautions have been instituted to assist the dentist in protecting himself, his staff, and other patients in situations where the office may be involved in treating a patient that is HIV positive.

As in the management of all medically-compromised patients, the appropriate care of HIV patients begins with a complete and thorough history. This history must allow the dentist to identify risk factors in the development of HIV as well as identify those patients known to be HIV positive. Knowledge of all medications prescribed to patients at risk is also important.

The current antiretroviral therapy used to treat patients with HIV infection and/or AIDS includes three primary classifications of drugs. These are the nucleoside analogs, protease inhibitors, and the non-nucleoside/nucleotide analogs (analogs refers to chemicals that can substitute competitively for naturally produced cell components such as found in DNA, RNA, or proteins). The newest drugs include several nucleoside analogs, abacavir (Ziagen), sub protease inhibitors, amprenavir, several non-nucleoside analogs, efavirenz (Sustiva), and adefovir, as well as the latest combination drugs, such as elvitegravir, cobicistat, emtricitabine, and tenofovir disoproxil fumarate (Stribild; formerly Quad). Finding the perfect "cocktail" of anti-HIV medications still eludes clinicians. This is partly due to the fact that therapies are still too novel and the patient's years too few to study. Numerous studies have indicated that combinations of drugs are far better than individual drug therapy. Several of these studies have looked at two drug combinations, particularly between nucleoside analogs in combination with protease inhibitors. The newer drugs (non-nucleoside analogs) have added the possibility of a triple "cocktail". Recently several studies indicated that this three-drug combination may be the best in managing HIV infection.

When HIV was first discovered, the efforts for monitoring HIV infection focused on the CD4 blood levels and the ratios between the helper cells, suppressor cells within the patient's immune system. These markers were used to indicate success or failure of drug therapies as patients moved through HIV pathogenesis toward AIDS. More recently, however, the advent of protease inhibitors has allowed clinicians to monitor the actual presence of viral RNA within the patient and the term viral load has become the focus of therapy monitoring. The availability of better therapies and our rapidly expanding knowledge of molecular biology of the HIV virus have created new opportunities to control the AIDS epidemic. Cases can be monitored closely looking at the number of copy units or virions within the patient's bloodstream as an indication in combination with other infections and/or declining or increasing CD4 numbers to establish prognostic values for the patient's success. Long-term survival of patients infected with HIV has been accomplished by monitoring and adjusting therapy to these numbers.

Comprehensive coordinated approaches, that have been advocated by researchers, have sought to establish national standards for HIV reporting, greater access to effective newly approved medications, improved access to individual physicians treating HIV patients, and continued protection of patient's privacy. These goals allow the reporting of studies that suggest that combination therapies, some of which have been tried in less controlled individual patient treatments, may prove useful in larger populations of HIV-infected individuals. As these studies are reported, the dental clinician should be aware that patients' drug therapies change rapidly, various combinations may be tried, and the side effects and interactions as described in the chapter on drug interactions and the CYP system will also emerge. The dentist must be aware of these potential interactions with seemingly innocuous drugs such as clarithromycin, erythromycin, and some of the sedative drugs that a dentist may utilize in their practice as well as some of the analgesics. These drug interactions may be the most important part of monitoring that the dentist provides in helping to manage a situation. Some of the antiviral drugs more commonly used for HIV, AIDS, Asymptomatic, CD4 <500, and the newer drugs (ie, protease inhibitors, nucleoside analogs, and non-nucleoside nucleotide analogs) are listed in Table 2.

Table 2. Examples of Drugs

Nucleoside Analogs	Protease Inhibitors	Non-nucleoside Analogs	Nucleotide Analogs	Fusion Protein Inhibitor	CCR5 Antagonist	Integrase Inhibitor
Zidovudine (Retrovir, AZT, SDV)	**Saquinavir** (Invirase)	**Nevirapine** (Viramune)	**Tenofovir disoproxil fumarate** (Viread)	**Enfuvirtide** (Fuzeon)	**Maraviroc** (Selzentry)	**Raltegravir** (Isentress)
Didanosine (Videx, ddi)	**Ritonavir** (Norvir)	**Delavirdine** (Rescriptor)				**Dolutegravir** (Tivicay)
Entecavir (Baraclude)	**Indinavir** (Crixivan)	**Efavirenz** (Sustiva)				
Stavudine (Zerit, d4T)	**Nelfinavir** (Viracept)	**Etravirine** (Intelence)				
LamiVUDine (Epivir)	**Fosamprenavir** (Lexiva)	**Rilpivirine** (Edurant)				
Abacavir (Ziagen)	**Atazanavir** (Reyataz)					
Emtricitabine (Emtriva)	**Darunavir** (Prezista)					
	Tipranavir (Aptivus)					

The presence of other infections is an important part of the health history. Appropriate medical consultation may be mandated after a health history in order to accomplish a complete evaluation of the patients at risk. Uniformity in the taking of a history from a patient is the dentist's best plan for all patients so that no selectivity or discrimination can be implicated.

An appropriate review of symptoms may also identify oral and systemic conditions that may be present in aggressive HIV disease. Medical physical examination may reveal pre-existing or developing intra- or extra-oral signs/symptoms of progressive disease. Aggressive herpes simplex, herpes zoster, papillomavirus, Kaposi's sarcoma or lymphoma are among the disorders that might be identified. In addition to these, intra-oral examination may raise suspicion regarding fungal infections, angular cheilitis, squamous cell carcinoma, and recurrent aphthous ulcers. The dentist should be vigilant in all patients regardless of HIV risk.

It will always be up to the dental practitioner to determine whether testing for HIV should be recommended following the history and physical examination of a new patient. Because of the severe psychological implications of learning of HIV positivity for a patient, the dentist should be aware that there are appropriate referral sites where psychological counseling and appropriate discrete testing for the patient is available. The dentist's office should have these sites available for referral should the patient be interested. Candid discussions, however, with the patient regarding risk factors and/or other signs or symptoms in their history and physical condition that may indicate a higher HIV risk than the normal population, should be an area the dentist feels comfortable in broaching with any new patient. Oftentimes, it is appropriate to recommend testing for other infectious diseases should risk factors be present. For example, testing for hepatitis B and hepatitis C may be appropriate for the patient and along with this the dentist could recommend that the patient consider HIV testing. Because of the legal issues involved, anonymity for HIV testing may be appropriate and it is always up to the patient to follow the doctor's recommendations. Currently there are national projects underway to expand HIV disease awareness and included in these initiatives are increased training for dental professionals and in-office screening for HIV. HIV-related oral conditions occur in a large proportion of patients, and frequently are misdiagnosed or inadequately treated. Dental expertise is necessary for appropriate management of oral manifestations of HIV infection or AIDS, but many patients do not receive adequate dental care. Common notable HIV-related oral conditions include xerostomia, candidiasis, oral hairy leukoplakia, periodontal diseases such as linear gingival erythema and necrotizing ulcerative periodontitis, Kaposi's sarcoma, human papilloma virus-associated warts, and ulcerative conditions including herpes simplex virus lesions, recurrent aphthous ulcers, and neutropenic ulcers.

When a patient has either given a positive history of knowing that they are HIV positive or it has been determined after referral for consultation, the dentist should be aware of the AIDS-defining illnesses. Of course, current medical status and drug therapy that the patient may be undergoing is of equal importance. The dentist, through medical consultation and regular follow-up with the patient's physician, should be made aware of the CD4 count (Table 3), the viral load, and the drugs that the patient is taking. The presence of other AIDS-defining illnesses as well as complications, such as higher risk of endocarditis and the risk of other systemic infections such as tuberculosis, are extremely important for the dentist. These may make an impact on the dental treatment plan in terms of the selection of preprocedural antibiotics or the use of oral medications to treat opportunistic infections in or around the oral cavity.

Table 3. CD4+ Lymphocyte Count and Percentage as Related to the Risk of Opportunistic Infection

CD4+ Cells/mm^3	CD4+ Percentage[a]	Risk of Opportunistic Infection
>600	32 to 60	No increased risk
400 to 500	<29	Initial immune suppression
200 to 400	14 to 28	Appearance of opportunistic infections, some may be major
<200	<14	Severe immune suppression. AIDS diagnosis. Major opportunistic infections. Although variable, prognosis for surviving >3 years is poor
<50	—	Although variable, prognosis for surviving >1 year is poor

[a]Several studies have suggested that the CD4+ percentage demonstrates less variability between measurements, as compared to the absolute CD4+ cell count. CD4+ percentages may therefore give a clearer impression of the course of disease.

Adapted from: Glick M, Silverman S. Dental management of HIV-infected patients. *J Am Dent Assoc* (supplement to reviewers). 1995.

AIDS-defining illnesses, such as oral-pharyngeal candidiasis, herpes infections lasting >30 days, recurrent pneumonia, or lymphoma are clearly important to the dentist. Chemotherapy that might be being given to the patient for treatment for any or all of these disorders can have implications in terms of the patient's response to simple dental procedures.

Drug therapies have become complex in the treatment of HIV/AIDS. Because of the moderate successes with protease inhibitors and the drug combination therapies, more patients are living longer and receiving more dental care throughout their lives. Drug therapies are often tailored to the current CD4 count in combination with the viral load. In general, patients with high CD4 counts are usually at lower risk for complications in the dental office than patients with low CD4 counts. However, the presence of a high viral load with or without a stable CD4 count may be indicative or a more rapid progression of the HIV/AIDS disease process than had previously been thought. Patients with a high viral load and a declining CD4 count are considered to have the greatest risk and the poorest prognosis of all the groups.

In HIV infections, a new drug known as raltegravir is an integrase inhibitor which works by interrupting HIV integration into the host cell DNA. In addition, in 2007, a new class of anti-HIV drugs was introduced, these are the chemokine receptor 5 antagonists or the CCR5 receptor blockers. The drug of interest for this class is maraviroc. This antiviral drug has shown great promise as an adjuvant therapy along with other anti-HIV drugs.

Other organ damage, such as liver compromise potentially leading to bleeding disorders, can be found as the disease progresses to AIDS. Liver dysfunction may be related to pre-existing hepatic diseases due to previous infection with a hepatitis virus such as hepatitis B or other drug toxicities associated with the treatment of AIDS. The dentist must have available current prothrombin and partial thromboplastin times (PT and PTT) in order to accurately evaluate any risk of bleeding abnormality. Platelet count and liver function studies are also important. Potential drug interactions include some antibiotics, as well as any anticoagulating drugs, which may be contraindicated in such patients. It may be necessary to avoid NSAIDs, as well as aspirin. (See Drug Interactions: Metabolism/Transport Effects on page 1899).

The use of preprocedural antibiotics is another issue in the HIV patient. As the absolute neutrophil count declines during the progression of AIDS, the use of antibiotics as a preprocedural step prior to dental care may be necessary. If protracted treatment plans are necessary, the dentist should receive updated information as the patient receives such from their physician. It is always important that the dentist have current CD4 counts, viral load assay, as well as liver function studies, AST and ALT, and bleeding indicators including platelet count, PT, and PTT. If any other existing conditions such as cardiac involvement or joint prostheses are involved, antibiotic coverage may also be necessary. However, these determinations are no different than in the non-HIV population and this subject is covered in Antibiotic Prophylaxis - Preprocedural Guidelines for Dental Patients on page 1812. See Laboratory Values/Body Measurements on page 1901 as a general guideline for provision of dental care.

The consideration of current blood values is important in long-term care of any medically compromised patient and in particular the HIV-positive patient. Preventive dental care is likewise valuable in these patients, however, the dentist's approach should be no different than as with all patients. See Table 4 for oral lesions commonly associated with HIV disease and a brief description of their usual treatment (see Part II of this Oral Medicine chapter for more detailed descriptions of these common oral lesions).

The clinician should be aware that several of the protease inhibitors have now been associated with drug interactions. Some of these drug interactions include therapies that the dentist may be utilizing. The basis for these drug interactions with protease inhibitors is the inhibition of cytochrome P450 isoforms, which are important in normal liver function and metabolism of drugs. A detailed description of the mechanisms of inhibition can be found in Drug Interactions: Metabolism/Transport Effects on page 1899, as well as a table illustrating some known drug interactions with antiviral therapy and drugs commonly prescribed in the dental office. The metabolism of these drugs could be affected by the patient's antiviral therapy.

Every dental office should have in place protocols for standard/universal precautions during patient care and for emergency procedures in case of occupational exposure to blood-borne pathogens.

Table 4. Oral Lesions Commonly Seen in HIV/AIDS

Condition	Management
Oral candidiasis	See Fungal Infections on page 1847
Angular cheilitis	
Oral hairy leukoplakia	See Systemic Viral Diseases on page 1806
Periodontal diseases Linear gingivitis Ulcerative periodontitis	See Bacterial Infections on page 1835
Herpes simplex	See Systemic Viral Diseases on page 1806
Herpes zoster	
Chronic aphthous ulceration	Palliation/Thalidomide (Thalomid)
Salivary gland disease	Referral
Human papillomavirus	Laser/Surgical excision
Kaposi's sarcoma	See Antibiotic Prophylaxis on page 1812; Biopsy/Laser
Non-Hodgkin's lymphoma	Biopsy/Referral
Tuberculosis	Referral

Abacavir on page 48
Abacavir and Lamivudine on page 49
Abacavir, Lamivudine, and Zidovudine on page 50
Atazanavir on page 177
Dapsone (Systemic) on page 449
Darunavir on page 453
Delavirdine on page 462
Didanosine on page 503
Dolutegravir on page 527
Efavirenz on page 558
Efavirenz, Emtricitabine, and Tenofovir Disoproxil Fumarate on page 559
Elvitegravir, Cobicistat, Emtricitabine, and Tenofovir Disoproxil Fumarate on page 566
Emtricitabine on page 568
Emtricitabine and Tenofovir Disoproxil Fumarate on page 570
Emtricitabine, Rilpivirine, and Tenofovir Disoproxil Fumarate on page 571
Enfuvirtide on page 575
Entecavir on page 578
Etravirine on page 673
Fosamprenavir on page 767
Indinavir on page 881
LamiVUDine on page 956
Lamivudine and Zidovudine on page 958

Lopinavir and Ritonavir on page 1017
Maraviroc on page 1037
Nelfinavir on page 1180
Nevirapine on page 1185
Raltegravir on page 1419
Rilpivirine on page 1436
Ritonavir on page 1443
Saquinavir on page 1463
Stavudine on page 1501
Tenofovir Disoproxil Fumarate on page 1539
Thalidomide on page 1553
Tipranavir on page 1573
Zidovudine on page 1672

Several new classes of drugs have been developed as antiretroviral drug classifications in the management of HIV infection. These are fusion inhibitors, CCR5 receptor blockers, and integrase inhibitors. The prototype fusion inhibitor is enfuvirtide (Fuzeon). There are no significant drug interactions; however, there are numerous side effects and toxicities including Guillain-Barré syndrome, as well as taste aberrations with this drug. The prototype CCR5 receptor blocker is maraviroc (Selzentry) and the integrase inhibitor is raltegravir (Isentress) both with no specific oral side effects.

First FDA-Approved Medication to Reduce HIV Risk

The FDA has approved a new indication for the existing drug emtricitabine and tenofovir disoproxil fumarate (Truvada) as a once daily dose used in combination with safer sex practices to reduce the risk of sexually-acquired HIV infection in high-risk adults not currently infected with HIV. The drug, first approved for treating HIV infection in 2004, is a combination of the cytosine analogue nucleoside reverse transcriptase inhibitor emtricitabine and the nucleotide reverse transcriptase inhibitor tenofovir disoproxil fumarate, an analog of adenosine 5'-monophosphate. Each drug interferes with HIV viral RNA dependent DNA polymerase, resulting in inhibition of viral replication. In two large clinical trials, daily use of Truvada was shown to significantly reduce the risk of contracting HIV. In a study sponsored by the National Institutes of Health (NIH) of about 2,500 HIV-negative gay and bisexual men and transgender women, Truvada reduced the risk of infection by ~42%. In a study sponsored by the University of Washington, risk was reduced by 75% in about 4,800 heterosexual couples in which one partner was HIV-positive and the other was not.

It is important that patients recognize that Truvada is not a substitute for safer sex practices. The drug is meant to be used as an adjunct to a comprehensive HIV prevention plan that includes consistent and correct condom use, risk reduction counseling, regular HIV testing, and treatment of any other sexually-transmitted infections. Health care providers must stress that healthy patients adhere to the pill's daily-dose regimen, which is necessary for it to work, and not discontinue other prevention measures, such as condom use. Truvada must be taken every day in order to help prevent HIV infection. One fear is that high-risk patients will not take this medication correctly, become infected, and develop a drug-resistant strain of HIV infection that may be more difficult to treat. These patients may then spread the infection to others, believing they are still HIV-negative.

Common side effects of Truvada include gastrointestinal problems (eg, nausea, abdominal pain, decreased appetite, weight loss, cramping, diarrhea). Joint or muscle pain, pain or tingling in the hands or feet, headache, dizziness, and fatigue are also possible. Obviously, such side effects can compromise daily compliance. Serious side effects may include fatal lactic acidosis and liver disease, as well as muscle weakness, blood disorders, renal failure, and pancreatitis.

The approval of this new indication is not without controversy. The AIDS Healthcare Foundation, a global AIDS organization that provides medical care and services to HIV-infected people, called the FDA's approval of Truvada for HIV prevention "reckless" and criticized the agency for not requiring proof of a negative HIV test in users. In March, the group had filed a petition with the agency urging it to reject Truvada's application, citing concerns about drug side effects, the nearly $14,000 annual cost of the drug and the difficulty of sticking with a daily pill regimen.

FDA Approves HIV Home Test Kit

With the CDC estimating that of the 1.2 million people living with HIV in this country, one-fifth or ~240,000 are unaware of their status. Furthermore, there are ~50,000 new cases of HIV infection added to that number annually. Because of these statistics, many people are unaware they are HIV positive may be transmitting the virus unknowingly. Testing helps slow new infections. In that regard, the FDA approved the first over-the-counter HIV test kit that allows people to test for HIV infection in the privacy of their own homes. The OraQuick In-Home HIV Test detects the presence of antibodies to human immunodeficiency virus type 1 (HIV-1) and type 2 (HIV-2). In essence, the kit is an OTC version of a test used in the clinical setting that was approved by the FDA in 2004. The idea is not for the home test kit to replace medical testing but to provide another route for people to find out their HIV status. In this test, the user takes an oral swab and places it in a specially prepared vial that comes with the kit. The result is ready in 20 to 40 minutes. However, the newly approved OTC kit is not as reliable as being tested by a trained clinician.

The FDA stressed in its approval announcement that the test is not 100% accurate in identifying people with the virus. A trial conducted by test maker OraSure showed OraQuick detected HIV in those carrying the virus only 92% of the time, though it was 99.9% accurate in ruling out HIV in patients not carrying the virus. That means the test could miss one in 12 HIV-infected people (false-negative) who use it but would incorrectly identify only one patient as having HIV for every 5,000 HIV-negative people tested (false-positive). As with other HIV tests performed by trained personnel, a positive result does not necessarily mean that the user is definitely infected with HIV, but that they should then go and be tested in a medical setting to confirm the result. Similarly, a negative result does not necessarily mean the user is definitely not infected, particularly if they may have picked up the virus in the previous 2 to 3 months and have not yet seroconverted.

Updated US Public Health Service Guidelines for the Management of Occupational Exposures to Human Immunodeficiency Virus and Recommendations for Postexposure Prophylaxis

The US Public Health Service has updated its recommendations for the management of health care personnel (HCP) who experience occupational exposure to blood and/or other body fluids that might contain human immunodeficiency virus (HIV). Although the principles of exposure management remain unchanged, recommended HIV postexposure prophylaxis (PEP) regimens and the duration of HIV followup testing for exposed personnel have been updated. This report emphasizes the importance of primary prevention strategies, the prompt reporting and management of occupational exposures, adherence to recommended HIV PEP regimens when indicated for an exposure, expert consultation in management of exposures, follow-up of exposed HCP to improve adherence to PEP, and careful monitoring for adverse events related to treatment, as well as for virologic, immunologic, and serologic signs of infection. To ensure timely postexposure management and administration of HIV PEP, clinicians should consider occupational exposures as urgent medical concerns, and institutions should take steps to ensure that staff are aware of both the importance of and the institutional mechanisms available for reporting and seeking care for such exposures. Summary of recommendations: (1) PEP is recommended when occupational exposures to HIV occur; (2) the HIV status of the exposure source patient should be determined, if possible, to guide need for HIV PEP; (3) PEP medication regimens should be started as soon as possible after occupational exposure to HIV, and they should be continued for a 4-week duration; (4) new recommendation—PEP medication regimens should contain 3 (or more) antiretroviral drugs for all occupational exposures to HIV; (5) expert consultation is recommended for any occupational exposures to HIV and at a minimum for situations described in Box 1; (6) close follow-up for exposed personnel (Box 2) should be provided that includes counseling, baseline and follow-up HIV testing, and monitoring for drug toxicity; follow-up appointments should begin within 72 hours of an HIV exposure; and (7) new recommendation—if a newer fourth-generation combination HIV p24 antigen–HIV antibody test is utilized for follow-up HIV testing of exposed HCP, HIV testing may be concluded 4 months after exposure (Box 2); if a newer testing platform is not available, follow-up HIV testing is typically concluded 6 months after an HIV exposure.

FREQUENTLY ASKED QUESTIONS

How does one get AIDS, aside from having unprotected sex?

Our current knowledge about the immunodeficiency virus is that it is carried via semen, contaminated needles, blood products, transfusion products not tested, and potentially in other fluids of the body. Patients at highest risk include IV drug-abusers, those receiving multiple transfusions with blood that has not been screened for HIV, or patients practicing unprotected sex with multiple partners, where the history of the partner may not be as clear as the patient would like.

Are patients safe from AIDS or HIV infection when they present to the dentist office?

Our current knowledge indicates that the answer is an unequivocal "yes". The patient is protected because dental offices are practicing standard/universal precautions, using antimicrobial handwashing agents, gloves, face masks, eye protection, special clothing, aerosol control, and instrument soaking and autoclaving. All of these procedures stop potential transmission to a new patient, as well as, allow for easy disposal of contaminated office supplies for elimination of microbes by an antimicrobial technique, should they be contaminated through treatment of another patient. These precautions are mandated by OSHA requirements.

What is the most common opportunistic infection that HIV-positive patients suffer that may be important in dentistry?

The most common opportunistic infection important to dentistry is oral candidiasis. This disease can present as white plaques, red areas, or angular cheilitis occurring at the corners of the mouth. Management of such lesions is appropriate by the dentist and is described in this handbook (see Fungal Infections on page 1847). Other oral complications include HIV-associated periodontal disease, as well as the other conditions outlined in Table 4. Of great concern to the dentist is the risk of tuberculosis. In many HIV-positive patients, tuberculosis has become a serious, life-threatening opportunistic infection. The dentist should be aware that appropriate referral for anyone showing such respiratory signs and symptoms would be prudent.

Can one patient infect another through unprotected sex if the other patient has tested negative for HIV?

Yes, there is always the possibility that a sexual partner may be in the early window of time when plasma viremia is not at a detectable level. The antibody response to plasma viremia may be slightly delayed and diagnostic testing may not indicate HIV positivity. This window of time represents a period when the patient may be infectious but not show up yet on normal diagnostic testing.

Can HIV be passed by oral fluids?

As our knowledge about HIV has evolved, we have thought that HIV is inactivated in saliva by an agent possibly associated with secretory leukocyte protease inhibitors known as SLPI. There is, however, a current resurgence in our interest in oral transmission because some research indicates that in moderate to advanced periodontal lesions or other oral lesions where there is tissue damage, the presence of a serous exudate may increase the risk of transmission. The dentist should be aware of this ongoing research and attempt to renew knowledge regularly so that any future breakthroughs will be noted.

REFERENCES AND SELECTED READINGS

Barouch DH, Baden LR, Dolin R. Human immunodeficiency virus vaccines. *Principles and Practice of Infectious Disease*. 6th ed. Mandell GL, Bennett JE, Dolin R, eds. Philadelphia, PA: Churchhill Livingstone; 2005;1707-1717.

Bodhade AS, Ganvir SM, Hazarey VK. Oral manifestations of HIV infection and their correlation with CD4 count. *J Oral Sci*. 2011;53(2):203–211.

DHHS Panel on Antiretroviral Guidelines for Adults and Adolescents. Guidelines for the use of antiretroviral agents in HIV-1-infected adults and adolescents, Department of Health and Human Services. 2013;1-267. Available at http://aidsinfo.nih.gov/contentfiles/lvguidelines/adultandadolescentgl.pdf

DHHS Panel on Antiretroviral Therapy and Medical Management of HIV-Infected Children. Guidelines for the use of antiretroviral agents in pediatric HIV infection, Department of Health and Human Services. 2011;1-268. Available at http://www.aidsinfo.nih.gov

DHHS Panel on Treatment of HIV-Infected Pregnant Women and Prevention of Perinatal Transmission. Recommendations for use of antiretroviral drugs in pregnant HIV-1-infected women for maternal health and interventions to reduce perinatal HIV transmission in the United States. 2012. Available at http://aidsinfo.nih.gov/contentfiles/lvguidelines/perinatalgl.pdf

Kuhar DT, Henderson DK, Struble KA, et al. Updated US Public Health Service guidelines for the management of occupational exposures to human immunodeficiency virus and recommendations for postexposure prophylaxis. *Infect Control Hosp Epidemiol.* 2013; 34(9):875-892.

Merson MH. The HIV-AIDS pandemic at 25-The Global Response. *N Engl J Med.* 2006;354(23):2414-2417.

Petersen PE. Policy for prevention of oral manifestations in HIV/AIDS - The approach of the WHO Global Oral Health Programme. *Adv Dent Res.* 2006;19:17-20.

Petersen PE. World Health Organization global policy for improvement of oral health – World Health Assembly 2007. *Int Dent J.* 2008;58(3):115-121.

Sax PE, Walker BD. Immunology related to AIDS. *Cecil Textbook of Medicine*. 22nd ed. Goldman L, Ausiello D, eds. Philadelphia, PA: Saunders; 2004;2137-2138.

Workowski KA, Berman S, Centers for Disease Control and Prevention (CDC). Sexually transmitted diseases treatment guidelines, 2010. *MMWR Recomm Rep.* 2010;59(RR-12):1-110. Available at http://www.cdc.gov/std/treatment/2010/STD-Treatment-2010-RR5912.pdf

RHEUMATOID ARTHRITIS, OSTEOARTHRITIS, AND OSTEOPOROSIS

RA AND OSTEOARTHRITIS MANAGEMENT

Arthritis and its variations represent the most common chronic musculoskeletal disorders of man. The conditions can essentially be divided into rheumatoid, osteoarthritic, and polyarthritic presentations. Differences in age of onset and joint involvement exist and it is now currently believed that the diagnosis of each may be less clear than previously thought. These degenerative and autoinflammatory diseases have now been shown to affect young and old alike. Criteria for a diagnosis of rheumatoid arthritis include a positive serologic test for rheumatoid factor, subcutaneous nodules, affected joints on opposite sides of the body, and clear radiographic changes. The hematologic picture includes moderate normocytic hypochromic anemia, mild leukocytosis, and mild thrombocytopenia. During acute inflammatory periods, C-reactive protein and tumor-necrosis-factor alpha (TNF-alpha) are elevated and IgG and IgM (rheumatoid factors) can be detected. Osteoarthritis is a degenerative joint disease and lacks these diagnostic features.

Other systemic conditions, such as gout, psoriasis, systemic lupus erythematosus and Sjögren's syndrome, are often found simultaneously with some of the arthritic conditions. The treatment of arthritis includes the use of slow-acting and rapid-acting anti-inflammatory agents ranging from the gold salts to aspirin (see following listings). Long-term usage of these drugs can lead to numerous adverse effects including bone marrow suppression, platelet suppression, and oral ulcerations. The dentist should be aware that steroids (usually prednisone) are often prescribed together with the listed drugs and are often used in dosages sufficient to induce adrenal suppression. Adjustment of dosing prior to invasive dental procedures may be indicated along with consultation with the managing physician. Alteration of steroid dosage, usually increasing the steroid dosage prior to and during the stressful procedures and then gradually returning the patient to the original dosage over several days. Even in the absence of evidence of adrenal suppression, consultation with the prescribing physician for appropriate dosing and timing of procedures is advisable.

Nonsteroidal anti-inflammatory drugs (including meloxicam) may rarely increase the risk of a heart attack or stroke. The risk may be greater if you have heart disease or increased risk for heart disease (for example, due to smoking, family history of heart disease, or conditions such as high blood pressure or diabetes), or with longer use. This drug should not be taken right before or after heart bypass surgery (CABG).

Antirheumatic, Disease Modifying

Abatacept on page 50
Adalimumab on page 79
Anakinra on page 144
Certolizumab Pegol on page 336
Etanercept on page 622
Golimumab on page 804
InFLIXimab on page 886
Tocilizumab on page 1576
Tofacitinib on page 1577

Gold Salts

Auranofin

Metabolic Inhibitor

Leflunomide on page 966
Methotrexate on page 1080

Nonsteroidal Anti-inflammatory Agents

Diclofenac (Systemic) on page 496
Diflunisal on page 506
Etodolac on page 668
Fenoprofen on page 696
Floctafenine on page 720
Flurbiprofen (Systemic) on page 746
Ibuprofen on page 851
Indomethacin on page 882
Ketoprofen on page 945
Ketorolac (Systemic) on page 948
Meclofenamate on page 1042
Mefenamic Acid on page 1044
Meloxicam on page 1046
Nabumetone on page 1157
Naproxen on page 1169
Oxaprozin on page 1250
Piroxicam on page 1346
Sulindac on page 1509

Tiaprofenic Acid
Tolmetin

COX-2 Inhibitor NSAID

Celecoxib on page 328

Combination NSAID Product to Prevent GI Distress

Diclofenac and Misoprostol on page 501
Naproxen and Esomeprazole on page 1173

Acetylated Salicylates

Aspirin on page 168

Other

Hydroxychloroquine on page 841
PredniSONE on page 1377

OSTEOPOROSIS MANAGEMENT

Prevalence

Osteoporosis effects 25 million Americans of which 80% are women; 27% of American women >80 years of age have osteopenia and 70% of American women >80 years of age have osteoporosis.

Consequences of Osteoporosis

1.3 million bone fractures annually (low impact/nontraumatic) and pain, pulmonary insufficiency, decreased quality of life, and economic costs; >250,000 hip fractures per year with a 20% mortality rate.

Risk Factors of Osteoporosis

Advanced age, female gender, chronic renal disease, hyperparathyroidism, Cushing's disease, hypogonadism/anorexia, hyperprolactinemia, cancer, large and prolonged dose heparin or glucocorticoids, anticonvulsants, hyperthyroidism (current or history, or excessive thyroid supplements), sedentary lifestyle, excessive exercise, early menopause, oophorectomy without hormone replacement, excessive aluminum-containing antacids, smoking, and methotrexate have all been at some time associated with risk of osteoporosis.

Diagnosis/Monitoring of Osteoporosis

DXA bone density, history of fracture (low impact or nontraumatic), compressed vertebrae, decreased height, hump-back appearance. Osteomark urine assay measures bone breakdown fragments and may help assess therapy response earlier than DXA but diagnostic value is uncertain as Osteomark does not reveal extent of bone loss. The clinician is referred to Osteonecrosis of the Jaw on page 1796 since the bisphosphonates are associated with this adverse event and its incidence associated with bisphosphonates for osteoporosis management is greater than previously estimated.

Prevention of Osteoporosis

1. Adequate dietary calcium (eg, dairy products)
2. Vitamin D (eg, fortified dairy products, cod, fatty fish)
3. Weight-bearing exercise (eg, walking) as tolerated
4. Fall prevention (eg, visual/hearing checks, minimizing pharmacologic agents that contribute to fall risk, checking environment for safety hazards)
5. Avoidance of tobacco use and excessive alcohol intake
6. Calcium: Adequate intake of at least 1,200 mg **elemental** calcium daily in the form of dietary calcium or calcium supplementation, particularly women ≥50 years of age. Intakes exceeding 1,200 to 1,500 mg offer limited additional benefit and may increase the risk for cardiovascular disease or kidney stones. To minimize constipation add fiber and start with 500 mg/day for several months, then increase to 500 mg twice daily taken at different times than fiber. Chewable and liquid products are available. Calcium carbonate is given with food to enhance bioavailability. Calcium citrate may be given without regards to meals.
   - Contraindications: Hypercalcemia, ventricular fibrillation
   - Side effects: Constipation, anorexia
   - Drug interactions: Fiber, tetracycline, iron supplement, minerals

7. Vitamin D Supplement: Adequate intake of at least 800 to 1,000 int. units of vitamin D for adults ≥50 years of age. Measuring serum vitamin D concentrations may be warranted, particularly in those at greatest risk for deficiency, to allow for the administration of vitamin D replacement. **Note:** Certain patients at risk for vitamin D deficiency (eg, elderly patients, diseases associated with malabsorption, chronic renal insufficiency) may require higher intakes. Some elderly patients, especially with significant renal or liver disease cannot metabolize (activate) vitamin D and require calcitriol 0.25 mcg orally twice daily or adjusted per serum calcium level, the active form of vitamin D.
   - Contraindications: Hypercalcemia (weakness, headache, drowsiness, nausea, diarrhea), hypercalciuria and renal stones
   - Side effects (uncommon): Hypercalcemia (see above)
   - Monitor 24-hour urine and serum calcium if using >1,000 units/day
8. Bisphosphonates: Osteoporosis prevention: Postmenopausal Females:
   (See chapter on risk of medication related osteonecrosis of the jaw on page 1796 [MRONJ])
   - Alendronate: Oral: 5 mg once daily **or** 35 mg once weekly
   - Ibandronate: Oral: 2.5 mg once daily **or** 150 mg once per month
   - Risedronate: Oral: 5 mg once daily **or** 35 mg once weekly **or** one 75 mg tablet once daily on two consecutive days per month (total: 2 tablets/month) or 150 mg once per month
   - Zoledronic acid (Reclast): IV: 5 mg infused over at least 15 minutes every 2 years
9. Glucocorticoid-induced osteoporosis prevention: Males and Females:
   - Alendronate: Oral: 5 to 10 mg once daily
   - Risedronate: Oral: 5 mg once daily
   - Zoledronic acid (Reclast): IV: 5 mg every 12 months
10. Estrogen agonist/antagonist (previously known as selective estrogen receptor modulators):
   - Postmenopausal Females: Raloxifene: Oral: 60 mg once daily; may be taken any time of the day without regard to meals but should be stopped 72 hours prior to or during immobilization due to risk of thromboembolic events.
11. Parathyroid hormone: Initial administration of teriparatide should occur under circumstances in which the patient may sit or lie down, in the event of orthostasis
   - Glucocorticoid-induced osteoporosis prevention: Males and Females: Teriparatide: SubQ: 20 mcg once daily
12. Estrogens/hormone therapy: Should not be considered first agents for preventing osteoporosis due to increased risk of breast cancer, heart disease, stroke, and deep-vein thrombosis (DVT) found in the Women's Health Initiative study. Estrogens, as well as various combination therapies, including ethinyl estradiol and norethindrone (femhrt) and estradiol and norgestimate (Prefest), have been approved for the prevention of osteoporosis. The FDA recommends that approved nonestrogen treatments should be considered before the use of estrogen/hormone therapy for the sole purpose of prevention of osteoporosis. **Note:** In women with an intact uterus, administer estrogen with oral progesterone; unopposed estrogen can cause endometrial cancer.
13. Bone-modifying agent: Osteoporosis in postmenopausal female: Denosumab: SubQ: 60 mg once every 6 months. Also used to treat bone loss caused by specific cancers or treatments of specific cancers (See chapter on risk of medication related osteonecrosis of the jaw on page 1796 [MRONJ]).

Treatment of Osteoporosis

1. Calcium, vitamin D, exercise, and estrogen: As above
2. Bisphosphonates: Oral bisphosphonates should be administered ≥30 minutes before first food or drink (except water) with 6 to 8 ounces tap water (**not** mineral water) and patients should remain upright (or raise head of bed to at least a 30° angle) to avoid ulcerative esophagitis. Consult individual monographs for details regarding use, precautions, dosing, and administration (See chapter on risk of medication related osteonecrosis of the jaw on page 1796 [MRONJ]).
3. Fall prevention: Minimize psychoactive and cardiovascular drugs (monitor BP for orthostasis), give diuretics early in the day, environmental safety check.

	% Elemental Calcium	Elemental Calcium
Calcium gluconate (various)	9	500 mg = 45 mg
Calcium glubionate (Calcionate)	6.5	1.8 g = 115 g per 5 mL
Calcium lactate (various)	13	325 mg = 42.25 mg
Calcium citrate (Citracal)	21	950 mg = 200 mg
Effervescent tabs (Citracal Liquitab)		2,376 mg = 500 mg
Calcium acetate (Phos-Lo)		667 mg = 169 mg
Calcium phosphate, tribasic (Posture)	39	1,565.2 mg = 600 mg
Calcium carbonate		
Tums	40	1.2 g = 500 mg
Oral suspension		1.25 g per 5 mL = 500 mg
Caltrate 600		1.5 g = 600 mg

REFERENCES AND SELECTED READINGS

National Osteoporosis Foundation. Clinician's guide to prevention and treatment of osteoporosis. Washington, DC; 2010. Available at http://www.nof.org/files/nof/public/content/file/344/upload/159.pdf

Singh JA, Furst DE, Bharat A, et al. 2012 update of the 2008 American College of Rheumatology recommendations for the use of disease-modifying antirheumatic drugs and biologic agents in the treatment of rheumatoid arthritis. *Arthritis Care Res (Hoboken)*. 2012;64(5):625-639.

OSTEONECROSIS OF THE JAW

Osteonecrosis of the jaw (ONJ), is relevant to the discussion of osteoporosis as well as Perioral Premalignant Lesions and Management of Patients Undergoing Cancer Therapy. on page 1875 It is an uncommon condition that results in exposure of bone in the oral cavity. Other signs and symptoms may be associated with changes in bone metabolism and/or poor wound healing, but the ONJ defined condition can also develop spontaneously, such as along the mylohyoid ridge, away from teeth, or any site where acute or chronic trauma could have occurred. It is defined as an area of exposed bone in the maxillofacial region that does not heal within 8 weeks after identification by a health care provider in a patient who is receiving (or been exposed to) a bisphosphonate or other antiresorptive therapy and has not received radiation therapy (Ruggiero 2009; Ruggiero 2013).

Cases of ONJ began to emerge in approximately 2003 and were linked primarily with patients with cancer and those receiving the intravenous bisphosphonate drugs such as zoledronic acid (Zometa) and/or pamidronate (Aredia). Patients receiving clodronate (Bonefos) appeared initially to develop this adverse reaction less frequently. Data has continued to emerge related to oral bisphosphonates and the risk of ONJ in patients who are receiving a significantly lower dosage of bisphosphonate via the oral route. Also refer to Perioral Premalignant Lesions and Management of Patients Undergoing Cancer Therapy on page 1875. As this adverse reaction became more familiar in the dental and oncology communities, it became known as bisphosphonate-related ONJ (BRONJ).

Nonbisphosphonate antiresorptive agents denosumab on page 464 (Prolia and Xgeva) and bevacizumab (Avastin) have also been associated with ONJ. Some researchers are using the term antiresorptive osteonecrosis of the jaw (ARONJ) or medication-related osteonecrosis of the jaw (MRONJ) to refer to ONJ caused by agents other than bisphosphonates. Despite the various terms used, the clinical finding of exposed and necrotic bone of the jaw is accepted as the consistent hallmark in diagnosis (Ruggiero 2013). The American Dental Association recently updated and clarified its guidelines (Hellstein 2011). **In this handbook, the acronym ONJ will continue to be used regardless of the etiology.**

Bone disease occurs in many patients with cancer, particularly those with multiple myeloma and metastatic lesions associated with breast cancer, prostate cancer, and other cancers. These changes are often associated with pain and pathologic fractures. This bone destruction often results from changes in the osteoclast and osteoblast activities related to bone remodeling and healing following trauma. Bisphosphonates act at sites of active bone remodeling, changing the activity of the cells necessary for osteoclastic activity. There are no data that indicate that bisphosphonates directly change mineralization of the bone; however, these drugs do result in changes in the vascularity of the bone and cell activity.

Of the 2,408 cases of bisphosphonate-associated ONJ published since 2003, bisphosphonate therapy was used to treat malignancies in 89% and nonmalignant conditions in 11% (Filleul 2010). Tooth extraction preceded 67% of the reported cases and 35% of these patients' cases resolved. The specific bisphosphonate drug used was provided in 1,694 of the cases. Eighty-eight percent of the patients received intravenous therapy, primarily zoledronic acid, and 12% received oral treatment, primarily alendronate (Fosamax) (Filleul 2010).

Bisphosphonates

Alendronate (Fosamax) on page 90
Clodronate (Clasteon) (Canada only) on page 391
Etidronate (Didronel) on page 666
Ibandronate (Boniva) on page 846
Pamidronate on page 1282
Risedronate (Actonel) on page 1439
Zoledronic acid (Aclasta, Zometa) on page 1676

Antiangiogenic drugs

Bevacizumab (Avastin) on page 224
Cabozantinib (Cometriq)
Everolimus (Afinitor, Zortress) on page 674
SORAfenib (NexAVAR) on page 1497
SUNItinib (Sutent) on page 1512

Nonbisphosphonate antiresorptive drug (Anti-RANKL drug)

Denosumab (Prolia, Xgeva) on page 464
Bevacizumab (Avastin) on page 224

The most comprehensive review to date on osteonecrosis of the jaw bone (ONJ) has been published in the Journal of Bone and Mineral Research and written by an International Task Force of authors (Khan 2015). The American Association of Oral and Maxillofacial Surgeons also has published a position paper in October of 2014 that essentially agrees with the report (Salvatore 2014).

ONJ continues to be defined by the Task Force as (1) exposed bone in the maxillofacial region that does not heal within 8 weeks after identification by a health care provider, (2) exposure to an antiresorptive agent, and (3) no history of radiation therapy to the craniofacial region. Antiresorptive agents include bisphosphonate drugs (BPs), the monoclonal antibody denosumab (Prolia, Xgeva) and antiangiogenic agents such as bevacizumab (Avastin). The clinical staging system currently being used was developed by Ruggiero 2006. The Task Force concurs with this description. Patients with Stage 1 disease have exposed bone but are asymptomatic with no evidence of significant adjacent or regional soft tissue inflammation or infection. Stage 2 disease is characterized by exposed bone with associated pain, adjacent or regional soft tissue inflammatory swelling, or secondary infection. Stage 3 disease is characterized by exposed bone associated with pain, adjacent or regional soft tissue inflammatory swelling, or secondary infection, in addition to a pathologic fracture, an extraoral fistula or oral-antral fistula, or radiographic evidence of osteolysis extending to the inferior border of the mandible or the floor of the maxillary sinus.

After reviewing all literature reports on this subject, the Task Force concluded that the prevalence of ONJ in patients prescribed oral BPs for the treatment of osteoporosis ranges from 0% to to 0.04% with the majority being below 0.001%. However, the Task Force does cite the study of Lo 2010 that evaluated the Kaiser Permanente database and found the prevalence of ONJ in those receiving BPs for >2 years to range from 0.05% to 0.21% and appeared to be related to duration of exposure. The American Dental Association has previously reported that the prevalence of ONJ in osteoporosis patients using oral BPs to be 1 out of 1,000 or 0.1% (Hellstein 2011).

From currently available data, the incidence of ONJ in the osteoporosis patient population appears to be low, ranging from 0.15% to <0.001% person-years drug exposure. In terms of the osteoporosis patient population taking oral BPs, the incidence ranges from 1.04 to 69 per 100,000 patient years of drug exposure. In a trial evaluating the BP known as Reclast (IV zoledronic acid) involving 7,765 patients receiving either zoledronic acid 5 mg or placebo over 3 years, one case of ONJ was identified in each arm.

The incidence of ONJ ranges from 1% to 15% in the oncology patient population in which high doses of BPs are used at frequent intervals. The oncology patient with bone metastasis is exposed to more osteoclastic inhibition than those with osteoporosis, thus the incidence of ONJ is much higher. Clinical studies comparing zoledronic acid 4 mg with denosumab 120 mg dosed monthly for the management of bone metastasis described the incidence of ONJ as ~1% to 2%.

In the osteoporosis patient population, the significant risk factors for the development of ONJ in declining order of importance include local suppuration, BP use, dental extractions and anemia. In the oncology patient population, the significant risk factors for the development of ONJ in declining order of importance are exposure to intravenous zoledronic acid (Zometa), exposure to intravenous pamidronate (Aredia), exposure to denosumab, radiation therapy, dental extraction, chemotherapy, periodontal disease, oral BP use, osteoporosis, local suppuration, glucocorticoid therapy, diabetes, denture use, erythropoietin therapy, tobacco use, hyperthyroidism, renal dialysis, cyclophosphamide therapy, and increasing age.

Management of Those at Risk

- **General dentistry:** Inform patients of the risk of developing ONJ, but treatment should continue as planned.
- **Oral and maxillofacial surgery:** Inform patients of the risk of developing ONJ and discuss alternative treatment plans, including endodontic treatment, followed by removal of the clinical crown, allowing the roots to exfoliate rather than tooth extraction. Before and after any surgical procedures involving bone, patients should rinse with chlorhexidine twice daily for 4 to 8 weeks after surgery. In addition, antibiotic prophylaxis starting one day before the procedure and for 3 to 7 days after may be effective in preventing ONJ.
- **Restorative dentistry and prosthodontics:** There is no evidence that malocclusion or masticatory forces increase the risk of developing ONJ. Treatment should continue as planned.
- **Orthodontics:** Reports have shown an increase in tooth movement in patients taking bisphosphonates; patients should be advised of this potential complication; the duration of orthodontic treatment may be prolonged and uniform tooth movement may be compromised.
- **Implant placement and maintenance:** Bisphosphonate treatment does not impact implant placement or maintenance, except in extensive cases; treatment should continue as planned.
- **Management of periodontal disease:** Patients who have active periodontal disease should receive appropriate forms of nonsurgical therapy. There is no evidence that periodontal procedures, such as guided tissue regeneration or bone replacement grafts, increase the risk of developing ONJ.
- **Endodontics:** Endodontic treatment is preferable to surgical manipulation if the tooth is salvageable. Limited evidence shows that periapical healing after endodontic therapy is similar regardless of bisphosphonate use.

FREQUENTLY ASKED QUESTIONS

According to the latest literature, what is the incidence of ONJ in oral bisphosphonates users?

Presently, the current estimates of the frequency of occurrence of ONJ in oral bisphosphonate users are the following: Merck drug company, the manufacturer of Fosamax calculated the incidence of ONJ to be 0.7 cases per 100,000 person-years of exposure to oral bisphosphonates. The Medical Consultants of Consumer Reports On-Health Bulletin reported an incidence of one case for every 20,000 users of oral bisphosphonates (0.005%). A recent report from Australia estimated that the frequency of ONJ in osteoporotic patients mainly on weekly oral alendronate (Fosamax) ranged from a minimum of 1 in 8,470 to a maximum of 1 in 2,260 (0.01% to 0.04%) patients. If extractions were performed, the frequency increased to 0.09% to 0.34%. The risk of developing ONJ in patients taking bisphosphonates or denosumab remains low with a prevalence of ~0.1% (1:1,000) (Hellstein 2011).

What numbers can practitioners use to tell the dental patient their risk of developing ONJ with oral bisphosphonates?

The recommendations from the Expert Panel of the American Dental Association suggest that the patient be informed that there is a very low risk of developing ONJ. The true risk posed by oral bisphosphonates remains uncertain but appears to be very small. All the data seem to point to a risk of ~0.1% of total users and that the risk increases with dental extractions to ~0.3%. The risks of developing ONJ can be minimized but never totally eliminated. Good oral hygiene along with regular dental care is the best way to lower the risk of developing ONJ. The current data on incidence of ONJ in patients taking oral bisphosphonates is retrospective information derived primarily from surveys and the number of reported cases in patients taking the drugs. More meaningful assessment of incidence of ONJ in the population at risk must come from prospective cohort investigations.

Is the risk of acquiring osteonecrosis of the jaw bone diminished with the use of other oral bisphosphonates compared to Fosamax?

In addition to alendronate (Fosamax), cases of ONJ, albeit rare, have been reported in patients taking either risedronate (Actonel) or ibandronate (Boniva). Among the class of oral bisphosphonates, more cases have been associated with Fosamax than with Actonel or Boniva. Also, there is no evidence to suggest that the risk of ONJ is less when taking monthly doses of Boniva. Zoledronic acid under the band name of Reclast has recently been approved as a once-annual, 15-minute intravenous infusion of a dose of 5 mg to prevent osteoporosis. This dosing was associated with a significant improvement in bone mineral density and bone metabolism markers. It is unknown whether this dosing schedule places the patient at risk for ONJ; however, data do show a higher risk of serious atrial fibrillation in patients receiving Reclast compared to patients receiving placebo.

Will Fosamax or the other oral bisphosphonates continue to be the standard treatment for osteoporosis?

Yes. The oral bisphosphonates continue to be the most effective class of drugs in reducing the risk of osteoporotic fractures and are the first-line therapy in the treatment of osteoporosis. Fosamax has been shown to prevent bone loss at the spine and hip in postmenopausal women and to reduce fractures by ~50%. Risedronate (Actonel) produced a 30% reduction in hip fractures. Fosamax continues to be in the top 50 of the most widely prescribed drugs in the US.

Do we know the pathogenesis of ONJ?

This question has not been answered and information is only speculative at this time. Osteoporosis can occur due to age-related changes in the number of osteoclasts and bone resorption sites. This overwhelms the production of new bone by osteoblasts and a decrease in bone mass occurs. By inhibiting osteoclastic activity, the oral bisphosphonates seemingly arrest the osteoporotic syndrome. In the process, however, the maxilla and mandible, upon continued exposure to the bisphosphonates, exhibit delayed wound healing following injury from mechanical forces or invasive surgery, such as tooth extraction. This coupled with the antiangiogenic effect (ie, a reduction in bone blood supply by the bisphosphonates) may contribute to jaw bone necrosis. Ruggiero and Drew have suggested that a preferential deposition of the bisphosphonates in the mandible and maxilla may contribute to the necrosis appearing within the jaw rather than within bones outside the craniofacial skeleton.

What are the factors that increase the risk of ONJ in oral bisphosphonate users?

Patients with a history of periodontal disease and dental abscesses are at increased risk of developing ONJ if taking oral bisphosphonates. Also, dentoalveolar trauma will increase the risk. The use of chronic steroids such as prednisone has been identified as a risk factor. Other factors are periodontitis, smoking, wearing dentures, diabetes, and the duration of exposure and age, with longer treatment regimens and age >65 years associated with a greater risk of developing the disease (Hellstein 2011). Patients identified with jaw bone necrosis typically were exposed to oral bisphosphonates for 2 years or longer.

What are the symptoms that an oral bisphosphonates patient would experience which could indicate necrotic jaw bone?

Tooth mobility, mucosal swelling, and/or ulceration. Clinical symptoms would include a nonhealing extraction site, exposed bone surrounded by inflamed soft tissue, and purulent discharge at site of exposed bone. Exposed bone is usually more prevalent in areas such as the tori and the mylohyoid ridge.

What kind of dental procedures can be performed in oral bisphosphonate users with no increase in risk for ONJ?

According to the American Dental Association, all routine procedures can be carried out. Routine dental treatment should not be modified on the basis of oral bisphosphonate use. However, the presence of risk factors, such as steroid use, >65 years of age, or prolonged exposure to oral bisphosphonates, may require consultation with an expert in metabolic bone disease prior to routine dental treatment.

Is dentoalveolar surgery contraindicated in Fosamax users?

According to both Ruggiero et al and Marx et al, no alteration or delay in planned surgery is typically necessary in patients taking an oral bisphosphonate for <3 years and having no other risk factors for ONJ. In asymptomatic patients receiving oral bisphosphonate therapy, dentoalveolar surgery is not contraindicated. Also surgery common to periodontists and other dental providers need not be delayed.

In addition, Marx suggested that if dental implants are placed, informed consent should be obtained related to the potential for implant failure and possible ONJ if the patient continues to take an oral bisphosphonate.

Is a so-called "drug holiday" an effective way to reduce the risks of ONJ?

Although a "drug holiday" would seem logical and has been suggested by some groups, there is no statistically significant evidence indicating in the cancer patient population that this is beneficial in reducing ONJ risk and in fact may be detrimental if the chance of a skeletal-related event increases. The data in oral bisphosphonates use are even less compelling since the incidence is so low to begin with that subjective drug holidays cannot be documented with any degree of confidence. As mentioned earlier, for individuals who have taken a bisphosphonate for <3 years and have no other risk factors for ONJ, no alteration or delay in the planned surgery is recommended, but the caveat is that the risk remains unknown.

In patients about to begin oral bisphosphonate therapy, should the bisphosphonate be delayed until dental health is optimized?

No. It does not appear necessary for patients to initiate prophylactic dental treatment prior to initiating oral bisphosphonate therapy for osteoporosis. It would be prudent, however, to encourage these patients to maintain an optimal level of dental health.

Is diagnostic imaging useful in assessing oral bisphosphonate individuals at risk for ONJ?

Imaging modalities have proved helpful in determining the extent of existing necrotic process, but have not been able to demonstrate any efficacy in assessing patients at risk for ONJ. It has been reported that panoramic and periapical radiographs probably will not reveal significant changes in early stages of osteonecrosis and they are poor screening tools for prediction. Computerized tomography (CT) scan also has not proved helpful with early identification of osteonecrosis in asymptomatic patients.

Do the Fosamax-type drugs increase the risk of ONJ in patients receiving dental implants?

A conclusive cause and effect relationship between bisphosphonate therapy and ONJ still has not been established. Evidence does suggest, however, that such an association may exist, particularly with intravenous bisphosphonate use in cancer patients. Oral bisphosphonates are widely used for the treatment of osteoporosis. It is estimated that 22 to 30 million prescriptions were written for alendronate (Fosamax), the most widely used oral bisphosphonate in the United States, between May 2003 and April 2004. For many years, dental implants have been placed in many patients taking oral bisphosphonates. Prior to the reports on the risk of bisphosphonate-associated ONJ, these patients were treated without any modification of the surgically placed implant procedure. Recently, however, guidelines from the American Dental Association (ADA) and the American Association of Oral and Maxillofacial Surgeons (AAOMS) have suggested a cautious approach to implant surgery and extractions for patients receiving bisphosphonate therapy.

Regarding dental implants, the ADA report cautions practitioners that patients may be at increased risk of developing osteonecrosis of the jaw bone when extensive implant placement or guided bone regeneration is necessary.

If dental implants are to be placed, the AAOMS Task Force suggested contacting the physician who prescribed the oral bisphosphonate prior to surgery to suggest an alternate dosing schedule, a drug holiday (discontinuance of the drug for a short time period), or an alternative to bisphosphonate therapy. It is important to remember that any beneficial or detrimental effects of these drug holidays have not been prospectively studied.

In addition, Marx has suggested the following precautions. Dental implant, if elected, can be placed in the patient about to begin oral bisphosphonate therapy. However, informed consent concerning the potential for implant loss and/or exposed bone related to the bisphosphonates should be obtained as the patient continues bisphosphonate therapy and exceeds 3 years of continuous use. For individuals who have taken an oral bisphosphonate for <3 years and have no clinical or radiographic risk factors, no alteration or delay is necessary for planned dental surgeries. If dental implants are placed, informed consent should be obtained related to the potential for implant failure and possible ONJ if the patient continues to take the bisphosphonate.

For patients who have taken an oral bisphosphonates for >3 years, it is advised that the prescribing physician be contacted and a recommendation made to discontinue the oral bisphosphonate for 3 months prior to the procedure and refrain from reinstating use until 3 months after the procedure.

One report from the UK suggested an even more conservative approach. Scully et al, suggested that when possible, extractions should be avoided in patients receiving oral bisphosphonates and it is best to avoid all elective surgery in these patients, including endosseous implant placement, or treatment should be performed well in advance prior to bisphosphonate therapy. If surgery is performed on patients taking bisphosphonates, they must be counseled about the risk.

A new report showed that implant surgery on patients receiving Fosamax-type drugs did not result in bisphosphonate-associated ONJ. This study, out of the Dentistry/Oral Surgery Group at Montefiore Medical Center, Albert Einstein College of Medicine, reported that of 115 patients taking oral bisphosphonates, none showed evidence or had symptoms of osteonecrosis after implant placement. This report had findings similar to a previous report by Dr Jeffcoat, who showed success in implant placement and no signs of necrosis in patients taking oral bisphosphonates.

The Montefiore study, by Grant et al, used a survey to collect information from patients who had received dental implants and were taking oral bisphosphonates. The study, reported in the *Journal of Oral and Maxillofacial Surgery*, identified 1,319 female patients >40 years of age who had implant surgery between January 1998 and December 2006. A survey was mailed to each of these individuals asking about current and past use of oral bisphosphonates. Of the 1,319 surveys mailed out, 458 (35%) were returned. From those returned, 115 individuals reported taking oral bisphosphonates before or after implant surgery. None reported receiving intravenous bisphosphonates. In this population, it was then determined that a total of 468 implants had been placed in the 115 individuals. This population that responded to the survey was then compared to a random sample of individuals who did not respond with regard to age and number of implants. It was found that only five among 100 nonresponders to the survey had a history of bisphosphonate use compared to the 115 of the 458 responders. The remaining 343 patients indicated that they had not received bisphosphonate therapy. From the pool of 458 responders, there were 1,450 implants placed in these patients and 1,436 had integrated successfully. Implant success was defined using criteria which included the absence of symptoms, such as pain, infection, paresthesia, or neuropathies, and that the dental implant should provide functional service for 5 years in 75% of the cases.

The results were the following:

1. None of the 458 responders to the survey reported symptoms of bisphosphonate-associated ONJ.
2. Since 115 of the 458 responders indicated they were treated with bisphosphonates, it was assumed that none of the 115 responders treated with bisphosphonates had ONJ.
3. Out of the pool of 115 patients, there was a total of 468 implants placed. It was found that 466 of those implants were in function and were considered successful. Only two implants failed. In one case of failure, the patient had taken oral bisphosphonates for 3 years prior to implant placement but no longer was taking any drug at the time of implant placement or thereafter. The investigators removed and replaced the implant and it was still in function for >4 years. In the second case, the patient had been taking bisphosphonates for >8 years and the failure occurred in one implant out of a total of 13 in place. The failed implant was removed, not replaced, and the area healed uneventfully.
4. There were no reports of ONJ from any of the 861 patients who did not return the survey.

This report from Montefiore is consistent with that of the findings of Jeffcoat. She also reported success in implant placement and no signs of necrosis in patients taking oral bisphosphonates. Her method was a single blind controlled study using 50 postmenopausal female dental implant patients. Twenty-five had taken oral bisphosphonates for 1-4 years and the other 25 patients did not take oral bisphosphonates prior to or during the study. In the bisphosphonate group, there was a total of 102 implants that were placed and in the nondrug group, there were 108 implants that were placed. After 3 years, there was 100% success rate with no evidence of infection, pain, or necrosis in patients receiving bisphosphonates. There was 99.2% success rate in the group not taking oral bisphosphonates.

A further review of the literature found only two cases of dental implant failure associated with oral bisphosphonate use. One was a case report from 1995 that suggested that failure of five implants was caused by bisphosphonate therapy. In that case, five implants were placed and successfully integrated in the mandible. The patient then began bisphosphonate therapy 28 months after implant placement and after 4 months, a panoramic radiograph revealed osteolysis around all implants and all five were removed one month later.

In the report by Wang et al, a patient developed a significant bone defect with necrosis after proper implant placement. The patient was a 65-year-old female who had taken Fosamax for 10 years. She received five implants in the mandible. Ten days after surgery, healing appeared to be progressing uneventfully. Four weeks later, upon evaluation, bone defects were observed and noted around two of the implants. The defects were repaired with mineralized human cancellous bone mixed with tetracycline and covered with collagen membrane. Eventually after some further antibiotics and chlorhexidine daily rinsing, complete uneventful healing occurred.

Is the CTX bone marker useful to assess the risk of ONJ in oral bisphosphonate users?

CTX is an acronym for C-terminal telopeptide. During bone resorption, the dominant type 1 collagen is degraded and, during this collagen breakdown, the telopeptide (CTX) is released. Thus, serum levels of CTX can be used as an indicator of bone breakdown/resorption. The CTX blood test, as a risk marker for ONJ, first proposed by Marx in 2007, was used in an Australian study to determine its effectiveness in the prevention and management of ONJ in patients taking bisphosphonates. Essentially, this test was found to be able to identify groups of those individuals in the "risk zone" for developing ONJ, which was defined as a blood level of 150 picograms/mL (pg/mL) to 200 picograms/mL (pg/mL). It was, however, not found to be predictive of the development of ONJ in any individual patient. The CTX test requires a 1 mL sample of whole blood drawn in the morning in fasted individuals. Marx used Quest Diagnostics Nichols East Lab in San Juan Capistrano California to perform the analysis on the samples. Values lower than 100 pg/mL were correlated with a high risk of ONJ; values between 100 pg/mL and 150 pg/mL correlated to a moderate risk and values >150 pg/mL associated with minimal or no risk. According to Ruggiero and Drew, low bone turnover in the jaw due to osteoclastic inhibition by bisphosphonates results in the inability of the bone to repair local microdamage from normal mechanical loading or injury. This ultimately results in bone necrosis. Thus, individuals with low CTX values while taking bisphosphonates are assumed to have jaw bones which may not be able to normally repair themselves and these individuals would have a relatively higher risk of developing ONJ compared to individuals having higher CTX serum values.

Rigorous prospective studies on greater numbers of individuals are required before the use of the CTX serum test could be suggested with any confidence. In 2011, the American Dental Association (ADA) reaffirmed its earlier position that CTX cannot be recommended as a predictive tool for ONJ risk assessment.

Are there other bone markers that may be useful?

Researchers have been seeking screening tools to predict and allow prevention of ONJ. A recent study by the Memorial Sloan-Kettering Cancer Center of New York investigated specific bone turnover markers as predictive models to assess risks of ONJ in patients exposed to bisphosphonates (Morris 2012). This retrospective study showed that N-telopeptide of type-I collagen (NTX) and bone-specific alkaline phosphatase (BAP) did not predict for the development of ONJ. No significant trend for either biomarker was detected. Thus, to date, there is insufficient evidence to recommend the use of serum tests as predictors of ONJ.

Do the new anti-RANK-L drugs such as denosumab (Prolia, Xgeva) increase the risk of ONJ?

ONJ has been reported in clinical studies in patients receiving denosumab at FDA-approved doses for osteoporosis. In clinical studies, patients with advanced cancer treated with 120 mg denosumab administered monthly, have reported a 2% incidence of ONJ. Known risk factors for ONJ include a diagnosis of cancer with bone lesions, concomitant therapies (eg, chemotherapy, antiangiogenic biologics, corticosteroids, radiotherapy to the head and neck), poor oral hygiene, dental extractions, comorbid disorders (eg, preexisting dental disease, anaemia, coagulopathy, infection) and previous treatment with bisphosphonates.

A dental examination with appropriate preventive dentistry should be considered prior to initiating denosumab treatment in patients with concomitant risk factors. These patients should avoid invasive dental procedures if possible during treatment with denosumab. Patients should maintain good oral hygiene during treatment. For patients who develop ONJ while on denosumab therapy, dental surgery may exacerbate the condition. Use clinical judgement and guide the management plan of each patient based on individual risk:benefit evaluation.

Denosumab on page 464

CLINICAL DENTAL MANAGEMENT CONSIDERATIONS

Suggested Preventive Dentistry Before Initiating Chemotherapy, Immunotherapy, or Antiresorptive Therapy

- Remove abscessed and nonrestorable teeth and teeth with severe periodontal disease involvement
- Remove teeth with poor long-term prognosis
- Functionally rehabilitate salvageable dentition, including endodontic therapy
- Perform dental prophylaxis, caries control, and stabilizing restorative dental care
- Examine dentures to ensure proper fit (dentures should be removed at night)
- Educate patients on oral self-care hygiene

Patients at Risk of ONJ Due to Antiresorptive Therapy (Without Any Signs of ONJ):

Invasive dental procedures should be avoided in patients receiving intravenous bisphosphonate therapy. These procedures should also be performed ideally prior to a patient starting bisphosphonate I.V. therapy. The treating physician should guide the management plan of each patient based on individual benefit:risk assessment and communication with the dentist. For patients requiring dental procedures, there are no prospective data available to suggest whether discontinuation of bisphosphonate treatment reduces the risk of ONJ.

There are five primary actions in this management plan:

1. Patients should be educated on maintaining excellent oral hygiene to reduce the risk of need for invasive procedures in the future.
2. Patients should check and adjust removable appliances such as prostheses to avoid soft tissue injury.
3. Routine cleaning should be performed with care, attempting to reduce any soft tissue injury; however, since hygiene is important, the normal recall planning and treatment should continue.
4. Dental infection should be managed aggressively and nonsurgically when possible. Alternatives such as endodontic therapy over extraction may be advisable.
5. Endodontic therapy is preferable to extractions; treatment with endodontics followed by coronal amputation and root canal therapy on the retained roots may be necessary.

If a Patient Develops Osteonecrosis of the Jaw: Consultations between oral surgeons/dental oncologists and the treating physician are strongly recommended:

- A nonsurgical approach is recommended to prevent further osseous injury.
- Only minimal bony debridement to reduce sharp and rough surfaces to prevent further trauma to adjacent or opposing tissues is recommended.
- A removable appliance or protective stent may be used to protect exposed bone or adjacent tissues.
- Before discontinuing bisphosphonate therapy, patient should be evaluated for potential risk of further osteonecrosis versus the risk of skeletal complications.
- Hyperbaric oxygen therapy is not recommended.
- Biopsy is not recommended unless metastasis to the jaw is suspected.
- Cultures should be taken for directed antimicrobial therapy.
- Prophylactic antibiotic therapy may be considered for pain and disease control.

SAMPLE PRESCRIPTIONS FOR PROPHYLACTIC ANTIBIOTIC THERAPY IF AN INVASIVE PROCEDURE IS PLANNED IN A PATIENT AT HIGH RISK FOR ONJ OR ALREADY HAS A DEFINED ONJ LESION

Rx:
Amoxicillin 875 mg tablets
Disp: 60 tablets
Sig: Take 1 tablet twice daily

Note: Alternatively, 500 mg tablet 3 times daily can be prescribed and may be continued for >1 month. Patients should be cautioned regarding gastrointestinal side effects with long-term use of any antibiotic. Probiotics may help, but evidence is conflicted on true efficacy.

Rx:
Clindamycin (Systemic) 300 mg capsules
Disp: 40 capsules
Sig: Take 1 capsule 3 or 4 times/day for 7 to 10 days

Note: Prescription usually selected for patients allergic to penicillin; may be prescribed for 3 or 4 times/day. This prescription can be continued for >1 month; however, risk of *Clostridium difficile* colitis increases. Patients should be cautioned to take clindamycin with food and monitor for gastrointestinal side effects with long-term use. Probiotics may help, but evidence is conflicted on true efficacy.

Rx:
Chlorhexidine Oral Rinse
Disp: 1 bottle
Sig: Rinse with 20 cc twice daily for 30 seconds and expectorate

ONJ Diagnosis and Definition

- Intraoral pain is variable
- Complaint of roughness along the teeth or ridge
- History of dental procedures (eg, extractions) but may occur on tissues
- Complaint of ill-fitting denture(s)
- Diagnosis of ONJ made clinically with presence of exposed bone in maxillofacial region (>8 weeks duration [with no history of radiation therapy])
- If the presence of exposed bone in maxillofacial region is noted but is <8 weeks duration (with no history of radiation therapy), the clinician must consider other differential diagnoses of:
  - Spontaneous lingual mandibular sequestration with ulceration
  - Trauma
  - Advanced periodontal disease with dehiscence
  - Local malignancy
  - Metastatic cancer

REFERENCES AND SELECTED READINGS

Almubarak H, Jones A, Chaisuparat R, et al. Zoledronic acid directly suppresses cell proliferation and induces apoptosis in highly tumorigenic prostate and breast cancers. *J Carcinog*. 2011;10:2.

American Dental Association Council on Scientific Affairs. Dental management of patients receiving oral bisphosphonate therapy: expert panel recommendations. *J Am Dent Assoc*. 2006;137(8):1144-1150.

Badros A, Weikel D, Salama A, et al. Osteonecrosis of the jaw in multiple myeloma patients: clinical features and risk factors. *J Clin Oncol*. 2006;24 (6):945-952.

Filleul O, Crompot E, Saussez S. Bisphosphonate-induced osteonecrosis of the jaw: a review of 2,400 patient cases. *J Cancer Res Clin Oncol*. 2010;136(8):1117-1124.

Grant BT, Amenedo C, Freeman K, Kraut RA. Outcomes of placing dental implants in patients taking oral bisphosphonates: a review of 115 cases. *J Oral Maxillofac Surg*. 2008;66(2):223-230.

Hellstein JW, Adler RA, Edwards B, et al. Managing the care of patients receiving antiresorptive therapy for prevention and treatment of osteoporosis: executive summary of recommendations from the American Dental Association Council on Scientific Affairs. *J Am Dent Assoc*. 2011;142 (11):1243-1251. Available at http://www.ada.org/sections/professionalResources/pdfs/topics_ARONJ_report.pdf. Accessed November 25, 2011.

Hinchy NV et al. Osteonecrosis of the jaw – prevention and treatment strategies for oral health professionals. *Oral Oncology*. 2013;49:878-886.

Katsarelis H, Shah NP, Dhariwal DK, Pazianas M. Infection and medication-related osteonecrosis of the jaw. *J Dent Res*. 2015;94(4):534-539.

Khan AA, Morrison A, Hanley DA, et al. Diagnosis and management of osteonecrosis of the jaw: a systematic review and international consensus. *J Bone Miner Res*. 2015; 30(1):3-23.

Kyrgidis A, Toulis KA. Denosumab-related osteonecrosis of the jaws. *Osteoporos Int*. 2011;22(1):369-370.

Marx RE, Cillo JE Jr, Ulloa JJ. Oral bisphosphonate-induced osteonecrosis: risk factors, prediction of risk using serum CTX testing, prevention, and treatment. *J Oral Maxillofac Surg*. 2007;65(12):2397-2410.

Marx RE. *Oral and Intravenous Bisphosphonate-Induced Osteonecrosis of the Jaws: History, Etiology, Prevention and Treatment*. Chicago, IL: Quintessence Publishing Company; 2007;87-91.

Marx RE, Sawatari Y, Fortin M, Broumand V. Bisphosphonate-induced exposed bone (osteonecrosis/osteopetrosis) of the jaws: risk factors, recognition, prevention, and treatment. *J Oral Maxillofac Surg*. 2005;63(11):1567-1575.

Mavrokokki T, Cheng A, Stein B, Goss A. Nature and frequency of bisphosphonate-associated osteonecrosis of the jaws in Australia. *J Oral Maxillofac Surg*. 2007;65(3):415-423.

Migliorati CA, Casiglia J, Epstein J, Jacobsen PL, Siegel MA, Woo SB. Managing the care of patients with bisphosphonate-associated osteonecrosis: an American Academy of Oral Medicine position paper. *J Am Dent Assoc*. 2005;136(12):1658-1668.

Morris PG, Fazio M, Farooki A, et al. Serum N-telopeptide and bone-specific alkaline phosphatase levels in patients with osteonecrosis of the jaw receiving bisphosphonates for bone metastases. *J Oral Maxillofac Surg*. 2012;70(12):2768-2775.

Mücke T, Deppe H, Hein J, et al. Prevention of bisphosphonate-related osteonecrosis of the jaws in patients with prostate cancer treated with zoledronic acid - a prospective study over 6 years. *J Craniomaxillofac Surg.* 2016;44(10):1689-1693.
Ruggiero SL. Diagnosis and management of antiresorptive-related osteonecrosis of the jaw. *Gen Dent.* 2013;61(7):24-29.
Ruggiero SL, Dodson TB, Fantasia J, et al. American Association of Oral and Maxillofacial Surgeons position paper on medication-related osteonecrosis of the jaw–2014 update. *J Oral Maxillofac Surg.* 2014;72(10):1938-1956.
Ruggiero SL, Dodson TB, Assael LA, et al. American Association of Oral and Maxillofacial Surgeons position paper on bisphosphonate-related osteonecrosis of the jaw – 2009 update. *Aust Endod J.* 2009;35(3):119-130.
Ruggiero SL, Drew SJ. Osteonecrosis of the jaws and bisphosphonate therapy. *J Dent Res.* 2007;86(11):1013-1021.
Ruggiero S, Gralow J, Marx RE. Practical guidelines for the prevention, diagnosis, and treatment of osteonecrosis of the jaw in patients with cancer. *J Oncol Pract.* 2006;2(1):7-14.
Ruggiero SL, Fantasia J, Carlson E. Bisphosphonate-related osteonecrosis of the jaw: background and guidelines for diagnosis, staging and management. *Oral Surg Oral Med Oral Pathol Oral Radiol Endod.* 2006;102(4):433-441.
Ruggiero SL, Mehrotra B, Rosenberg TJ, et al. Osteonecrosis of the jaws associated with the use of bisphosphonates: a review of 63 cases. *J Oral Maxillofac Surg.* 2004;62(5):527-534.
Scheper MA, Badros A, Chaisuparat R, et al. Effect of zoledronic acid on oral fibroblasts and epithelial cells: a potential mechanism of bisphosphonate-associated osteonecrosis. *Br J Haematol.* 2009;144(5):667-676.
Scheper MA, Badros A, Salama AR, et al. A novel bioassay model to determine clinically significant bisphosphonate levels. *Support Care Cancer.* 2009;17(12):1553-1557.
Scheper M, Chaisuparat R, Cullen K, et al. A novel soft-tissue in vitro model for bisphosphonate-associated osteonecrosis. *Fibrogenesis Tissue Repair.* 2010;3:6.
Scully C, Madrid C, Bagan J. Dental endosseous implants in patients on bisphosphonate therapy. *Implant Dent.* 2006;15(3):212-218.
Taylor KH, Middlefell LS, Mizen KD. Osteonecrosis of the jaws induced by anti-RANK ligand therapy. *Br J Oral Maxillofac Surg.* 2010;48(3):221-223.
Wang HL, Weber D, McCauley LK. Effect of long-term oral bisphosphonates on implant wound healing: literature review and a case report. *J Periodontol.* 2007;78(3):584-594.

SEXUALLY-TRANSMITTED DISEASES

Sexually transmitted diseases (STDs) represent a group of infectious diseases that include bacterial, fungal, and viral etiologies. Several related infections are covered elsewhere. Several viral STDs can be effectively prevented through vaccination with widely available vaccines, including hepatitis A, hepatitis B, and human papilloma virus vaccines.

Human papilloma virus is widespread and serotypes 16 and 18 have been associated with cervical cancer. Although most types that cause oral HPV lesions are not of these serotypes, the clinician should recommend appropriate surgical removal of all such lesions. Lesions in the posterior oral pharyngeal region are of particular concern. Pre-exposure vaccination is one of the most effective methods for preventing transmission of some STDs. Quadrivalent HPV vaccine (Gardasil) and the bivalent HPV vaccine (Cervarix) are available.

Gardasil is a vaccine indicated in girls and women 9 to 26 years of age for the prevention of the following diseases caused by Human Papillomavirus (HPV) types included in the vaccine:

- Cervical, vulvar, vaginal, and anal cancer caused by HPV types 16 and 18
- Genital warts (condyloma acuminata) caused by HPV types 6 and 11

And the following precancerous or dysplastic lesions caused by HPV types 6, 11, 16, and 18:

- Cervical intraepithelial neoplasia (CIN) grade 2/3 and cervical adenocarcinoma in situ (AIS)
- Cervical intraepithelial neoplasia (CIN) grade 1
- Vulvar intraepithelial neoplasia (VIN) grade 2 and grade 3
- Vaginal intraepithelial neoplasia (VaIN) grade 2 and grade 3
- Anal intraepithelial neoplasia (AIN) grades 1, 2, and 3

Gardasil is also indicated in boys and men 9 to 26 years of age for the prevention of the following diseases caused by HPV types included in the vaccine:

- Anal cancer caused by HPV types 16 and 18
- Genital warts (condyloma acuminata) caused by HPV types 6 and 11

And the following precancerous or dysplastic lesions caused by HPV types 6, 11, 16, and 18:

- Anal intraepithelial neoplasia (AIN) grades 1, 2, and 3

Cervarix is a vaccine indicated for the prevention of the following diseases caused by oncogenic human papillomavirus (HPV) types 16 and 18:

- Cervical cancer
- Cervical intraepithelial neoplasia (CIN) grade 2 or worse and adenocarcinoma *in situ*
- Cervical intraepithelial neoplasia (CIN) grade 1

Cervarix is approved for use in females 9 to 25 years of age.

Details regarding HPV vaccination are available at www.cdc.gov/std/hpv. Vaccines for other STDs (eg, HIV and herpes simplex virus) are under development or undergoing clinical trials. Vaccines are not available for bacterial or fungal STDs.

The management of a patient with an STD begins with identification. Paramount to the correct management of patients with a history of gonorrhea or syphilis is when the condition was diagnosed, how and with what agent it was treated, did the condition recur, and are there any residual signs and symptoms potentially indicating active or recurrent disease. With standard/universal precautions, the patient with *Neisseria gonorrhoea* or *Treponema pallidum* infection poses little threat to the dentist; however, diagnosis of oral lesions may be problematic. Gonococcal pharyngitis, primary syphilitic lesions (chancre), secondary syphilitic lesions (mucous patch), and tertiary lesions (gumma) may be identified by the dentist. All patients who have gonorrhea should also be tested for other STDs, including chlamydia, syphilis, and HIV. Most gonococcal infections of the pharynx are asymptomatic and can be relatively common in some populations. Gonococcal infections of the pharynx are more difficult to eradicate than urogenital and anorectal infections. Few antimicrobial regimens, including those involving oral cephalosporins, can reliably cure >90% of gonococcal pharyngeal infections. Chlamydial coinfection of the pharynx is unusual; however, because coinfection at genital sites sometimes occurs, treatment for both gonorrhea and chlamydia is recommended.

Gonorrhea is the second most commonly reported bacterial STD. The majority of urethral infections caused by *N. gonorrhoeae* among men produce symptoms that cause them to seek curative treatment soon enough to prevent serious sequelae, but treatment may not be soon enough to prevent transmission to others. Among women, gonococcal infections may not produce recognizable symptoms until complications (eg, pelvic inflammatory disease [PID]) have occurred. PID can result in tubal scarring that can lead to infertility or ectopic pregnancy. Treatment of uncomplicated gonococcal infections of the cervix, urethra, and rectum include ceftriaxone, cefixime, azithromycin, and doxycycline.

Chlamydial genital infection is the most frequently reported infectious disease in the United States and is found more commonly in patients ≤25 years of age. Several important sequelae can result from *C. trachomatous* infection in women including PID, infertility, and ectopic pregnancy. Chlamydia treatment should be provided promptly for all patients testing positive for infection. Coinfection with *C. trachomatous* frequently occurs among patients who have gonococcal infection; therefore, concurrent treatment for both infections is recommended. Chlamydial infections can be treated with azithromycin or doxycycline. Alternative treatments include erythromycin, levofloxacin, or ofloxacin (systemic). If treating gonorrhea concurrently, would not consider use of a fluoroquinolone as resistance is high.

DRUGS USED IN TREATMENT OF CHLAMYDIA, GONORRHEA/SYPHILIS INCLUDE:

Azithromycin (Systemic) on page 194
Cefixime on page 318
CefTRIAXone on page 326
Doxycycline on page 540
Penicillin G Benzathine on page 1309
Penicillin G (Parenteral/Aqueous) on page 1310

The drugs listed above are often used alone or in stepped regimens, particularly when there is concomitant *Chlamydia* infection or when there is evidence of disseminated disease. The proper treatment for syphilis depends on the state of the disease.

HPV PREVENTION:

Papillomavirus (Types 6, 11, 16, 18) Vaccine (Human, Recombinant) (Gardasil) on page 1287
Papillomavirus (Types 16, 18) Vaccine (Human, Recombinant) (Cervarix) on page 1288

REFERENCES AND SELECTED READINGS

Centers for Disease Control and Prevention (CDC). Update to CDC's sexually transmitted diseases treatment guidelines, 2006: fluoroquinolones no longer recommended for treatment of gonococcal infections. *MMWR Morb Mortal Wkly Rep.* 2007;56(14):332-336.

Centers for Disease Control and Prevention (CDC). Update to CDC's sexually transmitted diseases treatment guidelines, 2010: oral cephalosporins no longer a recommended treatment for gonococcal infections. *MMWR Morb Mortal Wkly Rep.* 2012;61(31):590-594.

Corstjens PL, Abrams WR, Malamud D. Detecting viruses by using salivary diagnostics. *J Am Dent Assoc.* 2012;143(10 Suppl):12S-8S.

Little JW. Syphilis: an update. *Oral Surg Oral Med Oral Pathol Oral Radiol Endod.* 2005;100(1):3-9.

Miller WC, Zenilman JM. Epidemiology of chlamydial infection, gonorrhea, and trichomoniasis in the United States – 2005. *Infect Dis Clin North Am.* 2005;19(2):281-296.

Workowski KA, Berman S, Centers for Disease Control and Prevention (CDC). Sexually transmitted diseases treatment guidelines, 2010. *MMWR Recomm Rep.* 2010;59(RR-12):1-110. Available at http://www.cdc.gov/std/treatment/2010/STD-Treatment-2010-RR5912.pdf

SYSTEMIC VIRAL DISEASES

HEPATITIS

The hepatitis viruses are a group of DNA and RNA viruses that produce symptoms associated with inflammation of the liver. Currently, hepatitis A through G have been identified by immunological testing; however, hepatitis A through E have received most attention in terms of disease identification. Recently, there has been increased interest in hepatitis viruses F and G, particularly as related to health care professionals. Our knowledge is expanding rapidly in this area and the clinician should be alert to changes in the literature that might update their knowledge. Hepatitis F, for instance, remains a diagnosis of exclusion, effectively being non-A, B, C, D, E, or G. Hepatitis G has serologic testing available; however, it is not commercially at this time. Research evaluations of various antibody and RT-PCR tests for hepatitis G are under development at this time.

Signs and symptoms of viral hepatitis in general are quite variable. Patients infected may range from asymptomatic to experiencing flu-like symptoms only. In addition, fever, nausea, joint muscle pain, jaundice, and hepatomegaly along with abdominal pain can result from infection with one of the hepatitis viruses. The virus also can create an acute or chronic infection. Usually following these early symptoms or the asymptomatic period, the patient may recover or may go on to develop chronic liver dysfunction. Liver dysfunction may be represented primarily by changes in liver function tests known as LFTs and these primarily include aspartate aminotransferase known as AST and alanine aminotransferase known as ALT. In addition, for A, B, C, D, and E, there are serologic tests for either antigen, antibody, or both. Of hepatitis A through G, five forms have both acute and chronic forms whereas A and E appear to only create acute disease. There are differences in the way clinicians may approach a known postexposure to one of the hepatitis viruses. In many instances, gamma globulin may be used; however, the indications for gamma globulin as a drug limit their use to several of the viruses only. The dental clinician should be aware that the gastroenterologist may choose to give gamma globulin off-label.

Hepatitis A

Hepatitis A virus is an enteric virus that is a member of the Picornavirus family along with Coxsackie viruses and poliovirus. Previously known as infectious hepatitis, hepatitis A has been detected in humans for centuries. It causes acute hepatitis, often transmitted by oral-fecal contamination and having an incubation period of approximately 30 days. Typically, constitutional symptoms are present and jaundice may occur. Drug therapy that the dentist may encounter in a patient being treated for hepatitis A would primarily include immunoglobulin. Hepatitis A vaccine (inactivated) is an FDA-approved vaccine indicated in the prevention of contracting hepatitis A in exposed or high-risk individuals. Candidates at high-risk for HAV infection include persons traveling internationally to highly endemic areas, individuals with chronic liver disease, individuals engaging in high-risk sexual behavior, illicit drug users, persons with high-risk occupational exposure, hemophiliacs or other persons receiving blood products, and pediatric populations. Hepatitis A, caused by infection with HAV, has an incubation period of ~28 days (range: 15 to 50 days). HAV replicates in the liver and is shed in high concentrations in feces from 2 weeks before to 1 week after the onset of clinical illness. HAV infection produces a self-limited disease that does not result in chronic infection or chronic liver disease; however, 10% to 15% of patients experience relapse symptoms during the 6 months after acute illness. Patients with acute hepatitis A usually require only supportive care with no restrictions in diet or activity. Hospitalization may be necessary for patients who become dehydrated due to nausea and vomiting, but is critical for patients with signs or symptoms of acute liver failure. Medications that may cause liver damage or are metabolized by the liver should be used with caution among patients with hepatitis A.

Two products are available for the prevention of HAV infection: Hepatitis A vaccine and immune globulin (IG) for IM administration. Patients recently exposed (within 14 days and prior to development of illness) to HAV and have not received a hepatitis A vaccine should be administered a single dose of the vaccine or IG ([GamaSTAN S/D] 0.02 mL/kg) as soon as possible.

Hepatitis B

Hepatitis B virus is previously known as serum hepatitis and has particular trophism for liver cells. Hepatitis B virus causes both acute and chronic disease in susceptible patients. The incubation period is often long and the diagnosis might be made by serologic markers even in the absence of symptoms.

Hepatitis B is caused by infection with the hepatitis B virus (HBV). The incubation period from the time of exposure to onset of symptoms is 6 weeks to 6 months. The highest concentrations of HBV are found in blood with lower concentrations found in other body fluids.

HBV infection can be self-limited or chronic. In adults, only ~1/2 of newly acquired HBV infections are symptomatic and ~1% of reported cases result in acute liver failure. HBV is efficiently transmitted by percutaneous or mucous membrane exposure to blood or body fluids that contain blood. Preventing disease after exposure in a person without previous hepatitis B vaccine protection is important. Passive-active postexposure prophylaxis (PEP) occurs with administration of hepatitis B immune globulin and hepatitis B vaccine.

Hepatitis C

In the United States, an estimated 4.1 million persons have been infected with hepatitis C virus (HCV), of whom an estimated 3.2 million are living with the infection. The hepatitis C virus (HCV) is an RNA virus. HCV is a major cause of both acute and chronic hepatitis. Persons become infected mainly through parenteral exposure to infected material by blood transfusions or injections with nonsterile needles. Persons who inject illegal drugs and health care workers who are at risk for needlestick and other exposures are at highest risk for HCV infection. Another major risk factor for HCV is high-risk sexual behavior. Cutaneous symptoms or findings relevant to HCV infection manifest in 20% to 40% of patients presenting to dermatologists and in a significant percentage (15% to 20%) of general patients. HCV is suggested and must appear in the differential diagnosis of these patients to avoid missing this important but occult factor in clinical disease in the appropriate setting. HCV has been considered in the differential diagnosis for the causes of oral lichen planus; however, no concrete relationship has been established.

Extrahepatic manifestations of hepatitis C virus are numerous. The most prevalent and most closely linked with HCV is essential mixed cryoglobulins with dermatologic, neurologic, renal, and rheumatologic complications. A less definite relationship to HCV is observed with systemic vasculitis, porphyria cutanea tarda, and the sicca syndromes, which could also affect the oral cavity. HCV is a major public health problem because it causes chronic hepatitis, cirrhosis, and hepatocellular carcinoma (HCC).

Treatment of acute hepatitis C infection has been primarily supportive up to now with monitoring to assess the need for antiviral therapy. Treatment regimens are typically based upon hepatitis C genome, whether the patient is treatment-naïve, has cirrhosis, or has other comorbid conditions, such as HIV. Individuals with Genotype-1 of Hepatitis-C are less likely to respond to standard-of-care HepC medications. Standard-of-care is pegylated interferon (PegIFN) with or without ribavirin. About 50% with genotype-1 and about 80% with genotype-2 or genotype-3 can be virologically cured, but for the others the options to now have been limited. The remaining nonresponders are left with no other treatment options to cure their infection. CDC recommends that all baby boomers (defined as born between 1945 and 1965) be tested for HCV based on the current data that ~2.7 to 3.9 million are infected and most do not know they carry the virus. Recently, Sofosbuvir (Solvaldi) has been approved for the treatment of genotype 1, 2, 3, or 4 chronic hepatitis C in combination with ribavirin or with peginterferon alfa and ribavirin. It is a nucleotide analog polymerase inhibitor, which stops the HCV virus from replicating. Also Sofosbuvir, in combination with ledipasvir (Harvoni), claims a 90% to 99% cure of Hepatitis C.

No vaccine is available for hepatitis C and prophylaxis with immune globulin is not effective in preventing HCV infection after exposure. The OraQuick HCV Rapid Antibody Test (OraSure Technologies) is a rapid assay for the presumptive detection of HCV antibody in fingerstick capillary blood and venipuncture whole blood. Its sensitivity and specificity are similar to those of FDA-approved, laboratory-conducted HCV antibody assays. The Chiron RIBA HCV 3.0 Strip Immunoblot Assay (Novartis Vaccines and Diagnostics) that was recommended for supplemental testing of blood samples after initial HCV antibody testing is no longer available. Testing to determine whether HCV infection has developed is recommended for health care workers after percutaneous or perimucosal exposure to HCV-positive blood.

Historically, HCV treatment was less effective for African Americans than for Caucasians. Researchers identified a gene that was linked with response to pegylated interferon-based treatment, called IL-28B. However, clinical trials of new generation of HCV drugs did not find any difference in cure rates between black and non-black study participants. Hepatitis C also seemed to progress more rapidly in Latinos than in people from other racial and ethnic groups. However, in the clinical trials of several new HCV antivirals, there was no apparent difference in success rates with the drug among Latinos than among non-Latinos.

Hepatitis C, with at least 6 genotypes, is a complex disease also in part because often other liver compromising issues such as cirrhosis and even previous treatments can inhibit the success of newly emerging therapies. Development and approval of a wide variety of drugs to treat selected groups of patients over the last decade has been nothing short of remarkable. In June of 2016 the FDA approved a new combination medicine, the first therapy approved to treat all HCV genotypes (1, 2, 3, 4, 5, or 6). It is also the first single tablet regimen approved for the treatment of patients with HCV genotype 2 and 3, without the need for ribavirin. **EPCLUSA (sofosbuvir 400 mg/velpatasvir 100 mg)** is a once-daily, fixed-dose combination tablet approved for the treatment of adults with chronic HCV genotype 1 to 6. Epclusa for 12 weeks was approved in patients without cirrhosis or with compensated cirrhosis, and in combination with ribavirin for patients with decompensated (advanced) cirrhosis.

Clinicians are advised to refer to liver disease sources such as AASLD-IDSA. See recommendations for testing, managing, and treating hepatitis C at www.hcvguidelines.org in order to assess the data on emerging therapies important in HCV.

Hepatitis D

Hepatitis D, previously known as the delta agent, is a virus that is incomplete in that it requires previous infection with hepatitis B in order to be manifested. Antiviral therapy is not indicated for an acute infection.

Hepatitis E

Hepatitis E virus is an RNA virus that represents a proportion of the previously classified non-A/non-B diagnoses. There is currently no antiviral therapy against hepatitis E.

Hepatitis F

Hepatitis F remains a diagnosis of exclusion. There are no known immunological tests available for identification of hepatitis F at present and currently the Centers for Disease Control have not come out with specific guidelines or recommendations. It is thought that hepatitis F is a blood-borne virus and it has been used as a diagnosis in several cases of post-transfusion hepatitis.

Hepatitis G

Hepatitis G virus (HGV) is the newest hepatitis and is also assumed to be a blood-borne virus. Similar in family to hepatitis C, it is thought to occur concomitantly with hepatitis C and appears to be even more prevalent in some blood donors than hepatitis C. Occupational transmission of HGV is currently under study (see the references for updated information) and currently there are no specific CDC recommendations for postexposure to an HGV individual as the testing for identification remains experimental.

For further information, refer to the following:

Adefovir on page 81
Boceprevir on page 233
Entecavir on page 578
Hepatitis A Vaccine on page 814
Hepatitis A and Hepatitis B Recombinant Vaccine on page 814
Hepatitis B Immune Globulin (Human) on page 815
Hepatitis B Vaccine (Recombinant) on page 816
Immune Globulin on page 870
Interferon Alfa-2b on page 904
LamiVUDine on page 956
Peginterferon Alfa-2a on page 1300
Peginterferon Alfa-2a and Ribavirin on page 1301
Peginterferon Alfa-2b on page 1303
Peginterferon Alfa-2b and Ribavirin
Ribavirin (Systemic) on page 1430
Simeprevir on page 1478
Sofosbuvir on page 1494
Telaprevir
Telbivudine on page 1533
Tenofovir Disoproxil Fumarate on page 1539

Types of Hepatitis Virus

Features	A	B	C	D	E	F	G
Incubation Period	2 to 6 weeks	8 to 24 weeks	2 to 52 weeks	3 to 13 weeks	3 to 6 weeks	Unknown	Unknown
Onset	Abrupt	Insidious	Insidious	Abrupt	Abrupt	Insidious	Insidious
Symptoms							
Jaundice	Adults: 70% to 80% Children: 10%	25%	25%	Varies	Unknown	Unknown	Unknown
Asymptomatic patients	Adults: 50% Children: Most	~75%	~75%	Rare	Rare	Common	Common
Routes of Transmission							
Fecal/Oral	Yes	No	No	No	Yes	Unknown	Unknown
Parenteral	Rare	Yes	Yes	Yes	No		
Sexual	No	Yes	Possible	Yes	No		
Perinatal	No	Yes	Possible	Possible	No		
Water/Food	Yes	No	No	No	Yes		
Sequelae (% of patients)							
Chronic state	No	Adults: 6% to 10% Children: 25% to 50% Infants: 70% to 90%	>75%	10% to 15%	No	Unknown	Likely
Case-Fatality Rate	0.6%	1.4%	1% to 2%	30%	1% to 2% Pregnant women: 20%	Unknown	Unknown

Preexposure Risk Factors for Hepatitis B

Health care factors:
Health care workers[a]
Special patient groups (eg, adolescents, infants born to HBsAg–positive mothers, military personnel, etc)
Hemodialysis patients[b]
Recipients of certain blood products[c]
Lifestyle factors:
Homosexual and bisexual men
IV drug-abusers
Heterosexually active persons with multiple sexual partners or recently acquired sexually transmitted diseases
Environmental factors:
Household and sexual contacts of HBV carriers
Prison inmates
Clients and staff of institutions for the mentally handicapped
Residents, immigrants, and refugees from areas with endemic HBV infection
International travelers at increased risk of acquiring HBV infection

[a]The risk of hepatitis B virus (HBV) infection for health care workers varies both between hospitals and within hospitals. Hepatitis B vaccination is recommended for all health care workers with blood exposure.

[b]Hemodialysis patients often respond poorly to hepatitis B vaccination; higher vaccine doses or increased number of doses are required. A special formulation of one vaccine is now available for such persons (Recombivax HB, 40 mcg/mL). The anti-HBs (antibody to hepatitis B surface antigen) response of such persons should be tested after they are vaccinated, and those who have not responded should be revaccinated with 1 to 3 additional doses.

Patients with chronic renal disease should be vaccinated as early as possible, ideally before they require hemodialysis. In addition, their anti-HBs levels should be monitored at 6- to 12-month intervals to assess the need for revaccination.

[c]Patients with hemophilia should be immunized SubQ, not IM

PREEXPOSURE VACCINATION

Preexposure vaccination is one of the most effective methods for preventing transmission of some STDs. Human papilloma virus is widespread and serotypes 16 and 18 have been associated with cervical cancer. Although most types that cause oral HPV lesions are not of these serotypes, the clinician should recommend appropriate surgical removal of all such lesions. Lesions in the posterior oral pharyngeal region are of particular concern. Preexposure vaccination is one of the most effective methods for preventing transmission of some STDs. Quadrivalent HPV vaccine (Gardasil) and the bivalent HPV vaccine (Cervarix) are available.

Gardasil is a vaccine indicated in girls and women 9 to 26 years of age for the prevention of the following diseases caused by Human Papillomavirus (HPV) types included in the vaccine:

- Cervical, vulvar, vaginal, and anal cancer caused by HPV types 16 and 18
- Genital warts (condyloma acuminata) caused by HPV types 6 and 11

And the following precancerous or dysplastic lesions caused by HPV types 6, 11, 16, and 18:

- Cervical intraepithelial neoplasia (CIN) grade 2/3 and cervical adenocarcinoma *in situ* (AIS)
- Cervical intraepithelial neoplasia (CIN) grade 1
- Vulvar intraepithelial neoplasia (VIN) grade 2 and grade 3
- Vaginal intraepithelial neoplasia (VaIN) grade 2 and grade 3
- Anal intraepithelial neoplasia (AIN) grades 1, 2, and 3

Gardasil is also indicated in boys and men 9 to 26 years of age for the prevention of the following diseases caused by HPV types included in the vaccine:

- Anal cancer caused by HPV types 16 and 18
- Genital warts (condyloma acuminata) caused by HPV types 6 and 11

And the following precancerous or dysplastic lesions caused by HPV types 6, 11, 16, and 18:

- Anal intraepithelial neoplasia (AIN) grades 1, 2, and 3

Cervarix is a vaccine indicated for the prevention of the following diseases caused by oncogenic human papillomavirus (HPV) types 16 and 18:

- Cervical cancer
- Cervical intraepithelial neoplasia (CIN) grade 2 or worse and adenocarcinoma *in situ*
- Cervical intraepithelial neoplasia (CIN) grade 1

Cervarix is approved for use in females 9 to 25 years of age.
Details regarding HPV vaccination are available at www.cdc.gov/std/hpv. Vaccines for other STDs (eg, HIV and herpes simplex virus) are under development or undergoing clinical trials. Vaccines are not available for bacterial or fungal STDs.

Hepatitis B vaccination is recommended for all unvaccinated and uninfected patients being evaluated for an STD. In addition, hepatitis A and B vaccines are recommended for men who have sex with men and injection drug users; each of these vaccines should also be administered to HIV-infected patients not yet infected with one or both types of hepatitis virus. Details regarding hepatitis A and B vaccination are available at http://www.cdc.gov/hepatitis.

HPV PREVENTION:

Papillomavirus (Types 6, 11, 16, 18) Vaccine (Human, Recombinant) on page 1287
Papillomavirus (Types 16, 18) Vaccine (Human, Recombinant) on page 1288

HERPES

The herpes viruses not only represent a topic of specific interest to the dentist due to oral manifestations, but are widespread as systemic infections. Herpes simplex virus is also of interest because of its central nervous system infections and its relationship as one of the viral infections commonly found in AIDS patients. Oral herpes infections will be covered elsewhere. Current recommended drug therapy includes acyclovir, valacyclovir, or famciclovir. Epstein-Barr virus is a member of the herpesvirus family and produces syndromes important in dentistry, including infectious mononucleosis with the commonly found oral pharyngitis and petechial hemorrhages, as well as being the causative agent of Burkitt's lymphoma. The relationship between Epstein-Barr virus to oral hairy leukoplakia in AIDS patients has not been shown to be one of cause and effect; however, the presence of Epstein-Barr in these lesions is consistent. Currently, there is no accepted treatment for Epstein-Barr virus, although acyclovir has been shown in in vitro studies to have some efficacy.

Varicella-zoster virus is another member of the herpesvirus family and is the causative agent of two clinical entities, chickenpox and shingles, or herpes zoster. Oral manifestations of both chickenpox and herpes zoster include vesicular eruptions often leading to confluent mucosal ulcerations. Although the thoracic region is a common site for shingles, the face and/or oral cavity are not rare areas affected. The dentist should be concerned if lesions are confined to one side of the face or oral cavity. Rapid intervention can result in significant reduction in the pain and eruptions of an adult zoster infection. Acyclovir, valacyclovir, or famciclovir are the drugs of choice for treatment of herpes zoster infections.

The vaccine for shingles (Zostavax) is recommended for use in persons ≥60 years of age to prevent shingles. The older a person is, the more severe the effects of shingles typically are. The shingles vaccine is specifically designed to protect people against shingles and will **not** protect people against other forms of herpes, such as genital herpes. The shingles vaccine is **not** recommended to treat active shingles or postherpetic neuralgia (pain after the rash is gone) once it develops. At this time, the CDC does recommend that health care providers within the recommended age group (≥50 years of age) receive the zoster vaccine.

There are other herpes viruses that produce disease in man and animals. These viruses have no specific treatment; therefore, incidence is thought to be less common than those mentioned and the specific treatment is not determined at present. The role of some of these viruses in concomitant infection with the HIV and other coinfection viruses is still under study.

Acyclovir (Systemic) on page 73
Acyclovir (Topical) on page 77
Amantadine on page 109
Atovaquone on page 185
Cidofovir on page 360
Famciclovir on page 686
Foscarnet on page 769
Ganciclovir (Systemic) on page 785
Hepatitis B Immune Globulin (Human) on page 815
Imiquimod on page 867
Immune Globulin on page 870
Interferon Alfa-2b on page 904
Interferon Alfa-n3 on page 909
Oseltamivir on page 1246
Peginterferon Alfa-2a on page 1300
Peginterferon Alfa-2b on page 1303
Penciclovir on page 1307
Ribavirin on page 1430
Rifabutin on page 1433
RiMANTAdine on page 1438
Trifluridine on page 1609
ValACYclovir on page 1622
Zanamivir on page 1670
Zoster Vaccine on page 1687

REFERENCES

AASLD-IDSA HCV Guidance Panel. Hepatitis C guidance: AASLD-IDSA recommendations for testing, managing, and treating adults infected with hepatitis C virus. *Hepatology*. 2015;62(3):932-954. www.hcvguidelines.org.

ACIP Adult Immunization Work Group, Bridges CB, Woods L, Coyne-Beasley T; Centers for Disease Control and Prevention (CDC). Advisory Committee on Immunization Practices (ACIP) recommended immunization schedule for adults aged 19 years and older – United States, 2013. *MMWR Surveill Summ*. 2013;62(Suppl 1):9-19.

Advisory Committee on Immunization Practices (ACIP) Centers for Disease Control and Prevention (CDC). Update: prevention of hepatitis A after exposure to hepatitis A virus and in international travelers. Updated recommendations of the Advisory Committee on Immunization Practices (ACIP). *MMWR Morb Mortal Wkly Rep*. 2007;56(41):1080-1084.

Advisory Committee on Immunization Practices (ACIP). Prevention of hepatitis A through active or passive immunization: recommendations of the Advisory Committee on Immunization Practices (ACIP). *MMWR Recomm Rep*. 2006;55(RR-7):1-23.

Centers for Disease Control and Prevention (CDC). Recommendations of the Advisory Committee on Immunization Practices (ACIP): general recommendations on immunization. *MMWR Recomm Rep*. 2011;60(2):1-64.

Centers for Disease Control and Prevention (CDC). Update on herpes zoster vaccine: licensure for persons aged 50 through 59 years. *MMWR Morb Mortal Wkly Rep*. 2011;60(44):1528.

Cooper C, Lester R, Thorlund K, et al. Direct-acting antiviral therapies for hepatitis C genotype 1 infection: a multiple treatment comparison meta-analysis. *QJM*. 2013;106:153–163.
Corey L, Wald A, Patel R, et al. Once-daily valacyclovir to reduce the risk of transmission of genital herpes. *N Engl J Med*. 2004;350(1):11-20.
Corstjens PL, Abrams WR, Malamud D. Detecting viruses by using salivary diagnostics. *J Am Dent Assoc*. 2012;143(10 Suppl):12S-8S.
Ghany MG, Nelson DR, Strader DB, Thomas DL, Seeff LB; American Association for Study of Liver Diseases. An update on treatment of genotype 1 chronic hepatitis C virus infection: 2011 practice guideline by the American Association for the Study of Liver Diseases. *Hepatology*. 2011;54 (4):1433-1444.
Ghany MG, Strader DB, Thomas DL, Seeff LB; American Association for the Study of Liver Diseases. Diagnosis, management, and treatment of hepatitis C: an update. *Hepatology*. 2009;49(4):1335-1374.
Kaplan JE, Benson C, Holmes KH, et al. Guidelines for prevention and treatment of opportunistic infections in HIV-infected adults and adolescents: recommendations from CDC, the National Institutes of Health, and the HIV Medicine Association of the Infectious Diseases Society of America. *MMWR Recomm Rep*. 2009;58(RR-4):1-207.
Mast EE, Margolis HS, Fiore AE, et al. A comprehensive immunization strategy to eliminate transmission of hepatitis B virus infection in the United States: recommendations of the Advisory Committee on Immunization Practices (ACIP) part 1: immunization of infants, children, and adolescents. *MMWR Recomm Rep*. 2005;54(RR-16):1-31.
Miller CS, Avdiushko SA, Kryscio RJ, Danaher RJ, Jacob RJ. Effect of prophylactic valacyclovir on the presence of human herpesvirus DNA in saliva of healthy individuals after dental treatment. *J Clin Microbiol* . 2005;43(5):2173-2180.
Mofenson LM, Brady MT, Danner SP, et al. Guidelines for the prevention and treatment of opportunistic infections among HIV-exposed and HIV-infected children: recommendations from CDC, the National Institutes of Health, the HIV Medicine Association of The Infectious Diseases Society of America, the Pediatric Infectious Diseases Society, and the American Academy of Pediatrics. *MMWR Recomm Rep*. 2009;58(RR-11):1-166.
Morgan RL, Baack B, Smith BD, Yartel A, Pitasi M, Falck-Yttor Y. Eradication of hepatitis C virus Infection and the development of hepatocellular carcinoma. A meta-analysis of observational studies. *Ann Intern Med*. 2013;158:329–337.
Niro GA, Gioffreda D, Fontana R. Hepatitis delta virus infection: open issues. *Dig Liver Dis*. 2011;43(Suppl 1):S19-S24.
Pascarella S, Negro F. Hepatitis D virus: an update. *Liver Int*. 2011;31(1):7-21.
Sherman KE. Hepatitis E virus infection: more common than previously realized? *Gastroenterol Hepatol (N Y)*. 2011;7(11):759-761.
Shivkumar S, Peeling R, Jafari Y, Joseph L, Pant Pai N. Accuracy of rapid and point-of-care screening tests for hepatitis C: a systematic review and meta-analysis. *Ann Intern Med*. 2012;157:558–566.
Teshale EH, Hu DJ. Hepatitis E: epidemiology and prevention. *World J Hepatol*. 2011;3(12):285-291.
Triantos C, Kalafateli M, Nikolopoulou V, Burroughs A. Meta-analysis: antiviral treatment for hepatitis D. *Aliment Pharmacol Ther*. 2012;35 (6):663-673.
Workowski KA, Berman S, Centers for Disease Control and Prevention (CDC). Sexually transmitted diseases treatment guidelines, 2010. *MMWR Recomm Rep*. 2010;59(RR-12):1-110. Available at http://www.cdc.gov/std/treatment/2010/STD-Treatment-2010-RR5912.pdf

ANTIBIOTIC PROPHYLAXIS

PREPROCEDURAL GUIDELINES FOR DENTAL PATIENTS

INTRODUCTION

Historically, in dental practice, antibiotic prophylaxis has been mandated for certain at-risk patients to prevent infective endocarditis, orthopedic implant late infection, or contamination through any oral surgical site. Clinical practice guidelines are generally provided through a joint effort of medical and dental organizations and are reviewed and rewritten periodically based upon clinical and scientific evidence. In this section, these guidelines are reviewed.

ANTIMICROBIAL STEWARDSHIP

Antimicrobial stewardship refers to coordinated interventions designed to improve and measure the appropriate use of antimicrobials by promoting the selection of the optimal antimicrobial drug regimen, dose, duration of therapy, and route of administration. Antimicrobial stewards seek to achieve optimal clinical outcomes related to antimicrobial use, minimize toxicity and other adverse events, reduce the costs of health care for infections, and limit the selection for antimicrobial resistant strains. Currently, there are no national or coordinated legislative or regulatory mandates designed to optimize use of antimicrobial therapy through antimicrobial stewardship. Given the societal value of antimicrobials and their diminishing effectiveness due to antimicrobial resistance, groups like the ADA support broad implementation of antimicrobial stewardship programs across all health care settings (eg, hospitals, long-term care facilities, long-term acute care facilities, ambulatory surgical centers, dialysis centers, and private practices).

The American Dental Association (ADA) supports the responsible use of antibiotics. As part of this effort toward antibiotic stewardship, the ADA has adopted an evidence-based approach to guideline development, which has resulted in recommendations for decreased indications for, and use of prophylactic antibiotics in people with heart conditions and those who have had joint replacements. Although there are some studies evaluating the appropriateness of antibiotic prescribing in dentistry, a recent paper in *JADA* suggests that it is likely that there are opportunities to improve prescribing practices.

PREVENTION OF INFECTIVE ENDOCARDITIS

In 2007, the American Heart Association (AHA), in conjunction with the American Dental Association (ADA) and other experts in both medicine and dentistry, performed an extensive evidence-based literature review and provided the most recent guidelines regarding the use of antibiotic prophylaxis to prevent infective endocarditis (IE) related to dental procedures. Since the mid-1950s, it has been recommended that patients at risk for IE from a variety of medical conditions should be premedicated with antibiotics prior to dental and other procedures. Earlier changes in the guidelines (1984, 1990, 1997) focused on the recommended antibiotics, dose, and dosing frequency. While indicating a minor modification of recommended antibiotics, the most recent change (2007) focused primarily on the patients for whom prophylaxis is recommended.

Infective endocarditis is the consequence of a sequence of events. This sequence is initiated by the formation of nonbacterial thrombotic endocarditis (NBTE) on the surface of a cardiac valve or elsewhere that endothelial damage occurs within the heart. Turbulent blood flow produced by congenital or acquired heart disease, including flow from high- to low-flow chambers and flow across a narrowed orifice, traumatizes the endothelium. This predisposes for deposition of platelets and fibrin on the endothelial surface and results in NBTE. If bacteremia then occurs following invasion of the bloodstream with a microbial species that has the pathogenic potential to colonize this site, IE can occur. Mucosal surfaces are populated by dense endogenous microflora. Trauma to a mucosal surface releases many different microbial species transiently into the blood stream. Transient bacteremia caused by oral microflora occurs commonly with dental extractions or other dental procedures or with routine daily activities. The frequency and intensity of the resulting bacteremias are related to the nature and magnitude of the trauma, density of the microbial flora, and degree of inflammation or infection at the site. The microbial species entering circulation depends on the unique endogenous microflora that colonize the traumatized site. The ability of the bacteria in the blood stream to adhere to specific NBTE sites determines the anatomic localization of the infection. Mediators of bacterial adherence serve as virulence factors. Common oral flora, including viridans group Streptococci and Staphylococci have cellular components that serve as adhesions to the NBTE and these adhesions are immunogenic. Microorganisms adherent to the vegetation stimulate further deposition of fibrin and platelets on their surface. The buried microorganisms multiply as rapidly as bacteria in broth cultures to reach maximal densities within a short time on the left side of the heart, apparently uninhibited by host defenses in left-sided lesions. Right-sided vegetations have lower bacterial densities due to host defense, such as PMN activity or platelet-derived antibacterial proteins. More than 90% of microorganisms in mature valvular vegetations are metabolically inactive and are therefore less responsive to the bacterial effects of antibiotics.

Viridans group Streptococci are normal oral tract flora and cause more than 50% of cases of community-acquired native valve IE that is not associated with IV drug use. As early as 1935, a report indicated that 11% of patients with poor oral hygiene had positive blood cultures, yet 61% of patients experienced bacteremia with dental extractions. Historically, the additional assumptions associated with antibiotic prophylaxis for IE are that these microorganisms are susceptible to antibiotics recommended for prophylaxis, that antibiotic prophylaxis prevents experimental endocarditis in animals, that a temporal relationship exists between dental procedures and the onset of symptoms of IE, that the risk of adverse drugs reactions is low, and that morbidity and mortality of IE are high.

A primary determinant of the changes for the 2007 guidelines are that the estimated absolute risk for IE from a dental procedure in patients with underlying cardiac conditions increases from 1:1.1 million for mitral valve prolapsed (MVP) to

1:475,000 for congenital heart disease (CHD). The absolute risk increases further for rheumatic heart disease (RHD) (1:142,000), prosthetic valve (1:114,000), and previous IE (1:95,000). Cardiac conditions with predisposition for IE show similar trends. Additionally, mortality associated with prosthetic valve endocarditis (PVE) is >20% and PVE increases the risk of heart failure.

As a result, antibiotic prophylaxis with certain dental procedures is recommended for patients at highest risk of IE due to specific cardiac conditions:

- Prosthetic cardiac valve
- A prior incidence of IE
- Heart transplant patients who develop cardiac valvulopathy
- Patients with CHD are required prophylaxis with the following conditions:
  - Unrepaired cyanotic CHD, including palliative shunts and conduits
  - Completely repaired CHD with prosthetic material or device during the first 6 months after the surgical or catheter intervention procedure
  - Repaired CHD with residual defects at the site or adjacent to the site of a prosthetic patch (which inhibits endothelialization)

These patients with high-risk cardiac conditions are recommended for prophylaxis for all dental procedures involving manipulation of gingival tissue or the periapical region of teeth or perforation of the oral mucosa.

Common dental procedures that **do not** require prophylaxis but do require sound clinical judgement include:

- Routine anesthetic injection into noninfected tissue
- Taking dental radiographs
- Placement of removable prosthodontic or orthodontic appliances
- Adjustment of orthodontic appliances
- Placement of orthodontic brackets
- Shedding of deciduous teeth
- Bleeding from trauma to the lips or oral mucosa

ANTIBIOTIC SELECTION

For examples of sample prescriptions see Prevention of Endocarditis and to Reduce the Risk of Late Infections of Joint Prostheses - Sample Prescriptions on page 37. Dentists should be vigilant in reviewing all current literature for updates.

Table 1 provides the recommended antibiotics and doses. Specific dosage forms available for each antibiotic can be found in the drug monographs. Extended or delayed release dosage formulations should not be used for antibiotic prophylaxis because they will not produce high immediate peak concentrations.

For those patients able to take oral antibiotics and those not allergic to beta-lactam antibiotics (penicillins, cephalosporins, monobactams, and carbapenems), the antibiotic of choice is amoxicillin, an amino penicillin. Aminopenicillins have an extended spectrum of antibacterial action compared to penicillin VK-treating gram-positive aerobes, such as staph and strep, but also some gram-aerobes, such as *Haemophilus influenza*. Aminopenicillins are more stable in the gastro-intestinal tract, allowing them to be taken with food or beverages, providing higher plasma concentrations following oral administration.

For individuals unable to take oral medications and not allergic to beta-lactam antibiotics, intramuscular (IM) or intravenous (IV) ampicillin, also an aminopenicillin, is recommended.

Table 1. Prophylactic Regimens for Infective Endocarditis for Dental Procedures

Situation	Drug	Single Dosage 30 to 60 minutes prior to procedure
Oral	Amoxicillin on page 121	Children: 50 mg/kg Adults: 2 g
Unable to take oral medications	Ampicillin on page 136 **or**	Children: 50 mg/kg IM or IV Adults: 2 g IM or IV
	CeFAZolin on page 312 **or** CefTRIAXone on page 326	Children: 50 mg/kg IM or IV Adults: 1 g IM or IV

(continued)

Table 1. Prophylactic Regimens for Infective Endocarditis for Dental Procedures *(continued)*

Situation	Drug	Single Dosage 30 to 60 minutes prior to procedure
Allergic to penicillins or ampicillin (oral)	Cephalexin on page 333[a,b] **or**	Children: 50 mg/kg Adults: 2 g
	Clindamycin (Systemic) on page 382 **or**	Children: 20 mg/kg Adults: 600 mg
	Azithromycin (Systemic) on page 194 **or** Clarithromycin on page 377	Children: 15 mg/kg Adults: 500 mg
Allergic to penicillins or ampicillin and unable to take oral medications	CeFAZolin on page 312 **or** CefTRIAXone on page 326[b]	Children: 50 mg/kg IM or IV Adults: 1 g IM or IV
	Clindamycin (Systemic) on page 382	Children: 20 mg/kg IM or IV Adults: 600 mg IM or IV

Note: Intramuscular injections should be avoided in patients receiving anticoagulant therapy.

[a]Can use first or second generation oral cephalosporins in equivalent doses.

[b]Cephalosporins should not be used in individuals with immediate-type hypersensitivity reaction (urticaria, angioedema, or anaphylaxis) to penicillins.

Individuals who are allergic to the penicillins, such as amoxicillin or ampicillin, should be treated with an alternate antibiotic. The 2007 guidelines suggest a number of alternate agents, including clindamycin, cephalosporins, azithromycin, and clarithromycin. Patients who do not have a Type I (immediate) allergic (hypersensitivity) reaction to penicillins (urticaria, bronchospasm, angioedema, anaphylaxis) may receive a first or second generation cephalosporin. Oral first generation cephalosporins include cephalexin (Keflex) and cefadroxil (Duricef). First generation cephalosporins have an antibacterial spectrum of activity similar to amoxicillin and ampicillin. Oral second generation cephalosporins include cefaclor (Ceclor), cefprozil, or cefuroxime axetil (Ceftin). Second generation cephalosporins have an antibacterial spectrum of activity broader than aminopenicillins and first generation cephalosporins and similar to amoxicillin with clavulanic acid. For patients unable to take oral cephalosporins, the first generation cephalosporin cefazolin (Ancef) is recommended for IM or IV administration. A third generation cephalosporin, ceftriaxone (Rocephin), is also listed as a parenteral option. Third generation cephalosporins have a broader antibacterial spectrum of activity than first and second generation cephalosporins and should generally be reserved for more serious gram infections or for gram-positive infections not responsive to first-line therapy.

Penicillin and cephalosporin antibiotics have a bactericidal mechanism of action by inhibiting synthesis of the bacterial cell wall. They are most effective in bacteria that are actively growing and reproducing. The most common adverse reaction is a Type I or immediate hypersensitivity reaction which generally produces urticaria, bronchospasm, angioedema, or anaphylaxis. Because both penicillins and cephalosporins are beta-lactam antibiotics, patients with Type I immediate hypersensitivity reactions can be cross-allergic.

Clindamycin (Cleocin) is a lincosamide antibiotic effective against gram-positive aerobes and many anaerobic bacteria. Clindamycin is an option both orally or IM or IV for patients with any penicillin allergy. Clindamycin is a bacteriostatic antibiotic that inhibits bacterial protein synthesis. Adverse effects of clindamycin after a single dose are rare. Although it is estimated that 1% of patients taking clindamycin will develop symptoms of pseudomembranous colitis, these symptoms usually develop after 9 to 14 days of clindamycin therapy. These symptoms are rare and only one case has been reported in a patient taking an acute dose for the prevention of endocarditis.

Azithromycin (Zithromax) and clarithromycin (Biaxin) are members of the class of antibiotics known as macrolides. The pharmacology of these drugs has been reviewed previously in *General Dentistry*. Erythromycins have been available for use in dentistry and medicine since the mid-1950s. Azithromycin and clarithromycin represent the first additions to this class in more than 40 years. The adult prophylactic dose for either drug is 500 mg 30 to 60 minutes before the procedure with no follow-up dose. The pediatric prophylactic dose of azithromycin and clarithromycin is 15 mg/kg orally 30 to 60 minutes before the procedure. Although the erythromycin family of drugs is known to inhibit the hepatic metabolism of theophylline and carbamazepine to enhance their effects, azithromycin has not been shown to affect the liver metabolism of these drugs.

Azithromycin is well-absorbed from the gastrointestinal tract and is extensively taken up from circulation into tissues with a slow release from those tissues. It reaches peak serum levels in 2 to 4 hours and serum half-life is 68 hours. Zithromax is supplied as 250 mg, 500 mg, and 600 mg tablets. It is also available for oral suspension at concentrations of 100 mg per 5 mL, 200 mg per 5 mL, and single-dose packets containing 1 g. In May 2012, the FDA notified health care providers that they are reviewing the results of an azithromycin study published in the *New England Journal of Medicine*. This study reported a small increase in cardiovascular deaths and in the risk of death from any cause in persons treated with a 5-day course of azithromycin (Zithromax) compared to persons treated with amoxicillin, ciprofloxacin, or no medication. The FDA will communicate any new information on azithromycin and this study or the potential risk of QT interval prolongation after the agency has completed its review. Patients taking azithromycin should not stop taking their medicine without talking to their health care provider. Health care providers should be aware of the potential for QT interval prolongation and heart arrhythmias when prescribing or administering any macrolide antibiotic.

Clarithromycin (Biaxin) achieves peak plasma concentrations in 3 hours and maintains effective serum concentrations over a 12-hour period. Reports indicate that it probably interacts with theophylline and carbamazepine by elevating the plasma concentrations of the two drugs. Biaxin is supplied as 250 mg and 500 mg tablets and 500 mg extended release tablets. It is also available as granules for oral suspension at concentrations of 125 mg per 5 mL and 250 mg per 5 mL.

Clinical Considerations for Dentistry

See Figure 1.

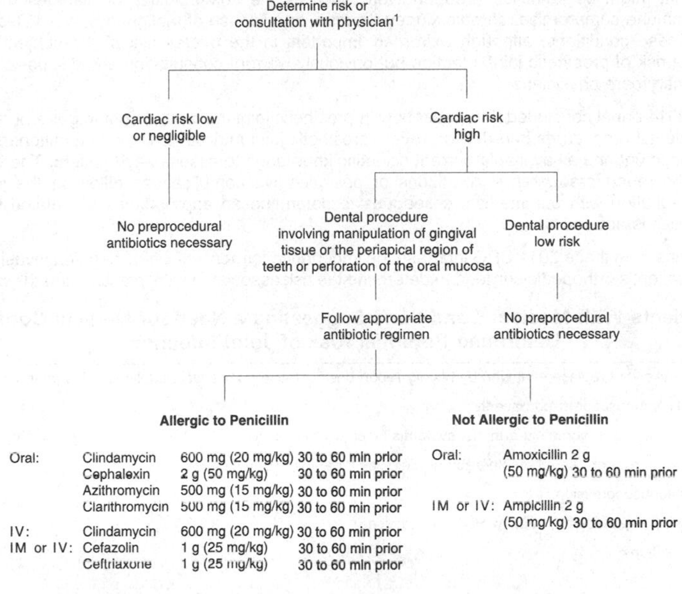

An antibiotic for prophylaxis should be administered in a single dose before the procedure. If the dosage of antibiotic is inadvertently not administered before the procedure, the dosage may be administered up to 2 hours after the procedure. However, administration of the dosage after the procedure should be considered only when the patient did not receive the preprocedural dose.

PREPROCEDURAL ANTIBIOTICS FOR PROSTHETIC IMPLANTS

A significant number of dental patients have had total joint replacements or other implanted prosthetic devices. Prior to performing dental procedures that might induce bacteremia, the dentist has historically been advised to consider the use of antibiotic prophylaxis in these patients. In December 2012, the American Academy of Orthopedic Surgeons (AAOS) and the ADA released an Evidence-Based Guideline and Evidence Report entitled "Prevention of Orthopaedic Implant Infection in Patients Undergoing Dental Procedures". The report concludes that the groups found insufficient evidence to recommend the routine use of antibiotics for joint replacement patients. They advised that there is no direct evidence that routine dental procedures cause prosthetic joint infections. **After 2012, the CPG stated that most patients no longer needed antibiotic prophylaxis, but based on a patient's medical history, consultation with the individuals' health care providers was often recommended.**

Recently the American Dental Association Council on Scientific Affairs convened a panel of experts to provide clarification of Clinical Practice Guidelines (CPG) for dental practitioners, related to the subject of prophylactic antibiotics prior to dental procedures in patients with prosthetic joints. This panel reviewed and supported all of the previous CPG implemented in 2012, related to evidence-based guidelines.

The goal of the new 2014 CPG is to provide additional information and they are published in the Journal of the American Dental Association (Sollecito 2015). The CPG state that in general, there is little or no evidence to support the use of preprocedural antibiotics in prosthetic joint replacement patients. These CPG were developed after an exhaustive re-review and update of those previous 2012 guidelines. Hence, prophylactic antibiotics are not routinely recommended prior to dental procedures in order to prevent prosthetic joint infection.

Regarding clinical conditions that might elevate the risk of late joint infections in this patient population, the panel evaluated the existing evidence related to preoperative conditions and peri/postoperative history of the joint replacement. Berbari EF, et al, published the most significant data in this evidence-based review, which evaluated those preoperative and postoperative factors that have been associated epidemiologically with late prosthetic joint infection. The most clinically relevant of these factors were postoperative problems, especially evidence of multiple joint surgeries, as well as wound drainage, hematoma, or infection postoperatively. History of any of these complications mandate discussion with the orthopedist to determine if antibiotics may be appropriate prior to dental procedures that produce bacteremia.

Other conditions that might be identified preoperatively, such as the comorbidities of diabetes mellitus, rheumatoid arthritis, levels of immune compromise, chronic kidney disease, or evidence of malignancy, were also considered in the risk assessment. These conditions, although extremely important in the overall risk of the subject, do not associate significantly with the risk of prosthetic joint infection but obviously warrant consultation and discussion with the patient's orthopedic and primary care physicians.

In conclusion, the 2014 panel concluded that patients with prosthetic joint implants do not in general require prophylactic antibiotics prior to dental procedures in order to prevent prosthetic joint infections. Dental practitioners must always use their best clinical judgment and all available current scientific knowledge to assess each patient. Therefore, as a general rule, in patients who report preoperative conditions or postoperative complications following the joint implant, open communication/consultation with our medical colleagues to determine an appropriate plan related to possible use of prophylactic antibiotics is advised.

The recommendations from these 2014 CPG increase the importance for dentists when planning invasive oral procedures to consult with the patient's orthopedic surgeon to determine the risk associated with infection and the need for antibiotics.

Table 2. Patients With Medical Conditions Suggesting a Need for Medical Consultation to Determine Potential Risk of Joint Infection

All patients with prosthetic joint replacement who by history report postoperative complications following the joint surgery
Immunocompromised/immunosuppressed patients
Inflammatory arthropathies (eg, rheumatoid arthritis, systemic lupus erythematosus)
Drug-induced immunosuppression (eg, chemotherapy or biologics for autoimmune diseases)
Radiation-induced immunosuppression
Patients with comorbidity (eg, diabetes, obesity, HIV, and smoking)
Previous prosthetic infections
Malnourishment
Hemophilia
HIV infection
Type 1 diabetes mellitus (insulin dependent, IDDM)
Malignancy
Megaprosthesis

Source: January 2013 AAOS Information Statement. Available at http://www.aaos.org/about/papers/advistmt/1033.asp. Original source: American Dental Association; American Academy of Orthopedic Surgeons. Antibiotic prophylaxis for dental patients with total joint replacements. *J Am Dent Assoc.* 2003;134(7):895-899.

Even in these patients, the new 2014 CPG stating that preprocedural antibiotics are not generally necessary should be seriously considered and a medical consultation with the physician will ultimately determine whether or not to use antibiotics. Late infections of implanted prosthetic devices have rarely been associated with microbial organisms of oral origin. Also, since late infections in such patients are often not reported, data is lacking to substantiate or refute this potential.

ANTIBIOTIC REGIMENS

The 2014 CPG should be carefully reviewed for any patient with a prosthetic joint. Clinical judgement decisions can always be made on a case-by-case basis. If using preprocedural antibiotics is found to be appropriate after careful consideration, the antibiotic prophylaxis regimens, as suggested by the advisory panel, are listed in Table 3. These regimens are not exactly the same as those listed in Table 1 (for prevention of endocarditis) and must be reviewed carefully to avoid confusion.

Please review the new Clinical Practice Guidelines (CPG), December 2014, for assessing the need for preprocedural antibiotics to prevent prosthetic joint late infections. The current CPG state that there is no direct evidence linking dental procedures to prostheses infections and that antibiotic prophylaxis is not warranted in most patients. Decisions must be made on a case-by-case basis. If after careful consideration, and/or consultation with the orthopedist, preprocedural antibiotics are found to be appropriate, the following example prescriptions apply. Prescription dispensing amounts are for three visits. These numbers can be adjusted for each patient treatment plan. Clinicians will be advised if and when any more specific guidelines are forthcoming.

The American Association of Orthopedic Surgeons (AAOS) has also developed Appropriate Use Criteria (AUC) for thirteen selected situations encountered by orthopedists, including, "Management of patients with orthopedic implants undergoing dental procedures". This was added as of November 2016.

Regarding antibiotic selection, when after consultation preprocedural antibiotics are deemed necessary, one important change occurred. In the latest release from the AAOS, clindamycin is no longer recommended as the suggested alternative in patients allergic to penicillins. The AAOS now recommends, in allergic patients still able to take oral medication, 2 g cephalexin, or 500 mg of azithromycin or clarithromycin in that order of selection. Since this release the ADA and the AHA have not taken any steps to alter their endocarditis recommendations. Terico AT, Gallagher JC. Beta-lactam hypersensitivity and cross-reactivity. *J Pharm Pract*. 2014; 27(6):530-544 is cited as the reference for considerations of cross allergenicity of cephalosporins and penicillins.

Cephalexin or amoxicillin may be used in patients not allergic to penicillin. The selected antibiotic is given as a single 2 g dose 30 to 60 minutes before the procedure. A follow-up dose is not recommended. Cephalexin (Keflex) and amoxicillin were described earlier in this section.

Parenteral ceftriaxone or ampicillin is the recommended antibiotic for patients unable to take oral medications (see Table 3 for doses). Ceftriaxone is a third generation cephalosporin, effective against anaerobes and aerobic gram-positive bacteria. Ampicillin is an aminopenicillin (described earlier). For patients allergic to penicillin, cephalexin is the recommended antibiotic of choice.

Table 3. Antibiotic Regimens for Patients With Prosthetic Implants

Patients not allergic to penicillin:	Cephalexin or amoxicillin:	2 g orally 1 hour prior to the procedure
Patients not allergic to penicillin and unable to take oral medications:	CefTRIAXone:	1 g IM or IV 1 hour prior to the procedure
	or Ampicillin:	2 g IM or IV 1 hour prior to the procedure
Patients allergic to penicillin:	Cephalexin:	2 g orally 1 hour prior to the procedure
Second choice:	or Azithromycin (Systemic)	500 mg 1 hour prior to the procedure
Third choice:	or Clarithromycin	500 mg 1 hour prior to the procedure
Patients allergic to penicillin and unable to take oral medications:	CefTRIAXone:	1 g IM or IV 1 hour prior to procedure

Please review the new guidelines for prevention of prosthetic joint late infections. Decisions must be made on a case-by-case basis.

Cephalexin on page 333

As more evidence and data are collected, these recommendations may be revised; however, it is thought to be prudent for the dental clinician to fully evaluate all patients with respect to history and/or physical findings and a medical consultation prior to determining the risk.

In patients in whom concern exists over joint complications and a medical consultation cannot be immediately obtained, the patient should be treated as though antibiotic coverage is necessary until such time that an appropriate consultation can be completed.

Clinical Considerations for Dentistry

See Figure 2.

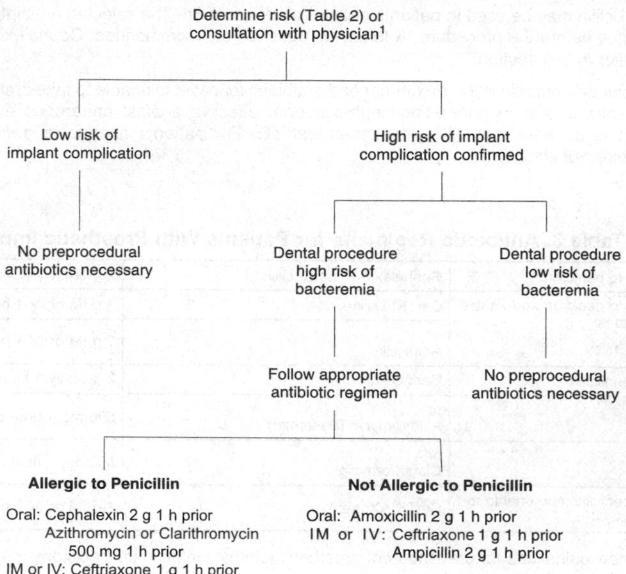

Cephalosporins should be avoided in patients with previous Type I hypersensitivity reactions to penicillin due to some evidence of cross allergenicity. Other risk of cross allergenicity ~1% to 5% (Terico 2014).

[1]For Emergency Dental Care the clinician should attempt phone consultation. If unable to contact patient's physician or determine risk, the patient should be treated as though there is high risk of implant complication and follow the algorithm.

FREQUENTLY ASKED QUESTIONS FOR INFECTIVE ENDOCARDITIS (IE) AND PROSTHETIC IMPLANTS

When should we start following the new prevention of IE and Prosthetic Joint guidelines?

Immediately, since the previous update was from June 2010 for IE and 2014 for Prosthetic Joints.

What should we do for patients who have been premedicated for IE in the past but are no longer recommended for prophylaxis?

If the patient does not fall into one of the highest risk groups, premedication should not be used unless an updated medical consultation suggests additional risks based on previously undisclosed comorbitities.

Should I just premedicate to be safe?

No, the new guidelines are based on evidence which documents that the risk of adverse side effects from the antibiotics (allergy, GI upset, development of microbial resistance, etc) outweigh the benefits in many patients who previously received SBE/IE prophylaxis. The new guidelines clearly recommend the use of prophylactic antibiotics only for those at the highest risk after consultation.

What if a patient did not meet the new high-risk criteria outlined in the new Guidelines and the patient's physician still recommends IE prophylaxis?

Please contact the physician to see if there are compelling medical reasons for continuing IE prophylaxis.

*What if a patient who has received IE prophylaxis in the past for a condition that is now deemed as **not** being high risk for IE prophylaxis still insists on being premedicated?*

Recommend that the patient contacts the physician to see if there are compelling medical reasons for continuing IE prophylaxis.

If the patient is presently taking antibiotics for some other ailment, is prophylaxis still necessary?

If a patient is already taking antibiotics for another condition, prophylaxis (when deemed necessary under the new guidelines) should be accomplished with a drug recommendation from another class. For example, in the patient who is not allergic to penicillin and is taking a macrolide antibiotic for a medical condition, amoxicillin would be the drug of choice for prophylaxis. Also, in the penicillin-allergic patient taking clindamycin, prophylaxis would best be accomplished with azithromycin or clarithromycin.

What should I do if medical consultation results in a recommendation that differs from the published guidelines endorsed by the American Dental Association?

The dentist is ultimately responsible for treatment recommendations. Ideally, by communicating with the physician, a consensus can be achieved that is either in agreement with the guidelines or is based on other established medical reasoning.

Is there cross-allergenicity between the cephalosporins and penicillin?

According to a recent study by Terico, the incidence of cross-allergenicity is 5% for first generation drugs and 1% for third generation drugs in the overall population. If a patient has demonstrated a Type I hypersensitivity reaction to penicillin, including urticaria, bronchospasm, angioedema, or anaphylaxis, then this incidence increases to 20%.

Is there definitely an interaction between contraceptive agents and antibiotics?

There are well-founded interactions between contraceptives and antibiotics. The best instructions that a patient could be given by his/her dentist are that should an antibiotic be necessary and the dentist is aware that the patient is on contraceptives, and if the patient is using chemical contraceptives, the patient should seriously consider additional means of contraception during the antibiotic management.

Are PROBIOTICS important in patients receiving long-term or repeated care with antibiotics?

There is always concern regarding disruption of healthy microflora of the gastrointestinal system when antibiotics are prescribed for an extended period of time or on closely repeated occasions. GI symptoms often occur and do not represent any direct drug allergy or toxicity but rather are the effects of this gut flora alteration.

Cultures of direct-fed microorganisms or probiotics are able to multiply in the intestinal tract to create a balance of microflora. Some lactobacillus species used in probiotic applications include *L. acidophilus, L. casei, L. reuteri, L. rhamnosus,* and *Bifidobacterium bifidum*. These and other organisms form a symbiotic or mutual relationship with their host. Each species develops a resistance to the disease-causing potential of such organisms and form mutual beneficial relationships with these organisms. The familiar *L. acidophilus* produces lactic acid, reduces gut pH, and acts as a colonizer. Some forms of antibiotics, such as cephalosporins, clindamycin, or fluoroquinolones, induce colitis, an inflammation of the large intestine, in some individuals. This type of colitis is caused by a toxin produced by the bacteria *Clostridium difficile*, which is resistant to many antibiotics and proliferates in the intestines when other normal bacterial flora in the intestine are altered by the antibiotics.

It is usually recommended to take probiotics at least 3 hours apart from antibiotics. Taking both at the same time defeats the purpose as the friendly bacteria will be totally destroyed by the drug. During antibiotic therapy, a good dose of viable probiotic cells is 6 to 25 billion colony-forming units per day. Probiotics are also being studied as adjunctive therapy to periodontal treatment and treatment of other bacterial infections.

Has there been any change in the guidelines for prophylaxis for patients with prosthetic joint replacements?

Yes, the 2012 Clinical Practice Guidelines and the 2014 panel concluded that patients with prosthetic joint implants do not in general require prophylactic antibiotics prior to dental procedures in order to prevent prosthetic joint infections. Dental practitioners must always use their best clinical judgment and all available current scientific knowledge to assess each patient. Therefore, as a general rule, in patients who report preoperative conditions or postoperative complications following the joint implant, open communication/consultation with our medical colleagues to determine an appropriate plan related to possible use of prophylactic antibiotics is advised. If concern over joint complications exists and a medical consultation cannot be immediately obtained, the dentist should treat the patient as though antibiotic coverage is necessary until an appropriate consultation can be completed.

REFERENCES

American Academy of Orthopaedic Surgeons and American Association of Orthopaedic Surgeons. Statement release for new 2012 clinical practice guideline – new guideline includes shared decision-making tool, implications for practice. 2013. Available at http://www6.aaos.org/news/PDFopen/PDFopen.cfm?page_url=http://www.aaos.org/news/aaosnow/jan13/cover1.asp

American Academy of Orthopaedic Surgeons; American Dental Association. Prevention of orthopaedic implant infection in patients undergoing dental procedures: Evidence-based guideline and evidence report. Rosemont, IL: American Academy of Orthopaedic Surgeons; 2012. Available at www.aaos.org/research/guidelines/PUDP/PUDP_guideline.pdf.

American Dental Association-Appointed Members of the Expert Writing and Voting Panels Contributing to the Development of American Academy of Orthopedic Surgeons Appropriate Use Criteria. American Dental Association guidance for utilizing appropriate use criteria in the management of the care of patients with orthopedic implants undergoing dental procedures. *J Am Dent Assoc.* 2017;148(2):57-59.

Berbari EF, Osmon DR, Carr A, et al. Dental procedures as risk factors for prosthetic hip or knee infection: A hospital-based prospective case-control study (published correction appears in *Clin Infect Dis.* 2010;50(6):944). *Clin Infect Dis.* 2010;50(1):8-16.

Centers for Disease Control and Prevention. Antibiotic/antimicrobial resistance: Threat report 2013. Atlanta: Centers for Disease Control and Prevention; 2013:6,51. Available at: https://www.cdc.gov/drugresistance/threat-report-2013/. Accessed September 21, 2014.

Centers for Disease Control and Prevention. Antibiotic/antimicrobial resistance. U.S. Department of Health & Human Services. Accessed May 20, 2016.

Fluent MT, Jacobsen PL, Hicks LA, OSAP. Considerations for responsible antibiotic use in dentistry. *J Am Dent Assoc.* 2016;147(8):683-686.

Legout L, Beltrand E, Migaud H, Senneville E. Antibiotic prophylaxis to reduce the risk of joint implant contamination during dental surgery seems unnecessary. *Orthop Traumatol Surg Res.* 2012;98(8):910-914.

Lockhart PB, Blizzard J, Maslow AL, Brennan MT, Sasser H, Carew J. Drug cost implications for antibiotic prophylaxis for dental procedures. *Oral Surg Oral Med Oral Pathol Oral Radiol.* 2013;115(3):345-353.

Meurman JH, Stamatova I. Probiotics: contributions to oral health. *Oral Dis.* 2007;13(5):443-445.

Palmer C. ADA News: ADA supports responsible antibiotic use. American Dental Association. June 15, 2015.

Quinn RH, Murray JN, Pezold R, Sevarino KS. The American Academy of Orthopaedic Surgeons Appropriate Use Criteria for the Management of Patients with Orthopaedic Implants Undergoing Dental Procedures. *J Bone Joint Surg Am.* 2017;99(2):161-63.

Rethman MP, Watters W 3rd, Abt E, et al; American Academy of Orthopaedic Surgeons; American Dental Association. The American Academy of Orthopaedic Surgeons and the American Dental Association clinical practice guideline on the prevention of orthopaedic implant infection in patients undergoing dental procedures. *J Bone Joint Surg Am.* 2013;95(8):745-747.

Sollecito TP, Abt E, Lockhart PB, et al. The use of prophylactic antibiotics prior to dental procedures in patients with prosthetic joints: Evidence-based clinical practice guideline for dental practitioners-a report of the American Dental Association Council on Scientific Affairs. *J Am Dent Assoc.* 2015;146(1):11-16.

Swan J, Dowsey M, Babazadeh S, Mandaleson A, Choong PF. Significance of sentinel infective events in haematogenous prosthetic knee infections. *ANZ J Surg.* 2011;81(1-2):40-45.

Terico AT, Gallagher JC. Beta-lactam hypersensitivity and cross-reactivity. *J Pharm Pract.* 2014; 27(6):530-544.

Teughels W, Van Essche M, Sliepen I, Quirynen M. Probiotics and oral healthcare. *Periodontol 2000.* 2008;48:111-147.

Watters W 3rd. Rethman MP, Hanson NB, et al; American Academy of Orthopaedic Surgeons; American Dental Association. Prevention of orthopaedic implant infection in patients undergoing dental procedures. *J Am Acad Orthop Surg.* 2013;21(3):180-189.

Wilson W, Chair, Taubert KA, Gewitz M, et al. Prevention of infective endocarditis: guidelines from the American Heart Association: a guideline from the American Heart Association Rheumatic Fever, Endocarditis, and Kawasaki Disease Committee, Council on Cardiovascular Disease in the Young, and the Council on Clinical Cardiology, Council on Cardiovascular Surgery and Anesthesia, and the Quality of Care and Outcomes Research Interdisciplinary Working Group. *Circulation.* 2007;116:1736-1754.

Wilson W, Taubert KA, Gewitz M, et al. Prevention of infective endocarditis: guidelines from the American Heart Association: a guideline from the American Heart Association Rheumatic Fever, Endocarditis and Kawasaki Disease Committee, Council on Cardiovascular Disease in the Young, and the Council on Clinical Cardiology, Council on Cardiovascular Surgery and Anesthesia, and the Quality of Care and Outcomes Research Interdisciplinary Working Group. *J Am Dent Assoc.* 2008;139 Suppl:3S-24S.

MANAGEMENT OF THE CHEMICALLY DEPENDENT PATIENT

INTRODUCTION

As long as history has been recorded, man has used drugs to alter mood, thought, and feeling. The financial and emotional cost to society due to the abuse and addiction of these substances is staggering. Some reports place the cost to society of alcoholism and alcohol abuse as high as $185 billion dollars annually. Increased on-the-job accidents, absenteeism, welfare costs, and alcohol-related auto fatalities contribute to this cost.

In 1986, the American Dental Association (ADA) passed a policy statement recognizing chemical dependency as a disease. In recognizing this disease, the Association mandated that dentists have a responsibility to include questions relating to a history of chemical dependency, or more broadly, substance abuse in their health history questionnaire. This policy statement included patients who are actively abusing drugs as well as patients who are in recovery. An affirmative response was an alert to the dentist and dental team to use caution with certain medications and that the treatment plan may have to be altered. This policy statement was revised in 1989 and 1991 with minor changes. In October 2005 at the annual ADA session, the House of Delegates passed several resolutions encompassing the use of opioids in management of dental pain, alcohol, and other substance use by pregnant and postpartum patients, and guidelines related to alcohol, nicotine, and/or drug use by child or adolescent patients. The House of Delegates in 2005 reaffirmed the disease concept of alcoholism and other substance use disorders and provided a more current statement on provision of dental treatment for patients with substance use disorders. For an in-depth review of these resolutions, refer to www.ada.org. At the minimum, the patient's past medical history questionnaire should include a question asking if there is a history of chemical dependency and if so, how long they have been in recovery. The dental office should have a list available of local resources for drug counseling in the event the patient admits drug use and seeks some help.

This chapter reviews common substances of abuse, where they come from, signs and symptoms of the substance abuser, and some of the dental implications of treating patients actively using or in recovery from these substances. There are many books and articles devoted to this topic that provide greater detail. The reader is referred to several comprehensive texts on this disease. The intent of this chapter is to provide an overview of some of the most prevalent drugs, how abuse of these substances by patients may influence dental treatment, and how to recognize some signs and symptoms of substance abuse and withdrawal.

Substances of abuse originate from many sources. They may be naturally occurring, semisynthetic, synthetic, over-the-counter, or prescription drugs. There is a paucity of information in the dental literature correlating substance abuse with dental manifestations for a simple reason. Most substance abusers do not seek routine dental care because obtaining their drug of choice is their top priority. Most often they will be episodic patients. In fact, that is one of the cardinal signs of addiction, a preoccupation with obtaining the drug or sex or gambling or whatever the addiction. Patients presenting to the dental office solely to obtain opiates or other controlled substances are referred to as "doctor shoppers" because they literally go from doctors' office to office seeking these medications. It can be difficult to distinguish between these drug seekers or the patient that is truly in need of pain medication. Most often these patients have multiple areas of decay and would appear to be in pain, but their main goal is to obtain the opiate medication.

What are some of the warning signs of a "doctor shopper"?

- They can name the medication or may ask for a brand name opiate.
- The patient may be very knowledgeable about contraindications of medications and health problems in order to direct the dentist to prescribe the opiate, for example, the patient may state they have an ulcer and cannot take NSAIDs limiting the prescription choice to opiates.
- The patient may request a prescription over the phone and is not willing to come into the office. Good dental practice dictates that prescriptions for medication never be prescribed over the phone unless the patient has been seen in the office to determine the problem.
- The patient may request to come into the office after hours when the dentist is alone and threaten the dentist to provide the prescription.
- The patient may call and say they are from out of town and need just enough medication to hold them over until they can get to their own dentist.
- The patient may exhibit cutaneous indications of prior drug use.

What can the dentist do to identify a "doctor shopper"?

- Evaluate for signs of drug use. Take the patient's blood pressure, giving you an opportunity to examine the bare arm.
- Check your state's **Prescription Drug Monitoring Program** (PDMP) data base: This information can be accessed to review prescription abuse trends, identify diversion locations, and identify patients who go from doctor to doctor to obtain these prescriptions. These programs are supported mostly by state funds and therefore vary widely in their effectiveness and reliability. However, several states now require the prescriber to consult the PDMP before prescribing an opiate or benzodiazepine. Failure to consult the PDMP by the prescriber can result in suspension of their license or a fine. In a PDMP, the dentist is provided with a password which allows them to check the name of a patient whom they suspect as a "doctor shopper" and to see how many prescriptions, and quantity of controlled substance, the patient has received within a certain period of time. If the dentist finds that the patient has visited other doctors within a short period of time, the dentist can refuse prescribing the controlled substance. Some states will have a telephone number to alert authorities to have the patient removed from the office.

How to manage the "doctor shopper"

- Perform a thorough examination.
- Document all that you see.
- Prescribe NSAIDs.
  An NSAID in combination with acetaminophen will be much more effective than an opiate analgesic because of the inflammatory nature of dental pain. Opiates are **not** anti-inflammatory. If you must prescribe an opioid analgesic do so in limited amounts. Routine dental pain (eg, extraction) only requires a two day supply of medication. If the patient requests a refill by phone, schedule an appointment for follow-up examination. If a dental cause of the pain cannot be identified, the patient should be referred to a pain management center.

As a general rule, the central nervous system (CNS) stimulant (uppers) abusing dental patient most likely will not be going to the dentist while under the influence of the drug because the stimulant will amplify their already existing anxiety. It is more likely that a patient will use or abuse a CNS depressant (downer) substance to self-medicate their anxiety. This is important to the dentist because stimulants such as cocaine, methamphetamine, and ecstacy are sympathomimetics and in combination with vasoconstrictor could result in a hypertensive crisis (stroke). **Plain local anesthetic without vasoconstrictor is not contraindicated in that patient.** Patients who self-medicate with depressant drugs such as alcohol, opioids, barbiturates, or marijuana are generally more compliant while in the dental chair, and the drug combination does not pose a serious threat.

ALCOHOL

Ethyl alcohol (referred to as alcohol) is the most abused drug in the United States today and the most abused drug by dentists. As mentioned above, the cost to society for the treatment of alcoholism and alcohol abuse is billions of dollars annually. Alcohol is a CNS depressant and not a stimulant as many people (particularly the adolescent population) believe. Its effect on the central nervous system is dose-dependent and correlated with the rising blood alcohol concentration rather than the falling concentration. Cognitive ability, reaction time, memory, psychomotor, and perceptual ability are impaired to varying degrees.

The majority of consumed alcohol is absorbed from the small intestine and is, therefore, affected by the gastric emptying time and the consumption of food. Alcohol is metabolized by the liver via acetaldehyde and eventually to carbon dioxide and water. Excess consumption of alcohol can result in hepatic damage that may affect the patient's ability to metabolize medications. Doses of medications that are metabolized by the liver, such as acetaminophen, may have to be reduced when treating a patient with confirmed hepatic damage from alcohol or other substance abuse. Alcohol readily crosses the placental barrier and has the potential of producing fetal alcohol syndrome (FAS), the most severe form of the fetal alcohol spectrum disorders (FASD). It has been estimated that 9 out of every 1,000 live births in the US suffer from some form of FASD resulting in mental retardation, supernumerary teeth, and facial deformities to name a few. These effects are not limited to physical changes but can influence social interactions, and the propensity for substance abuse later in life as well. The two classic signs of FAS in children are the absence of a philtrum and a thin upper lip. The American Dental Association addresses this problem with their resolution passed in 2005 entitled Statement on Alcohol and Other Substance Use by Pregnant and Postpartum Patients. There are many other resources that provide greater detail about this preventable syndrome and the reader is referred to those sources as well.

Excessive alcohol use has been associated with an increased incidence of periodontal disease, poor wound healing, chronic orofacial infections, iatrogenic injury, and an increased incidence of oral cancer. Since alcohol is a CNS depressant, any medication that causes respiratory depression should be prescribed or administered with caution or not at all for patients suspected of alcohol abuse. Patients who present to the dental office and are obviously intoxicated should not be provided dental treatment. The major concern with the intoxicated patient is a failure to follow directions while in the chair, and the inability to follow postoperative instructions. An additional concern is the aggressive, combative behavior exhibited by some that are intoxicated.

Signs and Symptoms of Alcohol Use or Abuse	
Lethargic, slow to respond	Odor on breath and/or clothes
Slurred speech	Inability to respond to commands
Telangiectasia	Psychomotor impairment

MARIJUANA

The most abused illegal drug by high school students today is marijuana. Marijuana is a plant that grows throughout the world, but is particularly suited for a warm, humid environment. There are three species of plants but the two most frequently cited are *Cannabis sativa* and *Cannabis indica*. All species possess a female and male plant. Approximately 450 chemicals have been isolated of which approximately 125 are described as cannabinoids. Of these, 23 are thought to be psychoactive. The major psychoactive cannabinoid is delta-9-tetrahydrocannabinol and also the most abundant. The highest concentration of THC is found in hashish which is derived from the bud of the female plant. The concentration of THC varies according to growing conditions and the part of the plant but has increased from ~2% to 3% in marijuana sold in the 1950s to ~40% sold on the streets today. The term sinsemilla (Hispanic for "without seed") is used to describe marijuana from the unpollinated tops of the female flowers and is associated with a higher concentration of THC. Marijuana can be smoked in cigarettes (joints, spliffs), pipes, water pipes (bongs), or baked in brownies, cakes, candies, etc, and then ingested. However, smoking marijuana is more efficient and the "high" has a quicker onset than oral forms. There are new street terms and forms of marijuana that are now used to describe the more potent forms of marjijuana such "scat", "dab", "wax", and the use of these forms such as "satting", "dabbing", etc. Descriptions of these new forms are beyond the scope of this chapter and the reader is directed to current literature. Marijuana is a Schedule I controlled substance but has been promoted as medicinal for the treatment of glaucoma (according to the Glaucoma Research Foundation, "the number of significant side effects generated by long-term oral use of marijuana or long-term inhalation of marijuana smoke make marijuana a poor choice in the treatment of glaucoma, a chronic disease requiring proven and effective treatment"), for increasing appetite in patients who have HIV disease, to prevent the nausea associated with cancer chemotherapy, and as an analgesic for chronic pain. In response to this request, the FDA approved dronabinol (Marinol), a synthetic THC, and placed this drug in Schedule III to be prescribed by physicians for the indicated medical conditions. The synthetic THC does not produce a "high" and in fact is not well-absorbed from the gastrointestinal tract. Twenty-eight states have passed legislation to allow marijuana for medical purposes. The laws passed or pending by these states differ in the allowable quantity of usable marijuana, as well as the quantity of plants possessed and the cannabinoid allowed. For instance, the cannabinoid cannabidiol (CBD) has been approved for treating medication-resistant types of epilepsy but does not produce a psychoactive effect. Recently, the medical indications for the use of marijuana have been expanded to include multiple sclerosis-induced spasticity, including the neuropathic pain associated with this condition. Eight states, including Alaska, California, Colorado, Maine, Massachusetts, Nevada, Oregon, Washington state, and the District of Columbia, have passed legislation to allow marijuana use for recreational purposes in spite of the DEA classification as a Schedule I Controlled Substance which states possession, distribution, and manufacturing of marijuana is a violation. Although Washington DC has passed legislation allowing recreational use, Congress has blocked the sale of marijuana for this purpose. On August 29, 2013, the Department of Justice issued a statement stating that it would not stand in the way of marijuana legalization in the states of Colorado and Washington. They added that it would not be a priority to close down recreational marijuana stores thus temporarily resolving the conflict between the states and the federal government.

An individual under the influence of marijuana may exhibit no signs or symptoms of intoxication. The pharmacologic effects are dose-dependent and depend to a large extent on the set and setting of the intoxicated individual. As the dose of THC increases, the person experiences euphoria or a state of well-being, often referred to as "mellowing out". Everything becomes comical, problems disappear, and their appetite for snack foods increases. This is called the "munchies". Additionally, marijuana produces time and spatial distortion, which contribute, as the dose increases, to a dysphoria characterized by paranoia, fear, and anxiety. Although there has never been a death reported from marijuana overdose, certainly the higher doses may produce such bizarre circumstances as to increase the chances of accidental death. Since THC is fat soluble, daily consumption of marijuana may result in THC being stored in body fat which will result in detectable amounts of THC being found in the urine for as long as 60 days in some cases. According to the National Institute of Drug Abuse, it is estimated that 9% of marijuana users will become dependent on it and this percentage increases to 17% when marijuana smokers began using in the teenage years. Recent research suggests that heavy marijuana smokers function at a lower intellectual level compared to nonsmokers affecting attention span, memory, cognitive ability, and psychomotor skills. Additional research is needed to ascertain a causal relationship as well as the impact on the dental practice. Studies have indicated that the psychomotor impairment associated with marijuana can extend for up to 24 hours after smoking marijuana.

An endogenous cannabinoid system has been identified in the human and receptors have been located. This system is referred to as the endocannabinoid system with an endogenous cannabinoid identified as anandamide. A detailed description and its medical implications and potential is not within the scope of this chapter and the reader is referred elsewhere for more detailed descriptions and current research regarding this innate system.

Because of anxiety associated with dental visits, marijuana would be the most likely drug, after alcohol, to be used when coming to the dental office. But, unlike alcohol, marijuana may not produce any detectable odor on the breath nor signs of intoxication. Fortunately, local anesthetics, analgesics, and antibiotics used by the general dentist do not interact with marijuana. The major concern with the marijuana-intoxicated patient, similar to the alcohol-intoxicated patient, is a failure to follow directions while in the chair, and the inability to follow postoperative instructions.

Signs and Symptoms of Marijuana Use	
Blood shot eyes	Odor on breath and clothes
Lethargic, slow to respond	Inability to respond to commands
Slurred speech	Memory impairment

Synthetic Cannabinoids: These chemicals are synthetic versions of delta 9-tetrahydrocannabinol (THC), the major psychoactive ingredient in marijuana. They are reported to be 200 to 800 times more potent than THC. The effects of these chemicals are similar to marijuana: Increased heart rate, increased blood pressure, paranoia, agitation, giddiness, and increased appetite. Synthetic cannabinoids are advertised as being undetectable in urine drug tests for THC; however, this is untrue. The chemicals can be detected by urinalysis, but it takes a very sophisticated system for detection, testing is expensive, and most laboratories do not routinely test for synthetic cannabinoids.

Internet sales of the chemicals have been connected to sources in China, Pakistan, and India. Once the chemicals have been purchased, the final product can be assembled in the United States. It is sold in small packets labeled as herbal incense or potpourri, which contain dried herbal materials that are sprayed with the synthetic cannabinoids. The product is typically smoked, and has various street names such as "Spice Diamond," "Dream," "Essence," and "K-2." Packets vary in cost from $20 to $50 and weigh 100 to 300 mg. Liquid synthetic cannabinoids can be vaporized in e-cigarettes.

These "designer" drugs are intended to circumvent the Controlled Substances Act of 1970. The problem for law enforcement is that underground chemists continue to modify chemicals into new ones that are not illegal to possess or use. According to the US Drug Enforcement Administration (DEA) there are 22 of these chemicals that have been placed on the Controlled Substances list and possibly another 75 that have been identified as being sold on the streets in the US but have not been placed on the Controlled Substances list. These synthetic cannabinoids have been implicated as the causative agent in renal and liver failure among our population. And yet they can be purchased over the internet or hand to hand sales on the streets. According to the DEA, a 15 state raid early 2016 seized approximately 16,000 pounds of these packaged synthetic cannabinoids for distribution to the streets. Go to www.DEA.gov for more information about these deadly chemicals.

OPIOIDS

The opioids are often called narcotics and include a variety of commonly prescribed drugs including morphine, oxycodone, and hydrocodone. Other illicit opioids are available such as heroin and acetyl fentanyl. Prescription opioid pain relievers are now the second most abused drugs after marijuana. Over 70% of people who abuse prescription pain relievers acquire them from friends or relatives. Nearly 1/3 of people ≥12 years of age who abuse these drugs began by using a prescription drug for nonmedical purposes. From 1999 to 2010, the number of people in the United States dying annually from prescription opioid related overdoses quadrupled, from 4,030 to 16,651 (*JAMA* 2013). The number of reported drug overdose deaths in the United States in 2010 was 22,134 and the top three classes of prescribed drugs involved in these deaths were opioids (16,651 deaths), benzodiazepines (6,497 deaths), and antidepressants (3,889 deaths).

According to the American Society for Addiction Medicine, 94% of people who were being treated for opioid addiction claimed they switched to heroin because of the cost and difficulty obtaining prescription opioids. According to the Center for Disease Control (CDC) from 2000 to 2015 more than half a million people died from drug overdoses. It is estimated that 91 Americans die every day from an opioid overdose. Influencing this increased overdose rate is the introduction of newer synthetics such as fentanyl (50 to 100 times more potent than heroin) and carfentanil (referred to as elephant tranquilizer on the street and is 10,000 times more potent than morphine) in the heroin sold on the street. Again according to the CDC, more people die from opioid overdose every day than die from automobile accidents. The American Medical Association (AMA), the Amerian Dental Association (ADA), the American Pharmaceutical Association (APhA), and the Food and Drug Association (FDA) have called for greater restrictions on opioid prescribing and approval of new opioid entities.

As noted previously in the dental office opioids should be the last choice to relieve postoperative pain. The nature of dental pain is a dull, aching, inflammatory pain and is best controlled by the NSAIDs with acetaminophen as a rescue analgesic. Opioids are **not** anti-inflammatory. Four hundred to 600 mg of ibuprofen every 6 hours by itself or alternating with acetaminophen 500 mg will control 90% of dental pain. Do not exceed 3,000 mg of acetaminophen or 3,200 mg of ibuprofen in 24 hours.

Many patients who have been abusing opioids will exhibit multiple carious lesions, particularly class V lesions. This increased caries rate is probably a result of xerostomia, high intake of sweets, and lack of daily oral hygiene. Patients who are recovering from heroin or other opioid addiction should not be prescribed any kind of opioid analgesic because of the increased chance of relapse. Nonsteroidal anti-inflammatory drugs (NSAIDs) should be used to control any postoperative discomfort in these patients. Patients with a past history of intravenous drug abuse may be at higher risk of subacute bacterial endocarditis (SBE), HIV disease, hepatitis, and certainly increased infection postoperatively. The clinician might consider or at least be aware of the increased possibility of postoperative infection in these patients.

Signs and Symptoms of Opioid Use	
Pin point pupils	Glazed eyes
Lethargic, slow to respond	Inability to respond to commands
Slurred speech	Xerostomia

METHAMPHETAMINE

Methamphetamine has been available clinically for 60 years as a medication to curb appetite. Today it is one of the most widely abused drugs on the street. Methamphetamine can be smoked in the form of "ice" (crystal meth), snorted, injected, or consumed orally. The onset of action varies with the route of administration, smoking providing the most rapid onset of action. Clandestine methamphetamine is usually synthesized from pseudoephedrine or ephedrine. Because of this avenue for the production of methamphetamine, Congress enacted the Combat Methamphetamine Epidemic Act of 2005 (CMEA) which placed restrictions on the sale of pseudoephedrine. Some states require a prescription for pseudoephedrine and others require identification and limits how much can be purchased over the counter without a prescription. According to the DEA, the majority of methamphetamine is imported to the US from Mexico with very little produced by small clandestine labs within the US According to the most recent surveys from the Monitoring the Future Study for 2014, the abuse of methamphetamine in the last year, the last 30 days, or lifetime in the 8th, 10th, and 12th grades has dramatically decreased.

The methamphetamine molecule can exist in either the "D" isomer or the "L" isomer. The latter isomer has its greatest effect on the cardiovascular system and, in fact, is available commercially over-the-counter as a nasal decongestant. The "D" isomer has its principle effects on the central nervous system as a stimulant (upper) and can not be converted from the "L" form. It is a sympathomimetic and as such raises blood pressure. This effect on the autonomic nervous system results in increased basal metabolic rate (BMR) and increased body temperature, resulting in the "sweats". Methamphetamine users crave sweets possibly as a source of energy to fuel the increased BMR. As a consequence of the increased sweating the individual becomes dehydrated and thirsty. The sympathetic stimulation produces thick, ropey saliva. This lack of saliva, increased consumption of sweets in the form of soda pop, and lack of routine dental care no doubt is the primary cause of "meth mouth". Initially the meth user experiences a feeling of exhilaration, alertness, and incredible energy. With successive uses, tolerance occurs and the user abuses increasing amounts of methamphetamine looking for the same high they experienced on the first time. They never quite attain it. This has been referred to on the street as "chasing the monkey". As a substitute, the user continues their high for several hours or days in some cases. This is called bingeing. A binge may last for 5 or 6 days. The user becomes very paranoid, develops psychotic episodes, and has the potential of becoming violent. stereotypical behavior develops such as rocking back and forth in a chair, picking their fingernails, or other behavior. During this stage the user begins "tweaking", using small amounts to stay high, and begins to hallucinate. Characteristically, they will describe the feeling that bugs are crawling under their skin and they scratch their arms, face, and any other exposed part of their body. The street term for this hallucination is called "coke bugs". Usually, the user will collapse from the physical exhaustion. Withdrawal can take weeks after the last use. As mentioned above, vasoconstrictor is contraindicated if there has been methamphetamine use within the last 24 hours.

Methamphetamine Signs and Symptoms in the Dental Office	
Dilated pupils	Jittery, irritable behavior
Rapid speech	Unable to sit still, twitching
Tremendous anxiety	Difficult to anesthetize

BENZODIAZEPINES AND OTHER NONALCOHOL SEDATIVES

These drugs are used mainly for treatment of anxiety disorders and, in some instances, insomnia. These drugs are commonly abused, either by themselves or as adjunct to the opioids. They have the ability to produce a strong physical dependency on the use of the medication. As tolerance builds up to the drug, the physical dependency increases dramatically. Unlike street drugs, where addiction is a primary consideration, the overuse of benzodiazepine lies in their ability to induce physical dependency. When these drugs are taken for several weeks, there is relatively little tolerance induced. However, after several months, the proportion of patients who become tolerant increases and reducing the dose or stopping the medication produces severe withdrawal symptoms often resulting in death.

It is extremely difficult for the physician to distinguish between the withdrawal symptoms and the reappearance of the myriad anxiety symptoms that cause the drug to be prescribed initially. Many patients increase their dose over time because tolerance develops to at least the sedative effects of the drug. The antianxiety benefits of the benzodiazepines continue to occur long after tolerance to the sedating effects. Patients often take these drugs for many years with relatively few ill effects other than the risk of withdrawal. The dentist should be keenly aware of the signs and symptoms and the historical pattern in patients taking benzodiazepines. On the street, the abuser will often mix a benzodiazepine with an opioid to enhance the opioid-induced euphoria. In particular the benzodiazepines are used with methadone to induce a heroin-like high. The dentist should be aware of "doctor shoppers" asking for the benzodiazepines who will then use these medications in conjunction with their opiates or other drugs of abuse. On the street this is referred to as a "benzo boost". The benzodiazepines are also taken along with ecstacy or MDMA to mitigate the crash or coming down from the MDMA. This is referred to as "parachuting" on the street. The most common dental side effect of the benzodiaaepines is xerostomia occurring in approximately 10% of the patients who consume these either therapeutically or abusers

NICOTINE

Cigarette (nicotine) addiction is influenced by multiple variables. Nicotine itself produces reinforcement; users compare nicotine to stimulants such as cocaine or amphetamine, although its effects are of lower magnitude.

Nicotine is absorbed readily through the skin, mucous membranes, and of course, through the lungs. The pulmonary route produces discernible central nervous system effects in as little as 7 seconds. Thus, each puff produces some discrete reinforcement. With 10 puffs per cigarette, the 1 pack per day smoker reinforces the habit 200 times daily. The timing, setting, situation, and preparation all become associated repetitively with the effects of nicotine.

Nicotine has both stimulant and depressant actions. The smoker feels alert, yet there is some muscle relaxation. Nicotine activates the nucleus accumbens reward system in the brain. Increased extracellular dopamine has been found in this region after nicotine injections in rats. Nicotine affects other systems as well, including the release of endogenous opioids and glucocorticoids.

Nicotine Withdrawal Syndrome Signs and Symptoms	
Irritability, impatience, hostility	Restlessness
Anxiety	Decreased heart rate
Dysphoric or depressed mood	Increased appetite or weight gain
Difficulty concentrating	

SMOKING CESSATION PRODUCTS

Several years ago, the journal, *Science* stated that ~80% of smokers say they want to quit, but each year <1 in 10 actually succeed. Nicotine transdermal delivery preparations (or nicotine patches) were approved by the US Food and Drug Administration in 1992 as aids to smoking cessation for the relief of nicotine withdrawal symptoms. Four preparations were approved simultaneously: Habitrol, Nicoderm, Nicotrol, and ProStep. These products differ in how much nicotine is released and whether they provide a 24- or 16-hour release time.

Studies are still being reported on the effectiveness of nicotine patches on tobacco cessation. Most previous studies had good entry criteria including definition of the Fagerstrom score. Dr Fred Cowan of Oregon Health Sciences University described these Fagerstrom criteria in a previous report on nicotine substitutes in AGD *Impact*. Abstinence of smoking cessation has usually been assessed by self-report, measurement of carbon monoxide in breath, and plasma or urine nicotine products.

In numerous protocols, percentages of study subjects who abstained from smoking after 3 to 10 weeks of patch treatment with nicotine compared to placebo, have never exceeded 40%. After the initial assessment, six studies continued to follow the study subjects through 24 to 52 weeks of patch treatment. The results were even poorer with <25% sustained success. A review of these and additional studies, reveals some general conclusions regarding the effectiveness of nicotine patches in tobacco cessation. In every study, many smokers abstained after treatment with placebo patches; nicotine treatment was initially more effective than placebo; and improved abstinence rates were more marked in the short term (10 weeks) than in the long term (52 weeks). Subjects undergoing tobacco cessation trials tended to gain weight irrespective of whether placebo or nicotine patches were worn. Patients often favor the nicotine polacrilex gum (Nicorette) which releases nicotine into the blood stream via the oral mucosa.

Data are now available from tobacco cessation studies carried out in general medical practices. The effectiveness of nicotine patch substitution under these conditions is similar to the results described previous. Most patch systems and gum are now available as over-the-counter products; only Habitrol remains prescription. Bupropion (Zyban) is another approach to the treatment of tobacco cessation. This drug is a norepinephrine/serotonin/dopamine reuptake inhibitor and its action directly affects the craving for tobacco. Another new product just introduced is varenicline (Chantix). This product targets certain nicotine receptors to prevent nicotine access and diminishes the mesolimbic dopamine reward associated with nicotine use. The reader is referred to more comprehensive information about these products and the treatment of tobacco cessation. In addition, the reader should familiarize themselves with the supportive ADA posture on the role of the dental team in tobacco cessation treatment.

Many patients have tried traditional therapies to quit smoking. Battery operated E-cigarettes are gaining in popularity, allowing the user to inhale vapors containing nicotine without the tar and carbon monoxide found in cigarettes. A new study indicates that subjects, with no immediate intention of quitting who switched to e-cigarettes demonstrated quitting behavior. They found 10.7% of the subjects who switched to nicotine containing e-cigarettes had completely quit smoking at week 12 and 8.7% were still not smoking 1 year later. Although the US Food and Drug Administration has not approved e-cigarettes for smoking cessation treatment, it is worth considering for patients who want to reduce the harmful effects of smoking but have failed in previous efforts to quit.

Therefore in patients who smoke but do not intend to quit, the use of e-cigarettes, with or without nicotine (but more successfully with nicotine), decreased cigarette consumption with lasting results, reducing the harmful side effects of smoking (Caponnetto 2013).

The most recent statistics from the 2015 Monitoring the Future Study indicate that 8th, 10th, and 12th graders prefer and more heavily abuse e-cigarettes compared to traditional tobacco products. These e-cigarettes cause a heated source to vaporize the nicotine-containing material giving the perception that they are safer than tobacco products. The reader should be reminded that these e-cigarettes can be used to vaporize other drugs as well such as "crack", methamphetamine, etc. and are not as innocent as they are portrayed. And lastly, nicotine is a very addictive substance regardless of how it is ingested.

COCAINE

Cocaine, referred to on the street as "snow", "nose candy", "girl", and many other euphemisms, has created an epidemic. This drug is like no other local anesthetic. Known for about the last 2,000 years, cocaine has been used and abused by politicians, scientists, farmers, warriors, and of course, on the street. Cocaine is derived from the leaves of a plant called *Erythroxylon* coca which grows in South America. Ninety percent of the world's supply of cocaine originates in Peru, Bolivia, and Colombia. At last estimate, the United States consumes 75% of the world's supply. The plant grows to a height of ~4 feet and produces a red berry. Farmers go through the fields stripping the leaves from the plant three times a year. During the working day, the farmers chew the coca leaves to suppress appetite and fight the fatigue of working the fields. The leaves are transported to a laboratory site where the cocaine is extracted by a process called maceration. It takes ~7 to 8 pounds of leaves to produce 1 ounce of cocaine.

On the streets of the United States, cocaine can be found in two forms - one is the hydrochloride salt which can be "snorted" or dissolved in water and injected intravenously, the other is the free base form which can be smoked and is sometimes referred to as "crack", "rock", or "free base". It is called crack because it cracks or pops when large pieces are smoked. It is called rock because it is hard and difficult to break into smaller pieces. The most popular method of administration of cocaine is "snorting" in which small amounts of cocaine hydrochloride are divided into segments or "lines" and any straw-like device can be used to inhale one or more lines of the cocaine into the nose. Although cocaine does not reach the lungs, enough cocaine is absorbed through nasal mucosa to provide a "high" within 3 to 5 minutes. Rock or crack, on the other hand, is heated and inhaled from any device available. This form of cocaine does reach the lungs and provides a much faster onset of action as well as a more intense stimulation. There are dangers to the user with any form of cocaine. Undoubtedly, the most dangerous form is the intravenous route.

Signs and Symptoms of Cocaine Use	
Dilated pupils	Tremors
Jitteriness	Talkative
Irritability	Increased blood pressure

The cocaine user, regardless of how the cocaine was administered, presents a potential life-threatening situation in the dental operatory. The patient under the influence of cocaine could be compared to a car going 100 miles per hour. Blood pressure is elevated and heart rate is likely increased. Use of a local anesthetic with epinephrine in such a patient may result in a medical emergency. Such patients can be identified by jitteriness, irritability, talkativeness, tremors, and short abrupt speech patterns. These same signs and symptoms may also be seen in a normal dental patient with preoperative dental anxiety; therefore, the dentist must be particularly alert to identify the potential cocaine abuser. If a patient is suspected, they should never be given a local anesthetic with vasoconstrictor for fear of exacerbating cocaine-induced sympathetic response. Life-threatening episodes of cardiac arrhythmias and hypertensive crises have been reported when local anesthetic with vasoconstrictor was administered to a patient under the influence of cocaine. No local anesthetic used by any dentist can interfere with, nor test positive for cocaine in any urine testing screen. Therefore, the dentist need not be concerned with any false drug use accusations associated with dental anesthesia.

CLUB DRUGS

Perceptual distortions that include hallucinations, illusions, and disorders of thinking such as paranoia can be produced by toxic doses of many drugs. These phenomena also may be seen during toxic withdrawal from sedatives such as alcohol. There are, however, certain drugs that have as their primary effect the production of perception, thought, or mood disturbances at low doses with minimal effects on memory and orientation. These are commonly called *hallucinogenic drugs*, but their use does not always result in frank hallucinations.

Ecstasy (MDMA) and Phenylethylamines (MDA): MDA and MDMA have stimulant, as well as, psychedelic effects and produce degeneration of serotonergic nerve cells and axons. While nerve degeneration has not been well-demonstrated in human beings, the potential remains. Thus, there is possible neurotoxicity with overuse of these drugs. Ecstasy became popular during the 1980s on college campuses and was used by some psychotherapists as an aid to the process of therapy, although very little controlled data is available. These drugs are now classified as Schedule I Controlled Substances and are no longer prescribed. They are, however, a popular street drug of abuse. Acute effects are dose-dependent and include dry mouth, jaw clinching, muscle aches, and tachycardia. At higher doses, effects include agitation, hyperthermia, panic attacks, and visual hallucinations. Frequent, repeated use of psychedelic drugs is unusual and, therefore, tolerance is not commonly seen. However, tolerance does develop to the behavioral effects of various psychedelic drugs, and after numerous doses, the tendency towards behavioral tolerance can be observed. Pure MDMA is referred to as "molly" on the street. Folk lore claims this name comes from "molecule" because of the purity of the drug. These drugs are sympathomimetics and therefore might amplify the effects of vasoconstrictor. Patients who admit to using these drugs within the last 24 hours should not be administered vasoconstrictor. Plain local anesthetic is acceptable.

Lysergic Acid Diethylamide (LSD): LSD is the most potent hallucinogenic drug and produces significant psychedelic effects with a total dose of as little as 25 to 50 mcg. This drug is over 3,000 times more potent than mescaline. It is sold on the illicit market in a variety of forms, as a tablet, capsule, sugar cube, or on blotting paper, a popular contemporary system involving postage stamp-sized papers impregnated with varying doses of LSD (50 to 300 mcg). A majority of street samples sold as LSD actually do contain LSD, while mushrooms and other botanicals sold as sources of psilocybin and other psychedelics have a low probability of containing the advertised hallucinogenics. Adverse effects which may affect treatment include visual and auditory hallucinations, tachycardia, psychosis, fear, tremors, delirium, hyperglycemia, fever, sweating, flushing, euphoria, hypertonia, nausea, vomiting, coma, seizures, tachypnea, and respiratory arrest.

Bath Salts (synthetic cathinones): These potentially deadly street drugs acquired the name bath salts, because they were packaged in containers that resemble the scented soaps that can be added to bath water. The term "bath salt" is a generic term which originally described three distinct synthetic chemicals: Mephedrone; 3,4-methylenedioxypyrovalerone (MDPV); and methylone. As of October 21, 2011, these substances were designated as Schedule I Controlled Substances by the US Drug Enforcement Administration (DEA). This action makes possession or selling of these chemicals illegal in the United States. These chemicals are synthetic forms of cathinone which is derived from the shrub Catha edulis (khat). There are several street terms for these crystalline chemicals; some of the more popular are "Ivory Wave," "Red Dove," "Vanilla Sky," and "White Lightning." The packages are usually labeled "Not Intended for Human Consumption," to protect the manufacturer, but users will snort, swallow, or inject the contents. A package may weigh from 300 to 500 mg and can cost ~$25 to $40 on the street.

The effects of the chemicals in "bath salts" have been described as a combination of cocaine, ecstasy, and methamphetamine. Psychological effects include insomnia, suicidal ideation, paranoia, agitation, and seizures. The user describes heightened awareness, euphoria, and enhanced sexual ability. Since these medications are sympathomimetics, vasoconstrictors should **not** be used in individuals suspected to be under the influence of "bath salts." Newer drugs have emerged on the street that resemble the synthetic cathinones and are considered more potent, more unpredictable, and therefore more dangerous to the user and law enforcement. These newer drugs are referred to as "flakka", "gravel", etc.

INHALANTS

Anesthetic gases such as nitrous oxide or halothane are sometimes used as intoxicants by medical personnel. Nitrous oxide also is abused by food service employees because it is supplied for use as a propellant in disposable aluminum mini tanks for whipping cream canisters. Nitrous oxide produces euphoria and analgesia and then loss of consciousness. Compulsive use and chronic toxicity rarely are reported, but there are obvious risks of overdose associated with the abuse of this anesthetic. Chronic use has been reported to cause peripheral neuropathy. Glue, correction fluid, gasoline, aerosol key board cleaners, model paint, in fact, any volatile substance has the potential to cause a "high" and like all of the above can become very addictive and deadly.

According to the Monitoring the Future Surveys, abuse of inhalants peaks in the 8th grade and less so in the 10th or 12th grades. Inhalants are CNS depressants and can cause respiratory failure, long-term use results in liver failure, and suffocation.

The dental team should be alert to the signs and symptoms of drug abuse and withdrawal. Further reading is recommended.

REFERENCES AND SELECTED READINGS

American Medical Association. *JAMA*. 2013;309.

Caponnetto P, Campagna D, Cibella F, et al. Efficiency and safety of an electronic cigarette (ECLAT) as tobacco cigarettes substitute: a prospective 12-month randomized control design study. *PLoS One*. 2013;8(6):e66317.

Okie S. A flood of opioids, a rising tide of deaths. *New Engl J Med*. 2010;363(21):1981-1985.

ORAL MEDICINE TOPICS

PART II:

DENTAL MANAGEMENT AND THERAPEUTIC CONSIDERATIONS IN PATIENTS WITH SPECIFIC ORAL CONDITIONS AND OTHER MEDICINE TOPICS

The second part of the chapter focuses on therapies the dentist may choose to prescribe for patients suffering from oral disease or who are in need of special care. Some overlap between these sections has resulted from systemic conditions that have oral manifestations and vice-versa. Cross-references to the descriptions and the monographs for individual drugs described elsewhere in this handbook allow for easy retrieval of information. Example prescriptions of selected drug therapies for each condition are presented so that the clinician can evaluate alternate approaches to treatment, since there is seldom a single drug of choice.

Drug prescriptions shown represent prototype drugs and popular prescriptions and are examples only. The pharmacologic category index is available for cross-referencing if alternatives and additional drugs are sought.

TABLE OF CONTENTS

ORAL PAIN

PAIN PREVENTION

For the dental patient, the prevention of pain aids in relieving anxiety and reduces the probability of stress during dental care. For the practitioner, dental procedures can be accomplished more efficiently in a "painless" situation. Appropriate selection and use of local anesthetics is one of the foundations for success in this arena. Local anesthetics listed below include drugs for the most commonly confronted dental procedures. Ester anesthetics are no longer available in dose form for dental injections, and historically had a higher incidence of allergic manifestations due to the formation of the metabolic byproduct, para-aminobenzoic acid. Articaine, which has an ester side chain, is rapidly metabolized to a non-PABA acid and functions as an amide and has a low allergic potential. The amides, in general, have a nearly negligible incidence of true allergic reactions, and only one well-documented case of amide allergy has been reported by Seng, et al. Although injectable diphenhydramine (Benadryl) has been used in an attempt to provide anesthesia in patients allergic to all the local anesthetics, it is no longer recommended in this context. The vehicle for injectable diphenhydramine can cause tissue necrosis.

Local Anesthetics

Articaine and Epinephrine on page 162
Bupivacaine on page 251
Bupivacaine and Epinephrine on page 252
Chloroprocaine on page 346
Lidocaine and Epinephrine on page 994
Lidocaine (Systemic) on page 987
Mepivacaine on page 1060
Mepivacaine and Levonordefrin on page 1062
Prilocaine on page 1385
Prilocaine and Epinephrine
Ropivacaine on page 1452
Tetracaine (Topical) on page 1548

The selection of a vasoconstrictor with the local anesthetic must be based on the length of the procedure to be performed, the patient's medical status (epinephrine is contraindicated in patients with uncontrolled hyperthyroidism), and the need for hemorrhage control. The following table lists some of the common drugs with their duration of action. The long-acting amide injectable, Ropivacaine (Naropin) may be useful for postoperative pain management.

Dental Anesthetics (Average Duration by Route)

Product	Infiltration	Inferior Alveolar Block
Articaine HCl 4% and epinephrine 1:100,000	60 minutes	~60 minutes
Articaine HCl 4% and epinephrine 1:200,000	40 minutes	50 minutes
Carbocaine HCl 2% with Neo-Cobefrin 1:20,000 (mepivacaine HCl and levonordefrin)	50 minutes	60 to 75 minutes
Carbocaine Plain 3%	20 minutes	40 minutes
Citanest Plain 4% (prilocaine)	20 minutes	2.5 hours
Citanest Forte with epinephrine 1:200,000 (prilocaine with epinephrine)	2.25 hours	3 hours
Lidocaine HCl 2% and epinephrine 1:100,000	60 minutes	90 minutes
Marcaine HCl 0.5% with epinephrine 1:200,000 (bupivacaine and epinephrine)	60 minutes	5 to 7 hours
Vivacaine 0.5% with epinephrine 1:200,000 (bupivacaine and epinephrine)	60 minutes	5 to 7 hours

The use of articaine 4% with epinephrine 1:100,000 solution for mandibular blocks has been associated occasionally with paresthesia (*J Am Dent Assoc*, 2001, 132(2):177-85).

The use of preinjection topical anesthetics can assist in pain prevention (see also Viral Infections on page 1849 and Ulcerative, Erosive, and Painful Oral Mucosal Disorders on page 1853). It should be noted that the FDA recently warned health care professionals regarding potential risks associated with unsupervised patient cutaneous use of topical anesthetic products. Life-threatening adverse events such as arrhythmias, seizures, coma, and respiratory complications have been reported. Thus, health care professionals are advised to prescribe FDA-approved topical anesthetics in the lowest concentration consistent with pain relief goals. It is not known if oral mucosa misuse may pose the same risk factors.

Clinicians are also using a eutectic mixture of 2.5% lidocaine with 2.5% prilocaine in a periodontal gel form in adults who require localized anesthesia in periodontal pockets during scaling and/or root planing. However, the same mixture available as a skin patch (EMLA) from Astra is not currently approved for oral use.

OraVerse (phentolamine mesylate) injection is a local anesthetic reversal agent that accelerates the return to normal sensation and function following restorative and periodontal maintenance procedures. OraVerse is indicated for the reversal of soft tissue anesthesia (ie, anesthesia of the lip, tongue, and the associated functional deficits resulting from an intraoral submucosal injection of a local anesthetic containing a vasoconstrictor. OraVerse is not recommended for use in children <6 years of age or weighing <15 kg (33 lbs).

Phentolamine (OraVerse), as used in its original context as a medical hypotensive agent, could be expected to cause significant hypotension and reflex tachycardia when used as the anesthetic reversal agent in children. Studies have shown, however, that neither of these reactions occurred in the children receiving the drug. According to the authors of the study, there was an impressive benefit:risk ratio suggesting a safe approach in accelerating recovery from soft tissue anesthesia in children (Tavares, et al. *JADA*. 2008;139(8):1095-1104). There were no serious adverse events observed. The adverse reactions were observed from study populations of 484 adults and 152 children. It should be anticipated that more adverse effects could occur as OraVerse is used in a larger number of patients. The clinical studies used a maximum of 2 cartridges of OraVerse (0.8 mg phentolamine). There is no information published on effects that occur with higher doses of OraVerse. Phentolamine is a very powerful alpha-adrenergic receptor blocker which can cause cardiovascular effects if inadvertently injected in high doses. The manufacturer advises to adhere to the recommended dosing for the OraVerse formulation. The dosing for OraVerse is based on the number of cartridges of local anesthetic with vasoconstrictor administered, with 1 cartridge of OraVerse containing 0.4 mg of phentolamine and 2 cartridges containing 0.8 mg phentolamine. Dosing is as a 1:1 cartridge ratio to local anesthetic using the same injection site and administration technique as that used for the local anesthetic.

Benzocaine on page 213
Lidocaine (Systemic) on page 987
Phentolamine on page 1328
Tetracaine (Topical) on page 1548

PAIN MANAGEMENT

The patient with existing acute or chronic oral pain requires appropriate treatment and sensitivity on the part of the dentist, all for the purpose of achieving relief from the oral source of pain. Pain can be divided into mild, moderate, and severe levels and requires a subjective assessment by the dentist based on knowledge of the dental procedures to be performed, the presenting signs and symptoms of the patient, and the realization that most dental procedures are invasive often leading to pain once the patient has left the dental office. The practitioner must be aware that the treatment of the source of the pain is usually the best management. If infection is present, treatment of the infection will directly alleviate the patient's discomfort. However, a patient who is not in pain tends to heal better and it is wise to adequately cover the patient for any residual or recurrent discomfort suffered. Likewise, many of the procedures that the dentist performs have pain associated with them. Much of this pain occurs after leaving the dentist office due to an inflammatory process or a healing process that has been initiated. It is difficult to assign specific pain levels (mild, moderate, or severe) for specific procedures; however, the dentist should use his or her prescribing capacity judiciously so that overmedication is avoided.

The potential interaction between acetaminophen and warfarin has been recently raised in the literature. The cytochrome P450 system of drug metabolism for these vitamin K-dependent metabolic pathways has raised the possibility that prolonged use of acetaminophen may inadvertently enhance, to dangerous levels, the anticoagulation effect of warfarin. As monitored by the INR, the effects of these drugs may be one and one-half to two times greater than as expected from the warfarin dosage alone. This potential interaction could be of importance in selecting an analgesic/antipyretic drug for the dental patient.

The following categories of drugs and appropriate example prescriptions for each can be found in the Oral Pain - Sample Prescriptions chart. These include management of mild pain with aspirin products, acetaminophen, and some of the nonsteroidal noninflammatory agents (eg, ibuprofen). Management of moderate pain includes codeine, Toradol, Vicodin, Vicodin ES, Opana; and Motrin in the 800 mg dosage. Etodolac is approved as an NSAID for mild-to-moderate acute and chronic pain, as well as, for pain of osteo and rheumatoid arthritis. Severe pain may require treatment with Percodan or Percocet. A new drug, tapentadol is similar to tramadol in its actions and was approved in November 2008 for moderate to severe acute pain. Tapentadol is classified as an opioid analgesic having a unique ability to bind to μ-opiate receptors and inhibit the reuptake of norepinephrine. It shares many properties of traditional opioid drugs including addiction liability. A report by Kleinert et al, showed that a single dose of tapentadol ≥75 mg effectively reduced moderate to severe postoperative dental pain in a dose related fashion and was well tolerated compared to 60 mg morphine. Their study showed that tapentadol was a highly effective, central-acting analgesic with a favorable side effect profile with rapid onset of action (Kleinert 2008). All prescription pain preparations should be closely monitored for efficacy and discontinued if the pain persists or requires a higher level formulation. Combination drugs such as the recently released Combunox containing 5 mg of oxycodone and 400 mg of ibuprofen have proven usefulness in acute moderately severe to severe pain management.

The chronic pain patient represents a particular challenge for the practitioner. Some additional drugs that may be useful in managing the patient with chronic pain of neuropathic origin are covered in the temporomandibular dysfunction section and in the section on Burning Mouth Syndrome within Ulcerative, Erosive, and Painful Oral Mucosal Disorders on page 1853. It is always incumbent on the practitioner to reevaluate the diagnosis, source of pain, and treatment, whenever prolonged use of analgesics is contemplated. Drugs such as Dilaudid are not recommended for management of dental pain in most states. Fibromyalgia, postherpetic and diabetic neuropathies may also require consideration when dealing with the patient with chronic pain although direct oral involvement is uncommon. The dentist may also be confronted with patients being managed at pain centers offering nonsurgical management of acute and chronic pain conditions.

Recently, the FDA has formally requested manufacturers to limit the amount of acetaminophen in prescription combination products to no more than 325 mg in each tablet or capsule. Manufacturers had until January 2014 to limit the amount of acetaminophen in their oral prescription drug products. The FDA is also requiring manufacturers to update labeling of all prescription combination acetaminophen products to warn of the potential risk for severe liver injury. The over-the-counter acetaminophen products are not affected by this ruling. Some manufacturers have already reduced acetaminophen amounts to 300 to 325 mg per tablet in

combination prescription products. Examples include the very popular hydrocodone and acetaminophen products such as Norco, Vicodin, and Xodol.

Effective August 18, 2014, Tramadol was classified as a Schedule IV controlled dangerous substance (CDS) under federal regulation. If you dispense Tramadol to your patients, you are required to report this to the Prescription Drug Monitoring Program (PDMP). If you write a prescription for Tramadol, but do **not** dispense this medication, you are not required to report to the PDMP. The Division of Drug Control (DDC) has posted the following information on its web site: USDOJ/DEA, 21 CFR (Federal Register) Part 1308: Schedules of Controlled Dangerous Substances: Placement of Tramadol Into Schedule IV (Final Rule). The link is: DEA (CFR Final Rule) Tramadol Schedule IV Placement (Effective: 8/18/14) (http://dhmh.maryland.gov/laboratories/drugcont/docs/DEA%20%28CFR%20Final%20Rule%29%20Tramadol%20Schedule%20IV%20Placement%20%28Eff.8-18-2014%29.pdf).

Overdose from prescription combination products containing acetaminophen account for nearly half of all cases of acetaminophen-related liver failure in the United States. Many cases result in liver transplant or death. There is no immediate danger to patients taking these combination pain medications. Patients should continue to take them as directed by health care provider. The risk of liver injury primarily occurs when patients take multiple products containing acetaminophen at one time and exceed the current maximum adult dose of 4,000 mg within a 24-hour period. For more information and a complete list of affected products see www.fda.gov/Drugs/DrugSafety/InformationbyDrugClass/ucm239874.htm

Opioid analgesics can be used on a short-term basis or intermittently in combination with non-opioid therapy in the chronic pain patient. Judicious prescribing, monitoring, and maintenance by the practitioner are imperative, particularly whenever considering the use of an opioid analgesic due to the abuse and addiction liabilities. For all prescribers of extended release and long-acting opioid analgesics, patient information as noted below is required. The CDC has released guidelines for opioid prescriptions. Numerous states have adopted prescription monitoring programs particularly targeting opioids and benzodiazapines. In general opioids should not be the first line therapy choice for chronic pain except for active cancer, palliative therapy or end of life care. Please visit www.cdc.gov/drugoverdose/prescribing/guideline.html for more specific details.

DOs and DON'Ts of Extended Release/Long-Acting Opioid Analgesics

DO:

- Read the **Medication Guide**
- Take your medicine exactly as prescribed
- Store your medicine away from children and in a safe place
- Check with pharmacy about disposal of unused medicine.
- Call your health care provider for medical advice about side effects. You may report side effects to the FDA at (800) FDA-1088

Call 911 or your local emergency service right away if:

- You take too much medicine
- You have trouble breathing or shortness of breath
- A child has taken this medicine

Talk to your health care provider:

- If the dose you are taking does not control your pain
- About any side effects you may be having
- About all the medicines you take, including over-the-counter medicines, vitamins, and dietary supplements

DON'T:

- **Do not** give your medicine to others
- **Do not** take medicine unless it was prescribed for you
- **Do not** stop taking your medicine without talking to your health care provider
- **Do not** break, chew, crush, dissolve, or inject your medicine. If you cannot swallow your medicine whole, talk to your health care provider
- **Do not** drink alcohol while taking this medicine

MILD PAIN

Acetaminophen on page 56
Aspirin (various products) on page 168
Diflunisal on page 506
Etodolac on page 668
Ibuprofen on page 851
Ketoprofen on page 945
Naproxen on page 1169

MODERATE/MODERATELY SEVERE PAIN

Dihydrocodeine, Aspirin, and Caffeine
HYDROcodone
Hydrocodone and Acetaminophen on page 825
Hydrocodone and Ibuprofen on page 828
Acetaminophen and Tramadol on page 65
Ibuprofen (various products) on page 851
Ketorolac (Systemic) on page 948
OxyMORphone on page 1274
Tapentadol on page 1526

An additional class of NSAIDs has been approved and indicated in the treatment of arthritis, COX-2 inhibitors. Celecoxib (Celebrex) has been approved for use in oral pain management.

The following is a guideline to use when prescribing codeine with either aspirin or acetaminophen (Tylenol):

Codeine No. 2 = codeine 15 mg
Codeine No. 3 = codeine 30 mg
Codeine No. 4 = codeine 60 mg

Example: ASA No. 3 = aspirin 325 mg + codeine 30 mg

HYDROCODONE PRODUCTS

Available hydrocodone oral products are listed in the following table and are scheduled as C-II controlled substances, indicating that prescriptions may either be oral or written. Thus, the prescriber may call in a prescription to the pharmacy for any of these hydrocodone products. All the formulations are combined with acetaminophen except for Vicoprofen, which contains ibuprofen. Most of these brand name drugs are available generically and the pharmacist will dispense the generic equivalent if available, unless the prescriber indicates otherwise.

Hydrocodone Analgesic Combination Oral Products (All Products DEA Schedule C-II)

HYDROcodone is available under numerous brand names with varying dosages and in combination with aspirin or ibuprofen.					
HYDROcodone Bitartrate	**Acetaminophen (APAP[a])**	**Other**	**Brand Name**	**Generic Available**	**Form**
5 mg	300 mg	–	Vicodin	Yes	Tablet
7.5 mg	300 mg	–	Vicodin ES	Yes	Tablet
7.5 mg	325 mg	–	Norco	Yes	Tablet
10 mg	325 mg	–	Norco	Yes	Tablet
10 mg	300 mg	–	Vicodin HP	Yes	Tablet
7.5 mg per 15 mL	325 mg per 15 mL	–	–	Yes	Elixir
7.5 mg	–	Ibuprofen 200 mg	Vicoprofen	Yes	Tablet
5 mg	–	Ibuprofen 200 mg	Ibudone; Reprexain	Yes	Tablet

Note: Although there are products still available with >325 mg of acetaminophen per dosage form, the deadline for reduction of acetaminophen was January 2014. The FDA will institute proceedings to withdraw approval of prescription combinations with >325 mg of acetaminophen.
[a]APAP is the common acronym for acetaminophen and is the abbreviation of the chemical name N-acetyl-para-aminophenol.

SEVERE PAIN

HYDROmorphone on page 839
OxyCODONE on page 1255
Oxycodone and Acetaminophen on page 1261
Oxycodone and Aspirin
Oxycodone and Ibuprofen

Oxycodone is available in a variety of dosages and combinations under numerous brand names.

SAMPLE PRESCRIPTIONS

Rx:

Ibuprofen 800 mg tablets
Disp: 16 tablets
Sig: Take 1 tablet 3 times/day as needed for pain

Note: For severe pain, can be given up to 4 times/day. Also available as 600 mg tablets

Rx:

Norco 10 mg hydrocodone/325 mg acetaminophen
Disp: 16 tablets
Sig: Take 1 or 2 tablets every 4 hours as needed for pain; not to exceed 8 tablets in 24 hours

Note: Restrictions: C-II; no refills
Ingredients: Hydrocodone 10 mg and acetaminophen 325 mg; available as generic equivalent

For additional sample prescriptions see Oral Pain - Sample Prescriptions on page 28

BACTERIAL INFECTIONS

Dental infection can occur for any number of reasons, primarily involving pulpal and periodontal infections. Secondary infections of the soft tissues as well as sinus infections pose special treatment challenges. The drugs of choice in treating most oral infections have been selected because of their efficacy in providing adequate blood levels for delivery to the oral tissues and their proven usefulness in managing dental infections. Penicillin remains the primary drug for treatment of dental infections of pulpal origin. The management of soft tissue infections may require the use of additional drugs.

ANTIMICROBIAL STEWARDSHIP

Antimicrobial stewardship refers to coordinated interventions designed to improve and measure the appropriate use of antimicrobials by promoting the selection of the optimal antimicrobial drug regimen, dose, duration of therapy, and route of administration. Antimicrobial stewards seek to achieve optimal clinical outcomes related to antimicrobial use, minimize toxicity and other adverse events, reduce the costs of health care for infections, and limit the selection for antimicrobial resistant strains. Currently, there are no national or coordinated legislative or regulatory mandates designed to optimize use of antimicrobial therapy through antimicrobial stewardship. Given the societal value of antimicrobials and their diminishing effectiveness due to antimicrobial resistance, groups like the ADA support broad implementation of antimicrobial stewardship programs across all health care settings (eg, hospitals, long-term care facilities, long-term acute care facilities, ambulatory surgical centers, dialysis centers, and private practices).

The American Dental Association (ADA) supports the responsible use of antibiotics. As part of this effort toward antibiotic stewardship, the ADA has adopted an evidence-based approach to guideline development, which has resulted in recommendations for decreased indications for and use of prophylactic antibiotics in people with heart conditions and those who have had joint replacements. Although there are some studies evaluating the appropriateness of antibiotic prescribing in dentistry, a recent paper in *JADA* suggests that it is likely that there are opportunities to improve prescribing practices.

OROFACIAL INFECTIONS

The basis of all infections is the successful multiplication of a microbial pathogen on or within a host. The pathogen is usually defined as any microorganism that has the capacity to cause disease. If the pathogen is bacterial in nature, antibiotic therapy is often indicated.

DIFFERENTIAL DIAGNOSIS OF ODONTOGENIC INFECTIONS

In choosing the appropriate antibiotic for therapy of a given infection, a number of important factors must be considered. First, the identity of the organism must be known. In odontogenic infections involving dental or periodontal structures, this is seldom the case. Secondly, accurate information regarding antibiotic susceptibility is required. Again, unless the organism has been identified, this is not possible. And thirdly, host factors must be taken into account, in terms of ability to absorb an antibiotic, to achieve appropriate host response. When clinical evidence of cellulitis or odontogenic infection has been found and the cardinal signs of swelling, inflammation, pain, and perhaps fever are present, the selection by the clinician of the appropriate antibiotic agent may lead to eradication.

CAUSES OF ODONTOGENIC INFECTIONS

Most acute orofacial infections are of odontogenic origin. Dental caries, resulting in infection of dental pulp, is the leading cause of odontogenic infection.

The major causative organisms involved in dental caries have been identified as members of the viridans (alpha-hemolytic) streptococci and include *Streptococcus mutans, Streptococcus sobrinus,* and *Streptococcus milleri*. Once the bacteria have breached the enamel they invade the dentin and eventually the dental pulp. An inflammatory reaction occurs in the pulp tissue resulting in necrosis and a lower tissue oxidation-reduction potential. At this point, the bacterial flora changes from predominantly aerobic to a more obligate anaerobic flora. The anaerobic gram-positive cocci *(Peptostreptococcus* species), and the anaerobic gram-negative rods, including *Bacteroides, Prevotella, Porphyromonas,* and *Fusobacterium* are most frequently present. An abscess usually forms at the apex of the involved tooth resulting in destruction of bone. Depending on the effectiveness of the host resistance and the virulence of the bacteria, the infection may spread through the marrow spaces, perforate the cortical plate, and enter the surrounding soft tissues.

The other major source of odontogenic infection arises from the anaerobic bacterial flora that inhabits the periodontal and supporting structures of the teeth. The most important potential pathogenic anaerobes within these structures are *Actinobacillus actinomycetemcomitans, Prevotella intermedius, Porphyromonas gingivalis, Fusobacterium nucleatum,* and *Eikenella corrodens*.

Most odontogenic infections (70%) have mixed aerobic and anaerobic flora. Pure aerobic infections are much less common and comprise ~5% incidence. Pure anaerobic infections make up the remaining 25% of odontogenic infections. Clinical correlates suggest that early odontogenic infections are characterized by rapid spreading and cellulitis with the absence of abscess formation. The bacteria are predominantly aerobic with gram-positive, alpha-hemolytic streptococci *(S. viridans)* the predominant pathogen. As the infection matures and becomes more severe, the microbial flora becomes a mix of aerobes and anaerobes. The anaerobes present are determined by the characteristic flora associated with the site of origin, whether it is pulpal or periodontal. Finally, as the infectious process becomes controlled by host defenses, the flora becomes primarily anaerobic. For example, Lewis and MacFarlane found a predominance of facultative oral streptococci in the early infections (<3 days of symptoms) with the later predominance of obligate anaerobes.

In a review of severe odontogenic infections, it was reported that Brook, et al, observed that 50% of odontogenic deep facial space infections yielded anaerobic bacteria only. Also, 44% of these infections yielded a mix of aerobic and anaerobic flora. The results of a study published in 1998 by Sakamoto, et al, were also described in the review. The study confirmed that odontogenic infections usually result from a synergistic interaction among several bacterial species and usually consist of an oral streptococcus and an oral anaerobic gram-negative rod. Sakamoto and his group reported a high level of the *Streptococcus milleri* group of aerobic gram-positive cocci, and high levels of oral anaerobes, including the *Peptostreptococcus* species and the *Prevotella, Porphyromonas,* and *Fusobacterium* species.

Oral streptococci, especially of the *Streptococcus milleri* group, can invade soft tissues initially, thus preparing an environment conducive to growth of anaerobic bacteria. Obligate oral anaerobes are dependent on nutrients synthesized by the aerobes. Thus the anaerobes appear ~3 days after onset of symptoms. Early infections are thus caused primarily by the aerobic streptococci (exquisitely sensitive to penicillin) and late infections are caused by the anaerobes (frequently resistant to penicillin).

It appears logical, as Flynn has noted, to separate infections presenting early in their course from those presenting later when selecting empiric antibiotics of choice for odontogenic infections.

If the patient is not allergic to penicillin, penicillin VK still remains the empiric antibiotic of first choice to treat mild or early odontogenic infections (see Table 1). In patients allergic to penicillin, clindamycin clearly remains the alternative antibiotic for treatment of mild or early infections. Secondary alternative antibiotics still recognized as useful in these conditions are cephalexin (Keflex), or other first generation cephalosporins available in oral dose forms. The first generation cephalosporins can be used in both penicillin-allergic and nonallergic patients, providing that the penicillin allergy is not the anaphylactoid type.

PENICILLIN VK

The spectrum of antibacterial action of penicillin VK is consistent with most of the organisms identified in odontogenic infections (see Table 2). Penicillin VK is a beta-lactam antibiotic, as are all the penicillins and cephalosporins, and is bactericidal against gram-positive cocci and the major pathogens of mixed anaerobic infections. It elicits virtually no adverse effects in the absence of allergy and is relatively low in cost. Adverse drug reactions occurring in >10% of patients include mild diarrhea, nausea, and oral candidiasis. To treat odontogenic infections and other orofacial infections, the usual dose for adults and children >12 years of age is 500 mg every 6 hours for at least 7 days (see Table 4). The daily dose for children ≤12 years of age is 25 to 50 mg/kg of body weight in divided doses every 6 to 8 hours (see Table 4). The patient must be instructed to take the penicillin continuously for the duration of therapy.

After oral dosing, penicillin VK achieves peak serum levels within 1 hour. Penicillin VK may be given with meals; however, blood concentrations may be slightly higher when penicillin is given on an empty stomach. The preferred dosing is 1 hour before meals or 2 hours after meals to ensure maximum serum levels. Penicillin VK diffuses into most body tissues, including oral tissues, soon after dosing. Hepatic metabolism accounts for <30% of the elimination of penicillins. Elimination is primarily renal. The nonmetabolized penicillin is excreted largely unchanged in the urine by glomerular filtration and active tubular secretion. Penicillins cross the placenta and are distributed in breast milk. Penicillin VK, like all beta-lactam antibiotics, causes death of bacteria by inhibiting synthesis of the bacterial cell wall during cell division. This action is dependent on the ability of penicillins to reach and bind to penicillin-binding proteins (PBPs) located on the inner membrane of the bacterial cell wall. PBPs (which include transpeptidases, carboxypeptidases, and endopeptidases) are enzymes that are involved in the terminal stages of assembling and reshaping the bacterial cell wall during growth. Penicillins and beta-lactams bind to and inactivate PBPs resulting in lysis of the cell due to weakening of the cell wall.

Penicillin VK is considered a "narrow spectrum" antibiotic. This class of antibiotics produces less alteration of normal microflora thereby reducing the incidence of superinfection. Also, its bactericidal action will reduce the numbers of microorganisms resulting in less reliance on host-phagocyte mechanisms for eradication of the pathogen.

Among patients, 0.7% to 10% are allergic to penicillins. There is no evidence that any single penicillin derivative differs from others in terms of incidence or severity when administered orally. About 85% of allergic reactions associated with penicillin VK are delayed and take >2 days to develop. This allergic response manifests as skin rashes characterized as erythema and bullous eruptions. This type of allergic reaction is mild, reversible, and usually responds to concurrent antihistamine therapy, such as diphenhydramine (Benadryl). Severe reactions of angioedema have occurred, characterized by marked swelling of the lips, tongue, face, and periorbital tissues. Patients with a history of penicillin allergy must never be given penicillin VK for treatment of infections. The alternative antibiotic is clindamycin. If the allergy is the delayed type and not the anaphylactoid type, a first generation cephalosporin may be used as an alternate antibiotic.

CLINDAMYCIN

In the event of penicillin allergy, clindamycin is clearly an alternative of choice in treating mild or early odontogenic infections (see Table 1). It is highly effective against almost all oral pathogens. Clindamycin is active against most aerobic gram-positive cocci, including staphylococci, *S. pneumoniae*, other streptococci, and anaerobic gram-negative and gram-positive organisms, including bacteroides (see Table 3). Clindamycin is not effective against mycoplasma or gram-negative aerobes. It inhibits protein synthesis in bacteria through binding to the 50 S subunit of bacterial ribosomes. Clindamycin has bacteriostatic actions at low concentrations, but is known to elicit bactericidal effects against susceptible bacteria at higher concentrations of drug at the site of infection.

The usual adult oral dose of clindamycin to treat orofacial infections of odontogenic origin is 150 to 450 mg every 6 hours for 7 to 10 days. The usual daily oral dose for children is 8 to 25 mg/kg in 3 to 4 equally divided doses (see Table 4).

Following oral administration of a 150 mg or a 300 mg dose on an empty stomach, 90% of the dose is rapidly absorbed into the bloodstream and peak serum concentrations are attained in 45 to 60 minutes. Administration with food does not markedly impair absorption into the bloodstream. Clindamycin serum levels exceed the minimum inhibitory concentration for bacterial growth for at least 6 hours after the recommended doses. The serum half-life is 2 to 3 hours. Clindamycin is distributed effectively to most body tissues, including saliva and bone. Its small molecular weight enables it to more readily enter bacterial cytoplasm and to penetrate bone. It is partially metabolized in the liver to active and inactive metabolites and is excreted in the urine, bile, and feces.

Adverse effects caused by clindamycin can include abdominal pain, nausea, vomiting, and diarrhea. Hypersensitivity reactions are rare, but have resulted in skin rash. Approximately 1% of clindamycin users develop pseudomembranous colitis characterized by severe diarrhea, abdominal cramps, and excretion of blood or mucus in the stools. The mechanism is disruption of normal bacterial flora of the colon, which leads to colonization of the bacterium *Clostridium difficile*. This bacterium releases endotoxins that cause mucosal damage and inflammation. Symptoms usually develop 2 to 9 days after initiation of therapy, but may not occur until several weeks after taking the drug. If significant diarrhea develops, clindamycin therapy should be discontinued immediately. Theoretically, any antibiotic can cause antibiotic-associated colitis and clindamycin probably has an undeserved reputation associated with this condition.

Sandor, et al, also notes that odontogenic infections are typically polymicrobial and that anaerobes outnumber aerobes by at least four-fold. The penicillins have historically been used as the first-line therapy in these cases, but increasing rates of resistance have lowered their usefulness. Bacterial resistance to penicillins is predominantly achieved through production of beta-lactamases. Clindamycin, because of its relatively broad spectrum of activity and resistance to beta-lactamase degradation, is an attractive first-line therapy in treatment of odontogenic infections. Recently, researchers have established a causal link between exposure to antibiotics and antibiotic resistance and they also have established evidence that the development of resistance to one class of antibiotic may confer persistent increased resistance to other antibiotic classes.

FIRST GENERATION CEPHALOSPORINS

Antibiotics of this class, which are available in oral dosage forms, include cefadroxil (Duricef) and cephalexin (Keflex). The first generation cephalosporins are alternates to penicillin VK in the treatment of odontogenic infections based on bactericidal effectiveness against the oral streptococci. These drugs are most active against gram-positive cocci, but are not very active against many anaerobes. First generation cephalosporins are indicated as alternatives in early infections because they are effective in killing the aerobes. First generation cephalosporins are active against gram-positive staphylococci and streptococci, but not enterococci. They are active against many gram-negative aerobic bacilli, including *E. coli, Klebsiella*, and *Proteus mirabilis*. They are inactive against methicillin-resistant *S. aureus* and penicillin-resistant *S. pneumoniae*. The gram-negative aerobic cocci, *Moraxella catarrhalis*, portrays variable sensitivity to first generation cephalosporins.

Cephalexin (Keflex) is the first generation cephalosporin often used to treat odontogenic infections. The usual adult dose is 250 to 1,000 mg every 6 hours with a maximum of 4 g/day. Children's dose is 25 to 50 mg/kg/day in divided doses every 6 hours; for severe infections: 50 to 100 mg/kg/day in divided doses every 6 hours with a maximum dose of 3 g/day (see Table 4).

Cephalexin (Keflex) causes diarrhea in about 1% to 10% of patients. About 90% of the cephalexin is excreted unchanged in urine.

SECOND GENERATION CEPHALOSPORINS

The second generation cephalosporins such as cefaclor (Ceclor) have better activity against some of the anaerobes including some *Bacteroides, Peptococcus*, and *Peptostreptococcus* species. Cefaclor (Ceclor) and cefuroxime (Ceftin) have been used to treat early stage infections. These antibiotics have the advantage of twice-a-day dosing. The usual oral adult dose of cefaclor is 250 to 500 mg every 8 hours (or daily dose can be given in 2 divided doses) for at least 7 days. Children's dose is 20 to 40 mg/kg/day divided every 8 to 12 hours with a maximum dose of 2 g/day. The usual adult oral dose of cefuroxime is 250 to 500 mg twice daily. Children's dose is 20 mg/kg/day (maximum: 500 mg/day) in 2 divided doses.

The cephalosporins inhibit bacterial cell wall synthesis by binding to one or more of the penicillin-binding proteins (PBPs), which in turn inhibit the final transpeptidation step of peptidoglycan synthesis in bacterial cell walls, thus inhibiting cell wall biosynthesis. Bacteria eventually lyse due to ongoing activity of cell wall autolytic enzymes while cell wall assembly is arrested.

BACTERIAL RESISTANCE TO ANTIBIOTICS

If a patient with an early stage odontogenic infection does not respond to penicillin VK within 24 to 36 hours, it is evidence of the presence of resistant bacteria. Bacterial resistance to the penicillins is predominantly achieved through the production of beta-lactamase. A switch to beta-lactamase-stable antibiotics should be made. For example, Kuriyama, et al, reported that past beta-lactam administration increases the emergence of beta-lactamase-producing bacteria and that beta-lactamase-stable antibiotics should be prescribed to patients with unresolved infections who have received beta-lactams. These include either clindamycin or amoxicillin/clavulanic acid (Augmentin). Doses are listed in Table 4.

In the past, all *S. viridans* species were uniformly susceptible to beta-lactam antibiotics. However, over the years, there has been a significant increase in resistant strains. Resistance may also be due to alteration of penicillin-binding proteins. Consequently, drugs which combine a beta-lactam antibiotic with a beta-lactamase inhibitor, such as amoxicillin/clavulanic acid (Augmentin), may no longer be more effective than the penicillin VK alone. In these situations, clindamycin is the recommended alternate antibiotic.

Evidence suggests that empirical use of penicillin VK as the first-line drug in treating early odontogenic infections is still the best way to ensure the minimal production of resistant bacteria to other classes of antibiotics, since any overuse of clindamycin or amoxicillin/clavulanic acid (Augmentin) is minimized in these situations. There is concern that overuse of clindamycin could contribute to development of clindamycin-resistant pathogens.

In late odontogenic infections, it is suggested that clindamycin be considered the first-line antibiotic to treat these infections. The dose of clindamycin would be the same as that used to treat early infections (see Table 4). In these infections, anaerobic bacteria usually predominate. Since penicillin spectrum includes anaerobes, penicillin VK is also useful as an empiric drug of first choice in these infections. It has been reported, however, that the penicillin resistance rate among patients with serious and late infections is in the 35% to 50% range. Therefore, if penicillin is the drug of first choice and the patient does not respond within 24 to 36 hours, a resistant pathogen should be suspected and a switch to clindamycin be made. Clindamycin, because of its relatively broad spectrum of activity and resistance to beta-lactamase degradation, is an attractive first-line therapy in the treatment of these infections. Another alternative is to add a second drug to the penicillin (eg, metronidazole [Flagyl]). Consequently, for those infections not responding to treatment with penicillin, the addition of a second drug (eg, metronidazole), not a beta-lactam or macrolide, is likely to be more effective. Bacterial resistance to metronidazole is very rare. The metronidazole dose is listed in Table 4.

Nonionized metronidazole is readily taken up by anaerobic organisms. Its selectivity for anaerobic bacteria is a result of the ability of these organisms to reduce metronidazole to its active form within the bacterial cell. The electron transport proteins necessary for this reaction are found only in anaerobic bacteria. Reduced metronidazole then disrupts DNA's helical structure, thereby inhibiting bacterial nucleic acid synthesis leading to death of the organism. Consequently, metronidazole is not effective against gram-positive aerobic cocci and most *Actinomyces, Lactobacillus,* and *Propionibacterium* species. Since most odontogenic infections are mixed aerobic and anaerobic, metronidazole should rarely be used as a single agent but it can be useful when combined with penicillins. Alternatively, one can switch to a beta-lactamase resistant drug (eg, amoxicillin/clavulanic acid [Augmentin]). The beta-lactamase resistant penicillins including methicillin, oxacillin, cloxacillin, dicloxacillin, and nafcillin, are only effective against gram-positive cocci and have no activity against anaerobes, hence, should not be used to treat the late stage odontogenic infections.

RESISTANCE IN ODONTOGENIC INFECTIONS

Recently, there has been an alarming increase in the incidence of resistant bacterial isolates in odontogenic infections. Many anaerobic bacteria have developed resistance to beta-lactam antibiotics via production of beta-lactamase enzymes. These include several species of *Prevotella, Porphyromonas, Fusobacterium nucleatum,* and *Campylobacter gracilis. Fusobacterium*, especially in combination with *S. viridans* species, has been associated with severe odontogenic infections. Often, they are resistant to macrolides. Clindamycin is the empiric drug of first choice in these patients.

SEVERE INFECTIONS

In patients hospitalized for severe odontogenic infections, IV antibiotics are indicated and clindamycin is the clear empiric antibiotic of choice. Alternative antibiotics include an IV combination of penicillin and metronidazole or IV ampicillin-sulbactam (Unasyn). Clindamycin, IV cephalosporins (if penicillin allergy is not the anaphylactoid type), and ciprofloxacin have been used in patients allergic to penicillins. Flynn notes that *Eikenella corrodens*, an occasional oral pathogen, is resistant to clindamycin. Ciprofloxacin is an excellent antibiotic for this organism.

Recently approved telavancin (Vibativ) has been approved for severe antibiotic resistant infections. Brand new mechanism of antibacterial effect:

1. Works like vancomycin and penicillins to block bacterial cell wall synthesis at D-alanine-D-alanine portion of cell wall.
2. Disrupts bacterial cell membrane potential due to presence of a lipophilic side chain of telavancin molecule.

Scheduled for use in complicated skin and skin structure infections caused by MRSA, and vancomycin-susceptible enterococcus, strept pyogenes, and strept anginosus.

ERYTHROMYCIN, CLARITHROMYCIN, AND AZITHROMYCIN

In the past, erythromycins were considered highly effective antibiotics for treating odontogenic infections, especially in penicillin allergy. At the present time, however, the current high resistance rates of both oral streptococci and oral anaerobes have rendered the entire macrolide family of antibiotics obsolete for odontogenic infections. Montgomery has noted that resistance develops rapidly to macrolides and there may be cross-resistance between erythromycin and newer macrolides, particularly among streptococci and staphylococci. Hardee has stated that erythromycin is no longer very useful because of resistant pathogens. The antibacterial spectrum of the erythromycin family is similar to penicillin VK. Erythromycins are effective against streptococcus, staphylococcus, and gram-negative aerobes, such as *H. influenzae, M. catarrhalis, N. gonorrhoeae, Bordetella pertussis,* and *Legionella pneumophilia*. Erythromycins are considered narrow spectrum antibiotics.

Both azithromycin and clarithromycin have been used to treat acute odontogenic infections. This is because of the following spectrum of actions: Clarithromycin shows good activity against many gram-positive and gram-negative aerobic and anaerobic organisms. It is active against methicillin-sensitive *S. aureus* and most streptococcus species. *S. aureus* strains resistant to erythromycin are resistant to clarithromycin. Clarithromycin is active against *H. influenzae*. It is similar to erythromycin in effectiveness against anaerobic gram-positive cocci and *Bacteroides sp.* Clarithromycin has been suggested as an alternative antibiotic if the prescriber wants to give an antibiotic from the macrolide family (see Table 3). The recommended oral adult dose is 500 mg twice daily for 7 days.

Azithromycin is active against staphylococci, including *S. aureus* and *S. epidermitis*, as well as streptococci, such as *S. pyogenes* and *S. pneumoniae*. Erythromycin-resistant strains of staphylococcus, enterococcus, and streptococcus, including methicillin-resistant *S. aureus*, are also resistant to azithromycin. It has excellent activity against *H. influenzae*. Inhibition of anaerobes, such as *Clostridium perfringens*, is better with azithromycin than with erythromycin. Inhibition of

Bacteroides fragilis and other bacteroides species by azithromycin is comparable to erythromycin. Both azithromycin and clarithromycin are presently recommended as alternatives in the prophylactic regimen for prevention of bacterial endocarditis. This past May, the FDA notified health care professionals that it is aware of the study published in the *New England Journal of Medicine* (Ray 2012) reporting a small increase in cardiovascular deaths and in the risk of death from any cause in persons treated with a 5-day course of azithromycin (Zithromax) compared to persons treated with amoxicillin, ciprofloxacin, or no drug. The FDA is reviewing the results from this study and will communicate any new information on azithromycin and this study or the potential risk of QT interval prolongation after the agency has completed its review.

Patients taking azithromycin should not stop taking their medicine without talking to their health care provider. Health care providers should be aware of the potential for QT interval prolongation and heart arrhythmias when prescribing or administering any macrolide antibiotic.

AMOXICILLIN

Some clinicians select amoxicillin over penicillin VK as the penicillin of choice to empirically treat odontogenic infections. Except for coverage of *Haemophilus influenzae* in acute sinus and otitis media infections, amoxicillin does not offer any advantage over penicillin VK for treatment of odontogenic infections. It is less effective than penicillin VK for aerobic gram-positive cocci, and similar to penicillin for coverage of anaerobes. Although it does provide coverage against gram-negative enteric bacteria, this is not needed to treat odontogenic infections, except in immunosuppressed patients where these organisms may be present. If one adheres to the principle of using the most effective narrow spectrum antibiotic, amoxicillin should not be favored over penicillin VK.

Note: The ADA Council on Scientific Affairs has published a review on the subject of antibiotic interaction with oral contraceptives in which a clear statement of the dental professional's responsibility was made. In essence, it was concluded that in any situation where a dentist is planning to prescribe a course of antibiotics, alternative/additional means of contraception should be recommended to the oral contraceptive users. Specifically, patients should be told about the potential for antibiotics to lower the usefulness of oral contraceptives and advised to consult their physician about nonhormonal contraceptive techniques while continuing their oral contraceptive regimen. Even though there is minimal scientific data supporting this position, the risk of possible unwanted pregnancies warrants this simple approach for professionals licensed to prescribe antibiotics (*JADA*. 2002;133:880).

The following tables have been adapted from Wynn RL, Bergman SA, Meiller TF, Crossley HL. Antibiotics in treating orofacial infections of odontogenic origin. *Gen Dent*. 2001;47(3):238-252.

Amoxicillin on page 121
Amoxicillin and Clavulanate on page 126
Cephalexin on page 333
Cefditoren on page 316
Ceftibuten on page 325
Chlorhexidine Gluconate on page 344
Chlorpheniramine on page 377
Clarithromycin on page 377
Clindamycin (Systemic) on page 382
Dicloxacillin on page 502
Erythromycin (Systemic) on page 596
Gemifloxacin on page 792
Loratadine and Pseudoephedrine on page 1019
MetroNIDAZOLE (Systemic) on page 1110
Mouthwash (Antiseptic) on page 1150
Moxifloxacin (Systemic) on page 1151
Oxymetazoline (Nasal) on page 1273
Penicillin V Potassium on page 1311
Pseudoephedrine on page 1404
Tetracycline on page 1550

Table 1. Empiric Antibiotics of Choice for Odontogenic Infections

Type of Infection	Antibiotic of Choice
Early (first 3 days of symptoms)	Penicillin VK, amoxicillin Clindamycin Cephalexin (or other first generation cephalosporin)[a]
No improvement in 24 to 36 hours	Beta-lactamase-stable antibiotic: Clindamycin or amoxicillin/clavulanic acid
Penicillin allergy	Clindamycin Cephalexin (if penicillin allergy is not anaphylactoid type) Clarithromycin (Biaxin)[b]
Late (>3 days)	Clindamycin Penicillin VK-metroNIDAZOLE, amoxicillin-metroNIDAZOLE
Penicillin allergy	Clindamycin

[a]For better patient compliance, second generation cephalosporins (cefaclor; cefuroxime) at twice daily dosing have been used; see text.

[b]A macrolide useful in patients allergic to penicillin, given as twice daily dosing for better patient compliance; see text.

Table 2. Penicillin VK: Antibacterial Spectrum

Gram-Positive Cocci	Oral Anaerobes
Streptococci	*Bacteroides*
Nonresistant staphylococci[a]	*Porphyromonas*
Pneumococci	*Prevotella*
	Peptococci
Gram-Negative Cocci	Peptostreptococci
Neisseria meningitides	*Actinomyces*
Neisseria gonorrhoeae	*Veillonella*
	Eubacterium
Gram-Positive Rods	*Eikenella*
Bacillus	*Capnocytophaga*
Corynebacterium	*Campylobacter*
Clostridium	*Fusobacterium*
	Others

[a]Nonresistant staphylococcus represents a small portion of community-acquired strains of *S. aureus* (5% to 15%). Most strains of *S. aureus* and *S. epidermitis* produce beta-lactamases, which destroy penicillins.

Table 3. Clindamycin: Antibacterial Spectrum[a]

Gram-Positive Cocci	Anaerobes[b]
Streptococci[c]	**Gram-Negative Bacilli**
S. aureus[d]	*Bacteroides* species including *B. fragilis*
Penicillinase and nonpenicillinase-producing staphylococcus	*B. melaninogenicus* *Fusobacterium species*
S. epidermitis	**Gram-Positive Nonspore-Forming Bacilli**
Pneumococci	*Propionibacterium*
	Eubacterium
	Actinomyces species
	Gram-Positive Cocci
	Peptococcus
	Peptostreptococcus
	Microaerophilic streptococci

[a]In vitro activity against isolates; information from manufacturer's package insert

[b] *Clostridia* are more resistant than most anaerobes to clindamycin. Most *Clostridium perfringens* are susceptible but *C. sporogens* and *C. tertium* are frequently resistant.

[c]Except *S. faecalis*

[d]Some staph strains originally resistant to erythromycin rapidly develop resistance to clindamycin.

Table 4. Oral Dose Ranges of Antibiotics Useful in Treating Odontogenic Infections[a]

Clinicians must select specific dose and regimen from ranges available to be prescribed based on clinical judgment		
Antibiotic	**Dosage**	
	Children	**Adults**
Penicillin VK	≤12 years: 25 to 50 mg/kg body weight in equally divided doses every 6 to 8 hours for at least 7 days; maximum dose: 3 g/day	>12 years: 500 mg q6h for at least 7 days
Clindamycin	8 to 25 mg/kg in 3 to 4 equally divided doses	150 to 450 mg q6h for at least 7 days; maximum dose: 1.8 g/day
Cephalexin (Keflex)	25 to 50 mg/kg/day in divided doses q6h Severe infection: 50 to 100 mg/kg/day in divided doses q6h; maximum dose: 3 g per 24 hours	250 to 1,000 mg q6h; maximum dose: 4 g/day
Amoxicillin	<40 kg: 20 to 40 mg (amoxicillin)/kg/day in divided doses q8h >40 kg: 250 to 500 mg q8h or 875 mg q12h for at least 7 days; maximum dose 2 g/day	>40 kg: 250 to 500 mg q8h or 875 mg q12h for at least 7 days; maximum dose: 2 g/day

Table 4. Oral Dose Ranges of Antibiotics Useful in Treating Odontogenic Infections[a] *(continued)*

Clinicians must select specific dose and regimen from ranges available to be prescribed based on clinical judgment		
Antibiotic	Dosage	
	Children	Adults
Amoxicillin/clavulanic acid (Augmentin)	<40 kg: 20 to 40 mg (amoxicillin)/kg/day in divided doses q8h >40 kg: 250 to 500 mg q8h or 875 mg q12h for at least 7 days; maximum dose 2 g/day	>40 kg: 250 to 500 mg q8h or 875 mg q12h for at least 7 days; maximum dose: 2 g/day
MetroNIDAZOLE (Flagyl)		500 mg every 6 to 8 hours for 7 to 10 days; maximum dose: 4 g/day

[a]For doses of other antibiotics, see monographs

SAMPLE PRESCRIPTIONS

Rx:

Penicillin V potassium 500 mg
Disp: 40 tablets
Sig: Take 1 tablet 4 times/day for 7 to 10 days (consider a loading dose of 1 g for acute infection)

Rx:

Clindamycin 300 mg
Disp: 40 capsules
Sig: Take 1 capsule 4 times/day for 7 to 10 days

Note: Prescription usually selected for patients allergic to penicillin; may be prescribed for 3 or 4 times/day. This prescription can be continued for treatment of some infections >1 month; however, risk of *Clostridium difficile* infection increases with long-term clindamycin use. Patient should be cautioned to take clindamycin with food and contact health care provider if diarrhea develops even after antibiotic course is completed. Probiotics may help but evidence is conflicted on true efficacy.

Rx:

Amoxicillin 500 mg
Disp: 30 capsules or tablets
Sig: Take 1 capsule or tablet 3 times/day for 7 to 10 days

For additional sample prescriptions see Bacterial Infections and Periodontal Diseases - Sample Prescriptions on page 32

SINUSITIS TREATMENT

Sinusitis represents a common condition which may present with confounding dental complaints. Sinusitis (or rhinosinusitis) is an inflammation of the mucous membrane that lines the paranasal sinuses. It is classified into several categories:

- Acute rhinosinusitis: A new episode that may last ≤4 weeks
- Recurrent acute rhinosinusitis: ≥4 separate episodes of acute sinusitis that occur within 1 year
- Chronic rhinosinusitis: Signs and symptoms last for >12 weeks

All of these types of sinusitis have similar symptoms and are often difficult to distinguish. Acute sinusitis is very common. It has been estimated that 90% of adults have had sinusitis at some point in their lives.

Treatment is sometimes instituted by the dentist, but due to the often chronic and recurrent nature of sinusitis, early involvement of an otolaryngologist is advised. Most sinusitis is brought on by a nasopharyngeal viral infection best treated by sinus lavage, but some infections may require antibiotics of varying spectrum as well as requiring the management of sinus congestion. Although amoxicillin is usually adequate, many otolaryngologists initially prescribe Augmentin. Second-generation cephalosporins and clarithromycin are sometimes used, depending on the chronicity of the problem. Although not the ideal drug for general dental and/or periodontal infections, levofloxacin (Levoquin) is approved for treatment of acute bacterial rhinosinusitis.

For examples of sample prescriptions see Sinus Infection Treatment - Sample Prescriptions on page 38

LYME DISEASE

Lyme disease is a challenging infectious, toxic disease that may exhibit many different symptoms. The clinical picture of Lyme disease can be similar to fibromyalgia, including chronic fatigue, joint pain (arthralgia), or muscle, fibrous tissue, and tendon pain. Lyme disease can also manifest primarily as a neurological disorder, including fatigue and other neurological symptoms. Early, aggressive, and comprehensive treatment improves the prognosis tremendously.

Chronic Persistent Infection

Some symptoms and signs of Lyme disease may not appear until weeks, months, or years after a tick bite. This typically involves intermittent episodes of joint pain or numerous neurological symptoms such as meningitis, Bell's palsy, dysfunction of cardiac rhythm, and migratory pain to joints, tendons, muscle, and bone. Arthritis is most likely to appear as brief bouts of pain and swelling, usually in one or more large joints; however, any combination of symptoms can be present.

In a minority of individuals (~11%), development of chronic Lyme arthritis may lead to erosion of cartilage and/or bone. Other clinical manifestations associated with chronic Lyme arthritis include neurologic complications, such as disturbances in memory, mood, or sleep patterns, and sensations of numbness and tingling.

Oral symptoms can occur as a mimic to atypical facial pain, burning mouth, or other orofacial symptoms with little or no organic basis identified. Although symptoms similar to fibromyalgia are common, the two conditions are not currently thought to be directly connected.

Diagnosis of Lyme Disease

Lyme disease is diagnosed based on history, clinical symptoms, and response to therapy. No test can conclusively rule out lyme disease since routine laboratory tests are usually normal. Liver enzymes may be slightly elevated. The erythrocyte sediment rate (ESR) is most often normal, distinguishing Lyme disease from some of the purely inflammatory disorders such as rheumatoid arthritis or lupus; however, overlap between Lyme disease and autoimmune diseases frequently occurs. A prompt biopsy of the erythema migrans rash can confirm *Borrelia burgdorferi* in the culture. Serological (blood) tests currently available for Lyme disease caused by *B. burgdorferi* include, the immunologically based ELISA and Western blot assays. Clinically, over 75% of patients with Lyme disease are negative by ELISA but positive by Western blot, adding to the complexity of diagnosis (Honegr 2001).

Treatment

Antibiotics are the foundation of Lyme disease therapy. Oral therapy with doxycycline, cefuroxime, or amoxicillin is appropriate for early cases of Lyme disease. Parenteral therapy, usually IV administration, may be used for patients with neurologic involvement, severe arthritis, or any life-threatening manifestation of Lyme disease, such as complete heart block.

Treatment of 2 to 4 weeks is usually effective if initiated at the first appearance of a erythema migrans rash. In patients with symptoms present for more than 6 months, the treatment course may need to be more prolonged or a retreatment course of varying length may be needed. Consult the American Lyme Disease Foundation for treatment suggestions (available at http://www.aldf.com/raad.shtml).

FREQUENTLY ASKED QUESTIONS

What is the best antibiotic modality for treating dental infections?

Penicillin is still the drug of choice for treatment of infections in and around the oral cavity. Phenoxymethyl penicillin (Pen VK) long has been the most commonly selected antibiotic. In penicillin-allergic individuals, clindamycin may be an appropriate consideration, prescribing 300 mg as a loading dose followed by 150 mg 4 times/day would be an appropriate regimen for a dental infection. In general, if there is no response to Pen VK, then Augmentin may be a good alternative in the nonpenicillin-allergic patient because of its slightly altered spectrum. Recommendations would include that the patient should take the drug with food.

Is there cross-allergenicity between the cephalosporins and penicillin?

The incidence of cross-allergenicity is 5% to 8% in the overall population. If a patient has demonstrated a Type I hypersensitivity reaction to penicillin, namely urticaria or anaphylaxis, then this incidence would increase to 20%.

Is there definitely an interaction between contraception agents and antibiotics?

There are well founded interactions between contraceptives and antibiotics. The best instructions that a patient could be given by their dentist are that should an antibiotic be necessary and the dentist is aware that the patient is on contraceptives, and if the patient is using chemical contraceptives, the patient should seriously consider additional means of contraception during the antibiotic management.

Are antibiotics necessary in diabetic mellitus patients?

In the management of diabetes, control of the diabetic status is the key factor relative to all morbidity issues. If a patient is well controlled, then antibiotics will likely not be necessary. However, in patients where the control is questionable or where they have recently been given a different drug regimen for their diabetes or if they are being titrated to an appropriate level of either insulin or oral hypoglycemic agents during these periods of time, the dentist might consider preprocedural antibiotics to be efficacious.

Do nonsteroidal anti-inflammatory drugs interfere with blood pressure medication?

At the current time there is no clear evidence that NSAIDs interfere with any of the blood pressure medications that are currently in usage.

REFERENCES AND SELECTED READINGS

American Dental Association-Appointed Members of the Expert Writing and Voting Panels Contributing to the Development of American Academy of Orthopedic Surgeons Appropriate Use Criteria. American Dental Association guidance for utilizing appropriate use criteria in the management of the care of patients with orthopedic implants undergoing dental procedures. *J Am Dent Assoc.* 2017;148(2):57-59.

Centers for Disease Control and Prevention. Antibiotic/Antimicrobial Resistance U.S. Department of Health & Human Services. Accessed May 20, 2016.

Fluent MT, Jacobsen PL, Hicks LA, OSAP. Considerations for responsible antibiotic use in dentistry. *J Am Dent Assoc.* 2016;147(8):683-686

Flynn TR. What are the antibiotics of choice for odontogenic infections, and how long should the treatment course last? *Oral Maxillofac Surg Clin North Am.* 2011;23(4):519-536.

Hayward G, Heneghan C, Perera R, Thompson M. Intranasal corticosteroids in management of acute sinusitis: a systematic review and meta-analysis. *Ann Fam Med.* 2012;10(3):241-249.

Honegr K, Hulínská D, Dostál V, et al. Persistence of *Borrelia burgdorferi* sensu lato in patients with *Lyme borreliosis*. *Epidemiol Mikrobiol Imunol*. 2001;50(1):10-16.

Mayer G. Antibiotics – protein synthesis, nucleic acid synthesis and metabolism. *Medical Microbiology*. 6th ed. Murray PR, Rosenthal KS, Pfaller MA, eds. Elseiver; 2010;Chapter 20.

Palmer C. ADA News: ADA supports responsible antibiotic use. American Dental Association. June 15, 2015. Accessed May 20, 2016.

Quinn RH, Murray JN, Pezold R, Sevarino KS. The American Academy of Orthopaedic Surgeons Appropriate Use Criteria for the Management of Patients with Orthopaedic Implants Undergoing Dental Procedures. *J Bone Joint Surg Am*. 2017;99(2):161-163.

Ray WA, Murray KT, Hall K, et al. Azithromycin and the risk of cardiovascular death. *N Engl J Med*. 2012;366:1881-1890.

Rosenfeld RM, Andes D, Bhattacharyya N, et al. Clinical practice guideline: adult sinusitis. *Otolaryngol Head Neck Surg*. 2007;137(3 Suppl):S1-S31.

Smith SR, Montgomery LG, Williams JW Jr. Treatment of mild to moderate sinusitis. *Arch Intern Med*. 2012;172(6):510-513.

Sollecito TP, Abt E, Lockhart PB, et al. The use of prophylactic antibiotics prior to dental procedures in patients with prosthetic joints: Evidence-based clinical practice guideline for dental practitioners–a report of the American Dental Association Council on Scientific Affairs. *J Am Dent Assoc*. 2015;146(1):11-16 e8.

Wilson W, Taubert KA, Gewitz M, et al. Prevention of infective endocarditis: guidelines from the American Heart Association: a guideline from the American Heart Association Rheumatic Fever, Endocarditis and Kawasaki Disease Committee, Council on Cardiovascular Disease in the Young, and the Council on Clinical Cardiology, Council on Cardiovascular Surgery and Anesthesia, and the Quality of Care and Outcomes Research Interdisciplinary Working Group. *J Am Dent Assoc*. 2008;139 Suppl:3S-24S.

Wormser GP, Dattwyler RJ, Shapiro ED, et al. The clinical assessment, treatment, and prevention of lyme disease, human granulocytic anaplasmosis, and babesiosis: clinical practice guidelines by the Infectious Diseases Society of America. *Clin Infect Dis*. 2006;43(9):1089-1134.

Zalmanovici A, Yaphe J. Intranasal steroids for acute sinusitis. *Cochrane Database Syst Rev*. 2009;(4):CD005149.

PERIODONTAL DISEASES

Periodontal diseases are common to mankind affecting, according to some epidemiologic studies, greater than 80% of the worldwide population. The conditions refer primarily to diseases that are caused by accumulations of dental plaque and the subsequent immune response of the host to the bacteria and toxins present in this plaque. Although most of the organisms that have been implicated in advanced periodontal diseases are anaerobic in nature, some aerobes contribute by either coaggregation with the anaerobic species or direct involvement with specific disease types.

As a group of diseases, the soft tissues are affected, supporting the teeth (ie, gingiva) leading to the term gingivitis or inflammation of gingival structures and those conditions that affect the bone and ligament supporting the teeth (ie, periodontitis) result from the infection and/or inflammation of these structures. Diseases of the periodontia can be further subdivided into various types including chronic periodontitis (localized and generalized, mainly in adults), aggressive periodontitis (localized and generalized, including previously classified), early onset periodontitis, prepubertal periodontitis, and rapidly progressing periodontitis. In addition, periodontitis as a manifestation of systemic diseases (hematologic, genetic disorders, not otherwise specified) as well as a necrotizing type due to specific conditions associated with predisposing immunodeficiency disease, such as those found in HIV-infected patients, create further subclassifications of the periodontal diseases, some of which are covered in those chapters associated with those conditions.

It is well accepted that control of most periodontal diseases requires, at the very minimum, appropriate mechanical cleansing of the dentition and the supporting structures by the patient. These efforts include brushing, some type of interdental cleaning, preferably with either floss or other aids, as well as appropriate sulcular cleaning usually with a brush.

Following appropriate dental treatment by the general dental practitioner and/or the periodontist, aids to these efforts by the patient might include the use of chemical agents to assist in the control of the periodontal diseases, or to prevent periodontal diseases. There are many available chemical agents on the market, only some of which are approved by the American Dental Association (ADA). Several have been tested utilizing guidelines published in 1986 by the ADA for assessment of agents that claim efficacy in the management of periodontal diseases. These chemical agents, including chlorhexidine (Peridex, PerioGard), a quaternary compound, are bisbiguanides. Chlorhexidine, in various concentrations, has shown efficacy in reducing plaque and gingivitis in patients with short-term utilization. Some side effects include staining of the dentition, which is reversible by dental prophylaxis. Chlorhexidine demonstrates the concept of substantivity, indicating that after its use, it has a continued effect in reducing the ability of plaque to form. It has been shown to be useful in a variety of periodontal conditions including acute necrotizing ulcerative gingivitis and healing studies. Some disturbances in taste and accumulation of calculus have been reported; however, chlorhexidine is the most applicable chemical agent of the bisbiguanides that has been studied to date.

Other chemical agents available as mouthwashes include the phenol compound Listerine Antiseptic. These compounds are primarily restricted to prototype agents; the first to be approved by the ADA being Listerine Antiseptic. Listerine Antiseptic has been shown to be effective against plaque and gingivitis in long-term studies and comparable to chlorhexidine in these long-term investigations. However, chlorhexidine performs better than Listerine Antiseptic in short-term investigations. Triclosan, the chemical agent found in the toothpaste Total, has been recently approved by the FDA and is an aid in the prevention of gingivitis. Antiplaque activity of triclosan is enhanced with the addition of zinc citrate and there are no serious side effects to the use of triclosan in the dose found in the dentifrice. Sanguinarine is a principle herbal extract used for antiplaque activity. It is an alkaloid from the plant *Sanguinaria canadensis* and has some antimicrobial properties perhaps due to its enzyme activity although a relationship was found between epithelial mucosa premalignant changes and sanguinarine use in mouth rinse. Zinc citrate and zinc chloride have often been added to toothpastes as well as enzymes such as mucinase, mutanase, and dextrinase which have demonstrated varying results in studies. Some commercial anionic surfactants are available on the market, which include amino alcohols and the agent Plax which essentially is comprised of sodium thiosulfate as a surfactant. Recent studies have shown Plax to have some efficacy when it is added to triclosan.

Long-term use of prescription medications, including antibiotics, is seldom recommended and is not in any way a substitute for general dental/periodontal therapies. As adjunctive therapy, however, benefit has been shown and the new formulations of doxycycline (Periostat [available in Canada] and Atridox), are recommended for long-term or repetitive treatments. It should be noted that the manufacturer's claims indicate that Periostat functions as a collagenase inhibitor not as an antibiotic at recommended low doses for long-term therapy. Atridox functions as an antibiotic and is not recommended for constant long-term therapy, but rather in repetitive applications as necessary. Prescription medications used in efforts to treat periodontal diseases have historically included the use of antibiotics such as tetracycline although complications with use with young patients (ie, teeth intrinsic staining) have often precluded their prescription. Doxycycline is often preferred to tetracycline in low doses. This broad-spectrum bacteriostatic agent has shown efficacy against a wide variety of bacterial organisms found in periodontal disease. Minocycline slow-release (Arestin) has recently been approved.

The drug metronidazole is a nitroimidazole, an agent that was originally used in treatment of protozoan infections and some anaerobic bacteria. It is bactericidal and has a good absorption and distribution throughout the body. The studies using metronidazole have suggested that it has a variety of uses in periodontal treatment and can be used as adjunct in both acute necrotizing ulcerative gingivitis and has specific efficacy against spirochetes, bacteria, and some *Porphyromonas* species. Metronidazole has also been useful alone or with clavulanic acid when combined with amoxicillin for management of acute periodontal infections and in cases of gingival hyperplasia. Recently, it has been used in combination with amoxicillin alone or with clavulanic acid in the management of osteomyelitis associated with bisphosphonate use.

Clindamycin is a derivative of vancomycin and has been useful in treatment of suppurative periodontal lesions. Long-term use is precluded by its complicating toxicities associated with colitis and gastrointestinal problems; however, recent studies have shown that a variety of antibiotics can result in colitis, thus, clindamycin should not be singled out as the sole or main culprit of this reported complication.

When severe gingival inflammation appears to be refractory to routine periodontal therapies the clinician should consider a biopsy since autoimmune conditions that comprise desquamative gingivitis diseases must be considered.

Research has also shown that various combination therapies of metronidazole and tetracycline for localized aggressive periodontitis and metronidazole with amoxicillin for rapidly progressive disease can be useful. The use of other prescription drugs including nonsteroidal anti-inflammatory, as well as other antibacterial agents, have been under study. Effects on prostaglandins of NSAIDs may indirectly slow periodontal disease progression. New research is currently underway in this regard. Perhaps, in combination therapy with some of the antibiotics, these drugs may assist in reducing the patient's immune response or inflammatory response to the presence of disease-causing bacteria.

Of greatest interest has been the improvement in technology for delivery of chemical agents to the periodontally-diseased site. These systems include biodegradable gelatins and biodegradable chips that can be placed under the gingiva and deliver antibacterial agents directly to the site as an adjunct to periodontal treatment. The initial therapy of mechanical debridement by the periodontal therapist is essential prior to using any chemical agent, and the dentist should be aware that the development of newer agents does not substitute for appropriate periodontal therapy and maintenance. The trade names of the gelatin chips and subgingival delivery systems include Periochip, Atridox, and Periostat (available in Canada).

In addition to the periodontal therapy, consideration of the patient's pre-existing or developing medical conditions are important in the management of the periodontal patient. Several diseases illustrate these points most acutely. The reader is referred to the chapters on Diabetes, Cardiovascular Disease, Pregnancy, Respiratory Disease, HIV, and Cancer Chemotherapy. It has long been accepted that uncontrolled diabetes mellitus may predispose to periodontal lesions. Now, under current investigation is the hypothesis that pre-existing periodontal diseases may make it more difficult for a diabetic patient to come under control. In addition, the inflammatory response and immune challenge that is ongoing in periodontal disease appears to be implicated in the development of coronary artery disease as well as an increased risk of myocardial infarction and/or stroke. The accumulation of intra-arterial plaques appears enhanced by the presence of the inflammatory response often seen systemically in patients suffering with periodontal disease. In addition, the clinician is referred to the section on preprocedural antibiotics in the text for a consideration of antibiotic usage in patients that may be at risk for infective endocarditis. Other conditions including pregnancy and respiratory diseases such as COPD, HIV, and cancer therapy must be considered in the overall view of periodontal diseases. The reader is referred to the sections within the text.

TISSUE REGENERATION

Periodontal therapies rely on disease control and the success of surgery followed by medicinal therapeutics to stabilize and manage patients with advanced periodontal diseases. Efforts in tissue regeneration have largely consisted of free gingival graft procedures, transplanting host tissue from one site to another, or placing lyophilized bone into defects. Recently, the FDA approved a new living cell construct, called GINTUIT, that is made up of an allogeneic cellularized scaffold (McGuire 2011). GINTUIT is intended for use as keratinized tissue to be added to surgical sites to enhance the success and stability of attached gingival surgery and implant placement. Use of this product would not require a donor site surgery, such as a free gingival graft procedure, which may reduce pain and the risk of postoperative infection. It is not known if this product offers long-term improvement in outcomes of periodontal surgery over conventional techniques and materials.

Stem cell research offers a particularly effective potential method for cell transplantation and tissue regeneration (Nguyen 2013). Conventional tissue transplantation solutions are limited by factors, such as insufficient donor tissue and graft rejection and failure. In contrast, stem cells may be able to regenerate new tissue and restore function. A tissue engineering approach to periodontal therapy has been proposed, whereby periodontal tissue would be constructed in the laboratory and then surgically implanted into defects. A promising technique involves harvesting stem cells from the PDL, culturing periodontal cell sheets in vitro and transplanting the tissue into periodontal defects. This has resulted in PDL tissue regeneration in animal models.

REFERENCE

Bulgin D, Hodzic E, Komljenovic-Blitva D. Advanced and prospective technologies for potential use in craniofacial tissues regeneration by stem cells and growth factors. *J Craniofac Surg.* 2011; 22(1):342-348.
McGuire MK, Scheyer FT, Nevins ML, et al. Living cellular construct for increasing the width of keratinized gingiva: results from a randomized, within-patient, controlled trial. *J Periodontol.* 2011;82(10):1414-1423.
Nguyen TT, Mui B, Mehrabzadeh M, et al. Regeneration of tissues of the oral complex: current clinical trends and research advances. *J Can Dent Assoc.* 2013; 79.
Trounson A, Thakar RG, Lomax G, Gibbons D. Clinical trials for stem cell therapies. *BMC Med.* 2011; 9:52.

NECROTIZING ULCERATING PERIODONTITIS (HIV Periodontal Disease)

Initial Treatment *(In-Office)*

Gentle debridement
Note: Ensure patient has no iodine allergies

Betadine rinse on page 1364

At-Home Treatment

Listerine antiseptic rinse (20 mL for 30 seconds twice daily)
Peridex rinse on page 344
MetroNIDAZOLE (Systemic) (Flagyl) 7 to 10 days on page 1110

Follow-Up Therapy

Proper dental cleaning, including scaling and root planing (repeat as needed)
Continue Peridex and Listerine rinse (indefinitely)

Amoxicillin on page 121
Chlorhexidine Gluconate on page 344
Clindamycin (Systemic) on page 382
Doxycycline Hyclate Periodontal Extended-Release Liquid on page 547
Listerine Antiseptic on page 1150
MetroNIDAZOLE (Systemic) on page 1110
Minocycline Hydrochloride (Periodontal)
NSAIDs see Oral Pain section on page 1830
Tetracycline on page 1550
Triclosan and Fluoride

For examples of sample prescriptions seeBacterial Infections and Periodontal Diseases on page 32

Pharmacologic Management of Periodontal Diseases

Antibiotic	Adult Dosage
Azithromycin	500 mg once daily for 4 to 7 days
Clindamycin (Systemic)	300 mg tid for 8 days
Doxycycline or minocycline	100 to 200 mg once daily for 21 days
MetroNIDAZOLE (Systemic)	500 mg tid for 8 days
Metronidazole + amoxicillin	250 mg tid for 8 days of each drug

Adapted from: Recommendations from the American Academy of Periodontology. Available at: www.perio.org.

FUNGAL INFECTIONS

Oral fungal infections can result from alteration in oral flora, immunosuppression, and underlying systemic diseases that may allow the overgrowth of these otherwise common but highly opportunistic organisms. These systemic conditions might include infection with the human immunodeficiency virus (and its treatments), diabetes mellitus, long-term xerostomia, adrenal suppression, anemia, and chemotherapy-induced myelosuppression for the management of cancer. Long-term administration of antibiotics such as doripenem used to treat advanced systemic infections, has been implicated in elevating the risk of fungal infections. Also, the use of oral inhalers that include steroids, such as Advair Diskus, have been implicated in the enhancing of the risk of fungal overgrowth. Clinical presentation might include pseudomembranous, erythematous, and hyperkeratotic forms.

Fungus has also been implicated in denture stomatitis, angular cheilitis, and symptomatic geographic tongue (erythema migrans). Patients being treated for fungal skin infections or common oral conditions (eg, angular cheilitis) may also be using topical antifungal preparations coupled with a steroid, such as triamcinolone. *Candida albicans* is the fungal species most commonly isolated from the oral cavity, but other species can be found, some of which are azole resistant, such as *Candida glabrata*.

Nystatin (Mycostatin) is effective topically in the treatment of candidal infections of the skin and mucous membrane. The drug is extremely well tolerated and appears to be nonsensitizing although gastrointestinal upset and nausea are fairly common side effects. Clotrimazole troches are also useful as a topical therapy. Due to the significant sucrose content in nystatin suspension, patients with salivary gland hypofunction may be prescribed an alternative medication, such as clotrimazole troches which do contain dextrose, in order to lessen the caries risk. Clotrimazole is also available as vaginal suppository/troche formulations which do not contain any sugars.

In persons with denture stomatitis in which *Candida albicans* plays at least a contributory role, it is important to soak the prosthesis (laden with organisms) overnight in a nystatin liquid suspension besides treatment of the affected oral mucosa. Nystatin ointment can be placed in the denture during the daytime much like a denture adhesive. Antifungal medication should be continued for at least 14 days in order to prevent relapse and the patient must be reevaluated. Predisposing systemic factors must be reconsidered if the oral fungal infection persists and remake of any prosthesis may be necessary.

Topical applications rely on contact of the drug with the organism within the lesions; therefore, 4 to 5 times daily with a dissolving troche or a nystatin rinse is appropriate. Chronically recurring oral mucosal fungal infections are often seen in patients who use systemic steroids or steroid inhalers for respiratory disease, such as asthma or COPD. Dental prosthesis wearers also often experience recurrent fungal colonization coupled with denture stomatitis. These predisposing conditions may be more resistant to antifungal therapy, possibly requiring a combination of topical and systemic drugs.

Several drugs of different classes can be used in treating systemic and localized fungal infections including, amphotericin B, anidulafungin, caspofungin, ciclopirox olamine, clotrimazole, fluconazole, itraconazole, ketoconazole, micafungin, miconazole, naftifine hydrochloride, nystatin, oxiconazole, posaconazole, and voriconazole. Many of these drugs however are not commonly utilized as topical oral therapies. Clotrimazole, fluconazole, and nystatin are the most commonly prescribed oral topical treatments.

MANAGEMENT OF FUNGAL INFECTIONS REQUIRING SYSTEMIC MEDICATION

If the patient is refractory to topical treatment, consideration of a systemic route usually includes fluconazole (Diflucan) or ketoconazole. Also, when the patient cannot tolerate topical therapy, these choices are effective, well-tolerated, systematic drugs for mucocutaneous candidiasis. Concern over liver function and possible drug interactions must be considered.

In patients who appear to be refractory to ketoconazole, itraconazole, or fluconazole related to the treatment of oropharyngeal candidiasis, posaconazole has been approved for usage. Anidulafungin (Eraxis), caspofungin (Cancidas), micafungin (Mycamine), or voriconazole (VFEND) are also indicated for treatment of serious fungal infections in patients intolerant of, or refractory to, other therapy.

Amphotericin B (Conventional) on page 134
Anidulafungin on page 146
Caspofungin on page 308
Clotrimazole (Oral) on page 404
Fluconazole on page 721
Ketoconazole (Systemic) on page 940
Micafungin on page 1116
Nystatin (Oral) on page 1214
Nystatin (Topical) on page 1215
Nystatin and Triamcinolone
Posaconazole on page 1358
Voriconazole on page 1655

Note: Consider Peridex oral rinse or Listerine antiseptic oral rinse for long-term control in immunosuppressed patients.

SAMPLE PRESCRIPTIONS FOR SYSTEMIC TREATMENT

Rx:

Diflucan 100 mg tablets
Disp: 16 tablets
Sig: Take 2 tablets day 1, then 1 tablet/day until gone

Note: Sometimes a shorter course is adequate; however, oral infections commonly are more difficult to eradicate. Often a 21-day (3-week) course, or and even a second course, may be necessary.

Ingredient: Fluconazole

Rx:

Ketoconazole (Systemic) 200 mg
Disp: 14 tablets
Sig: Take 1 tablet daily, with a meal, for 2 weeks

Note: May cause irreversible liver damage; liver function should be monitored with long-term use (ie, >3 weeks)

Ingredient: Ketoconazole

SAMPLE PRESCRIPTIONS FOR TOPICAL TREATMENT

Rx:

Nystatin 100,000 units/mL oral suspension
Disp: 300 mL
Sig: Rinse with 1 teaspoon (5 mL) for 2 minutes 4 to 5 times/day and expectorate

Rx:

Mycelex 10 mg troches
Disp: 70 troches
Sig: Dissolve 1 troche in mouth 4 to 5 times/day until gone; leave any prostheses out during treatment and soak prosthesis in nystatin liquid suspension overnight

Ingredient: Clotrimazole (Oral)

For additional sample prescriptions see Fungal Infections on page 35

MANAGEMENT OF ANGULAR CHEILITIS

Angular cheilitis may represent the clinical manifestation of a multitude of etiologic factors. Cheilitis-like lesions may result from local habits, from a decrease in the intermaxillary space, or from nutritional deficiency. More commonly, angular cheilitis represents a mixed infection coupled with an inflammatory response involving *Candida albicans* and other organisms (most frequently *Staphylococcus aureus*).

The drug of choice is now formulated to contain nystatin and triamcinolone (formerly known as Mycolog and Mycolog II) and the effect is excellent. In addition, an off-label use of iodoquinol and hydrocortisone has also been reported to be effective in the treatment of angular cheilitis.

VIRAL INFECTIONS

Oropharyngeal viral infections are most commonly caused by herpes simplex viruses and Coxsackie viruses. Infections of the oropharynx and upper respiratory infections are commonly caused by the Coxsackie group A viruses. Oral cavity proper soft tissue viral infections, on the other hand, are most often caused by the herpes simplex viruses. Herpes zoster or varicella-zoster virus, which is one of the herpes family of viruses, can likewise cause similar viral eruptions involving the oral mucosa. Oral manifestations of mononucleosis caused by Epstein-Barr virus (another Herpes family virus) can lead to petechiae on the soft palate during mononucleosis but usually do not require direct therapy and resolve as the systemic condition improves. When EBV causes hairy leukoplakia in HIV/AIDS patients, the lesions usually respond to the anti-retroviral therapies.

Human *Papillomavirus* is causative in a number of oral lesions, the most common of which are *Condyloma acuminatum* and Verruca vulgaris. Within the past few years, certain subtypes of human *Papillomavirus* already proven to cause uterine cervical carcinoma are suspected of also being responsible for some posterior oral cavity squamous cell carcinomas. Human papillomavirus (HPV) is the broad term for a large group of viruses comprised of more than 150 serotypes. Certain serotypes of HPV cause warts on the skin and others cause warts in the genital region. Some types of HPV are known to cause cervical cancers, as well as cancers of the anus, penis, vulva, vagina, and ***head and neck***.

HPV-related head and neck cancers occur primarily in the oropharynx (posterior to the tonsillar pillars and on the base of the tongue). Oropharyngeal cancers are more common in white men. Most head and neck cancers are caused by tobacco and alcohol use, but researchers believe that up to 80% of oropharyngeal cancers in the US may be related to long term infection with the HPV virus. HPV-related head and neck cancer occurs in both people who smoke and those who do not smoke.

Salivary diagnostic tests are available for HPV, and essentially they involve the use of Polymeras Chain Reaction PCR tests; thus, they are not point of care tests. Kits containing a salivary collector are placed in transport media and sent to a central laboratory for analysis. Investigators in the field have used oral swabs, expectorated saliva or an expectorated oral rinse with mouthwash (OraRisk HPV test, OralDNA Labs, Brentwood, TN, which, to our knowledge, is the only salivary diagnostic test for HPV commercially available in the United States). The latter collection technique probably has the highest sensitivity, because it samples the entire oral cavity and the swishing of the solution dislodges mucosal cells. Investigators in the laboratory use a variety of primers to detect as many HPV types as possible. Early diagnosis is critical for survival of patients with oral squamous cell carcinoma (OSCC), and, thus, it is likely that use of salivary HPV analyses will continue to increase.

Human papilloma virus is widespread and serotypes 16 and 18 have been associated with cervical cancer. Although most types that cause oral HPV lesions are not of these serotypes, the clinician should recommend appropriate surgical removal of all such lesions. Lesions in the posterior oral pharyngeal region are of particular concern. Long-term infection with HPV is still being studied and data regarding oral risk of malignancy is improving. All suspicious lesions should be removed and serotyping performed if counselling the patient seems appropriate. Preexposure vaccination is one of the most effective methods for preventing transmission of some serotypes of HPV. Quadrivalent HPV vaccine (Gardasil) and the bivalent HPV vaccine (Cervarix) are available.

Gardasil is a vaccine indicated in girls and women 9 to 26 years of age for the prevention of the following diseases caused by Human Papillomavirus (HPV) types included in the vaccine:

- Cervical, vulvar, vaginal, and anal cancer caused by HPV types 16 and 18
- Genital warts (condyloma acuminata) caused by HPV types 6 and 11

And the following precancerous or dysplastic lesions caused by HPV types 6, 11, 16, and 18:

- Cervical intraepithelial neoplasia (CIN) grade 2/3 and Cervical adenocarcinoma *in situ* (AIS)
- Cervical intraepithelial neoplasia (CIN) grade 1
- Vulvar intraepithelial neoplasia (VIN) grade 2 and grade 3
- Vaginal intraepithelial neoplasia (VaIN) grade 2 and grade 3
- Anal intraepithelial neoplasia (AIN) grades 1, 2, and 3

Gardasil is also indicated in boys and men 9 to 26 years of age for the prevention of the following diseases caused by HPV types included in the vaccine:

- Anal cancer caused by HPV types 16 and 18
- Genital warts (condyloma acuminata) caused by HPV types 6 and 11

And the following precancerous or dysplastic lesions caused by HPV types 6, 11, 16, and 18:

- Anal intraepithelial neoplasia (AIN) grades 1, 2, and 3

Cervarix is a vaccine indicated for the prevention of the following diseases caused by oncogenic human papillomavirus (HPV) types 16 and 18:

- Cervical cancer
- Cervical intraepithelial neoplasia (CIN) grade 2 or worse and adenocarcinoma *in situ*
- Cervical intraepithelial neoplasia (CIN) grade 1

Cervarix is approved for use in females 9 to 25 years of age.

Details regarding HPV vaccination are available at www.cdc.gov/std/hpv. Vaccines for other STDs (eg, HIV and herpes simplex virus) are under development or undergoing clinical trials. Vaccines are not available for bacterial or fungal STDs.

The diagnosis of an acute viral infection begins by ruling out bacterial etiology and having an awareness of the presenting signs and symptoms associated with viral infection. Acute onset and vesicular eruption on the soft tissues generally favors a diagnosis of viral infection. Unfortunately, vesicles do not remain for a great length of time in the oral cavity; therefore, the short-lived vesicles rupture leaving ulcerated bases as the only indication of their presence. These ulcers are generally small in size and only when left unmanaged, coalesce to form larger, irregular ulcerations. Distinction must be made between the commonly recurring intraoral atraumatic ulcers (aphthous ulcerations) which do not have a viral etiology and the lesions associated with intraoral recurrent herpes since their effective treatment is distinctly different.

The management of an oral viral infection may be palliative for the most part; however, with the advent of improved antiviral prescription medications there now exists a family of drugs that can assist in managing primary and secondary infection. Aldara has been approved for treatment of genital warts (superficial basal cell carcinomas and actinic keratosis); oral mucosa use is still under study.

It should be noted that herpes can present as a primary infection (gingivostomatitis or pharyngo stomatitis), recurrent lip lesions (herpes labialis of the skin and adjacent vermilion border), and intraoral ulcers (recurrent intraoral herpes), involving the oral and perioral tissues. Primary infection is a systemic infection that leads to acute gingivostomatitis that may involve all moveable and nonmovable sites of the oral cavity (buccal mucosa, lips, tongue, floor of the mouth, palate, and the gingiva). Treatment of primary infections utilizes prescription antivirals such as acyclovir in combination with supportive care. Topical anesthetics, such as lidocaine 1% or dyclonine HCl 1%, used in combination with Benadryl 0.5% in a saline vehicle was found to be an effective oral rinse in the symptomatic treatment of primary herpetic gingivostomatitis. Other agents for symptomatic and supportive treatment include commercially available elixir of Benadryl, Xylocaine viscous, Orajel (OTC), and antibiotics to prevent secondary infections. Systemic supportive therapy should include forced fluids, high concentration protein, vitamin and mineral food supplements, and rest.

Antivirals

Abreva (OTC) on page 524
Acyclovir (Systemic) on page 73
Acyclovir (Topical) on page 77
Famciclovir on page 686
Imiquimod on page 867
L-Lysine on page 1014
Nelfinavir on page 1180
Penciclovir on page 1307
ValACYclovir on page 1622

HPV Prevention

Papillomavirus (Types 6, 11, 16, 18); Vaccine (Human, Recombinant) on page 1287
Papillomavirus (Types 16, 18); Vaccine (Human, Recombinant) on page 1288

Supportive Therapy

DiphenhydrAMINE (Systemic) on page 517
Lidocaine (Topical) on page 990

Prevention of Secondary Bacterial Infection

Penicillin V Potassium on page 1311

SUPPORTIVE CARE FOR PAIN AND PREVENTION OF SECONDARY INFECTION

Primary infections often become secondarily infected with bacteria, requiring antibiotics. Dietary supplement may be necessary. Options are presented due to variability in patient compliance and response.

RECURRENT HERPETIC INFECTIONS

Following the primary herpetic infection, the herpesvirus remains latent until such time as it has the opportunity to recur. The etiology of this latent period and the degree of viral shedding present during latency is currently under study; however, it is thought that some trigger in the mucosa or the skin causes the virus to begin to replicate. This process may involve Langerhans cells which are immunocompetent antigen-presenting cells resident in all epidermal and epithelial surfaces. The virus replication then leads to physical movement of the virus along the sensory axon leading to eruptions in innervated tissues surrounding the mouth or within. The most common form of recurrence is the lip lesion or herpes labialis; however, intraoral recurrent herpes also occurs with some frequency (attached gingival and hard palate preferentially).

Prevention of recurrences has been attempted with lysine (OTC) 500 to 1,000 mg/day and acyclovir but response has been variable. Herpes zoster outbreaks can also involve the oral and facial tissues, although this is less common. The zoster vaccine (Zostavax) is approved for individuals >50 years of age and may protect against VZV outbreaks. Valacyclovir or famciclovir are the drugs of choice in the event of a shingles outbreak. Of the two medications, famciclovir is reported to be more effective against postherpetic neuralgia. Valacyclovir HCl in 500 mg and 1 g tablets has recently been approved by the FDA for first time generic formulations.

Water-soluble bioflavonoid-ascorbic acid complex, now available as Peridin-C, may be helpful in reducing the signs and symptoms associated with recurrent herpes simplex virus infections. As with all agents used, the therapy is more effective when instituted in the early prodromal stage of the disease process.

PREVENTATIVE SAMPLE PRESCRIPTIONS

Rx:
L-Lysine (OTC) 500 mg
Sig: Take 2 tablets/day as preventive; increase to 4 tablets/day if prodrome or recurrence begins

Rx:
Citrus bioflavonoids and ascorbic acid tablets 400 mg (Peridin-C)
Disp: 10 tablets
Sig: Take 2 tablets at once, then 1 tablet 3 times/day for 3 days

Where a recurrence is usually precipitated by exposure to sunlight, the lesion may be prevented by the application to the area of a sunscreen, with a high skin protection factor (SPF) in the range of ≥25.

SUPPORTIVE CARE FOR PAIN AND MAINTENANCE OF NUTRITION DURING ORAL VIRAL INFECTIONS

Rx:
Benadryl liquid 12.5 mg per 5 mL
Disp: 4 oz bottle
Sig: Rinse with 1 to 2 teaspoonfuls every 2 hours and expectorate

Note: Benadryl is available as a generic diphenhydramine liquid.

Rx:
Benadryl liquid 12.5 mg per 5 mL (mix 50/50) with Kaopectate
Disp: 8 oz total
Sig: Rinse with 1 to 2 teaspoonfuls every 2 hours and expectorate.

Note: Maalox can be used in place of Kaopectate if constipation is a problem. Benadryl is available as a generic diphenhydramine liquid.

Rx:
Xylocaine viscous 2%
Disp: 450 mL bottle
Sig: Swish with 1 tablespoon 4 times/day and spit out

Ingredient: Lidocaine (Topical)

Rx:
Merilene
Disp: 1 lb can (plain, chocolate, eggnog flavors)
Sig: Take 3 servings daily; prepare as indicated on can

Ingredient: Protein-vitamin-mineral food supplement

PRESCRIPTIVE TREATMENT

Acyclovir (Zovirax) possesses antiviral activity against herpes simplex types 1 and 2. Historically, ophthalmic ointments were used topically to treat recurrent mucosal and skin lesions. These do not penetrate well on the skin lesions, thereby providing questionable relief of symptoms. If recommended, use should be closely monitored. Penciclovir, an active metabolite of famciclovir, has been specifically approved in a cream for treatment of recurrent herpes lesions. Valacyclovir and famciclovir have also been approved for treatment of herpes labialis (see monograph for dosing).

The FDA has also approved acyclovir cream 5% for treatment of herpes labialis in adults and adolescents. Other over-the-counter preparations include 2% tetracaine gel and L-lysine 500 mg tablets.

SAMPLE PRESCRIPTIONS

Rx:
Zovirax 200 mg capsules
Disp: 50 or 60 capsules
Sig: Take 1 capsule 5 times/day for 10 days or 2 capsules 3 times/day for 10 days

Ingredient: Acyclovir (Systemic)

Rx:
Valtrex 500 mg caplets
Disp: 42 caplets
Sig: Take 2 caplets 3 times/day for 7 days without regard to meals

Ingredient: ValACYclovir

Rx:
Famvir 500 mg tablets
Disp: 3 tablets
Sig: Take 1,500 mg as a single dose

Ingredient: Famciclovir; available as generic equivalent

Rx:
Denavir topical cream 1%
Disp: 1.5 g tube
Sig: Apply locally as directed to lesion every 2 hours during waking hours (begin when symptoms first occur)

Ingredient: Penciclovir

For additional sample prescriptions see Viral Infections - Sample Prescriptions on page 40

REFERENCES

ADA Council on Scientific Affairs. Statement on Human Papillomavirus and Squamous Cell Cancers of the Oropharynx (adopted November 2012). Available at: http://www.ada.org/1749.aspx.

Andrews E, Seaman WT, Webster-Cyriaque J. Oropharyngeal carcinoma in nonsmokers and nondrinkers: a role for HPV. *Oral Oncol.* 2009;45(6):486-491.

Chaturvedi AK, Engels EA, Pfeiffer RM, et al. Human papillomavirus and rising oropharyngeal cancer incidence in the United States. *J Clin Oncol.* 2011;29(32):4294-4301.

Cleveland JL, Junger ML, Saraiya M, Markowitz LE, Dunne EF, Epstein JB. The connection between human papillomavirus and oropharyngeal squamous cell carcinomas in the United States: implications for dentistry. *J Am Dent Assoc.* 2011;142(8):915-924.

Corstjens PL, Abrams WR, Malamud D. Detecting viruses by using salivary diagnostics. *J Am Dent Assoc.* 2012;143(10 Suppl):12S-18S.

Gillison ML, Broutian T, Pickard RK, et al. Prevalence of oral HPV infection in the United States, 2009-2010. *JAMA.* 2012;307(7):693-703.

Jemal A, Simard EP, Dorell C, et al. Annual Report to the Nation on the Status of Cancer, 1975-2009, featuring the burden and trends in human papillomavirus (HPV)-associated cancers and HPV vaccination coverage levels. *J Natl Cancer Inst.* 2013;105(3):175-201. http://jnci.oxfordjournals.org/content/early/2013/01/03/jnci.djs491.full.pdf+html

Kulkarni SS1, Kulkarni SS, Vastrad PP, et al. Prevalence and distribution of high risk human papillomavirus (HPV) Types 16 and 18 in carcinoma of cervix, saliva of patients with oral squamous cell carcinoma and in the general population in Karnataka, India. *Asian Pac J Cancer Prev.* 2011;12(3):645-648.

Marur S, D'Souza G, Westra WH, Forastiere AA. HPV-associated head and neck cancer: a virus-related cancer epidemic. *Lancet Oncol.* 2010;11(8):781-789.

Pfister DG and Fury MG. New chapter in our understanding of human papillomavirus-related head and neck cancer. *J Clin Oncol.* 2014;32(30):3349-3352.

ULCERATIVE, EROSIVE, AND PAINFUL ORAL MUCOSAL DISORDERS

RECURRENT APHTHOUS STOMATITIS - MINOR, MAJOR, AND HERPETIFORM TYPES

Recurrent aphthous stomatitis is an extremely common mucosal disease. Although it is not considered a classic autoimmune disorder, the conditions that have been termed minor, major, and herpetiform types have in common a cellular-mediated event with underlying T-cells activation. This cytotoxicity leads to a destruction of the mucosal surface and is mediated by inflammatory cytokines throughout the oral tissues. The term herpetiform ulcerations is a misnomer and implies a herpes-type appearance to the ulcers when they are present. This is as far as the connection goes since there has never been a viral or bacterial etiology cited for any of the aphthous forms of ulcerations. The different subsets of patients have different triggering factors (eg, stress, hormonal, fluctuations and minor chemical irritations) and thus no one product or treatment technique is universally effective in all patients.

For minor or major aphthous ulcers that severely affect daily living and quality of life, corticosteroids seem to be the mainstay drug. It is believed that the immunomodulating effect of a short-term regimen of corticosteroids in an immunocompetent sufferer is effective without creating the well-known side effects of long-term or high-dose corticosteroid therapy. Sufferers of the herpetiform type of aphthae, in which as many as a hundred small ulcers appear per outbreak, may also obtain relief from an oral suspension corticosteroid (eg, dexamethasone) although management may be more protracted.

Triamcinolone dental paste (Oralone) is indicated for the temporary relief of minor symptoms associated with infrequent recurrences of minor aphthous lesions and ulcerative lesions resulting from trauma. Some clinicians prescribe a soothing rinse containing corticosteroid (eg, dexamethasone), an antifungal agent (eg, nystatin), a topical anesthetic (eg, viscous lidocaine), an antihistamine (eg, diphenhydramine), an antimicrobial/antibiotic (chlorhexidine), and/or coating agent such as attapulgite creating a so-called "magic elixir." The most popular combination contains 1.5 g tetracycline; 60 mg hydrocortisone; nystatin 6 million international units and an equal volume elixir of Benadryl and has been called Mary's Magic potion. Numerous other "Magic Mouthwash" mixtures have been formulated by clinicians, but there are insufficient data to provide evidence for selection of any of these combinations over others. All of the combinations do, however, have reasonable anecdotal evidence of palliative effects.

More severe forms of recurrent aphthous stomatitis may be treated with topical corticosteroids of higher strength (eg, fluocinonide, clobetasol) alone or mixed with Orabase. An oral suspension of tetracycline may be prescribed for avoidance of secondary infection. Tetracycline use is contraindicated during pregnancy, infancy, and childhood to the age of 8 years due to intrinsic staining of teeth. *Lactobacillus acidophilus* preparations (Bacid, Lactinex) are occasionally effective for reducing the frequency and severity of the minor lesions.

With professional oversight, a cauterizing agent, such as Debacterol may markedly decrease the pain associated with the aphthous ulcer. Clinician and patient must be extremely careful in using cauterizing agents within the oral cavity. Patients with long-standing history of recurrent aphthous stomatitis should be evaluated for iron, folic acid, and vitamin B_{12} deficiencies as well as hematological assessments for anemia. One subset of recurrent aphthous stomatitis sufferers markedly improve when tooth dentifrices lacking sodium lauryl sulfate are used.

In patients with medical contraindications for corticosteroid use, alternatives (eg, colchicine, dapsone, immune globulin [intravenous], methotrexate, misoprostol, mycophenolate mofetil, pentoxifylline, tacrolimus, and tretinoin) have had anecdotal reports of effectiveness. These alternative drugs should only be considered in consultation with the patient's physician.

Regular use of Listerine antiseptic has been shown in clinical trials to reduce the severity, duration, and frequency of aphthous stomatitis. An antimicrobial such as chlorhexidine oral rinses (20 mL for 30 seconds 2 to 3 times/day) has also demonstrated efficacy in reducing the duration of aphthae. With both of these products, however, patient intolerance of the burning from the alcohol content is of concern. The newer alcohol-free antimicrobial rinses have not been evaluated. Immunocompromised patients, such as those with AIDS, may have severe ulcer recurrences and thalidomide has been approved for these patients on an FDA orphan drug approved basis. See Periodontal Diseases on page 1844 for HIV-related periodontal considerations.

Two other conditions should be mentioned here since their diagnosis and management requires consideration of all of the ulcerative, erosive, and painful oral mucosal disorders. Necrotizing ulcerative gingivitis (NUG) is a condition that has been recognized for many years. The name historically included the term "acute"; however, most investigators have discontinued this because there is not a chronic form of the disease and it is unnecessary to consider it as anything other than necrotizing gingivitis. The organism *Fusobacterium nucleatum* has been implicated with several other organisms particularly Spirochetes in this condition. The infections seem to occur primarily following periods of psychological stress and this is the most common unifying factor in patients who suffer with NUG. In addition, immunosuppression, smoking, and local trauma have also been implicated. Generally, the classical appearance of NUG includes punched-out interdental papillae that are inflamed and appear blunted, somewhat necrotic at their tips. A pseudomembrane often is present and a strong fetor oris is usually present. The patient sometimes has fever and malaise as well. The treatment is generally conservative using gentle debridement. There is some benefit in using antibiotics such metronidazole, tetracycline, or amoxicillin. Historically, some clinicians have also chosen to add a vitamin supplement, generally a vitamin B complex with vitamin C, to help with the mucosal healing.

Another condition occasionally encountered is plasma cell gingivitis, a diffuse but intense erythema of the gingival complex, including a rapid onset and soreness to the oral gingival tissues. The implicated etiologies in plasma cell gingivitis include various chewing gums, toothpastes with herbal additives, as well as spicy candies, mints, peppers, and other potential allergens. The treatment of plasma cell gingivitis is local use of topical steroids; although by removing the dietary stimulant, generally the condition will resolve spontaneously. If plasma cell gingivitis is being considered as a diagnosis, the autoimmune desquamative gingival diseases must also be considered, including lichen planus, mucous membrane pemphigoid, and pemphigus. A biopsy is usually necessary to determine a diagnosis.

MILD TO MODERATE FORMS OF ULCERATIONS AND EROSIONS

There are several over-the-counter preparations that may give the patient some or total relief, including Ulcerease, BetaCell oral rinse, Cankermelts-GX, Gelclair Bioadherent Oral Gel, Orabase Sooth-N-Seal, OraMoist Dry Mouth Patch, OraPatch, Ricinol P.R.N., Zilactin gel, Canker Cover, Avamin Melts, Benzoin tincture saturated swabsticks, and Orajel Protective Mouth Sore Discs.

Aloclair (Ameseal) is now available as a spray. It is marketed by OMNI Preventive Care as an oral lesion pain relief spray, useful for indications related to aphthous ulcerations and other mild-to-moderate oral erosions. Its prescription companion preparation Gelclair has been suggested for use in the management of mucositis. Oralone is a new formulation of triamcinolone acetonide dental paste which had previously been available as Kenalog in Orabase.

A prescription viscous, mucoadhesive polymer rinse, MuGard, provides a protective coating to the oral mucosa and can help protect against oral mucositis.

SYMPTOMATIC GEOGRAPHIC TONGUE (BENIGN MIGRATORY GLOSSITIS, ERYTHEMA MIGRANS)

Geographic tongue is a localized, transitory loss of the tongue's filiform papillae. Although disconcerting in appearance, it usually is asymptomatic; however, occasionally patients will report a burning sensation. Fungal colonization has been implicated in symptomatic geographic tongue and this condition needs to be ruled out as a contributing factor (see Fungal Infections on page 1847).

After infection has been ruled out, palliation for symptomatic geographic tongue can sometimes be achieved with an approach similar to managing minor oral ulcerations. Benadryl elixir, a potent antihistamine, is used in the oral cavity primarily as a mild topical anesthetic agent for the symptomatic relief of certain allergic deficiencies which should be ruled out as possible etiologies for the oral condition under treatment. It is often used alone as well as in 50:50 solutions with agents such as Kaopectate or Maalox to assist in coating the oral mucosa. Benadryl can also be used systemically in capsule form although the elixir mixed with a coating agent as above provides excellent palliation prior to meals. Frequently, Benadryl alone or in combination with the above agents will be very effective in the relief of symptomatic geographic tongue.

Attapulgite on page 188
Chlorhexidine Gluconate on page 344
Clobetasol on page 390
Debacterol
Dexamethasone (Systemic) on page 474
DiphenhydrAMINE (Systemic) on page 517
Fluocinonide ointment with Orabase on page 734
Lactobacillus on page 955
MetroNIDAZOLE (Systemic) on page 1110
Mouthwash (Antiseptic) on page 1150
PredniSONE on page 1377
Sulfonated Phenolics and Aqueous Solution
Tetracaine (Topical) on page 1548
Tetracycline on page 1550
Thalidomide on page 1553
Triamcinolone (Topical) on page 1604

EROSIVE LICHEN PLANUS AND OTHER VESICULOEROSIVE DISEASES

Lichen planus is a chronic dermatologic disease that often affects the oral tissues. The name was first selected in 1869 because of the flat appearance of the white lesions on the oral mucosa. The etiology of lichen planus is unknown but significant associations have been made with Hepatitis C and the drug induced form called lichenoid mucositis. Clinically the lesions are identical to the dermatologic form of lichen planus but significant treatment response may be more difficult to achieve.

Lichen planus ranges from being totally asymptomatic to severely painful when present in its erosive forms. Reticular forms of lichen planus with no erosions show a white lacy pattern that has become pathognomic for the condition. The lesions on the skin often have a purplish hue and form slightly raised, pruritic papules, with an occasional white lacy or silvery appearance to the borders of the lesions. Patients do not need to have the skin lesions in order to suffer with oral lichen planus. The diagnosis of lichen planus is best performed by histopathology; however, often the pathognomic appearance and distribution of the lesions allows a presumptive diagnosis to be made from the clinical appearance. Generally the erosive forms of lichen planus require treatment based on the extent, severity, and pain level of the patient in question. Autoimmune desquamative gingival diseases, including pemphigoid and pemphigus, must also be considered. A biopsy is necessary to determine a diagnosis and systemic work-up for related disease effects must be completed in consultation with patient's physicians. Occasionally, an additional biopsy specimen is needed for diagnostic confirmation; the specimen is placed in Michel's transport media and then direct immunofluorescent studies are performed.

Elixir of dexamethasone, a potent steroidal anti-inflammatory agent, is used topically (as a 2-minute rinse and expectorate) in the management of acute episodes of erosive lichen planus and other vesiculo-erosive disease processes such as benign mucous membrane pemphigoid and pemphigus vulgaris. Some patients will not achieve relief from topical agents and systemic delivery either by swish and swallow or tablets may be necessary. Prednisone corticosteroid tablet is a popular and often effective starting point with a regimen consisting of burst therapy (eg, 6 to 80 mg) for several days followed by 7 to 10 days of a maintenance and tapering dose.

Immunosuppressant agents, such as tacrolimus (Protopic), hydroxychloroquine (Plaquenil), and pimecrolimus (Elidel), have shown some efficacy in off-label applications for severe cases. Prolonged use should be carried out in consult with the patient's physician and with a periodical Plaquenil-related ophthalmologic examination. Continued supervision of the patient during treatment is essential and the dentist must be aware that treatment of any secondary infections such as fungal overgrowth may be essential in gaining control of the erosive lesions. Also, patients should be counseled that maximum benefit of the medication will be achieved when oral hygiene is maintained at excellent levels.

For examples of sample prescriptions see Ulcerative and Erosive Disorders - Sample Prescriptions on page 43

BURNING MOUTH SYNDROME

Burning mouth syndrome (BMS) is a relatively common condition, of unknown etiology, and is a significant problem when it occurs, both in diagnosis and in management. Individuals often experience a burning or a scalding pain on the lips, tongue, and sometimes other parts of the oral cavity (eg, anterior hard palate). There are often no visible signs of irritation that the clinician can identify. The etiology of burning mouth syndrome remains unknown. The syndrome has been associated with everything ranging from vitamin deficiencies to the onset of menopause. It is estimated that nearly 5% of the population around the age of 60 may suffer with this condition. The symptoms often include burning mouth, dry mouth, a bitter or metallic taste, other taste alterations, changes in the patient's ability to eat, and onset of pain while attempting to sleep. Systemic conditions associated with BMS are abnormal hormonal fluctuations, diabetes, deficiencies in iron, zinc, and vitamins such as thiamine, B_{12}, niacin, complications associated with cancer therapy, and some patients report that the burning mouth syndrome symptoms occur after dental procedures. Three patterns of pain are reported:

- Type 1: pain absent on waking and developing during the day
- Type 2: pain present day and night
- Type 3: intermittent pain, with pain-free days

Abnormal taste (dysgeusia, parageusia) is either a metallic or bitter taste in the mouth or altered perception of taste particularly of salty or sweet/sour foods. Although the patient may perceive a dryness of the mouth, reduced saliva production is not confirmed on testing.

The evaluation of a patient complaining of burning mouth begins with a detailed history/process of elimination and may lead to a biopsy to determine if any organic reason for the condition is identifiable. Dry mouth often accompanies burning mouth. The clinician should culture the tongue or oral mucosa to rule out oral fungal colonization. A normal hematologic work up will ensure that there is no developing diabetes, allergy, or abnormal liver or thyroid condition. The clinician should carefully examine all of the surfaces of the tissues to see if there are any abrasive components caused by rough teeth or prostheses. It is often necessary to have the patient evaluated by their primary care physician because of the common association of BMS with high stress situations, common in the process of aging. The condition has the features of a neuropathy and could be related to the production of toxic radicals that may be released at the cellular level during times of stress.

These widely divergent hypotheses related to the etiology of BMS have led to equally broad therapeutic suggestions. A variety of drugs have been suggested, including: Topical rinses and anesthetics for palliative management, clonazepam 0.25 to 3 mg/day, amitriptyline 25 to 100 mg/day, nortriptyline 10 to 50 mg/day, gabapentin 900 to 1,500 mg/day, and doxepin cream, applied to the areas affected. Various studies indicate that alpha-lipoic acid in an initial dose of 600 mg may be used with a dose reduction to 200 mg after the initial 20 days. The rationale for attempting alpha-lipoic acid is the relationship between its antioxidant effects and the levels of glutathione and reduction of free radicals cellularly. In addition to alpha-lipoic acid, capsaicin has been used with some success. Capsaicin has been a prescription drug useful in arthritis care as a topical skin product. It has also been prescribed to assist with patients who have had shingles, post herpetic pain neuropathies associated with diabetes and other neuralgias. Its applications in oral use have been studied in very limited trials; however, it has recently been reevaluated in a 0.75% topical application for use in BMS and oral mucositis. Curcumin, the active agent in turmeric, has been recommended to treat BMS, although placebo-controlled trials have not been completed to suggest any consistent response to these products. All of the medications suggested for managing burning mouth are off-label uses and there are limited data from placebo controlled clinical trials.

During a Cochrane analysis, nine clinical trials were reviewed. Of the nine trials, three interventions demonstrated reduction in BMS and all of these included varying effects of clonazepam and alpha-lipoic acid. Although the other trials considered randomized double-blind trials, study designs were small and lacked power to draw and define conclusions. There is little evidence to provide a clear standard of care for treating patients with burning mouth syndrome to date. The clinician must always be aware of this lack of conclusive evidence. These drugs should be selected and managed in collaboration with the patient's physician, particularly since many of these patients suffering with burning mouth syndrome have complicated medical histories including the use of additional medications that could be affected.

REFERENCES AND SELECTED READINGS

Aggarwal BB, Sundaram C, Malani N, Ichikawa H. Curcumin: the Indian solid gold. *Adv Exp Med Biol*. 2007;595:1-75.

Baud CM, Colon LE, Gerberich J, et al. Protection from radiation-induced oral mucositis by MuGard oral rinse a clinical study and *in silico* analysis. Poster presentation at the 18th International MASCC/ISOO supportive care in cancer symposium. 2006. Available at http://www.accesspharma.com/downloads/product-programs/MuGard-Poster.pdf

Buchanan J, Zakrzewska J. Burning mouth syndrome. *Clin Evid (online)*. 2008. Available at http://www.ncbi.nlm.nih.gov/pmc/articles/PMC2907957/pdf/2008-1301.pdf.

Carrozzo M, Thorpe R. Oral lichen planus: a review. *Minerva Stomatol*. 2009;58(10):519-537.

Chakrabarty AK, Mraz S, Geisse JK, Anderson NJ. Aphthous ulcers associated with imiquimod and the treatment of actinic cheilitis. *J Am Acad Dermatol*. 2005;52(2 Suppl 1):35-37.

Donovan JC, Hayes RC, Burgess K, Leong IT, Rosen CF. Refractory erosive oral lichen planus associated with hepatitis C: response to topical tacrolimus ointment. *J Cutan Med Surg*. 2005;9(2):43-46.

Femiano F, Gombos F, Scully C. Burning mouth syndrome: open trial of psychotherapy alone, medication with alpha-lipoic acid (thioctic acid), and combination therapy. *Med Oral*. 2004;9(1):8-13.

Goel A, Kunnumakkara AB, Aggarwal BB. Curcumin as "Curecumin": from kitchen to clinic. *Biochem Pharmacol*. 2008;75(4):787-809.

Gremeau-Richard C, Woda A, Navez ML, et al. Topical clonazepam in stomatodynia: a randomised placebo-controlled study. *Pain*. 2004;108(1-2):51-57.

Hatcher H, Planalp R, Cho J, Torti FM, Torti SV. Curcumin: from ancient medicine to current clinical trials. *Cell Mol Life Sci*. 2008;65(11):1631-1652.

Heckmann SM, Heckmann JG, Ungethüm A, Hujoel P, Hummel T. Gabapentin has little or no effect in the treatment of burning mouth syndrome – results of an open-label pilot study. *Eur J Neurol*. 2006;13(7):e6-e7.

Hens MJ, Alonso-Ferreira V, Villaverde-Hueso A, Abaitua I, Posada de la Paz M. Cost-effectiveness analysis of burning mouth syndrome therapy. *Community Dent Oral Epidemiol*. 2012;40(2):185-192.

Kutluay SB, Doroghazi J, Roemer ME, Triezenberg SJ. Curcumin inhibits herpes simplex virus immediate-early gene expression by a mechanism independent of p300/CBP histone acetyltransferase activity. *Virology*. 2008;373(2):239-247.

Lodi G, Pellicano R, Carrozzo M. Hepatitis C virus infection and lichen planus: a systematic review with meta-analysis. *Oral Dis*. 2010;16(7):601-612.

Mínguez Serra MP, Salort Llorca C, Silvestre Donat FJ. Pharmacological treatment of burning mouth syndrome: a review and update. *Med Oral Patol Oral Cir Bucal*. 2007;12(4):E299-E304.

Olivier V, Lacour JP, Mousnier A, Garraffo R, Monteil RA, Ortonne JP. Treatment of chronic erosive oral lichen planus with low concentrations of topical tacrolimus: an open prospective study. *Arch Dermatol*. 2002;138(10):1335-1338.

Patton LL, Siegel MA, Benoliel R, De Laat A. Management of burning mouth syndrome: systematic review and management recommendations. *Oral Surg Oral Med Oral Pathol Oral Radiol Endod*. 2007;103(Suppl S39):e1-e13.

Petruzzi M, Lauritano D, De Benedittis M, Baldoni M, Serpico R. Systemic capsaicin for burning mouth syndrome: short-term results of a pilot study. *J Oral Pathol Med*. 2004;33(2):111-114.

Petti S, Rabiei M, De Luca M, Scully C. The magnitude of the association between hepatitis C virus infection and oral lichen planus: meta-analysis and case control study. *Odontology*. 2011;99(2):168-178.

Thomson MA, Hamburger J, Stewart DG, Lewis HM. Treatment of erosive oral lichen planus with topical tacrolimus. *J Dermatolog Treat*. 2004;15(5):308-314.

Vidal MA, Martinez-Fernandez E, Martinez-Vazquez de Castro J, et al. Diabetic neuropathy: effectiveness of amitriptyline and gabapentin. *Rev Soc Esp Dolor*. 2004;11(8):38-52.

White TL, Kent PF, Kurtz DB, Emko P. Effectiveness of gabapentin for treatment of burning mouth syndrome. *Arch Otolaryngol Head Neck Surg*. 2004;130(6):786-788.

Yeon KY, Kim SA, Kim YH, et al. Curcumin produces an antihyperalgesic effect via antagonism of TRPV1. *J Dent Res*. 2010;89(2):170-174.

Zakrzewska JM, Forssell H, Glenny AM. Interventions for the treatment of burning mouth syndrome. *Cochrane Database Syst Rev*. 2005.

DENTIN HYPERSENSITIVITY, ACID EROSION, HIGH CARIES INDEX, MANAGEMENT OF ALVEOLAR OSTEITIS, AND XEROSTOMIA

DENTIN HYPERSENSITIVITY

Suggested steps in resolving dentin hypersensitivity when a thorough exam has ruled-out any other source for the problem:

Treatment Steps

- Home treatment with a desensitizing toothpaste containing potassium nitrate (used to brush teeth as well as a thin layer applied, each night for 2 weeks)
- If needed, in office potassium oxalate (Protect by Butler) and/or in office fluoride iontophoresis
- If sensitivity is still not tolerable to the patient, consider pumice then dentin adhesive and unfilled resin or composite restoration overlaying a glass ionomer base
- The use of 5% sodium fluoride varnishes (Duraflor and Duraphat) have been encouraged for the prevention of decay in persons of high-risk populations and also show some efficacy for reducing sensitivity following multiple applications.
- Gluma is a brand name desensitizer used in dentistry to treat sensitivity. The product is manufactured by Heraeus Kulzer. Its formula of 5% glutaraldehyde and 35% HEMA (hydroxyethyl methacrylate) in water is used to help control both hypersensitive dentin and reduce the incidence of postoperative sensitivity in restorative dentistry procedures.

Home Products (all contain nitrate as active ingredient):

Promise
Denquel
Sensodyne
THERADENT

Other major brand name companies have added ingredients to their dentifrice product lines that also make hypersensitivity claims.

REFERENCE

Miglani S, Aggarwal V, Ahuja B. Dentin hypersensitivity: Recent trends in management. *J Conserv Dent*. 2010;13(4):218–224.

ACID EROSION

Acid erosion is the loss of tooth enamel through prolonged exposure to acid rich foods, beverages, and even fruits. The problem has been raised primarily in pediatric patients and can be significant. Several oral care products claim surface remineralization efficacy and should be coupled with dietary counseling to achieve a desirable reduction in tooth damage.

ReNew Remineralizing and Desensitizing Paste
Sensodyne ProNamel for Children
Recaldent, found in GC America's Prospec MI Paste with Recaldent and Trident XTRA CARE chewing gum
Amorphous calcium phosphate (ACP) found in Arm & Hammer Enamel Care Toothpaste
Premier Dental's Enamel Pro polishing paste
SensiStat, found in Ortek Therapeutic's ProClude and DenClude products
NovaMin, a synthetic mineral composed of calcium, sodium, phosphorus, and silica

ANTICARIES AGENTS

Fluoride (Gel 0.4%, Rinse 0.05%) on page 735

New toothpastes with triclosan such as Colgate Total show promise for combined treatment/prevention of caries, plaque, and gingivitis. The use of 5% sodium fluoride varnishes (Duraflor and Duraphat) have been encouraged for the prevention of decay in persons of high-risk populations.

FLUORIDES

Used for the prevention of demineralization of the tooth structure secondary to xerostomia. For patients with long-term or permanent xerostomia, daily application is accomplished using custom applicator trays, such as omnivac. Patients with porcelain crowns should use a neutral pH fluoride (see Fluoride monograph on page 735). Final selection of a fluoride product and/or saliva replacement/stimulant product must be based on patient comfort, taste, and ultimately, compliance. Experience has demonstrated that, often times, patients must try various combinations to achieve the greatest effect and their highest comfort levels. The presence of mucositis during cancer management complicates the clinician's selection of products.

Over-the-Counter (OTC) Products

Form	Brand Name	Strength/Size
Gel, topical (stannous fluoride)	Gel-Kam (cinnamon, fruit, mint flavors)	0.4% [0.1%] (65 g, 105 g, 122 g)
	Gel-Tin (lime, grape, cinnamon, raspberry, mint, orange flavors)	0.4% [0.1%] (60 g, 120 g)
	Stop (grape, cinnamon, bubblegum, piña colada, mint flavors)	0.4% [0.1%] (60 g, 120 g)
Rinse, topical (as sodium)	ACT, Fluorigard	0.05% [0.02%] (90 mL, 180 mL, 300 mL, 360 mL, 480 mL)
	Listermint with Fluoride	0.02% [0.01%] (180 mL, 300 mL, 360 mL, 480 mL, 540 mL, 720 mL, 960 mL, 1740 mL)

Adapted from: Newland JR, Meiller TF, Wynn RL, Crossley HL. *Oral Soft Tissue Diseases*. 6th ed. Hudson, OH: Lexi-Comp, Inc; 2013.

Prescription Only (Rx) Products

Form	Brand Name	Strength/Size
Drops, oral (as sodium)		0.275 mg/drop [0.125 mg/drop]
	Fluoritab, Flura-Drops	0.55 mg/drop [0.25 mg/drop] (22.8 mL, 24 mL)
	Karidium, Luride	0.275 mg/drop [0.125 mg/drop] (30 mL, 60 mL)
	Pediaflor	1.1 mg/mL [0.5 mg/mL] (50 mL)
Gel-Drops	Thera-Flur (lime flavor), Thera-Flur-N	1.1% [0.55%] (24 mL)
Gel, topical		
Acidulated phosphate fluoride	Minute-Gel (spearmint, strawberry, grape, apple-cinnamon, cherry cola, bubblegum flavors)	1.23% (480 mL)
Sodium fluoride	Karigel (orange flavor)	1.1% [0.5%]
	Karigel-N	1.1% [0.5%]
	PreviDent (mint, berry, cherry, fruit sherbet flavors)	1.1% [0.5%] (24 g, 30 g, 60 g, 120 g, 130 g, 250 g)
Lozenge (as sodium)	Flura-Loz (raspberry flavor)	2.2 mg [1 mg]
Rinse, topical (as sodium)	Fluorinse, Point-Two	0.2% [0.09%] (240 mL, 480 mL, 3780 mL)
Solution, oral (as sodium)	Phos-Flur (cherry, cinnamon, grape, wintergreen flavors)	0.44 mg/mL [0.2 mg/mL] (250 mL, 500 mL, 3780 mL)
Tablet (as sodium)		1.1 mg [0.5 mg]; 2.2 mg [1 mg]
Chewable	Fluor-A-Day	0.55 mg [0.25 mg]
	Fluor-A-Day, Fluoritab, Luride Lozi-Tab, Pharmaflur	1.1 mg [0.5 mg]
	Fluor-A-Day, Fluoritab, Karidium, Luride Lozi-Tab, Luride-SF Lozi-Tab, Pharmaflur	2.2 mg [1 mg]
Oral	Flura, Karidium	2.2 mg [1 mg]
Varnish	Duraflor	5% [50 mg/mL] (10 mL)

Adapted from: Newland JR, Meiller TF, Wynn RL, Crossley HL. *Oral Soft Tissue Diseases*. 6th ed. Hudson, OH: Lexi-Comp, Inc; 2013.

In-Office-Only Products

Form	Brand Name	Strength/Size
Gel, topical (as acidulated phosphate)	60 Second Taste Gel (bubblegum, chocolate and vanilla, groovy grape, marshmallow, mint, orange twist, strawberry flavors)	1.23% (16 oz bottle) [equivalent to 1.23% F ion]
	Denti-Care 60 Second Fluoride Gel (bubblegum, cherry, grape, mint, orange, strawberry, raspberry flavors)	1.23% (16 oz bottle) [equivalent to 1.23% F ion]
	Iris 60-second (orange smoothie, bubblegum, summer strawberry, California grape, fresh mint flavors)	1.23% (16 oz bottle) [equivalent to 1.23% F ion]
	Kolorz Sixty Second Fluoride Gel (blue raspberry, cherry cheesecake, cotton candy, pina colada, triple mint flavors)	1.23% (16 oz bottle) [equivalent to 1.23% F ion]
	Nupro Fluoride Gel (bubblegum, wild cherry flavors)	1.23% (12 oz bottle) [equivalent to 1.23% F ion]
	PCxx (banana berry, Bazooka bubblegum, grape explosion, mocha cappuccino, marshmallow float, crème de menthe, pina colada, cool peppermint, rootbeer float, raspberry blast, screamin' strawberry, vanilla orange, watermelon splash, wild cherry flavors)	1.23% (16.6 oz bottle) [equivalent 1.23% F ion]
	PediaGel (bubblegum, goofy grape, super strawberry flavors)	1.23% (12 oz bottle) [equivalent to 1.23% F ion]
	Perfect Choice One Minute APF Gel (creamy marshmallow, juicy grape, peppermint stick, pink bubblegum, strawberry delight, vanilla orange, way out watermelon flavors)	1.23% (17½ oz bottle) [equivalent to 1.23% F ion]
	Topex 00:60 APF Second Gel (bubble fun, cherry, mint, orange cream, pina colada flavors)	1.23% (16 oz bottle) [equivalent to 1.23% F ion]
	Zap Gel (bubblegum, cotton candy, grape, marshmallow, orange vanilla, strawberry, watermelon, dye-free mint flavors)	1.23% with xylitol (gluten free) (16 oz bottle) [equivalent to 1.23% F ion]
Gel, topical (as neutral sodium)	Denti-Care Neutral Sodium Fluoride Gel (mint, strawberry, raspberry flavors)	2% (16 oz bottle) [equivalent to 0.9% F ion]
	Nupro (apple cinnamon, mandarin orange, mint flavors)	2% (12 oz bottle) [equivalent to 0.9% F ion]
	PCxx (Bazooka bubblegum, mocha cappuccino, crème de menthe, cool peppermint, raspberry blast, vanilla orange, watermelon splash flavors)	2% (16.6 oz bottle) [equivalent 0.9% F ion]
	PediaGel (apple cinnamon, orange vanilla, way cool spearmint flavors)	2% (12 oz bottle) [equivalent to 0.9% F ion]
	pH 7 Neutral Fluoride Gel (mint flavor)	2% (16 oz bottle) [equivalent to 0.9% F ion]
	Topex Neutral pH (clearly strawberry [dye-free], mint, pina colada flavors)	2% (16 oz bottle) [equivalent 0.9% F ion]
	Zap Gel (mint flavor)	2% (16 oz bottle) [equivalent to 0.9% F ion]
Foam, topical (as acidulated phosphate)	Denti-Care Denti-Foam (bubblegum, grape, mint, orange, strawberry flavors)	1.23% APF [equivalent to 1.23% F ion]
	Kolorz Sixty Second (blue raspberry, cherry cheesecake, cotton candy, triple mint flavors)	1.23% (125 g) [equivalent to 1.23% F ion]
	Nupro (bubblegum, orange vanilla, spearmint, strawberry flavors)	1.23% (125 g) [equivalent to 1.23% F ion]
	Oral B Minute-Foam (banana splitz, bubblegum, grape punch, mellow mint, orange-A Tangy, strawberry flavors)	1.23% (105 g) [equivalent to 1.23% F]
	PCxx (wild cherry, Bazooka bubblegum, cool peppermint, screamin' strawberry, grape explosion, luscious lime, mocha cappuccino, raspberry blast, vanilla orange flavors)	1.23% [equivalent 1.23% F ion]
	P.U.F.F Fluoride Foam (cotton candy, peppy mint, tropical blast, very berry, wild strawberry flavors)	1.23% (210 g) [equivalent to 1.23% F ion]
	Topex 00:60 Second Foam (bubble fun, grape, orange dream, spearmint, strawberry flavors)	1.23% (125 g) [equivalent to 1.23% F]
	Waterpik UltraControl (bubblegum, melon, mint, strawberry flavors)	1.23% (125 g) [equivalent to 1.23% F]

(continued)

In-Office-Only Products *(continued)*

Form	Brand Name	Strength/Size
Foam, topical (as sodium)	DentiCare Pro-Foam Neutral (mint, raspberry flavors)	2% (125 g) [equivalent to 0.9% F]
	Kolorz Neutral (triple mint flavor)	2% (125 g) [equivalent to 0.9% F]
	Oral B Neutra-Foam (mint flavor)	2% (165 g) [equivalent to 0.9% F]
	PCxx (Bazooka bubblegum, cool peppermint, vanilla orange, screamin' strawberry, neutral [no flavor] flavors)	2% (210 g) [equivalent to 0.9% F]
	Topex Neutral (mixed berry flavor)	2% (125 g) [equivalent to 0.9% F]
Varnish, topical (as sodium)	Butler (bubblegum, melon madness flavors)	5% (0.5 mL/dose) (36/pkg) [equivalent to 2.26% F]
	CavityShield (bubblegum flavor)	5% (0.25 mL/dose) (32/pkg, 200/pkg) [equivalent to 2.26% F]
	CavityShield (bubblegum flavor)	5% (0.4 mL/dose) (32/pkg, 200/pkg) [equivalent to 2.26% F]
	Colgate Duraphat	5% (1 mL/dose) (10 mL/tube) [equivalent to 2.26% F]
	Colgate PreviDent (mint, raspberry flavors)	5% (0.40 mL/dose) (50/pkg) [equivalent to 2.26% F]
	Duraflor (bubblegum flavor)	5% (1 mL/dose) (10 mL/tube) [equivalent to 2.26% F]
	Duraflor (bubblegum flavor)	5% (0.25 mL/dose) (32/pkg, 200/pkg) [equivalent to 2.26% F]
	Duraflor (rasberry flavor)	5% (0.40 mL/dose) (32/pkg, 200/pkg) [equivalent to 2.26% F]
	Duraflor Halo (spearment, wildberry flavors)	5% (0.50 mL/dose) (32/pkg, 250/pkg) [equivalent to 2.26% F]
	DuraShield Clear (strawberry, watermelon flavors)	5% (0.40 mL/dose) (50/pkg, 200/pkg) [equivalent to 2.26% F]
	Embrace (bubblegum flavor)	5% (0.40 mL/dose) (50/pkg, 200/pkg) [equivalent to 2.26% F]
	Enamel Pro (bubblegum, strawberries n cream, vanilla mint flavors)	5% (0.40 mL/dose) (35/pkg, 200/pkg) [equivalent to 2.26% F]
	Enamel Pro Clear (bubblegum flavor)	5% (0.25 mL/dose) (35/pkg) [equivalent to 2.26% F]
	FluoroDose (bubblegum, cherry, melon, mint flavors)	5% (0.30 mL/dose) (120/pkg, 600/pkg, 1200/pkg) [equivalent to 2.26% F]
	Flor-Opal (bubblegum, white mint flavors)	5% (0.50 mL/dose) (40/pkg) [equivalent to 2.26% F]
	Iris (bubblegum, mint, raspberry flavors)	5% sodium fluoride (0.40 mL/dose) [equivalent to 2.26% F]
	Kolorz ClearShield (bubblegum, mint, watermelon flavors)	5% (0.40 mL/dose) (35/pkg, 200/pkg) [equivalent to 2.26% F]
	MI Varnish with RECALDENT (fresh strawberry flavor)	5% (0.50 mL/dose) (50/pkg) [equivalent to 2.26% F]
	Nupro (raspberry flavor)	5% (0.25 mL/dose) [equivalent to 2.26% F]
	Nupro White Varnish (grape, raspberry flavors)	5% (0.40 mL/dose) (50/pkg,100/pkg, 500/pkg) [equivalent to 2.26% F]
	Profluorid (caramel, cherry, melon, mint flavors)	5% (1 mL/dose) (10 mL/tube) [equivalent to 2.26% F]
	Profluorid (caramel, cherry, melon, mint, mixed flavors)	5% (0.40 mL/dose) (48/pkg, 50/pkg, 200/pkg) [equivalent to 2.26% F]
	Profluorid (melon flavor)	5% (0.25 mL) (kids) (50/pkg) [equivalent to 2.26% F]
	Sparkle V (bubblegum, mint flavors)	5% (0.40 mL/dose) (120/pkg) [equivalent to 2.26% F]
	Ultra Thin (bubblegum, melon, mint, strawberry, mixed flavors)	5% (0.40 mL/dose) (25/pkg, 30/pkg, 100/pkg) [equivalent to 2.26% F]
	Vanish (cherry, melon, mint, mixed flavors)	5% Sodium Fluoride White Varnish with TCP (0.50 mL/dose) (50/pkg, 100/pkg, 1000/pkg) [equivalent to 2.26% F]
	Vella (bubblegum, melon, mint, strawberry flavors)	5% Sodium Fluoride Varnish with Xylitol (0.5 mL/dose) (35/pkg, 100/pkg) [equivalent to 2.26% F]
Other fluoride varnishes	Fluor Protector	1% (0.9% difluorsilane) (0.4 mL/dose) (20/pkg) [equivalent to 0.10% F]

ANTIMICROBIAL ORAL RINSE

Chlorhexidine Gluconate (Peridex) on page 344
Chlorhexidine Gluconate alcohol-free (CHX) on page 344
Mouthwash (Antiseptic) (Listerine) on page 1150

For examples of sample prescriptions see Antimicrobial Oral Rinse on page 31

MANAGEMENT OF ALVEOLAR OSTEITIS

Alveolar osteitis, as compared to simple postoperative pain, occurs in about 2% to 5% of extractions. Factors affecting risk include the complexity of the extraction and other factors, such as smoking, excessive spitting, or poor wound care in the first 5 to 7 days after extraction. Wound healing is a complex process and can be affected by many factors. Alveolar osteitis is the most common healing disturbance of extraction sockets.

Several types of alveolar osteitis can result from disturbances in the healing process. The type that is commonly referred to as dry socket occurs when the initial blood clot that forms after tooth extraction is disturbed or lost during early healing. The healing tissue that normally replaces the blood clot (granulation tissue) fails to grow or is disrupted after beginning to grow, leading to alveolar osteitis. Alveolar osteitis is characterized by grayish slough, moderate to severe pain, and foul odor. The foul odor is a result of a breakdown of the blood clot by putrefaction, rather than by orderly retraction, leaving bare bone visible in the socket. Suppurative osteitis results when the disturbance of extraction socket wound healing is later (usually after day 14), results in infection, and exhibits a purulence in the extraction socket. Disruption of the clot can also result in necrotizing osteitis with bony sequestra.

Signs and Symptoms of Dry Socket or Postop Infection

1. Moderate to severe pain beginning 2 to 5 days after tooth extraction
2. Loss of the blood clot or visible bone in extraction site
3. Foul odor or unpleasant taste in mouth
4. Tenderness or swelling of lymph nodes around jaw
5. At the first signs of suppurative osteitis, antibiotics must be considered.

Treatments of Dry Socket

Irrigation and medicated dressings are primary ways to treat dry socket. Active ingredients in these sedative dressings usually include substances like soluble aspirin, zinc oxide, and eugenol made from oil of cloves. It is usually necessary to repeat treatment for 2 to 5 consecutive days, although it may take longer.

Resorbable dry socket products in the market include:

- Eugenol-soaked Gelfoam can be a one-time treatment with as needed follow-up if necessary
- Alvogyl by Septodont is resorbable but cannot be used on patients having a history of allergic reactions to procaine-type anesthetics or iodine

Nonresorbable dry socket products: **Note:** Must be removed and some have radiopaque markers; thus, patient compliance to return daily must be considered.

- Sultan Dry Socket Paste or Dry Socket Remedy is placed on a gauze strip and packed into the socket, follow-up and removal is needed (guaiacol, balsam peru, eugenol, 1.6% chlorobutanol); used to treat alveolitis and provides instant pain relief. Paste is introduced into socket with flat-bladed instrument, tamped down to cover exposed bone, and allowed to remain in the socket for 3 to 5 days. This is nonresorbable but is claimed to wash out gradually as socket heals.
- Dressol-X by Rainbow is another nonresorbable packing material with radiopaque marker; it contains aspirin and must not be used on patients with ASA allergy or G6PD deficiency.

REFERENCES

Benko P. Emergency dental procedures. Roberts J, et al, eds. *Clinical Procedures in Emergency Medicine*. 5th ed. Philadelphia, Pa.: Saunders Elsevier; 2009.

Cardoso CL, Rodrigues MT, Ferreira Júnior O, Garlet GP, de Carvalho PS. Clinical concepts of dry socket. *J Oral Maxillofac Surg*. 2010;68(8):1922-1932.

Noroozi AR, Philbert RF. Modern concepts in understanding and management of the "dry socket" syndrome: comprehensive review of the literature. *Oral Surg Oral Med Oral Pathol Oral Radiol Endod*. 2009;107(1):30-35.

MANAGEMENT OF SIALORRHEA

In patients suffering with medical conditions that result in hypersalivation, the dentist may determine that it is appropriate to use an atropine sulfate medication to achieve a dry field for dental procedures or to reduce excessive drooling. Currently there is one ADA approved medication sold under the name of Sal Tropine. Pro-Banthine (propantheline bromide), an antimuscarinic used for excessive stomach acid production is advocated by some for off-label use. See Atropine (Systemic) on page 186

XEROSTOMIA

Xerostomia refers to the subjective sensation of a dry mouth while salivary gland hypofunction can be objectively measured. Numerous factors can play a role in the patient's perception of xerostomia. Changes in salivary function caused by drugs, surgical intervention, or treatment of cancer are among the leading causes of xerostomia. Other factors including aging, smoking, mouth breathing, and autoimmune disorders such as Sjögren's syndrome, can also be implicated in a patient's perception of xerostomia. Human immunodeficiency virus (HIV) may produce xerostomia when viral changes in salivary glands are present. Xerostomia often occurs in patients taking antianxiety and antidepressant medication and often accompanies burning mouth syndrome. Xerostomia affects women more frequently than men and is also more common in older individuals. Some alteration in salivary function naturally occurs with age, but it is extremely difficult to quantify the effects. Xerostomia and salivary gland hypofunction in the elderly population are contributory to deterioration in the quality of life.

Once a diagnosis of xerostomia or salivary gland hypofunction is made and possible causes confirmed, treatment for the condition usually involves management of the underlying disease and avoidance of unnecessary medications. In addition, good hydration is essential and water is the drink of choice. Also, the use of artificial saliva substitutes, selected chewing gums, and/or toothpastes formulated to treat xerostomia, is often warranted. In more difficult cases, such as patients receiving radiotherapy for cancer of the head and neck regions or patients with Sjögren's syndrome, systemic cholinergic stimulants may be administered if no contraindications exist. The clinician must also rule out and treat concomitant conditions such as fungal colonization and overgrowth which often occur subsequent to xerostomia.

XEROSTOMIA TREATMENTS

Because of the complex nature of xerostomia, management by the dental clinician is difficult. Treatment success is also difficult to assess and is often unsatisfactory. The salivary stimulants, pilocarpine and cevimeline, may aid in some conditions but are only approved for use as sialogogues in patients receiving radiotherapy and in Sjögren's patients, specifically as described above. Artificial salivas are available as over-the-counter products and represent the potential for continuous application by the patient to achieve comfort for their xerostomic condition. Coenzyme Q_{10} (ubiquinone) has recently been proven successful with increasing saliva (100 mg daily) (Ryo 2011).

The role of the clinician in attempting treatment of dry mouth is to first achieve a differential diagnosis and to ensure that other conditions are not simultaneously present. For example, many patients suffer burning mouth syndrome or painful oral tissues with no obvious etiology accompanying dry mouth. Also, higher caries incidence may be associated with changes in salivary flow. As previously mentioned, Sjögren's syndrome represents an immune complex of disorders that can affect the eyes, oral tissues, and other organ systems. The reader is referred to current oral pathology or oral medicine textbooks for review of signs and symptoms of Sjögren's syndrome.

Treatment of cancer often leads to dry mouth. Surgical intervention removing salivary tissue due to the presence of a salivary gland tumor results in loss of salivary function. Also, many of the chemotherapeutic agents produce transitory changes in salivary flow, such that the patient may perceive a dry mouth during chemotherapy. Most notably related to salivary dysfunction is the use of radiation regimens to head and neck tissues. Tumors in or about salivary gland tissue, the oral cavity, and oropharynx are most notably sensitive to radiation therapy and subsequent dry mouth. In the head and neck, therapeutic radiation is commonly used in treatment of squamous cell carcinomas and lymphomas. The radiation level necessary to destroy malignant cells ranges from 40 to 70 Gy. Salivary tissue is extremely sensitive to radiation changes. Radiation dosages >30 Gy are sufficient to permanently change salivary function. In addition to the mucositis and subsequent secondary infection by fungal colonization or viral exacerbation, oral tissues can become exceptionally dry due to the effects of radiation on salivary glands. In fact, permanent damage to salivary gland tissue within the beam path produces significant levels of xerostomia in most patients. Some recovery may be noted by the patient. Most often, the effects are permanent and even progressive as the radiation dosage increases.

Artificial salivas do not produce any protectant or stimulation of the salivary gland. The use of pilocarpine and cevimeline as salivary stimulants in pre-emptive treatment, as well as postradiation treatment, have been shown to have some efficacy in management of dry mouth. The success rate, however, still is often unsatisfactory and post-treatment management by the dentist usually requires fluoride supplements to prevent radiation-induced caries due to dry mouth. Also, management of dry mouth through patient use of the artificial salivary gel, solutions and sprays, or other over-the-counter products for dry mouth (eg, chewing gum, toothpaste, mouthwash, swabsticks, sugar-free candy) is highly recommended. The use of pilocarpine or cevimeline should only be considered by the dentist in consultation with the managing physician. The oftentimes severe and widespread cholinergic side effects of pilocarpine and cevimeline mandate close monitoring of the patient and certain medical conditions contraindicated their use.

The use of artificial salivary substitutes is less problematic for the dentist. The dentist should, in considering selection of a drug, base his or her decision on patient compliance and comfort. Salivary substitutes presently on the market may have some benefit in terms of electrolyte balance and salivary consistency. However, the ultimate decision needs to be based on patients' taste, their willingness to use the medication ad libitum, and improvement in their comfort related to dry mouth. Many of the drugs are pH balanced to reduce additional risk of dental demineralization or caries. Oftentimes, the dentist must try numerous medications, one at a time, prior to finding one which gives the patient some comfort. Another gauge of acceptability is to investigate whether the artificial saliva substitute has the American Dental Association's seal of approval. Most of the currently accepted saliva substitute products have been evaluated by the ADA.

In general, considerations that the clinician might use in a prescribed regimen would be that saliva substitutes are meant to be used regularly throughout the day by the patient to achieve comfort during meals, reduce tissue abrasion, and prevent salivary stagnation on teeth. Other than these, there are no specific recommendations for patients. Recommendations by the dentist need to be tailored to the patient's acceptance. Salivary substitutes may provide an allergic potential in patients who are sensitive to some of the preservatives present in artificial saliva products. In addition to this allergic potential, there is a risk of microbial contamination by placement of the salivary substitute container in close contact with the oral cavity.

Patient education regarding the use of saliva substitutes is also part of the clinical approach. The patient with chronic xerostomia should be educated about regular professional care, high performance in dental hygiene, the need to reevaluate oral soft tissue pathology, and any changes that might occur long term. In patients with severe xerostomia, artificial salivary medications should be given in combination with topical fluoride treatment programs designed by the dentist to reduce caries (see Saliva Substitute monograph on page 1460).

REFERENCE

Ryo K, Ito A, Takatori R, et al. Effects of coenzyme Q_{10} on salivary secretion. *Clin Biochem*. 2011;44(8-9):669-674.

Products and Drugs to Treat Dry Mouth

Medication	Manufacturer and Phone Number	Product Type	Manufacturer's Description	Indication	Ingredients	Directions for Use	Form and Availability
Artificial Salivas (OTC)							
Biotene OralBalance Mouth Moisturizing Gel	Laclede Professional Products, Inc (800) 922-5856	Gel	Sugar-free oral lubricant; relieves dry mouth symptoms up to 8 hours; soothes and protects oral tissue to promote healing; helps to inhibit harmful bacteria; improves retention under dentures	Relieves symptoms of dry mouth: burning, itching, cotton palate, sore tissue swallowing difficulties	Contains the "Biotene" protective salivary enzyme system Active: Glucose oxidase (2,000 units), lactoperoxidase (3,000 units), lysozyme (5 mg), lactoferrin (5 mg) Other: Hydrogenated starch, xylitol, hydroxyethyl cellulose, glycerate polyhydrate, aloe vera	Using a clean fingertip, apply a 1" ribbon of gel on tongue; add additional amount of gel on other dry; use as needed	1.4 oz tube; available at mass merchandise stores, food stores, and drugstores
BreathTech Plaque Fighter Mouth Spray	Omnii Oral Pharmaceuticals (800) 445-3386	Pump dispenser	Plaque inhibitor in vanilla-mint flavor for breath malodor or reduced salivary flow	Treats the discomfort of oral dryness	Microdent patented plaque-inhibitor formula	Spray directly into mouth; spread over teeth and tissue with tongue	18 mL pump dispenser; order directly from manufacturer
Moi-Stir Moistening Solution	Kingswood Laboratories, Inc (800) 968-7772	Pump spray	Saliva supplement for moistening of mouth and mucosal area	Nontherapeutic treatment of dry mouth; intended for comfort only	Water, sorbitol, sodium carboxymethylcellulose, methylparaben, propylparaben, potassium chloride, sodium chloride, flavoring	Spray directly into mouth as necessary to treat drying conditions	4 oz spray bottle; order directly from manufacturer or various distributors
MouthKote Oral Moisturizer	Parnell Pharmaceuticals, Inc (800) 457-4276	Aqueous solution	Pleasant lemon-lime-flavored oral moisturizer to lubricate and protect oral tissue	Treats the discomfort of oral dryness caused by medications, disease, surgery, irradiation, aging	Water, xylitol, sorbitol, yerba santa, citric acid, ascorbic acid, flavor, sodium benzoate, sodium saccharin	Swirl 1 or 2 teaspoonfuls in mouth for 8 to 10 seconds; swallow or spit out; shake well before using	2 oz and 8 oz bottles; available at drugstores or order directly from manufacturer
Oasis Moisturizing Mouthwash	GlaxoSmithKline (800) 777-2500	Oral moisturizer, aqueous solution	Moisturizing mouthwash for a dry mouth indication	Moisturizes mouth and helps it from drying out	Active: Glycerin Other: Water, sorbitol, poloxamer 338, PEG-60 hydrogenated castor oil, cellulose gum, cetylpyridinium chloride, copovidone, disodium phosphate, flavor, methylparaben, propylparaben, sodium benzoate, sodium phosphate, sodium saccharin, xanthan gum, FD&C blue #1	Rinse for 30 seconds with 1 ounce of mouthwash first thing in the morning and before going to bed or as needed; do not swallow; use as part of an effective oral hygiene program	16 oz bottle
Optimoist Oral Moisturizer	Colgate Oral Pharmaceuticals (800) 225-3756	Oral moisturizer, aqueous solution	Pleasant tasting saliva substitute for instant relief of dry mouth and throat without demineralizing tooth enamel	Treats the discomfort of oral dryness	Deionized water, xylitol, calcium phosphate monobasic, citric acid, sodium hydroxide, sodium benzoate, flavoring, acesulfame potassium, hydroxyethylcellulose, polysorbate 20 and sodium monofluorophosphate (fluoride concentration is 2 parts per million)	Spray directly into mouth to relieve dry mouth discomfort; may be swallowed or expectorated; use as needed	2 oz and 12 oz bottles; available at mass merchandise stores, food stores, and drugstores
Salivart Synthetic Saliva, Aqueous Solution	Gebauer Co (800) 321-9348	Aerosol aqueous spray	Oral moisturizer for patients with reduced salivary flow	Replacement therapy for patients complaining of xerostomia	Sodium carboxymethylcellulose, sorbitol, sodium chloride, potassium chloride, calcium chloride dihydrate, magnesium chloride hexahydrate, potassium phosphate dibasic, purified water, nitrogen (propellant)	Spray directly into mouth or throat for 1 to 2 seconds; use as needed	2.48 fl oz (75 g); available at most drugstores or directly from manufacturer
Other Dry Mouth Products (OTC)							
Biotene Dry Mouth Gum	Laclede Professional Products, Inc (800) 922-9348	Chewing gum	Sugar-free; helps stimulate saliva flow; fights cause/effect of bad breath; reduces plaque	Treats oral dryness	Active: Lactoperoxidase (0.11 Units), glucose oxidase (0.15 Units) Other: Sorbitol, gum base, xylitol, hydrogenated glucose, potassium thiocyanate	Chew 1 or 2 pieces; use as needed	Each package contains 17 pieces; available at drugstores or directly from manufacturer

Products and Drugs to Treat Dry Mouth *continued*

Medication	Manufacturer and Phone Number	Product Type	Manufacturer's Description	Indication	Ingredients	Directions for Use	Form and Availability
Biotene Dry Mouth Toothpaste	Laclede Professional Products, Inc (800) 922-9348	Toothpaste	Reduces harmful bacteria which cause cavities, periodontal disease, and oral infections	Use in place of regular toothpaste for dry mouth	Active: Lactoperoxidase (15,000 Units), glucose oxidase (10,000 Units), lysozyme (16 mg), sodium monofluorophosphate Other: Sorbitol, glycerin, calcium pyrophosphate, hydrated silica, xylitol, isoceteth-20, cellulose gum, flavoring, sodium benzoate, beta-d-glucose, potassium thiocyanate	Use in place of regular toothpaste; rinse toothbrush before applying; brush for 2 minutes; rinse lightly	4.5 oz tube; available at drugstores or directly from manufacturer
Biotene Gentle Mouthwash	Laclede Professional Products, Inc (800) 922-9348	Mouthwash	Alcohol-free; strong antibacterial formula neutralizes mouth odors; soothes as it cleans to protect teeth and oral tissue	Treats dry mouth or oral irritations	Lysozyme, lactoferrin, glucose oxidase, lactoperoxidase	Use 15 mL (1 tablespoonful); swish thoroughly for 30 seconds and spit out; for dry throat, sip 1 tablespoonful of mouthwash 2 to 3 times/day	Available at drugstores or directly from manufacturer
Moi-Stir Oral Swabsticks	Kingswood Laboratories, Inc (800) 968-7772	Swabsticks	Lubricates and moistens mouth and mucosal area	Lubricates and moistens mouth and mucosal area	Water, sorbitol, sodium carboxymethylcellulose, methylparaben, propylparaben, potassium chloride, sodium chloride, flavoring	Gently swab all intraoral surfaces of mouth, gums, tongue, palate, buccal mucosa, gingival, teeth, and lips where uncomfortable dryness exists	3 swabsticks/packet, 100 packets/case; order directly from manufacturer or from various distributors.
Oasis Moisturizing Mouth Spray	GlaxoSmithKline (800) 777-2500	Oral moisturizer	Moisturizing mouth spray for a dry mouth indication	Moisturizes mouth and helps it from drying out	Active: Glycerin 35% (prediluted) Other: Cetylpyridinium chloride, copovidone, flavor, methylparaben, PEG-60 hydrogenated castor oil propylparaben, sodium benzoate, sodium saccharin, water, xanthan gum, xylitol	Use as required up to a maximum of 30 times or 60 sprays a day; spray 1 to 2 times into the affected area of mouth; do not rinse out	1 oz bottle
XyliMelts Discs	OraHealth (877) 672-6541	Time-release adhering discs	Lubricant	Treats dry mouth, reduces plaque	Xylitol 500 mg, cellulose gum	Use 2 discs as needed	120 tablets
Saliva Substitute (Rx)							
Aquoral	Auriga Laboratories (877) 287-4428	Pump spray	Lipid-based solution designed to moisten and lubricate the oral cavity and oropharynx by formation of lipid film which limits loss of water and restores the viscoelasticity of the oral mucosa	Chronic and temporary xerostomia which may be the result of Sjögren's syndrome, oral inflammation, medication, chemo- or radiotherapy, and stress or aging. **Note:** Contraindicated if patient has a known history of hypersensitivity to any of its ingredients. No known interactions with medicinal or other products.	Oxidized glycerol triesters (TGO), silicon dioxide, aspartame, and artificial flavoring	Shake gently; 1 dose (2 sprays) into the mouth 3-4 times/day; spread product onto inflamed and/or dry areas of the mouth with the tongue.	1 bottle (40 mL = 400 sprays)

Products and Drugs to Treat Dry Mouth *continued*

Medication	Manufacturer and Phone Number	Product Type	Manufacturer's Description	Indication	Ingredients	Directions for Use	Form and Availability
Cholinergic Salivary Stimulants (Rx)							
Cevimeline (Evoxac)	Snow Brand Pharmaceuticals (800) 475-6473			Treats symptoms of dry mouth in patients with Sjögren's syndrome	Active: Cevimeline 30 mg Other: Lactose monohydrate, hydroxypropyl cellulose, magnesium stearate	1 capsule (30 mg) 3 times/day	30 mg capsules
Pilocarpine (Salagen)	MGI Pharmaceuticals, Inc (800) 562-5580			Treats xerostomia caused by radiation therapy in patients with head/neck cancer, Sjögren's syndrome	Active: Pilocarpine 5 mg Other: Carnauba wax, hydroxypropyl methylcellulose, iron oxide, microcrystalline cellulose, stearic acid, titanium dioxide	1 to 2 tablets (5 mg) 3 to 4 times/day, not to exceed 30 mg/day	5 mg tablets

CHOLINERGIC SALIVARY STIMULANTS (PRESCRIPTION ONLY)

Pilocarpine (Systemic) (Salagen on page 1337) and cevimeline (Evoxac on page 341) are cholinergic drugs which stimulate salivary flow. They stimulate muscarinic-type acetylcholine receptors in salivary glands within the parasympathetic division of the autonomic nervous system, causing an increase in serous-type saliva. Thus, they are considered cholinergic, muscarinic-type (parasympathomimetic) drugs. Due to significant side effects caused by these drugs, they are available by prescription only.

Pilocarpine (Salagen) is indicated for the treatment of xerostomia caused by radiation therapy in patients with head and neck cancer and xerostomia in patients suffering from Sjögren's syndrome. The usual adult dosage is 1 to 2 tablets (5 mg or 7.5 mg/tablet) 3 to 4 times/day, not to exceed 30 mg/day. Patients should be treated for a minimum of 90 days for optimum effect. The most frequent adverse side effect is perspiration, which occurs in about 30% of patients who use 5 mg 3 times/day. Other adverse effects (in about 10% of patients) are nausea, rhinitis, chills, frequent urination, dizziness, headache, lacrimation, and pharyngitis. Salagen is contraindicated for patients with uncontrolled asthma and narrow-angle glaucoma.

Pilocarpine has been documented to overcome xerostomia from different causes. More recent studies confirm its effectiveness in improving salivary flow in patients undergoing irradiation therapy for head and neck cancer. A capstone study by Johnson, et al, reported the effects of pilocarpine in 208 irradiation patients at 39 different treatment sites. Salagen, at a dose of 5 mg 3 times/day, improved salivation in 44% of patients, compared with 25% in the placebo group. They concluded that treatment with pilocarpine (Salagen) produced the best overall outcome with respect to saliva production and relief of symptoms of xerostomia in patients undergoing irradiation therapy.

Additional studies have been published showing the effectiveness of pilocarpine (Salagen) in stimulating salivary flow in patients suffering from Sjögren's syndrome and the FDA has approved the use of Salagen for this indication.

Recent reports suggest that pre-emptive use of pilocarpine may be effective in protecting salivary glands during therapeutic irradiation; further studies are needed to confirm this. As of this publication date, the use of pilocarpine has not been approved to treat xerostomia induced by chronic medication. Pilocarpine could be used as a sialagogue for individuals with xerostomia induced by antidepressants and other medications. However, the potential for serious drug interactions is a concern and more studies are needed to clarify the safety and effectiveness of pilocarpine when given in the presence of other medications.

Cevimeline (Evoxac) is indicated for treatment of symptoms of dry mouth in patients with Sjögren's syndrome. The usual dosage in adults is 1 capsule (30 mg) 3 times/day. Cevimeline (Evoxac) is supplied in 30 mg capsules. Some adverse effects reported for Evoxac include increased sweating (19%), nausea (14%), rhinitis (11%), sinusitis (12%), and upper respiratory infection (11%). Evoxac is contraindicated for patients with uncontrolled asthma, narrow-angle glaucoma, acute iritis, and other conditions where miosis is undesirable. Cevimeline's half-life elimination is significantly slower than pilocarpine (0.76 hours versus 5 hours).

Other Drugs Implicated in Xerostomia

>10%	1% to 10%
ALPRAZolam	Acrivastine and Pseudoephedrine
Amitriptyline hydrochloride	Albuterol
Amoxapine	Almotriptan
Anisotropine methylbromide	Amantadine hydrochloride
AtoMOXetine	Amphetamine sulfate
Atropine sulfate	Anastrozole
Belladonna and Opium	Armodafinil
Benztropine mesylate	Astemizole (withdrawn from market)
Boceprevir	Azatadine maleate
BuPROPion	Beclomethasone dipropionate
ChlordiazePOXIDE	Bendamustine
ClomiPRAMINE hydrochloride	Bepridil hydrochloride
ClonazePAM	Bevacizumab
CloNIDine	Bitolterol mesylate
Clorazepate dipotassium	Brompheniramine maleate
Cyclobenzaprine	Carbinoxamine and Pseudoephedrine
Desipramine hydrochloride	Chlorpheniramine maleate
Desvenlafaxine	Clemastine fumarate
DiazePAM	CloZAPine
Dicyclomine hydrochloride	Cromolyn sodium
Diphenoxylate and Atropine	Cyproheptadine hydrochloride

Other Drugs Implicated in Xerostomia *(continued)*

>10%	1% to 10%
Doxepin hydrochloride	Dexchlorpheniramine maleate
DULoxetine	Dextroamphetamine sulfate
Ergotamine	DimenhyDRINATE
Estazolam	DiphenhydrAMINE hydrochloride
Everolimus	Disopyramide phosphate
FlavoxATE	Doxazosin
Flurazepam hydrochloride	Dronabinol
Glycopyrrolate	EPHEDrine sulfate
Guanabenz acetate	Escitalopram
GuanFACINE hydrochloride	Flumazenil
Hyoscyamine sulfate	FluvoxaMINE
IncobotulinumtoxinA	Gabapentin
Interferon alfa-2a	Guaifenesin and Codeine
Interferon alfa-2b	Guanadrel sulfate
Interferon alfa-N3	Guanethidine sulfate
Ipratropium bromide	HydrOXYzine
Isoproterenol	Hyoscyamine, Atropine, Scopolamine, and Phenobarbital
ISOtretinoin	Iloperidone
Loratadine	Imipramine
LORazepam	Isoetharine
Loxapine	LamoTRIgine
Maprotiline hydrochloride	Levocabastine hydrochloride
Methscopolamine bromide	Levodopa
Molindone hydrochloride	Levodopa and Carbidopa
Nabilone	Levorphanol tartrate
Nefazodone	Meclizine hydrochloride
Oxazepam	Meperidine hydrochloride
Oxybutynin chloride	Methadone hydrochloride
PARoxetine	Methamphetamine hydrochloride
Phenelzine sulfate	Methyldopa
Prochlorperazine	Metoclopramide
Propafenone hydrochloride	Milnacipran
Protriptyline hydrochloride	Morphine sulfate
Quazepam	Nortriptyline hydrochloride
Reserpine	Ondansetron
RimabotulinumtoxinB	OxyCODONE and Acetaminophen
Selegiline hydrochloride	OxyCODONE and Aspirin
Temazepam	Peginterferons
Thiethylperazine maleate	Pentazocine
Tiotropium	Phenylpropanolamine hydrochloride
TiZANidine	Prazosin hydrochloride
Trihexyphenidyl hydrochloride	Promethazine hydrochloride
Trimipramine maleate	Propoxyphene
Trospium	Pseudoephedrine
Venlafaxine	RisperiDONE
Zuclopenthixol	ROPINIRole
	Sertraline hydrochloride
	Tapentadol
	Terazosin
	Terbutaline sulfate
	Varenicline

TEMPOROMANDIBULAR DYSFUNCTION (TMD), CHRONIC PAIN, AND FIBROMYALGIA

Temporomandibular dysfunction comprises a broad spectrum of signs and symptoms and is the most common cause of chronic nondental facial pain. TMD usually involves the muscles of mastication uni- or bilaterally. Although TMD presents in patterns, diagnosis is often difficult. Evaluation and treatment is time-intensive and no single therapy or drug regimen has been shown to be universally beneficial.

The thorough diagnostician should perform a screening examination for temporomandibular dysfunction on all patients. Ideally, a baseline maximum mandibular opening along with lateral and protrusive movement evaluation should be performed. Secondly, the joint area should be palpated and an adequate exam of the muscles of mastication and the muscles of the neck and shoulders should be made. These muscles include the elevators of the mandible (masseter, internal pterygoid, and temporalis); the depressors of the mandible (including the external pterygoid and digastric); extrusive muscles (including the temporalis and digastric), and protrusive muscles (including the external and internal pterygoids). These muscles also account for lateral movement of the mandible.

The clinician should also be alert to indicators of dysfunction, primarily a history of pain with jaw function, chronic history of joint noise (although this can often be misinterpreted), pain in the muscles of the neck, limited jaw movement, pain in the actual muscles of mastication, and headache or even earache. The signs and symptoms are extremely variable and the clinician should be alert for any or all of these areas of interest. Because of the complexity of both evaluation and diagnosis, the general dentist often finds it too time consuming to spend the countless hours evaluating and treating the temporomandibular dysfunction patient. Therefore, oral medicine specialists trained in temporomandibular evaluation and treatment often accept referrals for the management of these complicated patients. Effective treatment therapies are listed in Tables 1 and 2.

TMD often accompanies other chronic pain conditions, such as facial neuralgia, fibromyalgia, chronic headache, and even Burning Mouth Syndrome. Neuropathic pain is usually unilateral with on and off episodes. A common example of neuropathic pain is trigeminal neuralgia. This presents as pain described as an electric shock often in response to a light touch. Finding the underlying cause of chronic facial pain can be challenging for the diagnostician. Other diagnostic pearls including, giant cell arteritis must be ruled out, especially in patients >50 years of age. Cancer may be the underlying cause of progressive neuropathic pain. While rarely recognized as a neuropathic pain, burning mouth syndrome is most common in perimenopausal women.

Chronic Headache

The lifetime prevalence of headache is >90% for chronic headache patients. Most patients who present with headache have one of three main headache syndromes: Migraine, cluster headache, or tension headache. However, headache and facial pain can have numerous other etiologies that are important for the clinician to consider (eg, pain associated with chronic sinusitis). Two main idiopathic disorders that cause headache and facial pain are midfacial segment pain and atypical facial pain. Midfacial segment pain is a form of tension-type headache of the midface. This pain consists of a symmetric pressure sensation in the nasion, nasal dorsum, periorbital, or malar region. Hyperesthesia of the skin and soft tissues is also found. Treatment consists of low-dose amitriptyline at 10 mg for 6 months and may take up to 6 weeks to show effect. Atypical facial pain is also known as persistent idiopathic facial pain and is constant, deep, and ill-defined, usually crossing recognized dermatomes. The distribution is often unilateral. It occurs most commonly in women older than 40 years of age. The pain may alter in location and psychological factors may play a role. The treatment is similar to that for midfacial segment pain.

Fibromyalgia (Fibromyositis; Fibrositis)

Fibromyalgia is a common syndrome in which a patient has long-term, body-wide pain and tenderness in the joints, muscles, tendons, and other soft tissues. Fibromyalgia has also been linked to fatigue, sleep problems, headaches, depression, and anxiety. The cause of fibromyalgia is unknown; however, suggested causes or triggers include physical or emotional trauma, abnormal pain response, sleep disturbances, or infection (ie, unidentified virus). Fibromyalgia is most common among women 20 to 50 years of age.

Conditions that have been associated with fibromyalgia or mimic its symptoms include chronic neck or back pain, systemic exertion intolerance disease (formerly known as chronic fatigue syndrome), depression, hypothyroidism, Lyme disease, sleep disorders, and atypical facial pain. Patients with fibromyalgia tend to wake up with body aches and stiffness. For some patients, pain improves during the day and gets worse at night, while others experience pain all day long. The pain may get worse with activity, cold or damp weather, anxiety, and stress. Fatigue, depressed mood, and sleep problems (sleep interruption is often reported) are seen in almost all patients with fibromyalgia.

A patient must have at least 3 months of widespread pain and tenderness in at least 11 of 18 areas to be diagnosed with fibromyalgia. These areas may include arms (elbows), buttocks, chest, knees, lower back, neck, rib cage, shoulders, or thighs. Blood and urine tests are usually normal; however, tests may be done to rule out other conditions that may have similar symptoms.

Treatment:

While acute facial pain may be more easily treated by one practitioner, patients with chronic facial pain are best managed by a multidisciplinary team of health professionals (Zakrzewska 2013).

The goal of treatment is to help relieve pain and other symptoms and to help the patient cope with symptoms. The first type of treatment may involve physical therapy, exercise and fitness programs, or stress-relief methods (eg, light massage and relaxation techniques). If these treatments fail, an antidepressant or muscle relaxant may be prescribed. The goal of medication is to improve sleep and pain tolerance. All medications should be used along with exercise and behavior therapy. Duloxetine, pregabalin, and milnacipran are medications that are approved specifically for treating fibromyalgia. People with fibromyalgia are typically treated with pain medicines, antidepressants, muscle relaxants, and sleep medicines. In June 2007, Lyrica (pregabalin) became the first FDA-approved drug for specifically treating fibromyalgia; a year later, in June 2008, Cymbalta (duloxetine) became the second; and in January 2009, Savella (milnacipran) became the third.

Lyrica, Cymbalta, and Savella reduce pain and improve function in some people with fibromyalgia. While those with fibromyalgia have been shown to experience pain differently from other people, the mechanism by which these drugs produce their effects is unknown. There is data suggesting that these drugs affect the release of neurotransmitters in the brain. Lyrica, marketed by Pfizer Inc, was previously approved to treat seizures, as well as pain in people with diabetes (diabetic peripheral neuropathy) and in those who develop pain associated with post-herpetic neuropathy. Side effects of Lyrica including sleepiness, dizziness, blurry vision, weight gain, trouble concentrating, swelling of the hands and feet, and dry mouth. Allergic reactions, although rare, can occur. Cymbalta, marketed by Eli Lilly and Co, was previously approved to treat depression, anxiety, and diabetic peripheral neuropathy. Cymbalta's side effects include nausea, dry mouth, sleepiness, constipation, decreased appetite, and increased sweating. Like some other antidepressants, Cymbalta may increase the risk of suicidal thinking and behavior in people who take the drug for depression. Some people with fibromyalgia also experience depression. Savella, marketed by Forest Pharmaceuticals, Inc, is the first drug introduced primarily for treating fibromyalgia. Savella is not used to treat depression in the United States, but acts like medicines that are used to treat depression. Antidepressants may increase suicidal thoughts or actions in some people. Side effects include nausea, constipation, dizziness, insomnia, excessive sweating, vomiting, palpitations or increased heart rate, dry mouth, and high blood pressure.

Other medications that have been suggested to treat this condition include antiseizure drugs, other antidepressants, muscle relaxants, pain relievers, or sleeping aids. Severe cases of fibromyalgia may require a referral to a pain management clinic.

Some health care providers may recommend an injection in the temporomandibular joint to help alleviate TMJ problems. It is important to note that these treatments have NOT been approved by the Food and Drug Administration (FDA) for treating TMJ disorders.

Botulinum toxin type A (Botox) is a drug made from the same bacterium that causes food poisoning. Used in small dosages, Botox injections can actually help alleviate some health problems and are approved by the Food and Drug Administration (FDA) for certain disorders. However, Botox is currently not approved by the FDA for use in TMJ disorders. Results from recent clinical studies are inconclusive regarding the effectiveness of Botox for treatment of chronic TMJ disorders. Additional research is under way to learn how Botox specifically affects jaw muscles and their nerves.

Steroid injection can be of help in reducing inflammation in cases of an acute flair-up of degenerative joint disease or rheumatoid arthritis. However, it is only a temporary palliative measure and does not address the cause of the problem. Controversy still exists regarding steroid injections as a TMJ treatment.

Hyaluronan (Hyaluronic acid/Hyaluronate) is sometimes used to treat osteoarthritis in the knees or hips; however, there is not enough evidence to judge whether it is helpful for people with TMJ problems. According to the FDA, hyaluronic acid has not been approved to treat TMJ disorders.

Local anesthetics are sometimes injected into the TM joint or jaw muscles for diagnostic purposes to determine the source of the pain. They are also used therapeutically to inject trigger points in the muscles. Such procedures do not need FDA approval as long as the anesthetic agent is an approved drug.

Ozone therapy involves the injection of ozone gas into the temporomandibular joint. Its use is based on the false theory that ozone can kill such bacteria, viruses, and fungi, as well as reduce inflammation and stimulate cartilage growth. Thus, there is no scientific basis for its use in the TM joint and ozone therapy is not approved by the FDA.

Prolotherapy (Sclerotherapy) is a technique in which an irritating solution is injected into a ligament or muscle tendon near a painful area with the intent of inducing the proliferation of new cells and thus strengthening these structures, supporting the weakened muscles, and eliminating the pain. Although it has been used mainly to treat chronic low back pain, it has also been recommended for patients with temporomandibular disorders. However, there is no scientific evidence to show that weakened ligaments and tendons are the cause of pain in TMD patients, or to substantiate the effectiveness of this procedure in eliminating the pain. Moreover, there are no studies to elucidate the risks of collateral tissue effects and prolotherapy should be avoided for TMJ treatments.

Studies are currently being performed to determine the efficacy of chronic pain medications in the specific management of TMD.

The oral medicine specialist in TMD management, the physical therapist interested in head and neck pain, and the oral and maxillofacial surgeon will all work together with the referring general dentist to accomplish successful patient treatment. Table 1 lists the wide variety of treatment alternatives available to the team. Depending on the diagnosis, one or more of the therapies might be selected. For organic diseases of the joint not responding to nonsurgical approaches, a wide variety of surgical techniques are available (Table 2).

ACUTE TMD

Acute TMD oftentimes presents alone or as an episode during a chronic pattern of signs and symptoms. Trauma, such as a blow to the chin or the side of the face, can result in acute TMD. Occasionally, similar symptoms will follow a lengthy wide open mouth dental procedure.

The condition usually presents as continuous deep pain in the TMJ. If edema is present in the joint, the condyle sometimes can be displaced which will cause abnormal occlusion of the posterior teeth on the affected side. The diagnosis is usually based on the history and clinical presentation. Management of the patient includes:

1. Explaining the problem and reassuring the patient
2. Restriction of all mandibular movement to function in a pain-free range of motion
3. Recommending a soft diet (eg, eggs, yogurt, casseroles, soup, ground meat). Avoid chewing gum or eating salads, large sandwiches or fruit that is hard or not sliced into small bites.
4. NSAIDs (eg, Anaprox DS 1 tablet every 12 hours for 7 to 10 days)
5. Moist heat applications to the affected area for 15 to 20 minutes, 4 to 6 times/day
6. Consideration of a muscle relaxant, such as Methocarbamol (Robaxin) on page 1077, adult patient of average height/weight, two (500 mg) tablets at bedtime; daytime dose can be tailored to patient

Additional therapies could include referral to a physical therapist for ultrasound therapy 2 to 4 times/week and a single injection of steroid in the joint space. A team approach with an oral maxillofacial surgeon for this procedure may be helpful.

CHRONIC TMD

The most common therapeutic modalities include:

- As with acute TMD: Reassuring the patient, soft diet, applying moist heat, and consideration of muscle relaxants are useful.
- Reducing stress; a monitored exercise program will be beneficial. Usually, working with a physical therapist is ideal.
- Medications include analgesics, anti-inflammatories, and tranquilizers

MEDICATION OPTIONS

Most commonly used medication (NSAIDs)

Choline Magnesium Trisalicylate on page 356
Diclofenac (Systemic) on page 496
Diflunisal on page 506
Etodolac on page 668
Fenoprofen on page 696
Flurbiprofen (Systemic) on page 746
Ibuprofen on page 851
Indomethacin on page 882
Ketoprofen on page 945
Ketorolac (Systemic) on page 948
Magnesium Salicylate on page 1035
Meclofenamate on page 1042
Mefenamic Acid on page 1044
Nabumetone on page 1157
Naproxen on page 1169
Oxaprozin on page 1250
Piroxicam on page 1346
Salsalate on page 1462
Sulindac on page 1509
Tolmetin

Tranquilizers and muscle relaxants, when used appropriately, can provide excellent adjunctive therapy. These drugs should be primarily used for a short period of time to manage acute pain. In low dosages, amitriptyline is often used to treat chronic pain and occasionally migraine headache. Two drugs similar to the prototype drug, amitriptyline, have been approved for use in adults only, for treatment of acute migraine with or without aura: Almotriptan malate (Axert [tablets]; Pharmacia Corp) and frovatriptan succinate (Frova [tablets]; Endo Pharmaceuticals). Other approved abortive (but not preventative) antimigraine triptan drugs include eletriptan (Relpax), naratriptan (Amerge), rizatriptan (Maxalt), sumatriptan (Imitrex), and zolmitriptan (Zomig). Selective serotonin reuptake inhibitors (SSRIs) are sometimes used in the management of chronic neuropathic pain, particularly in patients not responding to amitriptyline. Gabapentin (Neurontin) has been approved for chronic pain. Problems of inducing bruxism with SSRIs, however, have been reported and may preclude their use. Clinicians attempting to evaluate any patient with bruxism or involuntary muscle movement, who is simultaneously being treated with an SSRI, should be aware of this potential association.

Botox (botulinum toxin type A) is a drug made from the same bacterium that causes food poisoning. Used in small doses, Botox injections can actually help alleviate some health problems and have been approved by the Food and Drug Administration (FDA) for certain disorders. However, Botox is currently not approved by the FDA for use in TMJ disorders. Results from recent clinical studies are inconclusive regarding the effectiveness of Botox for treatment of chronic TMJ disorders. Additional research is under way to learn how Botox specifically affects jaw muscles and their nerves. The findings will help determine if this drug may be useful in treating TMJ disorders.

See individual monographs for dosing instructions.

Common minor tranquilizers include:

ALPRAZolam on page 101
DiazePAM on page 491
LORazepam on page 1020

Chronic neuropathic pain management:

Effective treatment usually involves medications. If the patient is unresponsive to medical management then a neurosurgery consultation may be necessary.

Amitriptyline on page 116
CarBAMazepine on page 293
Gabapentin on page 780
OXcarbazepine on page 1252

Acute migraine management:

Almotriptan on page 99
Eletriptan on page 561
Frovatriptan on page 776
Naratriptan on page 1174
Rizatriptan on page 1448
SUMAtriptan on page 1510
ZOLMitriptan on page 1682

Fibromyalgia management:

DULoxetine on page 552
Milnacipran on page 1126
Pregabalin on page 1382

Other non-FDA approved options:

AbobotulinumtoxinA on page 53
Hyaluronate and Derivatives on page 818

Common muscle relaxants include:

Chlorzoxazone on page 354
Cyclobenzaprine on page 427
Methocarbamol on page 1077
Orphenadrine on page 1245

Note: Muscle relaxants and tranquilizers should generally be prescribed with an analgesic or NSAID to relieve pain as well.

Opioid analgesics can be used on a short-term basis or intermittently in combination with non-opioid therapy in the chronic pain patient. Judicious prescribing, monitoring, and maintenance by the practitioner is imperative whenever considering the use of opioid analgesics due to the abuse and addiction liabilities.

Table 1. TMD – Nonsurgical Therapies

1. Moist heat and cold spray
2. Injections in muscle trigger areas (procaine)
3. Exercises (passive, active)
4. Medications
    a. Muscle relaxants
    b. Minerals (magnesium, glucosamine, chondroitin)
    c. Multiple vitamins (Ca, B_6, B_{12})
    d. NSAIDs, opioid combinations, antidepressants
5. Orthopedic craniomandibular repositioning appliance (splints)
6. Biofeedback, acupuncture
7. Physiotherapy: TMJ muscle therapy
8. Myofunctional therapy (occasionally)
9. TENS (transcutaneous electrical neural stimulation), Myo-Monitor (occasionally)

10. Dental therapy
    a. Equilibration (coronoplasty) (occasionally)
    b. Restoring occlusion to proper vertical dimension of maxilla to mandible by orthodontics, dental restorative procedures, orthognathic surgery, permanent splint, or any combination of these

Table 2. TMD – Surgical Therapies

1. Cortisone injection into joint (with local anesthetic)
2. Bony and/or fibrous ankylosis: Requires surgery (osteoarthrotomy with prosthetic appliance)
3. Chronic subluxation: Requires surgery, depending on problem (possibly eminectomy and/or prosthetic implant)
4. Osteoarthritis: Requires surgery (arthroscopy), depending on problem
    a. Arthroplasty
    b. Meniscectomy
    c. Arthroplasty with repair of disc
    d. Arthrocentesis
5. Rheumatoid arthritis
    a. Arthroplasty
    b. "Total" TMJ replacement
6. Tumors: Require osteoarthrotomy – removal of tumor and restoring of joint when possible
7. Chronic disc displacement: Arthroscopy with arthrocentesis; possible removal of bone from condyle

REFERENCES

Abeles M, Solitar BM, Pillinger MH, Abeles AM. Update on fibromyalgia therapy. *Am J Med*. 2008;121(7):555-561.

Ernberg M, Hedenberg-Magnusson B, List T, Svensson P. Efficacy of botulinum toxin type A for treatment of persistent myofascial TMD pain: a randomized, controlled, double-blind multicenter study. *Pain*. 2011;152(9):1988-1996.

Fedorowicz Z, van Zuuren EJ, Schoones J. Botulinum toxin for masseter hypertrophy. *Cochrane Database of Systematic Reviews 2013*. Issue 9. Art. No: CD007510.

Häuser W, Bernardy K, Uçeyler N, Sommer C. Treatment of fibromyalgia syndrome with antidepressants: a meta-analysis. *JAMA*. 2009;301(2):198-209.

Stoustrup P, Kristensen KD, Verna C, Küseler A, Pedersen TK, Herlin T. Intra-articular steroid injection for temporomandibular joint arthritis in juvenile idiopathic arthritis: a systematic review on efficacy and safety. *Semin Arthritis Rheum*. 2013;43(1):63-70.

Wolfe F, Rasker JJ. Fibromyalgia. *Kelley's Textbook of Rheumatology*. 8th ed. Chapter 38. Firestein GS, Budd RC, Harris ED Jr, et al, eds. Philadelphia, PA: Saunders Elsevier; 2008.

Wolfe F, Clauw DJ, Fitzcharles MA, et al. The American College of Rheumatology preliminary diagnostic criteria for fibromyalgia and measurement of symptom severity. *Arthritis Care Res (Hoboken)*. 2010;62(5):600-610.

Zakrzewska JM. Differential diagnosis of facial pain and guidelines for management. *Br J Anaesth*. 2013;111(1):95-104.

MANAGEMENT OF THE PATIENT WITH ANXIETY OR DEPRESSION

ANXIETY AND DEPRESSION

Over the past two decades, there has been a gradual, but steady, increase in the number of patients who are taking antianxiety and antidepressant medications. Much of this is driven by the emergence of new medications for management of these conditions and an increasing awareness on the part of medical clinicians in recognizing signs and symptoms of depression and anxiety. In addition, society has now accepted that the quality of life for these patients can be improved on an outpatient basis.

Anxiety is characterized by apprehension or fear of impending actual or imagined danger, vulnerability, or uncertainty and may be accompanied by restlessness, tension, tachycardia, and dyspnea unattached to a clearly identifiable stimulus. (ICD 10 code F41.1, F41.9, and F43.23)

Depression is an unpleasant, but not necessarily irrational or pathological, mood state characterized by sadness, despair, or discouragement; it may also involve low self-esteem, social withdrawal, and somatic symptoms such as eating and sleep disturbance. (ICD 10 code F32.9 and F33.1)

Oral Manifestations and Considerations

Oral

- Neglect of oral hygiene leading to increased risk of dental caries and periodontal disease
- Poor nutrition
- Drug-induced xerostomia (chronic xerostomia is associated with fungal overgrowth, burning mouth syndrome, caries, and mucosal irritations and is difficult to manage when it is drug induced)
- Some studies report a positive correlation with temporomandibular disorders and atypical facial pain

Other Potential Disorders/Concerns

- Mitral valve prolapse and GERD
- Children with depression are at increased risk for engaging in high-risk behaviors (promiscuity, smoking, alcohol and drug abuse)

Oral Side Effects of Commonly Prescribed Medications

Depression: SSRIs, Atypical Antidepressants: Xerostomia, dysphagia, sialadenitis; Tricyclic Antidepressants (TCA's): Dysgeusia, stomatitis, gingivitis, glossitis, tongue edema, discolored tongue, and bruxism

Anxiety: SSRIs, Atypical Antidepressants: Xerostomia, dysphagia, sialadenitis; Benzodiazepines: Dysgeusia, stomatitis, gingivitis, glossitis, tongue edema

The dentist often encounters patients taking medications that have the potential to induce mild to moderate adverse oral side effects and may create additional risk based on the types of medication used in the dental practice. In addition to a wide variety of depression-indicated signs and symptoms, antidepressant medications are prescribed for psychiatric disorders, pain control, sleep deprivation, smoking cessation, substance abuse, and eating disorders.

The side effects of these drugs primarily fall into several categories. Xerostomia or altered salivary flow has long been known as a side effect of tricyclic antidepressants. Newer antidepressants, although the effects may be lessened, also have similar side effects. Coupled with xerostomia is an increased risk of fungal infections and a significant association with burning mouth syndrome (BMS). The reader is referred to Fungal Infections on page 1847 and Ulcerative, Erosive, and Painful Oral Mucosal Disorders on page 1853 for management if an infection is suspected. In addition, some drugs, including the selective serotonin reuptake inhibitors (SSRIs), have effects on orthostatic hypotension and there have been rare reports of increased bruxism with chronic use of the drugs. Many of the antianxiety and antidepressant medications have shown some efficacy in the management of chronic pain and some have approval for use in atypical facial pain and temporomandibular dysfunction (TMD). Generally, the dosing for these chronic pain conditions is lower than the dosing for the management of depression or anxiety, but the approved dosing should always be verified before prescribing.

Another potential adverse reaction is cardiotoxicity associated with the use of combination drugs, including the antidepressant medication classes, and the use of a vasoconstrictor in local anesthetics. The reader is referred to Vasoconstrictor Interactions With Antidepressants on page 1913 in the appendix which discusses the classes of antidepressant and antianxiety medications and the potential risk of interactions with local anesthetics.

In reviewing the epidemiology of antidepressant and antianxiety medications, female subjects outnumber males by ~2.3:1 ratio with selective serotonin reuptake inhibitors being the most commonly prescribed medications. Tricyclic antidepressants, atypical third-generation antidepressants, and monoamine oxidase inhibitors are also used. Some of the drugs used for smoking cessation also fall into this atypical antidepressant class.

BIPOLAR DISORDER

Many advances have occurred in the treatment of bipolar illness and a number of drugs have been FDA-approved for use, including some of the atypical antipsychotics (eg, aripiprazole, olanzapine, risperidone, ziprasidone). Treatment options include mood stabilizers (eg, lithium, valproic acid, carbamazepine, oxcarbazepine), antidepressants, electroconvulsive therapy, and antipsychotics (adjunctive therapy). Most people with bipolar disorder take combinations of lithium, valproate, and carbamazepine to manage symptoms and prevent recurrence of bipolar episodes. These medications are often called mood stabilizers, to even out emotional highs and lows. These patients may also be prescribed other medications to treat the agitation, anxiety, and sleep disturbances that may accompany their illness. In patients with concomitant depression, antidepressants can help manage the feelings of sadness, guilt, worthlessness, or hopelessness. Dry mouth, constipation, and nausea are the most common side effects.

SEDATION

Anxiety constitutes the most frequently found psychiatric problem in the general population. Anxiety can range from a simple phobia to a severe debilitating disorder. Functional results of this anxiety can, therefore, range from simple avoidance of dental procedures to panic attacks when confronting stressful situations, such as seen in some patients regarding dental visits. Many patients claim to be anxious over dental care, when in reality, they simply have not been managed with modern techniques of local anesthesia, the availability of sedation, or the caring dental practitioner.

The dentist may detect anxiety in patients during the treatment planning and evaluation phases of care. The anxious person may appear overly alert, may lean forward in the dental chair during conversation, or may appear concerned over time, possibly using this as a guise to cut short the dental visit. Anxious persons may also show signs of being nervous by demonstrating sweating; muscle tension, including their temporomandibular musculature; or they may complain of being tired due to an inability to obtain an adequate night's sleep.

The management of these patients requires a methodical approach to relaxation, discussing their dental needs, and then planning, along with the patient, the best way to accomplish dental treatment in the presence of their fears, either real or imagined. Consideration may be given to sedation. This sedation can be oral or parenteral, or inhalation in the case of nitrous oxide. The dentist must be adequately trained in administering the sedative of choice, as well as in monitoring the patient during the sedated procedures. Numerous medications are available to achieve the level of sedation usually necessary in the dental office: Valium, Ativan, Xanax, Vistaril, Serax, and BuSpar represent a few. These oral sedatives can be given prior to dental visits as outlined in the following prescriptions. They have the advantage of allowing the patient a good night's sleep prior to the day of the procedure and provide on-the-spot sedation during the procedure. Nitrous oxide is an in-the-office administered sedative that is relatively safe, but requires additional training and carefully planned monitoring protocols of auxiliary personnel during inhalation. Both oral and inhalation techniques can be used to manage the anxious patient in the dental office.

It is recommended that patients not drive themselves to or from dental appointments following use of these medications. Also, these medications should not be prescribed during pregnancy. For pediatric patients, oral preprocedural sedatives include primarily hydroxyzine and liquid meperidine. Dosing suggestions are described in each of the respective monographs.

ALPRAZolam on page 101
BusPIRone on page 267
DiazePAM on page 491
HydrOXYzine on page 844
LORazepam on page 1020
Meperidine on page 1055
Nitrous Oxide on page 1206
Prochlorperazine on page 1389
Triazolam on page 1606

Note: Although various antidepressants have been used for preprocedure sedation, no specific regimens or protocols have been established. Guidelines for use are still under study.

Doxepin (Systemic) on page 533
FLUoxetine on page 738
FluvoxaMINE on page 759
PARoxetine on page 1291
Sertraline on page 1471
TraZODone on page 1597

For examples of sample prescriptions see Sedation (Prior to Dental Treatment) - Sample Prescriptions on page 42

REFERENCES

Anttila S, Knuuttila M, Ylöstalo P, Joukamaa M. Symptoms of depression and anxiety in relation to dental health behavior and self-perceived dental treatment need. *Eur J Oral Sci.* 2006;114(2):109-114.

Armfield JM, Stewart JF, Spencer AJ. The vicious cycle of dental fear: exploring the interplay between oral health, service utilization and dental fear. *BMC Oral Health.* 2007;14;7:1.

Brodine AH, Hartshorn MA. Recognition and management of somatoform disorders. *J Prosthet Dent.* 2004;91(3):268-273.

Coulson NS, Buchanan H. Self-reported efficacy of an online dental anxiety support group: a pilot study. *Community Dent Oral Epidemiol.* 2008;36(1):43-46.

Keene JJ Jr, Galasko GT, Land MF. Antidepressant use in psychiatry and medicine: importance for dental practice. *J Am Dent Assoc.* 2003;134(1):71-79.

Klingberg G, Broberg AG. Dental fear/anxiety and dental behaviour management problems in children and adolescents: a review of prevalence and concomitant psychological factors. *Int J Paediatr Dent.* 2007;17(6):391-406.

Lundgren J, Carlsson SG, Berggren U. Relaxation versus cognitive therapies for dental fear – a psychophysiological approach. *Health Psychol.* 2006;25(3):267-273.

Merry SN, Hetrick SE, Cox GR, et al. Cochrane review: psychological and educational interventions for preventing depression in children and adolescents. *Cochrane Database Syst Rev.* 2012;7(5):1409-1685.

Stenebrand A, Boman UW, Hakeberg M. Dental anxiety and symptoms of general anxiety and depression in 15-year-olds. *Int J Dent Hyg.* 2012.

PERIORAL PREMALIGNANT LESIONS AND MANAGEMENT OF PATIENTS UNDERGOING CANCER THERAPY

PERIORAL PREMALIGNANT LESIONS

Oral mucosal abnormalities present to the dentist in 5% to 15% of patients. The vast majority of these mucosal changes are benign; however, similar presentations are common making differentiation of relatively benign lesions or reactive conditions from premalignancy very difficult. It is very challenging to discriminate between progressive or nonprogressive lesions. Some precancerous lesions may be hidden within mucosa and appear normal clinically.

Oral squamous cell carcinoma (OSCC) is the most common oral cancer. The 5-year survival rate is 81% (early stages), 30% (late-stage), and 52% of all patients die within 5 years. The overall 5-year survival rate in whites in US and Europe has increased from 40%, in the 1950's, to 59%, but in black patients, only from 36% to 39%. These survival rates have not significantly changed in many decades.

Dentists are often the first to recognize early changes in the skin, lips, or oral mucosal tissues that could represent potential premalignancies. The general dentist may refer such patients to an oral and maxillofacial surgeon, oral pathology/oral medicine specialist, or otolaryngologist for biopsy. There are numerous drugs under study to manage premalignancies by preventing the progression of lesions from dysplasia to frank cancer. The condition actinic keratosis on the skin, and the equivalent condition of the lips, actinic cheilitis, create a diagnostic and management challenge for clinicians. Until now 5-fluorouracil preparations have been used with mixed success, but recently, imiquimod (Zyclara) has been approved for actinic keratosis.

For lesions that do not fit these criteria, additional diagnostic steps are often necessary. New approaches are available to aid the dentist in the proper timely management of patients with premalignant lesions or at risk for human papillomas virus infection.

ESTABLISHING A DIFFERENTIAL DIAGNOSIS

For many oral mucosal lesions, a precise diagnosis can be made based solely on patient history and clinical presentation and no additional diagnostic procedures are necessary; however, many lesions share similar clinical features. In order to determine the final diagnosis, additional diagnostic procedures may be necessary. These procedures most often require removal of some or all of the lesion for microscopic examination. Diagnostic procedures readily available to the dental team include conventional biopsy, brush biopsy, and exfoliative cytology.

DIAGNOSTIC PROCEDURES

Conventional Biopsy: The microscopic examination of tissue removed from an area of suspected disease. The purpose is to establish an accurate diagnosis so that the disease can be appropriately treated. A conventional biopsy is indicated when:

- Clinical examination fails to lead to a precise diagnosis.
- A lesion fails to respond to conservative therapy within a reasonable period of time.
- A lesion is thought to be premalignant.
- A lesion exhibits clinical features of malignancy.

Incisional Biopsy: The surgical removal of only a sample of the lesion for the purpose of microscopic examination. Once a microscopic diagnosis has been made, it may be necessary to remove the remainder of the lesion.

Excisional Biopsy: The removal of the entire lesion with a margin of clinically uninvolved tissue. The procedure is meant to be both diagnostic and therapeutic. If microscopic examination shows that some of the lesion remains, additional surgery may be necessary.

Punch Biopsy for Oral Mucosal Lesions: Punch biopsy is a convenient method for performing incisional biopsies of oral mucosal lesions. This technique employs a disposable instrument called a biopsy punch that makes a circular incision. A disposable biopsy punch with a diameter of 4 mm is preferred for incisional biopsies of most oral mucosal lesions.

Considerations for selection of the biopsy site:

- The biopsy site should be representative of the disease.
- Important anatomic structures in the submucosa (eg, salivary gland ducts and large blood vessels), should be avoided.
- Tissue that appears to be necrotic should not be included in the biopsy specimen.
- It may be beneficial to include a margin of clinically uninvolved tissue in the biopsy specimen.

Oral Brush Biopsy: The removal of all layers of the epithelium (including the basal cell layer) using a biopsy brush (a small brush with very firm bristles). Oral CDX is a service available to assess brush samples. In contrast to conventional exfoliative cytology which only provides cells from the surface of the lesion, brush biopsy generates a transepithelial specimen. If abnormal epithelial cells are detected, a conventional biopsy is indicated.

Indications for oral brush biopsy:

- Brush biopsy is especially suited for the early detection of precancerous and cancerous oral mucosal lesions.

Advantages of oral brush biopsy:
- Requires only a few instruments and supplies
- Easy to perform
- Well tolerated by patient
- Associated with little or no morbidity

Limitations of oral brush biopsy:
- Since only individual cells are examined, the cells cannot be evaluated in their proper tissue relationships.
- If atypical epithelial cells are detected, a conventional biopsy is indicated to confirm the diagnosis.

ORAL EXFOLIATIVE CYTOLOGY

Oral exfoliative cytology is the microscopic examination of cells from the surface of an oral mucosal lesion. Oral exfoliative cytology is a useful adjunct in the diagnosis of surface lesion of oral mucosa.

Indications for oral exfoliative cytology:
- Premalignant / malignant lesions (dysplasia, carcinoma *in situ*)
- Vesiculoulcerative diseases (herpes simplex virus, varicella-zoster virus)
- Superficial fungal infections (candidiasis, geotrichosis)

Advantages of oral exfoliative cytology:
- Requires only a few instruments and supplies
- Easy to perform
- Well tolerated by the patient
- Associated with no morbidity

Limitations of oral exfoliative cytology:
- Because only surface cells are examined, the disease process must involve the mucosal surface.
- Since only individual cells are examined, the cells cannot be evaluated in their proper tissue relationships.
- If atypical epithelial cells are detected, a conventional biopsy is indicated to confirm the diagnosis.

DIRECT OPTICAL FLUORESCENCE VISUALIZATION

Direct optical fluorescence visualization is the process of examining tissue directly with the human eye to assess its autofluorescence properties. In order to detect the fluorescent pattern of the tissue, it must be exposed to a light of specific wavelength and intensity that excites the cells and viewed through special filters that remove all unwanted light normally reflected from the tissue. The fluorescent pattern produced by the cells enables the clinician to differentiate between tissues composed of normal cells and abnormal tissue, specifically premalignant and malignant epithelial neoplasms.

In the oral cavity, direct optical fluorescence visualization is accomplished using the VELscope, a handheld, field-of- view device that provides the clinician with an easy-to-use, adjunctive, screening instrument for early clinical detection of oral premalignant and malignant lesions. The device emits a safe blue light into the oral cavity which excites cells beneath the epithelial surface causing them to fluoresce. Tissue composed of normal cells emits an apple-green fluorescence, while abnormal tissue exhibits a loss of fluorescence and appears dark.

Indications for Use of the Direct Optical Fluorescence Visualization (VELscope):
- Adjunct to routine oral mucosal examination procedures.
- Aid in early clinical detection of oral premalignant and malignant lesions.

Advantages of direct optical fluorescence visualization (VELscope)
- Simple and easy to use.
- Field-of-view technology facilitates efficient screening of oral mucosa and requires the addition of only a few minutes to the examination procedure.
- Noninvasive.

Limitations of direct optical fluorescence visualization (VELscope)
- When viewed through the VELscope, normal tissue exhibits apple-green fluorescence, while abnormal tissue exhibits loss of fluorescence and appears dark.
- If an area of concern is noted, a conventional biopsy is necessary to confirm the diagnosis of premalignancy or malignancy.

HPV AND HEAD & NECK CANCER

Human papillomavirus (HPV) is the broad term for a large group of viruses comprised of more than 150 serotypes. Certain serotypes of HPV cause warts on the skin and others cause warts in the genital region. Some types of HPV are known to cause cervical cancers, as well as cancers of the anus, penis, vulva, vagina and *head and neck.*

HPV-related head and neck cancers occur primarily in the oropharynx (posterior to the tonsillar pillars and on the base of the tongue). Oropharyngeal cancers are more common in white men. Most head and neck cancers have been shown to be clearly associated with tobacco and alcohol use, but researchers believe more than 80% of oropharyngeal cancers in the US may be related to long-term infection with the HPV virus. HPV-related head and neck cancer occurs in both people who smoke and those who do not smoke and it is assumed that smoking and alcohol use only increase the chances of cancer transformation.

Salivary diagnostic tests are available for HPV, and involve the use of Polymerase Chain Reaction PCR tests; thus, they are not point of care tests. Kits containing a salivary collector are placed in transport media and sent to a central laboratory for analysis. Various investigators have used oral swabs, expectorated saliva, or an expectorated oral rinse with mouthwash, to collect virions and cells for analysis (OraRisk HPV test, OralDNA Labs, Brentwood, TN, is the only salivary diagnostic test for HPV commercially available in the United States). The expectorated oral rinse with mouthwash collection technique has the highest sensitivity, because it samples the entire oral cavity and the swishing of the solution dislodges mucosal cells. Investigators in the laboratory use a variety of primers to detect as many HPV types as possible. Early diagnosis is critical for survival of patients with OSCC and use of salivary HPV analyses is likely to increase.

Human papilloma virus is widespread and serotypes 16 and 18 have clearly been associated with cervical cancer and are also the serotypes associated with the oropharyngeal cancers described above. Although most serotypes that cause commonly encountered oral HPV lesions in the anterior oral cavity are not 16 or 18, the clinician should recommend appropriate surgical removal of all such lesions. Lesions in the posterior oral pharyngeal region are, however, of the greatest concern. Pre-exposure vaccination is one of the most effective methods for preventing transmission of some serotypes of HPV. Quadrivalent HPV vaccine (Gardasil) and the bivalent HPV vaccine (Cervarix) are available.

Gardasil is a vaccine indicated in girls and women 9 to 26 years of age for the prevention of the following diseases caused by Human Papillomavirus (HPV) types included in the vaccine:

- Cervical, vulvar, vaginal, and anal cancer caused by HPV types 16 and 18
- Genital warts (condyloma acuminata) caused by HPV types 6 and 11

And the following precancerous or dysplastic lesions caused by HPV types 6, 11, 16, and 18:

- Cervical intraepithelial neoplasia (CIN) grade 2/3 and Cervical adenocarcinoma *in situ* (AIS)
- Cervical intraepithelial neoplasia (CIN) grade 1
- Vulvar intraepithelial neoplasia (VIN) grade 2 and grade 3
- Vaginal intraepithelial neoplasia (VaIN) grade 2 and grade 3
- Anal intraepithelial neoplasia (AIN) grades 1, 2, and 3

Gardasil is also indicated in boys and men 9 to 26 years of age for the prevention of the following diseases caused by HPV types included in the vaccine:

- Anal cancer caused by HPV types 16 and 18
- Genital warts (condyloma acuminata) caused by HPV types 6 and 11

And the following precancerous or dysplastic lesions caused by HPV types 6, 11, 16, and 18:

- Anal intraepithelial neoplasia (AIN) grades 1, 2, and 3

Cervarix is a vaccine indicated for the prevention of the following diseases caused by oncogenic human papillomavirus (HPV) types 16 and 18:

- Cervical cancer
- Cervical intraepithelial neoplasia (CIN) grade 2 or worse and adenocarcinoma *in situ*
- Cervical intraepithelial neoplasia (CIN) grade 1

Cervarix is approved for use in females 9 to 25 years of age.

Details regarding HPV vaccination are available at www.cdc.gov/std/hpv. Vaccines for other STDs (eg, HIV and herpes simplex virus) are under development or undergoing clinical trials. Vaccines are not available for bacterial or fungal STDs.

CANCER PATIENT DENTAL PROTOCOL

As in OSCC, the objective in treatment of any patient with cancer is eradication of the disease. In addition to surgery many cancer patients receive other modalities of treatment including chemotherapy, targeted molecular therapies, and radiation treatment. These treatments often lead to oral complications, such as mucosal ulceration, xerostomia, bleeding, and infections which can cause significant morbidity and may compromise systemic cancer treatment of the patient. With proper oral evaluation before systemic treatment, many of the complications can be minimized or prevented.

MUCOSITIS

Normal oral mucosa acts as a barrier against chemical and food irritants and oral micro-organisms. Disruption of the mucosal barrier can lead to secondary infection, increased pain, delayed healing, and decreased nutritional intake.

Mucositis is an inflammation of the mucous membranes; however, its pathogenesis is more complicated, resulting from cytokine signals that lead to surface cell necrosis and delayed new cell proliferation. It is a common reaction to chemotherapy and radiation therapy. It is first seen as an erythematous patch. The mucosal epithelium becomes thin as a result of the killing of the rapidly dividing basal layer mucosal cells. Seven to ten days after cytoreduction chemotherapy and between 1,000 cGy and 3,000 cGy of radiation to the head and neck, mucosal tissues begin to desquamate and eventually develop into frank ulcerations. The mucosal integrity is broken and is often secondarily infected by normal oral flora. The resultant ulcerations can also act as a portal of entry for pathogenic organisms into the patient's bloodstream and may lead to systemic infections. These ulcerations often force interruption of therapy. A specific type of ulcerative stomatitis is encountered in patients treated for cancer with mTOR inhibitors such as everolimus (Afinitor). These ulcers resemble aphthous ulcers and occur on tissues that are freely movable (most commonly the tongue and lips). The lesions are self-limiting but can interrupt chemotherapy. The pathogenesis of the lesions is not well understood, but they appear to respond to steroid rinses.

Prevention of radiation mucositis is difficult. Stents can be constructed to prevent irradiation of uninvolved tissues. Most recently, intensity-modulated radiotherapy has been used as an advanced approach to 3D conformal radiotherapy; it optimizes the delivery of irradiation to irregularly shaped volumes and thus spares normal tissue while delivering an adequate dose to the tumor volumes. The use of multiple ports and fractionation of therapy into smaller doses over a longer period of time can also reduce the severity. Fractured restorations, sharp teeth, and ill-fitted prostheses can damage soft tissues and lead to additional interruption of mucosal barriers. Correction of these problems before radiation therapy can diminish these complications.

CHEMOTHERAPY

Chemotherapy for neoplasia also frequently results in oral complications. Infections and mucositis are the most common complications seen in patients receiving chemotherapy. Also occurring frequently are pain, altered nutrition, and xerostomia, which can significantly affect the quality of life.

Certain chemotherapeutic agents, such as melphalan, 5-fluorouracil, methotrexate, and doxorubicin, are more commonly associated with the development of oral mucositis. Treatment of oral mucositis is mainly palliative, but steps should be taken to minimize secondary pathogenic infections. Culture and sensitivity data should be obtained to select appropriate therapy for the bacterial, viral, or fungal organisms found.

RADIATION CARIES

Dental caries that sometimes follow radiation therapy is called radiation caries. It usually develops in the cervical smooth surface region of the teeth adjacent to the gingiva, often affecting many teeth. It is secondary to the irreversible damage done to the salivary glands and is initiated by dental plaque, but its rapid progress is due to changes in saliva. In addition to the diminution in the amount of saliva, both the salivary pH and buffering capacity are diminished, which decreases anticaries activity of saliva. Oral bacterial flora also change with xerostomia leading to the increase in caries activity. Typically patients that receive a cumulative radiation dose of 30 Gy or more will suffer significant loss of saliva production, some of which will be irreversible.

Osteonecrosis of the jaw (ONJ) is pertinent to cancer patient management and patients with osteoporosis, as well as antiresorptive agents used secondary to multiple myeloma and breast cancer to prevent metastases to the skeleton (see Osteonecrosis of the Jaw on page 1796).

SALIVARY CHANGES

Chemotherapy is not thought to directly alter salivary flow, but alterations in taste and subjective sensations of dry mouth are relatively common complaints. Patients with mucositis and graft-vs-host disease following bone marrow or stem cell transplantation often demonstrate signs and symptoms of xerostomia. Radiation does directly affect salivary production. Radiation to the salivary glands produces fibrosis and alters the production of saliva. If all the major salivary glands are in the field, the decrease in saliva can be dramatic and the serous portion of the glands seems to be most severely affected. The saliva produced is increased in viscosity, which contributes to food retention, increased plaque formation, and difficulty swallowing. These xerostomia patients have difficulty in managing a normal diet. Normal saliva also has bacteriostatic properties that are diminished in these patients.

The dental management recommendations for patients undergoing chemotherapy, bone marrow transplantation, and/or radiation therapy for the treatment of cancer are based primarily on clinical observations. The following protocols will provide a conservative, consistent approach to the dental management of patients undergoing chemotherapy or bone marrow transplantation. Many of the cancer chemotherapy drugs produce oral side effects including mucositis, oral ulceration, dry mouth, acute infections, and taste aberrations. Cancer drugs include antibiotics, alkylating agents, antimetabolites, DNA inhibitors, hormones, and cytokines.

All patients undergoing chemotherapy or bone marrow transplantation for malignant disease should have the following baseline:

A. Panoramic radiograph

B. Dental consultation and examination

C. Dental prophylaxis and cleaning (if the neutrophil count is >1,500/mm^3 and the platelet count is >50,000/mm^3)

- Prophylaxis and cleaning will be deferred if the patient's neutrophil count is <1,500 and the platelet count is <50,000. Oral hygiene recommendations will be made. These levels are arbitrary guidelines and the dentist should consider the patient's oral condition and planned procedure relative to hemorrhage and level of bacteremia.

D. Oral Hygiene: Patients should be encouraged to follow normal hygiene procedures. Addition of a chlorhexidine mouth rinse such as Peridex or PerioGard on page 344 is usually helpful. If the patient develops oral mucositis, tolerance of such alcohol-based products may be limited. A nonalcohol-containing chlorhexidine mouth rinse CHX is also available. Biotène products including Oralbalance are also useful since many patients report alteration of quality and quantity of saliva.

PREVENTION AND TREATMENT OF MUCOSITIS

A. If the patient develops mucositis, bacterial, viral, and fungal cultures should be obtained. There are no standard of care recommendations for prevention of oral mucositis. The intravenous biologic product keratinocyte growth factor, palifermin (Kepivance) is approved to help reduce the chance that certain cancer patients, those with blood cancers undergoing chemotherapy, would develop mucositis. Most therapies are palliative only or help in reducing secondary infection. Sucralfate suspension in a pharmacy-prepared form or Carafate suspension, as well as Benadryl on page 517 or Xylocaine viscous on page 990 solution can assist in helping the patient to tolerate food. In addition to the mucosal-coating drugs described below, various emollients and lubricants can be tried. A cost-effective approach is to rinse with a solution of 1/2 teaspoon of baking soda (and/or 1/2 teaspoon of table salt) in 1 cup of lukewarm water several times a day. Lastly, multiple studies have indicated that lower-level laser therapy can reduce the severity of chemotherapy and radiation-induced oral mucositis.

B. Aloclair is now available as an oral lesion relief spray. It indicated for aphthous ulcerations and other mild to moderate oral erosions.

C. The oral barrier Gelclair and the mucositis treatment aid Caphosol are FDA approved for mucositis. Gargle and spit Gelclair mixture of one single-use packet (15 mL) and water 3 times/day or as needed; follow mixing and administration instructions on packet.

D. Mix contents of 1 blue (A) and 1 clear (B) Caphosol ampul in clean container, swish thoroughly with 1/2 of mixture (15 mL) for 1 minute and spit; repeat. Use immediately after mixing ampuls. Use 4 doses/day from the onset of high dose chemotherapy or radiation treatment. Patients may also require systemic and topical analgesics for pain relief depending on the presence of mucositis. Systemic treatments currently being used with variable success include antioxidants, immunomodulatory drugs, anticholinergic drugs, pentoxifylline, cytokines antiviral drugs, and glutamic acid; a topical analgesic commonly used is lidocaine. Positive fungal cultures may require a nystatin swish-and-swallow prescription or the selection of another antifungal agent (see Fungal Infections on page 1847).

E. The determination of performing dental procedures must be based on the goal of preventing infection during periods of neutropenia and reducing the risk of bleeding when platelet counts are low. Timing of procedures must be coordinated with the patient's hematologic status.

F. If oral surgery is required, at least 7 to 10 days of healing should be allowed before the anticipated date of bone marrow suppression (eg, ANC <1,000/mm^3 and/or platelet count of ≥50,000/mm^3).

G. Daily use of topical fluorides is recommended for those who have received radiation therapy to the head and neck region involving salivary glands. Any patients with prolonged xerostomia subsequent to graft-vs-host disease and/or chemotherapy can also be considered for fluoride supplement. Use the fluoride-containing mouthwashes (Act, Fluorigard, etc) each night before going to sleep; swish, hold 1 to 2 minutes, spit out or use prescription fluorides (gels or rinses); apply daily for 1 to 4 minutes as directed; if mouth is sore (mucositis), use flavorless/colorless gels (Thera-Flur, Gel-Kam, or Prevident). Custom trays for fluoride applications can be produced by the clinician for the patient's home use using heat-formed materials such as omnivac. Patients with porcelain crowns, resin, or glass ionomer restorations should use a neutral pH fluoride. Improvement in salivary flow following radiation therapy to the head and neck has been noted with prescription sialogogue Salagen on page 1337 or Evoxac on page 341. Salagen, containing the nonselective analogue cholinergic agonist, pilocarpine, is currently the sole sialogogic agent approved by the FDA for radiation-induced xerostomia. Evoxac, containing the quinuclidine analogue of acetylcholine, cevimeline, has been found safe and effective in treating xerostomia in patients with Sjögren's syndrome and may have merit for the treatment of radiation-induced xerostomia.

Benzonatate on page 215
Cevimeline on page 341
Chlorhexidine Gluconate on page 344
DiphenhydrAMINE (Systemic) on page 517
Gelclair Bioadherent Oral Gel on page 1154
Lidocaine (Topical) on page 990
MuGard on page 1154
Pilocarpine (Systemic) on page 1337
Povidone-Iodine (Topical) on page 1364
Sucralfate on page 1504

ORAL CARE PRODUCTS

Bacterial Plaque Control

Patients should use an extra soft bristle toothbrush and dental floss for removal of plaque. Sponge/foam sticks and lemon-glycerine swabs do not adequately remove bacterial plaque.

Cholinergic Agents

See Products for Xerostomia on page 1857

Used for the treatment of xerostomia caused by radiation therapy in patients with head and neck cancer and from Sjögren's syndrome

Cevimeline on page 341
Pilocarpine (Systemic) on page 1337

Fluorides

See Fluorides in the Dentin Hypersensitivity, High Caries Index, and Xerostomia section.

Used for the prevention of demineralization of the tooth structure secondary to xerostomia. For patients with long-term or permanent xerostomia, daily application is accomplished using custom gel applicator trays, such as omnivac. Patients with porcelain crowns should use a neutral pH fluoride (see Fluoride monograph on page 735). Final selection of a fluoride product and/or saliva replacement/stimulant product must be based on patient comfort, taste, and ultimately, compliance. Experience has demonstrated that, often times, patients must try various combinations to achieve the greatest effect and their highest comfort levels. The presence of mucositis during cancer management complicates the clinician's selection of products.

Saliva Substitutes

See Products for Xerostomia on page 1857
Saliva Substitute on page 1460

Oral and Lip Moisturizers/Lubricants

Note: Water-based gels should first be used to provide moisture to dry oral tissues.

Surgilube
K-Y Jelly
Oralbalance
Mouth Moisturizer
Caphosol

PALLIATION OF PAIN

Note: Palliative pain preparations should be monitored for efficacy.

- For relief of pain associated with isolated mucositis or ulcerations, topical anesthetic and protective preparations may be used.
  - Orabase-B with 20% benzocaine on page 213
  - Zilactin-B gel with 10% benzocaine
- For generalized oral pain:
  - Chloraseptic Spray (OTC) anesthetic spray without alcohol
  - Ulcer-Ease anesthetic/analgesic mouthrinse
  - BetaCell oral rinse
  - Xylocaine 2% viscous on page 990

    Note: May anesthetize swallowing mechanism and cause aspiration of food; caution patient against using too close to eating; lack of sensation may also allow patient to damage intact mucosa
  - Tantum Mouthrinse (benzydamine hydrochloride); may be diluted as required

    Note: Available only in Canada and Europe

Patient-Prepared Palliative Mixtures

Coating agents:
Maalox on page 108
Mylanta on page 108
Kaopectate on page 188

These products can be mixed with Benadryl elixir (50:50):

DiphenhydrAMINE (Systemic) (Benadryl) on page 517

Topical anesthetics (diphenhydrAMINE chloride):
Benadryl elixir or Benylin cough syrup on page 517
Note: Choose product with lowest alcohol and sucrose content; ask pharmacist for assistance
Mucotrol gel wafer

Pharmacy Preparations

A pharmacist may also prepare the following solutions for relief of generalized oral pain:

Benadryl-Lidocaine Solution
DiphenhydrAMINE injectable 1.5 mL (50 mg/mL) on page 517
Xylocaine viscous 2% (45 mL) on page 990
Magnesium aluminum hydroxide solution (45 mL)
Swish and hold 1 teaspoonful in mouth for 30 seconds; do not use too close to eating

REFERENCES

ADA Council on Scientific Affairs. Statement on Human Papillomavirus and Squamous Cell Cancers of the Oropharynx (adopted November 2012). Available at: http://www.ada.org/1749.aspx.

Andrews E, Seaman WT, Webster-Cyriaque J. Oropharyngeal carcinoma in nonsmokers and nondrinkers: a role for HPV. *Oral Oncol.* 2009;45(6):486-491.

California-Catalonia Program for Engineering Innovation. Oral cancer detection using optical coherence tomography. 2007-2008 Progress Report.

Chaturvedi AK, Engels EA, Pfeiffer RM, et al. Human papillomavirus and rising oropharyngeal cancer incidence in the United States. *J Clin Oncol.* 2011;29(32):4294-4301.

Cleveland JL, Junger ML, Saraiya M, Markowitz LE, Dunne EF, Epstein JB. The connection between human papillomavirus and oropharyngeal squamous cell carcinomas in the United States: implications for dentistry. *J Am Dent Assoc.* 2011;142(8):915-924.

Corstjens PL, Abrams WR, Malamud D. Detecting viruses by using salivary diagnostics. *J Am Dent Assoc.* 2012;143(10 Suppl):12S-18S.

Eisen T, Sternberg CN, Robert C, et al. Targeted therapies for renal cell carcinoma: review of adverse event management strategies. *J Natl Cancer Inst.* 2012;104(2):93-113.

Gillison ML, Broutian T, Pickard RK, et al. Prevalence of oral HPV infection in the United States, 2009-2010. *JAMA.* 2012;307(7):693-703.

Jaitley S, Agarwal P, Upadhyay R. Role of oral exfoliative cytology in predicting premalignant potential of oral submucous fibrosis: a short study. *J Cancer Res Ther.* 2015;11(2):471-474.

Jemal A, Simard EP, Dorell C, et al. Annual Report to the Nation on the Status of Cancer, 1975-2009, featuring the burden and trends in human papillomavirus (HPV)-associated cancers and HPV vaccination coverage levels. *J Natl Cancer Inst.* 2013;105(3):175-201. http://jnci.oxfordjournals.org/content/early/2013/01/03/jnci.djs491.full.pdf+html

Kulkarni SS1, Kulkarni SS, Vastrad PP, et al. Prevalence and distribution of high risk human papillomavirus (HPV) Types 16 and 18 in Carcinoma of cervix, saliva of patients with oral squamous cell carcinoma and in the general population in Karnataka, India. *Asian Pac J Cancer Prev.* 2011;12 (3):645-648.

Marur S, D'Souza G, Westra WH, Forastiere AA. HPV-associated head and neck cancer: a virus-related cancer epidemic. *Lancet Oncol.* 2010;11 (8):781-789.

Mehrotra R, Gupta A, Singh M, Ibrahim R. Application of cytology and molecular biology in diagnosing premalignant or malignant oral lesions. *Mol Cancer.* 2006;5:11.

Messada, D. Diagnostic aids for detection of oral precancerous conditions. *Int J Oral Sci.* 2013;5(2):59-65.

Patton LL, Epstein JB, Kerr AR. Adjunctive techniques for oral cancer examination and lesion diagnosis. *JADA.* 2008;139:1-10.

Pilotte AP, Hohos MB, Polson KM, et al. Managing stomatitis in patients treated with mammalian target of rapamycin inhibitors. *Clin J Oncol Nurs.* 2011;15(5):E83-E89.

Poh CF, MacAulay CE, Laronde DM, Williams PM. Squamous cell carcinoma and precursor lesions: Diagnosis and screening in a technical era. *Periodontol 2000.* 2011; 57(1): 73–88.

Porta C, Osanto S, Ravaud A, et al. Management of adverse events associated with the use of everolimus in patients with advanced renal cell carcinoma. *Eur J Cancer.* 2011;47(9):1287-1298.

Sonis S, Treister N, Chawla S, et al. Preliminary characterization of oral lesions associated with inhibitors of mammalian target of rapamycin in cancer patients. *Cancer.* 2010;116(1):210-215.

Warnakulasuriya S, Ariyawardana A. Malignant transformation of oral leukoplakia: a systematic review of observational studies. *J Oral Pathol Med.* 2015.

DENTIST'S ROLE IN RECOGNIZING DOMESTIC VIOLENCE, ABUSE, AND NEGLECT

Recognition of the signs and symptoms of domestic violence is an important topic for dental and medical professionals throughout the world. Unfortunately, statistics related to domestic abuse and/or neglect of women, children, and elderly patients appear to be on the rise, perhaps, in part, due to increased recognition.

Statistics are indeed staggering; one in four women will experience domestic violence in her lifetime (CDC 2008). In the United States, a woman, child, or elder is physically abused every 5 to 15 seconds. In fact, violence is cited as one of the common causes of emergency room admissions for women 15 to 44 years of age. Furthermore, 50,000 deaths occur annually, which are attributable to violence in the form of homicide or suicide.

The dentist's responsibilities and professional role in this arena are not clear in all states. The literature, however, is clear regarding how each professional has the responsibility to understand current state laws regarding the reporting of domestic violence, abuse of children or elderly patients, and/or neglect. Many states have existing codes defining the role of the professional in these regards. Many other states, such as Maryland, have adopted continuing education requirements specific to the subject. The overall problem of domestic violence, including child abuse, neglect, and other forms of abuse, are indeed public health issues. Likewise, the costs (eg, medical, dental, psychiatric, hospital, and emergency care fees) are borne to a great extent by the community as well as the individual.

Domestic abuse is defined as "controlling behavior." Neglect can take on a myriad of presentations. Although this often includes physical injury, the primary focus of domestic abuse is one person being in control of another person, making that person do something against his/her will. Women are often abused both physically and mentally in relationships that have existed for many years. Children are often the focus of domestic violence; however, the pattern for an entire family's abuse may be present. Abuse comes in many forms and many victims do not even realize that abuse is occurring. Some victims simply "chalk it up" to things that happen within families. Abuse may include battery and physical assault, such as throwing objects, pushing, hitting, slapping, kicking, or attacking with a weapon; sexual assault including the abuser forcing sexual activities upon another; and psychological abuse, such as forcing a victim to perform degrading or humiliating acts, threatening harm to a female or male partner or child, or destroying valued possessions of another. Verbal abuse can also be included; however, psychological forms of abuse are very difficult to ascertain and signs and symptoms may be difficult to separate from other psychological traits. Abuse tends to have a cyclic pattern, often where a partner or the controlling individual is extremely friendly, intimate, and a good household member; however, due to unknown reasons, as tension develops, family violence often erupts. Once battering has begun, it often increases in frequency and in severity with time. Early recognition can often prevent serious effects; however, until physical violence becomes part of the domestic abuse situation, recognition is usually difficult.

It is estimated that nearly 65% of abuse cases (where physical injury is involved) include injury to the head, neck, or mouth; therefore, dental professionals are in a unique position to detect and perhaps, if appropriate in that state, report suspected abuse. In children, these percentages are even higher. Being wards of adults, children are vulnerable. Child abuse includes any act that is not accidental, endangering or impairing a child's safety or emotional health. Types of child abuse may include physical abuse, emotional abuse and neglect, including neglect of proper health care. Any child suspected of suffering from an emotional injury, including sexual abuse or neglect, should be brought to the attention of the social welfare system. Occasionally, "Munchausen syndrome," which is defined as the guardians fabricating or inducing illness in the child, may be observed. Intentional poisoning and safety neglect are also included in this syndrome.

From a medical point-of-view, neglect is much more difficult to determine than abuse. The role of the dentist may be to define the state of normal and customary pediatric or elderly patient health within a locality; however, due to parents and families moving about the country, sometimes one standard may not be appropriate for all locations.
Several key behavioral indicators:

- Child, adult, or elderly patient:
  - Avoids eye contact
  - Is wary of a guardian or spouse
  - Demonstrates fear when touched
  - Exhibits dramatic mood changes (eg, hostile or aggressive behavior)
- History or reports of suicide attempts or running away
- Unexplained injuries or injuries inconsistent with explanation or delay in seeking treatment
- Inappropriate use of prescription drugs (ie, responsible adult controls compliance of a child or elderly patient)
- Individual decides to change practitioner when questioned too intensely

For the dentist, head-neck examination is important and includes gathering an overall visual impression of general cleanliness, dress, and stature and examining for any specific physical indicators such as bruises, welts, bite marks, abrasions, lacerations, or other injuries to the head or neck. Contusions or bruises represent the highest percentage of abuse injuries to the young child. The extremely young child or infant often suffers fractures, which fall to second place in terms of incidence as the child matures. In the adult, fractures are much less common. The dentist needs to document the location since this often represents the characteristic that may be difficult for the person to explain. Common areas for injuries include the bony eminences over the knees, shins, and elbows but could also be on the face, including the zygomatic arch and the chin. Burns are rarer, but represent one of the most serious types of injuries. Intraoral injuries, including trauma to the oral mucosa, tooth fractures, palatal lesions, ecchymoses, and fractures, represent serious evidence of domestic or child abuse. Physical indicators of sexual abuse may not be obvious to the dentist; however, bruising of the hard palate or other evidence of sexual dysfunction may sometimes be found.

The dentist has the responsibility to document, from a forensic point-of-view, the characteristics of abuse that are observed. As with all diagnostic considerations, the dentist must form a differential diagnosis to rule in or out oral and dental pathologies before suspecting abuse or neglect. History and probability are key to making these determinations. If necessary, evidence including impressions for bite marks or photographs to document unexplained injuries to the head, neck, and face may be necessary. The legal liability for the dentist is determined by the state laws governing the dental practice. The dental practitioner's failure to diagnose child abuse and neglect is another consideration which goes along with ethical and legal considerations. States are generally much clearer in the area of child abuse than they are regarding spousal or elderly abuse or overall domestic violence. The dentist has a responsibility to refer a patient for a second opinion, such as to their primary care pediatrician or internist, if there are concerns of abuse.

Under the Federal Child Abuse Prevention and Treatment Act (CAPTA) passed in 1974, all 50 states have passed laws mandating the reporting of child abuse and neglect. CAPTA provides a foundation for states by identifying a minimum set of acts or behaviors that characterize physical abuse, neglect, and sexual abuse. These laws vary from state to state. Each states responsible for the following:

- Providing its own definition of child abuse and neglect
- Describing the circumstances and conditions that obligate mandated individuals to report known or suspected child abuse
- Providing definitions for juvenile/family courts when to take custody of the child
- Specifying the forms of maltreatment that are criminally punishable

Unfortunately, there is little uniformity in the state laws regarding either the responsibility for reporting adult domestic violence or abuse or in protecting the health care professional by reporting, in good faith, abuse situations. When spousal or elderly abuse or other domestic violence is suspected, the definitions become even less clear. They are very similar in ambiguity to those that are faced by the professional regarding neglect as opposed to direct physical or mental abuse. The American Dental Association code is clear on principles and ethics regarding professional conduct regarding the responsibility for recognition of child abuse. They are much less clear on spousal or other abuse and it is likely that in the future, as some consistency is noted between and among the various state laws, the ADA Council will undoubtedly take a stronger position.

It is clearly up to the individual states to take the lead in establishing strict guidelines for recognition and reporting of domestic abuse, including protection under the "good faith" statutes for the practitioner. Rules and regulations regarding malicious reporting should also be better defined. The national position is difficult to define because of the extreme variation among states. Dentists are encouraged to use their best judgment in proceeding in any situation of suspected domestic abuse or neglect. They should primarily know their state laws and join in the discussion of the topic so that appropriate state actions and formation of legal codes can be undertaken. The current move by some states toward requiring continuing education on these subjects is an excellent sign that there is movement in a constructive direction.

RESOURCES

The National Health Resource Center on Domestic Violence, a project of the FVPF, provides support to thousands of health care professionals, policy makers and domestic violence advocates through its four main program areas: Model training strategies, practical tools, technical assistance, and public policy. **Contact information:** 383 Rhode Island St., Suite 304, San Francisco, CA 94103-5133; Phone: (888) Rx-ABUSE; TTY: (800) 595-4889; Fax: (415) 252-8991; email: health@endabuse.org; website: www.endabuse.org/health.

The **American Dental Association (ADA)** has developed a code of ethics and position statements on addressing adult domestic violence and child abuse in the dental health setting. **Contact information:** Phone: (312) 440-2500; website: www.ada.org/

Dental Professionals Against Violence (California Dental Association Foundation) DPAV's training program and print materials are designed to assist dental professionals and their teams to recognize and respond to child abuse/neglect, domestic/intimate partner violence, and elder abuse/neglect. The goal of DPAV is to raise the dental community's awareness of family violence using the most current information regarding patient risk assessment, clinical signs and symptoms, and dental professional's legal obligation to identify and report family violence situations. Dentists, registered dental hygienists, and registered dental assistants are mandated reporters in the state of California. The program includes definitive action steps for dental professionals to use within their practices and communities. **Contact information:** 1201 K Street, Suite 1511, Sacramento, CA 95814; Toll-free: (866) 232-6362 ext. 4921; Phone: (916) 554-4921; Fax: (916) 498-6182; email: foundationinfo@cda.org; website: www.cda.org/public/dpav.

Prevent Abuse and Neglect through Dental Awareness (PANDA) coalition educates dentists about how to effectively intervene in cases of child abuse and neglect and other forms of family violence, including intimate partner violence (domestic violence) and elder abuse and neglect. **Contact information:** Lynn Douglas Mouden, DDS, MPH Director, Office of Oral Health Arkansas Department of Health 4815 W. Markham Street, Slot 41, Little Rock, Arkansas 72205; Phone: (501) 661-2595; Fax: (501) 661-2055; email: Lmouden@healthyarkansas.com.

REFERENCES

American Academy of Pediatric Dentistry. Clinical guideline on oral and dental aspects of child abuse and neglect. *Pediatr Dent*. 2004;26(7 Suppl):63-66.

American Dental Association Council on Ethics, Bylaws and Judicial Affairs. American Dental Association principles of ethics and code of professional conduct, with official advisory opinions. 2012. Available at http://www.ada.org/sections/about/pdfs/code_of_ethics_2012.pdf

Centers for Disease Control and Prevention (CDC). Adverse health conditions and health risk behaviors associated with intimate partner violence – United States, 2005. *MMWR Morb Mortal Wkly Rep*. 2008;57(5):113-117.

Dubowitz H, Kim J, Black MM, Weisbart C, Semiatin J, Magder LS. Identifying children at high risk for a child maltreatment report. *Child Abuse Negl*. 2011;35(2):96-104.

Katner DR, Brown CE. Mandatory reporting of oral injuries indicating possible child abuse. *J Am Dent Assoc*. 2012;143(10):1087-1092.

Kellogg ND, American Academy of Pediatrics Committee on Child Abuse and Neglect. Evaluation of suspected child physical abuse. *Pediatrics*. 2007;119(6):1232-1241.

Kenney JP. Domestic violence: a complex health care issue for dentistry today. *Forensic Sci Int*. 2006;159(Suppl 1):S121–S125.

Manea S, Favero GA, Stellini E, Romoli L, Mazzucato M, Facchin P. Dentists' perceptions, attitudes, knowledge, and experience about child abuse and neglect in Northeast Italy. *J Clin Pediatr Dent*. 2007;32(1):19-25.

Nelms AP, Gutmann ME, Solomon ES, Dewald JP, Campbell PR. What victims of domestic violence need from the dental profession. *J Dent Educ*. 2009;73(4):490-498.

Stechey F. P.A.N.D.A. A dentist's introduction to recognizing child abuse. *Dental Practice Management*. 2001. Available at http://www.rcdso.org/life/ll_learning_pdf/DPM_PANDA.pdf

US Department of Health and Human Services, Administration for Children and Families, Child Welfare Information Gateway. Mandatory reporters of child abuse and neglect. 2012. Available at https://www.childwelfare.gov/systemwide/laws_policies/statutes/manda.pdf

Wiseman M. The role of the dentist in recognizing elder abuse. *J Can Dent Assoc*. 2008;74(8):715-720.

APPENDIX TABLE OF CONTENTS

ABBREVIATIONS, ACRONYMS, AND SYMBOLS

Abbreviations Which May Be Used in This Reference

Abbreviation	Meaning
½NS	0.45% sodium chloride
5-HT	5-hydroxytryptamine
AACT	American Academy of Clinical Toxicology
AAP	American Academy of Pediatrics
AAPC	antibiotic-associated pseudomembranous colitis
ABCB1	ATP-binding cassette sub-family B member 1 (also known as P-gP or MDR1)
ABCC2	ATP-binding cassette sub-family C member 2 (also known as MRP2)
ABCG2	ATP-binding cassette sub-family G member 2 (also known as BCRP)
ABG	arterial blood gases
ABMT	autologous bone marrow transplant
ABW	adjusted body weight
ACC	American College of Cardiology
ACE	angiotensin-converting enzyme
ACLS	advanced cardiac life support
ACOG	American College of Obstetricians and Gynecologists
ACTH	adrenocorticotrophic hormone
ADH	antidiuretic hormone
ADHD	attention-deficit/hyperactivity disorder
ADI	adequate daily intake
ADLs	activities of daily living
AED	antiepileptic drug
AHA	American Heart Association
AHCPR	Agency for Health Care Policy and Research
AIDS	acquired immunodeficiency syndrome
AIMS	Abnormal Involuntary Movement Scale
ALL	acute lymphoblastic leukemia
ALS	amyotrophic lateral sclerosis
ALT	alanine aminotransferase (formerly called SGPT)
AMA	American Medical Association
AML	acute myeloblastic leukemia
ANA	antinuclear antibodies
ANC	absolute neutrophil count
ANLL	acute nonlymphoblastic leukemia
APL	acute promyelocytic leukemia
aPTT	activated partial thromboplastin time
ARB	angiotensin receptor blocker
ARDS	acute respiratory distress syndrome
ASA-PS	American Society of Anesthesiologists – Physical Status (ASA-PS) I: Normal, healthy patient II: Patient having mild systemic disease III: Patient having severe systemic disease IV: Patient having severe systemic disease which is a constant threat to life V: Moribund patient; not expected to survive without the procedure VI: Patient declared brain-dead; organs being removed for donor purposes
AST	aspartate aminotransferase (formerly called SGOT)
ATP	adenosine triphosphate
AUC	area under the curve (area under the serum concentration-time curve)
A-V	atrial-ventricular
AVNRT	atrioventricular nodal reentrant tachycardia
AVRT	atrioventricular reentrant tachycardia
BCRP	breast cancer resistance protein
BDI	Beck Depression Inventory
BEC	blood ethanol concentration
BLS	basic life support
BMI	body mass index

Abbreviations Which May Be Used in This Reference *(continued)*

Abbreviation	Meaning
BMT	bone marrow transplant
BP	blood pressure
BPD	bronchopulmonary disease or dysplasia
BPH	benign prostatic hyperplasia
BPRS	Brief Psychiatric Rating Scale
BSA	body surface area
BSEP	bile salt export pump
BUN	blood urea nitrogen
CABG	coronary artery bypass graft
CAD	coronary artery disease
CADD	computer ambulatory drug delivery
cAMP	cyclic adenosine monophosphate
CAN	Canadian
CAPD	continuous ambulatory peritoneal dialysis
CAS	chemical abstract service
CBC	complete blood cell count
CBT	cognitive behavioral therapy
CDC	Centers for Disease Control and Prevention
CF	cystic fibrosis
CFC	chlorofluorocarbons
CGI	Clinical Global Impression
CHD	coronary heart disease
CHF	congestive heart failure; chronic heart failure
CI	cardiac index
CIE	chemotherapy-induced emesis
C-II	schedule two controlled substance
C-III	schedule three controlled substance
C-IV	schedule four controlled substance
C-V	schedule five controlled substance
CIV	continuous IV infusion
CLL	chronic lymphocytic leukemia
C_{max}	maximum plasma concentration
C_{min}	minimum plasma concentration
CML	chronic myelogenous leukemia
CMV	cytomegalovirus
CNS	central nervous system or coagulase negative staphylococcus
COLD	chronic obstructive lung disease
COMT	Catechol-*O*-methyltransferase
COPD	chronic obstructive pulmonary disease
COX	cyclooxygenase
CPK	creatine phosphokinase
CPR	cardiopulmonary resuscitation
CrCl	creatinine clearance
CRF	chronic renal failure
CRP	C-reactive protein
CRRT	continuous renal replacement therapy
CSF	cerebrospinal fluid
CSII	continuous subcutaneous insulin infusion
CT	computed tomography
CVA	cerebrovascular accident
CVP	central venous pressure
CVVH	continuous venovenous hemofiltration
CVVHD	continuous venovenous hemodialysis
CVVHDF	continuous venovenous hemodiafiltration
CYP	cytochrome
D5$^1/_4$NS	dextrose 5% in sodium chloride 0.2%
D5$^1/_2$NS	dextrose 5% in sodium chloride 0.45%

Abbreviations Which May Be Used in This Reference *(continued)*

Abbreviation	Meaning
D5LR	dextrose 5% in lactated Ringer's
D5NS	dextrose 5% in sodium chloride 0.9%
D5W	dextrose 5% in water
D10W	dextrose 10% in water
DBP	diastolic blood pressure
DEHP	di(3-ethylhexyl)phthalate
DIC	disseminated intravascular coagulation
DL_{co}	pulmonary diffusion capacity for carbon monoxide
DM	diabetes mellitus
DMARD	disease modifying antirheumatic drug
DNA	deoxyribonucleic acid
DSC	discontinued
DSM-IV	Diagnostic and Statistical Manual
DVT	deep vein thrombosis
EBV	Epstein-Barr virus
ECG	electrocardiogram
ECHO	echocardiogram
ECMO	extracorporeal membrane oxygenation
ECT	electroconvulsive therapy
ED	emergency department
EEG	electroencephalogram
EF	ejection fraction
EG	ethylene glycol
EGA	estimated gestational age
eGFR	estimated glomerular filtration rate
EIA	enzyme immunoassay
ELBW	extremely low birth weight
ELISA	enzyme-linked immunosorbent assay
EPS	extrapyramidal side effects
ESA	erythropoiesis-stimulating agent
ESR	erythrocyte sedimentation rate
ESRD	end stage renal disease
E.T.	endotracheal
EtOH	alcohol
FDA	Food and Drug Administration (United States)
FEV_1	forced expiratory volume exhaled after 1 second
FMO	Flavin-containing monooxygenase
FSH	follicle-stimulating hormone
FTT	failure to thrive
FVC	forced vital capacity
G-6-PD	glucose-6-phosphate dehydrogenase
GA	gestational age
GABA	gamma-aminobutyric acid
GAD	generalized anxiety disorder
GE	gastroesophageal
GERD	gastroesophageal reflux disease
GFR	glomerular filtration rate
GGT	gamma-glutamyltransferase
GI	gastrointestinal
GIST	gastrointestinal stromal tumor
GU	genitourinary
GVHD	graft versus host disease
HAM-A	Hamilton Anxiety Scale
HAM-D	Hamilton Depression Scale
HARS	HIV-associated adipose redistribution syndrome
HCAHPS	Hospital Consumer Assessment of Healthcare Providers and Systems
HCM	hypertrophic cardiomyopathy

Abbreviations Which May Be Used in This Reference *(continued)*

Abbreviation	Meaning
Hct	hematocrit
HCV	hepatitis C virus
HDL-C	high density lipoprotein cholesterol
HF	heart failure
HFA	hydrofluoroalkane
HFSA	Heart Failure Society of America
Hgb	hemoglobin
HIV	human immunodeficiency virus
HMG-CoA	3-hydroxy-3-methylglutaryl-coenzyme A
HOCM	hypertrophic obstructive cardiomyopathy
HPA	hypothalamic-pituitary-adrenal
HPLC	high performance liquid chromatography
HSV	herpes simplex virus
HTC	hematopoietic cell transplantation
HTN	hypertension
HUS	hemolytic uremic syndrome
IBD	inflammatory bowel disease
IBS	irritable bowel syndrome
IBW	ideal body weight
ICD	implantable cardioverter defibrillator
ICH	intracranial hemorrhage
ICP	intracranial pressure
IDDM	insulin-dependent diabetes mellitus
IDSA	Infectious Diseases Society of America
IgG	immune globulin G
ILCOR	International Liaison Committee on Resuscitation
IM	intramuscular
INR	international normalized ration
Int. unit	international unit
I.O.	Intraosseous
I & O	input and output
IOP	intraocular pressure
IQ	intelligence quotient
ITP	immune thrombocytopenia (formerly known as idiopathic thrombocytopenic purpura)
IUGR	intrauterine growth retardation
IV	intravenous
IVH	intraventricular hemorrhage
IVP	intravenous push
IVPB	intravenous piggyback
JIA	juvenile idiopathic arthritis
JNC	Joint National Committee
JRA	juvenile rheumatoid arthritis
kg	kilogram
KIU	kallikrein inhibitor unit
KOH	potassium hydroxide
LAMM	L-α-acetyl methadol
LDH	lactate dehydrogenase
LDL-C	low density lipoprotein cholesterol
LE	lupus erythematosus
LFT	liver function test
LGA	large for gestational age
LH	luteinizing hormone
LP	lumbar posture
LR	lactated Ringer's
LV	left ventricular
LVEF	left ventricular ejection fraction
LVH	left ventricular hypertrophy

Abbreviations Which May Be Used in This Reference *(continued)*

Abbreviation	Meaning
MAC	*Mycobacterium avium* complex
MADRS	Montgomery Asbery Depression Rating Scale
MAO	monoamine oxidase
MAOIs	monamine oxidase inhibitors
MAP	mean arterial pressure
MDD	major depressive disorder
MDR1	multidrug resistence protein 1
MDRD	modification of diet in renal disease
MDRSP	multidrug resistant *streptococcus pneumoniae*
MI	myocardial infarction
MMSE	mini mental status examination
MOPP	mustargen (mechlorethamine), Oncovin (vinCRIStine), procarbazine, and prednisone
M/P	milk to plasma ratio
MPS I	mucopolysaccharidosis I
MRHD	maximum recommended human dose
MRI	magnetic resonance imaging
MRP2	multidrug resistance-associated protein 2
MRSA	methicillin-resistant *Staphylococcus aureus*
MUGA	multiple gated acquisition scan
NAEPP	National Asthma Education and Prevention Program
NAS	neonatal abstinence syndrome
NCI	National Cancer Institute
ND	nasoduodenal
NF	National Formulary
NFD	nephrogenic fibrosing dermopathy
NG	nasogastric
NHL	Non-Hodgkin lymphoma
NIDDM	noninsulin-dependent diabetes mellitus
NIH	National Institute of Health
NIOSH	National Institute for Occupational Safety and Health
NKA	no known allergies
NKDA	no known drug allergies
NMDA	n-methyl-d-aspartate
NMS	neuroleptic malignant syndrome
NNRTI	non-nucleoside reverse transcriptase inhibitor
NRTI	nucleoside reverse transcriptase inhibitor
NS	normal saline (0.9% sodium chloride)
NSAID	nonsteroidal anti-inflammatory drug
NSCLC	non-small cell lung cancer
NSF	nephrogenic systemic fibrosis
NSTEMI	Non-ST-elevation myocardial infarction
NYHA	New York Heart Association
OA	osteoarthritis
OAT	Organic anion transporter
OCD	obsessive-compulsive disorder
OCT	Organic cation transporter
OCT2	Organic cation transporter 2
OHSS	ovarian hyperstimulation syndrome
O.R.	operating room
OTC	over-the-counter (nonprescription)
PABA	para-aminobenzoic acid
PACTG	Pediatric AIDS Clinical Trials Group
PALS	pediatric advanced life support
PAT	paroxysmal atrial tachycardia
PCA	patient-controlled analgesia
PCI	percutaneous coronary intervention
PCP	*Pneumocystis jiroveci* pneumonia (also called *Pneumocystis carinii* pneumonia)

Abbreviations Which May Be Used in This Reference *(continued)*

Abbreviation	Meaning
PCWP	pulmonary capillary wedge pressure
PD	Parkinson's disease; peritoneal dialysis
PDA	patent ductus arteriosus
PDE-5	phosphodiesterase-5
PE	pulmonary embolism
PEG tube	percutaneous endoscopic gastrostomy tube
P-gP	P-glycoprotein
PHN	post-herpetic neuralgia
PICU	Pediatric Intensive Care Unit
PID	pelvic inflammatory disease
PIP	peak inspiratory pressure
PMA	postmenstrual age
PMDD	premenstrual dysphoric disorder
PNA	postnatal age
PONV	postoperative nausea and vomiting
PPHN	persistent pulmonary hypertension of the neonate
PPN	peripheral parenteral nutrition
PROM	premature rupture of membranes
PSVT	paroxysmal supraventricular tachycardia
PT	prothrombin time
PTH	parathyroid hormone
PTSD	post-traumatic stress disorder
PTT	partial thromboplastin time
PUD	peptic ulcer disease
PVC	premature ventricular contraction
PVD	peripheral vascular disease
PVR	peripheral vascular resistance
QTc	corrected QT interval
QTcF	corrected QT interval by Fridericia's formula
R	Ringer's Injection
RA	rheumatoid arthritis
RAP	right arterial pressure
RDA	recommended daily allowance
REM	rapid eye movement
REMS	risk evaluation and mitigation strategies
RIA	radioimmunoassay
RNA	ribonucleic acid
RPLS	reversible posterior leukoencephalopathy syndrome
RSV	respiratory syncytial virus
SA	sinoatrial
SAD	seasonal affective disorder
SAH	subarachnoid hemorrhage
SBE	subacute bacterial endocarditis
SBP	systolic blood pressure
SCLC	small cell lung cancer
SCr	serum creatinine
SERM	selective estrogen receptor modulator
SGA	small for gestational age
SGOT	serum glutamic oxaloacetic aminotransferase
SGPT	serum glutamic pyruvate transaminase
SI	International System of Units or Systeme international d'Unites
SIADH	syndrome of inappropriate antidiuretic hormone secretion
SIDS	sudden infant death syndrome
SL	sodium lactate
SLCO1B1	Solute carrier organic anion transporter family member 1B1
SLE	systemic lupus erythematosus
SLEDD	sustained low-efficiency daily diafiltration

Abbreviations Which May Be Used in This Reference *(continued)*

Abbreviation	Meaning
SNRI	serotonin norepinephrine reuptake inhibitor
SSKI	saturated solution of potassium iodide
SSRIs	selective serotonin reuptake inhibitors
STD	sexually transmitted disease
STEM I	ST-elevation myocardial infarction
SubQ	subcutaneous
SVR	systemic vascular resistance
SVT	supraventricular tachycardia
SWFI	sterile water for injection
SWI	sterile water for injection
$T_{1/2}$	half-life
T_3	triiodothyronine
T_4	thyroxine
TB	tuberculosis
TC	total cholesterol
TCA	tricyclic antidepressant
TD	tardive dyskinesia
TG	triglyceride
TIA	transient ischemic attack
TIBC	total iron binding capacity
TMA	thrombotic microangiopathy
T_{max}	time to maximum observed concentration, plasma
TNF	tumor necrosis factor
TPN	total parenteral nutrition
TSH	thyroid stimulating hormone
TT	thrombin time
TTP	thrombotic microangiopathy
UA	urine analysis
UC	ulcerative colitis
UGT	UDP-glucuronosyltransferase
ULN	upper limits of normal
URI	upper respiratory infection
USAN	United States Adopted Names
USP	United States Pharmacopeia
UTI	urinary tract infection
UV	ultraviolet
V_d	volume of distribution
V_{dss}	volume of distribution at steady-state
VEGF	vascular endothelial growth factor
VF	ventricular fibrillation
VLBW	very low birth weight
VMA	vanillylmandelic acid
VT	ventricular tachycardia
VTE	venous thromboembolism
vWD	von Willebrand disease
VZV	varicella zoster virus
WHO	World Health Organization
w/v	weight for volume
w/w	weight for weight
YBOC	Yale Brown Obsessive-Compulsive Scale
YMRS	Young Mania Rating Scale

Common Weights, Measures, or Apothecary Abbreviations

Abbreviation	Meaning
<[a]	less than
>[a]	greater than
≤	less than or equal to
≥	greater than or equal to
ac	before meals or food
ad	to, up to
ad lib	at pleasure
AM	morning
AMA	against medical advice
amp	ampul
amt	amount
aq	water
aq. dest.	distilled water
ASAP	as soon as possible
a.u.[a]	each ear
bid	twice daily
bm	bowel movement
C	Celsius, centigrade
cal	calorie
cap	capsule
cc[a]	cubic centimeter
cm	centimeter
comp	compound
cont	continue
d	day
d/c[a]	discharge
dil	dilute
disp	dispense
div	divide
dtd	give of such a dose
Dx	diagnosis
elix, el	elixir
emp	as directed
et	and
ex aq	in water
F	Fahrenheit
g	gram
gr	grain
gtt	a drop
h	hour
hs[a]	at bedtime
kcal	kilocalorie
kg	kilogram
L	liter
liq	a liquor, solution
M	molar
mcg	microgram
m. dict	as directed
mEq	milliequivalent
mg	milligram
microL	microliter
min	minute
mL	milliliter
mm	millimeter

Common Weights, Measures, or Apothecary Abbreviations *(continued)*

Abbreviation	Meaning
mM	millimole
mm Hg	millimeters of mercury
mo	month
mOsm	milliosmoles
ng	nanogram
nmol	nanomole
no.	number
noc	in the night
non rep	do not repeat, no refills
NPO	nothing by mouth
NV	nausea and vomiting
O, Oct	a pint
o.d.[a]	right eye
o.l.	left eye
o.s.[a]	left eye
o.u.[a]	each eye
pc, post cib	after meals
PM	afternoon or evening
PO	by mouth
P.R.	rectally
prn	as needed
pulv	a powder
q	every
qad	every other day
qh	every hour
qid	four times a day
qs	a sufficient quantity
qs ad	a sufficient quantity to make
Rx	take, a recipe
S.L.	sublingual
stat	at once, immediately
SubQ	subcutaneous
supp	suppository
syr	syrup
tab	tablet
tal	such
tid	three times a day
tr, tinct	tincture
trit	triturate
tsp	teaspoon
u.d.	as directed
ung	ointment
v.o.	verbal order
w.a.	while awake
x3	3 times
x4	4 times
y	year

[a]ISMP error-prone abbreviation

Additional abbreviations used and defined within a specific monograph or text piece may only apply to that text.

REFERENCES

The Institute for Safe Medication Practices (ISMP) list of Error-Prone Abbreviations, Symbols, and Dose Designations. Available at http://www.ismp.org/Tools/errorproneabbreviations.pdf

AVERAGE WEIGHTS AND SURFACE AREAS

Average Height, Weight, and Surface Area by Age and Gender

Age	Girls			Boys		
	Height (cm)	Weight (kg)	BSA (m^2)	Height (cm)	Weight (kg)	BSA (m^2)
Birth	49.5	3.4	0.22	50	3.6	0.22
3 months	59	5.6	0.3	61	6	0.32
6 months	65	7.2	0.36	67	7.9	0.38
9 months	70	8.3	0.4	72	9.3	0.43
12 months	74.5	9.5	0.44	75.5	10.3	0.46
15 months	77	10.3	0.47	79	11.1	0.49
18 months	80	11	0.49	82	11.7	0.52
21 months	83	11.6	0.52	85	12.2	0.54
2 years	86	12	0.54	87.5	12.6	0.55
2.5 years	91	13	0.57	92	13.5	0.59
3 years	94.5	13.8	0.6	96	14.3	0.62
3.5 years	97	15	0.64	98	15	0.64
4 years	101	16	0.67	102	16	0.67
4.5 years	104	17	0.7	105	17	0.7
5 years	107.5	18	0.73	109	18.5	0.75
6 years	115	20	0.8	115	21	0.82
7 years	121.5	23	0.88	122	23	0.88
8 years	127.5	25.5	0.95	127.5	26	0.96
9 years	133	29	1.04	133.5	28.5	1.03
10 years	138	33	1.12	138.5	32	1.1
11 years	144	37	1.22	143.5	36	1.2
12 years	151	41.5	1.32	149	40.5	1.29
13 years	157	46	1.42	156	45.5	1.4
14 years	160.5	49.5	1.49	163.5	51	1.52
15 years	162	52	1.53	170	56	1.63
16 years	162.5	54	1.56	173.5	61	1.71
17 years	163	55	1.58	175	64.5	1.77
Adult[a]	163.5	58	1.62	177	83.5	2.03

Data extracted from the CDC growth charts based on the 50th percentile height and weight for a given age[b]

Body surface area calculation[c]: Square root of [(Ht x Wt) / 3,600]

[a]McDowell MA, Fryar CD, Hirsch R, Ogden CL. Anthropometric reference data for children and adults: U.S. population, 1999-2002. *Adv Data.* 2005;(361):1-5.

[b]Centers for Disease Control and Prevention (CDC). 2000 CDC growth charts: United States. Available at http://www.cdc.gov/growthcharts. Accessed November 16, 2007.

[c]Mosteller RD. Simplified calculation of body-surface area *N Engl J Med.* 1987;317(17):1098.

BODY SURFACE AREA OF CHILDREN AND ADULTS

Calculating Body Surface Area in Children

In a child of average size, find weight and corresponding surface area on the boxed scale to the left or use the nomogram to the right. Lay a straightedge on the correct height and weight points for the child, then read the intersecting point on the surface area scale. (**Note:** 2.2 lb = 1 kg)

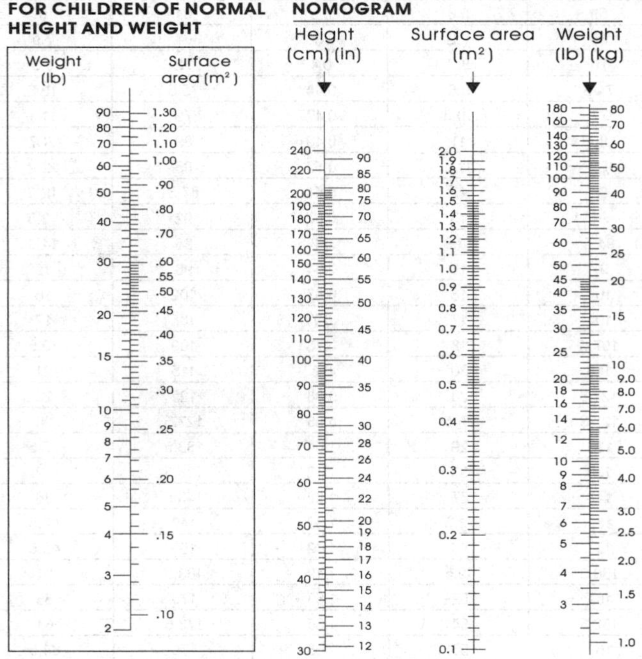

BODY SURFACE AREA FORMULA
(Adult and Pediatric)

BSA $(m^2) = \sqrt{\dfrac{\text{ht (in)} \times \text{wt (lb)}}{3131}}$ or, in metric: BSA $(m^2) = \sqrt{\dfrac{\text{ht (cm)} \times \text{wt (kg)}}{3600}}$

References

Lam TK and Leung DT, "More on Simplified Calculation of Body Surface Area," *N Engl J Med*, 1988, 318(17):1130 (letter).

Mosteller RD, "Simplified Calculation of Body Surface Area," *N Engl J Med*, 1987, 317(17):1098 (letter).

METRIC CONVERSIONS

Weight Conversion: Pounds/Kilograms

1 pound = 0.45359 kilograms

1 kilogram = 2.2 pounds

Temperature Conversion: Fahrenheit/Celsius

Fahrenheit to Celsius = (°F - 32) x 5/9 = °C

Celsius to Fahrenheit = (°C x 9/5) + 32 = °F

Apothecary-Metric Exact Equivalents

1 gram (g)	=	15.43 grains (gr)	0.1 mg	=	1/600 gr
1 milliliter (mL)	=	16.23 minims	0.12 mg	=	1/500 gr
1 minim	=	0.06 mL	0.15 mg	=	1/400 gr
1 gr	=	64.8 milligrams (mg)	0.2 mg	=	1/300 gr
1 fluid ounce (fl oz)	=	29.57 mL	0.3 mg	=	1/200 gr
1 pint (pt)	=	473.2 mL	0.4 mg	=	1/150 gr
1 ounce (oz)	=	28.35 g	0.5 mg	=	1/120 gr
1 pound (lb)	=	453.6 g	0.6 mg	=	1/100 gr
1 kilogram (kg)	=	2.2 lb	0.8 mg	=	1/80 gr
1 quart (qt)	=	946.4 mL	1 mg	=	1/65 gr

Apothecary-Metric Approximate Equivalents[a]

Liquids			Solids		
1 teaspoonful	=	5 mL	1/4 grain	=	15 mg
1 tablespoonful	=	15 mL	1/2 grain	=	30 mg
			1 grain	=	60 mg
			1 1/2 grain	=	100 mg
			5 grains	=	300 mg
			10 grains	=	600 mg

[a]Use exact equivalents for compounding and calculations requiring a high degree of accuracy.

POUNDS/KILOGRAMS CONVERSION

1 pound = 0.45359 kilograms
1 kilogram = 2.2 pounds

lb	=	kg	lb	=	kg	lb	=	kg
1 lb		0.45 kg	70 lbs		31.75 kg	140 lbs		63.5 kg
5 lbs		2.27 kg	75 lbs		34.02 kg	145 lbs		65.77 kg
10 lbs		4.54 kg	80 lbs		36.29 kg	150 lbs		68.04 kg
15 lbs		6.8 kg	85 lbs		38.56 kg	155 lbs		70.31 kg
20 lbs		9.07 kg	90 lbs		40.82 kg	160 lbs		72.58 kg
25 lbs		11.34 kg	95 lbs		43.09 kg	165 lbs		74.84 kg
30 lbs		13.61 kg	100 lbs		45.36 kg	170 lbs		77.11 kg
35 lbs		15.88 kg	105 lbs		47.63 kg	175 lbs		79.38 kg
40 lbs		18.14 kg	110 lbs		49.9 kg	180 lbs		81.65 kg
45 lbs		20.41 kg	115 lbs		52.16 kg	185 lbs		83.92 kg
50 lbs		22.68 kg	120 lbs		54.43 kg	190 lbs		86.18 kg
55 lbs		24.95 kg	125 lbs		56.7 kg	195 lbs		88.45 kg
60 lbs		27.22 kg	130 lbs		58.91 kg	200 lbs		90.72 kg
65 lbs		29.48 kg	135 lbs		61.24 kg			

DRUG INTERACTIONS: METABOLISM/TRANSPORT EFFECTS

Most drugs are eliminated from the body, at least in part, by being chemically altered to less lipid-soluble products (ie, metabolized), and thus are more likely to be excreted via the kidneys or the bile. Phase I metabolism includes drug hydrolysis, oxidation, and reduction, and results in drugs that are more polar in their chemical structure, while Phase II metabolism involves the attachment of an additional molecule onto the drug (or partially metabolized drug) in order to create an inactive and/or more water soluble compound. Phase II processes include (primarily) glucuronidation, sulfation, glutathione conjugation, acetylation, and methylation.

Virtually any of the Phase I and II enzymes can be inhibited by some xenobiotic or drug. Some of the Phase I and II enzymes can be induced. Inhibition of the activity of metabolic enzymes will result in increased concentrations of the substrate (drug), whereas induction of the activity of metabolic enzymes will result in decreased concentrations of the substrate. For example, the well-documented enzyme-inducing effects of phenobarbital may include a combination of Phase I and II enzymes. Phase II glucuronidation may be increased via induced UDP-glucuronosyltransferase (UGT) activity, whereas Phase I oxidation may be increased via induced cytochrome P450 (CYP) activity. However, for most drugs, the primary route of metabolism (and the primary focus of drug-drug interaction) is Phase I oxidation, and specifically, metabolism.

CYP enzymes may be responsible for the metabolism (at least partial metabolism) of ~75% of all drugs, with the CYP3A subfamily responsible for nearly half of this activity. Found throughout plant, animal, and bacterial species, CYP enzymes represent a superfamily of xenobiotic metabolizing proteins. There have been several hundred CYP enzymes identified in nature, each of which has been assigned to a family (1, 2, 3, etc), subfamily (A, B, C, etc), and given a specific enzyme number (1, 2, 3, etc) according to the similarity in amino acid sequence that it shares with other enzymes. Of these many enzymes, only a few are found in humans, and even fewer appear to be involved in the metabolism of xenobiotics (eg, drugs). The key human enzyme subfamilies include CYP1A, CYP2A, CYP1B, CYP2B, CYP2C, CYP2D, CYP2E, and CYP3A.

CYP enzymes are found in the endoplasmic reticulum of cells in a variety of human tissues (eg, skin, kidneys, brain, lungs), but their predominant sites of concentration and activity are the liver and intestine. Though the abundance of CYP enzymes throughout the body is relatively equally distributed among the various subfamilies, the relative contribution to drug metabolism is (in decreasing order of magnitude) CYP3A4/5 (nearly 50%), CYP2D6 (nearly 25%), CYP2C8/9 (nearly 15%), then CYP1A1/2, CYP2C19, CYP2A6, CYP2E1, CYP1B1, and CYP2B6. Owing to their potential for numerous drug-drug interactions, those drugs that are identified in preclinical studies as substrates of CYP3A enzymes are often given a lower priority for continued research and development in favor of drugs that appear to be less affected by (or less likely to affect) this enzyme subfamily.

Each enzyme subfamily possesses unique selectivity toward potential substrates. For example, CYP1A1/2 preferentially binds medium-sized, planar, lipophilic molecules, while CYP2D6 preferentially binds molecules that possess a basic nitrogen atom. Some CYP subfamilies exhibit polymorphism (ie, multiple allelic variants that manifest differing catalytic properties). The best described polymorphisms involve CYP2C8/9, CYP2C19, and CYP2D6. Individuals possessing "wild type" gene alleles exhibit normal functioning CYP capacity. Others, however, possess allelic variants that leave the person with a subnormal level of catalytic potential (so called "poor metabolizers"). Poor metabolizers would be more likely to experience toxicity from drugs metabolized by the affected enzymes (or less effects if the enzyme is responsible for converting a prodrug to it's active form as in the case of codeine). The percentage of people classified as poor metabolizers varies by enzyme and population group. As an example, ~7% of white patients and only about 1% of Asian patients appear to be CYP2D6 poor metabolizers.

CYP enzymes can be both inhibited and induced by other drugs, leading to increased or decreased serum concentrations (along with the associated effects), respectively. Induction occurs when a drug causes an increase in the amount of smooth endoplasmic reticulum, secondary to increasing the amount of the affected CYP enzymes in the tissues. This "revving up" of the CYP enzyme system may take several days to reach peak activity, and likewise, may take several days, even months, to return to normal following discontinuation of the inducing agent.

CYP inhibition occurs via several potential mechanisms. Most commonly, a CYP inhibitor competitively (and reversibly) binds to the active site on the enzyme, thus preventing the substrate from binding to the same site, and preventing the substrate from being metabolized. The affinity of an inhibitor for an enzyme may be expressed by an inhibition constant (Ki) or IC50 (defined as the concentration of the inhibitor required to cause 50% inhibition under a given set of conditions). In addition to reversible competition for an enzyme site, drugs may inhibit enzyme activity by binding to sites on the enzyme other than that to which the substrate would bind, and thereby cause a change in the functionality or physical structure of the enzyme. A drug may also bind to the enzyme in an irreversible (ie, "suicide") fashion. In such a case, it is not the concentration of drug at the enzyme site that is important (constantly binding and releasing), but the number of molecules available for binding (once bound, always bound).

Although an inhibitor or inducer may be known to affect a variety of CYP subfamilies, it may only inhibit one or two in a clinically important fashion. Likewise, although a substrate is known to be at least partially metabolized by a variety of CYP enzymes, only one or two enzymes may contribute significantly enough to its overall metabolism to warrant concern when used with potential inducers or inhibitors. Therefore, when attempting to predict the level of risk of using two drugs that may affect each other via altered CYP function, it is important to identify the relative effectiveness of the inhibiting/inducing drug on the CYP subfamilies that significantly contribute to the metabolism of the substrate. The contribution of a specific CYP pathway to substrate metabolism should be considered not only in light of other known CYP pathways, but also other nonoxidative pathways for substrate metabolism (eg, glucuronidation) and transporter proteins (eg, P-glycoprotein) that may affect the presentation of a substrate to a metabolic pathway.

SMOKING AND DRUG METABOLISM

A nonpharmaceutical interaction may be equally important because of its constant occurrence in users (tobacco). Smoking induces CYP1A2 activity, possibly causing a reduced effect of its substrates (eg, estradiol). Among postmenopausal women receiving 1 or 2 mg daily of oral estrogen, it has been found that the serum estradiol level in smokers was half that in nonsmokers. The effect was manifested by about a 50% reduction in breast tenderness in smokers. Thus, smoking may affect drugs metabolized by CYP1A2, with various consequences on target organs. A review of the literature suggests that at least a dozen drugs interact with cigarette smoke in a clinically significant manner. Polycyclic aromatic hydrocarbons (PAHs) are largely responsible for enhancing drug metabolism. Cigarette smoke induces an increase in the concentration of CYP1A2, the isoenzyme responsible for metabolism of theophylline. Theophylline is, therefore, eliminated more quickly in smokers than in nonsmokers. As a result of hepatic induction of CYP1A2, serum concentrations of theophylline have been shown to be reduced in smokers. Cigarette smoking may substantially reduce tacrine plasma concentrations. The manufacturer states that mean plasma tacrine concentrations in smokers are about one-third of the concentration in nonsmokers (presumably after multiple doses of tacrine).

Patients with insulin-dependent diabetes who smoke heavily may require a higher dosage of insulin than nonsmokers. Cigarette smoking may also reduce serum concentrations of flecainide. Although the mechanism of this interaction is unknown, enhanced hepatic metabolism is possible. Propoxyphene, a pain reliever, has been found to be less effective in smokers than in nonsmokers. The mechanism for the inefficacy of propoxyphene in smokers compared with nonsmokers may be enhanced biotransformation.

The norepinephrine and serotonin reuptake inhibitors, as a new class of smoking cessation drugs, have also received attention relative to metabolic interactions. In vitro studies indicate that bupropion (Zyban) is primarily metabolized to hydroxybupropion by the CYP2B6 isoenzyme. Therefore, the potential exists for a drug interaction between Zyban and drugs that affect the CYP2B6 isoenzyme metabolism [eg, orphenadrine (Norflex) and cyclophosphamide (Cytoxan)]. The hydroxybupropion metabolite of bupropion does not appear to be metabolized by the cytochrome P450 isoenzymes. No systemic data have been collected on the metabolism of Zyban following concomitant administration with other drugs, or alternatively, the effect of concomitant administration of Zyban on the metabolism of other drugs.

SUMMARY

Once a drug has been metabolized in the liver, it is eliminated through several different mechanisms. One is directly through bile, into the intestine, and eventually excreted in feces. More commonly, the metabolites and the original drug pass back into the liver from the general circulation and are carried to other organs and tissues. Eventually, these metabolites are excreted through the kidney. In the kidney, the drug and its metabolites may be filtered by the glomerulus or secreted by the renal tubules into the urine. From the kidney, some of the drug may be reabsorbed and pass back into the blood. The drug may also be carried to the lung. If the drug or its metabolite is volatile, it can pass from the blood into the alveolar air and be eliminated in the breath. To a minor extent, drugs and metabolites can be excreted by sweat and saliva. In nursing mothers, drugs are also excreted in mother's milk.

The clinical considerations of drug metabolism may affect which other drugs can and should be administered. Drug tolerance may be a consideration, in that larger doses of a drug may be necessary to obtain effect in patients in which the metabolism is extremely rapid. These interactions, via cytochrome P450 or its isoforms, can occasionally be used beneficially to increase/maintain blood levels of one drug by administering a second drug. Dental clinicians should attempt to stay current on this topic of drug interactions as knowledge evolves.

SELECTED READINGS

Bjarnason NH, Christiansen C. The influence of thinness and smoking on bone loss and response to hormone replacement therapy in early postmenopausal women. *J Clin Endocrinol Metab*. 2000;85(2):590-596.

Bjarnason NH, Jørgensen C, Kremmer H, Alexandersen P, Christiansen C. Smoking reduces breast tenderness during oral estrogen-progestogen therapy. *Climacteric*. 2004;7(4):390-396.

Bjornsson TD, Callaghan JT, Einolf HJ, et al. The conduct of in vitro and in vivo drug-drug interaction studies: a PhRMA perspective. *J Clin Pharmacol*. 2003;43(5):443-469.

Drug-Drug Interactions. Rodrigues AD, ed. New York, NY: Marcel Dekker, Inc; 2002.

Hersh EV, Moore PA. Drug interactions in dentistry: the importance of knowing your CYP's. *J Am Dent Assoc*. 2004;135(3):298-311.

Metabolic Drug Interactions. Levy RH, Thummel KE, Trager WF, et al, eds. Philadelphia, PA: Lippincott Williams & Wilkins; 2000.

Wilkinson GR. Drug metabolism and variability among patients in drug response. *N Engl J Med*. 2005;352(21):2211-2221.

Wynn RL, Meiller TF. CYP enzymes and adverse drug reactions. *Gen Dent*. 1998;46(5):436-438.

Zhang Y, Benet LZ. The gut as a barrier to drug absorption: combined role of cytochrome P450 3A and P-glycoprotein. *Clin Pharmacokinet*. 2001;40(3):159-168.

SELECTED WEBSITES

http://www.bdbiosciences.com/
http://www.cypalleles.ki.se/
http://medicine.iupui.edu/clinpharm/ddis/
http://mhc.com/Cytochromes/

LABORATORY VALUES/BODY MEASUREMENTS

In the following laboratory tests, normal reference values for commonly requested laboratory tests are listed in traditional units and in SI units. The tables are a guideline only. Values are method-dependent and "normal values" may vary between laboratories.

Reference Values for Blood, Plasma, or Serum Laboratory Tests

Determination	Reference Value	
	Conventional Units	SI Units
Alpha-fetoprotein	*Adult:* <15 ng/mL *Pregnant (16 to 18 weeks):* 38 to 45 ng/mL	*Adult:* <15 mcg/L *Pregnant (16 to 18 weeks):* 38 to 45 mcg/L
Ammonia (NH_3) - diffusion	20 to 120 mcg/dL	12 to 70 mcmol/L
Ammonia Nitrogen	15 to 45 µg/dL	11 to 32 µmol/L
Amylase	35 to 118 IU/L	0.58 to 1.97 mckat/L
Anion gap (Na^+-\[Cl^- + HCO_3^-]) (P)	7 to 16 mEq/L	7 to 16 mmol/L
Antithrombin III (AT III)	80 to 120 U/dL	800 to 1,200 U/L
Bicarbonate: Arterial	21 to 28 mEq/L	21 to 28 mmol/L
Venous	22 to 29 mEq/L	22 to 29 mmol/L
Bilirubin: Conjugated (direct)	≤0.2 mg/dL	≤4 mcmol/L
Total	0.1 to 1 mg/dl	2 to 18 mcmol/L
Calcitonin	<100 pg/mL	<100 ng/L
Calcium: Total	8.6 to 10.3 mg/dL	2.2 to 2.74 mmol/L
Ionized	4.4 to 5.1 mg/dL	1 to 1.3 mmol/L
Carbon dioxide content (plasma)	21 to 32 mmol/L	21 to 32 mmol/L
Carcinoembryonic antigen	<3 ng/mL	<3 mcg/L
Chloride	95 to 110 mEq/L	95 to 110 mmol/L
Coagulation screen:		
Bleeding time	3 to 9.5 minutes	180 to 570 seconds
Prothrombin time	10 to 13 seconds	10 to 13 seconds
Partial thromboplastin time (activated)	22 to 37 seconds	22 to 37 seconds
Protein C	0.7 to 1.4 µ/mL	700 to 1,400 U/mL
Protein S	0.7 to 1.4 µ/mL	700 to 1,400 U/mL
Copper, total	70 to 160 mcg/dL	11 to 25 mcmol/L
Corticotropin (ACTH) - 800 hours	<60 pg/mL	<13.2 pmol/L
Cortisol		
800 hours	5 to 30 mcg/dL	138 to 810 nmol/L
1,800 hours	2 to 15 mcg/dL	50 to 410 nmol/L
2,000 hours	≤50% of 800 hours	≤50% of 800 hours
Creatine kinase: Female	20 to 170 IU/L	0.33 to 2.83 mckat/L
Male	30 to 220 IU/L	0.5 to 3.67 mckat/L
Creatinine kinase isoenzymes, MB fraction	0 to 12 IU/L	0 to 0.2 mckat/L
Creatinine	0.5 to 1.7 mg/dL	44 to 150 mcmol/L
Fibrinogen (coagulation factor I)	150 to 360 mg/dL	1.5 to 3.6 g/L
Follicle-stimulating hormone (FSH):		
Female	2 to 13 mIU/mL	2 to 13 IU/L
Midcycle	5 to 22 mIU/mL	5 to 22 IU/L
Male	1 to 8 mIU/mL	1 to 8 IU/L
Glucose, fasting	65 to 115 mg/dL	3.6 to 6.3 mmol/L
Glucose Tolerance Test (Oral)	mg/dL	mmol/L

Reference Values for Blood, Plasma, or Serum Laboratory Tests *(continued)*

Determination	Reference Value			
	Conventional Units		SI Units	
	Normal	*Diabetic*	*Normal*	*Diabetic*
Fasting	70 to 105	\g 140	3.9 to 5.8	\g 7.8
60 minutes	120 to 170	≥200	6.7 to 9.4	≥11.1
90 minutes	100 to 140	≥200	5.6 to 7.8	≥11.1
120 minutes	70 to 120	≥140	3.9 to 6.7	≥7.8
(γ) -Glutamyltransferase (GGT): Male	9 to 50 units/L		9 to 50 units/L	
Female	8 to 40 units/L		8 to 40 units/L	
Haptoglobin	44 to 303 mg/dL		0.44 to 3.03 g/L	
Hematologic tests:				
Fibrinogen	200 to 400 mg/dL		2 to 4 g/L	
Hematocrit (Hct), female	36% to 44.6%		0.36 to 0.446 fraction of 1	
male	40.7% to 50.3%		0.4 to 0.503 fraction of 1	
Hemoglobin A_{1c}	5.3% to 7.5% of total Hgb		0.053 to 0.075	
Hemoglobin (Hb), female	12.1 to 15.3 g/dL		121 to 153 g/L	
male	13.8 to 17.5 g/dL		138 to 175 g/L	
Leukocyte count (WBC)	3,800 to 9,800/mcl		3.8 to 9.8 × 10^9/L	
Erythrocyte count (RBC), female	3.5 to 5 × 10^6/mcl		3.5 to 5 × 10^{12}/L	
male	4.3 to 5.9 × 10^6/mcl		4.3 to 5.9 × 10^{12}/L	
Mean corpuscular volume (MCV)	80 to 97.6 mcm^3		80 to 97.6 fl	
Mean corpuscular hemoglobin (MCH)	27 to 33 pg/cell		1.66 to 2.09 fmol/cell	
Mean corpuscular hemoglobin concentrate (MCHC)	33 to 36 g/dL		20.3 to 22 mmol/L	
Erythrocyte sedimentation rate (sedrate, ESR)	≤30 mm/hour		≤30 mm/hour	
Erythrocyte enzymes				
Glucose-6-phosphate dehydrognase (G-6-PD)	250 to 5,000 units per 10^6 cells		250 to 5,000 mcunits/cell	
Ferritin	10 to 383 ng/mL		23 to 862 pmol/L	
Folic acid: normal	>3.1 to 12.4 ng/mL		7 to 28.1 nmol/L	
Platelet count	150 to 450 × 10^3/mcl		150 to 450 × 10^9/L	
Reticulocytes	0.5% to 1.5% of erythrocytes		0.005 to 0.015	
Vitamin B_{12}	223 to 1,132 pg/mL		165 to 835 pmol/L	
Iron: Female	30 to 160 mcg/dL		5.4 to 31.3 mcmol/L	
Male	45 to 160 mcg/dL		8.1 to 31.3 mcmol/L	
Iron binding capacity	220 to 420 mcg/dL		39.4 to 75.2 mcmol/L	
Isocitrate dehydrogenase	1.2 to 7 units/L		1.2 to 7 units/L	
Isoenzymes				
Fraction 1	14% to 26% of total		0.14 to 0.26 fraction of total	
Fraction 2	29% to 39% of total		0.29 to 0.39 fraction of total	
Fraction 3	20% to 26% of total		0.20 to 0.26 fraction of total	
Fraction 4	8% to 16% of total		0.08 to 0.16 fraction of total	
Fraction 5	6% to 16% of total		0.06 to 0.16 fraction of total	
Lactate dehydrogenase	100 to 250 IU/L		1.67 to 4.17 mckat/L	
Lactic acid (lactate)	6 to 19 mg/dL		0.7 to 2.1 mmol/L	
Lead	≤50 mcg/dL		≤2.41 mcmol/L	
Lipase	10 to 150 units/L		10 to 150 units/L	

Reference Values for Blood, Plasma, or Serum Laboratory Tests *(continued)*

Determination	Reference Value	
	Conventional Units	**SI Units**
Lipids:		
Total Cholesterol		
Desirable	<200 mg/dL	<5.2 mmol/L
Borderline-high	200 to 239 mg/dL	<5.2 to 6.2 mmol/L
High	>239 mg/dL	>6.2 mmol/L
LDL		
Desirable	<130 mg/dL	<3.36 mmol/L
Borderline-high	130 to 159 mg/dL	3.36 to 4.11 mmol/L
High	>159 mg/dL	>4.11 mmol/L
HDL		
Low	<40 mg/dL	
Desirable	≥60 mg/dL	
Triglycerides		
Desirable	<150 mg/dL	
Borderline-high	150 to 199 mg/dL	
High	200 to 499 mg/dL	
Very high	≥500 mg/dL	
Magnesium	1.3 to 2.2 mEq/L	0.65 to 1.1 mmol/L
Osmolality	280 to 300 mOsm/kg	280 to 300 mmol/kg
Oxygen saturation (arterial)	94% to 100%	0.94 - fraction of 1
PCO_2, arterial	35 to 45 mm Hg	4.7 to 6 kPa
pH, arterial	7.35 to 7.45	7.35 to 7.45
PO_2, arterial: Breathing room air[a]	80 to 105 mm Hg	10.6 to 14 kPa
On 100% O_2	>500 mm Hg	
Phosphatase (acid), total at 37°C	0.13 to 0.63 IU/L	2.2 to 10.5 IU/L or 2.2 to 10.5 mckat/L
Phosphatase alkaline[b]	20 to 130 IU/L	20 to 130 IU/L or 0.33 to 2.17 mckat/L
Phosphorus, inorganic,[c] (phosphate)	2.5 to 5 mg/dL	0.8 to 1.6 mmol/L
Potassium	3.5 to 5 mEq/L	3.5 to 5 mmol/L
Progesterone		
Female	0.1 to 1.5 ng/mL	0.32 to 4.8 nmol/L
Follicular phase	0.1 to 1.5 ng/mL	0.32 to 4.8 nmol/L
Luteal phase	2.5 to 28 ng/mL	8 to 89 nmol/L
Male	<0.5 ng/mL	<1.6 nmol/L
Prolactin	1.4 to 24.2 ng/mL	1.4 to 24.2 mcg/L
Prostate-specific antigen	0 to 4 ng/mL	0 to 4 ng/mL
Protein: Total	6 to 8 g/dL	60 to 80 g/L
Albumin	3.6 to 5 g/dL	36 to 50 g/L
Globulin	2.3 to 3.5 g/dL	23 to 35 g/L
Rheumatoid factor	<60 IU/mL	<60 kIU/L
Sodium	135 to 147 mEq/L	135 to 147 mmol/L
Testosterone: Female	6 to 86 ng/dL	0.21 to 3 nmol/L
Male	270 to 1,070 ng/dL	9.3 to 37 nmol/L

Reference Values for Blood, Plasma, or Serum Laboratory Tests *(continued)*

Determination	Reference Value	
	Conventional Units	SI Units
Thyroid Hormone Function Tests:		
Thyroid-stimulating hormone (TSH)	0.35 to 6.2 mcU/mL	0.35 to 6.2 mU/L
Thyroxine-binding globulin capacity	10 to 26 mcg/dL	100 to 260 mcg/L
Total triiodothyronine (T_3)	75 to 220 ng/dL	1.2 to 3.4 nmol/L
Total thyroxine by RIA (T_4)	4 to 11 mcg/dL	51 to 142 nmol/L
T_3 resin uptake	25% to 38%	0.25 to 0.38 fraction of 1
Transaminase, AST (aspartate aminotransferase, SGOT)	11 to 47 IU/L	0.18 to 0.78 mckat/L
Transaminase, ALT (alanine aminotransferase, SGPT)	7 to 53 IU/L	0.12 to 0.88 mckat/L
Transferrin	220 to 400 mg/dL	2.2 to 4 g/L
Urea nitrogen (BUN)	8 to 25 mg/dL	2.9 to 8.9 mmol/L
Uric acid	3 to 8 mg/dL	179 to 476 mcmol/L
Vitamin A (retinol)	15 to 60 mcg/dL	0.52 to 2.09 mcmol/L
Zinc	50 to 150 mcg/dL	7.7 to 23 mcmol/L

[a]Age-dependent
[b]Infants and adolescents up to 104 U/L
[c]Infants in the first year up to 6 mg/dL

Reference Values for Urine Laboratory Tests

Determination	Reference Value	
	Conventional Units	SI Units
Calcium[a]	50 to 250 mcg/day	1.25 to 6.25 mmol/day
Catecholamines:		
EPINEPHrine	<20 mcg/day	<109 nmol/day
Norepinephrine	<100 mcg/day	<590 nmol/day
Catecholamines, 24-hour	<110 µg	<650 nmol
Copper[a]	15 to 60 mcg/day	0.24 to 0.95 mcmol/day
Creatinine: Child	8 to 22 mg/kg	71 to 195 µmol/kg
Adolescent	8 to 30 mg/kg	71 to 265 µmol/kg
Female	0.6 to 1.5 g/day	5.3 to 13.3 mmol/day
Male	0.8 to 1.8 g/day	7.1 to 15.9 mmol/day
pH	4.5 to 8	4.5 to 8
Phosphate[a]	0.9 to 1.3 g/day	29 to 42 mmol/day
Potassium[a]	25 to 100 mEq/day	25 to 100 mmol/day
Protein		
Total	1 to 14 mg/dL	10 to 140 mg/L
At rest	50 to 80 mg/day	50 to 80 mg/day
Protein, quantitative	<150 mg/day	<0.15 g/day
Sodium[a]	100 to 250 mEq/day	100 to 250 mmol/day
Specific gravity, random	1.002 to 1.03	1.002 to 1.03
Uric acid, 24-hour	250 to 750 mg	1.48 to 4.43 mmol

[a]Diet-dependent

Drug Levels[a]

Drug Determination		Reference Value	
		Conventional Units	**SI Units**
Animoglycosides	Amikacin (trough) (peak)	1 to 8 mcg/mL 20 to 30 mcg/mL	1.7 to 13.7 mcmol/L 34 to 51 mcmol/L
	Gentamicin (trough) (peak)	0.5 to 2 mcg/mL 6 to 10 mcg/mL	1 to 4.2 mcmol/L 12.5 to 20.9 mcmol/L
	Kanamycin (trough) (peak)	5 to 10 mcg/mL 20 to 25 mcg/mL	nd[b] nd
	Netilmicin (trough) (peak)	0.5 to 2 mcg/mL 6 to 10 mcg/mL	nd nd
	Streptomycin (trough) (peak)	<5 mcg/mL 5 to 20 mcg/mL	nd nd
	Tobramycin (trough) (peak)	0.5 to 2 mcg/mL 5 to 20 mcg/mL	1.1 to 4.3 mcmol/L 12.8 to 21.8 mcmol/L
Antiarrhythmics	Amiodarone	0.5 to 2.5 mcg/mL	1.5 to 4 mcmol/L
	Bretylium	0.5 to 1.5 mcg/mL	nd
	Digitoxin	9 to 25 mcg/L	11.8 to 32.8 nmol/L
	Digoxin	0.8 to 2 ng/mL	0.9 to 2.5 nmol/L
	Disopyramide	2 to 8 mcg/mL	6 to 18 mcmol/L
	Flecainide	0.2 to 1 mcg/mL	nd
	Lidocaine	1.5 to 6 mcg/ml	4.5 to 21.5 mcmol/L
	Mexiletine	0.5 to 2 mcg/mL	nd
	Procainamide	4 to 8 mcg/mL	17 to 34 mcmol/mL
	Propranolol	50 to 200 ng/mL	190 to 770 nmol/L
	QuiNIDine	2 to 6 mcg/mL	4.6 to 9.2 mcmol/L
	Tocainide	4 to 10 mcg/mL	nd
	Verapamil	0.08 to 0.3 mcg/mL	nd
Anticonvulsants	CarBAMazepine	4 to 12 mcg/mL	17 to 51 mcmol/L
	PHENobarbital	10 to 40 mcg/mL	43 to 172 mcmol/L
	Phenytoin	10 to 20 mcg/mL	40 to 80 mcmol/L
	Primidone	4 to 12 mcg/mL	18 to 55 mcmol/L
	Valproic Acid	40 to 100 mcg/mL	280 to 700 mcmol/L

Drug Levels[a] *(continued)*

Drug Determination		Reference Value	
		Conventional Units	SI Units
Antidepressants	Amitriptyline	110 to 250 ng/mL[c]	500 to 900 nmol/L
	Amoxapine	200 to 500 ng/mL	nd
	BuPROPion	25 to 100 ng/mL	nd
	ClomiPRAMINE	80 to 100 ng/mL	nd
	Desipramine	115 to 300 ng/mL	nd
	Doxepin	110 to 250 ng/mL[c]	nd
	Imipramine	225 to 350 ng/mL[c]	nd
	Maprotiline	200 to 300 ng/mL	nd
	Nortriptyline	50 to 150 ng/mL	nd
	Protriptyline	70 to 250 ng/mL	nd
	TraZODone	800 to 1,600 ng/mL	nd
Antipsychotics	ChlorproMAZINE	50 to 300 ng/mL	150 to 950 nmol/L
	FluPHENAZine	0.13 to 2.8 ng/mL	nd
	Haloperidol	5 to 20 ng/mL	nd
	Perphenazine	0.8 to 1.2 ng/mL	nd
	Thiothixene	2 to 57 ng/mL	nd
Miscellaneous	Amantadine	300 ng/mL	nd
	Amrinone	3.7 mcg/mL	nd
	Chloramphenicol	10 to 20 mcg/mL	31 to 62 mcmol/L
	CycloSPORINE[d]	250 to 800 ng/mL (whole blood, RIA) 50 to 300 ng/mL (plasma, RIA)	nd nd
	Ethanol[e]	0 mg/dL	0 mmol/L
	HydrALAZINE	100 ng/mL	nd
	Lithium	0.6 to 1.2 mEq/L	0.6 to 1.2 mmol/L
	Salicylate	100 to 300 mg/L	724 to 2,172 mcmol/L
	Sulfonamide	5 to 15 mg/dL	nd
	Terbutaline	0.5 to 4.1 ng/mL	nd
	Theophylline	10 to 20 mcg/mL	55 to 110 mcmol/L
	Vancomycin (trough) (peak)	10 to 20 mcg/mL 20 to 40 mcg/mL	nd nd

[a]The values given are generally accepted as desirable for treatment without toxicity for most patients. However, exceptions are not uncommon.
[b]nd = No data available
[c]Parent drug plus N-desmethyl metabolite
[d]24-hour trough values
[e]Toxic: 50 to 100 mg/dL (10.9 to 21.7 mmol/L)

The following is adopted from the Seventh Report of the Joint National Committee on Prevention, Detection, Evaluation, and Treatment of High Blood Pressure, National Institutes of Health.

Classification of Blood Pressure[a]

Category	Reference Value		
	Systolic (mm Hg)		Diastolic (mm Hg)
Normal	<120	and	<80
Prehypertension	120 to 139	or	80 to 89
Stage 1 hypertension	140 to 159	or	90 to 99
Stage 2 hypertension	≥160	or	≥100

[a]For adults age 18 and older who are not taking antihypertensive drugs and not acutely ill. When systolic and diastolic blood pressures fall into different categories, the higher category should be selected to classify the individual's blood pressure status.

The classification is based on the average of 2 or more readings properly measured taken at each of 2 or more visits after an initial reading.

Source: The seventh report of the Joint National Committee on Prevention, Detection, Evaluation, and Treatment of High Blood Pressure. *JAMA*. 2003; 289:2560-2571.

Average Height, Weight, and Surface Area by Age and Gender

Age	Girls[a]			Boys[a]		
	Height (cm)	Weight (kg)	BSA[b] (m^2)	Height (cm)	Weight (kg)	BSA[b] (m^2)
Birth	49.5	3.4	0.22	50	3.6	0.22
3 months	59	5.6	0.3	61	6	0.32
6 months	65	7.2	0.36	67	7.9	0.38
9 months	70	8.3	0.4	72	9.3	0.43
12 months	74.5	9.5	0.44	75.5	10.3	0.46
15 months	77	10.3	0.47	79	11.1	0.49
18 months	80	11	0.49	82	11.7	0.52
21 months	83	11.6	0.52	85	12.2	0.54
2 years	86	12	0.54	87.5	12.6	0.55
2.5 years	91	13	0.57	92	13.5	0.59
3 years	94.5	13.8	0.6	96	14.3	0.62
3.5 years	97	15	0.64	98	15	0.64
4 years	101	16	0.67	102	16	0.67
4.5 years	104	17	0.7	105	17	0.7
5 years	107.5	18	0.73	109	18.5	0.75
6 years	115	20	0.80	115	21	0.82
7 years	121.5	23	0.88	122	23	0.88
8 years	127.5	25.5	0.95	127.5	26	0.96
9 years	133	29	1.04	133.5	28.5	1.03
10 years	138	33	1.12	138.5	32	1.1
11 years	144	37	1.22	143.5	36	1.2
12 years	151	41.5	1.32	149	40.5	1.29
13 years	157	46	1.42	156	45.5	1.4
14 years	160.5	49.5	1.49	163.5	51	1.52
15 years	162	52	1.53	170	56	1.63
16 years	162.5	54	1.56	173.5	61	1.71
17 years	163	55	1.58	175	64.5	1.77
Adult	163.5	58	1.62	177	83.5	2.03

[a]Data extracted from the CDC growth charts based on the 50th percentile height and weight for a given age
[b]Body surface area calculation: Square root of [(height (cm) × weight (kg)) / 3,600].

REFERENCES

Centers for Disease Control and Prevention. 2000 CDC growth charts for the United States: Methods and Development. http://www.cdc.gov/growthcharts/2000growthchart-us.pdf. Published May 2002. Accessed November 16, 2007.

Chobanian AV, Bakris GL, Black HR, et al. The Seventh Report of the Joint National Committee on Prevention, Detection, Evaluation, and Treatment of High Blood Pressure: the JNC 7 report. *JAMA*. 2003;289(19):2560-2571.

McDowell MA, Fryar CD, Hirsch R, Ogden CL. Anthropometric reference data for children and adults: U.S. population, 1999-2002. *Adv Data*. 2005;(361):1-5.

Mosteller RD. Simplified calculation of body-surface area. *N Engl J Med*. 1987;317(17):1098.

CALCIUM CHANNEL BLOCKERS AND GINGIVAL HYPERPLASIA

The last published report on calcium channel blocker-induced gingival hyperplasia (GH) by this author was in 2009 (Wynn 2009). This present update reviews the reports up through 2014, relative to the incidence of GH in patients taking calcium channel blockers (CCBs) and the mechanisms by which these drugs cause GH.

The first reported cases of gingival hyperplasia induced by nifedipine were reported by Ramon et al, in 1984 (Ramon 1984). Since that report, additional reports and case studies have been published describing gingival hyperplasia caused by nifedipine and other calcium channel blockers. The following table lists the number of reported cases up through 2014. It lists the specific drug involved and the number of cases from 1995 to the present.

FDA Approval	General Preparation	Cases of Gingival Hyperplasia in Clinical Literature Through 1995	Cases Reported in Literature 1996 to Present	Total Reported Cases
1982	Verapamil	7	9	16
1982	DiltiaZEM	20	33	53
1982	NIFEdipine	120	171	291
1989	NiCARdipine	0	0	0
1989	NiMODipine	0	0	0
1991	Isradipine	0	0	0
1992	AmLODIPine	0	42	42
1992	Felodipine	1	3	4
1993	Nisoldipine	0	0	0
2008	Nitrendipine[a]	1	0	1
	Clevidipine	0	0	0
	Pinaverium[a]	0	0	0

[a]Not approved in the United States

Calcium channel blockers are so named because of their effects on calcium at the cellular level. Contractile cells of the myocardium and smooth muscle cells of coronary and systemic arteries are influenced by the movement of calcium across their membranes. Part of this influence is in the regulation of contractile processes in these cells by way of movement of calcium ions through specific membrane channels. By blocking this channel movement of calcium, these drugs cause depression of the mechanical contraction of the myocardial cells, depression of electrical impulse formation and conduction velocity within the myocardium, and depression of smooth muscle contraction in coronary and systemic arteries. Thus, these drugs are useful in cardiovascular diseases, such as angina and hypertension, in which relaxation of these cells to cause vasodilatation is desired. These agents are sometimes referred to as calcium antagonists.

CLINICAL FINDINGS

Typical clinical findings of CCB-induced GH are hyperplastic gingiva around the maxillary and mandibular anterior teeth (Lederman 1984). The hyperplastic gingiva usually originates in the interdental papilla, and in many areas, bleeding upon probing and small ulcerations are present. False periodontal pockets may be present with no evidence of bone loss. Histopathological analysis usually shows a thick layer of stratified squamous epithelium with parakeratosis and elongated rete pegs (Lederman 1984; Lucas 1985). In the submucosa, a proliferation of collagen fibers together with lymphocytic and plasma cell infiltration can be noticed (Lucas 1985). The connective tissue usually shows large bundles of dense collagenous fibers with a moderate increase in fibroblasts. In addition, signs of inflammation are present with lymphocytes and plasma cells located perivascularly (Lucas 1985).

MECHANISMS

Theories abound on the mechanism of CCB-induced gingival hyperplasia, but none have been proven. An early report using cell culture showed that the CCBs may lead to proliferation of selected fibroblasts, leading to an imbalance between regeneration and degeneration of those cells (Pernu 1989). Brown et al, proposed that CCBs influence calcium/sodium flux in gingival fibroblast to result in decreased uptake of folic acid (Brown 1990). The lack of intracellular folic acid then sets off a chain of events resulting in lack of production of active collagenases with no resultant catabolism of interstitial ground substance. The overabundance of ground substance manifests as gingival enlargement. Another theory suggests that these drugs elicit their effects indirectly through mediators which simulate proliferation and/or collagen synthesis by gingival fibroblasts (Giustiniani 1987). Two of the mediators are reported to be Interleukin-2 from T cells and the testosterone metabolite 5-dihydrotestosterone (Nishikawa 1991; Sooriyamoorthy 1990). The report by Sooriyamoorthy et al, showed convincing evidence in controlled experiments that increased levels of 5-dihydrotestosterone occurred in gingival hyperplasia induced by nifedipine (Sooriyamoorthy 1990). Their earlier work also showed that this testosterone metabolite had a stimulatory effect on the synthetic activity of fibroblasts (Sooriyamoorthy 1988). In another theory, Nishikawa et al, suggests that alteration of the intracellular calcium level in gingival cells by nifedipine in combination with some local inflammatory factors is important in eliciting gingival hyperplasia (Nishikawa 1991). Preexisting gingival inflammation may be essential for onset of drug-induced gingival hyperplasia and that strict plaque control would be effective for preventing onset (Nishikawa 1991). A more recent study using rats suggests that CCBs induce epithelial hyperplasia in gingival overgrowth not by an increase in keratinocyte proliferation, but by prolongation of cell life through reduction of apoptosis (controlled cell death) before epithelial hyperplasia is detected (Shimizu 2002). Harel-Raviv et al, have argued that CCB-induced GH must be a calcium-dependent process because drugs, such as phenytoin and cyclosporin, which cause GH, also affect calcium ion cellular flux (Harel-Raviv 1995). For example, phenytoin increases total intracellular calcium accumulation in gingival fibroblasts (Harel-Raviv 1995).

INCIDENCE AND TREATMENT

The frequency and incidence of gingival hyperplasia caused by calcium channel blockers is difficult to assess. Literature numbers tell us that the effect by the calcium blockers is most prevalent with nifedipine (See table). The incidence of nifedipine-induced GH as currently reported are 28 cases out of 442 patients (6.3%), 11 cases out 29 patients (38%), and 79 cases out of 181 patients (44%) (Ellis 1999; Nery 1995; Steele 1994). The other agents are diltiazem, 7 cases out of 33 patients (21%) and 4 cases out of 186 patients (2.2%), and amlodipine, 5 cases out of 150 patients (3.3%) and 3 cases out of 181 patients (1.7%) (Ellis 1999; Jorgensen 1997; Steele 1994). For verapamil, the incidence has been reported as 5 cases out of 26 patients (19%) (Steele 1994). A report from the Mayo clinic described the incidence of verapamil-induced GH as ranging between 4% to 19% (Meraw 1998). Thus to summarize these values, nifedipine incidence ranged from 6.3% to 44%; diltiazem incidence ranged from 2.2% to 21%; amlodipine incidence ranged from 1.7% to 3.3%; and verapamil incidence ranged from 4% to 19%. In a more recent report, 20,636 patients taking a CCB or a non-CCB for treatment of various cardiovascular conditions were evaluated for incidence of gingival hyperplasia (Kaur 2010). The report identified 103 patients with definite CCB-induced gingival hyperplasia. The number of CCB-identified cases included amlodipine (12), nifedipine (13), felodipine (1), verapamil (4), and diltiazem (8). Another three cases of GH associated with amlodipine were reported by Srivastava in 2010. Sharma and Sharma reported one case of amlodipine-associated enlargement in 2012. Sanz 2012, reported that the current use of calcium channel blockers compared to no use of calcium channel blockers doubles the risk of gingival hyperplasia. Nifedipine use alone was shown to nearly triple the risk of gingival hyperplasia. Joshi and Bansal reported a case of amlodipine-induced gingival enlargement in a 45 year old hypertensive patient taking a low dose of 5 mg. According to these authors, there are few reports of gingival enlargement at the dose of 5 mg.

Treatment of CCB-induced GH includes the reinforcement and maintenance of good oral hygiene, along with frequent professional plaque removal (Camargo 2000). The ideal treatment of choice; however, is the discontinuation of the suspected medication. Regression of GH has been demonstrated after discontinuation of the offending CCB (Meraw 1998). In some situations, the use of another drug in the same class of medications has provided similar medical outcomes with reduced incidence of GH (Westbrook 1997). If the nonsurgical approach is ineffective, then gingivectomy or periodontal flap procedures can reduce the enlarged gingival tissues (Camargo 2000).

The following case report is an example of a three-step treatment approach to nifedipine-induced gingival overgrowth (Alandia-Roman 2012). A 61-year old man had severe gingival overgrowth associated with nifedipine use for the management of hypertension. For step one, the treatment protocol was based on a consistent oral health hygiene program and nonsurgical techniques to reduce inflammation. Professional prophylaxis occurred over multiple visits. The patient also received printed and verbal information about oral hygiene and periodontal disease and was given toothbrushes, dental floss, therapeutic dentifrices, and mouthwashes formulated with 0.5% chloramine-T. Chlorhexidine was not used because of its tooth-staining properties. For the second step, the health care provider changed to a different antihypertension medication, in this case an angiotensin-converting enzyme inhibitor. The change in medication controlled the hypertension and the gingival overgrowth showed an expressive but not complete reduction in 4 weeks. Finally, surgical correction of the gingival overgrowth was still necessary and scalpel gingivectomy was conducted at six sites with one site treated per month for 6 months. Per the authors, the measures used to achieve a successful resolution were based on the most commonly cited and discussed techniques found in the literature.

REFERENCES

Alandia-Roman CC, Tirapelli C, Ribas P, Panzeri H. Drug-induced gingival overgrowth: a case report. *Gen Dent.* 2012;60(4):312-315.

Aral CA, Dilber E, Aral K, Sarica Y, Sivrikoz ON. Management of cyclosporine and nifedipine-induced gingival hypeplasia. *J Clin Diagn Res.* 2015; 9 (12):ZD12-15.

Brochet MS, Harry M, Morin F. Nifedipine induced gingival hyperplasia in pregnancy: a case report. *Curr Drug Saf.* 2016.

Brown RS, Sein P, Corio R, Bottomley WK. Nitrendipine-induced gingival hyperplasia. First case report. *Oral Surg Oral Med Oral Pathol.* 1990;70 (5):593-596.

Camargo PM, Melnick PR, Pirih FQ, Lagos R, Takei HH. Treatment of drug-induced gingival enlargement: aesthetic and functional considerations. *Periodontol 2000.* 2001;27:131-138.

Carty O, Walsh E, Abdelsalem A, MaCarthy D. Case report: drug-induced gingival overgrowth associated with the use of a calcium channel blocker (amlodipine). *J Ir Dent Assoc.* 2015; 61(5):248-251.

Ellis JS, Seymour RA, Steele JG, Robertson P, Butler TJ, Thomason JM. Prevalence of gingival overgrowth induced by calcium channel blockers: a community-based study. *J Periodontol.* 1999;70(1):63-67.

Giustiniani S, Robustelli della Cuna F, Marieni M. Hyperplastic gingivitis during diltiazem therapy. *Int J Cardiol.* 1987;15(2):247-249.

Harel-Raviv M, Eckler M, Lalani K, Raviv E, Gornitsky M. Nifedipine-induced gingival hyperplasia. A comprehensive review and analysis. *Oral Surg Oral Med Oral Pathol Oral Radiol Endod.* 1995;79(6):715-722.

Jorgensen MG. Prevalence of amlodipine-related gingival hyperplasia. *J Periodontol.* 1997;68(7):676-678.

Joshi S, Bansal S. A rare case report of amlodipine-induced gingival enlargement and review of its pathogenesis. *Case Rep Dent 2013.* 2013:138248.doi:10.1155/2013/138248.

Kaur G, Verhamme KM, Dieleman JP, et al. Association between calcium channel blockers and gingival hyperplasia. *J Clin Periodontol.* 2010;37 (7):625-630.

Lederman D, Lumerman H, Reuben S, Freedman PD. Gingival hyperplasia associated with nifedipine therapy. Report of a case. *Oral Surg Oral Med Oral Pathol.* 1984;57(6):620-622.

Livada R, Shiloah J. Calcium channel blocker-induced gingival enlargement. *J Hum Hypertens.* 2014;28(1):10-14.

Lucas RM, Howell LP, Wall BA. Nifedipine-induced gingival hyperplasia. A histochemical and ultrastructural study. *J Periodontol.* 1985;56(4):211-215.

Madi M, Shetty SR, Babu SG, Achalli S. Amlodipine-induced gingival hyperplasia – a case report and review. *West Indian Med J.* 2015;64 (3):279-282.

Meraw SJ, Sheridan PJ. Medically induced gingival hyperplasia. *Mayo Clin Proc.* 1998;73(12):1196-1199.

Nery EB, Edson RG, Lee KK, Pruthi VK, Watson J. Prevalence of nifedipine-induced gingival hyperplasia. *J Periodontol.* 1995;66(7):572-578.

Nishikawa S, Tada H, Hamasaki A, et al. Nifedipine-induced gingival hyperplasia: a clinical and in vitro study. *J Periodontol.* 1991;62(1):30-35.

Pavlic V, Zubovic N, Ilic S, Adamovic T. Untypical amlodipine-induced gingival hyperplasia. *Case Rep Dent.* 2015; 20215:756976.

Pernu HE, Oikarinen K, Hietanen J, Knuuttila M. Verapamil-induced gingival overgrowth: a clinical, histologic, and biochemic approach. *J Oral Pathol Med*. 1989;18(7):422-425.
Ramon Y, Behar S, Kishon Y, Engelberg IS. Gingival hyperplasia caused by nifedipine – a preliminary report. *Int J Cardiol*. 1984;5(2):195-206.
Sanz M. Current ise of calcium channel blockers (CCBs) is associated with an increased risk of gingival hyperplasia. *J Evid Based Dent Pract*. 2012;12(3 Suppl):147-148.
Sharma S, Sharma A. Amlodipine-induced gingival; enlargement – a clinical report. *Compend Contin Educ Dent*. 2012;33(5):e78-82.
Shimizu Y, Kataoka M, Seto H, Kido J, Nagata T. Nifedipine induces gingival epithelial hyperplasia in rats through inhibition of apoptosis. *J Periodontol*. 2002;73(8):861-867.
Sooriyamoorthy M, Gower DB, Eley BM. Androgen metabolism in gingival hyperplasia induced by nifedipine and cyclosporin. *J Periodontal Res*. 1990;25(1):25-30.
Sooriyamoorthy M, Harvey W, Gower DB. The use of human gingival fibroblasts in culture for studying the effects of phenytoin on testosterone metabolism. *Arch Oral Biol*. 1988;33(5):353-359.
Srivastava AK, Kundu D, Bandyopadhyay P, Pal AK. Management of amlodipine-induced gingival enlargement: series of three cases. *J Indian Soc Periodontol*. 2010;14(4):279-281.
Steele RM, Schuna AA, Schreiber RT. Calcium antagonist-induced gingival hyperplasia. *Ann Intern Med*. 1994;120(8):663-664.
Tejnani A, Mani A, Sodhi NK, et al. Incidence of amlodipine-induced gingival overgrowth in the rural population of Loni. *J Indian Soc Peridontol*. 2014;18(2):226-228.
Westbrook P, Bednarczyk EM, Carlson M, Sheehan H, Bissada NF. Regression of nifedipine-induced gingival hyperplasia following switch to a same class calcium channel blocker, isradipine. *J Periodontol*. 1997;68(7):645-650.
Wynn RL. Calcium channel blockers and gingival hyperplasia – an update. *Gen Dent*. 2009;57(2):105-107.

DENTIFRICES WITHOUT SODIUM LAURYL SULFATE (SLS)[a]

Brand Name	Active Ingredient
Arm & Hammer Advance White for Sensitive Teeth	Sodium fluoride 0.24%, triclosan 0.3%
Auromere Toothpaste, Foam Free, Cardamom, Fennel, Foam Free mint	Herbal extract blend, no fluoride, gluten-free
Orajel Tooth and Gum Cleanser (4 to 18 months of age)	Fluoride-, dairy-, and gluten-free
Burt's Bees Natural	Sodium monofluorophosphate 0.77% (0.14% w/v fluoride ion)
Biotene Sensitive	Potassium nitrate[b] 5%, sodium monofluorophosphate 0.14% w/v fluoride ion, anticavity
Desert Essence Natural Tea Oil Toothpaste	Calcium carbonate, glycerin (vegetable-derived), water, fluoride, gluten-free
Dr. Collins Natural	Xylitol 25%[c]
Hello	Aloe vera, erythritol, fluoride, no dyes or artificial sweeteners
Kiss My Face Triple Action Gel	Sorbitol, glycerin, hydrated silica, water, xylitol among other natural ingredients, gluten-free
Lush USA Toothy Tabs	Baking soda
MyntSmile Cosmetic Dental Tooth Cream, formulated for veneers, crowns, and bonding[d]	Sodium monofluorophosphate 0.83%, xylitol, sorbitol, gluten free
Sensodyne[e], Original and Fresh Mint, Fresh Impact, Cool Gel, Tartar Control plus Whitening, Full Protection plus Whitening	Potassium nitrate 5%, sodium fluoride 0.13% w/v fluoride ion, anticavity, gluten-free
Sensodyne ProNamel Mint Essence, Gentle Whitening, Fresh Breath Fresh Wave, Multi-Action	Potassium nitrate 5%, sodium fluoride 0.15% w/v fluoride ion, anticavity, gluten-free
Squigle Tooth Builder	Xylitol 36%, calcium, water, glycerin, gluten-free
Tom's of Maine Clean and Gentle, SLS Free	Sodium monofluorophosphate 0.76% (0.13% w/v fluoride ion)
Tom's of Maine Fluoride-Free Botanically Bright Whitening	Naturally derived ingredients
Tom's of Maine toddler training	Natural Ingredients
The Natural Dentist Whitening	Sodium fluoride 0.24%, gluten-free
The Natural Dentist Fluoride Free	Peppermint oil (0.10%), Sage oil (0.02%), gluten-free
The Natural Dentist Cavity Zapper Groovy Grape - Berry Blast	Sodium fluoride 0.24%, gluten-free
Spry	Xylitol, sorbitol, sodium fluoride, all natural ingredients
Uncle Harry's Toothpaste, Jar Formula (peppermint, cinnamon, spearmint, anise)	Natural ingredients, gluten-free
Verve Ultra Available online: www.verveultra.com or www.amazon.com	Sodium fluoride 0.24%
Xyliwhite platinum mint	Xylitol 25%, sodium bicarbonate (baking soda, whitening) 9%, papain (whitening), gluten-free

[a]**Note:** Studies have suggested that SLS may affect the structural integrity of the oral mucosa and demonstrate an increased incidence of recurrent aphthous ulcers (www.ncbi.nim.gov) and perioral irritation.

[b]Potassium nitrate is used as an antihypersensitivity agent.

[c]Recent studies indicate that xylitol can induce remineralization of tooth enamel. https://www.ncbi.nlm.nih.gov/pubmed/14700079

[d]Combination of ingredients exclusively formulated for veneers, crowns, implants, and bonding

[e]All Sensodyne products without SLS have potassium nitrate as a desensitizing agent

This chart represents a listing of products that have been researched, although it may not be inclusive of all products presently available in the marketplace.

DESENSITIZATION AND REMINERALIZATION PRODUCTS

Brand Name	Category	Formula	Availability
Arm & Hammer Age Defying Arm & Hammer Complete Care Plus Enamel Strengthening	Remineralization	ACP: <5% Sodium fluoride: 0.24%	OTC
Arm & Hammer Sensitive Whitening Arm & Hammer Sensitive Freshening Arm & Hammer Sensitive Multi-Protection	Desensitization	Potassium nitrate[a]: 5% Sodium fluoride: 0.24%	OTC
Burt's Bees Natural Toothpastes	Remineralization	Sodium monofluorophosphate: 0.77% Calcium sodium phosphosilicate:% not indicated	OTC
Colgate Sensitive Pro-Relief Desensitizing Paste	Desensitization	Calcium carbonate and arginine (Pro-Argin Technology[b])	OD (rotary cup paste used before and after scaling)
Colgate Sensitive Pro-Relief Colgate Sensitive Pro-Relief Plus Whitening	Desensitization	Potassium nitrate: 5% Sodium monofluorophosphate: 1.4%	OTC
Colgate Sensitivity Pro-Relief Enamel Repair	Desensitization	Potassium nitrate: 5% Sodium monofluorophosphate: 0.24%	OTC
Colgate Enamel Health, Mineral Repair	Remineralization	Potassium nitrate: 5% Sodium monofluorophosphate: 0.24%	OTC
Clinpro 5000	Remineralization	Sodium fluoride: 1.1% Tri-calcium phosphate	OD, Rx
DayWhite ACP Gel	Desensitization Remineralization Whitening	ACP: 0.5% Hydrogen peroxide: 7.5%, 9.5%	OD
Dr. Collins Restore Toothpaste	Remineralization	Calcium sodium phosphosilicate (NovaMin Technology[d])	Online, OD
MI Paste, various flavors[c]	Desensitization Remineralization	CPP-ACP (Recaldent): 10%	OD, Online
MI Paste Plus	Desensitization Remineralization[c]	CPP-ACP (Recaldent): 10% Sodium fluoride: 0.2%	OD, Online
MyntSmile Cosmetic Dental Tooth Cream, formulated for veneers, crowns, and bonding	Remineralization[c]	Xylitol, sorbitol[e], gluten-free, sodium monoflurophosphate 0.83%	Online
NiteWhite ACP Gel	Desensitization Remineralization Whitening	ACP: 0.5% Carbamide peroxide: 10%, 16%, 22%	OD
Relief ACP Oral Care Gel	Desensitization Remineralization	ACP: 0.375% Sodium fluoride: 0.22% Potassium nitrate: 5%	OD, Rx
Sensodyne Fresh Impact, Cool Gel, Fresh Mint, Original, Extra Whitening, Full Protection, Tartar Control	Desensitization	Potassium nitrate 5%, sodium fluoride 0.15% w/v fluoride ion	
Spry Chewing Gum[e]	Remineralization	Xylitol	OTC, Online
Spry Xylitol Toothpaste, varying flavors	Remineralization	Xylitol	OTC, Online
Topex ReNew Toothpaste	Remineralization	Calcium sodium phosphosilicate (NovaMin Technology): 5% Neutral sodium fluoride: 1.1%	OD
Trident Xtra Care with Recaldent	Remineralization	CPP-ACP (Recaldent): 1% Xylitol	OTC
Uncle Harry's Unscented Remineralization Powder	Remineralization	Calcium carbonate, pink sea salt, bamboo silica, alkalizing ionic minerals	Online

ACP = amorphous calcium phosphate; may contain properties that rebuild enamel and remineralize teeth; **ACP technology** = calcium ions, phosphate ions; **CPP** = casein phosphopeptide; **OD** = office dispensed; **Rx** = prescription only; **OTC** = over-the-counter

[a]Potassium nitrate decreases sensitivity.

[b]Pro-Arginine is proven to be effective in occluding tubules.

[c]Clinical cases available from GC America

[d]NovaMin is a synthetic mineral composed of calcium, sodium, phosphorus, and silica; also known to possess antibacterial properties

[e]Clinical trials have shown that dentifrices and chewing gum with xylitol and sorbitol may reduce tooth mineral loss. https://www.ncbi.nlm.nih.gov/pubmed/14700079

This chart represents a listing of products that have been researched, although it may not be inclusive of all products presently available in the marketplace.

VASOCONSTRICTOR INTERACTIONS WITH ANTIDEPRESSANTS

Antidepressant	Effects with EPINEPHrine, Levonordefrin	Contraindicated	Recommendation
Tricyclics			
Amitriptyline (Elavil [DSC])	EPINEPHrine = increased pressor response; cardiac dysrhythmias Levonordefrin = increased pressor response	No	Potentially dangerous; use minimal amounts with caution in local anesthetics
Amitriptyline and Chlordiazepoxide			
Amitriptyline and Perphenazine			
Amoxapine			
ClomiPRAMINE (Anafranil)			
Desipramine (Norpramin)			
Doxepin (Systemic) (Prudoxin, SINEquan, Zonalon)			
Imipramine (Tofranil-PM, Tofranil)			
Nortriptyline (Pamelor)			
Protriptyline (Vivactil)			
Trimipramine (Surmontil)			
Serotonin/Norepinephrine Reuptake Inhibitor			
Desvenlafaxine (Pristiq)	No adverse interactions reported	No	Suggest caution since serotonin/norepinephrine reuptake inhibitors block norepinephrine reuptake in CNS
Milnacipran (Savella)			
Venlafaxine (Effexor XR, Effexor)			
Serotonin-Only Reuptake Inhibitors			
Citalopram (CeleXA)	No adverse interactions reported	No	No precautions appear to be necessary
Escitalopram (Lexapro)			
FLUoxetine (PROzac Weekly, PROzac, Sarafem)			
FluvoxaMINE			
Olanzapine and Fluoxetine (Symbyax)			
PARoxetine (Paxil CR, Paxil, Pexeva)			
Sertraline (Zoloft)			
Central Alpha-2 Antagonist			
Mirtazapine (Remeron SolTab, Remeron)	No adverse interactions reported	No	Suggest caution since mirtazapine increases release of norepinephrine
DOPamine Reuptake Inhibitor			
BuPROPion (Wellbutrin SR, Wellbutrin XL, Wellbutrin, Zyban)	No adverse interactions reported	No	Part of the mechanism of bupropion is to block norepinephrine reuptake within CNS; it has been suggested that vasoconstrictor be administered with caution
Others			
DULoxetine (Cymbalta)	No adverse interactions reported	No	Part of the mechanism of duloxetine is to block norepinephrine reuptake within CNS; it has been suggested that vasoconstrictor be administered with caution
Maprotiline	Potential for increased pressor response	No	Blocks norepinephrine synaptic reuptake in the CNS; potentially dangerous; use minimal amounts with caution in local anesthetics

(continued)

Antidepressant	Effects with EPINEPHrine, Levonordefrin	Contraindicated	Recommendation
MAO Inhibitors			
Isocarboxazid (Marplan)	No effects on blood pressure or heart rate reported; however, potential exists for slight increase in pressor response	No	Use vasoconstrictor with caution
Moclobemide			
Phenelzine (Nardil)			
Tranylcypromine (Parnate)			
Serotonin Reuptake Inhibitor/Serotonin Antagonist			
Nefazodone (Serzone [DSC])	No adverse interactions reported	No	No precautions appear to be necessary
TraZODone (Desyrel)			
Serotonin Reuptake Inhibitor/5-HT_{1A} Receptor Partial Agonist			
Vilazodone (Viibryd)	No adverse interactions reported	No	No precautions appear to be necessary
Serotonin Reuptake Inhibitor/5-HT_{1A} Receptor Agonist/5-HT_3 Receptor Antagonist			
Vortioxetine (Brintellix)	No adverse interactions reported	No	No precautions appear to be necessary

REFERENCES

Boakes AL, Laurence DR, Teoh PC, Barar FS, Benedikter LT, Prichard BN. Interactions between sympathomimetic amines and antidepressant agents in man. *Br Med J.* 1973;1(5849):311-315.

Moore PA. Adverse drug interactions associated with local anesthetics, sedatives and anxiolytics. *JADA.* 1999; 130(4):541-554.

Naftalin LW, Yagiela JA. Vasoconstrictors: indications and precautions. *Dent Clin North Am.* 2002;46(4):733-746.

Svedmyr N. The influence of a tricyclic antidepressive agent (protriptyline) on some of the circulatory effects or noradrenalin and adrenalin in man. *Life Sci.* 1968;7(1):77-84.

Wahl MJ, Brown RS. Dentistry's wonder drugs: Local anesthetics and vasoconstrictors. *Gen Dent.* 2010; 58(2):114-23.

Waits J, Cretton-Scott E, Childers NK, Sims PJ. Pediatric pyschopharmacology and local anesthesia: potential adverse drug reactions with vasoconstrictor use in dental practice. *Pediatr Dent.* 2014; 36(1):18-23.

Yagiela JA. Adverse drug interactions in dental practice: interactions associated with vasoconstrictors. Part V of a series. *J Am Dent Assoc.* 1999;130 (5):701-709.

Yagiela JA. Chapter 1. Injectable and topical anesthetics. *ADA/PDR Guide to Dental Therapeutics.* 5th ed. ADA American Dental Association: Chicago. 2009; 1-23.

Yagiela JA. Local anesthetics. In Yagiela JA, Dowd FJ, Neidle EA, eds. *Pharmacology and Therapeutics for Dentistry.* 5th ed. St Louis: Mosby; 2004.

Yagiela JA, Duffin SR, Hunt LM. Drug interactions and vasoconstrictors used in local anesthetic solutions. *Oral Surg Oral Med Oral Pathol.* 1985;59 (6):565-571.

PHARMACOLOGIC CATEGORY INDEX

Vitamin, Water Soluble

Xanthine Oxidase Inhibitor

ALPHABETICAL INDEX

Deltasone *see* PredniSONE 1377

Demadex *see* Torsemide 1586

Exparel *see* Bupivacaine (Liposomal) ... 253

Glatopa *see* Glatiramer Acetate 795

NOTES

NOTES

NOTES

NOTES

NOTES

NOTES

Other Offerings from Lexicomp

Advanced Protocols for Medical Emergencies

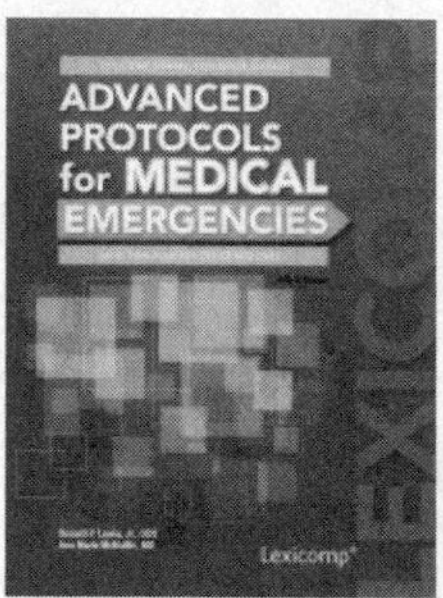

by Donald P. Lewis, Jr., DDS, and Ann Marie McMullin, MD

Advanced Protocols for Medical Emergencies is a valuable guide for offices that administer nitrous oxide, conscious sedation, and general anesthesia. This manual addresses specific medical emergency situations, which are presented in tabbed chapters for quick reference, to help ensure preparation for, and management of, office emergencies. Includes staff training guidelines.

Dental Office Medical Emergencies

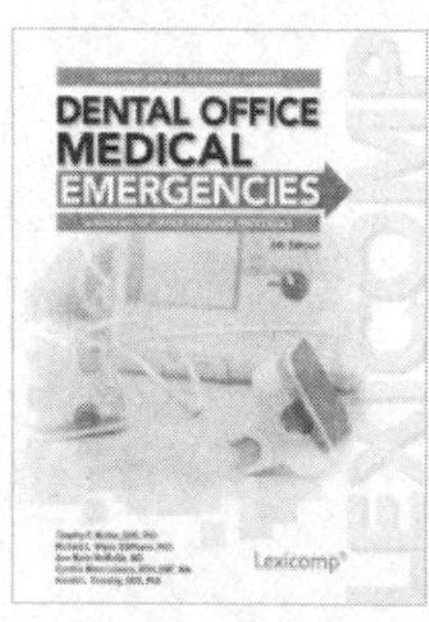

by Timothy F. Meiller, DDS, PhD; Richard L. Wynn, BSPharm, PhD; Ann Marie McMullin, MD; Cynthia Biron Leiseca, RDH, EMT, MA; Harold L. Crossley, DDS, PhD

The *Dental Office Medical Emergencies* manual facilitates dental office emergency treatment and assists the dentist in addressing any developing situation by reinforcing basic life support techniques. This handy reference is intended for use by the entire dental office staff for preparedness training as well as during times of crisis.

Clinician's Endodontic Handbook

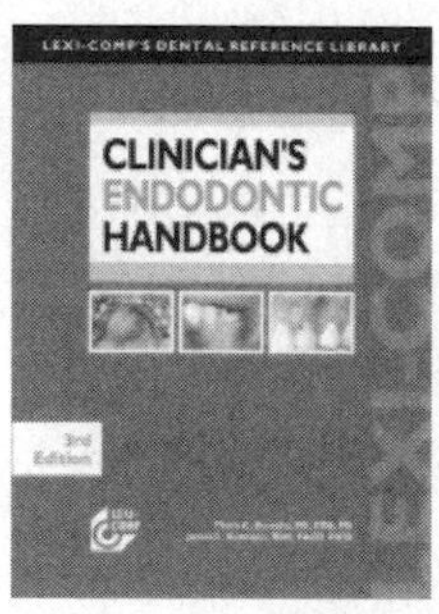

by Thom C. Dumsha, MS, DDS, MS, and James L. Gutmann, DDS, FACD, FICD

The *Clinician's Endodontic Handbook* is a fully illustrated guide to key issues in endodontic therapy. Here, the latest techniques, procedures, and materials are presented, eliminating the need for multiple textbooks. This is a valuable reference for all dental practitioners with an interest in endodontics.

Illustrated Handbook of Clinical Dentistry

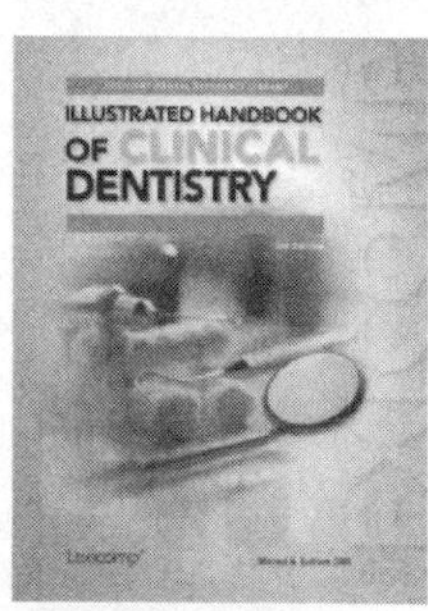

by Michael A. Sullivan, DDS

The *Illustrated Handbook of Clinical Dentistry* is a concise, yet wide-ranging, resource for dental professionals and students. This manual summarizes many basic dental principles and procedures and is designed to be used when transitioning into clinical practice or as a refresher for the seasoned dental professional.

www.wolterskluwerCDI.com/markets/dentistry • 1-866-397-3433

Offerings from Lexicomp

ual of Clinical Periodontics

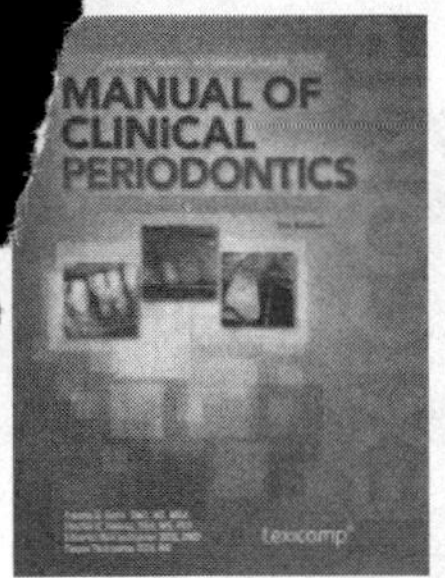

by Francis G. Serio, DMD, MS, MBA; Charles E. Hawley, DDS, MS, PhD; Eduardo Marcuschamer, BDS, DMD; Teppei Tsukiyama, DDS, MS.

The *Manual of Clinical Periodontics* is a quick reference for general dentists, dental hygienists, and students. The manual is a practical resource for both clinical and educational settings, stressing patient-centered, evidence-based diagnosis, treatment planning, and accepted modalities of periodontic therapy.

Manual of Dental Implants

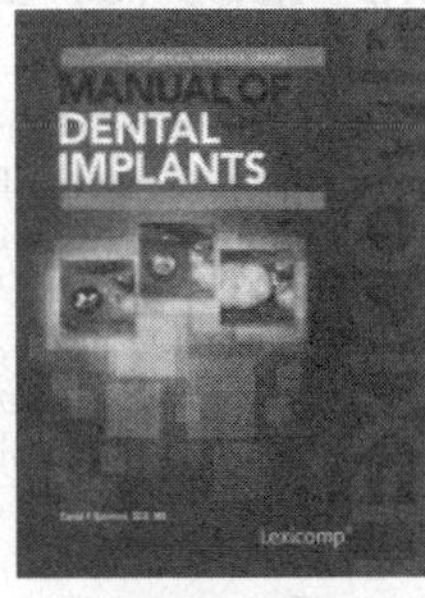

by David P. Sarment, DDS, MS; Beth Peshman, RDH; and Robert F. Faulkner, DDS

The *Manual of Dental Implants* introduces dental professionals to the world of restorative implant dentistry. More than 280 color photographs, diagrams and decision trees help illustrate the diagnosis, treatment, and maintenance of implants. This reference is valuable for increasing levels of knowledge and training, so the user can continue to benefit as he or she gains implant experience.

Oral Hard Tissue Diseases

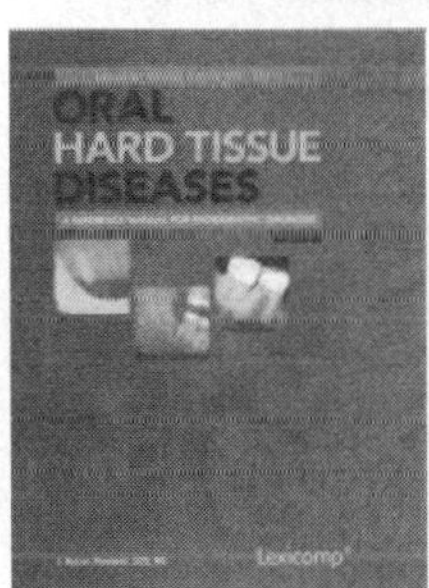

by J. Robert Newland, DDS, MS

Oral Hard Tissue Diseases is a handy reference for visual recognition and diagnosis of common bone lesions. Each section of this manual is devoted to a specific diagnostic category and illustrated with high-quality black-and-white photographs. Recommendations for treatment and follow-up and an alphabetical index are included.

Oral Soft Tissue Diseases

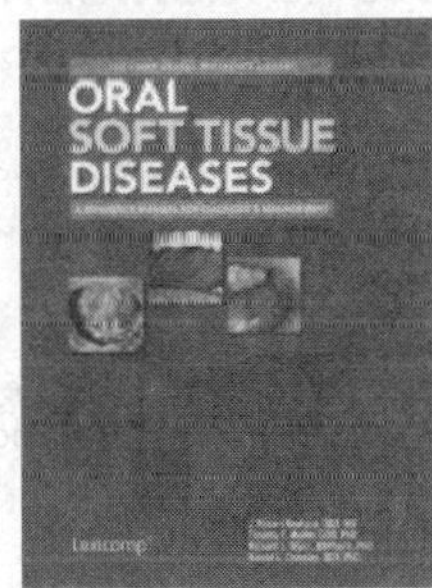

by J. Robert Newland, DDS, MS; Timothy F. Meiller, DDS, PhD; Richard L. Wynn, BSPharm, PhD; Harold L.Crossley, DDS, MS, PhD

In this visually cued manual, each lesion associated with soft tissue disease is illustrated by one or more color photographs depicting typical clinical features and common variations. Recommendations for treatment and follow-up, including sample prescriptions and concise drug monographs, are presented.

The Little Dental Drug Booklet

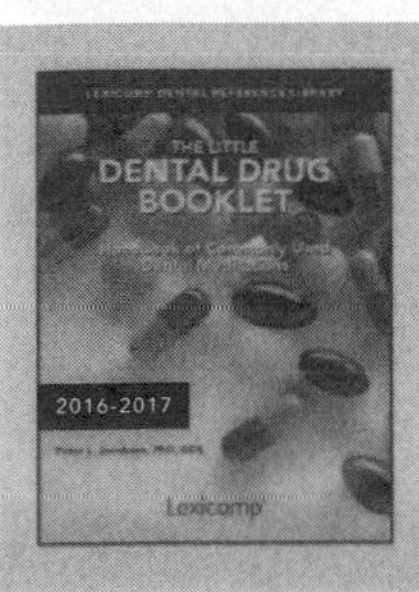

by Peter L. Jacobsen, PhD, DDS

The Little Dental Drug Booklet is a pocket-sized reference to the drugs most commonly used in dental practice. The information provided in this booklet includes practical, practice-oriented suggestions made by dental professionals. A section on prescription writing and prescription requirements is included.

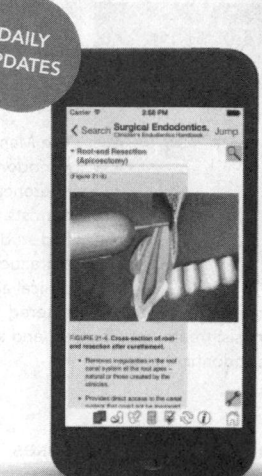